ST/ESA/STAT/SER.G/45

DEPARTMENT OF ECONOMIC AND SOCIAL AFFAIRS
STATISTICS DIVISION

DÉPARTEMENT DES AFFAIRES ÉCONOMIQUES ET SOCIALES
DIVISION DE STATISTIQUE

1996
INTERNATIONAL TRADE STATISTICS YEARBOOK
ANNUAIRE STATISTIQUE DU COMMERCE INTERNATIONAL

VOLUME I

TRADE BY COUNTRY

COMMERCE PAR PAYS

UNITED NATIONS/NATIONS UNIES
New York, 1997

NOTE

Symbols of United Nations documents are composed of capital letters combined with figures.

General disclaimer

The designations employed and the presentation of material in this publication do not imply the expression of any opinion whatsoever on the part of the Secretariat of the United Nations concerning the legal status of any country, territory, city or area, or of its authorities, or concerning the delimitation of its frontiers or boundaries.

Where the designation "country or area" appears in this publication, it covers countries, territories, cities or areas. In previous issues of this publication, where the designation "country" appears in the headings of tables, it should be interpreted to cover countries, territories, cities or areas.

In some tables, the designation "developed" or "developing" economies is intended for statistical convenience and does not necessarily express a judgment about the stage reached by a particular country or area in the development process.

NOTE

Les cotes des documents de l'Organisation des Nations Unies se composent de lettres majuscules et de chiffres.

Déni de responsabilité

Les appellations employées dans cette publication et la présentation des données qui y figurent n'impliquent de la part du Secrétariat de l'Organisation des Nations Unies aucune prise de position quant au statut juridique des pays, territoires, villes ou zones, ou de leurs autorités, ni quant au tracé de leurs frontières ou limites.

L'appellation "pays ou zone", figurant dans cette publication, désigne des pays, des territoires, des villes ou des zones. L'appellation "pays" figurant dans certaines rubriques des tableaux de numéros antérieurs de cette publication doit être interprétée comme désignant des pays, des territoires, des villes ou des zones.

L'appellation économie "développée" ou économie "en voie de développement" qui figure dans certains tableaux est utilisée pour plus de commodité dans la présentation des statistiques et n'implique pas nécessairement un jugement quant au stade de développement auquel est parvenu un pays ou une zone donné.

ST/ESA/STAT/SER.G/45

UNITED NATIONS PUBLICATION
Sales No. E/F.98.XVII.2, vol. I

PUBLICATION DES NATIONS UNIES
Numéro de vente : E/F.98.XVII.2, vol. I

ISBN 92-1-061172-1

Inquiries should be directed to:
PUBLISHING DIVISION
UNITED NATIONS
NEW YORK, N.Y. 10017

Adresser toutes demandes de renseignements à la :
DIVISION DES PUBLICATIONS
NATIONS UNIES
NEW YORK, N.Y. 10017

Printed by the United Nations Reproduction Section, New York
Imprimé par la Section de la reproduction des Nations Unies, New York

TABLE OF CONTENTS

Volume I

COUNTRY TABLES

TABLE DES MATIERES

Volume I

TABLEAUX PAR PAYS

ABBREVIATIONS AND COUNTRY NOMENCLATURE

Names of some countries or groups of countries and of some commodities or groups of commodities have been abbreviated. Exact titles will be found in the following publications referred to in the introduction:

(i) United Nations Standard Country Code (Annex II, Country classification for international trade statistics)

(ii) United Nations Standard Country or Area Code for Statistical Use, (Revision 1)

(iii) Standard Country or Area Codes for Statistical Use, (Revision 2)

(iv) Standard Country or Area Codes for Statistical Use, (Revision 3)

(v) Standard International Trade Classification, Revised (SITC, Revised)

(vi) Standard International Trade Classification, Revision 2, (SITC, Revision 2)

(vii) Classification by Broad Economic Categories (BEC)

(viii) Classification of Commodities by Industrial Origin

(ix) International Standard Industrial Classification of all Economic Activities (ISIC)

1. Data relating to the People's Republic of China generally include those for Taiwan Province in the field of statistics relating to population, area, natural resources, natural conditions such as climate, etc. In other fields of statistics, they do not include Taiwan Province unless otherwise stated. Therefore, in this publication the data published under the heading China exclude those for Taiwan Province. Figures representing the trade with Taiwan Province which may have been reported by any reporting country or area are included in the grouping Asia. Pursuant to a Joint Declaration signed on 19 December 1984, the United Kingdom restored Hong Kong to the People's Republic of China with effect from 1 July 1997; the People's Republic of China resumed the exercise of sovereignty over the territory with effect from that date. For statistical purposes, the data for China do not include those for Hong Kong Special Administrative Region.

2. On 22 May 1990 Democratic Yemen and Yemen merged to form a single State. Since that date they have been represented as one Member with the name "Yemen". All data shown in this publication relating to the period prior to 1990 refer to the former Democratic Yemen and the former Yemen.

3. Through accession of the German Democratic Republic to the Federal Republic of Germany with effect from 3 October 1990, the two German States have united to form one sovereign State. As from the date of unification, the Federal Republic of Germany acts in the United Nations under

the designation of "Germany". All data shown which pertain to Germany prior to 3 October 1990 are indicated separately for the Federal Republic of Germany and the former German Democratic Republic based on their respective territories at the time indicated. Where data for united Germany (subsequent to 3 October 1990) are not available, they are shown separately and pertain to the territorial boundaries prior to 3 October 1990.

4. In 1991, the Union of Soviet Socialist Republics formally dissolved into fifteen independent republics (Armenia, Azerbaijan, Belarus, Estonia, Georgia, Kazakhstan, Kyrgyzstan, Latvia, Lithuania, Republic of Moldova, Russian Federation, Tajikistan, Turkmenistan, Ukraine and Uzbekistan). From 1992 onwards data are shown for the individual republics. Prior to 1992 data are shown for the former USSR.

5. Unless otherwise indicated, data provided for Yugoslavia prior to 1 January 1992 refer to the Socialist Federal Republic of Yugoslavia which was composed of six republics, whereas data provided for Yugoslavia after that date refer to the Federal Republic of Yugoslavia which is composed of two republics (Serbia and Montenegro).

6. Data for the Czech Republic and Slovakia, where available, are shown separately under the appropriate country name. For periods prior to 1 January 1993, where no separate data are available for the Czech Republic and Slovakia, unless otherwise indicated, data for the former Czechoslovakia are shown under the country name "former Czechoslovakia".

7. Beginning 1 January 1997, the overseas departments of France were included in the statistical territory of France for the purposes of international trade statistics. Values on this basis have been provided by France for 1996 also, and values are published on that basis in this publication.

ABREVIATIONS ET CODES DES PAYS.

Les noms de certains pays ou groupes de pays et de certains produits ou groupes de produits ont dû être abrégés. On trouvera les intitulés exacts de ces noms dans les publications suivantes qui figurent dans l'Introduction:

(i) United Nations Standard Country Code (Annex V, 'Standardized Abbreviated French Country Names')

(ii) United Nations Standard Country or Area Code for Statistical Use, (Révision 1)

(iii) Standard Country or Area Codes for Statistical Use, (Révision 2)

(iv) Codes standard des pays et des zones à usage statistique, (Révision 3)

(v) Classification type pour le commerce international révisée, (CTCI révisée)

(vi) Classification type pour le commerce international (deuxième version révisée), (CTCI, Révision 2)

(vii) Classification par grandes catégories économiques (CGCE)

(viii) Classification des marchandises par origine industrielle

(ix) Classification internationale type, par industrie, de toutes les branches d'activité économique (CITI)

1. Les données relatives à la République populaire de Chine comprennent en général les données relatives à la province de Taïwan lorsqu'il s'agit de statistiques concernant la population, la superficie, les ressources naturelles, les conditions naturelles tel que le climat, etc. Dans les statistiques relevant d'autres domaines, la province de Taïwan n'est pas comprise, sauf indication contraire. C'est le cas dans cet Annuaire où les données pour la Chine ne comprennent pas celles de la province de Taïwan. Lorsque des pays partenaires ont déclaré des échanges avec Taïwan ceux-ci sont inclus dans Asie. Conformément à une Déclaration commune signée le 19 décembre 1984, le Royaume-Uni a rétrocédé Hong-kong à la République populaire de Chine, avec effet au ler juillet 1997; la souveraineté de la République populaire de Chine s'exerce à nouveau sur le territoire à compter de cette date. Pour les statistiques, les données de la Chine ne comprennent pas celles de la région administrative spéciale de Hong Kong.

2. Le Yémen et le Yémen démocratique ont fusionné le 22 mai 1990 pour ne plus former qu'un seul Etat, qui est depuis lors représenté comme tel à l'Organisation, sous le nom 'Yémen'. Toutes les données présentées dans cet Annuaire qui se rapportent à la période antérieure à l'année 1990 se réfèrent aux anciens Yémen démocratique et Yémen.

3. En vertu de l'adhésion de la République démocratique allemande à la République fédérale d'Allemagne, prenant effet le 3 octobre 1990, les deux Etats allemands se sont unis pour former un seul Etat souverain. A compter de la date de l'unification, la République fédérale d'Allemagne est désignée à l'ONU sous le nom 'Allemagne'. Toutes les données se rapportant à l'Allemagne avant le 3 octobre 1990 figurent dans deux rubriques séparées, basées sur les territoires respectifs de la République fédérale d'Allemagne et l'ancienne République démocratique allemande selon la période indiquée. En l'absence de données pour l'Allemagne unifiée (à compter du 3 octobre 1990), les données sont fournies séparément sous les rubriques Allemagne (République fédérale d') et Allemagne (ancienne République démocratique) et se rapportent aux limites territoriales antérieures au 3 octobre 1990 lorsqu'elles sont disponibles.

4. En 1991, l'ex Union Soviétique a été scindée officiellement en quinze républiques indépendantes (Arménie, Azerbaïdjan, Bélarus, Estonie, Fédération de Russie, Géorgie, Kazakstan, Kirghizistan, Lettonie, Lituanie, Ouzbékistan, République de Moldova, Tadjikistan, Turkménistan et Ukraine). A partir de 1992 les données sont indiquées pour chaque république individuellement. Avant 1992, les données sont indiquées pour l'ancienne URSS.

5. Sauf indication contraire, les données fournies pour la Yougoslavie avant le 1er janvier 1992 se rapportent à la République fédérative socialiste de Yougoslavie, qui était composée de six républiques; les données fournies pour la Yougoslavie après cette date se rapportent à la République fédérative de Yougoslavie, qui est composée de deux républiques (Serbie et Monténégro).

6. Les données relatives à la République tchèque, et à la Slovaquie, lorsqu'elles sont disponibles, sont présentées séparément sous le nom de chacun des pays. En ce qui concerne la période antérieure au 1er janvier 1993, pour laquelle on ne possède pas de données séparées pour les deux Républiques, les données relatives à l'ancienne Tchécoslovaquie sont, sauf indication contraire, présentées sous le titre 'ancienne Tchécoslovaquie'.

7. A partir de ler janvier 1997, pour les statistiques du commerce international, le territoire statistique de la France comprend les départements d'outre-mer. Les valeurs ont été fournies aussi sur cette base par la France pour 1996, et sont publiées dans cet annuaire.

EXPLANATION OF SYMBOLS
EXPLICATION DES SIGNES

Category not applicable .... Ne s'applique pas	. or ..
Not available........ Aucune donnée disponible	blank or ...
Magnitude of less than half the unit used........ Grandeur inférieure à la moitié de l'unité utilisée	0 or 0.0
Provisional or estimated figures........ Donnée provisoire ou estimation	X
Area (1,000 square metres)........ Superficie (1,000 mètres carrés)	A
1,000 kilowatt-hours........ 1,000 kilowatts-heures	H
Weight (kilograms)........ Poids (kilogrammes)	K
Length (1,000 metres)........ Longueur (1,000 mètres)	L
1,000 times unit shown........ 1,000 fois l'unité indiquée	M
Number........ Nombre	N
Other........ Autres	O
Number of pairs........ Paires	P
Volume (cubic metres)........ Volume (mètre cube)	V
Weight (metric tons)........ Poids (tonnes métriques)	W
1,000,000 times unit shown........ 1 million de fois l'unité indiquée	Y
Decimal figures are always preceded by a period except for the Country Notes in French where they are preceded by a comma........ Les décimales sont toujours précédées d'un point, à l'exception des notes de pays en français où elles sont précédées par une virgule.	(.)

MAGNETIC TAPES AND DISKETTES

External trade data, for the majority of countries from 1962 to the latest year, are available in machine readable form. Detailed information on coverage and price is available, on request, from the United Nations Statistics Division, New York, N.Y. 10017, USA.

BANDES MAGNETIQUES ET DISQUES

Les données du commerce extérieur pour la majorité des pays de 1962 à la dernière année écoulée sont disponibles sous forme de supports magnétiques. Les informations détaillées sur la nature, le volume, les dates et les prix de ces supports magnétiques peuvent être obtenues auprès Division de Statistique des Nations Unies, New York, N.Y. 10017, Etats Unis.

INTRODUCTION

The forty-fifth edition of the International Trade Statistics Yearbook provides the basic information for individual countries' external trade performances in terms of the overall trends in current value, as well as in volume and price, the importance of trading partners and the significance of individual commodities imported and exported. This edition shows annual statistics for 174 countries or reporting customs areas. It is published in two volumes.

VOLUME I

Volume I contains detailed data for individual countries. For each country the following tables usually appear:

(a) Table 1, showing ten series, five for imports and five for exports. The five are: total merchandise trade and trade in gold (generally in national currency, but in US dollars for some countries), conversion factors for converting total merchandise trade from national currency into United States dollars, quantum index numbers and unit value index numbers for total imports and exports.

(b) Table 2, showing for the years 1990 to the latest year available, percentage breakdowns of imports by broad economic categories and of exports by industrial origin. Data for the years 1970 to 1989 were shown in previous issues of this Yearbook. The analysis for imports is based on the Classification by Broad Economic Categories[1/] and for exports on the Classification of Commodities by Industrial Origin[2/]. Reclassification of foreign trade according to broad economic categories or industrial origin requires statistical information at the five-digit level of the Standard International Trade Classification, Revised. (For history and background of the SITC, see pages xx-xxii). When such details are not available, approximate allocations are made, using the three-digit level of the SITC Revised. In comparing statistics of international trade with statistics of production, problems of limitation exist in addition to those of classification. Exports of products which are obviously not produced in the reporting countries (e.g., exports of tea and cocoa from the Netherlands or the United Kingdom) have been allocated to the industrial origin in which they would have been classified in the producing countries; in the case of tea and cocoa: Agriculture. The industrial origin in the reporting country of these exports is, in fact, the wholesale trade. In the Classification of Commodities by Industrial Origin, SITC, Revised headings are subdivided to correspond, roughly, to groups of the International Standard Industrial Classification of All Economic Activities, (Revision 1)[3/]. The breakdown of exports by industrial origin is derived as much as possible from national or special exports.

(c) Table 3, showing up to the most recent five years available, the value in United States dollars of import and export trade analyzed by the principal countries or areas and regions of provenance and destination. The analysis is made according to the United Nations Standard Country or Area Codes for Statistical Use[4/]. In some instances, owing to the nature of the national country classification, the conversion to the United Nations country classification could not be done precisely. A maximum of 50 trading partners are shown, in order of magnitude, based on the sum of the values over the years included in the table, with imports and exports ranked separately. Below the value table is a listing showing the percentage breakdown of trade by regions and the percent of trade accounted for by each of the first ten trading partners for the latest available ten years. The lines for the European Union (EU) and European Free Trade Area (EFTA) are calculated for all years on the basis of the 1996 membership (fifteen countries for EU and three countries for EFTA). The lines for former USSR comprises the former USSR for years prior to 1992 and the aggregate of the subsequent fifteen independent republics from 1992 to date.

(d) Tables 4 and 5, showing up to the most recent four years available, the quantity and the value in United States dollars of imports and exports analyzed by commodities. Data for a commodity will appear if the value in any year is greater than or equal to 0.3 per cent of the total trade for that year. The commodities are shown in terms of SITC headings (abbreviated). An asterisk (*) preceding the description indicates that these are the only codes belonging to the next higher level of the SITC, and the next higher level is, therefore, not shown.

In some instances the figures shown in United States dollars in the tables indicated under (c) and (d) above may not correspond to those in United States dollars in the table described under (a) above or to those in national currency in that table after the application of the currency conversion factors. These discrepancies arise in large part from revisions to the more recent data at the total level and these revisions were not broken down for the more detailed data by commodity and partner. It was felt that a partial revision of the tables referred to under (c) and (d) above to make the totals consistent with those in (a) should not be made.

For all countries, the data in Tables 3, 4 and 5 are presented according to the Standard International Trade Classification (SITC)[5/] Revision 2. Many countries report data according to the SITC, Revision 3 or the Harmonized Commodity Description and Coding System (HS). The data so reported for these countries, were converted to SITC Revision 2. This is a difficult conversion and results in data for some SITC Revision 2 codes which are not comparable with data reported in terms of SITC, Revision 2 to a very significant extent.

In a few cases, the conversion to SITC from the national commodity classification systems could not be done precisely and, therefore, some of the SITC codes are not exact in their coverage.

When available, more detailed data by commodity and partner country according to the SITC, Revised, Revision 2 or Revision 3 are published in the Commodity Trade Statistics[6/] on microfiches.

Detailed descriptions of the current concepts and definitions applied by countries are available in the United Nations mimeograph "National Reporting Practices in International Merchandise Trade Statistics" (ST/ESA/STAT/112), issued February 1996 and available from the United Nations Statistics Division.

VOLUME II

Volume II contains commodity tables showing the total trade of certain commodities analyzed by regions and countries. Liked-named regions have the same composition as in Volumes I. In Volume II, the heading Eur.X E.Eur.& F.USSR, comprises Europe excluding East Europe and the Former USSR.

Commodity tables. These tables show imports and exports of commodities at the group (3-digit) level of the SITC, Revision 2 (all groups except for 351, 675 and 688). The years covered are the five years 1992 to 1996. The values are in U.S. dollars and both imports and exports are analyzed by regions and principal trading countries. A maximum of 50 countries are shown in order of magnitude, based on the sum of the values over the years 1993, 1994 and 1995 included in the table, with imports and exports ranked separately. No quantity data are shown.

In preparing these tables, in many cases estimates were made for countries whose data were not yet available and these are shown with an 'x'. In some cases, estimates were made for particular countries, and they were considered adequate to include in regional and world totals but not sufficiently explained to be published separately for the country. Consequently, they have been suppressed and a blank with an 'x' appearing in the table. Strictly speaking, an 'x' should appear against a regional or world total that contains estimates. However, in general, virtually all the regional and world totals include estimates. The 'x's have been omitted for cosmetic purposes.

Volume II also contains special tables showing, inter alia, (a) the contribution of the trade of each country to the trade of its region and of the world, (b) the flow of trade between countries and regions and (c) the fluctuations of the prices at which goods moved internationally. The special tables are:

A. Total imports and exports by regions and countries or areas;
B. World exports by commodity classes and by regions;
C. Growth of world exports by commodity classes and by regions;
D. Structure of world exports by commodity classes and by regions;
E. Total imports and exports: index numbers by countries or areas;
F. Total exports and imports: index numbers of quantum, unit value and terms of trade by regions;
G. Manufactured goods exports;
H. Fuel imports: developed economies;
I. Some indicators on fuel imports: developed economies;
J. Export price index numbers of primary commodities and non-ferrous base metals.

Special Tables

The economic and geographic groupings in all the special tables are in accordance with those of Special Table A in this issue, although Special Table A sometimes includes more detailed geographic sub-groups. (See Special Table A for the details.)

(A) Total imports and exports by regions and countries or areas. The regional, economic and world totals have been adjusted: (a) to include estimates for countries or areas for which full data are not available; (b) to include insurance and freight for imports valued f.o.b.; (c) to include countries or areas not listed separately; (d) to approximate special trade; (e) to approximate calendar years; and (f) where possible, to eliminate incomparabilities owing to geographical changes, by adjusting the figures for periods before the change to be comparable to those for periods after the change, for example, the European Union and the European Free Trade Association. The figures shown for individual countries correspond to the national currency figures which appear and are described in table 1 of the country tables. The letters in the first and last columns of the table indicate the system of trade used: G: General trade; S: Special trade. For footnotes see the end of the table.

Monthly and quarterly data appear in the Monthly Bulletin of Statistics.

(B) World exports by commodity classes and by regions. For the general note and footnotes, see the end of the table.

(C) Growth of world exports by commodity classes and by regions. The annual average rates of change in percentage terms given in this table have been uniformly calculated by the use of the compound interest formula:

$$r = \left(\sqrt[t]{\frac{Vn}{Vo}} -1 \right) 100$$

r = Annual average rate of change in percentage terms.
Vn = Value of exports during the last year of the period.
Vo = Value of exports during the first year of the period.
t = Number of years in period.

For the general note and footnotes, see the end of Special Table D.

(D) Structure of world exports by commodity classes and by regions. The figures shown under the heading 'Origin of Exports' refer to the exports of the region or country appearing in the 'Area' column; those shown under the heading 'Destination of

Exports' refer to the exports of the world to the region or country appearing in the 'Area' column. For the general note and footnotes, see the end of the table.

(E) Total imports and exports: index numbers by countries or areas. Unless otherwise stated in the footnotes, the unit value indices are in terms of national currencies. For the general note and footnotes, see the end of the table.

Monthly and quarterly data appear in the Monthly Bulletin of Statistics.

(F) Total exports and imports: index numbers of quantum, unit value and terms of trade by regions. For the footnotes, see the end of the table.

Quarterly data appear in the Monthly Bulletin of Statistics.

(G) Manufactured goods exports. For the general note and footnotes, see the end of the table.

Quarterly data appear in the Monthly Bulletin of Statistics.

(H) Fuel imports: developed economies. For the general note and footnotes, see the end of the table.

Quarterly data appear in the Monthly Bulletin of Statistics.

(I) Some indicators on fuel imports: developed economies. This table shows the share of fuel imports in the total value of imports and in the total value of exports, and the ratio of unit value indices of manufactured goods exports to those of fuel imports. For the general note and footnotes, see the end of the table.

Quarterly data appear in the Monthly Bulletin of Statistics.

(J) Export price index numbers of primary commodities and non-ferrous base metals. For the general note and footnote, see the end of the table.

Monthly and quarterly data appear in the Monthly Bulletin of Statistics.

SOURCES AND PRESENTATION

The figures for Volumes I and II are obtained from national published sources, from data supplied by the Governments for use in this publication, the United Nations publications: Monthly Bulletin of Statistics, and Statistical Yearbook, and from publications specially prepared by other United Nations agencies. Estimates for some missing data are made by the United Nations Statistics Division.

The country and regional names used by various countries are not uniform for their trade statistics. Also, where former geographical entities commonly referred to in national statistics have changed, countries may introduce the corresponding changes in their statistics at different times. Wherever possible, however, parts of the world have been designated by the names they currently bear.

The country aggregates shown throughout this publication are based on those set forth in the United Nations Standard Country or Area Codes for Statistical Use[4/], except where indicated.

NATIONAL INDEX NUMBERS

National index numbers of unit value in national currencies or United States dollars and of quantum are shown in Table 1. They are the official indices which show the changes in the volume, (quantum index) and the average price (unit value index) of the aggregate merchandise imports or exports. Each index number represents a change between the period to which the number refers, called the current period, and a fixed period, called the publication base, in which the index is represented by the percentage 100. In order to facilitate comparison, the indices shown have been adjusted, where possible, so that the calendar year 1990 is the publication base. When changes are made in the coverage, formula or base period of an index, the two series are linked together if they have an overlapping period and are sufficiently comparable.

Quarterly and monthly figures in these index series appear in the United Nations Monthly Bulletin of Statistics and a more detailed description of their compilation is given in the 1977 Supplement to the Statistical Yearbook and the Monthly Bulletin of Statistics[7/].

TRANSITION COUNTRIES

For the period covered by this Yearbook, countries formerly classified for statistical purposes as centrally planned economies had systems of official rates between their currencies and other currencies, all consistent with rates of 0.90 new roubles to the United States dollar prior to 24 December 1971 and 0.829 new roubles to the United States dollar until February 1973; since then these rates have been fluctuating. They generally used these rates when it was necessary to convert foreign into domestic currencies for the purpose of compiling external trade statistics. The resulting data are for comparison with the external transactions of the rest of the world rather than with domestic monetary transactions.

The trade statistics of these countries had definitions somewhat different from those which exist in other countries. Differences in definition contribute to the discrepancies which can be observed between statistical records referring to the same flow of goods but kept by two trading partners having different economic systems. The trade among these countries was carried out on a basis not comparable to that governing trade with other countries. The concept of transaction value, for instance, as applied outside those countries is based on the existence of a market between exporters and importers in which the interaction of supply and demand has more effect than it can be assumed to have had in those countries; in the absence of data on the unit values of specific commodities entering the trade of those countries with one another, it is difficult to assess the possible effects on the trade statistics of this kind of incomparability. Increasingly since 1992, the transition countries have adopted similar concepts and definitions for international trade statistics as are in effect in other countries.

GENERAL STATEMENTS[8/]

1. Territory. The statistics reported by a country generally refer to the customs area of the country. In most cases this coincides with the geographical area of the country. Unless otherwise stated, the combination of two territories, formerly separate, results in the elimination from the statistics of their trade with each other. The separation of two territories, formerly together, results in the appearance of their trade with each other in the statistics for each territory.

2. System of trade. Two systems of recording trade are in common use, differing mainly in the way warehoused and re-exported goods are recorded:

(a) Special trade: special imports are the combined total of imports for direct domestic consumption (including transformation and repair) and withdrawals from bonded warehouses or free zones for domestic consumption. Special exports comprise exports of national merchandise, namely, goods wholly or partly produced or manufactured in the country, together with exports of nationalized goods (nationalized goods are goods which, having been included in special imports, are then exported without transformation).

(b) General trade: general imports are the combined total of imports for direct domestic consumption and imports into bonded warehouses or free zones. General exports are the combined total of national exports and re-exports. Re-exports, in the general trade system, consist of the outward movement of nationalized goods plus goods which, after importation, move outward from bonded warehouses or free zones without having been transformed.

Direct transit trade, i.e., goods merely being trans-shipped or moving through the country for purposes of transport only, is excluded from the statistics of both special and general trade.

Each of the tables indicates in its heading the system of trade to which the figures relate.

3. Valuation. At its fifteenth session, in 1953, the Economic and Social Council, taking the view that trade statistics must reflect economic realities, recommended that the Governments of Member States of the United Nations, wherever possible, use transaction values in the compilation of their national statistics of external trade or, when national practices are based on other values, endeavour to provide supplementary statistical data based on transaction values (Economic and Social Council resolution 469 B (XV)). In the case of imports, the transaction value is the value at which the goods were purchased

by the importer plus the cost of transportation and insurance to the frontier of the importing country (a c.i.f. valuation). In the case of exports, the transaction value is the value at which the goods were sold by the exporter, including the cost of transportation and insurance, to bring the goods onto the transporting vehicle at the frontier of the exporting country (a f.o.b. valuation).

4. Currency conversion. For data in this publication, conversion of values from national currencies into United States dollars is done by means of currency conversion factors based on official exchange rates. Values in currencies subject to fluctuation (such currencies increased in number beginning December 1971) are converted into United States dollars using weighted average exchange rates specially calculated for this purpose. The weighted average exchange rate for a given currency for a given year is the component monthly factors, mostly furnished by the International Monetary Fund, weighted by the value of the relevant trade in each month. A monthly factor is the exchange rate (or the simple average rate) in effect during that month. These factors are applicable to total imports and exports respectively, but not necessarily to trade in individual commodities or with individual countries.

5. Merchandise. In order that external trade statistics shall be suited to the measurement of the influence of national economies upon one another, merchandise trade is defined to include, as far as possible, all goods which add to or subtract from the material resources of a country as a result of their movements into or out of the country. Unless, therefore, statements to the contrary are made in footnotes to the country tables, the treatment of the classes of goods listed below are as indicated:

(a) Gold. Gold traded internationally is usually defined as encompassing the three following types:

i) Gold coins (issued and unissued) and bullion, including banking and monetary gold;
ii) Unrefined gold, including gold ores and concentrates;
iii) Partly-worked gold in which the value of the gold is 80 per cent or more of the total value, including scrap, jewellers' sweepings, dust, primary shapes (such as rods, wire and gold leaf) and gold alloys (crude or in primary shapes).

Of the types of gold listed above, those belonging to the category of monetary gold are excluded from merchandise trade, and those classified as non-monetary gold are included, except as indicated below. Any gold shipment received by the central monetary authority of a country is treated as monetary gold. All other gold shipments (whether to commercial banks or to individuals), on the other hand, are considered non-monetary. SITC, Revised, treated all types of gold as non-merchandise trade. In compliance with the SITC, Revised, as well as for practical reasons, all types of gold listed above are in general excluded from the merchandise trade statistics compiled under this version of the classification. However, data compiled under SITC, Revision 2, Revision 3, and the Harmonized Commodity Description and coding system, include non-monetary gold.

(b) Silver ore, concentrates, bullion, unissued coin (as noted below), scrap and partly-worked and manufactured silver are all included in merchandise trade statistics.

(c) Currency and titles of ownership which have been issued into circulation, e.g., issued silver and base metal coins, bank notes, other paper currency and securities, are excluded from merchandise trade statistics. Unissued currency and titles of ownership are included at their intrinsic value as stamped metal or printed paper rather than at face value.

(d) Trade on government account is included as merchandise trade. Movements under government foreign aid programmes (civil and military), war reparations and restitutions and military goods[9/] moving internationally are therefore included. When goods are destined for use of national agencies (including embassies and military forces) stationed abroad they are, however, not considered to have moved in external trade and are excluded.

(e) Temporary imports and exports. Tourists' and travellers' effects not acquired abroad (including vehicles), goods for exhibitions or study, animals admitted to a country temporarily, merely for racing or breeding, returnable containers, etc., the movements of all of which are expected to be reversed within a limited time, are excluded.

(f) Improvement and repair trade. Countries sending goods abroad for improvement or repair and later returned are said to be engaging in the passive improvement and repair trade; countries receiving goods from other countries for improvement or repair and eventual return engage in the active improvement and repair trade. Inward and outward movement in this trade are generally excluded from imports and exports.

(g) Postal trade is included in merchandise trade.

(h) Trade in fish, etc. Fish and salvage sold abroad or to foreign vessels off national vessels, and fish and salvage landed from foreign vessels in national ports are excluded from merchandise trade statistics.

(i) Trade in ships and aircraft. New ships and aircraft bought and sold are included. Second-hand ships and aircraft entering or leaving the registers of the reporting country as a result of transfer of ownership are excluded.

(j) Bunkers and stores for ships and aircraft. In general, bunkers and stores should be included in aggregate merchandise exports.

6. Partner country. The following terms describe methods that may be used by reporting countries in determining, for each shipment of goods, the partner country under whose name it should be recorded: (a) for imports: country of origin or production, country of consignment, country of purchase or country of provenance; (b) for exports: country of consumption or consignment, or country of sale.

7. Trade analyzed by commodity. Analysis is according to the Standard International Trade Classification.

THE STANDARD INTERNATIONAL TRADE CLASSIFICATION (SITC) AND THE HARMONIZED COMMODITY DESCRIPTION AND CODING SYSTEM (HS)

In July 1950, the United Nations Economic and Social Council, on the advice of its Statistical Commission, recommended that Governments compile trade by commodity statistics according to the original SITC[5/] in order to have available data in internationally comparable categories suitable for the economic analysis of trade. The original SITC had been prepared by the United Nations Secretariat with the assistance of expert consultants and in co-operation with Member Governments and interested international organizations.

In May 1960, the Statistical Commission approved a revision, similarly prepared, of the original SITC, known as the SITC, Revised, designed to take account of the changes in the pattern of trade since 1950 and to simplify the relation between the SITC and internationally agreed customs tariff nomenclatures. The SITC, Revised, is a rearrangement into statistical order of the items of the 1955 Tariff Nomenclature (CCCN) of the Customs Co-operation Council.

The SITC, Revised, is based on 625 subgroups (identified by code numbers of four digits), most of which correspond to items of the original SITC. A number of subgroups are further subdivided either to distinguish commodities of statistical importance or to permit exact correspondence with the CCCN; this results in a basic (5-digit code) level for the SITC, Revised, consisting of 1,312 items. The subgroups are combined, progressively, into 177 groups, 56 divisions and 10 sections.

The headings of the SITC, Revised, are fully determined by their code numbers. The precise composition of each number is defined in the SITC, Revised, itself. In comparing data according to the SITC, Revised, with data according to a national commodity classification it must be remembered that the same brief description may refer to aggregates differing somewhat in composition.

Although the SITC, Revised, of 1960 represented a great improvement on the original SITC, basically the same reasons which led to the creation of the SITC and its first revision were found, in the late nineteen-sixties, to be once more valid. Since 1960 the volume of trade had increased rapidly and its geographic and commodity patterns had changed fundamentally. Consequently, a second revision of the SITC was undertaken. In October 1974 the Statistical Commission approved of this revision, known as SITC, Revision 2[5/], and in May 1975 the Economic and Social Council recommended that Member States of the United Nations should report data on external trade according to the SITC, Revision 2, as far and as soon as possible. Starting with data for 1976, some countries began reporting trade statistics based on the SITC, Revision 2.

The basic headings of the SITC, Revision 2 had a one-to-one correspondence with the subdivisions of the Customs Co-operation Council Nomenclature (CCCN). However, there were a number of users who found the subdivisions of CCCN (and thus SITC, Revision 2) insufficient for their needs[10/]. There was also an expressed need for the harmonization of economic classifications[11/]. Partly to satisfy these needs, the Customs Co-operation Council in May 1973 undertook responsibility for the development and completion of the Harmonized Commodity Description and Coding System (HS)[12/].

At its twenty-first session, in January 1981, the Statistical Commission had taken note of the fact that a third revision of SITC would have to be made available when both the revised CCCN and HS came into force[13/]. Accordingly, later that year, the United Nations Secretariat commenced work on the revision of SITC, Revision 2, based on the principle that every effort should be made to maintain its general character and structure but taking into account the need for its harmonization with the revised CCCN, the International Standard Industrial Classification (ISIC) Revision 3[14/] and a Central Product Classification[15/] which was developed jointly by the United Nations Statistics Division and the Statistical Office of the European Communities.

The final draft was revised and approved by the Statistical Commission at its twenty-third session, in February 1985,[16/] and a resolution was adopted by the Economic and Social Council on internationally data on external trade statistics according to the Standard International Trade 28 May 1985 (resolution 1985/7) which, inter alia, recommended that Member States should report Classification, Revision 3.

The Harmonized System was adopted by the Customs Cooperation Council in June 1993, and the International Convention on the Harmonized System (HS Convention) entered into force 1 January 1988 (HS88). As of 18 April 1997 there were 88 Contracting Parties, and another 64 countries or territories which were not contracting parties but were using the HS for Customs/statistical purposes.

The United Nations Statistical Commission, at its twenty-seventh session, held from 22 February to 3 March 1993, recommended that countries "adopt the HS for compilation and dissemination of their international trade statistics"[17/].

In accordance with the preamble of the HS Convention, which recognized the importance of ensuring that the HS be kept up-to-date in the light of changes in technology or in patterns of international trade, the HS is regularly reviewed and revised. The United Nations Statistical Commission at its twenty-seventh session "recommended that the Customs Cooperation Council take fully into account the statistical implications of any changes proposed for HS and the statistical needs and capacities of developing countries"[18/]. Some minor revisions to the HS88, which also resulted in the deletion of one six-digit code, were made in 1992 (HS92). A more comprehensive set of amendments was adopted in 1993 and these amendments entered into force 1 January 1996 (HS96).

The Statistical Commission, at its twenty-eighth session, 27 February - 3 March 1995 considered changes that would be required to the SITC, Rev. 3 to bring it into correlation with HS96; the Commission decided that the changes required in SITC, Rev. 3 to make it fully correlated with HS96 were minor in scale. The Commission therefore decided that it would not be necessary to issue a fourth revision of the SITC[19/].

1/ Classification by Broad Economic Categories (in terms of the SITC Revised), Statistical Papers, Series M No.53, (United Nations publication, Sales No. 71.XVII.12).

2/ Classification of Commodities by Industrial Origin (Relationship of the Standard International Trade Classification Revised to the International Standard Industrial Classification of All Economic Activities, Revision 1), Statistical Papers, Series M No.43, (United Nations publication, Sales No. 66.XVII.7).

3/ International Standard Industrial Classification of All Economic Activities (Revision 1), Statistical Papers, Series M No. 4, Rev. 1, (United Nations publication, Sales No. 58.XVII.7).

4/ United Nations Standard Country Codes, Statistical Papers, Series M No. 49, (United Nations publication, Sales No. E.70.XVII.13).

United Nations Standard Country or Area Codes for Statistical Use, Statistical Papers, Series M No. 49, Rev. 1, (United Nations publication, Sales No. E.75.XVII.8).

Standard Country or Area Codes for Statistical Use, Statistical Papers, Series M No. 49, Rev.2, (United Nations publication, Sales No. E.82.XVII.8).

Standard Country or Area Codes for Statistical Use, Series M No. 49, Rev. 3.

5/ Standard International Trade Classification Revision 2, Statistical Papers, Series M No.34/Rev.2, (United Nations publication, Sales No. E.75.XVII.6).

Standard International Trade Classification Revision 3, Statistical Papers, Series M No.34/Rev.3, (United Nations publication, Sales No. E.86.XVII.12).

6/ Commodity Trade Statistics, on microfiche (CTS SER.DCOM), carries annual figures showing the provenance and destination of trade for a large number of headings of the SITC, Revised, SITC, Revision 2, and SITC, Revision 3.

7/ 1977 Supplement to the Statistical Yearbook and Monthly Bulletin of Statistics, ST/ESA/STAT/SER.S/SUPPL.2, ST/ESA/STAT/SER.Q/SUPPL.2, (United Nations publication, Sales No. E.78.XVII.10).

8/ The treatment of items 1 to 7 is drawn mainly from International Trade Statistics Concepts and Definitions, Statistical Papers, Series M No. 52, Rev.1, (United Nations publication, Sales No. E.82.XVII.14).

9/ Countries excluding military goods from imports or exports use varying definitions of this category of merchandise, but for most countries concerned, weapons and their ammunition constitute a major part of the military goods excluded.

10/ United Nations Statistics Division and Statistical Office of the European Communities Joint Working Group on World Level Classifications, "A Harmonized Commodity Description and Coding System for Use in International Trade" (UNSO/SOEC/1/2).

11/ United Nations Secretariat, "The Harmonization of Statistical Classifications: report of an expert group meeting". (ST/ESA/STAT/78).

12/ Customs Co-operation Council, "The Harmonized Commodity Description and Coding System", Brussels, 1985.

13/ Official Records of the Economic and Social Council, 1981, Supplement No. 2, (E/1981/12), para. 41.

14/ International Standard Industrial Classification of All Economic Activities, Statistical Papers, Series M No.4, Rev.3, (United Nations publication, Sales No.E.90.XVII.11).

15/ Provisional Central Product Classification, Statistical Papers, Series M No.77, (United Nations publication, Sales No.E.91.XVII.7).

16/ Official Records of the Economic and Social Council, 1985, Supplement No. 6, (E/1985/26), para. 57 (d).

17/ Official Records of the Economic and Social Council, 1993, Supplement No. 6, (E/1993/26), para. 162 (d).

18/ Official Records of the Economic and Social Council, 1993, Supplement No. 6, (E/1993/26), para. 162 (e).

19/ Official Records of the Economic and Social Council, 1995, Supplement No. 8, (E/CN.3/1995/28), para. 19 (e).

INTRODUCTION

La quarante cinquième édition de l' annuaire statistique du commerce international présente les informations nécessaires à l'étude des échanges de chaque pays, en termes de valeur courante, de volume et de prix ainsi que l'importance des différents pays partenaires et des principaux produits importés et exportés. Cette édition présente des données annuelles pour 174 pays ou zones douanières déclarants. L'annuaire est publié en deux volumes.

VOLUME I

Le Volume I fournit des renseignements détaillés sur chaque pays au sujet duquel on trouvera généralement les tableaux suivants:

a) Tableau 1, donnant 10 séries, 5 à l'importation, 5 à l'exportation. Ces cinq séries sont: échanges de marchandises et échanges portant sur l'or (généralement en monnaie nationale mais pour quelques pays, en dollars des Etats-Unis), facteurs pour convertir les monnaies nationales en dollars des Etats-Unis, indices du quantum et de la valeur unitaire pour les importations et exportations totales.

b) Tableau 2, présentant de l'année 1990 jusqu'à la dernière année disponible, les pourcentages par rapport au commerce total des importations par grandes catégories économiques et les exportations par branches d'origine. Les pourcentages pour 1970 à 1989 ont été publiés dans les éditions précédentes de cet Annuaire. L'analyse pour les importations est basée sur la Classification par grandes catégories économiques;[1/] pour les exportations sur la Classification des marchandises par origine industrielle[2/]. Toute reclassification du commerce extérieur par grandes catégories économiques ou par origine industrielle nécessite le détail au niveau des 5 chiffres de la CTCI, révisée. (Se référer aux pages xxxiii à xxxv pour l'histoire et le fond de la CTCI). Lorsque les statistiques n'étaient pas disponibles à ce niveau on a utilisé les données au niveau des trois chiffres de la CTCI, révisée. En comparant des statistiques du commerce extérieur avec des statistiques de production on se heurte à certaines incohérences qui s'ajoutent aux problèmes de classification. Les exportations de marchandises qui de toute évidence n'ont pas été produites dans les pays exportateurs (exportation de thé et de cacao des Pays-Bas ou du Royaume-Uni) ont été classées dans la branche où elles auraient été classées dans le pays d'origine; dans le cas du thé et du cacao: l'agriculture. La branche dans le pays déclarant est en fait dans ce cas le commerce de gros. Pour obtenir la Classification des marchandises par origine industrielle, les postes de la CTCI, révisée sont regroupés afin de correspondre approximativement aux groupes de la Classification international type, par industrie, de toutes les branches d'activité économique (révisée) (CITI, Révision 1)[3/]. Dans toute la mesure du possible les exportations nationales ou spéciales ont été utilisées.

c) Tableau 3, présentant jusqu'aux cinq années les plus récentes la valeur en dollars des Etats-Unis des importations et des exportations selon les principaux pays ou zones et régions d'origine et de destination. La distribution géographique est faite selon le Standard Country or Area Codes for Statistical Use[4/] des Nations Unies. Parfois, étant donné la nature des codes géographiques nationaux, la conversion des données selon le code des Nations Unies n'a pu être effectuée que moyennant quelques imprécisions. Dans ces tableaux figurent les 50 pays partenaires les plus importants classés par ordre d'importance selon la somme des valeurs sur les années comprises dans le tableau. Une classification différente est effectuée pour les importations et les exportations. La ventilation en pourcentage est également indiquée pour les zones d'origine et de destination et pour les 10 premiers pays partenaires pour les dix plus récentes années. Les totaux pour l'Union européenne (UE) et l'Association européenne de Libre-Echange (AELE) sont calculés pour toutes les années sur la base des pays qui étaient membres en 1996 (quinze pays pour l'UE et trois pays pour l'AETE). Les totaux pour l'ancienne URSS comprennent l'ancienne URSS pour les années avant 1992 et l'agrégat des quinze républiques indépendantes à partir de 1992.

d) Tableaux 4 et 5, présentant les quantités et les valeurs en dollars des Etats-Unis des importations et des exportations par marchandises jusqu'aux quatre plus récentes années. Les chiffres sont publiés pour une marchandise donnée si sa valeur pour une année donnée est égale ou supérieure à 0,3 pour cent de la valeur totale pour ladite année. Les marchandises sont présentées selon les titres de la CTCI (en abrégé); lorsque les descriptions sont précédées d'un astérisque (*) cela indique que les chiffres donnés sont égaux à ceux du niveau de la CTCI immédiatement supérieur qui dans ce cas n'est pas publié.

Parfois les données en dollars des tableaux décrits en (c) et (d) ci-dessus peuvent ne pas correspondre à celles en dollars des Etats Unis du tableau décrit en (a) ou à celles en monnaies nationales de ce tableau après l'application des facteurs de conversion. Les différences sont dues pour la plupart à des révisions au niveau du total du commerce qui parfois ne sont pas disponibles à un plus grand niveau de détail par produit et partenaire et qui n'ont donc pas été apportées aux tableaux décrits en (c) et (d).

Pour tous les pays, les données présentées aux tableaux 3, 4 et 5 sont fondées sur la Classification type du commerce international (CTCI)[5/], Révision 2.. De nombreux pays déclarent leurs données fondées sur la CTCI, Révision 3 ou le Système harmonisé de désignation et de codification des marchandises (SH). Les données ainsi déclarées ont été converties en CTCI, Révision 2. C'est une conversion difficile qui, pour certains codes de la CTCI, Révision 2 produit des données qui ne sont pas comparables avec celles déclarées en termes de CTCI, Révision 2, de façon très substantielle.

Dans quelques cas, la conversion en CTCI à partir des nomenclatures nationales n'ayant pu se faire avec suffisante précision, certains codes de la CTCI ne couvrent pas exactement les échanges qui devraient leur être imputables.

Lorsqu'elles sont disponibles, des données plus détaillées par produit et pays partenaire du commerce extérieur, en CTCI, révisée, en CTCI, Révision 2 ou en CTCI, Révision 3 sont publiées dans Commodity Trade Statistics[6/] sous forme de microfiches.

Des descriptions détaillées des concepts et définitions actuels appliqués par les pays sont disponibles dans le document miméographé des Nations Unies "Pratiques nationales en matière de statistiques du commerce international des marchandises (ST/ESA/STAT/112), publié en février 1996 et disponible auprès de la Division de statistique des Nations Unies.

VOLUME II

Le volume II contient des tableaux présentant le commerce total de certains produits de base, analysé par régions et pays. Les régions aux noms identiques ont la même composition que celles du Volume I. Dans le volume II Eur. E.l'Est & l'URSS ex. l'en-tête désigne l'Europe sauf l'Europe de l'Est et l'ancienne URSS.

Tableaux par produits. Ces tableaux comprennent les importations et les exportations au niveau du groupe à 3 chiffres de la CTCI, Révision 2, (tous les groupes à l'exception de 351, 675 et 688). Les années couvertes sont les cinq années de 1992 à 1996. Les valeurs sont exprimées en dollars des Etats-Unis et les échanges sont analysés par pays et régions. Dans ces tableaux figurent les 50 pays les plus importants classés selon la somme des valeurs sur les années 1993, 1994 et 1995 inclus dans le tableau. Les quantités ne figurent pas dans ces tableaux.

Lors de la préparation de ces tableaux, on a eu recours à des estimations pour les pays dont les données n'étaient pas encore disponibles et ces estimations sont signalées par la lettre 'x'. Dans quelques cas, des estimations ont été faites pour certains pays qui ont été jugées adéquates pour être incluses dans les totaux régionaux et du monde mais non suffisamment élaborées pour être publiées séparément pour ces pays. Elles ont de ce fait été éliminées et remplacées par un 'x' dans les tableaux. A vrai dire, un 'x' devrait signaler que les totaux régionaux et du monde comprennent des estimations. Cependant, et en général, pratiquement tous les totaux régionaux et du monde comprennent des estimations. La lettre 'x' a été omise pour des raisons d'esthétique.

Le Volume II aussi fournit des tableaux spéciaux où est indiquée la contribution des échanges de chaque pays et région dans le commerce international. Les titres des tableaux spéciaux sont:

A. Importations et exportations totales par régions et pays ou zones;
B. Exportations mondiales p ar classes de marchandises et par régions;
C. Croissance des exportations mondiales par catégories de marchandises et par régions;
D. Structure des exportations mondiales par catégories de marchandises et par régions;
E. Importations et exportations totales: indices par pays ou zones;
F. Exportations et importations totales: indices du quantum, de la valeur unitaire et des termes de l'échange par régions;
G. Exportations des produits manufacturés;

H. Importations des produits énergétiques: pays à économies développées;
I. Quelques indicateurs sur les importations des produits énergétiques: pays à économies développées;
J. Indices des prix des exportations des matières premières et des métaux non-ferreux.

Tableaux spéciaux.

Les groupes économiques et géographiques dans tous les tableaux spéciaux sont conformes aux groupes de pays ou zones sont présentés dans le Tableau Spécial A de ce numéro, bien que le Tableau Spécial A comprend quelquefois plus de détails en ce qui concerne les sous-groupes géographiques. (Voir le Tableau Spécial A pour les détails).

(A) Importations et exportations totales par régions et pays ou zones. Les totaux régionaux, économiques et mondiaux, ont été ajustés: a) pour y inclure des estimations pour les données non disponibles; b) pour transformer le cas échéant les importations f.o.b. en importations c.a.f.; c) pour y inclure les pays ou zones pour lesquels il n'existe pas de liste séparée; d) pour ramener les données au commerce spécial; e) pour ramener les données à l'année civile; et f) autant que possible, éliminer les incompatibilités dues à des modifications géographiques pour obtenir des séries comparables par exemple, la union européenne et l'Association européenne de libre-échange. Les données pour chaque pays correspondent aux données en monnaie nationale sont présentés dans le tableau 1 des tableaux par pays. Les lettres des premières et dernières colonnes de ce tableau indiquent le système du commerce utilisé: G: Commerce général; S: Commerce spécial; Voir la fin du tableau pour les notes.

Le Bulletin Mensuel de Statistique présente des données mensuelles et trimestrielles.

(B) Exportations mondiales par classes de marchandises et par régions. Voir la fin du tableau pour la remarque générale et les notes.

(C) Croissance des exportations mondiales par catégories de marchandises et par régions. Les taux annuels de croissance ont tous été calculés à l'aide de la formule des intérêts composés:

$$r = \left(\sqrt[t]{\frac{Vn}{Vo}} - 1 \right) 100$$

r = Le taux annuel de croissance en pourcentage.
Vn = La valeur des exportations durant la dernière année de la période.
Vo = La valeur des exportations durant la première année de la période.
t = Le nombre d'années.

Voir la fin du Tableau Spécial D pour la remarque générale et les notes.

(D) Structure des exportations mondiales par catégories de marchandises et par régions. Les chiffres publiés sous le titre 'Origine des exportations' se réfèrent aux exportations de la région ou du pays indiqués dans la colonne zone. Il en est de même pour les 'Destinations des exportations'. Voir la fin du tableau pour la remarque générale et les notes.

(E) Importations et exportations totales: indices par pays ou zones. Sauf indication contraire, les indices de la valeur unitaire sont exprimés en monnaie nationale. Voir la fin du tableau pour la remarque générale et les notes.

Le Bulletin Mensuel de Statistique présente des données mensuelles et trimestrielles.

(F) Exportations et importations totales: indices du quantum, de la valeur unitaire et des termes de l'échange par régions. Voir la fin du tableau pour les notes.

Le Bulletin Mensuel de Statistique présente des données trimestrielles.

(G) Exportations des produits manufacturés. Voir la fin du tableau pour la remarque générale et les notes.

Le Bulletin Mensuel de Statistique présente des données trimestrielles.

(H) Importations des produits énergétiques: pays à économies développées. Voir la fin du tableau pour la remarque générale et les notes.

Le Bulletin Mensuel de Statistique présente des données trimestrielles.

(I) Quelques indicateurs sur les importations des produits énergétiques: pays à économies développées. Ce tableau indique la part des importations de combustibles dans la valeur totale des importations et des exportations ainsi que le rapport de l'indice de la valeur unitaire des produits manufacturés qu'ils exportent et de l'indice de la valeur unitaire des combustibles qu'ils importent. Voir la fin du tableau pour la remarque générale et les notes.

Le Bulletin Mensuel de Statistique présente des données trimestrielles.

(J) Indices des prix des exportations des matières et des métaux non-ferreux: économies de marché. Voir la fin du tableau pour la remarque générale et les notes.

Le Bulletin Mensuel de Statistique présente des données mensuelles et trimestrielles.

SOURCE ET PRESENTATION

Les données pour les Volumes I et II sont obtenues à partir de publications nationales, d'états soumis par les gouvernements pour cet ouvrage, autres publications des Nations Unies telles que: Bulletin Mensuel de Statistique, et Annuaire Statistique, et parfois de publications préparées par certaines agences spécialisées des Nations Unies. Des estimations pour quelques données faisant défaut sont préparées par la Division de Statistique des Nations Unies.

Les noms de pays et régions utilisés par divers pays pour leurs statistiques du commerce extérieur ne sont pas uniformes. Aussi, lorsque d'anciennes entités géographiques généralement indiquées dans les statistiques nationales ont changé, les pays peuvent avoir introduit les changements correspondants dans leurs statistiques à différentes époques. Dans la mesure du possible toutefois, les pays ou zones ont été désignés par leur nom actuel.

Sauf indication contraire, les groupements de pays sont conformes à ceux du Standard Country or Area Code for Statistical Use[4/] des Nations Unies.

INDICES NATIONAUX

Les indices nationaux, exprimés en monnaies nationales, ou en dollars des Etat Unis sont présentés dans le tableau 1. Ils indiquent les modifications dans le quantum et dans les prix (valeur unitaire) des agrégats des importations et des exportations. Chaque indice représente une modification entre la période à laquelle l'indice se réfère, la période courante, et une période fixe, la base de publication pour laquelle l'indice est représenté par 100. Pour faciliter les comparaisons, chaque fois qu'il était possible de le faire, les indices ont été ramenés à la base de publication 1990. Lorsque des modifications sont faites dans la couverture, la formule ou la période de base d'un indice, si cela est techniquement possible les deux séries s'enchaînent.

Les indices mensuels et trimestriels sont publiés dans le Bulletin Mensuel de Statistique des Nations Unies. On trouvera également dans le Supplément de 1977 à l'Annuaire Statistique et au Bulletin Mensuel de Statistique[7/] des notes plus détaillées sur les méthodes de calcul des indices nationaux.

PAYS EN TRANSITION

Pour la période couverte par l'Annuaire les pays classifiés antérieurement pour des raisons statistiques à économies planifiées centralement avaient un système de taux de change officiel entre leurs monnaies et celles des pays extérieurs consistant avec le taux de 0,90 nouveau roubles pour 1 dollar des Etats-Unis avant le 24 décembre 1971 et 0,829 jusqu'à février 1973; depuis cette date le taux a fluctué. Les pays d'Europe orientale utilisaient généralement ces taux lorsqu'il était nécessaire de convertir des devises en monnaie nationale pour préparer les statistiques du commerce extérieur. Les données qui en résultent permettent davantage une comparaison avec les transactions des autres pays qu'une comparaison avec les transactions monétaires intérieures.

Les statistiques du commerce extérieur de ces pays ont des définitions différentes de celles qui peuvent exister dans les autres pays. Les différentes définitions peuvent être la source des divergences observées pour le même flux de marchandise enregistré par deux pays partenaires ayant un système économique différent. Les échanges entre ces pays peuvent être conduits sur une base différente de celle qui régit les échanges entre autres pays. Le concept de la valeur de transaction, par exemple, est basé sur l'existence d'un prix de marché entre l'importateur et l'exportateur sur lequel les variations de l'offre et de la demande ont plus d'influence qu'ils ne peuvent en avoir dans les échanges de ces pays. Faute de données précises sur les valeurs unitaires des produits de base échangés entre ces pays, il est difficile de connaître les effets possibles de ces différences sur les statistiques du commerce extérieur. De plus en plus, depuis 1992, les pays en transition ont adopté les concepts et définitions pour la statistique du commerce international comparables à celles qui sont en vigueur dans les autres pays.

NOTE GENERALE[8/]

1. Territoire. Les statistiques rapportées par un pays s'appliquent en général au territoire douanier de cet état. Généralement territoire douanier et territoire géographique coïncident, le cas contraire étant indiqué dans les notes par pays. Les modifications dans le territoire douanier sont également indiquées dans les notes par pays. Sauf information contraire, l'unification de deux territoires séparés auparavant donne lieu à l'élimination des échanges entre ces deux territoires. Dans le cas d'une séparation d'un territoire en deux, les échanges entre ces deux territoires viennent à apparaître.

2. Système du commerce. Deux systèmes sont généralement utilisés ne différant que par la façon dont le commerce d'entrepôt et les réexportations sont enregistrés.

a) Commerce spécial. Les importations spéciales comprennent les marchandises entrées directement pour la consommation (y compris les transformations et réparations) et les marchandises sorties des entrepôts douaniers ou des zones franches pour être mises à la consommation. Les exportations spéciales comprennent les exportations de produits nationaux, c'est-à-dire les marchandises entièrement ou partiellement produites ou fabriquées dans le pays, ainsi que les exportations nationalisées (ces dernières sont des biens qui ayant été inclus dans les importations spéciales sont réexportés en l'état.)

b) Commerce général. Les importations générales comprennent les importations pour la consommation et les importations en entrepôt douanier ou en zone franche. Les exportations générales comprennent les exportations de produits nationaux et les réexportations. Ces dernières, dans le système du commerce général, comprennent les exportations nationalisées et les marchandises exportées des entrepôts douaniers et des zones franches sans avoir été transformées depuis leur importation.

Le transit direct, c'est-à-dire les marchandises uniquement transbordées ou traversant le pays pour des raisons de transport, est exclu du commerce général aussi bien que du commerce spécial.

Les titres de chaque tableau indiquent le système du commerce auquel se réfèrent les données. Des notes plus détaillées figurent, si nécessaire dans les notes par pays.

3. Evaluation. Lors de sa quinzième session en 1953, le Conseil Economique et Social, tenant compte du fait que les statistiques du commerce extérieur doivent refléter la réalité économique, a recommandé que les gouvernements des pays membres des Nations Unies utilisent, dans la mesure du possible, les valeurs de transaction en préparant leurs statistiques du commerce international ou qu'ils fournissent des informations supplémentaires basées sur les valeurs de transaction quand les politiques nationales font état d'autres valeurs (Résolution 469 B (XV) du Conseil Economique et Social). La valeur de transaction à l'importation est la valeur à laquelle les marchandises ont été achetées par l'importateur plus le coût de l'assurance et du fret jusqu'à la frontière des pays importateurs (valeur c.a.f.). A l'exportation, la valeur de transaction représente la valeur à laquelle les marchandises ont été vendues par l'exportateur y compris le coût de l'assurance du transport pour amener les marchandises à la frontière des pays exportateurs (valeur f.o.b.).

4. Conversion des monnaies. Pour les données dans cet Annuaire la conversion des valeurs nationales en dollars des Etats-Unis est effectuée au moyen de taux de conversion basés sur les taux de change officiels. Pour les monnaies sujettes à de larges marges de fluctuations par rapport au dollar, dont le nombre s'est accru considérablement depuis 1971, on utilise des moyennes pondérées des taux de change calculées spécialement dans ce but. La moyenne pondérée est le résultat des taux de change mensuels, généralement fournis par le Fonds Monétaire International, pondérés par les valeurs des importations et des exportations correspondantes. Les facteurs de conversion s'appliquent aux totaux des échanges mais pas nécessairement aux importations ou à l'exportation d'une marchandise donnée.

5. Marchandises. Dans la défin ition du commerce extérieur on entend par marchandises tous les biens dont l'importation ou l'exportation contribue à l'accroissement ou à la diminution du stock des ressources matérielles dans un pays. Sauf information contraire dans les notes par pays, le traitement des catégories de marchandises suit les règles énoncées ci-dessous:

a) Or. L'or dans le commerce international se présente sous trois formes:

i) Pièces d'or et lingots y compris l'or monétaire;
ii) Or non raffiné y compris les minerais et les concentrés;
iii) Or semi-ouvré dont la valeur de l'or représente au moins 80% de la valeur totale, y compris la limaille et les poussières et les formes primaires telles que feuilles et barres et les alliages d'or.

De ces différents types d'or, l'or monétaire est exclu du commerce des marchandises tandis que les autres types sont inclus, à l'exception de ceux indiqués ci-dessous. Tout transfert d'or entre les autorités monétaires doit être traité comme échange d'or monétaire, les autres échanges portant sur l'or sont classés comme or non-monétaire. A la différence de la CTCI, révisée, la CTCI, Révision 2, Révision 3, et le système harmonisé de désignation et de codification des marchandises, incluent l'or non- monétaire.

b) Minerai d'argent. Concentrés, lingots, pièces non émises, limailles et argent ouvré ou semi-ouvré sont tous inclus dans les échanges de marchandises.

c) Monnaie et titres de propriété. Pièces de monnaie d'argent et de métal, billets de banque et titres en circulation sont exclus du commerce. Les pièces, billets et titres non en circulation sont inclus à la valeur intrinsèque du papier ou du métal frappé.

d) Le commerce pour le compte de l'Etat. Il est inclus dans le commerce des marchandises. Les échanges au titre des programmes d'aide civile et militaire, les réparations de guerre et les équipements militaires[9/] sont donc inclus. Quand les marchandises sont destinées à des institutions nationales (ambassades ou forces armées) stationnées à l'étranger, elles ne sont pas comprises dans les statistiques.

e) Importations et exportations temporaires. Les effets des touristes et des voyageurs (y compris les véhicules) qui n'ont pas été acquis à l'étranger, les objets pour expositions ou études, les animaux pour la course ou la reproduction, les échantillons et les emballages en retour qui sont considérés comme devant être retournés dans un intervalle de temps assez court sont exclus.

f) Trafic de perfectionnement et de réparation. Les pays qui envoient à l'étranger temporairement des marchandises pour réparation ou complément d'ouvraison effectuent un trafic passif de réparation. Les pays recevant des marchandises dans les mêmes conditions effectuent un trafic actif de réparation. Les mouvements d'entrée et de sortie sont généralement exclus des importations et des exportations.

g) Commerce par poste. Il est inclus dans le commerce des marchandises.

h) Poisson. Le poisson et les épaves débarqués dans des ports étrangers par des navires nationaux et ceux débarqués dans des ports du pays par des navires étrangers sont exclus des statistiques.

i) Vente et achat de navires et d'aéronefs. La vente et l'achat de navires et d'aéronefs neufs sont inclus. Les navires et les aéronefs d'occasion inscrits sur le registre d'immatriculation du pays ou radiés de ce registre sont exclus du commerce quand ces mouvements sont dûs à un transfert de propriété.

j) Avitaillement des navires et des avions. Ils doivent être généralement inclus dans les exportations de marchandises.

6. Pays Partenaire. Les pays partenaires peuvent être distingués: a) à l'importation, suivant: l'origine ou la production, la consignation ou la provenance ou l'achat; b) à l'exportation, suivant: la consommation, la dernière destination connue ou la vente.

7. Echanges par produits. L'analyse est selon la Classification Type pour le Commerce International.

CLASSIFICATION TYPE POUR LE COMMERCE INTERNATIONAL (CTCI) ET UN SYSTEME HARMONISE DE DESIGNATION ET DE CODIFICATION DES MARCHANDISES (SH)

En juillet 1950, le Conseil Economique et Social des Nations Unies, sur avis de la Commission de Statistique, a recommandé aux pays de rassembler leurs statistiques des échanges par produits selon la CTCI originale[5/] afin de disposer au niveau mondial de données comparables pour l'analyse du commerce extérieur. La CTCI originale a été préparée par le Secrétariat des Nations Unies avec l'aide d'experts et en coopération avec les gouvernements et les organisations internationales concernées.

En mai 1960 la Commission de Statistique a approuvé une révision de la CTCI appelée la CTCI, révisée, qui tenait compte des modifications dans les courants commerciaux intervenus depuis 1950 et qui permettait un passage plus facile entre la CTCI et les nomenclatures internationales. La CTCI, révisée présentait selon une classification statistique les positions de la nomenclature tarifaire NCCD du Conseil de Coopération Douanière.

La CTCI, révisée comprend 625 sous-groupes (identifiés par un code à quatre chiffres) qui correspondent pour l'essentiel aux postes de la CTCI originale. Un certain nombre de sous-groupes ont été subdivisés soit pour obtenir des détails supplémentaires soit pour assurer une concordance exacte avec la NCCD. La CTCI, révisée comporte donc 1312 rubriques de base (niveau des 5 chiffres de la CTCI). Les sous-groupes sont rassemblés en 177 groupes, 56 divisions et 10 sections.

Les positions de la CTCI sont individualisées par leur numéro de code. Le contenu précis de chaque code est défini dans la CTCI, révisée. Si l'on compare les données selon la CTCI, révisée avec des données classées selon une nomenclature nationale, il faut tenir compte de ce que la même description, généralement abrégée, peut s'appliquer à des groupes de marchandises légèrement différents.

La révision de 1960 représentait par rapport à la CTCI initiale une amélioration considérable. Néanmoins vers la fin des années 1960 on a constaté que, pour l'essentiel, les raisons qui avaient conduit à l'établissement de la CTCI puis à sa première révision, se retrouvaient à nouveau valables. Depuis 1960 le volume des échanges commerciaux s'est accru rapidement tandis que leur répartition géographique et leur composition par produits se modifiaient radicalement. Une nouvelle révision de la CTCI fut donc entreprise. En octobre 1974, la Commission Statistique a approuvé cette révision, la désignation de la nouvelle révision est CTCI, Révision 2[5/]. En mai 1975 le Conseil Economique et Social a recommandé aux Etats membres des Nations Unies de communiquer les données sur les statistiques du commerce extérieur en se conformant autant que possible et le plus tôt possible à la CTCI, Révision 2. A partir des données pour 1976, certains pays ont commencé à communiquer leurs données selon la CTCI, Révision 2.

Il y avait entre les titres de base de la Classification type pour le commerce international, Révision 2 et les subdivisions de la Nomenclature du Conseil de Coopération Douanière une correspondance biunivoque. Toutefois, un certain nombre d'utilisateurs ont estimé que les subdivisions des positions de la NCCD (et par conséquent celles de la CTCI, Révision 2) ne suffisaient pas à leurs besoins[10/]. La nécessité d'une harmonisation des classifications économiques a également été signalée[11/]. En partie pour répondre à ces besoins, le Conseil de coopération douanière a assumé en mai 1973 la responsabilité d'élaborer et de mettre au point un système harmonisé de désignation et de codification des marchandises (SH)[12/].

A sa vingt et unième session, en janvier 1981, la Commission de statistique a pris note du fait qu'une troisième révision de la CTCI devait être disponible lorsque la NCCD révisée et le SH entreraient tous deux en vigueur[13/]. En conséquence, dans le courant de la même année, le Secrétariat de l'ONU a commencé à travailler à la révision de la CTCI, Révision 2 en partant du principe que le maximum devait être fait pour en conserver le caractère général et la structure, tout en tenant compte de la nécessité de son harmonisation avec la NCCD révisée, avec la Classification internationale type, par industrie, de toutes les branches d'activité économique (CITI), Révision 3[14/] et avec une Classification des produits centrale (CPC)[15/] dont l'élaboration était menée conjointement par la Division de statistique des Nations Unies et l'Office statistique des Communautés européennes.

Le projet final a été révisé et approuvé par la Commission de statistique à sa vingt-troisième session, en février 1985[16/], et une résolution a été adoptée par le Conseil économique et social le 28 mai 1985 (résolution 1985/7) qui, inter-alia, a recommandé aux Etats Membres de communiquer des données sur les statistiques du commerce extérieur aux institutions internationales en se conformant autant que possible et le plus rapidement possible à la Classification type pour le commerce international (troisième version révisée).

Le système harmonisé de désignation et de codification des marchandises (appelé système harmonisé) (SH) a été adopté par le Conseil de coopération douanière en juin 1983, tandis que la Convention internationale sur le système harmonisé de désignation et de codification des marchandises (Convention SH) est entré en vigueur le ler janvier 1988 (SH88). Au ler 18 avril 1997, les parties contractantes étaient au nombre de 88 et 64 autres pays ou territoires ne figuraient pas parmi les parties contractantes, mais utilisaient le système harmonisé à des fins douanières/statistiques.

Lors de la vingt-septième session, qui s'est tenue à New York du 22 février au 3 mars 1993, la Commission de statistique des Nations Unies a recommandé "que les pays adoptent le SH pour l'établissement et la diffusion de leurs statistiques du commerce international"[17/].

Conformément au préambule à la Convention SH, qui reconnaissait l'importance d'une actualisation effective du système harmonisé compte tenu de l'évolution de la technologie ou des courants commerciaux internationaux, le système harmonisé est régulièrement passé en revue et corrigé. Lors de sa vingt-septième session, la Commission de statistique des Nations Unies a "recommendé que le Conseil de coopération douanière tienne pleinement compte des effets que les modifications proposées pourraient avoir sur le plan statistique et de prendre dûment en considération les besoins et les capacités des pays en développement"[18/]. Quelques corrections mineures du système harmonisé de 1988, résultant par ailleurs de la suppression d'un code à 6 chiffres, ont été introduites en 1992 (SH92). Une série plus complète de modifications a été adoptée en 1993 et celles-ci sont entrées en vigueur le ler janvier 1996 (SH96).

A sa vingt-huitième session (27 février - 3 mars 1995), la Commission de statistique a examiné les changements qu'il faudrait apporter à la troisième version révisée de la CTCI pour l'adapter au SH96. La Commission a décidé que les changements à apporter à la troisième version révisée de la CTCI pour préserver une parfaite correspondance avec le système harmonisé étaient simplement des modifications mineures. La Commission a donc décidé qu'il serait inutile de publier une quatrième version révisée de la CTCI[19/].

1/ Classification par grandes catégories économiques, (selon les définitions de la CTCI, révisée), Etudes statistiques, Série M N° 53, (publication des Nations Unies, numéro de vente 71.XVII.12).

2/ Classification des marchandises par origine industrielle (Relation entre la Classification type pour le commerce international et la Classification internationale type, par industrie, de toutes les branches d'activité économique), Etudes statistiques, Série M N° 43, (publication des Nations Unies, numéro de vente 66.XVII.7).

3/ Classification internationale type, par industrie, de toutes les branches d'activité économique (révisée), Etudes statistiques, Série M N° 4, Rev. 1. (publication des Nations Unies, numéro de vente 58.XVII.7).

4/ United Nations Standard Country Code, Statistical Papers, Series M N° 49, (United Nations publication, Sales No. E.70.XVII.13).

United Nations Standard Country or Area Code for Statistical Use, Statistical Papers, Series M N° 49, Rev. 1, (United Nations publication, Sales No. E.75.XVII.8).

Standard Country or Area Codes for Statistical Use, Statistical Papers Series M N° 49, Rev.2, (United Nations publication, Sales No. E.82.XVII.8).

Codes standard des pays et des zones à usage statistique, Documents statistiques, Series M N° 49, Rev. 3.

5/ Classification type pour le commerce international, (deuxième version révisée), Etudes statistiques, Série M N° 34/Rev. 2, (publication des Nations Unies, numéro de vente F.75.XVII.6).

Classification type pour le commerce international (troisième version révisée), Etudes statistiques, Série M N° 34/Rev. 3, (publication des Nations Unies, numéro de vente F.86.XVII.12).

6/ Commodity Trade Statistics, Sous forme de microfiches (CTS SER.D COM), présentent annuellement les échanges par origine et destination pour un grand nombre de positions de la CTCI, révisée, de la CTCI, Révision 2 et CTCI, Révision 3.

7/ Supplément de 1977 à l'Annuaire Statistique et au Bulletin mensuel de statistique, ST/ESA/STAT/SER.S/SUPPL.2, ST/ESA/STAT/SER.Q/SUPPL.2, (publication des Nations Unies, numéro de vente F.78.XVII.10).

8/ Le traitement des articles 1 à 7 est dérivé principalement de Statistiques du commerce international concepts et définitions, Etudes statistiques, Série M N° 52 Révision 1, (publication des Nations Unies, numéro de vente F.82.XVII.14).

9/ Les pays qui excluent l'équipement militaire utilisent des définitions différentes pour cette catégorie de marchandise, pour la majorité des pays cependant, armes et munitions constituent la plupart de l'équipement militaire exclu des statistiques.

10/ Groupe de travail commun Division de statistique de l'ONU - Office statistique des communautés européennes sur les nomenclatures au niveau mondial, "Système harmonisé de désignation et de codification des marchandises pour les besoins du commerce international" (UNSO/SOEC/1/2).

11/ Secrétariat de l'ONU, "L'harmonisation des classifications statistiques : compte rendu d'une réunion d'un groupe d'experts" (ST/ESA/STAT/78).

12/ Conseil de coopération douanière, "Système harmonisé de désignation et de codification des marchandises", 1985.

13/ Documents officiels du Conseil économique et social, 1981, Supplément N° 2. (E/1981/12).

14/ Classification International Type, par industrie, de toutes les branches d'activité économique, Etudes statistiques, Série M N° 4, Révision 3 (publication des Nations Unies, numéro de vente F.90.XVII.11).

15/ Classification centrale de produits (CPC) provisoire, Etudes statistiques, Série M N° 77 (publication des Nations Unies, numéro de vente F.91.XVII.7).

16/ Documents officiels du Conseil économique et social, 1985, Supplément N° 6 (E/1985/26), para. 57 (d).

17/ Documents officiels du Conseil économique et social, 1993, Supplément N° 6 (E/1993/26), para. 162 (d).

18/ Documents officiels du Conseil économique et social, 1993, Supplément N° 6 (E/1993/26), para. 162 (e).

19/ Documents officiels du Conseil économique et social, 1995, Supplément N° 8 (E/CN.3/1995/28), para. 19 (e).

1996 INTERNATIONAL TRADE STATISTICS YEARBOOK

VOLUME I

COUNTRY TABLES

ANNUAIRE DE STATISTIQUE DU COMMERCE INTERNATIONAL 1996

VOLUME I

TABLEAUX PAR PAYS

FOOTNOTES

Footnotes relating to each set of country tables are located at the bottom of Table 5.

NOTES

Les notes relatives à chaque ensemble de tableau par pays sont situées à la fin du tableau 5.

1. HISTORICAL SERIES, 1958–1995 GENERAL TRADE, IMPORTS C.I.F., EXPORTS F.O.B.
SERIES HISTORIQUES, 1958–1995 COMMERCE GENERAL, IMPORTATIONS C.A.F., EXPORTATIONS F.O.B

YEAR ANNEE	VALUE IN MILLION U.S. DOLLARS VALEUR EN MILLION U.S. DOLLARS MERCHANDISE –MARCHANDISE		GOLD –OR		CONVERSION FACTORS U.S. CENTS PER LEK FACTEURS DE CONVERSION CENTS E.U. PAR LEK		INDEX NUMBERS –INDICES QUANTUM		UNIT VALUE VALEUR UNITAIRE	
	IMPORTS	EXPORTS	IMPORTS	EXPORTS	IMPORTS	EXPORTS	IMPORTS	EXPORTS	IMPORTS	EXPORTS
1958	79.00	29.00								
1960	81.00	49.00								
1963	71.00	48.00								
1965	90.00	60.00								
1967	105.00	66.00								
1968	115.00	70.00								
1969	125.00	75.00								
1970	135.00	76.00								
1971	146.00	77.00								
1972	154.00	85.00								
1973	175.00	100.90								
1974	197.00	142.20								
1975	222.00	175.00								
1976	245.00	200.00								
1977	280.00	235.00								
1978	325.00	260.00								
1979	370.00	350.00								
1985	360.14	300.14								
1986	380.86	355.71								
1987	378.57	355.71								
1988	536.17	424.83								
1989	592.50	473.28								
1990	253.00	151.53								
1995	650.01	201.96								

2. IMPORTS BY BROAD ECONOMIC CATEGORY AND EXPORTS BY INDUSTRIAL ORIGIN. (PERCENTAGE OF TOTAL VALUE)
IMPORTATIONS PAR CATEGORIES ECONOMIQUES ET EXPORTATIONS PAR BRANCHE D'ACTIVITE.(EN POURCENTAGE DE LA VALEUR TOTALE)

IMPORTS – IMPORTATIONS

	1990	1991	1992	1993	1994	1995	1996
TOTAL IMPORTS–IMPORTATIONS TOTALES							
1 FOOD BEV–ALIMENTATION BOISSONS							
11 PRIMARY–PRODUITS DE BASE							
111 FOR INDUSTRY–POUR L'INDUSTRIE							
112 FOR HOUSEHOLDS–POUR LES MENAGES							
12 PROCESSED–PRODUITS ELABORES							
121 FOR INDUSTRY–POUR L'INDUSTRIE							
122 FOR HOUSEHOLDS–POUR LES MENAGES							
2 IND SUPPLIES–APPROV INDUSTRIELS							
21 PRIMARY–PRODUITS DE BASE							
22 PROCESSED–PRODUITS ELABORES							
3 FUELS–COMBUSTIBLES							
31 PRIMARY–PRODUITS DE BASE							
32 PROCESSED–PRODUITS ELABORES							
321 MOTOR SPIRIT–ESSENCE							
322 OTHER–AUTRES							
4 MACHINERY–EQUIPEMENT							
41 CAPITAL EQUIPMENT–MACHINES							
42 PARTS–PIECES ACCESSOIRES							
5 TRANSPORT–TRANSPORT							
51 PASSENGER CARS–AUTOMOBILES							
52 OTHER–AUTRES							
521 INDUSTRIAL–INDUSTRIELS							
522 NON INDUSTRIAL–NON INDUSTRIEL							
53 PARTS–PIECES ACCESSOIRES							
6 CONSUM GOODS–BIENS CONSOMMATION							
61 DURABLE–DURABLES							
62 SEMI DURABLE–SEMI DURABLES							
63 NON DURABLE–NON DURABLES							
7 GOODS NES–BIENS NDA							

EXPORTS – EXPORTATIONS

	1990	1991	1992	1993	1994	1995	1996
TOTAL EXPORTS–EXPORTATIONS TOTALES							
1 AGRICULTURE							
2 MINING QUARRY–INDUS EXTRACTIVES							
3 MANUFACTURING–IND MANUFACTUR							
31 FOOD BEV TOBACCO–ALIM BOISS TAB							
32 TEXTILES–INDUSTRIES TEXTILES							
33 WOOD & PRODUCTS–BOIS & PRODUITS							
34 PAPER & PRODUCTS–PAPIER & PRODT							
35 CHEMICALS–INDUSTRIES CHIMIQUES							
36 NON METAL MIN–MIN NON METAL							
37 BASIC METAL–IND METAL BASE							
38 METAL MANUF–MANUF METAL							
39 OTH MANUF IND–AUTRES MANUF							

3. TRADE BY PRINCIPAL COUNTRIES OF ORIGIN AND DESTINATION (VALUE IN THOUSAND U.S. DOLLARS)
ECHANGES SELON LES PRINCIPAUX PAYS D'ORIGINE ET DE DESTINATION (VALEUR EN MILLIERS DE DOLLARS EU)

COUNTRIES–PAYS	GENERAL IMPORTS C.I.F. IMPORTATIONS GENERALES C.A.F 1985	1986	1987	1988	1989
World	360142	380857	378571	536168	592500
Africa		857	6714	9667	7031
Americas					
Northern America					
LAIA					
CACM					
Caribbean					
Rest of America					
As.ex F.USSR	8429	16857	29571	50833	33281
Eur.x F.USSR	312000	324714	313714	408501	468906
EU	97571	83000	86571	131167	197656
EFTA					
East Europe	174143	189571	190286	254501	242969
Other Europe					
Former USSR					
Oceania					
Czechoslovakia	41000	47000	54571	60333	51562
Romania/Roumanie	40000	32429	35714	43167	41406
Fm Yugoslav	40286	52143	36857	22833	28281
Bulgaria/Bulgarie	14286	30714	30143	49667	43281
Germany/Allemagne	23429	27571	25429	32667	55312
Former GDR	23571	22286	24429	39333	50625
Poland/Pologne	30143	28714	24000	37167	35937
Italy/Italie	16571	17857	20571	38667	51719
Greece/Grèce	26857	14429	13714	26167	42969
China/Chine	7143	15143	27714	46833	26094
Hungary/Hongrie	25143	28429	21429	24833	20156
Austria/Autriche	9143	9429	9857	13667	22344
Netherlands/Pays–Bas	5857	7143	9143	12333	15000
France, Monac	15714	6571	7857	7667	10312
Egypt/Egypte		857	6714	9667	7031
Turkey/Turquie	429	571	1286	3333	6094
Japan/Japon	857	1143	571	667	1094

COUNTRIES–PAYS	GENERAL EXPORTS F.O.B. EXPORTATIONS GENERALES F.O.B. 1985	1986	1987	1988	1989
Monde	300143	355714	355714	424834	473281
Afrique	143	3714	5429	5167	5312
Amériques					
Amérique du Nord					
ALAI					
MCAC					
Caraïbes					
Autre Amérique					
Asie l'URSS exclus	16000	22286	27714	30167	35937
Europe l'URSS exclus	238428	276285	279714	328834	363594
UE	44286	60143	68714	82667	101875
AELE					
Europe de l'Est	155000	166571	171428	216000	238437
Autre de l'Europe					
Ancienne URSS					
Océanie					
Czechoslovakia	37000	43000	44000	42833	54062
Fm Yugoslav	39143	49571	39571	30167	23281
Romania/Roumanie	28857	33714	33143	41167	42969
Bulgaria/Bulgarie	15857	26714	26714	39833	48906
Former GDR	22286	20143	24143	34833	43437
Poland/Pologne	25000	25000	21429	32000	31562
Hungary/Hongrie	26000	18000	22000	25333	17500
Italy/Italie	5857	12286	15571	26833	37187
China/Chine	6429	17571	21571	21833	26719
Greece/Grèce	16714	24286	19429	7833	14062
Germany/Allemagne	10714	11429	14143	18167	23125
Austria/Autriche	5429	5286	12571	22833	19375
France, Monac	5571	6857	7000	7000	8125
Japan/Japon	8571	4429	5571	7667	8125
Egypt/Egypte	143	3714	5429	5167	5312
Turkey/Turquie	1000	286	571	667	1094

(VALUE AS PERCENTAGE OF WORLD TOTAL)(VALEURS EN POURCENTAGE DU TOTAL MONDIAL)

	1980	1981	1982	1983	1984	1985	1986	1987	1988	1989
Africa							0.2	1.8	1.8	1.2
Americas										
Northern America										
LAIA										
CACM										
Caribbean										
Rest of America										
As.ex F.USSR						2.3	4.4	7.8	9.5	5.6
Eur.x F.USSR						86.6	85.3	82.9	76.2	79.1
EU						27.1	21.8	22.9	24.5	33.4
EFTA										
East Europe						48.4	49.8	50.3	47.5	41.0
Other Europe										
Former USSR										
Oceania										
Czechoslovakia						11.4	12.3	14.4	11.3	8.7
Romania/Roumanie						11.1	8.5	9.4	8.1	7.0
Fm Yugoslav						11.2	13.7	9.7	4.3	4.8
Bulgaria/Bulgarie						4.0	8.1	8.0	9.3	7.3
Germany/Allemagne						6.5	7.2	6.7	6.1	9.3
Former GDR						6.5	5.9	6.5	7.3	8.5
Poland/Pologne						8.4	7.5	6.3	6.9	6.1
Italy/Italie						4.6	4.7	5.4	7.2	8.7
Greece/Grèce						7.5	3.8	3.6	4.9	7.3
China/Chine						2.0	4.0	7.3	8.7	4.4

	1980	1981	1982	1983	1984	1985	1986	1987	1988	1989
Afrique						0.0	1.0	1.5	1.2	1.1
Amériques										
Amérique du Nord										
ALAI										
MCAC										
Caraïbes										
Autre Amérique										
Asie l'URSS exclus						5.3	6.3	7.8	7.1	7.6
Europe l'URSS exclus						79.4	77.7	78.6	77.4	76.8
UE						14.8	16.9	19.3	19.5	21.5
AELE										
Europe de l'Est						51.6	46.8	48.2	50.8	50.4
Autre de l'Europe										
Ancienne URSS										
Océanie										
Czechoslovakia						12.3	12.1	12.4	10.1	11.4
Fm Yugoslav						13.0	13.9	11.1	7.1	4.9
Romania/Roumanie						9.6	9.5	9.3	9.7	9.1
Bulgaria/Bulgarie						5.3	7.5	7.5	9.4	10.3
Former GDR						7.4	5.7	6.8	8.2	9.2
Poland/Pologne						8.3	7.0	6.0	7.5	6.7
Hungary/Hongrie						8.7	5.1	6.2	6.0	3.7
Italy/Italie						2.0	3.5	4.4	6.3	7.9
China/Chine						2.1	4.9	6.1	5.1	5.6
Greece/Grèce						5.6	6.8	5.5	1.8	3.0

4. General Imports C.I.F. by Commodities according to the S.I.T.C. (Rev. 2) in thousand U.S. Dollars
Importations Générales C.A.F. par Produits d'après la C.T.C.I. (Rév. 2) en milliers de Dollars E.U.

SITC CTCI	COMMODITY	1986 WEIGHT POIDS	1986 VALUE VALEUR	1987 WEIGHT POIDS	1987 VALUE VALEUR	1988 WEIGHT POIDS	1988 VALUE VALEUR	1989 WEIGHT POIDS	1989 VALUE VALEUR	PRODUIT
	ALL COMMODITIES		380857		378571		536168		592500	TOUS PRODUITS

5. General Exports F.O.B. by Commodities according to the S.I.T.C. (Rev. 2) in thousand U.S. Dollars
Exportations Générales F.O.B. par Produits d'après la C.T.C.I. (Rév. 2) en milliers de Dollars E.U.

SITC CTCI	COMMODITY	1986		1987		1988		1989		PRODUIT
		WEIGHT POIDS	VALUE VALEUR	WEIGHT POIDS	VALUE VALEUR	WEIGHT POIDS	VALUE VALEUR	WEIGHT POIDS	VALUE VALEUR	
	ALL COMMODITIES		355714		355714		424834		473281	TOUS PRODUITS

1. HISTORICAL SERIES, 1960–1995 SPECIAL TRADE, IMPORTS C.I.F., EXPORTS F.O.B.
SERIES HISTORIQUES, 1960–1995 COMMERCE SPECIAL, IMPORTATIONS C.A.F., EXPORTATIONS F.O.B

YEAR ANNEE	VALUE IN MILLION ALGERIAN DINARS VALEUR EN MILLION ALGERIAN DINARS MERCHANDISE –MARCHANDISE		GOLD –OR		CONVERSION FACTORS U.S. CENTS PER ALGERIAN DINAR FACTEURS DE CONVERSION CENTS E.U. PAR ALGERIAN DINAR		INDEX NUMBERS –INDICES QUANTUM		UNIT VALUE VALEUR UNITAIRE	
	IMPORTS	EXPORTS	IMPORTS	EXPORTS	IMPORTS	EXPORTS	IMPORTS	EXPORTS	IMPORTS	EXPORTS
1960	6241.40	1946.00	3.50	0.50	20.2600	20.2600				
1961	5054.50	1814.00	2.50	6.40	20.2600	20.2600				
1962	1938.30	948.70	0.50		20.2600	20.2600				
1963	3371.70	3746.20			20.2600	20.2600				
1964	3471.20	3588.80	0.20		20.2600	20.2600				
1965	3309.40	3145.80			20.2600	20.2600				
1966	3152.90	3067.20			20.2600	20.2600				
1967	3154.10	3571.80			20.2600	20.2600				
1968	4022.60	4097.90			20.2600	20.2600				
1969	4981.10	4610.70			20.2600	20.2600				
1970	6204.80	4980.40			20.2600	20.2600				
1971	6027.90	4207.60			20.3615	20.3615				
1972	6693.60	5853.80			22.3062	22.3080				
1973	9535.00	7478.60			25.4507	25.4863				
1974	17754.00	19584.00			23.9914	23.9273				
1975	23755.10	18563.00			25.2517	25.3113				
1976	22226.70	22205.00			24.0283	24.0259				
1977	29534.50	25356.00			24.1245	24.1339				
1978	34437.00	25125.00			25.2102	25.2497				
1979	32376.10	36870.00			26.0332	26.2131				
1980	40519.00	59952.80			26.0221	26.0512				
1981	48636.60	57383.50			23.2238	23.2127				
1982	49311.60	52699.50			21.7621	21.6594				
1983	49781.60	53457.10			20.8857	20.9086				
1984	51257.10	59106.50			20.0731	20.1089				
1985	49491.40	51027.70			19.8847	19.8884				
1986	43393.34	36828.02			21.2804	21.2625				
1987	34152.99	41736.00			20.5768	20.5203				
1988	43426.99	45420.99			17.0384	16.9678				
1989	70072.00	71936.99			13.1423	13.1423				
1990	87018.00	114392.00			11.0017	11.0804				
1991	139241.00	233589.00			5.3416	5.4186				
1992	188406.00	243087.00			4.5903	4.5815				
1993	181389.50	238817.80			4.2836	4.2836				
1994	328402.90	306820.30			2.8532	2.8942				
1995	487585.70	488517.80			2.1022	2.0961				

2. IMPORTS BY BROAD ECONOMIC CATEGORY AND EXPORTS BY INDUSTRIAL ORIGIN. (PERCENTAGE OF TOTAL VALUE)
IMPORTATIONS PAR CATEGORIES ECONOMIQUES ET EXPORTATIONS PAR BRANCHE D'ACTIVITE.(EN POURCENTAGE DE LA VALEUR TOTALE)

IMPORTS – IMPORTATIONS

	1990	1991	1992	1993	1994	1995	1996
TOTAL IMPORTS–IMPORTATIONS TOTALES	100.	100.	100.	100.	100.	100.	
1 FOOD BEV–ALIMENTATION BOISSONS	19.4	21.7	25.5	23.9	29.1	26.6	
11 PRIMARY–PRODUITS DE BASE	8.1	8.1	9.5	7.4	13.4	11.4	
111 FOR INDUSTRY–POUR L'INDUSTRIE	6.0	5.6	5.3	6.5	11.3	9.0	
112 FOR HOUSEHOLDS–POUR LES MENAGES	2.1	2.5	4.2	0.9	2.1	2.3	
12 PROCESSED–PRODUITS ELABORES	11.3	13.6	16.0	16.5	15.7	15.3	
121 FOR INDUSTRY–POUR L'INDUSTRIE	2.4	3.0	7.0	7.7	6.5	5.6	
122 FOR HOUSEHOLDS–POUR LES MENAGES	9.0	10.6	9.0	8.7	9.2	9.7	
2 IND SUPPLIES–APPROV INDUSTRIELS	30.8	35.0	33.1	34.0	33.5	31.1	
21 PRIMARY–PRODUITS DE BASE	3.5	3.6	3.8	3.7	4.0	2.6	
22 PROCESSED–PRODUITS ELABORES	27.4	31.3	29.3	30.3	29.4	28.5	
3 FUELS–COMBUSTIBLES	1.0	2.4	1.3	1.3	0.5	1.0	
31 PRIMARY–PRODUITS DE BASE	0.7	0.8	0.6	0.8	0.2	0.4	
32 PROCESSED–PRODUITS ELABORES	0.3	1.5	0.7	0.5	0.3	0.6	
321 MOTOR SPIRIT–ESSENCE	0.0	0.0	0.0	0.0	0.0	0.0	
322 OTHER–AUTRES	0.3	1.5	0.7	0.5	0.3	0.6	
4 MACHINERY–EQUIPEMENT	29.0	28.7	24.7	25.8	22.3	25.2	
41 CAPITAL EQUIPMENT–MACHINES	25.1	24.9	21.1	22.0	18.3	19.9	
42 PARTS–PIECES ACCESSOIRES	3.9	3.8	3.6	3.8	4.0	5.3	
5 TRANSPORT–TRANSPORT	14.9	7.9	7.3	7.3	6.7	7.3	
51 PASSENGER CARS–AUTOMOBILES	0.6	0.5	1.2	1.2	0.7	1.4	
52 OTHER–AUTRES	5.9	2.6	2.2	1.9	1.8	1.5	
521 INDUSTRIAL–INDUSTRIELS	5.9	2.6	2.2	1.8	1.8	1.4	
522 NON INDUSTRIAL–NON INDUSTRIEL	0.0	0.0	0.0	0.1	0.0	0.0	
53 PARTS–PIECES ACCESSOIRES	8.4	4.8	3.9	4.3	4.2	4.4	
6 CONSUM GOODS–BIENS CONSOMMATION	4.8	4.3	8.0	7.6	7.9	8.7	
61 DURABLE–DURABLES	0.6	0.6	1.7	1.7	1.0	1.3	
62 SEMI DURABLE–SEMI DURABLES	0.5	0.7	1.0	1.5	1.2	1.6	
63 NON DURABLE–NON DURABLES	3.8	2.9	5.3	4.5	5.6	5.7	
7 GOODS NES–BIENS NDA	0.0	0.0	0.1	0.0	0.1	0.1	

EXPORTS – EXPORTATIONS

	1990	1991	1992	1993	1994	1995	1996
TOTAL EXPORTS–EXPORTATIONS TOTALES	100.	100.	100.	100.	100.	100.	
1 AGRICULTURE	0.2	0.2	0.6	0.6	0.2	0.9	
2 MINING QUARRY–INDUS EXTRACTIVES	75.8	77.2	76.1	77.2	77.0	76.6	
3 MANUFACTURING–IND MANUFACTUR	24.0	22.6	23.3	22.2	22.8	22.5	
31 FOOD BEV TOBACCO–ALIM BOISS TAB	0.3	0.3	0.1	0.4	0.2	0.3	
32 TEXTILES–INDUSTRIES TEXTILES	0.4	0.3	0.1	0.3	0.1	0.4	
33 WOOD & PRODUCTS–BOIS & PRODUITS	0.1	0.1	0.1	0.0	0.0	0.0	
34 PAPER & PRODUCTS–PAPIER & PRODT	0.0	0.0	0.0	0.0	0.0	0.0	
35 CHEMICALS–INDUSTRIES CHIMIQUES	21.4	20.6	20.8	20.3	20.5	19.9	
36 NON METAL MIN–MIN NON METAL	0.0	0.0	0.0	0.0	0.0	0.0	
37 BASIC METAL–IND METAL BASE	0.8	0.5	0.6	0.7	0.7	1.0	
38 METAL MANUF–MANUF METAL	1.0	0.8	0.9	0.3	0.3	0.6	
39 OTH MANUF IND–AUTRES MANUF	0.0	0.0	0.6	0.1	0.9	0.1	

3. TRADE BY PRINCIPAL COUNTRIES OF PRODUCTION AND LAST CONSIGNMENT (VALUE IN THOUSAND U.S. DOLLARS)
ECHANGES SELON LES PRINCIPAUX PAYS DE PRODUCTION ET DE DERNIERE CONSIGNATION (VALEUR EN MILLIERS DE DOLLARS EU)

COUNTRIES–PAYS	SPECIAL IMPORTS C.I.F. IMPORTATIONS SPECIALES C.A.F					COUNTRIES–PAYS	SPECIAL EXPORTS F.O.B. EXPORTATIONS SPECIALES F.O.B.				
	1991	1992	1993	1994	1995		1991	1992	1993	1994	1995
World	7683298	8647832	8785287	9598686	9830584	Monde	11790026	11136803	10097666	8593807	8555509
Africa	240686	296588	303870	375259	275956	Afrique	217039	247166	191977	260063	213605
Americas	1172858	1319214	1719266	1976155	2039655	Amériques	2317956	1973482	2283905	1819910	1873714
Northern America	963234	1133750	1559632	1755021	1705576	Amérique du Nord	2037772	1586592	1766894	1588132	1631027
LAIA	153111	117186	110639	181809	264531	ALAI	269799	385989	506462	228819	241447
CACM	3210	3904	57	4667	10538	MCAC	0	762	19	0	
Caribbean	52753	63546	48796	30866	58771	Caraïbes	10354	110	10421	2957	1225
Rest of America	551	829	142	3791	239	Autre Amérique	31	29	110	0	15
As.ex F.USSR	748352	929563	1036025	1144573	1206252	Asie l'URSS exclus	293765	302409	311969	267466	528651
Eur.x F.USSR	5363009	5991251	5588859	5962551	6133576	Europe l'URSS exclus	8830751	8487496	7180587	6203497	5818322
EU	5020973	5752565	5397061	5730830	5829809	UE	8733037	8386145	7117904	6104888	5547535
EFTA	106741	118260	92542	118182	108992	AELE	3356	15520	8758	10581	115251
East Europe	140828	89124	87855	107255	173970	Europe de l'Est	29312	72932	36114	61153	106233
Other Europe	94467	126	55	92	4	Autre de l'Europe	65045	4843	4178	2529	41144
Former USSR	21252	12542	8708	53196	72608	Ancienne URSS	130515	126249	126341	42171	121217
Oceania	137141	98674	128560	86953	102537	Océanie	1		2887	700	
France, Monac	1584506	2097008	2240647	2376303	2449692	Italy/Italie	2794003	2414619	2219708	1535128	1918996
USA/Etats–Unis d'Amer	763583	954246	1311454	1371868	1292795	France, Monac	2215146	2037822	1688571	1326227	1202986
Italy/Italie	1186869	1242389	952076	931441	947342	USA/Etats–Unis d'Amer	2037633	1553403	1608691	1414039	1429388
Spain/Espagne	647121	832225	926222	901254	841921	Netherlands/Pays–Bas	991191	895998	784517	884999	889182
Germany/Allemagne	750717	752147	469100	517125	672218	Spain/Espagne	800143	846122	679235	650176	571537
Japan/Japon	371311	385029	375867	253990	333546	Belgium–Luxembourg	733495	795975	627835	528449	335686
Canada	199649	179501	247985	383118	412693	Germany/Allemagne	275079	524035	504192	524847	156779
Belgium–Luxembourg	253698	256677	164635	214660	225880	Brazil/Brésil	232235	351016	443760	195157	205959
Turkey/Turquie	188298	131017	108474	250404	278109	United Kingdom	308951	377425	192370	139996	186547
Austria/Autriche	120495	174719	172526	286574	200185	Portugal	237889	157830	284746	285041	130227
Indonesia/Indonésie	76282	55161	216520	240236	106359	Austria/Autriche	273748	206921	67183	161207	106301
China/Chine	9890	157060	120038	156453	230479	Canada	139	33189	158202	174093	201639
Netherlands/Pays–Bas	116653	121093	159496	109637	131877	Tunisia/Tunisie	101029	78305	62179	113063	99029
Tunisia/Tunisie	98650	123670	122484	138472	130192	Morocco/Maroc	50754	136506	70660	101348	74224
United Kingdom	104652	96884	119101	132021	141896	Turkey/Turquie	53714	27335	7216	49502	287475
Brazil/Brésil	87048	41041	79407	126420	123983	Russian Federation		126249	126341	40014	121094
Switz.Liecht	95648	87452	69810	91831	79465	Japan/Japon	81590	80088	48203	79459	60913
Morocco/Maroc	65019	96937	84777	120588	46940	Singapore/Singapour	34181	58095	154211	59936	42069
New Zealand	88629	59082	96728	76913	71053	Korea, Republic of	295	49544	34212	20703	111506
Sweden/Suède	93815	85073	71506	67548	74413	Greece/Grèce	47489	52386	45480	24597	32577
Cuba	52714	54258	48691	30586	45416	Bulgaria/Bulgarie	8103	54625	33382	40192	57451
Egypt/Egypte	5349	51531	48247	62360	53626	Sweden/Suède	38652	70917	19823	23271	4107
Korea, Republic of	25967	48752	42577	38449	42625	Paraguay	37555	22881	47248	27259	12122
Poland/Pologne	42294	27564	37301	48095	39532	Former USSR/Anc. URSS	130515				
Finland/Finlande	55663	19368	30890	21394	54365	Switz.Liecht	3295	1988	3143	4288	100667
Argentina/Argentine	31766	21661	7539	36664	60794	Mauritania/Mauritanie	29898	16239	31325	15810	18079
Australia/Australie	48512	37934	31803	9698	29060	Cyprus/Chypre	30721	22138	9410	14361	3144
Greece/Grèce	23171	13902	19795	69053	28134	Iran (Islamic Rp. of)	60290		10850		5
Portugal	20641	13032	38491	48371	27909	Yugoslavia/Yougoslavie		8057	13633	24345	8160
Denmark/Danemark	48480	38405	21357	22175	17198	Malta/Malte	160	3839	4178	2529	41144
Russian Federation		12528	8687	53196	69060	Poland/Pologne	939	1130	1804	15121	29949
Norway, SVD, JM	11005	30738	22732	26342	29508	Fm Yugoslav	46088				
Mexico/Mexique	32547	10572	5920	16034	55191	Liberia/Libéria	1	10105	10495	10126	12637
Viet Nam	5178	14936	13147	39118	41043	Thailand/Thaïlande	3529	23032	16620	0	
Syrian Arab Republic	22151	18143	11233	27178	28388	Norway, SVD, JM	61	13531	5605	6293	14584
Romania/Roumanie	9806	5097	5762	20435	58697	Egypt/Egypte	10969	1492	13570	5304	4977
Fm Yugoslav	94463					India/Inde	1347	1749	1633	26829	2637
Malaysia/Malaisie	4206	21143	36533	10547	13491	Finland/Finlande	8682	17		11263	12583
Ireland/Irlande	14491	9644	11221	33274	16778	Ecuador/Equateur		1823	14598	4611	9332
India/Inde	6091	13876	20294	28484	14779	Indonesia/Indonésie		23765	2926	1085	831
Hungary/Hongrie	28087	10202	8182	12459	23891	China/Chine	3856	1982	11349	3544	7317
Czechoslovakia	45394	34174				Denmark/Danemark	8559	5436	4243	9688	26
Bulgaria/Bulgarie	14948	12085	10039	16267	22685	Argentina/Argentine		10240			13496
Yugoslavia/Yougoslavie		31176	11346	6191	19587	Libyan Arab Jamahiriya	7131	2686	2540	7438	1867
Czech Republic			26500	9995	29162	Korea Dem People's Rp	1	13971		6657	
Saudi Arabia	3963	13175	15801	13786	14639	Romania/Roumanie	3074	2661	680	5797	8289
Cote d'Ivoire	28946	1314	14015	6245	10600	Hungary/Hongrie	5512	14516	229		
Singapore/Singapour	8178	21328	13022	2850	5969	Andorra/Andorre	18797	1004			
Peru/Pérou		23797	12457	2576	911	Un. Rep. of Tanzania	13039				
Jordan/Jordanie	883	2818	1599	19332	13087	Cuba	10300	68	1022		1225

(VALUE AS PERCENTAGE OF WORLD TOTAL)(VALEURS EN POURCENTAGE DU TOTAL MONDIAL)

	1986	1987	1988	1989	1990	1991	1992	1993	1994	1995		1986	1987	1988	1989	1990	1991	1992	1993	1994	1995
Africa	2.2	2.8	2.1	2.6	2.1	3.1	3.4	3.5	3.9	2.8	Afrique	0.6	1.7	2.4	1.9	2.6	1.8	2.2	1.9	3.0	2.5
Americas	14.0	14.0	16.9	19.3	17.6	15.3	15.3	19.6	20.6	20.7	Amériques	19.2	21.3	20.2	21.3	21.6	19.7	17.7	22.6	21.2	21.9
Northern America	9.9	8.9	13.2	15.5	14.8	12.5	13.1	17.8	18.3	17.3	Amérique du Nord	17.4	19.4	18.8	19.2	19.6	17.3	14.2	17.5	18.5	19.1
LAIA	3.8	4.9	3.0	2.8	2.0	2.0	1.4	1.3	1.9	2.7	ALAI	1.8	1.8	1.4	2.1	2.0	2.3	3.5	5.0	2.7	2.8
CACM	0.0	0.0		0.0	0.1	0.0	0.0	0.0	0.0	0.1	MCAC			0.0			0.0	0.0	0.0	0.0	
Caribbean	0.3	0.1	0.7	0.9	0.7	0.7	0.7	0.6	0.3	0.6	Caraïbes	0.0	0.1		0.0		0.1	0.0	0.1	0.0	0.0
Rest of America	0.0	0.1	0.0	0.0	0.0	0.0	0.0	0.0	0.0	0.0	Autre Amérique	0.0	0.0	0.0	0.0	0.1	0.0	0.0	0.0	0.0	0.0
As.ex F.USSR	8.7	10.4	9.1	10.3	8.7	9.7	10.7	11.8	11.9	12.3	Asie l'URSS exclus	2.6	3.2	5.1	4.7	3.6	2.5	2.7	3.1	3.1	6.2
Eur.x F.USSR	73.7	71.4	70.3	65.5	69.5	69.8	69.3	63.6	62.1	62.4	Europe l'URSS exclus	77.4	73.4	70.9	70.7	70.9	74.9	76.2	71.1	72.2	68.0
EU	67.7	65.1	63.5	58.5	64.3	65.3	66.5	61.4	59.7	59.3	UE	74.5	72.3	69.7	69.6	69.7	74.1	75.3	70.5	71.0	64.8
EFTA	2.0	1.5	1.9	1.5	1.3	1.4	1.4	1.1	1.2	1.1	AELE	0.0	0.2	0.1	0.4	0.0	0.0	0.1	0.1	0.1	1.3
East Europe	2.5	3.3	3.1	4.0	2.7	1.8	1.0	1.0	1.1	1.8	Europe de l'Est	0.9	0.3	1.0	0.6	0.3	0.2	0.7	0.4	0.7	1.2
Other Europe	1.5	1.6	1.6	1.5	1.1	1.2	0.0	0.0	0.0	0.0	Autre de l'Europe	1.9	0.6	0.0	0.1	0.8	0.6	0.0	0.0	0.0	0.5
Former USSR	0.2	0.4	0.8	1.8	1.0	0.3	0.1	0.1	0.6	0.7	Ancienne URSS	0.2	0.3	1.4	1.4	1.3	1.1	1.1	1.3	0.5	1.4
Oceania	1.2	1.0	0.9	0.4	1.1	1.8	1.1	1.5	0.9	1.0	Océanie	0.0	0.0	0.0	0.0	0.0	0.0		0.0	0.0	
France, Monac	24.0	22.9	18.9	17.4	23.1	20.6	24.2	25.5	24.8	24.9	Italy/Italie	19.9	15.3	17.1	20.5	20.5	23.7	21.7	22.0	17.9	22.4
USA/Etats–Unis d'Amer	7.7	7.0	10.8	12.0	11.5	9.9	11.0	14.9	14.3	13.2	France, Monac	21.6	22.1	19.6	18.6	17.3	18.8	18.3	16.7	15.4	14.1
Italy/Italie	12.9	11.2	10.0	13.3	12.3	15.4	14.4	10.8	9.7	9.6	USA/Etats–Unis d'Amer	17.4	19.2	18.7	19.1	19.2	17.3	13.9	15.9	16.5	16.7
Spain/Espagne	4.6	4.6	4.6	4.0	6.2	8.4	9.6	10.5	9.4	8.6	Netherlands/Pays–Bas	14.2	15.1	10.5	8.9	9.3	8.4	8.0	7.8	10.3	10.4
Germany/Allemagne	11.1	10.5	13.2	9.7	10.7	9.8	8.7	5.3	5.4	6.8	Spain/Espagne	5.7	4.4	6.2	5.5	6.0	6.8	7.6	6.7	7.6	6.7
Japan/Japon	4.6	3.9	4.3	3.8	4.6	4.8	4.5	4.3	2.6	3.4	Belgium–Luxembourg	6.3	6.4	7.1	7.0	6.9	6.2	7.1	6.2	6.1	3.9
Canada	2.2	1.9	2.4	3.5	3.3	2.6	2.1	2.8	4.0	4.2	Germany/Allemagne	3.2	4.1	4.4	4.2	2.1	2.3	4.7	5.0	6.1	1.8
Belgium–Luxembourg	3.0	4.5	4.5	3.2	3.7	3.3	3.0	1.9	2.2	2.3	Brazil/Brésil	1.4	1.3	0.9	1.7	1.5	2.0	3.2	4.4	2.3	2.4
Turkey/Turquie	2.2	2.3	2.9	2.9	2.1	2.5	1.5	1.2	2.6	2.8	United Kingdom	1.1	1.6	2.1	1.3	2.2	2.6	3.4	1.9	1.6	2.2
Austria/Autriche	2.6	2.2	3.1	2.1	1.5	1.6	2.0	2.0	3.0	2.0	Portugal	1.1	1.0	1.2	1.6	2.0	2.0	1.4	2.8	3.3	1.5

4. Special Imports C.I.F. by Commodities according to the S.I.T.C. (Rev. 2) in thousand U.S. Dollars
Importations Spéciales C.A.F. par Produits d'après la C.T.C.I. (Rév. 2) en milliers de Dollars E.U.

SITC CTCI	COMMODITY	1992 WEIGHT POIDS	1992 VALUE VALEUR	1993 WEIGHT POIDS	1993 VALUE VALEUR	1994 WEIGHT POIDS	1994 VALUE VALEUR	1995 WEIGHT POIDS	1995 VALUE VALEUR	PRODUIT
	ALL COMMODITIES		8647832		8785287		9598686		9830584	TOUS PRODUITS
0	FOOD AND LIVE ANIMALS		2121063		2155537		2848860		2462405	ALIMENTS,ANIMAUX VIVANTS
001	*LIVE ANIMALS FOR FOOD	W 21107	45572	W 5158	22168	W 6453	26558	W 5374	14433	ANIMAUX VIVANTS
01	MEAT AND PREPARATIONS		42918		25510		41232		57325	VIANDES ET PREPARATIONS
011	MEAT FRESH,CHILLD,FROZEN	W 19273	42859	W 20933	25311	W 20306	40987	W 30361	56963	VIANDES FRAICHES,REF,CONGE
0111	BOVINE MEAT FRESH,FROZEN	W 18293	40858	W 20921	25292	W 20256	40918	W 28138	52088	VIANDES BOVIN FRAI,REF
01112	BOVINE MEAT BONELESS	W 7384	18685	W 16868	18645	W 16457	33078	W 17545	32721	VIANDES BOVIN DESOSSEES
02	DAIRY PRODCTS,BIRDS'EGGS		641584		654023		540840		434792	PRODUITS LAITIERS,OEUFS
022	MILK AND CREAM	W 222244	558721	W 264174	569404	W 227923	493657	W 185762	374984	LAIT ET CREME
0223	MILK AND CREAM FRESH	W 61619	139199	W 4335	11586	W 4696	8596	W 1673	1595	LAIT,CREME FRAIS
0224	MILK,CREAM PRESERVED ETC	W 160625	419522	W 259839	557818	W 223226	485062	W 184089	373388	LAIT,CREME CONS,CONC
02242	MILK DRY,1.5% FAT OR LES	W 52509	130905	W 139265	282792	W 110766	197154	W 108108	210582	LAIT POUDRE INF 1.5%
02243	MILK DRY,OVER 1.5% FAT	W 103544	282353	W 118835	272936	W 112296	287572	W 74719	161291	LAIT POUDRE SUP 1.5%
023	BUTTER	W 32882	63868	W 38447	74010	W 22188	37343	W 21584	37078	BEURRE
04	CEREALS AND PREPARATIONS		772796		904191		1324087		1142234	CEREALES ET PRODUITS
041	WHEAT ETC UNMILLED	W 2329171	320911	W 2588227	353785	W 3511937	602387	W 3504679	662672	FROMENT,EPEAUTRE
0411	DURUM WHEAT UNMILLED	W 2180931	295228	W 2380941	327137	W 3297721	577062	W 3271708	617888	FROMENT DUR NON MOULU
0412	OTHER WHEAT ETC UNMILLED	W 148239	25683	W 207286	26648	W 214216	25325	W 232971	44785	AUTRE FROMENT NON MOULU
043	BARLEY UNMILLED	W 110223	16981	W 500169	70273	W 666566	113557	W 154986	15492	ORGE NON MONDEE
044	MAIZE UNMILLED	W 990785	136956	W 1154617	142493	W 1378024	186099	W 895146	121473	MAIS NON MOULU
046	WHEAT ETC MEAL OR FLOUR	W 1045768	231814	W 1130789	281254	W 1224556	323197	W 1116301	305986	SEMOULE FARINE,FROMENT
04601	FLOUR OF WHEAT OR MESLIN	W 235138	55716	W 385363	83958	W 585956	133075	W 762417	194646	FARINE DE FROMENT
04602	MEAL,GROATS OF WHEAT ETC	W 810630	176098	W 745426	197296	W 638599	190122	W 353885	111340	GRUAUX,SEMOULES FROMENT
047	OTHER CEREAL MEALS,FLOUR	W 183998	40943	W 63202	22247	W 38347	11187	W 15655	4418	AUTRES SEMOULES,FARINES
048	CEREAL ETC PREPARATIONS	W 13293	5827	W 14677	16686	W 40272	36058	W 35990	26168	PREPTNS A BASE CEREALES
05	VEGETABLES AND FRUIT		115527		38567		136654		192816	LEGUMES ET FRUITS
054	VEG ETC FRSH,SMPLY PRSVD	W 198708	103722		37326	W 315610	133534	W 254984	147066	LEGUMES FRAIS,CONG,SECS
0541	POTATOES FRSH EXCL SWEET	W 73685	30542	W 50579	13354	W 150778	55087	W 91324	35390	POMMES DE TERRE
0542	LEGUMINOUS VEGETBLES DRY	W 87358	38512	W 49510	22605	W 160089	74127	W 129824	76942	LEGUMES A COSSE SECS
0546	VEGETABLES SIMPLY PRESVD	W 36918	33288		560	W 3683	3666	W 33087	34023	LEGUMES CONG,CONSER
05461	VEGETABLES FROZEN	W 36918	33288		560	W 3683	3666	W 33072	34007	LEGUMES CONGELES
057	FRUIT,NUTS,FRESH,DRIED	W 16190	10754	W 1015	1164	W 3274	2925	W 43858	36263	FRUITS FRAIS OU SECS
06	SUGAR AND PREPS,HONEY		178314		253340		298135		295844	SUCRES ET PRODUITS
061	SUGAR AND HONEY	W 509935	177322	W 780922	253291	W 836921	297283	W 701550	290477	SUCRES ET MIEL
0611	RAW BEET AND CANE SUGAR	W 450405	158084	W 659798	216230	W 393884	107382	W 214688	87281	SUCRES BRUTS
0612	REFINED SUGAR ETC	W 47594	17138	W 93610	33411	W 415089	182359	W 472545	199063	SUCRES RAFFINES
07	COFFEE,TEA,COCOA,SPICES		165792		113925		336746		185304	CAFE,THE,CACAO,EPICES
071	COFFEE AND SUBSTITUTES	W 48614	56914	W 88203	105822	W 104446	308163	W 53673	158150	CAFE ET SUCCEDANES
0711	COFFEE GREEN,ROASTED,SUB	W 48563	56095	W 88203	105821	W 104391	307467	W 53624	157863	CAFE TORREFIE OU DECAFEINE
07111	COFFEE GREEN,HUSKS,SKINS	W 48560	56082	W 88195	105783	W 103722	306097	W 52273	153166	CAFE NON TORREFIE
074	TEA AND MATE	W 20980	94937	W 922	1955	W 8473	20096	W 3521	9764	THE ET MATE
0741	TEA	W 20980	94937	W 922	1955	W 8473	20096	W 3521	9764	THE
081	*FEEDING STUFF FOR ANIML	W 238397	66083	W 286990	89324	W 204138	65394	W 238157	54432	NOURRITURE POUR ANIMAUX
0813	OILCAKE AND OTH RESIDUES	W 235853	60823	W 284202	83987	W 200358	59328	W 234914	51140	TOURTEAUX
08131	— OF SOYA BEANS	W 235853	60823	W 284003	83913	W 200358	59328	W 234914	51138	TOURTEAUX DE SOJA
09	MISC EDIBLE PRODUCTS		92326		54277		77861		66556	PREP ALIMENTAIRES DIVERSES
091	MARGARINE AND SHORTENING	W 18534	19754	W 24123	25929	W 39392	39745	W 32623	33789	MARGARINE ET GRAISSES
0914	MARGARINE,EDIBLE FAT NES	W 18534	19754	W 24118	25920	W 39392	39745	W 32623	33789	MARGARINES,SIMILI SAINDOUX
09141	MARGARINE	W 18514	19723	W 24111	25913	W 34407	33952	W 31866	32913	MARGARINE
098	EDIBLE PRODCTS,PREPS NES	W 15744	72572	W 12369	28348	W 18453	38115	W 26964	32767	PREP ALIMENTAIRES NDA
09806	YEASTS,BAKING POWDERS	W 15320	70122	W 12074	26705	W 17666	35152	W 16852	29583	LEVURES
1	BEVERAGES AND TOBACCO		37218		45371		75806		76983	BOISSONS ET TABACS
12	TOBACCO AND MANUFACTURES		33306		44868		75341		63845	TABACS BRUTS FABRIQUES
121	TOBACCO UNMNFCTRD,REFUSE	W 14846	33276	W 23784	44867	W 29459	69324	W 22406	40930	TABACS BRUTS,DECHETS
1211	TOBACCO,NOT STRIPPED	W 14846	33276	W 23784	44867	W 29459	69324	W 22022	39844	TABACS NON ECOTES
2	CRUDE MATERLS,EXCL FUELS		330965		386024		378614		378628	MAT BRUTES NON COMESTIBLES
22	OIL SEEDS,OLEAGINOUS FRT		14222		18363		23486		35326	GRAINES,FRUITS OLEAGINEUX
222	SEEDS FOR'SOFT'FIXED OIL	W 22593	13367	W 22560	18006	W 25172	23028	W 33381	35147	GRAINES HUILES FIXES
2221	GROUNDNUTS,GREEN	W 21326	12099	W 21876	17172	W 24206	21231	W 32907	34634	ARACHIDES NON GRILLEES
24	CORK AND WOOD		93720		172480		168932		199413	LIEGE ET BOIS
248	WOOD SHAPED,SLEEPERS	W 148845	74063	W 375254	157484	W 335492	154559	W 384017	185210	BOIS SIMPLEMENT TRAVAILLES
2482	LUMBER SHAPED CONIFER	W 116918	60966	W 320546	136345	W 300218	137128	W 306973	144370	CONIFERES SCIES,RABOTES
24821	LUMBER SAWN ETC CONIFER	W 116905	60940	W 320510	136309	W 300204	137100	W 306869	144295	CONIFERES SCIES LONGITUD
2483	LUMBER SHAPED NON–CONIFR	W 28136	11799	W 54041	20646	W 34442	16816	W 76173	40279	NON CONIFERES SCIES,RABOTES
24831	LUMBER SAWN ETC NON–CON	W 28070	11720	W 53975	20573	W 34345	16722	W 76128	40212	SCIES LONGITUDINALEMENT
251	*PULP AND WASTE PAPER	W 50565	26809	W 54614	30183	W 57843	50019	W 38969	32526	PATES A PAPIER,DECHETS
2517	SODA,SULPHATE WOOD PULP	W 41387	22342	W 53244	28961	W 56638	49127	W 37577	31134	PATES CHIMIQUES AU SULFATE
25172	— BLEACHED,NONDISSOLVNG	W 28932	16348	W 33221	18824	W 31020	40561	W 30709	26117	PATES BLANCHIES
26	TEXTILE FIBRES AND WASTE		104522		100697		75774		54476	FIBRES TEXTILES
263	COTTON	W 25730	48168	W 27789	59647	W 24467	35697	W 14457	32777	COTON
2631	RAW COTTON,EXCL LINTERS	W 24120	46050	W 26233	57220	W 23170	34123	W 13346	26116	COTON EN MASSE
266	SYNTHETIC FIBRES TO SPIN	W 40322	50388	W 21798	36038	W 19722	37922	W 8007	17687	FIBRES SYNTHETIQUES
2665	DISCN SYNTH FIBRE UNCMBD	W 33635	35170	W 19186	30611	W 14327	27042	W 7164	15262	DISCONTINUES EN MASSE
27	CRUDE FERTLZR,MINRLS NES		27534		23504		24862		18092	ENGRAIS MINERAUX BRUTS
28	METALLIFEROUS ORES,SCRAP		37726		19140		9936		12903	MINERAIS METAL,DECHETS
287	BASE METAL ORES,CONC NES	W 63850	37451	W 46014	18805	W 9918	9837	W 6108	9792	MINERAIS METAUX COMMUNS
2875	ZINC ORES,CONCENTRATES	W 63768	37224	W 41929	17193	W 6566	2956	W 3498	1106	MINERAIS DE ZINC
3	MINERAL FUELS ETC		125132		126515		58540		108091	COMBUSTIBLES MINERAUX LUB
32	COAL,COKE AND BRIQUETTES		52025		70732		23131		42898	HOUILLES,COKES,BRIQUETTES
322	COAL,LIGNITE AND PEAT	W 803439	51991	W 1092054	70509	W 425326	23085	W 711526	42805	HOUILLES,LIGNITES,TOURBE
3222	OTH COAL,NOT AGGLOMERATD	W 802612	51457	W 1091555	70303	W 424543	22783	W 710364	42320	AUTRES HOUILLES
33	PETROLEUM AND PRODUCTS		73032		55704		35349		65066	PETROLE ET DERIVES
334	PETROLEUM PRODUCTS,REFIN		56980	W 420963	43958	W 255135	26610	W 400561	55675	PRODUITS RAFFINES
3345	LUBS,PETROLEUM OILS NES		34267	W 146444	19739	W 136913	16312	W 126016	29452	HUILES LUBRIFIANTES
33451	LUBS(HIGH PETR CONT) ETC		29519	W 145306	16378	W 135206	13697	W 124964	26834	HUILES LUBRIF,H LOURDES
4	ANIMAL,VEGETABLE OIL,FAT		292768		184222		222880		320767	HUILES,GRAISSES ANIM,VEG
411	*ANIMAL OILS AND FATS	W 47839	23884	W 48030	23269	W 51555	27333	W 74045	43836	HUILES,GRAISSES ANIMALES
4113	ANIML OIL,FAT,GREASE NES	W 39835	16400	W 42004	18616	W 43515	20636	W 59835	32569	HUILES,GRAISSES ANIMALES NDA
41132	FATS OF BOVINE,SHEEP,ETC	W 37340	15422	W 41980	18487	W 43401	20433	W 56750	31091	SUIFS BRUTS FONDUS
42	FIXED VEGETABLE OIL,FAT		248898		153089		188663		268800	HUILES VEGETALES FIXES
423	FIXED VEG OILS,SOFT	W 289592	227217	W 246521	115190	W 281951	176946	W 390525	254018	HUILES VEGET DOUCES FIXES
4232	SOYA BEAN OIL	W 57879	28677	W 177089	75642	W 177509	103644	W 116551	69879	HUILE DE SOJA
4236	SUNFLOWER SEED OIL	W 199436	181710	W 69415	39514	W 98642	69337	W 262077	175105	HUILE DE TOURNESOL
424	FIXED VEG OIL NONSOFT	W 58439	21682	W 76631	37899	W 21479	11716	W 28289	14782	AUTRES HUILES VEG FIXES
4242	PALM OIL	W 51323	17683	W 68519	34011	W 16757	8645	W 9668	7819	HUILE DE PALME
5	CHEMCLS,RELATED PROD NES		922339		895426		1027037		1094584	PRODUITS CHIMIQUES
51	ORGANIC CHEMICALS		74396		67933		67039		79874	PROD CHIMIQ ORGANIQUES
513	CARBOXYLIC ACIDS ETC	W 26378	31321	W 17552	21465	W 15048	17556	W 20284	34275	ACIDES CARBOXYLIQUES
52	INORGANIC CHEMICALS		89213		92075		79601		86902	PROD CHIM INORGANIQUES
522	INORG ELEMNTS,OXIDES,ETC		30512	W 27421	30101	W 30441	26259	W 28834	31812	ELEMENTS INORGANIQUES
523	OTHR INORG CHEMICALS ETC	W 192784	57736	W 173223	60785	W 165297	51927	W 166583	53913	AUT PRODUITS CHIMIQUES INORG

4. Special Imports C.I.F. by Commodities according to the S.I.T.C. (Rev. 2) in thousand U.S. Dollars
Importations Spéciales C.A.F. par Produits d'après la C.T.C.I. (Rév. 2) en milliers de Dollars E.U.

SITC CTCI	COMMODITY	1992 WEIGHT POIDS	1992 VALUE VALEUR	1993 WEIGHT POIDS	1993 VALUE VALEUR	1994 WEIGHT POIDS	1994 VALUE VALEUR	1995 WEIGHT POIDS	1995 VALUE VALEUR	PRODUIT
5232	OTH MTL CMPD OF INRG ACD	W 137941	36890	W 95907	38269	W 92549	33164	W 94624	36364	SELS METALLIQUES
52322	PHOSPHITES,PHOSPHATES	W 76073	20384	W 42674	26758	W 38407	20937	W 43401	24310	PHOSPHITES,PHOSPHATES
53	DYES,TANNING,COLOUR PROD		35835		40812		40661		40850	PROD TEINTURE,COLORANTS
541	*MEDICINAL,PHARM PRODUCT		442632	MK 27466	366734	MK 31804	509755	MK 37287	517558	PROD MEDICINAUX PHARMACEUT
5417	MEDICAMENTS	MK 31678	406638	MK 26470	334696	MK 30314	473931	MK 36102	460013	MEDICAMENTS
54171	— CONTAINNG ANTIBIOTICS	K 1262603	29834	K 977054	23807	K 2947719	81793	K 4512954	96011	MED CONTN ANTIBIOTIQUES
54172	— CONTAINING HORMONES	K 5979296	49875	K 128788	1926	K 435673	19072	K 506531	13065	MED CONTENANT HORMONES
54179	— CONTNG OTH SUBSTANCES	MK 23063	319315	MK 24404	303394	MK 25642	367173	MK 30551	348221	MED CONT AUT SUBSTANCES
55	PERFUME,CLEANING ETC PRD		17672		24253		25602		34083	PROD POUR PARFUM,TOILETTE
562	*FERTILIZERS,MANUFACTURE		12857	W 64673	14410	W 84194	17245	W 135852	31787	ENGRAIS MANUFACTURES
58	PLASTIC MATERIALS ETC		145638		134753		160053		172693	MAT PLAST ARTIFICIELLES
582	PROD OF CONDENSATION ETC	W 13555	26611	W 10167	19553	W 15557	25989	W 11712	25641	PROD CONDENS,POLYCOND
583	POLYMERIZATION ETC PRODS		94226		97662	W 82351	120047	W 89660	130050	PROD POLYMERISATION
5831	POLYETHYLENE	W 32874	42414	W 44322	41431	W 32143	27989	W 45783	57247	POLYETHYLENE
58311	— IN PRIMARY FORMS	W 27142	29260	W 41916	35951	W 30670	24742	W 38781	41105	POLYETHYLENE PRIMAIRES
5833	POLYSTYRENE,ITS COPOLYMR	W 13394	16469	W 6669	8616	W 11598	30289	W 7399	12809	POLYPROPYLENE COPOLYMERES
5839	OTH POLYMRZTION ETC PROD		12435	W 38385	22666	W 18445	35063	W 15011	28988	AUT PROD POLYMER COPOLYM
59	CHEMICAL MATERIALS NES		96643		143942		126177		126979	MAT PROD CHIMIQUES NDA
598	MISCEL CHEM PRODUCTS NES		65748		107403	W 53552	95066	W 35686	99418	PROD DIV INDUST CHIM NDA
5982	ANTI-KNOCK PREPARTNS ETC	W 13410	8612	W 7809	26070	W 8329	29288	W 5125	26958	PREPARAT ANTIDETONANTES
5989	CHEM PRODUCTS,PREPS NES	W 19865	52836		75606	W 42414	61326	W 28558	69049	PROD PREP CHIMIQUES NDA
59899	OTH CHEM PRODS,PREPS,NES	W 15289	38146		57622	W 37955	51338	W 24889	55217	AUT PRODUITS CHIMIQUES NDA
6	BASIC MANUFACTURES		1859310		1905565		2087434		2038112	ART MANUFACTURES
62	RUBBER MANUFACTURES NES		130353		180278		140829		164783	CAOUTCHOUC MANUFACTURE
625	RUBBER TYRES, TUBES ETC	W 23054	89481	W 43318	119295	W 51984	92262	W 56023	119199	PNEUS CAOUTCHOUC VULCANISE
6252	TYRES,NEW,BUS OR LORRY	W 11929	49716	W 25159	74051	W 13583	45390	W 29808	67557	PNEUS POUR AUTOBUS,CAMIONS
6259	OTH TYRES,TYRE CASES,ETC	W 7994	21905	W 12710	22734	W 31775	26096	W 17777	29542	AUTRES PNEUS RECHAPES FLAPS
628	RUBBER ARTICLES NES	W 3300	28164	W 2994	37957	W 3144	34851	W 3109	30706	OUVRAGES CAOUTCHOUC NDA
63	WOOD,CORK MANUFACTRS NES		39441		164558		77922		41537	OUVRAGES LIEGE ET BOIS
634	VENEERS,PLYWOOD,ETC	W 34160	19644		156264		48201	W 35313	28745	PLACAGES,CONTRE-PLAQUES
6342	PLYWOOD OF WOOD SHEETS	W 32410	17686	W 53135	151936	W 63267	46832	W 30183	23057	BOIS CONTRE-PLAQUES
635	WOOD MANUFACTURES NES	W 8100	19792	W 1800	8241	W 7088	29711	W 1999	12768	ART MANUF EN BOIS NDA
64	PAPER,PAPERBOARD AND MFR		151199		147984		157634		150397	PAPIERS,CARTONS & OUVRAGES
641	PAPER AND PAPERBOARD		112599	W 145149	105828	W 143492	143496	W 237802	120025	PAPIERS ET CARTONS
6413	KRAFT PAPER,PAPERBOARD	W 114602	28004	W 33517	19251	W 45078	28678	W 32698	27957	PAPIER ET CARTON KRAFT
6415	PAPER,PAPERBRD,BULK,NES		23551	W 21396	15688	W 31400	53327	W 39986	29017	PAPIERS,CARTONS ROULEAUX
64159	OTHER PAPER ETC,BULK,NES	W 24044	19932	W 18186	13717	W 27934	51091	W 34167	25093	AUT PAPIER ROULEAUX FEUILLES
6418	COATED ETC PAPER NES BLK	W 9521	20846	W 25719	27555	W 16661	22332	W 18711	23140	PAP,CARTONS COUCHES,ENDUITS
642	PAPER,ETC,PRECUT,ARTS OF	W 123407	38599	W 25536	42156	W 7222	14139	W 14193	30372	PAP,CARTONS DECOUPES
65	TEXTILE YARN,FABRICS,ETC		121989		96796		169917		160334	FILS,TISSUS,ARTICLES TEXTILE
651	TEXTILE YARN	W 19468	82634		60538	W 27737	81248	W 11540	52467	FILS TEXTILES
6514	SYN FIB YRN,BULK,MONOFIL	W 3668	10949	W 10067	13900	W 11885	30244	W 4887	18002	FILS CONT 85% FIB TEXT SYNTH
6516	DISCON SYN FIB BLEND YRN	W 6519	32769		26935	W 12140	33709	W 4045	17692	FILS FIBR TEX SYNT DIS MOINS
653	WOVN MAN-MADE FIB FABRIC	W 3730	9237		3500	W 11753	44254	W 11821	46649	TISSUS FIBRES SYNTH,ARTIF
66	NONMETAL MINERAL MFS NES		206210		194688		246045		226357	ART MIN NON METALLIQUES
661	LIME,CEMENT,BLDG PRODS	W 1645654	98650	W 1429056	82754	W 2175234	119325	W 2030104	105523	CHAUX,CIMENTS MAT CONSTR
6612	CEMENT	W 1644176	94442	W 1426559	78794	W 2174887	119059	W 2026918	102480	CIMENTS HYDRAULIQUES
662	CLAY,REFRACTORY BLDG PRD		34696	W 50179	21538	W 64552	43147	W 81062	43169	MAT CONST REFRACTAIRES
6623	REFRACTORY BUILDING PROD	W 32218	32570	W 46292	19836	W 43127	36763	W 27457	25729	BRIQUES REFRACTAIRES
663	MINERAL MANUFCTURES NES	W 12074	22672	W 22423	28759	W 13812	30487	W 7841	23349	ART MIN MANUF NDA
664	GLASS	W 21314	36742	W 27562	43733	W 42239	37847	W 39873	33326	VERRE
6649	GLASS NES	W 2700	17767	W 6244	28430	W 4002	8321	W 5323	8181	VERRE NDA
67	IRON AND STEEL		824185		740278		913648		820226	FER ET ACIER
672	IRON,STEEL PRIMARY FORMS	W 63170	25957	W 126237	53504	W 136970	44502	W 44790	21799	LINGOTS FER,ACIER
6727	IRN,STL COIL FR REROLLNG	W 44509	20165	W 119779	50793	W 97730	34306	W 43388	20066	EBAUCHES POUR TOLES FER
67271	IRON,SIMPLE STEEL COILS	W 40213	18268	W 119698	50567	W 97688	34152	W 41955	18806	EBAUCHES NON EN ACIER
673	IRON,STEEL SHAPES ETC	W 866846	313166	W 699129	254047	W 1299641	418180	W 969422	258279	BARRES,PROFIL FER,ACIER
6731	IRON,STEEL WIRE ROD	W 135600	54785	W 178999	68121	W 165002	58454	W 129401	40643	FIL MACHINE FER,ACIER
67311	IRON,SIMPLE STL WIRE ROD	W 105319	43826	W 147755	55320	W 138796	50453	W 115894	36658	FIL MACH AUT ACIER FIN
6732	IRON,STEEL BARS ETC	W 639432	218824	W 462499	161003	W 1086364	335922	W 670957	180364	BARRES FER,ACIER
67322	HIGH CARBON STL BARS ETC	W 181337	60168	W 182044	64618	W 174814	55199	W 81339	20298	BARRES ACIER FIN CARBONE
67326	IRN,OTH STL BARS HOTROLD	W 425581	142299	W 240991	81287	W 854121	258518	W 531481	140550	BARRES PLEINES FER,ACIER
6733	IRON,STEEL PROFILES ETC	W 91815	39558	W 57630	24924	W 48276	23804	W 169065	37272	PROFILES,PALPLAN FER,ACIER
67331	SMALL U,I,H SECTIONS ETC	W 65948	27163	W 25983	10604	W 27002	11545	W 111227	16228	PROFILES MOINS 80MM
674	IRN,STL UNIV,PLATE,SHEET	W 159835	125136	W 174055	142183	W 100924	102255	W 120516	105522	LARGES PLATS,TOLES
6744	IRN,STL HVY PLATE,ROLLED	W 41725	30085	W 30912	20303	W 16674	11565	W 30310	20368	TOLES LAMINEES PLUS 4.75 MM
67441	— OF IRON OR SIMPLE STL	W 40229	27109	W 29978	19105	W 16571	11255	W 29954	19730	TOLES NON ACIER FIN CARB
6746	IRN,STL THIN PLATE,ROLLD	W 50401	45388	W 60598	62029	W 32897	37683	W 25640	23321	TOLES LAM MOINS 3MM
67461	— OF IRON OR SIMPLE STL	W 46836	34733	W 58985	57724	W 31155	33295	W 24555	19828	TOL NON AC FIN MOINS 3 MM
6747	TINNED PLATES,SHEETS	W 11144	13540	W 18965	23133	W 27012	34215	W 31947	33786	TOLES ETAMEES EN ACIER
676	RAILWY RAILS ETC IRN,STL	W 27174	25920	W 32453	28370	W 5729	3621	W 3275	3686	RAILS,ELEMENTS VOIES FERREE
677	IRN,STL WIRE(EXCL W ROD)	W 43813	45096	W 27360	20516	W 6331	5166	W 5130	5194	FILS EN FER,ACIER
67701	IRON, SIMPLE STEEL WIRE	W 34374	28868	W 22708	16495	W 3752	2674	W 1431	1608	FILS NON ACIER FIN CARBONE
678	IRON,STL TUBES,PIPES,ETC	W 178348	271256	W 114283	224832	W 238704	325331	W 375411	408136	TUBES,TUYAUX EN FONTE,FER
6782	IRON,STL SEAMLESS TUBES	W 139778	209370	W 94447	157748	W 91091	176402	W 142993	161230	TUBES,TUYAUX SANS SOUDURE
6783	IRON,STL TUBES,PIPES NES	W 22214	27658	W 13030	23782	W 120990	100292	W 227542	218328	AUT TUBES,TUYAUX FER,ACIER
6785	IRON,STEEL TUBE FITTINGS	W 2908	23756	W 5907	42262	W 5878	32336	W 4174	27902	ACCESSOIRES DE TUYAUTERIE
68	NON-FERROUS METALS		124141		110825		105344		123431	METAUX NON FERREUX
682	COPPER EXC CEMENT COPPER	W 21435	57892	W 11665	37750	W 16660	50491	W 23424	56927	CUIVRE
6822	COPPER,ALLOYS WORKED	W 20388	54971	W 10870	35483	W 15443	47445	W 18204	52436	CUIVRE,ALLIAGES OUVRES
68221	COPPER BARS,WIRE,ETC	W 11730	32643	W 7903	21637	W 11705	31641	W 10443	30724	BARRES,PROFILES ET FILS
684	ALUMINIUM	W 18775	54222	W 44423	52194	W 17390	46326	W 20481	57566	ALUMINIUM
6842	ALUMINIUM,ALLOYS WORKED	W 13103	44925	W 37379	40935	W 11405	34114	W 14136	44236	ALUMINIUM,ALLIAGES OUVRE
69	METAL MANUFACTURES NES		257353		262759		270609		343044	ART MANUFACT EN METAL NDA
691	STRUCTURES AND PARTS NES	W 15863	41388	W 16078	42792	W 17809	63167	W 49841	116274	CONSTRUCT FER,ACIER,ALU
6911	STRUCTURES,PARTS IRN,STL	W 15808	41189	W 10118	42256	W 17638	62270	W 48782	115089	CONSTRUCT FER,ACIER,FONTE
692	METAL TANKS,BOXES,ETC	W 2456	4994	W 11198	22262	W 8720	46747	W 8276	48442	RECIPIENTS METALLIQUES
6924	MTL TRANSPORT BOXES ETC	W 2078	3093	W 6239	10833	W 6185	38097	W 7819	44474	FUTS,TAMBOURS,BIDONS
69243	IRN,STL COMP GAS CYLINDR	W 114	1285	W 674	4459	W 3407	28437	W 3599	35267	RECIP FER,ACIER GAZ COMP
693	WIRE PRODUCTS NON ELECTR	W 20920	26357	W 13986	26145	W 4253	13596	W 6142	17015	OUVRAGES FILS METALLIQUES
694	STL,COPPR NAILS,NUTS,ETC	W 9403	26120	W 37281	35314	W 3389	19647	W 5064	22861	CLOUS,VIS,ECROUS
69402	IRN,STL NUTS,BOLTS,ETC	W 6561	21221	W 4334	32429	W 2538	18245	W 3233	20651	BOULONS,VIS,ECROUS FER,AC
695	TOOLS	W 3191	46042	W 3547	52911	W 3531	51752	W 5279	56192	OUTILS A MAIN
6954	BLADES,TIPS,ETC FR TOOLS	W 753	25062	W 1038	32026	W 985	33388	W 836	31848	OUTILS POUR MACHINE-OUTIL
69541	PARTS TO INSERT IN TOOLS	W 622	18904	W 909	26444	W 899	29923	W 684	27225	OUTILS DE FORAGE
697	BASE MTL HOUSEHOLD EQUIP	W 10196	55332	W 4506	21371	W 4128	17468	W 5177	15428	ART MENAGE MET COMMUNS
6973	DMSTC HEATG,COOKG APPARA	W 9118	49807	W 1960	8304	W 2622	12182	W 3040	9416	APPS CHAUF NON ELECTRIQ
69732	IRN,STL DOM HEATG APPARA	W 3857	26160	W 831	3395	W 1264	4947	W 606	2638	POELES,RECHAUDS NON ELECTRS
699	BASE METAL MFRS NES	W 91935	55358		56579		53358	W 17464	61330	ART MANUFACTURES MET NDA
7	MACHINES,TRANSPORT EQUIP		2646597		2784115		2572230		2990335	MACHINES MATERIEL TRANSPORT
71	POWER GENERATING EQUIPMT		199455		355557		398504		273086	MACHINES GENERATRICES

4. Special Imports C.I.F. by Commodities according to the S.I.T.C. (Rev. 2) in thousand U.S. Dollars
Importations Spéciales C.A.F. par Produits d'après la C.T.C.I. (Rév. 2) en milliers de Dollars E.U.

SITC CTCI	COMMODITY	1992 WEIGHT POIDS	1992 VALUE VALEUR	1993 WEIGHT POIDS	1993 VALUE VALEUR	1994 WEIGHT POIDS	1994 VALUE VALEUR	1995 WEIGHT POIDS	1995 VALUE VALEUR	PRODUIT
711	STEAM BOILERS & AUX PLNT		11499	W 11061	117825	W 1613	16912	W 500	6015	GENERATEURS VAPEUR EAU ETC
7111	STEAM BOILERS ETC	W 434	6410	W 6727	88368	W 534	6068	W 361	3579	GENERATEURS VAPEUR EAU
712	STEAM ENGINES,TURBINES	W 32	6330	W 600	32008	W 922	16179	W 78	4670	MACHINES A VAPEUR D'EAU PIEC
713	INTRNL COMBUS PSTN ENGIN		87132	W 6868	90823	W 6487	106807	W 7371	104032	MOTEURS EXPL COMB INT, PIECE
7139	PISTON ENGINE PARTS NES	W 3412	39780	W 4342	56059	W 3680	69459	W 5007	69181	PIECES POUR 713.2,3,8
714	ENGINES AND MOTORS NES	W 217	32170	W 1096	56721	W 4069	196214	W 3502	115377	MOTEURS NON ELECTRIQUES
7148	GAS TURBINES NES	W 19	2826	W 950	24038	W 2444	100359	W 676	27709	TURBINES A GAZ
71488	OTHER GAS TURBINES NES	W 19	2822	W 948	24010	W 2266	95449	W 672	27146	AUTRES TURBINES A GAZ
7149	ENGINE & MOTOR PARTS NES	W 191	29314	W 129	30987	W 1618	93697	W 2800	83076	PIECES 714 ET 718.88
71499	PARTS NES,OF 71488,71888	W 188	26051	W 128	30562	W 1607	92862	W 2524	80519	PIECES 714.88 ET 718.88
716	ROTATING ELECTRIC PLANT	W 3100	60076	W 3137	52350	W 3208	59988	W 2348	36371	APP ELECTR ROTATIFS,PIECES
7162	AC MTRS,GENRTRS,GEN SETS	W 1448	24396	W 1981	31513	W 2252	41293	W 1697	24492	MOTEURS ELECTRIQUES
72	MACHS FOR SPCL INDUSTRYS		418025		241188		232945		239402	MAC SPECIALES POUR INDUST
723	CIVIL ENGNEERG EQUIP ETC	W 8195	78300	W 6135	57047	W 5984	58357	W 6258	45425	APPAREILS DE GENIE CIVIL
7234	CONST,MINING MACHNRY NES	W 6944	54080	W 5046	37492	W 4719	38850	W 5253	26988	MACH POUR LA CONST, MINES
724	TEXTILE,LEATHER MACHNRY		63655	W 8925	30988	W 10548	42597	W 7559	31149	MACH POUR INDUSTRIE TEXTILE
727	FOOD MACHRY NON-DOMESTIC	W 3185	39415	W 2723	28996	W 1926	22606	W 2692	26447	MACH INDUSTRIES ALIMENT
728	OTH MACHY FOR SPCL INDUS	W 17110	189062	W 10141	95479	W 7723	89241	W 19533	100475	AUT MACH IND PARTICULIERES
7283	OTHR MINERAL WORKG MACHY	W 9590	83422	W 4766	37987	W 3609	35001	W 3712	32218	MACH TRIER,CRIBLER,BROYER
72839	PTS NES OF MACHY OF 7283	W 4035	45140	W 1825	15756	W 1335	12886	W 974	12997	PIECES MACH DU 728.3
7284	MACHY FOR SPCL INDUS NES	W 4896	82079	W 4343	43304	W 3503	46538	W 14716	58164	MACH SPEC IND PARTICUL.
72842	RUBBER,PLASTICS WRKG MCH	W 2007	48955	W 1619	14417	W 1740	12319	W 1427	19085	MACH IND CAOUT MAT PLAST
73	METALWORKING MACHINERY		118115		80815		42227		60495	MACH TRAVAIL DES METAUX
736	METALWORKING MACH-TOOLS		84519	W 4684	60242	W 2062	23328	W 2524	31130	MACH-OUTILS TRAVAIL METAUX
7361	METAL CUTTING MACH-TOOLS		36315	W 2872	32792	W 939	8826	W 756	7401	MACH-OUT ENLEVEMENT METAL
737	METALWORKING MACHNRY NES	W 4479	33596	W 1158	20573	W 2590	18899	W 3634	29364	MACH TRAV METAUX PIECES
74	GENRL INDUSTRL MACHY NES		767039		974145		739543		981074	MACH APP INDUSTRIE
741	HEATING,COOLING EQUIPMNT		190099	W 35288	251352	W 14167	158177	W 22048	145076	MACH CHAUFFAGE,PIECES
7413	INDUS FURNACES ETC,PARTS	W 12122	93064	W 10813	56036	W 4672	26293	W 5625	34260	FOURS IND,LABOR,PIECES
74132	INDUST FURNACES NONELECT	W 11799	89900	W 10421	52654	W 3776	22575	W 5271	30231	FOURS NON ELECTRIQUES
7416	HEATING,COOLING EQU NES	W 7143	62974	W 19490	168138	W 6202	92964	W 7836	65431	APP CHANGEMENT TEMP
742	PUMPS FOR LIQUIDS ETC	W 4074	80518	W 5643	92486	W 5150	83538	W 6049	78460	POMPES MOTO-POMPES
7428	OTHER PUMPS FOR LIQUIDS	W 2787	47972	W 3798	50382	W 3771	52962	W 4660	47737	AUTRES POMPES POUR LIQ
74288	PUMPS FR LIQUIDS NES ETC	W 2765	47254	W 3793	50273	W 3721	52151	W 4621	47306	POMPES POUR LIQUIDES NDA
743	PUMPS NES,CENTRFUGES ETC	W 12402	116199	W 9630	219151	W 17744	125187	W 12424	235182	POMPES COMPRES,VENT ETC
7431	PUMPS FOR GASES ETC	W 8379	54320	W 4801	104873	W 3066	24874	W 6127	142296	POMPES AIR A VIDE,COMPRES
7436	GAS,LIQUID FILTERS ETC	W 2560	32883	W 3239	52322	W 3067	36503	W 4263	44041	APP POUR FILT DES LIQUIDES
7439	PTS NES OF APP OF 7435,6	W 919	25617	W 1000	54349	W 11424	60664	W 1554	38803	PIECES 743.5 ET 743.6
744	MECHANICAL HANDLING EQU		124770	W 13890	98374	W 9895	74780	W 7956	80678	EQUIP MANUTENTION PIECES
7441	FORK LIFT TRCKS,ETC,PTS		35309	W 4582	23687	W 2220	14479	W 1132	7923	CHARIOTS POUR USINES ETC
74411	FORK LIFT TRUCKS ETC		30832	W 2571	17791	W 1999	13716	W 1032	7111	CHARIOTS POUR LES GARES
7442	LIFTING,LOADING MACH NES	W 5971	68011	W 6255	48637	W 4122	37014	W 5601	59177	APP LEVAGE,MANUTENTION
74428	OTH HANDLING ETC MCH NES	W 4409	59313	W 4343	34323	W 2976	25639	W 4431	49079	AUT APP LEVAGE ETC
745	NONELEC MACHY,TOOLS NES	W 2500	65180		104841	W 2878	54965	W 4260	47873	AUT MACH NON ELEC,PIECES
7452	OTH NONELEC MCHS,PTS NES	W 2437	62718		102013	W 2761	51720	W 4069	43496	AUT MACH NON ELEC,PIECES
74522	PACKAGNG,BOTTLNG,ETC MCH	W 1158	46538	W 571	18637	W 598	14897	W 529	13751	MACH NETT BOUTEILLES,ETC
74527	SPRAYING MACHINERY	W 605	8058		74975	W 1834	30981	W 2745	16765	APP PROJETER ETC LIQUID
749	NONELEC MACH PTS,ACC NES	W 10097	190272	W 13213	207943	W 14517	242896	W 53598	393804	PIECES MACH NON ELEC NDA
7492	COCKS,VALVES ETC NES	W 4398	92921	W 6823	103775	W 8905	141745	W 47360	277238	ART ROB,SIM POUR TUYAUX
7493	SHAFT,CRANK,PULLEY ETC	W 2962	57073	W 2799	57645	W 2456	50780	W 2362	58520	ARBRES TRANS,VILEBREQUINS
7499	OTH NONELEC MCHY PTS NES	W 1517	20776	W 2280	25578	W 1812	29353	W 1333	29476	PIECES NON ELECT NDA
75	OFFICE MACHNES,ADP EQUIP		82261		90059		102733		200318	MACH BUREAU TRAIT AUTOM
752	AUTOMTIC DATA PROC EQUIP	W 545	45703	W 1296	55646	W 1046	63928	W 2577	156536	MACH TRAIT INFORMATION
7522	DIGITAL COMPUTERS	W 333	23506	W 360	29419	W 373	30828	W 1231	96858	MACH DIGITALES COMPLETES
7528	OFF-LINE DATA PROC EQUIP	W 32	3670	W 76	5478	W 345	9463	W 883	31976	MACH AUXIL TRAIT INFORM
76	TELECOMM,SOUND EQUIPMENT		178964		135921		134082		295117	EQUIPMENT DE TELECOM
761	TELEVISION RECEIVERS	W 1468	15209	W 3903	32244	W 8580	20766	W 4467	36822	RECEPTEURS DE TELEVISION
7611	COLOUR TV RECEIVERS	W 1422	14936	W 3517	30175	W 5544	18578	W 3118	31008	RECEPTEURS COULEUR
764	TELECOM EQPT,PTS,ACC NES		149471	W 1969	93383	W 1928	103363	W 4715	242214	EQUIP TELECOM,PIECES
7641	LINE TELEPHONE,ETC EQUIP	W 593	63049	W 469	40692	W 584	56999	W 864	67458	APP TELEPHON PAR FIL
7643	TV,RADIO TRANSMITTRS ETC	W 520	50884	W 226	24014	W 93	22250	W 316	28702	APP EMET TELE RADIO
7649	PTS NES OF EQUIPMT OF 76	W 1086	26821	W 1089	22529	W 1071	20739	W 3286	137735	PIECES DE LA DIV 76
76493	TELECOMM EQUIPMT PTS NES	W 769	15539	W 995	15494	W 955	12311	W 3229	132084	PIECES 761,762,764.3,8
77	ELECTRIC MACHNRY NES ETC		452036		508445		507902		481449	MACH APP ELECT NDA
771	ELECTRIC POWER MACHY NES	W 10474	75617	W 3927	57286	W 3228	51847	W 2992	34838	MACH PROD,TRANS ELECTR
7711	TRANSFORMERS,ELECTRICAL	W 8996	50367	W 2419	35546	W 1949	35293	W 1406	16287	TRANSFO ELECTRIQUES
77111	LIQUID DIELEC TRANSFRMRS	W 4307	39831	W 1484	17244	W 1294	16467	W 819	5574	TRANSFO DIELEC LIQUIDE
772	SWITCHGEAR ETC,PARTS NES		122658	W 12607	164039		217261	W 8346	206287	APP COUPURE,SECT ETC
7721	SWITCHGEAR ETC		115350	W 12397	157967		210629	W 8183	199382	APP COUPURE,SECTIONMNT
773	ELECTR DISTRIBUTNG EQUIP	W 16873	98141	W 19488	81202	W 12010	73326	W 8992	46587	EQUIPMT DISTRIBUTION ELECT
7731	INSULATED WIRE,CABLE ETC	W 14350	87689	W 18238	75288	W 8533	66114	W 7385	40404	FILS,CABLES ISOLES ELECT
775	HOUSEHOLD TYPE EQUIP NES	W 7527	34267	W 8717	57237	W 8871	24063	W 10148	37690	MACH,APP USAGE DOMESTQUE
7757	DOMESTIC ELECTRC EQU NES	W 1039	4372	W 2483	31419	W 861	8157	W 1710	7752	APP ELECTR DOMEST NDA
77572	DOM ELEC ROOM FANS ETC	W 794	3171	W 1863	26649	W 594	3027	W 1283	5286	HOTTES ASPIRANTES,VENTIL
776	TRANSISTORS,VALVES,ETC		42056	W 3016	38392	W 1901	32944	W 2456	38686	LAMPES,TUBES,VALVES
778	ELECTRICAL MACHINERY NES	W 38506	73432	W 18433	102469	W 16938	91394	W 14304	105163	AUTRES MACH ELECT NDA
7783	AUTOMOTIVE ELECTR EQUIP	W 2506	19163	W 8891	35103	W 8306	26095	W 2571	30861	EQUIP ELECT MOTEURS EXPL
7788	OTH ELEC MACHY,EQUIP NES	W 2319	25079	W 1487	30970	W 1840	32927	W 1438	34513	AUT MACH APP ELEC NDA
78	ROAD VEHICLES		394061		351701		348241		408839	VEHICULES ROUTIERS
781	PASS MOTOR VEH EXC BUSES	W 6542	99760	W 11448	105400	W 4700	68943	W 10799	140534	AUTO TRANSPORT PERSONNES
782	LORRIES,SPCL MTR VEH NES	W 9304	88466	W 7610	64757	W 7904	83390	W 6654	78680	VEHICULES SPECIAUX,MARCH
7821	LORRIES,TRUCKS	W 7298	59132	W 6362	48359	W 5590	39492	W 5281	37769	VEHICULES TRANSP MARCHAND
7822	SPECIAL MOTOR VEHCLS NES	W 2006	29333	W 1248	16399	W 2314	43897	W 1373	40911	VEHICULES USAGES SPECIAUX
783	ROAD MOTOR VEHICLES NES	W 12031	62020	W 10731	41007	W 12477	48235	W 9971	27047	VEHICULES ROUTIERS NDA
7831	BUSES	W 1649	18079	W 2066	23009	W 2713	37441	W 1709	20594	VOITURES TRANSPORT COMMUN
7832	TRACTORS FOR TR-TRAILERS	W 10382	43941	W 8665	17997	W 9763	10794	W 8262	6453	TRACTEURS ROUTIERS
784	MOTOR VEH PRTS,ACCES NES		106023	W 42099	102094	W 25749	129619	W 15531	135792	PIECES 722,781,782,783
7849	OTHER MOTOR VEHCL PARTS	W 11753	104212	W 42060	101561	W 25710	129376	W 15465	135226	PIECES 722,781,782,783
786	TRAILERS,NONMOTR VEH,NES	W 14289	26971	W 60112	31167	W 15419	15178	W 42876	19370	REMORQUES,CADRES,CONTAIN
79	OTHR TRANSPORT EQUIPMENT		36642		46283		66053		50558	AUTRE MATERIEL TRANSPORT
791	RAILWAY VEHICLES	W 5693	20224	W 6919	32463	W 10087	54842	W 3214	22725	VEHIC MAT CHEMINS DE FER
7919	RY TRACK FIXT,ETC,PARTS	W 5320	15774	W 5912	14208	W 8848	32677	W 3172	22628	MATER FIXE VOIES FERREES
8	MISC MANUFACTURED GOODS		307216		299943		321807		353602	ART MANUFACTURES DIVERS
87	PRECISION INSTRUMNTS NES		171947		138924		154130		136738	INSTRUM,APPAR SCIENT NDA
872	MEDICAL INSTRUMENTS NES	W 1518	33866		27732	W 1115	23193	W 2981	27801	INSTR,APP MEDIC-CHIR NDA
87202	OTH MEDICAL INSTRUMENTS	W 1463	31011		22903	W 1026	20447	W 2887	24737	INSTRUM,APP MEDECINE
873	METERS AND COUNTERS NES	W 2250	41460	W 537	9528	W 452	7663	W 86	3780	COMPTEURS,INST DE MESURE
8731	GAS SUPPLY METERS ETC	W 2192	39194	W 514	8303	W 418	5284	W 65	1731	COMPTEURS GAZ,LIQ ELECT
874	MEASURNG,CONTROLNG INSTR		95546		99101		120430	W 3728	101654	INSTRUMENTS DE MESURE
8743	GAS,LIQUID CONTROL INSTR	W 548	24317	W 680	29099	W 1138	36930	W 2077	39514	APP,INSTR MESURE FLUIDES
8748	ELEC MEAS,CONTRL EQU NES	W 239	22305	W 140	17273		29561	W 224	18149	APP ELEC ELECTRO MESURE

4. Special Imports C.I.F. by Commodities according to the S.I.T.C. (Rev. 2) in thousand U.S. Dollars
Importations Spéciales C.A.F. par Produits d'après la C.T.C.I. (Rév. 2) en milliers de Dollars E.U.

SITC CTCI	COMMODITY	1992		1993		1994		1995		PRODUIT
		WEIGHT POIDS	VALUE VALEUR	WEIGHT POIDS	VALUE VALEUR	WEIGHT POIDS	VALUE VALEUR	WEIGHT POIDS	VALUE VALEUR	
88	PHOTO EQU,OPTICL GDS ETC		23702		20875		29330		29121	APP,FOURN PHOTO,OP,MONTR
89	MISC MANUFCTRD GOODS NES		76193		111702		114367		116302	ART MANUFACTURES DIVERS
893	ARTICLES OF PLASTIC NES		37695		60946		52183		40090	OUVRAGES EN MAT DIVIS 58
8939	MISC PLASTIC ARTICLES		33660		54142	W 9599	43986	W 8428	31920	ART DIVERS EN MAT DIV 58
89399	OTHR PLASTC ARTICLES NES		32782	W 10276	53119	W 9498	43661	W 8008	31037	AUT OUV MAT DIV 58

5. Special Exports F.O.B. by Commodities according to the S.I.T.C. (Rev. 2) in thousand U.S. Dollars
Exportations Spéciales F.O.B. par Produits d'après la C.T.C.I. (Rév. 2) en milliers de Dollars E.U.

SITC CTCI	COMMODITY	1992 WEIGHT POIDS	1992 VALUE VALEUR	1993 WEIGHT POIDS	1993 VALUE VALEUR	1994 WEIGHT POIDS	1994 VALUE VALEUR	1995 WEIGHT POIDS	1995 VALUE VALEUR	PRODUIT
	ALL COMMODITIES		11136803		10097666		8593807		8555509	TOUS PRODUITS
0	FOOD AND LIVE ANIMALS		74364		94003		32632		91300	ALIMENTS,ANIMAUX VIVANTS
05	VEGETABLES AND FRUIT		63890		88500		28391		73902	LEGUMES ET FRUITS
057	FRUIT,NUTS,FRESH,DRIED	W 20879	58821	W 19876	55378	W 3916	12065	W 21964	72055	FRUITS FRAIS OU SECS
0579	FRUIT FRESH OR DRIED NES	W 20802	58754	W 19820	55331	W 3763	11988	W 21856	71919	FRUITS FRAIS,SECS NDA
05796	DATES,FRESH OR DRIED	W 20793	58744	W 19809	55318	W 3763	11988	W 21852	71907	DATTES FRAICHES OU SECHES
2	CRUDE MATERLS,EXCL FUELS		32053		25953		22934		36879	MAT BRUTES NON COMESTIBLES
3	MINERAL FUELS ETC		10759056		9679204		8341998		8146170	COMBUSTIBLES MINERAUX LUB
33	PETROLEUM AND PRODUCTS		7051932		6339670		5585511		5537426	PETROLE ET DERIVES
333	CRUDE PETROLEUM	MW 30338	4806712	MW 39108	4448707	MW 31492	3924450	MW 32287	3940738	HUILES BRUTES DE PETROLE
334	PETROLEUM PRODUCTS,REFIN	MW 13850	2161214	MW 13588	1828798	MW 12648	1617020	MW 12592	1540327	PRODUITS RAFFINES
3341	GASOLINE,OTH LIGHT OILS	W 3809202	691440	W 3496501	539813	W 3849867	564234	W 3539241	498392	ESSENCES POUR MOTEURS
33411	MOTOR,AVIATION SPIRIT	W 28726	5383	W 31942	5458	W 372650	64506	W 231830	37827	ESSENCES MOTEURS D'AVIONS
33412	SPIRIT TYPE JET FUEL			W 98313	13431	W 708507	106625	W 425470	71714	CARBUREACTEURS
33419	OTH LIGHT PETROLEUM OILS	W 3780476	686057	W 3366246	520925	W 2768709	393103	W 2881941	388851	AUTRES HUILES LEGERES
3342	KEROSENE,OTH MEDIUM OILS	W 41936	8128	W 129568	18863	W 434227	63428	W 353005	50498	PETR LAMPANTS,AUT HUIL
33421	KEROSENE INCL JET FUEL	W 41936	8128	W 129568	18863	W 434227	63428	W 353005	50498	PETROLES LAMPANTS
3343	GAS OILS	W 4400420	779726	W 4057442	676998	W 3436500	494124	W 3384114	477938	GAS OILS
3344	FUEL OILS,NES	W 5585066	669143	W 5879350	587814	W 4886914	485191	W 5287350	504875	FUEL OILS
335	RESIDUAL PETRLM PROD NES	W 458291	84005	W 403057	62165	W 366601	44041	W 408972	56361	PRODUITS RESIDUELS NDA
3352	MINERAL TARS AND PRODCTS	W 458187	83973	W 403057	62165	W 366601	44041	W 408972	56361	GOUDRONS MINERAUX
33525	MINERAL TAR OILS ETC NES	W 428587	81956	W 378319	60325	W 351990	42393	W 398752	55425	AUTRES PRODUITS NDA
341	*GAS,NATURAL AND MANUFCT		3643596		3329871		2677562		2597389	GAZ NATUREL,GAZ MANUFACT
3413	PETROLM GASES,LIQUEFIED	MW 19184	2574848	MW 18348	2198823	MW 18378	1773898	MW 13709	1404650	GAZ DE PETROLE LIQUEFIE
34131	LIQUEFIED PROPANE,BUTANE	W 3627183	675383	W 3377424	508852	W 3757483	459358	W 2866824	401927	PROPANE,BUTANE LIQUEFIES
34139	OTH HYDROCARBON GAS LQFD	MW 15557	1899466	MW 14971	1689971	MW 14621	1314540	MW 10843	1002723	HYDROCARBURES GAZEUX NDA
3414	PETROLEUM GASES, GASEOUS		1068747		1131048		903664		1192739	GAZ DE PETROLE GAZEUX
351	*ELECTRIC CURRENT	MH 238435	63528		9663		78177		11356	ENERGIE ELECTRIQUE
5	CHEMCLS,RELATED PROD NES		72331		148038		95525		104223	PRODUITS CHIMIQUES
51	ORGANIC CHEMICALS		26571		19797		44050		42536	PROD CHIMIQ ORGANIQUES
511	HYDROCARBONS NES,DERIVS	W 66226	16906	W 44393	10999	W 85502	28541	W 76514	25301	HYDROCARBURES NDA
52	INORGANIC CHEMICALS		32863		112786		27617		39875	PROD CHIM INORGANIQUES
522	INORG ELEMNTS,OXIDES,ETC	W 382092	31430	W 296307	112772	W 193314	27587	W 181096	39875	ELEMENTS INORGANIQUES
5225	INORGANIC BASES ETC NES	W 341631	28784	W 275867	111332	W 167893	25227	W 167032	28457	AUTRES BASES OXYDES METAL
52251	AMMONIA,ANHYDROUS ETC	W 341631	28784	W 275867	111332	W 167893	25227	W 167032	28457	AMMONIAC LIQUEFIE
6	BASIC MANUFACTURES		84155		101057		77245		124349	ART MANUFACTURES
67	IRON AND STEEL		54171		63153		56056		67325	FER ET ACIER
672	IRON,STEEL PRIMARY FORMS	W 58725	26712	W 125817	28741	W 114180	29996	W 117672	27527	LINGOTS FER,ACIER
6727	IRN,STL COIL FR REROLLNG	W 32225	7808	W 125817	28741	W 114005	29925	W 53404	12700	EBAUCHES POUR TOLES FER
67271	IRON,SIMPLE STEEL COILS	W 32225	7808	W 95317	22106	W 113359	29799	W 51504	12269	EBAUCHES NON EN ACIER
7	MACHINES,TRANSPORT EQUIP		90477		19834		14063		32225	MACHINES MATERIEL TRANSPORT

1. HISTORICAL SERIES, 1956–1992 SPECIAL TRADE, IMPORTS C.I.F., EXPORTS F.O.B.
SERIES HISTORIQUES, 1956–1992 COMMERCE SPECIAL, IMPORTATIONS C.A.F., EXPORTATIONS F.O.B

YEAR ANNEE	VALUE IN MILLION U.S. DOLLARS VALEUR EN MILLION U.S. DOLLARS MERCHANDISE –MARCHANDISE		GOLD –OR		CONVERSION FACTORS FACTEURS DE CONVERSION CENTS E.U. PAR		INDEX NUMBERS –INDICES QUANTUM		UNIT VALUE VALEUR UNITAIRE	
	IMPORTS	EXPORTS	IMPORTS	EXPORTS	IMPORTS	EXPORTS	IMPORTS	EXPORTS	IMPORTS	EXPORTS
1956	109.97	114.39								
1957	122.98	116.96								
1958	130.01	128.27								
1959	131.05	124.76								
1960	127.61	123.99								
1961	113.66	134.74								
1962	135.57	148.30								
1963	146.49	162.91								
1964	163.95	204.09								
1965	194.80	199.88								
1966	206.87	221.17								
1967	275.07	237.83								
1968	302.93	270.87								
1969	322.10	326.48								
1970	368.51	423.38								
1971	428.93	429.19								
1972	397.41	515.59								
1973	542.02	779.45								
1974	625.09	1227.33								
1978	893.71	977.60								
1979	1123.39	1101.64								
1980	1340.99	1901.66								
1981	1645.57	1837.78								
1982	877.78	1627.49								
1983	679.18	1808.15								
1984	713.20	2017.68								
1985	671.10	2223.66								
1986	618.67	1319.10								
1987	442.61	2146.93								
1988	988.85	2494.45								
1989	1139.51	2988.83								
1990		3910.00								
1991		3413.00								
1992		3714.00								

2. IMPORTS BY BROAD ECONOMIC CATEGORY AND EXPORTS BY INDUSTRIAL ORIGIN. (PERCENTAGE OF TOTAL VALUE)
IMPORTATIONS PAR CATEGORIES ECONOMIQUES ET EXPORTATIONS PAR BRANCHE D'ACTIVITE.(EN POURCENTAGE DE LA VALEUR TOTALE)

IMPORTS – IMPORTATIONS

	1990	1991	1992	1993	1994	1995	1996
TOTAL IMPORTS–IMPORTATIONS TOTALES							
1 FOOD BEV–ALIMENTATION BOISSONS							
11 PRIMARY–PRODUITS DE BASE							
111 FOR INDUSTRY–POUR L'INDUSTRIE							
112 FOR HOUSEHOLDS–POUR LES MENAGES							
12 PROCESSED–PRODUITS ELABORES							
121 FOR INDUSTRY–POUR L'INDUSTRIE							
122 FOR HOUSEHOLDS–POUR LES MENAGES							
2 IND SUPPLIES–APPROV INDUSTRIELS							
21 PRIMARY–PRODUITS DE BASE							
22 PROCESSED–PRODUITS ELABORES							
3 FUELS–COMBUSTIBLES							
31 PRIMARY–PRODUITS DE BASE							
32 PROCESSED–PRODUITS ELABORES							
321 MOTOR SPIRIT–ESSENCE							
322 OTHER–AUTRES							
4 MACHINERY–EQUIPEMENT							
41 CAPITAL EQUIPMENT–MACHINES							
42 PARTS–PIECES ACCESSOIRES							
5 TRANSPORT–TRANSPORT							
51 PASSENGER CARS–AUTOMOBILES							
52 OTHER–AUTRES							
521 INDUSTRIAL–INDUSTRIELS							
522 NON INDUSTRIAL–NON INDUSTRIEL							
53 PARTS–PIECES ACCESSOIRES							
6 CONSUM GOODS–BIENS CONSOMMATION							
61 DURABLE–DURABLES							
62 SEMI DURABLE–SEMI DURABLES							
63 NON DURABLE–NON DURABLES							
7 GOODS NES–BIENS NDA							

EXPORTS – EXPORTATIONS

	1990	1991	1992	1993	1994	1995	1996
TOTAL EXPORTS–EXPORTATIONS TOTALES	100.	100.					
1 AGRICULTURE	0.2	0.3					
2 MINING QUARRY–INDUS EXTRACTIVES	98.4	97.9					
3 MANUFACTURING–IND MANUFACTUR	1.4	1.8					
31 FOOD BEV TOBACCO–ALIM BOISS TAB		0.0					
32 TEXTILES–INDUSTRIES TEXTILES							
33 WOOD & PRODUCTS–BOIS & PRODUITS	0.0						
34 PAPER & PRODUCTS–PAPIER & PRODT							
35 CHEMICALS–INDUSTRIES CHIMIQUES	1.3	1.8					
36 NON METAL MIN–MIN NON METAL	0.1	0.0					
37 BASIC METAL–IND METAL BASE	0.0						
38 METAL MANUF–MANUF METAL	0.0	0.0					
39 OTH MANUF IND–AUTRES MANUF	0.0	0.0					

3. TRADE BY PRINCIPAL COUNTRIES OF PRODUCTION AND LAST CONSIGNMENT (VALUE IN THOUSAND U.S. DOLLARS)
ECHANGES SELON LES PRINCIPAUX PAYS DE PRODUCTION ET DE DERNIERE CONSIGNATION (VALEUR EN MILLIERS DE DOLLARS EU)

COUNTRIES–PAYS	SPECIAL IMPORTS C.I.F. IMPORTATIONS SPECIALES C.A.F				
	1988	1989	1990	1991	1992
World	987869	1139579			
Africa					
Americas	132102	109246			
Northern America					
LAIA	119193	104011			
CACM					
Caribbean	12909	5235			
Rest of America					
As.ex F.USSR	64777	57622			
Eur.x F.USSR	633832	915156			
EU	616487	894214			
EFTA					
East Europe	17344	20941			
Other Europe					
Former USSR					
Oceania					
Portugal	171359	206796			
Germany/Allemagne	149016	178366			
Netherlands/Pays-Bas	148255	160506			
Brazil/Brésil	119193	104011			
Belgium–Luxembourg	22938	99902			
France,Monac	8771	114051			
Spain/Espagne	53192	55601			
Japan/Japon	39720	34527			
United Kingdom	26679	32870			
Italy/Italie	19297	35189			
United Arab Emirates	25057	23095			
Former GDR	17344	20941			
Sweden/Suède	16980	10935			
Cuba	12909	5235			

COUNTRIES–PAYS	SPECIAL EXPORTS F.O.B. EXPORTATIONS SPECIALES F.O.B.				
	1988	1989	1990	1991	1992
Monde			3910328	3409670	3697520
Afrique			39131	38765	16000
Amériques			2264575	2364170	2517000
Amérique du Nord			2095709	2131762	2460000
ALAI			168866	232408	46000
MCAC					
Caraïbes					11000
Autre Amérique					
Asie l'URSS exclus			38246	125	112000
Europe l'URSS exclus			1566045	1000519	1051700
UE			1475962	918851	1051700
AELE				7013	
Europe de l'Est			17308		
Autre de l'Europe			72775	74654	
Ancienne URSS					
Océanie					
USA/Etats-Unis d'Amer			2067636	2094626	2460000
France,Monac			456301	290448	300000
Netherlands/Pays-Bas			414049	206182	167100
United Kingdom			21483	144277	316000
Belgium–Luxembourg			231940	45942	106000
Brazil/Brésil			79961	210211	46000
Italy/Italie			143876	82623	37000
Portugal			88765	87846	75500
Chile/Chili			76745	22196	
Spain/Espagne			2527	40542	50100
Gibraltar			72775	12482	
Canada			28073	37136	
China/Chine					63000
Austria/Autriche			62841		
Fm Yugoslav				62173	
Germany/Allemagne			40442	20987	
Singapore/Singapour					49000
Japan/Japon			38213	125	
Liberia/Libéria			34097		
Nigeria/Nigéria				18125	
Former GDR			17308		
Senegal/Sénégal					16000
Sweden/Suède			13738		
Mexico/Mexique			12160		
Martinique					11000
Un. Rep. of Tanzania				9136	
Cameroon/Cameroun				8830	
Norway,SVD,JM				7013	
Sao Tome and Principe			2051	1129	
Togo			1985		
Dem. Rep. of the Congo				868	
Cote d'Ivoire			684		
Morocco/Maroc				676	
So. Africa Customs Un			288		
India/Inde			33		
Congo			26		
Denmark/Danemark				2	

(VALUE AS PERCENTAGE OF WORLD TOTAL)(VALEURS EN POURCENTAGE DU TOTAL MONDIAL)

	1983	1984	1985	1986	1987	1988	1989	1990	1991	1992
Africa		0.6	0.8	1.3	1.4					
Americas		15.1	24.9	27.2	26.5	13.4	9.6			
Northern America		6.6	7.1	5.1	6.5					
LAIA		8.0	15.5	21.4	19.6	12.1	9.1			
CACM			0.0							
Caribbean		0.4	2.3	0.7	0.4	1.3	0.5			
Rest of America			0.0	0.0	0.0					
As.ex F.USSR		10.4	5.4	8.8	8.7	6.6	5.1			
Eur.x F.USSR		66.5	67.3	57.8	60.7	64.2	80.3			
EU		62.5	60.9	54.5	55.7	62.4	78.5			
EFTA		0.9	1.2	0.9	2.1					
East Europe		2.7	4.7	1.1	1.5	1.8	1.8			
Other Europe		0.5	0.6	1.3	1.4					
Former USSR		0.0	0.9							
Oceania			0.1	0.0	0.0					
Portugal		16.5	13.7	8.9	9.9	17.3	18.1			
Germany/Allemagne		6.3	6.9	5.3	6.5	15.1	15.7			
Netherlands/Pays-Bas		7.6	7.2	6.5	6.6	15.0	14.1			
Brazil/Brésil		6.5	11.3	20.6	19.3	12.1	9.1			
Belgium–Luxembourg		1.1	2.7	3.5	3.5	2.3	8.8			
France,Monac		10.9	11.7	13.1	12.4	0.9	10.0			
Spain/Espagne		5.4	3.0	3.6	4.5	5.4	4.9			
Japan/Japon		2.7	2.8	2.6	2.0	4.0	3.0			
United Kingdom		4.7	4.6	4.0	3.8	2.7	2.9			
Italy/Italie		5.1	3.8	5.2	5.6	2.0	3.1			

	1983	1984	1985	1986	1987	1988	1989	1990	1991	1992
Afrique		0.0		0.0	0.9			1.0	1.1	0.4
Amériques		33.1		38.7	38.3			57.9	69.3	68.1
Amérique du Nord		26.2		24.7	30.4			53.6	62.5	66.5
ALAI		6.3		8.2	4.5			4.3	6.8	1.2
MCAC										
Caraïbes		0.6		5.8	3.3					0.3
Autre Amérique				0.0						
Asie l'URSS exclus		20.0		17.2	27.5			1.0	0.0	3.0
Europe l'URSS exclus		37.7		33.5	22.4			40.0	29.3	28.4
UE		35.8		31.4	21.2			37.7	26.9	28.4
AELE		0.2		0.1	0.1				0.2	
Europe de l'Est		1.7		1.0	0.2			0.4		
Autre de l'Europe		0.0		0.9	0.9			1.9	2.2	
Ancienne URSS										
Océanie										
USA/Etats-Unis d'Amer		26.2		24.6	30.4			52.9	61.4	66.5
France,Monac		0.0		2.9	2.2			11.7	8.5	8.1
Netherlands/Pays-Bas		8.3		3.8	8.4			10.6	6.0	4.5
United Kingdom		13.6		3.4	0.1			0.5	4.2	8.5
Belgium–Luxembourg		0.7		3.7	4.8			5.9	1.3	2.9
Brazil/Brésil		6.3		8.2	4.4			2.0	6.2	1.2
Italy/Italie		0.7		2.1	2.3			3.7	2.4	1.0
Portugal		1.5		4.3	1.5			2.3	2.6	2.0
Chile/Chili								2.0	0.7	
Spain/Espagne		9.2		10.2	0.8			0.1	1.2	1.4

Angola

4. Special Imports C.I.F. by Commodities according to the S.I.T.C. (Rev. 2) in thousand U.S. Dollars
Importations Spéciales C.A.F. par Produits d'après la C.T.C.I. (Rév. 2) en milliers de Dollars E.U.

SITC CTCI	COMMODITY	1986		1987		1988		1989		PRODUIT
		WEIGHT POIDS	VALUE VALEUR	WEIGHT POIDS	VALUE VALEUR	WEIGHT POIDS	VALUE VALEUR	WEIGHT POIDS	VALUE VALEUR	
	ALL COMMODITIES		618672		442613		987869		1139579	TOUS PRODUITS

5. Special Exports F.O.B. by Commodities according to the S.I.T.C. (Rev. 2) in thousand U.S. Dollars
Exportations Spéciales F.O.B. par Produits d'après la C.T.C.I. (Rév. 2) en milliers de Dollars E.U.

SITC CTCI	COMMODITY	1989		1990		1991		1992		PRODUIT
		WEIGHT POIDS	VALUE VALEUR	WEIGHT POIDS	VALUE VALEUR	WEIGHT POIDS	VALUE VALEUR	WEIGHT POIDS	VALUE VALEUR	
	ALL COMMODITIES		2988828		3910328		3409670		3697520	TOUS PRODUITS
0	FOOD AND LIVE ANIMALS				9184		10431		3520	ALIMENTS,ANIMAUX VIVANTS
2	CRUDE MATERLS,EXCL FUELS				243397		165575		270000	MAT BRUTES NON COMESTIBLES
27	CRUDE FERTLZR,MINRLS NES				242793		165533		270000	ENGRAIS MINERAUX BRUTS
277	NATURAL ABRASIVES NES				242762		165270		270000	ABRASIFS NATURELS NDA
2771	INDUSTRIAL DIAMONDS				242762		165270		270000	DIAMANTS INDUSTRIELS
3	MINERAL FUELS ETC				3655284		3233443		3424000	COMBUSTIBLES MINERAUX LUB
33	PETROLEUM AND PRODUCTS				3647872		3182341		3424000	PETROLE ET DERIVES
333	CRUDE PETROLEUM	MW 21100	2383983	MW 22068	3598837	MW 23742	3120909	MW 25243	3424000	HUILES BRUTES DE PETROLE
334	PETROLEUM PRODUCTS,REFIN			W 391925	49035	W 495263	61432			PRODUITS RAFFINES
3344	FUEL OILS,NES			W 355162	42057	W 433547	44967			FUEL OILS
341	*GAS,NATURAL AND MANUFCT			W 65795	7412	W 203470	51102			GAZ NATUREL,GAZ MANUFACT
3414	PETROLEUM GASES, GASEOUS			W 65795	7412	W 203470	51102			GAZ DE PETROLE GAZEUX

1. HISTORICAL SERIES, 1956–1991 GENERAL TRADE, IMPORTS C.I.F., EXPORTS F.O.B.
SERIES HISTORIQUES, 1956–1991 COMMERCE GENERAL, IMPORTATIONS C.A.F., EXPORTATIONS F.O.B

YEAR ANNEE	VALUE IN MILLION E.C. DOLLARS VALEUR EN MILLION E.C. DOLLARS MERCHANDISE –MARCHANDISE IMPORTS	EXPORTS	GOLD –OR IMPORTS	EXPORTS	CONVERSION FACTORS U.S. CENTS PER E.C. DOLLAR FACTEURS DE CONVERSION CENTS E.U. PAR E.C. DOLLAR IMPORTS	EXPORTS	INDEX NUMBERS –INDICES QUANTUM IMPORTS	EXPORTS	UNIT VALUE VALEUR UNITAIRE IMPORTS	EXPORTS
1956	10.37	6.28			58.3300	58.3300				
1957	11.44	7.18			58.3300	58.3300				
1958	13.44	5.70			58.3300	58.3300				
1959	14.05	5.22			58.3300	58.3300				
1960	15.63	4.27			58.3300	58.3300				
1961	19.53	4.55			58.3300	58.3300				
1962	21.63	5.28			58.3300	58.3300				
1963	23.00	7.14			58.3300	58.3300				
1964	23.05	4.66			58.3300	58.3300				
1965	32.40	6.34			58.3300	58.3300				
1966	43.91	12.37			58.3300	58.3300				
1967	39.99	4.97			57.6500	57.6500				
1968	49.74	16.04			50.0000	50.0000				
1969	57.58	16.87			50.0000	50.0000				
1970	72.65	27.26			50.0000	50.0000				
1971	86.77	32.23			50.7160	50.7166				
1972	90.98	34.64			52.1210	52.1216				
1973	94.50	59.45			51.0800	51.0808				
1974	143.75	66.47			48.7300	48.7301				
1975	145.14	59.92			46.2870	46.2878				
1976	91.84	23.61			38.0480	38.0480				
1977	92.89	17.69			37.0370	37.0370				
1978	110.22	33.05			37.0370	37.0370				
1979	169.02	27.44			37.0370	37.0370				
1980	233.63	70.95			37.0370	37.0370				
1981	368.55	102.87			37.0370	37.0370				
1982	368.82	92.34			37.0370	37.0370				
1983	401.49	98.55			37.0370	37.0370				
1984	446.04	95.04			37.0370	37.0370				
1985	518.94	76.41			37.0370	37.0370				
1986	560.23	52.88			37.0370	37.0370				
1987	600.09	46.48			37.0370	37.0370				
1988	608.79	60.04			37.0370	37.0370				
1989	615.85	53.95			37.0370	37.0370				
1990	600.48	51.00			37.0370	37.0370				
1991	664.01	107.48			37.0400	37.0400				

2. IMPORTS BY BROAD ECONOMIC CATEGORY AND EXPORTS BY INDUSTRIAL ORIGIN. (PERCENTAGE OF TOTAL VALUE)
IMPORTATIONS PAR CATEGORIES ECONOMIQUES ET EXPORTATIONS PAR BRANCHE D'ACTIVITE.(EN POURCENTAGE DE LA VALEUR TOTALE)

IMPORTS – IMPORTATIONS

	1990	1991	1992	1993	1994	1995	1996
TOTAL IMPORTS–IMPORTATIONS TOTALES							
1 FOOD BEV–ALIMENTATION BOISSONS							
11 PRIMARY–PRODUITS DE BASE							
111 FOR INDUSTRY–POUR L'INDUSTRIE							
112 FOR HOUSEHOLDS–POUR LES MENAGES							
12 PROCESSED–PRODUITS ELABORES							
121 FOR INDUSTRY–POUR L'INDUSTRIE							
122 FOR HOUSEHOLDS–POUR LES MENAGES							
2 IND SUPPLIES–APPROV INDUSTRIELS							
21 PRIMARY–PRODUITS DE BASE							
22 PROCESSED–PRODUITS ELABORES							
3 FUELS–COMBUSTIBLES							
31 PRIMARY–PRODUITS DE BASE							
32 PROCESSED–PRODUITS ELABORES							
321 MOTOR SPIRIT–ESSENCE							
322 OTHER–AUTRES							
4 MACHINERY–EQUIPEMENT							
41 CAPITAL EQUIPMENT–MACHINES							
42 PARTS–PIECES ACCESSOIRES							
5 TRANSPORT–TRANSPORT							
51 PASSENGER CARS–AUTOMOBILES							
52 OTHER–AUTRES							
521 INDUSTRIAL–INDUSTRIELS							
522 NON INDUSTRIAL–NON INDUSTRIEL							
53 PARTS–PIECES ACCESSOIRES							
6 CONSUM GOODS–BIENS CONSOMMATION							
61 DURABLE–DURABLES							
62 SEMI DURABLE–SEMI DURABLES							
63 NON DURABLE–NON DURABLES							
7 GOODS NES–BIENS NDA							

EXPORTS – EXPORTATIONS

	1990	1991	1992	1993	1994	1995	1996
TOTAL EXPORTS–EXPORTATIONS TOTALES							
1 AGRICULTURE							
2 MINING QUARRY–INDUS EXTRACTIVES							
3 MANUFACTURING–IND MANUFACTUR							
31 FOOD BEV TOBACCO–ALIM BOISS TAB							
32 TEXTILES–INDUSTRIES TEXTILES							
33 WOOD & PRODUCTS–BOIS & PRODUITS							
34 PAPER & PRODUCTS–PAPIER & PRODT							
35 CHEMICALS–INDUSTRIES CHIMIQUES							
36 NON METAL MIN–MIN NON METAL							
37 BASIC METAL–IND METAL BASE							
38 METAL MANUF–MANUF METAL							
39 OTH MANUF IND–AUTRES MANUF							

3. TRADE BY PRINCIPAL COUNTRIES OF ORIGIN AND DESTINATION (VALUE IN THOUSAND U.S. DOLLARS)
ECHANGES SELON LES PRINCIPAUX PAYS D'ORIGINE ET DE DESTINATION (VALEUR EN MILLIERS DE DOLLARS EU)

COUNTRIES–PAYS	GENERAL IMPORTS C.I.F. IMPORTATIONS GENERALES C.A.F				
	1987	1988	1989	1990	1991
World	247014	250164	228092	222400	245929
Africa					
Americas	106306	12727	18404	20580	6100
Northern America	81555				
LAIA					
CACM					
Caribbean	24494	12258	17953	19921	5836
Rest of America	257	470	451	659	265
As.ex F.USSR					
Eur.x F.USSR	101898				
EU	101898				
EFTA					
East Europe					
Other Europe					
Former USSR					
Oceania					
USA/Etats–Unis d'Amer	72973				
Italy/Italie	61654				
Trinidad and Tobago	15734	2757	6619	7824	2130
United Kingdom	26160				
Jamaica/Jamaïque	3113	2574	3019	2520	924
Barbados/Barbade	2082	2386	2768	3188	847
St Vincent & Grenadines	1260	1988	2660	2794	636
France,Monac	9086				
Canada	8581				
Saint Lucia/St. Lucie	960	1050	1317	1790	497
Saint–Kitts–Nevis	704	865	669	793	268
Dominica/Dominique	412	519	808	817	221
Guyana	215	451	451	659	239
Denmark/Danemark	1823				
Germany/Allemagne	1536				
Netherlands/Pays–Bas	1267				
Grenada/Grenade	36	13	42	157	300
Montserrat	76	106	51	39	12
Belgium–Luxembourg	149				
Spain/Espagne	119				
Guadeloupe	90				
Portugal	68				
Ireland/Irlande	26				
British Virgin Islds	13				
Bahamas	13				

COUNTRIES–PAYS	GENERAL EXPORTS F.O.B. EXPORTATIONS GENERALES F.O.B.				
	1987	1988	1989	1990	1991
Monde	19448	22237	19981	18889	
Afrique					
Amériques	13222	4613	9049	10815	
Amérique du Nord	3365				
ALAI					
MCAC					
Caraïbes	8943	4369	8320	10166	
Autre Amérique	914	244	729	649	
Asie l'URSS exclus					
Europe l'URSS exclus	2923				
UE	2923				
AELE					
Europe de l'Est					
Autre de l'Europe					
Ancienne URSS					
Océanie					
Dominica/Dominique	3193	626	1107	1361	
Barbados/Barbade	1347	1230	1406	2167	
Saint–Kitts–Nevis	1213	647	1544	1197	
Montserrat	795	254	1854	1573	
Saint Lucia/St. Lucie	669	677	987	1184	
USA/Etats–Unis d'Amer	3001				
Trinidad and Tobago	450	620	459	1321	
Guyana	914	244	729	649	
United Kingdom	1753				
Jamaica/Jamaïque	188	147	406	660	
Italy/Italie	1096				
Grenada/Grenade	219	60	260	372	
St Vincent & Grenadines	142	109	298	332	
Guadeloupe	537				
Canada	364				
British Virgin Islds	170				
France,Monac	37				
Bahamas	21				
Spain/Espagne	9				
Netherlands/Pays–Bas	9				
Germany/Allemagne	8				
Denmark/Danemark	8				
Ireland/Irlande	3				

(VALUE AS PERCENTAGE OF WORLD TOTAL)(VALEURS EN POURCENTAGE DU TOTAL MONDIAL)

	1982	1983	1984	1985	1986	1987	1988	1989	1990	1991
Africa	0.0		0.0	0.0						
Americas	73.9	72.1	66.9	60.7	43.2	43.0	5.1	8.1	9.3	2.5
Northern America	22.6	47.1	45.7	33.9	29.7	33.0				
LAIA	0.8	0.5	0.2	0.2	0.4					
CACM	1.2	0.3	0.3	0.3	0.4					
Caribbean	45.4	22.8	19.5	26.2	12.5	9.9	4.9	7.9	9.0	2.4
Rest of America	4.0	1.4	1.2	0.1	0.2	0.1	0.2	0.2	0.3	0.1
As.ex F.USSR	6.4	2.0	5.1	6.5	10.9					
Eur.x F.USSR	9.1	17.8	17.0	13.8	22.7	41.3				
EU	9.1	14.3	14.6	13.8	22.6	41.3				
EFTA	0.1	0.0	0.0	0.1	0.0					
East Europe										
Other Europe		3.5	2.4							
Former USSR	0.1	0.1	0.0	0.0						
Oceania	0.1	0.0	0.0	0.1	0.1					
USA/Etats–Unis d'Amer	19.8	42.4	41.9	30.6	26.7	29.5				
Italy/Italie	0.3	0.7	0.5	0.9	11.3	25.0				
Trinidad and Tobago	36.3	17.4	15.2	21.6	7.2	6.4	1.1	2.9	3.5	0.9
United Kingdom	5.2	11.2	11.7	8.3	7.3	10.6				
Jamaica/Jamaïque	0.8	1.3	1.0	1.3	1.9	1.3	1.0	1.3	1.1	0.4
Barbados/Barbade	4.7	1.8	1.7	0.8	1.8	0.8	1.0	1.2	1.4	0.3
St Vincent & Grenadines	0.4	0.7	0.7	0.8	0.6	0.5	0.8	1.2	1.3	0.3
France,Monac	0.3	0.5	0.5	1.2	1.0	3.7				
Canada	2.7	4.7	3.7	3.4	3.0	3.5				
Saint Lucia/St. Lucie	1.1	0.5	0.1	0.3	0.3	0.4	0.4	0.6	0.8	0.2

	1982	1983	1984	1985	1986	1987	1988	1989	1990	1991
Afrique	0.1	0.2	0.0	0.0	0.0					
Amériques	85.9	83.6	84.9	80.1	64.7	68.0	20.7	45.3	57.3	
Amérique du Nord	10.4	18.3	23.1	10.2	18.0	17.3				
ALAI	0.0	0.0			0.5					
MCAC					0.0					
Caraïbes	72.5	62.1	58.9	67.8	43.8	46.0	19.6	41.6	53.8	
Autre Amérique	3.0	3.2	2.9	2.1	2.3	4.7	1.1	3.6	3.4	
Asie l'URSS exclus	0.1	0.3	0.2	0.3	0.4					
Europe l'URSS exclus	6.1	7.4	4.3	15.9	9.7	15.0				
UE	6.1	7.4	4.3	15.8	9.7	15.0				
AELE			0.1	0.1						
Europe de l'Est										
Autre de l'Europe										
Ancienne URSS	0.0									
Océanie	0.0				0.0					
Dominica/Dominique	6.3	6.9	7.1	13.5	10.5	16.4	2.8	5.5	7.2	
Barbados/Barbade	4.3	4.8	6.1	6.6	13.1	6.9	5.5	7.0	11.5	
Saint–Kitts–Nevis	1.6	1.9	1.9	4.0	4.8	6.2	2.9	7.7	6.3	
Montserrat	0.7	1.0	1.3	2.2	2.1	4.1	1.1	9.3	8.3	
Saint Lucia/St. Lucie	5.4	5.0	2.7	2.8	4.2	3.4	3.0	4.9	6.3	
USA/Etats–Unis d'Amer	9.5	13.6	21.1	8.8	15.6	15.4				
Trinidad and Tobago	42.7	35.9	31.9	32.9	2.3	2.3	2.8	2.3	7.0	
Guyana	0.7	1.0	0.2	2.1	2.3	4.7	1.1	3.6	3.4	
United Kingdom	5.0	7.2	4.2	15.4	6.7	9.0				
Jamaica/Jamaïque	1.2	2.1	1.1	0.6	0.4	1.0	0.7	2.0	3.5	

4. General Imports C.I.F. by Commodities according to the S.I.T.C. (Rev. 2) in thousand U.S. Dollars
Importations Générales C.A.F. par Produits d'après la C.T.C.I. (Rév. 2) en milliers de Dollars E.U.

SITC CTCI	COMMODITY	1988		1989		1990		1991		PRODUIT
		WEIGHT POIDS	VALUE VALEUR	WEIGHT POIDS	VALUE VALEUR	WEIGHT POIDS	VALUE VALEUR	WEIGHT POIDS	VALUE VALEUR	
	ALL COMMODITIES				228092		222400		245929	TOUS PRODUITS
0	FOOD AND LIVE ANIMALS				28155		27453		30357	ALIMENTS,ANIMAUX VIVANTS
1	BEVERAGES AND TOBACCO				7609		7419		8204	BOISSONS ET TABACS
2	CRUDE MATERLS,EXCL FUELS				4470		4359		4820	MAT BRUTES NON COMESTIBLES
3	MINERAL FUELS ETC				22532		21969		24294	COMBUSTIBLES MINERAUX LUB
5	CHEMCLS,RELATED PROD NES				14209		13854		15320	PRODUITS CHIMIQUES
6	BASIC MANUFACTURES				61690		60150		66514	ART MANUFACTURES
7	MACHINES,TRANSPORT EQUIP				61018		59495		65790	MACHINES MATERIEL TRANSPORT
8	MISC MANUFACTURED GOODS				28041		27341		30234	ART MANUFACTURES DIVERS

5. General Exports F.O.B. by Commodities according to the S.I.T.C. (Rev. 2) in thousand U.S. Dollars
Exportations Générales F.O.B. par Produits d'après la C.T.C.I. (Rév. 2) en milliers de Dollars E.U.

SITC CTCI	COMMODITY	1988		1989		1990		1991		PRODUIT
		WEIGHT POIDS	VALUE VALEUR	WEIGHT POIDS	VALUE VALEUR	WEIGHT POIDS	VALUE VALEUR	WEIGHT POIDS	VALUE VALEUR	
	ALL COMMODITIES				19981		18889		39807	TOUS PRODUITS
0	FOOD AND LIVE ANIMALS				1124		1138		1126	ALIMENTS,ANIMAUX VIVANTS
1	BEVERAGES AND TOBACCO				389		389		477	BOISSONS ET TABACS
2	CRUDE MATERLS,EXCL FUELS				87		85		139	MAT BRUTES NON COMESTIBLES
3	MINERAL FUELS ETC				3297		2886		9961	COMBUSTIBLES MINERAUX LUB
5	CHEMCLS,RELATED PROD NES				1976		1945		2810	PRODUITS CHIMIQUES
6	BASIC MANUFACTURES				2017		1953		3335	ART MANUFACTURES
7	MACHINES,TRANSPORT EQUIP				4556		4107		12021	MACHINES MATERIEL TRANSPORT
8	MISC MANUFACTURED GOODS				6527		6380		9925	ART MANUFACTURES DIVERS

1. HISTORICAL SERIES, 1961–1996 SPECIAL TRADE, IMPORTS C.I.F., EXPORTS F.O.B.
SERIES HISTORIQUES, 1961–1996 COMMERCE SPECIAL, IMPORTATIONS C.A.F., EXPORTATIONS F.O.B

YEAR ANNEE	VALUE IN MILLION U.S. DOLLARS VALEUR EN MILLION U.S. DOLLARS MERCHANDISE – MARCHANDISE		GOLD – OR		CONVERSION FACTORS FACTEURS DE CONVERSION CENTS E.U. PAR		INDEX NUMBERS – INDICES QUANTUM		UNIT VALUE VALEUR UNITAIRE	
	IMPORTS	EXPORTS	IMPORTS	EXPORTS	IMPORTS	EXPORTS	IMPORTS	EXPORTS	IMPORTS	EXPORTS
1961	1460.00	964.00								
1962	1357.00	1216.00								
1963	981.00	1365.00								
1964	1077.00	1410.00								
1965	1199.00	1493.00								
1966	1124.00	1593.00								
1967	1096.00	1465.00								
1968	1169.00	1368.00								
1969	1576.00	1612.00								
1970	1694.00	1773.20								
1971	1868.00	1740.40								
1972	1905.00	1941.20								
1973	2230.00	3266.00								
1974	3635.00	3930.70								
1975	3947.00	2961.30								
1976	3034.00	3916.00								
1977	4165.00	5655.00								
1978	3834.00	6399.00								
1979	6711.00	7813.00								
1980	10541.00	8020.00								
1981	9430.00	9143.00								
1982	5337.00	7626.00								
1983	4501.00	7835.00								
1984	4584.70	8107.40								
1985	3814.10	8396.00								
1986	4724.10	6852.20								
1987	5817.80	6360.20								
1988	5321.60	9134.80								
1989	4203.20	9579.30								
1990	4076.70	12352.50								
1991	8275.30	11977.80								
1992	14871.80	12235.00								
1993	16783.50	13117.80								
1994	21527.30	15659.30								
1995	20121.70	20967.41								
1996	23761.81	23811.41								

2. IMPORTS BY BROAD ECONOMIC CATEGORY AND EXPORTS BY INDUSTRIAL ORIGIN. (PERCENTAGE OF TOTAL VALUE)
IMPORTATIONS PAR CATEGORIES ECONOMIQUES ET EXPORTATIONS PAR BRANCHE D'ACTIVITE.(EN POURCENTAGE DE LA VALEUR TOTALE)

IMPORTS – IMPORTATIONS

	1990	1991	1992	1993	1994	1995	1996
TOTAL IMPORTS–IMPORTATIONS TOTALES	100.	100.	100.	100.	100.	100.	100.
1 FOOD BEV–ALIMENTATION BOISSONS	3.7	5.1	5.8	5.2	5.0	5.2	4.5
11 PRIMARY–PRODUITS DE BASE	2.5	2.4	2.4	2.2	1.9	1.9	1.9
111 FOR INDUSTRY–POUR L'INDUSTRIE	1.2	0.8	0.6	0.4	0.5	0.7	0.5
112 FOR HOUSEHOLDS–POUR LES MENAGES	1.3	1.6	1.8	1.8	1.4	1.2	1.4
12 PROCESSED–PRODUITS ELABORES	1.2	2.7	3.4	3.0	3.1	3.2	2.6
121 FOR INDUSTRY–POUR L'INDUSTRIE	0.6	0.5	0.4	0.4	0.4	0.5	0.4
122 FOR HOUSEHOLDS–POUR LES MENAGES	0.6	2.2	3.0	2.6	2.7	2.7	2.1
2 IND SUPPLIES–APPROV INDUSTRIELS	50.0	40.0	30.7	28.9	27.3	33.6	33.5
21 PRIMARY–PRODUITS DE BASE	6.5	3.3	2.2	1.8	1.6	2.1	2.1
22 PROCESSED–PRODUITS ELABORES	43.5	36.7	28.5	27.1	25.7	31.5	31.4
3 FUELS–COMBUSTIBLES	7.9	5.5	2.8	2.3	2.8	4.0	3.6
31 PRIMARY–PRODUITS DE BASE	7.3	3.8	1.4	0.9	1.0	1.3	1.2
32 PROCESSED–PRODUITS ELABORES	0.6	1.7	1.4	1.4	1.8	2.7	2.3
321 MOTOR SPIRIT–ESSENCE	0.2	0.0				0.5	0.4
322 OTHER–AUTRES	0.5	1.7	1.4	1.4	1.8	2.2	1.9
4 MACHINERY–EQUIPEMENT	23.5	24.4	26.0	28.3	30.5	29.1	28.5
41 CAPITAL EQUIPMENT–MACHINES	17.5	19.3	21.2	24.2	26.4	24.9	24.4
42 PARTS–PIECES ACCESSOIRES	6.0	5.1	4.7	4.1	4.0	4.3	4.1
5 TRANSPORT–TRANSPORT	8.3	10.7	18.1	18.8	20.1	15.3	17.5
51 PASSENGER CARS–AUTOMOBILES	0.3	2.4	5.3	5.0	6.5	3.8	5.0
52 OTHER–AUTRES	2.2	2.2	4.8	5.4	6.2	3.8	4.3
521 INDUSTRIAL–INDUSTRIELS	2.0	1.1	3.1	3.9	5.3	3.4	4.0
522 NON INDUSTRIAL–NON INDUSTRIEL	0.2	1.1	1.7	1.5	0.9	0.4	0.3
53 PARTS–PIECES ACCESSOIRES	5.8	6.0	8.0	8.3	7.5	7.7	8.2
6 CONSUM GOODS–BIENS CONSOMMATION	6.0	14.1	16.5	16.4	14.2	12.6	12.3
61 DURABLE–DURABLES	1.5	5.5	6.5	6.0	4.7	3.1	3.3
62 SEMI DURABLE–SEMI DURABLES	2.2	5.8	7.6	7.6	6.6	6.2	5.8
63 NON DURABLE–NON DURABLES	2.3	2.7	2.4	2.8	2.9	3.4	3.3
7 GOODS NES–BIENS NDA	0.6	0.3	0.1	0.1	0.1	0.1	0.0

EXPORTS – EXPORTATIONS

	1990	1991	1992	1993	1994	1995	1996
TOTAL EXPORTS–EXPORTATIONS TOTALES	100.	100.	100.	100.	100.	100.	100.
1 AGRICULTURE	27.3	29.5	30.3	26.7	25.1	24.3	25.5
2 MINING QUARRY–INDUS EXTRACTIVES	1.5	1.7	3.4	4.7	7.7	8.1	10.4
3 MANUFACTURING–IND MANUFACTUR	71.2	68.8	66.3	68.6	67.2	67.6	64.1
31 FOOD BEV TOBACCO–ALIM BOISS TAB	31.5	33.2	32.2	29.4	28.9	28.5	29.1
32 TEXTILES–INDUSTRIES TEXTILES	7.5	7.3	6.6	8.2	8.3	7.9	6.3
33 WOOD & PRODUCTS–BOIS & PRODUITS	0.2	0.1	0.0	0.1	0.1	0.2	0.3
34 PAPER & PRODUCTS–PAPIER & PRODT	1.8	1.0	1.1	1.2	1.3	2.0	1.7
35 CHEMICALS–INDUSTRIES CHIMIQUES	13.7	11.5	12.3	11.4	9.8	9.9	9.5
36 NON METAL MIN–MIN NON METAL	0.8	0.7	0.6	0.7	0.5	0.6	0.5
37 BASIC METAL–IND METAL BASE	8.6	6.8	4.6	4.3	4.1	4.9	4.3
38 METAL MANUF–MANUF METAL	6.9	8.1	8.7	12.8	12.5	13.0	12.3
39 OTH MANUF IND–AUTRES MANUF	0.2	0.1	0.2	0.5	1.6	0.7	0.2

3. TRADE BY PRINCIPAL COUNTRIES OF ORIGIN AND LAST CONSIGNMENT (VALUE IN THOUSAND U.S. DOLLARS)
ECHANGES SELON LES PRINCIPAUX PAYS D'ORIGINE ET DE DERNIERE CONSIGNATION (VALEUR EN MILLIERS DE DOLLARS EU)

COUNTRIES–PAYS	SPECIAL IMPORTS C.I.F. IMPORTATIONS SPECIALES C.A.F				
	1992	1993	1994	1995	1996
World	14863687	16772936	21581084	20121670	23761588
Africa	106586	131487	189194	255882	281358
Americas	8457952	9556210	11871713	10369181	12454035
Northern America	3294675	3946633	5061022	4480183	5024597
LAIA	4974426	5427099	6604346	5859946	7352316
CACM	5384	9719	19143	5461	15311
Caribbean	22828	18595	71699	21228	33561
Rest of America	160638	154165	115503	2363	28249
As.ex F.USSR	2118260	2358378	2591480	2506713	2959851
Eur.x F.USSR	4036079	4586437	6763865	6429762	7388460
EU	3801614	4327174	6476621	6024687	6901653
EFTA	167068	186398	182305	287615	326223
East Europe	61772	69698	83087	110862	147912
Other Europe	227	101	17297	1710	79
Former USSR	30498	45349	69675	104560	128692
Oceania	114265	95075	95104	150864	122294
USA/Etats–Unis d'Amer	3225932	3858599	4928321	4206624	4749168
Brazil/Brésil	3338794	3568453	4285915	4175976	5327116
Germany/Allemagne	1083443	1023548	1382433	1250655	1427343
Italy/Italie	760879	980918	1431177	1259041	1503540
France,Monac	573730	738662	1072187	1040048	1181320
Spain/Espagne	405871	509760	865760	929733	1063575
Japan/Japon	697176	668488	619847	710822	725304
Chile/Chili	639025	701981	828851	513815	559380
Uruguay	351166	570815	789099	286888	299827
Korea, Republic of	467491	525590	503344	362145	428089
China/Chine	170415	214839	217081	607890	697888
United Kingdom	197186	258271	351843	412900	563036
Belgium–Luxembourg	349355	331610	591830	231440	226585
Mexico/Mexique	201080	235489	260723	376424	541004
Hong Kong	272430	387049	489686	75869	89288
Netherlands/Pays–Bas	193460	224821	352064	210807	223169
Switz.Liecht	162234	164060	177854	236078	269361
Sweden/Suède	104523	116120	168283	252632	304447
Singapore/Singapour	167366	200897	265826	109072	103139
Canada	68496	87875	132701	273529	275430
Bolivia/Bolivie	145452	107907	144964	135112	136294
Paraguay	64709	72873	71604	139841	182112
So. Africa Customs Un	88996	95583	99594	124526	105048
Panama	160607	154165	115503	2357	3248
Australia/Australie	70614	73595	66065	121795	96372
Ecuador/Equateur	39450	63179	92403	100818	108720
Finland/Finlande	39136	43783	67882	110369	110355
Russian Federation	30498	45349	59490	85642	96679
Denmark/Danemark	28713	31058	47634	97692	84535
Israel/Israël	39665	37083	54472	62164	91280
Colombia/Colombie	80444	41922	60415	50927	48966
Austria/Autriche	24619	26663	33783	91541	100561
Venezuela	26349	40107	46250	46284	111861
India/Inde	28913	35466	50926	62353	81556
Malaysia/Malaisie	5764	13313	19659	98848	117882
Indonesia/Indonésie	14232	26321	40786	68928	78580
Ireland/Irlande	18020	19346	35261	71240	69008
Peru/Pérou	87957	24371	24123	33861	37036
Thailand/Thaïlande	10159	22528	24739	51782	71526
Portugal	8101	12220	56241	54584	34980
Poland/Pologne	44895	25534	25803	24103	31496
New Zealand	43639	21479	29038	29066	25916
Norway,SVD,JM	4804	22288	4451	51271	56773
Romania/Roumanie	4607	34905	37588	19874	36055
Nigeria/Nigéria	3890	37	40336	42307	23021
Cote d'Ivoire	485	1144	93	21885	71669
Bulgaria/Bulgarie	6615	5172	14789	29496	25971
Pakistan	11203	17405	18975	14771	15920
Saudi Arabia	16215	193	12440	16535	22878
Cuba	1847	1909	47613	6998	8396

COUNTRIES–PAYS	SPECIAL EXPORTS F.O.B. EXPORTATIONS SPECIALES F.O.B.				
	1992	1993	1994	1995	1996
Monde	12234949	13117758	15838665	20962590	23809643
Afrique	675363	394194	532970	872957	1099309
Amériques	5634524	6928821	9026017	11783408	13525881
Amérique du Nord	1403893	1343476	1815532	1885940	2079117
ALAI	3917560	5287300	6956616	9624901	11097658
MCAC	40172	39932	46153	73752	79079
Caraïbes	246670	215533	187646	163570	227126
Autre Amérique	26228	42580	20070	35244	42902
Asie l'URSS exclus	1797007	1800394	2096116	3342711	4026716
Europe l'URSS exclus	3976122	3816744	4076888	4793339	4862980
UE	3799171	3684677	3930498	4484056	4590241
AELE	53070	43044	85300	226408	87962
Europe de l'Est	108711	75498	35963	40566	134524
Autre de l'Europe	3618	4316	10025	14539	11726
Ancienne URSS	106884	109527	47255	99927	178670
Océanie	42606	68078	59419	58259	72997
Brazil/Brésil	1671350	2814207	3654849	5484131	6614832
USA/Etats–Unis d'Amer	1349202	1278714	1736949	1803414	1974387
Netherlands/Pays–Bas	1212037	1270067	1179560	1191261	1225394
Chile/Chili	580922	591892	998849	1475133	1765848
Germany/Allemagne	730872	625144	605481	649865	565459
Italy/Italie	527058	505098	654365	736475	721601
Spain/Espagne	500870	504437	592399	714048	736716
Uruguay	383630	511960	649841	662833	725191
Paraguay	271937	357800	498494	631378	584224
Japan/Japon	374972	466792	445246	457289	512455
Iran (Islamic Rp. of)	324022	248168	228755	509563	637297
China/Chine	128296	163250	224671	285741	607446
Venezuela	203616	229096	211197	377736	351316
France,Monac	266547	208341	215621	318513	311508
Peru/Pérou	235779	222246	288602	275578	254212
United Kingdom	169250	162021	222427	310126	355075
Mexico/Mexique	234450	219392	273672	144380	248210
So. Africa Customs Un	226014	80481	184762	339970	251005
Bolivia/Bolivie	160778	177989	192372	254024	291632
Egypt/Egypte	156002	135418	151493	228526	323328
Belgium–Luxembourg	154128	165391	153274	237457	269542
Hong Kong	106133	155831	204818	288960	215927
Malaysia/Malaisie	61363	73417	132584	259267	303150
Colombia/Colombie	105255	112832	123210	233408	182566
Indonesia/Indonésie	80180	73986	105130	167121	222440
Turkey/Turquie	129359	118150	35716	155389	139038
Denmark/Danemark	31795	91442	140618	107500	180637
Korea, Republic of	81630	49124	48929	133148	204002
Russian Federation	106884	109527	41265	90211	152226
India/Inde	20560	37942	51768	153162	183330
Greece/Grèce	67354	61046	74319	79945	95893
Canada	54656	64352	72920	81745	104730
Cuba	62770	71554	48213	65242	124879
Switz.Liecht	25884	32477	65375	190489	56149
Singapore/Singapour	66760	38431	70325	143597	43596
Ecuador/Equateur	69843	49886	65530	86301	79627
Thailand/Thaïlande	24236	28997	28468	124381	144806
Portugal	85015	60914	53229	85589	65358
Morocco/Maroc	34285	30009	56128	45138	147138
Netherlands Antilles	141526	82021	41720	6987	17686
Bangladesh	57577	25874	22217	98401	72160
Pakistan	39047	48379	41754	61856	68008
Dominican Republic	29941	51861	60358	57445	58696
Israel/Israël	47263	43301	45754	59492	60557
Australia/Australie	35794	58599	45238	48480	64685
Syrian Arab Republic	24700	40187	53890	37315	62981
Tunisia/Tunisie	34037	30707	29268	26162	90477
Algeria/Algérie	13545	8313	30213	61061	80642
Romania/Roumanie	34805	33368	14018	27618	70356
Saudi Arabia	39507	33230	17634	24520	49711

(VALUE AS PERCENTAGE OF WORLD TOTAL)(VALEURS EN POURCENTAGE DU TOTAL MONDIAL)

	1987	1988	1989	1990	1991	1992	1993	1994	1995	1996
Africa	1.3	1.4	0.6	0.6	1.4	0.7	0.8	0.9	1.3	1.2
Americas	48.2	50.6	55.4	54.0	50.1	56.9	57.0	55.0	51.5	52.4
Northern America	17.4	17.4	21.8	20.9	18.9	22.2	23.5	23.5	22.3	21.1
LAIA	29.6	32.7	33.1	33.0	30.6	33.5	32.4	30.6	29.1	30.9
CACM	0.1	0.0	0.1	0.0	0.0	0.0	0.1	0.1	0.0	0.1
Caribbean	0.6	0.5	0.1	0.1	0.4	0.2	0.1	0.3	0.1	0.1
Rest of America	0.4	0.0	0.3	0.0	0.0	1.1	0.9	0.5	0.0	0.1
As.ex F.USSR	10.8	11.8	8.5	10.3	17.0	14.3	14.1	12.0	12.5	12.5
Eur.x F.USSR	37.2	34.0	32.2	31.4	26.6	27.2	27.3	31.3	32.0	31.1
EU	33.7	29.4	28.9	27.5	24.2	25.6	25.8	30.0	29.9	29.0
EFTA	2.0	2.5	2.0	2.8	1.5	1.1	1.1	0.8	1.4	1.4
East Europe	1.2	2.1	1.2	1.0	0.8	0.4	0.4	0.4	0.6	0.6
Other Europe	0.3	0.0	0.0	0.1	0.0	0.0	0.0	0.1	0.0	0.0
Former USSR	1.6	0.4	0.6	0.4	0.3	0.2	0.3	0.3	0.5	0.5
Oceania	1.0	1.1	2.7	2.2	1.4	0.8	0.6	0.4	0.7	0.5
USA/Etats–Unis d'Amer	16.5	16.7	21.2	20.1	18.1	21.7	23.0	22.8	20.9	20.0
Brazil/Brésil	14.1	18.2	17.2	17.5	18.5	22.5	21.3	19.9	20.8	22.4
Germany/Allemagne	13.2	10.5	9.4	9.2	7.9	7.3	6.1	6.4	6.2	6.0
Italy/Italie	6.4	6.0	5.8	5.2	4.5	5.1	5.8	6.6	6.3	6.3
France,Monac	4.1	5.6	4.5	4.3	3.6	3.9	4.4	5.0	5.2	5.0
Spain/Espagne	2.1	1.9	2.2	2.7	2.4	2.7	3.0	4.0	4.6	4.5
Japan/Japon	7.6	7.3	4.3	4.4	7.3	4.7	4.0	2.9	3.5	3.1
Chile/Chili	2.6	2.7	2.6	2.3	2.8	4.3	4.2	3.8	2.6	2.4
Uruguay	2.0	2.0	2.4	1.9	2.0	2.4	3.4	3.7	1.4	1.3
Korea, Republic of	0.8	1.6	1.6	2.2	3.3	3.1	3.1	2.3	1.8	1.8

	1987	1988	1989	1990	1991	1992	1993	1994	1995	1996
Afrique	2.4	3.6	2.5	3.2	3.2	5.5	3.0	3.4	4.2	4.6
Amériques	39.6	36.9	41.2	42.0	42.1	46.1	52.8	57.0	56.2	56.8
Amérique du Nord	15.8	14.2	13.2	14.4	11.0	11.5	10.2	11.5	9.0	8.7
ALAI	20.7	19.3	25.0	25.3	28.1	32.0	40.3	43.9	45.9	46.6
MCAC	0.4	0.5	0.4	0.3	0.3	0.3	0.3	0.3	0.4	0.3
Caraïbes	2.4	2.7	2.5	1.8	2.4	2.0	1.6	1.2	0.8	1.0
Autre Amérique	0.2	0.2	0.1	0.1	0.2	0.2	0.3	0.1	0.2	0.2
Asie l'URSS exclus	14.9	15.8	16.5	16.9	16.6	14.7	13.7	13.2	15.9	16.9
Europe l'URSS exclus	32.3	33.6	29.6	33.3	35.7	32.5	29.1	25.7	22.9	20.4
UE	28.7	30.4	26.8	30.8	33.6	31.1	28.1	24.8	21.4	19.3
AELE	0.6	0.6	0.5	0.6	0.5	0.4	0.3	0.5	1.1	0.4
Europe de l'Est	2.9	2.3	2.2	1.7	1.2	0.9	0.6	0.2	0.2	0.6
Autre de l'Europe	0.1	0.3	0.1	0.2	0.4	0.0	0.0	0.1	0.1	0.0
Ancienne URSS	10.1	9.4	8.7	4.0	1.9	0.9	0.8	0.3	0.5	0.8
Océanie	0.8	0.8	1.5	0.6	0.5	0.3	0.5	0.4	0.3	0.3
Brazil/Brésil	8.5	6.7	11.8	11.5	12.4	13.7	21.5	23.1	26.2	27.8
USA/Etats–Unis d'Amer	14.6	13.3	12.4	13.8	10.4	11.0	9.7	11.0	8.6	8.3
Netherlands/Pays–Bas	9.7	11.9	10.3	11.1	11.1	9.9	9.7	7.4	5.7	5.1
Chile/Chili	2.3	2.8	3.7	3.7	4.1	4.7	4.5	6.3	7.0	7.4
Germany/Allemagne	6.0	5.3	4.3	5.2	6.1	6.0	4.8	3.8	3.1	2.4
Italy/Italie	3.7	3.7	3.0	4.3	4.8	4.3	3.9	4.1	3.5	3.0
Spain/Espagne	2.1	2.2	2.1	2.7	4.0	4.1	3.8	3.7	3.4	3.1
Uruguay	2.6	2.1	2.2	2.1	2.6	3.1	3.9	4.1	3.2	3.0
Paraguay	1.0	0.9	1.0	1.2	1.5	2.2	2.7	3.1	3.0	2.5
Japan/Japon	3.5	3.6	2.8	3.2	3.8	3.1	3.6	2.8	2.2	2.2

4. Special Imports C.I.F. by Commodities according to the S.I.T.C. (Rev. 2) in thousand U.S. Dollars
Importations Spéciales C.A.F. par Produits d'après la C.T.C.I. (Rév. 2) en milliers de Dollars E.U.

SITC CTCI	COMMODITY	1993 WEIGHT POIDS	1993 VALUE VALEUR	1994 WEIGHT POIDS	1994 VALUE VALEUR	1995 WEIGHT POIDS	1995 VALUE VALEUR	1996 WEIGHT POIDS	1996 VALUE VALEUR	PRODUIT
	ALL COMMODITIES		16772936		21581084		20121670		23761588	TOUS PRODUITS
0	FOOD AND LIVE ANIMALS		792386		992607		969714		1025634	ALIMENTS,ANIMAUX VIVANTS
01	MEAT AND PREPARATIONS		143811		157207		125464		168903	VIANDES ET PREPARATIONS
011	MEAT FRESH,CHILLD,FROZEN	W 88444	127960	W 86533	125088	W 42384	82581	W 67469	123804	VIANDES FRAICHES,REF,CONGE
0113	PIG MEAT FRESH,CHLD,FRZN	W 25654	57127	W 20811	50800	W 13582	40223	W 24795	63791	VIANDE DE PORC
0114	POULTRY FRESH CHLLD,FRZN	W 51467	55366	W 55866	60795	W 21603	31368	W 30006	42529	VOLAILLES MORTES
02	DAIRY PRODCTS,BIRDS'EGGS		66760		66242		53487		56489	PRODUITS LAITIERS,OEUFS
03	FISH AND PREPARATIONS		44671		65193		70052		70959	POISSONS ET PREPARATIONS
04	CEREALS AND PREPARATIONS		40341		54850		73294		90623	CEREALES ET PRODUITS
05	VEGETABLES AND FRUIT		258273		235948		249475		289345	LEGUMES ET FRUITS
054	VEG ETC FRSH,SMPLY PRSVD	W 95833	54856	W 45690	31616	W 81954	41579	W 79107	45294	LEGUMES FRAIS,CONG,SECS
057	FRUIT,NUTS,FRESH,DRIED	W 295139	111529	W 320500	121075	W 270539	108445	W 332014	138302	FRUITS FRAIS OU SECS
0573	BANANA,PLANTAIN,FRSH,DRY	W 212653	53115	W 247101	63564	W 201864	56071	W 248376	72548	BANANES FRAICHES,SECHEES
058	FRUIT PRESERVED,PREPARED	W 72912	70115	W 67966	62636	W 65641	77113	W 65287	78731	CONSERVES DE FRUITS
0589	FRUIT PREPRD,PRESRVD,NES	W 50924	55631	W 34199	40870	W 42103	51962	W 39425	53294	FRUITS PREPARES CONSERV
05899	FRUIT,NUTS NES,PRESERVED	W 50740	54740	W 33920	39685	W 41900	50827	W 38951	51002	FRUITS PREP CONSERV NDA
06	SUGAR AND PREPS,HONEY		26029		109550		82122		23883	SUCRES ET PRODUITS
061	SUGAR AND HONEY	W 10586	5567	W 281370	91552	W 184922	64594	W 16203	7440	SUCRES ET MIEL
0612	REFINED SUGAR ETC	W 523	263	W 253372	81285	W 177667	60424	W 9802	2896	SUCRES RAFFINES
07	COFFEE,TEA,COCOA,SPICES		137696		210124		224741		210402	CAFE,THE,CACAO,EPICES
071	COFFEE AND SUBSTITUTES	W 36995	51130	W 36796	95550	W 36295	118321	W 41164	106196	CAFE ET SUCCEDANES
0711	COFFEE GREEN,ROASTED,SUB	W 35717	44541	W 35484	87658	W 35105	109838	W 40203	100421	CAFE TORREFIE OU DECAFEINE
07111	COFFEE GREEN,HUSKS,SKINS	W 35674	44417	W 35449	87456	W 35057	109529	W 40170	100099	CAFE NON TORREFIE
09	MISC EDIBLE PRODUCTS		45427		64503		59999		75059	PREP ALIMENTAIRES DIVERSES
098	EDIBLE PRODCTS,PREPS NES	W 15400	44195	W 17144	63015	W 16543	58153	W 21991	73157	PREP ALIMENTAIRES NDA
1	BEVERAGES AND TOBACCO		95956		97090		92276		89100	BOISSONS ET TABACS
11	BEVERAGES		81450		87853		70624		64157	BOISSONS
112	ALCOHOLIC BEVERAGES	W 76960	61397	W 91359	75954	W 60581	59001	W 46553	58134	BOISSONS ALCOOLIQUES
2	CRUDE MATERLS,EXCL FUELS		540243		591619		714088		787308	MAT BRUTES NON COMESTIBLES
23	RUBBER, CRUDE		59154		64879		86136		89013	CAOUTCHOUC BRUT
24	CORK AND WOOD		62542		70276		56026		63545	LIEGE ET BOIS
248	WOOD SHAPED,SLEEPERS	W 150136	56429	W 161969	63898	W 119365	51188	W 130835	58787	BOIS SIMPLEMENT TRAVAILLES
251	*PULP AND WASTE PAPER	W 105410	47160	W 112750	54357	W 115639	86734	W 152619	80088	PATES A PAPIER,DECHETS
2517	SODA,SULPHATE WOOD PULP	W 84240	43603	W 93447	50120	W 87729	78121	W 128842	74097	PATES CHIMIQUES AU SULFATE
25172	— BLEACHED,NONDISSOLVNG	W 83691	43337	W 92834	49877	W 87492	77920	W 128599	73982	PATES BLANCHIES
26	TEXTILE FIBRES AND WASTE		83343		63358		80447		77011	FIBRES TEXTILES
28	METALLIFEROUS ORES,SCRAP		174318		193939		248486		277069	MINERAIS METAL,DECHETS
281	IRON ORE,CONCENTRATES	W 3204605	110082	W 3819660	117583	W 4361701	146394	W 4947040	174647	MINERAIS DE FER
2815	IRON ORE,CONC,NOT AGGLOM	W 1425812	41572	W 1869726	48074	W 2333398	64695	W 2363846	70086	MINERAIS NON AGGLOMERES
2816	IRON ORE AGGLOMERATES	W 1778793	68510	W 1949935	69509	W 2028303	81698	W 2583194	104561	MINERAIS AGGLOMERES
287	BASE METAL ORES,CONC NES	W 389606	62249		75607	W 551216	101441	W 529721	100890	MINERAIS METAUX COMMUNS
2873	ALUMINIUM ORES,ALUMINA	W 331656	55104	W 370834	63158	W 410927	88037	W 407930	85716	MINERAIS D'ALUMINIUM
28732	ALUMINA(ALUMINIUM OXIDE)	W 293426	51238	W 330666	59116	W 367947	84219	W 371768	81592	ALUMINE (OXYDE ALUMINIUM)
29	CRUDE ANIMAL,VEG MAT NES		69039		93724		97117		133637	MATIERES BRUTES ANIM,VEGET
292	CRUDE VEG MATERIALS NES	W 16844	63311	W 21053	82655	W 21332	82936	W 28686	110354	MAT BRUTES VEGETALES NDA
3	MINERAL FUELS ETC		410621		645657		859002		885800	COMBUSTIBLES MINERAUX LUB
32	COAL,COKE AND BRIQUETTES		52658		65204		69583		67335	HOUILLES,COKES,BRIQUETTES
322	COAL,LIGNITE AND PEAT	W 967099	52658	W 1278798	63814	W 1156134	69577	W 1030023	66539	HOUILLES,LIGNITES,TOURBE
3222	OTH COAL,NOT AGGLOMERATD	W 966477	52381	W 1278076	63433	W 1154762	68891	W 1028682	65966	AUTRES HOUILLES
33	PETROLEUM AND PRODUCTS		273393		487133		623960		616694	PETROLE ET DERIVES
333	CRUDE PETROLEUM	W 147814	18823	W 493402	65440	W 699756	98577	W 780149	126966	HUILES BRUTES DE PETROLE
334	PETROLEUM PRODUCTS,REFIN	W 1560755	230181	W 2153296	382372	W 2464062	475807	W 2040490	448530	PRODUITS RAFFINES
3341	GASOLINE,OTH LIGHT OILS					W 812996	170866	W 424860	96591	ESSENCES POUR MOTEURS
33411	MOTOR,AVIATION SPIRIT					W 465735	93626	W 340879	78226	ESSENCES MOTEURS D'AVIONS
33412	SPIRIT TYPE JET FUEL					W 282671	64975			CARBUREACTEURS
3342	KEROSENE,OTH MEDIUM OILS					W 1548038	243515	W 218569	48377	PETR LAMPANTS,AUT HUIL
33421	KEROSENE INCL JET FUEL					W 1548038	243515	W 218569	48377	PETROLES LAMPANTS
3343	GAS OILS					W 80934	37260	W 1241945	212745	GAS OILS
3345	LUBS,PETROLEUM OILS NES	W 2430	8200	W 4400	12795	W 21268	23886	W 155099	90774	HUILES LUBRIFIANTES
341	*GAS,NATURAL AND MANUFCT	W 627819	79556	W 474639	92325	W 182348	97811	W 208463	97047	GAZ NATUREL,GAZ MANUFACT
3414	PETROLEUM GASES, GASEOUS	W 627801	79506	W 473930	92051	W 174990	95233	W 205005	95585	GAZ DE PETROLE GAZEUX
351	*ELECTRIC CURRENT		5014		996		67648		104724	ENERGIE ELECTRIQUE
5	CHEMCLS,RELATED PROD NES		2299714		2933092		3482324		4264041	PRODUITS CHIMIQUES
51	ORGANIC CHEMICALS		679783		866994		1053378		1226892	PROD CHIMIQ ORGANIQUES
511	HYDROCARBONS NES,DERIVS		43121		75966		110589	W 194717	107361	HYDROCARBURES NDA
512	ALCOHOLS,PHENOLS ETC	W 62065	44545	W 63377	52963	W 62335	67344	W 110120	83421	PHENOLS,PHENOLS-ALCOOLS
513	CARBOXYLIC ACIDS ETC	W 85847	106408	W 111475	134747	W 105834	161801	W 118134	185355	ACIDES CARBOXYLIQUES
5137	MONOACIDS AND DERIVATIVS	W 42208	48247	W 55270	62526	W 46762	74213	W 50456	84973	ACIDES MONOCARBOXYLIQUES
514	NITROGEN-FNCTN COMPOUNDS	W 39333	206234	W 52124	251388	W 55270	291915	W 70281	336966	COMPOSES FONCT AZOTEES
5148	OTH NITROGN-FNCTN CMPNDS	W 15683	121692	W 17253	138894	W 17790	154830	W 22884	166131	AUTRES COMPOSES AZOTES
51482	IMIDE-,IMIDE-FNCT CMPNDS	W 5386	82632	W 5498	89471	W 6758	99454	W 7948	102644	COMPOSES A FONCTION IMIDE
515	ORG-INORG COMPOUNDS ETC	W 17942	219598	W 20795	266951	W 23244	305378	W 30596	375414	COMPOSES ORGANO-MINERAUX
5156	HETEROCYCLIC CMPDS ETC	W 6883	150977	W 7446	177976	W 7631	202157	W 10969	245889	COMPOSES HETEROCYCLIQUES
51569	OTH HETEROCYC CMPDS,ETC	W 4008	146393	W 4237	173122	W 4845	196786	W 5691	234478	AUT COMP HETEROCYCLIQUES
516	OTHER ORGANIC CHEMICALS	W 60691	59877	W 89587	84978	W 129034	116351	W 153021	138375	AUTRES PROD ORGANIQUES
5161	ETHERS,EPOXIDES,ACETALS	W 32878	26950	W 81326	44094	W 120314	64243	W 142456	74191	ETHERS-OXYDES,ALCOOLS
52	INORGANIC CHEMICALS		130708		153142		168124		203265	PROD CHIM INORGANIQUES
522	INORG ELEMNTS,OXIDES,ETC		49548	W 186163	62907	W 139195	62683	W 203288	81690	ELEMENTS INORGANIQUES
523	OTHR INORG CHEMICALS ETC	W 286596	78073	W 301670	85788		100405	W 363539	115441	AUT PRODUITS CHIMIQUES INORG
5232	OTH MTL CMPD OF INRG ACD	W 235451	50286	W 240958	54589	W 250054	60891	W 284805	75144	SELS METALLIQUES
53	DYES,TANNING,COLOUR PROD		148283		185613		191283		248001	PROD TEINTURE,COLORANTS
533	PIGMENTS,PAINTS,ETC	W 37843	101128	W 52430	128604	W 44244	131695	W 57695	170296	PIGMENTS,PEINTURES,VERNIS
541	*MEDICINAL,PHARM PRODUCT		356371	K 5513668	495061		488826	K 8462090	582580	PROD MEDICINAUX PHARMACEUT
5413	ANTIBIOTICS IN BULK	K 686585	74374	K 690165	79443	K 596632	74753	K 692529	89960	ANTIBIOTIQUES NDA
54139	OTHER ANTIBIOTICS	K 315068	52393	K 333926	58080	K 276180	54687	K 337745	68364	AUTRES ANTIBIOTIQUES
5416	GLYCOSIDES,GLANDS,SERA	K 451811	68367	K 485299	134631	K 969473	93659	K 432066	103096	HETEROSIDES
54164	ANTISERA,MICROB VACCINES	K 169810	39373	K 237365	93050	K 215910	51315	K 223980	75523	SERUMS,VACCINS
5417	MEDICAMENTS	K 1558848	130681	K 2399771	181432	K 4154774	224030	K 4860096	273495	MEDICAMENTS
54179	— CONTNG OTH SUBSTANCES	K 1291240	68678	K 1802162	101811	K 3466004	123677	K 3997950	166593	MED CONT AUT SUBSTANCES
55	PERFUME,CLEANING ETC PRD		116890		175752		191672		229458	PROD POUR PARFUM,TOILETTE
553	PERFUMERY,COSMETICS,ETC	W 6387	40828	W 8958	61012	W 10609	63045	W 14190	89121	PRODUITS DE PARFUMERIE
554	SOAP,CLEANSING ETC PREPS	W 29576	55717	W 51300	85369	W 50840	91529	W 60110	103359	SAVONS,PRODUITS DETERSIFS
5542	WASHING PREPARATIONS ETC	W 24399	43527	W 42904	67846	W 46132	80716	W 54413	90570	PROD ORG TENSIO-ACT NDA
562	*FERTILIZERS,MANUFACTURE	W 492420	73132	W 773682	123096	W 1055705	226612	W 1970285	429100	ENGRAIS MANUFACTURES
5621	CHEM NITROGENOUS FERTLZR	W 211268	27430	W 407806	53751	W 527589	107380	W 1007812	205674	ENGRAIS AZOTES
56216	UREA	W 184940	23048	W 365735	48058	W 417071	90620	W 838590	175643	UREE
5629	FERTILIZERS NES	W 227410	37416	W 313600	61613	W 433212	102682	W 854233	203053	ENGRAIS NDA
56292	NITROG-PHOS FERTILZR NES	W 207032	32293	W 289522	56127	W 409956	95564	W 830516	194926	ENGRAIS NDA CONT N P
58	PLASTIC MATERIALS ETC		446934		535438		679265		770889	MAT PLAST ARTIFICIELLES
582	PROD OF CONDENSATION ETC	W 51726	112611	W 74537	152369	W 83661	203177	W 113533	239454	PROD CONDENS,POLYCOND
5823	ALKYDS,OTHER POLYESTERS	W 27691	58268	W 46820	87602	W 58043	134991	W 80643	151762	ALKYDES ET AUT POLYESTERS

4. Special Imports C.I.F. by Commodities according to the S.I.T.C. (Rev. 2) in thousand U.S. Dollars
Importations Spéciales C.A.F. par Produits d'après la C.T.C.I. (Rév. 2) en milliers de Dollars E.U.

SITC CTCI	COMMODITY	1993			1994			1995			1996			PRODUIT
			WEIGHT POIDS	VALUE VALEUR		WEIGHT POIDS	VALUE VALEUR		WEIGHT POIDS	VALUE VALEUR		WEIGHT POIDS	VALUE VALEUR	
58231	— IN PRIMARY FORMS	W	22400	37319	W	41128	60598	W	53347	112860	W	76496	130158	SOUS FORMES PRIMAIRES
583	POLYMERIZATION ETC PRODS	W	244194	295188	W	275714	337577	W	255970	426948	W	337945	479527	PROD POLYMERISATION
5831	POLYETHYLENE	W	119614	90717	W	145473	113298	W	128106	150725	W	172817	176721	POLYETHYLENE
58311	— IN PRIMARY FORMS	W	116491	82845	W	141003	101545	W	122725	134765	W	165281	156524	POLYETHYLENE PRIMAIRES
5839	OTH POLYMRZTION ETC PROD	W	27962	78132	W	25652	73693	W	32218	99991	W	38772	105471	AUT PROD POLYMER COPOLYM
59	CHEMICAL MATERIALS NES			336961			387322			473906			562102	MAT PROD CHIMIQUES NDA
591	PESTICIDES,DISINFECTANTS	W	21015	118435	W	24430	154166	W	31044	207170	W	39085	240311	DESINF,INSECT,FONG,HERB
5913	HERBICIDES,FOR RETAIL	W	11837	75766	W	13808	97011	W	18748	137721	W	25169	155116	HERBICIDES VENTE AU DET
598	MISCEL CHEM PRODUCTS NES	W	81135	189818	W	91189	201432	W	98785	231092	W	116929	280830	PROD DIV INDUST CHIM NDA
5982	ANTI–KNOCK PREPARTNS ETC	W	23166	56386	W	25729	52546	W	22979	48043	W	28779	55703	PREPARAT ANTIDETONANTES
5989	CHEM PRODUCTS,PREPS NES	W	47284	119466	W	52877	130515	W	62285	161406	W	72650	201793	PROD PREP CHIMIQUES NDA
59899	OTH CHEM PRODS,PREPS,NES	W	35079	84253	W	36407	90815	W	42782	111397	W	48120	130681	AUT PRODUITS CHIMIQUES NDA
6	BASIC MANUFACTURES			2284408			2854621			3023690			3544722	ART MANUFACTURES
62	RUBBER MANUFACTURES NES			176077			207005			212360			307692	CAOUTCHOUC MANUFACTURE
625	RUBBER TYRES, TUBES ETC	W	31689	94948	W	36532	115025	W	35211	116774	W	50976	176109	PNEUS CAOUTCHOUC VULCANISE
6252	TYRES,NEW,BUS OR LORRY	W	12539	37991	W	16019	49438	W	16236	55209	W	23074	81653	PNEUS POUR AUTOBUS,CAMIONS
628	RUBBER ARTICLES NES	W	5301	52361	W	6672	65108	W	6640	66524	W	8408	88347	OUVRAGES CAOUTCHOUC NDA
63	WOOD,CORK MANUFACTRS NES			46678			80797			117097			144445	OUVRAGES LIEGE ET BOIS
635	WOOD MANUFACTURES NES	W	8318	14609	W	20587	37781	W	39983	80235	W	35733	101538	ART MANUF EN BOIS NDA
6353	BUILDERS WOODWRK,PREFABS	W	4211	7689	W	14792	27446	W	32559	71117	W	29705	90490	OUVRAGES DE MENUISERIE
64	PAPER,PAPERBOARD AND MFR			450844			524493			665674			721732	PAPIERS,CARTONS & OUVRAGES
641	PAPER AND PAPERBOARD	W	520063	351590	W	534720	410841	W	521473	544382	W	569517	583032	PAPIERS ET CARTONS
6411	NEWSPRINT	W	153451	75057	W	117077	58973	W	105298	81758	W	64419	50437	PAPIER JOURNAL
6412	PRINTG,WRITING PAPER NES	W	97589	79909	W	129485	109662	W	130228	150710	W	156471	166156	PAPIERS POUR L'IMPRESSION
64122	— COATED,IMPREGNATD ETC	W	80545	65194	W	114588	96215	W	113297	127188	W	128521	134948	PAPIERS IMPRESSION COUCHES
6413	KRAFT PAPER,PAPERBOARD	W	75475	43427	W	108782	64528	W	119184	95127	W	148877	105963	PAPIER ET CARTON KRAFT
6415	PAPER,PAPERBRD,BULK,NES	W	1[illegible]0344	87602	W	111775	86698	W	86555	97103	W	103688	113168	PAPIERS,CARTONS ROULEAUX
64159	OTHER PAPER ETC,BULK,NES	W	86089	67876	W	82581	69957	W	75019	84375	W	85787	96208	AUT PAPIER ROULEAUX FEUILLES
6418	COATED ETC PAPER NES BLK	W	38466	44920	W	29231	55849	W	57006	94842	W	73862	123001	PAP,CARTONS COUCHES,ENDUITS
64181	PLASTIC COATED PAPER ETC	W	7426	14605	W	13891	31148	W	37254	63729	W	47695	84894	PAP,CARTONS ENDUITS,RESINES
642	PAPER,ETC,PRECUT,ARTS OF	W	41889	99254	W	57829	113653	W	57847	121293	W	67004	138700	PAP,CARTONS DECOUPES
65	TEXTILE YARN,FABRICS,ETC			444106			485520			428685			609698	FILS,TISSUS,ARTICLES TEXTILE
651	TEXTILE YARN			80857	W	21344	87297	W	21376	89918	W	35173	144443	FILS TEXTILES
652	COTTON FABRICS,WOVEN	W	12656	64613	W	10798	60243	W	8998	54190	W	13801	86002	TISSUS DE COTON
6522	WOVEN COTTON BLEACHD,ETC	W	11528	60015	W	9714	55609	W	7812	49088	W	11268	74895	TISSUS COTON BLANCHIS ETC
653	WOVN MAN–MADE FIB FABRIC	W	18379	128564	W	17386	121546	W	12910	90827	W	18239	125143	TISSUS FIBRES SYNTH,ARTIF
657	SPECIAL TXTL FABRC,PRODS	W	9197	55044	W	11987	71805	W	13112	76293	W	16198	96809	TISSUS SPECIAUX
658	TEXTILE ARTICLES NES	W	9113	51549	W	10471	63529	W	9583	60374	W	10894	73763	ART FACONNES MAT TEXTILES
66	NONMETAL MINERAL MFS NES			198671			262009			231886			269043	ART MIN NON METALLIQUES
664	GLASS	W	46632	57777	W	28801	76160	W	17003	59702	W	21499	66672	VERRE
67	IRON AND STEEL			368755			487569			514292			524908	FER ET ACIER
672	IRON,STEEL PRIMARY FORMS	W	344931	98368	W	624673	163705	W	485402	152563	W	363846	114732	LINGOTS FER,ACIER
6725	IRN,STL BLOOMS,SLABS,ETC	W	180846	46560	W	497456	120666	W	396136	112815	W	270454	76405	BLOOMS,BILLETTES FER ACIER
67251	IRN,SMPLE STL BLOOMS,ETC	W	180393	46286	W	481335	113387	W	372293	99855	W	263849	72136	BLOOMS ETC NON ACIER FIN
6727	IRN,STL COIL FR REROLLNG	W	163831	51681	W	125282	42352	W	88524	39485	W	93192	38282	EBAUCHES POUR TOLES FER
67271	IRON,SIMPLE STEEL COILS	W	163686	51549	W	125145	42151	W	88378	39282	W	93108	38084	EBAUCHES NON EN ACIER
673	IRON,STEEL SHAPES ETC	W	102349	45310	W	116435	57128	W	87335	48821	W	142271	75210	BARRES,PROFIL FER,ACIER
674	IRN,STL UNIV,PLATE,SHEET	W	224748	159653	W	246253	166081	W	232661	178859	W	258133	192521	LARGES PLATS,TOLES
6746	IRN,STL THIN PLATE,ROLLD	W	95512	70476	W	105175	73245	W	78034	71931	W	112971	90433	TOLES LAM MOINS 3MM
678	IRON,STL TUBES,PIPES,ETC	W	19620	37410	W	41659	64793	W	54628	92359	W	39239	89369	TUBES,TUYAUX EN FONTE,FER
68	NON–FERROUS METALS			170915			214857			247304			285183	METAUX NON FERREUX
682	COPPER EXC CEMENT COPPER	W	48473	107857	W	51757	125590	W	42832	139433	W	48938	134332	CUIVRE
6821	COPPER NES,ALLOYS,UNWRT	W	40594	81942	W	40640	92065	W	31804	96914	W	33900	86087	CUIVRE BRUT
68212	COPPER REFINED,UNWROUGHT	W	40591	81927	W	40601	91965	W	31787	96844	W	33864	85939	CUIVRE AFFINE BRUT
684	ALUMINIUM	W	11599	37670	W	20521	58430	W	22538	73616	W	36541	114735	ALUMINIUM
6842	ALUMINIUM,ALLOYS WORKED	W	10847	36429	W	19789	57520	W	21196	70297	W	35382	112366	ALUMINIUM,ALLIAGES OUVRE
69	METAL MANUFACTURES NES			417126			575504			591851			647308	ART MANUFACT EN METAL NDA
691	STRUCTURES AND PARTS NES	W	8390	17476	W	15212	29529	W	24810	67345	W	27536	67299	CONSTRUCT FER,ACIER,ALU
692	METAL TANKS,BOXES,ETC	W	17645	61562	W	23711	88521	W	26438	87286	W	23950	63492	RECIPIENTS METALLIQUES
6924	MTL TRANSPORT BOXES ETC	W	15373	57838	W	18804	70405	W	24900	80401	W	18505	48979	FUTS,TAMBOURS,BIDONS
695	TOOLS	W	10383	77821	W	17686	120243	W	11306	107155	W	11935	119816	OUTILS A MAIN
6954	BLADES,TIPS,ETC FR TOOLS	W	1835	38208	W	6688	71477	W	3033	68391	W	2960	73777	OUTILS POUR MACHINE–OUTIL
697	BASE MTL HOUSEHOLD EQUIP	W	15900	59867	W	17751	64403	W	11843	43308	W	15387	55259	ART MENAGE MET COMMUNS
699	BASE METAL MFRS NES			109640	W	34486	156604	W	32425	170813	W	35531	190862	ART MANUFACTURES MET NDA
7	MACHINES,TRANSPORT EQUIP			8439424			11188152			8930585			10901953	MACHINES MATERIEL TRANSPORT
71	POWER GENERATING EQUIPMT			533023			660762			767264			887448	MACHINES GENERATRICES
713	INTRNL COMBUS PSTN ENGIN	W	37503	298875	W	39610	359689	W	37750	402358	W	45787	506814	MOTEURS EXPL COMB INT, PIECE
7132	MOTOR VEHCL PISTN ENGINS	W	12373	114735	W	14890	147465	W	22130	228745	W	28538	302469	MOTEURS EXPL POUR VEHICULES
7139	PISTON ENGINE PARTS NES	W	22988	156982	W	22266	176542	W	13881	145344	W	15061	170677	PIECES POUR 713.2,3,8
716	ROTATING ELECTRIC PLANT	W	15768	164829	W	18960	233487	W	19379	288390	W	23398	295680	APP ELECTR ROTATIFS,PIECES
7161	DC MOTORS AND GENERATORS	W	6090	86657	W	4728	98258	W	4859	147225	W	2436	55740	MOTEURS COURANT CONTINU
7162	AC MTRS,GENRTRS,GEN SETS	W	9293	59064	W	12495	84371	W	11662	91421	W	13702	98837	MOTEURS ELECTRIQUES
7169	PTS NES OF ROT ELEC PLNT	W	375	18843	W	1730	50699	W	2847	49620	W	7257	140966	PIECES MAC APP ROTATIFS
72	MACHS FOR SPCL INDUSTRYS			931568			1132190			814516			1090943	MAC SPECIALES POUR INDUST
721	AGRIC MACHY,EXC TRACTORS	W	13313	73770	W	22570	129091	W	18386	119029	W	28665	186049	MACHINES AGRICOLES
7212	HARVESTING ETC MACHINES	W	7010	44996	W	15084	89575	W	13816	91444	W	21803	149858	ENGINS POUR LA RECOLTE
72122	COMBINE HARVESTR–THRESHR	W	3433	18632	W	8832	50679	W	6018	35046	W	11354	73273	MOISSONNEUSES–BATTEUSES
722	TRACTORS NON–ROAD	W	7639	32844	W	11870	55708	W	7795	42872	W	16826	102406	TRACTEURS
7224	WHEELED TRACTORS NES	W	6993	28623	W	11440	52131	W	6961	35615	W	14898	85761	TRACTEURS A ROUES
723	CIVIL ENGNEERG EQUIP ETC	W	24274	119953	W	43971	211524	W	18462	112876	W	15504	119367	APPAREILS DE GENIE CIVIL
7234	CONST,MINING MACHNRY NES	W	22201	105481	W	39598	181425	W	15809	87454	W	13318	97723	MACH POUR LA CONST, MINES
72342	SLFPRP SHOVELS,EXCAVATRS	W	16768	68419	W	23053	102869	W	9397	49817	W	8371	53139	PELLES MECANIQUES
724	TEXTILE,LEATHER MACHNRY	W	13089	184631	W	12220	165969	W	9076	93067	W	13409	154368	MACH POUR INDUSTRIE TEXTILE
726	PRINTG,BKBINDG MACHY,PTS	W	7532	145285	W	6484	129830	W	2970	79284	W	3458	80684	MACHINES POUR IMPRIMERIE
7264	PRINTING PRESSES	W	6483	108854	W	4960	79922	W	2072	44413	W	2713	48480	MACHINES A IMPRIMER
72641	ROTARY PRINTING PRESSES	W	6483	108854	W	4960	79922	W	2072	44413	W	2713	48480	MACH IMPRIMER ROTATIVES
727	FOOD MACHRY NON–DOMESTIC	W	4109	76371	W	3738	73357	W	2709	64240	W	2605	52417	MACH INDUSTRIES ALIMENT
7272	OTH FOOD PROC MCHY,PARTS	W	3690	72119	W	3310	68514	W	2346	58464	W	1914	43834	AUT MACH IND ALIMENTAIRE
72722	INDUS FOOD PROC MACH NES	W	3494	68012	W	2877	60101	W	1967	51747	W	1607	40198	MACHINES BOULANGERIE
728	OTH MACHY FOR SPCL INDUS	W	16345	251282	W	22402	319476	W	20218	266010	W	31067	356313	AUT MACH IND PARTICULIERES
7284	MACHY FOR SPCL INDUS NES	W	11035	211533	W	12877	247718	W	14606	220068	W	18673	268148	MACH SPEC IND PARTICUL.
72842	RUBBER,PLASTICS WRKG MCH	W	5109	100217	W	6093	114797	W	3413	67292	W	4212	64264	MACH IND CAOUT MAT PLAST
72848	OTH MCHY WITH INDIV FNCT	W	2810	59837	W	4263	83321	W	8472	102428	W	12540	167870	AUTRES MACHINES NDA
73	METALWORKING MACHINERY			129204			177052			145287			231524	MACH TRAVAIL DES METAUX
736	METALWORKING MACH–TOOLS	W	10216	99880	W	13952	131278	W	8406	97879	W	13698	161331	MACH–OUTILS TRAVAIL METAUX
7361	METAL CUTTING MACH–TOOLS	W	3987	43705	W	7533	65563	W	4191	34440	W	4554	56147	MACH–OUT ENLEVEMENT METAL
74	GENRL INDUSTRL MACHY NES			1050495			1559845			1691779			1866929	MACH APP INDUSTRIE
741	HEATING,COOLING EQUIPMNT	W	18763	189139	W	35744	314963	W	33887	346495	W	35072	346900	MACH CHAUFFAGE,PIECES
7414	NONDOM REFRIG EQUIPT,PTS	W	5896	51908	W	11600	96919	W	10098	92529	W	11528	99796	MAT PRODUCTION DU FROID
74141	REFRIG EQUIP NONDOMESTIC	W	5101	44808	W	10338	86673	W	8978	81818	W	10285	89247	REFIG INDUSTRIELS
7415	AIR–CONDITIONING MACHNRY	W	5244	51677	W	5946	58625	W	6943	65573	W	10078	96201	GROUPES CONDITION AIR

4. Special Imports C.I.F. by Commodities according to the S.I.T.C. (Rev. 2) in thousand U.S. Dollars
Importations Spéciales C.A.F. par Produits d'après la C.T.C.I. (Rév. 2) en milliers de Dollars E.U.

SITC CTCI	COMMODITY	1993			1994			1995			1996			PRODUIT
		WEIGHT POIDS		VALUE VALEUR	WEIGHT POIDS		VALUE VALEUR	WEIGHT POIDS		VALUE VALEUR	WEIGHT POIDS		VALUE VALEUR	
7416	HEATING,COOLING EQU NES	W	5863	61679	W	11791	113244	W	13032	145563	W	10147	118285	APP CHANGEMENT TEMP
742	PUMPS FOR LIQUIDS ETC	W	7313	103093	W	10092	124280	W	9058	128039	W	11374	172651	POMPES MOTO–POMPES
7428	OTHER PUMPS FOR LIQUIDS	W	2819	50702	W	2962	57854	W	3152	58221	W	4272	83505	AUTRES POMPES POUR LIQ
743	PUMPS NES,CENTRFUGES ETC	W	22990	194370	W	25293	270330	W	25624	277265	W	27200	292388	POMPES COMPRES,VENT ETC
7431	PUMPS FOR GASES ETC	W	17129	118290	W	16763	160257	W	15482	132556	W	14979	123290	POMPES AIR A VIDE,COMPRES
7436	GAS,LIQUID FILTERS ETC	W	2559	36485	W	4630	58243	W	4980	69113	W	7220	91882	APP POUR FILT DES LIQUIDES
744	MECHANICAL HANDLING EQU	W	21444	116087	W	37579	225082	W	36761	307810	W	36981	294481	EQUIP MANUTENTION PIECES
7441	FORK LIFT TRCKS,ETC,PTS	W	9021	31299	W	16426	76512	W	12687	70505	W	12104	62271	CHARIOTS POUR USINES ETC
74411	FORK LIFT TRUCKS ETC	W	9017	31238	W	16412	76410	W	12681	70403	W	12096	62206	CHARIOTS POUR LES GARES
7442	LIFTING,LOADING MACH NES	W	9370	72412	W	17093	127879	W	19010	192958	W	17425	175614	APP LEVAGE,MANUTENTION
74428	OTH HANDLING ETC MCH NES	W	7481	60031	W	12902	100023	W	14246	151940	W	12252	126324	AUT APP LEVAGE ETC
745	NONELEC MACHY,TOOLS NES	W	10981	201023	W	15626	288363	W	17617	268125	W	29628	331446	AUT MACH NON ELEC,PIECES
7452	OTH NONELEC MCHS,PTS NES	W	9901	177191	W	14612	263884	W	16784	251667	W	28664	306281	AUT MACH NON ELEC,PIECES
74522	PACKAGNG,BOTTLNG,ETC MCH	W	2812	110675	W	4093	147861	W	3354	118418	W	2938	119484	MACH NETT BOUTEILLES,ETC
74527	SPRAYING MACHINERY	W	4731	35337	W	8008	63571	W	11525	86005	W	24120	146475	APP PROJETER ETC LIQUID
749	NONELEC MACH PTS,ACC NES	W	21822	246783	W	32011	336827	W	35978	364045	W	41288	429064	PIECES MACH NON ELEC NDA
7491	BALL,ROLLER,ETC BEARINGS	W	6450	81109	W	7398	92875	W	7876	100848	W	9217	115371	ROULEMENTS BILLES ETC
7492	COCKS,VALVES ETC NES	W	4352	63157	W	7344	99359	W	8217	110453	W	8840	130691	ART ROB,SIM POUR TUYAUX
7493	SHAFT,CRANK,PULLEY ETC	W	9717	70329	W	14952	91328	W	17989	105523	W	20551	114226	ARBRES TRANS,VILEBREQUINS
75	OFFICE MACHNES,ADP EQUIP			666400			927403			707632			815211	MACH BUREAU TRAIT AUTOM
751	OFFICE MACHINES	W	5129	95986	W	5127	134080	W	3484	86832	W	4575	103819	MACH,APPAREILS DE BUREAU
7518	OFFICE MACHINES NES	W	2925	53449	W	3110	63645	W	2048	49492	W	3130	67823	MACH,APP DE BUREAU NDA
752	AUTOMTIC DATA PROC EQUIP	W	11944	482350	W	14927	670504	W	9819	469076	W	13444	543049	MACH TRAIT INFORMATION
7523	DIGITL CENTRL PROCESSORS	W	3611	180933	W	4121	228977	W	1850	145084	W	2109	162200	UNITES CENTRALES
7525	ADP PERIPHERAL UNITS	W	7229	205588	W	9200	277865	W	6511	186521	W	9888	215854	UNITES PERIPHERIQUES
759	OFFICE,ADP MCH PTS,ACCES	W	1678	88064	W	2100	122819	W	3888	151725	W	6701	168343	PIECES DU 751 ET 752
7599	ACCTG,ETC,ADP MCH PTS,AC	W	1267	74677	W	1719	108633	W	3470	136558	W	6226	150270	PIECES DU 751 ET 752
76	TELECOMM,SOUND EQUIPMENT			1151088			1495055			1028652			1083050	EQUIPMENT DE TELECOM
761	TELEVISION RECEIVERS	W	11221	128873	W	8563	122281	W	1699	27307	W	1547	29350	RECEPTEURS DE TELEVISION
7611	COLOUR TV RECEIVERS	W	10132	122573	W	8036	119183	W	1507	26043	W	1376	28230	RECEPTEURS COULEUR
762	RADIO BROADCAST RECEIVRS	W	16232	220879	W	15654	214190	W	8809	121514	W	11285	131371	RECEPTEURS RADIODIFFUSION
7628	OTHER RADIO RECEIVERS	W	12722	177635	W	12616	175639	W	5715	78673	W	6323	69586	AUTRES RECEPT RADIO
763	SOUND RECORDRS,PHONOGRPH	W	2742	73219	W	1754	56535	W	978	29529	W	1073	39048	PHONO,APP ENREGISTREMENT
7638	OTHR SOUND APPARATUS ETC	W	2452	68954	W	1622	54445	W	926	29062	W	1051	38898	AUT APP D'ENREGIS,REPROD
764	TELECOM EQPT,PTS,ACC NES	W	18454	728117	W	24597	1102049	W	13729	850302	W	15446	883281	EQUIP TELECOM,PIECES
7641	LINE TELEPHONE,ETC EQUIP	W	4095	202376	W	4813	278565	W	3559	261110	W	4033	265033	APP TELEPHON PAR FIL
7643	TV,RADIO TRANSMITTRS ETC	W	1199	168478	W	5145	363648	W	1387	248645	W	1638	281359	APP EMET TELE RADIO
7649	PTS NES OF EQUIPMT OF 76	W	9502	276635	W	10631	370824	W	6100	285693	W	6513	272620	PIECES DE LA DIV 76
76491	PTS NES OF APPAR OF 7641	W	629	89599	W	610	65649	W	626	88569	W	430	79385	PIECES POUR 764.1
76493	TELECOMM EQUIPMT PTS NES	W	6680	116940	W	8561	260117	W	4841	176949	W	5385	173688	PIECES 761,762,764.3,8
76499	PARTS ETC OF SOUND EQUIP	W	2107	69139	W	1302	43146	W	512	19019	W	567	18172	PIECES NDA POUR 763
77	ELECTRIC MACHNRY NES ETC			1332950			1504753			1338292			1604211	MACH APP ELECT NDA
771	ELECTRIC POWER MACHY NES	W	5122	75425	W	12506	121942	W	7311	102305	W	11814	132620	MACH PROD,TRANS ELECTR
7712	OTH ELEC POWER MACHY NES	W	2563	44201	W	4645	71933	W	3682	68621	W	4889	77544	AUT APP PROD TRANSF ELEC
772	SWITCHGEAR ETC,PARTS NES	W	8966	192504	W	10351	227042	W	9168	232695	W	11525	289036	APP COUPURE,SECT ETC
7721	SWITCHGEAR ETC	W	7780	156730	W	9273	192899	W	8332	205469	W	10600	265462	APP COUPURE,SECTIONMNT
773	ELECTR DISTRIBUTNG EQUIP	W	29187	142986	W	29389	138500	W	27152	149915	W	18751	144340	EQUIPMT DISTRIBUTION ELECT
7731	INSULATED WIRE,CABLE ETC	W	27014	134182	W	27043	127785	W	24852	137689	W	16533	129695	FILS,CABLES ISOLES ELECT
774	ELECTRO–MEDCL,XRAY EQUIP	W	955	38109	W	1123	69935	W	661	64483	W	598	61716	APPAREILS MEDICAUX
775	HOUSEHOLD TYPE EQUIP NES	W	71181	312895	W	66091	311472	W	47848	221106	W	64809	296040	MACH,APP USAGE DOMESTQUE
7751	HOUSEHOLD LDRY EQUIP NES	W	22055	73939	W	25965	93295	W	16190	60571	W	27537	101816	MACH A LAVER ET SECHOIRS
77511	DOMESTIC WASHING MACHNES	W	21771	72229	W	25703	91752	W	16084	59989	W	27419	101109	MACH LAVER LINGE MOINS 6 KG
7752	DOM REFRIGERATRS,FREEZRS	W	19465	77896	W	13144	59489	W	12358	54306	W	13432	63162	REFRIG,CONGEL MENAGER
77521	DOMESTIC REFRIGERATORS	W	14851	58922	W	10693	49319	W	10008	44751	W	11355	53703	REFRIGERATEURS
7757	DOMESTIC ELECTRC EQU NES	W	19027	77320	W	13355	60840	W	10618	45538	W	13105	56371	APP ELECTR DOMEST NDA
7758	ELECTRO–THERMIC APPL NES	W	10013	73642	W	12960	88000	W	8107	51839	W	9959	64549	APP ELECTROTHERMIQ NDA
776	TRANSISTORS,VALVES,ETC	W	22223	255859	W	21764	250453	W	13276	182706	W	15772	202207	LAMPES,TUBES,VALVES
7761	TV PICTURE TUBES	W	19067	131895	W	18916	125171	W	11156	76282	W	12832	91929	TUBES CATHODIQUES
7764	ELECTRONIC MICROCIRCUITS	W	1801	81978	W	1680	84463	W	1321	77319	W	1737	78209	MICROSTRUCTURES ELECTRON
778	ELECTRICAL MACHINERY NES	W	40895	315171	W	48627	385409	W	46703	385081	W	53775	478251	AUTRES MACH ELECT NDA
7781	BATTERIES,ACCUMULATORS	W	15936	66114	W	19433	75258	W	19744	77464	W	24073	93442	PILES ET ACCUMULATEURS
7783	AUTOMOTIVE ELECTR EQUIP	W	7020	79650	W	9123	104413	W	7836	93643	W	9054	109797	EQUIP ELECT MOTEURS EXPL
77831	IGNITION,STARTING EQUIP	W	3941	49873	W	5264	67885	W	4838	62959	W	5049	65859	APP ELEC ALLUM,DEMARRAGE
7788	OTH ELEC MACHY,EQUIP NES	W	11015	86784	W	12735	116801	W	12419	136105	W	12720	186254	AUT MACH APP ELEC NDA
77886	OTH ELEC MACHINERY NES	W	819	21706	W	1475	35949	W	2500	62408	W	2952	100243	AUT MACH APP ELECTRIQUES
78	ROAD VEHICLES			2328285			3330590			2118971			2983694	VEHICULES ROUTIERS
781	PASS MOTOR VEH EXC BUSES	W	90155	844534	W	141497	1394468	W	79048	773204	W	127638	1198389	AUTO TRANSPORT PERSONNES
782	LORRIES,SPCL MTR VEH NES	W	36511	264650	W	75889	558680	W	40974	310998	W	69430	532857	VEHICULES SPECIAUX,MARCH
7821	LORRIES,TRUCKS	W	32494	242385	W	69133	519705	W	35753	284389	W	65972	509322	VEHICULES TRANSP MARCHAND
783	ROAD MOTOR VEHICLES NES	W	10060	54921	W	16867	137619	W	4541	35405	W	5035	39589	VEHICULES ROUTIERS NDA
7831	BUSES	W	6546	32119	W	10340	93421	W	2570	21061	W	3061	24069	VOITURES TRANSPORT COMMUN
784	MOTOR VEH PRTS,ACCES NES	W	145133	876185	W	166620	968052	W	134310	867733	W	153894	1061325	PIECES 722,781,782,783
7841	MOTOR VEHICLE CHASSIS	W	10979	66617	W	1957	13245	W	488	4175	W	591	4923	CHASSIS 722,781,782,783
7849	OTHER MOTOR VEHCL PARTS	W	129733	786242	W	160022	919517	W	128939	826151	W	146219	999010	PIECES 722,781,782,783
785	CYCLES,ETC MOTRZD OR NOT	W	33399	268500	W	30983	225825	W	15687	104678	W	18098	111675	MOTOCYCLES SCOOTERS
7851	MOTORCYCLES ETC	W	20095	218922	W	15558	164491	W	6171	62666	W	4685	53713	MOTO VELO MOTEUR AUXIL
79	OTHR TRANSPORT EQUIPMENT			316411			400502			318191			338941	AUTRE MATERIEL TRANSPORT
792	AIRCRAFT ETC	W	517	208980	W	1043	329338	W	561	175263	W	1088	204933	APP NAVIGATION AERIENNE
7923	AIRCRFT NES2000–15000KG	W	148	60825	W	196	74665	W	142	49844	W	158	86922	AERODYNES 2000 A 15000 KG
7924	AIRCRFT NES OVER 15000KG	W	276	136889	W	736	236198	W	186	98310	W	867	104636	AERODYNES PLUS 15000 KG
793	SHIPS AND BOATS ETC			104243	W	23225	64610	W	25329	104167	W	47550	114415	NAVIRES BATEAUX,ETC
7932	SHIPS AND BOATS NES			103343	W	22933	62257	W	24877	102200	W	46390	109752	NAVIRES ET BATEAUX
79324	FISHING VESSELS ETC	W	14951	66736	W	18606	42386	W	18914	68714	W	19157	73185	BATEAUX DE PECHE
8	MISC MANUFACTURED GOODS			1873078			2236232			1996846			2209614	ART MANUFACTURES DIVERS
821	*FURNITURE,PARTS THEREOF	W	31259	76105	W	40835	115241	W	28630	94558	W	34961	124368	MEUBLES ET PIECES
84	CLOTHING AND ACCESSORIES			314765			315437			229143			232205	VETEMENTS
842	MENS OUTERWEAR NOT KNIT	W	6942	72497	W	5483	81808	W	2457	49110	W	1896	46120	VET DESSUS POUR HOMMES
843	WOMENS OUTERWEAR NONKNIT	W	3303	51087	W	2874	58914	W	1746	43421	W	1456	41074	VET DESSUS FEMMES MAT TEX
846	UNDER GARMENTS KNITTED	W	4240	56611	W	2567	50398	W	1827	39233	W	1296	37291	SOUS VETS DE BONNETERIE
851	*FOOTWEAR	W	11641	128691	W	11204	141479	W	8719	114238	W	8142	116601	CHAUSSURES
85102	FOOTWEAR LEATHER	W	8372	100087	W	6142	96469	W	4588	72716	W	4505	69935	CHAUS SEMELLES EN CUIR
87	PRECISION INSTRUMNTS NES			284598			403309			367334			439092	INSTRUM,APPAR SCIENT NDA
872	MEDICAL INSTRUMENTS NES	W	2318	75030	W	2640	110342	W	2278	60545	W	2400	73697	INSTR,APP MEDIC–CHIR NDA
87202	OTH MEDICAL INSTRUMENTS	W	2144	68908	W	2375	102407	W	1980	54604	W	2106	67202	INSTRUM,APP MEDECINE
874	MEASURNG,CONTROLNG INSTR	W	4112	173252	W	6159	251281	W	6534	270720	W	8055	332277	INSTRUMENTS DE MESURE
8742	MEASUR,DRAW ETC INST,PTS	W	964	31558	W	1520	53935	W	1691	54708	W	2387	87544	INST DESSIN,TRACAGE,PCS
87421	MEASURNG,DRAWNG ETC INST	W	917	27908	W	1445	48796	W	1615	48731	W	2295	81433	INSTRUM DESSIN,TRACAGE
8743	GAS,LIQUID CONTROL INSTR	W	1530	49737	W	2128	64009	W	2142	77536	W	3166	97067	APP,INSTR MESURE FLUIDES
8748	ELEC MEAS,CONTRL EQU NES	W	464	52899	W	920	78399	W	640	83382	W	634	83875	APP ELEC ELECTRO MESURE
87483	OTH ELCTRNC MEAS ETC EQU	W	410	49913	W	798	74535	W	511	77256	W	547	79331	AUT APP ELECTRO DE MESURE
88	PHOTO EQU,OPTICL GDS ETC			206426			232074			199568			219381	APP,FOURN PHOTO,OP,MONTR

4. Special Imports C.I.F. by Commodities according to the S.I.T.C. (Rev. 2) in thousand U.S. Dollars
Importations Spéciales C.A.F. par Produits d'après la C.T.C.I. (Rév. 2) en milliers de Dollars E.U.

SITC CTCI	COMMODITY	1993			1994			1995			1996			PRODUIT
		WEIGHT POIDS		VALUE VALEUR	WEIGHT POIDS		VALUE VALEUR	WEIGHT POIDS		VALUE VALEUR	WEIGHT POIDS		VALUE VALEUR	
882	PHOTO,CINEMA SUPPLIES	W	8169	100990	W	7833	115052	W	7147	118591	W	7466	120827	PRODUITS PHOTO,CINEMA
8822	PHOTO FILM EXC DEV CINMA	W	5665	76436	W	5343	90417	W	4837	93093	W	4865	95591	PLAQUES,PELLICULES,FILMS
885	WATCHES AND CLOCKS			50891			54354			38772			48498	HORLOGERIE
89	MISC MANUFCTRD GOODS NES			808110			951328			916521			994454	ART MANUFACTURES DIVERS
892	PRINTED MATTER	W	19134	91016	W	22924	121496	W	24147	148345	W	21431	137424	IMPRIMES
8921	PRINTED BOOKS,GLOBES,ETC	W	7799	36399	W	9604	54808	W	13016	81922	W	10911	68444	LIVRES,BROCHURES,CARTES
89211	PRINTED BOOKS,PAMPHLETS	W	7535	35122	W	9052	52132	W	12110	77995	W	10271	66050	LIVRES,BROCHURES
893	ARTICLES OF PLASTIC NES			241189			294373			324122			332538	OUVRAGES EN MAT DIVIS 58
8931	PLSTC PACKG CONTNRS,LIDS	W	24115	70068	W	36913	97110	W	36467	116642	W	25805	83333	ART TRANSP EMBALLAGE ETC
8939	MISC PLASTIC ARTICLES	W	29673	169184	W	34619	194589	W	36462	202712	W	44320	244025	ART DIVERS EN MAT DIV 58
89399	OTHR PLASTC ARTICLES NES	W	28231	163146	W	32572	186205	W	33964	194236	W	40769	233114	AUT OUV MAT DIV 58
894	TOYS,SPORTING GOODS,ETC	W	36029	195134	W	43797	224991	W	37100	176627	W	43231	188278	VOITURES ENFANTS,JOUETS
8942	TOYS,INDOOR GAMES ETC	W	28341	152953	W	34765	168991	W	27409	124330	W	34687	140136	JOUETS,JEUX ETC
89423	TOYS NES	W	16524	85844	W	19417	99303	W	15409	68814	W	19279	80922	JOUETS,MODELES REDUITS
898	MUSICAL INSTRUMENTS,PTS	W	10082	137407	W	10135	151488	W	8054	135857			183810	INSTRUMENTS DE MUSIQUE
8983	SOUND RECRDNG TAPE,DISCS	W	8686	114159	W	8778	130007	W	7182	123174			166819	SUPPORTS SON POUR 763
89831	PREPD SND RECORDNG MEDIA	W	5940	58907	W	6425	58061	W	5003	43711	W	5395	48740	SUPPORTS PREPARES
89832	RECORDED DISCS,TAPES ETC	W	2746	55252	W	2353	71947	W	2179	79463			118079	DISQUES,PHONO,BANDES
899	OTHER MANUFACTURED GOODS			89609			98586			79021			91812	AUT ART MANUF DIVERS NDA

5. Special Exports F.O.B. by Commodities according to the S.I.T.C. (Rev. 2) in thousand U.S. Dollars
Exportations Spéciales F.O.B. par Produits d'après la C.T.C.I. (Rév. 2) en milliers de Dollars E.U.

SITC CTCI	COMMODITY	1993			1994			1995			1996			PRODUIT
			WEIGHT POIDS	VALUE VALEUR		WEIGHT POIDS	VALUE VALEUR		WEIGHT POIDS	VALUE VALEUR		WEIGHT POIDS	VALUE VALEUR	
	ALL COMMODITIES			13117758			15838665			20962590			23809643	TOUS PRODUITS
0	FOOD AND LIVE ANIMALS			5338956			5584425			7214582			9241573	ALIMENTS,ANIMAUX VIVANTS
001	*LIVE ANIMALS FOR FOOD	W	10215	13102	W	71563	50628	W	140998	97313	W	60764	44319	ANIMAUX VIVANTS
0011	BOVINE SPECIES,LIVE	W	5062	5002	W	70062	43785	W	138724	86973	W	58810	33122	ESPECE BOVINE
00119	— OTHR THAN FR BREEDING	W	4477	3700	W	69104	41605	W	137490	85241	W	58084	32234	BOVINS NON REPRODUCTEURS
01	MEAT AND PREPARATIONS			748198			918088			1229138			1073840	VIANDES ET PREPARATIONS
011	MEAT FRESH,CHILLD,FROZEN	W	135801	472591	W	217192	627906	W	303463	848098	W	303822	780996	VIANDES FRAICHES,REF,CONGE
0111	BOVINE MEAT FRESH,FROZEN	W	67790	331430	W	140423	494381	W	217585	695161	W	216948	627022	VIANDES BOVIN FRAI,REF
01112	BOVINE MEAT BONELESS	W	65031	327903	W	116601	470400	W	174873	653341	W	174293	583536	VIANDES BOVIN DESOSSEES
0115	HORSE MEAT FRSH,CHLD,FRN	W	30300	67098	W	31826	66088	W	30979	68189	W	35298	81727	VIANDES DE CHEVAL
014	MEAT PREPD,PRSVD,NES ETC	W	98561	275593	W	106156	289991	W	129128	381013	W	109165	292733	CONSERVES DE VIANDES
0149	OTH PREPARD,PRESRVD MEAT	W	97058	260451	W	104668	280396	W	127545	371041	W	106899	283777	AUTRES PREP DE VIANDES
02	DAIRY PRODCTS,BIRDS'EGGS			75837			135329			260062			280562	PRODUITS LAITIERS,OEUFS
022	MILK AND CREAM	W	21553	53061	W	45900	87266	W	111896	195221	W	124303	215057	LAIT ET CREME
0224	MILK,CREAM PRESERVED ETC	W	21191	52692	W	38791	83779	W	75621	175246	W	77954	186159	LAIT,CREME CONS,CONC
02243	MILK DRY,OVER 1.5% FAT	W	13532	39925	W	26334	62202	W	57267	135915	W	56437	138684	LAIT POUDRE SUP 1.5%
03	FISH AND PREPARATIONS			706597			725169			914291			1003813	POISSONS ET PREPARATIONS
034	FISH,FRESH,CHILLED,FROZN	W	244380	302256	W	299925	365653	W	351369	501564	W	365829	494855	POISSON FRAIS, REFRIG,CONG
0342	FISH FROZEN,EXCL FILLETS	W	114830	97931	W	160113	144470	W	166304	174746	W	168032	168396	POISSONS CONGELES
0344	FISH FILLETS,FROZEN	W	118729	194114	W	128674	209146	W	171129	311408	W	179085	299670	FILETS CONGELES
036	SHELL FISH FRESH,FROZEN	W	221165	330842	W	201577	291977	W	196825	319920	W	258825	432665	CRUSTACES,MOLLUSQUES
037	FISH ETC PREPD,PRSVD NES	W	31187	57165	W	23925	52703	W	27432	75644	W	27529	58731	POIS,CRUST,MOL PREPARES
0371	FISH PREPARD,PRESRVD NES	W	30788	55610	W	23408	50194	W	26866	71458	W	26280	53726	CONSERVES DE POISSONS
04	CEREALS AND PREPARATIONS			1536630			1456331			2017775			2802887	CEREALES ET PRODUITS
041	WHEAT ETC UNMILLED	W	5777230	734865	W	5172297	669979	W	6913286	1005372	W	5921995	1065647	FROMENT,EPEAUTRE
0412	OTHER WHEAT ETC UNMILLED	W	5671915	720615	W	5142921	666006	W	6837418	994602	W	5914223	1064462	AUTRE FROMENT NON MOULU
042	RICE	W	279889	75846	W	221386	79840	W	403205	138006	W	379591	139381	RIZ
0422	RICE SEMI–MILLED,MILLED	W	207716	61657	W	198278	74165	W	355630	128120	W	310170	120815	RIZ POLI,GLACE INCL BRISURES
04221	RICE MILLED UNBROKEN	W	192139	58778	W	180075	70670	W	311014	118843	W	281826	114532	RIZ POLI,GLACE EXCL BRISURES
044	MAIZE UNMILLED	W	4870802	525341	W	4153740	491845	W	6000872	682289	W	7079801	1239350	MAIS NON MOULU
045	CEREALS NES UNMILLED	W	1051417	100412	W	544784	78659	W	242169	33158	W	728209	114029	AUTRES CEREALES NON MOULUES
0459	OTHER CEREALS UNMILLED	W	1042721	99414	W	524794	76181	W	234172	32044	W	727889	113922	SARRASIN,MILLET,SORGHO
04592	SORGHUM UNMILLED	W	951593	79432	W	428896	42623	W	188620	17888	W	672064	99203	SORGHO NON MOULU
046	WHEAT ETC MEAL OR FLOUR	W	174231	36971	W	287723	59176	W	227604	57602	W	328532	107295	SEMOULE FARINE,FROMENT
04601	FLOUR OF WHEAT OR MESLIN	W	170763	35986	W	283642	57851	W	223926	56335	W	323929	105150	FARINE DE FROMENT
048	CEREAL ETC PREPARATIONS	W	93137	45337	W	140648	63952	W	134064	96722	W	183774	134350	PREPTNS A BASE CEREALES
05	VEGETABLES AND FRUIT			594487			699238			1034940			1180466	LEGUMES ET FRUITS
054	VEG ETC FRSH,SMPLY PRSVD	W	371433	187102	W	589573	262618	W	490821	266924	W	586906	291565	LEGUMES FRAIS,CONG,SECS
0542	LEGUMINOUS VEGETBLES DRY	W	216906	99014	W	214715	139746	W	201058	140123	W	203956	147712	LEGUMES A COSSE SECS
0545	OTHER FRESH VEGETABLES	W	141496	84199	W	195533	93494	W	234889	113611	W	331587	113449	AUTRES LEGUMES FRAIS,REF
05451	ALLIACEOUS VEGTBLS,FRESH	W	140168	82768	W	194053	91983	W	232206	110583	W	326238	110535	OIGNONS,ECHALOTES,AULX
056	VEGTBLES ETC PRSVD,PREPD	W	42465	45774	W	41655	49681	W	45421	77639	W	43170	78824	CONSERVES DE LEGUMES
0565	VEGTBLES PRSVD,PREPD NES	W	40926	40804	W	40424	45575	W	43325	70691	W	41308	73013	LEGUMES PREPARES CONSERVE
05659	OTH VEG PRESVD,PREPD NES	W	40227	40107	W	38438	43961	W	41180	68955	W	39665	71547	LEGUM PREPAP,CONSERV NDA
057	FRUIT,NUTS,FRESH,DRIED	W	459530	237191	W	548792	275728	W	763295	444813	W	818528	508676	FRUITS FRAIS OU SECS
0572	LEMONS,GRAPEFRUIT ETC	W	62798	22185	W	120568	50877	W	147279	77550	W	195687	109154	AUTRES AGRUMES FRAIS,SECS
05721	LEMONS,LIMES,FRESH,DRIED	W	34121	12210	W	93022	41606	W	110785	61527	W	161253	93033	CITRONS ET LIMES
0574	APPLES FRESH	W	145487	73686	W	146800	70722	W	243320	137126	W	209534	126008	POMMES FRAICHES
0579	FRUIT FRESH OR DRIED NES	W	156452	101152	W	161849	101896	W	245359	164779	W	262097	184238	FRUITS FRAIS,SECS NDA
05792	PEARS, QUINCES FRESH	W	142229	78223	W	142568	71232	W	222403	132072	W	237787	148439	POIRES ET COINGS FRAIS
058	FRUIT PRESERVED,PREPARED	W	127696	124420	W	132248	111211	W	254855	245564	W	263764	301401	CONSERVES DE FRUITS
0585	FRUIT OR VEGETABLE JUICE	W	97312	94827	W	104700	83132	W	223606	214452	W	219839	255819	JUS DE FRUITS
05857	JUICE OF OTHER FRUIT,VEG	W	72694	71047	W	85443	66361	W	187525	172488	W	194729	219504	JUS AUTRES FRUITS,LEGUMES
06	SUGAR AND PREPS,HONEY			93443			112479			192406			235101	SUCRES ET PRODUITS
061	SUGAR AND HONEY	W	126524	71746	W	128269	76484	W	238306	132012	W	263685	169225	SUCRES ET MIEL
0616	NATURAL HONEY	W	55000	50157	W	62437	53783	W	63511	70456	W	53559	90646	MIEL NATUREL
07	COFFEE,TEA,COCOA,SPICES			66234			80439			122019			145516	CAFE,THE,CACAO,EPICES
074	TEA AND MATE	W	63805	60781	W	64743	59993	W	81804	65934	W	84259	63294	THE ET MATE
081	*FEEDING STUFF FOR ANIML	W	8421021	1451123	W	8546943	1348966	MW	9538	1254639	MW	11204	2366909	NOURRITURE POUR ANIMAUX
0813	OILCAKE AND OTH RESIDUES	W	8112656	1401727	W	8236372	1301788	MW	9228	1196120	MW	10868	2293308	TOURTEAUX
08131	— OF SOYA BEANS	W	6621145	1238727	W	6670928	1145873	W	6887996	1022243	W	8345207	1984047	TOURTEAUX DE SOJA
08135	— OF SUNFLOWER SEEDS	W	1181878	123937	W	1285949	119997	W	1910256	125883	W	2096781	245448	TOURTEAUX DE TOURNESOL
09	MISC EDIBLE PRODUCTS			53304			57759			92000			108160	PREP ALIMENTAIRES DIVERSES
098	EDIBLE PRODCTS,PREPS NES	W	13858	38055	W	15539	43852	W	22680	74133	W	29365	88777	PREP ALIMENTAIRES NDA
1	BEVERAGES AND TOBACCO			162235			159696			269383			283467	BOISSONS ET TABACS
11	BEVERAGES			44644			59939			147013			121027	BOISSONS
112	ALCOHOLIC BEVERAGES	W	42117	42090	W	46522	47418	W	254641	97194	W	166310	104290	BOISSONS ALCOOLIQUES
1121	WINE OF FRESH GRAPES ETC	W	33301	32758	W	33966	35255	W	231575	78597	W	141339	83733	VINS DE RAISINS FRAIS
11212	WINE OF FRESH GRAPES	W	32896	32187	W	33093	34184	W	217967	73825	W	138137	81777	VINS DE MOUTS DE RAISINS
12	TOBACCO AND MANUFACTURES			117591			99757			122370			162441	TABACS BRUTS FABRIQUES
121	TOBACCO UNMNFCTRD,REFUSE	W	41360	116980	W	37995	87413	W	43440	100779	W	55781	145943	TABACS BRUTS,DECHETS
1212	TOBACCO STRIPPED OR PART	W	26439	104744	W	25337	76970	W	29644	87398	W	35133	130189	TABACS PART ECOTES
2	CRUDE MATERLS,EXCL FUELS			938493			1446894			1767938			1869110	MAT BRUTES NON COMESTIBLES
22	OIL SEEDS,OLEAGINOUS FRT			687816			943600			875059			955076	GRAINES,FRUITS OLEAGINEUX
222	SEEDS FOR'SOFT'FIXED OIL	W	2745783	687216	W	3610218	943123	W	3593880	874284	W	2962635	954302	GRAINES HUILES FIXES
2221	GROUNDNUTS,GREEN	W	119314	93151	W	104432	84769	W	165126	123329	W	264575	203201	ARACHIDES NON GRILLEES
2222	SOYA BEANS	W	2428304	547150	W	2909527	690463	W	2549840	535966	W	2055882	588186	FEVES DE SOJA
2224	SUNFLOWER SEEDS	W	181788	43014	W	585214	163293	W	845095	208269	W	586106	152801	GRAINES DE TOURNESOL
24	CORK AND WOOD			20090			39317			73488			67791	LIEGE ET BOIS
251	*PULP AND WASTE PAPER	W	144935	42827	W	177583	63480	W	162808	120952	W	192801	83469	PATES A PAPIER,DECHETS
2517	SODA,SULPHATE WOOD PULP	W	144746	42799	W	177126	63347	W	152266	115350	W	181415	79237	PATES CHIMIQUES AU SULFATE
25172	— BLEACHED,NONDISSOLVNG	W	144490	42718	W	176926	63265	W	151816	115092	W	180515	78895	PATES BLANCHIES
26	TEXTILE FIBRES AND WASTE			130504			318971			582196			625426	FIBRES TEXTILES
263	COTTON	W	24385	26509	W	127168	179153	W	249012	437489	W	363344	500701	COTON
2631	RAW COTTON,EXCL LINTERS	W	23338	25682	W	124081	176325	W	243474	432788	W	357447	497018	COTON EN MASSE
268	WOOL(EXC TOPS),ANML HAIR	W	49662	99462	W	57282	132305	W	42502	134974	W	41709	114681	LAINES ET POILS
2681	WOOL GREASY,FLEECE–WSHED	W	28189	49149	W	35717	74620	W	26584	86163	W	24810	64680	LAINE EN SUINT
2682	WOOL DEGREASED,UNCOMBED	W	17502	42682	W	17270	46128	W	10220	33980	W	10108	33748	LAINE DEGRAISSEE
3	MINERAL FUELS ETC			1241843			1657123			2175369			3096115	COMBUSTIBLES MINERAUX LUB
33	PETROLEUM AND PRODUCTS			1174738			1580964			2088659			2973320	PETROLE ET DERIVES
333	CRUDE PETROLEUM	W	4523323	527361	MW	10526	1125573	MW	14010	1591855	MW	16473	2319964	HUILES BRUTES DE PETROLE
334	PETROLEUM PRODUCTS,REFIN	W	4213371	606179	W	3249097	413556	W	2915078	435540	W	3135450	584876	PRODUITS RAFFINES
3341	GASOLINE,OTH LIGHT OILS							W	1240712	185645	W	1614807	301725	ESSENCES POUR MOTEURS
33411	MOTOR,AVIATION SPIRIT							W	1174978	174323	W	796375	151788	ESSENCES MOTEURS D'AVIONS
33419	OTH LIGHT PETROLEUM OILS							W	28318	5309	W	818432	149938	AUTRES HUILES LEGERES
3342	KEROSENE,OTH MEDIUM OILS							W	980367	131445	W	28510	6563	PETR LAMPANTS,AUT HUIL
33421	KEROSENE INCL JET FUEL							W	980367	131445	W	28510	6563	PETROLES LAMPANTS
3343	GAS OILS							W	61442	27921	W	1046435	179054	GAS OILS
3345	LUBS,PETROLEUM OILS NES	W	2757	6681	W	2717	6548	W	65728	88909	W	26888	65166	HUILES LUBRIFIANTES
33451	LUBS(HIGH PETR CONT) ETC							W	62455	81039	W	23243	56925	HUILES LUBRIF,H LOURDES
335	RESIDUAL PETRLM PROD NES	W	629743	41198	W	548141	41835	W	623665	61264	W	613742	68480	PRODUITS RESIDUELS NDA

5. Special Exports F.O.B. by Commodities according to the S.I.T.C. (Rev. 2) in thousand U.S. Dollars
Exportations Spéciales F.O.B. par Produits d'après la C.T.C.I. (Rév. 2) en milliers de Dollars E.U.

SITC CTCI	COMMODITY	1993		1994		1995		1996		PRODUIT
		WEIGHT POIDS	VALUE VALEUR	WEIGHT POIDS	VALUE VALEUR	WEIGHT POIDS	VALUE VALEUR	WEIGHT POIDS	VALUE VALEUR	
341	*GAS,NATURAL AND MANUFCT	W 422207	65852	W 502313	71806	W 461261	75758	W 550749	109614	GAZ NATUREL,GAZ MANUFACT
3413	PETROLM GASES,LIQUEFIED	W 422206	65845	W 502313	71806	W 461261	75758	W 548350	109480	GAZ DE PETROLE LIQUEFIE
34131	LIQUEFIED PROPANE,BUTANE	W 211154	33344	W 430498	61686	W 282048	44825	W 278330	55510	PROPANE,BUTANE LIQUEFIES
4	ANIMAL,VEGETABLE OIL,FAT		1063123		1518934		2077340		1882531	HUILES,GRAISSES ANIM,VEG
42	FIXED VEGETABLE OIL,FAT		1048045		1498542		2043852		1857181	HUILES VEGETALES FIXES
423	FIXED VEG OILS,SOFT	W 2244149	1024445	W 2523463	1481141	W 3234164	2007671	W 3287955	1828820	HUILES VEGET DOUCES FIXES
4232	SOYA BEAN OIL	W 1371680	599590	W 1502120	859437	W 1546358	942993	W 1694060	900771	HUILE DE SOJA
4234	GROUNDNUT(PEANUT) OIL	W 73469	43944	W 46547	42597	W 44295	40446	W 50860	41995	HUILE D'ARACHIDE
4236	SUNFLOWER SEED OIL	W 765478	355579	W 927690	546835	W 1578502	973681	W 1482974	832082	HUILE DE TOURNESOL
5	CHEMCLS,RELATED PROD NES		694678		918947		1314779		1320071	PRODUITS CHIMIQUES
51	ORGANIC CHEMICALS		178269		225442		335703		335575	PROD CHIMIQ ORGANIQUES
511	HYDROCARBONS NES,DERIVS	W 79218	32785	W 94562	56226	W 117301	87876	W 150828	64326	HYDROCARBURES NDA
5112	CYCLIC HYDROCARBONS	W 77036	29918	W 75255	42835	W 94489	71430	W 94085	39109	HYDROCARBURES CYCLIQUES
513	CARBOXYLIC ACIDS ETC	W 20069	30241	W 30139	38445	W 38384	63388	W 37601	53892	ACIDES CARBOXYLIQUES
514	NITROGEN–FNCTN COMPOUNDS	W 16183	37718	W 20596	47479	W 20235	61753	W 22168	72512	COMPOSES FONCT AZOTEES
52	INORGANIC CHEMICALS		62175		97933		124498		77113	PROD CHIM INORGANIQUES
523	OTHR INORG CHEMICALS ETC	W 51970	34028		70807	W 70481	82387	W 80643	41981	AUT PRODUITS CHIMIQUES INORG
5233	METALLIC ACID SALTS ETC	W 6787	13029	W 11137	48669	W 13890	55866	W 13788	12292	SELS ACIDES D'OXYDES METAL E
53	DYES,TANNING,COLOUR PROD		88907		95597		104391		123135	PROD TEINTURE,COLORANTS
532	DYES NES,TANNING PROD	W 48669	45564	W 60147	45038	W 58825	42471	W 55042	46146	EXTRAITS TEINTURE,TANNAGE
5322	DYE,TANN EXTRCTS,TANNINS	W 47311	44159	W 58077	43207	W 55778	39608	W 50533	41453	EXT TAN ORIG VEG,TANNINS
53221	VEG TANN EXTRCTS,TANNINS	W 47271	43815	W 58034	42755	W 55742	39374	W 50511	40712	EXTR TANNANTS ORIG VEGET
541	*MEDICINAL,PHARM PRODUCT		87531	K 2667599	111923		140878	K 4522979	198821	PROD MEDICINAUX PHARMACEUT
5417	MEDICAMENTS	K 1841530	59133	K 2092046	75928	K 3155362	107151	K 3471319	152080	MEDICAMENTS
54179	— CONTNG OTH SUBSTANCES	K 1503524	38612	K 1728091	46315	K 2712126	71569	K 2775292	96906	MED CONT AUT SUBSTANCES
55	PERFUME,CLEANING ETC PRD		87569		130098		172435		138425	PROD POUR PARFUM,TOILETTE
553	PERFUMERY,COSMETICS,ETC	W 7135	36791	W 9218	71797	W 12239	91931	W 13823	54360	PRODUITS DE PARFUMERIE
58	PLASTIC MATERIALS ETC		93686		135967		272671		254123	MAT PLAST ARTIFICIELLES
583	POLYMERIZATION ETC PRODS	W 90402	76337	W 138413	118141	W 209394	239054	W 199710	207222	PROD POLYMERISATION
5832	POLYPROPYLENE	W 38512	29080	W 61066	43647	W 80961	93560	W 61239	64048	POLYPROPYLENE
58321	— IN PRIMARY FORMS	W 35589	20591	W 56911	32261	W 75023	71489	W 53333	42349	POLYPROPYLENE PRIMAIRES
59	CHEMICAL MATERIALS NES		93805		119552		161753		189196	MAT PROD CHIMIQUES NDA
598	MISCEL CHEM PRODUCTS NES	W 37011	42191	W 41261	52053	W 48558	64913	W 58430	78575	PROD DIV INDUST CHIM NDA
6	BASIC MANUFACTURES		1796615		2095484		2972490		2851956	ART MANUFACTURES
61	LEATHER,DRESSED FUR,ETC		721522		876354		989161		926412	CUIRS,PELLETERIES
611	LEATHER	W 68015	598760	W 88050	733416	W 106001	893786	W 107663	823788	CUIRS,PEAUX PREPARES
6114	LEATHR BOVINE NES,EQUINE	W 67763	588110	W 87810	726607	W 105606	884380	W 107340	818261	CUIRS DE BOVINS
612	LEATHER ETC MANUFACTURES	W 6562	107898	W 5273	122201	W 5575	63052	W 4934	44627	OUVRAGES EN CUIRS NDA
6123	PREPRD PARTS OF FOOTWEAR	W 4313	61570	W 2739	53096	W 3493	31831	W 2208	22169	PARTIES DE CHAUSSURES
6129	LEATHER MANUFACTURES NES	W 2056	40361	W 2295	63155	W 1848	22472	W 2464	11818	AUT OUV CUIR NAT,ARTIF
62	RUBBER MANUFACTURES NES		41632		66872		100799		97938	CAOUTCHOUC MANUFACTURE
625	RUBBER TYRES, TUBES ETC	W 11077	31052	W 20237	56274	W 28873	85246	W 27226	81862	PNEUS CAOUTCHOUC VULCANISE
64	PAPER,PAPERBOARD AND MFR		45673		68983		188776		177413	PAPIERS,CARTONS & OUVRAGES
641	PAPER AND PAPERBOARD		23008	W 45808	35425	W 135143	112863	W 123748	85418	PAPIERS ET CARTONS
6415	PAPER,PAPERBRD,BULK,NES	W 10589	9771	W 12379	10869	W 76756	65604	W 45778	30381	PAPIERS,CARTONS ROULEAUX
642	PAPER,ETC,PRECUT,ARTS OF	W 19285	22665	W 24998	33557	W 32858	75913	W 35659	91995	PAP,CARTONS DECOUPES
65	TEXTILE YARN,FABRICS,ETC		192100		238466		359340		329461	FILS,TISSUS,ARTICLES TEXTILE
651	TEXTILE YARN	W 27723	114894	W 33556	140783	W 42397	200779	W 38928	177923	FILS TEXTILES
6512	WOOL,HAIR YARN,INCL TOPS	W 12281	50475	W 13435	60245	W 11690	69452	W 14190	73542	FILS DE LAINE,DE POILS
65121	WOOL TOPS	W 11986	45860	W 13089	56023	W 11566	67153	W 14093	71551	RUBANS LAINE PEIGN,TOPS
6514	SYN FIB YRN,BULK,MONOFIL	W 11415	46746	W 13353	52081	W 16930	73463	W 16602	71267	FILS CONT 85% FIB TEXT SYNTH
652	COTTON FABRICS,WOVEN	W 8153	32019	W 12827	51054	W 16620	75617	W 12540	63198	TISSUS DE COTON
6522	WOVEN COTTON BLEACHD,ETC	W 7898	31024	W 11203	45258	W 14303	65776	W 11144	56387	TISSUS COTON BLANCHIS ETC
66	NONMETAL MINERAL MFS NES		83244		77020		119516		115889	ART MIN NON METALLIQUES
67	IRON AND STEEL		432468		467998		731961		797759	FER ET ACIER
673	IRON,STEEL SHAPES ETC	W 89946	32423	W 152609	52574	W 242366	89380	W 209821	76423	BARRES,PROFIL FER,ACIER
674	IRN,STL UNIV,PLATE,SHEET	W 172589	70298	W 264761	115016	W 527311	256006	W 438631	185310	LARGES PLATS,TOLES
6746	IRN,STL THIN PLATE,ROLLD	W 108895	39626	W 193317	78466	W 388948	177599	W 324021	124874	TOLES LAM MOINS 3MM
67461	— OF IRON OR SIMPLE STL	W 108730	39296	W 192977	77605	W 388662	176826	W 323826	124206	TOL NON AC FIN MOINS 3 MM
678	IRON,STL TUBES,PIPES,ETC	W 503232	290907	W 440563	273386	W 509292	334442	W 616593	457840	TUBES,TUYAUX EN FONTE,FER
6782	IRON,STL SEAMLESS TUBES	W 477965	267706	W 424766	261574	W 483330	315006	W 570013	417163	TUBES,TUYAUX SANS SOUDURE
68	NON–FERROUS METALS		135635		179585		293873		213904	METAUX NON FERREUX
684	ALUMINIUM	W 102117	127270	W 103707	160914	W 130754	260495	W 115272	189671	ALUMINIUM
6841	ALUMINIUM,ALLOYS,UNWRGHT	W 86012	100678	W 81423	118860	W 100765	186784	W 93852	145137	ALUMINIUM,ALLIAGES BRUTS
6842	ALUMINIUM,ALLOYS WORKED	W 16105	26592	W 22284	42054	W 29989	73711	W 21420	44534	ALUMINIUM,ALLIAGES OUVRE
69	METAL MANUFACTURES NES		133720		105860		169146		153147	ART MANUFACT EN METAL NDA
695	TOOLS		53326	W 878	32657	W 1489	44347	W 1453	24199	OUTILS A MAIN
6954	BLADES,TIPS,ETC FR TOOLS	W 1155	44550	W 201	23527	W 877	37013	W 917	16998	OUTILS POUR MACHINE–OUTIL
69541	PARTS TO INSERT IN TOOLS	W 1051	42916	W 162	22410	W 808	34914	W 861	14790	OUTILS DE FORAGE
7	MACHINES,TRANSPORT EQUIP		1443895		1770733		2275227		2592458	MACHINES MATERIEL TRANSPORT
71	POWER GENERATING EQUIPMT		173463		165205		223181		289423	MACHINES GENERATRICES
713	INTRNL COMBUS PSTN ENGIN	W 22804	163938	W 23019	148838	W 22356	187678	W 23735	253085	MOTEURS EXPL COMB INT, PIECE
7132	MOTOR VEHCL PISTN ENGINS	W 8690	97259	W 9284	99719	W 9635	129316	W 11877	173865	MOTEURS EXPL POUR VEHICULES
7139	PISTON ENGINE PARTS NES	W 14059	65896	W 13675	48047	W 12594	56442	W 11712	76501	PIECES POUR 713.2,3,8
72	MACHS FOR SPCL INDUSTRYS		52795		52046		70076		77053	MAC SPECIALES POUR INDUST
74	GENRL INDUSTRL MACHY NES		253835		213930		331463		332419	MACH APP INDUSTRIE
744	MECHANICAL HANDLING EQU	W 3550	35079	W 1674	19068	W 4888	64365	W 4149	54454	EQUIP MANUTENTION PIECES
749	NONELEC MACH PTS,ACC NES	W 8033	91729	W 8833	73732	W 12115	105569	W 9793	105748	PIECES MACH NON ELEC NDA
75	OFFICE MACHNES,ADP EQUIP		81574		82956		68832		45396	MACH BUREAU TRAIT AUTOM
752	AUTOMTIC DATA PROC EQUIP	W 493	42867	W 415	39123	W 388	27914	W 219	18894	MACH TRAIT INFORMATION
76	TELECOMM,SOUND EQUIPMENT		9901		47211		84567		57693	EQUIPMENT DE TELECOM
77	ELECTRIC MACHNRY NES ETC		136482		284801		167660		132918	MACH APP ELECT NDA
772	SWITCHGEAR ETC,PARTS NES		69114	W 1974	204419	W 903	53416	W 900	25673	APP COUPURE,SECT ETC
7721	SWITCHGEAR ETC		65621	W 1958	203698	W 897	52892	W 894	24880	APP COUPURE,SECTIONMNT
78	ROAD VEHICLES		662187		863390		1233141		1514509	VEHICULES ROUTIERS
781	PASS MOTOR VEH EXC BUSES	W 23755	185457	W 25011	180897	W 24552	238719	W 89744	803840	AUTO TRANSPORT PERSONNES
782	LORRIES,SPCL MTR VEH NES	W 14143	98455	W 26004	206958	W 54429	426975	W 31437	253054	VEHICULES SPECIAUX,MARCH
7821	LORRIES,TRUCKS	W 13925	96921	W 25936	206681	W 54377	426431	W 31245	250571	VEHICULES TRANSP MARCHAND
784	MOTOR VEH PRTS,ACCES NES	W 52143	369747	W 70871	456722	W 83691	546161	W 65287	440791	PIECES 722,781,782,783
7841	MOTOR VEHICLE CHASSIS	W 2768	16237	W 9595	53769	W 13432	83579	W 13318	84552	CHASSIS 722,781,782,783
7849	OTHER MOTOR VEHCL PARTS	W 49350	353254	W 61245	402684	W 70084	460855	W 51620	354251	PIECES 722,781,782,783
79	OTHR TRANSPORT EQUIPMENT		55517		51210		70072		123047	AUTRE MATERIEL TRANSPORT
792	AIRCRAFT ETC	W 200	22705	W 31	2501	W 108	23650	W 1106	97441	APP NAVIGATION AERIENNE
7924	AIRCRFT NES OVER 15000KG	W 132	11400				9363	W 997	79825	AERODYNES PLUS 15000 KG
8	MISC MANUFACTURED GOODS		429793		642324		889997		666930	ART MANUFACTURES DIVERS
821	*FURNITURE,PARTS THEREOF	W 2183	14682	W 4019	20214	W 8799	56280	W 9800	85117	MEUBLES ET PIECES
84	CLOTHING AND ACCESSORIES		79423		101132		188782		157244	VETEMENTS
848	HEADGEAR,NONTXTL CLOTHNG	W 1248	64852	W 1276	80723	W 1380	106573	W 1615	120650	VET ACCES MAT AUT QUE TEX
8483	FUR ETC,CLOTHES,PRODUCTS	W 232	28685	W 255	36964	W 395	62378	W 534	85015	VETEMENTS DE FOURRURE
84831	ARTICLES OF FURSKIN,NES	W 232	28685	W 255	36964	W 395	62376	W 534	85015	PELLETERIES OUVREES NDA
851	*FOOTWEAR	W 2472	30778	W 2667	33654	W 3205	70544	W 2506	50566	CHAUSSURES

5. Special Exports F.O.B. by Commodities according to the S.I.T.C. (Rev. 2) in thousand U.S. Dollars
Exportations Spéciales F.O.B. par Produits d'après la C.T.C.I. (Rév. 2) en milliers de Dollars E.U.

SITC CTCI	COMMODITY	1993		1994		1995		1996		PRODUIT
		WEIGHT POIDS	VALUE VALEUR	WEIGHT POIDS	VALUE VALEUR	WEIGHT POIDS	VALUE VALEUR	WEIGHT POIDS	VALUE VALEUR	
85102	FOOTWEAR LEATHER	W 2026	27390	W 2148	27109	W 2768	65816	W 2220	47946	CHAUS SEMELLES EN CUIR
88	PHOTO EQU,OPTICL GDS ETC		46856		51101		169887		40100	APP,FOURN PHOTO,OP,MONTR
882	PHOTO,CINEMA SUPPLIES	W 2797	42935	W 2349	37844	W 2746	38145	W 2179	28901	PRODUITS PHOTO,CINEMA
8822	PHOTO FILM EXC DEV CINMA	W 2601	42576	W 2183	37233	W 2228	37355	W 1713	28218	PLAQUES,PELLICULES,FILMS
885	WATCHES AND CLOCKS		1412		10728		125022		2771	HORLOGERIE
8851	WATCHES,MOVEMENTS,CASES		68		9384		123524		576	MONTRES,MOUVEMENTS,BOITES
88514	WATCH CASES,CASE PARTS				9326		111141			BOITES DU 885.11,PIECES
89	MISC MANUFCTRD GOODS NES		207950		397120		362302		284544	ART MANUFACTURES DIVERS
892	PRINTED MATTER	W 7145	66364	W 8839	78465	W 16171	115917	W 21712	138241	IMPRIMES
893	ARTICLES OF PLASTIC NES	W 8386	39258		44522		68002		85494	OUVRAGES EN MAT DIVIS 58
897	GOLD,SILVER WARE,JEWELRY		48092		236586		109637		3404	BIJOUTERIE,ORFEVRERIE
8973	PREC JEWLRY,GLD–SILVWARE		33158		148681		104800		1553	BIJOUX OR,ARGENT ORFEVRE
89731	PRECIOUS METAL JEWELLERY		31034		132745		87618		871	ART BIJOUTERIE,JOAILLER

1. HISTORICAL SERIES, 1992–1996 GENERAL TRADE, IMPORTS C.I.F., EXPORTS F.O.B.
SERIES HISTORIQUES, 1992–1996 COMMERCE GENERAL, IMPORTATIONS C.A.F., EXPORTATIONS F.O.B

YEAR ANNEE	VALUE IN MILLION U.S. DOLLARS VALEUR EN MILLION U.S. DOLLARS MERCHANDISE –MARCHANDISE IMPORTS	EXPORTS	GOLD –OR IMPORTS	EXPORTS	CONVERSION FACTORS FACTEURS DE CONVERSION CENTS E.U. PAR IMPORTS	EXPORTS	INDEX NUMBERS –INDICES QUANTUM IMPORTS	EXPORTS	UNIT VALUE VALEUR UNITAIRE IMPORTS	EXPORTS
1992	50.00	26.00								
1993	86.00	30.00								
1994	415.00	232.00								
1995	661.00	248.00								
1996	855.80	290.31								

2. IMPORTS BY BROAD ECONOMIC CATEGORY AND EXPORTS BY INDUSTRIAL ORIGIN. (PERCENTAGE OF TOTAL VALUE)
IMPORTATIONS PAR CATEGORIES ECONOMIQUES ET EXPORTATIONS PAR BRANCHE D'ACTIVITE.(EN POURCENTAGE DE LA VALEUR TOTALE)

IMPORTS – IMPORTATIONS

	1990	1991	1992	1993	1994	1995	1996
TOTAL IMPORTS–IMPORTATIONS TOTALES							
1 FOOD BEV–ALIMENTATION BOISSONS							
11 PRIMARY–PRODUITS DE BASE							
111 FOR INDUSTRY–POUR L'INDUSTRIE							
112 FOR HOUSEHOLDS–POUR LES MENAGES							
12 PROCESSED–PRODUITS ELABORES							
121 FOR INDUSTRY–POUR L'INDUSTRIE							
122 FOR HOUSEHOLDS–POUR LES MENAGES							
2 IND SUPPLIES–APPROV INDUSTRIELS							
21 PRIMARY–PRODUITS DE BASE							
22 PROCESSED–PRODUITS ELABORES							
3 FUELS–COMBUSTIBLES							
31 PRIMARY–PRODUITS DE BASE							
32 PROCESSED–PRODUITS ELABORES							
321 MOTOR SPIRIT–ESSENCE							
322 OTHER–AUTRES							
4 MACHINERY–EQUIPEMENT							
41 CAPITAL EQUIPMENT–MACHINES							
42 PARTS–PIECES ACCESSOIRES							
5 TRANSPORT–TRANSPORT							
51 PASSENGER CARS–AUTOMOBILES							
52 OTHER–AUTRES							
521 INDUSTRIAL–INDUSTRIELS							
522 NON INDUSTRIAL–NON INDUSTRIEL							
53 PARTS–PIECES ACCESSOIRES							
6 CONSUM GOODS–BIENS CONSOMMATION							
61 DURABLE–DURABLES							
62 SEMI DURABLE–SEMI DURABLES							
63 NON DURABLE–NON DURABLES							
7 GOODS NES–BIENS NDA							

EXPORTS – EXPORTATIONS

	1990	1991	1992	1993	1994	1995	1996
TOTAL EXPORTS–EXPORTATIONS TOTALES							
1 AGRICULTURE							
2 MINING QUARRY–INDUS EXTRACTIVES							
3 MANUFACTURING–IND MANUFACTUR							
31 FOOD BEV TOBACCO–ALIM BOISS TAB							
32 TEXTILES–INDUSTRIES TEXTILES							
33 WOOD & PRODUCTS–BOIS & PRODUITS							
34 PAPER & PRODUCTS–PAPIER & PRODT							
35 CHEMICALS–INDUSTRIES CHIMIQUES							
36 NON METAL MIN–MIN NON METAL							
37 BASIC METAL–IND METAL BASE							
38 METAL MANUF–MANUF METAL							
39 OTH MANUF IND–AUTRES MANUF							

3. TRADE BY PRINCIPAL COUNTRIES OF CONSIGNMENT AND LAST DESTINATION(VALUE IN THOUSAND U.S. DOLLARS)
ECHANGES SELON LES PRINCIPAUX PAYS DE CONSIGNATION ET DE DESTINATION FINALE (VALEUR EN MILLIERS DE DOLLARS EU)

COUNTRIES–PAYS	GENERAL IMPORTS C.I.F. IMPORTATIONS GENERALES C.A.F				
	1992	1993	1994	1995	1996
World			415000	661000	855801
Africa			100		42660
Americas			96300	144600	104884
Northern America			96300	144600	104760
LAIA					124
CACM					
Caribbean					
Rest of America					
As.ex F.USSR			5300	4000	194542
Eur.x F.USSR			31170	103600	176622
EU			27470	83100	132708
EFTA			2400	7400	21551
East Europe			1200	12900	21802
Other Europe					
Former USSR			132200	201300	281959
Oceania					278
Russian Federation			112200	135100	125497
USA/Etats–Unis d'Amer			96100	144400	103565
Iran (Islamic Rp. of)					149794
Georgia/Géorgie			17800	61900	51240
Turkmenistan/Turkménistn					86440
Belgium–Luxembourg			1400	15600	49567
Italy/Italie			8900	22400	26177
So. Africa Customs Un					41953
Germany/Allemagne			6900	11300	17365
United Arab Emirates					33450
France, Monac			1070	16300	12021
Switz.Liecht			2400	6300	17898
Netherlands/Pays–Bas			8300	6000	5730
Bulgaria/Bulgarie			900	4600	14295
Ukraine			100	100	11991
United Kingdom			500	2100	7105
Turkey/Turquie			500	2600	6255
Denmark/Danemark				4900	2710
Czech Republic			100	6300	765
Lithuania/Lituanie			700	2000	3461
Romania/Roumanie				1400	4750
Greece/Grèce					5263
Norway,SVD,JM				1100	3653
Belarus/Bélarus			400	1900	2206
Ireland/Irlande				1700	2425
Austria/Autriche				2100	1861
China/Chine			1600	400	829
India/Inde			1800	200	733
Finland/Finlande			400	700	989
Canada			200	200	1195
Korea Dem People's Rp			1400		142
Sweden/Suède					1416
Hungary/Hongrie				200	1184
Poland/Pologne			200	400	759
Lebanon/Liban					1231
Syrian Arab Republic				600	412
Estonia/Estonie			300	100	543
Yugoslavia/Yougoslavie			100	200	427
Latvia/Lettonie			500		212
Egypt/Egypte					646
Cyprus/Chypre					520
Japan/Japon					516
Korea, Republic of				200	92
Kazakhstan			100	100	85
New Zealand					278
Uzbekistan/Ouzbékistan					232
Singapore/Singapour					186
Jordan/Jordanie					145
Slovenia/Slovénia					134
Pakistan					57

COUNTRIES–PAYS	GENERAL EXPORTS F.O.B. EXPORTATIONS GENERALES F.O.B.				
	1992	1993	1994	1995	1996
Monde			232000	248000	290314
Afrique			100	300	36488
Amériques			400	600	4481
Amérique du Nord			400	600	4401
ALAI					80
MCAC					
Caraïbes					
Autre Amérique					
Asie l'URSS exclus			400	3000	52589
Europe l'URSS exclus			38300	51700	62607
UE			35300	48300	61909
AELE			2500	3100	272
Europe de l'Est			500	300	324
Autre de l'Europe					
Ancienne URSS			154500	161300	128499
Océanie					
Russian Federation			83900	88500	96141
Turkmenistan/Turkménistn			65700	68600	17510
Belgium–Luxembourg			25900	30800	44835
Iran (Islamic Rp. of)					43913
So. Africa Customs Un					36416
Germany/Allemagne			6600	10100	3683
Netherlands/Pays–Bas			700	5300	8732
Georgia/Géorgie			2900	2700	6880
Turkey/Turquie			200	2600	6031
Switz.Liecht			2500	3100	272
USA/Etats–Unis d'Amer			400	600	4366
Ukraine			100	300	4854
United Kingdom			500	1300	3199
Belarus/Bélarus			700	900	1174
Kazakhstan			900	100	1035
United Arab Emirates					1907
Ireland/Irlande			1200	500	163
France, Monac			400	200	421
Syrian Arab Republic			200	300	200
Greece/Grèce					459
Uzbekistan/Ouzbékistan					433
Poland/Pologne			400		
Egypt/Egypte				300	72
Lithuania/Lituanie			200	100	51
Czech Republic			100	200	
Latvia/Lettonie			100		199
Bulgaria/Bulgarie				100	198
Spain/Espagne					296
Pakistan					281
Italy/Italie				100	99
Estonia/Estonie					160
Lebanon/Liban					159
India/Inde				100	28
Yugoslavia/Yougoslavie					102
Romania/Roumanie					71
Canada					35
Japan/Japon					34
China/Chine					25
Austria/Autriche					18
Hungary/Hongrie					17
Finland/Finlande					4

(VALUE AS PERCENTAGE OF WORLD TOTAL)(VALEURS EN POURCENTAGE DU TOTAL MONDIAL)

	1987	1988	1989	1990	1991	1992	1993	1994	1995	1996
Africa								0.0		5.0
Americas								23.2	21.9	12.3
Northern America								23.2	21.9	12.2
LAIA										0.0
CACM										
Caribbean										
Rest of America										
As.ex F.USSR								1.3	0.6	22.7
Eur.x F.USSR								7.5	15.7	20.6
EU								6.6	12.6	15.5
EFTA								0.6	1.1	2.5
East Europe								0.3	2.0	2.5
Other Europe										
Former USSR								31.9	30.5	32.9
Oceania										0.0
Russian Federation								27.0	20.4	14.7
USA/Etats–Unis d'Amer								23.2	21.8	12.1
Iran (Islamic Rp. of)										17.5
Georgia/Géorgie								4.3	9.4	6.0
Turkmenistan/Turkménistn										10.1
Belgium–Luxembourg								0.3	2.4	5.8
Italy/Italie								2.1	3.4	3.1
So. Africa Customs Un										4.9
Germany/Allemagne								1.7	1.7	2.0
United Arab Emirates										3.9

	1987	1988	1989	1990	1991	1992	1993	1994	1995	1996
Afrique								0.0	0.1	12.6
Amériques								0.2	0.2	1.5
Amérique du Nord								0.2	0.2	1.5
ALAI										0.0
MCAC										
Caraïbes										
Autre Amérique										
Asie l'URSS exclus								0.2	1.2	18.1
Europe l'URSS exclus								16.5	20.8	21.6
UE								15.2	19.5	21.3
AELE								1.1	1.2	0.1
Europe de l'Est								0.2	0.1	0.1
Autre de l'Europe										
Ancienne URSS								66.6	65.0	44.3
Océanie										
Russian Federation								36.2	35.7	33.1
Turkmenistan/Turkménistn								28.3	27.7	6.0
Belgium–Luxembourg								11.2	12.4	15.4
Iran (Islamic Rp. of)										15.1
So. Africa Customs Un										12.5
Germany/Allemagne								2.8	4.1	1.3
Netherlands/Pays–Bas								0.3	2.1	3.0
Georgia/Géorgie								1.2	1.1	2.4
Turkey/Turquie								0.1	1.0	2.1
Switz.Liecht								1.1	1.2	0.1

4. General Imports C.I.F. by Commodities according to the S.I.T.C. (Rev. 2) in thousand U.S. Dollars
Importations Générales C.A.F. par Produits d'après la C.T.C.I. (Rév. 2) en milliers de Dollars E.U.

SITC CTCI	COMMODITY	1992		1993		1994		1995		PRODUIT
		WEIGHT POIDS	VALUE VALEUR	WEIGHT POIDS	VALUE VALEUR	WEIGHT POIDS	VALUE VALEUR	WEIGHT POIDS	VALUE VALEUR	
	ALL COMMODITIES						415000		661000	TOUS PRODUITS

5. General Exports F.O.B. by Commodities according to the S.I.T.C. (Rev. 2) in thousand U.S. Dollars
Exportations Générales F.O.B. par Produits d'après la C.T.C.I. (Rév. 2) en milliers de Dollars E.U.

SITC CTCI	COMMODITY	1992 WEIGHT POIDS	1992 VALUE VALEUR	1993 WEIGHT POIDS	1993 VALUE VALEUR	1994 WEIGHT POIDS	1994 VALUE VALEUR	1995 WEIGHT POIDS	1995 VALUE VALEUR	PRODUIT
	ALL COMMODITIES						232000		248000	TOUS PRODUITS

1. HISTORICAL SERIES, 1988–1991 GENERAL TRADE, IMPORTS C.I.F., EXPORTS F.O.B.
SERIES HISTORIQUES, 1988–1991 COMMERCE GENERAL, IMPORTATIONS C.A.F., EXPORTATIONS F.O.B

YEAR ANNEE	VALUE IN MILLION FLORINS VALEUR EN MILLION FLORINS MERCHANDISE – MARCHANDISE IMPORTS	EXPORTS	GOLD – OR IMPORTS	EXPORTS	CONVERSION FACTORS U.S. CENTS PER FLORIN FACTEURS DE CONVERSION CENTS E.U. PAR FLORIN IMPORTS	EXPORTS	INDEX NUMBERS – INDICES QUANTUM IMPORTS	EXPORTS	UNIT VALUE VALEUR UNITAIRE IMPORTS	EXPORTS
1988	602.10	54.60			55.8657	55.8657				
1989	693.00	41.00			55.8659	55.8659				
1990	960.00	50.00			55.8658	55.8658				
1991	861.00	46.70			55.8658	55.8658				

2. IMPORTS BY BROAD ECONOMIC CATEGORY AND EXPORTS BY INDUSTRIAL ORIGIN. (PERCENTAGE OF TOTAL VALUE)
IMPORTATIONS PAR CATEGORIES ECONOMIQUES ET EXPORTATIONS PAR BRANCHE D'ACTIVITE.(EN POURCENTAGE DE LA VALEUR TOTALE)

IMPORTS – IMPORTATIONS

	1990	1991	1992	1993	1994	1995	1996
TOTAL IMPORTS–IMPORTATIONS TOTALES	100.	100.					
1 FOOD BEV–ALIMENTATION BOISSONS	17.1	21.0					
11 PRIMARY–PRODUITS DE BASE	5.9	6.9					
111 FOR INDUSTRY–POUR L'INDUSTRIE	0.4	0.4					
112 FOR HOUSEHOLDS–POUR LES MENAGES	5.5	6.5					
12 PROCESSED–PRODUITS ELABORES	11.2	14.1					
121 FOR INDUSTRY–POUR L'INDUSTRIE	0.8	1.1					
122 FOR HOUSEHOLDS–POUR LES MENAGES	10.4	13.0					
2 IND SUPPLIES–APPROV INDUSTRIELS	26.9	22.0					
21 PRIMARY–PRODUITS DE BASE	1.4	0.6					
22 PROCESSED–PRODUITS ELABORES	25.5	21.4					
3 FUELS–COMBUSTIBLES	0.3	0.3					
31 PRIMARY–PRODUITS DE BASE	0.0	0.0					
32 PROCESSED–PRODUITS ELABORES	0.3	0.3					
321 MOTOR SPIRIT–ESSENCE	0.0	0.0					
322 OTHER–AUTRES	0.3	0.3					
4 MACHINERY–EQUIPEMENT	18.6	17.4					
41 CAPITAL EQUIPMENT–MACHINES	16.4	15.6					
42 PARTS–PIECES ACCESSOIRES	2.2	1.8					
5 TRANSPORT–TRANSPORT	8.8	8.6					
51 PASSENGER CARS–AUTOMOBILES	4.6	4.2					
52 OTHER–AUTRES	2.5	2.6					
521 INDUSTRIAL–INDUSTRIELS	2.4	2.5					
522 NON INDUSTRIAL–NON INDUSTRIEL	0.1	0.1					
53 PARTS–PIECES ACCESSOIRES	1.7	1.8					
6 CONSUM GOODS–BIENS CONSOMMATION	28.2	30.6					
61 DURABLE–DURABLES	10.0	9.4					
62 SEMI DURABLE–SEMI DURABLES	12.0	14.3					
63 NON DURABLE–NON DURABLES	6.2	6.9					
7 GOODS NES–BIENS NDA	0.1	0.1					

EXPORTS – EXPORTATIONS

	1990	1991	1992	1993	1994	1995	1996
TOTAL EXPORTS–EXPORTATIONS TOTALES	100.	100.					
1 AGRICULTURE	6.1	2.2					
2 MINING QUARRY–INDUS EXTRACTIVES	1.2	1.0					
3 MANUFACTURING–IND MANUFACTUR	92.6	96.8					
31 FOOD BEV TOBACCO–ALIM BOISS TAB	36.6	16.1					
32 TEXTILES–INDUSTRIES TEXTILES	3.7	2.8					
33 WOOD & PRODUCTS–BOIS & PRODUITS	0.2	0.2					
34 PAPER & PRODUCTS–PAPIER & PRODT	1.5	0.9					
35 CHEMICALS–INDUSTRIES CHIMIQUES	5.2	10.1					
36 NON METAL MIN–MIN NON METAL	0.4	0.9					
37 BASIC METAL–IND METAL BASE	0.0	0.1					
38 METAL MANUF–MANUF METAL	20.3	21.7					
39 OTH MANUF IND–AUTRES MANUF	24.6	43.9					

3. TRADE BY PRINCIPAL COUNTRIES OF ORIGIN AND DESTINATION (VALUE IN THOUSAND U.S. DOLLARS)
ECHANGES SELON LES PRINCIPAUX PAYS D'ORIGINE ET DE DESTINATION (VALEUR EN MILLIERS DE DOLLARS EU)

COUNTRIES–PAYS	GENERAL IMPORTS C.I.F. IMPORTATIONS GENERALES C.A.F				
	1987	1988	1989	1990	1991
World		334173	387316	536388	481297
Africa		1	3	13	3
Americas		224752	241103	376745	359801
Northern America		146336	161353	301945	282688
LAIA		25155	35312	37664	39895
CACM		2183	2325	921	658
Caribbean		43798	33829	27368	26999
Rest of America		7280	8284	8846	9561
As.ex F.USSR		22221	20584	29585	26609
Eur.x F.USSR		77803	116316	120171	85374
EU		75658	113478	115797	81391
EFTA		1944	2451	3917	3784
East Europe		119	50	37	6
Other Europe		82	337	420	194
Former USSR		52	16	17	34
Oceania		186	207	278	431
USA/Etats–Unis d'Amer		142668	158288	295716	278898
Netherlands/Pays–Bas		42411	46758	70684	59334
Netherlands Antilles		41966	32188	24911	24150
Italy/Italie		17860	51331	26860	7639
Venezuela		16492	21470	23416	22657
Japan/Japon		12085	11391	18409	16710
Panama		7008	8207	8692	9370
Colombia/Colombie		4046	5764	6580	8064
Hong Kong		4331	3961	5068	4834
Germany/Allemagne		4778	4897	4305	3851
Canada		3544	2974	6108	3699
United Kingdom		3385	3378	4798	3774
Argentina/Argentine		2378	2759	3084	3667
Switz.Liecht		1750	2389	3770	3611
France,Monac		2864	2578	2954	2303
Mexico/Mexique		761	3526	1819	3146
Korea, Republic of		2736	2211	1975	1435
Brazil/Brésil		951	1542	2197	1897
Spain/Espagne		1319	1140	1988	970
Belgium–Luxembourg		1201	1035	1014	1418
Denmark/Danemark		861	1051	1275	1373
Costa Rica		864	1464	607	515
Philippines		513	341	923	1117
Trinidad and Tobago		574	360	713	700
Guatemala		1237	770	98	44
Singapore/Singapour		559	333	371	687
Ireland/Irlande		392	402	640	449
Sweden/Suède		139	513	875	215
China/Chine		188	596	658	182
Israel/Israël		225	296	388	655
Dominican Republic		363	315	394	467
Antigua and Barbuda		121	242	327	690
Peru/Pérou		306	161	454	320
Bahamas		199	284	286	321
Jamaica/Jamaïque		290	218	277	234
Barbados/Barbade		107	184	271	369
Thailand/Thaïlande		278	180	178	113
India/Inde		104	228	254	96
New Zealand		88	133	206	200
Norway,SVD,JM		194	61	142	173
Ecuador/Equateur		209	84	84	109
Australia/Australie		98	74	72	231
Austria/Autriche		172	231	36	13
Portugal		202	109	114	24
Malaysia/Malaisie		1	164	270	3
Bermuda/Bermudes		124	91	121	91
Suriname/Suriname		8	68	153	190
Greece/Grèce		38	56	196	18
Guyana		264	4	2	1
Cayman Is/Is Caïmans		158		1	

COUNTRIES–PAYS	GENERAL EXPORTS F.O.B. EXPORTATIONS GENERALES F.O.B.				
	1987	1988	1989	1990	1991
Monde		30621	22782	28276	26091
Afrique					
Amériques		22283	15593	18741	11437
Amérique du Nord		7562	3934	3675	3698
ALAI		1127	1053	3770	2665
MCAC		105	16	8	3
Caraïbes		13195	10499	11220	5029
Autre Amérique		294	91	68	42
Asie l'URSS exclus		1		6	1
Europe l'URSS exclus		1880	1229	1868	2495
UE		1712	1126	1861	2492
AELE		7			3
Europe de l'Est			1	6	
Autre de l'Europe		161	103		
Ancienne URSS					
Océanie					1
Netherlands Antilles		13097	10477	11110	4641
USA/Etats–Unis d'Amer		7532	3932	3634	3646
Netherlands/Pays–Bas		900	1104	1813	1373
Colombia/Colombie		665	536	2470	881
Venezuela		455	514	1290	1728
Denmark/Danemark		59			1088
Belgium–Luxembourg		531	1		1
Suriname/Suriname		223	18		18
Panama		71	70	44	24
Italy/Italie		197	6	1	1
Saint Lucia/St. Lucie				11	165
Bahamas		1		56	82
Dominican Republic		90	4	2	38
Bermuda/Bermudes		30		42	51
Guatemala		84		3	2
Trinidad and Tobago			1	21	65
Germany/Allemagne		6	13	26	2
Peru/Pérou		4	2	1	35
France,Monac				15	15
Guyana		1	3	25	
United Kingdom		10	1	3	13
Mexico/Mexique				1	20
Jamaica/Jamaïque		1	6	1	3
Brazil/Brésil			1	8	1
Antigua and Barbuda		1		8	1
Switz.Liecht		4			3
Costa Rica		1		5	
Cayman Is/Is Caïmans		2	2	1	
Japan/Japon		1		5	
Sweden/Suède				4	
Argentina/Argentine		3			
Canada			2	0	1
Norway,SVD,JM		3			
Dominica/Dominique		1	1		1
Spain/Espagne		2			
Australia/Australie					1
Austria/Autriche			1		
China/Chine				1	
Israel/Israël					1
Portugal				1	
Barbados/Barbade					1

(VALUE AS PERCENTAGE OF WORLD TOTAL)(VALEURS EN POURCENTAGE DU TOTAL MONDIAL)

	1982	1983	1984	1985	1986	1987	1988	1989	1990	1991
Africa							0.0	0.0	0.0	0.0
Americas							67.3	62.2	70.2	74.8
Northern America							43.8	41.7	56.3	58.7
LAIA							7.5	9.1	7.0	8.3
CACM							0.7	0.6	0.2	0.1
Caribbean							13.1	8.7	5.1	5.6
Rest of America							2.2	2.1	1.6	2.0
As.ex F.USSR							6.6	5.3	5.5	5.5
Eur.x F.USSR							23.3	30.0	22.4	17.7
EU							22.6	29.3	21.6	16.9
EFTA							0.6	0.6	0.7	0.8
East Europe							0.0	0.0	0.0	0.0
Other Europe							0.0	0.1	0.1	0.0
Former USSR							0.0	0.0	0.0	0.0
Oceania							0.1	0.1	0.1	0.1
USA/Etats–Unis d'Amer							42.7	40.9	55.1	57.9
Netherlands/Pays–Bas							12.7	12.1	13.2	12.3
Netherlands Antilles							12.6	8.3	4.6	5.0
Italy/Italie							5.3	13.3	5.0	1.6
Venezuela							4.9	5.5	4.4	4.7
Japan/Japon							3.6	2.9	3.4	3.5
Panama							2.1	2.1	1.6	1.9
Colombia/Colombie							1.2	1.5	1.2	1.7
Hong Kong							1.3	1.0	0.9	1.0
Germany/Allemagne							1.4	1.3	0.8	0.8

	1982	1983	1984	1985	1986	1987	1988	1989	1990	1991
Afrique										
Amériques							72.8	68.4	66.3	43.8
Amérique du Nord							24.7	17.3	13.0	14.2
ALAI							3.7	4.6	13.3	10.2
MCAC							0.3	0.1	0.0	0.0
Caraïbes							43.1	46.1	39.7	19.3
Autre Amérique							1.0	0.4	0.2	0.2
Asie l'URSS exclus							0.0		0.0	0.0
Europe l'URSS exclus							6.1	5.4	6.6	9.6
UE							5.6	4.9	6.6	9.6
AELE							0.0			0.0
Europe de l'Est								0.0	0.0	
Autre de l'Europe							0.5	0.5		
Ancienne URSS										
Océanie										0.0
Netherlands Antilles							42.8	46.0	39.3	17.8
USA/Etats–Unis d'Amer							24.6	17.3	12.9	14.0
Netherlands/Pays–Bas							2.9	4.8	6.4	5.3
Colombia/Colombie							2.2	2.4	8.7	3.4
Venezuela							1.5	2.3	4.6	6.6
Denmark/Danemark							0.2			4.2
Belgium–Luxembourg							1.7	0.0		0.0
Suriname/Suriname							0.7	0.1		0.1
Panama							0.2	0.3	0.2	0.1
Italy/Italie							0.6	0.0	0.0	0.0

4. General Imports C.I.F. by Commodities according to the S.I.T.C. (Rev. 2) in thousand U.S. Dollars
Importations Générales C.A.F. par Produits d'après la C.T.C.I. (Rév. 2) en milliers de Dollars E.U.

SITC CTCI	COMMODITY	1988 WEIGHT POIDS	1988 VALUE VALEUR	1989 WEIGHT POIDS	1989 VALUE VALEUR	1990 WEIGHT POIDS	1990 VALUE VALEUR	1991 WEIGHT POIDS	1991 VALUE VALEUR	PRODUIT
	ALL COMMODITIES # 1		334173		387316		536388		481297	TOUS PRODUITS
0	FOOD AND LIVE ANIMALS		58773		66374		78920		87449	ALIMENTS,ANIMAUX VIVANTS
01	MEAT AND PREPARATIONS		14476		16908		20490		22594	VIANDES ET PREPARATIONS
011	MEAT FRESH,CHILLD,FROZEN		10556		12754	W 6738	15347	W 6908	15797	VIANDES FRAICHES,REF,CONGE
0111	BOVINE MEAT FRESH,FROZEN		5413	W 1512	5471	W 1801	6433	W 2030	7887	VIANDES BOVIN FRAI,REF
0113	PIG MEAT FRESH,CHLD,FRZN	W 749	1598	W 944	2330	W 1043	3055	W 722	2008	VIANDE DE PORC
0114	POULTRY FRESH CHLLD,FRZN	W 2330	2954		4082	W 3546	4751	W 3830	4901	VOLAILLES MORTES
012	MEAT DRIED,SALTED,SMOKED		721		991	W 473	1470	W 810	2032	VIANDE,ABATS SALES,SECHES
0121	PIG MEAT DRIED,SLTD,SMKD		654		918	W 451	1388	W 769	1928	LARD,JAMBONS
014	MEAT PREPD,PRSVD,NES ETC		3198		3164	W 1178	3672	W 1573	4766	CONSERVES DE VIANDES
0142	SAUSAGES INCLDING TINNED		1327		1370	W 552	1852	W 765	2240	SAUCISSES,SAUCISSONS
0149	OTH PREPARD,PRESRVD MEAT		1810		1697	W 612	1749	W 790	2429	AUTRES PREP DE VIANDES
02	DAIRY PRODCTS,BIRDS'EGGS		5995		7682		10431		12332	PRODUITS LAITIERS,OEUFS
022	MILK AND CREAM	W 2172	3259		3882	W 3256	5410	W 3887	6296	LAIT ET CREME
0224	MILK,CREAM PRESERVED ETC	W 1606	2742		3607	W 3038	5057	W 3628	5904	LAIT,CREME CONS,CONC
02241	WHEY	W 654	720	W 1380	1344	W 1511	1680	W 1528	1707	LACTOSERUM (PETIT LAIT)
02242	MILK DRY,1.5% FAT OR LES	W 952	2022		2263	W 1527	3377	W 2100	4197	LAIT POUDRE INF 1.5%
024	CHEESE AND CURD		2300		3266	W 1256	4063	W 1781	5308	FROMAGE ET CAILLEBOTTE
03	FISH AND PREPARATIONS		4574		5428		5630		6645	POISSONS ET PREPARATIONS
034	FISH,FRESH,CHILLED,FROZN		1493		2393	W 475	1970	W 895	5460	POISSON FRAIS, REFRIG,CONG
036	SHELL FISH FRESH,FROZEN		1814		1996	W 301	2297			CRUSTACES,MOLLUSQUES
04	CEREALS AND PREPARATIONS		6977		5678		7592		8865	CEREALES ET PRODUITS
042	RICE		3014	W 1576	1150	W 1805	1440	W 2152	1644	RIZ
0421	RICE IN HUSK OR HUSKED		2779	W 381	286	W 136	104	W 738	592	RIZ SANS AUTRE PREPARATION
046	WHEAT ETC MEAL OR FLOUR	W 3325	1308		1491	W 3110	1266	W 25	14	SEMOULE FARINE,FROMENT
047	OTHER CEREAL MEALS,FLOUR	W 268	206		296	W 1042	617	W 4119	2146	AUTRES SEMOULES,FARINES
04701	CEREAL FLOUR(NON-WHEAT)	W 2	1					W 3832	1944	FARINES DE CEREALES
048	CEREAL ETC PREPARATIONS		2227		2372	W 1575	3426	W 1852	4245	PREPTNS A BASE CEREALES
0484	BAKERY PRODUCTS		1153		1389	W 721	1815	W 955	2497	PRODUITS DE BOULANGERIE
05	VEGETABLES AND FRUIT		11735		13783		17733		18910	LEGUMES ET FRUITS
054	VEG ETC FRSH,SMPLY PRSVD		3925		4551	W 7225	5811		6055	LEGUMES FRAIS,CONG,SECS
0545	OTHER FRESH VEGETABLES		1490		1871	W 3219	2440	W 3326	2663	AUTRES LEGUMES FRAIS,REF
05451	ALLIACEOUS VEGTBLS,FRESH		1490		1871	W 3219	2440	W 3326	2663	OIGNONS,ECHALOTES,AULX
0546	VEGETABLES SIMPLY PRESVD		1001		1150	W 1320	1578	W 1669	1659	LEGUMES CONG,CONSER
056	VEGTBLES ETC PRSVD,PREPD		1453		1687	W 1553	2256	W 1724	2530	CONSERVES DE LEGUMES
0565	VEGTBLES PRSVD,PREPD NES		1375		1616	W 1360	1999	W 1605	2360	LEGUMES PREPARES CONSERVE
05659	OTH VEG PRESVD,PREPD NES		1220	W 1053	1391	W 1216	1772	W 1427	2037	LEGUM PREPAP,CONSERV NDA
057	FRUIT,NUTS,FRESH,DRIED		3012		3408		4070		4491	FRUITS FRAIS OU SECS
0579	FRUIT FRESH OR DRIED NES		1158		1433		1708	W 2276	1789	FRUITS FRAIS,SECS NDA
058	FRUIT PRESERVED,PREPARED		3345		4137	W 5007	5596	W 5380	5835	CONSERVES DE FRUITS
0585	FRUIT OR VEGETABLE JUICE		2222		2863	W 4015	3970	W 4262	3855	JUS DE FRUITS
06	SUGAR AND PREPS,HONEY		1807		2476		3114		3469	SUCRES ET PRODUITS
061	SUGAR AND HONEY		1102		1443		1836	W 2615	2066	SUCRES ET MIEL
0612	REFINED SUGAR ETC	W 1703	894		1280	W 1679	1072	W 1889	1261	SUCRES RAFFINES
07	COFFEE,TEA,COCOA,SPICES		5943		6409		4054		3372	CAFE,THE,CACAO,EPICES
071	COFFEE AND SUBSTITUTES		4619		4985	W 812	2041	W 214	1178	CAFE ET SUCCEDANES
0711	COFFEE GREEN,ROASTED,SUB		4092		4939	W 764	1708	W 182	966	CAFE TORREFIE OU DECAFEINE
081	*FEEDING STUFF FOR ANIML	W 5908	2339		2363	W 6090	2941	W 6547	3566	NOURRITURE POUR ANIMAUX
0811	HAY, FODDER, GREEN, DRY	W 5908	2339		2363	W 6090	2941			FOIN ET FOURRAGE
08119	FODDER OF VEG ORIGIN NES	W 3214	1074							AUTRES FOURRAGES
09	MISC EDIBLE PRODUCTS		4860		5448		6777		7516	PREP ALIMENTAIRES DIVERSES
098	EDIBLE PRODCTS,PREPS NES		3899		4350	W 2899	5609	W 2721	6205	PREP ALIMENTAIRES NDA
09804	SAUCES,MIXED SEASONINGS		1072		1276	W 1186	1704	W 1131	1802	SAUCES,ASSAISONNEMENTS
09809	MISC FOOD PREPRTIONS NES		1735		1922	W 1209	2645	W 1030	2962	PREP ALIMENTAIRES NDA
1	BEVERAGES AND TOBACCO		11912		13473		18156		18865	BOISSONS ET TABACS
11	BEVERAGES		9555		11603		15597		16680	BOISSONS
111	NON-ALCOHL BEVERAGES NES	W 7532	1056		1087	W 4902729	2053	W 3215	2464	BOISSONS NON ALCOOLIQUES
11102	FLAVORED WATERS NON-ALCO	W 1375	898		983	W 1910	1534	W 2585	2153	LIMONADES,EAUX GAZEUSES
112	ALCOHOLIC BEVERAGES	W 6090	8499		10516	W 8603	13544	W 8374	14216	BOISSONS ALCOOLIQUES
1121	WINE OF FRESH GRAPES ETC	W 435	1163		1469	W 652	1787	W 569	1965	VINS DE RAISINS FRAIS
11212	WINE OF FRESH GRAPES	W 433	1158		1453	W 650	1775	W 567	1959	VINS DE MOUTS DE RAISINS
1123	BEER,ALE,STOUT,PORTER	W 5067	5640		6855	W 7294	9101	W 7232	9394	BIERES
1124	DISTILLED ALCOHOLIC BEVS	W 521	1585		2080	W 600	2551	W 511	2749	ALCOOLS,EAUX-DE-VIE
12	TOBACCO AND MANUFACTURES		2357		1870		2560		2185	TABACS BRUTS FABRIQUES
121	TOBACCO UNMNFCTRD,REFUSE	W 239	2212		986	W 16	180	W 1	27	TABACS BRUTS,DECHETS
122	TOBACCO,MANUFACTURED		145		884		2379		2158	TABACS FABRIQUES
1223	OTH MANUFACTURED TOBACCO		69	W 76	797	W 209	2171	W 80	1972	TABACS FUMER,CHIQUER,PRISER
2	CRUDE MATERLS,EXCL FUELS		3325		3046		4340		2866	MAT BRUTES NON COMESTIBLES
24	CORK AND WOOD		2335		1802		720		1259	LIEGE ET BOIS
248	WOOD SHAPED,SLEEPERS		2168		1626		531		1131	BOIS SIMPLEMENT TRAVAILLES
2483	LUMBER SHAPED NON-CONIFR		1521		509		266		677	NON CONIFERES SCIES,RABOTES
27	CRUDE FERTLZR,MINRLS NES		208		474		2286		500	ENGRAIS MINERAUX BRUTS
273	STONE,SAND AND GRAVEL		119	W 1290	344	W 22116	2092	W 13023	375	PIERRES,SABLES,GRAVIERS
3	MINERAL FUELS ETC		25317		14457		1725		2023	COMBUSTIBLES MINERAUX LUB
33	PETROLEUM AND PRODUCTS		24134		12855		1683		2012	PETROLE ET DERIVES
334	PETROLEUM PRODUCTS,REFIN		23785		12458	W 1327	1359	W 1558	1734	PRODUITS RAFFINES
3341	GASOLINE,OTH LIGHT OILS		8574	W 35470	6009	W 224	31	W 170	28	ESSENCES POUR MOTEURS
33411	MOTOR,AVIATION SPIRIT		6865	W 18201	2757	W 80	9	W 150	18	ESSENCES MOTEURS D'AVIONS
33412	SPIRIT TYPE JET FUEL		1709	W 17269	3252	W 144	22	W 20	10	CARBUREACTEURS
3343	GAS OILS	W 11737	2163	W 15210	2761	W 7	5	W 72	18	GAS OILS
3344	FUEL OILS,NES	W 132303	12342	W 30786	2642			W 100	5	FUEL OILS
3345	LUBS,PETROLEUM OILS NES		706		1045	W 1096	1322	W 1216	1682	HUILES LUBRIFIANTES
33451	LUBS(HIGH PETR CONT) ETC		706		1045	W 1096	1322	W 1216	1682	HUILES LUBRIF,H LOURDES
341	*GAS,NATURAL AND MANUFCT	W 10000	1181	W 4919	1602	W 48	42	W 9	11	GAZ NATUREL,GAZ MANUFACT
3413	PETROLM GASES,LIQUEFIED	W 10000	1181	W 4806	1583					GAZ DE PETROLE LIQUEFIE
5	CHEMCLS,RELATED PROD NES		26663		31653		45907		41632	PRODUITS CHIMIQUES
52	INORGANIC CHEMICALS		330		731		670		1516	PROD CHIM INORGANIQUES
53	DYES,TANNING,COLOUR PROD		2026		3091		4373		4008	PROD TEINTURE,COLORANTS
533	PIGMENTS,PAINTS,ETC		2004		2940		4262		3987	PIGMENTS,PEINTURES,VERNIS
5334	VARNISHES,DISTEMPERS ETC		1307		1727	W 993	2891	W 1513	2632	PEINTURES A L'EAU
541	*MEDICINAL,PHARM PRODUCT		6422		6273	K 501933	7314	K 398512	8161	PROD MEDICINAUX PHARMACEUT
55	PERFUME,CLEANING ETC PRD		12656		12888		15709		15526	PROD POUR PARFUM,TOILETTE
553	PERFUMERY,COSMETICS,ETC		10531		10170	W 789	12072	W 731	11728	PRODUITS DE PARFUMERIE
554	SOAP,CLEANSING ETC PREPS		1960		2470	W 1638	3444	W 1686	3674	SAVONS,PRODUITS DETERSIFS
5542	WASHING PREPARATIONS ETC	W 835	999		1344	W 1149	1944	W 1232	2258	PROD ORG TENSIO-ACT NDA
58	PLASTIC MATERIALS ETC		1454		3583		3757		3317	MAT PLAST ARTIFICIELLES
59	CHEMICAL MATERIALS NES		3132		4499		13539		8532	MAT PROD CHIMIQUES NDA
591	PESTICIDES,DISINFECTANTS		1310		1532	W 738	1864	W 775	2127	DESINF,INSECT,FONG,HERB
598	MISCEL CHEM PRODUCTS NES		1285		2017		10229	W 2362	5696	PROD DIV INDUST CHIM NDA
5989	CHEM PRODUCTS,PREPS NES		1271		1995	W 2839	10101	W 2345	5677	PROD PREP CHIMIQUES NDA
59899	OTH CHEM PRODS,PREPS,NES		1169		1902	W 2789	9987	W 2258	5538	AUT PRODUITS CHIMIQUES NDA

4. General Imports C.I.F. by Commodities according to the S.I.T.C. (Rev. 2) in thousand U.S. Dollars
Importations Générales C.A.F. par Produits d'après la C.T.C.I. (Rév. 2) en milliers de Dollars E.U.

SITC CTCI	COMMODITY	1988 WEIGHT POIDS	1988 VALUE VALEUR	1989 WEIGHT POIDS	1989 VALUE VALEUR	1990 WEIGHT POIDS	1990 VALUE VALEUR	1991 WEIGHT POIDS	1991 VALUE VALEUR	PRODUIT
6	BASIC MANUFACTURES		62681		95433		117335		86544	ART MANUFACTURES
62	RUBBER MANUFACTURES NES		1837		2269		3749		3536	CAOUTCHOUC MANUFACTURE
625	RUBBER TYRES, TUBES ETC	N 68407	1067		1064	N 68576	1500	N 73899	1579	PNEUS CAOUTCHOUC VULCANISE
628	RUBBER ARTICLES NES		561		731		1944		1850	OUVRAGES CAOUTCHOUC NDA
6289	OTH RUBBER ARTICLES NES		504		690	W 205	1904	W 210	1808	AUT OUVR CAOUTCHOUC NDA
63	WOOD,CORK MANUFACTRS NES		4888		6661		10501		7922	OUVRAGES LIEGE ET BOIS
634	VENEERS,PLYWOOD,ETC		3259		4196		5869		1689	PLACAGES,CONTRE–PLAQUES
6342	PLYWOOD OF WOOD SHEETS	V 4158	1653	V 2195	1655	V 7191	2620	V 4471	1688	BOIS CONTRE–PLAQUES
6343	IMPROVED,RECONSTIT WOOD		1606		2524	W 4743	3240			BOIS AMELIORES,RECONST
635	WOOD MANUFACTURES NES		1621		2458	W 3380	4621		6219	ART MANUF EN BOIS NDA
6353	BUILDERS WOODWRK,PREFABS		1189		1925	W 1292	2498	W 950	1680	OUVRAGES DE MENUISERIE
6359	OTHER WOOD MANUFACTURES		279		336	W 1885	1634	W 6014	4168	OUVRAGES EN BOIS NDA
63591	TOOLS,HANDLES ETC WOOD		279			W 1885	1634	W 398	934	OUTILS MANCHES D'OUTILS
63599	OTHER WOOD ARTICLES NES							W 5616	3235	AUTRES OUVRAGES EN BOIS NDA
64	PAPER,PAPERBOARD AND MFR		7579		8691		11034		11455	PAPIERS,CARTONS & OUVRAGES
641	PAPER AND PAPERBOARD		2291		2727	W 1471	2591		2515	PAPIERS ET CARTONS
6419	CONVERTED PAPER ETC NES		993		1588	W 460	1132	W 735	878	PAP,CART TRANSFORMES NDA
642	PAPER,ETC,PRECUT,ARTS OF		5288		5964	W 3887	8444	W 3167	8940	PAP,CARTONS DECOUPES
6424	PAPER ETC CT TO SIZE NES		1835		1946	W 1358	2540	W 1230	2811	PAP,CARTONS DECOUPES
64243	TOILET PAPER CUT TO SIZE		1620		1683	W 977	1954	W 822	2091	PAPIER HYGIENIQUE
6428	PAPER ETC ARTICLES NES		2042		2283	W 1717	3853	W 1119	3704	OUVRAGES EN PATE A PAPIER
64282	PUNCHED CARD MACH CARDS		2042		2283	W 1717	3853	W 1119	3704	CARTES POUR MACHINES
65	TEXTILE YARN,FABRICS,ETC		7372		8041		10226		8572	FILS,TISSUS,ARTICLES TEXTILE
658	TEXTILE ARTICLES NES		3975		3636		5256		4987	ART FACONNES MAT TEXTILES
6584	LINENS ETC		3389		3060		4198	W 265	3761	LINGE DE MAISON
659	FLOOR COVERINGS,ETC		1302		2077	W 457	2579	W 315	1588	COUVRE–PARQUETS,TAPIS ETC
66	NONMETAL MINERAL MFS NES		13130		25278		21440		16379	ART MIN NON METALLIQUES
661	LIME,CEMENT,BLDG PRODS		3361		5506	W 50422	6752	W 43906	4312	CHAUX,CIMENTS MAT CONSTR
6612	CEMENT		2813	W 52836	4366	W 47690	5143	W 42392	3554	CIMENTS HYDRAULIQUES
662	CLAY,REFRACTORY BLDG PRD		3664		5165		5399		3289	MAT CONST REFRACTAIRES
6623	REFRACTORY BUILDING PROD	W 1252	1186	W 1223	901	W 598	339	W 67	71	BRIQUES REFRACTAIRES
6624	BRICKS ETC NONREFRACTORY		2478		4264		5060	MN 11170	3218	BRIQUES ETC CERAM NON REFR
66243	PIPING ETC,CERAMIC	N 2525000	904		1702		3161			TUYAUX DE CANALISATION
66245	GLAZED CERAMIC SETTS ETC	W 1521	1019	W 1368	1570	W 1417	898			AUT CARREAUX CERAMIQUE
663	MINERAL MANUFCTURES NES		1510		7064		1284		699	ART MIN MANUF NDA
6633	MINRL MFS NES NONCERAMIC		1232		6617		837	W 496	368	OUVR MAT MINERALE NDA
664	GLASS		1376		3037	W 847	2192	W 601	1431	VERRE
6649	GLASS NES	W 340	972		2153	W 608	1346	W 491	1121	VERRE NDA
665	GLASSWARE		1767		3059		3394	W 1230	3068	OUVRAGES EN VERRE
6658	GLASS ARTICLES NES		995		1636		1788	W 53	1745	ARTICLES FAB EN VERRE NDA
66582	GLASS ORNAMENTS NES		809		1588	W 33	1579	W 29	1523	PERLES DE VERRE
666	POTTERY		1334		1434	W 317	1995	W 335	2416	POTERIE
6666	CERAMIC ORNAMENTS ETC		1334		1434	W 317	1995			OBJETS PORCELAINE,CERAM
67	IRON AND STEEL		8473		15189		22390		15741	FER ET ACIER
673	IRON,STEEL SHAPES ETC		6341	W 5844	6447	W 10749	4944	W 2780	2437	BARRES,PROFIL FER,ACIER
674	IRN,STL UNIV,PLATE,SHEET		1133		6275	W 6194	6436	W 1292	2149	LARGES PLATS,TOLES
678	IRON,STL TUBES,PIPES,ETC		920		2341	W 5870	10018	W 5084	10896	TUBES,TUYAUX EN FONTE,FER
68	NON–FERROUS METALS		2748		2987		3343		2666	METAUX NON FERREUX
682	COPPER EXC CEMENT COPPER		640		1202	W 286	1555	W 166	789	CUIVRE
684	ALUMINIUM		1794		1340	W 423	1453	W 515	1483	ALUMINIUM
69	METAL MANUFACTURES NES		16574		26183		34517		20094	ART MANUFACT EN METAL NDA
691	STRUCTURES AND PARTS NES		9051		14421	W 3061	8107	W 791	2956	CONSTRUCT FER,ACIER,ALU
6911	STRUCTURES,PARTS IRN,STL		8459		11323	W 2681	4979			CONSTRUCT FER,ACIER,FONTE
6912	STRUCTURES,PARTS ALUMNM		592		3097	W 380	3128			CONSTRUCT ALUMINIUM
692	METAL TANKS,BOXES,ETC		536		892	W 925	1850	W 536	794	RECIPIENTS METALLIQUES
694	STL,COPPR NAILS,NUTS,ETC		728		1389	W 806	2585	W 496	1615	CLOUS,VIS,ECROUS
69402	IRN,STL NUTS,BOLTS,ETC		413		908	W 603	2086	W 352	1350	BOULONS,VIS,ECROUS FER,AC
695	TOOLS		826		1285	W 382	3484	W 200	2132	OUTILS A MAIN
6953	OTHER HAND TOOLS		803		1236	W 375	3447	W 167	2060	AUTRES OUTILS A MAIN
697	BASE MTL HOUSEHOLD EQUIP		1614		2617		2984		2607	ART MENAGE MET COMMUNS
699	BASE METAL MFRS NES		2953		4702	W 3165	14095		8839	ART MANUFACTURES MET NDA
6991	LOCKSMITHS WARES,ETC		755		1251	W 253	2090	W 130	1417	ARTICLES DE SERRURERIE
6998	MFRS NES OF CPR,NIKL,ETC		1768		2542	W 2537	10403		5801	OUVRAGES EN CU,NI,AL,PB,ZN
69986	TIN MANUFACTURES NES		1697		2472	W 2382	10038	W 1763	5795	OUVRAGES EN ETAIN
7	MACHINES,TRANSPORT EQUIP		66813		80129		160221		133653	MACHINES MATERIEL TRANSPORT
71	POWER GENERATING EQUIPMT		2554		2718		6726		22118	MACHINES GENERATRICES
711	STEAM BOILERS & AUX PLNT		334		456	W 168	1169	W 301	3747	GENERATEURS VAPEUR EAU ETC
7111	STEAM BOILERS ETC		55		218	W 96	526	W 285	3134	GENERATEURS VAPEUR EAU
712	STEAM ENGINES,TURBINES		17	W 1	17	W 131	1479	W 374	15469	MACHINES A VAPEUR D'EAU PIEC
7126	STEAM POWR UNITS,ENGINES		17	W 1	17	W 131	1479	W 374	15469	MACHINES A VAPEUR D EAU
713	INTRNL COMBUS PSTN ENGIN		1011		740		941	W 55	764	MOTEURS EXPL COMB INT, PIECE
716	ROTATING ELECTRIC PLANT		1177		1475	W 324	3003	W 138	2118	APP ELECTR ROTATIFS,PIECES
72	MACHS FOR SPCL INDUSTRYS		3442		3066		11060		6439	MAC SPECIALES POUR INDUST
724	TEXTILE,LEATHER MACHNRY		513		278		1679		353	MACH POUR INDUSTRIE TEXTILE
728	OTH MACHY FOR SPCL INDUS		1765		1804	W 1219	7561	W 302	3415	AUT MACH IND PARTICULIERES
7283	OTHR MINERAL WORKG MACHY		908		479	W 463	1775	W 64	507	MACH TRIER,CRIBLER,BROYER
7284	MACHY FOR SPCL INDUS NES		808		1220	W 697	5407	W 228	2694	MACH SPEC IND PARTICUL.
73	METALWORKING MACHINERY		235		422		1874		832	MACH TRAVAIL DES METAUX
737	METALWORKING MACHNRY NES		160		343	W 193	1772	W 57	755	MACH TRAV METAUX PIECES
74	GENRL INDUSTRL MACHY NES		9433		16874		43841		29025	MACH APP INDUSTRIE
741	HEATING,COOLING EQUIPMNT		3569		8784		19827		12301	MACH CHAUFFAGE,PIECES
7414	NONDOM REFRIG EQUIPT,PTS		994		3156		2055	W 247	1940	MAT PRODUCTION DU FROID
74141	REFRIG EQUIP NONDOMESTIC		994		3156		2055	W 247	1940	REFIG INDUSTRIELS
7415	AIR–CONDITIONING MACHNRY		2354		5374		4805		3789	GROUPES CONDITION AIR
7416	HEATING,COOLING EQU NES		84		117	W 602	12528	W 140	6327	APP CHANGEMENT TEMP
742	PUMPS FOR LIQUIDS ETC		1159		1474	W 409	6366	W 498	4631	POMPES MOTO–POMPES
743	PUMPS NES,CENTRFUGES ETC		512		727	W 143	1673	W 175	2244	POMPES COMPRES,VENT ETC
7431	PUMPS FOR GASES ETC		512		727	W 143	1673	W 175	2244	POMPES AIR A VIDE,COMPRES
744	MECHANICAL HANDLING EQU		2718		1751	W 1311	5003	W 253	1403	EQUIP MANUTENTION PIECES
7441	FORK LIFT TRCKS,ETC,PTS		1878		1459	W 579	2430			CHARIOTS POUR USINES ETC
7442	LIFTING,LOADING MACH NES		840		292	W 731	2573			APP LEVAGE,MANUTENTION
749	NONELEC MACH PTS,ACC NES		1476		4138	W 1137	10972		8446	PIECES MACH NON ELEC NDA
7499	OTH NONELEC MCHY PTS NES		1305		3968	W 1124	10446	W 1104	7935	PIECES NON ELECT NDA
75	OFFICE MACHNES,ADP EQUIP		3208		4616		7720		5312	MACH BUREAU TRAIT AUTOM
752	AUTOMTIC DATA PROC EQUIP		2475		3598		6518		4151	MACH TRAIT INFORMATION
76	TELECOMM,SOUND EQUIPMENT		10735		5943		12969		9193	EQUIPMENT DE TELECOM
761	TELEVISION RECEIVERS	N 6554	1534		1773	N 10658	2724	N 7512	2058	RECEPTEURS DE TELEVISION
763	SOUND RECORDRS,PHONOGRPH	N 4705	482		823	N 10878	1226	N 14345	1779	PHONO,APP ENREGISTREMENT
7631	ELECTRIC GRAMOPHONES ETC	N 4705	482		823	N 10878	1226	N 14345	1779	ELECTROPHON,TOURNE–DISQ
764	TELECOM EQPT,PTS,ACC NES		8558		2985		8564		4753	EQUIP TELECOM,PIECES
7641	LINE TELEPHONE,ETC EQUIP		1741		679	W 38	1558	W 28	1009	APP TELEPHON PAR FIL

4. General Imports C.I.F. by Commodities according to the S.I.T.C. (Rev. 2) in thousand U.S. Dollars
Importations Générales C.A.F. par Produits d'après la C.T.C.I. (Rév. 2) en milliers de Dollars E.U.

SITC CTCI	COMMODITY	1988 WEIGHT POIDS	1988 VALUE VALEUR	1989 WEIGHT POIDS	1989 VALUE VALEUR	1990 WEIGHT POIDS	1990 VALUE VALEUR	1991 WEIGHT POIDS	1991 VALUE VALEUR	PRODUIT
7643	TV,RADIO TRANSMITTRS ETC		6486		1754	W 234	6197	W 29	2804	APP EMET TELE RADIO
77	ELECTRIC MACHNRY NES ETC		12144		19530		31616		21960	MACH APP ELECT NDA
772	SWITCHGEAR ETC,PARTS NES		1330		2695	W 283	5355	W 204	4052	APP COUPURE,SECT ETC
773	ELECTR DISTRIBUTNG EQUIP		3508		5120	W 2089	10604	W 1138	6617	EQUIPMT DISTRIBUTION ELECT
7731	INSULATED WIRE,CABLE ETC		2277		3091	W 1327	7534	W 968	5365	FILS,CABLES ISOLES ELECT
7732	ELECTRC INSULATING EQUIP		1231		2029	W 762	3071	W 169	1252	EQUIP ISOL ELECTRIQUE
775	HOUSEHOLD TYPE EQUIP NES		2410		3916		6194		5640	MACH,APP USAGE DOMESTQUE
7752	DOM REFRIGERATRS,FREEZRS		903		1496		2096	N 4443	1945	REFRIG,CONGEL MENAGER
7757	DOMESTIC ELECTRC EQU NES		573		1021	W 359	1908	W 217	1795	APP ELECTR DOMEST NDA
778	ELECTRICAL MACHINERY NES		4623		7536		9202		5479	AUTRES MACH ELECT NDA
7788	OTH ELEC MACHY,EQUIP NES		3264		5870	W 569	7377	W 274	3584	AUT MACH APP ELEC NDA
78	ROAD VEHICLES		21934		25735		38391		34749	VEHICULES ROUTIERS
781	PASS MOTOR VEH EXC BUSES	N 2153	14112	W 2437	15594	N 3491	24758	N 2903	20217	AUTO TRANSPORT PERSONNES
782	LORRIES,SPCL MTR VEH NES	N 456	3503	W 1053	4943	N 466	4435	N 587	7096	VEHICULES SPECIAUX,MARCH
7821	LORRIES,TRUCKS	N 448	3281	W 972	4518	N 452	4092	N 556	5521	VEHICULES TRANSP MARCHAND
7822	SPECIAL MOTOR VEHCLS NES	N 8	222	W 81	425	N 14	343	N 31	1575	VEHICULES USAGES SPECIAUX
783	ROAD MOTOR VEHICLES NES	N 36	355		870	N 145	1709	N 130	1656	VEHICULES ROUTIERS NDA
784	MOTOR VEH PRTS,ACCES NES		2641		3412		3737		4088	PIECES 722,781,782,783
7849	OTHER MOTOR VEHCL PARTS		2622		3285	W 293	3705	W 395	4082	PIECES 722,781,782,783
786	TRAILERS,NONMOTR VEH,NES		784		380	W 964	3133	W 240	972	REMORQUES,CADRES,CONTAIN
7861	TRAILERS,TRANSP CONTAINR		784		380	W 964	3133	W 240	972	REMORQUES TOUS VEHICULES
78611	HOUSING,CAMPING TRAILERS		784		380	W 964	3133	W 240	972	REMORQUES POUR CAMPING
79	OTHR TRANSPORT EQUIPMENT		3128		1224		6024		4025	AUTRE MATERIEL TRANSPORT
792	AIRCRAFT ETC		2516		269		2277		1674	APP NAVIGATION AERIENNE
7921	HELICOPTERS	N 2	1508				141			HELICOPTERES
7929	AIRCRAFT PARTS NES		1007		263	W 17	2131		1673	PIECES DU 792
793	SHIPS AND BOATS ETC		612		955		3690		2351	NAVIRES BATEAUX,ETC
7932	SHIPS AND BOATS NES		501		782		3537	N 92	2170	NAVIRES ET BATEAUX
8	MISC MANUFACTURED GOODS		77595		81519		108380		106522	ART MANUFACTURES DIVERS
812	*PLUMBG,HEATNG,LGHTNG EQ		2797		4307		5406		3724	APPAR SANITAIRES CHAUFFAGE
8122	CERAMIC PLUMBNG FIXTURES		580		1699	W 393	1862	W 179	745	EVIERS,LAVABOS,CUVETTES
8124	LIGHTING EQUIPMENT NES		2135		2289		3531		2969	APPAREILS ECLAIRAGE ETC
81242	LAMPS,FITTINGS BASE METL		1761		2203	W 203	3411	W 227	2902	APPAREILS D'ECLAIRAGE
821	*FURNITURE,PARTS THEREOF		15403		10882		19080		12339	MEUBLES ET PIECES
8219	FURNITURE AND PARTS NES		14913					W 2138	11790	AUTRES MEUBLES ET PIECES
831	*TRAVEL GOODS,HANDBAGS		1759		2695	W 140	4055	W 133	3999	ARTICLES DE VOYAGE ETC
84	CLOTHING AND ACCESSORIES		17864		20664		24762		27765	VETEMENTS
842	MENS OUTERWEAR NOT KNIT		9200		11270		13208		21849	VET DESSUS POUR HOMMES
843	WOMENS OUTERWEAR NONKNIT		4371		5351		6869			VET DESSUS FEMMES MAT TEX
845	OUTERWEAR KNIT NONELASTC		878		817		1192	N 126418	1701	VET DESSOUS,ACCES BONNET
846	UNDER GARMENTS KNITTED		1002		1208		1265		1516	SOUS VETS DE BONNETERIE
847	TEXTILE CLTHNG ACCES NES		1804		1233		1091		1299	ACCES VET MAT TEXT NDA
8471	— NOT KNITTED		1364		702		383		536	ACCES VET MAT TEX NON BON
84719	MADE–UP CLTHG ACCESS NES		1255		513		144		155	AUT ACCES VET MAT TEXTIL
851	*FOOTWEAR		3130		3445		4482		5461	CHAUSSURES
85101	FOOTWEAR RUBBER,PLASTIC		1079		1146	W 71	1291			CHAUS SEMELLES CAOUTCH
85102	FOOTWEAR LEATHER	P 103716	1106		1573	P 184080	1965			CHAUS SEMELLES EN CUIR
87	PRECISION INSTRUMNTS NES		1178		1963		4114		5798	INSTRUM,APPAR SCIENT NDA
872	MEDICAL INSTRUMENTS NES		570		841		1380	W 126	2672	INSTR,APP MEDIC–CHIR NDA
874	MEASURNG,CONTROLNG INSTR		535		1036	W 35	2640	W 57	2933	INSTRUMENTS DE MESURE
88	PHOTO EQU,OPTICL GDS ETC		10552		10489		13018		14280	APP,FOURN PHOTO,OP,MONTR
881	PHOTO APPARAT,EQUIPT NES		1482		1384		1971		3104	APP,EQUIP PHOTO NDA
8812	CINEMA CAMERAS,PROJ,ETC		185		186		491		1610	APPAREILS CINEMA,PIECES
885	WATCHES AND CLOCKS		7154		7116		8679		8495	HORLOGERIE
8851	WATCHES,MOVEMENTS,CASES		6948		6938		8473		8274	MONTRES,MOUVEMENTS,BOITES
88511	WATCHES		6940		6937		8473			MONTRES POCHE,BRACELET
89	MISC MANUFCTRD GOODS NES		24912		27073		33461		33156	ART MANUFACTURES DIVERS
892	PRINTED MATTER		2607		3411		4412		4699	IMPRIMES
8921	PRINTED BOOKS,GLOBES,ETC		1145		1424		1782		1902	LIVRES,BROCHURES,CARTES
89211	PRINTED BOOKS,PAMPHLETS		1133		1384	W 162	1750	W 217	1811	LIVRES,BROCHURES
8928	PRINTED MATTER NES		802		1091		1689	W 138	1637	IMPRIMES NDA
893	ARTICLES OF PLASTIC NES		4548		5888		8298	W 2198	7846	OUVRAGES EN MAT DIVIS 58
894	TOYS,SPORTING GOODS,ETC		3264		5766		5535		6001	VOITURES ENFANTS,JOUETS
8942	TOYS,INDOOR GAMES ETC		2652		5097	W 283	4494	W 311	4971	JOUETS,JEUX ETC
89424	INDOOR GAME EQUIPMENT		1481		3663	W 80	2598			ART,JEUX DE SOCIETE
897	GOLD,SILVER WARE,JEWELRY		11867		8840		10834		10077	BIJOUTERIE,ORFEVRERIE
8973	PREC JEWLRY,GLD–SILVWARE		11251		8213		10117		9388	BIJOUX OR,ARGENT ORFEVRE
899	OTHER MANUFACTURED GOODS		1196		1371		1703		1699	AUT ART MANUF DIVERS NDA

5. General Exports F.O.B. by Commodities according to the S.I.T.C. (Rev. 2) in thousand U.S. Dollars
Exportations Générales F.O.B. par Produits d'après la C.T.C.I. (Rév. 2) en milliers de Dollars E.U.

SITC CTCI	COMMODITY	1988 WEIGHT POIDS	1988 VALUE VALEUR	1989 WEIGHT POIDS	1989 VALUE VALEUR	1990 WEIGHT POIDS	1990 VALUE VALEUR	1991 WEIGHT POIDS	1991 VALUE VALEUR	PRODUIT
	ALL COMMODITIES # 1		30621		22782		28276		26091	TOUS PRODUITS
0	FOOD AND LIVE ANIMALS		6709		3244		3463		2496	ALIMENTS,ANIMAUX VIVANTS
01	MEAT AND PREPARATIONS		45		19		70		106	VIANDES ET PREPARATIONS
011	MEAT FRESH,CHILLD,FROZEN		29		9	W 13	46	W 41	82	VIANDES FRAICHES,REF,CONGE
02	DAIRY PRODCTS,BIRDS'EGGS		316		380		1083		1764	PRODUITS LAITIERS,OEUFS
022	MILK AND CREAM		203	W 131	232	W 440	732	W 903	1317	LAIT ET CREME
0224	MILK,CREAM PRESERVED ETC			W 131	232	W 440	732			LAIT,CREME CONS,CONC
02241	WHEY			W 131	232	W 440	732			LACTOSERUM (PETIT LAIT)
024	CHEESE AND CURD	W 36	107		148	W 137	346	W 287	440	FROMAGE ET CAILLEBOTTE
03	FISH AND PREPARATIONS		123		65		84		33	POISSONS ET PREPARATIONS
04	CEREALS AND PREPARATIONS		39		222		1309		281	CEREALES ET PRODUITS
044	MAIZE UNMILLED	W 32	18	W 347	197	W 638	317	W 277	144	MAIS NON MOULU
045	CEREALS NES UNMILLED			W 32	15	W 570	563	W 212	115	AUTRES CEREALES NON MOULUES
046	WHEAT ETC MEAL OR FLOUR				3	W 196	410	W 12	5	SEMOULE FARINE,FROMENT
05	VEGETABLES AND FRUIT		208		122		149		147	LEGUMES ET FRUITS
057	FRUIT,NUTS,FRESH,DRIED		183	W 66	75	W 37	39	W 38	41	FRUITS FRAIS OU SECS
0579	FRUIT FRESH OR DRIED NES		183	W 66	75	W 37	39	W 38	41	FRUITS FRAIS,SECS NDA
07	COFFEE,TEA,COCOA,SPICES		5629		2324		665		121	CAFE,THE,CACAO,EPICES
071	COFFEE AND SUBSTITUTES	W 1286	5625		2313	W 438	652	W 54	97	CAFE ET SUCCEDANES
0711	COFFEE GREEN,ROASTED,SUB				2313	W 438	652			CAFE TORREFIE OU DECAFEINE
09	MISC EDIBLE PRODUCTS		344		70		95		20	PREP ALIMENTAIRES DIVERSES
098	EDIBLE PRODCTS,PREPS NES		344		70	W 108	94		20	PREP ALIMENTAIRES NDA
09809	MISC FOOD PREPRTIONS NES				70	W 108	94			PREP ALIMENTAIRES NDA
1	BEVERAGES AND TOBACCO		9724		8037		8544		2028	BOISSONS ET TABACS
12	TOBACCO AND MANUFACTURES		9718		7975		8521		1989	TABACS BRUTS FABRIQUES
122	TOBACCO,MANUFACTURED	W 253	9718		7975	N 20900	8521	W 60	1989	TABACS FABRIQUES
1221	CIGARS,CHEROOTS,ETC	W 253	9718		7975	N 20900	8521			CIGARES
2	CRUDE MATERLS,EXCL FUELS		385		78		328		117	MAT BRUTES NON COMESTIBLES
28	METALLIFEROUS ORES,SCRAP		358		47		305		115	MINERAIS METAL,DECHETS
282	IRON AND STEEL SCRAP	W 854	134	W 86	27	W 4600	305	W 1103	109	FERRAILLES
288	NONFERR METAL SCRAP NES	W 816	224	W 69	20			W 35	6	DECHETS NON FERREUX
3	MINERAL FUELS ETC		65		165		1		1165	COMBUSTIBLES MINERAUX LUB
33	PETROLEUM AND PRODUCTS		65		165		1		1165	PETROLE ET DERIVES
335	RESIDUAL PETRLM PROD NES				153			W 24150	1161	PRODUITS RESIDUELS NDA
3351	PETRLM JELLY,MINERAL WAX			W 2500	152					VASELINE,CIRES MINERALES
33511	PETROLATUM			W 2500	152					VASELINE (PETROLATUM)
3353	MIN TAR PITCH,PITCH COKE							W 24150	1161	BRAI,COKE DE BRAI
33531	PITCH FROM MINERAL TARS							W 24150	1161	BRAI DE GOUDRON
4	ANIMAL,VEGETABLE OIL,FAT		61		63		33		189	HUILES,GRAISSES ANIM,VEG
42	FIXED VEGETABLE OIL,FAT		61		63		33		189	HUILES VEGETALES FIXES
423	FIXED VEG OILS,SOFT	W 23	53	W 17	39	W 15	32	W 144	189	HUILES VEGET DOUCES FIXES
5	CHEMCLS,RELATED PROD NES		2175		2334		1266		1350	PRODUITS CHIMIQUES
541	*MEDICINAL,PHARM PRODUCT		88		30	K 2319	45		108	PROD MEDICINAUX PHARMACEUT
55	PERFUME,CLEANING ETC PRD		1808		1755		809		799	PROD POUR PARFUM,TOILETTE
553	PERFUMERY,COSMETICS,ETC		1608		1497	W 44	381		440	PRODUITS DE PARFUMERIE
554	SOAP,CLEANSING ETC PREPS	W 140	198	W 210	258	W 305	428	W 335	359	SAVONS,PRODUITS DETERSIFS
5543	POLISHES,CREAMS,ETC			W 210	258	W 305	428			CIRAGES,ENCAUSTIQUES
59	CHEMICAL MATERIALS NES		255		508		398		383	MAT PROD CHIMIQUES NDA
598	MISCEL CHEM PRODUCTS NES	W 248	255		508	W 373	398	W 299	383	PROD DIV INDUST CHIM NDA
5989	CHEM PRODUCTS,PREPS NES	W 248	255		508	W 373	398	W 299	383	PROD PREP CHIMIQUES NDA
59899	OTH CHEM PRODS,PREPS,NES	W 248	255		508	W 373	398	W 299	383	AUT PRODUITS CHIMIQUES NDA
6	BASIC MANUFACTURES		802		940		1687		1298	ART MANUFACTURES
64	PAPER,PAPERBOARD AND MFR		304		135		84		96	PAPIERS,CARTONS & OUVRAGES
642	PAPER,ETC,PRECUT,ARTS OF		299	W 69	123	W 69	77	W 100	84	PAP,CARTONS DECOUPES
6421	PAPER ETC CONTAINERS			W 69	123	W 69	77			BOITES,SACS EMBALLAGES
66	NONMETAL MINERAL MFS NES		189		506		466		489	ART MIN NON METALLIQUES
665	GLASSWARE		145		326	W 64	60	W 415	147	OUVRAGES EN VERRE
6651	BOTTLES ETC OF GLASS				326	W 64	60			RECIPIENTS EN VERRE
667	PEARL,PREC–,SEMI–P STONE		17		149		342		254	PERLES, PIERRES GEMMES
6673	PREC–,SEMI–PR STONES NES				149		342			AUTRES PIERRES NON SERTIES
67	IRON AND STEEL		100		79		9		6	FER ET ACIER
678	IRON,STL TUBES,PIPES,ETC		98		12		1		6	TUBES,TUYAUX EN FONTE,FER
69	METAL MANUFACTURES NES		117		181		943		594	ART MANUFACT EN METAL NDA
691	STRUCTURES AND PARTS NES		3	W 10	56	W 143	287	W 56	44	CONSTRUCT FER,ACIER,ALU
6911	STRUCTURES,PARTS IRN,STL			W 10	56	W 143	287			CONSTRUCT FER,ACIER,FONTE
692	METAL TANKS,BOXES,ETC		49		31	W 86	357	W 61	135	RECIPIENTS METALLIQUES
6921	METAL STORAGE TANKS ETC				31	W 86	357			CUVES EN FONTE,FER,ALU
695	TOOLS		17		63	W 8	87	W 22	206	OUTILS A MAIN
6953	OTHER HAND TOOLS				63	W 8	87			AUTRES OUTILS A MAIN
697	BASE MTL HOUSEHOLD EQUIP		21		3		17	W 20	134	ART MENAGE MET COMMUNS
699	BASE METAL MFRS NES		22		21	W 18	185	W 13	72	ART MANUFACTURES MET NDA
7	MACHINES,TRANSPORT EQUIP		2442		1578		3989		4458	MACHINES MATERIEL TRANSPORT
71	POWER GENERATING EQUIPMT		127		283		58		306	MACHINES GENERATRICES
716	ROTATING ELECTRIC PLANT		96					W 14	108	APP ELECTR ROTATIFS,PIECES
718	OTH POWER GENERATG MACHY		31		283	W 19	58	W 25	197	AUTRES MOTEURS PARTIES
7188	WIND,WATER,ETC ENGINES				283	W 19	58			MOT MACHINES MOTRICES NDA
72	MACHS FOR SPCL INDUSTRYS		42		11		145		272	MAC SPECIALES POUR INDUST
725	PAPER ETC MILL MACHINERY		10		10	W 52	144		271	MACHINES FABR PATE PAPIER
73	METALWORKING MACHINERY		4		45		89		385	MACH TRAVAIL DES METAUX
736	METALWORKING MACH–TOOLS	W 6	4	W 5	45	W 13	89	W 58	385	MACH–OUTILS TRAVAIL METAUX
74	GENRL INDUSTRL MACHY NES		415		194		1395		1733	MACH APP INDUSTRIE
749	NONELEC MACH PTS,ACC NES				194	W 265	1395			PIECES MACH NON ELEC NDA
7499	OTH NONELEC MCHY PTS NES				194	W 265	1395			PIECES NON ELECT NDA
75	OFFICE MACHNES,ADP EQUIP		567		65		218		163	MACH BUREAU TRAIT AUTOM
751	OFFICE MACHINES		567		65		218		163	MACH,APPAREILS DE BUREAU
7518	OFFICE MACHINES NES				65		218			MACH,APP DE BUREAU NDA
75181	DUPLICAT MCH,HECTO,STNCL				65		218			DUPLICATEURS A STENCILS
76	TELECOMM,SOUND EQUIPMENT		27		49		61		83	EQUIPMENT DE TELECOM
761	TELEVISION RECEIVERS		27		49		61		83	RECEPTEURS DE TELEVISION
77	ELECTRIC MACHNRY NES ETC		304		336		809		335	MACH APP ELECT NDA
772	SWITCHGEAR ETC,PARTS NES				22	W 15	485			APP COUPURE,SECT ETC
776	TRANSISTORS,VALVES,ETC		31		54	W 93	31	W 44	101	LAMPES,TUBES,VALVES
778	ELECTRICAL MACHINERY NES		168		227	W 49	229	W 90	186	AUTRES MACH ELECT NDA
7788	OTH ELEC MACHY,EQUIP NES		168		227	W 49	229	W 90	186	AUT MACH APP ELEC NDA
78	ROAD VEHICLES		718		459		469		728	VEHICULES ROUTIERS
784	MOTOR VEH PRTS,ACCES NES				410	W 58	446			PIECES 722,781,782,783
7849	OTHER MOTOR VEHCL PARTS				410	W 58	446			PIECES 722,781,782,783
79	OTHR TRANSPORT EQUIPMENT		239		137		745		455	AUTRE MATERIEL TRANSPORT
792	AIRCRAFT ETC		54		113		689	W 10	366	APP NAVIGATION AERIENNE
7921	HELICOPTERS				106		685			HELICOPTERES
793	SHIPS AND BOATS ETC		185		23	W 33	55		89	NAVIRES BATEAUX,ETC

5. General Exports F.O.B. by Commodities according to the S.I.T.C. (Rev. 2) in thousand U.S. Dollars
Exportations Générales F.O.B. par Produits d'après la C.T.C.I. (Rév. 2) en milliers de Dollars E.U.

SITC CTCI	COMMODITY	1988 WEIGHT POIDS	1988 VALUE VALEUR	1989 WEIGHT POIDS	1989 VALUE VALEUR	1990 WEIGHT POIDS	1990 VALUE VALEUR	1991 WEIGHT POIDS	1991 VALUE VALEUR	PRODUIT
8	MISC MANUFACTURED GOODS		3812		1248		2069		1634	ART MANUFACTURES DIVERS
84	CLOTHING AND ACCESSORIES		1163		725		909		689	VETEMENTS
842	MENS OUTERWEAR NOT KNIT		1088		684		655	N 233293	667	VET DESSUS POUR HOMMES
845	OUTERWEAR KNIT NONELASTC	N 1092	8		7		175	N 132	1	VET DESSOUS,ACCES BONNET
87	PRECISION INSTRUMNTS NES		42		82		93		263	INSTRUM,APPAR SCIENT NDA
871	OPTICAL INSTRUMENTS		42						263	APPAR,INSTRUM D'OPTIQUE
874	MEASURNG,CONTROLNG INSTR				82		93			INSTRUMENTS DE MESURE
88	PHOTO EQU,OPTICL GDS ETC		651		59		207		39	APP,FOURN PHOTO,OP,MONTR
885	WATCHES AND CLOCKS		608		22		187		9	HORLOGERIE
8852	CLOCKS,CLOCK,WATCH PARTS				22		187			HORLOGES,MOUV,PARTIES
89	MISC MANUFCTRD GOODS NES		1853		307		716		568	ART MANUFACTURES DIVERS
892	PRINTED MATTER		320		88	W 14	340	W 9	146	IMPRIMES
8928	PRINTED MATTER NES				88	W 14	340			IMPRIMES NDA
893	ARTICLES OF PLASTIC NES		79		66		147	W 25	80	OUVRAGES EN MAT DIVIS 58
894	TOYS,SPORTING GOODS,ETC		165		66	W 13	154	W 47	159	VOITURES ENFANTS,JOUETS
8947	OTH SPORT GDS,FAIR AMUSM				66	W 13	154			AUT ART DE SPORT
89473	AMUSEMENTS ETC FOR FAIRS				66	W 13	154			MANEGES,BALANCOIRES
897	GOLD,SILVER WARE,JEWELRY		1238		72		41		59	BIJOUTERIE,ORFEVRERIE
8972	IMITATION JEWELLERY				72		41			BIJOUTERIE DE FANTAISIE
9	GOODS NOT CLASSD BY KIND		4445		5094		6896		11355	ART TRANSACT NON CLASSES
911	*MAIL NOT CLASSED BY KIN		59	W 4	43	W 15	103	W 11	77	COLIS POSTAUX
931	*SPECIAL TRANSACTIONS	W 29987	4292	W 33243	5001	W 41478	6761	W 58875	11214	TRANS.SPECIALES
941	*ZOO ANIMALS,PETS ETC		94		50	W 8	31	W 8	64	ANIMAUX DE ZOO ETC

FOOT NOTES – NOTES

TABLE 4 –
1 The data presented according to SITC, Revision 2 have been estimated from data reported according to the national classification.
TABLE 5 –
1 The data presented according to SITC, Revision 2 have been estimated from data reported according to the national classification.
TABLEAU 4 –
1 Les données qui se présentent conformément à C TCI, Révision 2 sont les estimations des données rapportées d'après la classification nationale.
TABLEAU 5 –
1 Les données qui se présentent conformément à C TCI, Révision 2 sont les estimations des données rapportées d'après la classification nationale.

1. HISTORICAL SERIES, 1961–1996 GENERAL TRADE, IMPORTS F.O.B., EXPORTS F.O.B. # 1
SERIES HISTORIQUES, 1961–1996 COMMERCE GENERAL, IMPORTATIONS F.O.B., EXPORTATIONS F.O.B

YEAR ANNEE	VALUE IN MILLION ASTL. DOLLARS VALEUR EN MILLION ASTL. DOLLARS MERCHANDISE –MARCHANDISE		GOLD –OR		CONVERSION FACTORS U.S. CENTS PER ASTL. DOLLAR FACTEURS DE CONVERSION CENTS E.U. PAR ASTL. DOLLAR		INDEX NUMBERS –INDICES QUANTUM		UNIT VALUE VALEUR UNITAIRE	
	IMPORTS	EXPORTS	IMPORTS	EXPORTS	IMPORTS	EXPORTS	IMPORTS	EXPORTS	IMPORTS	EXPORTS
1961	2147.30	1834.30	4.40	79.00	112.0000	112.0000	20	21	19	19
1962	1738.80	2100.20	4.30	18.00	112.0000	112.0000	16	24	19	20
1963	2128.30	2102.40	5.00	12.00	112.0000	112.0000	19	24	19	21
1964	2329.60	2725.60	4.60	14.00	112.0000	112.0000	22	28	19	23
1965	2841.30	2579.20	4.10	18.00	112.0000	112.0000	26	27	19	21
1966	2853.90	2742.30	4.20	24.00	112.0000	112.0000	26	28	20	22
1967	3083.30	3001.80	4.20	18.00	112.0000	112.0000	27	31	21	21
1968	3444.40	3037.20	4.40	15.00	112.0000	112.0000	29	32	20	20
1969	3573.80	3610.20	4.00	22.00	112.0000	112.0000	31	35	20	20
1970	4056.00	4259.00	6.90	29.00	112.0000	112.0000	34	42	21	21
1971	4139.00	4599.00	3.80	20.00	113.3598	113.3800	35	45	22	20
1972	3876.00	5419.00	4.60	19.00	119.0998	119.0998	32	50	23	21
1973	4781.00	6590.00	5.80	24.00	142.2887	141.7039	27	30	13	16
1974	7769.00	7684.00	8.70	34.00	143.8411	143.8174	33	28	17	19
1975	7637.00	9118.00			130.8722	131.0039	45	51	32	36
1976	9134.00	10743.00			122.4246	122.4827	51	56	35	39
1977	11036.00	12036.00			110.8736	110.9228	51	58	42	43
1978	12329.00	12591.00			114.5297	114.4904	53	56	45	46
1979	14801.00	16715.00			111.7402	111.6801	55	63	51	55
1980	17826.00	19341.00			114.0842	113.9083	58	64	60	62
1981	20693.00	18938.00			114.8582	114.9408	66	60	61	63
1982	23775.10	21718.10			101.7311	101.4743	70	64	65	65
1983	21539.90	22927.60			90.0350	90.2287	61	62	71	70
1984	26711.00	27374.00			87.6945	87.6682	80	72	72	71
1985	33631.00	32865.00			69.7270	69.6287	77	81	86	79
1986	39033.01	33716.00			66.8895	66.9509	74	84	94	80
1987	41816.00	37947.01			70.1184	70.1614	76	94	99	84
1988	45925.01	42369.01			78.6084	78.4488	89	89	97	94
1989	56801.01	47005.01			79.1259	79.0011	108	94	96	98
1990	53785.01	50892.00			78.1337	78.1257	100	100	100	100
1991	53427.01	53728.00			77.9592	77.9015	99	115	101	91
1992	59732.00	58383.01			73.3416	73.3766	107	121	106	93
1993	66910.00	62840.00			67.9686	67.9575	115	128	114	94
1994	72881.01	64899.01			73.3049	73.2297	133	139	111	92
1995	81370.00	71637.01			74.1266	74.1191	148	141	115	99
1996	83543.01	77275.01			78.3165	78.3364	162	159	109	95

2. IMPORTS BY BROAD ECONOMIC CATEGORY AND EXPORTS BY INDUSTRIAL ORIGIN. (PERCENTAGE OF TOTAL VALUE)
IMPORTATIONS PAR CATEGORIES ECONOMIQUES ET EXPORTATIONS PAR BRANCHE D'ACTIVITE.(EN POURCENTAGE DE LA VALEUR TOTALE)

IMPORTS – IMPORTATIONS

	1990	1991	1992	1993	1994	1995	1996
TOTAL IMPORTS–IMPORTATIONS TOTALES	100.	100.	100.	100.	100.	100.	100.
1 FOOD BEV–ALIMENTATION BOISSONS	4.2	4.5	4.4	4.4	4.5	4.5	4.4
11 PRIMARY–PRODUITS DE BASE	1.1	1.2	1.1	1.1	1.2	1.3	1.2
111 FOR INDUSTRY–POUR L'INDUSTRIE	0.3	0.3	0.2	0.2	0.3	0.4	0.3
112 FOR HOUSEHOLDS–POUR LES MENAGES	0.9	0.9	0.8	0.9	0.9	0.9	0.9
12 PROCESSED–PRODUITS ELABORES	3.1	3.3	3.3	3.3	3.3	3.2	3.2
121 FOR INDUSTRY–POUR L'INDUSTRIE	0.4	0.4	0.4	0.5	0.5	0.6	0.5
122 FOR HOUSEHOLDS–POUR LES MENAGES	2.7	2.9	2.9	2.8	2.7	2.6	2.7
2 IND SUPPLIES–APPROV INDUSTRIELS	22.5	22.4	22.3	23.6	24.1	24.2	22.9
21 PRIMARY–PRODUITS DE BASE	1.5	1.3	1.3	1.2	1.3	1.3	1.3
22 PROCESSED–PRODUITS ELABORES	21.0	21.1	21.0	22.5	22.8	22.9	21.6
3 FUELS–COMBUSTIBLES	5.5	5.7	5.7	6.1	4.9	5.1	6.3
31 PRIMARY–PRODUITS DE BASE	2.6	3.0	3.3	3.8	3.2	3.4	4.6
32 PROCESSED–PRODUITS ELABORES	2.8	2.6	2.4	2.3	1.6	1.7	1.7
321 MOTOR SPIRIT–ESSENCE							
322 OTHER–AUTRES	2.8	2.6	2.4	2.3	1.6	1.7	1.7
4 MACHINERY–EQUIPEMENT	26.5	26.3	25.7	27.9	30.4	31.6	31.3
41 CAPITAL EQUIPMENT–MACHINES	21.2	20.8	20.2	21.8	23.8	24.9	24.9
42 PARTS–PIECES ACCESSOIRES	5.4	5.5	5.5	6.1	6.6	6.7	6.4
5 TRANSPORT–TRANSPORT	17.6	17.3	15.9	16.0	17.1	16.5	16.6
51 PASSENGER CARS–AUTOMOBILES	4.3	4.4	5.1	5.3	5.7	5.6	5.4
52 OTHER–AUTRES	7.0	7.0	4.9	4.3	4.6	4.7	4.9
521 INDUSTRIAL–INDUSTRIELS	6.6	6.7	4.6	4.0	4.2	4.3	4.5
522 NON INDUSTRIAL–NON INDUSTRIEL	0.3	0.3	0.3	0.4	0.4	0.4	0.4
53 PARTS–PIECES ACCESSOIRES	6.3	5.8	5.9	6.3	6.8	6.1	6.2
6 CONSUM GOODS–BIENS CONSOMMATION	16.4	16.8	17.5	17.8	18.4	17.4	17.9
61 DURABLE–DURABLES	4.5	4.2	4.1	4.4	4.6	4.5	4.7
62 SEMI DURABLE–SEMI DURABLES	7.7	8.3	8.8	8.9	9.1	8.5	8.5
63 NON DURABLE–NON DURABLES	4.2	4.3	4.6	4.5	4.7	4.5	4.7
7 GOODS NES–BIENS NDA	7.2	7.1	8.4	4.2	0.6	0.7	0.6

EXPORTS – EXPORTATIONS

	1990	1991	1992	1993	1994	1995	1996
TOTAL EXPORTS–EXPORTATIONS TOTALES	100.	100.	100.	100.	100.	100.	100.
1 AGRICULTURE	14.8	13.2	12.6	13.3	14.2	12.0	16.5
2 MINING QUARRY–INDUS EXTRACTIVES	22.3	23.7	23.5	25.3	23.4	23.9	24.7
3 MANUFACTURING–IND MANUFACTUR	62.9	63.1	63.9	61.4	62.4	64.1	58.8
31 FOOD BEV TOBACCO–ALIM BOISS TAB	11.4	11.3	11.9	14.9	16.4	15.1	14.2
32 TEXTILES–INDUSTRIES TEXTILES	2.5	2.7	3.1	3.4	4.0	4.2	3.8
33 WOOD & PRODUCTS–BOIS & PRODUITS	0.1	0.1	0.2	0.9	1.0	1.1	1.0
34 PAPER & PRODUCTS–PAPIER & PRODT	0.7	0.8	0.7	0.8	0.9	0.9	0.9
35 CHEMICALS–INDUSTRIES CHIMIQUES	5.4	6.2	6.2	10.6	10.7	11.2	11.2
36 NON METAL MIN–MIN NON METAL	0.3	0.4	0.4	0.4	0.5	0.6	0.6
37 BASIC METAL–IND METAL BASE	9.4	9.0	9.0	9.3	9.8	11.0	9.8
38 METAL MANUF–MANUF METAL	10.4	11.9	12.3	14.2	15.6	16.6	13.7
39 OTH MANUF IND–AUTRES MANUF	22.8	20.9	20.1	6.8	3.5	3.4	3.5

3. TRADE BY PRINCIPAL COUNTRIES OF PRODUCTION AND LAST CONSIGNMENT (VALUE IN THOUSAND U.S. DOLLARS)
ECHANGES SELON LES PRINCIPAUX PAYS DE PRODUCTION ET DE DERNIERE CONSIGNATION (VALEUR EN MILLIERS DE DOLLARS EU)

COUNTRIES–PAYS	GENERAL IMPORTS F.O.B. IMPORTATIONS GENERALES F.O.B.					COUNTRIES–PAYS	GENERAL EXPORTS F.O.B. EXPORTATIONS GENERALES F.O.B.				
	1992	1993	1994	1995	1996		1992	1993	1994	1995	1996
World	42949141	44135226	49918074	57422838	61400173	Monde	45146366	44316359	47253847	53000584	60203900
Africa	150135	220393	272395	361013	496257	Afrique	429980	674738	688283	764241	1377830
Americas	10889846	10858383	12380315	14361735	16113237	Amériques	5866652	5184119	4802836	4907579	5645265
Northern America	10435459	10348840	11857513	13683434	15465508	Amérique du Nord	5427958	4615727	4184781	4326363	4914978
LAIA	388533	427512	493174	641250	618754	ALAI	422275	553158	601328	552549	706364
CACM	2317	3355	6275	9105	7855	MCAC	2607	3005	1641	1990	2148
Caribbean	27778	25489	22317	25916	19970	Caraïbes	11557	10655	11489	23968	18896
Rest of America	35760	53188	1037	2031	1150	Autre Amérique	2255	1575	3597	2709	2880
As.ex F.USSR	17491370	18719362	21026704	23385685	24246394	Asie l'URSS exclus	26619318	27886886	30628038	34745470	38846031
Eur.x F.USSR	10957207	10702306	12630104	15417416	16255868	Europe l'URSS exclus	6702798	5710902	5497296	6395988	7145474
EU	10132510	9980819	11747328	14407024	15256435	UE	6128379	5335315	5253622	5885074	6536096
EFTA	716826	617693	752993	869614	866296	AELE	427940	292100	142499	341862	430568
East Europe	78120	78465	98485	106183	99998	Europe de l'Est	117590	76005	87866	137796	156363
Other Europe	6712	745	2793	4202	5836	Autre de l'Europe	25631	1890	4496	7904	8368
Former USSR	137140	19396	19744	31685	19605	Ancienne URSS	75368	139787	214846	149603	79743
Oceania	3289692	3576026	3519758	3791820	4116618	Océanie	3587589	4002508	4586438	5377033	6317107
USA/Etats–Unis d'Amer	9754133	9623886	11049203	12577207	14327650	Japan/Japon	10595620	10624419	11701308	12260942	12184292
Japan/Japon	7417503	8121653	8869569	8869092	7998448	Korea, Republic of	2538432	2979461	3447297	4488821	5721642
United Kingdom	2659589	2515529	2974202	3451339	3939681	USA/Etats–Unis d'Amer	4547118	3729083	3375937	3427529	3896829
Germany/Allemagne	2408930	2481633	2988789	3828896	3681800	New Zealand	2360549	2725400	3214436	3929514	4432415
China/Chine	1703522	1995835	2472586	2862376	3228184	Singapore/Singapour	3159370	2768256	2494820	2839626	2478990
New Zealand	1878886	2082083	2479322	2672559	2874119	China/Chine	1325745	1649052	2061525	2321026	3037219
Singapore/Singapour	1096737	1101769	1513834	1854970	2092060	Hong Kong	1754922	1857015	1894903	2132522	2359287
Korea, Republic of	1114372	1293845	1294780	1672782	1820646	United Kingdom	1862441	2059054	1732275	1851116	2160043
Italy/Italie	965908	1002945	1345417	1604318	1808143	Indonesia/Indonésie	1103875	1299536	1447921	1773586	2468819
France,Monac	1127709	1105073	1200364	1403526	1530877	Malaysia/Malaisie	850185	1086815	1426493	1650648	1733149
Indonesia/Indonésie	923468	833884	760917	995923	1340626	Thailand/Thaïlande	779162	858008	1001042	1287424	1314781
Malaysia/Malaisie	711654	707435	894147	1158649	1335435	Canada	880769	886435	808473	898661	1018047
Sweden/Suède	752784	681174	898420	1173609	1205636	Italy/Italie	810098	643068	838592	965966	977196
Canada	681307	724784	808211	1106228	1137857	Germany/Allemagne	843667	641255	712459	800247	805986
Papua New Guinea	818521	903701	822079	865200	925718	India/Inde	616923	628380	640097	816138	958978
Thailand/Thaïlande	526882	522022	642563	751968	847007	Papua New Guinea	641417	650465	709005	688101	971145
Hong Kong	591700	522834	616758	752875	710161	France,Monac	777628	572087	558726	564875	540381
Switz.Liecht	510279	514775	639875	759967	730824	Philippines	403541	448803	530381	740754	887957
Netherlands/Pays–Bas	721626	708243	507790	510116	579073	Netherlands/Pays–Bas	658786	523143	539432	504293	519317
Saudi Arabia	526702	485450	411599	659642	669444	Belgium–Luxembourg	493456	371324	318471	406907	646457
Belgium–Luxembourg	347715	355255	427415	573021	580578	So. Africa Customs Un	230411	242870	320067	492811	748078
United Arab Emirates	434309	502129	403068	414130	514664	United Arab Emirates	242133	287604	290456	317586	449620
Finland/Finlande	262310	310291	371671	552436	454560	Iran (Islamic Rp. of)	173213	296270	306494	258629	509774
India/Inde	235579	285475	348978	410093	441763	Fiji/Fidji	204609	229815	257020	312644	398998
Brazil/Brésil	227294	238707	285556	356770	300756	Saudi Arabia	228738	207435	229140	277881	366503
Spain/Espagne	177908	155339	289539	374246	394620	Switz.Liecht	353018	205652	92815	291452	330657
Ireland/Irlande	207366	215539	243428	346792	341664	Brazil/Brésil	175428	255857	200960	243084	310162
Denmark/Danemark	254741	215642	237042	245811	282326	Spain/Espagne	258878	190734	208526	221629	216719
So. Africa Customs Un	111545	160723	212560	274828	359579	Turkey/Turquie	147215	170709	165956	210110	298383
Viet Nam	148094	170856	212111	212617	307625	Egypt/Egypte	44789	253964	196420	90574	340955
Austria/Autriche	164377	155816	171358	225722	308330	Pakistan	113201	195361	147235	142782	204188
Israel/Israël	115254	126579	170130	222147	221186	Finland/Finlande	107687	64625	118800	235089	251134
Philippines	121121	126206	169531	171876	222012	Sweden/Suède	124878	107495	98630	132834	202913
Fiji/Fidji	84732	107613	121166	142267	211573	New Caledonia	106611	122621	109960	136855	166511
Norway,SVD,JM	205687	101892	111910	108352	132203	Russian Federation	74721	131054	200988	108366	58383
Pakistan	81846	97365	107402	92496	113806	Viet Nam	37863	79917	82840	139764	159486
Mexico/Mexique	62737	67816	86803	115995	128284	Sri Lanka	45718	55241	112120	83960	180185
Qatar	2919	57304	132093	126891	112458	Mexico/Mexique	72091	102664	146932	57175	94496
Kuwait/Koweït	34976	43515	62361	64297	91082	Bangladesh	57249	53147	88375	89937	175784
Portugal	42691	43253	52595	64164	80703	Chile/Chili	45493	76802	82994	107820	139264
Argentina/Argentine	44617	67390	44200	56147	68895	Argentina/Argentine	57818	74224	68186	99029	78320
Chile/Chili	27016	22232	37142	74529	78122	Kuwait/Koweït	60501	61207	61199	61521	127073
Greece/Grèce	38857	35086	39298	53028	68446	Oman	56019	86424	66352	74020	85838
Samoa	25295	47360	48045	50710	50225	Norway,SVD,JM	74418	86276	49258	49250	97740
Russian Federation	136719	16712	15734	26583	14678	Denmark/Danemark	59023	39777	47993	82618	92576
Turkey/Turquie	33510	26929	35800	50324	58505	Israel/Israël	49293	55649	55896	61735	85386
Sri Lanka	28776	30637	36346	38439	44120	French Polynesia	61381	43978	54944	62116	60444
Czech Republic		32899	39972	38017	41520	Romania/Roumanie	65964	32534	34113	63868	82083
New Caledonia	25912	23972	30218	36656	34788	Mauritius/Maurice	41262	48249	48305	57113	80218
Hungary/Hongrie	21136	20679	25601	28882	23595	Solomon Isls	40476	45307	46454	62653	66455

(VALUE AS PERCENTAGE OF WORLD TOTAL)(VALEURS EN POURCENTAGE DU TOTAL MONDIAL)

	1987	1988	1989	1990	1991	1992	1993	1994	1995	1996		1987	1988	1989	1990	1991	1992	1993	1994	1995	1996
Africa	1.4	0.5	0.4	0.4	0.3	0.3	0.5	0.5	0.6	0.8	Afrique	1.5	1.4	1.6	1.4	1.2	1.0	1.5	1.5	1.4	2.3
Americas	24.2	25.3	26.7	27.7	26.9	25.4	24.6	24.8	25.0	26.2	Amériques	11.0	13.5	13.0	14.0	12.9	13.0	11.7	10.2	9.3	9.4
Northern America	23.1	23.9	25.1	26.5	25.8	24.3	23.4	23.8	23.8	25.2	Amérique du Nord	10.2	12.5	12.1	13.0	11.9	12.0	10.4	8.9	8.2	8.2
LAIA	1.0	1.3	1.5	1.2	1.1	0.9	1.0	1.0	1.1	1.0	ALAI	0.7	0.9	0.8	1.0	0.9	0.9	1.2	1.3	1.0	1.2
CACM	0.0	0.0	0.0	0.0	0.0	0.0	0.0	0.0	0.0	0.0	MCAC	0.0	0.0	0.0	0.0	0.0	0.0	0.0	0.0	0.0	0.0
Caribbean	0.0	0.0	0.0	0.0	0.0	0.1	0.1	0.0	0.0	0.0	Caraïbes	0.1	0.1	0.0	0.0	0.1	0.0	0.0	0.0	0.0	0.0
Rest of America	0.0	0.0	0.0	0.0	0.0	0.1	0.1	0.0	0.0	0.0	Autre Amérique	0.0	0.0	0.0	0.0	0.0	0.0	0.0	0.0	0.0	0.0
As.ex F.USSR	39.2	40.3	41.2	38.3	39.2	40.7	42.4	42.1	40.7	39.5	Asie l'URSS exclus	50.0	56.9	57.2	57.3	61.0	59.0	62.9	64.8	65.6	64.5
Eur.x F.USSR	28.3	28.7	26.8	27.4	25.3	25.5	24.2	25.3	26.8	26.5	Europe l'URSS exclus	17.9	17.0	16.7	16.5	14.4	14.8	12.9	11.6	12.1	11.9
EU	26.3	26.5	24.8	25.3	23.5	23.6	22.6	23.5	25.1	24.8	UE	15.5	15.0	14.5	13.8	12.5	13.6	12.0	11.1	11.1	10.9
EFTA	1.6	1.6	1.5	1.7	1.5	1.7	1.4	1.5	1.5	1.4	AELE	1.2	0.6	1.1	2.1	1.6	0.9	0.7	0.3	0.6	0.7
East Europe	0.3	0.4	0.3	0.2	0.2	0.2	0.2	0.2	0.2	0.2	Europe de l'Est	0.9	1.1	0.8	0.5	0.2	0.3	0.2	0.2	0.3	0.3
Other Europe	0.1	0.1	0.1	0.1	0.1	0.0	0.0	0.0	0.0	0.0	Autre de l'Europe	0.2	0.3	0.3	0.2	0.1	0.1	0.0	0.0	0.0	0.0
Former USSR	0.0	0.1	0.1	0.1	0.1	0.3	0.0	0.0	0.1	0.0	Ancienne URSS	1.7	1.7	2.2	0.8	0.9	0.2	0.3	0.5	0.3	0.1
Oceania	4.9	5.1	4.9	6.1	7.0	7.7	8.1	7.1	6.6	6.7	Océanie	8.2	8.1	8.0	8.2	8.0	7.9	9.0	9.7	10.1	10.5
USA/Etats–Unis d'Amer	21.1	21.7	22.7	24.4	24.1	22.7	21.8	22.1	21.9	23.3	Japan/Japon	24.0	27.1	26.7	25.2	27.1	23.5	24.0	24.8	23.1	20.2
Japan/Japon	19.3	20.1	20.3	18.3	16.9	17.3	18.4	17.8	15.4	13.0	Korea, Republic of	3.8	4.7	5.2	5.6	6.1	5.6	6.7	7.3	8.5	9.5
United Kingdom	7.1	7.5	6.8	6.9	6.2	6.2	5.7	6.0	6.0	6.4	USA/Etats–Unis d'Amer	9.4	10.7	10.8	11.4	10.4	10.1	8.4	7.1	6.5	6.5
Germany/Allemagne	7.1	6.7	6.3	6.5	6.0	5.6	5.6	6.0	6.7	6.0	New Zealand	5.1	5.0	5.2	5.2	5.1	5.2	6.1	6.8	7.4	7.4
China/Chine	1.9	2.1	2.4	2.6	3.4	4.0	4.5	5.0	5.0	5.3	Singapore/Singapour	2.2	3.2	3.6	5.0	5.8	7.0	6.2	5.3	5.4	4.1
New Zealand	4.0	4.4	4.1	4.3	4.4	4.4	4.7	5.0	4.7	4.7	China/Chine	3.6	2.6	2.5	2.5	2.8	2.9	3.7	4.4	4.4	5.0
Singapore/Singapour	2.0	2.3	2.5	2.4	2.6	2.6	2.5	3.0	3.2	3.4	Hong Kong	3.6	5.2	3.5	2.5	3.5	3.9	4.2	4.0	4.0	3.9
Korea, Republic of	2.5	2.6	2.6	2.3	2.4	2.6	2.9	2.6	2.9	3.0	United Kingdom	4.2	3.6	3.6	3.7	3.3	4.1	4.6	3.7	3.5	3.6
Italy/Italie	3.2	3.1	3.0	2.9	2.5	2.2	2.3	2.7	2.8	2.9	Indonesia/Indonésie	1.1	1.5	2.0	2.6	2.6	2.4	2.9	3.1	3.3	4.1
France,Monac	2.1	2.4	2.5	2.8	3.1	2.6	2.5	2.4	2.4	2.5	Malaysia/Malaisie	1.2	1.7	1.9	2.1	1.9	1.9	2.5	3.0	3.1	2.9

4. General Imports F.O.B. by Commodities according to the S.I.T.C. (Rev. 2) in thousand U.S. Dollars
Importations Générales F.O.B. par Produits d'après la C.T.C.I. (Rév. 2) en milliers de Dollars E.U.

SITC CTCI	COMMODITY	1993 WEIGHT POIDS	1993 VALUE VALEUR	1994 WEIGHT POIDS	1994 VALUE VALEUR	1995 WEIGHT POIDS	1995 VALUE VALEUR	1996 WEIGHT POIDS	1996 VALUE VALEUR	PRODUIT
	ALL COMMODITIES		44135226		49918074		57422838		61400173	TOUS PRODUITS
0	FOOD AND LIVE ANIMALS		1618180		1887961		2158965		2276723	ALIMENTS,ANIMAUX VIVANTS
03	FISH AND PREPARATIONS		365708		427322		443907		473578	POISSONS ET PREPARATIONS
037	FISH ETC PREPD,PRSVD NES		157231	W 43239	165661	W 40506	162493	W 43540	174770	POIS,CRUST,MOL PREPARES
04	CEREALS AND PREPARATIONS		115536		128437		190637		164999	CEREALES ET PRODUITS
05	VEGETABLES AND FRUIT		334343		364140		419423		459590	LEGUMES ET FRUITS
07	COFFEE,TEA,COCOA,SPICES		242415		318341		387252		379379	CAFE,THE,CACAO,EPICES
071	COFFEE AND SUBSTITUTES		89541	W 47286	138059		200179		158953	CAFE ET SUCCEDANES
09	MISC EDIBLE PRODUCTS		283336		320742		351684		398519	PREP ALIMENTAIRES DIVERSES
098	EDIBLE PRODCTS,PREPS NES		278871		316289		347985		394193	PREP ALIMENTAIRES NDA
09809	MISC FOOD PREPRTIONS NES		211276		237428		258333		295948	PREP ALIMENTAIRES NDA
1	BEVERAGES AND TOBACCO		307968		366113		373641		399796	BOISSONS ET TABACS
11	BEVERAGES		217500		247295		252625		266876	BOISSONS
112	ALCOHOLIC BEVERAGES		206409	W 40329	234808	W 53087	241891	W 49889	258413	BOISSONS ALCOOLIQUES
1124	DISTILLED ALCOHOLIC BEVS		160307	W 17294	177520	W 17613	173912	W 18731	188570	ALCOOLS,EAUX–DE–VIE
2	CRUDE MATERLS,EXCL FUELS		1051446		1208283		1296696		1183164	MAT BRUTES NON COMESTIBLES
24	CORK AND WOOD		442864		442860		387471		328654	LIEGE ET BOIS
248	WOOD SHAPED,SLEEPERS		441507		441548	W 597178	385759	W 513169	326349	BOIS SIMPLEMENT TRAVAILLES
2482	LUMBER SHAPED CONIFER		320298	W 523405	300184	W 467301	261453	W 403478	225847	CONIFERES SCIES,RABOTES
24821	LUMBER SAWN ETC CONIFER		294105	W 497979	271364	W 444221	237073	W 380334	203683	CONIFERES SCIES LONGITUD
3	MINERAL FUELS ETC		2640768		2425739		2915849		3871864	COMBUSTIBLES MINERAUX LUB
33	PETROLEUM AND PRODUCTS		2613325		2386868		2867242		3793299	PETROLE ET DERIVES
333	CRUDE PETROLEUM		1628944	MW 13434	1567775	MW 14842	1882169	MW 18226	2749426	HUILES BRUTES DE PETROLE
334	PETROLEUM PRODUCTS,REFIN		881257	W 5464289	703130	W 6509980	876563	W 5259825	868963	PRODUITS RAFFINES
4	ANIMAL,VEGETABLE OIL,FAT		138303		160517		193349		213514	HUILES,GRAISSES ANIM,VEG
42	FIXED VEGETABLE OIL,FAT		120751		137243		167525		185538	HUILES VEGETALES FIXES
5	CHEMCLS,RELATED PROD NES		4499938		5152164		6112161		6840088	PRODUITS CHIMIQUES
51	ORGANIC CHEMICALS		1011468		1212653		1332337		1517562	PROD CHIMIQ ORGANIQUES
513	CARBOXYLIC ACIDS ETC		140502		166709	W 124019	227999		244237	ACIDES CARBOXYLIQUES
514	NITROGEN–FNCTN COMPOUNDS		323880	W 89772	371066	W 89955	395379	W 95528	497288	COMPOSES FONCT AZOTEES
5148	OTH NITROGN–FNCTN CMPNDS		226582	W 55699	258913	W 58196	270161	W 54465	335647	AUTRES COMPOSES AZOTES
51482	IMIDE–,IMIDE–FNCT CMPNDS		171659	W 28741	180054	W 29042	187565	W 27301	237584	COMPOSES A FONCTION IMIDE
515	ORG–INORG COMPOUNDS ETC		292756	W 34324	355570	W 35119	390111	W 67882	468958	COMPOSES ORGANO–MINERAUX
5156	HETEROCYCLIC CMPDS ETC		142857	W 7668	154811	W 6317	161936	W 7246	189857	COMPOSES HETEROCYCLIQUES
51569	OTH HETEROCYC CMPDS,ETC		140897	W 6916	152053	W 5692	159572	W 6508	185232	AUT COMP HETEROCYCLIQUES
52	INORGANIC CHEMICALS		395102		324698		589966		622855	PROD CHIM INORGANIQUES
522	INORG ELEMNTS,OXIDES,ETC		217994	W 1260514	163331	W 1618562	398595	W 1613861	410095	ELEMENTS INORGANIQUES
5225	INORGANIC BASES ETC NES		147888	W 1105822	79749	W 1265418	304213	W 1298032	309580	AUTRES BASES OXYDES METAL
52253	SODIUM HYDROXIDE, OTHER		127090	W 1010023	50781	W 1174153	266808	W 1127558	260547	HYDROXYDE SODIUM AQUEUX
523	OTHR INORG CHEMICALS ETC		165241		151105		181688		202201	AUT PRODUITS CHIMIQUES INORG
53	DYES,TANNING,COLOUR PROD		224636		257509		271846		314116	PROD TEINTURE,COLORANTS
541	*MEDICINAL,PHARM PRODUCT		946906		1100693		1252209		1516496	PROD MEDICINAUX PHARMACEUT
5417	MEDICAMENTS		662210		802187		934880		1164855	MEDICAMENTS
54179	— CONTNG OTH SUBSTANCES		577746		686767		781159		954777	MED CONT AUT SUBSTANCES
55	PERFUME,CLEANING ETC PRD		334449		403074		443082		486260	PROD POUR PARFUM,TOILETTE
553	PERFUMERY,COSMETICS,ETC		211853		248810		259420		279858	PRODUITS DE PARFUMERIE
562	*FERTILIZERS,MANUFACTURE		254814	W 2123129	323212	W 2257960	432249	W 2806650	584237	ENGRAIS MANUFACTURES
5621	CHEM NITROGENOUS FERTLZR		73833	W 740990	109178	W 678586	143432	W 966724	201999	ENGRAIS AZOTES
5629	FERTILIZERS NES		114097	W 776796	136933	W 869868	188410	W 1190756	279098	ENGRAIS NDA
56292	NITROG–PHOS FERTILZR NES		104666	W 743454	124373	W 833279	173615	W 1162472	262265	ENGRAIS NDA CONT N P
58	PLASTIC MATERIALS ETC		785088		921424		1120566		1062742	MAT PLAST ARTIFICIELLES
582	PROD OF CONDENSATION ETC		256558	W 124682	283259	W 143325	374449	W 142250	344812	PROD CONDENS,POLYCOND
5823	ALKYDS,OTHER POLYESTERS		128601	W 68125	137242	W 85661	213246	W 84855	183286	ALKYDES ET AUT POLYESTERS
583	POLYMERIZATION ETC PRODS		471679		574331	W 353706	685787		659663	PROD POLYMERISATION
5839	OTH POLYMRZTION ETC PROD		192464		219653	W 75352	243534	W 78428	242676	AUT PROD POLYMER COPOLYM
59	CHEMICAL MATERIALS NES		531052		587961		649095		706248	MAT PROD CHIMIQUES NDA
598	MISCEL CHEM PRODUCTS NES		410957		430653		456953		473359	PROD DIV INDUST CHIM NDA
5989	CHEM PRODUCTS,PREPS NES		251537		270616		315186		324558	PROD PREP CHIMIQUES NDA
59899	OTH CHEM PRODS,PREPS,NES		177529		188701		221941		235775	AUT PRODUITS CHIMIQUES NDA
6	BASIC MANUFACTURES		6264785		7406644		8495162		8414493	ART MANUFACTURES
62	RUBBER MANUFACTURES NES		601881		732898		806476		876912	CAOUTCHOUC MANUFACTURE
625	RUBBER TYRES, TUBES ETC		375969	MN 17772	457082	MN 17741	516906	MN 17988	565455	PNEUS CAOUTCHOUC VULCANISE
6259	OTH TYRES,TYRE CASES,ETC		126089	MN 10302	159311	MN 9958	176926	MN 10326	209574	AUTRES PNEUS RECHAPES FLAPS
62599	TYRES NES,TYRE CASES,ETC		113639	N 4921581	146089	N 4789688	164695	N 5132324	195775	PNEUS,FLAPS
628	RUBBER ARTICLES NES		149348		183405		193208		212672	OUVRAGES CAOUTCHOUC NDA
63	WOOD,CORK MANUFACTRS NES		159539		192844		205993		217651	OUVRAGES LIEGE ET BOIS
64	PAPER,PAPERBOARD AND MFR		1037461		1236148		1558237		1423356	PAPIERS,CARTONS & OUVRAGES
641	PAPER AND PAPERBOARD		850124		1023450		1323419		1181945	PAPIERS ET CARTONS
6411	NEWSPRINT		92061	W 234042	119454	W 288677	193387	W 266785	205545	PAPIER JOURNAL
6412	PRINTG,WRITING PAPER NES		316083	W 440910	375131	W 488219	522871	W 395354	403483	PAPIERS POUR L'IMPRESSION
64122	— COATED,IMPREGNATD ETC		289868	W 394630	334301	W 422955	449497	W 328086	335113	PAPIERS IMPRESSION COUCHES
6415	PAPER,PAPERBRD,BULK,NES		140200	W 210453	173131	W 231627	224018	W 190232	200159	PAPIERS,CARTONS ROULEAUX
64159	OTHER PAPER ETC,BULK,NES		118715	W 189329	148144	W 196499	196662	W 168299	171778	AUT PAPIER ROULEAUX FEUILLES
6418	COATED ETC PAPER NES BLK		162687	W 166473	199315		216939	W 125537	204038	PAP,CARTONS COUCHES,ENDUITS
64189	COATED PAPER ETC NES		128469	W 127254	152430	W 87493	155305	W 82327	144731	PAPIERS,CARTONS COUCHES
642	PAPER,ETC,PRECUT,ARTS OF		187336		212697		234818		241411	PAP,CARTONS DECOUPES
65	TEXTILE YARN,FABRICS,ETC		1502109		1735988		1791468		1819574	FILS,TISSUS,ARTICLES TEXTILE
651	TEXTILE YARN		398875	W 122096	474617	W 95010	420213	W 93897	394919	FILS TEXTILES
6514	SYN FIB YRN,BULK,MONOFIL		157581	W 41160	171233	W 36710	162113	W 37525	152186	FILS CONT 85% FIB TEXT SYNTH
652	COTTON FABRICS,WOVEN		201175	A 212315	223196	A 184368	216985	A 211896	240806	TISSUS DE COTON
6522	WOVEN COTTON BLEACHD,ETC		182761	A 175803	197660	A 146912	186945	A 169829	207631	TISSUS COTON BLANCHIS ETC
65224	BLCHED COTTON FABRIC NES		165478	A 167251	180361	A 134916	163123	A 154245	177012	AUT TIS PLUS 85% COT BLANCHI
653	WOVN MAN–MADE FIB FABRIC		284308	A 232366	336223	A 250224	365238		325984	TISSUS FIBRES SYNTH,ARTIF
6531	CONT SYNT WEAVES NONPILE		124896	A 109719	157846	A 120766	170284	A 113908	151744	TISSUS FIBRES SYNTH CONTINUE
657	SPECIAL TXTL FABRC,PRODS		152146		173153		198840		205603	TISSUS SPECIAUX
658	TEXTILE ARTICLES NES		187595		199652		220786		245743	ART FACONNES MAT TEXTILES
66	NONMETAL MINERAL MFS NES		710201		842611		910047		970466	ART MIN NON METALLIQUES
662	CLAY,REFRACTORY BLDG PRD		164365		200509		213210		199192	MAT CONST REFRACTAIRES
6624	BRICKS ETC NONREFRACTORY		130197		161697		167739		151982	BRIQUES ETC CERAM NON REFR
66245	GLAZED CERAMIC SETTS ETC		122384	A 20336	151894	A 20623	154637	A 18641	139383	AUT CARREAUX CERAMIQUE
67	IRON AND STEEL		715260		820763		1097892		1008670	FER ET ACIER
674	IRN,STL UNIV,PLATE,SHEET		275557	W 704792	298296	W 420627	344884	W 385544	347790	LARGES PLATS,TOLES
6749	OTH IRN,STL PLATES,SHEET		133991	W 221874	130032	W 189868	139257	W 199960	155515	AUTRES TOLES FER,ACIER
678	IRON,STL TUBES,PIPES,ETC		183650		211717		318279		312059	TUBES,TUYAUX EN FONTE,FER
68	NON–FERROUS METALS		323265		430606		510251		471610	METAUX NON FERREUX
682	COPPER EXC CEMENT COPPER		94804		143512		211361		151048	CUIVRE
684	ALUMINIUM		127502	W 48159	157744	W 54089	196609	W 68413	228074	ALUMINIUM
6842	ALUMINIUM,ALLOYS WORKED		119005	W 44561	150901	W 47188	181291	W 55327	199286	ALUMINIUM,ALLIAGES OUVRE
69	METAL MANUFACTURES NES		1098494		1273455		1454634		1456849	ART MANUFACT EN METAL NDA
694	STL,COPPR NAILS,NUTS,ETC		136430		159469		182610		169850	CLOUS,VIS,ECROUS
695	TOOLS		226975		261841		315223		312894	OUTILS A MAIN

4. General Imports F.O.B. by Commodities according to the S.I.T.C. (Rev. 2) in thousand U.S. Dollars
Importations Générales F.O.B. par Produits d'après la C.T.C.I. (Rév. 2) en milliers de Dollars E.U.

SITC CTCI	COMMODITY	1993		1994		1995		1996		PRODUIT
		WEIGHT POIDS	VALUE VALEUR	WEIGHT POIDS	VALUE VALEUR	WEIGHT POIDS	VALUE VALEUR	WEIGHT POIDS	VALUE VALEUR	
699	BASE METAL MFRS NES		458720		536635		598064		582260	ART MANUFACTURES MET NDA
6991	LOCKSMITHS WARES,ETC		167443		203848		213383		201699	ARTICLES DE SERRURERIE
7	MACHINES,TRANSPORT EQUIP		18671516		23008278		26938647		28777356	MACHINES MATERIEL TRANSPORT
71	POWER GENERATING EQUIPMT		1131566		1289104		1368513		1595154	MACHINES GENERATRICES
713	INTRNL COMBUS PSTN ENGIN		560977		685617		694957		771106	MOTEURS EXPL COMB INT, PIECE
7138	PISTON ENGINES NES		108293	N 320036	138087	N 301831	132117	N 320031	190334	MOTEURS A PISTONS NDA
7139	PISTON ENGINE PARTS NES		210849		279152		313972		314650	PIECES POUR 713.2,3,8
714	ENGINES AND MOTORS NES		201219		186185		218189		276152	MOTEURS NON ELECTRIQUES
716	ROTATING ELECTRIC PLANT		305752		294264		363838		415999	APP ELECTR ROTATIFS,PIECES
7162	AC MTRS,GENRTRS,GEN SETS		226165		218378	N 8438164	219523	MN 17953	216963	MOTEURS ELECTRIQUES
72	MACHS FOR SPCL INDUSTRYS		1794469		2375141		2801441		3085059	MAC SPECIALES POUR INDUST
721	AGRIC MACHY,EXC TRACTORS		173078		233291		241442		397661	MACHINES AGRICOLES
7212	HARVESTING ETC MACHINES		122875		163641		159976		289900	ENGINS POUR LA RECOLTE
722	TRACTORS NON–ROAD		144993	N 25118	222337	N 10680	248166	N 13095	353162	TRACTEURS
7224	WHEELED TRACTORS NES		143029	N 25063	218768	N 10608	241809	N 12941	336369	TRACTEURS A ROUES
723	CIVIL ENGNEERG EQUIP ETC		458383		663391		690339		762304	APPAREILS DE GENIE CIVIL
7234	CONST,MINING MACHNRY NES		403971	N 163772	612899	N 195336	634991	N 35019	687593	MACH POUR LA CONST, MINES
72342	SLFPRP SHOVELS,EXCAVATRS		261525	N 5379	393940	N 4976	412432	N 4736	368048	PELLES MECANIQUES
724	TEXTILE,LEATHER MACHNRY		188816		237768		230656		188516	MACH POUR INDUSTRIE TEXTILE
726	PRINTG,BKBINDG MACHY,PTS		192262		290428		455601		279134	MACHINES POUR IMPRIMERIE
7264	PRINTING PRESSES		109970	N 17594	139631	N 81858	207389	N 6717	128687	MACHINES A IMPRIMER
72641	ROTARY PRINTING PRESSES		109970	N 17594	139631	N 81858	207389	N 6717	128687	MACH IMPRIMER ROTATIVES
728	OTH MACHY FOR SPCL INDUS		482742		544238		698146		900267	AUT MACH IND PARTICULIERES
7284	MACHY FOR SPCL INDUS NES		386128		401746		531633		705862	MACH SPEC IND PARTICUL.
72848	OTH MCHY WITH INDIV FNCT		215367	N 1064612	215226	N 1369773	279671		443855	AUTRES MACHINES NDA
73	METALWORKING MACHINERY		216780		315538		406880		462613	MACH TRAVAIL DES METAUX
736	METALWORKING MACH–TOOLS		159103	N 1789566	218670	N 1718326	299939	N 2036860	357770	MACH–OUTILS TRAVAIL METAUX
74	GENRL INDUSTRL MACHY NES		2350740		2884666		3295332		3669297	MACH APP INDUSTRIE
741	HEATING,COOLING EQUIPMNT		319959		438136		469664		526949	MACH CHAUFFAGE,PIECES
7415	AIR–CONDITIONING MACHNRY		119058	N 344306	157698	N 431858	190549		178090	GROUPES CONDITION AIR
7416	HEATING,COOLING EQU NES		122837		151596		151573		214340	APP CHANGEMENT TEMP
742	PUMPS FOR LIQUIDS ETC		172973		219200		249365		271495	POMPES MOTO–POMPES
743	PUMPS NES,CENTRFUGES ETC		457166		540009		596622		645249	POMPES COMPRES,VENT ETC
7431	PUMPS FOR GASES ETC		210071	N 3086763	255686	N 3172215	284246	N 3379538	306438	POMPES AIR A VIDE,COMPRES
744	MECHANICAL HANDLING EQU		300788		421128		559441		685879	EQUIP MANUTENTION PIECES
7441	FORK LIFT TRCKS,ETC,PTS		84547		134046		188562		190817	CHARIOTS POUR USINES ETC
74411	FORK LIFT TRUCKS ETC		84398	N 7858	133867	N 9189	188348	N 9316	190547	CHARIOTS POUR LES GARES
7442	LIFTING,LOADING MACH NES		102217	N 688090	160879	N 610230	190770	N 625582	280785	APP LEVAGE,MANUTENTION
74428	OTH HANDLING ETC MCH NES		76246	N 496726	117994	N 408927	137841	N 417308	203716	AUT APP LEVAGE ETC
7449	PTS NES OF MACHY OF 7442		114024		126202		180109		214278	PIECES DU 744.2
745	NONELEC MACHY,TOOLS NES		353560		374061		424712		445562	AUT MACH NON ELEC,PIECES
7452	OTH NONELEC MCHS,PTS NES		275501		291527		350362		355703	AUT MACH NON ELEC,PIECES
749	NONELEC MACH PTS,ACC NES		746293		892132		995529		1094165	PIECES MACH NON ELEC NDA
7491	BALL,ROLLER,ETC BEARINGS		138140	MN 43118	164146	MN 51682	179075	MN 60507	195917	ROULEMENTS BILLES ETC
7492	COCKS,VALVES ETC NES		301498	MN 67649	352961	MN 87800	375948	MN 104266	402590	ART ROB,SIM POUR TUYAUX
7493	SHAFT,CRANK,PULLEY ETC		200394	MN 18748	258611	MN 29573	299867	MN 28874	347999	ARBRES TRANS,VILEBREQUINS
75	OFFICE MACHNES,ADP EQUIP		3110949		3812998		4424522		4587113	MACH BUREAU TRAIT AUTOM
751	OFFICE MACHINES		235586	N 7077236	281457	N 7077293	303775	N 8079831	265389	MACH,APPAREILS DE BUREAU
7518	OFFICE MACHINES NES		186653	N 3579859	232351	N 3527860	251082	N 4051497	206816	MACH,APP DE BUREAU NDA
75182	PHOTO,THERMOCOPY APPARAT		147628	N 82399	176484	N 117524	194465	N 71836	159048	APPAREILS DE PHOTOCOPIE
752	AUTOMTIC DATA PROC EQUIP		1684091	N 5781916	2094030	N 7096906	2578260	N 8648220	2791495	MACH TRAIT INFORMATION
7522	DIGITAL COMPUTERS		605414	N 444811	701886	N 459949	801274	N 4387058	1757206	MACH DIGITALES COMPLETES
7523	DIGITL CENTRL PROCESSORS		184354	N 243865	290881	N 342604	411403	N 409800	250060	UNITES CENTRALES
7524	DIGITL CENTRL STOR UNITS		389494	N 2696014	473776	N 3190185	587664	N 1466769	272955	UNITES MEMOIRE CENTRALES
7525	ADP PERIPHERAL UNITS		406774	N 1855174	511564	N 2553951	634814	N 1632528	356417	UNITES PERIPHERIQUES
759	OFFICE,ADP MCH PTS,ACCES		1191272		1437512		1542487		1530229	PIECES DU 751 ET 752
7599	ACCTG,ETC,ADP MCH PTS,AC		1088612		1310189		1403451		1399167	PIECES DU 751 ET 752
76	TELECOMM,SOUND EQUIPMENT		1692039		2106348		2731325		2916463	EQUIPMENT DE TELECOM
761	TELEVISION RECEIVERS		191620	N 936631	221327	N 1341436	285264	N 1697571	376207	RECEPTEURS DE TELEVISION
7611	COLOUR TV RECEIVERS		189535	N 916078	218683	N 1313917	282514	N 1672607	373557	RECEPTEURS COULEUR
762	RADIO BROADCAST RECEIVRS		231545	N 5227619	297514	N 4934476	296312	N 5401623	319980	RECEPTEURS RADIODIFFUSION
763	SOUND RECORDRS,PHONOGRPH		214442	N 1872970	258523	N 2176817	284316	N 2421520	346877	PHONO,APP ENREGISTREMENT
7638	OTHR SOUND APPARATUS ETC		212002	N 1838510	257123	N 2154568	282913	N 2388417	345137	AUT APP D'ENREGIS,REPROD
76381	TV IMAGE,SND RECRDRS ETC		141322	N 773386	176196	N 857379	192261	N 1088890	248083	APP ENREG,REPRO IMAG,SON
764	TELECOM EQPT,PTS,ACC NES		1054432		1328984		1865434		1873399	EQUIP TELECOM,PIECES
7641	LINE TELEPHONE,ETC EQUIP		301099		326048		368367		400980	APP TELEPHON PAR FIL
7643	TV,RADIO TRANSMITTRS ETC		244523		431165		745718		692434	APP EMET TELE RADIO
7648	TELECOMM EQUIPMENT NES		177031		182792		216231		181709	APP TELECOM NDA
7649	PTS NES OF EQUIPMT OF 76		270709		312109		446059		498663	PIECES DE LA DIV 76
76491	PTS NES OF APPAR OF 7641		118979		125336		234148		240666	PIECES POUR 764.1
76493	TELECOMM EQUIPMT PTS NES		135282		167740		191013		236219	PIECES 761,762,764.3,8
77	ELECTRIC MACHNRY NES ETC		2570477		3237084		3944522		4012263	MACH APP ELECT NDA
771	ELECTRIC POWER MACHY NES		117152		151114		201670		246678	MACH PROD,TRANS ELECTR
7712	OTH ELEC POWER MACHY NES		92446		119947		161142		207219	AUT APP PROD TRANSF ELEC
772	SWITCHGEAR ETC,PARTS NES		489738		601529	MN 1453125	626789		653466	APP COUPURE,SECT ETC
7721	SWITCHGEAR ETC		425931		525741	MN 580170	539869		576782	APP COUPURE,SECTIONMNT
773	ELECTR DISTRIBUTNG EQUIP		206296		236187		313712		297370	EQUIPMT DISTRIBUTION ELECT
7731	INSULATED WIRE,CABLE ETC		187945		217524		293664		276786	FILS,CABLES ISOLES ELECT
774	ELECTRO–MEDCL,XRAY EQUIP		165395		211983		230119		235180	APPAREILS MEDICAUX
775	HOUSEHOLD TYPE EQUIP NES		396764		478435		524185		570576	MACH,APP USAGE DOMESTQUE
7758	ELECTRO–THERMIC APPL NES		173894		202290		232091		238939	APP ELECTROTHERMIQ NDA
776	TRANSISTORS,VALVES,ETC		481013	MN 445988	678797		967571		887028	LAMPES,TUBES,VALVES
7764	ELECTRONIC MICROCIRCUITS		386509	MN 150867	578534	MN 168280	853965	MN 146322	783613	MICROSTRUCTURES ELECTRON
778	ELECTRICAL MACHINERY NES		714119		879039		1080475		1121964	AUTRES MACH ELECT NDA
7781	BATTERIES,ACCUMULATORS		114612		143619		170585		191128	PILES ET ACCUMULATEURS
7783	AUTOMOTIVE ELECTR EQUIP		118787	MN 47223	149850	MN 43905	152794		156693	EQUIP ELECT MOTEURS EXPL
7788	OTH ELEC MACHY,EQUIP NES		299328		381517		528103		547262	AUT MACH APP ELEC NDA
77886	OTH ELEC MACHINERY NES		155556	N 6906729	201727	MN 20580	326374	MN 34921	321976	AUT MACH APP ELECTRIQUES
78	ROAD VEHICLES		4551349		5838921		6251975		6455264	VEHICULES ROUTIERS
781	PASS MOTOR VEH EXC BUSES		2309978	N 247018	2802413	N 283542	3208575	N 305869	3312092	AUTO TRANSPORT PERSONNES
782	LORRIES,SPCL MTR VEH NES		906930	N 128026	1336788	N 119853	1383776	N 112214	1392252	VEHICULES SPECIAUX,MARCH
7821	LORRIES,TRUCKS		902212	N 127926	1322532	N 119671	1355322	N 111990	1353150	VEHICULES TRANSP MARCHAND
783	ROAD MOTOR VEHICLES NES		99642		161921		154480		144308	VEHICULES ROUTIERS NDA
784	MOTOR VEH PRTS,ACCES NES		989466		1244279		1168537		1239313	PIECES 722,781,782,783
7849	OTHER MOTOR VEHCL PARTS		940150		1195873		1117947		1187838	PIECES 722,781,782,783
785	CYCLES,ETC MOTRZD OR NOT		196892		238122		281959		302344	MOTOCYCLES SCOOTERS
7851	MOTORCYCLES ETC		122439	N 47895	152679	N 48652	188016	N 51050	189238	MOTO VELO MOTEUR AUXIL
79	OTHR TRANSPORT EQUIPMENT		1253146		1148478		1714137		1994129	AUTRE MATERIEL TRANSPORT
792	AIRCRAFT ETC		661193		981153		1111268		1708901	APP NAVIGATION AERIENNE
7923	AIRCRFT NES2000–15000KG		87230	N 91	88764	N 90	123502	N 110	208069	AERODYNES 2000 A 15000 KG
7924	AIRCRFT NES OVER 15000KG		118470	N 17	279328	N 13	285411	N 25	795986	AERODYNES PLUS 15000 KG

4. General Imports F.O.B. by Commodities according to the S.I.T.C. (Rev. 2) in thousand U.S. Dollars
Importations Générales F.O.B. par Produits d'après la C.T.C.I. (Rév. 2) en milliers de Dollars E.U.

SITC CTCI	COMMODITY	1993		1994		1995		1996		PRODUIT
		WEIGHT POIDS	VALUE VALEUR	WEIGHT POIDS	VALUE VALEUR	WEIGHT POIDS	VALUE VALEUR	WEIGHT POIDS	VALUE VALEUR	
7929	AIRCRAFT PARTS NES		419997		542530		629443		665295	PIECES DU 792
793	SHIPS AND BOATS ETC		555653	N 46838	86748	N 102669	524691	N 80412	240371	NAVIRES BATEAUX,ETC
7932	SHIPS AND BOATS NES		428858	N 35368	34577	N 65510	311560	N 63996	78846	NAVIRES ET BATEAUX
79322	TANKERS OF ALL KINDS		213571			N 1	268338			BATEAUX-CITERNES
79323	OTHER CARGO VESSELS		202082	N 96	16948	N 200	10146	N 92	27508	AUT BATEAUX TRANS MARCH
7938	TUGS,SPECIAL VESSELS ETC		126445	N 10567	27216	N 36980	188937	N 16239	125299	REMORQUEURS,BATEAUX SPEC
79382	SPECL PURPOSE VESSLS ETC		123030	N 1862	21161	N 12993	180892		120882	BAT-PHARES,-POMPES,DRAGUES
8	MISC MANUFACTURED GOODS		6470315		7513513		8096496		8657701	ART MANUFACTURES DIVERS
821	*FURNITURE,PARTS THEREOF		279700		345773		369643		423027	MEUBLES ET PIECES
8219	FURNITURE AND PARTS NES		117762		146706		168877		195323	AUTRES MEUBLES ET PIECES
831	*TRAVEL GOODS,HANDBAGS		184727		230008		265510		267837	ARTICLES DE VOYAGE ETC
83109	OTHER TRAVEL BAGS,CASES		121851		150436		177066		177574	AUT CONTENANTS SIMILAIRES
84	CLOTHING AND ACCESSORIES		992472		1140236		1268456		1418590	VETEMENTS
842	MENS OUTERWEAR NOT KNIT		138100	MN 25653	165466		194472	MN 29060	223687	VET DESSUS POUR HOMMES
843	WOMENS OUTERWEAR NONKNIT		181107		187638		220507	MN 48214	278949	VET DESSUS FEMMES MAT TEX
845	OUTERWEAR KNIT NONELASTC		245110		267733	MN 72068	277553	MN 68608	302119	VET DESSOUS,ACCES BONNET
8451	— JERSEYS,PULLOVERS ETC		142693	MN 23730	154521	MN 24306	157195	MN 23148	165775	CHANDAILS,PULL-OVERS ETC
846	UNDER GARMENTS KNITTED		153672		196097		211471		231058	SOUS VETS DE BONNETERIE
851	*FOOTWEAR		327616	MP 58881	382055	MP 53434	384190	MP 51717	431791	CHAUSSURES
85102	FOOTWEAR LEATHER		241586	MP 35638	295725	MP 31566	291917	MP 31429	339061	CHAUS SEMELLES EN CUIR
87	PRECISION INSTRUMNTS NES		1108894		1292490		1408252		1489775	INSTRUM,APPAR SCIENT NDA
872	MEDICAL INSTRUMENTS NES		226744		277577		310102		356280	INSTR,APP MEDIC-CHIR NDA
87202	OTH MEDICAL INSTRUMENTS		199109		243836		266359		311124	INSTRUM,APP MEDECINE
874	MEASURNG,CONTROLNG INSTR		797816		903923		978245		1008845	INSTRUMENTS DE MESURE
8743	GAS,LIQUID CONTROL INSTR		274718	MN 11700	310193	MN 13126	323102	MN 15134	341947	APP,INSTR MESURE FLUIDES
8748	ELEC MEAS,CONTRL EQU NES		182358	N 3107897	211047	N 3244316	225761	N 3628332	235822	APP ELEC ELECTRO MESURE
87483	OTH ELCTRNC MEAS ETC EQU		168815	N 2625727	194703	N 2719295	206068	N 3190616	215035	AUT APP ELECTRO DE MESURE
88	PHOTO EQU,OPTICL GDS ETC		689186		796712		867096		922890	APP,FOURN PHOTO,OP,MONTR
882	PHOTO,CINEMA SUPPLIES		308200		365501		392358		436210	PRODUITS PHOTO,CINEMA
8822	PHOTO FILM EXC DEV CINMA		242946		294043		314457		359703	PLAQUES,PELLICULES,FILMS
88222	PHOTO FILM ROLL UNEXPOSD		106427	A 25071	155597	A 23244	178764	A 24671	215939	PEL SENSIB PERF OU NON
885	WATCHES AND CLOCKS		142471		165949		181493		167880	HORLOGERIE
89	MISC MANUFCTRD GOODS NES		2769705		3181474		3378045		3537996	ART MANUFACTURES DIVERS
892	PRINTED MATTER		576037		656988		662090		666438	IMPRIMES
8921	PRINTED BOOKS,GLOBES,ETC		348838	MN 157313	379100	MN 181478	390776	MN 186878	401466	LIVRES,BROCHURES,CARTES
89211	PRINTED BOOKS,PAMPHLETS		340374	MN 152262	371200	MN 176198	383344	MN 181308	393059	LIVRES,BROCHURES
8922	NEWSPAPERS,PERIODICALS		145614	MN 107447	162247	MN 100997	158104	MN 98441	148536	JOURNAUX ET PERIODIQUES
893	ARTICLES OF PLASTIC NES		579628		670588		768738		783717	OUVRAGES EN MAT DIVIS 58
8931	PLSTC PACKG CONTNRS,LIDS		129293		152823		189221		192612	ART TRANSP EMBALLAGE ETC
8939	MISC PLASTIC ARTICLES		440368		503439		563452		575290	ART DIVERS EN MAT DIV 58
89399	OTHR PLASTC ARTICLES NES		372860		429331		483343		497592	AUT OUV MAT DIV 58
894	TOYS,SPORTING GOODS,ETC		507479		554571		618589		736311	VOITURES ENFANTS,JOUETS
8942	TOYS,INDOOR GAMES ETC		352008		380749		429794		503216	JOUETS,JEUX ETC
89423	TOYS NES		184074	MN 301477	192134	MN 360268	199013		233742	JOUETS,MODELES REDUITS
89424	INDOOR GAME EQUIPMENT		115118		132878		168210		200573	ART,JEUX DE SOCIETE
898	MUSICAL INSTRUMENTS,PTS		582025		706673		677206		643480	INSTRUMENTS DE MUSIQUE
8983	SOUND RECRDNG TAPE,DISCS		529879	MN 214691	649585	MN 214611	612521	MN 198776	576225	SUPPORTS SON POUR 763
89832	RECORDED DISCS,TAPES ETC		403170	MN 55340	520089	MN 50603	478702	MN 40455	436085	DISQUES,PHONO,BANDES
899	OTHER MANUFACTURED GOODS		245679		270141		313117		335764	AUT ART MANUF DIVERS NDA
9	GOODS NOT CLASSD BY KIND		2472007		788861		841872		765475	ART TRANSACT NON CLASSES
931	*SPECIAL TRANSACTIONS		1747382		109657		112061		126602	TRANS.SPECIALES
971	*GOLD,NON MONETARY NES		681505		566778		542317		503369	OR NON MONETAIRE
97101	NONMON GLD UNWRT,SEMIMFD		680185		565512		538757		501185	OR,ALLIAGES D'OR BRUTS

5. General Exports F.O.B. by Commodities according to the S.I.T.C. (Rev. 2) in thousand U.S. Dollars
Exportations Générales F.O.B. par Produits d'après la C.T.C.I. (Rév. 2) en milliers de Dollars E.U.

SITC CTCI	COMMODITY	1993 WEIGHT POIDS	1993 VALUE VALEUR	1994 WEIGHT POIDS	1994 VALUE VALEUR	1995 WEIGHT POIDS	1995 VALUE VALEUR	1996 WEIGHT POIDS	1996 VALUE VALEUR	PRODUIT
	ALL COMMODITIES		44316359		47253847		53000584		60203900	TOUS PRODUITS
0	FOOD AND LIVE ANIMALS		8450335		9801244		9678005		12365652	ALIMENTS,ANIMAUX VIVANTS
001	*LIVE ANIMALS FOR FOOD	W 352981	190072	W 391625	256227	W 481207	417169	W 558625	503328	ANIMAUX VIVANTS
0011	BOVINE SPECIES,LIVE	W 72232	70549	W 102615	111320	W 181920	216666	W 264920	306627	ESPECE BOVINE
00119	— OTHR THAN FR BREEDING	W 60625	57324	W 99508	105696	W 169089	198135	W 258525	294476	BOVINS NON REPRODUCTEURS
0012	SHEEP AND GOATS,LIVE	W 279557	94776	W 287762	120184	W 297892	164044	W 292477	164179	ESPECES OVINE ET CAPRINE
00121	SHEEP,LIVE	W 278825	93774	W 286735	119191	W 297352	163320	W 291078	162387	ESPECE OVINE
01	MEAT AND PREPARATIONS		2689773		2783033		2622881		2264467	VIANDES ET PREPARATIONS
011	MEAT FRESH,CHILLD,FROZEN	W 1191935	2662489	W 1182681	2749541	W 1114350	2578292	W 1059243	2218986	VIANDES FRAICHES,REF,CONGE
0111	BOVINE MEAT FRESH,FROZEN	W 844779	2146832	W 823141	2184043	W 796621	2019127	W 737681	1621138	VIANDES BOVIN FRAI,REF
01112	BOVINE MEAT BONELESS	W 780152	2026413	W 764411	2061607	W 739010	1901597	W 685059	1520316	VIANDES BOVIN DESOSSEES
0112	MUTTON ETC FRSH,CHLD,FRN	W 240748	345188	W 253902	396305	W 215333	375375	W 216687	413072	VIANDE DE MOUTON
02	DAIRY PRODCTS,BIRDS'EGGS		783504		1013274		1077418		1344254	PRODUITS LAITIERS,OEUFS
022	MILK AND CREAM	W 301474	427541	W 441676	597552	W 398375	624768	W 481697	810103	LAIT ET CREME
0224	MILK,CREAM PRESERVED ETC	W 234344	373216	W 353213	527174	W 303359	542870	W 377956	709152	LAIT,CREME CONS,CONC
02242	MILK DRY,1.5% FAT OR LES	W 127652	214674	W 202000	309059	W 152901	295849	W 198174	403688	LAIT POUDRE INF 1.5%
02243	MILK DRY,OVER 1.5% FAT	W 75445	139235	W 109134	186690	W 97693	200024	W 110500	242040	LAIT POUDRE SUP 1.5%
024	CHEESE AND CURD	W 100710	231383	W 123176	282863	W 133950	329530	W 135257	368317	FROMAGE ET CAILLEBOTTE
03	FISH AND PREPARATIONS		719971		799303		859069		821798	POISSONS ET PREPARATIONS
036	SHELL FISH FRESH,FROZEN	W 39674	538872	W 36875	623526	W 41562	659283	W 38523	622271	CRUSTACES,MOLLUSQUES
04	CEREALS AND PREPARATIONS		2133638		2479118		2022181		4547222	CEREALES ET PRODUITS
041	WHEAT ETC UNMILLED	MW 11038	1511210	MW 12931	1670747		1308267		3124646	FROMENT,EPEAUTRE
0412	OTHER WHEAT ETC UNMILLED	MW 11036	1510609	MW 12927	1669727		1308197		3118685	AUTRE FROMENT NON MOULU
042	RICE	W 497669	165902	W 627660	267974	W 513479	203150	W 566669	244004	RIZ
0422	RICE SEMI–MILLED,MILLED	W 440315	150550	W 390554	152984	W 408574	159899	W 432488	183084	RIZ POLI,GLACE INCL BRISURES
04221	RICE MILLED UNBROKEN	W 440315	150550	W 390554	152984	W 408574	159899	W 432488	183084	RIZ POLI,GLACE EXCL BRISURES
043	BARLEY UNMILLED	W 1797741	217557	W 2520450	249016	W 1345006	212930	W 3712270	669632	ORGE NON MONDEE
048	CEREAL ETC PREPARATIONS	W 372047	172558	W 433231	210028	W 440566	240896	W 476578	292341	PREPTNS A BASE CEREALES
05	VEGETABLES AND FRUIT		624481		682209		690290		856192	LEGUMES ET FRUITS
054	VEG ETC FRSH,SMPLY PRSVD	W 813989	248585	W 846601	296573	W 481254	253434	W 889777	361326	LEGUMES FRAIS,CONG,SECS
0542	LEGUMINOUS VEGETBLES DRY	W 646083	133647	W 634937	144933	W 249801	77635	W 660007	181729	LEGUMES A COSSE SECS
057	FRUIT,NUTS,FRESH,DRIED	W 293225	259854	W 241766	240274	W 253301	278458		340706	FRUITS FRAIS OU SECS
06	SUGAR AND PREPS,HONEY		818001		1217697		1383667		1284420	SUCRES ET PRODUITS
061	SUGAR AND HONEY	W 3614425	794107	W 4756777	1189847		1340654		1233436	SUCRES ET MIEL
0611	RAW BEET AND CANE SUGAR	W 3235226	761372	W 4197341	1124638		1222383		1084230	SUCRES BRUTS
081	*FEEDING STUFF FOR ANIML	W 1143146	291921	W 805889	294964	W 769315	305505	W 945800	390513	NOURRITURE POUR ANIMAUX
0819	FOOD WASTE AND FEED NES	W 233514	131265	W 266655	188190	W 243299	190341	W 280067	236586	DECHETS,ALIMENTS NDA
08199	FODDER NES,INCL SWEETNED	W 233437	131200	W 266535	188061	W 243206	190220	W 279889	236353	PREPARATIONS FOURRAGERES
09	MISC EDIBLE PRODUCTS		99445		149150		167133		202067	PREP ALIMENTAIRES DIVERSES
1	BEVERAGES AND TOBACCO		339966		389982		431378		577381	BOISSONS ET TABACS
11	BEVERAGES		310021		361780		400560		528144	BOISSONS
112	ALCOHOLIC BEVERAGES	W 261466	299503	W 266507	345414	W 272005	374281	W 307702	496541	BOISSONS ALCOOLIQUES
1121	WINE OF FRESH GRAPES ETC	W 187237	243066	W 185401	281011	W 185286	307303	W 235205	433022	VINS DE RAISINS FRAIS
11212	WINE OF FRESH GRAPES	W 187013	242736	W 185000	280518	W 184607	306147	W 234177	430496	VINS DE MOUTS DE RAISINS
2	CRUDE MATERLS,EXCL FUELS		8510179		9023703		10130610		10955318	MAT BRUTES NON COMESTIBLES
21	HIDES,SKINS,FURS UNDRSSD		257321		330249		364437		388087	CUIRS,PEAUX BRUTS
211	HIDES,SKINS,EXC FURS,RAW	W 208337	256079	W 211273	328871	W 195158	364080	W 206650	386225	CUIRS ET PEAUX
2111	BOVINE,EQUINE HIDES,RAW	W 111498	153091	W 93099	155987	W 82632	145729	W 79437	128762	PEAUX DE BOVINS
2116	SHEEP SKIN WITH WOOL	W 82974	70482	W 104568	125723	W 101078	165689	W 110701	204271	PEAUX LAINEES D'OVINS
24	CORK AND WOOD		360159		389987		479153		485696	LIEGE ET BOIS
246	PULPWOOD,CHIPS,WOODWASTE	W 5425261	314693	W 6270803	345664	W 7216591	421110	W 6676480	418183	BOIS DE TRITURATION
24602	PULPWOOD CHIPS,PARTICLES	W 5425222	314660	W 6270757	345614	W 7216579	421039	W 6676277	418118	EN FORME DE PLAQUETTES
26	TEXTILE FIBRES AND WASTE		2330941		2924409		2914812		2995871	FIBRES TEXTILES
263	COTTON	W 350681	462729	W 317720	491332	W 307873	570567	W 400940	680463	COTON
2631	RAW COTTON,EXCL LINTERS	W 346518	457225	W 316823	489851	W 307097	568974	W 400541	678617	COTON EN MASSE
268	WOOL(EXC TOPS),ANML HAIR	W 687391	1848767	W 689828	2411666	W 544815	2318950	W 639335	2283500	LAINES ET POILS
2681	WOOL GREASY,FLEECE–WSHED	W 552987	1326887	W 541119	1753137	W 419893	1662681	W 506814	1651815	LAINE EN SUINT
2682	WOOL DEGREASED,UNCOMBED	W 125800	500468	W 134823	604670	W 113686	607117	W 119157	587570	LAINE DEGRAISSEE
27	CRUDE FERTLZR,MINRLS NES		571622		257422		316879		301288	ENGRAIS MINERAUX BRUTS
278	OTHER CRUDE MINERALS		509069	W 7778500	202257	W 8320590	226738	W 8484196	223969	AUTRES MINERAUX BRUTS
2786	SLAG,SCALINGS,DROSS,ETC		314787	W 12305	390	W 21891	993	W 18551	1401	SCORIES,LAITIERS
27862	SLAG,ASH,NES(INCL KELP)		314440	W 346	95	W 705	209	W 2806	419	SCORIES ET CENDRES
28	METALLIFEROUS ORES,SCRAP		4775853		4844393		5756949		6421387	MINERAIS METAL,DECHETS
281	IRON ORE,CONCENTRATES	MW 116903	1966333	MW 125018	1898327	MW 137075	2173459	MW 135502	2278644	MINERAIS DE FER
2815	IRON ORE,CONC,NOT AGGLOM	MW 116263	1955288	MW 124615	1887906	MW 136581	2159685	MW 135096	2266054	MINERAIS NON AGGLOMERES
286	URANIUM,THORIUM ORE,CONC		128344		124702		130560		194417	MINERAIS URANIUM,THORIUM
287	BASE METAL ORES,CONC NES	MW 13076	2491853	MW 14188	2615920	MW 14222	3173325	MW 14740	3666103	MINERAIS METAUX COMMUNS
2871	CPR ORE ETC,CEMENT COPPR	W 414579	183972	W 463291	221596	W 406523	282164	W 796545	500477	MINERAIS DE CUIVRE,MATTES
28711	COPPER ORES,EXCL MATTE	W 411225	182766	W 460277	220119	W 406283	282048	W 796513	500446	MINERAIS DE CUIVRE
2872	NICKEL ORES,CONCENTRATES	W 40124	183737	W 100288	196393	W 158818	343275	W 189025	331413	MINERAIS DE NICKEL
28722	NICKEL MATTE,SINTERS,ETC	W 34270	168956	W 32082	169658	W 32452	233174	W 28145	193583	MATTES,SINTERS
2873	ALUMINIUM ORES,ALUMINA	MW 9470	1588208	MW 10235	1578383	MW 10269	1809623	MW 10367	1994489	MINERAIS D'ALUMINIUM
28732	ALUMINA(ALUMINIUM OXIDE)	MW 9470	1588208	MW 10235	1578383	MW 10269	1809623	MW 10367	1994489	ALUMINE (OXYDE ALUMINIUM)
2875	ZINC ORES,CONCENTRATES	W 1432628	297608	W 1400297	296592	W 1386492	318296	W 1512334	348540	MINERAIS DE ZINC
2879	OTH NONFER ORE,CONCNTRTE	W 1504128	179118	W 1819881	257798	W 1832959	340050	W 1688078	404974	MINERAIS D'AUTRES METAUX
28793	MOLYBD, NIOBIUM ETC ORES	W 1501765	177081	W 1818004	256432	W 1830717	336665	W 1685584	402257	MINERAIS DE MOLYBDENE,TITANE
288	NONFERR METAL SCRAP NES	W 139922	92664	W 164807	132903	W 171580	162767	W 180419	175932	DECHETS NON FERREUX
29	CRUDE ANIMAL,VEG MAT NES		140096		155755		167198		173876	MATIERES BRUTES ANIM,VEGET
3	MINERAL FUELS ETC		8155476		7819972		8881542		10188989	COMBUSTIBLES MINERAUX LUB
32	COAL,COKE AND BRIQUETTES		5300247		4943960		5509213		6123550	HOUILLES,COKES,BRIQUETTES
322	COAL,LIGNITE AND PEAT	MW 133110	5240985	MW 131160	4902978	MW 136480	5472775	MW 140839	6081138	HOUILLES,LIGNITES,TOURBE
3222	OTH COAL,NOT AGGLOMERATD	MW 132845	5231718	MW 130888	4893891	MW 136078	5456470	MW 140436	6063678	AUTRES HOUILLES
33	PETROLEUM AND PRODUCTS		2027302		1985021		2248548		2752317	PETROLE ET DERIVES
333	CRUDE PETROLEUM	W 7297521	1055314	W 8146753	1058021	W 8542001	1202628	W 8283699	1336941	HUILES BRUTES DE PETROLE
334	PETROLEUM PRODUCTS,REFIN	W 5233369	956349	W 4273811	911517	W 4651717	1022612	W 5670863	1382187	PRODUITS RAFFINES
341	*GAS,NATURAL AND MANUFCT		827928		890991		1123782		1313121	GAZ NATUREL,GAZ MANUFACT
3413	PETROLM GASES,LIQUEFIED		827660		890802		1123608		1312397	GAZ DE PETROLE LIQUEFIE
34131	LIQUEFIED PROPANE,BUTANE	W 793586	112573	W 708300	99219	W 625633	115070	W 1177566	223203	PROPANE,BUTANE LIQUEFIES
34139	OTH HYDROCARBON GAS LQFD		715086		791583		1008538		1089194	HYDROCARBURES GAZEUX NDA
4	ANIMAL,VEGETABLE OIL,FAT		143727		163996		190052		186442	HUILES,GRAISSES ANIM,VEG
411	*ANIMAL OILS AND FATS	W 301604	117717	W 349265	134796	W 312294	160363	W 348496	151266	HUILES,GRAISSES ANIMALES
4113	ANIML OIL,FAT,GREASE NES	W 300898	116638	W 348550	133797	W 311947	159148	W 348150	149573	HUILES,GRAISSES ANIMALES NDA
5	CHEMCLS,RELATED PROD NES		1444243		1756533		2093477		2286621	PRODUITS CHIMIQUES
52	INORGANIC CHEMICALS		149804		201551		263558		260380	PROD CHIM INORGANIQUES
522	INORG ELEMNTS,OXIDES,ETC		128741		136868		166432		164577	ELEMENTS INORGANIQUES
53	DYES,TANNING,COLOUR PROD		239544		271074		313099		327029	PROD TEINTURE,COLORANTS
533	PIGMENTS,PAINTS,ETC	W 134091	221676	W 140643	251112	W 145245	289735	W 156796	295448	PIGMENTS,PEINTURES,VERNIS
5331	COLOURING MATERIAL NES	W 119238	176232	W 121560	191847	W 127498	237405	W 136157	229230	AUT MATIERES COLORANTES
541	*MEDICINAL,PHARM PRODUCT	MK 17876	433836	MK 17912	534339	MK 19008	618811	MK 21304	737654	PROD MEDICINAUX PHARMACEUT
5417	MEDICAMENTS	MK 14147	287688	MK 13991	379805	MK 14754	453025	MK 15919	567007	MEDICAMENTS
54179	— CONTNG OTH SUBSTANCES	MK 11724	225119	MK 11349	294984	MK 12097	344347	MK 13273	434104	MED CONT AUT SUBSTANCES

5. General Exports F.O.B. by Commodities according to the S.I.T.C. (Rev. 2) in thousand U.S. Dollars
Exportations Générales F.O.B. par Produits d'après la C.T.C.I. (Rév. 2) en milliers de Dollars E.U.

SITC CTCI	COMMODITY	1993		1994		1995		1996		PRODUIT
		WEIGHT POIDS	VALUE VALEUR	WEIGHT POIDS	VALUE VALEUR	WEIGHT POIDS	VALUE VALEUR	WEIGHT POIDS	VALUE VALEUR	
55	PERFUME,CLEANING ETC PRD		130149		172275		207089		234857	PROD POUR PARFUM,TOILETTE
58	PLASTIC MATERIALS ETC		179959		196369		311820		295056	MAT PLAST ARTIFICIELLES
583	POLYMERIZATION ETC PRODS		134046	W 150759	144712	W 173146	208506	W 180892	204059	PROD POLYMERISATION
59	CHEMICAL MATERIALS NES		231677		283516		276309		323573	MAT PROD CHIMIQUES NDA
6	BASIC MANUFACTURES		5333162		6316359		7651019		7816599	ART MANUFACTURES
61	LEATHER,DRESSED FUR,ETC		226347		316018		377523		374282	CUIRS,PELLETERIES
611	LEATHER	W 67997	202303	W 74775	289575	W 85427	344610	W 85623	331608	CUIRS,PEAUX PREPARES
6114	LEATHR BOVINE NES,EQUINE	W 66759	184527	W 71902	255993	W 84003	318198	W 84355	306686	CUIRS DE BOVINS
64	PAPER,PAPERBOARD AND MFR		196030		214291		230233		284488	PAPIERS,CARTONS & OUVRAGES
641	PAPER AND PAPERBOARD		142804		147425		156730	W 380431	193640	PAPIERS ET CARTONS
65	TEXTILE YARN,FABRICS,ETC		397823		521880		732534		802767	FILS,TISSUS,ARTICLES TEXTILE
651	TEXTILE YARN	W 42609	191517		270370		420694		432721	FILS TEXTILES
6512	WOOL,HAIR YARN,INCL TOPS	W 32453	162193	W 37066	226190	W 44613	358230	W 51619	367334	FILS DE LAINE,DE POILS
65121	WOOL TOPS	W 31496	156372	W 35479	215952	W 43399	349999	W 50713	360117	RUBANS LAINE PEIGN,TOPS
66	NONMETAL MINERAL MFS NES		406208		589526		524570		633273	ART MIN NON METALLIQUES
667	PEARL,PREC–,SEMI–P STONE		231774		360976		255929		319666	PERLES, PIERRES GEMMES
6671	PEARLS UNSET,UNSTRUNG		80961		152531		115539		174173	PERLES FINES NON SERTIES
67	IRON AND STEEL		966996		1142000		1358539		1335012	FER ET ACIER
672	IRON,STEEL PRIMARY FORMS	W 1726519	427830	W 2236601	532713	W 2006387	613753	W 2015124	497884	LINGOTS FER,ACIER
6725	IRN,STL BLOOMS,SLABS,ETC	W 963643	220098	W 1412600	309140	W 999981	262144	W 1024114	229411	BLOOMS,BILLETTES FER ACIER
67251	IRN,SMPLE STL BLOOMS,ETC	W 963507	219569	W 1412485	308596	W 999822	261460	W 1023088	227600	BLOOMS ETC NON ACIER FIN
6727	IRN,STL COIL FR REROLLNG	W 761954	206889	W 823668	223257	W 857159	308016	W 729282	202806	EBAUCHES POUR TOLES FER
67271	IRON,SIMPLE STEEL COILS	W 760841	206399	W 823558	223153	W 856292	306701	W 728426	201862	EBAUCHES NON EN ACIER
674	IRN,STL UNIV,PLATE,SHEET	W 572710	283308	W 523063	290532	W 562221	353379	W 707423	389972	LARGES PLATS,TOLES
6749	OTH IRN,STL PLATES,SHEET	W 297278	162289	W 310421	186864	W 328639	219981	W 406104	249400	AUTRES TOLES FER,ACIER
67491	— OF IRON OR SIMPLE STL	W 294759	159817	W 308807	183857	W 326073	214822	W 400622	239107	AUT TOLES AUTRES ACIER FIN
68	NON–FERROUS METALS		2645508		2924676		3775356		3618833	METAUX NON FERREUX
682	COPPER EXC CEMENT COPPER	W 249634	514265	W 271780	602134	W 219967	680242	W 250247	644217	CUIVRE
6821	COPPER NES,ALLOYS,UNWRT	W 169013	327785	W 183279	389239	W 107748	316327	W 118507	279303	CUIVRE BRUT
68212	COPPER REFINED,UNWROUGHT	W 160020	311682	W 178550	379978	W 107728	316232	W 118463	279218	CUIVRE AFFINE BRUT
6822	COPPER,ALLOYS WORKED	W 80622	186479	W 88500	212895	W 112219	363915	W 131741	364914	CUIVRE,ALLIAGES OUVRES
68221	COPPER BARS,WIRE,ETC	W 68304	145811	W 74489	165978	W 93914	291949	W 113015	292369	BARRES,PROFILES ET FILS
683	NICKEL		141023	W 39123	234524	W 50448	410805	W 53828	390232	NICKEL
6831	NICKEL,ALLOYS UNWROUGHT		140500	W 36024	215959	W 46195	375915	W 49992	361253	NICKEL ET ALLIAGES BRUTS
684	ALUMINIUM	W 1168676	1466511	W 1067439	1555020	W 1075693	2101894	W 1159247	1910079	ALUMINIUM
6841	ALUMINIUM,ALLOYS,UNWRGHT	W 1060298	1237873	W 952339	1321180	W 960700	1801601	W 1071174	1676840	ALUMINIUM,ALLIAGES BRUTS
6842	ALUMINIUM,ALLOYS WORKED	W 108379	228638	W 115100	233840	W 114993	300293	W 88073	233239	ALUMINIUM,ALLIAGES OUVRE
68422	ALUMNM PLATE,SHEET,STRIP	W 92476	191381	W 89188	174900	W 97456	248506	W 70515	184239	TOLES, PLANCHES EN ALU
685	LEAD	W 372854	192428	W 359426	203497	W 368224	253244	W 356637	307626	PLOMB
6851	LEAD,ALLOYS UNWROUGHT	W 371322	191341	W 358471	202610	W 367530	252221	W 355169	305977	PLOMB,ALLIAGES BRUTS
686	ZINC	W 256430	282745	W 259677	280978	W 227382	274536	W 241803	286251	ZINC
6861	ZINC,ALLOYS UNWROUGHT	W 254092	280499	W 257052	278540	W 224754	272326	W 239722	284060	ZINC ET ALLIAGES BRUTS
69	METAL MANUFACTURES NES		366996		463204		468183		553220	ART MANUFACT EN METAL NDA
691	STRUCTURES AND PARTS NES	W 117744	114287	W 138311	144170	W 131794	122725	W 124596	147148	CONSTRUCT FER,ACIER,ALU
699	BASE METAL MFRS NES	W 33958	119511	W 32931	145309	W 34725	152446	W 43480	192076	ART MANUFACTURES MET NDA
7	MACHINES,TRANSPORT EQUIP		4755103		5552753		6768993		7769379	MACHINES MATERIEL TRANSPORT
71	POWER GENERATING EQUIPMT		424130		439582		592062		688367	MACHINES GENERATRICES
713	INTRNL COMBUS PSTN ENGIN	W 41156	294033	W 43872	328310	W 55628	446387	W 54554	442362	MOTEURS EXPL COMB INT, PIECE
7132	MOTOR VEHCL PISTN ENGINS	W 22488	144499	W 23220	166477	W 36440	238704	W 28334	215484	MOTEURS EXPL POUR VEHICULES
72	MACHS FOR SPCL INDUSTRYS		513206		534967		737777		800571	MAC SPECIALES POUR INDUST
728	OTH MACHY FOR SPCL INDUS	W 25496	213242	W 23603	245221	W 40085	363825	W 38726	413525	AUT MACH IND PARTICULIERES
7284	MACHY FOR SPCL INDUS NES	W 12474	136238	W 12803	167288	W 25634	238888	W 24078	278410	MACH SPEC IND PARTICUL.
74	GENRL INDUSTRL MACHY NES		593608		747639		815919		1037493	MACH APP INDUSTRIE
741	HEATING,COOLING EQUIPMNT	W 17170	135452	W 21282	182110	W 24072	199124	W 30513	254482	MACH CHAUFFAGE,PIECES
744	MECHANICAL HANDLING EQU	W 26899	143685	W 27080	165886	W 42369	182990	W 39904	247994	EQUIP MANUTENTION PIECES
749	NONELEC MACH PTS,ACC NES	W 13232	130562	W 15253	164974	W 17283	173196	W 21108	206104	PIECES MACH NON ELEC NDA
75	OFFICE MACHNES,ADP EQUIP		794865		1105867		1299785		1394595	MACH BUREAU TRAIT AUTOM
752	AUTOMTIC DATA PROC EQUIP	W 5714	218845	W 3110	304114	W 3169	295827	W 3478	301447	MACH TRAIT INFORMATION
7523	DIGITL CENTRL PROCESSORS	W 2526	88856	W 1806	145810	W 681	82310	W 1259	87814	UNITES CENTRALES
759	OFFICE,ADP MCH PTS,ACCES	W 8421	561162	W 6788	783851	W 8150	985790	W 8862	1066166	PIECES DU 751 ET 752
7599	ACCTG,ETC,ADP MCH PTS,AC	W 7593	519190	W 5848	743425	W 7007	912973	W 7475	989247	PIECES DU 751 ET 752
76	TELECOMM,SOUND EQUIPMENT		296668		504066		510413		512665	EQUIPMENT DE TELECOM
764	TELECOM EQPT,PTS,ACC NES	W 10240	280107	W 10490	480855	W 15422	489329	W 17092	488089	EQUIP TELECOM,PIECES
7641	LINE TELEPHONE,ETC EQUIP	W 7842	132035	W 7988	268842	W 12111	226654	W 11815	164208	APP TELEPHON PAR FIL
7649	PTS NES OF EQUIPMT OF 76	W 1535	70755	W 1483	108802	W 2102	149642	W 4239	224438	PIECES DE LA DIV 76
77	ELECTRIC MACHNRY NES ETC		590020		787141		990257		1028311	MACH APP ELECT NDA
772	SWITCHGEAR ETC,PARTS NES	W 7163	180992	W 7291	214301	W 8963	296922	W 11894	302282	APP COUPURE,SECT ETC
7721	SWITCHGEAR ETC	W 7120	137566	W 7257	180647	W 8924	263436	W 11832	297091	APP COUPURE,SECTIONMNT
778	ELECTRICAL MACHINERY NES	W 10363	131884		229225		280974	W 23538	274401	AUTRES MACH ELECT NDA
7788	OTH ELEC MACHY,EQUIP NES	W 2945	83902	W 5816	173791	W 10323	224805	W 5361	212731	AUT MACH APP ELEC NDA
78	ROAD VEHICLES		743969		742140		834930		1208211	VEHICULES ROUTIERS
781	PASS MOTOR VEH EXC BUSES	W 41967	405366	W 38350	361219	W 41248	389854	W 68309	690271	AUTO TRANSPORT PERSONNES
784	MOTOR VEH PRTS,ACCES NES	W 35980	249150	W 34777	278720	W 38504	302039	W 47278	383140	PIECES 722,781,782,783
7849	OTHER MOTOR VEHCL PARTS	W 35392	246322	W 34555	277408	W 37935	297581	W 46087	373983	PIECES 722,781,782,783
79	OTHR TRANSPORT EQUIPMENT		743471		617102		902388		978052	AUTRE MATERIEL TRANSPORT
792	AIRCRAFT ETC	W 2588	408635	W 1559	388633	W 1840	482938	W 2238	498380	APP NAVIGATION AERIENNE
7929	AIRCRAFT PARTS NES	W 1528	301133	W 1222	358695	W 1482	405694	W 1721	427682	PIECES DU 792
793	SHIPS AND BOATS ETC		313401	W 26781	206322	W 99236	286419	W 90285	416200	NAVIRES BATEAUX,ETC
7932	SHIPS AND BOATS NES	W 31463	220661	W 22264	194738	W 95841	245063	W 88632	404019	NAVIRES ET BATEAUX
79323	OTHER CARGO VESSELS	W 19616	154133	W 17484	142126	W 74200	172940	W 27328	317540	AUT BATEAUX TRANS MARCH
8	MISC MANUFACTURED GOODS		1373534		1661534		1880865		2220293	ART MANUFACTURES DIVERS
84	CLOTHING AND ACCESSORIES		151006		211068		224166		266332	VETEMENTS
87	PRECISION INSTRUMNTS NES		301042		365219		393411		501927	INSTRUM,APPAR SCIENT NDA
874	MEASURNG,CONTROLNG INSTR	W 2470	168039	W 2135	204995	W 2012	207014	W 2817	272508	INSTRUMENTS DE MESURE
88	PHOTO EQU,OPTICL GDS ETC		261464		307126		337413		393775	APP,FOURN PHOTO,OP,MONTR
882	PHOTO,CINEMA SUPPLIES	W 19233	198330	W 20632	234334	W 23253	260529	W 29675	310148	PRODUITS PHOTO,CINEMA
8822	PHOTO FILM EXC DEV CINMA	W 8495	175164	W 9372	208543	W 11388	229344	W 13789	259662	PLAQUES,PELLICULES,FILMS
88222	PHOTO FILM ROLL UNEXPOSD	W 4287	129784	W 4245	153355	W 4375	152824	W 5227	180814	PEL SENSIB PERF OU NON
89	MISC MANUFCTRD GOODS NES		550080		650953		772700		858811	ART MANUFACTURES DIVERS
892	PRINTED MATTER	W 25155	140320	W 22804	177465	W 22268	187713	W 23613	226759	IMPRIMES
893	ARTICLES OF PLASTIC NES		119382		158350		192000		206725	OUVRAGES EN MAT DIVIS 58
9	GOODS NOT CLASSD BY KIND		5810633		4767772		5294642		5837225	ART TRANSACT NON CLASSES
931	*SPECIAL TRANSACTIONS # 1		2614236	MW 10503	1335703		1379606		1708980	TRANS.SPECIALES
971	*GOLD,NON MONETARY NES	K 286232	3184947	K 281641	3421829	K 337164	3900897	K 337737	4101202	OR NON MONETAIRE
97101	NONMON GLD UNWRT,SEMIMFD	K 285045	3183658	K 281139	3421671	K 320910	3898323	K 331185	4098808	OR,ALLIAGES D'OR BRUTS

FOOT NOTES – NOTES

Foot Notes (Continued) – Notes (Suite)

TABLE 1 –

1 Years ending 30 June of years stated for all data except merchandise trade and conversion factors which, beginning 1966, are on a calendar year basis.

TABLE 5 –

1 Some confidential data are included in SITC 931.

TABLEAU 1 –

1 Années se terminant le 30 juin des années indiquées pour toutes les données, sauf pour le commerce de marchandise et les taux de conversion qui, à partir de 1966, sont basés sur les années grégoriennes.

TABLEAU 5 –

1 Des données confidentielles sont comprises dans le groupe 931 de la CTCI.

1. HISTORICAL SERIES, 1961–1996 SPECIAL TRADE, IMPORTS C.I.F., EXPORTS F.O.B.
SERIES HISTORIQUES, 1961–1996 COMMERCE SPECIAL, IMPORTATIONS C.A.F., EXPORTATIONS F.O.B

YEAR ANNEE	VALUE IN MILLION SCHILLINGS / VALEUR EN MILLION SCHILLINGS — MERCHANDISE – MARCHANDISE IMPORTS	MERCHANDISE – MARCHANDISE EXPORTS	GOLD – OR IMPORTS	GOLD – OR EXPORTS	CONVERSION FACTORS U.S. CENTS PER SCHILLING FACTEURS DE CONVERSION CENTS E.U. PAR SCHILLING IMPORTS	CONVERSION FACTORS EXPORTS	INDEX NUMBERS – INDICES QUANTUM IMPORTS	QUANTUM EXPORTS	UNIT VALUE VALEUR UNITAIRE IMPORTS	UNIT VALUE EXPORTS
1961	38604.00	31262.00	677.40	579.90	3.8460	3.8460	31	27	61	63
1962	40348.00	32851.00	873.00	746.00	3.8460	3.8460	33	28	61	62
1963	43557.00	34475.00	686.70	479.40	3.8460	3.8460	36	32	61	62
1964	48433.00	37601.00	619.40	293.10	3.8460	3.8460	41	34	60	63
1965	54614.00	41600.00	904.60	275.60	3.8460	3.8460	46	36	58	61
1966	60519.00	43773.00	1060.10	366.20	3.8460	3.8460	51	39	59	60
1967	60046.00	47029.00	1480.60	316.60	3.8460	3.8460	51	42	58	60
1968	64896.00	51707.00	961.10	163.80	3.8460	3.8460	58	48	55	57
1969	73460.00	62723.00	648.90	67.00	3.8460	3.8460	24	24	55	56
1970	92266.00	74270.00	864.70	73.50	3.8460	3.8460	29	26	58	61
1971	104476.00	78997.00	1306.20	89.00	4.0110	4.0120	31	27	61	63
1972	120576.00	89747.00	1191.60	105.10	4.3261	4.3270	36	30	61	64
1973	137863.00	101977.00	482.00	89.00	5.1650	5.1820	40	32	63	68
1974	168281.00	133356.00			5.3616	5.3701	41	36	75	79
1975	163376.00	130884.00			5.7488	5.7441	38	34	78	82
1976	206081.00	152114.00			5.5910	5.5924	47	39	80	82
1977	234841.00	161781.00			6.0670	6.0623	51	41	83	84
1978	231888.00	176112.00			6.9093	6.9139	50	44	83	84
1979	269862.00	206253.00			7.5055	7.5064	56	50	87	88
1980	315846.00	226169.00			7.7410	7.7344	59	53	96	92
1981	334510.10	251769.00			6.2921	6.2933	57	55	107	98
1982	332550.90	266860.00			5.8808	5.8776	56	56	107	102
1983	348338.90	277139.70			5.5591	5.5670	60	59	106	102
1984	392094.00	314504.40			5.0067	5.0050	65	64	110	106
1985	430969.10	353962.00			4.8581	4.8667	69	70	113	109
1986	407954.90	342479.10			6.5821	6.5782	71	71	103	105
1987	411852.00	342432.00			7.9357	7.9360	75	72	99	103
1988	451440.10	383219.90			8.0995	8.1055	82	80	100	103
1989	514692.10	429312.00			7.5648	7.5668	90	90	103	100
1990	556233.90	466066.90			8.8258	8.8267	100	100	100	100
1991	591898.10	479028.90			8.5833	8.5852	101	106	100	97
1992	593924.10	487556.10			9.1127	9.1019	107	111	99	95
1993	565556.90	467655.90			8.5962	8.5960	106	108	96	91
1994	629421.00	511888.10			8.7922	8.7971	119	119	108	102
1995	668029.90	580008.90			9.9205	9.9205			89	86
1996	712759.60	612189.80			9.4399	9.4465			90	90

2. IMPORTS BY BROAD ECONOMIC CATEGORY AND EXPORTS BY INDUSTRIAL ORIGIN. (PERCENTAGE OF TOTAL VALUE)
IMPORTATIONS PAR CATEGORIES ECONOMIQUES ET EXPORTATIONS PAR BRANCHE D'ACTIVITE.(EN POURCENTAGE DE LA VALEUR TOTALE)

IMPORTS – IMPORTATIONS

	1990	1991	1992	1993	1994	1995	1996
TOTAL IMPORTS–IMPORTATIONS TOTALES	100.	100.	100.	100.	100.	100.	100.
1 FOOD BEV–ALIMENTATION BOISSONS	4.6	4.6	4.5	4.8	4.9	5.6	5.5
11 PRIMARY–PRODUITS DE BASE	2.3	2.3	2.1	2.1	2.2	2.6	2.4
111 FOR INDUSTRY–POUR L'INDUSTRIE	0.5	0.5	0.4	0.4	0.5	0.6	0.5
112 FOR HOUSEHOLDS–POUR LES MENAGES	1.8	1.8	1.7	1.7	1.6	2.0	1.9
12 PROCESSED–PRODUITS ELABORES	2.3	2.4	2.4	2.7	2.7	3.0	3.1
121 FOR INDUSTRY–POUR L'INDUSTRIE	0.3	0.3	0.3	0.3	0.4	0.4	0.4
122 FOR HOUSEHOLDS–POUR LES MENAGES	2.0	2.0	2.1	2.3	2.4	2.6	2.7
2 IND SUPPLIES–APPROV INDUSTRIELS	30.7	29.2	29.2	29.3	30.3	30.6	28.8
21 PRIMARY–PRODUITS DE BASE	3.0	2.9	2.8	2.6	2.8	3.1	2.5
22 PROCESSED–PRODUITS ELABORES	27.7	26.2	26.4	26.7	27.5	27.5	26.3
3 FUELS–COMBUSTIBLES	6.2	5.9	5.1	5.0	4.4	4.5	5.3
31 PRIMARY–PRODUITS DE BASE	4.3	4.0	3.6	3.6	3.0	3.0	3.4
32 PROCESSED–PRODUITS ELABORES	1.9	1.9	1.5	1.4	1.4	1.5	1.9
321 MOTOR SPIRIT–ESSENCE	0.3	0.3	0.3	0.3	0.0		0.3
322 OTHER–AUTRES	1.6	1.6	1.2	1.1	1.4	1.5	1.7
4 MACHINERY–EQUIPEMENT	24.1	24.3	23.6	23.4	23.8	22.3	22.4
41 CAPITAL EQUIPMENT–MACHINES	18.5	18.7	18.3	18.0	18.1	16.9	17.4
42 PARTS–PIECES ACCESSOIRES	5.6	5.6	5.3	5.4	5.6	5.3	5.0
5 TRANSPORT–TRANSPORT	14.1	15.1	16.6	15.0	14.9	15.4	16.1
51 PASSENGER CARS–AUTOMOBILES	7.0	7.6	7.9	7.0	6.6	6.6	7.0
52 OTHER–AUTRES	3.0	3.0	3.5	2.8	2.9	3.0	3.1
521 INDUSTRIAL–INDUSTRIELS	2.7	2.6	3.1	2.4	2.4	2.7	2.7
522 NON INDUSTRIAL–NON INDUSTRIEL	0.3	0.4	0.4	0.4	0.5	0.3	0.3
53 PARTS–PIECES ACCESSOIRES	4.1	4.6	5.2	5.2	5.3	5.8	6.1
6 CONSUM GOODS–BIENS CONSOMMATION	20.3	20.8	20.8	22.4	21.5	21.5	21.2
61 DURABLE–DURABLES	5.6	5.6	5.3	5.7	5.5	5.2	5.6
62 SEMI DURABLE–SEMI DURABLES	10.5	10.9	11.1	11.9	11.2	11.6	10.9
63 NON DURABLE–NON DURABLES	4.2	4.3	4.4	4.8	4.8	4.6	4.7
7 GOODS NES–BIENS NDA	0.1	0.1	0.2	0.2	0.4	0.1	0.7

EXPORTS – EXPORTATIONS

	1990	1991	1992	1993	1994	1995	1996
TOTAL EXPORTS–EXPORTATIONS TOTALES	100.	100.	100.	100.	100.	100.	100.
1 AGRICULTURE	1.1	1.1	1.1	0.9	1.1	1.6	1.0
2 MINING QUARRY–INDUS EXTRACTIVES	0.5	0.4	0.4	0.5	0.4	0.5	0.4
3 MANUFACTURING–IND MANUFACTUR	98.4	98.5	98.5	98.6	98.5	97.9	98.6
31 FOOD BEV TOBACCO–ALIM BOISS TAB	2.6	2.6	2.6	2.9	3.1	3.5	3.8
32 TEXTILES–INDUSTRIES TEXTILES	9.2	8.8	8.8	8.4	7.7	7.2	7.2
33 WOOD & PRODUCTS–BOIS & PRODUITS	4.4	3.9	3.7	3.6	3.8	3.6	3.4
34 PAPER & PRODUCTS–PAPIER & PRODT	7.2	7.4	7.1	6.9	7.1	7.6	6.8
35 CHEMICALS–INDUSTRIES CHIMIQUES	12.4	12.8	12.6	13.1	13.3	12.0	13.3
36 NON METAL MIN–MIN NON METAL	3.3	3.2	3.2	3.1	3.1	2.9	2.8
37 BASIC METAL–IND METAL BASE	9.4	8.3	7.8	7.5	7.8	8.8	7.6
38 METAL MANUF–MANUF METAL	47.2	48.7	49.7	50.0	49.7	49.2	50.9
39 OTH MANUF IND–AUTRES MANUF	2.7	2.8	3.0	3.1	3.0	2.9	2.8

3. TRADE BY PRINCIPAL COUNTRIES OF PRODUCTION AND LAST CONSIGNMENT (VALUE IN THOUSAND U.S. DOLLARS)
ECHANGES SELON LES PRINCIPAUX PAYS DE PRODUCTION ET DE DERNIERE CONSIGNATION (VALEUR EN MILLIERS DE DOLLARS EU)

COUNTRIES–PAYS	SPECIAL IMPORTS C.I.F. IMPORTATIONS SPECIALES C.A.F					COUNTRIES–PAYS	SPECIAL EXPORTS F.O.B. EXPORTATIONS SPECIALES F.O.B.				
	1992	1993	1994	1995	1996		1992	1993	1994	1995	1996
World	54115552	48561265	55290451	65662454	67283792	Monde	44434839	40159112	45072235	57141495	57830507
Africa	1003566	972421	908954	786563	1183034	Afrique	586087	554469	691899	613905	594971
Americas	2907392	2740152	3354008	2626533	3899645	Amériques	1824110	1971456	2336962	2460187	2911885
Northern America	2412281	2327823	2815767	2314095	3443864	Amérique du Nord	1430448	1583705	1868988	1946481	2254496
LAIA	405592	322279	429757	225541	323445	ALAI	343147	339982	419402	458354	614675
CACM	70635	73124	91152	75670	111767	MCAC	20649	15614	18951	15277	17591
Caribbean	6514	4690	6540	2355	5832	Caraïbes	23973	21838	25100	34534	22345
Rest of America	12370	12236	10791	8872	14738	Autre Amérique	5892	10316	4521	5540	2777
As.ex F.USSR	5731201	5290248	6035991	3655202	5195736	Asie l'URSS exclus	3455993	3330525	3353809	3830588	4433528
Eur.x F.USSR	43621805	38739911	43870138	56397862	55622504	Europe l'URSS exclus	37634085	33468903	37658988	44027292	48393006
EU	38097402	33657242	37803731	49558718	47654404	UE	30275833	26316401	29218458	33508484	37102428
EFTA	2337435	2139846	2431543	2482509	2562458	AELE	2923201	2713803	3127236	3575833	3509398
East Europe	2710386	2512447	3115371	3652872	4564927	Europe de l'Est	3560001	3536723	4123948	5319158	6012238
Other Europe	8911	6966	12705	4344	9068	Autre de l'Europe	25891	7848	12060	11551	13758
Former USSR	789443	762655	1053260	545012	1329519	Ancienne URSS	739379	670729	831663	1100793	1131551
Oceania	62146	55877	68101	32993	53341	Océanie	195186	163030	198668	276535	365560
Germany/Allemagne	23201024	20132161	22133187	31395835	28844518	Germany/Allemagne	17693192	15666448	17177411	19901445	21636435
Italy/Italie	4668014	4379633	4881832	5541135	5923910	Italy/Italie	3911151	3171133	3657949	4526929	4819226
France, Monac	2402908	2132357	2604813	3092249	3230288	Switz.Liecht	2636258	2475974	2868981	3309178	3144865
USA/Etats–Unis d'Amer	2136344	2141919	2418601	2044450	3000143	France, Monac	1947245	1779744	2051426	2078173	2477021
Switz.Liecht	2166944	1983633	2253367	2384556	2442202	Hungary/Hongrie	1417802	1422612	1763735	2072863	2299097
Japan/Japon	2557326	2131185	2366466	1129764	1624750	United Kingdom	1587395	1312279	1427145	1630297	2045101
Netherlands/Pays–Bas	1461933	1405171	1667832	2875186	2160714	USA/Etats–Unis d'Amer	1172602	1327303	1568578	1609333	1840938
United Kingdom	1472397	1326945	1602487	1643100	2027455	Netherlands/Pays–Bas	1295908	1189797	1343905	1453788	1495753
Belgium–Luxembourg	1631072	1386944	1599398	1767533	1541292	Czech Republic		975162	1181082	1540710	1676916
Hungary/Hongrie	1089658	930630	1128055	1198218	1807888	Spain/Espagne	1053159	836371	965752	1059940	1291939
Sweden/Suède	975161	808956	969792	1052178	1036442	Belgium–Luxembourg	876599	762226	849124	861526	1115284
Czech Republic		784919	992609	1216696	1355910	Slovenia/Slovénia	514104	585297	703716	958519	931832
Spain/Espagne	679604	660872	745629	702522	968392	Japan/Japon	682762	616434	696039	712441	893426
Russian Federation	682480	658907	895084	441118	1064058	Russian Federation	625774	533707	657327	830914	750645
China/Chine	543753	668811	851205	589100	848676	Poland/Pologne	643222	553077	529640	746271	855647
Poland/Pologne	456545	402198	454145	560126	534605	Sweden/Suède	658739	559368	628558	692564	763494
Denmark/Danemark	428999	390511	444135	461363	505188	Slovakia		351809	395254	555821	730956
Slovenia/Slovénia	272974	290120	356848	506442	561035	Denmark/Danemark	400234	352355	385517	420588	461813
Finland/Finlande	378964	311930	378199	388633	447714	Croatia/Croatie	174644	243618	367825	523768	577855
Slovakia		270204	362805	505596	617254	China/Chine	236422	315281	327589	431140	341996
Portugal	323830	285365	310480	239011	432731	Canada	252643	256259	298946	336650	413494
Canada	275919	185862	397066	269643	443608	Turkey/Turquie	286170	259768	173642	246337	483185
Turkey/Turquie	238126	248838	293057	293386	374747	Finland/Finlande	257936	209596	233979	316248	353522
Ireland/Irlande	259300	247274	270868	233393	357472	Norway, SVD, JM	277141	226404	250074	257893	343459
Korea, Republic of	306161	288903	271916	221216	240567	Hong Kong	212393	222810	247187	308896	283516
Nigeria/Nigéria	280747	334695	164383	258265	275879	Czechoslovakia	1259007				
Hong Kong	259576	234811	257817	201501	216949	Iran (Islamic Rp. of)	384060	289389	240558	133698	205997
Algeria/Algérie	244871	205071	236569	117552	269876	Greece/Grèce	282895	202416	206754	268386	276146
Czechoslovakia	1009321					Korea, Republic of	136458	192863	231908	298696	307070
Greece/Grèce	214198	189122	195079	166581	178287	Saudi Arabia	308879	218623	173858	185705	182334
Saudi Arabia	143114	182077	196573	162536	172177	Portugal	227019	194311	194156	183108	241395
So. Africa Customs Un	177554	158022	166803	116185	176816	Australia/Australie	165699	140148	169819	230697	321212
Libyan Arab Jamahiriya	138406	101870	164550	196888	190591	Indonesia/Indonésie	180328	210967	138769	208162	268275
India/Inde	132337	146002	178586	128021	180273	Romania/Roumanie	108985	111242	131353	242397	308600
Singapore/Singapour	183242	158879	202761	66097	153470	Singapore/Singapour	110489	111030	198255	235331	191799
Croatia/Croatie	85405	118661	132372	174431	236595	Brazil/Brésil	62520	74081	127438	234795	281780
Brazil/Brésil	156953	141392	207013	86958	141138	So. Africa Customs Un	102596	110043	163686	159319	176961
Norway, SVD, JM	166840	153411	173507	94649	116780	Thailand/Thaïlande	122460	160759	80892	122673	182883
Malaysia/Malaisie	110030	127252	156828	90229	185030	Bulgaria/Bulgarie	126100	116693	117139	146349	133934
Thailand/Thaïlande	134362	141887	164635	84855	132260	Israel/Israël	88597	101794	123241	120839	135853
Romania/Roumanie	89800	73537	113808	120180	180875	Ukraine	74789	55112	60432	116745	235625
Ukraine	88362	75470	114657	35716	173803	India/Inde	103499	74427	77903	118245	166112
Iran (Islamic Rp. of)	123112	81377	84305	47031	83054	Algeria/Algérie	123294	104645	181550	80352	32045
Indonesia/Indonésie	59099	68837	85514	57693	140037	Ireland/Irlande	84361	80358	96783	115491	125298
Israel/Israël	79974	79492	97271	59639	84034	Malaysia/Malaisie	89252	80021	139451	74062	93170
Bulgaria/Bulgarie	62888	49708	61872	50626	65815	Mexico/Mexique	97909	84431	100744	55372	91990
Mexico/Mexique	88521	46693	55689	28897	37553	Egypt/Egypte	76591	72428	102068	98034	81178
Pakistan	45740	43154	54544	42425	49873	United Arab Emirates	53478	59323	59386	97803	113143
Syrian Arab Republic	49943	47154	40088	54945	41351	Yugoslavia/Yougoslavie	150544	15410	25215	27059	141625
Philippines	34443	39848	53741	20132	48079	Libyan Arab Jamahiriya	60494	63800	53657	66952	102628

(VALUE AS PERCENTAGE OF WORLD TOTAL) (VALEURS EN POURCENTAGE DU TOTAL MONDIAL)

	1987	1988	1989	1990	1991	1992	1993	1994	1995	1996		1987	1988	1989	1990	1991	1992	1993	1994	1995	1996
Africa	2.2	1.7	2.2	2.4	2.1	1.9	2.0	1.6	1.2	1.8	Afrique	2.1	1.9	1.8	1.6	1.6	1.3	1.4	1.5	1.1	1.0
Americas	5.2	5.1	5.4	5.2	5.4	5.4	5.6	6.1	4.0	5.8	Amériques	5.3	5.0	5.2	4.7	4.2	4.1	4.9	5.2	4.3	5.0
Northern America	3.8	3.8	4.1	4.1	4.4	4.5	4.8	5.1	3.5	5.1	Amérique du Nord	4.3	4.2	4.5	4.0	3.4	3.2	3.9	4.1	3.4	3.9
LAIA	1.1	1.0	1.0	0.8	0.8	0.7	0.7	0.8	0.3	0.5	ALAI	0.8	0.6	0.6	0.6	0.7	0.8	0.8	0.9	0.8	1.1
CACM	0.2	0.2	0.2	0.2	0.2	0.1	0.2	0.2	0.1	0.2	MCAC	0.1	0.0	0.0	0.0	0.0	0.0	0.0	0.0	0.0	0.0
Caribbean	0.0	0.0	0.0	0.0	0.0	0.0	0.0	0.0	0.0	0.0	Caraïbes	0.1	0.1	0.1	0.1	0.0	0.1	0.1	0.1	0.1	0.0
Rest of America	0.1	0.1	0.0	0.1	0.0	0.0	0.0	0.0	0.0	0.0	Autre Amérique	0.0	0.0	0.0	0.0	0.0	0.0	0.0	0.0	0.0	0.0
As.ex F.USSR	8.8	10.1	10.0	9.7	10.6	10.6	10.9	10.9	5.6	7.7	Asie l'URSS exclus	6.5	6.9	6.9	7.4	7.8	7.8	8.3	7.4	6.7	7.7
Eur.x F.USSR	81.5	81.0	80.6	80.7	80.1	80.6	79.8	79.3	85.9	82.7	Europe l'URSS exclus	83.1	82.9	83.0	83.7	84.1	84.7	83.3	83.6	77.0	83.7
EU	70.6	70.6	70.4	71.1	70.2	70.4	69.3	68.4	75.5	70.8	UE	66.2	66.7	66.6	67.9	68.0	68.1	65.5	64.8	58.6	64.2
EFTA	5.3	4.9	4.5	4.6	4.5	4.3	4.4	4.4	3.8	3.8	AELE	8.3	7.9	7.9	7.5	7.0	6.6	6.8	6.9	6.3	6.1
East Europe	4.7	4.5	4.4	3.9	4.4	5.0	5.2	5.6	5.6	6.8	Europe de l'Est	6.5	6.3	6.4	5.6	7.0	8.0	8.8	9.1	9.3	10.4
Other Europe	1.0	1.0	1.2	1.2	1.0	0.0	0.0	0.0	0.0	0.0	Autre de l'Europe	2.0	2.1	2.2	2.7	2.0	0.1	0.0	0.0	0.0	0.0
Former USSR	2.1	1.9	1.7	1.8	1.6	1.5	1.6	1.9	0.8	2.0	Ancienne URSS	2.5	2.9	2.7	2.2	1.9	1.7	1.7	1.8	1.9	2.0
Oceania	0.2	0.2	0.1	0.1	0.1	0.1	0.1	0.1	0.1	0.1	Océanie	0.5	0.5	0.5	0.5	0.4	0.4	0.4	0.4	0.5	0.6
Germany/Allemagne	44.2	44.5	43.6	44.0	43.0	42.9	41.5	40.0	47.8	42.9	Germany/Allemagne	34.8	35.0	34.5	37.4	39.0	39.8	39.0	38.1	34.8	37.4
Italy/Italie	9.4	8.9	9.0	9.1	8.8	8.6	9.0	8.8	8.4	8.8	Italy/Italie	10.4	10.4	10.5	9.8	9.4	8.8	7.9	8.1	7.9	8.3
France, Monac	4.1	3.9	4.4	4.2	4.4	4.4	4.4	4.7	4.7	4.8	Switz.Liecht	7.4	7.2	7.3	6.9	6.4	5.9	6.2	6.4	5.8	5.4
USA/Etats–Unis d'Amer	3.5	3.4	3.6	3.6	4.0	3.9	4.4	4.4	3.1	4.5	France, Monac	4.5	4.6	4.7	4.8	4.3	4.4	4.4	4.6	3.6	4.3
Switz.Liecht	4.7	4.4	4.1	4.3	4.2	4.0	4.1	4.1	3.6	3.6	Hungary/Hongrie	1.9	1.8	2.0	2.2	3.0	3.2	3.5	3.9	3.6	4.0
Japan/Japon	4.4	5.1	4.9	4.5	4.8	4.7	4.4	4.3	1.7	2.4	United Kingdom	4.6	4.7	4.5	3.9	3.6	3.6	3.3	3.2	2.9	3.5
Netherlands/Pays–Bas	2.8	2.8	2.8	2.8	2.7	2.7	2.9	3.0	4.4	3.2	USA/Etats–Unis d'Amer	3.6	3.5	3.5	3.2	2.8	2.6	3.3	3.5	2.8	3.2
United Kingdom	2.4	2.5	2.5	2.6	2.7	2.7	2.7	2.9	2.5	3.0	Netherlands/Pays–Bas	2.7	2.6	3.0	2.9	3.0	2.9	3.0	3.0	2.5	2.6
Belgium–Luxembourg	2.4	2.7	2.7	2.9	3.0	3.0	2.9	2.9	2.7	2.3	Czech Republic							2.4	2.6	2.7	2.9
Hungary/Hongrie	1.5	1.4	1.5	1.6	1.9	2.0	1.9	2.0	1.8	2.7	Spain/Espagne	1.8	1.9	2.2	2.2	2.2	2.4	2.1	2.1	1.9	2.2

4. Special Imports C.I.F. by Commodities according to the S.I.T.C. (Rev. 2) in thousand U.S. Dollars
Importations Spéciales C.A.F. par Produits d'après la C.T.C.I. (Rév. 2) en milliers de Dollars E.U.

SITC CTCI	COMMODITY	1993 WEIGHT POIDS	1993 VALUE VALEUR	1994 WEIGHT POIDS	1994 VALUE VALEUR	1995 WEIGHT POIDS	1995 VALUE VALEUR	1996 WEIGHT POIDS	1996 VALUE VALEUR	PRODUIT
	ALL COMMODITIES		48561265		55290451		65662454		67283792	TOUS PRODUITS
0	FOOD AND LIVE ANIMALS		2324203		2663553		3575658		3639519	ALIMENTS,ANIMAUX VIVANTS
01	MEAT AND PREPARATIONS		107964		115529		345924		381327	VIANDES ET PREPARATIONS
011	MEAT FRESH,CHILLD,FROZEN	W 24617	91030	W 25115	94367	W 78274	274593	W 88388	297750	VIANDES FRAICHES,REF,CONGE
02	DAIRY PRODCTS,BIRDS'EGGS		156138		170347		240628		290881	PRODUITS LAITIERS,OEUFS
03	FISH AND PREPARATIONS		145828		182536		176783		190542	POISSONS ET PREPARATIONS
04	CEREALS AND PREPARATIONS		246391		302556		395666		467899	CEREALES ET PRODUITS
048	CEREAL ETC PREPARATIONS	W 98673	185618	W 91298	214833	W 119821	323850	W 145436	342026	PREPTNS A BASE CEREALES
0484	BAKERY PRODUCTS	W 41382	123417	W 48230	145347	W 66181	213319	W 78560	234574	PRODUITS DE BOULANGERIE
05	VEGETABLES AND FRUIT		875265		958371		1202878		1107963	LEGUMES ET FRUITS
054	VEG ETC FRSH,SMPLY PRSVD	W 232023	235184	W 241894	245563	W 379179	460939	W 362909	334082	LEGUMES FRAIS,CONG,SECS
0545	OTHER FRESH VEGETABLES	W 112058	134317	W 124053	136991	W 156614	278185	W 170181	192390	AUTRES LEGUMES FRAIS,REF
05459	FRESH VEGETABLES NES	W 100396	120515	W 111370	123718	W 135549	252019	W 146168	174157	LEGUMES FRAIS,REFRI NDA
057	FRUIT,NUTS,FRESH,DRIED	W 784090	446299		477097	W 599024	475338	W 628091	507223	FRUITS FRAIS OU SECS
0579	FRUIT FRESH OR DRIED NES	W 148424	144000	W 164545	166765	W 145026	153660	W 160742	166213	FRUITS FRAIS,SECS NDA
058	FRUIT PRESERVED,PREPARED	W 141263	152310	W 169793	193131	W 126553	202181	W 155589	207238	CONSERVES DE FRUITS
07	COFFEE,TEA,COCOA,SPICES		332979		434610		556239		502204	CAFE,THE,CACAO,EPICES
071	COFFEE AND SUBSTITUTES	W 105071	158826	W 82091	237914	W 67008	270284	W 69777	211385	CAFE ET SUCCEDANES
0711	COFFEE GREEN,ROASTED,SUB	W 101300	135144	W 79050	208399	W 64554	240615	W 67456	186940	CAFE TORREFIE OU DECAFEINE
07111	COFFEE GREEN,HUSKS,SKINS	W 99236	126927	W 76222	197392	W 62602	228994	W 63818	169034	CAFE NON TORREFIE
081	*FEEDING STUFF FOR ANIML	W 658984	187319	W 647336	189210	W 632114	212098	W 560794	217241	NOURRITURE POUR ANIMAUX
09	MISC EDIBLE PRODUCTS		174512		197995		254706		247257	PREP ALIMENTAIRES DIVERSES
098	EDIBLE PRODCTS,PREPS NES	W 43403	168096	W 44738	190278	W 55748	241658	W 56630	234587	PREP ALIMENTAIRES NDA
1	BEVERAGES AND TOBACCO		187061		216914		278806		261359	BOISSONS ET TABACS
11	BEVERAGES		127374		144479		208379		201764	BOISSONS
2	CRUDE MATERLS,EXCL FUELS		1875103		2323131		3055962		2513590	MAT BRUTES NON COMESTIBLES
24	CORK AND WOOD		526195		655434		785533		650839	LIEGE ET BOIS
247	OTH WOOD ROUGH,SQUARED	W 3611196	247569	W 3849815	303459	W 3909305	391623	W 3684318	322635	BOIS BRUTS EQUARRIS
2471	SAW–,VENEER–LOGS CONIFER	W 2755158	196927	W 3105946	254873	W 3061634	322598	W 2850943	265887	CONIFERES POUR SCIAGE,PLACAG
24711	— IN THE ROUGH	W 2755158	196927	W 3105946	254873	W 3061634	322598	W 2850943	265887	ECORCES OU DEGROSSIS
248	WOOD SHAPED,SLEEPERS	W 550631	239079	W 689997	297560	W 726143	332651	W 626448	270867	BOIS SIMPLEMENT TRAVAILLES
2482	LUMBER SHAPED CONIFER	W 421078	158744	W 518990	197376	W 544463	221697	W 468647	175947	CONIFERES SCIES,RABOTES
24821	LUMBER SAWN ETC CONIFER	W 399380	134003	W 500617	174322	W 527886	201022	W 452591	156775	CONIFERES SCIES LONGITUD
251	*PULP AND WASTE PAPER	W 953359	244612	W 1067044	348656	W 1132536	587485	W 1131185	347682	PATES A PAPIER,DECHETS
2517	SODA,SULPHATE WOOD PULP	W 383607	155112	W 425385	217342	W 422415	357048	W 437786	234624	PATES CHIMIQUES AU SULFATE
25172	— BLEACHED,NONDISSOLVNG	W 383132	154935	W 421823	215974	W 415552	352420	W 437252	234347	PATES BLANCHIES
27	CRUDE FERTLZR,MINRLS NES		202213		223030		289319		263062	ENGRAIS MINERAUX BRUTS
278	OTHER CRUDE MINERALS	W 723571	142460		164947	W 1023428	207307	W 1087990	180859	AUTRES MINERAUX BRUTS
28	METALLIFEROUS ORES,SCRAP		327333		432721		628875		508644	MINERAIS METAL,DECHETS
288	NONFERR METAL SCRAP NES	W 122027	111851	W 145302	173678	W 175699	282711	W 165497	215953	DECHETS NON FERREUX
2882	OTHER BASE MTL SCRAP NES	W 95128	102046	W 119748	163362	W 156537	271000	W 63859	107140	AUTRES DECHETS
29	CRUDE ANIMAL,VEG MAT NES		292944		325501		354697		367604	MATIERES BRUTES ANIM,VEGET
292	CRUDE VEG MATERIALS NES	W 67650	244059		271089	W 87140	292961	W 69579	303416	MAT BRUTES VEGETALES NDA
3	MINERAL FUELS ETC		2474467		2469546		3018687		3638280	COMBUSTIBLES MINERAUX LUB
32	COAL,COKE AND BRIQUETTES		299369		276529		326992		366811	HOUILLES,COKES,BRIQUETTES
322	COAL,LIGNITE AND PEAT	W 3282634	202949	W 3123076	186139	W 3084458	212905	W 3830131	262497	HOUILLES,LIGNITES,TOURBE
3222	OTH COAL,NOT AGGLOMERATD	W 3173276	189048	W 2996596	170973	W 2976773	198461	W 3659783	241566	AUTRES HOUILLES
33	PETROLEUM AND PRODUCTS		1567457		1588323		1832434		2227779	PETROLE ET DERIVES
333	CRUDE PETROLEUM	W 7453315	979824	W 7789848	970358	W 7599280	1031240	W 7728454	1245677	HUILES BRUTES DE PETROLE
334	PETROLEUM PRODUCTS,REFIN	W 2690760	533309	W 2903390	562437	W 3316547	730360	W 3723206	905513	PRODUITS RAFFINES
3343	GAS OILS	W 1275309	240423	W 432431	84067			W 2244270	521304	GAS OILS
3345	LUBS,PETROLEUM OILS NES	W 184134	92386	W 2008793	436652	W 146680	42887	W 193066	141410	HUILES LUBRIFIANTES
33451	LUBS(HIGH PETR CONT) ETC	W 174440	64993	W 1997286	403523			W 178059	97798	HUILES LUBRIF,H LOURDES
341	*GAS,NATURAL AND MANUFCT	W 4090941	514798	W 3769158	469874	W 4793688	683707	W 4963796	725220	GAZ NATUREL,GAZ MANUFACT
3413	PETROLM GASES,LIQUEFIED	W 166212	32991	W 135308	27884	W 161974	37895	W 155701	42161	GAZ DE PETROLE LIQUEFIE
34139	OTH HYDROCARBON GAS LQFD	W 22336	3010	W 17526	3536	W 13161	2022	W 700	90	HYDROCARBURES GAZEUX NDA
3414	PETROLEUM GASES, GASEOUS	W 3924729	481808	W 3633850	441990	W 4631672	645771	W 4807312	682893	GAZ DE PETROLE GAZEUX
351	*ELECTRIC CURRENT		92843		134819		175554		318470	ENERGIE ELECTRIQUE
5	CHEMCLS,RELATED PROD NES		4843685		5495438		6642220		6658273	PRODUITS CHIMIQUES
51	ORGANIC CHEMICALS		492720		576935		702194		693807	PROD CHIMIQ ORGANIQUES
52	INORGANIC CHEMICALS		286255		335918		405355		406732	PROD CHIM INORGANIQUES
522	INORG ELEMNTS,OXIDES,ETC	W 400392	164122		204240	W 418068	254603	W 472427	249391	ELEMENTS INORGANIQUES
53	DYES,TANNING,COLOUR PROD		424803		483515		535127		538256	PROD TEINTURE,COLORANTS
533	PIGMENTS,PAINTS,ETC	W 158937	334147	W 181709	386447	W 183678	426211	W 173708	428151	PIGMENTS,PEINTURES,VERNIS
5334	VARNISHES,DISTEMPERS ETC	W 49029	157625	W 55243	182395	W 66851	192018	W 51635	199223	PEINTURES A L'EAU
541	*MEDICINAL,PHARM PRODUCT		1228777		1341013		1647854		1842195	PROD MEDICINAUX PHARMACEUT
5416	GLYCOSIDES,GLANDS,SERA	K 1742100	214242		211054	K 2317581	270884	K 2755917	285169	HETEROSIDES
54164	ANTISERA,MICROB VACCINES	K 1538700	189385		188225	K 1581046	235804	K 1453858	241561	SERUMS,VACCINS
5417	MEDICAMENTS	MK 15440	787662		892373	MK 13586	1078173	MK 15913	1121888	MEDICAMENTS
54179	— CONTNG OTH SUBSTANCES	MK 13803	630363		715445	MK 11886	841466	MK 14283	892270	MED CONT AUT SUBSTANCES
55	PERFUME,CLEANING ETC PRD		511242		580588		677343		684420	PROD POUR PARFUM,TOILETTE
553	PERFUMERY,COSMETICS,ETC	W 32497	284648		335086	W 47803	387958	W 47474	413413	PRODUITS DE PARFUMERIE
554	SOAP,CLEANSING ETC PREPS	W 124476	186903		198452	W 130336	231438	W 145021	216069	SAVONS,PRODUITS DETERSIFS
5542	WASHING PREPARATIONS ETC	W 108498	151900	W 113595	163083	W 116423	197237	W 130245	182550	PROD ORG TENSIO–ACT NDA
58	PLASTIC MATERIALS ETC		1235926		1468763		1766129		1620514	MAT PLAST ARTIFICIELLES
582	PROD OF CONDENSATION ETC	W 231155	375131	W 276212	456269	W 274675	564545	W 315448	520546	PROD CONDENS,POLYCOND
5823	ALKYDS,OTHER POLYESTERS	W 66281	144668	W 88385	179525	W 84561	229925	W 75873	188321	ALKYDES ET AUT POLYESTERS
58231	— IN PRIMARY FORMS	W 62824	122725	W 84726	156339	W 79991	197959	W 71757	159744	SOUS FORMES PRIMAIRES
583	POLYMERIZATION ETC PRODS	W 577851	825316	W 678678	973974	W 790777	1155949	W 1070858	1050970	PROD POLYMERISATION
5831	POLYETHYLENE	W 188524	179246	W 188535	186471	W 158734	208865	W 307389	193760	POLYETHYLENE
5839	OTH POLYMRZTION ETC PROD	W 49949	192400	W 94422	269860	W 193073	304921	W 178938	307926	AUT PROD POLYMER COPOLYM
59	CHEMICAL MATERIALS NES		589209		624903		815927		774848	MAT PROD CHIMIQUES NDA
598	MISCEL CHEM PRODUCTS NES	W 332088	439425		461478	W 564027	607013	W 460340	552407	PROD DIV INDUST CHIM NDA
5989	CHEM PRODUCTS,PREPS NES	W 278455	382963		396037	W 502480	532977	W 398572	480637	PROD PREP CHIMIQUES NDA
59899	OTH CHEM PRODS,PREPS,NES	W 210189	298201	W 218853	319326	W 455288	438380	W 204052	383387	AUT PRODUITS CHIMIQUES NDA
6	BASIC MANUFACTURES		9191578		10807055		12737698		12482906	ART MANUFACTURES
61	LEATHER,DRESSED FUR,ETC		232108		267509		299179		326753	CUIRS,PELLETERIES
62	RUBBER MANUFACTURES NES		599199		624621		791191		755403	CAOUTCHOUC MANUFACTURE
625	RUBBER TYRES, TUBES ETC	W 75580	351695	W 76833	342826	W 99187	441837	W 90583	416120	PNEUS CAOUTCHOUC VULCANISE
6251	TYRES NEW FOR MOTOR CARS	W 39505	215655	W 37889	197741	W 45799	240910	W 47307	242210	PNEUS POUR VOITURES
628	RUBBER ARTICLES NES	W 13225	142295		160577	W 18481	206198	W 16331	192758	OUVRAGES CAOUTCHOUC NDA
63	WOOD,CORK MANUFACTRS NES		478253		568263		668946		659644	OUVRAGES LIEGE ET BOIS
634	VENEERS,PLYWOOD,ETC	W 157276	145271	W 183050	173961	W 174953	216525	W 169706	197034	PLACAGES,CONTRE–PLAQUES
635	WOOD MANUFACTURES NES	W 179938	310280	W 212633	371425	W 235806	420335	W 243774	431288	ART MANUF EN BOIS NDA
6353	BUILDERS WOODWRK,PREFABS	W 95295	232427	W 109181	279703	W 106302	308223	W 125300	320031	OUVRAGES DE MENUISERIE
64	PAPER,PAPERBOARD AND MFR		1032801		1202885		1471000		1467292	PAPIERS,CARTONS & OUVRAGES
641	PAPER AND PAPERBOARD	W 677626	637885		751401	W 826131	998397	W 875227	980610	PAPIERS ET CARTONS
6412	PRINTG,WRITING PAPER NES	W 165139	154393	W 195489	187388	W 198595	256838	W 233452	254793	PAPIERS POUR L'IMPRESSION
64122	— COATED,IMPREGNATD ETC	W 155043	142071	W 179847	169411	W 173860	220224	W 208907	221834	PAPIERS IMPRESSION COUCHES
6415	PAPER,PAPERBRD,BULK,NES	W 255149	195522		215261	W 272821	291029	W 279417	256256	PAPIERS,CARTONS ROULEAUX
64159	OTHER PAPER ETC,BULK,NES	W 236049	179240		194345	W 257311	273120	W 265038	238513	AUT PAPIER ROULEAUX FEUILLES

4. Special Imports C.I.F. by Commodities according to the S.I.T.C. (Rev. 2) in thousand U.S. Dollars
Importations Spéciales C.A.F. par Produits d'après la C.T.C.I. (Rév. 2) en milliers de Dollars E.U.

SITC CTCI	COMMODITY	1993 WEIGHT POIDS	1993 VALUE VALEUR	1994 WEIGHT POIDS	1994 VALUE VALEUR	1995 WEIGHT POIDS	1995 VALUE VALEUR	1996 WEIGHT POIDS	1996 VALUE VALEUR	PRODUIT
6418	COATED ETC PAPER NES BLK	W 91161	165078		203979	W 155294	244399	W 121132	255066	PAP,CARTONS COUCHES,ENDUITS
642	PAPER,ETC,PRECUT,ARTS OF	W 174051	394915		451484	W 196509	472603	W 204933	486681	PAP,CARTONS DECOUPES
6428	PAPER ETC ARTICLES NES	W 79831	185517		203301	W 80847	206366	W 88186	211867	OUVRAGES EN PATE A PAPIER
65	TEXTILE YARN,FABRICS,ETC		1709676		1817910		1972686		1910888	FILS,TISSUS,ARTICLES TEXTILE
651	TEXTILE YARN	W 69509	411652	W 73148	446456	W 69754	478909	W 65997	457889	FILS TEXTILES
652	COTTON FABRICS,WOVEN	W 13049	177140	W 14356	181741	W 12892	192682		190813	TISSUS DE COTON
653	WOVN MAN-MADE FIB FABRIC	W 11431	192587	W 12295	201968	W 26150	215876	W 14340	203512	TISSUS FIBRES SYNTH,ARTIF
657	SPECIAL TXTL FABRC,PRODS	W 21347	182739		202955	W 25400	223553	W 23539	224097	TISSUS SPECIAUX
658	TEXTILE ARTICLES NES	W 17873	179882		209484	W 24194	252623	W 23032	276986	ART FACONNES MAT TEXTILES
659	FLOOR COVERINGS,ETC	W 32300	218427	W 33678	218068	W 39543	231184	W 33540	213749	COUVRE-PARQUETS,TAPIS ETC
66	NONMETAL MINERAL MFS NES		1029130		1172404		1375950		1363234	ART MIN NON METALLIQUES
661	LIME,CEMENT,BLDG PRODS	W 726598	138674		178254	W 1529326	196536	W 1561476	195180	CHAUX,CIMENTS MAT CONSTR
662	CLAY,REFRACTORY BLDG PRD	W 473427	239675		268611	W 498313	293819	W 492915	272036	MAT CONST REFRACTAIRES
6624	BRICKS ETC NONREFRACTORY	W 430487	206130	W 513323	231983	W 429201	236916	W 427655	227194	BRIQUES ETC CERAM NON REFR
66245	GLAZED CERAMIC SETTS ETC	W 233668	156462	W 248923	171402	W 216487	173445	W 224798	159577	AUT CARREAUX CERAMIQUE
663	MINERAL MANUFCTURES NES	W 326555	221761		252434	W 387995	298708	W 386190	284333	ART MIN MANUF NDA
664	GLASS	W 141629	186289		196782	W 168927	250355	W 184677	277758	VERRE
67	IRON AND STEEL		1191092		1492512		1980814		1743892	FER ET ACIER
673	IRON,STEEL SHAPES ETC	W 522674	253924	W 575756	294331	W 547892	379025	W 560702	335024	BARRES,PROFIL FER,ACIER
6732	IRON,STEEL BARS ETC	W 258005	129854	W 280335	154689	W 291192	224218	W 322139	211870	BARRES FER,ACIER
674	IRN,STL UNIV,PLATE,SHEET	W 576947	407181	W 727562	532935	W 696114	675744	W 678308	551268	LARGES PLATS,TOLES
6746	IRN,STL THIN PLATE,ROLLD	W 138140	120185	W 178185	156779	W 170148	214753	W 166516	155401	TOLES LAM MOINS 3MM
6749	OTH IRN,STL PLATES,SHEET	W 184398	123178	W 253706	176202	W 234944	196279	W 228090	164552	AUTRES TOLES FER,ACIER
678	IRON,STL TUBES,PIPES,ETC	W 237545	290336	W 277690	346519	W 291134	455210	W 260307	406827	TUBES,TUYAUX EN FONTE,FER
68	NON-FERROUS METALS		1041335		1485744		1584628		1486870	METAUX NON FERREUX
682	COPPER EXC CEMENT COPPER	W 122451	342011		420938	W 261940	546121	W 158652	494434	CUIVRE
6822	COPPER,ALLOYS WORKED	W 100543	299115		338480	W 216740	416780	W 110257	379553	CUIVRE,ALLIAGES OUVRES
68221	COPPER BARS,WIRE,ETC	W 70731	165859		192812	W 61145	200370	W 74620	193607	BARRES,PROFILES ET FILS
684	ALUMINIUM	W 270161	521289	W 417575	833424	W 279772	780590	W 312487	725853	ALUMINIUM
6841	ALUMINIUM,ALLOYS,UNWRGHT	W 178783	224739	W 299027	456131	W 163730	336159	W 195481	334958	ALUMINIUM,ALLIAGES BRUTS
6842	ALUMINIUM,ALLOYS WORKED	W 91378	296550	W 118548	377293	W 116043	444432	W 117006	390895	ALUMINIUM,ALLIAGES OUVRE
69	METAL MANUFACTURES NES		1877984		2175208		2593302		2768931	ART MANUFACT EN METAL NDA
691	STRUCTURES AND PARTS NES	W 116796	317392	W 130863	352691	W 133805	418081	W 153043	442258	CONSTRUCT FER,ACIER,ALU
6911	STRUCTURES,PARTS IRN,STL	W 105253	227678	W 118214	255745	W 116999	296015	W 134256	312239	CONSTRUCT FER,ACIER,FONTE
694	STL,COPPR NAILS,NUTS,ETC	W 45054	179557		217733	W 63876	281574	W 62062	269270	CLOUS,VIS,ECROUS
69402	IRN,STL NUTS,BOLTS,ETC	W 37253	159041		194098	W 53646	252853	W 53174	242725	BOULONS,VIS,ECROUS FER,AC
695	TOOLS	W 15138	265962		295878	W 21100	379956	W 20492	387271	OUTILS A MAIN
6954	BLADES,TIPS,ETC FR TOOLS	W 4830	165813		174361	W 7110	222801	W 6055	223462	OUTILS POUR MACHINE-OUTIL
697	BASE MTL HOUSEHOLD EQUIP	W 29490	176387	W 30925	201696	W 31737	204379	W 38026	227031	ART MENAGE MET COMMUNS
699	BASE METAL MFRS NES	W 117819	681823		799195		959312	W 187977	1079390	ART MANUFACTURES MET NDA
6991	LOCKSMITHS WARES,ETC	W 29638	249108		288016	W 43162	355516	W 46090	372936	ARTICLES DE SERRURERIE
69913	BASE MTL DOOR,ETC FITTNG	W 24341	205353		240816	W 37168	297472	W 39844	310859	GARNITURES POUR MEUBLES
6997	IRON,STEEL ARTICLES NES	W 56164	202321		224758	W 70884	254112	W 93864	369431	OUV FONTE,FER,ACIER NDA
69979	IRN,STL MANUFACTURES NES	W 56144	202264		224690	W 70850	253954	W 93850	369371	AUT OUVRAGES EN FER NDA
7	MACHINES,TRANSPORT EQUIP		18290641		20979463		24045597		25438556	MACHINES MATERIEL TRANSPORT
71	POWER GENERATING EQUIPMT		1149830		1326878		1602208		1617143	MACHINES GENERATRICES
713	INTRNL COMBUS PSTN ENGIN	W 82873	753420		859412	W 110332	1044157	W 120815	1129497	MOTEURS EXPL COMB INT, PIECE
7132	MOTOR VEHCL PISTN ENGINS	W 13786	243149	W 15728	222332	W 18176	280175	W 25282	320307	MOTEURS EXPL POUR VEHICULES
7139	PISTON ENGINE PARTS NES	W 65846	466298		589218	W 86789	704040	W 91419	755600	PIECES POUR 713.2,3,8
716	ROTATING ELECTRIC PLANT	W 17606	237613	W 21372	268643	W 21083	278025	W 18938	250955	APP ELECTR ROTATIFS,PIECES
7162	AC MTRS,GENRTRS,GEN SETS	W 11860	151183	W 14654	184147	W 12605	187309	W 12014	165481	MOTEURS ELECTRIQUES
72	MACHS FOR SPCL INDUSTRYS		1645468		1825179		1972729		2117173	MAC SPECIALES POUR INDUST
721	AGRIC MACHY,EXC TRACTORS	W 26626	162897		187856	W 36292	258050	W 40896	281642	MACHINES AGRICOLES
723	CIVIL ENGNEERG EQUIP ETC	W 32777	211747	W 41060	262261	W 34901	267804	W 39809	277266	APPAREILS DE GENIE CIVIL
7234	CONST,MINING MACHNRY NES	W 28762	188251	W 35480	232684	W 29589	224821	W 34687	241173	MACH POUR LA CONST, MINES
72342	SLFPRP SHOVELS,EXCAVATRS	W 23818	141900	W 29455	181099	W 24555	175392	W 28323	177569	PELLES MECANIQUES
726	PRINTG,BKBINDG MACHY,PTS	W 8529	184971	W 6401	163852	W 31041	145396	W 6837	198991	MACHINES POUR IMPRIMERIE
728	OTH MACHY FOR SPCL INDUS	W 48111	644073	W 57109	721863	W 47578	806620	W 54418	793116	AUT MACH IND PARTICULIERES
7281	MACH-TOOLS FR SPCL INDUS	W 12354	141110	W 15089	173982	W 13067	177607	W 13984	182197	MACH-OUTILS SPEC IND PART
7284	MACHY FOR SPCL INDUS NES	W 24998	427770	W 29019	464965	W 22037	510840	W 28393	509426	MACH SPEC IND PARTICUL.
72848	OTH MCHY WITH INDIV FNCT	W 9904	202084	W 10308	224943	W 10603	206465	W 7983	189858	AUTRES MACHINES NDA
72849	PTS OF MACHS OF 7284 ETC	W 10661	136118	W 14125	139496	W 7207	198654	W 15847	195840	PIECES DU 728.4 ETC
73	METALWORKING MACHINERY		451099		454872		604076		694745	MACH TRAVAIL DES METAUX
736	METALWORKING MACH-TOOLS	W 21436	374385	W 24765	364308	W 21923	501474	W 22408	551718	MACH-OUTILS TRAVAIL METAUX
74	GENRL INDUSTRL MACHY NES		2873850		3309803		4030616		3920922	MACH APP INDUSTRIE
741	HEATING,COOLING EQUIPMNT	W 33980	421113		444707	W 40217	509747	W 47472	563880	MACH CHAUFFAGE,PIECES
7416	HEATING,COOLING EQU NES	W 13549	193006		196666	W 11824	188089	W 15251	213014	APP CHANGEMENT TEMP
742	PUMPS FOR LIQUIDS ETC	W 13121	271771	W 15533	336404	W 16742	408891	W 16479	375584	POMPES MOTO-POMPES
7428	OTHER PUMPS FOR LIQUIDS	W 6149	151052	W 7354	195669	W 5743	163935	W 5911	166948	AUTRES POMPES POUR LIQ
74288	PUMPS FR LIQUIDS NES ETC	W 5718	137576	W 6670	173792	W 5538	156088	W 5502	149994	POMPES POUR LIQUIDES NDA
743	PUMPS NES,CENTRFUGES ETC	W 32695	384150		438556	W 46204	512972	W 45248	527165	POMPES COMPRES,VENT ETC
744	MECHANICAL HANDLING EQU	W 65692	439710	W 86730	512728	W 98580	639026	W 91761	620138	EQUIP MANUTENTION PIECES
7442	LIFTING,LOADING MACH NES	W 26409	210633	W 30233	233032	W 38867	248474	W 31390	261419	APP LEVAGE,MANUTENTION
7449	PTS NES OF MACHY OF 7442	W 29361	162496	W 44861	204354	W 48308	293942	W 48984	270480	PIECES DU 744.2
745	NONELEC MACHY,TOOLS NES	W 21435	375817		445603	W 30781	558109	W 30447	518014	AUT MACH NON ELEC,PIECES
7452	OTH NONELEC MCHS,PTS NES	W 20277	347517		407681	W 29054	509587	W 28517	464660	AUT MACH NON ELEC,PIECES
749	NONELEC MACH PTS,ACC NES	W 72201	981289		1131804	W 121531	1401870	W 105584	1316141	PIECES MACH NON ELEC NDA
7491	BALL,ROLLER,ETC BEARINGS	W 10564	126743		168454	W 18996	211373	W 21625	210539	ROULEMENTS BILLES ETC
7492	COCKS,VALVES ETC NES	W 17765	359152		407556	W 25154	611162	W 24772	496148	ART ROB,SIM POUR TUYAUX
7493	SHAFT,CRANK,PULLEY ETC	W 37451	325146		370064	W 68815	396994	W 50840	417396	ARBRES TRANS,VILEBREQUINS
7499	OTH NONELEC MCHY PTS NES	W 6420	170248		185730	W 8567	182341	W 8347	192058	PIECES NON ELECT NDA
75	OFFICE MACHNES,ADP EQUIP		1683677		1979013		1998470		2029266	MACH BUREAU TRAIT AUTOM
751	OFFICE MACHINES	W 4453	146819	W 5910	196304	W 4759	165186	W 4999	165929	MACH,APPAREILS DE BUREAU
752	AUTOMTIC DATA PROC EQUIP	W 12251	916864	W 14332	1083822	W 16884	1195711	W 13740	1192196	MACH TRAIT INFORMATION
7523	DIGITL CENTRL PROCESSORS	W 2764	321409	W 3291	390734	W 3276	396757	W 2884	358836	UNITES CENTRALES
7525	ADP PERIPHERAL UNITS	W 7736	343092	W 9081	387414	W 8536	361265	W 8415	332118	UNITES PERIPHERIQUES
759	OFFICE,ADP MCH PTS,ACCES	W 5822	619994		698887	W 8493	637572	W 7677	671141	PIECES DU 751 ET 752
7599	ACCTG,ETC,ADP MCH PTS,AC	W 4676	563643		629192	W 7235	583567	W 6554	607766	PIECES DU 751 ET 752
76	TELECOMM,SOUND EQUIPMENT		1294842		1450470		1373762		1649602	EQUIPMENT DE TELECOM
761	TELEVISION RECEIVERS	W 11792	188913	W 13090	203323	W 12198	219494	W 14478	232459	RECEPTEURS DE TELEVISION
7611	COLOUR TV RECEIVERS	W 11706	185420	W 13021	201254	W 12076	214448	W 14389	229948	RECEPTEURS COULEUR
764	TELECOM EQPT,PTS,ACC NES	W 22181	876186		1001806	W 14369	869560	W 20449	1051762	EQUIP TELECOM,PIECES
7641	LINE TELEPHONE,ETC EQUIP	W 1521	135488	W 1683	155990	W 1914	207974	W 2013	203431	APP TELEPHON PAR FIL
7649	PTS NES OF EQUIPMT OF 76	W 15299	517942		606622	W 7829	428212	W 11949	539050	PIECES DE LA DIV 76
76493	TELECOMM EQUIPMT PTS NES	W 5552	189879	W 6638	239099	W 3134	147432	W 6280	239687	PIECES 761,762,764.3,8
76499	PARTS ETC OF SOUND EQUIP	W 7918	213164		221544	W 3166	85328	W 3786	115687	PIECES NDA POUR 763
77	ELECTRIC MACHNRY NES ETC		3290514		3901876		4321788		4574039	MACH APP ELECT NDA
771	ELECTRIC POWER MACHY NES	W 10799	224020		283443	W 11863	276661	W 15248	280590	MACH PROD,TRANS ELECTR
7712	OTH ELEC POWER MACHY NES	W 6285	159157		207330	W 8128	207596	W 10393	198997	AUT APP PROD TRANSF ELEC
772	SWITCHGEAR ETC,PARTS NES	W 22779	686906		809912	W 45245	913138	W 35302	926421	APP COUPURE,SECT ETC
7721	SWITCHGEAR ETC	W 21606	608242		718800	W 43588	818768	W 33428	817729	APP COUPURE,SECTIONMNT

4. Special Imports C.I.F. by Commodities according to the S.I.T.C. (Rev. 2) in thousand U.S. Dollars
Importations Spéciales C.A.F. par Produits d'après la C.T.C.I. (Rév. 2) en milliers de Dollars E.U.

SITC CTCI	COMMODITY	1993 WEIGHT POIDS	1993 VALUE VALEUR	1994 WEIGHT POIDS	1994 VALUE VALEUR	1995 WEIGHT POIDS	1995 VALUE VALEUR	1996 WEIGHT POIDS	1996 VALUE VALEUR	PRODUIT
773	ELECTR DISTRIBUTNG EQUIP	W 44481	272143		303609	W 105960	443182	W 66498	580600	EQUIPMT DISTRIBUTION ELECT
7731	INSULATED WIRE,CABLE ETC	W 42129	239230		267777	W 103552	394143	W 63684	531918	FILS,CABLES ISOLES ELECT
775	HOUSEHOLD TYPE EQUIP NES	W 78452	616926		672199	W 83931	783136	W 92934	823350	MACH,APP USAGE DOMESTQUE
7758	ELECTRO–THERMIC APPL NES	W 26893	254023		280335	W 29112	305694	W 32608	344946	APP ELECTROTHERMIQ NDA
77586	ELECTROTHERM DOM APP NES	W 15569	145709	W 16677	168460	W 16609	191774	W 19408	217693	APP ELECTRO THERMIQUES
776	TRANSISTORS,VALVES,ETC	W 29565	627785		860082	W 22067	830485	W 25559	759476	LAMPES,TUBES,VALVES
7761	TV PICTURE TUBES	W 16716	110765		193713	W 15022	110409	W 19751	147345	TUBES CATHODIQUES
7764	ELECTRONIC MICROCIRCUITS	W 542	329237		427437	W 1917	445754	W 666	358651	MICROSTRUCTURES ELECTRON
778	ELECTRICAL MACHINERY NES	W 42544	719480		816056	W 57822	941596	W 66366	1049297	AUTRES MACH ELECT NDA
7783	AUTOMOTIVE ELECTR EQUIP	W 9662	184431		197829	W 12701	252620	W 12691	246745	EQUIP ELECT MOTEURS EXPL
7788	OTH ELEC MACHY,EQUIP NES	W 8924	280917		330678	W 11413	350221	W 15437	464174	AUT MACH APP ELEC NDA
78	ROAD VEHICLES		5610374		6326874		7436244		8134255	VEHICULES ROUTIERS
781	PASS MOTOR VEH EXC BUSES	W 305858	3388306	W 318639	3670438	W 324500	4290063	W 373374	4673522	AUTO TRANSPORT PERSONNES
782	LORRIES,SPCL MTR VEH NES	W 60618	577106	W 67523	663805	W 65807	683404	W 66384	679450	VEHICULES SPECIAUX,MARCH
7821	LORRIES,TRUCKS	W 54233	502122	W 60726	580035	W 61369	630971	W 61552	632343	VEHICULES TRANSP MARCHAND
783	ROAD MOTOR VEHICLES NES	W 14443	194088	W 16809	219744	W 20722	313710	W 31152	368656	VEHICULES ROUTIERS NDA
7832	TRACTORS FOR TR–TRAILERS	W 9389	87182	W 12204	124685	W 13088	170661	W 25313	265976	TRACTEURS ROUTIERS
784	MOTOR VEH PRTS,ACCES NES	W 149322	1047973		1263692	W 202290	1640708	W 229408	1847717	PIECES 722,781,782,783
7849	OTHER MOTOR VEHCL PARTS	W 143212	976653		1194390	W 195719	1545873	W 223544	1768874	PIECES 722,781,782,783
785	CYCLES,ETC MOTRZD OR NOT	W 15894	245974		309863	W 13680	253955	W 17707	315838	MOTOCYCLES SCOOTERS
786	TRAILERS,NONMOTR VEH,NES	W 45858	156928		199331	W 61263	254404	W 63251	249072	REMORQUES,CADRES,CONTAIN
79	OTHR TRANSPORT EQUIPMENT		290988		404498		705704		701411	AUTRE MATERIEL TRANSPORT
792	AIRCRAFT ETC	W 360	135045	W 441	213806	W 1008	519434	W 882	557305	APP NAVIGATION AERIENNE
7924	AIRCRFT NES OVER 15000KG	W 74	68877	W 29	42012	W 505	394411	W 351	368247	AERODYNES PLUS 15000 KG
8	MISC MANUFACTURED GOODS		9180975		10021047		11856450		11956925	ART MANUFACTURES DIVERS
812	*PLUMBG,HEATNG,LGHTNG EQ	W 51683	354351	W 58385	404441	W 67337	449908	W 72584	486275	APPAR SANITAIRES CHAUFFAGE
8124	LIGHTING EQUIPMENT NES	W 19558	219604	W 21523	246550	W 31510	287708	W 28569	299587	APPAREILS ECLAIRAGE ETC
81242	LAMPS,FITTINGS BASE METL	W 12667	165012	W 15359	193767	W 17389	219908	W 18178	220652	APPAREILS D'ECLAIRAGE
821	*FURNITURE,PARTS THEREOF	W 238948	1100054		1244947	W 306466	1401037	W 354729	1596322	MEUBLES ET PIECES
8211	CHAIRS,SEATS AND PARTS	W 46138	307973		350114	W 59534	381918	W 67616	450561	SIEGES ET PIECES
82111	CHAIRS AND OTHER SEATS	W 40504	279628	W 46426	313129	W 50927	322863	W 54302	354739	SIEGES
8219	FURNITURE AND PARTS NES	W 181254	658148	W 208572	751137	W 233630	879270	W 270021	984218	AUTRES MEUBLES ET PIECES
82192	WOOD FURNITURE NES	W 133757	472965	W 152604	536567	W 171222	616306	W 199682	700973	MEUBLES NDA EN BOIS
84	CLOTHING AND ACCESSORIES		2525770		2666607		3050859		3186296	VETEMENTS
842	MENS OUTERWEAR NOT KNIT	W 10266	377765	W 10783	387524	W 13172	462506	W 12800	498816	VET DESSUS POUR HOMMES
8423	— TROUSERS,BREECHES ETC	W 5091	160664	W 5569	167686	W 6080	205088	W 6909	224404	PANTALONS HOMMES MAT TEX
843	WOMENS OUTERWEAR NONKNIT	W 14296	751039	W 16079	802512	W 20776	920339	W 18200	897140	VET DESSUS FEMMES MAT TEX
8431	— COATS AND JACKETS	W 2167	152730	W 2172	150183	W 3250	185297	W 2771	176322	MANT,VEST FEM MAT TEXTIL
8439	— OTHER OUTER GARMENTS	W 8193	319522	W 9283	352050	W 10773	352201	W 9605	362466	AUT VET DES FEM MAT TEXT
845	OUTERWEAR KNIT NONELASTC	W 17543	623301		641160	W 20057	691363	W 20787	744587	VET DESSOUS,ACCES BONNET
8451	— JERSEYS,PULLOVERS ETC	W 10364	371112		384361	W 7503	364889	W 10998	415801	CHANDAILS,PULL–OVERS ETC
8459	— OTHER,CLTHG ACCESRYS	W 6486	213917		218155	W 11399	266702	W 8564	268372	AUT VET DESSUS DE BONNE
846	UNDER GARMENTS KNITTED	W 12987	353908		383060	W 11468	464768	W 17308	515312	SOUS VETS DE BONNETERIE
8462	— OF COTTON NON ELASTIC	W 9629	233062		250516	W 7305	304769	W 12623	319431	SOUS–VET BONNET COTON
84629	—— OTHER	W 9629	233062		250516	W 7305	304769	W 12623	319431	AUT SOUS–VET BONNET COTON
848	HEADGEAR,NONTXTL CLOTHNG	W 6992	185759		210361	W 15879	214799	W 10295	230242	VET ACCES MAT AUT QUE TEX
851	*FOOTWEAR	W 28040	540212		568440	W 35350	658440	W 27709	696134	CHAUSSURES
85102	FOOTWEAR LEATHER	W 20990	465722	W 21917	490213	W 27712	556753	W 20986	599689	CHAUS SEMELLES EN CUIR
87	PRECISION INSTRUMNTS NES		914672		1047740		1193818		1225673	INSTRUM,APPAR SCIENT NDA
872	MEDICAL INSTRUMENTS NES	W 4581	241189		263636	W 6735	279700	W 6339	295994	INSTR,APP MEDIC–CHIR NDA
87202	OTH MEDICAL INSTRUMENTS	W 3908	214490		237300	W 5310	241887	W 5349	253305	INSTRUM,APP MEDECINE
874	MEASURNG,CONTROLNG INSTR		572014		657358	W 12322	775420	W 13397	791845	INSTRUMENTS DE MESURE
8743	GAS,LIQUID CONTROL INSTR	W 3691	189948		227728	W 4267	242636	W 5724	260729	APP,INSTR MESURE FLUIDES
88	PHOTO EQU,OPTICL GDS ETC		574124		607298		595196		625630	APP,FOURN PHOTO,OP,MONTR
882	PHOTO,CINEMA SUPPLIES	W 12340	201271		211022	W 10890	169994	W 14441	230934	PRODUITS PHOTO,CINEMA
8822	PHOTO FILM EXC DEV CINMA	W 7920	161125		167663	W 6307	124613	W 8493	177752	PLAQUES,PELLICULES,FILMS
885	WATCHES AND CLOCKS		158359		172610		184503		172182	HORLOGERIE
89	MISC MANUFCTRD GOODS NES		3035057		3338042		4342628		3983982	ART MANUFACTURES DIVERS
892	PRINTED MATTER	W 111846	758182		842716	W 96716	921016	W 107360	964544	IMPRIMES
8921	PRINTED BOOKS,GLOBES,ETC	W 24644	279618	W 25260	315362	W 11311	349125	W 29105	370243	LIVRES,BROCHURES,CARTES
89211	PRINTED BOOKS,PAMPHLETS	W 23621	269068	W 24194	304964	W 9837	335470	W 27914	356365	LIVRES,BROCHURES
8922	NEWSPAPERS,PERIODICALS	W 41690	230571	W 45590	250820	W 41864	290376	W 38073	255805	JOURNAUX ET PERIODIQUES
8928	PRINTED MATTER NES	W 44244	225950		256047	W 42385	260238	W 39082	319759	IMPRIMES NDA
893	ARTICLES OF PLASTIC NES		836338		937703		1683240		1180321	OUVRAGES EN MAT DIVIS 58
8931	PLSTC PACKG CONTNRS,LIDS	W 37823	147267	W 45756	165175	W 54935	199192	W 57429	192059	ART TRANSP EMBALLAGE ETC
8939	MISC PLASTIC ARTICLES	W 111536	640065		716356	W 204147	1416791	W 191613	903734	ART DIVERS EN MAT DIV 58
89399	OTHR PLASTC ARTICLES NES	W 98322	585902		656089	W 186771	1347041	W 174708	840409	AUT OUV MAT DIV 58
894	TOYS,SPORTING GOODS,ETC	W 36681	422854		495217	W 46124	545765	W 53440	624442	VOITURES ENFANTS,JOUETS
8942	TOYS,INDOOR GAMES ETC	W 24394	280311		311210	W 29569	336227	W 33948	381093	JOUETS,JEUX ETC
8947	OTH SPORT GDS,FAIR AMUSM	W 11123	133597	W 14086	140330	W 13992	176931	W 17285	211301	AUT ART DE SPORT
897	GOLD,SILVER WARE,JEWELRY		209372		209519		269774		260361	BIJOUTERIE,ORFEVRERIE
8973	PREC JEWLRY,GLD–SILVWARE		167173		162178		208708		211241	BIJOUX OR,ARGENT ORFEVRE
89731	PRECIOUS METAL JEWELLERY		153839		147487		181116		180464	ART BIJOUTERIE,JOAILLER
898	MUSICAL INSTRUMENTS,PTS	W 17318	463783		469182	W 20665	449895	W 15221	413683	INSTRUMENTS DE MUSIQUE
8983	SOUND RECRDNG TAPE,DISCS	W 15834	419028		419168	W 19084	391579	W 13620	358750	SUPPORTS SON POUR 763
89832	RECORDED DISCS,TAPES ETC	W 5878	302423		322720	W 11763	310178	W 5947	265907	DISQUES,PHONO,BANDES
899	OTHER MANUFACTURED GOODS		235047		268274		315625		333609	AUT ART MANUF DIVERS NDA
9	GOODS NOT CLASSD BY KIND		107087		214379		327662		563707	ART TRANSACT NON CLASSES
911	*MAIL NOT CLASSED BY KIN								347983	COLIS POSTAUX
951	*WAR FIREARMS,AMMUNITION	W 1909	72209	W 2794	184173	W 135	7336		69572	VEHIC BLINDES ARMES
971	*GOLD,NON MONETARY NES		28609		25363		248137		141367	OR NON MONETAIRE
97101	NONMON GLD UNWRT,SEMIMFD	K 1800	28430		25218	K 34705	247435	K 23933	139641	OR,ALLIAGES D'OR BRUTS

5. Special Exports F.O.B. by Commodities according to the S.I.T.C. (Rev. 2) in thousand U.S. Dollars
Exportations Spéciales F.O.B. par Produits d'après la C.T.C.I. (Rév. 2) en milliers de Dollars E.U.

SITC CTCI	COMMODITY	1993		1994		1995		1996		PRODUIT
		WEIGHT POIDS	VALUE VALEUR	WEIGHT POIDS	VALUE VALEUR	WEIGHT POIDS	VALUE VALEUR	WEIGHT POIDS	VALUE VALEUR	
	ALL COMMODITIES		40159112		45072235		57141495		57830507	TOUS PRODUITS
0	FOOD AND LIVE ANIMALS		1148038		1316332		1889768		2166066	ALIMENTS,ANIMAUX VIVANTS
01	MEAT AND PREPARATIONS		169399		189597		324527		393039	VIANDES ET PREPARATIONS
011	MEAT FRESH,CHILLD,FROZEN	W 47543	141280	W 45308	134287	W 91277	264631	W 113132	321918	VIANDES FRAICHES,REF,CONGE
02	DAIRY PRODCTS,BIRDS'EGGS		169302		171315		242451		285797	PRODUITS LAITIERS,OEUFS
04	CEREALS AND PREPARATIONS		189474		241031		305868		352525	CEREALES ET PRODUITS
048	CEREAL ETC PREPARATIONS	W 72389	112855	W 83970	125844	W 78341	164160	W 96084	198771	PREPTNS A BASE CEREALES
05	VEGETABLES AND FRUIT		169550		230622		342106		395208	LEGUMES ET FRUITS
058	FRUIT PRESERVED,PREPARED	W 82485	108826	W 134284	152665	W 142027	218178	W 133483	227708	CONSERVES DE FRUITS
07	COFFEE,TEA,COCOA,SPICES		156119		174558		215606		232098	CAFE,THE,CACAO,EPICES
073	CHOCOLATE AND PRODUCTS	W 31307	96971	W 30103	107307	W 38112	149881	W 50413	186505	CHOCOLAT
1	BEVERAGES AND TOBACCO		219248		311913		392925		367859	BOISSONS ET TABACS
11	BEVERAGES		181754		270274		335920		309017	BOISSONS
111	NON–ALCOHL BEVERAGES NES	W 210889	94179	W 301237	144664	W 272959	210124	W 281281	209871	BOISSONS NON ALCOOLIQUES
11102	FLAVORED WATERS NON–ALCO	W 203921	92463	W 290739	142085	W 263818	205967	W 272325	207232	LIMONADES,EAUX GAZEUSES
2	CRUDE MATERLS,EXCL FUELS		1581305		1933199		2770801		2100177	MAT BRUTES NON COMESTIBLES
23	RUBBER, CRUDE		7859		8537		410451		15488	CAOUTCHOUC BRUT
233	RUBBER,SYNTHTIC,RECLAIMD	W 14791	7354	W 13838	7821	W 1093310	409889	W 18900	14970	LATEX CAOUTCH SYNTH REGEN
24	CORK AND WOOD		820453		1050375		1241601		1080082	LIEGE ET BOIS
248	WOOD SHAPED,SLEEPERS	W 2338046	748205	W 2662823	961477	W 2740106	1139071	W 2475249	986285	BOIS SIMPLEMENT TRAVAILLES
2482	LUMBER SHAPED CONIFER	W 2247175	703154	W 2565037	907248	W 2599080	1076190	W 2391698	932954	CONIFERES SCIES,RABOTES
24821	LUMBER SAWN ETC CONIFER	W 2190451	649827	W 2489262	831727	W 2533466	1000190	W 2327218	863480	CONIFERES SCIES LONGITUD
251	*PULP AND WASTE PAPER		88484	W 318502	137281	W 233953	137573	W 372127	144745	PATES A PAPIER,DECHETS
26	TEXTILE FIBRES AND WASTE		283694		294723		332550		315348	FIBRES TEXTILES
266	SYNTHETIC FIBRES TO SPIN	W 33755	56793	W 38617	69170		309755		74771	FIBRES SYNTHETIQUES
267	OTHER MAN–MADE FIBRES	W 101687	215970	W 95652	212999	W 2455	3280	W 103830	221067	AUTR FIBR TEXT ARTIF SYNTH
2671	REGENERATD FIBRE TO SPIN	W 99229	214765	W 93080	211552	W 347	1515	W 101820	219536	FIBRES TEXT ARTIFIC
26711	DISCN REGEN FIBRE UNCMBD	W 99226	214724	W 93049	211452	W 244	1130	W 101685	219072	FIBRES TEX ARTIF DISCONT
27	CRUDE FERTLZR,MINRLS NES		168622		188155		252677		238995	ENGRAIS MINERAUX BRUTS
28	METALLIFEROUS ORES,SCRAP		127961		150762		265879		186282	MINERAIS METAL,DECHETS
3	MINERAL FUELS ETC		463873		603386		535020		736644	COMBUSTIBLES MINERAUX LUB
33	PETROLEUM AND PRODUCTS		170327		233576		256088		339965	PETROLE ET DERIVES
334	PETROLEUM PRODUCTS,REFIN	W 601919	146748		206651	W 848197	227443	W 1101102	305966	PRODUITS RAFFINES
3341	GASOLINE,OTH LIGHT OILS	W 311932	64705	W 639722	122455			W 830011	182105	ESSENCES POUR MOTEURS
33411	MOTOR,AVIATION SPIRIT	W 300142	62587	W 158	68			W 829889	181890	ESSENCES MOTEURS D'AVIONS
351	*ELECTRIC CURRENT		292526		366424		273191		392248	ENERGIE ELECTRIQUE
5	CHEMCLS,RELATED PROD NES		3464338		3948084		4733456		5157306	PRODUITS CHIMIQUES
51	ORGANIC CHEMICALS		487584		531147		643426		710289	PROD CHIMIQ ORGANIQUES
511	HYDROCARBONS NES,DERIVS	W 36736	12036	W 43275	15509	W 141220	178287	W 39773	18740	HYDROCARBURES NDA
513	CARBOXYLIC ACIDS ETC		219990	W 140251	217433	W 35952	80949	W 203032	272385	ACIDES CARBOXYLIQUES
5139	OXY–FNCT ACIDS,DERIVATVS	W 106120	166594	W 97742	167332	W 12006	47760	W 115013	156521	ACIDES CARBOXYLIQUES
514	NITROGEN–FNCTN COMPOUNDS	W 34722	97073		107243		96578		174371	COMPOSES FONCT AZOTEES
515	ORG–INORG COMPOUNDS ETC	W 7869	114136	W 8563	136512	W 10099	151502	W 9434	168155	COMPOSES ORGANO–MINERAUX
52	INORGANIC CHEMICALS		216563		259981		181348		306793	PROD CHIM INORGANIQUES
522	INORG ELEMNTS,OXIDES,ETC	W 281245	113810	W 278495	139005		128029		148745	ELEMENTS INORGANIQUES
53	DYES,TANNING,COLOUR PROD		192145		219228		285763		278389	PROD TEINTURE,COLORANTS
533	PIGMENTS,PAINTS,ETC	W 232502	175023		199771	W 255435	240023	W 234635	230225	PIGMENTS,PEINTURES,VERNIS
541	*MEDICINAL,PHARM PRODUCT		890345		1053973		1230486		1374537	PROD MEDICINAUX PHARMACEUT
5413	ANTIBIOTICS IN BULK	K 1958200	149263	K 2267915	162710	K 2324635	166744	K 2658608	179290	ANTIBIOTIQUES NDA
5416	GLYCOSIDES,GLANDS,SERA	K 867300	309413		339249	K 1127502	492633	K 2095014	481390	HETEROSIDES
54164	ANTISERA,MICROB VACCINES	K 615500	289292	K 648599	312496	K 814391	458320	K 944317	454040	SERUMS,VACCINS
5417	MEDICAMENTS	MK 16924	364226		472607	MK 15942	494092		634695	MEDICAMENTS
54171	— CONTAINNG ANTIBIOTICS	K 4693000	137499	K 5199242	157291	K 6369780	208737	K 5233895	146533	MED CONTN ANTIBIOTIQUES
54179	— CONTNG OTH SUBSTANCES	MK 12148	194017		206939	MK 9241	271772	MK 17278	339634	MED CONT AUT SUBSTANCES
55	PERFUME,CLEANING ETC PRD		189850		195683		257856		234889	PROD POUR PARFUM,TOILETTE
58	PLASTIC MATERIALS ETC		1056095		1237082		1551300		1579959	MAT PLAST ARTIFICIELLES
582	PROD OF CONDENSATION ETC	W 226437	194555		240444	W 64823	234015	W 240536	295004	PROD CONDENS,POLYCOND
5823	ALKYDS,OTHER POLYESTERS	W 39268	104899		121574	W 46836	175224	W 50664	153436	ALKYDES ET AUT POLYESTERS
583	POLYMERIZATION ETC PRODS	W 695561	841076		970770	W 743003	1286494	W 817976	1251734	PROD POLYMERISATION
5831	POLYETHYLENE	W 307281	246045	W 333360	291092	W 47340	111595	W 52404	103619	POLYETHYLENE
58311	— IN PRIMARY FORMS			W 284632	204031					POLYETHYLENE PRIMAIRES
5832	POLYPROPYLENE	W 201296	152366	W 119396	115207	W 15834	49665	W 14255	41598	POLYPROPYLENE
5839	OTH POLYMRZTION ETC PROD	W 57791	208788		328673	W 595883	881505	W 640610	851125	AUT PROD POLYMER COPOLYM
59	CHEMICAL MATERIALS NES		314774		321760		413732		489061	MAT PROD CHIMIQUES NDA
598	MISCEL CHEM PRODUCTS NES	W 156130	212610		230886	W 217761	368389	W 193557	320904	PROD DIV INDUST CHIM NDA
5989	CHEM PRODUCTS,PREPS NES	W 142670	199196		216807	W 200435	349090	W 175642	300759	PROD PREP CHIMIQUES NDA
59899	OTH CHEM PRODS,PREPS,NES	W 110992	162805		180022	W 159863	300467	W 135797	256318	AUT PRODUITS CHIMIQUES NDA
6	BASIC MANUFACTURES		11669302		13112757		16490906		15832338	ART MANUFACTURES
61	LEATHER,DRESSED FUR,ETC		210370		234889		358419		370647	CUIRS,PELLETERIES
611	LEATHER	W 8651	145975	W 8392	162963	W 12963	243294	W 12533	246224	CUIRS,PEAUX PREPARES
6114	LEATHR BOVINE NES,EQUINE	W 8312	138643	W 7845	155045	W 11857	205731	W 11624	219490	CUIRS DE BOVINS
62	RUBBER MANUFACTURES NES		545018		561860		276110		687314	CAOUTCHOUC MANUFACTURE
625	RUBBER TYRES, TUBES ETC	W 71520	324254		321993			W 92466	396406	PNEUS CAOUTCHOUC VULCANISE
6251	TYRES NEW FOR MOTOR CARS	W 34076	203074	W 32281	184730					PNEUS POUR VOITURES
6259	OTH TYRES,TYRE CASES,ETC	W 11342	20860		21967			W 92466	396406	AUTRES PNEUS RECHAPES FLAPS
62599	TYRES NES,TYRE CASES,ETC	W 11132	19524	W 13947	20915			W 90838	387934	PNEUS,FLAPS
63	WOOD,CORK MANUFACTRS NES		672522		762301		929289		953484	OUVRAGES LIEGE ET BOIS
634	VENEERS,PLYWOOD,ETC	W 706035	347640	W 721284	388174	W 792891	477230	W 859095	469212	PLACAGES,CONTRE–PLAQUES
6343	IMPROVED,RECONSTIT WOOD	W 630765	228553	W 638838	247398	W 720485	336750	W 773815	326021	BOIS AMELIORES,RECONST
63432	RECONSTITUTED WOOD	W 630604	228212	W 638271	246707	W 719929	335985	W 772971	324786	BOIS RECONSTITUES
635	WOOD MANUFACTURES NES	W 156379	322469		370882	W 212222	444145	W 266796	474213	ART MANUF EN BOIS NDA
6353	BUILDERS WOODWRK,PREFABS	W 117752	265169	W 139684	305018	W 167291	367642	W 193649	384933	OUVRAGES DE MENUISERIE
64	PAPER,PAPERBOARD AND MFR		2299985		2656400		3758294		3337487	PAPIERS,CARTONS & OUVRAGES
641	PAPER AND PAPERBOARD	W 2625272	1746771		2066932	W 3107106	3135790	W 3052018	2771315	PAPIERS ET CARTONS
6412	PRINTG,WRITING PAPER NES	W 1218913	948307	W 1311102	1087287	W 1306376	1502414	W 1364981	1414823	PAPIERS POUR L'IMPRESSION
64121	— UNCOATED	W 201226	184767	W 175544	175246	W 53498	76983	W 241769	376335	PAPIERS IMPRES NON COUCHES
64122	— COATED,IMPREGNATD ETC	W 1017687	763540	W 1135558	912041	W 1252878	1425431	W 1123212	1038488	PAPIERS IMPRESSION COUCHES
6413	KRAFT PAPER,PAPERBOARD	W 313539	172010	W 348301	196938	W 386394	300251	W 352394	242747	PAPIER ET CARTON KRAFT
6415	PAPER,PAPERBRD,BULK,NES	W 981727	508162	W 1128139	626748	W 1196408	950080	W 1148010	896265	PAPIERS,CARTONS ROULEAUX
64159	OTHER PAPER ETC,BULK,NES	W 914583	486505	W 1078028	608035	W 1143557	918338	W 1089667	872541	AUT PAPIER ROULEAUX FEUILLES
642	PAPER,ETC,PRECUT,ARTS OF	W 277473	553214		589468	W 286702	622503	W 276314	566173	PAP,CARTONS DECOUPES
6421	PAPER ETC CONTAINERS	W 165389	280607		309346	W 187154	413796	W 194465	387279	BOITES,SACS EMBALLAGES
6424	PAPER ETC CT TO SIZE NES	W 56827	145282		149195	W 28074	41313	W 28221	40369	PAP,CARTONS DECOUPES
65	TEXTILE YARN,FABRICS,ETC		1781690		1836793		2009400		1996751	FILS,TISSUS,ARTICLES TEXTILE
651	TEXTILE YARN	W 80173	370312		411804		394358	W 86964	424000	FILS TEXTILES
6517	REGEN FIBRE YARN,MONOFIL	W 38507	159516	W 42011	174757		130176	W 35194	137574	FILS TEXT ART NON VENTE DT
652	COTTON FABRICS,WOVEN	W 15436	272488		242964		304162	W 16630	285302	TISSUS DE COTON
6522	WOVEN COTTON BLEACHD,ETC	W 9435	236704		204840		257825	W 9579	244438	TISSUS COTON BLANCHIS ETC
65224	BLCHED COTTON FABRIC NES	W 6414	163426		144772	W 8094	188809	W 6986	187483	AUT TIS PLUS 85% COT BLANCHI
653	WOVN MAN–MADE FIB FABRIC	W 14791	253752		255050	W 18066	296948	W 14167	283606	TISSUS FIBRES SYNTH,ARTIF
655	KNITTED,ETC FABRICS	W 13922	228832		242116	W 11444	238883	W 13331	257787	ETOF BONNETERIE PIECES ETC

5. Special Exports F.O.B. by Commodities according to the S.I.T.C. (Rev. 2) in thousand U.S. Dollars
Exportations Spéciales F.O.B. par Produits d'après la C.T.C.I. (Rév. 2) en milliers de Dollars E.U.

SITC CTCI	COMMODITY	1993		1994		1995		1996		PRODUIT
		WEIGHT POIDS	VALUE VALEUR	WEIGHT POIDS	VALUE VALEUR	WEIGHT POIDS	VALUE VALEUR	WEIGHT POIDS	VALUE VALEUR	
6552	OTHER KNIT ETC FAB NONEL	W 13922	228832		242116	W 11444	238883	W 13331	257787	ETOF BON NON ELAS NON SYNT
656	LACE,RIBBONS,TULLE,ETC	W 3578	202083		196522	W 3723	212197	W 3979	193085	TULLES,BRODERIE
65606	EMBROIDERY	W 2047	158858		151882	W 2093	160088	W 1707	128279	BRODERIES PIECES,BANDES
657	SPECIAL TXTL FABRC,PRODS		163990		181700		253980		276326	TISSUS SPECIAUX
66	NONMETAL MINERAL MFS NES		1179443		1317547		1589083		1532954	ART MIN NON METALLIQUES
662	CLAY,REFRACTORY BLDG PRD	W 388122	253613	W 487068	296885	W 414630	373873	W 385708	343079	MAT CONST REFRACTAIRES
6623	REFRACTORY BUILDING PROD	W 307043	235087	W 413612	280249	W 372330	362294	W 350350	334294	BRIQUES REFRACTAIRES
66232	REFRACTRY BRICKS ETC NES	W 156166	155021	W 183143	183558	W 181208	230611	W 181934	224818	BRIQUES ETC REFRACTAIRES
663	MINERAL MANUFCTURES NES	W 472114	379376		421791	W 558558	523226	W 550547	471916	ART MIN MANUF NDA
6633	MINRL MFS NES NONCERAMIC	W 372650	188872		204984	W 447856	251759	W 459536	231658	OUVR MAT MINERALE NDA
66339	OTH MINRL MFS NONCERAMIC	W 80983	121234		136281	W 92901	162606	W 82802	139293	OUVRAGES EN PIERRES
665	GLASSWARE	W 114269	351217		394886	W 144804	451352		450760	OUVRAGES EN VERRE
6658	GLASS ARTICLES NES	W 8701	168787		195448	W 8127	225446	W 7933	216142	ARTICLES FAB EN VERRE NDA
66582	GLASS ORNAMENTS NES	W 6022	154418	W 5732	180361	W 6781	213641	W 6668	204799	PERLES DE VERRE
67	IRON AND STEEL		2120471		2420587		3499271		2858669	FER ET ACIER
671	PIG IRON ETC	W 28422	73049	W 30036	93077	W 34822	186986	W 25779	119612	FONTE,SPIEGEL,POUDRES
6716	FERRO-ALLOYS	W 20084	71543	W 19077	91083	W 32208	184911	W 20802	116509	FERRO-ALLIAGES
67169	OTHER FERRO-ALLOYS	W 20084	71543	W 17516	90358	W 21056	177784	W 16259	113509	AUTRES FERRO-ALLIAGES
672	IRON,STEEL PRIMARY FORMS	W 316270	117812		158256	W 617661	279946	W 436648	172753	LINGOTS FER,ACIER
673	IRON,STEEL SHAPES ETC	W 299921	294542		355836	W 354825	479502	W 303925	456646	BARRES,PROFIL FER,ACIER
6732	IRON,STEEL BARS ETC	W 125806	191048		223039	W 103153	288020	W 108508	308895	BARRES FER,ACIER
67325	OTH ALLOY STEEL BARS ETC	W 64610	134265		148505	W 74603	217936	W 74468	219813	BARRES NON ACIERS ALLIES
674	IRN,STL UNIV,PLATE,SHEET	W 1691885	934728	W 1861637	1090959	W 2128720	1541298	W 1579910	1101482	LARGES PLATS,TOLES
6744	IRN,STL HVY PLATE,ROLLED	W 209064	130815	W 268852	166116	W 346048	264982	W 220121	183200	TOLES LAMINEES PLUS 4.75 MM
67441	— OF IRON OR SIMPLE STL	W 199094	84245	W 258943	119142	W 332141	193148	W 205661	112882	TOLES NON ACIER FIN CARB
6745	IRN,STL MED PLATE,ROLLED	W 229105	109266	W 289666	144862	W 368751	233434	W 244382	147716	TOLES 3 A 4.75 MM
67451	— OF IRON OR SIMPLE STL	W 196057	75775	W 242875	103815	W 318469	172523	W 195891	94130	TOLES AUT NON ACIER FIN
6746	IRN,STL THIN PLATE,ROLLD	W 622492	294405	W 629892	333609	W 655334	459219	W 409610	281413	TOLES LAM MOINS 3MM
67461	— OF IRON OR SIMPLE STL	W 537477	224307	W 554466	256251	W 580269	328212	W 352480	187079	TOL NON AC FIN MOINS 3 MM
6749	OTH IRN,STL PLATES,SHEET	W 629974	398897	W 672145	445159	W 757632	581999	W 704581	487579	AUTRES TOLES FER,ACIER
67491	— OF IRON OR SIMPLE STL	W 623862	373699	W 663688	419187	W 754842	576363	W 701614	482579	AUT TOLES AUTRES ACIER FIN
676	RAILWY RAILS ETC IRN,STL	W 219267	166825	W 249707	170663	W 237045	191816	W 196034	148167	RAILS,ELEMENTS VOIES FERREE
67601	RAILWAY RAILS IRN,STL	W 200807	138344	W 237782	153555	W 229600	172652	W 187639	131651	RAILS,ELEMENTS FER,ACIER
678	IRON,STL TUBES,PIPES,ETC	W 441914	436875		444320	W 510023	657463	W 554596	705517	TUBES,TUYAUX EN FONTE,FER
6782	IRON,STL SEAMLESS TUBES	W 202423	187646	W 165316	151431	W 197898	247176	W 263500	298749	TUBES,TUYAUX SANS SOUDURE
6783	IRON,STL TUBES,PIPES NES	W 204675	141107		172237	W 283481	273175	W 248508	223683	AUT TUBES,TUYAUX FER,ACIER
68	NON-FERROUS METALS		772920		938568		1441096		1293673	METAUX NON FERREUX
682	COPPER EXC CEMENT COPPER	W 85562	242143		294685	W 125520	483235	W 121294	390311	CUIVRE
6821	COPPER NES,ALLOYS,UNWRT	W 61036	122926	W 64992	148399	W 84837	251979	W 79834	191181	CUIVRE BRUT
68212	COPPER REFINED,UNWROUGHT	W 61033	122911	W 64991	148388	W 84777	251748	W 79817	191116	CUIVRE AFFINE BRUT
6822	COPPER,ALLOYS WORKED	W 24527	119217		146286	W 40683	231256	W 41460	199130	CUIVRE,ALLIAGES OUVRES
684	ALUMINIUM	W 172452	483036		590229	W 205241	717674	W 219130	727970	ALUMINIUM
6841	ALUMINIUM,ALLOYS,UNWRGHT	W 56495	72081	W 68078	105636	W 80159	177415	W 75411	132676	ALUMINIUM,ALLIAGES BRUTS
6842	ALUMINIUM,ALLOYS WORKED	W 115957	410955		484593	W 125083	540259	W 143719	595294	ALUMINIUM,ALLIAGES OUVRE
68421	ALUMINIUM BARS,WIRE,ETC	W 40829	131057	W 53940	172639	W 57197	244792	W 59606	225744	BARRES,PROFILES FILS ALU
68422	ALUMNM PLATE,SHEET,STRIP	W 42365	112100	W 45595	135632	W 47318	179702	W 47298	162227	TOLES, PLANCHES EN ALU
68423	ALUMINIUM FOIL	W 25208	147164	W 26163	152151	W 11047	83358			FEUILLES,BANDES MINCES AL
689	NON-FER BASE METALS NES		14774		16200	W 5713	180510		36562	AUT METAUX NON FERREUX
69	METAL MANUFACTURES NES		2086883		2383812		2629944		2801358	ART MANUFACT EN METAL NDA
691	STRUCTURES AND PARTS NES	W 166557	459807		475683	W 175228	573816	W 187028	581434	CONSTRUCT FER,ACIER,ALU
6911	STRUCTURES,PARTS IRN,STL	W 154210	340675		359793	W 164995	450360	W 174401	439861	CONSTRUCT FER,ACIER,FONTE
692	METAL TANKS,BOXES,ETC	W 26015	107288	W 34185	140901		182055	W 43445	186532	RECIPIENTS METALLIQUES
695	TOOLS	W 17782	332886		395769	W 123572	481477	W 21160	455224	OUTILS A MAIN
6954	BLADES,TIPS,ETC FR TOOLS	W 11686	253696		293473	W 10739	310327	W 12787	300871	OUTILS POUR MACHINE-OUTIL
69541	PARTS TO INSERT IN TOOLS	W 4897	151635		177331	W 3403	152082	W 4752	148454	OUTILS DE FORAGE
699	BASE METAL MFRS NES	W 178289	961034		1127948		1082214		1282756	ART MANUFACTURES MET NDA
6991	LOCKSMITHS WARES,ETC	W 82047	471798		545743	W 89673	562063	W 81365	523260	ARTICLES DE SERRURERIE
69913	BASE MTL DOOR,ETC FITTNG	W 79983	437404		508076	W 67855	522160	W 79396	476960	GARNITURES POUR MEUBLES
6997	IRON,STEEL ARTICLES NES	W 49742	159039		163154	W 39111	162135	W 59076	204641	OUV FONTE,FER,ACIER NDA
69979	IRN,STL MANUFACTURES NES	W 49723	158982		163068	W 39099	162091	W 59073	204623	AUT OUVRAGES EN FER NDA
6998	MFRS NES OF CPR,NIKL,ETC	W 21185	135515		167832	W 111512	164727	W 27036	205074	OUVRAGES EN CU,NI,AL,PB,ZN
6999	OTHR BASE METAL MFRS NES	W 3606	94139		128087		51031		210441	OUVRAGES EN TUNGST,MOLYB
69999	BASE MTLS NES WRGHT,MFRS	W 135	2837		4255	W 2284	20626	W 9048	210440	MET COMMUNS OUVRES NDA
7	MACHINES,TRANSPORT EQUIP		15666686		17544804		22589124		23474090	MACHINES MATERIEL TRANSPORT
71	POWER GENERATING EQUIPMT		2387114		2758660		3287823		3624497	MACHINES GENERATRICES
713	INTRNL COMBUS PSTN ENGIN	W 154037	1883158		2220569	W 161820	2537700	W 187797	2939341	MOTEURS EXPL COMB INT, PIECE
7132	MOTOR VEHCL PISTN ENGINS	W 124594	1489345	W 137207	1726886	W 111384	1769262	W 136187	2104014	MOTEURS EXPL POUR VEHICULES
7139	PISTON ENGINE PARTS NES	W 26645	329937		409340	W 44907	637344	W 45135	679345	PIECES POUR 713.2,3,8
716	ROTATING ELECTRIC PLANT	W 25252	281694		337376	W 30087	368470	W 33582	412037	APP ELECTR ROTATIFS,PIECES
7162	AC MTRS,GENRTRS,GEN SETS	W 14837	187554		211116	W 19098	272725	W 21574	311156	MOTEURS ELECTRIQUES
72	MACHS FOR SPCL INDUSTRYS		2355466		2579084		3280674		3106754	MAC SPECIALES POUR INDUST
721	AGRIC MACHY,EXC TRACTORS	W 25538	165540	W 28767	185010	W 30251	220194	W 30671	232598	MACHINES AGRICOLES
723	CIVIL ENGNEERG EQUIP ETC	W 40986	303359	W 54439	389940	W 78312	619457	W 47726	364563	APPAREILS DE GENIE CIVIL
7234	CONST,MINING MACHNRY NES	W 36641	265705	W 49210	359248	W 45508	400172	W 42291	320125	MACH POUR LA CONST, MINES
72342	SLFPRP SHOVELS,EXCAVATRS	W 25992	160680	W 35745	235000	W 32870	255363	W 30750	206470	PELLES MECANIQUES
724	TEXTILE,LEATHER MACHNRY	W 15288	184625		158628	W 16470	202699	W 15554	215757	MACH POUR INDUSTRIE TEXTILE
725	PAPER ETC MILL MACHINERY	W 10973	184157		201618	W 14466	248284	W 13301	201918	MACHINES FABR PATE PAPIER
7259	PTS NES OF MACHS OF 725	W 8857	155353		169151	W 8505	145401	W 9537	142109	PIECES GROUPE 725
72591	PTS NES OF MACHS OF 7251	W 8714	152160	W 9040	162837	W 8329	140713	W 9333	137761	PIECES DU 725.1
726	PRINTG,BKBINDG MACHY,PTS	W 9107	185122		200999	W 8879	200162	W 8587	205100	MACHINES POUR IMPRIMERIE
727	FOOD MACHRY NON-DOMESTIC	W 5594	120499	W 5276	128541	W 5498	176147		191965	MACH INDUSTRIES ALIMENT
7272	OTH FOOD PROC MCHY,PARTS	W 5155	117255	W 4994	125557	W 5228	172480		187786	AUT MACH IND ALIMENTAIRE
72722	INDUS FOOD PROC MACH NES	W 5125	117032	W 4983	125443	W 5227	172461	W 5880	187778	MACHINES BOULANGERIE
728	OTH MACHY FOR SPCL INDUS	W 80117	1139705		1228138	W 71066	1511844	W 80418	1548408	AUT MACH IND PARTICULIERES
7281	MACH-TOOLS FR SPCL INDUS	W 17744	205720		229776	W 14170	223800	W 15761	216546	MACH-OUTILS SPEC IND PART
72812	MACH-TOOLS TO WORK WOOD	W 13285	154678	W 16727	172906	W 10768	163179	W 12485	162575	MACH-OUT POUR TRAVAIL BOIS
7284	MACHY FOR SPCL INDUS NES	W 43455	827195		899813	W 44773	1176728	W 50834	1194015	MACH SPEC IND PARTICUL.
72842	RUBBER,PLASTICS WRKG MCH	W 22015	369335	W 20488	367025	W 21671	507058	W 27802	492727	MACH IND CAOUT MAT PLAST
72848	OTH MCHY WITH INDIV FNCT	W 9487	234704	W 17138	271448	W 9337	283228	W 8586	305715	AUTRES MACHINES NDA
72849	PTS OF MACHS OF 7284 ETC	W 11071	210521		243431	W 12714	359975	W 13076	349449	PIECES DU 728.4 ETC
73	METALWORKING MACHINERY		536785		463747		657156		573147	MACH TRAVAIL DES METAUX
736	METALWORKING MACH-TOOLS		337587		279512	W 20855	390115	W 19138	358996	MACH-OUTILS TRAVAIL METAUX
737	METALWORKING MACHNRY NES	W 18646	199199		184235	W 18008	267041	W 19165	214151	MACH TRAV METAUX PIECES
74	GENRL INDUSTRL MACHY NES		2588910		2914478		3771996		3840061	MACH APP INDUSTRIE
741	HEATING,COOLING EQUIPMNT	W 38421	396952		418329	W 41464	549025	W 50381	609699	MACH CHAUFFAGE,PIECES
7416	HEATING,COOLING EQU NES	W 12833	128821	W 12716	141751	W 18009	213249	W 19914	202904	APP CHANGEMENT TEMP
742	PUMPS FOR LIQUIDS ETC	W 13144	199063		242544	W 12714	264889	W 14365	295006	POMPES MOTO-POMPES
743	PUMPS NES,CENTRFUGES ETC	W 43451	352985		388221	W 52365	540747	W 52288	515135	POMPES COMPRES,VENT ETC
7436	GAS,LIQUID FILTERS ETC	W 13263	128350		153601	W 17633	251233	W 16909	242308	APP POUR FILT DES LIQUIDES
744	MECHANICAL HANDLING EQU	W 79928	658906		730003	W 83108	819720	W 87868	878835	EQUIP MANUTENTION PIECES
7442	LIFTING,LOADING MACH NES	W 39302	316683	W 44961	349372	W 43916	449877	W 45183	455817	APP LEVAGE,MANUTENTION

5. Special Exports F.O.B. by Commodities according to the S.I.T.C. (Rev. 2) in thousand U.S. Dollars
Exportations Spéciales F.O.B. par Produits d'après la C.T.C.I. (Rév. 2) en milliers de Dollars E.U.

SITC CTCI	COMMODITY	1993 WEIGHT POIDS	1993 VALUE VALEUR	1994 WEIGHT POIDS	1994 VALUE VALEUR	1995 WEIGHT POIDS	1995 VALUE VALEUR	1996 WEIGHT POIDS	1996 VALUE VALEUR	PRODUIT
74428	OTH HANDLING ETC MCH NES	W 17964	191022	W 24688	213077	W 22652	300722	W 27539	322497	AUT APP LEVAGE ETC
7449	PTS NES OF MACHY OF 7442	W 32709	288261		310110	W 31857	309434	W 32400	342614	PIECES DU 744.2
745	NONELEC MACHY,TOOLS NES	W 14978	213992		279338	W 21116	362998	W 24139	362731	AUT MACH NON ELEC,PIECES
7452	OTH NONELEC MCHS,PTS NES	W 14770	204538		266608	W 20759	346606	W 23634	347709	AUT MACH NON ELEC,PIECES
749	NONELEC MACH PTS,ACC NES	W 44092	767013		856042	W 66684	1234617	W 66989	1178655	PIECES MACH NON ELEC NDA
7491	BALL,ROLLER,ETC BEARINGS	W 10234	136840		163477	W 20378	262235	W 20776	208461	ROULEMENTS BILLES ETC
7492	COCKS,VALVES ETC NES	W 12104	247045		260217	W 15116	364154	W 16139	394969	ART ROB,SIM POUR TUYAUX
7493	SHAFT,CRANK,PULLEY ETC	W 15243	216194		243374	W 22850	383978	W 20506	340677	ARBRES TRANS,VILEBREQUINS
7499	OTH NONELEC MCHY PTS NES	W 6510	166933		188975	W 8339	224250	W 9569	234548	PIECES NON ELECT NDA
74991	FOUNDRY MOULDS ETC NES	W 5563	137735	W 6363	155400	W 7294	185213	W 8424	194689	MOULES POUR METAUX
75	OFFICE MACHNES,ADP EQUIP		520792		501827		746966		603708	MACH BUREAU TRAIT AUTOM
752	AUTOMTIC DATA PROC EQUIP	W 3695	194940		189264	W 2510	365144	W 2038	295431	MACH TRAIT INFORMATION
759	OFFICE,ADP MCH PTS,ACCES	W 2487	297414		282580	W 2859	345620	W 2789	257071	PIECES DU 751 ET 752
7599	ACCTG,ETC,ADP MCH PTS,AC	W 2191	284970		266882	W 2256	324176	W 2110	237250	PIECES DU 751 ET 752
76	TELECOMM,SOUND EQUIPMENT		1406157		1549698		1974669		1764698	EQUIPMENT DE TELECOM
761	TELEVISION RECEIVERS	W 25246	408804	W 30509	483938	W 792	18627	W 35117	572433	RECEPTEURS DE TELEVISION
7611	COLOUR TV RECEIVERS	W 25238	408363	W 30493	483359	W 692	16799	W 35102	572112	RECEPTEURS COULEUR
763	SOUND RECORDRS,PHONOGRPH	W 11921	456066		438831	W 10504	426312	W 7987	302626	PHONO,APP ENREGISTREMENT
7638	OTHR SOUND APPARATUS ETC	W 11910	455721		438643	W 10486	425637	W 7931	301736	AUT APP D'ENREGIS,REPROD
76381	TV IMAGE,SND RECRDRS ETC				390309	W 10372	404440	W 7720	269413	APP ENREG,REPRO IMAG,SON
764	TELECOM EQPT,PTS,ACC NES	W 7005	482947		603164		1521197	W 11338	876160	EQUIP TELECOM,PIECES
7641	LINE TELEPHONE,ETC EQUIP	W 1500	169597		233890	W 590	108366	W 1766	229025	APP TELEPHON PAR FIL
7649	PTS NES OF EQUIPMT OF 76	W 4333	247307		301549	W 6813	185206	W 7817	506141	PIECES DE LA DIV 76
76491	PTS NES OF APPAR OF 7641	W 858	70768		110052			W 886	202205	PIECES POUR 764.1
76499	PARTS ETC OF SOUND EQUIP	W 2502	103107		108943	W 4855	132720	W 5249	176607	PIECES NDA POUR 763
77	ELECTRIC MACHNRY NES ETC		2909392		3440122		4001991		4318970	MACH APP ELECT NDA
771	ELECTRIC POWER MACHY NES	W 21929	277801		332404	W 27573	397663	W 30329	467614	MACH PROD,TRANS ELECTR
7712	OTH ELEC POWER MACHY NES	W 14228	208425		255570	W 16554	262399	W 17428	336176	AUT APP PROD TRANSF ELEC
772	SWITCHGEAR ETC,PARTS NES	W 16167	716685		855074	W 20102	1008603	W 26180	1055870	APP COUPURE,SECT ETC
7721	SWITCHGEAR ETC	W 13394	506284		595104	W 16565	659745	W 18199	706364	APP COUPURE,SECTIONMNT
7723	FIXED,VARIABLE RESISTORS	W 1286	120516		132853	W 1544	178181	W 5355	177309	POTENTIOMETRES PIECES
773	ELECTR DISTRIBUTNG EQUIP	W 54292	420850		502471	W 62614	507166	W 76473	644296	EQUIPMT DISTRIBUTION ELECT
7731	INSULATED WIRE,CABLE ETC	W 48394	369132		443035	W 55339	425258	W 68713	553473	FILS,CABLES ISOLES ELECT
775	HOUSEHOLD TYPE EQUIP NES	W 254674	413572		429180	W 22814	336616	W 45747	533153	MACH,APP USAGE DOMESTQUE
7758	ELECTRO–THERMIC APPL NES	W 26984	212039		213274	W 15549	155057	W 19795	230155	APP ELECTROTHERMIQ NDA
776	TRANSISTORS,VALVES,ETC	W 10702	511552		634773	W 12257	974008	W 14600	807084	LAMPES,TUBES,VALVES
7763	DIODES,TRANSISTORS,ETC	W 727	93031		98300	W 1254	308565	W 3188	204571	DIODES,TRANSISTORS
7764	ELECTRONIC MICROCIRCUITS	W 186	307782		397562	W 1018	533318	W 421	431717	MICROSTRUCTURES ELECTRON
778	ELECTRICAL MACHINERY NES		506644		622395	W 73172	685892		718926	AUTRES MACH ELECT NDA
7788	OTH ELEC MACHY,EQUIP NES		259498		353088	W 16139	345878		366040	AUT MACH APP ELEC NDA
78	ROAD VEHICLES		2558312		2866595		4260336		5115861	VEHICULES ROUTIERS
781	PASS MOTOR VEH EXC BUSES	W 78898	892287	W 83339	993245	W 114788	1739013	W 264291	2435810	AUTO TRANSPORT PERSONNES
782	LORRIES,SPCL MTR VEH NES	W 62121	595577	W 57268	513995	W 68963	673733	W 69058	647839	VEHICULES SPECIAUX,MARCH
7821	LORRIES,TRUCKS	W 55649	474020	W 50998	415990	W 63237	588677	W 63161	568717	VEHICULES TRANSP MARCHAND
7822	SPECIAL MOTOR VEHCLS NES	W 6471	121558	W 6269	98004	W 5725	85056	W 5896	79122	VEHICULES USAGES SPECIAUX
783	ROAD MOTOR VEHICLES NES	W 10402	80169	W 13484	91509	W 17818	147093	W 72856	338733	VEHICULES ROUTIERS NDA
7832	TRACTORS FOR TR–TRAILERS	W 5793	38474	W 7129	41887	W 10267	91199	W 63441	268654	TRACTEURS ROUTIERS
784	MOTOR VEH PRTS,ACCES NES	W 83683	802999		1042531	W 128062	1380068	W 112739	1341332	PIECES 722,781,782,783
7849	OTHER MOTOR VEHCL PARTS	W 80823	771776		953788	W 122583	1278491	W 107598	1261423	PIECES 722,781,782,783
786	TRAILERS,NONMOTR VEH,NES	W 32999	122328		154738	W 42337	207584	W 58266	226076	REMORQUES,CADRES,CONTAIN
79	OTHR TRANSPORT EQUIPMENT		403758		470594		607513		526394	AUTRE MATERIEL TRANSPORT
791	RAILWAY VEHICLES	W 21864	337082	W 23984	366722	W 22061	491118	W 21650	399438	VEHIC MAT CHEMINS DE FER
7915	FRT,MAINT CARS NOT POWRD	W 9399	220085	W 7991	178586	W 10310	215407	W 9834	214841	WAGONS DE SERVICE
79151	RY SERV CARS NOT POWERED	W 9266	218935	W 7186	176713	W 7843	205958	W 8146	210664	WAGONS–ATELIERS,–GRUES
7919	RY TRACK FIXT,ETC,PARTS	W 11718	107590	W 12920	101098	W 8292	133242	W 11270	179312	MATER FIXE VOIES FERREES
8	MISC MANUFACTURED GOODS		5743314		6144534		7533747		7705933	ART MANUFACTURES DIVERS
812	*PLUMBG,HEATNG,LGHTNG EQ	W 58958	371235		409981	W 43189	426835	W 69774	484198	APPAR SANITAIRES CHAUFFAGE
8124	LIGHTING EQUIPMENT NES	W 23749	271440		300857	W 26195	352424	W 29227	357444	APPAREILS ECLAIRAGE ETC
81242	LAMPS,FITTINGS BASE METL	W 13113	178112		207053	W 13151	226524	W 16869	248884	APPAREILS D'ECLAIRAGE
821	*FURNITURE,PARTS THEREOF	W 85655	650647		714824	W 114800	868749	W 143905	1040619	MEUBLES ET PIECES
8211	CHAIRS,SEATS AND PARTS	W 21821	161618	W 24769	196271	W 22747	211018	W 30747	303917	SIEGES ET PIECES
82111	CHAIRS AND OTHER SEATS	W 20347	149438	W 23448	183830	W 20382	173001	W 25175	182718	SIEGES
8212	MED FURN,STUFFD FURNSHGS	W 10228	124591		120124	W 11031	134781	W 7884	135500	MOB MEDICO–CHIRUR,PIECES
8219	FURNITURE AND PARTS NES	W 53606	364438	W 63715	398429	W 81022	522950	W 105274	601202	AUTRES MEUBLES ET PIECES
82192	WOOD FURNITURE NES	W 32254	258607	W 41463	291977	W 34552	318087	W 41138	355229	MEUBLES NDA EN BOIS
84	CLOTHING AND ACCESSORIES		1058892		1063722		1282988		1390463	VETEMENTS
842	MENS OUTERWEAR NOT KNIT	W 2004	135455		135344	W 2111	145071	W 2899	155893	VET DESSUS POUR HOMMES
843	WOMENS OUTERWEAR NONKNIT	W 2555	202142		184002	W 14559	232969	W 3585	248087	VET DESSUS FEMMES MAT TEX
845	OUTERWEAR KNIT NONELASTC	W 3691	241923		238669	W 3935	299640	W 4805	308777	VET DESSOUS,ACCES BONNET
8451	— JERSEYS,PULLOVERS ETC	W 1821	121132		108324	W 1746	123950	W 1978	108843	CHANDAILS,PULL–OVERS ETC
846	UNDER GARMENTS KNITTED	W 5373	333556		337532	W 5454	415271	W 5568	463449	SOUS VETS DE BONNETERIE
8462	— OF COTTON NON ELASTIC	W 2962	164259		174765	W 3398	202802	W 3395	216529	SOUS–VET BONNET COTON
84629	—— OTHER	W 2962	164259		174765	W 3398	202802	W 3395	216529	AUT SOUS–VET BONNET COTON
851	*FOOTWEAR	W 9910	362645	W 10144	389279	W 13599	543394	W 11974	481902	CHAUSSURES
85102	FOOTWEAR LEATHER	W 6989	288171	W 7013	309007	W 10088	448108	W 9031	409090	CHAUS SEMELLES EN CUIR
87	PRECISION INSTRUMNTS NES		573723		618049		900755		836780	INSTRUM,APPAR SCIENT NDA
872	MEDICAL INSTRUMENTS NES	W 634	44553		57614	W 1475	193537	W 1322	104884	INSTR,APP MEDIC–CHIR NDA
874	MEASURNG,CONTROLNG INSTR		444566		454542		594122	W 5430	612172	INSTRUMENTS DE MESURE
8742	MEASUR,DRAW ETC INST,PTS	W 1893	154076		149782	W 2206	180395	W 2197	195143	INST DESSIN,TRACAGE,PCS
87421	MEASURNG,DRAWNG ETC INST	W 1714	132857		120251	W 1753	136423	W 1850	146583	INSTRUM DESSIN,TRACAGE
8743	GAS,LIQUID CONTROL INSTR	W 1629	110456		117916	W 2088	183527	W 1650	152093	APP,INSTR MESURE FLUIDES
88	PHOTO EQU,OPTICL GDS ETC		259638		223935		328175		283461	APP,FOURN PHOTO,OP,MONTR
884	OPTICAL GOODS NES	W 2054	152121		107411		185001		137810	ELEMENTS OPTIQ,ART LUNET
8842	SPECTACLES AND FRAMES	W 2033	143781		99059	W 457	174103	W 369	129265	LUNETTES ET MONTURES
89	MISC MANUFCTRD GOODS NES		2451973		2707778		3163229		3168210	ART MANUFACTURES DIVERS
892	PRINTED MATTER	W 96578	392903		393796		456416	W 87445	446684	IMPRIMES
8928	PRINTED MATTER NES	W 37970	178359		191492		214417	W 34428	198001	IMPRIMES NDA
893	ARTICLES OF PLASTIC NES		714093		836134		1007591		1010975	OUVRAGES EN MAT DIVIS 58
8931	PLSTC PACKG CONTNRS,LIDS	W 54207	183585		226463	W 67183	237133	W 84382	297269	ART TRANSP EMBALLAGE ETC
8939	MISC PLASTIC ARTICLES	W 76993	470271		537620	W 246693	686926	W 111930	651634	ART DIVERS EN MAT DIV 58
89399	OTHR PLASTC ARTICLES NES	W 71227	441177		508194	W 240450	652270	W 106306	622845	AUT OUV MAT DIV 58
894	TOYS,SPORTING GOODS,ETC	W 24471	577858		653382	W 28340	825688	W 26542	659806	VOITURES ENFANTS,JOUETS
8942	TOYS,INDOOR GAMES ETC	W 6339	123747		126804	W 6452	191449	W 7695	139817	JOUETS,JEUX ETC
8947	OTH SPORT GDS,FAIR AMUSM	W 17823	450929		491270	W 21333	608621	W 17879	483427	AUT ART DE SPORT
89472	OTH OUTDOOR SPORT GOODS	W 17392	447570		486764	W 21063	604620	W 17563	478946	ART POUR JEUX PLEIN AIR
895	OFFICE SUPPLIES NES	W 22352	128694		138229		158593		159792	ART PAPET NDA
897	GOLD,SILVER WARE,JEWELRY		145506		151460		191496		187758	BIJOUTERIE,ORFEVRERIE
898	MUSICAL INSTRUMENTS,PTS	W 18031	372579		413483		359297		540204	INSTRUMENTS DE MUSIQUE
8983	SOUND RECRDNG TAPE,DISCS	W 17772	347874		388780	W 10154	339692	W 11769	447171	SUPPORTS SON POUR 763
89832	RECORDED DISCS,TAPES ETC	W 7254	235753		283060	W 9544	319975	W 10791	422905	DISQUES,PHONO,BANDES
9	GOODS NOT CLASSD BY KIND		180958		127256		156411		254064	ART TRANSACT NON CLASSES

5. Special Exports F.O.B. by Commodities according to the S.I.T.C. (Rev. 2) in thousand U.S. Dollars
Exportations Spéciales F.O.B. par Produits d'après la C.T.C.I. (Rév. 2) en milliers de Dollars E.U.

SITC CTCI	COMMODITY	1993		1994		1995		1996		PRODUIT
		WEIGHT POIDS	VALUE VALEUR	WEIGHT POIDS	VALUE VALEUR	WEIGHT POIDS	VALUE VALEUR	WEIGHT POIDS	VALUE VALEUR	
951	*WAR FIREARMS,AMMUNITION	W 2458	143316		113404	W 136	9248	W 1019	88269	VEHIC BLINDES ARMES
95101	ARMORED FIGHTNG VEHICLES	W 2458	143316	W 410	17644					CHARS DE COMBAT

1. HISTORICAL SERIES, 1992–1996 GENERAL TRADE, IMPORTS C.I.F., EXPORTS F.O.B.
SERIES HISTORIQUES, 1992–1996 COMMERCE GENERAL, IMPORTATIONS C.A.F., EXPORTATIONS F.O.B

YEAR ANNEE	VALUE IN MILLION U.S. DOLLARS / VALEUR EN MILLION U.S. DOLLARS — MERCHANDISE –MARCHANDISE IMPORTS	EXPORTS	GOLD –OR IMPORTS	EXPORTS	CONVERSION FACTORS FACTEURS DE CONVERSION CENTS E.U. PAR IMPORTS	EXPORTS	INDEX NUMBERS –INDICES — QUANTUM IMPORTS	EXPORTS	UNIT VALUE VALEUR UNITAIRE IMPORTS	EXPORTS
1992	332.53	754.15								
1993	241.00	350.90								
1994	791.00	637.00								
1995	681.00	550.00								
1996	960.63	631.25								

2. IMPORTS BY BROAD ECONOMIC CATEGORY AND EXPORTS BY INDUSTRIAL ORIGIN. (PERCENTAGE OF TOTAL VALUE)
IMPORTATIONS PAR CATEGORIES ECONOMIQUES ET EXPORTATIONS PAR BRANCHE D'ACTIVITE.(EN POURCENTAGE DE LA VALEUR TOTALE)

IMPORTS – IMPORTATIONS

	1990	1991	1992	1993	1994	1995	1996
TOTAL IMPORTS–IMPORTATIONS TOTALES							
1 FOOD BEV–ALIMENTATION BOISSONS							
11 PRIMARY–PRODUITS DE BASE							
111 FOR INDUSTRY–POUR L'INDUSTRIE							
112 FOR HOUSEHOLDS–POUR LES MENAGES							
12 PROCESSED–PRODUITS ELABORES							
121 FOR INDUSTRY–POUR L'INDUSTRIE							
122 FOR HOUSEHOLDS–POUR LES MENAGES							
2 IND SUPPLIES–APPROV INDUSTRIELS							
21 PRIMARY–PRODUITS DE BASE							
22 PROCESSED–PRODUITS ELABORES							
3 FUELS–COMBUSTIBLES							
31 PRIMARY–PRODUITS DE BASE							
32 PROCESSED–PRODUITS ELABORES							
321 MOTOR SPIRIT–ESSENCE							
322 OTHER–AUTRES							
4 MACHINERY–EQUIPEMENT							
41 CAPITAL EQUIPMENT–MACHINES							
42 PARTS–PIECES ACCESSOIRES							
5 TRANSPORT–TRANSPORT							
51 PASSENGER CARS–AUTOMOBILES							
52 OTHER–AUTRES							
521 INDUSTRIAL–INDUSTRIELS							
522 NON INDUSTRIAL–NON INDUSTRIEL							
53 PARTS–PIECES ACCESSOIRES							
6 CONSUM GOODS–BIENS CONSOMMATION							
61 DURABLE–DURABLES							
62 SEMI DURABLE–SEMI DURABLES							
63 NON DURABLE–NON DURABLES							
7 GOODS NES–BIENS NDA							

EXPORTS – EXPORTATIONS

	1990	1991	1992	1993	1994	1995	1996
TOTAL EXPORTS–EXPORTATIONS TOTALES							
1 AGRICULTURE							
2 MINING QUARRY–INDUS EXTRACTIVES							
3 MANUFACTURING–IND MANUFACTUR							
31 FOOD BEV TOBACCO–ALIM BOISS TAB							
32 TEXTILES–INDUSTRIES TEXTILES							
33 WOOD & PRODUCTS–BOIS & PRODUITS							
34 PAPER & PRODUCTS–PAPIER & PRODT							
35 CHEMICALS–INDUSTRIES CHIMIQUES							
36 NON METAL MIN–MIN NON METAL							
37 BASIC METAL–IND METAL BASE							
38 METAL MANUF–MANUF METAL							
39 OTH MANUF IND–AUTRES MANUF							

3. TRADE BY PRINCIPAL COUNTRIES OF ORIGIN AND DESTINATION (VALUE IN THOUSAND U.S. DOLLARS)
ECHANGES SELON LES PRINCIPAUX PAYS D'ORIGINE ET DE DESTINATION (VALEUR EN MILLIERS DE DOLLARS EU)

COUNTRIES–PAYS	GENERAL IMPORTS C.I.F. IMPORTATIONS GENERALES C.A.F				
	1991	1992	1993	1994	1995
World				777911	667600
Africa				1780	1300
Americas				11507	14300
Northern America				9987	14100
LAIA				1520	100
CACM					
Caribbean					100
Rest of America					
As.ex F.USSR				184953	301800
Eur.x F.USSR				81238	109700
EU				69865	86000
EFTA				2385	3300
East Europe				8745	19600
Other Europe					200
Former USSR				498140	240400
Oceania				272	
Turkmenistan/Turkménistn				195600	51400
Turkey/Turquie				76027	140500
Russian Federation				117511	88300
Iran (Islamic Rp. of)				66766	80300
Ukraine				86264	33500
United Arab Emirates				8968	68700
Germany/Allemagne				31949	43700
Kazakhstan				51900	17400
Georgia/Géorgie				7960	18900
USA/Etats–Unis d'Amer				9971	13100
Republic of Moldova				13477	4500
Belgium–Luxembourg				8939	8900
Korea, Republic of				14242	1900
United Kingdom				6929	8900
Belarus/Bélarus				7900	4700
France,Monac				5608	5800
Uzbekistan/Ouzbékistan				2600	7600
Poland/Pologne				2466	7700
Israel/Israël				6975	2700
Lithuania/Lituanie				4648	4400
Latvia/Lettonie				4935	4000
Finland/Finlande				7344	1400
Bulgaria/Bulgarie				1298	6900
Cyprus/Chypre				6302	700
Estonia/Estonie				2745	3700
Italy/Italie				3898	2400
Switz.Liecht				2385	3300
Hungary/Hongrie				4060	1500
Netherlands/Pays–Bas				1291	3200
Austria/Autriche				925	3400
Kyrgyzstan/Kirghizistan				2400	1900
Denmark/Danemark				463	3700
Czech Republic				694	3300
India/Inde				3254	500
Greece/Grèce				244	3100
China/Chine					2800
Dem. Rep. of the Congo				1740	
Ireland/Irlande				1414	300
Afghanistan				1169	200
Argentina/Argentine				1354	
Sierra Leone					1300
Japan/Japon				166	1100
Sweden/Suède				861	300
Bangladesh					1100
Canada				16	1000
Spain/Espagne					900
Yugoslavia/Yougoslavie				243	600
Lebanon/Liban				551	100
Singapore/Singapour				76	400
Romania/Roumanie				227	200

COUNTRIES–PAYS	GENERAL EXPORTS F.O.B. EXPORTATIONS GENERALES F.O.B.				
	1991	1992	1993	1994	1995
Monde				636769	542800
Afrique					
Amériques				20	1200
Amérique du Nord				20	1200
ALAI					
MCAC					
Caraïbes					
Autre Amérique					
Asie l'URSS exclus				262085	194600
Europe l'URSS exclus				92516	121600
UE				83399	91200
AELE				3966	28200
Europe de l'Est				5151	1400
Autre de l'Europe					700
Ancienne URSS				281359	224600
Océanie				691	800
Iran (Islamic Rp. of)				242065	163300
Russian Federation				139721	99000
United Kingdom				61699	48500
Ukraine				57984	33400
Georgia/Géorgie				16610	41400
Turkey/Turquie				16463	26300
Kazakhstan				16500	16600
Switz.Liecht				3966	28200
Turkmenistan/Turkménistn				17100	13100
Italy/Italie				79	26400
Republic of Moldova				12554	3000
Austria/Autriche				9517	3600
Belarus/Bélarus				7600	2700
Lithuania/Lituanie				3738	6300
Greece/Grèce				1161	7500
Germany/Allemagne				4086	3900
Uzbekistan/Ouzbékistan				2700	4000
Poland/Pologne				4282	300
Tajikistan/Tadjikistan				1100	3300
Latvia/Lettonie				3369	900
Finland/Finlande				3563	
Kyrgyzstan/Kirghizistan				2200	600
United Arab Emirates				851	1600
Belgium–Luxembourg				957	800
China/Chine					1700
Australia/Australie				691	800
Afghanistan				1090	200
Cyprus/Chypre				1272	
USA/Etats–Unis d'Amer				20	1200
Ireland/Irlande				1202	
Oman					1100
Bulgaria/Bulgarie				283	800
France,Monac				987	
Gibraltar					700
Hungary/Hongrie				346	300
Spain/Espagne					500
Estonia/Estonie				183	300
India/Inde				257	
Czech Republic				240	
Viet Nam					200
Lebanon/Liban					200
Sweden/Suède				129	
Yugoslavia/Yougoslavie					100
Japan/Japon				66	
Israel/Israël				21	
Netherlands/Pays–Bas				19	

(VALUE AS PERCENTAGE OF WORLD TOTAL)(VALEURS EN POURCENTAGE DU TOTAL MONDIAL)

	1986	1987	1988	1989	1990	1991	1992	1993	1994	1995
Africa									0.2	0.2
Americas									1.5	2.1
Northern America									1.3	2.1
LAIA									0.2	0.0
CACM										
Caribbean										0.0
Rest of America										
As.ex F.USSR									23.8	45.2
Eur.x F.USSR									10.4	16.4
EU									9.0	12.9
EFTA									0.3	0.5
East Europe									1.1	2.9
Other Europe										0.0
Former USSR									64.0	36.0
Oceania									0.0	
Turkmenistan/Turkménistn									25.1	7.7
Turkey/Turquie									9.8	21.0
Russian Federation									15.1	13.2
Iran (Islamic Rp. of)									8.6	12.0
Ukraine									11.1	5.0
United Arab Emirates									1.2	10.3
Germany/Allemagne									4.1	6.5
Kazakhstan									6.7	2.6
Georgia/Géorgie									1.0	2.8
USA/Etats–Unis d'Amer									1.3	2.0

	1986	1987	1988	1989	1990	1991	1992	1993	1994	1995
Afrique										
Amériques									0.0	0.2
Amérique du Nord									0.0	0.2
ALAI										
MCAC										
Caraïbes										
Autre Amérique										
Asie l'URSS exclus									41.2	35.9
Europe l'URSS exclus									14.5	22.4
UE									13.1	16.8
AELE									0.6	5.2
Europe de l'Est									0.8	0.3
Autre de l'Europe										0.1
Ancienne URSS									44.2	41.4
Océanie									0.1	0.1
Iran (Islamic Rp. of)									38.0	30.1
Russian Federation									21.9	18.2
United Kingdom									9.7	8.9
Ukraine									9.1	6.2
Georgia/Géorgie									2.6	7.6
Turkey/Turquie									2.6	4.8
Kazakhstan									2.6	3.1
Switz.Liecht									0.6	5.2
Turkmenistan/Turkménistn									2.7	2.4
Italy/Italie									0.0	4.9

4. General Imports C.I.F. by Commodities according to the S.I.T.C. (Rev. 2) in thousand U.S. Dollars
Importations Générales C.A.F. par Produits d'après la C.T.C.I. (Rév. 2) en milliers de Dollars E.U.

SITC CTCI	COMMODITY	1992		1993		1994		1995		PRODUIT
		WEIGHT POIDS	VALUE VALEUR	WEIGHT POIDS	VALUE VALEUR	WEIGHT POIDS	VALUE VALEUR	WEIGHT POIDS	VALUE VALEUR	
	ALL COMMODITIES						777911		667600	TOUS PRODUITS
01	MEAT AND PREPARATIONS						16513			VIANDES ET PREPARATIONS
023	BUTTER					W 5700	6632			BEURRE
044	MAIZE UNMILLED					W 124840	10184			MAIS NON MOULU
04601	FLOUR OF WHEAT OR MESLIN					W 246544	31869			FARINE DE FROMENT
061	SUGAR AND HONEY					W 46459	14458			SUCRES ET MIEL
12	TOBACCO AND MANUFACTURES						12800			TABACS BRUTS FABRIQUES
24	CORK AND WOOD						5479			LIEGE ET BOIS
333	CRUDE PETROLEUM					W 852600	31434			HUILES BRUTES DE PETROLE
341	*GAS,NATURAL AND MANUFCT					MV 2478300	192550			GAZ NATUREL,GAZ MANUFACT
4	ANIMAL,VEGETABLE OIL,FAT						31408			HUILES,GRAISSES ANIM,VEG
51216	ETHYL ALC,DENATRD SPIRIT					V 2259	2685			ALCOOL ETHYLIQUE NON DENAT
6252	TYRES,NEW,BUS OR LORRY					N 37800	4009			PNEUS POUR AUTOBUS,CAMIONS
66	NONMETAL MINERAL MFS NES						4753			ART MIN NON METALLIQUES
761	TELEVISION RECEIVERS						2902			RECEPTEURS DE TELEVISION
781	PASS MOTOR VEH EXC BUSES					N 1091	9033			AUTO TRANSPORT PERSONNES
782	LORRIES,SPCL MTR VEH NES					N 348	2923			VEHICULES SPECIAUX,MARCH
821	*FURNITURE,PARTS THEREOF						5899			MEUBLES ET PIECES

5. General Exports F.O.B. by Commodities according to the S.I.T.C. (Rev. 2) in thousand U.S. Dollars
Exportations Générales F.O.B. par Produits d'après la C.T.C.I. (Rév. 2) en milliers de Dollars E.U.

SITC CTCI	COMMODITY	1992		1993		1994		1995		PRODUIT
		WEIGHT POIDS	VALUE VALEUR	WEIGHT POIDS	VALUE VALEUR	WEIGHT POIDS	VALUE VALEUR	WEIGHT POIDS	VALUE VALEUR	
	ALL COMMODITIES						636769		542800	TOUS PRODUITS
054	VEG ETC FRSH,SMPLY PRSVD					W 29700	9957			LEGUMES FRAIS,CONG,SECS
0565	VEGTBLES PRSVD,PREPD NES					W 1000	5526			LEGUMES PREPARES CONSERVE
11242	DISTILLD WINE,GRAPE MARC						9306			EAUX-DE-VIE NATURELLES
1223	OTH MANUFACTURED TOBACCO					W 12900	10845			TABACS FUMER,CHIQUER,PRISER
2631	RAW COTTON,EXCL LINTERS					W 74800	98520			COTON EN MASSE
334	PETROLEUM PRODUCTS,REFIN					W 1804000	207058			PRODUITS RAFFINES
5157	SULPHONAMIDES,ETC					W 4500	3067			SULFAMIDES,SULTONES ETC
5542	WASHING PREPARATIONS ETC					W 172100	3653			PROD ORG TENSIO-ACT NDA
659	FLOOR COVERINGS,ETC						2562			COUVRE-PARQUETS,TAPIS ETC
678	IRON,STL TUBES,PIPES,ETC					W 5900	1974			TUBES,TUYAUX EN FONTE,FER
684	ALUMINIUM						10317			ALUMINIUM
69781	DOMSTC FOOD MACH NONELEC						2270			MOULINS A CAFE ETC
716	ROTATING ELECTRIC PLANT						11133			APP ELECTR ROTATIFS,PIECES
72343	SLFPRP CONST ETC MCH NES						25213			AUT MACH EXTR,TERRASSEM
7415	AIR-CONDITIONING MACHNRY					N 112536	20543			GROUPES CONDITION AIR
77521	DOMESTIC REFRIGERATORS					N 59255	9189			REFRIGERATEURS

1. HISTORICAL SERIES, 1960–1995 GENERAL TRADE, IMPORTS C.I.F., EXPORTS F.O.B.
SERIES HISTORIQUES, 1960–1995 COMMERCE GENERAL, IMPORTATIONS C.A.F., EXPORTATIONS F.O.B

YEAR ANNEE	VALUE IN MILLION BAHAMIAN DOLLARS VALEUR EN MILLION BAHAMIAN DOLLARS MERCHANDISE –MARCHANDISE		GOLD –OR		CONVERSION FACTORS U.S. CENTS PER BAHAMIAN DOLLAR FACTEURS DE CONVERSION CENTS E.U. PAR BAHAMIAN DOLLAR		INDEX NUMBERS –INDICES QUANTUM		UNIT VALUE VALEUR UNITAIRE	
	IMPORTS	EXPORTS	IMPORTS	EXPORTS	IMPORTS	EXPORTS	IMPORTS	EXPORTS	IMPORTS	EXPORTS
1960	66.90	5.90			98.0000	98.0000				
1961	86.90	8.50			98.0000	98.0000				
1962	70.10	9.20			98.0000	98.0000				
1963	80.80	9.90			98.0000	98.0000				
1964	102.00	16.00			98.0000	98.0000				
1965	107.00	19.00			98.0000	98.0000				
1966	141.60	22.80			98.0000	98.0000				
1967	165.50	32.30			98.0000	98.0000				
1968	180.00	51.80			98.0000	98.0000				
1969	302.30	54.30			98.0000	98.0000				
1970	337.50	89.60			100.0000	100.0000				
1971	511.30	266.60			100.0000	100.0000				
1972	484.90	343.40			100.0000	100.0000				
1973	764.30	529.80			100.0000	100.0000				
1974	1908.40	1443.60			100.0000	100.0000				
1975	2696.90	2508.30			100.0000	100.0000				
1976	3124.50	2992.30			100.0000	100.0000				
1977	3568.20	3260.70			100.0000	100.0000				
1978	3149.60	3058.40			100.0000	100.0000				
1979	3513.90	3786.00			100.0000	100.0000				
1980	7545.60	5009.40			100.0000	100.0000				
1981	7284.50	6189.20			100.0000	100.0000				
1982	6348.80	4534.40			100.0000	100.0000				
1983	4616.30	3970.30			100.0000	100.0000				
1984	4097.90	3392.70			100.0000	100.0000				
1985	3077.90	2629.50			100.0000	100.0000				
1986	3288.90	2701.00			100.0000	100.0000				
1987	3041.00	2727.70			100.0000	100.0000				
1988	2263.50	2163.80			100.0000	100.0000				
1989	3001.00	2786.00			100.0000	100.0000				
1990	2919.90	2678.00			100.0000	100.0000				
1991	1091.10	225.10			100.0000	100.0000				
1992	1037.50	192.30			100.0000	100.0000				
1993	953.90	162.30			100.0000	100.0000				
1994	1055.90	167.00			100.0000	100.0000				
1995	1243.10	175.90			100.0000	100.0000				

2. IMPORTS BY BROAD ECONOMIC CATEGORY AND EXPORTS BY INDUSTRIAL ORIGIN. (PERCENTAGE OF TOTAL VALUE)
IMPORTATIONS PAR CATEGORIES ECONOMIQUES ET EXPORTATIONS PAR BRANCHE D'ACTIVITE.(EN POURCENTAGE DE LA VALEUR TOTALE)

IMPORTS – IMPORTATIONS

	1990	1991	1992	1993	1994	1995	1996
TOTAL IMPORTS–IMPORTATIONS TOTALES		100.					
1 FOOD BEV–ALIMENTATION BOISSONS		20.1					
11 PRIMARY–PRODUITS DE BASE		6.5					
111 FOR INDUSTRY–POUR L'INDUSTRIE		0.3					
112 FOR HOUSEHOLDS–POUR LES MENAGES		6.2					
12 PROCESSED–PRODUITS ELABORES		13.7					
121 FOR INDUSTRY–POUR L'INDUSTRIE		1.1					
122 FOR HOUSEHOLDS–POUR LES MENAGES		12.5					
2 IND SUPPLIES–APPROV INDUSTRIELS		19.8					
21 PRIMARY–PRODUITS DE BASE		1.3					
22 PROCESSED–PRODUITS ELABORES		18.5					
3 FUELS–COMBUSTIBLES		10.9					
31 PRIMARY–PRODUITS DE BASE		0.8					
32 PROCESSED–PRODUITS ELABORES		10.2					
321 MOTOR SPIRIT–ESSENCE		3.4					
322 OTHER–AUTRES		6.7					
4 MACHINERY–EQUIPEMENT		16.2					
41 CAPITAL EQUIPMENT–MACHINES		14.6					
42 PARTS–PIECES ACCESSOIRES		1.6					
5 TRANSPORT–TRANSPORT		7.7					
51 PASSENGER CARS–AUTOMOBILES		2.8					
52 OTHER–AUTRES		2.3					
521 INDUSTRIAL–INDUSTRIELS		2.3					
522 NON INDUSTRIAL–NON INDUSTRIEL		0.1					
53 PARTS–PIECES ACCESSOIRES		2.5					
6 CONSUM GOODS–BIENS CONSOMMATION		24.7					
61 DURABLE–DURABLES		6.1					
62 SEMI DURABLE–SEMI DURABLES		11.2					
63 NON DURABLE–NON DURABLES		7.3					
7 GOODS NES–BIENS NDA		0.6					

EXPORTS – EXPORTATIONS

	1990	1991	1992	1993	1994	1995	1996
TOTAL EXPORTS–EXPORTATIONS TOTALES		100.					
1 AGRICULTURE		25.3					
2 MINING QUARRY–INDUS EXTRACTIVES		11.1					
3 MANUFACTURING–IND MANUFACTUR		63.6					
31 FOOD BEV TOBACCO–ALIM BOISS TAB		16.4					
32 TEXTILES–INDUSTRIES TEXTILES		0.9					
33 WOOD & PRODUCTS–BOIS & PRODUITS		0.0					
34 PAPER & PRODUCTS–PAPIER & PRODT		0.1					
35 CHEMICALS–INDUSTRIES CHIMIQUES		30.4					
36 NON METAL MIN–MIN NON METAL		3.4					
37 BASIC METAL–IND METAL BASE		0.7					
38 METAL MANUF–MANUF METAL		11.1					
39 OTH MANUF IND–AUTRES MANUF		0.5					

3. TRADE BY PRINCIPAL COUNTRIES OF PRODUCTION AND LAST CONSIGNMENT (VALUE IN THOUSAND U.S. DOLLARS)
ECHANGES SELON LES PRINCIPAUX PAYS DE PRODUCTION ET DE DERNIERE CONSIGNATION (VALEUR EN MILLIERS DE DOLLARS EU)

COUNTRIES–PAYS	GENERAL IMPORTS C.I.F. IMPORTATIONS GENERALES C.A.F				
	1991	1992	1993	1994	1995
World	1091191	1037535	953904	1055875	1243081
Africa	52				
Americas	964780	780145	771984	966629	1020029
Northern America	887425	780145	771984	966629	1020029
LAIA	13283				
CACM	2824				
Caribbean	55483				
Rest of America	5766				
As.ex F.USSR	20600				
Eur.x F.USSR	104036	22215	15129	7117	8691
EU	91003	22215	15129	7117	8691
EFTA	12509				
East Europe	452				
Other Europe	72				
Former USSR	59				
Oceania	1232				
USA/Etats–Unis d'Amer	865954	759900	757290	960450	1008691
United Kingdom	23914	22215	15129	7117	8691
Canada	21215	20245	14694	6179	11338
Aruba	52209				
Denmark/Danemark	23698				
France,Monac	20816				
Japan/Japon	14560				
Switz.Liecht	12473				
Panama	5765				
Germany/Allemagne	5593				
Netherlands/Pays–Bas	4951				
Argentina/Argentine	4368				
Austria/Autriche	3708				
Spain/Espagne	3509				
Italy/Italie	3295				
Hong Kong	3116				
Venezuela	2894				
Brazil/Brésil	2308				
Mexico/Mexique	1677				
Guatemala	1467				
Peru/Pérou	1280				
Trinidad and Tobago	1238				
El Salvador	951				
Barbados/Barbade	881				
Australia/Australie	777				
Colombia/Colombie	699				
Jamaica/Jamaïque	606				
Korea, Republic of	557				
Belgium–Luxembourg	530				
China/Chine	507				
New Zealand	447				
Costa Rica	406				
Sweden/Suède	355				
Ireland/Irlande	348				
Thailand/Thaïlande	333				
Czechoslovakia	273				
Bermuda/Bermudes	255				
Philippines	242				
Korea Dem People's Rp	186				
Israel/Israël	185				
Cuba	184				
Hungary/Hongrie	154				
Portugal	130				
Singapore/Singapour	126				
Greece/Grèce	122				
Saint Lucia/St. Lucie	90				
India/Inde	81				
Netherlands Antilles	81				
Haiti/Haïti	75				
Dominican Republic	64				

COUNTRIES–PAYS	GENERAL EXPORTS F.O.B. EXPORTATIONS GENERALES F.O.B.				
	1991	1992	1993	1994	1995
Monde	225070	192350	162307	167033	175916
Afrique					
Amériques	174114	113580	110348	126279	146002
Amérique du Nord	149795	113580	110348	126279	146002
ALAI	8346				
MCAC	995				
Caraïbes	12262				
Autre Amérique	2716				
Asie l'URSS exclus	56				
Europe l'URSS exclus	50831	9256	5786	10451	3966
UE	50500	9256	5786	10451	3966
AELE	322				
Europe de l'Est	9				
Autre de l'Europe					
Ancienne URSS					
Océanie	11				
USA/Etats–Unis d'Amer	142454	105135	105595	122560	142614
United Kingdom	27203	9256	5786	10451	3966
Canada	6742	8445	4753	3719	3388
France,Monac	14544				
Germany/Allemagne	6191				
Mexico/Mexique	4005				
Grenada/Grenade	2905				
Aruba	2636				
Panama	2605				
Brazil/Brésil	2305				
Netherlands Antilles	1593				
Jamaica/Jamaïque	1409				
Haiti/Haïti	1034				
Italy/Italie	977				
Dominican Republic	722				
Netherlands/Pays–Bas	635				
Venezuela	606				
Bermuda/Bermudes	600				
Cayman Is/Is Caïmans	545				
Belgium–Luxembourg	509				
Uruguay	404				
Barbados/Barbade	332				
Switz.Liecht	322				
Honduras	309				
Guatemala	294				
Trinidad and Tobago	286				
Antigua and Barbuda	268				
Ireland/Irlande	240				
Costa Rica	225				
Paraguay	208				
Bolivia/Bolivie	196				
Turks and Caicos Isls	165				
Colombia/Colombie	162				
Spain/Espagne	150				
Argentina/Argentine	145				
Chile/Chili	124				
Peru/Pérou	113				
Saint Lucia/St. Lucie	106				
Nicaragua	106				
British Antarctic Ter	103				
Ecuador/Equateur	79				
Martinique	77				
El Salvador	61				
Guadeloupe	52				
British Virgin Islds	43				
Greece/Grèce	30				
Hong Kong	14				
Japan/Japon	12				
Austria/Autriche	11				
Hungary/Hongrie	9				

(VALUE AS PERCENTAGE OF WORLD TOTAL)(VALEURS EN POURCENTAGE DU TOTAL MONDIAL)

	1986	1987	1988	1989	1990	1991	1992	1993	1994	1995
Africa		0.0	17.1	8.5	4.8	0.0				
Americas		47.4	46.6	43.1	47.0	88.4	75.2	80.9	84.7	82.1
Northern America		39.6	41.0	34.5	36.7	81.3	75.2	80.9	84.7	82.1
LAIA		7.5	4.8	6.8	7.5	1.2				
CACM		0.0	0.1	0.1	0.1	0.3				
Caribbean		0.3	0.5	1.4	2.4	5.1				
Rest of America		0.0	0.2	0.3	0.2	0.5				
As.ex F.USSR		7.2	26.5	43.4	40.8	1.9				
Eur.x F.USSR		45.3	8.6	4.7	7.0	9.5	2.1	1.6	0.7	0.7
EU		10.8	8.0	4.0	5.9	8.3	2.1	1.6	0.7	0.7
EFTA		34.6	0.6	0.5	1.1	1.1				
East Europe			0.0	0.2		0.0				
Other Europe		0.0	0.0	0.0		0.0				
Former USSR			0.0	0.1	0.3	0.0				
Oceania		0.1	0.0	0.0	0.0	0.1				
USA/Etats–Unis d'Amer		38.3	40.1	33.7	36.2	79.4	73.2	79.4	84.2	81.1
United Kingdom		2.1	5.0	1.4	3.7	2.2	2.1	1.6	0.7	0.7
Canada		1.2	0.9	0.7	0.6	1.9	2.0	1.5	0.6	0.9
Aruba			0.0	0.0	0.4	4.8				
Denmark/Danemark		0.8	0.1	0.1	0.1	2.2				
France,Monac		3.0	0.7	0.5	0.6	1.9				
Japan/Japon		4.0	0.6	0.4	0.5	1.3				
Switz.Liecht		1.0	0.6	0.5	0.4	1.1				
Panama		0.0	0.2	0.3	0.2	0.5				
Germany/Allemagne		0.8	0.6	0.5	0.4	0.5				

	1986	1987	1988	1989	1990	1991	1992	1993	1994	1995
Afrique		0.2	0.1	0.2	0.0					
Amériques		68.2	95.2	95.6	96.0	77.4	59.0	68.0	75.6	83.0
Amérique du Nord		66.1	92.9	94.3	94.7	66.6	59.0	68.0	75.6	83.0
ALAI		1.6	0.5	0.3	0.3	3.7				
MCAC		0.0	0.0	0.0	0.0	0.4				
Caraïbes		0.5	0.8	0.9	0.5	5.4				
Autre Amérique		0.0	0.9	0.1	0.3	1.2				
Asie l'URSS exclus		10.0	2.2	1.4	0.9	0.0				
Europe l'URSS exclus		20.9	2.3	2.6	2.6	22.6	4.8	3.6	6.3	2.3
UE		13.0	2.2	2.6	2.6	22.4	4.8	3.6	6.3	2.3
AELE		7.8	0.1	0.0	0.0	0.1				
Europe de l'Est			0.0	0.0		0.0				
Autre de l'Europe		0.1	0.0	0.0						
Ancienne URSS					0.3					
Océanie		0.7	0.2	0.2	0.1	0.0				
USA/Etats–Unis d'Amer		61.7	90.9	92.6	93.8	63.3	54.7	65.1	73.4	81.1
United Kingdom		3.6	0.8	0.9	0.8	12.1	4.8	3.6	6.3	2.3
Canada		4.4	1.9	1.6	0.9	3.0	4.4	2.9	2.2	1.9
France,Monac		1.5	0.2	0.1	0.4	6.5				
Germany/Allemagne		1.1	0.2	0.2	0.2	2.8				
Mexico/Mexique		0.4	0.1	0.2	0.2	1.8				
Grenada/Grenade			0.0	0.0	0.0	1.3				
Aruba			0.1	0.0	0.0	1.2				
Panama		0.0	0.9	0.1	0.3	1.2				
Brazil/Brésil		0.7	0.3	0.0	0.1	1.0				

4. General Imports C.I.F. by Commodities according to the S.I.T.C. (Rev. 2) in thousand U.S. Dollars
Importations Générales C.A.F. par Produits d'après la C.T.C.I. (Rév. 2) en milliers de Dollars E.U.

SITC CTCI	COMMODITY	1992		1993		1994		1995		PRODUIT
		WEIGHT POIDS	VALUE VALEUR	WEIGHT POIDS	VALUE VALEUR	WEIGHT POIDS	VALUE VALEUR	WEIGHT POIDS	VALUE VALEUR	
	ALL COMMODITIES		1037535		953904		1055875		1243081	TOUS PRODUITS
0	FOOD AND LIVE ANIMALS		184285		189995		196844		208972	ALIMENTS,ANIMAUX VIVANTS
1	BEVERAGES AND TOBACCO		24701		22059		19537		20382	BOISSONS ET TABACS
2	CRUDE MATERLS,EXCL FUELS		18147		19419		23017		26190	MAT BRUTES NON COMESTIBLES
3	MINERAL FUELS ETC		116706		76263		98617		156431	COMBUSTIBLES MINERAUX LUB
33411	MOTOR,AVIATION SPIRIT		42398		37409		36176		40776	ESSENCES MOTEURS D'AVIONS
33421	KEROSENE INCL JET FUEL		3077		3072		3211		3606	PETROLES LAMPANTS
3343	GAS OILS		35194		25573		29059		32923	GAS OILS
3345	LUBS,PETROLEUM OILS NES		2856		2863		3567		4322	HUILES LUBRIFIANTES
4	ANIMAL,VEGETABLE OIL,FAT		2241		2862		3473		3797	HUILES,GRAISSES ANIM,VEG
5	CHEMCLS,RELATED PROD NES		100339		94281		89281		100651	PRODUITS CHIMIQUES
6	BASIC MANUFACTURES		170854		154345		177740		194031	ART MANUFACTURES
7	MACHINES,TRANSPORT EQUIP		223754		198804		245875		308628	MACHINES MATERIEL TRANSPORT
8	MISC MANUFACTURED GOODS		172577		173938		188592		202922	ART MANUFACTURES DIVERS
9	GOODS NOT CLASSD BY KIND		23931		21938		12899		21077	ART TRANSACT NON CLASSES

5. General Exports F.O.B. by Commodities according to the S.I.T.C. (Rev. 2) in thousand U.S. Dollars
Exportations Générales F.O.B. par Produits d'après la C.T.C.I. (Rév. 2) en milliers de Dollars E.U.

SITC CTCI	COMMODITY	1992		1993		1994		1995		PRODUIT
		WEIGHT POIDS	VALUE VALEUR	WEIGHT POIDS	VALUE VALEUR	WEIGHT POIDS	VALUE VALEUR	WEIGHT POIDS	VALUE VALEUR	
	ALL COMMODITIES		192350		162307		167033		175916	TOUS PRODUITS
0	FOOD AND LIVE ANIMALS		63079		48507		66053		64825	ALIMENTS,ANIMAUX VIVANTS
036	SHELL FISH FRESH,FROZEN								56148	CRUSTACES,MOLLUSQUES
05	VEGETABLES AND FRUIT		5661		4347		3133		2842	LEGUMES ET FRUITS
1	BEVERAGES AND TOBACCO		21863		12099		8961		3472	BOISSONS ET TABACS
11249	OTH ALCOHOLC BEVS,CMPNDS		21110		11937		8581		3239	BOISSONS ALCOOLIQUES NDA
2	CRUDE MATERLS,EXCL FUELS		18820		26324		33008		31200	MAT BRUTES NON COMESTIBLES
2783	COMMON SALT,ETC		8163		14764		15511		13463	SEL
27899	MINERAL SUBSTANCES NES		1077		1276		851		343	MATIERES MINERALES NDA
3	MINERAL FUELS ETC		5060		14		3329		26	COMBUSTIBLES MINERAUX LUB
5	CHEMCLS,RELATED PROD NES		37260		44485		22007		16793	PRODUITS CHIMIQUES
54199	OTH PHARMACEUTICAL GOODS		767		351		78			AUT PREP PHARMACEUTIQUES
553	PERFUMERY,COSMETICS,ETC		1414		5					PRODUITS DE PARFUMERIE
6	BASIC MANUFACTURES		9521		8652		4167		7436	ART MANUFACTURES
7	MACHINES,TRANSPORT EQUIP		29403		14534		22714		45953	MACHINES MATERIEL TRANSPORT
8	MISC MANUFACTURED GOODS		6899		7298		6632		5983	ART MANUFACTURES DIVERS

1. HISTORICAL SERIES, 1961–1996 GENERAL TRADE, IMPORTS C.I.F., EXPORTS F.O.B. # 1
SERIES HISTORIQUES, 1961–1996 COMMERCE GENERAL, IMPORTATIONS C.A.F., EXPORTATIONS F.O.B

YEAR ANNEE	VALUE IN MILLION BAHRAINI DINARS / VALEUR EN MILLION BAHRAINI DINARS — MERCHANDISE – MARCHANDISE		GOLD – OR		CONVERSION FACTORS U.S. CENTS PER BAHRAINI DINAR FACTEURS DE CONVERSION CENTS E.U. PAR BAHRAINI DINAR		INDEX NUMBERS – INDICES — QUANTUM		UNIT VALUE VALEUR UNITAIRE	
	IMPORTS	EXPORTS	IMPORTS	EXPORTS	IMPORTS	EXPORTS	IMPORTS	EXPORTS	IMPORTS	EXPORTS
1961		9.40			210.0000	210.0000				
1962	31.20	11.00			210.0000	210.0000				
1963	33.00	10.60			210.0000	210.0000				
1964	37.90	10.50			210.0000	210.0000				
1965	38.80	10.70			210.0000	210.0000				
1966	42.00	12.60			210.0000	210.0000				
1967	45.50	14.70			210.0000	210.0000				
1968	52.00	18.50			210.0000	210.0000				
1969	99.50	121.30			210.0000	210.0000				
1970	117.70	130.60			210.0000	210.0000				
1971	148.00	151.60			210.0000	210.0000				
1972	165.60	141.70			228.0000	228.0000				
1973	212.60	162.40			250.7580	250.7620				
1974	473.30	459.00			253.3320	253.3320				
1975	458.10	453.70			252.8400	252.8400				
1976	660.50	548.50			252.7750	252.7750				
1977	802.80	730.10			252.7500	252.7500				
1978	792.30	733.10			258.2230	258.1640				
1979	945.30	948.00			262.4090	262.4520				
1980	1313.10	1355.90			265.3140	265.3320				
1981	1550.60	1634.60			265.9598	265.9595				
1982	1358.90	1424.80			265.9598	265.9596				
1983	1256.60	1202.80			265.9599	265.9598				
1984	1308.30	1204.70			265.9465	265.9597				
1985	1168.10	1089.20			265.9598	265.9597				
1986	904.30	827.00			265.9597	265.9596				
1987	1020.30	913.50			265.9596	265.9597				
1988	975.10	906.70			265.9597	265.9596				
1989	1178.20	1064.50			265.9597	265.9597				
1990	1395.60	1414.00			265.9597	265.9597				
1991	1547.30	1320.00			265.9597	265.9597				
1992	1602.90	1302.60			265.9596	265.9598				
1993	1450.60	1400.00			265.9591	265.9591				
1994	1409.20	1359.90			265.9578	265.9577				
1995	1397.10	1546.40			265.9579	265.9579				
1996	1530.80	1775.00			265.9576	265.9576				

2. IMPORTS BY BROAD ECONOMIC CATEGORY AND EXPORTS BY INDUSTRIAL ORIGIN. (PERCENTAGE OF TOTAL VALUE)
IMPORTATIONS PAR CATEGORIES ECONOMIQUES ET EXPORTATIONS PAR BRANCHE D'ACTIVITE.(EN POURCENTAGE DE LA VALEUR TOTALE)

IMPORTS – IMPORTATIONS

	1990	1991	1992	1993	1994	1995	1996
TOTAL IMPORTS–IMPORTATIONS TOTALES	100.	100.	100.	100.	100.		
1 FOOD BEV–ALIMENTATION BOISSONS	7.6	7.3	7.6	8.9	9.6		
11 PRIMARY–PRODUITS DE BASE	3.5	3.3	3.4	4.1	4.9		
111 FOR INDUSTRY–POUR L'INDUSTRIE	0.9	0.7	0.8	0.8	1.4		
112 FOR HOUSEHOLDS–POUR LES MENAGES	2.6	2.6	2.7	3.3	3.5		
12 PROCESSED–PRODUITS ELABORES	4.1	4.1	4.2	4.9	4.7		
121 FOR INDUSTRY–POUR L'INDUSTRIE	0.6	0.7	0.7	0.7	0.8		
122 FOR HOUSEHOLDS–POUR LES MENAGES	3.5	3.4	3.5	4.1	3.9		
2 IND SUPPLIES–APPROV INDUSTRIELS	19.4	19.0	19.3	24.3	23.4		
21 PRIMARY–PRODUITS DE BASE	1.0	1.0	0.8	1.1	1.3		
22 PROCESSED–PRODUITS ELABORES	18.4	18.0	18.5	23.2	22.0		
3 FUELS–COMBUSTIBLES	48.4	42.0	35.7	35.8	32.2		
31 PRIMARY–PRODUITS DE BASE	48.2	41.7	35.4	35.5	31.7		
32 PROCESSED–PRODUITS ELABORES	0.3	0.3	0.3	0.3	0.5		
321 MOTOR SPIRIT–ESSENCE	0.0	0.0	0.0	0.0	0.0		
322 OTHER–AUTRES	0.3	0.3	0.3	0.3	0.5		
4 MACHINERY–EQUIPEMENT	6.8	13.8	16.5	10.0	11.6		
41 CAPITAL EQUIPMENT–MACHINES	5.1	8.9	7.4	7.4	10.3		
42 PARTS–PIECES ACCESSOIRES	1.7	4.9	9.1	2.6	1.4		
5 TRANSPORT–TRANSPORT	7.2	6.4	9.4	8.8	10.1		
51 PASSENGER CARS–AUTOMOBILES	2.5	2.3	3.4	3.7	3.4		
52 OTHER–AUTRES	0.9	1.1	1.4	1.0	3.2		
521 INDUSTRIAL–INDUSTRIELS	0.9	1.0	1.4	1.0	3.2		
522 NON INDUSTRIAL–NON INDUSTRIEL	0.0	0.0	0.0	0.0	0.0		
53 PARTS–PIECES ACCESSOIRES	3.8	3.0	4.5	4.1	3.5		
6 CONSUM GOODS–BIENS CONSOMMATION	8.5	8.9	10.5	11.8	11.1		
61 DURABLE–DURABLES	3.2	3.3	4.3	4.8	3.4		
62 SEMI DURABLE–SEMI DURABLES	3.9	4.0	4.5	5.0	5.2		
63 NON DURABLE–NON DURABLES	1.5	1.6	1.7	2.0	2.5		
7 GOODS NES–BIENS NDA	2.1	2.6	1.0	0.4	1.9		

EXPORTS – EXPORTATIONS

	1990	1991	1992	1993	1994	1995	1996
TOTAL EXPORTS–EXPORTATIONS TOTALES	100.	100.	100.	100.	100.		
1 AGRICULTURE	0.1	0.3	0.3	0.5	0.5		
2 MINING QUARRY–INDUS EXTRACTIVES	78.2	77.6	75.2	65.7	59.5		
3 MANUFACTURING–IND MANUFACTUR	21.7	22.1	24.5	33.8	39.9		
31 FOOD BEV TOBACCO–ALIM BOISS TAB	0.6	1.1	1.6	1.9	1.8		
32 TEXTILES–INDUSTRIES TEXTILES	0.6	0.7	1.3	1.8	2.4		
33 WOOD & PRODUCTS–BOIS & PRODUITS	0.0	0.0	0.0	0.0	0.0		
34 PAPER & PRODUCTS–PAPIER & PRODT	0.2	0.2	0.1	0.4	0.5		
35 CHEMICALS–INDUSTRIES CHIMIQUES	3.7	4.7	3.0	3.2	6.0		
36 NON METAL MIN–MIN NON METAL	0.3	0.2	0.1	0.1	0.1		
37 BASIC METAL–IND METAL BASE	12.5	12.4	15.2	21.9	25.5		
38 METAL MANUF–MANUF METAL	3.7	2.6	3.0	4.1	3.5		
39 OTH MANUF IND–AUTRES MANUF	0.2	0.2	0.2	0.3	0.1		

3. TRADE BY PRINCIPAL COUNTRIES OF PRODUCTION AND LAST CONSIGNMENT (VALUE IN THOUSAND U.S. DOLLARS)
ECHANGES SELON LES PRINCIPAUX PAYS DE PRODUCTION ET DE DERNIERE CONSIGNATION (VALEUR EN MILLIERS DE DOLLARS EU)

COUNTRIES–PAYS	GENERAL IMPORTS C.I.F. IMPORTATIONS GENERALES C.A.F				
	1992	1993	1994	1995	1996
World	4272059	3858003	3761756	3624769	4092557
Africa	18613	27418	27871	22928	689
Americas	420603	415891	485363	395467	347716
Northern America	368921	357703	416632	316187	281748
LAIA	49600	57160	67073	77857	65287
CACM	1260	666	1176	904	681
Caribbean	791	331	461	503	
Rest of America	31	31	21	16	
As.ex F.USSR	997638	934125	982996	876958	729878
Eur.x F.USSR	1102788	794857	842659	776047	735668
EU	1017862	747469	767561	715345	693027
EFTA	67651	41663	69484	51774	42641
East Europe	14984	3544	3562	6322	
Other Europe	727	484	351	532	
Former USSR	631	786	1253	4811	
Oceania	172559	250309	191890	183262	230325
USA/Etats–Unis d'Amer	355081	349691	407719	298229	261426
United Kingdom	287560	234995	233457	212598	219851
Japan/Japon	275199	244690	209578	147887	150505
Australia/Australie	160239	241599	181731	172643	218077
Germany/Allemagne	269750	159650	137538	145219	169373
Saudi Arabia	147957	133263	161795	178855	166787
France,Monac	146059	92905	125392	84700	115466
Italy/Italie	112060	96515	97805	79176	86495
India/Inde	72555	87447	98006	89254	95511
United Arab Emirates	78662	81166	97545	96089	87806
Brazil/Brésil	45581	51167	60936	72921	65287
Netherlands/Pays–Bas	61774	50706	56881	52378	47537
China/Chine	35763	46735	54100	51532	48718
Switz.Liecht	55197	35518	39794	45062	42641
Korea. Republic of	32030	39735	53571	39878	41114
Malaysia/Malaisie	40057	35664	46589	41141	
Hong Kong	83820	21270	22771	17939	17162
Thailand/Thaïlande	32755	31638	25994	31686	26428
Pakistan	22695	23750	21483	34508	33098
Belgium–Luxembourg	37368	18880	23040	22253	20064
Denmark/Danemark	23151	21377	18757	24037	24574
Iran (Islamic Rp. of)	19379	20400	25941	17617	14508
Spain/Espagne	28656	20621	19959	22726	
Sweden/Suède	22525	19482	17909	30452	
Indonesia/Indonésie	20100	21430	25019	22811	
Singapore/Singapour	22409	22229	13439	12458	11668
Turkey/Turquie	14153	16152	21831	17383	
Canada	13840	8012	8907	17952	20322
Jordan/Jordanie	12321	17277	15675	17551	
Kuwait/ Koweït	8486	12746	11287	14713	12245
Austria/Autriche	10270	8612	9448	18976	9668
Norway,SVD,JM	12398	6087	29489	6508	
New Zealand	12316	8682	10081	10556	12247
Ireland/Irlande	7690	10746	13183	12755	
Qatar	8226	8793	9298	9348	8266
Lebanon/Liban	10480	8736	8417	7646	7343
Oman	6746	7800	7522	9088	8718
Egypt/Egypte	8001	9271	8851	7620	
Tunisia/Tunisie	7510	10075	9388	6378	
Philippines	5413	7409	8061	8170	
So. Africa Customs Un	953	7137	7842	7255	
Finland/Finlande	3703	6705	6180	4662	
Syrian Arab Republic	3163	3640	4407	4335	
Greece/Grèce	3370	4301	4923	2676	
Hungary/Hongrie	10695	1007	452	505	
Chile/Chili	1824	3952	3153	3596	
Cyprus/Chypre	3400	3268	3076	2309	
Portugal	3926	1976	3089	2734	
Romania/Roumanie	2517	1007	1430	2636	
Sri Lanka	1842	1934	2001	1753	

COUNTRIES–PAYS	GENERAL EXPORTS F.O.B. EXPORTATIONS GENERALES F.O.B.				
	1992	1993	1994	1995	1996
Monde	3464376	3710051	3452132	4092061	4602396
Afrique	5907	12124	15951	14724	753
Amériques	72347	104766	152513	134485	106431
Amérique du Nord	72176	104356	152102	131592	106431
ALAI	106	410	372	2894	
MCAC					
Caraïbes	65		39		
Autre Amérique					
Asie l'URSS exclus	609613	970504	1090713	1192408	988179
Europe l'URSS exclus	104431	100594	85397	123762	57702
UE	100834	98570	81192	117669	57702
AELE	2031	680	2624	5965	
Europe de l'Est	54	9	125	3	
Autre de l'Europe	1491	1327		125	
Ancienne URSS		60	284	582	
Océanie	5988	6267	2477	5886	15032
Saudi Arabia	142584	200576	219547	250728	246011
Japan/Japon	76119	192056	193088	142249	193630
Korea, Republic of	100460	115892	119678	157528	117253
USA/Etats–Unis d'Amer	69070	102644	150444	130743	105229
India/Inde	32849	62319	101926	103583	85910
United Arab Emirates	36200	69956	58471	74142	82665
Kuwait/ Koweït	41687	45453	42071	58309	47654
Iran (Islamic Rp. of)	20922	49375	55847	46631	40364
Singapore/Singapour	20125	20116	32338	79014	26787
Netherlands/Pays–Bas	43692	18444	34577	46937	13535
Qatar	25891	23991	27879	31511	42370
United Kingdom	18244	40676	16683	23657	17763
Malaysia/Malaisie	12285	24846	18370	42296	
Indonesia/Indonésie	16104	14578	26986	35745	
Jordan/Jordanie	11498	13984	21734	41391	
Pakistan	17377	8719	12138	14641	27309
Hong Kong	4010	10946	13313	19420	21205
Oman	4222	11980	20731	10963	17199
Thailand/Thaïlande	4200	6412	8181	21889	18894
China/Chine	959	4592	13476	22301	17423
Italy/Italie	16660	10678	9132	11245	
Belgium–Luxembourg	3320	2690	2921	12745	20008
Philippines	3857	7451	6434	19888	
Germany/Allemagne	5313	8600	7030	5021	4293
Turkey/Turquie	13219	6504	256	8896	
Australia/Australie	4748	5036	1147	4024	10856
Sweden/Suède	7734	12696	3251	436	96
France,Monac	4049	3538	4754	7213	1864
Tunisia/Tunisie	3200	6149	4839	6726	
Spain/Espagne	1166	861	2167	7226	
New Zealand	1240	1227	1330	1824	4176
Norway,SVD,JM	1152	496	2216	5567	
Lebanon/Liban	593	1290	1574	2098	3505
Canada	3106	1711	1658	848	1202
Sri Lanka	1643	905	1246	2926	
Egypt/Egypte	881	2500	2679	125	
Kenya	187	464	557	3875	737
Libyan Arab Jamahiriya	503	34	2767	928	
Syrian Arab Republic	656	491	1447	1492	
Brazil/Brésil	106	335		2668	
Malta/Malte	1491	1327		125	
Viet Nam		36	217	2221	
Portugal	97	27	49	2114	
Mauritius/Maurice	68	717	1465		
Yemen/Yémen	220	235	562	973	
Bangladesh	785	690	55	359	
So. Africa Customs Un	262	174	818	622	
Algeria/Algérie	130	31	1197	426	
Switz.Liecht	785	184	409		
Bosnia and Herzegovina			1255		

(VALUE AS PERCENTAGE OF WORLD TOTAL)(VALEURS EN POURCENTAGE DU TOTAL MONDIAL)

	1987	1988	1989	1990	1991	1992	1993	1994	1995	1996
Africa	0.3	0.3	0.2	0.3	0.2	0.4	0.7	0.7	0.6	0.0
Americas	13.5	26.5	8.8	8.4	9.4	9.8	10.8	12.9	10.9	8.5
Northern America	12.0	25.4	7.7	7.2	8.7	8.6	9.3	11.1	8.7	6.9
LAIA	1.3	1.1	1.1	1.1	0.7	1.2	1.5	1.8	2.1	1.6
CACM	0.2		0.0	0.0	0.0	0.0	0.0	0.0	0.0	0.0
Caribbean	0.0	0.0	0.0	0.0	0.0	0.0	0.0	0.0	0.0	
Rest of America			0.0	0.0	0.0	0.0	0.0	0.0	0.0	
As.ex F.USSR	28.3	23.0	21.4	17.8	19.4	23.4	24.2	26.1	24.2	17.8
Eur.x F.USSR	55.4	48.0	24.0	18.5	24.7	25.8	20.6	22.4	21.4	18.0
EU	49.2	42.7	23.0	17.6	23.2	23.8	19.4	20.4	19.7	16.9
EFTA	5.8	5.0	0.8	0.6	1.2	1.6	1.1	1.8	1.4	1.0
East Europe	0.1	0.0	0.2	0.1	0.2	0.4	0.1	0.1	0.2	
Other Europe	0.3	0.3	0.1	0.1	0.1	0.0	0.0	0.0	0.0	
Former USSR			0.0	0.1	0.1	0.0	0.0	0.0	0.1	
Oceania	2.5	2.1	4.4	5.4	3.4	4.0	6.5	5.1	5.1	5.6
USA/Etats–Unis d'Amer	11.1	24.6	7.5	7.1	8.4	8.3	9.1	10.8	8.2	6.4
United Kingdom	21.3	18.5	9.8	5.7	6.2	6.7	6.1	6.2	5.9	5.4
Japan/Japon	12.3	10.7	6.4	5.0	4.9	6.4	6.3	5.6	4.1	3.7
Australia/Australie	2.0	1.7	4.2	5.1	3.2	3.8	6.3	4.8	4.8	5.3
Germany/Allemagne	7.2	6.3	4.2	3.1	5.1	6.3	4.1	3.7	4.0	4.1
Saudi Arabia			2.8	2.7	3.3	3.5	3.5	4.3	4.9	4.1
France,Monac	4.2	3.6	1.8	1.9	3.5	3.4	2.4	3.3	2.3	2.8
Italy/Italie	6.0	5.2	2.8	1.7	2.6	2.6	2.5	2.6	2.2	2.1
India/Inde	3.1		2.3	1.5	1.5	1.7	2.3	2.6	2.5	2.3
United Arab Emirates			1.8	1.6	2.2	1.8	2.1	2.6	2.7	2.1

	1987	1988	1989	1990	1991	1992	1993	1994	1995	1996
Afrique	5.9	5.0	0.6	0.5	0.2	0.2	0.3	0.5	0.4	0.0
Amériques	6.0	10.5	1.8	2.0	2.0	2.1	2.8	4.4	3.3	2.3
Amérique du Nord	6.0	10.4	1.8	1.9	2.0	2.1	2.8	4.4	3.2	2.3
ALAI	0.0	0.1	0.0	0.0	0.0	0.0	0.0	0.0	0.1	
MCAC	0.0									
Caraïbes			0.0		0.0	0.0		0.0		
Autre Amérique										
Asie l'URSS exclus	70.7	65.8	17.6	15.3	15.9	17.6	26.2	31.6	29.1	21.5
Europe l'URSS exclus	16.2	17.5	2.5	2.2	2.5	3.0	2.7	2.5	3.0	1.3
UE	12.8	13.8	2.5	2.2	2.4	2.9	2.7	2.4	2.9	1.3
AELE	3.4	3.7	0.0	0.0	0.0	0.1	0.0	0.1	0.1	
Europe de l'Est			0.0		0.0	0.0	0.0	0.0	0.0	
Autre de l'Europe	0.0	0.0		0.0	0.1	0.0	0.0		0.0	
Ancienne URSS							0.0	0.0	0.0	
Océanie	1.2	1.3	0.1	0.0	0.0	0.2	0.2	0.1	0.1	0.3
Saudi Arabia	5.4	5.8	4.5	2.9	3.4	4.1	5.4	6.4	6.1	5.3
Japan/Japon	26.3	28.5	1.5	1.9	2.4	2.2	5.2	5.6	3.5	4.2
Korea, Republic of	2.7	2.9	1.0	1.4	1.8	2.9	3.1	3.5	3.8	2.5
USA/Etats–Unis d'Amer	5.9	10.3	1.8	1.9	1.9	2.0	2.8	4.4	3.2	2.3
India/Inde	9.9		1.1	1.1	1.4	0.9	1.7	3.0	2.5	1.9
United Arab Emirates			1.7	0.7	0.7	1.0	1.9	1.7	1.8	1.8
Kuwait/ Koweït			1.1	0.4	1.4	1.2	1.2	1.2	1.4	1.0
Iran (Islamic Rp. of)			0.1	0.2	0.5	0.6	1.3	1.6	1.1	0.9
Singapore/Singapour	21.3	22.6	0.5	0.4	0.5	0.6	0.5	0.9	1.9	0.6
Netherlands/Pays–Bas	0.2	0.3	0.6	0.7	0.7	1.3	0.5	1.0	1.1	0.3

4. General Imports C.I.F. by Commodities according to the S.I.T.C. (Rev. 2) in thousand U.S. Dollars
Importations Générales C.A.F. par Produits d'après la C.T.C.I. (Rév. 2) en milliers de Dollars E.U.

SITC CTCI	COMMODITY	1993 WEIGHT POIDS	1993 VALUE VALEUR	1994 WEIGHT POIDS	1994 VALUE VALEUR	1995 WEIGHT POIDS	1995 VALUE VALEUR	1996 WEIGHT POIDS	1996 VALUE VALEUR	PRODUIT
	ALL COMMODITIES # 1		3858003		3761756		3624769		4092557	TOUS PRODUITS
0	FOOD AND LIVE ANIMALS		308487		308333		319950		322341	ALIMENTS,ANIMAUX VIVANTS
001	*LIVE ANIMALS FOR FOOD		17205	W 20398	20543					ANIMAUX VIVANTS
0012	SHEEP AND GOATS,LIVE	W 15313	15017	W 19651	19226					ESPECES OVINE ET CAPRINE
01	MEAT AND PREPARATIONS		37529		40182					VIANDES ET PREPARATIONS
011	MEAT FRESH,CHILLD,FROZEN	W 21533	36092	W 22215	35300					VIANDES FRAICHES,REF,CONGE
0111	BOVINE MEAT FRESH,FROZEN	W 6388	11697	W 5082	9194					VIANDES BOVIN FRAI,REF
0114	POULTRY FRESH CHLLD,FRZN	W 12686	18230	W 4296	7099					VOLAILLES MORTES
0118	MEAT NES FRESH,CHLD,FRZN	W 438	1496	W 10592	13378					AUTRES VIANDES,ABATS
01181	POULTRY LIVER FRESH,ETC			W 10577	13307					FOIES DE VOLAILLES
02	DAIRY PRODCTS,BIRDS'EGGS		42891		48702					PRODUITS LAITIERS,OEUFS
022	MILK AND CREAM	W 13954	24727	W 15806	27659					LAIT ET CREME
0224	MILK,CREAM PRESERVED ETC	W 8011	18135	W 8011	17665					LAIT,CREME CONS,CONC
02242	MILK DRY,1.5% FAT OR LES	W 4705	13667	W 7824	17373					LAIT POUDRE INF 1.5%
024	CHEESE AND CURD	W 3638	11206	W 4192	12185					FROMAGE ET CAILLEBOTTE
04	CEREALS AND PREPARATIONS		61080		45837					CEREALES ET PRODUITS
042	RICE	W 39616	20156	W 35470	18606					RIZ
0421	RICE IN HUSK OR HUSKED	W 22	13	W 34747	18288					RIZ SANS AUTRE PREPARATION
04212	RICE HUSKED			W 34074	17875					RIZ CARGO
0422	RICE SEMI–MILLED,MILLED	W 39594	20143	W 723	318					RIZ POLI,GLACE INCL BRISURES
048	CEREAL ETC PREPARATIONS	W 6421	15093	W 5312	11876					PREPTNS A BASE CEREALES
05	VEGETABLES AND FRUIT		88241		86784					LEGUMES ET FRUITS
054	VEG ETC FRSH,SMPLY PRSVD	W 105236	36839	W 95614	34168					LEGUMES FRAIS,CONG,SECS
0545	OTHER FRESH VEGETABLES	W 47432	17764	W 48290	17313					AUTRES LEGUMES FRAIS,REF
05451	ALLIACEOUS VEGTBLS,FRESH	W 47432	17764	W 16340	4650					OIGNONS,ECHALOTES,AULX
05459	FRESH VEGETABLES NES			W 31950	12662					LEGUMES FRAIS,REFRI NDA
057	FRUIT,NUTS,FRESH,DRIED	W 78226	31541	W 91005	34632					FRUITS FRAIS OU SECS
0579	FRUIT FRESH OR DRIED NES	W 34924	12012	W 41512	12523					FRUITS FRAIS,SECS NDA
06	SUGAR AND PREPS,HONEY		16094		16426					SUCRES ET PRODUITS
07	COFFEE,TEA,COCOA,SPICES		18983		21982					CAFE,THE,CACAO,EPICES
09	MISC EDIBLE PRODUCTS		14850		18527					PREP ALIMENTAIRES DIVERSES
098	EDIBLE PRODCTS,PREPS NES	W 4311	12880	W 7514	17950					PREP ALIMENTAIRES NDA
1	BEVERAGES AND TOBACCO		57211		60406		63033		65692	BOISSONS ET TABACS
11	BEVERAGES		37990		42043					BOISSONS
111	NON–ALCOHL BEVERAGES NES	W 18412	6854	W 22533	11658					BOISSONS NON ALCOOLIQUES
112	ALCOHOLIC BEVERAGES	W 33015	31136	W 26853	30386					BOISSONS ALCOOLIQUES
1123	BEER,ALE,STOUT,PORTER	W 19121	15764	W 22718	15044					BIERES
12	TOBACCO AND MANUFACTURES		19221		18363					TABACS BRUTS FABRIQUES
122	TOBACCO,MANUFACTURED	W 1074	18643	W 1176	17889					TABACS FABRIQUES
1222	CIGARETTES	W 991	17856	W 1140	17229					CIGARETTES
2	CRUDE MATERLS,EXCL FUELS		240662		190188		63033		42287	MAT BRUTES NON COMESTIBLES
24	CORK AND WOOD		22630		22867					LIEGE ET BOIS
247	OTH WOOD ROUGH,SQUARED	W 64324	18477	W 48915	22034					BOIS BRUTS EQUARRIS
2472	SAW–,VENEER–LOGS NON–CON			W 29029	16209					NON CONIFERES SCIAGE,PLAC
24721	— IN THE ROUGH			W 29029	16209					BRUTS ECORCES DEGROSSIS
2479	PTPROPS,POLES,PILING,ETC	W 64324	18477							POTEAUX DE MINES
27	CRUDE FERTLZR,MINRLS NES		8425		13847					ENGRAIS MINERAUX BRUTS
28	METALLIFEROUS ORES,SCRAP		202598		143701					MINERAIS METAL,DECHETS
287	BASE METAL ORES,CONC NES	W 955740	200525	W 865069	141069					MINERAIS METAUX COMMUNS
2873	ALUMINIUM ORES,ALUMINA	W 943696	199931	W 864560	140003					MINERAIS D'ALUMINIUM
28732	ALUMINA(ALUMINIUM OXIDE)	W 943653	199885	W 864412	139550					ALUMINE (OXYDE ALUMINIUM)
3	MINERAL FUELS ETC		1429310		1247002		1382194		1834576	COMBUSTIBLES MINERAUX LUB
33	PETROLEUM AND PRODUCTS		1429281		1246911					PETROLE ET DERIVES
333	CRUDE PETROLEUM		1370505		1192020		1330066			HUILES BRUTES DE PETROLE
334	PETROLEUM PRODUCTS,REFIN	W 9744	10438	W 30455	17254					PRODUITS RAFFINES
3345	LUBS,PETROLEUM OILS NES	W 9676	10383	W 30180	16990					HUILES LUBRIFIANTES
33451	LUBS(HIGH PETR CONT) ETC	W 9544	10152	W 30121	16825					HUILES LUBRIF,H LOURDES
335	RESIDUAL PETRLM PROD NES	W 255195	48339	W 172681	37637					PRODUITS RESIDUELS NDA
3353	MIN TAR PITCH,PITCH COKE	W 255193	48328	W 44304	12031					BRAI,COKE DE BRAI
33532	PITCH COKE	W 253463	46836	W 36302	9890					COKE DE BRAI
3354	PETROLM BITUMEN,COKE ETC			W 128307	25457					BITUME,COKE DE PETROLE
33542	PETROLEUM COKE			W 127404	24842					COKE DE PETROLE
4	ANIMAL,VEGETABLE OIL,FAT		33904		31250		37766		32979	HUILES,GRAISSES ANIM,VEG
42	FIXED VEGETABLE OIL,FAT		33822		31122					HUILES VEGETALES FIXES
424	FIXED VEG OIL NONSOFT	W 45915	31455	W 41258	28216					AUTRES HUILES VEG FIXES
4242	PALM OIL	W 4408	2061	W 21045	11917					HUILE DE PALME
4249	FIXED VEGETABLE OILS NES	W 41366	29184	W 19966	16009					HUILES VEGET FIXES NDA
5	CHEMCLS,RELATED PROD NES		164773		173572		316226		363298	PRODUITS CHIMIQUES
52	INORGANIC CHEMICALS		22002		19174					PROD CHIM INORGANIQUES
523	OTHR INORG CHEMICALS ETC	W 21698	17405	W 19132	11223					AUT PRODUITS CHIMIQUES INORG
5231	METAL CMPD OF INORG ACID	W 14836	12386	W 13606	9198					SELS METALLIQUES
52311	FLUORIDES ETC	W 14836	12386	W 12521	8881					FLUORURES
53	DYES,TANNING,COLOUR PROD		24520		21596					PROD TEINTURE,COLORANTS
531	SYNT DYE,NAT INDGO,LAKES			W 8695	15697					MAT COLOR ORGAN,LAQUES
5311	SYNTHIC ORGNIC DYESTUFFS			W 8695	15697					MAT COLOR ORGAN SYNTHET
533	PIGMENTS,PAINTS,ETC	W 15990	24520	W 2742	5897					PIGMENTS,PEINTURES,VERNIS
5334	VARNISHES,DISTEMPERS ETC	W 14457	21681	W 1189	2260					PEINTURES A L'EAU
541	*MEDICINAL,PHARM PRODUCT	K 1474866	22522	K 1615042	27112					PROD MEDICINAUX PHARMACEUT
5417	MEDICAMENTS			K 720439	18993					MEDICAMENTS
54171	— CONTAINNG ANTIBIOTICS			K 641788	17279					MED CONTN ANTIBIOTIQUES
5419	PHARMACEUTICAL GOODS NES	K 1450856	22238	K 810057	6783					PREP,ART PHARMACEUTIQUES
54199	OTH PHARMACEUTICAL GOODS	K 1344741	20974	K 734255	5889					AUT PREP PHARMACEUTIQUES
55	PERFUME,CLEANING ETC PRD		49307		49015					PROD POUR PARFUM,TOILETTE
553	PERFUMERY,COSMETICS,ETC	W 4159	31126	W 3567	30478					PRODUITS DE PARFUMERIE
554	SOAP,CLEANSING ETC PREPS	W 12356	17115	W 11242	16904					SAVONS,PRODUITS DETERSIFS
5542	WASHING PREPARATIONS ETC	W 10170	11929	W 9527	11616					PROD ORG TENSIO–ACT NDA
59	CHEMICAL MATERIALS NES		38067		46053					MAT PROD CHIMIQUES NDA
598	MISCEL CHEM PRODUCTS NES	W 25930	33684	W 31524	41017					PROD DIV INDUST CHIM NDA
5981	CHEMCLS FROM WOOD,RESIN	W 7	11	W 14365	14499					PROD CHIM BASE BOIS RESIN
59814	ROSIN,RESIN ACIDS,ETC			W 14365	14497					COLOPHANES RESINIQUES
5989	CHEM PRODUCTS,PREPS NES	W 25913	33635	W 17042	26180					PROD PREP CHIMIQUES NDA
59899	OTH CHEM PRODS,PREPS,NES	W 25151	32779	W 15546	24331					AUT PRODUITS CHIMIQUES NDA
6	BASIC MANUFACTURES		521486		555495		557452		538032	ART MANUFACTURES
62	RUBBER MANUFACTURES NES		19136		20376					CAOUTCHOUC MANUFACTURE
625	RUBBER TYRES, TUBES ETC	W 5601	16170	W 6319	17482					PNEUS CAOUTCHOUC VULCANISE
63	WOOD,CORK MANUFACTRS NES		23563		29288					OUVRAGES LIEGE ET BOIS
634	VENEERS,PLYWOOD,ETC	W 27381	20091	W 29621	23295					PLACAGES,CONTRE–PLAQUES
6342	PLYWOOD OF WOOD SHEETS	W 26663	19311	W 28842	22778					BOIS CONTRE–PLAQUES
64	PAPER,PAPERBOARD AND MFR		59994		67821					PAPIERS,CARTONS & OUVRAGES
641	PAPER AND PAPERBOARD	W 16865	16995	W 24056	24503					PAPIERS ET CARTONS
642	PAPER,ETC,PRECUT,ARTS OF	W 20216	42999	W 20362	43318					PAP,CARTONS DECOUPES

4. General Imports C.I.F. by Commodities according to the S.I.T.C. (Rev. 2) in thousand U.S. Dollars
Importations Générales C.A.F. par Produits d'après la C.T.C.I. (Rév. 2) en milliers de Dollars E.U.

SITC CTCI	COMMODITY	1993 WEIGHT POIDS	1993 VALUE VALEUR	1994 WEIGHT POIDS	1994 VALUE VALEUR	1995 WEIGHT POIDS	1995 VALUE VALEUR	1996 WEIGHT POIDS	1996 VALUE VALEUR	PRODUIT
6421	PAPER ETC CONTAINERS	W 7124	11880	W 8138	11487					BOITES,SACS EMBALLAGES
6428	PAPER ETC ARTICLES NES	W 8570	22246	W 9345	23950					OUVRAGES EN PATE A PAPIER
64282	PUNCHED CARD MACH CARDS	W 8570	22246	W 90	277					CARTES POUR MACHINES
65	TEXTILE YARN,FABRICS,ETC		109087		111718					FILS,TISSUS,ARTICLES TEXTILE
652	COTTON FABRICS,WOVEN	W 3889	28098	W 6521	34996					TISSUS DE COTON
6521	GREY WOVEN COTTON FABRIC	W 3889	28098	W 2074	12609					TISSUS COT ECRUS NON MERCER
65214	GREY WOVEN COTTON NES	W 3889	28098							AUT TISSUS 85% COTON ECRUS
65215	GREY WOVN COTN BLEND NES			W 2074	12609					AUT TIS MOINS 85% COT ECRUS
6522	WOVEN COTTON BLEACHD,ETC			W 4447	22387					TISSUS COTON BLANCHIS ETC
65224	BLCHED COTTON FABRIC NES			W 4221	22106					AUT TIS PLUS 85% COT BLANCHI
653	WOVN MAN–MADE FIB FABRIC	W 3044	35671	W 4159	36195					TISSUS FIBRES SYNTH,ARTIF
6531	CONT SYNT WEAVES NONPILE			W 4078	35663					TISSUS FIBRES SYNTH CONTINUE
65315	CONT SYN TXTL FABRIC NES			W 4078	35663					TIS PLUS 85% TEXT SYNT CONT
658	TEXTILE ARTICLES NES	W 3577	15595	W 6193	10214					ART FACONNES MAT TEXTILES
659	FLOOR COVERINGS,ETC	W 4786	19042	W 4255	18062					COUVRE–PARQUETS,TAPIS ETC
66	NONMETAL MINERAL MFS NES		90879		104579					ART MIN NON METALLIQUES
661	LIME,CEMENT,BLDG PRODS	W 719274	48171	W 733377	55828					CHAUX,CIMENTS MAT CONSTR
6612	CEMENT	W 708259	38352	W 703284	43954					CIMENTS HYDRAULIQUES
6613	BUILDING STONE ETC WORKD	W 8191	7906	W 27520	11684					PIERRES A BATIR
66132	BUILDING STONE WORKED	W 8118	7806	W 27507	11669					OUVR EN PIERRES DE TAILLE
662	CLAY,REFRACTORY BLDG PRD	W 36850	18579	W 40895	24178					MAT CONST REFRACTAIRES
6624	BRICKS ETC NONREFRACTORY	W 29799	12883	W 31858	14589					BRIQUES ETC CERAM NON REFR
66245	GLAZED CERAMIC SETTS ETC	W 20510	10908	W 23841	12259					AUT CARREAUX CERAMIQUE
67	IRON AND STEEL		112837		121944					FER ET ACIER
671	PIG IRON ETC	W 182778	41844	W 259210	52693					FONTE,SPIEGEL,POUDRES
6713	IRON,STL POWDER,SHOT,ETC	W 420	223	W 258630	52345					POUDRES,GREN FER,ACIER
672	IRON,STEEL PRIMARY FORMS	W 74681	28505	W 14054	8103					LINGOTS FER,ACIER
6725	IRN,STL BLOOMS,SLABS,ETC	W 74681	28505	W 125	103					BLOOMS,BILLETTES FER ACIER
67251	IRN,SMPLE STL BLOOMS,ETC	W 74681	28505							BLOOMS ETC NON ACIER FIN
673	IRON,STEEL SHAPES ETC			W 86557	33266					BARRES,PROFIL FER,ACIER
6732	IRON,STEEL BARS ETC			W 55950	20576					BARRES FER,ACIER
67324	STNLESS STL ETC BARS ETC			W 55950	20576					BARRES ACIER INOXYDABLE
678	IRON,STL TUBES,PIPES,ETC	W 18083	26428	W 14481	19425					TUBES,TUYAUX EN FONTE,FER
68	NON–FERROUS METALS		24406		20905					METAUX NON FERREUX
684	ALUMINIUM	W 2482	8102	W 3357	11317					ALUMINIUM
69	METAL MANUFACTURES NES		80769		77649					ART MANUFACT EN METAL NDA
691	STRUCTURES AND PARTS NES	W 23457	16615	W 12967	13854					CONSTRUCT FER,ACIER,ALU
6911	STRUCTURES,PARTS IRN,STL	W 23353	16122	W 12359	11710					CONSTRUCT FER,ACIER,FONTE
692	METAL TANKS,BOXES,ETC	W 3113	6935	W 2995	12065					RECIPIENTS METALLIQUES
6924	MTL TRANSPORT BOXES ETC	W 2257	6220	W 2995	12065					FUTS,TAMBOURS,BIDONS
697	BASE MTL HOUSEHOLD EQUIP	W 1850	12998	W 1761	11033					ART MENAGE MET COMMUNS
699	BASE METAL MFRS NES	W 11124	28424	W 10107	23342					ART MANUFACTURES MET NDA
6997	IRON,STEEL ARTICLES NES	W 7238	11631	W 4637	4166					OUV FONTE,FER,ACIER NDA
7	MACHINES,TRANSPORT EQUIP		792482		835350		588304		598937	MACHINES MATERIEL TRANSPORT
71	POWER GENERATING EQUIPMT		29725		21649					MACHINES GENERATRICES
716	ROTATING ELECTRIC PLANT	W 1898	14259	W 269	3287					APP ELECTR ROTATIFS,PIECES
72	MACHS FOR SPCL INDUSTRYS		62736		76818					MAC SPECIALES POUR INDUST
723	CIVIL ENGNEERG EQUIP ETC	W 2751	21584	W 1703	24228					APPAREILS DE GENIE CIVIL
7234	CONST,MINING MACHNRY NES	W 2745	21557	W 1690	24065					MACH POUR LA CONST, MINES
72343	SLFPRP CONST ETC MCH NES			W 913	18484					AUT MACH EXTR,TERRASSEM
724	TEXTILE,LEATHER MACHNRY	W 299	2202	W 2413	16753					MACH POUR INDUSTRIE TEXTILE
728	OTH MACHY FOR SPCL INDUS	W 1436	26530	W 1410	12364					AUT MACH IND PARTICULIERES
7284	MACHY FOR SPCL INDUS NES	W 663	19893	W 282	3726					MACH SPEC IND PARTICUL.
73	METALWORKING MACHINERY		14330		18145					MACH TRAVAIL DES METAUX
736	METALWORKING MACH–TOOLS	W 945	12589	W 1224	11903					MACH–OUTILS TRAVAIL METAUX
74	GENRL INDUSTRL MACHY NES		103607		106948					MACH APP INDUSTRIE
741	HEATING,COOLING EQUIPMNT	W 1954	26250	W 6087	52225					MACH CHAUFFAGE,PIECES
7414	NONDOM REFRIG EQUIPT,PTS	W 1084	12012	W 654	4958					MAT PRODUCTION DU FROID
74141	REFRIG EQUIP NONDOMESTIC	W 1084	12012	W 555	3820					REFIG INDUSTRIELS
7415	AIR–CONDITIONING MACHNRY	W 566	4525	W 4875	37077					GROUPES CONDITION AIR
743	PUMPS NES,CENTRFUGES ETC	W 528	5471	W 1428	12585					POMPES COMPRES,VENT ETC
744	MECHANICAL HANDLING EQU	W 3231	16758	W 3119	20879					EQUIP MANUTENTION PIECES
7442	LIFTING,LOADING MACH NES	W 2913	14859	W 2185	12148					APP LEVAGE,MANUTENTION
749	NONELEC MACH PTS,ACC NES	W 1872	39570	W 34	388					PIECES MACH NON ELEC NDA
7499	OTH NONELEC MCHY PTS NES	W 1872	39570	W 34	388					PIECES NON ELECT NDA
75	OFFICE MACHNES,ADP EQUIP		40117		42715					MACH BUREAU TRAIT AUTOM
759	OFFICE,ADP MCH PTS,ACCES	W 508	32301	W 423	30274					PIECES DU 751 ET 752
7591	OFFICE MACHINE PARTS NES	W 508	32301							PIECES DU 7511,7518
75911	TYPEWRTR PARTS,ACCES NES	W 508	32301							PIECES DU 7511
7599	ACCTG,ETC,ADP MCH PTS,AC			W 423	30274					PIECES DU 751 ET 752
76	TELECOMM,SOUND EQUIPMENT		73384		67880					EQUIPMENT DE TELECOM
764	TELECOM EQPT,PTS,ACC NES	W 3057	53580	W 818	49146					EQUIP TELECOM,PIECES
7643	TV,RADIO TRANSMITTRS ETC	W 710	50392	W 184	11814					APP EMET TELE RADIO
7649	PTS NES OF EQUIPMT OF 76	W 16	521	W 274	26108					PIECES DE LA DIV 76
76491	PTS NES OF APPAR OF 7641			W 194	20138					PIECES POUR 764.1
77	ELECTRIC MACHNRY NES ETC		149426		151741					MACH APP ELECT NDA
771	ELECTRIC POWER MACHY NES			W 3232	46235					MACH PROD,TRANS ELECTR
7711	TRANSFORMERS,ELECTRICAL			W 2692	25408					TRANSFO ELECTRIQUES
77118	OTHER ELEC TRANSFORMERS			W 2692	25408					AUTRES TRANSFO ELECTRIQ
7712	OTH ELEC POWER MACHY NES			W 540	20827					AUT APP PROD TRANSF ELEC
77129	PTS NES OF MACHY OF 771			W 425	18715					PIECES MACH DU 771
772	SWITCHGEAR ETC,PARTS NES	W 979	21296	W 1198	28890					APP COUPURE,SECT ETC
7721	SWITCHGEAR ETC			W 1172	27377					APP COUPURE,SECTIONMNT
773	ELECTR DISTRIBUTNG EQUIP	W 18856	30236	W 6345	22312					EQUIPMT DISTRIBUTION ELECT
7731	INSULATED WIRE,CABLE ETC	W 17048	23720	W 6166	20511					FILS,CABLES ISOLES ELECT
775	HOUSEHOLD TYPE EQUIP NES	W 10576	56840		21193					MACH,APP USAGE DOMESTQUE
7757	DOMESTIC ELECTRC EQU NES	W 6078	33663	W 221	3169					APP ELECTR DOMEST NDA
778	ELECTRICAL MACHINERY NES	W 2705	39742	W 4033	31198					AUTRES MACH ELECT NDA
7788	OTH ELEC MACHY,EQUIP NES	W 1010	31500	W 2131	21186					AUT MACH APP ELEC NDA
77889	ELEC PARTS OF MACHY NES	W 579	27609	W 65	2615					PIECES ELEC DE MACH NDA
78	ROAD VEHICLES		215861		212686					VEHICULES ROUTIERS
781	PASS MOTOR VEH EXC BUSES	W 18049	141473	W 10754	127747					AUTO TRANSPORT PERSONNES
782	LORRIES,SPCL MTR VEH NES	W 5070	21226	W 1647	15049					VEHICULES SPECIAUX,MARCH
7821	LORRIES,TRUCKS	W 3577	15041	W 1110	7363					VEHICULES TRANSP MARCHAND
784	MOTOR VEH PRTS,ACCES NES	W 3524	44057	W 7754	57059					PIECES 722,781,782,783
7849	OTHER MOTOR VEHCL PARTS	W 3451	43820	W 7633	56427					PIECES 722,781,782,783
79	OTHR TRANSPORT EQUIPMENT		103297		136770					AUTRE MATERIEL TRANSPORT
792	AIRCRAFT ETC		86170	W 331	98722					APP NAVIGATION AERIENNE
7921	HELICOPTERS		1	W 64	61170					HELICOPTERES
7929	AIRCRAFT PARTS NES	W 416	86119	W 265	37498					PIECES DU 792
793	SHIPS AND BOATS ETC	W 5473	17127		37885					NAVIRES BATEAUX,ETC

4. General Imports C.I.F. by Commodities according to the S.I.T.C. (Rev. 2) in thousand U.S. Dollars
Importations Générales C.A.F. par Produits d'après la C.T.C.I. (Rév. 2) en milliers de Dollars E.U.

SITC CTCI	COMMODITY	1993		1994		1995		1996		PRODUIT
		WEIGHT POIDS	VALUE VALEUR	WEIGHT POIDS	VALUE VALEUR	WEIGHT POIDS	VALUE VALEUR	WEIGHT POIDS	VALUE VALEUR	
7932	SHIPS AND BOATS NES	W 1096	8984	W 3516	28503					NAVIRES ET BATEAUX
79323	OTHER CARGO VESSELS			W 2603	24811					AUT BATEAUX TRANS MARCH
8	MISC MANUFACTURED GOODS		293534		286271		279790		263564	ART MANUFACTURES DIVERS
812	*PLUMBG,HEATNG,LGHTNG EQ	W 3407	21827	W 4232	26083					APPAR SANITAIRES CHAUFFAGE
8124	LIGHTING EQUIPMENT NES	W 1805	16494	W 2176	18594					APPAREILS ECLAIRAGE ETC
81242	LAMPS,FITTINGS BASE METL	W 1761	16137	W 868	10574					APPAREILS D'ECLAIRAGE
821	*FURNITURE,PARTS THEREOF	W 12019	53596	W 10610	44463					MEUBLES ET PIECES
8211	CHAIRS,SEATS AND PARTS	W 9557	42831	W 343	1987					SIEGES ET PIECES
8219	FURNITURE AND PARTS NES	W 1475	7118	W 9532	39534					AUTRES MEUBLES ET PIECES
82192	WOOD FURNITURE NES			W 7124	30971					MEUBLES NDA EN BOIS
84	CLOTHING AND ACCESSORIES		60288		60744					VETEMENTS
842	MENS OUTERWEAR NOT KNIT	W 1843	21779	W 765	11908					VET DESSUS POUR HOMMES
843	WOMENS OUTERWEAR NONKNIT	W 1612	24236	W 1995	25975					VET DESSUS FEMMES MAT TEX
8439	— OTHER OUTER GARMENTS			W 1209	12707					AUT VET DES FEM MAT TEXT
844	UNDER GARMENTS NOT KNIT	W 489	6481	W 1155	15379					VETEMENT DESSOUS MAT TEX
8441	— MENS SHIRTS	W 251	3148	W 803	11735					CHEMISES HOMMES MAT TEXT
851	*FOOTWEAR	W 1622	14208	W 9253	14854					CHAUSSURES
87	PRECISION INSTRUMNTS NES		15849		17094					INSTRUM,APPAR SCIENT NDA
88	PHOTO EQU,OPTICL GDS ETC		33929		31458					APP,FOURN PHOTO,OP,MONTR
885	WATCHES AND CLOCKS		19340		17561					HORLOGERIE
8851	WATCHES,MOVEMENTS,CASES		18991		16373					MONTRES,MOUVEMENTS,BOITES
88511	WATCHES		18066		16067					MONTRES POCHE,BRACELET
89	MISC MANUFCTRD GOODS NES		89062		86282					ART MANUFACTURES DIVERS
893	ARTICLES OF PLASTIC NES	W 14282	37971	W 16015	40837					OUVRAGES EN MAT DIVIS 58
8939	MISC PLASTIC ARTICLES			W 11630	31929					ART DIVERS EN MAT DIV 58
89399	OTHR PLASTC ARTICLES NES			W 9568	29277					AUT OUV MAT DIV 58
894	TOYS,SPORTING GOODS,ETC	W 2847	12134	W 1853	13085					VOITURES ENFANTS,JOUETS
9	GOODS NOT CLASSD BY KIND		16156		73888		17021		30851	ART TRANSACT NON CLASSES
931	*SPECIAL TRANSACTIONS	W 2301	15759	W 763	7001					TRANS.SPECIALES
951	*WAR FIREARMS,AMMUNITION	W 6	117	W 2423	62411					VEHIC BLINDES ARMES
95106	AMMUNITION NES			W 2423	62411					PROJECTILES,MUNITIONS

5. General Exports F.O.B. by Commodities according to the S.I.T.C. (Rev. 2) in thousand U.S. Dollars
Exportations Générales F.O.B. par Produits d'après la C.T.C.I. (Rév. 2) en milliers de Dollars E.U.

SITC CTCI	COMMODITY	1993		1994		1995		1996		PRODUIT
		WEIGHT POIDS	VALUE VALEUR	WEIGHT POIDS	VALUE VALEUR	WEIGHT POIDS	VALUE VALEUR	WEIGHT POIDS	VALUE VALEUR	
	ALL COMMODITIES # 1		3710051		3452132		4092061		4602396	TOUS PRODUITS
0	FOOD AND LIVE ANIMALS		42989		28759		26862		30053	ALIMENTS,ANIMAUX VIVANTS
04	CEREALS AND PREPARATIONS		14829		1831					CEREALES ET PRODUITS
05	VEGETABLES AND FRUIT		15218		15665					LEGUMES ET FRUITS
2	CRUDE MATERLS,EXCL FUELS		12362		15386		19149		16489	MAT BRUTES NON COMESTIBLES
28	METALLIFEROUS ORES,SCRAP		10753		13035					MINERAIS METAL,DECHETS
3	MINERAL FUELS ETC		2439522		2055347		2455609		3157183	COMBUSTIBLES MINERAUX LUB
33	PETROLEUM AND PRODUCTS		2439517		2055333		2454545			PETROLE ET DERIVES
333	CRUDE PETROLEUM		2439100		2054660		2454545			HUILES BRUTES DE PETROLE
4	ANIMAL,VEGETABLE OIL,FAT		37023		42249		41756		36436	HUILES,GRAISSES ANIM,VEG
42	FIXED VEGETABLE OIL,FAT		36851		42140					HUILES VEGETALES FIXES
424	FIXED VEG OIL NONSOFT	W 37467	36815	W 39757	41872					AUTRES HUILES VEG FIXES
4249	FIXED VEGETABLE OILS NES	W 31862	31602	W 31607	36172					HUILES VEGET FIXES NDA
5	CHEMCLS,RELATED PROD NES		89739		174541		206385		112766	PRODUITS CHIMIQUES
51	ORGANIC CHEMICALS		35885		99037					PROD CHIMIQ ORGANIQUES
512	ALCOHOLS,PHENOLS ETC	W 412848	35884	W 429352	99029					PHENOLS,PHENOLS–ALCOOLS
5121	ACYCLIC ALCOHOLS,DERIVS	W 412848	35884	W 429352	99029					ALCOOLS ACYCLIQUES
51211	METHYL ALCOHOL(METHANOL)	W 412848	35884	W 429352	99029					ALCOOLS METHYLIQUES
52	INORGANIC CHEMICALS		41335		66759					PROD CHIM INORGANIQUES
522	INORG ELEMNTS,OXIDES,ETC	W 459087	41088	W 435638	65190					ELEMENTS INORGANIQUES
5225	INORGANIC BASES ETC NES	W 425253	37898	W 402764	61452					AUTRES BASES OXYDES METAL
52251	AMMONIA,ANHYDROUS ETC	W 425253	37898	W 402684	61427					AMMONIAC LIQUEFIE
6	BASIC MANUFACTURES		854624		938608		1153734		1066224	ART MANUFACTURES
64	PAPER,PAPERBOARD AND MFR		14121		16213					PAPIERS,CARTONS & OUVRAGES
642	PAPER,ETC,PRECUT,ARTS OF	W 6486	12984	W 7603	14052					PAP,CARTONS DECOUPES
6428	PAPER ETC ARTICLES NES	W 4830	9321	W 5963	11869					OUVRAGES EN PATE A PAPIER
67	IRON AND STEEL		112264		141520					FER ET ACIER
671	PIG IRON ETC	W 1822850	106223	W 2801220	128804					FONTE,SPIEGEL,POUDRES
6713	IRON,STL POWDER,SHOT,ETC			W 2801220	128804					POUDRES,GREN FER,ACIER
68	NON–FERROUS METALS		701358		739389					METAUX NON FERREUX
684	ALUMINIUM	W 469151	701221	W 443176	738992					ALUMINIUM
6841	ALUMINIUM,ALLOYS,UNWRGHT	W 333449	411304	W 307925	455013					ALUMINIUM,ALLIAGES BRUTS
6842	ALUMINIUM,ALLOYS WORKED	W 135702	289917	W 135250	283979					ALUMINIUM,ALLIAGES OUVRE
68421	ALUMINIUM BARS,WIRE,ETC	W 67991	128912	W 63665	115163					BARRES,PROFILES FILS ALU
68422	ALUMNM PLATE,SHEET,STRIP	W 63751	149673	W 65438	152702					TOLES, PLANCHES EN ALU
68424	ALUMINIUM POWDERS,FLAKES	W 3815	10122	W 5035	11840					POUDRES ET PAILLETTES ALU
69	METAL MANUFACTURES NES		17895		27405					ART MANUFACT EN METAL NDA
691	STRUCTURES AND PARTS NES	W 3828	4188	W 5567	12541					CONSTRUCT FER,ACIER,ALU
6911	STRUCTURES,PARTS IRN,STL	W 3720	3715	W 5406	12003					CONSTRUCT FER,ACIER,FONTE
7	MACHINES,TRANSPORT EQUIP		96918		57313		53192		42819	MACHINES MATERIEL TRANSPORT
72	MACHS FOR SPCL INDUSTRYS		17674		7272					MAC SPECIALES POUR INDUST
723	CIVIL ENGNEERG EQUIP ETC	W 2739	16587		5528					APPAREILS DE GENIE CIVIL
7234	CONST,MINING MACHNRY NES	W 2722	16555		5523					MACH POUR LA CONST, MINES
78	ROAD VEHICLES		20439		19538					VEHICULES ROUTIERS
784	MOTOR VEH PRTS,ACCES NES	W 650	10515	W 776	11358					PIECES 722,781,782,783
7849	OTHER MOTOR VEHCL PARTS	W 606	10472	W 775	11349					PIECES 722,781,782,783
79	OTHR TRANSPORT EQUIPMENT		34000		10437					AUTRE MATERIEL TRANSPORT
792	AIRCRAFT ETC	W 116	29212		5					APP NAVIGATION AERIENNE
7929	AIRCRAFT PARTS NES	W 116	29212		5					PIECES DU 792
793	SHIPS AND BOATS ETC	W 4870	4788	W 3214	10432					NAVIRES BATEAUX,ETC
8	MISC MANUFACTURED GOODS		126883		131121		125533		131117	ART MANUFACTURES DIVERS
812	*PLUMBG,HEATNG,LGHTNG EQ	W 1863	9431	W 1858	11047					APPAR SANITAIRES CHAUFFAGE
8124	LIGHTING EQUIPMENT NES	W 1852	9314	W 1856	11023					APPAREILS ECLAIRAGE ETC
81242	LAMPS,FITTINGS BASE METL	W 1850	9302	W 1853	11001					APPAREILS D'ECLAIRAGE
84	CLOTHING AND ACCESSORIES		66810		79822					VETEMENTS
842	MENS OUTERWEAR NOT KNIT	W 2400	31322	W 621	6483					VET DESSUS POUR HOMMES
843	WOMENS OUTERWEAR NONKNIT	W 2927	34692	W 3357	47647					VET DESSUS FEMMES MAT TEX
8435	— BLOUSES			W 1545	21023					BLOUSES FEM MAT TEXTILES
8439	— OTHER OUTER GARMENTS			W 1461	21756					AUT VET DES FEM MAT TEXT
844	UNDER GARMENTS NOT KNIT	W 29	474	W 1731	22392					VETEMENT DESSOUS MAT TEX
8441	— MENS SHIRTS	W 10	146	W 1496	19875					CHEMISES HOMMES MAT TEXT
89	MISC MANUFCTRD GOODS NES		34612		28028					ART MANUFACTURES DIVERS
893	ARTICLES OF PLASTIC NES	W 14954	27617	W 15967	26260					OUVRAGES EN MAT DIVIS 58
8939	MISC PLASTIC ARTICLES			W 11563	17116					ART DIVERS EN MAT DIV 58
89399	OTHR PLASTC ARTICLES NES			W 8805	15435					AUT OUV MAT DIV 58

FOOT NOTES – NOTES

TABLE 1 –
1 Prior to 1979, special trade.
TABLE 4 –
1 In 1993 and 1994 the data presented according to SITC, Revision 2 have been estimated from data reported according to the national classification.
TABLE 5 –
1 In 1993 and 1994 the data presented according to SITC, Revision 2 have been estimated from data reported according to the national classification.
TABLEAU 1 –
1 Avant 1979, commerce spécial.
TABLEAU 4 –
1 En 1993 et 1994 les données qui se présentent confor mément à CTCI, Révision 2 sont les estimations des données rapportées d'après la classification nati onale.
TABLEAU 5 –
1 En 1993 et 1994 les données qui se présentent confor mément à CTCI, Révision 2 sont les estimations des données rapportées d'après la classification nati onale.

1. HISTORICAL SERIES, 1974–1996 GENERAL TRADE, IMPORTS C.I.F., EXPORTS F.O.B.
SERIES HISTORIQUES, 1974–1996 COMMERCE GENERAL, IMPORTATIONS C.A.F., EXPORTATIONS F.O.B

YEAR ANNEE	VALUE IN MILLION TAKA / VALEUR EN MILLION TAKA				CONVERSION FACTORS U.S. CENTS PER TAKA / FACTEURS DE CONVERSION CENTS E.U. PAR TAKA		INDEX NUMBERS – INDICES			
	MERCHANDISE – MARCHANDISE		GOLD – OR				QUANTUM		UNIT VALUE / VALEUR UNITAIRE	
	IMPORTS	EXPORTS	IMPORTS	EXPORTS	IMPORTS	EXPORTS	IMPORTS	EXPORTS	IMPORTS	EXPORTS
1974	6190.50	3083.40			12.3699	12.3213				
1975	10377.40	3595.30			8.4187	8.4246				
1976	11913.50	6586.60			6.6131	6.5592				
1977	18156.40	6916.30			6.5149	6.5223			35	35
1978	20222.00	8295.30			6.6750	6.6490			39	39
1979	23844.00	10000.00			6.4197	6.4092			40	45
1980	30439.30	11413.80			6.4823	6.4667			43	58
1981	32487.60	11889.70			5.5798	5.5692			48	55
1982	38359.90	14868.50			4.5281	4.4858			54	53
1983	39051.80	16982.60			4.0632	4.0603			67	60
1984	51760.00	23690.30			3.9442	3.9442			68	72
1985	59666.00	25906.30			3.6374	3.5798			77	
1986	77471.01	26761.01			3.2862	3.2879			86	89
1987	84087.01	33030.00			3.2287	3.2307			95	83
1988	96558.00	40967.01			3.1501	3.1514			89	97
1989	117797.00	42108.00			3.0990	3.0990			90	96
1990	124880.00	57885.01			2.8968	2.8873			100	100
1991	124857.00	61866.00			2.7325	2.7297			121	105
1992	145328.00	81724.00			2.5676	2.5669				105
1993	158123.00	90183.01			2.5259	2.5258				109
1994	185098.00	107013.00			2.4865	2.4863				110
1995	261878.00	127782.00			2.4826	2.4832				111
1996	276590.00	137944.00			2.3918	2.3903				111

2. IMPORTS BY BROAD ECONOMIC CATEGORY AND EXPORTS BY INDUSTRIAL ORIGIN. (PERCENTAGE OF TOTAL VALUE)
IMPORTATIONS PAR CATEGORIES ECONOMIQUES ET EXPORTATIONS PAR BRANCHE D'ACTIVITE.(EN POURCENTAGE DE LA VALEUR TOTALE)

IMPORTS – IMPORTATIONS

	1990	1991	1992	1993	1994	1995	1996
TOTAL IMPORTS–IMPORTATIONS TOTALES	100.	100.	100.	100.			
1 FOOD BEV–ALIMENTATION BOISSONS	18.7	17.1	17.7	15.3			
11 PRIMARY–PRODUITS DE BASE	8.1	9.6	9.4	8.2			
111 FOR INDUSTRY–POUR L'INDUSTRIE	5.3	7.3	6.7	6.0			
112 FOR HOUSEHOLDS–POUR LES MENAGES	2.9	2.4	2.7	2.1			
12 PROCESSED–PRODUITS ELABORES	10.6	7.5	8.2	7.1			
121 FOR INDUSTRY–POUR L'INDUSTRIE	4.3	4.3	5.7	4.2			
122 FOR HOUSEHOLDS–POUR LES MENAGES	6.3	3.2	2.6	2.9			
2 IND SUPPLIES–APPROV INDUSTRIELS	43.1	47.0	48.9	52.6			
21 PRIMARY–PRODUITS DE BASE	7.0	5.7	4.8	5.4			
22 PROCESSED–PRODUITS ELABORES	36.1	41.4	44.1	47.1			
3 FUELS–COMBUSTIBLES	16.4	11.4	12.1	10.9			
31 PRIMARY–PRODUITS DE BASE	10.1	6.8	5.7	5.3			
32 PROCESSED–PRODUITS ELABORES	6.3	4.5	6.5	5.6			
321 MOTOR SPIRIT–ESSENCE	0.0	0.0	0.0	0.0			
322 OTHER–AUTRES	6.3	4.5	6.5	5.6			
4 MACHINERY–EQUIPEMENT	12.4	15.2	14.4	12.5			
41 CAPITAL EQUIPMENT–MACHINES	11.4	13.5	13.1	11.5			
42 PARTS–PIECES ACCESSOIRES	1.1	1.7	1.3	1.0			
5 TRANSPORT–TRANSPORT	5.5	4.9	2.9	4.0			
51 PASSENGER CARS–AUTOMOBILES	0.8	0.7	0.4	0.8			
52 OTHER–AUTRES	0.9	1.6	0.7	1.0			
521 INDUSTRIAL–INDUSTRIELS	0.5	1.2	0.4	0.7			
522 NON INDUSTRIAL–NON INDUSTRIEL	0.3	0.4	0.3	0.3			
53 PARTS–PIECES ACCESSOIRES	3.8	2.5	1.8	2.3			
6 CONSUM GOODS–BIENS CONSOMMATION	3.6	4.1	3.8	4.5			
61 DURABLE–DURABLES	0.6	0.9	1.1	1.2			
62 SEMI DURABLE–SEMI DURABLES	2.1	2.2	1.8	2.2			
63 NON DURABLE–NON DURABLES	0.9	0.9	0.9	1.1			
7 GOODS NES–BIENS NDA	0.2	0.3	0.2	0.2			

EXPORTS – EXPORTATIONS

	1990	1991	1992	1993	1994	1995	1996
TOTAL EXPORTS–EXPORTATIONS TOTALES	100.	100.	100.	100.			
1 AGRICULTURE	20.6	17.8	15.6	15.0			
2 MINING QUARRY–INDUS EXTRACTIVES				0.1			
3 MANUFACTURING–IND MANUFACTUR	79.4	82.2	84.4	84.9			
31 FOOD BEV TOBACCO–ALIM BOISS TAB	0.5	0.2	0.2	0.1			
32 TEXTILES–INDUSTRIES TEXTILES	75.0	75.3	77.4	79.2			
33 WOOD & PRODUCTS–BOIS & PRODUITS	0.0	0.0	0.1	0.2			
34 PAPER & PRODUCTS–PAPIER & PRODT	0.0	0.0	0.0	0.0			
35 CHEMICALS–INDUSTRIES CHIMIQUES	2.4	4.2	2.0	3.5			
36 NON METAL MIN–MIN NON METAL	0.1	0.2	0.2	0.2			
37 BASIC METAL–IND METAL BASE	0.0		0.0	0.0			
38 METAL MANUF–MANUF METAL	1.1	2.0	4.1	1.2			
39 OTH MANUF IND–AUTRES MANUF	0.2	0.2	0.3	0.4			

3. TRADE BY PRINCIPAL COUNTRIES OF CONSIGNMENT AND LAST DESTINATION(VALUE IN THOUSAND U.S. DOLLARS)
ECHANGES SELON LES PRINCIPAUX PAYS DE CONSIGNATION ET DE DESTINATION FINALE (VALEUR EN MILLIERS DE DOLLARS EU)

COUNTRIES–PAYS	GENERAL IMPORTS C.I.F. IMPORTATIONS GENERALES C.A.F				
	1991	1992	1993	1994	1995
World	3136691	3467055	3525714	4602000	6501000
Africa	25528	52213	22114	14592	31566
Americas	401916	418949	330174	171850	437651
Northern America	304074	277601	249114	130069	258706
LAIA	94917	135478	76044	38580	169610
CACM	2438	2250	4876	2137	2436
Caribbean	67	249	116	809	5909
Rest of America	420	3372	23	255	989
As.ex F.USSR	2026437	2300709	2498570	2015726	2897060
Eur.x F.USSR	539278	572114	568249	319448	538108
EU	475174	488049	518285	267359	476463
EFTA	34208	38223	27627	29834	41322
East Europe	28466	42668	17497	18836	19840
Other Europe	1429	2216	4562		
Former USSR	68350	42434	36572	54165	91599
Oceania	75182	80636	70035	64172	79924
India/Inde	199869	228325	258699	411136	687168
Korea, Republic of	295451	308954	357080	282825	339155
Hong Kong	214001	255691	289074	329463	398537
Japan/Japon	329109	250695	277577	185166	256356
China/Chine	182032	251500	236279	218452	408465
Singapore/Singapour	205255	256916	289752	199334	274517
USA/Etats–Unis d'Amer	217823	217607	203302	99475	213232
Germany/Allemagne	111960	119901	108586	68258	128747
Pakistan	71629	113255	121307	79965	132136
United Kingdom	91769	111376	106621	76384	116431
United Arab Emirates	122659	160681	119067	37482	48515
Indonesia/Indonésie	52725	104203	132840	54329	63632
Saudi Arabia	79540	45313	89345	48065	81943
Australia/Australie	70712	75113	60511	54282	53928
Malaysia/Malaisie	45909	62432	80731	56297	40910
Brazil/Brésil	53850	37393	46298	27758	118309
Netherlands/Pays–Bas	58508	70441	51037	32125	61539
Canada	86246	59994	45812	30390	44834
France,Monac	41611	32522	95540	15457	57280
Thailand/Thaïlande	35117	33912	45102	40987	85685
Russian Federation		42434	36572	50930	86941
Argentina/Argentine	39760	90569	28931	8227	38550
Italy/Italie	52725	36592	52460	26589	30935
Denmark/Danemark	50700	58499	47723	17916	17786
Switz.Liecht	28884	28192	26923	28289	39428
Belgium–Luxembourg	33192	20210	19573	9645	17460
Former USSR/Anc. URSS	68350				
Iran (Islamic Rp. of)	19390	8817	11700	4580	5468
Spain/Espagne	6456	11781	6603	5239	16754
Korea Dem People's Rp	185			18970	24141
Poland/Pologne	13445	15785	4847	2701	5600
Jordan/Jordanie	12175	15398	5157	3192	6108
Sweden/Suède	7811	4055	14722	4251	9570
Sri Lanka	9049	7836	6313	6698	8212
Tunisia/Tunisie	2739	17766	7692	5856	2356
Finland/Finlande	10886	12592	3898	1014	3871
New Zealand	3955	4723	8328	3409	11618
Sudan/Soudan	12977	6516	4063	2028	4051
Egypt/Egypte	1949	1666	5113	1928	15966
Hungary/Hongrie	4444	5123	3800	8930	4268
Austria/Autriche	5000	3919	4931	6845	2826
Turkey/Turquie	3015	3595	11082	1435	3666
Myanmar	316	250	3700	6665	9084
Ireland/Irlande	3982	4598	5514	2410	2638
Bulgaria/Bulgarie	300	11469	481	549	6068
Norway,SVD,JM	5323	9891	703	1412	1505
Qatar	3938	8335	2083	1616	1883
Philippines	5795	5783	3447	365	2226
Cyprus/Chypre	10672	3358	194	1673	932
Morocco/Maroc	3801	11689	0		

COUNTRIES–PAYS	GENERAL EXPORTS F.O.B. EXPORTATIONS GENERALES F.O.B.				
	1991	1992	1993	1994	1995
Monde	1690208	1941608	2253095	2661000	3173000
Afrique	63208	59862	83582	39614	94362
Amériques	539896	713243	889934	856094	1106805
Amérique du Nord	516484	685366	857840	823819	1083196
ALAI	20384	27090	30506	29998	21170
MCAC	695	276	1223	1026	1407
Caraïbes	1516	193	172	1153	945
Autre Amérique	816	317	193	98	88
Asie l'URSS exclus	322116	410348	415645	358165	514268
Europe l'URSS exclus	707815	717467	818511	1012264	1272314
UE	658266	689849	790112	976739	1236434
AELE	12400	14653	12494	13008	18273
Europe de l'Est	31991	9521	15712	22193	17154
Autre de l'Europe	5158	321	194	295	229
Ancienne URSS	29065	18830	26937	27561	29134
Océanie	28109	21859	18484	17541	21724
USA/Etats–Unis d'Amer	488281	659221	819849	780557	1027027
Germany/Allemagne	162250	160291	185746	227257	257549
United Kingdom	130325	113660	161574	221727	283798
Italy/Italie	92136	118506	111139	130875	182157
France,Monac	90916	109842	115201	140703	166929
Belgium–Luxembourg	76525	79151	81408	93196	118144
Netherlands/Pays–Bas	54749	60908	71896	81649	114098
Japan/Japon	57671	54779	60221	59262	86571
Hong Kong	19071	37362	51608	65831	110913
Singapore/Singapour	63814	80063	64703	33748	27738
Canada	28203	26145	37988	43233	56088
Iran (Islamic Rp. of)	31774	55278	34953	33198	36369
Pakistan	27120	32655	28082	21936	21132
Spain/Espagne	12390	16675	21745	26691	40174
Russian Federation		18830	26937	27352	29096
Denmark/Danemark	11765	8853	14470	27600	34233
Sudan/Soudan	15911	6573	30499	5612	36420
Syrian Arab Republic	11072	16680	15365	3421	42408
Turkey/Turquie	14584	18865	23715	17752	13448
China/Chine	34257	18126	9926	10074	12727
Australia/Australie	20639	17442	13856	13703	17130
Brazil/Brésil	16453	21315	15382	16591	9097
Sweden/Suède	18210	14006	13830	11940	14456
United Arab Emirates	6853	24115	12079	7008	13778
Egypt/Egypte	16104	16494	11119	5498	12327
India/Inde	5494	1280	2418	21258	28566
Viet Nam	8176	2057	14009	229	31478
Norway,SVD,JM	9790	10441	8477	7728	11248
Poland/Pologne	6005	6244	13030	15150	6732
Thailand/Thaïlande	1302	11120	14470	11652	4254
Indonesia/Indonésie	1972	8923	13814	9960	7512
Sri Lanka	10014	9698	8075	3373	8593
Malaysia/Malaisie	1662	6947	8263	6340	12041
Nepal/Népal	6826	37	4346	10937	12643
Former USSR/Anc. URSS	29065				
Korea, Republic of	3571	8087	5696	4322	6648
Uruguay	1701	2252	11142	6264	5310
Saudi Arabia	6265	3895	4458	4297	6330
Mozambique	6609	7602	8669	1480	851
Un. Rep. of Tanzania	3769	2181	9563	6344	3139
Myanmar	264	1511	6851	10356	5067
Switz.Liecht	2610	4156	4010	5093	6849
Philippines	26	2118	8420	4985	6712
Jordan/Jordanie	1387	4611	7496	4460	2469
Austria/Autriche	2759	2061	3794	4991	6704
Cote d'Ivoire	2699	2686	4313	4006	6159
Greece/Grèce	3188	1811	2286	2943	6540
Kenya	959	2832	674	3046	8543
Bulgaria/Bulgarie	6490	84	28	4372	4706
Yemen/Yémen	2364	2280	3252	4702	1714

(VALUE AS PERCENTAGE OF WORLD TOTAL)(VALEURS EN POURCENTAGE DU TOTAL MONDIAL)

	1986	1987	1988	1989	1990	1991	1992	1993	1994	1995
Africa	0.7	1.6	0.3	1.0	1.5	0.8	1.5	0.6	0.3	0.5
Americas	10.4	15.6	5.1	17.5	10.3	12.8	12.1	9.4	3.7	6.7
Northern America	9.1	14.8	4.9	14.6	8.2	9.7	8.0	7.1	2.8	4.0
LAIA	1.0	0.8	0.2	2.9	2.0	3.0	3.9	2.2	0.8	2.6
CACM	0.3	0.0	0.0	0.0	0.1	0.1	0.1	0.1	0.0	0.0
Caribbean	0.0	0.0		0.0	0.0	0.0	0.0	0.0	0.0	0.1
Rest of America	0.0	0.0		0.0	0.0	0.0	0.1	0.0	0.0	0.0
As.ex F.USSR	65.1	61.2	70.3	59.6	66.5	64.6	66.4	70.9	43.8	44.6
Eur.x F.USSR	20.3	18.7	18.8	18.0	18.0	17.2	16.5	16.1	6.9	8.3
EU	16.2	15.7	13.7	15.6	15.8	15.1	14.1	14.7	5.8	7.3
EFTA	1.4	1.2	1.7	0.9	1.1	1.1	1.1	0.8	0.6	0.6
East Europe	2.6	1.6	3.3	1.4	1.1	0.9	1.2	0.5	0.4	0.3
Other Europe	0.1	0.2	0.0	0.1	0.1	0.0	0.1	0.1		
Former USSR	1.7	1.2	1.9	1.2	0.8	2.2	1.2	1.0	1.2	1.4
Oceania	1.8	1.7	3.6	2.8	2.9	2.4	2.3	2.0	1.4	1.2
India/Inde	5.6	4.9	4.8	5.7	6.2	6.4	6.6	7.3	8.9	10.6
Korea, Republic of	6.2	5.0	4.9	5.9	6.6	9.4	8.9	10.1	6.1	5.2
Hong Kong	1.5	3.3	6.7	3.7	5.0	6.8	7.4	8.2	7.2	6.1
Japan/Japon	13.1	12.0	10.4	10.7	9.2	10.5	7.2	7.9	4.0	3.9
China/Chine	4.6	3.7	4.9	4.1	4.4	5.8	7.3	6.7	4.7	6.3
Singapore/Singapour	12.3	7.4	8.7	5.4	5.9	6.5	7.4	8.2	4.3	4.2
USA/Etats–Unis d'Amer	6.9	9.1	3.8	11.8	5.7	6.9	6.3	5.8	2.2	3.3
Germany/Allemagne	5.0	3.9	2.5	3.2	3.7	3.6	3.5	3.1	1.5	2.0
Pakistan	2.2	3.3	3.9	2.5	2.5	2.3	3.3	3.4	1.7	2.0
United Kingdom	3.7	4.0	3.3	4.2	3.7	2.9	3.2	3.0	1.7	1.8

	1986	1987	1988	1989	1990	1991	1992	1993	1994	1995
Afrique	8.1	5.7	5.0	7.0	3.7	3.7	3.1	3.7	1.5	3.0
Amériques	29.8	35.0	30.4	29.1	34.9	31.9	36.7	39.5	32.2	34.9
Amérique du Nord	29.3	34.0	29.5	27.4	33.2	30.6	35.3	38.1	31.0	34.1
ALAI	0.5	0.9	0.9	1.3	1.5	1.2	1.4	1.4	1.1	0.7
MCAC	0.0	0.0	0.0	0.0	0.1	0.0	0.0	0.1	0.0	0.0
Caraïbes	0.0	0.0	0.0	0.0	0.0	0.1	0.0	0.0	0.0	0.0
Autre Amérique	0.0	0.0		0.4	0.1	0.0	0.0	0.0	0.0	0.0
Asie l'URSS exclus	29.0	24.7	24.9	25.4	20.3	19.1	21.1	18.4	13.5	16.2
Europe l'URSS exclus	29.6	30.0	34.0	34.5	36.1	41.9	37.0	36.3	38.0	40.1
UE	26.0	27.3	28.7	30.3	32.3	38.9	35.5	35.1	36.7	39.0
AELE	0.6	0.6	1.4	0.7	0.5	0.7	0.8	0.6	0.5	0.6
Europe de l'Est	2.5	1.7	3.5	3.0	3.0	1.9	0.5	0.7	0.8	0.5
Autre de l'Europe	0.6	0.3	0.4	0.5	0.4	0.3	0.0	0.0	0.0	0.0
Ancienne URSS	2.1	3.1	3.0	2.4	3.5	1.7	1.0	1.2	1.0	0.9
Océanie	1.4	1.6	2.7	1.6	1.5	1.7	1.1	0.8	0.7	0.7
USA/Etats–Unis d'Amer	27.6	31.9	27.9	26.2	31.7	28.9	34.0	36.4	29.3	32.4
Germany/Allemagne	3.7	4.5	4.6	5.2	5.4	9.6	8.3	8.2	8.5	8.1
United Kingdom	6.3	5.4	5.4	6.2	6.2	7.7	5.9	7.2	8.3	8.9
Italy/Italie	7.4	8.6	10.2	7.7	8.1	5.5	6.1	4.9	4.9	5.7
France,Monac	0.8	1.5	1.5	2.8	4.0	5.4	5.7	5.1	5.3	5.3
Belgium–Luxembourg	4.3	3.1	2.9	4.2	4.1	4.5	4.1	3.6	3.5	3.7
Netherlands/Pays–Bas	1.9	1.8	1.8	1.9	2.1	3.2	3.1	3.2	3.1	3.6
Japan/Japon	7.7	5.5	5.9	5.0	4.2	3.4	2.8	2.7	2.2	2.7
Hong Kong	0.8	0.7	1.3	1.0	0.9	1.1	1.9	2.3	2.5	3.5
Singapore/Singapour	4.2	4.3	3.0	6.3	4.2	3.8	4.1	2.9	1.3	0.9

4. General Imports C.I.F. by Commodities according to the S.I.T.C. (Rev. 2) in thousand U.S. Dollars
Importations Générales C.A.F. par Produits d'après la C.T.C.I. (Rév. 2) en milliers de Dollars E.U.

SITC CTCI	COMMODITY	1990 WEIGHT POIDS	1990 VALUE VALEUR	1991 WEIGHT POIDS	1991 VALUE VALEUR	1992 WEIGHT POIDS	1992 VALUE VALEUR	1993 WEIGHT POIDS	1993 VALUE VALEUR	PRODUIT
	ALL COMMODITIES # 1		3431783		3136691		3467055		3525714	TOUS PRODUITS
0	FOOD AND LIVE ANIMALS		475851		390078		366828		352779	ALIMENTS,ANIMAUX VIVANTS
02	DAIRY PRODCTS,BIRDS'EGGS		90819		78294		71385		78595	PRODUITS LAITIERS,OEUFS
022	MILK AND CREAM	W 62501	88022	W 60006	77613	W 45281	69376	W 37620	73233	LAIT ET CREME
0224	MILK,CREAM PRESERVED ETC	W 62501	88022	W 60006	77613	W 45281	69376	W 37618	73229	LAIT,CREME CONS,CONC
02242	MILK DRY,1.5% FAT OR LES	W 1478	1660	W 5212	8990	W 9057	17335	W 9541	21368	LAIT POUDRE INF 1.5%
02243	MILK DRY,OVER 1.5% FAT	W 22013	52151	W 19188	40582	W 15258	34037	W 16616	41004	LAIT POUDRE SUP 1.5%
02249	MILK(EX DRY) PRSVD,SWEET	W 39010	34210	W 35606	28042	W 20966	18004	W 11461	10857	LAIT CONS,CONC SUCRE
04	CEREALS AND PREPARATIONS		226512		219113		192841		167166	CEREALES ET PRODUITS
041	WHEAT ETC UNMILLED	W 1156549	149143	W 1605701	207619	W 1475253	182919	W 1033520	152543	FROMENT,EPEAUTRE
0411	DURUM WHEAT UNMILLED	W 919089	118414	W 504784	63397	W 472250	58226	W 244144	37986	FROMENT DUR NON MOULU
0412	OTHER WHEAT ETC UNMILLED	W 237460	30729	W 1100917	144223	W 1003003	124693	W 789376	114557	AUTRE FROMENT NON MOULU
042	RICE	W 380062	68532	W 16414	2662	W 17714	2656	W 20930	3548	RIZ
0422	RICE SEMI-MILLED,MILLED	W 380062	68532	W 14664	2387	W 17714	2656	W 20744	3516	RIZ POLI,GLACE INCL BRISURES
04221	RICE MILLED UNBROKEN	W 380062	68532	W 14664	2387	W 17714	2656	W 20744	3516	RIZ POLI,GLACE EXCL BRISURES
05	VEGETABLES AND FRUIT		97438		53731		56870		47446	LEGUMES ET FRUITS
054	VEG ETC FRSH,SMPLY PRSVD	W 296095	82254	W 168563	41761	W 175253	42569	W 130759	26783	LEGUMES FRAIS,CONG,SECS
0542	LEGUMINOUS VEGETBLES DRY	W 184283	60173	W 95343	26706	W 55569	14874	W 63521	15914	LEGUMES A COSSE SECS
0545	OTHER FRESH VEGETABLES	W 93654	13749	W 71631	14026	W 119021	27122	W 65823	10229	AUTRES LEGUMES FRAIS,REF
05451	ALLIACEOUS VEGTBLS,FRESH	W 92734	13415	W 71423	13967	W 118911	27069	W 65335	10041	OIGNONS,ECHALOTES,AULX
057	FRUIT,NUTS,FRESH,DRIED	W 37047	14062	W 21111	10308	W 31259	12928	W 30741	19106	FRUITS FRAIS OU SECS
06	SUGAR AND PREPS,HONEY		44569		10549		2972		26168	SUCRES ET PRODUITS
061	SUGAR AND HONEY	W 92564	44552	W 22896	10549	W 6836	2972	W 75405	26163	SUCRES ET MIEL
0611	RAW BEET AND CANE SUGAR	W 459	231	W 7081	2771	W 4456	1513	W 48030	15810	SUCRES BRUTS
0612	REFINED SUGAR ETC	W 90429	43161	W 10964	5356	W 1017	435	W 25212	8345	SUCRES RAFFINES
07	COFFEE,TEA,COCOA,SPICES		12907		22006		38041		26079	CAFE,THE,CACAO,EPICES
075	SPICES	W 11068	12801	W 24952	21932	W 33178	37959	W 13943	25935	EPICES
0751	PEPPER AND PIMENTO	W 796	651	W 16561	10109	W 21857	22041	W 2502	2522	POIVRE,PIMENTS
0752	SPICES,EX PEPPER,PIMENTO	W 10272	12150	W 8391	11823	W 11321	15918	W 11441	23414	AUTRES EPICES
07525	SEEDS OF ANISE,CUMIN,ETC	W 2703	2508	W 2506	2995	W 4782	6879	W 5839	12440	GRAINES ANIS,FENOUIL
1	BEVERAGES AND TOBACCO		7870		7069		14137		14243	BOISSONS ET TABACS
2	CRUDE MATERLS,EXCL FUELS		256022		188887		218893		247184	MAT BRUTES NON COMESTIBLES
22	OIL SEEDS,OLEAGINOUS FRT		26069		19845		50423		57791	GRAINES,FRUITS OLEAGINEUX
222	SEEDS FOR'SOFT'FIXED OIL	W 28354	9893	W 896	259	W 67296	18313	W 72255	21131	GRAINES HUILES FIXES
2226	RAPE AND COLZA SEEDS	W 28353	9890	W 896	259	W 67296	18313	W 72255	21130	GRAINES DE NAVETTE,COLZA
223	SEEDS FOR OTH FIXED OILS	W 45378	16176	W 67498	19586	W 91881	32110	W 102916	36659	GRAINES AUTRES HUILES FIXES
2231	COPRA	W 21316	6536	W 53887	15659	W 53672	20411	W 73808	28781	COPRAH
2238	OIL SEEDS AND FRUITS NES	W 24062	9641	W 13611	3927	W 38210	11699	W 29108	7878	GRAINES D'OLEAGINEUX NDA
24	CORK AND WOOD		19263		8661		5640		27222	LIEGE ET BOIS
247	OTH WOOD ROUGH,SQUARED	W 5835086	18696	W 612154	3204	W 839440	3268	W 2970085	25707	BOIS BRUTS EQUARRIS
2471	SAW-,VENEER-LOGS CONIFER	W 5424313	16108	W 46872	327	W 668432	1905	W 2372258	21276	CONIFERES POUR SCIAGE,PLACAG
24711	— IN THE ROUGH	W 5424313	16108	W 46872	327	W 668432	1905	W 2372258	21276	ECORCES OU DEGROSSIS
251	*PULP AND WASTE PAPER	W 22859	14470	W 10916	6344	W 13195	6774	W 21897	11205	PATES A PAPIER,DECHETS
26	TEXTILE FIBRES AND WASTE		142562		112202		114736		122530	FIBRES TEXTILES
263	COTTON	W 110611	116488	W 52242	93405	W 64352	94982	W 72459	95360	COTON
2631	RAW COTTON,EXCL LINTERS	W 110594	116453	W 51849	92836	W 64352	94981	W 72447	95329	COTON EN MASSE
266	SYNTHETIC FIBRES TO SPIN	W 6930	11356	W 8872	11714	W 8335	10532	W 14771	17545	FIBRES SYNTHETIQUES
2665	DISCN SYNTH FIBRE UNCMBD	W 5852	8945	W 8137	10117	W 8039	9602	W 14439	16321	DISCONTINUES EN MASSE
26652	— POLYESTER	W 5628	8509	W 7887	9745	W 7934	9407	W 14414	16242	FIBRES EN POLYESTERS
27	CRUDE FERTLZR,MINRLS NES		30010		32717		32424		18880	ENGRAIS MINERAUX BRUTS
271	FERTILIZERS,CRUDE	W 131521	10526	W 78676	6785	W 143429	8534	W 122440	6207	ENGRAIS BRUTS
278	OTHER CRUDE MINERALS	W 150932	9741	W 332577	16548	W 396284	17942	W 78231	6415	AUTRES MINERAUX BRUTS
2783	COMMON SALT,ETC	W 116985	4871	W 300352	12716	W 363487	13287	W 42592	1319	SEL
28	METALLIFEROUS ORES,SCRAP		15868		3612		2401		1815	MINERAIS METAL,DECHETS
282	IRON AND STEEL SCRAP	W 76071	14593	W 12635	2737	W 12808	1969	W 9483	1301	FERRAILLES
28209	— OF OTHR IRON OR STEEL	W 51864	10445	W 7009	1489	W 9713	1498	W 9381	1289	FERRAILLES DE FER
3	MINERAL FUELS ETC		567938		362781		425285		391505	COMBUSTIBLES MINERAUX LUB
32	COAL,COKE AND BRIQUETTES		30195		9731		9431		3903	HOUILLES,COKES,BRIQUETTES
322	COAL,LIGNITE AND PEAT	W 558149	28890	W 173449	8924	W 158833	7941	W 55946	2835	HOUILLES,LIGNITES,TOURBE
3222	OTH COAL,NOT AGGLOMERATD	W 541949	28151	W 173434	8918	W 153935	7676	W 55946	2835	AUTRES HOUILLES
33	PETROLEUM AND PRODUCTS		537697		352930		415619		387255	PETROLE ET DERIVES
333	CRUDE PETROLEUM	W 2192210	318029	W 1060013	205113	W 1043072	188215	W 1221286	183467	HUILES BRUTES DE PETROLE
334	PETROLEUM PRODUCTS,REFIN	W 924080	214256		141707		222639		195487	PRODUITS RAFFINES
3342	KEROSENE,OTH MEDIUM OILS	W 221789	55334	V 134578	34874	V 124644	22348	V 82377	17023	PETR LAMPANTS,AUT HUIL
33421	KEROSENE INCL JET FUEL	W 221789	55334	V 74441	16735	V 34796	6294	V 20443	4087	PETROLES LAMPANTS
33429	OTH MEDIUM PETROLEUM OIL			V 60137	18139	V 89848	16054	V 61934	12936	AUTRES HUILES MOYENNES
3343	GAS OILS	W 665285	144880	V 395533	95662	V 936020	184703	V 776675	154712	GAS OILS
3345	LUBS,PETROLEUM OILS NES	W 33717	13066		11078		15512		23686	HUILES LUBRIFIANTES
33451	LUBS(HIGH PETR CONT) ETC	W 32736	11430	V 29426	10694	V 38415	14869	V 40867	13017	HUILES LUBRIF,H LOURDES
33452	LUBS (LOW PETRLM CONTNT)	W 982	1636	W 242	384	W 527	643	W 5327	10669	PREPARATIONS LUBRIFIANTES
4	ANIMAL,VEGETABLE OIL,FAT		140676		126986		201979		136830	HUILES,GRAISSES ANIM,VEG
411	*ANIMAL OILS AND FATS	W 9431	3327	W 5979	2081	W 31850	10894	W 34769	11163	HUILES,GRAISSES ANIMALES
4113	ANIML OIL,FAT,GREASE NES	W 9431	3327	W 5979	2081	W 31381	10496	W 34767	11155	HUILES,GRAISSES ANIMALES NDA
41132	FATS OF BOVINE,SHEEP,ETC	W 7043	2772	W 3857	1410	W 28498	9576	W 33635	10676	SUIFS BRUTS FONDUS
42	FIXED VEGETABLE OIL,FAT		134104		123014		187314		124353	HUILES VEGETALES FIXES
423	FIXED VEG OILS,SOFT	W 178563	90100	W 199541	101045	W 329670	150439	W 195051	87050	HUILES VEGET DOUCES FIXES
4232	SOYA BEAN OIL	W 177475	88968	W 194997	97679	W 328148	149333	W 195044	87036	HUILE DE SOJA
424	FIXED VEG OIL NONSOFT	W 83833	44004	W 46885	21969	W 101339	36875	W 83464	37303	AUTRES HUILES VEG FIXES
4242	PALM OIL	W 53332	22083	W 37263	15913	W 96771	34027	W 79880	34722	HUILE DE PALME
4243	COCONUT (COPRA) OIL	W 29936	21520	W 8920	5709	W 3965	2578	W 2974	2170	HJUILE DE COPRAH
5	CHEMCLS,RELATED PROD NES		279756		276980		365982		369442	PRODUITS CHIMIQUES
51	ORGANIC CHEMICALS		44118		42260		49051		59653	PROD CHIMIQ ORGANIQUES
515	ORG-INORG COMPOUNDS ETC	W 5713	33062	W 4832	27912	W 4116	33414	W 3457	33439	COMPOSES ORGANO-MINERAUX
5155	OTH ORG-INORG COMPOUNDS	W 5551	31335	W 3966	25274	W 3866	28136	W 3066	25258	AUTR COMP ORG-MINERAUX
52	INORGANIC CHEMICALS		37513		36103		45918		37797	PROD CHIM INORGANIQUES
522	INORG ELEMNTS,OXIDES,ETC		19651		16675		15883		18726	ELEMENTS INORGANIQUES
523	OTHR INORG CHEMICALS ETC		17831		19416		30006		19050	AUT PRODUITS CHIMIQUES INORG
5232	OTH MTL CMPD OF INRG ACD	W 47836	10565	W 63473	12611	W 64201	21813	W 42905	8485	SELS METALLIQUES
52327	SILICATES	W 377	437	W 234	165	W 8630	10728	W 353	377	SILICATES
53	DYES,TANNING,COLOUR PROD		28387		30769		31874		38840	PROD TEINTURE,COLORANTS
531	SYNT DYE,NAT INDGO,LAKES	W 4049	15765	W 3935	17284	W 4471	16010	W 5446	21541	MAT COLOR ORGAN,LAQUES
5311	SYNTHIC ORGNIC DYESTUFFS	W 3764	15089	W 3515	16465	W 4117	15339	W 4770	19690	MAT COLOR ORGAN SYNTHET
541	*MEDICINAL,PHARM PRODUCT	K 3592141	32673	K 2269922	37290	K 1478322	33986	K 3489554	76801	PROD MEDICINAUX PHARMACEUT
5413	ANTIBIOTICS IN BULK	K 164044	4337	K 307867	8563	K 148070	6451	K 353354	20191	ANTIBIOTIQUES NDA
5417	MEDICAMENTS	K 2630568	15280	K 1260251	12642	K 547935	11093	K 1856793	20653	MEDICAMENTS
54179	— CONTNG OTH SUBSTANCES	K 2470247	14276	K 1200543	11758	K 517859	10224	K 1726416	17825	MED CONT AUT SUBSTANCES
5419	PHARMACEUTICAL GOODS NES	K 711377	9514	K 522330	12670	K 639482	12312	K 898884	26219	PREP,ART PHARMACEUTIQUES
54199	OTH PHARMACEUTICAL GOODS	K 608549	9002	K 426425	12242	K 574558	11894	K 810534	25785	AUT PREP PHARMACEUTIQUES
562	*FERTILIZERS,MANUFACTURE	W 255750	49512	W 281435	42610	W 583251	113450	W 342879	55348	ENGRAIS MANUFACTURES
5622	CHEM PHOSPHATIC FERTILZR	W 148621	31473	W 211518	32006	W 478551	95394	W 262523	44859	ENGRAIS PHOSPHATES
56222	SUPERPHOSPHATES	W 139096	29758	W 211518	32006	W 462884	92902	W 252773	43149	SUPERPHOSPHATES

4. General Imports C.I.F. by Commodities according to the S.I.T.C. (Rev. 2) in thousand U.S. Dollars
Importations Générales C.A.F. par Produits d'après la C.T.C.I. (Rév. 2) en milliers de Dollars E.U.

SITC CTCI	COMMODITY	1990 WEIGHT POIDS	1990 VALUE VALEUR	1991 WEIGHT POIDS	1991 VALUE VALEUR	1992 WEIGHT POIDS	1992 VALUE VALEUR	1993 WEIGHT POIDS	1993 VALUE VALEUR	PRODUIT
5623	CHEM POTASSIC FERTILIZER	W 50427	9517	W 53336	8556	W 81975	14296	W 68001	8628	ENGRAIS POTASSIQUES
56239	CHEM POTASS FERTILZR NES	W 50427	9517	W 53315	8554	W 69205	12150	W 2051	307	ENGRAIS POTASSIQUES NDA
58	PLASTIC MATERIALS ETC		54597		47975		54318		62376	MAT PLAST ARTIFICIELLES
583	POLYMERIZATION ETC PRODS	W 19140	20054	W 20055	20642	W 29141	25716	W 49162	38796	PROD POLYMERISATION
5831	POLYETHYLENE	W 4574	4802	W 7333	7078	W 10971	8753	W 17624	12576	POLYETHYLENE
58311	— IN PRIMARY FORMS	W 4120	4299	W 6742	6574	W 10874	8609	W 17525	12422	POLYETHYLENE PRIMAIRES
585	PLASTIC MATERIAL NES	W 34769	32211	W 23146	21452	W 29471	22626	W 19194	13778	RESINES ARTIFICIELLES
5852	OTH ART PLASTIC MTLS NES	W 34769	32211	W 23146	21452	W 29471	22626	W 19194	13778	AUT MAT PLAST ARTIFICIEL
58521	HARDENED PROTEINS	W 34753	32178	W 23146	21447	W 29470	22617	W 19188	13747	MAT ALBUMINOIDES DURCIES
59	CHEMICAL MATERIALS NES		29158		35695		33263		33801	MAT PROD CHIMIQUES NDA
591	PESTICIDES,DISINFECTANTS	W 4150	13420	W 5146	17878	W 4179	15394	W 3727	14545	DESINF,INSECT,FONG,HERB
5911	INSECTICIDES,FOR RETAIL	W 3123	9626	W 3747	10406	W 3083	10286	W 2591	9691	INSECTICIDES VENTE DET
598	MISCEL CHEM PRODUCTS NES	W 14338	13539	W 15846	15067	W 16973	15286	W 16490	16060	PROD DIV INDUST CHIM NDA
5989	CHEM PRODUCTS,PREPS NES	W 10596	9993	W 12416	11584	W 13441	11181	W 12911	11939	PROD PREP CHIMIQUES NDA
6	BASIC MANUFACTURES		935744		980381		1078993		1205466	ART MANUFACTURES
62	RUBBER MANUFACTURES NES		34532		34837		26890		24832	CAOUTCHOUC MANUFACTURE
625	RUBBER TYRES, TUBES ETC	N 1709308	19973	N 1596137	18148	N 1874564	17722	N 1774566	21748	PNEUS CAOUTCHOUC VULCANISE
6252	TYRES,NEW,BUS OR LORRY	N 181638	9895	N 166233	8925	N 184946	9731	N 204059	12695	PNEUS POUR AUTOBUS,CAMIONS
628	RUBBER ARTICLES NES		12522		15987		8627		2443	OUVRAGES CAOUTCHOUC NDA
6281	HYGIENIC UNHRDND RUBBER	MN 1633306	10811	MN 1278297	14564	MN 464413	7092	MN 21808	523	ART HYGIENE PHARM CAOUT
64	PAPER,PAPERBOARD AND MFR		36064		40272		37636		41733	PAPIERS,CARTONS & OUVRAGES
641	PAPER AND PAPERBOARD	W 25111	20680	W 39835	30081	W 52369	30718	W 55884	37409	PAPIERS ET CARTONS
6415	PAPER,PAPERBRD,BULK,NES	W 15834	12303	W 22981	17777	W 27779	14882	W 30512	18976	PAPIERS,CARTONS ROULEAUX
64159	OTHER PAPER ETC,BULK,NES	W 14590	11309	W 19057	16033	W 18973	11336	W 15812	13452	AUT PAPIER ROULEAUX FEUILLES
642	PAPER,ETC,PRECUT,ARTS OF	W 12449	15384	W 9386	10190	W 6852	6918	W 4587	4324	PAP,CARTONS DECOUPES
6424	PAPER ETC CT TO SIZE NES	W 8403	11465	W 4207	6624	W 2937	4325	W 1370	1974	PAP,CARTONS DECOUPES
64241	CIGARETTE PAPER PRECUT	W 8194	11205	W 3977	6354	W 2660	3836	W 1155	1618	PAPIER A CIGARETTES
65	TEXTILE YARN,FABRICS,ETC		451233		490883		630089		675566	FILS,TISSUS,ARTICLES TEXTILE
651	TEXTILE YARN	W 40434	115324	W 30067	88427	W 29923	86225	W 37476	115084	FILS TEXTILES
6513	COTTON YARN	W 9100	36851	W 3598	17418	W 4181	18604	W 7572	34965	FILS DE COTON
6514	SYN FIB YRN,BULK,MONOFIL	W 25660	62025	W 22331	57822	W 20831	52889	W 23941	59302	FILS CONT 85% FIB TEXT SYNTH
65141	— TEXTRD,CONT POLYAMIDE	W 4581	12733	W 5121	13702	W 5549	15604	W 4068	14604	FILS TEXT FIB CONT POLYAMID
65142	— NONTXT ETC CONT PAMID	W 289	746	W 1779	3473	W 3286	7220	W 7802	15967	FILS NON TEX FI CON POLYAMID
65144	— TEXTRD,CONT POLYESTER	W 19590	45433	W 14929	39471	W 11430	28452	W 11590	27252	FILS TEX FI CONT POLYESTERS
6516	DISCON SYN FIB BLEND YRN	W 3007	8014	W 2807	8674	W 3928	12336	W 5135	18074	FILS FIBR TEX SYNT DIS MOINS
65168	OTH DISC SYN BLEND YARN	W 2386	6697	W 2291	7494	W 3278	11136	W 4719	17164	FILS TEXT SYNT MELANGE AUT F
652	COTTON FABRICS,WOVEN		104803		129903		198087		232531	TISSUS DE COTON
6521	GREY WOVEN COTTON FABRIC	L 3507	10815	L 12009	11311	L 16217	15459	L 18893	22497	TISSUS COT ECRUS NON MERCER
65214	GREY WOVEN COTTON NES	L 2152	9740	L 7708	8001	L 9434	10217	L 14485	18862	AUT TISSUS 85% COTON ECRUS
6522	WOVEN COTTON BLEACHD,ETC		93989		118592		182628		210034	TISSUS COTON BLANCHIS ETC
65224	BLCHED COTTON FABRIC NES		71496		75817		91832		104390	AUT TIS PLUS 85% COT BLANCHI
65225	BLCHD COTN BLEND FAB NES	L 31590	22197	L 50825	42380	L 115048	90131	L 115290	104371	AUT TIS MOINS 85% COT BLANCH
653	WOVN MAN-MADE FIB FABRIC		177077		200283	L 282994	238250	L 250975	228916	TISSUS FIBRES SYNTH,ARTIF
6531	CONT SYNT WEAVES NONPILE		40633		55477	L 52150	62640	L 56653	68067	TISSUS FIBRES SYNTH CONTINUE
65314	CONT SYN TYRE CORD FABRC	L 43882	40036	L 51078	54656	L 50496	60707	L 35428	42385	TIS ARMATURE PNEUMATIQUES
65315	CONT SYN TXTL FABRIC NES		597		821	L 1655	1933	L 21226	25682	TIS PLUS 85% TEXT SYNT CONT
6532	DISC SYN TXTL FABRIC NES	L 9340	8647	L 14861	14012	L 17167	14177	L 10816	9932	TIS DISC MOINS 85% FIBR TEXT
6534	DISC SYN BLEND FABRC NES	L 183497	125765	L 158422	125002	L 203475	150271	L 176783	143192	TISSUS FIBRES SYNTH DISCONT
65341	DISC SYN FIB-COTTN FABRC	L 179591	122047	L 154048	120554	L 194966	140778	L 171342	137590	TISSUS FIB SYNT DIS MEL COTO
655	KNITTED,ETC FABRICS	L 19352	19767	L 21615	22986	L 38878	41175	L 41178	42502	ETOF BONNETERIE PIECES ETC
6552	OTHER KNIT ETC FAB NONEL	L 19352	19767	L 21615	22986	L 38878	41175	L 41178	42502	ETOF BON NON ELAS NON SYNT
656	LACE,RIBBONS,TULLE,ETC		21690		32375		35351		29937	TULLES,BRODERIE
65602	WOVEN LABELS ETC NES	W 13722	21077	W 21934	31694	W 25075	35060	W 20058	29247	ECUSSONS,ART SIMIL TISSES
657	SPECIAL TXTL FABRC,PRODS		7051		9904		20439		21418	TISSUS SPECIAUX
6573	COATED ETC TEXTILES NES		3990		7968		18538		19443	TISSUS,ART MATIERE TEXT NDA
65732	PLASTIC COATED TEXTILES	L 646	575	L 6180	5636	L 17401	15671	L 20180	16951	TISSUS IMPREGNES
66	NONMETAL MINERAL MFS NES		112322		123959		121564		156356	ART MIN NON METALLIQUES
661	LIME,CEMENT,BLDG PRODS	W 1606282	94859	W 1669407	109935	W 1673340	109534	W 2159669	140946	CHAUX,CIMENTS MAT CONSTR
6612	CEMENT	W 1606033	94786	W 1668759	109767	W 1673039	109462	W 2159036	140726	CIMENTS HYDRAULIQUES
67	IRON AND STEEL		182340		159316		142643		152850	FER ET ACIER
671	PIG IRON ETC	W 110891	22273	W 43039	9545	W 16049	3488	W 29068	5944	FONTE,SPIEGEL,POUDRES
6712	PIG IRN,SPIEGELEISEN ETC	W 79222	14055	W 25565	5092	W 13687	2143	W 24022	4370	FONTES BRUTES
674	IRN,STL UNIV,PLATE,SHEET	W 281458	123682	W 328092	103097	W 223459	106054	W 415418	119038	LARGES PLATS,TOLES
6744	IRN,STL HVY PLATE,ROLLED	W 12646	8053	W 32175	23154	W 27122	16325	W 7202	4233	TOLES LAMINEES PLUS 4.75 MM
67441	— OF IRON OR SIMPLE STL	W 9574	5879	W 31917	23028	W 27054	16249	W 7032	3922	TOLES NON ACIER FIN CARB
6746	IRN,STL THIN PLATE,ROLLD	W 116339	33589	W 95950	51018	W 152847	69575	W 368004	91956	TOLES LAM MOINS 3MM
67461	— OF IRON OR SIMPLE STL	W 47411	28249	W 90008	47388	W 150538	68029	W 367409	90941	TOL NON AC FIN MOINS 3 MM
6749	OTH IRN,STL PLATES,SHEET	W 129507	71155	W 180270	20696	W 19984	9690	W 25594	15938	AUTRES TOLES FER,ACIER
67491	— OF IRON OR SIMPLE STL	W 129352	70906	W 180021	20484	W 19810	9515	W 25505	15752	AUT TOLES AUTRES ACIER FIN
678	IRON,STL TUBES,PIPES,ETC	W 16241	18091	W 74555	36251	W 61276	15763	W 14671	10569	TUBES,TUYAUX EN FONTE,FER
6782	IRON,STL SEAMLESS TUBES	W 1579	2343	W 19411	13117	W 14072	8296	W 2197	1699	TUBES,TUYAUX SANS SOUDURE
6783	IRON,STL TUBES,PIPES NES	W 8026	8798	W 48086	18588	W 31525	5278	W 8577	5825	AUT TUBES,TUYAUX FER,ACIER
68	NON-FERROUS METALS		61446		48661		50566		63685	METAUX NON FERREUX
682	COPPER EXC CEMENT COPPER	W 3513	11016	W 1886	5612	W 2895	8550	W 3340	8047	CUIVRE
6822	COPPER,ALLOYS WORKED	W 3470	10910	W 1778	5469	W 2481	7944	W 3070	7903	CUIVRE,ALLIAGES OUVRES
684	ALUMINIUM	W 11299	24951	W 10900	22078	W 12374	21372	W 14742	25869	ALUMINIUM
6841	ALUMINIUM,ALLOYS,UNWRGHT	W 6693	12562	W 7989	13556	W 7851	11680	W 10310	14076	ALUMINIUM,ALLIAGES BRUTS
6842	ALUMINIUM,ALLOYS WORKED	W 4605	12389	W 2911	8523	W 4523	9692	W 4431	11793	ALUMINIUM,ALLIAGES OUVRE
686	ZINC	W 12003	21592	W 11885	18710	W 14653	18726	W 18525	23898	ZINC
6861	ZINC,ALLOYS UNWROUGHT	W 11999	21583	W 11880	18695	W 14645	18696	W 18521	23886	ZINC ET ALLIAGES BRUTS
69	METAL MANUFACTURES NES		54222		80624		68525		88686	ART MANUFACT EN METAL NDA
691	STRUCTURES AND PARTS NES	W 14362	17421	W 39162	36819	W 9201	34303	W 20703	53467	CONSTRUCT FER,ACIER,ALU
6911	STRUCTURES,PARTS IRN,STL	W 14168	16972	W 38868	35782	W 8822	32942	W 20341	52165	CONSTRUCT FER,ACIER,FONTE
693	WIRE PRODUCTS NON ELECTR	W 7556	13901	W 6509	13733	W 4357	7257	W 6625	10584	OUVRAGES FILS METALLIQUES
6931	WIRE CABLES, ROPES ETC	W 6307	12835	W 4339	9139	W 2984	5330	W 6275	10037	CORDAGES EN FILS DE FER
699	BASE METAL MFRS NES		9867		12167		11911		15028	ART MANUFACTURES MET NDA
7	MACHINES,TRANSPORT EQUIP		637095		662382		645439		639243	MACHINES MATERIEL TRANSPORT
71	POWER GENERATING EQUIPMT		101034		59299		58201		80367	MACHINES GENERATRICES
713	INTRNL COMBUS PSTN ENGIN		69087		34131		22811		29287	MOTEURS EXPL COMB INT, PIECE
7138	PISTON ENGINES NES	N 111732	47343	N 47340	20392	N 43539	14621	N 65063	20955	MOTEURS A PISTONS NDA
7139	PISTON ENGINE PARTS NES		10567		7830		4454		5616	PIECES POUR 713.2,3,8
714	ENGINES AND MOTORS NES		274		2077		732		25405	MOTEURS NON ELECTRIQUES
7149	ENGINE & MOTOR PARTS NES		260		1353		732		22254	PIECES 714 ET 718.88
71499	PARTS NES,OF 71488,71888		257		1349		732		22254	PIECES 714.88 ET 718.88
716	ROTATING ELECTRIC PLANT		8732		16988		15723		14450	APP ELECTR ROTATIFS,PIECES
7162	AC MTRS,GENRTRS,GEN SETS	N 9257	6278	N 26712	11721	N 38085	13612	N 26131	11029	MOTEURS ELECTRIQUES
718	OTH POWER GENERATG MACHY		19490		454		176	N 13	31	AUTRES MOTEURS PARTIES
7188	WIND,WATER,ETC ENGINES		19489		439		176	N 13	31	MOT MACHINES MOTRICES NDA
71889	PARTS NES OF 71881,71882		19484		320		171			PARTIES DES POS 718.81,82
72	MACHS FOR SPCL INDUSTRYS		136530		183776		182197		179246	MAC SPECIALES POUR INDUST
721	AGRIC MACHY,EXC TRACTORS		13769		21012		9974		8555	MACHINES AGRICOLES

4. General Imports C.I.F. by Commodities according to the S.I.T.C. (Rev. 2) in thousand U.S. Dollars
Importations Générales C.A.F. par Produits d'après la C.T.C.I. (Rév. 2) en milliers de Dollars E.U.

SITC CTCI	COMMODITY	1990 WEIGHT POIDS	1990 VALUE VALEUR	1991 WEIGHT POIDS	1991 VALUE VALEUR	1992 WEIGHT POIDS	1992 VALUE VALEUR	1993 WEIGHT POIDS	1993 VALUE VALEUR	PRODUIT
7211	CULTIVATING MACHINERY		12889		17902		9555		6704	MACH PREPARATION DU SOL
72118	OTH AGRIC,HORTIC MACHNRY	N 12548	11798	N 20039	16794	N 11017	8663	N 8297	6265	AUT MACHINES AGRICOLES
724	TEXTILE,LEATHER MACHNRY		42699		71702		95593		85211	MACH POUR INDUSTRIE TEXTILE
7243	SEWING MACHS,NEEDLES ETC	N 8172308	4432	MN 9047	13048		30604	MN 9436	32521	MACHINES A COUDRE,PIECES
72431	SEWING MACHINES	N 45236	3314	N 66589	11758	N 74277	28673	N 83277	30517	MACHINES A COUDRE
7244	SPINNING,EXTRDNG,ETC MCH		16124		31007		26977		25359	MACH POUR LE FILAGE
72442	FIBRE PROCESSNG MACH NES	N 184	6550	N 439	10806	N 786	10050	N 298	7032	MACH PREP MAT TEXTILES
72443	SPINNING,REELING,ETC MCH	N 2307	6555	N 2726	12194	N 2539	14362	N 663	12259	MACH POUR LA FILATURE
7245	WEAVING,FELT MFG,ETC MCH		3005	N 9459	6920	N 5128	14209	N 6830	11671	METIERS A TISSER,PIECES
7248	SKIN,LEATHER WORKNG MACH	N 395	6715	N 518	9122	N 345	12683	N 508	4186	MACHINES TRAVAIL DES CUIRS
727	FOOD MACHRY NON–DOMESTIC		6239		14072		13405		8212	MACH INDUSTRIES ALIMENT
7272	OTH FOOD PROC MCHY,PARTS	N 636	5092	N 1880	13331	N 1771	12419	N 671	7144	AUT MACH IND ALIMENTAIRE
728	OTH MACHY FOR SPCL INDUS		62441		53919		52491		61710	AUT MACH IND PARTICULIERES
7284	MACHY FOR SPCL INDUS NES		60249		46235		47664		56665	MACH SPEC IND PARTICUL.
72848	OTH MCHY WITH INDIV FNCT	N 514	38826	N 671	32988	N 360	38852	N 1041	46160	AUTRES MACHINES NDA
72849	PTS OF MACHS OF 7284 ETC		13436		5170		4098		4774	PIECES DU 728.4 ETC
73	METALWORKING MACHINERY		26648		7107		5093		4284	MACH TRAVAIL DES METAUX
737	METALWORKING MACHNRY NES		23030		2094		1221		1283	MACH TRAV METAUX PIECES
7373	WELDING,BRAZING,ETC MCHS		21564		975		821		295	MACH SOUDAGE ETC PIECES
73732	ELECTRIC WELDERS,ETC	N 92	21424	N 12	916		805		213	MACH ELECT POUR SOUDER
74	GENRL INDUSTRL MACHY NES		57852		77154		66970		60889	MACH APP INDUSTRIE
741	HEATING,COOLING EQUIPMNT		10660		14367		13166		12198	MACH CHAUFFAGE,PIECES
743	PUMPS NES,CENTRFUGES ETC		11571		8079		7806		8224	POMPES COMPRES,VENT ETC
744	MECHANICAL HANDLING EQU		6713		12615		8908		7590	EQUIP MANUTENTION PIECES
749	NONELEC MACH PTS,ACC NES		16374		29153		24927		21111	PIECES MACH NON ELEC NDA
7492	COCKS,VALVES ETC NES	N 33385	3313	N 228985	15454	N 190269	11986	N 224966	8126	ART ROB,SIM POUR TUYAUX
75	OFFICE MACHNES,ADP EQUIP		15719		12891		13029		13042	MACH BUREAU TRAIT AUTOM
76	TELECOMM,SOUND EQUIPMENT		73148		43575		29386		31017	EQUIPMENT DE TELECOM
764	TELECOM EQPT,PTS,ACC NES		66218		36964		26986		27791	EQUIP TELECOM,PIECES
7643	TV,RADIO TRANSMITTRS ETC	N 5542	38731		18066		13911	N 90	15103	APP EMET TELE RADIO
7649	PTS NES OF EQUIPMT OF 76		24669		13712		9603		9200	PIECES DE LA DIV 76
76493	TELECOMM EQUIPMT PTS NES		15270		8357		6685		5597	PIECES 761,762,764.3,8
77	ELECTRIC MACHNRY NES ETC		82394		137869		211918		150215	MACH APP ELECT NDA
771	ELECTRIC POWER MACHY NES		17362		61976		81512		68583	MACH PROD,TRANS ELECTR
7711	TRANSFORMERS,ELECTRICAL	N 8462	13343	N 11609	15195	N 22759	29273	N 19656	28789	TRANSFO ELECTRIQUES
77118	OTHER ELEC TRANSFORMERS	N 7542	9114	N 4360	8483	N 21584	24726	N 18288	19387	AUTRES TRANSFO ELECTRIQ
7712	OTH ELEC POWER MACHY NES		4018		46781		52239		39794	AUT APP PROD TRANSF ELEC
77129	PTS NES OF MACHY OF 771		3860		41432		49626		34700	PIECES MACH DU 771
772	SWITCHGEAR ETC,PARTS NES	N 2386787	33729	N 2438034	30460	N 3178361	68534	N 2502132	27690	APP COUPURE,SECT ETC
7721	SWITCHGEAR ETC	N 2361282	33523	N 2429763	30387	N 3177244	68464	N 2492015	27536	APP COUPURE,SECTIONMNT
773	ELECTR DISTRIBUTNG EQUIP	W 2518	6323	W 6433	25217	W 6705	44249	W 8242	36250	EQUIPMT DISTRIBUTION ELECT
7731	INSULATED WIRE,CABLE ETC	W 2328	4751	W 5087	21135	W 3469	34405	W 5898	30430	FILS,CABLES ISOLES ELECT
778	ELECTRICAL MACHINERY NES		13715		8981		10361		8396	AUTRES MACH ELECT NDA
78	ROAD VEHICLES		91136		68077		48076		74248	VEHICULES ROUTIERS
781	PASS MOTOR VEH EXC BUSES	N 6232	27550	N 9525	22625	N 2965	14687	N 5109	27367	AUTO TRANSPORT PERSONNES
783	ROAD MOTOR VEHICLES NES	N 1430	8843	N 785	4475	N 1069	6145	N 1431	11082	VEHICULES ROUTIERS NDA
7831	BUSES	N 1253	8463	N 780	4012	N 1066	6030	N 1430	11075	VOITURES TRANSPORT COMMUN
784	MOTOR VEH PRTS,ACCES NES		27951		14132		6936		11338	PIECES 722,781,782,783
7841	MOTOR VEHICLE CHASSIS	N 2478	18500	N 1610	8931	N 426	2239	N 577	5948	CHASSIS 722,781,782,783
785	CYCLES,ETC MOTRZD OR NOT		18436		17182		16126		16723	MOTOCYCLES SCOOTERS
7851	MOTORCYCLES ETC	N 12996	11342	N 13395	11978	N 11845	9958	N 10198	9439	MOTO VELO MOTEUR AUXIL
79	OTHR TRANSPORT EQUIPMENT		52634		72635		30570		45936	AUTRE MATERIEL TRANSPORT
791	RAILWAY VEHICLES		5455		6212		9736		10631	VEHIC MAT CHEMINS DE FER
793	SHIPS AND BOATS ETC		46930		64068		20616		35260	NAVIRES BATEAUX,ETC
7932	SHIPS AND BOATS NES	N 6	933	N 40	22646		411	N 7	3169	NAVIRES ET BATEAUX
79323	OTHER CARGO VESSELS		58	N 3	15847		95	N 1	2965	AUT BATEAUX TRANS MARCH
7933	VESSELS FOR BREAKING UP	W 169115	45819	W 152828	33485	W 92844	18876	W 190516	31926	BATEAUX A DEPECER
8	MISC MANUFACTURED GOODS		124306		136154		145889		165130	ART MANUFACTURES DIVERS
84	CLOTHING AND ACCESSORIES		14418		11152		9185		6456	VETEMENTS
845	OUTERWEAR KNIT NONELASTC	MN 25171	12371	MN 15214	7808	N 8888484	5217	N 4067088	2276	VET DESSOUS,ACCES BONNET
8451	— JERSEYS,PULLOVERS ETC	MN 22519	11414	MN 13941	7060	N 8090628	4878	N 3786192	2097	CHANDAILS,PULL–OVERS ETC
87	PRECISION INSTRUMNTS NES		27303		34106		32144		26285	INSTRUM,APPAR SCIENT NDA
874	MEASURNG,CONTROLNG INSTR		16335		21562		12687		12912	INSTRUMENTS DE MESURE
8749	INSTR PTS NES,ACCESSORYS		6399		9539		4715		4688	PIECES 873,874.3,54,874.8
88	PHOTO EQU,OPTICL GDS ETC		12304		12327		14779		11672	APP,FOURN PHOTO,OP,MONTR
882	PHOTO,CINEMA SUPPLIES		8199		9216		12899		9777	PRODUITS PHOTO,CINEMA
8822	PHOTO FILM EXC DEV CINMA		7389		7881		11757		8779	PLAQUES,PELLICULES,FILMS
89	MISC MANUFCTRD GOODS NES		68581		76936		86457		117630	ART MANUFACTURES DIVERS
892	PRINTED MATTER		7547		8241		9820		16055	IMPRIMES
893	ARTICLES OF PLASTIC NES		32403		34422		36531		60031	OUVRAGES EN MAT DIVIS 58
8931	PLSTC PACKG CONTNRS,LIDS	W 990	2063	W 5609	7678	W 11489	10426	W 20949	39090	ART TRANSP EMBALLAGE ETC
8939	MISC PLASTIC ARTICLES		30284		26740		26101		20929	ART DIVERS EN MAT DIV 58
89399	OTHR PLASTC ARTICLES NES		30233		26685		26084		20851	AUT OUV MAT DIV 58
899	OTHER MANUFACTURED GOODS		21148		26956		32307		32902	AUT ART MANUF DIVERS NDA
8998	SMALLWARES,TOILETRYS ETC		16188		24127		29814		30618	ART MERCERIE,TOILETTE
89983	BUTTONS,STUDS,ETC	MN 1053056	15088	MN 1542692	19361	MN 1798408	21386	MN 1586775	20761	BOUTONS,BOUTONS–PRESSION

5. General Exports F.O.B. by Commodities according to the S.I.T.C. (Rev. 2) in thousand U.S. Dollars
Exportations Générales F.O.B. par Produits d'après la C.T.C.I. (Rév. 2) en milliers de Dollars E.U.

SITC CTCI	COMMODITY	1990 WEIGHT POIDS	1990 VALUE VALEUR	1991 WEIGHT POIDS	1991 VALUE VALEUR	1992 WEIGHT POIDS	1992 VALUE VALEUR	1993 WEIGHT POIDS	1993 VALUE VALEUR	PRODUIT
	ALL COMMODITIES # 1		1556441		1690208		1941608		2253095	TOUS PRODUITS
0	FOOD AND LIVE ANIMALS		220638		211106		209440		263993	ALIMENTS,ANIMAUX VIVANTS
03	FISH AND PREPARATIONS		168563		160060		165644		211327	POISSONS ET PREPARATIONS
034	FISH,FRESH,CHILLED,FROZN	W 3806	8123	W 5395	12673	W 4967	13094	W 6418	17997	POISSON FRAIS, REFRIG,CONG
0342	FISH FROZEN,EXCL FILLETS	W 3806	8123	W 5395	12673	W 4967	13094	W 6418	17997	POISSONS CONGELES
035	FISH SALTED,DRIED,SMOKED	W 1606	7746	W 1263	5980	W 1770	10534	W 1260	8995	POISSON SECHE,SALE,FUME
03503	FISH(EX COD)DRIED,SALTED	W 1488	6076	W 1050	4087	W 1630	7596	W 960	5460	POISSONS SECHES,SALES
036	SHELL FISH FRESH,FROZEN	W 26043	152694	W 22561	141407	W 24884	142016	W 27574	184335	CRUSTACES,MOLLUSQUES
05	VEGETABLES AND FRUIT		9375		4834		7069		10718	LEGUMES ET FRUITS
054	VEG ETC FRSH,SMPLY PRSVD		8513		3825		6333		9462	LEGUMES FRAIS,CONG,SECS
0545	OTHER FRESH VEGETABLES		8122		3273		5320		7975	AUTRES LEGUMES FRAIS,REF
05459	FRESH VEGETABLES NES		8122		3273		5320		7926	LEGUMES FRAIS,REFRI NDA
07	COFFEE,TEA,COCOA,SPICES		36439		43332		34170		41552	CAFE,THE,CACAO,EPICES
074	TEA AND MATE	W 21126	36345	W 26875	43321	W 24990	33924	W 29620	39719	THE ET MATE
0741	TEA	W 21126	36345	W 26862	43305	W 24990	33924	W 29620	39719	THE
2	CRUDE MATERLS,EXCL FUELS		106013		91791		92167		74544	MAT BRUTES NON COMESTIBLES
26	TEXTILE FIBRES AND WASTE		104458		90718		91002		71448	FIBRES TEXTILES
264	JUTE,OTH TEX BAST FIBRES	W 325557	104272	W 238679	90613	W 292374	90916	W 266115	71383	JUTE
3	MINERAL FUELS ETC		19904		34856		17343		19270	COMBUSTIBLES MINERAUX LUB
33	PETROLEUM AND PRODUCTS		19904		34856		17343		19270	PETROLE ET DERIVES
334	PETROLEUM PRODUCTS,REFIN	W 173896	19904	V 192701	34856	V 112236	17343	V 146542	19270	PRODUITS RAFFINES
3341	GASOLINE,OTH LIGHT OILS	W 43420	7919	V 54574	13666	V 36083	6276	V 67108	11407	ESSENCES POUR MOTEURS
33419	OTH LIGHT PETROLEUM OILS	W 43096	7862	V 54538	13659	V 36083	6276	V 67108	11407	AUTRES HUILES LEGERES
3344	FUEL OILS,NES	W 126161	10808	V 133031	19682	V 73649	10196	V 72082	6364	FUEL OILS
5	CHEMCLS,RELATED PROD NES		17104		35211		21253		59015	PRODUITS CHIMIQUES
562	*FERTILIZERS,MANUFACTURE	W 115045	15244	W 240593	33718	W 140100	19286	W 423969	55971	ENGRAIS MANUFACTURES
5621	CHEM NITROGENOUS FERTLZR	W 115045	15244	W 240379	33710	W 140100	19286	W 423969	55971	ENGRAIS AZOTES
56216	UREA	W 115045	15244	W 240379	33710	W 140100	19286	W 423969	55971	UREE
6	BASIC MANUFACTURES		527260		435554		466817		483204	ART MANUFACTURES
61	LEATHER,DRESSED FUR,ETC		180780		124934		132790		136627	CUIRS,PELLETERIES
611	LEATHER	W 25044	180167	W 12079	123994	W 13254	130350	W 12105	134698	CUIRS,PEAUX PREPARES
6113	CALF LEATHER	W 1705	11467	W 471	6227	W 1202	13106	W 1037	15439	CUIRS,PEAUX DE VEAUX
6114	LEATHR BOVINE NES,EQUINE	W 21644	142271	W 9177	86051	W 9962	89386	W 9313	92968	CUIRS DE BOVINS
6116	LEATHER OF OTH HIDE,SKIN	W 1596	25227	W 2298	30195	W 2002	26801	W 1625	24864	PEAUX PREP D'AUTRES ANIMAUX
61161	LEATHER FROM GOAT,KID	W 1596	25227	W 2298	30195	W 2002	26801	W 1616	24761	PEAUX DE CAPRINS PREPAREES
65	TEXTILE YARN,FABRICS,ETC		342870		304670		323665		333777	FILS,TISSUS,ARTICLES TEXTILE
651	TEXTILE YARN	W 57807	43455	W 38890	29641	W 35895	28612	W 33076	26991	FILS TEXTILES
6519	TEXTILE FIBRE YARN NES	W 57750	43322	W 38464	29427	W 35820	28544	W 32982	26761	FILS TEXT NDA FILE FIB VER
65196	FLAX,RAMIE YARN IN BULK	W 57729	43317	W 38458	29425	W 35814	28542	W 32982	26761	FILS LIN,RAMIE NON POUR DET
652	COTTON FABRICS,WOVEN	L 11111	6287		6515		6573		13019	TISSUS DE COTON
6522	WOVEN COTTON BLEACHD,ETC	L 11111	6287		6515		6573		12873	TISSUS COTON BLANCHIS ETC
65222	BLCHD COTTON TERRY FABRC	L 9736	5448	L 12828	6161	L 13601	6433	L 26060	12465	TISSUS COT BOUCLES BLANCHIS
654	OTH WOVEN TEXTILE FABRIC		161892		106592		109953		84097	TISSUS AUT COTON SYNT,ARTIF
6545	WEAVES OF FIBRES OF 2640	W 224456	161774	W 157448	106431	W 160670	109798	W 133162	83519	TISSUS DE JUTE
657	SPECIAL TXTL FABRC,PRODS		9187		30955		46759		57197	TISSUS SPECIAUX
6575	CORDAGE AND MANUFACTURES		9187		30919		46755		56382	FICELLES,CORDES,CORDAGES
65751	CORDAGE,CABLE,ROPE,TWINE	W 10081	7275	W 34730	28416	W 54839	43953	W 65817	54020	CORDAGES TRESSES OU NON
658	TEXTILE ARTICLES NES		119382		128368		126893		146284	ART FACONNES MAT TEXTILES
6581	BAGS,SACKS OF TEXTILES	W 206137	113663	W 182594	112158	W 251883	107375	W 531052	122732	SACS EMBALLAGE TEXTILES
6582	MADE-UP CANVAS GOODS	W 44	44	W 294	166	W 5447	5742	W 14980	10862	BACHES,TENTES ETC
6584	LINENS ETC		5334		15820		13069	MN 28119	11980	LINGE DE MAISON
65841	BED LINEN OF COTTON	N 1187604	3270	N 3144960	11204	N 2132784	7820	N 3308976	7448	LINGE DE LIT DE COTON
7	MACHINES,TRANSPORT EQUIP		14397		30052		74937		23074	MACHINES MATERIEL TRANSPORT
72	MACHS FOR SPCL INDUSTRYS		5210		15999		40790		7207	MAC SPECIALES POUR INDUST
723	CIVIL ENGNEERG EQUIP ETC		2134	N 13	364		8888		1141	APPAREILS DE GENIE CIVIL
7234	CONST,MINING MACHNRY NES		1985	N 11	360		8888	N 10	577	MACH POUR LA CONST, MINES
72348	PUBLIC WORKS MACHNRY NES		539				6349			MACHINES TRAVAUX PUBLICS
728	OTH MACHY FOR SPCL INDUS		2993		13902		27640		5810	AUT MACH IND PARTICULIERES
7284	MACHY FOR SPCL INDUS NES		2993		13902		27640		5802	MACH SPEC IND PARTICUL.
72848	OTH MCHY WITH INDIV FNCT		966		9777		21138		3723	AUTRES MACHINES NDA
72849	PTS OF MACHS OF 7284 ETC		2027		4115		6502		2079	PIECES DU 728.4 ETC
73	METALWORKING MACHINERY		5971		3206		2164		10	MACH TRAVAIL DES METAUX
736	METALWORKING MACH-TOOLS		5971		2998		2146	N 8	10	MACH-OUTILS TRAVAIL METAUX
74	GENRL INDUSTRL MACHY NES		63		3750		22617		10015	MACH APP INDUSTRIE
744	MECHANICAL HANDLING EQU				3318		16363		9882	EQUIP MANUTENTION PIECES
7442	LIFTING,LOADING MACH NES			N 13	1128		16355		3602	APP LEVAGE,MANUTENTION
74422	SHIP DERRICKS,CRANES ETC			N 13	1128	N 579	16337	N 6	527	GRUES,PONTS ROULANTS
8	MISC MANUFACTURED GOODS		647390		847484		1053537		1326561	ART MANUFACTURES DIVERS
84	CLOTHING AND ACCESSORIES		642956		840383		1041736		1307393	VETEMENTS
842	MENS OUTERWEAR NOT KNIT	MN 33979	199460	MN 39947	258833	MN 56275	330933	MN 79382	431741	VET DESSUS POUR HOMMES
8421	— OVERCOATS,OTHER COATS	N 196452	666	N 2303112	2657	N 7218324	5852	MN 30701	28737	MANTEAUX HOMMES MAT TEXT
84219	—— OF OTHER FIBRES	N 196452	666	N 2285112	2628	N 7218324	5852	MN 30701	28737	MANTEAUX HOMMES AUT FIBR
8422	— SUITS	N 433836	1314	N 1183176	8893	N 3205872	18658	N 3828000	24945	COMPLETS HOMMES MAT TEXT
84223	—— OF MAN-MADE FIBRES	N 433836	1314	N 1183176	8893	N 3205872	18658	N 3828000	24945	COMPLETS HOMMES FIB SYNT
8423	— TROUSERS,BREECHES ETC	MN 22907	72814	MN 22671	81231	MN 31387	113590	MN 28413	105250	PANTALONS HOMMES MAT TEX
8424	— JACKETS,BLAZERS ETC	N 5933244	35754	N 6088788	39991	N 5784552	43030	MN 9489	78461	VESTES HOMMES MAT TEXTIL
8429	— OTHER OUTER GARMENTS	N 4508736	88912	N 7701396	126061	N 8678772	149804	N 6951180	194348	AUT VET DES HOM MAT TEX
843	WOMENS OUTERWEAR NONKNIT	MN 45037	148281	MN 41343	150274	MN 46703	166652	MN 71910	244333	VET DESSUS FEMMES MAT TEX
8431	— COATS AND JACKETS	N 3408864	18574	N 2625564	16851	N 3344220	20202	N 4679280	32800	MANT,VEST FEM MAT TEXTIL
8433	— DRESSES	N 1465116	4910	N 2355228	9727	N 2044092	6974	N 2396496	8474	ROBES EN MAT-TEXTILES
8434	— SKIRTS	N 1890876	5771	N 1120716	3527	N 1253052	4161	N 1619580	5865	JUPES EN MAT TEXTILES
8435	— BLOUSES	MN 20543	52532	MN 16861	45600	MN 20527	56573	MN 35531	104704	BLOUSES FEM MAT TEXTILES
8439	— OTHER OUTER GARMENTS	MN 17099	63998	MN 17713	70766	MN 18839	74307	MN 26616	87029	AUT VET DES FEM MAT TEXT
844	UNDER GARMENTS NOT KNIT	MN 83682	207203	MN 104408	276440	MN 127279	354323	MN 143763	400161	VETEMENT DESSOUS MAT TEX
8441	— MENS SHIRTS	MN 80393	198289	MN 98616	260570	MN 120280	336980	MN 133049	376611	CHEMISES HOMMES MAT TEXT
84411	—— OF COTTON	MN 30375	73621	MN 31938	87391	MN 49151	148202	MN 53093	174463	CHEMISES HOMMES DE COTON
84412	—— OF SYNTHETIC FIBRES	MN 50017	124668	MN 66678	173178	MN 71128	188778	MN 79955	202148	CHEMISES HOMMES FIB SYNT
8442	— MENS,OTHR THAN SHIRTS	N 2447856	6709	N 3247368	7854	N 2953308	7008	N 6538176	12223	SOUS-VET HOMMES MAT TEXT
8443	— WOMENS	N 841476	2205	N 2543868	8016	N 4046436	10335	N 4175964	11327	VET DESSOUS FEM MAT TEXT
845	OUTERWEAR KNIT NONELASTC	MN 19283	46872	MN 22325	59345	MN 35679	92215	MN 31465	76455	VET DESSOUS,ACCES BONNET
8451	— JERSEYS,PULLOVERS ETC	MN 9858	18277	MN 9782	23504	MN 17698	48604	MN 14967	39553	CHANDAILS,PULL-OVERS ETC
8452	— WOMENS DRESSES ETC	N 358908	2032	N 798864	4354	N 1375728	7369	N 1038876	5435	ROBES,JUPES BONNETERIE
8459	— OTHER,CLTHG ACCESRYS	MN 9067	26563	MN 11745	31487	MN 16605	36242	MN 15459	31467	AUT VET DESSUS DE BONNE
846	UNDER GARMENTS KNITTED	MN 40963	38958	MN 81862	92344	MN 90148	93268	MN 153523	150165	SOUS VETS DE BONNETERIE
8462	— OF COTTON NON ELASTIC	MN 35067	27198	MN 76810	79859	MN 82631	75022	MN 143677	125737	SOUS-VET BONNET COTON
84629	—— OTHER	MN 35067	27198	MN 76810	79859	MN 82631	75022	MN 143677	125737	AUT SOUS-VET BONNET COTON
8463	— OF SYNTH FBR NONELAST	N 5895624	11760	N 5047092	12457	N 7516356	18246	MN 9846	24427	SOUS-VET BONNET FIB SYNT
84632	—— MENS SHIRTS	N 5895624	11760	N 5047092	12457	N 7516356	18246	MN 9846	24427	CHEMISES DE BON FIB SYNMT
89	MISC MANUFCTRD GOODS NES		2620		2304		5106		9523	ART MANUFACTURES DIVERS

FOOT NOTES – NOTES

TABLE 4 –

Bangladesh

Foot Notes (Continued) – Notes (Suite)

1 Because of the conversion from SITC Rev.3 to SITC Rev.2, not all data for 1991, 1992 and 1993 are comparable with those for previous years. For further details see the Introduction.

TABLE 5 –

1 Because of the conversion from SITC Rev.3 to SITC Rev.2, not all data for 1991, 1992 and 1993 are comparable with those for previous years. For further details see the Introduction.

TABLEAU 4 –

1 A cause de la conversion de la CTCI Rev.3 à la CTCI Rev.2, toutes les données pour 1991, 1992 et 1993 ne sont pas comparables à celles des années précédentes. Se référer aux explications supplémentaires dans l'introduction.

TABLEAU 5 –

1 A cause de la conversion de la CTCI Rev.3 à la CTCI Rev.2, toutes les données pour 1991, 1992 et 1993 ne sont pas comparables à celles des années précédentes. Se référer aux explications supplémentaires dans l'introduction.

1. HISTORICAL SERIES, 1961–1996 GENERAL TRADE, IMPORTS C.I.F., EXPORTS F.O.B.
SERIES HISTORIQUES, 1961–1996 COMMERCE GENERAL, IMPORTATIONS C.A.F., EXPORTATIONS F.O.B

YEAR / ANNEE	VALUE IN MILLION BARBADOS DOLLARS / VALEUR EN MILLION BARBADOS DOLLARS — MERCHANDISE –MARCHANDISE: IMPORTS	EXPORTS	GOLD –OR: IMPORTS	EXPORTS	CONVERSION FACTORS U.S. CENTS PER BARBADOS DOLLAR / FACTEURS DE CONVERSION CENTS E.U. PAR BARBADOS DOLLAR: IMPORTS	EXPORTS	INDEX NUMBERS –INDICES — QUANTUM: IMPORTS	EXPORTS	UNIT VALUE / VALEUR UNITAIRE: IMPORTS	EXPORTS
1961	80.30	43.30			58.3300	58.3300				
1962	89.10	50.30			58.3300	58.3300				
1963	98.90	69.80			58.3300	58.3300				
1964	108.90	60.30			58.3300	58.3300				
1965	116.30	64.30			58.3300	58.3300				
1966	131.10	70.00			58.3300	58.3300				
1967	134.10	71.60			57.3100	57.7800				
1968	168.00	80.20			50.0000	50.0000				
1969	194.60	74.30			50.0000	50.0000				
1970	236.00	79.20			50.0000	50.0000				
1971	243.70	80.40			50.0000	50.0000				
1972	270.40	84.50			52.1438	52.9137				
1973	328.60	103.70			51.0097	51.5789				
1974	417.70	172.40			48.7561	49.1835				
1975	437.20	216.50			49.4897	49.2208				
1976	473.30	173.60			49.9052	49.9052				
1977	545.10	193.00			49.8273	49.8360				
1978	628.20	261.10			49.7199	49.7200				
1979	852.50	306.00			49.7199	49.7200				
1980	1049.10	455.40			49.7199	49.7200				
1981	1165.90	448.60			49.7200	49.7200				
1982	1106.60	519.60			49.7199	49.7200				
1983	1258.00	717.40			49.7191	49.7191				
1984	1324.60	787.40			49.7191	49.7191				
1985	1221.60	707.80			49.7191	49.7191				
1986	1181.10	552.30			49.7200	49.7200				
1987	1035.90	313.50			49.7200	49.7200				
1988	1163.90	354.20			49.7200	49.7200				
1989	1354.30	375.50			49.7200	49.7200				
1990	1407.90	430.20			49.7200	49.7200				
1991	1397.70	414.70			49.7200	49.7200				
1992	1048.50	380.30			49.7200	49.7200				
1993	1154.10	374.00			49.7200	49.7200				
1994	1228.60	363.10			49.7200	49.7200				
1995	1541.20	477.80			49.7200	49.7200				
1996	1667.30	561.30			49.7200	49.7200				

2. IMPORTS BY BROAD ECONOMIC CATEGORY AND EXPORTS BY INDUSTRIAL ORIGIN. (PERCENTAGE OF TOTAL VALUE)
IMPORTATIONS PAR CATEGORIES ECONOMIQUES ET EXPORTATIONS PAR BRANCHE D'ACTIVITE.(EN POURCENTAGE DE LA VALEUR TOTALE)

IMPORTS – IMPORTATIONS

	1990	1991	1992	1993	1994	1995	1996
TOTAL IMPORTS–IMPORTATIONS TOTALES	100.	100.	100.	100.	100.	100.	100.
1 FOOD BEV–ALIMENTATION BOISSONS	15.5	16.3	19.1	18.0	19.0	17.0	15.9
11 PRIMARY–PRODUITS DE BASE	4.9	5.8	6.2	6.1	6.9	6.3	5.9
111 FOR INDUSTRY–POUR L'INDUSTRIE	0.6	1.5	0.8	1.4	1.9	1.9	1.8
112 FOR HOUSEHOLDS–POUR LES MENAGES	4.3	4.3	5.4	4.7	5.0	4.4	4.0
12 PROCESSED–PRODUITS ELABORES	10.6	10.5	12.9	11.9	12.1	10.6	10.1
121 FOR INDUSTRY–POUR L'INDUSTRIE	1.5	1.6	2.8	2.3	1.8	1.6	1.9
122 FOR HOUSEHOLDS–POUR LES MENAGES	9.1	8.8	10.1	9.6	10.4	9.0	8.1
2 IND SUPPLIES–APPROV INDUSTRIELS	27.4	28.3	27.9	27.3	27.3	27.1	27.5
21 PRIMARY–PRODUITS DE BASE	1.6	1.9	2.1	1.5	1.6	1.5	2.3
22 PROCESSED–PRODUITS ELABORES	25.8	26.4	25.8	25.8	25.7	25.7	25.2
3 FUELS–COMBUSTIBLES	14.3	13.2	11.2	9.7	8.7	8.5	9.9
31 PRIMARY–PRODUITS DE BASE	0.6	0.9	0.7	0.8	0.6	0.5	0.6
32 PROCESSED–PRODUITS ELABORES	13.7	12.4	10.6	8.9	8.1	7.9	9.3
321 MOTOR SPIRIT–ESSENCE	0.1	0.1	0.2	0.0	0.1	0.1	0.1
322 OTHER–AUTRES	13.6	12.3	10.4	8.9	8.0	7.8	9.2
4 MACHINERY–EQUIPEMENT	16.3	15.1	14.4	15.6	16.2	15.4	17.3
41 CAPITAL EQUIPMENT–MACHINES	14.4	13.0	11.5	12.7	12.6	12.5	14.5
42 PARTS–PIECES ACCESSOIRES	2.0	2.1	3.0	2.9	3.5	3.0	2.8
5 TRANSPORT–TRANSPORT	7.5	7.6	4.9	6.3	6.7	10.2	9.6
51 PASSENGER CARS–AUTOMOBILES	2.6	3.5	1.5	2.4	2.6	4.8	4.9
52 OTHER–AUTRES	1.6	2.1	1.1	1.7	1.7	2.3	2.4
521 INDUSTRIAL–INDUSTRIELS	1.5	2.0	1.0	1.6	1.6	2.2	2.3
522 NON INDUSTRIAL–NON INDUSTRIEL	0.1	0.1	0.1	0.1	0.1	0.1	0.1
53 PARTS–PIECES ACCESSOIRES	3.3	2.1	2.3	2.2	2.3	3.1	2.4
6 CONSUM GOODS–BIENS CONSOMMATION	16.5	16.9	21.9	22.4	21.1	20.9	19.3
61 DURABLE–DURABLES	3.0	3.2	4.5	5.8	5.1	6.0	5.5
62 SEMI DURABLE–SEMI DURABLES	7.5	7.5	9.6	8.7	8.4	8.1	7.4
63 NON DURABLE–NON DURABLES	6.0	6.1	7.7	7.8	7.5	6.9	6.3
7 GOODS NES–BIENS NDA	2.4	2.6	0.6	0.6	1.1	0.8	0.5

EXPORTS – EXPORTATIONS

	1990	1991	1992	1993	1994	1995	1996
TOTAL EXPORTS–EXPORTATIONS TOTALES	100.	100.	100.	100.	100.	100.	100.
1 AGRICULTURE	1.6	1.2	1.9	1.6	1.8	2.2	1.5
2 MINING QUARRY–INDUS EXTRACTIVES	0.0	0.1	0.3	0.3	0.3	1.6	1.0
3 MANUFACTURING–IND MANUFACTUR	98.4	98.7	97.8	98.1	97.9	96.2	97.5
31 FOOD BEV TOBACCO–ALIM BOISS TAB	25.9	24.8	31.2	27.5	27.9	27.4	35.9
32 TEXTILES–INDUSTRIES TEXTILES	4.3	4.7	3.8	3.7	2.9	2.4	2.2
33 WOOD & PRODUCTS–BOIS & PRODUITS	0.1	0.5	0.5	0.4	0.3	0.6	0.6
34 PAPER & PRODUCTS–PAPIER & PRODT	4.3	3.8	4.4	4.6	5.2	7.6	8.1
35 CHEMICALS–INDUSTRIES CHIMIQUES	40.2	41.8	32.1	31.5	30.1	29.1	26.8
36 NON METAL MIN–MIN NON METAL	2.9	1.5	0.5	0.8	0.7	0.7	1.2
37 BASIC METAL–IND METAL BASE	0.4	0.5	0.2	0.5	0.4	0.2	0.4
38 METAL MANUF–MANUF METAL	18.2	19.3	23.5	28.2	28.8	28.0	21.4
39 OTH MANUF IND–AUTRES MANUF	2.0	1.8	1.6	0.8	1.4	0.3	0.9

3. TRADE BY PRINCIPAL COUNTRIES OF PRODUCTION AND LAST DESTINATION (VALUE IN THOUSAND U.S. DOLLARS)
ECHANGES SELON LES PRINCIPAUX PAYS DE PRODUCTION ET DE DERNIERE DESTINATION (VALEUR EN MILLIERS DE DOLLARS EU)

COUNTRIES–PAYS	GENERAL IMPORTS C.I.F. # 1 IMPORTATIONS GENERALES C.A.F				
	1992	1993	1994	1995	1996
World	552964	574036	614424	766034	828975
Africa	140	197	254	928	503
Americas	402659	402743	442935	528147	591375
Northern America	242730	248002	284841	350665	403314
LAIA	33138	31536	31590	43230	56181
CACM	6185	7181	5185	6106	5740
Caribbean	113226	107687	110562	117299	115879
Rest of America	7380	8336	10758	10846	10261
As.ex F.USSR	42913	53870	52072	81952	74127
Eur.x F.USSR	95965	106150	109136	143323	149620
EU	89124	97345	99213	130837	135262
EFTA	6221	8256	7668	10041	8590
East Europe	583	539	647	1514	2559
Other Europe	0	1	2	0	0
Former USSR	60	111	130	91	13
Oceania	11094	10793	9870	11581	13311
USA/Etats–Unis d'Amer	211377	219426	246981	312001	360846
Trinidad and Tobago	67275	76032	78709	82746	89336
United Kingdom	48776	53611	56305	73128	69363
Canada	31346	28528	37848	38639	42465
Japan/Japon	21825	31007	29795	51572	41877
Venezuela	21921	20933	19324	30859	37355
Jamaica/Jamaïque	14620	15019	18002	16583	13592
Germany/Allemagne	12175	10685	10455	17897	17397
New Zealand	9041	9024	8577	10175	11093
France,Monac	8293	8505	7690	10814	7954
Korea, Republic of	4820	5480	5445	9581	13194
Guyana	5486	6898	7874	9152	7539
Brazil/Brésil	6853	6923	7478	7619	6688
Netherlands/Pays–Bas	5405	8064	6780	6053	6539
China/Chine	6189	5043	6399	8488	6072
Netherlands Antilles	17899	5503	649	2321	125
Switz.Liecht	3646	5046	5539	7441	4806
Italy/Italie	3262	4104	3797	5777	7531
St Vincent & Grenadines	3364	2994	5577	5777	4884
Guatemala	5143	4171	2966	3677	4534
Belgium–Luxembourg	1883	2543	4385	4962	5100
Sweden/Suède	752	1103	1497	1003	9642
Norway,SVD,JM	2431	3111	1995	2537	3784
Spain/Espagne	1523	1782	1789	3287	3871
Saint Lucia/St. Lucie	3150	2448	1831	2130	2545
Denmark/Danemark	1935	1699	2010	2829	3493
Ireland/Irlande	2763	2462	2144	2251	1431
Dominica/Dominique	2031	3437	1713	1873	1621
Colombia/Colombie	1650	1352	1732	633	4531
Mexico/Mexique	850	766	1201	1309	5430
Australia/Australie	2054	1768	1290	1406	2217
Finland/Finlande	1305	1988	1496	1647	2194
Grenada/Grenade	1187	1380	1877	2404	1530
Hong Kong	1353	1574	1373	1617	1732
Dominican Republic	1266		1659	1982	1636
Thailand/Thaïlande	1129	1124	1210	1325	1424
Tfyr Macedonia			1587	908	3208
Malaysia/Malaisie	510	824	938	1525	1366
Honduras	296	1905	1368	1379	191
Belize/Bélize	1517	931	838	905	672
Indonesia/Indonésie	640	787	959	903	1348
Costa Rica	744	1062	824	1015	975
Argentina/Argentine	982	780	757	1007	881
Singapore/Singapour	834	1182	806	806	729
Panama	377	457	1808	610	570
Czech Republic		178	235	957	2191
Austria/Autriche	615	649	506	908	499
India/Inde	460	451	559	639	823
Chile/Chili	383	388	492	490	761
Israel/Israël	393	735	342	502	440

COUNTRIES–PAYS	GENERAL EXPORTS F.O.B. EXPORTATIONS GENERALES F.O.B.				
	1992	1993	1994	1995	1996
Monde	186753	180971	181811	237538	279049
Afrique	58	23	83	67	110
Amériques	106344	115640	112654	149401	183876
Amérique du Nord	37210	39925	43272	51120	51868
ALAI	210	168	233	3372	24536
MCAC	269	56	233	500	169
Caraïbes	63533	70160	63420	85100	93305
Autre Amérique	5122	5332	5495	9310	13999
Asie l'URSS exclus	2101	2143	1228	3388	2154
Europe l'URSS exclus	44502	33286	39669	50459	55332
UE	44141	32953	38706	48781	53597
AELE	342	332	473	682	531
Europe de l'Est	13	0	5	7	21
Autre de l'Europe	5	0	2		7
Ancienne URSS	26	3	0		
Océanie	100	173	153	257	343
United Kingdom	37569	29454	35399	38916	46401
USA/Etats–Unis d'Amer	31598	33712	34686	38099	39245
Trinidad and Tobago	20335	20674	17064	21672	20462
Jamaica/Jamaïque	5386	13234	11251	17454	24990
Saint Lucia/St. Lucie	9903	10071	9192	11946	12409
Canada	5135	5927	7986	12603	12177
St Vincent & Grenadines	6328	5822	5495	7355	8307
Venezuela	68	50	91	3084	24159
Guyana	3825	3539	3844	7179	8494
Antigua and Barbuda	3913	3946	4159	7443	5965
Grenada/Grenade	4612	3993	4033	4556	5363
Dominica/Dominique	4052	3921	3113	5413	4934
Saint–Kitts–Nevis	3021	3122	3609	3809	4010
Belize/Bélize	938	1518	1387	1324	1824
Netherlands Antilles	1430	1666	988	749	1683
Bahamas	1030	849	1067	1256	1523
Germany/Allemagne	1049	534	695	1785	1544
France, Monac	835	660	591	1686	1736
Japan/Japon	1588	1097	353	1465	432
Netherlands/Pays–Bas	1674	875	382	1142	810
British Virgin Islds	595	693	1210	885	954
Spain/Espagne	703	218	197	2249	471
Denmark/Danemark	622	586	428	948	1099
Suriname/Suriname	92	123	2	196	2856
Tfyr Macedonia			483	989	1176
Montserrat	727	475	460	547	424
Bermuda/Bermudes	476	285	600	418	447
Belgium–Luxembourg	801	153	246	604	409
Sweden/Suède	616	246	370	448	436
Panama	252	147	262	580	825
Anguilla	498	230	401	280	635
Switz.Liecht	342	271	357	610	375
Martinique	519	365	464	540	
Haiti/Haïti	117	169	125	358	939
Korea, Republic of	0	191	331	507	485
Guadeloupe	469	549	195	220	
Singapore/Singapour	101	162	319	383	450
Italy/Italie	170	98	286	423	427
Cayman Is/Is Caïmans	207	191	240	283	227
Aruba	256	168	228	176	315
China/Chine	184	21	19	625	30
Australia/Australie	88	151	132	134	309
Guatemala		1	172	461	109
Ireland/Irlande	19	30	26	460	21
Dominican Republic	119		103	129	140
Finland/Finlande	72	76	75	113	113
Malaysia/Malaisie	6	36	5	18	320
Costa Rica	267	4	36	17	51
Norway,SVD,JM	1	62	68	71	156
Mexico/Mexique	25	20	75	123	90

(VALUE AS PERCENTAGE OF WORLD TOTAL)(VALEURS EN POURCENTAGE DU TOTAL MONDIAL)

	1987	1988	1989	1990	1991	1992	1993	1994	1995	1996
Africa	0.0	0.0	0.0	0.0	0.0	0.0	0.0	0.0	0.1	0.1
Americas	64.8	65.0	67.3	67.3	68.8	72.8	70.2	72.1	68.9	71.3
Northern America	41.3	41.7	42.9	39.6	42.0	43.9	43.2	46.4	45.8	48.7
LAIA	6.8	5.9	6.8	5.9	5.9	6.0	5.5	5.1	5.6	6.8
CACM	1.1	1.0	0.7	1.0	0.6	1.1	1.3	0.8	0.8	0.7
Caribbean	14.9	15.6	16.2	20.2	19.3	20.5	18.8	18.0	15.3	14.0
Rest of America	0.6	0.7	0.7	0.7	1.0	1.3	1.5	1.8	1.4	1.2
As.ex F.USSR	10.6	10.4	9.7	8.6	9.8	7.8	9.4	8.5	10.7	8.9
Eur.x F.USSR	22.3	22.2	21.0	22.2	19.5	17.4	18.5	17.8	18.7	18.0
EU	21.0	20.7	19.8	20.9	18.3	16.1	17.0	16.1	17.1	16.3
EFTA	1.1	1.4	1.1	1.2	1.0	1.1	1.4	1.2	1.3	1.0
East Europe	0.2	0.1	0.1	0.1	0.1	0.1	0.1	0.1	0.2	0.3
Other Europe	0.0	0.0	0.0	0.0	0.1	0.0	0.0	0.0	0.0	0.0
Former USSR	0.0	0.1	0.1	0.0	0.0	0.0	0.0	0.0	0.0	0.0
Oceania	2.3	2.2	1.9	1.8	1.7	2.0	1.9	1.6	1.5	1.6
USA/Etats–Unis d'Amer	33.4	34.5	35.3	33.8	36.1	38.2	38.2	40.2	40.7	43.5
Trinidad and Tobago	9.2	8.7	9.2	10.8	10.4	12.2	13.2	12.8	10.8	10.8
United Kingdom	11.6	11.8	11.0	10.6	11.2	8.8	9.3	9.2	9.5	8.4
Canada	7.8	7.1	7.5	5.7	5.9	5.7	5.0	6.2	5.0	5.1
Japan/Japon	5.3	5.4	5.8	5.3	6.0	3.9	5.4	4.8	6.7	5.1
Venezuela	3.8	3.4	4.2	4.0	4.0	4.0	3.6	3.1	4.0	4.5
Jamaica/Jamaïque	2.6	2.6	2.3	2.4	2.3	2.6	2.6	2.9	2.2	1.6
Germany/Allemagne	2.6	2.4	2.2	2.1	1.7	2.2	1.9	1.7	2.3	2.1
New Zealand	1.6	1.7	1.5	1.5	1.4	1.6	1.6	1.4	1.3	1.3
France,Monac	1.4	1.9	1.4	1.3	1.3	1.5	1.5	1.3	1.4	1.0

	1987	1988	1989	1990	1991	1992	1993	1994	1995	1996
Afrique	0.0	0.0	0.0	0.0	0.1	0.0	0.0	0.0	0.0	0.0
Amériques	57.8	60.0	62.0	50.2	52.6	56.9	63.9	62.0	62.9	65.9
Amérique du Nord	31.1	28.5	25.6	16.3	16.9	19.9	22.1	23.8	21.5	18.6
ALAI	0.0	0.1	0.2	0.3	0.1	0.1	0.1	0.1	1.4	8.8
MCAC	0.1	0.0	0.0	0.0	0.0	0.1	0.0	0.1	0.2	0.1
Caraïbes	25.3	29.8	34.8	32.3	33.8	34.0	38.8	34.9	35.8	33.4
Autre Amérique	1.3	1.6	1.5	1.2	1.8	2.7	2.9	3.0	3.9	5.0
Asie l'URSS exclus	1.2	0.8	0.9	0.3	0.4	1.1	1.2	0.7	1.4	0.8
Europe l'URSS exclus	22.2	21.3	16.3	20.3	17.7	23.8	18.4	21.8	21.2	19.8
UE	22.0	21.0	16.1	20.1	17.5	23.6	18.2	21.3	20.5	19.2
AELE	0.2	0.3	0.2	0.1	0.2	0.2	0.2	0.3	0.3	0.2
Europe de l'Est	0.0	0.0	0.0			0.0	0.0	0.0	0.0	0.0
Autre de l'Europe	0.0	0.0				0.0	0.0	0.0		0.0
Ancienne URSS						0.0	0.0	0.0		
Océanie	0.1	0.0	0.1	0.1	0.0	0.1	0.1	0.1	0.1	0.1
United Kingdom	20.2	17.8	13.0	18.3	10.5	20.1	16.3	19.5	16.4	16.6
USA/Etats–Unis d'Amer	27.0	24.8	22.4	13.2	13.6	16.9	18.6	19.1	16.0	14.1
Trinidad and Tobago	5.9	7.2	10.4	8.6	10.8	10.9	11.4	9.4	9.1	7.3
Jamaica/Jamaïque	2.8	2.9	4.8	6.0	4.1	2.9	7.3	6.2	7.3	9.0
Saint Lucia/St. Lucie	3.3	4.2	4.3	4.6	5.0	5.3	5.6	5.1	5.0	4.4
Canada	3.9	3.5	2.9	2.9	3.1	2.7	3.3	4.4	5.3	4.4
St Vincent & Grenadines	3.0	3.0	3.1	2.9	3.4	3.4	3.2	3.0	3.1	3.0
Venezuela	0.0	0.0	0.1	0.3	0.1	0.0	0.0	0.1	1.3	8.7
Guyana	1.0	1.1	1.0	0.8	1.2	2.0	2.0	2.1	3.0	3.0
Antigua and Barbuda	1.7	2.1	2.1	1.8	1.7	2.1	2.2	2.3	3.1	2.1

4. General Imports C.I.F. by Commodities according to the S.I.T.C. (Rev. 2) in thousand U.S. Dollars
Importations Générales C.A.F. par Produits d'après la C.T.C.I. (Rév. 2) en milliers de Dollars E.U.

SITC CTCI	COMMODITY	1993 WEIGHT POIDS	1993 VALUE VALEUR	1994 WEIGHT POIDS	1994 VALUE VALEUR	1995 WEIGHT POIDS	1995 VALUE VALEUR	1996 WEIGHT POIDS	1996 VALUE VALEUR	PRODUIT
	ALL COMMODITIES # 1		574036		614424		766034		828975	TOUS PRODUITS
0	FOOD AND LIVE ANIMALS		94045		103841		112459		120881	ALIMENTS,ANIMAUX VIVANTS
01	MEAT AND PREPARATIONS		14209		15144		16867		14076	VIANDES ET PREPARATIONS
011	MEAT FRESH,CHILLD,FROZEN	W 6572	10371	W 6135	10576	W 6146	11262	W 4912	10211	VIANDES FRAICHES,REF,CONGE
0111	BOVINE MEAT FRESH,FROZEN	W 997	2779	W 1237	3364	W 1183	3200	W 1083	3050	VIANDES BOVIN FRAI,REF
01112	BOVINE MEAT BONELESS	W 830	2318	W 1087	2756	W 1057	2766	W 992	2774	VIANDES BOVIN DESOSSEES
0112	MUTTON ETC FRSH,CHLD,FRN	W 2277	3669	W 2276	3591	W 2009	3604	W 1822	3686	VIANDE DE MOUTON
0114	POULTRY FRESH CHLLD,FRZN	W 2238	1921	W 1284	1627	W 1519	2144	W 868	1221	VOLAILLES MORTES
014	MEAT PREPD,PRSVD,NES ETC	W 1274	2646	W 1898	3428	W 2181	4062	W 1688	2737	CONSERVES DE VIANDES
0149	OTH PREPARD,PRESRVD MEAT	W 1101	2083	W 1764	2874	W 2059	3757	W 1571	2469	AUTRES PREP DE VIANDES
02	DAIRY PRODCTS,BIRDS'EGGS		11200		10104		12734		13545	PRODUITS LAITIERS,OEUFS
022	MILK AND CREAM	W 2287	3854	W 1737	3010	W 2031	3678	W 2936	4674	LAIT ET CREME
0224	MILK,CREAM PRESERVED ETC	W 2273	3808	W 1718	2945	W 2010	3611	W 2635	4229	LAIT,CREME CONS,CONC
024	CHEESE AND CURD	W 1563	4246	W 1587	4154	W 1834	5437	W 1709	5061	FROMAGE ET CAILLEBOTTE
025	EGGS,BIRDS,FRESH,PRSRVD	W 597	1858	W 649	1889	W 726	2546	W 754	2901	OEUFS
0251	— IN SHELL	W 596	1857	W 649	1889	W 726	2544	W 754	2901	OEUFS EN COQUILLE
03	FISH AND PREPARATIONS		6129		6570		7727		7437	POISSONS ET PREPARATIONS
037	FISH ETC PREPD,PRSVD NES	W 1198	2271	W 1068	2132	W 1466	2744	W 1149	2293	POIS,CRUST,MOL PREPARES
0371	FISH PREPARD,PRESRVD NES	W 1192	2249	W 1059	2101	W 1455	2698	W 1139	2252	CONSERVES DE POISSONS
04	CEREALS AND PREPARATIONS		20957		24031		24772		31958	CEREALES ET PRODUITS
041	WHEAT ETC UNMILLED	W 12773	2598	W 40358	4322	W 9780	3376	W 18251	4789	FROMENT,EPEAUTRE
0412	OTHER WHEAT ETC UNMILLED	W 12773	2598	W 40358	4322	W 9780	3376	W 18251	4789	AUTRE FROMENT NON MOULU
042	RICE	W 8402	3336	W 3813	3030	W 7883	3704	W 10284	4735	RIZ
0421	RICE IN HUSK OR HUSKED	W 7189	2630	W 2129	1635	W 6391	2609	W 8632	3423	RIZ SANS AUTRE PREPARATION
04212	RICE HUSKED	W 7188	2629	W 2129	1635	W 6390	2608	W 8632	3423	RIZ CARGO
044	MAIZE UNMILLED	W 28906	4580	W 39817	4412	W 68125	4129	W 33427	7680	MAIS NON MOULU
046	WHEAT ETC MEAL OR FLOUR	W 2455	1138	W 1809	1155	W 2389	1334	W 7083	2535	SEMOULE FARINE,FROMENT
048	CEREAL ETC PREPARATIONS	W 4729	8998	W 5308	10662	W 6244	11612	W 5715	11360	PREPTNS A BASE CEREALES
0481	PREPD BREAKFAST FOOD ETC	W 804	2796	W 883	3049	W 1257	3440	W 1281	3433	CEREALES TRAVAILLEES
04812	CEREAL ROASTED, PUFFED	W 405	1589	W 480	2073	W 609	2273	W 613	2171	PRODTS BASE CEREALES
0484	BAKERY PRODUCTS	W 590	1534	W 894	2402	W 1001	2508	W 950	2793	PRODUITS DE BOULANGERIE
0488	OTH CEREAL PREPS,MALT EX	W 787	3129	W 946	3433	W 1000	3245	W 958	3512	EXTRAITS DE MALT
05	VEGETABLES AND FRUIT		15822		19153		20974		21216	LEGUMES ET FRUITS
054	VEG ETC FRSH,SMPLY PRSVD	W 14335	5973	W 13038	6764	W 13380	7565	W 14471	7787	LEGUMES FRAIS,CONG,SECS
0541	POTATOES FRSH EXCL SWEET	W 10331	3400	W 9031	3682	W 9177	3673	W 9438	3340	POMMES DE TERRE
057	FRUIT,NUTS,FRESH,DRIED	W 7298	4315	W 8647	6251	W 9905	7116	W 9282	6988	FRUITS FRAIS OU SECS
058	FRUIT PRESERVED,PREPARED	W 2395	4302	W 2808	4334	W 2965	4838	W 2783	4874	CONSERVES DE FRUITS
0585	FRUIT OR VEGETABLE JUICE	W 1684	2749	W 1738	2254	W 1846	2836	W 1666	2879	JUS DE FRUITS
06	SUGAR AND PREPS,HONEY		8039		9872		10495		12589	SUCRES ET PRODUITS
061	SUGAR AND HONEY	W 30069	6988	W 34314	8857	W 32344	9582	W 32806	11603	SUCRES ET MIEL
0611	RAW BEET AND CANE SUGAR	W 6018	2833	W 7519	2740	W 5593	2248	W 4881	2159	SUCRES BRUTS
0612	REFINED SUGAR ETC	W 9936	2370	W 6511	3551	W 8240	4372	W 8294	4584	SUCRES RAFFINES
0619	SUGARS AND SYRUPS NES	W 473	760	W 282	908	W 464	1172	W 586	2713	AUTRES SUCRES SIROPS
07	COFFEE,TEA,COCOA,SPICES		4267		5033		5109		4651	CAFE,THE,CACAO,EPICES
073	CHOCOLATE AND PRODUCTS	W 422	1957	W 418	2491	W 458	2248	W 434	2000	CHOCOLAT
081	*FEEDING STUFF FOR ANIML	W 13643	4117	W 6070	2711	W 5157	2441	W 7783	3053	NOURRITURE POUR ANIMAUX
0813	OILCAKE AND OTH RESIDUES	W 10474	2576	W 2312	878	W 1743	702	W 2542	1143	TOURTEAUX
08131	— OF SOYA BEANS	W 10117	2499	W 2236	845	W 1661	671	W 2476	1108	TOURTEAUX DE SOJA
09	MISC EDIBLE PRODUCTS		9142		10627		10946		11949	PREP ALIMENTAIRES DIVERSES
098	EDIBLE PRODCTS,PREPS NES	W 4822	8951	W 4787	10388	W 5818	10631	W 5756	11715	PREP ALIMENTAIRES NDA
09804	SAUCES,MIXED SEASONINGS	W 2493	3609	W 2362	4264	W 2879	4070	W 2769	4124	SAUCES,ASSAISONNEMENTS
09809	MISC FOOD PREPRTIONS NES	W 1885	4560	W 1941	5221	W 2482	5659	W 2547	6752	PREP ALIMENTAIRES NDA
1	BEVERAGES AND TOBACCO		10926		13964		14715		14096	BOISSONS ET TABACS
11	BEVERAGES		9730		12816		13021		11664	BOISSONS
111	NON-ALCOHL BEVERAGES NES	W 1910	1849	W 1913	3332	W 2394	3002	W 2361	2606	BOISSONS NON ALCOOLIQUES
11102	FLAVORED WATERS NON-ALCO	W 1637	1696	W 1579	3136	W 1969	2742	W 1686	2276	LIMONADES,EAUX GAZEUSES
112	ALCOHOLIC BEVERAGES	W 3466	7881	W 4104	9484	W 5511	10018	W 4920	9057	BOISSONS ALCOOLIQUES
1121	WINE OF FRESH GRAPES ETC	W 1121	3013	W 1223	3429	W 1225	3894	W 1484	3689	VINS DE RAISINS FRAIS
11212	WINE OF FRESH GRAPES	W 1082	2876	W 1119	3248	W 1145	3711	W 1399	3483	VINS DE MOUTS DE RAISINS
1123	BEER,ALE,STOUT,PORTER	W 1490	1691	W 1988	2133	W 3036	2442	W 2310	2157	BIERES
1124	DISTILLED ALCOHOLIC BEVS	W 712	2983	W 662	3532	W 956	3240	W 748	2621	ALCOOLS,EAUX-DE-VIE
2	CRUDE MATERLS,EXCL FUELS		17887		24805		29517		31941	MAT BRUTES NON COMESTIBLES
22	OIL SEEDS,OLEAGINOUS FRT		2713		5221		8180		5967	GRAINES,FRUITS OLEAGINEUX
222	SEEDS FOR'SOFT'FIXED OIL	W 8013	2393	W 12427	5124	W 9847	8142	W 16626	5934	GRAINES HUILES FIXES
2222	SOYA BEANS	W 7645	1917	W 11915	4468	W 9402	7643	W 16240	5399	FEVES DE SOJA
24	CORK AND WOOD		11869		14251		14474		14988	LIEGE ET BOIS
248	WOOD SHAPED,SLEEPERS	W 17983	11610	W 19920	14149	W 19488	13836	W 19680	13935	BOIS SIMPLEMENT TRAVAILLES
2482	LUMBER SHAPED CONIFER	W 15410	9830	W 15962	11726	W 14950	10824	W 13971	10442	CONIFERES SCIES,RABOTES
24822	LUMBER PLANED ETC CONIFR	W 14924	9539	W 14805	10973	W 13429	9751	W 12324	9038	CONIFER RABOTES,RAINES
2483	LUMBER SHAPED NON-CONIFR	W 2573	1779	W 3958	2423	W 4538	3013	W 5709	3493	NON CONIFERES SCIES,RABOTES
27	CRUDE FERTLZR,MINRLS NES		966		2375		3225		3898	ENGRAIS MINERAUX BRUTS
277	NATURAL ABRASIVES NES	W 15	10		1263		2166		2541	ABRASIFS NATURELS NDA
2771	INDUSTRIAL DIAMONDS				1262		2161		2539	DIAMANTS INDUSTRIELS
29	CRUDE ANIMAL,VEG MAT NES		1680		2095		2355		5562	MATIERES BRUTES ANIM,VEGET
292	CRUDE VEG MATERIALS NES		1559		1904		2081		5211	MAT BRUTES VEGETALES NDA
2929	OTH CRUDE VEG MATERIALS	W 42	427	W 33	438	W 56	858	W 301	3763	MATIERES VEGETALES NDA
29291	VEGETABLE SAPS,EXTRACTS	W 29	417	W 32	429	W 55	853	W 298	3753	SUCS,EXTRAITS VEGETAUX
3	MINERAL FUELS ETC		55995		53492		65134		82038	COMBUSTIBLES MINERAUX LUB
33	PETROLEUM AND PRODUCTS		51435		49884		60953		76958	PETROLE ET DERIVES
334	PETROLEUM PRODUCTS,REFIN	W 309382	51235	W 275894	49707	W 386264	60852	W 402478	76863	PRODUITS RAFFINES
3342	KEROSENE,OTH MEDIUM OILS	W 105999	21672	W 99965	20757	W 121103	23122	W 133634	31508	PETR LAMPANTS,AUT HUIL
33421	KEROSENE INCL JET FUEL	W 105999	21672	W 99965	20757	W 121102	23117	W 133634	31508	PETROLES LAMPANTS
3343	GAS OILS	W 13759	2287	W 20754	3181	W 12401	2341	W 13332	2324	GAS OILS
3344	FUEL OILS,NES	W 186836	24084	W 149918	20753	W 244912	30839	W 243357	36903	FUEL OILS
3345	LUBS,PETROLEUM OILS NES	W 2434	2985	W 2414	4554	W 2755	3555	W 8329	5207	HUILES LUBRIFIANTES
33451	LUBS(HIGH PETR CONT) ETC	W 2416	2921	W 2400	4509	W 2749	3528	W 8316	5150	HUILES LUBRIF,H LOURDES
341	*GAS,NATURAL AND MANUFCT	W 10850	4280	W 8018	3456	W 9403	4017	W 9634	4943	GAZ NATUREL,GAZ MANUFACT
3413	PETROLM GASES,LIQUEFIED	W 10719	4263	W 7914	3416	W 9403	4017	W 9631	4912	GAZ DE PETROLE LIQUEFIE
34131	LIQUEFIED PROPANE,BUTANE	W 3899	1717	W 3693	1600	W 4269	2010	W 4438	2698	PROPANE,BUTANE LIQUEFIES
34139	OTH HYDROCARBON GAS LQFD	W 6820	2546	W 4222	1816	W 5134	2007	W 5193	2214	HYDROCARBURES GAZEUX NDA
4	ANIMAL,VEGETABLE OIL,FAT		6517		3310		4536		5541	HUILES,GRAISSES ANIM,VEG
42	FIXED VEGETABLE OIL,FAT		2906		716		1068		937	HUILES VEGETALES FIXES
423	FIXED VEG OILS,SOFT	W 2031	2435	W 213	283	W 386	513	W 417	566	HUILES VEGET DOUCES FIXES
4232	SOYA BEAN OIL	W 1848	2126	W 39	55	W 27	38	W 5	6	HUILE DE SOJA
431	*PROCESD ANML VEG OIL,ET	W 4817	2940	W 2002	2039	W 3599	2580	W 4194	3918	HUILES,GRAISSES PREPAREES
4312	HYDROGENATED OIL,FAT	W 4755	2887	W 1958	1998	W 3546	2526	W 4087	3815	HUILES HYDROGENEES
5	CHEMCLS,RELATED PROD NES		70096		73590		90342		97383	PRODUITS CHIMIQUES
51	ORGANIC CHEMICALS		5445		5657		9293		9122	PROD CHIMIQ ORGANIQUES
511	HYDROCARBONS NES,DERIVS	W 1659	1868	W 1800	2105	W 1935	2260	W 2220	2252	HYDROCARBURES NDA
516	OTHER ORGANIC CHEMICALS	W 581	2235	W 691	2328	W 1330	5579	W 1394	4889	AUTRES PROD ORGANIQUES
5169	ORGANIC CHEMICALS,NES	W 509	2093	W 437	2116	W 595	4977	W 486	4083	PROD CHIM ORGANIQUES NDA

4. General Imports C.I.F. by Commodities according to the S.I.T.C. (Rev. 2) in thousand U.S. Dollars
Importations Générales C.A.F. par Produits d'après la C.T.C.I. (Rév. 2) en milliers de Dollars E.U.

SITC CTCI	COMMODITY	1993		1994		1995		1996		PRODUIT
		WEIGHT POIDS	VALUE VALEUR	WEIGHT POIDS	VALUE VALEUR	WEIGHT POIDS	VALUE VALEUR	WEIGHT POIDS	VALUE VALEUR	
51699	OTHER ORGANIC COMPOUNDS	W 406	1911	W 362	1981	W 542	4893	W 479	4022	AUTRES COMPOS ORGANIQUES
52	INORGANIC CHEMICALS		5737		6131		6642		6907	PROD CHIM INORGANIQUES
522	INORG ELEMNTS,OXIDES,ETC	W 1927	2325	W 1688	2451	W 2095	2916	W 1771	2526	ELEMENTS INORGANIQUES
523	OTHR INORG CHEMICALS ETC	W 5400	3374	W 6248	3643	W 5743	3240	W 8221	4314	AUT PRODUITS CHIMIQUES INORG
5232	OTH MTL CMPD OF INRG ACD	W 3624	2200	W 3822	2255	W 3210	2037	W 3626	2290	SELS METALLIQUES
53	DYES,TANNING,COLOUR PROD		3569		3987		4282		5263	PROD TEINTURE,COLORANTS
533	PIGMENTS,PAINTS,ETC	W 1305	3433	W 1452	3746	W 1467	4020	W 1585	4996	PIGMENTS,PEINTURES,VERNIS
5334	VARNISHES,DISTEMPERS ETC	W 504	2041	W 613	2242	W 678	2483	W 553	3166	PEINTURES A L'EAU
53344	DISTEMPERS,DYES NES ETC	W 282	1520	W 295	1496	W 382	1915	W 373	2627	PEINTURES A L'EAU
541	*MEDICINAL,PHARM PRODUCT	K 1073297	18283	K 878061	18129		20679		22227	PROD MEDICINAUX PHARMACEUT
5417	MEDICAMENTS	K 922642	16837	K 756971	16704	K 786884	18537	K 1267655	20454	MEDICAMENTS
54179	— CONTNG OTH SUBSTANCES	K 856130	14543	K 717690	14498	K 738232	16000	K 1208081	17667	MED CONT AUT SUBSTANCES
55	PERFUME,CLEANING ETC PRD		18881		17886		23060		24000	PROD POUR PARFUM,TOILETTE
551	ESSENTL OILS,PERFUME,ETC	W 171	2381	W 175	2304	W 260	3961	W 492	8664	HUILES ESSENTIELLES
5514	MIXED PERFUME SUBSTANCES	W 141	2231	W 154	2126	W 233	3796	W 464	8480	MELANGES SUBSTAN ODORIFER
553	PERFUMERY,COSMETICS,ETC	W 1189	10253	W 1117	8519	W 1408	11883	W 1169	9378	PRODUITS DE PARFUMERIE
554	SOAP,CLEANSING ETC PREPS	W 4387	6247	W 4278	7062	W 4591	7216	W 3863	5958	SAVONS,PRODUITS DETERSIFS
5541	SOAPS	W 980	2239	W 991	3014	W 948	2737	W 725	2002	SAVONS,PROD TENSIO–ACTIFS
5542	WASHING PREPARATIONS ETC	W 3214	3325	W 3107	3553	W 3435	4002	W 2972	3563	PROD ORG TENSIO–ACT NDA
58	PLASTIC MATERIALS ETC		7527		9095		11554		11384	MAT PLAST ARTIFICIELLES
582	PROD OF CONDENSATION ETC	W 867	1414	W 1055	1943	W 1529	2589	W 1370	2434	PROD CONDENS,POLYCOND
583	POLYMERIZATION ETC PRODS	W 3440	6029	W 4007	7083	W 4414	8849	W 4982	8825	PROD POLYMERISATION
5839	OTH POLYMRZTION ETC PROD	W 2462	3988	W 2922	4980	W 3031	6003	W 3810	6502	AUT PROD POLYMER COPOLYM
59	CHEMICAL MATERIALS NES		9199		11235		12506		16692	MAT PROD CHIMIQUES NDA
591	PESTICIDES,DISINFECTANTS	W 1126	4175	W 1359	4919	W 1400	5445	W 1172	4905	DESINF,INSECT,FONG,HERB
5913	HERBICIDES,FOR RETAIL	W 298	1438	W 358	1790	W 512	2342	W 339	1717	HERBICIDES VENTE AU DET
598	MISCEL CHEM PRODUCTS NES	W 974	4051	W 1235	5295	W 1205	5921	W 1461	10635	PROD DIV INDUST CHIM NDA
5989	CHEM PRODUCTS,PREPS NES	W 669	2940	W 882	3558	W 954	4397	W 1257	9297	PROD PREP CHIMIQUES NDA
59899	OTH CHEM PRODS,PREPS,NES	W 555	2562	W 702	3003	W 776	3695	W 1093	8864	AUT PRODUITS CHIMIQUES NDA
6	BASIC MANUFACTURES		103529		105188		132105		132153	ART MANUFACTURES
62	RUBBER MANUFACTURES NES		6116		6235		6792		6931	CAOUTCHOUC MANUFACTURE
625	RUBBER TYRES, TUBES ETC	W 949	3531	W 861	3748	W 882	3665	W 847	3831	PNEUS CAOUTCHOUC VULCANISE
6251	TYRES NEW FOR MOTOR CARS	W 355	1461	W 376	1940	W 319	1585	W 299	1388	PNEUS POUR VOITURES
628	RUBBER ARTICLES NES	W 148	1750	W 279	1710	W 166	2078	W 188	1841	OUVRAGES CAOUTCHOUC NDA
63	WOOD,CORK MANUFACTRS NES		6413		8701		9623		9724	OUVRAGES LIEGE ET BOIS
634	VENEERS,PLYWOOD,ETC	W 4284	3386	W 5797	4949	W 7329	5158	W 5307	4898	PLACAGES,CONTRE–PLAQUES
6342	PLYWOOD OF WOOD SHEETS	W 3646	2921	W 5008	4222	W 6661	4567	W 4491	4063	BOIS CONTRE–PLAQUES
635	WOOD MANUFACTURES NES	W 898	2949	W 1205	3627	W 1350	4371	W 1550	4771	ART MANUF EN BOIS NDA
6353	BUILDERS WOODWRK,PREFABS	W 492	1953	W 649	2568	W 703	2902	W 790	3113	OUVRAGES DE MENUISERIE
64	PAPER,PAPERBOARD AND MFR		19334		19280		26583		25054	PAPIERS,CARTONS & OUVRAGES
641	PAPER AND PAPERBOARD	W 11572	11348	W 8010	10820	W 30444	15811	W 19488	14793	PAPIERS ET CARTONS
6412	PRINTG,WRITING PAPER NES	W 4143	4108	W 2760	4437	W 2884	6887	W 3452	5857	PAPIERS POUR L'IMPRESSION
64121	— UNCOATED	W 3803	3564	W 2423	3853	W 2475	4530	W 2940	4861	PAPIERS IMPRES NON COUCHES
64122	— COATED,IMPREGNATD ETC	W 340	544	W 338	584	W 409	2357	W 512	996	PAPIERS IMPRESSION COUCHES
6418	COATED ETC PAPER NES BLK	W 1051	1627	W 908	1231	W 1407	2371	W 1662	3491	PAP,CARTONS COUCHES,ENDUITS
642	PAPER,ETC,PRECUT,ARTS OF	W 4073	7986	W 4003	8460	W 4672	10772	W 4677	10261	PAP,CARTONS DECOUPES
6421	PAPER ETC CONTAINERS	W 2500	2908	W 2412	3409	W 2793	4565	W 2944	4853	BOITES,SACS EMBALLAGES
6428	PAPER ETC ARTICLES NES	W 870	2670	W 907	2715	W 1073	3514	W 1003	3051	OUVRAGES EN PATE A PAPIER
65	TEXTILE YARN,FABRICS,ETC		14823		15285		17537		16663	FILS,TISSUS,ARTICLES TEXTILE
652	COTTON FABRICS,WOVEN	W 479	3132	W 494	3857	W 842	4751	W 467	3459	TISSUS DE COTON
6521	GREY WOVEN COTTON FABRIC	W 132	821	W 150	1135	W 498	2378	W 131	811	TISSUS COT ECRUS NON MERCER
6522	WOVEN COTTON BLEACHD,ETC	W 347	2311	W 344	2723	W 345	2373	W 336	2648	TISSUS COTON BLANCHIS ETC
653	WOVN MAN–MADE FIB FABRIC	W 611	4876	W 645	5485	W 724	6321	W 702	5522	TISSUS FIBRES SYNTH,ARTIF
6534	DISC SYN BLEND FABRC NES	W 225	1619	W 253	1934	W 260	2357	W 248	1615	TISSUS FIBRES SYNTH DISCONT
658	TEXTILE ARTICLES NES	W 210	1746	W 284	2122	W 267	2199	W 358	2665	ART FACONNES MAT TEXTILES
66	NONMETAL MINERAL MFS NES		15132		15956		19158		22230	ART MIN NON METALLIQUES
661	LIME,CEMENT,BLDG PRODS	W 75691	3374	W 54011	3582	W 57321	4540	W 96310	6015	CHAUX,CIMENTS MAT CONSTR
6612	CEMENT	W 71724	2624	W 53280	2823	W 56040	3461	W 95355	5099	CIMENTS HYDRAULIQUES
662	CLAY,REFRACTORY BLDG PRD	W 3037	1972	W 3772	3229	W 4004	2772	W 4031	4127	MAT CONST REFRACTAIRES
6624	BRICKS ETC NONREFRACTORY	W 2851	1797	W 3737	3175	W 3952	2719	W 3780	3857	BRIQUES ETC CERAM NON REFR
66245	GLAZED CERAMIC SETTS ETC	W 2699	1660	W 3328	2960	W 3542	2451	W 3009	2557	AUT CARREAUX CERAMIQUE
664	GLASS	W 940	1847	W 994	1736	W 906	2342	W 1420	2302	VERRE
665	GLASSWARE	W 6204	5421	W 4952	5044	W 4407	5237	W 4914	7126	OUVRAGES EN VERRE
6651	BOTTLES ETC OF GLASS	W 5928	3553	W 4573	3419	W 4029	3186	W 4606	5480	RECIPIENTS EN VERRE
66511	GLASS BOTTLES ETC NONVAC	W 5927	3507	W 4572	3412	W 4029	3184	W 4606	5476	BONBONNES,BOUTEILLES,ETC
666	POTTERY	W 233	1826	W 218	1337	W 239	2441	W 170	1374	POTERIE
67	IRON AND STEEL		16147		12225		18030		17077	FER ET ACIER
673	IRON,STEEL SHAPES ETC	W 6826	4299	W 6991	3737	W 8448	5953	W 8835	5031	BARRES,PROFIL FER,ACIER
6731	IRON,STEEL WIRE ROD	W 4648	1875	W 4057	1596	W 1984	779	W 5738	2217	FIL MACHINE FER,ACIER
67311	IRON,SIMPLE STL WIRE ROD	W 4648	1875	W 4057	1596	W 1984	779	W 4580	1690	FIL MACH AUT ACIER FIN
6732	IRON,STEEL BARS ETC	W 1082	1370	W 2211	1601	W 5682	4396	W 1944	1805	BARRES FER,ACIER
67322	HIGH CARBON STL BARS ETC	W 663	314	W 1893	843	W 5331	3486	W 1581	850	BARRES ACIER FIN CARBONE
674	IRN,STL UNIV,PLATE,SHEET	W 8014	8430	W 5135	6126	W 7978	8265	W 6140	7407	LARGES PLATS,TOLES
6747	TINNED PLATES,SHEETS	W 3582	4374	W 2029	3065	W 2024	1906	W 1744	2324	TOLES ETAMEES EN ACIER
6749	OTH IRN,STL PLATES,SHEET	W 4179	3819	W 2833	2863	W 5670	6115	W 3890	4618	AUTRES TOLES FER,ACIER
67491	— OF IRON OR SIMPLE STL	W 4070	3584	W 2826	2839	W 5669	6110	W 3865	4545	AUT TOLES AUTRES ACIER FIN
678	IRON,STL TUBES,PIPES,ETC	W 1434	2748	W 2420	1918	W 1279	3231	W 1565	3711	TUBES,TUYAUX EN FONTE,FER
68	NON–FERROUS METALS		4339		3345		5442		5537	METAUX NON FERREUX
684	ALUMINIUM	W 702	3291	W 654	2439	W 880	3930	W 3001	4369	ALUMINIUM
6842	ALUMINIUM,ALLOYS WORKED	W 490	2139	W 415	1709	W 451	1772	W 527	1915	ALUMINIUM,ALLIAGES OUVRE
69	METAL MANUFACTURES NES		20921		23943		28655		28684	ART MANUFACT EN METAL NDA
691	STRUCTURES AND PARTS NES	W 493	1389	W 662	2204	W 1001	4815	W 1268	3398	CONSTRUCT FER,ACIER,ALU
6912	STRUCTURES,PARTS ALUMNM	W 151	649	W 239	1087	W 326	3018	W 177	1036	CONSTRUCT ALUMINIUM
692	METAL TANKS,BOXES,ETC	W 1414	3979	W 859	2889	W 1079	3455	W 923	3953	RECIPIENTS METALLIQUES
6924	MTL TRANSPORT BOXES ETC	W 1277	3520	W 798	2703	W 1004	2691	W 724	3152	FUTS,TAMBOURS,BIDONS
69241	STL TRANSPORT BOXES ETC	W 663	1865	W 438	1222	W 785	1568	W 361	1217	FUTS,TAMBOURS,BIDONS FER
694	STL,COPPR NAILS,NUTS,ETC	W 460	2225	W 530	2889	W 597	3036	W 663	3262	CLOUS,VIS,ECROUS
69402	IRN,STL NUTS,BOLTS,ETC	W 152	1711	W 195	2315	W 241	2490	W 306	2647	BOULONS,VIS,ECROUS FER,AC
697	BASE MTL HOUSEHOLD EQUIP	W 724	3660	W 701	4030	W 742	4255	W 653	3595	ART MENAGE MET COMMUNS
6973	DMSTC HEATG,COOKG APPARA	W 375	2138	W 340	2033	W 382	2305	W 401	1992	APPS CHAUF NON ELECTRIQ
69731	IRN,STL DOM COOKG APPARA	W 348	2003	W 325	1926	W 365	2181	W 380	1844	APPS CUISSON FER,ACIER
699	BASE METAL MFRS NES	W 1448	6745	W 1857	8871		9553	W 2223	10600	ART MANUFACTURES MET NDA
6991	LOCKSMITHS WARES,ETC	W 283	2002	W 332	2465	W 363	2484	W 504	3065	ARTICLES DE SERRURERIE
6997	IRON,STEEL ARTICLES NES	W 353	1569	W 755	2778	W 672	2518	W 743	3201	OUV FONTE,FER,ACIER NDA
69979	IRN,STL MANUFACTURES NES	W 343	1468	W 729	2732	W 661	2508	W 719	3122	AUT OUVRAGES EN FER NDA
7	MACHINES,TRANSPORT EQUIP		131570		144275		204911		229361	MACHINES MATERIEL TRANSPORT
71	POWER GENERATING EQUIPMT		5239		4641		9944		16669	MACHINES GENERATRICES
713	INTRNL COMBUS PSTN ENGIN	W 374	2700	W 215	3084	W 325	6949	W 299	4854	MOTEURS EXPL COMB INT, PIECE
7139	PISTON ENGINE PARTS NES	W 129	2149	W 93	2470	W 108	3000	W 109	2549	PIECES POUR 713.2,3,8
716	ROTATING ELECTRIC PLANT	W 79	1081	W 92	1101	W 143	1738	W 306	9684	APP ELECTR ROTATIFS,PIECES
7162	AC MTRS,GENRTRS,GEN SETS	W 56	719	W 65	811	W 86	928	W 240	8597	MOTEURS ELECTRIQUES

4. General Imports C.I.F. by Commodities according to the S.I.T.C. (Rev. 2) in thousand U.S. Dollars
Importations Générales C.A.F. par Produits d'après la C.T.C.I. (Rév. 2) en milliers de Dollars E.U.

SITC CTCI	COMMODITY	1993 WEIGHT POIDS	1993 VALUE VALEUR	1994 WEIGHT POIDS	1994 VALUE VALEUR	1995 WEIGHT POIDS	1995 VALUE VALEUR	1996 WEIGHT POIDS	1996 VALUE VALEUR	PRODUIT
71623	GEN SETS WITH PISTN ENGN	W 18	171	W 32	363	W 47	385	W 199	8025	GROUPES MOTEUR EXPLOSION
72	MACHS FOR SPCL INDUSTRYS		14655		11759		16841		22051	MAC SPECIALES POUR INDUST
721	AGRIC MACHY,EXC TRACTORS	W 133	865	W 246	1765	W 262	1552	W 316	2878	MACHINES AGRICOLES
723	CIVIL ENGNEERG EQUIP ETC	W 287	3260	W 252	1923	W 178	1650	W 831	5232	APPAREILS DE GENIE CIVIL
7234	CONST,MINING MACHNRY NES	W 246	2666	W 230	1644	W 153	1376	W 717	4491	MACH POUR LA CONST, MINES
72342	SLFPRP SHOVELS,EXCAVATRS	W 101	811	W 141	1051	W 125	938	W 457	2744	PELLES MECANIQUES
726	PRINTG,BKBINDG MACHY,PTS	W 105	2547	W 125	2091	W 99	3837	W 130	3664	MACHINES POUR IMPRIMERIE
727	FOOD MACHRY NON-DOMESTIC	W 574	4437	W 99	1086	W 222	2538	W 278	3186	MACH INDUSTRIES ALIMENT
7272	OTH FOOD PROC MCHY,PARTS	W 545	4320	W 96	1024	W 217	2458	W 274	3120	AUT MACH IND ALIMENTAIRE
72722	INDUS FOOD PROC MACH NES	W 450	3292	W 94	1013	W 217	2458	W 274	3120	MACHINES BOULANGERIE
728	OTH MACHY FOR SPCL INDUS	W 195	2218	W 202	2771	W 246	4153	W 269	3935	AUT MACH IND PARTICULIERES
7284	MACHY FOR SPCL INDUS NES	W 83	1306	W 151	2159	W 130	2301	W 128	2367	MACH SPEC IND PARTICUL.
74	GENRL INDUSTRL MACHY NES		21962		22782		26667		31514	MACH APP INDUSTRIE
741	HEATING,COOLING EQUIPMNT	W 580	5769	W 1197	5799	W 992	7052	W 766	7678	MACH CHAUFFAGE,PIECES
7416	HEATING,COOLING EQU NES	W 268	2512	W 168	1864	W 356	2359	W 257	3097	APP CHANGEMENT TEMP
742	PUMPS FOR LIQUIDS ETC	W 124	1967	W 84	1863	W 197	2002	W 153	2543	POMPES MOTO-POMPES
743	PUMPS NES,CENTRFUGES ETC	W 293	2534	W 209	2481	W 289	3953	W 295	4039	POMPES COMPRES,VENT ETC
744	MECHANICAL HANDLING EQU	W 324	2340	W 441	3969	W 377	2753	W 755	5240	EQUIP MANUTENTION PIECES
7442	LIFTING,LOADING MACH NES	W 179	1180	W 312	2818	W 162	1286	W 273	2164	APP LEVAGE,MANUTENTION
7449	PTS NES OF MACHY OF 7442	W 83	704	W 55	837	W 42	706	W 411	2570	PIECES DU 744.2
745	NONELEC MACHY,TOOLS NES	W 340	4151	W 270	3230	W 318	4260	W 291	5312	AUT MACH NON ELEC,PIECES
7452	OTH NONELEC MCHS,PTS NES	W 313	3858	W 238	2942	W 278	3795	W 234	4767	AUT MACH NON ELEC,PIECES
74522	PACKAGNG,BOTTLNG,ETC MCH	W 155	1891	W 101	1159	W 145	1569	W 85	2082	MACH NETT BOUTEILLES,ETC
749	NONELEC MACH PTS,ACC NES	W 363	5202	W 375	5439	W 427	6646	W 468	6701	PIECES MACH NON ELEC NDA
7492	COCKS,VALVES ETC NES	W 209	2385	W 226	2650	W 300	3243	W 278	3291	ART ROB,SIM POUR TUYAUX
75	OFFICE MACHNES,ADP EQUIP		15286		18831		23227		26266	MACH BUREAU TRAIT AUTOM
751	OFFICE MACHINES	W 52	1329	W 70	1698	W 87	2532	W 64	1877	MACH,APPAREILS DE BUREAU
752	AUTOMTIC DATA PROC EQUIP	W 211	9336	W 261	10882	W 243	13863	W 470	16704	MACH TRAIT INFORMATION
7522	DIGITAL COMPUTERS	W 120	4226	W 116	6016	W 134	7594	W 248	8776	MACH DIGITALES COMPLETES
7523	DIGITL CENTRL PROCESSORS	W 28	1966	W 21	1351	W 19	1343	W 61	2218	UNITES CENTRALES
7525	ADP PERIPHERAL UNITS	W 54	2511	W 114	2737	W 77	3806	W 146	4246	UNITES PERIPHERIQUES
759	OFFICE,ADP MCH PTS,ACCES	W 74	4621	W 104	6251	W 119	6832	W 153	7685	PIECES DU 751 ET 752
7599	ACCTG,ETC,ADP MCH PTS,AC	W 60	3990	W 82	5512	W 96	6004	W 130	6622	PIECES DU 751 ET 752
76	TELECOMM,SOUND EQUIPMENT		13808		19917		20301		21035	EQUIPMENT DE TELECOM
761	TELEVISION RECEIVERS	W 245	2456	W 181	1910	W 250	2722	W 218	2645	RECEPTEURS DE TELEVISION
7611	COLOUR TV RECEIVERS	W 244	2428	W 174	1793	W 246	2681	W 214	2591	RECEPTEURS COULEUR
763	SOUND RECORDRS,PHONOGRPH	W 101	1775	W 112	1758	W 156	2111	W 130	1721	PHONO,APP ENREGISTREMENT
7638	OTHR SOUND APPARATUS ETC	W 100	1751	W 110	1731	W 154	2096	W 129	1709	AUT APP D'ENREGIS,REPROD
764	TELECOM EQPT,PTS,ACC NES	W 269	8616	W 369	14949	W 250	14425	W 328	15651	EQUIP TELECOM,PIECES
7641	LINE TELEPHONE,ETC EQUIP	W 110	5074	W 161	6366	W 122	9108	W 157	8911	APP TELEPHON PAR FIL
7649	PTS NES OF EQUIPMT OF 76	W 75	2006	W 118	5937	W 76	2868	W 112	3892	PIECES DE LA DIV 76
76491	PTS NES OF APPAR OF 7641	W 15	856	W 41	4104	W 24	1579	W 40	2540	PIECES POUR 764.1
77	ELECTRIC MACHNRY NES ETC		30981		33342		40393		40070	MACH APP ELECT NDA
771	ELECTRIC POWER MACHY NES	W 236	1522	W 133	1560	W 274	2625	W 178	2760	MACH PROD,TRANS ELECTR
772	SWITCHGEAR ETC,PARTS NES	W 312	7280	W 269	7032	W 411	9277	W 496	9537	APP COUPURE,SECT ETC
7721	SWITCHGEAR ETC	W 255	4129	W 202	3996	W 338	5439	W 419	6106	APP COUPURE,SECTIONMNT
7723	FIXED,VARIABLE RESISTORS	W 46	1558	W 55	1695	W 63	2413	W 65	1677	POTENTIOMETRES PIECES
773	ELECTR DISTRIBUTNG EQUIP		3849	W 1038	4514		6370	W 1396	7875	EQUIPMT DISTRIBUTION ELECT
7731	INSULATED WIRE,CABLE ETC	W 847	2916	W 993	4083	W 936	5664	W 1312	7237	FILS,CABLES ISOLES ELECT
775	HOUSEHOLD TYPE EQUIP NES	W 1249	7178	W 917	5780	W 1391	7807	W 1036	6433	MACH,APP USAGE DOMESTQUE
7752	DOM REFRIGERATRS,FREEZRS	W 647	3558	W 470	2789	W 706	3852	W 496	3000	REFRIG,CONGEL MENAGER
77521	DOMESTIC REFRIGERATORS	W 470	2734	W 407	2498	W 603	3381	W 430	2629	REFRIGERATEURS
776	TRANSISTORS,VALVES,ETC	W 86	5947	W 115	8975	W 151	8011	W 160	7530	LAMPES,TUBES,VALVES
7768	ELCTRNC COMP PTS,CRYSTLS	W 62	4177	W 98	7522	W 133	5817	W 137	5846	CRIST PIEZO-ELEC,PCS 776
77689	ELECTRNIC COMPON PTS NES	W 62	4176	W 98	7503	W 133	5816	W 137	5842	PIECES DU GROUPE 776
778	ELECTRICAL MACHINERY NES	W 603	4689	W 789	5191	W 594	5846	W 570	5674	AUTRES MACH ELECT NDA
78	ROAD VEHICLES		27390		31170		59416		62583	VEHICULES ROUTIERS
781	PASS MOTOR VEH EXC BUSES	W 1645	13876	W 1908	15987	W 4081	36921	W 4764	40434	AUTO TRANSPORT PERSONNES
782	LORRIES,SPCL MTR VEH NES	W 982	6432	W 994	7550	W 1875	13061	W 1852	12173	VEHICULES SPECIAUX,MARCH
7821	LORRIES,TRUCKS	W 932	6051	W 954	7383	W 1839	12295	W 1651	11268	VEHICULES TRANSP MARCHAND
784	MOTOR VEH PRTS,ACCES NES	W 544	4431	W 489	4974	W 488	6403		6729	PIECES 722,781,782,783
7849	OTHER MOTOR VEHCL PARTS	W 506	4368	W 482	4870	W 461	5917	W 702	6224	PIECES 722,781,782,783
79	OTHR TRANSPORT EQUIPMENT		1616		1159		7331		7783	AUTRE MATERIEL TRANSPORT
792	AIRCRAFT ETC	W 10	251	W 4	332	W 160	4324	W 90	2253	APP NAVIGATION AERIENNE
7929	AIRCRAFT PARTS NES	W 10	237	W 4	308	W 160	4318	W 90	2246	PIECES DU 792
793	SHIPS AND BOATS ETC	W 220	1345	W 110	796	W 200	2987	W 673	5518	NAVIRES BATEAUX,ETC
7932	SHIPS AND BOATS NES	W 149	1015	W 105	701	W 194	1961	W 644	4485	NAVIRES ET BATEAUX
79323	OTHER CARGO VESSELS			W 28	370	W 92	1174	W 320	3258	AUT BATEAUX TRANS MARCH
8	MISC MANUFACTURED GOODS		80747		89403		110240		112997	ART MANUFACTURES DIVERS
812	*PLUMBG,HEATNG,LGHTNG EQ	W 445	2685	W 792	3272	W 652	3795	W 690	4046	APPAR SANITAIRES CHAUFFAGE
8124	LIGHTING EQUIPMENT NES	W 221	1993	W 498	2256	W 332	2695	W 333	2784	APPAREILS ECLAIRAGE ETC
81242	LAMPS,FITTINGS BASE METL	W 203	1797	W 479	2072	W 315	2558	W 313	2505	APPAREILS D'ECLAIRAGE
821	*FURNITURE,PARTS THEREOF	W 1178	4658	W 1424	6288	W 1602	5814	W 1691	7090	MEUBLES ET PIECES
8211	CHAIRS,SEATS AND PARTS	W 451	1607	W 459	1904	W 483	1800	W 478	2003	SIEGES ET PIECES
8219	FURNITURE AND PARTS NES	W 617	2573	W 745	3884	W 867	3427	W 1016	4338	AUTRES MEUBLES ET PIECES
82192	WOOD FURNITURE NES	W 267	809	W 371	1897	W 392	1259	W 350	1402	MEUBLES NDA EN BOIS
831	*TRAVEL GOODS,HANDBAGS	W 89	1760	W 351	1168	W 139	1657	W 98	1725	ARTICLES DE VOYAGE ETC
84	CLOTHING AND ACCESSORIES		12731		12028		13578		12862	VETEMENTS
843	WOMENS OUTERWEAR NONKNIT	W 57	1834	W 85	2176	W 92	2856	W 150	3052	VET DESSUS FEMMES MAT TEX
845	OUTERWEAR KNIT NONELASTC	W 151	2906	W 59	1591	W 66	1676	W 62	1610	VET DESSOUS,ACCES BONNET
846	UNDER GARMENTS KNITTED	W 340	4946	W 235	5013	W 243	4910	W 207	4149	SOUS VETS DE BONNETERIE
8462	— OF COTTON NON ELASTIC	W 96	1509	W 136	2078	W 116	1546	W 105	1388	SOUS-VET BONNET COTON
84629	—— OTHER	W 96	1509	W 136	2078	W 116	1546	W 105	1388	AUT SOUS-VET BONNET COTON
8465	CORSETS,GARTERS,ETC	W 32	2632	W 29	2008	W 51	2290	W 47	1950	CORSETS,GAINES ART SIM
84652	CORSETS,BRACES ETC	W 20	2392	W 20	1828	W 29	2033	W 30	1777	CORSETS,GAINES,JARRETEL
851	*FOOTWEAR	W 442	5819	W 372	4862	W 581	6004	W 585	6933	CHAUSSURES
85102	FOOTWEAR LEATHER	W 272	4015	W 224	3338	W 412	4298	W 451	5832	CHAUS SEMELLES EN CUIR
87	PRECISION INSTRUMNTS NES		4192		5100		6095		6391	INSTRUM,APPAR SCIENT NDA
872	MEDICAL INSTRUMENTS NES	W 50	1058	W 65	1981	W 83	1680	W 78	1876	INSTR,APP MEDIC-CHIR NDA
87202	OTH MEDICAL INSTRUMENTS	W 47	987	W 61	1887	W 78	1569	W 71	1720	INSTRUM,APP MEDECINE
874	MEASURNG,CONTROLNG INSTR	W 84	2509	W 81	2768	W 130	3815	W 106	3979	INSTRUMENTS DE MESURE
88	PHOTO EQU,OPTICL GDS ETC		8848		8732		13199		12124	APP,FOURN PHOTO,OP,MONTR
882	PHOTO,CINEMA SUPPLIES	W 236	3000	W 210	2805	W 215	3294	W 399	3032	PRODUITS PHOTO,CINEMA
8822	PHOTO FILM EXC DEV CINMA	W 156	2381	W 148	2212	W 147	2502	W 95	2207	PLAQUES,PELLICULES,FILMS
885	WATCHES AND CLOCKS		4173		3941		7732		6832	HORLOGERIE
8851	WATCHES,MOVEMENTS,CASES		3802		3506		7032		6243	MONTRES,MOUVEMENTS,BOITES
88511	WATCHES		3747		3479		7000		6220	MONTRES POCHE,BRACELET
89	MISC MANUFCTRD GOODS NES		40055		47953		60098		61827	ART MANUFACTURES DIVERS
892	PRINTED MATTER	W 1249	9020	W 1929	14656	W 1822	13907	W 1991	12178	IMPRIMES
8921	PRINTED BOOKS,GLOBES,ETC	W 491	4132	W 1059	6030	W 1285	6268	W 1393	7368	LIVRES,BROCHURES,CARTES
89211	PRINTED BOOKS,PAMPHLETS	W 474	4003	W 1027	5868	W 1251	6059	W 1357	7174	LIVRES,BROCHURES

4. General Imports C.I.F. by Commodities according to the S.I.T.C. (Rev. 2) in thousand U.S. Dollars
Importations Générales C.A.F. par Produits d'après la C.T.C.I. (Rév. 2) en milliers de Dollars E.U.

SITC CTCI	COMMODITY	1993		1994		1995		1996		PRODUIT
		WEIGHT POIDS	VALUE VALEUR	WEIGHT POIDS	VALUE VALEUR	WEIGHT POIDS	VALUE VALEUR	WEIGHT POIDS	VALUE VALEUR	
8928	PRINTED MATTER NES	W 547	3193	W 551	6509	W 235	5395	W 305	2594	IMPRIMES NDA
89283	UNISSUED BANKNOTES ETC	W 16	819	W 13	4050	W 14	3086	W 8	550	TIMBRES–POSTE FISCAUX
893	ARTICLES OF PLASTIC NES		14836		16299		19633		21125	OUVRAGES EN MAT DIVIS 58
8931	PLSTC PACKG CONTNRS,LIDS	W 2043	6870	W 2305	7268	W 3613	10029	W 3068	9842	ART TRANSP EMBALLAGE ETC
8939	MISC PLASTIC ARTICLES	W 2500	7731	W 3709	8717	W 3196	9269	W 3026	11020	ART DIVERS EN MAT DIV 58
89399	OTHR PLASTC ARTICLES NES	W 1724	6659	W 3103	7813	W 2215	8239	W 2461	10012	AUT OUV MAT DIV 58
894	TOYS,SPORTING GOODS,ETC	W 519	2141	W 408	2917	W 670	3718	W 705	4031	VOITURES ENFANTS,JOUETS
897	GOLD,SILVER WARE,JEWELRY		7941		6681		13937		16777	BIJOUTERIE,ORFEVRERIE
8973	PREC JEWLRY,GLD–SILVWARE		7257		6415		13566		16414	BIJOUX OR,ARGENT ORFEVRE
89731	PRECIOUS METAL JEWELLERY		7177		6295		13355		16307	ART BIJOUTERIE,JOAILLER
898	MUSICAL INSTRUMENTS,PTS	W 124	2879	W 169	3699	W 212	4517	W 202	3425	INSTRUMENTS DE MUSIQUE
8983	SOUND RECRDNG TAPE,DISCS	W 86	2077	W 128	3250	W 189	3996	W 172	3059	SUPPORTS SON POUR 763
89832	RECORDED DISCS,TAPES ETC	W 35	1512	W 65	2553	W 152	3489	W 105	2603	DISQUES,PHONO,BANDES
899	OTHER MANUFACTURED GOODS		2048		2474		2845		2573	AUT ART MANUF DIVERS NDA
9	GOODS NOT CLASSD BY KIND		2725		2558		2076		2585	ART TRANSACT NON CLASSES

5. General Exports F.O.B. by Commodities according to the S.I.T.C. (Rev. 2) in thousand U.S. Dollars
Exportations Générales F.O.B. par Produits d'après la C.T.C.I. (Rév. 2) en milliers de Dollars E.U.

SITC CTCI	COMMODITY	1993 WEIGHT POIDS	1993 VALUE VALEUR	1994 WEIGHT POIDS	1994 VALUE VALEUR	1995 WEIGHT POIDS	1995 VALUE VALEUR	1996 WEIGHT POIDS	1996 VALUE VALEUR	PRODUIT
	ALL COMMODITIES		180971		181811		237538		279049	TOUS PRODUITS
0	FOOD AND LIVE ANIMALS		39951		45021		54005		87292	ALIMENTS,ANIMAUX VIVANTS
01	MEAT AND PREPARATIONS		1286		1181		1908		2363	VIANDES ET PREPARATIONS
014	MEAT PREPD,PRSVD,NES ETC	W 553	1282	W 939	1154	W 580	1487	W 904	2253	CONSERVES DE VIANDES
0142	SAUSAGES INCLDING TINNED	W 449	980	W 821	778	W 499	1163	W 740	1695	SAUCISSES,SAUCISSONS
03	FISH AND PREPARATIONS		255		351		875		589	POISSONS ET PREPARATIONS
034	FISH,FRESH,CHILLED,FROZN	W 58	250	W 84	319	W 208	841		494	POISSON FRAIS, REFRIG,CONG
04	CEREALS AND PREPARATIONS		3568		2705		4476		6043	CEREALES ET PRODUITS
042	RICE	W 266	70	W 30	15	W 690	288	W 1983	958	RIZ
0422	RICE SEMI-MILLED,MILLED	W 182	52	W 28	14	W 689	288	W 1945	939	RIZ POLI,GLACE INCL BRISURES
04221	RICE MILLED UNBROKEN	W 182	52	W 28	14	W 689	288	W 1945	939	RIZ POLI,GLACE EXCL BRISURES
048	CEREAL ETC PREPARATIONS	W 1362	3141	W 1208	2224	W 1716	3486	W 2101	4323	PREPTNS A BASE CEREALES
0481	PREPD BREAKFAST FOOD ETC	W 328	670	W 378	453	W 293	773	W 240	558	CEREALES TRAVAILLEES
04812	CEREAL ROASTED, PUFFED	W 325	664	W 378	453	W 258	699	W 230	506	PRODTS BASE CEREALES
0484	BAKERY PRODUCTS	W 864	2268	W 757	1452	W 1021	1943	W 1406	2858	PRODUITS DE BOULANGERIE
05	VEGETABLES AND FRUIT		2196		2306		3194		3036	LEGUMES ET FRUITS
054	VEG ETC FRSH,SMPLY PRSVD	W 927	866	W 1383	892		1296	W 1217	1238	LEGUMES FRAIS,CONG,SECS
058	FRUIT PRESERVED,PREPARED	W 190	452	W 238	580		917	W 418	760	CONSERVES DE FRUITS
06	SUGAR AND PREPS,HONEY		23781		29933		28701		35928	SUCRES ET PRODUITS
061	SUGAR AND HONEY	W 38008	23707	W 30865	29884	W 37345	28623	W 53542	35823	SUCRES ET MIEL
0611	RAW BEET AND CANE SUGAR	W 38006	23706	W 30863	29880	W 37343	28619	W 53523	35805	SUCRES BRUTS
09	MISC EDIBLE PRODUCTS		7819		7395		13353		37616	PREP ALIMENTAIRES DIVERSES
091	MARGARINE AND SHORTENING	W 2110	3068	W 2279	2909	W 2982	4657	W 3422	5754	MARGARINE ET GRAISSES
0914	MARGARINE,EDIBLE FAT NES	W 2110	3068	W 2279	2909	W 2982	4657	W 3421	5751	MARGARINES,SIMILI SAINDOUX
09141	MARGARINE	W 1686	2480	W 1996	2494	W 2546	3977	W 2941	4576	MARGARINE
09149	OTH PREPARED EDIBLE FATS	W 423	588	W 283	416	W 436	680	W 479	1175	SIMILI-SAINDOUX
098	EDIBLE PRODCTS,PREPS NES	W 526	4751	W 487	4486	W 906	8696	W 3254	31863	PREP ALIMENTAIRES NDA
09809	MISC FOOD PREPRTIONS NES	W 377	4445	W 390	4290	W 724	8354	W 2525	31493	PREP ALIMENTAIRES NDA
1	BEVERAGES AND TOBACCO		11942		8161		14141		15600	BOISSONS ET TABACS
11	BEVERAGES		11066		7220		13017		15062	BOISSONS
111	NON-ALCOHL BEVERAGES NES	W 3437	1902	W 1410	1474	W 1930	2086	W 2204	2510	BOISSONS NON ALCOOLIQUES
11102	FLAVORED WATERS NON-ALCO	W 3349	1868	W 1218	1406	W 1751	1992	W 2069	2445	LIMONADES,EAUX GAZEUSES
112	ALCOHOLIC BEVERAGES	W 6038	9164	W 2151	5747	W 4464	10931	W 5543	12552	BOISSONS ALCOOLIQUES
1124	DISTILLED ALCOHOLIC BEVS	W 5629	8718	W 1756	5048	W 4234	10179	W 5256	12230	ALCOOLS,EAUX-DE-VIE
11249	OTH ALCOHOLC BEVS,CMPNDS	W 5566	8384	W 1716	4784	W 4213	10054	W 5197	11973	BOISSONS ALCOOLIQUES NDA
12	TOBACCO AND MANUFACTURES		876		940		1124		537	TABACS BRUTS FABRIQUES
122	TOBACCO,MANUFACTURED	W 62	875	W 69	940	W 39	1041	W 15	537	TABACS FABRIQUES
1222	CIGARETTES	W 54	809	W 62	855	W 37	967	W 13	403	CIGARETTES
2	CRUDE MATERLS,EXCL FUELS		1401		1461		5765		2494	MAT BRUTES NON COMESTIBLES
26	TEXTILE FIBRES AND WASTE		369		275		1231		308	FIBRES TEXTILES
263	COTTON	W 31	358	W 37	275	W 268	1223		305	COTON
2631	RAW COTTON,EXCL LINTERS	W 31	357	W 37	275	W 268	1223		305	COTON EN MASSE
27	CRUDE FERTLZR,MINRLS NES		483		636		3177		367	ENGRAIS MINERAUX BRUTS
277	NATURAL ABRASIVES NES				292		2718			ABRASIFS NATURELS NDA
2771	INDUSTRIAL DIAMONDS				292		2718			DIAMANTS INDUSTRIELS
3	MINERAL FUELS ETC		29206		26217		34141		36965	COMBUSTIBLES MINERAUX LUB
33	PETROLEUM AND PRODUCTS		29206		26217		34141		36965	PETROLE ET DERIVES
334	PETROLEUM PRODUCTS,REFIN	W 130007	29163	W 127018	26202	W 161244	34131	W 161099	36955	PRODUITS RAFFINES
3341	GASOLINE,OTH LIGHT OILS	W 1145	506	W 1072	367	W 22713	4823	W 708	234	ESSENCES POUR MOTEURS
33411	MOTOR,AVIATION SPIRIT	W 1145	506	W 1072	367	W 22713	4823	W 708	234	ESSENCES MOTEURS D'AVIONS
3342	KEROSENE,OTH MEDIUM OILS	W 113682	25445	W 106774	21486	W 114973	25299	W 138119	31393	PETR LAMPANTS,AUT HUIL
33421	KEROSENE INCL JET FUEL	W 113682	25445	W 106774	21486	W 114973	25299	W 138119	31393	PETROLES LAMPANTS
3343	GAS OILS	W 8198	2069	W 13924	3411	W 10398	1641	W 8902	2475	GAS OILS
3344	FUEL OILS,NES	W 6936	1077	W 5235	899	W 13031	2194	W 13271	2665	FUEL OILS
5	CHEMCLS,RELATED PROD NES		25717		25719		32004		33966	PRODUITS CHIMIQUES
51	ORGANIC CHEMICALS		118		2982		1614		130	PROD CHIMIQ ORGANIQUES
512	ALCOHOLS,PHENOLS ETC	W 6	14	W 2452	2904	W 1167	1544	W 59	85	PHENOLS,PHENOLS-ALCOOLS
5121	ACYCLIC ALCOHOLS,DERIVS	W 5	9	W 2452	2900	W 1166	1536	W 59	83	ALCOOLS ACYCLIQUES
51216	ETHYL ALC,DENATRD SPIRIT	W 2	4	W 2451	2898	W 1166	1495	W 59	81	ALCOOL ETHYLIQUE NON DENAT
53	DYES,TANNING,COLOUR PROD		4884		4525		5261		5175	PROD TEINTURE,COLORANTS
533	PIGMENTS,PAINTS,ETC	W 1771	4869		4510	W 1592	5247		5148	PIGMENTS,PEINTURES,VERNIS
5334	VARNISHES,DISTEMPERS ETC	W 1512	4451	W 1235	4109	W 1451	4832	W 1282	4756	PEINTURES A L'EAU
53341	WATER-THINNED PAINTS	W 368	1088	W 310	1365	W 321	996	W 239	801	PEINTURES DILUEES
53342	OTH PAINTS,VARNISHES ETC	W 1134	3300	W 918	2685	W 1122	3796	W 1035	3922	AUTRES PEINTURES,VERNIS
541	*MEDICINAL,PHARM PRODUCT	K 397145	5536	K 293046	5417	K 356963	7169		8371	PROD MEDICINAUX PHARMACEUT
5417	MEDICAMENTS	K 390847	5413	K 283393	5188	K 339465	6960	K 578135	7891	MEDICAMENTS
54179	— CONTNG OTH SUBSTANCES	K 370342	4948	K 272080	4578	K 331310	6116	K 569170	6995	MED CONT AUT SUBSTANCES
55	PERFUME,CLEANING ETC PRD		8117		7726		9199		10807	PROD POUR PARFUM,TOILETTE
553	PERFUMERY,COSMETICS,ETC	W 140	1251	W 112	940	W 95	830	W 132	1009	PRODUITS DE PARFUMERIE
554	SOAP,CLEANSING ETC PREPS	W 5968	6768	W 5550	6709	W 6923	8240	W 8312	9565	SAVONS,PRODUITS DETERSIFS
5542	WASHING PREPARATIONS ETC	W 5961	6744	W 5541	6682	W 6916	8213	W 8308	9543	PROD ORG TENSIO-ACT NDA
59	CHEMICAL MATERIALS NES		6569		4546		8164		9084	MAT PROD CHIMIQUES NDA
591	PESTICIDES,DISINFECTANTS	W 1202	5824	W 868	4072	W 1440	7339	W 1704	8101	DESINF,INSECT,FONG,HERB
5911	INSECTICIDES,FOR RETAIL	W 1055	5377	W 774	3860	W 1336	7080	W 1547	7763	INSECTICIDES VENTE DET
598	MISCEL CHEM PRODUCTS NES	W 457	717	W 174	445	W 292	796	W 201	954	PROD DIV INDUST CHIM NDA
5989	CHEM PRODUCTS,PREPS NES	W 453	705	W 170	431	W 288	773	W 195	937	PROD PREP CHIMIQUES NDA
6	BASIC MANUFACTURES		26518		26085		33820		39623	ART MANUFACTURES
63	WOOD,CORK MANUFACTRS NES		748		607		1307		1561	OUVRAGES LIEGE ET BOIS
635	WOOD MANUFACTURES NES	W 374	706	W 230	582	W 443	1078	W 597	1496	ART MANUF EN BOIS NDA
6353	BUILDERS WOODWRK,PREFABS	W 370	658	W 221	523	W 426	1003	W 577	1426	OUVRAGES DE MENUISERIE
64	PAPER,PAPERBOARD AND MFR		5389		5598		10864		14168	PAPIERS,CARTONS & OUVRAGES
642	PAPER,ETC,PRECUT,ARTS OF	W 1664	5268	W 1424	5462	W 2526	10750		13912	PAP,CARTONS DECOUPES
6421	PAPER ETC CONTAINERS	W 1282	3384	W 724	2090	W 1250	4278	W 1647	4630	BOITES,SACS EMBALLAGES
6428	PAPER ETC ARTICLES NES	W 332	1425	W 624	2782	W 1197	5597		8293	OUVRAGES EN PATE A PAPIER
64285	PAPER ETC DIAPERS ETC	W 208	877	W 531	2242	W 975	4767	W 1552	7493	SERVIETTES HYGIENIQUES
65	TEXTILE YARN,FABRICS,ETC		1523		1893		2141		2023	FILS,TISSUS,ARTICLES TEXTILE
658	TEXTILE ARTICLES NES		1443		1512		1765		1893	ART FACONNES MAT TEXTILES
6582	MADE-UP CANVAS GOODS	W 28	1359	W 67	1448	W 23	1687	W 25	1817	BACHES,TENTES ETC
66	NONMETAL MINERAL MFS NES		1483		1232		2085		5687	ART MIN NON METALLIQUES
661	LIME,CEMENT,BLDG PRODS	W 1425	307	W 4082	311	W 2582	290	W 5603	2017	CHAUX,CIMENTS MAT CONSTR
6611	LIME,QUICK,SLKD,HYDRAULC	W 1041	151	W 4046	260	W 2469	266	W 1924	992	CHAUX ORDINAIRE,HYDRAUL
6612	CEMENT	W 379	140	W 1	1			W 3559	1009	CIMENTS HYDRAULIQUES
665	GLASSWARE	W 1255	941	W 1333	731	W 1764	1136		1028	OUVRAGES EN VERRE
6651	BOTTLES ETC OF GLASS	W 1233	907	W 1329	727	W 1762	1113	W 1856	1012	RECIPIENTS EN VERRE
66511	GLASS BOTTLES ETC NONVAC	W 1233	907	W 1329	727	W 1762	1113	W 1856	1012	BONBONNES,BOUTEILLES,ETC
667	PEARL,PREC-,SEMI-P STONE						515		2391	PERLES, PIERRES GEMMES
6672	DIAMONDS NONINDUST,UNSET						515		2364	DIAMANTS BRUTS
66721	— ROUGH,UNSORTED						515		2364	DIAMANTS BRUTS NON TRIES
67	IRON AND STEEL		948		686		538		942	FER ET ACIER
673	IRON,STEEL SHAPES ETC	W 1266	592	W 253	147	W 266	129	W 1613	252	BARRES,PROFIL FER,ACIER
69	METAL MANUFACTURES NES		16315		15971		16745		14707	ART MANUFACT EN METAL NDA

5. General Exports F.O.B. by Commodities according to the S.I.T.C. (Rev. 2) in thousand U.S. Dollars
Exportations Générales F.O.B. par Produits d'après la C.T.C.I. (Rév. 2) en milliers de Dollars E.U.

SITC CTCI	COMMODITY	1993		1994		1995		1996		PRODUIT
		WEIGHT POIDS	VALUE VALEUR	WEIGHT POIDS	VALUE VALEUR	WEIGHT POIDS	VALUE VALEUR	WEIGHT POIDS	VALUE VALEUR	
691	STRUCTURES AND PARTS NES	W 699	2474	W 508	2628	W 625	3015	W 816	3439	CONSTRUCT FER,ACIER,ALU
6911	STRUCTURES,PARTS IRN,STL	W 376	703	W 224	442	W 122	361	W 238	426	CONSTRUCT FER,ACIER,FONTE
6912	STRUCTURES,PARTS ALUMNM	W 323	1771	W 283	2186	W 503	2654	W 578	3013	CONSTRUCT ALUMINIUM
692	METAL TANKS,BOXES,ETC	W 4622	9532	W 4428	7421	W 2996	6215		5886	RECIPIENTS METALLIQUES
6924	MTL TRANSPORT BOXES ETC	W 4598	9502	W 4427	7413	W 2978	6182	W 2190	5875	FUTS,TAMBOURS,BIDONS
69241	STL TRANSPORT BOXES ETC	W 4510	9325	W 4335	7190	W 2856	5952	W 2015	5640	FUTS,TAMBOURS,BIDONS FER
695	TOOLS	W 248	3054	W 318	3174	W 300	5981	W 358	4045	OUTILS A MAIN
6953	OTHER HAND TOOLS	W 246	3039	W 317	3170	W 299	5959	W 353	3986	AUTRES OUTILS A MAIN
69539	HAND TOOLS ETC NES	W 245	3033	W 315	3154	W 299	5943	W 352	3978	OUTILLAGE A MAIN NDA
699	BASE METAL MFRS NES	W 151	625		2391		1125		962	ART MANUFACTURES MET NDA
6994	SPRINGS AND LEAVES	W 4	431	W 67	2199	W 11	845	W 7	710	RESSORTS FER,ACIER
69942	COPPER SPRINGS,LEAVES	W 3	426	W 65	2194	W 6	833	W 7	704	RESSORTS,LAMES EN CUIVRE
7	MACHINES,TRANSPORT EQUIP		32526		33977		46918		38938	MACHINES MATERIEL TRANSPORT
71	POWER GENERATING EQUIPMT		264		113		444		875	MACHINES GENERATRICES
72	MACHS FOR SPCL INDUSTRYS		1182		1443		6324		2002	MAC SPECIALES POUR INDUST
722	TRACTORS NON-ROAD		4			W 53	2587			TRACTEURS
7224	WHEELED TRACTORS NES		4			W 53	2587			TRACTEURS A ROUES
723	CIVIL ENGNEERG EQUIP ETC	W 51	449	W 68	448	W 86	780	W 64	564	APPAREILS DE GENIE CIVIL
7234	CONST,MINING MACHNRY NES	W 40	134	W 58	400	W 82	752	W 46	418	MACH POUR LA CONST, MINES
726	PRINTG,BKBINDG MACHY,PTS	W 18	110		422	W 345	2325	W 34	322	MACHINES POUR IMPRIMERIE
7263	TYPESET ETC MCH,TYPE ETC	W 13	76		239	W 116	921	W 31	277	MACH COMPOSER,CLICHER
7267	OTH PRINTG & ANCILL MACH		7	W 22	168	W 220	924		19	AUT MACH IMPRIMERIE,PIEC
72671	PRINTING MACHINERY NES		7	W 22	158	W 220	923		18	AUT MACH IMPRIMERIE
73	METALWORKING MACHINERY		633		23		74		74	MACH TRAVAIL DES METAUX
736	METALWORKING MACH-TOOLS	W 68	601	W 1	2	W 6	48		61	MACH-OUTILS TRAVAIL METAUX
74	GENRL INDUSTRL MACHY NES		1129		387		959		3390	MACH APP INDUSTRIE
745	NONELEC MACHY,TOOLS NES	W 20	99	W 23	78	W 66	487		2379	AUT MACH NON ELEC,PIECES
7452	OTH NONELEC MCHS,PTS NES	W 17	88	W 23	74	W 64	440		2353	AUT MACH NON ELEC,PIECES
74522	PACKAGNG,BOTTLNG,ETC MCH	W 15	52	W 20	34	W 60	355	W 177	2022	MACH NETT BOUTEILLES,ETC
75	OFFICE MACHNES,ADP EQUIP		2278		2723		1323		1325	MACH BUREAU TRAIT AUTOM
752	AUTOMTIC DATA PROC EQUIP	W 9	774	W 6	310	W 20	497	W 21	499	MACH TRAIT INFORMATION
759	OFFICE,ADP MCH PTS,ACCES	W 29	1404	W 28	2329	W 26	733	W 20	711	PIECES DU 751 ET 752
7599	ACCTG,ETC,ADP MCH PTS,AC	W 29	1398	W 28	2304	W 26	724	W 20	710	PIECES DU 751 ET 752
76	TELECOMM,SOUND EQUIPMENT		251		789		6034		406	EQUIPMENT DE TELECOM
764	TELECOM EQPT,PTS,ACC NES	W 14	206		559		5944		368	EQUIP TELECOM,PIECES
7641	LINE TELEPHONE,ETC EQUIP	W 2	63	W 2	150	W 43	988	W 4	189	APP TELEPHON PAR FIL
7643	TV,RADIO TRANSMITTRS ETC		32		14	W 21	4715	W 2	80	APP EMET TELE RADIO
77	ELECTRIC MACHNRY NES ETC		24630		25752		28399		27262	MACH APP ELECT NDA
772	SWITCHGEAR ETC,PARTS NES	W 194	13664	W 189	15083	W 229	17484	W 232	18782	APP COUPURE,SECT ETC
7721	SWITCHGEAR ETC	W 60	760	W 20	513	W 29	587	W 7	373	APP COUPURE,SECTIONMNT
7722	PRINTED CIRCUITS,PTS NES	W 13	1020	W 58	3189	W 77	3652	W 82	3922	CIRCUITS ET PIECES
7723	FIXED,VARIABLE RESISTORS	W 120	11884	W 111	11381	W 123	13245	W 142	14487	POTENTIOMETRES PIECES
776	TRANSISTORS,VALVES,ETC	W 144	7900	W 134	7155	W 135	6738	W 111	4465	LAMPES,TUBES,VALVES
7763	DIODES,TRANSISTORS,ETC	W 7	934	W 5	534	W 4	467	W 5	133	DIODES,TRANSISTORS
7764	ELECTRONIC MICROCIRCUITS	W 121	6550	W 128	6498	W 130	6214	W 106	4262	MICROSTRUCTURES ELECTRON
778	ELECTRICAL MACHINERY NES		2989	W 255	3442		3771	W 430	3815	AUTRES MACH ELECT NDA
7788	OTH ELEC MACHY,EQUIP NES	W 12	2538	W 6	3007	W 9	3160	W 5	3237	AUT MACH APP ELEC NDA
77884	ELECTRICAL CONDENSERS	W 11	2491	W 4	2946	W 4	3085	W 2	3176	CONDENSATEURS ELECTRIQUES
78	ROAD VEHICLES		930		2210		2364		2098	VEHICULES ROUTIERS
781	PASS MOTOR VEH EXC BUSES	W 55	504	W 46	620	W 77	966	W 83	1298	AUTO TRANSPORT PERSONNES
782	LORRIES,SPCL MTR VEH NES	W 14	121	W 285	1044	W 55	196	W 156	370	VEHICULES SPECIAUX,MARCH
7821	LORRIES,TRUCKS	W 12	70	W 285	1044	W 51	152	W 147	303	VEHICULES TRANSP MARCHAND
79	OTHR TRANSPORT EQUIPMENT		1228		537		997		1506	AUTRE MATERIEL TRANSPORT
792	AIRCRAFT ETC	W 12	1033	W 12	521	W 18	976	W 11	1187	APP NAVIGATION AERIENNE
7929	AIRCRAFT PARTS NES	W 12	1033	W 12	513	W 18	976	W 11	1187	PIECES DU 792
8	MISC MANUFACTURED GOODS		12386		12740		15698		22436	ART MANUFACTURES DIVERS
821	*FURNITURE,PARTS THEREOF	W 161	1171	W 177	661	W 162	647	W 260	901	MEUBLES ET PIECES
8219	FURNITURE AND PARTS NES	W 105	955	W 80	440	W 65	409	W 142	668	AUTRES MEUBLES ET PIECES
84	CLOTHING AND ACCESSORIES		4842		3487		3469		3905	VETEMENTS
842	MENS OUTERWEAR NOT KNIT	W 11	323	W 13	408	W 17	853	W 22	614	VET DESSUS POUR HOMMES
8423	— TROUSERS,BREECHES ETC	W 11	298	W 11	340	W 15	813	W 20	547	PANTALONS HOMMES MAT TEX
845	OUTERWEAR KNIT NONELASTC		2223		781	W 5	349	W 6	348	VET DESSOUS,ACCES BONNET
8452	— WOMENS DRESSES ETC	W 42	1836	W 5	251	W 1	54	W 1	46	ROBES,JUPES BONNETERIE
846	UNDER GARMENTS KNITTED	W 70	2037	W 57	2096	W 56	1902	W 62	2592	SOUS VETS DE BONNETERIE
8462	— OF COTTON NON ELASTIC	W 52	1044	W 38	1054	W 40	1077	W 37	882	SOUS-VET BONNET COTON
84629	—— OTHER	W 52	1044	W 38	1054	W 40	1077	W 37	882	AUT SOUS-VET BONNET COTON
8465	CORSETS,GARTERS,ETC	W 18	988	W 19	1038	W 15	816	W 25	1681	CORSETS,GAINES ART SIM
84651	BRASSIERES	W 18	960	W 18	1022	W 13	702	W 22	1481	SOUTIENS-GORGE,BUSTIERS
87	PRECISION INSTRUMNTS NES		329		342		1044		773	INSTRUM,APPAR SCIENT NDA
874	MEASURNG,CONTROLNG INSTR	W 7	232	W 13	215	W 23	756		382	INSTRUMENTS DE MESURE
88	PHOTO EQU,OPTICL GDS ETC		243		876		407		3756	APP,FOURN PHOTO,OP,MONTR
882	PHOTO,CINEMA SUPPLIES	W 8	127	W 61	584	W 8	123		317	PRODUITS PHOTO,CINEMA
885	WATCHES AND CLOCKS		18		263		104		3173	HORLOGERIE
8852	CLOCKS,CLOCK,WATCH PARTS		5		15		80		3050	HORLOGES,MOUV,PARTIES
88523	TIME-CLOCKS ETC				1		10		2700	COMPTEURS DE TEMPS,MINUT
89	MISC MANUFCTRD GOODS NES		5492		7296		10050		12919	ART MANUFACTURES DIVERS
892	PRINTED MATTER		2876	W 495	3884		6504	W 531	7738	IMPRIMES
8921	PRINTED BOOKS,GLOBES,ETC	W 52	509	W 108	681		498	W 91	693	LIVRES,BROCHURES,CARTES
89211	PRINTED BOOKS,PAMPHLETS	W 44	378	W 100	620	W 80	459	W 82	675	LIVRES,BROCHURES
8928	PRINTED MATTER NES		2016	W 185	2836	W 342	5495	W 343	6566	IMPRIMES NDA
89281	LABELS PAPER,PAPERBOARD	W 85	893	W 91	974	W 162	1797	W 178	2413	ETIQUETTES TOUS GENRES
89283	UNISSUED BANKNOTES ETC	W 5	574	W 7	1491	W 15	2997	W 16	3359	TIMBRES-POSTE FISCAUX
893	ARTICLES OF PLASTIC NES		1887		2167		2888		3249	OUVRAGES EN MAT DIVIS 58
8931	PLSTC PACKG CONTNRS,LIDS	W 349	1271	W 454	961	W 494	1710	W 587	1937	ART TRANSP EMBALLAGE ETC
8939	MISC PLASTIC ARTICLES	W 195	615	W 356	1185	W 587	1176	W 573	1309	ART DIVERS EN MAT DIV 58
89399	OTHR PLASTC ARTICLES NES	W 193	605	W 354	1172	W 585	1167	W 570	1301	AUT OUV MAT DIV 58
897	GOLD,SILVER WARE,JEWELRY		214		693		151		1476	BIJOUTERIE,ORFEVRERIE
8973	PREC JEWLRY,GLD-SILVWARE		52		651		47		1410	BIJOUX OR,ARGENT ORFEVRE
89731	PRECIOUS METAL JEWELLERY		43		647		47		1405	ART BIJOUTERIE,JOAILLER
9	GOODS NOT CLASSD BY KIND		1297		2425		699		1297	ART TRANSACT NON CLASSES
931	*SPECIAL TRANSACTIONS		982		1568		230		771	TRANS.SPECIALES

FOOT NOTES – NOTES

TABLE 3 –
1 Imports of crude petroleum are excluded.
TABLE 4 –

1 Imports of crude petroleum are excluded.
TABLEAU 3 –
1 Les importations du pétrole brut sont exclues.
TABLEAU 4 –
1 Les importations du pétrole brut sont exclues.

1. HISTORICAL SERIES, 1992–1996 GENERAL TRADE, IMPORTS C.I.F., EXPORTS F.O.B.
SERIES HISTORIQUES, 1992–1996 COMMERCE GENERAL, IMPORTATIONS C.A.F., EXPORTATIONS F.O.B

YEAR ANNEE	VALUE IN MILLION U.S. DOLLARS / VALEUR EN MILLION U.S. DOLLARS: MERCHANDISE – MARCHANDISE IMPORTS	MERCHANDISE – MARCHANDISE EXPORTS	GOLD – OR IMPORTS	GOLD – OR EXPORTS	CONVERSION FACTORS FACTEURS DE CONVERSION CENTS E.U. PAR IMPORTS	CONVERSION FACTORS EXPORTS	INDEX NUMBERS – INDICES: QUANTUM IMPORTS	QUANTUM EXPORTS	UNIT VALUE / VALEUR UNITAIRE IMPORTS	UNIT VALUE EXPORTS
1992	750.90	1060.90								
1993	779.00	758.00								
1994	4746.00	2509.00								
1995	4795.21	4362.97								
1996	6939.30	5462.70								

2. IMPORTS BY BROAD ECONOMIC CATEGORY AND EXPORTS BY INDUSTRIAL ORIGIN. (PERCENTAGE OF TOTAL VALUE)
IMPORTATIONS PAR CATEGORIES ECONOMIQUES ET EXPORTATIONS PAR BRANCHE D'ACTIVITE.(EN POURCENTAGE DE LA VALEUR TOTALE)

IMPORTS – IMPORTATIONS

	1990	1991	1992	1993	1994	1995	1996
TOTAL IMPORTS–IMPORTATIONS TOTALES							
1 FOOD BEV–ALIMENTATION BOISSONS							
11 PRIMARY–PRODUITS DE BASE							
111 FOR INDUSTRY–POUR L'INDUSTRIE							
112 FOR HOUSEHOLDS–POUR LES MENAGES							
12 PROCESSED–PRODUITS ELABORES							
121 FOR INDUSTRY–POUR L'INDUSTRIE							
122 FOR HOUSEHOLDS–POUR LES MENAGES							
2 IND SUPPLIES–APPROV INDUSTRIELS							
21 PRIMARY–PRODUITS DE BASE							
22 PROCESSED–PRODUITS ELABORES							
3 FUELS–COMBUSTIBLES							
31 PRIMARY–PRODUITS DE BASE							
32 PROCESSED–PRODUITS ELABORES							
321 MOTOR SPIRIT–ESSENCE							
322 OTHER–AUTRES							
4 MACHINERY–EQUIPEMENT							
41 CAPITAL EQUIPMENT–MACHINES							
42 PARTS–PIECES ACCESSOIRES							
5 TRANSPORT–TRANSPORT							
51 PASSENGER CARS–AUTOMOBILES							
52 OTHER–AUTRES							
521 INDUSTRIAL–INDUSTRIELS							
522 NON INDUSTRIAL–NON INDUSTRIEL							
53 PARTS–PIECES ACCESSOIRES							
6 CONSUM GOODS–BIENS CONSOMMATION							
61 DURABLE–DURABLES							
62 SEMI DURABLE–SEMI DURABLES							
63 NON DURABLE–NON DURABLES							
7 GOODS NES–BIENS NDA							

EXPORTS – EXPORTATIONS

	1990	1991	1992	1993	1994	1995	1996
TOTAL EXPORTS–EXPORTATIONS TOTALES							
1 AGRICULTURE							
2 MINING QUARRY–INDUS EXTRACTIVES							
3 MANUFACTURING–IND MANUFACTUR							
31 FOOD BEV TOBACCO–ALIM BOISS TAB							
32 TEXTILES–INDUSTRIES TEXTILES							
33 WOOD & PRODUCTS–BOIS & PRODUITS							
34 PAPER & PRODUCTS–PAPIER & PRODT							
35 CHEMICALS–INDUSTRIES CHIMIQUES							
36 NON METAL MIN–MIN NON METAL							
37 BASIC METAL–IND METAL BASE							
38 METAL MANUF–MANUF METAL							
39 OTH MANUF IND–AUTRES MANUF							

3. TRADE BY PRINCIPAL COUNTRIES OF ORIGIN AND DESTINATION (VALUE IN THOUSAND U.S. DOLLARS)
ECHANGES SELON LES PRINCIPAUX PAYS D'ORIGINE ET DE DESTINATION (VALEUR EN MILLIERS DE DOLLARS EU)

COUNTRIES–PAYS	GENERAL IMPORTS C.I.F. IMPORTATIONS GENERALES C.A.F					COUNTRIES–PAYS	GENERAL EXPORTS F.O.B. EXPORTATIONS GENERALES F.O.B.				
	1992	1993	1994	1995	1996		1992	1993	1994	1995	1996
World				4795212	6939288	Monde				4362974	5462675
Africa				6863	24240	Afrique				81303	110801
Americas				102930	232346	Amériques				131535	134703
Northern America				85006	159675	Amérique du Nord				76087	66813
LAIA				14604	35836	ALAI				52270	61067
CACM				1470	1720	MCAC					8
Caribbean				1825	34401	Caraïbes				2658	6815
Rest of America				25	714	Autre Amérique				520	
As.ex F.USSR				68780	153398	Asie l'URSS exclus				268681	153332
Eur.x F.USSR				1223869	1734498	Europe l'URSS exclus				977354	974625
EU				792045	1253619	UE				566014	448160
EFTA				48269	53033	AELE				81114	23784
East Europe				371997	359349	Europe de l'Est				311110	480899
Other Europe				18		Autre de l'Europe				30	42
Former USSR				3388751	4782667	Ancienne URSS				2861156	4070069
Oceania				207	1354	Océanie				5895	1332
Russian Federation				2950352	3522119	Russian Federation				2087710	2907590
Ukraine				226327	889382	Ukraine				389466	478129
Germany/Allemagne				411757	600597	Poland/Pologne				212016	324638
Poland/Pologne				195692	195008	Germany/Allemagne				280288	198173
Lithuania/Lituanie				84285	153436	Latvia/Lettonie				88299	240981
USA/Etats–Unis d'Amer				81587	151652	Lithuania/Lituanie				146638	167138
Italy/Italie				82198	110992	Netherlands/Pays–Bas				75888	63988
Netherlands/Pays–Bas				74389	116620	USA/Etats–Unis d'Amer				69034	60856
United Kingdom				40593	98653	Kazakhstan				43443	84757
Hungary/Hongrie				73587	48448	Egypt/Egypte				46601	74709
Czech Republic				45918	56971	Republic of Moldova				43729	68933
France,Monac				54304	47668	Italy/Italie				53781	57363
Kazakhstan				36634	58775	Uzbekistan/Ouzbékistan				32802	77502
Belgium–Luxembourg				20145	70840	Switz.Liecht				69301	19954
Latvia/Lettonie				39957	49038	Hungary/Hongrie				31350	56955
Austria/Autriche				28122	54484	Turkey/Turquie				45941	30080
Switz.Liecht				39770	38347	China/Chine				53129	21286
Slovakia				31642	34130	United Kingdom				36970	32106
Uzbekistan/Ouzbékistan				23635	36479	Slovakia				23404	36636
Republic of Moldova				11862	48080	Peru/Pérou				41	58383
Denmark/Danemark				14086	39811	Pakistan				37137	20599
Finland/Finlande				19254	33315	Belgium–Luxembourg				21221	25026
Ireland/Irlande				19268	24936	Brazil/Brésil				44821	933
Bulgaria/Bulgarie				21955	19008	Austria/Autriche				29031	15438
Slovenia/Slovénia				2705	37052	Romania/Roumanie				13144	29940
Sweden/Suède				10466	28183	France,Monac				21376	16947
Japan/Japon				10271	25310	Czech Republic				17182	20030
China/Chine				7380	25187	Hong Kong				14548	18410
Spain/Espagne				11025	20199	Bulgaria/Bulgarie				14014	12697
Croatia/Croatie				3989	23564	Estonia/Estonie				10790	15122
Cuba					27215	Finland/Finlande				14887	10347
Israel/Israël				11031	13401	Viet Nam				10374	14303
Turkey/Turquie				6853	16861	Iran (Islamic Rp. of)				7911	16126
Korea, Republic of				9786	13650	Algeria/Algérie				12327	11120
Brazil/Brésil				8965	13798	Croatia/Croatie				12113	11038
Norway,SVD,JM				8021	14218	Korea, Republic of				14646	4744
Singapore/Singapour				1367	19630	India/Inde				15277	3978
India/Inde				5457	14619	United Arab Emirates				15839	2852
Estonia/Estonie				8211	10122	Ireland/Irlande				14086	1945
Ghana				5922	9633	Morocco/Maroc				7627	8192
Greece/Grèce				6438	6990	Norway,SVD,JM				11636	3812
Ecuador/Equateur					11795	Cyprus/Chypre				10090	4448
Canada				3419	8023	Spain/Espagne				5242	8119
Cyprus/Chypre				7917	2972	Canada				7053	5957
Argentina/Argentine				3785	6299	Sweden/Suède				4896	7735
Romania/Roumanie				3203	5784	Azerbaijan				4411	8145
Tfyr Macedonia				3611	4746	Denmark/Danemark				5011	7525
British Virgin Islds				1599	6728	Nigeria/Nigéria				8488	1573
Indonesia/Indonésie				2915	5306	Mongolia/Mongolie				6067	3810
Malaysia/Malaisie				1318	5918	Kyrgyzstan/Kirghizistan				3045	6776

(VALUE AS PERCENTAGE OF WORLD TOTAL)(VALEURS EN POURCENTAGE DU TOTAL MONDIAL)

	1987	1988	1989	1990	1991	1992	1993	1994	1995	1996		1987	1988	1989	1990	1991	1992	1993	1994	1995	1996
Africa									0.1	0.3	Afrique									1.9	2.0
Americas									2.1	3.3	Amériques									3.0	2.5
Northern America									1.8	2.3	Amérique du Nord									1.7	1.2
LAIA									0.3	0.5	ALAI									1.2	1.1
CACM									0.0	0.0	MCAC										0.0
Caribbean									0.0	0.5	Caraïbes									0.1	0.1
Rest of America									0.0	0.0	Autre Amérique									0.0	
As.ex F.USSR									1.4	2.2	Asie l'URSS exclus									6.2	2.8
Eur.x F.USSR									25.5	25.0	Europe l'URSS exclus									22.4	17.8
EU									16.5	18.1	UE									13.0	8.2
EFTA									1.0	0.8	AELE									1.9	0.4
East Europe									7.8	5.2	Europe de l'Est									7.1	8.8
Other Europe									0.0		Autre de l'Europe									0.0	0.0
Former USSR									70.7	68.9	Ancienne URSS									65.6	74.5
Oceania									0.0	0.0	Océanie									0.1	0.0
Russian Federation									61.5	50.8	Russian Federation									47.9	53.2
Ukraine									4.7	12.8	Ukraine									8.9	8.8
Germany/Allemagne									8.6	8.7	Poland/Pologne									4.9	5.9
Poland/Pologne									4.1	2.8	Germany/Allemagne									6.4	3.6
Lithuania/Lituanie									1.8	2.2	Latvia/Lettonie									2.0	4.4
USA/Etats–Unis d'Amer									1.7	2.2	Lithuania/Lituanie									3.4	3.1
Italy/Italie									1.7	1.6	Netherlands/Pays–Bas									1.7	1.2
Netherlands/Pays–Bas									1.6	1.7	USA/Etats–Unis d'Amer									1.6	1.1
United Kingdom									0.8	1.4	Kazakhstan									1.0	1.6
Hungary/Hongrie									1.5	0.7	Egypt/Egypte									1.1	1.4

4. General Imports C.I.F. by Commodities according to the S.I.T.C. (Rev. 2) in thousand U.S. Dollars
Importations Générales C.A.F. par Produits d'après la C.T.C.I. (Rév. 2) en milliers de Dollars E.U.

SITC CTCI	COMMODITY	1993		1994		1995		1996		PRODUIT
		WEIGHT POIDS	VALUE VALEUR	WEIGHT POIDS	VALUE VALEUR	WEIGHT POIDS	VALUE VALEUR	WEIGHT POIDS	VALUE VALEUR	
	ALL COMMODITIES						4795212		6939288	TOUS PRODUITS

5. General Exports F.O.B. by Commodities according to the S.I.T.C. (Rev. 2) in thousand U.S. Dollars
Exportations Générales F.O.B. par Produits d'après la C.T.C.I. (Rév. 2) en milliers de Dollars E.U.

SITC CTCI	COMMODITY	1993		1994		1995		1996		PRODUIT
		WEIGHT POIDS	VALUE VALEUR	WEIGHT POIDS	VALUE VALEUR	WEIGHT POIDS	VALUE VALEUR	WEIGHT POIDS	VALUE VALEUR	
	ALL COMMODITIES						4362974		5462675	TOUS PRODUITS

1. HISTORICAL SERIES, 1961–1996 SPECIAL TRADE, IMPORTS C.I.F., EXPORTS F.O.B.
SERIES HISTORIQUES, 1961–1996 COMMERCE SPECIAL, IMPORTATIONS C.A.F., EXPORTATIONS F.O.B

YEAR ANNEE	VALUE IN MILLION BELGIAN FRANCS VALEUR EN MILLION BELGIAN FRANCS MERCHANDISE –MARCHANDISE		GOLD –OR		CONVERSION FACTORS U.S. CENTS PER BELGIAN FRANC FACTEURS DE CONVERSION CENTS E.U. PAR BELGIAN FRANC		INDEX NUMBERS –INDICES QUANTUM		UNIT VALUE VALEUR UNITAIRE	
	IMPORTS	EXPORTS	IMPORTS	EXPORTS	IMPORTS	EXPORTS	IMPORTS	EXPORTS	IMPORTS	EXPORTS
1961	211162.00	196500.00	1488.00	458.00	2.0000	2.0000	28	25	70	66
1962	228435.00	216613.00	1030.00	650.00	2.0000	2.0000	30	28	69	65
1963	256421.00	242012.00	1139.00	741.00	2.0000	2.0000	34	31	69	65
1964	296511.00	280028.00	1372.00	369.00	2.0000	2.0000	39	35	70	66
1965	325074.00	319684.00	3087.00	290.00	2.0000	2.0000	43	40	69	66
1966	359104.00	341578.00	2367.00	407.00	2.0000	2.0000	47	42	70	68
1967	364337.00	354132.00	3237.00	362.00	2.0000	2.0000	48	44	69	68
1968	419758.00	408559.00	2723.00	1358.00	2.0000	2.0000	55	51	69	67
1969	501053.00	504466.00	3881.00	1806.00	2.0000	2.0000	64	61	71	70
1970	570647.00	579981.00	1176.00	615.00	2.0000	2.0000	40	38	35	39
1971	629063.00	620238.00	1235.00	1131.00	2.0505	2.0525	43	42	36	38
1972	681773.00	710980.00	779.00	1633.00	2.2719	2.2717	47	47	36	39
1973	856129.00	870245.00	2310.00	2305.00	2.5785	2.5804	55	53	39	42
1974	1160685.00	1099825.00	10030.00	5280.00	2.5740	2.5758	56	54	51	53
1975	1130945.00	1056879.00			2.7225	2.7254	53	50	52	55
1976	1368961.00	1266457.00			2.5940	2.5969	60	57	56	58
1977	1447981.00	1344704.00			2.7913	2.7918	63	60	57	58
1978	1526044.00	1410258.00			3.1855	3.1882	65	62	58	59
1979	1784353.00	1661224.00			3.4140	3.4135	69	65	64	66
1980	2100807.00	1890359.00			3.4213	3.4207	70	67	74	73
1981	2309761.00	2062316.00			2.7044	2.7011	67	67	85	80
1982	2653362.00	2393153.00			2.1949	2.1881	68	68	96	91
1983	2820865.00	2651341.00			1.9609	1.9590	67	71	104	97
1984	3195769.00	2992116.00			1.7305	1.7305	71	74	112	104
1985	3317812.00	3167691.00			1.6942	1.6971	73	77	112	106
1986	3065200.00	3070299.00			2.2422	2.2460	80	83	94	96
1987	3110099.00	3100100.00			2.6864	2.6873	88	89	88	90
1988	3393600.00	3382299.00			2.7243	2.7245	88	90	94	98
1989	3883899.00	3943099.00			2.5386	2.5385	94	94	102	106
1990	4011600.00	3944499.00			2.9994	2.9998	100	100	100	100
1991	4116300.00	4023399.00			2.9410	2.9417	104	104	99	98
1992	4023300.00	3969799.00			3.1107	3.1126	105	104	95	97
1993	3875000.00	4128999.00			2.8968	2.8947	106	111	91	95
1994	4192000.00	4579000.00			2.9971	2.9979	115	123	91	94
1995	4568399.00	4996100.00			3.3953	3.3951			97	92
1996	4729098.00	5133099.00			3.2307	3.2301			98	93

2. IMPORTS BY BROAD ECONOMIC CATEGORY AND EXPORTS BY INDUSTRIAL ORIGIN. (PERCENTAGE OF TOTAL VALUE)
IMPORTATIONS PAR CATEGORIES ECONOMIQUES ET EXPORTATIONS PAR BRANCHE D'ACTIVITE.(EN POURCENTAGE DE LA VALEUR TOTALE)

IMPORTS – IMPORTATIONS

	1990	1991	1992	1993	1994	1995	1996
TOTAL IMPORTS–IMPORTATIONS TOTALES	100.	100.	100.	100.	100.	100.	100.
1 FOOD BEV–ALIMENTATION BOISSONS	8.4	9.0	9.4	9.5	9.6	9.7	9.0
11 PRIMARY–PRODUITS DE BASE	4.3	4.4	4.4	4.3	4.4	4.2	4.3
111 FOR INDUSTRY–POUR L'INDUSTRIE	2.0	2.2	2.1	1.9	1.9	1.9	1.7
112 FOR HOUSEHOLDS–POUR LES MENAGES	2.2	2.3	2.3	2.4	2.5	2.4	2.6
12 PROCESSED–PRODUITS ELABORES	4.2	4.6	5.0	5.2	5.1	5.4	4.7
121 FOR INDUSTRY–POUR L'INDUSTRIE	0.5	0.5	0.5	0.6	0.6	0.6	0.6
122 FOR HOUSEHOLDS–POUR LES MENAGES	3.7	4.1	4.5	4.6	4.5	4.8	4.1
2 IND SUPPLIES–APPROV INDUSTRIELS	38.7	36.8	36.5	37.8	38.8	39.3	38.4
21 PRIMARY–PRODUITS DE BASE	10.8	10.0	9.7	11.0	11.1	10.6	11.0
22 PROCESSED–PRODUITS ELABORES	27.9	26.8	26.8	26.9	27.7	28.8	27.4
3 FUELS–COMBUSTIBLES	8.0	8.3	7.6	7.4	6.8	6.1	7.0
31 PRIMARY–PRODUITS DE BASE	4.9	5.5	5.0	4.6	4.0	3.6	4.4
32 PROCESSED–PRODUITS ELABORES	3.0	2.9	2.6	2.8	2.8	2.5	2.6
321 MOTOR SPIRIT–ESSENCE	0.6	0.6	0.6	0.6	0.6	0.7	0.9
322 OTHER–AUTRES	2.4	2.3	2.0	2.2	2.2	1.8	1.8
4 MACHINERY–EQUIPEMENT	14.1	13.9	14.3	12.5	12.9	13.4	14.1
41 CAPITAL EQUIPMENT–MACHINES	11.5	11.3	11.6	10.3	10.5	10.8	11.1
42 PARTS–PIECES ACCESSOIRES	2.6	2.6	2.7	2.1	2.4	2.6	3.0
5 TRANSPORT–TRANSPORT	12.0	12.8	12.1	12.9	12.9	13.3	14.5
51 PASSENGER CARS–AUTOMOBILES	4.9	5.4	5.0	5.3	5.4	5.0	5.8
52 OTHER–AUTRES	2.0	2.4	1.7	1.3	1.4	1.6	1.6
521 INDUSTRIAL–INDUSTRIELS	1.8	2.2	1.5	1.6	1.2	1.4	1.5
522 NON INDUSTRIAL–NON INDUSTRIEL	0.1	0.2	0.2	0.2	0.2	0.2	0.2
53 PARTS–PIECES ACCESSOIRES	5.1	4.9	5.4	5.9	6.1	6.7	7.0
6 CONSUM GOODS–BIENS CONSOMMATION	12.9	13.4	14.1	14.6	13.9	13.0	13.2
61 DURABLE–DURABLES	3.3	3.4	3.5	3.5	3.3	3.1	3.1
62 SEMI DURABLE–SEMI DURABLES	6.7	7.1	7.6	7.8	7.2	6.8	6.9
63 NON DURABLE–NON DURABLES	2.8	2.9	3.1	3.3	3.4	3.1	3.1
7 GOODS NES–BIENS NDA	6.0	5.7	6.0	5.3	5.2	5.1	3.9

EXPORTS – EXPORTATIONS

	1990	1991	1992	1993	1994	1995	1996
TOTAL EXPORTS–EXPORTATIONS TOTALES	100.	100.	100.	100.	100.	100.	100.
1 AGRICULTURE	2.5	2.6	2.6	2.6	2.8	2.3	2.0
2 MINING QUARRY–INDUS EXTRACTIVES	7.2	7.1	6.8	7.7	7.5	7.1	7.8
3 MANUFACTURING–IND MANUFACTUR	90.3	90.3	90.6	89.7	89.7	90.6	90.2
31 FOOD BEV TOBACCO–ALIM BOISS TAB	7.8	8.5	9.1	9.0	8.6	8.7	8.4
32 TEXTILES–INDUSTRIES TEXTILES	7.5	7.5	7.5	7.3	6.8	6.6	6.9
33 WOOD & PRODUCTS–BOIS & PRODUITS	0.9	0.9	0.9	0.8	0.8	0.8	0.8
34 PAPER & PRODUCTS–PAPIER & PRODT	2.7	2.7	2.6	2.4	2.5	2.8	2.5
35 CHEMICALS–INDUSTRIES CHIMIQUES	20.4	21.0	21.4	22.0	23.1	22.0	22.4
36 NON METAL MIN–MIN NON METAL	2.4	2.2	2.4	2.3	2.3	2.2	2.0
37 BASIC METAL–IND METAL BASE	11.6	10.3	9.2	8.2	8.6	8.9	7.7
38 METAL MANUF–MANUF METAL	32.1	32.0	32.4	32.6	33.1	32.4	33.4
39 OTH MANUF IND–AUTRES MANUF	4.8	5.0	5.1	5.1	4.0	6.3	6.0

3. TRADE BY PRINCIPAL COUNTRIES OF PRODUCTION AND LAST CONSIGNMENT (VALUE IN THOUSAND U.S. DOLLARS)
ECHANGES SELON LES PRINCIPAUX PAYS DE PRODUCTION ET DE DERNIERE CONSIGNATION (VALEUR EN MILLIERS DE DOLLARS EU)

COUNTRIES–PAYS	SPECIAL IMPORTS C.I.F. IMPORTATIONS SPECIALES C.A.F					COUNTRIES–PAYS	SPECIAL EXPORTS F.O.B. EXPORTATIONS SPECIALES F.O.B.				
	1992	1993	1994	1995	1996		1992	1993	1994	1995	1996
World	125122093	111305866	125615616	153388375	149072935	Monde	123459924	120861926	137269874	168153671	162265643
Africa	4848207	3878193	4066752	5304409	5419376	Afrique	2798293	2639730	2829349	3433377	3243899
Americas	7858896	7948034	9330992	11890214	12565019	Amériques	6252179	7441664	9041951	8983430	9086431
Northern America	6069756	6435763	7381253	9603494	10053342	Amérique du Nord	5131967	6165968	7456087	6734583	7376781
LAIA	1576219	1265361	1676917	1966015	1984409	ALAI	935857	1014459	1355720	1928290	1505034
CACM	52173	48039	67838	70720	231697	MCAC	41433	64626	62994	60867	57441
Caribbean	120667	153191	167685	228497	262667	Caraïbes	111995	153651	117795	204251	109320
Rest of America	40080	45679	37299	21488	32903	Autre Amérique	30928	42959	49354	55439	37854
As.ex F.USSR	9807619	9113296	10388725	11834547	11750866	Asie l'URSS exclus	11365492	12950149	14298972	16209488	15699627
Eur.x F.USSR	100737368	88479088	98490017	120382250	115814570	Europe l'URSS exclus	101232464	96020208	108822908	127174014	122327755
EU	96047502	84740460	94256029	115229059	111002409	UE	96479933	91342008	103341431	120830908	115816056
EFTA	3686822	2894112	2894251	3325403	2994532	AELE	3328644	3128530	3494315	3669153	3464998
East Europe	811409	707116	1174609	1594477	1584158	Europe de l'Est	1202918	1333886	1697617	2313594	2589252
Other Europe	27633	40881	36177	82102	87243	Autre de l'Europe	47480	43207	46091	59126	60596
Former USSR	1239734	1284115	1726085	1725526	1567947	Ancienne URSS	541664	756137	1033378	1450446	1842360
Oceania	531528	406063	457601	515847	635520	Océanie	426094	470645	597448	722597	675589
Germany/Allemagne	29899921	23962780	25331705	32001785	29184128	Germany/Allemagne	28209777	25358556	28773372	34715767	31704449
Netherlands/Pays–Bas	21908640	19780444	22146927	27160413	27435265	France, Monac	23772987	23024223	26068322	29229861	27323684
France, Monac	20605276	17957992	20177952	23486817	21846369	Netherlands/Pays–Bas	16861554	15852316	18069487	21499407	20683457
United Kingdom	9629479	10330278	11806359	13540807	13772208	United Kingdom	9690398	10238501	11605100	13179769	14227122
USA/Etats–Unis d'Amer	5493822	5973392	6639688	8576912	9215448	Italy/Italie	7274129	6608585	7084223	8532226	8223454
Italy/Italie	5623605	4899523	5381243	6544449	6158136	USA/Etats–Unis d'Amer	4763199	5707971	6887567	6248827	6909650
Japan/Japon	2793562	3064546	3383028	3945483	3320938	Spain/Espagne	3483643	3484037	4148390	4680795	4737349
Sweden/Suède	2515724	2049851	2877149	4043394	4049117	Switz.Liecht	2728930	2549326	2838210	2973012	2810266
Spain/Espagne	2004562	1847466	2094762	2694108	2761965	Israel/Israël	2298487	2344807	2647904	2838705	2910258
Switz.Liecht	2174859	2161117	1977521	2154611	1971586	India/Inde	1411107	1837879	1863024	2580566	2433634
Ireland/Irlande	813145	1177163	1292345	1745883	2146242	Sweden/Suède	1718925	1509512	1820557	2297243	2196808
Russian Federation	1065933	1127633	1431350	1346600	1205517	Japan/Japon	1277900	1360728	1805677	2178925	2053580
Norway, SVD, JM	1484668	709120	889565	1134634	997424	Austria/Autriche	1633066	1396169	1427308	1671234	1642787
Israel/Israël	779686	918458	929396	1085789	1239207	Denmark/Danemark	1120417	1124864	1276917	1535187	1418629
China/Chine	396113	429274	1199568	1325530	1498995	Hong Kong	910221	1008432	1203998	1179110	1228568
India/Inde	630850	787419	940627	1117083	1186053	Portugal	970949	1071103	1115325	1178111	1187691
Finland/Finlande	635736	573499	801232	1243149	946830	Russian Federation	447849	579479	752916	1041798	1260616
Denmark/Danemark	839977	686768	789017	997182	863448	Greece/Grèce	745256	717379	810423	872569	932760
Austria/Autriche	893151	741647	755606	870529	872413	Turkey/Turquie	509620	686020	546331	922421	1128105
So. Africa Customs Un	801259	653152	625995	819060	851708	Poland/Pologne	513636	554914	655969	926554	1107197
Canada	574695	462343	741370	1026407	837678	China/Chine	439057	711619	929090	903068	697628
Brazil/Brésil	672781	486481	623722	762151	753858	Saudi Arabia	943282	766051	649854	555703	506957
Portugal	516175	578811	645553	708058	788597	Finland/Finlande	576816	518633	574371	826494	904384
Dem. Rep. of the Congo	635157	419074	651519	692216	699266	Thailand/Thaïlande	401951	586719	651174	824056	811963
Thailand/Thaïlande	402346	587160	654933	681107	712530	Norway, SVD, JM	574989	556473	632023	663385	621653
Hong Kong	629960	847479	274673	344160	313012	Ireland/Irlande	422016	438130	567635	612245	633483
Algeria/Algérie	536961	474362	387258	475482	452056	Singapore/Singapour	387328	464998	558553	581856	526109
Liberia/Libéria	315362	291362	316988	759446	526266	So. Africa Customs Un	372764	385467	545527	549492	548582
Poland/Pologne	335578	270638	434338	571640	506236	Australia/Australie	339583	382200	477219	595992	544805
Congo	337126	326837	248688	436226	608862	Canada	367843	452874	565517	482992	465779
Indonesia/Indonésie	256311	269358	400120	407387	517273	Brazil/Brésil	161215	222984	375646	969430	576868
Malaysia/Malaisie	244723	273970	375088	495756	454005	Korea, Republic of	331130	425528	520956	493617	509177
Australia/Australie	421136	298281	316364	349506	441231	Czech Republic		283059	429349	553833	635613
Turkey/Turquie	251945	238781	310141	381347	397755	Hungary/Hongrie	264492	319160	383855	421830	447464
Korea, Republic of	275891	235254	293344	352221	369817	Tunisia/Tunisie	317097	283007	293620	373948	359522
Tunisia/Tunisie	272569	225633	251228	365529	408288	Algeria/Algérie	308509	277307	314838	313616	265219
Hungary/Hongrie	196304	181862	264392	396975	405801	Mexico/Mexique	324491	286793	363886	183651	264549
Mexico/Mexique	277284	205143	260540	355115	321476	Iran (Islamic Rp. of)	381155	299210	268503	251796	217694
Argentina/Argentine	211549	220564	289681	251818	349401	Malaysia/Malaisie	222476	215403	294164	313336	316607
Iran (Islamic Rp. of)	1036597	35188	76039	65505	97245	Indonesia/Indonésie	216915	290350	228743	328308	292640
Singapore/Singapour	214027	353361	244576	240625	198551	United Arab Emirates	216203	297566	256892	284141	248525
Saudi Arabia	729455	57294	110063	99389	70648	Egypt/Egypte	172300	236817	274797	286138	249955
Czech Republic		124646	230871	298104	369362	Morocco/Maroc	224571	187838	207631	316229	259218
Cote d'Ivoire	168613	167555	153379	201626	294299	Lebanon/Liban	123159	138932	168130	218029	225868
Morocco/Maroc	191029	133035	184327	209707	244608	Argentina/Argentine	98347	129384	191031	219339	233458
Angola	296290	136057	110285	158213	239652	Dem. Rep. of the Congo	159780	126075	140208	190506	204060
Greece/Grèce	162114	154238	156180	192487	177691	Nigeria/Nigéria	212502	157788	112165	132594	122499
Sri Lanka	132495	169332	145812	182683	190313	Syrian Arab Republic	113050	133533	145735	171515	143557
New Zealand	98607	95222	121516	148685	182502	Chile/Chili	93640	129532	141544	178825	147407
Pakistan	83213	97791	142529	136616	141206	Libyan Arab Jamahiriya	96583	151909	91861	169595	165893

(VALUE AS PERCENTAGE OF WORLD TOTAL)(VALEURS EN POURCENTAGE DU TOTAL MONDIAL)

	1987	1988	1989	1990	1991	1992	1993	1994	1995	1996		1987	1988	1989	1990	1991	1992	1993	1994	1995	1996
Africa	4.1	4.1	4.7	4.0	3.8	3.9	3.5	3.2	3.5	3.6	Afrique	2.5	2.4	2.5	2.5	2.4	2.3	2.2	2.1	2.0	2.0
Americas	7.1	6.7	7.1	6.7	6.9	6.3	7.1	7.4	7.8	8.4	Amériques	6.6	6.2	6.1	5.5	5.0	5.1	6.2	6.6	5.3	5.6
Northern America	5.4	5.0	5.3	5.0	5.3	4.9	5.8	5.9	6.3	6.7	Amérique du Nord	5.7	5.4	5.3	4.8	4.1	4.2	5.1	5.4	4.0	4.5
LAIA	1.5	1.6	1.6	1.5	1.4	1.3	1.1	1.3	1.3	1.3	ALAI	0.7	0.6	0.6	0.6	0.7	0.8	0.8	1.0	1.1	0.9
CACM	0.1	0.0	0.0	0.0	0.0	0.0	0.0	0.1	0.0	0.2	MCAC	0.0	0.0	0.0	0.0	0.0	0.0	0.1	0.0	0.0	0.0
Caribbean	0.1	0.1	0.1	0.1	0.1	0.1	0.1	0.1	0.1	0.2	Caraïbes	0.1	0.1	0.1	0.1	0.1	0.1	0.1	0.1	0.1	0.1
Rest of America	0.0	0.0	0.0	0.0	0.0	0.0	0.0	0.0	0.0	0.0	Autre Amérique	0.0	0.0	0.0	0.0	0.0	0.0	0.0	0.0	0.0	0.0
As.ex F.USSR	7.3	7.5	8.2	7.3	7.8	7.8	8.2	8.3	7.7	7.9	Asie l'URSS exclus	8.0	8.6	9.0	8.5	9.1	9.2	10.7	10.4	9.6	9.7
Eur.x F.USSR	79.3	79.7	78.0	80.2	80.0	80.5	79.5	78.4	78.5	77.7	Europe l'URSS exclus	81.3	81.4	80.7	81.9	82.0	82.0	79.4	79.3	75.6	75.4
EU	75.9	76.4	74.8	76.8	76.5	76.8	76.1	75.0	75.1	74.5	UE	77.4	77.6	76.9	78.5	78.3	78.1	75.6	75.3	71.9	71.4
EFTA	2.6	2.4	2.5	2.6	2.8	2.9	2.6	2.3	2.2	2.0	AELE	3.0	2.9	2.9	2.6	2.6	2.7	2.6	2.5	2.2	2.1
East Europe	0.7	0.7	0.6	0.6	0.6	0.6	0.6	0.9	1.0	1.1	Europe de l'Est	0.7	0.7	0.7	0.6	0.8	1.0	1.1	1.2	1.4	1.6
Other Europe	0.1	0.2	0.2	0.2	0.2	0.0	0.0	0.0	0.1	0.1	Autre de l'Europe	0.2	0.2	0.3	0.3	0.2	0.0	0.0	0.0	0.0	0.0
Former USSR	1.5	1.4	1.2	1.2	1.1	1.0	1.2	1.4	1.1	1.1	Ancienne URSS	0.6	0.5	0.5	0.4	0.4	0.4	0.6	0.8	0.9	1.1
Oceania	0.5	0.6	0.7	0.5	0.4	0.4	0.4	0.4	0.3	0.4	Océanie	0.4	0.4	0.4	0.4	0.3	0.3	0.4	0.4	0.4	0.4
Germany/Allemagne	24.3	24.5	23.5	23.9	23.5	23.9	21.5	20.2	20.9	19.6	Germany/Allemagne	19.8	19.6	18.9	21.2	23.7	22.8	21.0	21.0	20.6	19.5
Netherlands/Pays–Bas	17.2	17.8	17.6	17.6	17.2	17.5	17.8	17.6	17.7	18.4	France, Monac	20.5	19.9	20.4	20.2	19.1	19.3	19.1	19.0	17.4	16.8
France, Monac	15.7	15.1	14.9	15.9	15.8	16.5	16.1	16.1	15.3	14.7	Netherlands/Pays–Bas	15.0	14.9	13.7	13.6	13.7	13.7	13.1	13.2	12.8	12.7
United Kingdom	7.8	7.7	7.9	8.3	8.4	7.7	9.3	9.4	8.8	9.2	United Kingdom	8.4	9.4	9.4	8.7	7.7	7.8	8.5	8.5	7.8	8.8
USA/Etats–Unis d'Amer	4.7	4.3	4.6	4.5	4.8	4.4	5.4	5.3	5.6	6.2	Italy/Italie	6.4	6.1	6.4	6.6	6.0	5.9	5.5	5.2	5.1	5.1
Italy/Italie	4.3	4.3	4.2	4.5	4.5	4.5	4.4	4.3	4.3	4.1	USA/Etats–Unis d'Amer	5.2	4.9	4.8	4.3	3.8	3.9	4.7	5.0	3.7	4.3
Japan/Japon	2.7	2.3	2.3	2.1	2.2	2.2	2.8	2.7	2.6	2.2	Spain/Espagne	1.9	2.2	2.4	2.4	2.6	2.8	2.9	3.0	2.8	2.9
Sweden/Suède	2.3	2.2	2.1	2.2	2.4	2.0	1.8	2.3	2.6	2.7	Switz.Liecht	2.3	2.3	2.3	2.1	2.2	2.2	2.1	2.1	1.8	1.7
Spain/Espagne	1.2	1.5	1.4	1.3	1.5	1.6	1.7	1.7	1.8	1.9	Israel/Israël	1.5	1.6	1.5	1.5	1.6	1.9	1.9	1.9	1.7	1.8
Switz.Liecht	1.9	1.8	1.6	1.6	1.5	1.7	1.9	1.6	1.4	1.3	India/Inde	1.2	1.6	1.6	1.2	1.2	1.1	1.5	1.4	1.5	1.5

4. Special Imports C.I.F. by Commodities according to the S.I.T.C. (Rev. 2) in thousand U.S. Dollars
Importations Spéciales C.A.F. par Produits d'après la C.T.C.I. (Rév. 2) en milliers de Dollars E.U.

SITC CTCI	COMMODITY	1993 WEIGHT POIDS	1993 VALUE VALEUR	1994 WEIGHT POIDS	1994 VALUE VALEUR	1995 WEIGHT POIDS	1995 VALUE VALEUR	1996 WEIGHT POIDS	1996 VALUE VALEUR	PRODUIT
	ALL COMMODITIES		111305866		125615616		153388375		149072935	TOUS PRODUITS
0	FOOD AND LIVE ANIMALS		9811189		11081964		13756002		12465302	ALIMENTS,ANIMAUX VIVANTS
001	*LIVE ANIMALS FOR FOOD	W 228920	351803	W 248812	407152	W 230362	385429	W 218257	349586	ANIMAUX VIVANTS
01	MEAT AND PREPARATIONS		858171		941526		1057311		1068504	VIANDES ET PREPARATIONS
011	MEAT FRESH,CHILLD,FROZEN	W 266122	683660	W 287689	746398	W 281973	809168	W 289872	812918	VIANDES FRAICHES,REF,CONGE
02	DAIRY PRODCTS,BIRDS'EGGS		1947637		1988061		2835382		2182219	PRODUITS LAITIERS,OEUFS
022	MILK AND CREAM	W 668383	782839	W 687728	804990	W 951946	1456737	W 805227	944837	LAIT ET CREME
0223	MILK AND CREAM FRESH	W 458974	382336	W 496381	442780	W 616318	582703	W 588879	547197	LAIT,CREME FRAIS
0224	MILK,CREAM PRESERVED ETC	W 209409	400503	W 191347	362211	W 335628	874034	W 216349	397640	LAIT,CREME CONS,CONC
02243	MILK DRY,OVER 1.5% FAT	W 69971	204225	W 66043	200178	W 135334	484504	W 66052	197588	LAIT POUDRE SUP 1.5%
023	BUTTER	W 110697	367691	W 113839	362430	W 108655	476648	W 96914	382415	BEURRE
024	CHEESE AND CURD	W 178210	740332	W 174573	756476	W 176035	842026	W 176834	790378	FROMAGE ET CAILLEBOTTE
03	FISH AND PREPARATIONS		702939		808235		925097		827672	POISSONS ET PREPARATIONS
04	CEREALS AND PREPARATIONS		1765306		1763017		2286586		2205131	CEREALES ET PRODUITS
041	WHEAT ETC UNMILLED	W 2125197	441286	W 1895057	365882	W 2818671	583427	W 2706880	542515	FROMENT,EPEAUTRE
0412	OTHER WHEAT ETC UNMILLED	W 1927989	393546	W 1558647	292787	W 2395145	475304	W 2262171	435864	AUTRE FROMENT NON MOULU
048	CEREAL ETC PREPARATIONS	W 429787	542732	W 489835	609318	W 515546	728612	W 490887	706576	PREPTNS A BASE CEREALES
05	VEGETABLES AND FRUIT		1833957		2217738		2556484		2853355	LEGUMES ET FRUITS
054	VEG ETC FRSH,SMPLY PRSVD	W 2578160	718964	W 2879218	812268	W 2609575	963533	W 2749113	868445	LEGUMES FRAIS,CONG,SECS
057	FRUIT,NUTS,FRESH,DRIED	W 827206	651444	W 928239	825017	W 808501	885699	W 1345884	1246516	FRUITS FRAIS OU SECS
058	FRUIT PRESERVED,PREPARED	W 292531	322320	W 365389	372399	W 420952	467731	W 515164	540157	CONSERVES DE FRUITS
06	SUGAR AND PREPS,HONEY		190382		418948		685867		419079	SUCRES ET PRODUITS
061	SUGAR AND HONEY	W 302833	106478	W 644097	329298	W 900411	568325	W 586351	310571	SUCRES ET MIEL
07	COFFEE,TEA,COCOA,SPICES		731736		967334		1292981		954927	CAFE,THE,CACAO,EPICES
071	COFFEE AND SUBSTITUTES	W 126674	281805	W 129305	421736	W 138173	610714	W 140647	427975	CAFE ET SUCCEDANES
0711	COFFEE GREEN,ROASTED,SUB	W 118779	243893	W 121508	381417	W 130862	560954	W 133215	384688	CAFE TORREFIE OU DECAFEINE
081	*FEEDING STUFF FOR ANIML	W 3838089	909181	W 4092173	983209	W 4161698	1088288	W 4009059	1029098	NOURRITURE POUR ANIMAUX
0819	FOOD WASTE AND FEED NES	W 1577685	503801	W 1615326	532441	W 1720562	638443	W 1721557	547596	DECHETS,ALIMENTS NDA
08199	FODDER NES,INCL SWEETNED	W 764515	411670	W 793922	435052	W 825818	517090	W 848795	437909	PREPARATIONS FOURRAGERES
09	MISC EDIBLE PRODUCTS		520077		586745		642577		575732	PREP ALIMENTAIRES DIVERSES
098	EDIBLE PRODCTS,PREPS NES	W 239627	470706	W 206931	507145	W 217820	570221	W 213463	504414	PREP ALIMENTAIRES NDA
1	BEVERAGES AND TOBACCO		1584908		1629296		1912740		1698631	BOISSONS ET TABACS
11	BEVERAGES		1228429		1236642		1459879		1248718	BOISSONS
112	ALCOHOLIC BEVERAGES	W 504638	939228	W 357609	899733	W 364458	1054040	W 360378	914770	BOISSONS ALCOOLIQUES
1121	WINE OF FRESH GRAPES ETC	W 410353	680336	W 254743	648319	W 255792	772700	W 243600	674182	VINS DE RAISINS FRAIS
11212	WINE OF FRESH GRAPES	W 386309	648821	W 232578	619662	W 231868	736618	W 217665	635312	VINS DE MOUTS DE RAISINS
12	TOBACCO AND MANUFACTURES		356479		392654		452860		449913	TABACS BRUTS FABRIQUES
2	CRUDE MATERLS,EXCL FUELS		5028351		6434594		7758548		6648751	MAT BRUTES NON COMESTIBLES
22	OIL SEEDS,OLEAGINOUS FRT		484253		649885		694622		669140	GRAINES,FRUITS OLEAGINEUX
222	SEEDS FOR'SOFT'FIXED OIL		443952		587236	W 2221086	622831	W 1973413	577002	GRAINES HUILES FIXES
23	RUBBER, CRUDE		370261		383667		540060		475433	CAOUTCHOUC BRUT
24	CORK AND WOOD		702130		819208		916221		751709	LIEGE ET BOIS
248	WOOD SHAPED,SLEEPERS	W 1063014	534981	W 1118779	601167	W 1143306	669196	W 1198848	565671	BOIS SIMPLEMENT TRAVAILLES
251	*PULP AND WASTE PAPER	W 545152	195316	W 647982	295560	W 703054	476616	W 751429	314996	PATES A PAPIER,DECHETS
26	TEXTILE FIBRES AND WASTE		478835		661990		691980		603453	FIBRES TEXTILES
27	CRUDE FERTLZR,MINRLS NES		714233		864802		893432		844440	ENGRAIS MINERAUX BRUTS
28	METALLIFEROUS ORES,SCRAP		1663414		2259329		2985017		2454603	MINERAIS METAL,DECHETS
281	IRON ORE,CONCENTRATES	MW 15766	340028	MW 17011	395372	MW 15331	398349	MW 12863	329087	MINERAIS DE FER
282	IRON AND STEEL SCRAP	W 2424474	319082	W 2990241	520600	W 3741418	835886	W 3810693	549958	FERRAILLES
287	BASE METAL ORES,CONC NES	W 818848	324849	W 974448	469600	W 956678	645193	W 1816437	632277	MINERAIS METAUX COMMUNS
288	NONFERR METAL SCRAP NES	W 647130	547954	W 746757	672206	W 724133	881270	W 678843	686436	DECHETS NON FERREUX
2882	OTHER BASE MTL SCRAP NES	W 389151	344793	W 466608	470599	W 431614	632148	W 353164	440525	AUTRES DECHETS
29	CRUDE ANIMAL,VEG MAT NES		351595		407720		469109		450576	MATIERES BRUTES ANIM,VEGET
3	MINERAL FUELS ETC		8374076		8641267		9489595		10685077	COMBUSTIBLES MINERAUX LUB
32	COAL,COKE AND BRIQUETTES		895224		965423		993650		846261	HOUILLES,COKES,BRIQUETTES
322	COAL,LIGNITE AND PEAT	MW 12968	693583	MW 13870	742320	MW 13745	777836	MW 12623	713525	HOUILLES,LIGNITES,TOURBE
3222	OTH COAL,NOT AGGLOMERATD	MW 11254	550599	MW 12392	608160	MW 12036	627570	MW 11102	571698	AUTRES HOUILLES
33	PETROLEUM AND PRODUCTS		5763164		5999486		6577712		7743084	PETROLE ET DERIVES
333	CRUDE PETROLEUM	MW 27064	3090931	MW 26349	3032220	MW 25797	3285904	MW 27320	4038701	HUILES BRUTES DE PETROLE
334	PETROLEUM PRODUCTS,REFIN	MW 16486	2507579	MW 18863	2793470	MW 18463	3102171	MW 18617	3498089	PRODUITS RAFFINES
3341	GASOLINE,OTH LIGHT OILS	W 3655299	629268	W 4559186	759279	W 6015786	1088308	W 6229656	1272618	ESSENCES POUR MOTEURS
33419	OTH LIGHT PETROLEUM OILS	W 2103375	358205	W 3250352	534639	W 4682058	841555	W 4110306	840849	AUTRES HUILES LEGERES
3343	GAS OILS	W 6028158	980313	W 6640029	996643	W 6510560	1042210			GAS OILS
3344	FUEL OILS,NES	W 5649392	515510	W 6595288	635838	W 4743855	505164	W 4681077	529105	FUEL OILS
3345	LUBS,PETROLEUM OILS NES	W 591687	278369	W 656924	319833	W 647866	353839	W 7263138	1594761	HUILES LUBRIFIANTES
33451	LUBS(HIGH PETR CONT) ETC	W 574491	231520	W 634296	264644	W 628268	293928	W 7242964	1532476	HUILES LUBRIF,H LOURDES
341	*GAS,NATURAL AND MANUFCT	MW 10835	1343961	MW 10762	1231966	MW 11505	1468204	MW 11672	1792053	GAZ NATUREL,GAZ MANUFACT
3413	PETROLM GASES,LIQUEFIED	W 4545054	622513	W 4111044	522077	W 4439551	629191	W 4222300	649486	GAZ DE PETROLE LIQUEFIE
34139	OTH HYDROCARBON GAS LQFD	W 3941554	524227	W 3540722	438218	W 3954384	533175	W 3749890	557008	HYDROCARBURES GAZEUX NDA
3414	PETROLEUM GASES, GASEOUS	W 6289198	720998	W 6626042	705415	W 7058438	832352	W 7447787	1136781	GAZ DE PETROLE GAZEUX
351	*ELECTRIC CURRENT	MH 9302	371727	MH 11817	444391		450028		303678	ENERGIE ELECTRIQUE
4	ANIMAL,VEGETABLE OIL,FAT		428775		606460		742210		660744	HUILES,GRAISSES ANIM,VEG
5	CHEMCLS,RELATED PROD NES		14220769		16282981		20596979		20304007	PRODUITS CHIMIQUES
51	ORGANIC CHEMICALS		4332604		4999585		6295674		6490114	PROD CHIMIQ ORGANIQUES
511	HYDROCARBONS NES,DERIVS	W 4347268	1393621	W 3926201	1640025	W 3290840	1727181	W 3639235	1547557	HYDROCARBURES NDA
5111	ACYCLIC HYDROCARBONS	W 1821709	625548	W 1662623	587493	W 1520920	766065	W 1528917	676425	HYDROCARBURES ACYCLIQUES
51111	ETHYLENE	W 1224191	438695	W 1065813	388797	W 958558	490216	W 970119	448734	ETHYLENE
5112	CYCLIC HYDROCARBONS	W 1265138	449674	W 1530354	639955	W 1623805	784214	W 1994550	729485	HYDROCARBURES CYCLIQUES
512	ALCOHOLS,PHENOLS ETC	W 657987	379067	W 772100	523353	W 666154	573591	W 850737	590403	PHENOLS,PHENOLS–ALCOOLS
513	CARBOXYLIC ACIDS ETC	W 704677	608072	W 749774	737617	W 748049	1029661	W 847761	996600	ACIDES CARBOXYLIQUES
5137	MONOACIDS AND DERIVATIVS	W 416232	310529	W 444465	376928	W 509456	587539	W 556601	566065	ACIDES MONOCARBOXYLIQUES
514	NITROGEN–FNCTN COMPOUNDS	W 297489	781495	W 270312	764240	W 316090	1076565	W 354764	1209268	COMPOSES FONCT AZOTEES
5148	OTH NITROGN–FNCTN CMPNDS	W 120555	381783	W 113129	369609	W 122252	580827	W 131142	588096	AUTRES COMPOSES AZOTES
515	ORG–INORG COMPOUNDS ETC	W 104046	680128	W 128348	762391	W 185779	1209652	W 203896	1536749	COMPOSES ORGANO–MINERAUX
5156	HETEROCYCLIC CMPDS ETC	W 55049	519812	W 65648	567312	W 125106	966115	W 117127	1202732	COMPOSES HETEROCYCLIQUES
51569	OTH HETEROCYC CMPDS,ETC	W 18685	434588	W 26221	492543	W 61317	827271	W 61120	1081924	AUT COMP HETEROCYCLIQUES
516	OTHER ORGANIC CHEMICALS	W 608714	490221	W 652790	571958	W 606502	679025	W 557910	609537	AUTRES PROD ORGANIQUES
52	INORGANIC CHEMICALS		813381		955535		1198295		1036251	PROD CHIM INORGANIQUES
522	INORG ELEMNTS,OXIDES,ETC	W 2001460	417325	W 2452325	493254	W 2423947	635597	W 2530609	559461	ELEMENTS INORGANIQUES
523	OTHR INORG CHEMICALS ETC	W 1045688	359660	W 959275	424834	W 1222161	522278	W 1075121	435360	AUT PRODUITS CHIMIQUES INORG
53	DYES,TANNING,COLOUR PROD		792653		860790		1098281		1042225	PROD TEINTURE,COLORANTS
533	PIGMENTS,PAINTS,ETC	W 228602	533968	W 243182	567859	W 270190	752183	W 272825	726068	PIGMENTS,PEINTURES,VERNIS
541	*MEDICINAL,PHARM PRODUCT		2151668		2569012	MK 60938	3128314		3335797	PROD MEDICINAUX PHARMACEUT
5416	GLYCOSIDES,GLANDS,SERA	K 1634600	266310	K 2398400	334096	K 2097062	404070	K 1743081	465277	HETEROSIDES
5417	MEDICAMENTS		1304033	MK 36435	1673647	MK 46545	1987086	MK 48541	2029792	MEDICAMENTS
54179	— CONTNG OTH SUBSTANCES	MK 25903	1066425	MK 31387	1269409	MK 42047	1555171	MK 43472	1532321	MED CONT AUT SUBSTANCES
55	PERFUME,CLEANING ETC PRD		1076405		1171267		1285122		1197067	PROD POUR PARFUM,TOILETTE
553	PERFUMERY,COSMETICS,ETC	W 84582	542591	W 74030	559500	W 73703	578571	W 69508	517323	PRODUITS DE PARFUMERIE
554	SOAP,CLEANSING ETC PREPS	W 371245	448976	W 421859	519416	W 424180	604328	W 404319	565519	SAVONS,PRODUITS DETERSIFS
5542	WASHING PREPARATIONS ETC	W 333755	374016	W 387558	451046	W 385500	520977	W 364581	485022	PROD ORG TENSIO–ACT NDA
562	*FERTILIZERS,MANUFACTURE	W 3891821	454606	W 3371643	416895	W 3509985	516851	W 3357319	498735	ENGRAIS MANUFACTURES

4. Special Imports C.I.F. by Commodities according to the S.I.T.C. (Rev. 2) in thousand U.S. Dollars
Importations Spéciales C.A.F. par Produits d'après la C.T.C.I. (Rév. 2) en milliers de Dollars E.U.

SITC CTCI	COMMODITY	1993		1994		1995		1996		PRODUIT
		WEIGHT POIDS	VALUE VALEUR	WEIGHT POIDS	VALUE VALEUR	WEIGHT POIDS	VALUE VALEUR	WEIGHT POIDS	VALUE VALEUR	
58	PLASTIC MATERIALS ETC		3092073		3641547		5039484		4690776	MAT PLAST ARTIFICIELLES
582	PROD OF CONDENSATION ETC	W 550048	753755	W 652760	1046660	W 714844	1565297	W 728473	1465852	PROD CONDENS,POLYCOND
5823	ALKYDS,OTHER POLYESTERS	W 146165	248740	W 161835	338204	W 195253	552322	W 200534	450708	ALKYDES ET AUT POLYESTERS
583	POLYMERIZATION ETC PRODS	W 2004095	2211652	W 2147179	2466546	W 2200854	3303785	W 2267375	3057639	PROD POLYMERISATION
5831	POLYETHYLENE	W 725623	547013	W 759853	600578	W 751346	811531	W 754529	698418	POLYETHYLENE
58311	— IN PRIMARY FORMS	W 658621	454170	W 680828	487976	W 653815	648942	W 645255	530671	POLYETHYLENE PRIMAIRES
5832	POLYPROPYLENE	W 439282	356021	W 453779	451662	W 473087	655175	W 489512	582682	POLYPROPYLENE
58321	— IN PRIMARY FORMS	W 387672	221540	W 400397	297350	W 425534	466500	W 437227	395378	POLYPROPYLENE PRIMAIRES
5839	OTH POLYMRZTION ETC PROD	W 330046	657963	W 352920	687736	W 420730	887632	W 442361	926184	AUT PROD POLYMER COPOLYM
59	CHEMICAL MATERIALS NES		1489694		1656444		2021586		1995462	MAT PROD CHIMIQUES NDA
598	MISCEL CHEM PRODUCTS NES	W 870446	1016499	W 825516	1115237	W 876795	1411694	W 934035	1420671	PROD DIV INDUST CHIM NDA
5989	CHEM PRODUCTS,PREPS NES	W 640177	695250	W 638805	837196	W 635225	1044192	W 634538	1007813	PROD PREP CHIMIQUES NDA
59899	OTH CHEM PRODS,PREPS,NES	W 519168	465858	W 517540	570345	W 517974	732496	W 486813	694359	AUT PRODUITS CHIMIQUES NDA
6	BASIC MANUFACTURES		24848255		28464051		34790503		33066188	ART MANUFACTURES
62	RUBBER MANUFACTURES NES		954884		1108806		1297608		1299390	CAOUTCHOUC MANUFACTURE
625	RUBBER TYRES, TUBES ETC	W 148852	615284	W 166180	711396	W 165388	772540	W 158679	718843	PNEUS CAOUTCHOUC VULCANISE
6251	TYRES NEW FOR MOTOR CARS	W 74883	356991	W 81608	407623	W 73478	402284	W 80158	415519	PNEUS POUR VOITURES
63	WOOD,CORK MANUFACTRS NES		604816		654985		761900		698905	OUVRAGES LIEGE ET BOIS
64	PAPER,PAPERBOARD AND MFR		2618458		3027132		4116341		3389235	PAPIERS,CARTONS & OUVRAGES
641	PAPER AND PAPERBOARD	W 2242668	1810131	W 2606002	2156457	W 2765422	3016011	W 2586757	2424859	PAPIERS ET CARTONS
6412	PRINTG,WRITING PAPER NES	W 616257	539038	W 689227	616563	W 694229	854602	W 555684	594014	PAPIERS POUR L'IMPRESSION
64122	— COATED,IMPREGNATD ETC	W 531374	456575	W 576618	499146	W 566915	676045	W 436813	454896	PAPIERS IMPRESSION COUCHES
6415	PAPER,PAPERBRD,BULK,NES	W 722530	463303	W 892312	604573	W 1029202	942353	W 977992	711606	PAPIERS,CARTONS ROULEAUX
64159	OTHER PAPER ETC,BULK,NES	W 688168	440575	W 849841	573590	W 969037	890188	W 915219	669523	AUT PAPIER ROULEAUX FEUILLES
6418	COATED ETC PAPER NES BLK	W 220618	368353	W 269986	441278	W 286953	557302	W 287093	523837	PAP,CARTONS COUCHES,ENDUITS
642	PAPER,ETC,PRECUT,ARTS OF	W 427180	808327	W 476888	870674	W 454533	1100330	W 418942	964376	PAP,CARTONS DECOUPES
6428	PAPER ETC ARTICLES NES	W 145870	369267	W 165923	414315	W 157791	506166	W 155272	430098	OUVRAGES EN PATE A PAPIER
65	TEXTILE YARN,FABRICS,ETC		3100387		3637324		4168015		3818550	FILS,TISSUS,ARTICLES TEXTILE
651	TEXTILE YARN	W 373113	1140151	W 467280	1431122	W 455342	1625652	W 434630	1417372	FILS TEXTILES
6514	SYN FIB YRN,BULK,MONOFIL	W 139623	517378	W 176368	646676	W 158681	718428	W 155060	624945	FILS CONT 85% FIB TEXT SYNTH
652	COTTON FABRICS,WOVEN	W 60069	409120	W 66952	435870	W 58328	486438	W 71371	512947	TISSUS DE COTON
653	WOVN MAN–MADE FIB FABRIC	W 56165	403556	W 63434	434562	W 57695	495968	W 57183	436691	TISSUS FIBRES SYNTH,ARTIF
657	SPECIAL TXTL FABRC,PRODS	W 65979	318256	W 74558	393492	W 72842	468150	W 72018	438008	TISSUS SPECIAUX
66	NONMETAL MINERAL MFS NES		9955066		10776859		12449522		13207139	ART MIN NON METALLIQUES
662	CLAY,REFRACTORY BLDG PRD	W 849349	372326	W 821096	404685	W 843153	465100	W 727491	370273	MAT CONST REFRACTAIRES
663	MINERAL MANUFCTURES NES	W 1037160	341742	W 1077508	394734	W 1168195	495827	W 1142838	457688	ART MIN MANUF NDA
667	PEARL,PREC–,SEMI–P STONE		8320666		8994178		10304081		11269679	PERLES, PIERRES GEMMES
6672	DIAMONDS NONINDUST,UNSET		8288718		8955412		10261433		11232403	DIAMANTS BRUTS
66721	— ROUGH,UNSORTED		409464		628694		664931		598825	DIAMANTS BRUTS NON TRIES
66722	— SRTD,ROUGH,SIMPLY WKD		4658003		4808099		5701285		6339929	DIAMANTS TRIES BRUTS
66729	— CUT ETC NOT SET		3221250		3518619		3895216		4293649	DIAMANTS TAILLES
67	IRON AND STEEL		2891247		3674211		4956135		4311703	FER ET ACIER
672	IRON,STEEL PRIMARY FORMS	W 1317090	663495	W 1960253	934483	W 2361730	1338488	W 2340943	1380489	LINGOTS FER,ACIER
6725	IRN,STL BLOOMS,SLABS,ETC	W 814904	328141	W 1391541	521865	W 1664329	727329	W 1665316	748479	BLOOMS,BILLETTES FER ACIER
6727	IRN,STL COIL FR REROLLNG	W 489422	319120	W 555374	394743	W 669667	584908	W 651547	606766	EBAUCHES POUR TOLES FER
67274	STNLESS STEEL ETC COILS	W 183315	218481	W 220021	270131	W 295932	414591	W 254718	466593	EBAUCHES ACIER INOXYDBLE
673	IRON,STEEL SHAPES ETC	W 1548032	592594	W 1515126	665552	W 1604877	863187	W 1407365	640552	BARRES,PROFIL FER,ACIER
674	IRN,STL UNIV,PLATE,SHEET	W 1555678	914807	W 1860227	1153044	W 2021455	1546458	W 1881075	1289752	LARGES PLATS,TOLES
6746	IRN,STL THIN PLATE,ROLLD	W 569961	309028	W 692245	399073	W 574440	453939	W 564829	372892	TOLES LAM MOINS 3MM
6749	OTH IRN,STL PLATES,SHEET	W 451521	304125	W 512688	378425	W 623874	519143	W 657977	473592	AUTRES TOLES FER,ACIER
67491	— OF IRON OR SIMPLE STL	W 433952	280176	W 496522	354100	W 619133	501126	W 648524	452852	AUT TOLES AUTRES ACIER FIN
678	IRON,STL TUBES,PIPES,ETC	W 302594	339643	W 350240	408739	W 396397	554390	W 391025	501460	TUBES,TUYAUX EN FONTE,FER
68	NON–FERROUS METALS		2209201		2686475		3496818		2920977	METAUX NON FERREUX
682	COPPER EXC CEMENT COPPER	W 382381	815302	W 406887	993466	W 320817	1039737	W 274884	767051	CUIVRE
6821	COPPER NES,ALLOYS,UNWRT	W 321181	612232	W 326902	721826	W 243879	704172	W 204880	492817	CUIVRE BRUT
68212	COPPER REFINED,UNWROUGHT	W 157569	294605	W 179237	390483	W 113298	320688	W 81847	186801	CUIVRE AFFINE BRUT
684	ALUMINIUM	W 477005	893648	W 550196	1098269	W 547459	1473604	W 520316	1224858	ALUMINIUM
6841	ALUMINIUM,ALLOYS,UNWRGHT	W 310887	419615	W 370417	564623	W 364208	760482	W 351495	605723	ALUMINIUM,ALLIAGES BRUTS
6842	ALUMINIUM,ALLOYS WORKED	W 166118	474033	W 179779	533646	W 183251	713122	W 168821	619135	ALUMINIUM,ALLIAGES OUVRE
69	METAL MANUFACTURES NES		2374177		2719002		3354144		3245100	ART MANUFACT EN METAL NDA
691	STRUCTURES AND PARTS NES	W 191582	324012	W 210668	388542	W 197510	425528	W 197403	410496	CONSTRUCT FER,ACIER,ALU
695	TOOLS	W 22336	311847	W 25088	351007	W 27300	466086	W 24786	477372	OUTILS A MAIN
699	BASE METAL MFRS NES	W 285980	858661	W 298249	971252	W 224853	1214908	W 214377	1171747	ART MANUFACTURES MET NDA
7	MACHINES,TRANSPORT EQUIP		27990329		32056459		40259782		41998349	MACHINES MATERIEL TRANSPORT
71	POWER GENERATING EQUIPMT		1603671		2138159		2786737		2994512	MACHINES GENERATRICES
713	INTRNL COMBUS PSTN ENGIN	W 98177	1027501	W 134367	1520620	W 146291	2063053	W 164898	2298137	MOTEURS EXPL COMB INT, PIECE
7132	MOTOR VEHCL PSTN ENGINS	W 69106	724253	W 99821	1108839	W 107999	1543713	W 121779	1752780	MOTEURS EXPL POUR VEHICULES
72	MACHS FOR SPCL INDUSTRYS		2048850		2409184		2935043		2802765	MAC SPECIALES POUR INDUST
724	TEXTILE,LEATHER MACHNRY	W 20584	336699	W 26853	437563	W 28280	441177	W 22242	398047	MACH POUR INDUSTRIE TEXTILE
728	OTH MACHY FOR SPCL INDUS	W 48183	670377	W 70381	722583	W 87524	929511	W 66568	909905	AUT MACH IND PARTICULIERES
7284	MACHY FOR SPCL INDUS NES	W 26261	463862	W 34785	495675	W 62201	623953	W 42712	624499	MACH SPEC IND PARTICUL.
73	METALWORKING MACHINERY		516820		608528		620416		643279	MACH TRAVAIL DES METAUX
736	METALWORKING MACH–TOOLS	W 26666	335762	W 28334	355710	W 23759	374658	W 24289	390130	MACH–OUTILS TRAVAIL METAUX
74	GENRL INDUSTRL MACHY NES		3476750		4102279		5209969		5619200	MACH APP INDUSTRIE
741	HEATING,COOLING EQUIPMNT	W 53151	599184	W 56295	641115	W 71452	797598	W 78168	998901	MACH CHAUFFAGE,PIECES
743	PUMPS NES,CENTRFUGES ETC	W 53201	532417	W 60168	570010	W 70782	740674	W 82954	908578	POMPES COMPRES,VENT ETC
744	MECHANICAL HANDLING EQU	W 157384	699297	W 181517	814331	W 189552	1018575	W 187386	951562	EQUIP MANUTENTION PIECES
7449	PTS NES OF MACHY OF 7442	W 91013	296519	W 111979	408557	W 114526	514677	W 111380	461238	PIECES DU 744.2
745	NONELEC MACHY,TOOLS NES	W 22376	471550	W 27623	595450	W 28013	703329	W 26351	664175	AUT MACH NON ELEC,PIECES
7452	OTH NONELEC MCHS,PTS NES	W 19883	377901	W 23806	434064	W 25601	526487	W 22683	461844	AUT MACH NON ELEC,PIECES
749	NONELEC MACH PTS,ACC NES	W 121826	931388	W 143603	1192420	W 183918	1590308	W 166715	1746264	PIECES MACH NON ELEC NDA
7491	BALL,ROLLER,ETC BEARINGS	W 10773	134961	W 16092	200042	W 35558	381987	W 48314	540624	ROULEMENTS BILLES ETC
7492	COCKS,VALVES ETC NES	W 33842	391287	W 32269	464699	W 29461	540665	W 32899	545442	ART ROB,SIM POUR TUYAUX
75	OFFICE MACHNES,ADP EQUIP		2117723		2512945		3493887		3683234	MACH BUREAU TRAIT AUTOM
752	AUTOMTIC DATA PROC EQUIP	W 16658	1402955	W 20607	1699293	W 27401	2377758	W 35572	2657092	MACH TRAIT INFORMATION
7523	DIGITL CENTRL PROCESSORS	W 3004	393062	W 3259	423729	W 3416	568085	W 5423	592230	UNITES CENTRALES
7524	DIGITL CENTRL STOR UNITS	W 1595	242479	W 2415	316546	W 3014	413363	W 2764	533413	UNITES MEMOIRE CENTRALES
7525	ADP PERIPHERAL UNITS	W 7972	366778	W 10628	484582	W 14427	647538	W 18492	652660	UNITES PERIPHERIQUES
759	OFFICE,ADP MCH PTS,ACCES	W 10713	564607	W 9578	645053	W 20194	875090	W 24878	827098	PIECES DU 751 ET 752
7599	ACCTG,ETC,ADP MCH PTS,AC	W 6384	441094	W 6007	544590	W 6604	704895	W 6648	708993	PIECES DU 751 ET 752
76	TELECOMM,SOUND EQUIPMENT		2074967		2127720		2632308		2553149	EQUIPMENT DE TELECOM
762	RADIO BROADCAST RECEIVRS	W 14518	374172	W 14742	414187	W 15519	490909	W 15990	491086	RECEPTEURS RADIODIFFUSION
763	SOUND RECORDRS,PHONOGRPH	W 12065	422581	W 9473	340730	W 8505	334644	W 7270	315284	PHONO,APP ENREGISTREMENT
7638	OTHR SOUND APPARATUS ETC	W 11547	413490	W 9047	332542	W 8174	327670	W 7019	311324	AUT APP D'ENREGIS,REPROD
764	TELECOM EQPT,PTS,ACC NES	W 29248	1042548	W 31445	1158769	W 31860	1583081	W 31436	1480338	EQUIP TELECOM,PIECES
7641	LINE TELEPHONE,ETC EQUIP	W 3462	242336	W 3319	278156	W 4713	460573	W 4019	434316	APP TELEPHON PAR FIL
7649	PTS NES OF EQUIPMT OF 76	W 9346	409030	W 11423	490569	W 11078	640614	W 9496	574782	PIECES DE LA DIV 76
77	ELECTRIC MACHNRY NES ETC		3968772		4672903		5617209		5889688	MACH APP ELECT NDA
772	SWITCHGEAR ETC,PARTS NES	W 28624	825066	W 30863	938690	W 32948	1134525	W 31798	1042184	APP COUPURE,SECT ETC
7721	SWITCHGEAR ETC	W 27068	712476	W 29203	809327	W 31022	994494	W 28995	920576	APP COUPURE,SECTIONMNT
773	ELECTR DISTRIBUTNG EQUIP	W 51926	417836	W 65719	570031	W 69410	652876	W 71105	696493	EQUIPMT DISTRIBUTION ELECT

4. Special Imports C.I.F. by Commodities according to the S.I.T.C. (Rev. 2) in thousand U.S. Dollars
Importations Spéciales C.A.F. par Produits d'après la C.T.C.I. (Rév. 2) en milliers de Dollars E.U.

SITC CTCI	COMMODITY	1993		1994		1995		1996		PRODUIT
		WEIGHT POIDS	VALUE VALEUR	WEIGHT POIDS	VALUE VALEUR	WEIGHT POIDS	VALUE VALEUR	WEIGHT POIDS	VALUE VALEUR	
7731	INSULATED WIRE,CABLE ETC	W 46170	356798	W 59960	503566	W 64924	588514	W 67344	636772	FILS,CABLES ISOLES ELECT
775	HOUSEHOLD TYPE EQUIP NES	W 110500	809821	W 106716	825347	W 114185	949995	W 113064	890124	MACH,APP USAGE DOMESTQUE
7758	ELECTRO–THERMIC APPL NES	W 37267	334415	W 38859	364899	W 39703	416524	W 40193	386914	APP ELECTROTHERMIQ NDA
776	TRANSISTORS,VALVES,ETC	W 17680	498945	W 22371	702495	W 24506	882736	W 21107	1224125	LAMPES,TUBES,VALVES
7764	ELECTRONIC MICROCIRCUITS	W 572	291142	W 895	443915	W 1711	516886	W 1047	850758	MICROSTRUCTURES ELECTRON
778	ELECTRICAL MACHINERY NES	W 98294	1072009	W 106395	1268149	W 119570	1532282	W 152474	1551945	AUTRES MACH ELECT NDA
7788	OTH ELEC MACHY,EQUIP NES	W 16733	313383	W 19181	372340	W 23146	483861	W 22489	445373	AUT MACH APP ELEC NDA
78	ROAD VEHICLES		10791279		12748766		16115379		16804900	VEHICULES ROUTIERS
781	PASS MOTOR VEH EXC BUSES	W 557385	5839817	W 622180	6799089	W 612612	7631715	W 700218	8626705	AUTO TRANSPORT PERSONNES
782	LORRIES,SPCL MTR VEH NES	W 103046	553806	W 112887	619237	W 137814	891053	W 145488	957007	VEHICULES SPECIAUX,MARCH
7821	LORRIES,TRUCKS	W 96590	517975	W 107400	590034	W 129690	845046	W 137288	891953	VEHICULES TRANSP MARCHAND
783	ROAD MOTOR VEHICLES NES	W 42929	352029	W 55292	430358	W 65490	628531	W 56933	540059	VEHICULES ROUTIERS NDA
784	MOTOR VEH PRTS,ACCES NES	W 673010	3525140	W 703202	4330856	W 826158	6230350	W 977564	6018524	PIECES 722,781,782,783
7849	OTHER MOTOR VEHCL PARTS	W 656541	3389770	W 681541	4107461	W 801319	5944806	W 952886	5747915	PIECES 722,781,782,783
79	OTHR TRANSPORT EQUIPMENT		1391497		735963		848834		1007622	AUTRE MATERIEL TRANSPORT
792	AIRCRAFT ETC	W 3149	1091023	W 1110	341448	W 2194	682077	W 2349	810600	APP NAVIGATION AERIENNE
7924	AIRCRFT NES OVER 15000KG	W 640	467019			W 587	239601	W 730	286290	AERODYNES PLUS 15000 KG
7929	AIRCRAFT PARTS NES	W 2412	615460	W 928	329365	W 1310	408400	W 1420	486873	PIECES DU 792
8	MISC MANUFACTURED GOODS		12889481		13780677		16041409		15693972	ART MANUFACTURES DIVERS
812	*PLUMBG,HEATNG,LGHTNG EQ	W 80528	472427	W 131712	509566	W 83784	588434	W 83744	570757	APPAR SANITAIRES CHAUFFAGE
821	*FURNITURE,PARTS THEREOF	W 301435	1340174	W 372545	1544284	W 347054	1886379	W 360727	1859321	MEUBLES ET PIECES
8211	CHAIRS,SEATS AND PARTS	W 83306	509203	W 121274	598765	W 99071	756229	W 99654	750404	SIEGES ET PIECES
82111	CHAIRS AND OTHER SEATS	W 47318	335691	W 54855	380958	W 52705	434170	W 58765	439166	SIEGES
8219	FURNITURE AND PARTS NES	W 205222	722733	W 237570	830420	W 234119	989647	W 248555	983096	AUTRES MEUBLES ET PIECES
82192	WOOD FURNITURE NES	W 132392	482368	W 150188	557194	W 152768	665303	W 149751	641608	MEUBLES NDA EN BOIS
84	CLOTHING AND ACCESSORIES		3857248		3843971		4379309		4333915	VETEMENTS
842	MENS OUTERWEAR NOT KNIT	W 43761	1050737	W 37950	915672	W 37534	990086	W 39959	976966	VET DESSUS POUR HOMMES
8423	— TROUSERS,BREECHES ETC	W 32552	706092	W 26240	555438	W 24585	558608	W 27231	574228	PANTALONS HOMMES MAT TEX
843	WOMENS OUTERWEAR NONKNIT	W 27299	961646	W 24156	988263	W 25010	1149943	W 28542	1084678	VET DESSUS FEMMES MAT TEX
8439	— OTHER OUTER GARMENTS	W 16278	388612	W 12670	398037	W 12280	434842	W 15487	456860	AUT VET DES FEM MAT TEXT
845	OUTERWEAR KNIT NONELASTC	W 24343	753187	W 149277	771752	W 26301	842048	W 30679	886507	VET DESSOUS,ACCES BONNET
8451	— JERSEYS,PULLOVERS ETC	W 11995	385945	W 74116	401273	W 12605	423432	W 14983	459145	CHANDAILS,PULL–OVERS ETC
846	UNDER GARMENTS KNITTED	W 26937	550548	W 23844	563695	W 27046	707407	W 30668	735268	SOUS VETS DE BONNETERIE
8462	— OF COTTON NON ELASTIC	W 19048	378954	W 19353	386624	W 22037	483575	W 25306	507429	SOUS–VET BONNET COTON
84629	—— OTHER	W 19048	378954	W 19353	386624	W 22037	483575	W 25306	507429	AUT SOUS–VET BONNET COTON
851	*FOOTWEAR	W 38171	707341	W 41921	757167	W 42965	855891	W 56021	1013302	CHAUSSURES
85102	FOOTWEAR LEATHER	W 29501	621971	W 31385	653817	W 32882	742248	W 42727	854508	CHAUS SEMELLES EN CUIR
87	PRECISION INSTRUMNTS NES		1207174		1382670		1741577		1726802	INSTRUM,APPAR SCIENT NDA
872	MEDICAL INSTRUMENTS NES	W 13347	429389	W 19780	539141	W 21326	701919	W 24167	758431	INSTR,APP MEDIC–CHIR NDA
87202	OTH MEDICAL INSTRUMENTS	W 12653	407621	W 18824	515591	W 20315	671455	W 22800	721715	INSTRUM,APP MEDECINE
874	MEASURNG,CONTROLNG INSTR	W 11564	666739	W 11733	712170	W 15839	874046	W 11244	778708	INSTRUMENTS DE MESURE
88	PHOTO EQU,OPTICL GDS ETC		731027		778985		1021740		865834	APP,FOURN PHOTO,OP,MONTR
882	PHOTO,CINEMA SUPPLIES	W 27645	355981	W 30123	374960	W 38244	519501	W 32674	452985	PRODUITS PHOTO,CINEMA
89	MISC MANUFCTRD GOODS NES		4363234		4743734		5302710		5066475	ART MANUFACTURES DIVERS
892	PRINTED MATTER	W 150744	872874	W 207118	976132	W 138599	953317	W 153750	930944	IMPRIMES
893	ARTICLES OF PLASTIC NES		1514803		1652149		2004345		1904345	OUVRAGES EN MAT DIVIS 58
8931	PLSTC PACKG CONTNRS,LIDS	W 168242	492255	W 171676	527790	W 232408	652667	W 262739	611304	ART TRANSP EMBALLAGE ETC
8939	MISC PLASTIC ARTICLES	W 257212	947529	W 206436	1033521	W 216094	1237367	W 226800	1197683	ART DIVERS EN MAT DIV 58
89399	OTHR PLASTC ARTICLES NES	W 235182	858497	W 182584	937664	W 194170	1129518	W 205113	1097637	AUT OUV MAT DIV 58
894	TOYS,SPORTING GOODS,ETC	W 84426	743710	W 100321	745291	W 82434	769923	W 79986	787861	VOITURES ENFANTS,JOUETS
8942	TOYS,INDOOR GAMES ETC	W 68950	613048	W 77314	604077	W 62848	623293	W 61659	605636	JOUETS,JEUX ETC
898	MUSICAL INSTRUMENTS,PTS	W 70918	556987	W 141220	606750	W 30310	759256	W 101169	676735	INSTRUMENTS DE MUSIQUE
8983	SOUND RECRDNG TAPE,DISCS	W 69381	516031	W 139751	565686	W 28632	709983	W 99531	631468	SUPPORTS SON POUR 763
89832	RECORDED DISCS,TAPES ETC	W 8310	327646	W 8938	366390	W 13008	470007	W 9001	436325	DISQUES,PHONO,BANDES
899	OTHER MANUFACTURED GOODS		348305		395767		426478		430173	AUT ART MANUF DIVERS NDA
9	GOODS NOT CLASSD BY KIND		6129734		6637867		8040607		5851913	ART TRANSACT NON CLASSES
931	*SPECIAL TRANSACTIONS	W 2258893	5855043	W 2087686	6415718	W 2537103	7811485	W 1580227	5692068	TRANS.SPECIALES

5. Special Exports F.O.B. by Commodities according to the S.I.T.C. (Rev. 2) in thousand U.S. Dollars
Exportations Spéciales F.O.B. par Produits d'après la C.T.C.I. (Rév. 2) en milliers de Dollars E.U.

SITC CTCI	COMMODITY	1993 WEIGHT POIDS	1993 VALUE VALEUR	1994 WEIGHT POIDS	1994 VALUE VALEUR	1995 WEIGHT POIDS	1995 VALUE VALEUR	1996 WEIGHT POIDS	1996 VALUE VALEUR	PRODUIT
	ALL COMMODITIES		120861926		137269874		168153671		162265643	TOUS PRODUITS
0	FOOD AND LIVE ANIMALS		11377138		12512504		15113157		14107786	ALIMENTS,ANIMAUX VIVANTS
001	*LIVE ANIMALS FOR FOOD	W 182472	394476	W 208709	458609	W 221086	524089	W 205446	458600	ANIMAUX VIVANTS
01	MEAT AND PREPARATIONS		2504507		2546518		2946674		3027084	VIANDES ET PREPARATIONS
011	MEAT FRESH,CHILLD,FROZEN	W 799090	1919965	W 812264	1936970	W 884576	2253420	W 933946	230[illegible]746	VIANDES FRAICHES,REF,CONGE
0111	BOVINE MEAT FRESH,FROZEN	W 163767	622007	W 140898	548327	W 140824	551646	W 138507	431868	VIANDES BOVIN FRAI,REF
01111	BOVINE MEAT WITH BONE IN	W 114908	493350	W 95785	427789	W 87947	401452	W 83647	295923	VIANDES BOVIN NON DESOSS
0113	PIG MEAT FRESH,CHLD,FRZN	W 411159	918629	W 433130	969348	W 480227	1233524	W 493024	1334576	VIANDE DE PORC
014	MEAT PREPD,PRSVD,NES ETC	W 138793	476420	W 148382	506056	W 150618	582899	W 174627	601386	CONSERVES DE VIANDES
0149	OTH PREPARD,PRESRVD MEAT	W 107622	393343	W 113944	420625	W 114724	478928	W 126005	484661	AUTRES PREP DE VIANDES
02	DAIRY PRODCTS,BIRDS'EGGS		1900382		1918834		2459703		2135901	PRODUITS LAITIERS,OEUFS
022	MILK AND CREAM	W 1289447	1010128	W 1414592	1019861	W 1581686	1438029	W 1423375	1176063	LAIT ET CREME
0223	MILK AND CREAM FRESH	W 924064	487587	W 1060657	529161	W 1100199	631250	W 1065267	600257	LAIT,CREME FRAIS
0224	MILK,CREAM PRESERVED ETC	W 365382	522541	W 353935	490700	W 481487	806779	W 358108	575805	LAIT,CREME CONS,CONC
023	BUTTER	W 133541	362827	W 127367	349171	W 125094	433668	W 105345	368329	BEURRE
024	CHEESE AND CURD	W 100271	426943	W 107516	428709	W 114834	455433	W 114010	451077	FROMAGE ET CAILLEBOTTE
04	CEREALS AND PREPARATIONS		1497576		1625152		2041921		2040083	CEREALES ET PRODUITS
048	CEREAL ETC PREPARATIONS	W 825446	906833	W 823882	998840	W 1077484	1316455	W 1086941	1311393	PREPTNS A BASE CEREALES
0484	BAKERY PRODUCTS	W 169249	476235	W 185417	544283	W 209473	678234	W 214421	653186	PRODUITS DE BOULANGERIE
04842	PASTRY, CAKES ETC	W 127300	386472	W 142984	449074	W 160189	557137	W 157910	516427	PATISSERIE ETC.
05	VEGETABLES AND FRUIT		1963840		2412297		2596119		2554284	LEGUMES ET FRUITS
054	VEG ETC FRSH,SMPLY PRSVD	W 2301741	1041402	W 2443801	1245518	W 2362141	1414550	W 2227203	1283632	LEGUMES FRAIS,CONG,SECS
0546	VEGETABLES SIMPLY PRESVD	W 664471	467335	W 754140	579198	W 744426	700365	W 796866	654942	LEGUMES CONG,CONSER
05461	VEGETABLES FROZEN	W 661348	462544	W 745858	569666	W 740174	696306	W 792423	649310	LEGUMES CONGELES
057	FRUIT,NUTS,FRESH,DRIED	W 607895	419561	W 671962	591017	W 507039	484275	W 495682	472815	FRUITS FRAIS OU SECS
06	SUGAR AND PREPS,HONEY		564129		669587		955688		674104	SUCRES ET PRODUITS
061	SUGAR AND HONEY	W 752959	358237	W 1138712	437456	W 1630147	686744	W 959554	450323	SUCRES ET MIEL
0612	REFINED SUGAR ETC	W 682439	322542	W 1029061	388505	W 1468016	591786	W 823704	361918	SUCRES RAFFINES
07	COFFEE,TEA,COCOA,SPICES		970881		1182857		1491261		1237703	CAFE,THE,CACAO,EPICES
073	CHOCOLATE AND PRODUCTS	W 188378	714212	W 194257	827819	W 212465	1035598	W 192437	888672	CHOCOLAT
081	*FEEDING STUFF FOR ANIML	W 2577145	684826	W 2413657	682565	W 3137095	878784	W 2862982	839326	NOURRITURE POUR ANIMAUX
0819	FOOD WASTE AND FEED NES	W 1087720	386305	W 1091941	417749	W 1346324	527825	W 1235100	476870	DECHETS,ALIMENTS NDA
08199	FODDER NES,INCL SWEETNED	W 735549	366239	W 791794	399918	W 1055660	510679	W 947069	458129	PREPARATIONS FOURRAGERES
09	MISC EDIBLE PRODUCTS		674658		756692		927533		849732	PREP ALIMENTAIRES DIVERSES
098	EDIBLE PRODCTS,PREPS NES	W 267339	507803	W 266643	558711	W 309461	635358	W 263737	591582	PREP ALIMENTAIRES NDA
09809	MISC FOOD PREPRTIONS NES	W 166565	369252	W 168392	398599	W 206210	448765	W 181472	449547	PREP ALIMENTAIRES NDA
1	BEVERAGES AND TOBACCO		1070665		1230234		1339850		1270789	BOISSONS ET TABACS
11	BEVERAGES		633691		764225		958182		857417	BOISSONS
112	ALCOHOLIC BEVERAGES	W 483124	377187	W 638255	460667	W 692989	593761	W 551444	501212	BOISSONS ALCOOLIQUES
12	TOBACCO AND MANUFACTURES		436975		466009		381669		413372	TABACS BRUTS FABRIQUES
122	TOBACCO,MANUFACTURED	W 23805	396885	W 21529	410954	W 18011	348826	W 23642	375839	TABACS FABRIQUES
2	CRUDE MATERLS,EXCL FUELS		2589351		3158291		3679048		3315068	MAT BRUTES NON COMESTIBLES
23	RUBBER, CRUDE		382648		468937		238079		238687	CAOUTCHOUC BRUT
233	RUBBER,SYNTHTIC,RECLAIMD	W 253701	380097	W 288957	467191	W 99190	236573	W 107698	236541	LATEX CAOUTCH SYNTH REGEN
26	TEXTILE FIBRES AND WASTE		400414		563219		609729		486944	FIBRES TEXTILES
27	CRUDE FERTLZR,MINRLS NES		499732		552147		625343		582221	ENGRAIS MINERAUX BRUTS
28	METALLIFEROUS ORES,SCRAP		449871		550373		890650		884168	MINERAIS METAL,DECHETS
29	CRUDE ANIMAL,VEG MAT NES		379666		413257		487178		467270	MATIERES BRUTES ANIM,VEGET
3	MINERAL FUELS ETC		4145879		4210151		4467359		5351596	COMBUSTIBLES MINERAUX LUB
33	PETROLEUM AND PRODUCTS		3795989		3837704		4011465		4890169	PETROLE ET DERIVES
334	PETROLEUM PRODUCTS,REFIN	MW 22114	3515413	MW 22545	3526225	MW 20840	3665566	MW 23601	4551620	PRODUITS RAFFINES
3341	GASOLINE,OTH LIGHT OILS	W 6041349	1157161	W 6270784	1121479	W 5548732	1054486	W 6120902	1298965	ESSENCES POUR MOTEURS
33411	MOTOR,AVIATION SPIRIT	W 4370229	820522	W 4337809	761929	W 3663349	659525	W 5665664	1156305	ESSENCES MOTEURS D'AVIONS
3343	GAS OILS	W 4896818	826695	W 5004383	791956	W 5508327	911176			GAS OILS
3344	FUEL OILS,NES	MW 9508	848352	MW 9637	919976	W 8403836	937876	MW 9452	1130649	FUEL OILS
3345	LUBS,PETROLEUM OILS NES	W 562543	440362	W 578933	481328	W 554303	585556	W 6905923	1848152	HUILES LUBRIFIANTES
33451	LUBS(HIGH PETR CONT) ETC	W 547283	395269	W 556918	428168	W 534458	514235	W 6881649	1765880	HUILES LUBRIF,H LOURDES
4	ANIMAL,VEGETABLE OIL,FAT		388831		528644		739339		659294	HUILES,GRAISSES ANIM,VEG
42	FIXED VEGETABLE OIL,FAT		288103		412678		594528		527522	HUILES VEGETALES FIXES
5	CHEMCLS,RELATED PROD NES		18468330		22933978		26781820		25652310	PRODUITS CHIMIQUES
51	ORGANIC CHEMICALS		4113004		5297053		4795601		4655122	PROD CHIMIQ ORGANIQUES
511	HYDROCARBONS NES,DERIVS	W 1504602	589200	W 2023982	883410	W 1959035	1142734	W 1960026	879602	HYDROCARBURES NDA
512	ALCOHOLS,PHENOLS ETC	W 363825	212095	W 563906	347331	W 683158	543774	W 676178	459019	PHENOLS,PHENOLS–ALCOOLS
513	CARBOXYLIC ACIDS ETC	W 1037655	890760		1147166	W 476014	646579	W 806057	950459	ACIDES CARBOXYLIQUES
5137	MONOACIDS AND DERIVATIVS	W 245630	235939	W 308703	359614	W 347770	507295	W 523015	664180	ACIDES MONOCARBOXYLIQUES
5139	OXY–FNCT ACIDS,DERIVATVS	W 770951	627763	W 793527	743949	W 106520	96910	W 85030	137221	ACIDES CARBOXYLIQUES
514	NITROGEN–FNCTN COMPOUNDS	W 319284	769286	W 436065	1013228	W 375226	1091458	W 399617	1022860	COMPOSES FONCT AZOTEES
5148	OTH NITROGN–FNCTN CMPNDS	W 135985	415017	W 162707	528045	W 153735	695171	W 178700	599336	AUTRES COMPOSES AZOTES
515	ORG–INORG COMPOUNDS ETC		1308981		1493506	W 124807	826620	W 126961	838367	COMPOSES ORGANO–MINERAUX
5156	HETEROCYCLIC CMPDS ETC	W 46818	483668		481435	W 74734	621194	W 78222	619614	COMPOSES HETEROCYCLIQUES
51569	OTH HETEROCYC CMPDS,ETC	W 42959	448906		452048	W 71414	584576	W 75221	584178	AUT COMP HETEROCYCLIQUES
516	OTHER ORGANIC CHEMICALS	W 418375	342681	W 554979	412412	W 535106	544436	W 585285	504816	AUTRES PROD ORGANIQUES
52	INORGANIC CHEMICALS		1159525		1298585		943557		857545	PROD CHIM INORGANIQUES
522	INORG ELEMNTS,OXIDES,ETC	W 3580557	622564	W 4010462	716999	W 3418092	625358	W 3837913	586333	ELEMENTS INORGANIQUES
523	OTHR INORG CHEMICALS ETC		497023	W 1558265	534789	W 510674	263018	W 533947	219507	AUT PRODUITS CHIMIQUES INORG
53	DYES,TANNING,COLOUR PROD		1091635		1373286		1615917		1613531	PROD TEINTURE,COLORANTS
533	PIGMENTS,PAINTS,ETC	W 361362	841696	W 429808	1057015	W 442554	1259199	W 451138	1268497	PIGMENTS,PEINTURES,VERNIS
5331	COLOURING MATERIAL NES	W 195432	345210	W 225354	432290	W 241154	549438	W 243354	511662	AUT MATIERES COLORANTES
541	*MEDICINAL,PHARM PRODUCT		2720307		3333085	MK 70788	4120562		4145509	PROD MEDICINAUX PHARMACEUT
5416	GLYCOSIDES,GLANDS,SERA	K 2077600	601167	K 1854200	786270	K 4479819	958043	K 2044679	791096	HETEROSIDES
54164	ANTISERA,MICROB VACCINES	K 1531200	590827	K 1606300	780186	K 3934356	943963	K 1703829	694243	SERUMS,VACCINS
5417	MEDICAMENTS	MK 39397	1848122	MK 44210	2248717	MK 60187	2776664	MK 48124	2917413	MEDICAMENTS
54171	— CONTAINNG ANTIBIOTICS	K 5409500	413545	K 6112100	459578	K 7401778	564863	K 6595967	578340	MED CONTN ANTIBIOTIQUES
54179	— CONTNG OTH SUBSTANCES	MK 32129	1274491	MK 35135	1538914	MK 49572	1957002	MK 38720	2083336	MED CONT AUT SUBSTANCES
55	PERFUME,CLEANING ETC PRD		1355477		1458837		1771781		1634445	PROD POUR PARFUM,TOILETTE
553	PERFUMERY,COSMETICS,ETC	W 120103	641914	W 107242	656835	W 104534	698768	W 93862	626967	PRODUITS DE PARFUMERIE
554	SOAP,CLEANSING ETC PREPS	W 507914	673605	W 567276	753675	W 617409	987737	W 634419	917884	SAVONS,PRODUITS DETERSIFS
5542	WASHING PREPARATIONS ETC	W 449206	594833	W 520170	685236	W 578741	910830	W 594991	852140	PROD ORG TENSIO–ACT NDA
562	*FERTILIZERS,MANUFACTURE	W 4688163	502418	W 5783359	633975	W 5727278	799419	W 5756232	819690	ENGRAIS MANUFACTURES
58	PLASTIC MATERIALS ETC		5756987		6959065		9484436		8709649	MAT PLAST ARTIFICIELLES
582	PROD OF CONDENSATION ETC	W 604164	1366967	W 832237	1786062	W 893897	2482789	W 867414	2262896	PROD CONDENS,POLYCOND
5823	ALKYDS,OTHER POLYESTERS	W 129556	422949	W 163044	535667	W 187845	778301	W 157771	593959	ALKYDES ET AUT POLYESTERS
5829	OTH CONDNSATION,ETC PROD	W 271172	392113	W 356517	490701	W 372187	693879	W 371102	686560	AUT PROD CONDENSATION
583	POLYMERIZATION ETC PRODS	W 4383918	4289445	W 4811992	5062336	W 4691015	6835500	W 5094664	6279710	PROD POLYMERISATION
5831	POLYETHYLENE	W 1671380	1367330	W 1770442	1524373	W 1675184	2038611	W 1794391	1785513	POLYETHYLENE
58311	— IN PRIMARY FORMS	W 1504386	1128769	W 1581138	1246729	W 1488456	1682671	W 1593338	1471606	POLYETHYLENE PRIMAIRES
5832	POLYPROPYLENE	W 1094164	885347	W 1038512	1036415	W 1028364	1476098	W 1059625	1242538	POLYPROPYLENE
58321	— IN PRIMARY FORMS	W 986558	566654	W 907731	661799	W 891607	937766	W 919876	776265	POLYPROPYLENE PRIMAIRES
58322	— PLATES,FILM,STRIP,ETC	W 107606	318693	W 130782	374616	W 136757	538332	W 139749	466273	POLYPROPYLENE PLAQUES
5833	POLYSTYRENE,ITS COPOLYMR	W 541081	528131	W 671545	695758	W 651417	923899	W 730902	811156	POLYPROPYLENE COPOLYMERES
58331	— IN PRIMARY FORMS	W 502201	446357	W 627101	611646	W 614921	816178	W 695849	721725	SOUS FORMES PRIMAIRES

5. Special Exports F.O.B. by Commodities according to the S.I.T.C. (Rev. 2) in thousand U.S. Dollars
Exportations Spéciales F.O.B. par Produits d'après la C.T.C.I. (Rév. 2) en milliers de Dollars E.U.

SITC CTCI	COMMODITY	1993 WEIGHT POIDS	1993 VALUE VALEUR	1994 WEIGHT POIDS	1994 VALUE VALEUR	1995 WEIGHT POIDS	1995 VALUE VALEUR	1996 WEIGHT POIDS	1996 VALUE VALEUR	PRODUIT
5834	POLYVINYL CHLORIDE	W 369986	352034	W 398692	402466	W 390678	513311	W 469635	445353	CHLORURE DE POLYVINYLE
5839	OTH POLYMRZTION ETC PROD	W 653499	1010804	W 883364	1269117	W 887729	1687350	W 967945	1771509	AUT PROD POLYMER COPOLYM
59	CHEMICAL MATERIALS NES		1748153		2557226		3227564		3200182	MAT PROD CHIMIQUES NDA
591	PESTICIDES,DISINFECTANTS	W 39139	149853	W 112374	698244	W 143215	935199	W 150878	996252	DESINF,INSECT,FONG,HERB
5913	HERBICIDES,FOR RETAIL	W 2847	3448	W 69720	521921	W 96980	708436	W 105420	755343	HERBICIDES VENTE AU DET
598	MISCEL CHEM PRODUCTS NES	W 2001488	1381446	W 2425112	1605174	W 2269542	1970264	W 1572162	1884500	PROD DIV INDUST CHIM NDA
5989	CHEM PRODUCTS,PREPS NES	W 1764117	985772	W 2152260	1153699	W 1980114	1428500	W 1275685	1332138	PROD PREP CHIMIQUES NDA
59899	OTH CHEM PRODS,PREPS,NES	W 1668634	706044	W 2056362	835581	W 1846567	1082500	W 1164865	1012905	AUT PRODUITS CHIMIQUES NDA
6	BASIC MANUFACTURES		33349668		37561121		45807722		42334339	ART MANUFACTURES
62	RUBBER MANUFACTURES NES		1016344		1117775		1401308		1281633	CAOUTCHOUC MANUFACTURE
625	RUBBER TYRES, TUBES ETC	W 156940	578253	W 170765	626448	W 197552	806563	W 176793	694338	PNEUS CAOUTCHOUC VULCANISE
63	WOOD,CORK MANUFACTRS NES		844059		918608		1152989		1116848	OUVRAGES LIEGE ET BOIS
634	VENEERS,PLYWOOD,ETC	W 1315359	469914	W 1338680	523992	W 1297492	629473	W 1433482	583551	PLACAGES,CONTRE–PLAQUES
635	WOOD MANUFACTURES NES	W 278863	371483	W 305451	391644	W 313701	518208	W 328464	529899	ART MANUF EN BOIS NDA
64	PAPER,PAPERBOARD AND MFR		1966595		2255721		3285982		2918484	PAPIERS,CARTONS & OUVRAGES
641	PAPER AND PAPERBOARD		1122952	W 1323388	1383318	W 1559961	2089323	W 1546985	1788627	PAPIERS ET CARTONS
6412	PRINTG,WRITING PAPER NES	W 460635	396537	W 646548	571325	W 794027	953210	W 789368	780982	PAPIERS POUR L'IMPRESSION
64122	— COATED,IMPREGNATD ETC	W 445781	374576	W 623305	536504	W 733829	855772	W 732575	702168	PAPIERS IMPRESSION COUCHES
6418	COATED ETC PAPER NES BLK	W 153118	392275	W 137482	371344	W 150061	460222	W 134689	394047	PAP,CARTONS COUCHES,ENDUITS
642	PAPER,ETC,PRECUT,ARTS OF	W 423790	843642	W 476781	872403	W 538212	1196659	W 546629	1129857	PAP,CARTONS DECOUPES
65	TEXTILE YARN,FABRICS,ETC		6280276		6816666		7887578		7302186	FILS,TISSUS,ARTICLES TEXTILE
651	TEXTILE YARN	W 314127	1081704	W 327475	1204928	W 332985	1371375	W 304822	1164186	FILS TEXTILES
652	COTTON FABRICS,WOVEN	W 66440	513773	W 72946	588675	W 74272	737080	W 82026	778019	TISSUS DE COTON
6522	WOVEN COTTON BLEACHD,ETC	W 55821	464334	W 58113	509030	W 58111	643415	W 60826	657573	TISSUS COTON BLANCHIS ETC
653	WOVN MAN–MADE FIB FABRIC	W 103929	997493	W 98047	1012956	W 99258	1129518	W 110302	1090069	TISSUS FIBRES SYNTH,ARTIF
657	SPECIAL TXTL FABRC,PRODS		805289		924051	W 148644	1177556	W 133431	1018127	TISSUS SPECIAUX
6573	COATED ETC TEXTILES NES	W 39356	323520	W 60571	483059	W 66490	587107	W 66653	554720	TISSUS,ART MATIERE TEXT NDA
659	FLOOR COVERINGS,ETC	W 716598	2273690	W 788754	2417262	W 778036	2680230	W 796775	2508428	COUVRE–PARQUETS,TAPIS ETC
6595	MAN–MADE TXTL CARPTS NES	W 540524	1729474	W 604671	1870263	W 599059	2059279	W 611795	1924304	TAPIS MAT TEXT SYNT ARTIF
65951	— TUFTED	W 429809	1300468	W 455708	1329514	W 456927	1486829	W 466561	1384091	TAPIS MAT TEXT SYNT TOUFFT
65952	— WOVEN	W 110715	429005	W 148963	540750	W 142132	572449	W 145234	540213	TAPIS MAT TEXT SYNT TISSES
66	NONMETAL MINERAL MFS NES		11166748		12354863		14223983		14443408	ART MIN NON METALLIQUES
661	LIME,CEMENT,BLDG PRODS	W 4744924	479430	W 5217687	524663	W 4119926	517085	W 3986441	463684	CHAUX,CIMENTS MAT CONSTR
663	MINERAL MANUFCTURES NES	W 1415955	468680	W 1671998	558386	W 1748202	704180	W 1736542	622967	ART MIN MANUF NDA
664	GLASS	W 1488055	1110637	W 1686266	1274421	W 1710615	1502757	W 1651247	1381922	VERRE
6644	GLASS SURFACE–GROUND ETC	W 865428	389455	W 982264	436507	W 973126	520396	W 887373	394903	VERRE COULE,LAMINE
667	PEARL,PREC–,SEMI–P STONE		8510219		9361338		10735013		11282201	PERLES, PIERRES GEMMES
6672	DIAMONDS NONINDUST,UNSET		8463428		9325490		10698208		11243503	DIAMANTS BRUTS
66722	— SRTD,ROUGH,SIMPLY WKD		4540522		4916402		5819116		6150877	DIAMANTS TRIES BRUTS
66729	— CUT ETC NOT SET		3919395		4408829		4878599		5091385	DIAMANTS TAILLES
67	IRON AND STEEL		6768717		8177351		10218055		8736224	FER ET ACIER
672	IRON,STEEL PRIMARY FORMS	W 4512631	1703486	W 4872102	2169184	W 4627977	2644282	W 5110010	2544708	LINGOTS FER,ACIER
6725	IRN,STL BLOOMS,SLABS,ETC	W 1205501	425320	W 1183523	520159	W 968974	597203	W 1006234	665269	BLOOMS,BILLETTES FER ACIER
6727	IRN,STL COIL FR REROLLNG	W 3280934	1263986	W 3670553	1634345	W 3611548	2028278	W 3989328	1811597	EBAUCHES POUR TOLES FER
67271	IRON,SIMPLE STEEL COILS	W 2982456	916940	W 3344118	1204131	W 3275111	1487122	W 3645987	1323236	EBAUCHES NON EN ACIER
67274	STNLESS STEEL ETC COILS	W 289725	344358	W 315237	426056	W 322051	534498	W 326153	481467	EBAUCHES ACIER INOXYDBLE
673	IRON,STEEL SHAPES ETC	W 3125484	1151298	W 3489390	1384299	W 3218509	1591693	W 2988908	1283332	BARRES,PROFIL FER,ACIER
6733	IRON,STEEL PROFILES ETC	W 1836154	732360	W 1974023	849912	W 1840531	997103	W 1665755	801342	PROFILES,PALPLAN FER,ACIER
67332	LARGE U,I,H SECTIONS ETC	W 1231774	441075	W 1311960	516277	W 1123715	563515	W 1031996	454605	PROFILES PLUS 80MM
674	IRN,STL UNIV,PLATE,SHEET	W 5422155	2963262	W 5877585	3530515	W 6273128	4995113	W 5862577	4031738	LARGES PLATS,TOLES
6744	IRN,STL HVY PLATE,ROLLED	W 1038385	522831	W 1105236	652707	W 1174528	994967	W 908323	693097	TOLES LAMINEES PLUS 4.75 MM
67441	— OF IRON OR SIMPLE STL	W 944325	349381	W 988846	419458	W 1009611	543067	W 786071	365445	TOLES NON ACIER FIN CARB
6746	IRN,STL THIN PLATE,ROLLD	W 1756502	941757	W 1811949	1077183	W 1884636	1507380	W 1940290	1250477	TOLES LAM MOINS 3MM
67461	— OF IRON OR SIMPLE STL	W 1587603	682687	W 1605222	745664	W 1619949	915249	W 1710047	820921	TOL NON AC FIN MOINS 3 MM
67463	— OF STAINLESS ETC STL	W 120270	223007	W 145349	274146	W 182602	506225	W 163773	358192	TOL ACIER INOX MOINS 3 MM
6749	OTH IRN,STL PLATES,SHEET	W 1946800	1100787	W 2270377	1353482	W 2455211	1846129	W 2224725	1507926	AUTRES TOLES FER,ACIER
67491	— OF IRON OR SIMPLE STL	W 1931468	1080710	W 2254743	1330808	W 2430105	1793368	W 2206654	1466454	AUT TOLES AUTRES ACIER FIN
677	IRN,STL WIRE(EXCL W ROD)	W 464503	417501	W 517254	491808	W 298760	266108	W 304515	239310	FILS EN FER,ACIER
68	NON–FERROUS METALS		2995189		3451584		4510009		3569812	METAUX NON FERREUX
682	COPPER EXC CEMENT COPPER	W 547852	1298504	W 544532	1453186	W 538165	1865280	W 474201	1338140	CUIVRE
6821	COPPER NES,ALLOYS,UNWRT	W 244888	547515	W 182420	438827	W 210921	647669	W 155812	378516	CUIVRE BRUT
68212	COPPER REFINED,UNWROUGHT	W 210622	461888	W 152751	363254	W 173527	529118	W 130717	309643	CUIVRE AFFINE BRUT
6822	COPPER,ALLOYS WORKED	W 302588	748392	W 361709	1011046	W 327244	1217611	W 318388	959624	CUIVRE,ALLIAGES OUVRES
68221	COPPER BARS,WIRE,ETC	W 234585	485844	W 297413	729341	W 258432	833116	W 251741	631483	BARRES,PROFILES ET FILS
684	ALUMINIUM	W 402550	952131	W 463530	1125171	W 482329	1564164	W 401511	1196192	ALUMINIUM
6842	ALUMINIUM,ALLOYS WORKED	W 314738	838066	W 356257	973141	W 368155	1327612	W 339196	1092645	ALUMINIUM,ALLIAGES OUVRE
68422	ALUMNM PLATE,SHEET,STRIP	W 158173	340307	W 196492	457554	W 191717	591086	W 181360	487034	TOLES, PLANCHES EN ALU
69	METAL MANUFACTURES NES		2182896		2310090		2957621		2801247	ART MANUFACT EN METAL NDA
691	STRUCTURES AND PARTS NES	W 311642	512467	W 313985	514598	W 366219	656770	W 323193	617801	CONSTRUCT FER,ACIER,ALU
6911	STRUCTURES,PARTS IRN,STL	W 296784	418318	W 298101	420641	W 351737	546450	W 309646	516597	CONSTRUCT FER,ACIER,FONTE
699	BASE METAL MFRS NES	W 141776	571878	W 137437	618358	W 184280	830893	W 195733	786858	ART MANUFACTURES MET NDA
7	MACHINES,TRANSPORT EQUIP		33047097		38548436		45924475		46015795	MACHINES MATERIEL TRANSPORT
71	POWER GENERATING EQUIPMT		1031220		914730		1253918		1088371	MACHINES GENERATRICES
713	INTRNL COMBUS PSTN ENGIN	W 25938	339921	W 34218	431399	W 43194	642463	W 35720	559225	MOTEURS EXPL COMB INT, PIECE
72	MACHS FOR SPCL INDUSTRYS		2282723		3053698		3675707		3343998	MAC SPECIALES POUR INDUST
721	AGRIC MACHY,EXC TRACTORS	W 39035	306644	W 50014	437998	W 57470	491111	W 67499	580554	MACHINES AGRICOLES
723	CIVIL ENGNEERG EQUIP ETC	W 137234	749970	W 205456	1251182	W 209888	1437003	W 174663	1092017	APPAREILS DE GENIE CIVIL
7234	CONST,MINING MACHNRY NES	W 133848	729238	W 202466	1235154	W 206014	1413970	W 170907	1067483	MACH POUR LA CONST, MINES
72342	SLFPRP SHOVELS,EXCAVATRS	W 125273	682229	W 196228	1209830	W 199028	1374775	W 163403	1031992	PELLES MECANIQUES
728	OTH MACHY FOR SPCL INDUS	W 57909	562484	W 49037	616222	W 59185	774226	W 100823	809359	AUT MACH IND PARTICULIERES
7284	MACHY FOR SPCL INDUS NES	W 34831	409885	W 23189	433630	W 25874	526044	W 30136	546709	MACH SPEC IND PARTICUL.
73	METALWORKING MACHINERY		530011		516320		658317		659284	MACH TRAVAIL DES METAUX
736	METALWORKING MACH–TOOLS	W 35872	367840	W 34440	351061	W 35993	416321	W 37012	442892	MACH–OUTILS TRAVAIL METAUX
74	GENRL INDUSTRL MACHY NES		3102582		3484180		4562465		4857574	MACH APP INDUSTRIE
741	HEATING,COOLING EQUIPMNT	W 61878	606005	W 72118	696790	W 81851	859392	W 89542	871202	MACH CHAUFFAGE,PIECES
743	PUMPS NES,CENTRFUGES ETC	W 40040	688163	W 44021	754357	W 53350	935543	W 57135	973534	POMPES COMPRES,VENT ETC
744	MECHANICAL HANDLING EQU	W 102536	706112	W 103131	707279	W 115821	830041	W 120066	839249	EQUIP MANUTENTION PIECES
7449	PTS NES OF MACHY OF 7442	W 60574	443717	W 60469	446175	W 66579	527255	W 59824	485792	PIECES DU 744.2
749	NONELEC MACH PTS,ACC NES	W 45330	698986	W 48688	831728	W 65253	1288349	W 80150	1510884	PIECES MACH NON ELEC NDA
75	OFFICE MACHNES,ADP EQUIP		1246885		1580803		2342725		2493992	MACH BUREAU TRAIT AUTOM
752	AUTOMTIC DATA PROC EQUIP	W 8701	803707	W 11629	1015787	W 22602	1484601	W 19685	1733515	MACH TRAIT INFORMATION
7525	ADP PERIPHERAL UNITS	W 4646	313649	W 5543	357416	W 9585	581088	W 11923	644890	UNITES PERIPHERIQUES
759	OFFICE,ADP MCH PTS,ACCES	W 6881	336123	W 7392	429877	W 11628	592685	W 9595	580981	PIECES DU 751 ET 752
76	TELECOMM,SOUND EQUIPMENT		2581855		2895568		3373913		3152583	EQUIPMENT DE TELECOM
761	TELEVISION RECEIVERS	W 25216	444588	W 31673	522463	W 31555	606901	W 32584	656584	RECEPTEURS DE TELEVISION
7611	COLOUR TV RECEIVERS	W 25015	440600	W 31582	519257	W 31393	602838	W 32489	653063	RECEPTEURS COULEUR
762	RADIO BROADCAST RECEIVRS	W 9473	366401	W 9183	392057	W 11089	526715	W 13732	558476	RECEPTEURS RADIODIFFUSION
763	SOUND RECORDRS,PHONOGRPH	W 10634	423212	W 7509	343417	W 6633	367089	W 6085	299051	PHONO,APP ENREGISTREMENT
7638	OTHR SOUND APPARATUS ETC	W 10190	414318	W 7224	336647	W 6427	360383	W 5920	295188	AUT APP D'ENREGIS,REPROD
764	TELECOM EQPT,PTS,ACC NES	W 34014	1347654	W 35579	1637632	W 35851	1873208	W 33498	1638471	EQUIP TELECOM,PIECES
7649	PTS NES OF EQUIPMT OF 76	W 12516	902612	W 15521	1154478	W 15988	1191140	W 14287	1001834	PIECES DE LA DIV 76

5. Special Exports F.O.B. by Commodities according to the S.I.T.C. (Rev. 2) in thousand U.S. Dollars
Exportations Spéciales F.O.B. par Produits d'après la C.T.C.I. (Rév. 2) en milliers de Dollars E.U.

SITC CTCI	COMMODITY	1993 WEIGHT POIDS	1993 VALUE VALEUR	1994 WEIGHT POIDS	1994 VALUE VALEUR	1995 WEIGHT POIDS	1995 VALUE VALEUR	1996 WEIGHT POIDS	1996 VALUE VALEUR	PRODUIT
76491	PTS NES OF APPAR OF 7641	W 3734	587854	W 5054	849061	W 4780	772006	W 3717	621281	PIECES POUR 764.1
77	ELECTRIC MACHNRY NES ETC		3267368		3782185		4840878		5005752	MACH APP ELECT NDA
772	SWITCHGEAR ETC,PARTS NES	W 16432	636512	W 17810	683465	W 21046	1029390	W 18760	866272	APP COUPURE,SECT ETC
7721	SWITCHGEAR ETC	W 14402	491626	W 15194	521748	W 18211	829926	W 16150	698366	APP COUPURE,SECTIONMNT
773	ELECTR DISTRIBUTNG EQUIP	W 61905	390828	W 73071	465794	W 79584	681981	W 75594	573086	EQUIPMT DISTRIBUTION ELECT
7731	INSULATED WIRE,CABLE ETC	W 54050	242597	W 65245	328704	W 71400	535944	W 67561	425496	FILS,CABLES ISOLES ELECT
776	TRANSISTORS,VALVES,ETC	W 6940	324984	W 7737	423558	W 8540	486474	W 8902	898564	LAMPES,TUBES,VALVES
7764	ELECTRONIC MICROCIRCUITS	W 438	236417	W 552	326942	W 602	338168	W 520	737978	MICROSTRUCTURES ELECTRON
778	ELECTRICAL MACHINERY NES	W 122744	1313365	W 133257	1560586	W 146961	1908580	W 173274	1975253	AUTRES MACH ELECT NDA
7781	BATTERIES,ACCUMULATORS	W 87377	521689	W 93095	564142	W 99640	631690	W 128799	666349	PILES ET ACCUMULATEURS
77811	PRIMARY BATTERIES,CELLS	W 51484	396044	W 51856	417393	W 55578	468603	W 57552	494622	PILES ELECTRIQUES,PIECES
78	ROAD VEHICLES		18113494		21695007		24503900		24739367	VEHICULES ROUTIERS
781	PASS MOTOR VEH EXC BUSES	W 1321698	14214186	W 1546352	16900890	W 1507210	18023407	W 1566263	18426464	AUTO TRANSPORT PERSONNES
782	LORRIES,SPCL MTR VEH NES	W 146004	1001898	W 180637	1380199	W 194595	1658556	W 191657	1478839	VEHICULES SPECIAUX,MARCH
7821	LORRIES,TRUCKS	W 141031	972931	W 176536	1363528	W 189393	1627512	W 185224	1449720	VEHICULES TRANSP MARCHAND
783	ROAD MOTOR VEHICLES NES	W 86126	875394	W 98206	998567	W 115338	1299414	W 115129	1255807	VEHICULES ROUTIERS NDA
7831	BUSES	W 41083	567233	W 34288	474191	W 32846	489383	W 33865	508186	VOITURES TRANSPORT COMMUN
7832	TRACTORS FOR TR–TRAILERS	W 45042	308161	W 63918	524376	W 82492	810031	W 81264	747621	TRACTEURS ROUTIERS
784	MOTOR VEH PRTS,ACCES NES	W 294546	1697412	W 305773	2039489	W 371362	3074635	W 448542	3080392	PIECES 722,781,782,783
7849	OTHER MOTOR VEHCL PARTS	W 285566	1622362	W 288294	1865163	W 348086	2805506	W 420864	2795285	PIECES 722,781,782,783
79	OTHR TRANSPORT EQUIPMENT		890891		625869		712651		674875	AUTRE MATERIEL TRANSPORT
792	AIRCRAFT ETC	W 1306	518726	W 709	272852	W 876	402297	W 848	407200	APP NAVIGATION AERIENNE
7929	AIRCRAFT PARTS NES	W 1259	513676	W 489	257841	W 750	367395	W 731	378238	PIECES DU 792
8	MISC MANUFACTURED GOODS		11057082		11657255		14471147		14556645	ART MANUFACTURES DIVERS
812	*PLUMBG,HEATNG,LGHTNG EQ	W 151639	532808	W 162065	598180	W 153960	713676	W 164189	703062	APPAR SANITAIRES CHAUFFAGE
821	*FURNITURE,PARTS THEREOF	W 285598	1409315	W 304996	1497329	W 308847	1706016	W 309096	1634581	MEUBLES ET PIECES
8211	CHAIRS,SEATS AND PARTS	W 52983	460337	W 55373	463937	W 53051	495944	W 51163	467094	SIEGES ET PIECES
82111	CHAIRS AND OTHER SEATS	W 44885	397372	W 47643	394516	W 48609	432742	W 46164	401227	SIEGES
8219	FURNITURE AND PARTS NES	W 174640	660514	W 190551	746582	W 198422	885189	W 197046	837253	AUTRES MEUBLES ET PIECES
82192	WOOD FURNITURE NES	W 121746	511183	W 134235	575995	W 140978	671531	W 131738	610753	MEUBLES NDA EN BOIS
84	CLOTHING AND ACCESSORIES		2146479		2161118		2722854		2885376	VETEMENTS
842	MENS OUTERWEAR NOT KNIT	W 37666	883101	W 33023	765947	W 31607	945408	W 35867	1007178	VET DESSUS POUR HOMMES
8423	— TROUSERS,BREECHES ETC	W 30626	702315	W 25551	586327	W 22494	677577	W 26549	723150	PANTALONS HOMMES MAT TEX
843	WOMENS OUTERWEAR NONKNIT	W 12389	463279	W 12896	512239	W 12849	577798	W 12701	539819	VET DESSUS FEMMES MAT TEX
845	OUTERWEAR KNIT NONELASTC	W 9728	285042	W 10514	302420	W 11883	421638	W 14584	501293	VET DESSOUS,ACCES BONNET
851	*FOOTWEAR	W 12515	156872		165685	W 12451	174382	W 28019	802302	CHAUSSURES
85102	FOOTWEAR LEATHER	W 8792	118540	W 9730	124634	W 8783	131859	W 20815	626602	CHAUS SEMELLES EN CUIR
87	PRECISION INSTRUMNTS NES		949242		1085482		1498376		1404896	INSTRUM,APPAR SCIENT NDA
872	MEDICAL INSTRUMENTS NES	W 16362	409132	W 18309	477069	W 26276	759532	W 33398	782773	INSTR,APP MEDIC–CHIR NDA
87202	OTH MEDICAL INSTRUMENTS	W 15976	398827	W 17792	465240	W 25594	744273	W 32480	766560	INSTRUM,APP MEDECINE
874	MEASURNG,CONTROLNG INSTR		475561		539308	W 16999	655336	W 12486	541706	INSTRUMENTS DE MESURE
88	PHOTO EQU,OPTICL GDS ETC		1407131		1550927		2104997		1989829	APP,FOURN PHOTO,OP,MONTR
882	PHOTO,CINEMA SUPPLIES	W 112758	1182416	W 123132	1292150	W 152453	1677850	W 132525	1451425	PRODUITS PHOTO,CINEMA
8822	PHOTO FILM EXC DEV CINMA	W 48486	1024713	W 59829	1122713	W 76326	1436334	W 61269	1213014	PLAQUES,PELLICULES,FILMS
88221	PHOTO FILM FLAT UNEXPOSD	W 19895	425886	W 20923	445242	W 26093	608878	W 20360	509384	PLAQUES PHOTO,FILMS SENS
88222	PHOTO FILM ROLL UNEXPOSD	W 21317	475783	W 25055	519851	W 30052	621129	W 28012	561712	PEL SENSIB PERF OU NON
89	MISC MANUFCTRD GOODS NES		4238309		4367185		5242118		4825452	ART MANUFACTURES DIVERS
892	PRINTED MATTER	W 221761	879030		991634	W 270899	1164646	W 251022	1028209	IMPRIMES
8928	PRINTED MATTER NES	W 114252	397381	W 145211	494202	W 136595	527940	W 120823	490566	IMPRIMES NDA
893	ARTICLES OF PLASTIC NES		1703151		1878431		2400514		2237659	OUVRAGES EN MAT DIVIS 58
8931	PLSTC PACKG CONTNRS,LIDS	W 144799	379593	W 172335	420365	W 174033	584272	W 218946	529273	ART TRANSP EMBALLAGE ETC
8939	MISC PLASTIC ARTICLES	W 298306	1255417	W 315057	1368473	W 295339	1707614	W 310093	1612407	ART DIVERS EN MAT DIV 58
89399	OTHR PLASTC ARTICLES NES	W 176964	1007065	W 188193	1088325	W 198955	1375362	W 192113	1321394	AUT OUV MAT DIV 58
894	TOYS,SPORTING GOODS,ETC	W 67489	637139	W 47689	447294	W 33825	370866	W 34102	370017	VOITURES ENFANTS,JOUETS
8942	TOYS,INDOOR GAMES ETC	W 57200	560066	W 38086	357451	W 23988	273764	W 24443	268088	JOUETS,JEUX ETC
89423	TOYS NES	W 46351	434151	W 26843	226953	W 12629	144381	W 12763	134975	JOUETS,MODELES REDUITS
898	MUSICAL INSTRUMENTS,PTS		552971		552578	W 44356	631947	W 40882	571674	INSTRUMENTS DE MUSIQUE
8983	SOUND RECRDNG TAPE,DISCS	W 38030	535680	W 38964	536995	W 43926	612320	W 40245	552384	SUPPORTS SON POUR 763
89831	PREPD SND RECORDNG MEDIA	W 35861	407175	W 35517	363335	W 40564	421923	W 36742	348260	SUPPORTS PREPARES
9	GOODS NOT CLASSD BY KIND		5367884		4929261		9829754		9002020	ART TRANSACT NON CLASSES
931	*SPECIAL TRANSACTIONS	W 3265834	4977374	W 3120230	4456938	W 7718048	9467957	W 7373310	8624665	TRANS.SPECIALES
971	*GOLD,NON MONETARY NES		356364		436833		312699	K 35490	329588	OR NON MONETAIRE
97101	NONMON GLD UNWRT,SEMIMFD	K 29100	355545	K 48600	436779	K 25173	311899	K 27892	326988	OR,ALLIAGES D'OR BRUTS

1. HISTORICAL SERIES, 1961–1996 GENERAL TRADE, IMPORTS C.I.F., EXPORTS F.O.B.
SERIES HISTORIQUES, 1961–1996 COMMERCE GENERAL, IMPORTATIONS C.A.F., EXPORTATIONS F.O.B

YEAR ANNEE	VALUE IN MILLION BELIZE DOLLARS VALEUR EN MILLION BELIZE DOLLARS MERCHANDISE –MARCHANDISE IMPORTS	EXPORTS	GOLD –OR IMPORTS	EXPORTS	CONVERSION FACTORS U.S. CENTS PER BELIZE DOLLAR FACTEURS DE CONVERSION CENTS E.U. PAR BELIZE DOLLAR IMPORTS	EXPORTS	INDEX NUMBERS –INDICES QUANTUM IMPORTS	EXPORTS	UNIT VALUE VALEUR UNITAIRE IMPORTS	EXPORTS
1961	22.70	12.40			70.0000	70.0000				
1962	31.20	12.40			70.0000	70.0000				
1963	27.60	18.60			70.0000	70.0000				
1964	31.30	19.20			70.0000	70.0000				
1965	35.00	17.50			70.0000	70.0000				
1966	38.80	19.20			70.0000	70.0000				
1967	37.00	20.50			69.1500	69.1500				
1968	44.20	25.20			60.0000	60.0000				
1969	49.40	28.10			60.0000	60.0000				
1970	55.60	31.30			60.0000	60.0000				
1971	58.60	31.70			60.8600	60.8600				
1972	69.30	40.20			62.6000	62.6000				
1973	72.30	52.70			61.3042	61.3042				
1974	109.20	76.90			58.4761	58.4761				
1975	159.20	120.40			55.5952	55.5952				
1976	161.50	94.00			45.1552	45.1552				
1977	180.20	124.20			43.6378	43.6378				
1978	213.00	159.60			47.9874	47.9875				
1979	263.70	173.50			53.0379	53.0380				
1980	300.00	221.30			50.0000	50.0000				
1981	323.90	238.00			50.0000	50.0000				
1982	256.00	182.00			50.0000	50.0000				
1983	223.60	155.50			50.0000	50.0000				
1984	260.30	186.40			50.0000	50.0000				
1985	227.60	173.20			50.0000	50.0000				
1986	243.93	185.21			50.0000	50.0000				
1987	285.89	205.66			50.0000	50.0000				
1988	361.95	232.51			50.0000	50.0000				
1989	431.39	249.07			50.0000	50.0000				
1990	422.59	265.92			50.0000	50.0000				
1991	512.49	243.44			50.0000	50.0000				
1992	548.06	281.01			50.0000	50.0000				
1993	561.92	272.97			50.0000	50.0000				
1994	519.86	301.97			50.0000	50.0000				
1995	511.11	323.25			50.0000	50.0000				
1996	511.11	335.27			50.0000	50.0000				

2. IMPORTS BY BROAD ECONOMIC CATEGORY AND EXPORTS BY INDUSTRIAL ORIGIN. (PERCENTAGE OF TOTAL VALUE)
IMPORTATIONS PAR CATEGORIES ECONOMIQUES ET EXPORTATIONS PAR BRANCHE D'ACTIVITE.(EN POURCENTAGE DE LA VALEUR TOTALE)

IMPORTS – IMPORTATIONS

	1990	1991	1992	1993	1994	1995	1996
TOTAL IMPORTS–IMPORTATIONS TOTALES	100.		100.	100.	100.	100.	
1 FOOD BEV–ALIMENTATION BOISSONS	21.2		18.6	15.6	15.1	16.2	
11 PRIMARY–PRODUITS DE BASE	4.1		4.0	2.6	3.2	3.4	
111 FOR INDUSTRY–POUR L'INDUSTRIE	1.6		1.4	1.2	1.7	1.6	
112 FOR HOUSEHOLDS–POUR LES MENAGES	2.4		2.7	1.4	1.5	1.8	
12 PROCESSED–PRODUITS ELABORES	17.1		14.5	12.9	11.9	12.8	
121 FOR INDUSTRY–POUR L'INDUSTRIE	0.9		0.7	0.7	0.7	0.7	
122 FOR HOUSEHOLDS–POUR LES MENAGES	16.2		13.9	12.2	11.3	12.1	
2 IND SUPPLIES–APPROV INDUSTRIELS	26.1		29.4	30.1	30.8	28.7	
21 PRIMARY–PRODUITS DE BASE	0.6		1.6	0.8	1.1	0.8	
22 PROCESSED–PRODUITS ELABORES	25.5		27.8	29.3	29.7	27.9	
3 FUELS–COMBUSTIBLES	12.5		11.8	11.1	11.3	11.5	
31 PRIMARY–PRODUITS DE BASE	0.6		0.8	0.7	0.8	0.9	
32 PROCESSED–PRODUITS ELABORES	11.9		11.0	10.3	10.5	10.5	
321 MOTOR SPIRIT–ESSENCE	3.6		3.2	3.2	3.5	2.9	
322 OTHER–AUTRES	8.3		7.8	7.1	7.0	7.7	
4 MACHINERY–EQUIPEMENT	14.0		14.5	16.2	16.9	16.2	
41 CAPITAL EQUIPMENT–MACHINES	12.3		13.0	14.4	14.9	14.3	
42 PARTS–PIECES ACCESSOIRES	1.7		1.5	1.8	2.0	1.9	
5 TRANSPORT–TRANSPORT	9.1		9.8	9.8	8.9	10.0	
51 PASSENGER CARS–AUTOMOBILES	1.4		2.4	1.9	1.7	2.2	
52 OTHER–AUTRES	4.5		4.1	4.5	3.9	4.6	
521 INDUSTRIAL–INDUSTRIELS	4.2		3.8	4.1	3.6	4.3	
522 NON INDUSTRIAL–NON INDUSTRIEL	0.3		0.2	0.4	0.3	0.3	
53 PARTS–PIECES ACCESSOIRES	3.2		3.4	3.4	3.3	3.2	
6 CONSUM GOODS–BIENS CONSOMMATION	16.4		15.3	17.1	16.8	17.1	
61 DURABLE–DURABLES	2.5		2.5	2.6	2.8	3.5	
62 SEMI DURABLE–SEMI DURABLES	9.2		8.8	10.3	8.5	8.7	
63 NON DURABLE–NON DURABLES	4.6		4.0	4.2	5.4	4.9	
7 GOODS NES–BIENS NDA	0.8		0.6	0.2	0.2	0.3	

EXPORTS – EXPORTATIONS

	1990	1991	1992	1993	1994	1995	1996
TOTAL EXPORTS–EXPORTATIONS TOTALES	100.		100.	100.	100.	100.	
1 AGRICULTURE	14.6		14.3	18.9	22.2	25.4	
2 MINING QUARRY–INDUS EXTRACTIVES			0.1	0.0	0.2	0.1	
3 MANUFACTURING–IND MANUFACTUR	85.4		85.6	81.1	77.6	74.4	
31 FOOD BEV TOBACCO–ALIM BOISS TAB	60.6		58.8	53.7	48.5	55.3	
32 TEXTILES–INDUSTRIES TEXTILES	12.0		14.4	16.3	13.0	9.7	
33 WOOD & PRODUCTS–BOIS & PRODUITS	2.0		2.9	2.8	3.7	1.5	
34 PAPER & PRODUCTS–PAPIER & PRODT	0.0		0.0	0.2	0.0	0.0	
35 CHEMICALS–INDUSTRIES CHIMIQUES	4.7		4.0	3.1	3.8	3.5	
36 NON METAL MIN–MIN NON METAL	0.0		0.0	0.0	0.0	0.0	
37 BASIC METAL–IND METAL BASE	0.0		0.0	0.0	0.0	0.0	
38 METAL MANUF–MANUF METAL	5.5		5.4	4.8	7.1	3.9	
39 OTH MANUF IND–AUTRES MANUF	0.5		0.0	0.1	1.6	0.4	

3. TRADE BY PRINCIPAL COUNTRIES OF ORIGIN AND DESTINATION (VALUE IN THOUSAND U.S. DOLLARS)
ECHANGES SELON LES PRINCIPAUX PAYS D'ORIGINE ET DE DESTINATION (VALEUR EN MILLIERS DE DOLLARS EU)

COUNTRIES–PAYS	GENERAL IMPORTS C.I.F. IMPORTATIONS GENERALES C.A.F				
	1991	1992	1993	1994	1995
World		274153	280913	259942	258324
Africa		82	86	51	84
Americas		214057	226614	198305	207087
Northern America		161603	168520	144534	147660
LAIA		30132	35017	28567	31136
CACM		10751	11322	12812	10022
Caribbean		10955	10948	11279	17322
Rest of America		617	807	1113	948
As.ex F.USSR		14688	16115	13743	9795
Eur.x F.USSR		44638	37240	47273	40930
EU		43597	36599	44921	40140
EFTA		907	457	2249	750
East Europe		134	184	103	40
Other Europe			0		
Former USSR			54	16	60
Oceania		611	746	553	367
USA/Etats–Unis d'Amer		156150	162739	138517	139736
Mexico/Mexique		24212	26926	24951	28516
United Kingdom		23222	16900	18902	16164
Netherlands/Pays–Bas		8572	11226	17120	15009
Guatemala		6381	7651	8852	6979
Canada		5452	5779	6017	7925
China/Chine		1997	8387	8276	1977
Jamaica/Jamaïque		4610	4617	4032	4624
Trinidad and Tobago		4199	2991	4390	5624
Japan/Japon		4551	3539	3034	3409
Venezuela		4519	5658	467	327
Denmark/Danemark		3512	1712	1779	1819
Barbados/Barbade		1597	2194	2436	2171
Germany/Allemagne		1864	2319	1164	2808
El Salvador		2316	1960	1881	1791
Brazil/Brésil		1062	1770	1919	1377
Ireland/Irlande		918	1236	1239	1585
Cuba			1		4578
Italy/Italie		2968	451	429	717
Costa Rica		1512	962	1029	835
Hong Kong		1503	1318	717	717
France,Monac		935	916	1489	812
Switz.Liecht		815	418	2190	713
Panama		591	798	1096	873
Spain/Espagne		123	352	1974	524
Honduras		452	594	1050	417
Colombia/Colombie		142	590	915	694
Korea, Republic of		617	1207		231
Austria/Autriche		776	772	194	59
Singapore/Singapour		446	445	470	427
Sweden/Suède		285	392	468	412
India/Inde		355	447	368	273
New Zealand		599	391	173	279
Dominica/Dominique		180	830	95	99
Thailand/Thaïlande		204	411	280	281
Saint Lucia/St. Lucie		219	280	223	193
Australia/Australie		3	355	380	88
Indonesia/Indonésie		209	105	121	130
Belgium–Luxembourg		152	173	93	131
Malaysia/Malaisie		14	29	38	301
Portugal		166	93	61	2
Argentina/Argentine		118	49	141	11
Korea Dem People's Rp				304	9
Israel/Israël		4	86	77	127
Ecuador/Equateur		5	4	125	138
Nicaragua		90	155		0
Norway,SVD,JM		92	39	58	38
Finland/Finlande		58	58	8	98
Philippines		102	25	2	18
Hungary/Hongrie		0	70	49	14

COUNTRIES–PAYS	GENERAL EXPORTS F.O.B. EXPORTATIONS GENERALES F.O.B.				
	1991	1992	1993	1994	1995
Monde		135939	126605	142931	161680
Afrique		3029	1		10
Amériques		93993	74561	91491	76982
Amérique du Nord		70119	56842	73602	66068
ALAI		17039	11963	12012	4614
MCAC		616	678	802	638
Caraïbes		6212	4858	5060	5536
Autre Amérique		6	220	15	126
Asie l'URSS exclus		1278	817	561	317
Europe l'URSS exclus		37629	51209	50846	84344
UE		37566	51146	50599	83793
AELE		63	49	248	548
Europe de l'Est			14		3
Autre de l'Europe					
Ancienne URSS					
Océanie		10	17	1	27
USA/Etats–Unis d'Amer		64171	48525	63366	59099
United Kingdom		32098	47068	43425	68472
Mexico/Mexique		17017	11947	11923	4531
Canada		5931	8299	10237	6938
Germany/Allemagne		3352	2837	3062	8417
Trinidad and Tobago		3847	1519	1981	2074
France,Monac		1175	977	3838	3300
Jamaica/Jamaïque		1079	2484	1965	2030
Barbados/Barbade		986	702	825	1050
Morocco/Maroc		3012			
Netherlands/Pays–Bas		480	195	113	1363
Japan/Japon		1142	626	113	163
Italy/Italie				0	2042
Guatemala		370	255	485	432
Switz.Liecht		56	37	248	548
Honduras		230	346	178	115
Dominica/Dominique		120	50	102	141
Belgium–Luxembourg		338	44		1
Antigua and Barbuda		80	56	95	147
Singapore/Singapour				302	
Panama		2	195	2	95
Spain/Espagne		106	0	44	99
China/Chine		74	74	51	1
Costa Rica		2	34	76	71
Saint Lucia/St. Lucie		80	9	15	39
Venezuela		8		79	53
Denmark/Danemark		2		117	
Hong Kong			112	0	
El Salvador		14	38	29	21
Malaysia/Malaisie					71
Israel/Israël					68
Sweden/Suède		7			58
Bermuda/Bermudes		17	17		31
Korea Dem People's Rp				56	
Portugal					41
India/Inde		1		39	
Nicaragua		0	4	35	
New Zealand		10	11	1	13
Australia/Australie			6		14
Norway,SVD,JM		6	12		
Cuba				18	
Ireland/Irlande			17		
Ecuador/Equateur		4	10		
Colombia/Colombie		7			7
Finland/Finlande			8		
Thailand/Thaïlande		7			
Korea, Republic of			5		
Austria/Autriche		4			
Brazil/Brésil			4		
British Virgin Islds		1	1		

(VALUE AS PERCENTAGE OF WORLD TOTAL)(VALEURS EN POURCENTAGE DU TOTAL MONDIAL)

	1986	1987	1988	1989	1990	1991	1992	1993	1994	1995
Africa	0.0	0.0	0.0	0.0	0.0		0.0	0.0	0.0	0.0
Americas	76.8	77.1	75.3	75.9	78.7		78.1	80.7	76.3	80.2
Northern America	60.8	62.0	57.7	59.4	60.1		58.9	60.0	55.6	57.2
LAIA	8.0	9.2	7.6	7.7	7.8		11.0	12.5	11.0	12.1
CACM	5.5	3.3	4.0	3.5	3.2		3.9	4.0	4.9	3.9
Caribbean	2.2	2.4	5.6	5.1	7.7		4.0	3.9	4.3	6.7
Rest of America	0.3	0.2	0.3	0.1	0.0		0.2	0.3	0.4	0.4
As.ex F.USSR	5.7	4.8	6.0	4.7	5.0		5.4	5.7	5.3	3.8
Eur.x F.USSR	17.2	17.6	18.4	19.0	15.9		16.3	13.2	18.2	15.8
EU	16.6	17.1	17.7	18.5	15.5		15.9	13.0	17.3	15.5
EFTA	0.4	0.4	0.2	0.2	0.2		0.3	0.2	0.9	0.3
East Europe	0.2	0.1	0.4	0.2	0.2		0.0	0.1	0.0	0.0
Other Europe	0.0	0.0	0.0	0.0	0.0			0.0		
Former USSR	0.0	0.0	0.0	0.0	0.0			0.0	0.0	0.0
Oceania	0.3	0.5	0.3	0.3	0.3		0.2	0.3	0.2	0.1
USA/Etats–Unis d'Amer	57.4	58.1	53.6	57.2	57.8		57.0	57.9	53.3	54.1
Mexico/Mexique	7.3	8.8	6.9	6.9	6.8		8.8	9.6	9.6	11.0
United Kingdom	8.1	8.2	8.9	9.2	8.2		8.5	6.0	7.3	6.3
Netherlands/Pays–Bas	4.3	4.4	4.4	5.2	3.7		3.1	4.0	6.6	5.8
Guatemala	1.8	1.3	1.2	1.5	1.6		2.3	2.7	3.4	2.7
Canada	3.4	3.9	4.1	2.2	2.3		2.0	2.1	2.3	3.1
China/Chine	2.0	0.0	0.0	0.1	0.7		0.7	3.0	3.2	0.8
Jamaica/Jamaïque	1.9	2.0	3.5	3.6	4.8		1.7	1.6	1.6	1.8
Trinidad and Tobago	0.2	0.3	1.1	0.8	0.8		1.5	1.1	1.7	2.2
Japan/Japon	2.4	1.4	1.3	1.1	1.2		1.7	1.3	1.2	1.3

	1986	1987	1988	1989	1990	1991	1992	1993	1994	1995
Afrique	0.0	0.0	0.0	0.0	0.0		2.2	0.0		0.0
Amériques	70.3	68.8	66.8	70.2	69.7		69.1	58.9	64.0	47.6
Amérique du Nord	56.8	51.0	45.1	45.3	50.1		51.6	44.9	51.5	40.9
ALAI	11.4	9.4	13.8	17.2	11.8		12.5	9.4	8.4	2.9
MCAC	0.4	0.4	0.7	0.6	1.1		0.5	0.5	0.6	0.4
Caraïbes	1.7	7.9	7.1	7.2	6.7		4.6	3.8	3.5	3.4
Autre Amérique	0.0	0.0	0.0	0.0	0.0		0.0	0.2	0.0	0.1
Asie l'URSS exclus	0.1	0.1	0.5	0.6	1.9		0.9	0.6	0.4	0.2
Europe l'URSS exclus	28.6	31.0	32.7	29.1	28.3		27.7	40.5	35.6	52.2
UE	28.4	31.0	32.4	29.1	28.2		27.6	40.4	35.4	51.8
AELE	0.0	0.0	0.2	0.1	0.0		0.0	0.0	0.2	0.3
Europe de l'Est	0.0	0.0						0.0		0.0
Autre de l'Europe	0.2		0.2							
Ancienne URSS	1.0									
Océanie	0.0	0.1		0.0	0.0		0.0	0.0	0.0	0.0
USA/Etats–Unis d'Amer	56.5	47.4	41.6	42.4	45.6		47.2	38.3	44.3	36.6
United Kingdom	27.6	30.4	30.2	26.3	27.1		23.6	37.2	30.4	42.4
Mexico/Mexique	11.4	9.4	13.8	17.1	11.7		12.5	9.4	8.3	2.8
Canada	0.2	3.4	3.5	2.9	4.4		4.4	6.6	7.2	4.3
Germany/Allemagne	0.0	0.0	0.9	1.0	0.6		2.5	2.2	2.1	5.2
Trinidad and Tobago	0.4	3.5	3.3	1.8	2.8		2.8	1.2	1.4	1.3
France,Monac	0.3	0.5	0.9	0.6	0.4		0.9	0.8	2.7	2.0
Jamaica/Jamaïque	0.9	3.5	2.8	4.4	3.0		0.8	2.0	1.4	1.3
Barbados/Barbade	0.3	0.8	1.0	0.7	0.7		0.7	0.6	0.6	0.6
Morocco/Maroc							2.2			

4. General Imports C.I.F. by Commodities according to the S.I.T.C. (Rev. 2) in thousand U.S. Dollars
Importations Générales C.A.F. par Produits d'après la C.T.C.I. (Rév. 2) en milliers de Dollars E.U.

SITC CTCI	COMMODITY	1992 WEIGHT POIDS	1992 VALUE VALEUR	1993 WEIGHT POIDS	1993 VALUE VALEUR	1994 WEIGHT POIDS	1994 VALUE VALEUR	1995 WEIGHT POIDS	1995 VALUE VALEUR	PRODUIT
	ALL COMMODITIES		274153		280913		259942		258324	TOUS PRODUITS
0	FOOD AND LIVE ANIMALS		50401		42110		39244		41303	ALIMENTS,ANIMAUX VIVANTS
01	MEAT AND PREPARATIONS		4795		3716		3339		3606	VIANDES ET PREPARATIONS
012	MEAT DRIED,SALTED,SMOKED	W 630	756	W 566	733	W 686	774	W 703	788	VIANDE,ABATS SALES,SECHES
014	MEAT PREPD,PRSVD,NES ETC	W 1730	3784	W 1375	2901	W 1196	2496	W 1254	2659	CONSERVES DE VIANDES
0142	SAUSAGES INCLDING TINNED	W 473	1104	W 451	1021	W 514	1098	W 547	1084	SAUCISSES,SAUCISSONS
0149	OTH PREPARD,PRESRVD MEAT	W 1257	2681	W 924	1880	W 681	1398	W 707	1575	AUTRES PREP DE VIANDES
02	DAIRY PRODCTS,BIRDS'EGGS		14613		12245		9249		9971	PRODUITS LAITIERS,OEUFS
022	MILK AND CREAM	W 4412	6761	W 4590	7025	W 3859	5933	W 4024	6591	LAIT ET CREME
0224	MILK,CREAM PRESERVED ETC	W 3842	6174	W 4363	6740	W 3706	5722	W 3948	6454	LAIT,CREME CONS,CONC
02243	MILK DRY,OVER 1.5% FAT	W 1163	3323	W 1167	3345	W 1152	3078	W 1005	3035	LAIT POUDRE SUP 1.5%
02249	MILK(EX DRY) PRSVD,SWEET	W 2640	2755	W 3132	3229	W 2541	2611	W 2900	3315	LAIT CONS,CONC SUCRE
024	CHEESE AND CURD	W 2356	7087	W 1501	4818	W 1071	2822	W 893	2819	FROMAGE ET CAILLEBOTTE
03	FISH AND PREPARATIONS		935		776		706		968	POISSONS ET PREPARATIONS
04	CEREALS AND PREPARATIONS		8393		7769		8216		7963	CEREALES ET PRODUITS
041	WHEAT ETC UNMILLED	W 15574	2681	W 14911	2670	W 12524	3325	W 3771	3223	FROMENT,EPEAUTRE
0411	DURUM WHEAT UNMILLED	W 10412	1785	W 14911	2670	W 12524	3325	W 3771	3223	FROMENT DUR NON MOULU
0412	OTHER WHEAT ETC UNMILLED	W 5161	896							AUTRE FROMENT NON MOULU
042	RICE	W 2628	1164	W 1516	645	W 129	76	W 1267	732	RIZ
0422	RICE SEMI–MILLED,MILLED	W 2610	1149	W 1449	613	W 41	35	W 1157	627	RIZ POLI,GLACE INCL BRISURES
04221	RICE MILLED UNBROKEN	W 2610	1149	W 1431	605	W 22	18			RIZ POLI,GLACE EXCL BRISURES
048	CEREAL ETC PREPARATIONS	W 2582	4105	W 3006	4023	W 2915	4051	W 3123	3510	PREPTNS A BASE CEREALES
0484	BAKERY PRODUCTS	W 537	1032	W 658	997	W 755	1034	W 719	767	PRODUITS DE BOULANGERIE
0488	OTH CEREAL PREPS,MALT EX	W 722	1732	W 779	1789	W 703	1831	W 620	1463	EXTRAITS DE MALT
05	VEGETABLES AND FRUIT		6873		4491		3768		4550	LEGUMES ET FRUITS
054	VEG ETC FRSH,SMPLY PRSVD	W 5130	4913	W 4459	2729		2438	W 4553	2768	LEGUMES FRAIS,CONG,SECS
0541	POTATOES FRSH EXCL SWEET	W 2297	1317	W 2151	1284	W 2289	1245	W 2236	1451	POMMES DE TERRE
0542	LEGUMINOUS VEGETBLES DRY	W 1012	2580	W 391	355	W 193	179	W 191	144	LEGUMES A COSSE SECS
0545	OTHER FRESH VEGETABLES	W 1684	837	W 1712	871		857	W 1985	1014	AUTRES LEGUMES FRAIS,REF
07	COFFEE,TEA,COCOA,SPICES		2570		1721		1775		1777	CAFE,THE,CACAO,EPICES
071	COFFEE AND SUBSTITUTES	W 271	915	W 255	693	W 262	929	W 227	814	CAFE ET SUCCEDANES
0711	COFFEE GREEN,ROASTED,SUB	W 266	900	W 229	591	W 236	831	W 143	544	CAFE TORREFIE OU DECAFEINE
07112	COFFEE ROASTED	W 264	892	W 229	590	W 236	829	W 143	544	CAFE TORREFIE
073	CHOCOLATE AND PRODUCTS	W 363	1065	W 184	605	W 175	551	W 193	626	CHOCOLAT
081	*FEEDING STUFF FOR ANIML	W 10218	5094	W 8213	4240	W 11668	5026	W 10045	4188	NOURRITURE POUR ANIMAUX
0819	FOOD WASTE AND FEED NES	W 9961	4992	W 7852	4107	W 11380	4920	W 9831	4117	DECHETS,ALIMENTS NDA
08199	FODDER NES,INCL SWEETNED	W 9961	4992	W 7852	4107	W 11379	4920	W 9831	4117	PREPARATIONS FOURRAGERES
09	MISC EDIBLE PRODUCTS		6553		6539		6537		7351	PREP ALIMENTAIRES DIVERSES
091	MARGARINE AND SHORTENING	W 2922	2877	W 2618	2498	W 2807	2621	W 3060	3020	MARGARINE ET GRAISSES
0913	PIG,POULTRY FAT RENDERED	W 1667	1422	W 1283	1055	W 1296	1072	W 1310	1154	SAINDOUX
0914	MARGARINE,EDIBLE FAT NES	W 1255	1454	W 1335	1443	W 1511	1548	W 1750	1866	MARGARINES,SIMILI SAINDOUX
09141	MARGARINE	W 515	725	W 437	620	W 514	645	W 685	791	MARGARINE
09149	OTH PREPARED EDIBLE FATS	W 740	730	W 898	823	W 996	904	W 1065	1075	SIMILI–SAINDOUX
098	EDIBLE PRODCTS,PREPS NES		3676		4041		3916		4332	PREP ALIMENTAIRES NDA
09804	SAUCES,MIXED SEASONINGS	W 845	1166	W 889	1177	W 930	1077	W 967	1200	SAUCES,ASSAISONNEMENTS
09809	MISC FOOD PREPRTIONS NES	W 399	1725	W 515	2091	W 549	1949	W 621	2359	PREP ALIMENTAIRES NDA
1	BEVERAGES AND TOBACCO		6477		6923		7703		7195	BOISSONS ET TABACS
11	BEVERAGES		5399		5497		4942		4200	BOISSONS
111	NON–ALCOHL BEVERAGES NES	W 1110	941	W 1168	818	W 2400	518	W 2286	512	BOISSONS NON ALCOOLIQUES
11102	FLAVORED WATERS NON–ALCO	W 1084	922	W 1123	799	W 2317	487	W 2218	461	LIMONADES,EAUX GAZEUSES
112	ALCOHOLIC BEVERAGES		4458	W 1178	4680	W 829	4424	W 735	3688	BOISSONS ALCOOLIQUES
1124	DISTILLED ALCOHOLIC BEVS		3212	W 437	3310	W 302	3346	W 278	2808	ALCOOLS,EAUX–DE–VIE
11241	WHISKY	W 209	2485	W 318	2694	W 206	2673	W 180	2168	WHISKY
12	TOBACCO AND MANUFACTURES		1078		1426		2762		2995	TABACS BRUTS FABRIQUES
122	TOBACCO,MANUFACTURED	W 25	628	W 36	927	W 97	2186	W 466	2440	TABACS FABRIQUES
1222	CIGARETTES	W 25	619	W 35	906	W 96	2178	W 465	2422	CIGARETTES
2	CRUDE MATERLS,EXCL FUELS		4201		2752		2358		1720	MAT BRUTES NON COMESTIBLES
24	CORK AND WOOD		391		1076		239		87	LIEGE ET BOIS
27	CRUDE FERTLZR,MINRLS NES		1134		809		1025		670	ENGRAIS MINERAUX BRUTS
278	OTHER CRUDE MINERALS		1070		785	W 301811	978		643	AUTRES MINERAUX BRUTS
2789	MINERALS CRUDE NES		883	W 94362	623	W 300963	817		522	MINERAUX BRUTS NDA
27896	NATURAL ASPHALT,BITUMEN	W 173002	870	W 94299	576	W 300936	790	W 805	498	BITUMES,ASPHALTES NATURELS
29	CRUDE ANIMAL,VEG MAT NES		2208		249		390		345	MATIERES BRUTES ANIM,VEGET
292	CRUDE VEG MATERIALS NES	W 358	2206		243	W 303	381	W 190	338	MAT BRUTES VEGETALES NDA
2925	SEEDS,ETC FOR PLANTING	W 301	2153	W 122	172	W 266	279	W 138	307	SEMENCES NDA
3	MINERAL FUELS ETC		32636		31239		29377		29719	COMBUSTIBLES MINERAUX LUB
33	PETROLEUM AND PRODUCTS		30362		29125		27279		27264	PETROLE ET DERIVES
334	PETROLEUM PRODUCTS,REFIN	W 123297	30090	W 125242	29013	W 126089	27249	W 120578	27244	PRODUITS RAFFINES
3341	GASOLINE,OTH LIGHT OILS	W 34256	8713	W 38484	8942	W 42964	9185	W 31411	7405	ESSENCES POUR MOTEURS
33411	MOTOR,AVIATION SPIRIT	W 34098	8621	W 38434	8942	W 42964	9185	W 31411	7405	ESSENCES MOTEURS D'AVIONS
3342	KEROSENE,OTH MEDIUM OILS	W 23678	5401	W 17180	3647	W 18639	3735	W 15877	3348	PETR LAMPANTS,AUT HUIL
33421	KEROSENE INCL JET FUEL	W 23678	5400	W 17179	3647	W 18638	3734	W 15876	3346	PETROLES LAMPANTS
3343	GAS OILS	W 60295	12971	W 64095	12968	W 59893	11247	W 68125	13145	GAS OILS
3345	LUBS,PETROLEUM OILS NES	W 3013	2711	W 3411	3216	W 2967	2822	W 2686	2897	HUILES LUBRIFIANTES
33451	LUBS(HIGH PETR CONT) ETC	W 2977	2598	W 3381	3168	W 2946	2771	W 2674	2832	HUILES LUBRIF,H LOURDES
341	*GAS,NATURAL AND MANUFCT	W 8160	2274	W 7340	2094	W 9013	2094	W 9869	2444	GAZ NATUREL,GAZ MANUFACT
3413	PETROLM GASES,LIQUEFIED	W 8160	2273	W 7340	2094	W 9013	2094	W 9869	2443	GAZ DE PETROLE LIQUEFIE
34131	LIQUEFIED PROPANE,BUTANE	W 8143	2272	W 7338	2091	W 8755	2092	W 9760	2441	PROPANE,BUTANE LIQUEFIES
5	CHEMCLS,RELATED PROD NES		23169		24319		26307		25044	PRODUITS CHIMIQUES
52	INORGANIC CHEMICALS		859		994		852		930	PROD CHIM INORGANIQUES
53	DYES,TANNING,COLOUR PROD		3120		3370		3144		3213	PROD TEINTURE,COLORANTS
533	PIGMENTS,PAINTS,ETC		3116	W 1333	3355		3141		3211	PIGMENTS,PEINTURES,VERNIS
5334	VARNISHES,DISTEMPERS ETC	W 1108	2684	W 1075	2913	W 1228	2691	W 953	2714	PEINTURES A L'EAU
53341	WATER–THINNED PAINTS	W 380	1005	W 483	1135	W 543	1234	W 387	983	PEINTURES DILUEES
53342	OTH PAINTS,VARNISHES ETC	W 719	1654	W 581	1751	W 678	1433	W 544	1679	AUTRES PEINTURES,VERNIS
541	*MEDICINAL,PHARM PRODUCT		4475	K 511508	4761	K 547873	4364	K 485062	4118	PROD MEDICINAUX PHARMACEUT
5417	MEDICAMENTS		3955	K 473407	4147	K 529018	3825	K 452166	3736	MEDICAMENTS
54179	— CONTNG OTH SUBSTANCES	K 526099	3293	K 438514	3325	K 495381	3187	K 422576	3018	MED CONT AUT SUBSTANCES
55	PERFUME,CLEANING ETC PRD		4325		3868		5544		3810	PROD POUR PARFUM,TOILETTE
553	PERFUMERY,COSMETICS,ETC		1974	W 559	1945		3024	W 582	1673	PRODUITS DE PARFUMERIE
554	SOAP,CLEANSING ETC PREPS	W 1839	2316	W 1484	1880	W 2517	2475	W 2421	2076	SAVONS,PRODUITS DETERSIFS
5542	WASHING PREPARATIONS ETC	W 1461	1691	W 1194	1336	W 2042	1789	W 2086	1570	PROD ORG TENSIO–ACT NDA
562	*FERTILIZERS,MANUFACTURE		3513		2758		3979		4768	ENGRAIS MANUFACTURES
5621	CHEM NITROGENOUS FERTLZR		1003	W 5640	977	W 6113	1168	W 6866	1655	ENGRAIS AZOTES
56216	UREA	W 3013	637	W 3996	647	W 4806	901	W 4711	1128	UREE
5623	CHEM POTASSIC FERTILIZER	W 3368	647		638	W 4584	790		538	ENGRAIS POTASSIQUES
56239	CHEM POTASS FERTILZR NES	W 3107	573	W 3474	638	W 4584	790	W 2004	369	ENGRAIS POTASSIQUES NDA
5629	FERTILIZERS NES		1820		1138		2008	W 9861	2556	ENGRAIS NDA
56291	NIT–PHOS–POT FERTLZR NES		712	W 4638	240	W 16550	981	W 4332	1057	ENGRAIS CONT N P K
56292	NITROG–PHOS FERTILZR NES		900	W 4474	808		931	W 4087	995	ENGRAIS NDA CONT N P
572	*EXPLOSIVES,PYROTECH PRO	W 55	397	W 324	1173	W 91	252	W 29	107	EXPLOSIFS

4. General Imports C.I.F. by Commodities according to the S.I.T.C. (Rev. 2) in thousand U.S. Dollars
Importations Générales C.A.F. par Produits d'après la C.T.C.I. (Rév. 2) en milliers de Dollars E.U.

SITC CTCI	COMMODITY	1992 WEIGHT POIDS	1992 VALUE VALEUR	1993 WEIGHT POIDS	1993 VALUE VALEUR	1994 WEIGHT POIDS	1994 VALUE VALEUR	1995 WEIGHT POIDS	1995 VALUE VALEUR	PRODUIT
58	PLASTIC MATERIALS ETC		1042		1151		1201		1621	MAT PLAST ARTIFICIELLES
583	POLYMERIZATION ETC PRODS	W 552	889	W 625	973	W 690	944	W 471	1309	PROD POLYMERISATION
5839	OTH POLYMRZTION ETC PROD	W 124	293	W 160	372	W 68	194	W 190	807	AUT PROD POLYMER COPOLYM
59	CHEMICAL MATERIALS NES		5171		6019		6720		6257	MAT PROD CHIMIQUES NDA
591	PESTICIDES,DISINFECTANTS	W 1229	4111		4739	W 1532	5320	W 1536	4890	DESINF,INSECT,FONG,HERB
5911	INSECTICIDES,FOR RETAIL	W 595	1634	W 508	1626	W 601	1899	W 610	1917	INSECTICIDES VENTE DET
5912	FUNGICIDES,FOR RETAIL	W 119	1007	W 212	1522	W 313	1387	W 330	1142	FONGICIDES VENTE AU DET
5913	HERBICIDES,FOR RETAIL	W 273	1025	W 304	1173	W 370	1587	W 337	1403	HERBICIDES VENTE AU DET
598	MISCEL CHEM PRODUCTS NES		686		909		1018		1040	PROD DIV INDUST CHIM NDA
5989	CHEM PRODUCTS,PREPS NES	W 266	569	W 486	795	W 663	896	W 688	898	PROD PREP CHIMIQUES NDA
6	BASIC MANUFACTURES		54473		60002		53252		51780	ART MANUFACTURES
62	RUBBER MANUFACTURES NES		3818		4337		4130		4131	CAOUTCHOUC MANUFACTURE
625	RUBBER TYRES, TUBES ETC	N 146508	2906		3307	N 208772	3053	N 163139	3289	PNEUS CAOUTCHOUC VULCANISE
6252	TYRES,NEW,BUS OR LORRY	N 18503	1452	N 17548	1700	N 24734	1577	N 18704	1830	PNEUS POUR AUTOBUS,CAMIONS
6259	OTH TYRES,TYRE CASES,ETC	N 88063	877	N 106480	997	N 136047	904	N 106362	862	AUTRES PNEUS RECHAPES FLAPS
63	WOOD,CORK MANUFACTRS NES		8201		5331		2550		6807	OUVRAGES LIEGE ET BOIS
634	VENEERS,PLYWOOD,ETC		1536		1553		1831		1109	PLACAGES,CONTRE–PLAQUES
6342	PLYWOOD OF WOOD SHEETS	V 6723	1420	V 7378	1505	V 4718	1139	V 6410	1087	BOIS CONTRE–PLAQUES
635	WOOD MANUFACTURES NES		6655	W 1012	3763	W 91	712	W 1431	5690	ART MANUF EN BOIS NDA
6353	BUILDERS WOODWRK,PREFABS	W 3112	6593	W 984	3677	W 59	644	W 914	5313	OUVRAGES DE MENUISERIE
64	PAPER,PAPERBOARD AND MFR		7356		7400		7534		7586	PAPIERS,CARTONS & OUVRAGES
641	PAPER AND PAPERBOARD		2365	W 2565	2316	W 2323	2319	W 2093	2365	PAPIERS ET CARTONS
6412	PRINTG,WRITING PAPER NES	W 466	833	W 452	682	W 411	636	W 449	766	PAPIERS POUR L'IMPRESSION
64121	— UNCOATED	W 466	833	W 452	682	W 411	636	W 449	766	PAPIERS IMPRES NON COUCHES
642	PAPER,ETC,PRECUT,ARTS OF		4991	W 4648	5084	W 4418	5215	W 3817	5221	PAP,CARTONS DECOUPES
6421	PAPER ETC CONTAINERS	W 3050	3076	W 3710	3390	W 3235	3140	W 2787	3211	BOITES,SACS EMBALLAGES
6428	PAPER ETC ARTICLES NES		957	W 597	888	W 619	1166	W 636	1029	OUVRAGES EN PATE A PAPIER
64285	PAPER ETC DIAPERS ETC	W 320	626	W 379	536	W 383	836	W 352	647	SERVIETTES HYGIENIQUES
65	TEXTILE YARN,FABRICS,ETC		6112		7076		5081		5107	FILS,TISSUS,ARTICLES TEXTILE
652	COTTON FABRICS,WOVEN	A 176	1892		1694	A 146	677	A 26	432	TISSUS DE COTON
6522	WOVEN COTTON BLEACHD,ETC	A 175	1884		1672	A 144	659	A 26	431	TISSUS COTON BLANCHIS ETC
65224	BLCHED COTTON FABRIC NES	A 135	1138	A 532	1240	A 114	517	A 13	319	AUT TIS PLUS 85% COT BLANCHI
653	WOVN MAN–MADE FIB FABRIC		1101		1166		1011	A 95	851	TISSUS FIBRES SYNTH,ARTIF
655	KNITTED,ETC FABRICS		1127	A 964	1650	A 960	1129		499	ETOF BONNETERIE PIECES ETC
6552	OTHER KNIT ETC FAB NONEL		1127	A 964	1650	A 960	1129		499	ETOF BON NON ELAS NON SYNT
657	SPECIAL TXTL FABRC,PRODS		522		786		622		1424	TISSUS SPECIAUX
6577	TEXTILES FOR MACHINERY	W 78	193	W 105	308	W 106	263	W 177	1136	OUATES,MECHES ART TEXT
65773	TEXTLS FOR MACHINES NES	W 6	41	W 4	77	W 2	41	W 48	827	TISSUS USAGE TECH MAT TEX
658	TEXTILE ARTICLES NES		479		626		766		955	ART FACONNES MAT TEXTILES
66	NONMETAL MINERAL MFS NES		9031		10865		11204		8837	ART MIN NON METALLIQUES
661	LIME,CEMENT,BLDG PRODS	W 74419	5160	W 87824	6456	W 98308	6615	W 78256	5451	CHAUX,CIMENTS MAT CONSTR
6612	CEMENT	W 72729	4893	W 81882	6194	W 96875	6182	W 76760	5063	CIMENTS HYDRAULIQUES
662	CLAY,REFRACTORY BLDG PRD		565		939		1376		1164	MAT CONST REFRACTAIRES
6624	BRICKS ETC NONREFRACTORY		509		786		1282		1092	BRIQUES ETC CERAM NON REFR
66245	GLAZED CERAMIC SETTS ETC		442		601		1013		958	AUT CARREAUX CERAMIQUE
663	MINERAL MANUFCTURES NES		1144	W 2524	1079	W 1798	674		591	ART MIN MANUF NDA
665	GLASSWARE		1426		1717		1678		990	OUVRAGES EN VERRE
6651	BOTTLES ETC OF GLASS		1054		1363		1324		614	RECIPIENTS EN VERRE
66511	GLASS BOTTLES ETC NONVAC		1053	N 7092343	1361		1323		612	BONBONNES,BOUTEILLES,ETC
67	IRON AND STEEL		6884		7655		8094		4976	FER ET ACIER
673	IRON,STEEL SHAPES ETC		3506		3998		3007		2503	BARRES,PROFIL FER,ACIER
6732	IRON,STEEL BARS ETC		2714		3414		2654		2290	BARRES FER,ACIER
67322	HIGH CARBON STL BARS ETC		909	W 4514	1844	W 6159	1278	W 3451	1369	BARRES ACIER FIN CARBONE
67326	IRN,OTH STL BARS HOTROLD		1358	W 3742	1318	W 11277	1340	W 2371	890	BARRES PLEINES FER,ACIER
674	IRN,STL UNIV,PLATE,SHEET		1761		1703		1420		1279	LARGES PLATS,TOLES
6749	OTH IRN,STL PLATES,SHEET		1493		1563		1289	W 1170	969	AUTRES TOLES FER,ACIER
67491	— OF IRON OR SIMPLE STL		1475		1530		1241	W 1097	943	AUT TOLES AUTRES ACIER FIN
678	IRON,STL TUBES,PIPES,ETC		1239		1660		3222	W 694	892	TUBES,TUYAUX EN FONTE,FER
6783	IRON,STL TUBES,PIPES NES		477		382		1330	W 365	412	AUT TUBES,TUYAUX FER,ACIER
6785	IRON,STEEL TUBE FITTINGS		229		740		1346	W 132	239	ACCESSOIRES DE TUYAUTERIE
68	NON–FERROUS METALS		773		878		1132		1070	METAUX NON FERREUX
69	METAL MANUFACTURES NES		12251		16413		13489		13237	ART MANUFACT EN METAL NDA
691	STRUCTURES AND PARTS NES		2935	W 4083	5270	W 2201	3730	W 2409	3221	CONSTRUCT FER,ACIER,ALU
6911	STRUCTURES,PARTS IRN,STL		1934	W 3518	3981	W 2017	2501	W 2131	1969	CONSTRUCT FER,ACIER,FONTE
6912	STRUCTURES,PARTS ALUMNM		1001	W 565	1289	W 184	1229	W 277	1252	CONSTRUCT ALUMINIUM
692	METAL TANKS,BOXES,ETC		1007	W 1048	1145	W 864	1082	W 1310	1938	RECIPIENTS METALLIQUES
6924	MTL TRANSPORT BOXES ETC		921	W 840	789	W 724	993	W 1226	1516	FUTS,TAMBOURS,BIDONS
69241	STL TRANSPORT BOXES ETC		702	W 714	665	W 408	762	W 1063	1304	FUTS,TAMBOURS,BIDONS FER
693	WIRE PRODUCTS NON ELECTR		895	W 1172	1030		771		612	OUVRAGES FILS METALLIQUES
694	STL,COPPR NAILS,NUTS,ETC		1226	W 4071	1444	W 2331	1495	W 597	1297	CLOUS,VIS,ECROUS
69402	IRN,STL NUTS,BOLTS,ETC		690	W 733	916	W 1377	991	W 218	715	BOULONS,VIS,ECROUS FER,AC
695	TOOLS		1668	W 1032	1860		1710	W 910	1254	OUTILS A MAIN
6953	OTHER HAND TOOLS		1042	W 788	990	W 867	906	W 151	801	AUTRES OUTILS A MAIN
697	BASE MTL HOUSEHOLD EQUIP		1517	W 606	1685	W 696	1428	W 421	1546	ART MENAGE MET COMMUNS
6973	DMSTC HEATG,COOKG APPARA		815	W 448	1119	W 533	848	W 286	945	APPS CHAUF NON ELECTRIQ
69731	IRN,STL DOM COOKG APPARA		790	W 406	1080	W 475	816	W 280	905	APPS CUISSON FER,ACIER
699	BASE METAL MFRS NES		2710		3774	W 1736	3012	W 1271	3123	ART MANUFACTURES MET NDA
6991	LOCKSMITHS WARES,ETC		780	W 963	999	W 697	1027	W 192	838	ARTICLES DE SERRURERIE
6997	IRON,STEEL ARTICLES NES		521	W 381	1139	W 403	726	W 676	945	OUV FONTE,FER,ACIER NDA
69979	IRN,STL MANUFACTURES NES		512	W 372	1100	W 389	715	W 673	926	AUT OUVRAGES EN FER NDA
7	MACHINES,TRANSPORT EQUIP		67489		73805		66377		66401	MACHINES MATERIEL TRANSPORT
71	POWER GENERATING EQUIPMT		9587		4757		5739		4395	MACHINES GENERATRICES
713	INTRNL COMBUS PSTN ENGIN		3432	W 282	3263		2902		2518	MOTEURS EXPL COMB INT, PIECE
7133	MARINE PISTON ENGINES		1320	W 71	1020		1118		1226	MOTEURS EXPL POUR BATEAUX
71331	—— OUTBOARD	W 113	1119	W 55	947	W 158	981	W 55	1060	MOTEURS BATEAUX HORSBORD
7139	PISTON ENGINE PARTS NES		1545	W 170	1959		1469	W 31	1048	PIECES POUR 713.2,3,8
716	ROTATING ELECTRIC PLANT		5900	W 196	1170	W 236	1479	W 240	1643	APP ELECTR ROTATIFS,PIECES
7162	AC MTRS,GENRTRS,GEN SETS		5531	W 166	985	W 211	753	W 223	1412	MOTEURS ELECTRIQUES
71623	GEN SETS WITH PISTN ENGN	W 292	5197	W 76	648	W 136	519	W 191	1208	GROUPES MOTEUR EXPLOSION
718	OTH POWER GENERATG MACHY		5		10		1080		27	AUTRES MOTEURS PARTIES
7188	WIND,WATER,ETC ENGINES		5	W 1	10	W 214	1079		27	MOT MACHINES MOTRICES NDA
71889	PARTS NES OF 71881,71882					W 178	912		1	PARTIES DES POS 718.81,82
72	MACHS FOR SPCL INDUSTRYS		10607		12537		9112		8185	MAC SPECIALES POUR INDUST
721	AGRIC MACHY,EXC TRACTORS		944		1288	W 1286	903	W 417	1354	MACHINES AGRICOLES
722	TRACTORS NON–ROAD	N 374	1017	N 363	1668	N 116	1243	N 92	1219	TRACTEURS
7224	WHEELED TRACTORS NES	N 339	837	N 359	1615	N 91	1166	N 80	978	TRACTEURS A ROUES
723	CIVIL ENGNEERG EQUIP ETC		4905	W 1723	6141		2399		2347	APPAREILS DE GENIE CIVIL
7234	CONST,MINING MACHNRY NES		4764	W 1576	5799		2340		2279	MACH POUR LA CONST, MINES
72341	SELF–PROPELLD DOZERS,ETC	W 695	2480	W 676	1310	W 264	1143	W 329	1553	BULLDOZERS
72342	SLFPRP SHOVELS,EXCAVATRS	W 626	1367	W 592	2194	W 421	759	W 305	616	PELLES MECANIQUES
72343	SLFPRP CONST ETC MCH NES		237	W 221	2132		136		62	AUT MACH EXTR,TERRASSEM

4. General Imports C.I.F. by Commodities according to the S.I.T.C. (Rev. 2) in thousand U.S. Dollars
Importations Générales C.A.F. par Produits d'après la C.T.C.I. (Rév. 2) en milliers de Dollars E.U.

SITC CTCI	COMMODITY	1992 WEIGHT POIDS	1992 VALUE VALEUR	1993 WEIGHT POIDS	1993 VALUE VALEUR	1994 WEIGHT POIDS	1994 VALUE VALEUR	1995 WEIGHT POIDS	1995 VALUE VALEUR	PRODUIT
724	TEXTILE,LEATHER MACHNRY		876		880		282		461	MACH POUR INDUSTRIE TEXTILE
727	FOOD MACHRY NON–DOMESTIC		435	W 298	800	W 825	1920		1081	MACH INDUSTRIES ALIMENT
7272	OTH FOOD PROC MCHY,PARTS		365	W 257	637	W 412	1326		896	AUT MACH IND ALIMENTAIRE
72722	INDUS FOOD PROC MACH NES		365	W 255	628	W 412	1326	W 341	896	MACHINES BOULANGERIE
728	OTH MACHY FOR SPCL INDUS		2148		1625		2078	W 385	1546	AUT MACH IND PARTICULIERES
7283	OTHR MINERAL WORKG MACHY		1366	W 189	945	W 483	1244	W 272	841	MACH TRIER,CRIBLER,BROYER
72832	MINRL CRUSHING ETC MACHY	W 201	1056	W 93	520	W 11	103	W 62	138	MACH CONCASSER MAT MINER
74	GENRL INDUSTRL MACHY NES		9604		13342		13846		13642	MACH APP INDUSTRIE
741	HEATING,COOLING EQUIPMNT		1568		1850		3410	W 589	2651	MACH CHAUFFAGE,PIECES
7414	NONDOM REFRIG EQUIPT,PTS		569	W 189	664	W 431	935	W 165	1323	MAT PRODUCTION DU FROID
74141	REFRIG EQUIP NONDOMESTIC	W 120	520	W 183	617	W 420	899	W 152	1212	REFIG INDUSTRIELS
7415	AIR–CONDITIONING MACHNRY		676	W 224	718	W 312	1153	W 174	959	GROUPES CONDITION AIR
7416	HEATING,COOLING EQU NES		252		420		1282	W 242	331	APP CHANGEMENT TEMP
742	PUMPS FOR LIQUIDS ETC		1409		1600	W 267	1591	W 242	1705	POMPES MOTO–POMPES
7428	OTHER PUMPS FOR LIQUIDS		753	W 91	681	W 109	814	W 111	808	AUTRES POMPES POUR LIQ
743	PUMPS NES,CENTRFUGES ETC		1686		1989		1671	W 119	1735	POMPES COMPRES,VENT ETC
7436	GAS,LIQUID FILTERS ETC		837		788	W 103	732	W 60	730	APP POUR FILT DES LIQUIDES
744	MECHANICAL HANDLING EQU		1048	W 868	3286		2246	W 458	1571	EQUIP MANUTENTION PIECES
7441	FORK LIFT TRCKS,ETC,PTS	W 80	216	W 149	779	W 175	849	W 112	298	CHARIOTS POUR USINES ETC
74411	FORK LIFT TRUCKS ETC	W 65	215	W 148	773	W 174	833	W 112	297	CHARIOTS POUR LES GARES
7442	LIFTING,LOADING MACH NES		320	W 305	1891		764	W 193	717	APP LEVAGE,MANUTENTION
74422	SHIP DERRICKS,CRANES ETC		72	W 223	1129	W 34	207	W 23	28	GRUES,PONTS ROULANTS
745	NONELEC MACHY,TOOLS NES		947		1220		1377		3243	AUT MACH NON ELEC,PIECES
7452	OTH NONELEC MCHS,PTS NES		750		1019		1168		3071	AUT MACH NON ELEC,PIECES
74522	PACKAGNG,BOTTLNG,ETC MCH		72		467	W 48	609	W 68	2294	MACH NETT BOUTEILLES,ETC
749	NONELEC MACH PTS,ACC NES		2947	W 959	3397	W 2496	3550	W 376	2737	PIECES MACH NON ELEC NDA
7492	COCKS,VALVES ETC NES		740	W 424	1152	W 2134	1196	W 156	822	ART ROB,SIM POUR TUYAUX
7493	SHAFT,CRANK,PULLEY ETC		1064	W 422	1126	W 245	1123	W 67	879	ARBRES TRANS,VILEBREQUINS
75	OFFICE MACHNES,ADP EQUIP		2547		3073		2936		2683	MACH BUREAU TRAIT AUTOM
752	AUTOMTIC DATA PROC EQUIP		1530	N 3272	1904		1660		1361	MACH TRAIT INFORMATION
7522	DIGITAL COMPUTERS	N 1333	979	N 1173	1327	N 1501	903	N 593	857	MACH DIGITALES COMPLETES
76	TELECOMM,SOUND EQUIPMENT		3809		6396		4092		6198	EQUIPMENT DE TELECOM
764	TELECOM EQPT,PTS,ACC NES		3243		5538		3099		4710	EQUIP TELECOM,PIECES
7641	LINE TELEPHONE,ETC EQUIP	W 30	1495	W 65	3159	W 31	1246	W 52	3571	APP TELEPHON PAR FIL
7643	TV,RADIO TRANSMITTRS ETC		468	N 8161	1293		971	N 115	387	APP EMET TELE RADIO
7649	PTS NES OF EQUIPMT OF 76		1047		887	W 14	656	W 16	534	PIECES DE LA DIV 76
77	ELECTRIC MACHNRY NES ETC		11399		13361		13963		11262	MACH APP ELECT NDA
771	ELECTRIC POWER MACHY NES		776	W 502	1084	W 605	1969	W 149	833	MACH PROD,TRANS ELECTR
7711	TRANSFORMERS,ELECTRICAL		618	W 297	816	W 558	1690	W 128	537	TRANSFO ELECTRIQUES
77118	OTHER ELEC TRANSFORMERS		244	W 232	456	W 486	1146	W 82	342	AUTRES TRANSFO ELECTRIQ
772	SWITCHGEAR ETC,PARTS NES		2015		2945	W 265	3307	W 163	1814	APP COUPURE,SECT ETC
7721	SWITCHGEAR ETC		1794	W 214	2915	W 264	3279	W 163	1800	APP COUPURE,SECTIONMNT
773	ELECTR DISTRIBUTNG EQUIP		2962	W 925	4076	W 624	2268	W 537	2143	EQUIPMT DISTRIBUTION ELECT
7731	INSULATED WIRE,CABLE ETC		2817	W 865	3779	W 584	2018	W 529	2089	FILS,CABLES ISOLES ELECT
774	ELECTRO–MEDCL,XRAY EQUIP	W 4	204	W 4	151	W 8	951	W 10	700	APPAREILS MEDICAUX
7741	ELECTRO–MEDICAL EQUIPMNT	W 2	174	W 1	57	W 7	906		70	APP ELECTRICITE MEDICALE
775	HOUSEHOLD TYPE EQUIP NES		2967		2678		3052		3339	MACH,APP USAGE DOMESTQUE
7752	DOM REFRIGERATRS,FREEZRS		1749		1599		1841		1875	REFRIG,CONGEL MENAGER
77521	DOMESTIC REFRIGERATORS		1562		1399		1611		1633	REFRIGERATEURS
778	ELECTRICAL MACHINERY NES		2417		2327		2345		2345	AUTRES MACH ELECT NDA
7788	OTH ELEC MACHY,EQUIP NES		722		769		812		741	AUT MACH APP ELEC NDA
78	ROAD VEHICLES		18588		18537		14916		15591	VEHICULES ROUTIERS
781	PASS MOTOR VEH EXC BUSES	N 2710	6531	N 5152	5232	N 3431	4408	N 6668	5754	AUTO TRANSPORT PERSONNES
782	LORRIES,SPCL MTR VEH NES	N 3345	7778		8112	N 1628	4959	N 1872	5923	VEHICULES SPECIAUX,MARCH
7821	LORRIES,TRUCKS	N 3317	5908	N 8656	7073	N 1618	4582	N 1862	5646	VEHICULES TRANSP MARCHAND
7822	SPECIAL MOTOR VEHCLS NES	N 28	1870		1039	N 10	378	N 10	278	VEHICULES USAGES SPECIAUX
783	ROAD MOTOR VEHICLES NES	N 439	1129	N 710	1420	N 338	1031	N 243	1400	VEHICULES ROUTIERS NDA
7831	BUSES	N 318	674	N 610	942	N 276	659	N 193	1113	VOITURES TRANSPORT COMMUN
784	MOTOR VEH PRTS,ACCES NES		1525		1582		1300		1176	PIECES 722,781,782,783
7849	OTHER MOTOR VEHCL PARTS		1520	W 482	1573	W 572	1297	W 199	1174	PIECES 722,781,782,783
785	CYCLES,ETC MOTRZD OR NOT		825		1448		980		898	MOTOCYCLES SCOOTERS
786	TRAILERS,NONMOTR VEH,NES		800		742		2238		440	REMORQUES,CADRES,CONTAIN
7861	TRAILERS,TRANSP CONTAINR		427		488		1919		254	REMORQUES TOUS VEHICULES
78611	HOUSING,CAMPING TRAILERS	W 60	79	W 132	146	W 705	1708	W 26	27	REMORQUES POUR CAMPING
79	OTHR TRANSPORT EQUIPMENT		1032		1443		1365		3987	AUTRE MATERIEL TRANSPORT
792	AIRCRAFT ETC		416		702		398		2369	APP NAVIGATION AERIENNE
7923	AIRCRFT NES2000–15000KG	N 3	65	N 4	160	W 16	91	W 1	2092	AERODYNES 2000 A 15000 KG
793	SHIPS AND BOATS ETC		615	N 1454	741		967	N 518	1609	NAVIRES BATEAUX,ETC
7932	SHIPS AND BOATS NES	N 562	541	N 670	657		892	N 383	1134	NAVIRES ET BATEAUX
8	MISC MANUFACTURED GOODS		34563		39050		34551		34385	ART MANUFACTURES DIVERS
812	*PLUMBG,HEATNG,LGHTNG EQ		2071		1073		1151		1088	APPAR SANITAIRES CHAUFFAGE
8124	LIGHTING EQUIPMENT NES		1499		616	W 458	770	W 944	814	APPAREILS ECLAIRAGE ETC
81242	LAMPS,FITTINGS BASE METL	W 176	1417	W 105	516	W 104	652	W 118	692	APPAREILS D'ECLAIRAGE
821	*FURNITURE,PARTS THEREOF		1549	W 957	1597		2396	W 653	2569	MEUBLES ET PIECES
8212	MED FURN,STUFFD FURNSHGS		182	W 129	188	W 405	884	W 200	628	MOB MEDICO–CHIRUR,PIECES
8219	FURNITURE AND PARTS NES		903	W 681	1050	W 838	1146	W 353	1549	AUTRES MEUBLES ET PIECES
82191	METAL FURNITURE NES		494	W 229	597	W 453	805	W 218	939	MEUBLES NDA EN METAL
84	CLOTHING AND ACCESSORIES		12152		12034		11519		10408	VETEMENTS
842	MENS OUTERWEAR NOT KNIT		10117		9968	N 2082600	9839	N 2874924	9366	VET DESSUS POUR HOMMES
8422	— SUITS	N 615000	4508	N 557628	3403	N 9564	22	N 12912	22	COMPLETS HOMMES MAT TEXT
84223	—— OF MAN–MADE FIBRES	N 611880	4504	N 544536	3395	N 8868	21	N 4308	18	COMPLETS HOMMES FIB SYNT
8423	— TROUSERS,BREECHES ETC	N 1517196	5533		5747	N 1480656	6052	N 1784880	5191	PANTALONS HOMMES MAT TEX
8429	— OTHER OUTER GARMENTS	N 34368	42		783	N 546000	3730	N 1066440	4127	AUT VET DES HOM MAT TEX
843	WOMENS OUTERWEAR NONKNIT		978	N 514272	695		413		181	VET DESSUS FEMMES MAT TEX
851	*FOOTWEAR		1904	P 671883	1833		1696	P 277894	1288	CHAUSSURES
85103	SHOES WOOD–,CORK–SOLED	P 210585	707	P 249902	778	P 220020	848	P 137671	527	CHAUS SEMELLES BOIS,LIEGE
87	PRECISION INSTRUMNTS NES		2010		2230		1625		2057	INSTRUM,APPAR SCIENT NDA
872	MEDICAL INSTRUMENTS NES	W 21	472	W 18	359	W 11	390	W 18	803	INSTR,APP MEDIC–CHIR NDA
873	METERS AND COUNTERS NES		444	W 69	859	W 15	237	W 7	183	COMPTEURS,INST DE MESURE
8731	GAS SUPPLY METERS ETC	W 23	426	W 69	843	W 15	218	W 7	169	COMPTEURS GAZ,LIQ ELECT
874	MEASURNG,CONTROLNG INSTR		1052	W 44	957	W 44	912	W 54	1010	INSTRUMENTS DE MESURE
88	PHOTO EQU,OPTICL GDS ETC		1136		969		1119		1107	APP,FOURN PHOTO,OP,MONTR
89	MISC MANUFCTRD GOODS NES		13424		19036		14822		15590	ART MANUFACTURES DIVERS
892	PRINTED MATTER		3503	W 335	2934	W 357	3229	W 405	3327	IMPRIMES
8921	PRINTED BOOKS,GLOBES,ETC	W 175	1250	W 186	1497	W 179	1593	W 190	1587	LIVRES,BROCHURES,CARTES
89211	PRINTED BOOKS,PAMPHLETS	W 170	1191	W 176	1452	W 174	1560	W 180	1541	LIVRES,BROCHURES
8928	PRINTED MATTER NES		1900	W 114	1089	W 138	1187	W 164	1354	IMPRIMES NDA
89283	UNISSUED BANKNOTES ETC	W 11	1269	W 5	266	W 6	276	W 7	495	TIMBRES–POSTE FISCAUX
893	ARTICLES OF PLASTIC NES		5095		10937		5021		6647	OUVRAGES EN MAT DIVIS 58
8931	PLSTC PACKG CONTNRS,LIDS		1311	W 890	1396		1791		1871	ART TRANSP EMBALLAGE ETC
8939	MISC PLASTIC ARTICLES		3714	W 3275	9458		3157	W 1920	4702	ART DIVERS EN MAT DIV 58

4. General Imports C.I.F. by Commodities according to the S.I.T.C. (Rev. 2) in thousand U.S. Dollars
Importations Générales C.A.F. par Produits d'après la C.T.C.I. (Rév. 2) en milliers de Dollars E.U.

SITC CTCI	COMMODITY	1992		1993		1994		1995		PRODUIT
		WEIGHT POIDS	VALUE VALEUR	WEIGHT POIDS	VALUE VALEUR	WEIGHT POIDS	VALUE VALEUR	WEIGHT POIDS	VALUE VALEUR	
89399	OTHR PLASTC ARTICLES NES		3219	W 2899	9056		2827	W 1600	4316	AUT OUV MAT DIV 58
894	TOYS,SPORTING GOODS,ETC		963		981		986		1139	VOITURES ENFANTS,JOUETS
8942	TOYS,INDOOR GAMES ETC		697	W 167	642		642		800	JOUETS,JEUX ETC
899	OTHER MANUFACTURED GOODS		2846		3271		4735		3659	AUT ART MANUF DIVERS NDA
8998	SMALLWARES,TOILETRYS ETC	W 657	2082		2457	W 693	2264	W 1126	2816	ART MERCERIE,TOILETTE
89981	HAND SIEVES AND RIDDLES			W 696	1623					TAMIS ET CRIBLES
8999	OTHER MANUF GOODS NES		97		167	W 129	1955	W 24	270	OUVRAGES DIVERS NDA
89991	ARTICLES OF GUT,ETC			W 1	36	W 117	1897	W 13	194	OUVRAGES EN BOYAUX

5. General Exports F.O.B. by Commodities according to the S.I.T.C. (Rev. 2) in thousand U.S. Dollars
Exportations Générales F.O.B. par Produits d'après la C.T.C.I. (Rév. 2) en milliers de Dollars E.U.

SITC CTCI	COMMODITY	1992		1993		1994		1995		PRODUIT
		WEIGHT POIDS	VALUE VALEUR	WEIGHT POIDS	VALUE VALEUR	WEIGHT POIDS	VALUE VALEUR	WEIGHT POIDS	VALUE VALEUR	
	ALL COMMODITIES		135939		126605		142931		161680	TOUS PRODUITS
0	FOOD AND LIVE ANIMALS		95116		88238		96709		123998	ALIMENTS,ANIMAUX VIVANTS
01	MEAT AND PREPARATIONS		1266		574		358		27	VIANDES ET PREPARATIONS
014	MEAT PREPD,PRSVD,NES ETC	W 626	1255	W 267	571	W 127	356	W 11	27	CONSERVES DE VIANDES
0149	OTH PREPARD,PRESRVD MEAT	W 532	1033	W 192	393	W 89	266	W 8	21	AUTRES PREP DE VIANDES
02	DAIRY PRODCTS,BIRDS'EGGS		5184		2968		1224		319	PRODUITS LAITIERS,OEUFS
024	CHEESE AND CURD	W 1526	4692	W 796	2743	W 336	967	W 89	287	FROMAGE ET CAILLEBOTTE
03	FISH AND PREPARATIONS		7071		7827		13246		15752	POISSONS ET PREPARATIONS
036	SHELL FISH FRESH,FROZEN	W 849	6763	W 1018	7584	W 915	13067	W 1139	15504	CRUSTACES,MOLLUSQUES
04	CEREALS AND PREPARATIONS		570		370		158		27	CEREALES ET PRODUITS
048	CEREAL ETC PREPARATIONS	W 125	562	W 86	364	W 23	98	W 8	27	PREPTNS A BASE CEREALES
05	VEGETABLES AND FRUIT		39133		29689		35818		104694	LEGUMES ET FRUITS
054	VEG ETC FRSH,SMPLY PRSVD		389	W 1953	1814	W 2240	1950	W 2871	2205	LEGUMES FRAIS,CONG,SECS
0542	LEGUMINOUS VEGETBLES DRY	W 396	388	W 1900	1772	W 2230	1927	W 2835	2173	LEGUMES A COSSE SECS
057	FRUIT,NUTS,FRESH,DRIED		10933		13678		16253	W 139830	22802	FRUITS FRAIS OU SECS
0572	LEMONS,GRAPEFRUIT ETC	W 8	4		33	W 32	11	W 138830	22059	AUTRES AGRUMES FRAIS,SECS
05722	GRAPEFRUITS,FRESH,DRIED							W 138782	22037	PAMPLEMOUSSES,POMELOS
0573	BANANA,PLANTAIN,FRSH,DRY		10264		12094		14855			BANANES FRAICHES,SECHEES
0579	FRUIT FRESH OR DRIED NES	W 746	615	W 2238	1442	W 2161	1325	W 904	679	FRUITS FRAIS,SECS NDA
05798	OTHER FRESH FRUIT	W 687	441	W 2169	1225	W 2104	1058	W 800	473	AUTRES FRUITS FRAIS
058	FRUIT PRESERVED,PREPARED		27673	W 8985	14136	W 11154	17614	W 114930	79687	CONSERVES DE FRUITS
0585	FRUIT OR VEGETABLE JUICE		27566	W 8972	14101	W 11147	17601	W 114929	79684	JUS DE FRUITS
05851	ORANGE JUICE	W 8907	20645	W 6345	8819	W 8400	12324	W 16922	24799	JUS D'ORANGE
05852	GRAPEFRUIT JUICE	W 3284	6825	W 2558	5163	W 2708	5210	W 3912	6936	JUS DE PAMPLEMOUSSE
05858	MIXTURES OF DIFF JUICES		43	W 9	13	W 11	15	W 94006	47768	MELANGES JUS FRUITS,LEGUMES
06	SUGAR AND PREPS,HONEY		40965		46342		45563		2960	SUCRES ET PRODUITS
061	SUGAR AND HONEY		40876		46283		45543		2844	SUCRES ET MIEL
0611	RAW BEET AND CANE SUGAR	W 91477	37629	W 91839	41457	W 94335	40311			SUCRES BRUTS
0615	MOLASSES	V 35039	3185	V 36657	4812	V 41726	5214	V 29537	2843	MELASSES
07	COFFEE,TEA,COCOA,SPICES		643		280		78		57	CAFE,THE,CACAO,EPICES
1	BEVERAGES AND TOBACCO		3397		3008		4052		4771	BOISSONS ET TABACS
11	BEVERAGES		3251		2592		2403		1907	BOISSONS
112	ALCOHOLIC BEVERAGES		2911	W 322	2517	W 656	2380		1907	BOISSONS ALCOOLIQUES
1124	DISTILLED ALCOHOLIC BEVS		2649	W 220	2286	W 594	2234	W 178	1811	ALCOOLS,EAUX-DE-VIE
11241	WHISKY	W 184	2313	W 178	2018	W 552	1955	W 124	1549	WHISKY
12	TOBACCO AND MANUFACTURES		146		416		1649		2865	TABACS BRUTS FABRIQUES
122	TOBACCO,MANUFACTURED	W 6	146	W 14	416	W 37	1649	W 272	2865	TABACS FABRIQUES
1222	CIGARETTES	W 6	146	W 14	416	W 37	1649	W 272	2865	CIGARETTES
2	CRUDE MATERLS,EXCL FUELS		3785		3022		4218		2369	MAT BRUTES NON COMESTIBLES
24	CORK AND WOOD		3069		2324		3845		1965	LIEGE ET BOIS
248	WOOD SHAPED,SLEEPERS	W 7013	2923	W 5431	2289	W 7275	3753	W 2862	1771	BOIS SIMPLEMENT TRAVAILLES
2483	LUMBER SHAPED NON–CONIFR	W 7013	2923	W 5381	2276	W 7260	3749	W 2862	1771	NON CONIFERES SCIES,RABOTES
24831	LUMBER SAWN ETC NON–CON	W 6963	2902	W 5341	2267	W 7235	3728	W 2855	1767	SCIES LONGITUDINALEMENT
29	CRUDE ANIMAL,VEG MAT NES		421		508		96		10	MATIERES BRUTES ANIM,VEGET
292	CRUDE VEG MATERIALS NES	W 206	421		508	W 42	94	W 2	7	MAT BRUTES VEGETALES NDA
2929	OTH CRUDE VEG MATERIALS	W 76	358	W 104	492	W 8	85	W 1	4	MATIERES VEGETALES NDA
29291	VEGETABLE SAPS,EXTRACTS	W 76	357	W 104	490	W 8	83			SUCS,EXTRAITS VEGETAUX
3	MINERAL FUELS ETC		4089		2832		3477		5142	COMBUSTIBLES MINERAUX LUB
33	PETROLEUM AND PRODUCTS		3939		2832		3366		5072	PETROLE ET DERIVES
334	PETROLEUM PRODUCTS,REFIN	W 16931	3939	W 12370	2832	W 15857	3366		5068	PRODUITS RAFFINES
3341	GASOLINE,OTH LIGHT OILS	W 4941	1256	W 1401	368	W 1613	416	W 159	98	ESSENCES POUR MOTEURS
33411	MOTOR,AVIATION SPIRIT	W 4941	1256	W 1401	368	W 1613	416	W 159	98	ESSENCES MOTEURS D'AVIONS
3342	KEROSENE,OTH MEDIUM OILS	W 11877	2649	W 10909	2341	W 14155	2934	W 10578	4938	PETR LAMPANTS,AUT HUIL
33421	KEROSENE INCL JET FUEL	W 11877	2649	W 10909	2341	W 14155	2934	W 10578	4938	PETROLES LAMPANTS
4	ANIMAL,VEGETABLE OIL,FAT		4		1		5		1492	HUILES,GRAISSES ANIM,VEG
42	FIXED VEGETABLE OIL,FAT		4		1		5		1492	HUILES VEGETALES FIXES
424	FIXED VEG OIL NONSOFT		4		1	W 1	5	W 422	1492	AUTRES HUILES VEG FIXES
4243	COCONUT (COPRA) OIL	W 1	3		1	W 1	3	W 422	1492	HJUILE DE COPRAH
5	CHEMCLS,RELATED PROD NES		1443		987		1941		380	PRODUITS CHIMIQUES
55	PERFUME,CLEANING ETC PRD		1084		737		1761		324	PROD POUR PARFUM,TOILETTE
553	PERFUMERY,COSMETICS,ETC		638	W 81	422		1441	W 13	114	PRODUITS DE PARFUMERIE
6	BASIC MANUFACTURES		1626		1662		2252		1933	ART MANUFACTURES
63	WOOD,CORK MANUFACTRS NES		1080		1233		1517		691	OUVRAGES LIEGE ET BOIS
634	VENEERS,PLYWOOD,ETC		1004		1049		1443		246	PLACAGES,CONTRE–PLAQUES
6341	VENEER SHEETS ETC		979	V 440	344	V 1552	292	V 121	30	BOIS SIMPLEMENT SCIES
6342	PLYWOOD OF WOOD SHEETS			V 1045	704	V 1594	1150	V 412	208	BOIS CONTRE–PLAQUES
65	TEXTILE YARN,FABRICS,ETC		320		168		150		994	FILS,TISSUS,ARTICLES TEXTILE
658	TEXTILE ARTICLES NES	W 41	122	W 1	17	W 10	50	W 44	763	ART FACONNES MAT TEXTILES
6582	MADE–UP CANVAS GOODS		6					W 44	759	BACHES,TENTES ETC
69	METAL MANUFACTURES NES		191		200		547		127	ART MANUFACT EN METAL NDA
7	MACHINES,TRANSPORT EQUIP		4128		4222		8328		4832	MACHINES MATERIEL TRANSPORT
71	POWER GENERATING EQUIPMT		1203		632		236		1245	MACHINES GENERATRICES
713	INTRNL COMBUS PSTN ENGIN		600		378		159	W 10	152	MOTEURS EXPL COMB INT, PIECE
716	ROTATING ELECTRIC PLANT		595		121		65		1089	APP ELECTR ROTATIFS,PIECES
7162	AC MTRS,GENRTRS,GEN SETS		509	W 52	112		62	W 620	1088	MOTEURS ELECTRIQUES
71623	GEN SETS WITH PISTN ENGN		334	W 2	5	W 18	32	W 620	1088	GROUPES MOTEUR EXPLOSION
72	MACHS FOR SPCL INDUSTRYS		262		502		899		398	MAC SPECIALES POUR INDUST
74	GENRL INDUSTRL MACHY NES		222		851		1048		118	MACH APP INDUSTRIE
744	MECHANICAL HANDLING EQU		73	W 122	713	W 178	804	W 3	32	EQUIP MANUTENTION PIECES
7441	FORK LIFT TRCKS,ETC,PTS	W 8	55	W 120	681	W 87	573	W 1	1	CHARIOTS POUR USINES ETC
74411	FORK LIFT TRUCKS ETC	W 8	55	W 120	681	W 87	573	W 1	1	CHARIOTS POUR LES GARES
76	TELECOMM,SOUND EQUIPMENT		354		528		3946		109	EQUIPMENT DE TELECOM
764	TELECOM EQPT,PTS,ACC NES		345		523		3888		70	EQUIP TELECOM,PIECES
7643	TV,RADIO TRANSMITTRS ETC		96	N 129	267		2176		8	APP EMET TELE RADIO
7648	TELECOMM EQUIPMENT NES		14		13	N 11	1666		1	APP TELECOM NDA
76482	TELEVISION CAMERAS					N 9	1665		1	APP PRISE DE VUES TELE
78	ROAD VEHICLES		1489		1125		1449		1812	VEHICULES ROUTIERS
781	PASS MOTOR VEH EXC BUSES	N 20	94	N 46	330	N 30	503	N 63	1400	AUTO TRANSPORT PERSONNES
782	LORRIES,SPCL MTR VEH NES	N 120	1324	N 77	281	N 230	766	N 12	108	VEHICULES SPECIAUX,MARCH
7821	LORRIES,TRUCKS	N 20	237	N 69	182	N 220	712	N 9	75	VEHICULES TRANSP MARCHAND
7822	SPECIAL MOTOR VEHCLS NES	N 100	1087	N 8	99	N 10	54	N 3	33	VEHICULES USAGES SPECIAUX
79	OTHR TRANSPORT EQUIPMENT		251		159		352		1024	AUTRE MATERIEL TRANSPORT
792	AIRCRAFT ETC		120		112		144		894	APP NAVIGATION AERIENNE
7924	AIRCRFT NES OVER 15000KG							N 1	857	AERODYNES PLUS 15000 KG
8	MISC MANUFACTURED GOODS		22349		22611		21910		16763	ART MANUFACTURES DIVERS
84	CLOTHING AND ACCESSORIES		19167		20502		18356		14741	VETEMENTS
842	MENS OUTERWEAR NOT KNIT	N 2382420	15763	N 2273328	16074	N 2482620	16408	N 1736856	14570	VET DESSUS POUR HOMMES
8422	— SUITS	N 630960	7160	N 495732	5215	N 8220	1			COMPLETS HOMMES MAT TEXT
84223	—— OF MAN–MADE FIBRES	N 630960	7160	N 495732	5215	N 8220	1			COMPLETS HOMMES FIB SYNT
8423	— TROUSERS,BREECHES ETC	N 1747260	8543	N 1611660	9100	N 1823652	9923	N 1090224	7960	PANTALONS HOMMES MAT TEX
8429	— OTHER OUTER GARMENTS	N 4200	61	N 162288	1696	N 639756	6470	N 646632	6610	AUT VET DES HOM MAT TEX

 Belize

5. General Exports F.O.B. by Commodities according to the S.I.T.C. (Rev. 2) in thousand U.S. Dollars
Exportations Générales F.O.B. par Produits d'après la C.T.C.I. (Rév. 2) en milliers de Dollars E.U.

SITC CTCI	COMMODITY	1992		1993		1994		1995		PRODUIT
		WEIGHT POIDS	VALUE VALEUR	WEIGHT POIDS	VALUE VALEUR	WEIGHT POIDS	VALUE VALEUR	WEIGHT POIDS	VALUE VALEUR	
843	WOMENS OUTERWEAR NONKNIT	N 565380	987	N 83280	399		217	N 8472	5	VET DESSUS FEMMES MAT TEX
8439	— OTHER OUTER GARMENTS	N 557628	977	N 63264	347		156	N 8472	5	AUT VET DES FEM MAT TEXT
845	OUTERWEAR KNIT NONELASTC	N 319512	413	N 268524	784	N 24996	34	N 15432	21	VET DESSOUS,ACCES BONNET
8459	— OTHER,CLTHG ACCESRYS	N 318180	411	N 163152	449	N 23700	32	N 15432	21	AUT VET DESSUS DE BONNE
846	UNDER GARMENTS KNITTED	N 1071660	1803	N 1717872	3000	N 872616	1652	N 72732	143	SOUS VETS DE BONNETERIE
8462	— OF COTTON NON ELASTIC	N 1028352	1769	N 1686756	2973	N 872616	1652	N 22080	24	SOUS–VET BONNET COTON
84629	—— OTHER	N 1028352	1769	N 1686756	2973	N 872616	1652	N 22080	24	AUT SOUS–VET BONNET COTON
87	PRECISION INSTRUMNTS NES		2247		182		192		107	INSTRUM,APPAR SCIENT NDA
874	MEASURNG,CONTROLNG INSTR	W 37	2238	W 4	174		178		77	INSTRUMENTS DE MESURE
8741	SURVEYING INSTRUMENTS	W 29	682	W 4	137		18		20	INST GEODESIE,TOPO ETC
87412	SURVEY INSTR ETC NONELEC	W 29	678	W 3	118		17		7	INSTR GEODESIE,TOPO ETC
8748	ELEC MEAS,CONTRL EQU NES	W 7	1547		16		153		7	APP ELEC ELECTRO MESURE
87483	OTH ELCTRNC MEAS ETC EQU	W 7	1547		16		153		7	AUT APP ELECTRO DE MESURE
88	PHOTO EQU,OPTICL GDS ETC		293		603		385		395	APP,FOURN PHOTO,OP,MONTR
89	MISC MANUFCTRD GOODS NES		470		1087		2846		1439	ART MANUFACTURES DIVERS
899	OTHER MANUFACTURED GOODS	W 72	335		813		2722		1350	AUT ART MANUF DIVERS NDA
8998	SMALLWARES,TOILETRYS ETC	W 68	307		621	W 81	526	W 120	606	ART MERCERIE,TOILETTE
89981	HAND SIEVES AND RIDDLES			W 83	526					TAMIS ET CRIBLES
8999	OTHER MANUF GOODS NES	W 4	27	W 18	123	W 203	2130	W 105	609	OUVRAGES DIVERS NDA
89991	ARTICLES OF GUT,ETC				43	W 202	2123	W 105	609	OUVRAGES EN BOYAUX

1. HISTORICAL SERIES, 1960–1995 SPECIAL TRADE, IMPORTS C.I.F., EXPORTS F.O.B.
SERIES HISTORIQUES, 1960–1995 COMMERCE SPECIAL, IMPORTATIONS C.A.F., EXPORTATIONS F.O.B

YEAR ANNEE	VALUE IN MILLION C.F.A. FRANCS VALEUR EN MILLION C.F.A. FRANCS MERCHANDISE –MARCHANDISE		GOLD –OR		CONVERSION FACTORS U.S. CENTS PER C.F.A. FRANC FACTEURS DE CONVERSION CENTS E.U. PAR C.F.A. FRANC		INDEX NUMBERS –INDICES QUANTUM		UNIT VALUE VALEUR UNITAIRE	
	IMPORTS	EXPORTS	IMPORTS	EXPORTS	IMPORTS	EXPORTS	IMPORTS	EXPORTS	IMPORTS	EXPORTS
1960	7643.00	4513.00			0.4051	0.4051				
1961	6275.00	3579.00			0.4051	0.4051				
1962	6627.00	2699.00			0.4051	0.4051				
1963	8249.00	3155.00			0.4051	0.4051				
1964	7762.00	3254.00			0.4051	0.4051				
1965	8491.00	3367.00			0.4051	0.4051				
1966	8264.00	2585.00			0.4051	0.4051				
1967	10745.00	3750.00			0.4051	0.4051				
1968	12208.00	5508.00			0.4051	0.4051				
1969	14124.00	7067.00			0.3916	0.3909				
1970	17660.00	9062.00			0.3601	0.3601				
1971	21202.00	11648.00			0.3601	0.3601				
1972	23510.00	9189.00			0.3967	0.3969				
1973	24859.00	9794.00			0.4500	0.4453				
1974	35530.00	10240.00			0.4158	0.4158				
1975	42080.00	6791.00			0.4672	0.4672				
1976	50500.00	9053.00			0.4191	0.4191				
1977	60400.00	10120.00			0.4080	0.4080				
1978	70197.00	6140.00			0.4440	0.4440				
1979	68100.00	9770.00			0.4701	0.4701				
1980	69970.00	13270.00			0.4733	0.4733				
1981	147499.00	9141.00			0.3680	0.3680				
1982	152553.00	7837.00			0.3043	0.3043				
1983	112032.00	25351.00			0.2624	0.2624				
1984	125900.00	72820.00			0.2289	0.2289				
1985	148780.00	67350.00			0.2243	0.2243				
1986	133850.00	36012.99			0.2885	0.2897				
1987	104980.00	34270.00			0.3317	0.3326				
1988	97000.00	21000.00			0.3359	0.3368				
1989	66130.00	24580.00			0.3135	0.3135				
1990	72190.00	33250.00			0.3683	0.3683				
1991	68050.00	5980.00			0.3573	0.3573				
1992	162840.00	23260.00			0.3783	0.3783				
1993	173860.00	51380.00			0.3534	0.3534				
1994	273469.90	90550.00			0.1803	0.1803				
1995	345799.90	95800.00			0.2006	0.1976				

2. IMPORTS BY BROAD ECONOMIC CATEGORY AND EXPORTS BY INDUSTRIAL ORIGIN. (PERCENTAGE OF TOTAL VALUE)
IMPORTATIONS PAR CATEGORIES ECONOMIQUES ET EXPORTATIONS PAR BRANCHE D'ACTIVITE.(EN POURCENTAGE DE LA VALEUR TOTALE)

IMPORTS – IMPORTATIONS

	1990	1991	1992	1993	1994	1995	1996
TOTAL IMPORTS–IMPORTATIONS TOTALES							
1 FOOD BEV–ALIMENTATION BOISSONS							
11 PRIMARY–PRODUITS DE BASE							
111 FOR INDUSTRY–POUR L'INDUSTRIE							
112 FOR HOUSEHOLDS–POUR LES MENAGES							
12 PROCESSED–PRODUITS ELABORES							
121 FOR INDUSTRY–POUR L'INDUSTRIE							
122 FOR HOUSEHOLDS–POUR LES MENAGES							
2 IND SUPPLIES–APPROV INDUSTRIELS							
21 PRIMARY–PRODUITS DE BASE							
22 PROCESSED–PRODUITS ELABORES							
3 FUELS–COMBUSTIBLES							
31 PRIMARY–PRODUITS DE BASE							
32 PROCESSED–PRODUITS ELABORES							
321 MOTOR SPIRIT–ESSENCE							
322 OTHER–AUTRES							
4 MACHINERY–EQUIPEMENT							
41 CAPITAL EQUIPMENT–MACHINES							
42 PARTS–PIECES ACCESSOIRES							
5 TRANSPORT–TRANSPORT							
51 PASSENGER CARS–AUTOMOBILES							
52 OTHER–AUTRES							
521 INDUSTRIAL–INDUSTRIELS							
522 NON INDUSTRIAL–NON INDUSTRIEL							
53 PARTS–PIECES ACCESSOIRES							
6 CONSUM GOODS–BIENS CONSOMMATION							
61 DURABLE–DURABLES							
62 SEMI DURABLE–SEMI DURABLES							
63 NON DURABLE–NON DURABLES							
7 GOODS NES–BIENS NDA							

EXPORTS – EXPORTATIONS

	1990	1991	1992	1993	1994	1995	1996
TOTAL EXPORTS–EXPORTATIONS TOTALES							
1 AGRICULTURE							
2 MINING QUARRY–INDUS EXTRACTIVES							
3 MANUFACTURING–IND MANUFACTUR							
31 FOOD BEV TOBACCO–ALIM BOISS TAB							
32 TEXTILES–INDUSTRIES TEXTILES							
33 WOOD & PRODUCTS–BOIS & PRODUITS							
34 PAPER & PRODUCTS–PAPIER & PRODT							
35 CHEMICALS–INDUSTRIES CHIMIQUES							
36 NON METAL MIN–MIN NON METAL							
37 BASIC METAL–IND METAL BASE							
38 METAL MANUF–MANUF METAL							
39 OTH MANUF IND–AUTRES MANUF							

3. TRADE BY PRINCIPAL COUNTRIES OF PRODUCTION AND LAST DESTINATION (VALUE IN THOUSAND U.S. DOLLARS)
ECHANGES SELON LES PRINCIPAUX PAYS DE PRODUCTION ET DE DERNIERE DESTINATION (VALEUR EN MILLIERS DE DOLLARS EU)

COUNTRIES–PAYS	SPECIAL IMPORTS C.I.F. IMPORTATIONS SPECIALES C.A.F					COUNTRIES–PAYS	SPECIAL EXPORTS F.O.B. EXPORTATIONS SPECIALES F.O.B.				
	1991	1992	1993	1994	1995		1991	1992	1993	1994	1995
World		578874	571719	431558	647065	Monde		87980	181589	163260	164955
Africa		57262	33482	28108	62426	Afrique		30354	90164	45475	34839
Americas		42008	31792	24468	42962	Amériques		4133	13737	35265	35379
Northern America		35847	25373	21571	35325	Amérique du Nord		645	2741	2697	1360
LAIA		5796	5967	2790	6519	ALAI		3324	10662	32470	33106
CACM			4	0	106	MCAC		130	0		57
Caribbean		296	136	106	981	Caraïbes			167	8	12
Rest of America		69	312		30	Autre Amérique		33	167	89	845
As.ex F.USSR		205560	217268	156682	174842	Asie l'URSS exclus		18274	37729	26556	38899
Eur.x F.USSR		270419	284880	220337	363179	Europe l'URSS exclus		34088	39716	53714	51923
EU		256851	274770	210489	351085	UE		33667	39517	52506	49148
EFTA		7369	6034	5333	4694	AELE		420	95	1208	2774
East Europe		6162	3998	4483	7398	Europe de l'Est		0	104		
Other Europe			4	17	0	Autre de l'Europe		0			
Former USSR		1024	373	309	61	Ancienne URSS		13		1283	0
Oceania		150	915	110	1678	Océanie		137		349	392
France,Monac		134302	148499	111522	225347	Morocco/Maroc		11114	63923	15091	16801
Thailand/Thaïlande		102534	99249	69562	64459	Brazil/Brésil		3324	10662	31162	32914
Netherlands/Pays–Bas		42916	52046	22749	31125	Portugal		5384	9230	17868	24242
Japan/Japon		32062	33844	24772	28637	Italy/Italie		7005	13476	7141	7064
USA/Etats–Unis d'Amer		34641	24175	18519	31755	Nigeria/Nigéria		5143	5873	11654	4336
China/Chine		24223	33151	17730	20420	France,Monac		1597	5953	11586	4578
Germany/Allemagne		18994	16798	21588	22758	India/Inde		1162	7199	3635	10597
United Kingdom		20874	15502	14265	21833	Belgium–Luxembourg		12998	3836	2759	2383
Pakistan		25595	13170	15904	5631	Indonesia/Indonésie		3318	2579	7138	7258
Cote d'Ivoire		8877	10138	12506	23353	Thailand/Thaïlande		3557	3390	4806	8419
Spain/Espagne		8279	11499	13640	17695	China/Chine		775	13298	966	4147
Senegal/Sénégal		12025	8988	5675	21596	Niger		1691	2846	9001	2083
Belgium–Luxembourg		14045	9035	10776	11569	So. Africa Customs Un		1543	5199	2500	4291
Italy/Italie		9241	12313	9629	12342	Spain/Espagne		2080	844	6168	4105
India/Inde		6758	6227	6112	12208	Togo		2160	1544	2198	1630
Nigeria/Nigéria		25493	155	384	142	United Kingdom		1918	1390	2181	2039
Korea, Republic of		2584	3766	5750	11940	Cote d'Ivoire		2410	3359	1021	549
Brazil/Brésil		5701	5910	2218	6464	USA/Etats–Unis d'Amer		493	2490	2697	1360
Hong Kong		816	5450	4058	8511	Pakistan		3364	1835	72	893
Norway,SVD,JM		5665	5219	4059	3228	Germany/Allemagne		390	2274	1067	1850
Mauritania/Mauritanie		4482	6186	3196	3928	Netherlands/Pays–Bas		1003	623	1965	1564
Denmark/Danemark		4898	3844	2489	3597	Singapore/Singapour		2259	983	1309	442
Czechoslovakia		5394	3746	2226	2215	Switz.Liecht		393	71	1208	2774
Korea Dem People's Rp		1110	3144	3091	5436	Burkina Faso		1809	2134	286	174
Turkey/Turquie		975	783	1224	9286	Hong Kong		764	2354	417	806
Malaysia/Malaisie		1128	7587	807	1594	Viet Nam			1570	2162	20
Tunisia/Tunisie		2309	2486	2823	3030	Japan/Japon		1112	1433	787	370
Viet Nam		4419	3377	229	1448	Denmark/Danemark		847	546	1069	934
Canada		1206	1198	3052	3570	Bangladesh		141	470	964	1811
Singapore/Singapour		1478	4368	1133	1398	Cape Verde/Cap–Vert		1112			1621
Indonesia/Indonésie		726	1749	2983	1207	Saudi Arabia		146	5	970	1541
Romania/Roumanie		497	100	1369	4570	Malaysia/Malaisie		61	793	313	1178
Morocco/Maroc		1548	1652	706	2113	Korea, Republic of		639	233	1097	191
Austria/Autriche		1565	1513	1030	1267	Cameroon/Cameroun		69	56	1700	265
Switz.Liecht		1689	815	1265	1465	Gabon		201	723	550	582
Togo		401	362	342	3993	Senegal/Sénégal		700	652	225	446
Ireland/Irlande		581	1771	1115	1395	Congo		871	361	242	251
Bangladesh		907	760	679	1699	Mali		694	385	27	281
Saudi Arabia		2	4	2514	434	Philippines		246	337	763	
Sweden/Suède		354	587	1190	651	Austria/Autriche		186	761	0	375
So. Africa Customs Un		31	497	909	1221	Chad/Tchad		2	865	378	75
Portugal		488	545	391	741	Mauritius/Maurice			396		715
Zimbabwe		69	1233	482	0	Ghana		69	631	6	301
Russian Federation		1007	355	262	47	Korea Dem People's Rp		538	201	217	
Ghana		25		24	1586	Russian Federation		0		941	0
Finland/Finlande		191	652	88	195	Myanmar			940		
Australia/Australie		84	867	87	61	Turkey/Turquie					937
Bulgaria/Bulgarie		5	55	742	202	Sri Lanka				872	29
Gabon		379	347	73	177	Belize/Bélize					845
Rep. of the Marshall Islands					914	Mexico/Mexique				794	

(VALUE AS PERCENTAGE OF WORLD TOTAL)(VALEURS EN POURCENTAGE DU TOTAL MONDIAL)

	1986	1987	1988	1989	1990	1991	1992	1993	1994	1995		1986	1987	1988	1989	1990	1991	1992	1993	1994	1995
Africa	7.0	7.3	9.1	10.3			9.9	5.9	6.5	9.6	Afrique	5.3	8.1	11.1	14.6			34.5	49.7	27.9	21.1
Americas	8.4	5.5	7.8	7.2			7.3	5.6	5.7	6.6	Amériques	0.1	15.3	21.2	19.2			4.7	7.6	21.6	21.4
Northern America	4.9	4.4	5.5	6.1			6.2	4.4	5.0	5.5	Amérique du Nord	0.1	15.3	21.1	19.1			0.7	1.5	1.7	0.8
LAIA	3.1	1.1	2.4	1.0			1.0	1.0	0.6	1.0	ALAI	0.0	0.0	0.0	0.1			3.8	5.9	19.9	20.1
CACM								0.0	0.0	0.0	MCAC							0.1	0.0		0.0
Caribbean	0.5	0.0	0.0	0.0			0.1	0.0	0.0	0.2	Caraïbes	0.0		0.0	0.0				0.1	0.0	0.0
Rest of America							0.0	0.1		0.0	Autre Amérique							0.0	0.1	0.1	0.5
As.ex F.USSR	17.7	31.5	28.8	29.2			35.5	38.0	36.3	27.0	Asie l'URSS exclus	2.2	8.1	5.1	11.9			20.8	20.8	16.3	23.6
Eur.x F.USSR	56.9	47.6	47.3	49.0			46.7	49.8	51.1	56.1	Europe l'URSS exclus	89.3	60.9	57.9	38.5			38.7	21.9	32.9	31.5
EU	55.3	46.4	45.2	47.2			44.4	48.1	48.8	54.3	UE	87.5	60.4	57.1	37.6			38.3	21.8	32.2	29.8
EFTA	0.9	0.5	0.8	0.6			1.3	1.1	1.2	0.7	AELE	1.7	0.5	0.8	0.9			0.5	0.1	0.7	1.7
East Europe	0.7	0.7	1.3	1.1			1.1	0.7	1.0	1.1	Europe de l'Est	0.1						0.0	0.1		
Other Europe	0.0	0.1	0.1	0.1				0.0	0.0	0.0	Autre de l'Europe	0.0						0.0			
Former USSR	0.3	0.2	1.0	0.1			0.2	0.1	0.1	0.0	Ancienne URSS		0.1					0.0		0.8	0.0
Oceania	0.0						0.0	0.2	0.0	0.3	Océanie							0.2		0.2	0.2
France,Monac	26.3	21.1	22.3	22.2			23.2	26.0	25.8	34.8	Morocco/Maroc	0.1	0.7	0.3	2.3			12.6	35.2	9.2	10.2
Thailand/Thaïlande	2.2	15.3	14.7	12.8			17.7	17.4	16.1	10.0	Brazil/Brésil							3.8	5.9	19.1	20.0
Netherlands/Pays–Bas	7.0	6.9	6.3	7.6			7.4	9.1	5.3	4.8	Portugal	10.5	22.5	20.5	14.9			6.1	5.1	10.9	14.7
Japan/Japon	5.6	6.4	5.1	5.5			5.5	5.9	5.7	4.4	Italy/Italie	11.2	12.5	7.9	7.0			8.0	7.4	4.4	4.3
USA/Etats–Unis d'Amer	4.5	4.0	5.0	5.7			6.0	4.2	4.3	4.9	Nigeria/Nigéria	2.4	5.2	6.9	4.4			5.8	3.2	7.1	2.6
China/Chine	2.8	1.8	1.6	2.6			4.2	5.8	4.1	3.2	France,Monac	12.2	6.5	9.3	4.1			1.8	3.3	7.1	2.8
Germany/Allemagne	4.0	4.1	3.8	4.2			3.3	2.9	5.0	3.5	India/Inde				0.0			1.3	4.0	2.2	6.4
United Kingdom	4.8	3.6	3.3	3.3			3.6	2.7	3.3	3.4	Belgium–Luxembourg	1.6	0.8	0.6	1.4			14.8	2.1	1.7	1.4
Pakistan	1.1	0.7	0.7	0.0			4.4	2.3	3.7	0.9	Indonesia/Indonésie							3.8	1.4	4.4	4.4
Cote d'Ivoire	2.7	2.8	2.0	2.0			1.5	1.8	2.9	3.6	Thailand/Thaïlande	0.2	0.8	1.0	0.4			4.0	1.9	2.9	5.1

4. Special Imports C.I.F. by Commodities according to the S.I.T.C. (Rev. 2) in thousand U.S. Dollars
Importations Spéciales C.A.F. par Produits d'après la C.T.C.I. (Rév. 2) en milliers de Dollars E.U.

SITC CTCI	COMMODITY	1986		1987		1988		1989		PRODUIT
		WEIGHT POIDS	VALUE VALEUR	WEIGHT POIDS	VALUE VALEUR	WEIGHT POIDS	VALUE VALEUR	WEIGHT POIDS	VALUE VALEUR	
	ALL COMMODITIES		386157		348219		326492		207324	TOUS PRODUITS
0	FOOD AND LIVE ANIMALS		57348		81946		86419		40172	ALIMENTS,ANIMAUX VIVANTS
022	MILK AND CREAM	W 4273	4576	W 3991	4574	W 2672	3293	W 2089	2709	LAIT ET CREME
04	CEREALS AND PREPARATIONS		20573		59553		53125		21343	CEREALES ET PRODUITS
061	SUGAR AND HONEY	W 19935	6315	W 664	302	W 5161	1370	W 6067	2542	SUCRES ET MIEL
1	BEVERAGES AND TOBACCO		41307		26440		15587		14697	BOISSONS ET TABACS
2	CRUDE MATERLS,EXCL FUELS		11367		12518		15107		7678	MAT BRUTES NON COMESTIBLES
3	MINERAL FUELS ETC		30855		25458		44792		31704	COMBUSTIBLES MINERAUX LUB
334	PETROLEUM PRODUCTS,REFIN	W 107407	21170	W 86674	14260	W 82471	31405	W 123943	18167	PRODUITS RAFFINES
4	ANIMAL,VEGETABLE OIL,FAT		1688		952		822		1721	HUILES,GRAISSES ANIM,VEG
5	CHEMCLS,RELATED PROD NES		33746		19653		25936		14766	PRODUITS CHIMIQUES
6	BASIC MANUFACTURES		153026		133924		90800		63722	ART MANUFACTURES
7	MACHINES,TRANSPORT EQUIP		55753		47115		44655		30074	MACHINES MATERIEL TRANSPORT
77	ELECTRIC MACHNRY NES ETC		17723		12568		14230		7057	MACH APP ELECT NDA
78	ROAD VEHICLES		18473		17255		11595		11951	VEHICULES ROUTIERS
931	*SPECIAL TRANSACTIONS		1067		212	W 1137	2373	W 14519	2790	TRANS.SPECIALES

5. Special Exports F.O.B. by Commodities according to the S.I.T.C. (Rev. 2) in thousand U.S. Dollars
Exportations Spéciales F.O.B. par Produits d'après la C.T.C.I. (Rév. 2) en milliers de Dollars E.U.

SITC CTCI	COMMODITY	1986 WEIGHT POIDS	1986 VALUE VALEUR	1987 WEIGHT POIDS	1987 VALUE VALEUR	1988 WEIGHT POIDS	1988 VALUE VALEUR	1989 WEIGHT POIDS	1989 VALUE VALEUR	PRODUIT
	ALL COMMODITIES		104330		113969		70480		97467	TOUS PRODUITS
0	FOOD AND LIVE ANIMALS		32386		4916		1736		715	ALIMENTS,ANIMAUX VIVANTS
036	SHELL FISH FRESH,FROZEN	W 165	391	W 115	113	W 140	201	W 21	44	CRUSTACES,MOLLUSQUES
071	COFFEE AND SUBSTITUTES	W 767	1254	W 470	848	W 115	191	W 66	116	CAFE ET SUCCEDANES
0711	COFFEE GREEN,ROASTED,SUB	W 767	1254	W 470	848	W 115	191	W 66	116	CAFE TORREFIE OU DECAFEINE
072	COCOA	W 14148	27724	W 618	1044	W 4	3			CACAO
0721	COCOA BEANS,RAW,ROASTED	W 14148	27724	W 618	1044	W 4	3			CACAO EN FEVES
081	*FEEDING STUFF FOR ANIML	W 4823	594	W 7674	356	W 3766	258	W 1630	97	NOURRITURE POUR ANIMAUX
0813	OILCAKE AND OTH RESIDUES	W 4823	594	W 7674	356	W 3766	258	W 1630	97	TOURTEAUX
2	CRUDE MATERLS,EXCL FUELS		34164		65043		29448		62722	MAT BRUTES NON COMESTIBLES
2223	COTTON SEEDS	W 16363	970	W 60350	3871	W 28450	2407	W 55866	3508	GRAINES DE COTON
2238	OIL SEEDS AND FRUITS NES	W 2248	634							GRAINES D'OLEAGINEUX NDA
263	COTTON	W 38373	31041	W 59239	59545	W 19174	25933	W 49860	58565	COTON
2631	RAW COTTON,EXCL LINTERS	W 38373	31041	W 59239	59545	W 19174	25933	W 49860	58565	COTON EN MASSE
3	MINERAL FUELS ETC		21079		31361		21445		20804	COMBUSTIBLES MINERAUX LUB
4	ANIMAL,VEGETABLE OIL,FAT		8239		7640		7530		6116	HUILES,GRAISSES ANIM,VEG
4242	PALM OIL	W 107	32	W 11100	3027	W 11685	4149	W 10446	3458	HUILE DE PALME
4244	PALM KERNEL OIL	W 7243	1799	W 4875	1344	W 4294	1175	W 2654	1047	HUILE DE PALMISTE
5	CHEMCLS,RELATED PROD NES		805		1357		1407		398	PRODUITS CHIMIQUES
6	BASIC MANUFACTURES		4122		1989		4488		4320	ART MANUFACTURES
652	COTTON FABRICS,WOVEN	W 353	171	W 218	1194	W 140	634	W ·486	3160	TISSUS DE COTON
661	LIME,CEMENT,BLDG PRODS	W 15522	1257					W 4720	323	CHAUX,CIMENTS MAT CONSTR
6612	CEMENT	W 15522	1257					W 4720	323	CIMENTS HYDRAULIQUES
7	MACHINES,TRANSPORT EQUIP		3505		1357		4290		1922	MACHINES MATERIEL TRANSPORT
931	*SPECIAL TRANSACTIONS		26		226			W 4515	455	TRANS.SPECIALES

1. HISTORICAL SERIES, 1960–1995 GENERAL TRADE, IMPORTS C.I.F., EXPORTS F.O.B.
SERIES HISTORIQUES, 1960–1995 COMMERCE GENERAL, IMPORTATIONS C.A.F., EXPORTATIONS F.O.B

YEAR ANNEE	VALUE IN MILLION BERMUDA DOLLARS VALEUR EN MILLION BERMUDA DOLLARS MERCHANDISE –MARCHANDISE IMPORTS	EXPORTS	GOLD –OR IMPORTS	EXPORTS	CONVERSION FACTORS U.S. CENTS PER BERMUDA DOLLAR FACTEURS DE CONVERSION CENTS E.U. PAR BERMUDA DOLLAR IMPORTS	EXPORTS	INDEX NUMBERS –INDICES QUANTUM IMPORTS	EXPORTS	UNIT VALUE VALEUR UNITAIRE IMPORTS	EXPORTS
1960	47.20	21.30			116.6660	116.6660				
1961	52.70	22.90			116.6660	116.6660				
1962	48.70	22.50			116.6660	116.6660				
1963	47.30	33.00			116.6660	116.6660				
1964	50.40	31.70			116.6660	116.6660				
1965	50.20	46.70			116.6660	116.6660				
1966	56.80	46.10			116.6660	116.6660				
1967	59.10	52.10			114.5820	114.5820				
1968	72.70	66.10			98.0000	98.0000				
1969	85.00	78.80			98.0000	98.0000				
1970	105.10	97.10			100.0000	100.0000				
1971	108.50	91.60			100.0000	100.0000				
1972	109.40	34.10			100.0000	100.0000				
1973	122.90	29.80			100.0000	100.0000				
1974	149.80	34.30			100.0000	100.0000				
1975	162.40	36.20			100.0000	100.0000				
1976	165.50	46.30			100.0000	100.0000				
1977	185.60	38.60			100.0000	100.0000				
1978	211.60	41.20			100.0000	100.0000				
1979	234.00	31.30			100.0000	100.0000				
1980	311.50	36.70			100.0000	100.0000				
1981	322.70	29.40			100.0000	100.0000				
1982	351.00	16.90			100.0000	100.0000				
1983	377.70	22.80			100.0000	100.0000				
1984	414.10	40.50			100.0000	100.0000				
1985	402.50	23.10			100.0000	100.0000				
1986	492.00	65.00			100.0000	100.0000				
1987	420.00	29.00			100.0000	100.0000				
1988	488.00	30.81			100.0000	100.0000				
1989	535.00	50.40			100.0000	100.0000				
1990	594.69	59.81			100.0000	100.0000				
1991	510.12	54.53			100.0000	100.0000				
1992	562.25	84.98			100.0000	100.0000				
1993	534.00				100.0000					
1994	550.00				100.0000					
1995	629.88	52.78			100.0000	100.0000				

2. IMPORTS BY BROAD ECONOMIC CATEGORY AND EXPORTS BY INDUSTRIAL ORIGIN. (PERCENTAGE OF TOTAL VALUE)
IMPORTATIONS PAR CATEGORIES ECONOMIQUES ET EXPORTATIONS PAR BRANCHE D'ACTIVITE.(EN POURCENTAGE DE LA VALEUR TOTALE)

IMPORTS – IMPORTATIONS

	1990	1991	1992	1993	1994	1995	1996
TOTAL IMPORTS–IMPORTATIONS TOTALES							
1 FOOD BEV–ALIMENTATION BOISSONS							
11 PRIMARY–PRODUITS DE BASE							
111 FOR INDUSTRY–POUR L'INDUSTRIE							
112 FOR HOUSEHOLDS–POUR LES MENAGES							
12 PROCESSED–PRODUITS ELABORES							
121 FOR INDUSTRY–POUR L'INDUSTRIE							
122 FOR HOUSEHOLDS–POUR LES MENAGES							
2 IND SUPPLIES–APPROV INDUSTRIELS							
21 PRIMARY–PRODUITS DE BASE							
22 PROCESSED–PRODUITS ELABORES							
3 FUELS–COMBUSTIBLES							
31 PRIMARY–PRODUITS DE BASE							
32 PROCESSED–PRODUITS ELABORES							
321 MOTOR SPIRIT–ESSENCE							
322 OTHER–AUTRES							
4 MACHINERY–EQUIPEMENT							
41 CAPITAL EQUIPMENT–MACHINES							
42 PARTS–PIECES ACCESSOIRES							
5 TRANSPORT–TRANSPORT							
51 PASSENGER CARS–AUTOMOBILES							
52 OTHER–AUTRES							
521 INDUSTRIAL–INDUSTRIELS							
522 NON INDUSTRIAL–NON INDUSTRIEL							
53 PARTS–PIECES ACCESSOIRES							
6 CONSUM GOODS–BIENS CONSOMMATION							
61 DURABLE–DURABLES							
62 SEMI DURABLE–SEMI DURABLES							
63 NON DURABLE–NON DURABLES							
7 GOODS NES–BIENS NDA							

EXPORTS – EXPORTATIONS

	1990	1991	1992	1993	1994	1995	1996
TOTAL EXPORTS–EXPORTATIONS TOTALES							
1 AGRICULTURE							
2 MINING QUARRY–INDUS EXTRACTIVES							
3 MANUFACTURING–IND MANUFACTUR							
31 FOOD BEV TOBACCO–ALIM BOISS TAB							
32 TEXTILES–INDUSTRIES TEXTILES							
33 WOOD & PRODUCTS–BOIS & PRODUITS							
34 PAPER & PRODUCTS–PAPIER & PRODT							
35 CHEMICALS–INDUSTRIES CHIMIQUES							
36 NON METAL MIN–MIN NON METAL							
37 BASIC METAL–IND METAL BASE							
38 METAL MANUF–MANUF METAL							
39 OTH MANUF IND–AUTRES MANUF							

3. TRADE BY PRINCIPAL COUNTRIES OF PRODUCTION AND LAST CONSIGNMENT (VALUE IN THOUSAND U.S. DOLLARS)
ECHANGES SELON LES PRINCIPAUX PAYS DE PRODUCTION ET DE DERNIERE CONSIGNATION (VALEUR EN MILLIERS DE DOLLARS EU)

COUNTRIES–PAYS	GENERAL IMPORTS C.I.F. IMPORTATIONS GENERALES C.A.F					COUNTRIES–PAYS	GENERAL EXPORTS F.O.B. EXPORTATIONS GENERALES F.O.B.				
	1991	1992	1993	1994	1995		1991	1992	1993	1994	1995
World		511136			629883	Monde		84256			52785
Africa		111			843	Afrique					
Americas		386826			521208	Amériques		58869			33792
Northern America		356589			478902	Amérique du Nord		55944			33765
LAIA		20484			12326	ALAI		2270			
CACM		99			144	MCAC		101			
Caribbean		8822			29597	Caraïbes		552			27
Rest of America		832			239	Autre Amérique		2			
As.ex F.USSR		36886			32803	Asie l'URSS exclus		1383			
Eur.x F.USSR		84217			72119	Europe l'URSS exclus		22774			3897
EU		66013			68264	UE		22774			3897
EFTA		17532			3353	AELE					
East Europe		611			483	Europe de l'Est					
Other Europe		2			13	Autre de l'Europe					
Former USSR		7			163	Ancienne URSS					
Oceania		924			933	Océanie					
USA/Etats–Unis d'Amer		336391			451259	USA/Etats–Unis d'Amer		52529			33719
United Kingdom		34544			31179	United Kingdom		17350			3891
Japan/Japon		26664			23501	Italy/Italie		4990			
Canada		20198			27643	Canada		3415			46
Venezuela		18637			10807	Mexico/Mexique		1214			
Aruba					20370	Turkey/Turquie		900			
Switz.Liecht		17121			3192	Brazil/Brésil		612			
France,Monac		8336			7356	Spain/Espagne		430			
Netherlands Antilles		7021			4832	Venezuela		229			
Italy/Italie		5949			4994	Pakistan		225			
Hong Kong		5410			4506	Israel/Israël		179			
Sweden/Suède		536			8579	Netherlands Antilles		164			
Germany/Allemagne		5090			3869	Bahamas		115			27
Netherlands/Pays–Bas		3620			4881	Ecuador/Equateur		105			
Denmark/Danemark		3844			2557	Costa Rica		101			
Spain/Espagne		2012			1809	Trinidad and Tobago		72			
Ireland/Irlande		761			2082	Peru/Pérou		65			
Korea, Republic of		1083			1758	Lao People's Dem. Rp.		65			
Malaysia/Malaisie		1706			159	Jamaica/Jamaïque		55			
Antigua and Barbuda					1729	Argentina/Argentine		45			
China/Chine		663			949	Cuba		41			
Jamaica/Jamaïque		373			898	Barbados/Barbade		11			
New Zealand		717			549	Germany/Allemagne		3			5
Bahamas		569			659	India/Inde		6			
Barbados/Barbade		803			355	Antigua and Barbuda		2			
Mexico/Mexique		681			375	Japan/Japon		2			
Panama		818			214	Netherlands/Pays–Bas		1			
Hungary/Hongrie		535			368	Panama		1			
Peru/Pérou		246			538	France,Monac					1
Austria/Autriche		448			312	Malaysia/Malaisie		1			
Thailand/Thaïlande		393			362						
Belgium–Luxembourg		497			232						
Portugal		337			356						
Indonesia/Indonésie		164			488						
So. Africa Customs Un		52			583						
Brazil/Brésil		252			328						
Colombia/Colombie		471			100						
Norway,SVD,JM		411			132						
India/Inde		197			214						
Australia/Australie		113			271						
Dominica/Dominique		10			368						
Israel/Israël		124			143						
Philippines		153			98						
Korea Dem People's Rp		57			161						
Chile/Chili		26			152						
Argentina/Argentine		164			10						
Cuba		3			170						
Ukraine					159						
Turkey/Turquie		75			75						
Costa Rica		34			115						

(VALUE AS PERCENTAGE OF WORLD TOTAL)(VALEURS EN POURCENTAGE DU TOTAL MONDIAL)

	1986	1987	1988	1989	1990	1991	1992	1993	1994	1995		1986	1987	1988	1989	1990	1991	1992	1993	1994	1995
Africa			0.0	0.0			0.0			0.1	Afrique			0.1	0.0						
Americas			64.1	69.6	72.3		75.7			82.7	Amériques			2.6	2.0			69.9			64.0
Northern America			62.0	61.9	64.1		69.8			76.0	Amérique du Nord			1.2	1.1			66.4			64.0
LAIA			0.7	6.1	6.8		4.0			2.0	ALAI			1.4	0.7			2.7			
CACM				0.0			0.0			0.0	MCAC				0.1			0.1			
Caribbean			1.3	1.6	1.4		1.7			4.7	Caraïbes			0.0	0.1			0.7			0.1
Rest of America			0.0	0.0			0.2			0.0	Autre Amérique							0.0			
As.ex F.USSR			9.5	6.5	6.6		7.2			5.2	Asie l'URSS exclus			0.1	0.1			1.6			
Eur.x F.USSR			23.3	18.8	14.6		16.5			11.4	Europe l'URSS exclus			47.2	42.8			27.0			7.4
EU			19.9	16.8	13.5		12.9			10.8	UE			1.5	1.4			27.0			7.4
EFTA			3.4	2.0	1.1		3.4			0.5	AELE			44.9	41.0						
East Europe			0.0				0.1			0.1	Europe de l'Est			0.8	0.3						
Other Europe			0.0	0.0			0.0			0.0	Autre de l'Europe			0.0	0.0						
Former USSR							0.0			0.0	Ancienne URSS										
Oceania			0.4	0.2	0.3		0.2			0.1	Océanie			0.0	0.0						
USA/Etats–Unis d'Amer			56.2	57.1	59.4		65.8			71.6	USA/Etats–Unis d'Amer			0.7	0.7			62.3			63.9
United Kingdom			8.6	9.5	8.3		6.8			4.9	United Kingdom			0.2	0.2			20.6			7.4
Japan/Japon			7.1	4.4	5.2		5.2			3.7	Italy/Italie			0.0	0.0			5.9			
Canada			5.8	4.8	4.7		4.0			4.4	Canada			0.5	0.4			4.1			0.1
Venezuela			0.3	4.2	6.8		3.6			1.7	Mexico/Mexique			0.1	0.0			1.4			
Aruba										3.2	Turkey/Turquie							1.1			
Switz.Liecht			3.3	2.0	1.1		3.3			0.5	Brazil/Brésil							0.7			
France,Monac			3.1	1.6	1.9		1.6			1.2	Spain/Espagne							0.5			
Netherlands Antilles			0.9	1.5	1.4		1.4			0.8	Venezuela			0.1	0.0			0.3			
Italy/Italie			1.1	0.7	1.0		1.2			0.8	Pakistan			0.1	0.1			0.3			

4. General Imports C.I.F. by Commodities according to the S.I.T.C. (Rev. 2) in thousand U.S. Dollars
Importations Générales C.A.F. par Produits d'après la C.T.C.I. (Rév. 2) en milliers de Dollars E.U.

SITC CTCI	COMMODITY	1990		1991		1992		1993		PRODUIT
		WEIGHT POIDS	VALUE VALEUR	WEIGHT POIDS	VALUE VALEUR	WEIGHT POIDS	VALUE VALEUR	WEIGHT POIDS	VALUE VALEUR	
	ALL COMMODITIES		540631		463744		511136		535321	TOUS PRODUITS
0	FOOD AND LIVE ANIMALS		86862				87354		85042	ALIMENTS,ANIMAUX VIVANTS
01	MEAT AND PREPARATIONS		23789				22565		21165	VIANDES ET PREPARATIONS
02	DAIRY PRODCTS,BIRDS'EGGS		6497				6164		5934	PRODUITS LAITIERS,OEUFS
03	FISH AND PREPARATIONS		9794				9781		9321	POISSONS ET PREPARATIONS
04	CEREALS AND PREPARATIONS		8093				8723		8979	CEREALES ET PRODUITS
05	VEGETABLES AND FRUIT		18965				18778		18944	LEGUMES ET FRUITS
06	SUGAR AND PREPS,HONEY		2390				2325		2153	SUCRES ET PRODUITS
07	COFFEE,TEA,COCOA,SPICES		4110				4559		4353	CAFE,THE,CACAO,EPICES
081	*FEEDING STUFF FOR ANIML		2808				3132		2754	NOURRITURE POUR ANIMAUX
09	MISC EDIBLE PRODUCTS		10048				11088		11143	PREP ALIMENTAIRES DIVERSES
1	BEVERAGES AND TOBACCO		34294				23029		20057	BOISSONS ET TABACS
11	BEVERAGES		23850				19672		17037	BOISSONS
12	TOBACCO AND MANUFACTURES		10444				3357		3020	TABACS BRUTS FABRIQUES
2	CRUDE MATERLS,EXCL FUELS		4698				4310		4443	MAT BRUTES NON COMESTIBLES
24	CORK AND WOOD		2786				2706		2868	LIEGE ET BOIS
3	MINERAL FUELS ETC		46651				31591		30999	COMBUSTIBLES MINERAUX LUB
33	PETROLEUM AND PRODUCTS		45694				30494		30054	PETROLE ET DERIVES
5	CHEMCLS,RELATED PROD NES		53821				67861		74538	PRODUITS CHIMIQUES
53	DYES,TANNING,COLOUR PROD		4012				3714		3630	PROD TEINTURE,COLORANTS
541	*MEDICINAL,PHARM PRODUCT		25672				39918		46548	PROD MEDICINAUX PHARMACEUT
55	PERFUME,CLEANING ETC PRD		14026				14350		14171	PROD POUR PARFUM,TOILETTE
58	PLASTIC MATERIALS ETC		9185							MAT PLAST ARTIFICIELLES
59	CHEMICAL MATERIALS NES						9024		9082	MAT PROD CHIMIQUES NDA
6	BASIC MANUFACTURES		74054				66171		64327	ART MANUFACTURES
62	RUBBER MANUFACTURES NES		2302				2009		1701	CAOUTCHOUC MANUFACTURE
63	WOOD,CORK MANUFACTRS NES		10771				9009		8429	OUVRAGES LIEGE ET BOIS
64	PAPER,PAPERBOARD AND MFR		14768				13189		13314	PAPIERS,CARTONS & OUVRAGES
65	TEXTILE YARN,FABRICS,ETC		12785				11432		10992	FILS,TISSUS,ARTICLES TEXTILE
66	NONMETAL MINERAL MFS NES		15908				16302		18389	ART MIN NON METALLIQUES
69	METAL MANUFACTURES NES		15554				12112		10006	ART MANUFACT EN METAL NDA
7	MACHINES,TRANSPORT EQUIP		109165				111312		124934	MACHINES MATERIEL TRANSPORT
72	MACHS FOR SPCL INDUSTRYS		39523							MAC SPECIALES POUR INDUST
8	MISC MANUFACTURED GOODS		129515				118203		129369	ART MANUFACTURES DIVERS
812	*PLUMBG,HEATNG,LGHTNG EQ		5085				4862		5244	APPAR SANITAIRES CHAUFFAGE
821	*FURNITURE,PARTS THEREOF		16533				12672		15279	MEUBLES ET PIECES
831	*TRAVEL GOODS,HANDBAGS		1889				1728		1684	ARTICLES DE VOYAGE ETC
84	CLOTHING AND ACCESSORIES		40266				36244		36269	VETEMENTS
851	*FOOTWEAR		6224				5620		6104	CHAUSSURES
87	PRECISION INSTRUMNTS NES		10679							INSTRUM,APPAR SCIENT NDA
88	PHOTO EQU,OPTICL GDS ETC						11119		10663	APP,FOURN PHOTO,OP,MONTR
89	MISC MANUFCTRD GOODS NES		48839				45958		54126	ART MANUFACTURES DIVERS

5. General Exports F.O.B. by Commodities according to the S.I.T.C. (Rev. 2) in thousand U.S. Dollars
Exportations Générales F.O.B. par Produits d'après la C.T.C.I. (Rév. 2) en milliers de Dollars E.U.

SITC CTCI	COMMODITY	1989		1990		1991		1992		PRODUIT
		WEIGHT POIDS	VALUE VALEUR	WEIGHT POIDS	VALUE VALEUR	WEIGHT POIDS	VALUE VALEUR	WEIGHT POIDS	VALUE VALEUR	
	ALL COMMODITIES		49988		59730		48745		84256	TOUS PRODUITS
5	CHEMCLS,RELATED PROD NES		31541		48774		39652		75822	PRODUITS CHIMIQUES
541	*MEDICINAL,PHARM PRODUCT		31541		48774		39652		75822	PROD MEDICINAUX PHARMACEUT
9	GOODS NOT CLASSD BY KIND		18447		10956		9093		8140	ART TRANSACT NON CLASSES
931	*SPECIAL TRANSACTIONS		18447		10956		9093		8140	TRANS.SPECIALES

1. HISTORICAL SERIES, 1985–1994 GENERAL TRADE, IMPORTS C.I.F., EXPORTS F.O.B.
SERIES HISTORIQUES, 1985–1994 COMMERCE GENERAL, IMPORTATIONS C.A.F., EXPORTATIONS F.O.B

YEAR ANNEE	VALUE IN MILLION NGULTRUM VALEUR EN MILLION NGULTRUM MERCHANDISE –MARCHANDISE		GOLD –OR		CONVERSION FACTORS U.S. CENTS PER NGULTRUM FACTEURS DE CONVERSION CENTS E.U. PAR NGULTRUM		INDEX NUMBERS –INDICES QUANTUM		UNIT VALUE VALEUR UNITAIRE	
	IMPORTS	EXPORTS	IMPORTS	EXPORTS	IMPORTS	EXPORTS	IMPORTS	EXPORTS	IMPORTS	EXPORTS
1985	1041.60	272.00			8.0847	8.0847				
1986	1168.03	387.26			7.9296	7.9296				
1987	1124.16	714.99			7.7149	7.7149				
1988	1874.50	1041.30			7.1855	7.1855				
1989	1613.90	1132.30			6.1629	6.1629				
1990	1889.80	1306.40			5.7127	5.7127				
1991	2148.50	1631.90			4.5072	4.5072				
1992	3470.90	1837.30			3.8608	3.8608				
1993	3064.10	2097.90			3.3072	3.3070				
1994	3562.40	2225.00			3.1874	3.1874				

2. IMPORTS BY BROAD ECONOMIC CATEGORY AND EXPORTS BY INDUSTRIAL ORIGIN. (PERCENTAGE OF TOTAL VALUE)
IMPORTATIONS PAR CATEGORIES ECONOMIQUES ET EXPORTATIONS PAR BRANCHE D'ACTIVITE.(EN POURCENTAGE DE LA VALEUR TOTALE)

IMPORTS – IMPORTATIONS

	1990	1991	1992	1993	1994	1995	1996
TOTAL IMPORTS–IMPORTATIONS TOTALES		100.	100.	100.			
1 FOOD BEV–ALIMENTATION BOISSONS		23.3	11.9	8.5			
11 PRIMARY–PRODUITS DE BASE		3.1	3.7	4.6			
111 FOR INDUSTRY–POUR L'INDUSTRIE		1.0	2.1	3.6			
112 FOR HOUSEHOLDS–POUR LES MENAGES		2.1	1.6	1.0			
12 PROCESSED–PRODUITS ELABORES		20.2	8.2	3.9			
121 FOR INDUSTRY–POUR L'INDUSTRIE		6.5	0.8	2.0			
122 FOR HOUSEHOLDS–POUR LES MENAGES		13.7	7.4	1.9			
2 IND SUPPLIES–APPROV INDUSTRIELS		20.7	22.0	12.9			
21 PRIMARY–PRODUITS DE BASE		1.3	1.4	1.6			
22 PROCESSED–PRODUITS ELABORES		19.5	20.6	11.2			
3 FUELS–COMBUSTIBLES		11.9	8.2	4.9			
31 PRIMARY–PRODUITS DE BASE		1.2	1.0	0.8			
32 PROCESSED–PRODUITS ELABORES		10.7	7.1	4.1			
321 MOTOR SPIRIT–ESSENCE		3.1	1.5	1.0			
322 OTHER–AUTRES		7.6	5.6	3.1			
4 MACHINERY–EQUIPEMENT		20.4	17.8	11.9			
41 CAPITAL EQUIPMENT–MACHINES		19.0	16.0	11.6			
42 PARTS–PIECES ACCESSOIRES		1.4	1.8	0.2			
5 TRANSPORT–TRANSPORT		16.7	12.3	5.0			
51 PASSENGER CARS–AUTOMOBILES		4.6	2.5	1.1			
52 OTHER–AUTRES		4.7	5.1	0.3			
521 INDUSTRIAL–INDUSTRIELS		3.1	4.4	0.1			
522 NON INDUSTRIAL–NON INDUSTRIEL		1.6	0.7	0.3			
53 PARTS–PIECES ACCESSOIRES		7.4	4.7	3.6			
6 CONSUM GOODS–BIENS CONSOMMATION		6.4	5.4	4.5			
61 DURABLE–DURABLES		1.4	1.9	0.5			
62 SEMI DURABLE–SEMI DURABLES		2.6	1.9	2.3			
63 NON DURABLE–NON DURABLES		2.4	1.6	1.7			
7 GOODS NES–BIENS NDA		0.6	22.6	0.7			

EXPORTS – EXPORTATIONS

	1990	1991	1992	1993	1994	1995	1996
TOTAL EXPORTS–EXPORTATIONS TOTALES		100.	100.	100.			
1 AGRICULTURE		19.0	27.0	10.6			
2 MINING QUARRY–INDUS EXTRACTIVES		4.5	4.8	1.5			
3 MANUFACTURING–IND MANUFACTUR		76.4	68.2	39.8			
31 FOOD BEV TOBACCO–ALIM BOISS TAB		7.3	7.1	4.6			
32 TEXTILES–INDUSTRIES TEXTILES		0.0	0.0	0.0			
33 WOOD & PRODUCTS–BOIS & PRODUITS		11.4	10.6	5.5			
34 PAPER & PRODUCTS–PAPIER & PRODT		0.2	0.5	0.2			
35 CHEMICALS–INDUSTRIES CHIMIQUES		20.5	21.6	9.7			
36 NON METAL MIN–MIN NON METAL		10.1	8.0	5.7			
37 BASIC METAL–IND METAL BASE				0.0			
38 METAL MANUF–MANUF METAL		0.0	0.0	0.0			
39 OTH MANUF IND–AUTRES MANUF		26.9	20.4	14.0			

3. TRADE BY PRINCIPAL COUNTRIES OF ORIGIN AND DESTINATION (VALUE IN THOUSAND U.S. DOLLARS)
ECHANGES SELON LES PRINCIPAUX PAYS D'ORIGINE ET DE DESTINATION (VALEUR EN MILLIERS DE DOLLARS EU)

COUNTRIES–PAYS	GENERAL IMPORTS C.I.F. IMPORTATIONS GENERALES C.A.F				
	1989	1990	1991	1992	1993
World			96616	127986	90793
Africa			18	30	
Americas			1472	1194	426
Northern America			1420	1194	426
LAIA			53	0	0
CACM					
Caribbean					
Rest of America					
As.ex F.USSR			88723	82412	78124
Eur.x F.USSR			5587	43492	12196
EU			4677	33261	6053
EFTA			910	10231	6143
East Europe					
Other Europe					
Former USSR					
Oceania			518	220	48
India/Inde			72621	67345	63840
Japan/Japon			14207	13785	11927
United Kingdom			355	26398	2398
Norway,SVD,JM			697	10052	6084
Germany/Allemagne			2952	3634	1434
Denmark/Danemark			796	2176	724
Singapore/Singapour			620	781	1158
USA/Etats–Unis d'Amer			532	1083	342
Netherlands/Pays–Bas			77	703	524
Canada			887	112	84
Austria/Autriche			305	240	457
Malaysia/Malaisie			170	117	547
Korea, Republic of			536	1	208
Australia/Australie			516	90	46
Bangladesh			145	173	185
Switz.Liecht			214	179	59
Hong Kong			222	160	62
Italy/Italie			7	98	246
Belgium–Luxembourg			33		129
Sweden/Suède			74		81
Thailand/Thaïlande			134	0	2
New Zealand			2	130	2
France,Monac			57	11	61
Saudi Arabia			8	43	
Brazil/Brésil				0	

COUNTRIES–PAYS	GENERAL EXPORTS F.O.B. EXPORTATIONS GENERALES F.O.B.				
	1989	1990	1991	1992	1993
Monde			65029	67068	65820
Afrique					
Amériques					
Amérique du Nord					
ALAI					
MCAC					
Caraïbes					
Autre Amérique					
Asie l'URSS exclus			64830	66667	65493
Europe l'URSS exclus			94	84	60
UE			94	84	60
AELE					
Europe de l'Est					
Autre de l'Europe					
Ancienne URSS					10
Océanie					
India/Inde			58835	56172	59062
Bangladesh			5343	10444	6339
Singapore/Singapour			648		
Netherlands/Pays–Bas			77	38	42
Germany/Allemagne			16	46	12
Japan/Japon				16	47
Thailand/Thaïlande			5	3	4
United Kingdom					2

(VALUE AS PERCENTAGE OF WORLD TOTAL)(VALEURS EN POURCENTAGE DU TOTAL MONDIAL)

	1984	1985	1986	1987	1988	1989	1990	1991	1992	1993
Africa								0.0	0.0	
Americas			2.4	2.6	0.5			1.5	0.9	0.5
Northern America			2.4	2.4	0.4			1.5	0.9	0.5
LAIA				0.2	0.1			0.1	0.0	0.0
CACM										
Caribbean										
Rest of America										
As.ex F.USSR			85.0	80.2	68.2			91.8	64.4	86.0
Eur.x F.USSR			10.5	12.8	27.7			5.8	34.0	13.4
EU			8.7	8.0	26.7			4.8	26.0	6.7
EFTA			1.6	4.9	0.9			0.9	8.0	6.8
East Europe										
Other Europe			0.2							
Former USSR										
Oceania			0.9	0.4	0.0			0.5	0.2	0.1
India/Inde			60.0	71.3	57.2			75.2	52.6	70.3
Japan/Japon			20.5	5.7	7.8			14.7	10.8	13.1
United Kingdom			1.0	1.1	22.6			0.4	20.6	2.6
Norway,SVD,JM			1.5	4.6	0.6			0.7	7.9	6.7
Germany/Allemagne			4.2	4.0	2.9			3.1	2.8	1.6
Denmark/Danemark			0.2	0.6	0.0			0.8	1.7	0.8
Singapore/Singapour			4.1	0.3	1.2			0.6	0.6	1.3
USA/Etats–Unis d'Amer			2.1	1.9	0.4			0.6	0.8	0.4
Netherlands/Pays–Bas			0.0	0.1	0.2			0.1	0.5	0.6
Canada			0.3	0.5				0.9	0.1	0.1

	1984	1985	1986	1987	1988	1989	1990	1991	1992	1993
Afrique										
Amériques			0.3	0.1	0.7					
Amérique du Nord					0.7					
ALAI			0.0							
MCAC			0.2	0.1						
Caraïbes			0.0	0.0	0.0					
Autre Amérique										
Asie l'URSS exclus			97.6	98.0	94.3			99.7	99.4	99.5
Europe l'URSS exclus			0.3	0.2	0.1			0.1	0.1	0.1
UE			0.3	0.2	0.1			0.1	0.1	0.1
AELE				0.0	0.0					
Europe de l'Est										
Autre de l'Europe										
Ancienne URSS										0.0
Océanie										
India/Inde			94.5	95.9	92.5			90.5	83.8	89.7
Bangladesh								8.2	15.6	9.6
Singapore/Singapour			0.6	0.6	0.6			1.0		
Netherlands/Pays–Bas								0.1	0.1	0.1
Germany/Allemagne				0.1	0.0			0.0	0.1	0.0
Japan/Japon			0.1	0.0	0.0				0.0	0.1
Thailand/Thaïlande								0.0	0.0	0.0
United Kingdom				0.0	0.0					0.0

4. General Imports C.I.F. by Commodities according to the S.I.T.C. (Rev. 2) in thousand U.S. Dollars
Importations Générales C.A.F. par Produits d'après la C.T.C.I. (Rév. 2) en milliers de Dollars E.U.

SITC CTCI	COMMODITY	1990		1991		1992		1993		PRODUIT
		WEIGHT POIDS	VALUE VALEUR	WEIGHT POIDS	VALUE VALEUR	WEIGHT POIDS	VALUE VALEUR	WEIGHT POIDS	VALUE VALEUR	
	ALL COMMODITIES				96616		127986		90793	TOUS PRODUITS
0	FOOD AND LIVE ANIMALS				16791		13584		13002	ALIMENTS,ANIMAUX VIVANTS
001	*LIVE ANIMALS FOR FOOD			N 56013	223	N 34185	599	N 33043	191	ANIMAUX VIVANTS
0011	BOVINE SPECIES,LIVE			N 7022	202	N 18286	491	N 20796	176	ESPECE BOVINE
00111	— PURE BRED FR BREEDING			N 7012	202	N 18286	491	N 5422	136	BOVINS REPRODUCTEURS
02	DAIRY PRODCTS,BIRDS'EGGS				1393		2171		1711	PRODUITS LAITIERS,OEUFS
022	MILK AND CREAM				745		1374		1012	LAIT ET CREME
0224	MILK,CREAM PRESERVED ETC				682		1374		1005	LAIT,CREME CONS,CONC
02242	MILK DRY,1.5% FAT OR LES				532		562		899	LAIT POUDRE INF 1.5%
02243	MILK DRY,OVER 1.5% FAT						560			LAIT POUDRE SUP 1.5%
023	BUTTER			W 132	423	W 187	506	W 212	404	BEURRE
025	EGGS,BIRDS,FRESH,PRSRVD			N 8218644	212	N 8456988	224	W 729	278	OEUFS
0251	— IN SHELL			N 8218644	212	N 8456988	224	W 729	278	OEUFS EN COQUILLE
03	FISH AND PREPARATIONS				833		795		342	POISSONS ET PREPARATIONS
035	FISH SALTED,DRIED,SMOKED				829		774		304	POISSON SECHE,SALE,FUME
03503	FISH(EX COD)DRIED,SALTED				829		774		304	POISSONS SECHES,SALES
04	CEREALS AND PREPARATIONS				10651		7635		6739	CEREALES ET PRODUITS
041	WHEAT ETC UNMILLED					W 15915	2031	W 14694	1457	FROMENT,EPEAUTRE
0412	OTHER WHEAT ETC UNMILLED					W 15915	2031	W 14313	1414	AUTRE FROMENT NON MOULU
042	RICE				5654		3742	W 22250	4147	RIZ
0421	RICE IN HUSK OR HUSKED				2		2	W 22247	4146	RIZ SANS AUTRE PREPARATION
04212	RICE HUSKED							W 22226	4143	RIZ CARGO
0422	RICE SEMI–MILLED,MILLED			W 23800	5651	W 19568	3740			RIZ POLI,GLACE INCL BRISURES
04221	RICE MILLED UNBROKEN			W 23800	5651	W 19568	3740			RIZ POLI,GLACE EXCL BRISURES
046	WHEAT ETC MEAL OR FLOUR			W 25611	3765	W 1651	285		453	SEMOULE FARINE,FROMENT
04601	FLOUR OF WHEAT OR MESLIN			W 1109	207	W 1618	276	W 2216	290	FARINE DE FROMENT
04602	MEAL,GROATS OF WHEAT ETC			W 24502	3558	W 33	8		162	GRUAUX,SEMOULES FROMENT
048	CEREAL ETC PREPARATIONS				783		970	W 665	451	PREPTNS A BASE CEREALES
0488	OTH CEREAL PREPS,MALT EX				293		501	W 58	62	EXTRAITS DE MALT
05	VEGETABLES AND FRUIT				1325		855		2318	LEGUMES ET FRUITS
054	VEG ETC FRSH,SMPLY PRSVD				1010		479	W 7456	1582	LEGUMES FRAIS,CONG,SECS
0545	OTHER FRESH VEGETABLES			W 850	140	W 1875	217	W 3227	493	AUTRES LEGUMES FRAIS,REF
05459	FRESH VEGETABLES NES			W 653	102	W 1676	192	W 3070	470	LEGUMES FRAIS,REFRI NDA
0548	EDIBLE VEG NES FRESH,DRY				674		24	W 3028	787	RACINES,TUBERCULES
05482	SUGAR BEET FRSH DRY,CANE				673		1	W 3028	787	BETTERAVES,CANNES A SUCRE
057	FRUIT,NUTS,FRESH,DRIED				259		205	W 1244	281	FRUITS FRAIS OU SECS
06	SUGAR AND PREPS,HONEY				1891		949		1234	SUCRES ET PRODUITS
061	SUGAR AND HONEY			W 4731	1835	W 3184	887	W 4664	1171	SUCRES ET MIEL
0611	RAW BEET AND CANE SUGAR							W 4532	1132	SUCRES BRUTS
0612	REFINED SUGAR ETC			W 4725	1826	W 3130	871	W 110	33	SUCRES RAFFINES
1	BEVERAGES AND TOBACCO				3975		1719		1330	BOISSONS ET TABACS
11	BEVERAGES				3716		1689		1323	BOISSONS
112	ALCOHOLIC BEVERAGES				3674		1624		1315	BOISSONS ALCOOLIQUES
1123	BEER,ALE,STOUT,PORTER			V 685	2229	V 292	942	W 1427	856	BIERES
1124	DISTILLED ALCOHOLIC BEVS				1403		649		374	ALCOOLS,EAUX–DE–VIE
11241	WHISKY				126		114		366	WHISKY
11249	OTH ALCOHOLC BEVS,CMPNDS			W 2479	1277		535	W 6	9	BOISSONS ALCOOLIQUES NDA
2	CRUDE MATERLS,EXCL FUELS				1483		2157		3593	MAT BRUTES NON COMESTIBLES
24	CORK AND WOOD				669		1115		815	LIEGE ET BOIS
245	FUEL WOOD NES, CHARCOAL				327		683	W 4041	652	BOIS DE CHAUFFAGE
24502	WOOD CHARCOAL			W 3168	324	W 6900	678	W 4040	650	CHARBON DE BOIS
27	CRUDE FERTLZR,MINRLS NES				757		861		2377	ENGRAIS MINERAUX BRUTS
271	FERTILIZERS,CRUDE								2028	ENGRAIS BRUTS
2711	ANIMAL,VEG FERTLZR,CRUDE								2027	GUANO,ENGRAIS NATURELS
273	STONE,SAND AND GRAVEL				622		721	W 12467	246	PIERRES,SABLES,GRAVIERS
2732	CALCAREOUS STONE				561		677	W 11855	210	GYPSE,PLATRES,CASTINES
27322	CALCAREOUS STONE NES			V 181682	547	V 142052	661	W 11854	209	PIERRES A CHAUX
29	CRUDE ANIMAL,VEG MAT NES				24		113		273	MATIERES BRUTES ANIM,VEGET
292	CRUDE VEG MATERIALS NES				24		113		273	MAT BRUTES VEGETALES NDA
3	MINERAL FUELS ETC				11597		10371		8904	COMBUSTIBLES MINERAUX LUB
32	COAL,COKE AND BRIQUETTES				1822		1757		1581	HOUILLES,COKES,BRIQUETTES
322	COAL,LIGNITE AND PEAT			W 20891	875	W 30014	1042	W 26124	1271	HOUILLES,LIGNITES,TOURBE
3222	OTH COAL,NOT AGGLOMERATD			W 20891	875	W 30014	1042	W 26124	1271	AUTRES HOUILLES
323	BRIQUETS,COKE,SEMI–COKE			W 10140	947	W 10865	715	W 8628	310	BRIQUETTES
3232	COKE,SEMI–COKE,RTRT CRBN			W 10140	947	W 10865	715	W 8628	310	COKES ET SEMI–COKES
32321	COKE OF COAL,RETORT CRBN			W 10140	947	W 10865	715			COKES,SEMI–COKES HOUILLE
33	PETROLEUM AND PRODUCTS				9255		8127		6711	PETROLE ET DERIVES
334	PETROLEUM PRODUCTS,REFIN				8831		7508	W 24912	6366	PRODUITS RAFFINES
3341	GASOLINE,OTH LIGHT OILS			V 5478	2951	V 4557	2277	W 3499	1897	ESSENCES POUR MOTEURS
33411	MOTOR,AVIATION SPIRIT			V 5451	2939	V 3583	1852	W 3499	1897	ESSENCES MOTEURS D'AVIONS
3342	KEROSENE,OTH MEDIUM OILS			V 6245	660	V 6969	639	W 6956	602	PETR LAMPANTS,AUT HUIL
33421	KEROSENE INCL JET FUEL			V 6245	660	V 6969	639			PETROLES LAMPANTS
33429	OTH MEDIUM PETROLEUM OIL							W 6956	602	AUTRES HUILES MOYENNES
3343	GAS OILS			V 17478	3565	V 18553	3468	W 13856	2999	GAS OILS
3344	FUEL OILS,NES			V 2419	401	V 2595	484	W 193	329	FUEL OILS
3345	LUBS,PETROLEUM OILS NES				1255		640	W 407	538	HUILES LUBRIFIANTES
33451	LUBS(HIGH PETR CONT) ETC			W 34	37	W 26	12	W 392	517	HUILES LUBRIF,H LOURDES
33452	LUBS (LOW PETRLM CONTNT)			V 711	1218	V 636	628	W 15	21	PREPARATIONS LUBRIFIANTES
335	RESIDUAL PETRLM PROD NES				424		619	W 2225	345	PRODUITS RESIDUELS NDA
3354	PETROLM BITUMEN,COKE ETC				416		557	W 2174	338	BITUME,COKE DE PETROLE
33541	PETROLEUM BITUMEN, ETC							W 2104	326	BITUME DE PETROLE
33543	BITUMINOUS MIXTURES ETC				278		451	W 60	11	MELANGES BITUMINEUX
341	*GAS,NATURAL AND MANUFCT				294		264	W 1945	270	GAZ NATUREL,GAZ MANUFACT
3413	PETROLM GASES,LIQUEFIED				294		262	W 1945	270	GAZ DE PETROLE LIQUEFIE
351	*ELECTRIC CURRENT				226		223		341	ENERGIE ELECTRIQUE
4	ANIMAL,VEGETABLE OIL,FAT				3682		2635		3209	HUILES,GRAISSES ANIM,VEG
42	FIXED VEGETABLE OIL,FAT				3682		2635		3140	HUILES VEGETALES FIXES
423	FIXED VEG OILS,SOFT				2180		1429	W 1477	1384	HUILES VEGET DOUCES FIXES
4232	SOYA BEAN OIL			W 800	633			W 19	12	HUILE DE SOJA
4239	OTH FIXED VEG OILS,SOFT			W 936	1273	W 994	1117	W 1434	1344	AUTRES HUILES FIXES
42391	RAPE,COLZA,MUSTARD OILS			W 936	1273	W 114	136	W 1434	1344	H NAVETTE COLZA MOUTARDE
42392	SESAME OIL					W 880	981			HUILE DE SESAME
424	FIXED VEG OIL NONSOFT			W 674	1502	W 969	1206		1756	AUTRES HUILES VEG FIXES
4242	PALM OIL			W 65	27	W 130	38		547	HUILE DE PALME
4249	FIXED VEGETABLE OILS NES			W 593	1458	W 822	1143	W 1089	1146	HUILES VEGET FIXES NDA
5	CHEMCLS,RELATED PROD NES				5197		6239		7263	PRODUITS CHIMIQUES
51	ORGANIC CHEMICALS				420		275		3007	PROD CHIMIQ ORGANIQUES
511	HYDROCARBONS NES,DERIVS			V 690	344	V 386	231	W 1895	962	HYDROCARBURES NDA
5111	ACYCLIC HYDROCARBONS			V 690	344	V 386	231	W 1895	962	HYDROCARBURES ACYCLIQUES
51111	ETHYLENE			V 690	344	V 386	231			ETHYLENE
51119	OTH ACYCLIC HYDROCARBONS							W 1895	962	AUT HYDROCARBURES ACYCL

4. General Imports C.I.F. by Commodities according to the S.I.T.C. (Rev. 2) in thousand U.S. Dollars
Importations Générales C.A.F. par Produits d'après la C.T.C.I. (Rév. 2) en milliers de Dollars E.U.

SITC CTCI	COMMODITY	1990 WEIGHT POIDS	1990 VALUE VALEUR	1991 WEIGHT POIDS	1991 VALUE VALEUR	1992 WEIGHT POIDS	1992 VALUE VALEUR	1993 WEIGHT POIDS	1993 VALUE VALEUR	PRODUIT
512	ALCOHOLS,PHENOLS ETC				30		10	V 4817	1937	PHENOLS,PHENOLS–ALCOOLS
5121	ACYCLIC ALCOHOLS,DERIVS							V 4817	1937	ALCOOLS ACYCLIQUES
51216	ETHYL ALC,DENATRD SPIRIT							V 4817	1937	ALCOOL ETHYLIQUE NON DENAT
52	INORGANIC CHEMICALS				614		1159		811	PROD CHIM INORGANIQUES
522	INORG ELEMNTS,OXIDES,ETC				86		96		510	ELEMENTS INORGANIQUES
5221	CHEMICAL ELEMENTS				66		92		496	ELEMENTS CHIMIQUES
52217	ALKALI,RARE EARTH METALS							W 791	405	METAUX ALCALINS
523	OTHR INORG CHEMICALS ETC				67		20		301	AUT PRODUITS CHIMIQUES INORG
524	RADIOACTIVE ETC MATERIAL			W 1110	461	W 2354	1043			MATIERES RADIOACTIVES
5241	RADIOACTIVE ELEMENTS ETC			W 1110	461	W 2354	1043			RADIOELEMENTS,ISOTOPES
53	DYES,TANNING,COLOUR PROD				335		370		356	PROD TEINTURE,COLORANTS
533	PIGMENTS,PAINTS,ETC				335		369	W 284	356	PIGMENTS,PEINTURES,VERNIS
5334	VARNISHES,DISTEMPERS ETC			W 219	333	W 263	361	W 276	348	PEINTURES A L'EAU
53342	OTH PAINTS,VARNISHES ETC					W 190	346	W 276	348	AUTRES PEINTURES,VERNIS
53343	PIGMNTS IN PAINT ETC MED			W 209	325					PIGMENTS BROYES
541	*MEDICINAL,PHARM PRODUCT				1329		1345		1133	PROD MEDICINAUX PHARMACEUT
5415	HORMONES,NAT,SYN IN BULK				1000		963			HORMONES
54151	INSULIN				1000		963			INSULINE
5417	MEDICAMENTS				166		54		1093	MEDICAMENTS
54171	— CONTAINNG ANTIBIOTICS				38		32	K 329881	795	MED CONTN ANTIBIOTIQUES
54179	— CONTNG OTH SUBSTANCES				128		22		297	MED CONT AUT SUBSTANCES
55	PERFUME,CLEANING ETC PRD				899		957		966	PROD POUR PARFUM,TOILETTE
554	SOAP,CLEANSING ETC PREPS				683		736	W 773	802	SAVONS,PRODUITS DETERSIFS
5541	SOAPS				590		646	W 750	779	SAVONS,PROD TENSIO–ACTIFS
562	*FERTILIZERS,MANUFACTURE			W 2408	230	W 2869	319		374	ENGRAIS MANUFACTURES
5621	CHEM NITROGENOUS FERTLZR			W 15	2	W 551	63		374	ENGRAIS AZOTES
56216	UREA								370	UREE
572	*EXPLOSIVES,PYROTECH PRO				411		115	W 583	161	EXPLOSIFS
5721	PREPARED EXPLOSIVES				328		73	W 518	115	POUDRES,EXPLOSIFS
57211	PROPELLENT POWDERS				328		73	W 168	63	POUDRES A TIRER
59	CHEMICAL MATERIALS NES				828		1592		246	MAT PROD CHIMIQUES NDA
598	MISCEL CHEM PRODUCTS NES				524		1223		16	PROD DIV INDUST CHIM NDA
5989	CHEM PRODUCTS,PREPS NES				507		1208		1	PROD PREP CHIMIQUES NDA
59899	OTH CHEM PRODS,PREPS,NES				459		1195			AUT PRODUITS CHIMIQUES NDA
6	BASIC MANUFACTURES				15946		20910		16059	ART MANUFACTURES
62	RUBBER MANUFACTURES NES				2215		2298		1464	CAOUTCHOUC MANUFACTURE
625	RUBBER TYRES, TUBES ETC				2126		2163		1379	PNEUS CAOUTCHOUC VULCANISE
6251	TYRES NEW FOR MOTOR CARS				488		583	N 5653	283	PNEUS POUR VOITURES
6252	TYRES,NEW,BUS OR LORRY			N 10190	1421		1287	N 6173	790	PNEUS POUR AUTOBUS,CAMIONS
6259	OTH TYRES,TYRE CASES,ETC			N 15940	199	N 25964	259		294	AUTRES PNEUS RECHAPES FLAPS
63	WOOD,CORK MANUFACTRS NES				518		714		535	OUVRAGES LIEGE ET BOIS
634	VENEERS,PLYWOOD,ETC				480		471		117	PLACAGES,CONTRE–PLAQUES
6341	VENEER SHEETS ETC				463		329	V 83742	21	BOIS SIMPLEMENT SCIES
64	PAPER,PAPERBOARD AND MFR				1758		2053		1772	PAPIERS,CARTONS & OUVRAGES
641	PAPER AND PAPERBOARD				1023		1267		1084	PAPIERS ET CARTONS
6411	NEWSPRINT				353		536			PAPIER JOURNAL
6412	PRINTG,WRITING PAPER NES				634		707	W 32	32	PAPIERS POUR L'IMPRESSION
64121	— UNCOATED				634		707	W 32	32	PAPIERS IMPRES NON COUCHES
6413	KRAFT PAPER,PAPERBOARD							W 848	574	PAPIER ET CARTON KRAFT
64139	KRAFT PAPER PAPERBD,NES							W 343	355	PAPIER,CARTON KRAFT NDA
6419	CONVERTED PAPER ETC NES			N 82626	2	N 11190	4		467	PAP,CART TRANSFORMES NDA
64197	WALLPAPER,LINCRUSTA,ETC								467	PAPIERS DE TENTURE
642	PAPER,ETC,PRECUT,ARTS OF				734		786	W 1028	688	PAP,CARTONS DECOUPES
6423	EXERCISE BOOKS ETC				368		442	W 440	420	REGISTRES,CAHIERS,CARNETS
65	TEXTILE YARN,FABRICS,ETC				3188		3170		1971	FILS,TISSUS,ARTICLES TEXTILE
651	TEXTILE YARN				634		793	W 266	685	FILS TEXTILES
6513	COTTON YARN				307		152	W 156	113	FILS DE COTON
65131	— 14 KM PER KG OR LESS				307		152			FILS COT MOINS 14000 M KG
6514	SYN FIB YRN,BULK,MONOFIL						7	W 88	331	FILS CONT 85% FIB TEXT SYNTH
65142	— NONTXT ETC CONT PAMID							W 79	318	FILS NON TEX FI CON POLYAMID
652	COTTON FABRICS,WOVEN				1324		1250	A 1260	965	TISSUS DE COTON
6521	GREY WOVEN COTTON FABRIC				1324		1250	A 1236	949	TISSUS COT ECRUS NON MERCER
65211	GREY COTTON GAUZE				1324		1235			TISSUS COT POINT GAZE ECRUS
65214	GREY WOVEN COTTON NES						14	A 1236	949	AUT TISSUS 85% COTON ECRUS
658	TEXTILE ARTICLES NES				1016		950		135	ART FACONNES MAT TEXTILES
6581	BAGS,SACKS OF TEXTILES				449		559	W 24	24	SACS EMBALLAGE TEXTILES
6582	MADE–UP CANVAS GOODS				306		103		43	BACHES,TENTES ETC
66	NONMETAL MINERAL MFS NES				1623		1710		2912	ART MIN NON METALLIQUES
661	LIME,CEMENT,BLDG PRODS				78		47	W 3642	896	CHAUX,CIMENTS MAT CONSTR
6618	MNRL BLDG PRD UNFIRD NES							W 679	735	MAT CONST AMIANTE–CIMENT
66183	ASBESTOS–,FIBRE–CMNT PRD							W 674	733	OUVRAGES AMIANTE–CIMENT
662	CLAY,REFRACTORY BLDG PRD				300		583	W 20808	476	MAT CONST REFRACTAIRES
6624	BRICKS ETC NONREFRACTORY				300		583	W 8120	214	BRIQUES ETC CERAM NON REFR
664	GLASS				479		206	W 293	242	VERRE
6649	GLASS NES				399	N 218286	102	W 292	241	VERRE NDA
66491	GLASS IN SHAPES				298			W 216	114	VERRE A VITRES DECOUPES
665	GLASSWARE			MN 9909	676	MN 12053	788	W 8601	1204	OUVRAGES EN VERRE
6651	BOTTLES ETC OF GLASS			MN 9845	663	MN 11986	746	W 8559	1170	RECIPIENTS EN VERRE
66511	GLASS BOTTLES ETC NONVAC			MN 9845	663	MN 11986	746	W 8559	1170	BONBONNES,BOUTEILLES,ETC
67	IRON AND STEEL				3778		7128		4759	FER ET ACIER
673	IRON,STEEL SHAPES ETC				1065		3297	W 345101	2190	BARRES,PROFIL FER,ACIER
6732	IRON,STEEL BARS ETC				692		1313	W 2822	1108	BARRES FER,ACIER
67325	OTH ALLOY STEEL BARS ETC							W 2822	1108	BARRES NON ACIERS ALLIES
67326	IRN,OTH STL BARS HOTROLD			W 1424	643	W 2600	1257			BARRES PLEINES FER,ACIER
6733	IRON,STEEL PROFILES ETC			N 315977	359	N 584632	1936	W 342247	1066	PROFILES,PALPLAN FER,ACIER
67333	OTH PRFILES HOTROLLD ETC			N 292007	334	N 562793	1905	W 1659	818	AUT PROFILES LAMINES,FILES
674	IRN,STL UNIV,PLATE,SHEET				1127		2685		1501	LARGES PLATS,TOLES
6741	IRON OR STEEL UNIVERSALS				156	N 306367	608			LARGES PLATS FER,ACIER
67414	IRN,SMPL STL UNIVERSALS				147	N 306180	607			PLATS NON ACIER FIN
6747	TINNED PLATES,SHEETS			N 492185	972	N 190318	1473	W 8	3	TOLES ETAMEES EN ACIER
6749	OTH IRN,STL PLATES,SHEET						604		1497	AUTRES TOLES FER,ACIER
67491	— OF IRON OR SIMPLE STL						604		1497	AUT TOLES AUTRES ACIER FIN
675	IRON,STEEL HOOP,STRIP				827					FEUILLARDS LAMINES
67501	IRN,SMPLE STL HOOP,STRIP				827					FEUILLARDS NON ACIER FIN
678	IRON,STL TUBES,PIPES,ETC				610		1014	W 218259	997	TUBES,TUYAUX EN FONTE,FER
6782	IRON,STL SEAMLESS TUBES				44		156	W 155671	949	TUBES,TUYAUX SANS SOUDURE
6783	IRON,STL TUBES,PIPES NES			N 145861	374	N 180609	448			AUT TUBES,TUYAUX FER,ACIER
69	METAL MANUFACTURES NES				2770		3747		2441	ART MANUFACT EN METAL NDA
691	STRUCTURES AND PARTS NES			N 39327	159	N 73631	936		549	CONSTRUCT FER,ACIER,ALU
6911	STRUCTURES,PARTS IRN,STL			N 33074	144	N 57490	678	W 1078	535	CONSTRUCT FER,ACIER,FONTE
692	METAL TANKS,BOXES,ETC			N 1474779	494	N 736958	196		325	RECIPIENTS METALLIQUES

4. General Imports C.I.F. by Commodities according to the S.I.T.C. (Rev. 2) in thousand U.S. Dollars
Importations Générales C.A.F. par Produits d'après la C.T.C.I. (Rév. 2) en milliers de Dollars E.U.

SITC CTCI	COMMODITY	1990		1991		1992		1993		PRODUIT
		WEIGHT POIDS	VALUE VALEUR	WEIGHT POIDS	VALUE VALEUR	WEIGHT POIDS	VALUE VALEUR	WEIGHT POIDS	VALUE VALEUR	
6924	MTL TRANSPORT BOXES ETC			N 1474476	410	N 736678	183		281	FUTS,TAMBOURS,BIDONS
69241	STL TRANSPORT BOXES ETC			N 1452664	308	N 730016	178	W 9	22	FUTS,TAMBOURS,BIDONS FER
693	WIRE PRODUCTS NON ELECTR				392		398	W 644	404	OUVRAGES FILS METALLIQUES
6932	IRON,STEEL FENCING WIRE			W 146	99	W 284	162	W 561	326	RONCES DE FER OU ACIER
694	STL,COPPR NAILS,NUTS,ETC			W 603	272	W 249	192	W 378	277	CLOUS,VIS,ECROUS
697	BASE MTL HOUSEHOLD EQUIP				489		751	W 376	357	ART MENAGE MET COMMUNS
6978	BASE MTL HOUSE EQUIP NES			N 112630	174	N 130263	459			ART MENAGE MET COMMUNS
69781	DOMSTC FOOD MACH NONELEC			N 112630	174	N 130263	459			MOULINS A CAFE ETC
699	BASE METAL MFRS NES				522		1045	W 385	314	ART MANUFACTURES MET NDA
6997	IRON,STEEL ARTICLES NES			N 121661	231	N 719380	608	W 5	1	OUV FONTE,FER,ACIER NDA
69979	IRN,STL MANUFACTURES NES			N 121661	231	N 719380	608	W 5	1	AUT OUVRAGES EN FER NDA
7	MACHINES,TRANSPORT EQUIP				33648		59151		30602	MACHINES MATERIEL TRANSPORT
71	POWER GENERATING EQUIPMT				195		177		2391	MACHINES GENERATRICES
713	INTRNL COMBUS PSTN ENGIN						5		1295	MOTEURS EXPL COMB INT, PIECE
7131	AIRCRAFT PSTN ENGINS,PTS								1118	MOTEURS EXPL P.AVIATION, PIE
71311	AIRCRAFT PISTON ENGINES								1118	MOTEURS EXPL P.AVIATION
716	ROTATING ELECTRIC PLANT				175		170		1021	APP ELECTR ROTATIFS,PIECES
7162	AC MTRS,GENRTRS,GEN SETS				162		162		1013	MOTEURS ELECTRIQUES
71622	AC GENERATORS				52		74	W 47	917	GENER COURANT ALTERNATIF
72	MACHS FOR SPCL INDUSTRYS				9129		5364		1387	MAC SPECIALES POUR INDUST
721	AGRIC MACHY,EXC TRACTORS				7217		3079		549	MACHINES AGRICOLES
7219	AGRICULTURE MACHINES NES				7189		2987		486	ENGINS AGRICOLES NDA
72191	WINE–MAKING ETC MACHNERY				7158		2979	W 3	9	APPAREILS DE VINIFICATION
72199	PTS NES OF MCHY OF 72197						1		457	PIECES DES APP 721.97
723	CIVIL ENGNEERG EQUIP ETC				705		777		386	APPAREILS DE GENIE CIVIL
7234	CONST,MINING MACHNRY NES				49		111		290	MACH POUR LA CONST, MINES
7239	CONSTR ETC MACHY PTS NES				576		474	W 18	79	PIECES 723.41–723.46
728	OTH MACHY FOR SPCL INDUS				1019		1036		250	AUT MACH IND PARTICULIERES
7281	MACH–TOOLS FR SPCL INDUS				493		136		85	MACH–OUTILS SPEC IND PART
7284	MACHY FOR SPCL INDUS NES				271		774	W 24	46	MACH SPEC IND PARTICUL.
72848	OTH MCHY WITH INDIV FNCT				27		429	W 18	36	AUTRES MACHINES NDA
74	GENRL INDUSTRL MACHY NES				2500		8022		9776	MACH APP INDUSTRIE
741	HEATING,COOLING EQUIPMNT				689		3680		7923	MACH CHAUFFAGE,PIECES
7412	BURNERS,MECH STOKERS,ETC								5946	BRULEURS POUR FOYERS
7413	INDUS FURNACES ETC,PARTS				30		3588		82	FOURS IND,LABOR,PIECES
74131	INDUS FURNACES ETC ELCTR				30		3588		17	FOURS ELECTRIQUES
7414	NONDOM REFRIG EQUIPT,PTS				595		52		14	MAT PRODUCTION DU FROID
74149	PTS NES OF REFRIG EQUIPT				517		3			PIECES POUR MACH FROID
7416	HEATING,COOLING EQU NES				48		34	W 1095	1867	APP CHANGEMENT TEMP
744	MECHANICAL HANDLING EQU				364		914		1333	EQUIP MANUTENTION PIECES
7441	FORK LIFT TRCKS,ETC,PTS			N 1	26		123		275	CHARIOTS POUR USINES ETC
74411	FORK LIFT TRUCKS ETC			N 1	26	N 1	12	N 109	273	CHARIOTS POUR LES GARES
7442	LIFTING,LOADING MACH NES				73		779		710	APP LEVAGE,MANUTENTION
74422	SHIP DERRICKS,CRANES ETC							N 3	408	GRUES,PONTS ROULANTS
74428	OTH HANDLING ETC MCH NES				11		770	W 70	282	AUT APP LEVAGE ETC
7449	PTS NES OF MACHY OF 7442				265	N 106	13		349	PIECES DU 744.2
745	NONELEC MACHY,TOOLS NES				153		1357		131	AUT MACH NON ELEC,PIECES
7452	OTH NONELEC MCHS,PTS NES				153		1324	W 71	97	AUT MACH NON ELEC,PIECES
74522	PACKAGNG,BOTTLNG,ETC MCH				17		464	W 5	2	MACH NETT BOUTEILLES,ETC
74527	SPRAYING MACHINERY				41		816	W 55	77	APP PROJETER ETC LIQUID
749	NONELEC MACH PTS,ACC NES				1076		1835		206	PIECES MACH NON ELEC NDA
7492	COCKS,VALVES ETC NES				1042		40		33	ART ROB,SIM POUR TUYAUX
7493	SHAFT,CRANK,PULLEY ETC				33		1766	W 126	150	ARBRES TRANS,VILEBREQUINS
75	OFFICE MACHNES,ADP EQUIP				451		495		394	MACH BUREAU TRAIT AUTOM
751	OFFICE MACHINES				355		203		119	MACH,APPAREILS DE BUREAU
76	TELECOMM,SOUND EQUIPMENT				625		6320		7278	EQUIPMENT DE TELECOM
764	TELECOM EQPT,PTS,ACC NES				503		6138		7174	EQUIP TELECOM,PIECES
7648	TELECOMM EQUIPMENT NES				185		5932	W 12	5	APP TELECOM NDA
76481	RADIOTELEPHONE ETC RCVRS				185		5932	W 12	5	RECEP RADIOTELEPHONIE
7649	PTS NES OF EQUIPMT OF 76				9		56		7164	PIECES DE LA DIV 76
76491	PTS NES OF APPAR OF 7641				3		27		7117	PIECES POUR 764.1
77	ELECTRIC MACHNRY NES ETC				6529		2964		2457	MACH APP ELECT NDA
771	ELECTRIC POWER MACHY NES				3801		243		155	MACH PROD,TRANS ELECTR
7711	TRANSFORMERS,ELECTRICAL				3570		41	W 25	28	TRANSFO ELECTRIQUES
77111	LIQUID DIELEC TRANSFRMRS				3032					TRANSFO DIELEC LIQUIDE
77118	OTHER ELEC TRANSFORMERS				538		41	W 25	28	AUTRES TRANSFO ELECTRIQ
772	SWITCHGEAR ETC,PARTS NES				883		684		974	APP COUPURE,SECT ETC
7721	SWITCHGEAR ETC				880		683	W 612	931	APP COUPURE,SECTIONMNT
773	ELECTR DISTRIBUTNG EQUIP				463		378	W 171	398	EQUIPMT DISTRIBUTION ELECT
7731	INSULATED WIRE,CABLE ETC			L 564	427	L 449	263	W 164	332	FILS,CABLES ISOLES ELECT
774	ELECTRO–MEDCL,XRAY EQUIP				320		120		263	APPAREILS MEDICAUX
7742	X–RAY APPARATUS ETC				307		115		164	APPAREILS A RAYONS X
775	HOUSEHOLD TYPE EQUIP NES				362		666		260	MACH,APP USAGE DOMESTQUE
778	ELECTRICAL MACHINERY NES				663		824		400	AUTRES MACH ELECT NDA
7781	BATTERIES,ACCUMULATORS				479		459	W 172	323	PILES ET ACCUMULATEURS
77811	PRIMARY BATTERIES,CELLS				469		427	W 171	320	PILES ELECTRIQUES,PIECES
78	ROAD VEHICLES				12737		9990		6754	VEHICULES ROUTIERS
781	PASS MOTOR VEH EXC BUSES			N 428	4483	N 388	3169	N 185	2055	AUTO TRANSPORT PERSONNES
782	LORRIES,SPCL MTR VEH NES				1499		1358			VEHICULES SPECIAUX,MARCH
7821	LORRIES,TRUCKS			N 67	933	N 212	1037			VEHICULES TRANSP MARCHAND
7822	SPECIAL MOTOR VEHCLS NES				566		321			VEHICULES USAGES SPECIAUX
783	ROAD MOTOR VEHICLES NES				157		790	N 7	87	VEHICULES ROUTIERS NDA
7831	BUSES			N 46	101	N 40	600	N 7	87	VOITURES TRANSPORT COMMUN
784	MOTOR VEH PRTS,ACCES NES				5013		3671		4068	PIECES 722,781,782,783
7841	MOTOR VEHICLE CHASSIS				3820		2450	N 39	441	CHASSIS 722,781,782,783
7842	MOTOR VEHICLE BODIES							N 50599	1505	CARROS 722,781,782,783
7849	OTHER MOTOR VEHCL PARTS				1193		1221		2122	PIECES 722,781,782,783
785	CYCLES,ETC MOTRZD OR NOT				1556		934		492	MOTOCYCLES SCOOTERS
7851	MOTORCYCLES ETC				1554		834	N 656	468	MOTO VELO MOTEUR AUXIL
79	OTHR TRANSPORT EQUIPMENT				1294		25667		43	AUTRE MATERIEL TRANSPORT
792	AIRCRAFT ETC				1294		3469		43	APP NAVIGATION AERIENNE
7922	AIRCRFT NES 2000KG OR LS				363					AERODYNES MOINS 2000 KG
7924	AIRCRFT NES OVER 15000KG				849		3461			AERODYNES PLUS 15000 KG
793	SHIPS AND BOATS ETC					N 1	22198			NAVIRES BATEAUX,ETC
7931	WARSHIPS					N 1	22198			NAVIRES DE GUERRE
8	MISC MANUFACTURED GOODS				3720		4599		6009	ART MANUFACTURES DIVERS
821	*FURNITURE,PARTS THEREOF				379		767	W 296	437	MEUBLES ET PIECES
8219	FURNITURE AND PARTS NES				284		480	W 223	307	AUTRES MEUBLES ET PIECES
84	CLOTHING AND ACCESSORIES				657		564		911	VETEMENTS
842	MENS OUTERWEAR NOT KNIT			N 77351	217	N 128500	243		406	VET DESSUS POUR HOMMES
8429	— OTHER OUTER GARMENTS								392	AUT VET DES HOM MAT TEX

4. General Imports C.I.F. by Commodities according to the S.I.T.C. (Rev. 2) in thousand U.S. Dollars
Importations Générales C.A.F. par Produits d'après la C.T.C.I. (Rév. 2) en milliers de Dollars E.U.

SITC CTCI	COMMODITY	1990 WEIGHT POIDS	1990 VALUE VALEUR	1991 WEIGHT POIDS	1991 VALUE VALEUR	1992 WEIGHT POIDS	1992 VALUE VALEUR	1993 WEIGHT POIDS	1993 VALUE VALEUR	PRODUIT
847	TEXTILE CLTHNG ACCES NES								359	ACCES VET MAT TEXT NDA
8471	— NOT KNITTED							N 298016	345	ACCES VET MAT TEX NON BON
84712	SHAWLS,VEILS ETC,NOT KNT							N 298016	345	ECHARPES ETC MAT TEXT
851	*FOOTWEAR				552		661		995	CHAUSSURES
85101	FOOTWEAR RUBBER,PLASTIC			P 183726	346	P 187840	340		49	CHAUS SEMELLES CAOUTCH
85102	FOOTWEAR LEATHER				174		306	P 524374	946	CHAUS SEMELLES EN CUIR
87	PRECISION INSTRUMNTS NES				795		733		406	INSTRUM,APPAR SCIENT NDA
874	MEASURNG,CONTROLNG INSTR				578		278		349	INSTRUMENTS DE MESURE
8741	SURVEYING INSTRUMENTS				512		5	W 10	48	INST GEODESIE,TOPO ETC
87412	SURVEY INSTR ETC NONELEC				457		5	W 10	48	INSTR GEODESIE,TOPO ETC
89	MISC MANUFCTRD GOODS NES				930		1351		2924	ART MANUFACTURES DIVERS
892	PRINTED MATTER				369		617		1116	IMPRIMES
8921	PRINTED BOOKS,GLOBES,ETC				230		335	W 329	476	LIVRES,BROCHURES,CARTES
89211	PRINTED BOOKS,PAMPHLETS				230		334	W 329	474	LIVRES,BROCHURES
8928	PRINTED MATTER NES				135		272		623	IMPRIMES NDA
89283	UNISSUED BANKNOTES ETC								398	TIMBRES–POSTE FISCAUX
893	ARTICLES OF PLASTIC NES				191		245	W 2307	1367	OUVRAGES EN MAT DIVIS 58
8931	PLSTC PACKG CONTNRS,LIDS			N 70921	46	N 27502	36	W 1144	440	ART TRANSP EMBALLAGE ETC
8939	MISC PLASTIC ARTICLES				123		170	W 1023	789	ART DIVERS EN MAT DIV 58
89399	OTHR PLASTC ARTICLES NES				2			W 1013	783	AUT OUV MAT DIV 58
9	GOODS NOT CLASSD BY KIND				576		6621		822	ART TRANSACT NON CLASSES
931	*SPECIAL TRANSACTIONS				564		6580		816	TRANS.SPECIALES

5. General Exports F.O.B. by Commodities according to the S.I.T.C. (Rev. 2) in thousand U.S. Dollars
Exportations Générales F.O.B. par Produits d'après la C.T.C.I. (Rév. 2) en milliers de Dollars E.U.

SITC CTCI	COMMODITY	1990 WEIGHT POIDS	1990 VALUE VALEUR	1991 WEIGHT POIDS	1991 VALUE VALEUR	1992 WEIGHT POIDS	1992 VALUE VALEUR	1993 WEIGHT POIDS	1993 VALUE VALEUR	PRODUIT
	ALL COMMODITIES				65029		67068		65820	TOUS PRODUITS
0	FOOD AND LIVE ANIMALS				12244		16543		12973	ALIMENTS,ANIMAUX VIVANTS
04	CEREALS AND PREPARATIONS				1433		1700		1234	CEREALES ET PRODUITS
046	WHEAT ETC MEAL OR FLOUR			W 8947	1425	W 7909	1295	W 7257	993	SEMOULE FARINE,FROMENT
04601	FLOUR OF WHEAT OR MESLIN			W 8818	1403	W 7753	1276	W 7257	993	FARINE DE FROMENT
048	CEREAL ETC PREPARATIONS						396	W 487	147	PREPTNS A BASE CEREALES
0484	BAKERY PRODUCTS						396	W 487	147	PRODUITS DE BOULANGERIE
04842	PASTRY, CAKES ETC						396	W 475	135	PATISSERIE ETC.
05	VEGETABLES AND FRUIT				7182		11984		10230	LEGUMES ET FRUITS
054	VEG ETC FRSH,SMPLY PRSVD			W 6244	849	W 8984	995	W 11292	1312	LEGUMES FRAIS,CONG,SECS
0541	POTATOES FRSH EXCL SWEET			W 5808	736	W 8271	840	W 10829	1210	POMMES DE TERRE
057	FRUIT,NUTS,FRESH,DRIED				3944		9201	W 23571	6412	FRUITS FRAIS OU SECS
0571	ORANGES, MANDARINS ETC				2291		7528	W 1564	272	ORANGES,MAND,CLEMENTINES
05711	ORANGES,FRESH OR DRIED				2291		7528	W 1564	272	ORANGES FRAICHES,SECHEES
0574	APPLES FRESH			W 3203	1624	W 4012	1657	W 2473	1089	POMMES FRAICHES
0579	FRUIT FRESH OR DRIED NES			W 5	1	W 3	1	W 19367	4939	FRUITS FRAIS,SECS NDA
05797	OTH TROP FRUIT,FRESH,DRY							W 19310	4925	AVOCATS,MANGUES,GOYAVES
058	FRUIT PRESERVED,PREPARED				2389		1785	W 4603	2330	CONSERVES DE FRUITS
0583	FRUIT JAMS,JELLIES ETC				315		298	W 505	372	PATES DE FRUITS CONFITURES
0585	FRUIT OR VEGETABLE JUICE				1941		1379	W 4098	1958	JUS DE FRUITS
05858	MIXTURES OF DIFF JUICES				1807		1347	W 3517	1759	MELANGES JUS FRUITS,LEGUMES
07	COFFEE,TEA,COCOA,SPICES				3267		2653		1501	CAFE,THE,CACAO,EPICES
075	SPICES			W 2373	3267	W 1739	2653	W 1602	1501	EPICES
0752	SPICES,EX PEPPER,PIMENTO			W 2328	3221	W 1697	2621	W 1548	1483	AUTRES EPICES
07524	NUTMEG,MACE,CARDAMOMS			W 590	1532	W 858	2023	W 1099	1388	NOIX MUSCADES
07525	SEEDS OF ANISE,CUMIN,ETC			W 511	1309	W 173	503			GRAINES ANIS,FENOUIL
07526	GINGER (EXCPT SWEETENED)			W 1227	379	W 666	95	W 448	94	GINGEMBRE
081	*FEEDING STUFF FOR ANIML			W 2320	198	W 1423	114			NOURRITURE POUR ANIMAUX
1	BEVERAGES AND TOBACCO				588		1027		2142	BOISSONS ET TABACS
11	BEVERAGES				588		1027		2142	BOISSONS
111	NON-ALCOHL BEVERAGES NES				409		326	W 668	431	BOISSONS NON ALCOOLIQUES
11102	FLAVORED WATERS NON-ALCO				409		326	W 668	431	LIMONADES,EAUX GAZEUSES
112	ALCOHOLIC BEVERAGES				179		701	W 2824	1711	BOISSONS ALCOOLIQUES
1124	DISTILLED ALCOHOLIC BEVS				158		689	W 2812	1696	ALCOOLS,EAUX-DE-VIE
11249	OTH ALCOHOLC BEVS,CMPNDS			W 210	147	W 1130	674	W 2778	1650	BOISSONS ALCOOLIQUES NDA
2	CRUDE MATERLS,EXCL FUELS				6654		7526		5977	MAT BRUTES NON COMESTIBLES
24	CORK AND WOOD				4353		5162		4595	LIEGE ET BOIS
245	FUEL WOOD NES, CHARCOAL				136		242	W 8690	1171	BOIS DE CHAUFFAGE
24501	FUEL WOOD IN LOGS,ETC				39		208	W 7760	1170	RONDINS,BUCHES ETC.
247	OTH WOOD ROUGH,SQUARED				3989		4811	MW 11331	2796	BOIS BRUTS EQUARRIS
2471	SAW-,VENEER-LOGS CONIFER				2699		1871	MW 11331	2796	CONIFERES POUR SCIAGE,PLACAG
24711	— IN THE ROUGH				660		762	MW 11331	2796	ECORCES OU DEGROSSIS
24712	— RGHLY OR HALF SQUARED			V 12951	2040	V 9901	1109			BOIS SIMPLEMENT EQUARRIS
2472	SAW-,VENEER-LOGS NON-CON			V 8835	1267	V 26672	2785			NON CONIFERES SCIAGE,PLAC
24721	— IN THE ROUGH			V 4070	620	V 17647	1847			BRUTS ECORCES DEGROSSIS
24722	— RGHLY OR HALF SQUARED			V 4765	648	V 9024	938			BOIS SIMPLEMENT EQUARRIS
248	WOOD SHAPED,SLEEPERS				210		103	W 2759016	627	BOIS SIMPLEMENT TRAVAILLES
2483	LUMBER SHAPED NON-CONIFR				161		36	W 2277312	519	NON CONIFERES SCIES,RABOTES
24831	LUMBER SAWN ETC NON-CON						4	W 2276903	373	SCIES LONGITUDINALEMENT
27	CRUDE FERTLZR,MINRLS NES				2153		2111		1132	ENGRAIS MINERAUX BRUTS
273	STONE,SAND AND GRAVEL				995		1073		546	PIERRES,SABLES,GRAVIERS
2732	CALCAREOUS STONE				808		714	W 17877	496	GYPSE,PLATRES,CASTINES
27323	GYPSUM AND ANHYDRITE				695		598	W 17209	475	GYPSE ANHYDRITE
278	OTHER CRUDE MINERALS			V 1788603	1158		1038	W 190502	586	AUTRES MINERAUX BRUTS
2782	REFRACTORY MINERALS NES			V 1788603	1158	V 1418315	1037	W 190300	580	ARGILE MINERAUX REFRACTAIRES
27823	DOLOMITE			V 1788603	1158	V 1418315	1037	W 190300	580	DOLOMIE BRUTE
3	MINERAL FUELS ETC				18262		14795		18476	COMBUSTIBLES MINERAUX LUB
32	COAL,COKE AND BRIQUETTES				794		1089		708	HOUILLES,COKES,BRIQUETTES
322	COAL,LIGNITE AND PEAT			W 43008	794	W 58825	1089	W 55361	707	HOUILLES,LIGNITES,TOURBE
3222	OTH COAL,NOT AGGLOMERATD			W 43008	794	W 58825	1089	W 55361	707	AUTRES HOUILLES
351	*ELECTRIC CURRENT				17468		13703	H 1	17768	ENERGIE ELECTRIQUE
5	CHEMCLS,RELATED PROD NES				13319		14448		12119	PRODUITS CHIMIQUES
52	INORGANIC CHEMICALS				12726		13611		11789	PROD CHIM INORGANIQUES
523	OTHR INORG CHEMICALS ETC			W 25638	12723	W 26816	13606	W 25390	11777	AUT PRODUITS CHIMIQUES INORG
5239	INORG CHEM PRODUCTS NES			W 25638	12723	W 26816	13606	W 25390	11777	PROD CHIM INORGANIQ NDA
52393	CALCIUM CARBIDE			W 25638	12723	W 26816	13606	W 25390	11777	CARBURES DE CALCIUM
59	CHEMICAL MATERIALS NES				490		641		328	MAT PROD CHIMIQUES NDA
598	MISCEL CHEM PRODUCTS NES				490		641	W 304	328	PROD DIV INDUST CHIM NDA
5981	CHEMCLS FROM WOOD,RESIN				195		310	W 304	328	PROD CHIM BASE BOIS RESIN
59814	ROSIN,RESIN ACIDS,ETC			W 118	181	W 247	293	W 210	272	COLOPHANES RESINIQUES
5989	CHEM PRODUCTS,PREPS NES			W 342	295		331			PROD PREP CHIMIQUES NDA
59892	ACTIVTED NAT MINRL PROD			W 342	295	W 430	330			CHARBONS ACTIVES
6	BASIC MANUFACTURES				13827		12373		13641	ART MANUFACTURES
63	WOOD,CORK MANUFACTRS NES				7235		6976		6352	OUVRAGES LIEGE ET BOIS
634	VENEERS,PLYWOOD,ETC				7235		6965		6310	PLACAGES,CONTRE-PLAQUES
6342	PLYWOOD OF WOOD SHEETS			A 544	3150	A 1043	5448	A 111	439	BOIS CONTRE-PLAQUES
6343	IMPROVED,RECONSTIT WOOD							W 8003	5523	BOIS AMELIORES,RECONST
63432	RECONSTITUTED WOOD							W 7898	5485	BOIS RECONSTITUES
6344	WOOD-BASED PANELS NES				3897		1411			PANNEAUX SUPPORT BOIS NDA
63441	BLOCKBOARD,LAMINBRD, ETC				3897		1411			BOIS CONTRE-PLAQUES
6349	WOOD SIMPLY SHAPED NES				149		90	W 2770	342	BOIS SIMPL TRAVAILLES NDA
63491	HOOPWOOD,SPLIT POLES ETC			N 167475	77	N 67625	36	W 2770	342	BOIS ETC
66	NONMETAL MINERAL MFS NES				6553		5375		7267	ART MIN NON METALLIQUES
661	LIME,CEMENT,BLDG PRODS				6545		5371	W 108047	7215	CHAUX,CIMENTS MAT CONSTR
6612	CEMENT				6370		5245	W 106671	7172	CIMENTS HYDRAULIQUES
8	MISC MANUFACTURED GOODS				107		330		482	ART MANUFACTURES DIVERS
89	MISC MANUFCTRD GOODS NES				106		321		481	ART MANUFACTURES DIVERS
892	PRINTED MATTER				106		317		258	IMPRIMES
8928	PRINTED MATTER NES				106		317		258	IMPRIMES NDA
89283	UNISSUED BANKNOTES ETC								258	TIMBRES-POSTE FISCAUX
89289	OTHER PRINTED MATTER				106		317			GRAVURES,PHOTO AUT IMPR
893	ARTICLES OF PLASTIC NES							W 224	202	OUVRAGES EN MAT DIVIS 58
8939	MISC PLASTIC ARTICLES							W 222	201	ART DIVERS EN MAT DIV 58
89399	OTHR PLASTC ARTICLES NES							W 222	201	AUT OUV MAT DIV 58

1. HISTORICAL SERIES, 1961–1996 SPECIAL TRADE, IMPORTS C.I.F., EXPORTS F.O.B.
SERIES HISTORIQUES, 1961–1996 COMMERCE SPECIAL, IMPORTATIONS C.A.F., EXPORTATIONS F.O.B

YEAR ANNEE	VALUE IN MILLION U.S. DOLLARS VALEUR EN MILLION U.S. DOLLARS — MERCHANDISE – MARCHANDISE		GOLD – OR		CONVERSION FACTORS FACTEURS DE CONVERSION CENTS E.U. PAR		INDEX NUMBERS – INDICES — QUANTUM		UNIT VALUE VALEUR UNITAIRE	
	IMPORTS	EXPORTS	IMPORTS	EXPORTS	IMPORTS	EXPORTS	IMPORTS	EXPORTS	IMPORTS	EXPORTS
1961	77.70	73.30		2.83				77		74
1962	96.90	74.90		1.22				80		73
1963	103.30	81.00		5.36				85		74
1964	102.70	112.10		1.75				94		94
1965	133.80	128.90		2.94				96		106
1966	138.70	127.40		0.55				116		103
1967	151.70	149.90		0.04				133		99
1968	152.80	152.10		0.03				137		99
1969	165.00	172.30		1.50				144		188
1970	159.20	190.20		0.17				96		58
1971	169.60	181.10		0.02				119		45
1972	185.40	202.20						133		45
1973	229.40	260.50						144		57
1974	390.00	556.40						145		112
1975	557.90	444.70						133		99
1976	587.60	566.10						145		109
1977	665.90	634.30						134		131
1978	768.70	635.10						118		152
1979	894.70	857.20						119		169
1980	665.40	1037.20						113		176
1981	917.10	984.00						122		171
1982	554.10	898.50						112		162
1983	578.70	818.10						97		166
1984	488.50	781.50						100		164
1985	692.90	672.80						84		156
1986	674.00	637.80						94		131
1987	766.30	569.50						81		104
1988	590.50	600.20						82		99
1989	610.90	821.80						94		110
1990	687.20	926.10						100		64
1991	969.50	848.60						102		96
1992	1090.30	710.10						99		76
1993	1205.90	727.50						93		64
1994	1209.00	1032.40						95		66
1995	1423.80	1100.70						91		73
1996	1635.00	1137.10						90		72

2. IMPORTS BY BROAD ECONOMIC CATEGORY AND EXPORTS BY INDUSTRIAL ORIGIN. (PERCENTAGE OF TOTAL VALUE)
IMPORTATIONS PAR CATEGORIES ECONOMIQUES ET EXPORTATIONS PAR BRANCHE D'ACTIVITE.(EN POURCENTAGE DE LA VALEUR TOTALE)

IMPORTS – IMPORTATIONS

	1990	1991	1992	1993	1994	1995	1996
TOTAL IMPORTS–IMPORTATIONS TOTALES	100.	100.	100.	100.	100.	100.	100.
1 FOOD BEV–ALIMENTATION BOISSONS	10.9	10.3	10.7	8.9	9.6	9.0	10.8
11 PRIMARY–PRODUITS DE BASE	4.1	4.0	4.0	3.6	4.3	3.8	4.8
111 FOR INDUSTRY–POUR L'INDUSTRIE	3.5	3.5	3.5	3.1	3.8	3.4	4.4
112 FOR HOUSEHOLDS–POUR LES MENAGES	0.5	0.5	0.5	0.5	0.5	0.4	0.4
12 PROCESSED–PRODUITS ELABORES	6.8	6.4	6.7	5.4	5.3	5.2	6.0
121 FOR INDUSTRY–POUR L'INDUSTRIE	3.8	2.9	3.5	1.9	1.3	1.2	1.3
122 FOR HOUSEHOLDS–POUR LES MENAGES	3.0	3.5	3.2	3.4	4.0	4.0	4.7
2 IND SUPPLIES–APPROV INDUSTRIELS	29.8	30.5	27.5	27.8	29.7	29.8	28.8
21 PRIMARY–PRODUITS DE BASE	1.0	1.4	1.4	2.5	2.9	2.8	2.2
22 PROCESSED–PRODUITS ELABORES	28.8	29.1	26.1	25.4	26.8	27.0	26.7
3 FUELS–COMBUSTIBLES	0.5	0.7	2.9	4.6	4.9	4.2	3.4
31 PRIMARY–PRODUITS DE BASE	0.0	0.0	0.0	0.0	0.0	0.0	0.0
32 PROCESSED–PRODUITS ELABORES	0.5	0.7	2.9	4.6	4.9	4.2	3.4
321 MOTOR SPIRIT–ESSENCE	0.0	0.0	0.1	0.0	0.0	0.0	0.0
322 OTHER–AUTRES	0.5	0.7	2.8	4.6	4.9	4.2	3.4
4 MACHINERY–EQUIPEMENT	27.3	29.6	28.5	24.7	20.7	23.5	26.2
41 CAPITAL EQUIPMENT–MACHINES	25.0	27.3	26.3	22.7	18.8	21.7	24.4
42 PARTS–PIECES ACCESSOIRES	2.2	2.3	2.1	2.1	1.9	1.8	1.8
5 TRANSPORT–TRANSPORT	21.6	19.3	21.2	24.8	24.3	24.0	19.7
51 PASSENGER CARS–AUTOMOBILES	8.4	7.7	7.5	6.9	9.3	7.2	7.3
52 OTHER–AUTRES	9.3	8.2	10.1	14.0	11.2	13.3	9.6
521 INDUSTRIAL–INDUSTRIELS	9.1	7.9	9.8	13.6	10.7	12.9	9.2
522 NON INDUSTRIAL–NON INDUSTRIEL	0.3	0.3	0.4	0.4	0.5	0.4	0.4
53 PARTS–PIECES ACCESSOIRES	4.0	3.3	3.6	3.8	3.8	3.5	2.9
6 CONSUM GOODS–BIENS CONSOMMATION	9.8	9.4	8.9	8.9	10.4	9.4	11.0
61 DURABLE–DURABLES	2.2	1.9	1.7	1.5	1.8	1.8	2.3
62 SEMI DURABLE–SEMI DURABLES	3.9	3.7	4.1	3.8	4.2	3.8	3.6
63 NON DURABLE–NON DURABLES	3.6	3.8	3.1	3.6	4.3	3.9	5.2
7 GOODS NES–BIENS NDA	0.1	0.2	0.3	0.2	0.4	0.2	0.0

EXPORTS – EXPORTATIONS

	1990	1991	1992	1993	1994	1995	1996
TOTAL EXPORTS–EXPORTATIONS TOTALES	100.	100.	100.	100.	100.	100.	100.
1 AGRICULTURE	12.8	9.8	6.1	7.1	10.6	14.0	17.1
2 MINING QUARRY–INDUS EXTRACTIVES	53.3	53.7	52.5	39.4	28.2	36.6	37.1
3 MANUFACTURING–IND MANUFACTUR	33.9	36.5	41.4	53.5	61.2	49.4	45.8
31 FOOD BEV TOBACCO–ALIM BOISS TAB	9.0	9.5	9.4	11.3	14.0	11.0	17.5
32 TEXTILES–INDUSTRIES TEXTILES	3.4	2.8	3.3	4.2	3.2	2.9	4.3
33 WOOD & PRODUCTS–BOIS & PRODUITS	5.4	5.4	6.6	7.2	8.6	7.2	8.1
34 PAPER & PRODUCTS–PAPIER & PRODT	0.0	0.0	0.2	0.4	0.3	0.3	0.5
35 CHEMICALS–INDUSTRIES CHIMIQUES	0.7	0.6	0.6	1.7	1.5	2.4	1.6
36 NON METAL MIN–MIN NON METAL	0.0	0.0	0.1	0.1	0.1	0.2	0.3
37 BASIC METAL–IND METAL BASE	15.2	12.6	13.2	15.7	13.3	12.2	11.4
38 METAL MANUF–MANUF METAL	0.1	0.1	3.7	2.9	3.4	4.2	0.6
39 OTH MANUF IND–AUTRES MANUF	0.1	5.6	4.3	10.1	16.6	9.0	1.4

3. TRADE BY PRINCIPAL COUNTRIES OF PROVENANCE AND LAST CONSIGNMENT (VALUE IN THOUSAND U.S. DOLLARS)
ECHANGES SELON LES PRINCIPAUX PAYS DE PROVENANCE ET DE DERNIERE CONSIGNATION (VALEUR EN MILLIERS DE DOLLARS EU)

COUNTRIES–PAYS	SPECIAL IMPORTS C.I.F. IMPORTATIONS SPECIALES C.A.F					COUNTRIES–PAYS	SPECIAL EXPORTS F.O.B. EXPORTATIONS SPECIALES F.O.B.				
	1992	1993	1994	1995	1996		1992	1993	1994	1995	1996
World	1128608	1176941	1196345	1396260	1643051	Monde	765315	808939	1124232	1181213	1086945
Africa	1475	1979	1305	2372	1498	Afrique	67	89	653	194	190
Americas	700693	733596	773972	877080	1108627	Amériques	458823	523224	802225	776721	769008
Northern America	285269	271931	245676	335076	498465	Amérique du Nord	162826	220854	364192	341520	246177
LAIA	402401	448769	514946	532874	601433	ALAI	295724	301776	436484	422132	510063
CACM	638	595	1981	1749	745	MCAC	210	149	241	67	198
Caribbean	541	429	445	1001	2979	Caraïbes	9	280	735	8200	1813
Rest of America	11844	11872	10923	6381	5004	Autre Amérique	55	165	573	4801	10757
As.ex F.USSR	164523	157694	228775	221139	256798	Asie l'URSS exclus	12502	9164	11709	10850	7945
Eur.x F.USSR	256444	277590	185107	286825	269921	Europe l'URSS exclus	290530	274914	305832	388217	300234
EU	241142	256043	173160	273493	253974	UE	285287	271818	291274	306265	247404
EFTA	8400	8932	10082	10140	11789	AELE	5114	2907	14536	81038	52001
East Europe	6820	10888	1687	2416	3998	Europe de l'Est	129	177	21	899	727
Other Europe	15	23	54	24	70	Autre de l'Europe				14	
Former USSR						Ancienne URSS					
Oceania	1490	1941	3476	4478	4675	Océanie	143	147	444	636	965
USA/Etats–Unis d'Amer	275475	265224	235075	312647	455726	USA/Etats–Unis d'Amer	153712	214820	360919	331680	237423
Brazil/Brésil	164005	149914	178613	174202	181635	United Kingdom	127588	154188	150641	153297	155605
Japan/Japon	135419	128865	181826	171699	199118	Argentina/Argentine	153550	126793	160110	142657	143425
Argentina/Argentine	103210	114731	117483	117416	136637	Peru/Pérou	60822	79206	122916	144377	138745
Chile/Chili	78041	88545	93962	104786	110641	Colombia/Colombie	25155	36910	63940	64368	115995
Germany/Allemagne	85630	66453	59259	69937	60870	Belgium–Luxembourg	82468	48750	26592	40392	49349
Peru/Pérou	27127	54104	65060	73042	89141	Germany/Allemagne	31685	32040	54037	57076	24404
Sweden/Suède	25973	26589	32380	38752	48197	Switz.Liecht	5082	2831	14497	81003	51951
Italy/Italie	37177	23915	17192	36918	55622	France,Monac	32247	20627	47402	41233	2108
United Kingdom	27354	67240	13053	26253	12400	Brazil/Brésil	15343	22208	35369	23441	36316
Spain/Espagne	15868	36605	16869	19314	35004	Chile/Chili	18326	14857	19202	25834	43453
Colombia/Colombie	10527	15764	22729	22947	33779	Mexico/Mexique	6631	7747	13080	1398	11847
Canada	9794	6679	10591	22418	42722	Ecuador/Equateur	3806	6874	14562	7346	7755
Mexico/Mexique	10292	12820	16657	19457	25509	Netherlands/Pays–Bas	5774	7967	7363	4096	6178
Belgium–Luxembourg	7484	4632	6677	54727	9565	Canada	3345	2067	3273	5716	8754
France,Monac	24119	15860	9679	13453	11365	Venezuela	9578	1890	1522	5667	1329
Korea, Republic of	8981	8971	14453	18069	20350	Italy/Italie	1957	1084	3069	6785	6175
China/Chine	7514	4029	10044	14504	12446	Uruguay	1404	1536	4788	2047	8523
Venezuela	3496	6034	12621	10930	13172	Panama	49	165	573	4801	10757
Panama	11832	11872	10923	6379	5004	Spain/Espagne	2385	6643	1468	2531	2837
Switz.Liecht	7981	8768	9656	9386	9416	Malaysia/Malaisie	6738	2736	1105	2534	2169
Netherlands/Pays–Bas	6245	5016	4694	6076	8776	Bermuda/Bermudes	5769	3967		4125	
Denmark/Danemark	6008	4191	8179	1930	4402	Paraguay	1110	3754	997	4997	2676
Uruguay	3027	2653	3831	4657	4930	Japan/Japon	1628	2312	2068	3653	3791
Russian Federation	2149	4045	3299	3950	1434	Korea, Republic of	328	2095	4785	733	549
Ecuador/Equateur	1349	1551	2512	4114	4889	Bahamas				7690	
Czech Republic		9977	1219	1483	1339	Saudi Arabia	1837	484	768	1385	531
New Zealand	509	1547	2570	2672	4070	Dominican Republic	5	14	433	268	1575
Ireland/Irlande	1270	2196	2175	2419	3273	Australia/Australie	100	146	438	609	704
Austria/Autriche	2033	2545	1923	1441	2633	Syrian Arab Republic	141	178	269	966	38
Israel/Israël	187	1534	1404	1422	3821	Portugal	623	169	86	327	155
India/Inde	1428	926	1904	1638	2253	India/Inde	695	211	129	212	6
Paraguay	1328	2653	1478	1323	1101	Korea Dem People's Rp		256	649	28	20
Hong Kong	1806	1480	993	1058	1780	Hong Kong	17	236	516	100	2
Finland/Finlande	1742	743	986	1946	1561	Russian Federation	123	105	21	83	521
So. Africa Customs Un	1109	704	964	1995	1312	Turkey/Turquie			404	370	36
Australia/Australie	873	267	881	1730	583	Denmark/Danemark	26	206	292	137	83
Albania/Albanie	3707	399	48	17	34	China/Chine	16	1	271	169	273
Norway,SVD,JM	368	163	426	751	2373	Austria/Autriche	263	114	79	124	136
Indonesia/Indonésie	104	3	245	629	3018	Thailand/Thaïlande	246	172	207	12	16
Malaysia/Malaisie	213	963	685	270	1500	Poland/Pologne	85	20		410	113
Korea Dem People's Rp	386	1596	603	303	465	Czech Republic		27	18	401	101
Poland/Pologne	286	142	133	408	2334	Greece/Grèce		2	122	111	264
Cuba	431	194	214	369	1893	Romania/Roumanie	15	28			435
El Salvador	3	72	1473	1021	77	Sweden/Suède	194	19	90	107	39
Bosnia and Herzegovina		1658	107	711	18	Israel/Israël	2	147	5	113	176
Thailand/Thaïlande	53	22	92	445	1200	New Zealand	33		6	26	261
Costa Rica	181	228	335	543	455	Indonesia/Indonésie	297				25
Czechoslovakia	1741					Cyprus/Chypre	95	113	23	54	23
Singapore/Singapour	90	286	314	377	423	Seychelles			293		

(VALUE AS PERCENTAGE OF WORLD TOTAL)(VALEURS EN POURCENTAGE DU TOTAL MONDIAL)

	1987	1988	1989	1990	1991	1992	1993	1994	1995	1996		1987	1988	1989	1990	1991	1992	1993	1994	1995	1996
Africa	0.1	0.1	0.2	0.1	0.4	0.1	0.2	0.1	0.2	0.1	Afrique	0.1	0.0	0.0	0.0	0.0	0.0	0.0	0.1	0.0	0.0
Americas	68.1	68.8	69.6	70.2	64.7	62.1	62.3	64.7	62.8	67.5	Amériques	74.7	68.1	62.8	65.6	70.8	60.0	64.7	71.4	65.8	70.7
Northern America	22.1	22.2	25.3	23.1	26.6	25.3	23.1	20.5	24.0	30.3	Amérique du Nord	16.9	20.7	19.3	20.5	22.3	21.3	27.3	32.4	28.9	22.6
LAIA	43.6	45.3	43.2	46.0	37.0	35.7	38.1	43.0	38.2	36.6	ALAI	57.5	47.1	42.8	44.8	48.4	38.6	37.3	38.8	35.7	46.9
CACM	0.0	0.0	0.1	0.0	0.0	0.1	0.1	0.2	0.1	0.0	MCAC	0.0	0.0	0.2	0.0	0.0	0.0	0.0	0.0	0.0	0.0
Caribbean	0.0	0.0	0.0	0.1	0.0	0.0	0.0	0.0	0.1	0.2	Caraïbes	0.0	0.2	0.5	0.3	0.0	0.0	0.0	0.1	0.7	0.2
Rest of America	2.3	1.3	0.9	1.0	1.0	1.0	1.0	0.9	0.5	0.3	Autre Amérique	0.3	0.1	0.1	0.0	0.0	0.0	0.0	0.1	0.4	1.0
As.ex F.USSR	13.3	15.0	12.3	11.8	14.4	14.6	13.4	19.1	15.8	15.6	Asie l'URSS exclus	1.3	1.2	1.4	0.9	1.4	1.6	1.1	1.0	0.9	0.7
Eur.x F.USSR	18.1	15.7	17.8	17.3	19.7	22.7	23.6	15.5	20.5	16.4	Europe l'URSS exclus	23.9	30.7	35.8	33.4	27.8	38.0	34.0	27.2	32.9	27.6
EU	16.5	14.4	16.5	16.3	18.4	21.4	21.8	14.5	19.6	15.5	UE	21.7	27.7	30.9	29.0	26.5	37.3	33.6	25.9	25.9	22.8
EFTA	0.8	0.7	0.8	0.5	0.9	0.7	0.8	0.8	0.7	0.7	AELE	1.2	1.3	2.2	2.2	1.3	0.7	0.4	1.3	6.9	4.8
East Europe	0.8	0.5	0.5	0.3	0.4	0.6	0.9	0.1	0.2	0.2	Europe de l'Est	1.0	1.6	2.6	2.2	0.0	0.0	0.0	0.0	0.1	0.1
Other Europe	0.0	0.0		0.0	0.0	0.0	0.0	0.0	0.0	0.0	Autre de l'Europe				0.0					0.0	
Former USSR	0.4	0.3	0.2	0.3	0.5						Ancienne URSS					0.0					
Oceania	0.0	0.0	0.0	0.0	0.1	0.1	0.2	0.3	0.3	0.3	Océanie	0.0	0.0	0.0	0.0	0.0	0.0	0.0	0.0	0.1	0.1
USA/Etats–Unis d'Amer	21.0	21.8	24.4	22.2	25.9	24.4	22.5	19.6	22.4	27.7	USA/Etats–Unis d'Amer	16.9	20.7	19.2	20.0	21.9	20.1	26.6	32.1	28.1	21.8
Brazil/Brésil	20.3	19.1	20.7	16.8	14.3	14.5	12.7	14.9	12.5	11.1	United Kingdom	10.7	12.1	13.5	12.3	11.6	16.7	19.1	13.4	13.0	14.3
Japan/Japon	10.0	11.9	10.0	9.9	12.3	12.0	10.9	15.2	12.3	12.1	Argentina/Argentine	45.6	38.1	27.9	25.6	29.2	20.1	15.7	14.2	12.1	13.2
Argentina/Argentine	14.0	15.2	11.0	10.5	11.2	9.1	9.7	9.8	8.4	8.3	Peru/Pérou	4.2	3.8	5.5	5.7	6.0	7.9	9.8	10.9	12.2	12.8
Chile/Chili	6.0	6.2	6.6	12.5	6.4	6.9	7.5	7.9	7.5	6.7	Colombia/Colombie	0.7	0.7	0.5	0.4	3.4	3.3	4.6	5.7	5.4	10.7
Germany/Allemagne	6.9	5.4	7.6	7.9	8.4	7.6	5.6	5.0	5.0	3.7	Belgium–Luxembourg	3.1	5.9	7.7	7.3	9.1	10.8	6.0	2.4	3.4	4.5
Peru/Pérou	1.5	2.3	2.7	3.2	2.1	2.4	4.6	5.4	5.2	5.4	Germany/Allemagne	5.9	5.6	6.2	4.3	3.1	4.1	4.0	4.8	4.8	2.2
Sweden/Suède	1.4	1.6	1.3	1.3	1.8	2.3	2.3	2.7	2.8	2.9	Switz.Liecht	1.2	1.3	2.2	2.2	1.3	0.7	0.3	1.3	6.9	4.8
Italy/Italie	1.0	1.7	1.5	1.7	2.4	3.3	2.0	1.4	2.6	3.4	France,Monac	0.9	1.3	1.3	2.2	2.0	4.2	2.5	4.2	3.5	0.2
United Kingdom	0.9	1.5	1.3	1.3	0.9	2.4	5.7	1.1	1.9	0.8	Brazil/Brésil	3.4	1.8	5.6	8.4	4.6	2.0	2.7	3.1	2.0	3.3

4. Special Imports C.I.F. by Commodities according to the S.I.T.C. (Rev. 2) in thousand U.S. Dollars
Importations Spéciales C.A.F. par Produits d'après la C.T.C.I. (Rév. 2) en milliers de Dollars E.U.

SITC CTCI	COMMODITY	1993 WEIGHT POIDS	1993 VALUE VALEUR	1994 WEIGHT POIDS	1994 VALUE VALEUR	1995 WEIGHT POIDS	1995 VALUE VALEUR	1996 WEIGHT POIDS	1996 VALUE VALEUR	PRODUIT
	ALL COMMODITIES		1176941		1196345		1396260		1643051	TOUS PRODUITS
0	FOOD AND LIVE ANIMALS		99030		112395		124577		156606	ALIMENTS,ANIMAUX VIVANTS
02	DAIRY PRODCTS,BIRDS'EGGS		13043		11676		13484		19469	PRODUITS LAITIERS,OEUFS
022	MILK AND CREAM	W 7652	12454	W 6981	10419	W 6993	11788	W 10557	18743	LAIT ET CREME
0224	MILK,CREAM PRESERVED ETC	W 7370	12302	W 6202	10051	W 6304	11409	W 9391	18092	LAIT,CREME CONS,CONC
02242	MILK DRY,1.5% FAT OR LES	W 3872	6616	W 812	1609	W 500	922	W 626	744	LAIT POUDRE INF 1.5%
02243	MILK DRY,OVER 1.5% FAT	W 1815	3872	W 3077	6264	W 4199	8736	W 6360	14339	LAIT POUDRE SUP 1.5%
04	CEREALS AND PREPARATIONS		58076		63858		70205		86341	CEREALES ET PRODUITS
041	WHEAT ETC UNMILLED	W 183149	32244	W 202443	42385	W 183358	42928	W 200263	60233	FROMENT,EPEAUTRE
0411	DURUM WHEAT UNMILLED	W 172785	30314	W 162411	32769	W 97585	26132	W 91480	29214	FROMENT DUR NON MOULU
0412	OTHER WHEAT ETC UNMILLED	W 10364	1931	W 40032	9616	W 85773	16796	W 108784	31019	AUTRE FROMENT NON MOULU
046	WHEAT ETC MEAL OR FLOUR	W 32402	10126	W 25853	8006	W 12988	7712	W 26635	10139	SEMOULE FARINE,FROMENT
04601	FLOUR OF WHEAT OR MESLIN	W 32402	10126	W 25502	7872	W 12345	7364	W 26633	10137	FARINE DE FROMENT
047	OTHER CEREAL MEALS,FLOUR	W 14060	6226	W 3166	1434	W 9210	3809	W 2340	1068	AUTRES SEMOULES,FARINES
04701	CEREAL FLOUR(NON–WHEAT)	W 13531	5943	W 3166	1433	W 9206	3807	W 2327	1032	FARINES DE CEREALES
048	CEREAL ETC PREPARATIONS	W 16329	8343	W 18369	10925	W 21244	13327	W 18997	13704	PREPTNS A BASE CEREALES
0482	MALT INCLUDING FLOUR	W 11434	3990	W 12619	4601	W 10077	3848	W 12430	5737	MALT MEME TORREFIE
0484	BAKERY PRODUCTS	W 2293	2372	W 3259	3507	W 3851	4640	W 3734	4210	PRODUITS DE BOULANGERIE
05	VEGETABLES AND FRUIT		4448		5482		7017		7401	LEGUMES ET FRUITS
06	SUGAR AND PREPS,HONEY		3022		5544		7566		9537	SUCRES ET PRODUITS
062	SUGAR CANDY NON–CHOCLATE	W 2086	2580	W 3508	4945	W 4053	6697	W 5282	8678	SUCRERIES
07	COFFEE,TEA,COCOA,SPICES		3527		4624		4594		6030	CAFE,THE,CACAO,EPICES
09	MISC EDIBLE PRODUCTS		11407		13003		16128		19094	PREP ALIMENTAIRES DIVERSES
098	EDIBLE PRODCTS,PREPS NES	W 4731	10656	W 5767	12268	W 5249	15177	W 6117	17261	PREP ALIMENTAIRES NDA
09809	MISC FOOD PREPRTIONS NES	W 2267	7396	W 2827	8518	W 2326	10942	W 3088	12878	PREP ALIMENTAIRES NDA
1	BEVERAGES AND TOBACCO		5529		5350		6420		8721	BOISSONS ET TABACS
12	TOBACCO AND MANUFACTURES		3786		3503		3938		5728	TABACS BRUTS FABRIQUES
121	TOBACCO UNMNFCTRD,REFUSE	W 1206	3585	W 1230	3228	W 1506	3475	W 1694	5649	TABACS BRUTS,DECHETS
1212	TOBACCO STRIPPED OR PART	W 1206	3583	W 1223	3163	W 1506	3475	W 1668	5600	TABACS PART ECOTES
2	CRUDE MATERLS,EXCL FUELS		40011		43499		51175		51988	MAT BRUTES NON COMESTIBLES
26	TEXTILE FIBRES AND WASTE		16674		15861		19682		19937	FIBRES TEXTILES
266	SYNTHETIC FIBRES TO SPIN	W 7090	12686	W 6709	10574	W 7498	14064	W 9107	14857	FIBRES SYNTHETIQUES
2666	CONTIN FILAMNT TOW SYNTH	W 3778	7529	W 3356	5615	W 3153	6576	W 3912	6826	CABLES POUR DISCONTINUS
26663	— OF ACRYLIC FIBRES	W 3747	7439	W 3275	5520	W 3130	6562	W 3912	6825	DE FIBRES ACRYLIQUES
27	CRUDE FERTLZR,MINRLS NES		3771		5295		4605		3687	ENGRAIS MINERAUX BRUTS
278	OTHER CRUDE MINERALS	W 9831	3352	W 16846	4802	W 6919	3749	W 12120	3111	AUTRES MINERAUX BRUTS
2789	MINERALS CRUDE NES	W 7884	2196	W 15465	4043	W 5046	2725	W 10192	2042	MINERAUX BRUTS NDA
27896	NATURAL ASPHALT,BITUMEN	W 7653	2043	W 15243	3858	W 4478	2347	W 9966	1849	BITUMES,ASPHALTES NATURELS
28	METALLIFEROUS ORES,SCRAP		15764		18922		21993		23654	MINERAIS METAL,DECHETS
287	BASE METAL ORES,CONC NES	W 5846	7803	W 11370	18854	W 11076	21944	W 11509	23567	MINERAIS METAUX COMMUNS
2876	TIN ORES,CONCENTRATES	W 5268	7537	W 11340	18842	W 11011	21882	W 11479	23538	MINERAIS D'ETAIN
288	NONFERR METAL SCRAP NES	W 4878	7769	W 129	54	W 4	1	W 9	6	DECHETS NON FERREUX
2882	OTHER BASE MTL SCRAP NES	W 4878	7769	W 9	10					AUTRES DECHETS
28826	TIN WASTE AND SCRAP	W 4877	7766	W 9	10					DECHETS D'ETAIN
3	MINERAL FUELS ETC		57355		60441		63768		47979	COMBUSTIBLES MINERAUX LUB
33	PETROLEUM AND PRODUCTS		56642		59915		63728		47935	PETROLE ET DERIVES
334	PETROLEUM PRODUCTS,REFIN	W 178749	52595	W 185534	56989	W 202355	58306	W 112723	39771	PRODUITS RAFFINES
3343	GAS OILS	W 92160	24898	W 103195	30053	W 133069	36081	W 103427	30860	GAS OILS
3344	FUEL OILS,NES	W 65958	14822	W 69345	16241	W 59191	13190			FUEL OILS
3345	LUBS,PETROLEUM OILS NES	W 13115	11324	W 12747	10577	W 9929	8948	W 8882	8674	HUILES LUBRIFIANTES
33451	LUBS(HIGH PETR CONT) ETC	W 12678	10614	W 12254	9693	W 9367	8016	W 8171	7513	HUILES LUBRIF,H LOURDES
335	RESIDUAL PETRLM PROD NES	W 9913	4046	W 8170	2927	W 18356	5422	W 26488	8159	PRODUITS RESIDUELS NDA
3354	PETROLM BITUMEN,COKE ETC	W 9068	3434	W 6918	1765	W 17160	4158	W 24580	6387	BITUME,COKE DE PETROLE
33543	BITUMINOUS MIXTURES ETC	W 6346	1483	W 5864	1359	W 17160	4158	W 24575	6368	MELANGES BITUMINEUX
5	CHEMCLS,RELATED PROD NES		127225		152714		185488		202659	PRODUITS CHIMIQUES
51	ORGANIC CHEMICALS		11394		10104		12645		13429	PROD CHIMIQ ORGANIQUES
511	HYDROCARBONS NES,DERIVS	W 13843	4161	W 1662	992	W 1625	1126	W 1922	1241	HYDROCARBURES NDA
52	INORGANIC CHEMICALS		14098		21145		26306		29227	PROD CHIM INORGANIQUES
523	OTHR INORG CHEMICALS ETC	W 15569	10706	W 29891	18486	W 33939	22743	W 35901	25260	AUT PRODUITS CHIMIQUES INORG
5232	OTH MTL CMPD OF INRG ACD	W 11046	8245	W 21398	13787	W 23863	17405	W 25404	19345	SELS METALLIQUES
52325	CYANIDES,COMPLEX CYANIDE	W 6867	6534	W 10516	10281	W 10484	12405	W 9062	12891	CYANURES SIMPLES,COMPLEXES
53	DYES,TANNING,COLOUR PROD		9604		11395		12621		12898	PROD TEINTURE,COLORANTS
533	PIGMENTS,PAINTS,ETC	W 3506	5436	W 4491	6393	W 3499	7049	W 5073	7094	PIGMENTS,PEINTURES,VERNIS
541	*MEDICINAL,PHARM PRODUCT	K 1865511	20408	K 1723240	23466	K 1958007	28518	K 2251354	28228	PROD MEDICINAUX PHARMACEUT
5417	MEDICAMENTS	K 1330024	15753	K 1234185	17274	K 1394768	20020	K 1597505	20883	MEDICAMENTS
54179	— CONTNG OTH SUBSTANCES	K 911472	11650	K 1016286	13501	K 1078998	15142	K 1338486	16812	MED CONT AUT SUBSTANCES
55	PERFUME,CLEANING ETC PRD		19412		28503		23678		31252	PROD POUR PARFUM,TOILETTE
553	PERFUMERY,COSMETICS,ETC	W 2843	7030	W 5424	10625	W 3876	9235	W 4509	14161	PRODUITS DE PARFUMERIE
554	SOAP,CLEANSING ETC PREPS	W 12413	10526	W 17637	15352	W 12855	11578	W 14033	13915	SAVONS,PRODUITS DETERSIFS
5541	SOAPS	W 7038	2644	W 8604	3670	W 6534	3488	W 6433	4217	SAVONS,PROD TENSIO–ACTIFS
5542	WASHING PREPARATIONS ETC	W 5288	7719	W 8868	11361	W 6020	7319	W 7339	9054	PROD ORG TENSIO–ACT NDA
562	*FERTILIZERS,MANUFACTURE	W 11566	5384	W 5504	1937	W 14032	9531	W 18121	9037	ENGRAIS MANUFACTURES
5629	FERTILIZERS NES	W 3967	2189	W 1156	483	W 4723	3832	W 12200	6783	ENGRAIS NDA
58	PLASTIC MATERIALS ETC		24551		29590		41513		42631	MAT PLAST ARTIFICIELLES
582	PROD OF CONDENSATION ETC	W 1765	2312	W 3014	3045	W 3167	4172	W 4646	5327	PROD CONDENS,POLYCOND
583	POLYMERIZATION ETC PRODS	W 24274	20928	W 27306	24598	W 25692	33665	W 32535	34184	PROD POLYMERISATION
5831	POLYETHYLENE	W 9166	6900	W 11842	8146	W 9608	11155	W 12717	12552	POLYETHYLENE
58311	— IN PRIMARY FORMS	W 9043	6740	W 11721	7916	W 9456	10757	W 12449	11957	POLYETHYLENE PRIMAIRES
5832	POLYPROPYLENE	W 3304	2777	W 2849	2506	W 3035	4367	W 3423	3719	POLYPROPYLENE
5834	POLYVINYL CHLORIDE	W 4818	4161	W 5534	5664	W 6585	8466	W 9467	9385	CHLORURE DE POLYVINYLE
58341	— IN PRIMARY FORMS	W 4638	3985	W 5209	5301	W 6437	8210	W 9285	8961	SOUS FORMES PRIMAIRES
5839	OTH POLYMRZTION ETC PROD	W 4011	4064	W 3265	4015	W 3599	5870	W 2642	3676	AUT PROD POLYMER COPOLYM
59	CHEMICAL MATERIALS NES		20975		24436		28197		32828	MAT PROD CHIMIQUES NDA
591	PESTICIDES,DISINFECTANTS	W 3163	10005	W 3553	10471	W 3267	12135	W 4122	18134	DESINF,INSECT,FONG,HERB
5911	INSECTICIDES,FOR RETAIL	W 1284	4474	W 978	3194	W 1046	4396	W 1162	5460	INSECTICIDES VENTE DET
5913	HERBICIDES,FOR RETAIL	W 1455	4031	W 1732	4899	W 1666	5675	W 2367	10274	HERBICIDES VENTE AU DET
598	MISCEL CHEM PRODUCTS NES	W 6566	8313	W 7975	11024	W 9020	13384	W 7494	11408	PROD DIV INDUST CHIM NDA
5982	ANTI–KNOCK PREPARTNS ETC	W 210	685	W 1618	3832	W 1248	2678	W 682	1679	PREPARAT ANTIDETONANTES
5989	CHEM PRODUCTS,PREPS NES	W 6109	7088	W 6116	6726	W 7476	10185	W 6681	9409	PROD PREP CHIMIQUES NDA
59899	OTH CHEM PRODS,PREPS,NES	W 4129	4658	W 4040	4618	W 5246	7770	W 4381	6470	AUT PRODUITS CHIMIQUES NDA
6	BASIC MANUFACTURES		187221		203221		216809		229998	ART MANUFACTURES
62	RUBBER MANUFACTURES NES		13665		17667		16544		16748	CAOUTCHOUC MANUFACTURE
625	RUBBER TYRES, TUBES ETC	W 5666	10544	W 7846	14868	W 7637	12656	W 7808	12355	PNEUS CAOUTCHOUC VULCANISE
6251	TYRES NEW FOR MOTOR CARS	W 2386	3534	W 3361	5950	W 3998	5851	W 3555	4765	PNEUS POUR VOITURES
6252	TYRES,NEW,BUS OR LORRY	W 1828	4233	W 2604	5783	W 1440	3461	W 1490	3938	PNEUS POUR AUTOBUS,CAMIONS
64	PAPER,PAPERBOARD AND MFR		23109		26387		38696		35826	PAPIERS,CARTONS & OUVRAGES
641	PAPER AND PAPERBOARD	W 28946	19151	W 32004	20954	W 34227	30408	W 33361	25842	PAPIERS ET CARTONS
6411	NEWSPRINT	W 9181	5784	W 10048	6408	W 11267	9469	W 8395	7641	PAPIER JOURNAL
6413	KRAFT PAPER,PAPERBOARD	W 8158	4140	W 7192	3993	W 8179	6176	W 8859	5871	PAPIER ET CARTON KRAFT
6415	PAPER,PAPERBRD,BULK,NES	W 7655	5372	W 9366	5547	W 8653	7644	W 9741	6597	PAPIERS,CARTONS ROULEAUX
64159	OTHER PAPER ETC,BULK,NES	W 7383	5065	W 8898	5106	W 8411	7373	W 8580	5805	AUT PAPIER ROULEAUX FEUILLES

4. Special Imports C.I.F. by Commodities according to the S.I.T.C. (Rev. 2) in thousand U.S. Dollars
Importations Spéciales C.A.F. par Produits d'après la C.T.C.I. (Rév. 2) en milliers de Dollars E.U.

SITC CTCI	COMMODITY	1993		1994		1995		1996		PRODUIT
		WEIGHT POIDS	VALUE VALEUR	WEIGHT POIDS	VALUE VALEUR	WEIGHT POIDS	VALUE VALEUR	WEIGHT POIDS	VALUE VALEUR	
642	PAPER,ETC,PRECUT,ARTS OF	W 2279	3958	W 3552	5433	W 4517	8289	W 5305	9984	PAP,CARTONS DECOUPES
65	TEXTILE YARN,FABRICS,ETC		21991		28392		28753		29658	FILS,TISSUS,ARTICLES TEXTILE
651	TEXTILE YARN		6509	W 2618	8173	W 3033	9940	W 3203	10843	FILS TEXTILES
6514	SYN FIB YRN,BULK,MONOFIL		2946	W 1129	3287	W 1678	4849	W 1545	4338	FILS CONT 85% FIB TEXT SYNTH
652	COTTON FABRICS,WOVEN	W 1049	2581	W 1107	3693	W 1220	4784	W 1386	5916	TISSUS DE COTON
6522	WOVEN COTTON BLEACHD,ETC	W 827	2348	W 1049	3593	W 1112	4599	W 1315	5686	TISSUS COTON BLANCHIS ETC
653	WOVN MAN–MADE FIB FABRIC	W 3067	5303	W 3368	6778	W 3451	6300	W 3285	4680	TISSUS FIBRES SYNTH,ARTIF
66	NONMETAL MINERAL MFS NES		21013		19485		20462		26509	ART MIN NON METALLIQUES
661	LIME,CEMENT,BLDG PRODS	W 52133	3908	W 51624	3829	W 57435	4456	W 77181	5436	CHAUX,CIMENTS MAT CONSTR
662	CLAY,REFRACTORY BLDG PRD	W 16033	5031	W 14131	4867	W 10516	3673	W 12318	5379	MAT CONST REFRACTAIRES
664	GLASS	W 13144	5592	W 11293	6001	W 11029	6263	W 12674	9677	VERRE
665	GLASSWARE	W 7067	4492	W 3726	3041	W 3780	3971	W 1705	2564	OUVRAGES EN VERRE
67	IRON AND STEEL		58871		59703		60990		68861	FER ET ACIER
672	IRON,STEEL PRIMARY FORMS	W 11733	3187	W 8532	2501	W 14756	4305	W 11323	3745	LINGOTS FER,ACIER
673	IRON,STEEL SHAPES ETC	W 29775	11342	W 38941	14668	W 58397	21593	W 46820	18750	BARRES,PROFIL FER,ACIER
6732	IRON,STEEL BARS ETC	W 16932	6434	W 29882	11032	W 48595	17291	W 34706	13786	BARRES FER,ACIER
67326	IRN,OTH STL BARS HOTROLD	W 12263	4645	W 25826	9347	W 42333	14873	W 28949	11216	BARRES PLEINES FER,ACIER
674	IRN,STL UNIV,PLATE,SHEET	W 20475	11047	W 22337	11618	W 22247	14018	W 33836	20280	LARGES PLATS,TOLES
6746	IRN,STL THIN PLATE,ROLLD	W 4885	2845	W 7081	3574	W 4112	2832	W 8241	5079	TOLES LAM MOINS 3MM
6749	OTH IRN,STL PLATES,SHEET	W 12315	6095	W 9405	5508	W 9344	6577	W 13263	10011	AUTRES TOLES FER,ACIER
67491	— OF IRON OR SIMPLE STL	W 11858	5938	W 8764	5131	W 8791	6214	W 13108	9725	AUT TOLES AUTRES ACIER FIN
678	IRON,STL TUBES,PIPES,ETC	W 30023	26244	W 29623	24155	W 15756	15110	W 16593	18298	TUBES,TUYAUX EN FONTE,FER
6782	IRON,STL SEAMLESS TUBES	W 17571	14412	W 23450	18651	W 7819	6868	W 7635	8324	TUBES,TUYAUX SANS SOUDURE
6783	IRON,STL TUBES,PIPES NES	W 10863	10220	W 5656	4305	W 7422	7208	W 7054	7809	AUT TUBES,TUYAUX FER,ACIER
679	IRN,STL CASTINGS UNWORKD	W 6903	5810	W 8602	5772	W 6924	4602	W 8120	6220	OUVRAGES EN FONTE,FER,ACIER
6793	IRON,STL FORGINGS ROUGH	W 4181	3756	W 4303	2897	W 687	464	W 2030	1534	OUVRAGES FORGES,ESTAMPES
68	NON–FERROUS METALS		5657		5833		9353		6843	METAUX NON FERREUX
684	ALUMINIUM	W 1068	2551	W 1456	3266	W 1583	5801	W 1406	4065	ALUMINIUM
6842	ALUMINIUM,ALLOYS WORKED	W 982	2441	W 1446	3254	W 1553	5672	W 1303	3735	ALUMINIUM,ALLIAGES OUVRE
69	METAL MANUFACTURES NES		39109		42973		39353		42360	ART MANUFACT EN METAL NDA
691	STRUCTURES AND PARTS NES	W 19280	11759	W 18140	9399	W 4876	6071	W 3333	4416	CONSTRUCT FER,ACIER,ALU
6911	STRUCTURES,PARTS IRN,STL	W 19212	11594	W 18000	8983	W 4836	5835	W 3290	4288	CONSTRUCT FER,ACIER,FONTE
692	METAL TANKS,BOXES,ETC	W 3459	5648	W 4703	8357	W 3981	8331	W 4442	8306	RECIPIENTS METALLIQUES
6924	MTL TRANSPORT BOXES ETC	W 1793	3226	W 2809	4924	W 2550	5558	W 2311	3873	FUTS,TAMBOURS,BIDONS
695	TOOLS	W 2087	5793	W 1366	6147	W 1148	6364	W 1210	7029	OUTILS A MAIN
697	BASE MTL HOUSEHOLD EQUIP	W 1609	2595	W 1602	3136	W 1245	2760	W 2398	5619	ART MENAGE MET COMMUNS
699	BASE METAL MFRS NES	W 2958	6102	W 3103	6617	W 3732	6966	W 4192	7129	ART MANUFACTURES MET NDA
7	MACHINES,TRANSPORT EQUIP		553479		515972		645499		788775	MACHINES MATERIEL TRANSPORT
71	POWER GENERATING EQUIPMT		32715		18787		50284		47212	MACHINES GENERATRICES
713	INTRNL COMBUS PSTN ENGIN		8225	W 2288	8929	W 2199	9928	W 3566	9014	MOTEURS EXPL COMB INT, PIECE
7139	PISTON ENGINE PARTS NES	W 588	3963	W 466	5079	W 326	4712	W 1594	3606	PIECES POUR 713.2,3,8
714	ENGINES AND MOTORS NES	W 568	15769	W 88	2653	W 652	16746	W 251	6691	MOTEURS NON ELECTRIQUES
7148	GAS TURBINES NES	W 213	6787	W 7	733	W 187	6838	W 11	1025	TURBINES A GAZ
71488	OTHER GAS TURBINES NES	W 203	6759	W 7	733	W 185	6459	W 9	1013	AUTRES TURBINES A GAZ
7149	ENGINE & MOTOR PARTS NES	W 352	7718	W 78	1682	W 463	9778	W 233	3361	PIECES 714 ET 718.88
71499	PARTS NES,OF 71488,71888	W 352	7718	W 78	1672	W 456	8611	W 232	3358	PIECES 714.88 ET 718.88
716	ROTATING ELECTRIC PLANT	W 788	6732	W 896	5243	W 1636	21343	W 1714	23500	APP ELECTR ROTATIFS,PIECES
7161	DC MOTORS AND GENERATORS	W 101	1297	W 200	2151	W 690	12255	W 217	2449	MOTEURS COURANT CONTINU
7162	AC MTRS,GENRTRS,GEN SETS	W 654	4995	W 679	2640	W 911	8453	W 1430	20660	MOTEURS ELECTRIQUES
71622	AC GENERATORS	W 110	1669	W 50	296	W 74	1513	W 382	5046	GENER COURANT ALTERNATIF
71623	GEN SETS WITH PISTN ENGN	W 239	2469	W 172	886	W 397	5702	W 623	14676	GROUPES MOTEUR EXPLOSION
718	OTH POWER GENERATG MACHY	W 40	1304	W 43	1252	W 49	1568	W 264	6534	AUTRES MOTEURS PARTIES
7188	WIND,WATER,ETC ENGINES	W 40	1299	W 43	1251	W 49	1568	W 264	6534	MOT MACHINES MOTRICES NDA
71882	OTH HYDRAULIC ENGNS,MTRS	W 29	838	W 12	425	W 34	1154	W 246	6318	MACH MOTRICES HYDRAULQUES
72	MACHS FOR SPCL INDUSTRYS		87009		90731		107377		101431	MAC SPECIALES POUR INDUST
721	AGRIC MACHY,EXC TRACTORS	W 2610	5385	W 3312	6817	W 2746	5626	W 3351	6516	MACHINES AGRICOLES
722	TRACTORS NON–ROAD	W 2032	7063	W 2698	11105	W 2551	10177	W 2774	11944	TRACTEURS
7223	TRACK–LAYING TRACTORS	W 248	500	W 1163	4944	W 622	2292	W 921	4460	TRACTEURS A CHENILLES
7224	WHEELED TRACTORS NES	W 1784	6563	W 1535	6160	W 1929	7885	W 1853	7484	TRACTEURS A ROUES
723	CIVIL ENGNEERG EQUIP ETC	W 9555	30016	W 6216	28557	W 8233	43876	W 7117	35202	APPAREILS DE GENIE CIVIL
7234	CONST,MINING MACHNRY NES	W 5262	21132	W 5611	23320	W 6617	34554	W 4962	24428	MACH POUR LA CONST, MINES
72341	SELF–PROPELLD DOZERS,ETC	W 1895	6642	W 2682	10805	W 2110	9862	W 1531	7260	BULLDOZERS
72342	SLFPRP SHOVELS,EXCAVATRS	W 1962	10076	W 1355	5664	W 2556	11703	W 1861	9599	PELLES MECANIQUES
72343	SLFPRP CONST ETC MCH NES	W 932	2286	W 195	905	W 1229	8443	W 271	1828	AUT MACH EXTR,TERRASSEM
7239	CONSTR ETC MACHY PTS NES	W 4044	7689	W 374	4020	W 1295	8160	W 1899	9495	PIECES 723.41–723.46
724	TEXTILE,LEATHER MACHNRY	W 3586	11564	W 2613	13654	W 1933	11843	W 2505	12240	MACH POUR INDUSTRIE TEXTILE
7244	SPINNING,EXTRDNG,ETC MCH	W 1906	5115	W 1152	4607	W 334	1558	W 1051	4190	MACH POUR LE FILAGE
7245	WEAVING,FELT MFG,ETC MCH	W 402	1894	W 491	3937	W 484	4606	W 697	3516	METIERS A TISSER,PIECES
726	PRINTG,BKBINDG MACHY,PTS	W 466	5124	W 485	3221	W 432	3113	W 495	3116	MACHINES POUR IMPRIMERIE
7264	PRINTING PRESSES	W 314	3837	W 330	1970	W 315	1890	W 411	2194	MACHINES A IMPRIMER
72641	ROTARY PRINTING PRESSES	W 314	3837	W 330	1970	W 315	1890	W 411	2194	MACH IMPRIMER ROTATIVES
727	FOOD MACHRY NON–DOMESTIC	W 2457	10752	W 1594	6395	W 590	3714	W 2116	10614	MACH INDUSTRIES ALIMENT
7272	OTH FOOD PROC MCHY,PARTS	W 2204	9669	W 1458	5717	W 550	3338	W 2080	10165	AUT MACH IND ALIMENTAIRE
72722	INDUS FOOD PROC MACH NES	W 994	7785	W 928	4882	W 268	2106	W 603	7705	MACHINES BOULANGERIE
728	OTH MACHY FOR SPCL INDUS	W 3528	15986	W 4308	19645	W 5170	28243	W 4186	18843	AUT MACH IND PARTICULIERES
7283	OTHR MINERAL WORKG MACHY	W 1144	4724	W 2625	10424	W 3077	17463	W 2547	8536	MACH TRIER,CRIBLER,BROYER
72832	MINRL CRUSHING ETC MACHY	W 338	855	W 1166	3929	W 1486	9204	W 1032	1891	MACH CONCASSER MAT MINER
7284	MACHY FOR SPCL INDUS NES	W 2053	9224	W 1256	8071	W 853	7612	W 1089	7605	MACH SPEC IND PARTICUL.
72842	RUBBER,PLASTICS WRKG MCH	W 415	2787	W 473	3811	W 421	5015	W 647	5001	MACH IND CAOUT MAT PLAST
73	METALWORKING MACHINERY		3478		4211		4343		3791	MACH TRAVAIL DES METAUX
74	GENRL INDUSTRL MACHY NES		59872		62556		64803		67905	MACH APP INDUSTRIE
741	HEATING,COOLING EQUIPMNT	W 3631	16411	W 2049	8932	W 3218	10548	W 2221	11516	MACH CHAUFFAGE,PIECES
7411	GAS GENERATORS,PARTS NES	W 107	4387	W 45	305	W 240	2150	W 323	2392	GAZOGENES
7413	INDUS FURNACES ETC,PARTS	W 2492	7355	W 240	1406	W 768	1901	W 390	1615	FOURS IND,LABOR,PIECES
74132	INDUST FURNACES NONELECT	W 2480	7250	W 200	967	W 189	1211	W 344	1398	FOURS NON ELECTRIQUES
7416	HEATING,COOLING EQU NES	W 499	2292	W 1062	4081	W 568	3282	W 671	2885	APP CHANGEMENT TEMP
742	PUMPS FOR LIQUIDS ETC	W 1008	7397	W 930	8123	W 991	7143	W 1640	7472	POMPES MOTO–POMPES
743	PUMPS NES,CENTRFUGES ETC	W 1080	6768	W 1555	9501	W 1618	11054	W 3613	12604	POMPES COMPRES,VENT ETC
7431	PUMPS FOR GASES ETC	W 389	2883	W 638	4520	W 496	4454	W 624	6276	POMPES AIR A VIDE,COMPRES
7436	GAS,LIQUID FILTERS ETC	W 486	1749	W 622	2453	W 859	4336	W 1593	3421	APP POUR FILT DES LIQUIDES
744	MECHANICAL HANDLING EQU	W 1746	5579	W 2687	11199	W 2491	11336	W 2161	10649	EQUIP MANUTENTION PIECES
7442	LIFTING,LOADING MACH NES	W 1609	5054	W 1906	7329	W 1840	6695	W 1434	6060	APP LEVAGE,MANUTENTION
745	NONELEC MACHY,TOOLS NES		12796	W 1483	12177	W 1724	10829	W 1341	9623	AUT MACH NON ELEC,PIECES
7452	OTH NONELEC MCHS,PTS NES		9999	W 1178	9361	W 936	7425	W 1213	6555	AUT MACH NON ELEC,PIECES
74522	PACKAGNG,BOTTLNG,ETC MCH	W 970	7261	W 657	6902	W 329	3687	W 303	2781	MACH NETT BOUTEILLES,ETC
749	NONELEC MACH PTS,ACC NES	W 1506	10921	W 1473	12624	W 1500	13893	W 2235	16040	PIECES MACH NON ELEC NDA
7491	BALL,ROLLER,ETC BEARINGS	W 405	3108	W 354	4050	W 314	4350	W 461	4771	ROULEMENTS BILLES ETC
7492	COCKS,VALVES ETC NES	W 556	3777	W 696	4453	W 704	5031	W 1365	7484	ART ROB,SIM POUR TUYAUX
75	OFFICE MACHNES,ADP EQUIP		19970		16300		15498		17801	MACH BUREAU TRAIT AUTOM
751	OFFICE MACHINES	W 348	3371	W 525	3591	W 1256	2634	W 626	3644	MACH,APPAREILS DE BUREAU
752	AUTOMTIC DATA PROC EQUIP	W 2324	9748	W 451	8279	W 305	10114	W 249	9965	MACH TRAIT INFORMATION

4. Special Imports C.I.F. by Commodities according to the S.I.T.C. (Rev. 2) in thousand U.S. Dollars
Importations Spéciales C.A.F. par Produits d'après la C.T.C.I. (Rév. 2) en milliers de Dollars E.U.

SITC CTCI	COMMODITY	1993 WEIGHT POIDS	1993 VALUE VALEUR	1994 WEIGHT POIDS	1994 VALUE VALEUR	1995 WEIGHT POIDS	1995 VALUE VALEUR	1996 WEIGHT POIDS	1996 VALUE VALEUR	PRODUIT
7522	DIGITAL COMPUTERS	W 863	5055	W 268	4538	W 116	5304	W 130	5586	MACH DIGITALES COMPLETES
759	OFFICE,ADP MCH PTS,ACCES	W 509	6850	W 513	4430	W 319	2749	W 239	4192	PIECES DU 751 ET 752
7599	ACCTG,ETC,ADP MCH PTS,AC	W 469	6160	W 436	3846	W 292	2311	W 190	3412	PIECES DU 751 ET 752
76	TELECOMM,SOUND EQUIPMENT		42721		26852		48342		117202	EQUIPMENT DE TELECOM
764	TELECOM EQPT,PTS,ACC NES	W 1317	40607	W 760	22094	W 1431	43645	W 2088	109844	EQUIP TELECOM,PIECES
7641	LINE TELEPHONE,ETC EQUIP	W 565	21372	W 293	12842	W 474	22068	W 536	49591	APP TELEPHON PAR FIL
7643	TV,RADIO TRANSMITTRS ETC	W 85	5169	W 106	3604	W 86	5159	W 79	12773	APP EMET TELE RADIO
7648	TELECOMM EQUIPMENT NES	W 79	3573	W 23	672	W 10	85	W 84	9058	APP TELECOM NDA
76483	RADAR APPARATUS ETC	W 33	3171	W 2	391		14	W 63	8720	APP DE RADIOGUIDAGE ETC
7649	PTS NES OF EQUIPMT OF 76	W 507	10177	W 215	4354	W 687	15809	W 1118	37841	PIECES DE LA DIV 76
76491	PTS NES OF APPAR OF 7641	W 325	8355	W 54	2334	W 494	12730	W 905	34685	PIECES POUR 764.1
77	ELECTRIC MACHNRY NES ETC		46534		36091		50841		49725	MACH APP ELECT NDA
771	ELECTRIC POWER MACHY NES	W 1400	5087	W 791	2027	W 1274	6718	W 1260	5353	MACH PROD,TRANS ELECTR
7711	TRANSFORMERS,ELECTRICAL	W 1244	4421	W 685	1437	W 1200	6227	W 1211	5051	TRANSFO ELECTRIQUES
77111	LIQUID DIELEC TRANSFRMRS	W 570	2655	W 260	907	W 975	4488	W 924	3186	TRANSFO DIELEC LIQUIDE
772	SWITCHGEAR ETC,PARTS NES	W 833	9662	W 668	7030	W 1003	9529	W 620	8107	APP COUPURE,SECT ETC
7721	SWITCHGEAR ETC	W 813	9400	W 664	6858	W 998	9432	W 614	8001	APP COUPURE,SECTIONMNT
773	ELECTR DISTRIBUTNG EQUIP	W 2383	9369	W 2216	8446	W 2815	10698	W 2638	7613	EQUIPMT DISTRIBUTION ELECT
7731	INSULATED WIRE,CABLE ETC	W 2037	8848	W 2081	8166	W 2393	9910	W 2306	6979	FILS,CABLES ISOLES ELECT
775	HOUSEHOLD TYPE EQUIP NES	W 1917	4498	W 2083	4848	W 2647	4521	W 3055	9726	MACH,APP USAGE DOMESTQUE
7752	DOM REFRIGERATRS,FREEZRS	W 1222	2029	W 1197	2130	W 848	2004	W 2280	6324	REFRIG,CONGEL MENAGER
77521	DOMESTIC REFRIGERATORS	W 1070	1677	W 950	1569	W 698	1691	W 1928	5418	REFRIGERATEURS
778	ELECTRICAL MACHINERY NES	W 5689	13861	W 6169	11606	W 6458	16893	W 6637	14305	AUTRES MACH ELECT NDA
7781	BATTERIES,ACCUMULATORS	W 4459	7750	W 4931	5928	W 5172	7149	W 5382	8040	PILES ET ACCUMULATEURS
77811	PRIMARY BATTERIES,CELLS	W 3048	2958	W 3469	3500	W 3674	4125	W 3813	5080	PILES ELECTRIQUES,PIECES
77812	ELECTRIC ACCUMULATORS	W 1330	4554	W 1391	2239	W 1460	2872	W 1514	2846	ACCUMULATEURS ELECTRIQ
78	ROAD VEHICLES		183432		249390		234190		233284	VEHICULES ROUTIERS
781	PASS MOTOR VEH EXC BUSES	W 20886	80511	W 18108	109709	W 26612	100072	W 18420	107319	AUTO TRANSPORT PERSONNES
782	LORRIES,SPCL MTR VEH NES	W 17692	57477	W 17778	82734	W 16782	82263	W 15594	75663	VEHICULES SPECIAUX,MARCH
7821	LORRIES,TRUCKS	W 16910	52736	W 17247	78854	W 15777	75875	W 14643	69255	VEHICULES TRANSP MARCHAND
7822	SPECIAL MOTOR VEHCLS NES	W 782	4741	W 532	3880	W 1005	6388	W 951	6407	VEHICULES USAGES SPECIAUX
783	ROAD MOTOR VEHICLES NES	W 11941	23861	W 6987	31275	W 6273	26210	W 10141	32125	VEHICULES ROUTIERS NDA
7831	BUSES	W 9377	17169	W 4819	22341	W 4593	18631	W 9176	27581	VOITURES TRANSPORT COMMUN
7832	TRACTORS FOR TR–TRAILERS	W 2564	6692	W 2168	8934	W 1680	7579	W 965	4544	TRACTEURS ROUTIERS
784	MOTOR VEH PRTS,ACCES NES	W 4819	14195	W 3682	15897	W 4682	15719	W 3823	10442	PIECES 722,781,782,783
7841	MOTOR VEHICLE CHASSIS	W 692	2666	W 999	5231	W 797	4889	W 474	2986	CHASSIS 722,781,782,783
7849	OTHER MOTOR VEHCL PARTS	W 4092	11460	W 2588	10239	W 3769	10649	W 3318	7382	PIECES 722,781,782,783
785	CYCLES,ETC MOTRZD OR NOT	W 2011	5304	W 2643	7000	W 2153	6615	W 1683	6621	MOTOCYCLES SCOOTERS
7851	MOTORCYCLES ETC	W 491	2818	W 560	3761	W 418	3967	W 655	5183	MOTO VELO MOTEUR AUXIL
79	OTHR TRANSPORT EQUIPMENT		77747		11054		69821		150424	AUTRE MATERIEL TRANSPORT
792	AIRCRAFT ETC	W 296	77374	W 118	8628	W 479	68421	W 402	149945	APP NAVIGATION AERIENNE
7921	HELICOPTERS	W 6	2103	W 6	2103	W 30	9939	W 5	425	HELICOPTERES
7923	AIRCRFT NES2000–15000KG	W 40	13090	W 7	917	W 34	2185	W 15	21673	AERODYNES 2000 A 15000 KG
7924	AIRCRFT NES OVER 15000KG	W 177	58801	W 60	4000	W 363	54719	W 320	125035	AERODYNES PLUS 15000 KG
8	MISC MANUFACTURED GOODS		84361		83425		92451		113053	ART MANUFACTURES DIVERS
812	*PLUMBG,HEATNG,LGHTNG EQ	W 2378	3117	W 3307	3768	W 2724	5411	W 3376	7291	APPAR SANITAIRES CHAUFFAGE
821	*FURNITURE,PARTS THEREOF	W 1540	4204	W 2350	5138	W 2448	5927	W 3243	7195	MEUBLES ET PIECES
84	CLOTHING AND ACCESSORIES		7716		10141		6804		6934	VETEMENTS
851	*FOOTWEAR	W 1605	5040	W 2354	6369	W 4792	6727	W 1968	7521	CHAUSSURES
85102	FOOTWEAR LEATHER	W 1029	3824	W 1771	4705	W 1894	4180	W 1183	3401	CHAUS SEMELLES EN CUIR
87	PRECISION INSTRUMNTS NES		21551		13392		14806		19837	INSTRUM,APPAR SCIENT NDA
872	MEDICAL INSTRUMENTS NES	W 532	9805	W 237	3270	W 512	2653	W 1923	6173	INSTR,APP MEDIC–CHIR NDA
87202	OTH MEDICAL INSTRUMENTS	W 500	9455	W 210	2868	W 474	2308	W 1898	5705	INSTRUM,APP MEDECINE
874	MEASURNG,CONTROLNG INSTR	W 462	9518	W 429	8346	W 751	9831	W 586	11483	INSTRUMENTS DE MESURE
88	PHOTO EQU,OPTICL GDS ETC		6353		6781		6251		5814	APP,FOURN PHOTO,OP,MONTR
882	PHOTO,CINEMA SUPPLIES	W 617	3998	W 623	3908	W 647	4252	W 897	4136	PRODUITS PHOTO,CINEMA
89	MISC MANUFCTRD GOODS NES		35935		37116		45962		57795	ART MANUFACTURES DIVERS
892	PRINTED MATTER	W 3317	7184	W 2081	8302	W 2958	10274	W 4837	22480	IMPRIMES
8921	PRINTED BOOKS,GLOBES,ETC	W 2611	5331	W 1454	6099	W 2033	5921	W 4165	19922	LIVRES,BROCHURES,CARTES
89211	PRINTED BOOKS,PAMPHLETS	W 2603	5307	W 1441	6048	W 2012	5842	W 4146	19600	LIVRES,BROCHURES
893	ARTICLES OF PLASTIC NES		13948		12214		16623		15878	OUVRAGES EN MAT DIVIS 58
8931	PLSTC PACKG CONTNRS,LIDS	W 3255	5110	W 1933	4615	W 2306	6300	W 2783	8145	ART TRANSP EMBALLAGE ETC
8939	MISC PLASTIC ARTICLES	W 5051	8711	W 3259	7316	W 4331	10022	W 3186	7348	ART DIVERS EN MAT DIV 58
89399	OTHR PLASTC ARTICLES NES	W 4545	7970	W 2653	6350	W 3058	8753	W 2342	6233	AUT OUV MAT DIV 58
894	TOYS,SPORTING GOODS,ETC	W 2067	6019	W 3265	7525	W 3190	6493	W 3890	6373	VOITURES ENFANTS,JOUETS
8942	TOYS,INDOOR GAMES ETC	W 1777	4534	W 2547	5586	W 2159	4228	W 2029	4095	JOUETS,JEUX ETC
897	GOLD,SILVER WARE,JEWELRY		842		846		3084		5370	BIJOUTERIE,ORFEVRERIE
9	GOODS NOT CLASSD BY KIND		19664		18300		9313		42163	ART TRANSACT NON CLASSES
951	*WAR FIREARMS,AMMUNITION	W 695	1817	W 618	4277	W 18	263	W 8	129	VEHIC BLINDES ARMES
95102	MILITARY FIREARMS NES			W 580	4036				2	ARMES DE GUERRE
971	*GOLD,NON MONETARY NES	K 29420	17600	K 14583	13938	K 7085	9039	K 3486	41984	OR NON MONETAIRE
97101	NONMON GLD UNWRT,SEMIMFD	K 29420	17600	K 14583	13938	K 7085	9039	K 3486	41984	OR,ALLIAGES D'OR BRUTS

5. Special Exports F.O.B. by Commodities according to the S.I.T.C. (Rev. 2) in thousand U.S. Dollars
Exportations Spéciales F.O.B. par Produits d'après la C.T.C.I. (Rév. 2) en milliers de Dollars E.U.

SITC CTCI	COMMODITY	1993		1994		1995		1996		PRODUIT
		WEIGHT POIDS	VALUE VALEUR	WEIGHT POIDS	VALUE VALEUR	WEIGHT POIDS	VALUE VALEUR	WEIGHT POIDS	VALUE VALEUR	
	ALL COMMODITIES		808939		1124232		1181213		1086945	TOUS PRODUITS
0	FOOD AND LIVE ANIMALS		95542		157690		113616		179126	ALIMENTS,ANIMAUX VIVANTS
001	*LIVE ANIMALS FOR FOOD	W 960	630	W 5186	4351	W 5	20	W 699	513	ANIMAUX VIVANTS
0011	BOVINE SPECIES,LIVE	W 960	630	W 5183	4300			W 699	511	ESPECE BOVINE
01	MEAT AND PREPARATIONS		550		2585		3166		4045	VIANDES ET PREPARATIONS
011	MEAT FRESH,CHILLD,FROZEN	W 276	392	W 1567	2295	W 2764	3011	W 3260	3970	VIANDES FRAICHES,REF,CONGE
04	CEREALS AND PREPARATIONS		29273		28769		4757		4675	CEREALES ET PRODUITS
047	OTHER CEREAL MEALS,FLOUR	W 113421	26755	W 104364	23999	W 495	50	W 2	4	AUTRES SEMOULES,FARINES
04701	CEREAL FLOUR(NON–WHEAT)	W 113421	26755	W 104364	23999	W 495	50	W 2	4	FARINES DE CEREALES
05	VEGETABLES AND FRUIT		18922		28847		29879		42252	LEGUMES ET FRUITS
054	VEG ETC FRSH,SMPLY PRSVD		659	W 9707	5213	W 3713	3193	W 4196	3209	LEGUMES FRAIS,CONG,SECS
0542	LEGUMINOUS VEGETBLES DRY	W 1023	480	W 9628	5157	W 3490	3096	W 4010	3097	LEGUMES A COSSE SECS
057	FRUIT,NUTS,FRESH,DRIED	W 8445	15293	W 11305	17277	W 9159	19042	W 13327	29384	FRUITS FRAIS OU SECS
0577	NUTS EDIBLE,FRESH,DRIED	W 8246	15236	W 7488	15775	W 7666	18702	W 9961	28616	FRUITS A COQUES
05772	BRAZIL NUTS,FRESH,DRIED	W 1946	3509	W 1422	3153	W 869	2250	W 9679	27787	NOIX DU BRESIL
05779	NUTS EDIBLE,FRSH,DRY,NES	W 6300	11727	W 6065	12622	W 6797	16452	W 282	829	FRUITS A COQUES NDA
058	FRUIT PRESERVED,PREPARED	W 971	2956	W 2019	6351	W 1960	7627	W 3309	9635	CONSERVES DE FRUITS
0589	FRUIT PREPRD,PRESRVD,NES	W 943	2935	W 1947	6301	W 1834	7548	W 3161	9545	FRUITS PREPARES CONSERV
05899	FRUIT,NUTS NES,PRESERVED	W 943	2935	W 1947	6301	W 1834	7548	W 3161	9545	FRUITS PREP CONSERV NDA
06	SUGAR AND PREPS,HONEY		15781		45506		16968		28121	SUCRES ET PRODUITS
061	SUGAR AND HONEY	W 38292	15727	W 107318	45486	W 44159	16766	W 72328	27855	SUCRES ET MIEL
0611	RAW BEET AND CANE SUGAR			W 36	41	W 368	214	W 18998	8390	SUCRES BRUTS
0612	REFINED SUGAR ETC	W 38292	15727	W 107265	45430	W 43785	16545	W 53329	19465	SUCRES RAFFINES
07	COFFEE,TEA,COCOA,SPICES		5059		16023		17478		17054	CAFE,THE,CACAO,EPICES
071	COFFEE AND SUBSTITUTES	W 2788	3878	W 4995	15223	W 5781	16854	W 7390	16458	CAFE ET SUCCEDANES
0711	COFFEE GREEN,ROASTED,SUB	W 2788	3878	W 4995	15223	W 5781	16854	W 7390	16458	CAFE TORREFIE OU DECAFEINE
07111	COFFEE GREEN,HUSKS,SKINS	W 2712	3724	W 4932	15039	W 5738	16743	W 7389	16454	CAFE NON TORREFIE
081	*FEEDING STUFF FOR ANIML	W 96757	24958	W 130426	31046	W 203940	39346	W 354338	81708	NOURRITURE POUR ANIMAUX
0813	OILCAKE AND OTH RESIDUES	W 91719	23837	W 130323	30998	W 203473	39241	W 351168	81108	TOURTEAUX
08131	— OF SOYA BEANS	W 89801	23537	W 129645	30882	W 198447	38507	W 335240	78161	TOURTEAUX DE SOJA
1	BEVERAGES AND TOBACCO		1636		3702		6902		6918	BOISSONS ET TABACS
11	BEVERAGES		1134		1941		3705		3136	BOISSONS
112	ALCOHOLIC BEVERAGES	W 1634	1134	W 1868	1687	W 4076	3629	W 2939	2614	BOISSONS ALCOOLIQUES
12	TOBACCO AND MANUFACTURES		502		1761		3197		3782	TABACS BRUTS FABRIQUES
122	TOBACCO,MANUFACTURED	W 119	502	W 342	1761	W 527	3197	W 626	3782	TABACS FABRIQUES
1222	CIGARETTES	W 119	502	W 342	1761	W 527	3197	W 626	3782	CIGARETTES
2	CRUDE MATERLS,EXCL FUELS		277058		329889		415289		428712	MAT BRUTES NON COMESTIBLES
22	OIL SEEDS,OLEAGINOUS FRT		18889		44244		69509		84638	GRAINES,FRUITS OLEAGINEUX
222	SEEDS FOR'SOFT'FIXED OIL	W 72322	18852	W 191472	43972	W 209400	47118	W 272332	66319	GRAINES HUILES FIXES
2222	SOYA BEANS	W 71278	18182	W 189858	43174	W 208827	46716	W 265515	64794	FEVES DE SOJA
223	SEEDS FOR OTH FIXED OILS	W 105	37	W 1741	272	W 117748	22391	W 69951	18319	GRAINES AUTRES HUILES FIXES
2239	OIL SEED FLOUR AND MEAL		14	W 1241	201	W 117748	22391	W 69926	18315	FARINES GRAINES OLEAG
24	CORK AND WOOD		49711		78548		66115		68964	LIEGE ET BOIS
248	WOOD SHAPED,SLEEPERS	W 88137	49649	W 129243	78548	W 93312	66057	W 96183	68935	BOIS SIMPLEMENT TRAVAILLES
2481	RAILWAY SLEEPERS,TIES	W 8428	2147	W 12725	3677	W 1808	457	W 2980	866	TRAVERSES VOIES FERREES
2482	LUMBER SHAPED CONIFER	W 3227	3105	W 3842	4145	W 1564	1627	W 163	357	CONIFERES SCIES,RABOTES
24822	LUMBER PLANED ETC CONIFR	W 3227	3105	W 3723	4111	W 1483	1588	W 138	345	CONIFER RABOTES,RAINES
2483	LUMBER SHAPED NON–CONIFR	W 76481	44397	W 112677	70727	W 89941	63973	W 93041	67712	NON CONIFERES SCIES,RABOTES
24831	LUMBER SAWN ETC NON–CON	W 76334	44198	W 112532	70534	W 89244	63202	W 90209	64598	SCIES LONGITUDINALEMENT
26	TEXTILE FIBRES AND WASTE		9262		15373		31003		32385	FIBRES TEXTILES
263	COTTON	W 5153	8257	W 8428	13954	W 13902	29960	W 18188	31282	COTON
2631	RAW COTTON,EXCL LINTERS	W 5047	8088	W 8368	13876	W 13902	29960	W 18188	31282	COTON EN MASSE
27	CRUDE FERTLZR,MINRLS NES		3787		4283		3345		2451	ENGRAIS MINERAUX BRUTS
278	OTHER CRUDE MINERALS	W 22604	3703	W 23488	3623	W 28183	2890	W 17843	2025	AUTRES MINERAUX BRUTS
2789	MINERALS CRUDE NES	W 22236	3626	W 22196	3497	W 22161	2615	W 17461	1995	MINERAUX BRUTS NDA
27894	CRUDE NATURAL BORATES	W 22140	3595	W 18788	3102	W 10596	1556	W 12523	1522	BORATES NATURELS BRUTS
28	METALLIFEROUS ORES,SCRAP		189559		180852		240199		235042	MINERAIS METAL,DECHETS
287	BASE METAL ORES,CONC NES	W 288859	141058	W 256889	132709	W 334937	182758	W 334425	182485	MINERAIS METAUX COMMUNS
2874	LEAD ORES,CONCENTRATES	W 38366	9806	W 38220	12009	W 35076	12550	W 29417	11814	MINERAIS DE PLOMB
2875	ZINC ORES,CONCENTRATES	W 245539	119508	W 210031	105334	W 292812	151346	W 297973	151741	MINERAIS DE ZINC
2876	TIN ORES,CONCENTRATES	W 2896	8763	W 2533	7796	W 2440	8210	W 3769	12583	MINERAIS D'ETAIN
2879	OTH NONFER ORE,CONCNTRTE	W 1746	2737	W 5959	7416	W 4316	10397	W 2984	6194	MINERAIS D'AUTRES METAUX
28792	TUNGSTEN ORE,CONCENTRATE	W 677	1615	W 836	2407	W 1174	4847	W 1031	3471	MINERAIS DE TUNGSTENE
28799	OTH BASE MTL ORE,CON NES	W 1058	979	W 5119	4934	W 3142	5549	W 1953	2723	AUTRES MINERAIS
289	PREC MTAL ORES,WASTE NES	K 2745195	47759	K 2204298	48011	K 2627666	57374	K 3742531	52162	MINERAIS,DECHETS MET PREC
28901	PRECIOUS METAL ORES,CONC	K 2745195	47759	K 2204298	48011	K 2627666	57374	K 3742531	52162	MINERAIS METAUX PRECIEUX
3	MINERAL FUELS ETC		103045		107047		152875		142106	COMBUSTIBLES MINERAUX LUB
33	PETROLEUM AND PRODUCTS		12167		15144		60176		47346	PETROLE ET DERIVES
333	CRUDE PETROLEUM	W 68259	5787	W 64020	6577	W 338819	48109	W 218032	38494	HUILES BRUTES DE PETROLE
334	PETROLEUM PRODUCTS,REFIN	W 8780	6359	W 22578	8567	W 40293	12067	W 28592	8853	PRODUITS RAFFINES
3344	FUEL OILS,NES	W 8772	6347	W 22578	8567	W 34997	10757	W 28590	8849	FUEL OILS
341	*GAS,NATURAL AND MANUFCT	W 2784046	90621	W 2883107	91621	W 2729966	92407	W 2733123	94539	GAZ NATUREL,GAZ MANUFACT
3414	PETROLEUM GASES, GASEOUS	W 2781757	90203	W 2883107	91621	W 2729966	92407	W 2733123	94539	GAZ DE PETROLE GAZEUX
4	ANIMAL,VEGETABLE OIL,FAT		5858		21613		35559		40537	HUILES,GRAISSES ANIM,VEG
42	FIXED VEGETABLE OIL,FAT		5858		21561		35476		40500	HUILES VEGETALES FIXES
423	FIXED VEG OILS,SOFT	W 7792	5858	W 31780	21561	W 51455	35476	W 62153	40494	HUILES VEGET DOUCES FIXES
4232	SOYA BEAN OIL	W 7550	5658	W 30476	20451	W 50507	34679	W 61169	39484	HUILE DE SOJA
5	CHEMCLS,RELATED PROD NES		5770		6346		12888		16573	PRODUITS CHIMIQUES
51	ORGANIC CHEMICALS		3128		3527		3663		6273	PROD CHIMIQ ORGANIQUES
512	ALCOHOLS,PHENOLS ETC	W 11253	3026	W 10089	3491	W 10887	3642	W 22227	6273	PHENOLS,PHENOLS–ALCOOLS
5121	ACYCLIC ALCOHOLS,DERIVS	W 11253	3026	W 10089	3491	W 10887	3642	W 22227	6273	ALCOOLS ACYCLIQUES
51216	ETHYL ALC,DENATRD SPIRIT	W 11253	3026	W 10089	3491	W 10887	3642	W 22227	6273	ALCOOL ETHYLIQUE NON DENAT
52	INORGANIC CHEMICALS		2056		2010		7961		8629	PROD CHIM INORGANIQUES
522	INORG ELEMNTS,OXIDES,ETC	W 2874	1660	W 4192	1726	W 9098	7821	W 11484	8451	ELEMENTS INORGANIQUES
5225	INORGANIC BASES ETC NES					W 5497	6276	W 5508	6472	AUTRES BASES OXYDES METAL
52259	OTH OXIDES,BASES ETC NES					W 5497	6276	W 5508	6472	HYDRAZINE,HYDROXYLAMINE
6	BASIC MANUFACTURES		136822		157891		154103		144959	ART MANUFACTURES
61	LEATHER,DRESSED FUR,ETC		10728		8190		8180		7797	CUIRS,PELLETERIES
611	LEATHER	W 4010	10411	W 2189	8189	W 1820	7980	W 1660	7683	CUIRS,PEAUX PREPARES
6114	LEATHR BOVINE NES,EQUINE	W 3729	7752	W 1865	5120	W 1399	4432	W 1279	4065	CUIRS DE BOVINS
6118	LEATHER SPECIALLY FINSHD	W 262	2624	W 315	3043	W 291	3058	W 319	3130	CUIRS,PEAUX TANNES
63	WOOD,CORK MANUFACTRS NES		3678		7935		9713		12127	OUVRAGES LIEGE ET BOIS
634	VENEERS,PLYWOOD,ETC	W 1583	2506	W 1448	2180	W 949	1834	W 527	1416	PLACAGES,CONTRE–PLAQUES
635	WOOD MANUFACTURES NES	W 634	1172	W 3504	5755	W 3297	7878	W 4673	10711	ART MANUF EN BOIS NDA
6353	BUILDERS WOODWRK,PREFABS	W 628	1141	W 3404	5592	W 3264	7730	W 4497	10128	OUVRAGES DE MENUISERIE
64	PAPER,PAPERBOARD AND MFR		1402		1603		2490		3410	PAPIERS,CARTONS & OUVRAGES
65	TEXTILE YARN,FABRICS,ETC		3095		3550		1708		2846	FILS,TISSUS,ARTICLES TEXTILE
66	NONMETAL MINERAL MFS NES		1595		1899		2841		3365	ART MIN NON METALLIQUES
68	NON–FERROUS METALS		115422		133171		128022		113854	METAUX NON FERREUX
681	SILVER,PLATINUM,ETC		12921		14662		13477		11806	ARGENT ET PLATINE
6811	SILVER UNWKD,PARTLY WRKD		12921		14662		13477		11806	ARGENT BRUT MI–OUVRE

5. Special Exports F.O.B. by Commodities according to the S.I.T.C. (Rev. 2) in thousand U.S. Dollars
Exportations Spéciales F.O.B. par Produits d'après la C.T.C.I. (Rév. 2) en milliers de Dollars E.U.

SITC CTCI	COMMODITY	1993		1994		1995		1996		PRODUIT
		WEIGHT POIDS	VALUE VALEUR	WEIGHT POIDS	VALUE VALEUR	WEIGHT POIDS	VALUE VALEUR	WEIGHT POIDS	VALUE VALEUR	
68113	SILVER UNWROUGHT		12921		14662		13477		11806	ARGENT ET ALLIAGES BRUTS
687	TIN	W 18601	96004	W 20444	110032	W 18214	112926	W 16471	101223	ETAIN
6871	TIN,ALLOYS UNWROUGHT	W 18536	95708	W 20309	109631	W 18098	112386	W 16255	100226	ETAIN ET ALLIAGES BRUTS
689	NON–FER BASE METALS NES	W 5464	6432	W 6926	8389	W 464	1514	W 192	578	AUT METAUX NON FERREUX
6899	BASE METALS NES,CERMETS	W 5464	6432	W 6926	8389	W 464	1514	W 192	578	METAUX COMMUNS NDA
68999	BASE MTL NES UNWRT,WASTE	W 5464	6432	W 6926	8389	W 464	1514	W 192	578	AUT METAUX COM BRUTS NDA
7	MACHINES,TRANSPORT EQUIP		16266		28714		38134		76728	MACHINES MATERIEL TRANSPORT
72	MACHS FOR SPCL INDUSTRYS		6749		13045		12417		9284	MAC SPECIALES POUR INDUST
723	CIVIL ENGNEERG EQUIP ETC	W 703	6062	W 4683	11738	W 2252	8879	W 1084	6630	APPAREILS DE GENIE CIVIL
7234	CONST,MINING MACHNRY NES	W 375	1292	W 3805	9483	W 1835	6687	W 655	3878	MACH POUR LA CONST, MINES
72344	BORING,SINKING MACHINERY	W 171	843	W 3240	6584	W 604	1520	W 129	594	MACHINES DE FORAGE
7239	CONSTR ETC MACHY PTS NES	W 313	4748	W 816	1951	W 295	1695	W 361	2266	PIECES 723.41–723.46
78	ROAD VEHICLES		3794		3046		4083		2731	VEHICULES ROUTIERS
79	OTHR TRANSPORT EQUIPMENT		2480		8823		18531		59319	AUTRE MATERIEL TRANSPORT
792	AIRCRAFT ETC		2463	W 85	8789	W 102	18531	W 230	59310	APP NAVIGATION AERIENNE
7921	HELICOPTERS			W 11	4205			W 21	7994	HELICOPTERES
7924	AIRCRFT NES OVER 15000KG			W 60	4000	W 31	16675	W 195	48500	AERODYNES PLUS 15000 KG
8	MISC MANUFACTURED GOODS		94337		190360		117879		49602	ART MANUFACTURES DIVERS
821	*FURNITURE,PARTS THEREOF	W 1069	1147	W 1044	2446	W 876	3068	W 988	3393	MEUBLES ET PIECES
84	CLOTHING AND ACCESSORIES		12874		18333		17938		28543	VETEMENTS
844	UNDER GARMENTS NOT KNIT	W 129	1899	W 230	4307	W 215	4374	W 288	8475	VETEMENT DESSOUS MAT TEX
8441	— MENS SHIRTS	W 125	1836	W 230	4306	W 211	4311	W 277	8380	CHEMISES HOMMES MAT TEXT
84411	—— OF COTTON	W 116	1713	W 156	3303	W 198	4208	W 254	7199	CHEMISES HOMMES DE COTON
845	OUTERWEAR KNIT NONELASTC	W 1453	9717	W 3084	11237	W 1209	8071	W 646	12444	VET DESSOUS,ACCES BONNET
8451	— JERSEYS,PULLOVERS ETC	W 1367	7632	W 2280	10180	W 1149	6689	W 487	9479	CHANDAILS,PULL–OVERS ETC
846	UNDER GARMENTS KNITTED	W 54	659	W 157	1968	W 134	3574	W 164	2788	SOUS VETS DE BONNETERIE
87	PRECISION INSTRUMNTS NES		2885		1341		1428		1069	INSTRUM,APPAR SCIENT NDA
874	MEASURNG,CONTROLNG INSTR	W 119	2694	W 64	1329	W 34	1315	W 30	1052	INSTRUMENTS DE MESURE
89	MISC MANUFCTRD GOODS NES		73560		165419		92268		13285	ART MANUFACTURES DIVERS
897	GOLD,SILVER WARE,JEWELRY		72879		164314		90927		11400	BIJOUTERIE,ORFEVRERIE
8973	PREC JEWLRY,GLD–SILVWARE		72872		164279		90635		78	BIJOUX OR,ARGENT ORFEVRE
89731	PRECIOUS METAL JEWELLERY		72872		164148		90341		74	ART BIJOUTERIE,JOAILLER
8974	PREC MTL INDUS,LAB EQUIP						283		11297	AUT OUV METAUX PRECIEUX
9	GOODS NOT CLASSD BY KIND		72605		120978		133968		1684	ART TRANSACT NON CLASSES
971	*GOLD,NON MONETARY NES	K 6229	71612	K 10182	119088	K 10781	130802			OR NON MONETAIRE
97101	NONMON GLD UNWRT,SEMIMFD	K 6229	71612	K 10182	119088	K 10781	130802			OR,ALLIAGES D'OR BRUTS

1. HISTORICAL SERIES, 1961–1996 SPECIAL TRADE, IMPORTS C.I.F., EXPORTS F.O.B.
SERIES HISTORIQUES, 961–1996 COMMERCE PECIAL, IMPORTATIONS F.O.B., EXPORTATIONS F.O.B

YEAR ANNEE	VALUE IN MILLION U.S. DOLLARS VALEUR EN MILLION U.S. DOLLARS MERCHANDISE –MARCHANDISE IMPORTS	EXPORTS	GOLD –OR IMPORTS	EXPORTS	CONVERSION FACTORS FACTEURS DE CONVERSION CENTS E.U. PAR IMPORTS	EXPORTS	INDEX NUMBERS –INDICES QUANTUM IMPORTS	EXPORTS	UNIT VALUE VALEUR UNITAIRE IMPORTS	EXPORTS
1961	1460.00	1403.00					60	25	54	90
1962	1475.00	1214.00					60	25	55	78
1963	1487.00	1406.00					59	29	56	78
1964	1263.00	1430.00					52	25	54	94
1965	1096.00	1595.00	0.01				45	27	55	95
1966	1496.00	1741.00	0.01				60	31	56	91
1967	1667.00	1654.00	0.78				65	30	57	90
1968	2129.00	1881.00	3.17	0.01			80	34	59	89
1969	2265.00	2311.00	1.63				83	39	58	92
1970	2849.00	2739.00	4.59				48	23	25	39
1971	3701.00	2904.00	5.62				58	24	26	38
1972	4783.00	3990.00	7.68				71	30	28	42
1973	6999.00	6198.00	6.91	0.01			85	35	35	58
1974	14168.00	7951.00		0.11			116	36	54	74
1975	12210.00	8670.00					109	39	55	74
1976	13532.00	10128.00					108	40	57	85
1977	13069.00	12054.00					100	40	59	104
1978	14538.00	12527.00					105	45	63	95
1979	19372.00	15244.00					115	49	76	105
1980	24961.00	20132.00					115	61	97	111
1981	24079.00	23680.00					100	73	108	104
1982	21069.00	20213.00					91	66	104	98
1983	16801.00	21899.00					76	76	99	93
1984	13916.00	27005.00					73	93	94	95
1985	13153.00	25639.00					68	96	90	87
1986	15557.00	22349.01					92	79	70	93
1987	16581.00	26224.00					90	92	82	93
1988	16055.00	33494.00					80	109	89	102
1989	19875.01	34383.01					92	109	96	101
1990	22524.00	31414.00					100	100	111	100
1991	22950.00	31620.00					110	104	92	96
1992	23068.00	35793.01								86
1993	27740.00	38597.01								81
1994	35997.01	43558.00								106
1995	53783.01	46506.00								123
1996	56947.01	47762.00								124

2. IMPORTS BY BROAD ECONOMIC CATEGORY AND EXPORTS BY INDUSTRIAL ORIGIN. (PERCENTAGE OF TOTAL VALUE)
IMPORTATIONS PAR CATEGORIES ECONOMIQUES ET EXPORTATIONS PAR BRANCHE D'ACTIVITE.(EN POURCENTAGE DE LA VALEUR TOTALE)

IMPORTS – IMPORTATIONS

	1990	1991	1992	1993	1994	1995	1996
TOTAL IMPORTS–IMPORTATIONS TOTALES	100.	100.	100.	100.	100.	100.	
1 FOOD BEV–ALIMENTATION BOISSONS	8.7	10.4	8.8	8.6	10.0	10.0	
11 PRIMARY–PRODUITS DE BASE	4.3	5.3	5.0	2.6	3.8	3.6	
111 FOR INDUSTRY–POUR L'INDUSTRIE	0.8	2.7	3.0	0.9	1.4	1.2	
112 FOR HOUSEHOLDS–POUR LES MENAGES	3.4	2.6	2.0	1.7	2.3	2.4	
12 PROCESSED–PRODUITS ELABORES	4.4	5.1	3.8	6.0	6.2	6.4	
121 FOR INDUSTRY–POUR L'INDUSTRIE	0.8	1.2	1.1	1.0	1.2	1.0	
122 FOR HOUSEHOLDS–POUR LES MENAGES	3.6	3.9	2.7	5.0	5.0	5.4	
2 IND SUPPLIES–APPROV INDUSTRIELS	30.8	31.8	30.3	32.4	30.9	30.1	
21 PRIMARY–PRODUITS DE BASE	4.8	4.7	4.5	5.7	4.5	3.6	
22 PROCESSED–PRODUITS ELABORES	26.0	27.0	25.8	26.8	26.3	26.5	
3 FUELS–COMBUSTIBLES	26.8	23.6	24.5	20.5	14.7	12.0	
31 PRIMARY–PRODUITS DE BASE	25.2	20.6	20.0	12.2	9.7	7.3	
32 PROCESSED–PRODUITS ELABORES	1.5	3.0	4.4	8.3	5.0	4.7	
321 MOTOR SPIRIT–ESSENCE	0.2	0.5	1.7	4.1	2.2	2.6	
322 OTHER–AUTRES	1.3	2.5	2.7	4.2	2.8	2.1	
4 MACHINERY–EQUIPEMENT	23.3	22.6	23.8	23.6	26.0	25.5	
41 CAPITAL EQUIPMENT–MACHINES	16.8	16.8	18.1	18.0	20.6	19.9	
42 PARTS–PIECES ACCESSOIRES	6.5	5.8	5.8	5.6	5.4	5.6	
5 TRANSPORT–TRANSPORT	5.9	6.6	8.3	9.9	12.3	13.8	
51 PASSENGER CARS–AUTOMOBILES	0.1	0.5	1.3	2.6	4.3	5.8	
52 OTHER–AUTRES	0.8	1.4	1.7	1.2	1.7	2.1	
521 INDUSTRIAL–INDUSTRIELS	0.7	1.3	1.6	1.1	1.5	2.0	
522 NON INDUSTRIAL–NON INDUSTRIEL	0.0	0.1	0.1	0.2	0.2	0.1	
53 PARTS–PIECES ACCESSOIRES	5.1	4.7	5.4	6.0	6.3	5.8	
6 CONSUM GOODS–BIENS CONSOMMATION	4.4	4.9	4.2	4.9	6.1	8.5	
61 DURABLE–DURABLES	1.5	1.5	1.3	1.5	1.8	2.1	
62 SEMI DURABLE–SEMI DURABLES	1.4	1.6	1.2	1.6	2.1	3.5	
63 NON DURABLE–NON DURABLES	1.5	1.9	1.7	1.8	2.2	3.0	
7 GOODS NES–BIENS NDA	0.1	0.1	0.1	0.0	0.1	0.0	

EXPORTS – EXPORTATIONS

	1990	1991	1992	1993	1994	1995	1996
TOTAL EXPORTS–EXPORTATIONS TOTALES	100.	100.	100.	100.	100.	100.	100.
1 AGRICULTURE	10.8	10.6	9.3	9.1	11.6	9.6	9.8
2 MINING QUARRY–INDUS EXTRACTIVES	9.3	9.8	7.5	7.0	6.3	6.6	6.7
3 MANUFACTURING–IND MANUFACTUR	80.0	79.6	83.1	84.0	82.1	83.8	83.5
31 FOOD BEV TOBACCO–ALIM BOISS TAB	17.7	15.2	16.5	16.6	17.9	19.9	20.9
32 TEXTILES–INDUSTRIES TEXTILES	8.0	8.6	9.1	9.6	8.0	7.3	7.5
33 WOOD & PRODUCTS–BOIS & PRODUITS	1.1	1.2	1.3	1.9	2.2	2.1	2.1
34 PAPER & PRODUCTS–PAPIER & PRODT	4.2	4.2	4.4	4.4	4.4	6.1	4.3
35 CHEMICALS–INDUSTRIES CHIMIQUES	10.1	9.4	9.8	10.1	10.1	9.9	10.1
36 NON METAL MIN–MIN NON METAL	0.9	0.9	1.1	1.4	1.3	1.3	1.3
37 BASIC METAL–IND METAL BASE	16.1	17.9	16.1	14.7	13.1	13.4	12.5
38 METAL MANUF–MANUF METAL	20.4	20.8	23.6	24.2	23.7	22.0	22.9
39 OTH MANUF IND–AUTRES MANUF	1.5	1.4	1.2	1.1	1.4	1.7	1.7

3. TRADE BY PRINCIPAL COUNTRIES OF PURCHASE AND LAST CONSIGNMENT (VALUE IN THOUSAND U.S. DOLLARS)
ECHANGES SELON LES PRINCIPAUX PAYS D'ACHAT ET DE DERNIERE CONSIGNATION (VALEUR EN MILLIERS DE DOLLARS EU)

COUNTRIES–PAYS	SPECIAL IMPORTS C.I.F. IMPORTATIONS SPECIALES C.A.F				
	1992	1993	1994	1995	1996
World	22346268	27300226	35510426	53736718	
Africa	594716	1079184	994106	1459882	
Americas	10173055	12423992	16506119	25377775	
Northern America	5937381	7119512	9225359	14051575	
LAIA	3869634	4986168	6769586	10605668	
CACM	1559	7130	8359	11535	
Caribbean	241789	128926	257887	326201	
Rest of America	122692	182257	244929	382797	
As.ex F.USSR	5103733	5921389	6605025	9518674	
Eur.x F.USSR	6022036	7343743	10861463	16613325	
EU	5262622	6458886	9760432	14981721	
EFTA	565499	704394	901152	1326370	
East Europe	181774	172672	188303	293327	
Other Europe	9194	5919	7336	2310	
Former USSR	201977	240278	279483	305966	
Oceania	210275	280840	242913	329437	
USA/Etats–Unis d'Amer	5379480	6270423	8202790	12752111	
Argentina/Argentine	1832947	2816139	3828465	5749894	
Germany/Allemagne	2018546	2421966	3613655	5422733	
Japan/Japon	1260560	1663915	1937892	2726388	
Italy/Italie	876502	1004970	2066533	3159486	
Saudi Arabia	1653712	1666645	1416404	1266681	
France, Monac	631285	735582	932697	1411723	
Canada	546529	747159	894875	1219972	
Switz.Liecht	479377	593132	762085	1089874	
Chile/Chili	503607	470584	635455	1183319	
United Kingdom	434769	564666	780816	987610	
Uruguay	350222	439838	697212	999630	
Korea, Republic of	145705	355426	588442	1291437	
Netherlands/Pays--Bas	385189	452610	571332	822820	
Venezuela	345143	402025	580617	894863	
Iran (Islamic Rp. of)	1079726	338985	298695	254987	
Mexico/Mexique	379630	329704	360273	840596	
Belgium–Luxembourg	220711	305538	514852	772915	
Hong Kong	101532	269479	458538	907152	
Spain/Espagne	170937	258095	325959	818212	
Sweden/Suède	228845	240085	390397	600505	
Algeria/Algérie	340660	548923	278759	253473	
Paraguay	191377	282048	374588	530936	
Singapore/Singapour	112434	354101	312071	594587	
Kuwait/ Koweït	87534	321115	338915	299988	
Nigeria/Nigéria	32619	140945	246102	570620	
Australia/Australie	199893	266426	229938	271584	
China/Chine	57289	156981	196810	417928	
Panama	82595	127694	225194	353259	
Russian Federation	201977	185954	180442	184366	
So. Africa Customs Un	77555	122663	245444	296217	
Peru/Pérou	165380	132605	196150	218028	
Finland/Finlande	91990	121260	155258	234526	
Norway,SVD,JM	83439	108504	136640	227911	
Poland/Pologne	126093	118297	149947	158949	
Malaysia/Malaisie	37985	84017	119280	256153	
Denmark/Danemark	61957	89351	94007	186927	
Israel/Israël	69203	88565	122238	128078	
Austria/Autriche	55561	58885	98070	178585	
Portugal	37934	62619	91079	188925	
Netherlands Antilles	177060	60199	57641	70849	
Bermuda/Bermudes	11372	101930	127694	79474	
Ireland/Irlande	41060	64110	83037	119563	
Colombia/Colombie	61732	63928	66847	111787	
India/Inde	14419	65698	73293	137872	
United Arab Emirates	122742	70753	69560	23639	
Indonesia/Indonésie	11359	30611	82577	127233	
Thailand/Thaïlande	15215	30668	54415	116892	
Qatar	124019	47457	35964	96	
Greece/Grèce	7336	79150	42742	77190	

COUNTRIES–PAYS	SPECIAL EXPORTS F.O.B. EXPORTATIONS SPECIALES F.O.B.				
	1992	1993	1994	1995	1996
Monde	35975460	38700877	43557977	46505382	47746546
Afrique	1138577	1110040	1349611	1585822	1521506
Amériques	15633690	18274925	20099922	20040366	21475609
Amérique du Nord	7483751	8490617	9471414	9262083	9820809
ALAI	7592641	9144476	9745042	9974437	10927769
MCAC	207133	235552	241920	216381	161563
Caraïbes	273885	296733	529092	460090	435947
Autre Amérique	76279	107548	112453	127375	129521
Asie l'URSS exclus	7116012	7566820	8287011	9669735	9349002
Europe l'URSS exclus	11366977	10755327	12949366	13827796	14019216
UE	10868080	10201093	12202116	12911952	12882610
AELE	220608	274413	382088	504536	502599
Europe de l'Est	247275	232632	330244	360303	476365
Autre de l'Europe	6319	35840	11208	11771	9747
Ancienne URSS	126060	246768	231985	642873	580017
Océanie	236815	255574	291427	350441	296303
USA/Etats–Unis d'Amer	7081437	8030210	8968961	8799213	9312405
Argentina/Argentine	3041106	3658247	4135677	4041136	5170032
Netherlands/Pays–Bas	2339121	2488027	3077114	2917780	3548740
Japan/Japon	2311352	2313004	2586091	3101596	3047134
Germany/Allemagne	2073729	1823733	2048851	2158189	2082704
Italy/Italie	1597182	1312054	1646531	1713142	1530739
Belgium–Luxembourg	1174070	1130515	1355415	1610302	1431624
United Kingdom	1286694	1139587	1228783	1325572	1323659
Chile/Chili	922102	1110347	998944	1210470	1055274
Paraguay	543317	960646	1053622	1300733	1324582
France, Monac	844347	791429	900636	1038389	958866
China/Chine	460032	779395	822416	1203751	1113829
Mexico/Mexique	1113669	995359	1049973	496086	679346
Spain/Espagne	739072	675899	709386	876871	937495
Uruguay	514150	774844	731835	811060	810490
Korea, Republic of	571331	537629	634342	827455	838437
Canada	401489	455457	500533	460904	505768
Bolivia/Bolivie	332701	430594	469997	530083	531679
Venezuela	442292	392961	281641	480892	454419
Colombia/Colombie	347325	377264	400914	457200	431908
Saudi Arabia	455053	420887	357081	360110	409464
Hong Kong	311018	331119	376482	405146	432719
Thailand/Thaïlande	353710	289633	384108	419354	395600
Portugal	258595	270059	302030	412882	324270
Russian Federation	126060	228549	173341	569266	465741
Peru/Pérou	199574	273941	349691	438290	297969
Switz.Liecht	168352	218791	303521	388725	445531
Singapore/Singapour	203075	267132	308060	293665	333125
India/Inde	148699	124816	621181	319993	184916
Indonesia/Indonésie	136951	256938	218768	365919	290753
Iran (Islamic Rp. of)	336234	257850	184028	256271	184087
Nigeria/Nigéria	307798	239869	149295	243327	274540
Australia/Australie	206942	197719	251924	299142	257166
Philippines	182377	204918	217310	275129	322132
So. Africa Customs Un	177346	194653	226757	261948	296995
Malaysia/Malaisie	220114	243721	210962	244264	233236
Egypt/Egypte	156686	175692	179383	369666	224371
Turkey/Turquie	216014	209344	149426	197590	237108
Ecuador/Equateur	136405	170273	272749	208488	172071
Denmark/Danemark	82813	183417	231297	216831	167895
Greece/Grèce	142792	97742	193196	217046	188512
Sweden/Suède	114486	108289	173090	159473	146378
Morocco/Maroc	116556	114994	116441	175057	162103
United Arab Emirates	85916	93591	115539	109078	171701
Poland/Pologne	39885	106037	109014	86440	201273
Hungary/Hongrie	119241	68921	96705	86683	91765
Costa Rica	81270	98850	110629	84868	67012
Ireland/Irlande	113023	59750	118722	66146	75198
Panama	56203	85823	86079	91993	105262
Finland/Finlande	47096	68200	120391	107101	79888

(VALUE AS PERCENTAGE OF WORLD TOTAL)(VALEURS EN POURCENTAGE DU TOTAL MONDIAL)

	1987	1988	1989	1990	1991	1992	1993	1994	1995	1996
Africa	3.7	4.7	3.1	2.9	4.0	2.7	4.0	2.8	2.7	
Americas	35.1	36.1	41.1	40.0	45.0	45.5	45.5	46.5	47.2	
Northern America	23.1	23.3	23.0	22.2	26.1	26.6	26.1	26.0	26.1	
LAIA	11.4	12.2	17.5	16.9	17.2	17.3	18.3	19.1	19.7	
CACM	0.0	0.0	0.0	0.0	0.0	0.0	0.0	0.0	0.0	
Caribbean	0.4	0.3	0.3	0.7	1.0	1.1	0.5	0.7	0.6	
Rest of America	0.2	0.3	0.2	0.1	0.7	0.5	0.7	0.7	0.7	
As.ex F.USSR	31.6	29.9	28.6	30.2	22.2	22.8	21.7	18.6	17.7	
Eur.x F.USSR	28.0	28.3	26.2	25.7	27.4	26.9	26.9	30.6	30.9	
EU	23.4	23.4	21.6	21.7	23.5	23.6	23.7	27.5	27.9	
EFTA	2.4	2.7	2.8	2.3	2.7	2.5	2.6	2.5	2.5	
East Europe	2.3	2.2	1.7	1.7	1.1	0.8	0.6	0.5	0.5	
Other Europe	0.0	0.1	0.1	0.1	0.0	0.0	0.0	0.0	0.0	
Former USSR	0.7	0.3	0.4	0.6	0.6	0.9	0.9	0.8	0.6	
Oceania	0.9	0.7	0.5	0.6	0.7	0.9	1.0	0.7	0.6	
USA/Etats–Unis d'Amer	20.1	20.1	20.3	20.1	23.5	24.1	23.0	23.1	23.7	
Argentina/Argentine	3.7	4.6	6.5	6.7	7.6	8.2	10.3	10.8	10.7	
Germany/Allemagne	9.1	9.4	8.0	8.2	8.8	9.0	8.9	10.2	10.1	
Japan/Japon	6.1	7.1	7.6	7.2	5.9	5.6	6.1	5.5	5.1	
Italy/Italie	2.3	2.0	2.5	3.3	3.7	3.9	3.7	5.8	5.9	
Saudi Arabia	5.6	6.8	3.7	7.4	6.4	7.4	6.1	4.0	2.4	
France, Monac	4.1	3.9	3.0	2.8	2.8	2.8	2.7	2.6	2.6	
Canada	3.0	3.1	2.7	2.2	2.5	2.4	2.7	2.5	2.3	
Switz.Liecht	1.9	2.2	2.1	1.8	2.3	2.1	2.2	2.1	2.0	
Chile/Chili	2.3	2.3	2.7	2.3	2.3	2.3	1.7	1.8	2.2	

	1987	1988	1989	1990	1991	1992	1993	1994	1995	1996
Afrique	4.1	3.8	3.8	3.2	3.3	3.2	2.9	3.1	3.4	3.2
Amériques	43.1	40.4	39.6	38.1	38.5	43.5	47.2	46.1	43.1	45.0
Amérique du Nord	29.6	27.4	25.0	26.3	21.7	20.8	21.9	21.7	19.9	20.6
ALAI	11.5	11.1	11.0	10.2	15.6	21.1	23.6	22.4	21.4	22.9
MCAC	0.5	0.5	0.9	0.4	0.4	0.6	0.6	0.6	0.5	0.3
Caraïbes	0.8	1.0	2.4	1.1	0.7	0.8	0.8	1.2	1.0	0.9
Autre Amérique	0.7	0.3	0.4	0.2	0.2	0.2	0.3	0.3	0.3	0.3
Asie l'URSS exclus	16.5	18.8	20.0	20.7	22.0	19.8	19.6	19.0	20.8	19.6
Europe l'URSS exclus	32.9	34.4	33.8	35.4	34.0	31.6	27.8	29.7	29.7	29.4
UE	27.1	29.8	30.4	32.4	32.1	30.2	26.4	28.0	27.8	27.0
AELE	1.8	1.0	1.0	1.0	0.7	0.6	0.7	0.9	1.1	1.1
Europe de l'Est	3.4	2.1	2.1	1.6	0.9	0.7	0.6	0.8	0.8	1.0
Autre de l'Europe	0.6	1.4	0.4	0.4	0.3	0.0	0.1	0.0	0.0	0.0
Ancienne URSS	1.1	0.5	0.6	0.7	0.3	0.4	0.6	0.5	1.4	1.2
Océanie	1.5	1.4	1.2	0.7	0.8	0.7	0.7	0.7	0.8	0.6
USA/Etats–Unis d'Amer	27.4	24.9	22.5	24.6	20.2	19.7	20.7	20.6	18.9	19.5
Argentina/Argentine	2.3	2.2	1.7	2.1	4.7	8.5	9.5	9.5	8.7	10.8
Netherlands/Pays–Bas	5.9	7.5	7.6	7.9	6.8	6.5	6.4	7.1	6.3	7.4
Japan/Japon	6.1	6.7	7.0	7.5	8.1	6.4	6.0	5.9	6.7	6.4
Germany/Allemagne	4.4	4.3	4.5	5.7	6.8	5.8	4.7	4.7	4.6	4.4
Italy/Italie	4.8	4.2	3.6	5.1	4.3	4.4	3.4	3.8	3.7	3.2
Belgium–Luxembourg	2.5	2.7	2.9	3.1	3.4	3.3	2.9	3.1	3.5	3.0
United Kingdom	2.7	3.1	2.9	3.0	3.3	3.6	2.9	2.8	2.9	2.8
Chile/Chili	1.6	1.8	2.0	1.5	2.1	2.6	2.9	2.3	2.6	2.2
Paraguay	1.3	1.0	1.2	1.2	1.6	1.5	2.5	2.4	2.8	2.8

4. Special Imports C.I.F. by Commodities according to the S.I.T.C. (Rev. 2) in thousand U.S. Dollars
Importations Spéciales C.A.F. par Produits d'après la C.T.C.I. (Rév. 2) en milliers de Dollars E.U.

SITC CTCI	COMMODITY	1992 WEIGHT POIDS	1992 VALUE VALEUR	1993 WEIGHT POIDS	1993 VALUE VALEUR	1994 WEIGHT POIDS	1994 VALUE VALEUR	1995 WEIGHT POIDS	1995 VALUE VALEUR	PRODUIT
	ALL COMMODITIES		22346268		27300226		35510426		53736718	TOUS PRODUITS
0	FOOD AND LIVE ANIMALS		1801203		2323302		3197994		4795417	ALIMENTS,ANIMAUX VIVANTS
001	*LIVE ANIMALS FOR FOOD	W 6754	30313	W 24301	45036	W 113007	124750	W 135341	154547	ANIMAUX VIVANTS
0011	BOVINE SPECIES,LIVE	W 6377	14457	W 20870	29581	W 108077	108135	W 132760	130189	ESPECE BOVINE
01	MEAT AND PREPARATIONS		133716		53493		146590		231448	VIANDES ET PREPARATIONS
011	MEAT FRESH,CHILLD,FROZEN	W 109426	132834	W 45241	53080	W 103486	144680	W 148427	226721	VIANDES FRAICHES,REF,CONGE
0111	BOVINE MEAT FRESH,FROZEN	W 92255	120831	W 24580	36027	W 76602	116774	W 111148	178661	VIANDES BOVIN FRAI,REF
01111	BOVINE MEAT WITH BONE IN	W 64841	75020	W 8299	8071	W 44828	52780	W 60327	70717	VIANDES BOVIN NON DESOSS
02	DAIRY PRODCTS,BIRDS'EGGS		79382		159810		273725		647967	PRODUITS LAITIERS,OEUFS
022	MILK AND CREAM	W 35342	59253	W 70646	116149	W 106591	157453	W 350755	433107	LAIT ET CREME
0224	MILK,CREAM PRESERVED ETC	W 31628	57909	W 61867	110981	W 94668	151309	W 291555	400478	LAIT,CREME CONS,CONC
02243	MILK DRY,OVER 1.5% FAT	W 19926	38926	W 28835	56649	W 55076	91208	W 216913	276073	LAIT POUDRE SUP 1.5%
024	CHEESE AND CURD	W 2511	8133	W 8217	25115	W 31650	90616	W 89345	168759	FROMAGE ET CAILLEBOTTE
03	FISH AND PREPARATIONS		132250		199971		260965		440076	POISSONS ET PREPARATIONS
034	FISH,FRESH,CHILLED,FROZN	W 71252	52814	W 130184	90492	W 132455	117270	W 174500	192798	POISSON FRAIS, REFRIG,CONG
035	FISH SALTED,DRIED,SMOKED	W 11131	69401	W 16665	93557	W 22860	123588	W 31341	197918	POISSON SECHE,SALE,FUME
04	CEREALS AND PREPARATIONS		1040888		1400877		1604421		1927614	CEREALES ET PRODUITS
041	WHEAT ETC UNMILLED	W 2770248	390313	W 5732	783	W 32412	4332	W 34789	6160	FROMENT,EPEAUTRE
0411	DURUM WHEAT UNMILLED	W 2770245	390311	W 5732	783	W 25161	3499			FROMENT DUR NON MOULU
042	RICE	W 519185	156111	W 779235	214999	W 1077981	323815	W 995686	293560	RIZ
0422	RICE SEMI-MILLED,MILLED	W 372962	121065	W 525736	156356	W 746727	245050	W 562824	214577	RIZ POLI,GLACE INCL BRISURES
04221	RICE MILLED UNBROKEN	W 334151	113299	W 474096	146474	W 711285	237823	W 551713	212185	RIZ POLI,GLACE EXCL BRISURES
044	MAIZE UNMILLED	W 517483	72057	W 1329980	176009	W 1409985	199083	W 1309332	180818	MAIS NON MOULU
048	CEREAL ETC PREPARATIONS	W 2119751	372942	W 6095333	959347	W 6604925	995046	W 6857100	1340644	PREPTNS A BASE CEREALES
0481	PREPD BREAKFAST FOOD ETC	W 1686545	231944	W 5691269	833000	W 6109729	859015	W 6131439	1034053	CEREALES TRAVAILLEES
04811	CEREAL FLAKED,ROLLED,ETC	W 1686531	231877	W 5691225	832861	W 6109434	858428	W 6116319	1027361	GRAINS GERMES DE CEREALES
0482	MALT INCLUDING FLOUR	W 424986	131052	W 391816	110958	W 478020	114892	W 688226	230257	MALT MEME TORREFIE
05	VEGETABLES AND FRUIT		312776		371685		647202		1000959	LEGUMES ET FRUITS
054	VEG ETC FRSH,SMPLY PRSVD	W 328192	178138	W 306340	206537	W 755959	348360	W 1430394	435779	LEGUMES FRAIS,CONG,SECS
0542	LEGUMINOUS VEGETBLES DRY	W 123344	44155	W 81376	36393	W 258599	118110	W 205941	98450	LEGUMES A COSSE SECS
0546	VEGETABLES SIMPLY PRESVD	W 67836	77103	W 84995	91219	W 95327	107262	W 159973	165644	LEGUMES CONG,CONSER
057	FRUIT,NUTS,FRESH,DRIED	W 141902	119340	W 150646	138517	W 254283	223939	W 581066	414721	FRUITS FRAIS OU SECS
0579	FRUIT FRESH OR DRIED NES	W 66500	53308	W 74793	66239	W 106784	95116	W 227695	204248	FRUITS FRAIS,SECS NDA
07	COFFEE,TEA,COCOA,SPICES		14791		20980		40696		172236	CAFE,THE,CACAO,EPICES
1	BEVERAGES AND TOBACCO		77883		82723		141077		356911	BOISSONS ET TABACS
11	BEVERAGES		37024		50486		105597		295681	BOISSONS
112	ALCOHOLIC BEVERAGES	W 20533	36728	W 29064	49906	W 68383	96618	W 291371	208220	BOISSONS ALCOOLIQUES
2	CRUDE MATERLS,EXCL FUELS		1313392		1785149		2003628		2501234	MAT BRUTES NON COMESTIBLES
22	OIL SEEDS,OLEAGINOUS FRT		118940		38051		196738		208677	GRAINES,FRUITS OLEAGINEUX
222	SEEDS FOR'SOFT'FIXED OIL	W 478645	112786	W 135159	33870	W 813186	194150	W 887152	206317	GRAINES HUILES FIXES
2222	SOYA BEANS	W 472884	110462	W 127866	29975	W 801784	187372	W 878664	200764	FEVES DE SOJA
23	RUBBER, CRUDE		175135		203758		249503		345264	CAOUTCHOUC BRUT
232	NATURAL RUBBER,GUMS	W 88439	87364	W 105014	92665	W 99900	112553	W 110155	190756	LATEX CAOUTCHOUC NATUREL
233	RUBBER,SYNTHTIC,RECLAIMD	W 36939	87770	W 49040	111093	W 74007	136950	W 91034	154508	LATEX CAOUTCH SYNTH REGEN
2331	SYNTHETIC RUBBER ETC	W 36921	87758	W 49021	111084	W 73988	136942	W 91016	154497	LATEX CAOUTCH SYNTHETIQUE
251	*PULP AND WASTE PAPER	W 102730	55495	W 172880	76404	W 151519	83330	W 237306	189814	PATES A PAPIER,DECHETS
26	TEXTILE FIBRES AND WASTE		278632		779576		696589		747637	FIBRES TEXTILES
263	COTTON	W 167831	219877	W 504825	689131	W 393103	593022	W 294844	575768	COTON
2631	RAW COTTON,EXCL LINTERS	W 165113	218482	W 499034	686545	W 365729	584944	W 279027	563563	COTON EN MASSE
27	CRUDE FERTLZR,MINRLS NES		127816		139814		166554		214677	ENGRAIS MINERAUX BRUTS
28	METALLIFEROUS ORES,SCRAP		466973		433760		491568		628245	MINERAIS METAL,DECHETS
287	BASE METAL ORES,CONC NES	W 1513825	429473	W 1467267	403041	W 1290190	438517		571333	MINERAIS METAUX COMMUNS
2871	CPR ORE ETC,CEMENT COPPR	W 414517	219564	W 403490	196566	W 433968	233894	W 394034	346189	MINERAIS DE CUIVRE,MATTES
28711	COPPER ORES,EXCL MATTE	W 414517	219564	W 403490	196566	W 433968	233894	W 394034	346189	MINERAIS DE CUIVRE
2873	ALUMINIUM ORES,ALUMINA	W 911239	134427	W 851287	145338	W 688425	136619	W 444200	131216	MINERAIS D'ALUMINIUM
28732	ALUMINA(ALUMINIUM OXIDE)	W 728498	127919	W 851176	145316	W 683293	136017	W 443974	131150	ALUMINE (OXYDE ALUMINIUM)
3	MINERAL FUELS ETC		5531230		5672156		5294709		6519019	COMBUSTIBLES MINERAUX LUB
32	COAL,COKE AND BRIQUETTES		810164		761257		783594		941215	HOUILLES,COKES,BRIQUETTES
322	COAL,LIGNITE AND PEAT	MW 11942	669226	MW 12601	648479	MW 12379	618640	MW 12542	722596	HOUILLES,LIGNITES,TOURBE
3222	OTH COAL,NOT AGGLOMERATD	MW 11474	642899	MW 12225	632454	MW 11475	576494	MW 12082	696807	AUTRES HOUILLES
323	BRIQUETS,COKE,SEMI-COKE	W 1419342	140939	W 1331386	112778	W 1731627	164954	W 1830747	218619	BRIQUETTES
3232	COKE,SEMI-COKE,RTRT CRBN	W 1419342	140939	W 1331386	112778	W 1731627	164954	W 1830747	218619	COKES ET SEMI-COKES
33	PETROLEUM AND PRODUCTS		4404607		4642586		4250817		5140922	PETROLE ET DERIVES
333	CRUDE PETROLEUM	MW 26268	3491956	MW 22551	2414492	MW 23098	2562669	MW 22483	2756383	HUILES BRUTES DE PETROLE
334	PETROLEUM PRODUCTS,REFIN	W 5365091	845104	MW 14795	2158508	MW 12382	1616394	MW 11790	2298908	PRODUITS RAFFINES
3341	GASOLINE,OTH LIGHT OILS	W 2014919	374313	W 6844563	1116693	W 5580171	783851	W 6615998	1386193	ESSENCES POUR MOTEURS
33419	OTH LIGHT PETROLEUM OILS	W 2009194	373226	W 6812147	1110663	W 5542389	777763	W 5988132	1259651	AUTRES HUILES LEGERES
3343	GAS OILS	W 1856707	348544	W 3695880	631699	W 2824829	432146	W 3655856	621914	GAS OILS
3344	FUEL OILS,NES	W 535636	64785	W 3982233	332631	W 3523069	293637	W 804353	91985	FUEL OILS
335	RESIDUAL PETRLM PROD NES		67546	W 367450	69587	W 392212	71754	W 895520	85630	PRODUITS RESIDUELS NDA
341	*GAS,NATURAL AND MANUFCT	W 1680153	316458	W 1576729	268312	W 1592270	260265	W 2129834	436875	GAZ NATUREL,GAZ MANUFACT
3413	PETROLM GASES,LIQUEFIED	W 1675362	315428	W 1576726	268294	W 1576083	257555	W 2084647	428174	GAZ DE PETROLE LIQUEFIE
34131	LIQUEFIED PROPANE,BUTANE	W 1451425	267524	W 1008818	172433	W 1313057	213944	W 1818732	369461	PROPANE,BUTANE LIQUEFIES
34139	OTH HYDROCARBON GAS LQFD	W 223938	47904	W 567908	95861	W 263026	43611	W 265915	58713	HYDROCARBURES GAZEUX NDA
4	ANIMAL,VEGETABLE OIL,FAT		137860		212324		346947		396350	HUILES,GRAISSES ANIM,VEG
42	FIXED VEGETABLE OIL,FAT		108409		164543		284892		318234	HUILES VEGETALES FIXES
423	FIXED VEG OILS,SOFT	W 117228	82706	W 164127	113024	W 296125	223543		251105	HUILES VEGET DOUCES FIXES
4232	SOYA BEAN OIL	W 97443	43666	W 136879	64290	W 254522	155998	W 204520	136077	HUILE DE SOJA
5	CHEMCLS,RELATED PROD NES		3478321		4359696		5803891		8042305	PRODUITS CHIMIQUES
51	ORGANIC CHEMICALS		1331310		1695360		2409863		3227717	PROD CHIMIQ ORGANIQUES
511	HYDROCARBONS NES,DERIVS	W 187758	108336	W 200976	117018	W 193432	132341	W 287255	231449	HYDROCARBURES NDA
512	ALCOHOLS,PHENOLS ETC	W 646238	185114	W 904574	285612	W 1580605	661607	W 1801334	814358	PHENOLS,PHENOLS-ALCOOLS
5121	ACYCLIC ALCOHOLS,DERIVS	W 625186	140241	W 878461	228748	W 1549891	596698	W 1774907	738119	ALCOOLS ACYCLIQUES
51211	METHYL ALCOHOL(METHANOL)	W 417334	50032	W 403577	47082	W 493009	149632	W 573674	148153	ALCOOLS METHYLIQUES
51216	ETHYL ALC,DENATRD SPIRIT	W 191093	65879	W 429117	144446	W 1003697	400223	W 1130649	496581	ALCOOL ETHYLIQUE NON DENAT
513	CARBOXYLIC ACIDS ETC	W 92249	137816	W 125432	180166	W 176138	209766	W 308623	362442	ACIDES CARBOXYLIQUES
5137	MONOACIDS AND DERIVATIVS	W 68216	92452	W 79791	111125	W 124100	133122	W 156144	229040	ACIDES MONOCARBOXYLIQUES
51379	OTH MONOACIDS ETC,DERIVS	W 51495	73702	W 42819	81219	W 48978	86986	W 65404	146019	AUTRES MONOCARBOXYLIQUES
514	NITROGEN-FNCTN COMPOUNDS	W 85347	448674	W 109369	549473	W 119827	645186	W 163158	778271	COMPOSES FONCT AZOTEES
5145	AMINE-FUNCTION COMPOUNDS	W 19672	65287	W 22694	83329	W 25920	87082	W 54242	100438	COMPOSES FONCTION AMINE
5147	AMIDE-FNCT CMPD,EXC UREA	W 5770	74546	W 6372	76301	W 9113	103441	W 10165	126400	COMPOSES CARBOXYAMIDE
5148	OTH NITROGN-FNCTN CMPNDS	W 48119	245178	W 63988	314768	W 65725	360876	W 75979	448069	AUTRES COMPOSES AZOTES
51482	IMIDE-,IMIDE-FNCT CMPNDS	W 14585	146886	W 14846	179402	W 21123	221673	W 23167	269566	COMPOSES A FONCTION IMIDE
515	ORG-INORG COMPOUNDS ETC	W 36274	354329	W 46593	433111	W 58519	609232	W 77770	819518	COMPOSES ORGANO-MINERAUX
5154	ORGANO-SULPHUR CMPNDS	W 18797	74156	W 23608	87705	W 27644	114054	W 36470	152710	THIOCOMPOSES ORGANIQUES
5156	HETEROCYCLIC CMPDS ETC	W 11580	215257	W 15227	257385	W 18965	368581	W 22458	470498	COMPOSES HETEROCYCLIQUES
51569	OTH HETEROCYC CMPDS,ETC	W 11226	209318	W 12633	250538	W 15576	358988	W 17256	454478	AUT COMP HETEROCYCLIQUES
516	OTHER ORGANIC CHEMICALS		97041		129980		151731		221679	AUTRES PROD ORGANIQUES
52	INORGANIC CHEMICALS		320176		320215		417209		578123	PROD CHIM INORGANIQUES
522	INORG ELEMNTS,OXIDES,ETC	W 709997	173880	W 896169	161761	W 1023471	236285	W 1040104	313475	ELEMENTS INORGANIQUES
5222	INORGANIC ACIDS ETC	W 506364	91423	W 664652	83867	W 643744	109331	W 618553	129162	ACIDES INORGANIQUES

4. Special Imports C.I.F. by Commodities according to the S.I.T.C. (Rev. 2) in thousand U.S. Dollars
Importations Spéciales C.A.F. par Produits d'après la C.T.C.I. (Rév. 2) en milliers de Dollars E.U.

SITC CTCI	COMMODITY	1992 WEIGHT POIDS	1992 VALUE VALEUR	1993 WEIGHT POIDS	1993 VALUE VALEUR	1994 WEIGHT POIDS	1994 VALUE VALEUR	1995 WEIGHT POIDS	1995 VALUE VALEUR	PRODUIT
52224	PHOSPHORIC ACIDS ETC	W 414385	74134	W 401033	61513	W 420259	78789	W 397855	89785	ACIDES PHOSPHORIQUES
523	OTHR INORG CHEMICALS ETC	W 387739	134772	W 476123	147133	W 545744	169017	W 633229	245877	AUT PRODUITS CHIMIQUES INORG
53	DYES,TANNING,COLOUR PROD		187343		256608		289971		447515	PROD TEINTURE,COLORANTS
531	SYNT DYE,NAT INDGO,LAKES	W 5505	84702	W 9208	129581	W 8626	124375	W 12588	155326	MAT COLOR ORGAN,LAQUES
5311	SYNTHIC ORGNIC DYESTUFFS	W 4725	75861	W 8058	117392	W 8115	117403	W 11562	144010	MAT COLOR ORGAN SYNTHET
533	PIGMENTS,PAINTS,ETC	W 41346	96295	W 52391	119154	W 71121	157700	W 116125	279172	PIGMENTS,PEINTURES,VERNIS
541	*MEDICINAL,PHARM PRODUCT		381827		494356	MK 9465	734601		978864	PROD MEDICINAUX PHARMACEUT
5413	ANTIBIOTICS IN BULK	K 1375652	75128	K 2673112	98839	K 2608147	126262	K 3688480	168378	ANTIBIOTIQUES NDA
5416	GLYCOSIDES,GLANDS,SERA	K 339754	74111	K 338632	85215	K 377042	159676	K 620611	149907	HETEROSIDES
54164	ANTISERA,MICROB VACCINES	K 255004	55434	K 203221	58146	K 258125	123935	K 321422	90221	SERUMS,VACCINS
5417	MEDICAMENTS	K 753772	115913	K 1028403	153578	K 1835088	267674	K 5179929	397282	MEDICAMENTS
54179	— CONTNG OTH SUBSTANCES	K 557902	74826	K 617594	94263	K 955891	148118	K 3688490	224833	MED CONT AUT SUBSTANCES
55	PERFUME,CLEANING ETC PRD		61378		113197		144247		243660	PROD POUR PARFUM,TOILETTE
562	*FERTILIZERS,MANUFACTURE		510996	W 4931979	583148	W 5434972	711461	W 4658660	729913	ENGRAIS MANUFACTURES
5621	CHEM NITROGENOUS FERTLZR	W 942679	84219	W 1318594	122664	W 1378541	151233	W 1260981	167295	ENGRAIS AZOTES
5623	CHEM POTASSIC FERTILIZER	W 2174839	312824	W 2580251	320573	W 2792178	335856	W 2534869	383128	ENGRAIS POTASSIQUES
56231	POTASSIUM CHLORIDE	W 2117161	299552	W 2533703	309742	W 2752089	326861	W 2484865	371304	CHLORURE DE POTASSIUM
5629	FERTILIZERS NES	W 307225	79142	W 672686	101506	W 822842	162080	W 568433	133885	ENGRAIS NDA
56292	NITROG–PHOS FERTILZR NES	W 189772	55392	W 588496	85179	W 726216	143058	W 464475	111593	ENGRAIS NDA CONT N P
58	PLASTIC MATERIALS ETC		402442		574573		672325		1285571	MAT PLAST ARTIFICIELLES
582	PROD OF CONDENSATION ETC	W 60161	160237	W 90429	229171	W 114050	275932	W 211120	489076	PROD CONDENS,POLYCOND
5823	ALKYDS,OTHER POLYESTERS	W 25330	61090	W 42518	94734	W 50182	107394	W 126220	276792	ALKYDES ET AUT POLYESTERS
58231	— IN PRIMARY FORMS	W 21521	38038	W 36834	62450	W 45111	77202	W 120173	241640	SOUS FORMES PRIMAIRES
583	POLYMERIZATION ETC PRODS	W 134431	220567	W 218762	315181	W 227685	360742	W 539998	747821	PROD POLYMERISATION
5839	OTH POLYMRZTION ETC PROD	W 25012	86137	W 31204	110238	W 31951	133389	W 48211	193455	AUT PROD POLYMER COPOLYM
59	CHEMICAL MATERIALS NES		279906		319741		421516		549017	MAT PROD CHIMIQUES NDA
598	MISCEL CHEM PRODUCTS NES	W 68994	197982	W 90341	246146	W 108172	299397	W 141716	378131	PROD DIV INDUST CHIM NDA
5989	CHEM PRODUCTS,PREPS NES	W 37082	135321	W 49321	172209	W 62788	214194	W 80518	283922	PROD PREP CHIMIQUES NDA
59899	OTH CHEM PRODS,PREPS,NES	W 22316	87619	W 29227	118699	W 38229	152455	W 42013	204489	AUT PRODUITS CHIMIQUES NDA
6	BASIC MANUFACTURES		1946551		2408870		3176037		6169620	ART MANUFACTURES
61	LEATHER,DRESSED FUR,ETC		168127		209431		200545		188321	CUIRS,PELLETERIES
611	LEATHER	W 11128	158538	W 20608	197027	W 16724	183992	W 22974	171703	CUIRS,PEAUX PREPARES
6114	LEATHR BOVINE NES,EQUINE	W 9262	124283	W 17746	157771	W 13837	146207	W 19855	143584	CUIRS DE BOVINS
62	RUBBER MANUFACTURES NES		126287		183536		322930		802210	CAOUTCHOUC MANUFACTURE
625	RUBBER TYRES, TUBES ETC	W 12113	27091	W 27967	58927	W 67747	131158	W 203868	285434	PNEUS CAOUTCHOUC VULCANISE
628	RUBBER ARTICLES NES	W 2324	66335	W 2987	77830	W 5005	127182	W 27480	428785	OUVRAGES CAOUTCHOUC NDA
6289	OTH RUBBER ARTICLES NES	W 1337	53628	W 2219	65428	W 3384	107704	W 6570	398507	AUT OUVR CAOUTCHOUC NDA
62898	UNHARD RUBBER PRODS NES	W 1320	53014	W 2200	64596	W 3369	106854	W 6471	397726	OUV CAOUT VULC NON DURCI
64	PAPER,PAPERBOARD AND MFR		254001		312855		433817		1003513	PAPIERS,CARTONS & OUVRAGES
641	PAPER AND PAPERBOARD	W 218361	213544	W 309616	276653	W 467306	388235	W 848666	874027	PAPIERS ET CARTONS
6411	NEWSPRINT	W 104915	60323	W 151961	84692	W 287588	155766	W 377537	398771	PAPIER JOURNAL
6412	PRINTG,WRITING PAPER NES	W 41819	47891	W 56318	61524	W 70934	75465	W 162340	217096	PAPIERS POUR L'IMPRESSION
64122	— COATED,IMPREGNATD ETC	W 41559	46898	W 56155	60610	W 70807	74604	W 161654	214980	PAPIERS IMPRESSION COUCHES
65	TEXTILE YARN,FABRICS,ETC		264779		443969		629824		1371752	FILS,TISSUS,ARTICLES TEXTILE
651	TEXTILE YARN	W 18594	128871	W 37888	215496	W 44949	212072	W 386450	482461	FILS TEXTILES
6514	SYN FIB YRN,BULK,MONOFIL	W 9548	73323	W 17237	119273	W 22752	116421	W 136841	287646	FILS CONT 85% FIB TEXT SYNTH
653	WOVN MAN–MADE FIB FABRIC	W 3342	26694	W 10830	75523	W 32289	197923	W 85647	419334	TISSUS FIBRES SYNTH,ARTIF
6531	CONT SYNT WEAVES NONPILE	W 2286	15330	W 6786	42941	W 17020	103134	W 48967	203671	TISSUS FIBRES SYNTH CONTINUE
65315	CONT SYN TXTL FABRIC NES	W 2166	14697	W 6179	40931	W 15848	99111	W 45427	188396	TIS PLUS 85% TEXT SYNT CONT
66	NONMETAL MINERAL MFS NES		175226		209108		296039		483419	ART MIN NON METALLIQUES
67	IRON AND STEEL		268835		261006		284417		503019	FER ET ACIER
674	IRN,STL UNIV,PLATE,SHEET	W 87291	110500	W 127900	136287	W 80259	115569	W 153438	232138	LARGES PLATS,TOLES
68	NON–FERROUS METALS		413881		433303		546005		996282	METAUX NON FERREUX
682	COPPER EXC CEMENT COPPER	W 89971	234661	W 90175	211850	W 97673	255397	W 130609	456132	CUIVRE
6821	COPPER NES,ALLOYS,UNWRT	W 80539	194813	W 67428	140925	W 67313	153458	W 91814	288699	CUIVRE BRUT
68212	COPPER REFINED,UNWROUGHT	W 80537	194767	W 67419	140806	W 64330	144615	W 90805	285302	CUIVRE AFFINE BRUT
6822	COPPER,ALLOYS WORKED	W 9432	39847	W 22747	70925	W 30360	101939	W 38795	167433	CUIVRE,ALLIAGES OUVRES
684	ALUMINIUM	W 17785	67956	W 28560	89923	W 43826	125130	W 81091	274830	ALUMINIUM
6842	ALUMINIUM,ALLOYS WORKED	W 16470	65362	W 22067	81462	W 36535	113933	W 65841	241604	ALUMINIUM,ALLIAGES OUVRE
69	METAL MANUFACTURES NES		260279		342893		446045		782738	ART MANUFACT EN METAL NDA
695	TOOLS	W 3532	88124	W 4272	82237	W 5541	84885	W 19739	180382	OUTILS A MAIN
6954	BLADES,TIPS,ETC FR TOOLS	W 2312	72833	W 2402	65878	W 1933	61910	W 7029	123068	OUTILS POUR MACHINE–OUTIL
699	BASE METAL MFRS NES	W 10213	86143		148099	W 20260	165433		253059	ART MANUFACTURES MET NDA
7	MACHINES,TRANSPORT EQUIP		6858880		8986426		13516584		21020500	MACHINES MATERIEL TRANSPORT
71	POWER GENERATING EQUIPMT		564576		648131		1186729		1133148	MACHINES GENERATRICES
712	STEAM ENGINES,TURBINES	W 103	8695	W 63	5811	W 9223	431219	W 153	25944	MACHINES A VAPEUR D'EAU PIEC
7129	STM ENGINE ETC PARTS NES	W 39	6841	W 35	4753	W 9210	430270	W 151	25847	PARTIES,PIECES DU 712.6
713	INTRNL COMBUS PSTN ENGIN	W 30479	318228	W 36258	380177	W 45753	491631	W 75824	699392	MOTEURS EXPL COMB INT, PIECE
7132	MOTOR VEHCL PISTN ENGINS	W 13190	114111	W 16855	177423	W 22787	227408	W 26976	287179	MOTEURS EXPL POUR VEHICULES
7139	PISTON ENGINE PARTS NES	W 13839	148902	W 15033	137470	W 17951	187451	W 41526	291488	PIECES POUR 713.2,3,8
714	ENGINES AND MOTORS NES	W 301	121678	W 158	99405	W 175	87840	W 558	170858	MOTEURS NON ELECTRIQUES
7149	ENGINE & MOTOR PARTS NES	W 87	81087	W 104	57933	W 126	58979	W 281	100966	PIECES 714 ET 718.88
716	ROTATING ELECTRIC PLANT	W 3470	89680	W 4980	107145	W 6593	112766	W 19608	186846	APP ELECTR ROTATIFS,PIECES
72	MACHS FOR SPCL INDUSTRYS		1008038		1090697		1729388		2831215	MAC SPECIALES POUR INDUST
723	CIVIL ENGNEERG EQUIP ETC	W 7464	82974	W 8453	83178	W 7461	72001	W 15086	128258	APPAREILS DE GENIE CIVIL
7234	CONST,MINING MACHNRY NES	W 6104	68809	W 7645	71459	W 6875	60647	W 13441	111144	MACH POUR LA CONST, MINES
724	TEXTILE,LEATHER MACHNRY	W 13050	279729	W 28352	372414	W 31672	557031	W 44767	779948	MACH POUR INDUSTRIE TEXTILE
7243	SEWING MACHS,NEEDLES ETC	W 2510	45498	W 6139	85258	W 10255	107421	W 15133	158450	MACHINES A COUDRE,PIECES
7244	SPINNING,EXTRDNG,ETC MCH	W 3729	94452	W 5332	105206	W 6735	135231	W 8906	173283	MACH POUR LE FILAGE
7245	WEAVING,FELT MFG,ETC MCH	W 3799	75510	W 12906	96975	W 9425	207589	W 13020	304152	METIERS A TISSER,PIECES
726	PRINTG,BKBINDG MACHY,PTS	W 4444	167175	W 3279	135431	W 7826	292059	W 16999	561850	MACHINES POUR IMPRIMERIE
7264	PRINTING PRESSES	W 2615	87562	W 1703	59212	W 5452	170010	W 12074	339807	MACHINES A IMPRIMER
72641	ROTARY PRINTING PRESSES	W 2615	87562	W 1703	59212	W 5452	170010	W 12074	339807	MACH IMPRIMER ROTATIVES
728	OTH MACHY FOR SPCL INDUS	W 14019	337727	W 14420	381950	W 25746	623445	W 47880	1043009	AUT MACH IND PARTICULIERES
7284	MACHY FOR SPCL INDUS NES	W 8863	265584	W 10694	325961	W 17098	499075	W 35353	871583	MACH SPEC IND PARTICUL.
72842	RUBBER,PLASTICS WRKG MCH	W 3853	75545	W 5511	114264	W 6753	148446	W 15210	273050	MACH IND CAOUT MAT PLAST
72848	OTH MCHY WITH INDIV FNCT	W 3715	135994	W 3464	144317	W 6978	245815	W 17092	456646	AUTRES MACHINES NDA
73	METALWORKING MACHINERY		266697		306305		418140		758098	MACH TRAVAIL DES METAUX
736	METALWORKING MACH–TOOLS	W 9400	212816	W 8866	201836	W 16430	275030	W 32622	499065	MACH–OUTILS TRAVAIL METAUX
7361	METAL CUTTING MACH–TOOLS	W 3296	85766	W 3228	75003	W 5815	109694	W 11834	209468	MACH–OUT ENLEVEMENT METAL
737	METALWORKING MACHNRY NES	W 6031	53881	W 16020	104469	W 10254	143110	W 30203	259033	MACH TRAV METAUX PIECES
7373	WELDING,BRAZING,ETC MCHS	W 481	25475	W 593	31293	W 1838	59961	W 4453	175727	MACH SOUDAGE ETC PIECES
73732	ELECTRIC WELDERS,ETC	W 455	24255	W 556	28822	W 1772	56416	W 4365	171533	MACH ELECT POUR SOUDER
74	GENRL INDUSTRL MACHY NES		1033579		1189644		1608999		2656346	MACH APP INDUSTRIE
741	HEATING,COOLING EQUIPMNT	W 13065	121321	W 7199	148360	W 15871	228192	W 48074	398015	MACH CHAUFFAGE,PIECES
742	PUMPS FOR LIQUIDS ETC	W 3050	82241	W 3527	118158	W 5595	141234	W 16223	210333	POMPES MOTO–POMPES
743	PUMPS NES,CENTRFUGES ETC	W 7948	151888	W 11461	176303	W 16161	242289	W 39990	402346	POMPES COMPRES,VENT ETC
7431	PUMPS FOR GASES ETC	W 3937	47228	W 5736	55800	W 8709	94773	W 18146	173208	POMPES AIR A VIDE,COMPRES
744	MECHANICAL HANDLING EQU	W 6156	63333	W 10392	103114	W 14755	135363	W 39308	297501	EQUIP MANUTENTION PIECES
7442	LIFTING,LOADING MACH NES	W 3501	37268	W 4358	48006	W 6644	76470	W 13329	162848	APP LEVAGE,MANUTENTION
745	NONELEC MACHY,TOOLS NES	W 4417	144018	W 8044	155115	W 9155	263865	W 21468	455564	AUT MACH NON ELEC,PIECES

4. Special Imports C.I.F. by Commodities according to the S.I.T.C. (Rev. 2) in thousand U.S. Dollars
Importations Spéciales C.A.F. par Produits d'après la C.T.C.I. (Rév. 2) en milliers de Dollars E.U.

SITC CTCI	COMMODITY	1992 WEIGHT POIDS	1992 VALUE VALEUR	1993 WEIGHT POIDS	1993 VALUE VALEUR	1994 WEIGHT POIDS	1994 VALUE VALEUR	1995 WEIGHT POIDS	1995 VALUE VALEUR	PRODUIT
7452	OTH NONELEC MCHS,PTS NES	W 4292	137691	W 7850	145350	W 8778	247279	W 20734	429536	AUT MACH NON ELEC,PIECES
74522	PACKAGNG,BOTTLNG,ETC MCH	W 1716	70882	W 1890	81772	W 3605	155926	W 6362	246871	MACH NETT BOUTEILLES,ETC
749	NONELEC MACH PTS,ACC NES	W 27610	470778	W 26668	488595	W 33748	598056	W 68074	892588	PIECES MACH NON ELEC NDA
7491	BALL,ROLLER,ETC BEARINGS	W 15697	135054	W 11638	158296	W 15052	198927	W 22354	273891	ROULEMENTS BILLES ETC
7492	COCKS,VALVES ETC NES	W 2299	92900	W 3805	119554	W 4703	141129	W 14164	224680	ART ROB,SIM POUR TUYAUX
7493	SHAFT,CRANK,PULLEY ETC	W 7174	133249	W 9871	142198	W 12124	171334	W 25342	269453	ARBRES TRANS,VILEBREQUINS
7499	OTH NONELEC MCHY PTS NES	W 2440	109574	W 1354	68546	W 1869	86665	W 6215	124563	PIECES NON ELECT NDA
74991	FOUNDRY MOULDS ETC NES	W 1927	95942	W 1034	55993	W 1377	68783	W 3114	101787	MOULES POUR METAUX
75	OFFICE MACHNES,ADP EQUIP		747742		941294		1234372		1684390	MACH BUREAU TRAIT AUTOM
751	OFFICE MACHINES	W 1599	53595	W 2039	60734	W 3696	113704	W 6925	209580	MACH,APPAREILS DE BUREAU
7518	OFFICE MACHINES NES	W 1176	42629	W 1431	44332	W 2970	93926	W 5623	180181	MACH,APP DE BUREAU NDA
75182	PHOTO,THERMOCOPY APPARAT	W 1029	31566	W 593	25560	W 1554	60226	W 5317	169846	APPAREILS DE PHOTOCOPIE
752	AUTOMTIC DATA PROC EQUIP	W 3630	383547	W 5896	540012	W 9452	743255	W 17651	892070	MACH TRAIT INFORMATION
7522	DIGITAL COMPUTERS	W 463	85713	W 913	98349	W 1142	139196	W 972	102636	MACH DIGITALES COMPLETES
7523	DIGITL CENTRL PROCESSORS	W 607	102205	W 976	147525	W 1152	176506	W 1390	165719	UNITES CENTRALES
7524	DIGITL CENTRL STOR UNITS	W 4	2715	W 9	5880	W 733	116877	W 2487	204955	UNITES MEMOIRE CENTRALES
7525	ADP PERIPHERAL UNITS	W 2086	95724	W 3361	155305	W 5607	166069	W 11789	279724	UNITES PERIPHERIQUES
7528	OFF–LINE DATA PROC EQUIP	W 401	92930	W 593	127339	W 775	140964	W 858	132456	MACH AUXIL TRAIT INFORM
759	OFFICE,ADP MCH PTS,ACCES	W 5163	310601	W 6493	340549	W 8267	377412	W 15201	582740	PIECES DU 751 ET 752
7591	OFFICE MACHINE PARTS NES	W 2697	95522	W 2292	80525	W 2782	109294	W 4522	144452	PIECES DU 7511,7518
75919	COPY MACH PRTS,ACCES NES	W 2454	87397	W 2038	69851	W 2319	92558	W 3620	120832	PIECES DU 751.82
7599	ACCTG,ETC,ADP MCH PTS,AC	W 2466	215078	W 4202	260024	W 5485	268119	W 10679	438288	PIECES DU 751 ET 752
76	TELECOMM,SOUND EQUIPMENT		555019		884786		1360565		2215680	EQUIPMENT DE TELECOM
762	RADIO BROADCAST RECEIVRS	W 3160	45266	W 4990	52007	W 9086	111479	W 15106	179624	RECEPTEURS RADIODIFFUSION
764	TELECOM EQPT,PTS,ACC NES	W 5977	441977	W 13650	749407	W 20453	1114770	W 36591	1799350	EQUIP TELECOM,PIECES
7641	LINE TELEPHONE,ETC EQUIP	W 582	40569	W 1275	80102	W 1500	127900	W 2493	214503	APP TELEPHON PAR FIL
7643	TV,RADIO TRANSMITTRS ETC	W 511	93253	W 904	148182	W 1486	276613	W 2236	373252	APP EMET TELE RADIO
7649	PTS NES OF EQUIPMT OF 76	W 4567	279943	W 10501	462377	W 15478	626949	W 25725	1069510	PIECES DE LA DIV 76
76491	PTS NES OF APPAR OF 7641	W 480	64106	W 761	76986	W 816	89062	W 1597	165509	PIECES POUR 764.1
76493	TELECOMM EQUIPMT PTS NES	W 2307	130224	W 4385	186143	W 6359	255910	W 11143	445046	PIECES 761,762,764.3,8
76499	PARTS ETC OF SOUND EQUIP	W 1742	84688	W 5270	197659	W 7994	278632	W 12047	452831	PIECES NDA POUR 763
77	ELECTRIC MACHNRY NES ETC		1344980		1737560		2449735		3594232	MACH APP ELECT NDA
771	ELECTRIC POWER MACHY NES	W 8102	125086	W 7260	140972	W 7720	165539	W 14757	263765	MACH PROD,TRANS ELECTR
772	SWITCHGEAR ETC,PARTS NES	W 4164	284324	W 6734	324077	W 8746	621430	W 15815	596600	APP COUPURE,SECT ETC
7721	SWITCHGEAR ETC	W 3274	217204	W 5537	248572	W 6538	509270	W 12252	442705	APP COUPURE,SECTIONMNT
773	ELECTR DISTRIBUTNG EQUIP	W 3374	60192	W 5813	74204	W 7407	97351	W 14443	165632	EQUIPMT DISTRIBUTION ELECT
774	ELECTRO–MEDCL,XRAY EQUIP	W 1438	116712	W 1169	144039	W 1001	115771	W 1324	186428	APPAREILS MEDICAUX
7742	X–RAY APPARATUS ETC	W 1372	110130	W 1024	137143	W 859	108610	W 1100	152731	APPAREILS A RAYONS X
775	HOUSEHOLD TYPE EQUIP NES	W 5666	48128	W 10915	83913	W 17400	116524	W 32876	203465	MACH,APP USAGE DOMESTQUE
776	TRANSISTORS,VALVES,ETC	W 7221	380608	W 15487	561095	W 31396	807600	W 52315	1329459	LAMPES,TUBES,VALVES
7761	TV PICTURE TUBES	W 2909	28053	W 10008	84013	W 27096	198461	W 44967	329153	TUBES CATHODIQUES
7764	ELECTRONIC MICROCIRCUITS	W 373	236098	W 568	336754	W 844	448403	W 1293	742979	MICROSTRUCTURES ELECTRON
778	ELECTRICAL MACHINERY NES	W 126183	329929	W 31120	409261	W 39776	525521	W 184091	848883	AUTRES MACH ELECT NDA
7783	AUTOMOTIVE ELECTR EQUIP	W 3585	77758	W 4785	111179	W 6530	138521	W 27789	179512	EQUIP ELECT MOTEURS EXPL
77831	IGNITION,STARTING EQUIP	W 2999	62401	W 3209	89685	W 4522	111650	W 8490	134178	APP ELEC ALLUM,DEMARRAGE
7788	OTH ELEC MACHY,EQUIP NES	W 119330	202019	W 20817	222280	W 21713	268273	W 124203	432001	AUT MACH APP ELEC NDA
77886	OTH ELEC MACHINERY NES	W 1039	78346	W 1575	78066	W 2008	98267	W 4164	194450	AUT MACH APP ELECTRIQUES
78	ROAD VEHICLES		941110		1889336		3294962		5784027	VEHICULES ROUTIERS
781	PASS MOTOR VEH EXC BUSES	W 31705	281351	W 78960	710203	W 179221	1524002	W 359097	3143226	AUTO TRANSPORT PERSONNES
782	LORRIES,SPCL MTR VEH NES	W 6601	74903	W 18240	202128	W 37306	327903	W 94334	736174	VEHICULES SPECIAUX,MARCH
7821	LORRIES,TRUCKS	W 5334	45865	W 16090	121113	W 35358	268078	W 93874	724238	VEHICULES TRANSP MARCHAND
784	MOTOR VEH PRTS,ACCES NES	W 52777	539126	W 87540	828827	W 132681	1166295	W 302388	1486052	PIECES 722,781,782,783
7849	OTHER MOTOR VEHCL PARTS	W 49007	511692	W 83720	804175	W 118955	1080809	W 286757	1389208	PIECES 722,781,782,783
785	CYCLES,ETC MOTRZD OR NOT	W 5712	44341	W 21640	136109	W 36388	194542	W 57883	269432	MOTOCYCLES SCOOTERS
7853	INVAL CARR, PTS OF 785	W 4307	30929	W 15775	89638	W 25262	117048	W 49437	202265	FAUTEUILS INVALIDES,PIECES
78539	PARTS,ACCES NES OF 785	W 4295	30796	W 15760	89442	W 25243	116768	W 49389	201572	PIECES DU 785
79	OTHR TRANSPORT EQUIPMENT		397140		298672		233693		363364	AUTRE MATERIEL TRANSPORT
792	AIRCRAFT ETC	W 3086	355363	W 753	125852	W 842	200889	W 2094	271293	APP NAVIGATION AERIENNE
7924	AIRCRFT NES OVER 15000KG	W 2640	206128	W 127	8430	W 77	13116	W 350	28100	AERODYNES PLUS 15000 KG
7929	AIRCRAFT PARTS NES	W 224	90693	W 213	59156	W 345	65430	W 361	95596	PIECES DU 792
793	SHIPS AND BOATS ETC	W 2655	23688	W 16466	164051	W 881	19367	W 13047	78277	NAVIRES BATEAUX,ETC
7938	TUGS,SPECIAL VESSELS ETC	W 288	4618	W 15729	150697	W 55	1513	W 9311	56231	REMORQUEURS,BATEAUX SPEC
79382	SPECL PURPOSE VESSLS ETC	W 237	2894	W 14000	148400	W 17	642	W 9252	55103	BAT–PHARES,–POMPES,DRAGUES
8	MISC MANUFACTURED GOODS		1190907		1455658		2023041		3924222	ART MANUFACTURES DIVERS
84	CLOTHING AND ACCESSORIES		40261		53055		118494		372359	VETEMENTS
851	*FOOTWEAR	W 811	13279	W 3627	34796	W 5073	84280	W 14790	213812	CHAUSSURES
87	PRECISION INSTRUMNTS NES		558135		565783		700583		1035381	INSTRUM,APPAR SCIENT NDA
872	MEDICAL INSTRUMENTS NES	W 3469	134206	W 2483	155056	W 3077	160061	W 6186	225700	INSTR,APP MEDIC–CHIR NDA
87202	OTH MEDICAL INSTRUMENTS	W 3356	123053	W 2290	142888	W 2544	145820	W 3696	195599	INSTRUM,APP MEDECINE
874	MEASURNG,CONTROLNG INSTR	W 3419	390623	W 2975	369071	W 6665	472685	W 12778	693194	INSTRUMENTS DE MESURE
8742	MEASUR,DRAW ETC INST,PTS	W 1351	76190	W 734	70983	W 1388	99548	W 2443	153845	INST DESSIN,TRACAGE,PCS
87421	MEASURNG,DRAWNG ETC INST	W 1308	67525	W 667	62128	W 1319	89927	W 2360	142075	INSTRUM DESSIN,TRACAGE
8743	GAS,LIQUID CONTROL INSTR	W 994	89165	W 1030	95592	W 3694	105706	W 5961	160044	APP,INSTR MESURE FLUIDES
8748	ELEC MEAS,CONTRL EQU NES	W 587	136342	W 761	130544	W 947	175715	W 3091	235803	APP ELEC ELECTRO MESURE
87483	OTH ELCTRNC MEAS ETC EQU	W 480	124733	W 643	120245	W 827	162635	W 2694	221376	AUT APP ELECTRO DE MESURE
88	PHOTO EQU,OPTICL GDS ETC		240634		275251		336067		533484	APP,FOURN PHOTO,OP,MONTR
882	PHOTO,CINEMA SUPPLIES	W 7844	146260	W 9013	150933	W 12158	187816	W 18675	261546	PRODUITS PHOTO,CINEMA
8822	PHOTO FILM EXC DEV CINMA	W 6734	120880	W 7824	129662	W 10405	155379	W 14795	209207	PLAQUES,PELLICULES,FILMS
88222	PHOTO FILM ROLL UNEXPOSD	W 2590	73706	W 2509	71267	W 2945	86472	W 4492	128801	PEL SENSIB PERF OU NON
89	MISC MANUFCTRD GOODS NES		316521		490188		704377		1558089	ART MANUFACTURES DIVERS
892	PRINTED MATTER	W 7836	80837	W 8976	96315	W 12389	133904	W 45293	327423	IMPRIMES
8921	PRINTED BOOKS,GLOBES,ETC	W 3398	40351	W 3976	49464	W 6666	62042	W 23477	174646	LIVRES,BROCHURES,CARTES
89211	PRINTED BOOKS,PAMPHLETS	W 3347	39796	W 3840	47634	W 6354	60607	W 23024	172334	LIVRES,BROCHURES
893	ARTICLES OF PLASTIC NES		98838		139050		204417		454256	OUVRAGES EN MAT DIVIS 58
8931	PLSTC PACKG CONTNRS,LIDS	W 5319	21019	W 16002	36195	W 16270	58945	W 54045	192071	ART TRANSP EMBALLAGE ETC
8939	MISC PLASTIC ARTICLES	W 5565	77703	W 10357	102353	W 18366	145017	W 60526	259940	ART DIVERS EN MAT DIV 58
89399	OTHR PLASTC ARTICLES NES	W 5334	77032	W 9436	100244	W 14450	139200	W 52035	246717	AUT OUV MAT DIV 58
894	TOYS,SPORTING GOODS,ETC	W 2861	27833	W 6284	68981	W 17142	125759	W 65392	353697	VOITURES ENFANTS,JOUETS
8942	TOYS,INDOOR GAMES ETC	W 2113	23963	W 5046	61315	W 12648	105885	W 45820	263888	JOUETS,JEUX ETC
898	MUSICAL INSTRUMENTS,PTS	W 3324	56896	W 6178	101986	W 8984	132805	W 16773	193319	INSTRUMENTS DE MUSIQUE

5. Special Exports F.O.B. by Commodities according to the S.I.T.C. (Rev. 2) in thousand U.S. Dollars
Exportations Spéciales F.O.B. par Produits d'après la C.T.C.I. (Rév. 2) en milliers de Dollars E.U.

SITC CTCI	COMMODITY	1993 WEIGHT POIDS	1993 VALUE VALEUR	1994 WEIGHT POIDS	1994 VALUE VALEUR	1995 WEIGHT POIDS	1995 VALUE VALEUR	1996 WEIGHT POIDS	1996 VALUE VALEUR	PRODUIT
	ALL COMMODITIES		38700877		43557977		46505382		47746546	TOUS PRODUITS
0	FOOD AND LIVE ANIMALS		7433645		9203566		9975310		10737782	ALIMENTS,ANIMAUX VIVANTS
01	MEAT AND PREPARATIONS		1332158		1332997		1295606		1503125	VIANDES ET PREPARATIONS
011	MEAT FRESH,CHILLD,FROZEN	W 705295	994109	W 636436	1008660	W 532796	962291	W 706647	1228891	VIANDES FRAICHES,REF,CONGE
0111	BOVINE MEAT FRESH,FROZEN	W 99543	271645	W 78718	268090	W 37505	180780	W 46656	194305	VIANDES BOVIN FRAI,REF
01112	BOVINE MEAT BONELESS	W 99301	271322	W 78457	267645	W 37499	180770	W 46651	194297	VIANDES BOVIN DESOSSEES
0114	POULTRY FRESH CHLLD,FRZN	W 525062	596819	W 499482	646997	W 440825	667528	W 571646	876231	VOLAILLES MORTES
014	MEAT PREPD,PRSVD,NES ETC	W 136392	333323	W 119826	319200	W 106542	328078	W 100274	269136	CONSERVES DE VIANDES
0149	OTH PREPARD,PRESRVD MEAT	W 132657	308456	W 114832	301389	W 101468	311301	W 94537	253918	AUTRES PREP DE VIANDES
03	FISH AND PREPARATIONS		191607		178509		159802		133328	POISSONS ET PREPARATIONS
036	SHELL FISH FRESH,FROZEN	W 13814	122526	W 10637	124305	W 7216	111349	W 5856	89188	CRUSTACES,MOLLUSQUES
05	VEGETABLES AND FRUIT		1234242		1366679		1487340		1824565	LEGUMES ET FRUITS
057	FRUIT,NUTS,FRESH,DRIED	W 408070	273201	W 399839	266697	W 275935	276478	W 294268	291186	FRUITS FRAIS OU SECS
0577	NUTS EDIBLE,FRESH,DRIED	W 45698	140572	W 41362	138747	W 47877	173384	W 46798	185531	FRUITS A COQUES
05773	CASHEW NUTS,FRESH,DRIED	W 31190	119911	W 23079	109200	W 31877	147236	W 36222	167508	NOIX DE CAJOU
058	FRUIT PRESERVED,PREPARED	W 1251290	923717	W 1222853	1070708	W 1012281	1174389	W 1247446	1496795	CONSERVES DE FRUITS
0585	FRUIT OR VEGETABLE JUICE	W 1210465	866154	W 1189556	1019382	W 990193	1131880	W 1224518	1453664	JUS DE FRUITS
05851	ORANGE JUICE	W 1168722	827083	W 1154379	987734	W 968936	1108371	W 1189072	1396837	JUS D'ORANGE
06	SUGAR AND PREPS,HONEY		875141		1067645		2001859		1689760	SUCRES ET PRODUITS
061	SUGAR AND HONEY	W 3043909	791896	W 3414237	996923	W 6246198	1926264	W 5388845	1619732	SUCRES ET MIEL
0611	RAW BEET AND CANE SUGAR	W 2132977	550059	W 2716975	787861	W 4800099	1450654	W 4090398	1190735	SUCRES BRUTS
0612	REFINED SUGAR ETC	W 903891	236616	W 689936	204345	W 1439072	468806	W 1288496	420759	SUCRES RAFFINES
07	COFFEE,TEA,COCOA,SPICES		1694882		3018866		2748851		2461337	CAFE,THE,CACAO,EPICES
071	COFFEE AND SUBSTITUTES	W 1036184	1306395	W 938968	2585417	W 787595	2462395	W 842336	2135136	CAFE ET SUCCEDANES
0711	COFFEE GREEN,ROASTED,SUB	W 964524	1065997	W 871427	2220338	W 722150	1973508	W 778702	1722211	CAFE TORREFIE OU DECAFEINE
07111	COFFEE GREEN,HUSKS,SKINS	W 964153	1065185	W 871018	2218689	W 721313	1969877	W 777909	1718593	CAFE NON TORREFIE
0712	COFFEE EXTRACTS,ESSENCES	W 71660	240398	W 67541	365079	W 65445	488887	W 63634	412925	EXTRAITS DE CAFE
072	COCOA	W 211671	265010	W 187362	295215	W 77685	131219	W 95958	173550	CACAO
0723	COCOA BUTTER AND PASTE	W 97234	156019	W 78940	172877	W 40312	92115	W 46218	115235	BEURRE ET PATE DE CACAO
081	*FEEDING STUFF FOR ANIML		2001510		2152135		2184100		2930133	NOURRITURE POUR ANIMAUX
0811	HAY, FODDER, GREEN, DRY	W 1615387	123529	W 1160407	103582	W 1076615	114840	W 1226414	134652	FOIN ET FOURRAGE
08119	FODDER OF VEG ORIGIN NES	W 1571475	120159	W 1111637	100320	W 1040186	112276	W 1226409	134649	AUTRES FOURRAGES
0813	OILCAKE AND OTH RESIDUES	MW 9866	1865425	MW 11068	2029387	MW 12001	2044209	MW 11613	2771150	TOURTEAUX
08131	— OF SOYA BEANS	MW 9414	1816606	MW 10644	1982716	MW 11597	2000119	MW 11262	2730940	TOURTEAUX DE SOJA
1	BEVERAGES AND TOBACCO		981680		1123863		1272508		1636131	BOISSONS ET TABACS
12	TOBACCO AND MANUFACTURES		900782		1030708		1174961		1515392	TABACS BRUTS FABRIQUES
121	TOBACCO UNMNFCTRD,REFUSE	W 243474	697002	W 275543	693896	W 256270	768571	W 282364	1028521	TABACS BRUTS,DECHETS
1212	TOBACCO STRIPPED OR PART	W 157723	607358	W 190497	599951	W 170984	666120	W 190332	917958	TABACS PART ECOTES
122	TOBACCO,MANUFACTURED	W 35841	203780	W 60024	336812	W 65027	406390	W 82889	486871	TABACS FABRIQUES
1222	CIGARETTES	W 33848	193153	W 57818	327635	W 63417	402110	W 80262	481186	CIGARETTES
2	CRUDE MATERLS,EXCL FUELS		4744874		5447309		6091234		5938121	MAT BRUTES NON COMESTIBLES
22	OIL SEEDS,OLEAGINOUS FRT		949419		1320889		775467		1020111	GRAINES,FRUITS OLEAGINEUX
222	SEEDS FOR'SOFT'FIXED OIL	W 4188601	948394	W 5402858	1320199	W 3496290	774012	W 3648537	1019544	GRAINES HUILES FIXES
2222	SOYA BEANS	W 4184704	945500	W 5397589	1315979	W 3492525	770425	W 3646933	1017918	FEVES DE SOJA
24	CORK AND WOOD		260895		380243		480452		435021	LIEGE ET BOIS
248	WOOD SHAPED,SLEEPERS	W 576375	248180	W 928695	353457	W 884787	417522	W 883040	381494	BOIS SIMPLEMENT TRAVAILLES
2483	LUMBER SHAPED NON–CONIFR	W 472172	210555	W 730513	291778	W 689173	328482	W 653171	272042	NON CONIFERES SCIES,RABOTES
24831	LUMBER SAWN ETC NON–CON	W 438333	191277	W 715957	266185	W 673395	293735	W 633522	238383	SCIES LONGITUDINALEMENT
251	*PULP AND WASTE PAPER	W 2413463	718439	W 2074513	851333	W 1983775	1475408	W 2240084	999464	PATES A PAPIER,DECHETS
2517	SODA,SULPHATE WOOD PULP	W 2386238	711006	W 2044427	839729	W 1942495	1446695	W 2153709	954339	PATES CHIMIQUES AU SULFATE
25172	— BLEACHED,NONDISSOLVNG	W 2374244	707823	W 2021832	833473	W 1922000	1436098	W 2133993	947054	PATES BLANCHIES
26	TEXTILE FIBRES AND WASTE		60531		62134		172306		65261	FIBRES TEXTILES
27	CRUDE FERTLZR,MINRLS NES		135034		126218		135729		141032	ENGRAIS MINERAUX BRUTS
278	OTHER CRUDE MINERALS	W 983937	128192	W 986972	121467	W 1000364	132253	W 1006024	138265	AUTRES MINERAUX BRUTS
28	METALLIFEROUS ORES,SCRAP		2500334		2544283		2793600		3017615	MINERAIS METAL,DECHETS
281	IRON ORE,CONCENTRATES	MW 115131	2256905	MW 122801	2293992	MW 130178	2547781	MW 128990	2695207	MINERAIS DE FER
2815	IRON ORE,CONC,NOT AGGLOM	MW 92366	1590624	MW 96357	1532504	MW 103336	1701388	MW 100827	1740771	MINERAIS NON AGGLOMERES
2816	IRON ORE AGGLOMERATES	MW 22765	666281	MW 26445	761488	MW 26842	846393	MW 28163	954436	MINERAIS AGGLOMERES
287	BASE METAL ORES,CONC NES	W 7478577	240251		226502	W 6576406	241101	W 6102365	278548	MINERAIS METAUX COMMUNS
2873	ALUMINIUM ORES,ALUMINA	W 6687656	185561	W 4704836	158667	W 5293342	168446	W 4996673	211767	MINERAIS D'ALUMINIUM
28731	ALUMINIUM ORE,CONCNTRATE	W 6504263	151925	W 4416133	113880	W 5045710	122791	W 4569442	130013	MINERAIS D'ALUMINIUM
3	MINERAL FUELS ETC		646236		793109		413393		429014	COMBUSTIBLES MINERAUX LUB
33	PETROLEUM AND PRODUCTS		645017		792391		413187		425019	PETROLE ET DERIVES
334	PETROLEUM PRODUCTS,REFIN	W 3265611	615529	W 5693229	742995	W 2299816	316152	W 2538850	379031	PRODUITS RAFFINES
3341	GASOLINE,OTH LIGHT OILS	W 2378757	402788	W 2806113	422522	W 624244	100360	W 781468	138510	ESSENCES POUR MOTEURS
33411	MOTOR,AVIATION SPIRIT	W 2378753	402786	W 2806090	422487	W 624235	100341	W 781452	138484	ESSENCES MOTEURS D'AVIONS
3344	FUEL OILS,NES	W 318025	103727	W 1832755	155090	W 578651	55023	W 1422018	160494	FUEL OILS
4	ANIMAL,VEGETABLE OIL,FAT		412535		957031		1234210		880484	HUILES,GRAISSES ANIM,VEG
42	FIXED VEGETABLE OIL,FAT		346155		882254		1107743		749081	HUILES VEGETALES FIXES
423	FIXED VEG OILS,SOFT	W 784490	334173	W 1577264	867883	W 1811722	1084653	W 1352988	726222	HUILES VEGET DOUCES FIXES
4232	SOYA BEAN OIL	W 746044	313859	W 1533302	839078	W 1763959	1053014	W 1332257	713279	HUILE DE SOJA
5	CHEMCLS,RELATED PROD NES		2321753		2543153		3030959		3127751	PRODUITS CHIMIQUES
51	ORGANIC CHEMICALS		796967		892919		1078286		1064174	PROD CHIMIQ ORGANIQUES
511	HYDROCARBONS NES,DERIVS	W 732272	210781	W 771814	253218	W 794790	283252	W 765659	241725	HYDROCARBURES NDA
5112	CYCLIC HYDROCARBONS	W 361726	97322	W 338758	109411	W 431991	142957	W 395661	104044	HYDROCARBURES CYCLIQUES
512	ALCOHOLS,PHENOLS ETC	W 323659	153516	W 364861	181178	W 395558	244176	W 344666	209913	PHENOLS,PHENOLS–ALCOOLS
5121	ACYCLIC ALCOHOLS,DERIVS	W 307001	140510	W 348547	168234	W 381535	229438	W 332410	196338	ALCOOLS ACYCLIQUES
514	NITROGEN–FNCTN COMPOUNDS	W 126471	173254	W 148474	186667	W 139774	213481	W 164771	276057	COMPOSES FONCT AZOTEES
52	INORGANIC CHEMICALS		228508		221257		309337		388946	PROD CHIM INORGANIQUES
522	INORG ELEMNTS,OXIDES,ETC	W 299613	152698	W 357200	172742		246689	W 437447	297877	ELEMENTS INORGANIQUES
5221	CHEMICAL ELEMENTS	W 91135	85056	W 100778	90226	W 134291	144775	W 142746	188033	ELEMENTS CHIMIQUES
52212	NON–METALS NES	W 84710	81787	W 85158	84090	W 115287	139519	W 121011	180904	SELENIUM,PHOSPHORE
53	DYES,TANNING,COLOUR PROD		119265		133138		160026		184462	PROD TEINTURE,COLORANTS
541	*MEDICINAL,PHARM PRODUCT	K 5450371	110810	K o224320	132806	MK 9112	167588	MK 10083	189147	PROD MEDICINAUX PHARMACEUT
55	PERFUME,CLEANING ETC PRD		152633		161644		198882		212692	PROD POUR PARFUM,TOILETTE
58	PLASTIC MATERIALS ETC		594125		662102		693136		612210	MAT PLAST ARTIFICIELLES
583	POLYMERIZATION ETC PRODS	W 769044	494949	W 741284	533479	W 534683	534915	W 517722	460160	PROD POLYMERISATION
5831	POLYETHYLENE	W 367082	214783	W 362900	220555	W 236613	223668	W 222977	188729	POLYETHYLENE
58311	— IN PRIMARY FORMS	W 360599	203539	W 356824	210111	W 231279	212335	W 218412	178573	POLYETHYLENE PRIMAIRES
59	CHEMICAL MATERIALS NES		267647		296183		353242		404869	MAT PROD CHIMIQUES NDA
591	PESTICIDES,DISINFECTANTS	W 16128	89889	W 19294	102183	W 22351	127545	W 23893	146073	DESINF,INSECT,FONG,HERB
598	MISCEL CHEM PRODUCTS NES	W 103982	115052	W 106731	120856	W 120474	151585	W 113297	163391	PROD DIV INDUST CHIM NDA
6	BASIC MANUFACTURES		10330207		10751692		11741459		11283469	ART MANUFACTURES
61	LEATHER,DRESSED FUR,ETC		501500		558055		667241		770892	CUIRS,PELLETERIES
611	LEATHER	W 79056	401252	W 84914	457322	W 133106	560148	W 178473	658801	CUIRS,PEAUX PREPARES
6114	LEATHR BOVINE NES,EQUINE	W 75222	363493	W 79779	421895	W 129718	522388	W 174127	620357	CUIRS DE BOVINS
62	RUBBER MANUFACTURES NES		504756		550350		577998		615374	CAOUTCHOUC MANUFACTURE
625	RUBBER TYRES, TUBES ETC	W 157899	424436	W 168804	465442	W 158362	481649	W 161471	511961	PNEUS CAOUTCHOUC VULCANISE
6251	TYRES NEW FOR MOTOR CARS	W 66329	159717	W 69083	172202	W 59740	167327	W 62390	183461	PNEUS POUR VOITURES
6252	TYRES,NEW,BUS OR LORRY	W 61458	178349	W 68459	203557	W 63576	207726	W 63869	217222	PNEUS POUR AUTOBUS,CAMIONS
63	WOOD,CORK MANUFACTRS NES		489385		593957		565523		599680	OUVRAGES LIEGE ET BOIS

5. Special Exports F.O.B. by Commodities according to the S.I.T.C. (Rev. 2) in thousand U.S. Dollars
Exportations Spéciales F.O.B. par Produits d'après la C.T.C.I. (Rév. 2) en milliers de Dollars E.U.

SITC CTCI	COMMODITY	1993 WEIGHT POIDS	1993 VALUE VALEUR	1994 WEIGHT POIDS	1994 VALUE VALEUR	1995 WEIGHT POIDS	1995 VALUE VALEUR	1996 WEIGHT POIDS	1996 VALUE VALEUR	PRODUIT
634	VENEERS,PLYWOOD,ETC	W 765743	341361	W 891639	391308	W 701825	368405	W 1174102	403187	PLACAGES,CONTRE–PLAQUES
6342	PLYWOOD OF WOOD SHEETS	W 425606	274122	W 471638	293149	W 393281	259993	W 359638	247670	BOIS CONTRE–PLAQUES
635	WOOD MANUFACTURES NES	W 269801	147329	W 313266	201563	W 251899	195039	W 221019	194653	ART MANUF EN BOIS NDA
64	PAPER,PAPERBOARD AND MFR		894474		1040402		1326143		1016967	PAPIERS,CARTONS & OUVRAGES
641	PAPER AND PAPERBOARD	W 1629775	803531	W 1782094	968945	W 1475787	1249322	W 1439185	929094	PAPIERS ET CARTONS
6412	PRINTG,WRITING PAPER NES	W 192650	127981	W 348921	241200	W 327522	360518	W 321915	264323	PAPIERS POUR L'IMPRESSION
64121	— UNCOATED	W 130953	87927	W 200566	145990	W 220222	252146	W 209871	173762	PAPIERS IMPRES NON COUCHES
6413	KRAFT PAPER,PAPERBOARD	W 393356	120988	W 391095	148887	W 290535	179255	W 334634	161201	PAPIER ET CARTON KRAFT
64131	KRAFT LINER IN BULK	W 347596	94529	W 341980	120645	W 255869	148806	W 272329	110376	PAP KRAFT POUR COUVERTURES
6415	PAPER,PAPERBRD,BULK,NES	W 689577	413465	W 670904	424986	W 500476	544561	W 466902	354702	PAPIERS,CARTONS ROULEAUX
64159	OTHER PAPER ETC,BULK,NES	W 652791	392600	W 630964	402241	W 473748	519545	W 447018	333324	AUT PAPIER ROULEAUX FEUILLES
65	TEXTILE YARN,FABRICS,ETC		954573		1006743		1025996		1021707	FILS,TISSUS,ARTICLES TEXTILE
651	TEXTILE YARN	W 64115	250419	W 81534	304604	W 68446	302372	W 61005	290610	FILS TEXTILES
652	COTTON FABRICS,WOVEN	W 55525	209160	W 50999	207519	W 49132	230757		237909	TISSUS DE COTON
6522	WOVEN COTTON BLEACHD,ETC	W 40417	164164	W 36384	162055	W 41264	201872	W 41154	214110	TISSUS COTON BLANCHIS ETC
65224	BLCHED COTTON FABRIC NES	W 35998	146480	W 33333	139051	W 38274	176346	W 36705	177682	AUT TIS PLUS 85% COT BLANCHI
657	SPECIAL TXTL FABRC,PRODS	W 80920	112666	W 97717	149276	W 103734	161848	W 77959	143203	TISSUS SPECIAUX
658	TEXTILE ARTICLES NES	W 34432	283645	W 29519	247990	W 26519	245283	W 26291	242684	ART FACONNES MAT TEXTILES
6584	LINENS ETC	W 27368	248647	W 23062	211095	W 20288	206772	W 19286	201979	LINGE DE MAISON
65845	OTHER LINEN OF COTTON	W 17377	152180	W 15256	134104	W 14512	141968	W 14032	141655	LINGE DE TOILETTE COTON
66	NONMETAL MINERAL MFS NES		642365		651398		714323		727051	ART MIN NON METALLIQUES
661	LIME,CEMENT,BLDG PRODS	W 761898	125477	W 784732	132727	W 879067	152588	W 964035	173262	CHAUX,CIMENTS MAT CONSTR
6613	BUILDING STONE ETC WORKD	W 546637	107924	W 603549	119840	W 685148	136448	W 749451	153647	PIERRES A BATIR
662	CLAY,REFRACTORY BLDG PRD	W 483640	164038	W 491891	173149	W 461955	177834	W 463612	175198	MAT CONST REFRACTAIRES
6624	BRICKS ETC NONREFRACTORY	W 452206	144366	W 460011	151019	W 423128	149479	W 424980	146124	BRIQUES ETC CERAM NON REFR
66245	GLAZED CERAMIC SETTS ETC	W 425774	142232	W 413984	147904	W 382267	145570	W 390817	142018	AUT CARREAUX CERAMIQUE
67	IRON AND STEEL		4195812		4119744		4329381		4225945	FER ET ACIER
671	PIG IRON ETC	W 2388958	625664	W 3045727	735558	W 3012439	839841	W 2983284	873130	FONTE,SPIEGEL,POUDRES
6712	PIG IRN,SPIEGELEISEN ETC	W 1858954	238994	W 2632021	362672	W 2670446	427544	W 2538099	390022	FONTES BRUTES
6716	FERRO–ALLOYS	W 526931	384977	W 410869	371323	W 339106	410645	W 441783	481247	FERRO–ALLIAGES
67162	FERRO–SILICON	W 228539	121702	W 183907	108445	W 181093	141788	W 185794	163191	FERRO–SILICIUM
67169	OTHER FERRO–ALLOYS	W 233614	233859	W 147351	226186	W 127822	254728	W 150805	268061	AUTRES FERRO–ALLIAGES
672	IRON,STEEL PRIMARY FORMS	W 7467308	1743235	W 6416410	1566927	W 6103076	1740330	W 6907320	1690810	LINGOTS FER,ACIER
6725	IRN,STL BLOOMS,SLABS,ETC	W 5309248	1137422	W 4824860	1102908	W 5129999	1395424	W 5684277	1329661	BLOOMS,BILLETTES FER ACIER
67251	IRN,SMPLE STL BLOOMS,ETC	W 5266020	1122229	W 4741565	1071997	W 5081209	1368523	W 5607878	1294280	BLOOMS ETC NON ACIER FIN
6727	IRN,STL COIL FR REROLLNG	W 2158057	605810	W 1589264	463324	W 972743	344763	W 1222861	361053	EBAUCHES POUR TOLES FER
67271	IRON,SIMPLE STEEL COILS	W 2155066	602091	W 1571769	454328	W 941147	327866	W 1213741	351965	EBAUCHES NON EN ACIER
673	IRON,STEEL SHAPES ETC	W 2244773	713405	W 1977050	613846	W 1041257	401285	W 761665	295299	BARRES,PROFIL FER,ACIER
6731	IRON,STEEL WIRE ROD	W 902877	265625	W 852081	240301	W 568496	175171	479866	142940	FIL MACHINE FER,ACIER
67311	IRON,SIMPLE STL WIRE ROD	W 795813	228872	W 724471	200949	W 501587	149152	W 411904	118642	FIL MACH AUT ACIER FIN
6732	IRON,STEEL BARS ETC	W 1213477	407439	W 1040174	341896	W 419596	202543	W 231818	130685	BARRES FER,ACIER
67326	IRN,OTH STL BARS HOTROLD	W 1043898	294326	W 892879	241725	W 311620	96235	W 137923	46993	BARRES PLEINES FER,ACIER
674	IRN,STL UNIV,PLATE,SHEET	W 2172011	867519	W 2292660	934215	W 2131606	1052165	W 2205886	1049870	LARGES PLATS,TOLES
6744	IRN,STL HVY PLATE,ROLLED	W 1126329	337310	W 1019468	313798	W 989581	397688	W 983169	365026	TOLES LAMINEES PLUS 4.75 MM
67441	— OF IRON OR SIMPLE STL	W 1124270	333596	W 1016941	309846	W 985805	389825	W 974196	347170	TOLES NON ACIER FIN CARB
6746	IRN,STL THIN PLATE,ROLLD	W 437603	216803	W 643232	291201	W 510312	272166	W 603058	308080	TOLES LAM MOINS 3MM
67461	— OF IRON OR SIMPLE STL	W 387598	158401	W 581812	244121	W 467578	222711	W 533137	232214	TOL NON AC FIN MOINS 3 MM
6747	TINNED PLATES,SHEETS	W 212134	135850	W 240127	139999	W 218194	140419	W 219387	152678	TOLES ETAMEES EN ACIER
6749	OTH IRN,STL PLATES,SHEET	W 198364	95496	W 264691	132130	W 332965	198254	W 309743	177886	AUTRES TOLES FER,ACIER
67491	— OF IRON OR SIMPLE STL	W 198277	95201	W 264427	131400	W 324188	193119	W 294411	170188	AUT TOLES AUTRES ACIER FIN
678	IRON,STL TUBES,PIPES,ETC	W 282029	192644	W 320277	211172	W 313451	231048	W 323423	254620	TUBES,TUYAUX EN FONTE,FER
68	NON–FERROUS METALS		1490698		1536069		1853970		1636735	METAUX NON FERREUX
682	COPPER EXC CEMENT COPPER	W 96865	206251	W 67045	155299	W 72974	224773	W 61337	160453	CUIVRE
6821	COPPER NES,ALLOYS,UNWRT	W 80054	152930	W 55946	121449	W 58423	167604	W 41842	98565	CUIVRE BRUT
68212	COPPER REFINED,UNWROUGHT	W 80053	152914	W 55946	121438	W 58423	167587	W 41837	98536	CUIVRE AFFINE BRUT
684	ALUMINIUM	W 885703	1068513	W 864563	1189743	W 788682	1461653	W 800327	1296370	ALUMINIUM
6841	ALUMINIUM,ALLOYS,UNWRGHT	W 814696	943373	W 777840	1024900	W 703009	1255745	W 708973	1102817	ALUMINIUM,ALLIAGES BRUTS
6842	ALUMINIUM,ALLOYS WORKED	W 71007	125140	W 86723	164844	W 85673	205908	W 91354	193553	ALUMINIUM,ALLIAGES OUVRE
69	METAL MANUFACTURES NES		656644		694975		680884		669117	ART MANUFACT EN METAL NDA
697	BASE MTL HOUSEHOLD EQUIP	W 41008	116107	W 39999	119635	W 31237	110366	W 28297	103078	ART MENAGE MET COMMUNS
699	BASE METAL MFRS NES	W 59717	124743	W 83354	143108	W 55910	141959		152769	ART MANUFACTURES MET NDA
7	MACHINES,TRANSPORT EQUIP		8100364		8973851		8836737		9508069	MACHINES MATERIEL TRANSPORT
71	POWER GENERATING EQUIPMT		1046847		1278624		1305248		1403226	MACHINES GENERATRICES
713	INTRNL COMBUS PSTN ENGIN	W 185916	793513	W 217794	853972	W 205720	922871	W 207498	1029351	MOTEURS EXPL COMB INT, PIECE
7132	MOTOR VEHCL PISTN ENGINS	W 32685	273487	W 52237	254732	W 26614	260457	W 31115	332337	MOTEURS EXPL POUR VEHICULES
7139	PISTON ENGINE PARTS NES	W 145242	444768	W 157592	526268	W 175864	628188	W 172419	657007	PIECES POUR 713.2,3,8
714	ENGINES AND MOTORS NES	W 224	65942	W 562	198208	W 666	128422	W 167	92608	MOTEURS NON ELECTRIQUES
716	ROTATING ELECTRIC PLANT	W 33874	154698	W 41811	194150	W 50892	224764	W 50060	238829	APP ELECTR ROTATIFS,PIECES
7162	AC MTRS,GENRTRS,GEN SETS	W 25202	114798	W 29218	128302	W 35947	152679	W 33427	152447	MOTEURS ELECTRIQUES
72	MACHS FOR SPCL INDUSTRYS		778738		976437		900934		1011276	MAC SPECIALES POUR INDUST
721	AGRIC MACHY,EXC TRACTORS	W 41065	93234	W 46112	126181	W 46371	133373	W 56838	190462	MACHINES AGRICOLES
723	CIVIL ENGNEERG EQUIP ETC	W 48306	252465	W 69715	458346	W 54243	337029	W 57521	338803	APPAREILS DE GENIE CIVIL
7234	CONST,MINING MACHNRY NES	W 40656	224830	W 56087	393841	W 47718	310224	W 50149	309604	MACH POUR LA CONST, MINES
72341	SELF--PROPELLD DOZERS,ETC	W 22550	128436	W 25828	178984	W 25936	180986	W 28846	192514	BULLDOZERS
724	TEXTILE,LEATHER MACHNRY	W 16157	129110	W 14706	121603	W 16031	120142	W 13124	115847	MACH POUR INDUSTRIE TEXTILE
73	METALWORKING MACHINERY		126676		104251		177525		182961	MACH TRAVAIL DES METAUX
736	METALWORKING MACH–TOOLS	W 14848	96150	W 12575	74917	W 20526	142216	W 18530	148846	MACH–OUTILS TRAVAIL METAUX
74	GENRL INDUSTRL MACHY NES		1242040		1369246		1583476		1551224	MACH APP INDUSTRIE
741	HEATING,COOLING EQUIPMNT	W 28237	136793	W 27561	146719	W 29132	170290	W 29173	181681	MACH CHAUFFAGE,PIECES
742	PUMPS FOR LIQUIDS ETC	W 9775	152972	W 10857	216016	W 12369	271021	W 11781	281862	POMPES MOTO–POMPES
7428	OTHER PUMPS FOR LIQUIDS	W 3499	96075	W 4945	161131	W 5477	192341	W 5425	198784	AUTRES POMPES POUR LIQ
74288	PUMPS FR LIQUIDS NES ETC	W 3017	91424	W 4325	154914	W 4856	185994	W 5044	194097	POMPES POUR LIQUIDES NDA
743	PUMPS NES,CENTRFUGES ETC	W 108907	412232	W 111566	443568	W 118930	522235	W 101740	469405	POMPES COMPRES,VENT ETC
7431	PUMPS FOR GASES ETC	W 94025	326279	W 93369	347943	W 106108	429073	W 91545	386644	POMPES AIR A VIDE,COMPRES
744	MECHANICAL HANDLING EQU	W 31812	122883	W 29348	116179	W 34216	141419	W 34567	147579	EQUIP MANUTENTION PIECES
745	NONELEC MACHY,TOOLS NES	W 10638	145018	W 9928	137821	W 7828	125184	W 7632	113267	AUT MACH NON ELEC,PIECES
7452	OTH NONELEC MCHS,PTS NES	W 9843	122088	W 9324	120806	W 6901	96273	W 6755	85968	AUT MACH NON ELEC,PIECES
749	NONELEC MACH PTS,ACC NES	W 47699	272142	W 48674	308943	W 58145	353328	W 62106	357431	PIECES MACH NON ELEC NDA
7493	SHAFT,CRANK,PULLEY ETC	W 35331	139707	W 35339	148476	W 45374	185624	W 50531	192076	ARBRES TRANS,VILEBREQUINS
75	OFFICE MACHNES,ADP EQUIP		247921		217411		261440		353666	MACH BUREAU TRAIT AUTOM
752	AUTOMTIC DATA PROC EQUIP	W 717	85507	W 905	93615	W 1775	132776	W 3049	197445	MACH TRAIT INFORMATION
7523	DIGITL CENTRL PROCESSORS	W 109	34449	W 118	28371	W 912	62782	W 2406	163321	UNITES CENTRALES
759	OFFICE,ADP MCH PTS,ACCES	W 2797	123225	W 1873	80178	W 2504	86621	W 2133	110987	PIECES DU 751 ET 752
76	TELECOMM,SOUND EQUIPMENT		395730		409230		400195		452688	EQUIPMENT DE TELECOM
762	RADIO BROADCAST RECEIVRS	W 4183	336191	W 4017	339083	W 3844	343258	W 3830	357832	RECEPTEURS RADIODIFFUSION
7621	MTR VEHC RADIO RECEIVERS	W 4132	335537	W 3939	338295	W 3758	341625	W 3802	357169	RECEPTEURS RADIO AUTO
77	ELECTRIC MACHNRY NES ETC		882160		875123		948159		963914	MACH APP ELECT NDA
772	SWITCHGEAR ETC,PARTS NES	W 9774	136172	W 9137	151468	W 8135	181282	W 8385	192696	APP COUPURE,SECT ETC
7721	SWITCHGEAR ETC	W 8596	114017	W 8029	125745	W 6852	147059	W 7092	151836	APP COUPURE,SECTIONMNT
775	HOUSEHOLD TYPE EQUIP NES	W 79631	199831	W 61508	145725	W 31627	147576	W 29284	150693	MACH,APP USAGE DOMESTQUE
7752	DOM REFRIGERATRS,FREEZRS	W 69731	128899	W 53518	83806	W 23789	83672	W 18849	73916	REFRIG,CONGEL MENAGER

5. Special Exports F.O.B. by Commodities according to the S.I.T.C. (Rev. 2) in thousand U.S. Dollars
Exportations Spéciales F.O.B. par Produits d'après la C.T.C.I. (Rév. 2) en milliers de Dollars E.U.

SITC CTCI	COMMODITY	1993 WEIGHT POIDS	1993 VALUE VALEUR	1994 WEIGHT POIDS	1994 VALUE VALEUR	1995 WEIGHT POIDS	1995 VALUE VALEUR	1996 WEIGHT POIDS	1996 VALUE VALEUR	PRODUIT
778	ELECTRICAL MACHINERY NES	W 51465	262120	W 54858	284796	W 56785	305974	W 59381	317691	AUTRES MACH ELECT NDA
78	ROAD VEHICLES		2814408		2992723		2663379		2929363	VEHICULES ROUTIERS
781	PASS MOTOR VEH EXC BUSES	W 85337	597585	W 81668	533979	W 67549	455344	W 83550	619248	AUTO TRANSPORT PERSONNES
782	LORRIES,SPCL MTR VEH NES	W 86705	496327	W 102463	617650	W 81994	519088	W 83403	558904	VEHICULES SPECIAUX,MARCH
7821	LORRIES,TRUCKS	W 86058	494041	W 102032	612617	W 81757	517325	W 83325	558183	VEHICULES TRANSP MARCHAND
783	ROAD MOTOR VEHICLES NES	W 91370	382587	W 40655	327469	W 16890	147723	W 12404	107940	VEHICULES ROUTIERS NDA
7831	BUSES	W 84720	338076	W 31663	262151	W 10753	100714	W 7925	70704	VOITURES TRANSPORT COMMUN
784	MOTOR VEH PRTS,ACCES NES	W 376120	1239536	W 375286	1423802	W 350364	1470855	W 333250	1562343	PIECES 722,781,782,783
7841	MOTOR VEHICLE CHASSIS	W 28993	156852	W 27638	185439	W 20248	153328	W 18789	143868	CHASSIS 722,781,782,783
7842	MOTOR VEHICLE BODIES	W 23976	120501	W 21546	144528	W 12897	105707	W 11984	112803	CARROS 722,781,782,783
7849	OTHER MOTOR VEHCL PARTS	W 323151	962183	W 326101	1093835	W 317218	1211819	W 302477	1305671	PIECES 722,781,782,783
79	OTHR TRANSPORT EQUIPMENT		565844		750805		596383		659751	AUTRE MATERIEL TRANSPORT
792	AIRCRAFT ETC	W 700	299715	W 794	309846	W 413	276838	W 1216	457887	APP NAVIGATION AERIENNE
7923	AIRCRFT NES2000–15000KG	W 173	121906	W 103	92594	W 199	171364	W 204	226627	AERODYNES 2000 A 15000 KG
7929	AIRCRAFT PARTS NES	W 426	136887	W 322	105209	W 143	90152	W 199	97367	PIECES DU 792
793	SHIPS AND BOATS ETC	W 181224	223565	W 135868	411922	W 215190	274487	W 304618	186075	NAVIRES BATEAUX,ETC
7932	SHIPS AND BOATS NES	W 178285	220404	W 100555	183076	W 163569	122255	W 295274	154216	NAVIRES ET BATEAUX
79322	TANKERS OF ALL KINDS	W 74194	145351	W 50800	148712	W 60035	57788	W 181593	38001	BATEAUX–CITERNES
7938	TUGS,SPECIAL VESSELS ETC	W 2937	3156	W 35296	228832	W 34197	151186	W 9265	31479	REMORQUEURS,BATEAUX SPEC
79382	SPECL PURPOSE VESSLS ETC	W 22	638	W 31194	222791	W 10807	79452	W 6935	25137	BAT–PHARES,–POMPES,DRAGUES
8	MISC MANUFACTURED GOODS		3491282		3111067		2923696		2979215	ART MANUFACTURES DIVERS
821	*FURNITURE,PARTS THEREOF	W 144953	260101	W 138675	286903	W 140692	331361	W 146947	347663	MEUBLES ET PIECES
8219	FURNITURE AND PARTS NES	W 124067	198026	W 118851	215065	W 124703	267150	W 131450	278167	AUTRES MEUBLES ET PIECES
82192	WOOD FURNITURE NES	W 107009	167579	W 101783	184588	W 110320	237509	W 115539	244524	MEUBLES NDA EN BOIS
84	CLOTHING AND ACCESSORIES		407632		381156		298334		248207	VETEMENTS
846	UNDER GARMENTS KNITTED	W 15935	148758	W 7634	116378	W 6084	108730	W 4160	80615	SOUS VETS DE BONNETERIE
851	*FOOTWEAR	W 144458	1859611	W 92401	1537203	W 78815	1413693	W 84216	1567227	CHAUSSURES
85102	FOOTWEAR LEATHER	W 130488	1803333	W 85003	1488963	W 71402	1356494	W 74931	1480491	CHAUS SEMELLES EN CUIR
87	PRECISION INSTRUMNTS NES		166423		185251		149342		134528	INSTRUM,APPAR SCIENT NDA
88	PHOTO EQU,OPTICL GDS ETC		203631		234403		280813		235442	APP,FOURN PHOTO,OP,MONTR
882	PHOTO,CINEMA SUPPLIES	W 18901	183181	W 20969	213813	W 24344	259194	W 22096	218972	PRODUITS PHOTO,CINEMA
8822	PHOTO FILM EXC DEV CINMA	W 16633	172198	W 18299	202259	W 20422	244142	W 18701	205154	PLAQUES,PELLICULES,FILMS
88223	PHOTO SENSITZD CLOTH ETC	W 11480	108784	W 13863	132711	W 14813	145113	W 13729	136090	PAPIERS SENSIB NON DEVEL
89	MISC MANUFCTRD GOODS NES		561620		449957		415034		419062	ART MANUFACTURES DIVERS
894	TOYS,SPORTING GOODS,ETC	W 12443	126123	W 8594	117296	W 6676	95148	W 4620	84972	VOITURES ENFANTS,JOUETS
9	GOODS NOT CLASSD BY KIND		238301		653335		985874		1226510	ART TRANSACT NON CLASSES
931	*SPECIAL TRANSACTIONS	W 1135055	210444	W 2411022	442788	W 3428593	620110	W 3265132	637453	TRANS.SPECIALES
971	*GOLD,NON MONETARY NES	K 2000	21519	K 16427	202817		359578		583044	OR NON MONETAIRE
97101	NONMON GLD UNWRT,SEMIMFD	K 1935	21516	K 16422	202817	K 34777	359578	K 46970	583044	OR,ALLIAGES D'OR BRUTS

1. HISTORICAL SERIES, 1956–1992 GENERAL TRADE, IMPORTS C.I.F., EXPORTS F.O.B.
SERIES HISTORIQUES, 1956–1992 COMMERCE GENERAL, IMPORTATIONS C.A.F., EXPORTATIONS F.O.B

YEAR ANNEE	VALUE IN MILLION U.S. DOLLARS VALEUR EN MILLION U.S. DOLLARS MERCHANDISE –MARCHANDISE		GOLD –OR		CONVERSION FACTORS FACTEURS DE CONVERSION CENTS E.U. PAR		INDEX NUMBERS –INDICES QUANTUM		UNIT VALUE VALEUR UNITAIRE	
	IMPORTS	EXPORTS	IMPORTS	EXPORTS	IMPORTS	EXPORTS	IMPORTS	EXPORTS	IMPORTS	EXPORTS
1956	0.50	0.14								
1957	0.72	0.15								
1958	0.66	0.17								
1959	0.69	0.14								
1960	0.86	0.19								
1961	1.32	0.15								
1962	1.98	0.15								
1963	2.29	0.16								
1964	2.44	0.11								
1965	2.96	0.10								
1966	4.18	0.16								
1967	3.89	0.10								
1968	6.21	0.15								
1969	8.10	0.06								
1970	10.22	0.07								
1971	8.85	0.37								
1972	7.56	0.17								
1973	9.47	0.44								
1974	11.61	0.43								
1975	13.72	0.50								
1976	14.29	0.54								
1978	21.66	0.81								
1979	32.78	1.41								
1980	40.49	1.16								
1981	49.81	2.00								
1982	58.55	1.24								
1983	70.57	2.25								
1984	77.31	2.29								
1985	86.22	2.02								
1986	94.25	2.56								
1987	105.66	2.56								
1988	119.75	2.81								
1989	130.96									
1990	123.04									
1991	93.14									
1992	105.93									

2. IMPORTS BY BROAD ECONOMIC CATEGORY AND EXPORTS BY INDUSTRIAL ORIGIN. (PERCENTAGE OF TOTAL VALUE)
IMPORTATIONS PAR CATEGORIES ECONOMIQUES ET EXPORTATIONS PAR BRANCHE D'ACTIVITE.(EN POURCENTAGE DE LA VALEUR TOTALE)

IMPORTS – IMPORTATIONS

	1990	1991	1992	1993	1994	1995	1996
TOTAL IMPORTS–IMPORTATIONS TOTALES							
1 FOOD BEV–ALIMENTATION BOISSONS							
11 PRIMARY–PRODUITS DE BASE							
111 FOR INDUSTRY–POUR L'INDUSTRIE							
112 FOR HOUSEHOLDS–POUR LES MENAGES							
12 PROCESSED–PRODUITS ELABORES							
121 FOR INDUSTRY–POUR L'INDUSTRIE							
122 FOR HOUSEHOLDS–POUR LES MENAGES							
2 IND SUPPLIES–APPROV INDUSTRIELS							
21 PRIMARY–PRODUITS DE BASE							
22 PROCESSED–PRODUITS ELABORES							
3 FUELS–COMBUSTIBLES							
31 PRIMARY–PRODUITS DE BASE							
32 PROCESSED–PRODUITS ELABORES							
321 MOTOR SPIRIT–ESSENCE							
322 OTHER–AUTRES							
4 MACHINERY–EQUIPEMENT							
41 CAPITAL EQUIPMENT–MACHINES							
42 PARTS–PIECES ACCESSOIRES							
5 TRANSPORT–TRANSPORT							
51 PASSENGER CARS–AUTOMOBILES							
52 OTHER–AUTRES							
521 INDUSTRIAL–INDUSTRIELS							
522 NON INDUSTRIAL–NON INDUSTRIEL							
53 PARTS–PIECES ACCESSOIRES							
6 CONSUM GOODS–BIENS CONSOMMATION							
61 DURABLE–DURABLES							
62 SEMI DURABLE–SEMI DURABLES							
63 NON DURABLE–NON DURABLES							
7 GOODS NES–BIENS NDA							

EXPORTS – EXPORTATIONS

	1990	1991	1992	1993	1994	1995	1996
TOTAL EXPORTS–EXPORTATIONS TOTALES							
1 AGRICULTURE							
2 MINING QUARRY–INDUS EXTRACTIVES							
3 MANUFACTURING–IND MANUFACTUR							
31 FOOD BEV TOBACCO–ALIM BOISS TAB							
32 TEXTILES–INDUSTRIES TEXTILES							
33 WOOD & PRODUCTS–BOIS & PRODUITS							
34 PAPER & PRODUCTS–PAPIER & PRODT							
35 CHEMICALS–INDUSTRIES CHIMIQUES							
36 NON METAL MIN–MIN NON METAL							
37 BASIC METAL–IND METAL BASE							
38 METAL MANUF–MANUF METAL							
39 OTH MANUF IND–AUTRES MANUF							

3. TRADE BY PRINCIPAL COUNTRIES OF PURCHASE AND CONSUMPTION (VALUE IN THOUSAND U.S. DOLLARS)
ECHANGES SELON LES PRINCIPAUX PAYS D'ACHAT ET DE COMSOMMATION (VALEUR EN MILLIERS DE DOLLARS EU)

COUNTRIES–PAYS	GENERAL IMPORTS C.I.F. IMPORTATIONS GENERALES C.A.F					COUNTRIES–PAYS	GENERAL EXPORTS F.O.B. EXPORTATIONS GENERALES F.O.B.				
	1988	1989	1990	1991	1992		1988	1989	1990	1991	1992
World				93138	105931	Monde					
Africa						Afrique					
Americas				51244	60252	Amériques					
Northern America				49763	56513	Amérique du Nord					
LAIA						ALAI					
CACM						MCAC					
Caribbean				1256	3171	Caraïbes					
Rest of America				225	568	Autre Amérique					
As.ex F.USSR						Asie l'URSS exclus					
Eur.x F.USSR				2086	4347	Europe l'URSS exclus					
EU				2086	4347	UE					
EFTA						AELE					
East Europe						Europe de l'Est					
Other Europe						Autre de l'Europe					
Former USSR						Ancienne URSS					
Oceania						Océanie					
USA/Etats–Unis d'Amer				49513	56479						
United Kingdom				2031	4070						
Trinidad and Tobago				523	1489						
Antigua and Barbuda				201	827						
Barbados/Barbade				438	406						
Guyana				221	568						
St Vincent & Grenadines				45	333						
Canada				250	34						
France, Monac				42	194						

(VALUE AS PERCENTAGE OF WORLD TOTAL)(VALEURS EN POURCENTAGE DU TOTAL MONDIAL)

	1983	1984	1985	1986	1987	1988	1989	1990	1991	1992
Africa										
Americas									55.0	56.9
Northern America									53.4	53.3
LAIA										
CACM										
Caribbean									1.3	3.0
Rest of America									0.2	0.5
As.ex F.USSR										
Eur.x F.USSR									2.2	4.1
EU									2.2	4.1
EFTA										
East Europe										
Other Europe										
Former USSR										
Oceania										
USA/Etats–Unis d'Amer									53.2	53.3
United Kingdom									2.2	3.8
Trinidad and Tobago									0.6	1.4
Antigua and Barbuda									0.2	0.8
Barbados/Barbade									0.5	0.4
Guyana									0.2	0.5
St Vincent & Grenadines									0.0	0.3
Canada									0.3	0.0
France, Monac									0.0	0.2

	1983	1984	1985	1986	1987	1988	1989	1990	1991	1992
Afrique										
Amériques	80.7	39.7		19.4						
Amérique du Nord	80.5	38.8		18.0						
ALAI										
MCAC										
Caraïbes	0.3	0.9		1.2						
Autre Amérique		0.0		0.2						
Asie l'URSS exclus										
Europe l'URSS exclus	4.2	0.1		25.0						
UE	4.2	0.1		25.0						
AELE										
Europe de l'Est										
Autre de l'Europe										
Ancienne URSS										
Océanie										

4. General Imports C.I.F. by Commodities according to the S.I.T.C. (Rev. 2) in thousand U.S. Dollars
Importations Générales C.A.F. par Produits d'après la C.T.C.I. (Rév. 2) en milliers de Dollars E.U.

SITC CTCI	COMMODITY	1989 WEIGHT POIDS	1989 VALUE VALEUR	1990 WEIGHT POIDS	1990 VALUE VALEUR	1991 WEIGHT POIDS	1991 VALUE VALEUR	1992 WEIGHT POIDS	1992 VALUE VALEUR	PRODUIT
	ALL COMMODITIES		130963		123038		93138		105931	TOUS PRODUITS
0	FOOD AND LIVE ANIMALS		25579		22266		16001		21321	ALIMENTS,ANIMAUX VIVANTS
1	BEVERAGES AND TOBACCO		5887		7488		5966		6743	BOISSONS ET TABACS
2	CRUDE MATERLS,EXCL FUELS		2917		2169		3053		2937	MAT BRUTES NON COMESTIBLES
3	MINERAL FUELS ETC		7286		13699		5274		8758	COMBUSTIBLES MINERAUX LUB
4	ANIMAL,VEGETABLE OIL,FAT		297		306		175		324	HUILES,GRAISSES ANIM,VEG
5	CHEMCLS,RELATED PROD NES		13298		7364		6061		7121	PRODUITS CHIMIQUES
6	BASIC MANUFACTURES		12527		18213		16820		19015	ART MANUFACTURES
7	MACHINES,TRANSPORT EQUIP		52634		30666		28281		27023	MACHINES MATERIEL TRANSPORT
8	MISC MANUFACTURED GOODS		9610		16367		11446		12689	ART MANUFACTURES DIVERS
9	GOODS NOT CLASSD BY KIND		928		4500		61			ART TRANSACT NON CLASSES

5. General Exports F.O.B. by Commodities according to the S.I.T.C. (Rev. 2) in thousand U.S. Dollars
Exportations Générales F.O.B. par Produits d'après la C.T.C.I. (Rév. 2) en milliers de Dollars E.U.

SITC CTCI	COMMODITY	1984 WEIGHT POIDS	1984 VALUE VALEUR	1985 WEIGHT POIDS	1985 VALUE VALEUR	1986 WEIGHT POIDS	1986 VALUE VALEUR	1987 WEIGHT POIDS	1987 VALUE VALEUR	PRODUIT
	ALL COMMODITIES		2290		2024		2559			TOUS PRODUITS
0	FOOD AND LIVE ANIMALS		19		101		129			ALIMENTS,ANIMAUX VIVANTS
1	BEVERAGES AND TOBACCO		1116		1247		1543			BOISSONS ET TABACS
2	CRUDE MATERLS,EXCL FUELS		330		432		462			MAT BRUTES NON COMESTIBLES
6	BASIC MANUFACTURES		157		50		40			ART MANUFACTURES
7	MACHINES,TRANSPORT EQUIP		25		35		30			MACHINES MATERIEL TRANSPORT
8	MISC MANUFACTURED GOODS						11			ART MANUFACTURES DIVERS
9	GOODS NOT CLASSD BY KIND		644		156		343			ART TRANSACT NON CLASSES

1. HISTORICAL SERIES, 1959–1994 GENERAL TRADE, IMPORTS C.I.F., EXPORTS F.O.B.
SERIES HISTORIQUES, 1959–1994 COMMERCE GENERAL, IMPORTATIONS C.A.F., EXPORTATIONS F.O.B

YEAR / ANNEE	VALUE IN MILLION BRUNEI DOLLARS / VALEUR EN MILLION BRUNEI DOLLARS: MERCHANDISE – MARCHANDISE IMPORTS	EXPORTS	GOLD – OR IMPORTS	EXPORTS	CONVERSION FACTORS U.S. CENTS PER BRUNEI DOLLAR / FACTEURS DE CONVERSION CENTS E.U. PAR BRUNEI DOLLAR: IMPORTS	EXPORTS	INDEX NUMBERS – INDICES: QUANTUM IMPORTS	EXPORTS	UNIT VALUE / VALEUR UNITAIRE IMPORTS	EXPORTS
1959	57.10	309.00	0.03		32.6667	32.6667				
1960	53.50	254.70	0.07		32.6667	32.6667				
1961	49.10	235.60	0.56		32.6667	32.6667				
1962	48.70	199.30	0.39		32.6667	32.6667				
1963	63.40	182.60	2.56		32.6667	32.6667				
1964	96.30	187.40	5.87		32.6667	32.6667				
1965	109.80	199.80	4.25		32.6667	32.6667				
1966	150.00	225.50	6.54		32.6667	32.6667				
1967	130.90	248.30	6.76		32.6667	32.6667				
1968	206.60	281.40	3.12		32.6667	32.6667				
1969	218.70	270.10	3.30		32.6667	32.6667				
1970	256.10	281.90	3.39		32.6667	32.6667				
1971	456.60	310.70	2.79		32.6667	32.6667				
1972	300.20	469.70	1.85		35.4667	35.4667				
1973	323.20	852.10	0.10		41.0779	41.0779				
1974	450.90	2388.30			41.5581	41.5581				
1975	648.90	2494.80	0.22		41.5286	41.4834				
1976	642.50	3293.20	1.06		39.3513	39.3558				
1977	680.40	3996.00			40.6289	40.7006				
1978	639.20	4195.20			43.2205	43.2206				
1979	862.10	5796.50			45.7002	45.7002				
1980	1331.50	9852.50			45.8693	45.8693				
1981	1265.00	8591.70			47.3267	47.3267				
1982	1571.70	8153.30			46.7020	46.7020				
1983	1542.20	7170.70			47.2156	47.2156				
1984	1331.50	6813.90			47.0157	47.0157				
1985	1348.40	6532.90			45.5731	45.4886				
1986	1456.96	3990.10			45.0425	45.0425				
1987	1350.18	4005.61			47.4834	47.4834				
1988	1497.30	3436.45			49.6919	49.6919				
1989	1675.01	3672.61			51.2742	51.2742				
1990	1813.16	4010.15			55.1930	55.1930				
1991	1922.38	4266.97			62.8580	62.8580				
1992	1916.80	3863.20			61.3490	61.3490				
1993	2012.60	3684.50			59.6595	59.6595				
1994	2497.00	3383.20			67.8795	67.8795				

2. IMPORTS BY BROAD ECONOMIC CATEGORY AND EXPORTS BY INDUSTRIAL ORIGIN. (PERCENTAGE OF TOTAL VALUE)
IMPORTATIONS PAR CATEGORIES ECONOMIQUES ET EXPORTATIONS PAR BRANCHE D'ACTIVITE.(EN POURCENTAGE DE LA VALEUR TOTALE)

IMPORTS – IMPORTATIONS

	1990	1991	1992	1993	1994	1995	1996
TOTAL IMPORTS–IMPORTATIONS TOTALES	100.	100.	100.	100.	100.		
1 FOOD BEV–ALIMENTATION BOISSONS	17.2	13.7	11.0	8.2	12.8		
11 PRIMARY–PRODUITS DE BASE	6.3	5.3	4.2	3.4	5.1		
111 FOR INDUSTRY–POUR L'INDUSTRIE	0.8	0.7	0.4	0.4	0.4		
112 FOR HOUSEHOLDS–POUR LES MENAGES	5.5	4.6	3.7	2.9	4.7		
12 PROCESSED–PRODUITS ELABORES	10.9	8.3	6.8	4.9	7.7		
121 FOR INDUSTRY–POUR L'INDUSTRIE	0.4	0.3	0.5	0.4	0.6		
122 FOR HOUSEHOLDS–POUR LES MENAGES	10.5	8.0	6.3	4.5	7.1		
2 IND SUPPLIES–APPROV INDUSTRIELS	31.1	30.2	28.7	23.2	32.7		
21 PRIMARY–PRODUITS DE BASE	1.3	1.0	1.3	0.7	2.0		
22 PROCESSED–PRODUITS ELABORES	29.8	29.1	27.4	22.5	30.8		
3 FUELS–COMBUSTIBLES	0.9	0.6	0.6	1.1	0.4		
31 PRIMARY–PRODUITS DE BASE	0.0	0.0	0.0	0.0	0.0		
32 PROCESSED–PRODUITS ELABORES	0.9	0.6	0.6	1.1	0.4		
321 MOTOR SPIRIT–ESSENCE	0.4	0.1	0.1	0.5	0.0		
322 OTHER–AUTRES	0.5	0.5	0.5	0.6	0.4		
4 MACHINERY–EQUIPEMENT	20.9	24.6	22.3	27.7	21.4		
41 CAPITAL EQUIPMENT–MACHINES	14.2	17.6	16.0	17.6	18.8		
42 PARTS–PIECES ACCESSOIRES	6.6	7.0	6.4	10.1	2.6		
5 TRANSPORT–TRANSPORT	15.7	14.9	19.6	25.6	14.6		
51 PASSENGER CARS–AUTOMOBILES	8.3	7.4	7.6	5.6	4.3		
52 OTHER–AUTRES	1.0	1.5	8.1	16.4	5.5		
521 INDUSTRIAL–INDUSTRIELS	0.9	1.4	7.9	16.3	5.5		
522 NON INDUSTRIAL–NON INDUSTRIEL	0.0	0.1	0.2	0.1	0.1		
53 PARTS–PIECES ACCESSOIRES	6.4	6.0	4.0	3.6	4.7		
6 CONSUM GOODS–BIENS CONSOMMATION	13.8	15.5	17.5	13.9	17.8		
61 DURABLE–DURABLES	3.1	3.2	6.7	6.1	3.4		
62 SEMI DURABLE–SEMI DURABLES	6.4	8.3	6.8	4.7	6.7		
63 NON DURABLE–NON DURABLES	4.4	4.0	4.1	3.1	7.7		
7 GOODS NES–BIENS NDA	0.4	0.5	0.3	0.3	0.3		

EXPORTS – EXPORTATIONS

	1990	1991	1992	1993	1994	1995	1996
TOTAL EXPORTS–EXPORTATIONS TOTALES	100.	100.	100.	100.	100.		
1 AGRICULTURE	0.1	0.1					
2 MINING QUARRY–INDUS EXTRACTIVES	90.9	91.9	95.9	96.2	95.3		
3 MANUFACTURING–IND MANUFACTUR	9.0	8.0	4.1	3.8	4.7		
31 FOOD BEV TOBACCO–ALIM BOISS TAB	0.6	0.5	0.0	0.0	0.0		
32 TEXTILES–INDUSTRIES TEXTILES	0.5	0.6	0.7	0.3	1.3		
33 WOOD & PRODUCTS–BOIS & PRODUITS	0.0	0.0	0.0				
34 PAPER & PRODUCTS–PAPIER & PRODT	0.0	0.0	0.0	0.0	0.0		
35 CHEMICALS–INDUSTRIES CHIMIQUES	5.7	4.9	3.3	3.5	3.4		
36 NON METAL MIN–MIN NON METAL	0.1	0.0	0.0	0.0			
37 BASIC METAL–IND METAL BASE	0.1	0.0					
38 METAL MANUF–MANUF METAL	1.9	1.8	0.0	0.0	0.0		
39 OTH MANUF IND–AUTRES MANUF	0.1	0.1	0.0		0.0		

3. TRADE BY PRINCIPAL COUNTRIES OF PRODUCTION AND LAST CONSIGNMENT (VALUE IN THOUSAND U.S. DOLLARS)
ECHANGES SELON LES PRINCIPAUX PAYS DE PRODUCTION ET DE DERNIERE CONSIGNATION (VALEUR EN MILLIERS DE DOLLARS EU)

COUNTRIES–PAYS	GENERAL IMPORTS C.I.F. IMPORTATIONS GENERALES C.A.F				
	1990	1991	1992	1993	1994
World	1000738	1208372	1475663	1820541	1873637
Africa	329	1194	37470	51382	101293
Americas	157272	173165	275407	459394	216904
Northern America	154109	169732	274420	458545	215613
LAIA	2951	3297	212	289	533
CACM			10	2	7
Caribbean	23	16	330	239	352
Rest of America	189	120	434	318	399
As.ex F.USSR	627122	711133	514066	497248	668597
Eur.x F.USSR	185731	291149	635521	779667	864942
EU	181060	288207	305960	468310	335951
EFTA	4319	2375	508	188	6524
East Europe	201	531	329027	311152	522304
Other Europe	151	36	3	1	116
Former USSR	4	36	41	95	4
Oceania	29146	29819	13158	32755	21897
USA/Etats–Unis d'Amer	152894	165218	272399	457079	212420
Romania/Roumanie	34	114	328591	310792	521419
Japan/Japon	145783	190583	229310	170534	189081
Malaysia/Malaisie	102764	116236	135123	150790	244585
Singapore/Singapour	259034	266731			
United Kingdom	65437	85100	90567	77356	130105
Germany/Allemagne	39415	51273	59876	216857	77102
Italy/Italie	21466	53719	82737	94610	37588
Indonesia/Indonésie	18672	19967	25540	54763	67237
Thailand/Thaïlande	37209	32434	27829	29259	58454
Netherlands/Pays–Bas	20403	31610	21428	51996	41538
China/Chine	27057	34770	30732	22712	33398
Angola			29483	45602	65135
Hong Kong	15658	21402	27510	29866	19537
France,Monac	14373	12532	38256	12027	16161
Denmark/Danemark	7835	32620	6416	5651	17323
Korea, Republic of	6213	7647	12531	15832	17710
Australia/Australie	25785	26413	0	1	1
New Zealand	3360	3404	6062	7150	17248
So. Africa Customs Un			2348	1512	29654
Kiribati			5357	22579	3706
Sweden/Suède	4161	5949	4358	3679	12220
Canada	1215	4515	2013	1466	3194
India/Inde	1272	1808	2334	2805	3886
Belgium–Luxembourg	2735	4554	9	3427	123
Spain/Espagne	1628	1673	1287	1658	2552
Finland/Finlande	1063	6131	365	334	472
Norway,SVD,JM	582	421	469	184	6321
Guinea–Bissau			3005	2269	2559
United Arab Emirates	85	848	1456	1467	3633
Gambia/Gambie			1391	1585	2951
Switz.Liecht	3737	1951	14	3	202
Austria/Autriche	1655	2733			
Micronesia/Micronésie			1511	1332	562
Philippines	1553	1561			
Brazil/Brésil	1167	1647			
Ireland/Irlande	809	182	533	499	480
Argentina/Argentine	1236	1215			
Qatar	0		871	705	351
Nepal/Népal	6	4	216	1366	281
Chile/Chili	306	139	114	226	447
Falkland Isl (Malvinas)			419	317	396
Egypt/Egypte	6	13	689	59	95
Mali			96	174	576
Portugal	73	130	130	216	285
Iran (Islamic Rp. of)	61	121	75	157	370
Israel/Israël	25	36	615	42	64
Turkey/Turquie	40	30	569	35	46
Poland/Pologne	41	118	120	116	264
Czech Republic				81	517

COUNTRIES–PAYS	GENERAL EXPORTS F.O.B. EXPORTATIONS GENERALES F.O.B.				
	1990	1991	1992	1993	1994
Monde	2213320	2682129	2301218	2093947	2110310
Afrique	53	96	88618	48670	34533
Amériques	75922	29201	20811	8652	46631
Amérique du Nord	75911	29177	19854	8644	23595
ALAI		23			
MCAC					
Caraïbes			957	8	23036
Autre Amérique	11				
Asie l'URSS exclus	2102606	2562088	2137913	2019343	2028314
Europe l'URSS exclus	5475	14148	661	65	748
UE	5328	13670	434	65	746
AELE	148	470	227		2
Europe de l'Est		9			
Autre de l'Europe					
Ancienne URSS					
Océanie	29262	76597	53197	17218	84
Japan/Japon	1285903	1678644	1613032	1566957	1526514
Thailand/Thaïlande	170695	220328	214766	214691	245232
Viet Nam			235154	173747	196821
Korea, Republic of	274011	276182			
Singapore/Singapour	156524	179417			
Philippines	108278	104041			
Guinea–Bissau			88618	48670	34515
Australia/Australie	29225	70956	53197	17218	84
USA/Etats–Unis d'Amer	75577	28370	19559	8643	23286
Malaysia/Malaisie	27354	27380	1555	443	190
Antigua and Barbuda			957	8	23036
United Kingdom	2664	8847	366	65	708
China/Chine	3183	3813	4593		
New Zealand	35	5640			
France,Monac	1124	1609		0	
Netherlands/Pays–Bas	642	1622	21	0	0
Germany/Allemagne	602	1252	30		
Canada	318	807	295	1	309
Pakistan	1208	4			
Norway,SVD,JM	147	455	227		
Indonesia/Indonésie	353	272			
Hong Kong	139	258	143		14
Nepal/Népal	273	90			
United Arab Emirates	56	132			
Belgium–Luxembourg	185				
Spain/Espagne		145			
Italy/Italie	40	103			
Denmark/Danemark	11	26	17		34
Austria/Autriche		66			
India/Inde	16	28			
Sweden/Suède	42				
Nigeria/Nigéria	28				
Mexico/Mexique		23			
Finland/Finlande	18				4
Oman	19	1			
So. Africa Customs Un					17
Switz.Liecht	1	14			2
Hungary/Hongrie		9			
Turkey/Turquie	3				
Egypt/Egypte					0

(VALUE AS PERCENTAGE OF WORLD TOTAL)(VALEURS EN POURCENTAGE DU TOTAL MONDIAL)

	1985	1986	1987	1988	1989	1990	1991	1992	1993	1994
Africa		0.0	0.0	0.0	0.0	0.0	0.1	2.5	2.8	5.4
Americas	7.8	12.5	12.5	13.1	13.2	15.7	14.3	18.7	25.2	11.6
Northern America	7.8	12.3	12.2	12.7	12.9	15.4	14.0	18.6	25.2	11.5
LAIA	0.0	0.1	0.2	0.3	0.3	0.3	0.3	0.0	0.0	0.0
CACM			0.0					0.0	0.0	0.0
Caribbean		0.0	0.0	0.0	0.0	0.0	0.0	0.0	0.0	0.0
Rest of America		0.0	0.0	0.0		0.0	0.0	0.0	0.0	0.0
As.ex F.USSR	70.0	60.1	60.1	63.1	62.7	62.7	58.9	34.8	27.3	35.7
Eur.x F.USSR	21.0	24.6	23.0	19.8	21.4	18.6	24.1	43.1	42.8	46.2
EU	18.7	24.2	22.7	19.3	20.9	18.1	23.9	20.7	25.7	17.9
EFTA	2.4	0.4	0.3	0.4	0.5	0.4	0.2	0.0	0.0	0.3
East Europe		0.0	0.0	0.0	0.1	0.0	0.0	22.3	17.1	27.9
Other Europe		0.0	0.0	0.0	0.0	0.0	0.0	0.0	0.0	0.0
Former USSR	1.1	0.0	0.0	0.0	0.0	0.0	0.0	0.0	0.0	0.0
Oceania	0.1	2.8	3.9	3.7	2.4	2.9	2.5	0.9	1.8	1.2
USA/Etats–Unis d'Amer	7.8	12.2	12.1	12.6	12.7	15.3	13.7	18.5	25.1	11.3
Romania/Roumanie		0.0	0.0	0.0	0.0	0.0	0.0	22.3	17.1	27.8
Japan/Japon	13.8	17.7	14.4	16.0	14.7	14.6	15.8	15.5	9.4	10.1
Malaysia/Malaisie	6.3	5.9	8.2	7.9	9.1	10.3	9.6	9.2	8.3	13.1
Singapore/Singapour	44.7	25.8	24.1	26.5	26.9	25.9	22.1			
United Kingdom	13.7	7.9	8.3	7.8	8.8	6.5	7.0	6.1	4.2	6.9
Germany/Allemagne	0.9	6.0	3.4	4.7	4.4	3.9	4.2	4.1	11.9	4.1
Italy/Italie	0.8	2.2	2.7	1.6	1.8	2.1	4.4	5.6	5.2	2.0
Indonesia/Indonésie		0.7	0.9	1.3	1.7	1.9	1.7	1.7	3.0	3.6
Thailand/Thaïlande	1.5	3.1	4.4	4.0	3.8	3.7	2.7	1.9	1.6	3.1

	1985	1986	1987	1988	1989	1990	1991	1992	1993	1994
Afrique		0.0	0.0	0.0	0.0	0.0	0.0	3.9	2.3	1.6
Amériques	0.1	6.1	1.6	2.1	4.9	3.4	1.1	0.9	0.4	2.2
Amérique du Nord	0.1	6.1	1.6	2.1	4.9	3.4	1.1	0.9	0.4	1.1
ALAI		0.0		0.0	0.0		0.0			
MCAC										
Caraïbes	0.0							0.0	0.0	1.1
Autre Amérique				0.0		0.0				
Asie l'URSS exclus	98.7	92.9	97.1	96.5	94.0	95.0	95.5	92.9	96.4	96.1
Europe l'URSS exclus	1.2	0.2	0.2	0.1	0.2	0.2	0.5	0.0	0.0	0.0
UE	1.2	0.2	0.2	0.1	0.1	0.2	0.5	0.0	0.0	0.0
AELE	0.0	0.0	0.0	0.0	0.0	0.0	0.0	0.0		0.0
Europe de l'Est					0.0		0.0			
Autre de l'Europe										
Ancienne URSS				0.0						
Océanie		0.9	1.1	1.3	0.9	1.3	2.9	2.3	0.8	0.0
Japan/Japon	70.7	66.8	61.7	65.0	58.1	58.1	62.6	70.1	74.8	72.3
Thailand/Thaïlande	8.3	8.1	11.7	8.8	10.3	7.7	8.2	9.3	10.3	11.6
Viet Nam				0.0	0.0			10.2	8.3	9.3
Korea, Republic of	8.4	7.4	9.7	10.4	13.1	12.4	10.3			
Singapore/Singapour	9.1	6.7	6.7	5.7	4.8	7.1	6.7			
Philippines	2.2	0.7	3.2	2.0	2.6	4.9	3.9			
Guinea–Bissau								3.9	2.3	1.6
Australia/Australie		0.8	1.1	1.3	0.9	1.3	2.6	2.3	0.8	0.0
USA/Etats–Unis d'Amer	0.1	6.1	1.6	2.1	4.9	3.4	1.1	0.8	0.4	1.1
Malaysia/Malaisie	0.1	1.4	1.2	1.4	1.2	1.2	1.0	0.1	0.0	0.0

4. General Imports C.I.F. by Commodities according to the S.I.T.C. (Rev. 2) in thousand U.S. Dollars
Importations Générales C.A.F. par Produits d'après la C.T.C.I. (Rév. 2) en milliers de Dollars E.U.

SITC CTCI	COMMODITY	1991 WEIGHT POIDS	1991 VALUE VALEUR	1992 WEIGHT POIDS	1992 VALUE VALEUR	1993 WEIGHT POIDS	1993 VALUE VALEUR	1994 WEIGHT POIDS	1994 VALUE VALEUR	PRODUIT
	ALL COMMODITIES		1208372		1475663		1820541		1873637	TOUS PRODUITS
0	FOOD AND LIVE ANIMALS		155437		146698		136427		221531	ALIMENTS,ANIMAUX VIVANTS
001	*LIVE ANIMALS FOR FOOD	N 2441700	7165	W 6446	4779	W 7450	6697	W 5801	6035	ANIMAUX VIVANTS
0011	BOVINE SPECIES,LIVE	N 8178	5314	W 6441	4142	W 7446	6021	W 5794	5332	ESPECE BOVINE
00111	— PURE BRED FR BREEDING	N 690	451	W 4546	2969	W 7177	5846	W 5649	5229	BOVINS REPRODUCTEURS
00119	— OTHR THAN FR BREEDING	N 7488	4862	W 1895	1173	W 269	175	W 145	103	BOVINS NON REPRODUCTEURS
01	MEAT AND PREPARATIONS		26127		25307		24925		44018	VIANDES ET PREPARATIONS
011	MEAT FRESH,CHILLD,FROZEN	W 11307	21907	W 10240	21726	W 7732	20951	W 16156	37349	VIANDES FRAICHES,REF,CONGE
0111	BOVINE MEAT FRESH,FROZEN	W 1441	4278	W 1159	4266	W 1001	3853	W 1957	6629	VIANDES BOVIN FRAI,REF
01111	BOVINE MEAT WITH BONE IN			W 1159	4266	W 1001	3853	W 1957	6629	VIANDES BOVIN NON DESOSS
0114	POULTRY FRESH CHLLD,FRZN	W 8512	15231	W 7876	14018	W 5044	12656	W 10361	19989	VOLAILLES MORTES
0118	MEAT NES FRESH,CHLD,FRZN	W 103	252	W 394	1161	W 948	2572	W 2144	6131	AUTRES VIANDES,ABATS
014	MEAT PREPD,PRSVD,NES ETC	W 1184	3801	W 974	3437	W 1106	3154	W 1340	4092	CONSERVES DE VIANDES
02	DAIRY PRODCTS,BIRDS'EGGS		14652		14211		11237		12735	PRODUITS LAITIERS,OEUFS
022	MILK AND CREAM	W 5160	12001	W 4486	10748	W 3855	8228	W 3418	8699	LAIT ET CREME
0224	MILK,CREAM PRESERVED ETC	W 5111	11916	W 4313	10398	W 3556	7734	W 2699	7766	LAIT,CREME CONS,CONC
02243	MILK DRY,OVER 1.5% FAT	W 1595	7021	W 1578	5539	W 1500	3756	W 1417	3508	LAIT POUDRE SUP 1.5%
02249	MILK(EX DRY) PRSVD,SWEET	W 3260	4393	W 2528	4304	W 1873	3371	W 1072	3270	LAIT CONS,CONC SUCRE
03	FISH AND PREPARATIONS		12709		13470		12909		32565	POISSONS ET PREPARATIONS
034	FISH,FRESH,CHILLED,FROZN		4321	W 399	5035	W 959	4861	W 2052	8761	POISSON FRAIS, REFRIG,CONG
036	SHELL FISH FRESH,FROZEN	W 759	3675	W 966	3561	W 1854	3810	W 1920	6317	CRUSTACES,MOLLUSQUES
037	FISH ETC PREPD,PRSVD NES	W 804	3484	W 866	3655	W 771	3038	W 7979	15512	POIS,CRUST,MOL PREPARES
0371	FISH PREPARD,PRESRVD NES	W 493	1656	W 489	1779	W 506	1538	W 7454	13134	CONSERVES DE POISSONS
04	CEREALS AND PREPARATIONS		28248		28225		23364		41102	CEREALES ET PRODUITS
042	RICE	W 21324	9169	W 17069	7962	W 13058	4009	W 19334	9866	RIZ
0422	RICE SEMI–MILLED,MILLED	W 21324	9169	W 17069	7962	W 13058	4004	W 19334	9866	RIZ POLI,GLACE INCL BRISURES
04221	RICE MILLED UNBROKEN	W 21301	9162	W 17069	7959	W 13058	4003	W 19334	9837	RIZ POLI,GLACE EXCL BRISURES
048	CEREAL ETC PREPARATIONS	W 8408	15883	W 8177	17621	W 10456	16687	W 11317	27645	PREPTNS A BASE CEREALES
0483	MACARONI,SPAGHETTI ETC	W 1502	1728	W 2954	5340	W 5146	4593	W 2843	6608	PATES ALMENTAIRES
0484	BAKERY PRODUCTS	W 2422	7769	W 2702	7031	W 2259	6126	W 3379	10312	PRODUITS DE BOULANGERIE
04841	BREAD,BISCUIT,COM WAFERS	W 19	47	W 1673	4642	W 1467	4268	W 1920	6538	PAINS,BISCUITS DE MER
04842	PASTRY, CAKES ETC	W 2403	7722	W 1029	2388	W 792	1859	W 1458	3774	PATISSERIE ETC.
0488	OTH CEREAL PREPS,MALT EX	W 1166	3403	W 1210	2971	W 2069	3880	W 3202	7773	EXTRAITS DE MALT
05	VEGETABLES AND FRUIT		31158		29894		27886		41859	LEGUMES ET FRUITS
054	VEG ETC FRSH,SMPLY PRSVD		7700		7880		7520		10633	LEGUMES FRAIS,CONG,SECS
0545	OTHER FRESH VEGETABLES	W 5554	5471	W 3949	4948	W 5440	4433	W 5357	6532	AUTRES LEGUMES FRAIS,REF
05459	FRESH VEGETABLES NES	W 2897	3764	W 2670	3664	W 3564	3201	W 3255	4888	LEGUMES FRAIS,REFRI NDA
057	FRUIT,NUTS,FRESH,DRIED		14003	W 11031	12856	W 15326	12535	W 13064	19499	FRUITS FRAIS OU SECS
0579	FRUIT FRESH OR DRIED NES	W 5870	6155	W 2661	5362	W 4610	5364	W 3786	8231	FRUITS FRAIS,SECS NDA
05798	OTHER FRESH FRUIT	W 3907	4021	W 1477	2839	W 2842	3025	W 2242	4783	AUTRES FRUITS FRAIS
058	FRUIT PRESERVED,PREPARED	W 2985	6005		5794		4809		7032	CONSERVES DE FRUITS
0589	FRUIT PREPRD,PRESRVD,NES	W 1602	3988		3524		2515		3013	FRUITS PREPARES CONSERV
06	SUGAR AND PREPS,HONEY		6411		4425		4466		5068	SUCRES ET PRODUITS
061	SUGAR AND HONEY		3867	W 1327	1620	W 1754	1357	W 587	1608	SUCRES ET MIEL
0612	REFINED SUGAR ETC	W 6643	3720	W 1193	1336	W 1697	1128	W 461	821	SUCRES RAFFINES
07	COFFEE,TEA,COCOA,SPICES		7723		8370		8426		13003	CAFE,THE,CACAO,EPICES
073	CHOCOLATE AND PRODUCTS	W 500	3131	W 1034	3979	W 1170	4657	W 2937	8317	CHOCOLAT
081	*FEEDING STUFF FOR ANIML	W 14429	8231	W 7664	7311	W 5749	5925	W 11409	8712	NOURRITURE POUR ANIMAUX
0819	FOOD WASTE AND FEED NES	W 7958	5429	W 2372	4695	W 2912	3798	W 6820	6160	DECHETS,ALIMENTS NDA
08199	FODDER NES,INCL SWEETNED	W 7958	5429	W 2372	4680	W 2912	3797	W 6819	6111	PREPARATIONS FOURRAGERES
09	MISC EDIBLE PRODUCTS		13012		10705		10592		16434	PREP ALIMENTAIRES DIVERSES
098	EDIBLE PRODCTS,PREPS NES		12384	W 3852	10009		10112		15476	PREP ALIMENTAIRES NDA
09804	SAUCES,MIXED SEASONINGS	W 2302	3354	W 1327	3608	W 1542	3191	W 2536	7213	SAUCES,ASSAISONNEMENTS
09809	MISC FOOD PREPRTIONS NES	W 3329	7806	W 2027	5340		4992		5865	PREP ALIMENTAIRES NDA
1	BEVERAGES AND TOBACCO		28895		33424		31904		40827	BOISSONS ET TABACS
11	BEVERAGES		17515		19150		16860		21505	BOISSONS
111	NON–ALCOHL BEVERAGES NES	W 19846	17009	W 21821	17009	W 22567	14910	W 25941	19683	BOISSONS NON ALCOOLIQUES
11102	FLAVORED WATERS NON–ALCO	W 16328	14883	W 16444	14271	W 15503	12502	W 18236	15747	LIMONADES,EAUX GAZEUSES
12	TOBACCO AND MANUFACTURES		11379		14274		15044		19322	TABACS BRUTS FABRIQUES
122	TOBACCO,MANUFACTURED	W 420	11378	W 409	14274	W 424	15043	W 481	19321	TABACS FABRIQUES
1222	CIGARETTES	W 419	11366	W 125	3823	W 139	4423	W 184	6891	CIGARETTES
1223	OTH MANUFACTURED TOBACCO			W 281	10331	W 284	10588	W 293	12259	TABACS FUMER,CHIQUER,PRISER
2	CRUDE MATERLS,EXCL FUELS		14841		24564		16971		46819	MAT BRUTES NON COMESTIBLES
24	CORK AND WOOD		3058		4820		4929		10725	LIEGE ET BOIS
248	WOOD SHAPED,SLEEPERS		2888	W 33600	4496	W 14707	4617	W 29743	10239	BOIS SIMPLEMENT TRAVAILLES
2483	LUMBER SHAPED NON–CONIFR		2824	W 33599	4306	W 14707	4575	W 29741	9798	NON CONIFERES SCIES,RABOTES
24831	LUMBER SAWN ETC NON–CON	W 19536	2644	W 30797	4030	W 13357	4196	W 26716	8568	SCIES LONGITUDINALEMENT
27	CRUDE FERTLZR,MINRLS NES		7812		14984		9545		31647	ENGRAIS MINERAUX BRUTS
273	STONE,SAND AND GRAVEL	W 94945	4808		12421		7328		28999	PIERRES,SABLES,GRAVIERS
2731	BLDG,DIMENSION STONE	W 4230	3666	W 4331	9294	W 2301	4234	W 19970	16252	PIERRES DE TAILLE
27312	MARBLE,ETC BLDG STONE	W 863	1923	W 2270	7148	W 1387	3260	W 13551	11634	MARBRES,TRAVERTINS
2734	GRAVEL,CRUSHED STONE,ETC	W 83779	791	W 145949	2532	W 147945	2607	W 813504	11813	PIERRES CONCASSEES
3	MINERAL FUELS ETC		7356		8733		19707		7580	COMBUSTIBLES MINERAUX LUB
33	PETROLEUM AND PRODUCTS		7345		8664		19436		7316	PETROLE ET DERIVES
334	PETROLEUM PRODUCTS,REFIN	W 20276	7173	W 18306	8109	W 40728	19016	W 5215	6566	PRODUITS RAFFINES
3341	GASOLINE,OTH LIGHT OILS	W 13284	1236	W 13176	1199	W 32916	8910	W 156	77	ESSENCES POUR MOTEURS
33411	MOTOR,AVIATION SPIRIT	W 13253	1195	W 13173	1198	W 32915	8909	W 147	68	ESSENCES MOTEURS D'AVIONS
3345	LUBS,PETROLEUM OILS NES	W 6134	5337	W 2558	5892	W 6337	7770	W 4964	6440	HUILES LUBRIFIANTES
33451	LUBS(HIGH PETR CONT) ETC	W 5790	4802	W 1613	4172	W 1996	3147	W 2113	2367	HUILES LUBRIF,H LOURDES
4	ANIMAL,VEGETABLE OIL,FAT		4109		4953		4196		6298	HUILES,GRAISSES ANIM,VEG
42	FIXED VEGETABLE OIL,FAT		4076		3853		3144		3659	HUILES VEGETALES FIXES
424	FIXED VEG OIL NONSOFT	W 1619	3688	W 496	3431		2411	W 240	2754	AUTRES HUILES VEG FIXES
5	CHEMCLS,RELATED PROD NES		75892		77899		69917		86716	PRODUITS CHIMIQUES
52	INORGANIC CHEMICALS		7335		6691		6244		7119	PROD CHIM INORGANIQUES
522	INORG ELEMNTS,OXIDES,ETC		4140		4482		2637		2571	ELEMENTS INORGANIQUES
53	DYES,TANNING,COLOUR PROD		13315		16912		13560		15917	PROD TEINTURE,COLORANTS
533	PIGMENTS,PAINTS,ETC		13187		16789		13343		15816	PIGMENTS,PEINTURES,VERNIS
5334	VARNISHES,DISTEMPERS ETC		12012	W 5809	15457	W 4474	12668	W 4832	15063	PEINTURES A L'EAU
53342	OTH PAINTS,VARNISHES ETC	V 3143	10598	W 5779	15404	W 4464	12622	W 4634	14678	AUTRES PEINTURES,VERNIS
541	*MEDICINAL,PHARM PRODUCT		14010		16234		12948		20452	PROD MEDICINAUX PHARMACEUT
5417	MEDICAMENTS		10797		12527		9055		13112	MEDICAMENTS
54179	— CONTNG OTH SUBSTANCES		10727		8399		7944		9542	MED CONT AUT SUBSTANCES
55	PERFUME,CLEANING ETC PRD		12805		13217		13452		15355	PROD POUR PARFUM,TOILETTE
553	PERFUMERY,COSMETICS,ETC		5521		6227		5727		7383	PRODUITS DE PARFUMERIE
554	SOAP,CLEANSING ETC PREPS	W 5821	6944		6810		7542		7847	SAVONS,PRODUITS DETERSIFS
5542	WASHING PREPARATIONS ETC	W 5020	5068	W 3007	4152	W 3196	4588	W 2549	4148	PROD ORG TENSIO–ACT NDA
58	PLASTIC MATERIALS ETC		4733		2821		4233		5168	MAT PLAST ARTIFICIELLES
583	POLYMERIZATION ETC PRODS	W 2292	3888		2105		3447		3705	PROD POLYMERISATION
59	CHEMICAL MATERIALS NES		18661		16836		15560		18097	MAT PROD CHIMIQUES NDA
598	MISCEL CHEM PRODUCTS NES		15204		12787		11723		12789	PROD DIV INDUST CHIM NDA
5989	CHEM PRODUCTS,PREPS NES		13569		10670		10269		11331	PROD PREP CHIMIQUES NDA

4. General Imports C.I.F. by Commodities according to the S.I.T.C. (Rev. 2) in thousand U.S. Dollars
Importations Générales C.A.F. par Produits d'après la C.T.C.I. (Rév. 2) en milliers de Dollars E.U.

SITC CTCI	COMMODITY	1991 WEIGHT POIDS	1991 VALUE VALEUR	1992 WEIGHT POIDS	1992 VALUE VALEUR	1993 WEIGHT POIDS	1993 VALUE VALEUR	1994 WEIGHT POIDS	1994 VALUE VALEUR	PRODUIT
59899	OTH CHEM PRODS,PREPS,NES	W 4942	12506	W 3443	8171	W 7658	8979	W 3233	9246	AUT PRODUITS CHIMIQUES NDA
6	BASIC MANUFACTURES		331182		335756		360604		429903	ART MANUFACTURES
62	RUBBER MANUFACTURES NES		7689		11889		9288		10974	CAOUTCHOUC MANUFACTURE
621	MATERIALS OF RUBBER	W 375	2558	W 862	4624	W 331	1914	W 577	2423	PRODUITS EN CAOUTCHOUC
625	RUBBER TYRES, TUBES ETC	N 324782	4085	N 365182	4604	N 369033	4036	N 398572	5102	PNEUS CAOUTCHOUC VULCANISE
63	WOOD,CORK MANUFACTRS NES		8103		11466		9383		12350	OUVRAGES LIEGE ET BOIS
634	VENEERS,PLYWOOD,ETC		5239		6695		5769		7248	PLACAGES,CONTRE–PLAQUES
6342	PLYWOOD OF WOOD SHEETS	V 23138	4287	W 30	5961	W 26	5288	W 48	6641	BOIS CONTRE–PLAQUES
635	WOOD MANUFACTURES NES		2859		4743		3607		5091	ART MANUF EN BOIS NDA
64	PAPER,PAPERBOARD AND MFR		15650		15883		19049		27794	PAPIERS,CARTONS & OUVRAGES
641	PAPER AND PAPERBOARD		6689		4722		6177		8185	PAPIERS ET CARTONS
6412	PRINTG,WRITING PAPER NES	W 2257	3749		970		745		1057	PAPIERS POUR L'IMPRESSION
642	PAPER,ETC,PRECUT,ARTS OF		8961		11161		12872		19609	PAP,CARTONS DECOUPES
6428	PAPER ETC ARTICLES NES		2805		5284		6317		10119	OUVRAGES EN PATE A PAPIER
65	TEXTILE YARN,FABRICS,ETC		30917		38878		41167		43279	FILS,TISSUS,ARTICLES TEXTILE
652	COTTON FABRICS,WOVEN	A 1829	2198	A 1931	2862	A 3309	6240	A 11414	7525	TISSUS DE COTON
6522	WOVEN COTTON BLEACHD,ETC	A 1774	2107	A 1644	2598	A 2684	4863	A 9634	5947	TISSUS COTON BLANCHIS ETC
65224	BLCHED COTTON FABRIC NES	A 1707	2030	A 1429	2426	A 2544	4661	A 9342	5725	AUT TIS PLUS 85% COT BLANCHI
653	WOVN MAN–MADE FIB FABRIC		3084	W 2431	4606		3659	W 1300	3802	TISSUS FIBRES SYNTH,ARTIF
655	KNITTED,ETC FABRICS	A 3829	8487	A 2813	5498	A 281	867	A 1227	1453	ETOF BONNETERIE PIECES ETC
6552	OTHER KNIT ETC FAB NONEL	A 1988	4567	A 2813	5498	A 281	867	A 1227	1453	ETOF BON NON ELAS NON SYNT
65522	KNIT ETC COTTN FAB NONEL	A 1293	3682							ETOF BON NON ELAS COTON
656	LACE,RIBBONS,TULLE,ETC		579		3958		7268		9357	TULLES,BRODERIE
65601	NARROW FABRICS NES	L 905	103	L 29460	2683	L 60035	4625	L 63781	7106	RUBANS SANS TRAME EN FILS
657	SPECIAL TXTL FABRC,PRODS		6232		8338		11469		6245	TISSUS SPECIAUX
6571	FELT AND ARTICLES NES		19		2549		8082	W 178	2792	FEUTRES,ART EN FEUTRE
6577	TEXTILES FOR MACHINERY		4003		3263		1259		1054	OUATES,MECHES ART TEXT
65771	TEXTILE WADDING NES ETC		3917		3250		1210		833	OUATES,ARTICLES EN OUATE
658	TEXTILE ARTICLES NES		4345		5006		3801		4529	ART FACONNES MAT TEXTILES
659	FLOOR COVERINGS,ETC		5248		7020		5023	W 537	6823	COUVRE–PARQUETS,TAPIS ETC
66	NONMETAL MINERAL MFS NES		71672		70530		70875		97027	ART MIN NON METALLIQUES
661	LIME,CEMENT,BLDG PRODS	W 198607	33377	W 188812	23884	W 338982	28039	W 536632	39136	CHAUX,CIMENTS MAT CONSTR
6612	CEMENT	W 186295	18062	W 185058	17923	W 332625	24023	W 528923	32596	CIMENTS HYDRAULIQUES
6613	BUILDING STONE ETC WORKD	W 11415	14469	W 1792	4018	W 4536	2135	W 1050	1716	PIERRES A BATIR
66132	BUILDING STONE WORKED	W 11415	14469	W 1792	4016	W 4536	2114	W 1050	1607	OUVR EN PIERRES DE TAILLE
662	CLAY,REFRACTORY BLDG PRD		18629	W 22949	22809	W 46434	19566	W 30333	23454	MAT CONST REFRACTAIRES
6623	REFRACTORY BUILDING PROD	W 449	440	W 2712	3897	W 7229	4678	W 9093	5711	BRIQUES REFRACTAIRES
6624	BRICKS ETC NONREFRACTORY		18189	W 20238	18912	W 39205	14888	W 21240	17744	BRIQUES ETC CERAM NON REFR
66244	UNGLAZD CERAMC SETTS ETC	W 6051	4900	W 2839	2011	W 2140	2052	W 3646	4193	CARREAUX, NON VERNIS
66245	GLAZED CERAMIC SETTS ETC	W 16587	10523	W 12647	11458	W 14108	6584	W 6947	5775	AUT CARREAUX CERAMIQUE
663	MINERAL MANUFCTURES NES		6835		7368		11408		18910	ART MIN MANUF NDA
6633	MINRL MFS NES NONCERAMIC		5172		6058		9770		17055	OUVR MAT MINERALE NDA
66332	CEMENT,ARTFCL STONE PROD	W 9672	2142	W 14686	4408	W 44294	8553	W 90957	16050	OUVRAGES EN CIMENT
664	GLASS		4670		7983		5618		7800	VERRE
665	GLASSWARE		4853		4514		3318		4834	OUVRAGES EN VERRE
6652	HOUSEHLD,HOTEL ETC GLASS		3637		3259		2590		3667	OBJETS VERRE TABLE,CUISINE
67	IRON AND STEEL		77727		86236		64842		124496	FER ET ACIER
673	IRON,STEEL SHAPES ETC		20903	W 45864	22825	W 38674	26177	W 49324	43801	BARRES,PROFIL FER,ACIER
6731	IRON,STEEL WIRE ROD		763	W 20250	4570	W 18300	4466	W 15000	7111	FIL MACHINE FER,ACIER
67314	STNLESS STL ETC WIRE ROD				1591		2834		6709	FIL MACH ACIER INOXYDABLE
6732	IRON,STEEL BARS ETC	W 33369	14942	W 17355	7700	W 12444	6169	W 14055	10071	BARRES FER,ACIER
67322	HIGH CARBON STL BARS ETC	W 76	99	W 11477	5138	W 2744	1712	W 2407	1207	BARRES ACIER FIN CARBONE
67325	OTH ALLOY STEEL BARS ETC	W 53	33	W 5878	2560	W 9700	4216	W 11648	8766	BARRES NON ACIERS ALLIES
67326	IRN,OTH STL BARS HOTROLD	W 30392	13469							BARRES PLEINES FER,ACIER
6733	IRON,STEEL PROFILES ETC	W 6275	5198	W 8259	10555	W 7930	15542	W 20269	26619	PROFILES,PALPLAN FER,ACIER
67338	STNLESS STL ETC PROFILES	W 17	55	W 1078	4912	W 2558	10519	W 2510	19008	PROFILES ACIER INOXYDABLE
674	IRN,STL UNIV,PLATE,SHEET		6075		7360		3738		11278	LARGES PLATS,TOLES
6744	IRN,STL HVY PLATE,ROLLED	W 196	143		4380		1549		8210	TOLES LAMINEES PLUS 4.75 MM
67443	— OF STAINLESS ETC STL	W 4	12		1709		1029		6392	TOLES ACIER INOXYDABLE
6749	OTH IRN,STL PLATES,SHEET		4909	W 1334	2005	W 430	1330	W 497	1697	AUTRES TOLES FER,ACIER
67491	— OF IRON OR SIMPLE STL	W 4102	4907	W 1334	1302	W 428	592	W 495	562	AUT TOLES AUTRES ACIER FIN
678	IRON,STL TUBES,PIPES,ETC	W 53792	48548	W 47828	51428	W 33943	29850	W 95525	63558	TUBES,TUYAUX EN FONTE,FER
6781	CAST IRON TUBES,PIPES	W 1036	1055	W 876	951	W 2542	1782	W 7959	11325	TUBES,TUYAUX EN FONTE
6782	IRON,STL SEAMLESS TUBES	W 33599	20220	W 17668	21504	W 9195	6483	W 58240	19570	TUBES,TUYAUX SANS SOUDURE
6783	IRON,STL TUBES,PIPES NES	W 13395	14308	W 10725	10146	W 8735	8510	W 9712	12860	AUT TUBES,TUYAUX FER,ACIER
6785	IRON,STEEL TUBE FITTINGS	W 5526	12520	W 18560	18827	W 13472	13075	W 19613	19803	ACCESSOIRES DE TUYAUTERIE
68	NON–FERROUS METALS		4313		6226		7906		10583	METAUX NON FERREUX
69	METAL MANUFACTURES NES		114528		94282		137431		101900	ART MANUFACT EN METAL NDA
691	STRUCTURES AND PARTS NES	W 12994	21153	W 17908	31716	W 15338	65414	W 17106	32219	CONSTRUCT FER,ACIER,ALU
6911	STRUCTURES,PARTS IRN,STL	W 12457	18345	W 13772	27143	W 13734	62642	W 10736	24375	CONSTRUCT FER,ACIER,FONTE
6912	STRUCTURES,PARTS ALUMNM	W 537	2809	W 4137	4573	W 1604	2771	W 6370	7844	CONSTRUCT ALUMINIUM
692	METAL TANKS,BOXES,ETC		3195		4459		24248		3828	RECIPIENTS METALLIQUES
6924	MTL TRANSPORT BOXES ETC		2250		3894		23852		2570	FUTS,TAMBOURS,BIDONS
69242	ALUMNM TRNSPRT BOXES ETC		1786		1539		20373		294	FUTS,TAMBOURS,BIDONS ALU
693	WIRE PRODUCTS NON ELECTR		5926	W 3984	6581	W 2138	5392	W 2749	7267	OUVRAGES FILS METALLIQUES
694	STL,COPPR NAILS,NUTS,ETC	W 3893	4121	W 3554	4964	W 3239	4965	W 3768	7435	CLOUS,VIS,ECROUS
695	TOOLS		25531		15877		10089		11116	OUTILS A MAIN
6953	OTHER HAND TOOLS		3469		6182		4956		6125	AUTRES OUTILS A MAIN
6954	BLADES,TIPS,ETC FR TOOLS		21881		9424		4831		4512	OUTILS POUR MACHINE–OUTIL
69541	PARTS TO INSERT IN TOOLS		21832		9186		4601		4215	OUTILS DE FORAGE
697	BASE MTL HOUSEHOLD EQUIP		26540		6564		5928		9052	ART MENAGE MET COMMUNS
6978	BASE MTL HOUSE EQUIP NES		20905		973		813		775	ART MENAGE MET COMMUNS
69782	BASE MTL DECOR ARTICLES		20876		945		780		673	AUT OBJETS ORNEM INTERIEUR
699	BASE METAL MFRS NES		26400		22691		20001		28402	ART MANUFACTURES MET NDA
6991	LOCKSMITHS WARES,ETC		4655		5464		5055		5667	ARTICLES DE SERRURERIE
6997	IRON,STEEL ARTICLES NES		15484	W 6822	9123	W 2829	7477	W 3589	12641	OUV FONTE,FER,ACIER NDA
69979	IRN,STL MANUFACTURES NES		14924	W 6822	8785	W 2829	7091	W 3589	12455	AUT OUVRAGES EN FER NDA
6998	MFRS NES OF CPR,NIKL,ETC		3664		5065		4980		7726	OUVRAGES EN CU,NI,AL,PB,ZN
7	MACHINES,TRANSPORT EQUIP		462675		650421		902397		792929	MACHINES MATERIEL TRANSPORT
71	POWER GENERATING EQUIPMT		28675		49425		18122		106374	MACHINES GENERATRICES
712	STEAM ENGINES,TURBINES		8691		962		1421		12293	MACHINES A VAPEUR D'EAU PIEC
7126	STEAM POWR UNITS,ENGINES	N 583	775		144		51		10200	MACHINES A VAPEUR D EAU
7129	STM ENGINE ETC PARTS NES		7916		818		1370		2093	PARTIES,PIECES DU 712.6
713	INTRNL COMBUS PSTN ENGIN		7707		6308		4620		5970	MOTEURS EXPL COMB INT, PIECE
714	ENGINES AND MOTORS NES		243	W 84	2855	W 16	1125	W 300	8015	MOTEURS NON ELECTRIQUES
7149	ENGINE & MOTOR PARTS NES		228	W 84	2652	W 14	1013	W 300	7440	PIECES 714 ET 718.88
71499	PARTS NES,OF 71488,71888			W 84	2652	W 13	1010	W 300	7339	PIECES 714.88 ET 718.88
716	ROTATING ELECTRIC PLANT		9406		38193		9675		78450	APP ELECTR ROTATIFS,PIECES
7161	DC MOTORS AND GENERATORS	N 885	1740	N 1297	2156	N 2270	1117	N 8350	36793	MOTEURS COURANT CONTINU
7162	AC MTRS,GENRTRS,GEN SETS	N 1027	7204	N 4478	29816	N 2240	2069		2420	MOTEURS ELECTRIQUES
71622	AC GENERATORS	N 111	894	N 1766	28107	N 91	332		1162	GENER COURANT ALTERNATIF

4. General Imports C.I.F. by Commodities according to the S.I.T.C. (Rev. 2) in thousand U.S. Dollars
Importations Générales C.A.F. par Produits d'après la C.T.C.I. (Rév. 2) en milliers de Dollars E.U.

SITC CTCI	COMMODITY	1991 WEIGHT POIDS	1991 VALUE VALEUR	1992 WEIGHT POIDS	1992 VALUE VALEUR	1993 WEIGHT POIDS	1993 VALUE VALEUR	1994 WEIGHT POIDS	1994 VALUE VALEUR	PRODUIT
71623	GEN SETS WITH PISTN ENGN	N 291	6130	N 150	816	N 154	1088	N 54	246	GROUPES MOTEUR EXPLOSION
7169	PTS NES OF ROT ELEC PLNT		461		6149		6474		39208	PIECES MAC APP ROTATIFS
72	MACHS FOR SPCL INDUSTRYS		21462		15713		14657		18023	MAC SPECIALES POUR INDUST
723	CIVIL ENGNEERG EQUIP ETC		14341		5523		4480		7999	APPAREILS DE GENIE CIVIL
7234	CONST,MINING MACHNRY NES	N 98	3075		4271		2964		5897	MACH POUR LA CONST, MINES
7239	CONSTR ETC MACHY PTS NES		11063		919		1316		1576	PIECES 723.41–723.46
728	OTH MACHY FOR SPCL INDUS		4678		6171		4794		3495	AUT MACH IND PARTICULIERES
74	GENRL INDUSTRL MACHY NES		94805		123642		218793		87786	MACH APP INDUSTRIE
741	HEATING,COOLING EQUIPMNT		11265		16150		17450		21048	MACH CHAUFFAGE,PIECES
7415	AIR–CONDITIONING MACHNRY		6903		11046		9842		15689	GROUPES CONDITION AIR
742	PUMPS FOR LIQUIDS ETC		2328		5952		6264		5231	POMPES MOTO–POMPES
743	PUMPS NES,CENTRFUGES ETC		12632		16244		7909		8929	POMPES COMPRES,VENT ETC
7431	PUMPS FOR GASES ETC	N 10781	6055	N 7448	10277	N 10686	3266	N 11165	2729	POMPES AIR A VIDE,COMPRES
7433	FREE–PSTN GEN FR GAS TUR		3884							GENERATEURS A PISTONS LIBRES
744	MECHANICAL HANDLING EQU		17780		22079		18590		26034	EQUIP MANUTENTION PIECES
7441	FORK LIFT TRCKS,ETC,PTS		1734		2461		4555		7362	CHARIOTS POUR USINES ETC
74411	FORK LIFT TRUCKS ETC	N 69	1590		2309		4146		7305	CHARIOTS POUR LES GARES
7442	LIFTING,LOADING MACH NES	N 1063	11450	N 6972	6417	N 4432	7149	N 1988	9275	APP LEVAGE,MANUTENTION
74421	PULLEY TACKLE,WINCHS ETC	N 141	4109	N 296	680	N 629	307	N 349	272	PALANS,TREUILS
74422	SHIP DERRICKS,CRANES ETC	N 31	3664	N 169	3092	N 96	2376	N 127	4669	GRUES,PONTS ROULANTS
7449	PTS NES OF MACHY OF 7442		4596		13201		6886		9397	PIECES DU 744.2
745	NONELEC MACHY,TOOLS NES		4616		4153		3379		4037	AUT MACH NON ELEC,PIECES
749	NONELEC MACH PTS,ACC NES		46183		59063		165201		22507	PIECES MACH NON ELEC NDA
7491	BALL,ROLLER,ETC BEARINGS		905		24108		1241		1723	ROULEMENTS BILLES ETC
7492	COCKS,VALVES ETC NES		20004		23114		11206		12308	ART ROB,SIM POUR TUYAUX
7499	OTH NONELEC MCHY PTS NES		22084		9498		151779		6974	PIECES NON ELECT NDA
74999	MACH PARTS NONELEC NES		20622	W 649	7348	W 9003	150241	W 567	5778	PIECES MACHINES NDA
75	OFFICE MACHNES,ADP EQUIP		26681		23422		22073		30081	MACH BUREAU TRAIT AUTOM
751	OFFICE MACHINES	N 69641	3719	W 36	2224	W 30	1902	W 40	2645	MACH,APPAREILS DE BUREAU
752	AUTOMTIC DATA PROC EQUIP	N 9156	10034		9310		9915		17815	MACH TRAIT INFORMATION
7522	DIGITAL COMPUTERS	N 39	69	N 2989	4804	N 2587	2377	N 1958	4198	MACH DIGITALES COMPLETES
7528	OFF–LINE DATA PROC EQUIP	N 4447	6422	N 1508	1315	N 5444	2738	N 3285	5592	MACH AUXIL TRAIT INFORM
759	OFFICE,ADP MCH PTS,ACCES		12928		11888		10255		9620	PIECES DU 751 ET 752
7599	ACCTG,ETC,ADP MCH PTS,AC		12183		11121		9345		7682	PIECES DU 751 ET 752
76	TELECOMM,SOUND EQUIPMENT		30043		40470		59962		77710	EQUIPMENT DE TELECOM
761	TELEVISION RECEIVERS	N 12685	2571	N 20634	2027	N 19650	2161	N 119580	12895	RECEPTEURS DE TELEVISION
7611	COLOUR TV RECEIVERS	N 12212	2543	N 14014	1930	N 16670	2121	N 118710	12847	RECEPTEURS COULEUR
763	SOUND RECORDRS,PHONOGRPH	N 30593	2097	N 54223	3306	N 137191	3207	N 143891	7492	PHONO,APP ENREGISTREMENT
7638	OTHR SOUND APPARATUS ETC	N 30567	2094	N 50686	2522	N 130307	2003	N 124050	6670	AUT APP D'ENREGIS,REPROD
764	TELECOM EQPT,PTS,ACC NES		23646		33167		52470		55699	EQUIP TELECOM,PIECES
7641	LINE TELEPHONE,ETC EQUIP		9160	N 32311	13413	N 136621	29064	N 51133	17784	APP TELEPHON PAR FIL
7643	TV,RADIO TRANSMITTRS ETC	N 1083	253	N 2550	1012	N 3028	1589	N 68080	13271	APP EMET TELE RADIO
7649	PTS NES OF EQUIPMT OF 76		11691		14954		18720		18723	PIECES DE LA DIV 76
76491	PTS NES OF APPAR OF 7641		9211		9509		7425		11069	PIECES POUR 764.1
76493	TELECOMM EQUIPMT PTS NES		2223		5001		11028		7236	PIECES 761,762,764.3,8
77	ELECTRIC MACHNRY NES ETC		67850		117657		110620		203920	MACH APP ELECT NDA
771	ELECTRIC POWER MACHY NES		5735		13677		18425		23976	MACH PROD,TRANS ELECTR
7711	TRANSFORMERS,ELECTRICAL	N 19576	4193	N 20480	10632	N 10121	17368	N 16089	9964	TRANSFO ELECTRIQUES
77111	LIQUID DIELEC TRANSFRMRS			N 2452	5044	N 3204	14474	N 4626	7489	TRANSFO DIELEC LIQUIDE
77118	OTHER ELEC TRANSFORMERS	N 19576	4193	N 18028	5587	N 6917	2894	N 11463	2475	AUTRES TRANSFO ELECTRIQ
7712	OTH ELEC POWER MACHY NES		1543		3045		1058		14013	AUT APP PROD TRANSF ELEC
77122	INDUCTORS	N 16652	56	N 246100	1420	N 68595	384	N 2006000	12546	BOBINES REACTANCE,SELFS
772	SWITCHGEAR ETC,PARTS NES		17434		21363		22613		34029	APP COUPURE,SECT ETC
7721	SWITCHGEAR ETC		16226		21189		22485		30762	APP COUPURE,SECTIONMNT
773	ELECTR DISTRIBUTNG EQUIP		20503		42666		40814		107839	EQUIPMT DISTRIBUTION ELECT
7731	INSULATED WIRE,CABLE ETC		18710	W 29789	42163	W 23293	39736	W 46280	103412	FILS,CABLES ISOLES ELECT
775	HOUSEHOLD TYPE EQUIP NES		7776		9493		8232		9181	MACH,APP USAGE DOMESTQUE
778	ELECTRICAL MACHINERY NES		16028		27196		18084		22528	AUTRES MACH ELECT NDA
7788	OTH ELEC MACHY,EQUIP NES		10366		19361		9164		11734	AUT MACH APP ELEC NDA
77886	OTH ELEC MACHINERY NES		8443	W 1	8315		6189	W 3	3678	AUT MACH APP ELECTRIQUES
77889	ELEC PARTS OF MACHY NES		1324		10103		1542		6740	PIECES ELEC DE MACH NDA
78	ROAD VEHICLES		123764		144429		176047		164191	VEHICULES ROUTIERS
781	PASS MOTOR VEH EXC BUSES	N 6902	89556	N 7976	112062	N 6128	102144	N 5041	81326	AUTO TRANSPORT PERSONNES
782	LORRIES,SPCL MTR VEH NES	N 138	6861	N 314	9295	N 649	17217	N 1022	20526	VEHICULES SPECIAUX,MARCH
7821	LORRIES,TRUCKS	N 119	2554	N 265	5472	N 536	11018	N 916	15847	VEHICULES TRANSP MARCHAND
7822	SPECIAL MOTOR VEHCLS NES	N 19	4307	N 49	3823	N 113	6199	N 106	4679	VEHICULES USAGES SPECIAUX
783	ROAD MOTOR VEHICLES NES	N 174	3520	N 147	9415	N 1943	32321	N 522	47743	VEHICULES ROUTIERS NDA
7831	BUSES	N 174	3520	N 147	9415	N 1936	32180	N 521	47690	VOITURES TRANSPORT COMMUN
784	MOTOR VEH PRTS,ACCES NES		21902		9693		9911		11288	PIECES 722,781,782,783
7849	OTHER MOTOR VEHCL PARTS		21898		9436		9525		10411	PIECES 722,781,782,783
786	TRAILERS,NONMOTR VEH,NES		885		1480		12171		1826	REMORQUES,CADRES,CONTAIN
7861	TRAILERS,TRANSP CONTAINR	N 56	589		630		10749		830	REMORQUES TOUS VEHICULES
78613	CONTAINERS INC ROAD–RAIL	N 38	297		160		9728		353	CADRES ET CONTAINERS
79	OTHR TRANSPORT EQUIPMENT		66640		132984		279599		101543	AUTRE MATERIEL TRANSPORT
792	AIRCRAFT ETC		37541		120919		270232		90972	APP NAVIGATION AERIENNE
7923	AIRCRFT NES2000–15000KG								26629	AERODYNES 2000 A 15000 KG
7924	AIRCRFT NES OVER 15000KG				86281		227241		63	AERODYNES PLUS 15000 KG
7929	AIRCRAFT PARTS NES		34480		34638		42974		63738	PIECES DU 792
793	SHIPS AND BOATS ETC	N 1410	29074		12066		9367		10571	NAVIRES BATEAUX,ETC
7932	SHIPS AND BOATS NES	N 1376	2468	N 1553	10210	N 1106	8176	N 888	5728	NAVIRES ET BATEAUX
79323	OTHER CARGO VESSELS			N 13	7163	N 7	5922	N 40	2380	AUT BATEAUX TRANS MARCH
7938	TUGS,SPECIAL VESSELS ETC	N 29	26508	W 2	1273	W 3	882	W 1	4429	REMORQUEURS,BATEAUX SPEC
79382	SPECL PURPOSE VESSLS ETC	N 5	24458		873		525		3309	BAT–PHARES,–POMPES,DRAGUES
8	MISC MANUFACTURED GOODS		122184		190078		273128		236453	ART MANUFACTURES DIVERS
812	*PLUMBG,HEATNG,LGHTNG EQ		9151		18392		14088		26649	APPAR SANITAIRES CHAUFFAGE
8124	LIGHTING EQUIPMENT NES		6851		15922		12227		24164	APPAREILS ECLAIRAGE ETC
81242	LAMPS,FITTINGS BASE METL		5184	W 96	15224	W 618	10878	W 732	22906	APPAREILS D'ECLAIRAGE
821	*FURNITURE,PARTS THEREOF		16393		70580		79422		21404	MEUBLES ET PIECES
8219	FURNITURE AND PARTS NES		12371		64672		74650		13103	AUTRES MEUBLES ET PIECES
82191	METAL FURNITURE NES		2211		11149		45993		3152	MEUBLES NDA EN METAL
82192	WOOD FURNITURE NES		3653		51571		7372		8132	MEUBLES NDA EN BOIS
82199	OTHR FURN,FURN PARTS NES		6507		1952		21285		1819	MEUBLES NDA AUTRES MATIERES
84	CLOTHING AND ACCESSORIES		19106		16783		14816		17732	VETEMENTS
842	MENS OUTERWEAR NOT KNIT		7993		2551		1280		1557	VET DESSUS POUR HOMMES
8423	— TROUSERS,BREECHES ETC	N 731508	7032	N 656504	1728	N 484061	803	N 431762	997	PANTALONS HOMMES MAT TEX
84232	—— OF COTTON	N 720720	7008							PANTALONS HOMMES COTON
851	*FOOTWEAR		5709	W 266	6508	W 363	5521	W 272	7763	CHAUSSURES
87	PRECISION INSTRUMNTS NES		20343		12640		95176		12764	INSTRUM,APPAR SCIENT NDA
872	MEDICAL INSTRUMENTS NES		1602		2180		14402		1700	INSTR,APP MEDIC–CHIR NDA
87203	MECHANO–THERAPY APPARAT		261		1335		13636		293	APP DE MECANOTHERAPIE
874	MEASURNG,CONTROLNG INSTR		18311		9525		79839		9391	INSTRUMENTS DE MESURE

4. General Imports C.I.F. by Commodities according to the S.I.T.C. (Rev. 2) in thousand U.S. Dollars
Importations Générales C.A.F. par Produits d'après la C.T.C.I. (Rév. 2) en milliers de Dollars E.U.

SITC CTCI	COMMODITY	1991		1992		1993		1994		PRODUIT
		WEIGHT POIDS	VALUE VALEUR	WEIGHT POIDS	VALUE VALEUR	WEIGHT POIDS	VALUE VALEUR	WEIGHT POIDS	VALUE VALEUR	
8743	GAS,LIQUID CONTROL INSTR		7584		2962		1654		1376	APP,INSTR MESURE FLUIDES
8745	MEAS,CONTRL,SCI INST NES		916		485		74643		2723	APP SCIENT MESURE NDA
87452	INSTRMNTS ETC FR DEMONST		256		93		74017		93	INSTR POUR DEMONSTRATION
8748	ELEC MEAS,CONTRL EQU NES		4611		2533		1225		1701	APP ELEC ELECTRO MESURE
88	PHOTO EQU,OPTICL GDS ETC		3707		6143		4241		5163	APP,FOURN PHOTO,OP,MONTR
89	MISC MANUFCTRD GOODS NES		44591		55752		56971		140809	ART MANUFACTURES DIVERS
892	PRINTED MATTER		11206		13585		11388		83448	IMPRIMES
8921	PRINTED BOOKS,GLOBES,ETC		4756		5650		4438		6316	LIVRES,BROCHURES,CARTES
89211	PRINTED BOOKS,PAMPHLETS		4616		5480		4354	N 707153	6133	LIVRES,BROCHURES
8922	NEWSPAPERS,PERIODICALS		4261		4525		3531		3317	JOURNAUX ET PERIODIQUES
8928	PRINTED MATTER NES		1714		2972		2901		72888	IMPRIMES NDA
89289	OTHER PRINTED MATTER		814		1462		1668		70511	GRAVURES,PHOTO AUT IMPR
893	ARTICLES OF PLASTIC NES		15226		24380		20514		28974	OUVRAGES EN MAT DIVIS 58
8931	PLSTC PACKG CONTNRS,LIDS		1563	W 552	3785		4378	W 14428	6325	ART TRANSP EMBALLAGE ETC
8939	MISC PLASTIC ARTICLES		12976		19536		14833	W 2809	21278	ART DIVERS EN MAT DIV 58
89399	OTHR PLASTC ARTICLES NES		12276	W 1	18592		14102	W 2600	20041	AUT OUV MAT DIV 58
894	TOYS,SPORTING GOODS,ETC		8859		7090		7171		13525	VOITURES ENFANTS,JOUETS
8942	TOYS,INDOOR GAMES ETC		4522		4969		5581	W 519	8881	JOUETS,JEUX ETC
896	WORKS OF ART ETC		528		758		8650		1198	OBJETS D'ART
89601	HAND PAINTINGS ETC NES		417		348		8530		892	TABLEAUX,PEINTURES
9	GOODS NOT CLASSD BY KIND		5803		3137		5289		4582	ART TRANSACT NON CLASSES

5. General Exports F.O.B. by Commodities according to the S.I.T.C. (Rev. 2) in thousand U.S. Dollars
Exportations Générales F.O.B. par Produits d'après la C.T.C.I. (Rév. 2) en milliers de Dollars E.U.

SITC CTCI	COMMODITY	1991		1992		1993		1994		PRODUIT
		WEIGHT POIDS	VALUE VALEUR	WEIGHT POIDS	VALUE VALEUR	WEIGHT POIDS	VALUE VALEUR	WEIGHT POIDS	VALUE VALEUR	
	ALL COMMODITIES		2682129		2301218		2093947		2110310	TOUS PRODUITS
0	FOOD AND LIVE ANIMALS		9781		5		6			ALIMENTS,ANIMAUX VIVANTS
3	MINERAL FUELS ETC		2594565		2284168		2087855		2082743	COMBUSTIBLES MINERAUX LUB
33	PETROLEUM AND PRODUCTS		1402224		1325799		1138442		1123813	PETROLE ET DERIVES
333	CRUDE PETROLEUM	W 7443295	1272600	W 8124210	1249202	W 7896040	1065261	W 8043467	1052008	HUILES BRUTES DE PETROLE
334	PETROLEUM PRODUCTS,REFIN	W 649498	129624	W 414135	76598	W 485242	73181	W 489710	71805	PRODUITS RAFFINES
3341	GASOLINE,OTH LIGHT OILS	W 649438	129613							ESSENCES POUR MOTEURS
33411	MOTOR,AVIATION SPIRIT	W 645108	128176							ESSENCES MOTEURS D'AVIONS
3345	LUBS,PETROLEUM OILS NES	W 60	11	W 414135	76598	W 485242	73181	W 489350	71664	HUILES LUBRIFIANTES
33451	LUBS(HIGH PETR CONT) ETC	W 60	11	W 414135	76598	W 485242	73181	W 489350	71664	HUILES LUBRIF,H LOURDES
341	*GAS,NATURAL AND MANUFCT	W 5446911	1192342	W 5514125	958369	W 5639411	949413	W 5904588	958930	GAZ NATUREL,GAZ MANUFACT
3413	PETROLM GASES,LIQUEFIED	W 5446911	1192342	W 5514125	958369	W 5639411	949413	W 5904588	958930	GAZ DE PETROLE LIQUEFIE
34131	LIQUEFIED PROPANE,BUTANE	W 5446911	1192342							PROPANE,BUTANE LIQUEFIES
34139	OTH HYDROCARBON GAS LQFD			W 5514125	958369	W 5639411	949413	W 5904588	958930	HYDROCARBURES GAZEUX NDA
6	BASIC MANUFACTURES		11201		9		10			ART MANUFACTURES
69	METAL MANUFACTURES NES		8453		5					ART MANUFACT EN METAL NDA
7	MACHINES,TRANSPORT EQUIP		35232							MACHINES MATERIEL TRANSPORT
71	POWER GENERATING EQUIPMT		9349							MACHINES GENERATRICES
713	INTRNL COMBUS PSTN ENGIN		8853							MOTEURS EXPL COMB INT, PIECE
8	MISC MANUFACTURED GOODS		24322		16594		5966		27420	ART MANUFACTURES DIVERS
84	CLOTHING AND ACCESSORIES		16605		16526		5918		27318	VETEMENTS
845	OUTERWEAR KNIT NONELASTC	N 1668132	5410	N 2436991	8582	N 778837	2797	N 7260410	17254	VET DESSOUS,ACCES BONNET
8459	— OTHER,CLTHG ACCESRYS	N 143232	824	N 2325401	8169	N 359567	1101	N 3900525	11746	AUT VET DESSUS DE BONNE
846	UNDER GARMENTS KNITTED		2352	W 150	6155	W 72	3036		7755	SOUS VETS DE BONNETERIE
8462	— OF COTTON NON ELASTIC	N 693564	1904	W 125	4021	W 55	1766	W 166	6741	SOUS–VET BONNET COTON
84629	—— OTHER			W 125	4021	W 55	1766	W 166	6741	AUT SOUS–VET BONNET COTON

1. HISTORICAL SERIES, 1961–1996 GENERAL TRADE, IMPORTS C.I.F., EXPORTS F.O.B.
SERIES HISTORIQUES, 1961–1996 COMMERCE GENERAL, IMPORTATIONS C.A.F., EXPORTATIONS F.O.B

YEAR ANNEE	VALUE IN MILLION LEVA / VALEUR EN MILLION LEVA — MERCHANDISE –MARCHANDISE		GOLD –OR		CONVERSION FACTORS U.S. CENTS PER LEV FACTEURS DE CONVERSION CENTS E.U. PAR LEV		INDEX NUMBERS –INDICES — QUANTUM		UNIT VALUE VALEUR UNITAIRE	
	IMPORTS	EXPORTS	IMPORTS	EXPORTS	IMPORTS	EXPORTS	IMPORTS	EXPORTS	IMPORTS	EXPORTS
1961	779.20	775.20			85.4700	85.4700	15	10		
1962	918.10	903.90			85.4700	85.4700	18	12		
1963	1091.90	975.80			85.4700	85.4700	21	13		
1964	1243.00	1145.20			85.4700	85.4700	24	15		
1965	1377.90	1375.70			85.4700	85.4700	26	18		
1966	1729.60	1526.90			85.4700	85.4700	33	20		
1967	1839.10	1706.10			85.4700	85.4700	35	23		
1968	2085.30	1889.70			85.4700	85.4700	40	27		
1969	2046.70	2099.50			85.4700	85.4700	40	29		
1970	2142.30	2344.50			85.4700	85.4700	21	20		
1971	2480.00	2553.30			85.4700	85.4700	47	34		
1972	2772.20	2837.00			92.5900	92.5900	53	38		
1973	3171.70	3200.70			102.9856	103.1319	59	42		
1974	4195.80	3720.80			103.0926	103.0926	72	46		
1975	5235.60	4541.40			103.2929	103.3023	81	51		
1976	5436.00	5199.80			103.5011	103.5118	79	58		
1977	6061.70	6022.00			105.4628	105.4628	83	66		
1978	6800.90	6649.60			112.5013	112.4564	89	74		
1979	7363.40	7666.80			115.6286	115.6793	91	84		
1980	8282.90	8901.50			116.5039	116.5207	94	94		
1981	9957.90	9860.30			108.4716	108.4071	104	102		
1982	10975.90	10880.00			105.0243	105.0383	107	113		
1983	11966.00	11817.50			102.6506	102.6344	112	118		
1984	12842.30	12987.30			98.9998	98.9402	115	124		
1985	14066.50	13739.40			97.0834	97.1548	127	133		
1986	14353.30	13350.50			106.2375	106.3017	132	128		
1987	14067.30	13802.00			115.2415	115.2361	130	130		
1988	13820.40	14353.60			119.9853	119.9877	137	133		
1989	12551.70	13506.30			118.5546	118.5591	130	130		
1990	10160.30	10496.00			126.8922	127.1617	100	100		
1991	45132.42	57368.29			6.6845	6.6845	83	70		
1992	104424.70	86199.09			5.0423	4.9817				
1993	119288.10	99043.10			3.6169	3.6169				
1994	234120.00	225468.00			1.8435	1.8435				
1995	380012.00	359663.60			1.4897	1.4909				
1996	905612.80	818315.00			0.5915	0.5882				

2. IMPORTS BY BROAD ECONOMIC CATEGORY AND EXPORTS BY INDUSTRIAL ORIGIN. (PERCENTAGE OF TOTAL VALUE)
IMPORTATIONS PAR CATEGORIES ECONOMIQUES ET EXPORTATIONS PAR BRANCHE D'ACTIVITE.(EN POURCENTAGE DE LA VALEUR TOTALE)

IMPORTS – IMPORTATIONS

	1990	1991	1992	1993	1994	1995	1996
TOTAL IMPORTS–IMPORTATIONS TOTALES			100.				100.
1 FOOD BEV–ALIMENTATION BOISSONS			5.1				
11 PRIMARY–PRODUITS DE BASE			1.3				
111 FOR INDUSTRY–POUR L'INDUSTRIE			0.6				
112 FOR HOUSEHOLDS–POUR LES MENAGES			0.6				
12 PROCESSED–PRODUITS ELABORES			3.8				
121 FOR INDUSTRY–POUR L'INDUSTRIE			1.4				
122 FOR HOUSEHOLDS–POUR LES MENAGES			2.4				
2 IND SUPPLIES–APPROV INDUSTRIELS			27.8				
21 PRIMARY–PRODUITS DE BASE			4.2				
22 PROCESSED–PRODUITS ELABORES			23.6				
3 FUELS–COMBUSTIBLES			36.0				
31 PRIMARY–PRODUITS DE BASE			23.5				
32 PROCESSED–PRODUITS ELABORES			12.5				
321 MOTOR SPIRIT–ESSENCE							
322 OTHER–AUTRES			12.5				
4 MACHINERY–EQUIPEMENT			12.1				
41 CAPITAL EQUIPMENT–MACHINES			10.3				
42 PARTS–PIECES ACCESSOIRES			1.8				
5 TRANSPORT–TRANSPORT			9.2				
51 PASSENGER CARS–AUTOMOBILES			4.5				
52 OTHER–AUTRES			2.1				
521 INDUSTRIAL–INDUSTRIELS			2.0				
522 NON INDUSTRIAL–NON INDUSTRIEL			0.1				
53 PARTS–PIECES ACCESSOIRES			2.6				
6 CONSUM GOODS–BIENS CONSOMMATION			9.7				
61 DURABLE–DURABLES			3.5				
62 SEMI DURABLE–SEMI DURABLES			3.2				
63 NON DURABLE–NON DURABLES			3.0				
7 GOODS NES–BIENS NDA			0.2				

EXPORTS – EXPORTATIONS

	1990	1991	1992	1993	1994	1995	1996
TOTAL EXPORTS–EXPORTATIONS TOTALES	100.						
1 AGRICULTURE							
2 MINING QUARRY–INDUS EXTRACTIVES							
3 MANUFACTURING–IND MANUFACTUR							
31 FOOD BEV TOBACCO–ALIM BOISS TAB							
32 TEXTILES–INDUSTRIES TEXTILES							
33 WOOD & PRODUCTS–BOIS & PRODUITS							
34 PAPER & PRODUCTS–PAPIER & PRODT							
35 CHEMICALS–INDUSTRIES CHIMIQUES							
36 NON METAL MIN–MIN NON METAL							
37 BASIC METAL–IND METAL BASE							
38 METAL MANUF–MANUF METAL							
39 OTH MANUF IND–AUTRES MANUF							

3. TRADE BY PRINCIPAL COUNTRIES OF CONSIGNMENT (VALUE IN THOUSAND U.S. DOLLARS)
ECHANGES SELON LES PRINCIPAUX PAYS DE CONSIGNATION (VALEUR EN MILLIERS DE DOLLARS EU)

GENERAL IMPORTS C.I.F. IMPORTATIONS GENERALES C.A.F

COUNTRIES–PAYS	1991	1992	1993	1994	1995
World	3016849	4344862	5057551	4316002	5026209
Africa	122928	237128	143522	72415	88952
Americas	119719	228897	271282	240096	117580
Northern America	88503	130289	189410	124591	117580
LAIA	25735	59814	69719	69762	
CACM		14102			
Caribbean	5481	23717	7968	45107	
Rest of America		976	4185	636	
As.ex F.USSR	99399	558643	610041	318594	141977
Eur.x F.USSR	1008758	2037284	2232749	2114494	2399840
EU	786766	1559030	1693613	1676348	1912637
EFTA	63570	99011	226212	61890	90963
East Europe	99599	267616	215596	233555	210615
Other Europe		170			
Former USSR	1304079	1279401	1730256	1363244	1695583
Oceania	334	3509	15372	17310	32903
Russian Federation		1009873	1393440	1130897	1418597
Germany/Allemagne	210294	559786	549953	569057	635432
Former USSR/Anc. URSS	1304079				
Italy/Italie	125869	194538	218305	246749	295863
Greece/Grèce	26872	245127	168757	207860	234293
Ukraine		226832	252235	179015	170306
United Kingdom	109024	78430	280476	121968	125999
Austria/Autriche	141377	140949	125792	126112	142119
USA/Etats–Unis d'Amer	86564	125168	184339	118084	107454
France,Monac	64104	110345	116135	123935	140453
Switz.Liecht	62366	97504	222526	57698	85975
Iran (Islamic Rp. of)		161530	244126	81348	
Netherlands/Pays–Bas	31751	77456	81854	91255	102148
Tfyr Macedonia			77926	129347	169245
Romania/Roumanie	13035	120225	101559	82345	56803
Turkey/Turquie		76329	76747	85929	93178
Belgium–Luxembourg	26404	53105	46351	51620	69648
Japan/Japon	16310	82786	64428	41954	39873
Algeria/Algérie	14572	47983	38408	41123	75702
Czech Republic			63039	57031	70845
Poland/Pologne	34425	31788	26002	52890	28455
Sweden/Suède	15976	34065	36990	31924	45914
Finland/Finlande	14572	21144	24201	48029	55726
Syrian Arab Republic	11497	64796	70280	1604	2651
Libyan Arab Jamahiriya	75000	18710	42307	4841	90
Hungary/Hongrie	12901	28147	20327	29983	40012
Egypt/Egypte	6417	107890	5143	5300	2324
Czechoslovakia	35762	83343			
Tunisia/Tunisie	25401	50472	39247	79	158
Yugoslavia/Yougoslavie		105038	4163	697	1970
China/Chine	11163	44524	25792	22347	
Spain/Espagne	15040	16521	14431	25437	25809
Brazil/Brésil	3877	17519	28574	44412	
Denmark/Danemark		18971	23510	23669	27497
Cuba	5481	23152	7968	45107	
Argentina/Argentine	21858	23070	25210	10812	
Korea, Republic of		26748	28262	22832	
Australia/Australie	334	2883	15357	17228	32740
Republic of Moldova		17004	16063	11522	18532
Belarus/Bélarus		13946	17256	17347	14263
Fm Yugoslav	58824				
Pakistan	52808	303	861	715	
Singapore/Singapour		14309	21618	8699	
Israel/Israël		8058	13252	14595	
Slovenia/Slovénia		4203	10485	9570	10269
Peru/Pérou		14076	7614	9588	
Kazakhstan		686	19253	6589	4592
Saudi Arabia		23790	7053	83	83
Turkmenistan/Turkménistn		1750	828	1714	26242
Slovakia			4300	10661	14303

GENERAL EXPORTS F.O.B. EXPORTATIONS GENERALES F.O.B.

COUNTRIES–PAYS	1991	1992	1993	1994	1995
Monde	3834764	4563561	3720973	4156503	5091011
Afrique	200936	122249	62818	72512	134887
Amériques	140441	146330	169484	276123	175655
Amérique du Nord	134559	105896	143312	226999	175655
ALAI	4345	33903	20671	43886	
MCAC					
Caraïbes	1537	3540	2488	2205	
Autre Amérique		2991	3013	3033	
Asie l'URSS exclus	330014	898024	819043	572707	548829
Europe l'URSS exclus	1032555	2274676	1750305	2263243	2743144
UE	667113	1435632	1114671	1474813	1896374
AELE	60227	72791	46325	25689	80798
Europe de l'Est	199265	293708	201657	191565	223155
Autre de l'Europe					
Ancienne URSS	1908558	1023564	718190	720997	881264
Océanie	2005	3939	2749	4043	4064
Russian Federation		819151	505096	501576	513454
Former USSR/Anc. URSS	1908558				
Germany/Allemagne	182420	348650	245067	350236	431806
Italy/Italie	103543	263893	221144	289050	416412
Tfyr Macedonia		184521	227416	386549	424403
Greece/Grèce	83489	208053	229268	294975	353535
Turkey/Turquie		289121	283084	188620	371186
USA/Etats–Unis d'Amer	128677	93681	125969	199104	153998
United Kingdom	74398	142292	115263	118935	142011
Ukraine		167470	118895	124866	181507
Yugoslavia/Yougoslavie		200575	130342	137263	82522
France,Monac	55281	117712	95121	108400	146252
Romania/Roumanie	70187	129778	91945	63319	93307
Syrian Arab Republic	79278	127534	101356	70728	61410
Belgium–Luxembourg	36431	136060	48503	85892	77411
Netherlands/Pays–Bas	34693	73739	54814	92669	97126
China/Chine	47928	64565	104373	60788	
Switz.Liecht	59492	69551	44184	20673	74339
Lebanon/Liban	27741	73290	59531	36901	50397
Austria/Autriche	37634	56638	42130	53836	44223
Spain/Espagne	19853	27072	17752	36367	127466
Albania/Albanie	1604	61374	38133	56607	58661
Egypt/Egypte	44385	41232	27836	29763	39923
Poland/Pologne	79078	38240	24490	18404	22917
Iran (Islamic Rp. of)	29679	78325	19079	8508	
Jordan/Jordanie	14572	35249	24769	23361	23995
Hungary/Hongrie	15508	29914	22537	23018	22424
Libyan Arab Jamahiriya	80214	20342	4362	3289	1756
Fm Yugoslav	105949				
Saudi Arabia	16110	38141	23043	9564	17610
Thailand/Thaïlande		33105	38169	29848	
Japan/Japon	26604	18298	16327	19880	17657
Sweden/Suède	18316	20491	15686	16042	17073
Belarus/Bélarus		21738	20544	22039	21720
Canada	5882	12215	17343	27896	21658
India/Inde	37901	9622	21148	15867	
Republic of Moldova		10320	11708	17838	40338
Pakistan	42914	15555	5827	15025	
Bosnia and Herzegovina		64615	8923	114	86
Slovenia/Slovénia		5085	8402	35823	21234
Algeria/Algérie	24332	10320	2076	10672	22921
Czechoslovakia	32888	34401			
Israel/Israël		23931	18851	22437	
Tunisia/Tunisie	8155	17600	9805	10366	18304
Denmark/Danemark	6751	16353	12030	12580	15682
Nigeria/Nigéria	37032	14159	8058	3781	
Finland/Finlande	12166	17550	7733	10698	12332
Czech Republic			21271	17819	17912
Croatia/Croatie		17749	12569	11426	14573
Georgia/Géorgie		648	10464	5481	36919

(VALUE AS PERCENTAGE OF WORLD TOTAL) (VALEURS EN POURCENTAGE DU TOTAL MONDIAL)

Imports

	1986	1987	1988	1989	1990	1991	1992	1993	1994	1995
Africa				1.8	2.0	4.1	5.5	2.8	1.7	1.8
Americas				4.0	2.3	4.0	5.3	5.4	5.6	2.3
Northern America				1.5	0.6	2.9	3.0	3.7	2.9	2.3
LAIA				0.8	0.6	0.9	1.4	1.4	1.6	
CACM							0.3			
Caribbean				1.7	1.1	0.2	0.5	0.2	1.0	
Rest of America							0.0	0.1	0.0	
As.ex F.USSR				2.3	2.7	3.3	12.9	12.1	7.4	2.8
Eur.x F.USSR				33.8	32.0	33.4	46.9	44.1	49.0	47.7
EU				12.3	11.3	26.1	35.9	33.5	38.8	38.1
EFTA				1.7	1.3	2.1	2.3	4.5	1.4	1.8
East Europe				18.9	18.5	3.3	6.2	4.3	5.4	4.2
Other Europe							0.0			
Former USSR				52.9	56.5	43.2	29.4	34.2	31.6	33.7
Oceania				0.0	0.1	0.0	0.1	0.3	0.4	0.7
Russian Federation							23.2	27.6	26.2	28.2
Germany/Allemagne				5.0	3.7	7.0	12.9	10.9	13.2	12.6
Former USSR/Anc. URSS				52.9	56.5	43.2				
Italy/Italie				1.4	1.9	4.2	4.5	4.3	5.7	5.9
Greece/Grèce				0.4	0.3	0.9	5.6	3.3	4.8	4.7
Ukraine							5.2	5.0	4.1	3.4
United Kingdom				1.1	1.7	3.6	1.8	5.5	2.8	2.5
Austria/Autriche				1.5	1.6	4.7	3.2	2.5	2.9	2.8
USA/Etats–Unis d'Amer				1.5	0.6	2.9	2.9	3.6	2.7	2.1
France,Monac				1.0	0.7	2.1	2.5	2.3	2.9	2.8

Exports

	1986	1987	1988	1989	1990	1991	1992	1993	1994	1995
Afrique				2.2	5.1	5.2	2.7	1.7	1.7	2.6
Amériques				2.1	2.8	3.7	3.2	4.6	6.6	3.5
Amérique du Nord				0.7	1.8	3.5	2.3	3.9	5.5	3.5
ALAI				0.1	0.0	0.1	0.7	0.6	1.1	
MCAC										
Caraïbes				1.4	1.0	0.0	0.1	0.1	0.1	
Autre Amérique							0.1	0.1	0.1	
Asie l'URSS exclus				3.9	4.1	8.6	19.7	22.0	13.8	10.8
Europe l'URSS exclus				25.3	22.6	26.9	49.8	47.0	54.5	53.9
UE				6.0	5.6	17.4	31.5	30.0	35.5	37.2
AELE				1.0	0.9	1.6	1.6	1.2	0.6	1.6
Europe de l'Est				17.3	15.2	5.2	6.4	5.4	4.6	4.4
Autre de l'Europe										
Ancienne URSS				65.2	64.0	49.8	22.4	19.3	17.3	17.3
Océanie				0.0	0.0	0.1	0.1	0.1	0.1	0.1
Russian Federation							17.9	13.6	12.1	10.1
Former USSR/Anc. URSS				65.2	64.0	49.8				
Germany/Allemagne				1.4	1.4	4.8	7.6	6.6	8.4	8.5
Italy/Italie				0.7	0.8	2.7	5.8	5.9	7.0	8.2
Tfyr Macedonia							4.0	6.1	9.3	8.3
Greece/Grèce				1.3	0.8	2.2	4.6	6.2	7.1	6.9
Turkey/Turquie							6.3	7.6	4.5	7.3
USA/Etats–Unis d'Amer				0.6	1.7	3.4	2.1	3.4	4.8	3.0
United Kingdom				0.9	0.6	1.9	3.1	3.1	2.9	2.8
Ukraine							3.7	3.2	3.0	3.6

4. General Imports C.I.F. by Commodities according to the S.I.T.C. (Rev. 2) in thousand U.S. Dollars
Importations Générales C.A.F. par Produits d'après la C.T.C.I. (Rév. 2) en milliers de Dollars E.U.

SITC CTCI	COMMODITY	1992		1993		1994		1995		PRODUIT
		WEIGHT POIDS	VALUE VALEUR	WEIGHT POIDS	VALUE VALEUR	WEIGHT POIDS	VALUE VALEUR	WEIGHT POIDS	VALUE VALEUR	
	ALL COMMODITIES		4344862		5057551		4316002		5026209	TOUS PRODUITS
0	FOOD AND LIVE ANIMALS		211572		300622					ALIMENTS,ANIMAUX VIVANTS
01	MEAT AND PREPARATIONS		4316		21340					VIANDES ET PREPARATIONS
011	MEAT FRESH,CHILLD,FROZEN	W 2637	3113	W 33000	19318	W 33700	33139	W 30900	29369	VIANDES FRAICHES,REF,CONGE
0111	BOVINE MEAT FRESH,FROZEN	W 877	988	W 20694	10532	W 19375	17980	W 23788	24133	VIANDES BOVIN FRAI,REF
02	DAIRY PRODCTS,BIRDS'EGGS		6736		20519					PRODUITS LAITIERS,OEUFS
04	CEREALS AND PREPARATIONS		9638		35699					CEREALES ET PRODUITS
04702	MEAL OR GROATS NON–WHEAT	W 1	1	W 89000	20229	W 61100	14907	W 107400	26062	GRUAUX,SEMOULES DE CEREALES
05	VEGETABLES AND FRUIT		30087		52814					LEGUMES ET FRUITS
057	FRUIT,NUTS,FRESH,DRIED	W 45734	18126	W 147600	33442	W 207100	49192	W 160800	36433	FRUITS FRAIS OU SECS
0573	BANANA,PLANTAIN,FRSH,DRY	W 16015	7570	W 51200	14978	W 75100	22328	W 49500	14135	BANANES FRAICHES,SECHEES
06	SUGAR AND PREPS,HONEY		74135		73738		105588		110361	SUCRES ET PRODUITS
061	SUGAR AND HONEY	W 260538	70760	W 364000	6137	W 349500	92933	W 313300	103349	SUCRES ET MIEL
0611	RAW BEET AND CANE SUGAR	W 164526	50326							SUCRES BRUTS
0612	REFINED SUGAR ETC	W 40620	15345							SUCRES RAFFINES
07	COFFEE,TEA,COCOA,SPICES		31840		34502		34107		34059	CAFE,THE,CACAO,EPICES
0711	COFFEE GREEN,ROASTED,SUB	W 8093	9530	W 21100	12583	W 24900	15347	W 25200	15723	CAFE TORREFIE OU DECAFEINE
073	CHOCOLATE AND PRODUCTS	W 5834	13061	W 5400	7350	W 4200	3617	W 2900	2809	CHOCOLAT
081	*FEEDING STUFF FOR ANIML	W 106102	29084		31818		20887		36233	NOURRITURE POUR ANIMAUX
0813	OILCAKE AND OTH RESIDUES	W 94085	23885							TOURTEAUX
08131	— OF SOYA BEANS	W 94070	23858							TOURTEAUX DE SOJA
09	MISC EDIBLE PRODUCTS		16813		19488		13703		7539	PREP ALIMENTAIRES DIVERSES
1	BEVERAGES AND TOBACCO		117680		120020					BOISSONS ET TABACS
11	BEVERAGES		34286		14728		32989		30977	BOISSONS
112	ALCOHOLIC BEVERAGES	W 33513	30817							BOISSONS ALCOOLIQUES
1124	DISTILLED ALCOHOLIC BEVS	W 16124	23927							ALCOOLS,EAUX–DE–VIE
11241	WHISKY	W 6927	18509							WHISKY
12	TOBACCO AND MANUFACTURES		83395		105292		43809		20573	TABACS BRUTS FABRIQUES
121	TOBACCO UNMNFCTRD,REFUSE	W 11214	24486							TABACS BRUTS,DECHETS
1211	TOBACCO,NOT STRIPPED	W 9994	20211							TABACS NON ECOTES
122	TOBACCO,MANUFACTURED	W 8381	58909							TABACS FABRIQUES
1222	CIGARETTES	W 6539	56604	W 9200	83019	W 1700	25191	W 200	3206	CIGARETTES
2	CRUDE MATERLS,EXCL FUELS		227166		207672					MAT BRUTES NON COMESTIBLES
211	HIDES,SKINS,EXC FURS,RAW	W 3978	3126			W 8000	35782	W 7900	37867	CUIRS ET PEAUX
23	RUBBER, CRUDE		15388		9910					CAOUTCHOUC BRUT
233	RUBBER,SYNTHTIC,RECLAIMD	W 13213	14087							LATEX CAOUTCH SYNTH REGEN
2331	SYNTHETIC RUBBER ETC	W 12939	13752							LATEX CAOUTCH SYNTHETIQUE
24	CORK AND WOOD		8547		17278					LIEGE ET BOIS
251	*PULP AND WASTE PAPER	W 26230	8986	W 54100	15151	W 23300	11424	W 36500	24691	PATES A PAPIER,DECHETS
26	TEXTILE FIBRES AND WASTE		77896		56847					FIBRES TEXTILES
263	COTTON	W 20936	30473			W 37800	85479	W 35000	98545	COTON
2631	RAW COTTON,EXCL LINTERS	W 20551	30295							COTON EN MASSE
266	SYNTHETIC FIBRES TO SPIN	W 2838	6760			W 26200	127450	W 24500	146049	FIBRES SYNTHETIQUES
267	OTHER MAN–MADE FIBRES	W 7968	37945							AUTR FIBR TEXT ARTIF SYNTH
2671	REGENERATD FIBRE TO SPIN	W 7961	37930							FIBRES TEXT ARTIFIC
26712	CONTIN FILAMNT TOW REGEN	W 6799	35640							CABLES POUR DISCONTINUS
268	WOOL(EXC TOPS),ANML HAIR	W 348	1845			W 6900	30816	W 7200	34918	LAINES ET POILS
27	CRUDE FERTLZR,MINRLS NES		22035		25510					ENGRAIS MINERAUX BRUTS
28	METALLIFEROUS ORES,SCRAP		84220		72931					MINERAIS METAL,DECHETS
281	IRON ORE,CONCENTRATES	W 424316	10114	W 878500	30360	W 723300	15592	W 1362200	26213	MINERAIS DE FER
287	BASE METAL ORES,CONC NES	W 162996	72441							MINERAIS METAUX COMMUNS
2871	CPR ORE ETC,CEMENT COPPR	W 80777	39477							MINERAIS DE CUIVRE,MATTES
28711	COPPER ORES,EXCL MATTE	W 79755	38393							MINERAIS DE CUIVRE
2875	ZINC ORES,CONCENTRATES	W 68309	28637							MINERAIS DE ZINC
3	MINERAL FUELS ETC		1564908		1776657		1167743		1324197	COMBUSTIBLES MINERAUX LUB
32	COAL,COKE AND BRIQUETTES		125088		94057					HOUILLES,COKES,BRIQUETTES
322	COAL,LIGNITE AND PEAT	W 2748480	98524							HOUILLES,LIGNITES,TOURBE
3221	ANTHRACITE,NOT AGGLOMRTD	W 1118729	45422	W 1671700	48839	W 1064400	34433	W 621900	26948	ANTHRACITE
3222	OTH COAL,NOT AGGLOMERATD	W 1589572	52385							AUTRES HOUILLES
323	BRIQUETS,COKE,SEMI–COKE	W 254300	26564							BRIQUETTES
3231	BRIQUETTES,OVOIDS ETC	W 18228	783	W 1229900	39688	W 876300	24769	W 1244700	46922	BRIQUETTES ET BOULETS
3232	COKE,SEMI–COKE,RTRT CRBN	W 236072	25781	W 92200	5527	W 546900	33441	W 134100	14117	COKES ET SEMI–COKES
33	PETROLEUM AND PRODUCTS		953865		1272986					PETROLE ET DERIVES
333	CRUDE PETROLEUM	W 3562639	573108	W 8900000	1013745	W 5600000	598514	W 5800000	706078	HUILES BRUTES DE PETROLE
334	PETROLEUM PRODUCTS,REFIN	W 1923322	378524							PRODUITS RAFFINES
3341	GASOLINE,OTH LIGHT OILS			W 143200	30378	W 113100	17506	W 12600	1610	ESSENCES POUR MOTEURS
3343	GAS OILS			W 566200	98673	W 178300	17331	W 3100	535	GAS OILS
3344	FUEL OILS,NES			W 703700	58507	W 124100	7975	W 68200	7147	FUEL OILS
341	*GAS,NATURAL AND MANUFCT		347389		365701					GAZ NATUREL,GAZ MANUFACT
3413	PETROLM GASES,LIQUEFIED		347378							GAZ DE PETROLE LIQUEFIE
34139	OTH HYDROCARBON GAS LQFD		347376							HYDROCARBURES GAZEUX NDA
351	*ELECTRIC CURRENT	H 2592953	138567							ENERGIE ELECTRIQUE
431	*PROCESD ANML VEG OIL,ET	W 2440	2634		3367	W 28800	21678	W 25100	20500	HUILES,GRAISSES PREPAREES
5	CHEMCLS,RELATED PROD NES		415114		463502					PRODUITS CHIMIQUES
51	ORGANIC CHEMICALS		82344		65574		114114		130681	PROD CHIMIQ ORGANIQUES
511	HYDROCARBONS NES,DERIVS	W 22441	13167							HYDROCARBURES NDA
512	ALCOHOLS,PHENOLS ETC	W 40939	17446							PHENOLS,PHENOLS–ALCOOLS
5121	ACYCLIC ALCOHOLS,DERIVS	W 37961	13670							ALCOOLS ACYCLIQUES
514	NITROGEN–FNCTN COMPOUNDS	W 14116	22769							COMPOSES FONCT AZOTEES
52	INORGANIC CHEMICALS		38852		116222		26384		101480	PROD CHIM INORGANIQUES
522	INORG ELEMNTS,OXIDES,ETC	W 20400	14386							ELEMENTS INORGANIQUES
53	DYES,TANNING,COLOUR PROD		42098		38487		38559		44511	PROD TEINTURE,COLORANTS
531	SYNT DYE,NAT INDGO,LAKES	W 1001	13761							MAT COLOR ORGAN,LAQUES
533	PIGMENTS,PAINTS,ETC	W 12045	26090							PIGMENTS,PEINTURES,VERNIS
5334	VARNISHES,DISTEMPERS ETC	W 5893	15156							PEINTURES A L'EAU
541	*MEDICINAL,PHARM PRODUCT	K 3837490	72421		75402	K 2600000	50840	K 2100000	73270	PROD MEDICINAUX PHARMACEUT
5417	MEDICAMENTS	K 2353818	46173		55830		43531		64721	MEDICAMENTS
54179	— CONTNG OTH SUBSTANCES	K 1864950	34151							MED CONT AUT SUBSTANCES
55	PERFUME,CLEANING ETC PRD		27906		38090		24095		36301	PROD POUR PARFUM,TOILETTE
58	PLASTIC MATERIALS ETC		62041		45913		110597		135815	MAT PLAST ARTIFICIELLES
582	PROD OF CONDENSATION ETC	W 6555	16136							PROD CONDENS,POLYCOND
583	POLYMERIZATION ETC PRODS	W 41793	44640							PROD POLYMERISATION
5834	POLYVINYL CHLORIDE	W 20221	14220							CHLORURE DE POLYVINYLE
59	CHEMICAL MATERIALS NES		80160		76646					MAT PROD CHIMIQUES NDA
591	PESTICIDES,DISINFECTANTS	W 6369	41036	W 6100	31279	W 7300	24401	W 4800	29106	DESINF,INSECT,FONG,HERB
5913	HERBICIDES,FOR RETAIL	W 4415	24970							HERBICIDES VENTE AU DET
598	MISCEL CHEM PRODUCTS NES	W 15512	34486			W 33800	64661	W 34900	79994	PROD DIV INDUST CHIM NDA
5989	CHEM PRODUCTS,PREPS NES	W 11536	25311							PROD PREP CHIMIQUES NDA
59899	OTH CHEM PRODS,PREPS,NES	W 9017	17273							AUT PRODUITS CHIMIQUES NDA
6	BASIC MANUFACTURES		603495		625745					ART MANUFACTURES
61	LEATHER,DRESSED FUR,ETC		34361		17213					CUIRS,PELLETERIES

4. General Imports C.I.F. by Commodities according to the S.I.T.C. (Rev. 2) in thousand U.S. Dollars
Importations Générales C.A.F. par Produits d'après la C.T.C.I. (Rév. 2) en milliers de Dollars E.U.

SITC CTCI	COMMODITY	1992			1993			1994			1995			PRODUIT
		WEIGHT POIDS		VALUE VALEUR	WEIGHT POIDS		VALUE VALEUR	WEIGHT POIDS		VALUE VALEUR	WEIGHT POIDS		VALUE VALEUR	
611	LEATHER	W	796	13687										CUIRS,PEAUX PREPARES
612	LEATHER ETC MANUFACTURES	W	1444	19857										OUVRAGES EN CUIRS NDA
6123	PREPRD PARTS OF FOOTWEAR	W	1414	18906	P	1530000	5820	P	1514000	6607				PARTIES DE CHAUSSURES
62	RUBBER MANUFACTURES NES			31482			28744			43035			56724	CAOUTCHOUC MANUFACTURE
625	RUBBER TYRES, TUBES ETC	W	12202	22182										PNEUS CAOUTCHOUC VULCANISE
6252	TYRES,NEW,BUS OR LORRY	W	9097	16907										PNEUS POUR AUTOBUS,CAMIONS
64	PAPER,PAPERBOARD AND MFR			83449			77543			104921			171881	PAPIERS,CARTONS & OUVRAGES
641	PAPER AND PAPERBOARD	W	99460	68085										PAPIERS ET CARTONS
6411	NEWSPRINT	W	51961	18079	W	53200	14753	W	44000	15380	W	52600	34960	PAPIER JOURNAL
6412	PRINTG,WRITING PAPER NES	W	15870	23147										PAPIERS POUR L'IMPRESSION
64122	— COATED,IMPREGNATD ETC	W	11679	16049										PAPIERS IMPRESSION COUCHES
642	PAPER,ETC,PRECUT,ARTS OF	W	9763	15363										PAP,CARTONS DECOUPES
65	TEXTILE YARN,FABRICS,ETC			172223			177062							FILS,TISSUS,ARTICLES TEXTILE
651	TEXTILE YARN	W	5227	26720										FILS TEXTILES
652	COTTON FABRICS,WOVEN	W	2326	26181			83615	A	73700	35052	A	21100	38185	TISSUS DE COTON
6522	WOVEN COTTON BLEACHD,ETC	W	1703	21885										TISSUS COTON BLANCHIS ETC
65224	BLCHED COTTON FABRIC NES	W	1468	18050										AUT TIS PLUS 85% COT BLANCHI
653	WOVN MAN–MADE FIB FABRIC	W	2711	54761	W	14200	64609							TISSUS FIBRES SYNTH,ARTIF
6531	CONT SYNT WEAVES NONPILE	W	1192	16153										TISSUS FIBRES SYNTH CONTINUE
65315	CONT SYN TXTL FABRIC NES	W	1111	15303										TIS PLUS 85% TEXT SYNT CONT
6534	DISC SYN BLEND FABRC NES	W	619	15449										TISSUS FIBRES SYNTH DISCONT
654	OTH WOVEN TEXTILE FABRIC	W	921	13436										TISSUS AUT COTON SYNT,ARTIF
655	KNITTED,ETC FABRICS	W	620	13655	W	1100	12786	W	1300	11579	W	1400	14688	ETOF BONNETERIE PIECES ETC
6552	OTHER KNIT ETC FAB NONEL	W	620	13655										ETOF BON NON ELAS NON SYNT
657	SPECIAL TXTL FABRC,PRODS	W	2492	25126										TISSUS SPECIAUX
6573	COATED ETC TEXTILES NES	W	2139	19070										TISSUS,ART MATIERE TEXT NDA
65732	PLASTIC COATED TEXTILES	W	1984	17453										TISSUS IMPREGNES
66	NONMETAL MINERAL MFS NES			32689			39287							ART MIN NON METALLIQUES
662	CLAY,REFRACTORY BLDG PRD	W	15399	13300										MAT CONST REFRACTAIRES
666	POTTERY	W	524	875	W	34200	20862	W	43500	25391	W	54100	29063	POTERIE
67	IRON AND STEEL			134609			179579			138725			128110	FER ET ACIER
672	IRON,STEEL PRIMARY FORMS	W	48656	14085	W	5200	774	W	25600	4657	W	34500	5582	LINGOTS FER,ACIER
673	IRON,STEEL SHAPES ETC	W	139299	41589										BARRES,PROFIL FER,ACIER
6731	IRON,STEEL WIRE ROD	W	68250	20000										FIL MACHINE FER,ACIER
67311	IRON,SIMPLE STL WIRE ROD	W	67000	19388										FIL MACH AUT ACIER FIN
674	IRN,STL UNIV,PLATE,SHEET	W	66570	35872										LARGES PLATS,TOLES
6746	IRN,STL THIN PLATE,ROLLD	W	18941	13568										TOLES LAM MOINS 3MM
678	IRON,STL TUBES,PIPES,ETC	W	32613	29160	W	57700	19387	W	22500	12646	W	24000	16241	TUBES,TUYAUX EN FONTE,FER
6782	IRON,STL SEAMLESS TUBES	W	28847	24421										TUBES,TUYAUX SANS SOUDURE
68	NON–FERROUS METALS			71694			48246							METAUX NON FERREUX
682	COPPER EXC CEMENT COPPER	W	16427	35922				W	19800	38437	W	30700	78359	CUIVRE
6821	COPPER NES,ALLOYS,UNWRT	W	14810	32196										CUIVRE BRUT
68212	COPPER REFINED,UNWROUGHT	W	14611	31819										CUIVRE AFFINE BRUT
684	ALUMINIUM	W	13423	28312	W	21800	32125	W	20000	44648	W	29300	83090	ALUMINIUM
6841	ALUMINIUM,ALLOYS,UNWRGHT	W	9350	13501	W	9900	9285	W	9300	10849	W	13300	24938	ALUMINIUM,ALLIAGES BRUTS
6842	ALUMINIUM,ALLOYS WORKED	W	4073	14811										ALUMINIUM,ALLIAGES OUVRE
69	METAL MANUFACTURES NES			36946			49667							ART MANUFACT EN METAL NDA
699	BASE METAL MFRS NES	W	6843	13089										ART MANUFACTURES MET NDA
6997	IRON,STEEL ARTICLES NES	W	588	637	W	144000	46202	W	68700	41645	W	52500	47529	OUV FONTE,FER,ACIER NDA
7	MACHINES,TRANSPORT EQUIP			980947			952493							MACHINES MATERIEL TRANSPORT
71	POWER GENERATING EQUIPMT			34264			38234			432284			474190	MACHINES GENERATRICES
713	INTRNL COMBUS PSTN ENGIN	W	4034	20086										MOTEURS EXPL COMB INT, PIECE
72	MACHS FOR SPCL INDUSTRYS			134317			173919							MAC SPECIALES POUR INDUST
721	AGRIC MACHY,EXC TRACTORS	W	4624	16817										MACHINES AGRICOLES
722	TRACTORS NON–ROAD	W	10204	17542										TRACTEURS
7224	WHEELED TRACTORS NES	W	9924	16597										TRACTEURS A ROUES
724	TEXTILE,LEATHER MACHNRY	W	1997	26403										MACH POUR INDUSTRIE TEXTILE
727	FOOD MACHRY NON–DOMESTIC	W	2379	21627										MACH INDUSTRIES ALIMENT
7272	OTH FOOD PROC MCHY,PARTS	W	2290	20713										AUT MACH IND ALIMENTAIRE
72722	INDUS FOOD PROC MACH NES	W	2256	20553										MACHINES BOULANGERIE
728	OTH MACHY FOR SPCL INDUS	W	2118	32104										AUT MACH IND PARTICULIERES
7284	MACHY FOR SPCL INDUS NES	W	610	22810										MACH SPEC IND PARTICUL.
73	METALWORKING MACHINERY			17692			12952							MACH TRAVAIL DES METAUX
74	GENRL INDUSTRL MACHY NES			148863			131290							MACH APP INDUSTRIE
741	HEATING,COOLING EQUIPMNT	W	5285	55743										MACH CHAUFFAGE,PIECES
7413	INDUS FURNACES ETC,PARTS	W	1357	19949										FOURS IND,LABOR,PIECES
74131	INDUS FURNACES ETC ELCTR	W	829	17663										FOURS ELECTRIQUES
7416	HEATING,COOLING EQU NES	W	1761	23023										APP CHANGEMENT TEMP
743	PUMPS NES,CENTRFUGES ETC	W	2098	27375										POMPES COMPRES,VENT ETC
744	MECHANICAL HANDLING EQU	W	2623	16216										EQUIP MANUTENTION PIECES
745	NONELEC MACHY,TOOLS NES	W	752	16212										AUT MACH NON ELEC,PIECES
7452	OTH NONELEC MCHS,PTS NES	W	733	15574										AUT MACH NON ELEC,PIECES
749	NONELEC MACH PTS,ACC NES	W	2100	20398										PIECES MACH NON ELEC NDA
75	OFFICE MACHNES,ADP EQUIP			68848			94217							MACH BUREAU TRAIT AUTOM
752	AUTOMTIC DATA PROC EQUIP	W	572	33203										MACH TRAIT INFORMATION
759	OFFICE,ADP MCH PTS,ACCES	W	618	24491										PIECES DU 751 ET 752
7599	ACCTG,ETC,ADP MCH PTS,AC	W	591	22634										PIECES DU 751 ET 752
76	TELECOMM,SOUND EQUIPMENT			91779			67039							EQUIPMENT DE TELECOM
761	TELEVISION RECEIVERS	W	5547	47607										RECEPTEURS DE TELEVISION
7611	COLOUR TV RECEIVERS	W	4835	45154				N	113000	12823	N	205000	17929	RECEPTEURS COULEUR
763	SOUND RECORDRS,PHONOGRPH	W	986	19806										PHONO,APP ENREGISTREMENT
7638	OTHR SOUND APPARATUS ETC	W	967	19518										AUT APP D'ENREGIS,REPROD
76381	TV IMAGE,SND RECRDRS ETC	W	541	14692										APP ENREG,REPRO IMAG,SON
764	TELECOM EQPT,PTS,ACC NES	W	1175	21385										EQUIP TELECOM,PIECES
77	ELECTRIC MACHNRY NES ETC			132265			128678			205185			245662	MACH APP ELECT NDA
772	SWITCHGEAR ETC,PARTS NES	W	402	16252										APP COUPURE,SECT ETC
7721	SWITCHGEAR ETC	W	376	14825										APP COUPURE,SECTIONMNT
774	ELECTRO–MEDCL,XRAY EQUIP	W	171	18564										APPAREILS MEDICAUX
775	HOUSEHOLD TYPE EQUIP NES	W	19731	53588										MACH,APP USAGE DOMESTQUE
7752	DOM REFRIGERATRS,FREEZRS	W	11730	26301										REFRIG,CONGEL MENAGER
77521	DOMESTIC REFRIGERATORS	W	9872	20062										REFRIGERATEURS
778	ELECTRICAL MACHINERY NES	W	6153	26454										AUTRES MACH ELECT NDA
7788	OTH ELEC MACHY,EQUIP NES	W	3284	16032										AUT MACH APP ELEC NDA
78	ROAD VEHICLES			317259			294513			228906			222403	VEHICULES ROUTIERS
781	PASS MOTOR VEH EXC BUSES	W	26905	194566	N	59700	174458	N	33300	114172	N	15400	97366	AUTO TRANSPORT PERSONNES
782	LORRIES,SPCL MTR VEH NES	W	42821	42572										VEHICULES SPECIAUX,MARCH
7821	LORRIES,TRUCKS	W	41037	36520	N	10700	49251	N	5000	38052	N	3100	41489	VEHICULES TRANSP MARCHAND
783	ROAD MOTOR VEHICLES NES	W	17972	27064										VEHICULES ROUTIERS NDA
7831	BUSES	W	9921	20472	N	1218	18312	N	871	12551	N	697	15298	VOITURES TRANSPORT COMMUN
7832	TRACTORS FOR TR–TRAILERS	W	8051	6592	N	16000	31930	N	2800	17633	N	900	17116	TRACTEURS ROUTIERS
784	MOTOR VEH PRTS,ACCES NES	W	8657	36284										PIECES 722,781,782,783

4. General Imports C.I.F. by Commodities according to the S.I.T.C. (Rev. 2) in thousand U.S. Dollars
Importations Générales C.A.F. par Produits d'après la C.T.C.I. (Rév. 2) en milliers de Dollars E.U.

SITC CTCI	COMMODITY	1992		1993		1994		1995		PRODUIT
		WEIGHT POIDS	VALUE VALEUR	WEIGHT POIDS	VALUE VALEUR	WEIGHT POIDS	VALUE VALEUR	WEIGHT POIDS	VALUE VALEUR	
7849	OTHER MOTOR VEHCL PARTS	W 7900	35616							PIECES 722,781,782,783
79	OTHR TRANSPORT EQUIPMENT		35660		11650					AUTRE MATERIEL TRANSPORT
792	AIRCRAFT ETC	W 248	28769							APP NAVIGATION AERIENNE
7929	AIRCRAFT PARTS NES	W 241	23733							PIECES DU 792
8	MISC MANUFACTURED GOODS		213162		295975					ART MANUFACTURES DIVERS
821	*FURNITURE,PARTS THEREOF	W 4150	12525		14149		22489		32415	MEUBLES ET PIECES
84	CLOTHING AND ACCESSORIES		64974		56937		46547		52554	VETEMENTS
851	*FOOTWEAR	W 2859	13490	W 8600	37753	W 9900	39834	W 9600	44581	CHAUSSURES
87	PRECISION INSTRUMNTS NES		44017		61679					INSTRUM,APPAR SCIENT NDA
872	MEDICAL INSTRUMENTS NES	W 585	15507							INSTR,APP MEDIC–CHIR NDA
874	MEASURNG,CONTROLNG INSTR	W 429	25859							INSTRUMENTS DE MESURE
89	MISC MANUFCTRD GOODS NES		61106		100506					ART MANUFACTURES DIVERS
893	ARTICLES OF PLASTIC NES		18538		17372					OUVRAGES EN MAT DIVIS 58
899	OTHER MANUFACTURED GOODS		13873							AUT ART MANUF DIVERS NDA
9	GOODS NOT CLASSD BY KIND		5815		300492					ART TRANSACT NON CLASSES

5. General Exports F.O.B. by Commodities according to the S.I.T.C. (Rev. 2) in thousand U.S. Dollars
Exportations Générales F.O.B. par Produits d'après la C.T.C.I. (Rév. 2) en milliers de Dollars E.U.

SITC CTCI	COMMODITY	1992		1993		1994		1995		PRODUIT
		WEIGHT POIDS	VALUE VALEUR	WEIGHT POIDS	VALUE VALEUR	WEIGHT POIDS	VALUE VALEUR	WEIGHT POIDS	VALUE VALEUR	
	ALL COMMODITIES		4563561		3720973		4156503		5091011	TOUS PRODUITS
0	FOOD AND LIVE ANIMALS		598703		319466					ALIMENTS,ANIMAUX VIVANTS
001	*LIVE ANIMALS FOR FOOD	W 112300	118351	W 43200	41891	W 50900	45953	W 14400	22033	ANIMAUX VIVANTS
0011	BOVINE SPECIES,LIVE	N 197000	46925	N 57000	17444	N 63000	16167	N 5100	2368	ESPECE BOVINE
00121	SHEEP,LIVE	N 1477000	58996	N 693000	23492	N 936000	28646	N 259000	12313	ESPECE OVINE
01	MEAT AND PREPARATIONS		82493		36263					VIANDES ET PREPARATIONS
011	MEAT FRESH,CHILLD,FROZEN	W 98300	80629	W 10500	34462	W 13400	40688	W 12400	37490	VIANDES FRAICHES,REF,CONGE
0113	PIG MEAT FRESH,CHLD,FRZN	W 6008	14060	W 599	944	W 763	1178	W 1063	1702	VIANDE DE PORC
0114	POULTRY FRESH CHLLD,FRZN	W 16221	27122	W 4478	10088	W 6320	11623	W 7089	13022	VOLAILLES MORTES
02	DAIRY PRODCTS,BIRDS'EGGS		70508		39746					PRODUITS LAITIERS,OEUFS
024	CHEESE AND CURD	W 21900	53546	W 13300	34342	W 15400	34237	W 6100	15561	FROMAGE ET CAILLEBOTTE
04	CEREALS AND PREPARATIONS		107915		18989					CEREALES ET PRODUITS
041	WHEAT ETC UNMILLED	W 327400	41960	W 46600	5342	W 14800	1303	W 774200	98838	FROMENT,EPEAUTRE
05	VEGETABLES AND FRUIT		138662		95381					LEGUMES ET FRUITS
054	VEG ETC FRSH,SMPLY PRSVD	W 112600	58333	W 51000	22067	W 79000	43086	W 60900	37592	LEGUMES FRAIS,CONG,SECS
0565	VEGTBLES PRSVD,PREPD NES	W 62300	31255	W 55600	27601	W 48500	31247	W 46400	28895	LEGUMES PREPARES CONSERVE
057	FRUIT,NUTS,FRESH,DRIED	W 40500	21837	W 43000	20352	W 128800	63864	W 87700	35139	FRUITS FRAIS OU SECS
058	FRUIT PRESERVED,PREPARED					W 97400	59294	W 81600	52332	CONSERVES DE FRUITS
06	SUGAR AND PREPS,HONEY		23717		27590		25921		51195	SUCRES ET PRODUITS
07	COFFEE,TEA,COCOA,SPICES		15660		16240		20964		17648	CAFE,THE,CACAO,EPICES
09	MISC EDIBLE PRODUCTS		16004		25094		29679		26601	PREP ALIMENTAIRES DIVERSES
1	BEVERAGES AND TOBACCO		477575		352481					BOISSONS ET TABACS
11	BEVERAGES		113883		118504		149849		182776	BOISSONS
1121	WINE OF FRESH GRAPES ETC	W 87400	77253	W 119000	80060	W 147200	93901	W 189700	120389	VINS DE RAISINS FRAIS
12	TOBACCO AND MANUFACTURES		363692		233977		225405		295857	TABACS BRUTS FABRIQUES
121	TOBACCO UNMNFCTRD,REFUSE	W 29700	123456	W 15200	56467	W 21300	47686	W 29300	60940	TABACS BRUTS,DECHETS
122	TOBACCO,MANUFACTURED				177510					TABACS FABRIQUES
1222	CIGARETTES		239493	W 23100	177221	W 40100	177435	W 59200	234118	CIGARETTES
2	CRUDE MATERLS,EXCL FUELS		296375		212265					MAT BRUTES NON COMESTIBLES
21	HIDES,SKINS,FURS UNDRSSD		15860		8728					CUIRS,PEAUX BRUTS
211	HIDES,SKINS,EXC FURS,RAW					W 14800	23652	W 9100	20473	CUIRS ET PEAUX
22	OIL SEEDS,OLEAGINOUS FRT		33953		23676		37355		52644	GRAINES,FRUITS OLEAGINEUX
24	CORK AND WOOD		41192		54438					LIEGE ET BOIS
251	*PULP AND WASTE PAPER	W 56000	22540	W 43800	11509	W 51600	24683	W 36200	23557	PATES A PAPIER,DECHETS
2517	SODA,SULPHATE WOOD PULP	W 45100	21458	W 34900	9567	W 45600	23151	W 35100	23250	PATES CHIMIQUES AU SULFATE
26	TEXTILE FIBRES AND WASTE		29964		20099					FIBRES TEXTILES
263	COTTON					W 21500	38476	W 17400	38971	COTON
266	SYNTHETIC FIBRES TO SPIN					W 26000	76548	W 29100	93879	FIBRES SYNTHETIQUES
268	WOOL(EXC TOPS),ANML HAIR					W 5100	19936	W 4400	19324	LAINES ET POILS
27	CRUDE FERTLZR,MINRLS NES		19574		22146					ENGRAIS MINERAUX BRUTS
28	METALLIFEROUS ORES,SCRAP		92176		60207					MINERAIS METAL,DECHETS
2871	CPR ORE ETC,CEMENT COPPR	W 129100	46118	W 119000	31973	W 101300	35557	W 71500	33962	MINERAIS DE CUIVRE,MATTES
29	CRUDE ANIMAL,VEG MAT NES		27815		10131					MATIERES BRUTES ANIM,VEGET
3	MINERAL FUELS ETC		307383		323235		282957		312395	COMBUSTIBLES MINERAUX LUB
33	PETROLEUM AND PRODUCTS		290816		298792		282957		312395	PETROLE ET DERIVES
4	ANIMAL,VEGETABLE OIL,FAT		16732		30881					HUILES,GRAISSES ANIM,VEG
42	FIXED VEGETABLE OIL,FAT		13716		28877					HUILES VEGETALES FIXES
431	*PROCESD ANML VEG OIL,ET		708		991	W 35000	21726	W 66400	45414	HUILES,GRAISSES PREPAREES
5	CHEMCLS,RELATED PROD NES		562053		542531					PRODUITS CHIMIQUES
51	ORGANIC CHEMICALS		74177		72295		138699		181726	PROD CHIMIQ ORGANIQUES
52	INORGANIC CHEMICALS		122479		58500					PROD CHIM INORGANIQUES
52229	OTH INORGANIC ACIDS ETC					W 888000	82884	W 679800	117158	AUTRES ACIDES INORGANIQUES
52323	NEUTRAL SODIUM CARBONATE	W 344700	57580	W 127500	15379	W 300700	32792	W 543000	60919	CARBONATE NEUTRE SODIUM
541	*MEDICINAL,PHARM PRODUCT		94040		181832	MK 9500	87035	MK 10600	87456	PROD MEDICINAUX PHARMACEUT
5413	ANTIBIOTICS IN BULK		36021							ANTIBIOTIQUES NDA
5417	MEDICAMENTS		49633							MEDICAMENTS
54171	— CONTAINNG ANTIBIOTICS				26472		7846		10421	MED CONTN ANTIBIOTIQUES
55	PERFUME,CLEANING ETC PRD		19848		47421		41694		75239	PROD POUR PARFUM,TOILETTE
553	PERFUMERY,COSMETICS,ETC		6388	W 13600	21965	W 15900	24618	W 25900	42460	PRODUITS DE PARFUMERIE
562	*FERTILIZERS,MANUFACTURE		165096	W 1223700	98405	W 1541100	131412	W 1840500	231736	ENGRAIS MANUFACTURES
56211	AMMONIUM NITRATE	W 410200	43101	W 209000	20396	W 290400	27083	W 728100	78388	NITRATE D'AMMONIUM
58	PLASTIC MATERIALS ETC		55276		60221		112203		147552	MAT PLAST ARTIFICIELLES
5831	POLYETHYLENE	W 39500	30064	W 51600	28957	W 48900	28829	W 47700	41698	POLYETHYLENE
59	CHEMICAL MATERIALS NES		23468		20381					MAT PROD CHIMIQUES NDA
591	PESTICIDES,DISINFECTANTS	W 6200	12429	W 7400	14413	W 9200	16180	W 6800	13774	DESINF,INSECT,FONG,HERB
598	MISCEL CHEM PRODUCTS NES					W 26600	20041	W 12500	19380	PROD DIV INDUST CHIM NDA
6	BASIC MANUFACTURES		982462		934574					ART MANUFACTURES
61	LEATHER,DRESSED FUR,ETC		8850		14576					CUIRS,PELLETERIES
6123	PREPRD PARTS OF FOOTWEAR					P 5891000	53734			PARTIES DE CHAUSSURES
62	RUBBER MANUFACTURES NES		46417		30870		45850		55694	CAOUTCHOUC MANUFACTURE
625	RUBBER TYRES, TUBES ETC		24445	W 10300	13665	W 6300	10150	W 4700	10399	PNEUS CAOUTCHOUC VULCANISE
63	WOOD,CORK MANUFACTRS NES		22999		24457					OUVRAGES LIEGE ET BOIS
64	PAPER,PAPERBOARD AND MFR		30672		30751		46110		66209	PAPIERS,CARTONS & OUVRAGES
65	TEXTILE YARN,FABRICS,ETC		128262		113589					FILS,TISSUS,ARTICLES TEXTILE
652	COTTON FABRICS,WOVEN	W 74	12714		34878	A 28200	17386	A 37200	18523	TISSUS DE COTON
653	WOVN MAN–MADE FIB FABRIC	W 19500	53731	W 19400	51519					TISSUS FIBRES SYNTH,ARTIF
654	OTH WOVEN TEXTILE FABRIC	W 5200	22929	W 3700	21741					TISSUS AUT COTON SYNT,ARTIF
6584	LINENS ETC		23538							LINGE DE MAISON
66	NONMETAL MINERAL MFS NES		85106		64077					ART MIN NON METALLIQUES
6612	CEMENT	W 447800	13332	W 584200	16970	W 1149800	29017	W 1817800	44184	CIMENTS HYDRAULIQUES
663	MINERAL MANUFCTURES NES	W 93300	27371	W 54400	9241	W 47200	10226	W 38700	6704	ART MIN MANUF NDA
666	POTTERY	W 71900	23233	W 59000	22114	W 71000	25092	W 77600	31376	POTERIE
67	IRON AND STEEL		320266		362417		447912		519010	FER ET ACIER
674	IRN,STL UNIV,PLATE,SHEET	W 390600	136783	W 545000	131626	W 769800	208476	W 969900	261821	LARGES PLATS,TOLES
68	NON–FERROUS METALS		283058		234581					METAUX NON FERREUX
682	COPPER EXC CEMENT COPPER	W 102300	204912	W 78500	146463	W 91600	166267	W 96300	265260	CUIVRE
684	ALUMINIUM			W 14800	19915	W 23700	31948	W 17400	36616	ALUMINIUM
685	LEAD	W 35700	18397	W 35400	13223	W 50300	22188	W 57700	31938	PLOMB
686	ZINC	W 45900	55142	W 63100	53483	W 58600	43247	W 62600	56032	ZINC
6861	ZINC,ALLOYS UNWROUGHT	W 43600	53601	W 61800	52998	W 57400	42375	W 62400	55924	ZINC ET ALLIAGES BRUTS
69	METAL MANUFACTURES NES		56832		59252					ART MANUFACT EN METAL NDA
6997	IRON,STEEL ARTICLES NES			W 109100	54879	W 113600	52892	W 104400	67702	OUV FONTE,FER,ACIER NDA
7	MACHINES,TRANSPORT EQUIP		817994		641396					MACHINES MATERIEL TRANSPORT
71	POWER GENERATING EQUIPMT		55974		44036		239080		282825	MACHINES GENERATRICES
71621	AC MTRS,INC UNIVRSL MTRS		32357	N 650000	22280	N 581000	16188	N 674000	18314	MOT ELEC NON COUR CONTINU
72	MACHS FOR SPCL INDUSTRYS		35384		36328					MAC SPECIALES POUR INDUST
73	METALWORKING MACHINERY		70827		46336					MACH TRAVAIL DES METAUX
73613	LATHES,METALWORKING		24111	W 6300	14337	W 6600	13837	W 6000	14506	TOURS A METAUX
74	GENRL INDUSTRL MACHY NES		289171		265936					MACH APP INDUSTRIE
75	OFFICE MACHNES,ADP EQUIP		28264		25716					MACH BUREAU TRAIT AUTOM
76	TELECOMM,SOUND EQUIPMENT		27386		17198					EQUIPMENT DE TELECOM

5. General Exports F.O.B. by Commodities according to the S.I.T.C. (Rev. 2) in thousand U.S. Dollars
Exportations Générales F.O.B. par Produits d'après la C.T.C.I. (Rév. 2) en milliers de Dollars E.U.

SITC CTCI	COMMODITY	1992		1993		1994		1995		PRODUIT
		WEIGHT POIDS	VALUE VALEUR	WEIGHT POIDS	VALUE VALEUR	WEIGHT POIDS	VALUE VALEUR	WEIGHT POIDS	VALUE VALEUR	
77	ELECTRIC MACHNRY NES ETC		227024		142289		191600		179168	MACH APP ELECT NDA
7721	SWITCHGEAR ETC		23798							APP COUPURE,SECTIONMNT
7758	ELECTRO–THERMIC APPL NES		28262							APP ELECTROTHERMIQ NDA
77812	ELECTRIC ACCUMULATORS		46393		28932		57915		21865	ACCUMULATEURS ELECTRIQ
7784	ELECTRO–MECH HAND TOOLS		16950							OUTILS ELECTROMEC,PIECES
78	ROAD VEHICLES		37233		31058		40806		41916	VEHICULES ROUTIERS
79	OTHR TRANSPORT EQUIPMENT		46731		32494					AUTRE MATERIEL TRANSPORT
793	SHIPS AND BOATS ETC		31659		30353		20315		77540	NAVIRES BATEAUX,ETC
8	MISC MANUFACTURED GOODS		503675		363643					ART MANUFACTURES DIVERS
812	*PLUMBG,HEATNG,LGHTNG EQ		17325		8192					APPAR SANITAIRES CHAUFFAGE
821	*FURNITURE,PARTS THEREOF		32103		26526		38242		45228	MEUBLES ET PIECES
8219	FURNITURE AND PARTS NES		26338							AUTRES MEUBLES ET PIECES
84	CLOTHING AND ACCESSORIES		217691		176939		182313		226351	VETEMENTS
842	MENS OUTERWEAR NOT KNIT				20302		24743		33311	VET DESSUS POUR HOMMES
8441	— MENS SHIRTS		17561		16055		16125		16919	CHEMISES HOMMES MAT TEXT
8451	— JERSEYS,PULLOVERS ETC		20337							CHANDAILS,PULL–OVERS ETC
8459	— OTHER,CLTHG ACCESRYS		18880							AUT VET DESSUS DE BONNE
851	*FOOTWEAR		87354	W 7300	78385	W 9200	91784	W 7800	92590	CHAUSSURES
85102	FOOTWEAR LEATHER	P 4452000	49468					P 5159000	48273	CHAUS SEMELLES EN CUIR
89	MISC MANUFCTRD GOODS NES		125101		51769					ART MANUFACTURES DIVERS

1. HISTORICAL SERIES, 1961–1996 SPECIAL TRADE, IMPORTS C.I.F., EXPORTS F.O.B.
SERIES HISTORIQUES, 1961–1996 COMMERCE SPECIAL, IMPORTATIONS C.A.F., EXPORTATIONS F.O.B

YEAR ANNEE	VALUE IN MILLION C.F.A. FRANCS / VALEUR EN MILLION C.F.A. FRANCS — MERCHANDISE –MARCHANDISE		GOLD –OR		CONVERSION FACTORS U.S. CENTS PER C.F.A. FRANC FACTEURS DE CONVERSION CENTS E.U. PAR C.F.A. FRANC		INDEX NUMBERS –INDICES — QUANTUM		UNIT VALUE VALEUR UNITAIRE	
	IMPORTS	EXPORTS	IMPORTS	EXPORTS	IMPORTS	EXPORTS	IMPORTS	EXPORTS	IMPORTS	EXPORTS
1961	6992.00	812.00		70.00	0.4051	0.4051				
1962	8551.00	1654.00		290.00	0.4051	0.4051				
1963	9382.00	2769.00		288.00	0.4051	0.4051				
1964	9484.00	3087.00		227.00	0.4051	0.4051				
1965	9169.00	3432.00		248.00	0.4051	0.4051				
1966	9293.00	3869.00		116.00	0.4051	0.4051				
1967	8970.00	4429.00			0.4051	0.4051				
1968	10803.00	5288.00			0.4051	0.4051				
1969	13989.00	5329.00			0.3870	0.3865				
1970	13701.00	5056.00			0.3601	0.3601				
1971	15611.00	4408.00			0.3601	0.3601				
1972	17269.00	5141.00			0.4000	0.3980				
1973	21690.00	5596.00			0.4519	0.4532				
1974	34664.00	8702.00			0.4168	0.4142				
1975	32386.00	9368.00			0.4670	0.4647				
1976	34423.00	12690.00			0.4187	0.4237				
1977	51356.00	13614.00			0.4074	0.4057				
1978	51075.00	9600.00			0.4392	0.4460				
1979	63916.00	16240.00			0.4707	0.4726				
1980	75610.00	19070.00			0.4733	0.4733				
1981	91443.00	20066.00			0.3691	0.3737				
1982	113708.00	18109.00			0.3044	0.3103				
1983	109572.00	21712.00			0.2624	0.2624				
1984	91098.00	34871.00			0.2269	0.2256				
1985	146243.00	31156.00			0.2277	0.2262				
1986	139640.00	28665.01			0.2900	0.2881				
1987	130527.00	46593.01			0.3327	0.3327				
1988	134940.00	41947.01			0.3363	0.3380				
1989	125352.00	30280.00			0.3123	0.3128				
1990	145833.00	41282.00			0.3702	0.3661				
1991	169200.00	268999.90			0.3567	0.3526				
1992	144200.00	237300.00			0.3777	0.3777				
1993	156800.00	226100.00			0.3541	0.3541				
1994	216600.00	193700.00			0.1800	0.1800				
1995	265639.00	267600.00			0.2002	0.2002				
1996	278644.90	155800.00			0.1956	0.1956				

2. IMPORTS BY BROAD ECONOMIC CATEGORY AND EXPORTS BY INDUSTRIAL ORIGIN. (PERCENTAGE OF TOTAL VALUE)
IMPORTATIONS PAR CATEGORIES ECONOMIQUES ET EXPORTATIONS PAR BRANCHE D'ACTIVITE.(EN POURCENTAGE DE LA VALEUR TOTALE)

IMPORTS – IMPORTATIONS

	1990	1991	1992	1993	1994	1995	1996
TOTAL IMPORTS–IMPORTATIONS TOTALES							
1 FOOD BEV–ALIMENTATION BOISSONS							
11 PRIMARY–PRODUITS DE BASE							
111 FOR INDUSTRY–POUR L'INDUSTRIE							
112 FOR HOUSEHOLDS–POUR LES MENAGES							
12 PROCESSED–PRODUITS ELABORES							
121 FOR INDUSTRY–POUR L'INDUSTRIE							
122 FOR HOUSEHOLDS–POUR LES MENAGES							
2 IND SUPPLIES–APPROV INDUSTRIELS							
21 PRIMARY–PRODUITS DE BASE							
22 PROCESSED–PRODUITS ELABORES							
3 FUELS–COMBUSTIBLES							
31 PRIMARY–PRODUITS DE BASE							
32 PROCESSED–PRODUITS ELABORES							
321 MOTOR SPIRIT–ESSENCE							
322 OTHER–AUTRES							
4 MACHINERY–EQUIPEMENT							
41 CAPITAL EQUIPMENT–MACHINES							
42 PARTS–PIECES ACCESSOIRES							
5 TRANSPORT–TRANSPORT							
51 PASSENGER CARS–AUTOMOBILES							
52 OTHER–AUTRES							
521 INDUSTRIAL–INDUSTRIELS							
522 NON INDUSTRIAL–NON INDUSTRIEL							
53 PARTS–PIECES ACCESSOIRES							
6 CONSUM GOODS–BIENS CONSOMMATION							
61 DURABLE–DURABLES							
62 SEMI DURABLE–SEMI DURABLES							
63 NON DURABLE–NON DURABLES							
7 GOODS NES–BIENS NDA							

EXPORTS – EXPORTATIONS

	1990	1991	1992	1993	1994	1995	1996
TOTAL EXPORTS–EXPORTATIONS TOTALES							
1 AGRICULTURE							
2 MINING QUARRY–INDUS EXTRACTIVES							
3 MANUFACTURING–IND MANUFACTUR							
31 FOOD BEV TOBACCO–ALIM BOISS TAB							
32 TEXTILES–INDUSTRIES TEXTILES							
33 WOOD & PRODUCTS–BOIS & PRODUITS							
34 PAPER & PRODUCTS–PAPIER & PRODT							
35 CHEMICALS–INDUSTRIES CHIMIQUES							
36 NON METAL MIN–MIN NON METAL							
37 BASIC METAL–IND METAL BASE							
38 METAL MANUF–MANUF METAL							
39 OTH MANUF IND–AUTRES MANUF							

3. TRADE BY PRINCIPAL COUNTRIES OF PRODUCTION AND LAST DESTINATION (VALUE IN THOUSAND U.S. DOLLARS)
ECHANGES SELON LES PRINCIPAUX PAYS DE PRODUCTION ET DE DERNIERE DESTINATION (VALEUR EN MILLIERS DE DOLLARS EU)

COUNTRIES–PAYS	SPECIAL IMPORTS C.I.F. IMPORTATIONS SPECIALES C.A.F				
	1987	1988	1989	1990	1991
World	434263	455436	391098		535960
Africa	104435	104085	88021		153770
Americas	33942	23311	21662		33619
Northern America	30292	22275	20645		31397
LAIA	3650	1036	1017		2222
CACM					
Caribbean					
Rest of America					
As.ex F.USSR	41927	53787	61913		69492
Eur.x F.USSR	227567	236500	191322		219659
EU	222889	233736	186975		216560
EFTA	2306	2113	1585		1191
East Europe	2372	651	2761		1908
Other Europe					
Former USSR	4119	2207	537		378
Oceania	140				464
France,Monac	135569	140235	112707		130709
Cote d'Ivoire	70962	69657	56815		103907
USA/Etats–Unis d'Amer	27977	20496	17625		26378
Japan/Japon	21888	28870	18505		22593
Germany/Allemagne	17823	23986	18511		21473
Thailand/Thaïlande	14446	18404	36176		12324
Netherlands/Pays–Bas	19273	23497	13460		14625
Italy/Italie	17394	19750	16573		14161
Togo	15903	14813	11266		14065
China/Chine	5593	6514	4624		34575
United Kingdom	10713	7739	9138		9217
Belgium–Luxembourg	8763	8134	6143		11789
Nigeria/Nigéria	6072	6068	5738		14828
Spain/Espagne	5806	6267	7092		7088
Senegal/Sénégal	2612	2487	4434		8718
Ghana	4298	4414	2608		4448
Denmark/Danemark	4202	1910	2331		4409
Canada	2316	1779	3020		5019
Cameroon/Cameroun	1850	3453	1298		3321
Brazil/Brésil	3650	1036	1017		2222
Former USSR/Anc. URSS	4119	2207	537		378
Switz.Liecht	2306	2113	1585		1191
Mali	1371	1752	1120		1680
Portugal	802	1272	1020		1106
Czechoslovakia	572	651	1236		1388
Mauritania/Mauritanie			3413		
Benin/Bénin	396	300	746		1712
Austria/Autriche	2326	742			
Former GDR	915		1526		521
Niger	596	1050	321		571
Ireland/Irlande	183	202			1826
India/Inde			1707		
Romania/Roumanie	885				
Morocco/Maroc	299		243		221
Hong Kong			633		
Australia/Australie	140				464
Tunisia/Tunisie					300
Greece/Grèce	37				157
Korea Dem People's Rp			193		
Algeria/Algérie	77	91	16		
Pakistan			50		
Saudi Arabia			19		
Myanmar			6		

COUNTRIES–PAYS	SPECIAL EXPORTS F.O.B. EXPORTATIONS SPECIALES F.O.B.				
	1987	1988	1989	1990	1991
Monde	155015	141781	94742	151092	105399
Afrique	40283	25262	19951	21810	18705
Amériques	1258	1480			310
Amérique du Nord	1258	1480			310
ALAI					
MCAC					
Caraïbes					
Autre Amérique					
Asie l'URSS exclus	3889	6537	1512	1984	13589
Europe l'URSS exclus	77406	71068	31472	34968	59593
UE	70599	70733	30968	34968	38201
AELE	6807	335	504		21392
Europe de l'Est					
Autre de l'Europe					
Ancienne URSS					
Océanie					4
France,Monac	53295	52863	27694	34898	14164
Cote d'Ivoire	22547	12905	11885	17114	11816
Togo	7542	9052	5778	4696	3008
Switz.Liecht	6807	335	504		21392
Italy/Italie	3939	4387			10603
Portugal	3380	4269			9848
Japan/Japon	2934	5100	1512	1984	1943
Spain/Espagne	3680	3850			1604
Thailand/Thaïlande					8797
Germany/Allemagne	3287	1497	2100	70	610
United Kingdom	1504	2160	1174		367
China/Chine	639	1386			2849
Ghana	2801	612	654		575
Mali	842	1251	726		1291
Morocco/Maroc	3710	186			
Niger	1444	463	908		335
Denmark/Danemark	642	1315			529
Nigeria/Nigéria	622	81			1499
USA/Etats–Unis d'Amer	256	1467			296
Benin/Bénin	339	690			155
Canada	1001	14			14
Netherlands/Pays–Bas	519	281			42
Belgium–Luxembourg	349	10			405
Senegal/Sénégal	396	24			28
Hong Kong	316	51			
Greece/Grèce		101			
Cameroon/Cameroun	40				
Ireland/Irlande					28
Australia/Australie					4
Sweden/Suède	3				

(VALUE AS PERCENTAGE OF WORLD TOTAL)(VALEURS EN POURCENTAGE DU TOTAL MONDIAL)

	1982	1983	1984	1985	1986	1987	1988	1989	1990	1991
Africa	27.7	28.8	34.0	31.9	28.1	24.0	22.9	22.5		28.7
Americas	11.0	13.7	11.5	14.0	8.2	7.8	5.1	5.5		6.3
Northern America	8.7	10.8	10.9	13.7	6.8	7.0	4.9	5.3		5.9
LAIA	1.8	2.5	0.6	0.3	1.4	0.8	0.2	0.3		0.4
CACM	0.0									
Caribbean	0.5	0.4								
Rest of America	0.0	0.0								
As.ex F.USSR	10.9	11.0	5.3	5.3	5.8	9.7	11.8	15.8		13.0
Eur.x F.USSR	49.6	46.2	42.3	44.0	55.4	52.4	51.9	48.9		41.0
EU	48.8	45.5	41.9	43.1	54.8	51.3	51.3	47.8		40.4
EFTA	0.3	0.5	0.3	0.7	0.4	0.5	0.5	0.4		0.2
East Europe	0.3	0.2	0.0	0.1	0.2	0.5	0.1	0.7		0.4
Other Europe	0.1	0.0	0.0	0.1	0.0					
Former USSR	0.1	0.1	1.2	1.0	0.0	0.9	0.5	0.1		0.1
Oceania	0.0	0.0		0.0	0.0	0.0				0.1
France,Monac	32.0	27.9	28.5	27.7	32.9	31.2	30.8	28.8		24.4
Cote d'Ivoire	22.5	23.6	30.0	27.5	23.6	16.3	15.3	14.5		19.4
USA/Etats–Unis d'Amer	6.6	9.4	10.0	13.2	6.0	6.4	4.5	4.5		4.9
Japan/Japon	3.7	4.3	3.3	3.0	4.4	5.0	6.3	4.7		4.2
Germany/Allemagne	3.7	3.4	2.6	4.3	3.7	4.1	5.3	4.7		4.0
Thailand/Thaïlande	1.9	0.4	0.1	0.8	0.6	3.3	4.0	9.2		2.3
Netherlands/Pays–Bas	4.3	5.1	4.4	4.0	4.5	4.4	5.2	3.4		2.7
Italy/Italie	1.4	1.7	1.8	2.2	7.9	4.0	4.3	4.2		2.6
Togo	1.7	1.3	0.9	0.7	1.0	3.7	3.3	2.9		2.6
China/Chine	1.9	2.2	1.7	1.4	0.6	1.3	1.4	1.2		6.5

	1982	1983	1984	1985	1986	1987	1988	1989	1990	1991
Afrique	31.9	26.3	13.7	17.9	14.5	26.0	17.8	21.1	14.4	17.7
Amériques	0.1	1.1	0.7	1.3	1.0	0.8	1.0			0.3
Amérique du Nord	0.1	1.1	0.7	1.2	1.0	0.8	1.0			0.3
ALAI										
MCAC					0.0					
Caraïbes			0.0	0.0	0.0					
Autre Amérique										
Asie l'URSS exclus	23.9	43.2	17.7	7.2	2.9	2.5	4.6	1.6	1.3	12.9
Europe l'URSS exclus	43.9	29.1	51.1	62.6	68.1	49.9	50.1	33.2	23.1	56.5
UE	43.7	28.9	50.4	58.1	64.1	45.5	49.9	32.7	23.1	36.2
AELE	0.2	0.2	0.7	4.5	4.0	4.4	0.2	0.5		20.3
Europe de l'Est										
Autre de l'Europe	0.0		0.0	0.0	0.0					
Ancienne URSS										
Océanie										0.0
France,Monac	14.5	11.9	14.3	35.4	42.3	34.4	37.3	29.2	23.1	13.4
Cote d'Ivoire	21.0	9.0	9.5	10.4	8.9	14.5	9.1	12.5	11.3	11.2
Togo	1.4	2.6	0.6	0.7	0.4	4.9	6.4	6.1	3.1	2.9
Switz.Liecht	0.2	0.2	0.7	4.4	4.0	4.4	0.2	0.5		20.3
Italy/Italie	4.9	1.7	5.1	7.2	4.4	2.5	3.1			10.1
Portugal	0.0		0.0		1.4	2.2	3.0			9.3
Japan/Japon	5.2	4.3	13.9	3.3	2.4	1.9	3.6	1.6	1.3	1.8
Spain/Espagne	0.3	1.0	3.7	2.8	4.7	2.4	2.7			1.5
Thailand/Thaïlande	0.2		1.0	1.1	0.1					8.3
Germany/Allemagne	7.4	1.3	9.1	3.9	3.2	2.1	1.1	2.2	0.0	0.6

4. Special Imports C.I.F. by Commodities according to the S.I.T.C. (Rev. 2) in thousand U.S. Dollars
Importations Spéciales C.A.F. par Produits d'après la C.T.C.I. (Rév. 2) en milliers de Dollars E.U.

SITC CTCI	COMMODITY	1988 WEIGHT POIDS	1988 VALUE VALEUR	1989 WEIGHT POIDS	1989 VALUE VALEUR	1990 WEIGHT POIDS	1990 VALUE VALEUR	1991 WEIGHT POIDS	1991 VALUE VALEUR	PRODUIT
	ALL COMMODITIES		455436		391098		539582		535960	TOUS PRODUITS
0	FOOD AND LIVE ANIMALS		94726		91350		98453		104106	ALIMENTS,ANIMAUX VIVANTS
001	*LIVE ANIMALS FOR FOOD				84		170		3792	ANIMAUX VIVANTS
01	MEAT AND PREPARATIONS				643		2420			VIANDES ET PREPARATIONS
02	DAIRY PRODCTS,BIRDS'EGGS				10711		18082		18388	PRODUITS LAITIERS,OEUFS
022	MILK AND CREAM	W 16314	17803							LAIT ET CREME
0224	MILK,CREAM PRESERVED ETC			W 6254	7731	W 7622	11703			LAIT,CREME CONS,CONC
03	FISH AND PREPARATIONS				4490		5546			POISSONS ET PREPARATIONS
04	CEREALS AND PREPARATIONS		41755		55508		42272		38638	CEREALES ET PRODUITS
042	RICE			W 90453	37487	W 70	26444			RIZ
05	VEGETABLES AND FRUIT				9890		16084		28172	LEGUMES ET FRUITS
05771	COCONUTS FRESH OR DRIED			W 7551	7057	W 10919	12621			NOIX DE COCO
06	SUGAR AND PREPS,HONEY				874		4643		810	SUCRES ET PRODUITS
0612	REFINED SUGAR ETC			W 41	12	W 6595	3593			SUCRES RAFFINES
07	COFFEE,TEA,COCOA,SPICES				2062		3722			CAFE,THE,CACAO,EPICES
081	*FEEDING STUFF FOR ANIML				22		15		14307	NOURRITURE POUR ANIMAUX
09	MISC EDIBLE PRODUCTS				6465		5498			PREP ALIMENTAIRES DIVERSES
1	BEVERAGES AND TOBACCO		8697		8599		10493		11596	BOISSONS ET TABACS
12	TOBACCO AND MANUFACTURES				7812		9561			TABACS BRUTS FABRIQUES
1222	CIGARETTES			W 472	3884	W 126	2168			CIGARETTES
2	CRUDE MATERLS,EXCL FUELS		11863		8508		11400		10134	MAT BRUTES NON COMESTIBLES
24	CORK AND WOOD				1732		3064			LIEGE ET BOIS
26	TEXTILE FIBRES AND WASTE				3366		3419			FIBRES TEXTILES
27	CRUDE FERTLZR,MINRLS NES				2318		3189			ENGRAIS MINERAUX BRUTS
2783	COMMON SALT,ETC			W 16063	1616	W 23890	2168			SEL
3	MINERAL FUELS ETC		33196		33718		60506		62005	COMBUSTIBLES MINERAUX LUB
33	PETROLEUM AND PRODUCTS				32732		59514		62005	PETROLE ET DERIVES
334	PETROLEUM PRODUCTS,REFIN	W 145640	33196						62005	PRODUITS RAFFINES
33419	OTH LIGHT PETROLEUM OILS			W 59261	14446	W 64351	22807			AUTRES HUILES LEGERES
3342	KEROSENE,OTH MEDIUM OILS			W 13222	3001	W 17447	5206			PETR LAMPANTS,AUT HUIL
3343	GAS OILS			W 29880	6078	W 36665	10563			GAS OILS
4	ANIMAL,VEGETABLE OIL,FAT		4516		3781		7692		11411	HUILES,GRAISSES ANIM,VEG
431	*PROCESD ANML VEG OIL,ET				3772		7685			HUILES,GRAISSES PREPAREES
43143	VEGETABLE WAXES				855		2960			CIRES VEGETALES
5	CHEMCLS,RELATED PROD NES		53551		44532		73948		99088	PRODUITS CHIMIQUES
51	ORGANIC CHEMICALS				1454		3237			PROD CHIMIQ ORGANIQUES
52	INORGANIC CHEMICALS				2387		4514			PROD CHIM INORGANIQUES
53	DYES,TANNING,COLOUR PROD				1869		2179			PROD TEINTURE,COLORANTS
541	*MEDICINAL,PHARM PRODUCT				19041		29063			PROD MEDICINAUX PHARMACEUT
55	PERFUME,CLEANING ETC PRD				2596		3064			PROD POUR PARFUM,TOILETTE
562	*FERTILIZERS,MANUFACTURE				5866		16276			ENGRAIS MANUFACTURES
58	PLASTIC MATERIALS ETC				3295		4344			MAT PLAST ARTIFICIELLES
59	CHEMICAL MATERIALS NES				7728		10748			MAT PROD CHIMIQUES NDA
6	BASIC MANUFACTURES		120872		78911		117131		125894	ART MANUFACTURES
62	RUBBER MANUFACTURES NES				5201		7578			CAOUTCHOUC MANUFACTURE
62599	TYRES NES,TYRE CASES,ETC			W 1176	4015	W 1446	5169			PNEUS,FLAPS
63	WOOD,CORK MANUFACTRS NES				1229		1598			OUVRAGES LIEGE ET BOIS
64	PAPER,PAPERBOARD AND MFR				6895		12221			PAPIERS,CARTONS & OUVRAGES
6423	EXERCISE BOOKS ETC			W 395	1033	W 792	2431			REGISTRES,CAHIERS,CARNETS
65	TEXTILE YARN,FABRICS,ETC				11578		17479		1948	FILS,TISSUS,ARTICLES TEXTILE
652	COTTON FABRICS,WOVEN			W 3036	5054	W 4657	8458			TISSUS DE COTON
653	WOVN MAN–MADE FIB FABRIC			W 1221	1700	W 2079	4440			TISSUS FIBRES SYNTH,ARTIF
66	NONMETAL MINERAL MFS NES				22149		32775			ART MIN NON METALLIQUES
6612	CEMENT	W 186534	22464	W 157318	18336	W 192715	27606		23400	CIMENTS HYDRAULIQUES
67	IRON AND STEEL				16811		24261			FER ET ACIER
673	IRON,STEEL SHAPES ETC			W 7531	4271	W 11007	7056			BARRES,PROFIL FER,ACIER
674	IRN,STL UNIV,PLATE,SHEET			W 8171	7170	W 11583	12154			LARGES PLATS,TOLES
68	NON–FERROUS METALS				1326		2738			METAUX NON FERREUX
69	METAL MANUFACTURES NES				13581		18359			ART MANUFACT EN METAL NDA
697	BASE MTL HOUSEHOLD EQUIP			W 711	1934	W 1965	2442			ART MENAGE MET COMMUNS
7	MACHINES,TRANSPORT EQUIP		128014		102258		133185		111722	MACHINES MATERIEL TRANSPORT
744	MECHANICAL HANDLING EQU								44609	EQUIP MANUTENTION PIECES
745	NONELEC MACHY,TOOLS NES		49781	W 4911	38432	W 4830	45932			AUT MACH NON ELEC,PIECES
77	ELECTRIC MACHNRY NES ETC		26413		26654		40918		28436	MACH APP ELECT NDA
78	ROAD VEHICLES		50028		36797		46335			VEHICULES ROUTIERS
781	PASS MOTOR VEH EXC BUSES								38516	AUTO TRANSPORT PERSONNES
782	LORRIES,SPCL MTR VEH NES			W 4201	10218	W 3721	10497			VEHICULES SPECIAUX,MARCH
7831	BUSES			W 569	5975	W 358	5047			VOITURES TRANSPORT COMMUN
7849	OTHER MOTOR VEHCL PARTS			W 269	2530	W 347	3615			PIECES 722,781,782,783
7851	MOTORCYCLES ETC			W 628	5460	W 574	6005			MOTO VELO MOTEUR AUXIL
78539	PARTS,ACCES NES OF 785			W 1335	5969	W 1937	10933			PIECES DU 785
792	AIRCRAFT ETC	W 16	1438						68	APP NAVIGATION AERIENNE
8	MISC MANUFACTURED GOODS				18654		26355			ART MANUFACTURES DIVERS
812	*PLUMBG,HEATNG,LGHTNG EQ			W 383	1282	W 508	1757			APPAR SANITAIRES CHAUFFAGE
821	*FURNITURE,PARTS THEREOF				1373		3038			MEUBLES ET PIECES
84	CLOTHING AND ACCESSORIES				2109		2509			VETEMENTS
87	PRECISION INSTRUMNTS NES				3136		4958			INSTRUM,APPAR SCIENT NDA
89	MISC MANUFCTRD GOODS NES				7438		9983			ART MANUFACTURES DIVERS

5. Special Exports F.O.B. by Commodities according to the S.I.T.C. (Rev. 2) in thousand U.S. Dollars
Exportations Spéciales F.O.B. par Produits d'après la C.T.C.I. (Rév. 2) en milliers de Dollars E.U.

SITC CTCI	COMMODITY	1988		1989		1990		1991		PRODUIT
		WEIGHT POIDS	VALUE VALEUR	WEIGHT POIDS	VALUE VALEUR	WEIGHT POIDS	VALUE VALEUR	WEIGHT POIDS	VALUE VALEUR	
	ALL COMMODITIES		141781		94742		151092		105399	TOUS PRODUITS
0	FOOD AND LIVE ANIMALS		9765		9615		13784		13487	ALIMENTS,ANIMAUX VIVANTS
001	*LIVE ANIMALS FOR FOOD				5218		10006		10553	ANIMAUX VIVANTS
0011	BOVINE SPECIES,LIVE	W 5882	3857	W 5940	3574	W 11089	7115		7570	ESPECE BOVINE
0012	SHEEP AND GOATS,LIVE	W 349	483	W 440	601	W 1368	1636		1883	ESPECES OVINE ET CAPRINE
0014	LIVE POULTRY	W 1429	1369	W 1092	1039	W 1176	1241		1040	VOLAILLES VIVANTES
05	VEGETABLES AND FRUIT		2890		3315		3078		2352	LEGUMES ET FRUITS
054	VEG ETC FRSH,SMPLY PRSVD	W 7665	2295	W 3337	1095	W 5439	1914		1830	LEGUMES FRAIS,CONG,SECS
081	*FEEDING STUFF FOR ANIML				967		608		582	NOURRITURE POUR ANIMAUX
0813	OILCAKE AND OTH RESIDUES	W 22914	1088						568	TOURTEAUX
1	BEVERAGES AND TOBACCO		54		329		348		109	BOISSONS ET TABACS
2	CRUDE MATERLS,EXCL FUELS		74661		53457		97839		73313	MAT BRUTES NON COMESTIBLES
21	HIDES,SKINS,FURS UNDRSSD				6764		8638			CUIRS,PEAUX BRUTS
211	HIDES,SKINS,EXC FURS,RAW	W 1536	7453						5109	CUIRS ET PEAUX
2114	GOAT AND KID SKINS,RAW			W 1396	6764	W 1450	8638			PEAUX DE CAPRINS
22	OIL SEEDS,OLEAGINOUS FRT				1487		3082			GRAINES,FRUITS OLEAGINEUX
222	SEEDS FOR'SOFT'FIXED OIL					W 1264	776			GRAINES HUILES FIXES
2221	GROUNDNUTS,GREEN	W 3893	1413	W 1406	545	W 712	329		335	ARACHIDES NON GRILLEES
2225	SESAME SEEDS	W 2773	764	W 1237	592	W 552	447		762	GRAINES DE SESAME
223	SEEDS FOR OTH FIXED OILS	W 2676	243				2306			GRAINES AUTRES HUILES FIXES
2232	PALM NUTS AND KERNELS						2306			NOIX,AMANDES DE PALMISTE
26	TEXTILE FIBRES AND WASTE				44962		85761			FIBRES TEXTILES
263	COTTON	W 54550	64257	W 43062	44934	W 59239	85699			COTON
2631	RAW COTTON,EXCL LINTERS	W 54550	64257	W 43062	44934	W 59239	85699		66127	COTON EN MASSE
2714	NTRL POTASSIC SALTS,CRDE								557	SELS DE POTASSIUM
4	ANIMAL,VEGETABLE OIL,FAT		700		25		249		1657	HUILES,GRAISSES ANIM,VEG
6	BASIC MANUFACTURES		6239		5765		7525		15708	ART MANUFACTURES
61	LEATHER,DRESSED FUR,ETC				2038		2621			CUIRS,PELLETERIES
62	RUBBER MANUFACTURES NES		2160		1271		1614		1714	CAOUTCHOUC MANUFACTURE
625	RUBBER TYRES, TUBES ETC	W 434	2160							PNEUS CAOUTCHOUC VULCANISE
63	WOOD,CORK MANUFACTRS NES				16		18		8646	OUVRAGES LIEGE ET BOIS
69	METAL MANUFACTURES NES				623		889			ART MANUFACT EN METAL NDA
7	MACHINES,TRANSPORT EQUIP		8534		3296		1204		1008	MACHINES MATERIEL TRANSPORT
745	NONELEC MACHY,TOOLS NES			W 780	1687	W 68	516			AUT MACH NON ELEC,PIECES
77	ELECTRIC MACHNRY NES ETC				360		366			MACH APP ELECT NDA
78	ROAD VEHICLES				1249		318			VEHICULES ROUTIERS
8	MISC MANUFACTURED GOODS				485		586			ART MANUFACTURES DIVERS
9	GOODS NOT CLASSD BY KIND				21575		29382			ART TRANSACT NON CLASSES
961	*COIN NONGOLD,NONCURRENT				21575		29382			MONNAIES NON EMISES
971	*GOLD,NON MONETARY NES	K 4000	41598							OR NON MONETAIRE

1. HISTORICAL SERIES, 1966–1996 SPECIAL TRADE, IMPORTS C.I.F., EXPORTS F.O.B.
SERIES HISTORIQUES, 1966–1996 COMMERCE SPECIAL, IMPORTATIONS C.A.F., EXPORTATIONS F.O.B

YEAR ANNEE	VALUE IN MILLION BURUNDI FRANCS / VALEUR EN MILLION BURUNDI FRANCS — MERCHANDISE –MARCHANDISE		GOLD –OR		CONVERSION FACTORS U.S. CENTS PER BURUNDI FRANC / FACTEURS DE CONVERSION CENTS E.U. PAR BURUNDI FRANC		INDEX NUMBERS –INDICES — QUANTUM		UNIT VALUE / VALEUR UNITAIRE	
	IMPORTS	EXPORTS	IMPORTS	EXPORTS	IMPORTS	EXPORTS	IMPORTS	EXPORTS	IMPORTS	EXPORTS
1966	1698.00	1247.20			1.1429	1.1429				
1967	1693.50	1469.10			1.1429	1.1429				
1968	1993.90	1322.00			1.1429	1.1429				
1969	1880.10	1064.20			1.1429	1.1429				
1970	1956.10	2131.60			1.1429	1.1429				
1971	2617.80	1619.60			1.1429	1.1429				
1972	2736.40	2275.20			1.1429	1.1429				
1973	2495.10	2379.90			1.2613	1.2686				
1974	3395.60	2323.80			1.2698	1.2698				
1975	4855.60	2514.70			1.2698	1.2698				
1976	5027.10	5420.00			1.1524	1.1169				
1977	6678.00	8011.00			1.1111	1.1111				
1978	8841.70	6243.00			1.1111	1.1111				
1979	13721.00	9361.00			1.1111	1.1111				
1980	15109.00	5861.00			1.1111	1.1111				
1981	14509.00	6423.30			1.1111	1.1111				
1982	19280.00	7883.00			1.1111	1.1111				
1983	17074.90	7505.70			1.0737	1.0662				
1984	22233.50	11779.30			0.8352	0.8357				
1985	22433.00	13462.00			0.8284	0.8245				
1986	23195.01	17674.00			0.8724	0.8686				
1987	25465.01	11117.00			0.8094	0.8071				
1988	28885.01	18589.01			0.7132	0.7141				
1989	29910.00	12304.00			0.6294	0.6333				
1990	40179.01	12784.00			0.5860	0.5856				
1991	46154.00	16698.00			0.5516	0.5424				
1992	46106.00	15355.00			0.4801	0.4749				
1993	49702.00	15019.00			0.4129	0.4116				
1994	56468.00	30034.00			0.3958	0.4021				
1995	58200.00	25982.00			0.4026	0.4067				
1996	37332.00	11293.00			0.3488	0.3566				

2. IMPORTS BY BROAD ECONOMIC CATEGORY AND EXPORTS BY INDUSTRIAL ORIGIN. (PERCENTAGE OF TOTAL VALUE)
IMPORTATIONS PAR CATEGORIES ECONOMIQUES ET EXPORTATIONS PAR BRANCHE D'ACTIVITE.(EN POURCENTAGE DE LA VALEUR TOTALE)

IMPORTS – IMPORTATIONS

	1990	1991	1992	1993	1994	1995	1996
TOTAL IMPORTS–IMPORTATIONS TOTALES	100.						
1 FOOD BEV–ALIMENTATION BOISSONS	6.9						
11 PRIMARY–PRODUITS DE BASE	0.0						
111 FOR INDUSTRY–POUR L'INDUSTRIE	0.0						
112 FOR HOUSEHOLDS–POUR LES MENAGES	0.0						
12 PROCESSED–PRODUITS ELABORES	6.8						
121 FOR INDUSTRY–POUR L'INDUSTRIE	6.2						
122 FOR HOUSEHOLDS–POUR LES MENAGES	0.6						
2 IND SUPPLIES–APPROV INDUSTRIELS	14.4						
21 PRIMARY–PRODUITS DE BASE	0.9						
22 PROCESSED–PRODUITS ELABORES	13.5						
3 FUELS–COMBUSTIBLES	0.0						
31 PRIMARY–PRODUITS DE BASE	0.0						
32 PROCESSED–PRODUITS ELABORES							
321 MOTOR SPIRIT–ESSENCE							
322 OTHER–AUTRES							
4 MACHINERY–EQUIPEMENT	0.1						
41 CAPITAL EQUIPMENT–MACHINES	0.1						
42 PARTS–PIECES ACCESSOIRES							
5 TRANSPORT–TRANSPORT	7.4						
51 PASSENGER CARS–AUTOMOBILES							
52 OTHER–AUTRES	3.7						
521 INDUSTRIAL–INDUSTRIELS	3.7						
522 NON INDUSTRIAL–NON INDUSTRIEL							
53 PARTS–PIECES ACCESSOIRES	3.7						
6 CONSUM GOODS–BIENS CONSOMMATION	6.8						
61 DURABLE–DURABLES	0.4						
62 SEMI DURABLE–SEMI DURABLES	1.0						
63 NON DURABLE–NON DURABLES	5.3						
7 GOODS NES–BIENS NDA	3.6						

EXPORTS – EXPORTATIONS

	1990	1991	1992	1993	1994	1995	1996
TOTAL EXPORTS–EXPORTATIONS TOTALES	100.						
1 AGRICULTURE	85.4						
2 MINING QUARRY–INDUS EXTRACTIVES							
3 MANUFACTURING–IND MANUFACTUR	14.6						
31 FOOD BEV TOBACCO–ALIM BOISS TAB	4.7						
32 TEXTILES–INDUSTRIES TEXTILES	0.2						
33 WOOD & PRODUCTS–BOIS & PRODUITS							
34 PAPER & PRODUCTS–PAPIER & PRODT							
35 CHEMICALS–INDUSTRIES CHIMIQUES							
36 NON METAL MIN–MIN NON METAL	2.4						
37 BASIC METAL–IND METAL BASE							
38 METAL MANUF–MANUF METAL							
39 OTH MANUF IND–AUTRES MANUF	7.4						

3. TRADE BY PRINCIPAL COUNTRIES OF PURCHASE AND SALE (VALUE IN THOUSAND U.S. DOLLARS)
ECHANGES SELON LES PRINCIPAUX PAYS D'ACHAT ET DE VENTE (VALEUR EN MILLIERS DE DOLLARS EU)

COUNTRIES–PAYS	SPECIAL IMPORTS C.I.F. IMPORTATIONS SPECIALES C.A.F					COUNTRIES–PAYS	SPECIAL EXPORTS F.O.B. EXPORTATIONS SPECIALES F.O.B.				
	1989	1990	1991	1992	1993		1989	1990	1991	1992	1993
World	188132	235652	247087	229508	204525	Monde					
Africa	21979	25181	29414	38690	28013	Afrique					
Americas	2686	2719	4903	10289	4134	Amériques					
Northern America	2686	2719	4903	10289	4134	Amérique du Nord					
LAIA						ALAI					
CACM						MCAC					
Caribbean						Caraïbes					
Rest of America						Autre Amérique					
As.ex F.USSR	45159	61914	69695	42320	46921	Asie l'URSS exclus					
Eur.x F.USSR	94372	112231	104250	104281	95554	Europe l'URSS exclus					
EU	91067	108240	101539	102045	93157	UE					
EFTA	1768	2464	1874	1195	1657	AELE					
East Europe	1537	1290	726	1036	740	Europe de l'Est					
Other Europe						Autre de l'Europe					
Former USSR	335	148	88	100	140	Ancienne URSS					
Oceania	30	117	29	423	398	Océanie					
Belgium–Luxembourg	29123	34167	35781	34108	33809						
France,Monac	19097	23283	24145	25493	23676						
Germany/Allemagne	25534	30296	18695	17614	13865						
Japan/Japon	15271	17164	20876	18585	18754						
Iran (Islamic Rp. of)	18140	29479		7520	12578						
China/Chine	5767	8158	14562	8371	8176						
Italy/Italie	7458	8586	8773	8053	9246						
Un. Rep. of Tanzania	2232	2857	4024	20538	11752						
Kenya	5621	5886	6999	7520	6590						
Zambia/Zambie	4519	6697	7676	6648	5015						
Cyprus/Chypre			27123								
Netherlands/Pays–Bas	3075	2755	5728	6305	6319						
USA/Etats–Unis d'Amer	2301	2408	4346	9801	3638						
United Kingdom	3791	3839	4118	5289	3459						
Zimbabwe	4094	5947	4789	2151	2237						
United Arab Emirates	1792	1969	1553	3093	2068						
Korea, Republic of	1108	1755	2655	1828	1876						
Switz.Liecht	1768	2464	1874	1195	1657						
Dem. Rep. of the Congo	2013	1560	2058	1295	1476						
Denmark/Danemark	1225	1691	1845	1504	1575						
Malawi	2775	1229	2936	95	29						
India/Inde	1262	835	1687	1280	1698						
Hong Kong	1209	1840	1172	1116	1093						
Czechoslovakia	1274	482	726	891	663						
Austria/Autriche	166	2103	387	349	107						
Spain/Espagne	354	606	489	767	347						
Sweden/Suède	371	306	870	553	278						
Canada	385	311	557	488	496						
Djibouti	544	620	134	214	578						
Greece/Grèce	314	152	189	1066	303						
Rwanda	181	385	797	229	337						
Bangladesh		635	67	403	677						
Portugal	408	299	330	428	62						
Ireland/Irlande	150	158	189	518	112						
Former GDR	263	808									
Korea Dem People's Rp	609	78		124							
Australia/Australie	30	117	29	418	192						
Former USSR/Anc. URSS	335	148	88	100	51						
Fm Yugoslav		236	111	5							
Pitcairn					194						
Poland/Pologne				144							

(VALUE AS PERCENTAGE OF WORLD TOTAL)(VALEURS EN POURCENTAGE DU TOTAL MONDIAL)

	1984	1985	1986	1987	1988	1989	1990	1991	1992	1993
Africa	14.8	13.1	13.7	15.1	10.7	11.7	10.7	11.9	16.9	13.7
Americas	4.8	5.0	2.9	2.3	1.8	1.4	1.2	2.0	4.5	2.0
Northern America	4.8	5.0	2.9	2.1	1.5	1.4	1.2	2.0	4.5	2.0
LAIA			0.0	0.1	0.1					
CACM										
Caribbean										
Rest of America				0.1	0.3					
As.ex F.USSR	13.1	15.5	23.1	28.7	15.6	24.0	26.3	28.2	18.4	22.9
Eur.x F.USSR	44.7	48.4	56.5	49.8	68.5	50.2	47.6	42.2	45.4	46.7
EU	43.7	47.4	52.0	46.3	66.1	48.4	45.9	41.1	44.5	45.5
EFTA	0.8	0.9	2.5	1.4	0.7	0.9	1.0	0.8	0.5	0.8
East Europe	0.1	0.2	0.2	0.9	0.6	0.8	0.5	0.3	0.5	0.4
Other Europe	0.1	0.0	1.7	1.2	1.2					
Former USSR	12.8	12.8	0.3	0.7	0.3	0.2	0.1	0.0	0.0	0.1
Oceania	0.0	0.1	0.1	0.0	0.0	0.0	0.0	0.0	0.2	0.2
Belgium–Luxembourg	5.8	7.1	17.9	16.4	24.1	15.5	14.5	14.5	14.9	16.5
France,Monac	14.8	11.3	9.2	6.9	6.2	10.2	9.9	9.8	11.1	11.6
Germany/Allemagne	8.0	10.6	11.5	11.2	5.1	13.6	12.9	7.6	7.7	6.8
Japan/Japon	4.6	5.5	6.1	7.4	5.2	8.1	7.3	8.4	8.1	9.2
Iran (Islamic Rp. of)	7.6	7.3	12.3	15.0	6.7	9.6	12.5		3.3	6.1
China/Chine	2.7	1.2	1.8	2.9	1.9	3.1	3.5	5.9	3.6	4.0
Italy/Italie	3.6	5.0	4.3	3.1	2.1	4.0	3.6	3.6	3.5	4.5
Un. Rep. of Tanzania	2.6	1.4	1.0	0.9	0.5	1.2	1.2	1.6	8.9	5.7
Kenya	4.4	3.9	2.6	2.5	1.7	3.0	2.5	2.8	3.3	3.2
Zambia/Zambie	2.2	3.9	4.7	7.0	2.1	2.4	2.8	3.1	2.9	2.5

	1984	1985	1986	1987	1988	1989	1990	1991	1992	1993
Afrique	11.3		4.4	6.7	3.6					
Amériques	1.9		7.0	3.8	0.8					
Amérique du Nord	1.9		6.9	3.8	0.8					
ALAI			0.0	0.0	0.0					
MCAC										
Caraïbes										
Autre Amérique										
Asie l'URSS exclus	7.3		2.8	16.4	6.0					
Europe l'URSS exclus	63.6		84.6	70.9	69.1					
UE	63.3		84.6	70.6	68.8					
AELE	0.3		0.0	0.3	0.4					
Europe de l'Est										
Autre de l'Europe	0.0									
Ancienne URSS	0.0									
Océanie	0.0		0.0	0.0	0.1					

4. Special Imports C.I.F. by Commodities according to the S.I.T.C. (Rev. 2) in thousand U.S. Dollars
Importations Spéciales C.A.F. par Produits d'après la C.T.C.I. (Rév. 2) en milliers de Dollars E.U.

SITC CTCI	COMMODITY	1990		1991		1992		1993		PRODUIT
		WEIGHT POIDS	VALUE VALEUR	WEIGHT POIDS	VALUE VALEUR	WEIGHT POIDS	VALUE VALEUR	WEIGHT POIDS	VALUE VALEUR	
	ALL COMMODITIES		235652		247087		229508		204525	TOUS PRODUITS
0	FOOD AND LIVE ANIMALS		20396		22675		19706		20312	ALIMENTS,ANIMAUX VIVANTS
02	DAIRY PRODCTS,BIRDS'EGGS		2535		2599		3112		1983	PRODUITS LAITIERS,OEUFS
03	FISH AND PREPARATIONS		48		32		20		721	POISSONS ET PREPARATIONS
04	CEREALS AND PREPARATIONS		11642		14424		12520		13341	CEREALES ET PRODUITS
041	WHEAT ETC UNMILLED	W 198	93	W 3714	1244	W 2881	1011	W 3728	1255	FROMENT,EPEAUTRE
042	RICE	W 8	15	W 1058	280	W 1672	488	W 2434	747	RIZ
046	WHEAT ETC MEAL OR FLOUR	W 12952	5533	W 18786	6453	W 10305	3904			SEMOULE FARINE,FROMENT
04601	FLOUR OF WHEAT OR MESLIN	W 12952	5533	W 18741	6445	W 10233	3835	W 11331	3859	FARINE DE FROMENT
048	CEREAL ETC PREPARATIONS	W 9456	6002	W 10081	6447	W 8669	7116			PREPTNS A BASE CEREALES
0482	MALT INCLUDING FLOUR	W 9422	5875	W 9979	6290	W 8645	6962	W 10745	7365	MALT MEME TORREFIE
06	SUGAR AND PREPS,HONEY		3114		2798		334		881	SUCRES ET PRODUITS
061	SUGAR AND HONEY	W 5347	3114	W 2	2798	W 752	334			SUCRES ET MIEL
0612	REFINED SUGAR ETC							W 1590	767	SUCRES RAFFINES
09	MISC EDIBLE PRODUCTS		2772		2484		3366		2890	PREP ALIMENTAIRES DIVERSES
098	EDIBLE PRODCTS,PREPS NES	W 544	2667	W 462	2326	W 617	3282	W 308	2837	PREP ALIMENTAIRES NDA
1	BEVERAGES AND TOBACCO		1279		1123		1155		911	BOISSONS ET TABACS
11	BEVERAGES		1279		1108		1155		900	BOISSONS
112	ALCOHOLIC BEVERAGES	W 435	1279	W 366	1108	W 370	1155			BOISSONS ALCOOLIQUES
2	CRUDE MATERLS,EXCL FUELS		5308		8081		4915		5478	MAT BRUTES NON COMESTIBLES
26	TEXTILE FIBRES AND WASTE		3538		3694		3083		2623	FIBRES TEXTILES
269	WASTE OF TEXTILE FABRICS	W 3228	3208	W 2945	3089	W 3007	2744	W 2767	2115	FRIPERIE DRILLES,CHIFFONS
27	CRUDE FERTLZR,MINRLS NES		1174		3594		1081		1242	ENGRAIS MINERAUX BRUTS
278	OTHER CRUDE MINERALS	W 7911	1174	W 17746	3594		1081			AUTRES MINERAUX BRUTS
2783	COMMON SALT,ETC	W 7843	1116	W 17363	3211		837	W 8344	1147	SEL
29	CRUDE ANIMAL,VEG MAT NES		596		794		752		1613	MATIERES BRUTES ANIM,VEGET
292	CRUDE VEG MATERIALS NES	W 40	596	W 46	794	W 37	752			MAT BRUTES VEGETALES NDA
2929	OTH CRUDE VEG MATERIALS	W 40	596	W 46	794	W 37	752			MATIERES VEGETALES NDA
29291	VEGETABLE SAPS,EXTRACTS	W 40	596	W 46	794	W 37	752	W 72	1613	SUCS,EXTRAITS VEGETAUX
3	MINERAL FUELS ETC		32695		31183		27992		25387	COMBUSTIBLES MINERAUX LUB
33	PETROLEUM AND PRODUCTS		32578		31044		27888		25346	PETROLE ET DERIVES
334	PETROLEUM PRODUCTS,REFIN	W 66054	32034	W 56474	29603	W 62187	27248			PRODUITS RAFFINES
3341	GASOLINE,OTH LIGHT OILS	W 25326	13859	W 21475	12511	W 22893	10570	W 19548	8630	ESSENCES POUR MOTEURS
3342	KEROSENE,OTH MEDIUM OILS	W 3399	1782	W 4046	2328	W 8333	4026	W 9817	3999	PETR LAMPANTS,AUT HUIL
3343	GAS OILS	W 28646	12521	W 20729	9893	W 22420	8966	W 21218	7993	GAS OILS
3344	FUEL OILS,NES	W 7246	2294	W 8558	2913	W 6905	2189	W 5468	1577	FUEL OILS
3345	LUBS,PETROLEUM OILS NES	W 1437	1578	W 1666	1957	W 1636	1496	W 3138	2339	HUILES LUBRIFIANTES
335	RESIDUAL PETRLM PROD NES	W 1617	544	W 2854	1442	W 1675	640	W 2588	808	PRODUITS RESIDUELS NDA
3354	PETROLM BITUMEN,COKE ETC	W 1617	544	W 2854	1442	W 1675	640	W 2588	808	BITUME,COKE DE PETROLE
4	ANIMAL,VEGETABLE OIL,FAT		555		1159		896		1032	HUILES,GRAISSES ANIM,VEG
42	FIXED VEGETABLE OIL,FAT		331		967		812		739	HUILES VEGETALES FIXES
5	CHEMCLS,RELATED PROD NES		29184		33890		32475		28807	PRODUITS CHIMIQUES
51	ORGANIC CHEMICALS		1149		1518		1200		1523	PROD CHIMIQ ORGANIQUES
52	INORGANIC CHEMICALS		1877		3216		3043		2478	PROD CHIM INORGANIQUES
53	DYES,TANNING,COLOUR PROD		3359		2642		1743		1612	PROD TEINTURE,COLORANTS
531	SYNT DYE,NAT INDGO,LAKES	W 345	3359	W 261	2642	W 248	1743	W 210	1612	MAT COLOR ORGAN,LAQUES
541	*MEDICINAL,PHARM PRODUCT	K 607000	8972	K 566000	10289	K 555000	11554	K 465000	8523	PROD MEDICINAUX PHARMACEUT
55	PERFUME,CLEANING ETC PRD		1490		1904		1205		1704	PROD POUR PARFUM,TOILETTE
553	PERFUMERY,COSMETICS,ETC	W 105	487	W 71	606	W 113	632	W 125	816	PRODUITS DE PARFUMERIE
554	SOAP,CLEANSING ETC PREPS	W 667	1003	W 833	1298	W 272	573	W 594	888	SAVONS,PRODUITS DETERSIFS
562	*FERTILIZERS,MANUFACTURE	W 5029	2122	W 7888	3228	W 16660	4865	W 12959	4562	ENGRAIS MANUFACTURES
58	PLASTIC MATERIALS ETC		5506		4774		4721		5401	MAT PLAST ARTIFICIELLES
59	CHEMICAL MATERIALS NES		4709		6318		4143		3005	MAT PROD CHIMIQUES NDA
591	PESTICIDES,DISINFECTANTS	W 430	4037	W 440	5809	W 347	3581			DESINF,INSECT,FONG,HERB
5911	INSECTICIDES,FOR RETAIL	W 402	3949	W 406	5713	W 306	3451	W 193	2635	INSECTICIDES VENTE DET
6	BASIC MANUFACTURES		53641		52433		48948		42859	ART MANUFACTURES
62	RUBBER MANUFACTURES NES		3801		6641		5383		7077	CAOUTCHOUC MANUFACTURE
625	RUBBER TYRES, TUBES ETC	W 521	2581	W 1095	5334	W 1030	4059			PNEUS CAOUTCHOUC VULCANISE
62591	INNER TUBES	W 50	207	W 155	612	W 128	488	W 1354	5215	CHAMBRES A AIR
628	RUBBER ARTICLES NES	W 284	1219	W 336	1307	W 313	1325	W 334	1862	OUVRAGES CAOUTCHOUC NDA
64	PAPER,PAPERBOARD AND MFR		6084		6062		5777		5556	PAPIERS,CARTONS & OUVRAGES
65	TEXTILE YARN,FABRICS,ETC		2750		2373		2136		1156	FILS,TISSUS,ARTICLES TEXTILE
658	TEXTILE ARTICLES NES	W 1496	1528	W 303	761	W 894	1175			ART FACONNES MAT TEXTILES
6581	BAGS,SACKS OF TEXTILES	W 1318	916	W 174	230	W 740	543			SACS EMBALLAGE TEXTILES
66	NONMETAL MINERAL MFS NES		10902		13512		12898		9445	ART MIN NON METALLIQUES
661	LIME,CEMENT,BLDG PRODS	W 65719	8755	W 80046	11093	W 70586	10896			CHAUX,CIMENTS MAT CONSTR
6612	CEMENT	W 65633	8229	W 79788	10481	W 70260	10226	W 52275	6820	CIMENTS HYDRAULIQUES
663	MINERAL MANUFCTURES NES	W 414	753	W 612	1010	W 501	911			ART MIN MANUF NDA
6639	CERAMIC ARTICLES NES	W 414	753	W 612	1010	W 501	911	W 834	1283	ARTICLES EN CERAMIQUE NDA
665	GLASSWARE	W 729	1394	W 638	1408	W 489	1091			OUVRAGES EN VERRE
68	NON–FERROUS METALS		1490		744		1116		1218	METAUX NON FERREUX
684	ALUMINIUM	W 466	1490	W 232	744	W 425	1116	W 537	1218	ALUMINIUM
69	METAL MANUFACTURES NES		27648		22187		20991		17641	ART MANUFACT EN METAL NDA
695	TOOLS	W 1130	2081	W 1880	2979		2485		1940	OUTILS A MAIN
699	BASE METAL MFRS NES	W 460	1392	W 543	1647	W 569	1743			ART MANUFACTURES MET NDA
6991	LOCKSMITHS WARES,ETC	W 218	784	W 305	965	W 292	996			ARTICLES DE SERRURERIE
69911	LOCKS,KEYS AND PARTS	W 218	784	W 305	965	W 292	996	W 196	667	SERRURES,VERROUS,CADENAS
7	MACHINES,TRANSPORT EQUIP		70790		70144		63206		51673	MACHINES MATERIEL TRANSPORT
71	POWER GENERATING EQUIPMT		1226		1100		1220		786	MACHINES GENERATRICES
716	ROTATING ELECTRIC PLANT	W 204	1226	W 89	1100	W 54	1220	W 59	786	APP ELECTR ROTATIFS,PIECES
74	GENRL INDUSTRL MACHY NES		22886		29926		23147		20484	MACH APP INDUSTRIE
76	TELECOMM,SOUND EQUIPMENT		2257		1656		2082		2217	EQUIPMENT DE TELECOM
77	ELECTRIC MACHNRY NES ETC		19455		10695		12355		9747	MACH APP ELECT NDA
778	ELECTRICAL MACHINERY NES	W 170	497	W 443	1104	W 392	,026			AUTRES MACH ELECT NDA
7781	BATTERIES,ACCUMULATORS	W 170	497	W 443	1104	W 392	1026	W 342	780	PILES ET ACCUMULATEURS
78	ROAD VEHICLES		24712		26388		23999		18265	VEHICULES ROUTIERS
781	PASS MOTOR VEH EXC BUSES	W 1487	8098	W 1600	9687	W 1358	8202	W 991	5350	AUTO TRANSPORT PERSONNES
782	LORRIES,SPCL MTR VEH NES	W 1232	8742	W 1762	9557	W 1368	7530			VEHICULES SPECIAUX,MARCH
7821	LORRIES,TRUCKS	W 1232	8742	W 1762	9557	W 1368	7530	W 836	5984	VEHICULES TRANSP MARCHAND
784	MOTOR VEH PRTS,ACCES NES	W 483	5300	W 246	4326	W 346	5543			PIECES 722,781,782,783
7849	OTHER MOTOR VEHCL PARTS	W 483	5300	W 246	4326	W 346	5543	W 199	4194	PIECES 722,781,782,783
785	CYCLES,ETC MOTRZD OR NOT	W 239	1394	W 281	1060	W 410	1454	W 319	1165	MOTOCYCLES SCOOTERS
8	MISC MANUFACTURED GOODS		12812		12105		16798		8188	ART MANUFACTURES DIVERS
821	*FURNITURE,PARTS THEREOF	W 145	719	W 157	1072	W 125	1245	W 88	935	MEUBLES ET PIECES
84	CLOTHING AND ACCESSORIES		743		789		647		503	VETEMENTS
851	*FOOTWEAR	W 228	1816	W 190	897	W 260	1091	W 201	538	CHAUSSURES
88	PHOTO EQU,OPTICL GDS ETC		4821		6725		10154		4182	APP,FOURN PHOTO,OP,MONTR
882	PHOTO,CINEMA SUPPLIES	W 41	685	W 33	687	W 38	767	W 34	471	PRODUITS PHOTO,CINEMA
89	MISC MANUFCTRD GOODS NES		4356		2307		3182		1825	ART MANUFACTURES DIVERS
892	PRINTED MATTER	W 214	2768	W 102	1280	W 138	1758	W 86	1063	IMPRIMES
898	MUSICAL INSTRUMENTS,PTS	W 17	628	W 10	268	W 15	767	W 3	4	INSTRUMENTS DE MUSIQUE

 Burundi

4. Special Imports C.I.F. by Commodities according to the S.I.T.C. (Rev. 2) in thousand U.S. Dollars
Importations Spéciales C.A.F. par Produits d'après la C.T.C.I. (Rév. 2) en milliers de Dollars E.U.

SITC CTCI	COMMODITY	1990		1991		1992		1993		PRODUIT
		WEIGHT POIDS	VALUE VALEUR	WEIGHT POIDS	VALUE VALEUR	WEIGHT POIDS	VALUE VALEUR	WEIGHT POIDS	VALUE VALEUR	
9	GOODS NOT CLASSD BY KIND		8522		14291		13417		19877	ART TRANSACT NON CLASSES
931	*SPECIAL TRANSACTIONS	W 9426	8522	W 9325	14291		13417		19877	TRANS.SPECIALES

5. Special Exports F.O.B. by Commodities according to the S.I.T.C. (Rev. 2) in thousand U.S. Dollars
Exportations Spéciales F.O.B. par Produits d'après la C.T.C.I. (Rév. 2) en milliers de Dollars E.U.

SITC CTCI	COMMODITY	1990		1991		1992		1993		PRODUIT
		WEIGHT POIDS	VALUE VALEUR	WEIGHT POIDS	VALUE VALEUR	WEIGHT POIDS	VALUE VALEUR	WEIGHT POIDS	VALUE VALEUR	
	ALL COMMODITIES		74955		91536		74701		68703	TOUS PRODUITS
0	FOOD AND LIVE ANIMALS		63832		82477		59065		52300	ALIMENTS,ANIMAUX VIVANTS
03	FISH AND PREPARATIONS								240	POISSONS ET PREPARATIONS
0341	FISH FRSH,CHLLD,EX FILLT							W 1	240	POISSON FRAIS,REFRIGERE
07	COFFEE,TEA,COCOA,SPICES		63832		82477		59065		51936	CAFE,THE,CACAO,EPICES
071	COFFEE AND SUBSTITUTES	W 33501	56022		74149	W 39991	49665	W 27666	43262	CAFE ET SUCCEDANES
0711	COFFEE GREEN,ROASTED,SUB	W 33501	56022		74149	W 39991	49665	W 27666	43262	CAFE TORREFIE OU DECAFEINE
074	TEA AND MATE	W 3920	7810		8328	W 5696	9400	W 5216	8674	THE ET MATE
0741	TEA	W 3920	7810			W 5696	9400	W 5216	8674	THE
1	BEVERAGES AND TOBACCO		95		60		752		2097	BOISSONS ET TABACS
11	BEVERAGES		95		60		190		394	BOISSONS
112	ALCOHOLIC BEVERAGES	W 226	60		60	W 497	190	W 1205	394	BOISSONS ALCOOLIQUES
1123	BEER,ALE,STOUT,PORTER	W 226	60		60	W 497	190	W 1205	394	BIERES
12	TOBACCO AND MANUFACTURES						562		1703	TABACS BRUTS FABRIQUES
122	TOBACCO,MANUFACTURED					W 86	562			TABACS FABRIQUES
1222	CIGARETTES					W 86	562	W 244	1703	CIGARETTES
2	CRUDE MATERLS,EXCL FUELS		3563		2384		1676		4089	MAT BRUTES NON COMESTIBLES
21	HIDES,SKINS,FURS UNDRSSD		3399		2384		1676		844	CUIRS,PEAUX BRUTS
211	HIDES,SKINS,EXC FURS,RAW	W 1036	3399		2384	W 950	1676	W 563	844	CUIRS ET PEAUX
26	TEXTILE FIBRES AND WASTE		164						3245	FIBRES TEXTILES
263	COTTON	W 100	164					W 2445	3245	COTON
2631	RAW COTTON,EXCL LINTERS	W 100	164					W 2445	3245	COTON EN MASSE
5	CHEMCLS,RELATED PROD NES								984	PRODUITS CHIMIQUES
55	PERFUME,CLEANING ETC PRD								984	PROD POUR PARFUM,TOILETTE
5541	SOAPS							W 856	984	SAVONS,PROD TENSIO–ACTIFS
6	BASIC MANUFACTURES		1914		2464		4413		4402	ART MANUFACTURES
65	TEXTILE YARN,FABRICS,ETC		115		1340		1679		2442	FILS,TISSUS,ARTICLES TEXTILE
652	COTTON FABRICS,WOVEN	W 12	115		1340	W 198	1679	W 451	2442	TISSUS DE COTON
66	NONMETAL MINERAL MFS NES		1781		1051		2417		1909	ART MIN NON METALLIQUES
665	GLASSWARE	W 1788	1745		1002	W 3761	2390		1881	OUVRAGES EN VERRE
6651	BOTTLES ETC OF GLASS	W 1788	1745		1002	W 3761	2390	W 3370	1729	RECIPIENTS EN VERRE
69	METAL MANUFACTURES NES		19		73		318		51	ART MANUFACT EN METAL NDA
9	GOODS NOT CLASSD BY KIND		5550		4150		8795		4826	ART TRANSACT NON CLASSES
931	*SPECIAL TRANSACTIONS	W 3914	5550		4150		8795		4826	TRANS.SPECIALES

1. HISTORICAL SERIES, 1961–1996 SPECIAL TRADE, IMPORTS C.I.F., EXPORTS F.O.B.
SERIES HISTORIQUES, 1961–1996 COMMERCE SPECIAL, IMPORTATIONS C.A.F., EXPORTATIONS F.O.B

YEAR ANNEE	VALUE IN MILLION C.F.A. FRANCS VALEUR EN MILLION C.F.A. FRANCS MERCHANDISE –MARCHANDISE		GOLD –OR		CONVERSION FACTORS U.S. CENTS PER C.F.A. FRANC FACTEURS DE CONVERSION CENTS E.U. PAR C.F.A. FRANC		INDEX NUMBERS –INDICES QUANTUM		UNIT VALUE VALEUR UNITAIRE	
	IMPORTS	EXPORTS	IMPORTS	EXPORTS	IMPORTS	EXPORTS	IMPORTS	EXPORTS	IMPORTS	EXPORTS
1961	23716.30	24197.70		4.90	0.4051	0.4051				
1962	25141.40	25478.20		38.10	0.4051	0.4051				
1963	31562.90	33277.50			0.4051	0.4051				
1964	32835.70	34516.20		6.30	0.4051	0.4051				
1965	37396.00	34362.50		7.10	0.4051	0.4051				
1966	36114.00	35882.60		6.80	0.4051	0.4051				
1967	46419.00	39100.00	0.70	6.10	0.4051	0.4051				
1968	46220.00	46722.60	1.30	2.20	0.4051	0.4051				
1969	53000.00	58573.50	0.30		0.3866	0.3855				
1970	67241.40	64359.20			0.3601	0.3601				
1971	69351.60	57282.80	1.70		0.3601	0.3601				
1972	76382.50	55699.20	1.90		0.3912	0.3912				
1973	74487.00	78321.40			0.4494	0.4502				
1974	104825.20	114815.00			0.4168	0.4162				
1975	128104.00	96130.00			0.4676	0.4657				
1976	145963.00	122028.00			0.4175	0.4186				
1977	192401.00	172851.00			0.4073	0.4073				
1978	237247.00	181697.00			0.4455	0.4419				
1979	271160.00	238700.00			0.4686	0.4691				
1980	337607.00	290615.00			0.4745	0.4761				
1981	386089.00	303307.00			0.3700	0.3700				
1982	394574.80	326891.30			0.3069	0.3060				
1983	463888.60	358880.80			0.2624	0.2616				
1984	484431.10	381334.00			0.2284	0.2313				
1985	508730.40	321730.80			0.2263	0.2243				
1986	590449.90	271630.00			0.2886	0.2880				
1987	517280.00	241920.00			0.3332	0.3331				
1988	378729.90	275120.10			0.3357	0.3357				
1989	402240.00	405989.80			0.3135	0.3135				
1990	381149.90	545110.00			0.3673	0.3673				
1991	330960.10	517390.00			0.3545	0.3545				
1992	307790.00	487130.10			0.3778	0.3778				
1993	311960.00	533250.00			0.3545	0.3565				
1994	601499.90	825200.10			0.1812	0.1813				
1995	619399.90	1018200.00			0.2010	0.2011				
1996	616142.40	899455.70			0.1955	0.1954				

2. IMPORTS BY BROAD ECONOMIC CATEGORY AND EXPORTS BY INDUSTRIAL ORIGIN. (PERCENTAGE OF TOTAL VALUE)
IMPORTATIONS PAR CATEGORIES ECONOMIQUES ET EXPORTATIONS PAR BRANCHE D'ACTIVITE.(EN POURCENTAGE DE LA VALEUR TOTALE)

IMPORTS – IMPORTATIONS

	1990	1991	1992	1993	1994	1995	1996
TOTAL IMPORTS–IMPORTATIONS TOTALES	100.					100.	100.
1 FOOD BEV–ALIMENTATION BOISSONS	16.5					16.2	12.7
11 PRIMARY–PRODUITS DE BASE	3.7					3.8	2.8
111 FOR INDUSTRY–POUR L'INDUSTRIE	0.4					1.4	0.8
112 FOR HOUSEHOLDS–POUR LES MENAGES	3.4					2.4	2.0
12 PROCESSED–PRODUITS ELABORES	12.8					12.4	9.9
121 FOR INDUSTRY–POUR L'INDUSTRIE	6.3					4.7	3.4
122 FOR HOUSEHOLDS–POUR LES MENAGES	6.5					7.8	6.5
2 IND SUPPLIES–APPROV INDUSTRIELS	34.8					41.5	34.2
21 PRIMARY–PRODUITS DE BASE	1.5					3.5	3.5
22 PROCESSED–PRODUITS ELABORES	33.4					38.0	30.8
3 FUELS–COMBUSTIBLES	0.7					1.5	14.3
31 PRIMARY–PRODUITS DE BASE	0.1					0.0	12.5
32 PROCESSED–PRODUITS ELABORES	0.6					1.5	1.8
321 MOTOR SPIRIT–ESSENCE	0.6					0.1	0.0
322 OTHER–AUTRES	0.0					1.5	1.8
4 MACHINERY–EQUIPEMENT	19.5					17.4	17.5
41 CAPITAL EQUIPMENT–MACHINES	17.2					15.1	15.3
42 PARTS–PIECES ACCESSOIRES	2.3					2.3	2.2
5 TRANSPORT–TRANSPORT	10.3					13.8	12.1
51 PASSENGER CARS–AUTOMOBILES	3.1					3.5	3.8
52 OTHER–AUTRES	3.7					6.5	4.8
521 INDUSTRIAL–INDUSTRIELS	3.6					6.3	4.6
522 NON INDUSTRIAL–NON INDUSTRIEL	0.0					0.1	0.3
53 PARTS–PIECES ACCESSOIRES	3.5					3.8	3.6
6 CONSUM GOODS–BIENS CONSOMMATION	18.1					9.4	9.1
61 DURABLE–DURABLES	1.3					0.8	1.0
62 SEMI DURABLE–SEMI DURABLES	3.5					2.6	2.6
63 NON DURABLE–NON DURABLES	13.3					6.0	5.5
7 GOODS NES–BIENS NDA	0.0					0.1	0.0

EXPORTS – EXPORTATIONS

	1990	1991	1992	1993	1994	1995	1996
TOTAL EXPORTS–EXPORTATIONS TOTALES	100.					100.	100.
1 AGRICULTURE	28.8					43.3	40.0
2 MINING QUARRY–INDUS EXTRACTIVES	49.7					29.0	35.8
3 MANUFACTURING–IND MANUFACTUR	21.5					27.7	24.3
31 FOOD BEV TOBACCO–ALIM BOISS TAB	3.2					4.0	4.6
32 TEXTILES–INDUSTRIES TEXTILES	1.0					0.8	0.7
33 WOOD & PRODUCTS–BOIS & PRODUITS	4.0					9.1	6.3
34 PAPER & PRODUCTS–PAPIER & PRODT	0.1					0.3	0.3
35 CHEMICALS–INDUSTRIES CHIMIQUES	1.9					1.6	1.9
36 NON METAL MIN–MIN NON METAL	1.6					1.5	2.2
37 BASIC METAL–IND METAL BASE	6.8					8.6	6.4
38 METAL MANUF–MANUF METAL	2.8					1.9	1.7
39 OTH MANUF IND–AUTRES MANUF	0.0					0.0	0.0

3. TRADE BY PRINCIPAL COUNTRIES OF ORIGIN AND DESTINATION (VALUE IN THOUSAND U.S. DOLLARS)
ECHANGES SELON LES PRINCIPAUX PAYS D'ORIGINE ET DE DESTINATION (VALEUR EN MILLIERS DE DOLLARS EU)

COUNTRIES–PAYS	SPECIAL IMPORTS C.I.F. IMPORTATIONS SPECIALES C.A.F 1992	1993	1994	1995	1996
World		1106000	1090000	1078541	1204343
Africa		115000	132000	122962	253445
Americas				125744	135736
Northern America				106304	112676
LAIA				17069	15039
CACM				480	2457
Caribbean				1881	5562
Rest of America				10	1
As.ex F.USSR		13000	15000	138879	139321
Eur.x F.USSR		1000	2000	655383	665789
EU				633182	643482
EFTA				10378	6958
East Europe		1000	2000	11762	15334
Other Europe				6	10
Former USSR				5987	5771
Oceania				325	1323
France,Monac				337134	325085
USA/Etats–Unis d'Amer				83473	102291
Germany/Allemagne				78409	87705
Nigeria/Nigéria		10000	11000	1818	116572
Guinea/Guinée		32000	32000	40709	30004
Senegal/Sénégal		42000	54000	11919	13054
Japan/Japon				58897	60030
Belgium–Luxembourg				58985	57967
Italy/Italie				38717	44291
Netherlands/Pays–Bas				37138	33050
United Kingdom				33292	35500
Mauritania/Mauritanie		17000	21000	16941	
Tunisia/Tunisie		9000	8000	13181	10387
Spain/Espagne				16482	21430
Canada				22831	10386
Cote d'Ivoire				14111	14926
Pakistan			6000	13482	8806
Brazil/Brésil				15215	11835
China/Chine				11829	14945
India/Inde				9064	14825
So. Africa Customs Un				11501	11175
Finland/Finlande				12713	9440
Romania/Roumanie				7428	12145
Korea, Republic of				8383	9880
Malaysia/Malaisie		8000	3000	3136	2013
Indonesia/Indonésie		4000	5000	3183	3941
Morocco/Maroc		3000	3000	5155	4954
Ireland/Irlande				8435	6693
Switz.Liecht				8015	6312
Russian Federation				5541	5708
Viet Nam				4583	4815
Thailand/Thaïlande				5168	3673
Sweden/Suède				5341	3428
Mauritius/Maurice				0	7736
Dominican Republic				1866	5550
Turkey/Turquie				3987	3191
Bangladesh		1000	1000	3421	1590
Austria/Autriche				3948	2600
Gabon		1000	1000	2175	1812
Singapore/Singapour				4235	736
Hong Kong				2348	2163
Poland/Pologne				2577	1806
Denmark/Danemark				1287	2547
Egypt/Egypte		1000	2000	316	399
Israel/Israël				1290	2120
Albania/Albanie		1000	2000	35	2
Norway,SVD,JM				2307	641
Costa Rica				480	2457
Togo				7	2478
Congo				1051	1342

COUNTRIES–PAYS	SPECIAL EXPORTS F.O.B. EXPORTATIONS SPECIALES F.O.B. 1992	1993	1994	1995	1996
Monde		1901000	1496000	1538719	1757869
Afrique		303000	394000	144253	179768
Amériques				51068	49830
Amérique du Nord				36333	41753
ALAI				14571	7513
MCAC					
Caraïbes				164	564
Autre Amérique					
Asie l'URSS exclus		2000	8000	151342	164455
Europe l'URSS exclus				1191866	1363607
UE				1185730	1360714
AELE				235	43
Europe de l'Est				5881	2804
Autre de l'Europe				19	45
Ancienne URSS					125
Océanie				191	84
France,Monac				407294	311772
Italy/Italie				237089	358154
Spain/Espagne				187173	371906
Netherlands/Pays–Bas				206769	180257
Senegal/Sénégal		131000	196000	7566	5532
Nigeria/Nigéria		62000	75000	8437	17724
Gabon		39000	41000	24470	32175
Morocco/Maroc		37000	37000	5016	4150
Chad/Tchad		26000	33000	5720	9729
Belgium–Luxembourg				34462	38916
USA/Etats–Unis d'Amer				29010	40874
Germany/Allemagne				37177	31238
China/Chine				32759	30816
Portugal				35310	27698
Korea, Republic of				43599	17923
United Kingdom				26372	30493
Thailand/Thaïlande				16114	22999
Congo				17589	20994
Central African Rep.				12799	16310
Japan/Japon				12102	14025
Hong Kong				8379	11065
Singapore/Singapour				3420	13976
Cote d'Ivoire				9122	8062
Tunisia/Tunisie		3000	5000	1613	7501
Brazil/Brésil				9518	5183
Greece/Grèce				8676	5357
Malaysia/Malaisie		2000	2000	1000	8696
Turkey/Turquie			3000	5094	4917
Philippines				2572	9280
Algeria/Algérie		4000	4000	163	3185
So. Africa Customs Un				3744	6136
Ireland/Irlande				5013	4717
Poland/Pologne				5464	2804
Canada				7323	879
Indonesia/Indonésie			1000	1113	4875
Mexico/Mexique				4755	2115
Dem. Rep. of the Congo				3180	2951
Guinea/Guinée		1000	1000	1159	2837
Mauritius/Maurice				4914	131
Benin/Bénin				2043	2061
Saudi Arabia			2000	957	963
Angola				1795	1344
Togo				1379	1623
India/Inde				2591	199
Sao Tome and Principe				2005	623
Libyan Arab Jamahiriya				1500	1120
Reunion/Réunion				2050	
Gambia/Gambie			2000		
Bangladesh				141	1666
Mali				542	1142

(VALUE AS PERCENTAGE OF WORLD TOTAL)(VALEURS EN POURCENTAGE DU TOTAL MONDIAL)

	1987	1988	1989	1990	1991	1992	1993	1994	1995	1996
Africa	5.8		7.7	7.0			10.4	12.1	11.4	21.0
Americas	6.6		11.5	9.4					11.7	11.3
Northern America	3.8		8.9	5.4					9.9	9.4
LAIA	1.3		2.2	2.4					1.6	1.2
CACM	0.0		0.0	0.0					0.0	0.2
Caribbean	0.0		0.0	0.0					0.2	0.5
Rest of America	1.5		0.4	1.6					0.0	0.0
As.ex F.USSR	15.5		12.8	12.4			1.2	1.4	12.9	11.6
Eur.x F.USSR	69.7		65.0	70.3			0.1	0.2	60.8	55.3
EU	66.0		62.3	68.0					58.7	53.4
EFTA	2.7		1.8	1.5					1.0	0.6
East Europe	1.0		0.8	0.7			0.1	0.2	1.1	1.3
Other Europe	0.1		0.1	0.1					0.0	0.0
Former USSR	0.4		0.2	0.9					0.6	0.5
Oceania	0.1		0.1	0.0					0.0	0.1
France,Monac	37.5		36.5	37.7					31.3	27.0
USA/Etats–Unis d'Amer	3.5		5.1	4.4					7.7	8.5
Germany/Allemagne	9.2		5.6	9.0					7.3	7.3
Nigeria/Nigéria	0.2		0.4	0.3			0.9	1.0	0.2	9.7
Guinea/Guinée	1.6		2.7	2.5			2.9	2.9	3.8	2.5
Senegal/Sénégal	1.0		1.2	1.5			3.8	5.0	1.1	1.1
Japan/Japon	8.2		5.7	4.7					5.5	5.0
Belgium–Luxembourg	4.1		3.1	4.7					5.5	4.8
Italy/Italie	4.3		3.0	4.4					3.6	3.7
Netherlands/Pays–Bas	2.3		9.1	3.2					3.4	2.7

	1987	1988	1989	1990	1991	1992	1993	1994	1995	1996
Afrique	17.6		15.8	8.7			15.9	26.3	9.4	10.2
Amériques	9.1		11.4	8.2					3.3	2.8
Amérique du Nord	7.4		10.3	7.6					2.4	2.4
ALAI	1.8		1.2	0.6					0.9	0.4
MCAC										
Caraïbes	0.0		0.0	0.0					0.0	0.0
Autre Amérique										
Asie l'URSS exclus	3.2		4.4	4.9			0.1	0.5	9.8	9.4
Europe l'URSS exclus	68.5		67.8	78.0					77.5	77.6
UE	68.4		66.4	76.6					77.1	77.4
AELE	0.0		0.0	1.3					0.0	0.0
Europe de l'Est	0.0		1.4	0.0					0.4	0.2
Autre de l'Europe	0.0		0.0	0.0					0.0	0.0
Ancienne URSS	1.6		0.5	0.3						0.0
Océanie	0.0		0.0	0.0					0.0	0.0
France,Monac	17.5		23.5	40.6					26.5	17.7
Italy/Italie	13.8		1.4	7.0					15.4	20.4
Spain/Espagne	2.7		5.0	6.9					12.2	21.2
Netherlands/Pays–Bas	23.1		6.4	15.1					13.4	10.3
Senegal/Sénégal	0.3		1.0	0.2			6.9	13.1	0.5	0.3
Nigeria/Nigéria	3.1		2.4	1.7			3.3	5.0	0.5	1.0
Gabon	5.7		2.3	1.5			2.1	2.7	1.6	1.8
Morocco/Maroc	0.0		0.2	0.1			1.9	2.5	0.3	0.2
Chad/Tchad	2.2		0.5	0.6			1.4	2.2	0.4	0.6
Belgium–Luxembourg	3.2		19.3	1.5					2.2	2.2

4. Special Imports C.I.F. by Commodities according to the S.I.T.C. (Rev. 2) in thousand U.S. Dollars
Importations Spéciales C.A.F. par Produits d'après la C.T.C.I. (Rév. 2) en milliers de Dollars E.U.

SITC CTCI	COMMODITY	1993 WEIGHT POIDS	1993 VALUE VALEUR	1994 WEIGHT POIDS	1994 VALUE VALEUR	1995 WEIGHT POIDS	1995 VALUE VALEUR	1996 WEIGHT POIDS	1996 VALUE VALEUR	PRODUIT
	ALL COMMODITIES						1078541		1204343	TOUS PRODUITS
0	FOOD AND LIVE ANIMALS						174039		153054	ALIMENTS,ANIMAUX VIVANTS
02	DAIRY PRODCTS,BIRDS'EGGS						11576		12635	PRODUITS LAITIERS,OEUFS
022	MILK AND CREAM					W 5702	9781	W 6665	10873	LAIT ET CREME
0224	MILK,CREAM PRESERVED ETC					W 4815	9037	W 5767	10172	LAIT,CREME CONS,CONC
02243	MILK DRY,OVER 1.5% FAT					W 1700	4084	W 2071	4861	LAIT POUDRE SUP 1.5%
02249	MILK(EX DRY) PRSVD,SWEET					W 2875	4417	W 3382	4590	LAIT CONS,CONC SUCRE
03	FISH AND PREPARATIONS						27225		22034	POISSONS ET PREPARATIONS
034	FISH,FRESH,CHILLED,FROZN					W 46005	24240	W 41104	20731	POISSON FRAIS, REFRIG,CONG
0342	FISH FROZEN,EXCL FILLETS					W 45040	23718	W 41102	20725	POISSONS CONGELES
04	CEREALS AND PREPARATIONS						90477		77636	CEREALES ET PRODUITS
041	WHEAT ETC UNMILLED					W 65969	12987	W 34996	9482	FROMENT,EPEAUTRE
0411	DURUM WHEAT UNMILLED					W 18769	5025	W 10500	2917	FROMENT DUR NON MOULU
0412	OTHER WHEAT ETC UNMILLED					W 47200	7962	W 24496	6565	AUTRE FROMENT NON MOULU
042	RICE					W 124946	26916	W 81559	24338	RIZ
0422	RICE SEMI-MILLED,MILLED					W 124943	26915	W 81558	24337	RIZ POLI,GLACE INCL BRISURES
04221	RICE MILLED UNBROKEN					W 124943	26915	W 81557	24335	RIZ POLI,GLACE EXCL BRISURES
046	WHEAT ETC MEAL OR FLOUR					W 26985	7936	W 12500	4301	SEMOULE FARINE,FROMENT
04601	FLOUR OF WHEAT OR MESLIN					W 24921	6969	W 8335	2432	FARINE DE FROMENT
047	OTHER CEREAL MEALS,FLOUR					W 10297	4523	W 8836	4057	AUTRES SEMOULES,FARINES
04702	MEAL OR GROATS NON-WHEAT					W 10268	4517	W 8750	4045	GRUAUX,SEMOULES DE CEREALES
048	CEREAL ETC PREPARATIONS					W 58874	36664	W 46990	35346	PREPTNS A BASE CEREALES
0482	MALT INCLUDING FLOUR					W 56985	31936	W 44454	28757	MALT MEME TORREFIE
0488	OTH CEREAL PREPS,MALT EX					W 868	3462	W 1144	4842	EXTRAITS DE MALT
05	VEGETABLES AND FRUIT						6124		5967	LEGUMES ET FRUITS
054	VEG ETC FRSH,SMPLY PRSVD					W 2555	3827	W 3338	3985	LEGUMES FRAIS,CONG,SECS
06	SUGAR AND PREPS,HONEY						11697		12710	SUCRES ET PRODUITS
061	SUGAR AND HONEY					W 20549	11174	W 23407	11907	SUCRES ET MIEL
0612	REFINED SUGAR ETC					W 18636	9991	W 21881	10962	SUCRES RAFFINES
081	*FEEDING STUFF FOR ANIML					W 8773	4475	W 7800	4847	NOURRITURE POUR ANIMAUX
09	MISC EDIBLE PRODUCTS						19880		14074	PREP ALIMENTAIRES DIVERSES
098	EDIBLE PRODCTS,PREPS NES					W 6904	17054	W 5855	11524	PREP ALIMENTAIRES NDA
09806	YEASTS,BAKING POWDERS					W 1025	3328	W 932	2589	LEVURES
09809	MISC FOOD PREPRTIONS NES					W 5334	10840	W 4145	7643	PREP ALIMENTAIRES NDA
1	BEVERAGES AND TOBACCO						11579		11449	BOISSONS ET TABACS
11	BEVERAGES						5208		4119	BOISSONS
112	ALCOHOLIC BEVERAGES					W 4849	5063	W 3825	3979	BOISSONS ALCOOLIQUES
1121	WINE OF FRESH GRAPES ETC					W 4150	3423	W 3319	2761	VINS DE RAISINS FRAIS
11212	WINE OF FRESH GRAPES					W 4137	3386	W 3309	2747	VINS DE MOUTS DE RAISINS
12	TOBACCO AND MANUFACTURES						6371		7329	TABACS BRUTS FABRIQUES
121	TOBACCO UNMNFCTRD,REFUSE					W 325	1525	W 1204	5513	TABACS BRUTS,DECHETS
1212	TOBACCO STRIPPED OR PART					W 221	1038	W 1036	4910	TABACS PART ECOTES
122	TOBACCO,MANUFACTURED					W 512	4846	W 923	1816	TABACS FABRIQUES
1223	OTH MANUFACTURED TOBACCO					W 394	3758	W 134	1009	TABACS FUMER,CHIQUER,PRISER
2	CRUDE MATERLS,EXCL FUELS						77839		67822	MAT BRUTES NON COMESTIBLES
26	TEXTILE FIBRES AND WASTE						22548		25437	FIBRES TEXTILES
269	WASTE OF TEXTILE FABRICS					W 15917	20835	W 20180	23906	FRIPERIE DRILLES,CHIFFONS
26901	BULK TEXT WSTE,OLD CLTHG					W 15830	20735	W 20059	23785	ART ET ACCESS D'HABILLEMENT
27	CRUDE FERTLZR,MINRLS NES						8827		7493	ENGRAIS MINERAUX BRUTS
278	OTHER CRUDE MINERALS					W 60709	6674	W 52226	5471	AUTRES MINERAUX BRUTS
2783	COMMON SALT,ETC					W 47767	3324	W 38756	2498	SEL
28	METALLIFEROUS ORES,SCRAP						41573		30807	MINERAIS METAL,DECHETS
287	BASE METAL ORES,CONC NES					W 197952	41529	W 130563	30728	MINERAIS METAUX COMMUNS
2873	ALUMINIUM ORES,ALUMINA					W 196411	40747	W 128667	29825	MINERAIS D'ALUMINIUM
28732	ALUMINA(ALUMINIUM OXIDE)					W 196411	40747	W 128667	29825	ALUMINE (OXYDE ALUMINIUM)
29	CRUDE ANIMAL,VEG MAT NES						4190		3470	MATIERES BRUTES ANIM,VEGET
292	CRUDE VEG MATERIALS NES					W 153	4189	W 179	3469	MAT BRUTES VEGETALES NDA
2929	OTH CRUDE VEG MATERIALS					W 101	3624	W 100	2652	MATIERES VEGETALES NDA
29291	VEGETABLE SAPS,EXTRACTS					W 98	3615	W 99	2642	SUCS,EXTRAITS VEGETAUX
3	MINERAL FUELS ETC						27400		189502	COMBUSTIBLES MINERAUX LUB
33	PETROLEUM AND PRODUCTS						27260		188249	PETROLE ET DERIVES
333	CRUDE PETROLEUM							W 895366	149298	HUILES BRUTES DE PETROLE
334	PETROLEUM PRODUCTS,REFIN					W 29543	16570	W 38542	21924	PRODUITS RAFFINES
3345	LUBS,PETROLEUM OILS NES					W 23717	13834	W 20741	17331	HUILES LUBRIFIANTES
33451	LUBS(HIGH PETR CONT) ETC					W 22968	12785	W 20615	16821	HUILES LUBRIF,H LOURDES
335	RESIDUAL PETRLM PROD NES					W 50159	10689	W 66612	17028	PRODUITS RESIDUELS NDA
3353	MIN TAR PITCH,PITCH COKE					W 16233	3868	W 9439	2798	BRAI,COKE DE BRAI
3354	PETROLM BITUMEN,COKE ETC					W 33245	6182	W 56146	13359	BITUME,COKE DE PETROLE
33542	PETROLEUM COKE					W 22400	4301	W 51631	12278	COKE DE PETROLE
5	CHEMCLS,RELATED PROD NES						175080		173937	PRODUITS CHIMIQUES
51	ORGANIC CHEMICALS						8964		8344	PROD CHIMIQ ORGANIQUES
52	INORGANIC CHEMICALS						17498		17821	PROD CHIM INORGANIQUES
522	INORG ELEMNTS,OXIDES,ETC					W 19327	8360	W 14134	6465	ELEMENTS INORGANIQUES
5225	INORGANIC BASES ETC NES					W 17818	6224	W 12030	3633	AUTRES BASES OXYDES METAL
52252	SODIUM HYDROXIDE, SOLID					W 6835	3484	W 1701	931	HYDROXYDE DE SODIUM
523	OTHR INORG CHEMICALS ETC					W 13156	9056	W 19563	11200	AUT PRODUITS CHIMIQUES INORG
5231	METAL CMPD OF INORG ACID					W 7975	6428	W 11187	7423	SELS METALLIQUES
52311	FLUORIDES ETC					W 4187	3585	W 2400	2126	FLUORURES
53	DYES,TANNING,COLOUR PROD						7081		8687	PROD TEINTURE,COLORANTS
533	PIGMENTS,PAINTS,ETC					W 1980	4691	W 2849	5755	PIGMENTS,PEINTURES,VERNIS
541	*MEDICINAL,PHARM PRODUCT					K 1838803	45353	K 1846422	45494	PROD MEDICINAUX PHARMACEUT
5417	MEDICAMENTS					K 1674770	41951	K 1648274	42190	MEDICAMENTS
54171	— CONTAINNG ANTIBIOTICS					K 278370	8751	K 226916	6518	MED CONTN ANTIBIOTIQUES
54179	— CONTNG OTH SUBSTANCES					K 1274415	28710	K 1313427	31843	MED CONT AUT SUBSTANCES
55	PERFUME,CLEANING ETC PRD						13839		14654	PROD POUR PARFUM,TOILETTE
551	ESSENTL OILS,PERFUME,ETC					W 1136	8937	W 1070	9416	HUILES ESSENTIELLES
5514	MIXED PERFUME SUBSTANCES					W 1103	8883	W 1046	9327	MELANGES SUBSTAN ODORIFER
554	SOAP,CLEANSING ETC PREPS					W 2056	3801	W 2788	3906	SAVONS,PRODUITS DETERSIFS
562	*FERTILIZERS,MANUFACTURE					W 74990	19693	W 79258	22799	ENGRAIS MANUFACTURES
5621	CHEM NITROGENOUS FERTLZR					W 17480	4026	W 22084	6702	ENGRAIS AZOTES
56216	UREA					W 13771	3275	W 18687	5970	UREE
5623	CHEM POTASSIC FERTILIZER					W 20014	4792	W 9830	2073	ENGRAIS POTASSIQUES
5629	FERTILIZERS NES					W 35542	10342	W 45848	13647	ENGRAIS NDA
56291	NIT-PHOS-POT FERTLZR NES					W 33780	9905	W 39759	12014	ENGRAIS CONT N P K
58	PLASTIC MATERIALS ETC						24392		24985	MAT PLAST ARTIFICIELLES
582	PROD OF CONDENSATION ETC					W 3468	5552	W 3679	5961	PROD CONDENS,POLYCOND
583	POLYMERIZATION ETC PRODS					W 9297	17760	W 12031	17706	PROD POLYMERISATION
5831	POLYETHYLENE					W 3736	5666	W 4778	6026	POLYETHYLENE
58311	— IN PRIMARY FORMS					W 3579	4886	W 4516	4714	POLYETHYLENE PRIMAIRES
5834	POLYVINYL CHLORIDE					W 3576	6155	W 4912	6691	CHLORURE DE POLYVINYLE
58341	— IN PRIMARY FORMS					W 3405	5724	W 4703	6190	SOUS FORMES PRIMAIRES

4. Special Imports C.I.F. by Commodities according to the S.I.T.C. (Rev. 2) in thousand U.S. Dollars
Importations Spéciales C.A.F. par Produits d'après la C.T.C.I. (Rév. 2) en milliers de Dollars E.U.

SITC CTCI	COMMODITY	1993 WEIGHT POIDS	1993 VALUE VALEUR	1994 WEIGHT POIDS	1994 VALUE VALEUR	1995 WEIGHT POIDS	1995 VALUE VALEUR	1996 WEIGHT POIDS	1996 VALUE VALEUR	PRODUIT
59	CHEMICAL MATERIALS NES						37576		30539	MAT PROD CHIMIQUES NDA
591	PESTICIDES,DISINFECTANTS					W 4343	23148	W 3514	14817	DESINF,INSECT,FONG,HERB
5911	INSECTICIDES,FOR RETAIL					W 932	5481	W 949	4560	INSECTICIDES VENTE DET
5912	FUNGICIDES,FOR RETAIL					W 1747	10000	W 1471	5857	FONGICIDES VENTE AU DET
5913	HERBICIDES,FOR RETAIL					W 793	4127	W 618	3126	HERBICIDES VENTE AU DET
5914	DISINFECTANTS,ETC,FR RET					W 870	3540	W 477	1274	DESINFECTANTS VENTE DET
598	MISCEL CHEM PRODUCTS NES					W 4318	11199	W 4526	12761	PROD DIV INDUST CHIM NDA
5982	ANTI-KNOCK PREPARTNS ETC					W 987	3273	W 985	4310	PREPARAT ANTIDETONANTES
5989	CHEM PRODUCTS,PREPS NES					W 2782	7208	W 3338	8104	PROD PREP CHIMIQUES NDA
59899	OTH CHEM PRODS,PREPS,NES					W 1624	5011	W 1788	5290	AUT PRODUITS CHIMIQUES NDA
6	BASIC MANUFACTURES						229003		216271	ART MANUFACTURES
62	RUBBER MANUFACTURES NES						23142		26488	CAOUTCHOUC MANUFACTURE
625	RUBBER TYRES, TUBES ETC					W 6727	17539	W 7278	21029	PNEUS CAOUTCHOUC VULCANISE
6252	TYRES,NEW,BUS OR LORRY					W 2440	10795	W 3224	14026	PNEUS POUR AUTOBUS,CAMIONS
6259	OTH TYRES,TYRE CASES,ETC					W 4023	5640	W 3655	5372	AUTRES PNEUS RECHAPES FLAPS
62599	TYRES NES,TYRE CASES,ETC					W 3660	4730	W 3182	4179	PNEUS,FLAPS
628	RUBBER ARTICLES NES					W 238	3319	W 227	3408	OUVRAGES CAOUTCHOUC NDA
64	PAPER,PAPERBOARD AND MFR						51353		45861	PAPIERS,CARTONS & OUVRAGES
641	PAPER AND PAPERBOARD					W 44373	44232	W 40711	37771	PAPIERS ET CARTONS
6411	NEWSPRINT					W 3682	3528	W 4004	3596	PAPIER JOURNAL
6412	PRINTG,WRITING PAPER NES					W 3521	5032	W 3676	4909	PAPIERS POUR L'IMPRESSION
64122	— COATED,IMPREGNATD ETC					W 3028	4086	W 2885	3737	PAPIERS IMPRESSION COUCHES
6413	KRAFT PAPER,PAPERBOARD					W 20463	16761	W 15983	11941	PAPIER ET CARTON KRAFT
64131	KRAFT LINER IN BULK					W 15610	12531	W 11131	7272	PAP KRAFT POUR COUVERTURES
64139	KRAFT PAPER PAPERBD,NES					W 4716	4168	W 4773	4601	PAPIER,CARTON KRAFT NDA
6415	PAPER,PAPERBRD,BULK,NES					W 14523	14857	W 14524	12643	PAPIERS,CARTONS ROULEAUX
64151	SEMI-CHEM FLUTING PAPER					W 7166	4947	W 7551	4488	PAPIER FLUTING
64159	OTHER PAPER ETC,BULK,NES					W 7295	9750	W 6941	8039	AUT PAPIER ROULEAUX FEUILLES
642	PAPER,ETC,PRECUT,ARTS OF					W 3462	7122	W 3378	8091	PAP,CARTONS DECOUPES
65	TEXTILE YARN,FABRICS,ETC						17628		15639	FILS,TISSUS,ARTICLES TEXTILE
652	COTTON FABRICS,WOVEN						3417	W 673	2279	TISSUS DE COTON
658	TEXTILE ARTICLES NES					W 7006	5801	W 3247	4110	ART FACONNES MAT TEXTILES
6581	BAGS,SACKS OF TEXTILES					W 6689	4902	W 2882	2620	SACS EMBALLAGE TEXTILES
66	NONMETAL MINERAL MFS NES						36623		34082	ART MIN NON METALLIQUES
661	LIME,CEMENT,BLDG PRODS					W 364778	23157	W 319109	20758	CHAUX,CIMENTS MAT CONSTR
6612	CEMENT					W 360824	21670	W 315118	19102	CIMENTS HYDRAULIQUES
662	CLAY,REFRACTORY BLDG PRD					W 10786	5162	W 10664	4901	MAT CONST REFRACTAIRES
6624	BRICKS ETC NONREFRACTORY					W 8782	3470	W 8336	2841	BRIQUES ETC CERAM NON REFR
665	GLASSWARE					W 2726	3458	W 2418	3496	OUVRAGES EN VERRE
67	IRON AND STEEL						40918		41749	FER ET ACIER
672	IRON,STEEL PRIMARY FORMS					W 10728	4206	W 7157	2656	LINGOTS FER,ACIER
6725	IRN,STL BLOOMS,SLABS,ETC					W 9506	3582	W 6545	2275	BLOOMS,BILLETTES FER ACIER
67251	IRN,SMPLE STL BLOOMS,ETC					W 9253	3468	W 6527	2201	BLOOMS ETC NON ACIER FIN
673	IRON,STEEL SHAPES ETC					W 22742	9633	W 15365	6957	BARRES,PROFIL FER,ACIER
6732	IRON,STEEL BARS ETC					W 16441	5929	W 6736	2944	BARRES FER,ACIER
67326	IRN,OTH STL BARS HOTROLD					W 9237	3787	W 5553	2400	BARRES PLEINES FER,ACIER
6733	IRON,STEEL PROFILES ETC					W 5774	3447	W 6019	3214	PROFILES,PALPLAN FER,ACIER
674	IRN,STL UNIV,PLATE,SHEET					W 11784	9330	W 11807	7895	LARGES PLATS,TOLES
676	RAILWY RAILS ETC IRN,STL					W 1312	3435	W 3752	3790	RAILS,ELEMENTS VOIES FERREE
677	IRN,STL WIRE(EXCL W ROD)					W 6783	3451	W 1905	1986	FILS EN FER,ACIER
678	IRON,STL TUBES,PIPES,ETC					W 4629	10000	W 12095	17305	TUBES,TUYAUX EN FONTE,FER
6782	IRON,STL SEAMLESS TUBES					W 2640	6148	W 8425	12239	TUBES,TUYAUX SANS SOUDURE
68	NON-FERROUS METALS						10440		7692	METAUX NON FERREUX
684	ALUMINIUM					W 771	8920	W 625	6888	ALUMINIUM
6842	ALUMINIUM,ALLOYS WORKED					W 756	8868	W 620	6871	ALUMINIUM,ALLIAGES OUVRE
68423	ALUMINIUM FOIL					W 374	7596	W 331	5963	FEUILLES,BANDES MINCES AL
69	METAL MANUFACTURES NES						46797		42840	ART MANUFACT EN METAL NDA
691	STRUCTURES AND PARTS NES					W 1439	3850	W 1875	5957	CONSTRUCT FER,ACIER,ALU
6911	STRUCTURES,PARTS IRN,STL					W 1324	2544	W 1831	5739	CONSTRUCT FER,ACIER,FONTE
694	STL,COPPR NAILS,NUTS,ETC					W 1446	7707	W 970	2769	CLOUS,VIS,ECROUS
69402	IRN,STL NUTS,BOLTS,ETC					W 770	7127	W 478	2339	BOULONS,VIS,ECROUS FER,AC
695	TOOLS					W 1078	5567	W 759	5877	OUTILS A MAIN
6953	OTHER HAND TOOLS					W 450	3402	W 409	3151	AUTRES OUTILS A MAIN
699	BASE METAL MFRS NES					W 6627	20166	W 6526	18960	ART MANUFACTURES MET NDA
6996	BASE MTL MISC ARTICLES					W 2864	8840	W 2259	6875	ART DIVERS METAUX COMMUNS
69963	BASE METAL STOPPERS,ETC					W 2352	7361	W 1833	5480	BOUCHONS METALLIQUES
6998	MFRS NES OF CPR,NIKL,ETC					W 1625	4341	W 1669	4402	OUVRAGES EN CU,NI,AL,PB,ZN
69985	ZINC MANUFACTURES NES					W 1473	3787	W 1605	3861	OUVRAGES EN ZINC
7	MACHINES,TRANSPORT EQUIP						328500		331071	MACHINES MATERIEL TRANSPORT
71	POWER GENERATING EQUIPMT						14555		12407	MACHINES GENERATRICES
713	INTRNL COMBUS PSTN ENGIN					W 1061	6230	W 1167	6058	MOTEURS EXPL COMB INT, PIECE
7139	PISTON ENGINE PARTS NES					W 172	4427	W 181	4049	PIECES POUR 713.2,3,8
716	ROTATING ELECTRIC PLANT					W 310	5355	W 316	3637	APP ELECTR ROTATIFS,PIECES
72	MACHS FOR SPCL INDUSTRYS						55508		59622	MAC SPECIALES POUR INDUST
722	TRACTORS NON-ROAD					W 649	3976	W 1001	5384	TRACTEURS
7224	WHEELED TRACTORS NES					W 473	3627	W 808	5081	TRACTEURS A ROUES
723	CIVIL ENGNEERG EQUIP ETC					W 4777	30050	W 4120	31792	APPAREILS DE GENIE CIVIL
7234	CONST,MINING MACHNRY NES					W 4074	23207	W 2730	14200	MACH POUR LA CONST, MINES
72341	SELF-PROPELLD DOZERS,ETC					W 2042	10911	W 1461	8705	BULLDOZERS
72342	SLFPRP SHOVELS,EXCAVATRS					W 1995	12079	W 1092	4879	PELLES MECANIQUES
7239	CONSTR ETC MACHY PTS NES					W 364	4322	W 1179	17163	PIECES 723.41–723.46
728	OTH MACHY FOR SPCL INDUS					W 1546	11644	W 1575	11488	AUT MACH IND PARTICULIERES
7281	MACH-TOOLS FR SPCL INDUS					W 900	4809	W 833	4516	MACH–OUTILS SPEC IND PART
72812	MACH-TOOLS TO WORK WOOD					W 788	3927	W 628	3038	MACH–OUT POUR TRAVAIL BOIS
7284	MACHY FOR SPCL INDUS NES					W 515	6095	W 379	4785	MACH SPEC IND PARTICUL.
74	GENRL INDUSTRL MACHY NES						56807		67357	MACH APP INDUSTRIE
741	HEATING,COOLING EQUIPMNT					W 650	5862	W 1009	8898	MACH CHAUFFAGE,PIECES
7416	HEATING,COOLING EQU NES					W 217	1845	W 488	3903	APP CHANGEMENT TEMP
742	PUMPS FOR LIQUIDS ETC					W 292	6345	W 302	5451	POMPES MOTO–POMPES
7428	OTHER PUMPS FOR LIQUIDS					W 190	4005	W 186	3432	AUTRES POMPES POUR LIQ
743	PUMPS NES,CENTRFUGES ETC					W 623	8442	W 1130	14600	POMPES COMPRES,VENT ETC
7431	PUMPS FOR GASES ETC					W 302	2049	W 645	7043	POMPES AIR A VIDE,COMPRES
7436	GAS,LIQUID FILTERS ETC					W 189	3890	W 281	2972	APP POUR FILT DES LIQUIDES
7439	PTS NES OF APP OF 7435,6					W 83	1959	W 165	3678	PIECES 743.5 ET 743.6
744	MECHANICAL HANDLING EQU					W 2337	16830	W 2870	15328	EQUIP MANUTENTION PIECES
7441	FORK LIFT TRCKS,ETC,PTS					W 755	3723	W 622	3632	CHARIOTS POUR USINES ETC
74411	FORK LIFT TRUCKS ETC					W 749	3675	W 617	3598	CHARIOTS POUR LES GARES
7442	LIFTING,LOADING MACH NES					W 674	4160	W 605	4871	APP LEVAGE,MANUTENTION
7449	PTS NES OF MACHY OF 7442					W 908	8947	W 1643	6825	PIECES DU 744.2
745	NONELEC MACHY,TOOLS NES					W 378	5198	W 926	7411	AUT MACH NON ELEC,PIECES
7452	OTH NONELEC MCHS,PTS NES					W 316	4135	W 876	6174	AUT MACH NON ELEC,PIECES

4. Special Imports C.I.F. by Commodities according to the S.I.T.C. (Rev. 2) in thousand U.S. Dollars
Importations Spéciales C.A.F. par Produits d'après la C.T.C.I. (Rév. 2) en milliers de Dollars E.U.

SITC CTCI	COMMODITY	1993		1994		1995		1996		PRODUIT
		WEIGHT POIDS	VALUE VALEUR	WEIGHT POIDS	VALUE VALEUR	WEIGHT POIDS	VALUE VALEUR	WEIGHT POIDS	VALUE VALEUR	
749	NONELEC MACH PTS,ACC NES					W 685	14130	W 738	15669	PIECES MACH NON ELEC NDA
7492	COCKS,VALVES ETC NES					W 327	4777	W 346	5824	ART ROB,SIM POUR TUYAUX
7493	SHAFT,CRANK,PULLEY ETC					W 152	4176	W 169	4535	ARBRES TRANS,VILEBREQUINS
75	OFFICE MACHNES,ADP EQUIP						11578		10167	MACH BUREAU TRAIT AUTOM
752	AUTOMTIC DATA PROC EQUIP					W 128	7322	W 142	6239	MACH TRAIT INFORMATION
76	TELECOMM,SOUND EQUIPMENT						9548		16527	EQUIPMENT DE TELECOM
764	TELECOM EQPT,PTS,ACC NES					W 198	7821	W 215	13187	EQUIP TELECOM,PIECES
7643	TV,RADIO TRANSMITTRS ETC					W 13	1592	W 21	4453	APP EMET TELE RADIO
7649	PTS NES OF EQUIPMT OF 76					W 115	2982	W 106	4453	PIECES DE LA DIV 76
77	ELECTRIC MACHNRY NES ETC						57172		38778	MACH APP ELECT NDA
771	ELECTRIC POWER MACHY NES					W 574	6819	W 463	4810	MACH PROD,TRANS ELECTR
7711	TRANSFORMERS,ELECTRICAL					W 408	4355	W 374	3531	TRANSFO ELECTRIQUES
77111	LIQUID DIELEC TRANSFRMRS					W 343	3666	W 281	2801	TRANSFO DIELEC LIQUIDE
772	SWITCHGEAR ETC,PARTS NES					W 729	14271	W 583	13771	APP COUPURE,SECT ETC
7721	SWITCHGEAR ETC					W 715	13823	W 578	13491	APP COUPURE,SECTIONMNT
773	ELECTR DISTRIBUTNG EQUIP					W 3240	20826	W 1189	5593	EQUIPMT DISTRIBUTION ELECT
7731	INSULATED WIRE,CABLE ETC					W 3041	19904	W 1056	4593	FILS,CABLES ISOLES ELECT
778	ELECTRICAL MACHINERY NES					W 3179	12369	W 2374	9782	AUTRES MACH ELECT NDA
7781	BATTERIES,ACCUMULATORS					W 1142	3536	W 752	2893	PILES ET ACCUMULATEURS
7788	OTH ELEC MACHY,EQUIP NES					W 1585	5709	W 1234	3751	AUT MACH APP ELEC NDA
77887	ELECTRICAL CARBONS					W 1511	3641	W 1184	2711	PIECES CHARBON,GRAPHITE
78	ROAD VEHICLES						107955		109601	VEHICULES ROUTIERS
781	PASS MOTOR VEH EXC BUSES					W 7237	37377	W 10492	45220	AUTO TRANSPORT PERSONNES
782	LORRIES,SPCL MTR VEH NES					W 4298	24028	W 5020	18260	VEHICULES SPECIAUX,MARCH
7821	LORRIES,TRUCKS					W 3474	16978	W 4646	17042	VEHICULES TRANSP MARCHAND
7822	SPECIAL MOTOR VEHCLS NES					W 824	7049	W 374	1218	VEHICULES USAGES SPECIAUX
783	ROAD MOTOR VEHICLES NES					W 3762	27904	W 4469	26643	VEHICULES ROUTIERS NDA
7831	BUSES					W 1304	7960	W 2091	9575	VOITURES TRANSPORT COMMUN
7832	TRACTORS FOR TR–TRAILERS					W 2458	19944	W 2378	17068	TRACTEURS ROUTIERS
784	MOTOR VEH PRTS,ACCES NES					W 1302	10430	W 1247	9299	PIECES 722,781,782,783
7849	OTHER MOTOR VEHCL PARTS					W 1282	10232	W 1205	9073	PIECES 722,781,782,783
785	CYCLES,ETC MOTRZD OR NOT					W 476	1728	W 990	4319	MOTOCYCLES SCOOTERS
786	TRAILERS,NONMOTR VEH,NES					W 2340	6489	W 2161	5860	REMORQUES,CADRES,CONTAIN
7868	OTH NONMOTR VEHICLES ETC					W 1271	5005	W 996	3402	AUT VEHIC NON AUTO,PIECES
78689	PTS NES OF TRAILERS ETC					W 882	4177	W 795	3143	PIECES 786.11,12,786.81
79	OTHR TRANSPORT EQUIPMENT						12572		14614	AUTRE MATERIEL TRANSPORT
792	AIRCRAFT ETC					W 136	9055	W 11	1109	APP NAVIGATION AERIENNE
7923	AIRCRFT NES2000–15000KG					W 125	7557			AERODYNES 2000 A 15000 KG
793	SHIPS AND BOATS ETC					W 254	1715	W 2414	11689	NAVIRES BATEAUX,ETC
7938	TUGS,SPECIAL VESSELS ETC					W 226	1540	W 1378	9227	REMORQUEURS,BATEAUX SPEC
79382	SPECL PURPOSE VESSLS ETC							W 1170	7616	BAT–PHARES,–POMPES,DRAGUES
8	MISC MANUFACTURED GOODS						52787		60111	ART MANUFACTURES DIVERS
812	*PLUMBG,HEATNG,LGHTNG EQ					W 1312	3553	W 1182	3748	APPAR SANITAIRES CHAUFFAGE
87	PRECISION INSTRUMNTS NES						11113		12172	INSTRUM,APPAR SCIENT NDA
874	MEASURNG,CONTROLNG INSTR					W 279	6348	W 355	7968	INSTRUMENTS DE MESURE
89	MISC MANUFCTRD GOODS NES						28539		32014	ART MANUFACTURES DIVERS
892	PRINTED MATTER					W 1244	10302	W 1565	13779	IMPRIMES
8921	PRINTED BOOKS,GLOBES,ETC					W 590	3698	W 936	8685	LIVRES,BROCHURES,CARTES
89211	PRINTED BOOKS,PAMPHLETS					W 589	3655	W 929	8666	LIVRES,BROCHURES
8928	PRINTED MATTER NES					W 309	3411	W 231	1915	IMPRIMES NDA
893	ARTICLES OF PLASTIC NES						10714	W 3670	11036	OUVRAGES EN MAT DIVIS 58
8931	PLSTC PACKG CONTNRS,LIDS					W 1467	5059	W 1750	5448	ART TRANSP EMBALLAGE ETC
8939	MISC PLASTIC ARTICLES					W 1630	5476	W 1855	5429	ART DIVERS EN MAT DIV 58
89399	OTHR PLASTC ARTICLES NES					W 1481	5061	W 1483	4862	AUT OUV MAT DIV 58

5. Special Exports F.O.B. by Commodities according to the S.I.T.C. (Rev. 2) in thousand U.S. Dollars
Exportations Spéciales F.O.B. par Produits d'après la C.T.C.I. (Rév. 2) en milliers de Dollars E.U.

SITC CTCI	COMMODITY	1993 WEIGHT POIDS	1993 VALUE VALEUR	1994 WEIGHT POIDS	1994 VALUE VALEUR	1995 WEIGHT POIDS	1995 VALUE VALEUR	1996 WEIGHT POIDS	1996 VALUE VALEUR	PRODUIT
	ALL COMMODITIES						1538719		1757869	TOUS PRODUITS
0	FOOD AND LIVE ANIMALS						400080		393478	ALIMENTS,ANIMAUX VIVANTS
05	VEGETABLES AND FRUIT						80323		66488	LEGUMES ET FRUITS
057	FRUIT,NUTS,FRESH,DRIED					W 188422	77324	W 163265	63525	FRUITS FRAIS OU SECS
0573	BANANA,PLANTAIN,FRSH,DRY					W 187211	76945	W 160192	62836	BANANES FRAICHES,SECHEES
07	COFFEE,TEA,COCOA,SPICES						303828		310207	CAFE,THE,CACAO,EPICES
071	COFFEE AND SUBSTITUTES					W 63167	142487	W 74121	127043	CAFE ET SUCCEDANES
0711	COFFEE GREEN,ROASTED,SUB					W 63167	142487	W 74121	127043	CAFE TORREFIE OU DECAFEINE
07111	COFFEE GREEN,HUSKS,SKINS					W 62713	141204	W 74039	126835	CAFE NON TORREFIE
072	COCOA					W 119992	160652	W 141493	182099	CACAO
0721	COCOA BEANS,RAW,ROASTED					W 105636	133258	W 122217	151271	CACAO EN FEVES
0723	COCOA BUTTER AND PASTE					W 14356	27394	W 19277	30827	BEURRE ET PATE DE CACAO
07231	COCOA PASTE					W 10653	14642	W 15768	20490	CACAO EN MASSE
07232	COCOA BUTTER					W 3703	12752	W 3509	10338	BEURRE DE CACAO
09	MISC EDIBLE PRODUCTS						7971		8387	PREP ALIMENTAIRES DIVERSES
098	EDIBLE PRODCTS,PREPS NES					W 2660	7969	W 3078	8382	PREP ALIMENTAIRES NDA
09805	SOUPS AND BROTHS					W 1858	5854	W 1728	5490	SOUPES,POTAGES,BOUILLONS
1	BEVERAGES AND TOBACCO						8919		9765	BOISSONS ET TABACS
11	BEVERAGES						6134		6714	BOISSONS
112	ALCOHOLIC BEVERAGES					W 6422	4985	W 9074	5286	BOISSONS ALCOOLIQUES
2	CRUDE MATERLS,EXCL FUELS						424578		445032	MAT BRUTES NON COMESTIBLES
23	RUBBER, CRUDE						53223		78035	CAOUTCHOUC BRUT
232	NATURAL RUBBER,GUMS					W 33448	53221	W 62405	78035	LATEX CAOUTCHOUC NATUREL
23202	OTHER NATURAL RUBBER					W 27018	43085	W 39387	51237	CAOUTCHOUC NATUREL
23203	BALATA,GUTTA–PERCHA, ETC					W 3159	6846	W 18701	22706	BALATA,GUTTA–PERCHA
24	CORK AND WOOD						285684		248916	LIEGE ET BOIS
247	OTH WOOD ROUGH,SQUARED					W 821953	174573	W 925063	162868	BOIS BRUTS EQUARRIS
2472	SAW–,VENEER–LOGS NON–CON					W 821953	174573	W 924284	162517	NON CONIFERES SCIAGE,PLAC
24721	— IN THE ROUGH					W 821953	174573	W 924284	162517	BRUTS ECORCES DEGROSSIS
248	WOOD SHAPED,SLEEPERS					W 176283	111111	W 203561	86047	BOIS SIMPLEMENT TRAVAILLES
2483	LUMBER SHAPED NON–CONIFR					W 172600	110132	W 197705	84553	NON CONIFERES SCIES,RABOTES
24831	LUMBER SAWN ETC NON–CON					W 172288	109886	W 195667	82720	SCIES LONGITUDINALEMENT
26	TEXTILE FIBRES AND WASTE						78227		109788	FIBRES TEXTILES
263	COTTON					W 54300	78224	W 65834	109776	COTON
2631	RAW COTTON,EXCL LINTERS					W 54130	78172	W 65834	109776	COTON EN MASSE
29	CRUDE ANIMAL,VEG MAT NES						4404		5436	MATIERES BRUTES ANIM,VEGET
292	CRUDE VEG MATERIALS NES					W 1228	4367	W 2003	5409	MAT BRUTES VEGETALES NDA
3	MINERAL FUELS ETC						448755		635523	COMBUSTIBLES MINERAUX LUB
33	PETROLEUM AND PRODUCTS						448567		635255	PETROLE ET DERIVES
333	CRUDE PETROLEUM					W 3727760	445279	W 4982805	627958	HUILES BRUTES DE PETROLE
334	PETROLEUM PRODUCTS,REFIN					W 6858	3217	W 14656	7078	PRODUITS RAFFINES
4	ANIMAL,VEGETABLE OIL,FAT						6992		22557	HUILES,GRAISSES ANIM,VEG
42	FIXED VEGETABLE OIL,FAT						6992		22555	HUILES VEGETALES FIXES
424	FIXED VEG OIL NONSOFT					W 9118	6982	W 35897	22490	AUTRES HUILES VEG FIXES
4242	PALM OIL					W 8103	6290	W 35897	22490	HUILE DE PALME
5	CHEMCLS,RELATED PROD NES						14845		19514	PRODUITS CHIMIQUES
55	PERFUME,CLEANING ETC PRD						7227		13044	PROD POUR PARFUM,TOILETTE
554	SOAP,CLEANSING ETC PREPS					W 4325	4041	W 8522	9205	SAVONS,PRODUITS DETERSIFS
5541	SOAPS					W 4187	3725	W 7988	8105	SAVONS,PROD TENSIO–ACTIFS
6	BASIC MANUFACTURES						209539		203453	ART MANUFACTURES
63	WOOD,CORK MANUFACTRS NES						28502		24863	OUVRAGES LIEGE ET BOIS
634	VENEERS,PLYWOOD,ETC					W 27617	27946	W 27485	24116	PLACAGES,CONTRE–PLAQUES
6341	VENEER SHEETS ETC					W 20718	22269	W 19552	19047	BOIS SIMPLEMENT SCIES
6342	PLYWOOD OF WOOD SHEETS					W 6036	5533	W 5962	4627	BOIS CONTRE–PLAQUES
65	TEXTILE YARN,FABRICS,ETC						10131		9185	FILS,TISSUS,ARTICLES TEXTILE
652	COTTON FABRICS,WOVEN					W 1714	9661	W 1823	8589	TISSUS DE COTON
6521	GREY WOVEN COTTON FABRIC					W 1590	8209	W 1681	7199	TISSUS COT ECRUS NON MERCER
65214	GREY WOVEN COTTON NES					W 1489	7686	W 1634	6951	AUT TISSUS 85% COTON ECRUS
66	NONMETAL MINERAL MFS NES						22443		39290	ART MIN NON METALLIQUES
661	LIME,CEMENT,BLDG PRODS					W 141936	14841	W 255469	28358	CHAUX,CIMENTS MAT CONSTR
6612	CEMENT					W 141936	14840	W 255462	28347	CIMENTS HYDRAULIQUES
665	GLASSWARE					W 15513	7551	W 23264	10855	OUVRAGES EN VERRE
6651	BOTTLES ETC OF GLASS					W 15388	7525	W 23259	10838	RECIPIENTS EN VERRE
66511	GLASS BOTTLES ETC NONVAC					W 15388	7525	W 23259	10838	BONBONNES,BOUTEILLES,ETC
68	NON–FERROUS METALS						127562		110774	METAUX NON FERREUX
684	ALUMINIUM					W 63776	127524	W 68604	110755	ALUMINIUM
6841	ALUMINIUM,ALLOYS,UNWRGHT					W 59032	116236	W 64500	101050	ALUMINIUM,ALLIAGES BRUTS
6842	ALUMINIUM,ALLOYS WORKED					W 4744	11287	W 4104	9705	ALUMINIUM,ALLIAGES OUVRE
68422	ALUMNM PLATE,SHEET,STRIP					W 4743	11283	W 4104	9701	TOLES, PLANCHES EN ALU
69	METAL MANUFACTURES NES						10118		8991	ART MANUFACT EN METAL NDA
699	BASE METAL MFRS NES					W 2771	7949	W 6776	5388	ART MANUFACTURES MET NDA
6998	MFRS NES OF CPR,NIKL,ETC					W 2764	7918	W 1821	4836	OUVRAGES EN CU,NI,AL,PB,ZN
69983	ALUMINIUM MANUFACTS NES					W 2764	7917	W 1821	4836	OUVRAGES EN ALUMINIUM
7	MACHINES,TRANSPORT EQUIP						17269		19107	MACHINES MATERIEL TRANSPORT
72	MACHS FOR SPCL INDUSTRYS						2854		6257	MAC SPECIALES POUR INDUST
723	CIVIL ENGNEERG EQUIP ETC					W 557	2011	W 1971	5280	APPAREILS DE GENIE CIVIL
77	ELECTRIC MACHNRY NES ETC						7749		7107	MACH APP ELECT NDA
778	ELECTRICAL MACHINERY NES					W 2674	7298	W 2634	6874	AUTRES MACH ELECT NDA
7781	BATTERIES,ACCUMULATORS					W 2671	7280	W 2630	6850	PILES ET ACCUMULATEURS
77811	PRIMARY BATTERIES,CELLS					W 2670	7279	W 2630	6824	PILES ELECTRIQUES,PIECES
8	MISC MANUFACTURED GOODS						7743		9438	ART MANUFACTURES DIVERS
89	MISC MANUFCTRD GOODS NES						6288		7125	ART MANUFACTURES DIVERS

Canada

1. HISTORICAL SERIES, 1961–1996 GENERAL TRADE, IMPORTS F.O.B., EXPORTS F.O.B.
SERIES HISTORIQUES, 1961–1996 COMMERCE GENERAL, IMPORTATIONS F.O.B., EXPORTATIONS F.O.B

YEAR ANNEE	VALUE IN MILLION CANADIAN DOLLARS VALEUR EN MILLION CANADIAN DOLLARS MERCHANDISE –MARCHANDISE		GOLD # 1 –OR		CONVERSION FACTORS U.S. CENTS PER CANADIAN DOLLAR FACTEURS DE CONVERSION CENTS E.U. PAR CANADIAN DOLLAR		INDEX NUMBERS –INDICES QUANTUM		UNIT VALUE VALEUR UNITAIRE	
	IMPORTS	EXPORTS	IMPORTS	EXPORTS	IMPORTS	EXPORTS	IMPORTS	EXPORTS	IMPORTS	EXPORTS
1961	5781.00	5902.00		162.00	98.6700	98.5600	20	20	27	26
1962	6294.00	6357.00		155.00	93.4100	93.3500	20	21	28	27
1963	6578.00	6990.00		154.00	92.5000	92.5000	21	23	30	27
1964	7488.00	8303.00		145.00	92.5000	92.5000	23	27	30	27
1965	8633.00	8767.00		138.00	92.5000	92.5000	27	28	30	27
1966	10072.00	10325.00		127.00	92.5000	92.5000	30	32	30	29
1967	10872.00	11420.00		112.00	92.5000	92.5000	34	34	30	29
1968	12358.00	13624.00		120.00	92.5000	92.5000	31	33	29	28
1969	14130.00	14890.00		109.00	92.5000	92.5000	35	35	30	30
1970	13952.00	16820.00			95.7600	95.8300	34	38	30	30
1971	15617.00	17820.00			99.0400	99.0300	37	40	31	30
1972	18669.00	20150.00			100.9960	101.0040	43	44	32	31
1973	23324.00	25420.00			99.9960	100.0000	50	48	34	36
1974	31692.00	32441.00			102.2730	102.2830	55	47	42	47
1975	34691.00	32246.00			98.3110	98.3050	52	43	49	52
1976	37444.00	38397.00			101.4600	101.4590	56	48	49	53
1977	42332.00	44554.00			94.0370	93.9890	57	53	55	57
1978	50102.00	53183.00			87.5590	87.5600	58	58	62	62
1979	62871.00	65641.00			85.3900	85.3920	65	59	71	75
1980	69274.00	76159.00			85.4970	85.5100	61	58	83	88
1981	79481.70	83811.50			83.4196	83.5425	63	60	92	93
1982	67855.70	84530.30			81.1053	81.0310	53	60	94	94
1983	75608.40	90612.50			81.1319	81.1297	61	66	90	93
1984	95460.00	112383.60			77.2100	77.1726	73	80	95	94
1985	104355.20	119474.50			73.2242	73.2194	72	80	101	98
1986	118785.00	125497.00			71.9738	71.9738	80	84	101	95
1987	122718.00	130089.00			75.4542	75.4642	89	93	97	94
1988	138802.00	144038.00			81.2077	81.3062	95	94	98	98
1989	141866.00	144248.00			84.4429	84.4625	100	96	98	101
1990	143837.00	148912.00			85.6854	85.7107	100	100	100	100
1991	142913.00	145658.00			87.3136	87.3025	102	101	99	97
1992	156246.00	162596.00			82.7334	82.6838	110	110	103	99
1993	179425.00	187346.00			77.4913	77.4943	120	121	109	104
1994	211792.00	225908.00			73.2207	73.2069	139	140	116	111
1995	230602.00	263697.00			72.8757	72.8882	153	157	121	119
1996	238489.00	274884.10			73.3625	73.3531	162	164	122	122

2. IMPORTS BY BROAD ECONOMIC CATEGORY AND EXPORTS BY INDUSTRIAL ORIGIN. (PERCENTAGE OF TOTAL VALUE)
IMPORTATIONS PAR CATEGORIES ECONOMIQUES ET EXPORTATIONS PAR BRANCHE D'ACTIVITE.(EN POURCENTAGE DE LA VALEUR TOTALE)

IMPORTS – IMPORTATIONS

	1990	1991	1992	1993	1994	1995	1996
TOTAL IMPORTS–IMPORTATIONS TOTALES	100.	100.	100.	100.	100.	100.	100.
1 FOOD BEV–ALIMENTATION BOISSONS	5.7	5.9	5.8	5.7	5.5	5.2	5.3
11 PRIMARY–PRODUITS DE BASE	2.9	3.1	2.9	2.9	2.7	2.6	2.6
111 FOR INDUSTRY–POUR L'INDUSTRIE	0.5	0.5	0.4	0.4	0.5	0.5	0.5
112 FOR HOUSEHOLDS–POUR LES MENAGES	2.5	2.7	2.5	2.5	2.2	2.1	2.1
12 PROCESSED–PRODUITS ELABORES	2.8	2.8	2.9	2.8	2.8	2.6	2.7
121 FOR INDUSTRY–POUR L'INDUSTRIE	0.5	0.4	0.4	0.4	0.4	0.4	0.5
122 FOR HOUSEHOLDS–POUR LES MENAGES	2.2	2.4	2.5	2.4	2.4	2.2	2.2
2 IND SUPPLIES–APPROV INDUSTRIELS	21.3	20.8	21.1	21.6	22.2	23.0	22.4
21 PRIMARY–PRODUITS DE BASE	2.2	2.0	2.1	2.0	2.1	2.5	2.2
22 PROCESSED–PRODUITS ELABORES	19.1	18.8	18.9	19.6	20.1	20.5	20.2
3 FUELS–COMBUSTIBLES	6.2	4.8	4.3	3.9	3.4	3.5	4.2
31 PRIMARY–PRODUITS DE BASE	4.5	3.8	3.3	3.0	2.7	2.8	3.5
32 PROCESSED–PRODUITS ELABORES	1.7	1.0	1.0	0.9	0.7	0.7	0.8
321 MOTOR SPIRIT–ESSENCE	0.3	0.2	0.1	0.2	0.2	0.2	0.2
322 OTHER–AUTRES	1.4	0.8	0.8	0.7	0.5	0.5	0.5
4 MACHINERY–EQUIPEMENT	24.9	24.8	24.8	25.3	26.6	27.5	27.2
41 CAPITAL EQUIPMENT–MACHINES	19.4	18.7	18.3	18.6	19.1	19.5	19.5
42 PARTS–PIECES ACCESSOIRES	5.5	6.1	6.5	6.7	7.4	8.1	7.7
5 TRANSPORT–TRANSPORT	26.3	27.0	26.5	26.3	26.1	25.1	25.0
51 PASSENGER CARS–AUTOMOBILES	8.0	8.8	8.1	7.2	6.9	6.0	6.1
52 OTHER–AUTRES	3.6	4.1	3.9	3.3	3.6	3.8	3.8
521 INDUSTRIAL–INDUSTRIELS	3.4	4.0	3.8	3.2	3.4	3.7	3.6
522 NON INDUSTRIAL–NON INDUSTRIEL	0.1	0.1	0.1	0.1	0.1	0.1	0.1
53 PARTS–PIECES ACCESSOIRES	14.8	14.1	14.6	15.9	15.7	15.3	15.2
6 CONSUM GOODS–BIENS CONSOMMATION	12.7	13.4	14.2	14.1	13.4	12.9	12.3
61 DURABLE–DURABLES	3.6	3.8	4.0	4.0	3.8	3.6	3.3
62 SEMI DURABLE–SEMI DURABLES	6.3	6.4	6.7	6.6	6.3	6.0	5.7
63 NON DURABLE–NON DURABLES	2.9	3.2	3.4	3.4	3.3	3.3	3.3
7 GOODS NES–BIENS NDA	2.8	3.3	3.3	31	2.8	2.8	3.5

EXPORTS – EXPORTATIONS

	1990	1991	1992	1993	1994	1995	1996
TOTAL EXPORTS–EXPORTATIONS TOTALES	100.	100.	100.	100.	100.	100.	100.
1 AGRICULTURE	6.4	6.5	6.7	5.2	5.3	5.0	4.9
2 MINING QUARRY–INDUS EXTRACTIVES	10.9	11.2	10.7	10.2	9.4	9.0	9.7
3 MANUFACTURING–IND MANUFACTUR	82.7	82.3	82.6	84.6	85.3	860	85.4
31 FOOD BEV TOBACCO–ALIM BOISS TAB	3.0	3.1	3.4	3.6	3.1	3.0	3.3
32 TEXTILES–INDUSTRIES TEXTILES	0.9	1.0	1.1	1.2	1.3	1.4	1.6
33 WOOD & PRODUCTS–BOIS & PRODUITS	4.7	4.6	5.2	6.4	6.4	5.5	6.0
34 PAPER & PRODUCTS–PAPIER & PRODT	10.7	10.2	9.4	8.5	8.5	10.7	8.5
35 CHEMICALS–INDUSTRIES CHIMIQUES	8.9	9.0	8.8	8.6	8.6	8.8	9.2
36 NON METAL MIN–MIN NON METAL	0.7	0.7	0.7	0.7	0.8	0.8	0.8
37 BASIC METAL–IND METAL BASE	6.6	6.7	6.6	6.1	5.9	6.4	6.0
38 METAL MANUF–MANUF METAL	41.6	41.6	42.1	44.2	45.2	44.1	44.4
39 OTH MANUF IND–AUTRES MANUF	5.6	5.4	5.2	5.3	5.6	5.3	5.4

3. TRADE BY PRINCIPAL COUNTRIES OF ORIGIN AND DESTINATION (VALUE IN THOUSAND U.S. DOLLARS)
ECHANGES SELON LES PRINCIPAUX PAYS D'ORIGINE ET DE DESTINATION (VALEUR EN MILLIERS DE DOLLARS EU)

COUNTRIES–PAYS	GENERAL IMPORTS F.O.B. # 1 IMPORTATIONS GENERALES F.O.B.					COUNTRIES–PAYS	GENERAL EXPORTS F.O.B. EXPORTATIONS GENERALES F.O.B.				
	1992	1993	1994	1995	1996		1992	1993	1994	1995	1996
World	122440199	131331114	148185486	164326887	171007193	Monde	134462160	144631676	166254561	192160647	201573714
Africa	917755	1147863	1145656	1297102	1518762	Afrique	801706	808848	890287	1229466	1151547
Americas	84264870	92958447	106045282	116695952	123240318	Amériques	106791980	119550589	139209119	156852707	168470685
Northern America	79840636	88049595	100237731	109831206	115542373	Amérique du Nord	104132828	116755975	135924182	152884516	164628513
LAIA	3705282	4229572	5001753	5925992	6623163	ALAI	2168873	2294617	2808829	3281428	3189428
CACM	198701	175823	228910	262719	248329	MCAC	68219	99361	83939	101946	99526
Caribbean	477225	369770	405557	526194	634246	Caraïbes	392686	360943	358504	535031	505462
Rest of America	43025	133687	171331	149840	192206	Autre Amérique	29373	39694	33665	49785	47756
As.ex F.USSR	18881333	19265271	20398563	22685383	21687795	Asie l'URSS exclus	13542277	13135368	14895353	19562112	17631088
Eur.x F.USSR	15075110	14096417	16547405	19204689	19892904	Europe l'URSS exclus	11583475	9939645	10286623	13281837	13075920
EU	13057533	12544230	14394986	16449672	16674976	UE	9939889	8588532	8990655	12025879	11400648
EFTA	1800010	1331756	1813338	2387521	2820946	AELE	1453884	1148434	1128527	976382	1318107
East Europe	168944	167029	259489	279790	299325	Europe de l'Est	168098	169264	141622	241709	308106
Other Europe	1946	9115	21562	34808	42992	Autre de l'Europe	1827	12374	3154	3053	3913
Former USSR	222786	358781	331991	434293	386799	Ancienne URSS	1058947	462861	168446	210455	324446
Oceania	803930	1043547	1084951	1186445	1204240	Océanie	683774	734366	804733	1023993	915610
USA/Etats–Unis d'Amer	79822735	88041705	100226304	109826152	115537870	USA/Etats–Unis d'Amer	104064388	116696402	135879612	152827788	164575384
Japan/Japon	8908192	8284601	8320709	8820047	7661759	Japan/Japon	6204335	6555071	7082029	8738901	7711289
United Kingdom	3396933	3432424	3660716	3986106	4334852	United Kingdom	2575606	2266447	2399050	2820076	2932007
Mexico/Mexique	2278062	2785223	3274280	3892004	4426510	Germany/Allemagne	1894647	1925050	1669900	2400807	2428751
Germany/Allemagne	2924226	2715893	3216502	3498785	3536735	China/Chine	1869138	1300356	1681757	2465670	2090879
China/Chine	2026398	2393000	2826598	3380398	3613700	Korea, Republic of	1177951	1329075	1608232	1988637	1993313
France,Monac	2226398	1751572	1891751	2277168	2494437	France,Monac	1171619	995194	998888	1421995	1282649
Korea, Republic of	1663207	1701689	1836715	2334997	2001077	Netherlands/Pays–Bas	1221748	1048929	893508	1207531	1197337
Italy/Italie	1444630	1498772	1896050	2383296	1994816	Belgium–Luxembourg	909592	712450	985542	1351131	1120653
Norway,SVD,JM	1250701	795524	1218195	1686530	2037833	Italy/Italie	965411	737751	960756	1333385	993840
Hong Kong	939570	925150	873539	950828	838603	Hong Kong	680567	588874	853234	1279035	879430
Malaysia/Malaisie	495271	674567	890245	1128825	1159191	Brazil/Brésil	523806	594031	713213	943509	1008986
Australia/Australie	621853	825520	822173	934937	947246	Mexico/Mexique	649655	633192	769235	829184	888351
Sweden/Suède	655614	664699	827986	951370	881141	Australia/Australie	580385	625027	695242	880913	741153
Singapore/Singapour	533876	617316	845066	946707	873726	Switz.Liecht	977066	700172	657104	401133	684287
Brazil/Brésil	592235	610585	703974	756355	831608	Norway,SVD,JM	463753	443880	467455	562797	618106
Thailand/Thaïlande	477896	590905	657178	738765	765398	Venezuela	423334	448856	445776	582193	400578
Netherlands/Pays–Bas	495874	516076	629111	696984	683291	Indonesia/Indonésie	362846	347680	348609	472116	638803
Switz.Liecht	539352	516130	559860	657363	687902	Russian Federation	1058947	351005	138466	151419	234117
Belgium–Luxembourg	371596	410782	469232	558024	626432	Saudi Arabia	251075	382387	416586	379561	354440
Spain/Espagne	361225	388087	467268	513904	498661	Spain/Espagne	367973	259335	270379	453273	375578
Saudi Arabia	448952	412972	396775	365712	477396	Thailand/Thaïlande	274774	286513	299730	418670	411891
Nigeria/Nigéria	392391	533803	463364	426285	228227	Singapore/Singapour	274515	259300	276721	361816	414943
Indonesia/Indonésie	326625	340971	383047	435137	459130	Iran (Islamic Rp. of)	310507	210494	329008	307900	378556
Venezuela	276969	272038	371721	471976	532527	India/Inde	426720	208879	193110	316188	254905
Ireland/Irlande	325913	334208	342255	411862	433449	Malaysia/Malaisie	194547	172346	211982	416315	385958
Austria/Autriche	249115	270200	334303	390937	445506	Algeria/Algérie	127714	179516	335911	386373	299797
India/Inde	230431	274720	336740	394470	443086	Colombia/Colombie	198078	186968	331924	273592	307479
Philippines	228774	298849	344050	362487	405427	Chile/Chili	128218	163975	229075	281439	242685
Russian Federation	222786	334575	265603	363039	329514	Austria/Autriche	171759	109787	198019	214832	306217
Finland/Finlande	196605	197433	234861	331569	306361	Sweden/Suède	183196	145123	174940	249719	201343
So. Africa Customs Un	149835	124977	259035	340023	364913	Philippines	171272	150970	135779	233592	192777
Algeria/Algérie	81415	174575	186406	253086	541464	So. Africa Customs Un	116314	127722	177140	247183	181933
Denmark/Danemark	202024	180705	232520	244096	259827	Turkey/Turquie	115815	121760	102002	208775	193216
New Zealand	169183	196647	235420	217183	236381	Cuba	98218	108138	84256	199902	197271
Cuba	212105	132906	142611	233869	294304	Israel/Israël	103878	120298	120099	171548	171167
Chile/Chili	167293	161384	172898	203247	251069	Argentina/Argentine	87327	107536	146195	171885	148627
Colombia/Colombie	108080	132980	188811	271117	217857	Ireland/Irlande	75571	71862	130290	145611	169381
Jamaica/Jamaïque	143965	140729	155141	145876	175409	New Zealand	87754	92896	102568	135227	160649
Israel/Israël	108904	119437	133946	175546	196002	Finland/Finlande	82468	73164	101460	168107	146825
Portugal	153687	138604	131649	156806	129641	Morocco/Maroc	104438	71892	55416	137645	145921
Pakistan	116410	153201	145704	148909	121256	Denmark/Danemark	123654	91757	79747	103473	86224
Iran (Islamic Rp. of)	104390	185408	85573	88722	174496	Egypt/Egypte	87641	88278	78716	111642	108679
Guyana	32293	117724	149558	124794	149684	United Arab Emirates	47600	66116	72657	145394	122835
Costa Rica	109125	99530	110559	118872	107606	Peru/Pérou	75595	75367	62878	105575	114310
Argentina/Argentine	92880	89651	97368	123809	136773	Portugal	135967	81394	69254	67443	72716
Ecuador/Equateur	89326	100918	93303	100567	94444	Poland/Pologne	46255	66444	43894	130279	126937
Turkey/Turquie	55518	62481	87895	109392	111348	Greece/Grèce	60678	70288	58924	88492	87126
Poland/Pologne	47894	47067	74923	87845	105862	Jamaica/Jamaïque	56940	69408	66854	75147	66593
Peru/Pérou	78772	49181	70662	70043	92700	Libyan Arab Jamahiriya	66981	69652	48733	48758	100771

(VALUE AS PERCENTAGE OF WORLD TOTAL)(VALEURS EN POURCENTAGE DU TOTAL MONDIAL)

	1987	1988	1989	1990	1991	1992	1993	1994	1995	1996		1987	1988	1989	1990	1991	1992	1993	1994	1995	1996
Africa	0.6	0.7	0.9	0.8	0.8	0.7	0.9	0.8	0.8	0.9	Afrique	0.8	0.9	0.8	0.8	0.7	0.6	0.6	0.5	0.6	0.6
Americas	71.9	69.4	69.0	67.9	67.6	68.8	70.8	71.6	71.0	72.1	Amériques	78.8	75.4	75.5	76.9	77.2	79.4	82.7	83.7	81.6	83.6
Northern America	68.2	66.1	65.4	64.6	63.7	65.2	67.0	67.6	66.8	67.6	Amérique du Nord	75.5	73.4	73.6	75.1	75.4	77.4	80.7	81.8	79.6	81.7
LAIA	2.7	2.8	3.1	2.9	3.3	3.0	3.2	3.4	3.6	3.9	ALAI	1.8	1.4	1.3	1.3	1.4	1.6	1.6	1.7	1.7	1.6
CACM	0.2	0.2	0.2	0.1	0.2	0.2	0.1	0.2	0.2	0.1	MCAC	0.1	0.1	0.1	0.1	0.0	0.1	0.1	0.1	0.1	0.0
Caribbean	0.7	0.3	0.3	0.3	0.4	0.4	0.3	0.3	0.3	0.4	Caraïbes	1.4	0.5	0.4	0.4	0.3	0.3	0.2	0.2	0.3	0.3
Rest of America	0.1	0.0	0.0	0.0	0.0	0.0	0.1	0.1	0.1	0.1	Autre Amérique	0.0	0.0	0.0	0.0	0.0	0.0	0.0	0.0	0.0	0.0
As.ex F.USSR	13.0	14.0	14.5	14.4	15.4	15.4	14.7	13.8	13.8	12.7	Asie l'URSS exclus	10.7	12.6	12.2	11.1	11.2	10.1	9.1	9.0	10.2	8.7
Eur.x F.USSR	13.9	14.8	13.7	14.7	13.7	12.3	10.7	11.2	11.7	11.6	Europe l'URSS exclus	8.4	9.5	10.1	9.8	9.4	8.6	6.9	6.2	6.9	6.5
EU	12.8	13.5	12.3	12.7	11.8	10.7	9.6	9.7	10.0	9.8	UE	7.7	8.4	9.0	8.5	8.4	7.4	5.9	5.4	6.3	5.7
EFTA	0.8	0.9	1.0	1.7	1.6	1.5	1.0	1.2	1.5	1.6	AELE	0.5	0.9	1.0	1.1	0.9	1.1	0.8	0.7	0.5	0.7
East Europe	0.2	0.3	0.2	0.2	0.1	0.1	0.1	0.2	0.2	0.2	Europe de l'Est	0.2	0.1	0.1	0.1	0.1	0.1	0.1	0.1	0.1	0.2
Other Europe	0.1	0.1	0.1	0.1	0.1	0.0	0.0	0.0	0.0	0.0	Autre de l'Europe	0.0	0.0	0.0	0.0	0.0	0.0	0.0	0.0	0.0	0.0
Former USSR	0.0	0.1	0.1	0.2	0.2	0.2	0.3	0.2	0.3	0.2	Ancienne URSS	0.6	0.8	0.5	0.8	1.0	0.8	0.3	0.1	0.1	0.2
Oceania	0.7	0.7	0.6	0.7	0.6	0.7	0.8	0.7	0.7	0.7	Océanie	0.7	0.8	1.0	0.7	0.5	0.5	0.5	0.5	0.5	0.5
USA/Etats–Unis d'Amer	68.2	66.1	65.4	64.6	63.7	65.2	67.0	67.6	66.8	67.6	USA/Etats–Unis d'Amer	75.5	73.3	73.6	75.0	75.3	77.4	80.7	81.7	79.5	81.6
Japan/Japon	6.5	7.1	7.1	7.0	7.6	7.3	6.3	5.6	5.4	4.5	Japan/Japon	5.4	6.3	6.4	5.5	4.9	4.6	4.5	4.3	4.5	3.8
United Kingdom	3.7	3.5	3.4	3.6	3.1	2.8	2.6	2.5	2.4	2.5	United Kingdom	2.2	2.6	2.6	2.4	2.1	1.9	1.6	1.4	1.5	1.5
Mexico/Mexique	1.0	1.0	1.3	1.3	1.9	1.9	2.1	2.2	2.4	2.6	Germany/Allemagne	1.3	1.3	1.4	1.6	1.7	1.4	1.3	1.0	1.2	1.2
Germany/Allemagne	3.0	2.9	2.8	2.8	2.8	2.4	2.1	2.2	2.1	2.1	China/Chine	1.1	1.9	0.8	1.1	1.3	1.4	0.9	1.0	1.3	1.0
China/Chine	0.7	0.7	0.9	1.0	1.4	1.7	1.8	1.9	2.1	2.1	Korea, Republic of	0.9	0.9	1.2	1.1	1.3	0.9	0.9	1.0	1.0	1.0
France,Monac	1.3	2.2	1.5	1.8	2.0	1.8	1.3	1.3	1.4	1.5	France,Monac	0.9	0.9	1.0	0.9	1.0	0.9	0.7	0.6	0.7	0.6
Korea, Republic of	1.4	1.7	1.8	1.7	1.6	1.4	1.3	1.2	1.4	1.2	Netherlands/Pays–Bas	0.8	1.0	1.2	1.0	1.2	0.9	0.7	0.5	0.6	0.6
Italy/Italie	1.5	1.5	1.5	1.4	1.3	1.2	1.1	1.3	1.5	1.2	Belgium–Luxembourg	0.8	0.9	0.9	0.8	0.8	0.7	0.5	0.6	0.7	0.6
Norway,SVD,JM	0.2	0.4	0.6	1.2	1.1	1.0	0.6	0.8	1.0	1.2	Italy/Italie	0.7	0.7	0.8	0.8	0.7	0.7	0.5	0.6	0.7	0.5

4. General Imports F.O.B. by Commodities according to the S.I.T.C. (Rev. 2) in thousand U.S. Dollars
Importations Générales F.O.B. par Produits d'après la C.T.C.I. (Rév. 2) en milliers de Dollars E.U.

SITC CTCI	COMMODITY	1993		1994		1995		1996		PRODUIT
		WEIGHT POIDS	VALUE VALEUR	WEIGHT POIDS	VALUE VALEUR	WEIGHT POIDS	VALUE VALEUR	WEIGHT POIDS	VALUE VALEUR	
	ALL COMMODITIES		131331114		148185486		164326887		171007193	TOUS PRODUITS
0	FOOD AND LIVE ANIMALS		7266061		7905812		8228494		8621672	ALIMENTS,ANIMAUX VIVANTS
01	MEAT AND PREPARATIONS		849897		878544		838362		797483	VIANDES ET PREPARATIONS
011	MEAT FRESH,CHILLD,FROZEN	W 279318	698524	W 301779	726570	W 274016	681758	W 272032	625539	VIANDES FRAICHES,REF,CONGE
0111	BOVINE MEAT FRESH,FROZEN	W 188859	519485	W 201362	529179	W 178154	489178	W 163863	416865	VIANDES BOVIN FRAI,REF
01112	BOVINE MEAT BONELESS	W 179472	478378	W 192508	493368	W 171838	464553	W 157816	394836	VIANDES BOVIN DESOSSEES
03	FISH AND PREPARATIONS		795841		882332		994860		1105804	POISSONS ET PREPARATIONS
04	CEREALS AND PREPARATIONS		698103		777806		852837		940209	CEREALES ET PRODUITS
048	CEREAL ETC PREPARATIONS	W 318601	495260	W 351150	562258	W 367621	592069	W 361067	614182	PREPTNS A BASE CEREALES
05	VEGETABLES AND FRUIT		2671503		2601118		2762126		2867782	LEGUMES ET FRUITS
054	VEG ETC FRSH,SMPLY PRSVD	W 1581679	873187	W 1551312	839020	W 1557492	919032	W 1605597	877405	LEGUMES FRAIS,CONG,SECS
0545	OTHER FRESH VEGETABLES	W 1003188	544281	W 932533	501476	W 960413	573187	W 982310	520961	AUTRES LEGUMES FRAIS,REF
05459	FRESH VEGETABLES NES	W 854586	483251	W 805796	450091	W 827200	516767	W 855108	470711	LEGUMES FRAIS,REFRI NDA
057	FRUIT,NUTS,FRESH,DRIED	W 1592930	1221160	W 1588124	1159466	W 1588274	1203965	W 1630647	1257839	FRUITS FRAIS OU SECS
058	FRUIT PRESERVED,PREPARED		426028		439083		469920	W 1632225	554519	CONSERVES DE FRUITS
06	SUGAR AND PREPS,HONEY		434004		482760		489488		546861	SUCRES ET PRODUITS
07	COFFEE,TEA,COCOA,SPICES		673680		889512		1000519		962158	CAFE,THE,CACAO,EPICES
071	COFFEE AND SUBSTITUTES	W 136621	254534	W 155694	460406	W 138018	543341	W 154048	463306	CAFE ET SUCCEDANES
081	*FEEDING STUFF FOR ANIML	W 1206495	488531	W 1243683	514311	W 1492821	534956	W 1558476	582871	NOURRITURE POUR ANIMAUX
09	MISC EDIBLE PRODUCTS		376588		567395		466835		509925	PREP ALIMENTAIRES DIVERSES
098	EDIBLE PRODCTS,PREPS NES	W 196341	362483	W 240191	552156	W 259844	451506	W 268838	492516	PREP ALIMENTAIRES NDA
1	BEVERAGES AND TOBACCO		613398		686551		750586		816882	BOISSONS ET TABACS
11	BEVERAGES		566901		634845		696518		745718	BOISSONS
112	ALCOHOLIC BEVERAGES	W 225344	492890	W 243334	542080	W 256354	591226	W 263817	648982	BOISSONS ALCOOLIQUES
2	CRUDE MATERLS,EXCL FUELS		4112017		4686324		5856481		5548444	MAT BRUTES NON COMESTIBLES
23	RUBBER, CRUDE		303366		379000		502035		506163	CAOUTCHOUC BRUT
24	CORK AND WOOD		733324		810639		911293		863664	LIEGE ET BOIS
248	WOOD SHAPED,SLEEPERS		504982		508237		499274		539405	BOIS SIMPLEMENT TRAVAILLES
251	*PULP AND WASTE PAPER	W 1381146	276411	W 1940240	368135	W 2451104	615699	W 1516836	301596	PATES A PAPIER,DECHETS
28	METALLIFEROUS ORES,SCRAP		1677692		1947144		2489229		2455412	MINERAIS METAL,DECHETS
287	BASE METAL ORES,CONC NES	W 6510996	1046586	W 6748823	1171767	W 6321787	1453729	W 6921763	1464716	MINERAIS METAUX COMMUNS
2873	ALUMINIUM ORES,ALUMINA	W 6125714	651343	W 6262394	635855	W 5782154	705052	W 6146775	776798	MINERAIS D'ALUMINIUM
28732	ALUMINA(ALUMINIUM OXIDE)	W 3265189	568195	W 3332986	554289	W 3158540	628419	W 3572570	698349	ALUMINE (OXYDE ALUMINIUM)
288	NONFERR METAL SCRAP NES	W 274954	216080	W 369791	325993	W 497822	503729	W 465601	463925	DECHETS NON FERREUX
3	MINERAL FUELS ETC		5283768		5218649		6004190		7502741	COMBUSTIBLES MINERAUX LUB
32	COAL,COKE AND BRIQUETTES		374875		383210		459862		517166	HOUILLES,COKES,BRIQUETTES
33	PETROLEUM AND PRODUCTS		4714560		4663562		5348003		6725286	PETROLE ET DERIVES
333	CRUDE PETROLEUM	MW 28343	3473912	MW 31164	3491298	MW 34285	4159689	MW 37184	5332523	HUILES BRUTES DE PETROLE
334	PETROLEUM PRODUCTS,REFIN	W 7340290	1082483	W 6090874	1004175	W 5069098	913414	W 5133484	1106620	PRODUITS RAFFINES
3345	LUBS,PETROLEUM OILS NES	W 2940568	518409	W 1005539	308877	W 750648	315451	W 785174	368801	HUILES LUBRIFIANTES
33451	LUBS(HIGH PETR CONT) ETC	W 2918820	469682	W 978528	248933	W 722545	252738	W 756584	300723	HUILES LUBRIF,H LOURDES
5	CHEMCLS,RELATED PROD NES		9764364		11315539		12857972		14005819	PRODUITS CHIMIQUES
51	ORGANIC CHEMICALS		1741618		2107857		2433423		2627774	PROD CHIMIQ ORGANIQUES
514	NITROGEN–FNCTN COMPOUNDS	W 211026	566603	W 245534	682751	W 237244	798296	W 229983	803659	COMPOSES FONCT AZOTEES
52	INORGANIC CHEMICALS		634351		793813		943746		1035633	PROD CHIM INORGANIQUES
53	DYES,TANNING,COLOUR PROD		757276		872130		930859		971645	PROD TEINTURE,COLORANTS
533	PIGMENTS,PAINTS,ETC		563918		676489		724075		761136	PIGMENTS,PEINTURES,VERNIS
541	*MEDICINAL,PHARM PRODUCT		1475697		1608827		1807567		2024173	PROD MEDICINAUX PHARMACEUT
5417	MEDICAMENTS		982547		1052829		1203078		1364151	MEDICAMENTS
54179	— CONTNG OTH SUBSTANCES		722323		781845		897224		1054795	MED CONT AUT SUBSTANCES
55	PERFUME,CLEANING ETC PRD		884467		1004359		1137383		1284809	PROD POUR PARFUM,TOILETTE
553	PERFUMERY,COSMETICS,ETC		433487		513872		592786		694192	PRODUITS DE PARFUMERIE
58	PLASTIC MATERIALS ETC		2480605		2944778		3358073		3705838	MAT PLAST ARTIFICIELLES
582	PROD OF CONDENSATION ETC	W 354559	759428	W 439981	892684	W 487037	1038636	W 505259	1100551	PROD CONDENS,POLYCOND
583	POLYMERIZATION ETC PRODS		1602439		1935323		2202217	W 1722601	2490062	PROD POLYMERISATION
5839	OTH POLYMRZTION ETC PROD		536628		611970		699648	W 391128	770487	AUT PROD POLYMER COPOLYM
59	CHEMICAL MATERIALS NES		1510321		1710472		1937537		1995872	MAT PROD CHIMIQUES NDA
591	PESTICIDES,DISINFECTANTS	W 86551	325064	W 91757	421207	W 108985	506423	W 110989	506248	DESINF,INSECT,FONG,HERB
598	MISCEL CHEM PRODUCTS NES		999880		1087987		1208556		1226702	PROD DIV INDUST CHIM NDA
5989	CHEM PRODUCTS,PREPS NES		762024		835376		947069		986899	PROD PREP CHIMIQUES NDA
59899	OTH CHEM PRODS,PREPS,NES		512344		556356		607759	W 465620	648867	AUT PRODUITS CHIMIQUES NDA
6	BASIC MANUFACTURES		16705299		19295688		21760737		21587980	ART MANUFACTURES
62	RUBBER MANUFACTURES NES		1601711		1819290		2025179		2023853	CAOUTCHOUC MANUFACTURE
625	RUBBER TYRES, TUBES ETC	MN 26080	859103	MN 29758	931248	MN 29517	1056156	MN 28386	1017364	PNEUS CAOUTCHOUC VULCANISE
6251	TYRES NEW FOR MOTOR CARS	MN 13257	385430	MN 15648	446484	MN 15496	477870	MN 14710	459009	PNEUS POUR VOITURES
628	RUBBER ARTICLES NES		380242		487460		535221		535150	OUVRAGES CAOUTCHOUC NDA
63	WOOD,CORK MANUFACTRS NES		463553		497250		613252		522360	OUVRAGES LIEGE ET BOIS
64	PAPER,PAPERBOARD AND MFR		2007241		2256529		2794509		2913044	PAPIERS,CARTONS & OUVRAGES
641	PAPER AND PAPERBOARD	W 1433555	1274078	W 1596771	1427391	W 1773422	1780312	W 1955389	1826959	PAPIERS ET CARTONS
6412	PRINTG,WRITING PAPER NES	W 339476	332202	W 384284	380868	W 429474	522343	W 447657	509637	PAPIERS POUR L'IMPRESSION
642	PAPER,ETC,PRECUT,ARTS OF		733163		829137		1014197		1086085	PAP,CARTONS DECOUPES
65	TEXTILE YARN,FABRICS,ETC		2721842		2925470		3216522		3325952	FILS,TISSUS,ARTICLES TEXTILE
651	TEXTILE YARN	W 141979	500473	W 160734	552313	W 170113	637644		674475	FILS TEXTILES
653	WOVN MAN–MADE FIB FABRIC	W 53939	457999	W 56945	466125	W 59037	493757	W 55467	482037	TISSUS FIBRES SYNTH,ARTIF
657	SPECIAL TXTL FABRC,PRODS		490382		535217		616114		650546	TISSUS SPECIAUX
66	NONMETAL MINERAL MFS NES		1923277		2122410		2115061		2192345	ART MIN NON METALLIQUES
664	GLASS		723192		821731		824178		879449	VERRE
67	IRON AND STEEL		2423074		3194102		3636175		3424097	FER ET ACIER
672	IRON,STEEL PRIMARY FORMS	W 1439442	284385	W 2157096	641252	W 2148135	726262	W 1735850	525500	LINGOTS FER,ACIER
673	IRON,STEEL SHAPES ETC	W 773074	382534	W 1007625	486668	W 1183840	630523	W 1074944	582843	BARRES,PROFIL FER,ACIER
674	IRN,STL UNIV,PLATE,SHEET	W 1040151	828725	W 1319443	964675	W 1271311	1049674	W 1202297	1020115	LARGES PLATS,TOLES
678	IRON,STL TUBES,PIPES,ETC		583330		709122		784335		798646	TUBES,TUYAUX EN FONTE,FER
68	NON–FERROUS METALS		1588846		2017346		2516935		2273471	METAUX NON FERREUX
682	COPPER EXC CEMENT COPPER	W 113838	334803	W 135807	421990	W 167297	565961	W 143930	456016	CUIVRE
684	ALUMINIUM		940290		1199507		1475285		1310689	ALUMINIUM
6842	ALUMINIUM,ALLOYS WORKED		796107		986384		1254133		1116063	ALUMINIUM,ALLIAGES OUVRE
68422	ALUMNM PLATE,SHEET,STRIP	W 318839	627867	W 368220	785998	W 375154	994108	W 342532	844731	TOLES, PLANCHES EN ALU
69	METAL MANUFACTURES NES		3726263		4180432		4572306		4646290	ART MANUFACT EN METAL NDA
694	STL,COPPR NAILS,NUTS,ETC		521001		588359		636980		674719	CLOUS,VIS,ECROUS
69402	IRN,STL NUTS,BOLTS,ETC		485108		548967		598009		632199	BOULONS,VIS,ECROUS FER,AC
695	TOOLS		704262		771853		869987		860878	OUTILS A MAIN
6954	BLADES,TIPS,ETC FR TOOLS		423154		469332		554234		547487	OUTILS POUR MACHINE–OUTIL
699	BASE METAL MFRS NES		1547176		1843712		1994023		2037091	ART MANUFACTURES MET NDA
6991	LOCKSMITHS WARES,ETC		659586		789027		844606		899761	ARTICLES DE SERRURERIE
69913	BASE MTL DOOR,ETC FITTNG		476666		581335		623693		671981	GARNITURES POUR MEUBLES
6997	IRON,STEEL ARTICLES NES		348064		469668		490236		380320	OUV FONTE,FER,ACIER NDA
69979	IRN,STL MANUFACTURES NES		347184		468448		489232		379242	AUT OUVRAGES EN FER NDA
7	MACHINES,TRANSPORT EQUIP		66505508		76310427		84550676		87181521	MACHINES MATERIEL TRANSPORT
71	POWER GENERATING EQUIPMT		6290886		6945265		7895744		8263456	MACHINES GENERATRICES
713	INTRNL COMBUS PSTN ENGIN		4602810		5204530		5561333		5714885	MOTEURS EXPL COMB INT, PIECE
7132	MOTOR VEHCL PISTN ENGINS	N 2140220	3129223	N 1882972	3337704	N 1985553	3719428	N 1938913	3560281	MOTEURS EXPL POUR VEHICULES

4. General Imports F.O.B. by Commodities according to the S.I.T.C. (Rev. 2) in thousand U.S. Dollars
Importations Générales F.O.B. par Produits d'après la C.T.C.I. (Rév. 2) en milliers de Dollars E.U.

SITC CTCI	COMMODITY	1993 WEIGHT POIDS	1993 VALUE VALEUR	1994 WEIGHT POIDS	1994 VALUE VALEUR	1995 WEIGHT POIDS	1995 VALUE VALEUR	1996 WEIGHT POIDS	1996 VALUE VALEUR	PRODUIT
7139	PISTON ENGINE PARTS NES		1068995		1384069		1313975		1670043	PIECES POUR 713.2,3,8
714	ENGINES AND MOTORS NES		947344		816617		1101818		1514642	MOTEURS NON ELECTRIQUES
7149	ENGINE & MOTOR PARTS NES		681886		590848		815279		1045244	PIECES 714 ET 718.88
71491	PARTS NES OF 7144,71481		488515		413916		588558		744505	PIECES DES PROPULSEURS
716	ROTATING ELECTRIC PLANT		526348		685895		967556		780761	APP ELECTR ROTATIFS,PIECES
72	MACHS FOR SPCL INDUSTRYS		4308105		5091664		5593023		5501841	MAC SPECIALES POUR INDUST
721	AGRIC MACHY,EXC TRACTORS		816422		853248		853280		905424	MACHINES AGRICOLES
7212	HARVESTING ETC MACHINES		567735		578539		576366		612898	ENGINS POUR LA RECOLTE
722	TRACTORS NON-ROAD	N 22819	449555	N 63262	474554	N 25210	489111	N 25771	539168	TRACTEURS
7224	WHEELED TRACTORS NES	N 22653	437479	N 63040	456572	N 24968	470986	N 25558	515915	TRACTEURS A ROUES
723	CIVIL ENGNEERG EQUIP ETC		792905		1223631		1236906		1131565	APPAREILS DE GENIE CIVIL
7234	CONST,MINING MACHNRY NES	N 48845	701638	N 56957	1105123	N 49863	1100516	N 45797	991232	MACH POUR LA CONST, MINES
72342	SLFPRP SHOVELS,EXCAVATRS	N 7985	492433	N 11541	754257	N 11080	754391	N 9496	646354	PELLES MECANIQUES
728	OTH MACHY FOR SPCL INDUS		1392179		1551921		1818474		1784605	AUT MACH IND PARTICULIERES
7284	MACHY FOR SPCL INDUS NES		1100400		1208524		1424799		1402907	MACH SPEC IND PARTICUL.
72848	OTH MCHY WITH INDIV FNCT		633351	N 689549	583715	N 606870	695154	N 629141	699362	AUTRES MACHINES NDA
73	METALWORKING MACHINERY		779381		1214596		1262622		1307626	MACH TRAVAIL DES METAUX
736	METALWORKING MACH-TOOLS		558798		970762		965959		983059	MACH-OUTILS TRAVAIL METAUX
74	GENRL INDUSTRL MACHY NES		6815030		8066478		9149434		9360101	MACH APP INDUSTRIE
741	HEATING,COOLING EQUIPMNT		1265396		1496442		1660203		1785111	MACH CHAUFFAGE,PIECES
7415	AIR-CONDITIONING MACHNRY		739918		876558		924831		1015545	GROUPES CONDITION AIR
742	PUMPS FOR LIQUIDS ETC		677202		776052		822197		871789	POMPES MOTO-POMPES
743	PUMPS NES,CENTRFUGES ETC		1242324		1444641		1800696		1630409	POMPES COMPRES,VENT ETC
7436	GAS,LIQUID FILTERS ETC	MN 36569	530849	MN 38876	602840	MN 40069	846632	MN 44540	698244	APP POUR FILT DES LIQUIDES
744	MECHANICAL HANDLING EQU		883168		1080963		1271129		1331424	EQUIP MANUTENTION PIECES
7449	PTS NES OF MACHY OF 7442		428369		495101		556566		579633	PIECES DU 744.2
745	NONELEC MACHY,TOOLS NES		645984		756623		761804		794639	AUT MACH NON ELEC,PIECES
7452	OTH NONELEC MCHS,PTS NES		515607		596065		595086		645742	AUT MACH NON ELEC,PIECES
749	NONELEC MACH PTS,ACC NES		2100956		2511756		2833406		2946729	PIECES MACH NON ELEC NDA
7491	BALL,ROLLER,ETC BEARINGS		396001		461928		562645		534677	ROULEMENTS BILLES ETC
7492	COCKS,VALVES ETC NES		756779		907596		1004448		1067914	ART ROB,SIM POUR TUYAUX
7493	SHAFT,CRANK,PULLEY ETC		611526		773498		852114		881771	ARBRES TRANS,VILEBREQUINS
75	OFFICE MACHNES,ADP EQUIP		6841418		7784772		8722633		9177873	MACH BUREAU TRAIT AUTOM
751	OFFICE MACHINES		466724	N 7259954	437187	N 7475833	454184	N 7370710	472961	MACH,APPAREILS DE BUREAU
752	AUTOMTIC DATA PROC EQUIP		4203187		4711628		5422452		5995206	MACH TRAIT INFORMATION
7522	DIGITAL COMPUTERS		306237		480610		542788		977365	MACH DIGITALES COMPLETES
7523	DIGITL CENTRL PROCESSORS		1557822		1665769		2050145		2225609	UNITES CENTRALES
7524	DIGITL CENTRL STOR UNITS	N 3325067	873142	N 4226231	972689	N 4553078	1080108	N 5145875	1153644	UNITES MEMOIRE CENTRALES
7525	ADP PERIPHERAL UNITS	N 5217494	1278453	N 5695977	1336802	N 5746240	1421983	N 4856112	1164138	UNITES PERIPHERIQUES
759	OFFICE,ADP MCH PTS,ACCES		2171507		2635956		2845997		2709706	PIECES DU 751 ET 752
7599	ACCTG,ETC,ADP MCH PTS,AC		1891409		2345408		2533802		2384602	PIECES DU 751 ET 752
76	TELECOMM,SOUND EQUIPMENT		3856278		4216640		4815820		5247415	EQUIPMENT DE TELECOM
762	RADIO BROADCAST RECEIVRS		628155	MN 9067	701449	MN 9637	789559	N 8299136	685744	RECEPTEURS RADIODIFFUSION
763	SOUND RECORDRS,PHONOGRPH	N 4497946	525096	N 4438129	518008	N 4534614	518739	N 4147963	492699	PHONO,APP ENREGISTREMENT
7638	OTHR SOUND APPARATUS ETC	N 4466993	520345	N 4418292	514091	N 4510207	515402	N 4127870	489959	AUT APP D'ENREGIS,REPROD
764	TELECOM EQPT,PTS,ACC NES		2355450		2648709		3118711		3691415	EQUIP TELECOM,PIECES
7641	LINE TELEPHONE,ETC EQUIP		693629		797536		953349		1099548	APP TELEPHON PAR FIL
7643	TV,RADIO TRANSMITTRS ETC	N 1449899	323356	N 2251340	414718	N 2550191	541049	N 3266419	631378	APP EMET TELE RADIO
7649	PTS NES OF EQUIPMT OF 76		807385		910962		1047081		1354383	PIECES DE LA DIV 76
76491	PTS NES OF APPAR OF 7641		312533		356264		435094		646226	PIECES POUR 764.1
76493	TELECOMM EQUIPMT PTS NES		432454		479832		520298		617643	PIECES 761,762,764.3,8
77	ELECTRIC MACHNRY NES ETC		10589067		12671898		14815927		15003474	MACH APP ELECT NDA
771	ELECTRIC POWER MACHY NES		438153		503382		577564		624140	MACH PROD,TRANS ELECTR
772	SWITCHGEAR ETC,PARTS NES		2037778		2423065		2639347		2754052	APP COUPURE,SECT ETC
7721	SWITCHGEAR ETC		1414161		1672134		1867228		2034925	APP COUPURE,SECTIONMNT
7722	PRINTED CIRCUITS,PTS NES		560835		679018		691445		637699	CIRCUITS ET PIECES
773	ELECTR DISTRIBUTNG EQUIP		990406		1160198		1303034		1370940	EQUIPMT DISTRIBUTION ELECT
7731	INSULATED WIRE,CABLE ETC		916954		1102458		1238807		1306319	FILS,CABLES ISOLES ELECT
775	HOUSEHOLD TYPE EQUIP NES		988251		1039203		1043192		1067733	MACH,APP USAGE DOMESTQUE
776	TRANSISTORS,VALVES,ETC		3523785		4587779		6269517		6089123	LAMPES,TUBES,VALVES
7764	ELECTRONIC MICROCIRCUITS	MN 675302	3186201	MN 792526	4184284	MN 961431	5744906	MN 959748	5616174	MICROSTRUCTURES ELECTRON
778	ELECTRICAL MACHINERY NES		2327864		2679385		2725260		2806475	AUTRES MACH ELECT NDA
7783	AUTOMOTIVE ELECTR EQUIP		1052959		1208438		1107532		1174328	EQUIP ELECT MOTEURS EXPL
77831	IGNITION,STARTING EQUIP		594580		707844	MN 88440	602100	MN 84693	625138	APP ELEC ALLUM,DEMARRAGE
77832	ELECT VEHICLE LGHTNG EQU		458380		500594		505432		549190	APP ELEC ECLAIR,SIGNAL AUTO
7788	OTH ELEC MACHY,EQUIP NES		668689		783028		913543		892934	AUT MACH APP ELEC NDA
78	ROAD VEHICLES		25104801		28405884		29588325		30337978	VEHICULES ROUTIERS
781	PASS MOTOR VEH EXC BUSES	N 799044	9348136	N 832800	10113173	N 739278	9794998	N 732784	10347394	AUTO TRANSPORT PERSONNES
782	LORRIES,SPCL MTR VEH NES	N 198243	2241360	N 234254	2820167	N 232519	3100764	N 241888	3443247	VEHICULES SPECIAUX,MARCH
7821	LORRIES,TRUCKS	N 197539	2171545	N 233422	2745967	N 231577	3006075	N 239304	3341207	VEHICULES TRANSP MARCHAND
783	ROAD MOTOR VEHICLES NES	N 12970	718416	N 18996	1069346	N 18623	1099893	N 15670	971136	VEHICULES ROUTIERS NDA
7832	TRACTORS FOR TR-TRAILERS	N 11674	650371	N 16713	994639	N 15828	981473	N 12443	763288	TRACTEURS ROUTIERS
784	MOTOR VEH PRTS,ACCES NES		12115971		13645566		14714355		14716445	PIECES 722,781,782,783
7849	OTHER MOTOR VEHCL PARTS		11900950		13385301		14369529		14351260	PIECES 722,781,782,783
786	TRAILERS,NONMOTR VEH,NES		415821		483328		573788		535085	REMORQUES,CADRES,CONTAIN
79	OTHR TRANSPORT EQUIPMENT		1920542		1913231		2707147		2981756	AUTRE MATERIEL TRANSPORT
791	RAILWAY VEHICLES		206628		309116		551238		429502	VEHIC MAT CHEMINS DE FER
792	AIRCRAFT ETC		1559820		1441550		1978264		2392278	APP NAVIGATION AERIENNE
7924	AIRCRFT NES OVER 15000KG	N 15	405023	N 27	309056	N 20	686564	N 39	803323	AERODYNES PLUS 15000 KG
7929	AIRCRAFT PARTS NES		914049		901293		1040159		1290785	PIECES DU 792
8	MISC MANUFACTURED GOODS		16284313		17889860		19050871		18860717	ART MANUFACTURES DIVERS
812	*PLUMBG,HEATNG,LGHTNG EQ		446182		487151		481647		515268	APPAR SANITAIRES CHAUFFAGE
821	*FURNITURE,PARTS THEREOF		1738061		1912180		1985209		1951130	MEUBLES ET PIECES
8211	CHAIRS,SEATS AND PARTS		959686		1053737		1178059		1137909	SIEGES ET PIECES
82111	CHAIRS AND OTHER SEATS		526662		433490		339912		335125	SIEGES
82119	PTS NES OF CHAIRS ETC		433024		620247		838146		802784	PIECES DU 821.11
8219	FURNITURE AND PARTS NES		639095		719302		674838		681503	AUTRES MEUBLES ET PIECES
84	CLOTHING AND ACCESSORIES		2534555		2543584		2713581		2560977	VETEMENTS
843	WOMENS OUTERWEAR NONKNIT	MN 72920	668876	MN 66264	648055	MN 64826	666211	MN 61338	621408	VET DESSUS FEMMES MAT TEX
845	OUTERWEAR KNIT NONELASTC	MN 82810	490034	MN 83165	496995	MN 92547	532995	MN 78967	497913	VET DESSOUS,ACCES BONNET
851	*FOOTWEAR	MP 81795	700364	MP 87286	752050	MP 93891	821353	MP 84752	774427	CHAUSSURES
85102	FOOTWEAR LEATHER	MP 59040	576997	MP 62893	617777	MP 67472	670967	MP 57305	613790	CHAUS SEMELLES EN CUIR
87	PRECISION INSTRUMNTS NES		2758650		3374654		3656604		3744127	INSTRUM,APPAR SCIENT NDA
872	MEDICAL INSTRUMENTS NES		480956		511656		540638		561858	INSTR,APP MEDIC-CHIR NDA
87202	OTH MEDICAL INSTRUMENTS		403250		427470		450462		475284	INSTRUM,APP MEDECINE
874	MEASURNG,CONTROLNG INSTR		1993371		2467612		2709003		2734858	INSTRUMENTS DE MESURE
8743	GAS,LIQUID CONTROL INSTR		836031		1091811		1304591		1200124	APP,INSTR MESURE FLUIDES
88	PHOTO EQU,OPTICL GDS ETC		1136247		1194919		1258109		1266303	APP,FOURN PHOTO,OP,MONTR
882	PHOTO,CINEMA SUPPLIES		560358		582439		610383		616908	PRODUITS PHOTO,CINEMA
8822	PHOTO FILM EXC DEV CINMA		461365		468187		475649		478397	PLAQUES,PELLICULES,FILMS
89	MISC MANUFCTRD GOODS NES		6738621		7379927		7848514		7764984	ART MANUFACTURES DIVERS

4. General Imports F.O.B. by Commodities according to the S.I.T.C. (Rev. 2) in thousand U.S. Dollars
Importations Générales F.O.B. par Produits d'après la C.T.C.I. (Rév. 2) en milliers de Dollars E.U.

SITC CTCI	COMMODITY	1993 WEIGHT POIDS	1993 VALUE VALEUR	1994 WEIGHT POIDS	1994 VALUE VALEUR	1995 WEIGHT POIDS	1995 VALUE VALEUR	1996 WEIGHT POIDS	1996 VALUE VALEUR	PRODUIT
892	PRINTED MATTER		1852713		1973088		2144461		2092930	IMPRIMES
8921	PRINTED BOOKS,GLOBES,ETC		865396		939130		1006598		972886	LIVRES,BROCHURES,CARTES
89211	PRINTED BOOKS,PAMPHLETS		848428		922745		990642		955027	LIVRES,BROCHURES
8922	NEWSPAPERS,PERIODICALS		567343		615655		638761		645356	JOURNAUX ET PERIODIQUES
893	ARTICLES OF PLASTIC NES		1366976		1534081		1639808		1691291	OUVRAGES EN MAT DIVIS 58
8939	MISC PLASTIC ARTICLES		1030572		1158777		1208441		1248782	ART DIVERS EN MAT DIV 58
89399	OTHR PLASTC ARTICLES NES		897466		1021826		1086313		1126009	AUT OUV MAT DIV 58
894	TOYS,SPORTING GOODS,ETC		1444139		1541003		1614198		1627128	VOITURES ENFANTS,JOUETS
8942	TOYS,INDOOR GAMES ETC		1048478		1088396		1084782		1174410	JOUETS,JEUX ETC
89424	INDOOR GAME EQUIPMENT		523676		525352		449229		495876	ART,JEUX DE SOCIETE
898	MUSICAL INSTRUMENTS,PTS		1182539		1357540		1400459		1299825	INSTRUMENTS DE MUSIQUE
8983	SOUND RECRDNG TAPE,DISCS		1072177		1254674		1293407		1201714	SUPPORTS SON POUR 763
89832	RECORDED DISCS,TAPES ETC		849772		1037412		1087984		997886	DISQUES,PHONO,BANDES
899	OTHER MANUFACTURED GOODS		463029		499563		547245		556692	AUT ART MANUF DIVERS NDA
9	GOODS NOT CLASSD BY KIND		4633201		4679152		5034699		6615663	ART TRANSACT NON CLASSES
931	*SPECIAL TRANSACTIONS		3423168		3800761		4220713		5473969	TRANS.SPECIALES
971	*GOLD,NON MONETARY NES	K 3218821	939622	K 3179163	605917	K 1474256	511735	K 1416954	742171	OR NON MONETAIRE
97101	NONMON GLD UNWRT,SEMIMFD	K 55360	525068	K 36486	315300	K 23774	237818	K 229315	472238	OR,ALLIAGES D'OR BRUTS
97103	GOLD SWEEPINGS,WASTE ETC	K 3161985	414028	K 3142082	290259	K 1450377	273740	K 1187382	269606	CENDRES ORFEVR,DECHET OR

5. General Exports F.O.B. by Commodities according to the S.I.T.C. (Rev. 2) in thousand U.S. Dollars
Exportations Générales F.O.B. par Produits d'après la C.T.C.I. (Rév. 2) en milliers de Dollars E.U.

SITC CTCI	COMMODITY	1993 WEIGHT POIDS	1993 VALUE VALEUR	1994 WEIGHT POIDS	1994 VALUE VALEUR	1995 WEIGHT POIDS	1995 VALUE VALEUR	1996 WEIGHT POIDS	1996 VALUE VALEUR	PRODUIT
	ALL COMMODITIES		144631676		166254561		192160647		201573714	TOUS PRODUITS
0	FOOD AND LIVE ANIMALS		9277238		10173841		11473945		12663273	ALIMENTS,ANIMAUX VIVANTS
001	*LIVE ANIMALS FOR FOOD		1057957		955835		1082688		1371433	ANIMAUX VIVANTS
0011	BOVINE SPECIES,LIVE	N 1212459	934482	N 1017257	829900	N 1135555	884509	N 1514244	1027269	ESPECE BOVINE
00119	— OTHR THAN FR BREEDING	N 1202220	918990	N 1010573	817896	N 1132234	878040	N 1509658	1018308	BOVINS NON REPRODUCTEURS
01	MEAT AND PREPARATIONS		1084556		1112070		1274788		1518180	VIANDES ET PREPARATIONS
011	MEAT FRESH,CHILLD,FROZEN	W 436950	975894	W 472797	985691	W 554669	1116521	W 623680	1320122	VIANDES FRAICHES,REF,CONGE
0113	PIG MEAT FRESH,CHLD,FRZN	W 210018	483131	W 204478	458986	W 238391	548191	W 242854	626331	VIANDE DE PORC
03	FISH AND PREPARATIONS		2036690		2156426		2298904		2269046	POISSONS ET PREPARATIONS
034	FISH,FRESH,CHILLED,FROZN	W 295002	874852	W 245507	829683	W 225693	757688	W 247626	784021	POISSON FRAIS, REFRIG,CONG
036	SHELL FISH FRESH,FROZEN	W 88527	677356	W 110238	888240	W 120027	1063461	W 120202	935902	CRUSTACES,MOLLUSQUES
04	CEREALS AND PREPARATIONS		3159699		3714552		4110747		4391309	CEREALES ET PRODUITS
041	WHEAT ETC UNMILLED	MW 17901	2195029	MW 21290	2577985	MW 16503	2866375	MW 13781	2840290	FROMENT,EPEAUTRE
0411	DURUM WHEAT UNMILLED	W 2344579	319185	W 2904004	496516	W 3773923	812876	W 3191761	709315	FROMENT DUR NON MOULU
0412	OTHER WHEAT ETC UNMILLED	MW 15557	1875844	MW 18386	2081470	MW 12729	2053499	MW 10590	2130976	AUTRE FROMENT NON MOULU
048	CEREAL ETC PREPARATIONS	W 505432	414610	W 617300	471054	W 692478	567170	W 797048	714318	PREPTNS A BASE CEREALES
05	VEGETABLES AND FRUIT		639146		828400		1044733		1136549	LEGUMES ET FRUITS
054	VEG ETC FRSH,SMPLY PRSVD		440590		600816		793013	W 2312956	853276	LEGUMES FRAIS,CONG,SECS
081	*FEEDING STUFF FOR ANIML	W 2752590	453675	W 2981454	500068	W 3273514	576436	W 3259131	719915	NOURRITURE POUR ANIMAUX
1	BEVERAGES AND TOBACCO		1317504		896290		869830		985564	BOISSONS ET TABACS
11	BEVERAGES		686396		752120		734877		825378	BOISSONS
112	ALCOHOLIC BEVERAGES	W 373547	582029	W 441301	593861	W 421681	562391	W 397675	613168	BOISSONS ALCOOLIQUES
12	TOBACCO AND MANUFACTURES		631108		144170		134953		160186	TABACS BRUTS FABRIQUES
122	TOBACCO,MANUFACTURED	W 23087	539933	W 7736	78926	W 8641	66125	W 7719	53568	TABACS FABRIQUES
1222	CIGARETTES	W 18516	485974	W 4879	60183	W 4448	47085	W 1966	31469	CIGARETTES
2	CRUDE MATERLS,EXCL FUELS		16384836		19572213		23687697		21638555	MAT BRUTES NON COMESTIBLES
22	OIL SEEDS,OLEAGINOUS FRT		727202		1352042		1504633		1188592	GRAINES,FRUITS OLEAGINEUX
222	SEEDS FOR'SOFT'FIXED OIL	W 2558829	619604	W 4165847	1151722	W 4151923	1233167	W 2896540	915280	GRAINES HUILES FIXES
2226	RAPE AND COLZA SEEDS	W 2107267	496472	W 3670423	1025878	W 3436976	1043856	W 2416103	759862	GRAINES DE NAVETTE,COLZA
24	CORK AND WOOD		7847615		8843203		8446639		9674515	LIEGE ET BOIS
248	WOOD SHAPED,SLEEPERS		7552033		8587316		8178626		9407501	BOIS SIMPLEMENT TRAVAILLES
2482	LUMBER SHAPED CONIFER		7249703		8249645		7817691	MW 47535	9015727	CONIFERES SCIES,RABOTES
24821	LUMBER SAWN ETC CONIFER	MW 26841	7105830	MW 28091	8101073	MW 29722	7667082	MW 31034	8869229	CONIFERES SCIES LONGITUD
251	*PULP AND WASTE PAPER	MW 9547	3605215	MW 10777	4976280	MW 11302	8074351	MW 10900	5141735	PATES A PAPIER,DECHETS
2517	SODA,SULPHATE WOOD PULP	W 7438576	2873224	W 8333448	4022048	W 8546417	6552764	W 8237548	4202852	PATES CHIMIQUES AU SULFATE
25172	— BLEACHED,NONDISSOLVNG	W 7300603	2823398	W 8152745	3935188	W 8444154	6484026	W 8145514	4163281	PATES BLANCHIES
2519	OTHER CELLULOSIC PULPS	W 962373	301458	W 1188832	463545	W 1285574	801393	W 1284231	470529	AUTRES PATES CELLULOSE
25191	SEMI–CHEMICAL WOOD PULP	W 962366	301444	W 1185108	461842	W 1281692	799611	W 1266086	463578	PATES MI CHIMIQUES
27	CRUDE FERTLZR,MINRLS NES		635673		749475		868778		870122	ENGRAIS MINERAUX BRUTS
28	METALLIFEROUS ORES,SCRAP		2644043		2663687		3657975		3514462	MINERAIS METAL,DECHETS
281	IRON ORE,CONCENTRATES	MW 26140	621467	MW 30126	689270	MW 28967	677645	MW 28880	723914	MINERAIS DE FER
287	BASE METAL ORES,CONC NES	MW 86302	1319120	MW 88912	1164866	MW 799460	1911487	MW 890832	1872322	MINERAIS METAUX COMMUNS
2871	CPR ORE ETC,CEMENT COPPR	W 312304	488713	W 238628	402374	W 270133	668624	W 466800	472234	MINERAIS DE CUIVRE,MATTES
28711	COPPER ORES,EXCL MATTE	W 301560	446625	W 219423	370569	W 256654	634266	W 448485	429942	MINERAIS DE CUIVRE
2872	NICKEL ORES,CONCENTRATES	W 59440	456464	W 71778	409356	W 78707	675883	W 96242	790419	MINERAIS DE NICKEL
28722	NICKEL MATTE,SINTERS,ETC	W 59440	456464	W 71778	409356	W 78707	675883	W 96242	790413	MATTES,SINTERS
288	NONFERR METAL SCRAP NES	W 551076	443469	W 558574	527353	W 503662	657342	W 513018	542786	DECHETS NON FERREUX
2882	OTHER BASE MTL SCRAP NES	W 362173	397691	W 411490	497478	W 425427	612593	W 400942	514055	AUTRES DECHETS
3	MINERAL FUELS ETC		15195400		16112020		17270946		20513892	COMBUSTIBLES MINERAUX LUB
32	COAL,COKE AND BRIQUETTES		1600665		1676786		1789100		1741045	HOUILLES,COKES,BRIQUETTES
322	COAL,LIGNITE AND PEAT	MW 29081	1581143	MW 32037	1656628	MW 34543	1766597	MW 32262	1716362	HOUILLES,LIGNITES,TOURBE
3222	OTH COAL,NOT AGGLOMERATD	MW 28275	1430786	MW 31090	1493786	MW 33720	1609019	MW 31371	1567240	AUTRES HOUILLES
33	PETROLEUM AND PRODUCTS		7423350		7397006		9138781		11034475	PETROLE ET DERIVES
333	CRUDE PETROLEUM	MW 45022	5353667	MW 49007	5443258	MW 56312	7081755	MW 56733	8099160	HUILES BRUTES DE PETROLE
334	PETROLEUM PRODUCTS,REFIN	MW 12195	1973854	MW 11981	1794545	MW 11612	1879453	MW 14237	2731432	PRODUITS RAFFINES
3341	GASOLINE,OTH LIGHT OILS	W 3463474	581611	W 3692983	567721	W 3968711	682012	W 5198030	1010580	ESSENCES POUR MOTEURS
33411	MOTOR,AVIATION SPIRIT	W 3463474	581611	W 3692983	567721	W 3968711	682012	W 5198030	1010580	ESSENCES MOTEURS D'AVIONS
3343	GAS OILS	W 4748424	790363	W 4604102	691324	W 4418686	677652	W 5243056	996970	GAS OILS
341	*GAS,NATURAL AND MANUFCT		5506926		6076059		5486692		6848203	GAZ NATUREL,GAZ MANUFACT
3413	PETROLM GASES,LIQUEFIED	W 5168678	1009068	W 5569436	1049537	MW 10497	1466393	MW 9877	1790077	GAZ DE PETROLE LIQUEFIE
34131	LIQUEFIED PROPANE,BUTANE	W 4129678	652154	W 4204215	554954	W 4914735	638462	W 4445215	846227	PROPANE,BUTANE LIQUEFIES
34139	OTH HYDROCARBON GAS LQFD	W 1039000	356915	W 1365221	494583	W 5581886	827931	W 5431590	943849	HYDROCARBURES GAZEUX NDA
3414	PETROLEUM GASES, GASEOUS	MV 63602807	4497850	MV 72362572	5026522	MV 79264963	4020205	MV 80974561	5058126	GAZ DE PETROLE GAZEUX
351	*ELECTRIC CURRENT	MH 29364	664460	MH 44308	962170	MH 40378	856373	MH 41583	890170	ENERGIE ELECTRIQUE
5	CHEMCLS,RELATED PROD NES		7273767		8801121		10901951		11119454	PRODUITS CHIMIQUES
51	ORGANIC CHEMICALS		1354795		1651430		2263343		1987693	PROD CHIMIQ ORGANIQUES
511	HYDROCARBONS NES,DERIVS	W 1423592	523322	W 1427134	615685	W 1705491	940397	W 2115994	857357	HYDROCARBURES NDA
5112	CYCLIC HYDROCARBONS	W 951769	365509	W 966446	468713	W 1080648	728125	W 1096510	573504	HYDROCARBURES CYCLIQUES
512	ALCOHOLS,PHENOLS ETC		322526		516898		720138		560866	PHENOLS,PHENOLS–ALCOOLS
5121	ACYCLIC ALCOHOLS,DERIVS		319026		506117		709444		549652	ALCOOLS ACYCLIQUES
52	INORGANIC CHEMICALS		1329530		1550139		1720242		1950533	PROD CHIM INORGANIQUES
522	INORG ELEMNTS,OXIDES,ETC	W 3628114	570770	W 4186558	659438	W 4130104	774488	W 4165459	799978	ELEMENTS INORGANIQUES
524	RADIOACTIVE ETC MATERIAL		388963		475391		510117		702476	MATIERES RADIOACTIVES
5241	RADIOACTIVE ELEMENTS ETC		378543		452269		498809		613713	RADIOELEMENTS,ISOTOPES
541	*MEDICINAL,PHARM PRODUCT		394677		504696		611092		683353	PROD MEDICINAUX PHARMACEUT
55	PERFUME,CLEANING ETC PRD		381777		478268		580988		659247	PROD POUR PARFUM,TOILETTE
562	*FERTILIZERS,MANUFACTURE	MW 12841	1275902	MW 15865	1567183	MW 16587	1685517	MW 15683	1559037	ENGRAIS MANUFACTURES
5623	CHEM POTASSIC FERTILIZER	MW 10171	929792	MW 12996	1196618	MW 13803	1285588	MW 12942	1132094	ENGRAIS POTASSIQUES
56231	POTASSIUM CHLORIDE	MW 10147	926578	MW 12961	1189091	MW 13795	1283252	MW 12927	1129058	CHLORURE DE POTASSIUM
58	PLASTIC MATERIALS ETC		1758209		2223857		2993347		3064509	MAT PLAST ARTIFICIELLES
583	POLYMERIZATION ETC PRODS	W 1759705	1509582		1902794		2624747	W 2578188	2620458	PROD POLYMERISATION
5831	POLYETHYLENE	W 1131726	728745	W 1289365	923305	W 1404696	1336568	W 1642439	1334254	POLYETHYLENE
58311	— IN PRIMARY FORMS	W 1079650	631778	W 1225653	800771	W 1335628	1185130	W 1563317	1170728	POLYETHYLENE PRIMAIRES
59	CHEMICAL MATERIALS NES		463452		486898		612923		721208	MAT PROD CHIMIQUES NDA
6	BASIC MANUFACTURES		22601770		25485002		32273131		32789021	ART MANUFACTURES
62	RUBBER MANUFACTURES NES		1299156		1463320		1580018		1708942	CAOUTCHOUC MANUFACTURE
625	RUBBER TYRES, TUBES ETC	MN 19788	883598	MN 24415	939022	MN 23258	948946	MN 23863	1039518	PNEUS CAOUTCHOUC VULCANISE
6251	TYRES NEW FOR MOTOR CARS	MN 15797	529171	MN 19746	594818	MN 18009	594194	MN 18864	642249	PNEUS POUR VOITURES
63	WOOD,CORK MANUFACTRS NES		1413106		1785460		2221583		2503085	OUVRAGES LIEGE ET BOIS
634	VENEERS,PLYWOOD,ETC		860340		1103263		1368217		1427414	PLACAGES,CONTRE–PLAQUES
6343	IMPROVED,RECONSTIT WOOD		530924		721063		828697		882700	BOIS AMELIORES,RECONST
63432	RECONSTITUTED WOOD	W 1935960	530851	W 2240529	720937	W 2796108	828539	W 3377162	881793	BOIS RECONSTITUES
635	WOOD MANUFACTURES NES		551934		681219		852539		1074844	ART MANUF EN BOIS NDA
6353	BUILDERS WOODWRK,PREFABS		192865		315429		434256		631495	OUVRAGES DE MENUISERIE
64	PAPER,PAPERBOARD AND MFR		7851116		8297620		11463594		10922788	PAPIERS,CARTONS & OUVRAGES
641	PAPER AND PAPERBOARD	MW 13113	7429628	MW 14025	7742504	MW 14234	10654106	MW 13955	10002662	PAPIERS ET CARTONS
6411	NEWSPRINT	W 8995904	4688640	MW 9387	4592503	MW 9166	6061219	W 8593681	5633021	PAPIER JOURNAL
6412	PRINTG,WRITING PAPER NES	W 593530	485505	W 699757	592214	W 790876	932801	W 936307	940294	PAPIERS POUR L'IMPRESSION
64122	— COATED,IMPREGNATD ETC	W 469244	396176	W 569403	491991	W 615116	729230	W 667438	698617	PAPIERS IMPRESSION COUCHES
6413	KRAFT PAPER,PAPERBOARD	W 801971	379839	W 914187	444468	W 932530	641278	W 949326	553280	PAPIER ET CARTON KRAFT
6415	PAPER,PAPERBRD,BULK,NES	W 2182119	1272093	W 2412181	1430545	W 2713143	2219931	W 2761262	2052480	PAPIERS,CARTONS ROULEAUX

5. General Exports F.O.B. by Commodities according to the S.I.T.C. (Rev. 2) in thousand U.S. Dollars
Exportations Générales F.O.B. par Produits d'après la C.T.C.I. (Rév. 2) en milliers de Dollars E.U.

SITC CTCI	COMMODITY	1993		1994		1995		1996		PRODUIT
		WEIGHT POIDS	VALUE VALEUR	WEIGHT POIDS	VALUE VALEUR	WEIGHT POIDS	VALUE VALEUR	WEIGHT POIDS	VALUE VALEUR	
64159	OTHER PAPER ETC,BULK,NES	W 1877676	1179037	W 2070746	1309602	W 2413198	2061113	W 2429621	1939067	AUT PAPIER ROULEAUX FEUILLES
642	PAPER,ETC,PRECUT,ARTS OF		421489		555116		809489		920126	PAP,CARTONS DECOUPES
65	TEXTILE YARN,FABRICS,ETC		974224		1171419		1375775		1652930	FILS,TISSUS,ARTICLES TEXTILE
66	NONMETAL MINERAL MFS NES		1032862		1231206		1450497		1640985	ART MIN NON METALLIQUES
67	IRON AND STEEL		2647184		2776955		3129342		3201452	FER ET ACIER
672	IRON,STEEL PRIMARY FORMS	W 1276488	474798	W 847310	399787	W 1018757	522571	W 2619398	469025	LINGOTS FER,ACIER
673	IRON,STEEL SHAPES ETC		628993	W 1354097	664576	W 1437704	755204	W 1675659	841461	BARRES,PROFIL FER,ACIER
674	IRN,STL UNIV,PLATE,SHEET	W 1392083	765612	W 1373203	836656	W 1299183	827116	W 1369944	836025	LARGES PLATS,TOLES
678	IRON,STL TUBES,PIPES,ETC		419022		488392		566257		605708	TUBES,TUYAUX EN FONTE,FER
68	NON–FERROUS METALS		5420660		6377807		8211021		7896930	METAUX NON FERREUX
682	COPPER EXC CEMENT COPPER		957357		1121693		1718224		1532444	CUIVRE
6821	COPPER NES,ALLOYS,UNWRT	W 408606	807880	W 388843	906673	W 471895	1407100	W 465743	1202877	CUIVRE BRUT
68212	COPPER REFINED,UNWROUGHT	W 408553	807798	W 388787	906557	W 430666	1288268	W 460838	1190140	CUIVRE AFFINE BRUT
683	NICKEL		647160	W 94336	602458	W 98833	844044		889298	NICKEL
6831	NICKEL,ALLOYS UNWROUGHT	W 99595	555212	W 82467	492403	W 86234	711021	W 97155	757922	NICKEL ET ALLIAGES BRUTS
684	ALUMINIUM		2847851		3500118		4263951		3939014	ALUMINIUM
6841	ALUMINIUM,ALLOYS,UNWRGHT	W 1841116	2279390	W 1877362	2766036	W 1718805	3283731	W 1820450	2987892	ALUMINIUM,ALLIAGES BRUTS
6842	ALUMINIUM,ALLOYS WORKED		568461		734082		980220		951122	ALUMINIUM,ALLIAGES OUVRE
68422	ALUMNM PLATE,SHEET,STRIP	W 218453	407839	W 227494	454600	W 251442	600605	W 257137	552019	TOLES, PLANCHES EN ALU
686	ZINC	W 510334	528221	W 568445	575032	W 546810	608213	W 588932	656335	ZINC
6861	ZINC,ALLOYS UNWROUGHT	W 498164	509918	W 560237	561053	W 538783	591345	W 581770	641747	ZINC ET ALLIAGES BRUTS
69	METAL MANUFACTURES NES		1896259		2297582		2744942		3156124	ART MANUFACT EN METAL NDA
699	BASE METAL MFRS NES		908810		1076125		1252041		1480802	ART MANUFACTURES MET NDA
6991	LOCKSMITHS WARES,ETC		299083		368196		433090		615306	ARTICLES DE SERRURERIE
7	MACHINES,TRANSPORT EQUIP		57039752		66531256		75081047		78636800	MACHINES MATERIEL TRANSPORT
71	POWER GENERATING EQUIPMT		3741839		3664023		4122187		5272219	MACHINES GENERATRICES
713	INTRNL COMBUS PSTN ENGIN		1818535		1841873		1766439		2525963	MOTEURS EXPL COMB INT, PIECE
7132	MOTOR VEHCL PISTN ENGINS	N 797000	1200957	N 749163	1124122	N 628386	1004959	N 896794	1741529	MOTEURS EXPL POUR VEHICULES
7139	PISTON ENGINE PARTS NES		586527		689527		723142		692605	PIECES POUR 713.2,3,8
714	ENGINES AND MOTORS NES		1354199		1190355		1496078		1795783	MOTEURS NON ELECTRIQUES
7148	GAS TURBINES NES	N 1278	512392	N 1059	398057	N 1296	499179	N 1357	556565	TURBINES A GAZ
7149	ENGINE & MOTOR PARTS NES		642361		632051		765991		886771	PIECES 714 ET 718.88
71491	PARTS NES OF 7144,71481		509611		501002		602617		672492	PIECES DES PROPULSEURS
72	MACHS FOR SPCL INDUSTRYS		2062109		2521882		3134824		3242589	MAC SPECIALES POUR INDUST
728	OTH MACHY FOR SPCL INDUS		783443		1006756		1253535		1195184	AUT MACH IND PARTICULIERES
7284	MACHY FOR SPCL INDUS NES		670398		864774		1090075		997604	MACH SPEC IND PARTICUL.
73	METALWORKING MACHINERY		376557		459281		553232		632589	MACH TRAVAIL DES METAUX
74	GENRL INDUSTRL MACHY NES		3167836		4466807		5100740		5415585	MACH APP INDUSTRIE
741	HEATING,COOLING EQUIPMNT		474495		506128		533172		636340	MACH CHAUFFAGE,PIECES
743	PUMPS NES,CENTRFUGES ETC		401410		458844		601177		828982	POMPES COMPRES,VENT ETC
744	MECHANICAL HANDLING EQU		639412		826690		1004508		1114132	EQUIP MANUTENTION PIECES
749	NONELEC MACH PTS,ACC NES		1206289		2175155		2357670		2119170	PIECES MACH NON ELEC NDA
7499	OTH NONELEC MCHY PTS NES		443606		1214101		1270924		945126	PIECES NON ELECT NDA
74991	FOUNDRY MOULDS ETC NES		409993		1175502		1224563		901526	MOULES POUR METAUX
75	OFFICE MACHNES,ADP EQUIP		3573564		4643040		5901549		5178155	MACH BUREAU TRAIT AUTOM
752	AUTOMTIC DATA PROC EQUIP		1407140		1647695		1937051		1691752	MACH TRAIT INFORMATION
7523	DIGITL CENTRL PROCESSORS		550516		835580		899663		773028	UNITES CENTRALES
759	OFFICE,ADP MCH PTS,ACCES		2091974		2925466		3875728		3374727	PIECES DU 751 ET 752
7599	ACCTG,ETC,ADP MCH PTS,AC		1942077		2763634		3751002		3242142	PIECES DU 751 ET 752
76	TELECOMM,SOUND EQUIPMENT		2223253		2701034		3245539		4136708	EQUIPMENT DE TELECOM
764	TELECOM EQPT,PTS,ACC NES		2138163		2584436		3103197		3980771	EQUIP TELECOM,PIECES
7641	LINE TELEPHONE,ETC EQUIP		475279		537715		744000		943304	APP TELEPHON PAR FIL
7643	TV,RADIO TRANSMITTRS ETC		347196		517524		592340		780960	APP EMET TELE RADIO
7649	PTS NES OF EQUIPMT OF 76		1163146		1357844		1545781		1941073	PIECES DE LA DIV 76
76491	PTS NES OF APPAR OF 7641		1007607		1170662		1316538		1597149	PIECES POUR 764.1
77	ELECTRIC MACHNRY NES ETC		4054135		4605191		5535804		6565361	MACH APP ELECT NDA
772	SWITCHGEAR ETC,PARTS NES		917587		1032723		1069604		1103192	APP COUPURE,SECT ETC
7721	SWITCHGEAR ETC		503223		571156		598737		681432	APP COUPURE,SECTIONMNT
776	TRANSISTORS,VALVES,ETC		1708451		1891192		2405494		3018464	LAMPES,TUBES,VALVES
7764	ELECTRONIC MICROCIRCUITS	MN 197755	1562027	MN 289313	1725954	MN 287879	2206368	MN 298598	2797195	MICROSTRUCTURES ELECTRON
778	ELECTRICAL MACHINERY NES		559599		696452		794070		954504	AUTRES MACH ELECT NDA
78	ROAD VEHICLES		34850079		39876908		42966923		42978202	VEHICULES ROUTIERS
781	PASS MOTOR VEH EXC BUSES	N 1503336	19024322	N 1627162	23459009	N 1748876	26000495	N 1723845	26168170	AUTO TRANSPORT PERSONNES
782	LORRIES,SPCL MTR VEH NES	N 536194	7807078	N 502127	7029204	N 467285	6952140	N 437994	6710777	VEHICULES SPECIAUX,MARCH
7821	LORRIES,TRUCKS	N 535656	7754044	N 501630	6983953	N 466569	6897193	N 437283	6654152	VEHICULES TRANSP MARCHAND
783	ROAD MOTOR VEHICLES NES	N 29520	915023	N 43678	1724766	N 41284	2133449	N 45321	2099384	VEHICULES ROUTIERS NDA
7831	BUSES	N 20631	429243	N 23535	583396	N 14012	537305	N 22655	740478	VOITURES TRANSPORT COMMUN
7832	TRACTORS FOR TR–TRAILERS	N 8889	485781	N 20143	1141371	N 27272	1596144	N 22666	1358906	TRACTEURS ROUTIERS
784	MOTOR VEH PRTS,ACCES NES		6984555		7518984		7683279		7801567	PIECES 722,781,782,783
7849	OTHER MOTOR VEHCL PARTS		6825908		7384451		7542431		7655540	PIECES 722,781,782,783
79	OTHR TRANSPORT EQUIPMENT		2990381		3593090		4520249		5215393	AUTRE MATERIEL TRANSPORT
791	RAILWAY VEHICLES		582641		955394		965990		1014075	VEHIC MAT CHEMINS DE FER
792	AIRCRAFT ETC		2150915		2292709		3005556		3478719	APP NAVIGATION AERIENNE
7923	AIRCRFT NES2000–15000KG	N 86	951107	N 82	921263	N 108	1396251	N 137	1811160	AERODYNES 2000 A 15000 KG
7929	AIRCRAFT PARTS NES		744512		764412		852389		1013570	PIECES DU 792
793	SHIPS AND BOATS ETC		256825		344987		548703		722600	NAVIRES BATEAUX,ETC
7932	SHIPS AND BOATS NES	N 70499	242881	N 90927	329172	N 139565	540076	N 160664	707084	NAVIRES ET BATEAUX
79321	YACHTS,SPORTS VESSLS ETC	N 70348	240938	N 89449	308684	N 138947	532378	N 160584	704750	BATEAUX DE PLAISANCE
8	MISC MANUFACTURED GOODS		6675370		8058240		9614640		11208998	ART MANUFACTURES DIVERS
821	*FURNITURE,PARTS THEREOF		1693407		2179960		2619927		3112376	MEUBLES ET PIECES
8211	CHAIRS,SEATS AND PARTS		843687		1057801		1223546		1395709	SIEGES ET PIECES
82111	CHAIRS AND OTHER SEATS		277596		589322		570714		648388	SIEGES
82119	PTS NES OF CHAIRS ETC		566091		468479		652833		747321	PIECES DU 821.11
8219	FURNITURE AND PARTS NES		803954		1061080		1311064		1635493	AUTRES MEUBLES ET PIECES
82192	WOOD FURNITURE NES		473971		636870		746340		964435	MEUBLES NDA EN BOIS
84	CLOTHING AND ACCESSORIES		665447		830710		1019846		1242384	VETEMENTS
87	PRECISION INSTRUMNTS NES		1044622		1301437		1395584		1608503	INSTRUM,APPAR SCIENT NDA
874	MEASURNG,CONTROLNG INSTR		846007		979332		1084679		1210551	INSTRUMENTS DE MESURE
89	MISC MANUFCTRD GOODS NES		2600615		3043247		3774511		4330667	ART MANUFACTURES DIVERS
892	PRINTED MATTER		644205		662991		814059		895138	IMPRIMES
893	ARTICLES OF PLASTIC NES		925976		1176690		1448182		1671627	OUVRAGES EN MAT DIVIS 58
8939	MISC PLASTIC ARTICLES		635624		794432		955362		1126847	ART DIVERS EN MAT DIV 58
89399	OTHR PLASTC ARTICLES NES		579939		718389		851730		1007891	AUT OUV MAT DIV 58
894	TOYS,SPORTING GOODS,ETC		401755		507896		694515		823782	VOITURES ENFANTS,JOUETS
9	GOODS NOT CLASSD BY KIND		8544266		10213983		10496675		11442826	ART TRANSACT NON CLASSES
931	*SPECIAL TRANSACTIONS		6003065		7285007		8043046		8659731	TRANS.SPECIALES
971	*GOLD,NON MONETARY NES	K 204518	2300298	K 229942	2598915	K 172590	2076189	K 201749	2502843	OR NON MONETAIRE
97101	NONMON GLD UNWRT,SEMIMFD	K 201463	2286139	K 210476	2572335	K 170976	2060346	K 197288	2460175	OR,ALLIAGES D'OR BRUTS

FOOT NOTES – NOTES

TABLE 1 –

1 Gold exports refer to new gold production available for export.

Canada

Foot Notes (Continued) – Notes (Suite)

TABLE 3 –
1 Imports of Caribbean, Central and South American goods consigned from the United States are classified by countries of production.
TABLEAU 1 –
1 Les exportations d'or se réfèrent à l'or nouvellement produit pour l'exportation.
TABLEAU 3 –
1 Les importations de produits en provenance des Caraibes, de l'Amérique Centrale ou du Sud via une consignation aux Etats–Unis sont classées d'après le pays de production.

1. HISTORICAL SERIES, 1960–1995 SPECIAL TRADE, IMPORTS C.I.F., EXPORTS F.O.B.
SERIES HISTORIQUES, 1960–1995 COMMERCE SPECIAL, IMPORTATIONS C.A.F., EXPORTATIONS F.O.B

YEAR ANNEE	VALUE IN MILLION C. VERDE ESCUDOS / VALEUR EN MILLION C. VERDE ESCUDOS — MERCHANDISE –MARCHANDISE		GOLD –OR		CONVERSION FACTORS U.S. CENTS PER C. VERDE ESCUDO / FACTEURS DE CONVERSION CENTS E.U. PAR C. VERDE ESCUDO		INDEX NUMBERS –INDICES — QUANTUM		UNIT VALUE VALEUR UNITAIRE	
	IMPORTS	EXPORTS	IMPORTS	EXPORTS	IMPORTS	EXPORTS	IMPORTS	EXPORTS	IMPORTS	EXPORTS
1960	348.80	306.50			3.4780	3.4780				
1961	185.50	27.80			3.4780	3.4780				
1962	197.20	22.20			3.4780	3.4780				
1963	170.20	24.10			3.4780	3.4780				
1964	200.70	27.50			3.4780	3.4780				
1965	228.30	28.00			3.4780	3.4780				
1966	244.20	32.90			3.4780	3.4780				
1967	258.80	30.90			3.4780	3.4780				
1968	281.90	40.80			3.4780	3.4780				
1969	418.80	44.60			3.4780	3.4780				
1970	469.40	47.70			3.4780	3.4780				
1971	573.50	45.60			3.4780	3.4780				
1972	656.90	48.00			3.6700	3.6700				
1973	833.10	47.80			4.0636	4.0750				
1974	869.30	52.70			3.9381	3.9328				
1975	1010.90	61.30			3.9220	3.9220				
1976	913.60	48.50			3.3170	3.3170				
1977	1284.80	74.50			3.4190	3.3600				
1978	1908.20	75.10			2.2472	2.2700				
1979	1986.90	92.10			2.0408	2.0354				
1980	2742.30	170.50			2.4724	2.4764				
1981	3446.60	140.80			2.0563	2.0600				
1982	5086.00	191.00			1.7265	1.7265				
1983	6217.00	246.00			1.4018	1.4018				
1984	7011.00	212.00			1.1825	1.1825				
1985	7605.00	524.00			1.0926	1.0926				
1986	8601.00	355.00			1.2483	1.2483				
1987	8596.00	567.00			1.3777	1.3781				
1988	8626.00	237.00			1.3916	1.3557				
1989	8706.00	527.00			1.2857	1.3014				
1990	9495.00	398.00			1.4330	1.4734				
1991	10468.67	438.00			1.4043	1.4473				
1992	12233.62	327.00			1.4704	1.4538				
1993	12387.06	312.00			1.2440	1.2488				
1994	17110.91	407.87			1.2279	1.2266				
1995	19394.08	686.63			1.3015	1.3018				

2. IMPORTS BY BROAD ECONOMIC CATEGORY AND EXPORTS BY INDUSTRIAL ORIGIN. (PERCENTAGE OF TOTAL VALUE)
IMPORTATIONS PAR CATEGORIES ECONOMIQUES ET EXPORTATIONS PAR BRANCHE D'ACTIVITE.(EN POURCENTAGE DE LA VALEUR TOTALE)

IMPORTS – IMPORTATIONS

	1990	1991	1992	1993	1994	1995	1996
TOTAL IMPORTS–IMPORTATIONS TOTALES							
1 FOOD BEV–ALIMENTATION BOISSONS							
11 PRIMARY–PRODUITS DE BASE							
111 FOR INDUSTRY–POUR L'INDUSTRIE							
112 FOR HOUSEHOLDS–POUR LES MENAGES							
12 PROCESSED–PRODUITS ELABORES							
121 FOR INDUSTRY–POUR L'INDUSTRIE							
122 FOR HOUSEHOLDS–POUR LES MENAGES							
2 IND SUPPLIES–APPROV INDUSTRIELS							
21 PRIMARY–PRODUITS DE BASE							
22 PROCESSED–PRODUITS ELABORES							
3 FUELS–COMBUSTIBLES							
31 PRIMARY–PRODUITS DE BASE							
32 PROCESSED–PRODUITS ELABORES							
321 MOTOR SPIRIT–ESSENCE							
322 OTHER–AUTRES							
4 MACHINERY–EQUIPEMENT							
41 CAPITAL EQUIPMENT–MACHINES							
42 PARTS–PIECES ACCESSOIRES							
5 TRANSPORT–TRANSPORT							
51 PASSENGER CARS–AUTOMOBILES							
52 OTHER–AUTRES							
521 INDUSTRIAL–INDUSTRIELS							
522 NON INDUSTRIAL–NON INDUSTRIEL							
53 PARTS–PIECES ACCESSOIRES							
6 CONSUM GOODS–BIENS CONSOMMATION							
61 DURABLE–DURABLES							
62 SEMI DURABLE–SEMI DURABLES							
63 NON DURABLE–NON DURABLES							
7 GOODS NES–BIENS NDA							

EXPORTS – EXPORTATIONS

	1990	1991	1992	1993	1994	1995	1996
TOTAL EXPORTS–EXPORTATIONS TOTALES							
1 AGRICULTURE							
2 MINING QUARRY–INDUS EXTRACTIVES							
3 MANUFACTURING–IND MANUFACTUR							
31 FOOD BEV TOBACCO–ALIM BOISS TAB							
32 TEXTILES–INDUSTRIES TEXTILES							
33 WOOD & PRODUCTS–BOIS & PRODUITS							
34 PAPER & PRODUCTS–PAPIER & PRODT							
35 CHEMICALS–INDUSTRIES CHIMIQUES							
36 NON METAL MIN–MIN NON METAL							
37 BASIC METAL–IND METAL BASE							
38 METAL MANUF–MANUF METAL							
39 OTH MANUF IND–AUTRES MANUF							

3. TRADE BY PRINCIPAL COUNTRIES OF ORIGIN AND DESTINATION (VALUE IN THOUSAND U.S. DOLLARS)
ECHANGES SELON LES PRINCIPAUX PAYS D'ORIGINE ET DE DESTINATION (VALEUR EN MILLIERS DE DOLLARS EU)

COUNTRIES–PAYS	SPECIAL IMPORTS C.I.F. IMPORTATIONS SPECIALES C.A.F				
	1990	1991	1992	1993	1994
World	136310	146603	179858	154727	210128
Africa	6064	8321	15209	8712	6496
Americas	21662	11189	25992	19480	13425
Northern America	3348	2110	10398	5661	5246
LAIA	15553	5411	13261	11310	8114
CACM	305	842	285		29
Caribbean	2456	2826	2045	2490	36
Rest of America		0	3	18	1
As.ex F.USSR	7270	16743	10490	15252	18671
Eur.x F.USSR	97005	107411	125068	105854	164111
EU	92048	100864	116723	100360	159502
EFTA	614	435	3060	2326	2847
East Europe	3861	5160	5285	3168	1511
Other Europe	482		0		5
Former USSR	556			3629	3617
Oceania	39	1	5	9	354
Portugal	44551	50143	57875	51959	72559
Netherlands/Pays–Bas	15132	14348	18739	13153	16800
France,Monac	4184	3081	6431	6764	28972
Brazil/Brésil	14365	5390	10280	9213	7236
Japan/Japon	5185	7517	9004	9279	10444
Germany/Allemagne	4102	9349	6622	7651	8474
Belgium–Luxembourg	4327	6042	4675	5588	6553
USA/Etats–Unis d'Amer	3296	2082	10147	5425	4834
Sweden/Suède	3369	3787	4005	3611	8778
Spain/Espagne	7099	7864	3727	1150	1951
Denmark/Danemark	4548	2630	3052	2216	8126
Cote d'Ivoire	2360	5458	4759	4060	2236
Italy/Italie	1864	900	7677	2336	2247
United Kingdom	2360	2230	3325	3198	2933
Romania/Roumanie	223	3845	4858	3124	1387
Switz.Liecht	215	425	3043	2072	1935
Cuba	2433	1824	1718	422	0
So. Africa Customs Un	1201	458	2218	1100	1161
Pakistan	0	2228	650	0	3257
Argentina/Argentine	584	1	2837	1623	10
Nigeria/Nigéria	1051	725	1607	479	966
Albania/Albanie	3320	1087	78	1	
Former USSR/Anc. URSS	556			3629	
Israel/Israël	9	1625		268	2045
Viet Nam	807			2834	
Russian Federation					3617
Un. Rep. of Tanzania	887	350	907	413	806
Thailand/Thaïlande	2	497		2052	675
China/Chine	6	2650	203	77	104
Ireland/Irlande	7	258	8	2618	
Bahamas		338	307	2067	4
Senegal/Sénégal	212	487	820	1116	81
Austria/Autriche	478	188		110	1853
Turkey/Turquie	1	35	47	485	1553
Togo	193	192	941	297	321
Fm Yugoslav	482	952			246
Kenya		201	1368	1	
Gambia/Gambie		107	281	667	493
Malaysia/Malaisie	1021	1		34	323
Norway,SVD,JM	32	10	17	254	911
Guinea–Bissau	84	73	409	457	198
Colombia/Colombie			74	373	721
Cyprus/Chypre		984	58	6	0
Canada	53	28	251	236	412
Mauritius/Maurice		3	945		
Finland/Finlande	13	43	574		257
Honduras		824			29
Hong Kong	145	148	271	148	80
India/Inde		551	161	3	1
Bulgaria/Bulgarie	220	158	323		

COUNTRIES–PAYS	SPECIAL EXPORTS F.O.B. # 1 EXPORTATIONS SPECIALES F.O.B.				
	1990	1991	1992	1993	1994
Monde	28564	6128	4810	3826	5011
Afrique	1922	29	29	713	46
Amériques	366	124		1	16
Amérique du Nord	304	96		0	9
ALAI	59	27		0	7
MCAC	1			0	
Caraïbes	1	0			
Autre Amérique	1	0			0
Asie l'URSS exclus	9	34		40	18
Europe l'URSS exclus	3274	5931	4774	3070	4927
UE	3271	5928	4774	3070	4926
AELE		1		0	0
Europe de l'Est	1	2			0
Autre de l'Europe	1	1			0
Ancienne URSS	4				1
Océanie					
Portugal	2359	2541	3910	1868	2944
Netherlands/Pays–Bas	71	2616	463	129	104
Spain/Espagne	3	121	328	752	724
Algeria/Algérie	1821				
United Kingdom	428	15		3	730
France,Monac	172	81		223	254
Angola	61	25		615	
Italy/Italie	157	296		50	47
Canada	302	49			2
Germany/Allemagne	82	61	38	27	113
Belgium–Luxembourg		194	34	16	1
So. Africa Customs Un	1			72	3
Hong Kong				39	17
USA/Etats–Unis d'Amer	2	47		0	7
Guinea/Guinée				25	28
Japan/Japon	8	33			0
Brazil/Brésil	8	22			7
Guinea–Bissau			29	0	7
Togo	27				
Denmark/Danemark	0		0	2	6
Mauritania/Mauritanie	8				
Senegal/Sénégal		0		1	5
Argentina/Argentine	1	5			
Former USSR/Anc. URSS	4				
Romania/Roumanie	1	2			
Sweden/Suède	1	2			
Greece/Grèce		1			2
Cyprus/Chypre	0	1			1
Bahamas	1	0			
Russian Federation					1
Turkey/Turquie	1			0	
Bulgaria/Bulgarie	0				0
Fm Yugoslav	1				
Honduras	1			0	
India/Inde		1			
Iceland/Islande		1			
Cuba	0	0			
Korea Dem People's Rp	0				
Switz.Liecht				0	
Saudi Arabia	0				
Norway,SVD,JM					0

(VALUE AS PERCENTAGE OF WORLD TOTAL)(VALEURS EN POURCENTAGE DU TOTAL MONDIAL)

	1985	1986	1987	1988	1989	1990	1991	1992	1993	1994
Africa	1.8	3.2	3.4	1.5	2.5	4.4	5.7	8.5	5.6	3.1
Americas	19.3	20.4	11.5	11.5	14.5	15.9	7.6	14.5	12.6	6.4
Northern America	0.8	1.1	2.9	3.0	4.4	2.5	1.4	5.8	3.7	2.5
LAIA	8.3	10.4	7.7	8.2	6.6	11.4	3.7	7.4	7.3	3.9
CACM	0.2	0.0		0.0	1.2	0.2	0.6	0.2		0.0
Caribbean	10.0	8.9	0.8	0.3	2.3	1.8	1.9	1.1	1.6	0.0
Rest of America	0.0	0.0	0.0	0.0			0.0	0.0	0.0	0.0
As.ex F.USSR	1.3	1.6	3.7	4.7	7.2	5.3	11.4	5.8	9.9	8.9
Eur.x F.USSR	76.6	72.5	78.1	79.8	70.9	71.2	73.3	69.5	68.4	78.1
EU	74.8	71.3	77.5	77.8	66.1	67.5	68.8	64.9	64.9	75.9
EFTA	1.1	0.5	0.2	0.2	0.1	0.5	0.3	1.7	1.5	1.4
East Europe	0.6	0.6	0.4	1.7	4.6	2.8	3.5	2.9	2.0	0.7
Other Europe	0.0			0.0	0.0	0.4		0.0		0.0
Former USSR	0.7	0.4	0.3	0.7	1.4	0.4			2.3	1.7
Oceania		0.6	0.1	0.1	0.1	0.0	0.0	0.0	0.0	0.2
Portugal	26.9	29.0	33.5	34.5	30.5	32.7	34.2	32.2	33.6	34.5
Netherlands/Pays–Bas	16.0	14.8	12.9	11.6	8.8	11.1	9.8	10.4	8.5	8.0
France,Monac	5.1	7.4	4.1	4.2	3.2	3.1	2.1	3.6	4.4	13.8
Brazil/Brésil	6.5	9.5	6.5	7.2	5.0	10.5	3.7	5.7	6.0	3.4
Japan/Japon	0.9	1.3	2.8	4.1	6.2	3.8	5.1	5.0	6.0	5.0
Germany/Allemagne	4.7	4.4	4.3	4.6	4.1	3.0	6.4	3.7	4.9	4.0
Belgium–Luxembourg	0.6	1.7	2.6	2.0	2.6	3.2	4.1	2.6	3.6	3.1
USA/Etats–Unis d'Amer	0.8	1.0	2.9	3.0	4.1	2.4	1.4	5.6	3.5	2.3
Sweden/Suède	2.4	3.1	3.3	3.7	4.9	2.5	2.6	2.2	2.3	4.2
Spain/Espagne	5.9	2.5	5.9	6.3	2.6	5.2	5.4	2.1	0.7	0.9

	1985	1986	1987	1988	1989	1990	1991	1992	1993	1994
Afrique	40.5	12.3	34.1	21.0	13.5	6.7	0.5	0.6	18.6	0.9
Amériques	0.0	0.2	0.1	0.2	0.2	1.3	2.0		0.0	0.3
Amérique du Nord	0.0	0.0	0.0	0.1	0.2	1.1	1.6		0.0	0.2
ALAI		0.2	0.0	0.1	0.0	0.2	0.4		0.0	0.1
MCAC						0.0			0.0	
Caraïbes			0.0	0.0	0.0	0.0	0.0			
Autre Amérique					0.0	0.0	0.0			0.0
Asie l'URSS exclus	3.6		0.0	0.1	0.2	0.0	0.6		1.0	0.4
Europe l'URSS exclus	47.4	13.1	19.3	26.3	10.3	11.5	96.8	99.3	80.3	98.3
UE	47.4	13.1	19.2	26.2	10.2	11.5	96.7	99.3	80.2	98.3
AELE	0.0	0.0	0.1	0.1	0.1		0.0		0.0	0.0
Europe de l'Est					0.0	0.0	0.0			0.0
Autre de l'Europe						0.0	0.0			0.0
Ancienne URSS	7.3					0.0				0.0
Océanie										
Portugal	22.8	6.8	11.7	14.4	6.3	8.3	41.5	81.3	48.8	58.8
Netherlands/Pays–Bas	1.4	0.3	0.5	0.8	0.9	0.2	42.7	9.6	3.4	2.1
Spain/Espagne	1.4	0.2	0.3	3.3	0.1	0.0	2.0	6.8	19.6	14.5
Algeria/Algérie	21.3	10.7	27.6	20.2	12.8	6.4				
United Kingdom	5.2	1.2	1.3	1.6	0.1	1.5	0.3		0.1	14.6
France,Monac	5.4	1.7	2.7	2.9	0.8	0.6	1.3		5.8	5.1
Angola	18.1	0.6	6.4	0.2	0.1	0.2	0.4		16.1	
Italy/Italie	8.9	2.5	1.9	2.1	1.2	0.5	4.8		1.3	0.9
Canada					0.1	1.1	0.8			0.0
Germany/Allemagne	0.8	0.2	0.5	0.7	0.4	0.3	1.0	0.8	0.7	2.3

4. Special Imports C.I.F. by Commodities according to the S.I.T.C. (Rev. 2) in thousand U.S. Dollars
Importations Spéciales C.A.F. par Produits d'après la C.T.C.I. (Rév. 2) en milliers de Dollars E.U.

SITC CTCI	COMMODITY	1991		1992		1993		1994		PRODUIT
		WEIGHT POIDS	VALUE VALEUR	WEIGHT POIDS	VALUE VALEUR	WEIGHT POIDS	VALUE VALEUR	WEIGHT POIDS	VALUE VALEUR	
	ALL COMMODITIES		146603		179858		154727		210128	TOUS PRODUITS
0	FOOD AND LIVE ANIMALS		32257		59110		43304		48981	ALIMENTS,ANIMAUX VIVANTS
01	MEAT AND PREPARATIONS		963		3133		2505		2346	VIANDES ET PREPARATIONS
011	MEAT FRESH,CHILLD,FROZEN		440		575		641	W 272	639	VIANDES FRAICHES,REF,CONGE
014	MEAT PREPD,PRSVD,NES ETC		520		2556	W 944	1849		1677	CONSERVES DE VIANDES
0142	SAUSAGES INCLDING TINNED	W 5186	229	W 143	373	W 234	518		705	SAUCISSES,SAUCISSONS
0149	OTH PREPARD,PRESRVD MEAT	W 110	290	W 1224	2183	W 710	1331	W 472	972	AUTRES PREP DE VIANDES
02	DAIRY PRODCTS,BIRDS'EGGS		4973		6305		6414		7346	PRODUITS LAITIERS,OEUFS
022	MILK AND CREAM		4442		5828	W 2690	5762	W 2911	6551	LAIT ET CREME
0224	MILK,CREAM PRESERVED ETC		4363		5781	W 2527	5606	W 2663	6359	LAIT,CREME CONS,CONC
02242	MILK DRY,1.5% FAT OR LES	W 404	589	W 436	341	W 589	1518	W 548	1403	LAIT POUDRE INF 1.5%
02243	MILK DRY,OVER 1.5% FAT		3581		5153	W 1573	3589	W 1724	4433	LAIT POUDRE SUP 1.5%
02249	MILK(EX DRY) PRSVD,SWEET	W 151	192	W 194	287	W 365	499	W 391	523	LAIT CONS,CONC SUCRE
04	CEREALS AND PREPARATIONS		9818		25614		13616		14521	CEREALES ET PRODUITS
041	WHEAT ETC UNMILLED	W 17242	2277	W 17023	2042	W 17761	2215	W 19726	2057	FROMENT,EPEAUTRE
0411	DURUM WHEAT UNMILLED	W 17242	2277	W 17023	2042	W 17761	2215	W 19726	2057	FROMENT DUR NON MOULU
042	RICE		4592		6424	W 19895	5168		4866	RIZ
0422	RICE SEMI–MILLED,MILLED		4592	W 19773	6424	W 19895	5168		4866	RIZ POLI,GLACE INCL BRISURES
04221	RICE MILLED UNBROKEN	W 15489	4592	W 16767	5393	W 17876	4671	W 24122	4865	RIZ POLI,GLACE EXCL BRISURES
04222	RICE BROKEN			W 3006	1031	W 2019	497			BRISURES DE RIZ
044	MAIZE UNMILLED	W 9174	1384	W 89422	14414	W 31281	4109	W 32712	5216	MAIS NON MOULU
047	OTHER CEREAL MEALS,FLOUR		22		949		82	W 516	210	AUTRES SEMOULES,FARINES
04701	CEREAL FLOUR(NON–WHEAT)		21		948		82	W 515	208	FARINES DE CEREALES
048	CEREAL ETC PREPARATIONS		1530		1757		2019		2100	PREPTNS A BASE CEREALES
0483	MACARONI,SPAGHETTI ETC		284	W 493	436	W 844	674	W 579	455	PATES ALMENTAIRES
0484	BAKERY PRODUCTS		473		582		786		747	PRODUITS DE BOULANGERIE
04842	PASTRY, CAKES ETC		471		582		783		736	PATISSERIE ETC.
05	VEGETABLES AND FRUIT		4419		8262		7091		8341	LEGUMES ET FRUITS
054	VEG ETC FRSH,SMPLY PRSVD		1964		4517		3249		3584	LEGUMES FRAIS,CONG,SECS
0541	POTATOES FRSH EXCL SWEET	W 3049	1132	W 4486	1369	W 5486	1378	W 4406	1709	POMMES DE TERRE
0542	LEGUMINOUS VEGETBLES DRY	W 646	627	W 4159	2827	W 2353	1573	W 2070	1471	LEGUMES A COSSE SECS
056	VEGTBLES ETC PRSVD,PREPD		862		1229		1001		1189	CONSERVES DE LEGUMES
0565	VEGTBLES PRSVD,PREPD NES	W 647	820		1139		941		1129	LEGUMES PREPARES CONSERVE
05659	OTH VEG PRESVD,PREPD NES	W 621	804		1131	W 841	937		1119	LEGUM PREPAP,CONSERV NDA
057	FRUIT,NUTS,FRESH,DRIED		653		1106		1318		1658	FRUITS FRAIS OU SECS
0574	APPLES FRESH	W 104	164	W 122	205	W 520	492	W 792	768	POMMES FRAICHES
0579	FRUIT FRESH OR DRIED NES		243		627		380		365	FRUITS FRAIS,SECS NDA
058	FRUIT PRESERVED,PREPARED		940		1411		1522		1910	CONSERVES DE FRUITS
0585	FRUIT OR VEGETABLE JUICE		658		1001		1158		1524	JUS DE FRUITS
05857	JUICE OF OTHER FRUIT,VEG	W 467	583	W 516	814	W 745	908	W 965	1132	JUS AUTRES FRUITS,LEGUMES
06	SUGAR AND PREPS,HONEY		5007		5169		6216		5765	SUCRES ET PRODUITS
061	SUGAR AND HONEY		3929		4371		5209		4561	SUCRES ET MIEL
0612	REFINED SUGAR ETC		3902	W 13304	4340	W 13866	5195	W 11833	4521	SUCRES RAFFINES
062	SUGAR CANDY NON–CHOCLATE	W 542	1078	W 339	798	W 512	1006	W 638	1204	SUCRERIES
07	COFFEE,TEA,COCOA,SPICES		1597		1978		1649		1974	CAFE,THE,CACAO,EPICES
071	COFFEE AND SUBSTITUTES		1041	W 773	1500		1109		1372	CAFE ET SUCCEDANES
0711	COFFEE GREEN,ROASTED,SUB		874	W 691	1206		1015	W 409	1177	CAFE TORREFIE OU DECAFEINE
07111	COFFEE GREEN,HUSKS,SKINS		874	W 10	14		826	W 409	1177	CAFE NON TORREFIE
081	*FEEDING STUFF FOR ANIML	W 2550	1003	W 2705	1565	W 1901	1275	W 2275	1398	NOURRITURE POUR ANIMAUX
0813	OILCAKE AND OTH RESIDUES	W 1217	546	W 1458	638	W 1030	423	W 1221	531	TOURTEAUX
08131	— OF SOYA BEANS	W 1161	529	W 1210	568	W 980	412	W 1066	492	TOURTEAUX DE SOJA
0819	FOOD WASTE AND FEED NES	W 208	220	W 828	677	W 483	478	W 515	515	DECHETS,ALIMENTS NDA
08199	FODDER NES,INCL SWEETNED	W 208	220	W 828	677	W 483	478	W 515	515	PREPARATIONS FOURRAGERES
09	MISC EDIBLE PRODUCTS		4122		6818		4066		6540	PREP ALIMENTAIRES DIVERSES
091	MARGARINE AND SHORTENING		1589		3391	W 1529	1530		2712	MARGARINE ET GRAISSES
0913	PIG,POULTRY FAT RENDERED	W 1204	937	W 873	1281	W 917	753	W 1312	1107	SAINDOUX
0914	MARGARINE,EDIBLE FAT NES		652		2110	W 612	777		1606	MARGARINES,SIMILI SAINDOUX
09141	MARGARINE	W 519	652	W 1535	2110	W 611	776	W 1259	1605	MARGARINE
098	EDIBLE PRODCTS,PREPS NES		2533		3427		2536		3828	PREP ALIMENTAIRES NDA
09805	SOUPS AND BROTHS		754		1129	W 184	923	W 305	1307	SOUPES,POTAGES,BOUILLONS
09809	MISC FOOD PREPRTIONS NES		1196		1664		1134		1996	PREP ALIMENTAIRES NDA
1	BEVERAGES AND TOBACCO		5275		6197		7085		6712	BOISSONS ET TABACS
11	BEVERAGES		4479		5266		6325		5913	BOISSONS
111	NON–ALCOHL BEVERAGES NES		1378	W 2201	1646	W 2952	1999	W 2721	1974	BOISSONS NON ALCOOLIQUES
11101	WATERS,ICE AND SNOW		286	W 883	274	W 1505	480	W 1270	402	EAU,EAUX MINERALES
11102	FLAVORED WATERS NON–ALCO	W 1021	1092	W 1318	1372	W 1447	1519	W 1451	1572	LIMONADES,EAUX GAZEUSES
112	ALCOHOLIC BEVERAGES		3101		3621		4326		3938	BOISSONS ALCOOLIQUES
1121	WINE OF FRESH GRAPES ETC		2243		2436		2837		2734	VINS DE RAISINS FRAIS
11212	WINE OF FRESH GRAPES		2078	W 3958	2191		2582		2569	VINS DE MOUTS DE RAISINS
1123	BEER,ALE,STOUT,PORTER	W 532	415	W 630	547	W 755	634	W 730	611	BIERES
1124	DISTILLED ALCOHOLIC BEVS		443		637		855		593	ALCOOLS,EAUX–DE–VIE
11241	WHISKY	W 73	353	W 106	536	W 144	655	W 101	520	WHISKY
12	TOBACCO AND MANUFACTURES		796		931		760		800	TABACS BRUTS FABRIQUES
121	TOBACCO UNMNFCTRD,REFUSE	W 73	792	W 79	929	W 66	758	W 70	794	TABACS BRUTS,DECHETS
1212	TOBACCO STRIPPED OR PART	W 73	792	W 79	929	W 66	758	W 70	794	TABACS PART ECOTES
12129	— OTHER TYPES	W 73	792	W 79	929	W 66	758	W 68	787	AUTRES SECHES AIR CHAUD
2	CRUDE MATERLS,EXCL FUELS		4162		3951		3699		4274	MAT BRUTES NON COMESTIBLES
24	CORK AND WOOD		3707		3058		3207		3692	LIEGE ET BOIS
247	OTH WOOD ROUGH,SQUARED		33	W 419	129	W 378	109	W 2684	801	BOIS BRUTS EQUARRIS
248	WOOD SHAPED,SLEEPERS	W 7748	3674		2928	W 7285	3087	W 7050	2889	BOIS SIMPLEMENT TRAVAILLES
2482	LUMBER SHAPED CONIFER	W 3089	1321		1410	W 2265	863	W 2414	970	CONIFERES SCIES,RABOTES
24821	LUMBER SAWN ETC CONIFER	W 3085	1318	W 2670	1409	W 2264	862	W 2411	965	CONIFERES SCIES LONGITUD
2483	LUMBER SHAPED NON–CONIFR	W 4659	2353	W 3266	1518	W 5020	2224	W 4636	1919	NON CONIFERES SCIES,RABOTES
24831	LUMBER SAWN ETC NON–CON	W 4658	2350	W 3256	1511	W 5008	2206	W 4597	1866	SCIES LONGITUDINALEMENT
3	MINERAL FUELS ETC		11367		12767		8450		7536	COMBUSTIBLES MINERAUX LUB
33	PETROLEUM AND PRODUCTS		9007		10215		6998		6052	PETROLE ET DERIVES
334	PETROLEUM PRODUCTS,REFIN		8935		10093		6941		5964	PRODUITS RAFFINES
3341	GASOLINE,OTH LIGHT OILS	W 4605	1321	W 5232	2725		1147		1141	ESSENCES POUR MOTEURS
33411	MOTOR,AVIATION SPIRIT	W 4591	1312	W 5214	2715	W 5457	1131		1136	ESSENCES MOTEURS D'AVIONS
3342	KEROSENE,OTH MEDIUM OILS	W 3414	826		1366	W 2302	415		556	PETR LAMPANTS,AUT HUIL
33421	KEROSENE INCL JET FUEL	W 3414	826	W 6670	1366	W 2302	415	W 3132	554	PETROLES LAMPANTS
3343	GAS OILS	W 23356	4538	W 22610	4501	W 24367	4398	W 18148	3144	GAS OILS
3344	FUEL OILS,NES	W 8768	1203	W 4347	440	W 1985	201	W 692	88	FUEL OILS
3345	LUBS,PETROLEUM OILS NES		1047		1061		780		1036	HUILES LUBRIFIANTES
33451	LUBS(HIGH PETR CONT) ETC	W 792	1045	W 800	1058	W 553	772	W 805	1035	HUILES LUBRIF,H LOURDES
341	*GAS,NATURAL AND MANUFCT		2360		2551	W 5945	1452		1483	GAZ NATUREL,GAZ MANUFACT
3413	PETROLM GASES,LIQUEFIED		2360		2547	W 5945	1452	W 7318	1475	GAZ DE PETROLE LIQUEFIE
34131	LIQUEFIED PROPANE,BUTANE	W 7107	2360	W 8287	2547	W 5945	1452	W 7318	1475	PROPANE,BUTANE LIQUEFIES
4	ANIMAL,VEGETABLE OIL,FAT		3773		8551		2944		8938	HUILES,GRAISSES ANIM,VEG
42	FIXED VEGETABLE OIL,FAT		3688		8341		2747		8369	HUILES VEGETALES FIXES
423	FIXED VEG OILS,SOFT		3348	W 3371	4952	W 1102	1597	W 3304	4435	HUILES VEGET DOUCES FIXES

4. Special Imports C.I.F. by Commodities according to the S.I.T.C. (Rev. 2) in thousand U.S. Dollars
Importations Spéciales C.A.F. par Produits d'après la C.T.C.I. (Rév. 2) en milliers de Dollars E.U.

SITC CTCI	COMMODITY	1991		1992		1993		1994		PRODUIT
		WEIGHT POIDS	VALUE VALEUR	WEIGHT POIDS	VALUE VALEUR	WEIGHT POIDS	VALUE VALEUR	WEIGHT POIDS	VALUE VALEUR	
4232	SOYA BEAN OIL	W 99	116	W 369	429	W 90	92	W 1688	1755	HUILE DE SOJA
4235	OLIVE OIL	W 219	697	W 740	2168	W 432	954	W 705	1727	HUILE D'OLIVE
4239	OTH FIXED VEG OILS,SOFT	W 2804	2532	W 2253	2343	W 564	531	W 869	916	AUTRES HUILES FIXES
42391	RAPE,COLZA,MUSTARD OILS	W 2804	2532	W 2253	2343			W 869	916	H NAVETTE COLZA MOUTARDE
424	FIXED VEG OIL NONSOFT		340		3389		1151		3934	AUTRES HUILES VEG FIXES
4249	FIXED VEGETABLE OILS NES	W 389	335	W 3274	3377	W 1268	1142	W 3646	3920	HUILES VEGET FIXES NDA
5	CHEMCLS,RELATED PROD NES		9827		10859		10211		10813	PRODUITS CHIMIQUES
53	DYES,TANNING,COLOUR PROD		989		834		893		816	PROD TEINTURE,COLORANTS
533	PIGMENTS,PAINTS,ETC		982		820		889		797	PIGMENTS,PEINTURES,VERNIS
5334	VARNISHES,DISTEMPERS ETC		888	W 199	684		682	W 261	586	PEINTURES A L'EAU
53342	OTH PAINTS,VARNISHES ETC	W 139	652	W 116	569	W 108	442	W 72	272	AUTRES PEINTURES,VERNIS
541	*MEDICINAL,PHARM PRODUCT		1667		2405		2734		2823	PROD MEDICINAUX PHARMACEUT
5417	MEDICAMENTS		223		373		516		565	MEDICAMENTS
5419	PHARMACEUTICAL GOODS NES		1352		1779		2013		1819	PREP,ART PHARMACEUTIQUES
54191	BANDAGES PREPARED ETC	K 91000	1221		1578		1859		1657	OUATES,GAZES,BANDES
55	PERFUME,CLEANING ETC PRD		2848		2620		2340		2667	PROD POUR PARFUM,TOILETTE
553	PERFUMERY,COSMETICS,ETC		648		612		645		844	PRODUITS DE PARFUMERIE
554	SOAP,CLEANSING ETC PREPS		2155		1921		1612		1731	SAVONS,PRODUITS DETERSIFS
5541	SOAPS		1325		717		416		499	SAVONS,PROD TENSIO–ACTIFS
5542	WASHING PREPARATIONS ETC	W 728	759	W 1045	1088		1117	W 1247	1116	PROD ORG TENSIO–ACT NDA
58	PLASTIC MATERIALS ETC		2606		3444		1920		1867	MAT PLAST ARTIFICIELLES
582	PROD OF CONDENSATION ETC		643		922		621		182	PROD CONDENS,POLYCOND
5825	POLYURETHANES			W 123	817		520	W 16	94	POLYURETHANES
58259	— OTHER FORMS,INC WASTE			W 123	817	W 93	518	W 16	94	POLYURETHAN AUT FORMES
5826	EPOXIDE RESINS		569			W 3	10	W 17	32	RESINES EPOXYDES
58269	— OTHER FORMS,INC WASTE	W 89	568			W 1	4	W 13	23	EPOXYD AUTRES FORMES
583	POLYMERIZATION ETC PRODS		1915		2447		1244		1616	PROD POLYMERISATION
5834	POLYVINYL CHLORIDE		1258		2189	W 439	898	W 466	1127	CHLORURE DE POLYVINYLE
58342	— MONOFIL,TUBES,ETC	W 300	1167	W 1013	2077	W 428	852	W 393	983	SOUS FORME DE MONOFILS
59	CHEMICAL MATERIALS NES		1042		1030		1324		1997	MAT PROD CHIMIQUES NDA
591	PESTICIDES,DISINFECTANTS		416		399		468		579	DESINF,INSECT,FONG,HERB
592	STARCH,INULIN,GLUTEN,ETC		270		189		227		665	AMIDONS,INUL,GLUT FROM
5922	ALBUMINOID SUBSTAN,GLUES		264		186		221		648	MAT ALBUMIN,COLLES
59229	PREPARED GLUES NES,ETC	W 123	254	W 49	185	W 71	221	W 83	648	COLLES PREPAREES NDA
598	MISCEL CHEM PRODUCTS NES		356		442		629		753	PROD DIV INDUST CHIM NDA
5989	CHEM PRODUCTS,PREPS NES		339		387		590		676	PROD PREP CHIMIQUES NDA
6	BASIC MANUFACTURES		28757		28368		28926		32729	ART MANUFACTURES
62	RUBBER MANUFACTURES NES		1727		1959		1743		1671	CAOUTCHOUC MANUFACTURE
625	RUBBER TYRES, TUBES ETC		1347		1357		1257	N 31115	1135	PNEUS CAOUTCHOUC VULCANISE
6251	TYRES NEW FOR MOTOR CARS	W 123	537	W 124	548	W 123	531	N 13280	605	PNEUS POUR VOITURES
6252	TYRES,NEW,BUS OR LORRY	W 101	506	W 127	553	W 108	455	N 1734	290	PNEUS POUR AUTOBUS,CAMIONS
63	WOOD,CORK MANUFACTRS NES		446		1095		787		1038	OUVRAGES LIEGE ET BOIS
634	VENEERS,PLYWOOD,ETC		190		864		576		772	PLACAGES,CONTRE–PLAQUES
64	PAPER,PAPERBOARD AND MFR		2398		3169		2442		2463	PAPIERS,CARTONS & OUVRAGES
641	PAPER AND PAPERBOARD		718		700		597		500	PAPIERS ET CARTONS
642	PAPER,ETC,PRECUT,ARTS OF		1680		2469		1844		1964	PAP,CARTONS DECOUPES
6421	PAPER ETC CONTAINERS	W 277	365		589	W 202	332	W 188	301	BOITES,SACS EMBALLAGES
6423	EXERCISE BOOKS ETC	W 108	392	W 128	488	W 216	569	W 198	477	REGISTRES,CAHIERS,CARNETS
6424	PAPER ETC CT TO SIZE NES		583		793		558		637	PAP,CARTONS DECOUPES
65	TEXTILE YARN,FABRICS,ETC		2157		2208		2438		2159	FILS,TISSUS,ARTICLES TEXTILE
652	COTTON FABRICS,WOVEN		613		404		537		391	TISSUS DE COTON
6522	WOVEN COTTON BLEACHD,ETC		600		386		507		334	TISSUS COTON BLANCHIS ETC
65224	BLCHED COTTON FABRIC NES		447		11		359		225	AUT TIS PLUS 85% COT BLANCHI
657	SPECIAL TXTL FABRC,PRODS		211		497		638		372	TISSUS SPECIAUX
658	TEXTILE ARTICLES NES		748		693		613		702	ART FACONNES MAT TEXTILES
66	NONMETAL MINERAL MFS NES		10674		9741		10519		12731	ART MIN NON METALLIQUES
661	LIME,CEMENT,BLDG PRODS		8000		6026		7697		8977	CHAUX,CIMENTS MAT CONSTR
6612	CEMENT	W 112692	7392	W 89442	5662	W 118248	7349	W 135422	8598	CIMENTS HYDRAULIQUES
662	CLAY,REFRACTORY BLDG PRD		1063		2394		1508		1899	MAT CONST REFRACTAIRES
6624	BRICKS ETC NONREFRACTORY		1026		2391		1504		1896	BRIQUES ETC CERAM NON REFR
66245	GLAZED CERAMIC SETTS ETC	A 47731	872	A 2909	1880	A 4387	1258	A 2713	1509	AUT CARREAUX CERAMIQUE
664	GLASS		603		487		424		637	VERRE
665	GLASSWARE		633		537		434		520	OUVRAGES EN VERRE
67	IRON AND STEEL		4240		3358		3938		3590	FER ET ACIER
673	IRON,STEEL SHAPES ETC	W 6888	2948		2084	W 6562	2637		1976	BARRES,PROFIL FER,ACIER
6732	IRON,STEEL BARS ETC	W 6744	2789		1887	W 6265	2415	W 4509	1695	BARRES FER,ACIER
67327	IRN, OTH STL BARS FORGED	W 6729	2779	W 4088	1883	W 6243	2395	W 4267	1596	BARRES FORGEES CREUSES
674	IRN,STL UNIV,PLATE,SHEET		496		351		436		632	LARGES PLATS,TOLES
678	IRON,STL TUBES,PIPES,ETC		669		561		463	W 669	897	TUBES,TUYAUX EN FONTE,FER
69	METAL MANUFACTURES NES		6705		6642		6643		8761	ART MANUFACT EN METAL NDA
691	STRUCTURES AND PARTS NES		1645		1609		1193		2325	CONSTRUCT FER,ACIER,ALU
6911	STRUCTURES,PARTS IRN,STL		1073	W 354	1165	W 184	640	W 692	1613	CONSTRUCT FER,ACIER,FONTE
6912	STRUCTURES,PARTS ALUMNM		571	N 28318	444	N 17510	553		711	CONSTRUCT ALUMINIUM
692	METAL TANKS,BOXES,ETC		726		622		1022		1143	RECIPIENTS METALLIQUES
6924	MTL TRANSPORT BOXES ETC		665		620		992		974	FUTS,TAMBOURS,BIDONS
69243	IRN,STL COMP GAS CYLINDR	W 80	266	W 96	289	W 279	576	W 223	530	RECIP FER,ACIER GAZ COMP
694	STL,COPPR NAILS,NUTS,ETC		404		467		447		633	CLOUS,VIS,ECROUS
695	TOOLS		585		432		524		536	OUTILS A MAIN
697	BASE MTL HOUSEHOLD EQUIP		1345		1286		1437		1543	ART MENAGE MET COMMUNS
6973	DMSTC HEATG,COOKG APPARA		584		760		728		792	APPS CHAUF NON ELECTRIQ
69731	IRN,STL DOM COOKG APPARA	W 105	541	W 139	658		647	W 157	705	APPS CUISSON FER,ACIER
6974	BASE MTL DMSTC ARTIC NES		505		360	N 330828	468	N 298241	507	ARTICLES NDA FONTE,FER,ETC
699	BASE METAL MFRS NES		1776		1930		1751		2140	ART MANUFACTURES MET NDA
6991	LOCKSMITHS WARES,ETC		951		1012		924		1139	ARTICLES DE SERRURERIE
69913	BASE MTL DOOR,ETC FITTNG	W 54	482	W 48	507	W 59	449	W 93	612	GARNITURES POUR MEUBLES
7	MACHINES,TRANSPORT EQUIP		40082		37657		38668		75677	MACHINES MATERIEL TRANSPORT
71	POWER GENERATING EQUIPMT		6279		1663		2234		7601	MACHINES GENERATRICES
711	STEAM BOILERS & AUX PLNT		905	N 1	3		148		1835	GENERATEURS VAPEUR EAU ETC
7111	STEAM BOILERS ETC	N 5	878	N 1	3	N 2	138	N 1	1759	GENERATEURS VAPEUR EAU
713	INTRNL COMBUS PSTN ENGIN		1145		977		949		1053	MOTEURS EXPL COMB INT, PIECE
7139	PISTON ENGINE PARTS NES		579		656		758	W 16	818	PIECES POUR 713.2,3,8
716	ROTATING ELECTRIC PLANT		4197		650	N 483	1100		4704	APP ELECTR ROTATIFS,PIECES
7162	AC MTRS,GENRTRS,GEN SETS	N 240	4133	N 233	493	N 434	763	N 4882	3965	MOTEURS ELECTRIQUES
71622	AC GENERATORS	N 211	314	N 194	275	N 307	445	N 390	1755	GENER COURANT ALTERNATIF
71623	GEN SETS WITH PSTN ENGN	N 13	3811	N 18	210	N 69	298	N 4442	2150	GROUPES MOTEUR EXPLOSION
72	MACHS FOR SPCL INDUSTRYS		2627		1837		1114		2797	MAC SPECIALES POUR INDUST
723	CIVIL ENGNEERG EQUIP ETC		390		595		119		200	APPAREILS DE GENIE CIVIL
7234	CONST,MINING MACHNRY NES	N 5	181		571	N 5	29	N 10	142	MACH POUR LA CONST, MINES
724	TEXTILE,LEATHER MACHNRY		96		51		96		678	MACH POUR INDUSTRIE TEXTILE
727	FOOD MACHRY NON–DOMESTIC		792		104		187		550	MACH INDUSTRIES ALIMENT
7271	GRAIN WORKING MCHY,PARTS	W 22	538		65		15		167	MACH POUR MINOTERIE,PIEC

4. Special Imports C.I.F. by Commodities according to the S.I.T.C. (Rev. 2) in thousand U.S. Dollars
Importations Spéciales C.A.F. par Produits d'après la C.T.C.I. (Rév. 2) en milliers de Dollars E.U.

SITC CTCI	COMMODITY	1991		1992		1993		1994		PRODUIT
		WEIGHT POIDS	VALUE VALEUR	WEIGHT POIDS	VALUE VALEUR	WEIGHT POIDS	VALUE VALEUR	WEIGHT POIDS	VALUE VALEUR	
72719	PTS NES OF MCHY OF 72711	W 21	528		10		1	W 3	41	PIECES MACH DU 727.11
728	OTH MACHY FOR SPCL INDUS		782		488		527		704	AUT MACH IND PARTICULIERES
74	GENRL INDUSTRL MACHY NES		5085		6326		3828		9016	MACH APP INDUSTRIE
741	HEATING,COOLING EQUIPMNT		1613		2810		922		1870	MACH CHAUFFAGE,PIECES
7414	NONDOM REFRIG EQUIPT,PTS	N 371	143	N 1159	654	N 500	280	N 239	878	MAT PRODUCTION DU FROID
74149	PTS NES OF REFRIG EQUIPT	N 290	20	N 1090	577	N 377	92	N 135	491	PIECES POUR MACH FROID
7415	AIR–CONDITIONING MACHNRY		335		440		484		550	GROUPES CONDITION AIR
7416	HEATING,COOLING EQU NES		1083		1710		113		225	APP CHANGEMENT TEMP
742	PUMPS FOR LIQUIDS ETC		862		836		404		1314	POMPES MOTO–POMPES
7428	OTHER PUMPS FOR LIQUIDS	N 404	365	N 354	337	N 448	247	N 514	739	AUTRES POMPES POUR LIQ
74288	PUMPS FR LIQUIDS NES ETC	N 374	347	N 323	333	N 435	206	N 502	713	POMPES POUR LIQUIDES NDA
743	PUMPS NES,CENTRFUGES ETC		488		593		492		921	POMPES COMPRES,VENT ETC
744	MECHANICAL HANDLING EQU		417		371		872		3178	EQUIP MANUTENTION PIECES
7441	FORK LIFT TRCKS,ETC,PTS	N 4	102		128		265	N 29	746	CHARIOTS POUR USINES ETC
74411	FORK LIFT TRUCKS ETC	N 3	89	N 7	94	N 9	175	N 15	724	CHARIOTS POUR LES GARES
7442	LIFTING,LOADING MACH NES	N 131	252		193		581		2392	APP LEVAGE,MANUTENTION
74422	SHIP DERRICKS,CRANES ETC	N 6	4			N 2	195	N 31	697	GRUES,PONTS ROULANTS
74428	OTH HANDLING ETC MCH NES	N 109	123	N 224	154	N 216	194	N 288	1364	AUT APP LEVAGE ETC
745	NONELEC MACHY,TOOLS NES		640		559		328		705	AUT MACH NON ELEC,PIECES
7452	OTH NONELEC MCHS,PTS NES		605		527		297		645	AUT MACH NON ELEC,PIECES
749	NONELEC MACH PTS,ACC NES		1065		1158		810		1029	PIECES MACH NON ELEC NDA
7492	COCKS,VALVES ETC NES		547		560		447		624	ART ROB,SIM POUR TUYAUX
75	OFFICE MACHNES,ADP EQUIP		1517		2431		2041		2610	MACH BUREAU TRAIT AUTOM
752	AUTOMTIC DATA PROC EQUIP	N 487	1083	N 913	1900	N 1869	1493	N 1370	1927	MACH TRAIT INFORMATION
7522	DIGITAL COMPUTERS	N 118	391	N 209	562	N 276	419	N 338	619	MACH DIGITALES COMPLETES
7528	OFF–LINE DATA PROC EQUIP	N 78	246	N 154	562	N 225	350	N 93	305	MACH AUXIL TRAIT INFORM
76	TELECOMM,SOUND EQUIPMENT		1757		4371		3716		3129	EQUIPMENT DE TELECOM
764	TELECOM EQPT,PTS,ACC NES		1512		3848		3305		2476	EQUIP TELECOM,PIECES
7641	LINE TELEPHONE,ETC EQUIP		1033		865		1746		1168	APP TELEPHON PAR FIL
7643	TV,RADIO TRANSMITTRS ETC	N 34	142	N 75	518	N 130	666	N 214	475	APP EMET TELE RADIO
7649	PTS NES OF EQUIPMT OF 76		180		2375		758		706	PIECES DE LA DIV 76
76491	PTS NES OF APPAR OF 7641	W 2	53		2196	W 2	423	W 2	371	PIECES POUR 764.1
77	ELECTRIC MACHNRY NES ETC		6306		5884		5272		9184	MACH APP ELECT NDA
772	SWITCHGEAR ETC,PARTS NES		1281		1397		779		2489	APP COUPURE,SECT ETC
7721	SWITCHGEAR ETC		1267		1383		771		2460	APP COUPURE,SECTIONMNT
773	ELECTR DISTRIBUTNG EQUIP		571		771		548		726	EQUIPMT DISTRIBUTION ELECT
7731	INSULATED WIRE,CABLE ETC		555		745		538		665	FILS,CABLES ISOLES ELECT
775	HOUSEHOLD TYPE EQUIP NES		1397		1224		1461		1510	MACH,APP USAGE DOMESTQUE
7752	DOM REFRIGERATRS,FREEZRS		1092	N 3047	1060	N 3361	1096	N 3154	1005	REFRIG,CONGEL MENAGER
77521	DOMESTIC REFRIGERATORS	N 2283	829	N 2475	847	N 2662	866	N 2409	779	REFRIGERATEURS
776	TRANSISTORS,VALVES,ETC		1221		1150		301		2502	LAMPES,TUBES,VALVES
7761	TV PICTURE TUBES	W 170	1189	W 207	1098	W 50	229	W '366	1842	TUBES CATHODIQUES
778	ELECTRICAL MACHINERY NES		1539		943		1892		1516	AUTRES MACH ELECT NDA
7781	BATTERIES,ACCUMULATORS		824	W 201	564		702		948	PILES ET ACCUMULATEURS
77811	PRIMARY BATTERIES,CELLS	W 164	459	W 201	564	W 169	420	W 196	527	PILES ELECTRIQUES,PIECES
7788	OTH ELEC MACHY,EQUIP NES		224		138		729		149	AUT MACH APP ELEC NDA
77886	OTH ELEC MACHINERY NES		56		36		644		65	AUT MACH APP ELECTRIQUES
78	ROAD VEHICLES		10011		14021		14019		15846	VEHICULES ROUTIERS
781	PASS MOTOR VEH EXC BUSES	N 552	3634	N 4074	5646	N 648	4927	N 708	5812	AUTO TRANSPORT PERSONNES
782	LORRIES,SPCL MTR VEH NES	N 286	3876	N 371	5826	N 488	7166	N 470	6804	VEHICULES SPECIAUX,MARCH
7821	LORRIES,TRUCKS	N 284	3742	N 370	5822	N 482	6859	N 421	6632	VEHICULES TRANSP MARCHAND
783	ROAD MOTOR VEHICLES NES	N 94	1677	N 86	1522	N 68	1079	N 78	1440	VEHICULES ROUTIERS NDA
7831	BUSES	N 94	1677	N 86	1522	N 68	1079	N 78	1440	VOITURES TRANSPORT COMMUN
784	MOTOR VEH PRTS,ACCES NES	N 37	488	N 1139	542	N 7016	488	N 64	594	PIECES 722,781,782,783
7849	OTHER MOTOR VEHCL PARTS	N 33	484	N 1135	538	N 7012	464	N 60	576	PIECES 722,781,782,783
786	TRAILERS,NONMOTR VEH,NES		85	N 1221	275	N 9117	196		639	REMORQUES,CADRES,CONTAIN
79	OTHR TRANSPORT EQUIPMENT		6253		916		6186		25258	AUTRE MATERIEL TRANSPORT
792	AIRCRAFT ETC		4466		275	N 502	3405		21607	APP NAVIGATION AERIENNE
7923	AIRCRFT NES2000–15000KG	N 1	3900			N 1	2877			AERODYNES 2000 A 15000 KG
7924	AIRCRFT NES OVER 15000KG							W 2	21388	AERODYNES PLUS 15000 KG
7929	AIRCRAFT PARTS NES	N 2	566		275	N 1	524	N 1	220	PIECES DU 792
793	SHIPS AND BOATS ETC		1787	N 2688	642	N 232	2780	N 1054	3649	NAVIRES BATEAUX,ETC
7932	SHIPS AND BOATS NES	N 41	1532	N 21	635	N 30	2762	N 46	3648	NAVIRES ET BATEAUX
79322	TANKERS OF ALL KINDS					N 1	2067			BATEAUX–CITERNES
79323	OTHER CARGO VESSELS	N 1	981			N 2	94			AUT BATEAUX TRANS MARCH
79324	FISHING VESSELS ETC	N 3	25	N 12	591	N 8	533	N 20	3444	BATEAUX DE PECHE
79328	OTHER SHIPS AND BOATS	N 2	505	N 1	13	N 7	24	N 8	148	NAVIRES ET BATEAUX NDA
8	MISC MANUFACTURED GOODS		10545		12227		11397		14435	ART MANUFACTURES DIVERS
812	*PLUMBG,HEATNG,LGHTNG EQ		983		1036		874		1122	APPAR SANITAIRES CHAUFFAGE
8124	LIGHTING EQUIPMENT NES		707		580		536		646	APPAREILS ECLAIRAGE ETC
81242	LAMPS,FITTINGS BASE METL		617		490		425		523	APPAREILS D'ECLAIRAGE
821	*FURNITURE,PARTS THEREOF		1430		1620		1425		2067	MEUBLES ET PIECES
8219	FURNITURE AND PARTS NES		759		840		811		1297	AUTRES MEUBLES ET PIECES
82191	METAL FURNITURE NES	N 1139	532	N 4577	617	N 6634	573	N 7936	985	MEUBLES NDA EN METAL
84	CLOTHING AND ACCESSORIES		1257		1415		1443		1287	VETEMENTS
851	*FOOTWEAR		924		906		956		1368	CHAUSSURES
85102	FOOTWEAR LEATHER	P 114521	511		595	P 162669	660	P 200011	899	CHAUS SEMELLES EN CUIR
87	PRECISION INSTRUMNTS NES		1426		1148		1440		1936	INSTRUM,APPAR SCIENT NDA
874	MEASURNG,CONTROLNG INSTR		1006		742		1016		971	INSTRUMENTS DE MESURE
8748	ELEC MEAS,CONTRL EQU NES	N 539	600	N 714	342	N 694	538	N 845	316	APP ELEC ELECTRO MESURE
87483	OTH ELCTRNC MEAS ETC EQU	N 113	520	N 63	199	N 125	477	N 240	247	AUT APP ELECTRO DE MESURE
88	PHOTO EQU,OPTICL GDS ETC		513		561		474		658	APP,FOURN PHOTO,OP,MONTR
89	MISC MANUFCTRD GOODS NES		3747		5297		4516		5675	ART MANUFACTURES DIVERS
892	PRINTED MATTER		788		816		936		1069	IMPRIMES
8928	PRINTED MATTER NES		406		441		467		439	IMPRIMES NDA
893	ARTICLES OF PLASTIC NES		1685		2440		1935		2504	OUVRAGES EN MAT DIVIS 58
8939	MISC PLASTIC ARTICLES		1124		1737		1401		1623	ART DIVERS EN MAT DIV 58
89399	OTHR PLASTC ARTICLES NES		988		1564		1279		1447	AUT OUV MAT DIV 58
899	OTHER MANUFACTURED GOODS		684		1033		808		896	AUT ART MANUF DIVERS NDA

5. Special Exports F.O.B. by Commodities according to the S.I.T.C. (Rev. 2) in thousand U.S. Dollars
Exportations Spéciales F.O.B. par Produits d'après la C.T.C.I. (Rév. 2) en milliers de Dollars E.U.

SITC CTCI	COMMODITY	1991		1992		1993		1994		PRODUIT
		WEIGHT POIDS	VALUE VALEUR	WEIGHT POIDS	VALUE VALEUR	WEIGHT POIDS	VALUE VALEUR	WEIGHT POIDS	VALUE VALEUR	
	ALL COMMODITIES		6128		4810		3826		5011	TOUS PRODUITS
0	FOOD AND LIVE ANIMALS		3163		766		2857		2458	ALIMENTS,ANIMAUX VIVANTS
03	FISH AND PREPARATIONS		1497		765		2391		2406	POISSONS ET PREPARATIONS
034	FISH,FRESH,CHILLED,FROZN		246		568		919	W 1873	748	POISSON FRAIS, REFRIG,CONG
0341	FISH FRSH,CHLLD,EX FILLT		194		418		161	W 4	8	POISSON FRAIS,REFRIGERE
0342	FISH FROZEN,EXCL FILLETS		52	W 1481	150		759	W 1869	740	POISSONS CONGELES
036	SHELL FISH FRESH,FROZEN	W 70	1134	W 99	166		1447		1584	CRUSTACES,MOLLUSQUES
037	FISH ETC PREPD,PRSVD NES	W 27	117	W 32	31		24		75	POIS,CRUST,MOL PREPARES
0371	FISH PREPARD,PRESRVD NES	W 27	117	W 32	31		24		75	CONSERVES DE POISSONS
05	VEGETABLES AND FRUIT		1664		1		450		52	LEGUMES ET FRUITS
057	FRUIT,NUTS,FRESH,DRIED	W 2940	1664	W 2054	1		450	W 90	51	FRUITS FRAIS OU SECS
0573	BANANA,PLANTAIN,FRSH,DRY	W 2940	1664	W 2054	1		450	W 90	51	BANANES FRAICHES,SECHEES
07	COFFEE,TEA,COCOA,SPICES						16			CAFE,THE,CACAO,EPICES
071	COFFEE AND SUBSTITUTES						16			CAFE ET SUCCEDANES
0711	COFFEE GREEN,ROASTED,SUB						16			CAFE TORREFIE OU DECAFEINE
07111	COFFEE GREEN,HUSKS,SKINS						16			CAFE NON TORREFIE
1	BEVERAGES AND TOBACCO		19		2		7		12	BOISSONS ET TABACS
11	BEVERAGES		19		2		7		12	BOISSONS
2	CRUDE MATERLS,EXCL FUELS		77		30		59		93	MAT BRUTES NON COMESTIBLES
21	HIDES,SKINS,FURS UNDRSSD		67				40		42	CUIRS,PEAUX BRUTS
211	HIDES,SKINS,EXC FURS,RAW	W 55	67				40	W 49	42	CUIRS ET PEAUX
2111	BOVINE,EQUINE HIDES,RAW	W 49	62				39	W 47	41	PEAUX DE BOVINS
27	CRUDE FERTLZR,MINRLS NES		3		5				28	ENGRAIS MINERAUX BRUTS
278	OTHER CRUDE MINERALS							W 375	28	AUTRES MINERAUX BRUTS
2783	COMMON SALT,ETC							W 375	28	SEL
28	METALLIFEROUS ORES,SCRAP				24		14			MINERAIS METAL,DECHETS
288	NONFERR METAL SCRAP NES			W 26	24		14			DECHETS NON FERREUX
2882	OTHER BASE MTL SCRAP NES			W 26	24		14			AUTRES DECHETS
28821	COPPER WASTE AND SCRAP			W 26	24		12			DECHETS DE CUIVRE
29	CRUDE ANIMAL,VEG MAT NES		6		2		5		23	MATIERES BRUTES ANIM,VEGET
291	CRUDE ANIMAL MTRIALS NES	W 70	6	W 2940	2		4		23	MATIERES BRUTES ANIMALES
2911	BONES,IVORY,HORNS,ETC	W 70	6	W 2940	2		4	W 3	17	OS,CORNES,SABOTS
29116	IVORY,TORTOISE–SHELL ETC			W 2940	2		4	W 3	17	IVOIRE ECAILLE
4	ANIMAL,VEGETABLE OIL,FAT						54			HUILES,GRAISSES ANIM,VEG
411	*ANIMAL OILS AND FATS						54			HUILES,GRAISSES ANIMALES
4111	OILS OF FISH,WHALES ETC						54			GRAISSES,HUILES DE POISSONS
41111	FISH LIVER OIL						54			HUILES DE FOIES
5	CHEMCLS,RELATED PROD NES		34				620		5	PRODUITS CHIMIQUES
541	*MEDICINAL,PHARM PRODUCT		25				616			PROD MEDICINAUX PHARMACEUT
5417	MEDICAMENTS						616			MEDICAMENTS
5419	PHARMACEUTICAL GOODS NES	K 2400	25							PREP,ART PHARMACEUTIQUES
6	BASIC MANUFACTURES		113		18		144		1062	ART MANUFACTURES
61	LEATHER,DRESSED FUR,ETC		6				139		1055	CUIRS,PELLETERIES
612	LEATHER ETC MANUFACTURES						139	W 11	1055	OUVRAGES EN CUIRS NDA
6123	PREPRD PARTS OF FOOTWEAR						139	W 11	1055	PARTIES DE CHAUSSURES
69	METAL MANUFACTURES NES		104		18		5		4	ART MANUFACT EN METAL NDA
692	METAL TANKS,BOXES,ETC	W 40	91		7		2			RECIPIENTS METALLIQUES
6924	MTL TRANSPORT BOXES ETC	W 40	91		7		2			FUTS,TAMBOURS,BIDONS
69243	IRN,STL COMP GAS CYLINDR	W 40	91		7		2			RECIP FER,ACIER GAZ COMP
7	MACHINES,TRANSPORT EQUIP		2400		157		51		108	MACHINES MATERIEL TRANSPORT
74	GENRL INDUSTRL MACHY NES		28		65		5		12	MACH APP INDUSTRIE
749	NONELEC MACH PTS,ACC NES		1		56		5		4	PIECES MACH NON ELEC NDA
7492	COCKS,VALVES ETC NES		1		55		3		1	ART ROB,SIM POUR TUYAUX
78	ROAD VEHICLES		6		57				18	VEHICULES ROUTIERS
781	PASS MOTOR VEH EXC BUSES			W 1	29			W 3	18	AUTO TRANSPORT PERSONNES
782	LORRIES,SPCL MTR VEH NES			W 5	27					VEHICULES SPECIAUX,MARCH
7821	LORRIES,TRUCKS			W 5	27					VEHICULES TRANSP MARCHAND
79	OTHR TRANSPORT EQUIPMENT		2343		31		36		61	AUTRE MATERIEL TRANSPORT
792	AIRCRAFT ETC		110		31		11			APP NAVIGATION AERIENNE
7929	AIRCRAFT PARTS NES		110		31		11			PIECES DU 792
793	SHIPS AND BOATS ETC		2233				25	W 8	61	NAVIRES BATEAUX,ETC
7932	SHIPS AND BOATS NES	W 247	2230				25	W 8	61	NAVIRES ET BATEAUX
79321	YACHTS,SPORTS VESSLS ETC	W 13	46					W 8	61	BATEAUX DE PLAISANCE
79322	TANKERS OF ALL KINDS	W 234	2184							BATEAUX–CITERNES
79324	FISHING VESSELS ETC						25			BATEAUX DE PECHE
8	MISC MANUFACTURED GOODS		306		16		34		1267	ART MANUFACTURES DIVERS
84	CLOTHING AND ACCESSORIES		60				8			VETEMENTS
842	MENS OUTERWEAR NOT KNIT	W 9	60							VET DESSUS POUR HOMMES
8423	— TROUSERS,BREECHES ETC	W 9	60							PANTALONS HOMMES MAT TEX
84232	—— OF COTTON	W 9	60							PANTALONS HOMMES COTON
851	*FOOTWEAR	W 14	217					W 68	1260	CHAUSSURES
85102	FOOTWEAR LEATHER	W 14	217					W 68	1260	CHAUS SEMELLES EN CUIR
89	MISC MANUFCTRD GOODS NES		11		10		19		3	ART MANUFACTURES DIVERS
896	WORKS OF ART ETC		5		9		19		2	OBJETS D'ART
89605	COINS,NATURE COLLECTIONS		5		9		19		2	COLLECTIONS ZOOLOG,BOTAN

FOOT NOTES – NOTES

TABLE 3 –
1 Export data include re–exports in 1990.
TABLEAU 3 –
1 Y compris les réexportations en 1990.

1. HISTORICAL SERIES, 1971–1995 GENERAL TRADE, IMPORTS C.I.F., EXPORTS F.O.B.
SERIES HISTORIQUES, 1971–1995 COMMERCE GENERAL, IMPORTATIONS C.A.F., EXPORTATIONS F.O.B

YEAR ANNEE	VALUE IN MILLION C.I. DOLLARS VALEUR EN MILLION C.I. DOLLARS				CONVERSION FACTORS U.S. CENTS PER C.I. DOLLAR FACTEURS DE CONVERSION CENTS E.U. PAR C.I. DOLLAR		INDEX NUMBERS –INDICES			
	MERCHANDISE –MARCHANDISE		GOLD –OR				QUANTUM		UNIT VALUE VALEUR UNITAIRE	
	IMPORTS	EXPORTS	IMPORTS	EXPORTS	IMPORTS	EXPORTS	IMPORTS	EXPORTS	IMPORTS	EXPORTS
1971	8.90	0.50			128.2050	117.6470				
1972	12.50	0.50			117.6470	117.6470				
1973	16.50	0.70			117.6470	117.6470				
1974	21.90	0.30			117.6470	117.6470				
1975	25.70	0.20			117.6470	117.6470				
1976	29.80	0.60			117.6470	117.6470				
1977	35.70	1.30			117.6470	117.6470				
1978	41.70	2.90			117.6470	117.6470				
1979	51.00	2.50			117.6470	117.6470				
1980	85.80	2.20			117.6470	117.6470				
1981	100.42	0.65			117.6470	117.6470				
1982	107.00	1.00			117.6470	117.6470				
1983	110.00	1.00			117.6470	117.6470				
1984	118.00	1.00			117.6470	117.6470				
1985	122.71	1.50			117.6470	117.6470				
1986	134.00	2.20			120.0000	120.0000				
1987	162.60	1.80			120.0000	120.0000				
1988	192.60	1.90			120.0000	120.0000				
1989	215.60	2.10			120.0000	120.0000				
1990	239.70	3.07			120.0000	120.0000				
1991	222.90	2.45			120.0000	120.0000				
1992	278.40	3.70			120.0000	120.0000				
1993	266.10	1.76			120.0000	120.0000				
1994	272.90	2.17			120.0000	120.0000				
1995	332.50	3.43			120.0000	120.0000				

2. IMPORTS BY BROAD ECONOMIC CATEGORY AND EXPORTS BY INDUSTRIAL ORIGIN. (PERCENTAGE OF TOTAL VALUE)
IMPORTATIONS PAR CATEGORIES ECONOMIQUES ET EXPORTATIONS PAR BRANCHE D'ACTIVITE.(EN POURCENTAGE DE LA VALEUR TOTALE)

IMPORTS – IMPORTATIONS

	1990	1991	1992	1993	1994	1995	1996
TOTAL IMPORTS–IMPORTATIONS TOTALES							
1 FOOD BEV–ALIMENTATION BOISSONS							
11 PRIMARY–PRODUITS DE BASE							
111 FOR INDUSTRY–POUR L'INDUSTRIE							
112 FOR HOUSEHOLDS–POUR LES MENAGES							
12 PROCESSED–PRODUITS ELABORES							
121 FOR INDUSTRY–POUR L'INDUSTRIE							
122 FOR HOUSEHOLDS–POUR LES MENAGES							
2 IND SUPPLIES–APPROV INDUSTRIELS							
21 PRIMARY–PRODUITS DE BASE							
22 PROCESSED–PRODUITS ELABORES							
3 FUELS–COMBUSTIBLES							
31 PRIMARY–PRODUITS DE BASE							
32 PROCESSED–PRODUITS ELABORES							
321 MOTOR SPIRIT–ESSENCE							
322 OTHER–AUTRES							
4 MACHINERY–EQUIPEMENT							
41 CAPITAL EQUIPMENT–MACHINES							
42 PARTS–PIECES ACCESSOIRES							
5 TRANSPORT–TRANSPORT							
51 PASSENGER CARS–AUTOMOBILES							
52 OTHER–AUTRES							
521 INDUSTRIAL–INDUSTRIELS							
522 NON INDUSTRIAL–NON INDUSTRIEL							
53 PARTS–PIECES ACCESSOIRES							
6 CONSUM GOODS–BIENS CONSOMMATION							
61 DURABLE–DURABLES							
62 SEMI DURABLE–SEMI DURABLES							
63 NON DURABLE–NON DURABLES							
7 GOODS NES–BIENS NDA							

EXPORTS – EXPORTATIONS

	1990	1991	1992	1993	1994	1995	1996
TOTAL EXPORTS–EXPORTATIONS TOTALES							
1 AGRICULTURE							
2 MINING QUARRY–INDUS EXTRACTIVES							
3 MANUFACTURING–IND MANUFACTUR							
31 FOOD BEV TOBACCO–ALIM BOISS TAB							
32 TEXTILES–INDUSTRIES TEXTILES							
33 WOOD & PRODUCTS–BOIS & PRODUITS							
34 PAPER & PRODUCTS–PAPIER & PRODT							
35 CHEMICALS–INDUSTRIES CHIMIQUES							
36 NON METAL MIN–MIN NON METAL							
37 BASIC METAL–IND METAL BASE							
38 METAL MANUF–MANUF METAL							
39 OTH MANUF IND–AUTRES MANUF							

3. TRADE BY PRINCIPAL COUNTRIES OF ORIGIN AND LAST DESTINATION (VALUE IN THOUSAND U.S. DOLLARS)
ECHANGES SELON LES PRINCIPAUX PAYS D'ORIGINE ET DE DERNIERE DESTINATION (VALEUR EN MILLIERS DE DOLLARS EU)

COUNTRIES–PAYS	GENERAL IMPORTS C.I.F. IMPORTATIONS GENERALES C.A.F				
	1990	1991	1992	1993	1994
World	287674	267438	334087	313320	327432
Africa					
Americas	248760	234960	288000	277752	298800
Northern America	217200	203400	261480	241800	259440
LAIA	1200	360		1800	2280
CACM	2520	960		240	1200
Caribbean	27240	29880	26520	32952	34680
Rest of America	600	360		960	1200
As.ex F.USSR	9960	8640	10200	10560	10920
Eur.x F.USSR	22560	20880	16680	19704	15384
EU	19080	18240	14160	16224	12600
EFTA	3480	2640	2520	3480	2784
East Europe					
Other Europe					
Former USSR					
Oceania					
USA/Etats–Unis d'Amer	215280	201360	255120	240120	256920
Netherlands Antilles	24960	27000	22440	29400	30240
Japan/Japon	9000	8160	10200	9840	9360
United Kingdom	10080	10440	8880	8880	6120
Jamaica/Jamaïque	2280	2280	4080	2952	4200
Switz.Liecht	3480	2640	2520	3480	2784
Canada	1920	2040	6360	1680	2520
Netherlands/Pays–Bas	2760	3240	1920	2064	2040
France,Monac	2520	1920	1200	1080	720
Italy/Italie	1680	360		1920	1680
Mexico/Mexique	1200	360		1800	2280
Sweden/Suède	1080	1320	2160	600	360
Costa Rica	2520	960		240	1200
Korea, Republic of	960	480		720	1560
Panama	600	360		960	1200
Germany/Allemagne	960	480		240	720
Ireland/Irlande		480		1080	720
Barbados/Barbade		600		600	240
Spain/Espagne				360	240

COUNTRIES–PAYS	GENERAL EXPORTS F.O.B. EXPORTATIONS GENERALES F.O.B.				
	1990	1991	1992	1993	1994
Monde	3686	2945	4440	2113	2604
Afrique					
Amériques	2093	640	640	1642	898
Amérique du Nord	2093	640	640	1642	898
ALAI					
MCAC					
Caraïbes					
Autre Amérique					
Asie l'URSS exclus					
Europe l'URSS exclus					
UE					
AELE					
Europe de l'Est					
Autre de l'Europe					
Ancienne URSS					
Océanie					
USA/Etats–Unis d'Amer	2093	640	640	1642	898

(VALUE AS PERCENTAGE OF WORLD TOTAL)(VALEURS EN POURCENTAGE DU TOTAL MONDIAL)

	1985	1986	1987	1988	1989	1990	1991	1992	1993	1994
Africa										
Americas	82.1	88.8	83.1	61.6	90.3	86.5	87.9	86.2	88.6	91.3
Northern America	70.5	76.9	76.1	55.4	81.3	75.5	76.1	78.3	77.2	79.2
LAIA	0.1	1.8	1.1	2.0	0.8	0.4	0.1		0.6	0.7
CACM	0.5	1.9	0.4	0.2	0.8	0.9	0.4		0.1	0.4
Caribbean	10.9	8.0	5.3	4.0	7.2	9.5	11.2	7.9	10.5	10.6
Rest of America	0.1	0.2	0.2	0.1	0.2	0.2	0.1		0.3	0.4
As.ex F.USSR	6.8	8.1	6.3	3.5	3.2	3.5	3.2	3.1	3.4	3.3
Eur.x F.USSR	10.0	11.7	9.8	33.9	5.6	7.8	7.8	5.0	6.3	4.7
EU	9.2	9.4	8.7	33.4	4.9	6.6	6.8	4.2	5.2	3.8
EFTA	0.8	2.4	1.0	0.5	0.6	1.2	1.0	0.8	1.1	0.9
East Europe										
Other Europe										
Former USSR	0.0									
Oceania	0.0	0.0	0.0	0.0	0.0					
USA/Etats–Unis d'Amer	70.1	74.5	74.8	54.8	80.5	74.8	75.3	76.4	76.6	78.5
Netherlands Antilles	7.0	6.7	4.0	2.9	6.3	8.7	10.1	6.7	9.4	9.2
Japan/Japon	6.6	7.4	4.2	3.0	2.7	3.1	3.1	3.1	3.1	2.9
United Kingdom	4.5	4.1	3.2	3.7	2.3	3.5	3.9	2.7	2.8	1.9
Jamaica/Jamaïque	0.9	1.0	1.2	0.9	0.9	0.8	0.9	1.2	0.9	1.3
Switz.Liecht	0.8	2.3	1.0	0.5	0.6	1.2	1.0	0.8	1.1	0.9
Canada	0.4	2.4	1.3	0.6	0.8	0.7	0.8	1.9	0.5	0.8
Netherlands/Pays–Bas	0.5	0.8	2.9	2.2	0.6	1.0	1.2	0.6	0.7	0.6
France,Monac	1.2	1.6	1.1	1.8	0.7	0.9	0.7	0.4	0.3	0.2
Italy/Italie	1.4	0.3	0.3	0.4	0.4	0.6	0.1		0.6	0.5

	1985	1986	1987	1988	1989	1990	1991	1992	1993	1994
Afrique					0.1					
Amériques				78.2	72.1	56.8	21.7	14.4	77.7	34.5
Amérique du Nord				78.2	49.9	56.8	21.7	14.4	77.7	34.5
ALAI					22.1					
MCAC					0.0					
Caraïbes					0.1					
Autre Amérique										
Asie l'URSS exclus					2.4					
Europe l'URSS exclus					13.2					
UE					13.2					
AELE										
Europe de l'Est										
Autre de l'Europe										
Ancienne URSS										
Océanie					4.5					
USA/Etats–Unis d'Amer				78.2	49.9	56.8	21.7	14.4	77.7	34.5

4. General Imports C.I.F. by Commodities according to the S.I.T.C. (Rev. 2) in thousand U.S. Dollars
Importations Générales C.A.F. par Produits d'après la C.T.C.I. (Rév. 2) en milliers de Dollars E.U.

SITC CTCI	COMMODITY	1991 WEIGHT POIDS	1991 VALUE VALEUR	1992 WEIGHT POIDS	1992 VALUE VALEUR	1993 WEIGHT POIDS	1993 VALUE VALEUR	1994 WEIGHT POIDS	1994 VALUE VALEUR	PRODUIT
	ALL COMMODITIES		267438		334087		313320		327432	TOUS PRODUITS
0	FOOD AND LIVE ANIMALS		50536		59082		42535		49250	ALIMENTS,ANIMAUX VIVANTS
01	MEAT AND PREPARATIONS		16295		12935		8825		11104	VIANDES ET PREPARATIONS
0111	BOVINE MEAT FRESH,FROZEN		2020		3494		2798		2312	VIANDES BOVIN FRAI,REF
0114	POULTRY FRESH CHLLD,FRZN		2422		3457		2281		3374	VOLAILLES MORTES
0118	MEAT NES FRESH,CHLD,FRZN				3594		2267		3337	AUTRES VIANDES,ABATS
0149	OTH PREPARD,PRESRVD MEAT		2395		2389		1444		2080	AUTRES PREP DE VIANDES
02	DAIRY PRODCTS,BIRDS'EGGS		5015		6506		4526		5138	PRODUITS LAITIERS,OEUFS
022	MILK AND CREAM		3174		3430		2710		2977	LAIT ET CREME
0223	MILK AND CREAM FRESH		990							LAIT,CREME FRAIS
024	CHEESE AND CURD		1454		2502		1444		1822	FROMAGE ET CAILLEBOTTE
03	FISH AND PREPARATIONS		3214		3362		2914		3146	POISSONS ET PREPARATIONS
035	FISH SALTED,DRIED,SMOKED				1616		1418		1427	POISSON SECHE,SALE,FUME
036	SHELL FISH FRESH,FROZEN		1421							CRUSTACES,MOLLUSQUES
04	CEREALS AND PREPARATIONS		5371		8556		5662		5542	CEREALES ET PRODUITS
0481	PREPD BREAKFAST FOOD ETC		1703		2323		1411		1586	CEREALES TRAVAILLEES
0484	BAKERY PRODUCTS		2611		4406		2906		2563	PRODUITS DE BOULANGERIE
05	VEGETABLES AND FRUIT		9698		12172		9355		8924	LEGUMES ET FRUITS
054	VEG ETC FRSH,SMPLY PRSVD				4727		3290		2977	LEGUMES FRAIS,CONG,SECS
056	VEGTBLES ETC PRSVD,PREPD		1716		2215		1746		1985	CONSERVES DE LEGUMES
057	FRUIT,NUTS,FRESH,DRIED		750		1319		936		842	FRUITS FRAIS OU SECS
0585	FRUIT OR VEGETABLE JUICE		2501		3161		2687		2567	JUS DE FRUITS
06	SUGAR AND PREPS,HONEY		1512		1789		1386		1626	SUCRES ET PRODUITS
07	COFFEE,TEA,COCOA,SPICES		2124		3120		1898		2488	CAFE,THE,CACAO,EPICES
071	COFFEE AND SUBSTITUTES				1201		744		810	CAFE ET SUCCEDANES
081	*FEEDING STUFF FOR ANIML		1624		1996		1964		1120	NOURRITURE POUR ANIMAUX
09	MISC EDIBLE PRODUCTS		5563		8621		5975		10163	PREP ALIMENTAIRES DIVERSES
091	MARGARINE AND SHORTENING		892							MARGARINE ET GRAISSES
0914	MARGARINE,EDIBLE FAT NES		892		521		370		356	MARGARINES,SIMILI SAINDOUX
098	EDIBLE PRODCTS,PREPS NES		4670		8082		5605		9806	PREP ALIMENTAIRES NDA
1	BEVERAGES AND TOBACCO		13034		12707		12937		12061	BOISSONS ET TABACS
11	BEVERAGES		11753		11620		11632		10625	BOISSONS
11102	FLAVORED WATERS NON–ALCO		3422		3937		4154		2773	LIMONADES,EAUX GAZEUSES
1121	WINE OF FRESH GRAPES ETC		1918		1516		1320		1199	VINS DE RAISINS FRAIS
1123	BEER,ALE,STOUT,PORTER		3781		3220		3431		3828	BIERES
1124	DISTILLED ALCOHOLIC BEVS		1848		2432		2352		2386	ALCOOLS,EAUX–DE–VIE
12	TOBACCO AND MANUFACTURES		1282		1087		1306		1436	TABACS BRUTS FABRIQUES
1222	CIGARETTES		1178		925		1127		1165	CIGARETTES
2	CRUDE MATERLS,EXCL FUELS		6475		5255		4970		7906	MAT BRUTES NON COMESTIBLES
24	CORK AND WOOD		3574		2756		3113		4986	LIEGE ET BOIS
248	WOOD SHAPED,SLEEPERS		3137		2588		2856		4986	BOIS SIMPLEMENT TRAVAILLES
27	CRUDE FERTLZR,MINRLS NES		1193		992		278		1286	ENGRAIS MINERAUX BRUTS
29	CRUDE ANIMAL,VEG MAT NES		1709		1506		1579		1498	MATIERES BRUTES ANIM,VEGET
2926	LIVE PLANTS,BULBS,ETC				1183		1186		1181	BULBES,TUBERCULES
3	MINERAL FUELS ETC		26893		25244		30938		32351	COMBUSTIBLES MINERAUX LUB
33	PETROLEUM AND PRODUCTS		26642		24268		30040		30989	PETROLE ET DERIVES
3341	GASOLINE,OTH LIGHT OILS		6889		6407		7150		6787	ESSENCES POUR MOTEURS
3342	KEROSENE,OTH MEDIUM OILS				2164		2585		2622	PETR LAMPANTS,AUT HUIL
33421	KEROSENE INCL JET FUEL		17221							PETROLES LAMPANTS
3343	GAS OILS				13444		18802		20612	GAS OILS
335	RESIDUAL PETRLM PROD NES				2254		1504		967	PRODUITS RESIDUELS NDA
5	CHEMCLS,RELATED PROD NES		15743		19382		17820		17057	PRODUITS CHIMIQUES
53	DYES,TANNING,COLOUR PROD		1246		2963		2237		2142	PROD TEINTURE,COLORANTS
533	PIGMENTS,PAINTS,ETC				2647		2004		1879	PIGMENTS,PEINTURES,VERNIS
5334	VARNISHES,DISTEMPERS ETC		980							PEINTURES A L'EAU
541	*MEDICINAL,PHARM PRODUCT		3276		2494		3092		2921	PROD MEDICINAUX PHARMACEUT
55	PERFUME,CLEANING ETC PRD		8323		10075		9455		8134	PROD POUR PARFUM,TOILETTE
553	PERFUMERY,COSMETICS,ETC		4134		5228		5120		4640	PRODUITS DE PARFUMERIE
5541	SOAPS		1193		1386		1472		1338	SAVONS,PROD TENSIO–ACTIFS
5542	WASHING PREPARATIONS ETC		2822		3461		2862		2155	PROD ORG TENSIO–ACT NDA
59	CHEMICAL MATERIALS NES		2141		2840		2342		2824	MAT PROD CHIMIQUES NDA
591	PESTICIDES,DISINFECTANTS		1322		1158		797		1061	DESINF,INSECT,FONG,HERB
598	MISCEL CHEM PRODUCTS NES				1682		1546		1763	PROD DIV INDUST CHIM NDA
6	BASIC MANUFACTURES		34742		49364		42698		45334	ART MANUFACTURES
61	LEATHER,DRESSED FUR,ETC		664		1319		932		456	CUIRS,PELLETERIES
62	RUBBER MANUFACTURES NES		973		1162		1573		2008	CAOUTCHOUC MANUFACTURE
63	WOOD,CORK MANUFACTRS NES		5087		5368		4818		7031	OUVRAGES LIEGE ET BOIS
634	VENEERS,PLYWOOD,ETC		2372		1837		2477		3106	PLACAGES,CONTRE–PLAQUES
64	PAPER,PAPERBOARD AND MFR		4225		10564		5581		4625	PAPIERS,CARTONS & OUVRAGES
65	TEXTILE YARN,FABRICS,ETC		4711		6710		6392		5074	FILS,TISSUS,ARTICLES TEXTILE
6584	LINENS ETC		1836		2478		2378		2020	LINGE DE MAISON
659	FLOOR COVERINGS,ETC		1457		3185		2200		1685	COUVRE–PARQUETS,TAPIS ETC
66	NONMETAL MINERAL MFS NES		7333		13330		15316		11633	ART MIN NON METALLIQUES
6612	CEMENT		1231		1445		1249		1470	CIMENTS HYDRAULIQUES
662	CLAY,REFRACTORY BLDG PRD				7906		9324		7120	MAT CONST REFRACTAIRES
665	GLASSWARE				1660		1284		1465	OUVRAGES EN VERRE
6652	HOUSEHLD,HOTEL ETC GLASS		1456							OBJETS VERRE TABLE,CUISINE
6664	PORCELN,CHINA HOUSE WARE		628		674		1236		805	VAISSELLE,ARTS MEN PORC
6666	CERAMIC ORNAMENTS ETC		791		994		1848		631	OBJETS PORCELAINE,CERAM
67	IRON AND STEEL		4738		7914		4106		5750	FER ET ACIER
673	IRON,STEEL SHAPES ETC		2339		972		1523		3125	BARRES,PROFIL FER,ACIER
68	NON–FERROUS METALS		1349		125		95		145	METAUX NON FERREUX
69	METAL MANUFACTURES NES		5663		2874		3884		8612	ART MANUFACT EN METAL NDA
695	TOOLS		720		898		904		1249	OUTILS A MAIN
699	BASE METAL MFRS NES				1408		2624		6132	ART MANUFACTURES MET NDA
7	MACHINES,TRANSPORT EQUIP		69109		102714		81984		85529	MACHINES MATERIEL TRANSPORT
71	POWER GENERATING EQUIPMT		7226		11672		5334		3840	MACHINES GENERATRICES
716	ROTATING ELECTRIC PLANT		2086		890		594		116	APP ELECTR ROTATIFS,PIECES
718	OTH POWER GENERATG MACHY		5141		10782		4740		3724	AUTRES MOTEURS PARTIES
72	MACHS FOR SPCL INDUSTRYS		1484		1220		1889		1240	MAC SPECIALES POUR INDUST
722	TRACTORS NON–ROAD		937		937		251		386	TRACTEURS
7234	CONST,MINING MACHNRY NES		317				1430		566	MACH POUR LA CONST, MINES
74	GENRL INDUSTRL MACHY NES		6233		4841		7370		7142	MACH APP INDUSTRIE
75	OFFICE MACHNES,ADP EQUIP		6292		7543		6386		6668	MACH BUREAU TRAIT AUTOM
751	OFFICE MACHINES		1752		1458		770		787	MACH,APPAREILS DE BUREAU
752	AUTOMTIC DATA PROC EQUIP		4540		6085		5616		5881	MACH TRAIT INFORMATION
76	TELECOMM,SOUND EQUIPMENT		10756		9894		4964		6928	EQUIPMENT DE TELECOM
764	TELECOM EQPT,PTS,ACC NES		7596		7231		2053		3370	EQUIP TELECOM,PIECES
77	ELECTRIC MACHNRY NES ETC		10637		23419		13925		12282	MACH APP ELECT NDA
7752	DOM REFRIGERATRS,FREEZRS		973		731		853		1465	REFRIG,CONGEL MENAGER
7757	DOMESTIC ELECTRC EQU NES				22688		13070		10817	APP ELECTR DOMEST NDA

4. General Imports C.I.F. by Commodities according to the S.I.T.C. (Rev. 2) in thousand U.S. Dollars
Importations Générales C.A.F. par Produits d'après la C.T.C.I. (Rév. 2) en milliers de Dollars E.U.

SITC CTCI	COMMODITY	1991		1992		1993		1994		PRODUIT
		WEIGHT POIDS	VALUE VALEUR	WEIGHT POIDS	VALUE VALEUR	WEIGHT POIDS	VALUE VALEUR	WEIGHT POIDS	VALUE VALEUR	
7784	ELECTRO–MECH HAND TOOLS		3022							OUTILS ELECTROMEC,PIECES
7788	OTH ELEC MACHY,EQUIP NES		6642							AUT MACH APP ELEC NDA
78	ROAD VEHICLES		22163		31888		34933		41056	VEHICULES ROUTIERS
781	PASS MOTOR VEH EXC BUSES		14681		21715		22866		31370	AUTO TRANSPORT PERSONNES
782	LORRIES,SPCL MTR VEH NES				2454		2873		2262	VEHICULES SPECIAUX,MARCH
7831	BUSES		1880				610			VOITURES TRANSPORT COMMUN
784	MOTOR VEH PRTS,ACCES NES		3754							PIECES 722,781,782,783
7849	OTHER MOTOR VEHCL PARTS				6300		7649		6652	PIECES 722,781,782,783
7868	OTH NONMOTR VEHICLES ETC		1094							AUT VEHIC NON AUTO,PIECES
79	OTHR TRANSPORT EQUIPMENT		4319		12235		7182		6373	AUTRE MATERIEL TRANSPORT
8	MISC MANUFACTURED GOODS		47825		55884		74837		72378	ART MANUFACTURES DIVERS
8122	CERAMIC PLUMBNG FIXTURES		884							EVIERS,LAVABOS,CUVETTES
8124	LIGHTING EQUIPMENT NES		1404		1174		1715		1016	APPAREILS ECLAIRAGE ETC
821	*FURNITURE,PARTS THEREOF		7622		9248		16786		13139	MEUBLES ET PIECES
8211	CHAIRS,SEATS AND PARTS		1602		1753		966		875	SIEGES ET PIECES
8219	FURNITURE AND PARTS NES				2016		4123		3473	AUTRES MEUBLES ET PIECES
82191	METAL FURNITURE NES		1501		2016		4123		3473	MEUBLES NDA EN METAL
84	CLOTHING AND ACCESSORIES		9142		13692		17988		15409	VETEMENTS
851	*FOOTWEAR		1771		1291		1754		2347	CHAUSSURES
87	PRECISION INSTRUMNTS NES		593		752		1694		1594	INSTRUM,APPAR SCIENT NDA
874	MEASURNG,CONTROLNG INSTR				656		1666		1584	INSTRUMENTS DE MESURE
88	PHOTO EQU,OPTICL GDS ETC		4898		5984		7088		6072	APP,FOURN PHOTO,OP,MONTR
881	PHOTO APPARAT,EQUIPT NES				2435		2244		1246	APP,EQUIP PHOTO NDA
885	WATCHES AND CLOCKS		3312		3121		4547		4487	HORLOGERIE
89	MISC MANUFCTRD GOODS NES		21109		22295		26172		31374	ART MANUFACTURES DIVERS
892	PRINTED MATTER		3811				4861		4951	IMPRIMES
893	ARTICLES OF PLASTIC NES		4102		5382		4357		4154	OUVRAGES EN MAT DIVIS 58
8947	OTH SPORT GDS,FAIR AMUSM		1422		2808		2225		2959	AUT ART DE SPORT
8973	PREC JEWLRY,GLD–SILVWARE		2844		3065		3479		4640	BIJOUX OR,ARGENT ORFEVRE
9	GOODS NOT CLASSD BY KIND		2986		3640		3918		5042	ART TRANSACT NON CLASSES
911	*MAIL NOT CLASSED BY KIN		1579		1364		1165		863	COLIS POSTAUX
931	*SPECIAL TRANSACTIONS		1274		1757		2450		4130	TRANS.SPECIALES

5. General Exports F.O.B. by Commodities according to the S.I.T.C. (Rev. 2) in thousand U.S. Dollars
Exportations Générales F.O.B. par Produits d'après la C.T.C.I. (Rév. 2) en milliers de Dollars E.U.

SITC CTCI	COMMODITY	1991		1992		1993		1994		PRODUIT
		WEIGHT POIDS	VALUE VALEUR	WEIGHT POIDS	VALUE VALEUR	WEIGHT POIDS	VALUE VALEUR	WEIGHT POIDS	VALUE VALEUR	
	ALL COMMODITIES		2945		4440		2113		2604	TOUS PRODUITS
5	CHEMCLS,RELATED PROD NES						188		4	PRODUITS CHIMIQUES
9	GOODS NOT CLASSD BY KIND		2945		4440		1925		2600	ART TRANSACT NON CLASSES
931	*SPECIAL TRANSACTIONS		2945		4440		1925		2600	TRANS.SPECIALES

1. HISTORICAL SERIES, 1961–1996 SPECIAL TRADE, IMPORTS C.I.F., EXPORTS F.O.B.
SERIES HISTORIQUES, 1961–1996 COMMERCE SPECIAL, IMPORTATIONS C.A.F., EXPORTATIONS F.O.B

YEAR ANNEE	VALUE IN MILLION C.F.A. FRANCS / VALEUR EN MILLION C.F.A. FRANCS — MERCHANDISE –MARCHANDISE		GOLD –OR		CONVERSION FACTORS U.S. CENTS PER C.F.A. FRANC FACTEURS DE CONVERSION CENTS E.U. PAR C.F.A. FRANC		INDEX NUMBERS –INDICES — QUANTUM		UNIT VALUE VALEUR UNITAIRE	
	IMPORTS	EXPORTS	IMPORTS	EXPORTS	IMPORTS	EXPORTS	IMPORTS	EXPORTS	IMPORTS	EXPORTS
1961	5479.00	3389.00	1.20	1.10	0.4051	0.4051				
1962	6134.00	3641.00	0.10	0.70	0.4051	0.4051				
1963	6502.00	5430.00		0.50	0.4051	0.4051				
1964	7368.00	7139.00	0.10		0.4051	0.4051				
1965	6770.00	6507.00	0.30		0.4051	0.4051				
1966	7581.00	7591.00			0.4051	0.4051				
1967	9895.00	7166.00			0.4051	0.4051				
1968	8816.00	8816.00			0.4051	0.4051				
1969	9193.00	9196.00			0.3860	0.3871				
1970	9491.00	8494.00			0.3601	0.3601				
1971	9053.00	8939.00			0.3601	0.3601				
1972	8547.00	9930.00			0.3960	0.3966				
1973	11496.00	8328.00			0.4490	0.4490				
1974	11090.00	11622.00			0.4151	0.4153				
1975	14615.00	10112.00			0.4733	0.4701				
1976	13154.00	13997.00			0.4132	0.4157				
1977	15540.00	19764.00			0.4123	0.4130				
1978	12372.00	16182.00			0.4448	0.4428				
1979	14816.00	16937.00			0.4698	0.4693				
1980	17010.00	24384.00			0.4733	0.4733				
1981	25646.00	21323.00			0.3686	0.3686				
1982	41307.00	35454.00			0.3040	0.3040				
1983	32456.00	28402.00			0.2624	0.2624				
1984	38193.00	37482.00			0.2290	0.2290				
1985	50685.00	41216.00			0.2230	0.2230				
1986	57841.01	22975.01			0.2888	0.2888				
1987	61370.00	39180.00			0.3327	0.3327				
1988	42002.00	19769.01			0.3357	0.3357				
1989	47994.00	42866.00			0.3135	0.3135				
1990	42050.00	32770.00			0.3673	0.3673				
1991	26186.00	13209.00			0.3550	0.3550				
1992	38469.01	28328.00			0.3796	0.3796				
1993	35559.01	31079.01			0.3530	0.3530				
1994	77300.00	83900.00			0.1805	0.1805				
1995	86900.00	85300.00			0.2010	0.2010				
1996	92058.49				0.1955					

2. IMPORTS BY BROAD ECONOMIC CATEGORY AND EXPORTS BY INDUSTRIAL ORIGIN. (PERCENTAGE OF TOTAL VALUE)
IMPORTATIONS PAR CATEGORIES ECONOMIQUES ET EXPORTATIONS PAR BRANCHE D'ACTIVITE.(EN POURCENTAGE DE LA VALEUR TOTALE)

IMPORTS – IMPORTATIONS

	1990	1991	1992	1993	1994	1995	1996
TOTAL IMPORTS–IMPORTATIONS TOTALES						100.	100.
1 FOOD BEV–ALIMENTATION BOISSONS						12.1	8.6
11 PRIMARY–PRODUITS DE BASE						1.8	1.1
111 FOR INDUSTRY–POUR L'INDUSTRIE						1.6	0.9
112 FOR HOUSEHOLDS–POUR LES MENAGES						0.2	0.3
12 PROCESSED–PRODUITS ELABORES						10.3	7.4
121 FOR INDUSTRY–POUR L'INDUSTRIE						5.9	3.3
122 FOR HOUSEHOLDS–POUR LES MENAGES						4.4	4.1
2 IND SUPPLIES–APPROV INDUSTRIELS						27.0	29.4
21 PRIMARY–PRODUITS DE BASE						13.2	15.7
22 PROCESSED–PRODUITS ELABORES						13.8	13.6
3 FUELS–COMBUSTIBLES						8.7	8.1
31 PRIMARY–PRODUITS DE BASE						0.1	0.0
32 PROCESSED–PRODUITS ELABORES						8.6	8.0
321 MOTOR SPIRIT–ESSENCE						3.1	2.6
322 OTHER–AUTRES						5.4	5.4
4 MACHINERY–EQUIPEMENT						22.2	13.9
41 CAPITAL EQUIPMENT–MACHINES						20.4	12.6
42 PARTS–PIECES ACCESSOIRES						1.7	1.3
5 TRANSPORT–TRANSPORT						21.8	24.8
51 PASSENGER CARS–AUTOMOBILES						3.4	3.0
52 OTHER–AUTRES						11.7	11.6
521 INDUSTRIAL–INDUSTRIELS						11.1	10.9
522 NON INDUSTRIAL–NON INDUSTRIEL						0.5	0.8
53 PARTS–PIECES ACCESSOIRES						6.8	10.1
6 CONSUM GOODS–BIENS CONSOMMATION						8.3	10.6
61 DURABLE–DURABLES						0.7	1.2
62 SEMI DURABLE–SEMI DURABLES						1.5	1.8
63 NON DURABLE–NON DURABLES						6.0	7.6
7 GOODS NES–BIENS NDA						0.0	4.8

EXPORTS – EXPORTATIONS

	1990	1991	1992	1993	1994	1995	1996
TOTAL EXPORTS–EXPORTATIONS TOTALES						100.	100.
1 AGRICULTURE						22.6	24.6
2 MINING QUARRY–INDUS EXTRACTIVES						63.9	60.2
3 MANUFACTURING–IND MANUFACTUR						13.5	15.2
31 FOOD BEV TOBACCO–ALIM BOISS TAB						0.7	0.1
32 TEXTILES–INDUSTRIES TEXTILES						0.1	0.1
33 WOOD & PRODUCTS–BOIS & PRODUITS						0.9	1.0
34 PAPER & PRODUCTS–PAPIER & PRODT						0.1	0.1
35 CHEMICALS–INDUSTRIES CHIMIQUES						1.5	0.2
36 NON METAL MIN–MIN NON METAL						0.0	0.0
37 BASIC METAL–IND METAL BASE						0.0	0.0
38 METAL MANUF–MANUF METAL						10.3	13.7
39 OTH MANUF IND–AUTRES MANUF						0.0	

3. TRADE BY PRINCIPAL COUNTRIES OF PRODUCTION AND CONSUMPTION (VALUE IN THOUSAND U.S. DOLLARS)
ECHANGES SELON LES PRINCIPAUX PAYS DE PRODUCTION ET DE COMSOMMATION (VALEUR EN MILLIERS DE DOLLARS EU)

COUNTRIES–PAYS	SPECIAL IMPORTS C.I.F. IMPORTATIONS SPECIALES C.A.F				
	1992	1993	1994	1995	1996
World		143522	154162	265499	179942
Africa		14164	31527	25923	16546
Americas		2530	3205	6017	4140
Northern America		2150	2960	5162	3818
LAIA		289	228	449	54
CACM		1		59	
Caribbean		90	17	346	267
Rest of America					
As.ex F.USSR		16949	10195	56079	18635
Eur.x F.USSR		85337	71649	116062	87975
EU		84358	71280	115482	87378
EFTA		923	219	531	577
East Europe		47	124	47	20
Other Europe		2			
Former USSR			20	76	20
Oceania		15		36	17
France,Monac		70642	59149	90739	71137
Japan/Japon		15090	8586	52303	15676
Cameroon/Cameroun		7112	8448	12880	7103
Congo		1161	18047	4738	3371
Germany/Allemagne		4439	3213	7626	2792
Belgium–Luxembourg		3003	2675	6589	2805
USA/Etats–Unis d'Amer		1928	2447	4871	2971
Netherlands/Pays–Bas		1960	1685	2815	1845
United Kingdom		1374	1437	1563	3148
Italy/Italie		1077	1332	2921	1674
Dem. Rep. of the Congo		1416	1386	1841	1938
Chad/Tchad		737	1378	1391	1491
Spain/Espagne		688	872	1389	1182
Senegal/Sénégal		827	814	1895	182
Cote d'Ivoire		909	481	530	638
So. Africa Customs Un		323	198	954	1043
China/Chine		618	310	603	511
Canada		222	513	290	848
Sweden/Suède		167	26	70	1595
Nigeria/Nigéria		814	286	725	6
Denmark/Danemark		332	425	571	315
Switz.Liecht		426	218	515	261
Ireland/Irlande		163	255	593	356
Korea, Republic of		89	80	644	364
Korea Dem People's Rp		47	284	519	300
Portugal		258	145	353	309
Lebanon/Liban		197	302	385	145
Malaysia/Malaisie		3	15		934
Morocco/Maroc		449	60	254	185
Brazil/Brésil		279	203	411	54
Hong Kong		76	120	372	259
Norway,SVD,JM		462	1	17	316
British Virgin Islds		90	17	344	267
Turkey/Turquie		208	184	91	96
Thailand/Thaïlande		201	29	228	90
Afghanistan			133	174	115
Austria/Autriche		2	5	213	90
Finland/Finlande		253	56		0
Benin/Bénin		31	14	138	94
Viet Nam		273		1	
Jordan/Jordanie			44	195	24
India/Inde			43	151	
Gabon		48	72	42	27
Indonesia/Indonésie		3	57	82	37
Greece/Grèce		0	6	42	130
Myanmar				178	
Sudan/Soudan		45		78	45
Tunisia/Tunisie		0		126	12
Togo		75	2	7	8
Zimbabwe				53	13

COUNTRIES–PAYS	SPECIAL EXPORTS F.O.B. EXPORTATIONS SPECIALES F.O.B.				
	1992	1993	1994	1995	1996
Monde		91689	81451	119522	115128
Afrique		4548	3482	6690	5471
Amériques		97	57	582	38
Amérique du Nord		94	57	579	38
ALAI					
MCAC					
Caraïbes				3	
Autre Amérique		3			
Asie l'URSS exclus		176	804	1966	26
Europe l'URSS exclus		86862	76633	108735	109576
UE		86799	76569	108448	109516
AELE		62	64	286	43
Europe de l'Est					3
Autre de l'Europe		1			14
Ancienne URSS					
Océanie					
Belgium–Luxembourg		71105	64906	75487	69192
France,Monac		13924	9862	30207	35556
United Kingdom		321	270	2069	3996
Dem. Rep. of the Congo		1255	437	1917	1904
Sudan/Soudan		2545	810	447	160
Cameroon/Cameroun		306	226	1825	1184
Congo		9	1012	1374	850
Germany/Allemagne		761	185	373	655
Chad/Tchad		42	735	496	425
Japan/Japon		175	608	905	
Spain/Espagne		3	1154	4	
Italy/Italie		449	43	148	99
So. Africa Customs Un		7	2	273	360
Nigeria/Nigéria		222	188	211	12
Hong Kong				607	22
Israel/Israël			133	431	
Netherlands/Pays–Bas		236	144	150	12
USA/Etats–Unis d'Amer		81	31	282	38
Switz.Liecht		62	64	240	43
Togo		1		10	384
Canada		13	25	297	
Senegal/Sénégal		4	10	9	164
Benin/Bénin		73		4	17
Cote d'Ivoire		41	38	3	
China/Chine			33	20	4
Norway,SVD,JM				47	
India/Inde		1	30		
Gabon			22	0	6
Morocco/Maroc		17		8	
Portugal			6	10	
Greece/Grèce					5
British Virgin Islds				3	
Panama		3			
Korea Dem People's Rp				2	
Denmark/Danemark				1	
Finland/Finlande				0	

(VALUE AS PERCENTAGE OF WORLD TOTAL)(VALEURS EN POURCENTAGE DU TOTAL MONDIAL)

	1987	1988	1989	1990	1991	1992	1993	1994	1995	1996
Africa			20.9				9.9	20.5	9.8	9.2
Americas			1.8				1.8	2.1	2.3	2.3
Northern America			1.5				1.5	1.9	1.9	2.1
LAIA			0.3				0.2	0.1	0.2	0.0
CACM			0.0				0.0		0.0	
Caribbean			0.0				0.1	0.0	0.1	0.1
Rest of America										
As.ex F.USSR			12.0				11.8	6.6	21.1	10.4
Eur.x F.USSR			57.9				59.5	46.5	43.7	48.9
EU			57.0				58.8	46.2	43.5	48.6
EFTA			0.5				0.6	0.1	0.2	0.3
East Europe			0.3				0.0	0.1	0.0	0.0
Other Europe			0.2				0.0			
Former USSR			0.0					0.0	0.0	0.0
Oceania			0.2				0.0		0.0	0.0
France,Monac			42.5				49.2	38.4	34.2	39.5
Japan/Japon			7.6				10.5	5.6	19.7	8.7
Cameroon/Cameroun			9.1				5.0	5.5	4.9	3.9
Congo			3.2				0.8	11.7	1.8	1.9
Germany/Allemagne			5.0				3.1	2.1	2.9	1.6
Belgium–Luxembourg			2.5				2.1	1.7	2.5	1.6
USA/Etats–Unis d'Amer			1.3				1.3	1.6	1.8	1.7
Netherlands/Pays–Bas			2.1				1.4	1.1	1.1	1.0
United Kingdom			1.2				1.0	0.9	0.6	1.7
Italy/Italie			1.7				0.8	0.9	1.1	0.9

	1987	1988	1989	1990	1991	1992	1993	1994	1995	1996
Afrique			4.3				5.0	4.3	5.6	4.8
Amériques			1.2				0.1	0.1	0.5	0.0
Amérique du Nord			0.6				0.1	0.1	0.5	0.0
ALAI										
MCAC										
Caraïbes									0.0	
Autre Amérique			0.6				0.0			
Asie l'URSS exclus			0.0				0.2	1.0	1.6	0.0
Europe l'URSS exclus			94.4				94.7	94.1	91.0	95.2
UE			89.4				94.7	94.0	90.7	95.1
AELE			5.0				0.1	0.1	0.2	0.0
Europe de l'Est										0.0
Autre de l'Europe							0.0			0.0
Ancienne URSS										
Océanie										
Belgium–Luxembourg			50.9				77.6	79.7	63.2	60.1
France,Monac			34.4				15.2	12.1	25.3	30.9
United Kingdom			0.3				0.3	0.3	1.7	3.5
Dem. Rep. of the Congo			0.7				1.4	0.5	1.6	1.7
Sudan/Soudan			2.4				2.8	1.0	0.4	0.1
Cameroon/Cameroun			0.2				0.3	0.3	1.5	1.0
Congo			0.5				0.0	1.2	1.1	0.7
Germany/Allemagne			1.1				0.8	0.2	0.3	0.6
Chad/Tchad			0.1				0.0	0.9	0.4	0.4
Japan/Japon							0.2	0.7	0.8	

4. Special Imports C.I.F. by Commodities according to the S.I.T.C. (Rev. 2) in thousand U.S. Dollars
Importations Spéciales C.A.F. par Produits d'après la C.T.C.I. (Rév. 2) en milliers de Dollars E.U.

SITC CTCI	COMMODITY	1993		1994		1995		1996		PRODUIT
		WEIGHT POIDS	VALUE VALEUR	WEIGHT POIDS	VALUE VALEUR	WEIGHT POIDS	VALUE VALEUR	WEIGHT POIDS	VALUE VALEUR	
	ALL COMMODITIES		143522		154162		265499		179942	TOUS PRODUITS
0	FOOD AND LIVE ANIMALS		17709		24635		27587		12585	ALIMENTS,ANIMAUX VIVANTS
01	MEAT AND PREPARATIONS		1908		513		349		165	VIANDES ET PREPARATIONS
011	MEAT FRESH,CHILLD,FROZEN	W 238	1100	W 95	167	W 15	70	W 13	55	VIANDES FRAICHES,REF,CONGE
0111	BOVINE MEAT FRESH,FROZEN	W 85	547	W 29	84	W 1	6	W 3	11	VIANDES BOVIN FRAI,REF
01112	BOVINE MEAT BONELESS	W 81	529	W 28	80		2	W 2	10	VIANDES BOVIN DESOSSEES
0114	POULTRY FRESH CHLLD,FRZN	W 144	505	W 29	75	W 3	11	W 4	19	VOLAILLES MORTES
014	MEAT PREPD,PRSVD,NES ETC	W 269	791	W 151	342	W 124	275	W 47	104	CONSERVES DE VIANDES
0149	OTH PREPARD,PRESRVD MEAT	W 226	518	W 96	170	W 116	260	W 47	102	AUTRES PREP DE VIANDES
02	DAIRY PRODCTS,BIRDS'EGGS		2418		2217		1555		764	PRODUITS LAITIERS,OEUFS
022	MILK AND CREAM	W 1597	1998	W 1387	1968	W 829	1320	W 426	615	LAIT ET CREME
0223	MILK AND CREAM FRESH	W 223	377	W 601	1024	W 211	155	W 169	139	LAIT,CREME FRAIS
0224	MILK,CREAM PRESERVED ETC	W 1373	1622	W 786	945	W 618	1165	W 257	476	LAIT,CREME CONS,CONC
02243	MILK DRY,OVER 1.5% FAT	W 533	606	W 187	362	W 32	108	W 49	162	LAIT POUDRE SUP 1.5%
02249	MILK(EX DRY) PRSVD,SWEET	W 837	1007	W 598	582	W 585	1056	W 208	315	LAIT CONS,CONC SUCRE
03	FISH AND PREPARATIONS		1139		528		359		164	POISSONS ET PREPARATIONS
037	FISH ETC PREPD,PRSVD NES	W 403	773	W 245	383	W 203	313	W 24	59	POIS,CRUST,MOL PREPARES
0371	FISH PREPARD,PRESRVD NES	W 399	763	W 245	382	W 203	313	W 24	58	CONSERVES DE POISSONS
04	CEREALS AND PREPARATIONS		8892		17183		15010		5915	CEREALES ET PRODUITS
046	WHEAT ETC MEAL OR FLOUR	W 22393	5640	W 33624	14006	W 20892	7999	W 10190	3442	SEMOULE FARINE,FROMENT
04601	FLOUR OF WHEAT OR MESLIN	W 22392	5638	W 33616	13990	W 20892	7999	W 10190	3442	FARINE DE FROMENT
047	OTHER CEREAL MEALS,FLOUR	W 2510	674	W 1662	603	W 2546	2083	W 416	343	AUTRES SEMOULES,FARINES
04702	MEAL OR GROATS NON–WHEAT	W 1080	354	W 1150	426	W 2229	1437	W 416	343	GRUAUX,SEMOULES DE CEREALES
048	CEREAL ETC PREPARATIONS	W 3221	2253	W 3546	2256	W 3122	4374	W 1540	1732	PREPTNS A BASE CEREALES
0482	MALT INCLUDING FLOUR	W 2941	1510	W 3224	1747	W 2877	3767	W 1356	1352	MALT MEME TORREFIE
05	VEGETABLES AND FRUIT		1294		1839		2185		2286	LEGUMES ET FRUITS
054	VEG ETC FRSH,SMPLY PRSVD	W 676	712	W 608	1477	W 616	1855	W 439	1862	LEGUMES FRAIS,CONG,SECS
0546	VEGETABLES SIMPLY PRESVD	W 372	454	W 322	1367	W 487	1735	W 404	1756	LEGUMES CONG,CONSER
05461	VEGETABLES FROZEN	W 372	454	W 322	1367	W 463	1726	W 404	1756	LEGUMES CONGELES
06	SUGAR AND PREPS,HONEY		893		1376		2233		430	SUCRES ET PRODUITS
061	SUGAR AND HONEY	W 1791	817	W 2452	1300	W 3013	2128	W 611	382	SUCRES ET MIEL
0612	REFINED SUGAR ETC	W 1790	813	W 2450	1297	W 2997	2107	W 587	336	SUCRES RAFFINES
07	COFFEE,TEA,COCOA,SPICES		294		263		3911		1624	CAFE,THE,CACAO,EPICES
071	COFFEE AND SUBSTITUTES		12	W 1406	192	W 18919	3861	W 10160	1555	CAFE ET SUCCEDANES
0711	COFFEE GREEN,ROASTED,SUB		5	W 1386	173	W 18916	3839	W 10152	1528	CAFE TORREFIE OU DECAFEINE
07111	COFFEE GREEN,HUSKS,SKINS			W 1360	120	W 18894	3794	W 10147	1518	CAFE NON TORREFIE
09	MISC EDIBLE PRODUCTS		817		700		1942		1216	PREP ALIMENTAIRES DIVERSES
098	EDIBLE PRODCTS,PREPS NES	W 261	652	W 244	660	W 483	1701	W 242	1019	PREP ALIMENTAIRES NDA
09806	YEASTS,BAKING POWDERS	W 190	506	W 112	262	W 246	595	W 86	251	LEVURES
09809	MISC FOOD PREPRTIONS NES	W 48	97	W 94	329	W 138	947	W 121	665	PREP ALIMENTAIRES NDA
1	BEVERAGES AND TOBACCO		8043		14238		12128		8977	BOISSONS ET TABACS
11	BEVERAGES		2840		2022		2885		2268	BOISSONS
111	NON–ALCOHL BEVERAGES NES	W 866	698	W 937	362	W 737	343	W 1066	534	BOISSONS NON ALCOOLIQUES
112	ALCOHOLIC BEVERAGES	W 1339	2142	W 1275	1660	W 2605	2542	W 959	1734	BOISSONS ALCOOLIQUES
1121	WINE OF FRESH GRAPES ETC	W 1032	1076	W 955	833	W 2254	1336	W 685	922	VINS DE RAISINS FRAIS
11212	WINE OF FRESH GRAPES	W 1025	1043	W 951	816	W 2254	1334	W 676	890	VINS DE MOUTS DE RAISINS
1124	DISTILLED ALCOHOLIC BEVS	W 204	948	W 182	697	W 304	1113	W 198	704	ALCOOLS,EAUX–DE–VIE
11241	WHISKY	W 115	555	W 155	603	W 204	768	W 124	461	WHISKY
12	TOBACCO AND MANUFACTURES		5204		12216		9244		6709	TABACS BRUTS FABRIQUES
121	TOBACCO UNMNFCTRD,REFUSE	W 845	4638	W 801	4417	W 1074	8510	W 438	3632	TABACS BRUTS,DECHETS
1212	TOBACCO STRIPPED OR PART	W 827	4541	W 767	4174	W 1065	8441	W 420	3606	TABACS PART ECOTES
122	TOBACCO,MANUFACTURED	W 35	566	W 375	7799	W 43	734	W 187	3077	TABACS FABRIQUES
1222	CIGARETTES	W 35	562	W 375	7799	W 43	734	W 187	3077	CIGARETTES
2	CRUDE MATERLS,EXCL FUELS		1620		10353		27184		25177	MAT BRUTES NON COMESTIBLES
24	CORK AND WOOD				97		2466		4365	LIEGE ET BOIS
247	OTH WOOD ROUGH,SQUARED			W 170	90	W 13773	2038	W 12034	3906	BOIS BRUTS EQUARRIS
2471	SAW–,VENEER–LOGS CONIFER			W 170	90	W 12997	1921	W 11995	3901	CONIFERES POUR SCIAGE,PLACAG
24711	— IN THE ROUGH			W 170	90	W 12997	1921	W 11995	3901	ECORCES OU DEGROSSIS
26	TEXTILE FIBRES AND WASTE		1139		9361		22443		19132	FIBRES TEXTILES
263	COTTON			W 4346	7951	W 12522	20547	W 6008	17501	COTON
2631	RAW COTTON,EXCL LINTERS			W 4346	7951	W 12522	20547	W 6008	17501	COTON EN MASSE
269	WASTE OF TEXTILE FABRICS	W 700	1138	W 1074	1410	W 1493	1895	W 1416	1631	FRIPERIE DRILLES,CHIFFONS
26901	BULK TEXT WSTE,OLD CLTHG	W 697	1132	W 1049	1303	W 1484	1886	W 1407	1613	ART ET ACCESS D'HABILLEMENT
27	CRUDE FERTLZR,MINRLS NES		323		645		765		777	ENGRAIS MINERAUX BRUTS
278	OTHER CRUDE MINERALS	W 3067	320	W 5350	645	W 4979	742	W 3365	595	AUTRES MINERAUX BRUTS
2783	COMMON SALT,ETC	W 3009	294	W 5083	518	W 4764	595	W 3288	420	SEL
29	CRUDE ANIMAL,VEG MAT NES		149		182		1174		868	MATIERES BRUTES ANIM,VEGET
292	CRUDE VEG MATERIALS NES	W 100	148	W 140	182	W 1194	1174	W 1961	867	MAT BRUTES VEGETALES NDA
2922	NAT GUMS,RESINS,LACS,ETC					W 1139	409	W 1910	657	GOMME LAQUE
3	MINERAL FUELS ETC		24542		11606		23063		14594	COMBUSTIBLES MINERAUX LUB
33	PETROLEUM AND PRODUCTS		24251		11374		22755		14550	PETROLE ET DERIVES
334	PETROLEUM PRODUCTS,REFIN	W 91470	23994	W 73333	11223	W 135842	22715	W 95975	14447	PRODUITS RAFFINES
3341	GASOLINE,OTH LIGHT OILS	W 30002	7805	W 23368	3223	W 48858	8364	W 34827	4756	ESSENCES POUR MOTEURS
33411	MOTOR,AVIATION SPIRIT	W 19002	5017	W 12962	1827	W 27642	4975	W 20366	2767	ESSENCES MOTEURS D'AVIONS
33419	OTH LIGHT PETROLEUM OILS	W 11000	2788	W 10406	1396	W 21215	3388	W 14461	1989	AUTRES HUILES LEGERES
3342	KEROSENE,OTH MEDIUM OILS	W 28658	7200	W 29499	3948	W 30299	4239	W 21568	2973	PETR LAMPANTS,AUT HUIL
33421	KEROSENE INCL JET FUEL	W 28658	7200	W 29499	3948	W 30299	4239	W 21568	2973	PETROLES LAMPANTS
3343	GAS OILS	W 28960	6821	W 17663	2242	W 51362	7651	W 35999	4809	GAS OILS
3344	FUEL OILS,NES	W 3380	1392	W 1814	378	W 4581	1152	W 2859	639	FUEL OILS
3345	LUBS,PETROLEUM OILS NES	W 471	775	W 989	1432	W 743	1309	W 722	1270	HUILES LUBRIFIANTES
33451	LUBS(HIGH PETR CONT) ETC	W 470	771	W 989	1431	W 727	1262	W 722	1268	HUILES LUBRIF,H LOURDES
4	ANIMAL,VEGETABLE OIL,FAT		512		2811		1466		609	HUILES,GRAISSES ANIM,VEG
42	FIXED VEGETABLE OIL,FAT		512		2811		1392		554	HUILES VEGETALES FIXES
423	FIXED VEG OILS,SOFT	W 133	146	W 1612	1231	W 721	614	W 449	505	HUILES VEGET DOUCES FIXES
4233	COTTON SEED OIL	W 23	40	W 1076	822	W 662	524	W 208	120	HUILE DE COTON
424	FIXED VEG OIL NONSOFT	W 249	366	W 2207	1580	W 456	778	W 35	49	AUTRES HUILES VEG FIXES
4242	PALM OIL			W 490	483	W 400	684	W 23	20	HUILE DE PALME
4249	FIXED VEGETABLE OILS NES	W 234	344	W 1697	1069	W 56	92	W 12	29	HUILES VEGET FIXES NDA
5	CHEMCLS,RELATED PROD NES		15346		25037		20721		14056	PRODUITS CHIMIQUES
52	INORGANIC CHEMICALS		876		620		1501		563	PROD CHIM INORGANIQUES
522	INORG ELEMNTS,OXIDES,ETC	W 620	588	W 514	568	W 886	810	W 215	245	ELEMENTS INORGANIQUES
53	DYES,TANNING,COLOUR PROD		371		1242		1115		614	PROD TEINTURE,COLORANTS
533	PIGMENTS,PAINTS,ETC	W 115	324	W 465	1240	W 136	1049	W 119	503	PIGMENTS,PEINTURES,VERNIS
5334	VARNISHES,DISTEMPERS ETC	W 13	89	W 398	1051	W 80	745	W 15	218	PEINTURES A L'EAU
53341	WATER–THINNED PAINTS	W 11	72	W 381	884	W 54	734	W 10	54	PEINTURES DILUEES
541	*MEDICINAL,PHARM PRODUCT	K 504009	9078	K 921638	16759	K 375609	9522	K 325783	6416	PROD MEDICINAUX PHARMACEUT
5416	GLYCOSIDES,GLANDS,SERA	K 43413	763	K 55550	579	K 34348	750	K 8010	238	HETEROSIDES
54164	ANTISERA,MICROB VACCINES	K 43413	763	K 55550	579	K 32786	743	K 2754	156	SERUMS,VACCINS
5417	MEDICAMENTS	K 436121	7993	K 847721	15912	K 320603	8300	K 299334	5960	MEDICAMENTS
54179	— CONTNG OTH SUBSTANCES	K 389753	7861	K 801329	15720	K 307173	7644	K 294306	5538	MED CONT AUT SUBSTANCES
55	PERFUME,CLEANING ETC PRD		1244		964		980		654	PROD POUR PARFUM,TOILETTE

4. Special Imports C.I.F. by Commodities according to the S.I.T.C. (Rev. 2) in thousand U.S. Dollars
Importations Spéciales C.A.F. par Produits d'après la C.T.C.I. (Rév. 2) en milliers de Dollars E.U.

SITC CTCI	COMMODITY	1993 WEIGHT POIDS	1993 VALUE VALEUR	1994 WEIGHT POIDS	1994 VALUE VALEUR	1995 WEIGHT POIDS	1995 VALUE VALEUR	1996 WEIGHT POIDS	1996 VALUE VALEUR	PRODUIT
554	SOAP,CLEANSING ETC PREPS	W 396	746	W 690	670	W 513	748	W 185	482	SAVONS,PRODUITS DETERSIFS
562	*FERTILIZERS,MANUFACTURE	W 1534	1104	W 2546	593	W 3165	1100	W 1041	254	ENGRAIS MANUFACTURES
5629	FERTILIZERS NES	W 830	694	W 1591	371	W 2585	882	W 2	1	ENGRAIS NDA
56291	NIT–PHOS–POT FERTLZR NES	W 830	694	W 1591	371	W 2500	820	W 2	1	ENGRAIS CONT N P K
58	PLASTIC MATERIALS ETC		572		987		765		750	MAT PLAST ARTIFICIELLES
583	POLYMERIZATION ETC PRODS	W 88	318	W 229	721	W 195	603	W 324	530	PROD POLYMERISATION
5839	OTH POLYMRZTION ETC PROD	W 34	157	W 120	489	W 78	224	W 44	64	AUT PROD POLYMER COPOLYM
59	CHEMICAL MATERIALS NES		1802		3501		5199		4509	MAT PROD CHIMIQUES NDA
591	PESTICIDES,DISINFECTANTS	W 105	566	W 285	2824	W 390	3760	W 344	4039	DESINF,INSECT,FONG,HERB
5911	INSECTICIDES,FOR RETAIL	W 79	530	W 279	2802	W 358	3640	W 261	2692	INSECTICIDES VENTE DET
5914	DISINFECTANTS,ETC,FR RET	W 25	33	W 6	22	W 11	52	W 67	1189	DESINFECTANTS VENTE DET
59149	RAT POISONS ETC FR RTAIL	W 25	26	W 3	7	W 7	40	W 63	1185	ANTIPARASITES VENTE DET
598	MISCEL CHEM PRODUCTS NES	W 208	1024	W 218	531	W 111	922	W 78	422	PROD DIV INDUST CHIM NDA
5989	CHEM PRODUCTS,PREPS NES	W 194	1003	W 198	492	W 66	657	W 67	390	PROD PREP CHIMIQUES NDA
59899	OTH CHEM PRODS,PREPS,NES	W 116	869	W 152	393	W 35	415	W 46	306	AUT PRODUITS CHIMIQUES NDA
6	BASIC MANUFACTURES		16532		21404		29201		19118	ART MANUFACTURES
62	RUBBER MANUFACTURES NES		1508		2425		3775		2927	CAOUTCHOUC MANUFACTURE
625	RUBBER TYRES, TUBES ETC	W 346	1273	W 491	2058	W 561	3227	W 404	2621	PNEUS CAOUTCHOUC VULCANISE
6252	TYRES,NEW,BUS OR LORRY	W 145	696	W 229	1568	W 363	2263	W 215	1979	PNEUS POUR AUTOBUS,CAMIONS
63	WOOD,CORK MANUFACTRS NES		89		657		325		239	OUVRAGES LIEGE ET BOIS
634	VENEERS,PLYWOOD,ETC	W 74	57	W 970	608	W 380	105	W 287	176	PLACAGES,CONTRE–PLAQUES
6342	PLYWOOD OF WOOD SHEETS	W 66	53	W 967	606	W 338	97	W 267	172	BOIS CONTRE–PLAQUES
64	PAPER,PAPERBOARD AND MFR		3539		3483		4169		3970	PAPIERS,CARTONS & OUVRAGES
641	PAPER AND PAPERBOARD	W 628	1373	W 649	1013	W 709	1398	W 1305	2832	PAPIERS ET CARTONS
6412	PRINTG,WRITING PAPER NES	W 143	283	W 346	315	W 457	601	W 1057	2347	PAPIERS POUR L'IMPRESSION
64121	— UNCOATED	W 142	276	W 337	294	W 337	506	W 850	2132	PAPIERS IMPRES NON COUCHES
6415	PAPER,PAPERBRD,BULK,NES	W 452	953	W 289	657	W 213	403	W 150	221	PAPIERS,CARTONS ROULEAUX
64159	OTHER PAPER ETC,BULK,NES	W 450	943	W 288	643	W 212	397	W 145	217	AUT PAPIER ROULEAUX FEUILLES
642	PAPER,ETC,PRECUT,ARTS OF	W 648	2167	W 1258	2469	W 754	2771	W 333	1138	PAP,CARTONS DECOUPES
6421	PAPER ETC CONTAINERS	W 455	1305	W 813	1415	W 538	1749	W 174	521	BOITES,SACS EMBALLAGES
6423	EXERCISE BOOKS ETC	W 98	409	W 256	560	W 114	538	W 87	320	REGISTRES,CAHIERS,CARNETS
65	TEXTILE YARN,FABRICS,ETC		1210		1176		2627		1431	FILS,TISSUS,ARTICLES TEXTILE
652	COTTON FABRICS,WOVEN	W 32	366	W 67	430	W 185	840	W 85	826	TISSUS DE COTON
6522	WOVEN COTTON BLEACHD,ETC	W 31	364	W 60	390	W 86	821	W 71	772	TISSUS COTON BLANCHIS ETC
65224	BLCHED COTTON FABRIC NES	W 30	334	W 55	361	W 71	737	W 54	609	AUT TIS PLUS 85% COT BLANCHI
658	TEXTILE ARTICLES NES	W 134	552	W 85	416	W 372	720	W 183	390	ART FACONNES MAT TEXTILES
66	NONMETAL MINERAL MFS NES		3261		2102		2835		2625	ART MIN NON METALLIQUES
661	LIME,CEMENT,BLDG PRODS	W 15818	2493	W 17511	1434	W 14245	1377	W 10489	977	CHAUX,CIMENTS MAT CONSTR
6612	CEMENT	W 15727	2404	W 17414	1399	W 14033	1288	W 10357	901	CIMENTS HYDRAULIQUES
664	GLASS	W 66	202	W 112	237	W 98	401	W 91	927	VERRE
6647	SAFETY GLASS CUT OR NOT	W 6	99	W 21	154	W 30	283	W 25	829	GLACES DE SECURITE
67	IRON AND STEEL		1380		1469		1796		1367	FER ET ACIER
673	IRON,STEEL SHAPES ETC	W 921	520	W 1917	824	W 821	391	W 567	310	BARRES,PROFIL FER,ACIER
6732	IRON,STEEL BARS ETC	W 581	354	W 1598	716	W 672	313	W 324	165	BARRES FER,ACIER
67326	IRN,OTH STL BARS HOTROLD	W 301	143	W 1232	563	W 165	77	W 150	73	BARRES PLEINES FER,ACIER
674	IRN,STL UNIV,PLATE,SHEET	W 452	400	W 403	316	W 792	800	W 594	554	LARGES PLATS,TOLES
68	NON–FERROUS METALS		1144		4685		3548		1812	METAUX NON FERREUX
684	ALUMINIUM	W 295	1082	W 2003	4393	W 988	3204	W 437	1210	ALUMINIUM
6842	ALUMINIUM,ALLOYS WORKED	W 295	1082	W 2003	4393	W 988	3204	W 437	1210	ALUMINIUM,ALLIAGES OUVRE
68422	ALUMNM PLATE,SHEET,STRIP	W 166	550	W 1955	3985	W 941	2575	W 430	1066	TOLES, PLANCHES EN ALU
68423	ALUMINIUM FOIL	W 129	530	W 41	401	W 46	621	W 7	144	FEUILLES,BANDES MINCES AL
686	ZINC	W 4	9	W 133	251	W 210	312	W 695	570	ZINC
6863	ZINC,ALLOYS WKD,INC DUST	W 4	9	W 133	251	W 210	312	W 695	570	ZINC ET ALLIAGES OUVRES
68632	ZINC SHEETS,STRIP,FOIL	W 2	3	W 133	251	W 210	312	W 695	570	PLANCHES,FEUILLES EN ZINC
69	METAL MANUFACTURES NES		4400		5406		10126		4743	ART MANUFACT EN METAL NDA
693	WIRE PRODUCTS NON ELECTR	W 96	370	W 163	368	W 517	1364	W 25	126	OUVRAGES FILS METALLIQUES
6935	METAL FENCING,GAUZE,ETC	W 70	193	W 52	144	W 490	1303	W 22	87	TOILES EN FER,ACIER,CUIVRE
69351	IRN,STL FENCNG,GAUZE ETC	W 70	193	W 52	141	W 490	1303	W 22	86	TOILES EN FER,ACIER
695	TOOLS	W 214	1069	W 187	1138	W 422	4497	W 145	1313	OUTILS A MAIN
6951	HAND TOOLS,AGRIC,FOREST	W 134	429	W 97	259	W 241	860	W 64	194	BECHES,PELLES,PIOCHES
6953	OTHER HAND TOOLS	W 71	540	W 85	779	W 127	1939	W 75	1073	AUTRES OUTILS A MAIN
69539	HAND TOOLS ETC NES	W 44	260	W 58	540	W 97	1613	W 59	894	OUTILLAGE A MAIN NDA
6954	BLADES,TIPS,ETC FR TOOLS	W 9	100	W 4	100	W 54	1698	W 6	47	OUTILS POUR MACHINE–OUTIL
69541	PARTS TO INSERT IN TOOLS	W 7	69	W 3	55	W 52	1671	W 1	27	OUTILS DE FORAGE
696	CUTLERY		488	W 13	34	W 2	41	W 14	49	COUTELLERIE
69606	BASE METAL TABLEWARE NES		456	W 11	4		2	W 4	32	CUILLERS,FOURCHETTES
697	BASE MTL HOUSEHOLD EQUIP	W 66	256	W 436	1446	W 93	434	W 272	745	ART MENAGE MET COMMUNS
6974	BASE MTL DMSTC ARTIC NES	W 55	200	W 417	1387	W 60	256	W 227	585	ARTICLES NDA FONTE,FER,ETC
69743	— OF ALUMINIUM	W 17	42	W 363	1166	W 4	28	W 188	493	ARTICLES NDA EN ALUMINIUM
699	BASE METAL MFRS NES	W 245	1378	W 599	1545	W 786	2633	W 395	1536	ART MANUFACTURES MET NDA
6991	LOCKSMITHS WARES,ETC	W 36	432	W 29	150	W 92	411	W 39	275	ARTICLES DE SERRURERIE
6996	BASE MTL MISC ARTICLES	W 134	440	W 156	478	W 206	863	W 100	355	ART DIVERS METAUX COMMUNS
6998	MFRS NES OF CPR,NIKL,ETC	W 3	39	W 392	804	W 448	1212	W 211	594	OUVRAGES EN CU,NI,AL,PB,ZN
69983	ALUMINIUM MANUFACTS NES	W 3	31	W 392	798	W 448	1209	W 210	578	OUVRAGES EN ALUMINIUM
7	MACHINES,TRANSPORT EQUIP		48712		36668		112122		67289	MACHINES MATERIEL TRANSPORT
71	POWER GENERATING EQUIPMT		1435		1424		3897		3704	MACHINES GENERATRICES
713	INTRNL COMBUS PSTN ENGIN	W 21	360	W 72	730	W 91	2287	W 96	2811	MOTEURS EXPL COMB INT, PIECE
7138	PISTON ENGINES NES	W 2	36	W 21	190	W 55	1253	W 75	2240	MOTEURS A PISTONS NDA
7139	PISTON ENGINE PARTS NES	W 9	247	W ,45	459	W 28	940	W 17	406	PIECES POUR 713.2,3,8
716	ROTATING ELECTRIC PLANT	W 54	864	W 37	503	W 98	1465	W 68	839	APP ELECTR ROTATIFS,PIECES
7162	AC MTRS,GENRTRS,GEN SETS	W 43	563	W 21	251	W 55	640	W 45	568	MOTEURS ELECTRIQUES
71623	GEN SETS WITH PISTN ENGN	W 40	458	W 13	143	W 40	408	W 40	321	GROUPES MOTEUR EXPLOSION
72	MACHS FOR SPCL INDUSTRYS		3002		2809		26240		7912	MAC SPECIALES POUR INDUST
722	TRACTORS NON–ROAD	W 116	661	W 209	941	W 57	454	W 52	754	TRACTEURS
7224	WHEELED TRACTORS NES	W 116	661	W 166	821	W 37	365	W 52	754	TRACTEURS A ROUES
723	CIVIL ENGNEERG EQUIP ETC	W 179	291	W 166	876	W 1897	23753	W 322	4939	APPAREILS DE GENIE CIVIL
7233	MECHANICAL ROAD ROLLERS	W 44	92	W 56	276	W 281	3272	W 49	1098	ROULEAUX COMPRESSEURS
7234	CONST,MINING MACHNRY NES	W 101	186	W 98	460	W 1602	20437	W 265	3685	MACH POUR LA CONST, MINES
72341	SELF–PROPELLD DOZERS,ETC	W 48	98	W 76	366	W 1287	14872	W 70	472	BULLDOZERS
72342	SLFPRP SHOVELS,EXCAVATRS	W 52	75	W 22	93	W 186	1410	W 118	831	PELLES MECANIQUES
72343	SLFPRP CONST ETC MCH NES							W 30	877	AUT MACH EXTR,TERRASSEM
72344	BORING,SINKING MACHINERY					W 108	4025	W 40	1345	MACHINES DE FORAGE
728	OTH MACHY FOR SPCL INDUS	W 52	1072	W 46	569	W 106	790	W 595	1327	AUT MACH IND PARTICULIERES
7281	MACH–TOOLS FR SPCL INDUS	W 13	278	W 16	113	W 25	280	W 545	1154	MACH–OUTILS SPEC IND PART
72812	MACH–TOOLS TO WORK WOOD	W 7	102	W 6	36	W 16	118	W 489	1010	MACH–OUT POUR TRAVAIL BOIS
7284	MACHY FOR SPCL INDUS NES	W 18	719	W 24	417	W 57	455	W 15	94	MACH SPEC IND PARTICUL.
72843	TOBACCO WORKING MACH NES	W 4	609	W 12	373	W 10	231	W 4	65	MACH POUR IND DU TABAC
74	GENRL INDUSTRL MACHY NES		6132		5969		9441		5042	MACH APP INDUSTRIE
741	HEATING,COOLING EQUIPMNT	W 111	1051	W 80	804	W 220	3019	W 97	1231	MACH CHAUFFAGE,PIECES
7415	AIR–CONDITIONING MACHNRY	W 51	576	W 42	337	W 96	1091	W 46	474	GROUPES CONDITION AIR
7416	HEATING,COOLING EQU NES	W 4	17	W 21	282	W 70	1241	W 18	226	APP CHANGEMENT TEMP

4. Special Imports C.I.F. by Commodities according to the S.I.T.C. (Rev. 2) in thousand U.S. Dollars
Importations Spéciales C.A.F. par Produits d'après la C.T.C.I. (Rév. 2) en milliers de Dollars E.U.

SITC CTCI	COMMODITY	1993		1994		1995		1996		PRODUIT
		WEIGHT POIDS	VALUE VALEUR	WEIGHT POIDS	VALUE VALEUR	WEIGHT POIDS	VALUE VALEUR	WEIGHT POIDS	VALUE VALEUR	
742	PUMPS FOR LIQUIDS ETC	W 60	1358	W 20	350	W 63	1063	W 41	689	POMPES MOTO–POMPES
7428	OTHER PUMPS FOR LIQUIDS	W 56	1211	W 15	286	W 57	990	W 39	598	AUTRES POMPES POUR LIQ
74288	PUMPS FR LIQUIDS NES ETC	W 54	1161	W 12	255	W 57	986	W 32	416	POMPES POUR LIQUIDES NDA
743	PUMPS NES,CENTRFUGES ETC	W 33	598	W 36	314	W 96	1032	W 55	536	POMPES COMPRES,VENT ETC
744	MECHANICAL HANDLING EQU	W 164	832	W 54	446	W 132	1290	W 82	763	EQUIP MANUTENTION PIECES
7441	FORK LIFT TRCKS,ETC,PTS	W 127	479	W 2	21	W 43	109	W 14	99	CHARIOTS POUR USINES ETC
74411	FORK LIFT TRUCKS ETC	W 127	477			W 43	108	W 13	33	CHARIOTS POUR LES GARES
7449	PTS NES OF MACHY OF 7442	W 19	165	W 34	314	W 59	1061	W 39	585	PIECES DU 744.2
745	NONELEC MACHY,TOOLS NES	W 42	323	W 35	427	W 46	799	W 34	606	AUT MACH NON ELEC,PIECES
749	NONELEC MACH PTS,ACC NES	W 137	1970	W 266	3628	W 159	2238	W 46	1217	PIECES MACH NON ELEC NDA
7492	COCKS,VALVES ETC NES	W 55	533	W 194	2640	W 57	658	W 6	166	ART ROB,SIM POUR TUYAUX
7499	OTH NONELEC MCHY PTS NES	W 67	947	W 22	444	W 76	603	W 12	501	PIECES NON ELECT NDA
74992	METAL–PLASTIC GASKETS	W 22	631	W 21	395	W 26	517	W 8	317	JOINTS METALLOPLASTIQUES
75	OFFICE MACHNES,ADP EQUIP		2396		2155		3098		2784	MACH BUREAU TRAIT AUTOM
751	OFFICE MACHINES	W 21	622	W 26	725	W 24	908	W 44	717	MACH,APPAREILS DE BUREAU
7518	OFFICE MACHINES NES	W 18	513	W 17	576	W 15	653	W 38	626	MACH,APP DE BUREAU NDA
75182	PHOTO,THERMOCOPY APPARAT	W 9	410	W 11	487	W 13	563	W 17	360	APPAREILS DE PHOTOCOPIE
752	AUTOMTIC DATA PROC EQUIP	W 14	1315	W 21	1221	W 36	1818	W 30	1598	MACH TRAIT INFORMATION
7523	DIGITL CENTRL PROCESSORS	W 6	402	W 4	375	W 5	336	W 9	558	UNITES CENTRALES
759	OFFICE,ADP MCH PTS,ACCES	W 24	459	W 5	209	W 6	372	W 9	469	PIECES DU 751 ET 752
76	TELECOMM,SOUND EQUIPMENT		3897		3131		12119		4777	EQUIPMENT DE TELECOM
764	TELECOM EQPT,PTS,ACC NES	W 51	3691	W 45	3004	W 94	11734	W 42	4442	EQUIP TELECOM,PIECES
7641	LINE TELEPHONE,ETC EQUIP	W 11	1681	W 6	452	W 31	1841	W 15	1166	APP TELEPHON PAR FIL
7643	TV,RADIO TRANSMITTRS ETC	W 16	756	W 8	983	W 18	6170	W 13	2496	APP EMET TELE RADIO
7648	TELECOMM EQUIPMENT NES	W 1	88	W 11	932	W 25	2211		119	APP TELECOM NDA
76483	RADAR APPARATUS ETC		70	W 11	895	W 20	1462		110	APP DE RADIOGUIDAGE ETC
7649	PTS NES OF EQUIPMT OF 76	W 23	1148	W 16	446	W 19	1481	W 8	595	PIECES DE LA DIV 76
76491	PTS NES OF APPAR OF 7641	W 7	823	W 3	65	W 4	206	W 2	231	PIECES POUR 764.1
76493	TELECOMM EQUIPMT PTS NES	W 16	310	W 14	379	W 15	1273	W 5	327	PIECES 761,762,764.3,8
77	ELECTRIC MACHNRY NES ETC		4586		4120		5494		4180	MACH APP ELECT NDA
772	SWITCHGEAR ETC,PARTS NES	W 48	1328	W 120	1126	W 55	1569	W 103	1027	APP COUPURE,SECT ETC
7721	SWITCHGEAR ETC	W 48	1315	W 119	1117	W 55	1558	W 103	1017	APP COUPURE,SECTIONMNT
773	ELECTR DISTRIBUTNG EQUIP	W 171	834	W 183	477	W 150	744	W 163	856	EQUIPMT DISTRIBUTION ELECT
7731	INSULATED WIRE,CABLE ETC	W 171	830	W 182	463	W 148	721	W 150	732	FILS,CABLES ISOLES ELECT
775	HOUSEHOLD TYPE EQUIP NES	W 81	531	W 110	416	W 146	901	W 139	730	MACH,APP USAGE DOMESTQUE
778	ELECTRICAL MACHINERY NES	W 425	1648	W 527	1759	W 522	1918	W 216	945	AUTRES MACH ELECT NDA
7781	BATTERIES,ACCUMULATORS	W 381	1234	W 504	1473	W 492	1396	W 190	568	PILES ET ACCUMULATEURS
77811	PRIMARY BATTERIES,CELLS	W 268	690	W 325	699	W 322	891	W 126	318	PILES ELECTRIQUES,PIECES
77812	ELECTRIC ACCUMULATORS	W 107	529	W 179	774	W 159	475	W 64	250	ACCUMULATEURS ELECTRIQ
78	ROAD VEHICLES		25632		16456		49770		33043	VEHICULES ROUTIERS
781	PASS MOTOR VEH EXC BUSES	W 1031	7297	W 793	2948	W 1434	8935	W 1098	5473	AUTO TRANSPORT PERSONNES
782	LORRIES,SPCL MTR VEH NES	W 1208	7051	W 1435	4847	W 2693	17160	W 2147	13314	VEHICULES SPECIAUX,MARCH
7821	LORRIES,TRUCKS	W 1094	6352	W 1358	4500	W 2162	11006	W 1774	11387	VEHICULES TRANSP MARCHAND
7822	SPECIAL MOTOR VEHCLS NES	W 114	699	W 77	347	W 532	6154	W 373	1927	VEHICULES USAGES SPECIAUX
783	ROAD MOTOR VEHICLES NES	W 446	2885	W 518	1776	W 1191	9096	W 778	3808	VEHICULES ROUTIERS NDA
7831	BUSES	W 246	1989	W 213	1071	W 611	5987	W 386	2815	VOITURES TRANSPORT COMMUN
7832	TRACTORS FOR TR–TRAILERS	W 200	896	W 305	706	W 581	3110	W 392	993	TRACTEURS ROUTIERS
784	MOTOR VEH PRTS,ACCES NES	W 565	6323	W 244	4204	W 980	9836	W 543	7056	PIECES 722,781,782,783
7849	OTHER MOTOR VEHCL PARTS	W 540	6319	W 244	4204	W 979	9831	W 539	7002	PIECES 722,781,782,783
785	CYCLES,ETC MOTRZD OR NOT	W 205	1387	W 169	1551	W 147	1972	W 127	1520	MOTOCYCLES SCOOTERS
7851	MOTORCYCLES ETC	W 123	607	W 96	1061	W 80	1301	W 95	1298	MOTO VELO MOTEUR AUXIL
7853	INVAL CARR, PTS OF 785	W 65	770	W 46	389	W 33	517	W 23	153	FAUTEUILS INVALIDES,PIECES
78539	PARTS,ACCES NES OF 785	W 64	769	W 44	378	W 33	517	W 23	153	PIECES DU 785
786	TRAILERS,NONMOTR VEH,NES	W 434	689	W 310	1129	W 741	2770	W 465	1872	REMORQUES,CADRES,CONTAIN
7861	TRAILERS,TRANSP CONTAINR	W 387	455	W 241	813	W 550	2041	W 415	1703	REMORQUES TOUS VEHICULES
78612	OTHER TRAILERS	W 371	398	W 151	528	W 532	1795	W 401	1695	REMORQUES TRANSP MARCH
79	OTHR TRANSPORT EQUIPMENT		1233		557		1963		5771	AUTRE MATERIEL TRANSPORT
792	AIRCRAFT ETC	W 11	1230	W 7	548	W 33	1791	W 36	5771	APP NAVIGATION AERIENNE
7922	AIRCRFT NES 2000KG OR LS					W 2	16	W 20	595	AERODYNES MOINS 2000 KG
7929	AIRCRAFT PARTS NES	W 3	1150	W 2	395	W 17	1471	W 15	5168	PIECES DU 792
8	MISC MANUFACTURED GOODS		10478		7040		12019		10386	ART MANUFACTURES DIVERS
821	*FURNITURE,PARTS THEREOF	W 122	901	W 134	415	W 64	396	W 89	807	MEUBLES ET PIECES
8219	FURNITURE AND PARTS NES	W 111	787	W 97	260	W 41	225	W 68	595	AUTRES MEUBLES ET PIECES
82191	METAL FURNITURE NES	W 98	753	W 62	219	W 28	161	W 35	340	MEUBLES NDA EN METAL
84	CLOTHING AND ACCESSORIES		443		456		461		266	VETEMENTS
851	*FOOTWEAR	W 260	380	W 228	326	W 57	214	W 30	545	CHAUSSURES
87	PRECISION INSTRUMNTS NES		2126		860		2452		1577	INSTRUM,APPAR SCIENT NDA
872	MEDICAL INSTRUMENTS NES	W 57	855	W 27	416	W 24	890	W 20	526	INSTR,APP MEDIC–CHIR NDA
87202	OTH MEDICAL INSTRUMENTS	W 56	843	W 27	416	W 23	853	W 19	522	INSTRUM,APP MEDECINE
874	MEASURNG,CONTROLNG INSTR	W 10	1140	W 10	433	W 14	1186	W 17	512	INSTRUMENTS DE MESURE
89	MISC MANUFCTRD GOODS NES		6055		4300		7791		6779	ART MANUFACTURES DIVERS
892	PRINTED MATTER	W 329	2717	W 372	1544	W 232	2582	W 848	3890	IMPRIMES
8921	PRINTED BOOKS,GLOBES,ETC	W 193	861	W 282	798	W 81	1246	W 112	1412	LIVRES,BROCHURES,CARTES
89211	PRINTED BOOKS,PAMPHLETS	W 192	841	W 282	794	W 81	1237	W 111	1401	LIVRES,BROCHURES
8922	NEWSPAPERS,PERIODICALS	W 56	999	W 43	374	W 55	578	W 50	343	JOURNAUX ET PERIODIQUES
8928	PRINTED MATTER NES	W 81	854	W 47	372	W 95	751	W 686	2134	IMPRIMES NDA
89283	UNISSUED BANKNOTES ETC	W 29	183	W 2	5	W 22	41	W 630	1404	TIMBRES–POSTE FISCAUX
893	ARTICLES OF PLASTIC NES	W 432	1170	W 249	845	W 237	1146	W 192	760	OUVRAGES EN MAT DIVIS 58
8939	MISC PLASTIC ARTICLES	W 408	1047	W 189	590	W 178	806	W 124	509	ART DIVERS EN MAT DIV 58
89399	OTHR PLASTC ARTICLES NES	W 362	945	W 169	467	W 163	709	W 70	384	AUT OUV MAT DIV 58
894	TOYS,SPORTING GOODS,ETC	W 156	1317	W 269	1181	W 289	2907	W 224	1354	VOITURES ENFANTS,JOUETS
8946	NON–MILITARY ARMS,AMMO	W 115	1133	W 250	1086	W 245	2682	W 197	1244	ARMES NON MILITAIRES
89463	HUNTNG,SPORTNG AMMUNTION	W 115	1113	W 249	1083	W 244	2672	W 196	1237	MUNITIONS
899	OTHER MANUFACTURED GOODS		469		347		408		178	AUT ART MANUF DIVERS NDA
9	GOODS NOT CLASSD BY KIND		27		370		6		7153	ART TRANSACT NON CLASSES
951	*WAR FIREARMS,AMMUNITION	W 1	27		17		6	W 232	7152	VEHIC BLINDES ARMES
95101	ARMORED FIGHTNG VEHICLES							W 195	6830	CHARS DE COMBAT

5. Special Exports F.O.B. by Commodities according to the S.I.T.C. (Rev. 2) in thousand U.S. Dollars
Exportations Spéciales F.O.B. par Produits d'après la C.T.C.I. (Rév. 2) en milliers de Dollars E.U.

SITC CTCI	COMMODITY	1993 WEIGHT POIDS	1993 VALUE VALEUR	1994 WEIGHT POIDS	1994 VALUE VALEUR	1995 WEIGHT POIDS	1995 VALUE VALEUR	1996 WEIGHT POIDS	1996 VALUE VALEUR	PRODUIT
	ALL COMMODITIES		91689		81451		119522		115128	TOUS PRODUITS
0	FOOD AND LIVE ANIMALS		3918		2605		4142		1295	ALIMENTS,ANIMAUX VIVANTS
001	*LIVE ANIMALS FOR FOOD			W 894	490	W 643	871	W 537	312	ANIMAUX VIVANTS
0011	BOVINE SPECIES,LIVE			W 890	485	W 635	863	W 129	309	ESPECE BOVINE
00119	— OTHR THAN FR BREEDING			W 890	485	W 632	862	W 129	309	BOVINS NON REPRODUCTEURS
07	COFFEE,TEA,COCOA,SPICES		3909		2054		3109		872	CAFE,THE,CACAO,EPICES
071	COFFEE AND SUBSTITUTES	W 8281	3907	W 8215	2049	W 13674	3103	W 5023	872	CAFE ET SUCCEDANES
0711	COFFEE GREEN,ROASTED,SUB	W 8281	3907	W 8215	2049	W 13674	3103	W 5023	872	CAFE TORREFIE OU DECAFEINE
07111	COFFEE GREEN,HUSKS,SKINS	W 8281	3907	W 8215	2049	W 13674	3103	W 5023	872	CAFE NON TORREFIE
1	BEVERAGES AND TOBACCO		809		454		678		43	BOISSONS ET TABACS
12	TOBACCO AND MANUFACTURES		732		397		660		38	TABACS BRUTS FABRIQUES
122	TOBACCO,MANUFACTURED	W 26	732	W 22	397	W 29	643	W 4	24	TABACS FABRIQUES
1222	CIGARETTES	W 26	732	W 22	397	W 29	643	W 4	24	CIGARETTES
2	CRUDE MATERLS,EXCL FUELS		49483		42858		59829		57334	MAT BRUTES NON COMESTIBLES
22	OIL SEEDS,OLEAGINOUS FRT		27		308		160		52	GRAINES,FRUITS OLEAGINEUX
222	SEEDS FOR'SOFT'FIXED OIL	W 31	27	W 791	302	W 904	143	W 206	39	GRAINES HUILES FIXES
2221	GROUNDNUTS,GREEN			W 781	301	W 879	142	W 191	32	ARACHIDES NON GRILLEES
24	CORK AND WOOD		795		1299		2790		4756	LIEGE ET BOIS
247	OTH WOOD ROUGH,SQUARED	W 1184	233	W 3416	181	W 15204	1856	W 12390	3883	BOIS BRUTS EQUARRIS
2471	SAW–,VENEER–LOGS CONIFER	W 1126	230	W 1332	142	W 14227	1736	W 12390	3883	CONIFERES POUR SCIAGE,PLACAG
24711	— IN THE ROUGH	W 1126	230	W 1332	142	W 14227	1736	W 12390	3883	ECORCES OU DEGROSSIS
248	WOOD SHAPED,SLEEPERS	W 9740	563	W 9701	1118	W 6674	934	W 4416	873	BOIS SIMPLEMENT TRAVAILLES
2483	LUMBER SHAPED NON–CONIFR	W 9740	563	W 9701	1118	W 6674	934	W 4416	873	NON CONIFERES SCIES,RABOTES
24831	LUMBER SAWN ETC NON–CON	W 9740	563	W 9701	1118	W 6674	934	W 4416	873	SCIES LONGITUDINALEMENT
26	TEXTILE FIBRES AND WASTE		10584		7531		20351		22379	FIBRES TEXTILES
263	COTTON	W 7633	10584	W 5468	7528	W 11879	20309	W 12410	22379	COTON
2631	RAW COTTON,EXCL LINTERS	W 7633	10584	W 5468	7528	W 11879	20309	W 12410	22379	COTON EN MASSE
27	CRUDE FERTLZR,MINRLS NES		37427		33545		35998		29437	ENGRAIS MINERAUX BRUTS
277	NATURAL ABRASIVES NES		37427		33545		35998		29435	ABRASIFS NATURELS NDA
2771	INDUSTRIAL DIAMONDS		37427		33545		35998		29435	DIAMANTS INDUSTRIELS
29	CRUDE ANIMAL,VEG MAT NES		564		112		472		696	MATIERES BRUTES ANIM,VEGET
292	CRUDE VEG MATERIALS NES	W 346	564	W 313	112	W 1201	471	W 1930	696	MAT BRUTES VEGETALES NDA
2922	NAT GUMS,RESINS,LACS,ETC	W 164	98	W 300	95	W 1163	415	W 1900	653	GOMME LAQUE
2924	VEG USED IN PHARMACY ETC	W 182	467	W 12	16	W 36	55	W 29	43	PLANTES MEDICINALES
3	MINERAL FUELS ETC		157		320		930		219	COMBUSTIBLES MINERAUX LUB
33	PETROLEUM AND PRODUCTS		157		320		930		219	PETROLE ET DERIVES
334	PETROLEUM PRODUCTS,REFIN	W 1322	157	W 2251	320	W 4620	930	W 337	219	PRODUITS RAFFINES
3343	GAS OILS	W 1320	146	W 148	41	W 2584	607	W 290	181	GAS OILS
5	CHEMCLS,RELATED PROD NES		291		104		481		11	PRODUITS CHIMIQUES
6	BASIC MANUFACTURES		32562		31114		41776		40107	ART MANUFACTURES
66	NONMETAL MINERAL MFS NES		29819		30839		39887		39725	ART MIN NON METALLIQUES
667	PEARL,PREC–,SEMI–P STONE		29786		30836		39880		39715	PERLES, PIERRES GEMMES
6672	DIAMONDS NONINDUST,UNSET		29786		30836		39880		39715	DIAMANTS BRUTS
66722	— SRTD,ROUGH,SIMPLY WKD		13562		29877		39812		39663	DIAMANTS TRIES BRUTS
66729	— CUT ETC NOT SET		16225		959		68		51	DIAMANTS TAILLES
67	IRON AND STEEL		2663		150		12		2	FER ET ACIER
671	PIG IRON ETC	W 9506	2646							FONTE,SPIEGEL,POUDRES
6716	FERRO–ALLOYS	W 9506	2646							FERRO–ALLIAGES
67162	FERRO–SILICON	W 9506	2646							FERRO–SILICIUM
69	METAL MANUFACTURES NES		27		22		1586		80	ART MANUFACT EN METAL NDA
693	WIRE PRODUCTS NON ELECTR	W 4	6			W 500	1213			OUVRAGES FILS METALLIQUES
6935	METAL FENCING,GAUZE,ETC	W 1	3			W 500	1213			TOILES EN FER,ACIER,CUIVRE
69351	IRN,STL FENCNG,GAUZE ETC	W 1	3			W 500	1213			TOILES EN FER,ACIER
7	MACHINES,TRANSPORT EQUIP		1676		2239		10543		8663	MACHINES MATERIEL TRANSPORT
71	POWER GENERATING EQUIPMT		435		71		228		77	MACHINES GENERATRICES
713	INTRNL COMBUS PSTN ENGIN	W 36	338	W 8	53	W 3	23	W 6	49	MOTEURS EXPL COMB INT, PIECE
72	MACHS FOR SPCL INDUSTRYS		116		33		607		464	MAC SPECIALES POUR INDUST
723	CIVIL ENGNEERG EQUIP ETC	W 2	62	W 1	16	W 75	520	W 11	122	APPAREILS DE GENIE CIVIL
7234	CONST,MINING MACHNRY NES	W 2	47			W 65	458	W 11	122	MACH POUR LA CONST, MINES
74	GENRL INDUSTRL MACHY NES		18		33		32		838	MACH APP INDUSTRIE
741	HEATING,COOLING EQUIPMNT		1				3	W 60	801	MACH CHAUFFAGE,PIECES
7416	HEATING,COOLING EQU NES							W 60	801	APP CHANGEMENT TEMP
78	ROAD VEHICLES		881		2008		9259		7119	VEHICULES ROUTIERS
782	LORRIES,SPCL MTR VEH NES	W 75	350	W 105	527	W 344	1970	W 57	1540	VEHICULES SPECIAUX,MARCH
7821	LORRIES,TRUCKS	W 75	350	W 105	527	W 252	973	W 57	1141	VEHICULES TRANSP MARCHAND
7822	SPECIAL MOTOR VEHCLS NES					W 92	997		400	VEHICULES USAGES SPECIAUX
783	ROAD MOTOR VEHICLES NES	W 2	22	W 9	74	W 186	3397	W 325	1183	VEHICULES ROUTIERS NDA
7831	BUSES	W 2	22	W 9	74	W 171	3277	W 46	823	VOITURES TRANSPORT COMMUN
7832	TRACTORS FOR TR–TRAILERS					W 15	120	W 278	360	TRACTEURS ROUTIERS
784	MOTOR VEH PRTS,ACCES NES	W 76	344	W 128	1237	W 125	3351	W 175	4141	PIECES 722,781,782,783
7849	OTHER MOTOR VEHCL PARTS	W 76	344	W 118	1237	W 125	3351	W 170	4090	PIECES 722,781,782,783
8	MISC MANUFACTURED GOODS		402		424		397		171	ART MANUFACTURES DIVERS
89	MISC MANUFCTRD GOODS NES		207		289		189		141	ART MANUFACTURES DIVERS
892	PRINTED MATTER	W 30	201	W 31	283	W 11	124	W 12	128	IMPRIMES
8921	PRINTED BOOKS,GLOBES,ETC	W 29	200	W 31	283	W 11	119	W 12	125	LIVRES,BROCHURES,CARTES
89211	PRINTED BOOKS,PAMPHLETS	W 29	200	W 31	283	W 11	119	W 12	125	LIVRES,BROCHURES
9	GOODS NOT CLASSD BY KIND		2311		1303		691		7231	ART TRANSACT NON CLASSES
951	*WAR FIREARMS,AMMUNITION	W 9	1175	W 44	692			W 196	6992	VEHIC BLINDES ARMES
95101	ARMORED FIGHTNG VEHICLES							W 195	6829	CHARS DE COMBAT
95106	AMMUNITION NES			W 44	692					PROJECTILES,MUNITIONS
95109	PARTS OF ARMS NES	W 9	1175							PIECES POUR ARMES
971	*GOLD,NON MONETARY NES	K 153	1136	K 78	611	K 66	691	K 24	240	OR NON MONETAIRE
97101	NONMON GLD UNWRT,SEMIMFD	K 153	1136	K 78	611	K 66	691	K 24	240	OR,ALLIAGES D'OR BRUTS

1. HISTORICAL SERIES, 1960–1995 SPECIAL TRADE, IMPORTS C.I.F., EXPORTS F.O.B.
SERIES HISTORIQUES, 1960–1995 COMMERCE SPECIAL, IMPORTATIONS C.A.F., EXPORTATIONS F.O.B

YEAR ANNEE	VALUE IN MILLION C.F.A. FRANCS VALEUR EN MILLION C.F.A. FRANCS MERCHANDISE – MARCHANDISE		GOLD – OR		CONVERSION FACTORS U.S. CENTS PER C.F.A. FRANC FACTEURS DE CONVERSION CENTS E.U. PAR C.F.A. FRANC		INDEX NUMBERS – INDICES QUANTUM		UNIT VALUE VALEUR UNITAIRE	
	IMPORTS	EXPORTS	IMPORTS	EXPORTS	IMPORTS	EXPORTS	IMPORTS	EXPORTS	IMPORTS	EXPORTS
1960	6231.00	3271.00			0.4051	0.4051				
1961	6250.00	5293.00			0.4051	0.4051				
1962	7508.00	4178.00			0.4051	0.4051				
1963	7167.00	5605.00			0.4051	0.4051				
1964	8537.00	6544.00			0.4051	0.4051				
1965	7700.00	6722.00			0.4051	0.4051				
1966	7338.00	5848.00			0.4051	0.4051				
1967	9248.00	6635.00			0.4051	0.4051				
1968	8262.00	6824.00			0.4051	0.4051				
1969	13797.00	8020.00			0.3942	0.3938				
1970	17058.99	8205.00			0.3601	0.3601				
1971	17117.39	7786.00			0.3601	0.3601				
1972	15475.51	9028.30			0.3969	0.3969				
1973	18213.44	8483.22			0.4490	0.4490				
1974	20858.99	9052.65			0.4178	0.4128				
1975	28324.99	10183.00			0.4670	0.4670				
1976	27592.99	14861.00			0.4193	0.4261				
1977	46464.99	26176.99			0.4071	0.4071				
1978	49034.00	22328.99			0.4432	0.4432				
1979	18132.00	18776.00			0.4701	0.4701				
1980	15533.00	14999.00			0.4733	0.4733				
1981	29349.01	22665.01			0.3680	0.3680				
1982	35701.01	18968.00			0.3040	0.3040				
1983	59707.01	39824.00			0.2624	0.2624				
1984	79272.00	57384.00			0.2290	0.2290				
1985	74708.00	27781.01			0.2226	0.2226				
1986	73437.01	34145.01			0.2888	0.2888				
1987	67894.00	32892.00			0.3327	0.3327				
1988	68000.00	42900.00			0.3707	0.3707				
1989	75100.00	49570.00			0.3135	0.3135				
1990	77742.00	51202.00			0.3673	0.3673				
1991	70500.00	54600.00			0.3570	0.3570				
1992	64320.00	48250.00			0.3777	0.3777				
1993	56910.00	37330.00			0.3541	0.3541				
1994	98310.00	82160.00			0.1800	0.1800				
1995	109720.00	125600.00			0.2002	0.2002				

2. IMPORTS BY BROAD ECONOMIC CATEGORY AND EXPORTS BY INDUSTRIAL ORIGIN. (PERCENTAGE OF TOTAL VALUE)
IMPORTATIONS PAR CATEGORIES ECONOMIQUES ET EXPORTATIONS PAR BRANCHE D'ACTIVITE.(EN POURCENTAGE DE LA VALEUR TOTALE)

IMPORTS – IMPORTATIONS

	1990	1991	1992	1993	1994	1995	1996
TOTAL IMPORTS–IMPORTATIONS TOTALES						100.	
1 FOOD BEV–ALIMENTATION BOISSONS						21.2	
11 PRIMARY–PRODUITS DE BASE						1.1	
111 FOR INDUSTRY–POUR L'INDUSTRIE						0.1	
112 FOR HOUSEHOLDS–POUR LES MENAGES						1.0	
12 PROCESSED–PRODUITS ELABORES						20.1	
121 FOR INDUSTRY–POUR L'INDUSTRIE						5.2	
122 FOR HOUSEHOLDS–POUR LES MENAGES						14.8	
2 IND SUPPLIES–APPROV INDUSTRIELS						17.3	
21 PRIMARY–PRODUITS DE BASE						0.9	
22 PROCESSED–PRODUITS ELABORES						16.4	
3 FUELS–COMBUSTIBLES						17.9	
31 PRIMARY–PRODUITS DE BASE						0.0	
32 PROCESSED–PRODUITS ELABORES						17.9	
321 MOTOR SPIRIT–ESSENCE						3.0	
322 OTHER–AUTRES						14.9	
4 MACHINERY–EQUIPEMENT						15.5	
41 CAPITAL EQUIPMENT–MACHINES						13.2	
42 PARTS–PIECES ACCESSOIRES						2.3	
5 TRANSPORT–TRANSPORT						11.5	
51 PASSENGER CARS–AUTOMOBILES						0.7	
52 OTHER–AUTRES						3.7	
521 INDUSTRIAL–INDUSTRIELS						3.3	
522 NON INDUSTRIAL–NON INDUSTRIEL						0.4	
53 PARTS–PIECES ACCESSOIRES						7.1	
6 CONSUM GOODS–BIENS CONSOMMATION						10.0	
61 DURABLE–DURABLES						1.2	
62 SEMI DURABLE–SEMI DURABLES						3.0	
63 NON DURABLE–NON DURABLES						5.8	
7 GOODS NES–BIENS NDA						6.5	

EXPORTS – EXPORTATIONS

	1990	1991	1992	1993	1994	1995	1996
TOTAL EXPORTS–EXPORTATIONS TOTALES							
1 AGRICULTURE							
2 MINING QUARRY–INDUS EXTRACTIVES							
3 MANUFACTURING–IND MANUFACTUR							
31 FOOD BEV TOBACCO–ALIM BOISS TAB							
32 TEXTILES–INDUSTRIES TEXTILES							
33 WOOD & PRODUCTS–BOIS & PRODUITS							
34 PAPER & PRODUCTS–PAPIER & PRODT							
35 CHEMICALS–INDUSTRIES CHIMIQUES							
36 NON METAL MIN–MIN NON METAL							
37 BASIC METAL–IND METAL BASE							
38 METAL MANUF–MANUF METAL							
39 OTH MANUF IND–AUTRES MANUF							

3. TRADE BY PRINCIPAL COUNTRIES OF PRODUCTION AND CONSUMPTION (VALUE IN THOUSAND U.S. DOLLARS)
ECHANGES SELON LES PRINCIPAUX PAYS DE PRODUCTION ET DE COMSOMMATION (VALEUR EN MILLIERS DE DOLLARS EU)

COUNTRIES–PAYS	SPECIAL IMPORTS C.I.F. IMPORTATIONS SPECIALES C.A.F				
	1991	1992	1993	1994	1995
World			201000	178000	215171
Africa			41000	49000	64762
Americas					14233
Northern America					14045
LAIA					140
CACM					
Caribbean					48
Rest of America					
As.ex F.USSR					14635
Eur.x F.USSR					111674
EU					110325
EFTA					1332
East Europe					17
Other Europe					0
Former USSR					869
Oceania					41
Cameroon/Cameroun			29000	37000	33911
France,Monac					88887
Nigeria/Nigéria			11000	11000	25269
USA/Etats–Unis d'Amer					13966
Italy/Italie					6452
China/Chine					6251
Japan/Japon					5121
Belgium–Luxembourg					4771
Spain/Espagne					3402
Central African Rep.					3010
Germany/Allemagne					2988
Netherlands/Pays–Bas					2843
Malaysia/Malaisie					2234
Senegal/Sénégal			1000	1000	66
Russian Federation					857
Cote d'Ivoire					831
Switz.Liecht					799
Denmark/Danemark					602
So. Africa Customs Un					573
Norway,SVD,JM					533
Sudan/Soudan					471
Indonesia/Indonésie					380
Sweden/Suède					229
Congo					172
Afghanistan					154
Ethiopia/Ethiopie					132
Benin/Bénin					121
Saudi Arabia					119
India/Inde					100
Morocco/Maroc					3

COUNTRIES–PAYS	SPECIAL EXPORTS F.O.B. EXPORTATIONS SPECIALES F.O.B.				
	1991	1992	1993	1994	1995
Monde			132000	148000	
Afrique			3000	3000	
Amériques					
Amérique du Nord					
ALAI					
MCAC					
Caraïbes					
Autre Amérique					
Asie l'URSS exclus					
Europe l'URSS exclus					
UE					
AELE					
Europe de l'Est					
Autre de l'Europe					
Ancienne URSS					
Océanie					
Nigeria/Nigéria			2000	2000	
Morocco/Maroc			1000	1000	

(VALUE AS PERCENTAGE OF WORLD TOTAL)(VALEURS EN POURCENTAGE DU TOTAL MONDIAL)

	1986	1987	1988	1989	1990	1991	1992	1993	1994	1995
Africa								20.4	27.5	30.1
Americas										6.6
Northern America										6.5
LAIA										0.1
CACM										
Caribbean										0.0
Rest of America										
As.ex F.USSR										6.8
Eur.x F.USSR										51.9
EU										51.3
EFTA										0.6
East Europe										0.0
Other Europe										0.0
Former USSR										0.4
Oceania										0.0
Cameroon/Cameroun								14.4	20.8	15.8
France,Monac										41.3
Nigeria/Nigéria								5.5	6.2	11.7
USA/Etats–Unis d'Amer										6.5
Italy/Italie										3.0
China/Chine										2.9
Japan/Japon										2.4
Belgium–Luxembourg										2.2
Spain/Espagne										1.6
Central African Rep.										1.4

	1986	1987	1988	1989	1990	1991	1992	1993	1994	1995
Afrique								2.3	2.0	
Amériques										
Amérique du Nord										
ALAI										
MCAC										
Caraïbes										
Autre Amérique										
Asie l'URSS exclus										
Europe l'URSS exclus										
UE										
AELE										
Europe de l'Est										
Autre de l'Europe										
Ancienne URSS										
Océanie										
Nigeria/Nigéria								1.5	1.4	
Morocco/Maroc								0.8	0.7	

5. Special Exports C.I.F. by Commodities according to the S.I.T.C. (Rev. 2) in thousand U.S. Dollars
Exportations Spéciales C.A.F. par Produits d'après la C.T.C.I. (Rév. 2) en milliers de Dollars E.U.

SITC CTCI	COMMODITY	1992 WEIGHT POIDS	1992 VALUE VALEUR	1993 WEIGHT POIDS	1993 VALUE VALEUR	1994 WEIGHT POIDS	1994 VALUE VALEUR	1995 WEIGHT POIDS	1995 VALUE VALEUR	PRODUIT
	ALL COMMODITIES								215171	TOUS PRODUITS
0	FOOD AND LIVE ANIMALS								41182	ALIMENTS,ANIMAUX VIVANTS
01	MEAT AND PREPARATIONS								893	VIANDES ET PREPARATIONS
02	DAIRY PRODCTS,BIRDS'EGGS								2507	PRODUITS LAITIERS,OEUFS
022	MILK AND CREAM							W 712	1538	LAIT ET CREME
0224	MILK,CREAM PRESERVED ETC							W 690	1385	LAIT,CREME CONS,CONC
02243	MILK DRY,OVER 1.5% FAT							W 667	1339	LAIT POUDRE SUP 1.5%
024	CHEESE AND CURD							W 103	769	FROMAGE ET CAILLEBOTTE
03	FISH AND PREPARATIONS								953	POISSONS ET PREPARATIONS
037	FISH ETC PREPD,PRSVD NES							W 348	840	POIS,CRUST,MOL PREPARES
0371	FISH PREPARD,PRESRVD NES							W 345	814	CONSERVES DE POISSONS
04	CEREALS AND PREPARATIONS								16028	CEREALES ET PRODUITS
042	RICE							W 6208	4589	RIZ
0422	RICE SEMI-MILLED,MILLED							W 6208	4589	RIZ POLI,GLACE INCL BRISURES
04221	RICE MILLED UNBROKEN							W 6208	4589	RIZ POLI,GLACE EXCL BRISURES
046	WHEAT ETC MEAL OR FLOUR							W 22717	8945	SEMOULE FARINE,FROMENT
04601	FLOUR OF WHEAT OR MESLIN							W 22717	8945	FARINE DE FROMENT
047	OTHER CEREAL MEALS,FLOUR							W 4294	1360	AUTRES SEMOULES,FARINES
04701	CEREAL FLOUR(NON-WHEAT)							W 4190	1270	FARINES DE CEREALES
048	CEREAL ETC PREPARATIONS							W 699	778	PREPTNS A BASE CEREALES
05	VEGETABLES AND FRUIT								975	LEGUMES ET FRUITS
06	SUGAR AND PREPS,HONEY								17078	SUCRES ET PRODUITS
061	SUGAR AND HONEY							W 24203	16970	SUCRES ET MIEL
0612	REFINED SUGAR ETC							W 23970	16825	SUCRES RAFFINES
07	COFFEE,TEA,COCOA,SPICES								1102	CAFE,THE,CACAO,EPICES
074	TEA AND MATE							W 813	855	THE ET MATE
0741	TEA							W 813	855	THE
09	MISC EDIBLE PRODUCTS								1627	PREP ALIMENTAIRES DIVERSES
098	EDIBLE PRODCTS,PREPS NES							W 813	1620	PREP ALIMENTAIRES NDA
09809	MISC FOOD PREPRTIONS NES							W 444	1157	PREP ALIMENTAIRES NDA
1	BEVERAGES AND TOBACCO								7175	BOISSONS ET TABACS
11	BEVERAGES								4526	BOISSONS
111	NON-ALCOHL BEVERAGES NES							W 2518	1059	BOISSONS NON ALCOOLIQUES
11101	WATERS,ICE AND SNOW							W 2328	760	EAU,EAUX MINERALES
112	ALCOHOLIC BEVERAGES							W 4444	3467	BOISSONS ALCOOLIQUES
1123	BEER,ALE,STOUT,PORTER							W 4166	2995	BIERES
12	TOBACCO AND MANUFACTURES								2650	TABACS BRUTS FABRIQUES
122	TOBACCO,MANUFACTURED							W 224	2414	TABACS FABRIQUES
1223	OTH MANUFACTURED TOBACCO							W 217	2200	TABACS FUMER,CHIQUER,PRISER
2	CRUDE MATERLS,EXCL FUELS								2218	MAT BRUTES NON COMESTIBLES
27	CRUDE FERTLZR,MINRLS NES								931	ENGRAIS MINERAUX BRUTS
278	OTHER CRUDE MINERALS							W 4904	865	AUTRES MINERAUX BRUTS
2783	COMMON SALT,ETC							W 4801	772	SEL
3	MINERAL FUELS ETC								38592	COMBUSTIBLES MINERAUX LUB
33	PETROLEUM AND PRODUCTS								38574	PETROLE ET DERIVES
334	PETROLEUM PRODUCTS,REFIN							W 94019	38551	PRODUITS RAFFINES
3341	GASOLINE,OTH LIGHT OILS							W 15815	6490	ESSENCES POUR MOTEURS
33411	MOTOR,AVIATION SPIRIT							W 8817	3744	ESSENCES MOTEURS D'AVIONS
33419	OTH LIGHT PETROLEUM OILS							W 6998	2747	AUTRES HUILES LEGERES
3342	KEROSENE,OTH MEDIUM OILS							W 21658	8456	PETR LAMPANTS,AUT HUIL
33421	KEROSENE INCL JET FUEL							W 21595	8444	PETROLES LAMPANTS
3343	GAS OILS							W 56338	23318	GAS OILS
4	ANIMAL,VEGETABLE OIL,FAT								3302	HUILES,GRAISSES ANIM,VEG
42	FIXED VEGETABLE OIL,FAT								700	HUILES VEGETALES FIXES
431	*PROCESD ANML VEG OIL,ET							W 3596	2602	HUILES,GRAISSES PREPAREES
4313	FATTY ACIDS ETC,RESIDUES							W 3596	2601	ACIDES GRAS INDUST,RESIDUS
43131	FATTY ACIDS,ACID OILS							W 3596	2601	ACIDES GRAS INDUSTRIELS
5	CHEMCLS,RELATED PROD NES								15507	PRODUITS CHIMIQUES
541	*MEDICINAL,PHARM PRODUCT							K 617692	7789	PROD MEDICINAUX PHARMACEUT
5416	GLYCOSIDES,GLANDS,SERA							K 13301	663	HETEROSIDES
54164	ANTISERA,MICROB VACCINES							K 12216	652	SERUMS,VACCINS
5417	MEDICAMENTS							K 551938	6351	MEDICAMENTS
54179	— CONTNG OTH SUBSTANCES							K 499550	5877	MED CONT AUT SUBSTANCES
55	PERFUME,CLEANING ETC PRD								866	PROD POUR PARFUM,TOILETTE
562	*FERTILIZERS,MANUFACTURE							W 5031	2400	ENGRAIS MANUFACTURES
5621	CHEM NITROGENOUS FERTLZR							W 1391	820	ENGRAIS AZOTES
56213	AMMONIUM SULPHATE							W 1032	720	SULFATE D'AMMONIUM
5629	FERTILIZERS NES							W 2328	1305	ENGRAIS NDA
56299	OTHER FERTILIZERS NES							W 1418	716	AUTRES ENGRAIS NDA
58	PLASTIC MATERIALS ETC								1126	MAT PLAST ARTIFICIELLES
584	CELLULOSE DERIVATIVS ETC							W 109	703	CEL REGEN NIT ACETATE
5843	CELLULOSE ACETATES							W 109	703	ACETATES DE CELLULOSE
58431	— NON-PLASTICIZED							W 109	703	ACETAT CELLULOSE NON PLAST
59	CHEMICAL MATERIALS NES								2234	MAT PROD CHIMIQUES NDA
591	PESTICIDES,DISINFECTANTS							W 168	1559	DESINF,INSECT,FONG,HERB
5911	INSECTICIDES,FOR RETAIL							W 106	954	INSECTICIDES VENTE DET
6	BASIC MANUFACTURES								26190	ART MANUFACTURES
62	RUBBER MANUFACTURES NES								3053	CAOUTCHOUC MANUFACTURE
625	RUBBER TYRES, TUBES ETC							W 364	2500	PNEUS CAOUTCHOUC VULCANISE
6252	TYRES,NEW,BUS OR LORRY							W 184	1495	PNEUS POUR AUTOBUS,CAMIONS
6259	OTH TYRES,TYRE CASES,ETC							W 129	646	AUTRES PNEUS RECHAPES FLAPS
64	PAPER,PAPERBOARD AND MFR								3547	PAPIERS,CARTONS & OUVRAGES
641	PAPER AND PAPERBOARD							W 429	1225	PAPIERS ET CARTONS
642	PAPER,ETC,PRECUT,ARTS OF							W 1137	2322	PAP,CARTONS DECOUPES
6421	PAPER ETC CONTAINERS							W 930	1486	BOITES,SACS EMBALLAGES
65	TEXTILE YARN,FABRICS,ETC								2504	FILS,TISSUS,ARTICLES TEXTILE
653	WOVN MAN-MADE FIB FABRIC							W 206	978	TISSUS FIBRES SYNTH,ARTIF
658	TEXTILE ARTICLES NES							W 392	777	ART FACONNES MAT TEXTILES
66	NONMETAL MINERAL MFS NES								7654	ART MIN NON METALLIQUES
661	LIME,CEMENT,BLDG PRODS							W 52158	6394	CHAUX,CIMENTS MAT CONSTR
6612	CEMENT							W 51546	6247	CIMENTS HYDRAULIQUES
67	IRON AND STEEL								2736	FER ET ACIER
672	IRON,STEEL PRIMARY FORMS							W 1248	1239	LINGOTS FER,ACIER
6727	IRN,STL COIL FR REROLLNG							W 1247	1238	EBAUCHES POUR TOLES FER
67271	IRON,SIMPLE STEEL COILS							W 1049	1065	EBAUCHES NON EN ACIER
673	IRON,STEEL SHAPES ETC							W 2574	844	BARRES,PROFIL FER,ACIER
69	METAL MANUFACTURES NES								6068	ART MANUFACT EN METAL NDA
691	STRUCTURES AND PARTS NES							W 727	997	CONSTRUCT FER,ACIER,ALU
6911	STRUCTURES,PARTS IRN,STL							W 621	678	CONSTRUCT FER,ACIER,FONTE
694	STL,COPPR NAILS,NUTS,ETC							W 147	1002	CLOUS,VIS,ECROUS
695	TOOLS							W 102	1163	OUTILS A MAIN

5. Special Exports C.I.F. by Commodities according to the S.I.T.C. (Rev. 2) in thousand U.S. Dollars
Exportations Spéciales C.A.F. par Produits d'après la C.T.C.I. (Rév. 2) en milliers de Dollars E.U.

SITC CTCI	COMMODITY	1992 WEIGHT POIDS	1992 VALUE VALEUR	1993 WEIGHT POIDS	1993 VALUE VALEUR	1994 WEIGHT POIDS	1994 VALUE VALEUR	1995 WEIGHT POIDS	1995 VALUE VALEUR	PRODUIT
6953	OTHER HAND TOOLS							W 77	836	AUTRES OUTILS A MAIN
699	BASE METAL MFRS NES							W 199	1691	ART MANUFACTURES MET NDA
6996	BASE MTL MISC ARTICLES							W 101	792	ART DIVERS METAUX COMMUNS
7	MACHINES,TRANSPORT EQUIP								51246	MACHINES MATERIEL TRANSPORT
71	POWER GENERATING EQUIPMT								3831	MACHINES GENERATRICES
713	INTRNL COMBUS PSTN ENGIN							W 59	1861	MOTEURS EXPL COMB INT, PIECE
7139	PISTON ENGINE PARTS NES							W 29	1271	PIECES POUR 713.2,3,8
716	ROTATING ELECTRIC PLANT							W 127	1426	APP ELECTR ROTATIFS,PIECES
7162	AC MTRS,GENRTRS,GEN SETS							W 104	1038	MOTEURS ELECTRIQUES
72	MACHS FOR SPCL INDUSTRYS								3980	MAC SPECIALES POUR INDUST
724	TEXTILE,LEATHER MACHNRY							W 176	1973	MACH POUR INDUSTRIE TEXTILE
7244	SPINNING,EXTRDNG,ETC MCH							W 172	1943	MACH POUR LE FILAGE
72442	FIBRE PROCESSNG MACH NES							W 145	1318	MACH PREP MAT TEXTILES
727	FOOD MACHRY NON-DOMESTIC							W 182	776	MACH INDUSTRIES ALIMENT
74	GENRL INDUSTRL MACHY NES								8175	MACH APP INDUSTRIE
741	HEATING,COOLING EQUIPMNT							W 55	972	MACH CHAUFFAGE,PIECES
742	PUMPS FOR LIQUIDS ETC							W 116	1764	POMPES MOTO-POMPES
7428	OTHER PUMPS FOR LIQUIDS							W 102	1369	AUTRES POMPES POUR LIQ
74288	PUMPS FR LIQUIDS NES ETC							W 101	1343	POMPES POUR LIQUIDES NDA
743	PUMPS NES,CENTRFUGES ETC							W 84	1037	POMPES COMPRES,VENT ETC
744	MECHANICAL HANDLING EQU							W 61	777	EQUIP MANUTENTION PIECES
745	NONELEC MACHY,TOOLS NES							W 58	751	AUT MACH NON ELEC,PIECES
7452	OTH NONELEC MCHS,PTS NES							W 58	725	AUT MACH NON ELEC,PIECES
749	NONELEC MACH PTS,ACC NES							W 94	2875	PIECES MACH NON ELEC NDA
7493	SHAFT,CRANK,PULLEY ETC							W 53	1339	ARBRES TRANS,VILEBREQUINS
75	OFFICE MACHINES,ADP EQUIP								3629	MACH BUREAU TRAIT AUTOM
751	OFFICE MACHINES							W 28	714	MACH,APPAREILS DE BUREAU
752	AUTOMTIC DATA PROC EQUIP							W 23	2124	MACH TRAIT INFORMATION
7522	DIGITAL COMPUTERS							W 11	1275	MACH DIGITALES COMPLETES
759	OFFICE,ADP MCH PTS,ACCES							W 11	790	PIECES DU 751 ET 752
7599	ACCTG,ETC,ADP MCH PTS,AC							W 8	655	PIECES DU 751 ET 752
76	TELECOMM,SOUND EQUIPMENT								4572	EQUIPMENT DE TELECOM
764	TELECOM EQPT,PTS,ACC NES							W 68	4375	EQUIP TELECOM,PIECES
7641	LINE TELEPHONE,ETC EQUIP							W 23	1974	APP TELEPHON PAR FIL
7643	TV,RADIO TRANSMITTRS ETC							W 5	677	APP EMET TELE RADIO
7649	PTS NES OF EQUIPMT OF 76							W 40	1630	PIECES DE LA DIV 76
76493	TELECOMM EQUIPMT PTS NES							W 36	1332	PIECES 761,762,764.3,8
77	ELECTRIC MACHNRY NES ETC								8001	MACH APP ELECT NDA
771	ELECTRIC POWER MACHY NES							W 18	2630	MACH PROD,TRANS ELECTR
7711	TRANSFORMERS,ELECTRICAL							W 12	2381	TRANSFO ELECTRIQUES
77118	OTHER ELEC TRANSFORMERS							W 12	2380	AUTRES TRANSFO ELECTRIQ
772	SWITCHGEAR ETC,PARTS NES							W 90	994	APP COUPURE,SECT ETC
7721	SWITCHGEAR ETC							W 90	965	APP COUPURE,SECTIONMNT
773	ELECTR DISTRIBUTNG EQUIP							W 218	820	EQUIPMT DISTRIBUTION ELECT
778	ELECTRICAL MACHINERY NES							W 343	2786	AUTRES MACH ELECT NDA
7781	BATTERIES,ACCUMULATORS							W 268	803	PILES ET ACCUMULATEURS
7783	AUTOMOTIVE ELECTR EQUIP							W 32	1128	EQUIP ELECT MOTEURS EXPL
78	ROAD VEHICLES								17873	VEHICULES ROUTIERS
781	PASS MOTOR VEH EXC BUSES							W 529	1574	AUTO TRANSPORT PERSONNES
782	LORRIES,SPCL MTR VEH NES							W 2232	4444	VEHICULES SPECIAUX,MARCH
7821	LORRIES,TRUCKS							W 2185	4338	VEHICULES TRANSP MARCHAND
783	ROAD MOTOR VEHICLES NES							W 537	1774	VEHICULES ROUTIERS NDA
7831	BUSES							W 255	1661	VOITURES TRANSPORT COMMUN
784	MOTOR VEH PRTS,ACCES NES							W 522	8253	PIECES 722,781,782,783
7849	OTHER MOTOR VEHCL PARTS							W 476	8195	PIECES 722,781,782,783
785	CYCLES,ETC MOTRZD OR NOT							W 200	930	MOTOCYCLES SCOOTERS
786	TRAILERS,NONMOTR VEH,NES							W 352	897	REMORQUES,CADRES,CONTAIN
79	OTHR TRANSPORT EQUIPMENT								871	AUTRE MATERIEL TRANSPORT
792	AIRCRAFT ETC							W 5	862	APP NAVIGATION AERIENNE
7929	AIRCRAFT PARTS NES							W 4	855	PIECES DU 792
8	MISC MANUFACTURED GOODS								27335	ART MANUFACTURES DIVERS
821	*FURNITURE,PARTS THEREOF							W 177	2048	MEUBLES ET PIECES
8211	CHAIRS,SEATS AND PARTS							W 84	1203	SIEGES ET PIECES
82111	CHAIRS AND OTHER SEATS							W 84	1202	SIEGES
84	CLOTHING AND ACCESSORIES								2015	VETEMENTS
842	MENS OUTERWEAR NOT KNIT							W 64	908	VET DESSUS POUR HOMMES
87	PRECISION INSTRUMNTS NES								5073	INSTRUM,APPAR SCIENT NDA
872	MEDICAL INSTRUMENTS NES							W 149	1833	INSTR,APP MEDIC-CHIR NDA
87202	OTH MEDICAL INSTRUMENTS							W 63	1804	INSTRUM,APP MEDECINE
874	MEASURNG,CONTROLNG INSTR							W 41	2967	INSTRUMENTS DE MESURE
8741	SURVEYING INSTRUMENTS							W 16	1829	INST GEODESIE,TOPO ETC
87412	SURVEY INSTR ETC NONELEC							W 15	1789	INSTR GEODESIE,TOPO ETC
89	MISC MANUFCTRD GOODS NES								16966	ART MANUFACTURES DIVERS
892	PRINTED MATTER							W 219	13565	IMPRIMES
8921	PRINTED BOOKS,GLOBES,ETC							W 129	1031	LIVRES,BROCHURES,CARTES
89211	PRINTED BOOKS,PAMPHLETS							W 127	994	LIVRES,BROCHURES
8928	PRINTED MATTER NES							W 68	12035	IMPRIMES NDA
89283	UNISSUED BANKNOTES ETC							W 37	11622	TIMBRES-POSTE FISCAUX
893	ARTICLES OF PLASTIC NES							W 374	1731	OUVRAGES EN MAT DIVIS 58
8939	MISC PLASTIC ARTICLES							W 244	1368	ART DIVERS EN MAT DIV 58
89399	OTHR PLASTC ARTICLES NES							W 212	1260	AUT OUV MAT DIV 58
894	TOYS,SPORTING GOODS,ETC							W 35	960	VOITURES ENFANTS,JOUETS
9	GOODS NOT CLASSD BY KIND								2424	ART TRANSACT NON CLASSES
931	*SPECIAL TRANSACTIONS								1499	TRANS.SPECIALES
951	*WAR FIREARMS,AMMUNITION							W 22	924	VEHIC BLINDES ARMES
95106	AMMUNITION NES							W 14	720	PROJECTILES,MUNITIONS

1. HISTORICAL SERIES, 1961–1996 SPECIAL TRADE, IMPORTS C.I.F., EXPORTS F.O.B.
SERIES HISTORIQUES, 1961–1996 COMMERCE SPECIAL, IMPORTATIONS C.A.F., EXPORTATIONS F.O.B

YEAR ANNEE	VALUE IN MILLION U.S. DOLLARS VALEUR EN MILLION U.S. DOLLARS MERCHANDISE –MARCHANDISE		GOLD –OR		CONVERSION FACTORS FACTEURS DE CONVERSION CENTS E.U. PAR		INDEX NUMBERS –INDICES QUANTUM		UNIT VALUE VALEUR UNITAIRE	
	IMPORTS	EXPORTS	IMPORTS	EXPORTS	IMPORTS	EXPORTS	IMPORTS	EXPORTS	IMPORTS	EXPORTS
1961	590.50	508.10								
1962	511.70	532.10								
1963	637.30	542.00								
1964	607.20	625.80								
1965	603.60	687.90								
1966	749.20	875.50								
1967	722.50	907.70								
1968	743.60	935.90								
1969	907.90	1067.90								
1970	930.10	1233.60								
1971	979.80	961.20								
1972	941.20	855.40								
1973	1097.90	1230.50								
1974	1681.40	1247.50								
1975	1338.20	1552.10								
1976	1683.80	2082.60								
1977	2414.00	2190.30								
1978	3002.40	2477.70								
1979	4217.60	3894.20								
1980	5123.70	4670.70								
1981	6363.80	3906.30								
1982	3830.90	3709.50								
1983	2968.80	3835.50								
1984	3480.50	3657.20								
1985	3006.60	3822.90								
1986	3436.30	4191.20								
1987	4396.40	5223.70								
1988	5291.80	7051.80								
1989	7144.20	8080.00								
1990	7677.60	8372.70								
1991	8093.70	8941.50								
1992	10128.60	10007.40								
1993	11125.40	9198.70								
1994	11824.60	11604.10								
1995	15914.10	16136.50								
1996	17827.50	15353.00								

2. IMPORTS BY BROAD ECONOMIC CATEGORY AND EXPORTS BY INDUSTRIAL ORIGIN. (PERCENTAGE OF TOTAL VALUE)
IMPORTATIONS PAR CATEGORIES ECONOMIQUES ET EXPORTATIONS PAR BRANCHE D'ACTIVITE.(EN POURCENTAGE DE LA VALEUR TOTALE)

IMPORTS – IMPORTATIONS

	1990	1991	1992	1993	1994	1995	1996
TOTAL IMPORTS–IMPORTATIONS TOTALES	100.	100.	100.	100.	100.	100.	100.
1 FOOD BEV–ALIMENTATION BOISSONS	3.7	4.7	5.1	5.0	5.7	5.6	5.8
11 PRIMARY–PRODUITS DE BASE	1.1	1.6	2.5	2.5	2.9	2.7	3.0
111 FOR INDUSTRY–POUR L'INDUSTRIE	0.3	0.5	1.1	1.1	1.3	1.2	1.5
112 FOR HOUSEHOLDS–POUR LES MENAGES	0.8	1.1	1.4	1.5	1.6	1.5	1.5
12 PROCESSED–PRODUITS ELABORES	2.6	3.2	2.6	2.5	2.8	2.8	2.9
121 FOR INDUSTRY–POUR L'INDUSTRIE	0.8	0.6	0.7	0.7	0.8	0.7	0.6
122 FOR HOUSEHOLDS–POUR LES MENAGES	1.9	2.5	1.9	1.8	2.0	2.2	2.2
2 IND SUPPLIES–APPROV INDUSTRIELS	27.4	30.7	28.8	27.8	27.7	29.5	26.5
21 PRIMARY–PRODUITS DE BASE	1.8	2.5	2.1	2.0	2.5	2.9	2.0
22 PROCESSED–PRODUITS ELABORES	25.6	28.2	26.7	25.8	25.2	26.6	24.5
3 FUELS–COMBUSTIBLES	15.6	14.8	11.5	9.9	9.7	8.8	10.8
31 PRIMARY–PRODUITS DE BASE	13.5	12.7	9.8	8.6	8.0	7.5	8.7
32 PROCESSED–PRODUITS ELABORES	2.1	2.1	1.6	1.3	1.7	1.4	2.1
321 MOTOR SPIRIT–ESSENCE	1.9	2.1	1.6	0.1	0.4	0.2	0.4
322 OTHER–AUTRES	0.2	0.1	0.0	1.2	1.3	1.2	1.6
4 MACHINERY–EQUIPEMENT	32.1	24.9	25.0	28.1	28.7	26.6	26.5
41 CAPITAL EQUIPMENT–MACHINES	28.3	21.5	21.8	24.7	25.4	23.5	23.7
42 PARTS–PIECES ACCESSOIRES	3.7	3.4	3.2	3.3	3.3	3.1	2.9
5 TRANSPORT–TRANSPORT	11.8	12.7	16.2	14.9	13.8	15.1	15.5
51 PASSENGER CARS–AUTOMOBILES	3.0	3.8	5.6	4.6	4.0	5.0	5.1
52 OTHER–AUTRES	5.2	5.4	7.0	6.7	6.6	7.1	7.4
521 INDUSTRIAL–INDUSTRIELS	5.2	5.3	6.9	6.5	6.4	7.0	7.3
522 NON INDUSTRIAL–NON INDUSTRIEL	0.1	0.1	0.2	0.2	0.2	0.1	0.2
53 PARTS–PIECES ACCESSOIRES	3.6	3.6	3.6	3.7	3.3	3.0	2.9
6 CONSUM GOODS–BIENS CONSOMMATION	8.1	10.6	11.7	12.6	12.8	13.2	13.6
61 DURABLE–DURABLES	2.9	3.6	4.1	4.1	4.0	4.1	3.9
62 SEMI DURABLE–SEMI DURABLES	3.6	4.9	5.5	6.2	6.4	6.7	7.2
63 NON DURABLE–NON DURABLES	1.7	2.1	2.2	2.3	2.4	2.4	2.5
7 GOODS NES–BIENS NDA	1.3	1.6	1.6	1.7	1.5	1.3	1.3

EXPORTS – EXPORTATIONS

	1990	1991	1992	1993	1994	1995	1996
TOTAL EXPORTS–EXPORTATIONS TOTALES	100.	100.	100.	100.	100.	100.	100.
1 AGRICULTURE	16.2	17.1	17.2	18.3	17.0	14.4	16.1
2 MINING QUARRY–INDUS EXTRACTIVES	11.1	14.4	14.4	13.0	13.7	16.6	15.7
3 MANUFACTURING–IND MANUFACTUR	72.7	68.5	68.4	68.7	69.3	69.0	68.2
31 FOOD BEV TOBACCO–ALIM BOISS TAB	9.9	12.3	13.2	12.6	12.2	12.0	13.5
32 TEXTILES–INDUSTRIES TEXTILES	1.4	1.7	1.6	2.0	1.8	1.3	1.4
33 WOOD & PRODUCTS–BOIS & PRODUITS	3.8	4.3	3.8	4.4	4.3	4.0	4.1
34 PAPER & PRODUCTS–PAPIER & PRODT	5.3	5.5	7.3	7.5	8.9	10.5	7.4
35 CHEMICALS–INDUSTRIES CHIMIQUES	4.4	4.9	4.5	5.1	5.7	4.4	4.6
36 NON METAL MIN–MIN NON METAL	0.3	0.2	0.2	0.2	0.2	0.2	0.2
37 BASIC METAL–IND METAL BASE	44.3	35.7	33.2	30.7	30.2	32.4	31.1
38 METAL MANUF–MANUF METAL	1.8	2.1	2.7	3.7	4.0	2.7	3.8
39 OTH MANUF IND–AUTRES MANUF	1.5	1.9	2.0	2.3	2.1	1.5	2.0

3. TRADE BY PRINCIPAL COUNTRIES OF PURCHASE AND SALE (VALUE IN THOUSAND U.S. DOLLARS)
ECHANGES SELON LES PRINCIPAUX PAYS D'ACHAT ET DE VENTE (VALEUR EN MILLIERS DE DOLLARS EU)

COUNTRIES–PAYS	SPECIAL IMPORTS C.I.F. IMPORTATIONS SPECIALES C.A.F				
	1992	1993	1994	1995	1996
World	9455518	10541887	11149092	14903075	16810002
Africa	581558	596093	315154	315252	438035
Americas	4599968	5150960	5885279	8258361	9331545
Northern America	2146651	2680076	2902730	4107965	4517622
LAIA	2392486	2424329	2883446	4035531	4655639
CACM	11118	11173	25242	41958	41569
Caribbean	41180	26003	68352	63161	109659
Rest of America	8532	9380	5507	9747	7057
As.ex F.USSR	1784925	1941620	2097068	2640773	2817870
Eur.x F.USSR	2217743	2507378	2532466	3346062	3813033
EU	2026263	2312397	2347663	3155565	3538036
EFTA	131093	161519	139473	155825	222963
East Europe	33298	32516	44048	31703	49363
Other Europe	537	199	443	308	405
Former USSR	69208	58948	38220	44406	47009
Oceania	62443	113796	133246	173511	214995
USA/Etats–Unis d'Amer	1984247	2477064	2637895	3792872	4109518
Brazil/Brésil	995850	1059942	999759	1194632	1065653
Argentina/Argentine	633529	580194	954737	1384522	1634218
Japan/Japon	964664	882641	1007063	1012922	949707
Germany/Allemagne	630607	620004	506545	789673	729880
Mexico/Mexique	178288	209615	263675	600647	927213
Italy/Italie	273221	335503	350408	508697	550773
France,Monac	281919	345633	362506	445870	581994
Korea, Republic of	249483	343200	333413	527397	556771
Spain/Espagne	223455	278321	340783	444957	530349
China/Chine	146738	212511	280686	390333	515061
Canada	162404	203012	264836	315092	408104
Nigeria/Nigéria	324168	397336	134409	166608	154189
United Kingdom	187548	214713	243054	246977	281714
Venezuela	131628	141640	139850	226778	313210
Ecuador/Equateur	151756	129433	187142	209051	224892
Sweden/Suède	100723	112898	119050	193164	271297
Colombia/Colombie	106288	98185	118860	149863	222375
Belgium–Luxembourg	85439	105337	115009	125528	143345
Switz.Liecht	101235	107672	117110	124466	120607
Peru/Pérou	67779	72302	94490	147370	117903
Australia/Australie	44762	86142	95481	119059	153331
Netherlands/Pays–Bas	87580	87700	91154	106418	123861
Finland/Finlande	44383	77042	71356	90318	103714
Denmark/Danemark	40217	56493	56344	87270	94361
So. Africa Customs Un	67589	69773	51557	72041	70063
Gabon	169223	97173	20895		40997
Malaysia/Malaisie	83632	42441	44454	76363	80761
Paraguay	61378	68107	55593	57997	69354
Angola	18306	28962	69949	70470	116241
Hong Kong			63523	108128	120811
Indonesia/Indonésie	17815	27921	42429	82741	97125
Uruguay	49273	51789	43994	40001	44967
Norway,SVD,JM	29153	52017	16971	30497	100751
Russian Federation	69208	58948	38220	33144	27696
Netherlands Antilles	28438	14412	44438	41242	90086
Singapore/Singapour	30272	35205	38522	56997	44099
New Zealand	17632	27575	36955	54408	61662
Austria/Autriche	33201	37314	33657	41692	38444
Ireland/Irlande	24872	27124	35745	40086	50134
Israel/Israël	24362	26770	32257	41942	46736
Thailand/Thaïlande	19055	26238	31548	40978	50349
Iran (Islamic Rp. of)	40201	92874	4868	9480	1518
India/Inde	5867	12759	21172	34094	57979
Portugal	11943	13460	21472	32696	36521
Bolivia/Bolivie	16718	13123	25346	24669	35852
Trinidad and Tobago	10708	10714	22626	19933	16477
Philippines	10308	10243	10578	15667	20393
Guatemala	3793	1391	11943	25581	21458
Costa Rica	4964	9080	12764	15115	19371

COUNTRIES–PAYS	SPECIAL EXPORTS F.O.B. EXPORTATIONS SPECIALES F.O.B.				
	1992	1993	1994	1995	1996
Monde	9913297	9308266	11368688	15901147	15406833
Afrique	92586	40647	102369	129613	120433
Amériques	3345111	3457712	4374313	5320621	5572229
Amérique du Nord	1644809	1587457	1931748	2233199	2515434
ALAI	1614243	1798179	2337507	2984645	2928462
MCAC	45405	31972	37020	41107	52101
Caraïbes	24978	18566	29803	37892	51001
Autre Amérique	15676	21538	38235	23779	25231
Asie l'URSS exclus	2993857	2952616	3796838	5581033	5369194
Europe l'URSS exclus	3112047	2578866	2763654	4461481	3909213
UE	3015315	2532682	2705512	4241438	3731867
AELE	39537	38051	50599	137325	111415
Europe de l'Est	56265	7030	5021	73882	57911
Autre de l'Europe	715		637	5638	820
Ancienne URSS	34907	22484	51684	146722	139747
Océanie	38216	39578	50195	87347	108733
Japan/Japon	1714078	1542898	1972096	2840193	2530560
USA/Etats–Unis d'Amer	1581945	1525756	1861227	2138339	2372569
United Kingdom	619283	551925	505129	1044241	916616
Brazil/Brésil	451471	424157	616673	1063915	946758
Germany/Allemagne	609506	493110	547949	808214	758280
Korea, Republic of	242963	421396	594494	891175	892215
Argentina/Argentine	455808	588482	635618	584103	699856
Italy/Italie	376985	330517	351525	596310	490450
France,Monac	380868	375647	394115	500891	404227
Netherlands/Pays–Bas	263216	227666	293378	358896	345239
Peru/Pérou	173005	206158	328260	432321	324931
Spain/Espagne	360883	243371	220657	303981	274886
China/Chine	221297	183334	133342	287195	372925
Belgium–Luxembourg	185295	141170	203905	370328	283531
Bolivia/Bolivie	153225	162188	171587	196897	207805
Mexico/Mexique	90124	124378	202863	127374	146162
Colombia/Colombie	75212	71726	116754	188425	194057
Venezuela	74700	73939	72700	135110	140996
Indonesia/Indonésie	45969	49707	88653	158780	147478
Thailand/Thaïlande	34621	65173	112424	149675	119016
Ecuador/Equateur	64225	54570	82775	124220	143844
Canada	62864	61701	70520	94860	142865
Sweden/Suède	75324	62757	64932	82615	71609
Russian Federation	34907	22484	51684	116736	120120
So. Africa Customs Un	59576	31853	84044	96344	67901
Singapore/Singapour	57398	38939	54931	78621	88057
Philippines	43117	44132	54935	59183	103211
Paraguay	41386	48261	57471	75954	66356
Saudi Arabia	59008	52238	43878	56105	57440
India/Inde	1560	19615	57965	89014	99164
Finland/Finlande	46066	27300	38853	62802	87966
Uruguay	35087	44321	52805	56326	57696
Malaysia/Malaisie	17741	29820	40536	87412	69585
Switz.Liecht	31310	24864	23375	92637	72098
Australia/Australie	23393	27909	35932	59896	75748
Hong Kong			34020	81673	105382
Greece/Grèce	35965	43066	40380	52988	40015
United Arab Emirates	27889	36443	32058	52732	53757
Norway,SVD,JM	7969	13128	27146	44517	38847
Panama	15600	21398	37984	23429	25073
Poland/Pologne	55602	6438	3698	29364	15255
Denmark/Danemark	11914	15825	20403	26880	29161
Costa Rica	22197	14671	16225	13940	24963
Portugal	35844	9053	12172	15977	13814
Sri Lanka	9168	4641	13375	21278	15829
Guatemala	15378	10000	12060	15113	10832
Turkey/Turquie	18606	23439	3961	13343	1602
Dominican Republic	10765	11264	12034	12107	13059
Cuba	4074	4491	14873	17486	18069
Bulgaria/Bulgarie		98	69	35070	22576

(VALUE AS PERCENTAGE OF WORLD TOTAL)(VALEURS EN POURCENTAGE DU TOTAL MONDIAL)

	1987	1988	1989	1990	1991	1992	1993	1994	1995	1996
Africa	4.0	4.5	5.0	8.1	6.1	6.2	5.7	2.8	2.1	2.6
Americas	47.8	52.6	49.6	47.7	51.2	48.6	48.9	52.8	55.4	55.5
Northern America	22.1	23.5	22.4	22.7	23.3	22.7	25.4	26.0	27.6	26.9
LAIA	25.0	28.7	27.0	24.6	27.3	25.3	23.0	25.9	27.1	27.7
CACM	0.0	0.0	0.0	0.0	0.1	0.1	0.1	0.2	0.3	0.2
Caribbean	0.5	0.3	0.2	0.2	0.5	0.4	0.2	0.6	0.4	0.7
Rest of America	0.1	0.0	0.1	0.1	0.1	0.1	0.1	0.0	0.1	0.0
As.ex F.USSR	17.3	14.6	18.8	13.8	17.7	18.9	18.4	18.8	17.7	16.8
Eur.x F.USSR	29.7	27.1	25.3	29.0	23.0	23.5	23.8	22.7	22.5	22.7
EU	27.3	24.1	22.9	26.8	21.0	21.4	21.9	21.1	21.2	21.0
EFTA	2.1	2.5	2.0	1.7	1.7	1.4	1.5	1.3	1.0	1.3
East Europe	0.4	0.4	0.4	0.5	0.3	0.4	0.3	0.4	0.2	0.3
Other Europe	0.0	0.1	0.1	0.1	0.0	0.0	0.0	0.0	0.0	0.0
Former USSR	0.0	0.3	0.3	0.3	0.5	0.7	0.6	0.3	0.3	0.3
Oceania	0.9	0.5	0.5	0.6	0.9	0.7	1.1	1.2	1.2	1.3
USA/Etats–Unis d'Amer	20.4	21.2	20.7	19.5	21.2	21.0	23.5	23.7	25.5	24.4
Brazil/Brésil	10.0	11.7	10.8	8.0	9.4	10.5	10.1	9.0	8.0	6.3
Argentina/Argentine	4.2	5.9	6.1	7.2	7.4	6.7	5.5	8.6	9.3	9.7
Japan/Japon	10.2	8.3	11.3	8.1	8.7	10.2	8.4	9.0	6.8	5.6
Germany/Allemagne	8.8	7.7	7.4	7.4	6.7	6.7	5.9	4.5	5.3	4.3
Mexico/Mexique	1.2	1.5	1.8	1.4	1.9	1.9	2.0	2.4	4.0	5.5
Italy/Italie	2.5	2.5	2.4	2.8	2.4	2.9	3.2	3.1	3.4	3.3
France,Monac	3.4	3.2	3.4	4.2	3.2	3.0	3.3	3.3	3.0	3.5
Korea, Republic of	2.2	2.3	2.5	1.7	2.3	2.6	3.3	3.0	3.5	3.3
Spain/Espagne	3.1	2.5	2.4	2.3	2.0	2.4	2.6	3.1	3.0	3.2

	1987	1988	1989	1990	1991	1992	1993	1994	1995	1996
Afrique	1.1	0.7	1.4	1.3	1.3	0.9	0.4	0.9	0.8	0.8
Amériques	40.5	33.5	30.7	30.1	31.0	33.7	37.1	38.5	33.5	36.2
Amérique du Nord	23.1	20.1	18.5	17.4	16.1	16.6	17.1	17.0	14.0	16.3
ALAI	16.8	12.7	11.8	12.0	14.2	16.3	19.3	20.6	18.8	19.0
MCAC	0.2	0.2	0.1	0.4	0.3	0.5	0.3	0.3	0.3	0.3
Caraïbes	0.2	0.2	0.2	0.1	0.2	0.3	0.2	0.3	0.2	0.3
Autre Amérique	0.2	0.3	0.2	0.2	0.2	0.2	0.2	0.3	0.1	0.2
Asie l'URSS exclus	21.1	22.6	27.0	27.4	30.8	30.2	31.7	33.4	35.1	34.8
Europe l'URSS exclus	36.0	41.9	39.2	39.3	34.8	31.4	27.7	24.3	28.1	25.4
UE	34.5	39.6	37.6	38.3	34.0	30.4	27.2	23.8	26.7	24.2
AELE	0.3	0.3	0.3	0.2	0.4	0.4	0.4	0.4	0.9	0.7
Europe de l'Est	0.9	1.1	0.9	0.6	0.4	0.6	0.1	0.0	0.5	0.4
Autre de l'Europe	0.3	0.9	0.5	0.2	0.0	0.0		0.0	0.0	0.0
Ancienne URSS	0.0			0.0	0.0	0.4	0.2	0.5	0.9	0.9
Océanie	0.5	0.5	0.7	0.7	0.6	0.4	0.4	0.4	0.5	0.7
Japan/Japon	11.2	12.7	13.7	16.2	18.7	17.3	16.6	17.3	17.9	16.4
USA/Etats–Unis d'Amer	21.7	19.4	17.7	16.8	15.5	16.0	16.4	16.4	13.4	15.4
United Kingdom	6.5	5.8	6.0	6.5	6.2	6.2	5.9	4.4	6.6	5.9
Brazil/Brésil	7.0	5.1	6.4	5.8	5.3	4.6	4.6	5.4	6.7	6.1
Germany/Allemagne	9.5	11.6	11.2	11.2	8.0	6.1	5.3	4.8	5.1	4.9
Korea, Republic of	2.2	2.0	3.2	3.0	3.0	2.5	4.5	5.2	5.6	5.8
Argentina/Argentine	3.5	2.4	1.3	1.3	2.9	4.6	6.3	5.6	3.7	4.5
Italy/Italie	5.3	6.4	5.1	4.8	3.8	3.8	3.6	3.1	3.8	3.2
France,Monac	3.6	5.0	4.8	4.7	4.3	3.8	4.0	3.5	3.2	2.6
Netherlands/Pays–Bas	2.9	3.3	3.1	3.3	3.1	2.7	2.4	2.6	2.3	2.2

4. Special Imports C.I.F. by Commodities according to the S.I.T.C. (Rev. 2) in thousand U.S. Dollars
Importations Spéciales C.A.F. par Produits d'après la C.T.C.I. (Rév. 2) en milliers de Dollars E.U.

SITC CTCI	COMMODITY	1993 WEIGHT POIDS	1993 VALUE VALEUR	1994 WEIGHT POIDS	1994 VALUE VALEUR	1995 WEIGHT POIDS	1995 VALUE VALEUR	1996 WEIGHT POIDS	1996 VALUE VALEUR	PRODUIT
	ALL COMMODITIES		10541887		11149092		14903075		16810002	TOUS PRODUITS
0	FOOD AND LIVE ANIMALS		516735		634793		824529		1026235	ALIMENTS,ANIMAUX VIVANTS
01	MEAT AND PREPARATIONS		78543		93497		127328		148484	VIANDES ET PREPARATIONS
011	MEAT FRESH,CHILLD,FROZEN	W 38641	77135	W 43460	91393	W 52297	123670		143882	VIANDES FRAICHES,REF,CONGE
0111	BOVINE MEAT FRESH,FROZEN	W 35017	73987	W 40936	88795	W 49972	120829	W 61593	140501	VIANDES BOVIN FRAI,REF
01112	BOVINE MEAT BONELESS	W 35017	73987	W 40936	88795	W 49951	120769	W 61009	139706	VIANDES BOVIN DESOSSEES
02	DAIRY PRODCTS,BIRDS'EGGS		63026		43832		55932		76669	PRODUITS LAITIERS,OEUFS
022	MILK AND CREAM	W 30894	50506	W 19534	29151	W 21429	39102	W 26746	55304	LAIT ET CREME
0224	MILK,CREAM PRESERVED ETC	W 30056	49499	W 18775	28480	W 20530	38044	W 24950	52847	LAIT,CREME CONS,CONC
03	FISH AND PREPARATIONS		16655		27220		45234		35402	POISSONS ET PREPARATIONS
04	CEREALS AND PREPARATIONS		154646		205129		245693		337178	CEREALES ET PRODUITS
041	WHEAT ETC UNMILLED	W 481150	77298	W 672254	109091	W 633398	123565	W 714258	177555	FROMENT,EPEAUTRE
0412	OTHER WHEAT ETC UNMILLED	W 393271	60114	W 530504	78319	W 561064	105370	W 623804	153195	AUTRE FROMENT NON MOULU
044	MAIZE UNMILLED	W 323483	46316	W 459015	66840	W 508673	80783	W 404887	84856	MAIS NON MOULU
05	VEGETABLES AND FRUIT		56956		59978		79079		90273	LEGUMES ET FRUITS
057	FRUIT,NUTS,FRESH,DRIED	W 145157	38265	W 152668	36396	W 151078	38489		42046	FRUITS FRAIS OU SECS
0573	BANANA,PLANTAIN,FRSH,DRY	W 138775	35050	W 147946	33758	W 144923	35026	W 150653	37784	BANANES FRAICHES,SECHEES
06	SUGAR AND PREPS,HONEY		14988		36603		70404		85834	SUCRES ET PRODUITS
061	SUGAR AND HONEY	W 19795	7326	W 75924	26970	W 136027	56468	W 178579	70869	SUCRES ET MIEL
0612	REFINED SUGAR ETC	W 17046	5408	W 71214	24895	W 129840	53012	W 164102	65047	SUCRES RAFFINES
07	COFFEE,TEA,COCOA,SPICES		55255		76017		90689		88679	CAFE,THE,CACAO,EPICES
081	*FEEDING STUFF FOR ANIML	W 142864	46512	W 178281	56575	W 237068	71900	W 293700	117919	NOURRITURE POUR ANIMAUX
0813	OILCAKE AND OTH RESIDUES	W 137196	38786	W 153020	43281	W 216092	54744	W 255316	87706	TOURTEAUX
08131	— OF SOYA BEANS	W 123102	36028	W 131268	39081	W 188647	50492	W 217156	78710	TOURTEAUX DE SOJA
2	CRUDE MATERLS,EXCL FUELS		243113		278131		445547		317231	MAT BRUTES NON COMESTIBLES
23	RUBBER, CRUDE		32507		34435		50700		44187	CAOUTCHOUC BRUT
26	TEXTILE FIBRES AND WASTE		116827		111060		138589		122122	FIBRES TEXTILES
263	COTTON	W 22771	32367	W 24843	37595	W 24464	50947	W 26678	47877	COTON
2631	RAW COTTON,EXCL LINTERS	W 22329	31995	W 24195	37007	W 23871	50334	W 26187	47364	COTON EN MASSE
266	SYNTHETIC FIBRES TO SPIN	W 22081	43485	W 18467	35045	W 20656	46462	W 19122	37605	FIBRES SYNTHETIQUES
28	METALLIFEROUS ORES,SCRAP		28138		59304		160546		56106	MINERAIS METAL,DECHETS
287	BASE METAL ORES,CONC NES	W 28408	28011	W 32484	56736	W 111343	160324	W 78180	55981	MINERAIS METAUX COMMUNS
2879	OTH NONFER ORE,CONCNTRTE	W 18785	25446	W 27441	55299	W 38603	156751	W 23483	54100	MINERAIS D'AUTRES METAUX
28793	MOLYBD, NIOBIUM ETC ORES	W 11762	24024	W 16330	53812	W 18526	153427	W 12891	51796	MINERAIS DE MOLYBDENE,TITANE
3	MINERAL FUELS ETC		1057217		1101760		1340987		1847478	COMBUSTIBLES MINERAUX LUB
32	COAL,COKE AND BRIQUETTES		76818		84169		124605		206844	HOUILLES,COKES,BRIQUETTES
322	COAL,LIGNITE AND PEAT	W 1623105	76752	W 2344903	82878	W 2873841	123177	W 4674958	205052	HOUILLES,LIGNITES,TOURBE
3222	OTH COAL,NOT AGGLOMERATD	W 1621563	76172	W 2343237	82185	W 2871639	122322	W 4673570	204399	AUTRES HOUILLES
33	PETROLEUM AND PRODUCTS		926372		952861		1129280		1536128	PETROLE ET DERIVES
333	CRUDE PETROLEUM	W 4861073	779692	W 5127757	747950	W 5649080	905665	W 6085003	1158834	HUILES BRUTES DE PETROLE
334	PETROLEUM PRODUCTS,REFIN	W 440093	134416	W 810247	187816	W 793896	200348	W 1255400	349592	PRODUITS RAFFINES
3341	GASOLINE,OTH LIGHT OILS	W 57683	15570	W 155538	39695	W 78672	23153	W 231517	74313	ESSENCES POUR MOTEURS
33411	MOTOR,AVIATION SPIRIT	W 32233	8592	W 152345	38270	W 73473	21067	W 227753	72500	ESSENCES MOTEURS D'AVIONS
3343	GAS OILS	W 258143	59520	W 263030	56526	W 296378	65013	W 510195	134579	GAS OILS
3344	FUEL OILS,NES	W 34357	3496	W 296117	34390	W 307640	40309	W 358594	52348	FUEL OILS
3345	LUBS,PETROLEUM OILS NES	W 88650	55279	W 95346	57092	W 97185	68519	W 105580	75015	HUILES LUBRIFIANTES
33451	LUBS(HIGH PETR CONT) ETC	W 86787	50448	W 93442	52298	W 94446	61418	W 102144	67180	HUILES LUBRIF,H LOURDES
341	*GAS,NATURAL AND MANUFCT	W 269004	54027	W 338486	64730	W 414532	87101	W 443200	104506	GAZ NATUREL,GAZ MANUFACT
3413	PETROLM GASES,LIQUEFIED	W 269004	54025	W 338436	64710	W 414531	87098	W 429944	101181	GAZ DE PETROLE LIQUEFIE
34131	LIQUEFIED PROPANE,BUTANE	W 194491	39327	W 268643	52384	W 371437	78674	W 381624	90475	PROPANE,BUTANE LIQUEFIES
4	ANIMAL,VEGETABLE OIL,FAT		87398		108282		130660		131368	HUILES,GRAISSES ANIM,VEG
42	FIXED VEGETABLE OIL,FAT		72885		91705		111769		104597	HUILES VEGETALES FIXES
423	FIXED VEG OILS,SOFT	W 140025	70168	W 140891	88822	W 151607	108441	W 157496	99591	HUILES VEGET DOUCES FIXES
4232	SOYA BEAN OIL	W 99302	47478	W 93679	57000	W 91930	63539	W 92560	56341	HUILE DE SOJA
5	CHEMCLS,RELATED PROD NES		1173821		1309911		1763585		1959427	PRODUITS CHIMIQUES
51	ORGANIC CHEMICALS		176279		187658		262306		235663	PROD CHIMIQ ORGANIQUES
513	CARBOXYLIC ACIDS ETC	W 29939	33821	W 29541	34076	W 34831	54509	W 34836	47215	ACIDES CARBOXYLIQUES
514	NITROGEN–FNCTN COMPOUNDS	W 13843	44847	W 14755	47209	W 18316	65801	W 17978	64132	COMPOSES FONCT AZOTEES
5148	OTH NITROGN–FNCTN CMPNDS	W 10570	29349	W 11510	31377	W 14329	45242	W 12809	41526	AUTRES COMPOSES AZOTES
515	ORG–INORG COMPOUNDS ETC	W 6662	40478	W 7016	44783	W 7840	49733	W 6558	40703	COMPOSES ORGANO–MINERAUX
52	INORGANIC CHEMICALS		110245		118305		163926		188257	PROD CHIM INORGANIQUES
522	INORG ELEMNTS,OXIDES,ETC	W 172576	36283	W 147732	46078	W 265301	68355	W 458402	75129	ELEMENTS INORGANIQUES
523	OTHR INORG CHEMICALS ETC	W 168393	73065	W 163983	71362	W 214659	94665	W 245773	112035	AUT PRODUITS CHIMIQUES INORG
5232	OTH MTL CMPD OF INRG ACD	W 126456	49457	W 112332	44779	W 161131	61091	W 189921	75974	SELS METALLIQUES
53	DYES,TANNING,COLOUR PROD		107611		116729		146590		184145	PROD TEINTURE,COLORANTS
531	SYNT DYE,NAT INDGO,LAKES	W 2320	52804	W 2300	59017	W 2688	69564	W 2845	101766	MAT COLOR ORGAN,LAQUES
5311	SYNTHIC ORGNIC DYESTUFFS	W 2081	49463	W 1985	55401	W 2143	65415	W 2355	98327	MAT COLOR ORGAN SYNTHET
533	PIGMENTS,PAINTS,ETC	W 16108	48798	W 18346	53466	W 21408	72784	W 21702	76817	PIGMENTS,PEINTURES,VERNIS
541	*MEDICINAL,PHARM PRODUCT	K 3389499	117881	K 4254444	137418		182872		214068	PROD MEDICINAUX PHARMACEUT
5417	MEDICAMENTS	K 1357034	59685	K 1811072	78244	K 2444345	106314	K 3947311	128972	MEDICAMENTS
54179	— CONTNG OTH SUBSTANCES	K 1026352	35824	K 1335737	50263	K 1888954	67825	K 3199999	81998	MED CONT AUT SUBSTANCES
55	PERFUME,CLEANING ETC PRD		82108		94571		127944		152225	PROD POUR PARFUM,TOILETTE
553	PERFUMERY,COSMETICS,ETC	W 4145	33512	W 4319	38156	W 7745	56378	W 10423	79371	PRODUITS DE PARFUMERIE
562	*FERTILIZERS,MANUFACTURE	W 697893	102008	W 729404	122236	W 822156	167893	W 1065693	230514	ENGRAIS MANUFACTURES
5621	CHEM NITROGENOUS FERTLZR	W 384676	55215	W 383166	64409	W 436059	94261	W 582285	130181	ENGRAIS AZOTES
56216	UREA	W 280640	37055	W 272585	42986	W 303016	65114	W 401176	89722	UREE
58	PLASTIC MATERIALS ETC		278067		320196		449329		443435	MAT PLAST ARTIFICIELLES
582	PROD OF CONDENSATION ETC	W 32528	60096	W 33737	60836	W 41907	88477	W 38339	83728	PROD CONDENS,POLYCOND
5823	ALKYDS,OTHER POLYESTERS	W 14862	27177	W 16210	28220	W 21434	45820	W 17670	36948	ALKYDES ET AUT POLYESTERS
583	POLYMERIZATION ETC PRODS	W 202450	205059	W 224989	247533	W 234194	345911	W 288262	344950	PROD POLYMERISATION
5831	POLYETHYLENE	W 79036	62785	W 96448	82451	W 97254	116941	W 122869	125233	POLYETHYLENE
58311	— IN PRIMARY FORMS	W 74900	53953	W 90784	70817	W 90745	101175	W 114079	106226	POLYETHYLENE PRIMAIRES
5832	POLYPROPYLENE	W 29185	27738	W 31903	33649	W 36363	63322	W 36509	44837	POLYPROPYLENE
5834	POLYVINYL CHLORIDE	W 57751	47504	W 56409	56770	W 57440	68173	W 78614	73311	CHLORURE DE POLYVINYLE
58341	— IN PRIMARY FORMS	W 53308	35955	W 52028	44707	W 50945	49307	W 71889	54077	SOUS FORMES PRIMAIRES
5839	OTH POLYMRZTION ETC PROD	W 10857	31450	W 11624	34428	W 13834	44612	W 15276	48459	AUT PROD POLYMER COPOLYM
59	CHEMICAL MATERIALS NES		197686		210418		260139		308628	MAT PROD CHIMIQUES NDA
591	PESTICIDES,DISINFECTANTS	W 10464	69604	W 10199	65981	W 12143	80910	W 14042	93534	DESINF,INSECT,FONG,HERB
598	MISCEL CHEM PRODUCTS NES	W 54009	105969	W 56510	122894	W 69779	150526	W 74537	183083	PROD DIV INDUST CHIM NDA
5989	CHEM PRODUCTS,PREPS NES	W 36861	77527	W 37960	93017	W 48717	115628	W 53006	144413	PROD PREP CHIMIQUES NDA
59899	OTH CHEM PRODS,PREPS,NES	W 26501	60012	W 27824	75964	W 34839	92881	W 36422	114224	AUT PRODUITS CHIMIQUES NDA
6	BASIC MANUFACTURES		1721491		1689175		2473800		2471898	ART MANUFACTURES
62	RUBBER MANUFACTURES NES		147502		141797		193925		206946	CAOUTCHOUC MANUFACTURE
625	RUBBER TYRES, TUBES ETC	W 20852	92709	W 21046	95938	W 28988	134884	W 30060	146328	PNEUS CAOUTCHOUC VULCANISE
6252	TYRES,NEW,BUS OR LORRY	W 8292	32525	W 6757	27184	W 10655	43746	W 12193	53685	PNEUS POUR AUTOBUS,CAMIONS
6259	OTH TYRES,TYRE CASES,ETC	W 10018	48731	W 11664	57838	W 13525	70298	W 14102	76092	AUTRES PNEUS RECHAPES FLAPS
62599	TYRES NES,TYRE CASES,ETC	W 9184	45425	W 10809	54765	W 12588	66677	W 12811	70822	PNEUS,FLAPS
628	RUBBER ARTICLES NES	W 4351	34179	W 2645	24104	W 3520	34135	W 3227	34112	OUVRAGES CAOUTCHOUC NDA
63	WOOD,CORK MANUFACTRS NES		30322		36045		51185		58371	OUVRAGES LIEGE ET BOIS
64	PAPER,PAPERBOARD AND MFR		192546		233627		401358		337415	PAPIERS,CARTONS & OUVRAGES
641	PAPER AND PAPERBOARD	W 184642	154103	W 235512	186795	W 310875	336603	W 321868	268985	PAPIERS ET CARTONS

4. Special Imports C.I.F. by Commodities according to the S.I.T.C. (Rev. 2) in thousand U.S. Dollars
Importations Spéciales C.A.F. par Produits d'après la C.T.C.I. (Rév. 2) en milliers de Dollars E.U.

SITC CTCI	COMMODITY	1993 WEIGHT POIDS	1993 VALUE VALEUR	1994 WEIGHT POIDS	1994 VALUE VALEUR	1995 WEIGHT POIDS	1995 VALUE VALEUR	1996 WEIGHT POIDS	1996 VALUE VALEUR	PRODUIT
6412	PRINTG,WRITING PAPER NES	W 46883	47044	W 50725	47817	W 79928	104016	W 64088	73159	PAPIERS POUR L'IMPRESSION
64122	— COATED,IMPREGNATD ETC	W 39200	38684	W 44121	40678	W 67021	85077	W 52814	59466	PAPIERS IMPRESSION COUCHES
6413	KRAFT PAPER,PAPERBOARD	W 48835	21417	W 73705	35642	W 85173	59047	W 124735	62028	PAPIER ET CARTON KRAFT
6415	PAPER,PAPERBRD,BULK,NES	W 58512	43109	W 68793	51358	W 107247	108544	W 71817	54553	PAPIERS,CARTONS ROULEAUX
64159	OTHER PAPER ETC,BULK,NES	W 41760	35538	W 56248	44513	W 79061	87644	W 44047	41579	AUT PAPIER ROULEAUX FEUILLES
6418	COATED ETC PAPER NES BLK	W 17473	31009	W 17475	34813	W 23103	48183	W 25645	47424	PAP,CARTONS COUCHES,ENDUITS
642	PAPER,ETC,PRECUT,ARTS OF	W 20622	38443	W 21535	46832	W 30141	64755	W 32495	68430	PAP,CARTONS DECOUPES
65	TEXTILE YARN,FABRICS,ETC		406745		373031		487953		500184	FILS,TISSUS,ARTICLES TEXTILE
651	TEXTILE YARN	W 15691	72454	W 16389	69892	W 21909	100002	W 22859	96854	FILS TEXTILES
652	COTTON FABRICS,WOVEN	W 10742	58339	W 8136	44507	W 9293	59935	W 10113	67607	TISSUS DE COTON
6522	WOVEN COTTON BLEACHD,ETC	W 9808	55371	W 7820	43134	W 8836	57606	W 9596	64821	TISSUS COTON BLANCHIS ETC
65224	BLCHED COTTON FABRIC NES	W 9270	49423	W 7263	37100	W 8110	49776	W 8341	52043	AUT TIS PLUS 85% COT BLANCHI
653	WOVN MAN-MADE FIB FABRIC	W 13937	99864	W 13433	92662	W 14949	110220	W 15550	109798	TISSUS FIBRES SYNTH,ARTIF
6531	CONT SYNT WEAVES NONPILE	W 5681	41849	W 4914	34435	W 5282	39376	W 5856	42841	TISSUS FIBRES SYNTH CONTINUE
65315	CONT SYN TXTL FABRIC NES	W 5240	38865	W 4679	31975	W 4871	35285	W 5382	38753	TIS PLUS 85% TEXT SYNT CONT
6534	DISC SYN BLEND FABRC NES	W 5838	34883	W 4868	27351	W 5984	36491	W 6956	42775	TISSUS FIBRES SYNTH DISCONT
657	SPECIAL TXTL FABRC,PRODS	W 14886	95487	W 13370	84213	W 16976	109513	W 15173	105328	TISSUS SPECIAUX
6575	CORDAGE AND MANUFACTURES	W 6242	36853	W 4849	27588	W 6785	41273	W 5186	34730	FICELLES,CORDES,CORDAGES
66	NONMETAL MINERAL MFS NES		180179		161263		220964		260115	ART MIN NON METALLIQUES
662	CLAY,REFRACTORY BLDG PRD	W 45230	33589	W 41187	28682	W 69403	46149	W 88602	56973	MAT CONST REFRACTAIRES
664	GLASS	W 34828	50592	W 39686	50422	W 38217	69886	W 37402	61464	VERRE
67	IRON AND STEEL		355783		328164		538157		480923	FER ET ACIER
672	IRON,STEEL PRIMARY FORMS	W 87298	28543	W 91760	30535	W 127688	52490	W 152437	55564	LINGOTS FER,ACIER
6727	IRN,STL COIL FR REROLLNG	W 82305	27065	W 91181	30329	W 118507	50002	W 145639	53784	EBAUCHES POUR TOLES FER
67271	IRON,SIMPLE STEEL COILS	W 81815	26428	W 91027	30088	W 117971	48759	W 144423	52909	EBAUCHES NON EN ACIER
673	IRON,STEEL SHAPES ETC	W 232792	86559	W 153642	59834	W 213966	91086	W 222623	92801	BARRES,PROFIL FER,ACIER
6732	IRON,STEEL BARS ETC	W 118027	47122	W 79406	33994	W 107447	51720	W 84469	42702	BARRES FER,ACIER
67326	IRN,OTH STL BARS HOTROLD	W 100994	34651	W 56988	19081	W 83713	31599	W 44910	16993	BARRES PLEINES FER,ACIER
674	IRN,STL UNIV,PLATE,SHEET		136600	W 230041	136534	W 376394	247270	W 296495	188699	LARGES PLATS,TOLES
6744	IRN,STL HVY PLATE,ROLLED		38463	W 62651	26595	W 130674	62993	W 118203	55308	TOLES LAMINEES PLUS 4.75 MM
67441	— OF IRON OR SIMPLE STL		32073	W 59740	22293	W 127900	56133	W 112238	45950	TOLES NON ACIER FIN CARB
6746	IRN,STL THIN PLATE,ROLLD	W 53672	37661	W 88601	53646	W 150346	103988	W 82501	57880	TOLES LAM MOINS 3MM
67461	— OF IRON OR SIMPLE STL	W 42026	19961	W 75670	37180	W 133435	76844	W 63625	32582	TOL NON AC FIN MOINS 3 MM
6749	OTH IRN,STL PLATES,SHEET	W 49990	31817	W 43919	28735	W 66361	52683	W 58344	42937	AUTRES TOLES FER,ACIER
67491	— OF IRON OR SIMPLE STL	W 49906	31625	W 43774	28253	W 66268	52473	W 58233	42683	AUT TOLES AUTRES ACIER FIN
678	IRON,STL TUBES,PIPES,ETC	W 68796	76275	W 53920	70792	W 66727	97799	W 91239	107830	TUBES,TUYAUX EN FONTE,FER
6783	IRON,STL TUBES,PIPES NES	W 51507	42386	W 37562	37628	W 41630	46705	W 71457	66222	AUT TUBES,TUYAUX FER,ACIER
68	NON-FERROUS METALS		84620		81152		130425		116293	METAUX NON FERREUX
684	ALUMINIUM	W 22905	55190	W 22594	57535	W 29524	93336	W 28670	81234	ALUMINIUM
6842	ALUMINIUM,ALLOYS WORKED	W 8750	33990	W 8341	33376	W 13873	59773	W 14841	55582	ALUMINIUM,ALLIAGES OUVRE
69	METAL MANUFACTURES NES		294316		310161		414753		478918	ART MANUFACT EN METAL NDA
691	STRUCTURES AND PARTS NES	W 8523	17849	W 14030	25618	W 16836	36460	W 27958	53432	CONSTRUCT FER,ACIER,ALU
692	METAL TANKS,BOXES,ETC	W 12799	43328	W 15318	52974	W 19991	76406	W 16995	63749	RECIPIENTS METALLIQUES
6924	MTL TRANSPORT BOXES ETC	W 12008	39681	W 13393	45548	W 18221	71120	W 16429	60341	FUTS,TAMBOURS,BIDONS
69242	ALUMNM TRNSPRT BOXES ETC	W 6527	25267	W 8332	33249	W 12170	54559	W 10289	44277	FUTS,TAMBOURS,BIDONS ALU
695	TOOLS	W 5804	62208	W 5119	60899	W 5530	72950	W 6186	78188	OUTILS A MAIN
697	BASE MTL HOUSEHOLD EQUIP	W 6669	32518	W 5826	28351	W 8368	41421	W 9471	49726	ART MENAGE MET COMMUNS
699	BASE METAL MFRS NES	W 16718	81877		82495	W 17105	97799	W 22070	121625	ART MANUFACTURES MET NDA
7	MACHINES,TRANSPORT EQUIP		4567807		4738308		6273939		7147508	MACHINES MATERIEL TRANSPORT
71	POWER GENERATING EQUIPMT		256111		457510		314976		406731	MACHINES GENERATRICES
711	STEAM BOILERS & AUX PLNT	W 5921	50353	W 14058	207854	W 8621	75217	W 12472	115264	GENERATEURS VAPEUR EAU ETC
7111	STEAM BOILERS ETC	W 5665	47931	W 13827	204415	W 8347	71411	W 11998	109431	GENERATEURS VAPEUR EAU
712	STEAM ENGINES,TURBINES	W 46	757	W 2651	65420	W 854	21241	W 1424	32816	MACHINES A VAPEUR D'EAU PIEC
7126	STEAM POWR UNITS,ENGINES	W 37	206	W 2624	64426	W 831	20592	W 1405	31600	MACHINES A VAPEUR D EAU
713	INTRNL COMBUS PSTN ENGIN	W 6062	71144	W 3618	62827	W 3915	77595	W 4463	86334	MOTEURS EXPL COMB INT, PIECE
7139	PISTON ENGINE PARTS NES	W 1825	41078	W 1660	39857	W 2014	52932	W 2068	53565	PIECES POUR 713.2,3,8
716	ROTATING ELECTRIC PLANT	W 8557	115093	W 7414	103691	W 9740	114578	W 8751	113783	APP ELECTR ROTATIFS,PIECES
7162	AC MTRS,GENRTRS,GEN SETS	W 7200	82046	W 6688	90107	W 8523	97437	W 7306	80679	MOTEURS ELECTRIQUES
71621	AC MTRS,INC UNIVRSL MTRS	W 4460	35621	W 3347	25474	W 3820	31082	W 2806	25391	MOT ELEC NON COUR CONTINU
71622	AC GENERATORS	W 455	7563	W 1983	49945	W 2197	35228	W 1340	24589	GENER COURANT ALTERNATIF
71623	GEN SETS WITH PISTN ENGN	W 2284	38861	W 1357	14688	W 2507	31127	W 3160	30700	GROUPES MOTEUR EXPLOSION
72	MACHS FOR SPCL INDUSTRYS		722839		665479		1005031		1174214	MAC SPECIALES POUR INDUST
721	AGRIC MACHY,EXC TRACTORS	W 4398	38824	W 4831	40782	W 7017	60094	W 8001	85455	MACHINES AGRICOLES
722	TRACTORS NON-ROAD	W 5377	32112	W 4749	29898	W 5239	34676	W 5913	40068	TRACTEURS
723	CIVIL ENGNEERG EQUIP ETC	W 23042	195774	W 22123	202827	W 33156	297363	W 40883	378336	APPAREILS DE GENIE CIVIL
7234	CONST,MINING MACHNRY NES	W 21375	177532	W 20391	183525	W 30290	266817	W 37146	342905	MACH POUR LA CONST, MINES
72341	SELF-PROPELLD DOZERS,ETC	W 4189	35431	W 4282	36836	W 6323	53534	W 6332	59073	BULLDOZERS
72342	SLFPRP SHOVELS,EXCAVATRS	W 15182	112026	W 13912	114436	W 20949	172198	W 27429	229171	PELLES MECANIQUES
724	TEXTILE,LEATHER MACHNRY	W 4975	76099	W 2879	55634	W 3794	64897	W 2993	52715	MACH POUR INDUSTRIE TEXTILE
725	PAPER ETC MILL MACHINERY	W 3367	46787	W 1849	34533	W 2859	53186	W 2133	49071	MACHINES FABR PATE PAPIER
726	PRINTG,BKBINDG MACHY,PTS	W 2016	51597	W 1893	44714	W 2387	75323	W 1394	41637	MACHINES POUR IMPRIMERIE
7264	PRINTING PRESSES	W 1576	34032	W 1310	27325	W 1831	53176	W 843	19132	MACHINES A IMPRIMER
72641	ROTARY PRINTING PRESSES	W 1576	34032	W 1310	27325	W 1831	53176	W 843	19132	MACH IMPRIMER ROTATIVES
727	FOOD MACHRY NON-DOMESTIC	W 2071	39089	W 1274	28277	W 2667	50566	W 1823	45517	MACH INDUSTRIES ALIMENT
7272	OTH FOOD PROC MCHY,PARTS	W 1888	37010	W 1093	26109	W 2416	47983	W 1626	43303	AUT MACH IND ALIMENTAIRE
72722	INDUS FOOD PROC MACH NES	W 1743	34730	W 1082	25263	W 2383	47734	W 1571	42535	MACHINES BOULANGERIE
728	OTH MACHY FOR SPCL INDUS	W 20290	242558	W 20837	228814	W 42296	368927	W 38524	481415	AUT MACH IND PARTICULIERES
7281	MACH-TOOLS FR SPCL INDUS	W 3620	45323	W 2024	25228	W 2979	45816	W 2848	45507	MACH-OUTILS SPEC IND PART
72812	MACH-TOOLS TO WORK WOOD	W 3362	40098	W 1747	18920	W 2462	35089	W 2429	35551	MACH-OUT POUR TRAVAIL BOIS
7283	OTHR MINERAL WORKG MACHY	W 8939	66945	W 12409	97051	W 26323	166748	W 15044	108991	MACH TRIER,CRIBLER,BROYER
72831	MINRAL SORTING ETC MACHY	W 1267	13412	W 4035	36708	W 12252	69567	W 3561	24314	MACH TRIER MAT MINERALES
72832	MINRL CRUSHING ETC MACHY	W 4087	30032	W 3763	30452	W 8256	57227	W 5280	39158	MACH CONCASSER MAT MINER
7284	MACHY FOR SPCL INDUS NES	W 7731	130289	W 6405	106535	W 12994	156364	W 20633	326917	MACH SPEC IND PARTICUL.
72842	RUBBER,PLASTICS WRKG MCH	W 2798	40922	W 1949	35326	W 2706	36838	W 2344	49807	MACH IND CAOUT MAT PLAST
72848	OTH MCHY WITH INDIV FNCT	W 3142	59943	W 3477	46332	W 6271	70738	W 15059	224783	AUTRES MACHINES NDA
73	METALWORKING MACHINERY		94884		118142		73109		80457	MACH TRAVAIL DES METAUX
736	METALWORKING MACH-TOOLS	W 7461	57143	W 5738	43190	W 4791	43474	W 5438	47645	MACH-OUTILS TRAVAIL METAUX
737	METALWORKING MACHNRY NES	W 4205	37740	W 3948	74952	W 2675	29635	W 2566	32812	MACH TRAV METAUX PIECES
7372	ROLLING MILLS AND ROLLS	W 2192	15028	W 2439	52852	W 856	6117	W 1003	8264	LAMINOIRS CYLINDRES PIEC
73721	ROLLING MILLS	W 1268	10120	W 1620	45983	W 84	1491	W 92	1142	LAMINOIRS ET TRAINS
74	GENRL INDUSTRL MACHY NES		881118		841525		1152861		1236356	MACH APP INDUSTRIE
741	HEATING,COOLING EQUIPMNT	W 13072	173358	W 11580	147209	W 16289	186549	W 23026	255800	MACH CHAUFFAGE,PIECES
7414	NONDOM REFRIG EQUIPT,PTS	W 2527	28951	W 2458	30485	W 4095	45883	W 4734	52759	MAT PRODUCTION DU FROID
7416	HEATING,COOLING EQU NES	W 6324	80130	W 5561	59350	W 8518	86681	W 13490	131288	APP CHANGEMENT TEMP
742	PUMPS FOR LIQUIDS ETC	W 3730	66933	W 3763	69331	W 4851	89764	W 4997	92657	POMPES MOTO-POMPES
743	PUMPS NES,CENTRFUGES ETC	W 12013	152200	W 11068	136376	W 13875	169190	W 15520	190345	POMPES COMPRES,VENT ETC
7431	PUMPS FOR GASES ETC	W 4527	47371	W 4362	42146	W 5859	58204	W 4961	52883	POMPES AIR A VIDE,COMPRES
7436	GAS,LIQUID FILTERS ETC	W 3607	54398	W 3751	52610	W 4942	62807	W 7039	79230	APP POUR FILT DES LIQUIDES
744	MECHANICAL HANDLING EQU	W 24820	190488	W 22995	187360	W 44086	321901	W 37758	291382	EQUIP MANUTENTION PIECES
7441	FORK LIFT TRCKS,ETC,PTS	W 7192	43499	W 5302	31273	W 8172	53844	W 9957	60022	CHARIOTS POUR USINES ETC
74411	FORK LIFT TRUCKS ETC	W 7185	43405	W 5300	31209	W 8171	53801	W 9952	59996	CHARIOTS POUR LES GARES

4. Special Imports C.I.F. by Commodities according to the S.I.T.C. (Rev. 2) in thousand U.S. Dollars
Importations Spéciales C.A.F. par Produits d'après la C.T.C.I. (Rév. 2) en milliers de Dollars E.U.

SITC CTCI	COMMODITY	1993 WEIGHT POIDS	1993 VALUE VALEUR	1994 WEIGHT POIDS	1994 VALUE VALEUR	1995 WEIGHT POIDS	1995 VALUE VALEUR	1996 WEIGHT POIDS	1996 VALUE VALEUR	PRODUIT
7442	LIFTING,LOADING MACH NES	W 13498	115291	W 12840	120348	W 29591	224253	W 20938	170873	APP LEVAGE,MANUTENTION
74428	OTH HANDLING ETC MCH NES	W 7517	68961	W 8156	79931	W 23495	175131	W 13388	111884	AUT APP LEVAGE ETC
7449	PTS NES OF MACHY OF 7442	W 4130	31699	W 4853	35739	W 6323	43804	W 6863	60487	PIECES DU 744.2
745	NONELEC MACHY,TOOLS NES	W 3955	97964	W 4073	102516	W 5265	136389	W 5101	133258	AUT MACH NON ELEC,PIECES
7452	OTH NONELEC MCHS,PTS NES	W 3567	86106	W 3712	92035	W 4835	122470	W 4626	120054	AUT MACH NON ELEC,PIECES
74522	PACKAGNG,BOTTLNG,ETC MCH	W 1473	47721	W 1254	49193	W 1997	70335	W 1481	62288	MACH NETT BOUTEILLES,ETC
749	NONELEC MACH PTS,ACC NES	W 10519	200174	W 9663	198733	W 13071	249069	W 13679	272914	PIECES MACH NON ELEC NDA
7491	BALL,ROLLER,ETC BEARINGS	W 1602	32669	W 1479	32185	W 1870	39643	W 2089	44829	ROULEMENTS BILLES ETC
7492	COCKS,VALVES ETC NES	W 4150	74511	W 3918	75880	W 5040	94551	W 5553	99528	ART ROB,SIM POUR TUYAUX
7493	SHAFT,CRANK,PULLEY ETC	W 2951	62431	W 2827	59647	W 3792	73343	W 3881	82020	ARBRES TRANS,VILEBREQUINS
75	OFFICE MACHNES,ADP EQUIP		303717		350920		465937		529999	MACH BUREAU TRAIT AUTOM
751	OFFICE MACHINES	W 1439	43480	W 1260	38873	W 1697	53652	W 1929	60598	MACH,APPAREILS DE BUREAU
752	AUTOMTIC DATA PROC EQUIP	W 3327	198987	W 3748	237059	W 5187	319632	W 6303	369330	MACH TRAIT INFORMATION
7522	DIGITAL COMPUTERS	W 613	46112	W 831	71375	W 936	89083	W 1274	99781	MACH DIGITALES COMPLETES
7523	DIGITL CENTRL PROCESSORS	W 554	45696	W 426	34724	W 1029	76963	W 887	68702	UNITES CENTRALES
7525	ADP PERIPHERAL UNITS	W 1852	64623	W 2173	76329	W 2824	95204	W 3252	109390	UNITES PERIPHERIQUES
759	OFFICE,ADP MCH PTS,ACCES	W 628	61250	W 839	74989	W 1161	92654	W 1448	100071	PIECES DU 751 ET 752
7599	ACCTG,ETC,ADP MCH PTS,AC	W 462	52789	W 668	66027	W 881	79460	W 1139	86151	PIECES DU 751 ET 752
76	TELECOMM,SOUND EQUIPMENT		474291		426707		585629		699220	EQUIPMENT DE TELECOM
761	TELEVISION RECEIVERS	W 7738	109622	W 7450	105246	W 12269	156930	W 12101	153808	RECEPTEURS DE TELEVISION
7611	COLOUR TV RECEIVERS	W 7277	105412	W 7173	102140	W 11968	153841	W 11998	152516	RECEPTEURS COULEUR
762	RADIO BROADCAST RECEIVRS	W 4356	73772	W 4113	74109	W 5362	107939	W 5458	107016	RECEPTEURS RADIODIFFUSION
7628	OTHER RADIO RECEIVERS	W 3772	54156	W 3486	52682	W 4506	77529	W 4572	77109	AUTRES RECEPT RADIO
763	SOUND RECORDRS,PHONOGRPH	W 844	32681	W 706	30681	W 844	36410	W 738	30524	PHONO,APP ENREGISTREMENT
7638	OTHR SOUND APPARATUS ETC	W 841	32618	W 695	30522	W 832	36193	W 723	30221	AUT APP D'ENREGIS,REPROD
764	TELECOM EQPT,PTS,ACC NES	W 3542	258216	W 3322	216671	W 4314	284349	W 6357	407871	EQUIP TELECOM,PIECES
7641	LINE TELEPHONE,ETC EQUIP	W 1360	88978	W 1148	72452	W 1376	85036	W 2055	116951	APP TELEPHON PAR FIL
7643	TV,RADIO TRANSMITTRS ETC	W 349	57114	W 335	50558	W 499	82108	W 885	131169	APP EMET TELE RADIO
7649	PTS NES OF EQUIPMT OF 76	W 1084	88464	W 947	69296	W 1039	81153	W 1634	118640	PIECES DE LA DIV 76
76491	PTS NES OF APPAR OF 7641	W 573	68500	W 277	39676	W 451	57283	W 1045	93697	PIECES POUR 764.1
77	ELECTRIC MACHNRY NES ETC		472127		534435		695735		710412	MACH APP ELECT NDA
771	ELECTRIC POWER MACHY NES	W 2891	40565	W 3829	46630	W 5290	59263	W 4323	60573	MACH PROD,TRANS ELECTR
772	SWITCHGEAR ETC,PARTS NES	W 4631	113125	W 4680	124821	W 6241	156081	W 6610	166661	APP COUPURE,SECT ETC
7721	SWITCHGEAR ETC	W 4564	109961	W 4607	121580	W 6152	151845	W 6533	162554	APP COUPURE,SECTIONMNT
773	ELECTR DISTRIBUTNG EQUIP	W 8012	41819	W 10073	50976	W 12782	77060	W 16626	85322	EQUIPMT DISTRIBUTION ELECT
7731	INSULATED WIRE,CABLE ETC	W 7231	36176	W 8953	44338	W 11242	67103	W 15155	76591	FILS,CABLES ISOLES ELECT
775	HOUSEHOLD TYPE EQUIP NES	W 14521	105467	W 15430	118195	W 20501	159221	W 23063	176080	MACH,APP USAGE DOMESTQUE
7751	HOUSEHOLD LDRY EQUIP NES	W 3626	23226	W 5102	32038	W 6151	41484	W 8588	56963	MACH A LAVER ET SECHOIRS
77511	DOMESTIC WASHING MACHNES	W 3432	21511	W 4809	30124	W 5924	40169	W 8397	55640	MACH LAVER LINGE MOINS 6 KG
778	ELECTRICAL MACHINERY NES	W 13559	132565	W 13128	143346	W 14837	186359	W 16652	179980	AUTRES MACH ELECT NDA
7781	BATTERIES,ACCUMULATORS	W 8283	37344	W 7594	34753	W 8536	39888	W 9898	46041	PILES ET ACCUMULATEURS
7788	OTH ELEC MACHY,EQUIP NES	W 1398	31844	W 1854	49096	W 2010	73580	W 2025	55009	AUT MACH APP ELEC NDA
77886	OTH ELEC MACHINERY NES	W 238	12841	W 405	24326	W 548	47939	W 461	23343	AUT MACH APP ELECTRIQUES
78	ROAD VEHICLES		1269262		1236247		1824421		2043353	VEHICULES ROUTIERS
781	PASS MOTOR VEH EXC BUSES	W 50550	480697	W 45558	442680	W 73979	741941	W 84807	862025	AUTO TRANSPORT PERSONNES
782	LORRIES,SPCL MTR VEH NES	W 49878	428082	W 49805	445103	W 68941	633646	W 75436	715137	VEHICULES SPECIAUX,MARCH
7821	LORRIES,TRUCKS	W 47085	400963	W 48157	423450	W 64880	586787	W 70398	663528	VEHICULES TRANSP MARCHAND
7822	SPECIAL MOTOR VEHCLS NES	W 2792	27119	W 1648	21653	W 4061	46859	W 5038	51609	VEHICULES USAGES SPECIAUX
783	ROAD MOTOR VEHICLES NES	W 14446	139888	W 15392	141854	W 20423	211470	W 19341	200722	VEHICULES ROUTIERS NDA
7831	BUSES	W 9954	98310	W 12201	108901	W 10927	107870	W 11152	109774	VOITURES TRANSPORT COMMUN
7832	TRACTORS FOR TR–TRAILERS	W 4493	41578	W 3191	32953	W 9496	103600	W 8190	90949	TRACTEURS ROUTIERS
784	MOTOR VEH PRTS,ACCES NES	W 25440	160866	W 18352	154045	W 16331	156542	W 18242	174694	PIECES 722,781,782,783
7841	MOTOR VEHICLE CHASSIS	W 4414	39989	W 4093	38890	W 2298	24927	W 2817	32505	CHASSIS 722,781,782,783
7849	OTHER MOTOR VEHCL PARTS	W 18396	115136	W 13710	113073	W 13524	129819	W 14772	139862	PIECES 722,781,782,783
785	CYCLES,ETC MOTRZD OR NOT	W 5822	35316	W 5500	31265	W 6502	38912	W 6779	43314	MOTOCYCLES SCOOTERS
79	OTHR TRANSPORT EQUIPMENT		93458		107343		156241		266766	AUTRE MATERIEL TRANSPORT
791	RAILWAY VEHICLES	W 777	2707	W 561	2562	W 2890	17787	W 3316	107798	VEHIC MAT CHEMINS DE FER
7913	MECHAN–PROPELLED RY CARS					W 119	9279	W 1168	98642	AUTOMOTRICES,DRAISINES
793	SHIPS AND BOATS ETC	W 55984	76889	W 58338	94245	W 77527	117265	W 77290	143739	NAVIRES BATEAUX,ETC
7932	SHIPS AND BOATS NES	W 51632	66995	W 57619	92216	W 70667	109825	W 70253	137160	NAVIRES ET BATEAUX
79323	OTHER CARGO VESSELS	W 44529	36009	W 50725	68028	W 29661	47233	W 11620	17129	AUT BATEAUX TRANS MARCH
79324	FISHING VESSELS ETC	W 5974	22436	W 6244	15087	W 2044	11261	W 5155	65396	BATEAUX DE PECHE
8	MISC MANUFACTURED GOODS		974773		1099993		1419184		1663155	ART MANUFACTURES DIVERS
821	*FURNITURE,PARTS THEREOF	W 4639	30591	W 5697	38475	W 7927	55528	W 12808	74705	MEUBLES ET PIECES
84	CLOTHING AND ACCESSORIES		200478		219259		290477		416349	VETEMENTS
842	MENS OUTERWEAR NOT KNIT	W 2359	36139	W 2949	36643	W 4012	46270	W 5106	67983	VET DESSUS POUR HOMMES
843	WOMENS OUTERWEAR NONKNIT	W 1489	30642	W 2233	41742	W 3061	52959	W 4407	82847	VET DESSUS FEMMES MAT TEX
845	OUTERWEAR KNIT NONELASTC	W 1473	28369	W 1890	32656	W 2903	44831	W 3645	67906	VET DESSOUS,ACCES BONNET
846	UNDER GARMENTS KNITTED	W 3725	49401	W 3445	45284	W 4336	62802	W 5729	83724	SOUS VETS DE BONNETERIE
848	HEADGEAR,NONTXTL CLOTHNG	W 1836	21724	W 1843	20807	W 2637	31965	W 3390	50505	VET ACCES MAT AUT QUE TEX
851	*FOOTWEAR	W 3587	57746	W 5844	85962	W 8594	126110	W 10281	149269	CHAUSSURES
85102	FOOTWEAR LEATHER	W 2433	47006	W 3973	69309	W 5278	96221	W 5738	108806	CHAUS SEMELLES EN CUIR
87	PRECISION INSTRUMNTS NES		156624		193869		198655		200280	INSTRUM,APPAR SCIENT NDA
872	MEDICAL INSTRUMENTS NES	W 1096	41380	W 1239	44691	W 1739	54413	W 1728	58519	INSTR,APP MEDIC–CHIR NDA
87202	OTH MEDICAL INSTRUMENTS	W 977	34878	W 1090	38480	W 1503	46347	W 1506	50753	INSTRUM,APP MEDECINE
874	MEASURNG,CONTROLNG INSTR	W 2119	106180	W 2924	134416	W 2413	128058	W 2610	124679	INSTRUMENTS DE MESURE
8743	GAS,LIQUID CONTROL INSTR	W 643	27536	W 1335	48881	W 724	35718	W 711	31272	APP,INSTR MESURE FLUIDES
8748	ELEC MEAS,CONTRL EQU NES	W 236	31812	W 548	45193	W 337	41444	W 319	34546	APP ELEC ELECTRO MESURE
88	PHOTO EQU,OPTICL GDS ETC		117420		126114		144385		152866	APP,FOURN PHOTO,OP,MONTR
882	PHOTO,CINEMA SUPPLIES	W 3983	56564	W 4011	59601	W 4898	65452	W 5343	70119	PRODUITS PHOTO,CINEMA
8822	PHOTO FILM EXC DEV CINMA	W 2642	44951	W 2697	46431	W 2963	49079	W 3118	50080	PLAQUES,PELLICULES,FILMS
89	MISC MANUFCTRD GOODS NES		374359		395585		545321		599785	ART MANUFACTURES DIVERS
892	PRINTED MATTER	W 5611	53188	W 6331	57089	W 8830	80026	W 9023	82653	IMPRIMES
8921	PRINTED BOOKS,GLOBES,ETC	W 2822	31467	W 2937	32207	W 4720	48795	W 4924	50953	LIVRES,BROCHURES,CARTES
89211	PRINTED BOOKS,PAMPHLETS	W 2735	30767	W 2815	31538	W 4387	46885	W 4706	49035	LIVRES,BROCHURES
893	ARTICLES OF PLASTIC NES		99645		107332		151750		175635	OUVRAGES EN MAT DIVIS 58
8939	MISC PLASTIC ARTICLES	W 14565	70516	W 15522	75915	W 20291	107819	W 24492	126638	ART DIVERS EN MAT DIV 58
89399	OTHR PLASTC ARTICLES NES	W 9810	63385	W 10165	68410	W 14378	96751	W 18022	115456	AUT OUV MAT DIV 58
894	TOYS,SPORTING GOODS,ETC	W 11561	90831	W 13199	95892	W 18154	139678	W 21056	154227	VOITURES ENFANTS,JOUETS
8942	TOYS,INDOOR GAMES ETC	W 9461	72497	W 10549	75763	W 14108	108451	W 14528	107050	JOUETS,JEUX ETC
89423	TOYS NES	W 5560	37013	W 6094	40160	W 7613	53847	W 8022	56950	JOUETS,MODELES REDUITS
898	MUSICAL INSTRUMENTS,PTS	W 2364	57331	W 2364	60836	W 3130	70409	W 3439	76592	INSTRUMENTS DE MUSIQUE
8983	SOUND RECRDNG TAPE,DISCS	W 1953	49662	W 1975	53914	W 2701	62410	W 2995	68590	SUPPORTS SON POUR 763
89832	RECORDED DISCS,TAPES ETC	W 322	30227	W 435	35706	W 708	41031	W 849	46391	DISQUES,PHONO,BANDES
899	OTHER MANUFACTURED GOODS		37325		36236		49410		53343	AUT ART MANUF DIVERS NDA
9	GOODS NOT CLASSD BY KIND		176030		162860		188879		206012	ART TRANSACT NON CLASSES
931	*SPECIAL TRANSACTIONS		174346		160627		186388		204162	TRANS.SPECIALES

5. Special Exports F.O.B. by Commodities according to the S.I.T.C. (Rev. 2) in thousand U.S. Dollars
Exportations Spéciales F.O.B. par Produits d'après la C.T.C.I. (Rév. 2) en milliers de Dollars E.U.

SITC CTCI	COMMODITY	1993 WEIGHT POIDS	1993 VALUE VALEUR	1994 WEIGHT POIDS	1994 VALUE VALEUR	1995 WEIGHT POIDS	1995 VALUE VALEUR	1996 WEIGHT POIDS	1996 VALUE VALEUR	PRODUIT
	ALL COMMODITIES		9308266		11368688		15901147		15406833	TOUS PRODUITS
0	FOOD AND LIVE ANIMALS		2365860		2729484		3471921		3733605	ALIMENTS,ANIMAUX VIVANTS
01	MEAT AND PREPARATIONS		23954		36105		27639		33734	VIANDES ET PREPARATIONS
03	FISH AND PREPARATIONS		738602		806026		1021746		1042894	POISSONS ET PREPARATIONS
034	FISH,FRESH,CHILLED,FROZN	W 144415	502075	W 161988	571468	W 180429	716005	W 206872	736156	POISSON FRAIS, REFRIG,CONG
0341	FISH FRSH,CHLLD,EX FILLT	W 27823	107238	W 26319	98126	W 31362	119362	W 38926	130098	POISSON FRAIS,REFRIGERE
0342	FISH FROZEN,EXCL FILLETS	W 75059	246680	W 90650	284614	W 97777	349305	W 106134	333920	POISSONS CONGELES
0343	FISH FILLETS,FRESH,CHLLD	W 6141	42260	W 8789	55277	W 11773	72353	W 19698	103717	FILETS FRAIS,REFRIGERES
0344	FISH FILLETS,FROZEN	W 35392	105897	W 36230	133451	W 39517	174986	W 42114	168421	FILETS CONGELES
036	SHELL FISH FRESH,FROZEN	W 12331	53608	W 11723	69055	W 12356	89282	W 9599	80671	CRUSTACES,MOLLUSQUES
037	FISH ETC PREPD,PRSVD NES	W 45841	173867	W 55815	147016	W 72192	182979	W 68129	182408	POIS,CRUST,MOL PREPARES
0371	FISH PREPARD,PRESRVD NES	W 33147	38432	W 43916	50247	W 59522	71706	W 55740	72932	CONSERVES DE POISSONS
0372	SHELL FISH PREPRD,PRESVD	W 12693	135436	W 11899	96769	W 12671	111273	W 12389	109476	CRUSTACES,COQUIL PREPARES
04	CEREALS AND PREPARATIONS		67481		75794		94540		123415	CEREALES ET PRODUITS
048	CEREAL ETC PREPARATIONS	W 81131	42932	W 77503	43971	W 114987	67550	W 118926	82940	PREPTNS A BASE CEREALES
05	VEGETABLES AND FRUIT		1042191		1170747		1374847		1568578	LEGUMES ET FRUITS
054	VEG ETC FRSH,SMPLY PRSVD	W 183351	125082	W 217884	152359	W 279169	194774	W 220142	172164	LEGUMES FRAIS,CONG,SECS
0546	VEGETABLES SIMPLY PRESVD	W 95947	77769	W 115257	101572	W 145132	126328	W 129824	120446	LEGUMES CONG,CONSER
05461	VEGETABLES FROZEN	W 93573	75170	W 110730	96844	W 140956	121072	W 124199	113785	LEGUMES CONGELES
056	VEGTBLES ETC PRSVD,PREPD	W 15133	38972	W 18610	43228	W 15206	35933	W 12885	32033	CONSERVES DE LEGUMES
057	FRUIT,NUTS,FRESH,DRIED	W 1210146	734699	W 1268805	819615	W 1361641	907496	W 1492113	1083538	FRUITS FRAIS OU SECS
0574	APPLES FRESH	W 361268	131843	W 347103	139540	W 432522	197176	W 442095	223277	POMMES FRAICHES
0575	GRAPES FRESH OR DRIED	W 460160	351233	W 490006	386334	W 471695	376133	W 542776	463800	RAISINS FRAIS OU SECS
05751	GRAPES FRESH	W 440749	327481	W 458160	350022	W 442818	345344	W 513093	429390	RAISINS FRAIS
05752	GRAPES DRIED(RAISINS)	W 19411	23752	W 31845	36312	W 28877	30789	W 29682	34409	RAISINS SECS
0579	FRUIT FRESH OR DRIED NES	W 368037	223188	W 419443	266023	W 441977	299181	W 491402	353185	FRUITS FRAIS,SECS NDA
05792	PEARS, QUINCES FRESH	W 146526	53967	W 156871	59988	W 146841	58475	W 162419	73192	POIRES ET COINGS FRAIS
05793	STONE FRUIT FRESH NES	W 122091	89670	W 136846	103013	W 147248	116794	W 166689	144514	FRUITS A NOYAU NDA FRAIS
05798	OTHER FRESH FRUIT	W 76520	42723	W 86970	49462	W 113054	67459	W 121677	69499	AUTRES FRUITS FRAIS
05799	OTHER DRIED FRUIT	W 16156	30074	W 17446	34679	W 19523	38726	W 19241	41358	AUTRES FRUITS SECHES
058	FRUIT PRESERVED,PREPARED	W 132670	143438	W 148639	155545	W 179976	236644	W 193646	280843	CONSERVES DE FRUITS
0585	FRUIT OR VEGETABLE JUICE	W 57709	50339	W 59047	47039	W 73714	96854	W 81375	126134	JUS DE FRUITS
05857	JUICE OF OTHER FRUIT,VEG	W 56907	49761	W 57935	46244	W 71137	95152	W 79017	124590	JUS AUTRES FRUITS,LEGUMES
0586	FRUIT TEMPORARILY PRESVD	W 27219	40124	W 32683	49476	W 37695	67436	W 42101	70808	FRUITS CONSERV TEMPORAIRE
05861	FRUIT,FRZN WITHOUT SUGAR	W 25244	37428	W 30313	46625	W 36105	65333	W 40568	68055	FRUITS CONG SANS SUCRE
0589	FRUIT PREPRD,PRESRVD,NES	W 34868	39587	W 41736	44559	W 49516	52747	W 50885	61593	FRUITS PREPARES CONSERV
05899	FRUIT,NUTS NES,PRESERVED	W 34770	39114	W 41614	44039	W 49459	52416	W 50817	61101	FRUITS PREP CONSERV NDA
07	COFFEE,TEA,COCOA,SPICES		27318		31411		46993		62690	CAFE,THE,CACAO,EPICES
081	*FEEDING STUFF FOR ANIML	W 762102	386810	W 1010045	472836	W 1134282	657195	W 913102	639320	NOURRITURE POUR ANIMAUX
0814	MEAT OR FISH MEAL FODDER	W 692009	367055	W 897551	454133	W 1022293	633449	W 812735	612650	FARINES DE VIANDES,POISSONS
08142	FISH MEAL FODDER	W 692009	367055	W 897551	454133	W 1022192	633393	W 812666	612606	FARINES DE POISSONS
09	MISC EDIBLE PRODUCTS		37981		72071		176514		194456	PREP ALIMENTAIRES DIVERSES
098	EDIBLE PRODCTS,PREPS NES	W 18739	37679	W 29617	71767	W 67499	176189	W 61444	193590	PREP ALIMENTAIRES NDA
09809	MISC FOOD PREPRTIONS NES	W 9826	20516	W 21897	53004	W 59026	155295	W 51051	166834	PREP ALIMENTAIRES NDA
1	BEVERAGES AND TOBACCO		153432		173783		203533		319894	BOISSONS ET TABACS
11	BEVERAGES		137381		152148		189667		300379	BOISSONS
112	ALCOHOLIC BEVERAGES	W 97607	131273	W 121709	147345	W 146543	186365	W 206624	297325	BOISSONS ALCOOLIQUES
1121	WINE OF FRESH GRAPES ETC	W 96029	128580	W 118500	143688	W 142858	182433	W 203920	294372	VINS DE RAISINS FRAIS
11212	WINE OF FRESH GRAPES	W 95984	128513	W 118450	143609	W 142251	181789	W 203368	293742	VINS DE MOUTS DE RAISINS
2	CRUDE MATERLS,EXCL FUELS		2244753		2906476		4724372		3947493	MAT BRUTES NON COMESTIBLES
24	CORK AND WOOD		479403		518976		704010		619562	LIEGE ET BOIS
246	PULPWOOD,CHIPS,WOODWASTE	W 2557251	137326	W 3018189	163514	W 4076520	232833	W 2906174	170912	BOIS DE TRITURATION
24602	PULPWOOD CHIPS,PARTICLES	W 2557229	137324	W 3018189	163514	W 4076496	232829	W 2906147	170897	EN FORME DE PLAQUETTES
247	OTH WOOD ROUGH,SQUARED	W 1158462	149890	W 1302549	125224	W 1626312	160012	W 1158469	116119	BOIS BRUTS EQUARRIS
2471	SAW–,VENEER–LOGS CONIFER	W 1084898	143167	W 1216932	117361	W 1447707	142886	W 1099183	109485	CONIFERES POUR SCIAGE,PLACAG
24711	— IN THE ROUGH	W 1084898	143167	W 1216932	117361	W 1447707	142886	W 1099183	109485	ECORCES OU DEGROSSIS
248	WOOD SHAPED,SLEEPERS	W 439600	192180	W 537294	230237	W 742549	311162	W 657465	332531	BOIS SIMPLEMENT TRAVAILLES
2482	LUMBER SHAPED CONIFER	W 423363	181182	W 513436	210261	W 719701	293043	W 641008	318144	CONIFERES SCIES,RABOTES
24821	LUMBER SAWN ETC CONIFER	W 402079	154712	W 483940	170356	W 679182	237195	W 582123	231480	CONIFERES SCIES LONGITUD
24822	LUMBER PLANED ETC CONIFR	W 21284	26471	W 29496	39905	W 40519	55848	W 58884	86663	CONIFER RABOTES,RAINES
251	*PULP AND WASTE PAPER	W 1399147	468894	W 1603347	720056	W 1641259	1274178	W 1657847	764853	PATES A PAPIER,DECHETS
2517	SODA,SULPHATE WOOD PULP	W 1394480	468367	W 1584218	717692	W 1625171	1270398	W 1653166	764354	PATES CHIMIQUES AU SULFATE
25171	— UNBLEACHED	W 257419	80395	W 341098	132148	W 272184	193031	W 272938	106679	PATES ECRUES
25172	— BLEACHED,NONDISSOLVNG	W 1137061	387971	W 1243120	585544	W 1352987	1077367	W 1380227	657675	PATES BLANCHIES
27	CRUDE FERTLZR,MINRLS NES		65104		63597		62953		84461	ENGRAIS MINERAUX BRUTS
271	FERTILIZERS,CRUDE	W 375919	51588	W 223949	31428	W 315010	45060	W 260185	42955	ENGRAIS BRUTS
2712	NATURAL SODIUM NITRATE	W 375318	51518	W 223552	31384	W 314843	45015	W 259671	42897	NITRATE SODIUM NATUREL
28	METALLIFEROUS ORES,SCRAP		1112798		1455000		2501274		2278204	MINERAIS METAL,DECHETS
281	IRON ORE,CONCENTRATES	W 5756787	114732	W 6938960	125827	W 6096077	123292	W 6982429	147561	MINERAIS DE FER
2815	IRON ORE,CONC,NOT AGGLOM	W 2578072	34576	W 3528814	43400	W 3099451	39360	W 3568952	46987	MINERAIS NON AGGLOMERES
2816	IRON ORE AGGLOMERATES	W 3178715	80156	W 3410146	82427	W 2996626	83932	W 3413477	100574	MINERAIS AGGLOMERES
287	BASE METAL ORES,CONC NES	W 718234	953120	W 761009	1262525	W 911679	2312458	W 1116138	2045907	MINERAIS METAUX COMMUNS
2871	CPR ORE ETC,CEMENT COPPR	W 624411	862166	W 678765	1129972	W 787046	1928650	W 1020569	1881500	MINERAIS DE CUIVRE,MATTES
28711	COPPER ORES,EXCL MATTE	W 623295	860978	W 678765	1129971	W 783877	1920327	W 1019778	1879515	MINERAIS DE CUIVRE
2879	OTH NONFER ORE,CONCNTRTE	W 27662	80853	W 29933	125289	W 33911	368451	W 29311	153504	MINERAIS D'AUTRES METAUX
28793	MOLYBD, NIOBIUM ETC ORES	W 27574	80821	W 29933	125289	W 33911	368451	W 29311	153504	MINERAIS DE MOLYBDENE,TITANE
289	PREC MTAL ORES,WASTE NES	MK 55658	42787	MK 62674	59353	MK 63088	58470	MK 85935	77200	MINERAIS,DECHETS MET PREC
28901	PRECIOUS METAL ORES,CONC	MK 55657	42787	MK 62674	59353	MK 63088	58470	MK 85935	77137	MINERAIS METAUX PRECIEUX
29	CRUDE ANIMAL,VEG MAT NES		108410		129469		157448		179043	MATIERES BRUTES ANIM,VEGET
292	CRUDE VEG MATERIALS NES		103989	W 51014	124734	W 58124	151507	W 61849	173425	MAT BRUTES VEGETALES NDA
2925	SEEDS,ETC FOR PLANTING		35798	W 2750	37227	W 2424	37656	W 1715	41172	SEMENCES NDA
2929	OTH CRUDE VEG MATERIALS	W 26261	46522	W 35977	60866	W 41236	77314	W 44457	88753	MATIERES VEGETALES NDA
29291	VEGETABLE SAPS,EXTRACTS	W 2121	32579	W 2913	40082	W 3546	50556	W 4009	58605	SUCS,EXTRAITS VEGETAUX
4	ANIMAL,VEGETABLE OIL,FAT		21963		48524		76056		62483	HUILES,GRAISSES ANIM,VEG
411	*ANIMAL OILS AND FATS	W 72256	19483	W 167929	44810	W 151649	49637	W 129090	42845	HUILES,GRAISSES ANIMALES
4111	OILS OF FISH,WHALES ETC	W 71171	19023	W 165720	43820	W 150587	49174	W 127189	41712	GRAISSES,HUILES DE POISSONS
41112	OTHER FISH OILS AND FATS	W 71165	18978	W 165714	43776	W 150587	49174	W 127189	41712	AUTRES HUILES ET GRAISSES
5	CHEMCLS,RELATED PROD NES		359821		521377		541335		545233	PRODUITS CHIMIQUES
51	ORGANIC CHEMICALS		71778		196528		169846		129917	PROD CHIMIQ ORGANIQUES
512	ALCOHOLS,PHENOLS ETC	W 714505	63153	W 875489	188645	W 723324	151305	W 852563	106230	PHENOLS,PHENOLS–ALCOOLS
5121	ACYCLIC ALCOHOLS,DERIVS	W 714462	63008	W 875453	188522	W 723315	151273	W 852523	106122	ALCOOLS ACYCLIQUES
51211	METHYL ALCOHOL(METHANOL)	W 705691	53801	W 867172	179007	W 715334	134866	W 844034	92199	ALCOOLS METHYLIQUES
52	INORGANIC CHEMICALS		168861		193751		226069		253443	PROD CHIM INORGANIQUES
522	INORG ELEMNTS,OXIDES,ETC	W 52716	58850	W 186827	67281	W 110752	108756	W 85271	131630	ELEMENTS INORGANIQUES
5221	CHEMICAL ELEMENTS	W 8731	37607	W 12562	40088	W 14408	62856	W 16730	90875	ELEMENTS CHIMIQUES
52214	FLUORINE,BROMINE,IODINE	W 4459	35878	W 4883	37999	W 6401	60791	W 6332	88781	FLUOR,BROME ET IODE
523	OTHR INORG CHEMICALS ETC	W 179108	110011	W 213897	126468	W 238206	117313	W 221640	121811	AUT PRODUITS CHIMIQUES INORG
5232	OTH MTL CMPD OF INRG ACD	W 163852	71955	W 193247	77360	W 217536	91673	W 204098	94677	SELS METALLIQUES
52321	NITRITES AND NITRATES	W 150332	40189	W 179867	44784	W 203215	52771	W 189245	54906	NITRITES ET NITRATES
52324	CARBONATE NES,PERCBONATE	W 10682	30818	W 10765	31684	W 13109	38107	W 13703	39164	CARBONATES,PERCARBONATES
5233	METALLIC ACID SALTS ETC		25666	W 258	34351	W 218	7591	W 668	8365	SELS ACIDES D'OXYDES METAL E

5. Special Exports F.O.B. by Commodities according to the S.I.T.C. (Rev. 2) in thousand U.S. Dollars
Exportations Spéciales F.O.B. par Produits d'après la C.T.C.I. (Rév. 2) en milliers de Dollars E.U.

SITC CTCI	COMMODITY	1993 WEIGHT POIDS	1993 VALUE VALEUR	1994 WEIGHT POIDS	1994 VALUE VALEUR	1995 WEIGHT POIDS	1995 VALUE VALEUR	1996 WEIGHT POIDS	1996 VALUE VALEUR	PRODUIT
55	PERFUME,CLEANING ETC PRD		35833		34172		32967		34672	PROD POUR PARFUM,TOILETTE
562	*FERTILIZERS,MANUFACTURE	W 138435	25024	W 179671	35118	W 162459	30205	W 175784	35411	ENGRAIS MANUFACTURES
5629	FERTILiZERS NES	W 135221	23938	W 177341	34372	W 159475	29287	W 161707	33146	ENGRAIS NDA
6	BASIC MANUFACTURES		3163876		3810429		5614827		5339303	ART MANUFACTURES
62	RUBBER MANUFACTURES NES		48565		53722		70543		64862	CAOUTCHOUC MANUFACTURE
625	RUBBER TYRES, TUBES ETC	W 12551	45498	W 14021	50712	W 16945	65632	W 14971	60049	PNEUS CAOUTCHOUC VULCANISE
63	WOOD,CORK MANUFACTRS NES		65375		79623		82645		109629	OUVRAGES LIEGE ET BOIS
635	WOOD MANUFACTURES NES	W 32953	42846	W 36692	54925	W 38739	55842	W 53352	76876	ART MANUF EN BOIS NDA
6353	BUILDERS WOODWRK,PREFABS	W 27376	35154	W 31633	47363	W 30776	45951	W 35016	62467	OUVRAGES DE MENUISERIE
64	PAPER,PAPERBOARD AND MFR		141451		184479		239901		238238	PAPIERS,CARTONS & OUVRAGES
641	PAPER AND PAPERBOARD	W 244933	115972	W 276354	150329	W 252980	186600	W 291935	186885	PAPIERS ET CARTONS
6411	NEWSPRINT	W 143008	69024	W 151019	76974	W 135713	110876	W 138134	97973	PAPIER JOURNAL
6416	FIBRE BUILDING BOARD	W 93491	38895	W 108750	59444	W 97119	54933	W 127640	65699	PLAQUES CONSTRUCT EN PATE
64162	INSULATING BOARD, ETC	W 67120	28787	W 82991	48994	W 65769	41650	W 95587	51996	PLAQUES CONST NON COMPR
642	PAPER,ETC,PRECUT,ARTS OF	W 10564	25479	W 16070	34150	W 24779	53301	W 26913	51353	PAP,CARTONS DECOUPES
65	TEXTILE YARN,FABRICS,ETC		67860		81198		94531		122708	FILS,TISSUS,ARTICLES TEXTILE
67	IRON AND STEEL		51459		58761		97217		92835	FER ET ACIER
671	PIG IRON ETC	W 5176	14659	W 6046	28484	W 6806	60758	W 6933	42458	FONTE,SPIEGEL,POUDRES
6716	FERRO–ALLOYS	W 5176	14659	W 6045	28483	W 6797	60750	W 6931	42457	FERRO–ALLIAGES
67169	OTHER FERRO–ALLOYS	W 3292	13420	W 4947	27737	W 6586	60590	W 6904	42425	AUTRES FERRO–ALLIAGES
68	NON–FERROUS METALS		2733844		3281142		4928616		4563192	METAUX NON FERREUX
681	SILVER,PLATINUM,ETC		82076		114499		134028		153046	ARGENT ET PLATINE
6811	SILVER UNWKD,PARTLY WRKD		82060		114457		134002		153033	ARGENT BRUT MI–OUVRE
68113	SILVER UNWROUGHT		72939		104963		130253		150855	ARGENT ET ALLIAGES BRUTS
682	COPPER EXC CEMENT COPPER	W 1381009	2646062	W 1437940	3160453	W 1619048	4782812	W 1883569	4401010	CUIVRE
6821	COPPER NES,ALLOYS,UNWRT	W 1345477	2559874	W 1392497	3041363	W 1569532	4611569	W 1836663	4263822	CUIVRE BRUT
68211	COPPER UNREF,EXC CEMENT	W 128065	231138	W 196936	418603	W 175824	509790	W 230606	532761	CUIVRE POUR AFFINAGE
68212	COPPER REFINED,UNWROUGHT	W 1217407	2328720	W 1195552	2622732	W 1393704	4101762	W 1606051	3731038	CUIVRE AFFINE BRUT
6822	COPPER,ALLOYS WORKED	W 35531	86187	W 45443	119090	W 49516	171243	W 46906	137187	CUIVRE,ALLIAGES OUVRES
68221	COPPER BARS,WIRE,ETC	W 25289	57719	W 33986	85463	W 36379	121349	W 33092	92037	BARRES,PROFILES ET FILS
69	METAL MANUFACTURES NES		39996		51614		69766		110947	ART MANUFACT EN METAL NDA
699	BASE METAL MFRS NES	W 5198	18041	W 8007	23962		32027		48110	ART MANUFACTURES MET NDA
7	MACHINES,TRANSPORT EQUIP		246989		312155		285863		372239	MACHINES MATERIEL TRANSPORT
72	MACHS FOR SPCL INDUSTRYS		20739		20587		28040		64334	MAC SPECIALES POUR INDUST
74	GENRL INDUSTRL MACHY NES		22993		37118		52848		55893	MACH APP INDUSTRIE
77	ELECTRIC MACHNRY NES ETC		33550		37156		38289		52800	MACH APP ELECT NDA
78	ROAD VEHICLES		132767		147819		115576		105578	VEHICULES ROUTIERS
781	PASS MOTOR VEH EXC BUSES	W 3166	45630	W 2151	29286	W 1217	15983	W 595	7099	AUTO TRANSPORT PERSONNES
782	LORRIES,SPCL MTR VEH NES	W 2695	27616	W 4766	47165	W 6449	57837	W 4979	54895	VEHICULES SPECIAUX,MARCH
7821	LORRIES,TRUCKS	W 2621	27313	W 4668	46873	W 6249	56518	W 4870	53921	VEHICULES TRANSP MARCHAND
784	MOTOR VEH PRTS,ACCES NES	W 3467	45762	W 4123	54970	W 2497	31828	W 3047	36088	PIECES 722,781,782,783
7849	OTHER MOTOR VEHCL PARTS	W 3463	45699	W 4018	54706	W 2367	31462	W 2832	35688	PIECES 722,781,782,783
79	OTHR TRANSPORT EQUIPMENT		25161		51684		33025		71775	AUTRE MATERIEL TRANSPORT
793	SHIPS AND BOATS ETC	W 44747	19022	W 47246	48490	W 51498	30657	W 103462	60174	NAVIRES BATEAUX,ETC
7932	SHIPS AND BOATS NES	W 44654	18460	W 45761	46210	W 50525	28075	W 101373	45239	NAVIRES ET BATEAUX
8	MISC MANUFACTURED GOODS		332339		345661		356900		344844	ART MANUFACTURES DIVERS
821	*FURNITURE,PARTS THEREOF	W 13768	35383	W 15927	40378	W 13268	39467	W 21481	43204	MEUBLES ET PIECES
8219	FURNITURE AND PARTS NES	W 11883	28738	W 13948	32144	W 10399	29322	W 16396	31198	AUTRES MEUBLES ET PIECES
84	CLOTHING AND ACCESSORIES		76511		75000		66241		60731	VETEMENTS
851	*FOOTWEAR	W 2424	41233	W 1835	31444	W 1451	26397	W 1227	22205	CHAUSSURES
85102	FOOTWEAR LEATHER	W 2020	36830	W 1532	28608	W 1185	24108	W 978	19168	CHAUS SEMELLES EN CUIR
89	MISC MANUFCTRD GOODS NES		153705		175223		202950		196770	ART MANUFACTURES DIVERS
892	PRINTED MATTER	W 17434	69534	W 19838	79652	W 25951	123906	W 27763	110650	IMPRIMES
8921	PRINTED BOOKS,GLOBES,ETC	W 6952	26349	W 9133	36646	W 11537	55876	W 13660	46621	LIVRES,BROCHURES,CARTES
89211	PRINTED BOOKS,PAMPHLETS	W 6672	25200	W 8684	35255	W 11443	55425	W 13647	46549	LIVRES,BROCHURES
8922	NEWSPAPERS,PERIODICALS	W 9425	36167	W 9179	34272	W 13065	56591	W 12949	53679	JOURNAUX ET PERIODIQUES
897	GOLD,SILVER WARE,JEWELRY		37104		30586		7492		4862	BIJOUTERIE,ORFEVRERIE
9	GOODS NOT CLASSD BY KIND		402610		496990		586422		712613	ART TRANSACT NON CLASSES
931	*SPECIAL TRANSACTIONS		155926		183422		211199		272178	TRANS.SPECIALES
971	*GOLD,NON MONETARY NES	K 23223	239579	K 26680	308928	K 30634	371017	K 34261	427612	OR NON MONETAIRE
97101	NONMON GLD UNWRT,SEMIMFD	K 20506	229604	K 24784	303782	K 30076	369678	K 34261	427612	OR,ALLIAGES D'OR BRUTS

1. HISTORICAL SERIES, 1962–1996 SPECIAL TRADE, IMPORTS C.I.F., EXPORTS F.O.B.
SERIES HISTORIQUES, 1962–1996 COMMERCE SPECIAL, IMPORTATIONS C.A.F., EXPORTATIONS F.O.B

YEAR ANNEE	VALUE IN MILLION YUAN RENMINBI / VALEUR EN MILLION YUAN RENMINBI: MERCHANDISE –MARCHANDISE		GOLD –OR		CONVERSION FACTORS U.S. CENTS PER YUAN RENMINBI / FACTEURS DE CONVERSION CENTS E.U. PAR YUAN RENMINBI		INDEX NUMBERS –INDICES: QUANTUM		UNIT VALUE / VALEUR UNITAIRE	
	IMPORTS	EXPORTS	IMPORTS	EXPORTS	IMPORTS	EXPORTS	IMPORTS	EXPORTS	IMPORTS	EXPORTS
1962	3380.00	4710.00			40.6207	40.6207				
1963	3570.00	5000.00			40.6207	40.6207				
1964	4210.00	5540.00			40.6207	40.6207				
1965	6310.00	5530.00			40.6504	40.6504				
1966	6110.00	6600.00			40.6504	40.6504				
1967	5340.00	5880.00			40.6504	40.6504				
1968	5090.00	5760.00			40.6504	40.6504				
1969	4720.00	5980.00			40.6504	40.6504				
1970	5610.00	5680.00			41.5330	39.7887				
1971	5240.00	6850.00			42.1756	38.5401				
1972	6400.00	8290.00			44.6875	41.4958				
1973	10360.00	11690.00			49.8069	49.7861				
1974	15280.00	13940.00			49.8691	49.8565				
1975	14740.00	14300.00			50.8141	50.7692				
1976	12930.00	13480.00			50.8894	50.8902				
1977	13280.00	13970.00			54.2922	54.3307				
1978	18739.00	16765.00			58.1110	58.1395				
1979	24290.00	21168.00			64.5121	64.5253				
1980	29140.00	27240.00			67.0899	67.0705				
1981	36773.00	36761.00			59.8646	59.8651				
1982	35769.20	41433.10			52.9487	52.8883				
1983	42182.50	43832.70			50.5510	50.5342				
1984	62047.30	58055.70			42.1989	42.8399				
1985	125783.50	80931.50			33.7809	33.7854				
1986	149826.00	108210.50			28.6391	28.5926				
1987	161421.00	146995.00			26.8665	26.8665				
1988	205507.00	176672.00			26.8665	26.8665				
1989	219986.00	195606.00			26.5597	26.5597				
1990	254934.30	296731.20			20.9250	20.9250				
1991	339530.60	382744.30			18.7880	18.7880				
1992	444263.80	468272.80			18.1390	18.1390				
1993	593961.60	524141.40			17.3560	17.3560				
1994	996906.30	1043149.00			11.6040	11.6040				
1995	1077052.00	1241769.00			11.9876	11.9827				
1996	1155209.00	1257084.00			12.0276	12.0276				

2. IMPORTS BY BROAD ECONOMIC CATEGORY AND EXPORTS BY INDUSTRIAL ORIGIN. (PERCENTAGE OF TOTAL VALUE)
IMPORTATIONS PAR CATEGORIES ECONOMIQUES ET EXPORTATIONS PAR BRANCHE D'ACTIVITE.(EN POURCENTAGE DE LA VALEUR TOTALE)

IMPORTS – IMPORTATIONS

	1990	1991	1992	1993	1994	1995	1996
TOTAL IMPORTS–IMPORTATIONS TOTALES	100.	100.	100.	100.	100.	100.	100.
1 FOOD BEV–ALIMENTATION BOISSONS	7.7	4.8	4.0	2.3	4.0	5.6	4.5
11 PRIMARY–PRODUITS DE BASE	4.8	3.0	2.7	1.5	1.7	2.6	2.6
111 FOR INDUSTRY–POUR L'INDUSTRIE	4.4	2.6	2.2	1.0	1.1	2.0	1.9
112 FOR HOUSEHOLDS–POUR LES MENAGES	0.4	0.4	0.6	0.5	0.6	0.6	0.7
12 PROCESSED–PRODUITS ELABORES	2.9	1.9	1.2	0.8	2.3	3.0	1.8
121 FOR INDUSTRY–POUR L'INDUSTRIE	2.4	1.5	0.9	0.6	1.9	2.4	1.4
122 FOR HOUSEHOLDS–POUR LES MENAGES	0.5	0.4	0.3	0.3	0.4	0.6	0.4
2 IND SUPPLIES–APPROV INDUSTRIELS	44.0	46.4	48.1	44.9	44.0	45.5	46.6
21 PRIMARY–PRODUITS DE BASE	5.3	5.1	5.3	4.1	4.5	5.9	5.3
22 PROCESSED–PRODUITS ELABORES	38.7	41.4	42.9	40.8	39.5	39.6	41.3
3 FUELS–COMBUSTIBLES	2.4	3.3	4.4	5.6	3.5	3.9	4.9
31 PRIMARY–PRODUITS DE BASE	1.0	1.6	2.3	2.4	1.6	2.2	3.1
32 PROCESSED–PRODUITS ELABORES	1.4	1.7	2.1	3.1	1.8	1.7	1.8
321 MOTOR SPIRIT–ESSENCE	0.1	0.0	0.1		0.2		0.1
322 OTHER–AUTRES	1.3	1.6	2.0	3.1	1.6	1.7	1.7
4 MACHINERY–EQUIPEMENT	27.6	26.8	29.1	33.0	34.5	34.8	34.4
41 CAPITAL EQUIPMENT–MACHINES	24.4	23.2	24.4	28.6	29.4	29.0	27.7
42 PARTS–PIECES ACCESSOIRES	3.2	3.6	4.7	4.4	5.2	5.7	6.7
5 TRANSPORT–TRANSPORT	11.6	12.6	8.4	8.8	8.8	4.3	4.7
51 PASSENGER CARS–AUTOMOBILES	0.6	0.9	1.7	2.0	1.4	0.7	0.3
52 OTHER–AUTRES	3.0	2.6	3.4	4.2	5.6	1.8	2.1
521 INDUSTRIAL–INDUSTRIELS	3.0	2.6	3.4	3.9	5.3	1.8	2.1
522 NON INDUSTRIAL–NON INDUSTRIEL	0.0	0.0	0.0	0.4	0.4	0.0	0.0
53 PARTS–PIECES ACCESSOIRES	8.0	9.1	3.3	2.5	1.8	1.8	2.2
6 CONSUM GOODS–BIENS CONSOMMATION	6.1	5.7	5.1	4.7	4.5	4.7	4.4
61 DURABLE–DURABLES	2.6	2.3	1.9	1.9	1.9	1.7	1.4
62 SEMI DURABLE–SEMI DURABLES	2.6	2.5	2.2	2.0	2.0	2.2	2.2
63 NON DURABLE–NON DURABLES	0.9	0.9	0.9	0.7	0.5	0.8	0.9
7 GOODS NES–BIENS NDA	0.5	0.3	0.8	0.7	0.7	1.3	0.6

EXPORTS – EXPORTATIONS

	1990	1991	1992	1993	1994	1995	1996
TOTAL EXPORTS–EXPORTATIONS TOTALES	100.	100.	100.	100.	100.	100.	100.
1 AGRICULTURE	8.9	8.4	7.5	6.7	6.4	4.5	4.0
2 MINING QUARRY–INDUS EXTRACTIVES	8.1	6.2	5.2	4.5	3.3	3.5	3.8
3 MANUFACTURING–IND MANUFACTUR	83.0	85.4	87.3	88.8	90.3	92.0	92.2
31 FOOD BEV TOBACCO–ALIM BOISS TAB	6.3	5.9	5.4	5.5	5.2	5.1	5.3
32 TEXTILES–INDUSTRIES TEXTILES	30.9	32.3	35.9	36.2	35.7	31.1	30.1
33 WOOD & PRODUCTS–BOIS & PRODUITS	0.5	0.6	0.8	0.8	0.8	0.9	0.9
34 PAPER & PRODUCTS–PAPIER & PRODT	0.5	0.5	0.6	0.7	0.6	0.8	0.7
35 CHEMICALS–INDUSTRIES CHIMIQUES	9.9	9.4	9.5	9.6	9.5	10.6	10.7
36 NON METAL MIN–MIN NON METAL	1.8	2.2	1.9	1.6	1.8	2.0	2.1
37 BASIC METAL–IND METAL BASE	3.0	3.1	2.6	2.2	2.8	5.0	3.8
38 METAL MANUF–MANUF METAL	22.2	24.3	22.8	24.6	26.0	29.1	31.5
39 OTH MANUF IND–AUTRES MANUF	7.9	7.1	7.8	7.6	7.8	7.5	7.1

3. TRADE BY PRINCIPAL COUNTRIES OF ORIGIN AND CONSUMPTION (VALUE IN THOUSAND U.S. DOLLARS)
ECHANGES SELON LES PRINCIPAUX PAYS D'ORIGINE ET DE COMSOMMATION (VALEUR EN MILLIERS DE DOLLARS EU)

COUNTRIES–PAYS	SPECIAL IMPORTS C.I.F. IMPORTATIONS SPECIALES C.A.F				
	1992	1993	1994	1995	1996
World	80585333	103958979	115613642	132083539	138832776
Africa	503773	1001439	891936	1424659	1464468
Americas	12727434	14001366	17989821	21766755	22335398
Northern America	10827931	12070717	15742609	18799849	18727999
LAIA	1707338	1841699	2117966	2657462	3463170
CACM	1901	2407	2771	69271	3316
Caribbean	186698	75598	121808	229660	138898
Rest of America	3567	10946	4666	10513	2015
As.ex F.USSR	48841498	61419153	66992268	75799285	81023567
Eur.x F.USSR	12170260	18053781	20360627	22898588	21398105
EU	10854007	15719022	18581403	21256819	19867428
EFTA	689795	1139839	1139139	1166522	1150892
East Europe	554863	1095513	623457	452408	315190
Other Europe	843	1949	75	759	22680
Former USSR	3917046	5920073	4658691	4912927	6255846
Oceania	2058571	2360447	2915623	3021582	3936277
Japan/Japon	13682461	23288653	26326910	29004529	29180841
USA/Etats–Unis d'Amer	8900999	10687375	13893735	16118483	16155168
Hong Kong	20533589	10446461	9441714	8590713	7826688
Korea, Republic of	2622799	5360063	7319144	10293234	12481622
Germany/Allemagne	4015042	6040717	7137391	8037859	7324132
Russian Federation	3526076	4980901	3495201	3798640	5151769
Italy/Italie	1748288	2737352	3068521	3115049	3245949
Singapore/Singapour	1235994	2645835	2491675	3397831	3600890
Australia/Australie	1671164	1949492	2451819	2584548	3433801
Canada	1926567	1375226	1848746	2681312	2572591
France,Monac	1495511	1640916	1938808	2648400	2240018
Indonesia/Indonésie	1554259	1468562	1589044	2052173	2280424
United Kingdom	1013632	1663673	1769891	1972063	1880939
Malaysia/Malaisie	830178	1083639	1622035	2070595	2243573
Thailand/Thaïlande	424543	601456	864402	1610768	1890360
Brazil/Brésil	519322	863085	1058803	1231546	1484083
Belgium–Luxembourg	470136	816840	1066455	1146948	1058609
Switz.Liecht	523691	1004821	986592	938694	932105
Sweden/Suède	475753	670702	827242	999751	1379739
Netherlands/Pays–Bas	508206	713927	707431	817999	918584
Spain/Espagne	355695	475171	902491	908611	517382
Oman	446907	561057	413290	481516	811218
Ukraine	134143	485782	742800	539622	507335
So. Africa Customs Un	7995	414724	537814	689553	672069
Finland/Finlande	252301	322362	447613	621672	549550
India/Inde	180984	416576	321764	397534	719174
Peru/Pérou	310075	249107	384306	459520	517564
Saudi Arabia	127414	118637	248948	551113	829047
Austria/Autriche	321433	315867	364843	562593	301122
New Zealand	279004	264083	316491	346353	403078
Argentina/Argentine	200121	219910	268565	370398	517634
Chile/Chili	409642	281660	183100	230490	455251
Yemen/Yémen	73903	255062	149192	344188	570325
Turkey/Turquie	108550	497552	463837	143889	94107
Philippines	155109	212857	272414	275767	372931
Kazakhstan	141173	263053	196965	315545	364596
Denmark/Danemark	139250	225490	277400	318489	318507
Iran (Islamic Rp. of)	100977	310016	181534	226561	386146
Romania/Roumanie	211460	378844	286446	194147	73474
Viet Nam	72711	122634	191319	332061	309370
Pakistan	91127	96406	161939	223059	342274
Norway,SVD,JM	165125	132439	149780	224816	212868
Mexico/Mexique	113985	124823	93860	194491	297242
Korea Dem People's Rp	155463	297294	199219	63609	68638
Cuba	182842	73642	120686	213555	137638
Myanmar	131272	164789	143339	149532	137407
Macau/Macao	165384	153832	131839	128578	120879
Angola	29409	180711	47985	136907	243752
Papua New Guinea	97672	139198	141357	77764	98993
Poland/Pologne	90203	223689	105056	83586	47417

COUNTRIES–PAYS	SPECIAL EXPORTS F.O.B. EXPORTATIONS SPECIALES F.O.B.				
	1992	1993	1994	1995	1996
Monde	84940062	91744005	121006321	148779565	151047526
Afrique	1277569	1509868	1723105	2465033	2534625
Amériques	10323264	19940116	25314606	29394011	31416151
Amérique du Nord	9252855	18171905	22873548	26262098	28322123
ALAI	635166	1057567	1466155	2107029	2196749
MCAC	42528	79220	119031	141540	129752
Caraïbes	249697	266083	274007	275484	269297
Autre Amérique	143017	365340	581866	607860	498230
Asie l'URSS exclus	61066963	52617690	73447878	92002245	91242141
Europe l'URSS exclus	8644800	13352254	16901742	20998284	21884986
UE	8004400	12255325	15414415	19126743	19859649
AELE	304695	403539	516702	640524	804063
Europe de l'Est	300869	663166	935076	1178617	1164341
Autre de l'Europe	21883	17873	18849	21063	19884
Ancienne URSS	2743216	3092723	1895152	2018008	2008116
Océanie	795405	1231354	1723838	1901982	1961508
Hong Kong	37512229	22049707	32360964	35983427	32906258
Japan/Japon	11678713	15776654	21578615	28466685	30886224
USA/Etats–Unis d'Amer	8599389	16972686	21474852	24728644	26705643
Korea, Republic of	2404912	2860501	4402450	6687805	7499856
Germany/Allemagne	2447990	3967507	4761157	5671451	5842688
Singapore/Singapour	2030869	2245322	2558058	3500636	3748787
Netherlands/Pays–Bas	1200333	1608775	2267067	3232066	3536863
United Kingdom	922839	1928673	2413926	2797665	3200910
Russian Federation	2336321	2691754	1580794	1664663	1692715
Italy/Italie	1095477	1305389	1590941	2067581	1836583
France,Monac	764215	1292355	1426557	1843707	1912753
Australia/Australie	660812	1060753	1487871	1626187	1672962
Canada	653195	1197778	1396969	1532529	1615959
Thailand/Thaïlande	894807	750494	1159279	1751751	1254749
Malaysia/Malaisie	645444	704369	1117673	1280995	1370321
Indonesia/Indonésie	471439	691719	1051699	1438148	1427569
United Arab Emirates	542963	711405	864732	1101097	1076887
Belgium–Luxembourg	540989	611276	822038	1045612	1056723
Spain/Espagne	353492	551196	774644	1013296	996248
Pakistan	551435	751933	605701	788620	623018
Saudi Arabia	444257	578843	624857	733907	747804
Macau/Macao	528687	524717	666055	793396	572714
Philippines	209557	280466	475691	1030143	1014842
Korea Dem People's Rp	541108	602340	424495	486037	497014
India/Inde	158436	259191	573013	765275	686024
Viet Nam	106360	274652	341536	720294	842153
Brazil/Brésil	64756	192171	362400	759067	762941
Panama	132004	350140	569034	594850	488186
Myanmar	259166	324660	369110	617815	521138
Bangladesh	214776	202908	370446	632955	653049
So. Africa Customs Un	7717	250037	366255	637435	688220
Sweden/Suède	215247	322468	500471	396030	392001
Poland/Pologne	119239	248530	294183	471958	568469
Iran (Islamic Rp. of)	335646	402705	265745	277894	394588
Switz.Liecht	159879	278946	357639	413546	460996
Egypt/Egypte	174564	199601	279611	439652	404450
Chile/Chili	128152	204132	285326	410421	463664
Argentina/Argentine	124146	247687	291127	273602	336631
Turkey/Turquie	68918	165695	184549	430692	406615
Denmark/Danemark	152051	198674	259654	308515	287832
Hungary/Hongrie	44997	165023	389558	325473	218782
Norway,SVD,JM	143327	120640	156799	222693	339478
Mexico/Mexique	157742	155693	201473	195071	221099
New Zealand	87405	130969	188087	232025	231348
Sri Lanka	107064	136987	145722	239187	191555
Cuba	200232	177044	147244	146329	100501
Greece/Grèce	82354	115028	134183	192675	204180
Finland/Finlande	92633	103597	155650	175750	199396
Kazakhstan	227121	171692	107036	75447	95306
Austria/Autriche	69540	117223	150563	169692	167919

(VALUE AS PERCENTAGE OF WORLD TOTAL)(VALEURS EN POURCENTAGE DU TOTAL MONDIAL)

	1987	1988	1989	1990	1991	1992	1993	1994	1995	1996
Africa	0.4	0.5	0.7	0.7	0.7	0.6	1.0	0.8	1.1	1.1
Americas	17.2	19.3	19.1	17.9	17.6	15.8	13.5	15.6	16.5	16.1
Northern America	14.4	15.4	15.0	15.0	15.1	13.4	11.6	13.6	14.2	13.5
LAIA	2.7	3.4	3.7	2.2	2.1	2.1	1.8	1.8	2.0	2.5
CACM	0.0	0.0	0.0	0.0	0.0	0.0	0.0	0.0	0.1	0.0
Caribbean	0.2	0.5	0.4	0.6	0.3	0.2	0.1	0.1	0.2	0.1
Rest of America	0.0	0.0	0.0	0.0	0.0	0.0	0.0	0.0	0.0	0.0
As.ex F.USSR	51.0	52.3	51.5	53.9	58.6	60.6	59.1	57.9	57.4	58.4
Eur.x F.USSR	24.2	21.0	21.3	19.9	16.6	15.1	17.4	17.6	17.3	15.4
EU	18.3	15.8	16.5	16.4	14.5	13.5	15.1	16.1	16.1	14.3
EFTA	1.4	1.2	1.2	1.1	1.1	0.9	1.1	1.0	0.9	0.8
East Europe	4.1	3.8	3.3	2.3	0.9	0.7	1.1	0.5	0.3	0.2
Other Europe	0.4	0.2	0.2	0.1	0.1	0.0	0.0	0.0	0.0	0.0
Former USSR	2.9	3.2	3.6	4.0	3.2	4.9	5.7	4.0	3.7	4.5
Oceania	3.7	2.8	3.0	2.8	2.7	2.6	2.3	2.5	2.3	2.8
Japan/Japon	23.3	20.0	17.8	14.2	15.7	17.0	22.4	22.8	22.0	21.0
USA/Etats–Unis d'Amer	11.1	12.0	13.3	12.3	12.5	11.0	10.3	12.0	12.2	11.6
Hong Kong	19.4	21.5	21.1	26.5	27.3	25.5	10.0	8.2	6.5	5.6
Korea, Republic of	0.0	0.4	0.7	1.3	1.7	3.3	5.2	6.3	7.8	9.0
Germany/Allemagne	7.2	6.2	5.7	5.0	4.8	5.0	5.8	6.2	6.1	5.3
Russian Federation						4.4	4.8	3.0	2.9	3.7
Italy/Italie	2.9	2.8	3.1	2.0	2.3	2.2	2.6	2.7	2.4	2.3
Singapore/Singapour	1.4	1.8	2.5	1.6	1.6	1.5	2.5	2.2	2.6	2.6
Australia/Australie	3.1	2.0	2.5	2.5	2.4	2.1	1.9	2.1	2.0	2.5
Canada	3.2	3.3	1.8	2.7	2.6	2.4	1.3	1.6	2.0	1.9

	1987	1988	1989	1990	1991	1992	1993	1994	1995	1996
Afrique	1.5	1.4	1.2	1.1	1.2	1.5	1.6	1.4	1.7	1.7
Amériques	9.9	8.7	10.2	10.3	10.4	12.2	21.7	20.9	19.8	20.8
Amérique du Nord	8.7	7.9	9.2	9.0	9.3	10.9	19.8	18.9	17.7	18.8
ALAI	0.9	0.4	0.5	0.6	0.6	0.7	1.2	1.2	1.4	1.5
MCAC	0.1	0.0	0.0	0.0	0.0	0.1	0.1	0.1	0.1	0.1
Caraïbes	0.2	0.4	0.4	0.5	0.4	0.3	0.3	0.2	0.2	0.2
Autre Amérique	0.1	0.1	0.1	0.2	0.1	0.2	0.4	0.5	0.4	0.3
Asie l'URSS exclus	62.6	66.8	70.0	70.8	73.4	71.9	57.4	60.7	61.8	60.4
Europe l'URSS exclus	15.2	14.5	13.2	11.4	10.6	10.2	14.6	14.0	14.1	14.5
UE	10.4	10.5	9.7	9.6	9.8	9.4	13.4	12.7	12.9	13.1
AELE	0.8	0.5	0.4	0.3	0.4	0.4	0.4	0.4	0.4	0.5
Europe de l'Est	3.9	3.4	3.0	1.5	0.3	0.4	0.7	0.8	0.8	0.8
Autre de l'Europe	0.1	0.1	0.1	0.1	0.1	0.0	0.0	0.0	0.0	0.0
Ancienne URSS	3.2	3.1	3.5	3.6	2.5	3.2	3.4	1.6	1.4	1.3
Océanie	0.9	0.9	0.9	0.9	0.9	0.9	1.3	1.4	1.3	1.3
Hong Kong	34.9	38.4	41.7	42.9	44.7	44.2	24.0	26.7	24.2	21.8
Japan/Japon	16.2	16.6	16.0	14.5	14.2	13.7	17.2	17.8	19.1	20.4
USA/Etats–Unis d'Amer	7.7	7.1	8.4	8.3	8.6	10.1	18.5	17.7	16.6	17.7
Korea, Republic of	0.0	0.2	0.9	2.0	3.0	2.8	3.1	3.6	4.5	5.0
Germany/Allemagne	3.1	3.1	3.1	3.0	3.3	2.9	4.3	3.9	3.8	3.9
Singapore/Singapour	3.4	3.1	3.2	3.2	2.8	2.4	2.4	2.1	2.4	2.5
Netherlands/Pays–Bas	1.5	1.6	1.4	1.5	1.5	1.4	1.8	1.9	2.2	2.3
United Kingdom	1.3	1.4	1.2	1.0	1.0	1.1	2.1	2.0	1.9	2.1
Russian Federation						2.8	2.9	1.3	1.1	1.1
Italy/Italie	1.4	1.6	1.4	1.3	1.3	1.3	1.4	1.3	1.4	1.2

4. Special Imports C.I.F. by Commodities according to the S.I.T.C. (Rev. 2) in thousand U.S. Dollars
Importations Spéciales C.A.F. par Produits d'après la C.T.C.I. (Rév. 2) en milliers de Dollars E.U.

SITC CTCI	COMMODITY	1993		1994		1995		1996		PRODUIT
		WEIGHT POIDS	VALUE VALEUR	WEIGHT POIDS	VALUE VALEUR	WEIGHT POIDS	VALUE VALEUR	WEIGHT POIDS	VALUE VALEUR	
	ALL COMMODITIES		103958979		115613642		132083539		138832776	TOUS PRODUITS
0	FOOD AND LIVE ANIMALS		2203894		3132071		6122401		5648888	ALIMENTS,ANIMAUX VIVANTS
03	FISH AND PREPARATIONS		367058		578310		607868		600366	POISSONS ET PREPARATIONS
034	FISH,FRESH,CHILLED,FROZN		212419	W 497764	368533	W 528606	388848	W 370544	380812	POISSON FRAIS, REFRIG,CONG
04	CEREALS AND PREPARATIONS		1034137		1332542		3637055		2601294	CEREALES ET PRODUITS
041	WHEAT ETC UNMILLED	W 6423919	834076	W 7299283	960577	MW 11586	2026390	W 8245961	1890396	FROMENT,EPEAUTRE
0411	DURUM WHEAT UNMILLED	W 2842042	359099	W 1821773	238729	W 5603643	1013955	W 4512381	1023059	FROMENT DUR NON MOULU
0412	OTHER WHEAT ETC UNMILLED	W 3581877	474977	W 5477509	721847	W 5981937	1012435	W 3733580	867337	AUTRE FROMENT NON MOULU
042	RICE	W 96266	34969	W 513816	141488	W 1642201	433529	W 761398	286467	RIZ
0422	RICE SEMI–MILLED,MILLED	W 95759	34920	W 492544	138893	W 1623169	429370	W 751308	283578	RIZ POLI,GLACE INCL BRISURES
04221	RICE MILLED UNBROKEN	W 95729	34917	W 492522	138890	W 1610034	426374	W 701507	270685	RIZ POLI,GLACE EXCL BRISURES
044	MAIZE UNMILLED	W 291	184	W 618	179	W 5181023	816077	W 441130	73056	MAIS NON MOULU
06	SUGAR AND PREPS,HONEY		132614		446160		935461		427690	SUCRES ET PRODUITS
061	SUGAR AND HONEY	W 460123	114528	W 1556059	411279	W 3052177	907406	W 1265803	399655	SUCRES ET MIEL
0611	RAW BEET AND CANE SUGAR	W 419636	101924	W 1484427	385212	W 2572053	777953	W 1204662	374263	SUCRES BRUTS
081	*FEEDING STUFF FOR ANIML	W 582275	308164	W 768941	349213	W 884248	422557	W 3478237	1299516	NOURRITURE POUR ANIMAUX
0813	OILCAKE AND OTH RESIDUES	W 60936	13182	W 3182	347	W 12147	1183	W 1883561	520677	TOURTEAUX
08131	— OF SOYA BEANS	W 54818	12001	W 1380	159	W 1003	195	W 1876478	519545	TOURTEAUX DE SOJA
0814	MEAT OR FISH MEAL FODDER	W 447475	211412	W 675600	276742	W 699846	330221	W 916284	581991	FARINES DE VIANDES,POISSONS
08142	FISH MEAL FODDER	W 434197	206202	W 668792	275232	W 693301	328086	W 884478	569341	FARINES DE POISSONS
1	BEVERAGES AND TOBACCO		245320		67936		393433		497345	BOISSONS ET TABACS
12	TOBACCO AND MANUFACTURES		200262		32343		358944		456987	TABACS BRUTS FABRIQUES
2	CRUDE MATERLS,EXCL FUELS		5227757		7200333		9868806		10447163	MAT BRUTES NON COMESTIBLES
21	HIDES,SKINS,FURS UNDRSSD		189373		268241		410867		369303	CUIRS,PEAUX BRUTS
23	RUBBER, CRUDE		423699		586722		757188		1123513	CAOUTCHOUC BRUT
232	NATURAL RUBBER,GUMS	W 266976	222162	W 341964	332769	W 321295	424740	W 554021	723072	LATEX CAOUTCHOUC NATUREL
23202	OTHER NATURAL RUBBER	W 176087	145955	W 185495	183035	W 177132	244299	W 337627	464163	CAOUTCHOUC NATUREL
24	CORK AND WOOD		634028		595764		544004		652543	LIEGE ET BOIS
247	OTH WOOD ROUGH,SQUARED	W 2515486	459041	W 2435817	430371	W 1906091	368372	V 3185492	457780	BOIS BRUTS EQUARRIS
251	*PULP AND WASTE PAPER	W 1120429	294053	W 1520763	494431	W 1730327	844519	W 2839852	967880	PATES A PAPIER,DECHETS
2517	SODA,SULPHATE WOOD PULP	W 359481	152220	W 558166	270753	W 647086	526643	W 1035054	539221	PATES CHIMIQUES AU SULFATE
25172	— BLEACHED,NONDISSOLVNG	W 295492	128548	W 431380	217406	W 553295	452829	W 941825	495669	PATES BLANCHIES
26	TEXTILE FIBRES AND WASTE		1360925		2782780		3827949		3528055	FIBRES TEXTILES
263	COTTON	W 44775	25199	W 615757	936140	W 1003367	1486726	W 751460	1276438	COTON
2631	RAW COTTON,EXCL LINTERS	W 13374	15964	W 502142	880147	W 741055	1377819	W 650512	1196668	COTON EN MASSE
266	SYNTHETIC FIBRES TO SPIN	W 524398	721503	W 684449	972214	W 756424	1316001	W 974250	1399283	FIBRES SYNTHETIQUES
2665	DISCN SYNTH FIBRE UNCMBD	W 436512	582355	W 527842	744592	W 600853	1049439	W 748932	1076791	DISCONTINUES EN MASSE
26652	— POLYESTER	W 236037	268331	W 262008	330854	W 316303	502374	W 403743	502807	FIBRES EN POLYESTERS
26653	— ACRYLIC	W 181285	285242	W 239468	378240	W 256658	498337	W 318252	534825	FIBRES ACRYLIQUES
268	WOOL(EXC TOPS),ANML HAIR	W 198119	550597	W 277014	634245	W 243421	743771	W 190392	642817	LAINES ET POILS
2681	WOOL GREASY,FLEECE–WSHED	W 145088	382217	W 204006	427499	W 173933	477232	W 128633	416526	LAINE EN SUINT
28	METALLIFEROUS ORES,SCRAP		2058692		2150716		3059579		3069738	MINERAIS METAL,DECHETS
281	IRON ORE,CONCENTRATES	MW 33047	926981	MW 37343	1025483	MW 41154	1226912	MW 43874	1320589	MINERAIS DE FER
2815	IRON ORE,CONC,NOT AGGLOM	MW 30927	852665	MW 35401	956085	MW 37624	1076097	MW 39451	1130201	MINERAIS NON AGGLOMERES
282	IRON AND STEEL SCRAP	W 2751192	422408	W 1924466	273027	W 1296699	169051	W 1259597	170824	FERRAILLES
28209	— OF OTHR IRON OR STEEL	W 2078043	318092	W 1618039	223054	W 1068206	131000	W 960656	118936	FERRAILLES DE FER
287	BASE METAL ORES,CONC NES	W 2632468	453216	W 4070307	572910	W 4774364	1001896	W 5136448	1114942	MINERAIS METAUX COMMUNS
288	NONFERR METAL SCRAP NES	W 708899	255889	W 955384	278965	W 1611823	660776	W 1037996	461662	DECHETS NON FERREUX
2882	OTHER BASE MTL SCRAP NES	W 649344	244209	W 912461	270766	W 1575557	652474	W 1032745	459955	AUTRES DECHETS
28821	COPPER WASTE AND SCRAP	W 568642	218719	W 773881	232390	W 1188926	492600	W 710983	318295	DECHETS DE CUIVRE
3	MINERAL FUELS ETC		5856049		4080214		5172152		6930341	COMBUSTIBLES MINERAUX LUB
33	PETROLEUM AND PRODUCTS		5412882		3641404		4612924		5973993	PETROLE ET DERIVES
333	CRUDE PETROLEUM	MW 15671	2323412	MW 12346	1573387	MW 17090	2356427	MW 22617	3406548	HUILES BRUTES DE PETROLE
334	PETROLEUM PRODUCTS,REFIN	MW 17318	3023361	MW 12917	2001883	MW 14419	2110797	MW 15860	2437492	PRODUITS RAFFINES
3343	GAS OILS			W 6238433	1044827			W 4624981	901480	GAS OILS
3344	FUEL OILS,NES			W 3980870	347452			W 8541815	829937	FUEL OILS
341	*GAS,NATURAL AND MANUFCT		157018	W 1407675	296305	W 2358320	452851	W 3695456	806728	GAZ NATUREL,GAZ MANUFACT
3413	PETROLM GASES,LIQUEFIED	W 679168	155657	W 1403736	295458	W 2339791	448691	W 3691625	806112	GAZ DE PETROLE LIQUEFIE
34139	OTH HYDROCARBON GAS LQFD	W 652945	149785	W 1026044	222773	W 951188	186645	W 1962139	449149	HYDROCARBURES GAZEUX NDA
4	ANIMAL,VEGETABLE OIL,FAT		498527		1804168		2592441		1692045	HUILES,GRAISSES ANIM,VEG
42	FIXED VEGETABLE OIL,FAT		456566		1744289		2436130		1571241	HUILES VEGETALES FIXES
423	FIXED VEG OILS,SOFT	W 236019	117439	W 1622958	984391	W 2128812	1449446	W 1626360	964647	HUILES VEGET DOUCES FIXES
4232	SOYA BEAN OIL	W 75708	37570	W 1063518	651243	W 1481815	1023915	W 1295396	764488	HUILE DE SOJA
4239	OTH FIXED VEG OILS,SOFT	W 150200	73123	W 545180	319606	W 631218	414034	W 316602	188502	AUTRES HUILES FIXES
42391	RAPE,COLZA,MUSTARD OILS	W 150067	72926	W 544930	319210	W 630672	413166	W 316047	187314	H NAVETTE COLZA MOUTARDE
424	FIXED VEG OIL NONSOFT	W 838279	339127	W 1586171	759898	W 1606760	986684	W 1134320	606593	AUTRES HUILES VEG FIXES
4242	PALM OIL	W 792519	318424	W 1456671	690126	W 1396840	865305	W 1009184	527067	HUILE DE PALME
5	CHEMCLS,RELATED PROD NES		9610219		11967920		16849519		17898736	PRODUITS CHIMIQUES
51	ORGANIC CHEMICALS		1568170		1982076		3156237		3057842	PROD CHIMIQ ORGANIQUES
511	HYDROCARBONS NES,DERIVS	W 697818	331694	W 1077955	471145	W 1639562	779102	W 1490238	644700	HYDROCARBURES NDA
5112	CYCLIC HYDROCARBONS	W 528693	235781	W 889701	380183	W 1338207	610359	W 1246081	501020	HYDROCARBURES CYCLIQUES
512	ALCOHOLS,PHENOLS ETC		263406		306685		501582		558909	PHENOLS,PHENOLS–ALCOOLS
5121	ACYCLIC ALCOHOLS,DERIVS		182426		233749		382068		430175	ALCOOLS ACYCLIQUES
513	CARBOXYLIC ACIDS ETC	W 561545	366889	W 619627	442737	W 875009	876158	W 1132198	814132	ACIDES CARBOXYLIQUES
5138	POLYACIDS AND DERIVATIVS	W 433891	251642	W 448082	310768	W 629619	646462	W 797007	561802	ACIDES POLYCARBOXYLIQUES
51389	OTH POLYACIDS ETC,DERIVS	W 284583	172610	W 279213	205776	W 435173	489249	W 512760	362844	ACIDES POLYCARBOXYLIQUES
514	NITROGEN–FNCTN COMPOUNDS	W 225882	284252	W 320580	366500	W 354834	446490	W 340968	435867	COMPOSES FONCT AZOTEES
52	INORGANIC CHEMICALS		257232		303994		371691		507405	PROD CHIM INORGANIQUES
53	DYES,TANNING,COLOUR PROD		585920		702163		791004		856124	PROD TEINTURE,COLORANTS
533	PIGMENTS,PAINTS,ETC	W 173842	375335	W 248112	476958	W 305357	561798	W 355152	603236	PIGMENTS,PEINTURES,VERNIS
541	*MEDICINAL,PHARM PRODUCT		416124	MK 17238	402973	MK 20747	407241	MK 19479	351081	PROD MEDICINAUX PHARMACEUT
562	*FERTILIZERS,MANUFACTURE	MW 10159	1469733	MW 12602	1925516	MW 19843	3731976	MW 18365	3538879	ENGRAIS MANUFACTURES
5621	CHEM NITROGENOUS FERTLZR	W 4103867	506182	W 3844718	494648	W 8024152	1548418	W 7253204	1398569	ENGRAIS AZOTES
56216	UREA	W 3607022	457654	W 3133315	423096	W 6962529	1426975	W 6009741	1242021	UREE
5623	CHEM POTASSIC FERTILIZER	W 2293968	334012	W 3502276	437983	W 4396298	541915	W 3855466	471165	ENGRAIS POTASSIQUES
56231	POTASSIUM CHLORIDE	W 1727246	203930	W 2846045	306192	W 3858241	437795	W 3438962	386648	CHLORURE DE POTASSIUM
5629	FERTILIZERS NES	W 3577479	597746	W 5194366	982366	W 7385865	1635938	W 7242871	1667083	ENGRAIS NDA
56291	NIT–PHOS–POT FERTLZR NES	W 1041476	196240	W 1013350	188912	W 1331350	278059	W 2128430	462724	ENGRAIS CONT N P K
56292	NITROG–PHOS FERTILZR NES	W 2521776	398329	W 4114703	777962	W 5964180	1338718	W 5084582	1197946	ENGRAIS NDA CONT N P
58	PLASTIC MATERIALS ETC		4310075		5402310		7111366		7918177	MAT PLAST ARTIFICIELLES
582	PROD OF CONDENSATION ETC	W 549143	625332	W 720797	807903	W 778917	1065633	W 867761	1130382	PROD CONDENS,POLYCOND
5823	ALKYDS,OTHER POLYESTERS	W 351162	356453	W 471323	473455	W 488359	621673	W 520079	579949	ALKYDES ET AUT POLYESTERS
58231	— IN PRIMARY FORMS	W 341078	334945	W 452597	439869	W 471355	582938	W 499300	536904	SOUS FORMES PRIMAIRES
583	POLYMERIZATION ETC PRODS	W 4369353	3607249	W 5699022	4527931	W 6940115	6006968	W 7918562	6681436	PROD POLYMERISATION
5831	POLYETHYLENE	W 1127250	770192	W 1456296	942068	W 1976387	1533678	W 2262718	1655973	POLYETHYLENE
58311	— IN PRIMARY FORMS	W 1035153	712587	W 1337170	877180	W 1825347	1444610	W 2194554	1581931	POLYETHYLENE PRIMAIRES
5832	POLYPROPYLENE	W 627798	433834	W 882527	594393	W 1165687	892161	W 1264136	920353	POLYPROPYLENE
58321	— IN PRIMARY FORMS	W 583201	379082	W 811964	527889	W 1070428	813065	W 1127276	814075	POLYPROPYLENE PRIMAIRES
5833	POLYSTYRENE,ITS COPOLYMR	W 1399349	1207804	W 1884901	1579937	W 2112571	1930317	W 2490436	2232039	POLYPROPYLENE COPOLYMERES
58331	— IN PRIMARY FORMS	W 1311603	1178301	W 1776747	1541502	W 2000936	1895265	W 2436148	2211910	SOUS FORMES PRIMAIRES
5834	POLYVINYL CHLORIDE	W 654793	547108	W 757396	629162	W 866829	758205	W 1149692	923063	CHLORURE DE POLYVINYLE

4. Special Imports C.I.F. by Commodities according to the S.I.T.C. (Rev. 2) in thousand U.S. Dollars
Importations Spéciales C.A.F. par Produits d'après la C.T.C.I. (Rév. 2) en milliers de Dollars E.U.

SITC CTCI	COMMODITY	1993 WEIGHT POIDS	1993 VALUE VALEUR	1994 WEIGHT POIDS	1994 VALUE VALEUR	1995 WEIGHT POIDS	1995 VALUE VALEUR	1996 WEIGHT POIDS	1996 VALUE VALEUR	PRODUIT
58341	— IN PRIMARY FORMS	W 421485	312105	W 488742	368204	W 576237	473874	W 860909	625062	SOUS FORMES PRIMAIRES
5839	OTH POLYMRZTION ETC PROD	W 514758	596735	W 656836	716211	W 752305	813172	W 662967	841081	AUT PROD POLYMER COPOLYM
59	CHEMICAL MATERIALS NES		840123		1038159		1078071		1444270	MAT PROD CHIMIQUES NDA
598	MISCEL CHEM PRODUCTS NES		553253	W 468116	696587	W 425424	661882	W 654012	1003656	PROD DIV INDUST CHIM NDA
5989	CHEM PRODUCTS,PREPS NES		458896	W 418387	602303	W 358105	545691	W 581229	882084	PROD PREP CHIMIQUES NDA
59899	OTH CHEM PRODS,PREPS,NES		278750	W 258349	377504	W 168404	253590	W 349466	527962	AUT PRODUITS CHIMIQUES NDA
6	BASIC MANUFACTURES		29191585		28732420		29142219		32065095	ART MANUFACTURES
61	LEATHER,DRESSED FUR,ETC		1931690		2202934		2313825		2483032	CUIRS,PELLETERIES
611	LEATHER	W 300138	1465010	W 340507	1762839	W 404896	1881933	W 483455	2029238	CUIRS,PEAUX PREPARES
6114	LEATHR BOVINE NES,EQUINE	W 244081	867552	W 271574	1060102	W 338610	1241623	W 418624	1345344	CUIRS DE BOVINS
612	LEATHER ETC MANUFACTURES		359519	W 111932	307399	W 111458	330098	W 106914	351268	OUVRAGES EN CUIRS NDA
6123	PREPRD PARTS OF FOOTWEAR	W 120057	355484	W 110890	300318	W 110036	320801	W 106026	345408	PARTIES DE CHAUSSURES
63	WOOD,CORK MANUFACTRS NES		943431		1016829		990679		875237	OUVRAGES LIEGE ET BOIS
634	VENEERS,PLYWOOD,ETC		860746		914135		875191		777843	PLACAGES,CONTRE–PLAQUES
6342	PLYWOOD OF WOOD SHEETS		762163	V 2108870	816257	V 2082926	773676	V 1775113	643835	BOIS CONTRE–PLAQUES
64	PAPER,PAPERBOARD AND MFR		1554383		1976309		2215078		2846043	PAPIERS,CARTONS & OUVRAGES
641	PAPER AND PAPERBOARD	W 2559179	1246271	W 3389041	1634096	W 3264491	1826364	W 4776657	2423730	PAPIERS ET CARTONS
6412	PRINTG,WRITING PAPER NES	W 363272	225305	W 595968	379996	W 719144	496106	W 931531	582773	PAPIERS POUR L'IMPRESSION
64122	— COATED,IMPREGNATD ETC	W 319650	199961	W 537981	346598	W 646372	455125	W 873670	551270	PAPIERS IMPRESSION COUCHES
6413	KRAFT PAPER,PAPERBOARD	W 750476	313324	W 935746	375590	W 790965	377635	W 1258798	548987	PAPIER ET CARTON KRAFT
64139	KRAFT PAPER PAPERBD,NES	W 604534	250240	W 744427	297348	W 661346	316178	W 1057434	460901	PAPIER,CARTON KRAFT NDA
6415	PAPER,PAPERBRD,BULK,NES	W 809968	352525	W 1021838	426513	W 976401	467504	W 1360194	629607	PAPIERS,CARTONS ROULEAUX
64159	OTHER PAPER ETC,BULK,NES	W 503140	269127	W 672193	330828	W 652198	366869	W 823308	457494	AUT PAPIER ROULEAUX FEUILLES
642	PAPER,ETC,PRECUT,ARTS OF	W 339532	308112	W 396594	342213	W 395223	388715	W 428113	422313	PAP,CARTONS DECOUPES
65	TEXTILE YARN,FABRICS,ETC		7789846		9524030		11176596		12206940	FILS,TISSUS,ARTICLES TEXTILE
651	TEXTILE YARN	W 670956	1719224	W 971225	2140610	W 1088045	2461174	W 1234394	2881274	FILS TEXTILES
6512	WOOL,HAIR YARN,INCL TOPS	W 90737	450160	W 106559	483660	W 98121	542876	W 99593	490375	FILS DE LAINE,DE POILS
6513	COTTON YARN	W 103371	237047	W 180256	366550	W 230092	467289	W 318335	627589	FILS DE COTON
6514	SYN FIB YRN,BULK,MONOFIL	W 300531	507717	W 448135	651443	W 503980	739239	W 568493	1052164	FILS CONT 85% FIB TEXT SYNTH
65142	— NONTXT ETC CONT PAMID	W 90084	145464	W 107166	159705	W 127418	249512	W 283313	543466	FILS NON TEX FI CON POLYAMID
652	COTTON FABRICS,WOVEN		1019133		1288464	L 1435115	1528600	L 1678012	1697490	TISSUS DE COTON
6522	WOVEN COTTON BLEACHD,ETC		945980		1165130	L 1217195	1348173	L 1405571	1503481	TISSUS COTON BLANCHIS ETC
65224	BLCHED COTTON FABRIC NES		806966		994860	L 1080955	1152531	L 1272967	1295385	AUT TIS PLUS 85% COT BLANCHI
653	WOVN MAN–MADE FIB FABRIC		2566625		3146424	L 3613368	3744690	L 3567035	3960561	TISSUS FIBRES SYNTH,ARTIF
6531	CONT SYNT WEAVES NONPILE	L 1810087	1638755	L 2140124	1963320	L 2338496	2338043	L 2384358	2528856	TISSUS FIBRES SYNTH CONTINUE
65315	CONT SYN TXTL FABRIC NES	L 1741160	1552073	L 2070140	1866027	L 2266626	2227884	L 2305697	2412212	TIS PLUS 85% TEXT SYNT CONT
6532	DISC SYN TXTL FABRIC NES	L 452051	295800	L 680659	431792	L 550044	477432	L 454370	483866	TIS DISC MOINS 85% FIBR TEXT
6534	DISC SYN BLEND FABRC NES	L 304968	370498	L 380526	445267	L 456498	565245	L 469660	582045	TISSUS FIBRES SYNTH DISCONT
65341	DISC SYN FIB–COTTN FABRC	L 247912	255321	L 326730	330471	L 390097	414089	L 403964	427896	TISSUS FIB SYNT DIS MEL COTO
654	OTH WOVEN TEXTILE FABRIC		482016		625082		699444		690725	TISSUS AUT COTON SYNT,ARTIF
655	KNITTED,ETC FABRICS	W 245850	689126	W 288817	820773	W 322736	975172	W 365939	1118040	ETOF BONNETERIE PIECES ETC
6552	OTHER KNIT ETC FAB NONEL	W 245850	689126	W 288817	820773	W 322736	975172	W 365939	1118040	ETOF BON NON ELAS NON SYNT
657	SPECIAL TXTL FABRC,PRODS		1018855	W 471413	1146639	W 528873	1321312	W 550088	1415109	TISSUS SPECIAUX
6573	COATED ETC TEXTILES NES	W 279720	738849	W 324579	818733	W 358097	915219	W 380312	998602	TISSUS,ART MATIERE TEXT NDA
65732	PLASTIC COATED TEXTILES	W 268767	693829	W 315058	771776	W 346597	856231	W 367206	934183	TISSUS IMPREGNES
66	NONMETAL MINERAL MFS NES		881486		1066051		1212801		1254682	ART MIN NON METALLIQUES
664	GLASS		287461		393412		488518		480170	VERRE
67	IRON AND STEEL		12767443		9534909		6583035		7309822	FER ET ACIER
672	IRON,STEEL PRIMARY FORMS	MW 13053	3481362	W 5962337	1648777	W 2657625	1016255	W 3590627	1272557	LINGOTS FER,ACIER
6725	IRN,STL BLOOMS,SLABS,ETC	W 5504711	1257415	W 1908983	437434	W 418469	105890	W 301720	81665	BLOOMS,BILLETTES FER ACIER
67251	IRN,SMPLE STL BLOOMS,ETC	W 5495694	1244128	W 1865197	414464	W 396170	86419	W 292364	61421	BLOOMS ETC NON ACIER FIN
6727	IRN,STL COIL FR REROLLNG	W 6444991	1993915	W 3132042	1004897	W 1974574	843536	W 3168520	1159358	EBAUCHES POUR TOLES FER
67271	IRON,SIMPLE STEEL COILS	W 6239241	1876383	W 3003955	925999	W 1869374	736957	W 2993034	970772	EBAUCHES NON EN ACIER
673	IRON,STEEL SHAPES ETC	MW 14721	4543983	MW 11706	3432965	W 3891138	1205942	W 4850378	1495706	BARRES,PROFIL FER,ACIER
6731	IRON,STEEL WIRE ROD	W 4494277	1359600	W 4389363	1237980	W 642869	169583	W 2596525	739825	FIL MACHINE FER,ACIER
67311	IRON,SIMPLE STL WIRE ROD	W 3761510	1113875	W 3808239	1059660	W 515261	126989	W 2479114	690068	FIL MACH AUT ACIER FIN
6732	IRON,STEEL BARS ETC	W 6307006	1908535	W 5660790	1644829	W 2718280	778724	W 1908550	577717	BARRES FER,ACIER
67326	IRN,OTH STL BARS HOTROLD	W 5276402	1549412	W 5053145	1417356	W 2454225	653058	W 1666360	448692	BARRES PLEINES FER,ACIER
6733	IRON,STEEL PROFILES ETC	W 3919588	1275848	W 1656008	550156	W 529989	257635	W 345303	178165	PROFILES,PALPLAN FER,ACIER
67331	SMALL U,I,H SECTIONS ETC	W 1863068	591018	W 573132	170272	W 79355	30707	W 56966	27434	PROFILES MOINS 80MM
67332	LARGE U,I,H SECTIONS ETC	W 1781666	584935	W 930829	310967	W 288792	125922	W 179192	83950	PROFILES PLUS 80MM
674	IRN,STL UNIV,PLATE,SHEET	W 7425752	3315300	W 5944955	2684930	W 5458173	2948037	W 7268528	3700504	LARGES PLATS,TOLES
6744	IRN,STL HVY PLATE,ROLLED	W 2679413	900747	W 1444842	495904	W 541727	272904	W 624970	317589	TOLES LAMINEES PLUS 4.75 MM
67441	— OF IRON OR SIMPLE STL	W 2635373	833488	W 1408001	451293	W 502485	231554	W 569300	271510	TOLES NON ACIER FIN CARB
6745	IRN,STL MED PLATE,ROLLED	W 927546	485639	W 681203	314478	W 425720	263851	W 823564	421741	TOLES 3 A 4.75 MM
6746	IRN,STL THIN PLATE,ROLLD	W 2395024	1152777	W 2446869	1128002	W 186706	261227	W 3516525	1638587	TOLES LAM MOINS 3MM
67461	— OF IRON OR SIMPLE STL	W 2202074	872792	W 2200800	847349	W 23583	17155	W 3306313	1373725	TOL NON AC FIN MOINS 3 MM
6747	TINNED PLATES,SHEETS	W 522740	325142	W 466913	272221	W 596242	366448	W 551029	355554	TOLES ETAMEES EN ACIER
6749	OTH IRN,STL PLATES,SHEET	W 901029	450994	W 905129	474325	W 3707777	1783606	W 1752439	967032	AUTRES TOLES FER,ACIER
67491	— OF IRON OR SIMPLE STL	W 822171	379963	W 829747	383534	W 3639129	1692319	W 1615192	836642	AUT TOLES AUTRES ACIER FIN
678	IRON,STL TUBES,PIPES,ETC	W 1188942	998455	W 1406486	1271599	W 930602	998176	W 532796	602957	TUBES,TUYAUX EN FONTE,FER
6782	IRON,STL SEAMLESS TUBES	W 721576	647462	W 997351	897138	W 666865	679070	W 279475	317498	TUBES,TUYAUX SANS SOUDURE
68	NON–FERROUS METALS		1862287		1658786		2680247		3001585	METAUX NON FERREUX
682	COPPER EXC CEMENT COPPER	W 570562	1211555	W 404286	889655	W 537879	1356401	W 714243	1673126	CUIVRE
6821	COPPER NES,ALLOYS,UNWRT	W 362396	695504	W 121408	224215	W 187504	406441	W 290940	571402	CUIVRE BRUT
68212	COPPER REFINED,UNWROUGHT	W 259696	511996	W 78629	148675	W 107681	232328	W 157820	328420	CUIVRE AFFINE BRUT
6822	COPPER,ALLOYS WORKED	W 208167	516051	W 282878	665440	W 350375	949960	W 423303	1101724	CUIVRE,ALLIAGES OUVRES
68221	COPPER BARS,WIRE,ETC	W 124405	251077	W 167586	321713	W 201829	448971	W 262092	555316	BARRES,PROFILES ET FILS
684	ALUMINIUM	W 290647	492531	W 346022	588395	W 615749	1089131	W 634518	1052766	ALUMINIUM
6841	ALUMINIUM,ALLOYS,UNWRGHT	W 165640	178161	W 168853	189124	W 387925	513895	W 366733	457778	ALUMINIUM,ALLIAGES BRUTS
6842	ALUMINIUM,ALLOYS WORKED	W 125007	314370	W 177169	399271	W 227823	575236	W 267785	594988	ALUMINIUM,ALLIAGES OUVRE
69	METAL MANUFACTURES NES		1262984		1542068		1725957		1766469	ART MANUFACT EN METAL NDA
699	BASE METAL MFRS NES		587264	W 331086	686198	W 320888	799431	W 315976	792386	ART MANUFACTURES MET NDA
7	MACHINES,TRANSPORT EQUIP		44468249		51384705		52435805		54705137	MACHINES MATERIEL TRANSPORT
71	POWER GENERATING EQUIPMT		2519718		3185172		3111685		3211507	MACHINES GENERATRICES
711	STEAM BOILERS & AUX PLNT		333049		331912		404006		379496	GENERATEURS VAPEUR EAU ETC
713	INTRNL COMBUS PSTN ENGIN		803512		688509		608361		698939	MOTEURS EXPL COMB INT, PIECE
7139	PISTON ENGINE PARTS NES		386788	W 42543	370043	W 39027	359998	W 44789	426555	PIECES POUR 713.2,3,8
716	ROTATING ELECTRIC PLANT		1155894		1728456		1687376		1556456	APP ELECTR ROTATIFS,PIECES
7162	AC MTRS,GENRTRS,GEN SETS	MN 303788	704362	MN 438415	1058959	MN 531079	947252	MN 565921	936318	MOTEURS ELECTRIQUES
71623	GEN SETS WITH PISTN ENGN	N 17561	479440	N 28672	719495	N 22990	508738	N 23073	476806	GROUPES MOTEUR EXPLOSION
7169	PTS NES OF ROT ELEC PLNT		371236	W 60772	525934	W 46459	508861	W 43578	392866	PIECES MAC APP ROTATIFS
72	MACHS FOR SPCL INDUSTRYS		13157867		12739851		13247390		14218858	MAC SPECIALES POUR INDUST
723	CIVIL ENGNEERG EQUIP ETC		783442		501559		690862		467064	APPAREILS DE GENIE CIVIL
7234	CONST,MINING MACHNRY NES	N 19061	632835	N 8257	392990	N 6723	472767	N 6897	321170	MACH POUR LA CONST, MINES
72342	SLFPRP SHOVELS,EXCAVATRS	N 11013	356687	N 4872	204230	N 4474	232292	N 5109	190059	PELLES MECANIQUES
724	TEXTILE,LEATHER MACHNRY		4475203		3352382		3181467		3294755	MACH POUR INDUSTRIE TEXTILE
7243	SEWING MACHS,NEEDLES ETC		532509		454810		408290		405652	MACHINES A COUDRE,PIECES
72431	SEWING MACHINES	N 620986	489829	N 423506	396254	N 349789	324480	N 382606	337201	MACHINES A COUDRE
7244	SPINNING,EXTRDNG,ETC MCH		1049880		955310		767565		827510	MACH POUR LE FILAGE
72443	SPINNING,REELING,ETC MCH	N 6062	318244	N 7578	270451	N 6644	268616	N 7607	265302	MACH POUR LA FILATURE

4. Special Imports C.I.F. by Commodities according to the S.I.T.C. (Rev. 2) in thousand U.S. Dollars
Importations Spéciales C.A.F. par Produits d'après la C.T.C.I. (Rév. 2) en milliers de Dollars E.U.

SITC CTCI	COMMODITY	1993 WEIGHT POIDS	1993 VALUE VALEUR	1994 WEIGHT POIDS	1994 VALUE VALEUR	1995 WEIGHT POIDS	1995 VALUE VALEUR	1996 WEIGHT POIDS	1996 VALUE VALEUR	PRODUIT
7245	WEAVING,FELT MFG,ETC MCH		1684572		1044735		1135947		1154524	METIERS A TISSER,PIECES
72451	WEAVING MACHINES (LOOMS)	N 27067	677805	N 20897	413089	N 18603	498915	N 21567	481518	METIERS A TISSER
72452	KNITTING MACHINES	N 96457	408931	N 117151	263989	N 83523	328616	N 57513	313544	METIERS A BONNETERIE
72453	GIMPING,WARPING ETC MCHS	N 28356	557299	N 16230	321590	N 24149	278300	N 18634	342275	METIERS A TULLE ETC
7247	TEXTILE MACHINERY NES		688797		540304		558146		577294	MACH LAVAGE,TEINTURE TEX
72474	OTH TEXTILE MACHNERY NES	N 45060	607892	N 38325	470641	N 34365	482594	N 31287	502617	MACH LAVAGE ETC MAT TEXT
7248	SKIN,LEATHER WORKNG MACH		326385		237920	N 43691	175692	N 42066	197742	MACHINES TRAVAIL DES CUIRS
725	PAPER ETC MILL MACHINERY		325282		366071		489209		499102	MACHINES FABR PATE PAPIER
726	PRINTG,BKBINDG MACHY,PTS		737352		662684		646156		796959	MACHINES POUR IMPRIMERIE
7267	OTH PRINTG & ANCILL MACH	N 21338	376298	N 18379	374497	N 15338	367519	N 15174	418837	AUT MACH IMPRIMERIE,PIEC
72671	PRINTING MACHINERY NES	N 9697	322266	N 12337	323004	N 10706	329025	N 9799	353116	AUT MACH IMPRIMERIE
727	FOOD MACHRY NON-DOMESTIC		592078		567575		640145		797476	MACH INDUSTRIES ALIMENT
7272	OTH FOOD PROC MCHY,PARTS		492125		474683		575782	N 30577	736420	AUT MACH IND ALIMENTAIRE
72722	INDUS FOOD PROC MACH NES		462792	N 19703	386914	N 21342	473826	N 29598	680280	MACHINES BOULANGERIE
728	OTH MACHY FOR SPCL INDUS		6035279		7103665		7450426		8185962	AUT MACH IND PARTICULIERES
7281	MACH-TOOLS FR SPCL INDUS		532290		591873		509649		705939	MACH-OUTILS SPEC IND PART
72812	MACH-TOOLS TO WORK WOOD	N 32200	290683	N 35807	345512	N 32301	311165	N 40803	468566	MACH-OUT POUR TRAVAIL BOIS
7283	OTHR MINERAL WORKG MACHY		448634		487105		508599		511790	MACH TRIER,CRIBLER,BROYER
7284	MACHY FOR SPCL INDUS NES		5054355		6024688		6432179		6968233	MACH SPEC IND PARTICUL.
72842	RUBBER,PLASTICS WRKG MCH	N 60441	1492619	N 54904	1400067	N 47287	1272833	N 45358	1818129	MACH IND CAOUT MAT PLAST
72843	TOBACCO WORKING MACH NES	N 912	251771	N 1651	418181	N 484	505238	N 284	340809	MACH POUR IND DU TABAC
72848	OTH MCHY WITH INDIV FNCT	N 172800	2415278	N 420288	3419634	N 329161	3579189	N 253089	3730289	AUTRES MACHINES NDA
72849	PTS OF MACHS OF 7284 ETC		520331	W 31545	422013	W 24703	410289	W 29291	542398	PIECES DU 728.4 ETC
73	METALWORKING MACHINERY		2498136		3002826		3341883		3637639	MACH TRAVAIL DES METAUX
736	METALWORKING MACH-TOOLS		2079811		2218117		2344292		2742415	MACH-OUTILS TRAVAIL METAUX
7361	METAL CUTTING MACH-TOOLS	N 72860	826132	N 86233	827562	N 76872	915825	N 68875	1143787	MACH-OUT ENLEVEMENT METAL
73619	OTH MTL CUTTNG MCH-TOOLS	N 28822	313129	N 43017	297010	N 34919	316065	N 25960	392950	MACH A AFFUTER ETC METAL
7362	METAL FORMING MACH-TOOLS	N 41265	635947	N 53279	730387	N 43835	718132	N 42335	812478	MACH-OUTILS DEFORM METAL
7367	OTH METALWRKG MACH-TOOLS	N 15593	472046	N 16586	487314	N 13530	553371	N 13756	545367	AUT MACH-OUT POUR METAUX
737	METALWORKING MACHNRY NES		418325		784709		997591		895224	MACH TRAV METAUX PIECES
7372	ROLLING MILLS AND ROLLS		144693		359416		520833		352931	LAMINOIRS CYLINDRES PIEC
74	GENRL INDUSTRL MACHY NES		4820083		6254336		7196626		7781016	MACH APP INDUSTRIE
741	HEATING,COOLING EQUIPMNT		1352572		1854958		1837850		1723263	MACH CHAUFFAGE,PIECES
7415	AIR-CONDITIONING MACHNRY		389037		449957	N 295569	398674		298590	GROUPES CONDITION AIR
7416	HEATING,COOLING EQU NES		484643		802706	N 404382	785603	N 244303	652366	APP CHANGEMENT TEMP
743	PUMPS NES,CENTRFUGES ETC		636398		864326		1074545		1036141	POMPES COMPRES,VENT ETC
7431	PUMPS FOR GASES ETC	N 2654564	304032	N 2462814	415306	N 2606282	497890	N 2461418	443848	POMPES AIR A VIDE,COMPRES
744	MECHANICAL HANDLING EQU		902770		1233744		1667071		1898055	EQUIP MANUTENTION PIECES
7442	LIFTING,LOADING MACH NES	N 72744	594403	N 73929	860274	N 68429	1194483	N 71684	1360157	APP LEVAGE,MANUTENTION
74424	LIFTS AND SKIP HOISTS	N 2796	161066	N 4202	307345	N 5486	497314	N 6936	598785	ASCENSEURS,MONTE-CHARGE
74428	OTH HANDLING ETC MCH NES	N 54947	246359	N 57084	336788	N 53110	416327	N 54730	458849	AUT APP LEVAGE ETC
7449	PTS NES OF MACHY OF 7442		214439	W 29143	279592	W 36166	353824	W 57494	419691	PIECES DU 744.2
745	NONELEC MACHY,TOOLS NES		570880		660101		723892		1059350	AUT MACH NON ELEC,PIECES
7452	OTH NONELEC MCHS,PTS NES		561301		650617		712545		1047669	AUT MACH NON ELEC,PIECES
74522	PACKAGNG,BOTTLNG,ETC MCH	N 31144	350984	N 27964	428398	N 27640	488249	N 48373	701739	MACH NETT BOUTEILLES,ETC
749	NONELEC MACH PTS,ACC NES		1164773		1339304		1519149		1718370	PIECES MACH NON ELEC NDA
7499	OTH NONELEC MCHY PTS NES		776804	W 58486	813637	W 53510	844075	W 65542	1026637	PIECES NON ELECT NDA
74991	FOUNDRY MOULDS ETC NES		655013	W 52437	726612	W 46776	739348	W 59169	893104	MOULES POUR METAUX
75	OFFICE MACHNES,ADP EQUIP		1592981		2072878		2857853		3420946	MACH BUREAU TRAIT AUTOM
752	AUTOMTIC DATA PROC EQUIP	N 2130801	697404	N 3322149	831545	MN 9036	1050559	N 8882547	964722	MACH TRAIT INFORMATION
7522	DIGITAL COMPUTERS	N 64450	379466	N 75494	421361	N 82897	211870	N 32103	242528	MACH DIGITALES COMPLETES
7528	OFF-LINE DATA PROC EQUIP	N 137154	31642	N 472323	48477	N 3637840	397830	N 499690	64602	MACH AUXIL TRAIT INFORM
759	OFFICE,ADP MCH PTS,ACCES		801474	W 68604	1133328	W 72197	1725580		2374705	PIECES DU 751 ET 752
7599	ACCTG,ETC,ADP MCH PTS,AC		705921	W 56132	998969	W 52503	1451666	MN 62079	2023569	PIECES DU 751 ET 752
76	TELECOMM,SOUND EQUIPMENT		5453707		6805449		7616359		5833304	EQUIPMENT DE TELECOM
763	SOUND RECORDRS,PHONOGRPH	N 1766845	339091	N 3082829	379213	N 2294999	227179	N 1119845	93612	PHONO,APP ENREGISTREMENT
7638	OTHR SOUND APPARATUS ETC	N 1597953	336754	N 2839866	375806	N 2167569	225077	N 1018005	91643	AUT APP D'ENREGIS,REPROD
764	TELECOM EQPT,PTS,ACC NES		4850379		5960875		6897636		5415719	EQUIP TELECOM,PIECES
7641	LINE TELEPHONE,ETC EQUIP	MN 38119	1296190	MN 36482	2112348	MN 38790	2176966	MN 35687	409709	APP TELEPHON PAR FIL
7643	TV,RADIO TRANSMITTRS ETC		818983	N 524445	793998	N 531622	941369	N 475519	1169078	APP EMET TELE RADIO
7649	PTS NES OF EQUIPMT OF 76		2431148	W 198312	2798836		3446140		3587666	PIECES DE LA DIV 76
76491	PTS NES OF APPAR OF 7641		806139	W 40474	763379	W 35818	933583	W 30859	1025383	PIECES POUR 764.1
76493	TELECOMM EQUIPMT PTS NES		985662	W 124985	1069815	W 72450	1311932	MN 109627	1378531	PIECES 761,762,764.3,8
76499	PARTS ETC OF SOUND EQUIP		578257	W 657	885070		1095494	MN 286160	1082328	PIECES NDA POUR 763
77	ELECTRIC MACHNRY NES ETC		5941860		7702268		9741274		11274172	MACH APP ELECT NDA
771	ELECTRIC POWER MACHY NES		457056		700705		796672		932883	MACH PROD,TRANS ELECTR
7712	OTH ELEC POWER MACHY NES		346279		465223		555570		608919	AUT APP PROD TRANSF ELEC
772	SWITCHGEAR ETC,PARTS NES		1111672	W 147003	1519922	W 122348	1888105		2093179	APP COUPURE,SECT ETC
7721	SWITCHGEAR ETC		698936	W 79669	1025834	W 76660	1277046		1430751	APP COUPURE,SECTIONMNT
7722	PRINTED CIRCUITS,PTS NES		269801	W 47656	316281	W 31630	398418	MN 1917680	439453	CIRCUITS ET PIECES
773	ELECTR DISTRIBUTNG EQUIP	W 172957	566660	W 194290	640111	W 204106	740360	W 207192	795873	EQUIPMT DISTRIBUTION ELECT
7731	INSULATED WIRE,CABLE ETC	W 168815	522734	W 188704	588048	W 199107	685346	W 202146	734105	FILS,CABLES ISOLES ELECT
776	TRANSISTORS,VALVES,ETC		2128099		2917573		3878053		4685439	LAMPES,TUBES,VALVES
7761	TV PICTURE TUBES	N 8960248	469170	MN 10759	604977	MN 10851	576113	N 7525848	474182	TUBES CATHODIQUES
7763	DIODES,TRANSISTORS,ETC	MN 9566289	220561	MN 13454129	335242	MN 18580600	467289	MN 23031630	687149	DIODES,TRANSISTORS
7764	ELECTRONIC MICROCIRCUITS	MN 3944154	1117421	MN 5236467	1544400	MN 6133268	2190964	MN 6911463	2605099	MICROSTRUCTURES ELECTRON
7768	ELCTRNC COMP PTS,CRYSTLS		293371		391114		526264		559715	CRIST PIEZO-ELEC,PCS 776
77689	ELECTRNIC COMPON PTS NES		269678	W 25024	349958	W 18794	455140	W 22263	459793	PIECES DU GROUPE 776
778	ELECTRICAL MACHINERY NES		1172962		1429844		1814910		2150068	AUTRES MACH ELECT NDA
7788	OTH ELEC MACHY,EQUIP NES		884087		1109385		1422757		1510317	AUT MACH APP ELEC NDA
77884	ELECTRICAL CONDENSERS		256337	W 24770	339387	W 24453	429594	W 27122	517747	CONDENSATEURS ELECTRIQUES
77886	OTH ELEC MACHINERY NES		242251		310711	N 3461404	410451	N 5582834	446154	AUT MACH APP ELECTRIQUES
78	ROAD VEHICLES		5285859		4774317		2685398		2190244	VEHICULES ROUTIERS
781	PASS MOTOR VEH EXC BUSES	N 222336	2130720	N 188050	1637553	N 139745	932953	N 63637	403533	AUTO TRANSPORT PERSONNES
782	LORRIES,SPCL MTR VEH NES	N 80543	1275005	N 71896	1226720	N 16563	538292	N 9913	371712	VEHICULES SPECIAUX,MARCH
7821	LORRIES,TRUCKS	N 78092	1082639	N 69159	974503	N 12566	152762	N 6606	121968	VEHICULES TRANSP MARCHAND
783	ROAD MOTOR VEHICLES NES	N 8160	195007	N 21501	550489	N 1815	38320	N 1757	55216	VEHICULES ROUTIERS NDA
7831	BUSES	N 6263	141060	N 20086	498356	N 1277	22396	N 1254	33297	VOITURES TRANSPORT COMMUN
784	MOTOR VEH PRTS,ACCES NES		999755		740153		896813		1102581	PIECES 722,781,782,783
7849	OTHER MOTOR VEHCL PARTS		784211	W 30107	506517	W 111585	748115	W 116858	1043933	PIECES 722,781,782,783
785	CYCLES,ETC MOTRZD OR NOT		552745		586975		251504		236641	MOTOCYCLES SCOOTERS
7851	MOTORCYCLES ETC	N 240601	365585	N 336399	407053	N 46248	23824	N 2911	1510	MOTO VELO MOTEUR AUXIL
79	OTHR TRANSPORT EQUIPMENT		3198039		4847608		2637338		3137452	AUTRE MATERIEL TRANSPORT
792	AIRCRAFT ETC		2269764		3397005		1359465		2648545	APP NAVIGATION AERIENNE
7922	AIRCRFT NES 2000KG OR LS	N 22	350572	N 36	6060	N 8	1359	N 27	551700	AERODYNES MOINS 2000 KG
7924	AIRCRFT NES OVER 15000KG	N 76	1369582	N 56	2847145	N 14	891906	N 27	1419499	AERODYNES PLUS 15000 KG
7929	AIRCRAFT PARTS NES		312813	W 704	171981	W 947	237742	W 2631	498044	PIECES DU 792
793	SHIPS AND BOATS ETC		843076	N 4266	1346466		1090917	N 2188	425751	NAVIRES BATEAUX,ETC
7932	SHIPS AND BOATS NES	N 18543	431505	N 2640	1043616	N 1151	557570	N 1066	347040	NAVIRES ET BATEAUX
79323	OTHER CARGO VESSELS	N 693	299885	N 480	989310	N 339	361125	N 345	258499	AUT BATEAUX TRANS MARCH
7933	VESSELS FOR BREAKING UP	N 2051	328036	N 375	151039	N 214	47538	N 108	15879	BATEAUX A DEPECER

4. Special Imports C.I.F. by Commodities according to the S.I.T.C. (Rev. 2) in thousand U.S. Dollars
Importations Spéciales C.A.F. par Produits d'après la C.T.C.I. (Rév. 2) en milliers de Dollars E.U.

SITC CTCI	COMMODITY	1993 WEIGHT POIDS	1993 VALUE VALEUR	1994 WEIGHT POIDS	1994 VALUE VALEUR	1995 WEIGHT POIDS	1995 VALUE VALEUR	1996 WEIGHT POIDS	1996 VALUE VALEUR	PRODUIT
7938	TUGS,SPECIAL VESSELS ETC		70625	N 1179	140745		483176	N 859	35865	REMORQUEURS,BATEAUX SPEC
79382	SPECL PURPOSE VESSLS ETC	N 156	62102	N 37	133006	N 340	469157	N 37	29167	BAT–PHARES,–POMPES,DRAGUES
8	MISC MANUFACTURED GOODS		5928845		6496824		7904715		8164859	ART MANUFACTURES DIVERS
84	CLOTHING AND ACCESSORIES		551547		622096		969333		1044731	VETEMENTS
844	UNDER GARMENTS NOT KNIT		295057		303526		592791		661695	VETEMENT DESSOUS MAT TEX
8441	— MENS SHIRTS		292688		301851		591121		660885	CHEMISES HOMMES MAT TEXT
84412	—— OF SYNTHETIC FIBRES		278719		272100	W 43891	563334	W 44928	620968	CHEMISES HOMMES FIB SYNT
87	PRECISION INSTRUMNTS NES		1568318		1736224		2231328		2278224	INSTRUM,APPAR SCIENT NDA
874	MEASURNG,CONTROLNG INSTR		1288174		1470314		1893965		1853844	INSTRUMENTS DE MESURE
8742	MEASUR,DRAW ETC INST,PTS		389615		458965		582798		653097	INST DESSIN,TRACAGE,PCS
87421	MEASURNG,DRAWNG ETC INST	N 3388415	362909	N 5855053	426188	MN 16654	546282	N 8291979	616733	INSTRUM DESSIN,TRACAGE
8748	ELEC MEAS,CONTRL EQU NES	N 416270	400858	N 675310	414237	N 714286	505581	N 610266	503026	APP ELEC ELECTRO MESURE
87483	OTH ELCTRNC MEAS ETC EQU	N 377867	360201	N 617768	369090	N 658721	448635	N 548822	460175	AUT APP ELECTRO DE MESURE
88	PHOTO EQU,OPTICL GDS ETC		1449072		1543297		1729067		1721137	APP,FOURN PHOTO,OP,MONTR
881	PHOTO APPARAT,EQUIPT NES		331685		346746		425546		522493	APP,EQUIP PHOTO NDA
8811	CAMERAS STILL,FLASH APP		282563		303045		382058		444607	APPAREILS PHOTO,PIECES
88119	PTS NES OF APPAR OF 8811		230825	W 9629	249789	W 7155	347193	W 6730	420499	PIECES POUR 881.1
885	WATCHES AND CLOCKS		971031		1033467		1094861		979025	HORLOGERIE
8851	WATCHES,MOVEMENTS,CASES		592924		661977		748914		667496	MONTRES,MOUVEMENTS,BOITES
88513	WATCH MOVEMENTS ASSEMBLD		437826		504685		568846		509116	MOUVEMENTS TERMINES
8852	CLOCKS,CLOCK,WATCH PARTS		378107		371490		345947		311529	HORLOGES,MOUV,PARTIES
88529	CLOCK,WATCH PARTS NES		340301		322564		295229		262296	FOURNIT D HORLOG NDA
89	MISC MANUFCTRD GOODS NES		2033445		2235128		2647640		2873538	ART MANUFACTURES DIVERS
892	PRINTED MATTER	W 160765	228050	W 156678	247874	W 178114	341750	W 252296	492753	IMPRIMES
8928	PRINTED MATTER NES	W 130624	169985	W 136163	196082	W 149578	266391	W 221218	417811	IMPRIMES NDA
893	ARTICLES OF PLASTIC NES		643639		759831		895208		894843	OUVRAGES EN MAT DIVIS 58
8939	MISC PLASTIC ARTICLES	W 265292	493840	W 300910	606288	W 299002	683588	W 282923	677979	ART DIVERS EN MAT DIV 58
89399	OTHR PLASTC ARTICLES NES	W 238993	471127	W 269802	582502	W 257414	658594	W 244873	655113	AUT OUV MAT DIV 58
894	TOYS,SPORTING GOODS,ETC		348312		342249		471919		575288	VOITURES ENFANTS,JOUETS
8942	TOYS,INDOOR GAMES ETC		264620		253644		373151		461897	JOUETS,JEUX ETC
899	OTHER MANUFACTURED GOODS		372653		411370		454740		435517	AUT ART MANUF DIVERS NDA
9	GOODS NOT CLASSD BY KIND		728534		747052		1602048		783166	ART TRANSACT NON CLASSES
931	*SPECIAL TRANSACTIONS		712211		735319		1583675		755623	TRANS.SPECIALES

5. Special Exports F.O.B. by Commodities according to the S.I.T.C. (Rev. 2) in thousand U.S. Dollars
Exportations Spéciales F.O.B. par Produits d'après la C.T.C.I. (Rév. 2) en milliers de Dollars E.U.

SITC CTCI	COMMODITY	1993 WEIGHT POIDS	1993 VALUE VALEUR	1994 WEIGHT POIDS	1994 VALUE VALEUR	1995 WEIGHT POIDS	1995 VALUE VALEUR	1996 WEIGHT POIDS	1996 VALUE VALEUR	PRODUIT
	ALL COMMODITIES		91744005		121006321		148779565		151047526	TOUS PRODUITS
0	FOOD AND LIVE ANIMALS		8380720		9993123		9923994		10206708	ALIMENTS,ANIMAUX VIVANTS
001	*LIVE ANIMALS FOR FOOD	MN 54469	434165	MN 55404	445157	MN 55501	473248	MN 56319	462213	ANIMAUX VIVANTS
01	MEAT AND PREPARATIONS		661388		910045		1371766		1437757	VIANDES ET PREPARATIONS
011	MEAT FRESH,CHILLD,FROZEN	W 229721	344950	W 356925	630582	W 498535	1022759	W 526519	1083566	VIANDES FRAICHES,REF,CONGE
0114	POULTRY FRESH CHLLD,FRZN	W 107434	185034	W 184486	377412	W 282133	620823	W 326795	690880	VOLAILLES MORTES
014	MEAT PREPD,PRSVD,NES ETC	W 193010	310587	W 154369	268278	W 166693	336632	W 154378	344834	CONSERVES DE VIANDES
0149	OTH PREPARD,PRESRVD MEAT	W 185500	298307	W 145092	251344	W 154409	314703	W 143715	324301	AUTRES PREP DE VIANDES
03	FISH AND PREPARATIONS		1541713		2319422		2852601		2855306	POISSONS ET PREPARATIONS
034	FISH,FRESH,CHILLED,FROZN		424911	W 272937	660904	W 317403	906390	W 350796	866680	POISSON FRAIS, REFRIG,CONG
0341	FISH FRSH,CHLLD,EX FILLT		201349	W 109951	306895	W 118357	447866	W 115783	324867	POISSON FRAIS,REFRIGERE
036	SHELL FISH FRESH,FROZEN	W 239234	758227	W 280820	1002223	W 270294	1024766	W 269530	781830	CRUSTACES,MOLLUSQUES
037	FISH ETC PREPD,PRSVD NES	W 42785	295857	W 62119	523103	W 71899	788140	W 104158	1131189	POIS,CRUST,MOL PREPARES
0371	FISH PREPARD,PRESRVD NES	W 23439	242049	W 33724	428144	W 41407	648660	W 64798	954023	CONSERVES DE POISSONS
04	CEREALS AND PREPARATIONS		1637144		1739444		351200		604266	CEREALES ET PRODUITS
042	RICE	W 1432221	252760	W 1519255	514608	W 46800	16237	W 265162	111638	RIZ
044	MAIZE UNMILLED	MW 11097	1153992	W 8740013	944270	W 112536	13233	W 158656	30269	MAIS NON MOULU
05	VEGETABLES AND FRUIT		2216543		2935815		3399371		3178633	LEGUMES ET FRUITS
054	VEG ETC FRSH,SMPLY PRSVD	W 2653879	1001316	W 3432519	1361670	W 2411748	1373573	W 2043929	1357810	LEGUMES FRAIS,CONG,SECS
0542	LEGUMINOUS VEGETBLES DRY	W 799242	261238	W 1461394	437359	W 1041229	358565	W 547117	248171	LEGUMES A COSSE SECS
0545	OTHER FRESH VEGETABLES	W 733821	307012	W 725484	350450	W 678276	411462	W 807139	457505	AUTRES LEGUMES FRAIS,REF
0546	VEGETABLES SIMPLY PRESVD	W 339887	270508	W 410786	336450	W 450222	407618	W 477621	453663	LEGUMES CONG,CONSER
056	VEGTBLES ETC PRSVD,PREPD	W 556421	633846	W 636585	848677	W 738252	1148486	W 710252	944893	CONSERVES DE LEGUMES
0561	VEG DRIED EXC LEGUMINOUS	W 81704	214898	W 108818	373916	W 130033	508419	W 112964	349411	LEGUM DESSECH,DESHYDRAT
0565	VEGTBLES PRSVD,PREPD NES	W 470100	413860	W 521415	467422	W 602636	632339	W 588609	581591	LEGUMES PREPARES CONSERVE
05659	OTH VEG PRESVD,PREPD NES	W 465727	411163	W 516399	464190	W 592283	623586	W 575492	571319	LEGUM PREPAP,CONSERV NDA
057	FRUIT,NUTS,FRESH,DRIED	W 420347	331614	W 494550	396530	W 493785	444705	W 562728	417572	FRUITS FRAIS OU SECS
058	FRUIT PRESERVED,PREPARED	W 263689	249768	W 319628	328938	W 387633	432607	W 403164	458359	CONSERVES DE FRUITS
06	SUGAR AND PREPS,HONEY		724603		437928		321060		415275	SUCRES ET PRODUITS
061	SUGAR AND HONEY	W 1989557	674162	W 1060300	402665	W 581473	285115	W 764970	374384	SUCRES ET MIEL
0612	REFINED SUGAR ETC	W 1793386	578127	W 918966	311567	W 456525	176958	W 642071	238565	SUCRES RAFFINES
07	COFFEE,TEA,COCOA,SPICES		511112		490999		511942		547297	CAFE,THE,CACAO,EPICES
074	TEA AND MATE	W 201435	355678	W 179671	294359	W 166581	274763	W 169678	282540	THE ET MATE
0741	TEA	W 201435	355678	W 179667	294350	W 166572	274748	W 169670	282500	THE
081	*FEEDING STUFF FOR ANIML	W 3590457	455841	W 2948266	466439	W 2046172	351015	W 2266987	365461	NOURRITURE POUR ANIMAUX
0813	OILCAKE AND OTH RESIDUES	W 2575245	311348	W 1945072	329189	W 1243281	213862	W 1112549	159285	TOURTEAUX
1	BEVERAGES AND TOBACCO		901456		1001665		1369146		1341935	BOISSONS ET TABACS
12	TOBACCO AND MANUFACTURES		640352		686359		999011		975690	TABACS BRUTS FABRIQUES
122	TOBACCO,MANUFACTURED		505511		592543		899217		864724	TABACS FABRIQUES
1222	CIGARETTES		484955		562181	W 66211	864153	MN 58816441	832530	CIGARETTES
2	CRUDE MATERLS,EXCL FUELS		3041217		4093429		4347860		4019613	MAT BRUTES NON COMESTIBLES
22	OIL SEEDS,OLEAGINOUS FRT		434348		666016		522277		478379	GRAINES,FRUITS OLEAGINEUX
222	SEEDS FOR'SOFT'FIXED OIL	W 999710	407368	W 1486288	635318	W 908817	494270	W 690196	452366	GRAINES HUILES FIXES
24	CORK AND WOOD		284890		318802		481148		466026	LIEGE ET BOIS
26	TEXTILE FIBRES AND WASTE		813126		1076473		737712		694690	FIBRES TEXTILES
261	SILK	W 17801	244704	W 24774	404547	W 18404	352891	W 18069	312500	SOIE
268	WOOL(EXC TOPS),ANML HAIR	W 19720	293402	W 24946	447825	W 19525	267146	W 22309	314122	LAINES ET POILS
27	CRUDE FERTLZR,MINRLS NES		600516		696696		979770		953404	ENGRAIS MINERAUX BRUTS
278	OTHER CRUDE MINERALS	MW 9144	451757	MW 9989	529922	MW 11306	798046	MW 10223	749239	AUTRES MINERAUX BRUTS
2782	REFRACTORY MINERALS NES	W 4617434	242606	W 4885564	296585	W 5521107	483556	W 4389486	410245	ARGILE MINERAUX REFRACTAIRES
29	CRUDE ANIMAL,VEG MAT NES		744628		1117385		1339680		1236557	MATIERES BRUTES ANIM,VEGET
291	CRUDE ANIMAL MTRIALS NES	W 184558	354419	W 175540	520817	W 170994	690566	W 174921	662668	MATIERES BRUTES ANIMALES
2919	OTH ANIMAL MATERIALS NES	W 78544	332382	W 90851	502712	W 90771	669355	W 86589	637232	MAT ORIGINE ANIMALE NDA
292	CRUDE VEG MATERIALS NES	W 339914	390209	W 392385	596568	W 379539	649114	W 380979	573889	MAT BRUTES VEGETALES NDA
2924	VEG USED IN PHARMACY ETC	W 126028	235760	W 155434	410050	W 142532	415416	W 165023	327847	PLANTES MEDICINALES
3	MINERAL FUELS ETC		4112012		4072206		5335222		5937543	COMBUSTIBLES MINERAUX LUB
32	COAL,COKE AND BRIQUETTES		874439		1053989		1694537		1720877	HOUILLES,COKES,BRIQUETTES
322	COAL,LIGNITE AND PEAT	MW 19814	702238	MW 24302	770982	MW 28618	1010801	MW 29001	1109243	HOUILLES,LIGNITES,TOURBE
3222	OTH COAL,NOT AGGLOMERATD	MW 17899	614504	MW 22437	691418	MW 26087	904357	MW 27268	1034327	AUTRES HOUILLES
323	BRIQUETS,COKE,SEMI-COKE	W 2613324	172201	W 4049898	283007	W 8872356	683736	W 7688114	611635	BRIQUETTES
3232	COKE,SEMI-COKE,RTRT CRBN	W 2610787	171808	W 4048838	282753	W 8871959	683620	W 7687363	611444	COKES ET SEMI-COKES
33	PETROLEUM AND PRODUCTS		3226098		2799809		3243647		3920451	PETROLE ET DERIVES
333	CRUDE PETROLEUM	MW 19434	2408801	MW 18552	2000305	MW 18827	2236367	MW 20403	2789286	HUILES BRUTES DE PETROLE
334	PETROLEUM PRODUCTS,REFIN	W 3719174	632346	W 3794744	624411	W 4151740	795432	W 4179271	874815	PRODUITS RAFFINES
4	ANIMAL,VEGETABLE OIL,FAT		205113		495301		453316		375917	HUILES,GRAISSES ANIM,VEG
42	FIXED VEGETABLE OIL,FAT		196488		485132		438879		351105	HUILES VEGETALES FIXES
5	CHEMCLS,RELATED PROD NES		4576245		6176384		8945515		8771268	PRODUITS CHIMIQUES
51	ORGANIC CHEMICALS		1104171		1600951		2284795		2262186	PROD CHIMIQ ORGANIQUES
513	CARBOXYLIC ACIDS ETC	W 231817	255860	W 309396	332296	W 322580	478187	W 239241	367679	ACIDES CARBOXYLIQUES
514	NITROGEN-FNCTN COMPOUNDS	W 88471	239632	W 136040	389697	W 162690	539379	W 157236	543999	COMPOSES FONCT AZOTEES
515	ORG-INORG COMPOUNDS ETC	W 79113	274798	W 98671	363754	W 109974	496629	W 151289	645318	COMPOSES ORGANO-MINERAUX
52	INORGANIC CHEMICALS		1140580		1349448		2225033		2106167	PROD CHIM INORGANIQUES
522	INORG ELEMNTS,OXIDES,ETC	W 923262	535774	W 1164495	689635	W 1545080	1067267		1021427	ELEMENTS INORGANIQUES
5221	CHEMICAL ELEMENTS	W 247452	213422	W 306322	266246	W 408878	409135		470290	ELEMENTS CHIMIQUES
523	OTHR INORG CHEMICALS ETC	W 1945678	424800	W 2252465	566913	W 2853949	917597		842652	AUT PRODUITS CHIMIQUES INORG
53	DYES,TANNING,COLOUR PROD		371428		537191		726515		726459	PROD TEINTURE,COLORANTS
531	SYNT DYE,NAT INDGO,LAKES	W 75201	245429	W 96451	351174	W 123106	468844	W 125522	480181	MAT COLOR ORGAN,LAQUES
5311	SYNTHC ORGNIC DYESTUFFS	W 74135	241679	W 94464	342495	W 121274	457656	W 124564	473533	MAT COLOR ORGAN SYNTHET
541	*MEDICINAL,PHARM PRODUCT		905057	MK 127362	1185298	MK 146642	1581968	MK 136158	1516115	PROD MEDICINAUX PHARMACEUT
5413	ANTIBIOTICS IN BULK	MK 12800	224541	MK 17216	352936	MK 19987	513579	MK 17301	479579	ANTIBIOTIQUES NDA
55	PERFUME,CLEANING ETC PRD		283036		292378		384465		368362	PROD POUR PARFUM,TOILETTE
58	PLASTIC MATERIALS ETC		240167		449157		732364		554977	MAT PLAST ARTIFICIELLES
583	POLYMERIZATION ETC PRODS	W 174070	171908	W 318780	322964	W 337040	466009	W 335018	397131	PROD POLYMERISATION
59	CHEMICAL MATERIALS NES		355383		542051		698439		826839	MAT PROD CHIMIQUES NDA
598	MISCEL CHEM PRODUCTS NES		230248	W 652646	323969		381372	W 797760	484965	PROD DIV INDUST CHIM NDA
6	BASIC MANUFACTURES		16776684		23780289		32831542		29209618	ART MANUFACTURES
61	LEATHER,DRESSED FUR,ETC		454220		823676		926681		830986	CUIRS,PELLETERIES
612	LEATHER ETC MANUFACTURES		244186	W 62396	445139	W 74126	483160	W 69172	462415	OUVRAGES EN CUIRS NDA
62	RUBBER MANUFACTURES NES		316056		422360		693892		752986	CAOUTCHOUC MANUFACTURE
625	RUBBER TYRES, TUBES ETC		199449		258730	MN 110726	484657	MN 118378	524483	PNEUS CAOUTCHOUC VULCANISE
63	WOOD,CORK MANUFACTRS NES		545679		705402		927238		940102	OUVRAGES LIEGE ET BOIS
635	WOOD MANUFACTURES NES		491976	W 519119	650298	W 611875	849005		834373	ART MANUF EN BOIS NDA
64	PAPER,PAPERBOARD AND MFR		502098		611406		916469		796325	PAPIERS,CARTONS & OUVRAGES
642	PAPER,ETC,PRECUT,ARTS OF	W 363648	363528	W 499720	444829	W 540506	542990	W 595343	613656	PAP,CARTONS DECOUPES
65	TEXTILE YARN,FABRICS,ETC		8807334		11942522		14059236		12317578	FILS,TISSUS,ARTICLES TEXTILE
651	TEXTILE YARN	W 465341	1335390	W 525162	1778054	W 553191	2111404	W 504106	1935188	FILS TEXTILES
6513	COTTON YARN	W 198787	416373	W 194927	514410	W 179895	576313	W 142044	458520	FILS DE COTON
652	COTTON FABRICS,WOVEN		2248452		2711262	L 3772663	3457442	L 3063018	2957360	TISSUS DE COTON
6521	GREY WOVEN COTTON FABRIC	L 1502238	672460	L 1285053	745502	L 1288748	860460	L 1161670	789850	TISSUS COT ECRUS NON MERCER
65214	GREY WOVEN COTTON NES	L 1218531	553871	L 1012279	605670	L 975296	676149	L 889585	632064	AUT TISSUS 85% COTON ECRUS
6522	WOVEN COTTON BLEACHD,ETC		1575992		1965760	L 2483915	2596982	L 1901348	2167510	TISSUS COTON BLANCHIS ETC

5. Special Exports F.O.B. by Commodities according to the S.I.T.C. (Rev. 2) in thousand U.S. Dollars
Exportations Spéciales F.O.B. par Produits d'après la C.T.C.I. (Rév. 2) en milliers de Dollars E.U.

SITC CTCI	COMMODITY	1993		1994		1995		1996		PRODUIT
		WEIGHT POIDS	VALUE VALEUR	WEIGHT POIDS	VALUE VALEUR	WEIGHT POIDS	VALUE VALEUR	WEIGHT POIDS	VALUE VALEUR	
65224	BLCHED COTTON FABRIC NES		1332560		1636016	L 2012835	2164303	L 1494366	1732173	AUT TIS PLUS 85% COT BLANCHI
653	WOVN MAN-MADE FIB FABRIC		1291993		2148477	L 3516165	2474047	L 3232562	2114243	TISSUS FIBRES SYNTH,ARTIF
6531	CONT SYNT WEAVES NONPILE	L 96886	62816	L 284952	399680	L 278752	287154	L 391065	299955	TISSUS FIBRES SYNTH CONTINUE
65315	CONT SYN TXTL FABRIC NES	L 67086	46227	L 247240	376315	L 240097	250135	L 368633	281297	TIS PLUS 85% TEXT SYNT CONT
6534	DISC SYN BLEND FABRC NES	L 1491939	691340	L 1596696	897357	L 1779785	1107346	L 1814948	1113986	TISSUS FIBRES SYNTH DISCONT
65341	DISC SYN FIB-COTTN FABRC	L 1169945	536926	L 1206575	659882	L 1283234	778565	L 1320867	797713	TISSUS FIB SYNT DIS MEL COTO
6536	DISC REGN TXTL FABRC NES	L 836043	383937	L 1104495	628525	L 1086077	716340	L 675308	377942	TISSUS 85% TEXT ART DISC
654	OTH WOVEN TEXTILE FABRIC		734220		1140961		1141627		826019	TISSUS AUT COTON SYNT,ARTIF
6541	SILK FABRICS WOVEN	L 157739	408306	L 194719	676034	L 187405	656462	L 145529	431843	TISSUS DE SOIE
655	KNITTED,ETC FABRICS	W 187850	543660	W 211888	745158	W 231776	907312	W 214192	785614	ETOF BONNETERIE PIECES ETC
6552	OTHER KNIT ETC FAB NONEL	W 187850	543660	W 211888	745158	W 231776	907312	W 214192	785614	ETOF BON NON ELAS NON SYNT
657	SPECIAL TXTL FABRC,PRODS		183808	W 121483	288458	W 132924	463022	W 131296	361730	TISSUS SPECIAUX
658	TEXTILE ARTICLES NES		1741523		2186445		2560621		2466850	ART FACONNES MAT TEXTILES
6584	LINENS ETC	MN 2052626	1126613	MN 2094066	1398253	MN 2426798	1596904	MN 2176058	1482751	LINGE DE MAISON
65841	BED LINEN OF COTTON	MN 159078	325397	MN 161576	416025	MN 156211	466602	MN 120187	383136	LINGE DE LIT DE COTON
65845	OTHER LINEN OF COTTON	MN 1380732	383046	MN 1384488	452444	MN 1702584	553083	MN 1606258	555454	LINGE DE TOILETTE COTON
659	FLOOR COVERINGS,ETC		631237		762267		722448		647668	COUVRE-PARQUETS,TAPIS ETC
6592	CARPETS ETC KNOTTED	A 11370	445641	A 14439	504192	A 11207	427546	A 6137	306668	TAPIS POINTS NOUES,ENROULES
65921	— OF WOOL OR FINE HAIR	A 8622	322159	A 11269	363447	A 7997	293915	A 4552	212648	TAP NOUES,ENROULES LAINE
66	NONMETAL MINERAL MFS NES		1559774		2523169		3425028		3297029	ART MIN NON METALLIQUES
661	LIME,CEMENT,BLDG PRODS	W 3780777	369690	W 5702371	533321	MW 9802	883246	MW 13591	1105435	CHAUX,CIMENTS MAT CONSTR
6613	BUILDING STONE ETC WORKD	W 1191813	263647	W 1044658	362746	W 1446643	568126	W 1632429	634505	PIERRES A BATIR
66132	BUILDING STONE WORKED	W 1028798	247083	W 869182	341153	W 1222113	533009	W 1400147	596893	OUVR EN PIERRES DE TAILLE
666	POTTERY		562803	W 780917	981656	W 850988	1029015	W 918593	1013430	POTERIE
6664	PORCELN,CHINA HOUSE WARE		287072	W 497784	488830	W 519979	505951	W 565757	496195	VAISSELLE,ARTS MEN PORC
6666	CERAMIC ORNAMENTS ETC		256668	W 249615	468115	W 277356	482325	W 292887	466363	OBJETS PORCELAINE,CERAM
667	PEARL,PREC-,SEMI-P STONE		149669		385727		515061		241883	PERLES, PIERRES GEMMES
67	IRON AND STEEL		1202810		1867129		5467472		4067923	FER ET ACIER
671	PIG IRON ETC	W 1214208	496865	W 2479859	758112	W 6850331	1770843	W 4621266	1223838	FONTE,SPIEGEL,POUDRES
6712	PIG IRN,SPIEGELEISEN ETC	W 336436	51752	W 1541334	215994	W 5330778	796957	W 3553051	512146	FONTES BRUTES
6716	FERRO-ALLOYS	W 873881	442524	W 922717	536174	W 1475438	961748	W 1031280	699403	FERRO-ALLIAGES
67169	OTHER FERRO-ALLOYS	W 439308	238048	W 520641	340860	W 906394	661728	W 604754	446461	AUTRES FERRO-ALLIAGES
672	IRON,STEEL PRIMARY FORMS	W 250706	63434	W 836019	197110	W 6353041	1699605	W 3630883	920001	LINGOTS FER,ACIER
6725	IRN,STL BLOOMS,SLABS,ETC	W 108622	24443	W 657122	145661	W 4432879	1071465	W 2698954	636553	BLOOMS,BILLETTES FER ACIER
67251	IRN,SMPLE STL BLOOMS,ETC	W 102704	21999	W 656178	143526	W 4411460	1037766	W 2692936	622740	BLOOMS ETC NON ACIER FIN
6727	IRN,STL COIL FR REROLLNG	W 114400	32103	W 137796	41639	W 1742933	586643	W 860249	267099	EBAUCHES POUR TOLES FER
67271	IRON,SIMPLE STEEL COILS	W 113306	31576	W 136752	39010	W 1710162	568585	W 853252	261773	EBAUCHES NON EN ACIER
674	IRN,STL UNIV,PLATE,SHEET		84655	W 289338	115537	W 2051506	768730	W 1312762	474464	LARGES PLATS,TOLES
678	IRON,STL TUBES,PIPES,ETC	W 255561	189789	W 350152	253685	W 589891	422897	W 744445	544747	TUBES,TUYAUX EN FONTE,FER
68	NON-FERROUS METALS		813226		1430632		1929466		1663836	METAUX NON FERREUX
684	ALUMINIUM	W 97998	125686	W 170708	242108	W 256744	453641	W 169170	288228	ALUMINIUM
69	METAL MANUFACTURES NES		2575486		3453994		4486060		4542851	ART MANUFACT EN METAL NDA
695	TOOLS		495602	W 339831	635415	W 389995	801793	W 321064	752114	OUTILS A MAIN
6953	OTHER HAND TOOLS		363127	W 254210	434700	W 288223	546286	W 249784	528855	AUTRES OUTILS A MAIN
697	BASE MTL HOUSEHOLD EQUIP		412890		587150		743162		826517	ART MENAGE MET COMMUNS
6974	BASE MTL DMSTC ARTIC NES	W 126076	280414	W 171256	428201	W 212727	555492	W 228638	592570	ARTICLES NDA FONTE,FER,ETC
69741	— OF IRON OR STEEL	W 115941	242455	W 156109	367142	W 194008	477577	W 212140	515676	ART NDA EN FONTE,FER
699	BASE METAL MFRS NES		839638	W 777834	1162278	W 938452	1446218	W 934690	1454870	ART MANUFACTURES MET NDA
6991	LOCKSMITHS WARES,ETC		395297	W 223654	468398	W 264266	563097	W 268688	569437	ARTICLES DE SERRURERIE
69911	LOCKS,KEYS AND PARTS		284364	W 116596	311774	W 131003	355549	W 114937	333040	SERRURES,VERROUS,CADENAS
7	MACHINES,TRANSPORT EQUIP		15220414		21830429		31296804		35239176	MACHINES MATERIEL TRANSPORT
71	POWER GENERATING EQUIPMT		889427		980904		1438879		1543238	MACHINES GENERATRICES
716	ROTATING ELECTRIC PLANT		712892		778361		1080420		1156482	APP ELECTR ROTATIFS,PIECES
7162	AC MTRS,GENRTRS,GEN SETS	MN 887411	460217	MN 1297431	673246	MN 1549398	888213	MN 1472263	953034	MOTEURS ELECTRIQUES
71621	AC MTRS,INC UNIVRSL MTRS	MN 887347	437263	MN 1297362	627101	MN 1549311	845567	MN 1472183	926766	MOT ELEC NON COUR CONTINU
72	MACHS FOR SPCL INDUSTRYS		763999		820540		1140466		1169095	MAC SPECIALES POUR INDUST
724	TEXTILE,LEATHER MACHNRY		307210		304131		404440		389928	MACH POUR INDUSTRIE TEXTILE
73	METALWORKING MACHINERY		286599		321826		417235		409989	MACH TRAVAIL DES METAUX
74	GENRL INDUSTRL MACHY NES		977896		1305408		1748930		2093643	MACH APP INDUSTRIE
749	NONELEC MACH PTS,ACC NES		419071		537484		770444		907830	PIECES MACH NON ELEC NDA
75	OFFICE MACHNES,ADP EQUIP		1646658		2664410		4802717		6716757	MACH BUREAU TRAIT AUTOM
751	OFFICE MACHINES	MN 190144	318197	MN 259244	553651		850747	MN 320883	1117132	MACH,APPAREILS DE BUREAU
7518	OFFICE MACHINES NES	MN 34397	87116	MN 41333	236764	MN 44930	472912	MN 48485	633019	MACH,APP DE BUREAU NDA
75182	PHOTO,THERMOCOPY APPARAT	N 135603	54230	N 358970	163556	N 831234	392289	N 945621	500867	APPAREILS DE PHOTOCOPIE
752	AUTOMTIC DATA PROC EQUIP	MN 9471	558646	MN 26225	987379	MN 66073	2301505	MN 114857	3690397	MACH TRAIT INFORMATION
7524	DIGITL CENTRL STOR UNITS	N 1015312	29439	N 5436367	217349	MN 20554	821961	MN 23619	1113778	UNITES MEMOIRE CENTRALES
7525	ADP PERIPHERAL UNITS	N 7755204	470510	MN 16512	620187	MN 36304	1060963	MN 87071	1984923	UNITES PERIPHERIQUES
759	OFFICE,ADP MCH PTS,ACCES		769816	W 68030	1123379	W 112547	1650466		1909227	PIECES DU 751 ET 752
7599	ACCTG,ETC,ADP MCH PTS,AC		734533	W 60696	1063455	W 95835	1518577	MN 164623	1679195	PIECES DU 751 ET 752
76	TELECOMM,SOUND EQUIPMENT		4521687		6743785		8408599		9004087	EQUIPMENT DE TELECOM
761	TELEVISION RECEIVERS	MN 11309	761348	MN 10788	711449	MN 11513	807884	MN 10323	794335	RECEPTEURS DE TELEVISION
7611	COLOUR TV RECEIVERS	N 4353476	535811	N 4422106	514028	N 5660404	601804	N 5371004	622067	RECEPTEURS COULEUR
762	RADIO BROADCAST RECEIVRS	MN 200371	1610028	MN 254134	2305340	MN 275499	2555296	MN 270306	2396693	RECEPTEURS RADIODIFFUSION
7622	PORTABLE RADIO RECEIVERS	MN 62963	299805	MN 84370	351971	MN 102187	410493	MN 112915	479661	RECEPT PORTATIFS RADIO
7628	OTHER RADIO RECEIVERS	MN 126176	1157968	MN 154134	1724853	MN 157393	1829829	MN 138928	1557142	AUTRES RECEPT RADIO
763	SOUND RECORDRS,PHONOGRPH	MN 37774	395229	MN 56733	790214	MN 63259	1001407	MN 61040	1125427	PHONO,APP ENREGISTREMENT
7638	OTHR SOUND APPARATUS ETC	MN 37547	390709	MN 56549	787725	MN 62841	997443	MN 60477	1119495	AUT APP D'ENREGIS,REPROD
76388	DICTATING MACHINES ETC	MN 37048	355174	MN 54237	633808	MN 59133	783266	MN 55302	734838	MACHINES A DICTER
764	TELECOM EQPT,PTS,ACC NES		1755082		2936782		4044012		4687632	EQUIP TELECOM,PIECES
7641	LINE TELEPHONE,ETC EQUIP	MN 217450	474980	MN 321074	962394	MN 396293	1230426	MN 368489	1259062	APP TELEPHON PAR FIL
7642	MICROPH,LOUDSPKR,AMPLIFR	MN 531965	164588	MN 855228	386283	MN 898271	509116	MN 851009	574051	MICRO,HAUT-PARLEUR,AMPLI
7643	TV,RADIO TRANSMITTRS ETC		126113	N 5375193	159745	N 6398771	260602	N 6502083	489484	APP EMET TELE RADIO
7649	PTS NES OF EQUIPMT OF 76		919053	W 76846	1307131		1828509		2199101	PIECES DE LA DIV 76
76493	TELECOMM EQUIPMT PTS NES		505746	W 57106	593740	W 57692	812061	MN 78442	986598	PIECES 761,762,764.3,8
76499	PARTS ETC OF SOUND EQUIP		333812	W 55	622127		858531	MN 311818	951180	PIECES NDA POUR 763
77	ELECTRIC MACHNRY NES ETC		4433961		6436695		9555660		10335870	MACH APP ELECT NDA
771	ELECTRIC POWER MACHY NES		681697		1087040		1545276		1648436	MACH PROD,TRANS ELECTR
7711	TRANSFORMERS,ELECTRICAL	MN 1272634	276874	MN 1537952	402328	MN 2582754	633433	MN 2754724	590227	TRANSFO ELECTRIQUES
77118	OTHER ELEC TRANSFORMERS	MN 1272565	240903	MN 1536012	370225	MN 2581028	586260	MN 2753834	541931	AUTRES TRANSFO ELECTRIQ
7712	OTH ELEC POWER MACHY NES		404823		684712		911844		1058209	AUT APP PROD TRANSF ELEC
77121	STATIC CONVERTERS ETC	MN 86180	226976	MN 117650	379220	MN 152937	518111	MN 177631	629629	CONVERTISSEURS STATIQUES
772	SWITCHGEAR ETC,PARTS NES		725232	W 179814	1053068	W 195231	1630104		1500066	APP COUPURE,SECT ETC
7721	SWITCHGEAR ETC		429674	W 136378	584473	W 156372	920739	MN 6014286	879102	APP COUPURE,SECTIONMNT
7722	PRINTED CIRCUITS,PTS NES		224577	W 33760	316073	W 27615	415200	MN 941564	504784	CIRCUITS ET PIECES
773	ELECTR DISTRIBUTNG EQUIP	W 144273	282341	W 188543	390907	W 229300	545744	W 256573	745360	EQUIPMT DISTRIBUTION ELECT
7731	INSULATED WIRE,CABLE ETC	W 122557	259038	W 162664	361308	W 198425	509587	W 229585	700061	FILS,CABLES ISOLES ELECT
775	HOUSEHOLD TYPE EQUIP NES		1274314		1566018		2108417		2464077	MACH,APP USAGE DOMESTQUE
7757	DOMESTIC ELECTRC EQU NES		658706		779944		1045461		1175067	APP ELECTR DOMEST NDA
77572	DOM ELEC ROOM FANS ETC	MN 41393	458725	MN 56522	510623	MN 90446	717007	MN 121884	794176	HOTTES ASPIRANTES,VENTIL
7758	ELECTRO-THERMIC APPL NES		551486		683266		883786		1060386	APP ELECTROTHERMIQ NDA
77586	ELECTROTHERM DOM APP NES	MN 42738	258860	MN 57691	336345	MN 73447	464622	MN 88425	617685	APP ELECTRO THERMIQUES

5. Special Exports F.O.B. by Commodities according to the S.I.T.C. (Rev. 2) in thousand U.S. Dollars
Exportations Spéciales F.O.B. par Produits d'après la C.T.C.I. (Rév. 2) en milliers de Dollars E.U.

SITC CTCI	COMMODITY	1993 WEIGHT POIDS	1993 VALUE VALEUR	1994 WEIGHT POIDS	1994 VALUE VALEUR	1995 WEIGHT POIDS	1995 VALUE VALEUR	1996 WEIGHT POIDS	1996 VALUE VALEUR	PRODUIT
776	TRANSISTORS,VALVES,ETC		359850		614374		1294618		1476900	LAMPES,TUBES,VALVES
7764	ELECTRONIC MICROCIRCUITS	MN 204497	54189	MN 441543	141273	MN 903602	407216	MN 1282054	539581	MICROSTRUCTURES ELECTRON
778	ELECTRICAL MACHINERY NES		1099652		1700936		2391047		2450388	AUTRES MACH ELECT NDA
7781	BATTERIES,ACCUMULATORS		300323		348908		452593		579959	PILES ET ACCUMULATEURS
7788	OTH ELEC MACHY,EQUIP NES		501656		902592		1152930		1117508	AUT MACH APP ELEC NDA
78	ROAD VEHICLES		1240870		1790694		2699370		2568494	VEHICULES ROUTIERS
785	CYCLES,ETC MOTRZD OR NOT		596153		740534		880065		882084	MOTOCYCLES SCOOTERS
7852	CYCLES, ETC NON-MOTOR	MN 10539	427330	MN 13578	507082	MN 12823	538772	MN 12239	465274	VELOCIPEDES SANS MOTEUR
786	TRAILERS,NONMOTR VEH,NES		324690		692192		1286763		1156006	REMORQUES,CADRES,CONTAIN
7861	TRAILERS,TRANSP CONTAINR	N 100239	277744	N 222062	631892	N 409311	1211435	N 368208	1079647	REMORQUES TOUS VEHICULES
78613	CONTAINERS INC ROAD-RAIL	N 88707	265211	N 217797	615661	N 406170	1195832	N 353120	1062390	CADRES ET CONTAINERS
79	OTHR TRANSPORT EQUIPMENT		459318		766167		1084948		1398003	AUTRE MATERIEL TRANSPORT
793	SHIPS AND BOATS ETC		241560		552191		878890	N 84930	1153988	NAVIRES BATEAUX,ETC
7932	SHIPS AND BOATS NES	N 58351	188071	N 60699	401521	N 8146	616898	N 16811	978869	NAVIRES ET BATEAUX
79323	OTHER CARGO VESSELS	N 343	147013	N 483	329940	N 583	585185	N 534	890251	AUT BATEAUX TRANS MARCH
8	MISC MANUFACTURED GOODS		38134774		49199409		53726145		55723545	ART MANUFACTURES DIVERS
812	*PLUMBG,HEATNG,LGHTNG EQ		574390		820142		1000955		1012803	APPAR SANITAIRES CHAUFFAGE
8124	LIGHTING EQUIPMENT NES		566378		808802		983981		999138	APPAREILS ECLAIRAGE ETC
81242	LAMPS,FITTINGS BASE METL		397567	W 234488	601577	W 316864	733128	W 357665	752672	APPAREILS D'ECLAIRAGE
821	*FURNITURE,PARTS THEREOF		1082512		1495573		1764656		1892198	MEUBLES ET PIECES
8212	MED FURN,STUFFD FURNSHGS		479673		651724		658988		596924	MOB MEDICO-CHIRUR,PIECES
82122	MATTRESSES ETC		476714		649249	W 90691	654426		591806	SOMMIERS,ARTICLES DE LITERIE
8219	FURNITURE AND PARTS NES		368001		543669		700373		850418	AUTRES MEUBLES ET PIECES
82192	WOOD FURNITURE NES	MN 10895	248760	MN 16659	372021	MN 20457	439421	MN 25553	515352	MEUBLES NDA EN BOIS
831	*TRAVEL GOODS,HANDBAGS		1726966		2364895		2869573		2725353	ARTICLES DE VOYAGE ETC
83101	HANDBAGS NES	MN 241750	310024	MN 293948	419331	MN 290249	512941	MN 270642	402590	SACS A MAIN
83102	TRAVEL GDS,TOILET-CASES	MN 837267	1083746	MN 1077288	1563665	MN 1309413	1886182	MN 1390247	1871174	ARTICLES DE VOYAGE
83109	OTHER TRAVEL BAGS,CASES		333196		381899		470450		451589	AUT CONTENANTS SIMILAIRES
84	CLOTHING AND ACCESSORIES		18479112		23793477		24123367		25100918	VETEMENTS
842	MENS OUTERWEAR NOT KNIT	MN 845788	3857613	MN 1095498	5464734	MN 1087932	5168099	MN 1118004	5476419	VET DESSUS POUR HOMMES
8423	— TROUSERS,BREECHES ETC	MN 477547	1277123	MN 609473	1866504	MN 634053	1899448	MN 625607	1851218	PANTALONS HOMMES MAT TEX
8424	— JACKETS,BLAZERS ETC	MN 145193	941787	MN 204405	1376430	MN 166079	1147676	MN 142833	1067439	VESTES HOMMES MAT TEXTIL
8429	— OTHER OUTER GARMENTS	MN 193053	1252821	MN 242811	1751252	MN 242197	1631853	MN 294964	2025041	AUT VET DES HOM MAT TEX
843	WOMENS OUTERWEAR NONKNIT		5252478		6613213	MN 1622059	6306137	MN 1639646	6269416	VET DESSUS FEMMES MAT TEX
8431	— COATS AND JACKETS	MN 170862	1093034	MN 187153	1196056	MN 185377	1286947	MN 199700	1395516	MANT,VEST FEM MAT TEXTIL
8433	— DRESSES	MN 45254	263701	MN 61622	373692	MN 71171	375101	MN 73473	393101	ROBES EN MAT-TEXTILES
8434	— SKIRTS	MN 78348	284541	MN 88540	351154	MN 116011	436445	MN 113512	439188	JUPES EN MAT TEXTILES
8435	— BLOUSES	MN 247160	1107475	MN 242670	1058292	MN 222686	980146	MN 214934	936047	BLOUSES FEM MAT TEXTILES
8439	— OTHER OUTER GARMENTS		2436216		3479247	MN 1020798	3121991	MN 1033544	3037766	AUT VET DES FEM MAT TEXT
844	UNDER GARMENTS NOT KNIT		2019284		2357228	MN 773917	2133849	MN 725698	2074771	VETEMENT DESSOUS MAT TEX
8441	— MENS SHIRTS		1455497		1638560	MN 491736	1458923	MN 456486	1386321	CHEMISES HOMMES MAT TEXT
84411	—— OF COTTON	MN 182866	464914	MN 225716	665480	MN 218537	677028	MN 198132	639770	CHEMISES HOMMES DE COTON
84412	—— OF SYNTHETIC FIBRES		990583		973080	MN 273199	781895	MN 258354	746551	CHEMISES HOMMES FIB SYNT
8443	— WOMENS	MN 98675	299506	MN 108289	409903	MN 100213	348153	MN 99444	354989	VET DESSOUS FEM MAT TEXT
845	OUTERWEAR KNIT NONELASTC		3123163		3908284	MN 1316941	3948723	MN 1382633	4252064	VET DESSOUS,ACCES BONNET
8451	— JERSEYS,PULLOVERS ETC	MN 465175	1721860	MN 542703	2099665	MN 637678	2366349	MN 729816	2535559	CHANDAILS,PULL-OVERS ETC
8459	— OTHER,CLTHG ACCESRYS		1127571		1449891	MN 585948	1332360	MN 560170	1466256	AUT VET DESSUS DE BONNE
846	UNDER GARMENTS KNITTED	MN 2775869	1810439	MN 2938698	2332318	MN 3270058	2913451	MN 3220308	3290193	SOUS VETS DE BONNETERIE
8462	— OF COTTON NON ELASTIC	MN 2441325	1550698	MN 2523266	2014657	MN 2804635	2513897	MN 2733839	2813029	SOUS-VET BONNET COTON
84629	—— OTHER	MN 2441325	1550698	MN 2508633	1980475	MN 2789255	2476204	MN 2733839	2813029	AUT SOUS-VET BONNET COTON
847	TEXTILE CLTHNG ACCES NES		510741		664851		812232		834148	ACCES VET MAT TEXT NDA
8471	— NOT KNITTED		291112		380484		446436		439882	ACCES VET MAT TEX NON BON
848	HEADGEAR,NONTXTL CLOTHNG		1905394		2452848		2840877		2903907	VET ACCES MAT AUT QUE TEX
8481	LEATHER CLOTHES,ACCESSOR		1156086		1674655		1950150	MN 570197	1947516	VET ACCES MAT CUIR ARTIF
8483	FUR ETC,CLOTHES,PRODUCTS		303979	W 8915	230195	W 11363	244777	W 10616	262144	VETEMENTS DE FOURRURE
84831	ARTICLES OF FURSKIN,NES		300042	W 7484	223017	W 8528	224376	W 9701	257054	PELLETERIES OUVREES NDA
851	*FOOTWEAR	MP 2061460	5053850	MP 2368580	5706857	MP 2540059	6273600	MN 2634211	6704884	CHAUSSURES
85101	FOOTWEAR RUBBER,PLASTIC	MP 811965	1561735	MP 977685	1851681	MP 1148324	2214588	MN 1281532	2476309	CHAUS SEMELLES CAOUTCH
85102	FOOTWEAR LEATHER	MP 1124716	3267630	MP 1247913	3637336	MP 1238209	3812002	MN 1179380	3969873	CHAUS SEMELLES EN CUIR
87	PRECISION INSTRUMNTS NES		482054		635056		914803		1063332	INSTRUM,APPAR SCIENT NDA
88	PHOTO EQU,OPTICL GDS ETC		1979727		2455393		2929839		3055882	APP,FOURN PHOTO,OP,MONTR
881	PHOTO APPARAT,EQUIPT NES		402066		486491		670297		810758	APP,EQUIP PHOTO NDA
8811	CAMERAS STILL,FLASH APP		392579		474777		654847		789694	APPAREILS PHOTO,PIECES
88111	STILL CAMERAS	MN 38819	343226	MN 43209	398855	MN 61504	571777	MN 61804	695793	APPAREILS PHOTOGRAPHIQ
885	WATCHES AND CLOCKS		1414254		1741801		1904453		1822586	HORLOGERIE
8851	WATCHES,MOVEMENTS,CASES		1095502		1328797		1408898		1292595	MONTRES,MOUVEMENTS,BOITES
88511	WATCHES		782960		957186		1038606		974037	MONTRES POCHE,BRACELET
8852	CLOCKS,CLOCK,WATCH PARTS		318753		413004		495555		529991	HORLOGES,MOUV,PARTIES
89	MISC MANUFCTRD GOODS NES		8756162		11928016		13849350		14168175	ART MANUFACTURES DIVERS
893	ARTICLES OF PLASTIC NES		1429539		2022315		2565640		2791077	OUVRAGES EN MAT DIVIS 58
8931	PLSTC PACKG CONTNRS,LIDS	W 270490	300480	W 358551	416539	W 421722	527504	W 512435	609596	ART TRANSP EMBALLAGE ETC
8939	MISC PLASTIC ARTICLES	W 744908	1122804	W 998333	1593416	W 1198375	2024219	W 1409690	2164207	ART DIVERS EN MAT DIV 58
89399	OTHR PLASTC ARTICLES NES	W 692889	1055167	W 929083	1500081	W 1117480	1912721	W 1321094	2042743	AUT OUV MAT DIV 58
894	TOYS,SPORTING GOODS,ETC		4050083		5093089		5861950		6444712	VOITURES ENFANTS,JOUETS
8942	TOYS,INDOOR GAMES ETC		3590572		4519076		5116671		5578682	JOUETS,JEUX ETC
89422	DOLLS		330023		400172	MN 729791	516180	MN 853756	577043	POUPEES
89423	TOYS NES	W 976219	2276500	W 1055970	2635136	W 1170489	2895234	W 1312921	3332735	JOUETS,MODELES REDUITS
89424	INDOOR GAME EQUIPMENT		420965		718786		820468		737229	ART,JEUX DE SOCIETE
89425	XMAS DECORATIONS ETC		540137	W 302604	736462	W 356695	865533	W 384791	916988	ART DIVERTIS,FETES
8947	OTH SPORT GDS,FAIR AMUSM		337943		473372		620286		715653	AUT ART DE SPORT
89472	OTH OUTDOOR SPORT GOODS		270452		387904		493863	MN 456587	556146	ART POUR JEUX PLEIN AIR
897	GOLD,SILVER WARE,JEWELRY		801983		1254779		1399275		1150977	BIJOUTERIE,ORFEVRERIE
8973	PREC JEWLRY,GLD-SILVWARE		707994		1130801		1267024		1012249	BIJOUX OR,ARGENT ORFEVRE
89731	PRECIOUS METAL JEWELLERY		595983		829739		950385		878545	ART BIJOUTERIE,JOAILLER
898	MUSICAL INSTRUMENTS,PTS		502859		711453		765689		689448	INSTRUMENTS DE MUSIQUE
8983	SOUND RECRDNG TAPE,DISCS		420344		606024		585962	MN 1899277	456014	SUPPORTS SON POUR 763
89831	PREPD SND RECORDNG MEDIA		408850		574531		552084	MN 1891278	411681	SUPPORTS PREPARES
899	OTHER MANUFACTURED GOODS		1612696		2421850		2719348		2474098	AUT ART MANUF DIVERS NDA
8994	UMBRELLAS,CANES ETC		334071		457126		490531		438374	PARAPLUIES,CANNES ETC
89941	UMBRELLAS,SUNSHADES	MN 329826	322116	MN 404539	418009	MN 404918	454409	MN 373672	414413	PARAPLUIES,PARASOLS ETC
8997	BASKETWORK,BROOMS ETC		432918		624903		768449		634090	OUVRAGES VANNERIE NDA
89971	BASKETWORK,WICKERWRK,ETC	W 167061	304401	W 187599	462326	W 200515	565964	W 174830	414656	OUVRAGES DE VANNERIE
8998	SMALLWARES,TOILETRYS ETC		126076		380376		352131		258004	ART MERCERIE,TOILETTE
8999	OTHER MANUF GOODS NES		501910		657268		746903		704759	OUVRAGES DIVERS NDA
89993	ARTIFICIAL FLOWERS ETC	W 107347	341874	W 125342	468805	W 127956	483651	W 124177	413231	FLEURS ARTIFICIELLES
9	GOODS NOT CLASSD BY KIND		395372		364087		550019		222204	ART TRANSACT NON CLASSES
931	*SPECIAL TRANSACTIONS		358604		324030		507333		184848	TRANS.SPECIALES

1. HISTORICAL SERIES, 1961–1996 SPECIAL TRADE, IMPORTS C.I.F., EXPORTS F.O.B.
SERIES HISTORIQUES, 1961–1996 COMMERCE SPECIAL, IMPORTATIONS C.A.F., EXPORTATIONS F.O.B

YEAR ANNEE	VALUE IN MILLION U.S. DOLLARS VALEUR EN MILLION U.S. DOLLARS MERCHANDISE –MARCHANDISE		GOLD –OR		CONVERSION FACTORS FACTEURS DE CONVERSION CENTS E.U. PAR		INDEX NUMBERS –INDICES QUANTUM		UNIT VALUE VALEUR UNITAIRE	
	IMPORTS	EXPORTS	IMPORTS	EXPORTS	IMPORTS	EXPORTS	IMPORTS	EXPORTS	IMPORTS	EXPORTS
1961	556.80	434.50	0.30						2	2
1962	540.40	463.40							2	2
1963	506.00	446.70							2	2
1964	586.30	548.10							2	2
1965	453.50	539.10							2	2
1966	674.10	507.60							3	3
1967	496.90	509.90							4	3
1968	643.30	558.30							4	3
1969	685.30	607.50		4.60					3	3
1970	843.00	727.20		7.90					3	4
1971	929.40	688.90		0.90					3	4
1972	858.90	969.00							4	4
1973	1061.50	1177.30							4	6
1974	1597.20	1416.90							5	7
1975	1494.80	1465.20							6	6
1976	1708.10	1745.20							7	9
1977	2028.30	2443.20							7	15
1978	2836.30	3002.70							7	12
1979	3233.20	3300.40							8	11
1980	4662.60	3945.00							10	14
1981	5199.20	2956.40							10	11
1982	5477.70	3095.00							14	16
1983	4968.10	3080.90							17	20
1984	4492.40	3483.10							22	28
1985	4130.70	3551.90							30	37
1986	3861.50	5101.60							38	57
1987	4321.90	4642.20							47	54
1988	5001.80	5037.00							60	70
1989	5004.10	5716.50							80	73
1990	5589.50	6765.80							100	100
1991	4906.10	7232.10							121	117
1992	6516.40	6916.50							130	118
1993	9831.50	7115.90							145	134
1994	11882.90	8418.50							159	174
1995	13852.90	10125.70							191	204
1996	13683.70	10587.00							209	217

2. IMPORTS BY BROAD ECONOMIC CATEGORY AND EXPORTS BY INDUSTRIAL ORIGIN. (PERCENTAGE OF TOTAL VALUE)
IMPORTATIONS PAR CATEGORIES ECONOMIQUES ET EXPORTATIONS PAR BRANCHE D'ACTIVITE.(EN POURCENTAGE DE LA VALEUR TOTALE)

IMPORTS – IMPORTATIONS

	1990	1991	1992	1993	1994	1995	1996
TOTAL IMPORTS–IMPORTATIONS TOTALES	100.	100.	100.	100.	100.	100.	
1 FOOD BEV–ALIMENTATION BOISSONS	5.9	5.2	6.7	5.7	6.4	7.1	
11 PRIMARY–PRODUITS DE BASE	4.0	3.4	4.5	3.2	3.3	3.7	
111 FOR INDUSTRY–POUR L'INDUSTRIE	2.9	2.3	3.2	2.3	2.1	2.1	
112 FOR HOUSEHOLDS–POUR LES MENAGES	1.1	1.0	1.3	0.9	1.2	1.6	
12 PROCESSED–PRODUITS ELABORES	2.0	1.8	2.3	2.5	3.1	3.4	
121 FOR INDUSTRY–POUR L'INDUSTRIE	1.0	0.7	0.7	0.9	0.9	0.9	
122 FOR HOUSEHOLDS–POUR LES MENAGES	0.9	1.1	1.6	1.6	2.2	2.5	
2 IND SUPPLIES–APPROV INDUSTRIELS	43.8	46.6	44.6	36.1	35.7	38.7	
21 PRIMARY–PRODUITS DE BASE	2.5	2.6	3.9	3.0	3.2	3.3	
22 PROCESSED–PRODUITS ELABORES	41.3	43.9	40.8	33.1	32.5	35.4	
3 FUELS–COMBUSTIBLES	5.9	5.8	5.2	3.7	2.6	2.7	
31 PRIMARY–PRODUITS DE BASE	0.0	0.0	0.4	0.3	0.0	0.0	
32 PROCESSED–PRODUITS ELABORES	5.9	5.8	4.9	3.5	2.5	2.7	
321 MOTOR SPIRIT–ESSENCE	4.9	4.8	4.1	2.7	1.9	1.7	
322 OTHER–AUTRES	0.9	1.0	0.7	0.8	0.7	1.0	
4 MACHINERY–EQUIPEMENT	26.7	25.3	24.9	24.3	25.9	27.1	
41 CAPITAL EQUIPMENT–MACHINES	23.2	22.0	22.1	21.5	23.2	24.4	
42 PARTS–PIECES ACCESSOIRES	3.5	3.3	2.8	2.8	2.8	2.7	
5 TRANSPORT–TRANSPORT	10.8	9.4	9.7	22.7	22.1	11.7	
51 PASSENGER CARS–AUTOMOBILES	3.0	2.3	2.3	8.2	7.6	3.8	
52 OTHER–AUTRES	3.2	3.1	4.3	10.0	10.7	4.3	
521 INDUSTRIAL–INDUSTRIELS	2.8	2.6	4.1	9.2	9.7	4.2	
522 NON INDUSTRIAL–NON INDUSTRIEL	0.4	0.5	0.1	0.8	1.0	0.1	
53 PARTS–PIECES ACCESSOIRES	4.6	4.1	3.1	4.4	3.8	3.6	
6 CONSUM GOODS–BIENS CONSOMMATION	3.5	4.5	5.2	6.0	7.0	7.6	
61 DURABLE–DURABLES	0.8	1.1	1.4	1.7	1.8	1.8	
62 SEMI DURABLE–SEMI DURABLES	1.2	1.9	2.3	2.5	2.8	3.2	
63 NON DURABLE–NON DURABLES	1.5	1.6	1.4	1.8	2.4	2.6	
7 GOODS NES–BIENS NDA	3.3	3.2	3.7	1.4	0.4	5.1	

EXPORTS – EXPORTATIONS

	1990	1991	1992	1993	1994	1995	1996
TOTAL EXPORTS–EXPORTATIONS TOTALES	100.	100.	100.	100.	100.	100.	
1 AGRICULTURE	32.5	33.0	33.9	29.5	36.3	30.2	
2 MINING QUARRY–INDUS EXTRACTIVES	32.5	26.4	27.4	27.2	21.6	26.6	
3 MANUFACTURING–IND MANUFACTUR	35.0	40.6	38.8	43.3	42.1	43.2	
31 FOOD BEV TOBACCO–ALIM BOISS TAB	4.5	4.4	5.2	4.6	5.2	5.2	
32 TEXTILES–INDUSTRIES TEXTILES	11.5	14.0	12.3	13.2	10.8	10.3	
33 WOOD & PRODUCTS–BOIS & PRODUITS	0.1	0.2	0.2	0.2	0.1	0.1	
34 PAPER & PRODUCTS–PAPIER & PRODT	1.8	2.4	2.7	2.7	2.4	2.5	
35 CHEMICALS–INDUSTRIES CHIMIQUES	10.0	9.7	10.2	10.3	10.4	12.1	
36 NON METAL MIN–MIN NON METAL	1.1	1.7	1.5	1.5	1.4	1.4	
37 BASIC METAL–IND METAL BASE	2.6	2.5	2.2	1.8	2.2	2.4	
38 METAL MANUF–MANUF METAL	2.1	4.1	4.1	7.7	8.0	8.0	
39 OTH MANUF IND–AUTRES MANUF	1.1	1.6	0.4	1.3	1.6	1.2	

3. TRADE BY PRINCIPAL COUNTRIES OF PURCHASE AND DESTINATION (VALUE IN THOUSAND U.S. DOLLARS)
ECHANGES SELON LES PRINCIPAUX PAYS D'ACHAT ET DE DESTINATION (VALEUR EN MILLIERS DE DOLLARS EU)

COUNTRIES–PAYS	SPECIAL IMPORTS C.I.F. IMPORTATIONS SPECIALES C.A.F				
	1991	1992	1993	1994	1995
World	4966991	6683944	9840821	11937088	13863079
Africa	32418	30516	50136	88011	46792
Americas	3022425	4260771	5940829	7094499	8678983
Northern America	1872467	2612485	3520398	4275258	5233809
LAIA	986258	1432031	2315110	2680120	3274915
CACM	11900	9956	15595	15858	21357
Caribbean	126995	173165	67568	94798	120968
Rest of America	24806	33133	22157	28465	27935
As.ex F.USSR	642114	836238	1603412	1827590	1987438
Eur.x F.USSR	1222404	1486304	2090887	2673152	2892554
EU	1012289	1304564	1859114	2416908	2571569
EFTA	165306	141590	170592	182074	216012
East Europe	36465	32925	56476	65986	90800
Other Europe	8344	1118	364	1717	5658
Former USSR	14681	13500	49998	66078	86212
Oceania	11791	13595	93469	57709	23675
USA/Etats–Unis d'Amer	1737035	2394545	3278180	3837318	4692289
Japan/Japon	505373	583739	1096089	1141939	1230522
Venezuela	342498	435390	944260	1149597	1382597
Germany/Allemagne	271401	417588	578063	638553	756842
Brazil/Brésil	158532	277534	456463	427585	452547
Canada	135361	217604	242006	437897	541472
Mexico/Mexique	163746	192740	264344	341775	505424
Italy/Italie	113872	163499	272248	363938	391104
France,Monac	230743	209154	230909	271204	329486
United Kingdom	145638	131482	175057	389467	248474
Argentina/Argentine	89135	202171	232135	204736	241085
Spain/Espagne	69133	112681	221076	261959	282307
Ecuador/Equateur	33994	89818	186398	259493	272210
Switz.Liecht	149594	132436	161580	173460	194550
Korea, Republic of	23455	54146	131556	223851	229057
Sweden/Suède	51515	57541	86516	159327	180232
Chile/Chili	47184	78358	74307	128899	199737
Peru/Pérou	115167	91867	90679	101755	125593
Netherlands/Pays–Bas	46271	61568	140828	122032	94236
Belgium–Luxembourg	31487	68750	55241	65709	105315
China/Chine	8747	26729	54616	91177	118913
Trinidad and Tobago	93387	31011	37619	47352	51671
Bolivia/Bolivie	25035	54476	48454	49754	64257
Israel/Israël	21604	24697	58501	44736	62704
So. Africa Customs Un	26957	21945	35718	65644	31300
Finland/Finlande	13742	22702	29414	43276	66164
Russian Federation		13500	35115	49617	71991
Denmark/Danemark	12081	33390	25293	39069	50947
Hong Kong	9871	21559	31672	37503	43438
Panama	24667	32460	21868	27023	26664
Netherlands Antilles	32027	64258	4975	9496	15901
Austria/Autriche	18013	16825	25192	27640	28075
Indonesia/Indonésie	9327	13928	21213	30258	37346
Australia/Australie	4311	5377	18245	55991	16140
Romania/Roumanie	15934	9868	26458	18892	21555
American Samoa	3512	4224	73473	190	3746
Aruba	4	57222	10591	7225	9525
Ireland/Irlande	6239	8146	14347	23326	28726
India/Inde	4049	4757	13820	21196	35287
Uruguay	10284	8283	16513	15562	23128
Malaysia/Malaisie	9882	10808	13036	14934	20558
Singapore/Singapour	6948	7640	10720	12048	28051
Norway,SVD,JM	15557	8889	8453	7663	20304
Poland/Pologne	5963	7454	6579	15131	23072
Viet Nam		122	332	41726	7131
Thailand/Thaïlande	2965	6016	8297	12912	16155
Czech Republic			11456	11502	22123
Korea Dem People's Rp	1752	4682	21662	11129	4225
Antigua and Barbuda		13642	6520	11424	11161
Cuba	195	3259	2930	13486	22830

COUNTRIES–PAYS	SPECIAL EXPORTS F.O.B. EXPORTATIONS SPECIALES F.O.B.				
	1991	1992	1993	1994	1995
Monde	7268642	6916051	7454865	8916833	10327778
Afrique	5676	10395	21145	10917	35952
Amériques	4694553	4548423	5065945	5347400	6770780
Amérique du Nord	2905180	2779124	3075180	3286371	3705312
ALAI	1108772	1321355	1474441	1577498	2454599
MCAC	108738	132320	144461	164663	178228
Caraïbes	275356	199038	209936	171475	294745
Autre Amérique	296507	116586	161926	147393	137896
Asie l'URSS exclus	359500	333682	410547	571479	647929
Europe l'URSS exclus	2160769	1964926	1868070	2875218	2753164
UE	1991471	1877914	1758558	2739554	2634002
AELE	88429	50529	91075	108097	84475
Europe de l'Est	64097	32996	14720	24102	21303
Autre de l'Europe	16772	318	628	746	10738
Ancienne URSS	1165	6628	27486	11904	27809
Océanie	7916	9656	11330	10793	14336
USA/Etats–Unis d'Amer	2823832	2722519	3014798	3191260	3539538
Germany/Allemagne	547419	592334	562579	909660	745082
Venezuela	429766	587492	716850	561961	962419
Netherlands/Pays–Bas	312498	277895	212784	357858	344934
Peru/Pérou	212599	246697	210057	235717	566920
Japan/Japon	231725	197432	237962	353579	363917
Ecuador/Equateur	126884	152358	223059	325810	423318
Belgium–Luxembourg	171262	181763	220820	359070	296140
France,Monac	174088	128597	121741	220767	277751
United Kingdom	189772	186435	146372	196653	197879
Spain/Espagne	151949	146239	124405	169316	260549
Panama	295029	115595	160659	144629	133274
Italy/Italie	110013	127662	115628	177996	187924
Chile/Chili	180625	103701	95290	119906	165478
Mexico/Mexique	55290	69861	83574	150282	99931
Canada	80633	55508	60116	94916	165668
Costa Rica	65786	74004	84320	92702	93034
Denmark/Danemark	116048	68221	76492	69623	70712
Brazil/Brésil	53389	56604	60860	63534	136508
Netherlands Antilles	153133	82482	42710	33542	39183
Sweden/Suède	64570	51220	51308	92038	89261
Argentina/Argentine	35450	85816	62331	92242	63107
Switz.Liecht	64878	29603	68125	66028	53267
Finland/Finlande	56377	36738	39771	70193	56766
Hong Kong	10895	25295	61141	54836	97713
Aruba	43189	23778	32549	10965	105215
Portugal	20078	27871	29648	68228	60400
Dominican Republic	27496	37572	40594	40167	47669
Ireland/Irlande	28443	34933	47762	33386	35164
Israel/Israël	26490	25793	30344	30397	38336
Saudi Arabia	28433	43355	31525	40730	4975
Norway,SVD,JM	23208	20752	22693	41786	30730
Guatemala	14384	27416	26958	29360	34936
Trinidad and Tobago	3734	4086	50084	16685	55755
Korea, Republic of	17244	13111	18055	33377	45717
Cuba	20088	14443	20315	35150	18138
Bolivia/Bolivie	9160	15757	18362	23065	24737
El Salvador	7719	9521	14701	24498	17283
Austria/Autriche	42349	12088	7093	5905	4312
Honduras	8536	13047	14748	13031	20530
Russian Federation		6628	21129	11358	25976
Poland/Pologne	12630	10085	5705	16192	15882
China/Chine	17250	3508	3879	1815	30765
Hungary/Hongrie	27840	13540	3084	771	721
Jamaica/Jamaïque	3308	19545	8447	6475	7993
Australia/Australie	6226	7787	9332	8228	11113
Nicaragua	12313	8332	3734	5072	12445
Morocco/Maroc	1797	4967	8577	3209	17268
Bahamas	7587	5771	1677	18057	2289
Czechoslovakia	22816	8003			

(VALUE AS PERCENTAGE OF WORLD TOTAL)(VALEURS EN POURCENTAGE DU TOTAL MONDIAL)

	1986	1987	1988	1989	1990	1991	1992	1993	1994	1995
Africa	0.1	0.4	0.0	0.2	0.1	0.7	0.5	0.5	0.7	0.3
Americas	59.5	55.9	61.1	62.2	60.5	60.9	63.7	60.4	59.4	62.6
Northern America	39.3	39.1	40.0	39.7	39.0	37.7	39.1	35.8	35.8	37.8
LAIA	17.0	15.8	18.7	20.2	18.4	19.9	21.4	23.5	22.5	23.6
CACM	0.2	0.2	0.2	0.1	0.1	0.2	0.1	0.2	0.1	0.2
Caribbean	0.8	0.5	0.2	0.5	1.7	2.6	2.6	0.7	0.8	0.9
Rest of America	2.2	0.4	2.0	1.6	1.4	0.5	0.5	0.2	0.2	0.2
As.ex F.USSR	10.3	14.2	12.1	11.8	11.8	12.9	12.5	16.3	15.3	14.3
Eur.x F.USSR	29.2	27.6	26.0	24.9	26.5	24.6	22.2	21.2	22.4	20.9
EU	25.4	24.0	22.0	20.9	22.4	20.4	19.5	18.9	20.2	18.5
EFTA	2.2	2.2	2.8	2.7	3.0	3.3	2.1	1.7	1.5	1.6
East Europe	1.3	1.1	1.0	1.2	1.0	0.7	0.5	0.6	0.6	0.7
Other Europe	0.3	0.3	0.2	0.1	0.1	0.2	0.0	0.0	0.0	0.0
Former USSR	0.3	0.2	0.2	0.2	0.2	0.3	0.2	0.5	0.6	0.6
Oceania	0.3	0.3	0.3	0.3	0.2	0.2	0.2	0.9	0.5	0.2
USA/Etats–Unis d'Amer	36.1	34.5	36.2	36.0	35.4	35.0	35.8	33.3	32.1	33.8
Japan/Japon	9.1	11.0	10.8	9.4	8.9	10.2	8.7	11.1	9.6	8.9
Venezuela	3.1	2.8	3.5	4.1	5.8	6.9	6.5	9.6	9.6	10.0
Germany/Allemagne	6.6	7.6	6.8	6.9	8.5	5.5	6.2	5.9	5.3	5.5
Brazil/Brésil	3.6	3.7	4.6	4.2	3.3	3.2	4.2	4.6	3.6	3.3
Canada	3.0	4.6	3.6	3.6	3.5	2.7	3.3	2.5	3.7	3.9
Mexico/Mexique	3.1	3.6	4.1	2.5	2.1	3.3	2.9	2.7	2.9	3.6
Italy/Italie	2.6	2.0	1.7	1.8	1.9	2.3	2.4	2.8	3.0	2.8
France,Monac	4.0	4.2	3.7	3.1	2.8	4.6	3.1	2.3	2.3	2.4
United Kingdom	2.7	2.6	2.4	2.8	2.6	2.9	2.0	1.8	3.3	1.8

	1986	1987	1988	1989	1990	1991	1992	1993	1994	1995
Afrique	0.2	0.5	1.3	0.1	0.1	0.1	0.2	0.3	0.1	0.3
Amériques	42.8	58.4	57.0	61.2	62.9	64.6	65.8	68.0	60.0	65.6
Amérique du Nord	31.4	41.1	40.5	44.7	45.5	40.0	40.2	41.3	36.9	35.9
ALAI	7.8	11.4	11.1	9.2	9.6	15.3	19.1	19.8	17.7	23.8
MCAC	0.5	0.8	1.0	0.9	0.9	1.5	1.9	1.9	1.8	1.7
Caraïbes	1.5	2.5	1.9	2.4	2.3	3.8	2.9	2.8	1.9	2.9
Autre Amérique	1.5	2.6	2.5	4.0	4.5	4.1	1.7	2.2	1.7	1.3
Asie l'URSS exclus	5.4	4.8	7.0	5.8	5.1	4.9	4.8	5.5	6.4	6.3
Europe l'URSS exclus	50.7	33.2	34.3	31.5	30.0	29.7	28.4	25.1	32.2	26.7
UE	45.5	30.1	30.3	28.1	27.3	27.4	27.2	23.6	30.7	25.5
AELE	1.7	0.9	0.8	0.7	0.7	1.2	0.7	1.2	1.2	0.8
Europe de l'Est	3.4	2.0	3.1	2.6	1.7	0.9	0.5	0.2	0.3	0.2
Autre de l'Europe	0.2	0.2	0.1	0.1	0.3	0.2	0.0	0.0	0.0	0.1
Ancienne URSS	0.0	0.1	0.3	1.3	0.2	0.0	0.1	0.4	0.1	0.3
Océanie	0.1	0.1	0.1	0.1	0.1	0.1	0.1	0.2	0.1	0.1
USA/Etats–Unis d'Amer	30.0	39.8	39.3	43.2	44.5	38.8	39.4	40.4	35.8	34.3
Germany/Allemagne	20.6	11.8	10.4	8.6	8.4	7.5	8.6	7.5	10.2	7.2
Venezuela	2.9	4.4	4.4	3.2	3.0	5.9	8.5	9.6	6.3	9.3
Netherlands/Pays–Bas	5.2	4.2	5.0	5.7	4.3	4.3	4.0	2.9	4.0	3.3
Peru/Pérou	1.4	2.4	1.7	1.1	1.3	2.9	3.6	2.8	2.6	5.5
Japan/Japon	4.9	4.1	5.2	4.4	3.8	3.2	2.9	3.2	4.0	3.5
Ecuador/Equateur	1.2	1.3	0.9	1.0	1.1	1.7	2.2	3.0	3.7	4.1
Belgium–Luxembourg	2.2	1.4	1.5	1.4	1.7	2.4	2.6	3.0	4.0	2.9
France,Monac	2.6	2.2	2.6	2.5	2.8	2.4	1.9	1.6	2.5	2.7
United Kingdom	2.6	2.0	1.8	1.8	2.8	2.6	2.7	2.0	2.2	1.9

4. Special Imports C.I.F. by Commodities according to the S.I.T.C. (Rev. 2) in thousand U.S. Dollars
Importations Spéciales C.A.F. par Produits d'après la C.T.C.I. (Rév. 2) en milliers de Dollars E.U.

SITC CTCI	COMMODITY	1992 WEIGHT POIDS	1992 VALUE VALEUR	1993 WEIGHT POIDS	1993 VALUE VALEUR	1994 WEIGHT POIDS	1994 VALUE VALEUR	1995 WEIGHT POIDS	1995 VALUE VALEUR	PRODUIT
	ALL COMMODITIES		6683944		9840821		11937088		13863079	TOUS PRODUITS
0	FOOD AND LIVE ANIMALS		505105		570232		868959		1064622	ALIMENTS,ANIMAUX VIVANTS
03	FISH AND PREPARATIONS		31794		44787		64471		92594	POISSONS ET PREPARATIONS
037	FISH ETC PREPD,PRSVD NES	W 21040	27869	W 27307	33973	W 37144	44427	W 43139	55235	POIS,CRUST,MOL PREPARES
0371	FISH PREPARD,PRESRVD NES	W 20955	27391	W 27257	33747	W 36762	43902	W 43035	54706	CONSERVES DE POISSONS
04	CEREALS AND PREPARATIONS		267374		286649		423340		506231	CEREALES ET PRODUITS
041	WHEAT ETC UNMILLED	W 863690	140600	W 852752	132807	W 851207	135224	W 990847	192801	FROMENT,EPEAUTRE
0411	DURUM WHEAT UNMILLED	W 787552	128091	W 768838	119867	W 762528	121114	W 857324	168216	FROMENT DUR NON MOULU
042	RICE	W 70824	21642	W 61707	15505	W 237852	74901	W 123077	38818	RIZ
0422	RICE SEMI–MILLED,MILLED	W 56263	17517	W 45348	10685	W 236560	74494	W 120835	38165	RIZ POLI,GLACE INCL BRISURES
04221	RICE MILLED UNBROKEN	W 44739	14749	W 13269	4366	W 221951	71191	W 97220	33316	RIZ POLI,GLACE EXCL BRISURES
044	MAIZE UNMILLED	W 505902	70918	W 569751	79041	W 1052942	145366	W 1153541	176107	MAIS NON MOULU
048	CEREAL ETC PREPARATIONS	W 3486	5154	W 11186	18424	W 22070	27652	W 53811	51798	PREPTNS A BASE CEREALES
05	VEGETABLES AND FRUIT		79837		73954		130631		172348	LEGUMES ET FRUITS
054	VEG ETC FRSH,SMPLY PRSVD	W 144005	47219	W 95714	29460	W 156208	59020	W 134700	64170	LEGUMES FRAIS,CONG,SECS
0542	LEGUMINOUS VEGETBLES DRY	W 129784	39503	W 82951	20549	W 120416	42671	W 107489	44154	LEGUMES A COSSE SECS
057	FRUIT,NUTS,FRESH,DRIED	W 63900	25436	W 81231	33485	W 109188	56885	W 181761	87915	FRUITS FRAIS OU SECS
06	SUGAR AND PREPS,HONEY		9694		10913		28963		50500	SUCRES ET PRODUITS
081	*FEEDING STUFF FOR ANIML	W 161698	63666		75046		109866	W 332274	104875	NOURRITURE POUR ANIMAUX
0813	OILCAKE AND OTH RESIDUES	W 92205	29973	W 135701	34755	W 260899	63287	W 262157	62407	TOURTEAUX
08131	— OF SOYA BEANS	W 91328	29699	W 133321	34507	W 260736	63269	W 261940	62377	TOURTEAUX DE SOJA
0814	MEAT OR FISH MEAL FODDER	W 52163	23842	W 71136	27907	W 75423	29433	W 50597	24466	FARINES DE VIANDES,POISSONS
08142	FISH MEAL FODDER	W 42294	21373	W 65224	26309	W 72856	28466	W 47712	22636	FARINES DE POISSONS
09	MISC EDIBLE PRODUCTS		11507		22458		34030		47635	PREP ALIMENTAIRES DIVERSES
1	BEVERAGES AND TOBACCO		17756		27139		33711		64422	BOISSONS ET TABACS
11	BEVERAGES		13957		23626		28547		54965	BOISSONS
112	ALCOHOLIC BEVERAGES	W 6513	13897	W 13922	22691	W 13763	25114	W 47671	42043	BOISSONS ALCOOLIQUES
2	CRUDE MATERLS,EXCL FUELS		352298		400027		430725		489973	MAT BRUTES NON COMESTIBLES
22	OIL SEEDS,OLEAGINOUS FRT		45473		70024		67044		56520	GRAINES,FRUITS OLEAGINEUX
222	SEEDS FOR'SOFT'FIXED OIL	W 133266	35861	W 151746	41657	W 159734	42944	W 129262	35875	GRAINES HUILES FIXES
2222	SOYA BEANS	W 131292	34759	W 150982	41080	W 158283	42419	W 128847	35385	FEVES DE SOJA
23	RUBBER, CRUDE		67772		69735		70562		97067	CAOUTCHOUC BRUT
232	NATURAL RUBBER,GUMS	W 24412	23855	W 25620	25595	W 24245	25705	W 28072	44349	LATEX CAOUTCHOUC NATUREL
233	RUBBER,SYNTHTIC,RECLAIMD	W 40854	43917	W 37717	44140	W 40997	44858	W 37272	52718	LATEX CAOUTCH SYNTH REGEN
2331	SYNTHETIC RUBBER ETC	W 40836	43915	W 37518	44050	W 40706	44613	W 37118	52603	LATEX CAOUTCH SYNTHETIQUE
23315	POLYBUTADIENE–STYRN(SBR)	W 26754	24887	W 24421	24107	W 26801	25188	W 24114	30404	POLYBUTADIENE–STYRENE
251	*PULP AND WASTE PAPER	W 103246	48163	W 90736	38031	W 117880	57463	W 114850	73191	PATES A PAPIER,DECHETS
2517	SODA,SULPHATE WOOD PULP	W 59034	36877	W 49533	27363	W 75961	45209	W 62171	57476	PATES CHIMIQUES AU SULFATE
25172	— BLEACHED,NONDISSOLVNG	W 57378	35990	W 46867	26212	W 73770	43990	W 60507	56116	PATES BLANCHIES
26	TEXTILE FIBRES AND WASTE		71380		88770		101356		133183	FIBRES TEXTILES
263	COTTON	W 11081	17044	W 28338	39301	W 37047	56267	W 38108	81174	COTON
2631	RAW COTTON,EXCL LINTERS	W 11061	17028	W 28294	39223	W 35371	55613	W 37747	80909	COTON EN MASSE
266	SYNTHETIC FIBRES TO SPIN	W 14730	29114	W 14884	28290	W 15780	28438	W 15703	33171	FIBRES SYNTHETIQUES
27	CRUDE FERTLZR,MINRLS NES		48014		56526		58577		58370	ENGRAIS MINERAUX BRUTS
278	OTHER CRUDE MINERALS	W 102336	32745	W 196306	40071	W 300543	38154	W 278065	35362	AUTRES MINERAUX BRUTS
28	METALLIFEROUS ORES,SCRAP		25089		27797		28817		27293	MINERAIS METAL,DECHETS
29	CRUDE ANIMAL,VEG MAT NES		40610		32812		32326		38704	MATIERES BRUTES ANIM,VEGET
292	CRUDE VEG MATERIALS NES	W 3854	36165	W 4173	26097	W 4252	27430	W 5120	34278	MAT BRUTES VEGETALES NDA
3	MINERAL FUELS ETC		366603		378103		321601		395930	COMBUSTIBLES MINERAUX LUB
33	PETROLEUM AND PRODUCTS		360673		354083		315687		388939	PETROLE ET DERIVES
334	PETROLEUM PRODUCTS,REFIN		324752	W 1795291	332672	W 1731854	301912	W 1953175	370074	PRODUITS RAFFINES
3341	GASOLINE,OTH LIGHT OILS	W 1408592	275654	W 1510862	267215	W 1462188	224262	W 1424299	239154	ESSENCES POUR MOTEURS
33411	MOTOR,AVIATION SPIRIT	W 1408463	275591	W 1510706	267124	W 1461298	223989	W 1423650	238856	ESSENCES MOTEURS D'AVIONS
3343	GAS OILS	W 45440	7234	W 80051	15155	W 165324	26636	W 393044	61785	GAS OILS
3345	LUBS,PETROLEUM OILS NES		37200	W 195555	48089	W 101088	50000	W 130828	67543	HUILES LUBRIFIANTES
33451	LUBS(HIGH PETR CONT) ETC		32800	W 193370	41468	W 98853	43628	W 127877	58421	HUILES LUBRIF,H LOURDES
4	ANIMAL,VEGETABLE OIL,FAT		53778		80883		85805		114136	HUILES,GRAISSES ANIM,VEG
411	*ANIMAL OILS AND FATS	W 60889	22936	W 48736	20896	W 53693	21003	W 43844	21261	HUILES,GRAISSES ANIMALES
4113	ANIML OIL,FAT,GREASE NES	W 60633	22456	W 48439	20374	W 45361	18097	W 35686	18038	HUILES,GRAISSES ANIMALES NDA
42	FIXED VEGETABLE OIL,FAT		27549		56259		56699		84217	HUILES VEGETALES FIXES
423	FIXED VEG OILS,SOFT	W 49945	25083	W 89426	43406	W 78895	50202	W 118309	81189	HUILES VEGET DOUCES FIXES
4232	SOYA BEAN OIL	W 42969	20767	W 78257	36951	W 63641	39929	W 93958	62859	HUILE DE SOJA
5	CHEMCLS,RELATED PROD NES		1394778		1593919		1936468		2484057	PRODUITS CHIMIQUES
51	ORGANIC CHEMICALS		537301		608227		714946		952544	PROD CHIMIQ ORGANIQUES
511	HYDROCARBONS NES,DERIVS		126599	W 316609	139978	W 337160	189431	W 407376	279110	HYDROCARBURES NDA
5111	ACYCLIC HYDROCARBONS	W 89713	35071	W 84115	32159	W 99055	39777	W 121980	69840	HYDROCARBURES ACYCLIQUES
51112	PROPYLENE	W 88567	34394	W 81090	30850	W 96758	38598	W 118120	67239	PROPYLENE
5112	CYCLIC HYDROCARBONS		22634	W 67772	34182	W 79401	51137	W 78472	76246	HYDROCARBURES CYCLIQUES
51125	STYRENE		17995	W 57680	32107	W 72314	46886	W 75513	73956	STYRENE
5113	HALOG DERIV OF HYDROCARB	W 168792	68250	W 164319	72810	W 158171	97701	W 203837	130074	DERIVES HALOGENES HYDROCAR
51131	VINYL CHLORIDE	W 157693	60195	W 154495	63724	W 151371	89988	W 198060	121890	CHLORURE DE VINYLE
512	ALCOHOLS,PHENOLS ETC	W 76352	45468	W 75347	40329	W 87174	53880	W 81103	77643	PHENOLS,PHENOLS–ALCOOLS
5121	ACYCLIC ALCOHOLS,DERIVS	W 69803	36915	W 69633	34406	W 80848	46765	W 74785	69221	ALCOOLS ACYCLIQUES
513	CARBOXYLIC ACIDS ETC	W 124661	101829	W 128063	110104	W 138187	126634	W 145100	184698	ACIDES CARBOXYLIQUES
5137	MONOACIDS AND DERIVATIVS	W 32108	34123	W 36408	35233	W 41460	40709	W 36275	52973	ACIDES MONOCARBOXYLIQUES
5138	POLYACIDS AND DERIVATIVS	W 90595	55374	W 88686	58182	W 94642	69488	W 105827	108883	ACIDES POLYCARBOXYLIQUES
51384	TEREPHTHALIC ACID ESTERS	W 72579	41258	W 71446	44379	W 75343	51728	W 84351	82609	ESTERS DE L'ACIDE TEREPHTALI
514	NITROGEN–FNCTN COMPOUNDS		116881	W 27557	135019	W 28530	143518	W 36914	174717	COMPOSES FONCT AZOTEES
5145	AMINE–FUNCTION COMPOUNDS	W 6900	21519	W 5460	16835	W 5426	15991	W 11630	20502	COMPOSES FONCTION AMINE
5146	OXYGEN–FNCT AMINO–CMPNDS	W 8016	26064	W 8527	30553	W 9240	33921	W 10356	37483	COMP AMINES FONCT OXYGEN
5148	OTH NITROGN–FNCTN CMPNDS		51605	W 11619	69565	W 11947	73709	W 12551	92592	AUTRES COMPOSES AZOTES
51482	IMIDE–,IMIDE–FNCT CMPNDS		28007	W 3149	41413	W 2790	41907	W 3480	50952	COMPOSES A FONCTION IMIDE
515	ORG–INORG COMPOUNDS ETC	W 10234	107811	W 13201	137870	W 14355	148278	W 11591	172137	COMPOSES ORGANO–MINERAUX
5154	ORGANO–SULPHUR CMPNDS	W 5805	26207	W 6249	28596	W 7253	34613	W 5351	37396	THIOCOMPOSES ORGANIQUES
5156	HETEROCYCLIC CMPDS ETC	W 3588	73075	W 5951	98335	W 5924	101357	W 4756	118567	COMPOSES HETEROCYCLIQUES
51569	OTH HETEROCYC CMPDS,ETC	W 3534	71369	W 5902	97798	W 4914	98458	W 4662	116494	AUT COMP HETEROCYCLIQUES
516	OTHER ORGANIC CHEMICALS	W 26848	38713	W 30163	44928	W 31678	53204	W 31022	64240	AUTRES PROD ORGANIQUES
52	INORGANIC CHEMICALS		111173		107895		127077		157937	PROD CHIM INORGANIQUES
522	INORG ELEMNTS,OXIDES,ETC		51432	W 141377	39562	W 170762	53323	W 195602	72236	ELEMENTS INORGANIQUES
5225	INORGANIC BASES ETC NES	W 145363	28314	W 113605	15039	W 136324	25648	W 157864	41256	AUTRES BASES OXYDES METAL
523	OTHR INORG CHEMICALS ETC		59415	W 167323	67371	W 193430	72322	W 233323	84282	AUT PRODUITS CHIMIQUES INORG
5232	OTH MTL CMPD OF INRG ACD		38837	W 136963	44056	W 154763	45632	W 191178	52993	SELS METALLIQUES
52322	PHOSPHITES,PHOSPHATES	W 36610	22892	W 33960	21004	W 43856	23117	W 50145	24602	PHOSPHITES,PHOSPHATES
53	DYES,TANNING,COLOUR PROD		108105		130427		139489		145988	PROD TEINTURE,COLORANTS
531	SYNT DYE,NAT INDGO,LAKES	W 3962	54325	W 7648	72106	W 5062	65607	W 4807	64393	MAT COLOR ORGAN,LAQUES
5311	SYNTHIC ORGNIC DYESTUFFS	W 3408	46991	W 6667	63537	W 4550	58559	W 4171	56275	MAT COLOR ORGAN SYNTHET
533	PIGMENTS,PAINTS,ETC	W 19825	48247	W 20821	52265	W 28228	68328	W 27974	75919	PIGMENTS,PEINTURES,VERNIS
5331	COLOURING MATERIAL NES	W 13097	25336	W 13676	26306	W 17335	33498	W 15037	38611	AUT MATIERES COLORANTES
541	*MEDICINAL,PHARM PRODUCT		76278	MK 9127	145100	K 4082238	203997	K 4847406	268541	PROD MEDICINAUX PHARMACEUT
5413	ANTIBIOTICS IN BULK	K 298760	22357	K 5913121	35411	K 409285	33408	K 616298	38425	ANTIBIOTIQUES NDA
5417	MEDICAMENTS	K 1089613	27428	K 1974227	57203	K 2420875	102086	K 2543849	138180	MEDICAMENTS

4. Special Imports C.I.F. by Commodities according to the S.I.T.C. (Rev. 2) in thousand U.S. Dollars
Importations Spéciales C.A.F. par Produits d'après la C.T.C.I. (Rév. 2) en milliers de Dollars E.U.

SITC CTCI	COMMODITY	1992 WEIGHT POIDS	1992 VALUE VALEUR	1993 WEIGHT POIDS	1993 VALUE VALEUR	1994 WEIGHT POIDS	1994 VALUE VALEUR	1995 WEIGHT POIDS	1995 VALUE VALEUR	PRODUIT
54179	— CONTNG OTH SUBSTANCES	K 816069	13412	K 1190342	30065	K 1045053	55357	K 1656541	80284	MED CONT AUT SUBSTANCES
55	PERFUME,CLEANING ETC PRD		46782		60700		81125		108852	PROD POUR PARFUM,TOILETTE
551	ESSENTL OILS,PERFUME,ETC	W 1449	20477	W 4037	27927	W 2281	37703	W 2443	45403	HUILES ESSENTIELLES
554	SOAP,CLEANSING ETC PREPS		22770	W 11897	24115	W 13558	26317	W 19413	35649	SAVONS,PRODUITS DETERSIFS
5542	WASHING PREPARATIONS ETC	W 10733	22362	W 11358	23113	W 11964	23632	W 15766	29830	PROD ORG TENSIO–ACT NDA
562	*FERTILIZERS,MANUFACTURE	W 932259	141781	W 792380	110062	W 987262	159752	W 934549	184745	ENGRAIS MANUFACTURES
5621	CHEM NITROGENOUS FERTLZR	W 409893	63821	W 372467	53311	W 450141	73955	W 448632	99131	ENGRAIS AZOTES
56216	UREA	W 382478	56961	W 352216	44705	W 407164	63813	W 381047	82068	UREE
5623	CHEM POTASSIC FERTILIZER	W 293442	36834	W 231816	29216	W 305289	39819	W 265016	35339	ENGRAIS POTASSIQUES
56231	POTASSIUM CHLORIDE	W 281008	34394	W 217679	26424	W 298059	38687	W 252310	33000	CHLORURE DE POTASSIUM
5629	FERTILIZERS NES	W 218084	39656	W 179551	26428	W 221650	44394	W 211972	48707	ENGRAIS NDA
56292	NITROG–PHOS FERTILZR NES	W 185082	33077	W 175402	24685	W 209817	41135	W 210284	47029	ENGRAIS NDA CONT N P
58	PLASTIC MATERIALS ETC		229868		249867		297683		400529	MAT PLAST ARTIFICIELLES
582	PROD OF CONDENSATION ETC	W 20843	44537	W 21015	46060	W 33242	65677	W 32256	77492	PROD CONDENS,POLYCOND
583	POLYMERIZATION ETC PRODS	W 145098	153347	W 181512	173909	W 191875	203395	W 210213	292376	PROD POLYMERISATION
5831	POLYETHYLENE	W 91434	73890	W 114202	83475	W 117799	95284	W 145775	167884	POLYETHYLENE
58311	— IN PRIMARY FORMS	W 90476	72610	W 112975	81121	W 116224	92023	W 142703	162224	POLYETHYLENE PRIMAIRES
584	CELLULOSE DERIVATIVS ETC	W 9338	29191	W 11474	26370	W 8119	24461	W 8675	25872	CEL REGEN NIT ACETATE
59	CHEMICAL MATERIALS NES		140927		177842		207693		260145	MAT PROD CHIMIQUES NDA
591	PESTICIDES,DISINFECTANTS	W 6847	33600	W 8687	41435	W 6657	47249	W 7780	55954	DESINF,INSECT,FONG,HERB
598	MISCEL CHEM PRODUCTS NES	W 83305	97791	W 105067	124732	W 112273	143543	W 137234	178759	PROD DIV INDUST CHIM NDA
5989	CHEM PRODUCTS,PREPS NES	W 62077	66015	W 81686	86712	W 84752	100642	W 106254	127710	PROD PREP CHIMIQUES NDA
59899	OTH CHEM PRODS,PREPS,NES	W 45513	44731	W 64459	59548	W 67306	72463	W 84940	91857	AUT PRODUITS CHIMIQUES NDA
6	BASIC MANUFACTURES		1176086		1610133		1896112		2426867	ART MANUFACTURES
61	LEATHER,DRESSED FUR,ETC		25199		38644		22883		27092	CUIRS,PELLETERIES
611	LEATHER	W 8925	22760	W 10307	33708	W 3695	18618	W 4627	22492	CUIRS,PEAUX PREPARES
62	RUBBER MANUFACTURES NES		53084		102453		114213		157738	CAOUTCHOUC MANUFACTURE
625	RUBBER TYRES, TUBES ETC		31323	W 20172	67180	W 31688	81422	W 36482	121277	PNEUS CAOUTCHOUC VULCANISE
6252	TYRES,NEW,BUS OR LORRY		4673	W 5601	21374	W 8694	26009	W 13829	43888	PNEUS POUR AUTOBUS,CAMIONS
63	WOOD,CORK MANUFACTRS NES		25979		13694		25360		32593	OUVRAGES LIEGE ET BOIS
634	VENEERS,PLYWOOD,ETC	W 48665	23778	W 16909	9457	W 29233	19773	W 32555	20808	PLACAGES,CONTRE–PLAQUES
64	PAPER,PAPERBOARD AND MFR		170732		219978		277022		352701	PAPIERS,CARTONS & OUVRAGES
641	PAPER AND PAPERBOARD	W 219633	158588	W 290542	198458	W 345524	240702	W 299847	293550	PAPIERS ET CARTONS
6411	NEWSPRINT	W 63358	39137	W 81508	50337	W 96547	56213	W 107548	79378	PAPIER JOURNAL
6412	PRINTG,WRITING PAPER NES	W 20065	19587	W 26172	22991	W 44767	38736	W 39263	47917	PAPIERS POUR L'IMPRESSION
64122	— COATED,IMPREGNATD ETC	W 19962	19509	W 25127	22104	W 40453	34864	W 36022	42622	PAPIERS IMPRESSION COUCHES
6413	KRAFT PAPER,PAPERBOARD	W 52978	24884	W 96735	44806	W 102692	51607	W 71646	50954	PAPIER ET CARTON KRAFT
64139	KRAFT PAPER PAPERBD,NES	W 35837	16608	W 77832	35196	W 74026	37764	W 51850	38895	PAPIER,CARTON KRAFT NDA
6415	PAPER,PAPERBRD,BULK,NES	W 73313	56426	W 73617	55246	W 80799	59116	W 63136	75867	PAPIERS,CARTONS ROULEAUX
64159	OTHER PAPER ETC,BULK,NES	W 35027	36830	W 39573	37804	W 42749	38637	W 35239	51399	AUT PAPIER ROULEAUX FEUILLES
642	PAPER,ETC,PRECUT,ARTS OF		12144	W 13999	21521	W 21927	36320	W 30106	59151	PAP,CARTONS DECOUPES
65	TEXTILE YARN,FABRICS,ETC		172466		295540		319272		387354	FILS,TISSUS,ARTICLES TEXTILE
651	TEXTILE YARN		52411	W 18546	85655	W 20227	84040	W 21982	109314	FILS TEXTILES
6514	SYN FIB YRN,BULK,MONOFIL	W 5023	32249	W 8887	52715	W 12130	54053	W 11579	63150	FILS CONT 85% FIB TEXT SYNTH
65142	— NONTXT ETC CONT PAMID	W 2560	20356	W 4995	32359	W 5609	27930	W 5089	33028	FILS NON TEX FI CON POLYAMID
652	COTTON FABRICS,WOVEN	W 6131	34272	W 10772	55256		60317	W 15495	81585	TISSUS DE COTON
6522	WOVEN COTTON BLEACHD,ETC	W 6089	34079	W 10605	54680		59227	W 14998	79117	TISSUS COTON BLANCHIS ETC
65224	BLCHED COTTON FABRIC NES	W 5430	28713	W 10022	49082	W 10544	51906	W 14229	71348	AUT TIS PLUS 85% COT BLANCHI
653	WOVN MAN–MADE FIB FABRIC	W 3307	30553	W 7670	61190	W 8842	68446	W 7572	69158	TISSUS FIBRES SYNTH,ARTIF
657	SPECIAL TXTL FABRC,PRODS	W 3624	23576	W 6883	34209	W 7179	35190	W 9499	41709	TISSUS SPECIAUX
66	NONMETAL MINERAL MFS NES		63530		105104		161186		183819	ART MIN NON METALLIQUES
662	CLAY,REFRACTORY BLDG PRD	W 17086	14998	W 39775	26350	W 83471	45486	W 103291	48607	MAT CONST REFRACTAIRES
665	GLASSWARE		11216	W 16837	15864	W 61224	37212	W 61994	44895	OUVRAGES EN VERRE
67	IRON AND STEEL		384193		478110		547799		751504	FER ET ACIER
672	IRON,STEEL PRIMARY FORMS		27581	W 153069	45004	W 265325	68886	W 181347	51894	LINGOTS FER,ACIER
6725	IRN,STL BLOOMS,SLABS,ETC	W 64826	16140	W 120518	29621	W 211454	50000	W 147110	37224	BLOOMS,BILLETTES FER ACIER
67251	IRN,SMPLE STL BLOOMS,ETC	W 64823	16090	W 120504	29510	W 211443	49974	W 147055	37095	BLOOMS ETC NON ACIER FIN
673	IRON,STEEL SHAPES ETC		45031	W 189831	78025	W 254016	97199	W 214477	88204	BARRES,PROFIL FER,ACIER
6731	IRON,STEEL WIRE ROD	W 69327	25158	W 112013	39714	W 131295	46237	W 97600	37261	FIL MACHINE FER,ACIER
6732	IRON,STEEL BARS ETC		12474	W 50580	25436	W 95957	38916	W 80401	34646	BARRES FER,ACIER
674	IRN,STL UNIV,PLATE,SHEET	W 355876	201590	W 441011	232849	W 499661	252376	W 492265	293263	LARGES PLATS,TOLES
6745	IRN,STL MED PLATE,ROLLED	W 52836	30816	W 69742	39321	W 79303	41906	W 69391	43204	TOLES 3 A 4.75 MM
67451	— OF IRON OR SIMPLE STL	W 47370	22488	W 63202	29109	W 70381	29252	W 60279	28283	TOLES AUT NON ACIER FIN
6746	IRN,STL THIN PLATE,ROLLD	W 255812	143902	W 281184	148518	W 295325	148686	W 334763	197906	TOLES LAM MOINS 3MM
67461	— OF IRON OR SIMPLE STL	W 249503	129538	W 271665	129094	W 284094	130274	W 324574	172363	TOL NON AC FIN MOINS 3 MM
678	IRON,STL TUBES,PIPES,ETC	W 97099	90332	W 117266	101295	W 77291	99142	W 237099	280279	TUBES,TUYAUX EN FONTE,FER
6782	IRON,STL SEAMLESS TUBES	W 38459	42980	W 49956	49179	W 31095	45840	W 44681	56782	TUBES,TUYAUX SANS SOUDURE
6783	IRON,STL TUBES,PIPES NES	W 56589	40642	W 61978	39866	W 34923	26480	W 186465	204426	AUT TUBES,TUYAUX FER,ACIER
68	NON–FERROUS METALS		175027		185964		214527		263962	METAUX NON FERREUX
682	COPPER EXC CEMENT COPPER		64748	W 27029	72148	W 32537	88727	W 26625	99396	CUIVRE
6822	COPPER,ALLOYS WORKED		62680	W 26274	70389	W 31838	86886	W 25449	95363	CUIVRE,ALLIAGES OUVRES
68221	COPPER BARS,WIRE,ETC	W 16992	46474	W 20683	49954	W 26424	67270	W 21253	72179	BARRES,PROFILES ET FILS
684	ALUMINIUM		78136	W 48721	79028	W 53662	92136	W 53951	125299	ALUMINIUM
6841	ALUMINIUM,ALLOYS,UNWRGHT	W 31242	42508	W 30010	38484	W 35606	49815	W 34335	65431	ALUMINIUM,ALLIAGES BRUTS
6842	ALUMINIUM,ALLOYS WORKED		35628	W 18711	40544	W 18056	42321	W 19616	59868	ALUMINIUM,ALLIAGES OUVRE
686	ZINC	W 17328	21687	W 19659	20787	W 16880	17134	W 21551	24966	ZINC
6861	ZINC,ALLOYS UNWROUGHT	W 15063	20206	W 18097	19592	W 16099	16487	W 20867	24236	ZINC ET ALLIAGES BRUTS
69	METAL MANUFACTURES NES		105876		170646		213850		270104	ART MANUFACT EN METAL NDA
695	TOOLS		25710	W 4768	50134	W 9222	68367	W 9142	78347	OUTILS A MAIN
6954	BLADES,TIPS,ETC FR TOOLS		16942	W 1228	32113	W 2411	41363	W 1306	49556	OUTILS POUR MACHINE–OUTIL
69541	PARTS TO INSERT IN TOOLS	W 603	13827	W 825	27369	W 1732	35678	W 813	44786	OUTILS DE FORAGE
699	BASE METAL MFRS NES		33997	W 12506	47289	W 12121	57118	W 16436	71679	ART MANUFACTURES MET NDA
7	MACHINES,TRANSPORT EQUIP		2231502		4467508		5552245		5170907	MACHINES MATERIEL TRANSPORT
71	POWER GENERATING EQUIPMT		288286		281526		260743		255666	MACHINES GENERATRICES
713	INTRNL COMBUS PSTN ENGIN	W 12938	62467	W 26156	83031	W 21094	92623	W 20406	88337	MOTEURS EXPL COMB INT, PIECE
7139	PISTON ENGINE PARTS NES	W 3385	27309	W 10322	47127	W 4754	44323	W 4682	50942	PIECES POUR 713.2,3,8
714	ENGINES AND MOTORS NES		36827	W 1570	18847	W 261	16760	W 1437	36838	MOTEURS NON ELECTRIQUES
7148	GAS TURBINES NES	W 712	33257	W 32	1125	W 44	1873	W 1327	25588	TURBINES A GAZ
71488	OTHER GAS TURBINES NES	W 706	32577	W 3	151	W 33	789	W 1313	24859	AUTRES TURBINES A GAZ
716	ROTATING ELECTRIC PLANT		150428	W 17163	148210	W 11276	116184	W 9039	86578	APP ELECTR ROTATIFS,PIECES
7161	DC MOTORS AND GENERATORS	W 1017	13326	W 3021	94025	W 3941	59283	W 824	8450	MOTEURS COURANT CONTINU
7162	AC MTRS,GENRTRS,GEN SETS	W 13372	132078	W 12438	44809	W 5434	41325	W 6535	66446	MOTEURS ELECTRIQUES
71623	GEN SETS WITH PISTN ENGN	W 10343	106799	W 4941	22599	W 1958	19051	W 2872	29518	GROUPES MOTEUR EXPLOSION
72	MACHS FOR SPCL INDUSTRYS		450163		619473		655295		826670	MAC SPECIALES POUR INDUST
722	TRACTORS NON–ROAD	W 3282	21310	W 3615	21388	W 4067	27802	W 4722	32204	TRACTEURS
723	CIVIL ENGNEERG EQUIP ETC	W 24516	120472	W 22602	119350	W 35362	176043	W 41314	235079	APPAREILS DE GENIE CIVIL
7234	CONST,MINING MACHNRY NES	W 21845	101754	W 21117	105092	W 32202	152155	W 37412	209796	MACH POUR LA CONST, MINES
72342	SLFPRP SHOVELS,EXCAVATRS	W 10070	48101	W 12722	60489	W 20380	95899	W 19190	100283	PELLES MECANIQUES
72344	BORING,SINKING MACHINERY	W 7434	34610	W 2129	16445	W 1376	8400	W 9553	57649	MACHINES DE FORAGE
724	TEXTILE,LEATHER MACHNRY		120775	W 15045	171966	W 9061	104258	W 7655	97130	MACH POUR INDUSTRIE TEXTILE
7243	SEWING MACHS,NEEDLES ETC	W 1207	18580	W 2643	33420	W 1734	25981	W 1887	24625	MACHINES A COUDRE,PIECES

4. Special Imports C.I.F. by Commodities according to the S.I.T.C. (Rev. 2) in thousand U.S. Dollars
Importations Spéciales C.A.F. par Produits d'après la C.T.C.I. (Rév. 2) en milliers de Dollars E.U.

SITC CTCI	COMMODITY	1992 WEIGHT POIDS	1992 VALUE VALEUR	1993 WEIGHT POIDS	1993 VALUE VALEUR	1994 WEIGHT POIDS	1994 VALUE VALEUR	1995 WEIGHT POIDS	1995 VALUE VALEUR	PRODUIT
72431	SEWING MACHINES	W 1152	17435	W 1979	31345	W 1665	24043	W 1783	22578	MACHINES A COUDRE
7244	SPINNING,EXTRDNG,ETC MCH	W 2123	24852	W 4423	47307	W 2307	22693	W 1548	24524	MACH POUR LE FILAGE
7245	WEAVING,FELT MFG,ETC MCH	W 2570	40020	W 3172	40171	W 1280	16657	W 1244	19291	METIERS A TISSER,PIECES
72451	WEAVING MACHINES (LOOMS)	W 1211	20132	W 1649	14630	W 531	3929	W 644	5915	METIERS A TISSER
7247	TEXTILE MACHINERY NES	W 1890	25414	W 3696	33828	W 2793	26710	W 2337	17179	MACH LAVAGE,TEINTURE TEX
72474	OTH TEXTILE MACHNERY NES	W 1356	20209	W 1603	25150	W 1890	19164	W 977	11085	MACH LAVAGE ETC MAT TEXT
725	PAPER ETC MILL MACHINERY	W 2011	21445	W 5442	29229	W 2338	24995	W 3469	40718	MACHINES FABR PATE PAPIER
726	PRINTG,BKBINDG MACHY,PTS		35166	W 4961	68966	W 3799	69928	W 2652	53936	MACHINES POUR IMPRIMERIE
7264	PRINTING PRESSES	W 1941	19508	W 3736	42355	W 2716	42025	W 1870	30022	MACHINES A IMPRIMER
72641	ROTARY PRINTING PRESSES	W 1941	19508	W 3736	42355	W 2716	42025	W 1870	30022	MACH IMPRIMER ROTATIVES
727	FOOD MACHRY NON-DOMESTIC		17274	W 2277	32315	W 2451	39975	W 4684	66475	MACH INDUSTRIES ALIMENT
7272	OTH FOOD PROC MCHY,PARTS		16212	W 1991	28255	W 2227	36826	W 4343	62782	AUT MACH IND ALIMENTAIRE
72722	INDUS FOOD PROC MACH NES	W 1613	13540	W 1962	27936	W 2079	34563	W 4172	61033	MACHINES BOULANGERIE
728	OTH MACHY FOR SPCL INDUS		105208	W 33693	160909	W 20766	196523	W 26240	279941	AUT MACH IND PARTICULIERES
7283	OTHR MINERAL WORKG MACHY	W 4581	23277	W 10066	33595	W 8221	50439	W 12556	79870	MACH TRIER,CRIBLER,BROYER
7284	MACHY FOR SPCL INDUS NES		77204	W 22690	120023	W 10933	133719	W 12587	190264	MACH SPEC IND PARTICUL.
72842	RUBBER,PLASTICS WRKG MCH	W 3201	32673	W 5219	46048	W 4884	47148	W 4098	53415	MACH IND CAOUT MAT PLAST
72848	OTH MCHY WITH INDIV FNCT	W 2155	26666	W 16220	49682	W 4324	59036	W 4908	72309	AUTRES MACHINES NDA
73	METALWORKING MACHINERY		36926		63048		80335		62683	MACH TRAVAIL DES METAUX
736	METALWORKING MACH-TOOLS		26245	W 10975	42853	W 9767	58360	W 7515	42650	MACH-OUTILS TRAVAIL METAUX
74	GENRL INDUSTRL MACHY NES		337148		535493		709346		793887	MACH APP INDUSTRIE
741	HEATING,COOLING EQUIPMNT		42633	W 9230	76786	W 14044	102385	W 16775	140016	MACH CHAUFFAGE,PIECES
7416	HEATING,COOLING EQU NES	W 1452	20835	W 3449	34958	W 5320	43846	W 5019	63170	APP CHANGEMENT TEMP
742	PUMPS FOR LIQUIDS ETC	W 3227	31976	W 5801	53411	W 5437	77937	W 4429	69932	POMPES MOTO-POMPES
743	PUMPS NES,CENTRFUGES ETC		65240	W 15204	103066	W 13632	146195	W 16090	143041	POMPES COMPRES,VENT ETC
7431	PUMPS FOR GASES ETC	W 4316	34636	W 6470	50238	W 7448	74625	W 9536	68950	POMPES AIR A VIDE,COMPRES
744	MECHANICAL HANDLING EQU		48351	W 17976	78038	W 20367	103743	W 19615	111604	EQUIP MANUTENTION PIECES
7442	LIFTING,LOADING MACH NES		28648	W 7204	36449	W 9567	54184	W 8263	52745	APP LEVAGE,MANUTENTION
745	NONELEC MACHY,TOOLS NES	W 2227	38785	W 7514	76154	W 4779	103927	W 5904	141661	AUT MACH NON ELEC,PIECES
7452	OTH NONELEC MCHS,PTS NES	W 1859	30753	W 6586	62506	W 4022	84296	W 4972	116653	AUT MACH NON ELEC,PIECES
74522	PACKAGNG,BOTTLNG,ETC MCH	W 645	16040	W 1594	37658	W 2049	55518	W 2830	83177	MACH NETT BOUTEILLES,ETC
749	NONELEC MACH PTS,ACC NES		110164	W 24976	148039	W 14164	175158	W 15973	187633	PIECES MACH NON ELEC NDA
7491	BALL,ROLLER,ETC BEARINGS	W 2546	27689	W 3586	37899	W 3521	40005	W 4619	44590	ROULEMENTS BILLES ETC
7492	COCKS,VALVES ETC NES	W 5556	41376	W 7283	44746	W 5531	71895	W 5392	67548	ART ROB,SIM POUR TUYAUX
7493	SHAFT,CRANK,PULLEY ETC	W 2031	25155	W 9914	40567	W 3423	39953	W 3795	42695	ARBRES TRANS,VILEBREQUINS
75	OFFICE MACHNES,ADP EQUIP		124751		297480		415865		469645	MACH BUREAU TRAIT AUTOM
751	OFFICE MACHINES	W 983	17308	W 2672	46117	W 3961	62681	W 3237	62003	MACH,APPAREILS DE BUREAU
7518	OFFICE MACHINES NES	W 467	9773	W 1249	33338	W 1791	46486	W 1663	45176	MACH,APP DE BUREAU NDA
752	AUTOMTIC DATA PROC EQUIP	W 1948	89772	W 5183	210584	W 5904	298520	W 6339	339843	MACH TRAIT INFORMATION
7522	DIGITAL COMPUTERS	W 519	35775	W 1513	95286	W 2042	151355	W 1612	143766	MACH DIGITALES COMPLETES
7523	DIGITL CENTRL PROCESSORS	W 174	12996	W 277	33768	W 523	47918	W 770	72226	UNITES CENTRALES
7525	ADP PERIPHERAL UNITS	W 1127	22738	W 3031	56324	W 2998	65359	W 3580	80311	UNITES PERIPHERIQUES
759	OFFICE,ADP MCH PTS,ACCES	W 693	17671	W 1686	40779	W 2144	54664	W 2275	67799	PIECES DU 751 ET 752
7599	ACCTG,ETC,ADP MCH PTS,AC	W 624	15132	W 1458	33382	W 1857	44412	W 1916	56895	PIECES DU 751 ET 752
76	TELECOMM,SOUND EQUIPMENT		223832		321386		595189		853802	EQUIPMENT DE TELECOM
764	TELECOM EQPT,PTS,ACC NES		195135	W 4970	277874	W 7774	536093	W 10061	785678	EQUIP TELECOM,PIECES
7641	LINE TELEPHONE,ETC EQUIP	W 1363	116461	W 2427	174060	W 2512	206504	W 3851	309709	APP TELEPHON PAR FIL
7643	TV,RADIO TRANSMITTRS ETC		20829	W 401	38598	W 2466	240956	W 2365	346272	APP EMET TELE RADIO
7648	TELECOMM EQUIPMENT NES	W 233	29378	W 189	18809	W 131	22863	W 417	44137	APP TELECOM NDA
7649	PTS NES OF EQUIPMT OF 76	W 842	25564	W 1374	42640	W 2160	61076	W 2655	79035	PIECES DE LA DIV 76
77	ELECTRIC MACHNRY NES ETC		209065		289085		404265		531364	MACH APP ELECT NDA
771	ELECTRIC POWER MACHY NES	W 2476	21037	W 3777	26908	W 2900	27772	W 4448	45091	MACH PROD,TRANS ELECTR
772	SWITCHGEAR ETC,PARTS NES		60125	W 5667	69307	W 4363	85015	W 5467	121356	APP COUPURE,SECT ETC
7721	SWITCHGEAR ETC	W 3505	54744	W 5243	61865	W 3865	74147	W 5086	109422	APP COUPURE,SECTIONMNT
773	ELECTR DISTRIBUTNG EQUIP		21748	W 3930	21966	W 8882	38652	W 17791	77956	EQUIPMT DISTRIBUTION ELECT
7731	INSULATED WIRE,CABLE ETC	W 2070	11220	W 2929	15650	W 7802	31396	W 16883	67849	FILS,CABLES ISOLES ELECT
774	ELECTRO-MEDCL,XRAY EQUIP	W 211	9050	W 472	23393	W 548	39358	W 640	44226	APPAREILS MEDICAUX
775	HOUSEHOLD TYPE EQUIP NES	W 5549	26767	W 8016	36483	W 14888	55928	W 17118	64617	MACH,APP USAGE DOMESTQUE
778	ELECTRICAL MACHINERY NES		55824	W 24883	90529	W 16908	130947	W 19854	150767	AUTRES MACH ELECT NDA
7788	OTH ELEC MACHY,EQUIP NES		22571	W 5777	27437	W 4169	41969	W 4935	51827	AUT MACH APP ELEC NDA
78	ROAD VEHICLES		356952		1645868		1824811		1115735	VEHICULES ROUTIERS
781	PASS MOTOR VEH EXC BUSES	W 16316	155158	W 105033	811864	W 107788	903729	W 56394	525621	AUTO TRANSPORT PERSONNES
782	LORRIES,SPCL MTR VEH NES	W 7210	46359	W 43164	280262	W 70522	459782	W 43774	291623	VEHICULES SPECIAUX,MARCH
7821	LORRIES,TRUCKS	W 4565	26330	W 39408	262188	W 66253	434811	W 40850	272995	VEHICULES TRANSP MARCHAND
783	ROAD MOTOR VEHICLES NES	W 7073	55570	W 40546	235803	W 17967	127560	W 11221	77974	VEHICULES ROUTIERS NDA
7831	BUSES	W 2983	22569	W 16185	108132	W 10547	69909	W 6784	40549	VOITURES TRANSPORT COMMUN
7832	TRACTORS FOR TR-TRAILERS	W 4089	33000	W 24361	127671	W 7420	57651	W 4436	37425	TRACTEURS ROUTIERS
784	MOTOR VEH PRTS,ACCES NES	W 36772	76757	W 56512	209149	W 36828	189107	W 34360	173031	PIECES 722,781,782,783
7841	MOTOR VEHICLE CHASSIS	W 625	4090	W 12299	87181	W 6569	49193	W 1711	10923	CHASSIS 722,781,782,783
7849	OTHER MOTOR VEHCL PARTS	W 35844	72078	W 43299	120698	W 28382	136322	W 29077	147338	PIECES 722,781,782,783
785	CYCLES,ETC MOTRZD OR NOT	W 4020	16564	W 11915	96264	W 15562	137981	W 8142	35492	MOTOCYCLES SCOOTERS
7851	MOTORCYCLES ETC	W 455	7598	W 6900	80038	W 9824	119400	W 1157	10652	MOTO VELO MOTEUR AUXIL
79	OTHR TRANSPORT EQUIPMENT		204381		414148		606396		261455	AUTRE MATERIEL TRANSPORT
791	RAILWAY VEHICLES	W 3760	27759	W 1789	62855	W 1196	37513	W 2152	14445	VEHIC MAT CHEMINS DE FER
7914	RY COACHES NES NOT POWRD	W 621	23714	W 1494	60281	W 1038	35963			VOITURES A VOYAGEURS
792	AIRCRAFT ETC		131385	W 2232	317471	W 2026	520694	W 1681	223657	APP NAVIGATION AERIENNE
7921	HELICOPTERS		5454	W 418	61184	W 55	30063	W 117	63370	HELICOPTERES
7923	AIRCRFT NES2000-15000KG	W 93	37416	W 283	116177	W 341	113131	W 153	44783	AERODYNES 2000 A 15000 KG
7924	AIRCRFT NES OVER 15000KG	W 949	80266	W 1238	113286	W 1484	352914	W 904	67497	AERODYNES PLUS 15000 KG
793	SHIPS AND BOATS ETC	W 17733	45237	W 38021	33823	W 30575	48189	W 24809	23354	NAVIRES BATEAUX,ETC
7938	TUGS,SPECIAL VESSELS ETC	W 4972	36977	W 666	3477	W 4261	14200	W 5689	18445	REMORQUEURS,BATEAUX SPEC
79382	SPECL PURPOSE VESSLS ETC	W 2676	27567	W 169	612	W 1902	6667	W 5037	10531	BAT-PHARES,-POMPES,DRAGUES
8	MISC MANUFACTURED GOODS		342446		585817		772376		950512	ART MANUFACTURES DIVERS
821	*FURNITURE,PARTS THEREOF	W 832	4130	W 2873	18683	W 5554	27697	W 8516	44492	MEUBLES ET PIECES
84	CLOTHING AND ACCESSORIES		47029		53048		69986		83088	VETEMENTS
87	PRECISION INSTRUMNTS NES		113560		184450		225504		257288	INSTRUM,APPAR SCIENT NDA
872	MEDICAL INSTRUMENTS NES	W 708	17864	W 1416	53230	W 1710	60149	W 2119	73647	INSTR,APP MEDIC-CHIR NDA
87202	OTH MEDICAL INSTRUMENTS	W 651	16494	W 1241	48189	W 1468	54145	W 1712	65904	INSTRUM,APP MEDECINE
874	MEASURNG,CONTROLNG INSTR		79836	W 4759	112881	W 3541	138858	W 3673	156446	INSTRUMENTS DE MESURE
8743	GAS,LIQUID CONTROL INSTR	W 605	15570	W 2458	22990	W 1282	36511	W 960	28697	APP,INSTR MESURE FLUIDES
8748	ELEC MEAS,CONTRL EQU NES	W 334	24799	W 431	30294	W 492	39029	W 587	48656	APP ELEC ELECTRO MESURE
87483	OTH ELCTRNC MEAS ETC EQU	W 206	18737	W 374	27325	W 405	34596	W 503	43709	AUT APP ELECTRO DE MESURE
88	PHOTO EQU,OPTICL GDS ETC		40004		83209		111907		122745	APP,FOURN PHOTO,OP,MONTR
882	PHOTO,CINEMA SUPPLIES	W 2870	28090	W 4489	52941	W 6478	74117	W 6615	79313	PRODUITS PHOTO,CINEMA
8822	PHOTO FILM EXC DEV CINMA	W 2325	24471	W 3690	45800	W 4595	61342	W 4930	65424	PLAQUES,PELLICULES,FILMS
89	MISC MANUFCTRD GOODS NES		125820		228178		304828		392449	ART MANUFACTURES DIVERS
892	PRINTED MATTER		27568	W 13895	50363	W 10653	69794	W 11389	88015	IMPRIMES
8921	PRINTED BOOKS,GLOBES,ETC	W 2257	19117	W 10761	33776	W 7682	51312	W 7913	57873	LIVRES,BROCHURES,CARTES
89211	PRINTED BOOKS,PAMPHLETS	W 2245	19046	W 10712	33521	W 7592	50945	W 7816	57123	LIVRES,BROCHURES
893	ARTICLES OF PLASTIC NES		35057		54081		69182		97784	OUVRAGES EN MAT DIVIS 58
8939	MISC PLASTIC ARTICLES	W 4615	21192	W 8255	36822	W 11351	47171	W 12494	62433	ART DIVERS EN MAT DIV 58

4. Special Imports C.I.F. by Commodities according to the S.I.T.C. (Rev. 2) in thousand U.S. Dollars
Importations Spéciales C.A.F. par Produits d'après la C.T.C.I. (Rév. 2) en milliers de Dollars E.U.

SITC CTCI	COMMODITY	1992 WEIGHT POIDS	1992 VALUE VALEUR	1993 WEIGHT POIDS	1993 VALUE VALEUR	1994 WEIGHT POIDS	1994 VALUE VALEUR	1995 WEIGHT POIDS	1995 VALUE VALEUR	PRODUIT
89399	OTHR PLASTC ARTICLES NES	W 4184	20299	W 7615	34999	W 10510	44735	W 11376	59148	AUT OUV MAT DIV 58
894	TOYS,SPORTING GOODS,ETC	W 3475	17753	W 10970	33730	W 8590	42215	W 14456	60809	VOITURES ENFANTS,JOUETS
8942	TOYS,INDOOR GAMES ETC	W 2484	14030	W 9906	27285	W 7071	33622	W 12516	48826	JOUETS,JEUX ETC
898	MUSICAL INSTRUMENTS,PTS	W 949	20828	W 2503	47926	W 3553	71627	W 3651	84571	INSTRUMENTS DE MUSIQUE
8983	SOUND RECRDNG TAPE,DISCS	W 758	18477	W 2233	44668	W 3172	66915	W 3256	80558	SUPPORTS SON POUR 763
89832	RECORDED DISCS,TAPES ETC	W 213	15199	W 788	37070	W 1193	57084	W 1102	69778	DISQUES,PHONO,BANDES
9	GOODS NOT CLASSD BY KIND		243591		127060		39086		701653	ART TRANSACT NON CLASSES
931	*SPECIAL TRANSACTIONS	W 30730	187682			W 4	39	W 72857	651322	TRANS.SPECIALES
951	*WAR FIREARMS,AMMUNITION	W 1093	55900	W 3176	127002	W 2268	38816	W 1816	50199	VEHIC BLINDES ARMES
95102	MILITARY FIREARMS NES	W 126	18191	W 1342	51570	W 38	8689	W 42	10557	ARMES DE GUERRE
95109	PARTS OF ARMS NES	W 383	29937	W 810	57701	W 10	1523	W 168	12771	PIECES POUR ARMES

5. Special Exports F.O.B. by Commodities according to the S.I.T.C. (Rev. 2) in thousand U.S. Dollars
Exportations Spéciales F.O.B. par Produits d'après la C.T.C.I. (Rév. 2) en milliers de Dollars E.U.

SITC CTCI	COMMODITY	1992 WEIGHT POIDS	1992 VALUE VALEUR	1993 WEIGHT POIDS	1993 VALUE VALEUR	1994 WEIGHT POIDS	1994 VALUE VALEUR	1995 WEIGHT POIDS	1995 VALUE VALEUR	PRODUIT
	ALL COMMODITIES		6916051		7454865		8916833		10327778	TOUS PRODUITS
0	FOOD AND LIVE ANIMALS		2212893		2090494		3158334		3027059	ALIMENTS,ANIMAUX VIVANTS
001	*LIVE ANIMALS FOR FOOD	W 20487	21410	W 2171	3386	W 553	1588	W 8685	12882	ANIMAUX VIVANTS
03	FISH AND PREPARATIONS		167141		159841		257346		247694	POISSONS ET PREPARATIONS
034	FISH,FRESH,CHILLED,FROZN	W 49900	51383	W 44798	47801	W 55083	62555	W 55593	65648	POISSON FRAIS, REFRIG,CONG
0342	FISH FROZEN,EXCL FILLETS	W 49106	44455	W 43837	39374	W 54037	53138	W 54095	54741	POISSONS CONGELES
035	FISH SALTED,DRIED,SMOKED	W 8962	28939	W 4412	15761	W 5045	20994	W 270	1458	POISSON SECHE,SALE,FUME
03504	FISH SMOKED	W 8911	27153	W 4377	13857	W 4937	16263			POISSONS FUMES
036	SHELL FISH FRESH,FROZEN	W 10566	76670	W 9992	82284	W 12863	124462	W 11869	118787	CRUSTACES,MOLLUSQUES
037	FISH ETC PREPD,PRSVD NES	W 4353	10149	W 5592	13995	W 17525	49335	W 20124	61801	POIS,CRUST,MOL PREPARES
0371	FISH PREPARD,PRESRVD NES	W 4353	10149	W 5592	13995	W 17525	49335	W 20121	61782	CONSERVES DE POISSONS
04	CEREALS AND PREPARATIONS		24541		13843		22351		32037	CEREALES ET PRODUITS
048	CEREAL ETC PREPARATIONS	W 47274	23606	W 7114	11966	W 21165	20437	W 28313	30994	PREPTNS A BASE CEREALES
05	VEGETABLES AND FRUIT		493343		481565		543332		497010	LEGUMES ET FRUITS
054	VEG ETC FRSH,SMPLY PRSVD	W 92422	30801	W 104517	24071	W 91461	29065	W 77052	30282	LEGUMES FRAIS,CONG,SECS
057	FRUIT,NUTS,FRESH,DRIED		423724	W 1591555	438619	W 1708127	501072	W 1370174	447210	FRUITS FRAIS OU SECS
0573	BANANA,PLANTAIN,FRSH,DRY	W 1414760	407237	W 1580541	424738	W 1704078	490237	W 1360278	431240	BANANES FRAICHES,SECHEES
058	FRUIT PRESERVED,PREPARED	W 16899	37976	W 11571	17788	W 6711	9667	W 7367	13467	CONSERVES DE FRUITS
0585	FRUIT OR VEGETABLE JUICE	W 12865	31195	W 6678	11416	W 3163	4210	W 5344	9145	JUS DE FRUITS
05857	JUICE OF OTHER FRUIT,VEG	W 12708	31029	W 6203	10838	W 2195	2939	W 4326	7644	JUS AUTRES FRUITS,LEGUMES
06	SUGAR AND PREPS,HONEY		139322		182937		186263		216953	SUCRES ET PRODUITS
061	SUGAR AND HONEY	W 467729	124804	W 761042	162580	W 696459	162835	W 618803	181056	SUCRES ET MIEL
0611	RAW BEET AND CANE SUGAR	W 108464	34583	W 351742	87341	W 198996	52505	W 263947	85444	SUCRES BRUTS
0612	REFINED SUGAR ETC	W 308470	87088	W 267789	68023	W 339447	99696	W 245511	88609	SUCRES RAFFINES
062	SUGAR CANDY NON–CHOCLATE	W 12213	14519	W 13551	20358	W 15547	23429	W 21610	35896	SUCRERIES
07	COFFEE,TEA,COCOA,SPICES		1340418		1230791		2125327		1979283	CAFE,THE,CACAO,EPICES
071	COFFEE AND SUBSTITUTES	W 978064	1324495	W 798513	1209398	W 687046	2102925	W 569967	1953656	CAFE ET SUCCEDANES
0711	COFFEE GREEN,ROASTED,SUB	W 968241	1261277	W 788033	1152336	W 674967	1998651	W 559560	1840735	CAFE TORREFIE OU DECAFEINE
07111	COFFEE GREEN,HUSKS,SKINS	W 967536	1260070	W 784585	1143083	W 673399	1993104	W 558745	1837243	CAFE NON TORREFIE
0712	COFFEE EXTRACTS,ESSENCES	W 9823	63218	W 10480	57062	W 12079	104274	W 10408	112921	EXTRAITS DE CAFE
1	BEVERAGES AND TOBACCO		69661		41833		33110		30803	BOISSONS ET TABACS
12	TOBACCO AND MANUFACTURES		64401		35827		25715		22925	TABACS BRUTS FABRIQUES
121	TOBACCO UNMNFCTRD,REFUSE	W 18964	34221	W 9529	19972	W 13675	25287	W 11783	22722	TABACS BRUTS,DECHETS
1211	TOBACCO,NOT STRIPPED	W 14126	24292	W 6373	13255	W 9446	16051	W 7492	13407	TABACS NON ECOTES
122	TOBACCO,MANUFACTURED	W 6415	30180	W 3378	15854	W 88	428	W 127	203	TABACS FABRIQUES
1222	CIGARETTES	W 6413	30175	W 3378	15854	W 83	411	W 117	145	CIGARETTES
2	CRUDE MATERLS,EXCL FUELS		450167		437068		520353		584038	MAT BRUTES NON COMESTIBLES
26	TEXTILE FIBRES AND WASTE		78622		30528		23228		43889	FIBRES TEXTILES
263	COTTON	W 42351	56538	W 7508	9847	W 1918	3211	W 7421	13667	COTON
2631	RAW COTTON,EXCL LINTERS	W 41968	56381	W 6853	9550	W 1588	3063	W 5372	12776	COTON EN MASSE
29	CRUDE ANIMAL,VEG MAT NES		349123		392991		460977		488400	MATIERES BRUTES ANIM,VEGET
292	CRUDE VEG MATERIALS NES	W 125168	342925	W 133434	385034	W 139473	434607	W 139407	480195	MAT BRUTES VEGETALES NDA
2927	CUT FLOWERS AND FOLIAGE	W 124647	341014	W 132686	382493	W 138185	430261	W 138819	477330	FLEURS,FEUILLAGES COUPES
29271	CUT FLOWERS	W 124627	340896	W 132633	382265	W 138098	429802	W 138725	476718	FLEURS ET BOUTONS
3	MINERAL FUELS ETC		1972108		1888352		1788855		2523179	COMBUSTIBLES MINERAUX LUB
32	COAL,COKE AND BRIQUETTES		555430		564414		552921		595687	HOUILLES,COKES,BRIQUETTES
322	COAL,LIGNITE AND PEAT	MW 14614	545126	MW 17616	557393	MW 18437	545575	MW 18274	587426	HOUILLES,LIGNITES,TOURBE
3222	OTH COAL,NOT AGGLOMERATD	MW 14612	544970	MW 17616	557367	MW 18437	545536	MW 18274	587405	AUTRES HOUILLES
33	PETROLEUM AND PRODUCTS		1416678		1323933		1235934		1926956	PETROLE ET DERIVES
333	CRUDE PETROLEUM	MW 9505	1149486	MW 9692	1058570	MW 9141	936914	MW 14219	1637934	HUILES BRUTES DE PETROLE
334	PETROLEUM PRODUCTS,REFIN	W 2959974	263357	W 3044721	264166	W 3200091	295750	W 2743223	287803	PRODUITS RAFFINES
3343	GAS OILS	W 135313	18618	W 2605305	189933	W 2742687	221983	W 2367369	225000	GAS OILS
3344	FUEL OILS,NES	W 2560951	197184							FUEL OILS
3345	LUBS,PETROLEUM OILS NES	W 263681	47521	W 438935	73683	W 444943	71331	W 361979	59843	HUILES LUBRIFIANTES
33451	LUBS(HIGH PETR CONT) ETC	W 263510	47157	W 438785	73326	W 444671	70516	W 361750	59072	HUILES LUBRIF,H LOURDES
5	CHEMCLS,RELATED PROD NES		373290		417947		529663		805282	PRODUITS CHIMIQUES
51	ORGANIC CHEMICALS		37206		38485		41022		61624	PROD CHIMIQ ORGANIQUES
52	INORGANIC CHEMICALS		19687		16538		26577		39787	PROD CHIM INORGANIQUES
541	*MEDICINAL,PHARM PRODUCT	K 2736483	25262	K 4861116	35410	K 6339281	56844	K 8229459	95670	PROD MEDICINAUX PHARMACEUT
5417	MEDICAMENTS	K 2397777	20155	K 4381381	29249	K 5674015	49234	K 7455829	82619	MEDICAMENTS
54179	— CONTNG OTH SUBSTANCES	K 1855467	14897	K 3547620	21398	K 5236681	37987	K 6942159	62406	MED CONT AUT SUBSTANCES
55	PERFUME,CLEANING ETC PRD		9479		18151		38054		67594	PROD POUR PARFUM,TOILETTE
58	PLASTIC MATERIALS ETC		149967		169878		213819		326363	MAT PLAST ARTIFICIELLES
582	PROD OF CONDENSATION ETC	W 36005	41226	W 36942	45201	W 39642	48070	W 41569	67041	PROD CONDENS,POLYCOND
5823	ALKYDS,OTHER POLYESTERS	W 26905	29216	W 30184	35216	W 30409	36387	W 32582	55610	ALKYDES ET AUT POLYESTERS
58231	— IN PRIMARY FORMS	W 26904	29209	W 30184	35212	W 30408	36373	W 32582	55608	SOUS FORMES PRIMAIRES
583	POLYMERIZATION ETC PRODS	W 129124	102029	W 156388	118438	W 166251	158905	W 202124	251732	PROD POLYMERISATION
5832	POLYPROPYLENE	W 40411	34184	W 37691	28740	W 36048	32071	W 39377	55224	POLYPROPYLENE
58321	— IN PRIMARY FORMS	W 34750	23559	W 32571	19100	W 31109	22566	W 33859	39369	POLYPROPYLENE PRIMAIRES
5833	POLYSTYRENE,ITS COPOLYMR	W 22501	18511	W 23244	18719	W 36092	34131	W 41994	54129	POLYPROPYLENE COPOLYMERES
58331	— IN PRIMARY FORMS	W 22428	18339	W 23197	18612	W 36083	34106	W 41725	53516	SOUS FORMES PRIMAIRES
5834	POLYVINYL CHLORIDE	W 55446	35917	W 74462	49908	W 67520	63596	W 92380	96044	CHLORURE DE POLYVINYLE
58341	— IN PRIMARY FORMS	W 53561	31508	W 71966	43248	W 64928	56033	W 87689	82744	SOUS FORMES PRIMAIRES
5839	OTH POLYMRZTION ETC PROD	W 8028	8636	W 17395	14754	W 21169	20943	W 19912	31438	AUT PROD POLYMER COPOLYM
59	CHEMICAL MATERIALS NES		109562		121193		130370		179037	MAT PROD CHIMIQUES NDA
591	PESTICIDES,DISINFECTANTS	W 20460	87898	W 21510	96397	W 22279	101523	W 28600	141169	DESINF,INSECT,FONG,HERB
5911	INSECTICIDES,FOR RETAIL	W 1287	8599	W 1689	11866	W 2344	15576	W 3969	32596	INSECTICIDES VENTE DET
5912	FUNGICIDES,FOR RETAIL	W 12665	51989	W 14986	59368	W 14486	56097	W 16322	65441	FONGICIDES VENTE AU DET
5913	HERBICIDES,FOR RETAIL	W 6461	27171	W 4675	24643	W 5111	28383	W 7784	42163	HERBICIDES VENTE AU DET
6	BASIC MANUFACTURES		855229		1109717		1240502		1526934	ART MANUFACTURES
61	LEATHER,DRESSED FUR,ETC		87091		85512		94157		115615	CUIRS,PELLETERIES
611	LEATHER	W 3393	33009	W 3980	46943	W 4988	53999	W 6407	62606	CUIRS,PEAUX PREPARES
6118	LEATHER SPECIALLY FINSHD	W 1377	17653	W 1489	27827	W 1603	27248	W 1662	29046	CUIRS,PEAUX TANNES
61183	LEATHER PATENT,METALIZED	W 1375	17637	W 1458	27292	W 1586	26920	W 1634	28177	CUIRS,PEAUX VERNIS
612	LEATHER ETC MANUFACTURES	W 6350	54003	W 7471	38398	W 7680	40058	W 11189	52856	OUVRAGES EN CUIRS NDA
6123	PREPRD PARTS OF FOOTWEAR	W 1381	32525	W 1058	18926	W 1044	17775	W 3773	27275	PARTIES DE CHAUSSURES
6129	LEATHER MANUFACTURES NES	W 4925	20792	W 6379	18805	W 6611	21612	W 7387	23234	AUT OUV CUIR NAT,ARTIF
62	RUBBER MANUFACTURES NES		19109		18680		20458		37201	CAOUTCHOUC MANUFACTURE
625	RUBBER TYRES, TUBES ETC	W 6510	15501	W 5762	15203	W 6399	17142	W 11258	32969	PNEUS CAOUTCHOUC VULCANISE
64	PAPER,PAPERBOARD AND MFR		61055		75823		84253		137207	PAPIERS,CARTONS & OUVRAGES
641	PAPER AND PAPERBOARD		29380	W 44963	33808	W 53781	41190	W 66267	68890	PAPIERS ET CARTONS
6415	PAPER,PAPERBRD,BULK,NES		15360	W 28293	17488	W 32337	20979	W 42297	44271	PAPIERS,CARTONS ROULEAUX
64159	OTHER PAPER ETC,BULK,NES		15290	W 25248	16432	W 30798	20264	W 38983	42261	AUT PAPIER ROULEAUX FEUILLES
642	PAPER,ETC,PRECUT,ARTS OF	W 19567	31675	W 26062	42015	W 29448	43063	W 38442	68317	PAP,CARTONS DECOUPES
65	TEXTILE YARN,FABRICS,ETC		177013		203464		211492		279935	FILS,TISSUS,ARTICLES TEXTILE
651	TEXTILE YARN	W 5450	23936	W 7381	31552	W 7684	33960	W 14574	58078	FILS TEXTILES
6514	SYN FIB YRN,BULK,MONOFIL	W 2261	9589	W 3795	15102	W 3735	14588	W 9422	32914	FILS CONT 85% FIB TEXT SYNTH
652	COTTON FABRICS,WOVEN	W 8939	46764	W 8808	47301	W 9523	54442	W 11548	76912	TISSUS DE COTON
6522	WOVEN COTTON BLEACHD,ETC	W 4749	28074	W 7472	41245	W 8794	50451	W 11081	74300	TISSUS COTON BLANCHIS ETC
65224	BLCHED COTTON FABRIC NES	W 3964	21390	W 6722	34256	W 7442	39324	W 9563	59486	AUT TIS PLUS 85% COT BLANCHI
657	SPECIAL TXTL FABRC,PRODS		39057	W 12851	38258	W 13355	40136	W 13449	43677	TISSUS SPECIAUX

5. Special Exports F.O.B. by Commodities according to the S.I.T.C. (Rev. 2) in thousand U.S. Dollars
Exportations Spéciales F.O.B. par Produits d'après la C.T.C.I. (Rév. 2) en milliers de Dollars E.U.

SITC CTCI	COMMODITY	1992 WEIGHT POIDS	1992 VALUE VALEUR	1993 WEIGHT POIDS	1993 VALUE VALEUR	1994 WEIGHT POIDS	1994 VALUE VALEUR	1995 WEIGHT POIDS	1995 VALUE VALEUR	PRODUIT
6573	COATED ETC TEXTILES NES		30180	W 10578	28665	W 11049	30998	W 11056	33922	TISSUS,ART MATIERE TEXT NDA
65732	PLASTIC COATED TEXTILES	W 11469	29969	W 10539	28429	W 11034	30694	W 11001	33589	TISSUS IMPREGNES
658	TEXTILE ARTICLES NES		37237	W 4806	48201	W 5393	47970	W 5633	54999	ART FACONNES MAT TEXTILES
6584	LINENS ETC		33768	W 4476	44947	W 4685	43596	W 5321	50877	LINGE DE MAISON
65845	OTHER LINEN OF COTTON	W 2649	26931	W 3266	33210	W 3406	30399	W 3804	35089	LINGE DE TOILETTE COTON
66	NONMETAL MINERAL MFS NES		278099		504542		532429		580383	ART MIN NON METALLIQUES
661	LIME,CEMENT,BLDG PRODS	W 1330126	47129	W 1310500	49995	W 1252388	53137	W 1301840	58737	CHAUX,CIMENTS MAT CONSTR
6612	CEMENT	W 1310584	41658	W 1283096	41927	W 1225687	45295	W 1269566	49702	CIMENTS HYDRAULIQUES
667	PEARL,PREC–,SEMI–P STONE		180061		404090		426705		455906	PERLES, PIERRES GEMMES
6673	PREC–,SEMI–PR STONES NES		180037		403183		424274		455314	AUTRES PIERRES NON SERTIES
67	IRON AND STEEL		143224		113853		142249		217147	FER ET ACIER
671	PIG IRON ETC	W 48758	126632	W 49721	102010	W 51668	118859	W 56817	184937	FONTE,SPIEGEL,POUDRES
6716	FERRO–ALLOYS	W 48606	126592	W 49379	101899	W 51456	118786	W 56520	184808	FERRO–ALLIAGES
67169	OTHER FERRO–ALLOYS	W 48606	126592	W 49379	101898	W 51456	118785	W 56520	184808	AUTRES FERRO–ALLIAGES
68	NON–FERROUS METALS		5760		22427		54327		31255	METAUX NON FERREUX
681	SILVER,PLATINUM,ETC				15392		45774		15227	ARGENT ET PLATINE
6812	METALS OF PLATINUM GROUP				15392		45724		15022	PLATINE
68123	PLATINUM,ALLOYS UNWRGHT				15392		45724		15022	PLATINE,ALLIAGES BRUTS
69	METAL MANUFACTURES NES		73753		75715		92018		114738	ART MANUFACT EN METAL NDA
7	MACHINES,TRANSPORT EQUIP		161337		431014		514002		581276	MACHINES MATERIEL TRANSPORT
71	POWER GENERATING EQUIPMT		24564		62546		58813		53960	MACHINES GENERATRICES
714	ENGINES AND MOTORS NES	W 6	325	W 122	25812	W 111	17914	W 126	19345	MOTEURS NON ELECTRIQUES
72	MACHS FOR SPCL INDUSTRYS		16453		46145		68029		53993	MAC SPECIALES POUR INDUST
723	CIVIL ENGNEERG EQUIP ETC	W 676	2961	W 3135	17360	W 5816	29585	W 1604	14124	APPAREILS DE GENIE CIVIL
74	GENRL INDUSTRL MACHY NES		31994		38467		49418		56577	MACH APP INDUSTRIE
77	ELECTRIC MACHNRY NES ETC		56222		67709		76699		104856	MACH APP ELECT NDA
775	HOUSEHOLD TYPE EQUIP NES	W 4827	19967	W 4875	21329	W 5555	23057	W 8833	36115	MACH,APP USAGE DOMESTQUE
778	ELECTRICAL MACHINERY NES		15243	W 6492	21178	W 8737	26324	W 9951	34884	AUTRES MACH ELECT NDA
78	ROAD VEHICLES		21691		50060		53864		91818	VEHICULES ROUTIERS
781	PASS MOTOR VEH EXC BUSES	W 152	1873	W 1722	22113	W 1174	15365	W 2774	35142	AUTO TRANSPORT PERSONNES
782	LORRIES,SPCL MTR VEH NES	W 577	3982	W 1395	9764	W 2479	20119	W 3950	35620	VEHICULES SPECIAUX,MARCH
7821	LORRIES,TRUCKS	W 575	3968	W 1125	7195	W 2155	17659	W 3620	32575	VEHICULES TRANSP MARCHAND
79	OTHR TRANSPORT EQUIPMENT		5660		149548		191518		182018	AUTRE MATERIEL TRANSPORT
792	AIRCRAFT ETC	W 154	5546	W 484	96311	W 1014	137726	W 1077	166191	APP NAVIGATION AERIENNE
7924	AIRCRFT NES OVER 15000KG	W 136	4145	W 417	75560	W 883	104588	W 903	143685	AERODYNES PLUS 15000 KG
793	SHIPS AND BOATS ETC	W 15	114	W 9283	53174	W 12526	53740	W 11136	15719	NAVIRES BATEAUX,ETC
7938	TUGS,SPECIAL VESSELS ETC	W 1	10	W 9018	44815	W 11718	50476	W 11120	15611	REMORQUEURS,BATEAUX SPEC
79382	SPECL PURPOSE VESSLS ETC	W 1	6	W 8428	41764	W 11288	44598	W 11119	15553	BAT–PHARES,–POMPES,DRAGUES
8	MISC MANUFACTURED GOODS		815660		1034545		1060668		1046507	ART MANUFACTURES DIVERS
831	*TRAVEL GOODS,HANDBAGS	W 1575	65997	W 1934	81773	W 1702	69097	W 1366	56052	ARTICLES DE VOYAGE ETC
83101	HANDBAGS NES	W 541	28350	W 634	29778	W 527	24758	W 481	20786	SACS A MAIN
83102	TRAVEL GDS,TOILET–CASES	W 912	31693	W 919	29162	W 826	28059	W 694	25755	ARTICLES DE VOYAGE
83109	OTHER TRAVEL BAGS,CASES	W 122	5955	W 381	22833	W 349	16280	W 191	9511	AUT CONTENANTS SIMILAIRES
84	CLOTHING AND ACCESSORIES		446599		534311		522503		553103	VETEMENTS
842	MENS OUTERWEAR NOT KNIT	W 3792	85136	W 4269	90919	W 5157	103436	W 5754	107522	VET DESSUS POUR HOMMES
8423	— TROUSERS,BREECHES ETC	W 2767	48755	W 3041	49073	W 3917	59280	W 4419	68586	PANTALONS HOMMES MAT TEX
8424	— JACKETS,BLAZERS ETC	W 729	24012	W 926	29271	W 804	29279	W 761	23274	VESTES HOMMES MAT TEXTIL
843	WOMENS OUTERWEAR NONKNIT	W 8319	175592	W 9757	198149	W 8841	181397	W 5908	152041	VET DESSUS FEMMES MAT TEX
8431	— COATS AND JACKETS	W 955	26952	W 1026	26034	W 902	25053	W 931	28963	MANT,VEST FEM MAT TEXTIL
8439	— OTHER OUTER GARMENTS	W 5798	110468	W 7043	123515	W 6337	110532	W 3711	80096	AUT VET DES FEM MAT TEXT
844	UNDER GARMENTS NOT KNIT	W 941	20347	W 1445	29629	W 1475	29116	W 1967	40109	VETEMENT DESSOUS MAT TEX
845	OUTERWEAR KNIT NONELASTC	W 1719	35804	W 2072	55769	W 1994	52594	W 1550	49113	VET DESSOUS,ACCES BONNET
8459	— OTHER,CLTHG ACCESRYS	W 1238	27793	W 1613	45766	W 1605	43999	W 1213	40681	AUT VET DESSUS DE BONNE
846	UNDER GARMENTS KNITTED	W 4458	98762	W 4514	121653	W 4718	119632	W 5813	165391	SOUS VETS DE BONNETERIE
8462	— OF COTTON NON ELASTIC	W 3650	69329	W 3579	81498	W 3729	76995	W 4324	101746	SOUS–VET BONNET COTON
84629	—— OTHER	W 3650	69329	W 3579	81498	W 3729	76995	W 4324	101746	AUT SOUS–VET BONNET COTON
8465	CORSETS,GARTERS,ETC	W 349	16098	W 347	21875	W 394	25147	W 602	39009	CORSETS,GAINES ART SIM
84651	BRASSIERES	W 333	15493	W 322	20982	W 376	24215	W 576	36472	SOUTIENS–GORGE,BUSTIERS
851	*FOOTWEAR	W 4102	72361	W 4793	78618	W 3774	63377	W 2745	44028	CHAUSSURES
85102	FOOTWEAR LEATHER	W 3609	60862	W 4210	69251	W 3252	54215	W 2134	37813	CHAUS SEMELLES EN CUIR
87	PRECISION INSTRUMNTS NES		7939		25034		24319		30420	INSTRUM,APPAR SCIENT NDA
89	MISC MANUFCTRD GOODS NES		196622		276754		342285		322783	ART MANUFACTURES DIVERS
892	PRINTED MATTER		123300	W 20680	124185	W 22881	131933	W 19955	119275	IMPRIMES
8921	PRINTED BOOKS,GLOBES,ETC	W 14799	80275	W 16081	77930	W 18501	86776	W 16509	89257	LIVRES,BROCHURES,CARTES
89211	PRINTED BOOKS,PAMPHLETS	W 14686	79628	W 15731	76370	W 18227	85296	W 16267	87410	LIVRES,BROCHURES
8922	NEWSPAPERS,PERIODICALS	W 3576	33129	W 3570	34308	W 3519	30275	W 2550	16967	JOURNAUX ET PERIODIQUES
893	ARTICLES OF PLASTIC NES		23767		41986		50267		67745	OUVRAGES EN MAT DIVIS 58
8931	PLSTC PACKG CONTNRS,LIDS	W 1953	10619	W 4182	18778	W 5290	25322	W 7645	37757	ART TRANSP EMBALLAGE ETC
896	WORKS OF ART ETC		231		59477		100609		56690	OBJETS D'ART
89601	HAND PAINTINGS ETC NES		151		24997		1680		31184	TABLEAUX,PEINTURES
89606	ANTIQUES NES				34169		98058		25150	OBJETS D'ANTIQUITE
9	GOODS NOT CLASSD BY KIND		1777		2285		60849		187190	ART TRANSACT NON CLASSES
971	*GOLD,NON MONETARY NES		263	K 17	172	K 3369	36652	K 15106	175096	OR NON MONETAIRE
97101	NONMON GLD UNWRT,SEMIMFD		263	K 15	169	K 3369	36652	K 14875	174532	OR,ALLIAGES D'OR BRUTS

1. HISTORICAL SERIES, 1960–1995 SPECIAL TRADE, IMPORTS C.I.F., EXPORTS F.O.B.
SERIES HISTORIQUES, 1960–1995 COMMERCE SPECIAL, IMPORTATIONS C.A.F., EXPORTATIONS F.O.B

YEAR ANNEE	VALUE IN MILLION COMORIAN FRANCS VALEUR EN MILLION COMORIAN FRANCS — MERCHANDISE –MARCHANDISE		GOLD –OR		CONVERSION FACTORS U.S. CENTS PER COMORIAN FRANC FACTEURS DE CONVERSION CENTS E.U. PAR COMORIAN FRANC		INDEX NUMBERS –INDICES — QUANTUM		UNIT VALUE VALEUR UNITAIRE	
	IMPORTS	EXPORTS	IMPORTS	EXPORTS	IMPORTS	EXPORTS	IMPORTS	EXPORTS	IMPORTS	EXPORTS
1960	940.30	799.60			0.4051	0.4051				
1961	908.80	686.40			0.4051	0.4051				
1962	1008.00	626.00			0.4051	0.4051				
1963	1335.00	1161.00			0.4051	0.4051				
1964	1507.00	986.00			0.4051	0.4051				
1965	1623.00	915.00			0.4051	0.4051				
1966	1783.00	953.00			0.4051	0.4051				
1967	1850.00	938.00			0.4051	0.4051				
1968	1763.00	1008.00			0.4051	0.4051				
1969	2091.70	1289.00			0.3824	0.3824				
1970	2373.30	1278.10			0.3601	0.3601				
1971	2834.70	1572.10			0.3609	0.3609				
1972	2932.00	1511.00			0.3965	0.3965				
1973	2369.00	1106.00			0.4450	0.4450				
1974	6202.90	2143.80			0.4157	0.4157				
1975	4974.00	2036.00			0.4673	0.4673				
1976	3118.60	2223.70			0.4187	0.4201				
1977	4052.50	2022.90			0.4322	0.4322				
1978	4329.00	2099.00			0.4440	0.4440				
1979	6135.00	3701.00			0.4704	0.4704				
1980	6147.00	2364.00			0.4908	0.4908				
1981	8791.00	4461.00			0.3680	0.3680				
1982	10725.00	6435.00			0.3043	0.3043				
1983	13099.00	7419.00			0.2624	0.2624				
1984	18778.00	3079.00			0.2289	0.2289				
1985	16481.00	7048.00			0.2226	0.2226				
1986	12849.00	7053.00			0.2888	0.2888				
1987	15560.00	3485.00			0.3327	0.3327				
1988	15647.00	6398.00			0.3357	0.3357				
1989	13575.00	5758.00			0.3135	0.3135				
1990	14040.00	4883.00			0.3673	0.3673				
1991	16399.00	7028.00			0.3545	0.3545				
1992	18139.01	5847.00			0.3778	0.3778				
1993	16816.90	6188.60			0.4028	0.4049				
1994	21929.30	4688.40			0.2408	0.2429				
1995	23411.20	4235.90			0.2675	0.2682				

2. IMPORTS BY BROAD ECONOMIC CATEGORY AND EXPORTS BY INDUSTRIAL ORIGIN. (PERCENTAGE OF TOTAL VALUE)
IMPORTATIONS PAR CATEGORIES ECONOMIQUES ET EXPORTATIONS PAR BRANCHE D'ACTIVITE.(EN POURCENTAGE DE LA VALEUR TOTALE)

IMPORTS – IMPORTATIONS

	1990	1991	1992	1993	1994	1995	1996
TOTAL IMPORTS–IMPORTATIONS TOTALES							
1 FOOD BEV–ALIMENTATION BOISSONS							
11 PRIMARY–PRODUITS DE BASE							
111 FOR INDUSTRY–POUR L'INDUSTRIE							
112 FOR HOUSEHOLDS–POUR LES MENAGES							
12 PROCESSED–PRODUITS ELABORES							
121 FOR INDUSTRY–POUR L'INDUSTRIE							
122 FOR HOUSEHOLDS–POUR LES MENAGES							
2 IND SUPPLIES–APPROV INDUSTRIELS							
21 PRIMARY–PRODUITS DE BASE							
22 PROCESSED–PRODUITS ELABORES							
3 FUELS–COMBUSTIBLES							
31 PRIMARY–PRODUITS DE BASE							
32 PROCESSED–PRODUITS ELABORES							
321 MOTOR SPIRIT–ESSENCE							
322 OTHER–AUTRES							
4 MACHINERY–EQUIPEMENT							
41 CAPITAL EQUIPMENT–MACHINES							
42 PARTS–PIECES ACCESSOIRES							
5 TRANSPORT–TRANSPORT							
51 PASSENGER CARS–AUTOMOBILES							
52 OTHER–AUTRES							
521 INDUSTRIAL–INDUSTRIELS							
522 NON INDUSTRIAL–NON INDUSTRIEL							
53 PARTS–PIECES ACCESSOIRES							
6 CONSUM GOODS–BIENS CONSOMMATION							
61 DURABLE–DURABLES							
62 SEMI DURABLE–SEMI DURABLES							
63 NON DURABLE–NON DURABLES							
7 GOODS NES–BIENS NDA							

EXPORTS – EXPORTATIONS

	1990	1991	1992	1993	1994	1995	1996
TOTAL EXPORTS–EXPORTATIONS TOTALES							
1 AGRICULTURE							
2 MINING QUARRY–INDUS EXTRACTIVES							
3 MANUFACTURING–IND MANUFACTUR							
31 FOOD BEV TOBACCO–ALIM BOISS TAB							
32 TEXTILES–INDUSTRIES TEXTILES							
33 WOOD & PRODUCTS–BOIS & PRODUITS							
34 PAPER & PRODUCTS–PAPIER & PRODT							
35 CHEMICALS–INDUSTRIES CHIMIQUES							
36 NON METAL MIN–MIN NON METAL							
37 BASIC METAL–IND METAL BASE							
38 METAL MANUF–MANUF METAL							
39 OTH MANUF IND–AUTRES MANUF							

3. TRADE BY PRINCIPAL COUNTRIES OF PROVENANCE AND DESTINATION (VALUE IN THOUSAND U.S. DOLLARS)
ECHANGES SELON LES PRINCIPAUX PAYS DE PROVENANCE ET DE DESTINATION (VALEUR EN MILLIERS DE DOLLARS EU)

COUNTRIES–PAYS	SPECIAL IMPORTS C.I.F. IMPORTATIONS SPECIALES C.A.F 1991	1992	1993	1994	1995
World			67755	52784	62625
Africa				8804	
Americas					
Northern America					
LAIA					
CACM					
Caribbean					
Rest of America					
As.ex F.USSR					16721
Eur.x F.USSR			27644	21114	20040
EU			27644	21114	20040
EFTA					
East Europe					
Other Europe					
Former USSR					
Oceania					
France,Monac			27644	21114	20040
India/Inde					10834
Saudi Arabia					5887
Kenya				5463	
So. Africa Customs Un				3341	

COUNTRIES–PAYS	SPECIAL EXPORTS F.O.B. EXPORTATIONS SPECIALES F.O.B. 1991	1992	1993	1994	1995
Monde	24914	22135	25058	11388	11361
Afrique					
Amériques	10617	10498	11553	3273	3222
Amérique du Nord	10617	10498	11553	3273	3222
ALAI					
MCAC					
Caraïbes					
Autre Amérique					
Asie l'URSS exclus					
Europe l'URSS exclus	7615	10287	12555	5978	5063
UE	7615	10287	12555	5978	5063
AELE					
Europe de l'Est					
Autre de l'Europe					
Ancienne URSS					
Océanie					
USA/Etats–Unis d'Amer	10617	10498	11553	3273	3222
France,Monac	7615	9113	10450	5340	4150
Germany/Allemagne		1173	2105	638	913

(VALUE AS PERCENTAGE OF WORLD TOTAL)(VALEURS EN POURCENTAGE DU TOTAL MONDIAL)

	1986	1987	1988	1989	1990	1991	1992	1993	1994	1995
Africa					12.8				16.7	
Americas										
Northern America										
LAIA										
CACM										
Caribbean										
Rest of America										
As.ex F.USSR					19.5					26.7
Eur.x F.USSR					40.0			40.8	40.0	32.0
EU					40.0			40.8	40.0	32.0
EFTA										
East Europe										
Other Europe										
Former USSR										
Oceania										
France,Monac					40.0			40.8	40.0	32.0
India/Inde										17.3
Saudi Arabia										9.4
Kenya									10.4	
So. Africa Customs Un					12.8				6.3	

	1986	1987	1988	1989	1990	1991	1992	1993	1994	1995
Afrique	1.2	5.4	0.7	0.5						
Amériques	43.5	39.7	58.9	48.3	35.0	42.6	47.4	46.1	28.7	28.4
Amérique du Nord	43.5	39.7	58.8	48.2	35.0	42.6	47.4	46.1	28.7	28.4
ALAI	0.1	0.0	0.0	0.0						
MCAC				0.0						
Caraïbes	0.0	0.0	0.0	0.0						
Autre Amérique	0.0	0.0	0.0	0.0						
Asie l'URSS exclus	2.5	6.0	1.7	3.6						
Europe l'URSS exclus	49.0	48.0	37.9	46.3	41.2	30.6	46.5	50.1	52.5	44.6
UE	48.9	47.8	37.7	46.1	41.2	30.6	46.5	50.1	52.5	44.6
AELE	0.1	0.1	0.1	0.1						
Europe de l'Est										
Autre de l'Europe	0.0	0.1	0.1	0.1						
Ancienne URSS										
Océanie	0.0	0.0	0.0	0.0						
USA/Etats–Unis d'Amer	24.1	16.3	31.2	27.7	30.0	42.6	47.4	46.1	28.7	28.4
France,Monac	39.7	29.1	27.0	35.6	41.2	30.6	41.2	41.7	46.9	36.5
Germany/Allemagne	7.1	10.8	6.8	7.9			5.3	8.4	5.6	8.0

4. Special Imports C.I.F. by Commodities according to the S.I.T.C. (Rev. 2) in thousand U.S. Dollars
Importations Spéciales C.A.F. par Produits d'après la C.T.C.I. (Rév. 2) en milliers de Dollars E.U.

SITC CTCI	COMMODITY	1992 WEIGHT POIDS	1992 VALUE VALEUR	1993 WEIGHT POIDS	1993 VALUE VALEUR	1994 WEIGHT POIDS	1994 VALUE VALEUR	1995 WEIGHT POIDS	1995 VALUE VALEUR	PRODUIT
	ALL COMMODITIES		68620		67755		52784		62625	TOUS PRODUITS
01	MEAT AND PREPARATIONS		4432		5078		3139		4466	VIANDES ET PREPARATIONS
02	DAIRY PRODCTS,BIRDS'EGGS		2837		2082		2051		1317	PRODUITS LAITIERS,OEUFS
042	RICE	W 32493	8162	W 30271	6646	W 28518	6293	W 41650	14050	RIZ
04601	FLOUR OF WHEAT OR MESLIN	W 3617	1052	W 3767	1401	W 3911	1269	W 3918	1507	FARINE DE FROMENT
061	SUGAR AND HONEY	W 3939	2438	W 3854	2309	W 3629	1906	W 3665	2246	SUCRES ET MIEL
334	PETROLEUM PRODUCTS,REFIN	W 30536	7190	W 21148	7224	W 23816	6128	W 33962	7749	PRODUITS RAFFINES
541	*MEDICINAL,PHARM PRODUCT	K 91100	1198	K 99800	1369	K 89300	734	K 62000	633	PROD MEDICINAUX PHARMACEUT
6612	CEMENT	W 34568	3310	W 41980	4111	W 39212	4033	W 43315	4419	CIMENTS HYDRAULIQUES
67	IRON AND STEEL		2400		2521		2047		2375	FER ET ACIER
78	ROAD VEHICLES		7334		6095		3893		4412	VEHICULES ROUTIERS
84	CLOTHING AND ACCESSORIES		1391		1564		813		682	VETEMENTS
9	GOODS NOT CLASSD BY KIND		26876		27354		20478			ART TRANSACT NON CLASSES
931	*SPECIAL TRANSACTIONS		26876		27354		20478		18768	TRANS.SPECIALES

5. Special Exports F.O.B. by Commodities according to the S.I.T.C. (Rev. 2) in thousand U.S. Dollars
Exportations Spéciales F.O.B. par Produits d'après la C.T.C.I. (Rév. 2) en milliers de Dollars E.U.

SITC CTCI	COMMODITY	1992 WEIGHT POIDS	1992 VALUE VALEUR	1993 WEIGHT POIDS	1993 VALUE VALEUR	1994 WEIGHT POIDS	1994 VALUE VALEUR	1995 WEIGHT POIDS	1995 VALUE VALEUR	PRODUIT
	ALL COMMODITIES		22135		25058		11388		11361	TOUS PRODUITS
0	FOOD AND LIVE ANIMALS				20504		7991		6581	ALIMENTS,ANIMAUX VIVANTS
07	COFFEE,TEA,COCOA,SPICES				20504		7991		6581	CAFE,THE,CACAO,EPICES
075	SPICES	W 710	15996	W 1854	20504	W 2885	7991	W 642	6581	EPICES
0752	SPICES,EX PEPPER,PIMENTO	W 710	15996	W 1854	20504	W 2885	7991	W 642	6581	AUTRES EPICES
07521	VANILLA	W 236	15588	W 288	19420	W 131	6722	W 159	6223	VANILLE
07523	CLOVES	W 474	408	W 1566	1084	W 2754	1269	W 483	359	GIROFLES
5	CHEMCLS,RELATED PROD NES				3342		2264		2301	PRODUITS CHIMIQUES
55	PERFUME,CLEANING ETC PRD				3342		2264		2301	PROD POUR PARFUM,TOILETTE
551	ESSENTL OILS,PERFUME,ETC			W 39	3342	W 45	2264	W 44	2301	HUILES ESSENTIELLES
5513	ESSENTL OIL,RESINOID,ETC	W 46	4354	W 39	3342	W 45	2264	W 44	2301	HUILES ESSENTIELLES,RESIN
9	GOODS NOT CLASSD BY KIND		1786		1212		1134			ART TRANSACT NON CLASSES
931	*SPECIAL TRANSACTIONS		1786		1212		1134		2479	TRANS.SPECIALES

1. HISTORICAL SERIES, 1960–1995 SPECIAL TRADE, IMPORTS C.I.F., EXPORTS F.O.B.
SERIES HISTORIQUES, 1960–1995 COMMERCE SPECIAL, IMPORTATIONS C.A.F., EXPORTATIONS F.O.B

YEAR ANNEE	VALUE IN MILLION C.F.A. FRANCS / VALEUR EN MILLION C.F.A. FRANCS — MERCHANDISE –MARCHANDISE		GOLD –OR		CONVERSION FACTORS U.S. CENTS PER C.F.A. FRANC FACTEURS DE CONVERSION CENTS E.U. PAR C.F.A. FRANC		INDEX NUMBERS –INDICES — QUANTUM		UNIT VALUE VALEUR UNITAIRE	
	IMPORTS	EXPORTS	IMPORTS	EXPORTS	IMPORTS	EXPORTS	IMPORTS	EXPORTS	IMPORTS	EXPORTS
1960	17316.00	4399.00	0.10	29.20	0.4051	0.4051				
1961	19492.00	4830.00	0.20	39.40	0.4051	0.4051				
1962	16010.00	8404.00	0.10	29.10	0.4051	0.4051				
1963	15245.00	10277.00		18.80	0.4051	0.4051				
1964	16006.00	11690.00		12.60	0.4051	0.4051				
1965	15974.00	11512.00		5.70	0.4051	0.4051				
1966	17170.00	10659.00			0.4051	0.4051				
1967	20231.00	11730.00			0.4051	0.4051				
1968	20605.00	12189.00			0.4051	0.4051				
1969	20291.00	11384.00			0.3854	0.3874				
1970	15910.00	8564.00			0.3601	0.3601				
1971	21910.00	10300.00			0.3601	0.3601				
1972	22608.00	13212.00			0.3970	0.3966				
1973	27730.00	19600.00			0.4501	0.4501				
1974	29900.00	45090.00			0.4160	0.4160				
1975	36380.00	38400.00			0.4673	0.4673				
1976	40240.00	43380.00			0.4185	0.4184				
1977	50450.00	42560.00			0.4071	0.4071				
1978	60364.00	69545.00			0.4432	0.4432				
1979	77209.00	105440.00			0.4701	0.4701				
1980	115191.00	192393.00			0.4733	0.4733				
1981	218362.00	291488.00			0.3680	0.3680				
1982	244560.00	364260.00			0.3043	0.3043				
1983	262090.00	406280.00			0.2624	0.2624				
1984	259820.00	516700.00			0.2289	0.2289				
1985	260871.00	488515.00			0.2226	0.2226				
1986	206648.00	268989.90			0.2888	0.2888				
1987	159083.00	155440.00			0.3327	0.3327				
1988	167985.00	279200.00			0.3357	0.3357				
1989	165130.00	397700.10			0.3131	0.3131				
1990	169023.00	267100.00			0.3652	0.3652				
1991	167684.00	290500.10			0.3570	0.3552				
1992	119480.00	312000.00			0.3777	0.3790				
1993	164789.00	302629.80			0.3535	0.3534				
1994	352465.90	517580.00			0.1809	0.1810				
1995	334182.90	420379.90			0.2006	0.2003				

2. IMPORTS BY BROAD ECONOMIC CATEGORY AND EXPORTS BY INDUSTRIAL ORIGIN. (PERCENTAGE OF TOTAL VALUE)
IMPORTATIONS PAR CATEGORIES ECONOMIQUES ET EXPORTATIONS PAR BRANCHE D'ACTIVITE.(EN POURCENTAGE DE LA VALEUR TOTALE)

IMPORTS – IMPORTATIONS

	1990	1991	1992	1993	1994	1995	1996
TOTAL IMPORTS–IMPORTATIONS TOTALES				100.	100.		
1 FOOD BEV–ALIMENTATION BOISSONS				18.3	25.5		
11 PRIMARY–PRODUITS DE BASE				5.8	11.7		
111 FOR INDUSTRY–POUR L'INDUSTRIE				0.9	0.4		
112 FOR HOUSEHOLDS–POUR LES MENAGES				4.9	11.3		
12 PROCESSED–PRODUITS ELABORES				12.5	13.8		
121 FOR INDUSTRY–POUR L'INDUSTRIE				5.7	5.7		
122 FOR HOUSEHOLDS–POUR LES MENAGES				6.9	8.1		
2 IND SUPPLIES–APPROV INDUSTRIELS				22.7	28.4		
21 PRIMARY–PRODUITS DE BASE				1.7	2.0		
22 PROCESSED–PRODUITS ELABORES				21.0	26.4		
3 FUELS–COMBUSTIBLES				0.8	0.8		
31 PRIMARY–PRODUITS DE BASE				0.0	0.0		
32 PROCESSED–PRODUITS ELABORES				0.8	0.8		
321 MOTOR SPIRIT–ESSENCE							
322 OTHER–AUTRES				0.8	0.8		
4 MACHINERY–EQUIPEMENT				32.0	24.4		
41 CAPITAL EQUIPMENT–MACHINES				27.8	19.6		
42 PARTS–PIECES ACCESSOIRES				4.1	4.8		
5 TRANSPORT–TRANSPORT				7.3	7.1		
51 PASSENGER CARS–AUTOMOBILES				2.3	2.1		
52 OTHER–AUTRES				2.6	2.4		
521 INDUSTRIAL–INDUSTRIELS				2.5	2.3		
522 NON INDUSTRIAL–NON INDUSTRIEL				0.1	0.1		
53 PARTS–PIECES ACCESSOIRES				2.4	2.6		
6 CONSUM GOODS–BIENS CONSOMMATION				18.7	13.7		
61 DURABLE–DURABLES				1.5	0.9		
62 SEMI DURABLE–SEMI DURABLES				4.7	3.4		
63 NON DURABLE–NON DURABLES				12.6	9.4		
7 GOODS NES–BIENS NDA				0.1	0.1		

EXPORTS – EXPORTATIONS

	1990	1991	1992	1993	1994	1995	1996
TOTAL EXPORTS–EXPORTATIONS TOTALES				100.	100.		
1 AGRICULTURE				1.3	11.7		
2 MINING QUARRY–INDUS EXTRACTIVES				92.3	82.4		
3 MANUFACTURING–IND MANUFACTUR				6.4	5.9		
31 FOOD BEV TOBACCO–ALIM BOISS TAB				0.9	0.8		
32 TEXTILES–INDUSTRIES TEXTILES				0.0	0.0		
33 WOOD & PRODUCTS–BOIS & PRODUITS				2.4	1.9		
34 PAPER & PRODUCTS–PAPIER & PRODT				0.0	0.0		
35 CHEMICALS–INDUSTRIES CHIMIQUES				2.2	2.2		
36 NON METAL MIN–MIN NON METAL				0.0	0.0		
37 BASIC METAL–IND METAL BASE				0.2	0.0		
38 METAL MANUF–MANUF METAL				0.8	1.0		
39 OTH MANUF IND–AUTRES MANUF				0.0	0.0		

3. TRADE BY PRINCIPAL COUNTRIES OF ORIGIN AND DESTINATION (VALUE IN THOUSAND U.S. DOLLARS)
ECHANGES SELON LES PRINCIPAUX PAYS D'ORIGINE ET DE DESTINATION (VALEUR EN MILLIERS DE DOLLARS EU)

COUNTRIES–PAYS	SPECIAL IMPORTS C.I.F. IMPORTATIONS SPECIALES C.A.F				
	1990	1991	1992	1993	1994
World	594491			347064	408372
Africa	2272			15665	33870
Americas	67993			19283	43037
Northern America	66152			16585	41358
LAIA	1841			2682	1668
CACM				0	1
Caribbean				15	10
Rest of America					
As.ex F.USSR	25929			27181	25457
Eur.x F.USSR	346863			243247	225680
EU	346863			240373	220573
EFTA				2557	4889
East Europe				317	207
Other Europe					
Former USSR	3287			70	552
Oceania				5	372
France,Monac	218645			113953	131808
Italy/Italie	62559			66228	17652
USA/Etats–Unis d'Amer	66152			16091	40854
Netherlands/Pays–Bas	27175			27475	25428
Germany/Allemagne	29066			8364	9526
Japan/Japon	23877			11053	10526
Belgium–Luxembourg				9686	15401
United Kingdom				9030	13074
Spain/Espagne	9419			3151	3554
So. Africa Customs Un				2752	8444
Hong Kong				4496	4170
Senegal/Sénégal				1847	6241
Cote d'Ivoire				2875	3738
Singapore/Singapour				3023	3141
Norway,SVD,JM				1650	4157
Cameroon/Cameroun				2654	2391
Viet Nam				2888	1750
China/Chine	2052			1349	1014
Morocco/Maroc				822	2672
Former USSR/Anc. URSS	3287				
Nigeria/Nigéria				1960	1325
Brazil/Brésil	1841			995	448
Angola				173	3073
Dem. Rep. of the Congo	1304			822	650
Argentina/Argentine				1568	954
Indonesia/Indonésie				1018	1359
Portugal				1336	1029
Guinea–Bissau					2306
Korea, Republic of				943	1259
Ireland/Irlande				559	1590
Switz.Liecht				904	731
Thailand/Thaïlande				654	586
Benin/Bénin				454	743
Sweden/Suède				232	940
Tunisia/Tunisie	968			23	11
Canada				494	505
Gabon				293	573
Mauritania/Mauritanie				3	752
Myanmar				677	
Russian Federation				70	552
Denmark/Danemark				244	377
Togo				147	395
Zimbabwe				493	13
Egypt/Egypte				216	239
Turkey/Turquie				161	256
India/Inde				120	287
Czech Republic				238	123
New Zealand				4	354
Korea Dem People's Rp				179	107
Pakistan				1	273

COUNTRIES–PAYS	SPECIAL EXPORTS F.O.B. EXPORTATIONS SPECIALES F.O.B.				
	1990	1991	1992	1993	1994
Monde	977670			965339	948482
Afrique	10277			18223	22040
Amériques	354774			507871	440660
Amérique du Nord	354503			507572	399176
ALAI	270			64	30656
MCAC					
Caraïbes				235	10829
Autre Amérique					
Asie l'URSS exclus	464			79680	141040
Europe l'URSS exclus	443627			359546	344705
UE	443627			346130	340211
AELE				13416	4486
Europe de l'Est					8
Autre de l'Europe					
Ancienne URSS	1271			1	2
Océanie				13	32
USA/Etats–Unis d'Amer	354503			503409	399172
Italy/Italie	112803			226299	198201
France,Monac	240506			79493	58135
Netherlands/Pays–Bas	54196			16550	11403
Spain/Espagne	23727			17271	29023
Israel/Israël				12814	12244
Portugal				1587	22649
Germany/Allemagne	12395			2634	8392
Angola	3838			10183	5232
Japan/Japon	464			14350	3294
Chile/Chili					16135
Brazil/Brésil	270			64	14485
Switz.Liecht				12319	1
Dem. Rep. of the Congo	6431			1112	4355
Reunion/Réunion				4724	4194
Belgium–Luxembourg				465	8131
Morocco/Maroc				818	5540
Bahamas					5713
Norway,SVD,JM				1097	4485
Haiti/Haïti					5116
Bermuda/Bermudes				4163	
United Kingdom				1111	1763
Greece/Grèce				24	1887
Turkey/Turquie					1281
Denmark/Danemark				669	606
Former USSR/Anc. URSS	1271				
China/Chine				31	1228
So. Africa Customs Un				403	739
Guinea/Guinée				330	363
Algeria/Algérie					629
Tunisia/Tunisie	7			103	194
Singapore/Singapour				47	192
Trinidad and Tobago				235	
Nigeria/Nigéria				107	68
Korea, Republic of				162	11
Mauritius/Maurice				171	
Gabon				89	61
Zimbabwe				55	81
Togo				6	127
Chad/Tchad					105
Cote d'Ivoire				8	79
Benin/Bénin				22	62
Mauritania/Mauritanie					62
Un. Rep. of Tanzania				51	
Senegal/Sénégal				6	45
Australia/Australie				13	32
Argentina/Argentine					36
Lebanon/Liban				35	
Ireland/Irlande				25	
India/Inde					23

(VALUE AS PERCENTAGE OF WORLD TOTAL)(VALEURS EN POURCENTAGE DU TOTAL MONDIAL)

	1985	1986	1987	1988	1989	1990	1991	1992	1993	1994
Africa	5.6	4.4	3.9	3.0	3.3	0.4			4.5	8.3
Americas	10.4	8.2	4.7	8.2	6.0	11.4			5.6	10.5
Northern America	6.8	7.3	2.0	5.5	5.0	11.1			4.8	10.1
LAIA	3.5	0.9	2.7	2.7	1.1	0.3			0.8	0.4
CACM	0.0	0.0							0.0	0.0
Caribbean	0.1	0.0			0.0				0.0	0.0
Rest of America	0.0	0.0								
As.ex F.USSR	7.1	7.1	5.8	6.0	6.8	4.4			7.8	6.2
Eur.x F.USSR	75.2	78.2	72.4	69.6	73.3	58.3			70.1	55.3
EU	72.9	75.9	71.7	68.9	72.6	58.3			69.3	54.0
EFTA	1.9	1.8	0.7	0.7	0.7				0.7	1.2
East Europe	0.4	0.4							0.1	0.1
Other Europe	0.0	0.0	0.0	0.0	0.0					
Former USSR	0.7	1.0	0.6	0.6	0.6	0.6			0.0	0.1
Oceania	0.0	0.0							0.0	0.1
France,Monac	45.5	52.5	50.7	46.3	49.7	36.8			32.8	32.3
Italy/Italie	8.3	4.6	5.8	6.9	6.2	10.5			19.1	4.3
USA/Etats–Unis d'Amer	6.6	5.2	1.8	5.5	5.0	11.1			4.6	10.0
Netherlands/Pays–Bas	2.7	2.5	3.2	3.4	3.5	4.6			7.9	6.2
Germany/Allemagne	4.7	3.2	2.9	4.0	5.2	4.9			2.4	2.3
Japan/Japon	3.4	4.2	3.3	3.8	3.6	4.0			3.2	2.6
Belgium–Luxembourg	2.4	2.8	1.7	1.6	1.7				2.8	3.8
United Kingdom	3.4	3.3	3.5	3.5	3.7				2.6	3.2
Spain/Espagne	4.5	5.6	3.5	2.7	2.1	1.6			0.9	0.9
So. Africa Customs Un	0.1	0.2							0.8	2.1

	1985	1986	1987	1988	1989	1990	1991	1992	1993	1994
Afrique	3.5	2.8	1.3	1.8	1.8	1.1			1.9	2.3
Amériques	60.0	54.2	37.4	41.7	44.5	36.3			52.6	46.5
Amérique du Nord	60.0	54.2	37.2	41.6	44.0	36.3			52.6	42.1
ALAI	0.0	0.0	0.2	0.1	0.5	0.0			0.0	3.2
MCAC										
Caraïbes	0.0	0.0							0.0	1.1
Autre Amérique	0.0	0.0								
Asie l'URSS exclus	1.7	0.2	1.6	1.2	1.0	0.0			8.3	14.9
Europe l'URSS exclus	34.6	42.0	53.9	47.9	46.6	45.4			37.2	36.3
UE	34.5	41.7	53.4	47.5	46.3	45.4			35.9	35.9
AELE	0.0	0.1	0.3	0.3	0.2				1.4	0.5
Europe de l'Est	0.0	0.2								0.0
Autre de l'Europe	0.0	0.1	0.1	0.1	0.1					
Ancienne URSS	0.1	0.4	0.7	0.4	0.4	0.1			0.0	0.0
Océanie	0.0	0.2	0.0	0.0	0.0				0.0	0.0
USA/Etats–Unis d'Amer	60.0	54.2	37.2	41.6	44.0	36.3			52.1	42.1
Italy/Italie	1.8	9.0	11.5	7.2	8.3	11.5			23.4	20.9
France,Monac	10.9	12.9	18.0	18.1	17.3	24.6			8.2	6.1
Netherlands/Pays–Bas	6.1	4.3	4.2	5.8	5.0	5.5			1.7	1.2
Spain/Espagne	13.9	11.5	7.2	5.0	6.7	2.4			1.8	3.1
Israel/Israël	0.0								1.3	1.3
Portugal	0.2	0.9	1.4	1.3	1.0				0.2	2.4
Germany/Allemagne	0.3	0.9	5.9	5.4	4.4	1.3			0.3	0.9
Angola	1.1	0.3	0.1	0.2	0.2	0.4			1.1	0.6
Japan/Japon	0.0	0.1	1.1	0.9	0.7	0.0			1.5	0.3

4. Special Imports C.I.F. by Commodities according to the S.I.T.C. (Rev. 2) in thousand U.S. Dollars
Importations Spéciales C.A.F. par Produits d'après la C.T.C.I. (Rév. 2) en milliers de Dollars E.U.

SITC CTCI	COMMODITY	1991		1992		1993		1994		PRODUIT
		WEIGHT POIDS	VALUE VALEUR	WEIGHT POIDS	VALUE VALEUR	WEIGHT POIDS	VALUE VALEUR	WEIGHT POIDS	VALUE VALEUR	
	ALL COMMODITIES						347064		408372	TOUS PRODUITS
0	FOOD AND LIVE ANIMALS						59572		90831	ALIMENTS,ANIMAUX VIVANTS
01	MEAT AND PREPARATIONS						15816		24531	VIANDES ET PREPARATIONS
011	MEAT FRESH,CHILLD,FROZEN					W 15156	15042	W 23964	22419	VIANDES FRAICHES,REF,CONGE
0111	BOVINE MEAT FRESH,FROZEN					W 173	338	W 14125	12136	VIANDES BOVIN FRAI,REF
01112	BOVINE MEAT BONELESS							W 14055	12054	VIANDES BOVIN DESOSSEES
0113	PIG MEAT FRESH,CHLD,FRZN					W 1909	1371	W 2444	2047	VIANDE DE PORC
0114	POULTRY FRESH CHLLD,FRZN					W 12431	12385	W 6492	7209	VOLAILLES MORTES
014	MEAT PREPD,PRSVD,NES ETC					W 612	747	W 1228	2088	CONSERVES DE VIANDES
0149	OTH PREPARD,PRESRVD MEAT					W 612	747	W 963	1574	AUTRES PREP DE VIANDES
02	DAIRY PRODCTS,BIRDS'EGGS						10032		8970	PRODUITS LAITIERS,OEUFS
022	MILK AND CREAM					W 6325	7617	W 4568	7415	LAIT ET CREME
0224	MILK,CREAM PRESERVED ETC					W 5642	7219	W 4021	7009	LAIT,CREME CONS,CONC
02243	MILK DRY,OVER 1.5% FAT							W 1597	3798	LAIT POUDRE SUP 1.5%
02249	MILK(EX DRY) PRSVD,SWEET					W 5558	7062	W 2423	3208	LAIT CONS,CONC SUCRE
03	FISH AND PREPARATIONS						129		22514	POISSONS ET PREPARATIONS
034	FISH,FRESH,CHILLED,FROZN						11	W 17497	10302	POISSON FRAIS, REFRIG,CONG
0342	FISH FROZEN,EXCL FILLETS						4	W 17497	10299	POISSONS CONGELES
035	FISH SALTED,DRIED,SMOKED					W 24	73	W 5489	11422	POISSON SECHE,SALE,FUME
03503	FISH(EX COD)DRIED,SALTED					W 24	73	W 5488	11413	POISSONS SECHES,SALES
04	CEREALS AND PREPARATIONS						27507		24586	CEREALES ET PRODUITS
041	WHEAT ETC UNMILLED					W 19375	2989	W 7072	1389	FROMENT,EPEAUTRE
0411	DURUM WHEAT UNMILLED					W 19375	2989	W 7072	1389	FROMENT DUR NON MOULU
042	RICE					W 21069	5020	W 30907	7204	RIZ
0422	RICE SEMI–MILLED,MILLED					W 21068	5020	W 30906	7204	RIZ POLI,GLACE INCL BRISURES
04221	RICE MILLED UNBROKEN					W 21068	5020	W 29965	6879	RIZ POLI,GLACE EXCL BRISURES
046	WHEAT ETC MEAL OR FLOUR					W 65119	18105	W 34221	8431	SEMOULE FARINE,FROMENT
04601	FLOUR OF WHEAT OR MESLIN					W 65114	18092	W 34219	8429	FARINE DE FROMENT
047	OTHER CEREAL MEALS,FLOUR					W 1	1	W 3026	1555	AUTRES SEMOULES,FARINES
04702	MEAL OR GROATS NON–WHEAT							W 3023	1551	GRUAUX,SEMOULES DE CEREALES
048	CEREAL ETC PREPARATIONS					W 1349	1377	W 6188	6005	PREPTNS A BASE CEREALES
0482	MALT INCLUDING FLOUR							W 4819	3101	MALT MEME TORREFIE
0488	OTH CEREAL PREPS,MALT EX					W 34	78	W 423	1978	EXTRAITS DE MALT
05	VEGETABLES AND FRUIT						2704		4394	LEGUMES ET FRUITS
054	VEG ETC FRSH,SMPLY PRSVD					W 1897	1685	W 3571	3512	LEGUMES FRAIS,CONG,SECS
0546	VEGETABLES SIMPLY PRESVD					W 1714	1542	W 1830	2402	LEGUMES CONG,CONSER
05461	VEGETABLES FROZEN					W 1714	1542	W 1830	2402	LEGUMES CONGELES
06	SUGAR AND PREPS,HONEY						1084		1332	SUCRES ET PRODUITS
09	MISC EDIBLE PRODUCTS						1703		3776	PREP ALIMENTAIRES DIVERSES
098	EDIBLE PRODCTS,PREPS NES					W 1562	1703	W 1111	2563	PREP ALIMENTAIRES NDA
1	BEVERAGES AND TOBACCO						2987		6353	BOISSONS ET TABACS
11	BEVERAGES						2897		2947	BOISSONS
112	ALCOHOLIC BEVERAGES					W 3835	2363	W 4100	2616	BOISSONS ALCOOLIQUES
1121	WINE OF FRESH GRAPES ETC					W 3725	1977	W 3155	1694	VINS DE RAISINS FRAIS
11212	WINE OF FRESH GRAPES					W 3724	1971	W 3149	1676	VINS DE MOUTS DE RAISINS
12	TOBACCO AND MANUFACTURES						90		3405	TABACS BRUTS FABRIQUES
121	TOBACCO UNMNFCTRD,REFUSE					W 19	39	W 621	3369	TABACS BRUTS,DECHETS
1212	TOBACCO STRIPPED OR PART							W 591	3322	TABACS PART ECOTES
2	CRUDE MATERLS,EXCL FUELS						5920		5076	MAT BRUTES NON COMESTIBLES
26	TEXTILE FIBRES AND WASTE						147		1770	FIBRES TEXTILES
269	WASTE OF TEXTILE FABRICS					W 140	128	W 1001	1717	FRIPERIE DRILLES,CHIFFONS
26901	BULK TEXT WSTE,OLD CLTHG							W 954	1660	ART ET ACCESS D'HABILLEMENT
27	CRUDE FERTLZR,MINRLS NES						4179		2742	ENGRAIS MINERAUX BRUTS
278	OTHER CRUDE MINERALS					W 11586	2990	W 11520	2538	AUTRES MINERAUX BRUTS
2783	COMMON SALT,ETC					W 8248	1975	W 7910	1794	SEL
29	CRUDE ANIMAL,VEG MAT NES						1515		399	MATIERES BRUTES ANIM,VEGET
3	MINERAL FUELS ETC						2892		5092	COMBUSTIBLES MINERAUX LUB
33	PETROLEUM AND PRODUCTS						2784		5026	PETROLE ET DERIVES
334	PETROLEUM PRODUCTS,REFIN					W 4024	2717	W 5214	3171	PRODUITS RAFFINES
335	RESIDUAL PETRLM PROD NES						68	W 6720	1856	PRODUITS RESIDUELS NDA
3354	PETROLM BITUMEN,COKE ETC					W 17	11	W 6719	1855	BITUME,COKE DE PETROLE
33543	BITUMINOUS MIXTURES ETC					W 3	3	W 6432	1705	MELANGES BITUMINEUX
4	ANIMAL,VEGETABLE OIL,FAT						8290		11033	HUILES,GRAISSES ANIM,VEG
42	FIXED VEGETABLE OIL,FAT						8289		10809	HUILES VEGETALES FIXES
423	FIXED VEG OILS,SOFT					W 605	529	W 8932	8742	HUILES VEGET DOUCES FIXES
4232	SOYA BEAN OIL							W 7550	7309	HUILE DE SOJA
4236	SUNFLOWER SEED OIL							W 1372	1413	HUILE DE TOURNESOL
424	FIXED VEG OIL NONSOFT					W 10966	7760	W 2415	2067	AUTRES HUILES VEG FIXES
4242	PALM OIL					W 1620	532	W 1666	1364	HUILE DE PALME
4249	FIXED VEGETABLE OILS NES					W 9342	7220	W 746	698	HUILES VEGET FIXES NDA
5	CHEMCLS,RELATED PROD NES						54617		56535	PRODUITS CHIMIQUES
51	ORGANIC CHEMICALS						1987		1441	PROD CHIMIQ ORGANIQUES
514	NITROGEN–FNCTN COMPOUNDS					W 221	1180	W 155	353	COMPOSES FONCT AZOTEES
52	INORGANIC CHEMICALS						926		3470	PROD CHIM INORGANIQUES
522	INORG ELEMNTS,OXIDES,ETC					W 260	366	W 4824	2077	ELEMENTS INORGANIQUES
523	OTHR INORG CHEMICALS ETC					W 678	541	W 3034	1371	AUT PRODUITS CHIMIQUES INORG
53	DYES,TANNING,COLOUR PROD						838		1380	PROD TEINTURE,COLORANTS
533	PIGMENTS,PAINTS,ETC					W 478	758	W 422	1349	PIGMENTS,PEINTURES,VERNIS
541	*MEDICINAL,PHARM PRODUCT					K 2104827	39255	K 1322614	25325	PROD MEDICINAUX PHARMACEUT
5417	MEDICAMENTS					K 2019362	38451	K 1275690	24789	MEDICAMENTS
54179	— CONTNG OTH SUBSTANCES					K 2001822	37939	K 1260979	24548	MED CONT AUT SUBSTANCES
55	PERFUME,CLEANING ETC PRD						4423		5359	PROD POUR PARFUM,TOILETTE
554	SOAP,CLEANSING ETC PREPS					W 2226	2855	W 4551	3564	SAVONS,PRODUITS DETERSIFS
5541	SOAPS					W 1150	962	W 3872	2079	SAVONS,PROD TENSIO–ACTIFS
5542	WASHING PREPARATIONS ETC					W 851	1513	W 583	1269	PROD ORG TENSIO–ACT NDA
572	*EXPLOSIVES,PYROTECH PRO					W 147	1745	W 60	928	EXPLOSIFS
5721	PREPARED EXPLOSIVES					W 147	1716	W 53	847	POUDRES,EXPLOSIFS
57211	PROPELLENT POWDERS					W 89	1470	W 49	667	POUDRES A TIRER
58	PLASTIC MATERIALS ETC						1841		1944	MAT PLAST ARTIFICIELLES
59	CHEMICAL MATERIALS NES						3596		15916	MAT PROD CHIMIQUES NDA
598	MISCEL CHEM PRODUCTS NES					W 1323	3037	W 12647	14763	PROD DIV INDUST CHIM NDA
5989	CHEM PRODUCTS,PREPS NES					W 871	1982	W 12555	14485	PROD PREP CHIMIQUES NDA
59899	OTH CHEM PRODS,PREPS,NES					W 820	1800	W 12279	13791	AUT PRODUITS CHIMIQUES NDA
6	BASIC MANUFACTURES						61518		79212	ART MANUFACTURES
62	RUBBER MANUFACTURES NES						4186		7834	CAOUTCHOUC MANUFACTURE
621	MATERIALS OF RUBBER					W 93	1315	W 424	4781	PRODUITS EN CAOUTCHOUC
62105	UNHARD VULC RUBBER TUBES					W 88	1302	W 396	4735	TUBES,TUYAUX CAOUT VULC
625	RUBBER TYRES, TUBES ETC					W 994	2673	W 763	2413	PNEUS CAOUTCHOUC VULCANISE
6252	TYRES,NEW,BUS OR LORRY					W 621	1465	W 258	1001	PNEUS POUR AUTOBUS,CAMIONS
63	WOOD,CORK MANUFACTRS NES						6023		400	OUVRAGES LIEGE ET BOIS
635	WOOD MANUFACTURES NES					W 4498	5973	W 156	301	ART MANUF EN BOIS NDA

4. Special Imports C.I.F. by Commodities according to the S.I.T.C. (Rev. 2) in thousand U.S. Dollars
Importations Spéciales C.A.F. par Produits d'après la C.T.C.I. (Rév. 2) en milliers de Dollars E.U.

SITC CTCI	COMMODITY	1991		1992		1993		1994		PRODUIT
		WEIGHT POIDS	VALUE VALEUR	WEIGHT POIDS	VALUE VALEUR	WEIGHT POIDS	VALUE VALEUR	WEIGHT POIDS	VALUE VALEUR	
6353	BUILDERS WOODWRK,PREFABS					W 4450	5855	W 115	193	OUVRAGES DE MENUISERIE
64	PAPER,PAPERBOARD AND MFR						7924		4881	PAPIERS,CARTONS & OUVRAGES
641	PAPER AND PAPERBOARD					W 789	2205	W 1155	1813	PAPIERS ET CARTONS
6412	PRINTG,WRITING PAPER NES					W 400	1360	W 522	919	PAPIERS POUR L'IMPRESSION
64121	— UNCOATED					W 360	1258	W 513	895	PAPIERS IMPRES NON COUCHES
642	PAPER,ETC,PRECUT,ARTS OF					W 2242	5719	W 1028	3069	PAP,CARTONS DECOUPES
6421	PAPER ETC CONTAINERS					W 1451	3925	W 368	1273	BOITES,SACS EMBALLAGES
65	TEXTILE YARN,FABRICS,ETC						2631		2846	FILS,TISSUS,ARTICLES TEXTILE
658	TEXTILE ARTICLES NES					W 483	1074	W 479	945	ART FACONNES MAT TEXTILES
66	NONMETAL MINERAL MFS NES						5012		4064	ART MIN NON METALLIQUES
661	LIME,CEMENT,BLDG PRODS					W 5067	981	W 8859	1501	CHAUX,CIMENTS MAT CONSTR
662	CLAY,REFRACTORY BLDG PRD					W 2575	1216	W 1754	764	MAT CONST REFRACTAIRES
6624	BRICKS ETC NONREFRACTORY					W 2507	1136	W 1732	754	BRIQUES ETC CERAM NON REFR
665	GLASSWARE					W 1860	1782	W 312	557	OUVRAGES EN VERRE
6651	BOTTLES ETC OF GLASS					W 1406	1109	W 14	37	RECIPIENTS EN VERRE
66511	GLASS BOTTLES ETC NONVAC					W 1406	1109	W 14	37	BONBONNES,BOUTEILLES,ETC
67	IRON AND STEEL						17772		21226	FER ET ACIER
673	IRON,STEEL SHAPES ETC					W 4095	1738	W 3860	1802	BARRES,PROFIL FER,ACIER
6732	IRON,STEEL BARS ETC					W 3147	1235	W 2735	1179	BARRES FER,ACIER
678	IRON,STL TUBES,PIPES,ETC					W 16255	14606	W 15025	18234	TUBES,TUYAUX EN FONTE,FER
6782	IRON,STL SEAMLESS TUBES					W 15672	13215	W 14039	16337	TUBES,TUYAUX SANS SOUDURE
6785	IRON,STEEL TUBE FITTINGS					W 199	1125	W 168	1295	ACCESSOIRES DE TUYAUTERIE
68	NON-FERROUS METALS						2795		1209	METAUX NON FERREUX
684	ALUMINIUM					W 728	2730	W 416	1066	ALUMINIUM
6842	ALUMINIUM,ALLOYS WORKED					W 728	2730	W 416	1066	ALUMINIUM,ALLIAGES OUVRE
68422	ALUMNM PLATE,SHEET,STRIP					W 656	1759	W 383	726	TOLES, PLANCHES EN ALU
69	METAL MANUFACTURES NES						15169		36738	ART MANUFACT EN METAL NDA
691	STRUCTURES AND PARTS NES					W 108	220	W 4680	22346	CONSTRUCT FER,ACIER,ALU
6911	STRUCTURES,PARTS IRN,STL					W 58	107	W 4663	22278	CONSTRUCT FER,ACIER,FONTE
695	TOOLS					W 108	1459	W 396	5679	OUTILS A MAIN
6954	BLADES,TIPS,ETC FR TOOLS					W 34	828	W 285	4913	OUTILS POUR MACHINE–OUTIL
69541	PARTS TO INSERT IN TOOLS					W 29	801	W 252	4839	OUTILS DE FORAGE
696	CUTLERY					W 463	3194	W 56	314	COUTELLERIE
69603	RAZORS,RAZOR BLADES					W 450	3129	W 15	173	RASOIRS ET LAMES
697	BASE MTL HOUSEHOLD EQUIP					W 678	1318	W 338	809	ART MENAGE MET COMMUNS
699	BASE METAL MFRS NES					W 1716	6427	W 1741	5038	ART MANUFACTURES MET NDA
6996	BASE MTL MISC ARTICLES					W 823	3535	W 447	1821	ART DIVERS METAUX COMMUNS
69961	BASE MTL FLEXIBLE TUBING					W 276	1834	W 22	414	TUYAUX FLEXIBLES
69963	BASE METAL STOPPERS,ETC					W 379	1211	W 307	1044	BOUCHONS METALLIQUES
6997	IRON,STEEL ARTICLES NES					W 406	1298	W 661	696	OUV FONTE,FER,ACIER NDA
69979	IRN,STL MANUFACTURES NES					W 406	1298	W 659	687	AUT OUVRAGES EN FER NDA
6998	MFRS NES OF CPR,NIKL,ETC					W 347	1098	W 429	1314	OUVRAGES EN CU,NI,AL,PB,ZN
69983	ALUMINIUM MANUFACTS NES					W 304	947	W 422	1282	OUVRAGES EN ALUMINIUM
7	MACHINES,TRANSPORT EQUIP						127098		116315	MACHINES MATERIEL TRANSPORT
71	POWER GENERATING EQUIPMT						3032		5286	MACHINES GENERATRICES
713	INTRNL COMBUS PSTN ENGIN					W 65	1241	W 115	1842	MOTEURS EXPL COMB INT, PIECE
716	ROTATING ELECTRIC PLANT					W 100	1132	W 172	2081	APP ELECTR ROTATIFS,PIECES
7162	AC MTRS,GENRTRS,GEN SETS					W 58	809	W 125	1401	MOTEURS ELECTRIQUES
72	MACHS FOR SPCL INDUSTRYS						10730		17893	MAC SPECIALES POUR INDUST
722	TRACTORS NON-ROAD					W 18	67	W 153	1493	TRACTEURS
723	CIVIL ENGINEERG EQUIP ETC					W 1507	7231	W 1285	12336	APPAREILS DE GENIE CIVIL
7234	CONST,MINING MACHNRY NES					W 130	913	W 390	2495	MACH POUR LA CONST, MINES
72342	SLFPRP SHOVELS,EXCAVATRS					W 29	30	W 253	1251	PELLES MECANIQUES
7239	CONSTR ETC MACHY PTS NES					W 1376	6315	W 878	9813	PIECES 723.41–723.46
728	OTH MACHY FOR SPCL INDUS					W 223	2186	W 319	3127	AUT MACH IND PARTICULIERES
7284	MACHY FOR SPCL INDUS NES					W 76	930	W 196	1925	MACH SPEC IND PARTICUL.
72848	OTH MCHY WITH INDIV FNCT					W 53	468	W 177	1623	AUTRES MACHINES NDA
74	GENRL INDUSTRL MACHY NES						24891		31416	MACH APP INDUSTRIE
741	HEATING,COOLING EQUIPMNT					W 362	3038	W 259	2927	MACH CHAUFFAGE,PIECES
7413	INDUS FURNACES ETC,PARTS					W 121	1164	W 60	677	FOURS IND,LABOR,PIECES
7415	AIR-CONDITIONING MACHNRY					W 167	1166	W 117	1026	GROUPES CONDITION AIR
742	PUMPS FOR LIQUIDS ETC					W 117	2697	W 174	4523	POMPES MOTO–POMPES
7428	OTHER PUMPS FOR LIQUIDS					W 55	1163	W 73	1480	AUTRES POMPES POUR LIQ
74288	PUMPS FR LIQUIDS NES ETC					W 55	1161	W 59	1257	POMPES POUR LIQUIDES NDA
7429	PTS NES OF PUMPS OF 742					W 55	1382	W 44	1436	PIECES POUR GROUPE 742
743	PUMPS NES,CENTRFUGES ETC					W 192	5027	W 573	9464	POMPES COMPRES,VENT ETC
7431	PUMPS FOR GASES ETC					W 28	360	W 454	6518	POMPES AIR A VIDE,COMPRES
7436	GAS,LIQUID FILTERS ETC					W 89	2320	W 76	1041	APP POUR FILT DES LIQUIDES
7439	PTS NES OF APP OF 7435,6					W 35	2161	W 24	1164	PIECES 743.5 ET 743.6
744	MECHANICAL HANDLING EQU					W 395	3226	W 387	2841	EQUIP MANUTENTION PIECES
7442	LIFTING,LOADING MACH NES					W 186	1505	W 138	1119	APP LEVAGE,MANUTENTION
7449	PTS NES OF MACHY OF 7442					W 155	1540	W 108	1115	PIECES DU 744.2
745	NONELEC MACHY,TOOLS NES					W 83	1119		880	AUT MACH NON ELEC,PIECES
749	NONELEC MACH PTS,ACC NES					W 651	9784	W 665	10781	PIECES MACH NON ELEC NDA
7492	COCKS,VALVES ETC NES					W 386	5482	W 185	4398	ART ROB,SIM POUR TUYAUX
7499	OTH NONELEC MCHY PTS NES					W 118	2772	W 287	4357	PIECES NON ELECT NDA
74992	METAL-PLASTIC GASKETS					W 111	2536	W 279	3859	JOINTS METALLOPLASTIQUES
75	OFFICE MACHNES,ADP EQUIP						4552		4768	MACH BUREAU TRAIT AUTOM
752	AUTOMTIC DATA PROC EQUIP					W 34	2708	W 40	2916	MACH TRAIT INFORMATION
759	OFFICE,ADP MCH PTS,ACCES					W 15	1436	W 13	1217	PIECES DU 751 ET 752
7599	ACCTG,ETC,ADP MCH PTS,AC					W 15	1431	W 7	1037	PIECES DU 751 ET 752
76	TELECOMM,SOUND EQUIPMENT						3958		4028	EQUIPMENT DE TELECOM
764	TELECOM EQPT,PTS,ACC NES					W 86	2730	W 86	3171	EQUIP TELECOM,PIECES
77	ELECTRIC MACHNRY NES ETC						11711		24534	MACH APP ELECT NDA
771	ELECTRIC POWER MACHY NES					W 72	1097	W 84	745	MACH PROD,TRANS ELECTR
772	SWITCHGEAR ETC,PARTS NES					W 219	5895	W 536	11728	APP COUPURE,SECT ETC
7721	SWITCHGEAR ETC					W 218	5801	W 535	11639	APP COUPURE,SECTIONMNT
773	ELECTR DISTRIBUTNG EQUIP					W 52	403	W 726	6687	EQUIPMT DISTRIBUTION ELECT
7731	INSULATED WIRE,CABLE ETC					W 35	199	W 716	6340	FILS,CABLES ISOLES ELECT
775	HOUSEHOLD TYPE EQUIP NES					W 507	2029	W 267	1019	MACH,APP USAGE DOMESTQUE
7752	DOM REFRIGERATRS,FREEZRS					W 447	1771	W 173	604	REFRIG,CONGEL MENAGER
77522	DOMESTIC DEEP-FREEZERS					W 293	1290	W 96	316	MEUBLES CONGELATEURS
778	ELECTRICAL MACHINERY NES					W 192	1685	W 969	3591	AUTRES MACH ELECT NDA
7781	BATTERIES,ACCUMULATORS					W 69	376	W 801	1483	PILES ET ACCUMULATEURS
78	ROAD VEHICLES						20358		21349	VEHICULES ROUTIERS
781	PASS MOTOR VEH EXC BUSES					W 1536	8035	W 1697	8592	AUTO TRANSPORT PERSONNES
782	LORRIES,SPCL MTR VEH NES					W 1077	3579	W 1068	5371	VEHICULES SPECIAUX,MARCH
7821	LORRIES,TRUCKS					W 1048	3368	W 1019	4706	VEHICULES TRANSP MARCHAND
783	ROAD MOTOR VEHICLES NES					W 727	4341	W 541	2944	VEHICULES ROUTIERS NDA
7831	BUSES					W 601	3798	W 282	1231	VOITURES TRANSPORT COMMUN
7832	TRACTORS FOR TR-TRAILERS					W 126	543	W 260	1713	TRACTEURS ROUTIERS

4. Special Imports C.I.F. by Commodities according to the S.I.T.C. (Rev. 2) in thousand U.S. Dollars
Importations Spéciales C.A.F. par Produits d'après la C.T.C.I. (Rév. 2) en milliers de Dollars E.U.

SITC CTCI	COMMODITY	1991		1992		1993		1994		PRODUIT
		WEIGHT POIDS	VALUE VALEUR	WEIGHT POIDS	VALUE VALEUR	WEIGHT POIDS	VALUE VALEUR	WEIGHT POIDS	VALUE VALEUR	
784	MOTOR VEH PRTS,ACCES NES					W 347	3283	W 281	3058	PIECES 722,781,782,783
7849	OTHER MOTOR VEHCL PARTS					W 347	3283	W 270	3009	PIECES 722,781,782,783
79	OTHR TRANSPORT EQUIPMENT						47092		6709	AUTRE MATERIEL TRANSPORT
791	RAILWAY VEHICLES						8	W 175	2137	VEHIC MAT CHEMINS DE FER
7919	RY TRACK FIXT,ETC,PARTS						8	W 175	2137	MATER FIXE VOIES FERREES
79191	RY TRACK FIXTURES ETC							W 100	1677	APP DE SIGNALISATION
792	AIRCRAFT ETC					W 3	208	W 10	1573	APP NAVIGATION AERIENNE
7929	AIRCRAFT PARTS NES					W 3	199	W 8	1517	PIECES DU 792
793	SHIPS AND BOATS ETC					W 3185	46876	W 921	2999	NAVIRES BATEAUX,ETC
7938	TUGS,SPECIAL VESSELS ETC					W 3152	46662	W 890	2909	REMORQUEURS,BATEAUX SPEC
79382	SPECL PURPOSE VESSLS ETC					W 2929	45660			BAT–PHARES,–POMPES,DRAGUES
79383	FLOATING STRUCTURES NES					W 223	1001	W 890	2909	ENGINS FLOTTANTS DIVERS
8	MISC MANUFACTURED GOODS						24171		37552	ART MANUFACTURES DIVERS
812	*PLUMBG,HEATNG,LGHTNG EQ					W 277	352	W 307	1386	APPAR SANITAIRES CHAUFFAGE
821	*FURNITURE,PARTS THEREOF					W 287	1029	W 305	1360	MEUBLES ET PIECES
84	CLOTHING AND ACCESSORIES						6016		2384	VETEMENTS
843	WOMENS OUTERWEAR NONKNIT					W 1904	3300	W 149	370	VET DESSUS FEMMES MAT TEX
8439	— OTHER OUTER GARMENTS					W 1900	3210	W 128	264	AUT VET DES FEM MAT TEXT
846	UNDER GARMENTS KNITTED					W 371	1166	W 220	551	SOUS VETS DE BONNETERIE
851	*FOOTWEAR					W 558	1105	W 851	1609	CHAUSSURES
87	PRECISION INSTRUMNTS NES						8186		13660	INSTRUM,APPAR SCIENT NDA
874	MEASURNG,CONTROLNG INSTR					W 245	7538	W 564	11996	INSTRUMENTS DE MESURE
8742	MEASUR,DRAW ETC INST,PTS					W 83	1212	W 71	1294	INST DESSIN,TRACAGE,PCS
87421	MEASURNG,DRAWNG ETC INST					W 83	1160	W 67	1173	INSTRUM DESSIN,TRACAGE
8743	GAS,LIQUID CONTROL INSTR					W 88	2848	W 217	3744	APP,INSTR MESURE FLUIDES
8748	ELEC MEAS,CONTRL EQU NES					W 32	1355	W 196	3851	APP ELEC ELECTRO MESURE
87483	OTH ELCTRNC MEAS ETC EQU					W 3	267	W 88	2143	AUT APP ELECTRO DE MESURE
87489	ELEC MEASUR ETC INST NES					W 28	1055	W 108	1698	AUT INSTRUM ELEC NDA
8749	INSTR PTS NES,ACCESSORYS					W 14	1146	W 16	1475	PIECES 873,874.3,54,874.8
89	MISC MANUFCTRD GOODS NES						6357		15815	ART MANUFACTURES DIVERS
892	PRINTED MATTER					W 83	932	W 229	2082	IMPRIMES
8928	PRINTED MATTER NES					W 75	718	W 138	1294	IMPRIMES NDA
893	ARTICLES OF PLASTIC NES						1589	W 2511	4622	OUVRAGES EN MAT DIVIS 58
8939	MISC PLASTIC ARTICLES					W 173	707	W 1971	3855	ART DIVERS EN MAT DIV 58
89399	OTHR PLASTC ARTICLES NES					W 130	479	W 1946	3757	AUT OUV MAT DIV 58
894	TOYS,SPORTING GOODS,ETC					W 60	273	W 702	2836	VOITURES ENFANTS,JOUETS
8946	NON–MILITARY ARMS,AMMO					W 3	42	W 607	2426	ARMES NON MILITAIRES
89463	HUNTNG,SPORTNG AMMUNTION					W 3	42	W 607	2417	MUNITIONS
895	OFFICE SUPPLIES NES					W 109	1137	W 130	1276	ART PAPET NDA
899	OTHER MANUFACTURED GOODS						1638		4317	AUT ART MANUF DIVERS NDA
8997	BASKETWORK,BROOMS ETC					W 186	574	W 597	3116	OUVRAGES VANNERIE NDA
89972	BRUSHES,BROOMS,MOPS ETC					W 186	574	W 579	3108	BALAIS ET BALAYETTES

Congo

5. Special Exports F.O.B. by Commodities according to the S.I.T.C. (Rev. 2) in thousand U.S. Dollars
Exportations Spéciales F.O.B. par Produits d'après la C.T.C.I. (Rév. 2) en milliers de Dollars E.U.

SITC CTCI	COMMODITY	1991 WEIGHT POIDS	1991 VALUE VALEUR	1992 WEIGHT POIDS	1992 VALUE VALEUR	1993 WEIGHT POIDS	1993 VALUE VALEUR	1994 WEIGHT POIDS	1994 VALUE VALEUR	PRODUIT
	ALL COMMODITIES						965339		948482	TOUS PRODUITS
0	FOOD AND LIVE ANIMALS						12023		8356	ALIMENTS,ANIMAUX VIVANTS
03	FISH AND PREPARATIONS						3628		1277	POISSONS ET PREPARATIONS
036	SHELL FISH FRESH,FROZEN					W 1062	3604	W 660	1214	CRUSTACES,MOLLUSQUES
06	SUGAR AND PREPS,HONEY						8123		6439	SUCRES ET PRODUITS
061	SUGAR AND HONEY					W 18210	8123	W 11000	6430	SUCRES ET MIEL
0611	RAW BEET AND CANE SUGAR					W 18210	8123	W 11000	6430	SUCRES BRUTS
2	CRUDE MATERLS,EXCL FUELS						18367		128691	MAT BRUTES NON COMESTIBLES
24	CORK AND WOOD						17827		118371	LIEGE ET BOIS
247	OTH WOOD ROUGH,SQUARED					W 119351	8735	W 510522	109582	BOIS BRUTS EQUARRIS
2472	SAW–,VENEER–LOGS NON–CON					W 119351	8735	W 509783	109395	NON CONIFERES SCIAGE,PLAC
24721	— IN THE ROUGH					W 119351	8735	W 509783	109395	BRUTS ECORCES DEGROSSIS
248	WOOD SHAPED,SLEEPERS					W 22105	9091	W 15102	8787	BOIS SIMPLEMENT TRAVAILLES
2483	LUMBER SHAPED NON–CONIFR					W 22105	9091	W 15102	8787	NON CONIFERES SCIES,RABOTES
24831	LUMBER SAWN ETC NON–CON					W 22105	9091	W 14206	7805	SCIES LONGITUDINALEMENT
27	CRUDE FERTLZR,MINRLS NES						385		10003	ENGRAIS MINERAUX BRUTS
277	NATURAL ABRASIVES NES								9866	ABRASIFS NATURELS NDA
2771	INDUSTRIAL DIAMONDS								9866	DIAMANTS INDUSTRIELS
3	MINERAL FUELS ETC						911178		790823	COMBUSTIBLES MINERAUX LUB
33	PETROLEUM AND PRODUCTS						911178		790821	PETROLE ET DERIVES
333	CRUDE PETROLEUM					MW 9002	890867	W 8621539	771686	HUILES BRUTES DE PETROLE
334	PETROLEUM PRODUCTS,REFIN					W 267623	20312	W 226859	19135	PRODUITS RAFFINES
6	BASIC MANUFACTURES						16484		11726	ART MANUFACTURES
63	WOOD,CORK MANUFACTRS NES						13630		9176	OUVRAGES LIEGE ET BOIS
634	VENEERS,PLYWOOD,ETC					W 13501	13614	W 8564	9125	PLACAGES,CONTRE–PLAQUES
6341	VENEER SHEETS ETC					W 13490	13604	W 8515	9114	BOIS SIMPLEMENT SCIES
7	MACHINES,TRANSPORT EQUIP						5346		3949	MACHINES MATERIEL TRANSPORT
8	MISC MANUFACTURED GOODS						1149		3259	ART MANUFACTURES DIVERS

1. HISTORICAL SERIES, 1958–1993 GENERAL TRADE, IMPORTS C.I.F., EXPORTS F.O.B.
SERIES HISTORIQUES, 1958–1993 COMMERCE GENERAL, IMPORTATIONS C.A.F., EXPORTATIONS F.O.B

YEAR ANNEE	VALUE IN MILLION N.Z. DOLLARS VALEUR EN MILLION N.Z. DOLLARS MERCHANDISE –MARCHANDISE		GOLD –OR		CONVERSION FACTORS U.S. CENTS PER N.Z. DOLLAR FACTEURS DE CONVERSION CENTS E.U. PAR N.Z. DOLLAR		INDEX NUMBERS –INDICES QUANTUM		UNIT VALUE VALEUR UNITAIRE	
	IMPORTS	EXPORTS	IMPORTS	EXPORTS	IMPORTS	EXPORTS	IMPORTS	EXPORTS	IMPORTS	EXPORTS
1958	1.77	0.81			140.0000	140.0000				
1959	1.44	1.00			140.0000	140.0000				
1960	1.79	0.93			140.0000	140.0000				
1961	2.04	1.20			140.0000	140.0000				
1962	1.88	1.42			139.0000	139.0000				
1963	2.45	1.67			139.0000	139.0000				
1964	3.00	1.87			139.0000	139.0000				
1965	3.07	1.99			139.0000	139.0000				
1966	3.15	1.74			139.0000	139.0000				
1967	2.99	1.78			137.0000	137.0000				
1968	3.38	1.92			112.0000	112.0000				
1969	3.40	2.40			112.0000	112.0000				
1970	5.77	2.69			112.0000	112.0000				
1971	5.79	2.01			113.6080	113.6080				
1972	6.20	1.89			119.5000	119.5000				
1973	4.95	2.51			136.1970	136.3000				
1974	6.22	2.58			140.1000	140.1000				
1975	10.52	2.39			121.4560	121.4560				
1976	13.37	2.20			99.6380	99.4150				
1977	17.50	2.39			97.0830	96.9160				
1978	18.23	2.41			103.7760	104.0350				
1979	22.46	3.78			101.8410	102.0700				
1980	23.61	4.19			97.0800	97.2800				
1981	28.73	5.01			86.9619	86.8414				
1982	26.85	4.98			75.7608	75.5292				
1983	35.09	4.89			66.8717	66.6792				
1984	36.17	6.51			56.9005	57.6534				
1985	47.16	6.07			49.7975	50.8231				
1986	50.31	9.23			52.3131	52.3408				
1987	56.98	12.04			59.3850	58.9991				
1988	64.53	6.63			65.4367	65.9262				
1989	73.08	4.67			59.6126	59.5968				
1990	86.33	8.17			59.5778	59.8340				
1991	94.51	9.43			57.9200	57.9200				
1992	109.16	5.11			53.8119	53.8205				
1993	124.25	7.16			54.1631	53.9514				

2. IMPORTS BY BROAD ECONOMIC CATEGORY AND EXPORTS BY INDUSTRIAL ORIGIN. (PERCENTAGE OF TOTAL VALUE)
IMPORTATIONS PAR CATEGORIES ECONOMIQUES ET EXPORTATIONS PAR BRANCHE D'ACTIVITE.(EN POURCENTAGE DE LA VALEUR TOTALE)

IMPORTS – IMPORTATIONS

	1990	1991	1992	1993	1994	1995	1996
TOTAL IMPORTS–IMPORTATIONS TOTALES							
1 FOOD BEV–ALIMENTATION BOISSONS							
11 PRIMARY–PRODUITS DE BASE							
111 FOR INDUSTRY–POUR L'INDUSTRIE							
112 FOR HOUSEHOLDS–POUR LES MENAGES							
12 PROCESSED–PRODUITS ELABORES							
121 FOR INDUSTRY–POUR L'INDUSTRIE							
122 FOR HOUSEHOLDS–POUR LES MENAGES							
2 IND SUPPLIES–APPROV INDUSTRIELS							
21 PRIMARY–PRODUITS DE BASE							
22 PROCESSED–PRODUITS ELABORES							
3 FUELS–COMBUSTIBLES							
31 PRIMARY–PRODUITS DE BASE							
32 PROCESSED–PRODUITS ELABORES							
321 MOTOR SPIRIT–ESSENCE							
322 OTHER–AUTRES							
4 MACHINERY–EQUIPEMENT							
41 CAPITAL EQUIPMENT–MACHINES							
42 PARTS–PIECES ACCESSOIRES							
5 TRANSPORT–TRANSPORT							
51 PASSENGER CARS–AUTOMOBILES							
52 OTHER–AUTRES							
521 INDUSTRIAL–INDUSTRIELS							
522 NON INDUSTRIAL–NON INDUSTRIEL							
53 PARTS–PIECES ACCESSOIRES							
6 CONSUM GOODS–BIENS CONSOMMATION							
61 DURABLE–DURABLES							
62 SEMI DURABLE–SEMI DURABLES							
63 NON DURABLE–NON DURABLES							
7 GOODS NES–BIENS NDA							

EXPORTS – EXPORTATIONS

	1990	1991	1992	1993	1994	1995	1996
TOTAL EXPORTS–EXPORTATIONS TOTALES							
1 AGRICULTURE							
2 MINING QUARRY–INDUS EXTRACTIVES							
3 MANUFACTURING–IND MANUFACTUR							
31 FOOD BEV TOBACCO–ALIM BOISS TAB							
32 TEXTILES–INDUSTRIES TEXTILES							
33 WOOD & PRODUCTS–BOIS & PRODUITS							
34 PAPER & PRODUCTS–PAPIER & PRODT							
35 CHEMICALS–INDUSTRIES CHIMIQUES							
36 NON METAL MIN–MIN NON METAL							
37 BASIC METAL–IND METAL BASE							
38 METAL MANUF–MANUF METAL							
39 OTH MANUF IND–AUTRES MANUF							

3. TRADE BY PRINCIPAL COUNTRIES OF PROVENANCE AND DESTINATION (VALUE IN THOUSAND U.S. DOLLARS)
ECHANGES SELON LES PRINCIPAUX PAYS DE PROVENANCE ET DE DESTINATION (VALEUR EN MILLIERS DE DOLLARS EU)

COUNTRIES–PAYS	GENERAL IMPORTS C.I.F. IMPORTATIONS GENERALES C.A.F				
	1988	1989	1990	1991	1992
World			51647	54737	
Africa			6	3	
Americas			3622	3232	
Northern America			3511	3087	
LAIA			37	92	
CACM			0	1	
Caribbean			73	52	
Rest of America					
As.ex F.USSR			4602	5201	
Eur.x F.USSR			18713	1820	
EU			18507	1742	
EFTA			203	60	
East Europe			3	18	
Other Europe					
Former USSR				1	
Oceania			24704	29940	
New Zealand			19462	23035	
Italy/Italie			16773	783	
USA/Etats–Unis d'Amer			3298	2942	
Australia/Australie			2779	2957	
Fiji/Fidji			1976	2724	
Japan/Japon			1708	2782	
Singapore/Singapour			749	816	
France,Monac			766	666	
Hong Kong			745	501	
French Polynesia			130	707	
United Kingdom			562	212	
China/Chine			287	455	
Samoa			232	405	
Thailand/Thaïlande			229	209	
Canada			214	145	
Korea, Republic of			101	211	
Switz.Liecht			194	59	
Germany/Allemagne			210	37	
Spain/Espagne			119	10	
Denmark/Danemark			0	1	
Former USSR/Anc. URSS				1	

COUNTRIES–PAYS	GENERAL EXPORTS F.O.B. EXPORTATIONS GENERALES F.O.B.				
	1988	1989	1990	1991	1992
Monde				5476	3245
Afrique					
Amériques				192	187
Amérique du Nord				192	187
ALAI					
MCAC					
Caraïbes					
Autre Amérique					
Asie l'URSS exclus				3578	1351
Europe l'URSS exclus				2	34
UE				2	9
AELE					26
Europe de l'Est					
Autre de l'Europe					
Ancienne URSS					
Océanie				1526	1179
Japan/Japon				2794	612
New Zealand				1097	1100
Hong Kong				778	691
USA/Etats–Unis d'Amer				192	187
Australia/Australie				277	44
French Polynesia				102	23
Fiji/Fidji				36	4
Switz.Liecht					26
United Kingdom				2	1
Samoa					1

(VALUE AS PERCENTAGE OF WORLD TOTAL)(VALEURS EN POURCENTAGE DU TOTAL MONDIAL)

	1983	1984	1985	1986	1987	1988	1989	1990	1991	1992
Africa								0.0	0.0	
Americas	0.0	2.1						7.0	5.9	
Northern America		2.1						6.8	5.6	
LAIA								0.1	0.2	
CACM	0.0							0.0	0.0	
Caribbean								0.1	0.1	
Rest of America										
As.ex F.USSR	8.9	8.8						8.9	9.5	
Eur.x F.USSR	15.3	5.6						36.2	3.3	
EU	14.8	5.5						35.8	3.2	
EFTA	0.5	0.2						0.4	0.1	
East Europe								0.0	0.0	
Other Europe										
Former USSR	2.5	1.5							0.0	
Oceania	73.2	72.5						47.8	54.7	
New Zealand	57.8	58.4						37.7	42.1	
Italy/Italie	1.5	0.6						32.5	1.4	
USA/Etats–Unis d'Amer		2.1						6.4	5.4	
Australia/Australie		5.7						5.4	5.4	
Fiji/Fidji	13.9	7.6						3.8	5.0	
Japan/Japon	8.2	8.3						3.3	5.1	
Singapore/Singapour								1.5	1.5	
France,Monac	0.1	0.2						1.5	1.2	
Hong Kong	0.6	0.5						1.4	0.9	
French Polynesia								0.3	1.3	

	1983	1984	1985	1986	1987	1988	1989	1990	1991	1992
Afrique										
Amériques		0.1							3.5	5.8
Amérique du Nord		0.1							3.5	5.8
ALAI										
MCAC										
Caraïbes										
Autre Amérique										
Asie l'URSS exclus	2.3	9.1							65.3	41.6
Europe l'URSS exclus	33.5	9.1							0.0	1.1
UE	33.5	9.1							0.0	0.3
AELE		0.0								0.8
Europe de l'Est										
Autre de l'Europe										
Ancienne URSS	0.2	0.6								
Océanie	63.9	80.9							27.9	36.3
Japan/Japon	2.2	8.9							51.0	18.9
New Zealand	63.7	65.3							20.0	33.9
Hong Kong									14.2	21.3
USA/Etats–Unis d'Amer		0.1							3.5	5.8
Australia/Australie									5.1	1.3
French Polynesia		14.6							1.9	0.7
Fiji/Fidji		0.0							0.7	0.1
Switz.Liecht										0.8
United Kingdom	3.8	0.1							0.0	0.0
Samoa	0.2	0.6								0.0

4. General Imports C.I.F. by Commodities according to the S.I.T.C. (Rev. 2) in thousand U.S. Dollars
Importations Générales C.A.F. par Produits d'après la C.T.C.I. (Rév. 2) en milliers de Dollars E.U.

SITC CTCI	COMMODITY	1990 WEIGHT POIDS	1990 VALUE VALEUR	1991 WEIGHT POIDS	1991 VALUE VALEUR	1992 WEIGHT POIDS	1992 VALUE VALEUR	1993 WEIGHT POIDS	1993 VALUE VALEUR	PRODUIT
	ALL COMMODITIES		51647		54737		58741		67296	TOUS PRODUITS
0	FOOD AND LIVE ANIMALS		7395		11309		12136		13911	ALIMENTS,ANIMAUX VIVANTS
01	MEAT AND PREPARATIONS		2367							VIANDES ET PREPARATIONS
02	DAIRY PRODCTS,BIRDS'EGGS		804							PRODUITS LAITIERS,OEUFS
03	FISH AND PREPARATIONS		446							POISSONS ET PREPARATIONS
04	CEREALS AND PREPARATIONS		1202							CEREALES ET PRODUITS
05	VEGETABLES AND FRUIT		704							LEGUMES ET FRUITS
06	SUGAR AND PREPS,HONEY		417							SUCRES ET PRODUITS
07	COFFEE,TEA,COCOA,SPICES		252							CAFE,THE,CACAO,EPICES
09	MISC EDIBLE PRODUCTS		824							PREP ALIMENTAIRES DIVERSES
1	BEVERAGES AND TOBACCO		2275		3252		3495		3997	BOISSONS ET TABACS
11	BEVERAGES		2127							BOISSONS
2	CRUDE MATERLS,EXCL FUELS		1740		1150		1239		1413	MAT BRUTES NON COMESTIBLES
24	CORK AND WOOD		1505							LIEGE ET BOIS
3	MINERAL FUELS ETC		1606		6481		6926		7935	COMBUSTIBLES MINERAUX LUB
33	PETROLEUM AND PRODUCTS		1450							PETROLE ET DERIVES
4	ANIMAL,VEGETABLE OIL,FAT		101		306		329		383	HUILES,GRAISSES ANIM,VEG
5	CHEMCLS,RELATED PROD NES		5737		3875		4172		4765	PRODUITS CHIMIQUES
53	DYES,TANNING,COLOUR PROD		367							PROD TEINTURE,COLORANTS
55	PERFUME,CLEANING ETC PRD		729							PROD POUR PARFUM,TOILETTE
58	PLASTIC MATERIALS ETC		3782							MAT PLAST ARTIFICIELLES
59	CHEMICAL MATERIALS NES		221							MAT PROD CHIMIQUES NDA
6	BASIC MANUFACTURES		15343		10849		11642		13346	ART MANUFACTURES
62	RUBBER MANUFACTURES NES		323							CAOUTCHOUC MANUFACTURE
63	WOOD,CORK MANUFACTRS NES		2608							OUVRAGES LIEGE ET BOIS
64	PAPER,PAPERBOARD AND MFR		1049							PAPIERS,CARTONS & OUVRAGES
65	TEXTILE YARN,FABRICS,ETC		1799							FILS,TISSUS,ARTICLES TEXTILE
66	NONMETAL MINERAL MFS NES		2393							ART MIN NON METALLIQUES
67	IRON AND STEEL		2955							FER ET ACIER
68	NON–FERROUS METALS		1893							METAUX NON FERREUX
69	METAL MANUFACTURES NES		2305							ART MANUFACT EN METAL NDA
7	MACHINES,TRANSPORT EQUIP		12100		9853		10567		12128	MACHINES MATERIEL TRANSPORT
71	POWER GENERATING EQUIPMT		1127							MACHINES GENERATRICES
72	MACHS FOR SPCL INDUSTRYS		1614							MAC SPECIALES POUR INDUST
74	GENRL INDUSTRL MACHY NES		1240							MACH APP INDUSTRIE
75	OFFICE MACHNES,ADP EQUIP		549							MACH BUREAU TRAIT AUTOM
76	TELECOMM,SOUND EQUIPMENT		2498							EQUIPMENT DE TELECOM
77	ELECTRIC MACHNRY NES ETC		2009							MACH APP ELECT NDA
78	ROAD VEHICLES		2430							VEHICULES ROUTIERS
79	OTHR TRANSPORT EQUIPMENT		541							AUTRE MATERIEL TRANSPORT
8	MISC MANUFACTURED GOODS		5307		7515		8073		9234	ART MANUFACTURES DIVERS
84	CLOTHING AND ACCESSORIES		868							VETEMENTS
87	PRECISION INSTRUMNTS NES		574							INSTRUM,APPAR SCIENT NDA
88	PHOTO EQU,OPTICL GDS ETC		222							APP,FOURN PHOTO,OP,MONTR
89	MISC MANUFCTRD GOODS NES		2073							ART MANUFACTURES DIVERS

5. General Exports F.O.B. by Commodities according to the S.I.T.C. (Rev. 2) in thousand U.S. Dollars
Exportations Générales F.O.B. par Produits d'après la C.T.C.I. (Rév. 2) en milliers de Dollars E.U.

SITC CTCI	COMMODITY	1990 WEIGHT POIDS	1990 VALUE VALEUR	1991 WEIGHT POIDS	1991 VALUE VALEUR	1992 WEIGHT POIDS	1992 VALUE VALEUR	1993 WEIGHT POIDS	1993 VALUE VALEUR	PRODUIT
	ALL COMMODITIES		4890		5476		3245		3861	TOUS PRODUITS
0	FOOD AND LIVE ANIMALS		1246		920		995		1022	ALIMENTS,ANIMAUX VIVANTS
05	VEGETABLES AND FRUIT		1145		787		873		928	LEGUMES ET FRUITS
0542	LEGUMINOUS VEGETBLES DRY		164		30		25		6	LEGUMES A COSSE SECS
05459	FRESH VEGETABLES NES		44		13		12		9	LEGUMES FRAIS,REFRI NDA
05481	ROOTS,TUBERS FRESH,DRY		50		28		3			RACINES DE MANIOC ETC
05729	CITRUS NES, FRESH,DRIED		22		12		1			AGRUMES N.D.A
05797	OTH TROP FRUIT,FRESH,DRY		31		9		27		57	AVOCATS,MANGUES,GOYAVES
05798	OTHER FRESH FRUIT		784		681		793		839	AUTRES FRUITS FRAIS
0751	PEPPER AND PIMENTO		28		20		10		17	POIVRE,PIMENTS
2	CRUDE MATERLS,EXCL FUELS		339		241		123		111	MAT BRUTES NON COMESTIBLES
29115	CORAL, SHELLS, AND WASTE		339							CORAIL & SIMILAIRES
29199	ANIMAL PRODUCTS,NES				82		96		109	PROD ORIGINE ANIMALE NDA
5	CHEMCLS,RELATED PROD NES		2		1		8		15	PRODUITS CHIMIQUES
6	BASIC MANUFACTURES		2615		3843		1714		2068	ART MANUFACTURES
7	MACHINES,TRANSPORT EQUIP		358		32		42		93	MACHINES MATERIEL TRANSPORT
8	MISC MANUFACTURED GOODS		315		414		360		489	ART MANUFACTURES DIVERS

1. HISTORICAL SERIES, 1961–1996 SPECIAL TRADE, IMPORTS C.I.F., EXPORTS F.O.B.
SERIES HISTORIQUES, 1961–1996 COMMERCE SPECIAL, IMPORTATIONS C.A.F., EXPORTATIONS F.O.B

YEAR ANNEE	VALUE IN MILLION U.S. DOLLARS VALEUR EN MILLION U.S. DOLLARS MERCHANDISE –MARCHANDISE		GOLD –OR		CONVERSION FACTORS FACTEURS DE CONVERSION CENTS E.U. PAR		INDEX NUMBERS –INDICES QUANTUM		UNIT VALUE VALEUR UNITAIRE	
	IMPORTS	EXPORTS	IMPORTS	EXPORTS	IMPORTS	EXPORTS	IMPORTS	EXPORTS	IMPORTS	EXPORTS
1961	107.20	84.20								
1962	113.40	93.00								
1963	123.90	95.00								
1964	138.60	113.90								
1965	178.20	111.80								
1966	178.50	135.50								
1967	190.70	143.80								
1968	213.90	170.80								
1969	245.10	189.70								
1970	316.70	231.20								
1971	349.70	225.40								
1972	342.80	278.50								
1973	455.30	344.50								
1974	719.70	440.30								
1975	694.00	493.30								
1976	770.40	592.90								
1977	1026.20	828.20								
1978	1165.70	864.90								
1979	1396.80	934.30								
1980	1523.80	1001.70								
1981	1208.50	1008.10								
1982	893.10	871.00								
1983	987.80	866.10								
1984	1084.50	978.50								
1985	1098.20	988.90								
1986	1147.50	1120.50								
1987	1382.50	1158.30								
1988	1409.80	1245.70								
1989	1717.40	1414.60								
1990	1989.70	1448.20								
1991	1876.60	1597.70								
1992	2440.70	1840.80								
1993	2885.80	1995.30								
1994	3025.10	2242.50								
1995	3252.80	2701.60								
1996	3432.70	2946.10								

2. IMPORTS BY BROAD ECONOMIC CATEGORY AND EXPORTS BY INDUSTRIAL ORIGIN. (PERCENTAGE OF TOTAL VALUE)
IMPORTATIONS PAR CATEGORIES ECONOMIQUES ET EXPORTATIONS PAR BRANCHE D'ACTIVITE.(EN POURCENTAGE DE LA VALEUR TOTALE)

IMPORTS – IMPORTATIONS

	1990	1991	1992	1993	1994	1995	1996
TOTAL IMPORTS–IMPORTATIONS TOTALES	100.	100.	100.	100.	100.	100.	
1 FOOD BEV–ALIMENTATION BOISSONS	6.0	5.9	6.2	7.8	8.5	8.3	
11 PRIMARY–PRODUITS DE BASE	3.3	3.1	3.1	4.3	4.2	4.6	
111 FOR INDUSTRY–POUR L'INDUSTRIE	2.0	2.1	2.0	2.6	2.9	3.3	
112 FOR HOUSEHOLDS–POUR LES MENAGES	1.4	1.0	1.1	1.7	1.3	1.3	
12 PROCESSED–PRODUITS ELABORES	2.7	2.8	3.1	3.5	4.3	3.6	
121 FOR INDUSTRY–POUR L'INDUSTRIE	0.3	0.3	0.3	0.3	0.4	0.4	
122 FOR HOUSEHOLDS–POUR LES MENAGES	2.4	2.5	2.8	3.2	3.9	3.2	
2 IND SUPPLIES–APPROV INDUSTRIELS	36.3	37.6	35.4	36.3	37.7	41.2	
21 PRIMARY–PRODUITS DE BASE	2.6	2.9	2.4	2.6	2.6	2.7	
22 PROCESSED–PRODUITS ELABORES	33.7	34.7	33.0	33.6	35.1	38.4	
3 FUELS–COMBUSTIBLES	9.5	9.3	8.6	8.4	8.9	8.5	
31 PRIMARY–PRODUITS DE BASE	3.2	2.7	3.1	2.6	2.4	3.0	
32 PROCESSED–PRODUITS ELABORES	6.3	6.6	5.5	5.7	6.5	5.5	
321 MOTOR SPIRIT–ESSENCE	2.2	2.1	1.5	1.8	2.3	2.2	
322 OTHER–AUTRES	4.2	4.5	4.0	3.9	4.2	3.2	
4 MACHINERY–EQUIPEMENT	16.3	14.1	16.2	20.5	17.6	17.9	
41 CAPITAL EQUIPMENT–MACHINES	13.9	12.0	13.8	17.8	15.0	15.5	
42 PARTS–PIECES ACCESSOIRES	2.4	2.1	2.4	2.7	2.6	2.5	
5 TRANSPORT–TRANSPORT	7.5	6.0	9.8	11.1	10.9	8.6	
51 PASSENGER CARS–AUTOMOBILES	4.3	2.8	6.6	7.6	4.4	2.6	
52 OTHER–AUTRES	0.6	0.7	0.6	0.8	3.7	3.5	
521 INDUSTRIAL–INDUSTRIELS	0.5	0.5	0.4	0.5	3.3	3.2	
522 NON INDUSTRIAL–NON INDUSTRIEL	0.1	0.1	0.2	0.3	0.4	0.3	
53 PARTS–PIECES ACCESSOIRES	2.7	2.5	2.5	2.8	2.8	2.5	
6 CONSUM GOODS–BIENS CONSOMMATION	9.4	9.7	10.6	13.3	16.1	15.1	
61 DURABLE–DURABLES	1.6	1.7	2.2	3.1	4.1	3.3	
62 SEMI DURABLE–SEMI DURABLES	3.8	3.8	4.3	5.4	6.5	6.3	
63 NON DURABLE–NON DURABLES	4.0	4.2	4.2	4.9	5.4	5.5	
7 GOODS NES–BIENS NDA	15.0	17.5	13.2	2.7	0.3	0.4	

EXPORTS – EXPORTATIONS

	1990	1991	1992	1993	1994	1995	1996
TOTAL EXPORTS–EXPORTATIONS TOTALES	100.	100.	100.	100.	100.	100.	100.
1 AGRICULTURE	52.9	54.3	53.9	57.3	54.5	56.3	49.7
2 MINING QUARRY–INDUS EXTRACTIVES	0.1	0.0	0.1	0.2	0.2	0.1	0.2
3 MANUFACTURING–IND MANUFACTUR	47.0	45.7	46.0	42.6	45.3	43.6	50.1
31 FOOD BEV TOBACCO–ALIM BOISS TAB	10.7	11.5	11.7	13.7	11.7	12.0	14.5
32 TEXTILES–INDUSTRIES TEXTILES	6.3	5.4	5.8	5.9	5.8	4.0	3.4
33 WOOD & PRODUCTS–BOIS & PRODUITS	0.9	0.7	0.9	1.1	1.4	1.3	1.3
34 PAPER & PRODUCTS–PAPIER & PRODT	1.3	1.6	1.9	1.8	1.6	2.2	1.8
35 CHEMICALS–INDUSTRIES CHIMIQUES	9.3	8.9	9.6	10.1	9.8	9.8	10.4
36 NON METAL MIN–MIN NON METAL	1.2	1.1	1.1	1.1	1.1	1.2	1.3
37 BASIC METAL–IND METAL BASE	1.6	1.5	1.6	1.5	1.4	1.5	1.4
38 METAL MANUF–MANUF METAL	5.3	5.1	5.3	5.5	5.2	5.0	5.8
39 OTH MANUF IND–AUTRES MANUF	10.3	9.8	8.1	1.8	7.3	6.5	10.2

3. TRADE BY PRINCIPAL COUNTRIES OF PRODUCTION AND LAST DESTINATION (VALUE IN THOUSAND U.S. DOLLARS)
ECHANGES SELON LES PRINCIPAUX PAYS DE PRODUCTION ET DE DERNIERE DESTINATION (VALEUR EN MILLIERS DE DOLLARS EU)

COUNTRIES–PAYS	SPECIAL IMPORTS C.I.F. IMPORTATIONS SPECIALES C.A.F					COUNTRIES–PAYS	SPECIAL EXPORTS F.O.B. EXPORTATIONS SPECIALES F.O.B.				
	1992	1993	1994	1995	1996		1992	1993	1994	1995	1996
World	2789130	2938673	3024345	3205485	3885656	Monde	1833713	1941721	2220441	2701759	2881593
Africa	611	2884	2347	4005	8016	Afrique	1873	3396	12600	5898	7178
Americas	2104909	2124484	2273206	2496377	3131245	Amériques	1322135	1345669	1451784	1692194	1837068
Northern America	1411618	1340484	1384250	1492396	1989842	Amérique du Nord	917369	908415	991666	1118276	1177247
LAIA	445028	491997	571413	641141	764821	ALAI	50903	76927	80859	91137	138676
CACM	216289	206026	231179	235615	250407	MCAC	308709	269440	285851	349687	384284
Caribbean	10002	10980	21173	26613	25534	Caraïbes	29283	26514	26433	33007	47117
Rest of America	21972	74998	65191	100613	100642	Autre Amérique	15871	64372	66975	100088	89744
As.ex F.USSR	325836	400293	333688	272390	304271	Asie l'URSS exclus	40660	36569	41401	106359	105408
Eur.x F.USSR	340664	388828	381038	407486	433109	Europe l'URSS exclus	467469	552705	697861	858302	881991
EU	306210	357671	342557	374467	390761	UE	454167	541906	683409	830538	860151
EFTA	29961	27082	28328	20268	26238	AELE	9992	6720	12214	21723	14809
East Europe	4000	3362	9471	10205	11570	Europe de l'Est	3310	4040	2237	5921	7029
Other Europe	7	176	87	639	4166	Autre de l'Europe		38		3	0
Former USSR						Ancienne URSS					
Oceania	905	947	1443	6243	1405	Océanie	863	1628	3065	3812	3940
USA/Etats–Unis d'Amer	1385683	1306599	1341920	1453012	1940818	USA/Etats–Unis d'Amer	887462	871729	963045	1084662	1123968
Venezuela	113039	139057	164903	211285	252464	Germany/Allemagne	173262	187976	197843	172932	206534
Japan/Japon	168854	217783	166455	122863	146367	Belgium–Luxembourg	78254	124372	148147	177603	127068
Mexico/Mexique	123783	116462	136760	176757	252415	Italy/Italie	83319	87835	105366	132055	150510
Guatemala	96783	104165	109256	112079	116466	Guatemala	75271	84770	102621	116977	123563
Brazil/Brésil	98677	110342	124370	101591	79519	Nicaragua	134443	69418	67534	87295	101986
Germany/Allemagne	86502	101345	100250	99890	93669	El Salvador	55701	62935	72264	90862	93302
Colombia/Colombie	56512	77457	86828	98593	112647	Netherlands/Pays–Bas	35216	42382	59986	87594	111939
El Salvador	60803	69232	76388	84148	93380	United Kingdom	23987	38121	66591	101239	93189
Panama	21963	74918	65110	99380	98014	Panama	269	63443	65632	84601	85793
Italy/Italie	36532	47345	50810	61902	64814	Honduras	43295	52318	43432	54554	65433
Spain/Espagne	32412	46105	42580	57223	50080	France, Monac	19248	24151	35534	51131	61402
France, Monac	38309	55375	40727	33314	54942	Canada	29705	36504	28539	33408	53038
Canada	25918	33839	42024	39331	48096	Mexico/Mexique	17617	28705	22098	16451	52828
Netherlands/Pays–Bas	24075	25718	28231	43390	30706	Japan/Japon	13373	11609	19454	28054	35123
United Kingdom	29307	29875	30505	26031	34035	Spain/Espagne	14528	11502	21241	25867	27844
Korea, Republic of	56597	222	50205	2693	37030	Sweden/Suède	6710	7077	13162	24506	45194
Nicaragua	50528	21616	22735	17128	15364	Finland/Finlande	8656	7721	16699	35796	16497
Switz.Liecht	28620	26141	25009	18075	24356	Hong Kong	2564	5786	12814	22019	39619
Hong Kong	27395	32609	16735	23038	20495	Colombia/Colombie	6827	8825	10885	16516	21263
Belgium–Luxembourg	17492	22884	15411	28326	29340	Chile/Chili	4377	9367	12043	16281	18588
Chile/Chili	19011	15444	17555	12675	32342	Russian Federation	420	496	4147	33074	20805
Korea Dem People's Rp	58	51963	185	39814	2787	Dominican Republic	11219	7720	8301	12340	15730
Honduras	8176	11014	22799	22261	25197	Venezuela	7830	10797	7974	14494	11605
Argentina/Argentine	9434	9737	19358	27102	22390	Switz.Liecht	8338	5297	7854	16924	12368
China/Chine	287	375	20791	17153	24165	Portugal	8322	6062	10978	11872	11213
Sweden/Suède	11052	7913	9686	8361	11013	Jamaica/Jamaïque	5105	5718	9532	9043	11656
Ecuador/Equateur	15599	12705	10027	3435	3647	Argentina/Argentine	4773	6840	9939	5142	8487
Peru/Pérou	7800	8863	11065	8965	8348	China/Chine		150	277	32988	475
Israel/Israël	6280	7675	7242	7082	9651	Belize/Bélize	15399	614	908	14534	2334
Ireland/Irlande	5928	7338	7464	6134	8957	Peru/Pérou	1777	4404	5974	7072	13838
Trinidad and Tobago	7821	5589	10299	9503	1450	Ecuador/Equateur	4066	4098	7273	7235	7170
Denmark/Danemark	5683	4665	9119	3117	6385	Israel/Israël	4418	4552	2507	9509	7190
Austria/Autriche	12680	5032	4268	2599	4228	Denmark/Danemark	1063	1972	4286	5585	6485
Singapore/Singapour	5809	8141	4872	5161	3971	Poland/Pologne	1777	3705	1594	4286	5836
Russian Federation	3137	4822	7172	8535	2850	Norway,SVD,JM	1627	1391	4248	4793	2405
Jamaica/Jamaïque	99	68	35	8341	12060	Brazil/Brésil	2782	1169	260	6746	3391
Poland/Pologne	1198	1324	5264	5790	6083	Morocco/Maroc	578	748	10095	1258	535
Finland/Finlande	5154	2666	2219	2496	1920	Haiti/Haïti	656	724	1777	1604	8078
Thailand/Thaïlande	2114	2341	2736	2035	3615	Australia/Australie	724	1474	2840	3627	3841
Cuba	709	3506	6462	103	1535	Singapore/Singapour	1416	372	627	3818	6001
Dominican Republic	1110	912	2232	3358	4542	Netherlands Antilles	1893	5429	1254	1871	1341
So. Africa Customs Un	452	234	1502	2366	6840	Ireland/Irlande	979	1559	2570	3312	1369
Aruba	48	242	1492	3775	5264	So. Africa Customs Un	794	1897	1289	3412	2318
Norway,SVD,JM	1322	941	3250	2177	1882	Korea Dem People's Rp	115	4504	434	2117	2226
India/Inde	1156	1935	1503	1690	1893	Trinidad and Tobago	1504	1268	1137	989	3915
Malaysia/Malaisie	1490	1794	2142	1115	843	Aruba	3929	1856	607	1073	1043
Turkey/Turquie	201	1507	2953	888	1554	Turkey/Turquie	26	1469		153	4365
Czech Republic		1355	1412	1955	2153	Cameroon/Cameroun	433	710	919	976	2863
Indonesia/Indonésie	844	599	1516	2647	1261	Korea, Republic of	1279	52	1049	196	2675

(VALUE AS PERCENTAGE OF WORLD TOTAL)(VALEURS EN POURCENTAGE DU TOTAL MONDIAL)

	1987	1988	1989	1990	1991	1992	1993	1994	1995	1996
Africa	0.0	0.0	0.0	0.0	0.0	0.0	0.1	0.1	0.1	0.2
Americas	67.5	72.0	74.9	73.0	77.1	75.5	72.3	75.2	77.9	80.6
Northern America	39.2	40.4	48.3	48.6	52.6	50.6	45.6	45.8	46.6	51.2
LAIA	17.8	20.9	17.5	16.4	16.0	16.0	16.7	18.9	20.0	19.7
CACM	8.5	8.4	6.9	6.5	6.9	7.8	7.0	7.6	7.4	6.4
Caribbean	0.2	0.4	0.5	0.1	0.2	0.4	0.4	0.7	0.8	0.7
Rest of America	1.8	1.8	1.7	1.2	1.4	0.8	2.6	2.2	3.1	2.6
As.ex F.USSR	14.2	12.3	11.2	12.2	10.4	11.7	13.6	11.0	8.5	7.8
Eur.x F.USSR	17.1	14.9	12.9	13.6	11.3	12.2	13.2	12.6	12.7	11.1
EU	15.8	13.5	11.5	12.3	10.0	11.0	12.2	11.3	11.7	10.1
EFTA	1.1	1.1	0.8	1.0	1.1	1.1	0.9	0.9	0.6	0.7
East Europe	0.2	0.2	0.3	0.3	0.2	0.1	0.1	0.3	0.3	0.3
Other Europe	0.0	0.0	0.0	0.0	0.0	0.0	0.0	0.0	0.0	0.1
Former USSR	0.2	0.1	0.1	0.1	0.1					
Oceania	0.0	0.0	0.0	0.0	0.0	0.0	0.0	0.0	0.2	0.0
USA/Etats–Unis d'Amer	37.2	38.8	47.1	47.3	51.3	49.7	44.5	44.4	45.3	49.9
Venezuela	7.0	7.4	6.8	7.4	5.2	4.1	4.7	5.5	6.6	6.5
Japan/Japon	8.5	6.7	6.1	7.2	5.3	6.1	7.4	5.5	3.8	3.8
Mexico/Mexique	5.0	6.0	4.8	2.8	3.9	4.4	4.0	4.5	5.5	6.5
Guatemala	4.7	4.7	3.6	3.5	3.7	3.5	3.5	3.6	3.5	3.0
Brazil/Brésil	2.7	4.0	3.1	2.5	3.1	3.5	3.8	4.1	3.2	2.0
Germany/Allemagne	5.3	4.2	3.6	4.0	2.8	3.1	3.4	3.3	3.1	2.4
Colombia/Colombie	1.2	1.6	1.0	0.8	1.6	2.0	2.6	2.9	3.1	2.9
El Salvador	2.7	2.6	2.2	2.2	2.3	2.2	2.4	2.5	2.6	2.4
Panama	1.8	1.8	1.7	1.2	1.4	0.8	2.5	2.2	3.1	2.5

	1987	1988	1989	1990	1991	1992	1993	1994	1995	1996
Afrique	0.2	0.3	0.2	0.1	0.1	0.1	0.2	0.6	0.2	0.2
Amériques	63.4	61.5	66.5	66.0	68.0	72.1	69.3	65.4	62.6	63.8
Amérique du Nord	47.0	44.1	49.3	49.0	50.2	50.0	46.8	44.7	41.4	40.9
ALAI	1.1	2.0	2.1	1.9	1.8	2.8	4.0	3.6	3.4	4.8
MCAC	9.8	11.0	10.3	9.5	11.0	16.8	13.9	12.9	12.9	13.3
Caraïbes	1.2	1.5	1.7	2.0	1.5	1.6	1.4	1.2	1.2	1.6
Autre Amérique	4.3	3.0	3.0	3.6	3.4	0.9	3.3	3.0	3.7	3.1
Asie l'URSS exclus	2.4	3.4	1.9	2.6	2.9	2.2	1.9	1.9	3.9	3.7
Europe l'URSS exclus	32.1	32.9	29.0	30.3	28.4	25.5	28.5	31.4	31.8	30.6
UE	29.4	29.7	26.8	29.5	27.7	24.8	27.9	30.8	30.7	29.8
AELE	0.3	0.4	0.3	0.5	0.6	0.5	0.3	0.6	0.8	0.5
Europe de l'Est	1.7	2.8	1.9	0.3	0.2	0.2	0.2	0.1	0.2	0.2
Autre de l'Europe	0.0	0.0	0.0	0.0	0.0		0.0		0.0	0.0
Ancienne URSS	0.6	0.5	0.8	0.0	0.0					
Océanie	0.1	0.1	0.1	0.1	0.1	0.0	0.1	0.1	0.1	0.1
USA/Etats–Unis d'Amer	45.3	41.7	45.4	45.1	47.6	48.4	44.9	43.4	40.1	39.0
Germany/Allemagne	15.4	14.6	12.4	11.9	10.7	9.4	9.7	8.9	6.4	7.2
Belgium–Luxembourg	1.0	0.9	1.9	4.5	4.7	4.3	6.4	6.7	6.6	4.4
Italy/Italie	3.0	4.4	4.3	4.3	4.5	4.5	4.5	4.7	4.9	5.2
Guatemala	3.9	4.7	4.2	3.6	3.6	4.1	4.4	4.6	4.3	4.3
Nicaragua	1.1	1.4	1.7	2.1	3.6	7.3	3.6	3.0	3.2	3.5
El Salvador	3.2	3.7	3.2	2.5	2.7	3.0	3.2	3.3	3.4	3.2
Netherlands/Pays–Bas	2.7	3.0	2.3	3.0	2.6	1.9	2.2	2.7	3.2	3.9
United Kingdom	2.2	2.3	2.2	2.0	1.9	1.3	2.0	3.0	3.7	3.2
Panama	4.2	2.9	2.9	3.5	3.3	0.0	3.3	3.0	3.1	3.0

4. Special Imports C.I.F. by Commodities according to the S.I.T.C. (Rev. 2) in thousand U.S. Dollars
Importations Spéciales C.A.F. par Produits d'après la C.T.C.I. (Rév. 2) en milliers de Dollars E.U.

SITC CTCI	COMMODITY	1993			1994			1995			1996			PRODUIT
			WEIGHT POIDS	VALUE VALEUR		WEIGHT POIDS	VALUE VALEUR		WEIGHT POIDS	VALUE VALEUR		WEIGHT POIDS	VALUE VALEUR	
	ALL COMMODITIES			2938673			3024345			3205485			3885656	TOUS PRODUITS
0	FOOD AND LIVE ANIMALS			224846			252784			256164			367204	ALIMENTS,ANIMAUX VIVANTS
001	*LIVE ANIMALS FOR FOOD	W	13728	13408	W	10002	10297	W	1361	2090	W	149	1723	ANIMAUX VIVANTS
0011	BOVINE SPECIES,LIVE	W	13488	11529	W	9847	8584	W	1234	1067	W	44	66	ESPECE BOVINE
00119	— OTHR THAN FR BREEDING	W	13464	11460	W	9815	8344	W	1218	1030				BOVINS NON REPRODUCTEURS
02	DAIRY PRODCTS,BIRDS'EGGS			8978			9368			9889			10281	PRODUITS LAITIERS,OEUFS
03	FISH AND PREPARATIONS			33785			23111			21271			38041	POISSONS ET PREPARATIONS
034	FISH,FRESH,CHILLED,FROZN	W	22080	31133	W	59406	20874	W	20337	18596	W	31959	33479	POISSON FRAIS, REFRIG,CONG
0341	FISH FRSH,CHLLD,EX FILLT	W	22080	31133	W	415	577	W	514	690	W	414	368	POISSON FRAIS,REFRIGERE
0342	FISH FROZEN,EXCL FILLETS				W	58949	20239	W	19635	17812	W	31544	33105	POISSONS CONGELES
04	CEREALS AND PREPARATIONS			96755			126920			130758			206046	CEREALES ET PRODUITS
041	WHEAT ETC UNMILLED	W	113471	25364	W	152451	30047	W	162137	34430	W	246260	56541	FROMENT,EPEAUTRE
0411	DURUM WHEAT UNMILLED							W	56732	13002	W	156510	33979	FROMENT DUR NON MOULU
0412	OTHER WHEAT ETC UNMILLED				W	152451	30047	W	105405	21428	W	89750	22562	AUTRE FROMENT NON MOULU
042	RICE	W	36469	6375	W	52691	19817	W	156209	16219	W	87925	28601	RIZ
0421	RICE IN HUSK OR HUSKED	W	46	26	W	10199	1910	W	155248	15816	W	87577	28436	RIZ SANS AUTRE PREPARATION
04211	RICE IN THE HUSK				W	10195	1908	W	155233	15807	W	87572	28432	RIZ PADDY
0422	RICE SEMI–MILLED,MILLED	W	36423	6348	W	42493	17907	W	960	403	W	348	165	RIZ POLI,GLACE INCL BRISURES
04221	RICE MILLED UNBROKEN				W	42485	17900	W	960	402	W	348	165	RIZ POLI,GLACE EXCL BRISURES
044	MAIZE UNMILLED	W	336720	45843	W	383111	50084	W	345017	52181	W	451734	90635	MAIS NON MOULU
048	CEREAL ETC PREPARATIONS	W	20690	17626	W	24275	24593	W	25714	25498	W	24922	27996	PREPTNS A BASE CEREALES
0481	PREPD BREAKFAST FOOD ETC	W	5428	9436	W	5817	11078	W	6098	9788	W	6026	10969	CEREALES TRAVAILLEES
04812	CEREAL ROASTED, PUFFED	W	2558	7624	W	3205	9353	W	3735	8096	W	3388	8848	PRODTS BASE CEREALES
05	VEGETABLES AND FRUIT			26463			30759			37274			49226	LEGUMES ET FRUITS
054	VEG ETC FRSH,SMPLY PRSVD	W	6936	3157	W	10654	7727	W	21940	12216	W	33200	20130	LEGUMES FRAIS,CONG,SECS
0542	LEGUMINOUS VEGETBLES DRY	W	2149	1199	W	5461	3695	W	8052	4901	W	17986	12099	LEGUMES A COSSE SECS
057	FRUIT,NUTS,FRESH,DRIED	W	16259	7974	W	17207	8403	W	20897	10445	W	20412	13592	FRUITS FRAIS OU SECS
058	FRUIT PRESERVED,PREPARED	W	8538	10232	W	8805	10250	W	9250	10478	W	9909	10590	CONSERVES DE FRUITS
06	SUGAR AND PREPS,HONEY			8524			9902			9847			10720	SUCRES ET PRODUITS
07	COFFEE,TEA,COCOA,SPICES			6802			10238			12239			12859	CAFE,THE,CACAO,EPICES
09	MISC EDIBLE PRODUCTS			24726			23558			25476			28968	PREP ALIMENTAIRES DIVERSES
098	EDIBLE PRODCTS,PREPS NES	W	11391	24683	W	13814	23278	W	12930	24971	W	14017	28219	PREP ALIMENTAIRES NDA
09809	MISC FOOD PREPRTIONS NES	W	5729	17502	W	4605	7414	W	3899	9370	W	5096	12122	PREP ALIMENTAIRES NDA
1	BEVERAGES AND TOBACCO			16258			15432			17137			18133	BOISSONS ET TABACS
11	BEVERAGES			15054			15045			15308			14635	BOISSONS
112	ALCOHOLIC BEVERAGES	W	6052	11484	W	7157	11282	W	6496	11045	W	5736	10840	BOISSONS ALCOOLIQUES
2	CRUDE MATERLS,EXCL FUELS			80291			86554			96788			120240	MAT BRUTES NON COMESTIBLES
22	OIL SEEDS,OLEAGINOUS FRT			36538			41785			47204			67089	GRAINES,FRUITS OLEAGINEUX
222	SEEDS FOR'SOFT'FIXED OIL	W	130201	35954	W	143037	40544	W	161448	46129	W	203672	66326	GRAINES HUILES FIXES
2222	SOYA BEANS	W	129071	35421	W	141041	39391	W	159823	44938	W	201431	64716	FEVES DE SOJA
23	RUBBER, CRUDE			10534			13597			14954			14589	CAOUTCHOUC BRUT
233	RUBBER,SYNTHTIC,RECLAIMD	W	8274	7402	W	9453	9129	W	7909	9738	W	7622	9383	LATEX CAOUTCH SYNTH REGEN
2331	SYNTHETIC RUBBER ETC	W	8199	7319	W	9318	8985	W	7903	9716	W	7580	9338	LATEX CAOUTCH SYNTHETIQUE
27	CRUDE FERTLZR,MINRLS NES			9216			9653			9629			8595	ENGRAIS MINERAUX BRUTS
3	MINERAL FUELS ETC			248729			271654			273591			335790	COMBUSTIBLES MINERAUX LUB
33	PETROLEUM AND PRODUCTS			242321			263437			265409			322016	PETROLE ET DERIVES
333	CRUDE PETROLEUM	W	569026	71202	W	553852	64203	W	706133	88696	W	675988	101371	HUILES BRUTES DE PETROLE
334	PETROLEUM PRODUCTS,REFIN	W	856040	167897	W	1044246	196012	W	885215	173669	W	904336	216999	PRODUITS RAFFINES
3341	GASOLINE,OTH LIGHT OILS	W	347788	67917	W	387557	70128	W	380459	70729	W	419241	96651	ESSENCES POUR MOTEURS
33411	MOTOR,AVIATION SPIRIT	W	269613	52662										ESSENCES MOTEURS D'AVIONS
33412	SPIRIT TYPE JET FUEL	W	78080	15186										CARBUREACTEURS
33419	OTH LIGHT PETROLEUM OILS	W	95	69	W	387557	70128	W	380459	70729	W	419241	96651	AUTRES HUILES LEGERES
3343	GAS OILS	W	401613	66944										GAS OILS
3344	FUEL OILS,NES	W	83522	10183	W	614740	93582	W	459205	70513	W	437985	85939	FUEL OILS
3345	LUBS,PETROLEUM OILS NES	W	22820	22548	W	41292	31968	W	45145	32176	W	46586	34053	HUILES LUBRIFIANTES
33451	LUBS(HIGH PETR CONT) ETC	W	22371	21688	W	40700	30953	W	44552	31222	W	45947	33045	HUILES LUBRIF,H LOURDES
341	*GAS,NATURAL AND MANUFCT	W	29786	6298	W	31261	6488	W	42082	8084	W	44526	13084	GAZ NATUREL,GAZ MANUFACT
3413	PETROLM GASES,LIQUEFIED	W	29786	6298	W	31260	6482	W	42058	8048	W	44506	13049	GAZ DE PETROLE LIQUEFIE
34131	LIQUEFIED PROPANE,BUTANE				W	31253	6473	W	40953	7798	W	40101	11825	PROPANE,BUTANE LIQUEFIES
5	CHEMCLS,RELATED PROD NES			521459			537438			622138			657634	PRODUITS CHIMIQUES
51	ORGANIC CHEMICALS			58859			57516			67470			72004	PROD CHIMIQ ORGANIQUES
512	ALCOHOLS,PHENOLS ETC	W	37864	11811	W	35795	11172	W	55039	18717	W	32598	14321	PHENOLS,PHENOLS–ALCOOLS
5121	ACYCLIC ALCOHOLS,DERIVS	W	37732	11179	W	34197	9869	W	54773	17795	W	32182	13228	ALCOOLS ACYCLIQUES
51216	ETHYL ALC,DENATRD SPIRIT	W	34047	7886	W	29108	5569	W	50563	12738	W	27421	8477	ALCOOL ETHYLIQUE NON DENAT
513	CARBOXYLIC ACIDS ETC	W	8572	12947	W	9098	15041	W	6943	14077	W	8945	16268	ACIDES CARBOXYLIQUES
514	NITROGEN–FNCTN COMPOUNDS	W	2173	7483	W	2807	12228	W	3187	13441	W	3287	15547	COMPOSES FONCT AZOTEES
515	ORG–INORG COMPOUNDS ETC	W	1458	12698	W	1810	8296	W	1912	9000	W	1931	9626	COMPOSES ORGANO–MINERAUX
5156	HETEROCYCLIC CMPDS ETC	W	962	9138	W	1103	5627	W	1127	6047	W	1088	6164	COMPOSES HETEROCYCLIQUES
52	INORGANIC CHEMICALS			36603			38148			42896			46086	PROD CHIM INORGANIQUES
522	INORG ELEMNTS,OXIDES,ETC	W	72678	21933	W	56858	21689	W	63379	26384	W	82004	28047	ELEMENTS INORGANIQUES
5225	INORGANIC BASES ETC NES	W	59699	10734	W	43077	9971	W	49351	15242	W	62763	15856	AUTRES BASES OXYDES METAL
52251	AMMONIA,ANHYDROUS ETC	W	48662	8681	W	35014	7998	W	43572	11920	W	56019	13007	AMMONIAC LIQUEFIE
523	OTHR INORG CHEMICALS ETC	W	37859	14385	W	37453	16068	W	45096	16172	W	47767	17655	AUT PRODUITS CHIMIQUES INORG
5232	OTH MTL CMPD OF INRG ACD	W	22288	8412	W	20440	8649	W	30108	9893	W	27335	9858	SELS METALLIQUES
53	DYES,TANNING,COLOUR PROD			27057			25081			24903			28393	PROD TEINTURE,COLORANTS
533	PIGMENTS,PAINTS,ETC	W	5292	16705	W	5270	15959	W	6784	17204	W	7399	19974	PIGMENTS,PEINTURES,VERNIS
541	*MEDICINAL,PHARM PRODUCT	K	3769173	95473	K	3139377	98378	K	3686335	103151	K	5162707	117091	PROD MEDICINAUX PHARMACEUT
5417	MEDICAMENTS	K	2508286	74129	K	2342088	81232	K	2707163	85318	K	4165775	95648	MEDICAMENTS
54171	— CONTAINNG ANTIBIOTICS				K	640631	20189	K	551628	16496	K	456472	13181	MED CONTN ANTIBIOTIQUES
54179	— CONTNG OTH SUBSTANCES				K	1528530	53411	K	1890324	62325	K	3026259	73565	MED CONT AUT SUBSTANCES
55	PERFUME,CLEANING ETC PRD			46991			55475			64539			72029	PROD POUR PARFUM,TOILETTE
551	ESSENTL OILS,PERFUME,ETC	W	477	8822	W	598	10744	W	699	10293	W	550	10375	HUILES ESSENTIELLES
5514	MIXED PERFUME SUBSTANCES	W	399	8073	W	497	9468	W	617	9229	W	474	9455	MELANGES SUBSTAN ODORIFER
553	PERFUMERY,COSMETICS,ETC	W	3733	17220	W	4147	18942	W	5974	28482	W	6756	31535	PRODUITS DE PARFUMERIE
554	SOAP,CLEANSING ETC PREPS	W	15435	20950	W	19468	25789	W	22990	25763	W	22498	30119	SAVONS,PRODUITS DETERSIFS
5542	WASHING PREPARATIONS ETC	W	12364	15536	W	15854	18612	W	17222	19165	W	17551	21560	PROD ORG TENSIO–ACT NDA
562	*FERTILIZERS,MANUFACTURE	W	215754	36453	W	243540	40943	W	272784	59709	W	250761	57046	ENGRAIS MANUFACTURES
5621	CHEM NITROGENOUS FERTLZR	W	96882	15999	W	102026	17421	W	128095	30761	W	113306	27493	ENGRAIS AZOTES
56216	UREA				W	72890	11647	W	79468	19309	W	84742	21597	UREE
56219	CHEM NITROG FERTILZR NES	W	90462	15004	W	13093	3298	W	11729	5911	W	899	638	ENGRAIS AZOTES NDA
5623	CHEM POTASSIC FERTILIZER	W	86360	13283	W	98110	13833	W	94322	15595	W	90612	15124	ENGRAIS POTASSIQUES
56239	CHEM POTASS FERTILZR NES	W	86360	13283	W	38955	5702	W	13602	3124	W	12091	2884	ENGRAIS POTASSIQUES NDA
5629	FERTILIZERS NES	W	5137	3000	W	27463	6741	W	36154	10053	W	36566	11751	ENGRAIS NDA
58	PLASTIC MATERIALS ETC			114178			119243			141912			137017	MAT PLAST ARTIFICIELLES
582	PROD OF CONDENSATION ETC	W	15180	22734	W	13896	19097	W	13748	22750	W	19160	23656	PROD CONDENS,POLYCOND
5823	ALKYDS,OTHER POLYESTERS	W	13669	18206	W	7313	10172	W	7277	12748	W	7609	12375	ALKYDES ET AUT POLYESTERS
58231	— IN PRIMARY FORMS				W	7015	8712	W	6868	10649	W	7232	10528	SOUS FORMES PRIMAIRES
583	POLYMERIZATION ETC PRODS	W	85545	82874	W	96142	96223	W	90123	115806	W	107808	109419	PROD POLYMERISATION
5831	POLYETHYLENE	W	728	1885	W	42378	36104	W	37224	43713	W	38313	37676	POLYETHYLENE
58311	— IN PRIMARY FORMS				W	40456	32803	W	35460	40109	W	35802	32990	POLYETHYLENE PRIMAIRES
5832	POLYPROPYLENE				W	13217	12646	W	15276	19514	W	17010	19453	POLYPROPYLENE

4. Special Imports C.I.F. by Commodities according to the S.I.T.C. (Rev. 2) in thousand U.S. Dollars
Importations Spéciales C.A.F. par Produits d'après la C.T.C.I. (Rév. 2) en milliers de Dollars E.U.

SITC CTCI	COMMODITY	1993 WEIGHT POIDS	1993 VALUE VALEUR	1994 WEIGHT POIDS	1994 VALUE VALEUR	1995 WEIGHT POIDS	1995 VALUE VALEUR	1996 WEIGHT POIDS	1996 VALUE VALEUR	PRODUIT
58321	— IN PRIMARY FORMS			W 11614	8333	W 13646	14503	W 14725	13142	POLYPROPYLENE PRIMAIRES
5834	POLYVINYL CHLORIDE	W 20644	16065	W 23749	20940	W 18584	20422	W 32438	19082	CHLORURE DE POLYVINYLE
58341	— IN PRIMARY FORMS			W 22544	18540	W 17521	18046	W 31415	16320	SOUS FORMES PRIMAIRES
5839	OTH POLYMRZTION ETC PROD	W 63286	64022	W 7495	13798	W 9754	17079	W 9204	16094	AUT PROD POLYMER COPOLYM
59	CHEMICAL MATERIALS NES		105256		102151		117249		126443	MAT PROD CHIMIQUES NDA
591	PESTICIDES,DISINFECTANTS	W 13184	69427	W 13742	71993	W 15861	85224	W 16247	89444	DESINF,INSECT,FONG,HERB
5911	INSECTICIDES,FOR RETAIL	W 3093	14400	W 2392	12493	W 4158	16996	W 3647	18606	INSECTICIDES VENTE DET
5912	FUNGICIDES,FOR RETAIL	W 5592	34575	W 5385	34065	W 5777	41149	W 7007	46227	FONGICIDES VENTE AU DET
5913	HERBICIDES,FOR RETAIL	W 2414	12971	W 3193	16415	W 3211	16688	W 3098	17939	HERBICIDES VENTE AU DET
5914	DISINFECTANTS,ETC,FR RET	W 2085	7482	W 2772	9021	W 2715	10390	W 2496	6671	DESINFECTANTS VENTE DET
59149	RAT POISONS ETC FR RTAIL	W 1843	6860	W 2385	8208	W 2337	9773	W 1626	5618	ANTIPARASITES VENTE DET
598	MISCEL CHEM PRODUCTS NES	W 10017	28798	W 10600	21856	W 11782	22990	W 12015	26819	PROD DIV INDUST CHIM NDA
5989	CHEM PRODUCTS,PREPS NES	W 8407	23338	W 8618	15583	W 8604	18094	W 10319	21950	PROD PREP CHIMIQUES NDA
59899	OTH CHEM PRODS,PREPS,NES	W 6353	19081	W 6260	12152	W 5797	14162	W 7555	17761	AUT PRODUITS CHIMIQUES NDA
6	BASIC MANUFACTURES		580985		640326		744213		725056	ART MANUFACTURES
62	RUBBER MANUFACTURES NES		31004		33436		34909		40209	CAOUTCHOUC MANUFACTURE
625	RUBBER TYRES, TUBES ETC	W 5657	18845	W 6402	20969	W 6048	20072	W 6829	23118	PNEUS CAOUTCHOUC VULCANISE
6251	TYRES NEW FOR MOTOR CARS	W 3884	13436	W 2299	7462	W 2153	6783	W 2324	7039	PNEUS POUR VOITURES
63	WOOD,CORK MANUFACTRS NES		6312		9678		9547		8933	OUVRAGES LIEGE ET BOIS
64	PAPER,PAPERBOARD AND MFR		155094		202112		259179		244690	PAPIERS,CARTONS & OUVRAGES
641	PAPER AND PAPERBOARD	W 179969	125919	W 311140	157553	W 264573	208218	W 271372	182114	PAPIERS ET CARTONS
6411	NEWSPRINT			W 27511	16940	W 19579	15918	W 21839	18675	PAPIER JOURNAL
6412	PRINTG,WRITING PAPER NES	W 20242	13180	W 9209	8811	W 10861	13116	W 9883	9932	PAPIERS POUR L'IMPRESSION
64121	— UNCOATED	W 20242	13180	W 1328	1404	W 1522	2536	W 1359	1674	PAPIERS IMPRES NON COUCHES
64122	— COA[illegible] IMPREGNATD ETC			W 7882	7407	W 9339	10580	W 8524	8258	PAPIERS IMPRESSION COUCHES
6413	KRAFT [illegible],PAPERBOARD	W 119459	54768	W 199213	88831	W 188199	128394	W 202469	105329	PAPIER ET CARTON KRAFT
64131	KRAF[illegible] IN BULK			W 139321	60215	W 125848	87724	W 145208	74576	PAP KRAFT POUR COUVERTURES
64139	KRA[illegible]PER PAPERBD,NES			W 55848	25602	W 56980	35909	W 53480	27434	PAPIER,CARTON KRAFT NDA
6415	PA[illegible],PAPERBRD,BULK,NES	W 19820	15933	W 59382	16965	W 22515	23360	W 23445	21109	PAPIERS,CARTONS ROULEAUX
64159	OT[illegible]R PAPER ETC,BULK,NES	W 19666	15512	W 58871	16087	W 21424	21849	W 21962	19658	AUT PAPIER ROULEAUX FEUILLES
6418	COATED ETC PAPER NES BLK	W 18735	40343	W 11112	22896	W 20653	24744	W 9472	23773	PAP,CARTONS COUCHES,ENDUITS
64181	PLASTIC COATED PAPER ETC			W 4620	14052	W 4608	14528	W 4877	16280	PAP,CARTONS ENDUITS,RESINES
64189	COATED PAPER ETC NES			W 6405	8787	W 16031	10209	W 4578	7483	PAPIERS,CARTONS COUCHES
642	PAPER,ETC,PRECUT,ARTS OF	W 21610	29175	W 43534	44559	W 44492	50961	W 35022	62576	PAP,CARTONS DECOUPES
6421	PAPER ETC CONTAINERS	W 9807	10557	W 31065	23817	W 31489	28832	W 21981	35992	BOITES,SACS EMBALLAGES
6428	PAPER ETC ARTICLES NES	W 4711	7585	W 7821	11763	W 7929	12324	W 7703	14717	OUVRAGES EN PATE A PAPIER
65	TEXTILE YARN,FABRICS,ETC		102268		79861		87621		98236	FILS,TISSUS,ARTICLES TEXTILE
651	TEXTILE YARN	W 4014	14018	W 6949	9324	W 2299	9004	W 2768	11614	FILS TEXTILES
652	COTTON FABRICS,WOVEN	W 6433	27453	W 3840	16812	W 4017	21022	W 4650	26074	TISSUS DE COTON
6521	GREY WOVEN COTTON FABRIC	W 5032	22618	W 515	2938	W 333	1827	W 188	2363	TISSUS COT ECRUS NON MERCER
65215	GREY WOVN COTN BLEND NES	W 4991	22406	W 36	193	W 110	655	W 80	1942	AUT TIS MOINS 85% COT ECRUS
6522	WOVEN COTTON BLEACHD,ETC	W 1401	4835	W 3325	13874	W 3684	19195	W 4462	23711	TISSUS COTON BLANCHIS ETC
65224	BLCHED COTTON FABRIC NES	W 1381	4738	W 2117	9485	W 2360	11597	W 3452	18539	AUT TIS PLUS 85% COT BLANCHI
653	WOVN MAN-MADE FIB FABRIC	W 4270	23712	W 2647	15472	W 3367	17762	W 3256	16278	TISSUS FIBRES SYNTH,ARTIF
6531	CONT SYNT WEAVES NONPILE	W 2539	13373	W 797	4202	W 1155	5434	W 1294	5068	TISSUS FIBRES SYNTH CONTINUE
6534	DISC SYN BLEND FABRC NES	W 1680	10060	W 1023	7105	W 1266	7530	W 1175	7578	TISSUS FIBRES SYNTH DISCONT
657	SPECIAL TXTL FABRC,PRODS	W 3340	12419	W 4326	16706	W 4532	17025	W 4495	20751	TISSUS SPECIAUX
6573	COATED ETC TEXTILES NES	W 1230	3559	W 1985	9414	W 2388	8931	W 1931	10770	TISSUS,ART MATIERE TEXT NDA
658	TEXTILE ARTICLES NES	W 1811	8949	W 1757	9419	W 2557	11055	W 2798	13123	ART FACONNES MAT TEXTILES
66	NONMETAL MINERAL MFS NES		46210		53081		53522		52411	ART MIN NON METALLIQUES
662	CLAY,REFRACTORY BLDG PRD	W 24787	12211	W 38398	14339	W 48097	18598	W 58569	17121	MAT CONST REFRACTAIRES
6624	BRICKS ETC NONREFRACTORY	W 23307	11022	W 37171	13388	W 47225	17869	W 56862	15927	BRIQUES ETC CERAM NON REFR
66245	GLAZED CERAMIC SETTS ETC	W 21965	10521	W 32984	12398	W 42529	16890	W 53313	15170	AUT CARREAUX CERAMIQUE
664	GLASS	W 15414	8875	W 19842	11203	W 14164	10279	W 15844	12116	VERRE
665	GLASSWARE	W 13175	12615	W 14785	12051	W 9337	9966	W 7594	8921	OUVRAGES EN VERRE
67	IRON AND STEEL		114760		116308		144966		122429	FER ET ACIER
672	IRON,STEEL PRIMARY FORMS	W 95033	28509	W 144352	41817	W 104897	39337	W 84882	26058	LINGOTS FER,ACIER
6724	IRN,STL INGOTS,LUMPS,ETC	W 58257	17031	W 75678	19574	W 50816	13872	W 53282	13896	FER,ACIER LINGOTS,MASSES
67241	IRON,SIMPLE STEEL INGOTS			W 75669	19514	W 50688	13642	W 53209	13692	LINGOTS EN FER ET ACIER
67245	IRN,STL BLOCKS,LUMPS,ETC	W 58257	17031	W 7	28	W 120	154	W 8	14	FER,ACIER EN MASSES
6727	IRN,STL COIL FR REROLLNG	W 36775	11470	W 68667	22239	W 53953	25428	W 31571	12132	EBAUCHES POUR TOLES FER
67271	IRON,SIMPLE STEEL COILS	W 36775	11470	W 68429	22021	W 53793	25300	W 31502	11985	EBAUCHES NON EN ACIER
673	IRON,STEEL SHAPES ETC	W 36994	15837	W 34960	15149	W 44387	20957	W 37326	18298	BARRES,PROFIL FER,ACIER
6731	IRON,STEEL WIRE ROD	W 13299	5571	W 16405	5807	W 25914	11407	W 13553	4409	FIL MACHINE FER,ACIER
67311	IRON,SIMPLE STL WIRE ROD	W 7225	2355	W 16404	5798	W 25913	11396	W 13238	4258	FIL MACH AUT ACIER FIN
674	IRN,STL UNIV,PLATE,SHEET	W 108338	51121	W 83028	41773	W 106732	65480	W 93307	55580	LARGES PLATS,TOLES
6746	IRN,STL THIN PLATE,ROLLD			W 44684	19311	W 67155	37898	W 53978	26548	TOLES LAM MOINS 3MM
67461	— OF IRON OR SIMPLE STL			W 43449	18018	W 65691	35848	W 53225	25093	TOL NON AC FIN MOINS 3 MM
6747	TINNED PLATES,SHEETS			W 7976	6352	W 11726	10024	W 13370	11729	TOLES ETAMEES EN ACIER
6749	OTH IRN,STL PLATES,SHEET	W 106222	49814	W 12196	8467	W 11288	8635	W 10229	9158	AUTRES TOLES FER,ACIER
67491	— OF IRON OR SIMPLE STL	W 106222	49814	W 11539	7737	W 10476	7816	W 8232	7170	AUT TOLES AUTRES ACIER FIN
678	IRON,STL TUBES,PIPES,ETC	W 13457	9362	W 9233	12908	W 8133	13140	W 15591	16794	TUBES,TUYAUX EN FONTE,FER
68	NON-FERROUS METALS		40563		43766		53056		50531	METAUX NON FERREUX
682	COPPER EXC CEMENT COPPER	W 4997	12847	W 6391	16429	W 4661	16426	W 6871	20219	CUIVRE
6822	COPPER,ALLOYS WORKED	W 4996	12846	W 6354	16225	W 4649	16372	W 6869	20205	CUIVRE,ALLIAGES OUVRES
68221	COPPER BARS,WIRE,ETC	W 4558	10794	W 5905	14151	W 4198	14100	W 6375	17572	BARRES,PROFILES ET FILS
684	ALUMINIUM	W 10652	20277	W 10036	21379	W 13357	29422	W 11071	25092	ALUMINIUM
6841	ALUMINIUM,ALLOYS,UNWRGHT	W 7206	9095	W 6620	9604	W 7891	14738	W 7448	12067	ALUMINIUM,ALLIAGES BRUTS
6842	ALUMINIUM,ALLOYS WORKED	W 3446	11182	W 3416	11775	W 5466	14684	W 3623	13025	ALUMINIUM,ALLIAGES OUVRE
69	METAL MANUFACTURES NES		82104		94544		92828		98777	ART MANUFACT EN METAL NDA
692	METAL TANKS,BOXES,ETC	W 5161	9999	W 4913	13255	W 5029	13049	W 7206	15694	RECIPIENTS METALLIQUES
6924	MTL TRANSPORT BOXES ETC	W 4983	9392	W 4403	11704	W 4536	11822	W 6601	14165	FUTS,TAMBOURS,BIDONS
695	TOOLS	W 1960	15632	W 2091	15810	W 2348	15920	W 2551	17723	OUTILS A MAIN
6953	OTHER HAND TOOLS	W 1201	8873	W 1292	9361	W 1311	9878	W 1600	9986	AUTRES OUTILS A MAIN
699	BASE METAL MFRS NES	W 6371	25959	W 7579	29184	W 8095	30820	W 7479	28106	ART MANUFACTURES MET NDA
6991	LOCKSMITHS WARES,ETC	W 1735	9673	W 2319	10851	W 1806	10634	W 1390	8703	ARTICLES DE SERRURERIE
7	MACHINES,TRANSPORT EQUIP		922988		889478		850482		925362	MACHINES MATERIEL TRANSPORT
71	POWER GENERATING EQUIPMT		67311		37375		72304		41111	MACHINES GENERATRICES
711	STEAM BOILERS & AUX PLNT	W 908	12199	W 416	1456	W 674	2141	W 337	1390	GENERATEURS VAPEUR EAU ETC
7111	STEAM BOILERS ETC	W 868	11879	W 245	945	W 427	1279	W 121	814	GENERATEURS VAPEUR EAU
713	INTRNL COMBUS PSTN ENGIN	W 1842	14031	W 1641	14317	W 1596	13897	W 1543	14911	MOTEURS EXPL COMB INT, PIECE
7139	PISTON ENGINE PARTS NES			W 539	10359	W 593	9856	W 638	11161	PIECES POUR 713.2,3,8
714	ENGINES AND MOTORS NES	W 7	368	W 37	1410	W 968	21003	W 154	2659	MOTEURS NON ELECTRIQUES
7148	GAS TURBINES NES			W 9	40	W 549	12727	W 1	45	TURBINES A GAZ
71488	OTHER GAS TURBINES NES			W 8	26	W 549	12708		16	AUTRES TURBINES A GAZ
716	ROTATING ELECTRIC PLANT	W 3124	26790	W 1610	18024	W 1979	18642	W 1218	12752	APP ELECTR ROTATIFS,PIECES
7162	AC MTRS,GENRTRS,GEN SETS			W 1411	15389	W 1583	14382	W 964	8661	MOTEURS ELECTRIQUES
71622	AC GENERATORS			W 889	11273	W 954	9692	W 347	3798	GENER COURANT ALTERNATIF
718	OTH POWER GENERATG MACHY	W 432	13571	W 77	2064	W 653	15122	W 202	2341	AUTRES MOTEURS PARTIES
7188	WIND,WATER,ETC ENGINES	W 432	13571	W 77	2063	W 649	15097	W 202	2341	MOT MACHINES MOTRICES NDA
71882	OTH HYDRAULIC ENGNS,MTRS	W 432	13571	W 9	223	W 391	6751	W 5	44	MACH MOTRICES HYDRAULQUES

4. Special Imports C.I.F. by Commodities according to the S.I.T.C. (Rev. 2) in thousand U.S. Dollars
Importations Spéciales C.A.F. par Produits d'après la C.T.C.I. (Rév. 2) en milliers de Dollars E.U.

SITC CTCI	COMMODITY	1993		1994		1995		1996		PRODUIT
		WEIGHT POIDS	VALUE VALEUR	WEIGHT POIDS	VALUE VALEUR	WEIGHT POIDS	VALUE VALEUR	WEIGHT POIDS	VALUE VALEUR	
72	MACHS FOR SPCL INDUSTRYS		147242		105069		99870		110011	MAC SPECIALES POUR INDUST
721	AGRIC MACHY,EXC TRACTORS	W 1599	9701	W 1568	10286	W 1554	9404	W 2011	13040	MACHINES AGRICOLES
722	TRACTORS NON–ROAD	W 7240	26781	W 2005	10128	W 1777	9303	W 1714	10531	TRACTEURS
723	CIVIL ENGNEERG EQUIP ETC	W 5402	26401	W 3575	17336	W 3149	17750	W 3010	20529	APPAREILS DE GENIE CIVIL
7234	CONST,MINING MACHNRY NES	W 5376	26084	W 3405	16457	W 2927	16048	W 2624	16220	MACH POUR LA CONST, MINES
72342	SLFPRP SHOVELS,EXCAVATRS			W 1965	9806	W 1788	9643	W 1624	10039	PELLES MECANIQUES
724	TEXTILE,LEATHER MACHNRY	W 5428	29356	W 962	8552	W 859	9282	W 1126	12849	MACH POUR INDUSTRIE TEXTILE
7247	TEXTILE MACHINERY NES	W 4388	18415	W 395	3087	W 310	2461	W 272	2814	MACH LAVAGE,TEINTURE TEX
726	PRINTG,BKBINDG MACHY,PTS	W 874	13807	W 660	12793	W 595	9756	W 549	7715	MACHINES POUR IMPRIMERIE
7264	PRINTING PRESSES	W 673	10649	W 378	6695	W 247	3652	W 217	2260	MACHINES A IMPRIMER
727	FOOD MACHRY NON–DOMESTIC	W 1138	10257	W 1100	9991	W 1347	12610	W 1960	12275	MACH INDUSTRIES ALIMENT
7272	OTH FOOD PROC MCHY,PARTS	W 915	8251	W 1067	9476	W 1225	11396	W 1854	11356	AUT MACH IND ALIMENTAIRE
728	OTH MACHY FOR SPCL INDUS	W 2827	25236	W 3150	31919	W 3150	27970	W 2694	27592	AUT MACH IND PARTICULIERES
7284	MACHY FOR SPCL INDUS NES	W 1099	14863	W 1002	18492	W 1191	21955	W 1205	19150	MACH SPEC IND PARTICUL.
72842	RUBBER,PLASTICS WRKG MCH			W 453	9504	W 394	6030	W 599	8450	MACH IND CAOUT MAT PLAST
72848	OTH MCHY WITH INDIV FNCT	W 1032	12937	W 352	4380	W 345	5071	W 348	4787	AUTRES MACHINES NDA
73	METALWORKING MACHINERY		11586		9453		10719		9526	MACH TRAVAIL DES METAUX
736	METALWORKING MACH–TOOLS	W 1223	9967	W 914	6810	W 945	8170	W 950	7525	MACH–OUTILS TRAVAIL METAUX
74	GENRL INDUSTRL MACHY NES		147545		122399		132092		133236	MACH APP INDUSTRIE
741	HEATING,COOLING EQUIPMNT	W 5234	34875	W 2949	24953	W 3281	29178	W 3406	26089	MACH CHAUFFAGE,PIECES
7414	NONDOM REFRIG EQUIPT,PTS	W 3701	19557	W 1464	10008	W 1257	8951	W 1940	11861	MAT PRODUCTION DU FROID
7416	HEATING,COOLING EQU NES	W 686	6984	W 606	7824	W 1001	9876	W 570	7275	APP CHANGEMENT TEMP
742	PUMPS FOR LIQUIDS ETC	W 772	11913	W 780	10618	W 1004	13399	W 901	13091	POMPES MOTO–POMPES
7428	OTHER PUMPS FOR LIQUIDS			W 663	8643	W 851	10748	W 762	9853	AUTRES POMPES POUR LIQ
74288	PUMPS FR LIQUIDS NES ETC			W 596	7496	W 812	10003	W 728	9251	POMPES POUR LIQUIDES NDA
743	PUMPS NES,CENTRFUGES ETC	W 2768	22558	W 2548	18185	W 3072	19254	W 3309	20528	POMPES COMPRES,VENT ETC
7431	PUMPS FOR GASES ETC	W 1757	14265	W 1195	6245	W 1681	8783	W 1879	8861	POMPES AIR A VIDE,COMPRES
744	MECHANICAL HANDLING EQU	W 2462	13023	W 3125	16465	W 4023	16489	W 3095	17824	EQUIP MANUTENTION PIECES
745	NONELEC MACHY,TOOLS NES	W 1586	24703	W 1309	20294	W 1269	19964	W 1219	18474	AUT MACH NON ELEC,PIECES
7452	OTH NONELEC MCHS,PTS NES	W 1431	21174	W 1172	17262	W 1126	17272	W 1099	16104	AUT MACH NON ELEC,PIECES
74522	PACKAGNG,BOTTLNG,ETC MCH	W 578	12234	W 372	7599	W 237	6567	W 246	5675	MACH NETT BOUTEILLES,ETC
749	NONELEC MACH PTS,ACC NES	W 2611	40472	W 2269	31883	W 2449	33808	W 3339	37230	PIECES MACH NON ELEC NDA
7492	COCKS,VALVES ETC NES	W 1088	18283	W 999	11888	W 1048	13186	W 1808	13845	ART ROB,SIM POUR TUYAUX
7499	OTH NONELEC MCHY PTS NES	W 629	8993	W 497	7635	W 533	8147	W 556	8746	PIECES NON ELECT NDA
75	OFFICE MACHNES,ADP EQUIP		58688		70894		78062		90165	MACH BUREAU TRAIT AUTOM
751	OFFICE MACHINES	W 335	5273	W 506	10225	W 520	9672	W 517	9414	MACH,APPAREILS DE BUREAU
752	AUTOMTIC DATA PROC EQUIP	W 832	38321	W 945	41761	W 1127	47593	W 1512	61687	MACH TRAIT INFORMATION
7522	DIGITAL COMPUTERS			W 258	16589	W 475	19872	W 606	24142	MACH DIGITALES COMPLETES
7525	ADP PERIPHERAL UNITS			W 445	11396	W 294	7397	W 383	7256	UNITES PERIPHERIQUES
759	OFFICE,ADP MCH PTS,ACCES	W 373	15095	W 500	18907	W 479	20797	W 536	19064	PIECES DU 751 ET 752
7591	OFFICE MACHINE PARTS NES	W 373	15095	W 50	1642	W 59	1751	W 53	1763	PIECES DU 7511,7518
75911	TYPEWRTR PARTS,ACCES NES	W 373	15095	W 1	52	W 3	57	W 1	31	PIECES DU 7511
7599	ACCTG,ETC,ADP MCH PTS,AC			W 450	17265	W 420	19045	W 483	17300	PIECES DU 751 ET 752
76	TELECOMM,SOUND EQUIPMENT		93623		94383		82005		91740	EQUIPMENT DE TELECOM
761	TELEVISION RECEIVERS	W 1544	14613	W 1931	19214	W 1544	15200	W 1565	13092	RECEPTEURS DE TELEVISION
7611	COLOUR TV RECEIVERS			W 1859	18698	W 1472	14757	W 1406	11769	RECEPTEURS COULEUR
762	RADIO BROADCAST RECEIVRS	W 1199	13255	W 1250	12849	W 1087	10530	W 944	9903	RECEPTEURS RADIODIFFUSION
7628	OTHER RADIO RECEIVERS			W 988	9717	W 905	8455	W 759	7069	AUTRES RECEPT RADIO
764	TELECOM EQPT,PTS,ACC NES	W 1635	58495	W 1517	54304	W 1504	50263	W 1673	64502	EQUIP TELECOM,PIECES
7641	LINE TELEPHONE,ETC EQUIP	W 872	43471	W 549	18925	W 665	26847	W 629	31689	APP TELEPHON PAR FIL
7643	TV,RADIO TRANSMITTRS ETC	W 18	159	W 117	11700	W 46	3772	W 198	6305	APP EMET TELE RADIO
7648	TELECOMM EQUIPMENT NES	W 271	9383	W 21	1717	W 22	2625	W 36	2957	APP TELECOM NDA
7649	PTS NES OF EQUIPMT OF 76	W 183	2651	W 480	18674	W 414	13497	W 467	19742	PIECES DE LA DIV 76
76491	PTS NES OF APPAR OF 7641			W 169	12668	W 210	10185	W 169	13850	PIECES POUR 764.1
77	ELECTRIC MACHNRY NES ETC		99456		170564		147062		144268	MACH APP ELECT NDA
771	ELECTRIC POWER MACHY NES			W 3320	18800	W 2367	13310	W 2135	11777	MACH PROD,TRANS ELECTR
7711	TRANSFORMERS,ELECTRICAL			W 2490	15003	W 1683	8702	W 1461	7530	TRANSFO ELECTRIQUES
77111	LIQUID DIELEC TRANSFRMRS			W 1540	9416	W 985	5196	W 736	3487	TRANSFO DIELEC LIQUIDE
772	SWITCHGEAR ETC,PARTS NES	W 1803	22709	W 1887	25709	W 2228	31809	W 1502	24699	APP COUPURE,SECT ETC
7721	SWITCHGEAR ETC	W 1594	20144	W 1882	25371	W 2219	31285	W 1480	23290	APP COUPURE,SECTIONMNT
773	ELECTR DISTRIBUTNG EQUIP	W 2637	9023	W 6924	21184	W 3213	12591	W 2935	12021	EQUIPMT DISTRIBUTION ELECT
7731	INSULATED WIRE,CABLE ETC	W 2022	7495	W 6474	20097	W 2803	11564	W 2467	10613	FILS,CABLES ISOLES ELECT
775	HOUSEHOLD TYPE EQUIP NES	W 4768	28192	W 10969	53153	W 9964	44355	W 8698	40917	MACH,APP USAGE DOMESTQUE
7751	HOUSEHOLD LDRY EQUIP NES			W 3344	13928	W 3824	12642	W 2344	10035	MACH A LAVER ET SECHOIRS
77511	DOMESTIC WASHING MACHNES			W 3235	13473	W 3736	12288	W 2238	9619	MACH LAVER LINGE MOINS 6 KG
7752	DOM REFRIGERATRS,FREEZRS			W 3155	12558	W 2176	9938	W 1820	8525	REFRIG,CONGEL MENAGER
77521	DOMESTIC REFRIGERATORS			W 2503	10966	W 1914	8554	W 1641	7732	REFRIGERATEURS
7758	ELECTRO–THERMIC APPL NES	W 3170	19238	W 2866	17509	W 2540	15085	W 2578	15551	APP ELECTROTHERMIQ NDA
77586	ELECTROTHERM DOM APP NES	W 1747	11733	W 2110	12675	W 1808	10095	W 1889	10336	APP ELECTRO THERMIQUES
776	TRANSISTORS,VALVES,ETC	W 418	9658	W 452	12955	W 357	9555	W 406	12831	LAMPES,TUBES,VALVES
778	ELECTRICAL MACHINERY NES	W 4288	29091	W 4926	32352	W 5131	31023	W 6039	37377	AUTRES MACH ELECT NDA
78	ROAD VEHICLES		273779		274152		209889		299654	VEHICULES ROUTIERS
781	PASS MOTOR VEH EXC BUSES	W 51043	221662	W 30936	131521	W 15686	82439	W 21329	185227	AUTO TRANSPORT PERSONNES
782	LORRIES,SPCL MTR VEH NES	W 491	2467	W 13257	57061	W 12049	53102	W 9502	42904	VEHICULES SPECIAUX,MARCH
7821	LORRIES,TRUCKS			W 12586	54403	W 11504	50674	W 9258	41986	VEHICULES TRANSP MARCHAND
783	ROAD MOTOR VEHICLES NES			W 8470	32463	W 6572	25292	W 7339	22873	VEHICULES ROUTIERS NDA
7831	BUSES			W 4116	20565	W 3212	16590	W 2663	14733	VOITURES TRANSPORT COMMUN
7832	TRACTORS FOR TR–TRAILERS			W 4354	11898	W 3361	8702	W 4676	8140	TRACTEURS ROUTIERS
784	MOTOR VEH PRTS,ACCES NES	W 5028	31609	W 4647	30204	W 4389	28047	W 4944	29123	PIECES 722,781,782,783
7849	OTHER MOTOR VEHCL PARTS	W 4086	28311	W 3971	26487	W 3830	25345	W 4155	25000	PIECES 722,781,782,783
785	CYCLES,ETC MOTRZD OR NOT	W 2979	13034	W 3451	17584	W 3127	16211	W 2910	15850	MOTOCYCLES SCOOTERS
79	OTHR TRANSPORT EQUIPMENT		23758		5191		18478		5650	AUTRE MATERIEL TRANSPORT
793	SHIPS AND BOATS ETC	W 7752	18167	W 1529	3492	W 2030	15953	W 946	2811	NAVIRES BATEAUX,ETC
7932	SHIPS AND BOATS NES	W 1177	2339	W 1518	3408	W 2021	15897	W 923	2675	NAVIRES ET BATEAUX
7938	TUGS,SPECIAL VESSELS ETC	W 6575	15828	W 9	65	W 9	51	W 23	133	REMORQUEURS,BATEAUX SPEC
79382	SPECL PURPOSE VESSLS ETC	W 6571	15756	W 4	29		2	W 16	79	BAT–PHARES,–POMPES,DRAGUES
8	MISC MANUFACTURED GOODS		319673		300279		315747		711016	ART MANUFACTURES DIVERS
812	*PLUMBG,HEATNG,LGHTNG EQ	W 3355	6956	W 3507	9646	W 3556	8613	W 2970	8438	APPAR SANITAIRES CHAUFFAGE
821	*FURNITURE,PARTS THEREOF	W 3806	8725	W 6540	16102	W 6489	15618	W 6940	21888	MEUBLES ET PIECES
8219	FURNITURE AND PARTS NES	W 2705	5170	W 5087	10274	W 5124	10137	W 5326	12527	AUTRES MEUBLES ET PIECES
84	CLOTHING AND ACCESSORIES		28505		38152		37411		307829	VETEMENTS
842	MENS OUTERWEAR NOT KNIT	W 736	5478	W 509	3762	W 597	3289	W 5088	52995	VET DESSUS POUR HOMMES
8423	— TROUSERS,BREECHES ETC			W 348	2606	W 462	2375	W 4444	42643	PANTALONS HOMMES MAT TEX
843	WOMENS OUTERWEAR NONKNIT	W 662	5720	W 779	6776	W 904	7028	W 5662	52330	VET DESSUS FEMMES MAT TEX
8439	— OTHER OUTER GARMENTS			W 501	4186	W 446	4059	W 5259	47507	AUT VET DES FEM MAT TEXT
844	UNDER GARMENTS NOT KNIT	W 560	4698	W 463	4601	W 530	3572	W 6640	81310	VETEMENT DESSOUS MAT TEX
8441	— MENS SHIRTS			W 299	3304	W 299	2680	W 5726	72580	CHEMISES HOMMES MAT TEXT
84411	—— OF COTTON			W 149	2061	W 144	1839	W 5051	61113	CHEMISES HOMMES DE COTON
845	OUTERWEAR KNIT NONELASTC	W 162	1804	W 721	6565	W 605	6325	W 5425	55597	VET DESSOUS,ACCES BONNET
8459	— OTHER,CLTHG ACCESRYS			W 569	5372	W 467	4916	W 4898	45666	AUT VET DESSUS DE BONNE
846	UNDER GARMENTS KNITTED	W 557	5879	W 992	10398	W 1243	11263	W 2559	57919	SOUS VETS DE BONNETERIE

Costa Rica

4. Special Imports C.I.F. by Commodities according to the S.I.T.C. (Rev. 2) in thousand U.S. Dollars
Importations Spéciales C.A.F. par Produits d'après la C.T.C.I. (Rév. 2) en milliers de Dollars E.U.

SITC CTCI	COMMODITY	1993 WEIGHT POIDS	1993 VALUE VALEUR	1994 WEIGHT POIDS	1994 VALUE VALEUR	1995 WEIGHT POIDS	1995 VALUE VALEUR	1996 WEIGHT POIDS	1996 VALUE VALEUR	PRODUIT
8462	— OF COTTON NON ELASTIC			W 641	5471	W 872	5589	W 1388	24345	SOUS–VET BONNET COTON
84629	—— OTHER			W 598	5030	W 800	5299	W 1043	20651	AUT SOUS–VET BONNET COTON
8465	CORSETS,GARTERS,ETC	W 66	1156	W 85	1903	W 113	2601	W 925	30583	CORSETS,GAINES ART SIM
84651	BRASSIERES			W 56	1724	W 88	2359	W 895	30113	SOUTIENS–GORGE,BUSTIERS
851	*FOOTWEAR	W 2274	14715	W 3181	20941	W 4399	24237	W 4462	30309	CHAUSSURES
85102	FOOTWEAR LEATHER	W 1582	11091	W 2242	16209	W 3084	17522	W 2848	22797	CHAUS SEMELLES EN CUIR
87	PRECISION INSTRUMNTS NES		40233		41359		46815		52688	INSTRUM,APPAR SCIENT NDA
872	MEDICAL INSTRUMENTS NES	W 548	14680	W 673	14209	W 857	17646	W 841	18751	INSTR,APP MEDIC–CHIR NDA
87202	OTH MEDICAL INSTRUMENTS	W 501	13861	W 587	13175	W 780	16314	W 786	17516	INSTRUM,APP MEDECINE
874	MEASURNG,CONTROLNG INSTR	W 783	19887	W 759	21469	W 1016	23977	W 844	25585	INSTRUMENTS DE MESURE
88	PHOTO EQU,OPTICL GDS ETC		27395		19770		20082		23333	APP,FOURN PHOTO,OP,MONTR
882	PHOTO,CINEMA SUPPLIES	W 795	10754	W 875	11519	W 879	12076	W 965	12695	PRODUITS PHOTO,CINEMA
89	MISC MANUFCTRD GOODS NES		191015		151062		159978		263514	ART MANUFACTURES DIVERS
892	PRINTED MATTER	W 2669	93966	W 3790	33412	W 4155	38291	W 4803	130643	IMPRIMES
8921	PRINTED BOOKS,GLOBES,ETC	W 1522	16179	W 1979	21909	W 1927	17056	W 2095	17338	LIVRES,BROCHURES,CARTES
89211	PRINTED BOOKS,PAMPHLETS	W 1484	16011	W 1862	20861	W 1797	16388	W 1995	16916	LIVRES,BROCHURES
8928	PRINTED MATTER NES	W 655	75794	W 1058	7769	W 1159	16346	W 1057	108585	IMPRIMES NDA
89283	UNISSUED BANKNOTES ETC	W 96	70940	W 95	1953	W 105	9759	W 86	102651	TIMBRES–POSTE FISCAUX
893	ARTICLES OF PLASTIC NES	W 8524	33566		48008		51942		56505	OUVRAGES EN MAT DIVIS 58
8931	PLSTC PACKG CONTNRS,LIDS	W 4432	14861	W 5679	17744	W 5603	18728	W 6274	19654	ART TRANSP EMBALLAGE ETC
8939	MISC PLASTIC ARTICLES	W 2957	14302	W 7303	29096	W 8662	31873	W 10699	35317	ART DIVERS EN MAT DIV 58
89399	OTHR PLASTC ARTICLES NES	W 2042	10896	W 6304	27608	W 7677	30187	W 9769	33709	AUT OUV MAT DIV 58
894	TOYS,SPORTING GOODS,ETC	W 5106	26673	W 5883	29617	W 5934	28542	W 5894	26554	VOITURES ENFANTS,JOUETS
8942	TOYS,INDOOR GAMES ETC	W 4095	22357	W 4610	24387	W 4726	23559	W 4348	20776	JOUETS,JEUX ETC
89423	TOYS NES	W 2804	14806	W 2788	14995	W 2957	15226	W 2493	12530	JOUETS,MODELES REDUITS
898	MUSICAL INSTRUMENTS,PTS	W 748	14981	W 760	14788	W 878	16848	W 941	22623	INSTRUMENTS DE MUSIQUE
8983	SOUND RECRDNG TAPE,DISCS	W 543	12433	W 585	12404	W 675	14641	W 762	20403	SUPPORTS SON POUR 763
89832	RECORDED DISCS,TAPES ETC	W 268	11020	W 241	8252	W 316	11433	W 376	16934	DISQUES,PHONO,BANDES
899	OTHER MANUFACTURED GOODS		8263		12967		11774		12419	AUT ART MANUF DIVERS NDA
9	GOODS NOT CLASSD BY KIND		19083		25188		23427		18682	ART TRANSACT NON CLASSES
971	*GOLD,NON MONETARY NES	K 33736	11827	K 121622	19031	K 16246	20474	K 1277	14852	OR NON MONETAIRE
97101	NONMON GLD UNWRT,SEMIMFD	K 33736	11827	K 121130	19027	K 16212	20284	K 1266	14851	OR,ALLIAGES D'OR BRUTS

5. Special Exports F.O.B. by Commodities according to the S.I.T.C. (Rev. 2) in thousand U.S. Dollars
Exportations Spéciales F.O.B. par Produits d'après la C.T.C.I. (Rév. 2) en milliers de Dollars E.U.

SITC CTCI	COMMODITY	1993 WEIGHT POIDS	1993 VALUE VALEUR	1994 WEIGHT POIDS	1994 VALUE VALEUR	1995 WEIGHT POIDS	1995 VALUE VALEUR	1996 WEIGHT POIDS	1996 VALUE VALEUR	PRODUIT
	ALL COMMODITIES		1941721		2220441		2701759		2881593	TOUS PRODUITS
0	FOOD AND LIVE ANIMALS		1255640		1326611		1673311		1776659	ALIMENTS,ANIMAUX VIVANTS
01	MEAT AND PREPARATIONS		68201		55735		49150		46281	VIANDES ET PREPARATIONS
011	MEAT FRESH,CHILLD,FROZEN	W 26975	65350	W 23980	53055	W 23582	46623	W 22457	44292	VIANDES FRAICHES,REF,CONGE
0111	BOVINE MEAT FRESH,FROZEN	W 25745	63745	W 22604	51186	W 21242	43775	W 20916	42426	VIANDES BOVIN FRAI,REF
01112	BOVINE MEAT BONELESS			W 22470	50963	W 21158	43633	W 20777	42157	VIANDES BOVIN DESOSSEES
02	DAIRY PRODCTS,BIRDS'EGGS		13082		7318		8958		17193	PRODUITS LAITIERS,OEUFS
022	MILK AND CREAM	W 9165	12042	W 8286	6494	W 11400	7758	W 14448	15562	LAIT ET CREME
0224	MILK,CREAM PRESERVED ETC	W 3493	9009	W 1442	2867	W 1133	2611	W 4886	10250	LAIT,CREME CONS,CONC
03	FISH AND PREPARATIONS		134907		104795		125890		215724	POISSONS ET PREPARATIONS
034	FISH,FRESH,CHILLED,FROZN	W 6748	41180	W 7288	35487	W 18979	35109	W 17518	59934	POISSON FRAIS, REFRIG,CONG
0341	FISH FRSH,CHLLD,EX FILLT	W 6748	41180	W 4441	20793	W 15424	20816	W 6230	29321	POISSON FRAIS,REFRIGERE
0342	FISH FROZEN,EXCL FILLETS			W 136	739	W 794	1117	W 7954	14447	POISSONS CONGELES
0343	FISH FILLETS,FRESH,CHLLD			W 2534	12758	W 2538	11821	W 2963	14023	FILETS FRAIS,REFRIGERES
035	FISH SALTED,DRIED,SMOKED	W 232	16395	W 117	12430	W 151	23977	W 243	46534	POISSON SECHE,SALE,FUME
03503	FISH(EX COD)DRIED,SALTED	W 232	16395	W 114	12362	W 150	23810	W 242	46476	POISSONS SECHES,SALES
036	SHELL FISH FRESH,FROZEN	W 3219	48568	W 3765	30967	W 3824	32955	W 7064	63612	CRUSTACES,MOLLUSQUES
037	FISH ETC PREPD,PRSVD NES	W 10563	28765	W 9871	25911	W 13073	33849	W 16931	45644	POIS,CRUST,MOL PREPARES
0371	FISH PREPARD,PRESRVD NES	W 10563	28765	W 9871	25911	W 13073	33849	W 16930	45639	CONSERVES DE POISSONS
04	CEREALS AND PREPARATIONS		12706		13889		21560		27140	CEREALES ET PRODUITS
048	CEREAL ETC PREPARATIONS	W 8791	11434	W 9383	12489	W 13891	17962	W 15781	19721	PREPTNS A BASE CEREALES
0484	BAKERY PRODUCTS	W 7090	9623	W 7455	10124	W 11457	15191	W 11971	15500	PRODUITS DE BOULANGERIE
04842	PASTRY, CAKES ETC	W 7081	9606	W 7141	9530	W 10975	14275	W 11366	14999	PATISSERIE ETC.
05	VEGETABLES AND FRUIT		750394		757890		942837		946772	LEGUMES ET FRUITS
054	VEG ETC FRSH,SMPLY PRSVD	W 95133	46300	W 88871	52310	W 133938	67168	W 112843	72633	LEGUMES FRAIS,CONG,SECS
0545	OTHER FRESH VEGETABLES	W 30016	11860	W 26656	13658	W 28679	17505	W 26647	18353	AUTRES LEGUMES FRAIS,REF
05459	FRESH VEGETABLES NES	W 30016	11860	W 23249	12425	W 26718	14599	W 25228	14543	LEGUMES FRAIS,REFRI NDA
0548	EDIBLE VEG NES FRESH,DRY	W 57821	29881	W 60286	38126	W 72901	46240	W 83506	52194	RACINES,TUBERCULES
05481	ROOTS,TUBERS FRESH,DRY	W 57783	29823	W 60264	38097	W 72832	46141	W 83468	52143	RACINES DE MANIOC ETC
056	VEGTBLES ETC PRSVD,PREPD	W 6365	13318	W 2703	5516	W 746	1166	W 1229	2839	CONSERVES DE LEGUMES
0565	VEGTBLES PRSVD,PREPD NES	W 6166	13198	W 2398	5232	W 408	852	W 836	2535	LEGUMES PREPARES CONSERVE
05651	VEGTBLS,FRUIT IN VINEGAR	W 5996	12976	W 2325	5159	W 357	797	W 781	2473	LEGUM CONSERV AU VINAIGRE
057	FRUIT,NUTS,FRESH,DRIED	W 2073558	656425	W 2172690	650340	W 2322018	800836	W 2428661	778012	FRUITS FRAIS OU SECS
0573	BANANA,PLANTAIN,FRSH,DRY			W 1891050	543388	W 2038411	686617	W 2125368	644351	BANANES FRAICHES,SECHEES
0579	FRUIT FRESH OR DRIED NES	W 2072558	653909	W 278493	103165	W 280732	109951	W 297091	126444	FRUITS FRAIS,SECS NDA
05795	PINEAPPLES,FRESH,DRIED			W 160526	56533	W 177604	58621	W 179451	68933	ANANAS FRAIS OU SECS
05797	OTH TROP FRUIT,FRESH,DRY	W 1991940	621068	W 2072	2383	W 2500	3497	W 3713	5114	AVOCATS,MANGUES,GOYAVES
05798	OTHER FRESH FRUIT	W 80282	31873	W 115563	43150	W 100331	46910	W 113511	51205	AUTRES FRUITS FRAIS
058	FRUIT PRESERVED,PREPARED	W 42553	34351	W 57053	49723	W 76468	73668	W 89137	93287	CONSERVES DE FRUITS
0583	FRUIT JAMS,JELLIES ETC	W 26644	18081	W 34929	22233	W 45259	28102	W 56665	35416	PATES DE FRUITS CONFITURES
0585	FRUIT OR VEGETABLE JUICE	W 11343	10782	W 13169	14584	W 18232	22533	W 16927	26574	JUS DE FRUITS
05851	ORANGE JUICE			W 4643	6432	W 10005	12872	W 8642	13320	JUS D'ORANGE
05854	PINEAPPLE JUICE			W 6234	6271	W 6158	7671	W 6186	11391	JUS D'ANANAS
05857	JUICE OF OTHER FRUIT,VEG	W 11343	10782	W 627	734	W 625	749	W 696	813	JUS AUTRES FRUITS,LEGUMES
0589	FRUIT PREPRD,PRESRVD,NES	W 1117	1750	W 5189	8823	W 9202	18167	W 11460	25440	FRUITS PREPARES CONSERV
05899	FRUIT,NUTS NES,PRESERVED	W 1117	1750	W 4047	6727	W 8066	15922	W 10408	23123	FRUITS PREP CONSERV NDA
06	SUGAR AND PREPS,HONEY		34048		36293		53630		57816	SUCRES ET PRODUITS
061	SUGAR AND HONEY	W 96279	27918	W 96290	28840	W 146046	46176	W 148741	48016	SUCRES ET MIEL
0611	RAW BEET AND CANE SUGAR	W 96263	27884	W 90010	28312	W 145823	46054	W 113054	44404	SUCRES BRUTS
062	SUGAR CANDY NON–CHOCLATE	W 3461	6130	W 4302	7453	W 3651	7454	W 4302	9800	SUCRERIES
07	COFFEE,TEA,COCOA,SPICES		220480		327038		443259		426532	CAFE,THE,CACAO,EPICES
071	COFFEE AND SUBSTITUTES	W 145350	203971	W 132540	308506	W 128728	418608	W 158178	385672	CAFE ET SUCCEDANES
0711	COFFEE GREEN,ROASTED,SUB	W 145350	203971	W 132539	308504	W 128728	418608	W 158178	385672	CAFE TORREFIE OU DECAFEINE
07111	COFFEE GREEN,HUSKS,SKINS			W 132417	307602	W 128495	417434	W 157816	384099	CAFE NON TORREFIE
072	COCOA	W 2548	4133	W 2403	5327	W 4286	8687	W 3530	7759	CACAO
075	SPICES	W 4621	5871	W 4297	10045	W 6197	12927	W 13287	29153	EPICES
0752	SPICES,EX PEPPER,PIMENTO	W 2973	4344	W 2617	8526	W 4456	10983	W 11371	26988	AUTRES EPICES
07526	GINGER (EXCPT SWEETENED)			W 2366	3221	W 4217	5471	W 10794	18482	GINGEMBRE
09	MISC EDIBLE PRODUCTS		18285		19565		24894		34659	PREP ALIMENTAIRES DIVERSES
098	EDIBLE PRODCTS,PREPS NES	W 6684	16809	W 6000	19497	W 7473	24757	W 9832	34269	PREP ALIMENTAIRES NDA
09809	MISC FOOD PREPRTIONS NES	W 2274	11640	W 1423	14266	W 2018	18115	W 2500	25277	PREP ALIMENTAIRES NDA
1	BEVERAGES AND TOBACCO		7898		4249		1583		3066	BOISSONS ET TABACS
2	CRUDE MATERLS,EXCL FUELS		100928		125864		146369		201228	MAT BRUTES NON COMESTIBLES
21	HIDES,SKINS,FURS UNDRSSD		8131		32		313		377	CUIRS,PEAUX BRUTS
211	HIDES,SKINS,EXC FURS,RAW	W 3891	8131	W 14	32	W 196	313	W 532	377	CUIRS ET PEAUX
2111	BOVINE,EQUINE HIDES,RAW	W 1127	7855	W 11	23	W 125	130	W 299	189	PEAUX DE BOVINS
28	METALLIFEROUS ORES,SCRAP		3005		7218		7022		8158	MINERAIS METAL,DECHETS
29	CRUDE ANIMAL,VEG MAT NES		87606		112595		129917		183871	MATIERES BRUTES ANIM,VEGET
291	CRUDE ANIMAL MTRIALS NES	W 1183	3001	W 1500	7484	W 1631	7359	W 3699	33915	MATIERES BRUTES ANIMALES
2919	OTH ANIMAL MATERIALS NES	W 1162	2795	W 1446	6945	W 1525	6836	W 3661	33408	MAT ORIGINE ANIMALE NDA
29198	AMBERGRIS,CIVET,MUSK,ETC	W 813	503	W 812	1286	W 1066	958	W 1429	17841	AMBRE GRIS,CIVETTE,MUSC
292	CRUDE VEG MATERIALS NES	W 48815	84606		105111	W 68964	122559	W 76754	149956	MAT BRUTES VEGETALES NDA
2924	VEG USED IN PHARMACY ETC	W 124	4948	W 253	2312	W 1739	4035	W 3084	10211	PLANTES MEDICINALES
2925	SEEDS,ETC FOR PLANTING	W 483	7216	W 533	5937	W 248	6228	W 502	5867	SEMENCES NDA
2926	LIVE PLANTS,BULBS,ETC	W 28110	30490	W 35035	36041	W 36702	40926	W 40676	47904	BULBES,TUBERCULES
29269	LIVE PLANTS NES	W 28076	30481	W 34961	35953	W 36610	40784	W 40593	47753	AUTRES PLANTES VIVANTES
2927	CUT FLOWERS AND FOLIAGE	W 20076	41900	W 25764	60763	W 30202	71232	W 32416	85745	FLEURS,FEUILLAGES COUPES
29271	CUT FLOWERS	W 5051	11778	W 7432	20995	W 7617	22320	W 8676	24526	FLEURS ET BOUTONS
29272	CUT FOLIAGE	W 15024	30122	W 18332	39768	W 22585	48912	W 23740	61219	FEUILLAGES,RAMEAUX ETC
3	MINERAL FUELS ETC		7644		12894		20970		24161	COMBUSTIBLES MINERAUX LUB
33	PETROLEUM AND PRODUCTS		7637		12893		20970		24161	PETROLE ET DERIVES
334	PETROLEUM PRODUCTS,REFIN	W 33492	7620	W 100130	12875	W 163086	20940	W 160722	24091	PRODUITS RAFFINES
3344	FUEL OILS,NES	W 3744	393	W 81311	7563	W 145482	15611	W 143494	18195	FUEL OILS
4	ANIMAL,VEGETABLE OIL,FAT		17682		24292		33955		37987	HUILES,GRAISSES ANIM,VEG
42	FIXED VEGETABLE OIL,FAT		17511		21752		29059		34943	HUILES VEGETALES FIXES
424	FIXED VEG OIL NONSOFT	W 37259	15097	W 34704	16657	W 40579	22969	W 55943	31087	AUTRES HUILES VEG FIXES
4242	PALM OIL	W 20	6	W 34703	16654	W 40579	22968	W 55942	31085	HUILE DE PALME
4249	FIXED VEGETABLE OILS NES	W 37220	15075						1	HUILES VEGET FIXES NDA
5	CHEMCLS,RELATED PROD NES		118771		130136		164495		179350	PRODUITS CHIMIQUES
51	ORGANIC CHEMICALS		14030		11927		19392		20147	PROD CHIMIQ ORGANIQUES
512	ALCOHOLS,PHENOLS ETC	W 37420	13825	W 77521	11553	W 77308	18697	W 98859	19008	PHENOLS,PHENOLS–ALCOOLS
5121	ACYCLIC ALCOHOLS,DERIVS	W 37420	13825	W 77520	11551	W 77308	18696	W 98840	18980	ALCOOLS ACYCLIQUES
51216	ETHYL ALC,DENATRD SPIRIT	W 37407	13810	W 77489	11533	W 77194	18457	W 98579	18675	ALCOOL ETHYLIQUE NON DENAT
53	DYES,TANNING,COLOUR PROD		6616		7940		11893		14582	PROD TEINTURE,COLORANTS
541	*MEDICINAL,PHARM PRODUCT	K 2690683	46024	K 2904204	48761	K 2990975	54402	K 2683278	51752	PROD MEDICINAUX PHARMACEUT
5417	MEDICAMENTS	K 2586956	44868	K 2724717	47831	K 2945305	52434	K 2644872	50443	MEDICAMENTS
54171	— CONTAINNG ANTIBIOTICS			K 1493255	16114	K 1382289	19507	K 247655	6946	MED CONTN ANTIBIOTIQUES
54179	— CONTNG OTH SUBSTANCES			K 1167171	30381	K 1500791	31989	K 2241739	42290	MED CONT AUT SUBSTANCES
55	PERFUME,CLEANING ETC PRD		10868		13809		18066		21774	PROD POUR PARFUM,TOILETTE
554	SOAP,CLEANSING ETC PREPS	W 4142	4865	W 9216	7317	W 8144	9308	W 8378	15421	SAVONS,PRODUITS DETERSIFS
562	*FERTILIZERS,MANUFACTURE	W 83001	15121	W 139784	15699	W 94542	22057	W 110278	30673	ENGRAIS MANUFACTURES

5. Special Exports F.O.B. by Commodities according to the S.I.T.C. (Rev. 2) in thousand U.S. Dollars
Exportations Spéciales F.O.B. par Produits d'après la C.T.C.I. (Rév. 2) en milliers de Dollars E.U.

SITC CTCI	COMMODITY	1993 WEIGHT POIDS	1993 VALUE VALEUR	1994 WEIGHT POIDS	1994 VALUE VALEUR	1995 WEIGHT POIDS	1995 VALUE VALEUR	1996 WEIGHT POIDS	1996 VALUE VALEUR	PRODUIT
5621	CHEM NITROGENOUS FERTLZR	W 82646	14942	W 138338	15060	W 91122	20822	W 97023	27287	ENGRAIS AZOTES
56211	AMMONIUM NITRATE	W 1253	258	W 927	184	W 939	204	W 51479	11751	NITRATE D'AMMONIUM
56212	AMMONIUM SULPHONITRATE			W 135313	14401	W 87093	19805	W 41987	14567	SULFONITRATE D'AMMONIUM
56219	CHEM NITROG FERTILZR NES	W 81393	14684	W 1156	255	W 1586	397	W 173	78	ENGRAIS AZOTES NDA
58	PLASTIC MATERIALS ETC		15062		18048		18524		18234	MAT PLAST ARTIFICIELLES
583	POLYMERIZATION ETC PRODS	W 6572	10681	W 8372	13737	W 7054	14248	W 7672	13989	PROD POLYMERISATION
59	CHEMICAL MATERIALS NES		9530		12529		18091		19773	MAT PROD CHIMIQUES NDA
591	PESTICIDES,DISINFECTANTS	W 3359	7042	W 4056	9357	W 4507	14309	W 3465	13908	DESINF,INSECT,FONG,HERB
6	BASIC MANUFACTURES		191537		226672		267751		283589	ART MANUFACTURES
61	LEATHER,DRESSED FUR,ETC		8271		22440		22309		26594	CUIRS,PELLETERIES
611	LEATHER	W 497	5242	W 14502	18683	W 3269	18240	W 4396	21068	CUIRS,PEAUX PREPARES
6114	LEATHR BOVINE NES,EQUINE			W 12030	9822	W 1713	9236	W 1858	7754	CUIRS DE BOVINS
6118	LEATHER SPECIALLY FINSHD	W 492	5237	W 1525	8082	W 1125	8528	W 1168	11305	CUIRS,PEAUX TANNES
61183	LEATHER PATENT,METALIZED	W 486	5178	W 1510	8042	W 1087	8449	W 1113	11065	CUIRS,PEAUX VERNIS
62	RUBBER MANUFACTURES NES		43813		45939		45582		52951	CAOUTCHOUC MANUFACTURE
625	RUBBER TYRES, TUBES ETC	W 5032	14475	W 6133	17185	W 5691	18070	W 6996	22432	PNEUS CAOUTCHOUC VULCANISE
6251	TYRES NEW FOR MOTOR CARS	W 4392	13175	W 2513	7625	W 2279	7443	W 2962	9590	PNEUS POUR VOITURES
6252	TYRES,NEW,BUS OR LORRY			W 2663	7607	W 2601	8504	W 3281	10834	PNEUS POUR AUTOBUS,CAMIONS
628	RUBBER ARTICLES NES	W 6725	28477	W 7376	27820	W 7698	26568	W 8307	29440	OUVRAGES CAOUTCHOUC NDA
6289	OTH RUBBER ARTICLES NES	W 6724	28456	W 7375	27810	W 7694	26529	W 8305	29426	AUT OUVR CAOUTCHOUC NDA
62898	UNHARD RUBBER PRODS NES	W 6723	28444	W 7374	27807	W 7682	26514	W 8297	29415	OUV CAOUT VULC NON DURCI
63	WOOD,CORK MANUFACTRS NES		21810		30868		34805		38172	OUVRAGES LIEGE ET BOIS
634	VENEERS,PLYWOOD,ETC	W 17615	8528	W 17554	8677	W 20218	9873	W 18904	9088	PLACAGES,CONTRE–PLAQUES
635	WOOD MANUFACTURES NES	W 3541	13282	W 6387	22191	W 9373	24932	W 10431	29085	ART MANUF EN BOIS NDA
6353	BUILDERS WOODWRK,PREFABS	W 1531	6643	W 2060	9459	W 2885	8300	W 1371	7706	OUVRAGES DE MENUISERIE
6354	WOOD MFRS DOMESTIC ETC	W 154	3053	W 117	5766	W 109	6459	W 429	8867	ART MANUF USAGE DOMESTIQUE
63549	WOOD MFRS,DOMESTIC NES	W 139	3007	W 113	5743	W 105	6438	W 425	8825	OUVRAGES DE TABLETTERIE
6359	OTHER WOOD MANUFACTURES	W 1799	3534	W 1037	5759	W 1178	8568	W 996	9303	OUVRAGES EN BOIS NDA
63599	OTHER WOOD ARTICLES NES	W 1728	3327	W 968	5517	W 1131	8332	W 979	9252	AUTRES OUVRAGES EN BOIS NDA
64	PAPER,PAPERBOARD AND MFR		26609		27883		44221		42993	PAPIERS,CARTONS & OUVRAGES
642	PAPER,ETC,PRECUT,ARTS OF	W 13213	23837	W 16977	25515	W 24801	38811	W 23913	37723	PAP,CARTONS DECOUPES
6421	PAPER ETC CONTAINERS	W 3972	4119	W 7080	5606	W 13791	16044	W 12622	13632	BOITES,SACS EMBALLAGES
6424	PAPER ETC CT TO SIZE NES	W 4314	6567	W 4553	7201	W 4725	7492	W 4550	7995	PAP,CARTONS DECOUPES
6428	PAPER ETC ARTICLES NES	W 4384	12044	W 4738	11458	W 5641	13476	W 5656	13433	OUVRAGES EN PATE A PAPIER
64285	PAPER ETC DIAPERS ETC		1	W 2918	8242	W 3420	9486	W 3931	10275	SERVIETTES HYGIENIQUES
64289	OTHER ARTICLES OF PAPER	W 4363	12005	W 61	391	W 171	221	W 125	234	ARTICLES,OUVRAGES EN PAPIER
65	TEXTILE YARN,FABRICS,ETC		25409		27178		28276		29493	FILS,TISSUS,ARTICLES TEXTILE
651	TEXTILE YARN	W 5267	12929	W 4942	12782	W 5165	14424	W 5116	13060	FILS TEXTILES
6514	SYN FIB YRN,BULK,MONOFIL	W 4797	12172	W 4609	11571	W 4797	12738	W 4986	12551	FILS CONT 85% FIB TEXT SYNTH
65142	— NONTXT ETC CONT PAMID	W 1	9	W 4255	10407	W 4531	12009	W 4795	12201	FILS NON TEX FI CON POLYAMID
65145	— NONTXT ETC CONT PESTR	W 4715	11950							FILS NON TEX CONT POLYESTER
653	WOVN MAN–MADE FIB FABRIC	W 926	6790	W 1036	7814	W 801	6525	W 744	6872	TISSUS FIBRES SYNTH,ARTIF
6534	DISC SYN BLEND FABRC NES	W 672	4909	W 822	6740	W 672	6147	W 728	6806	TISSUS FIBRES SYNTH DISCONT
65341	DISC SYN FIB–COTTN FABRC			W 822	6740	W 672	6147	W 717	6706	TISSUS FIB SYNT DIS MEL COTO
66	NONMETAL MINERAL MFS NES		17067		17702		24239		25177	ART MIN NON METALLIQUES
665	GLASSWARE	W 27204	14071	W 26397	13905	W 36137	18882	W 37545	19527	OUVRAGES EN VERRE
6651	BOTTLES ETC OF GLASS	W 26164	13387	W 25720	13144	W 36093	18766	W 37369	19417	RECIPIENTS EN VERRE
66511	GLASS BOTTLES ETC NONVAC	W 26164	13387	W 25720	13144	W 36093	18766	W 37369	19417	BONBONNES,BOUTEILLES,ETC
67	IRON AND STEEL		13551		17114		18785		15803	FER ET ACIER
674	IRN,STL UNIV,PLATE,SHEET	W 7181	6258	W 9474	7591	W 9976	9045	W 11050	9827	LARGES PLATS,TOLES
6749	OTH IRN,STL PLATES,SHEET	W 1358	1648	W 9470	7583	W 9962	9002	W 10977	9702	AUTRES TOLES FER,ACIER
67491	— OF IRON OR SIMPLE STL	W 1358	1648	W 9470	7583	W 9962	9001	W 10967	9687	AUT TOLES AUTRES ACIER FIN
678	IRON,STL TUBES,PIPES,ETC	W 8739	6099	W 11833	7425	W 9375	6487	W 5838	4220	TUBES,TUYAUX EN FONTE,FER
6783	IRON,STL TUBES,PIPES NES	W 8551	5819	W 11651	7203	W 9216	6188	W 5693	3907	AUT TUBES,TUYAUX FER,ACIER
68	NON–FERROUS METALS		16104		13498		20782		24115	METAUX NON FERREUX
684	ALUMINIUM	W 7248	14895	W 5855	13408	W 7286	20580	W 9010	23719	ALUMINIUM
6842	ALUMINIUM,ALLOYS WORKED	W 6116	14094	W 5855	13408	W 7245	20552	W 9010	23719	ALUMINIUM,ALLIAGES OUVRE
68423	ALUMINIUM FOIL	W 5523	12413	W 4847	10592	W 5192	14945	W 7027	18691	FEUILLES,BANDES MINCES AL
69	METAL MANUFACTURES NES		18904		24050		28753		28290	ART MANUFACT EN METAL NDA
692	METAL TANKS,BOXES,ETC	W 2971	9994	W 3068	11045	W 4338	15741	W 3295	13518	RECIPIENTS METALLIQUES
6924	MTL TRANSPORT BOXES ETC	W 2907	9780	W 3005	10792	W 4329	15687	W 3271	13496	FUTS,TAMBOURS,BIDONS
69242	ALUMNM TRNSPRT BOXES ETC	W 390	4050	W 687	5633	W 1084	8333	W 839	7023	FUTS,TAMBOURS,BIDONS ALU
7	MACHINES,TRANSPORT EQUIP		55960		72394		85861		115609	MACHINES MATERIEL TRANSPORT
72	MACHS FOR SPCL INDUSTRYS		2047		4328		5736		13849	MAC SPECIALES POUR INDUST
74	GENRL INDUSTRL MACHY NES		10720		4300		5737		9605	MACH APP INDUSTRIE
741	HEATING,COOLING EQUIPMNT	W 1749	6679	W 214	759	W 156	744	W 263	825	MACH CHAUFFAGE,PIECES
77	ELECTRIC MACHNRY NES ETC		38821		59119		66597		73440	MACH APP ELECT NDA
772	SWITCHGEAR ETC,PARTS NES	W 1603	18896	W 1701	21866	W 1834	25547	W 1837	22309	APP COUPURE,SECT ETC
7721	SWITCHGEAR ETC	W 1453	18350	W 1699	21823	W 1793	24036	W 1837	22302	APP COUPURE,SECTIONMNT
773	ELECTR DISTRIBUTNG EQUIP	W 2016	6210	W 3118	9597	W 3567	12546	W 5814	18913	EQUIPMT DISTRIBUTION ELECT
7731	INSULATED WIRE,CABLE ETC	W 2015	6199	W 3116	9595	W 3567	12542	W 5810	18855	FILS,CABLES ISOLES ELECT
775	HOUSEHOLD TYPE EQUIP NES	W 137	540	W 2005	7488	W 2394	9040	W 2626	10726	MACH,APP USAGE DOMESTQUE
7752	DOM REFRIGERATRS,FREEZRS			W 1927	7178	W 2270	8519	W 2265	9673	REFRIG,CONGEL MENAGER
77521	DOMESTIC REFRIGERATORS			W 1926	7172	W 2268	8508	W 2263	9662	REFRIGERATEURS
778	ELECTRICAL MACHINERY NES	W 3799	12015	W 4698	20001	W 5519	16045	W 5655	17005	AUTRES MACH ELECT NDA
7781	BATTERIES,ACCUMULATORS	W 3487	6584	W 4303	7330	W 5197	7692	W 5263	8444	PILES ET ACCUMULATEURS
77811	PRIMARY BATTERIES,CELLS	W 3403	6522	W 3779	7237	W 3948	7554	W 4124	8305	PILES ELECTRIQUES,PIECES
7783	AUTOMOTIVE ELECTR EQUIP	W 39	3929	W 141	9381	W 110	6989	W 210	7675	EQUIP ELECT MOTEURS EXPL
77831	IGNITION,STARTING EQUIP	W 39	3929	W 137	9336	W 109	6982	W 203	7661	APP ELEC ALLUM,DEMARRAGE
8	MISC MANUFACTURED GOODS		171809		179887		179620		150318	ART MANUFACTURES DIVERS
812	*PLUMBG,HEATNG,LGHTNG EQ	W 3341	5485	W 3987	7706	W 4136	9643	W 4578	11543	APPAR SANITAIRES CHAUFFAGE
821	*FURNITURE,PARTS THEREOF	W 2925	11352	W 2693	9829	W 3039	11567	W 2775	12268	MEUBLES ET PIECES
8219	FURNITURE AND PARTS NES	W 2485	10374	W 2417	9128	W 2603	10336	W 2412	11199	AUTRES MEUBLES ET PIECES
82199	OTHR FURN,FURN PARTS NES			W 1835	7547	W 2005	7990	W 1736	8189	MEUBLES NDA AUTRES MATIERES
84	CLOTHING AND ACCESSORIES		75237		70620		50325		31853	VETEMENTS
842	MENS OUTERWEAR NOT KNIT	W 1667	19787	W 1045	11960	W 971	11447	W 826	11159	VET DESSUS POUR HOMMES
8423	— TROUSERS,BREECHES ETC			W 646	7285	W 816	9489	W 717	9754	PANTALONS HOMMES MAT TEX
843	WOMENS OUTERWEAR NONKNIT	W 3322	42704	W 2350	27070	W 1026	12459	W 541	7205	VET DESSUS FEMMES MAT TEX
8439	— OTHER OUTER GARMENTS			W 2330	26841	W 962	11719	W 452	5996	AUT VET DES FEM MAT TEXT
844	UNDER GARMENTS NOT KNIT	W 579	7564	W 304	4367	W 646	9912	W 220	3966	VETEMENT DESSOUS MAT TEX
8441	— MENS SHIRTS			W 286	3912	W 635	9775	W 211	3835	CHEMISES HOMMES MAT TEXT
8442	— MENS,OTHR THAN SHIRTS	W 516	6373	W 16	398	W 11	138	W 9	127	SOUS–VET HOMMES MAT TEXT
845	OUTERWEAR KNIT NONELASTC	W 150	1992	W 840	14064	W 404	4966	W 94	1887	VET DESSOUS,ACCES BONNET
8459	— OTHER,CLTHG ACCESRYS			W 616	11744	W 248	4079	W 63	1395	AUT VET DESSUS DE BONNE
846	UNDER GARMENTS KNITTED	W 66	1799	W 747	10677	W 508	8259	W 316	4788	SOUS VETS DE BONNETERIE
8462	— OF COTTON NON ELASTIC			W 741	10607	W 488	7918	W 304	4534	SOUS–VET BONNET COTON
84629	—— OTHER			W 545	8005	W 486	7839	W 300	4434	AUT SOUS–VET BONNET COTON
851	*FOOTWEAR	W 682	5628	W 690	7934	W 673	8173	W 659	8879	CHAUSSURES
85102	FOOTWEAR LEATHER	W 314	4364	W 456	6940	W 522	7325	W 577	8605	CHAUS SEMELLES EN CUIR
88	PHOTO EQU,OPTICL GDS ETC		10048		1852		3131		2711	APP,FOURN PHOTO,OP,MONTR
885	WATCHES AND CLOCKS		9980		1680		2974		2385	HORLOGERIE

Costa Rica

5. Special Exports F.O.B. by Commodities according to the S.I.T.C. (Rev. 2) in thousand U.S. Dollars
Exportations Spéciales F.O.B. par Produits d'après la C.T.C.I. (Rév. 2) en milliers de Dollars E.U.

SITC CTCI	COMMODITY	1993		1994		1995		1996		PRODUIT
		WEIGHT POIDS	VALUE VALEUR	WEIGHT POIDS	VALUE VALEUR	WEIGHT POIDS	VALUE VALEUR	WEIGHT POIDS	VALUE VALEUR	
8851	WATCHES,MOVEMENTS,CASES		9979		1679		2974		2355	MONTRES,MOUVEMENTS,BOITES
88511	WATCHES		9979		307					MONTRES POCHE,BRACELET
89	MISC MANUFCTRD GOODS NES		59086		80224		95762		81597	ART MANUFACTURES DIVERS
892	PRINTED MATTER	W 2969	7243	W 4132	6599	W 2920	12996		9257	IMPRIMES
8921	PRINTED BOOKS,GLOBES,ETC	W 2758	5859	W 2775	5251	W 2463	7407	W 2566	6810	LIVRES,BROCHURES,CARTES
893	ARTICLES OF PLASTIC NES	W 11212	24431		27876		33082		34018	OUVRAGES EN MAT DIVIS 58
8931	PLSTC PACKG CONTNRS,LIDS	W 5925	13138	W 5771	12955	W 6553	17045	W 6961	16669	ART TRANSP EMBALLAGE ETC
8939	MISC PLASTIC ARTICLES	W 4792	10166	W 6245	14713	W 6299	15811	W 7278	17222	ART DIVERS EN MAT DIV 58
89391	PVC FLOORING TILES ETC	W 2737	5947	W 1	3	W 1	6			CHLORURE POLYVINYL PLAQ
89399	OTHR PLASTC ARTICLES NES	W 2054	4207	W 6242	14697	W 6296	15790	W 7278	17207	AUT OUV MAT DIV 58
897	GOLD,SILVER WARE,JEWELRY		18700		39707		42196		25380	BIJOUTERIE,ORFEVRERIE
8973	PREC JEWLRY,GLD--SILVWARE		17795		39018		42064		24741	BIJOUX OR,ARGENT ORFEVRE
89731	PRECIOUS METAL JEWELLERY		17795		39011		42064		24740	ART BIJOUTERIE,JOAILLER
898	MUSICAL INSTRUMENTS,PTS	W 41	5877	W 53	2006	W 57	1665	W 46	1685	INSTRUMENTS DE MUSIQUE
8983	SOUND RECRDNG TAPE,DISCS	W 40	5860	W 38	1931	W 37	1407	W 37	1542	SUPPORTS SON POUR 763
89832	RECORDED DISCS,TAPES ETC	W 40	5860	W 35	1605	W 36	1351	W 36	1437	DISQUES,PHONO,BANDES
9	GOODS NOT CLASSD BY KIND		13853		117442		127842		109625	ART TRANSACT NON CLASSES
931	*SPECIAL TRANSACTIONS	W 4288	13750	W 36558	117193	W 43669	127495	W 44527	109256	TRANS.SPECIALES

1. HISTORICAL SERIES, 1992–1996 GENERAL TRADE, IMPORTS C.I.F., EXPORTS F.O.B.
SERIES HISTORIQUES, 1992–1996 COMMERCE GENERAL, IMPORTATIONS C.A.F., EXPORTATIONS F.O.B

YEAR ANNEE	VALUE IN MILLION U.S. DOLLARS VALEUR EN MILLION U.S. DOLLARS MERCHANDISE –MARCHANDISE		GOLD –OR		CONVERSION FACTORS FACTEURS DE CONVERSION CENTS E.U. PAR		INDEX NUMBERS –INDICES QUANTUM		UNIT VALUE VALEUR UNITAIRE	
	IMPORTS	EXPORTS	IMPORTS	EXPORTS	IMPORTS	EXPORTS	IMPORTS	EXPORTS	IMPORTS	EXPORTS
1992	4460.70	4597.00								
1993	4666.80	3913.50								
1994	5229.30	4260.40								
1995	7509.90	4632.70								
1996	7787.90	4511.80								

2. IMPORTS BY BROAD ECONOMIC CATEGORY AND EXPORTS BY INDUSTRIAL ORIGIN. (PERCENTAGE OF TOTAL VALUE)
IMPORTATIONS PAR CATEGORIES ECONOMIQUES ET EXPORTATIONS PAR BRANCHE D'ACTIVITE.(EN POURCENTAGE DE LA VALEUR TOTALE)

IMPORTS – IMPORTATIONS

	1990	1991	1992	1993	1994	1995	1996
TOTAL IMPORTS–IMPORTATIONS TOTALES			100.	100.	100.	100.	100.
1 FOOD BEV–ALIMENTATION BOISSONS			11.2	7.7	10.0	10.9	10.3
11 PRIMARY–PRODUITS DE BASE			5.6	3.5	4.6	5.3	4.8
111 FOR INDUSTRY–POUR L'INDUSTRIE			2.5	0.9	1.4	1.7	1.6
112 FOR HOUSEHOLDS–POUR LES MENAGES			3.1	2.6	3.2	3.6	3.2
12 PROCESSED–PRODUITS ELABORES			5.6	4.3	5.5	5.6	5.5
121 FOR INDUSTRY–POUR L'INDUSTRIE			0.9	0.7	0.8	0.9	0.9
122 FOR HOUSEHOLDS–POUR LES MENAGES			4.7	3.6	4.7	4.7	4.6
2 IND SUPPLIES–APPROV INDUSTRIELS			39.2	40.8	35.8	28.2	29.1
21 PRIMARY–PRODUITS DE BASE			3.6	2.9	2.2	1.8	1.7
22 PROCESSED–PRODUITS ELABORES			35.5	37.8	33.6	26.4	27.4
3 FUELS–COMBUSTIBLES			9.6	9.8	11.2	11.5	11.0
31 PRIMARY–PRODUITS DE BASE			8.7	9.1	9.6	9.6	9.7
32 PROCESSED–PRODUITS ELABORES			0.9	0.8	1.6	1.9	1.3
321 MOTOR SPIRIT–ESSENCE			0.0	0.0	0.1	0.1	0.1
322 OTHER–AUTRES			0.9	0.7	1.5	1.9	1.2
4 MACHINERY–EQUIPEMENT			12.6	16.3	16.8	18.0	18.4
41 CAPITAL EQUIPMENT–MACHINES			10.5	13.5	14.7	15.8	16.4
42 PARTS–PIECES ACCESSOIRES			2.1	2.8	2.1	2.2	2.0
5 TRANSPORT–TRANSPORT			4.7	9.0	9.6	8.9	9.3
51 PASSENGER CARS–AUTOMOBILES			1.5	3.1	2.7	2.0	2.4
52 OTHER–AUTRES			1.2	3.8	4.7	4.3	4.5
521 INDUSTRIAL–INDUSTRIELS			1.1	3.7	4.6	4.1	4.3
522 NON INDUSTRIAL–NON INDUSTRIEL			0.1	0.1	0.2	0.2	0.1
53 PARTS–PIECES ACCESSOIRES			2.0	2.1	2.1	2.5	2.4
6 CONSUM GOODS–BIENS CONSOMMATION			16.0	16.3	16.6	16.7	17.2
61 DURABLE–DURABLES			2.1	2.2	3.1	3.8	3.8
62 SEMI DURABLE–SEMI DURABLES			11.0	11.7	10.7	9.6	9.9
63 NON DURABLE–NON DURABLES			2.9	2.4	2.9	3.4	3.5
7 GOODS NES–BIENS NDA			6.8	0.0	0.0	5.8	4.8

EXPORTS – EXPORTATIONS

	1990	1991	1992	1993	1994	1995	1996
TOTAL EXPORTS–EXPORTATIONS TOTALES			100.	100.	100.	100.	100.
1 AGRICULTURE			4.4	3.4	3.0	3.2	3.0
2 MINING QUARRY–INDUS EXTRACTIVES			2.4	2.0	1.4	1.1	1.3
3 MANUFACTURING–IND MANUFACTUR			93.2	94.6	95.6	95.7	95.7
31 FOOD BEV TOBACCO–ALIM BOISS TAB			9.2	9.5	9.1	8.7	9.7
32 TEXTILES–INDUSTRIES TEXTILES			18.6	25.1	24.9	22.6	22.0
33 WOOD & PRODUCTS–BOIS & PRODUITS			4.3	5.3	4.5	4.4	4.4
34 PAPER & PRODUCTS–PAPIER & PRODT			2.5	2.8	3.3	2.9	1.9
35 CHEMICALS–INDUSTRIES CHIMIQUES			22.6	23.7	22.4	26.1	23.1
36 NON METAL MIN–MIN NON METAL			2.9	2.8	3.1	2.9	3.1
37 BASIC METAL–IND METAL BASE			7.0	2.9	2.9	2.9	2.7
38 METAL MANUF–MANUF METAL			23.9	20.9	24.0	23.7	27.6
39 OTH MANUF IND–AUTRES MANUF			2.1	1.6	1.5	1.4	1.4

3. TRADE BY PRINCIPAL COUNTRIES OF ORIGIN AND DESTINATION (VALUE IN THOUSAND U.S. DOLLARS)
ECHANGES SELON LES PRINCIPAUX PAYS D'ORIGINE ET DE DESTINATION (VALEUR EN MILLIERS DE DOLLARS EU)

COUNTRIES–PAYS	GENERAL IMPORTS C.I.F. IMPORTATIONS GENERALES C.A.F				
	1992	1993	1994	1995	1996
World	4460729	4666365	5229137	7509210	7787787
Africa	106121	109310	110631	265893	291922
Americas	171484	203984	273865	359214	372849
Northern America	110126	146170	192760	214284	229938
LAIA	59538	52345	67231	121948	129093
CACM	791	2523	6229	7743	6334
Caribbean	480	616	7116	12558	6558
Rest of America	549	2330	528	2681	925
As.ex F.USSR	338157	361665	493376	439598	606099
Eur.x F.USSR	3593018	3723619	4090494	6205822	6242062
EU	2118315	2630337	3096079	4663313	4625403
EFTA	77130	85807	111964	219257	179300
East Europe	377395	235198	306778	464925	567514
Other Europe	509	104	3414	8444	3629
Former USSR	230883	261099	254087	223940	252932
Oceania	9534	6196	6684	14736	21871
Germany/Allemagne	767587	990737	1109769	1508989	1601803
Italy/Italie	761198	881714	994628	1365981	1421608
Slovenia/Slovénia	874296	712470	540882	804753	769169
Austria/Autriche	189680	310553	352723	574086	597426
Iran (Islamic Rp. of)	231864	236549	292390	89570	165225
United Kingdom	64549	89668	179087	455295	225402
Russian Federation	202255	226943	182993	156974	214050
USA/Etats–Unis d'Amer	105937	123803	173239	202252	212829
France,Monac	71867	97580	117579	188558	198988
Netherlands/Pays–Bas	88592	91672	114638	174206	176496
Hungary/Hongrie	102737	78188	100124	158011	192646
Switz.Liecht	69737	81119	103693	174636	151675
Libyan Arab Jamahiriya	27235	32609	67658	189728	242452
Czech Republic		93476	91934	147097	207138
Sweden/Suède	53473	60202	81431	147514	117147
Belgium–Luxembourg	51046	47753	55639	88082	105205
Japan/Japon	31769	42146	54071	79849	104517
Slovakia		24355	53074	77911	83680
Czechoslovakia	214586				
Brazil/Brésil	25639	23878	29124	56708	64710
Poland/Pologne	31742	25179	37622	45254	49712
Denmark/Danemark	31039	16130	30973	51178	47984
Spain/Espagne	11463	20052	30711	50896	62143
Bosnia and Herzegovina	80632	13942	4055	8718	63480
China/Chine	6896	16698	30021	44314	54665
Syrian Arab Republic	133	237	11834	32661	102442
Tfyr Macedonia		45558	27321	36412	33566
Ukraine	9446	11796	50495	40604	11273
Korea, Republic of	5701	8423	13881	35518	32364
Turkey/Turquie	14742	8627	15752	27916	27140
Belarus/Bélarus	17184	19648	13172	21667	19489
Norway,SVD,JM	7172	4608	7963	44078	26637
Morocco/Maroc	22972	15694	11536	15502	13832
Finland/Finlande	12477	8429	6917	24499	26293
India/Inde	7800	8168	14611	23511	21866
Ecuador/Equateur	8501	7258	14191	22506	21768
Bulgaria/Bulgarie	19669	8180	10714	21283	13406
Ireland/Irlande	4500	7915	13227	16634	28137
Yugoslavia/Yougoslavie	64741	202	1		1
Canada	4189	10374	19429	11707	16821
So. Africa Customs Un	10957	31884	4905	5400	6103
Egypt/Egypte	12164	13701	10865	14056	8095
Hong Kong	2766	4434	11781	18650	17952
Greece/Grèce	9675	7018	6871	15929	14563
Argentina/Argentine	12272	4728	8633	12914	13256
Romania/Roumanie	3941	3718	10649	12569	19137
Israel/Israël	12895	5234	5620	13761	10679
Australia/Australie	8840	5138	4761	8500	17272
Peru/Pérou	6637	7943	5771	9216	9584
Colombia/Colombie	4347	5048	5357	11038	9010

COUNTRIES–PAYS	GENERAL EXPORTS F.O.B. EXPORTATIONS GENERALES F.O.B.				
	1992	1993	1994	1995	1996
Monde	4597492	3903818	4260374	4632666	4511739
Afrique	90567	77132	94273	151027	311173
Amériques	109808	122461	161228	144608	127683
Amérique du Nord	76128	88911	99958	96139	100746
ALAI	11853	10415	20696	13560	18836
MCAC	161	1162	722	923	640
Caraïbes	455	2203	4132	31857	5366
Autre Amérique	21211	19770	35719	2129	2096
Asie l'URSS exclus	178656	110885	67383	119071	142880
Europe l'URSS exclus	4027695	3413439	3756556	4026223	3753464
UE	2414684	2245092	2530654	2671925	2302589
AELE	60803	44716	65229	59128	40609
Europe de l'Est	111873	133688	177803	190201	190101
Autre de l'Europe	510	24870	15130	44203	1192
Ancienne URSS	155475	173262	175744	185491	171796
Océanie	4927	5814	5191	6246	4742
Italy/Italie	909151	828449	910156	1098220	949683
Germany/Allemagne	773267	895103	941482	996884	839477
Slovenia/Slovénia	1100944	711619	555897	607792	611442
Bosnia and Herzegovina	192365	188887	338465	383241	548535
Austria/Autriche	104979	130101	149430	200335	198066
Russian Federation	144783	144475	151021	152082	130545
Sweden/Suède	338886	25318	163840	14219	12806
Liberia/Libéria	50874	39461	54761	104886	265741
France,Monac	57824	133859	112010	112134	84471
Netherlands/Pays–Bas	98238	92233	94057	80186	68793
USA/Etats–Unis d'Amer	71575	83883	94594	88660	92435
United Kingdom	56242	73053	67717	57335	70230
Hungary/Hongrie	42045	54039	68353	71081	55299
Tfyr Macedonia		62789	73368	69733	58987
Switz.Liecht	37517	41887	61313	54183	37529
Poland/Pologne	32248	37224	45149	48607	55992
China/Chine	113197	28768	12897	27082	30441
Belgium–Luxembourg	32439	29146	37872	43318	41075
Yugoslavia/Yougoslavie	146515	1777	11		10
Czech Republic		24156	34239	35621	40341
Panama	21155	19716	35640	2056	2009
Malta/Malte	440	24811	14645	38899	1077
Cyprus/Chypre	879	2997	1561	19832	53877
Greece/Grèce	14626	15939	12456	18932	7031
Slovakia		8062	16169	21488	22287
Spain/Espagne	11947	6117	17208	20511	9619
Turkey/Turquie	11408	20491	13875	4623	12740
Egypt/Egypte	12248	10218	12472	13661	13852
Belarus/Bélarus	2869	12400	4592	8982	21716
Ukraine	5632	9885	11721	12779	8594
Ireland/Irlande	2736	5655	4968	16298	13709
Ecuador/Equateur	7785	7108	9746	9485	5519
Norway,SVD,JM	23262	2818	3827	4882	3003
Iran (Islamic Rp. of)	6624	3700	2644	18730	4290
Denmark/Danemark	6707	7028	9916	6785	4324
India/Inde	6222	10241	1378	6612	8197
Czechoslovakia	31839				
Canada	4530	5023	5193	7473	8267
Nigeria/Nigéria	2041	9467	11660	5568	1246
Saudi Arabia	3077	4787	6315	8312	6547
Morocco/Maroc	3325	3079	2925	6185	11649
Bahamas	0	18	53	26874	111
Australia/Australie	4734	5530	4738	5674	4388
Israel/Israël	3043	2333	3814	10871	3770
Algeria/Algérie	3834	4332	4124	8602	2623
Bulgaria/Bulgarie	1978	3581	4969	6279	4779
Romania/Roumanie	1899	3382	5098	4617	5670
Lebanon/Liban	1868	6108	2490	7540	2261
Albania/Albanie	1865	3243	3825	2508	5732
Finland/Finlande	4678	2348	2039	4922	2061

(VALUE AS PERCENTAGE OF WORLD TOTAL)(VALEURS EN POURCENTAGE DU TOTAL MONDIAL)

	1987	1988	1989	1990	1991	1992	1993	1994	1995	1996
Africa						2.4	2.3	2.1	3.5	3.7
Americas						3.8	4.4	5.2	4.8	4.8
Northern America						2.5	3.1	3.7	2.9	3.0
LAIA						1.3	1.1	1.3	1.6	1.7
CACM						0.0	0.1	0.1	0.1	0.1
Caribbean						0.0	0.0	0.1	0.2	0.1
Rest of America						0.0	0.0	0.0	0.0	0.0
As.ex F.USSR						7.6	7.8	9.4	5.9	7.8
Eur.x F.USSR						80.5	79.8	78.2	82.6	80.2
EU						47.5	56.4	59.2	62.1	59.4
EFTA						1.7	1.8	2.1	2.9	2.3
East Europe						8.5	5.0	5.9	6.2	7.3
Other Europe						0.0	0.0	0.1	0.1	0.0
Former USSR						5.2	5.6	4.9	3.0	3.2
Oceania						0.2	0.1	0.1	0.2	0.3
Germany/Allemagne						17.2	21.2	21.2	20.1	20.6
Italy/Italie						17.1	18.9	19.0	18.2	18.3
Slovenia/Slovénia						19.6	15.3	10.3	10.7	9.9
Austria/Autriche						4.3	6.7	6.7	7.6	7.7
Iran (Islamic Rp. of)						5.2	5.1	5.6	1.2	2.1
United Kingdom						1.4	1.9	3.4	6.1	2.9
Russian Federation						4.5	4.9	3.5	2.1	2.7
USA/Etats–Unis d'Amer						2.4	2.7	3.3	2.7	2.7
France,Monac						1.6	2.1	2.2	2.5	2.6
Netherlands/Pays–Bas						2.0	2.0	2.2	2.3	2.3

	1987	1988	1989	1990	1991	1992	1993	1994	1995	1996
Afrique						2.0	2.0	2.2	3.3	6.9
Amériques						2.4	3.1	3.8	3.1	2.8
Amérique du Nord						1.7	2.3	2.3	2.1	2.2
ALAI						0.3	0.3	0.5	0.3	0.4
MCAC						0.0	0.0	0.0	0.0	0.0
Caraïbes						0.0	0.1	0.1	0.7	0.1
Autre Amérique						0.5	0.5	0.8	0.0	0.0
Asie l'URSS exclus						3.9	2.8	1.6	2.6	3.2
Europe l'URSS exclus						87.6	87.4	88.2	86.9	83.2
UE						52.5	57.5	59.4	57.7	51.0
AELE						1.3	1.1	1.5	1.3	0.9
Europe de l'Est						2.4	3.4	4.2	4.1	4.2
Autre de l'Europe						0.0	0.6	0.4	1.0	0.0
Ancienne URSS						3.4	4.4	4.1	4.0	3.8
Océanie						0.1	0.1	0.1	0.1	0.1
Italy/Italie						19.8	21.2	21.4	23.7	21.0
Germany/Allemagne						16.8	22.9	22.1	21.5	18.6
Slovenia/Slovénia						23.9	18.2	13.0	13.1	13.6
Bosnia and Herzegovina						4.2	4.8	7.9	8.3	12.2
Austria/Autriche						2.3	3.3	3.5	4.3	4.4
Russian Federation						3.1	3.7	3.5	3.3	2.9
Sweden/Suède						7.4	0.6	3.8	0.3	0.3
Liberia/Libéria						1.1	1.0	1.3	2.3	5.9
France,Monac						1.3	3.4	2.6	2.4	1.9
Netherlands/Pays–Bas						2.1	2.4	2.2	1.7	1.5

4. General Imports C.I.F. by Commodities according to the S.I.T.C. (Rev. 2) in thousand U.S. Dollars
Importations Générales C.A.F. par Produits d'après la C.T.C.I. (Rév. 2) en milliers de Dollars E.U.

SITC CTCI	COMMODITY	1993 WEIGHT POIDS	1993 VALUE VALEUR	1994 WEIGHT POIDS	1994 VALUE VALEUR	1995 WEIGHT POIDS	1995 VALUE VALEUR	1996 WEIGHT POIDS	1996 VALUE VALEUR	PRODUIT
	ALL COMMODITIES		4666365		5229137		7509210		7787787	TOUS PRODUITS
0	FOOD AND LIVE ANIMALS		359717		498937		780189		767460	ALIMENTS,ANIMAUX VIVANTS
001	*LIVE ANIMALS FOR FOOD		9127		17846	W 14172	26915	W 24733	45053	ANIMAUX VIVANTS
0011	BOVINE SPECIES,LIVE	W 5344	4979	W 10761	15833	W 13102	23084	W 18779	33846	ESPECE BOVINE
01	MEAT AND PREPARATIONS		60987		75871		114452		97999	VIANDES ET PREPARATIONS
011	MEAT FRESH,CHILLD,FROZEN		40208		49606	W 34709	77862		63177	VIANDES FRAICHES,REF,CONGE
0111	BOVINE MEAT FRESH,FROZEN		17006		24584	W 10176	23695	W 6974	16192	VIANDES BOVIN FRAI,REF
01111	BOVINE MEAT WITH BONE IN	W 8007	15656	W 8548	15649	W 4552	10315	W 2399	5853	VIANDES BOVIN NON DESOSS
0113	PIG MEAT FRESH,CHLD,FRZN	W 8217	14071		18289	W 17909	40821	W 16417	39262	VIANDE DE PORC
014	MEAT PREPD,PRSVD,NES ETC	W 5906	18195		24187	W 9647	33614	W 10032	30688	CONSERVES DE VIANDES
0142	SAUSAGES INCLDING TINNED	W 3452	11715		17260	W 6887	25200	W 6628	22063	SAUCISSES,SAUCISSONS
02	DAIRY PRODCTS,BIRDS'EGGS		34479		34410		65632		76651	PRODUITS LAITIERS,OEUFS
022	MILK AND CREAM		19286		22446	W 108683	44918	W 118124	50300	LAIT ET CREME
0223	MILK AND CREAM FRESH	W 37099	12897		16604	W 70408	30755	W 91167	38420	LAIT,CREME FRAIS
024	CHEESE AND CURD	W 4596	12093		10784	W 6408	19209	W 9382	23367	FROMAGE ET CAILLEBOTTE
03	FISH AND PREPARATIONS		12720		18953		23276		28098	POISSONS ET PREPARATIONS
04	CEREALS AND PREPARATIONS		19211		42712		52789		66737	CEREALES ET PRODUITS
048	CEREAL ETC PREPARATIONS	W 26396	12818		30150	W 46608	42349	W 61244	51248	PREPTNS A BASE CEREALES
05	VEGETABLES AND FRUIT		92395		131437		221851		194219	LEGUMES ET FRUITS
054	VEG ETC FRSH,SMPLY PRSVD		27285		30101		62317	W 95654	44479	LEGUMES FRAIS,CONG,SECS
056	VEGTBLES ETC PRSVD,PREPD		13991		19046	W 15834	26021	W 15941	26614	CONSERVES DE LEGUMES
057	FRUIT,NUTS,FRESH,DRIED		31732		60929		93555		84366	FRUITS FRAIS OU SECS
0573	BANANA,PLANTAIN,FRSH,DRY	W 23019	9470		18239	W 67373	27985	W 58037	27750	BANANES FRAICHES,SECHEES
0579	FRUIT FRESH OR DRIED NES		4927		13617	W 36120	23385	W 37698	18357	FRUITS FRAIS,SECS NDA
058	FRUIT PRESERVED,PREPARED		19387		21361	W 42032	39958		38760	CONSERVES DE FRUITS
0585	FRUIT OR VEGETABLE JUICE	W 14912	9708		12937	W 32230	25118	W 27410	23785	JUS DE FRUITS
06	SUGAR AND PREPS,HONEY		28208		47555		62573		39336	SUCRES ET PRODUITS
061	SUGAR AND HONEY	W 111783	22614		34314	W 129941	45906	W 75427	27864	SUCRES ET MIEL
07	COFFEE,TEA,COCOA,SPICES		25287		51687		97864		88905	CAFE,THE,CACAO,EPICES
071	COFFEE AND SUBSTITUTES	W 9806	13169		29999	W 19033	63987	W 18907	56192	CAFE ET SUCCEDANES
0711	COFFEE GREEN,ROASTED,SUB	W 9792	13093		29639	W 18960	62833	W 18698	52788	CAFE TORREFIE OU DECAFEINE
07111	COFFEE GREEN,HUSKS,SKINS	W 9553	12595		26950	W 18221	58909	W 18196	49565	CAFE NON TORREFIE
081	*FEEDING STUFF FOR ANIML		41161		34083		38199	W 108023	53059	NOURRITURE POUR ANIMAUX
0813	OILCAKE AND OTH RESIDUES	W 75580	21136	W 67376	15310		9977	W 65461	21280	TOURTEAUX
08131	— OF SOYA BEANS	W 72103	20580	W 50425	11610	W 33449	7846	W 59394	18680	TOURTEAUX DE SOJA
09	MISC EDIBLE PRODUCTS		36141		44384		76637		77402	PREP ALIMENTAIRES DIVERSES
098	EDIBLE PRODCTS,PREPS NES		33066		41631		72036		73325	PREP ALIMENTAIRES NDA
09809	MISC FOOD PREPRTIONS NES	W 6775	28667		34496	W 13736	61492	W 15294	61416	PREP ALIMENTAIRES NDA
1	BEVERAGES AND TOBACCO		37470		62825		66270		57609	BOISSONS ET TABACS
11	BEVERAGES		24146		47964		44310		41079	BOISSONS
112	ALCOHOLIC BEVERAGES		16116		33461		24985	W 33210	26219	BOISSONS ALCOOLIQUES
1123	BEER,ALE,STOUT,PORTER	W 20205	8921		26479	W 23392	14406	W 22028	13743	BIERES
2	CRUDE MATERLS,EXCL FUELS		174047		147710		191598		214536	MAT BRUTES NON COMESTIBLES
24	CORK AND WOOD		16240		19490		26819		51984	LIEGE ET BOIS
248	WOOD SHAPED,SLEEPERS	W 42285	13869		16011	W 65355	22701	W 145951	48553	BOIS SIMPLEMENT TRAVAILLES
2482	LUMBER SHAPED CONIFER	W 31186	9463		11993	W 57769	17382	W 131711	39375	CONIFERES SCIES,RABOTES
24821	LUMBER SAWN ETC CONIFER	W 30414	8776		11353	W 55606	15907	W 128371	36860	CONIFERES SCIES LONGITUD
251	*PULP AND WASTE PAPER		13012		13088	W 74716	22554	W 51913	9074	PATES A PAPIER,DECHETS
26	TEXTILE FIBRES AND WASTE		33938		25101		25614		23989	FIBRES TEXTILES
267	OTHER MAN–MADE FIBRES	W 3447	15453		8439	W 3612	9886	W 2886	8464	AUTR FIBR TEXT ARTIF SYNTH
2671	REGENERATD FIBRE TO SPIN	W 3011	15192		7970	W 3009	9416	W 2089	7836	FIBRES TEXT ARTIFIC
27	CRUDE FERTLZR,MINRLS NES		45202		38080		50596		55695	ENGRAIS MINERAUX BRUTS
271	FERTILIZERS,CRUDE	W 240928	15679		11409		14237		14556	ENGRAIS BRUTS
2713	NAT CALCM PHOSPHATES ETC	W 240482	15647		11363	W 259310	14123		13462	PHOSPHATES DE CALCIUM
27131	— UNGROUND	W 240481	15644	W 242381	11351	W 259286	14120	W 239512	13459	PHOSPHATES NON MOULUS
278	OTHER CRUDE MINERALS	W 310269	18529		15268	W 394651	18632	W 439593	23265	AUTRES MINERAUX BRUTS
28	METALLIFEROUS ORES,SCRAP		30772		7382		2688		7086	MINERAIS METAL,DECHETS
287	BASE METAL ORES,CONC NES		28889		7012		2325	W 62450	6161	MINERAIS METAUX COMMUNS
2877	MANGANESE ORE,CONCENTRTE	W 29766	24752	W 3933	4769			W 21	7	MINERAIS DE MANGANESE
29	CRUDE ANIMAL,VEG MAT NES		20112		25282		38711		42704	MATIERES BRUTES ANIM,VEGET
292	CRUDE VEG MATERIALS NES		11605		16453	W 9340	26610		28077	MAT BRUTES VEGETALES NDA
3	MINERAL FUELS ETC		464141		591386		874122		860683	COMBUSTIBLES MINERAUX LUB
32	COAL,COKE AND BRIQUETTES		47235		29704		17382		16109	HOUILLES,COKES,BRIQUETTES
322	COAL,LIGNITE AND PEAT	W 739439	45919	W 481553	27098	W 245467	13504	W 204577	12120	HOUILLES,LIGNITES,TOURBE
3222	OTH COAL,NOT AGGLOMERATD	W 576146	35849	W 350570	21194	W 89387	4780	W 61406	4245	AUTRES HOUILLES
33	PETROLEUM AND PRODUCTS		304692		437738		739163		710041	PETROLE ET DERIVES
333	CRUDE PETROLEUM	W 1890190	273743		381813	W 4929170	674854	W 4098141	635214	HUILES BRUTES DE PETROLE
334	PETROLEUM PRODUCTS,REFIN	W 154118	25917		50565	W 324659	56981		67211	PRODUITS RAFFINES
3343	GAS OILS	W 29772	4457	W 107151	17613	W 151496	11060	W 77139	14474	GAS OILS
3345	LUBS,PETROLEUM OILS NES	W 14108	11915		14640	W 28419	22902	W 51219	28303	HUILES LUBRIFIANTES
33451	LUBS(HIGH PETR CONT) ETC	W 13480	9370		12511	W 27473	19847	W 50328	25087	HUILES LUBRIF,H LOURDES
341	*GAS,NATURAL AND MANUFCT		103361		94921		33787		107001	GAZ NATUREL,GAZ MANUFACT
3414	PETROLEUM GASES, GASEOUS		103342		91953	W 143032	32203	W 509725	105705	GAZ DE PETROLE GAZEUX
351	*ELECTRIC CURRENT		8853		29023		83789		27532	ENERGIE ELECTRIQUE
4	ANIMAL,VEGETABLE OIL,FAT		14101		11664		25113		36817	HUILES,GRAISSES ANIM,VEG
42	FIXED VEGETABLE OIL,FAT		9026		5990		16467		27225	HUILES VEGETALES FIXES
5	CHEMCLS,RELATED PROD NES		561324		521707		776902		818616	PRODUITS CHIMIQUES
51	ORGANIC CHEMICALS		102072		80756		113945		118675	PROD CHIMIQ ORGANIQUES
511	HYDROCARBONS NES,DERIVS		25890		9142		14072		14217	HYDROCARBURES NDA
5111	ACYCLIC HYDROCARBONS	W 53476	16151		703	W 4113	2267		3627	HYDROCARBURES ACYCLIQUES
51111	ETHYLENE	W 53329	15994		435	W 3238	1884	W 6191	3332	ETHYLENE
513	CARBOXYLIC ACIDS ETC		18450		17361	W 11630	20359	W 12804	19635	ACIDES CARBOXYLIQUES
514	NITROGEN–FNCTN COMPOUNDS		31385		27429	W 10723	37848		48236	COMPOSES FONCT AZOTEES
52	INORGANIC CHEMICALS		50756		35102		50861		46417	PROD CHIM INORGANIQUES
522	INORG ELEMNTS,OXIDES,ETC		15430		9828		14707		15640	ELEMENTS INORGANIQUES
523	OTHR INORG CHEMICALS ETC		33796		24153		34216		28527	AUT PRODUITS CHIMIQUES INORG
5232	OTH MTL CMPD OF INRG ACD		22809		17223	W 104786	25614	W 66941	19774	SELS METALLIQUES
53	DYES,TANNING,COLOUR PROD		44921		43815		64263		68233	PROD TEINTURE,COLORANTS
533	PIGMENTS,PAINTS,ETC	W 15472	33570		34151	W 26964	50680	W 36089	55466	PIGMENTS,PEINTURES,VERNIS
5334	VARNISHES,DISTEMPERS ETC	W 7980	19943		19598	W 12924	29461	W 13402	30649	PEINTURES A L'EAU
53342	OTH PAINTS,VARNISHES ETC	W 3899	15441		14204	W 5364	21464	W 5587	22163	AUTRES PEINTURES,VERNIS
541	*MEDICINAL,PHARM PRODUCT		97979		98697		176547		188268	PROD MEDICINAUX PHARMACEUT
5413	ANTIBIOTICS IN BULK	K 155000	10555		9788	K 432000	22699	K 289622	26374	ANTIBIOTIQUES NDA
5417	MEDICAMENTS	K 1255000	71037		69267	K 1739000	122693	K 1870611	125589	MEDICAMENTS
54171	— CONTAINNG ANTIBIOTICS	K 263000	9007		12234	K 310000	23855	K 275477	21650	MED CONTN ANTIBIOTIQUES
54179	— CONTNG OTH SUBSTANCES	K 875000	51736		49595	K 1298000	79727	K 1406207	86237	MED CONT AUT SUBSTANCES
55	PERFUME,CLEANING ETC PRD		41906		69334		105524		122770	PROD POUR PARFUM,TOILETTE
553	PERFUMERY,COSMETICS,ETC	W 2588	14499		30182	W 8043	51801	W 8347	56796	PRODUITS DE PARFUMERIE
554	SOAP,CLEANSING ETC PREPS	W 16815	22594		33052	W 34668	46566	W 40432	52950	SAVONS,PRODUITS DETERSIFS
5542	WASHING PREPARATIONS ETC	W 15194	19620		27907	W 31920	39521	W 37424	45232	PROD ORG TENSIO–ACT NDA
562	*FERTILIZERS,MANUFACTURE	W 191106	24276		15167		22447	W 172595	20256	ENGRAIS MANUFACTURES

4. General Imports C.I.F. by Commodities according to the S.I.T.C. (Rev. 2) in thousand U.S. Dollars
Importations Générales C.A.F. par Produits d'après la C.T.C.I. (Rév. 2) en milliers de Dollars E.U.

SITC CTCI	COMMODITY	1993 WEIGHT POIDS	1993 VALUE VALEUR	1994 WEIGHT POIDS	1994 VALUE VALEUR	1995 WEIGHT POIDS	1995 VALUE VALEUR	1996 WEIGHT POIDS	1996 VALUE VALEUR	PRODUIT
5623	CHEM POTASSIC FERTILIZER	W 149442	18843		11622	W 181385	19280	W 170999	19175	ENGRAIS POTASSIQUES
56231	POTASSIUM CHLORIDE	W 145890	17998		11523	W 178418	18458	W 163127	17476	CHLORURE DE POTASSIUM
58	PLASTIC MATERIALS ETC		82296		97029		118014		118489	MAT PLAST ARTIFICIELLES
582	PROD OF CONDENSATION ETC	W 19216	24490		17792	W 18081	26801	W 19644	29327	PROD CONDENS,POLYCOND
583	POLYMERIZATION ETC PRODS		53931		75880	W 49611	86042	W 50119	84435	PROD POLYMERISATION
5831	POLYETHYLENE	W 10914	8207		21652	W 19106	22655	W 20018	23071	POLYETHYLENE
58311	— IN PRIMARY FORMS	W 9070	6352	W 17695	19653	W 17535	18903	W 17411	17616	POLYETHYLENE PRIMAIRES
5834	POLYVINYL CHLORIDE	W 7933	8209		21462	W 12120	19873	W 10084	16098	CHLORURE DE POLYVINYLE
5839	OTH POLYMRZTION ETC PROD		16211		15800	W 6582	19463	W 6954	20447	AUT PROD POLYMER COPOLYM
59	CHEMICAL MATERIALS NES		113005		78893		121040		130839	MAT PROD CHIMIQUES NDA
591	PESTICIDES,DISINFECTANTS	W 2051	14879		11589	W 2510	20031	W 2791	22926	DESINF,INSECT,FONG,HERB
598	MISCEL CHEM PRODUCTS NES		86245		56667		86572	W 58089	92924	PROD DIV INDUST CHIM NDA
5982	ANTI-KNOCK PREPARTNS ETC	W 6195	14766		11947	W 4742	17898	W 4712	18219	PREPARAT ANTIDETONANTES
5989	CHEM PRODUCTS,PREPS NES		68839		41939	W 31959	64567	W 51423	70860	PROD PREP CHIMIQUES NDA
59899	OTH CHEM PRODS,PREPS,NES		49289		26128	W 24078	35953	W 43644	39664	AUT PRODUITS CHIMIQUES NDA
6	BASIC MANUFACTURES		1274067		1321884		1395210		1481472	ART MANUFACTURES
61	LEATHER,DRESSED FUR,ETC		149502		83076		87082		88783	CUIRS,PELLETERIES
612	LEATHER ETC MANUFACTURES	W 96780	136913		69044	W 3669	68164	W 3414	70001	OUVRAGES EN CUIRS NDA
6123	PREPRD PARTS OF FOOTWEAR	W 96757	136301		68378	W 3633	67245	W 3375	69191	PARTIES DE CHAUSSURES
62	RUBBER MANUFACTURES NES		45298		53347		85999		88603	CAOUTCHOUC MANUFACTURE
625	RUBBER TYRES, TUBES ETC		27412		32825	W 13247	52728	W 13475	58057	PNEUS CAOUTCHOUC VULCANISE
6252	TYRES,NEW,BUS OR LORRY	W 3933	13393		15902	W 5489	23645	W 5744	25612	PNEUS POUR AUTOBUS,CAMIONS
63	WOOD,CORK MANUFACTRS NES		23539		34628		50916		62277	OUVRAGES LIEGE ET BOIS
635	WOOD MANUFACTURES NES	W 8770	11182		22353	W 17006	33068	W 18221	38483	ART MANUF EN BOIS NDA
6353	BUILDERS WOODWRK,PREFABS	W 6590	9166		18909	W 13881	27287	W 13794	32232	OUVRAGES DE MENUISERIE
64	PAPER,PAPERBOARD AND MFR		168216		136257		238739		252749	PAPIERS,CARTONS & OUVRAGES
641	PAPER AND PAPERBOARD		133264		90415	W 132977	155315	W 150638	159368	PAPIERS ET CARTONS
6411	NEWSPRINT	W 18317	8331		11034	W 34119	25936	W 33645	26685	PAPIER JOURNAL
6412	PRINTG,WRITING PAPER NES	W 15836	67638		17072	W 19786	32497	W 22307	26639	PAPIERS POUR L'IMPRESSION
64121	— UNCOATED	W 1400	34597		1881	W 3548	5879	W 3781	5391	PAPIERS IMPRES NON COUCHES
64122	— COATED,IMPREGNATD ETC	W 14436	33041		15191	W 16238	26618	W 18526	21248	PAPIERS IMPRESSION COUCHES
6415	PAPER,PAPERBRD,BULK,NES	W 26009	24705		23777	W 34543	39762	W 37754	34877	PAPIERS,CARTONS ROULEAUX
64159	OTHER PAPER ETC,BULK,NES	W 25213	23596		22121	W 32569	37079	W 34725	32066	AUT PAPIER ROULEAUX FEUILLES
6418	COATED ETC PAPER NES BLK		15815		22233	W 17714	36222	W 23062	45801	PAP,CARTONS COUCHES,ENDUITS
642	PAPER,ETC,PRECUT,ARTS OF	W 150752	34952		45842		83425		93381	PAP,CARTONS DECOUPES
6421	PAPER ETC CONTAINERS	W 111873	14628		17303	W 14770	26263	W 15561	29917	BOITES,SACS EMBALLAGES
6428	PAPER ETC ARTICLES NES	W 32340	11050		14465		30822		37725	OUVRAGES EN PATE A PAPIER
64285	PAPER ETC DIAPERS ETC	W 28131	5726		7439	W 4668	17247	W 6239	23626	SERVIETTES HYGIENIQUES
65	TEXTILE YARN,FABRICS,ETC		475446		581939		216468		209150	FILS,TISSUS,ARTICLES TEXTILE
651	TEXTILE YARN		46856		48516		55107		53395	FILS TEXTILES
6513	COTTON YARN		19153		22064	W 4070	18872	W 4330	19785	FILS DE COTON
6514	SYN FIB YRN,BULK,MONOFIL	W 3429	14512		12256	W 3816	15330	W 3308	13550	FILS CONT 85% FIB TEXT SYNTH
652	COTTON FABRICS,WOVEN		346199		449555		34713		32684	TISSUS DE COTON
6521	GREY WOVEN COTTON FABRIC	W 1007625	327394		432553	W 1218	6347	W 625	2956	TISSUS COT ECRUS NON MERCER
65215	GREY WOVN COTN BLEND NES	W 1006837	325351		430645	W 262	1242	W 41	317	AUT TIS MOINS 85% COT ECRUS
6522	WOVEN COTTON BLEACHD,ETC		18806		17002		28366		29728	TISSUS COTON BLANCHIS ETC
65224	BLCHED COTTON FABRIC NES	W 26019	14047		12500	W 2909	21551	W 3161	22911	AUT TIS PLUS 85% COT BLANCHI
653	WOVN MAN-MADE FIB FABRIC		18547		18473	W 2072	27266	W 1931	26624	TISSUS FIBRES SYNTH,ARTIF
657	SPECIAL TXTL FABRC,PRODS		20717		21409		30830		33569	TISSUS SPECIAUX
659	FLOOR COVERINGS,ETC		10640		11513		26037		18873	COUVRE-PARQUETS,TAPIS ETC
66	NONMETAL MINERAL MFS NES		76635		84018		131134		153382	ART MIN NON METALLIQUES
661	LIME,CEMENT,BLDG PRODS	W 63259	7127		12221	W 220797	24954	W 187832	26416	CHAUX,CIMENTS MAT CONSTR
662	CLAY,REFRACTORY BLDG PRD	W 33363	14662		18493	W 63750	28099	W 145655	38359	MAT CONST REFRACTAIRES
6624	BRICKS ETC NONREFRACTORY	W 25752	9818		13463	W 51880	23356	W 130267	32877	BRIQUES ETC CERAM NON REFR
66245	GLAZED CERAMIC SETTS ETC	W 17469	8176		11486	W 35254	19900	W 46105	24645	AUT CARREAUX CERAMIQUE
663	MINERAL MANUFCTURES NES		16247		15567	W 54204	24977		28599	ART MIN MANUF NDA
664	GLASS	W 28173	19364		19817	W 27709	27271	W 28730	34111	VERRE
665	GLASSWARE		15434		12376		17127		16571	OUVRAGES EN VERRE
67	IRON AND STEEL		163181		145266		248124		260839	FER ET ACIER
672	IRON,STEEL PRIMARY FORMS		27503		21177		19334		16865	LINGOTS FER,ACIER
6725	IRN,STL BLOOMS,SLABS,ETC	W 95150	22240		14022	W 51052	12156		7942	BLOOMS,BILLETTES FER ACIER
67251	IRN,SMPLE STL BLOOMS,ETC	W 95135	22204		13978	W 51018	12062	W 29491	7334	BLOOMS ETC NON ACIER FIN
673	IRON,STEEL SHAPES ETC	W 55594	48251		23458	W 83230	41410		52173	BARRES,PROFIL FER,ACIER
6732	IRON,STEEL BARS ETC	W 27633	37753		10401	W 33498	19483	W 57195	25228	BARRES FER,ACIER
67326	IRN,OTH STL BARS HOTROLD	W 21208	31470		4501	W 22667	9298	W 44863	15557	BARRES PLEINES FER,ACIER
674	IRN,STL UNIV,PLATE,SHEET	W 93084	53162		48161	W 156291	95846	W 169190	108549	LARGES PLATS,TOLES
6744	IRN,STL HVY PLATE,ROLLED	W 36467	17181		14362	W 90176	41667	W 85350	42009	TOLES LAMINEES PLUS 4.75 MM
67441	— OF IRON OR SIMPLE STL	W 35779	15769		13161	W 89136	39556	W 84778	40465	TOLES NON ACIER FIN CARB
6746	IRN,STL THIN PLATE,ROLLD	W 24419	14640		11384	W 22023	19179	W 22483	19309	TOLES LAM MOINS 3MM
678	IRON,STL TUBES,PIPES,ETC	W 18579	20145		29638	W 53859	61250	W 43635	48494	TUBES,TUYAUX EN FONTE,FER
6781	CAST IRON TUBES,PIPES	W 2017	1466		7227	W 27583	27099	W 13874	12038	TUBES,TUYAUX EN FONTE
68	NON-FERROUS METALS		64337		81235		137000		133462	METAUX NON FERREUX
682	COPPER EXC CEMENT COPPER	W 7349	20267		20279	W 10076	40283	W 11876	40678	CUIVRE
6822	COPPER,ALLOYS WORKED	W 7254	19967		20049	W 9877	39403	W 11687	39906	CUIVRE,ALLIAGES OUVRES
68221	COPPER BARS,WIRE,ETC	W 5559	12860		12274	W 6986	23759	W 7540	20970	BARRES,PROFILES ET FILS
684	ALUMINIUM	W 22836	36564		55793	W 35512	88146	W 35928	82778	ALUMINIUM
6841	ALUMINIUM,ALLOYS,UNWRGHT	W 15416	17784	W 26895	34335	W 25129	48781	W 23558	39390	ALUMINIUM,ALLIAGES BRUTS
6842	ALUMINIUM,ALLOYS WORKED	W 7420	18780		21459	W 10383	39365	W 12370	43388	ALUMINIUM,ALLIAGES OUVRE
69	METAL MANUFACTURES NES		107913		122119		199749		232225	ART MANUFACT EN METAL NDA
691	STRUCTURES AND PARTS NES		11854		13952	W 12560	26820	W 18956	30675	CONSTRUCT FER,ACIER,ALU
695	TOOLS	W 2481	16165		17071	W 2081	27745		29435	OUTILS A MAIN
697	BASE MTL HOUSEHOLD EQUIP		13855		22425	W 4859	35354		42014	ART MENAGE MET COMMUNS
6974	BASE MTL DMSTC ARTIC NES	W 584	7852		13112	W 2054	21849		25245	ARTICLES NDA FONTE,FER,ETC
69741	— OF IRON OR STEEL	W 560	7671		12593	W 1956	21189	W 2367	24574	ART NDA EN FONTE,FER
699	BASE METAL MFRS NES		38051		38112		62552		72480	ART MANUFACTURES MET NDA
6991	LOCKSMITHS WARES,ETC	W 1568	12367		12920	W 2553	23463	W 3069	26706	ARTICLES DE SERRURERIE
7	MACHINES,TRANSPORT EQUIP		1125329		1358593		1999902		2115617	MACHINES MATERIEL TRANSPORT
71	POWER GENERATING EQUIPMT		56564		50496		48405		44388	MACHINES GENERATRICES
713	INTRNL COMBUS PSTN ENGIN	W 1015	14102		17426	W 1297	28336		22496	MOTEURS EXPL COMB INT, PIECE
716	ROTATING ELECTRIC PLANT		28883		19542	W 712	8336		8591	APP ELECTR ROTATIFS,PIECES
7162	AC MTRS,GENRTRS,GEN SETS	W 2063	25351		17257	W 319	4453		4919	MOTEURS ELECTRIQUES
71623	GEN SETS WITH PSTN ENGN	W 1942	23445		15050	W 175	1763	W 239	1803	GROUPES MOTEUR EXPLOSION
72	MACHS FOR SPCL INDUSTRYS		147415		175013		279308		315141	MAC SPECIALES POUR INDUST
721	AGRIC MACHY,EXC TRACTORS		20654		13955		36861		24340	MACHINES AGRICOLES
7212	HARVESTING ETC MACHINES	W 850	14525		7003	W 1610	11708	W 2164	15229	ENGINS POUR LA RECOLTE
723	CIVIL ENGNEERG EQUIP ETC	W 2838	14002		26656	W 9052	45675		65386	APPAREILS DE GENIE CIVIL
7234	CONST,MINING MACHNRY NES	W 2361	12107		23114	W 8319	40058	W 13437	58815	MACH POUR LA CONST, MINES
72342	SLFPRP SHOVELS,EXCAVATRS	W 1739	6313		16741	W 6476	27838	W 11023	42636	PELLES MECANIQUES
724	TEXTILE,LEATHER MACHNRY		32870		21578	W 2107	28772		31320	MACH POUR INDUSTRIE TEXTILE
726	PRINTG,BKBINDG MACHY,PTS		8282		11853	W 3387	30871		27438	MACHINES POUR IMPRIMERIE
727	FOOD MACHRY NON-DOMESTIC	W 414	6808		15789	W 907	17415		29655	MACH INDUSTRIES ALIMENT

4. General Imports C.I.F. by Commodities according to the S.I.T.C. (Rev. 2) in thousand U.S. Dollars
Importations Générales C.A.F. par Produits d'après la C.T.C.I. (Rév. 2) en milliers de Dollars E.U.

SITC CTCI	COMMODITY	1993 WEIGHT POIDS	1993 VALUE VALEUR	1994 WEIGHT POIDS	1994 VALUE VALEUR	1995 WEIGHT POIDS	1995 VALUE VALEUR	1996 WEIGHT POIDS	1996 VALUE VALEUR	PRODUIT
7272	OTH FOOD PROC MCHY,PARTS	W 283	6026		13256	W 797	16327		27325	AUT MACH IND ALIMENTAIRE
72722	INDUS FOOD PROC MACH NES	W 253	5885		13110	W 742	15805	W 1319	27303	MACHINES BOULANGERIE
728	OTH MACHY FOR SPCL INDUS	W 9124	43772		63054	W 11251	90502	W 18969	112117	AUT MACH IND PARTICULIERES
7284	MACHY FOR SPCL INDUS NES	W 6490	27751		42063	W 7524	61592	W 13134	72015	MACH SPEC IND PARTICUL.
72848	OTH MCHY WITH INDIV FNCT	W 4553	11293		16592	W 5876	29667	W 11464	51417	AUTRES MACHINES NDA
73	METALWORKING MACHINERY		22684		23246		26663		29679	MACH TRAVAIL DES METAUX
736	METALWORKING MACH–TOOLS		17087		18544	W 2976	18592		22021	MACH–OUTILS TRAVAIL METAUX
74	GENRL INDUSTRL MACHY NES		169582		217487		330464		371883	MACH APP INDUSTRIE
741	HEATING,COOLING EQUIPMNT		36635		52532	W 7221	86069	W 9906	104646	MACH CHAUFFAGE,PIECES
7414	NONDOM REFRIG EQUIPT,PTS	W 1239	7506		15115	W 2966	24319	W 3867	26458	MAT PRODUCTION DU FROID
74141	REFRIG EQUIP NONDOMESTIC	W 1116	6581		13671	W 2525	21365	W 3366	23476	REFIG INDUSTRIELS
7416	HEATING,COOLING EQU NES	W 1214	12794		18850	W 2103	31715	W 3433	45968	APP CHANGEMENT TEMP
742	PUMPS FOR LIQUIDS ETC	W 340218	16051		16923	W 1351	26769	W 1562	25061	POMPES MOTO–POMPES
743	PUMPS NES,CENTRFUGES ETC		23143		29238	W 3286	40034	W 3553	47954	POMPES COMPRES,VENT ETC
744	MECHANICAL HANDLING EQU		18100		26909	W 6545	33117	W 8785	41445	EQUIP MANUTENTION PIECES
745	NONELEC MACHY,TOOLS NES		28961		41212	W 2495	63538		76470	AUT MACH NON ELEC,PIECES
7452	OTH NONELEC MCHS,PTS NES		25985		37101	W 2308	56819		67571	AUT MACH NON ELEC,PIECES
74522	PACKAGNG,BOTTLNG,ETC MCH	W 626	16580		27481	W 992	36563	W 1607	46866	MACH NETT BOUTEILLES,ETC
749	NONELEC MACH PTS,ACC NES		46692		50673	W 5160	80938	W 5003	76307	PIECES MACH NON ELEC NDA
7492	COCKS,VALVES ETC NES	W 6090	24667		28386	W 2368	41658	W 2963	43984	ART ROB,SIM POUR TUYAUX
75	OFFICE MACHNES,ADP EQUIP		135975		120261		183674		185075	MACH BUREAU TRAIT AUTOM
751	OFFICE MACHINES		27300		15233		20233		19580	MACH,APPAREILS DE BUREAU
7512	CALCULATNG,ACCTG,ETC MCH		20549		4940		5817		5120	MACHINE A CALCULER ETC
75121	CALCULATING MACHINES	W 32	19368		1975	W 58	2081		1828	MACHINES A CALCULER
752	AUTOMTIC DATA PROC EQUIP	W 58172	63156		82140		129652		130736	MACH TRAIT INFORMATION
7523	DIGITL CENTRL PROCESSORS	W 159	16496		19352	W 250	36320	W 241	32345	UNITES CENTRALES
7524	DIGITL CENTRL STOR UNITS	W 37084	12169		14689	W 148	24697	W 156	22194	UNITES MEMOIRE CENTRALES
7525	ADP PERIPHERAL UNITS	W 20797	21047		31458	W 1062	40644	W 1456	49304	UNITES PERIPHERIQUES
759	OFFICE,ADP MCH PTS,ACCES	W 264	45519		22888		33790		34759	PIECES DU 751 ET 752
7599	ACCTG,ETC,ADP MCH PTS,AC	W 222	44115		20245	W 536	29286	W 657	29380	PIECES DU 751 ET 752
76	TELECOMM,SOUND EQUIPMENT		70162		108289		200117		161591	EQUIPMENT DE TELECOM
761	TELEVISION RECEIVERS	W 327	4866		14370	W 1615	24314		24281	RECEPTEURS DE TELEVISION
7611	COLOUR TV RECEIVERS	W 324	4773		14329	W 1610	24213	W 1736	24127	RECEPTEURS COULEUR
764	TELECOM EQPT,PTS,ACC NES		59854		83527	W 1897	157532		114815	EQUIP TELECOM,PIECES
7641	LINE TELEPHONE,ETC EQUIP		30788		37356	W 494	42072	W 380	25496	APP TELEPHON PAR FIL
7643	TV,RADIO TRANSMITTRS ETC	W 101	13379		17537	W 108	24926	W 75	28453	APP EMET TELE RADIO
7649	PTS NES OF EQUIPMT OF 76		13216		22596	W 1021	77566		50654	PIECES DE LA DIV 76
76491	PTS NES OF APPAR OF 7641	W 53	9290		16215	W 476	64207	W 295	41225	PIECES POUR 764.1
77	ELECTRIC MACHNRY NES ETC		159411		234453		370170		387743	MACH APP ELECT NDA
771	ELECTRIC POWER MACHY NES	W 11271	17918		14790	W 3020	38004	W 1911	19819	MACH PROD,TRANS ELECTR
7711	TRANSFORMERS,ELECTRICAL	W 742	3871		6209	W 474	27696	W 866	9670	TRANSFO ELECTRIQUES
77118	OTHER ELEC TRANSFORMERS	W 191	3707		6136	W 400	27573	W 537	7836	AUTRES TRANSFO ELECTRIQ
7712	OTH ELEC POWER MACHY NES	W 10529	14047		8581	W 2546	10308	W 1045	10150	AUT APP PROD TRANSF ELEC
772	SWITCHGEAR ETC,PARTS NES		37021		49516	W 3319	77196		86181	APP COUPURE,SECT ETC
7721	SWITCHGEAR ETC	W 11619	32734		45515	W 3275	71882	W 3910	80293	APP COUPURE,SECTIONMNT
773	ELECTR DISTRIBUTNG EQUIP	W 4662	25931		52445	W 11576	68878	W 13463	62332	EQUIPMT DISTRIBUTION ELECT
7731	INSULATED WIRE,CABLE ETC	W 3771	17202		42963	W 10351	54697	W 12030	51588	FILS,CABLES ISOLES ELECT
774	ELECTRO–MEDCL,XRAY EQUIP		7825		8852	W 133	17768	W 339	38383	APPAREILS MEDICAUX
7742	X–RAY APPARATUS ETC		4002		5727	W 91	11148	W 213	24976	APPAREILS A RAYONS X
775	HOUSEHOLD TYPE EQUIP NES		27386		49098		88113		95605	MACH,APP USAGE DOMESTQUE
7752	DOM REFRIGERATRS,FREEZRS	W 1847	7592		13775	W 4959	25022	W 5314	24972	REFRIG,CONGEL MENAGER
7758	ELECTRO–THERMIC APPL NES	W 1838	8489		15500		26475		31584	APP ELECTROTHERMIQ NDA
778	ELECTRICAL MACHINERY NES		34689		47018		64464		71245	AUTRES MACH ELECT NDA
78	ROAD VEHICLES		291548		390360		438481		476957	VEHICULES ROUTIERS
781	PASS MOTOR VEH EXC BUSES	W 53179	146631	W 17271	142958	W 21929	153190	W 33390	187902	AUTO TRANSPORT PERSONNES
782	LORRIES,SPCL MTR VEH NES	W 20802	49115		115860	W 32421	139034	W 42212	136133	VEHICULES SPECIAUX,MARCH
7821	LORRIES,TRUCKS	W 19756	44681		103965	W 29090	113034	W 37635	112722	VEHICULES TRANSP MARCHAND
7822	SPECIAL MOTOR VEHCLS NES	W 1046	4434	W 2217	11895	W 3331	25999	W 4578	23411	VEHICULES USAGES SPECIAUX
783	ROAD MOTOR VEHICLES NES	W 5447	35118	W 14425	72307	W 7643	49492	W 10071	54675	VEHICULES ROUTIERS NDA
7831	BUSES	W 2328	18092	W 10644	51715	W 5584	37245	W 5945	35422	VOITURES TRANSPORT COMMUN
7832	TRACTORS FOR TR–TRAILERS	W 3119	17026	W 3781	20592	W 2059	12247	W 4126	19253	TRACTEURS ROUTIERS
784	MOTOR VEH PRTS,ACCES NES	W 9701	38260		32300	W 6903	63893	W 8574	65418	PIECES 722,781,782,783
7849	OTHER MOTOR VEHCL PARTS	W 9589	37322		30118	W 6379	57961	W 8206	63006	PIECES 722,781,782,783
786	TRAILERS,NONMOTR VEH,NES	W 5433	17519		17072	W 5853	14574	W 8808	18043	REMORQUES,CADRES,CONTAIN
7861	TRAILERS,TRANSP CONTAINR	W 4457	14847		13339	W 4500	10163	W 6994	12786	REMORQUES TOUS VEHICULES
78612	OTHER TRAILERS	W 4424	14769		13289	W 4323	9865	W 6920	12714	REMORQUES TRANSP MARCH
79	OTHR TRANSPORT EQUIPMENT		71989		38987		122621		143160	AUTRE MATERIEL TRANSPORT
792	AIRCRAFT ETC		54058		13589		22879		31162	APP NAVIGATION AERIENNE
7924	AIRCRFT NES OVER 15000KG	W 131	52510		4313	W 3	777	W 21	14797	AERODYNES PLUS 15000 KG
793	SHIPS AND BOATS ETC		12062		20888	W 86364	82329	W 42068	98216	NAVIRES BATEAUX,ETC
7932	SHIPS AND BOATS NES	W 4118	9567		18687	W 85548	79364	W 41770	96138	NAVIRES ET BATEAUX
79322	TANKERS OF ALL KINDS	W 576	1084		8898	W 81608	60095	W 22701	70718	BATEAUX–CITERNES
8	MISC MANUFACTURED GOODS		654310		713929		967169		1065949	ART MANUFACTURES DIVERS
812	*PLUMBG,HEATNG,LGHTNG EQ		10732		19186	W 7854	38404	W 7803	44501	APPAR SANITAIRES CHAUFFAGE
821	*FURNITURE,PARTS THEREOF		33340		56362	W 28024	97483	W 28903	96825	MEUBLES ET PIECES
8211	CHAIRS,SEATS AND PARTS		14444		14972	W 6159	26070	W 7140	26080	SIEGES ET PIECES
82111	CHAIRS AND OTHER SEATS		12412		11939	W 4413	22696	W 6254	22865	SIEGES
8219	FURNITURE AND PARTS NES	W 6438	16164		33653	W 20069	62173	W 19783	59113	AUTRES MEUBLES ET PIECES
82192	WOOD FURNITURE NES	W 3331	9178		21249	W 13318	39435	W 13638	38765	MEUBLES NDA EN BOIS
84	CLOTHING AND ACCESSORIES		173012		231526		271271		285670	VETEMENTS
842	MENS OUTERWEAR NOT KNIT	W 3591	47141		68540	W 2961	64481	W 2712	59514	VET DESSUS POUR HOMMES
8423	— TROUSERS,BREECHES ETC	W 2103	18685		23205	W 1421	22719	W 1406	24214	PANTALONS HOMMES MAT TEX
8424	— JACKETS,BLAZERS ETC	W 839	18099		28036	W 830	22010	W 635	17424	VESTES HOMMES MAT TEXTIL
843	WOMENS OUTERWEAR NONKNIT	W 2485	52869		71919	W 2582	78463	W 2944	81711	VET DESSUS FEMMES MAT TEX
8431	— COATS AND JACKETS	W 786	19867		25273	W 697	25620	W 733	23370	MANT,VEST FEM MAT TEXTIL
8439	— OTHER OUTER GARMENTS	W 833	15144		26805	W 1083	27437	W 1433	34288	AUT VET DES FEM MAT TEXT
844	UNDER GARMENTS NOT KNIT	W 1046	8628		15398	W 1285	17994	W 1348	26094	VETEMENT DESSOUS MAT TEX
845	OUTERWEAR KNIT NONELASTC		37385		29971	W 1714	37680		32846	VET DESSOUS,ACCES BONNET
8451	— JERSEYS,PULLOVERS ETC	W 1155	30409		19837	W 834	20246	W 808	15795	CHANDAILS,PULL–OVERS ETC
846	UNDER GARMENTS KNITTED		15428		24540	W 2633	38044	W 2603	51790	SOUS VETS DE BONNETERIE
8462	— OF COTTON NON ELASTIC		10131		14788	W 2121	23323	W 2073	34794	SOUS–VET BONNET COTON
84629	—— OTHER		10131		14788	W 2121	23323	W 2073	34794	AUT SOUS–VET BONNET COTON
848	HEADGEAR,NONTXTL CLOTHNG		8846		16878	W 1564	27833		27485	VET ACCES MAT AUT QUE TEX
851	*FOOTWEAR		221892		133156	W 10976	147202	W 12070	171221	CHAUSSURES
85102	FOOTWEAR LEATHER		214617		117815	W 9006	131068	W 9993	151492	CHAUS SEMELLES EN CUIR
87	PRECISION INSTRUMNTS NES		57808		77513		110508		129582	INSTRUM,APPAR SCIENT NDA
872	MEDICAL INSTRUMENTS NES	W 725	20215		26270	W 800	33246	W 1020	47478	INSTR,APP MEDIC–CHIR NDA
87202	OTH MEDICAL INSTRUMENTS	W 662	19221		24121	W 677	28030	W 873	38204	INSTRUM,APP MEDECINE
874	MEASURNG,CONTROLNG INSTR		30208		43264		66478		68542	INSTRUMENTS DE MESURE
8743	GAS,LIQUID CONTROL INSTR	W 326	9786		18431	W 1056	25854	W 827	23630	APP,INSTR MESURE FLUIDES
88	PHOTO EQU,OPTICL GDS ETC		27921		30944		43579		58118	APP,FOURN PHOTO,OP,MONTR

4. General Imports C.I.F. by Commodities according to the S.I.T.C. (Rev. 2) in thousand U.S. Dollars
Importations Générales C.A.F. par Produits d'après la C.T.C.I. (Rév. 2) en milliers de Dollars E.U.

SITC CTCI	COMMODITY	1993 WEIGHT POIDS	1993 VALUE VALEUR	1994 WEIGHT POIDS	1994 VALUE VALEUR	1995 WEIGHT POIDS	1995 VALUE VALEUR	1996 WEIGHT POIDS	1996 VALUE VALEUR	PRODUIT
89	MISC MANUFCTRD GOODS NES		126134		156447		246369		264933	ART MANUFACTURES DIVERS
892	PRINTED MATTER		6634		11197		23474		23188	IMPRIMES
893	ARTICLES OF PLASTIC NES		34767		54489		100039		112342	OUVRAGES EN MAT DIVIS 58
8931	PLSTC PACKG CONTNRS,LIDS	W 3803	6780		11244	W 6257	18912	W 8281	24496	ART TRANSP EMBALLAGE ETC
8939	MISC PLASTIC ARTICLES		25006		39595	W 16264	74880	W 16841	79972	ART DIVERS EN MAT DIV 58
89399	OTHR PLASTC ARTICLES NES	W 5928	23788		36891	W 15079	70169	W 15354	74620	AUT OUV MAT DIV 58
894	TOYS,SPORTING GOODS,ETC		58437		46473	W 7538	54687		52655	VOITURES ENFANTS,JOUETS
8942	TOYS,INDOOR GAMES ETC	W 4908	55267		40471	W 6504	44457	W 6800	40325	JOUETS,JEUX ETC
89423	TOYS NES	W 4417	52581		30121	W 5183	33165	W 3520	24236	JOUETS,MODELES REDUITS
898	MUSICAL INSTRUMENTS,PTS		9564		14280		23086		26439	INSTRUMENTS DE MUSIQUE
899	OTHER MANUFACTURED GOODS		10010		17445		26017		28164	AUT ART MANUF DIVERS NDA
9	GOODS NOT CLASSD BY KIND		1860		503		432735		369030	ART TRANSACT NON CLASSES
931	*SPECIAL TRANSACTIONS	W 598	932		8	W 724372	431327	W 228957	367633	TRANS.SPECIALES

5. General Exports F.O.B. by Commodities according to the S.I.T.C. (Rev. 2) in thousand U.S. Dollars
Exportations Générales F.O.B. par Produits d'après la C.T.C.I. (Rév. 2) en milliers de Dollars E.U.

SITC CTCI	COMMODITY	1993		1994		1995		1996		PRODUIT
		WEIGHT POIDS	VALUE VALEUR	WEIGHT POIDS	VALUE VALEUR	WEIGHT POIDS	VALUE VALEUR	WEIGHT POIDS	VALUE VALEUR	
	ALL COMMODITIES		3903818		4260374		4632666		4511739	TOUS PRODUITS
0	FOOD AND LIVE ANIMALS		369198		400783		396069		411507	ALIMENTS,ANIMAUX VIVANTS
001	*LIVE ANIMALS FOR FOOD	W 6721	22390		5201	W 3481	5990	W 3961	6692	ANIMAUX VIVANTS
0015	EQUINE SPECIES, LIVE	W 1902	12698	W 2196	3550	W 2477	3819	W 3081	5069	CHEVAUX,ANES,MULETS
01	MEAT AND PREPARATIONS		49402		60680		50535		47469	VIANDES ET PREPARATIONS
011	MEAT FRESH,CHILLD,FROZEN		28154		31653	W 5757	19941	W 3698	12227	VIANDES FRAICHES,REF,CONGE
0111	BOVINE MEAT FRESH,FROZEN	W 2250	10294		18043	W 2187	11836	W 1374	7059	VIANDES BOVIN FRAI,REF
01111	BOVINE MEAT WITH BONE IN	W 2054	9505	W 3643	17264	W 2126	11661	W 1178	6620	VIANDES BOVIN NON DESOSS
0114	POULTRY FRESH CHLLD,FRZN	W 9231	16576	W 5795	11562	W 2444	5382	W 1244	2895	VOLAILLES MORTES
014	MEAT PREPD,PRSVD,NES ETC	W 7928	21057		28169	W 8178	29982	W 9892	33874	CONSERVES DE VIANDES
0149	OTH PREPARD,PRESRVD MEAT	W 7146	18575		22431	W 6694	23931	W 7817	26033	AUTRES PREP DE VIANDES
02	DAIRY PRODCTS,BIRDS'EGGS		10036		16170		18244		23579	PRODUITS LAITIERS,OEUFS
03	FISH AND PREPARATIONS		49254		50238		44702		48996	POISSONS ET PREPARATIONS
034	FISH,FRESH,CHILLED,FROZN		24902		25485	W 6163	20472	W 5886	19751	POISSON FRAIS, REFRIG,CONG
0341	FISH FRSH,CHLLD,EX FILLT	W 38178	24370		25345	W 6104	20314	W 5782	19515	POISSON FRAIS,REFRIGERE
037	FISH ETC PREPD,PRSVD NES	W 13061	18503		18943	W 8213	19766		22518	POIS,CRUST,MOL PREPARES
0371	FISH PREPARD,PRESRVD NES	W 13058	18472		18927	W 8212	19763	W 9804	22517	CONSERVES DE POISSONS
04	CEREALS AND PREPARATIONS		76982		68526		79238		69211	CEREALES ET PRODUITS
041	WHEAT ETC UNMILLED	W 9808	2491	W 28312	5427	W 226856	32283	W 138943	22010	FROMENT,EPEAUTRE
0412	OTHER WHEAT ETC UNMILLED	W 2605	786	W 17561	2303	W 221411	31168	W 125377	19517	AUTRE FROMENT NON MOULU
044	MAIZE UNMILLED	W 125123	23954	W 19522	11969	W 35526	11271	W 68829	14436	MAIS NON MOULU
046	WHEAT ETC MEAL OR FLOUR	W 21591	10343		22187	W 19875	5879	W 8049	2749	SEMOULE FARINE,FROMENT
04601	FLOUR OF WHEAT OR MESLIN	W 20847	10203		22106	W 19808	5805	W 7392	2386	FARINE DE FROMENT
048	CEREAL ETC PREPARATIONS		37187		26936	W 11195	28491	W 11180	28476	PREPTNS A BASE CEREALES
0484	BAKERY PRODUCTS	W 9905	25215		21393	W 8543	22512	W 8278	22189	PRODUITS DE BOULANGERIE
04842	PASTRY, CAKES ETC	W 7937	20401		16430	W 7125	18253	W 6841	18122	PATISSERIE ETC.
05	VEGETABLES AND FRUIT		39986		40012		41591		39508	LEGUMES ET FRUITS
054	VEG ETC FRSH,SMPLY PRSVD		13306		11572	W 16092	10110		10644	LEGUMES FRAIS,CONG,SECS
058	FRUIT PRESERVED,PREPARED		16160		16157		13643		12078	CONSERVES DE FRUITS
07	COFFEE,TEA,COCOA,SPICES		24725		29701		34339		30693	CAFE,THE,CACAO,EPICES
073	CHOCOLATE AND PRODUCTS	W 4017	17301		18576	W 4529	20415	W 4512	20954	CHOCOLAT
081	*FEEDING STUFF FOR ANIML	W 58896	10445		20917	W 83235	14514		15362	NOURRITURE POUR ANIMAUX
0819	FOOD WASTE AND FEED NES	W 22883	4391		17493	W 61259	11543	W 47450	11984	DECHETS,ALIMENTS NDA
08199	FODDER NES,INCL SWEETNED	W 12085	3370		15538	W 16389	6578	W 16177	8442	PREPARATIONS FOURRAGERES
09	MISC EDIBLE PRODUCTS		77560		100937		99115		117729	PREP ALIMENTAIRES DIVERSES
098	EDIBLE PRODCTS,PREPS NES		69956		94494	W 37533	94790	W 43465	112951	PREP ALIMENTAIRES NDA
09804	SAUCES,MIXED SEASONINGS	W 15842	43535		60027	W 23194	59726	W 27666	72229	SAUCES,ASSAISONNEMENTS
09809	MISC FOOD PREPRTIONS NES		15561		20666	W 5606	18001	W 6579	20736	PREP ALIMENTAIRES NDA
1	BEVERAGES AND TOBACCO		100770		68430		90010		91555	BOISSONS ET TABACS
11	BEVERAGES		56740		39962		67646		74313	BOISSONS
111	NON-ALCOHL BEVERAGES NES	W 27838	2880		5446	W 23472	10175	W 39202	14817	BOISSONS NON ALCOOLIQUES
112	ALCOHOLIC BEVERAGES	W 74714	53859		34517	W 61600	57471		59496	BOISSONS ALCOOLIQUES
1121	WINE OF FRESH GRAPES ETC	W 39422	20981		12091	W 24907	25997	W 27066	17665	VINS DE RAISINS FRAIS
11212	WINE OF FRESH GRAPES	W 29182	18517		9376	W 19294	23888	W 21664	15380	VINS DE MOUTS DE RAISINS
1123	BEER,ALE,STOUT,PORTER	W 22770	8133		8835	W 24747	12284	W 39552	19198	BIERES
1124	DISTILLED ALCOHOLIC BEVS	W 12463	24628		13585	W 11930	19180		22598	ALCOOLS,EAUX-DE-VIE
11242	DISTILLD WINE,GRAPE MARC	W 8100	16540		9950	W 8429	14154	W 9358	17091	EAUX-DE-VIE NATURELLES
12	TOBACCO AND MANUFACTURES		44030		28467		22365		17242	TABACS BRUTS FABRIQUES
121	TOBACCO UNMNFCTRD,REFUSE	W 3341	5836	W 8223	14364	W 3471	4288	W 4179	4850	TABACS BRUTS,DECHETS
122	TOBACCO,MANUFACTURED	W 9081	38194	W 1639	14103	W 2011	18076	W 1476	12393	TABACS FABRIQUES
1222	CIGARETTES	W 9079	38191	W 1609	14048	W 1627	17894	W 1035	11983	CIGARETTES
2	CRUDE MATERLS,EXCL FUELS		237774		214067		250397		247404	MAT BRUTES NON COMESTIBLES
21	HIDES,SKINS,FURS UNDRSSD		2893		6230		9729		14446	CUIRS,PEAUX BRUTS
211	HIDES,SKINS,EXC FURS,RAW	W 1843	2893		6166	W 4557	9726	W 7013	14440	CUIRS ET PEAUX
24	CORK AND WOOD		168118		143750		160869		166333	LIEGE ET BOIS
247	OTH WOOD ROUGH,SQUARED	W 101763	8191		17836	W 189363	24167	W 194670	22362	BOIS BRUTS EQUARRIS
2472	SAW-,VENEER-LOGS NON-CON	W 99423	7900	W 134330	16913	W 171879	22805	W 192842	22074	NON CONIFERES SCIAGE,PLAC
24721	— IN THE ROUGH	W 99423	7900	W 134330	16913	W 171879	22805	W 192842	22074	BRUTS ECORCES DEGROSSIS
248	WOOD SHAPED,SLEEPERS	W 412201	154893		121905	W 294184	133797	W 292260	140663	BOIS SIMPLEMENT TRAVAILLES
2483	LUMBER SHAPED NON-CONIFR	W 406230	152967	W 304909	120223	W 291486	132706	W 290277	140013	NON CONIFERES SCIES,RABOTES
24831	LUMBER SAWN ETC NON-CON	W 393025	137023	W 289634	101461	W 281404	117590	W 279507	124513	SCIES LONGITUDINALEMENT
24832	LUMBER PLANED ETC NONCON	W 13205	15944	W 15275	18763	W 10082	15116	W 10770	15500	RABOTES,RAINES,LANGUETES
251	*PULP AND WASTE PAPER	W 55949	24421	W 44571	10998	W 50810	17126	W 48113	12971	PATES A PAPIER,DECHETS
2512	MECHANICAL WOOD PULP	W 42469	23286	W 32717	9583	W 36750	13941	W 36406	11269	PATES MECANIQUES DE BOIS
27	CRUDE FERTLZR,MINRLS NES		12428		12705		13410		13388	ENGRAIS MINERAUX BRUTS
28	METALLIFEROUS ORES,SCRAP		9696		20397		21643		19522	MINERAIS METAL,DECHETS
282	IRON AND STEEL SCRAP	W 45354	3463	W 59584	13313	W 100206	9573	W 106093	9036	FERRAILLES
29	CRUDE ANIMAL,VEG MAT NES		13080		12181		17184		15834	MATIERES BRUTES ANIM,VEGET
3	MINERAL FUELS ETC		377689		386628		396505		416460	COMBUSTIBLES MINERAUX LUB
32	COAL,COKE AND BRIQUETTES		36780		23222		767		125	HOUILLES,COKES,BRIQUETTES
323	BRIQUETS,COKE,SEMI-COKE		36620		23110	W 7232	742		51	BRIQUETTES
3232	COKE,SEMI-COKE,RTRT CRBN	W 354855	36620		23109	W 7227	739	W 710	50	COKES ET SEMI-COKES
33	PETROLEUM AND PRODUCTS		322957		343791		371991		371166	PETROLE ET DERIVES
333	CRUDE PETROLEUM	W 85709	10042	W 46761	5820	W 123039	15788	W 117526	17699	HUILES BRUTES DE PETROLE
334	PETROLEUM PRODUCTS,REFIN	W 1986141	299158		320261	W 1978659	335915		331270	PRODUITS RAFFINES
3341	GASOLINE,OTH LIGHT OILS	W 718339	125617		146484	W 964533	160869	W 692470	140373	ESSENCES POUR MOTEURS
33411	MOTOR,AVIATION SPIRIT				109763	W 607424	103048	W 457794	103883	ESSENCES MOTEURS D'AVIONS
33419	OTH LIGHT PETROLEUM OILS				36721	W 357109	57821	W 234676	36490	AUTRES HUILES LEGERES
3342	KEROSENE,OTH MEDIUM OILS	W 294294	44565		23758	W 133139	20418		42975	PETR LAMPANTS,AUT HUIL
33429	OTH MEDIUM PETROLEUM OIL			W 157717	23758	W 133125	20406	W 233467	42975	AUTRES HUILES MOYENNES
3343	GAS OILS	W 339596	57354	W 435577	80057	W 533479	85124	W 468508	97854	GAS OILS
3344	FUEL OILS,NES	W 362759	45279	W 433443	43963	W 289062	33046	W 142694	19951	FUEL OILS
3345	LUBS,PETROLEUM OILS NES	W 271153	26342		25998	W 58446	36458	W 50986	30116	HUILES LUBRIFIANTES
33451	LUBS(HIGH PETR CONT) ETC	W 270962	25973		25715	W 54287	30608	W 50851	29689	HUILES LUBRIF,H LOURDES
335	RESIDUAL PETRLM PROD NES		13757		17711		20288	W 157910	22197	PRODUITS RESIDUELS NDA
3354	PETROLM BITUMEN,COKE ETC	W 104537	8552		12832	W 177453	15275	W 146977	17109	BITUME,COKE DE PETROLE
33541	PETROLEUM BITUMEN, ETC	W 95461	7698	W 132234	10722	W 104265	11294	W 116195	14531	BITUME DE PETROLE
341	*GAS,NATURAL AND MANUFCT	W 137830	17953		16440		22221		28369	GAZ NATUREL,GAZ MANUFACT
3413	PETROLM GASES,LIQUEFIED	W 137829	17947		16437	W 161768	22199	W 149377	28368	GAZ DE PETROLE LIQUEFIE
34131	LIQUEFIED PROPANE,BUTANE	W 50468	7065	W 50006	6456	W 60374	8454	W 66152	13587	PROPANE,BUTANE LIQUEFIES
34139	OTH HYDROCARBON GAS LQFD	W 87361	10882		9981	W 101394	13745	W 83225	14781	HYDROCARBURES GAZEUX NDA
351	*ELECTRIC CURRENT				3174		1525		16800	ENERGIE ELECTRIQUE
5	CHEMCLS,RELATED PROD NES		549442		526316		784797		626089	PRODUITS CHIMIQUES
51	ORGANIC CHEMICALS		60733		42881		53201		43652	PROD CHIMIQ ORGANIQUES
511	HYDROCARBONS NES,DERIVS		27033		19099	W 58977	27482		20072	HYDROCARBURES NDA
5112	CYCLIC HYDROCARBONS	W 16415	4110		7	W 38603	13934		13548	HYDROCARBURES CYCLIQUES
5113	HALOG DERIV OF HYDROCARB		20510		18758	W 19913	13109	W 16163	6165	DERIVES HALOGENES HYDROCAR
51131	VINYL CHLORIDE	W 57745	20493	W 47780	18725	W 19877	13008	W 16145	6120	CHLORURE DE VINYLE
515	ORG-INORG COMPOUNDS ETC		13289		11791		11318		10642	COMPOSES ORGANO-MINERAUX
5157	SULPHONAMIDES,ETC	W 312	12286		9099	W 258	8957	W 234	9079	SULFAMIDES,SULTONES ETC
51571	SULPHONAMIDES	W 312	12286		9099	W 258	8957	W 234	9079	SULFAMIDES

5. General Exports F.O.B. by Commodities according to the S.I.T.C. (Rev. 2) in thousand U.S. Dollars
Exportations Générales F.O.B. par Produits d'après la C.T.C.I. (Rév. 2) en milliers de Dollars E.U.

SITC CTCI	COMMODITY	1993 WEIGHT POIDS	1993 VALUE VALEUR	1994 WEIGHT POIDS	1994 VALUE VALEUR	1995 WEIGHT POIDS	1995 VALUE VALEUR	1996 WEIGHT POIDS	1996 VALUE VALEUR	PRODUIT
52	INORGANIC CHEMICALS		79889		12639		21936		17162	PROD CHIM INORGANIQUES
522	INORG ELEMNTS,OXIDES,ETC		77676		11626		21244		16409	ELEMENTS INORGANIQUES
5221	CHEMICAL ELEMENTS		76270		10550		20414		15546	ELEMENTS CHIMIQUES
52218	CARBON NES, CARBON BLACK	W 183550	75124	W 21081	9731	W 26738	14904	W 25723	14845	CARBONE NDA
53	DYES,TANNING,COLOUR PROD		15478		13733		18118		22448	PROD TEINTURE,COLORANTS
533	PIGMENTS,PAINTS,ETC		14485		13000	W 11427	17399	W 16443	21798	PIGMENTS,PEINTURES,VERNIS
541	*MEDICINAL,PHARM PRODUCT		99664		133365		137167		139368	PROD MEDICINAUX PHARMACEUT
5411	PROVITAMINS AND VITAMINS		15896		16939	K 1423000	15702	K 616286	5808	PROVITAMINES,VITAMINES
5413	ANTIBIOTICS IN BULK		17460		16867		33106		56517	ANTIBIOTIQUES NDA
54139	OTHER ANTIBIOTICS	K 37000	13799		10878	K 49000	27679	K 90110	51804	AUTRES ANTIBIOTIQUES
5417	MEDICAMENTS		54456		86965	K 2253000	73382	K 2212363	65342	MEDICAMENTS
54171	— CONTAINNG ANTIBIOTICS		12735		31712	K 533000	30322	K 479903	26280	MED CONTN ANTIBIOTIQUES
54179	— CONTNG OTH SUBSTANCES	K 1472000	37600		47874	K 1663000	37375	K 1648718	34663	MED CONT AUT SUBSTANCES
55	PERFUME,CLEANING ETC PRD		26885		20068		18351		20995	PROD POUR PARFUM,TOILETTE
554	SOAP,CLEANSING ETC PREPS		18584		11883	W 9749	11109	W 10634	13262	SAVONS,PRODUITS DETERSIFS
5542	WASHING PREPARATIONS ETC	W 9646	18044		10972	W 9313	10090	W 9629	11646	PROD ORG TENSIO–ACT NDA
562	*FERTILIZERS,MANUFACTURE		77240		86189		112198		118144	ENGRAIS MANUFACTURES
5621	CHEM NITROGENOUS FERTLZR		33130		38250		60586	W 415610	67013	ENGRAIS AZOTES
56216	UREA	W 216710	19369	W 232338	22502	W 234984	38038	W 269295	47403	UREE
56219	CHEM NITROG FERTILZR NES	W 132782	11755		13948	W 161986	20935	W 142415	18643	ENGRAIS AZOTES NDA
5629	FERTILIZERS NES		44019		47937	W 324853	51594	W 282296	51122	ENGRAIS NDA
56291	NIT–PHOS–POT FERTLZR NES	W 265605	43586	W 365850	47811	W 323840	51236	W 282133	51029	ENGRAIS CONT N P K
58	PLASTIC MATERIALS ETC		156851		190477		387561		226145	MAT PLAST ARTIFICIELLES
583	POLYMERIZATION ETC PRODS		146008		184898		373376		217678	PROD POLYMERISATION
5831	POLYETHYLENE		79480		78605	W 125891	142816		98588	POLYETHYLENE
58311	— IN PRIMARY FORMS	W 122331	74035	W 104664	75354	W 124285	138542	W 126135	94656	POLYETHYLENE PRIMAIRES
5833	POLYSTYRENE,ITS COPOLYMR	W 86495	43200	W 61811	49752		138900	W 56166	82368	POLYPROPYLENE COPOLYMERES
58331	— IN PRIMARY FORMS	W 86474	43158	W 61776	49715	W 48854	138878	W 56127	82264	SOUS FORMES PRIMAIRES
5834	POLYVINYL CHLORIDE	W 33136	19757		51399	W 83328	85008	W 41980	29676	CHLORURE DE POLYVINYLE
58341	— IN PRIMARY FORMS	W 31122	15831		45896	W 79818	68977	W 38598	22906	SOUS FORMES PRIMAIRES
58343	— PLATES,STRIP,ETC NES	W 1711	3250		4797	W 3135	14883	W 2982	5865	SOUS FORME DE PLAQUES
59	CHEMICAL MATERIALS NES		32672		26774		35788		37513	MAT PROD CHIMIQUES NDA
591	PESTICIDES,DISINFECTANTS	W 2074	13840		10398	W 2417	12808	W 3054	14021	DESINF,INSECT,FONG,HERB
598	MISCEL CHEM PRODUCTS NES		17665		15159		21376		21773	PROD DIV INDUST CHIM NDA
5989	CHEM PRODUCTS,PREPS NES		15566		13798		20675		19447	PROD PREP CHIMIQUES NDA
6	BASIC MANUFACTURES		611231		762243		760692		684701	ART MANUFACTURES
61	LEATHER,DRESSED FUR,ETC		91595		128217		100815		96307	CUIRS,PELLETERIES
611	LEATHER		13968		21043		12871		9414	CUIRS,PEAUX PREPARES
6114	LEATHR BOVINE NES,EQUINE	W 156461	8363		16928	W 1689	11119	W 966	7620	CUIRS DE BOVINS
612	LEATHER ETC MANUFACTURES		77626		106897		87869		86646	OUVRAGES EN CUIRS NDA
6123	PREPRD PARTS OF FOOTWEAR	W 5678	77547		106830	W 2610	87786	W 2808	86580	PARTIES DE CHAUSSURES
62	RUBBER MANUFACTURES NES		10647		12994		9112		9384	CAOUTCHOUC MANUFACTURE
63	WOOD,CORK MANUFACTRS NES		52502		67844		67668		57520	OUVRAGES LIEGE ET BOIS
634	VENEERS,PLYWOOD,ETC	W 19744	22487		37021	W 18175	31644	W 16559	27933	PLACAGES,CONTRE–PLAQUES
6341	VENEER SHEETS ETC	W 9955	14252		28945	W 9347	21494	W 7933	18139	BOIS SIMPLEMENT SCIES
635	WOOD MANUFACTURES NES	W 42379	29966		30811	W 21779	36005	W 16222	29552	ART MANUF EN BOIS NDA
6353	BUILDERS WOODWRK,PREFABS	W 37055	26298		26958	W 14917	31208	W 12100	25759	OUVRAGES DE MENUISERIE
64	PAPER,PAPERBOARD AND MFR		80404		97623		107537		62330	PAPIERS,CARTONS & OUVRAGES
641	PAPER AND PAPERBOARD		35702		62992	W 111748	65410	W 82107	30932	PAPIERS ET CARTONS
6415	PAPER,PAPERBRD,BULK,NES		26586		53577	W 105107	56864	W 78453	25546	PAPIERS,CARTONS ROULEAUX
64151	SEMI–CHEM FLUTING PAPER	W 85580	20227	W 106860	35312	W 92683	50558	W 64646	19884	PAPIER FLUTING
64159	OTHER PAPER ETC,BULK,NES		6278		18191	W 12363	6124	W 13746	5526	AUT PAPIER ROULEAUX FEUILLES
642	PAPER,ETC,PRECUT,ARTS OF		44701		34631		42127		31398	PAP,CARTONS DECOUPES
6421	PAPER ETC CONTAINERS	W 32054	19828		15085	W 9897	16617	W 9797	15146	BOITES,SACS EMBALLAGES
6424	PAPER ETC CT TO SIZE NES	W 7372	15368		13436	W 6841	14534	W 1923	4389	PAP,CARTONS DECOUPES
64241	CIGARETTE PAPER PRECUT	W 7051	14712		12778	W 6415	13825	W 1502	3810	PAPIER A CIGARETTES
65	TEXTILE YARN,FABRICS,ETC		95368		129222		123893		110336	FILS,TISSUS,ARTICLES TEXTILE
651	TEXTILE YARN		26928		45432		35878		25209	FILS TEXTILES
6513	COTTON YARN	W 1957	11315		15512	W 2315	18157	W 1542	15285	FILS DE COTON
6514	SYN FIB YRN,BULK,MONOFIL		6898		15989	W 2254	7929		5872	FILS CONT 85% FIB TEXT SYNTH
652	COTTON FABRICS,WOVEN		11145		13730		13476		9102	TISSUS DE COTON
653	WOVN MAN–MADE FIB FABRIC		13743		14874	W 1337	13387		13495	TISSUS FIBRES SYNTH,ARTIF
654	OTH WOVEN TEXTILE FABRIC		9228		12868		17064		20664	TISSUS AUT COTON SYNT,ARTIF
657	SPECIAL TXTL FABRC,PRODS		10149		13206		16231		16380	TISSUS SPECIAUX
658	TEXTILE ARTICLES NES		20718		25632	W 2641	23548		20405	ART FACONNES MAT TEXTILES
6584	LINENS ETC	W 1741	14120		19503	W 1453	14201	W 1118	12681	LINGE DE MAISON
66	NONMETAL MINERAL MFS NES		102304		125759		126297		135721	ART MIN NON METALLIQUES
661	LIME,CEMENT,BLDG PRODS	W 772994	34689		44325	W 638249	37831	W 411089	35168	CHAUX,CIMENTS MAT CONSTR
6612	CEMENT	W 742417	29998		37906	W 613559	31257	W 372043	25916	CIMENTS HYDRAULIQUES
662	CLAY,REFRACTORY BLDG PRD	W 130216	18053		25184	W 120035	17299	W 125966	19497	MAT CONST REFRACTAIRES
6624	BRICKS ETC NONREFRACTORY	W 117308	17366		24516	W 110116	16644	W 123854	18931	BRIQUES ETC CERAM NON REFR
66245	GLAZED CERAMIC SETTS ETC	W 24925	13415		13024	W 22433	10470	W 21335	8381	AUT CARREAUX CERAMIQUE
663	MINERAL MANUFCTURES NES		11651		13305		15950		20242	ART MIN MANUF NDA
665	GLASSWARE		31495		34108	W 105461	44067		36525	OUVRAGES EN VERRE
6651	BOTTLES ETC OF GLASS	W 93923	21376		25650	W 104086	35050	W 75575	29636	RECIPIENTS EN VERRE
66511	GLASS BOTTLES ETC NONVAC	W 93923	21376	W 92713	25646	W 104086	35050	W 75575	29636	BONBONNES,BOUTEILLES,ETC
666	POTTERY		4527		4921	W 2499	6535	W 2568	15228	POTERIE
6664	PORCELN,CHINA HOUSE WARE	W 1456	3366		4372	W 1694	5240	W 1638	14001	VAISSELLE,ARTS MEN PORC
67	IRON AND STEEL		70858		73216		62680		54168	FER ET ACIER
671	PIG IRON ETC		12362		24714		21227		8083	FONTE,SPIEGEL,POUDRES
6716	FERRO–ALLOYS		12345		24701		21169		8039	FERRO–ALLIAGES
67169	OTHER FERRO–ALLOYS		12345	W 27556	23965	W 27655	21168	W 12608	8038	AUTRES FERRO–ALLIAGES
678	IRON,STL TUBES,PIPES,ETC		46343		39833	W 39582	31756	W 34874	31245	TUBES,TUYAUX EN FONTE,FER
6782	IRON,STL SEAMLESS TUBES		18216		9139	W 8035	6135	W 13763	9975	TUBES,TUYAUX SANS SOUDURE
6783	IRON,STL TUBES,PIPES NES		16717		20882	W 27502	14306	W 16310	10983	AUT TUBES,TUYAUX FER,ACIER
68	NON–FERROUS METALS		40681		50387		73261		65476	METAUX NON FERREUX
684	ALUMINIUM	W 20130	37985		47870	W 21480	70473	W 24245	62002	ALUMINIUM
6842	ALUMINIUM,ALLOYS WORKED	W 18274	35874		45375	W 20749	69145	W 21367	58008	ALUMINIUM,ALLIAGES OUVRE
68422	ALUMNM PLATE,SHEET,STRIP	W 10845	17994		21824	W 11950	35639	W 12067	29514	TOLES, PLANCHES EN ALU
68423	ALUMINIUM FOIL	W 3518	9843		12253	W 4417	17681	W 5300	17044	FEUILLES,BANDES MINCES AL
69	METAL MANUFACTURES NES		66873		76981		89429		93459	ART MANUFACT EN METAL NDA
691	STRUCTURES AND PARTS NES	W 17996	13481		25476	W 11356	22351	W 11467	20654	CONSTRUCT FER,ACIER,ALU
6911	STRUCTURES,PARTS IRN,STL	W 17421	8145		20033	W 10843	16470	W 10837	15455	CONSTRUCT FER,ACIER,FONTE
699	BASE METAL MFRS NES		21011		23939		34991		37830	ART MANUFACTURES MET NDA
6997	IRON,STEEL ARTICLES NES	W 5969	9800		11227	W 6583	16359	W 7345	17024	OUV FONTE,FER,ACIER NDA
69979	IRN,STL MANUFACTURES NES	W 5298	9116		10566	W 6190	15629	W 7111	16582	AUT OUVRAGES EN FER NDA
7	MACHINES,TRANSPORT EQUIP		552683		731376		777066		963438	MACHINES MATERIEL TRANSPORT
71	POWER GENERATING EQUIPMT		53903		66640		60805		58229	MACHINES GENERATRICES
713	INTRNL COMBUS PSTN ENGIN		7401		15740		13042		10022	MOTEURS EXPL COMB INT, PIECE
714	ENGINES AND MOTORS NES	W 1135	13158		15798	W 2029	15077		19445	MOTEURS NON ELECTRIQUES
7149	ENGINE & MOTOR PARTS NES	W 1135	13158		15791	W 2029	15077		19445	PIECES 714 ET 718.88

5. General Exports F.O.B. by Commodities according to the S.I.T.C. (Rev. 2) in thousand U.S. Dollars
Exportations Générales F.O.B. par Produits d'après la C.T.C.I. (Rév. 2) en milliers de Dollars E.U.

SITC CTCI	COMMODITY	1993 WEIGHT POIDS	1993 VALUE VALEUR	1994 WEIGHT POIDS	1994 VALUE VALEUR	1995 WEIGHT POIDS	1995 VALUE VALEUR	1996 WEIGHT POIDS	1996 VALUE VALEUR	PRODUIT
71499	PARTS NES,OF 71488,71888	W 1135	13158		15791	W 2029	15077	W 2223	19010	PIECES 714.88 ET 718.88
716	ROTATING ELECTRIC PLANT		18542		19937		18342		19453	APP ELECTR ROTATIFS,PIECES
7162	AC MTRS,GENRTRS,GEN SETS	W 4287	16008		15962	W 2869	14755	W 2846	15441	MOTEURS ELECTRIQUES
72	MACHS FOR SPCL INDUSTRYS		28515		40358		37428		45525	MAC SPECIALES POUR INDUST
728	OTH MACHY FOR SPCL INDUS		11013		27764	W 10111	20822		26183	AUT MACH IND PARTICULIERES
7284	MACHY FOR SPCL INDUS NES		8804		26011	W 8181	17204		20798	MACH SPEC IND PARTICUL.
72848	OTH MCHY WITH INDIV FNCT	W 3721	4353		22872	W 6935	12881	W 8604	14318	AUTRES MACHINES NDA
73	METALWORKING MACHINERY		16799		14072		27623		23027	MACH TRAVAIL DES METAUX
736	METALWORKING MACH-TOOLS		14451		11119		18658		19882	MACH-OUTILS TRAVAIL METAUX
74	GENRL INDUSTRL MACHY NES		42555		48179		60191		59772	MACH APP INDUSTRIE
744	MECHANICAL HANDLING EQU		10248		14303		20787		17293	EQUIP MANUTENTION PIECES
749	NONELEC MACH PTS,ACC NES		13944		15303	W 4583	16750		19323	PIECES MACH NON ELEC NDA
76	TELECOMM,SOUND EQUIPMENT		48922		47530		57201		80135	EQUIPMENT DE TELECOM
764	TELECOM EQPT,PTS,ACC NES		48785		47432		56963		79875	EQUIP TELECOM,PIECES
7641	LINE TELEPHONE,ETC EQUIP		29620		19533	W 459	23887	W 902	21054	APP TELEPHON PAR FIL
7649	PTS NES OF EQUIPMT OF 76		18877		26177		32357		54932	PIECES DE LA DIV 76
76491	PTS NES OF APPAR OF 7641	W 346	18127		25521	W 451	31205	W 655	54040	PIECES POUR 764.1
77	ELECTRIC MACHNRY NES ETC		143354		171816		211120		219058	MACH APP ELECT NDA
771	ELECTRIC POWER MACHY NES	W 4856	25569		35944	W 6561	48907	W 7954	52493	MACH PROD,TRANS ELECTR
7711	TRANSFORMERS,ELECTRICAL	W 2270	14198		25887	W 5366	41885	W 7235	46611	TRANSFO ELECTRIQUES
77111	LIQUID DIELEC TRANSFRMRS	W 2040	9306		17082	W 4853	29147	W 6739	34610	TRANSFO DIELEC LIQUIDE
772	SWITCHGEAR ETC,PARTS NES		45799		55040	W 4600	75638		78779	APP COUPURE,SECT ETC
7721	SWITCHGEAR ETC		40107		49021	W 4570	68088	W 4902	70569	APP COUPURE,SECTIONMNT
773	ELECTR DISTRIBUTNG EQUIP		43343		52357	W 8788	52586	W 9285	53046	EQUIPMT DISTRIBUTION ELECT
7731	INSULATED WIRE,CABLE ETC	W 5913	42771		51718	W 8688	51724	W 9154	51902	FILS,CABLES ISOLES ELECT
775	HOUSEHOLD TYPE EQUIP NES		14253		15617		16885		17370	MACH,APP USAGE DOMESTQUE
7758	ELECTRO-THERMIC APPL NES		13862		15198		16516		16822	APP ELECTROTHERMIQ NDA
778	ELECTRICAL MACHINERY NES		13416		11740		15293		15235	AUTRES MACH ELECT NDA
78	ROAD VEHICLES		53398		36221		57595		61606	VEHICULES ROUTIERS
784	MOTOR VEH PRTS,ACCES NES		50638		29578	W 7653	49109	W 7890	53586	PIECES 722,781,782,783
7841	MOTOR VEHICLE CHASSIS	W 2500	28356			W 7	37	W 9	60	CHASSIS 722,781,782,783
7849	OTHER MOTOR VEHCL PARTS		21618		29016	W 7614	48984	W 7716	52915	PIECES 722,781,782,783
79	OTHR TRANSPORT EQUIPMENT		164220		304293		261466		410406	AUTRE MATERIEL TRANSPORT
793	SHIPS AND BOATS ETC		162342		302791	W 184248	260386	W 226668	409640	NAVIRES BATEAUX,ETC
7932	SHIPS AND BOATS NES	W 74894	160989		301519	W 183335	258100	W 226554	408052	NAVIRES ET BATEAUX
79322	TANKERS OF ALL KINDS	W 24358	37282		62118	W 119897	225937	W 90014	296630	BATEAUX-CITERNES
79323	OTHER CARGO VESSELS	W 50371	122310		237998	W 63251	30664	W 136352	110030	AUT BATEAUX TRANS MARCH
8	MISC MANUFACTURED GOODS		1099841		1165032		1166083		1059761	ART MANUFACTURES DIVERS
812	*PLUMBG,HEATNG,LGHTNG EQ		15955		16210	W 5974	17464	W 5162	15259	APPAR SANITAIRES CHAUFFAGE
821	*FURNITURE,PARTS THEREOF		148076		138368	W 45133	151581	W 38149	120173	MEUBLES ET PIECES
8211	CHAIRS,SEATS AND PARTS		73106		66008	W 17960	71497	W 15906	55725	SIEGES ET PIECES
82111	CHAIRS AND OTHER SEATS		66020		57556	W 14272	63964	W 12925	49870	SIEGES
8219	FURNITURE AND PARTS NES	W 1933778	71097		68933	W 26113	76410	W 21191	60356	AUTRES MEUBLES ET PIECES
82192	WOOD FURNITURE NES	W 1923953	50697		50398	W 16302	46078	W 12530	37195	MEUBLES NDA EN BOIS
82199	OTHR FURN,FURN PARTS NES	W 9688	19825		17722	W 9158	28278	W 8117	21041	MEUBLES NDA AUTRES MATIERES
84	CLOTHING AND ACCESSORIES		644438		629041		672881		632687	VETEMENTS
842	MENS OUTERWEAR NOT KNIT	W 414130	244128		227109	W 5152	241827	W 5202	236259	VET DESSUS POUR HOMMES
8421	— OVERCOATS,OTHER COATS	W 439	19964		16674	W 255	12826	W 207	10677	MANTEAUX HOMMES MAT TEXT
84211	—— OF WOOL,FINE HAIR	W 264	12939		10685	W 158	7537	W 156	7325	MANTEAUX HOMMES DE LAINE
8422	— SUITS	W 805	31993		33767	W 554	35277	W 708	37660	COMPLETS HOMMES MAT TEXT
84221	—— OF WOOL,FINE HAIR	W 383	16660		18199	W 273	19475	W 364	21050	COMPLETS HOMMES LAINE
84223	—— OF MAN-MADE FIBRES	W 422	15332		15568	W 281	15802	W 344	16610	COMPLETS HOMMES FIB SYNT
8423	— TROUSERS,BREECHES ETC	W 2136	58291		57913	W 1974	56761	W 1996	52806	PANTALONS HOMMES MAT TEX
8424	— JACKETS,BLAZERS ETC	W 410483	118454		108211	W 2035	119576	W 1945	115584	VESTES HOMMES MAT TEXTIL
8429	— OTHER OUTER GARMENTS	W 267	15426		10543	W 334	17387	W 347	19531	AUT VET DES HOM MAT TEX
843	WOMENS OUTERWEAR NONKNIT		236216		192190	W 4011	215193	W 3779	190068	VET DESSUS FEMMES MAT TEX
8431	— COATS AND JACKETS	W 381813	87943		72378	W 1455	80972	W 1289	70303	MANT,VEST FEM MAT TEXTIL
8433	— DRESSES	W 245	12026		9751	W 259	16280	W 291	16431	ROBES EN MAT-TEXTILES
8434	— SKIRTS	W 3538	34494		26607	W 552	29244	W 450	23658	JUPES EN MAT TEXTILES
8435	— BLOUSES	W 3325	25397		23817	W 404	22244	W 307	16754	BLOUSES FEM MAT TEXTILES
8439	— OTHER OUTER GARMENTS		68233		54090	W 1195	57436	W 1296	54316	AUT VET DES FEM MAT TEXT
844	UNDER GARMENTS NOT KNIT	W 1100	30923		28487	W 1121	34392	W 780	23850	VETEMENT DESSOUS MAT TEX
8441	— MENS SHIRTS	W 917	25421		24750	W 814	30245	W 614	20507	CHEMISES HOMMES MAT TEXT
84411	—— OF COTTON	W 623	19304		17607	W 495	20878	W 406	16637	CHEMISES HOMMES DE COTON
845	OUTERWEAR KNIT NONELASTC	W 5236	65601		67163	W 2446	61125	W 2491	66008	VET DESSOUS,ACCES BONNET
8451	— JERSEYS,PULLOVERS ETC	W 977	23367		33833	W 1469	29879	W 1524	34541	CHANDAILS,PULL-OVERS ETC
8459	— OTHER,CLTHG ACCESRYS	W 4178	39574		30926	W 854	26994	W 835	26828	AUT VET DESSUS DE BONNE
846	UNDER GARMENTS KNITTED	W 5992	51429		77761	W 2820	95490		94900	SOUS VETS DE BONNETERIE
8462	— OF COTTON NON ELASTIC	W 5623	43071		60955	W 2430	58958	W 2993	64756	SOUS-VET BONNET COTON
84629	—— OTHER	W 5623	43071		60955	W 2430	58958	W 2993	64756	AUT SOUS-VET BONNET COTON
8463	— OF SYNTH FBR NONELAST	W 359	7434		5954	W 317	6345		20673	SOUS-VET BONNET FIB SYNT
84631	—— PANTY HOSE (TIGHTS)	W 290	5354		5161	W 309	6018		20154	COLLANTS BON FIBR SYNT
8465	CORSETS,GARTERS,ETC	W 10	925		10852	W 73	30187	W 101	9472	CORSETS,GAINES ART SIM
84651	BRASSIERES	W 4	484		5617	W 47	28459	W 78	7774	SOUTIENS-GORGE,BUSTIERS
848	HEADGEAR,NONTXTL CLOTHNG		10930		31070		18521		17016	VET ACCES MAT AUT QUE TEX
8481	LEATHER CLOTHES,ACCESSOR		7667		26192	W 104	13994	W 135	10631	VET ACCES MAT CUIR ARTIF
851	*FOOTWEAR	W 8345	147453		171692	W 6627	145912	W 6193	148612	CHAUSSURES
85102	FOOTWEAR LEATHER	W 7096	139988		161480	W 5532	135384	W 5423	141906	CHAUS SEMELLES EN CUIR
87	PRECISION INSTRUMNTS NES		13157		17012		28072		21783	INSTRUM,APPAR SCIENT NDA
874	MEASURNG,CONTROLNG INSTR		9413		13464		23712		17896	INSTRUMENTS DE MESURE
8743	GAS,LIQUID CONTROL INSTR		7106		11575	W 813	20509	W 562	15730	APP,INSTR MESURE FLUIDES
88	PHOTO EQU,OPTICL GDS ETC		12377		23087		13998		12135	APP,FOURN PHOTO,OP,MONTR
885	WATCHES AND CLOCKS		8483		19867		8425		5240	HORLOGERIE
8852	CLOCKS,CLOCK,WATCH PARTS		8434		19838		8386		5178	HORLOGES,MOUV,PARTIES
88524	TIME SWITCHES		8338		19661		8137		5107	APP DECLENC MECANISME
89	MISC MANUFCTRD GOODS NES		116154		166245		129990		103553	ART MANUFACTURES DIVERS
892	PRINTED MATTER		5150		31814		10226		8890	IMPRIMES
8928	PRINTED MATTER NES		1466		26195		3548		3994	IMPRIMES NDA
89283	UNISSUED BANKNOTES ETC		18		23999		40	W 23	479	TIMBRES-POSTE FISCAUX
893	ARTICLES OF PLASTIC NES	W 21524	42105		68692	W 19138	48844	W 18272	43120	OUVRAGES EN MAT DIVIS 58
8931	PLSTC PACKG CONTNRS,LIDS	W 13475	15656		39742	W 8245	12559	W 8242	11834	ART TRANSP EMBALLAGE ETC
8939	MISC PLASTIC ARTICLES	W 7806	25347		28058	W 10363	33869	W 9066	27215	ART DIVERS EN MAT DIV 58
89399	OTHR PLASTC ARTICLES NES	W 7725	24767		27520	W 10263	33248	W 8862	26042	AUT OUV MAT DIV 58
894	TOYS,SPORTING GOODS,ETC		31076		33263		28003		16185	VOITURES ENFANTS,JOUETS
8942	TOYS,INDOOR GAMES ETC		30934		33013	W 5760	27422	W 3141	15769	JOUETS,JEUX ETC
89423	TOYS NES		27355		27673	W 5282	25384	W 2735	14123	JOUETS,MODELES REDUITS
899	OTHER MANUFACTURED GOODS		28864		23318		27934		20741	AUT ART MANUF DIVERS NDA
8997	BASKETWORK,BROOMS ETC	W 3065	17721		12164	W 2295	14286	W 1868	8720	OUVRAGES VANNERIE NDA
89971	BASKETWORK,WICKERWRK,ETC	W 2865	16803		10673	W 2090	12972	W 1613	7533	OUVRAGES DE VANNERIE

1. HISTORICAL SERIES, 1961–1996 GENERAL TRADE, IMPORTS C.I.F., EXPORTS F.O.B.
SERIES HISTORIQUES, 1961–1996 COMMERCE GENERAL, IMPORTATIONS C.A.F., EXPORTATIONS F.O.B

YEAR ANNEE	VALUE IN MILLION CYPRUS POUNDS / VALEUR EN MILLION CYPRUS POUNDS: MERCHANDISE – MARCHANDISE IMPORTS	MERCHANDISE – MARCHANDISE EXPORTS	GOLD – OR IMPORTS	GOLD – OR EXPORTS	CONVERSION FACTORS U.S. CENTS PER CYPRUS POUND / FACTEURS DE CONVERSION CENTS E.U. PAR CYPRUS POUND: IMPORTS	CONVERSION FACTORS EXPORTS	INDEX NUMBERS – INDICES: QUANTUM IMPORTS	QUANTUM EXPORTS	UNIT VALUE / VALEUR UNITAIRE IMPORTS	UNIT VALUE / VALEUR UNITAIRE EXPORTS
1961	38.30	17.80			280.0000	280.0000				29
1962	44.90	20.80			280.0000	280.0000				32
1963	47.00	21.90			280.0000	280.0000				30
1964	37.50	20.60			280.0000	280.0000				30
1965	51.20	25.30			280.0000	280.0000				33
1966	55.20	29.20			280.0000	280.0000				37
1967	59.50	29.70			275.8700	276.2700				29
1968	70.70	37.00			240.0000	240.0000				36
1969	86.20	40.90			240.0000	240.0000				39
1970	98.00	45.20			240.0000	240.0000				41
1971	106.50	47.30			243.2200	242.8800				40
1972	121.00	51.30			260.7410	260.7940				43
1973	157.40	60.50			286.2230	286.1890				46
1974	148.00	55.30			274.7380	275.2740				52
1975	113.70	56.00			270.8630	271.1040				62
1976	177.80	106.30			243.1160	242.4900				66
1977	254.00	129.80			245.2150	244.7970				66
1978	282.70	128.40			268.1270	267.7890				66
1979	357.60	161.90			282.1910	281.7830				71
1980	424.30	188.00			283.3130	283.3600				77
1981	489.50	234.80			238.0484	236.6654				94
1982	577.60	263.80			210.4190	210.2771				92
1983	642.00	260.50			189.8973	189.6373				91
1984	796.50	336.80			171.2021	170.6190				101
1985	762.30	290.60			163.5775	163.9238				97
1986	659.07	260.16			193.3665	193.6711				92
1987	711.42	297.99			208.5753	208.4327				95
1988	866.76	330.86			214.2754	214.9259				
1989	1130.30	393.05			202.1515	202.3059				
1990	1174.54	435.60			218.7020	217.7073				100
1991	1215.83	441.79			215.6854	215.8765				96
1992	1490.75	443.72			221.4602	221.7269				96
1993	1260.05	431.40			201.1368	200.9395				101
1994	1481.66	475.47			203.6779	203.5009				100
1995	1668.40	554.71			221.1538	221.5009				101
1996	1855.94	647.20			214.2868	214.2309				100

2. IMPORTS BY BROAD ECONOMIC CATEGORY AND EXPORTS BY INDUSTRIAL ORIGIN. (PERCENTAGE OF TOTAL VALUE)
IMPORTATIONS PAR CATEGORIES ECONOMIQUES ET EXPORTATIONS PAR BRANCHE D'ACTIVITE. (EN POURCENTAGE DE LA VALEUR TOTALE)

IMPORTS – IMPORTATIONS

	1990	1991	1992	1993	1994	1995	1996
TOTAL IMPORTS–IMPORTATIONS TOTALES	100.	100.	100.	100.	100.	100.	100.
1 FOOD BEV–ALIMENTATION BOISSONS	9.4	9.0	8.5	9.6	9.1	8.9	8.6
11 PRIMARY–PRODUITS DE BASE	4.2	3.9	3.3	3.4	3.5	3.3	3.6
111 FOR INDUSTRY–POUR L'INDUSTRIE	2.5	2.1	1.4	1.6	1.7	1.6	2.4
112 FOR HOUSEHOLDS–POUR LES MENAGES	1.7	1.9	1.9	1.8	1.8	1.7	1.2
12 PROCESSED–PRODUITS ELABORES	5.2	5.1	5.2	6.2	5.6	5.6	5.0
121 FOR INDUSTRY–POUR L'INDUSTRIE	0.7	0.8	0.7	1.2	0.9	0.8	0.6
122 FOR HOUSEHOLDS–POUR LES MENAGES	4.5	4.3	4.5	5.0	4.6	4.8	4.4
2 IND SUPPLIES–APPROV INDUSTRIELS	32.5	32.1	29.6	30.1	27.8	27.3	23.7
21 PRIMARY–PRODUITS DE BASE	1.7	2.0	1.7	2.1	1.9	1.6	1.7
22 PROCESSED–PRODUITS ELABORES	30.8	30.1	27.9	28.0	25.8	25.8	22.0
3 FUELS–COMBUSTIBLES	10.5	10.3	8.5	10.1	8.4	7.7	8.4
31 PRIMARY–PRODUITS DE BASE	4.6	4.9	3.6	3.8	3.8	3.1	3.2
32 PROCESSED–PRODUITS ELABORES	5.9	5.4	4.9	6.4	4.6	4.6	5.2
321 MOTOR SPIRIT–ESSENCE	5.9	5.3	4.8	6.3	0.4	0.4	0.6
322 OTHER–AUTRES	0.0	0.0	0.0	0.1	4.2	4.1	4.6
4 MACHINERY–EQUIPEMENT	14.6	15.0	16.2	15.7	16.7	15.0	13.9
41 CAPITAL EQUIPMENT–MACHINES	13.4	13.6	14.9	14.3	15.5	13.8	12.7
42 PARTS–PIECES ACCESSOIRES	1.3	1.4	1.3	1.3	1.3	1.2	1.2
5 TRANSPORT–TRANSPORT	14.6	12.2	15.3	10.8	10.0	11.6	10.0
51 PASSENGER CARS–AUTOMOBILES	6.1	5.7	5.9	3.5	4.5	5.1	4.8
52 OTHER–AUTRES	6.1	4.3	7.2	4.8	3.3	4.3	3.3
521 INDUSTRIAL–INDUSTRIELS	5.9	4.0	6.9	4.6	3.1	4.1	3.1
522 NON INDUSTRIAL–NON INDUSTRIEL	0.2	0.3	0.3	0.2	0.2	0.2	0.2
53 PARTS–PIECES ACCESSOIRES	2.4	2.1	2.2	2.5	2.2	2.2	1.9
6 CONSUM GOODS–BIENS CONSOMMATION	18.3	21.4	21.8	23.7	23.6	26.2	29.8
61 DURABLE–DURABLES	5.4	5.1	5.0	5.5	4.4	4.5	3.6
62 SEMI DURABLE–SEMI DURABLES	6.2	7.1	6.9	7.8	7.3	7.5	7.8
63 NON DURABLE–NON DURABLES	6.7	9.2	9.9	10.5	11.9	14.2	18.5
7 GOODS NES–BIENS NDA	0.1	0.1	0.1	0.1	4.5	3.3	5.6

EXPORTS – EXPORTATIONS

	1990	1991	1992	1993	1994	1995	1996
TOTAL EXPORTS–EXPORTATIONS TOTALES	100.	100.	100.	100.	100.	100.	100.
1 AGRICULTURE	15.9	14.2	11.1	10.5	10.1	12.7	8.7
2 MINING QUARRY–INDUS EXTRACTIVES	0.3	0.5	0.9	1.1	1.5	0.4	0.7
3 MANUFACTURING–IND MANUFACTUR	83.8	85.3	88.0	88.4	88.4	86.9	90.7
31 FOOD BEV TOBACCO–ALIM BOISS TAB	18.0	22.3	26.7	28.5	33.5	38.1	48.6
32 TEXTILES–INDUSTRIES TEXTILES	27.9	29.0	26.6	22.7	19.3	15.6	11.4
33 WOOD & PRODUCTS–BOIS & PRODUITS	0.3	0.1	0.1	0.0	0.0	0.1	0.1
34 PAPER & PRODUCTS–PAPIER & PRODT	1.9	1.9	1.4	1.4	1.6	1.7	1.4
35 CHEMICALS–INDUSTRIES CHIMIQUES	13.5	11.9	12.7	13.3	13.0	12.0	11.6
36 NON METAL MIN–MIN NON METAL	2.0	1.5	1.7	1.5	2.6	1.6	1.6
37 BASIC METAL–IND METAL BASE	0.3	0.2	0.3	0.3	0.3	0.8	0.7
38 METAL MANUF–MANUF METAL	19.1	17.1	17.3	19.7	17.4	16.4	14.8
39 OTH MANUF IND–AUTRES MANUF	0.7	1.2	1.1	1.0	0.8	0.6	0.5

3. TRADE BY PRINCIPAL COUNTRIES OF CONSIGNMENT AND LAST DESTINATION(VALUE IN THOUSAND U.S. DOLLARS)
ECHANGES SELON LES PRINCIPAUX PAYS DE CONSIGNATION ET DE DESTINATION FINALE (VALEUR EN MILLIERS DE DOLLARS EU)

COUNTRIES–PAYS	GENERAL IMPORTS C.I.F. IMPORTATIONS GENERALES C.A.F				
	1992	1993	1994	1995	1996
World	3300428	2535948	3014070	3693786	3981887
Africa	46555	26793	37409	35567	89009
Americas	319099	278318	379713	553307	743375
Northern America	294958	250403	335436	506139	684384
LAIA	22751	26988	43599	46059	57676
CACM	266	76	181	156	156
Caribbean	869	848	455	807	863
Rest of America	254	3	42	145	296
As.ex F.USSR	757340	550249	636806	770802	706960
Eur.x F.USSR	2011808	1543516	1677543	2024366	2056513
EU	1848783	1436060	1587628	1907821	1934197
EFTA	72101	46795	44482	51922	44137
East Europe	81252	55960	41319	57936	65703
Other Europe	398	127	181	890	1996
Former USSR	154734	128167	140611	177426	153432
Oceania	8781	7520	10067	12663	10199
USA/Etats–Unis d'Amer	277005	235411	311643	480861	670720
United Kingdom	373092	319034	343577	434664	447636
Italy/Italie	318770	264393	297916	361784	364367
Germany/Allemagne	297594	204846	247848	301354	280854
Japan/Japon	347283	205596	205268	246937	237485
Greece/Grèce	224767	211007	205144	265513	287095
France,Monac	260324	146452	128002	151875	156691
Russian Federation	154734	125730	121123	146885	111922
Netherlands/Pays–Bas	77938	63829	90540	75653	68012
Spain/Espagne	63501	53095	71482	78905	93306
Korea, Republic of	56890	37093	67143	101222	53223
Belgium–Luxembourg	54622	48391	60353	68811	59711
China/Chine	43541	45898	57139	69808	59187
Syrian Arab Republic	52229	42963	45840	54529	69007
Switz.Liecht	66363	41913	39019	46263	39750
Sweden/Suède	42380	29873	37688	55375	63870
Israel/Israël	27013	34774	38412	53768	66740
Denmark/Danemark	33486	28784	30932	31884	29919
Austria/Autriche	49129	21598	17014	22126	21241
Ireland/Irlande	24550	23185	25811	30388	24866
India/Inde	30694	12777	17751	29205	28037
Malaysia/Malaisie	15609	19872	22969	36093	23627
Egypt/Egypte	13645	7899	9607	15684	66264
Hong Kong	25394	20039	16808	21823	21533
Thailand/Thaïlande	16453	15978	19407	24837	27327
Canada	17931	14991	23768	25235	13572
Argentina/Argentine	8767	15384	25688	21867	23491
Indonesia/Indonésie	13092	14070	17676	20980	21343
Romania/Roumanie	14969	16687	10461	14643	23107
Finland/Finlande	13100	10754	18417	14759	20083
Singapore/Singapour	17346	15053	12631	13704	12608
Portugal	15531	10823	12903	14731	16548
Ukraine		2107	15109	17033	27983
Brazil/Brésil	10951	7975	13691	14563	14732
Saudi Arabia	11190	10264	11466	12234	9015
Algeria/Algérie	23716	10028	15945	2295	0
Bulgaria/Bulgarie	16232	7604	7935	9521	9341
Pakistan	13654	7898	9187	9044	6265
Hungary/Hongrie	10243	9372	5517	8610	11930
Czech Republic		14259	10267	12793	8139
Lebanon/Liban	11345	10162	5845	10018	6753
Poland/Pologne	18195	8038	3655	4941	8680
Mexico/Mexique	1134	1111	1538	7648	16953
Iran (Islamic Rp. of)	2909	2923	16102	2794	2243
Australia/Australie	4395	3874	5299	6226	7065
Norway,SVD,JM	5429	4506	5367	5520	4363
Republic of Moldova		94	378	10993	10999
New Zealand	4224	3607	4655	6238	2999
Czechoslovakia	21602				
Korea Dem People's Rp	2843	3261	13452		

COUNTRIES–PAYS	GENERAL EXPORTS F.O.B. EXPORTATIONS GENERALES F.O.B.				
	1992	1993	1994	1995	1996
Monde	1005173	867302	961225	1230550	1390620
Afrique	91350	59447	63185	71212	68472
Amériques	18072	22740	18662	18303	15437
Amérique du Nord	16325	18038	15949	15927	10696
ALAI	1333	1337	2353	1524	996
MCAC	89	758	22	131	908
Caraïbes	323	2575	266	542	410
Autre Amérique	2	31	72	178	2428
Asie l'URSS exclus	281756	263366	225140	222455	250963
Europe l'URSS exclus	484088	402527	460256	635109	684141
UE	423920	335781	354180	426925	394798
AELE	10482	8207	12736	18360	12550
Europe de l'Est	41693	54137	87555	184598	247563
Autre de l'Europe	1709	1763	3599	1245	1189
Ancienne URSS	25822	28852	105574	181404	258374
Océanie	567	739	1099	850	1343
United Kingdom	192960	136121	142534	164128	144489
Russian Federation	25822	26390	97952	168125	243705
Bulgaria/Bulgarie	16621	34520	55979	112375	209380
Lebanon/Liban	121537	111365	82942	53075	54621
Greece/Grèce	83670	66614	72816	73856	80536
Germany/Allemagne	45763	44796	56601	65441	60970
Egypt/Egypte	64959	26418	25993	28030	34040
United Arab Emirates	22003	20139	21429	47715	38482
Saudi Arabia	28877	27271	19461	13492	40084
Israel/Israël	19696	21278	26280	22968	33640
Romania/Roumanie	11420	11117	19575	58792	22731
Syrian Arab Republic	17783	19427	20515	22356	21111
Belgium–Luxembourg	16407	13665	15215	23112	17606
Netherlands/Pays–Bas	17472	14566	13593	20581	18415
France,Monac	18770	14304	14765	17406	18558
Italy/Italie	16330	10805	10507	15676	22141
USA/Etats–Unis d'Amer	15275	17022	15031	15284	10066
Libyan Arab Jamahiriya	13003	16779	17015	13636	9127
Jordan/Jordanie	17135	9784	10299	13709	10265
Spain/Espagne	10846	14080	10693	[illegible]	8306
Switz.Liecht	7813	7679	9752	10250	8443
Kuwait/ Koweït	10266	8984	8117	7808	7763
Austria/Autriche	6373	6090	4852	14532	6722
Hong Kong	7012	4866	5650	8691	9176
Morocco/Maroc	818	4666	5727	13570	6760
Ireland/Irlande	5271	4906	5273	6628	6395
Ukraine		891	5039	8760	11732
Yugoslavia/Yougoslavie	6284	1911	180	1445	16457
Poland/Pologne	2902	2928	6571	6252	4247
Sweden/Suède	5352	3542	2322	4081	4081
Yemen/Yémen	4725	5278	2535	2962	3730
Turkey/Turquie	650	9542	2666	2626	3730
Denmark/Danemark	1761	3792	3000	6373	3682
Singapore/Singapour	2368	2110	5337	1996	6745
Norway,SVD,JM	2613	442	2929	8078	4000
Nigeria/Nigéria	2826	4988	3495	3125	2848
Oman	3651	4230	2835	3002	3326
Tunisia/Tunisie	1085	2057	3350	4704	3455
Sudan/Soudan	3226	1743	3001	3244	2574
Bahrain/Bahreïn	3486	3090	2505	2121	1641
Czech Republic		3426	1980	3305	3714
Iran (Islamic Rp. of)	4246	1165	683	3006	2083
Japan/Japon	2771	2416	1874	2188	1721
Finland/Finlande	2339	1521	1290	2371	2426
Malta/Malte	1689	1762	3597	1218	1183
Slovenia/Slovénia		472	268	670	7882
Thailand/Thaïlande	1514	1283	2216	2259	1740
Hungary/Hongrie	2918	1875	1280	877	1624
Malaysia/Malaisie	1385	1713	2062	1439	1933
Czechoslovakia	7679				

(VALUE AS PERCENTAGE OF WORLD TOTAL)(VALEURS EN POURCENTAGE DU TOTAL MONDIAL)

	1987	1988	1989	1990	1991	1992	1993	1994	1995	1996
Africa	1.6	2.2	1.6	1.9	2.0	1.4	1.1	1.2	1.0	2.2
Americas	6.1	6.0	7.0	8.3	9.2	9.7	11.0	12.6	15.0	18.7
Northern America	5.2	4.8	5.9	7.5	8.4	8.9	9.9	11.1	13.7	17.2
LAIA	0.8	1.1	1.0	0.8	0.7	0.7	1.1	1.4	1.2	1.4
CACM	0.0	0.1	0.0	0.0	0.0	0.0	0.0	0.0	0.0	0.0
Caribbean	0.0	0.0	0.0	0.0	0.1	0.0	0.0	0.0	0.0	0.0
Rest of America	0.0	0.0	0.0	0.0	0.0	0.0	0.0	0.0	0.0	0.0
As.ex F.USSR	22.7	22.6	23.2	24.2	23.6	22.9	21.7	21.1	20.9	17.8
Eur.x F.USSR	67.3	66.1	65.5	62.4	60.1	61.0	60.9	55.7	54.8	51.6
EU	60.4	58.7	58.7	56.5	54.4	56.0	56.6	52.7	51.6	48.6
EFTA	2.2	2.1	1.6	1.8	1.9	2.2	1.8	1.5	1.4	1.1
East Europe	4.0	4.4	4.6	3.5	3.1	2.5	2.2	1.4	1.6	1.7
Other Europe	0.8	0.9	0.6	0.7	0.7	0.0	0.0	0.0	0.0	0.1
Former USSR	1.9	2.8	2.5	2.9	4.8	4.7	5.1	4.7	4.8	3.9
Oceania	0.4	0.2	0.2	0.2	0.2	0.3	0.3	0.3	0.3	0.3
USA/Etats–Unis d'Amer	4.5	4.6	5.6	7.1	7.9	8.4	9.3	10.3	13.0	16.8
United Kingdom	14.3	13.9	11.4	12.7	13.0	11.3	12.6	11.4	11.8	11.2
Italy/Italie	11.5	10.3	9.5	10.0	10.1	9.7	10.4	9.9	9.8	9.2
Germany/Allemagne	9.2	9.3	9.1	9.0	9.6	9.0	8.1	8.2	8.2	7.1
Japan/Japon	10.2	11.6	10.8	11.5	11.4	10.5	8.1	6.8	6.7	6.0
Greece/Grèce	7.7	7.3	6.1	7.0	6.9	6.8	8.3	6.8	7.2	7.2
France,Monac	5.0	5.0	11.8	6.5	3.7	7.9	5.8	4.2	4.1	3.9
Russian Federation						4.7	5.0	4.0	4.0	2.8
Netherlands/Pays–Bas	2.6	2.6	2.2	2.5	2.1	2.4	2.5	3.0	2.0	1.7
Spain/Espagne	2.5	2.0	1.9	2.2	1.6	1.9	2.1	2.4	2.1	2.3

	1987	1988	1989	1990	1991	1992	1993	1994	1995	1996
Afrique	13.6	13.8	6.6	5.1	8.2	9.1	6.9	6.6	5.8	4.9
Amériques	2.1	3.0	2.1	2.7	1.8	1.8	2.6	1.9	1.5	1.1
Amérique du Nord	2.1	2.5	1.8	1.7	1.5	1.6	2.1	1.7	1.3	0.8
ALAI	0.0	0,3	0.0	0.9	0.2	0.1	0.2	0.2	0.1	0.1
MCAC	0.0		0.0	0.0		0.0	0.1	0.0	0.0	0.1
Caraïbes	0.0	0.1	0.0	0.0	0.0	0.0	0.3	0.0	0.0	0.0
Autre Amérique		0.2	0.2	0.0	0.0	0.0	0.0	0.0	0.0	0.2
Asie l'URSS exclus	25.5	24.2	25.8	23.5	28.7	28.0	30.4	23.4	18.1	18.0
Europe l'URSS exclus	46.7	47.6	51.5	54.4	50.8	48.2	46.4	47.9	51.6	49.2
UE	43.0	44.4	48.0	49.0	45.1	42.2	38.7	36.8	34.7	28.4
AELE	1.4	1.1	0.7	1.1	1.1	1.0	0.9	1.3	1.5	0.9
Europe de l'Est	1.9	1.9	1.8	2.3	3.2	4.1	6.2	9.1	15.0	17.8
Autre de l'Europe	0.4	0.2	1.0	2.0	1.4	0.2	0.2	0.4	0.1	0.1
Ancienne URSS	3.1	2.2	3.9	3.2	1.7	2.6	3.3	11.0	14.7	18.6
Océanie	0.1	0.1	0.1	0.1	0.2	0.1	0.1	0.1	0.1	0.1
United Kingdom	22.3	21.6	23.4	23.1	21.0	19.2	15.7	14.8	13.3	10.4
Russian Federation						2.6	3.0	10.2	13.7	17.5
Bulgaria/Bulgarie	0.5	0.6	0.5	0.6	0.8	1.7	4.0	5.8	9.1	15.1
Lebanon/Liban	7.5	6.3	8.6	9.7	12.7	12.1	12.8	8.6	4.3	3.9
Greece/Grèce	6.5	8.3	10.2	9.9	8.4	8.3	7.7	7.6	6.0	5.8
Germany/Allemagne	4.2	3.7	4.2	5.2	5.2	4.6	5.2	5.9	5.3	4.4
Egypt/Egypte	3.9	3.3	3.0	2.4	4.8	6.5	3.0	2.7	2.3	2.4
United Arab Emirates	2.3	2.5	2.2	1.5	2.0	2.2	2.3	2.2	3.9	2.8
Saudi Arabia	5.8	5.0	4.3	2.9	3.3	2.9	3.1	2.0	1.1	2.9
Israel/Israël	0.6	0.9	1.3	1.2	1.5	2.0	2.5	2.7	1.9	2.4

4. General Imports C.I.F. by Commodities according to the S.I.T.C. (Rev. 2) in thousand U.S. Dollars
Importations Générales C.A.F. par Produits d'après la C.T.C.I. (Rév. 2) en milliers de Dollars E.U.

SITC CTCI	COMMODITY	1993 WEIGHT POIDS	1993 VALUE VALEUR	1994 WEIGHT POIDS	1994 VALUE VALEUR	1995 WEIGHT POIDS	1995 VALUE VALEUR	1996 WEIGHT POIDS	1996 VALUE VALEUR	PRODUIT
	ALL COMMODITIES		2535948		3014070		3693786		3981887	TOUS PRODUITS
0	FOOD AND LIVE ANIMALS		227335		258523		311477		339818	ALIMENTS,ANIMAUX VIVANTS
01	MEAT AND PREPARATIONS		18514		19240		22627		11859	VIANDES ET PREPARATIONS
011	MEAT FRESH,CHILLD,FROZEN	W 4296	14605	W 4212	15483	W 3561	18020	W 1910	7507	VIANDES FRAICHES,REF,CONGE
0111	BOVINE MEAT FRESH,FROZEN	W 2895	11353	W 2613	11652	W 1911	13945	W 1340	5819	VIANDES BOVIN FRAI,REF
01112	BOVINE MEAT BONELESS	W 2894	11332	W 2613	11651	W 1911	13941	W 1321	5783	VIANDES BOVIN DESOSSEES
02	DAIRY PRODCTS,BIRDS'EGGS		19896		18107		21800		21909	PRODUITS LAITIERS,OEUFS
024	CHEESE AND CURD	W 3258	10951	W 3287	11082	W 3356	13283	W 2900	13031	FROMAGE ET CAILLEBOTTE
03	FISH AND PREPARATIONS		24153		25902		33107		29260	POISSONS ET PREPARATIONS
034	FISH,FRESH,CHILLED,FROZN	W 2894	10240	W 2591	9518	W 3062	12458	W 2519	9876	POISSON FRAIS, REFRIG,CONG
04	CEREALS AND PREPARATIONS		75854		82794		100144		139593	CEREALES ET PRODUITS
041	WHEAT ETC UNMILLED	W 61699	8043	W 89025	13211	W 77605	13754	W 104891	24050	FROMENT,EPEAUTRE
0412	OTHER WHEAT ETC UNMILLED	W 27999	3342	W 48048	6753	W 22354	3441	W 70247	15207	AUTRE FROMENT NON MOULU
043	BARLEY UNMILLED	W 253937	25702	W 323781	26395	W 270806	32189	W 323985	53122	ORGE NON MONDEE
044	MAIZE UNMILLED		18085	W 130987	16799	W 168873	23213	W 144256	30061	MAIS NON MOULU
048	CEREAL ETC PREPARATIONS	W 9324	21103	W 9267	22675	W 10575	27036	W 10783	28248	PREPTNS A BASE CEREALES
05	VEGETABLES AND FRUIT		17500		25499		30445		31349	LEGUMES ET FRUITS
054	VEG ETC FRSH,SMPLY PRSVD	W 14433	6734		14058	W 14411	12994	W 17284	11007	LEGUMES FRAIS,CONG,SECS
0541	POTATOES FRSH EXCL SWEET	W 10413	3456	W 16546	9299	W 8996	6426	W 11876	5778	POMMES DE TERRE
06	SUGAR AND PREPS,HONEY		13207		15119		18543		17202	SUCRES ET PRODUITS
061	SUGAR AND HONEY	W 27576	8873	W 31616	11908	W 32996	14467	W 32278	13622	SUCRES ET MIEL
0612	REFINED SUGAR ETC	W 26220	8181	W 30430	11156	W 31662	13537	W 31152	12780	SUCRES RAFFINES
07	COFFEE,TEA,COCOA,SPICES		15945		20979		24472		23542	CAFE,THE,CACAO,EPICES
071	COFFEE AND SUBSTITUTES	W 2242	6745	W 2706	11068	W 2489	13098	W 2664	13351	CAFE ET SUCCEDANES
081	*FEEDING STUFF FOR ANIML	W 59243	22567	W 79094	28693	W 86911	32025	W 75905	33191	NOURRITURE POUR ANIMAUX
0813	OILCAKE AND OTH RESIDUES	W 34347	8513	W 54820	14475	W 60836	13925	W 50721	14873	TOURTEAUX
08131	— OF SOYA BEANS	W 31367	8055	W 53020	14199	W 58317	13368	W 47770	14400	TOURTEAUX DE SOJA
0819	FOOD WASTE AND FEED NES	W 11247	8679	W 11575	8712	W 13082	11784	W 12855	11782	DECHETS,ALIMENTS NDA
08199	FODDER NES,INCL SWEETNED	W 11247	8679	W 11575	8712	W 13063	11770	W 12854	11780	PREPARATIONS FOURRAGERES
09	MISC EDIBLE PRODUCTS		17883		20931		26781		30688	PREP ALIMENTAIRES DIVERSES
098	EDIBLE PRODCTS,PREPS NES		15331		18258		23472		27495	PREP ALIMENTAIRES NDA
09809	MISC FOOD PREPRTIONS NES		9436		11450	W 1553	16018	W 3897	19946	PREP ALIMENTAIRES NDA
1	BEVERAGES AND TOBACCO		179791		256705		397528		598396	BOISSONS ET TABACS
11	BEVERAGES		22412		27945		31357		30486	BOISSONS
112	ALCOHOLIC BEVERAGES		19487	W 6247	23325	W 5602	26001	W 6496	25140	BOISSONS ALCOOLIQUES
1124	DISTILLED ALCOHOLIC BEVS		14677	W 3038	18254	W 2380	19986	W 2529	18054	ALCOOLS,EAUX–DE–VIE
11241	WHISKY	W 1481	10344	W 1768	12501	W 1630	15612	W 1594	13335	WHISKY
12	TOBACCO AND MANUFACTURES		157379		228760		366171		567910	TABACS BRUTS FABRIQUES
122	TOBACCO,MANUFACTURED	W 13425	152804	W 17504	224346	W 26021	363174	W 41745	563277	TABACS FABRIQUES
1222	CIGARETTES	W 10923	140703	W 16497	216025	W 24577	350471	W 40463	552125	CIGARETTES
1223	OTH MANUFACTURED TOBACCO	W 1676	9951	W 970	6746	W 1406	10437	W 1185	8371	TABACS FUMER,CHIQUER,PRISER
2	CRUDE MATERLS,EXCL FUELS		55715		60696		69206		64163	MAT BRUTES NON COMESTIBLES
22	OIL SEEDS,OLEAGINOUS FRT		14317		9391		11802		15828	GRAINES,FRUITS OLEAGINEUX
223	SEEDS FOR OTH FIXED OILS	W 51090	12719	W 29611	7243	W 33906	7896	W 26826	8242	GRAINES AUTRES HUILES FIXES
2239	OIL SEED FLOUR AND MEAL	W 50869	12305	W 29489	7084	W 33678	7443	W 26501	7703	FARINES GRAINES OLEAG
24	CORK AND WOOD		20797		26841		33217		27178	LIEGE ET BOIS
248	WOOD SHAPED,SLEEPERS		18875		23080		29328	W 73105	23576	BOIS SIMPLEMENT TRAVAILLES
2482	LUMBER SHAPED CONIFER		11797		13744		19250	W 57114	12111	CONIFERES SCIES,RABOTES
24821	LUMBER SAWN ETC CONIFER		10555		11813		16406	W 54395	9456	CONIFERES SCIES LONGITUD
2483	LUMBER SHAPED NON–CONIFR		7078		9332		10078	W 15991	11465	NON CONIFERES SCIES,RABOTES
27	CRUDE FERTLZR,MINRLS NES		8901		11780		8167		7046	ENGRAIS MINERAUX BRUTS
3	MINERAL FUELS ETC		258351		254045		286553		338701	COMBUSTIBLES MINERAUX LUB
33	PETROLEUM AND PRODUCTS		247300		243457		270816		322035	PETROLE ET DERIVES
333	CRUDE PETROLEUM	W 706267	85394	W 875423	103138	W 808725	100152	W 748947	113336	HUILES BRUTES DE PETROLE
334	PETROLEUM PRODUCTS,REFIN		158820		136638		166864	W 1224083	204712	PRODUITS RAFFINES
3341	GASOLINE,OTH LIGHT OILS		158200	W 59427	12202	W 72978	15916	W 101122	23319	ESSENCES POUR MOTEURS
33411	MOTOR,AVIATION SPIRIT			W 57876	11635	W 72449	15621	W 98598	22442	ESSENCES MOTEURS D'AVIONS
3342	KEROSENE,OTH MEDIUM OILS			W 401393	55041	W 436219	58140	W 285911	60183	PETR LAMPANTS,AUT HUIL
33421	KEROSENE INCL JET FUEL			W 401367	55010	W 436217	58134	W 285892	60163	PETROLES LAMPANTS
3343	GAS OILS			W 84734	13334	W 151624	24726	W 224509	43674	GAS OILS
3344	FUEL OILS,NES			W 545737	46081	W 538783	56713	W 599181	65316	FUEL OILS
3345	LUBS,PETROLEUM OILS NES		620		9979		11369	W 13360	12220	HUILES LUBRIFIANTES
33451	LUBS(HIGH PETR CONT) ETC				9377	W 10634	10590	W 13131	11496	HUILES LUBRIF,H LOURDES
4	ANIMAL,VEGETABLE OIL,FAT		20419		23381		31621		20880	HUILES,GRAISSES ANIM,VEG
42	FIXED VEGETABLE OIL,FAT		17714		20755		28295		18954	HUILES VEGETALES FIXES
423	FIXED VEG OILS,SOFT	W 23383	14598	W 20988	17389	W 23007	22416	W 16636	15085	HUILES VEGET DOUCES FIXES
4232	SOYA BEAN OIL	W 13909	7616	W 13487	10534	W 8459	7766	W 6773	5783	HUILE DE SOJA
4236	SUNFLOWER SEED OIL	W 7267	4693	W 4969	4246	W 11438	11232	W 7944	7159	HUILE DE TOURNESOL
5	CHEMCLS,RELATED PROD NES		214083		245645		313188		298616	PRODUITS CHIMIQUES
51	ORGANIC CHEMICALS		15613		19519		23963		22500	PROD CHIMIQ ORGANIQUES
514	NITROGEN–FNCTN COMPOUNDS		7683		9670	W 1177	11634		10991	COMPOSES FONCT AZOTEES
52	INORGANIC CHEMICALS		10443		11142		13992		13173	PROD CHIM INORGANIQUES
53	DYES,TANNING,COLOUR PROD		12530		14413		17399		16773	PROD TEINTURE,COLORANTS
533	PIGMENTS,PAINTS,ETC	W 3957	9956	W 4608	11477	W 5815	14347	W 6562	14165	PIGMENTS,PEINTURES,VERNIS
541	*MEDICINAL,PHARM PRODUCT		55574		61849		77608		84070	PROD MEDICINAUX PHARMACEUT
5413	ANTIBIOTICS IN BULK	K 132219	8287	K 158893	9719	K 174222	12354	K 179523	13727	ANTIBIOTIQUES NDA
54139	OTHER ANTIBIOTICS	K 103021	7821	K 54586	5091	K 56494	5301	K 61045	6998	AUTRES ANTIBIOTIQUES
5417	MEDICAMENTS		41370		46539		58820	K 2127823	63360	MEDICAMENTS
54179	— CONTNG OTH SUBSTANCES		30491		34674		45078	K 1704712	47942	MED CONT AUT SUBSTANCES
55	PERFUME,CLEANING ETC PRD		34718		42004		50769		51442	PROD POUR PARFUM,TOILETTE
553	PERFUMERY,COSMETICS,ETC		21415		27804		33061	W 3332	33646	PRODUITS DE PARFUMERIE
554	SOAP,CLEANSING ETC PREPS		8867		9409		12278	W 7038	13503	SAVONS,PRODUITS DETERSIFS
562	*FERTILIZERS,MANUFACTURE		12442	W 71917	11564	W 91018	19148	W 58958	14559	ENGRAIS MANUFACTURES
5629	FERTILIZERS NES	W 42487	8932	W 45180	8222	W 60398	13673	W 45839	11680	ENGRAIS NDA
58	PLASTIC MATERIALS ETC		45440		52378		71590		60564	MAT PLAST ARTIFICIELLES
582	PROD OF CONDENSATION ETC	W 5702	9285	W 6514	10885	W 7422	14127	W 6320	11970	PROD CONDENS,POLYCOND
583	POLYMERIZATION ETC PRODS		34711		39632	W 35073	55199	W 35139	46653	PROD POLYMERISATION
5831	POLYETHYLENE	W 12669	10077	W 14598	12028	W 16808	20011	W 17668	16950	POLYETHYLENE
58311	— IN PRIMARY FORMS	W 12172	8961	W 13948	10644	W 15947	17511	W 16787	14766	POLYETHYLENE PRIMAIRES
5834	POLYVINYL CHLORIDE		8265	W 8823	10758	W 8764	13503	W 8347	10069	CHLORURE DE POLYVINYLE
5839	OTH POLYMRZTION ETC PROD		7777		7871	W 2483	9595	W 2651	9522	AUT PROD POLYMER COPOLYM
59	CHEMICAL MATERIALS NES		25651		30898		36842		33655	MAT PROD CHIMIQUES NDA
591	PESTICIDES,DISINFECTANTS	W 2351	8920	W 2932	12822	W 2790	16032	W 2485	12983	DESINF,INSECT,FONG,HERB
598	MISCEL CHEM PRODUCTS NES		13522		14501		16469		16384	PROD DIV INDUST CHIM NDA
5989	CHEM PRODUCTS,PREPS NES		11618		11756		13479		13066	PROD PREP CHIMIQUES NDA
59899	OTH CHEM PRODS,PREPS,NES		10030		9945		11694	W 4403	11450	AUT PRODUITS CHIMIQUES NDA
6	BASIC MANUFACTURES		577323		621629		727499		687705	ART MANUFACTURES
61	LEATHER,DRESSED FUR,ETC		17560		21360		19750		17654	CUIRS,PELLETERIES
611	LEATHER	A 818	13299	A 930	15444	A 707	13591	W 675	11859	CUIRS,PEAUX PREPARES
6114	LEATHR BOVINE NES,EQUINE	A 524	9060	A 613	10804	A 428	9154	W 555	8841	CUIRS DE BOVINS
62	RUBBER MANUFACTURES NES		27490		31114		37546		33911	CAOUTCHOUC MANUFACTURE

4. General Imports C.I.F. by Commodities according to the S.I.T.C. (Rev. 2) in thousand U.S. Dollars
Importations Générales C.A.F. par Produits d'après la C.T.C.I. (Rév. 2) en milliers de Dollars E.U.

SITC CTCI	COMMODITY	1993 WEIGHT POIDS	1993 VALUE VALEUR	1994 WEIGHT POIDS	1994 VALUE VALEUR	1995 WEIGHT POIDS	1995 VALUE VALEUR	1996 WEIGHT POIDS	1996 VALUE VALEUR	PRODUIT
625	RUBBER TYRES, TUBES ETC	N 573884	17982	N 608715	20300	N 657700	25792	N 641073	22339	PNEUS CAOUTCHOUC VULCANISE
6251	TYRES NEW FOR MOTOR CARS	N 264662	10257	N 288163	12706	N 352498	15691	N 308829	14231	PNEUS POUR VOITURES
63	WOOD,CORK MANUFACTRS NES		15091		16479		21683		23496	OUVRAGES LIEGE ET BOIS
634	VENEERS,PLYWOOD,ETC		9953		10712		13335		13038	PLACAGES,CONTRE–PLAQUES
64	PAPER,PAPERBOARD AND MFR		73185		85795		113027		103498	PAPIERS,CARTONS & OUVRAGES
641	PAPER AND PAPERBOARD		52005		62241		83830	W 72609	72488	PAPIERS ET CARTONS
6412	PRINTG,WRITING PAPER NES		8341		8108		14602	W 10268	11193	PAPIERS POUR L'IMPRESSION
64122	— COATED,IMPREGNATD ETC	W 8217	6890	W 7838	6605	W 9852	11165	W 7856	8254	PAPIERS IMPRESSION COUCHES
6415	PAPER,PAPERBRD,BULK,NES		7865		9226	W 12677	14514	W 11346	11139	PAPIERS,CARTONS ROULEAUX
64159	OTHER PAPER ETC,BULK,NES		6532		7809	W 8958	11568	W 6176	8094	AUT PAPIER ROULEAUX FEUILLES
6416	FIBRE BUILDING BOARD	V 29500	8828		10710	V 29650	10194	W 17377	8419	PLAQUES CONSTRUCT EN PATE
64162	INSULATING BOARD, ETC	V 27908	8260		10000	V 24029	9113	W 16475	7524	PLAQUES CONST NON COMPR
6418	COATED ETC PAPER NES BLK	W 5318	12358	W 7628	17682	W 8205	21174	W 6882	18435	PAP,CARTONS COUCHES,ENDUITS
64181	PLASTIC COATED PAPER ETC	W 1801	6376	W 3232	10579	W 3616	14074	W 3267	12475	PAP,CARTONS ENDUITS,RESINES
642	PAPER,ETC,PRECUT,ARTS OF		21180		23554		29197	W 10077	31010	PAP,CARTONS DECOUPES
6428	PAPER ETC ARTICLES NES		8877		10023		13478	W 4211	14991	OUVRAGES EN PATE A PAPIER
65	TEXTILE YARN,FABRICS,ETC		177196		194353		204039		166077	FILS,TISSUS,ARTICLES TEXTILE
651	TEXTILE YARN		25470		26278		27883	W 3333	18228	FILS TEXTILES
6513	COTTON YARN	W 2303	7871		9184	W 2650	10029	W 1371	5936	FILS DE COTON
6516	DISCON SYN FIB BLEND YRN	W 2287	9917	W 2116	9257	W 1702	8171	W 1205	6732	FILS FIBR TEX SYNT DIS MOINS
652	COTTON FABRICS,WOVEN		21451		24201	A 10460	23872	W 2808	20520	TISSUS DE COTON
6522	WOVEN COTTON BLEACHD,ETC		21227		23865	A 10095	23254	W 2697	19842	TISSUS COTON BLANCHIS ETC
65224	BLCHED COTTON FABRIC NES		14520		16972	A 8517	17826	W 2290	15202	AUT TIS PLUS 85% COT BLANCHI
653	WOVN MAN–MADE FIB FABRIC		73977		86197	A 62260	93951	W 9194	71188	TISSUS FIBRES SYNTH,ARTIF
6531	CONT SYNT WEAVES NONPILE		14421	A 8365	12202	A 7161	11033	W 1077	11683	TISSUS FIBRES SYNTH CONTINUE
65315	CONT SYN TXTL FABRIC NES		12721	A 7054	9572	A 5268	8422	W 841	9516	TIS PLUS 85% TEXT SYNT CONT
6532	DISC SYN TXTL FABRIC NES		10053	A 17694	23541	A 19533	29561	W 3505	22236	TIS DISC MOINS 85% FIBR TEXT
6534	DISC SYN BLEND FABRC NES		38261	A 31651	39181	A 29544	39437	W 3686	25669	TISSUS FIBRES SYNTH DISCONT
65341	DISC SYN FIB–COTTN FABRC		10721	A 10224	9526	A 8617	10071	W 908	6501	TISSUS FIB SYNT DIS MEL COTO
65349	OTH DISC SYN BLEND FABRC		19820	A 15720	18375	A 16215	19689	W 2033	11862	TISSUS FIB SYNT MEL MAT AUT
654	OTH WOVEN TEXTILE FABRIC		9320		8979	A 1762	7297	W 437	7184	TISSUS AUT COTON SYNT,ARTIF
655	KNITTED,ETC FABRICS		13380		15118	A 6071	14363	W 1450	13291	ETOF BONNETERIE PIECES ETC
6552	OTHER KNIT ETC FAB NONEL		13380		15118	A 6071	14363	W 1450	13291	ETOF BON NON ELAS NON SYNT
657	SPECIAL TXTL FABRC,PRODS		11684		11471		12912	W 2426	12133	TISSUS SPECIAUX
658	TEXTILE ARTICLES NES		9821		8625		10065	W 1498	11242	ART FACONNES MAT TEXTILES
659	FLOOR COVERINGS,ETC		8471		8910		9474		9061	COUVRE–PARQUETS,TAPIS ETC
66	NONMETAL MINERAL MFS NES		69563		81152		93356		99999	ART MIN NON METALLIQUES
661	LIME,CEMENT,BLDG PRODS		10516		12501		17900		18309	CHAUX,CIMENTS MAT CONSTR
6613	BUILDING STONE ETC WORKD		5157		8104		11135	W 20819	13057	PIERRES A BATIR
66132	BUILDING STONE WORKED		5066		7983		10866	W 20329	12891	OUVR EN PIERRES DE TAILLE
662	CLAY,REFRACTORY BLDG PRD		15500		18940		23812		28190	MAT CONST REFRACTAIRES
6624	BRICKS ETC NONREFRACTORY		14434		17599		22462		26543	BRIQUES ETC CERAM NON REFR
66245	GLAZED CERAMIC SETTS ETC		12151		15375		20071	A 5030	23821	AUT CARREAUX CERAMIQUE
664	GLASS		8610		9879		11643		10712	VERRE
665	GLASSWARE		10889		11733		15133		15640	OUVRAGES EN VERRE
666	POTTERY		7907		8536		9594	W 3166	10328	POTERIE
667	PEARL,PREC–,SEMI–P STONE		10426		12317		7921		9822	PERLES, PIERRES GEMMES
6672	DIAMONDS NONINDUST,UNSET		9469		11315		6238		8378	DIAMANTS BRUTS
66729	— CUT ETC NOT SET		8265		9305		4737		6734	DIAMANTS TAILLES
67	IRON AND STEEL		84157		75958		99842		98059	FER ET ACIER
673	IRON,STEEL SHAPES ETC		42764		42634	W 167050	51264	W 158703	50143	BARRES,PROFIL FER,ACIER
6732	IRON,STEEL BARS ETC		35846		32390	W 130165	38313	W 124360	38663	BARRES FER,ACIER
67326	IRN,OTH STL BARS HOTROLD	W 111852	31531		25627	W 114681	31724	W 122996	37218	BARRES PLEINES FER,ACIER
674	IRN,STL UNIV,PLATE,SHEET	W 35132	18195		19121	W 38818	28476	W 28727	22086	LARGES PLATS,TOLES
6749	OTH IRN,STL PLATES,SHEET	W 18878	10444	W 16070	11191	W 20173	15944	W 16247	13707	AUTRES TOLES FER,ACIER
67491	— OF IRON OR SIMPLE STL	W 18480	9636	W 15594	9980	W 19733	14787	W 15906	12813	AUT TOLES AUTRES ACIER FIN
678	IRON,STL TUBES,PIPES,ETC	W 21132	18452	W 7681	7962	W 9222	9184	W 18219	17220	TUBES,TUYAUX EN FONTE,FER
6781	CAST IRON TUBES,PIPES	W 12739	10070	W 460	616	W 827	705	W 9360	6319	TUBES,TUYAUX EN FONTE
68	NON–FERROUS METALS		26062		25997		37770		37653	METAUX NON FERREUX
682	COPPER EXC CEMENT COPPER		8831		7329	W 2656	10587		11952	CUIVRE
6822	COPPER,ALLOYS WORKED		8686	W 2075	7192	W 2607	10508	W 2947	11288	CUIVRE,ALLIAGES OUVRES
684	ALUMINIUM	W 7544	14465	W 7376	14940	W 7980	22061	W 8083	19477	ALUMINIUM
6841	ALUMINIUM,ALLOYS,UNWRGHT	W 5077	7073	W 5013	7765	W 5389	11866	W 5280	9683	ALUMINIUM,ALLIAGES BRUTS
69	METAL MANUFACTURES NES		87018		89422		100485		107356	ART MANUFACT EN METAL NDA
691	STRUCTURES AND PARTS NES		11881		9706	W 7257	13846	W 8420	15045	CONSTRUCT FER,ACIER,ALU
6911	STRUCTURES,PARTS IRN,STL	W 6628	10443	W 4627	7070	W 7010	11565	W 8056	12710	CONSTRUCT FER,ACIER,FONTE
692	METAL TANKS,BOXES,ETC		14428		17597		17081	W 4387	18357	RECIPIENTS METALLIQUES
6924	MTL TRANSPORT BOXES ETC		14110		15286		16576	W 3774	17118	FUTS,TAMBOURS,BIDONS
69242	ALUMNM TRNSPRT BOXES ETC		11192		12377		13420	W 2425	13158	FUTS,TAMBOURS,BIDONS ALU
695	TOOLS		8460		9525		9925	W 778	8222	OUTILS A MAIN
697	BASE MTL HOUSEHOLD EQUIP		17685		17041		17836		19318	ART MENAGE MET COMMUNS
6974	BASE MTL DMSTC ARTIC NES		7937		8211		8137	W 1339	9050	ARTICLES NDA FONTE,FER,ETC
699	BASE METAL MFRS NES		23410		23797		27820	W 5482	30566	ART MANUFACTURES MET NDA
6991	LOCKSMITHS WARES,ETC		10648		10847		12528	W 1764	13123	ARTICLES DE SERRURERIE
69913	BASE MTL DOOR,ETC FITTNG		8464		8632		9661	W 1440	10034	GARNITURES POUR MEUBLES
7	MACHINES,TRANSPORT EQUIP		695071		820534		1018792		963467	MACHINES MATERIEL TRANSPORT
71	POWER GENERATING EQUIPMT		23109		38064		28091		23022	MACHINES GENERATRICES
712	STEAM ENGINES,TURBINES		1510		11727		1970		641	MACHINES A VAPEUR D'EAU PIEC
7126	STEAM POWR UNITS,ENGINES	N 34	470		9376				25	MACHINES A VAPEUR D EAU
713	INTRNL COMBUS PSTN ENGIN		11600		11293		12618		10302	MOTEURS EXPL COMB INT, PIECE
716	ROTATING ELECTRIC PLANT		8372		13984		12278		10851	APP ELECTR ROTATIFS,PIECES
7162	AC MTRS,GENRTRS,GEN SETS		7644	N 244490	12678	N 164399	10872	N 155434	9969	MOTEURS ELECTRIQUES
72	MACHS FOR SPCL INDUSTRYS		72254		64863		75126		71343	MAC SPECIALES POUR INDUST
723	CIVIL ENGNEERG EQUIP ETC		13788		9185		9731		10843	APPAREILS DE GENIE CIVIL
7234	CONST,MINING MACHNRY NES		12337		7871		8550	N 357	9144	MACH POUR LA CONST, MINES
72342	SLFPRP SHOVELS,EXCAVATRS	N 251	8691		5594	N 200	6714	N 199	7516	PELLES MECANIQUES
724	TEXTILE,LEATHER MACHNRY		8036		6860		5484		4627	MACH POUR INDUSTRIE TEXTILE
728	OTH MACHY FOR SPCL INDUS		25841		24654		28213		25576	AUT MACH IND PARTICULIERES
7284	MACHY FOR SPCL INDUS NES		13502		10906		13830		14089	MACH SPEC IND PARTICUL.
74	GENRL INDUSTRL MACHY NES		114911		132847		161929		176461	MACH APP INDUSTRIE
741	HEATING,COOLING EQUIPMNT		33612		43626		59234		74849	MACH CHAUFFAGE,PIECES
7414	NONDOM REFRIG EQUIPT,PTS		6062		9164		13128		20405	MAT PRODUCTION DU FROID
74141	REFRIG EQUIP NONDOMESTIC	N 34690	4974	N 24196	8026	N 33834	11294		18571	REFIG INDUSTRIELS
7415	AIR–CONDITIONING MACHNRY		15197		20686	N 83699	29399	N 106352	36133	GROUPES CONDITION AIR
7416	HEATING,COOLING EQU NES		6785		7171		12074	N 28981	12755	APP CHANGEMENT TEMP
742	PUMPS FOR LIQUIDS ETC		8736		9605		10846		15132	POMPES MOTO–POMPES
743	PUMPS NES,CENTRFUGES ETC		16782		24221		20455		25897	POMPES COMPRES,VENT ETC
7436	GAS,LIQUID FILTERS ETC	N 581747	5622	N 628833	8441	N 734059	7704	N 791279	13395	APP POUR FILT DES LIQUIDES
744	MECHANICAL HANDLING EQU		17499		17723		27728		17962	EQUIP MANUTENTION PIECES
7442	LIFTING,LOADING MACH NES	N 32181	10561		7412	N 32881	19634	N 16628	7626	APP LEVAGE,MANUTENTION
74422	SHIP DERRICKS,CRANES ETC	N 470	4688	N 41	645	N 1994	12604	N 123	580	GRUES,PONTS ROULANTS

4. General Imports C.I.F. by Commodities according to the S.I.T.C. (Rev. 2) in thousand U.S. Dollars
Importations Générales C.A.F. par Produits d'après la C.T.C.I. (Rév. 2) en milliers de Dollars E.U.

SITC CTCI	COMMODITY	1993 WEIGHT POIDS	1993 VALUE VALEUR	1994 WEIGHT POIDS	1994 VALUE VALEUR	1995 WEIGHT POIDS	1995 VALUE VALEUR	1996 WEIGHT POIDS	1996 VALUE VALEUR	PRODUIT
745	NONELEC MACHY,TOOLS NES		19054		17503		20086		20094	AUT MACH NON ELEC,PIECES
7452	OTH NONELEC MCHS,PTS NES		17651		16389		18685		18690	AUT MACH NON ELEC,PIECES
74522	PACKAGNG,BOTTLNG,ETC MCH	N 1585	11106	N 2665	9015	N 2514	9314	N 3586	10621	MACH NETT BOUTEILLES,ETC
749	NONELEC MACH PTS,ACC NES		19226		20169		23579		22527	PIECES MACH NON ELEC NDA
7492	COCKS,VALVES ETC NES		10048		12016		14197	W 1201	12778	ART ROB,SIM POUR TUYAUX
75	OFFICE MACHNES,ADP EQUIP		42637		55427		69956		74827	MACH BUREAU TRAIT AUTOM
752	AUTOMTIC DATA PROC EQUIP		29394		39129		50077	N 133324	50670	MACH TRAIT INFORMATION
7522	DIGITAL COMPUTERS		4409		8395		11094	N 3149	4542	MACH DIGITALES COMPLETES
7523	DIGITL CENTRL PROCESSORS		4889		6242		11211	N 11244	16356	UNITES CENTRALES
7528	OFF-LINE DATA PROC EQUIP	N 33201	14691	N 36942	13354	N 47457	14128	N 53206	12310	MACH AUXIL TRAIT INFORM
759	OFFICE,ADP MCH PTS,ACCES		6900		8392		10953	W 249	16003	PIECES DU 751 ET 752
7599	ACCTG,ETC,ADP MCH PTS,AC		5067		6581		8570	W 202	13507	PIECES DU 751 ET 752
76	TELECOMM,SOUND EQUIPMENT		102543		110122		121428		114671	EQUIPMENT DE TELECOM
761	TELEVISION RECEIVERS	N 99380	33710	N 92911	28523	N 100610	30300	N 112871	18395	RECEPTEURS DE TELEVISION
7611	COLOUR TV RECEIVERS	N 98388	33386	N 92818	28492	N 100425	30251	N 111846	18338	RECEPTEURS COULEUR
762	RADIO BROADCAST RECEIVRS	N 240817	15243	N 216074	11948	N 324178	19359	N 239688	12863	RECEPTEURS RADIODIFFUSION
7628	OTHER RADIO RECEIVERS	N 111086	8429	N 112758	7178	N 189516	12499	N 114897	8758	AUTRES RECEPT RADIO
764	TELECOM EQPT,PTS,ACC NES		46870		63463		62585		76125	EQUIP TELECOM,PIECES
7641	LINE TELEPHONE,ETC EQUIP		9844		13182	N 146206	12836	N 332335	12342	APP TELEPHON PAR FIL
7643	TV,RADIO TRANSMITTRS ETC	N 23658	8994	N 18591	9936	N 40385	17496	N 39759	16185	APP EMET TELE RADIO
7649	PTS NES OF EQUIPMT OF 76		18900		31512		23464	W 716	41655	PIECES DE LA DIV 76
76491	PTS NES OF APPAR OF 7641	N 156635	7191	N 956892	16759	N 251865	12659	W 190	19942	PIECES POUR 764.1
76493	TELECOMM EQUIPMT PTS NES		11182		14387		10370	W 515	21316	PIECES 761,762,764.3,8
77	ELECTRIC MACHNRY NES ETC		99725		152976		177722		144638	MACH APP ELECT NDA
771	ELECTRIC POWER MACHY NES		4650		9151		8967		10294	MACH PROD,TRANS ELECTR
772	SWITCHGEAR ETC,PARTS NES		23635		19815		25675	W 1679	31632	APP COUPURE,SECT ETC
7721	SWITCHGEAR ETC		23409		19537		25388	W 1674	31318	APP COUPURE,SECTIONMNT
773	ELECTR DISTRIBUTNG EQUIP		12546		11765		22222	W 6985	20099	EQUIPMT DISTRIBUTION ELECT
7731	INSULATED WIRE,CABLE ETC		12169		11261		21272	W 6837	19765	FILS,CABLES ISOLES ELECT
775	HOUSEHOLD TYPE EQUIP NES		35103		39119		51510		45751	MACH,APP USAGE DOMESTQUE
7752	DOM REFRIGERATRS,FREEZRS	N 24881	8300	N 27727	9268	N 34553	13557	N 31696	12786	REFRIG,CONGEL MENAGER
77521	DOMESTIC REFRIGERATORS	N 21072	7174	N 23618	8071	N 29288	11922	N 26742	11197	REFRIGERATEURS
7758	ELECTRO-THERMIC APPL NES		15101		16620		21320		18429	APP ELECTROTHERMIQ NDA
77586	ELECTROTHERM DOM APP NES	N 191101	8091	N 208613	10801	N 290918	13819	N 213747	11575	APP ELECTRO THERMIQUES
778	ELECTRICAL MACHINERY NES		21957		67432		63330		30921	AUTRES MACH ELECT NDA
7788	OTH ELEC MACHY,EQUIP NES		5920		50890		43446		10001	AUT MACH APP ELEC NDA
77886	OTH ELEC MACHINERY NES		3990		47414		40571	N 108256	6571	AUT MACH APP ELECTRIQUES
78	ROAD VEHICLES		186930		247763		360412		340021	VEHICULES ROUTIERS
781	PASS MOTOR VEH EXC BUSES	N 8729	87616	N 12840	134281	N 18740	187230	N 23562	188807	AUTO TRANSPORT PERSONNES
782	LORRIES,SPCL MTR VEH NES	N 5277	63227	N 6990	77252	N 10020	123100	N 8149	100390	VEHICULES SPECIAUX,MARCH
7821	LORRIES,TRUCKS	N 5182	58079	N 6939	74146	N 9960	119083	N 8075	94111	VEHICULES TRANSP MARCHAND
784	MOTOR VEH PRTS,ACCES NES		20976		24223		30012		29265	PIECES 722,781,782,783
7849	OTHER MOTOR VEHCL PARTS		19708		22117		27061	W 2317	27216	PIECES 722,781,782,783
79	OTHR TRANSPORT EQUIPMENT		47423		11912		17985		11853	AUTRE MATERIEL TRANSPORT
792	AIRCRAFT ETC		38801		2387		2711		3502	APP NAVIGATION AERIENNE
7924	AIRCRFT NES OVER 15000KG	N 1	34970							AERODYNES PLUS 15000 KG
793	SHIPS AND BOATS ETC	N 7743	8308	N 7823	9430	N 6161	15235	N 7259	8193	NAVIRES BATEAUX,ETC
8	MISC MANUFACTURED GOODS		283034		310502		388919		423306	ART MANUFACTURES DIVERS
812	*PLUMBG,HEATNG,LGHTNG EQ		24617		23738		29933		31006	APPAR SANITAIRES CHAUFFAGE
8121	CENTRAL HEATING EQUIPMNT		9786		7505		8867		8656	CHAUDIERES,RADIATEURS
8124	LIGHTING EQUIPMENT NES		9724		10476		14532		16227	APPAREILS ECLAIRAGE ETC
81242	LAMPS,FITTINGS BASE METL		9065		9640		13325	W 1679	14593	APPAREILS D'ECLAIRAGE
821	*FURNITURE,PARTS THEREOF		14352		16201		23257		30926	MEUBLES ET PIECES
8219	FURNITURE AND PARTS NES		7748		9195		14076		19210	AUTRES MEUBLES ET PIECES
84	CLOTHING AND ACCESSORIES		45984		49801		70464		95618	VETEMENTS
842	MENS OUTERWEAR NOT KNIT	N 519871	5925	N 428187	5765	N 554398	8089		12223	VET DESSUS POUR HOMMES
843	WOMENS OUTERWEAR NONKNIT	N 1119686	10343	N 1379340	13424	N 1512917	18085	N 2029234	28222	VET DESSUS FEMMES MAT TEX
845	OUTERWEAR KNIT NONELASTC		7157		10418	N 1236981	15221	N 1460425	19375	VET DESSOUS,ACCES BONNET
846	UNDER GARMENTS KNITTED		14017		11264		15230		17840	SOUS VETS DE BONNETERIE
8462	— OF COTTON NON ELASTIC	N 7115381	9039	N 4703903	7135	N 4487786	9680	N 3438348	10928	SOUS-VET BONNET COTON
84629	—— OTHER	N 7115381	9039	N 4703903	7135	N 4487786	9680	N 3438348	10928	AUT SOUS-VET BONNET COTON
851	*FOOTWEAR	P 1093989	14026	P 1141952	16906	P 1557463	23109	P 1570766	26334	CHAUSSURES
85102	FOOTWEAR LEATHER	P 769659	11298	P 787817	13012	P 1269221	19908	P 1274344	22803	CHAUS SEMELLES EN CUIR
87	PRECISION INSTRUMNTS NES		24950		23192		27646		27751	INSTRUM,APPAR SCIENT NDA
872	MEDICAL INSTRUMENTS NES		7667		6499		10009		8968	INSTR,APP MEDIC-CHIR NDA
874	MEASURNG,CONTROLNG INSTR		14731		13670		14712		16360	INSTRUMENTS DE MESURE
88	PHOTO EQU,OPTICL GDS ETC		37076		35773		41281		34822	APP,FOURN PHOTO,OP,MONTR
882	PHOTO,CINEMA SUPPLIES		9932		12617		13651		11353	PRODUITS PHOTO,CINEMA
8822	PHOTO FILM EXC DEV CINMA		8194		10529		11220		8992	PLAQUES,PELLICULES,FILMS
884	OPTICAL GOODS NES		9305		8172		10235		10077	ELEMENTS OPTIQ,ART LUNET
885	WATCHES AND CLOCKS		14886		11364		12623		8850	HORLOGERIE
8851	WATCHES,MOVEMENTS,CASES		13513		9839		10936		7273	MONTRES,MOUVEMENTS,BOITES
88511	WATCHES		13331		9612		10819		7120	MONTRES POCHE,BRACELET
89	MISC MANUFCTRD GOODS NES		118355		139944		167492		168947	ART MANUFACTURES DIVERS
892	PRINTED MATTER		25145		30331		37426	W 5130	41586	IMPRIMES
8921	PRINTED BOOKS,GLOBES,ETC		10025		12498		15816	W 2444	21931	LIVRES,BROCHURES,CARTES
89211	PRINTED BOOKS,PAMPHLETS		9766		12208		15452	W 2382	21587	LIVRES,BROCHURES
8922	NEWSPAPERS,PERIODICALS		8918		10152		11692	W 1756	10726	JOURNAUX ET PERIODIQUES
893	ARTICLES OF PLASTIC NES		30420		34181		43923		43792	OUVRAGES EN MAT DIVIS 58
8939	MISC PLASTIC ARTICLES		24088		26310		34642	W 6962	34747	ART DIVERS EN MAT DIV 58
89399	OTHR PLASTC ARTICLES NES		22301		24268		32083	W 6323	32192	AUT OUV MAT DIV 58
894	TOYS,SPORTING GOODS,ETC		25962		32587		37448		34528	VOITURES ENFANTS,JOUETS
8942	TOYS,INDOOR GAMES ETC		15259		20026		24964		21526	JOUETS,JEUX ETC
89423	TOYS NES		8737		10766		13845	N 7764918	10756	JOUETS,MODELES REDUITS
898	MUSICAL INSTRUMENTS,PTS		15057		18821		20794		20868	INSTRUMENTS DE MUSIQUE
8983	SOUND RECRDNG TAPE,DISCS	N 6398780	13185	N 5620779	16324	N 6879190	18281	N 5295831	18207	SUPPORTS SON POUR 763
89832	RECORDED DISCS,TAPES ETC	N 2329452	8866	N 2380792	13171	N 3781017	14817	N 3093078	15666	DISQUES,PHONO,BANDES
899	OTHER MANUFACTURED GOODS		13281		13492		16090		15045	AUT ART MANUF DIVERS NDA
9	GOODS NOT CLASSD BY KIND		24826		162410		149003		246835	ART TRANSACT NON CLASSES
951	*WAR FIREARMS,AMMUNITION		333		131427		119163		221488	VEHIC BLINDES ARMES
95102	MILITARY FIREARMS NES				130987	N 11821	118505	N 34471	220896	ARMES DE GUERRE
971	*GOLD,NON MONETARY NES	K 2190	24276	K 2696	30106	K 2451	29562	K 3406	24539	OR NON MONETAIRE
97101	NONMON GLD UNWRT,SEMIMFD	K 2190	24276	K 2696	30106	K 2400	29470	K 3382	24536	OR,ALLIAGES D'OR BRUTS

5. General Exports F.O.B. by Commodities according to the S.I.T.C. (Rev. 2) in thousand U.S. Dollars
Exportations Générales F.O.B. par Produits d'après la C.T.C.I. (Rév. 2) en milliers de Dollars E.U.

SITC CTCI	COMMODITY	1993 WEIGHT POIDS	1993 VALUE VALEUR	1994 WEIGHT POIDS	1994 VALUE VALEUR	1995 WEIGHT POIDS	1995 VALUE VALEUR	1996 WEIGHT POIDS	1996 VALUE VALEUR	PRODUIT
	ALL COMMODITIES		867302		961225		1230550		1390620	TOUS PRODUITS
0	FOOD AND LIVE ANIMALS		132990		139472		205053		168885	ALIMENTS,ANIMAUX VIVANTS
01	MEAT AND PREPARATIONS		4731		3360		3190		5060	VIANDES ET PREPARATIONS
011	MEAT FRESH,CHILLD,FROZEN	W 2052	3590	W 1823	2321	W 1583	2764	W 2918	4780	VIANDES FRAICHES,REF,CONGE
02	DAIRY PRODCTS,BIRDS'EGGS		10306		10238		12326		12405	PRODUITS LAITIERS,OEUFS
024	CHEESE AND CURD	W 2108	7924	W 2154	9288	W 2291	11029	W 2419	11187	FROMAGE ET CAILLEBOTTE
03	FISH AND PREPARATIONS		3423		2310		3393		2528	POISSONS ET PREPARATIONS
04	CEREALS AND PREPARATIONS		2964		2805		3078		2564	CEREALES ET PRODUITS
048	CEREAL ETC PREPARATIONS	W 1673	2837	W 1934	2704	W 2324	2913	W 2187	2331	PREPTNS A BASE CEREALES
05	VEGETABLES AND FRUIT		98785		110844		171167		135314	LEGUMES ET FRUITS
054	VEG ETC FRSH,SMPLY PRSVD		50330		57704	W 198328	104929	W 189721	68664	LEGUMES FRAIS,CONG,SECS
0541	POTATOES FRSH EXCL SWEET	W 153217	40510	W 96224	47976	W 186969	95442	W 178287	59308	POMMES DE TERRE
0545	OTHER FRESH VEGETABLES	W 5921	5530	W 6883	6273	W 6598	6059	W 6291	6291	AUTRES LEGUMES FRAIS,REF
05459	FRESH VEGETABLES NES	W 5879	5508	W 6554	6101	W 6589	6048	W 6282	6281	LEGUMES FRAIS,REFRI NDA
0548	EDIBLE VEG NES FRESH,DRY	W 9732	3587	W 8556	2810	W 4132	2694	W 4761	2601	RACINES,TUBERCULES
05488	VEG PRODTS NES FRESH,DRY	W 9585	3368	W 8407	2650	W 3988	2566	W 4642	2444	PROD VEGET ALIM HUMAINE
057	FRUIT,NUTS,FRESH,DRIED		35507		33301	W 98136	43449	W 91965	45025	FRUITS FRAIS OU SECS
0571	ORANGES, MANDARINS ETC		5871		6436	W 25629	10172	W 27169	12223	ORANGES,MAND,CLEMENTINES
05711	ORANGES,FRESH OR DRIED		5497		6124	W 24149	9233	W 24591	10193	ORANGES FRAICHES,SECHEES
0572	LEMONS,GRAPEFRUIT ETC		21277		21376	W 65702	27074	W 57877	26557	AUTRES AGRUMES FRAIS,SECS
05721	LEMONS,LIMES,FRESH,DRIED		6701	W 19781	7528	W 16099	7552	W 17124	9085	CITRONS ET LIMES
05722	GRAPEFRUITS,FRESH,DRIED	W 41445	12540	W 33204	10370	W 41409	14736	W 33233	12979	PAMPLEMOUSSES,POMELOS
05729	CITRUS NES, FRESH,DRIED		2036		3478	W 8194	4786	W 7519	4492	AGRUMES N.D.A
0575	GRAPES FRESH OR DRIED	W 6373	6575	W 5423	4723	W 5554	5382	W 5251	5325	RAISINS FRAIS OU SECS
05751	GRAPES FRESH	W 6095	6258	W 5039	4293	W 4958	4617	W 4635	4610	RAISINS FRAIS
058	FRUIT PRESERVED,PREPARED	W 15492	12768	W 27597	19415	W 28361	22224	W 27069	21347	CONSERVES DE FRUITS
0585	FRUIT OR VEGETABLE JUICE	W 10008	6946	W 21924	13574	W 23641	17289	W 21728	15787	JUS DE FRUITS
05851	ORANGE JUICE	W 2710	1665	W 5946	3442	W 6844	3959	W 6040	3667	JUS D'ORANGE
05852	GRAPEFRUIT JUICE	W 1765	2052	W 3761	3287	W 3216	2888	W 2246	1971	JUS DE PAMPLEMOUSSE
05857	JUICE OF OTHER FRUIT,VEG	W 3569	2364	W 5941	4163	W 6456	6643	W 6989	6382	JUS AUTRES FRUITS,LEGUMES
0589	FRUIT PREPRD,PRESRVD,NES	W 4856	4919	W 5078	5173	W 4149	4313	W 4452	4734	FRUITS PREPARES CONSERV
05899	FRUIT,NUTS NES,PRESERVED	W 4751	4659	W 5069	5118	W 4147	4308	W 4437	4683	FRUITS PREP CONSERV NDA
07	COFFEE,TEA,COCOA,SPICES		3988		4763		4176		5228	CAFE,THE,CACAO,EPICES
073	CHOCOLATE AND PRODUCTS	W 445	3318	W 575	3755	W 359	3373	W 374	3127	CHOCOLAT
09	MISC EDIBLE PRODUCTS		3532		2011		3582		1755	PREP ALIMENTAIRES DIVERSES
098	EDIBLE PRODCTS,PREPS NES		3372		1888		3321		1496	PREP ALIMENTAIRES NDA
09809	MISC FOOD PREPRTIONS NES		2806		1502		3105	W 598	1320	PREP ALIMENTAIRES NDA
1	BEVERAGES AND TOBACCO		192930		262865		402879		612677	BOISSONS ET TABACS
11	BEVERAGES		29854		37635		43232		40978	BOISSONS
112	ALCOHOLIC BEVERAGES		28468	W 56258	35428	W 55125	42088	W 50039	40135	BOISSONS ALCOOLIQUES
1121	WINE OF FRESH GRAPES ETC	W 41878	10742	W 52831	17574	W 51691	21595	W 46512	22191	VINS DE RAISINS FRAIS
11212	WINE OF FRESH GRAPES	W 41858	10642	W 52805	17462	W 50389	20887	W 16187	10993	VINS DE MOUTS DE RAISINS
11213	VERMOUTHS ETC	W 19	101	W 23	108	W 1256	629	W 29469	10228	VERMOUTHS
1124	DISTILLED ALCOHOLIC BEVS		16058	W 1967	16151	W 1927	18611	W 1663	15794	ALCOOLS,EAUX–DE–VIE
11241	WHISKY	W 1078	9634	W 1004	9507	W 978	11999	W 888	9866	WHISKY
11249	OTH ALCOHOLC BEVS,CMPNDS		4871	W 816	5095	W 782	4963	W 636	4410	BOISSONS ALCOOLIQUES NDA
12	TOBACCO AND MANUFACTURES		163076		225230		359647		571699	TABACS BRUTS FABRIQUES
122	TOBACCO,MANUFACTURED	W 12193	162994	W 17386	224985	W 25607	358939	W 41523	571185	TABACS FABRIQUES
1222	CIGARETTES	W 12140	160418	W 17340	222271	W 25541	356090	W 41424	567871	CIGARETTES
2	CRUDE MATERLS,EXCL FUELS		11796		16933		18978		18778	MAT BRUTES NON COMESTIBLES
27	CRUDE FERTLZR,MINRLS NES		2836		3388		3153		4409	ENGRAIS MINERAUX BRUTS
28	METALLIFEROUS ORES,SCRAP		5254		7835		9192		8055	MINERAIS METAL,DECHETS
288	NONFERR METAL SCRAP NES	W 98633	2985	W 111937	5085	W 22538	5528	W 23436	4411	DECHETS NON FERREUX
2882	OTHER BASE MTL SCRAP NES	W 98633	2985	W 59826	4547	W 22538	5528	W 23436	4411	AUTRES DECHETS
3	MINERAL FUELS ETC		42443		37944		45893		60586	COMBUSTIBLES MINERAUX LUB
33	PETROLEUM AND PRODUCTS		42443		37944		45886		60484	PETROLE ET DERIVES
334	PETROLEUM PRODUCTS,REFIN		41436		37690	W 241289	45736	W 284810	60470	PRODUITS RAFFINES
3341	GASOLINE,OTH LIGHT OILS		41434							ESSENCES POUR MOTEURS
3342	KEROSENE,OTH MEDIUM OILS			W 140390	28579	W 164726	34797	W 160821	41994	PETR LAMPANTS,AUT HUIL
33421	KEROSENE INCL JET FUEL			W 140390	28579	W 164726	34797	W 160821	41994	PETROLES LAMPANTS
3343	GAS OILS			W 15866	2906	W 18203	3235	W 34352	7093	GAS OILS
3344	FUEL OILS,NES			W 123599	5059	W 54736	5886	W 85283	9714	FUEL OILS
4	ANIMAL,VEGETABLE OIL,FAT		9177		12026		12371		10555	HUILES,GRAISSES ANIM,VEG
42	FIXED VEGETABLE OIL,FAT		8324		11189		11537		9654	HUILES VEGETALES FIXES
423	FIXED VEG OILS,SOFT	W 11550	7653	W 14101	10523	W 10520	9867	W 10209	8506	HUILES VEGET DOUCES FIXES
4232	SOYA BEAN OIL	W 8374	5282	W 10834	7806	W 3542	3125	W 2964	2237	HUILE DE SOJA
4236	SUNFLOWER SEED OIL	W 3167	2352	W 3265	2713	W 6821	6278	W 7210	6213	HUILE DE TOURNESOL
5	CHEMCLS,RELATED PROD NES		51922		63475		76367		80837	PRODUITS CHIMIQUES
541	*MEDICINAL,PHARM PRODUCT		26389		33179		39828		43408	PROD MEDICINAUX PHARMACEUT
5417	MEDICAMENTS		26295		33143		39820	K 1178406	41751	MEDICAMENTS
54171	— CONTAINNG ANTIBIOTICS		4368		5120		6487	K 319108	8132	MED CONTN ANTIBIOTIQUES
54179	— CONTNG OTH SUBSTANCES		21927		27976		33277	K 858850	33577	MED CONT AUT SUBSTANCES
55	PERFUME,CLEANING ETC PRD		18635		22154		25697		22816	PROD POUR PARFUM,TOILETTE
553	PERFUMERY,COSMETICS,ETC		16328		19929		22641	W 1705	20449	PRODUITS DE PARFUMERIE
59	CHEMICAL MATERIALS NES		2946		4572		6586		7043	MAT PROD CHIMIQUES NDA
6	BASIC MANUFACTURES		95238		130132		128876		117804	ART MANUFACTURES
61	LEATHER,DRESSED FUR,ETC		3352		3487		3160		3223	CUIRS,PELLETERIES
64	PAPER,PAPERBOARD AND MFR		8278		11086		14685		13679	PAPIERS,CARTONS & OUVRAGES
642	PAPER,ETC,PRECUT,ARTS OF		7585		10658		13789	W 5103	13204	PAP,CARTONS DECOUPES
6421	PAPER ETC CONTAINERS		4514		4983		4328	W 1388	3008	BOITES,SACS EMBALLAGES
6428	PAPER ETC ARTICLES NES		2572		5300		9047	W 3537	9826	OUVRAGES EN PATE A PAPIER
64285	PAPER ETC DIAPERS ETC		1819		4961		8775	W 3399	9500	SERVIETTES HYGIENIQUES
65	TEXTILE YARN,FABRICS,ETC		52695		65316		67459		54995	FILS,TISSUS,ARTICLES TEXTILE
651	TEXTILE YARN		5588		5968		5850	W 1485	3321	FILS TEXTILES
6514	SYN FIB YRN,BULK,MONOFIL		2866		3013		3151	W 858	1653	FILS CONT 85% FIB TEXT SYNTH
652	COTTON FABRICS,WOVEN		6330	A 6770	5043		3579	W 1560	4315	TISSUS DE COTON
6522	WOVEN COTTON BLEACHD,ETC		5389	A 6202	4761		3456	W 1468	3917	TISSUS COTON BLANCHIS ETC
65224	BLCHED COTTON FABRIC NES		4442	A 4761	3803		3025	W 1432	3620	AUT TIS PLUS 85% COT BLANCHI
653	WOVN MAN–MADE FIB FABRIC		28241	A 39958	42999	A 37285	44556	W 7553	36520	TISSUS FIBRES SYNTH,ARTIF
6531	CONT SYNT WEAVES NONPILE	A 5248	6326	A 4265	5229	A 1371	2516	W 485	3025	TISSUS FIBRES SYNTH CONTINUE
65315	CONT SYN TXTL FABRIC NES	A 5074	6148	A 4241	5173	A 1257	2344	W 476	2944	TIS PLUS 85% TEXT SYNT CONT
6532	DISC SYN TXTL FABRIC NES		594	A 8441	10011	A 11524	14905	W 2052	14339	TIS DISC MOINS 85% FIBR TEXT
6534	DISC SYN BLEND FABRC NES		20816	A 26554	27028	A 23578	26061	W 4833	18508	TISSUS FIBRES SYNTH DISCONT
65341	DISC SYN FIB–COTTN FABRC		6335	A 6625	5697	A 6697	5319	W 642	2282	TISSUS FIB SYNT DIS MEL COTO
65343	DISC SYN–CONT MAN–MD FAB	A 1159	1678	A 2607	3654	A 3242	4566	W 419	3709	TISSUS FIB SYNT MEL TEXT SY
65349	OTH DISC SYN BLEND FABRC	A 11899	11905	A 16829	17147	A 13460	15906	W 3711	12340	TISSUS FIB SYNT MEL MAT AUT
655	KNITTED,ETC FABRICS	A 1177	2242		1271	A 1786	4075	W 481	2873	ETOF BONNETERIE PIECES ETC
6552	OTHER KNIT ETC FAB NONEL	A 1177	2242		1271	A 1786	4075	W 481	2873	ETOF BON NON ELAS NON SYNT
658	TEXTILE ARTICLES NES		6369		7632		6201	W 915	5744	ART FACONNES MAT TEXTILES
6589	OTH TEXTILE ARTICLES NES		5013		5856		5297	W 424	3434	AUT ART EN TEXTILES NDA
65898	KNITTED ETC ARTICLES NES		4963		5821		5243	W 415	3379	ART BONNET NON ELASTIQUE

5. General Exports F.O.B. by Commodities according to the S.I.T.C. (Rev. 2) in thousand U.S. Dollars
Exportations Générales F.O.B. par Produits d'après la C.T.C.I. (Rév. 2) en milliers de Dollars E.U.

SITC CTCI	COMMODITY	1993 WEIGHT POIDS	1993 VALUE VALEUR	1994 WEIGHT POIDS	1994 VALUE VALEUR	1995 WEIGHT POIDS	1995 VALUE VALEUR	1996 WEIGHT POIDS	1996 VALUE VALEUR	PRODUIT
66	NONMETAL MINERAL MFS NES		19419		35411		21407		25888	ART MIN NON METALLIQUES
661	LIME,CEMENT,BLDG PRODS		11813		23317		18108	W 529756	19430	CHAUX,CIMENTS MAT CONSTR
6612	CEMENT	W 378124	11729	W 699963	22593	W 528716	17279	W 529407	18826	CIMENTS HYDRAULIQUES
667	PEARL,PREC–,SEMI–P STONE		6822		11040		2316		4768	PERLES, PIERRES GEMMES
6672	DIAMONDS NONINDUST,UNSET		6677		10802		2264		4323	DIAMANTS BRUTS
66721	— ROUGH,UNSORTED		6470		10191		2204		4185	DIAMANTS BRUTS NON TRIES
68	NON–FERROUS METALS		1818		1894		2501		5729	METAUX NON FERREUX
69	METAL MANUFACTURES NES		7685		9227		13369		10205	ART MANUFACT EN METAL NDA
699	BASE METAL MFRS NES		2879		3307		8836		5129	ART MANUFACTURES MET NDA
6999	OTHR BASE METAL MFRS ETC				29	W 26	5371	W 9	1809	OUVRAGES EN TUNGST,MOLYB
69999	BASE MTLS NES WRGHT,MFRS				29	W 26	5371	W 9	1808	MET COMMUNS OUVRES NDA
7	MACHINES,TRANSPORT EQUIP		123728		117478		148839		153194	MACHINES MATERIEL TRANSPORT
71	POWER GENERATING EQUIPMT		5210		3123		3319		3023	MACHINES GENERATRICES
716	ROTATING ELECTRIC PLANT		2663		2485		2443		2346	APP ELECTR ROTATIFS,PIECES
7162	AC MTRS,GENRTRS,GEN SETS		2634	N 25046	2428	N 34017	2414	N 20041	2288	MOTEURS ELECTRIQUES
72	MACHS FOR SPCL INDUSTRYS		6418		6101		10595		7946	MAC SPECIALES POUR INDUST
728	OTH MACHY FOR SPCL INDUS		2611		2050		3294		1471	AUT MACH IND PARTICULIERES
74	GENRL INDUSTRL MACHY NES		17325		19825		21197		28287	MACH APP INDUSTRIE
741	HEATING,COOLING EQUIPMNT		4653		5532		6459		15652	MACH CHAUFFAGE,PIECES
7414	NONDOM REFRIG EQUIPT,PTS		869		1334		1828		9414	MAT PRODUCTION DU FROID
74141	REFRIG EQUIP NONDOMESTIC	N 1550	860	N 3467	1296	N 6610	1764	N 21623	9331	REFIG INDUSTRIELS
7415	AIR–CONDITIONING MACHNRY		3527		4047	N 11070	4476	N 23997	6067	GROUPES CONDITION AIR
742	PUMPS FOR LIQUIDS ETC		7377		6030		7884		5039	POMPES MOTO–POMPES
7422	CENTRIFUGAL PUMPS NES	N 4282	5074		4480	N 6890	6258	N 4644	3693	POMPES CENTRIF NON 742.81
743	PUMPS NES,CENTRFUGES ETC		1718		3157		3047		4230	POMPES COMPRES,VENT ETC
75	OFFICE MACHNES,ADP EQUIP		3339		2431		3462		5739	MACH BUREAU TRAIT AUTOM
76	TELECOMM,SOUND EQUIPMENT		48921		41447		48460		33363	EQUIPMENT DE TELECOM
761	TELEVISION RECEIVERS	N 61171	22990	N 47525	18834	N 60178	21620	N 35104	12583	RECEPTEURS DE TELEVISION
7611	COLOUR TV RECEIVERS	N 61163	22987	N 47512	18816	N 60172	21617	N 35102	12582	RECEPTEURS COULEUR
762	RADIO BROADCAST RECEIVRS	N 63067	8952	N 64742	8762	N 120435	10749	N 87537	8297	RECEPTEURS RADIODIFFUSION
7621	MTR VEHC RADIO RECEIVERS	N 25842	2675	N 31515	2884	N 81790	4799	N 6601	1054	RECEPTEURS RADIO AUTO
7628	OTHER RADIO RECEIVERS	N 33129	6035	N 29375	5625	N 34065	5722	N 75046	6939	AUTRES RECEPT RADIO
763	SOUND RECORDRS,PHONOGRPH	N 17171	3457		3798	N 35155	5292	N 26818	5442	PHONO,APP ENREGISTREMENT
7638	OTHR SOUND APPARATUS ETC	N 16709	3379		3689	N 35112	5279	N 26730	5417	AUT APP D'ENREGIS,REPROD
76381	TV IMAGE,SND RECRDRS ETC	N 8714	2718	N 8866	2671	N 19070	4523	N 20103	4909	APP ENREG,REPRO IMAG,SON
764	TELECOM EQPT,PTS,ACC NES		13522		10053		10799		7041	EQUIP TELECOM,PIECES
7641	LINE TELEPHONE,ETC EQUIP		3338		1488	N 14842	1586	N 41587	1840	APP TELEPHON PAR FIL
7648	TELECOMM EQUIPMENT NES	N 4102	2283	N 6768	3078	N 17725	2611	N 60015	1616	APP TELECOM NDA
7649	PTS NES OF EQUIPMT OF 76		5510		3669		2681	W 74	1750	PIECES DE LA DIV 76
76493	TELECOMM EQUIPMT PTS NES		5377		3331		2394	W 72	1572	PIECES 761,762,764.3,8
77	ELECTRIC MACHNRY NES ETC		21020		20608		46246		48037	MACH APP ELECT NDA
772	SWITCHGEAR ETC,PARTS NES		13004		6496		3462	W 219	3154	APP COUPURE,SECT ETC
7721	SWITCHGEAR ETC		12978		6462		3456	W 216	3083	APP COUPURE,SECTIONMNT
775	HOUSEHOLD TYPE EQUIP NES		4631		4265		4694		1439	MACH,APP USAGE DOMESTQUE
7752	DOM REFRIGERATRS,FREEZRS	N 11031	3852	N 8491	3577	N 8479	3958	N 2241	928	REFRIG,CONGEL MENAGER
77522	DOMESTIC DEEP–FREEZERS	N 10210	3535	N 7737	3371	N 8209	3786	N 2050	834	MEUBLES CONGELATEURS
778	ELECTRICAL MACHINERY NES		2729		9085		37563		42377	AUTRES MACH ELECT NDA
7788	OTH ELEC MACHY,EQUIP NES		1117		7160		35194		39028	AUT MACH APP ELEC NDA
77886	OTH ELEC MACHINERY NES		886		6643		34944	N 47171	38730	AUT MACH APP ELECTRIQUES
78	ROAD VEHICLES		20417		21703		14486		16115	VEHICULES ROUTIERS
781	PASS MOTOR VEH EXC BUSES	N 727	11084	N 543	10153	N 177	4767	N 354	6576	AUTO TRANSPORT PERSONNES
782	LORRIES,SPCL MTR VEH NES	N 347	5190	N 453	7800	N 340	6038	N 407	6338	VEHICULES SPECIAUX,MARCH
7821	LORRIES,TRUCKS	N 331	4339	N 438	7068	N 330	5485	N 397	5654	VEHICULES TRANSP MARCHAND
79	OTHR TRANSPORT EQUIPMENT		560		1708		457		9739	AUTRE MATERIEL TRANSPORT
793	SHIPS AND BOATS ETC		318	N 42	1688	N 85	419	N 220	9563	NAVIRES BATEAUX,ETC
7938	TUGS,SPECIAL VESSELS ETC	N 10	27	N 7	1525	N 10	18	N 36	8601	REMORQUEURS,BATEAUX SPEC
79381	TUGS			N 2	822			N 16	8569	BATEAUX REMORQUEURS
8	MISC MANUFACTURED GOODS		206835		180378		191149		166517	ART MANUFACTURES DIVERS
812	*PLUMBG,HEATNG,LGHTNG EQ		3221		3582		4340		4327	APPAR SANITAIRES CHAUFFAGE
8124	LIGHTING EQUIPMENT NES		3182		3470		4210		4252	APPAREILS ECLAIRAGE ETC
81242	LAMPS,FITTINGS BASE METL		3086		3155		3961	W 1228	3156	APPAREILS D'ECLAIRAGE
821	*FURNITURE,PARTS THEREOF		7965		10225		11933		11803	MEUBLES ET PIECES
8211	CHAIRS,SEATS AND PARTS		3579		4230		4325		4845	SIEGES ET PIECES
82111	CHAIRS AND OTHER SEATS		3515		4190		4273	N 122045	4811	SIEGES
8219	FURNITURE AND PARTS NES		4126		5650		7194		6555	AUTRES MEUBLES ET PIECES
82191	METAL FURNITURE NES		2024		3119		2972	W 723	3420	MEUBLES NDA EN METAL
82192	WOOD FURNITURE NES		2018		2414		4008	N 124609	2965	MEUBLES NDA EN BOIS
831	*TRAVEL GOODS,HANDBAGS		5955		3501		1143		1003	ARTICLES DE VOYAGE ETC
83102	TRAVEL GDS,TOILET–CASES		5764		3174		650	N 30385	412	ARTICLES DE VOYAGE
84	CLOTHING AND ACCESSORIES		119420		99645		109047		88496	VETEMENTS
842	MENS OUTERWEAR NOT KNIT	N 1792129	22166	N 1241367	12544	N 942837	8762		6634	VET DESSUS POUR HOMMES
8423	— TROUSERS,BREECHES ETC	N 1569429	17960	N 1092158	9554	N 801727	6666	N 567032	4698	PANTALONS HOMMES MAT TEX
843	WOMENS OUTERWEAR NONKNIT	N 6047946	55725		53167	N 5643861	65898	N 4619902	53015	VET DESSUS FEMMES MAT TEX
8432	— SUITS AND COSTUMES	N 337047	5756	N 326904	5043	N 204092	4290	N 214219	3944	COSTUMES–TAIL MAT TEXIL
8433	— DRESSES	N 638087	8571	N 478216	6293	N 658068	9774	N 535172	8311	ROBES EN MAT–TEXTILES
8434	— SKIRTS	N 515330	4653	N 514887	5097	N 544874	5983	N 344293	3602	JUPES EN MAT TEXTILES
8435	— BLOUSES	N 3937918	30259	N 3373009	29409	N 3585189	37657	N 3044985	30335	BLOUSES FEM MAT TEXTILES
8439	— OTHER OUTER GARMENTS	N 515786	4825	N 481939	5558	N 583601	6788	N 438034	6115	AUT VET DES FEM MAT TEXT
844	UNDER GARMENTS NOT KNIT		6425		4840		5250		4626	VETEMENT DESSOUS MAT TEX
8441	— MENS SHIRTS		5243		4441		4660	N 501369	4281	CHEMISES HOMMES MAT TEXT
84412	—— OF SYNTHETIC FIBRES		3742		2850		2715	N 258025	2100	CHEMISES HOMMES FIB SYNT
845	OUTERWEAR KNIT NONELASTC		23999		21988		20596		18559	VET DESSOUS,ACCES BONNET
8451	— JERSEYS,PULLOVERS ETC		16186		14018		12425	N 1644882	11180	CHANDAILS,PULL–OVERS ETC
8452	— WOMENS DRESSES ETC	N 183358	2481	N 371356	4680	N 211264	2693	N 165395	2018	ROBES,JUPES BONNETERIE
8459	— OTHER,CLTHG ACCESRYS		5332		3290	N 720041	5478		5361	AUT VET DESSUS DE BONNE
846	UNDER GARMENTS KNITTED		10144		5827		7214		3360	SOUS VETS DE BONNETERIE
8462	— OF COTTON NON ELASTIC	N 6892135	7663		4805	N 5078398	5839	N 2226786	2971	SOUS–VET BONNET COTON
84629	—— OTHER	N 6892135	7663		4805	N 5078398	5839	N 2226786	2971	AUT SOUS–VET BONNET COTON
851	*FOOTWEAR		22572	P 2397745	18957	P 1857762	15413	P 1822544	15562	CHAUSSURES
85101	FOOTWEAR RUBBER,PLASTIC	P 1541938	7020	P 1043599	5701	P 1032153	4687	P 911098	4212	CHAUS SEMELLES CAOUTCH
85102	FOOTWEAR LEATHER		15156	P 1324139	12994	P 818568	10601	P 907048	11221	CHAUS SEMELLES EN CUIR
87	PRECISION INSTRUMNTS NES		1076		1722		1609		4510	INSTRUM,APPAR SCIENT NDA
88	PHOTO EQU,OPTICL GDS ETC		20371		17113		17088		11539	APP,FOURN PHOTO,OP,MONTR
882	PHOTO,CINEMA SUPPLIES		3893		4604		5085		2517	PRODUITS PHOTO,CINEMA
8822	PHOTO FILM EXC DEV CINMA		3816		4524		4965		2423	PLAQUES,PELLICULES,FILMS
88222	PHOTO FILM ROLL UNEXPOSD		3489		4374		4808	L 1109	2311	PEL SENSIB PERF OU NON
884	OPTICAL GOODS NES		3298		3422		3046		2357	ELEMENTS OPTIQ,ART LUNET
8842	SPECTACLES AND FRAMES		2966		3012		2822	N 72654	2221	LUNETTES ET MONTURES
885	WATCHES AND CLOCKS		11788		8017		7268		5767	HORLOGERIE
8851	WATCHES,MOVEMENTS,CASES		11676		7813		7169		5635	MONTRES,MOUVEMENTS,BOITES
88511	WATCHES		11648		7775		7099		5631	MONTRES POCHE,BRACELET

5. General Exports F.O.B. by Commodities according to the S.I.T.C. (Rev. 2) in thousand U.S. Dollars
Exportations Générales F.O.B. par Produits d'après la C.T.C.I. (Rév. 2) en milliers de Dollars E.U.

SITC CTCI	COMMODITY	1993 WEIGHT POIDS	1993 VALUE VALEUR	1994 WEIGHT POIDS	1994 VALUE VALEUR	1995 WEIGHT POIDS	1995 VALUE VALEUR	1996 WEIGHT POIDS	1996 VALUE VALEUR	PRODUIT
89	MISC MANUFCTRD GOODS NES		26255		25632		30577		29278	ART MANUFACTURES DIVERS
892	PRINTED MATTER		3240		3488		4835	W 762	4011	IMPRIMES
893	ARTICLES OF PLASTIC NES		6287		6589		9901		9534	OUVRAGES EN MAT DIVIS 58
8931	PLSTC PACKG CONTNRS,LIDS		2932		2674		3636	W 1400	3092	ART TRANSP EMBALLAGE ETC
8939	MISC PLASTIC ARTICLES		3342		3903		6203	W 2307	6424	ART DIVERS EN MAT DIV 58
89399	OTHR PLASTC ARTICLES NES		3254		3844		6088	W 2286	6370	AUT OUV MAT DIV 58
894	TOYS,SPORTING GOODS,ETC		8129		6794		7152		6996	VOITURES ENFANTS,JOUETS
8946	NON-MILITARY ARMS,AMMO		5934		5537		5526		5433	ARMES NON MILITAIRES
89461	NON-MILITARY FIREARMS	N 49015	3511	N 39936	2823	N 37466	3128	N 39006	2865	ARMES A FEU
897	GOLD,SILVER WARE,JEWELRY		2929		2482		2042		1877	BIJOUTERIE,ORFEVRERIE
8973	PREC JEWLRY,GLD-SILVWARE		2799		2423		1810		1576	BIJOUX OR,ARGENT ORFEVRE
899	OTHER MANUFACTURED GOODS		3599		3278		3088		2491	AUT ART MANUF DIVERS NDA

1. HISTORICAL SERIES, 1993–1996 GENERAL TRADE, IMPORTS F.O.B., EXPORTS F.O.B.
SERIES HISTORIQUES, 1993–1996 COMMERCE GENERAL, IMPORTATIONS F.O.B., EXPORTATIONS F.O.B

YEAR ANNEE	VALUE IN MILLION CZECH. KORUNY / VALEUR EN MILLION CZECH. KORUNY: MERCHANDISE –MARCHANDISE		GOLD –OR		CONVERSION FACTORS U.S. CENTS PER CZECH. KORUNA FACTEURS DE CONVERSION CENTS E.U. PAR CZECH. KORUNA		INDEX NUMBERS –INDICES: QUANTUM		UNIT VALUE VALEUR UNITAIRE	
	IMPORTS	EXPORTS	IMPORTS	EXPORTS	IMPORTS	EXPORTS	IMPORTS	EXPORTS	IMPORTS	EXPORTS
1993	370396.90	384965.80			3.4271	3.4312				
1994	428638.90	410249.90			3.4892	3.4808				
1995	670407.90	574722.00			3.7744	3.7733				
1996	753911.00	594080.00			3.6845	3.6851				

2. IMPORTS BY BROAD ECONOMIC CATEGORY AND EXPORTS BY INDUSTRIAL ORIGIN. (PERCENTAGE OF TOTAL VALUE)
IMPORTATIONS PAR CATEGORIES ECONOMIQUES ET EXPORTATIONS PAR BRANCHE D'ACTIVITE.(EN POURCENTAGE DE LA VALEUR TOTALE)

IMPORTS – IMPORTATIONS

	1990	1991	1992	1993	1994	1995	1996
TOTAL IMPORTS–IMPORTATIONS TOTALES				100.	100.	100.	100.
1 FOOD BEV–ALIMENTATION BOISSONS				6.1	6.9	5.4	5.6
11 PRIMARY–PRODUITS DE BASE				3.3	3.5	2.6	2.6
111 FOR INDUSTRY–POUR L'INDUSTRIE				1.2	1.0	0.8	0.8
112 FOR HOUSEHOLDS–POUR LES MENAGES				2.1	2.4	1.8	1.8
12 PROCESSED–PRODUITS ELABORES				2.9	3.4	2.9	3.0
121 FOR INDUSTRY–POUR L'INDUSTRIE				0.4	0.4	0.4	0.4
122 FOR HOUSEHOLDS–POUR LES MENAGES				2.4	3.0	2.5	2.6
2 IND SUPPLIES–APPROV INDUSTRIELS				30.0	31.1	34.3	32.6
21 PRIMARY–PRODUITS DE BASE				4.1	4.0	3.5	3.0
22 PROCESSED–PRODUITS ELABORES				25.9	27.1	30.8	29.6
3 FUELS–COMBUSTIBLES				10.8	9.9	7.7	8.6
31 PRIMARY–PRODUITS DE BASE				8.4	7.6	6.1	7.0
32 PROCESSED–PRODUITS ELABORES				2.4	2.2	1.7	1.7
321 MOTOR SPIRIT–ESSENCE				2.2	1.8	1.2	1.3
322 OTHER–AUTRES				0.2	0.4	0.4	0.4
4 MACHINERY–EQUIPEMENT				30.3	29.0	28.8	28.5
41 CAPITAL EQUIPMENT–MACHINES				26.1	25.1	24.3	24.2
42 PARTS–PIECES ACCESSOIRES				4.3	3.9	4.6	4.4
5 TRANSPORT–TRANSPORT				6.7	6.8	7.9	9.4
51 PASSENGER CARS–AUTOMOBILES				2.2	2.7	2.5	3.0
52 OTHER–AUTRES				1.6	1.7	2.2	2.2
521 INDUSTRIAL–INDUSTRIELS				1.4	1.6	2.1	2.1
522 NON INDUSTRIAL–NON INDUSTRIEL				0.2	0.2	0.1	0.1
53 PARTS–PIECES ACCESSOIRES				3.0	2.3	3.3	4.1
6 CONSUM GOODS–BIENS CONSOMMATION				15.3	15.8	14.6	15.3
61 DURABLE–DURABLES				4.7	4.7	4.1	4.2
62 SEMI DURABLE–SEMI DURABLES				6.2	6.2	6.4	6.9
63 NON DURABLE–NON DURABLES				4.4	5.0	4.1	4.2
7 GOODS NES–BIENS NDA				0.7	0.5	1.2	0.0

EXPORTS – EXPORTATIONS

	1990	1991	1992	1993	1994	1995	1996
TOTAL EXPORTS–EXPORTATIONS TOTALES				100.	100.	100.	100.
1 AGRICULTURE				3.1	3.5	3.0	2.1
2 MINING QUARRY–INDUS EXTRACTIVES				5.7	4.7	3.6	3.7
3 MANUFACTURING–IND MANUFACTUR				91.2	91.8	93.5	94.1
31 FOOD BEV TOBACCO–ALIM BOISS TAB				6.2	5.5	4.3	4.3
32 TEXTILES–INDUSTRIES TEXTILES				9.0	9.2	10.6	9.1
33 WOOD & PRODUCTS–BOIS & PRODUITS				3.0	3.7	3.0	3.0
34 PAPER & PRODUCTS–PAPIER & PRODT				2.4	2.3	3.2	2.9
35 CHEMICALS–INDUSTRIES CHIMIQUES				13.0	14.2	13.5	13.7
36 NON METAL MIN–MIN NON METAL				6.2	6.4	5.1	5.6
37 BASIC METAL–IND METAL BASE				11.8	11.2	11.2	9.3
38 METAL MANUF–MANUF METAL				34.7	33.6	38.6	43.7
39 OTH MANUF IND–AUTRES MANUF				5.0	5.6	4.0	2.5

3. TRADE BY PRINCIPAL COUNTRIES OF ORIGIN AND DESTINATION (VALUE IN THOUSAND U.S. DOLLARS)
ECHANGES SELON LES PRINCIPAUX PAYS D'ORIGINE ET DE DESTINATION (VALEUR EN MILLIERS DE DOLLARS EU)

COUNTRIES–PAYS	GENERAL IMPORTS F.O.B. IMPORTATIONS GENERALES F.O.B.				
	1992	1993	1994	1995	1996
World		12703902	14950973	25303438	27717333
Africa		52195	71975	93411	144128
Americas		590610	755717	1172160	1297886
Northern America		435876	568110	930229	1028174
LAIA		125730	141679	188648	216351
CACM		23964	35029	40462	39173
Caribbean		1999	2274	4221	7197
Rest of America		3041	8624	8600	6990
As.ex F.USSR		783560	1005636	1513064	1850519
Eur.x F.USSR		9770957	11568069	20136915	21846518
EU		6720572	8307802	15454807	17300190
EFTA		329740	391207	568773	560488
East Europe		2646932	2753886	3922384	3772080
Other Europe		1150	3873	4793	3682
Former USSR		1443649	1474789	2229978	2361138
Oceania		55368	31601	35945	49643
Germany/Allemagne		3259894	3795473	8015731	8262104
Slovakia		2127229	2131165	2988361	2650718
Russian Federation		1268918	1256528	1879170	2059854
Austria/Autriche		1001235	1207057	1747492	1594043
Italy/Italie		605121	768501	1344522	1633429
France,Monac		394194	548020	1018475	1162110
United Kingdom		348795	452280	953438	1042956
USA/Etats–Unis d'Amer		386199	506767	853155	939984
Poland/Pologne		322460	426157	683061	806539
Netherlands/Pays–Bas		360241	437207	665529	630133
Switz.Liecht		295533	343376	494071	493109
Belgium–Luxembourg		210761	314762	507717	503005
Japan/Japon		225121	303084	442143	473645
Sweden/Suède		144154	203412	312891	336080
Spain/Espagne		98252	159203	275608	358024
Hungary/Hongrie		174345	170850	218455	275606
Finland/Finlande		94190	168287	213489	266930
Denmark/Danemark		118889	141984	203336	224692
China/Chine		76599	101881	209558	298237
Ukraine		115667	113912	216588	175435
Korea, Republic of		58141	95481	120038	179763
Slovenia/Slovénia		51312	72266	131109	153488
Ireland/Irlande		46308	66133	116353	129936
Hong Kong		64774	72984	104033	108825
Brazil/Brésil		33024	55760	90151	111717
Canada		49623	61237	76769	87982
Turkey/Turquie		42255	44211	61415	78550
India/Inde		34054	48453	61073	82702
Norway,SVD,JM		33394	46940	73435	66288
Singapore/Singapour		24616	39361	70252	54383
Greece/Grèce		32856	37300	63723	49510
Malaysia/Malaisie		21164	29361	48104	67543
Israel/Israël		20970	27214	40460	50055
Thailand/Thaïlande		20792	24493	42442	44851
Uzbekistan/Ouzbékistan		17267	32030	42330	40539
Croatia/Croatie		19372	29778	40637	36907
Indonesia/Indonésie		12842	20451	37320	47253
Colombia/Colombie		26319	22002	25718	34670
Australia/Australie		18199	19396	29592	41394
So. Africa Customs Un		11392	15014	26300	34077
Argentina/Argentine		36839	20167	11889	16115
Costa Rica		9556	19299	24184	23166
Bulgaria/Bulgarie		13560	14331	18118	22623
Belarus/Bélarus		6591	17688	20214	19849
Ecuador/Equateur		10833	19237	22321	11797
Kazakhstan		7634	19096	13482	22749
Portugal		5682	8182	16503	24402
Cyprus/Chypre		1514	14557	30600	7774
Iran (Islamic Rp. of)		3798	5472	7856	35396
Peru/Pérou		9436	9008	15679	17873

COUNTRIES–PAYS	GENERAL EXPORTS F.O.B. EXPORTATIONS GENERALES F.O.B.				
	1992	1993	1994	1995	1996
Monde		12892226	14081475	21685601	21907355
Afrique		255320	222534	230690	341555
Amériques		401761	483243	634684	693818
Amérique du Nord		279111	345717	471139	522297
ALAI		102204	112906	135205	140195
MCAC		6441	12749	9748	8694
Caraïbes		7260	8757	15524	19755
Autre Amérique		6745	3114	3067	2878
Asie l'URSS exclus		1149061	921968	1100435	1056762
Europe l'URSS exclus		10231356	11526394	18534487	18495184
UE		6410697	7633445	13217531	12762128
AELE		186302	243291	364292	354996
Europe de l'Est		3440012	3342081	4493861	4862295
Autre de l'Europe		7126	7525	11026	5347
Ancienne URSS		813634	873370	1091142	1202720
Océanie		37106	37796	45844	41766
Germany/Allemagne		3352368	4153127	8144949	7892013
Slovakia		2704914	2319447	3009443	3120936
Austria/Autriche		779421	1013149	1426396	1411172
Poland/Pologne		351935	548616	966854	1205395
Italy/Italie		666073	628592	809180	722400
Russian Federation		575366	548162	631991	692797
United Kingdom		388844	392610	687912	551813
France,Monac		250547	359312	570215	628228
Netherlands/Pays–Bas		307599	358109	517964	454600
Hungary/Hongrie		292822	363284	378260	390708
USA/Etats–Unis d'Amer		236151	302552	415548	463202
Belgium–Luxembourg		173101	218767	345632	373575
Switz.Liecht		152432	198267	290535	264927
Slovenia/Slovénia		111836	162342	244407	227816
Ukraine		98766	133625	223103	224579
Spain/Espagne		158996	130141	166257	161558
Sweden/Suède		84981	105693	162849	176008
China/Chine		251573	85519	94663	71428
Croatia/Croatie		68434	97347	139666	154125
Egypt/Egypte		149045	123790	81030	93068
Denmark/Danemark		80945	97713	132513	134972
Hong Kong		109341	117961	70843	103894
Japan/Japon		64738	88585	139733	95437
Turkey/Turquie		134996	53082	70603	90577
Greece/Grèce		75528	66408	91060	92798
Finland/Finlande		51983	68197	96833	90720
India/Inde		49741	56512	81103	83570
Singapore/Singapour		36552	32352	122260	70392
Bulgaria/Bulgarie		53409	61571	75848	66790
Thailand/Thaïlande		73843	82463	42286	48726
Iran (Islamic Rp. of)		57890	45131	58955	68293
Norway,SVD,JM		30404	42334	69825	85412
Syrian Arab Republic		38169	67161	58730	48880
Romania/Roumanie		32715	46435	57138	72578
Lithuania/Lituanie		13934	43677	59712	85835
Canada		42922	42930	55558	59073
Lebanon/Liban		50026	35386	53384	61381
So. Africa Customs Un		9085	10994	24139	130263
Belarus/Bélarus		17465	39931	54225	58950
Israel/Israël		40135	50427	43775	30483
Australia/Australie		33011	33615	42549	37850
Ireland/Irlande		25731	22363	40867	47827
Kazakhstan		25599	41189	31952	30418
Brazil/Brésil		15099	24436	42515	37768
Korea, Republic of		13560	13361	37871	45057
Tunisia/Tunisie		10912	17972	44411	36386
Yugoslavia/Yougoslavie		4441	9253	17176	74414
United Arab Emirates		19662	20492	18196	37287
Algeria/Algérie		27399	18095	23104	22854
Tfyr Macedonia			23961	37454	23780

(VALUE AS PERCENTAGE OF WORLD TOTAL)(VALEURS EN POURCENTAGE DU TOTAL MONDIAL)

	1987	1988	1989	1990	1991	1992	1993	1994	1995	1996
Africa							0.4	0.5	0.4	0.5
Americas							4.6	5.1	4.6	4.7
Northern America							3.4	3.8	3.7	3.7
LAIA							1.0	0.9	0.7	0.8
CACM							0.2	0.2	0.2	0.1
Caribbean							0.0	0.0	0.0	0.0
Rest of America							0.0	0.1	0.0	0.0
As.ex F.USSR							6.2	6.7	6.0	6.7
Eur.x F.USSR							76.9	77.4	79.6	78.8
EU							52.9	55.6	61.1	62.4
EFTA							2.6	2.6	2.2	2.0
East Europe							20.8	18.4	15.5	13.6
Other Europe							0.0	0.0	0.0	0.0
Former USSR							11.4	9.9	8.8	8.5
Oceania							0.4	0.2	0.1	0.2
Germany/Allemagne							25.7	25.4	31.7	29.8
Slovakia							16.7	14.3	11.8	9.6
Russian Federation							10.0	8.4	7.4	7.4
Austria/Autriche							7.9	8.1	6.9	5.8
Italy/Italie							4.8	5.1	5.3	5.9
France,Monac							3.1	3.7	4.0	4.2
United Kingdom							2.7	3.0	3.8	3.8
USA/Etats–Unis d'Amer							3.0	3.4	3.4	3.4
Poland/Pologne							2.5	2.9	2.7	2.9
Netherlands/Pays–Bas							2.8	2.9	2.6	2.3

	1987	1988	1989	1990	1991	1992	1993	1994	1995	1996
Afrique							2.0	1.6	1.1	1.6
Amériques							3.1	3.4	2.9	3.2
Amérique du Nord							2.2	2.5	2.2	2.4
ALAI							0.8	0.8	0.6	0.6
MCAC							0.0	0.1	0.0	0.0
Caraïbes							0.1	0.1	0.1	0.1
Autre Amérique							0.1	0.0	0.0	0.0
Asie l'URSS exclus							8.9	6.5	5.1	4.8
Europe l'URSS exclus							79.4	81.9	85.5	84.4
UE							49.7	54.2	61.0	58.3
AELE							1.4	1.7	1.7	1.6
Europe de l'Est							26.7	23.7	20.7	22.2
Autre de l'Europe							0.1	0.1	0.1	0.0
Ancienne URSS							6.3	6.2	5.0	5.5
Océanie							0.3	0.3	0.2	0.2
Germany/Allemagne							26.0	29.5	37.6	36.0
Slovakia							21.0	16.5	13.9	14.2
Austria/Autriche							6.0	7.2	6.6	6.4
Poland/Pologne							2.7	3.9	4.5	5.5
Italy/Italie							5.2	4.5	3.7	3.3
Russian Federation							4.5	3.9	2.9	3.2
United Kingdom							3.0	2.8	3.2	2.5
France,Monac							1.9	2.6	2.6	2.9
Netherlands/Pays–Bas							2.4	2.5	2.4	2.1
Hungary/Hongrie							2.3	2.6	1.7	1.8

4. General Imports F.O.B. by Commodities according to the S.I.T.C. (Rev. 2) in thousand U.S. Dollars
Importations Générales F.O.B. par Produits d'après la C.T.C.I. (Rév. 2) en milliers de Dollars E.U.

SITC CTCI	COMMODITY	1993 WEIGHT POIDS	1993 VALUE VALEUR	1994 WEIGHT POIDS	1994 VALUE VALEUR	1995 WEIGHT POIDS	1995 VALUE VALEUR	1996 WEIGHT POIDS	1996 VALUE VALEUR	PRODUIT
	ALL COMMODITIES		12703902		14950973		25303438		27717333	TOUS PRODUITS
0	FOOD AND LIVE ANIMALS		799495		1037747		1400829		1585069	ALIMENTS,ANIMAUX VIVANTS
01	MEAT AND PREPARATIONS		24529		53672		56629		60790	VIANDES ET PREPARATIONS
03	FISH AND PREPARATIONS		45223		62516		72376		84643	POISSONS ET PREPARATIONS
04	CEREALS AND PREPARATIONS		108253		91871		121426		184526	CEREALES ET PRODUITS
048	CEREAL ETC PREPARATIONS	W 26026	36423	W 35191	51092	W 50015	71277	W 65768	80718	PREPTNS A BASE CEREALES
05	VEGETABLES AND FRUIT		268616		370076		487861		535369	LEGUMES ET FRUITS
054	VEG ETC FRSH,SMPLY PRSVD	W 255886	80107	W 255393	104603	W 341283	156455	W 358124	155077	LEGUMES FRAIS,CONG,SECS
0545	OTHER FRESH VEGETABLES	W 127058	38095	W 155676	54566	W 153086	63265	W 169840	75517	AUTRES LEGUMES FRAIS,REF
057	FRUIT,NUTS,FRESH,DRIED	W 361714	142009	W 387383	180527	W 454254	219867	W 460857	255595	FRUITS FRAIS OU SECS
0573	BANANA,PLANTAIN,FRSH,DRY	W 103293	45727	W 121057	55046	W 161194	67559	W 148543	73645	BANANES FRAICHES,SECHEES
058	FRUIT PRESERVED,PREPARED	W 37006	34334	W 92572	68267	W 99891	87756	W 104573	99571	CONSERVES DE FRUITS
07	COFFEE,TEA,COCOA,SPICES		119599		166721		218844		214641	CAFE,THE,CACAO,EPICES
071	COFFEE AND SUBSTITUTES	W 29423	49606	W 30667	83647	W 30284	115647	W 33564	96117	CAFE ET SUCCEDANES
0711	COFFEE GREEN,ROASTED,SUB	W 28644	45649	W 29221	74520	W 28588	99598	W 31091	76500	CAFE TORREFIE OU DECAFEINE
07111	COFFEE GREEN,HUSKS,SKINS	W 26016	38733	W 26743	65614	W 25973	86441	W 28538	66753	CAFE NON TORREFIE
081	*FEEDING STUFF FOR ANIML	W 393321	115749	W 417639	121550	W 514736	157021		206261	NOURRITURE POUR ANIMAUX
0813	OILCAKE AND OTH RESIDUES	W 310016	68956	W 321174	67512	W 389167	78632	W 423230	117706	TOURTEAUX
08131	— OF SOYA BEANS	W 292518	66118	W 308613	65605	W 374711	76749	W 413809	116386	TOURTEAUX DE SOJA
09	MISC EDIBLE PRODUCTS		62688		96005		145264		157327	PREP ALIMENTAIRES DIVERSES
098	EDIBLE PRODCTS,PREPS NES	W 21614	54833	W 34578	91635	W 44255	139984		151521	PREP ALIMENTAIRES NDA
09809	MISC FOOD PREPRTIONS NES	W 11524	37391	W 19170	68212	W 24758	101042	W 31307	112901	PREP ALIMENTAIRES NDA
1	BEVERAGES AND TOBACCO		134376		191738		198349		241657	BOISSONS ET TABACS
11	BEVERAGES		56666		67569		75271		101278	BOISSONS
112	ALCOHOLIC BEVERAGES	W 47337	38961	W 69400	53478	W 64337	60154	W 95081	85355	BOISSONS ALCOOLIQUES
12	TOBACCO AND MANUFACTURES		77710		124169		123078		140380	TABACS BRUTS FABRIQUES
121	TOBACCO UNMNFCTRD,REFUSE	W 12214	32400	W 17502	46597	W 17030	59022	W 20648	87214	TABACS BRUTS,DECHETS
122	TOBACCO,MANUFACTURED	W 5368	45310	W 8000	77571	W 7863	64057	W 7593	53166	TABACS FABRIQUES
1222	CIGARETTES	W 4009	31589	W 5954	55298	W 6688	55185	W 4312	33967	CIGARETTES
2	CRUDE MATERLS,EXCL FUELS		635904		724027		1109017		1004313	MAT BRUTES NON COMESTIBLES
23	RUBBER, CRUDE		50836		56040		100973		89573	CAOUTCHOUC BRUT
24	CORK AND WOOD		42084		33890		74576		63278	LIEGE ET BOIS
251	*PULP AND WASTE PAPER	W 137291	53322	W 133545	72145	W 134877	110863	W 150732	81596	PATES A PAPIER,DECHETS
2517	SODA,SULPHATE WOOD PULP	W 96239	37756	W 91784	46152	W 83771	72836	W 85628	42988	PATES CHIMIQUES AU SULFATE
26	TEXTILE FIBRES AND WASTE		127969		161798		254380		237577	FIBRES TEXTILES
263	COTTON	W 45833	60362	W 54533	85160	W 61389	132465	W 59523	110528	COTON
2631	RAW COTTON,EXCL LINTERS	W 44663	58979	W 52149	83148	W 58757	129333	W 56949	107365	COTON EN MASSE
27	CRUDE FERTLZR,MINRLS NES		81897		79549		104142		102038	ENGRAIS MINERAUX BRUTS
278	OTHER CRUDE MINERALS	W 1077283	53097	W 1094484	51820	W 1309621	68837	W 1492307	72294	AUTRES MINERAUX BRUTS
28	METALLIFEROUS ORES,SCRAP		195341		209514		315940		257817	MINERAIS METAL,DECHETS
281	IRON ORE,CONCENTRATES	W 7551506	148944	W 7368775	157460	MW 9146	214620	W 8079384	186936	MINERAIS DE FER
2815	IRON ORE,CONC,NOT AGGLOM	W 2638076	51838	W 2443117	58816	W 2709980	71224	W 2569950	62845	MINERAIS NON AGGLOMERES
2816	IRON ORE AGGLOMERATES	W 4911161	97083	W 4925658	98643	W 6436127	143394	W 5509434	124091	MINERAIS AGGLOMERES
29	CRUDE ANIMAL,VEG MAT NES		47808		62554		89271		102128	MATIERES BRUTES ANIM,VEGET
292	CRUDE VEG MATERIALS NES	W 7717	35668	W 10330	49562	W 14047	67520	W 18570	78039	MAT BRUTES VEGETALES NDA
3	MINERAL FUELS ETC		1391463		1508580		1999117		2433498	COMBUSTIBLES MINERAUX LUB
32	COAL,COKE AND BRIQUETTES		60737		71373		113185		118160	HOUILLES,COKES,BRIQUETTES
322	COAL,LIGNITE AND PEAT	W 1951413	57762	W 1746431	56194	W 2683306	86290	W 3233878	107630	HOUILLES,LIGNITES,TOURBE
3222	OTH COAL,NOT AGGLOMERATD	W 1928737	56646	W 1730771	55601	W 2661238	85477	W 3174020	104577	AUTRES HOUILLES
33	PETROLEUM AND PRODUCTS		920211		992054		1174947		1453461	PETROLE ET DERIVES
333	CRUDE PETROLEUM	W 5609994	606123	W 6493361	672946	W 7072167	804910	W 7644963	1045538	HUILES BRUTES DE PETROLE
334	PETROLEUM PRODUCTS,REFIN	W 1505036	292229	W 1578295	286731	W 1505324	325060	W 1547760	368703	PRODUITS RAFFINES
3341	GASOLINE,OTH LIGHT OILS	W 1497300	280652	W 1571474	274767	W 1497688	306853	W 1541363	351117	ESSENCES POUR MOTEURS
341	*GAS,NATURAL AND MANUFCT		405566		412064	W 8114629	645791	MW 9537	782222	GAZ NATUREL,GAZ MANUFACT
3414	PETROLEUM GASES, GASEOUS		398000		402015	W 8049135	628751	MW 9439	758702	GAZ DE PETROLE GAZEUX
4	ANIMAL,VEGETABLE OIL,FAT		45684		53113		75847		76237	HUILES,GRAISSES ANIM,VEG
5	CHEMCLS,RELATED PROD NES		1462817		1869078		2826369		3063287	PRODUITS CHIMIQUES
51	ORGANIC CHEMICALS		200832		252885		373597		328104	PROD CHIMIQ ORGANIQUES
512	ALCOHOLS,PHENOLS ETC	W 77540	27995	W 95994	46732	W 99932	69506	W 94286	54266	PHENOLS,PHENOLS–ALCOOLS
514	NITROGEN–FNCTN COMPOUNDS	W 18683	57466	W 19404	63570	W 22770	88643	W 25156	85165	COMPOSES FONCT AZOTEES
516	OTHER ORGANIC CHEMICALS	W 68382	41798	W 66424	44874	W 80931	72317		64044	AUTRES PROD ORGANIQUES
52	INORGANIC CHEMICALS		158217		175128		253950		259543	PROD CHIM INORGANIQUES
522	INORG ELEMNTS,OXIDES,ETC	W 492725	72531	W 454100	88604	W 513828	122347	W 436118	124677	ELEMENTS INORGANIQUES
523	OTHR INORG CHEMICALS ETC	W 303591	81357	W 320041	82267	W 390040	125170		132805	AUT PRODUITS CHIMIQUES INORG
5232	OTH MTL CMPD OF INRG ACD	W 230448	47347	W 238375	47983	W 280844	72930	W 287807	78121	SELS METALLIQUES
53	DYES,TANNING,COLOUR PROD		146357		181841		277490		307506	PROD TEINTURE,COLORANTS
533	PIGMENTS,PAINTS,ETC	W 45474	120184	W 60936	153142	W 105808	242936	W 119628	267895	PIGMENTS,PEINTURES,VERNIS
5334	VARNISHES,DISTEMPERS ETC	W 26769	75191	W 32232	91088	W 42470	143797	W 46320	159294	PEINTURES A L'EAU
53342	OTH PAINTS,VARNISHES ETC	W 17160	50603	W 19239	56452	W 25186	94511	W 25692	103923	AUTRES PEINTURES,VERNIS
541	*MEDICINAL,PHARM PRODUCT	MK 44326	309337	MK 16556	450738	MK 18429	629236		711019	PROD MEDICINAUX PHARMACEUT
5416	GLYCOSIDES,GLANDS,SERA	K 247213	21542	K 477595	44090	K 1066272	80090	K 584797	82673	HETEROSIDES
5417	MEDICAMENTS	MK 11641	241861	MK 13455	343331	MK 14450	471285	MK 16309	542561	MEDICAMENTS
54171	— CONTAINNG ANTIBIOTICS	K 1104443	28680	K 1255763	48745	K 1572104	58684	K 1655803	64865	MED CONTN ANTIBIOTIQUES
54172	— CONTAINING HORMONES	K 1269141	33885	K 833529	48353	K 650825	69567	K 629332	73320	MED CONTENANT HORMONES
54179	— CONTNG OTH SUBSTANCES	K 8909207	171979	MK 11022	233344	MK 11724	320396	MK 13525	378393	MED CONT AUT SUBSTANCES
55	PERFUME,CLEANING ETC PRD		162350		190677		253803		290892	PROD POUR PARFUM,TOILETTE
553	PERFUMERY,COSMETICS,ETC	W 20457	70213	W 22037	88051	W 25933	117131	W 27518	130737	PRODUITS DE PARFUMERIE
554	SOAP,CLEANSING ETC PREPS	W 77024	74685	W 84398	78308	W 89925	100381	W 100104	109503	SAVONS,PRODUITS DETERSIFS
5542	WASHING PREPARATIONS ETC	W 66049	61452	W 75406	65533	W 80163	83830	W 89015	90926	PROD ORG TENSIO–ACT NDA
562	*FERTILIZERS,MANUFACTURE	W 384142	34357	W 627748	59376	W 705434	81270	W 749081	89740	ENGRAIS MANUFACTURES
58	PLASTIC MATERIALS ETC		277858		343524		636257		705062	MAT PLAST ARTIFICIELLES
582	PROD OF CONDENSATION ETC	W 42635	68847	W 62815	84999	W 89600	169933	W 104311	180508	PROD CONDENS,POLYCOND
5823	ALKYDS,OTHER POLYESTERS	W 7222	18924	W 14116	31504	W 27963	77699	W 31866	71350	ALKYDES ET AUT POLYESTERS
583	POLYMERIZATION ETC PRODS	W 134656	193539	W 157783	241378	W 238371	447544	W 297086	507670	PROD POLYMERISATION
5831	POLYETHYLENE	W 57042	47968	W 63684	57645	W 82197	103533	W 98957	111085	POLYETHYLENE
5834	POLYVINYL CHLORIDE	W 27792	36416	W 33509	47332	W 66330	109111	W 76977	113646	CHLORURE DE POLYVINYLE
5839	OTH POLYMRZTION ETC PROD	W 16214	45668	W 18406	61987	W 31748	116360	W 43361	135913	AUT PROD POLYMER COPOLYM
59	CHEMICAL MATERIALS NES		172002		213254		318165		363965	MAT PROD CHIMIQUES NDA
591	PESTICIDES,DISINFECTANTS	W 6066	48521	W 9250	68735	W 9142	86468	W 10509	104405	DESINF,INSECT,FONG,HERB
5913	HERBICIDES,FOR RETAIL	W 3610	30256	W 5705	45944	W 5263	56218	W 5705	66503	HERBICIDES VENTE AU DET
598	MISCEL CHEM PRODUCTS NES	W 68416	105243	W 82595	120194	W 128507	189913	W 160122	211312	PROD DIV INDUST CHIM NDA
5989	CHEM PRODUCTS,PREPS NES	W 55540	84100	W 70231	100511	W 112569	161634	W 140826	176668	PROD PREP CHIMIQUES NDA
59899	OTH CHEM PRODS,PREPS,NES	W 32799	48662	W 41871	58805	W 75060	102924	W 103265	117779	AUT PRODUITS CHIMIQUES NDA
6	BASIC MANUFACTURES		2050006		2520671		5282050		5481866	ART MANUFACTURES
61	LEATHER,DRESSED FUR,ETC		41582		64700		221452		203485	CUIRS,PELLETERIES
611	LEATHER	W 2249	20257	W 3185	31858	W 8707	113218	W 8490	111744	CUIRS,PEAUX PREPARES
6114	LEATHR BOVINE NES,EQUINE	W 754	10082	W 1608	19998	W 4928	87563	W 4889	77565	CUIRS DE BOVINS
612	LEATHER ETC MANUFACTURES	W 1960	16239	W 3275	24888	W 8052	88449	W 6547	75329	OUVRAGES EN CUIRS NDA
6123	PREPRD PARTS OF FOOTWEAR	W 1877	15418	W 3179	23785	W 7813	83746	W 6281	66737	PARTIES DE CHAUSSURES
62	RUBBER MANUFACTURES NES		130625		143034		261694		296870	CAOUTCHOUC MANUFACTURE
621	MATERIALS OF RUBBER	W 12174	31209	W 13211	34655	W 22906	68418	W 26168	85516	PRODUITS EN CAOUTCHOUC

4. General Imports F.O.B. by Commodities according to the S.I.T.C. (Rev. 2) in thousand U.S. Dollars
Importations Générales F.O.B. par Produits d'après la C.T.C.I. (Rév. 2) en milliers de Dollars E.U.

SITC CTCI	COMMODITY	1993 WEIGHT POIDS	1993 VALUE VALEUR	1994 WEIGHT POIDS	1994 VALUE VALEUR	1995 WEIGHT POIDS	1995 VALUE VALEUR	1996 WEIGHT POIDS	1996 VALUE VALEUR	PRODUIT
625	RUBBER TYRES, TUBES ETC	W 31076	55511	W 26954	63017	W 35736	94792	W 35775	110062	PNEUS CAOUTCHOUC VULCANISE
628	RUBBER ARTICLES NES	W 14790	43906	W 12451	45362	W 15114	98485	W 14533	101292	OUVRAGES CAOUTCHOUC NDA
63	WOOD,CORK MANUFACTRS NES		62304		72221		122380		137394	OUVRAGES LIEGE ET BOIS
64	PAPER,PAPERBOARD AND MFR		242312		313235		526441		594845	PAPIERS,CARTONS & OUVRAGES
641	PAPER AND PAPERBOARD	W 235849	164254	W 292496	216825	W 290153	329433	W 353019	359335	PAPIERS ET CARTONS
6412	PRINTG,WRITING PAPER NES	W 47222	51153	W 55549	64225	W 63105	90887	W 85516	96570	PAPIERS POUR L'IMPRESSION
64122	— COATED,IMPREGNATD ETC	W 45293	48132	W 52755	59979	W 56978	81386	W 75113	83533	PAPIERS IMPRESSION COUCHES
6415	PAPER,PAPERBRD,BULK,NES	W 74713	38515	W 103371	56464	W 125311	104860	W 132827	102068	PAPIERS,CARTONS ROULEAUX
64159	OTHER PAPER ETC,BULK,NES	W 61941	34224	W 80824	48004	W 102187	89350	W 103911	87083	AUT PAPIER ROULEAUX FEUILLES
6418	COATED ETC PAPER NES BLK	W 51983	43857	W 81125	66086	W 49523	88506	W 63841	106854	PAP,CARTONS COUCHES,ENDUITS
642	PAPER,ETC,PRECUT,ARTS OF	W 66447	78058	W 76246	96410	W 100799	197009	W 113477	235510	PAP,CARTONS DECOUPES
6421	PAPER ETC CONTAINERS	W 27441	32311	W 30924	34204	W 51968	94494	W 54371	117888	BOITES,SACS EMBALLAGES
65	TEXTILE YARN,FABRICS,ETC		285385		319405		955632		1022615	FILS,TISSUS,ARTICLES TEXTILE
651	TEXTILE YARN	W 38168	121104	W 40227	139975	W 55713	253783		252992	FILS TEXTILES
6514	SYN FIB YRN,BULK,MONOFIL	W 25983	81422	W 26505	90586	W 33306	140515	W 31766	135179	FILS CONT 85% FIB TEXT SYNTH
65142	— NONTXT ETC CONT PAMID	W 14481	41138	W 16150	52095	W 20800	75685	W 18547	65547	FILS NON TEX FI CON POLYAMID
652	COTTON FABRICS,WOVEN	W 4945	16610	W 4671	18699	W 13289	123347		115724	TISSUS DE COTON
6522	WOVEN COTTON BLEACHD,ETC	W 2420	10911	W 2418	12868	W 10010	105923		98675	TISSUS COTON BLANCHIS ETC
653	WOVN MAN–MADE FIB FABRIC	W 4459	41457	W 4132	41988	W 10851	162348	W 12413	176133	TISSUS FIBRES SYNTH,ARTIF
654	OTH WOVEN TEXTILE FABRIC	W 1183	7514	W 1082	8536	W 4270	89095	W 4104	80828	TISSUS AUT COTON SYNT,ARTIF
657	SPECIAL TXTL FABRC,PRODS	W 4043	27863	W 4790	33530	W 16076	137151		168656	TISSUS SPECIAUX
6573	COATED ETC TEXTILES NES	W 1107	9092	W 1282	11617	W 6532	67381	W 7766	92816	TISSUS,ART MATIERE TEXT NDA
66	NONMETAL MINERAL MFS NES		212711		284826		478682		535872	ART MIN NON METALLIQUES
662	CLAY,REFRACTORY BLDG PRD	W 161868	70383	W 187705	92368	W 223682	119967	W 217003	112361	MAT CONST REFRACTAIRES
6623	REFRACTORY BUILDING PROD	W 110289	50401	W 132488	69754	W 156186	91270	W 135621	76778	BRIQUES REFRACTAIRES
66232	REFRACTRY BRICKS ETC NES	W 91453	41266	W 103267	54825	W 110461	67814	W 85199	53215	BRIQUES ETC REFRACTAIRES
663	MINERAL MANUFCTURES NES	W 184837	49394	W 244609	70459	W 273403	105047	W 321608	119428	ART MIN MANUF NDA
664	GLASS	W 95126	39242	W 98260	51164	W 132434	117101	W 157979	135759	VERRE
67	IRON AND STEEL		455906		571338		1271153		1150104	FER ET ACIER
671	PIG IRON ETC	W 187188	63605	W 164805	72750	W 189994	110977	W 139446	85773	FONTE,SPIEGEL,POUDRES
6716	FERRO–ALLOYS	W 92518	54636	W 99228	63926	W 117200	98611	W 105213	79581	FERRO–ALLIAGES
672	IRON,STEEL PRIMARY FORMS	W 302854	70910	W 396666	95571	W 551824	178281		97279	LINGOTS FER,ACIER
6725	IRN,STL BLOOMS,SLABS,ETC	W 177268	35003	W 208185	45130	W 364661	107843	W 95524	39388	BLOOMS,BILLETTES FER ACIER
67251	IRN,SMPLE STL BLOOMS,ETC	W 176943	34242	W 207294	43381	W 357877	97663	W 91211	30878	BLOOMS ETC NON ACIER FIN
673	IRON,STEEL SHAPES ETC	W 36418	23106	W 58403	33954	W 154685	113441	W 192410	126750	BARRES,PROFIL FER,ACIER
674	IRN,STL UNIV,PLATE,SHEET	W 509376	223260	W 562582	248434	W 996711	601465	W 899938	559185	LARGES PLATS,TOLES
6744	IRN,STL HVY PLATE,ROLLED	W 82869	28327	W 115259	41204	W 183075	93877	W 161062	86460	TOLES LAMINEES PLUS 4.75 MM
67441	— OF IRON OR SIMPLE STL	W 80759	25484	W 112902	36119	W 178659	82314	W 147556	66960	TOLES NON ACIER FIN CARB
6745	IRN,STL MED PLATE,ROLLED	W 85098	26416	W 113982	37632	W 202247	92708	W 256495	122592	TOLES 3 A 4.75 MM
67451	— OF IRON OR SIMPLE STL	W 82580	23795	W 111900	33930	W 190799	80222	W 237192	103158	TOLES AUT NON ACIER FIN
6746	IRN,STL THIN PLATE,ROLLD	W 201722	93632	W 195012	90260	W 361250	227667	W 230132	163477	TOLES LAM MOINS 3MM
67461	— OF IRON OR SIMPLE STL	W 191595	76455	W 181937	71735	W 325634	172605	W 200515	114411	TOL NON AC FIN MOINS 3 MM
6749	OTH IRN,STL PLATES,SHEET	W 99678	48312	W 93856	50422	W 208700	153988	W 207885	151249	AUTRES TOLES FER,ACIER
67491	— OF IRON OR SIMPLE STL	W 96721	45767	W 91059	42614	W 203696	141014	W 204142	144371	AUT TOLES AUTRES ACIER FIN
678	IRON,STL TUBES,PIPES,ETC	W 46859	57556	W 88603	99206	W 143742	204144	W 150054	208834	TUBES,TUYAUX EN FONTE,FER
6783	IRON,STL TUBES,PIPES NES	W 17473	15151	W 54945	46300	W 84465	88199	W 84200	82210	AUT TUBES,TUYAUX FER,ACIER
68	NON–FERROUS METALS		266818		330190		635953		608957	METAUX NON FERREUX
682	COPPER EXC CEMENT COPPER	W 41778	98747	W 43210	110907	W 59414	192247	W 66632	189527	CUIVRE
6822	COPPER,ALLOYS WORKED	W 30874	75886	W 32652	86763	W 41270	140387	W 47393	148314	CUIVRE,ALLIAGES OUVRES
68221	COPPER BARS,WIRE,ETC	W 24838	54774	W 25175	60052	W 31498	94144	W 35228	90960	BARRES,PROFILES ET FILS
684	ALUMINIUM	W 78361	123659	W 94723	165850	W 116352	300887	W 116329	281115	ALUMINIUM
6841	ALUMINIUM,ALLOYS,UNWRGHT	W 58824	62099	W 71346	85233	W 82718	156022	W 76394	124908	ALUMINIUM,ALLIAGES BRUTS
6842	ALUMINIUM,ALLOYS WORKED	W 19537	61560	W 23377	80617	W 33635	144865	W 39934	156208	ALUMINIUM,ALLIAGES OUVRE
69	METAL MANUFACTURES NES		352363		421722		808662		931725	ART MANUFACT EN METAL NDA
691	STRUCTURES AND PARTS NES	W 27596	53454	W 36215	68308	W 63344	123707	W 71927	145480	CONSTRUCT FER,ACIER,ALU
6911	STRUCTURES,PARTS IRN,STL	W 25093	38342	W 33384	49598	W 60100	94709	W 68225	117734	CONSTRUCT FER,ACIER,FONTE
692	METAL TANKS,BOXES,ETC	W 25561	50438	W 23804	57981	W 28221	72304	W 28266	78367	RECIPIENTS METALLIQUES
6924	MTL TRANSPORT BOXES ETC	W 13240	36929	W 16880	47294	W 19731	58867	W 20637	62782	FUTS,TAMBOURS,BIDONS
695	TOOLS	W 4029	39029	W 6197	65228	W 14201	100857	W 8499	110604	OUTILS A MAIN
697	BASE MTL HOUSEHOLD EQUIP	W 9897	46480	W 8656	50423	W 11207	65111		74333	ART MENAGE MET COMMUNS
699	BASE METAL MFRS NES	W 105265	111940	W 31520	122969	W 72401	311763		367398	ART MANUFACTURES MET NDA
6991	LOCKSMITHS WARES,ETC	W 6868	49402	W 7197	54910	W 18747	138445	W 21660	147750	' ARTICLES DE SERRURERIE
69913	BASE MTL DOOR,ETC FITTNG	W 3066	23922	W 4752	35147	W 11470	79524	W 14435	91716	GARNITURES POUR MEUBLES
6997	IRON,STEEL ARTICLES NES	W 11854	19642	W 11870	20570	W 31817	62485	W 49687	93880	OUV FONTE,FER,ACIER NDA
69979	IRN,STL MANUFACTURES NES	W 11653	19306	W 11682	20013	W 31674	62214	W 49125	93322	AUT OUVRAGES EN FER NDA
7	MACHINES,TRANSPORT EQUIP		4555841		5162221		9107900		10534562	MACHINES MATERIEL TRANSPORT
71	POWER GENERATING EQUIPMT		142994		82596		330941		490817	MACHINES GENERATRICES
713	INTRNL COMBUS PSTN ENGIN	W 2700	30157	W 2535	28437	W 6245	71594	W 15709	146412	MOTEURS EXPL COMB INT, PIECE
716	ROTATING ELECTRIC PLANT	W 2357	18393	W 2034	20984	W 13628	134922	W 18227	154434	APP ELECTR ROTATIFS,PIECES
718	OTH POWER GENERATG MACHY	W 1057	57889	W 260	7916	W 1216	61393	W 2731	93921	AUTRES MOTEURS PARTIES
7187	NUCLEAR REACTORS,PTS NES	W 1001	56571	W 257	7791	W 351	43828	W 211	62871	REACTEURS NUCLEAIRES
72	MACHS FOR SPCL INDUSTRYS		820997		887677		1364435		1329233	MAC SPECIALES POUR INDUST
721	AGRIC MACHY,EXC TRACTORS	W 14895	83844	W 19789	108388	W 25213	184015		231067	MACHINES AGRICOLES
7212	HARVESTING ETC MACHINES	W 8645	38119	W 12573	57470	W 15735	107483	W 20982	151709	ENGINS POUR LA RECOLTE
723	CIVIL ENGNEERG EQUIP ETC	W 18828	105183	W 16939	106125	W 27656	180041	W 26753	161458	APPAREILS DE GENIE CIVIL
7234	CONST,MINING MACHNRY NES	W 17242	97101	W 15256	94944	W 22650	158023	W 22007	143670	MACH POUR LA CONST, MINES
72342	SLFPRP SHOVELS,EXCAVATRS	W 6995	28904	W 9418	42897	W 15308	86177	W 15713	84645	PELLES MECANIQUES
724	TEXTILE,LEATHER MACHNRY	W 9155	103718	W 10056	136100	W 17812	211730	W 19001	198529	MACH POUR INDUSTRIE TEXTILE
7247	TEXTILE MACHINERY NES	W 2132	27995	W 3910	45811	W 4099	36801	W 4556	40721	MACH LAVAGE,TEINTURE TEX
725	PAPER ETC MILL MACHINERY	W 1686	27251	W 2082	33548	W 5244	79532	W 3997	61413	MACHINES FABR PATE PAPIER
726	PRINTG,BKBINDG MACHY,PTS	W 3477	77190	W 4337	99316	W 4695	123574		84503	MACHINES POUR IMPRIMERIE
727	FOOD MACHRY NON–DOMESTIC	W 5253	95811	W 3892	73374	W 3806	66638	W 5543	80237	MACH INDUSTRIES ALIMENT
7272	OTH FOOD PROC MCHY,PARTS	W 5068	93364	W 3654	70672	W 3632	65914	W 5340	77524	AUT MACH IND ALIMENTAIRE
72722	INDUS FOOD PROC MACH NES	W 4340	83176	W 3186	60418	W 3008	51732	W 4428	60722	MACHINES BOULANGERIE
728	OTH MACHY FOR SPCL INDUS	W 25825	311495	W 28691	300910	W 42938	477737	W 36438	460013	AUT MACH IND PARTICULIERES
7281	MACH–TOOLS FR SPCL INDUS	W 6190	66859	W 7599	59981	W 7643	75074	W 6497	74036	MACH–OUTILS SPEC IND PART
7283	OTHR MINERAL WORKG MACHY	W 4897	40736	W 4843	36178	W 9140	63619	W 7333	55432	MACH TRIER,CRIBLER,BROYER
7284	MACHY FOR SPCL INDUS NES	W 14738	203900	W 16248	204751	W 26156	339045	W 22607	330545	MACH SPEC IND PARTICUL.
72842	RUBBER,PLASTICS WRKG MCH	W 2798	45656	W 5945	69268	W 6574	82230	W 7022	80510	MACH IND CAOUT MAT PLAST
72848	OTH MCHY WITH INDIV FNCT	W 6372	38774	W 6369	60202	W 13753	118622	W 8427	105629	AUTRES MACHINES NDA
72849	PTS OF MACHS OF 7284 ETC	W 3073	51667	W 2370	40107	W 3869	66129	W 5371	79374	PIECES DU 728.4 ETC
73	METALWORKING MACHINERY		158906		217196		300890		313604	MACH TRAVAIL DES METAUX
736	METALWORKING MACH–TOOLS	W 11675	116603	W 17096	154050	W 27883	225744	W 26337	241018	MACH–OUTILS TRAVAIL METAUX
7361	METAL CUTTING MACH–TOOLS	W 4570	48492	W 5505	51170	W 8823	76092	W 8257	70381	MACH–OUT ENLEVEMENT METAL
737	METALWORKING MACHNRY NES	W 3099	42303	W 3946	63146	W 8287	75146	W 7805	72587	MACH TRAV METAUX PIECES
7373	WELDING,BRAZING,ETC MCHS	W 1210	22541	W 1933	46220	W 2885	57340	W 3283	58186	MACH SOUDAGE ETC PIECES
74	GENRL INDUSTRL MACHY NES		966706		1025050		1641201		1794316	MACH APP INDUSTRIE
741	HEATING,COOLING EQUIPMNT	W 17369	193916	W 15251	202568	W 29457	325438		349935	MACH CHAUFFAGE,PIECES
7414	NONDOM REFRIG EQUIPT,PTS	W 7062	61443	W 3123	61739	W 12283	108836	W 11789	110957	MAT PRODUCTION DU FROID
74141	REFRIG EQUIP NONDOMESTIC	W 5708	49591	W 1954	52819	W 8275	70498	W 8271	75742	REFIG INDUSTRIELS
7415	AIR–CONDITIONING MACHNRY	W 2962	38975	W 2760	39208	W 4886	65955	W 5479	76701	GROUPES CONDITION AIR

4. General Imports F.O.B. by Commodities according to the S.I.T.C. (Rev. 2) in thousand U.S. Dollars
Importations Générales F.O.B. par Produits d'après la C.T.C.I. (Rév. 2) en milliers de Dollars E.U.

SITC CTCI	COMMODITY	1993			1994			1995			1996			PRODUIT
		WEIGHT POIDS		VALUE VALEUR	WEIGHT POIDS		VALUE VALEUR	WEIGHT POIDS		VALUE VALEUR	WEIGHT POIDS		VALUE VALEUR	
7416	HEATING,COOLING EQU NES	W	4055	49587	W	3196	42807	W	6292	84451	W	10684	92365	APP CHANGEMENT TEMP
742	PUMPS FOR LIQUIDS ETC	W	3570	53280	W	4030	61399	W	6623	125691	W	7929	164359	POMPES MOTO-POMPES
743	PUMPS NES,CENTRFUGES ETC	W	10296	190667	W	12478	216530	W	25992	274954	W	29664	322401	POMPES COMPRES,VENT ETC
7436	GAS,LIQUID FILTERS ETC	W	5068	107091	W	6153	132148	W	15132	150587	W	17600	195959	APP POUR FILT DES LIQUIDES
7439	PTS NES OF APP OF 7435,6	W	2920	50274	W	2672	35636	W	5911	46400	W	5324	51923	PIECES 743.5 ET 743.6
744	MECHANICAL HANDLING EQU	W	17499	103595	W	19196	126124	W	40935	217550	W	44443	232368	EQUIP MANUTENTION PIECES
7442	LIFTING,LOADING MACH NES	W	7722	42977	W	7748	51698	W	13204	72266	W	13096	89246	APP LEVAGE,MANUTENTION
7449	PTS NES OF MACHY OF 7442	W	6838	42384	W	7412	52993	W	22017	112455	W	23672	101800	PIECES DU 744.2
745	NONELEC MACHY,TOOLS NES	W	6437	179803	W	8023	177663	W	9910	222052	W	12240	239191	AUT MACH NON ELEC,PIECES
7452	OTH NONELEC MCHS,PTS NES	W	5811	161274	W	7374	159195	W	9214	197390	W	11448	212446	AUT MACH NON ELEC,PIECES
74522	PACKAGNG,BOTTLNG,ETC MCH	W	1994	92382	W	2702	83726	W	2497	98907	W	3129	96368	MACH NETT BOUTEILLES,ETC
749	NONELEC MACH PTS,ACC NES	W	20790	245444	W	20959	240766	W	34288	475516	W	39283	486062	PIECES MACH NON ELEC NDA
7491	BALL,ROLLER,ETC BEARINGS	W	4842	65672	W	5689	51996	W	7576	99924	W	7622	103812	ROULEMENTS BILLES ETC
7492	COCKS,VALVES ETC NES	W	10292	122326	W	9296	121688	W	11249	190291	W	13396	220559	ART ROB,SIM POUR TUYAUX
7493	SHAFT,CRANK,PULLEY ETC	W	3810	35354	W	3603	32237	W	10152	91452	W	12041	95202	ARBRES TRANS,VILEBREQUINS
7499	OTH NONELEC MCHY PTS NES	W	1846	22092	W	2372	34844	W	5310	93849	W	6225	66488	PIECES NON ELECT NDA
75	OFFICE MACHNES,ADP EQUIP			641827			729041			1024837			1035186	MACH BUREAU TRAIT AUTOM
751	OFFICE MACHINES	W	2170	70740	W	2327	73787	W	4235	86867	W	4167	84034	MACH,APPAREILS DE BUREAU
7518	OFFICE MACHINES NES	W	1328	42040	W	1617	52317	W	3473	63755	W	3540	65140	MACH,APP DE BUREAU NDA
752	AUTOMTIC DATA PROC EQUIP	W	13430	465808	W	7926	541864	W	10182	743092	W	11495	732792	MACH TRAIT INFORMATION
7522	DIGITAL COMPUTERS	W	1793	157862	W	1573	169164	W	1593	202279	W	1741	173202	MACH DIGITALES COMPLETES
7523	DIGITL CENTRL PROCESSORS	W	1001	69289	W	864	90776	W	902	137485	W	550	85432	UNITES CENTRALES
7524	DIGITL CENTRL STOR UNITS	W	376	54003	W	403	75560	W	513	92622	W	612	112038	UNITES MEMOIRE CENTRALES
7525	ADP PERIPHERAL UNITS	W	8796	121791	W	3629	138155	W	5342	224710	W	5327	202686	UNITES PERIPHERIQUES
7528	OFF-LINE DATA PROC EQUIP	W	1405	58387	W	1358	55495	W	1766	79157	W	3011	126123	MACH AUXIL TRAIT INFORM
759	OFFICE,ADP MCH PTS,ACCES	W	3348	105279	W	2845	113391	W	6517	194878	W	7125	218361	PIECES DU 751 ET 752
7599	ACCTG,ETC,ADP MCH PTS,AC	W	2415	86858	W	2162	85963	W	5220	153019	W	4940	154884	PIECES DU 751 ET 752
76	TELECOMM,SOUND EQUIPMENT			369048			478547			719381			985585	EQUIPMENT DE TELECOM
761	TELEVISION RECEIVERS	W	4852	42867	W	6639	51117	W	5732	56759	W	7451	78814	RECEPTEURS DE TELEVISION
7611	COLOUR TV RECEIVERS	W	4788	39985	W	6600	50572	W	5701	56088	W	7412	78195	RECEPTEURS COULEUR
762	RADIO BROADCAST RECEIVRS	W	2292	41610	W	3180	49066	W	3431	67543	W	4459	80751	RECEPTEURS RADIODIFFUSION
763	SOUND RECORDRS,PHONOGRPH	W	1788	41280	W	2004	48378	W	1225	55924			74805	PHONO,APP ENREGISTREMENT
7638	OTHR SOUND APPARATUS ETC	W	1772	41013	W	1985	48096	W	1205	55496	W	1512	74303	AUT APP D'ENREGIS,REPROD
764	TELECOM EQPT,PTS,ACC NES	W	5194	243292	W	7329	329985	W	9711	539154			751215	EQUIP TELECOM,PIECES
7641	LINE TELEPHONE,ETC EQUIP	W	1211	81769	W	1356	80035	W	1786	128920	W	2114	161186	APP TELEPHON PAR FIL
7643	TV,RADIO TRANSMITTRS ETC	W	118	18484	W	203	36302	W	253	55589	W	567	142758	APP EMET TELE RADIO
7649	PTS NES OF EQUIPMT OF 76	W	3008	118137	W	4821	190799	W	6117	314575	W	7299	367766	PIECES DE LA DIV 76
76491	PTS NES OF APPAR OF 7641	W	1071	80304	W	2179	134357	W	2060	194089	W	2096	220006	PIECES POUR 764.1
76493	TELECOMM EQUIPMT PTS NES	W	1889	36386	W	2563	55207	W	3530	103841	W	3841	128683	PIECES 761,762,764.3,8
77	ELECTRIC MACHNRY NES ETC			723344			853772			2024828			2441494	MACH APP ELECT NDA
771	ELECTRIC POWER MACHY NES	W	7169	46320	W	9737	60241	W	15394	140555	W	18791	176793	MACH PROD,TRANS ELECTR
7712	OTH ELEC POWER MACHY NES	W	1617	18198	W	3210	26469	W	7563	95443	W	10127	133065	AUT APP PROD TRANSF ELEC
772	SWITCHGEAR ETC,PARTS NES	W	33510	141637	W	7947	152197	W	110292	512547	W	26774	636084	APP COUPURE,SECT ETC
7721	SWITCHGEAR ETC	W	33442	139487	W	7853	148543	W	108666	459461	W	24923	566743	APP COUPURE,SECTIONMNT
773	ELECTR DISTRIBUTNG EQUIP	W	10231	56412	W	14864	57236	W	35730	250764	W	50066	342927	EQUIPMT DISTRIBUTION ELECT
7731	INSULATED WIRE,CABLE ETC	W	7867	45437	W	13150	46627	W	32507	214020	W	45951	284059	FILS,CABLES ISOLES ELECT
774	ELECTRO-MEDCL,XRAY EQUIP	W	421	56657	W	623	99385	W	626	82872	W	560	80674	APPAREILS MEDICAUX
7741	ELECTRO-MEDICAL EQUIPMNT	W	189	32041	W	332	61818	W	325	48337	W	247	41011	APP ELECTRICITE MEDICALE
775	HOUSEHOLD TYPE EQUIP NES	W	39739	199393	W	42427	218237	W	54044	317033	W	64242	388317	MACH,APP USAGE DOMESTQUE
7752	DOM REFRIGERATRS,FREEZRS	W	15402	74508	W	15265	61827	W	18809	84006	W	19923	90869	REFRIG,CONGEL MENAGER
77521	DOMESTIC REFRIGERATORS	W	9649	52215	W	10133	41411	W	12848	57673	W	14754	67709	REFRIGERATEURS
7758	ELECTRO-THERMIC APPL NES	W	13178	65327	W	13143	81577	W	16017	120369	W	17919	139944	APP ELECTROTHERMIQ NDA
776	TRANSISTORS,VALVES,ETC	W	1073	76445	W	1360	94790	W	2824	217819			221371	LAMPES,TUBES,VALVES
7764	ELECTRONIC MICROCIRCUITS	W	248	62449	W	417	79390	W	409	155569	W	350	151509	MICROSTRUCTURES ELECTRON
778	ELECTRICAL MACHINERY NES	W	17067	146481	W	18925	171686	W	34388	503239			595328	AUTRES MACH ELECT NDA
7781	BATTERIES,ACCUMULATORS	W	6047	22866	W	6525	25692	W	11467	95757	W	15194	131163	PILES ET ACCUMULATEURS
7788	OTH ELEC MACHY,EQUIP NES	W	7137	70138	W	7537	80736	W	14826	284257			315206	AUT MACH APP ELEC NDA
77884	ELECTRICAL CONDENSERS	W	204	3538	W	189	4838	W	5383	158483	W	1260	177731	CONDENSATEURS ELECTRIQUES
78	ROAD VEHICLES			688890			874955			1567768			1972546	VEHICULES ROUTIERS
781	PASS MOTOR VEH EXC BUSES	W	154065	273153	W	83012	406955	W	110239	621313	W	160790	823757	AUTO TRANSPORT PERSONNES
782	LORRIES,SPCL MTR VEH NES	W	17542	87218	W	24196	113445	W	37786	232383	W	38567	274385	VEHICULES SPECIAUX,MARCH
7821	LORRIES,TRUCKS	W	13102	65168	W	18126	91663	W	28614	191380	W	32433	234982	VEHICULES TRANSP MARCHAND
783	ROAD MOTOR VEHICLES NES	W	4166	33235	W	6913	69521	W	11772	118877	W	12620	114633	VEHICULES ROUTIERS NDA
7832	TRACTORS FOR TR-TRAILERS	W	3214	25133	W	5606	53155	W	9011	99122	W	10034	97435	TRACTEURS ROUTIERS
784	MOTOR VEH PRTS,ACCES NES	W	50368	207382	W	39957	185909	W	80588	437712	W	108381	582950	PIECES 722,781,782,783
7849	OTHER MOTOR VEHCL PARTS	W	42166	196402	W	36732	175618	W	73020	410088	W	103913	562440	PIECES 722,781,782,783
785	CYCLES,ETC MOTRZD OR NOT	W	7827	54787	W	7952	51805	W	14210	80922	W	15230	87252	MOTOCYCLES SCOOTERS
786	TRAILERS,NONMOTR VEH,NES	W	11761	33115	W	12690	47320	W	19883	76561	W	21672	89568	REMORQUES,CADRES,CONTAIN
79	OTHR TRANSPORT EQUIPMENT			43128			13388			133619			171780	AUTRE MATERIEL TRANSPORT
791	RAILWAY VEHICLES	W	16736	42409	W	9445	11152	W	42944	130246	W	30406	68558	VEHIC MAT CHEMINS DE FER
792	AIRCRAFT ETC	W	4	149	W	2	120	W	11	598			98870	APP NAVIGATION AERIENNE
8	MISC MANUFACTURED GOODS			1530392			1805672			3001488			3282791	ART MANUFACTURES DIVERS
812	*PLUMBG,HEATNG,LGHTNG EQ	W	62796	81257	W	19313	105898	W	24849	153117	W	30200	182307	APPAR SANITAIRES CHAUFFAGE
8124	LIGHTING EQUIPMENT NES	W	9847	56466	W	11108	72499	W	10960	92227	W	10714	97774	APPAREILS ECLAIRAGE ETC
81242	LAMPS,FITTINGS BASE METL	W	8186	42496	W	8423	48690	W	7131	55159	W	7027	62613	APPAREILS D'ECLAIRAGE
821	*FURNITURE,PARTS THEREOF	W	154661	157438	W	68788	175415	W	177736	258639	W	98193	308828	MEUBLES ET PIECES
8211	CHAIRS,SEATS AND PARTS	W	11406	38811	W	12988	47166	W	115891	97838	W	27178	132658	SIEGES ET PIECES
8219	FURNITURE AND PARTS NES	W	141881	103169	W	53795	107115	W	59536	136314	W	68430	150190	AUTRES MEUBLES ET PIECES
82192	WOOD FURNITURE NES	W	124217	55761	W	32039	57641	W	35704	73198	W	41491	83046	MEUBLES NDA EN BOIS
84	CLOTHING AND ACCESSORIES			196987			227542			462104			502206	VETEMENTS
843	WOMENS OUTERWEAR NONKNIT	W	4826	42319	W	6504	56093	W	6925	94054	W	7502	107179	VET DESSUS FEMMES MAT TEX
845	OUTERWEAR KNIT NONELASTC	W	4676	42266	W	6880	47712	W	8765	76099	W	9656	78043	VET DESSOUS,ACCES BONNET
846	UNDER GARMENTS KNITTED	W	6123	40063	W	8183	43694	W	10161	94563	W	10307	101535	SOUS VETS DE BONNETERIE
851	*FOOTWEAR	W	10508	81806	W	12029	93810	W	14994	132939	W	17286	167037	CHAUSSURES
85102	FOOTWEAR LEATHER	W	6429	55558	W	7203	63596	W	8839	88490	W	10531	117126	CHAUS SEMELLES EN CUIR
87	PRECISION INSTRUMNTS NES			338989			385062			623826			594701	INSTRUM,APPAR SCIENT NDA
872	MEDICAL INSTRUMENTS NES	W	1659	62334	W	2998	110707	W	4603	127509	W	5548	136084	INSTR,APP MEDIC-CHIR NDA
87202	OTH MEDICAL INSTRUMENTS	W	1300	53595	W	2080	93835	W	3085	108259	W	3645	112950	INSTRUM,APP MEDECINE
874	MEASURNG,CONTROLNG INSTR	W	4513	233687	W	3815	225588	W	6992	437508			398162	INSTRUMENTS DE MESURE
8742	MEASUR,DRAW ETC INST,PTS	W	920	46664	W	1182	58027	W	1880	118990	W	1887	96917	INST DESSIN,TRACAGE,PCS
87421	MEASURNG,DRAWNG ETC INST	W	793	40089	W	981	48902	W	1592	103515	W	1388	77747	INSTRUM DESSIN,TRACAGE
8743	GAS,LIQUID CONTROL INSTR	W	2169	76025	W	1105	55327	W	1818	97415	W	2035	92183	APP,INSTR MESURE FLUIDES
8748	ELEC MEAS,CONTRL EQU NES	W	450	59346	W	451	61564	W	720	107149	W	670	107275	APP ELEC ELECTRO MESURE
87483	OTH ELCTRNC MEAS ETC EQU	W	344	51826	W	348	52895	W	571	93932	W	530	88754	AUT APP ELECTRO DE MESURE
88	PHOTO EQU,OPTICL GDS ETC			93934			112205			157167			183515	APP,FOURN PHOTO,OP,MONTR
882	PHOTO,CINEMA SUPPLIES	W	2440	38858	W	3147	46158	W	4200	62923			64212	PRODUITS PHOTO,CINEMA
89	MISC MANUFCTRD GOODS NES			554099			680681			1175608			1302137	ART MANUFACTURES DIVERS
892	PRINTED MATTER	W	23128	104823	W	30156	119398	W	43873	188686			222058	IMPRIMES
8921	PRINTED BOOKS,GLOBES,ETC	W	11304	40947	W	12789	47109	W	16477	67614	W	17694	69317	LIVRES,BROCHURES,CARTES
89211	PRINTED BOOKS,PAMPHLETS	W	10676	38223	W	12222	42870	W	15797	62848	W	16579	62471	LIVRES,BROCHURES
8928	PRINTED MATTER NES	W	5869	44356	W	7844	48234	W	15195	80498			103603	IMPRIMES NDA

4. General Imports F.O.B. by Commodities according to the S.I.T.C. (Rev. 2) in thousand U.S. Dollars
Importations Générales F.O.B. par Produits d'après la C.T.C.I. (Rév. 2) en milliers de Dollars E.U.

SITC CTCI	COMMODITY	1993 WEIGHT POIDS	1993 VALUE VALEUR	1994 WEIGHT POIDS	1994 VALUE VALEUR	1995 WEIGHT POIDS	1995 VALUE VALEUR	1996 WEIGHT POIDS	1996 VALUE VALEUR	PRODUIT
893	ARTICLES OF PLASTIC NES		169217		227254		417194		518128	OUVRAGES EN MAT DIVIS 58
8931	PLSTC PACKG CONTNRS,LIDS	W 12800	38321	W 22348	62006	W 29563	110865	W 37218	114930	ART TRANSP EMBALLAGE ETC
8939	MISC PLASTIC ARTICLES	W 47938	120170	W 54484	151676	W 83445	285599	W 87490	382386	ART DIVERS EN MAT DIV 58
89399	OTHR PLASTC ARTICLES NES	W 42723	110925	W 49904	140454	W 78592	269523	W 82293	364482	AUT OUV MAT DIV 58
894	TOYS,SPORTING GOODS,ETC	W 11088	87564	W 12384	100122	W 17929	175225	W 22432	193402	VOITURES ENFANTS,JOUETS
8942	TOYS,INDOOR GAMES ETC	W 8456	67611	W 9197	73979	W 12313	106841	W 14194	108199	JOUETS,JEUX ETC
898	MUSICAL INSTRUMENTS,PTS	W 4489	88489	W 4082	98123	W 5375	126647		145828	INSTRUMENTS DE MUSIQUE
8983	SOUND RECRDNG TAPE,DISCS	W 4109	80145	W 3696	85940	W 4720	110333	W 5252	127217	SUPPORTS SON POUR 763
89832	RECORDED DISCS,TAPES ETC	W 1036	44019	W 1051	57158	W 1322	77069	W 1724	91706	DISQUES,PHONO,BANDES
899	OTHER MANUFACTURED GOODS		60225		80156		120656		130990	AUT ART MANUF DIVERS NDA
9	GOODS NOT CLASSD BY KIND		97923		78126		302471		14052	ART TRANSACT NON CLASSES
931	*SPECIAL TRANSACTIONS	W 4529	80328	W 4721	67743	W 12525	279192			TRANS.SPECIALES

5. General Exports F.O.B. by Commodities according to the S.I.T.C. (Rev. 2) in thousand U.S. Dollars
Exportations Générales F.O.B. par Produits d'après la C.T.C.I. (Rév. 2) en milliers de Dollars E.U.

SITC CTCI	COMMODITY	1993 WEIGHT POIDS	1993 VALUE VALEUR	1994 WEIGHT POIDS	1994 VALUE VALEUR	1995 WEIGHT POIDS	1995 VALUE VALEUR	1996 WEIGHT POIDS	1996 VALUE VALEUR	PRODUIT
	ALL COMMODITIES		12892226		14081475		21685601		21907355	TOUS PRODUITS
0	FOOD AND LIVE ANIMALS		834310		743261		1038453		875699	ALIMENTS,ANIMAUX VIVANTS
001	*LIVE ANIMALS FOR FOOD	W 60543	77151	W 37896	57330	W 25900	52292	W 17163	35728	ANIMAUX VIVANTS
0011	BOVINE SPECIES,LIVE	W 49851	62316	W 29897	45174	W 21580	39570	W 11666	20666	ESPECE BOVINE
00119	— OTHR THAN FR BREEDING	W 38301	44882	W 13449	17990	W 7194	12083	W 6632	11930	BOVINS NON REPRODUCTEURS
01	MEAT AND PREPARATIONS		70016		47559		53949		52232	VIANDES ET PREPARATIONS
011	MEAT FRESH,CHILLD,FROZEN	W 31481	50634	W 16871	30681	W 11699	31501		30831	VIANDES FRAICHES,REF,CONGE
02	DAIRY PRODCTS,BIRDS'EGGS		222898		180019		229231		212910	PRODUITS LAITIERS,OEUFS
022	MILK AND CREAM	W 113521	138058	W 117594	117724	W 111528	143675	W 104479	125636	LAIT ET CREME
0224	MILK,CREAM PRESERVED ETC	W 100865	130516	W 98996	110586	W 88751	135400	W 81286	117770	LAIT,CREME CONS,CONC
02242	MILK DRY,1.5% FAT OR LES	W 68714	93940	W 58376	71968	W 53930	94711	W 43504	75180	LAIT POUDRE INF 1.5%
023	BUTTER	W 32963	44045	W 19936	27377	W 26600	50373	W 26841	44402	BEURRE
04	CEREALS AND PREPARATIONS		110865		89430		263691		157328	CEREALES ET PRODUITS
041	WHEAT ETC UNMILLED	W 126787	16182	W 28722	3601	W 1018274	117405	W 145320	21452	FROMENT,EPEAUTRE
0412	OTHER WHEAT ETC UNMILLED	W 121500	15545	W 27259	3395	W 1000441	115186	W 144588	21336	AUTRE FROMENT NON MOULU
048	CEREAL ETC PREPARATIONS	W 168525	72783	W 214522	73872	W 254238	105483	W 234306	117256	PREPTNS A BASE CEREALES
05	VEGETABLES AND FRUIT		135531		137052		143657		147652	LEGUMES ET FRUITS
054	VEG ETC FRSH,SMPLY PRSVD	W 209563	90469	W 277726	90970	W 137294	76674		75876	LEGUMES FRAIS,CONG,SECS
0548	EDIBLE VEG NES FRESH,DRY	W 57161	59851	W 68228	55764	W 7413	48602		51225	RACINES,TUBERCULES
05484	HOP CONES AND LUPULIN	W 8090	57907	W 7483	54415	W 6723	48127	W 7286	49236	HOUBLON
06	SUGAR AND PREPS,HONEY		60185		58687		66276		42306	SUCRES ET PRODUITS
061	SUGAR AND HONEY	W 124013	39220	W 103597	37349	W 114827	43472	W 50806	21763	SUCRES ET MIEL
07	COFFEE,TEA,COCOA,SPICES		58306		60584		84136		76276	CAFE,THE,CACAO,EPICES
073	CHOCOLATE AND PRODUCTS	W 17833	44500	W 15428	45186	W 17162	53704	W 18949	54921	CHOCOLAT
081	*FEEDING STUFF FOR ANIML	W 283881	42238	W 287170	43669	W 342728	48374	W 342490	51822	NOURRITURE POUR ANIMAUX
09	MISC EDIBLE PRODUCTS		34859		43866		66508		67321	PREP ALIMENTAIRES DIVERSES
1	BEVERAGES AND TOBACCO		157812		173705		174151		223405	BOISSONS ET TABACS
11	BEVERAGES		124918		112470		116291		136796	BOISSONS
112	ALCOHOLIC BEVERAGES	W 259299	113044	W 313320	99525	W 211313	101897		114641	BOISSONS ALCOOLIQUES
1123	BEER,ALE,STOUT,PORTER	W 209017	80996	W 273720	67898	W 178385	79812	W 212148	98299	BIERES
12	TOBACCO AND MANUFACTURES		32894		61235		57860		86610	TABACS BRUTS FABRIQUES
122	TOBACCO,MANUFACTURED	W 6287	32892	W 6576	60979	W 8031	57417		85329	TABACS FABRIQUES
1222	CIGARETTES	W 3786	32806	W 6337	56829	W 8025	57389	W 11671	78947	CIGARETTES
2	CRUDE MATERLS,EXCL FUELS		744660		966608		1110447		1048391	MAT BRUTES NON COMESTIBLES
23	RUBBER, CRUDE		28795		62062		68600		63471	CAOUTCHOUC BRUT
233	RUBBER,SYNTHTIC,RECLAIMD	W 42729	26539	W 68681	45887	W 60072	68021		62989	LATEX CAOUTCH SYNTH REGEN
2331	SYNTHETIC RUBBER ETC	W 35278	24350	W 61140	43764	W 53972	65859		60715	LATEX CAOUTCH SYNTHETIQUE
24	CORK AND WOOD		216629		368128		424169		408572	LIEGE ET BOIS
247	OTH WOOD ROUGH,SQUARED	W 1097337	76819	W 1826532	135990	W 1674819	163103	W 1692751	138580	BOIS BRUTS EQUARRIS
2471	SAW–,VENEER–LOGS CONIFER	W 883475	67137	W 1570911	125513	W 1332723	146114	W 1335376	122204	CONIFERES POUR SCIAGE,PLACAG
24711	— IN THE ROUGH	W 883475	67137	W 1570911	125513	W 1332723	146114	W 1335376	122204	ECORCES OU DEGROSSIS
248	WOOD SHAPED,SLEEPERS	W 516737	127949	W 820998	218747	W 866596	242672	W 805878	250472	BOIS SIMPLEMENT TRAVAILLES
2482	LUMBER SHAPED CONIFER	W 487378	117929	W 782203	206756	W 820359	223057	W 770113	234000	CONIFERES SCIES,RABOTES
24821	LUMBER SAWN ETC CONIFER	W 479127	110624	W 763453	196725	W 798832	207271	W 748424	217065	CONIFERES SCIES LONGITUD
251	*PULP AND WASTE PAPER	W 207666	65465	W 253564	91551	W 240049	154972	W 270552	101065	PATES A PAPIER,DECHETS
2518	SULPHITE WOOD PULP	W 136400	47797	W 182406	75312	W 161096	120134	W 190654	77011	PATES AU BISULFITE
25182	— BLEACHED,NONDISSOLVNG	W 129725	46656	W 162924	71924	W 152895	116546	W 185260	75621	PATES BLANCHES
26	TEXTILE FIBRES AND WASTE		57537		103715		91691		60446	FIBRES TEXTILES
263	COTTON	W 8715	9304	W 36936	45700	W 5544	7555	W 4722	4655	COTON
2631	RAW COTTON,EXCL LINTERS	W 5896	8279	W 33312	44018	W 2583	5653	W 1482	2457	COTON EN MASSE
27	CRUDE FERTLZR,MINRLS NES		115814		73496		84867		150320	ENGRAIS MINERAUX BRUTS
273	STONE,SAND AND GRAVEL	W 3101496	58985	W 2703589	23854	W 2529730	26342	W 2083042	58249	PIERRES,SABLES,GRAVIERS
2734	GRAVEL,CRUSHED STONE,ETC	W 1929355	46046	W 1563887	11141	W 1264652	11126	W 1104581	44703	PIERRES CONCASSEES
278	OTHER CRUDE MINERALS	W 887259	55604	W 780660	48733	W 779003	57592		91033	AUTRES MINERAUX BRUTS
2782	REFRACTORY MINERALS NES	W 688712	45499	W 608901	38773	W 606525	44454	W 588257	42864	ARGILE MINERAUX REFRACTAIRES
27821	CLAY ETC	W 679527	43017	W 602322	36285	W 602476	42238	W 582726	40567	ARGILES
28	METALLIFEROUS ORES,SCRAP		195482		182684		181540		160065	MINERAIS METAL,DECHETS
282	IRON AND STEEL SCRAP	W 1086378	149553	W 994036	127316	W 826669	96057	W 906236	96614	FERRAILLES
28209	— OF OTHR IRON OR STEEL	W 936713	127393	W 919221	84537	W 767948	84509	W 807921	82065	FERRAILLES DE FER
288	NONFERR METAL SCRAP NES	W 52543	41066	W 50709	51718	W 54470	72521	W 49847	56159	DECHETS NON FERREUX
2882	OTHER BASE MTL SCRAP NES	W 50205	40198	W 46490	50636	W 50133	70637	W 46788	55123	AUTRES DECHETS
3	MINERAL FUELS ETC		785366		786740		927175		993790	COMBUSTIBLES MINERAUX LUB
32	COAL,COKE AND BRIQUETTES		565210		563896		652897		649781	HOUILLES,COKES,BRIQUETTES
322	COAL,LIGNITE AND PEAT	MW 9698	425714	MW 12660	422929	MW 13489	489077	MW 12373	480036	HOUILLES,LIGNITES,TOURBE
3222	OTH COAL,NOT AGGLOMERATD	W 5133761	284790	W 6449540	300903	W 6975637	357082	W 6730650	361717	AUTRES HOUILLES
3223	LIGNITE,NOT AGGLOMERATED	W 4555294	140550	W 6131627	118494	W 6455319	128763	W 5606695	115708	LIGNITES
323	BRIQUETS,COKE,SEMI–COKE	W 1755716	139496	W 1774278	140967	W 1848627	163821	W 1895907	169745	BRIQUETTES
3232	COKE,SEMI–COKE,RTRT CRBN	W 1337797	118398	W 1442295	125613	W 1406223	139989	W 1329646	139202	COKES ET SEMI–COKES
33	PETROLEUM AND PRODUCTS		145512		147072		192323		237678	PETROLE ET DERIVES
334	PETROLEUM PRODUCTS,REFIN	W 528327	88044	W 791222	106544	W 826940	122285	W 1507659	175358	PRODUITS RAFFINES
3341	GASOLINE,OTH LIGHT OILS	W 527144	86664	W 790011	104775	W 825997	120267	W 1506554	173751	ESSENCES POUR MOTEURS
335	RESIDUAL PETRLM PROD NES	W 236967	48863	W 325090	32351	W 347054	41076	W 356393	52099	PRODUITS RESIDUELS NDA
351	*ELECTRIC CURRENT		67466		68630	H 2020	71760		98358	ENERGIE ELECTRIQUE
5	CHEMCLS,RELATED PROD NES		1174727		1376437		1937397		1911412	PRODUITS CHIMIQUES
51	ORGANIC CHEMICALS		356318		413729		590029		555458	PROD CHIMIQ ORGANIQUES
511	HYDROCARBONS NES,DERIVS	W 273684	90961	W 367411	142248	W 421922	181213	W 476725	190203	HYDROCARBURES NDA
5111	ACYCLIC HYDROCARBONS	W 134378	45352	W 166434	76506	W 212743	106696	W 254916	127273	HYDROCARBURES ACYCLIQUES
5112	CYCLIC HYDROCARBONS	W 131605	37915	W 191515	59020	W 200577	67004	W 212737	56644	HYDROCARBURES CYCLIQUES
512	ALCOHOLS,PHENOLS ETC	W 82144	101929	W 93146	56620	W 94088	57532		52428	PHENOLS,PHENOLS–ALCOOLS
5121	ACYCLIC ALCOHOLS,DERIVS	W 64101	49675	W 77520	39579	W 50693	36411	W 63132	36908	ALCOOLS ACYCLIQUES
5123	PHENOLS,PHEN ALCS,DERIVS	W 18009	52093	W 15609	16775	W 43383	20830	W 12357	15352	PHENOLS,PHENOLS–ALCOOLS
513	CARBOXYLIC ACIDS ETC	W 60047	53277	W 74769	74480	W 95392	141660	W 105674	123637	ACIDES CARBOXYLIQUES
5137	MONOACIDS AND DERIVATIVS	W 39316	37005	W 36653	42162	W 57765	93244	W 59759	76660	ACIDES MONOCARBOXYLIQUES
51379	OTH MONOACIDS ETC,DERIVS	W 34266	33561	W 29223	37030	W 51224	86489	W 50655	68748	AUTRES MONOCARBOXYLIQUES
514	NITROGEN–FNCTN COMPOUNDS	W 60503	59412	W 70841	74937	W 81616	112406		101194	COMPOSES FONCT AZOTEES
5145	AMINE–FUNCTION COMPOUNDS	W 56864	49508	W 67167	58147	W 76704	80026	W 77150	70186	COMPOSES FONCTION AMINE
515	ORG–INORG COMPOUNDS ETC	W 28874	37810	W 36687	50327	W 74663	74684	W 43676	69652	COMPOSES ORGANO–MINERAUX
5156	HETEROCYCLIC CMPDS ETC	W 28728	36865	W 36553	49403	W 73961	72382	W 42658	66818	COMPOSES HETEROCYCLIQUES
52	INORGANIC CHEMICALS		92847		112447		150369		140798	PROD CHIM INORGANIQUES
522	INORG ELEMNTS,OXIDES,ETC	W 233796	55115	W 320514	68535	W 350791	74994		80223	ELEMENTS INORGANIQUES
523	OTHR INORG CHEMICALS ETC	W 106902	36977	W 131310	43043	W 168346	73935		56578	AUT PRODUITS CHIMIQUES INORG
53	DYES,TANNING,COLOUR PROD		121554		126772		182473		155447	PROD TEINTURE,COLORANTS
531	SYNT DYE,NAT INDGO,LAKES	W 5682	56870	W 6122	59327	W 6205	64859	W 6932	64078	MAT COLOR ORGAN,LAQUES
5311	SYNTHIC ORGNIC DYESTUFFS	W 5384	55615	W 5853	57739	W 5853	62551	W 6595	62052	MAT COLOR ORGAN SYNTHET
533	PIGMENTS,PAINTS,ETC	W 81658	63589	W 79658	66777	W 86213	116779	W 72998	90629	PIGMENTS,PEINTURES,VERNIS
541	*MEDICINAL,PHARM PRODUCT	K 8233553	123085	MK 9331	150339	MK 11743	185606		218060	PROD MEDICINAUX PHARMACEUT
5417	MEDICAMENTS	K 5562994	81260	K 5869966	96113	K 7072207	109799	K 5898324	127573	MEDICAMENTS
54179	— CONTNG OTH SUBSTANCES	K 4848937	68525	K 5097315	81998	K 6580630	89904	K 4738556	75581	MED CONT AUT SUBSTANCES
55	PERFUME,CLEANING ETC PRD		113088		147362		167977		214489	PROD POUR PARFUM,TOILETTE
554	SOAP,CLEANSING ETC PREPS	W 85559	79693	W 123309	107553	W 151438	118936	W 206099	164008	SAVONS,PRODUITS DETERSIFS
5542	WASHING PREPARATIONS ETC	W 69602	66496	W 106344	94803	W 130456	99443	W 184469	142463	PROD ORG TENSIO–ACT NDA

5. General Exports F.O.B. by Commodities according to the S.I.T.C. (Rev. 2) in thousand U.S. Dollars
Exportations Générales F.O.B. par Produits d'après la C.T.C.I. (Rév. 2) en milliers de Dollars E.U.

SITC CTCI	COMMODITY	1993 WEIGHT POIDS	1993 VALUE VALEUR	1994 WEIGHT POIDS	1994 VALUE VALEUR	1995 WEIGHT POIDS	1995 VALUE VALEUR	1996 WEIGHT POIDS	1996 VALUE VALEUR	PRODUIT
562	*FERTILIZERS,MANUFACTURE	W 554801	49010	W 590081	57405	W 761599	92567		102328	ENGRAIS MANUFACTURES
5621	CHEM NITROGENOUS FERTLZR	W 481816	37641	W 504085	44662	W 634517	70216		84017	ENGRAIS AZOTES
58	PLASTIC MATERIALS ETC		248686		295982		467988		413792	MAT PLAST ARTIFICIELLES
582	PROD OF CONDENSATION ETC	W 11536	16477	W 15482	22925	W 30660	71733	W 27686	50978	PROD CONDENS,POLYCOND
583	POLYMERIZATION ETC PRODS	W 290031	226306	W 520310	261998	W 333484	382097	W 364923	350080	PROD POLYMERISATION
5831	POLYETHYLENE	W 82239	67621	W 105347	60865	W 97223	87445	W 100553	84271	POLYETHYLENE
58311	— IN PRIMARY FORMS	W 72108	60391	W 97314	53513	W 81765	68446	W 89497	67990	POLYETHYLENE PRIMAIRES
5832	POLYPROPYLENE	W 62510	41939	W 75913	44550	W 59370	53031	W 58050	65252	POLYPROPYLENE
5833	POLYSTYRENE,ITS COPOLYMR	W 37377	32859	W 53756	51856	W 55529	74057	W 60534	59856	POLYPROPYLENE COPOLYMERES
58331	— IN PRIMARY FORMS	W 36852	32537	W 52855	51249	W 54381	71957	W 59188	57391	SOUS FORMES PRIMAIRES
5834	POLYVINYL CHLORIDE	W 90417	51998	W 268016	73426	W 90664	96440	W 117391	83016	CHLORURE DE POLYVINYLE
58341	— IN PRIMARY FORMS	W 84829	45042	W 260614	64407	W 73051	65644	W 105655	63911	SOUS FORMES PRIMAIRES
59	CHEMICAL MATERIALS NES		69675		71966		99586		92317	MAT PROD CHIMIQUES NDA
598	MISCEL CHEM PRODUCTS NES	W 100552	40189	W 137815	35282	W 201003	67686	W 172397	52139	PROD DIV INDUST CHIM NDA
6	BASIC MANUFACTURES		4086586		4444259		7252695		6570659	ART MANUFACTURES
61	LEATHER,DRESSED FUR,ETC		60391		74143		232559		150212	CUIRS,PELLETERIES
611	LEATHER	W 9705	33642	W 10838	41329	W 13596	120136		52503	CUIRS,PEAUX PREPARES
6114	LEATHR BOVINE NES,EQUINE	W 2861	12137	W 3690	21342	W 5977	83680	W 3586	29561	CUIRS DE BOVINS
612	LEATHER ETC MANUFACTURES	W 4996	24343	W 5159	29512	W 11884	102161	W 8268	91802	OUVRAGES EN CUIRS NDA
6123	PREPRD PARTS OF FOOTWEAR	W 4888	23176	W 4913	27224	W 11398	96466	W 7978	86349	PARTIES DE CHAUSSURES
62	RUBBER MANUFACTURES NES		129219		171908		328381		332523	CAOUTCHOUC MANUFACTURE
625	RUBBER TYRES, TUBES ETC	W 39673	88916	W 51093	118599	W 178379	202276	W 70964	205272	PNEUS CAOUTCHOUC VULCANISE
6251	TYRES NEW FOR MOTOR CARS	W 12091	35159	W 16560	45460	W 25280	79950	W 21078	75321	PNEUS POUR VOITURES
6252	TYRES,NEW,BUS OR LORRY	W 9077	20565	W 13659	33069	W 127586	69159	W 24186	71662	PNEUS POUR AUTOBUS,CAMIONS
628	RUBBER ARTICLES NES	W 9246	26227	W 11804	37220	W 16631	76672	W 16524	78014	OUVRAGES CAOUTCHOUC NDA
6289	OTH RUBBER ARTICLES NES	W 8275	20336	W 10630	30157	W 14963	65109	W 14781	65121	AUT OUVR CAOUTCHOUC NDA
63	WOOD,CORK MANUFACTRS NES		253963		299391		404743		408196	OUVRAGES LIEGE ET BOIS
634	VENEERS,PLYWOOD,ETC	W 187591	41883	W 199448	54851	W 262727	98086	W 285648	100015	PLACAGES,CONTRE–PLAQUES
635	WOOD MANUFACTURES NES	W 318241	211080	W 404253	243828	W 424064	305952	W 433001	307324	ART MANUF EN BOIS NDA
6351	BOXES,CASES,CRATES,ETC	W 158252	38174	W 201803	45436	W 240421	64859	W 248392	64452	CAISSES EMBALLAGES BOIS
6353	BUILDERS WOODWRK,PREFABS	W 149457	157872	W 185234	177676	W 161391	205571	W 163551	209054	OUVRAGES DE MENUISERIE
64	PAPER,PAPERBOARD AND MFR		197091		181530		438958		406179	PAPIERS,CARTONS & OUVRAGES
641	PAPER AND PAPERBOARD	W 240593	146380	W 271473	142024	W 371107	289555	W 354451	251943	PAPIERS ET CARTONS
6413	KRAFT PAPER,PAPERBOARD	W 48349	38762	W 73480	38529	W 68799	53605	W 51280	33838	PAPIER ET CARTON KRAFT
6415	PAPER,PAPERBRD,BULK,NES	W 93098	57712	W 87240	53368	W 133787	114729	W 128997	91090	PAPIERS,CARTONS ROULEAUX
64159	OTHER PAPER ETC,BULK,NES	W 66692	36929	W 64535	36955	W 98969	78004	W 99292	63030	AUT PAPIER ROULEAUX FEUILLES
642	PAPER,ETC,PRECUT,ARTS OF	W 39328	50711	W 39321	39505	W 108166	149402	W 101681	154237	PAP,CARTONS DECOUPES
6421	PAPER ETC CONTAINERS	W 18269	17780	W 19011	14378	W 68743	89561	W 53396	81285	BOITES,SACS EMBALLAGES
65	TEXTILE YARN,FABRICS,ETC		631497		671891		1352172		991390	FILS,TISSUS,ARTICLES TEXTILE
651	TEXTILE YARN	W 19315	58907	W 24827	71031	W 43677	172624		123778	FILS TEXTILES
652	COTTON FABRICS,WOVEN	W 23702	143690	W 24580	157215	W 37705	308311		216618	TISSUS DE COTON
6522	WOVEN COTTON BLEACHD,ETC	W 19034	126876	W 18358	127655	W 28755	257776		174497	TISSUS COTON BLANCHIS ETC
65224	BLCHED COTTON FABRIC NES	W 14472	98019	W 12901	94772	W 19661	182402	W 13927	129875	AUT TIS PLUS 85% COT BLANCHI
653	WOVN MAN–MADE FIB FABRIC	W 12990	85316	W 13909	90960	W 21524	210557	W 14515	124129	TISSUS FIBRES SYNTH,ARTIF
6534	DISC SYN BLEND FABRC NES	W 4154	34079	W 3570	31247	W 7333	70771	W 4641	53588	TISSUS FIBRES SYNTH DISCONT
654	OTH WOVEN TEXTILE FABRIC	W 12088	95203	W 16296	108492	W 18966	182498		100982	TISSUS AUT COTON SYNT,ARTIF
6542	WOVEN WOOL,HAIR NONPILE	W 2759	39723	W 2563	32457	W 3889	85415	W 2174	34976	TIS PLUS 85% LAINE,POILS
655	KNITTED,ETC FABRICS	W 4457	38339	W 4733	29416	W 7817	65343	W 5091	45079	ETOF BONNETERIE PIECES ETC
6552	OTHER KNIT ETC FAB NONEL	W 4457	38339	W 4733	29416	W 7817	65343	W 5091	45079	ETOF BON NON ELAS NON SYNT
657	SPECIAL TXTL FABRC,PRODS	W 25453	91095	W 28490	96750	W 47185	228017		167086	TISSUS SPECIAUX
6573	COATED ETC TEXTILES NES	W 11480	51316	W 13711	54197	W 23192	132725	W 18258	95121	TISSUS,ART MATIERE TEXT NDA
65732	PLASTIC COATED TEXTILES	W 3647	19037	W 4123	13253	W 11143	73324	W 7772	35568	TISSUS IMPREGNES
658	TEXTILE ARTICLES NES	W 17130	81283	W 20216	85983	W 27652	120560		158331	ART FACONNES MAT TEXTILES
6584	LINENS ETC	W 4506	33155	W 6432	37270	W 11234	48117	W 9073	77011	LINGE DE MAISON
66	NONMETAL MINERAL MFS NES		792637		882751		1034890		1158917	ART MIN NON METALLIQUES
661	LIME,CEMENT,BLDG PRODS	W 2103562	119002	W 2500024	140695	W 1847245	123034	W 1819996	193003	CHAUX,CIMENTS MAT CONSTR
6612	CEMENT	W 1817909	91861	W 2130974	107664	W 1469507	83451	W 1417898	152527	CIMENTS HYDRAULIQUES
662	CLAY,REFRACTORY BLDG PRD	W 566550	110981	W 1168351	138575	W 631064	116251	W 444342	120905	MAT CONST REFRACTAIRES
6624	BRICKS ETC NONREFRACTORY	W 469779	95112	W 1064206	119575	W 579978	102059	W 383568	104130	BRIQUES ETC CERAM NON REFR
66245	GLAZED CERAMIC SETTS ETC	W 71562	36870	W 84908	71824	W 97897	49746	W 98616	49803	AUT CARREAUX CERAMIQUE
663	MINERAL MANUFCTURES NES	W 449532	64434	W 536397	89871	W 572775	121808	W 557481	126388	ART MIN MANUF NDA
6633	MINRL MFS NES NONCERAMIC	W 382321	30519	W 456004	47733	W 497022	65821	W 468434	70283	OUVR MAT MINERALE NDA
66332	CEMENT,ARTFCL STONE PROD	W 371087	26785	W 446592	43290	W 470471	56064	W 427935	58235	OUVRAGES EN CIMENT
664	GLASS	W 197723	118961	W 234322	116668	W 302742	201026	W 323019	199894	VERRE
6644	GLASS SURFACE–GROUND ETC	W 110734	57417	W 120249	41759	W 140071	53650	W 143635	46112	VERRE COULE,LAMINE
665	GLASSWARE	W 157365	300951	W 209175	317442	W 226343	386865	W 169799	410006	OUVRAGES EN VERRE
6651	BOTTLES ETC OF GLASS	W 110469	29557	W 156714	45203	W 168703	56097	W 110513	41117	RECIPIENTS EN VERRE
66511	GLASS BOTTLES ETC NONVAC	W 110415	29376	W 156628	44930	W 168456	54936	W 110462	40872	BONBONNES,BOUTEILLES,ETC
6652	HOUSEHLD,HOTEL ETC GLASS	W 37696	181550	W 42616	175001	W 46141	193087	W 47750	204728	OBJETS VERRE TABLE,CUISINE
6658	GLASS ARTICLES NES	W 9200	89844	W 9845	97238	W 11499	137681	W 11535	164162	ARTICLES FAB EN VERRE NDA
66582	GLASS ORNAMENTS NES	W 3853	78238	W 4172	83277	W 3978	116234	W 3888	143500	PERLES DE VERRE
666	POTTERY	W 13729	39587	W 18369	46709	W 24554	82786	W 22784	106372	POTERIE
6664	PORCELN,CHINA HOUSE WARE	W 12911	35097	W 17335	42844	W 23027	77544	W 20665	99025	VAISSELLE,ARTS MEN PORC
667	PEARL,PREC–,SEMI–P STONE		38721		32791		3119		2348	PERLES, PIERRES GEMMES
67	IRON AND STEEL		1406128		1411916		2065927		1733542	FER ET ACIER
671	PIG IRON ETC	W 138596	24783	W 217098	51570	W 226982	79778	W 195131	79226	FONTE,SPIEGEL,POUDRES
672	IRON,STEEL PRIMARY FORMS	W 677634	143640	W 1172640	149165	W 390846	130591		108070	LINGOTS FER,ACIER
6725	IRN,STL BLOOMS,SLABS,ETC	W 620500	126021	W 1100078	130295	W 317874	102986	W 296995	77869	BLOOMS,BILLETTES FER ACIER
67251	IRN,SMPLE STL BLOOMS,ETC	W 605156	121065	W 1094674	127397	W 306320	89082	W 289530	68563	BLOOMS ETC NON ACIER FIN
673	IRON,STEEL SHAPES ETC	W 2085434	620858	W 2980650	585434	W 2320951	726957	W 1905557	592110	BARRES,PROFIL FER,ACIER
6731	IRON,STEEL WIRE ROD	W 668718	171757	W 1592913	207935	W 775856	229459	W 806739	221489	FIL MACHINE FER,ACIER
67311	IRON,SIMPLE STL WIRE ROD	W 665891	170836	W 1581592	203348	W 727385	208092	W 805574	219987	FIL MACH AUT ACIER FIN
6732	IRON,STEEL BARS ETC	W 1010013	295556	W 1038967	265750	W 925076	342182	W 760384	264654	BARRES FER,ACIER
67325	OTH ALLOY STEEL BARS ETC	W 89444	47920	W 84075	42378	W 170491	122360	W 98332	76495	BARRES NON ACIERS ALLIES
67326	IRN,OTH STL BARS HOTROLD	W 646077	171281	W 930226	210218	W 719452	192332	W 642881	171731	BARRES PLEINES FER,ACIER
67327	IRN, OTH STL BARS FORGED	W 260747	66696	W 17314	7575	W 24424	14547	W 3005	2264	BARRES FORGEES CREUSES
6733	IRON,STEEL PROFILES ETC	W 406704	153545	W 348769	111749	W 620020	155316	W 338434	105967	PROFILES,PALPLAN FER,ACIER
67331	SMALL U,I,H SECTIONS ETC	W 224752	94140	W 79865	21556	W 285508	30511	W 72953	21541	PROFILES MOINS 80MM
67332	LARGE U,I,H SECTIONS ETC	W 129078	39617	W 221001	60636	W 283754	93430	W 240069	69020	PROFILES PLUS 80MM
674	IRN,STL UNIV,PLATE,SHEET	W 531381	275627	W 771367	233120	W 879206	450334	W 639739	275792	LARGES PLATS,TOLES
6744	IRN,STL HVY PLATE,ROLLED	W 398352	227856	W 654035	165419	W 504892	222795	W 470903	179409	TOLES LAMINEES PLUS 4.75 MM
67441	— OF IRON OR SIMPLE STL	W 397521	226633	W 653224	164119	W 501193	215829	W 469079	175174	TOLES NON ACIER FIN CARB
6746	IRN,STL THIN PLATE,ROLLD	W 46907	20008	W 75384	29264	W 198011	117372	W 65671	38811	TOLES LAM MOINS 3MM
67461	— OF IRON OR SIMPLE STL	W 45934	18425	W 73903	27321	W 182519	100066	W 62413	33537	TOL NON AC FIN MOINS 3 MM
677	IRN,STL WIRE(EXCL W ROD)	W 144695	51637	W 155182	61564	W 201405	101910	W 211235	99778	FILS EN FER,ACIER
67701	IRON, SIMPLE STEEL WIRE	W 130814	44856	W 135309	49906	W 169257	74892	W 195103	83383	FILS NON ACIER FIN CARBONE
678	IRON,STL TUBES,PIPES,ETC	W 339836	179068	W 384102	187494	W 590506	346836	W 508301	333380	TUBES,TUYAUX EN FONTE,FER
6782	IRON,STL SEAMLESS TUBES	W 166907	89135	W 196096	97266	W 352883	188754	W 305912	200694	TUBES,TUYAUX SANS SOUDURE
6783	IRON,STL TUBES,PIPES NES	W 154588	66888	W 169709	69231	W 208469	116086	W 181276	92001	AUT TUBES,TUYAUX FER,ACIER
679	IRN,STL CASTINGS UNWORKD	W 85661	93433	W 105957	118561	W 147937	187832	W 140220	202729	OUVRAGES EN FONTE,FER,ACIER
6794	IRON,STL CASTINGS ROUGH	W 67410	66615	W 84410	93025	W 119939	144797	W 114788	162650	OUVRAGES COULES,MOULES

5. General Exports F.O.B. by Commodities according to the S.I.T.C. (Rev. 2) in thousand U.S. Dollars
Exportations Générales F.O.B. par Produits d'après la C.T.C.I. (Rév. 2) en milliers de Dollars E.U.

SITC CTCI	COMMODITY	1993			1994			1995			1996			PRODUIT
			WEIGHT POIDS	VALUE VALEUR		WEIGHT POIDS	VALUE VALEUR		WEIGHT POIDS	VALUE VALEUR		WEIGHT POIDS	VALUE VALEUR	
67941	IRON CASTINGS ROUGH	W	67410	66615	W	84410	93025	W	119939	144797	W	114788	162650	OUVRAGES A L'ETAT BRUT
68	NON-FERROUS METALS			109933			152712			336910			231242	METAUX NON FERREUX
684	ALUMINIUM	W	40385	66193	W	61951	106646	W	66413	179206	W	64963	161781	ALUMINIUM
6842	ALUMINIUM,ALLOYS WORKED	W	21746	46769	W	34237	70816	W	42552	135224	W	40348	128846	ALUMINIUM,ALLIAGES OUVRE
69	METAL MANUFACTURES NES			505727			598017			1058156			1158458	ART MANUFACT EN METAL NDA
691	STRUCTURES AND PARTS NES	W	94395	91088	W	177939	120586	W	230093	200407	W	214374	225499	CONSTRUCT FER,ACIER,ALU
6911	STRUCTURES,PARTS IRN,STL	W	93228	87745	W	176365	115756	W	227887	188801	W	212246	210641	CONSTRUCT FER,ACIER,FONTE
692	METAL TANKS,BOXES,ETC	W	50311	57380	W	53860	63733	W	66418	94349	W	68056	123360	RECIPIENTS METALLIQUES
6924	MTL TRANSPORT BOXES ETC	W	28003	33351	W	28433	36596	W	35420	56125	W	40445	82489	FUTS,TAMBOURS,BIDONS
694	STL,COPPR NAILS,NUTS,ETC	W	41941	36537	W	50375	42129	W	66816	89741	W	59622	75227	CLOUS,VIS,ECROUS
69402	IRN,STL NUTS,BOLTS,ETC	W	24764	25963	W	31982	32394	W	47597	73781	W	40439	60498	BOULONS,VIS,ECROUS FER,AC
695	TOOLS	W	7111	48336	W	11174	50163	W	11509	75772	W	10604	84192	OUTILS A MAIN
697	BASE MTL HOUSEHOLD EQUIP	W	24220	72858	W	22883	66786	W	30086	71284			77194	ART MENAGE MET COMMUNS
699	BASE METAL MFRS NES	W	183053	155755	W	137998	214241	W	208802	470482			506592	ART MANUFACTURES MET NDA
6991	LOCKSMITHS WARES,ETC	W	9711	29227	W	15203	46678	W	28880	133352	W	26134	122777	ARTICLES DE SERRURERIE
69911	LOCKS,KEYS AND PARTS	W	2220	11605	W	4203	23075	W	10073	74255	W	6472	57915	SERRURES,VERROUS,CADENAS
6997	IRON,STEEL ARTICLES NES	W	145822	64039	W	88121	85061	W	132846	166152	W	133330	181245	OUV FONTE,FER,ACIER NDA
69979	IRN,STL MANUFACTURES NES	W	145526	63742	W	87928	84812	W	132681	165884	W	133225	181056	AUT OUVRAGES EN FER NDA
7	MACHINES,TRANSPORT EQUIP			3364133			3428382			6336338			7147089	MACHINES MATERIEL TRANSPORT
71	POWER GENERATING EQUIPMT			281734			257575			453937			578499	MACHINES GENERATRICES
711	STEAM BOILERS & AUX PLNT	W	14520	62996	W	9805	26547	W	10432	27494	W	10390	35060	GENERATEURS VAPEUR EAU ETC
7119	PTS NES OF APP OF 711	W	10982	55789	W	6847	18586	W	6577	18775	W	6685	24903	PART,PIECES POUR 711
71191	PTS NES OF BOILERS	W	8353	49800	W	4804	13531	W	5526	14819	W	5732	20747	PART,PIECES POUR 711.1
713	INTRNL COMBUS PSTN ENGIN	W	7370	49307	W	9821	63500	W	13117	99930			131741	MOTEURS EXPL COMB INT, PIECE
7139	PISTON ENGINE PARTS NES	W	4309	36089	W	4957	43200	W	7370	62401	W	14595	87276	PIECES POUR 713.2,3,8
716	ROTATING ELECTRIC PLANT	W	35417	109579	W	46217	126562	W	64805	256026			278303	APP ELECTR ROTATIFS,PIECES
7162	AC MTRS,GENRTRS,GEN SETS	W	22474	74319	W	31302	86973	W	36839	133661	W	39850	143519	MOTEURS ELECTRIQUES
71621	AC MTRS,INC UNIVRSL MTRS	W	18921	57640	W	25663	63432	W	32806	115572	W	34526	116934	MOT ELEC NON COUR CONTINU
7169	PTS NES OF ROT ELEC PLNT	W	12444	32165	W	13510	33903	W	23591	72513	W	20135	83338	PIECES MAC APP ROTATIFS
72	MACHS FOR SPCL INDUSTRYS			452231			467049			783842			862885	MAC SPECIALES POUR INDUST
721	AGRIC MACHY,EXC TRACTORS	W	20542	59249	W	25790	63695	W	34507	86716	W	37654	95336	MACHINES AGRICOLES
722	TRACTORS NON-ROAD	W	23248	68497	W	11208	37117	W	31573	118566	W	28809	108098	TRACTEURS
7224	WHEELED TRACTORS NES	W	23222	68468	W	11103	36911	W	31427	118509	W	28742	108000	TRACTEURS A ROUES
723	CIVIL ENGNEERG EQUIP ETC	W	12719	30121	W	12565	31565	W	18583	47744	W	28820	66246	APPAREILS DE GENIE CIVIL
724	TEXTILE,LEATHER MACHNRY	W	16450	138378	W	19993	139855	W	26745	216006	W	23478	224868	MACH POUR INDUSTRIE TEXTILE
7244	SPINNING,EXTRDNG,ETC MCH	W	4981	43448	W	7316	46570	W	9853	80118	W	8970	77327	MACH POUR LE FILAGE
726	PRINTG,BKBINDG MACHY,PTS	W	3317	37771	W	7584	46599	W	5078	58658			71807	MACHINES POUR IMPRIMERIE
728	OTH MACHY FOR SPCL INDUS	W	28082	84608	W	26157	108743	W	39840	196563	W	40005	219006	AUT MACH IND PARTICULIERES
7284	MACHY FOR SPCL INDUS NES	W	8116	36036	W	7806	43731	W	15937	111979	W	15801	125711	MACH SPEC IND PARTICUL.
73	METALWORKING MACHINERY			213461			223418			351378			384669	MACH TRAVAIL DES METAUX
736	METALWORKING MACH-TOOLS	W	34407	157806	W	49056	175755	W	61588	271801	W	56284	326433	MACH-OUTILS TRAVAIL METAUX
7361	METAL CUTTING MACH-TOOLS	W	16066	89470	W	16516	75649	W	17256	105596	W	20271	150797	MACH-OUT ENLEVEMENT METAL
73614	REAMING ETC MCHS,MTLWRKG	W	8430	50220	W	7008	34764	W	6894	48513	W	10787	79804	MACH POUR ALESER FRAISER
7369	PTS NES OF TOOLS OF 736	W	10139	25991	W	22458	54828	W	33844	115188	W	26815	98301	PIECES GROUPE 736
737	METALWORKING MACHNRY NES	W	13266	55655	W	10257	47663	W	20491	79577	W	13897	58236	MACH TRAV METAUX PIECES
7372	ROLLING MILLS AND ROLLS	W	9357	39968	W	6705	32047	W	13243	54262	W	11156	39663	LAMINOIRS CYLINDRES PIEC
73729	ROLL-MILL PTS NES, ROLLS	W	9341	39818	W	6703	32039	W	12424	52258	W	11106	39074	CYLINDRES DE LAMINOIRS
74	GENRL INDUSTRL MACHY NES			480347			502330			957377			1065379	MACH APP INDUSTRIE
741	HEATING,COOLING EQUIPMNT	W	18693	62851	W	18220	79781	W	29082	168520	W	28120	218883	MACH CHAUFFAGE,PIECES
7414	NONDOM REFRIG EQUIPT,PTS	W	2934	17795	W	3956	31337	W	9533	84937	W	8333	85663	MAT PRODUCTION DU FROID
742	PUMPS FOR LIQUIDS ETC	W	9698	54922	W	8525	55471	W	11574	105889	W	10597	139997	POMPES MOTO-POMPES
7428	OTHER PUMPS FOR LIQUIDS	W	2050	14495	W	1979	14432	W	2631	25045	W	3515	73573	AUTRES POMPES POUR LIQ
743	PUMPS NES,CENTRFUGES ETC	W	11394	61813	W	11005	56745	W	17116	88653	W	21745	106926	POMPES COMPRES,VENT ETC
744	MECHANICAL HANDLING EQU	W	46423	110803	W	59569	112647	W	131776	195693	W	83673	197174	EQUIP MANUTENTION PIECES
7449	PTS NES OF MACHY OF 7442	W	28941	58641	W	40499	64832	W	70523	132302	W	66799	138849	PIECES DU 744.2
745	NONELEC MACHY,TOOLS NES	W	5924	42580	W	8142	38976	W	11748	64778	W	11569	68097	AUT MACH NON ELEC,PIECES
7452	OTH NONELEC MCHS,PTS NES	W	5769	38806	W	7996	36616	W	11406	60720	W	11390	63989	AUT MACH NON ELEC,PIECES
749	NONELEC MACH PTS,ACC NES	W	35667	147378	W	36550	158711	W	55369	333844	W	54227	334303	PIECES MACH NON ELEC NDA
7492	COCKS,VALVES ETC NES	W	17749	61314	W	16332	60804	W	19915	99831	W	20450	121094	ART ROB,SIM POUR TUYAUX
7493	SHAFT,CRANK,PULLEY ETC	W	8713	32309	W	11752	44510	W	23412	108929	W	21365	93833	ARBRES TRANS,VILEBREQUINS
7499	OTH NONELEC MCHY PTS NES	W	3717	19134	W	3917	28407	W	5996	65433	W	6106	63267	PIECES NON ELECT NDA
75	OFFICE MACHNES,ADP EQUIP			77605			116569			200842			227103	MACH BUREAU TRAIT AUTOM
752	AUTOMTIC DATA PROC EQUIP	W	1646	34014	W	4932	68325	W	3597	79363			85434	MACH TRAIT INFORMATION
759	OFFICE,ADP MCH PTS,ACCES	W	1677	15681	W	4136	24391	W	8760	99910	W	7579	117191	PIECES DU 751 ET 752
7599	ACCTG,ETC,ADP MCH PTS,AC	W	997	11687	W	2682	17387	W	6653	81644	W	5544	96261	PIECES DU 751 ET 752
76	TELECOMM,SOUND EQUIPMENT			54923			80570			139717			165307	EQUIPMENT DE TELECOM
764	TELECOM EQPT,PTS,ACC NES	W	2972	45845	W	4088	67317	W	6501	126095			160059	EQUIP TELECOM,PIECES
7649	PTS NES OF EQUIPMT OF 76	W	1389	18146	W	3011	41604	W	4178	96787	W	5220	125563	PIECES DE LA DIV 76
76493	TELECOMM EQUIPMT PTS NES	W	704	6448	W	1444	8780	W	2284	55108	W	1800	72304	PIECES 761,762,764.3,8
77	ELECTRIC MACHNRY NES ETC			533315			504413			1554498			1521718	MACH APP ELECT NDA
771	ELECTRIC POWER MACHY NES	W	4294	27089	W	7597	31957	W	11526	86946	W	9292	97292	MACH PROD,TRANS ELECTR
7712	OTH ELEC POWER MACHY NES	W	1815	18783	W	3758	18607	W	7945	73918	W	5425	72633	AUT APP PROD TRANSF ELEC
772	SWITCHGEAR ETC,PARTS NES	W	11187	83037	W	19427	114217	W	36230	458677	W	28025	459422	APP COUPURE,SECT ETC
7721	SWITCHGEAR ETC	W	10221	74597	W	17437	100316	W	33025	394055	W	26034	401944	APP COUPURE,SECTIONMNT
773	ELECTR DISTRIBUTNG EQUIP	W	28481	84749	W	28642	79594	W	92710	247131			308524	EQUIPMT DISTRIBUTION ELECT
7731	INSULATED WIRE,CABLE ETC	W	25671	79174	W	26172	73307	W	87617	222253	W	39238	284603	FILS,CABLES ISOLES ELECT
775	HOUSEHOLD TYPE EQUIP NES	W	13502	63987	W	16842	72969	W	18286	86800			95653	MACH,APP USAGE DOMESTQUE
776	TRANSISTORS,VALVES,ETC	W	3375	37651	W	6111	54359	W	10121	144485			116934	LAMPES,TUBES,VALVES
778	ELECTRICAL MACHINERY NES	W	16076	231169	W	21795	145286	W	43015	519708			436664	AUTRES MACH ELECT NDA
7781	BATTERIES,ACCUMULATORS	W	6379	15125	W	9957	21144	W	24216	84258	W	22612	87178	PILES ET ACCUMULATEURS
77812	ELECTRIC ACCUMULATORS	W	5375	11799	W	7319	13513	W	12021	39663	W	18955	71870	ACCUMULATEURS ELECTRIQ
7788	OTH ELEC MACHY,EQUIP NES	W	2517	152222	W	3857	62437	W	6799	327888			239149	AUT MACH APP ELEC NDA
77884	ELECTRICAL CONDENSERS	W	587	134633	W	726	38411	W	2315	271874	W	945	190831	CONDENSATEURS ELECTRIQUES
78	ROAD VEHICLES			1163057			1118943			1593203			2034480	VEHICULES ROUTIERS
781	PASS MOTOR VEH EXC BUSES	W	103861	560221	W	96556	536180	W	121339	720812	W	143435	948151	AUTO TRANSPORT PERSONNES
782	LORRIES,SPCL MTR VEH NES	W	90958	254380	W	63528	207658	W	44164	171672	W	44044	191757	VEHICULES SPECIAUX,MARCH
7821	LORRIES,TRUCKS	W	76796	228361	W	50505	182835	W	34800	141275	W	38519	178475	VEHICULES TRANSP MARCHAND
783	ROAD MOTOR VEHICLES NES	W	14829	49359	W	11065	38002	W	13848	60501	W	12402	75317	VEHICULES ROUTIERS NDA
7831	BUSES	W	11811	42139	W	8789	32677	W	11822	51875	W	10905	68261	VOITURES TRANSPORT COMMUN
784	MOTOR VEH PRTS,ACCES NES	W	49098	179106	W	106716	217914	W	126660	487493	W	143698	665436	PIECES 722,781,782,783
7842	MOTOR VEHICLE BODIES	W	2225	10102	W	3360	12754	W	6767	37330	W	12814	75624	CARROS 722,781,782,783
7849	OTHER MOTOR VEHCL PARTS	W	45585	162142	W	102322	189875	W	115945	430449	W	123541	563365	PIECES 722,781,782,783
785	CYCLES,ETC MOTRZD OR NOT	W	12766	57672	W	15093	61632	W	21698	85281	W	17392	83751	MOTOCYCLES SCOOTERS
786	TRAILERS,NONMOTR VEH,NES	W	42338	62319	W	41890	57557	W	52037	67443	W	47405	70068	REMORQUES,CADRES,CONTAIN
7861	TRAILERS,TRANSP CONTAINR	W	30636	42473	W	26845	25489	W	27855	32984	W	27766	35734	REMORQUES TOUS VEHICULES
79	OTHR TRANSPORT EQUIPMENT			107459			157514			301545			307049	AUTRE MATERIEL TRANSPORT
791	RAILWAY VEHICLES	W	68685	97017	W	69840	139329	W	114203	293312	W	84993	178640	VEHIC MAT CHEMINS DE FER
7919	RY TRACK FIXT,ETC,PARTS	W	34096	58378	W	41406	73905	W	69530	139694	W	60373	124216	MATER FIXE VOIES FERREES
79199	PARTS NES OF 7911-7915	W	30958	56917	W	40751	73283	W	67935	138033	W	59231	123190	PIECES 791.1 ET 5
792	AIRCRAFT ETC	W	41	2489	W	51	2481	W	49	1922			115540	APP NAVIGATION AERIENNE
8	MISC MANUFACTURED GOODS			1481454			1856609			2513553			3044962	ART MANUFACTURES DIVERS

5. General Exports F.O.B. by Commodities according to the S.I.T.C. (Rev. 2) in thousand U.S. Dollars
Exportations Générales F.O.B. par Produits d'après la C.T.C.I. (Rév. 2) en milliers de Dollars E.U.

SITC CTCI	COMMODITY	1993		1994		1995		1996		PRODUIT
		WEIGHT POIDS	VALUE VALEUR	WEIGHT POIDS	VALUE VALEUR	WEIGHT POIDS	VALUE VALEUR	WEIGHT POIDS	VALUE VALEUR	
812	*PLUMBG,HEATNG,LGHTNG EQ	W 48826	107228	W 50410	111643	W 57815	140545	W 68300	175591	APPAR SANITAIRES CHAUFFAGE
8124	LIGHTING EQUIPMENT NES	W 9512	57795	W 10170	53949	W 12015	70000	W 11691	81158	APPAREILS ECLAIRAGE ETC
821	*FURNITURE,PARTS THEREOF	W 111053	194006	W 140127	291611	W 208773	402182	W 149959	519014	MEUBLES ET PIECES
8211	CHAIRS,SEATS AND PARTS	W 34702	81166	W 46391	123297	W 108921	196248	W 51972	291717	SIEGES ET PIECES
82111	CHAIRS AND OTHER SEATS	W 26084	61793	W 33004	104856	W 30446	87839	W 22601	81912	SIEGES
82119	PTS NES OF CHAIRS ETC	W 8618	19373	W 13387	18442	W 78475	108409	W 29371	209805	PIECES DU 821.11
8219	FURNITURE AND PARTS NES	W 70940	100435	W 87733	150676	W 94970	184926	W 93198	200017	AUTRES MEUBLES ET PIECES
82191	METAL FURNITURE NES	W 22952	28231	W 30912	51738	W 24861	36704	W 20977	32457	MEUBLES NDA EN METAL
82192	WOOD FURNITURE NES	W 38276	60244	W 44111	83785	W 51151	115741	W 51790	126740	MEUBLES NDA EN BOIS
84	CLOTHING AND ACCESSORIES		303957		367748		523906		622499	VETEMENTS
842	MENS OUTERWEAR NOT KNIT	W 5198	62730	W 6395	103483	W 7466	95846	W 6242	127161	VET DESSUS POUR HOMMES
8429	— OTHER OUTER GARMENTS	W 1061	9938	W 1499	44673	W 1900	18877	W 1605	30873	AUT VET DES HOM MAT TEX
843	WOMENS OUTERWEAR NONKNIT	W 5345	62228	W 6761	77395	W 7673	101608	W 6287	154732	VET DESSUS FEMMES MAT TEX
845	OUTERWEAR KNIT NONELASTC	W 2946	42720	W 3810	44371	W 5313	63783	W 4319	86910	VET DESSOUS,ACCES BONNET
846	UNDER GARMENTS KNITTED	W 3864	51624	W 7266	47231	W 7343	86196	W 4446	93723	SOUS VETS DE BONNETERIE
847	TEXTILE CLTHNG ACCES NES	W 2085	25556	W 3234	27296	W 4432	74290	W 2920	49665	ACCES VET MAT TEXT NDA
851	*FOOTWEAR	W 17269	171796	W 20585	208755	W 16596	215169	W 14507	254136	CHAUSSURES
85102	FOOTWEAR LEATHER	W 12129	135628	W 15848	182151	W 12725	180693	W 10572	214963	CHAUS SEMELLES EN CUIR
87	PRECISION INSTRUMNTS NES		65974		82690		210036		186184	INSTRUM,APPAR SCIENT NDA
874	MEASURNG,CONTROLNG INSTR	W 25190	49058	W 5317	58934	W 9646	166003		129521	INSTRUMENTS DE MESURE
88	PHOTO EQU,OPTICL GDS ETC		29683		37330		57228		73811	APP,FOURN PHOTO,OP,MONTR
89	MISC MANUFCTRD GOODS NES		576627		724419		925092		1170468	ART MANUFACTURES DIVERS
892	PRINTED MATTER	W 16151	47597	W 23844	56383	W 41261	111565		133022	IMPRIMES
8928	PRINTED MATTER NES	W 3824	15007	W 8363	21326	W 20024	51188		68774	IMPRIMES NDA
893	ARTICLES OF PLASTIC NES		125166		147820		309880		356812	OUVRAGES EN MAT DIVIS 58
8931	PLSTC PACKG CONTNRS,LIDS	W 16682	35640	W 21255	30521	W 31297	76181	W 43008	90588	ART TRANSP EMBALLAGE ETC
8939	MISC PLASTIC ARTICLES	W 33891	87348	W 70511	112819	W 78823	224687	W 70001	256665	ART DIVERS EN MAT DIV 58
89399	OTHR PLASTC ARTICLES NES	W 27425	80991	W 62402	102824	W 69381	206305	W 61620	238761	AUT OUV MAT DIV 58
894	TOYS,SPORTING GOODS,ETC	W 13467	85532	W 17749	111256	W 21231	150830	W 24518	220895	VOITURES ENFANTS,JOUETS
8942	TOYS,INDOOR GAMES ETC	W 8515	47683	W 12004	61427	W 11135	73617	W 10300	80055	JOUETS,JEUX ETC
8947	OTH SPORT GDS,FAIR AMUSM	W 4633	27525	W 5364	36594	W 9779	67695	W 7668	91122	AUT ART DE SPORT
89472	OTH OUTDOOR SPORT GOODS	W 3581	24554	W 4767	33484	W 8071	63397	W 7173	84635	ART POUR JEUX PLEIN AIR
896	WORKS OF ART ETC		70477		208381		80591		17244	OBJETS D'ART
89601	HAND PAINTINGS ETC NES		26623		173627		22629		6958	TABLEAUX,PEINTURES
897	GOLD,SILVER WARE,JEWELRY		66321		49532		55777		55529	BIJOUTERIE,ORFEVRERIE
8972	IMITATION JEWELLERY		41133		39169		43103		40112	BIJOUTERIE DE FANTAISIE
898	MUSICAL INSTRUMENTS,PTS	W 5645	100596	W 6939	78050	W 8641	103089		239551	INSTRUMENTS DE MUSIQUE
8983	SOUND RECRDNG TAPE,DISCS	W 2135	36363	W 2752	28609	W 3532	44372		176449	SUPPORTS SON POUR 763
89832	RECORDED DISCS,TAPES ETC	W 1954	33937	W 2532	26443	W 3318	42400	W 2902	174751	DISQUES,PHONO,BANDES
899	OTHER MANUFACTURED GOODS		60295		46851		75297		89309	AUT ART MANUF DIVERS NDA
9	GOODS NOT CLASSD BY KIND		231974		263426		361736		57263	ART TRANSACT NON CLASSES
931	*SPECIAL TRANSACTIONS	W 11024	221615	W 19556	250911	W 17152	335257			TRANS.SPECIALES

1. HISTORICAL SERIES, 1961–1996 GENERAL TRADE, IMPORTS C.I.F., EXPORTS F.O.B.
SERIES HISTORIQUES, 1961–1996 COMMERCE GENERAL, IMPORTATIONS C.A.F., EXPORTATIONS F.O.B

YEAR ANNEE	VALUE IN MILLION DANISH KRONER / VALEUR EN MILLION DANISH KRONER: MERCHANDISE – MARCHANDISE: IMPORTS	EXPORTS	GOLD – OR: IMPORTS	EXPORTS	CONVERSION FACTORS U.S. CENTS PER DANISH KRONE / FACTEURS DE CONVERSION CENTS E.U. PAR DANISH KRONE: IMPORTS	EXPORTS	INDEX NUMBERS – INDICES: QUANTUM: IMPORTS	EXPORTS	UNIT VALUE / VALEUR UNITAIRE: IMPORTS	EXPORTS
1961	12938.00	10620.00	22.00		14.4778	14.4778	29	20	24	24
1962	14715.00	11525.00	26.50	1.00	14.4778	14.4778	33	22	24	25
1963	14703.00	13176.00	27.90	1.00	14.4778	14.4778	33	24	24	26
1964	18077.00	14651.00	35.20	1.00	14.4778	14.4778	39	26	24	26
1965	19495.00	16025.00	41.30	1.00	14.4778	14.4778	41	28	24	26
1966	20739.00	16944.00	40.60	1.00	14.4778	14.4778	44	28	25	27
1967	21940.00	17660.00	41.80	1.00	14.3395	14.3360	46	30	25	27
1968	24274.00	19799.00	43.90	3.00	13.3333	13.3333	47	33	26	27
1969	28594.00	22654.00	52.70	2.00	13.3333	13.3333	56	36	27	29
1970	32909.00	24673.00	45.40	3.00	13.3333	13.3333	62	38	28	30
1971	34013.00	26739.00	39.50	3.00	13.4939	13.4982	59	40	30	31
1972	35155.00	30136.00	54.50	4.00	14.3444	14.3436	62	43	30	33
1973	46734.00	36817.00	58.60	6.00	16.6115	16.6413	74	46	33	37
1974	60480.00	46922.00	51.40	8.00	16.4133	16.4515	70	49	45	43
1975	59708.00	50031.00			17.3671	17.4150	65	47	47	47
1976	75011.00	55034.00			16.5668	16.5625	77	49	50	51
1977	79637.00	60436.00			16.6572	16.6551	76	51	55	54
1978	81405.00	65308.00			18.1952	18.1981	78	54	55	56
1979	98292.00	78160.00			19.0034	19.0078	83	60	62	61
1980	111143.00	96986.00			17.7333	17.7333	76	65	77	69
1981	126274.20	115605.90			14.0445	14.0445	72	67	90	79
1982	141356.50	129996.00			11.9963	11.9963	75	68	99	88
1983	148896.00	146798.00			10.9313	10.9313	79	74	102	91
1984	171826.00	165346.00			9.6520	9.6520	84	77	111	99
1985	187701.20	174415.20			9.4340	9.4340	90	80	111	102
1986	184733.00	171720.00			12.3541	12.3541	96	82	103	98
1987	174033.00	175187.00			14.6118	14.6118	95	83	96	97
1988	174429.00	185819.00			14.8739	14.8836	94	87	97	96
1989	195328.00	205300.00			13.6822	13.6937	94	92	105	103
1990	198782.00	216444.00			16.2139	16.2329	100	100	100	100
1991	206799.00	229764.00			15.6727	15.6730	108	111	99	100
1992	212088.00	247254.00			16.5900	16.6091	113	116	96	98
1993	197957.00	241034.00			15.4304	15.4219	104	113	93	96
1994	220769.00	262365.00			15.8002	15.7878	118	122	95	97
1995	241936.00	274496.00			17.8687	17.8673	126	128	97	97
1996	250611.00	282831.10			17.2462	17.2453	125	130	98	99

2. IMPORTS BY BROAD ECONOMIC CATEGORY AND EXPORTS BY INDUSTRIAL ORIGIN. (PERCENTAGE OF TOTAL VALUE)
IMPORTATIONS PAR CATEGORIES ECONOMIQUES ET EXPORTATIONS PAR BRANCHE D'ACTIVITE.(EN POURCENTAGE DE LA VALEUR TOTALE)

IMPORTS – IMPORTATIONS

	1990	1991	1992	1993	1994	1995	1996
TOTAL IMPORTS–IMPORTATIONS TOTALES	100.	100.	100.	100.	100.	100.	100.
1 FOOD BEV–ALIMENTATION BOISSONS	9.5	10.1	10.5	10.6	10.1	10.0	10.1
11 PRIMARY–PRODUITS DE BASE	5.0	5.4	5.4	5.2	5.1	4.9	4.9
111 FOR INDUSTRY–POUR L'INDUSTRIE	0.5	0.6	0.8	0.9	0.9	0.9	0.8
112 FOR HOUSEHOLDS–POUR LES MENAGES	4.5	4.8	4.6	4.3	4.2	4.0	4.1
12 PROCESSED–PRODUITS ELABORES	4.5	4.7	5.2	5.4	5.0	5.2	5.2
121 FOR INDUSTRY–POUR L'INDUSTRIE	0.7	0.8	0.9	0.9	0.9	0.9	0.9
122 FOR HOUSEHOLDS–POUR LES MENAGES	3.7	3.9	4.3	4.5	4.2	4.3	4.4
2 IND SUPPLIES–APPROV INDUSTRIELS	34.3	32.3	33.3	30.5	30.4	31.0	28.4
21 PRIMARY–PRODUITS DE BASE	2.3	2.2	2.4	2.3	2.2	2.2	2.3
22 PROCESSED–PRODUITS ELABORES	32.0	30.1	30.9	28.1	28.2	28.8	26.2
3 FUELS–COMBUSTIBLES	6.8	5.1	4.6	4.9	4.1	3.3	3.7
31 PRIMARY–PRODUITS DE BASE	3.6	2.4	2.2	2.2	1.8	1.6	1.9
32 PROCESSED–PRODUITS ELABORES	3.2	2.7	2.5	2.7	2.3	1.6	1.8
321 MOTOR SPIRIT–ESSENCE	0.6	0.6	2.1	2.5	2.2	1.4	
322 OTHER–AUTRES	2.6	2.2	0.4	0.3	0.1	0.2	1.8
4 MACHINERY–EQUIPEMENT	20.4	19.9	20.0	20.0	20.0	21.5	21.4
41 CAPITAL EQUIPMENT–MACHINES	16.4	16.0	15.9	15.9	15.9	16.8	16.9
42 PARTS–PIECES ACCESSOIRES	4.0	3.9	4.1	4.1	4.2	4.6	4.5
5 TRANSPORT–TRANSPORT	11.1	11.6	9.7	9.1	11.1	10.6	10.8
51 PASSENGER CARS–AUTOMOBILES	2.4	2.5	2.8	2.8	4.1	3.9	4.0
52 OTHER–AUTRES	5.8	6.1	3.8	3.2	3.9	3.8	3.9
521 INDUSTRIAL–INDUSTRIELS	5.7	5.9	3.7	3.0	3.8	3.6	3.6
522 NON INDUSTRIAL–NON INDUSTRIEL	0.2	0.2	0.2	0.2	0.2	0.2	0.2
53 PARTS–PIECES ACCESSOIRES	2.9	3.0	3.0	3.1	3.0	3.0	3.0
6 CONSUM GOODS–BIENS CONSOMMATION	15.5	16.4	17.2	17.4	17.0	16.7	17.1
61 DURABLE–DURABLES	3.6	3.6	3.6	3.8	3.8	3.7	3.9
62 SEMI DURABLE–SEMI DURABLES	8.6	9.4	9.8	10.0	9.6	9.4	9.5
63 NON DURABLE–NON DURABLES	3.2	3.4	3.8	3.6	3.6	3.5	3.7
7 GOODS NES–BIENS NDA	2.5	4.7	4.6	7.5	7.4	6.9	8.4

EXPORTS – EXPORTATIONS

	1990	1991	1992	1993	1994	1995	1996
TOTAL EXPORTS–EXPORTATIONS TOTALES	100.	100.	100.	100.	100.	100.	100.
1 AGRICULTURE	9.7	9.7	8.4	7.9	7.5	7.1	7.2
2 MINING QUARRY–INDUS EXTRACTIVES	1.6	1.9	1.8	1.3	1.0	1.5	1.7
3 MANUFACTURING–IND MANUFACTUR	88.7	88.4	89.8	90.8	91.5	91.4	91.1
31 FOOD BEV TOBACCO–ALIM BOISS TAB	20.5	20.8	20.7	20.4	20.2	19.5	18.6
32 TEXTILES–INDUSTRIES TEXTILES	5.1	5.3	5.4	5.1	4.8	4.9	5.0
33 WOOD & PRODUCTS–BOIS & PRODUITS	1.6	1.6	1.6	1.6	1.7	1.9	1.7
34 PAPER & PRODUCTS–PAPIER & PRODT	2.2	2.2	2.0	2.1	2.1	2.2	2.0
35 CHEMICALS–INDUSTRIES CHIMIQUES	12.4	11.9	12.6	12.7	12.5	12.8	13.3
36 NON METAL MIN–MIN NON METAL	1.6	1.7	1.8	1.6	1.5	1.5	1.3
37 BASIC METAL–IND METAL BASE	2.1	2.0	1.9	1.6	1.8	2.1	1.9
38 METAL MANUF–MANUF METAL	37.5	36.5	37.6	35.0	35.4	36.2	36.2
39 OTH MANUF IND–AUTRES MANUF	5.8	6.3	6.1	10.6	11.5	10.4	11.1

3. TRADE BY PRINCIPAL COUNTRIES OF PRODUCTION AND LAST CONSIGNMENT (VALUE IN THOUSAND U.S. DOLLARS)
ECHANGES SELON LES PRINCIPAUX PAYS DE PRODUCTION ET DE DERNIERE CONSIGNATION (VALEUR EN MILLIERS DE DOLLARS EU)

COUNTRIES–PAYS	GENERAL IMPORTS C.I.F. IMPORTATIONS GENERALES C.A.F				
	1992	1993	1994	1995	1996
World	33590347	30535740	35436475	43141557	43110375
Africa	147425	143210	249196	201387	188395
Americas	2755308	2316625	2728685	3035875	3193887
Northern America	2120357	1743634	2120704	2396199	2522567
LAIA	502984	463433	572953	614047	635173
CACM	20147	13249	15157	20569	30304
Caribbean	106647	94286	18821	3798	5386
Rest of America	5173	2023	1049	1263	457
As.ex F.USSR	3406360	3183506	3756286	3895922	3822278
Eur.x F.USSR	26047779	23623739	27262501	34170559	34139842
EU	22701035	20625598	23805801	30113659	30018137
EFTA	2539527	2250999	2459625	3000149	3042773
East Europe	581368	533248	686721	857525	874134
Other Europe	173160	181667	154969	139496	152997
Former USSR	369756	511782	542463	675640	659066
Oceania	43878	41704	53300	93971	105740
Germany/Allemagne	7679094	6592349	7249522	9185960	8694344
Sweden/Suède	3614705	3180590	3891673	5024676	4967651
United Kingdom	2729290	2184079	2191438	2810567	2896398
Netherlands/Pays–Bas	1834598	1880296	2248398	3023663	2828477
France,Monac	1863230	1530526	1811491	2220736	2239659
Norway,SVD,JM	1789434	1506042	1709947	2120668	2204521
USA/Etats–Unis d'Amer	1719200	1383895	1715816	1942610	2032782
Italy/Italie	1381122	1106819	1310867	1756129	1739757
Belgium–Luxembourg	1087183	1055826	1187343	1509000	1427641
Japan/Japon	1374398	1008453	1160292	1122283	960432
Finland/Finlande	897230	840881	1040796	1222042	1148943
Switz.Liecht	648297	658818	640077	730130	692326
China/Chine	550007	569215	656359	758549	807285
Poland/Pologne	396120	388131	477215	591472	591245
Spain/Espagne	420827	332133	376164	488069	506364
Portugal	417641	324746	373083	470307	430638
Austria/Autriche	405156	345586	347486	407557	381554
Russian Federation	264422	307652	313140	431141	363078
Ireland/Irlande	292828	178055	251809	424661	511744
Greenland/Groenland	281589	241984	275963	307068	327815
Korea, Republic of	160385	234970	348926	232616	229127
Brazil/Brésil	196878	210847	243197	268267	219555
Argentina/Argentine	201642	150884	204018	174064	214970
Hong Kong	163448	153963	170708	204299	229257
Thailand/Thaïlande	138036	122709	157857	189753	202450
India/Inde	97779	111707	160384	205271	193917
Faeroe Islds/Is Féroé	165022	178412	151523	136292	135950
Indonesia/Indonésie	132442	135896	142889	170578	176823
Malaysia/Malaisie	110387	97320	140915	172075	161799
Canada	119547	117672	128906	146511	160929
Singapore/Singapour	101641	182519	199940	84349	93022
Iceland/Islande	101796	86138	109601	149351	145926
Turkey/Turquie	77630	78301	115755	144563	152669
Czech Republic		67880	105540	131873	133385
Lithuania/Lituanie	52096	44914	74524	94048	107425
Greece/Grèce	78132	50847	55906	55090	57582
Latvia/Lettonie	27665	85570	62226	51459	68506
Israel/Israël	47347	49117	57398	73357	45392
Hungary/Hongrie	50053	41015	47615	57561	68786
Pakistan	44437	44841	45437	62985	57474
Estonia/Estonie	16875	22688	38294	63221	73257
Bangladesh	26324	30357	43437	56979	56183
Colombia/Colombie	31191	30416	44088	53716	45216
Australia/Australie	14873	15477	19188	49616	67355
Croatia/Croatie	5196	8477	124847	19254	7050
New Zealand	27719	24888	31007	41414	37422
Philippines	31320	30092	29733	31391	34050
Chile/Chili	25879	21073	24753	33227	38301
Slovenia/Slovénia	18418	19725	26173	35565	36992
Bahamas	46838	83761	5087	210	767

COUNTRIES–PAYS	GENERAL EXPORTS F.O.B. EXPORTATIONS GENERALES F.O.B.				
	1992	1993	1994	1995	1996
Monde	39553141	37171027	41602403	48789163	48873242
Afrique	729476	456007	747563	850841	511174
Amériques	2667176	2748610	3156493	2986380	2973932
Amérique du Nord	2109147	2082069	2377216	2160691	2253143
ALAI	336983	337200	478101	507504	426774
MCAC	17542	16829	26240	28836	21252
Caraïbes	93587	297845	258887	205589	131601
Autre Amérique	109919	14667	16049	83759	141163
Asie l'URSS exclus	3700248	3614360	4124893	5009305	4922420
Europe l'URSS exclus	29385185	27021722	29619612	34971206	35475729
UE	25352783	22898070	25169569	29863549	29976707
AELE	3067224	3168085	3340862	3778761	3901700
Europe de l'Est	701769	712401	856525	1051340	1193365
Autre de l'Europe	182536	144874	160187	161191	279296
Ancienne URSS	374527	437976	636127	1044738	1198774
Océanie	185310	210230	265982	286190	295973
Germany/Allemagne	8809397	7987475	8302791	10219395	9697061
Sweden/Suède	3969573	3386727	3918197	4404250	4732974
United Kingdom	3781459	2941309	3036772	3537121	4006018
Norway,SVD,JM	2216664	2425915	2483287	2771362	2993951
France,Monac	2074527	1720988	1955414	2360702	2173786
USA/Etats–Unis d'Amer	1668473	1701378	1953372	1727604	1759542
Netherlands/Pays–Bas	1636745	1404257	1431114	1936208	1844630
Italy/Italie	1684502	1341848	1466477	1633640	1614000
Japan/Japon	1352671	1315022	1466862	1675768	1522981
Finland/Finlande	757333	644598	907253	1175526	1173179
Belgium–Luxembourg	766659	638381	664134	856822	822699
Spain/Espagne	742408	617698	659967	840491	862742
Switz.Liecht	694829	600624	697488	813525	706922
Poland/Pologne	483543	452245	533317	634305	798120
Russian Federation	242293	268404	409218	624610	702411
Austria/Autriche	377650	349533	385753	456221	449115
Greece/Grèce	326671	278175	287718	326767	331573
Hong Kong	214752	240337	303287	347203	443043
Korea, Republic of	202092	194326	315095	368028	460512
Saudi Arabia	231701	242379	242030	284274	234072
Greenland/Groenland	278411	217583	219153	239023	247652
Portugal	228869	168627	199560	301523	259943
Ireland/Irlande	196991	161903	182857	247531	242791
Australia/Australie	144910	162585	202268	217569	229293
Singapore/Singapour	216347	119576	182320	201938	216458
China/Chine	107139	126925	162470	245160	285982
Canada	160068	160839	186070	173552	182318
Iceland/Islande	155731	141546	160087	193874	200827
Thailand/Thaïlande	130609	164632	162303	205766	185633
Liberia/Libéria	235718	40424	284400	262636	3796
India/Inde	86068	70468	138967	338397	181417
Turkey/Turquie	97168	123986	119873	157007	145544
Faeroe Islds/Is Féroé	134801	92028	98704	136814	155291
Egypt/Egypte	102742	113736	120170	152868	126338
Czech Republic		107362	131421	172705	179209
United Arab Emirates	100937	103389	116300	129322	131773
Iran (Islamic Rp. of)	161944	165047	80027	80842	76775
Israel/Israël	128844	76670	99247	124374	118430
Bahamas	3096	234353	147873	85873	46335
Brazil/Brésil	51990	68798	91617	165921	124045
Indonesia/Indonésie	74346	94669	63945	98558	144433
Hungary/Hongrie	54135	71267	99385	105551	95138
Lithuania/Lituanie	42987	29504	67568	122388	159687
Mexico/Mexique	106333	88811	132827	40633	35094
Malaysia/Malaisie	65238	63447	70629	93749	106238
So. Africa Customs Un	42700	51501	82936	116598	98227
Panama	104413	10138	12057	77923	138196
Argentina/Argentine	41670	52107	75083	85564	76060
Pakistan	49073	36108	38303	58079	79890
Chile/Chili	38333	45863	46772	55230	71779

(VALUE AS PERCENTAGE OF WORLD TOTAL)(VALEURS EN POURCENTAGE DU TOTAL MONDIAL)

	1987	1988	1989	1990	1991	1992	1993	1994	1995	1996
Africa	0.7	0.6	0.9	0.7	0.5	0.4	0.5	0.7	0.5	0.4
Americas	8.2	8.9	9.7	8.9	8.4	8.2	7.6	7.7	7.0	7.4
Northern America	6.6	7.0	7.8	7.1	6.9	6.3	5.7	6.0	5.6	5.9
LAIA	1.4	1.4	1.6	1.3	1.4	1.5	1.5	1.6	1.4	1.5
CACM	0.1	0.1	0.1	0.1	0.1	0.1	0.0	0.0	0.0	0.1
Caribbean	0.1	0.3	0.2	0.2	0.0	0.3	0.3	0.1	0.0	0.0
Rest of America	0.0	0.1	0.0	0.2	0.0	0.0	0.0	0.0	0.0	0.0
As.ex F.USSR	10.4	10.9	11.2	10.5	10.5	10.1	10.4	10.6	9.0	8.9
Eur.x F.USSR	77.7	76.6	74.5	76.7	77.1	77.5	77.4	76.9	79.2	79.2
EU	68.6	67.3	65.6	67.2	67.0	67.6	67.5	67.2	69.8	69.6
EFTA	6.6	6.7	6.5	6.9	7.8	7.6	7.4	6.9	7.0	7.1
East Europe	1.7	1.8	1.8	1.8	1.6	1.7	1.7	1.9	2.0	2.0
Other Europe	0.8	0.7	0.7	0.7	0.7	0.5	0.6	0.4	0.3	0.4
Former USSR	0.7	0.5	0.8	0.7	0.8	1.1	1.7	1.5	1.6	1.5
Oceania	0.2	0.2	0.2	0.1	0.1	0.1	0.1	0.2	0.2	0.2
Germany/Allemagne	23.5	22.9	22.0	22.2	21.9	22.9	21.6	20.5	21.3	20.2
Sweden/Suède	12.3	12.2	12.0	11.5	10.8	10.8	10.4	11.0	11.6	11.5
United Kingdom	7.4	6.9	6.8	7.5	8.0	8.1	7.2	6.2	6.5	6.7
Netherlands/Pays–Bas	5.3	6.0	5.6	5.8	5.7	5.5	6.2	6.3	7.0	6.6
France,Monac	5.3	4.9	4.9	5.3	6.2	5.5	5.0	5.1	5.1	5.2
Norway,SVD,JM	4.2	4.4	4.3	4.6	5.6	5.3	4.9	4.8	4.9	5.1
USA/Etats–Unis d'Amer	5.1	5.5	6.3	5.7	5.6	5.1	4.5	4.8	4.5	4.7
Italy/Italie	4.0	3.9	3.9	4.1	4.2	4.1	3.6	3.7	4.1	4.0
Belgium–Luxembourg	3.4	3.3	3.2	3.3	3.1	3.2	3.5	3.4	3.5	3.3
Japan/Japon	4.4	4.2	3.8	4.1	3.8	4.1	3.3	3.3	2.6	2.2

	1987	1988	1989	1990	1991	1992	1993	1994	1995	1996
Afrique	1.8	2.3	1.8	2.7	1.1	1.8	1.2	1.8	1.7	1.0
Amériques	10.4	8.5	7.7	6.7	6.8	6.7	7.4	7.6	6.1	6.1
Amérique du Nord	9.4	7.5	6.5	5.8	5.2	5.3	5.6	5.7	4.4	4.6
ALAI	0.6	0.6	0.7	0.5	0.8	0.9	0.9	1.1	1.0	0.9
MCAC	0.1	0.1	0.1	0.1	0.1	0.0	0.0	0.1	0.1	0.0
Caraïbes	0.2	0.2	0.3	0.2	0.6	0.2	0.8	0.6	0.4	0.3
Autre Amérique	0.1	0.2	0.1	0.1	0.0	0.3	0.0	0.0	0.2	0.3
Asie l'URSS exclus	9.6	9.1	9.5	8.5	8.8	9.4	9.7	9.9	10.3	10.1
Europe l'URSS exclus	74.2	73.1	73.0	74.6	75.7	74.3	72.7	71.2	71.7	72.6
UE	61.4	60.9	62.6	64.7	64.9	64.1	61.6	60.5	61.2	61.3
AELE	10.5	9.6	8.1	7.9	7.7	7.8	8.5	8.0	7.7	8.0
Europe de l'Est	0.9	1.2	1.4	1.3	2.3	1.8	1.9	2.1	2.2	2.4
Autre de l'Europe	1.4	1.4	0.9	0.8	0.7	0.5	0.4	0.4	0.3	0.6
Ancienne URSS	0.4	0.5	0.8	1.0	0.6	0.9	1.2	1.5	2.1	2.5
Océanie	0.6	0.9	0.7	0.5	0.5	0.5	0.6	0.6	0.6	0.6
Germany/Allemagne	16.3	16.6	16.4	18.5	21.0	22.3	21.5	20.0	20.9	19.8
Sweden/Suède	11.5	11.1	11.7	12.3	10.9	10.0	9.1	9.4	9.0	9.7
United Kingdom	11.2	11.1	11.5	10.2	9.8	9.6	7.9	7.3	7.2	8.2
Norway,SVD,JM	7.5	6.9	5.6	5.6	5.4	5.6	6.5	6.0	5.7	6.1
France,Monac	5.3	5.3	5.6	5.6	5.4	5.2	4.6	4.7	4.8	4.4
USA/Etats–Unis d'Amer	7.0	5.4	5.0	4.6	4.2	4.2	4.6	4.7	3.5	3.6
Netherlands/Pays–Bas	4.2	3.8	3.9	4.5	4.5	4.1	3.8	3.4	4.0	3.8
Italy/Italie	4.7	4.4	4.5	4.7	4.6	4.3	3.6	3.5	3.3	3.3
Japan/Japon	3.7	3.9	4.1	3.2	3.4	3.4	3.5	3.5	3.4	3.1
Finland/Finlande	2.2	2.3	2.6	2.5	2.2	1.9	1.7	2.2	2.4	2.4

4. General Imports C.I.F. by Commodities according to the S.I.T.C. (Rev. 2) in thousand U.S. Dollars
Importations Générales C.A.F. par Produits d'après la C.T.C.I. (Rév. 2) en milliers de Dollars E.U.

SITC CTCI	COMMODITY	1993 WEIGHT POIDS	1993 VALUE VALEUR	1994 WEIGHT POIDS	1994 VALUE VALEUR	1995 WEIGHT POIDS	1995 VALUE VALEUR	1996 WEIGHT POIDS	1996 VALUE VALEUR	PRODUIT
	ALL COMMODITIES		30535740		35436475		43141557		43110375	TOUS PRODUITS
0	FOOD AND LIVE ANIMALS		3479804		3744413		4329832		4392935	ALIMENTS,ANIMAUX VIVANTS
01	MEAT AND PREPARATIONS		292841		327574		431321		436042	VIANDES ET PREPARATIONS
011	MEAT FRESH,CHILLD,FROZEN	W 72475	259999	W 78549	285091	W 99080	375278	W 106131	369755	VIANDES FRAICHES,REF,CONGE
0111	BOVINE MEAT FRESH,FROZEN	W 41855	169568	W 41274	173495	W 47984	227215	W 52341	213061	VIANDES BOVIN FRAI,REF
01111	BOVINE MEAT WITH BONE IN	W 32410	124922	W 27825	109481	W 29499	123110	W 31536	109607	VIANDES BOVIN NON DESOSS
02	DAIRY PRODCTS,BIRDS'EGGS		138916		159046		233546		228645	PRODUITS LAITIERS,OEUFS
03	FISH AND PREPARATIONS		957592		1076553		1225815		1242706	POISSONS ET PREPARATIONS
034	FISH,FRESH,CHILLED,FROZN	W 300780	508616	W 337416	550253	W 327366	620281	W 311099	607905	POISSON FRAIS, REFRIG,CONG
0341	FISH FRSH,CHLLD,EX FILLT	W 202255	280053	W 241007	314804	W 241600	370569	W 229874	364040	POISSON FRAIS,REFRIGERE
0342	FISH FROZEN,EXCL FILLETS	W 59073	102292	W 56883	101518	W 49748	99877	W 44055	94035	POISSONS CONGELES
0344	FISH FILLETS,FROZEN	W 31067	94615	W 32122	103009	W 31144	125179	W 30036	114152	FILETS CONGELES
036	SHELL FISH FRESH,FROZEN	W 61857	219460	W 66651	236262	W 59987	262304	W 71292	290953	CRUSTACES,MOLLUSQUES
037	FISH ETC PREPD,PRSVD NES	W 33439	191623	W 40434	229426	W 41014	278388	W 45270	277830	POIS,CRUST,MOL PREPARES
0372	SHELL FISH PREPRD,PRESVD	W 19102	130038	W 25537	170388	W 24227	209425	W 24433	197510	CRUSTACES,COQUIL PREPARES
04	CEREALS AND PREPARATIONS		334177		302691		374683		342433	CEREALES ET PRODUITS
048	CEREAL ETC PREPARATIONS	W 137338	161653	W 149268	169312	W 167558	217345	W 134915	203306	PREPTNS A BASE CEREALES
05	VEGETABLES AND FRUIT		482525		540736		596787		628011	LEGUMES ET FRUITS
054	VEG ETC FRSH,SMPLY PRSVD	W 237540	160284	W 233312	172898	W 213870	187749	W 227619	194045	LEGUMES FRAIS,CONG,SECS
057	FRUIT,NUTS,FRESH,DRIED	W 231605	186116	W 232295	225729	W 211086	232453	W 245945	264549	FRUITS FRAIS OU SECS
06	SUGAR AND PREPS,HONEY		155794		136818		173025		195616	SUCRES ET PRODUITS
061	SUGAR AND HONEY	W 526488	110578	W 420040	86276	W 453649	104947	W 457555	122793	SUCRES ET MIEL
07	COFFEE,TEA,COCOA,SPICES		267549		344375		407686		359680	CAFE,THE,CACAO,EPICES
071	COFFEE AND SUBSTITUTES	W 57716	97391	W 58922	169032	W 50613	192090	W 57925	170027	CAFE ET SUCCEDANES
0711	COFFEE GREEN,ROASTED,SUB	W 56465	85912	W 57142	152626	W 49528	178962	W 56439	154366	CAFE TORREFIE OU DECAFEINE
07111	COFFEE GREEN,HUSKS,SKINS	W 55567	83003	W 54974	145791	W 47477	168955	W 54692	144885	CAFE NON TORREFIE
073	CHOCOLATE AND PRODUCTS	W 35341	137528	W 33454	139685	W 35075	172318	W 32189	147365	CHOCOLAT
081	*FEEDING STUFF FOR ANIML	W 3290871	688362	W 3070948	670018	W 2924388	668936	W 2831323	743667	NOURRITURE POUR ANIMAUX
0813	OILCAKE AND OTH RESIDUES	W 2456727	444988	W 2388427	465158	W 2228836	421474	W 2098537	465514	TOURTEAUX
08131	— OF SOYA BEANS	W 1352241	278318	W 1518308	331191	W 1581610	324579	W 1355132	336853	TOURTEAUX DE SOJA
0819	FOOD WASTE AND FEED NES	W 605678	170620	W 517483	148412	W 437893	163270	W 453760	166807	DECHETS,ALIMENTS NDA
08199	FODDER NES,INCL SWEETNED	W 102187	95395	W 97167	86020	W 96844	106415	W 129445	107683	PREPARATIONS FOURRAGERES
09	MISC EDIBLE PRODUCTS		154302		174472		195689		196215	PREP ALIMENTAIRES DIVERSES
098	EDIBLE PRODCTS,PREPS NES	W 48372	136876	W 49777	152079	W 69622	166028	W 54361	171112	PREP ALIMENTAIRES NDA
09809	MISC FOOD PREPRTIONS NES	W 32261	97320	W 35701	115387	W 48338	115730	W 31558	120210	PREP ALIMENTAIRES NDA
1	BEVERAGES AND TOBACCO		432563		451792		546397		574142	BOISSONS ET TABACS
11	BEVERAGES		329288		340936		432449		462567	BOISSONS
112	ALCOHOLIC BEVERAGES	W 153501	316528	W 152147	327241	W 168832	413560	W 181464	444778	BOISSONS ALCOOLIQUES
1121	WINE OF FRESH GRAPES ETC	W 123030	229188	W 128452	258377	W 144529	341213	W 154511	368514	VINS DE RAISINS FRAIS
11212	WINE OF FRESH GRAPES	W 117936	220128	W 123422	249168	W 139332	330914	W 149489	359060	VINS DE MOUTS DE RAISINS
12	TOBACCO AND MANUFACTURES		103275		110856		113948		111575	TABACS BRUTS FABRIQUES
2	CRUDE MATERLS,EXCL FUELS		1052845		1344903		1609126		1477952	MAT BRUTES NON COMESTIBLES
24	CORK AND WOOD		425888		634915		685602		553339	LIEGE ET BOIS
248	WOOD SHAPED,SLEEPERS	W 1016978	395287	W 1316943	588085	W 1097042	596776	W 929912	469864	BOIS SIMPLEMENT TRAVAILLES
2482	LUMBER SHAPED CONIFER	W 968411	355001	W 1252465	530993	W 1025983	529202	W 870694	410550	CONIFERES SCIES,RABOTES
24821	LUMBER SAWN ETC CONIFER	W 966701	352587	W 1246801	525479	W 1016601	519248	W 856993	395719	CONIFERES SCIES LONGITUD
27	CRUDE FERTLZR,MINRLS NES		100912		111150		148029		170650	ENGRAIS MINERAUX BRUTS
29	CRUDE ANIMAL,VEG MAT NES		256413		263819		338684		327500	MATIERES BRUTES ANIM,VEGET
292	CRUDE VEG MATERIALS NES	W 59516	183285	W 65173	185982	W 65213	240184	W 64113	220889	MAT BRUTES VEGETALES NDA
3	MINERAL FUELS ETC		1548378		1484980		1454195		1666871	COMBUSTIBLES MINERAUX LUB
33	PETROLEUM AND PRODUCTS		1437777		1420896		1350584		1552437	PETROLE ET DERIVES
333	CRUDE PETROLEUM	W 5006197	634916	W 4986799	601971	W 5236573	689163	W 5174129	802857	HUILES BRUTES DE PETROLE
334	PETROLEUM PRODUCTS,REFIN	W 4711448	751701	W 5110345	769370	W 3645454	610534	W 3530037	684861	PRODUITS RAFFINES
4	ANIMAL,VEGETABLE OIL,FAT		152244		171064		208769		232358	HUILES,GRAISSES ANIM,VEG
42	FIXED VEGETABLE OIL,FAT		71137		98777		128026		148511	HUILES VEGETALES FIXES
5	CHEMCLS,RELATED PROD NES		3248916		3686967		4636480		4291499	PRODUITS CHIMIQUES
51	ORGANIC CHEMICALS		320616		379811		480946		461726	PROD CHIMIQ ORGANIQUES
514	NITROGEN–FNCTN COMPOUNDS	W 24998	83190	W 30000	99149	W 31697	129631	W 33604	123823	COMPOSES FONCT AZOTEES
52	INORGANIC CHEMICALS		237735		242482		321410		265359	PROD CHIM INORGANIQUES
522	INORG ELEMNTS,OXIDES,ETC	W 609961	122219	W 545968	128595	W 711410	187071	W 537846	140006	ELEMENTS INORGANIQUES
523	OTHR INORG CHEMICALS ETC	W 344222	104615	W 335367	106757	W 354569	128172	W 352843	119674	AUT PRODUITS CHIMIQUES INORG
53	DYES,TANNING,COLOUR PROD		304686		335812		425306		398162	PROD TEINTURE,COLORANTS
531	SYNT DYE,NAT INDGO,LAKES	W 6084	121970	W 6851	132147	W 7360	171413	W 8030	156770	MAT COLOR ORGAN,LAQUES
5311	SYNTHIC ORGNIC DYESTUFFS	W 4935	108743	W 6411	129271	W 6642	166436	W 7371	152156	MAT COLOR ORGAN SYNTHET
533	PIGMENTS,PAINTS,ETC	W 68924	176838	W 74393	195243	W 71096	238742	W 76649	225379	PIGMENTS,PEINTURES,VERNIS
541	*MEDICINAL,PHARM PRODUCT	MK 13003	605576	MK 17154	726884	MK 15981	897604	MK 19498	846805	PROD MEDICINAUX PHARMACEUT
5411	PROVITAMINS AND VITAMINS	K 4435309	95953	K 5851705	108372	K 6289336	134347	K 7137294	91556	PROVITAMINES,VITAMINES
5417	MEDICAMENTS	K 5911002	367929	K 8397754	475279	K 7026452	606521	MK 9455	583880	MEDICAMENTS
54179	— CONTNG OTH SUBSTANCES	K 4828088	278609	K 6570188	321209	K 4943992	347508	K 7150645	380422	MED CONT AUT SUBSTANCES
55	PERFUME,CLEANING ETC PRD		342103		380511		409187		438445	PROD POUR PARFUM,TOILETTE
553	PERFUMERY,COSMETICS,ETC	W 21985	193745	W 24680	220177	W 24404	228794	W 27291	268330	PRODUITS DE PARFUMERIE
554	SOAP,CLEANSING ETC PREPS	W 76991	117819	W 80975	124577	W 81580	136657	W 84018	130057	SAVONS,PRODUITS DETERSIFS
5542	WASHING PREPARATIONS ETC	W 68182	97167	W 70106	103082	W 69631	109984	W 73180	106592	PROD ORG TENSIO–ACT NDA
562	*FERTILIZERS,MANUFACTURE	W 1095244	149023	W 1278782	180395	W 1134785	202156	W 962460	177606	ENGRAIS MANUFACTURES
58	PLASTIC MATERIALS ETC		880357		1001785		1357967		1209388	MAT PLAST ARTIFICIELLES
582	PROD OF CONDENSATION ETC	W 86695	205161	W 96236	229175	W 105035	307441	W 110725	293587	PROD CONDENS,POLYCOND
5823	ALKYDS,OTHER POLYESTERS	W 37561	90497	W 39373	101981	W 41724	141517	W 42738	130827	ALKYDES ET AUT POLYESTERS
583	POLYMERIZATION ETC PRODS	W 541478	650249	W 580244	743547	W 594414	1014666	W 619995	883022	PROD POLYMERISATION
5831	POLYETHYLENE	W 195857	168206	W 207462	188528	W 208805	267396	W 214584	224538	POLYETHYLENE
58311	— IN PRIMARY FORMS	W 172007	135499	W 173113	142908	W 178224	213865	W 176565	171794	POLYETHYLENE PRIMAIRES
5832	POLYPROPYLENE	W 126763	107053	W 118057	109829	W 133040	178511	W 136464	150859	POLYPROPYLENE
5834	POLYVINYL CHLORIDE	W 75357	101127	W 80161	119842	W 66839	140122	W 80668	119756	CHLORURE DE POLYVINYLE
5839	OTH POLYMRZTION ETC PROD	W 57516	128365	W 72278	159314	W 80310	212151	W 77861	192608	AUT PROD POLYMER COPOLYM
59	CHEMICAL MATERIALS NES		401458		431638		532237		482927	MAT PROD CHIMIQUES NDA
591	PESTICIDES,DISINFECTANTS	W 10059	113428	W 8571	111338	W 12691	148665	W 12336	121889	DESINF,INSECT,FONG,HERB
598	MISCEL CHEM PRODUCTS NES	W 117667	204663	W 137574	232769	W 130555	273897	W 134266	252751	PROD DIV INDUST CHIM NDA
5989	CHEM PRODUCTS,PREPS NES	W 67385	138549	W 83038	159172	W 82602	195576	W 99404	190292	PROD PREP CHIMIQUES NDA
59899	OTH CHEM PRODS,PREPS,NES	W 49371	106629	W 59780	121099	W 62791	153157	W 76790	148341	AUT PRODUITS CHIMIQUES NDA
6	BASIC MANUFACTURES		5190835		6159386		7966666		7167287	ART MANUFACTURES
62	RUBBER MANUFACTURES NES		255135		293310		379766		358597	CAOUTCHOUC MANUFACTURE
625	RUBBER TYRES, TUBES ETC	W 39688	150812	W 46248	174302	W 52716	237078	W 51355	225464	PNEUS CAOUTCHOUC VULCANISE
63	WOOD,CORK MANUFACTRS NES		267863		332328		403526		363896	OUVRAGES LIEGE ET BOIS
634	VENEERS,PLYWOOD,ETC	W 291861	171143	W 332833	206817	W 335408	244813	W 309394	203425	PLACAGES,CONTRE–PLAQUES
635	WOOD MANUFACTURES NES	W 70473	91486	W 96898	120088	W 108585	153547	W 109112	155382	ART MANUF EN BOIS NDA
64	PAPER,PAPERBOARD AND MFR		1111691		1251878		1605614		1506296	PAPIERS,CARTONS & OUVRAGES
641	PAPER AND PAPERBOARD	W 1016996	773504	W 1175663	894843	W 1133034	1156851	W 1129742	1059215	PAPIERS ET CARTONS
6411	NEWSPRINT	W 223633	107347	W 267545	132264	W 262814	181490	W 256117	204370	PAPIER JOURNAL
6412	PRINTG,WRITING PAPER NES	W 146887	135601	W 168579	165917	W 223709	287525	W 190841	218806	PAPIERS POUR L'IMPRESSION
64122	— COATED,IMPREGNATD ETC	W 128901	116898	W 146676	140657	W 195948	241253	W 164259	183172	PAPIERS IMPRESSION COUCHES
6413	KRAFT PAPER,PAPERBOARD	W 170263	105343	W 187342	119146	W 158388	136277	W 175953	129524	PAPIER ET CARTON KRAFT
6415	PAPER,PAPERBRD,BULK,NES	W 266672	174526	W 327257	216349	W 286503	266678	W 297199	238681	PAPIERS,CARTONS ROULEAUX

4. General Imports C.I.F. by Commodities according to the S.I.T.C. (Rev. 2) in thousand U.S. Dollars
Importations Générales C.A.F. par Produits d'après la C.T.C.I. (Rév. 2) en milliers de Dollars E.U.

SITC CTCI	COMMODITY	1993 WEIGHT POIDS	1993 VALUE VALEUR	1994 WEIGHT POIDS	1994 VALUE VALEUR	1995 WEIGHT POIDS	1995 VALUE VALEUR	1996 WEIGHT POIDS	1996 VALUE VALEUR	PRODUIT
64159	OTHER PAPER ETC,BULK,NES	W 198535	139741	W 256804	180476	W 219070	216841	W 244598	205448	AUT PAPIER ROULEAUX FEUILLES
6418	COATED ETC PAPER NES BLK	W 126797	195252	W 129118	200093	W 115026	218225	W 128891	210448	PAP,CARTONS COUCHES,ENDUITS
64189	COATED PAPER ETC NES	W 79070	118394	W 78728	117228	W 79050	148892	W 86861	138484	PAPIERS,CARTONS COUCHES
642	PAPER,ETC,PRECUT,ARTS OF	W 174347	338187	W 176603	357035	W 188232	448763	W 207135	447081	PAP,CARTONS DECOUPES
6421	PAPER ETC CONTAINERS	W 54950	89080	W 52637	92437	W 67135	137347	W 73829	129929	BOITES,SACS EMBALLAGES
6428	PAPER ETC ARTICLES NES	W 64011	143096	W 64659	152374	W 64433	182173	W 70504	184598	OUVRAGES EN PATE A PAPIER
65	TEXTILE YARN,FABRICS,ETC		780889		861633		1061015		1004780	FILS,TISSUS,ARTICLES TEXTILE
651	TEXTILE YARN	W 38832	195081	W 49078	235129	W 51494	282492	W 54692	271467	FILS TEXTILES
6514	SYN FIB YRN,BULK,MONOFIL	W 17331	79499	W 24283	102344	W 26614	129775	W 30607	128620	FILS CONT 85% FIB TEXT SYNTH
653	WOVN MAN-MADE FIB FABRIC	W 12165	143614	W 10854	131479	W 12058	164922	W 11445	145919	TISSUS FIBRES SYNTH,ARTIF
657	SPECIAL TXTL FABRC,PRODS	W 20628	105886	W 21623	118157	W 22650	155333	W 26202	145994	TISSUS SPECIAUX
658	TEXTILE ARTICLES NES	W 14737	104255	W 15260	113144	W 17530	145619	W 16862	137548	ART FACONNES MAT TEXTILES
66	NONMETAL MINERAL MFS NES		380912		446033		568792		552545	ART MIN NON METALLIQUES
664	GLASS	W 130979	109349	W 158807	129260	W 191587	174601	W 176840	163119	VERRE
67	IRON AND STEEL		1063401		1371320		1869474		1425515	FER ET ACIER
672	IRON,STEEL PRIMARY FORMS	W 217405	78425	W 292990	112088	W 394185	186747	W 284383	135357	LINGOTS FER,ACIER
6727	IRN,STL COIL FR REROLLNG	W 211680	70632	W 272414	103586	W 281143	147632	W 262002	127401	EBAUCHES POUR TOLES FER
673	IRON,STEEL SHAPES ETC	W 296395	165853	W 400033	226788	W 398634	296347	W 351895	225410	BARRES,PROFIL FER,ACIER
6732	IRON,STEEL BARS ETC	W 124350	80722	W 175602	112738	W 165366	151536	W 144997	116115	BARRES FER,ACIER
674	IRN,STL UNIV,PLATE,SHEET	W 748796	483903	W 956695	632567	W 1001805	847608	W 792619	618489	LARGES PLATS,TOLES
6744	IRN,STL HVY PLATE,ROLLED	W 199206	107128	W 290805	151250	W 271335	194070	W 197490	121038	TOLES LAMINEES PLUS 4.75 MM
67441	— OF IRON OR SIMPLE STL	W 189268	89100	W 279843	129672	W 259586	158702	W 186613	94841	TOLES NON ACIER FIN CARB
6746	IRN,STL THIN PLATE,ROLLD	W 216733	138732	W 268714	192375	W 270889	244983	W 206313	172272	TOLES LAM MOINS 3MM
67461	— OF IRON OR SIMPLE STL	W 184579	79900	W 217950	102265	W 225629	134201	W 159969	85750	TOL NON AC FIN MOINS 3 MM
6749	OTH IRN,STL PLATES,SHEET	W 184179	120637	W 221869	151229	W 261942	223109	W 212391	171760	AUTRES TOLES FER,ACIER
67491	— OF IRON OR SIMPLE STL	W 181225	112794	W 218433	124483	W 256629	206627	W 209390	164016	AUT TOLES AUTRES ACIER FIN
678	IRON,STL TUBES,PIPES,ETC	W 238081	254682	W 267515	289616	W 305848	401524	W 255692	339074	TUBES,TUYAUX EN FONTE,FER
6783	IRON,STL TUBES,PIPES NES	W 190496	149507	W 218241	166801	W 255681	249508	W 206645	191976	AUT TUBES,TUYAUX FER,ACIER
68	NON-FERROUS METALS		393151		511105		654596		574549	METAUX NON FERREUX
682	COPPER EXC CEMENT COPPER	W 42499	125087	W 51005	159134	W 54419	209423	W 51188	181872	CUIVRE
6822	COPPER,ALLOYS WORKED	W 40737	121580	W 49120	155067	W 52527	204340	W 49130	175284	CUIVRE,ALLIAGES OUVRES
684	ALUMINIUM	W 74957	215515	W 100000	288129	W 101722	368656	W 98635	320831	ALUMINIUM
6842	ALUMINIUM,ALLOYS WORKED	W 53753	184612	W 70453	240914	W 66326	292101	W 65041	258849	ALUMINIUM,ALLIAGES OUVRE
69	METAL MANUFACTURES NES		847932		990016		1324699		1282866	ART MANUFACT EN METAL NDA
691	STRUCTURES AND PARTS NES	W 64479	132638	W 69683	142890	W 92267	248390	W 107346	266498	CONSTRUCT FER,ACIER,ALU
6911	STRUCTURES,PARTS IRN,STL	W 62321	121183	W 66791	126209	W 89871	230261	W 104029	245160	CONSTRUCT FER,ACIER,FONTE
692	METAL TANKS,BOXES,ETC	W 33945	100350	W 36804	115145	W 40478	162470	W 41771	147379	RECIPIENTS METALLIQUES
6924	MTL TRANSPORT BOXES ETC	W 32442	95603	W 34323	107832	W 38090	150013	W 36058	133930	FUTS,TAMBOURS,BIDONS
694	STL,COPPR NAILS,NUTS,ETC	W 23496	74492	W 29427	91340	W 37290	131723	W 46779	112129	CLOUS,VIS,ECROUS
695	TOOLS	W 7180	122578	W 8668	144836	W 9780	190990	W 10636	196072	OUTILS A MAIN
699	BASE METAL MFRS NES	W 61738	281965	W 70517	333050	W 72361	387859	W 73346	365784	ART MANUFACTURES MET NDA
6991	LOCKSMITHS WARES,ETC	W 17890	114310	W 22778	134940	W 22654	150833	W 22037	140724	ARTICLES DE SERRURERIE
69913	BASE MTL DOOR,ETC FITTNG	W 15264	92693	W 19677	111510	W 19509	123295	W 18619	112911	GARNITURES POUR MEUBLES
7	MACHINES,TRANSPORT EQUIP		8931089		11020512		13806272		13979306	MACHINES MATERIEL TRANSPORT
71	POWER GENERATING EQUIPMT		464951		511985		711597		669613	MACHINES GENERATRICES
713	INTRNL COMBUS PSTN ENGIN	W 19421	242526	W 16998	234492	W 22505	285861	W 22465	265371	MOTEURS EXPL COMB INT, PIECE
7133	MARINE PISTON ENGINES	W 7900	110081	W 7304	82017	W 10150	100970	W 9117	81708	MOTEURS EXPL POUR BATEAUX
71332	—— OTHER THAN OUTBOARD	W 7712	105820	W 7156	77985	W 9896	93245	W 8803	73689	MOT BATEAUX AUT HORSBORD
7139	PISTON ENGINE PARTS NES	W 7902	90789	W 5677	102569	W 8005	133173	W 9808	144041	PIECES POUR 713.2,3,8
716	ROTATING ELECTRIC PLANT	W 16650	134896	W 19108	182094	W 26318	260629	W 26029	248951	APP ELECTR ROTATIFS,PIECES
7162	AC MTRS,GENRTRS,GEN SETS	W 12697	95711	W 14716	126221	W 18021	174529	W 17156	157218	MOTEURS ELECTRIQUES
72	MACHS FOR SPCL INDUSTRYS		750933		888043		1226237		1272162	MAC SPECIALES POUR INDUST
721	AGRIC MACHY,EXC TRACTORS	W 16942	108876	W 21818	148693	W 31768	234753	W 33847	247932	MACHINES AGRICOLES
7212	HARVESTING ETC MACHINES	W 8615	57760	W 10324	77186	W 15330	125416	W 16949	131232	ENGINS POUR LA RECOLTE
722	TRACTORS NON-ROAD	W 8229	49652	W 14196	93831	W 18672	147374	W 22735	178042	TRACTEURS
7224	WHEELED TRACTORS NES	W 8195	49532	W 14196	93831	W 18559	146645	W 22735	178042	TRACTEURS A ROUES
723	CIVIL ENGNEERG EQUIP ETC	W 15788	130588	W 16648	128145	W 19298	186161	W 25098	216316	APPAREILS DE GENIE CIVIL
7234	CONST,MINING MACHNRY NES	W 10156	51120	W 13164	76136	W 15890	120557	W 21453	142572	MACH POUR LA CONST, MINES
726	PRINTG,BKBINDG MACHY,PTS	W 3561	107690	W 3477	118014	W 4497	145436	W 4303	150163	MACHINES POUR IMPRIMERIE
728	OTH MACHY FOR SPCL INDUS	W 14248	213238	W 16332	248352	W 18491	324132	W 17092	306820	AUT MACH IND PARTICULIERES
7284	MACHY FOR SPCL INDUS NES	W 7620	150097	W 7912	161764	W 9283	209117	W 8997	200931	MACH SPEC IND PARTICUL.
73	METALWORKING MACHINERY		127910		163444		246119		209229	MACH TRAVAIL DES METAUX
736	METALWORKING MACH-TOOLS	W 6980	99414	W 7843	128689	W 10314	197190	W 9520	172876	MACH-OUTILS TRAVAIL METAUX
74	GENRL INDUSTRL MACHY NES		1233644		1399910		1859437		1782889	MACH APP INDUSTRIE
741	HEATING,COOLING EQUIPMNT	W 14293	178292	W 14900	191533	W 16836	249344	W 18667	252726	MACH CHAUFFAGE,PIECES
742	PUMPS FOR LIQUIDS ETC	W 13593	128944	W 7337	147468	W 17574	208086	W 35642	204200	POMPES MOTO-POMPES
743	PUMPS NES,CENTRFUGES ETC	W 25058	229685	W 32158	276870	W 31889	315126	W 60508	302033	POMPES COMPRES,VENT ETC
7431	PUMPS FOR GASES ETC	W 15880	98928	W 18866	104211	W 19048	123028	W 47495	112558	POMPES AIR A VIDE,COMPRES
744	MECHANICAL HANDLING EQU	W 22537	173101	W 26257	206596	W 28752	250334	W 35957	271696	EQUIP MANUTENTION PIECES
745	NONELEC MACHY,TOOLS NES	W 7314	172105	W 7459	161691	W 9333	237323	W 9738	222100	AUT MACH NON ELEC,PIECES
7452	OTH NONELEC MCHS,PTS NES	W 6542	150634	W 6558	132982	W 8365	202514	W 8665	194174	AUT MACH NON ELEC,PIECES
749	NONELEC MACH PTS,ACC NES	W 34911	351518	W 34275	415752	W 47601	599224	W 41377	530134	PIECES MACH NON ELEC NDA
7492	COCKS,VALVES ETC NES	W 19206	154348	W 16868	180335	W 20592	248767	W 17031	234435	ART ROB,SIM POUR TUYAUX
7493	SHAFT,CRANK,PULLEY ETC	W 10037	82908	W 11941	109738	W 20721	204461	W 17007	159789	ARBRES TRANS,VILEBREQUINS
75	OFFICE MACHNES,ADP EQUIP		1612737		1863529		2319618		2319984	MACH BUREAU TRAIT AUTOM
751	OFFICE MACHINES	W 3556	114932	W 3236	112911	W 3036	121306	W 3202	118976	MACH,APPAREILS DE BUREAU
7518	OFFICE MACHINES NES	W 2996	93786	W 2706	93284	W 2550	97649	W 2756	98593	MACH,APP DE BUREAU NDA
752	AUTOMTIC DATA PROC EQUIP	W 13035	942212	W 15103	1097875	W 17040	1291184	W 20906	1321908	MACH TRAIT INFORMATION
7522	DIGITAL COMPUTERS	W 493	59953	W 626	85025	W 886	137574	W 693	132269	MACH DIGITALES COMPLETES
7523	DIGITL CENTRL PROCESSORS	W 4936	450897	W 4393	465469	W 4645	512360	W 4143	446039	UNITES CENTRALES
7524	DIGITL CENTRL STOR UNITS	W 844	106844	W 1038	123298	W 991	144479	W 4218	226566	UNITES MEMOIRE CENTRALES
7525	ADP PERIPHERAL UNITS	W 5982	239453	W 7855	333569	W 8503	332882	W 9859	342659	UNITES PERIPHERIQUES
7528	OFF-LINE DATA PROC EQUIP	W 716	74883	W 1132	85955	W 1885	139555	W 1635	132080	MACH AUXIL TRAIT INFORM
759	OFFICE,ADP MCH PTS,ACCES	W 6698	555593	W 7545	652743	W 10211	907129	W 11196	879100	PIECES DU 751 ET 752
7591	OFFICE MACHINE PARTS NES	W 1190	60466	W 1564	83055	W 2592	148032	W 2002	95216	PIECES DU 7511,7518
75919	COPY MACH PRTS,ACCES NES	W 1052	52256	W 1454	74593	W 2420	134946	W 1637	63618	PIECES DU 751.82
7599	ACCTG,ETC,ADP MCH PTS,AC	W 5508	495127	W 5981	569688	W 7620	759097	W 9194	783885	PIECES DU 751 ET 752
76	TELECOMM,SOUND EQUIPMENT		940715		1190919		1467541		1690328	EQUIPMENT DE TELECOM
761	TELEVISION RECEIVERS	W 10615	145604	W 11376	158724	W 11390	176219	W 14944	218874	RECEPTEURS DE TELEVISION
7611	COLOUR TV RECEIVERS	W 10579	144549	W 11345	157890	W 11346	174650	W 14906	217453	RECEPTEURS COULEUR
762	RADIO BROADCAST RECEIVRS	W 4798	96976	W 6039	128211	W 6191	144428	W 6304	135392	RECEPTEURS RADIODIFFUSION
763	SOUND RECORDRS,PHONOGRPH	W 3744	148107	W 4246	177157	W 4510	193447	W 4470	210815	PHONO,APP ENREGISTREMENT
7638	OTHR SOUND APPARATUS ETC	W 3591	145413	W 4146	175282	W 4439	192029	W 4375	209049	AUT APP D'ENREGIS,REPROD
76381	TV IMAGE,SND RECRDRS ETC	W 1764	83730	W 2089	106890	W 2089	111224	W 2321	136679	APP ENREG,REPRO IMAG,SON
764	TELECOM EQPT,PTS,ACC NES	W 13614	550028	W 15001	726827	W 18242	953448	W 23325	1125248	EQUIP TELECOM,PIECES
7641	LINE TELEPHONE,ETC EQUIP	W 1081	90292	W 1553	171793	W 1416	111394	W 1881	177137	APP TELEPHON PAR FIL
7642	MICROPH,LOUDSPKR,AMPLIFR	W 6535	83669	W 7620	96934	W 9731	112968	W 12972	142655	MICRO,HAUT-PARLEUR,AMPLI
7643	TV,RADIO TRANSMITTRS ETC	W 250	65263	W 379	108355	W 859	307566	W 1026	331553	APP EMET TELE RADIO
7649	PTS NES OF EQUIPMT OF 76	W 5552	264134	W 5180	293256	W 5921	341437	W 7297	440662	PIECES DE LA DIV 76
76491	PTS NES OF APPAR OF 7641	W 663	97270	W 855	126209	W 899	152339	W 1283	205079	PIECES POUR 764.1
76493	TELECOMM EQUIPMT PTS NES	W 3759	138131	W 2791	127520	W 3249	136620	W 3993	181872	PIECES 761,762,764.3,8

4. General Imports C.I.F. by Commodities according to the S.I.T.C. (Rev. 2) in thousand U.S. Dollars
Importations Générales C.A.F. par Produits d'après la C.T.C.I. (Rév. 2) en milliers de Dollars E.U.

SITC CTCI	COMMODITY	1993		1994		1995		1996		PRODUIT
		WEIGHT POIDS	VALUE VALEUR	WEIGHT POIDS	VALUE VALEUR	WEIGHT POIDS	VALUE VALEUR	WEIGHT POIDS	VALUE VALEUR	
77	ELECTRIC MACHNRY NES ETC		1368904		1605058		2039869		1992113	MACH APP ELECT NDA
771	ELECTRIC POWER MACHY NES	W 6368	103241	W 8279	124057	W 11822	186774	W 9380	132982	MACH PROD,TRANS ELECTR
772	SWITCHGEAR ETC,PARTS NES	W 7704	255675	W 8195	293580	W 10118	385684	W 12733	363236	APP COUPURE,SECT ETC
7721	SWITCHGEAR ETC	W 7388	226744	W 7758	258428	W 9682	336246	W 12274	313812	APP COUPURE,SECTIONMNT
773	ELECTR DISTRIBUTNG EQUIP	W 21854	114770	W 21066	120591	W 27584	167115	W 38426	177823	EQUIPMT DISTRIBUTION ELECT
7731	INSULATED WIRE,CABLE ETC	W 20856	101272	W 19993	107061	W 26274	150392	W 37052	160002	FILS,CABLES ISOLES ELECT
775	HOUSEHOLD TYPE EQUIP NES	W 37686	304869	W 46395	372631	W 49093	434523	W 49353	422422	MACH,APP USAGE DOMESTQUE
7758	ELECTRO–THERMIC APPL NES	W 11542	109072	W 13260	133068	W 13804	149847	W 14947	157589	APP ELECTROTHERMIQ NDA
776	TRANSISTORS,VALVES,ETC	W 2788	201427	W 2842	252044	W 2371	318534	W 3079	323103	LAMPES,TUBES,VALVES
7764	ELECTRONIC MICROCIRCUITS	W 196	129134	W 269	175008	W 320	228005	W 297	212822	MICROSTRUCTURES ELECTRON
778	ELECTRICAL MACHINERY NES	W 28173	333740	W 28938	377373	W 31617	471195	W 36389	500329	AUTRES MACH ELECT NDA
7788	OTH ELEC MACHY,EQUIP NES	W 5002	130704	W 5341	144664	W 5172	179861	W 5823	168282	AUT MACH APP ELEC NDA
78	ROAD VEHICLES		1792277		2626566		3284081		3308063	VEHICULES ROUTIERS
781	PASS MOTOR VEH EXC BUSES	W 108376	856370	W 180740	1469714	W 171656	1666175	W 177022	1718219	AUTO TRANSPORT PERSONNES
782	LORRIES,SPCL MTR VEH NES	W 44452	363684	W 56498	483316	W 74026	751360	W 67000	681254	VEHICULES SPECIAUX,MARCH
7821	LORRIES,TRUCKS	W 43824	357663	W 55887	478197	W 73348	745037	W 66387	675561	VEHICULES TRANSP MARCHAND
784	MOTOR VEH PRTS,ACCES NES	W 41762	314302	W 46681	375653	W 54396	449532	W 57907	456583	PIECES 722,781,782,783
7849	OTHER MOTOR VEHCL PARTS	W 40479	302046	W 45055	357958	W 52821	426550	W 56206	434761	PIECES 722,781,782,783
785	CYCLES,ETC MOTRZD OR NOT	W 8448	104571	W 10401	119645	W 13222	155216	W 13688	163615	MOTOCYCLES SCOOTERS
786	TRAILERS,NONMOTR VEH,NES	W 23844	111235	W 29012	125024	W 45328	204971	W 56001	245926	REMORQUES,CADRES,CONTAIN
7861	TRAILERS,TRANSP CONTAINR	W 15926	71441	W 17898	68521	W 31224	127459	W 38708	165750	REMORQUES TOUS VEHICULES
79	OTHR TRANSPORT EQUIPMENT		639019		771058		651771		734925	AUTRE MATERIEL TRANSPORT
792	AIRCRAFT ETC	W 628	151419	W 605	179968	W 1342	382243	W 819	405663	APP NAVIGATION AERIENNE
7924	AIRCRFT NES OVER 15000KG	W 241	72211	W 212	96186	W 894	282160	W 449	289018	AERODYNES PLUS 15000 KG
793	SHIPS AND BOATS ETC	W 185202	444457	W 239141	558942	W 65126	226952	W 127282	303716	NAVIRES BATEAUX,ETC
7932	SHIPS AND BOATS NES	W 169247	287193	W 237592	548357	W 60530	201701	W 122099	254782	NAVIRES ET BATEAUX
79322	TANKERS OF ALL KINDS	W 30570	139266	W 65601	221408			W 63118	82157	BATEAUX–CITERNES
79323	OTHER CARGO VESSELS	W 137308	134459	W 170523	312467	W 59504	189552	W 57651	152304	AUT BATEAUX TRANS MARCH
7938	TUGS,SPECIAL VESSELS ETC	W 10544	117052	W 1451	8566	W 143	1860	W 1380	7770	REMORQUEURS,BATEAUX SPEC
79382	SPECL PURPOSE VESSLS ETC	W 10028	114697	W 1177	7146	W 5	116	W 174	1168	BAT–PHARES,–POMPES,DRAGUES
8	MISC MANUFACTURED GOODS		4232665		4741646		5607242		5736722	ART MANUFACTURES DIVERS
812	*PLUMBG,HEATNG,LGHTNG EQ	W 15076	116820	W 17498	140947	W 18140	164322	W 22341	179215	APPAR SANITAIRES CHAUFFAGE
821	*FURNITURE,PARTS THEREOF	W 75517	293911	W 93743	359275	W 105556	442749	W 112008	472586	MEUBLES ET PIECES
8211	CHAIRS,SEATS AND PARTS	W 20382	103132	W 23131	121183	W 27046	155944	W 27543	160001	SIEGES ET PIECES
82111	CHAIRS AND OTHER SEATS	W 18434	88156	W 20605	104974	W 24420	136941	W 24243	136887	SIEGES
8219	FURNITURE AND PARTS NES	W 47003	130994	W 60300	164305	W 69133	205445	W 73874	224798	AUTRES MEUBLES ET PIECES
84	CLOTHING AND ACCESSORIES		1311652		1483490		1808724		1833901	VETEMENTS
842	MENS OUTERWEAR NOT KNIT	W 9167	198503	W 11757	248623	W 12622	310128	W 12372	310282	VET DESSUS POUR HOMMES
8423	— TROUSERS,BREECHES ETC	W 4832	88260	W 6109	110441	W 6321	136934	W 6558	149739	PANTALONS HOMMES MAT TEX
843	WOMENS OUTERWEAR NONKNIT	W 14204	332823	W 17926	406165	W 17859	486706	W 18090	481497	VET DESSUS FEMMES MAT TEX
8439	— OTHER OUTER GARMENTS	W 9336	173641	W 12106	225586	W 11055	246201	W 11030	241963	AUT VET DES FEM MAT TEXT
845	OUTERWEAR KNIT NONELASTC	W 17491	354549	W 19574	367209	W 21236	432625	W 22547	461063	VET DESSOUS,ACCES BONNET
8451	— JERSEYS,PULLOVERS ETC	W 7900	170468	W 8859	177190	W 10075	214492	W 10915	231230	CHANDAILS,PULL–OVERS ETC
8459	— OTHER,CLTHG ACCESRYS	W 8635	158751	W 9622	163539	W 9666	181151	W 10186	195225	AUT VET DESSUS DE BONNE
846	UNDER GARMENTS KNITTED	W 13814	220999	W 13077	230590	W 14532	288756	W 15433	307775	SOUS VETS DE BONNETERIE
8462	— OF COTTON NON ELASTIC	W 11806	158460	W 11091	164638	W 12414	212418	W 13095	220575	SOUS–VET BONNET COTON
84629	—— OTHER	W 11806	158460	W 11091	164638	W 12414	212418	W 13095	220575	AUT SOUS–VET BONNET COTON
851	*FOOTWEAR	W 14783	286069	W 18086	325377	W 18081	366732	W 17671	365706	CHAUSSURES
85102	FOOTWEAR LEATHER	W 11101	254486	W 13754	289901	W 13647	322079	W 13406	319101	CHAUS SEMELLES EN CUIR
87	PRECISION INSTRUMNTS NES		442925		538232		595969		569595	INSTRUM,APPAR SCIENT NDA
872	MEDICAL INSTRUMENTS NES	W 2937	127711	W 3811	146946	W 3390	153365	W 3347	157047	INSTR,APP MEDIC–CHIR NDA
87202	OTH MEDICAL INSTRUMENTS	W 2427	112523	W 3183	130851	W 2778	134123	W 2628	138505	INSTRUM,APP MEDECINE
874	MEASURNG,CONTROLNG INSTR	W 3054	257212	W 3485	324367	W 3885	364583	W 3677	326522	INSTRUMENTS DE MESURE
88	PHOTO EQU,OPTICL GDS ETC		271780		271135		321884		326347	APP,FOURN PHOTO,OP,MONTR
882	PHOTO,CINEMA SUPPLIES	W 11825	136117	W 8044	135391	W 8405	148812	W 8853	136330	PRODUITS PHOTO,CINEMA
8822	PHOTO FILM EXC DEV CINMA	W 5080	102073	W 4568	95355	W 4708	112397	W 5509	109607	PLAQUES,PELLICULES,FILMS
89	MISC MANUFCTRD GOODS NES		1452740		1557581		1826791		1870291	ART MANUFACTURES DIVERS
892	PRINTED MATTER	W 53027	228795	W 48239	233374	W 65063	271848	W 80229	298816	IMPRIMES
8928	PRINTED MATTER NES	W 31309	99385	W 28969	112495	W 41937	134767	W 58454	153827	IMPRIMES NDA
893	ARTICLES OF PLASTIC NES		459441		501532		630087		607058	OUVRAGES EN MAT DIVIS 58
8931	PLSTC PACKG CONTNRS,LIDS	W 39176	122401	W 46579	132057	W 52048	183177	W 71629	172008	ART TRANSP EMBALLAGE ETC
8939	MISC PLASTIC ARTICLES	W 61979	326924	W 69176	359869	W 76055	429713	W 102924	420559	ART DIVERS EN MAT DIV 58
89399	OTHR PLASTC ARTICLES NES	W 54720	300567	W 59149	325880	W 65454	389129	W 90622	381916	AUT OUV MAT DIV 58
894	TOYS,SPORTING GOODS,ETC	W 26666	259617	W 26752	249292	W 27941	285712	W 31579	315896	VOITURES ENFANTS,JOUETS
8942	TOYS,INDOOR GAMES ETC	W 20082	194058	W 20726	179574	W 21490	206426	W 23735	226365	JOUETS,JEUX ETC
89423	TOYS NES	W 13160	128667	W 11898	112351	W 12084	125883	W 13318	138669	JOUETS,MODELES REDUITS
898	MUSICAL INSTRUMENTS,PTS	W 10597	264926	W 12404	295541	W 12735	324251	W 15272	312310	INSTRUMENTS DE MUSIQUE
8983	SOUND RECRDNG TAPE,DISCS	W 9994	248551	W 11744	278218	W 11851	298036	W 14194	283721	SUPPORTS SON POUR 763
89832	RECORDED DISCS,TAPES ETC	W 4095	165849	W 4579	194293	W 4553	207368	W 5381	207865	DISQUES,PHONO,BANDES
899	OTHER MANUFACTURED GOODS		146873		164285		198801		218276	AUT ART MANUF DIVERS NDA
9	GOODS NOT CLASSD BY KIND		2266400		2630812		2976578		3591303	ART TRANSACT NON CLASSES
931	*SPECIAL TRANSACTIONS		2220110		2596257		2951403		3566559	TRANS.SPECIALES

5. General Exports F.O.B. by Commodities according to the S.I.T.C. (Rev. 2) in thousand U.S. Dollars
Exportations Générales F.O.B. par Produits d'après la C.T.C.I. (Rév. 2) en milliers de Dollars E.U.

SITC CTCI	COMMODITY	1993 WEIGHT POIDS	1993 VALUE VALEUR	1994 WEIGHT POIDS	1994 VALUE VALEUR	1995 WEIGHT POIDS	1995 VALUE VALEUR	1996 WEIGHT POIDS	1996 VALUE VALEUR	PRODUIT
	ALL COMMODITIES		37171027		41602403		48789163		48873242	TOUS PRODUITS
0	FOOD AND LIVE ANIMALS		8982489		9812241		10879333		10463092	ALIMENTS,ANIMAUX VIVANTS
01	MEAT AND PREPARATIONS		3377586		3875897		4118837		3994457	VIANDES ET PREPARATIONS
011	MEAT FRESH,CHILLD,FROZEN	W 982455	2445494	W 1089111	2877995	W 1053837	3055679	W 1007639	2887938	VIANDES FRAICHES,REF,CONGE
0111	BOVINE MEAT FRESH,FROZEN	W 129438	419483	W 127660	442386	W 111580	417467	W 98693	309360	VIANDES BOVIN FRAI,REF
01111	BOVINE MEAT WITH BONE IN	W 82557	253347	W 72841	256249	W 69296	242569	W 48922	152747	VIANDES BOVIN NON DESOSS
01112	BOVINE MEAT BONELESS	W 46882	166136	W 54819	186136	W 42284	174898	W 49771	156613	VIANDES BOVIN DESOSSEES
0113	PIG MEAT FRESH,CHLD,FRZN	W 676707	1810683	W 774202	2195796	W 739781	2374594	W 711103	2301976	VIANDE DE PORC
0114	POULTRY FRESH CHLLD,FRZN	W 105151	153608	W 103600	158427	W 105268	164453	W 102291	179066	VOLAILLES MORTES
012	MEAT DRIED,SALTED,SMOKED	W 106973	319597	W 127584	359367	W 120990	425427	W 121582	465166	VIANDE,ABATS SALES,SECHES
0121	PIG MEAT DRIED,SLTD,SMKD	W 106969	319566	W 127582	359354	W 120990	425427	W 121582	465166	LARD,JAMBONS
014	MEAT PREPD,PRSVD,NES ETC	W 211470	612494	W 216976	638535	W 191284	637731	W 191170	641353	CONSERVES DE VIANDES
0142	SAUSAGES INCLDING TINNED	W 50673	132269	W 52430	143086	W 50795	154953	W 55522	174170	SAUCISSES,SAUCISSONS
0149	OTH PREPARD,PRESRVD MEAT	W 160791	480181	W 164516	495118	W 140429	482216	W 135619	466796	AUTRES PREP DE VIANDES
02	DAIRY PRODCTS,BIRDS'EGGS		1327584		1362118		1623256		1595904	PRODUITS LAITIERS,OEUFS
022	MILK AND CREAM	W 166297	348050	W 177660	376092	W 168191	398534	W 158665	376298	LAIT ET CREME
0224	MILK,CREAM PRESERVED ETC	W 125360	297985	W 137009	324210	W 129479	345115	W 123836	325488	LAIT,CREME CONS,CONC
02243	MILK DRY,OVER 1.5% FAT	W 94785	245155	W 105905	272747	W 92650	271624	W 85886	252855	LAIT POUDRE SUP 1.5%
023	BUTTER	W 47982	155677	W 49412	169969	W 50978	190460	W 54593	199404	BEURRE
024	CHEESE AND CURD	W 260043	813146	W 236773	808390	W 254974	1014143	W 241724	998742	FROMAGE ET CAILLEBOTTE
03	FISH AND PREPARATIONS		2060845		2259410		2193244		2122429	POISSONS ET PREPARATIONS
034	FISH,FRESH,CHILLED,FROZN	W 372030	1054124	W 369985	1104216	W 339225	1052976	W 355167	964727	POISSON FRAIS, REFRIG,CONG
0341	FISH FRSH,CHLLD,EX FILLT	W 152281	497219	W 166551	540819	W 158134	510254	W 188290	429605	POISSON FRAIS,REFRIGERE
0342	FISH FROZEN,EXCL FILLETS	W 83461	175455	W 74581	145269	W 66065	131737	W 49812	122877	POISSONS CONGELES
0343	FISH FILLETS,FRESH,CHLLD	W 74490	154956	W 65441	165062	W 61982	172547	W 57871	175870	FILETS FRAIS,REFRIGERES
0344	FISH FILLETS,FROZEN	W 61798	226495	W 63413	253066	W 53044	238438	W 59193	236375	FILETS CONGELES
035	FISH SALTED,DRIED,SMOKED	W 37921	252283	W 56177	359108	W 40030	298287	W 42154	288929	POISSON SECHE,SALE,FUME
03504	FISH SMOKED	W 10341	156707	W 11676	158105	W 13192	187186	W 15032	186457	POISSONS FUMES
036	SHELL FISH FRESH,FROZEN	W 73809	284458	W 72421	313485	W 70061	330879	W 85389	385662	CRUSTACES,MOLLUSQUES
037	FISH ETC PREPD,PRSVD NES	W 107091	469979	W 113479	482601	W 102528	511102	W 96573	483110	POIS,CRUST,MOL PREPARES
0371	FISH PREPARD,PRESRVD NES	W 70687	260765	W 74554	265855	W 70580	285318	W 69963	273454	CONSERVES DE POISSONS
0372	SHELL FISH PREPRD,PRESVD	W 36404	209214	W 38925	216746	W 31948	225784	W 26609	209657	CRUSTACES,COQUIL PREPARES
04	CEREALS AND PREPARATIONS		807981		754503		1035098		953293	CEREALES ET PRODUITS
041	WHEAT ETC UNMILLED	W 1332167	174312	W 794429	103139	W 1585305	229098	W 823946	154599	FROMENT,EPEAUTRE
0412	OTHER WHEAT ETC UNMILLED	W 1332167	174312	W 770661	99159	W 1579196	227965	W 823436	154502	AUTRE FROMENT NON MOULU
043	BARLEY UNMILLED	W 575699	117496	W 691825	112686	W 791420	190528	W 699612	163439	ORGE NON MONDEE
048	CEREAL ETC PREPARATIONS	W 264153	490541	W 282995	512371	W 294136	574779	W 310574	550777	PREPTNS A BASE CEREALES
0484	BAKERY PRODUCTS	W 103914	273838	W 113574	301601	W 121549	340698	W 115323	324989	PRODUITS DE BOULANGERIE
04841	BREAD,BISCUIT,COM WAFERS	W 50964	108507	W 55874	120392	W 69444	159998	W 63854	151258	PAINS,BISCUITS DE MER
04842	PASTRY, CAKES ETC	W 52950	165330	W 57700	181209	W 52105	180700	W 51468	173732	PATISSERIE ETC.
05	VEGETABLES AND FRUIT		243747		231489		229507		213828	LEGUMES ET FRUITS
054	VEG ETC FRSH,SMPLY PRSVD	W 299250	114605	W 307532	104324	W 185171	91193	W 160723	73767	LEGUMES FRAIS,CONG,SECS
06	SUGAR AND PREPS,HONEY		249120		278303		312415		267839	SUCRES ET PRODUITS
062	SUGAR CANDY NON-CHOCLATE	W 41188	139958	W 45568	170143	W 45723	206345	W 38851	167125	SUCRERIES
081	*FEEDING STUFF FOR ANIML	W 768493	375939	W 851879	446617	W 994642	584425	W 920861	581383	NOURRITURE POUR ANIMAUX
0814	MEAT OR FISH MEAL FODDER	W 343151	171775	W 366270	190644	W 439261	254057	W 402307	251946	FARINES DE VIANDES,POISSONS
08142	FISH MEAL FODDER	W 267717	149253	W 285361	163710	W 355664	224411	W 331591	225141	FARINES DE POISSONS
0819	FOOD WASTE AND FEED NES	W 234217	181704	W 266860	228368	W 280627	290583	W 283617	290778	DECHETS,ALIMENTS NDA
08199	FODDER NES,INCL SWEETNED	W 208076	176405	W 246720	223679	W 259716	286444	W 267419	286050	PREPARATIONS FOURRAGERES
09	MISC EDIBLE PRODUCTS		368793		418856		543575		484742	PREP ALIMENTAIRES DIVERSES
098	EDIBLE PRODCTS,PREPS NES	W 101616	335000	W 104852	377357	W 109781	484615	W 113746	436334	PREP ALIMENTAIRES NDA
09809	MISC FOOD PREPRTIONS NES	W 80512	294914	W 76722	331182	W 85315	434668	W 83733	378001	PREP ALIMENTAIRES NDA
1	BEVERAGES AND TOBACCO		412031		430589		539457		483553	BOISSONS ET TABACS
11	BEVERAGES		275814		285776		356062		311289	BOISSONS
112	ALCOHOLIC BEVERAGES	W 279095	251666	W 288730	259736	W 331353	322979	W 301170	284068	BOISSONS ALCOOLIQUES
1123	BEER,ALE,STOUT,PORTER	W 254352	186702	W 265737	204051	W 311227	254030	W 283832	221267	BIERES
12	TOBACCO AND MANUFACTURES		136217		144813		183395		172263	TABACS BRUTS FABRIQUES
122	TOBACCO,MANUFACTURED	W 5958	125574	W 5628	132474	W 6331	166748	W 5821	156236	TABACS FABRIQUES
2	CRUDE MATERLS,EXCL FUELS		1292696		1460711		1760391		1778890	MAT BRUTES NON COMESTIBLES
21	HIDES,SKINS,FURS UNDRSSD		326608		396404		393062		534740	CUIRS,PEAUX BRUTS
212	FURSKINS,RAW	W 1975	278708	W 1587	344056	W 1625	330474	W 1523	482380	PELLETERIES BRUTES
21201	MINK SKINS,RAW	W 1552	243868	W 1245	293128	W 1289	276472	W 1120	406300	PEAUX DE VISON BRUTES
28	METALLIFEROUS ORES,SCRAP		119130		158831		245208		161844	MINERAIS METAL,DECHETS
288	NONFERR METAL SCRAP NES	W 89092	67137	W 103832	98398	W 118671	154663	W 77930	84842	DECHETS NON FERREUX
2882	OTHER BASE MTL SCRAP NES	W 85541	65522	W 98559	97268	W 115010	152873	W 72513	82461	AUTRES DECHETS
29	CRUDE ANIMAL,VEG MAT NES		598860		619438		767028		784211	MATIERES BRUTES ANIM,VEGET
292	CRUDE VEG MATERIALS NES	W 182521	507605	W 184031	511526	W 214920	665819	W 228352	672192	MAT BRUTES VEGETALES NDA
2925	SEEDS,ETC FOR PLANTING	W 54706	116150	W 57207	117382	W 68162	155129	W 77447	167350	SEMENCES NDA
2926	LIVE PLANTS,BULBS,ETC	W 81655	314594	W 80605	314577	W 101975	416538	W 108393	427476	BULBES,TUBERCULES
29269	LIVE PLANTS NES	W 81164	312283	W 80177	312535	W 101582	414273	W 108072	426405	AUTRES PLANTES VIVANTES
3	MINERAL FUELS ETC		1104844		1041567		1270675		2107641	COMBUSTIBLES MINERAUX LUB
33	PETROLEUM AND PRODUCTS		997755		890156		1151287		1538446	PETROLE ET DERIVES
333	CRUDE PETROLEUM	W 3161834	395362	W 2897144	338157	W 5130018	641343	W 4616379	717618	HUILES BRUTES DE PETROLE
334	PETROLEUM PRODUCTS,REFIN	W 3855941	598612	W 3769416	548378	W 3212929	505207	W 4340760	810250	PRODUITS RAFFINES
351	*ELECTRIC CURRENT		96865		143036		108004		547628	ENERGIE ELECTRIQUE
4	ANIMAL,VEGETABLE OIL,FAT		130998		174902		261209		248670	HUILES,GRAISSES ANIM,VEG
5	CHEMCLS,RELATED PROD NES		3282316		3701859		4587849		4555538	PRODUITS CHIMIQUES
51	ORGANIC CHEMICALS		553842		648668		680266		662025	PROD CHIMIQ ORGANIQUES
516	OTHER ORGANIC CHEMICALS	W 55223	423731	W 61468	475799	W 57042	475848	W 64587	473431	AUTRES PROD ORGANIQUES
5169	ORGANIC CHEMICALS,NES	W 54619	420319	W 59730	465092	W 56399	470756	W 64119	470196	PROD CHIM ORGANIQUES NDA
51691	ENZYMES	W 53838	417516	W 58682	461728	W 55312	467387	W 62393	465344	ENZYMES
53	DYES,TANNING,COLOUR PROD		324455		363424		467542		448908	PROD TEINTURE,COLORANTS
531	SYNT DYE,NAT INDGO,LAKES	W 12622	135378	W 15823	163477	W 19655	219244	W 26323	196124	MAT COLOR ORGAN,LAQUES
5311	SYNTHIC ORGNIC DYESTUFFS	W 12584	134900	W 15733	162943	W 19581	218726	W 26243	195657	MAT COLOR ORGAN SYNTHET
533	PIGMENTS,PAINTS,ETC	W 88372	182818	W 79602	190127	W 81919	231324	W 88656	232865	PIGMENTS,PEINTURES,VERNIS
5334	VARNISHES,DISTEMPERS ETC	W 56843	141588	W 56219	148909	W 59159	181939	W 59456	182148	PEINTURES A L'EAU
53342	OTH PAINTS,VARNISHES ETC	W 46345	114973	W 46608	119091	W 48996	147214	W 48464	145690	AUTRES PEINTURES,VERNIS
541	*MEDICINAL,PHARM PRODUCT	MK 14111	1378666	MK 15593	1615144	MK 16531	2160841		2214119	PROD MEDICINAUX PHARMACEUT
5417	MEDICAMENTS	MK 9018	1054156	MK 10324	1258870	MK 10945	1767397	MK 11620	1768058	MEDICAMENTS
54172	— CONTAINING HORMONES	K 2904315	717193	K 2911955	858374	K 3815242	1196169	K 3737229	1069014	MED CONTENANT HORMONES
54179	— CONTNG OTH SUBSTANCES	K 5030418	287634	K 6296014	348961	K 5905131	499339	K 6747460	632639	MED CONT AUT SUBSTANCES
55	PERFUME,CLEANING ETC PRD		262954		264485		291982		278929	PROD POUR PARFUM,TOILETTE
553	PERFUMERY,COSMETICS,ETC	W 17577	116294	W 15018	97251	W 14437	96928	W 15278	105746	PRODUITS DE PARFUMERIE
554	SOAP,CLEANSING ETC PREPS	W 113610	131428	W 111879	149751	W 114974	174167	W 117248	152898	SAVONS,PRODUITS DETERSIFS
5542	WASHING PREPARATIONS ETC	W 109962	119918	W 108546	137784	W 110130	157979	W 112562	138020	PROD ORG TENSIO-ACT NDA
58	PLASTIC MATERIALS ETC		301020		316858		397530		415581	MAT PLAST ARTIFICIELLES
583	POLYMERIZATION ETC PRODS	W 97235	253472	W 106685	266649	W 104546	333292	W 115900	355356	PROD POLYMERISATION
5839	OTH POLYMRZTION ETC PROD	W 36050	145297	W 35844	139459	W 37832	179595	W 43562	198882	AUT PROD POLYMER COPOLYM
59	CHEMICAL MATERIALS NES		355591		390862		457573		439124	MAT PROD CHIMIQUES NDA
592	STARCH,INULIN,GLUTEN,ETC	W 190693	159505	W 208518	159806	W 156615	172228	W 169225	188088	AMIDONS,INUL,GLUT FROM
5922	ALBUMINOID SUBSTAN,GLUES	W 81784	125362	W 88604	119584	W 91280	137945	W 83769	139946	MAT ALBUMIN,COLLES

5. General Exports F.O.B. by Commodities according to the S.I.T.C. (Rev. 2) in thousand U.S. Dollars
Exportations Générales F.O.B. par Produits d'après la C.T.C.I. (Rév. 2) en milliers de Dollars E.U.

SITC CTCI	COMMODITY	1993 WEIGHT POIDS	1993 VALUE VALEUR	1994 WEIGHT POIDS	1994 VALUE VALEUR	1995 WEIGHT POIDS	1995 VALUE VALEUR	1996 WEIGHT POIDS	1996 VALUE VALEUR	PRODUIT
598	MISCEL CHEM PRODUCTS NES	W 73517	180838	W 80505	214686	W 82881	261379	W 82218	223271	PROD DIV INDUST CHIM NDA
6	BASIC MANUFACTURES		3772757		4247549		5385174		5125167	ART MANUFACTURES
63	WOOD,CORK MANUFACTRS NES		517116		634072		797887		749736	OUVRAGES LIEGE ET BOIS
635	WOOD MANUFACTURES NES	W 179229	444106	W 187540	557023	W 204108	710204	W 196103	667849	ART MANUF EN BOIS NDA
6353	BUILDERS WOODWRK,PREFABS	W 123308	366043	W 148055	462018	W 157959	587388	W 148600	546302	OUVRAGES DE MENUISERIE
64	PAPER,PAPERBOARD AND MFR		441045		484838		610341		593220	PAPIERS,CARTONS & OUVRAGES
641	PAPER AND PAPERBOARD	W 235661	170686	W 293105	217732	W 279015	281952	W 274792	233547	PAPIERS ET CARTONS
6415	PAPER,PAPERBRD,BULK,NES	W 151270	77525	W 209293	120796	W 203787	179864	W 190690	124841	PAPIERS,CARTONS ROULEAUX
64159	OTHER PAPER ETC,BULK,NES	W 150690	76112	W 207873	117714	W 201792	176949	W 189977	122731	AUT PAPIER ROULEAUX FEUILLES
642	PAPER,ETC,PRECUT,ARTS OF	W 147695	270359	W 149807	267106	W 157607	328390	W 175230	359673	PAP,CARTONS DECOUPES
6421	PAPER ETC CONTAINERS	W 72373	121094	W 75082	123068	W 83815	159581	W 92199	168887	BOITES,SACS EMBALLAGES
6428	PAPER ETC ARTICLES NES	W 68806	127484	W 69064	125970	W 69933	152350	W 78634	162072	OUVRAGES EN PATE A PAPIER
65	TEXTILE YARN,FABRICS,ETC		609797		669057		819725		854876	FILS,TISSUS,ARTICLES TEXTILE
651	TEXTILE YARN	W 14529	104848	W 18171	128629	W 20783	171117	W 22149	183283	FILS TEXTILES
6514	SYN FIB YRN,BULK,MONOFIL	W 11077	77320	W 14047	97031	W 16181	132956	W 17908	147883	FILS CONT 85% FIB TEXT SYNTH
659	FLOOR COVERINGS,ETC	W 24575	122848	W 24317	124488	W 25960	146430	W 26855	148752	COUVRE–PARQUETS,TAPIS ETC
66	NONMETAL MINERAL MFS NES		564277		582939		675202		616073	ART MIN NON METALLIQUES
663	MINERAL MANUFCTURES NES	W 851588	236688	W 874178	226775	W 826367	253872	W 834885	248216	ART MIN MANUF NDA
6633	MINRL MFS NES NONCERAMIC	W 636020	129700	W 742273	169527	W 728670	182060	W 742639	181020	OUVR MAT MINERALE NDA
67	IRON AND STEEL		465734		560250		769784		701281	FER ET ACIER
674	IRN,STL UNIV,PLATE,SHEET	W 317854	146492	W 373766	188401	W 439442	268474	W 455374	268904	LARGES PLATS,TOLES
6744	IRN,STL HVY PLATE,ROLLED	W 262812	108427	W 293332	129973	W 343939	191532	W 366384	195515	TOLES LAMINEES PLUS 4.75 MM
67441	— OF IRON OR SIMPLE STL	W 262350	107656	W 290628	124747	W 339831	178532	W 358362	177537	TOLES NON ACIER FIN CARB
678	IRON,STL TUBES,PIPES,ETC	W 123737	177226	W 137978	204277	W 158281	281734	W 134190	254786	TUBES,TUYAUX EN FONTE,FER
6783	IRON,STL TUBES,PIPES NES	W 106530	112929	W 121542	134573	W 136779	182760	W 114543	157534	AUT TUBES,TUYAUX FER,ACIER
68	NON–FERROUS METALS		134108		169131		265040		208065	METAUX NON FERREUX
684	ALUMINIUM	W 38212	112467	W 42357	132555	W 53089	209562	W 44846	176016	ALUMINIUM
6842	ALUMINIUM,ALLOYS WORKED	W 19112	91473	W 25002	105403	W 29293	164037	W 24163	145416	ALUMINIUM,ALLIAGES OUVRE
69	METAL MANUFACTURES NES		896475		973987		1250401		1179025	ART MANUFACT EN METAL NDA
691	STRUCTURES AND PARTS NES	W 99682	333506	W 102906	342602	W 110971	441385	W 106762	385407	CONSTRUCT FER,ACIER,ALU
6911	STRUCTURES,PARTS IRN,STL	W 82889	213932	W 85151	208969	W 91163	274153	W 88162	235405	CONSTRUCT FER,ACIER,FONTE
6912	STRUCTURES,PARTS ALUMNM	W 16793	119574	W 17756	133633	W 19808	167232	W 18600	150002	CONSTRUCT ALUMINIUM
699	BASE METAL MFRS NES	W 53886	299347	W 53254	332068	W 62414	430330	W 69377	415626	ART MANUFACTURES MET NDA
7	MACHINES,TRANSPORT EQUIP		8976716		10259572		12248191		12483427	MACHINES MATERIEL TRANSPORT
71	POWER GENERATING EQUIPMT		550234		656491		933964		926490	MACHINES GENERATRICES
713	INTRNL COMBUS PSTN ENGIN	W 7808	161321	W 7123	120340	W 6293	143334	W 7560	174620	MOTEURS EXPL COMB INT, PIECE
7139	PISTON ENGINE PARTS NES	W 4090	127806	W 3140	82307	W 3872	106756	W 5485	145191	PIECES POUR 713.2,3,8
716	ROTATING ELECTRIC PLANT	W 25901	290635	W 36295	417359	W 55576	691728	W 55284	617692	APP ELECTR ROTATIFS,PIECES
7161	DC MOTORS AND GENERATORS	W 15632	161704	W 21076	229530	W 36705	439861	W 39524	412891	MOTEURS COURANT CONTINU
72	MACHS FOR SPCL INDUSTRYS		1357262		1550487		1911239		1946940	MAC SPECIALES POUR INDUST
721	AGRIC MACHY,EXC TRACTORS	W 28863	312929	W 41931	441969	W 43016	561184	W 50207	602913	MACHINES AGRICOLES
7212	HARVESTING ETC MACHINES	W 15350	103236	W 25480	207795	W 24364	222249	W 30335	273517	ENGINS POUR LA RECOLTE
7213	DAIRY MACHINERY NES	W 4470	153285	W 4833	165747	W 8337	267241	W 7117	248730	MACHINES DE LAITERIE NDA
72139	PTS NES OF MACHY OF 7213	W 2962	108183	W 3583	129322	W 4994	186026	W 3881	153488	PIECES POUR MACH 721.3
726	PRINTG,BKBINDG MACHY,PTS	W 4271	114969	W 3649	125575	W 4057	182437	W 4439	208903	MACHINES POUR IMPRIMERIE
727	FOOD MACHRY NON–DOMESTIC	W 13587	302378	W 12783	291518	W 13152	354236	W 14146	359216	MACH INDUSTRIES ALIMENT
7272	OTH FOOD PROC MCHY,PARTS	W 11696	279822	W 10885	274066	W 11239	328858	W 12333	336652	AUT MACH IND ALIMENTAIRE
72722	INDUS FOOD PROC MACH NES	W 11243	269200	W 10420	263121	W 10763	314812	W 11504	315556	MACHINES BOULANGERIE
728	OTH MACHY FOR SPCL INDUS	W 33742	454710	W 32112	478877	W 31370	568892	W 32514	536880	AUT MACH IND PARTICULIERES
7283	OTHR MINERAL WORKG MACHY	W 18994	252035	W 18607	247365	W 18408	308242	W 19307	288551	MACH TRIER,CRIBLER,BROYER
72839	PTS NES OF MACHY OF 7283	W 8875	148066	W 10814	155043	W 10308	189249	W 14060	199721	PIECES MACH DU 728.3
7284	MACHY FOR SPCL INDUS NES	W 13052	181921	W 11200	205671	W 10628	229477	W 11260	216219	MACH SPEC IND PARTICUL.
74	GENRL INDUSTRL MACHY NES		2591045		2789576		3534031		3430120	MACH APP INDUSTRIE
741	HEATING,COOLING EQUIPMNT	W 48713	687764	W 61518	793987	W 67354	1022178	W 69854	995271	MACH CHAUFFAGE,PIECES
7414	NONDOM REFRIG EQUIPT,PTS	W 25771	291778	W 34781	348989	W 37831	469418	W 38004	427115	MAT PRODUCTION DU FROID
74141	REFRIG EQUIP NONDOMESTIC	W 19525	203886	W 28713	265008	W 30335	339813	W 30788	317060	REFIG INDUSTRIELS
7416	HEATING,COOLING EQU NES	W 15830	288347	W 18983	320269	W 19702	378778	W 19506	375140	APP CHANGEMENT TEMP
742	PUMPS FOR LIQUIDS ETC	W 23773	318495	W 27765	375584	W 30001	456281	W 30482	478704	POMPES MOTO–POMPES
7422	CENTRIFUGAL PUMPS NES	W 11058	149437	W 12953	178498	W 13569	213418	W 14204	228211	POMPES CENTRIF NON 742.81
7429	PTS NES OF PUMPS OF 742	W 12005	149592	W 14064	179399	W 15705	218730	W 14948	222576	PIECES POUR GROUPE 742
743	PUMPS NES,CENTRFUGES ETC	W 22992	345257	W 22520	353884	W 28634	467842	W 27604	443117	POMPES COMPRES,VENT ETC
7439	PTS NES OF APP OF 7435,6	W 10808	150307	W 10306	142784	W 14407	200963	W 13072	188029	PIECES 743.5 ET 743.6
744	MECHANICAL HANDLING EQU	W 39284	422924	W 42641	416101	W 40190	450435	W 40881	430821	EQUIP MANUTENTION PIECES
7442	LIFTING,LOADING MACH NES	W 28200	326873	W 30543	315031	W 27934	320399	W 27768	297385	APP LEVAGE,MANUTENTION
74428	OTH HANDLING ETC MCH NES	W 24249	297613	W 25662	283555	W 23944	282289	W 24769	270381	AUT APP LEVAGE ETC
745	NONELEC MACHY,TOOLS NES	W 17842	324006	W 17219	310204	W 21739	449696	W 22311	445571	AUT MACH NON ELEC,PIECES
7452	OTH NONELEC MCHS,PTS NES	W 17687	319017	W 16990	303905	W 21559	441959	W 22120	438384	AUT MACH NON ELEC,PIECES
74527	SPRAYING MACHINERY	W 11804	138342	W 12550	142234	W 14593	192878	W 16094	209725	APP PROJETER ETC LIQUID
749	NONELEC MACH PTS,ACC NES	W 28305	492600	W 29286	539816	W 37254	687598	W 34060	636636	PIECES MACH NON ELEC NDA
7492	COCKS,VALVES ETC NES	W 21230	411236	W 20350	452811	W 26049	580549	W 22487	535796	ART ROB,SIM POUR TUYAUX
75	OFFICE MACHNES,ADP EQUIP		597637		875963		857124		901570	MACH BUREAU TRAIT AUTOM
752	AUTOMTIC DATA PROC EQUIP	W 3873	294041	W 5793	497907	W 4013	388679	W 9186	461643	MACH TRAIT INFORMATION
7523	DIGITL CENTRL PROCESSORS	W 1567	114638	W 1903	166265	W 799	102724	W 6022	138176	UNITES CENTRALES
7525	ADP PERIPHERAL UNITS	W 1085	58170	W 2192	152596	W 1434	82405	W 1418	89140	UNITES PERIPHERIQUES
759	OFFICE,ADP MCH PTS,ACCES	W 3356	271332	W 4160	349948	W 4514	432190	W 4999	409402	PIECES DU 751 ET 752
7599	ACCTG,ETC,ADP MCH PTS,AC	W 2926	258932	W 3642	334298	W 4074	416695	W 3711	378414	PIECES DU 751 ET 752
76	TELECOMM,SOUND EQUIPMENT		760579		944032		1323629		1394608	EQUIPMENT DE TELECOM
761	TELEVISION RECEIVERS	W 5193	88300	W 5031	96053	W 7602	170071	W 6197	125615	RECEPTEURS DE TELEVISION
7611	COLOUR TV RECEIVERS	W 5183	88001	W 5024	95932	W 7582	168643	W 6194	125464	RECEPTEURS COULEUR
762	RADIO BROADCAST RECEIVRS	W 1389	61462	W 2330	87818	W 4255	147356	W 6319	106937	RECEPTEURS RADIODIFFUSION
764	TELECOM EQPT,PTS,ACC NES	W 20562	565210	W 23040	711610	W 29252	921237	W 34355	1109784	EQUIP TELECOM,PIECES
7641	LINE TELEPHONE,ETC EQUIP	W 491	48947	W 658	132535	W 740	108439	W 802	114482	APP TELEPHON PAR FIL
7642	MICROPH,LOUDSPKR,AMPLIFR	W 11724	133596	W 14960	176930	W 19119	239290	W 22108	302914	MICRO,HAUT–PARLEUR,AMPLI
7643	TV,RADIO TRANSMITTRS ETC	W 629	151928	W 628	156666	W 745	246151	W 1229	335704	APP EMET TELE RADIO
7649	PTS NES OF EQUIPMT OF 76	W 7596	198503	W 6633	214763	W 8471	284483	W 10091	320473	PIECES DE LA DIV 76
76493	TELECOMM EQUIPMT PTS NES	W 6321	152149	W 5538	160887	W 7250	217358	W 7989	241220	PIECES 761,762,764.3,8
77	ELECTRIC MACHNRY NES ETC		1178386		1347765		1580723		1606815	MACH APP ELECT NDA
771	ELECTRIC POWER MACHY NES	W 6362	132241	W 5202	169402	W 7096	210137	W 7482	229818	MACH PROD,TRANS ELECTR
7712	OTH ELEC POWER MACHY NES	W 4321	109059	W 3844	145156	W 5259	173161	W 5713	192116	AUT APP PROD TRANSF ELEC
77121	STATIC CONVERTERS ETC	W 1693	86854	W 2075	117234	W 2630	142862	W 2842	156891	CONVERTISSEURS STATIQUES
772	SWITCHGEAR ETC,PARTS NES	W 5807	190913	W 6321	230016	W 7257	299566	W 8009	316511	APP COUPURE,SECT ETC
7721	SWITCHGEAR ETC	W 5307	131625	W 5817	159622	W 6645	204723	W 7396	220454	APP COUPURE,SECTIONMNT
774	ELECTRO–MEDCL,XRAY EQUIP	W 1031	128213	W 1145	154668	W 1246	189974	W 1106	168260	APPAREILS MEDICAUX
7741	ELECTRO–MEDICAL EQUIPMNT	W 791	103774	W 863	125207	W 865	142036	W 822	136902	APP ELECTRICITE MEDICALE
775	HOUSEHOLD TYPE EQUIP NES	W 70669	382065	W 71279	413281	W 74372	463957	W 61362	408765	MACH,APP USAGE DOMESTQUE
7752	DOM REFRIGERATRS,FREEZRS	W 61974	283373	W 62460	294505	W 64408	334438	W 49611	252108	REFRIG,CONGEL MENAGER
77522	DOMESTIC DEEP–FREEZERS	W 48742	219245	W 50108	234629	W 52095	266395	W 39164	194746	MEUBLES CONGELATEURS
778	ELECTRICAL MACHINERY NES	W 10653	181977	W 11565	203182	W 12282	241212	W 14085	276630	AUTRES MACH ELECT NDA
78	ROAD VEHICLES		715416		725859		902970		958908	VEHICULES ROUTIERS
781	PASS MOTOR VEH EXC BUSES	W 13794	141791	W 9519	96130	W 9394	114811	W 12334	143494	AUTO TRANSPORT PERSONNES
784	MOTOR VEH PRTS,ACCES NES	W 68688	306311	W 90062	372012	W 102873	457851	W 188329	470284	PIECES 722,781,782,783

5. General Exports F.O.B. by Commodities according to the S.I.T.C. (Rev. 2) in thousand U.S. Dollars
Exportations Générales F.O.B. par Produits d'après la C.T.C.I. (Rév. 2) en milliers de Dollars E.U.

SITC CTCI	COMMODITY	1993		1994		1995		1996		PRODUIT
		WEIGHT POIDS	VALUE VALEUR	WEIGHT POIDS	VALUE VALEUR	WEIGHT POIDS	VALUE VALEUR	WEIGHT POIDS	VALUE VALEUR	
7849	OTHER MOTOR VEHCL PARTS	W 65922	293504	W 86737	356256	W 99126	434497	W 185133	450043	PIECES 722,781,782,783
79	OTHR TRANSPORT EQUIPMENT		1125127		1254533		1071409		1189342	AUTRE MATERIEL TRANSPORT
792	AIRCRAFT ETC	W 548	133576	W 960	213671	W 631	101270	W 628	238523	APP NAVIGATION AERIENNE
7924	AIRCRFT NES OVER 15000KG	W 219	75724	W 508	126995	W 206	10753	W 273	141271	AERODYNES PLUS 15000 KG
793	SHIPS AND BOATS ETC	W 431900	977418	W 573615	1035769	W 390656	945798	W 317389	896702	NAVIRES BATEAUX,ETC
7932	SHIPS AND BOATS NES	W 428123	940807	W 550603	939278	W 378278	850638	W 310282	837270	NAVIRES ET BATEAUX
79322	TANKERS OF ALL KINDS	W 118387	122759	W 289993	388581	W 77251	271973	W 172672	529412	BATEAUX–CITERNES
79323	OTHER CARGO VESSELS	W 303173	773160	W 259210	524303	W 298503	545817	W 136301	272974	AUT BATEAUX TRANS MARCH
8	MISC MANUFACTURED GOODS		5583960		6078960		7196315		7045461	ART MANUFACTURES DIVERS
812	*PLUMBG,HEATNG,LGHTNG EQ	W 28672	164966	W 27697	181502	W 26596	218149	W 26772	222919	APPAR SANITAIRES CHAUFFAGE
8124	LIGHTING EQUIPMENT NES	W 7457	97681	W 7760	115251	W 8104	149711	W 9009	158136	APPAREILS ECLAIRAGE ETC
821	*FURNITURE,PARTS THEREOF	W 379446	1598916	W 432151	1786181	W 451407	2160220	W 449792	2023872	MEUBLES ET PIECES
8211	CHAIRS,SEATS AND PARTS	W 22357	228390	W 22350	237503	W 26754	313552	W 23350	279659	SIEGES ET PIECES
82111	CHAIRS AND OTHER SEATS	W 20413	212700	W 20597	223242	W 25217	298275	W 21447	260547	SIEGES
8212	MED FURN,STUFFD FURNSHGS	W 17545	112072	W 19669	140668	W 19153	171147	W 22241	168552	MOB MEDICO–CHIRUR,PIECES
8219	FURNITURE AND PARTS NES	W 339544	1258454	W 390132	1408010	W 405500	1675521	W 404201	1575660	AUTRES MEUBLES ET PIECES
82192	WOOD FURNITURE NES	W 292118	1076919	W 340323	1218259	W 353172	1439515	W 353238	1370181	MEUBLES NDA EN BOIS
82199	OTHR FURN,FURN PARTS NES	W 39495	138652	W 40757	140946	W 43494	181106	W 36835	142413	MEUBLES NDA AUTRES MATIERES
84	CLOTHING AND ACCESSORIES		1037346		1064844		1274286		1287431	VETEMENTS
842	MENS OUTERWEAR NOT KNIT	W 4029	113265	W 4242	138891	W 5001	177126	W 5552	200866	VET DESSUS POUR HOMMES
843	WOMENS OUTERWEAR NONKNIT	W 6628	273076	W 7347	296508	W 7765	369007	W 7608	350359	VET DESSUS FEMMES MAT TEX
8439	— OTHER OUTER GARMENTS	W 3932	128997	W 4859	146855	W 4797	175170	W 4321	151294	AUT VET DES FEM MAT TEXT
845	OUTERWEAR KNIT NONELASTC	W 14394	435932	W 12179	412156	W 14093	498074	W 14877	471362	VET DESSOUS,ACCES BONNET
8451	— JERSEYS,PULLOVERS ETC	W 7515	223582	W 6272	218696	W 7206	259799	W 7314	240726	CHANDAILS,PULL–OVERS ETC
8459	— OTHER,CLTHG ACCESRYS	W 5893	169572	W 4918	149281	W 5487	182665	W 6340	182190	AUT VET DESSUS DE BONNE
846	UNDER GARMENTS KNITTED	W 5777	137700	W 3640	122466	W 3779	125250	W 4884	166353	SOUS VETS DE BONNETERIE
851	*FOOTWEAR	W 5705	184062	W 6486	211483	W 6302	224455	W 6285	213070	CHAUSSURES
85102	FOOTWEAR LEATHER	W 5141	175986	W 5812	202178	W 5638	214191	W 5600	202903	CHAUS SEMELLES EN CUIR
87	PRECISION INSTRUMNTS NES		739138		837571		926270		964335	INSTRUM,APPAR SCIENT NDA
872	MEDICAL INSTRUMENTS NES	W 6334	201093	W 7953	235723	W 7394	256043	W 7084	295595	INSTR,APP MEDIC–CHIR NDA
87202	OTH MEDICAL INSTRUMENTS	W 6047	182055	W 7619	212583	W 6908	233163	W 6436	269981	INSTRUM,APP MEDECINE
874	MEASURNG,CONTROLNG INSTR	W 3773	505387	W 3842	568965	W 3977	622894	W 4562	587684	INSTRUMENTS DE MESURE
8742	MEASUR,DRAW ETC INST,PTS	W 895	128617	W 703	141951	W 808	157588	W 1136	142586	INST DESSIN,TRACAGE,PCS
87421	MEASURNG,DRAWNG ETC INST	W 706	121354	W 547	134203	W 729	150757	W 1018	132440	INSTRUM DESSIN,TRACAGE
8748	ELEC MEAS,CONTRL EQU NES	W 554	158925	W 839	182300	W 534	172116	W 495	147796	APP ELEC ELECTRO MESURE
87483	OTH ELCTRNC MEAS ETC EQU	W 451	147797	W 742	174777	W 408	160085	W 370	137058	AUT APP ELECTRO DE MESURE
88	PHOTO EQU,OPTICL GDS ETC		150144		191732		224645		237550	APP,FOURN PHOTO,OP,MONTR
89	MISC MANUFCTRD GOODS NES		1695908		1789177		2144727		2073041	ART MANUFACTURES DIVERS
892	PRINTED MATTER	W 45987	304629	W 48937	319315	W 51313	365007	W 63689	326792	IMPRIMES
8921	PRINTED BOOKS,GLOBES,ETC	W 18915	134003	W 20160	129414	W 19989	139510	W 16541	127127	LIVRES,BROCHURES,CARTES
89211	PRINTED BOOKS,PAMPHLETS	W 17993	122849	W 19334	118783	W 19207	128095	W 15621	116201	LIVRES,BROCHURES
8928	PRINTED MATTER NES	W 19022	115599	W 21792	132482	W 20116	156729	W 35256	149440	IMPRIMES NDA
893	ARTICLES OF PLASTIC NES		784128		837817		1047574		1009718	OUVRAGES EN MAT DIVIS 58
8931	PLSTC PACKG CONTNRS,LIDS	W 51656	210840	W 53008	230710	W 53999	273701	W 158647	264816	ART TRANSP EMBALLAGE ETC
8939	MISC PLASTIC ARTICLES	W 91292	566873	W 92996	596849	W 103229	764048	W 97830	735568	ART DIVERS EN MAT DIV 58
89399	OTHR PLASTC ARTICLES NES	W 79060	519515	W 78688	540507	W 84478	677696	W 79653	663115	AUT OUV MAT DIV 58
898	MUSICAL INSTRUMENTS,PTS	W 11205	216263	W 10316	197265	W 10425	248482	W 10243	184463	INSTRUMENTS DE MUSIQUE
8983	SOUND RECRDNG TAPE,DISCS	W 10939	209883	W 10180	192586	W 10171	236590	W 9876	171599	SUPPORTS SON POUR 763
89832	RECORDED DISCS,TAPES ETC	W 8496	170698	W 6277	146218	W 6194	182546	W 6394	139671	DISQUES,PHONO,BANDES
899	OTHER MANUFACTURED GOODS		195454		217594		259354		325045	AUT ART MANUF DIVERS NDA
8996	HEARING,ORTHOPAEDIC AIDS		133147		151567		168897		242800	APPAREILS D'ORTHOPEDIE
89961	HEARING AIDS		91881		108753		119937		183618	APPAREILS POUR LES SOURDS
9	GOODS NOT CLASSD BY KIND		3632220		4394452		4660569		4581804	ART TRANSACT NON CLASSES
931	*SPECIAL TRANSACTIONS		3599250		4376054		4643326		4567484	TRANS.SPECIALES

1. HISTORICAL SERIES, 1957–1992 SPECIAL TRADE, IMPORTS C.I.F., EXPORTS F.O.B.
SERIES HISTORIQUES, 1957–1992 COMMERCE SPECIAL, IMPORTATIONS C.A.F., EXPORTATIONS F.O.B

YEAR ANNEE	VALUE IN MILLION DJIB. FRANCS VALEUR EN MILLION DJIB. FRANCS MERCHANDISE –MARCHANDISE		GOLD –OR		CONVERSION FACTORS U.S. CENTS PER DJIB. FRANC FACTEURS DE CONVERSION CENTS E.U. PAR DJIB. FRANC		INDEX NUMBERS –INDICES QUANTUM		UNIT VALUE VALEUR UNITAIRE	
	IMPORTS	EXPORTS	IMPORTS	EXPORTS	IMPORTS	EXPORTS	IMPORTS	EXPORTS	IMPORTS	EXPORTS
1957	3926.00	2192.00			0.4665	0.4665				
1958	5091.00	3454.00			0.4665	0.4665				
1959	6659.00	4108.00			0.4665	0.4665				
1960	7157.00	4483.00			0.4665	0.4665				
1961	8075.00	4784.00			0.4665	0.4665				
1962	9318.80	5786.90			0.4665	0.4665				
1963	11437.00	4891.80			0.4665	0.4665				
1964	12201.60	4833.90			0.4665	0.4665				
1965	13116.80	5985.80			0.4665	0.4665				
1966	12628.60	5776.40			0.4665	0.4665				
1967	12289.80	4954.20			0.4665	0.4665				
1968	10752.80	2580.10			0.4665	0.4665				
1969	10475.10	2521.90			0.4665	0.4665				
1970	10592.90	4523.20			0.4665	0.4665				
1971	11335.00	3219.30			0.4664	0.4664				
1972	12934.90	3829.10			0.5138	0.5138				
1973	14495.60	5498.60			0.5836	0.5836				
1974	24932.70	6732.90			0.5382	0.5382				
1975	24166.30	2639.20			0.6082	0.6070				
1976	21284.40	2835.20			0.6063	0.6052				
1977	18948.60	3364.10			0.5269	0.5268				
1978	29117.40	3154.20			0.5592	0.5621				
1979	33454.30	2023.20			0.5630	0.5630				
1980	37890.00	2220.50			0.5630	0.5630				
1981	39865.00	1553.70			0.5630	0.5630				
1982	40197.50	2234.20			0.5630	0.5630				
1983	39306.90	1918.80			0.5630	0.5630				
1984	40462.00	2362.00			0.5630	0.5630				
1985	35670.00	2488.00			0.5630	0.5630				
1986	32731.01	3628.00			0.5627	0.5627				
1987	36487.01	4976.00			0.5627	0.5627				
1988	35771.01	4116.00			0.5627	0.5627				
1989	34920.00	4423.00			0.5627	0.5627				
1990	38174.00	4420.00			0.5627	0.5627				
1991	38103.01	3083.00			0.5627	0.5627				
1992	38860.00	2800.00			0.5627	0.5627				

2. IMPORTS BY BROAD ECONOMIC CATEGORY AND EXPORTS BY INDUSTRIAL ORIGIN. (PERCENTAGE OF TOTAL VALUE)
IMPORTATIONS PAR CATEGORIES ECONOMIQUES ET EXPORTATIONS PAR BRANCHE D'ACTIVITE.(EN POURCENTAGE DE LA VALEUR TOTALE)

IMPORTS – IMPORTATIONS

	1990	1991	1992	1993	1994	1995	1996
TOTAL IMPORTS–IMPORTATIONS TOTALES	100.	100.	100.				
1 FOOD BEV–ALIMENTATION BOISSONS	26.6	24.8	24.2				
11 PRIMARY–PRODUITS DE BASE	8.1	6.9	3.4				
111 FOR INDUSTRY–POUR L'INDUSTRIE	4.1	3.6	0.3				
112 FOR HOUSEHOLDS–POUR LES MENAGES	4.0	3.2	3.0				
12 PROCESSED–PRODUITS ELABORES	18.5	17.9	20.9				
121 FOR INDUSTRY–POUR L'INDUSTRIE	4.9	4.1	3.5				
122 FOR HOUSEHOLDS–POUR LES MENAGES	13.6	13.8	17.4				
2 IND SUPPLIES–APPROV INDUSTRIELS	24.8	26.2	27.9				
21 PRIMARY–PRODUITS DE BASE	11.6	10.4	10.4				
22 PROCESSED–PRODUITS ELABORES	13.2	15.8	17.5				
3 FUELS–COMBUSTIBLES	7.0	9.0	8.0				
31 PRIMARY–PRODUITS DE BASE	0.1	0.1	0.1				
32 PROCESSED–PRODUITS ELABORES	6.8	8.8	7.9				
321 MOTOR SPIRIT–ESSENCE	0.9	1.2	2.2				
322 OTHER–AUTRES	5.9	7.7	5.7				
4 MACHINERY–EQUIPEMENT	8.6	8.6	7.9				
41 CAPITAL EQUIPMENT–MACHINES	7.8	7.9	7.1				
42 PARTS–PIECES ACCESSOIRES	0.8	0.7	0.8				
5 TRANSPORT–TRANSPORT	8.7	7.5	8.6				
51 PASSENGER CARS–AUTOMOBILES	4.5	4.5	0.6				
52 OTHER–AUTRES	1.8	1.0	5.9				
521 INDUSTRIAL–INDUSTRIELS	1.6	0.8	5.7				
522 NON INDUSTRIAL–NON INDUSTRIEL	0.2	0.2	0.2				
53 PARTS–PIECES ACCESSOIRES	2.4	2.1	2.1				
6 CONSUM GOODS–BIENS CONSOMMATION	21.1	20.8	19.2				
61 DURABLE–DURABLES	2.6	2.1	2.1				
62 SEMI DURABLE–SEMI DURABLES	6.9	7.8	7.5				
63 NON DURABLE–NON DURABLES	11.5	10.9	9.6				
7 GOODS NES–BIENS NDA	3.3	3.1	4.1				

EXPORTS – EXPORTATIONS

	1990	1991	1992	1993	1994	1995	1996
TOTAL EXPORTS–EXPORTATIONS TOTALES	100.	100.	100.				
1 AGRICULTURE	39.3	25.1	21.4				
2 MINING QUARRY–INDUS EXTRACTIVES		0.1	0.1				
3 MANUFACTURING–IND MANUFACTUR	60.7	74.8	78.5				
31 FOOD BEV TOBACCO–ALIM BOISS TAB	5.0	7.1	3.3				
32 TEXTILES–INDUSTRIES TEXTILES	0.0	0.6	2.3				
33 WOOD & PRODUCTS–BOIS & PRODUITS	0.0	0.0	0.0				
34 PAPER & PRODUCTS–PAPIER & PRODT	0.2	0.2	0.2				
35 CHEMICALS–INDUSTRIES CHIMIQUES	0.4	0.5	0.8				
36 NON METAL MIN–MIN NON METAL	0.1	0.2	0.1				
37 BASIC METAL–IND METAL BASE	0.1	0.6	0.1				
38 METAL MANUF–MANUF METAL	7.1	10.6	10.5				
39 OTH MANUF IND–AUTRES MANUF	47.7	55.1	61.3				

3. TRADE BY PRINCIPAL COUNTRIES OF PROVENANCE AND DESTINATION (VALUE IN THOUSAND U.S. DOLLARS)
ECHANGES SELON LES PRINCIPAUX PAYS DE PROVENANCE ET DE DESTINATION (VALEUR EN MILLIERS DE DOLLARS EU)

COUNTRIES–PAYS	SPECIAL IMPORTS C.I.F. IMPORTATIONS SPECIALES C.A.F					COUNTRIES–PAYS	SPECIAL EXPORTS F.O.B. EXPORTATIONS SPECIALES F.O.B.				
	1988	1989	1990	1991	1992		1988	1989	1990	1991	1992
World	201286	196496	214805	214403	219926	Monde	23158	24890	24883	17347	15919
Africa	22460	27178	27106	20771	20494	Afrique	1763	1795	1631	1592	1407
Americas	6086	4243	7991	9337	8812	Amériques	38	112	69	162	
Northern America	5404	3468	7566	8586	7101	Amérique du Nord	28	109	60	153	
LAIA	675	760	425	698	1131	ALAI		0			
CACM	4	0		31		MCAC	8	0			
Caribbean		15		22		Caraïbes		2	2	9	
Rest of America	3	1			580	Autre Amérique	1		6		
As.ex F.USSR	64322	64913	66194	74499	56428	Asie l'URSS exclus	6414	9760	9032	4126	2628
Eur.x F.USSR	102889	95534	107230	104488	101112	Europe l'URSS exclus	13930	12630	13831	11086	9397
EU	98944	91747	102798	99944	98489	UE	13499	11843	13549	10868	9397
EFTA	456	1532	3114	3009	1992	AELE	55	27	5	217	
East Europe	900	829	780	967	281	Europe de l'Est	0	3		1	
Other Europe	2589	1426	538	568	90	Autre de l'Europe	376	756	276		
Former USSR	98	815	684	635	129	Ancienne URSS	5				
Oceania	485	59	155	312	467	Océanie	1	5	14	8	
France, Monac	57749	54676	62895	56006	58003	France, Monac	11672	10176	12181	9906	9144
Ethiopia/Ethiopie	20294	24781	23884	17750	17157	Former Yemen	5683	9027			
Japan/Japon	12582	9748	11647	15412	14810	Former Democratic Yemen	43	87	8325		
Italy/Italie	9999	12283	11333	13891	12064	Yemen/Yémen				2851	686
Saudi Arabia	11147	9781	10717	10806	8750	Saudi Arabia	258	323	281	964	1587
Netherlands/Pays-Bas	8868	7408	6178	7466	7771	Somalia/Somalie	656	885	433	715	664
Thailand/Thaïlande	6083	5288	6423	6476	6207	Italy/Italie	816	839	889	562	
USA/Etats-Unis d'Amer	5017	3096	6997	7906	6764	Ethiopia/Ethiopie	630	368	390	308	523
China/Chine	5582	6013	4808	6644	6724	Fm Yugoslav	374	756	276		
United Kingdom	5996	4928	5603	5785	6955	Belgium-Luxembourg	275	263	176	175	191
Bahrain/Bahreïn	5993	6055	5292	5697	3860	Greece/Grèce	461	314	128	54	
Singapore/Singapour	4744	5103	5277	5375	4355	Reunion/Réunion	84	171	264	205	146
Belgium-Luxembourg	4485	3818	6604	5150	3455	United Arab Emirates	100	203	284	27	
Korea, Republic of	4911	5476	4219	3342	1671	Madagascar	142	99	203	168	
Germany/Allemagne	3718	3146	3238	4627	4372	Thailand/Thaïlande	41	66	8	46	293
United Arab Emirates	2133	3262	5540	4869	1474	Germany/Allemagne	91	81	67	144	
Denmark/Danemark	4332	2880	3495	3261	2543	USA/Etats-Unis d'Amer	21	101	60	135	
Hong Kong	2704	3500	3216	2504	287	Japan/Japon	38	8	43	155	62
India/Inde	1651	1987	2619	2986	2240	Switz.Liecht	54	9	0	213	
Switz.Liecht	429	1430	3067	2893	1992	India/Inde	173	11	22	52	
Pakistan	809	1305	976	3178	518	United Kingdom	74	10	37	2	62
Kenya	1136	983	835	1503	1277	Kenya	37	0	6	45	73
Austria/Autriche	924	618	1280	1194	1114	Netherlands/Pays-Bas	47	43	44	17	
Yemen/Yémen				1954	3039	Egypt/Egypte	36	29	77	2	
Fm Yugoslav	2560	1403	515	508		Tunisia/Tunisie	43	31	38	25	
Ireland/Irlande	1144	851	810	734	900	Spain/Espagne	16	36	12		
Egypt/Egypte	213	652	364	638	1654	Denmark/Danemark	31	2	7	3	
Spain/Espagne	851	558	751	625	501	Un. Rep. of Tanzania	2	40	0		
Chile/Chili	602	713	421	586	242	Cote d'Ivoire	21	8	1	8	
Korea Dem People's Rp	347	663	353	403	793	Canada	7	8	1	18	
Canada	387	372	569	680	338	Bahrain/Bahreïn		0	29		
Former USSR/Anc. URSS	98	815	684	635		Lebanon/Liban	16			11	
Lebanon/Liban	329	198	619	434	568	Korea, Republic of	2	10	12		
Sweden/Suède	387	441	450	660	203	Iraq	9	2	10		
Former Yemen	907	851				Sudan/Soudan	2	11	7		
Romania/Roumanie	390	377	255	316	281	Australia/Australie			13	5	
Australia/Australie	388	59	154	285	467	Qatar				17	
Somalia/Somalie	368	360	413	117	79	Turkey/Turquie	17			0	
Un. Rep. of Tanzania	174	83	626	301	113	Jordan/Jordanie	16			1	
Czechoslovakia	319	245	301	421		Singapore/Singapour	13	3	0		
Greece/Grèce	283	75	36	285	400	Sweden/Suède	0	4	3	4	
Sri Lanka	107	242	225	282	169	Pakistan	1	8	2		
Brazil/Brésil	72	16	0	47	889	Oman	0	0	6		
Former Democratic Yemen	304	108	547			Ireland/Irlande	6				
Indonesia/Indonésie	157	116	157	419		Indonesia/Indonésie			6		
Finland/Finlande	204	63	63	229	208	Cyprus/Chypre		5	0		
Malaysia/Malaisie	281	246	107	45		Norway,SVD,JM	1	0	0	4	
Jordan/Jordanie	56	4	516	14		Former USSR/Anc. URSS	5				
Tunisia/Tunisie	3	32	549	0		Philippines	2		0	2	
Panama		1			580	Romania/Roumanie		3			

(VALUE AS PERCENTAGE OF WORLD TOTAL)(VALEURS EN POURCENTAGE DU TOTAL MONDIAL)

	1983	1984	1985	1986	1987	1988	1989	1990	1991	1992		1983	1984	1985	1986	1987	1988	1989	1990	1991	1992
Africa	11.5	12.9	11.6	12.1	11.5	11.2	13.8	12.6	9.7	9.3	Afrique				12.7	15.7	7.6	7.2	6.6	9.2	8.8
Americas	2.2	2.6	2.6	2.5	2.5	3.0	2.2	3.7	4.4	4.0	Amériques				0.9	0.6	0.2	0.4	0.3	0.9	
Northern America	2.1	2.4	2.6	2.5	2.3	2.7	1.8	3.5	4.0	3.2	Amérique du Nord				0.7	0.4	0.1	0.4	0.2	0.9	
LAIA	0.0	0.2	0.1	0.1	0.2	0.3	0.4	0.2	0.3	0.5	ALAI				0.0	0.0		0.0			
CACM	0.0	0.0	0.0	0.0	0.0	0.0	0.0		0.0		MCAC						0.0	0.0			
Caribbean	0.1	0.0	0.0	0.0	0.0		0.0		0.0		Caraïbes				0.1	0.1		0.0	0.0	0.1	
Rest of America	0.0	0.0				0.0	0.0			0.3	Autre Amérique				0.0		0.0		0.0		
As.ex F.USSR	24.8	24.2	31.3	26.2	29.9	32.0	33.0	30.8	34.7	25.7	Asie l'URSS exclus				33.4	23.3	27.7	39.2	36.3	23.8	16.5
Eur.x F.USSR	55.5	58.6	51.6	55.9	53.3	51.1	48.6	49.9	48.7	46.0	Europe l'URSS exclus				52.4	60.2	60.2	50.7	55.6	63.9	59.0
EU	54.6	57.3	49.9	53.8	51.1	49.2	46.7	47.9	46.6	44.8	UE				51.6	59.1	58.3	47.6	54.5	62.6	59.0
EFTA	0.1	0.4	0.6	0.3	0.3	0.2	0.8	1.4	1.4	0.9	AELE				0.2	0.0	0.2	0.1	0.0	1.3	
East Europe	0.5	0.4	0.4	0.4	0.5	0.4	0.4	0.4	0.5	0.1	Europe de l'Est				0.1	0.0	0.0	0.0		0.0	
Other Europe	0.3	0.3	0.7	1.4	1.4	1.3	0.7	0.3	0.3	0.0	Autre de l'Europe				0.5	1.1	1.6	3.0	1.1		
Former USSR	0.2	0.3	0.1	0.0	0.0	0.0	0.4	0.3	0.3	0.1	Ancienne URSS						0.0				
Oceania	0.1	0.1	0.2	0.6	0.1	0.2	0.0	0.1	0.1	0.2	Océanie				0.0	0.0	0.0	0.0	0.1	0.0	
France, Monac	35.6	37.5	28.6	30.7	28.7	28.7	27.8	29.3	26.1	26.4	France, Monac				45.3	53.1	50.4	40.9	49.0	57.1	57.4
Ethiopia/Ethiopie	10.4	12.2	10.8	11.4	9.5	10.1	12.6	11.1	8.3	7.8	Former Yemen				26.2	21.2	24.5	36.3			
Japan/Japon	7.8	6.9	7.0	4.7	6.3	6.3	5.0	5.4	7.2	6.7	Former Democratic Yemen				1.3	0.7	0.2	0.4	33.5		
Italy/Italie	4.5	7.1	6.2	7.9	6.0	5.0	6.3	5.3	6.5	5.5	Yemen/Yémen									16.4	4.3
Saudi Arabia	0.9	1.4	4.3	4.6	4.7	5.5	5.0	5.0	5.0	4.0	Saudi Arabia				0.6	0.5	1.1	1.3	1.1	5.6	10.0
Netherlands/Pays-Bas	4.4	3.6	2.9	3.4	4.5	4.4	3.8	2.9	3.5	3.5	Somalia/Somalie				6.5	9.4	2.8	3.6	1.7	4.1	4.2
Thailand/Thaïlande	0.5	1.5	3.8	2.3	1.3	3.0	2.7	3.0	3.0	2.8	Italy/Italie				3.8	3.5	3.5	3.4	3.6	3.2	
USA/Etats-Unis d'Amer	2.0	2.3	2.4	2.4	2.2	2.5	1.6	3.3	3.7	3.1	Ethiopia/Ethiopie				2.5	5.4	2.7	1.5	1.6	1.8	3.3
China/Chine	2.5	1.6	1.9	2.3	2.8	2.8	3.1	2.2	3.1	3.1	Fm Yugoslav				0.5	1.1	1.6	3.0	1.1		
United Kingdom	3.9	3.8	6.0	5.0	3.7	3.0	2.5	2.6	2.7	3.2	Belgium-Luxembourg				1.1	0.6	1.2	1.1	0.7	1.0	1.2

4. Special Imports C.I.F. by Commodities according to the S.I.T.C. (Rev. 2) in thousand U.S. Dollars
Importations Spéciales C.A.F. par Produits d'après la C.T.C.I. (Rév. 2) en milliers de Dollars E.U.

SITC CTCI	COMMODITY	1989 WEIGHT POIDS	1989 VALUE VALEUR	1990 WEIGHT POIDS	1990 VALUE VALEUR	1991 WEIGHT POIDS	1991 VALUE VALEUR	1992 WEIGHT POIDS	1992 VALUE VALEUR	PRODUIT
	ALL COMMODITIES		196496		214805		214403		219926	TOUS PRODUITS
0	FOOD AND LIVE ANIMALS		41427		49673		45028		43789	ALIMENTS,ANIMAUX VIVANTS
01	MEAT AND PREPARATIONS		2340		2501		2535		2808	VIANDES ET PREPARATIONS
011	MEAT FRESH,CHILLD,FROZEN	W 510	1765	W 436	1618	W 400	1636	W 455	1694	VIANDES FRAICHES,REF,CONGE
0111	BOVINE MEAT FRESH,FROZEN	W 85	542	W 121	848	W 121	802	W 32	293	VIANDES BOVIN FRAI,REF
014	MEAT PREPD,PRSVD,NES ETC	W 82	422	W 161	865	W 571	853	W 216	1114	CONSERVES DE VIANDES
0142	SAUSAGES INCLDING TINNED	W 63	371	W 148	804	W 100	701	W 143	928	SAUCISSES,SAUCISSONS
02	DAIRY PRODCTS,BIRDS'EGGS		5891		6835		7237		7400	PRODUITS LAITIERS,OEUFS
022	MILK AND CREAM	W 2844	4093	W 2822	4936	W 3001	5279	W 3124	5182	LAIT ET CREME
0223	MILK AND CREAM FRESH	W 591	640	W 539	613	W 518	545	W 627	625	LAIT,CREME FRAIS
0224	MILK,CREAM PRESERVED ETC	W 2253	3453	W 2283	4323	W 2483	4734	W 2497	4558	LAIT,CREME CONS,CONC
02242	MILK DRY,1.5% FAT OR LES	W 1618	2697	W 1742	3667	W 1343	3221	W 1661	3573	LAIT POUDRE INF 1.5%
02249	MILK(EX DRY) PRSVD,SWEET	W 636	756	W 541	655	W 1140	1513	W 485	585	LAIT CONS,CONC SUCRE
024	CHEESE AND CURD	W 161	859	W 142	909	W 151	1014	W 187	1137	FROMAGE ET CAILLEBOTTE
03	FISH AND PREPARATIONS		587		591		706		1097	POISSONS ET PREPARATIONS
037	FISH ETC PREPD,PRSVD NES	W 139	322	W 99	193	W 97	317	W 443	895	POIS,CRUST,MOL PREPARES
0371	FISH PREPARD,PRESRVD NES	W 135	303	W 96	175	W 96	302	W 425	737	CONSERVES DE POISSONS
04	CEREALS AND PREPARATIONS		12778		20228		17335		16307	CEREALES ET PRODUITS
042	RICE	W 15055	6065	W 23906	8389	W 18193	7211	W 16470	5734	RIZ
0421	RICE IN HUSK OR HUSKED	W 15055	6065	W 23906	8389	W 18193	7211			RIZ SANS AUTRE PREPARATION
046	WHEAT ETC MEAL OR FLOUR	W 8117	2220	W 29427	7313	W 16465	3918	W 17108	4423	SEMOULE FARINE,FROMENT
04601	FLOUR OF WHEAT OR MESLIN	W 8114	2216	W 29426	7311	W 16305	3879	W 17108	4423	FARINE DE FROMENT
047	OTHER CEREAL MEALS,FLOUR	W 11	16	W 18	41	W 439	840	W 299	568	AUTRES SEMOULES,FARINES
04701	CEREAL FLOUR(NON–WHEAT)	W 11	16	W 18	41	W 439	840	W 299	568	FARINES DE CEREALES
048	CEREAL ETC PREPARATIONS	W 5745	3931	W 6145	4111	W 5990	4676	W 6759	4867	PREPTNS A BASE CEREALES
0483	MACARONI,SPAGHETTI ETC	W 4844	2463	W 5510	2647	W 5152	2898	W 5956	3033	PATES ALMENTAIRES
0484	BAKERY PRODUCTS	W 732	1156	W 495	1063	W 657	1278	W 512	1159	PRODUITS DE BOULANGERIE
04842	PASTRY, CAKES ETC	W 334	686	W 201	578	W 275	646	W 147	585	PATISSERIE ETC.
05	VEGETABLES AND FRUIT		7151		7956		6713		6246	LEGUMES ET FRUITS
054	VEG ETC FRSH,SMPLY PRSVD	W 8706	1960	W 15975	2652	W 6512	1542	W 2291	833	LEGUMES FRAIS,CONG,SECS
0545	OTHER FRESH VEGETABLES	W 7492	1433	W 15066	2303	W 5889	1377	W 1593	551	AUTRES LEGUMES FRAIS,REF
05459	FRESH VEGETABLES NES	W 7484	1424	W 15050	2288	W 5708	1338			LEGUMES FRAIS,REFRI NDA
056	VEGTBLES ETC PRSVD,PREPD	W 3156	2648	W 2659	2401	W 2449	2388	W 2771	2639	CONSERVES DE LEGUMES
0565	VEGTBLES PRSVD,PREPD NES	W 2153	2356	W 2645	2381	W 2122	2290	W 2771	2639	LEGUMES PREPARES CONSERVE
05659	OTH VEG PRESVD,PREPD NES	W 2114	2320	W 2640	2357	W 2104	2277	W 2291	2358	LEGUM PREPAP,CONSERV NDA
057	FRUIT,NUTS,FRESH,DRIED	W 2596	1952	W 2597	2254	W 3424	2140	W 912	1643	FRUITS FRAIS OU SECS
0579	FRUIT FRESH OR DRIED NES	W 1694	1129	W 1417	1128	W 2798	1275	W 535	867	FRUITS FRAIS,SECS NDA
05796	DATES,FRESH OR DRIED	W 1032	537	W 733	566	W 2370	790			DATTES FRAICHES OU SECHES
058	FRUIT PRESERVED,PREPARED	W 678	590	W 546	649	W 519	642	W 897	1131	CONSERVES DE FRUITS
0589	FRUIT PREPRD,PRESRVD,NES	W 390	305	W 423	456	W 267	338	W 632	709	FRUITS PREPARES CONSERV
05899	FRUIT,NUTS NES,PRESERVED	W 390	305	W 423	456	W 267	338	W 632	709	FRUITS PREP CONSERV NDA
06	SUGAR AND PREPS,HONEY		6781		6622		5844		5171	SUCRES ET PRODUITS
061	SUGAR AND HONEY	W 17635	6394	W 14426	6090	W 15847	5516	W 14479	4789	SUCRES ET MIEL
0612	REFINED SUGAR ETC	W 17614	6353	W 14419	6062	W 15701	5423	W 13629	4496	SUCRES RAFFINES
07	COFFEE,TEA,COCOA,SPICES		1058		1916		1834		1682	CAFE,THE,CACAO,EPICES
074	TEA AND MATE	W 258	286	W 500	718	W 387	593	W 468	529	THE ET MATE
0741	TEA	W 258	286	W 500	718	W 385	591	W 468	529	THE
075	SPICES	W 303	420	W 318	582	W 417	738	W 461	658	EPICES
0752	SPICES,EX PEPPER,PIMENTO	W 288	387	W 277	509	W 375	679	W 413	596	AUTRES EPICES
09	MISC EDIBLE PRODUCTS		4704		2450		2749		3010	PREP ALIMENTAIRES DIVERSES
098	EDIBLE PRODCTS,PREPS NES	W 2982	4603	W 815	2343	W 1081	2676	W 1049	2943	PREP ALIMENTAIRES NDA
09801	HOMOGENZD COMPOSITE FOOD	W 2080	2521	W 6	16	W 26	63	W 133	141	PREP ALIM COMPOSITES
09809	MISC FOOD PREPRTIONS NES	W 655	1636	W 576	1761	W 847	2166	W 750	2346	PREP ALIMENTAIRES NDA
1	BEVERAGES AND TOBACCO		11099		11801		11603		12413	BOISSONS ET TABACS
11	BEVERAGES		4859		6079		5976		7259	BOISSONS
111	NON–ALCOHL BEVERAGES NES	W 4067	1918	W 4437	2531	W 4394	2307	W 5925	3432	BOISSONS NON ALCOOLIQUES
11101	WATERS,ICE AND SNOW	W 2363	570	W 2343	659	W 2529	694	W 3537	996	EAU,EAUX MINERALES
11102	FLAVORED WATERS NON–ALCO	W 1704	1348	W 2094	1873	W 1866	1613	W 2388	2436	LIMONADES,EAUX GAZEUSES
112	ALCOHOLIC BEVERAGES	W 2895	2942	W 3052	3547	W 3077	3669	W 2944	3826	BOISSONS ALCOOLIQUES
1121	WINE OF FRESH GRAPES ETC	W 536	599	W 568	760	W 601	778	W 455	754	VINS DE RAISINS FRAIS
11212	WINE OF FRESH GRAPES	W 524	578	W 556	738	W 589	754	W 455	754	VINS DE MOUTS DE RAISINS
1123	BEER,ALE,STOUT,PORTER	W 2131	1642	W 2293	2076	W 2323	2251	W 2209	2414	BIERES
1124	DISTILLED ALCOHOLIC BEVS	W 215	683	W 161	673	W 146	629	W 280	658	ALCOOLS,EAUX–DE–VIE
12	TOBACCO AND MANUFACTURES		6239		5723		5627		5154	TABACS BRUTS FABRIQUES
122	TOBACCO,MANUFACTURED	W 531	5957	W 492	5577	W 455	5497	W 405	5047	TABACS FABRIQUES
1222	CIGARETTES	W 514	5835	W 492	5570	W 455	5488	W 405	5047	CIGARETTES
2	CRUDE MATERLS,EXCL FUELS		24724		24853		22715		23448	MAT BRUTES NON COMESTIBLES
24	CORK AND WOOD		385		987		841		1002	LIEGE ET BOIS
248	WOOD SHAPED,SLEEPERS	W 539	321	W 1136	612	W 1520	732	W 1831	861	BOIS SIMPLEMENT TRAVAILLES
2483	LUMBER SHAPED NON–CONIFR	W 537	305	W 1010	549	W 1202	534	W 1831	861	NON CONIFERES SCIES,RABOTES
24831	LUMBER SAWN ETC NON–CON	W 432	249	W 1009	548	W 1199	517	W 1831	861	SCIES LONGITUDINALEMENT
26	TEXTILE FIBRES AND WASTE		4330		5487		7830		5171	FIBRES TEXTILES
269	WASTE OF TEXTILE FABRICS	W 4881	4047	W 6329	5406	W 8800	7787	W 5978	5126	FRIPERIE DRILLES,CHIFFONS
26901	BULK TEXT WSTE,OLD CLTHG	W 4604	3820	W 5749	4890	W 8327	7273	W 5634	4856	ART ET ACCESS D'HABILLEMENT
29	CRUDE ANIMAL,VEG MAT NES		19849		17961		13564		17140	MATIERES BRUTES ANIM,VEGET
292	CRUDE VEG MATERIALS NES	W 3802	19796	W 3476	17961	W 2695	13563		17140	MAT BRUTES VEGETALES NDA
2922	NAT GUMS,RESINS,LACS,ETC	W 668	807	W 598	803	W 609	761	W 380	563	GOMME LAQUE
2924	VEG USED IN PHARMACY ETC	W 3037	18776	W 2731	16855	W 2059	12694	W 2657	16436	PLANTES MEDICINALES
3	MINERAL FUELS ETC		13142		15044		19587		17708	COMBUSTIBLES MINERAUX LUB
33	PETROLEUM AND PRODUCTS		12861		14749		19263		17427	PETROLE ET DERIVES
334	PETROLEUM PRODUCTS,REFIN	W 82288	12592	W 84336	14680	W 86772	18947	W 97065	17337	PRODUITS RAFFINES
3341	GASOLINE,OTH LIGHT OILS	W 9125	1580	W 9499	2010	W 8732	2661	W 20356	4817	ESSENCES POUR MOTEURS
33411	MOTOR,AVIATION SPIRIT	W 9109	1568	W 9494	2004	W 8373	2550			ESSENCES MOTEURS D'AVIONS
33419	OTH LIGHT PETROLEUM OILS	W 16	13	W 5	6	W 4	5	W 20356	4817	AUTRES HUILES LEGERES
3342	KEROSENE,OTH MEDIUM OILS	W 10291	1827	W 10583	2184	W 10943	3315			PETR LAMPANTS,AUT HUIL
33421	KEROSENE INCL JET FUEL	W 10291	1827	W 10582	2181	W 10943	3313			PETROLES LAMPANTS
3343	GAS OILS	W 21033	3410	W 23490	4465	W 28700	6967	W 32787	5998	GAS OILS
3344	FUEL OILS,NES	W 39022	4556	W 39279	4627	W 36332	4350	W 41555	4248	FUEL OILS
3345	LUBS,PETROLEUM OILS NES	W 2817	1218	W 1486	1395	W 2064	1654	W 2367	2273	HUILES LUBRIFIANTES
33451	LUBS(HIGH PETR CONT) ETC	W 2816	1216	W 1486	1395	W 2062	1651	W 2367	2273	HUILES LUBRIF,H LOURDES
4	ANIMAL,VEGETABLE OIL,FAT		3053		2732		3312		3247	HUILES,GRAISSES ANIM,VEG
42	FIXED VEGETABLE OIL,FAT		2948		2643		3205		3179	HUILES VEGETALES FIXES
424	FIXED VEG OIL NONSOFT	W 4041	2772	W 4525	2505	W 4403	2747	W 4543	2943	AUTRES HUILES VEG FIXES
4242	PALM OIL	W 2981	1921	W 3457	1908	W 3174	1968	W 3504	2200	HUILE DE PALME
4249	FIXED VEGETABLE OILS NES	W 910	709	W 1027	563	W 1149	713	W 937	641	HUILES VEGET FIXES NDA
5	CHEMCLS,RELATED PROD NES		12557		12196		12797		14872	PRODUITS CHIMIQUES
53	DYES,TANNING,COLOUR PROD		1066		1001		1009		872	PROD TEINTURE,COLORANTS
533	PIGMENTS,PAINTS,ETC	W 1188	978	W 1012	999	W 997	1008	W 708	872	PIGMENTS,PEINTURES,VERNIS
5334	VARNISHES,DISTEMPERS ETC	W 1153	923	W 957	900	W 924	936	W 648	737	PEINTURES A L'EAU
541	*MEDICINAL,PHARM PRODUCT	K 423864	5402	K 345217	6023	K 361333	5872		8508	PROD MEDICINAUX PHARMACEUT
5417	MEDICAMENTS	K 405379	5045	K 303415	5596	K 332911	5326	K 445000	6814	MEDICAMENTS

4. Special Imports C.I.F. by Commodities according to the S.I.T.C. (Rev. 2) in thousand U.S. Dollars
Importations Spéciales C.A.F. par Produits d'après la C.T.C.I. (Rév. 2) en milliers de Dollars E.U.

SITC CTCI	COMMODITY	1989			1990			1991			1992			PRODUIT
		WEIGHT POIDS		VALUE VALEUR	WEIGHT POIDS		VALUE VALEUR	WEIGHT POIDS		VALUE VALEUR	WEIGHT POIDS		VALUE VALEUR	
54173	— CONTAINING ALKALOIDS	K	228078	1989	K	162428	2257	K	192860	2274	K	278000	2718	MED CONTEN ALCALOIDES
54179	— CONTNG OTH SUBSTANCES	K	172857	2951	K	140709	3333	K	140022	3049	K	167000	4096	MED CONT AUT SUBSTANCES
5419	PHARMACEUTICAL GOODS NES	K	16389	276	K	24935	301	K	20359	316	K	62000	1480	PREP,ART PHARMACEUTIQUES
54199	OTH PHARMACEUTICAL GOODS	K	10126	134	K	8444	109	K	4877	110	K	47000	1305	AUT PREP PHARMACEUTIQUES
55	PERFUME,CLEANING ETC PRD			4568			3564			3976			4006	PROD POUR PARFUM,TOILETTE
553	PERFUMERY,COSMETICS,ETC	W	413	1503	W	233	1110	W	386	1446	W	305	1502	PRODUITS DE PARFUMERIE
554	SOAP,CLEANSING ETC PREPS	W	3895	3036	W	2872	2433	W	3010	2482	W	2693	2504	SAVONS,PRODUITS DETERSIFS
5541	SOAPS	W	3186	2363	W	2533	1886	W	2665	1870	W	2266	1756	SAVONS,PROD TENSIO-ACTIFS
5542	WASHING PREPARATIONS ETC	W	689	613	W	321	473	W	303	488	W	400	658	PROD ORG TENSIO-ACT NDA
58	PLASTIC MATERIALS ETC			363			597			726			129	MAT PLAST ARTIFICIELLES
59	CHEMICAL MATERIALS NES			716			678			838			1002	MAT PROD CHIMIQUES NDA
6	BASIC MANUFACTURES			29321			31240			36703			35118	ART MANUFACTURES
62	RUBBER MANUFACTURES NES			1260			1159			1410			1519	CAOUTCHOUC MANUFACTURE
625	RUBBER TYRES, TUBES ETC	W	335	986	W	282	964	W	340	1101	W	342	1154	PNEUS CAOUTCHOUC VULCANISE
6252	TYRES,NEW,BUS OR LORRY	W	271	772	W	230	738	W	265	836	W	255	850	PNEUS POUR AUTOBUS,CAMIONS
63	WOOD,CORK MANUFACTRS NES			2514			2703			1851			2110	OUVRAGES LIEGE ET BOIS
634	VENEERS,PLYWOOD,ETC	W	3848	1615	W	3142	1626	W	3072	1426	W	1096	557	PLACAGES,CONTRE-PLAQUES
6342	PLYWOOD OF WOOD SHEETS	W	1750	843	W	1472	1007	W	1774	821				BOIS CONTRE-PLAQUES
635	WOOD MANUFACTURES NES	W	451	787	W	554	1072	W	163	421	W	931	1553	ART MANUF EN BOIS NDA
64	PAPER,PAPERBOARD AND MFR			2628			3073			2915			2960	PAPIERS,CARTONS & OUVRAGES
641	PAPER AND PAPERBOARD	W	375	488	W	461	805	W	565	589	W	238	478	PAPIERS ET CARTONS
642	PAPER,ETC,PRECUT,ARTS OF	W	782	2141	W	636	2268	W	673	2326	W	802	2482	PAP,CARTONS DECOUPES
6421	PAPER ETC CONTAINERS	W	275	434	W	305	602	W	296	832	W	176	619	BOITES,SACS EMBALLAGES
6423	EXERCISE BOOKS ETC	W	243	973	W	175	1040	W	241	994	W	288	1283	REGISTRES,CAHIERS,CARNETS
65	TEXTILE YARN,FABRICS,ETC			11909			11131			13120			9960	FILS,TISSUS,ARTICLES TEXTILE
651	TEXTILE YARN	W	1200	4326	W	1207	7021	W	967	5332	W	567	3078	FILS TEXTILES
6513	COTTON YARN	W	435	1320	W	104	552	W	36	127	W	44	191	FILS DE COTON
6514	SYN FIB YRN,BULK,MONOFIL	W	102	338	W	129	483	W	226	786	W	37	135	FILS CONT 85% FIB TEXT SYNTH
6515	YARN OF 6514 FOR RETAIL	W	591	2468	W	943	5831	W	701	4392	W	484	2729	FILS CONT 85% FI SYNTHETIQ
65152	— OF DISCONTIN FIBRES	W	555	2340	W	930	5794	W	692	4335	W	484	2729	FILS CONT 85% FI TEXT SYNT
652	COTTON FABRICS,WOVEN	W	191	559	W	192	753	W	183	879	W	232	1215	TISSUS DE COTON
6522	WOVEN COTTON BLEACHD,ETC	W	185	540	W	190	742	W	174	863	W	224	1064	TISSUS COTON BLANCHIS ETC
65224	BLCHED COTTON FABRIC NES	W	183	520	W	188	735	W	174	862				AUT TIS PLUS 85% COT BLANCHI
65225	BLCHD COTN BLEND FAB NES										W	224	1064	AUT TIS MOINS 85% COT BLANCH
653	WOVN MAN-MADE FIB FABRIC	W	1332	5370	W	420	1999	W	659	3194	W	361	1744	TISSUS FIBRES SYNTH,ARTIF
6531	CONT SYNT WEAVES NONPILE	W	1261	5162	W	363	1745	W	583	2825	W	340	1677	TISSUS FIBRES SYNTH CONTINUE
658	TEXTILE ARTICLES NES	W	368	1089	W	338	1055	W	605	2875	W	940	3129	ART FACONNES MAT TEXTILES
6582	MADE-UP CANVAS GOODS	W	2	9	W	2	13	W	302	1807	W	294	805	BACHES,TENTES ETC
65821	MADE-UP COTTN CANVAS GDS										W	294	805	BACHES,TENTES DE COTON
6583	BLANKETS ETC NON ELECTRC	W	85	222	W	50	138	W	65	308	W	281	1064	COUVERTURES
65839	BLANKETS ETC NES	W	18	72	W	24	55	W	16	61	W	211	709	COUVERTURES AUTRES FIBRES
6589	OTH TEXTILE ARTICLES NES	W	102	404	W	88	310	W	93	340	W	219	799	AUT ART EN TEXTILES NDA
65899	TXTL ARTCLES NONKNIT NES	W	101	401	W	83	293	W	93	338	W	219	799	ART TIS AUT QUE BONNETERIE
66	NONMETAL MINERAL MFS NES			3064			4276			4207			5683	ART MIN NON METALLIQUES
661	LIME,CEMENT,BLDG PRODS	W	24550	1430	W	28545	1881	W	37562	2704	W	29278	2082	CHAUX,CIMENTS MAT CONSTR
6612	CEMENT	W	24237	1307	W	28015	1699	W	37432	2562	W	29233	2020	CIMENTS HYDRAULIQUES
662	CLAY,REFRACTORY BLDG PRD	W	680	383	W	1198	605	W	837	423	W	1789	1030	MAT CONST REFRACTAIRES
6624	BRICKS ETC NONREFRACTORY	W	553	297	W	1085	546	W	804	391	W	1623	827	BRIQUES ETC CERAM NON REFR
66245	GLAZED CERAMIC SETTS ETC	W	268	135	W	535	349	W	456	283	W	1224	664	AUT CARREAUX CERAMIQUE
664	GLASS	W	161	262	W	152	231	W	80	167	W	1761	1317	VERRE
6649	GLASS NES	W	79	179	W	30	59	W	20	32	W	1680	1238	VERRE NDA
66494	GLASS FIBRE AND PROD NES	W	20	33	W	3	7	W	17	17	W	1680	1238	LAINE DE VERRE,FIBRES
665	GLASSWARE	W	586	625	W	829	643	W	670	495	W	667	658	OUVRAGES EN VERRE
67	IRON AND STEEL			1951			2089			5463			4715	FER ET ACIER
673	IRON,STEEL SHAPES ETC	W	2355	1193	W	2311	1163	W	4200	2099	W	3439	1874	BARRES,PROFIL FER,ACIER
6731	IRON,STEEL WIRE ROD	W	1917	847	W	1793	732	W	3689	1671				FIL MACHINE FER,ACIER
6732	IRON,STEEL BARS ETC	W	248	218	W	456	373	W	319	258	W	2734	1474	BARRES FER,ACIER
67326	IRN,OTH STL BARS HOTROLD										W	2348	1187	BARRES PLEINES FER,ACIER
674	IRN,STL UNIV,PLATE,SHEET	W	372	377	W	508	488	W	1577	1723	W	824	1035	LARGES PLATS,TOLES
6744	IRN,STL HVY PLATE,ROLLED										W	524	878	TOLES LAMINEES PLUS 4.75 MM
67441	— OF IRON OR SIMPLE STL										W	524	878	TOLES NON ACIER FIN CARB
678	IRON,STL TUBES,PIPES,ETC	W	227	256	W	248	389	W	612	1382	W	1148	1502	TUBES,TUYAUX EN FONTE,FER
6783	IRON,STL TUBES,PIPES NES										W	992	962	AUT TUBES,TUYAUX FER,ACIER
6785	IRON,STEEL TUBE FITTINGS	W	37	50	W	97	243	W	187	1122	W	156	540	ACCESSOIRES DE TUYAUTERIE
68	NON-FERROUS METALS			1053			1245			922			872	METAUX NON FERREUX
684	ALUMINIUM	W	152	625	W	261	1066	W	178	747	W	284	872	ALUMINIUM
6842	ALUMINIUM,ALLOYS WORKED	W	151	623	W	261	1066	W	178	747	W	284	872	ALUMINIUM,ALLIAGES OUVRE
68421	ALUMINIUM BARS,WIRE,ETC	W	44	270	W	91	716	W	101	492	W	206	720	BARRES,PROFILES FILS ALU
69	METAL MANUFACTURES NES			4883			5537			6794			7264	ART MANUFACT EN METAL NDA
691	STRUCTURES AND PARTS NES	W	528	1352	W	715	1698	W	1432	3010	W	1109	1699	CONSTRUCT FER,ACIER,ALU
6911	STRUCTURES,PARTS IRN,STL	W	293	653	W	501	1073	W	1148	2313	W	1018	1305	CONSTRUCT FER,ACIER,FONTE
6912	STRUCTURES,PARTS ALUMNM	W	235	699	W	215	625	W	285	698	W	91	394	CONSTRUCT ALUMINIUM
695	TOOLS	W	91	545	W	147	767	W	121	707	W	477	1919	OUTILS A MAIN
6953	OTHER HAND TOOLS	W	75	412	W	84	447	W	51	369	W	225	1013	AUTRES OUTILS A MAIN
69539	HAND TOOLS ETC NES										W	138	709	OUTILLAGE A MAIN NDA
697	BASE MTL HOUSEHOLD EQUIP	W	311	799	W	154	640	W	244	634	W	616	1356	ART MENAGE MET COMMUNS
6974	BASE MTL DMSTC ARTIC NES	W	243	650	W	88	415	W	194	502	W	569	1210	ARTICLES NDA FONTE,FER,ETC
69741	— OF IRON OR STEEL										W	532	1080	ART NDA EN FONTE,FER
699	BASE METAL MFRS NES	W	682	1151	W	567	1486	W	679	1272			1502	ART MANUFACTURES MET NDA
7	MACHINES,TRANSPORT EQUIP			33084			38049			33306			42157	MACHINES MATERIEL TRANSPORT
71	POWER GENERATING EQUIPMT			1742			2377			2807			3106	MACHINES GENERATRICES
716	ROTATING ELECTRIC PLANT	W	51	1414	W	60	1794	W	67	2358	W	65	2735	APP ELECTR ROTATIFS,PIECES
7162	AC MTRS,GENRTRS,GEN SETS	W	13	122	W	15	134	W	5	83	W	37	928	MOTEURS ELECTRIQUES
71623	GEN SETS WITH PISTN ENGN	W	11	108	W	10	98	W	4	57	W	34	777	GROUPES MOTEUR EXPLOSION
7169	PTS NES OF ROT ELEC PLNT	W	33	1260	W	41	1595	W	60	2253	W	28	1806	PIECES MAC APP ROTATIFS
72	MACHS FOR SPCL INDUSTRYS			1254			2798			1554			855	MAC SPECIALES POUR INDUST
723	CIVIL ENGNEERG EQUIP ETC	W	145	323	W	228	926	W	51	567	W	9	118	APPAREILS DE GENIE CIVIL
726	PRINTG,BKBINDG MACHY,PTS	W	4	78	W	36	725	W	6	150				MACHINES POUR IMPRIMERIE
74	GENRL INDUSTRL MACHY NES			3547			3805			3495			3736	MACH APP INDUSTRIE
741	HEATING,COOLING EQUIPMNT	W	273	2193	W	239	1776	W	187	1642	W	145	1356	MACH CHAUFFAGE,PIECES
7415	AIR-CONDITIONING MACHNRY	W	183	1238	W	182	1273	W	159	1198	W	137	1199	GROUPES CONDITION AIR
742	PUMPS FOR LIQUIDS ETC	W	15	177	W	29	381	W	24	471	W	73	1109	POMPES MOTO-POMPES
7429	PTS NES OF PUMPS OF 742	W	1	20	W	2	33	W	11	223	W	49	799	PIECES POUR GROUPE 742
743	PUMPS NES,CENTRFUGES ETC	W	35	505	W	68	733	W	64	757	W	33	535	POMPES COMPRES,VENT ETC
75	OFFICE MACHNES,ADP EQUIP			1901			2806			2299			2870	MACH BUREAU TRAIT AUTOM
752	AUTOMTIC DATA PROC EQUIP	W	7	535	W	7	1094	W	9	813	W	11	732	MACH TRAIT INFORMATION
759	OFFICE,ADP MCH PTS,ACCES	W	15	930	W	17	1248	W	14	1008	W	28	1621	PIECES DU 751 ET 752
7591	OFFICE MACHINE PARTS NES	W	15	930	W	17	1248	W	14	1008	W	28	1621	PIECES DU 7511,7518
75911	TYPEWRTR PARTS,ACCES NES	W	11	775	W	12	1069	W	11	870	W	15	1407	PIECES DU 7511
76	TELECOMM,SOUND EQUIPMENT			6242			2494			4264			6353	EQUIPMENT DE TELECOM
764	TELECOM EQPT,PTS,ACC NES	W	112	5766	W	34	1872	W	61	3780	W	78	6252	EQUIP TELECOM,PIECES

4. Special Imports C.I.F. by Commodities according to the S.I.T.C. (Rev. 2) in thousand U.S. Dollars
Importations Spéciales C.A.F. par Produits d'après la C.T.C.I. (Rév. 2) en milliers de Dollars E.U.

SITC CTCI	COMMODITY	1989		1990		1991		1992		PRODUIT
		WEIGHT POIDS	VALUE VALEUR	WEIGHT POIDS	VALUE VALEUR	WEIGHT POIDS	VALUE VALEUR	WEIGHT POIDS	VALUE VALEUR	
7641	LINE TELEPHONE,ETC EQUIP	W 83	4730	W 10	1111	W 23	1153	W 29	1024	APP TELEPHON PAR FIL
7643	TV,RADIO TRANSMITTRS ETC	W 8	535	W 7	347	W 13	1501	W 3	107	APP EMET TELE RADIO
7649	PTS NES OF EQUIPMT OF 76	W 9	314	W 4	130	W 12	534	W 29	5002	PIECES DE LA DIV 76
76499	PARTS ETC OF SOUND EQUIP							W 21	4800	PIECES NDA POUR 763
77	ELECTRIC MACHNRY NES ETC		4270		6998		4293		7827	MACH APP ELECT NDA
772	SWITCHGEAR ETC,PARTS NES	W 86	960	W 87	1270	W 84	1351	W 377	3978	APP COUPURE,SECT ETC
7721	SWITCHGEAR ETC	W 84	919	W 79	1205	W 78	1312	W 377	3978	APP COUPURE,SECTIONMNT
773	ELECTR DISTRIBUTNG EQUIP	W 91	470	W 164	775	W 89	416	W 234	1154	EQUIPMT DISTRIBUTION ELECT
7731	INSULATED WIRE,CABLE ETC	W 91	464	W 164	772	W 89	414	W 234	1154	FILS,CABLES ISOLES ELECT
775	HOUSEHOLD TYPE EQUIP NES	W 224	1186	W 371	3174	W 257	1331	W 268	1182	MACH,APP USAGE DOMESTQUE
7752	DOM REFRIGERATRS,FREEZRS	W 134	796	W 125	739	W 126	849	W 218	990	REFRIG,CONGEL MENAGER
77521	DOMESTIC REFRIGERATORS	W 115	670	W 112	704	W 116	760	W 202	883	REFRIGERATEURS
7753	DOMSTC DISHWASHING MACHS	W 2	32	W 118	1981	W 9	47			MACH A LAVER VAISSELLE
778	ELECTRICAL MACHINERY NES	W 726	1322	W 647	1531	W 382	998	W 406	1283	AUTRES MACH ELECT NDA
7781	BATTERIES,ACCUMULATORS	W 682	896	W 612	1076	W 347	662	W 334	805	PILES ET ACCUMULATEURS
77811	PRIMARY BATTERIES,CELLS	W 593	671	W 504	668	W 295	447	W 276	619	PILES ELECTRIQUES,PIECES
78	ROAD VEHICLES		13245		15558		13989		17072	VEHICULES ROUTIERS
781	PASS MOTOR VEH EXC BUSES	W 884	5666	W 1338	9705	W 1238	9548	W 440	1401	AUTO TRANSPORT PERSONNES
782	LORRIES,SPCL MTR VEH NES	W 286	1589	W 144	1747	W 109	546	W 1349	11699	VEHICULES SPECIAUX,MARCH
7821	LORRIES,TRUCKS	W 270	1312	W 108	983	W 98	466	W 1349	11699	VEHICULES TRANSP MARCHAND
7822	SPECIAL MOTOR VEHCLS NES	W 16	277	W 36	764	W 11	80			VEHICULES USAGES SPECIAUX
783	ROAD MOTOR VEHICLES NES	W 173	1258	W 97	631	W 77	444	W 130	585	VEHICULES ROUTIERS NDA
7831	BUSES	W 145	1198	W 96	620	W 61	404	W 80	518	VOITURES TRANSPORT COMMUN
784	MOTOR VEH PRTS,ACCES NES	W 225	2956	W 201	2431	W 198	2549	W 223	2633	PIECES 722,781,782,783
7849	OTHER MOTOR VEHCL PARTS	W 224	2946	W 200	2431	W 198	2549	W 223	2633	PIECES 722,781,782,783
786	TRAILERS,NONMOTR VEH,NES	W 128	1366	W 100	589	W 126	421	W 30	236	REMORQUES,CADRES,CONTAIN
7868	OTH NONMOTR VEHICLES ETC	W 117	1281	W 81	557	W 75	379	W 30	236	AUT VEHIC NON AUTO,PIECES
78681	OTH NONMOTORIZED VEHCLS	W 105	1004	W 56	205	W 10	44			AUTRES VEHIC NON AUTO
79	OTHR TRANSPORT EQUIPMENT		769		1166		405		338	AUTRE MATERIEL TRANSPORT
8	MISC MANUFACTURED GOODS		22115		22295		22719		18198	ART MANUFACTURES DIVERS
821	*FURNITURE,PARTS THEREOF	W 1120	2272	W 1069	3435	W 1090	2656	W 1195	2667	MEUBLES ET PIECES
8219	FURNITURE AND PARTS NES	W 912	1867	W 938	3118	W 950	2303	W 1032	2431	AUTRES MEUBLES ET PIECES
82191	METAL FURNITURE NES	W 88	273	W 222	1161	W 141	609	W 62	326	MEUBLES NDA EN METAL
82192	WOOD FURNITURE NES	W 784	1442	W 679	1510	W 788	1594	W 895	1699	MEUBLES NDA EN BOIS
831	*TRAVEL GOODS,HANDBAGS	W 392	802	W 273	613	W 262	636	W 258	613	ARTICLES DE VOYAGE ETC
84	CLOTHING AND ACCESSORIES		6320		4945		4324		3635	VETEMENTS
842	MENS OUTERWEAR NOT KNIT	W 480	2324	W 266	1240	W 259	1109	W 214	1148	VET DESSUS POUR HOMMES
8423	— TROUSERS,BREECHES ETC	W 181	926	W 117	415	W 45	247	W 58	270	PANTALONS HOMMES MAT TEX
8429	— OTHER OUTER GARMENTS	W 236	1108	W 101	608	W 166	639	W 156	878	AUT VET DES HOM MAT TEX
843	WOMENS OUTERWEAR NONKNIT	W 193	1032	W 173	1168	W 192	961	W 151	827	VET DESSUS FEMMES MAT TEX
8439	— OTHER OUTER GARMENTS	W 111	447	W 81	630	W 121	627	W 126	675	AUT VET DES FEM MAT TEXT
844	UNDER GARMENTS NOT KNIT	W 327	1102	W 215	624	W 370	748	W 280	461	VETEMENT DESSOUS MAT TEX
846	UNDER GARMENTS KNITTED	W 192	835	W 174	781	W 104	547	W 87	450	SOUS VETS DE BONNETERIE
847	TEXTILE CLTHNG ACCES NES	W 173	763	W 145	551	W 214	678	W 132	428	ACCES VET MAT TEXT NDA
8471	— NOT KNITTED	W 169	747	W 141	501	W 208	640	W 132	428	ACCES VET MAT TEX NON BON
851	*FOOTWEAR	W 1486	4620	W 1259	3800	W 1385	4269	W 935	3213	CHAUSSURES
85101	FOOTWEAR RUBBER,PLASTIC	W 735	2084	W 757	1830	W 781	2210	W 500	1395	CHAUS SEMELLES CAOUTCH
85102	FOOTWEAR LEATHER	W 689	2309	W 437	1721	W 500	1703	W 404	1682	CHAUS SEMELLES EN CUIR
87	PRECISION INSTRUMNTS NES		684		1050		2427		771	INSTRUM,APPAR SCIENT NDA
872	MEDICAL INSTRUMENTS NES	W 20	272	W 15	601	W 34	1721	W 21	478	INSTR,APP MEDIC–CHIR NDA
87202	OTH MEDICAL INSTRUMENTS	W 14	214	W 14	502	W 32	1636	W 21	478	INSTRUM,APP MEDECINE
88	PHOTO EQU,OPTICL GDS ETC		555		544		401		799	APP,FOURN PHOTO,OP,MONTR
89	MISC MANUFCTRD GOODS NES		6507		7334		7663		6043	ART MANUFACTURES DIVERS
892	PRINTED MATTER	W 506	2395	W 435	2565	W 250	2076	W 279	2037	IMPRIMES
8921	PRINTED BOOKS,GLOBES,ETC	W 146	941	W 247	1769	W 139	1542	W 141	1305	LIVRES,BROCHURES,CARTES
89211	PRINTED BOOKS,PAMPHLETS	W 131	824	W 244	1745	W 139	1533	W 141	1305	LIVRES,BROCHURES
8922	NEWSPAPERS,PERIODICALS	W 134	617	W 46	220	W 6	53	W 12	163	JOURNAUX ET PERIODIQUES
8928	PRINTED MATTER NES	W 223	795	W 138	497	W 103	442	W 126	568	IMPRIMES NDA
893	ARTICLES OF PLASTIC NES	W 533	1319	W 566	1492	W 773	2033	W 610	1705	OUVRAGES EN MAT DIVIS 58
8931	PLSTC PACKG CONTNRS,LIDS	W 222	590	W 180	550	W 303	768	W 238	653	ART TRANSP EMBALLAGE ETC
8939	MISC PLASTIC ARTICLES	W 273	604	W 353	780	W 380	951	W 283	793	ART DIVERS EN MAT DIV 58
894	TOYS,SPORTING GOODS,ETC	W 111	683	W 108	987	W 99	762	W 111	658	VOITURES ENFANTS,JOUETS
899	OTHER MANUFACTURED GOODS		1242		1154		1876	W 237	625	AUT ART MANUF DIVERS NDA
8993	COMBUSTIBLE PRODUCTS ETC	W 225	264	W 268	429	W 516	1017	W 21	39	BOUGIES,ALLUMETTES ETC
89932	MATCHES	W 220	242	W 255	347	W 502	946			ALLUMETTES
9	GOODS NOT CLASSD BY KIND		5974		6922		6634		8975	ART TRANSACT NON CLASSES
931	*SPECIAL TRANSACTIONS	W 1063	5521	W 908	6431	W 1140	5869	W 1073	7805	TRANS.SPECIALES
951	*WAR FIREARMS,AMMUNITION	W 10	447	W 14	406	W 108	765		490	VEHIC BLINDES ARMES
961	*COIN NONGOLD,NONCURRENT			W 5	84				681	MONNAIES NON EMISES

5. Special Exports F.O.B. by Commodities according to the S.I.T.C. (Rev. 2) in thousand U.S. Dollars
Exportations Spéciales F.O.B. par Produits d'après la C.T.C.I. (Rév. 2) en milliers de Dollars E.U.

SITC CTCI	COMMODITY	1989		1990		1991		1992		PRODUIT
		WEIGHT POIDS	VALUE VALEUR	WEIGHT POIDS	VALUE VALEUR	WEIGHT POIDS	VALUE VALEUR	WEIGHT POIDS	VALUE VALEUR	
	ALL COMMODITIES		24890		24883		17347		15919	TOUS PRODUITS
0	FOOD AND LIVE ANIMALS		10846		9717		4593		3292	ALIMENTS,ANIMAUX VIVANTS
001	*LIVE ANIMALS FOR FOOD	W 8193	9021	W 6990	7868	W 2382	2685	W 308	326	ANIMAUX VIVANTS
0011	BOVINE SPECIES,LIVE	W 8188	9004	W 6990	7867	W 2381	2680	W 307	326	ESPECE BOVINE
00111	— PURE BRED FR BREEDING							W 307	326	BOVINS REPRODUCTEURS
01	MEAT AND PREPARATIONS		95		59		121		34	VIANDES ET PREPARATIONS
014	MEAT PREPD,PRSVD,NES ETC	W 10	27	W 9	25	W 22	76	W 10	34	CONSERVES DE VIANDES
0149	OTH PREPARD,PRESRVD MEAT	W 4	10	W 5	16	W 20	71	W 10	34	AUTRES PREP DE VIANDES
02	DAIRY PRODCTS,BIRDS'EGGS		79		33		62		51	PRODUITS LAITIERS,OEUFS
022	MILK AND CREAM	W 16	19	W 11	14	W 23	29	W 28	51	LAIT ET CREME
0224	MILK,CREAM PRESERVED ETC	W 1	2	W 1	2	W 3	6	W 28	51	LAIT,CREME CONS,CONC
02242	MILK DRY,1.5% FAT OR LES					W 1	3	W 28	51	LAIT POUDRE INF 1.5%
03	FISH AND PREPARATIONS		165		248		187		73	POISSONS ET PREPARATIONS
034	FISH,FRESH,CHILLED,FROZN	W 54	158	W 66	225	W 44	181	W 18	73	POISSON FRAIS, REFRIG,CONG
0341	FISH FRSH,CHLLD,EX FILLT	W 54	158	W 65	223	W 44	181			POISSON FRAIS,REFRIGERE
04	CEREALS AND PREPARATIONS		960		957		410		777	CEREALES ET PRODUITS
042	RICE	W 2407	892	W 2653	929	W 998	322	W 2258	726	RIZ
0421	RICE IN HUSK OR HUSKED	W 2407	892	W 2653	929	W 998	322			RIZ SANS AUTRE PREPARATION
046	WHEAT ETC MEAL OR FLOUR	W 45	15	W 5	2	W 206	56			SEMOULE FARINE,FROMENT
04601	FLOUR OF WHEAT OR MESLIN	W 45	15	W 5	2	W 206	56			FARINE DE FROMENT
05	VEGETABLES AND FRUIT		383		252		271		118	LEGUMES ET FRUITS
054	VEG ETC FRSH,SMPLY PRSVD	W 162	155	W 104	89	W 215	102	W 228	90	LEGUMES FRAIS,CONG,SECS
0542	LEGUMINOUS VEGETBLES DRY	W 13	11			W 140	44	W 228	90	LEGUMES A COSSE SECS
057	FRUIT,NUTS,FRESH,DRIED	W 132	143	W 157	116	W 194	147	W 28	23	FRUITS FRAIS OU SECS
0574	APPLES FRESH	W 73	85	W 20	33	W 18	28			POMMES FRAICHES
0579	FRUIT FRESH OR DRIED NES	W 17	16	W 105	55	W 153	98	W 28	23	FRUITS FRAIS,SECS NDA
05796	DATES,FRESH OR DRIED		1	W 63	23	W 120	78			DATTES FRAICHES OU SECHES
07	COFFEE,TEA,COCOA,SPICES		10		95		846		1829	CAFE,THE,CACAO,EPICES
071	COFFEE AND SUBSTITUTES		3	W 162	95	W 1077	843	W 2000	1773	CAFE ET SUCCEDANES
0711	COFFEE GREEN,ROASTED,SUB		3	W 162	95	W 1077	843	W 2000	1773	CAFE TORREFIE OU DECAFEINE
07111	COFFEE GREEN,HUSKS,SKINS		1	W 162	95	W 1077	843			CAFE NON TORREFIE
075	SPICES	W 3	2			W 1	1		56	EPICES
0752	SPICES,EX PEPPER,PIMENTO								56	AUTRES EPICES
081	*FEEDING STUFF FOR ANIML	W 1500	125	W 1700	165					NOURRITURE POUR ANIMAUX
0812	BRAN,POLLARD,SHARPS,ETC	W 1500	125	W 1700	165					SONS
09	MISC EDIBLE PRODUCTS		5		33		9		73	PREP ALIMENTAIRES DIVERSES
098	EDIBLE PRODCTS,PREPS NES	W 3	5	W 12	32	W 2	9	W 15	73	PREP ALIMENTAIRES NDA
09801	HOMOGENZD COMPOSITE FOOD			W 1	2		1	W 15	73	PREP ALIM COMPOSITES
1	BEVERAGES AND TOBACCO		107		15		19		45	BOISSONS ET TABACS
2	CRUDE MATERLS,EXCL FUELS		1728		1203		948		867	MAT BRUTES NON COMESTIBLES
21	HIDES,SKINS,FURS UNDRSSD		1278		918		661		174	CUIRS,PEAUX BRUTS
211	HIDES,SKINS,EXC FURS,RAW	W 652	1278	W 486	918	W 381	661	W 158	174	CUIRS ET PEAUX
2111	BOVINE,EQUINE HIDES,RAW	W 20	39	W 92	102	W 6	5	W 144	124	PEAUX DE BOVINS
2114	GOAT AND KID SKINS,RAW	W 284	653	W 68	189	W 128	248			PEAUX DE CAPRINS
2116	SHEEP SKIN WITH WOOL	W 324	526	W 244	412	W 239	408			PEAUX LAINEES D'OVINS
2119	SKIN NES,WASTE,USED LTHR	W 22	59	W 76	209			W 14	51	CUIRS ET PEAUX NDA
21199	HIDES AND SKINS NES,RAW	W 22	59	W 76	209			W 14	51	CUIRS,PEAUX NDA
26	TEXTILE FIBRES AND WASTE		22		12		38		304	FIBRES TEXTILES
269	WASTE OF TEXTILE FABRICS	W 20	22	W 9	12	W 25	38	W 259	298	FRIPERIE DRILLES,CHIFFONS
26901	BULK TEXT WSTE,OLD CLTHG	W 17	15	W 6	8	W 6	9	W 250	276	ART ET ACCESS D'HABILLEMENT
29	CRUDE ANIMAL,VEG MAT NES		383		239		212		371	MATIERES BRUTES ANIM,VEGET
291	CRUDE ANIMAL MTRIALS NES	W 6	150	W 3	152	W 1	169		101	MATIERES BRUTES ANIMALES
2919	OTH ANIMAL MATERIALS NES	W 5	147	W 2	149	W 1	169		101	MAT ORIGINE ANIMALE NDA
29198	AMBERGRIS,CIVET,MUSK,ETC	W 5	147	W 1	147	W 1	164		101	AMBRE GRIS,CIVETTE,MUSC
292	CRUDE VEG MATERIALS NES	W 255	233	W 66	87	W 69	43	W 271	270	MAT BRUTES VEGETALES NDA
2922	NAT GUMS,RESINS,LACS,ETC	W 250	223	W 64	81	W 67	40	W 199	208	GOMME LAQUE
4	ANIMAL,VEGETABLE OIL,FAT		9		9		102		45	HUILES,GRAISSES ANIM,VEG
411	*ANIMAL OILS AND FATS		3			W 71	98			HUILES,GRAISSES ANIMALES
4113	ANIML OIL,FAT,GREASE NES		3			W 71	98			HUILES,GRAISSES ANIMALES NDA
41133	LARD STEARIN AND OIL,ETC					W 68	96			STEARINE SOLAIRE
5	CHEMCLS,RELATED PROD NES		107		41		49		28	PRODUITS CHIMIQUES
6	BASIC MANUFACTURES		262		275		457		771	ART MANUFACTURES
65	TEXTILE YARN,FABRICS,ETC		5		3		56		298	FILS,TISSUS,ARTICLES TEXTILE
658	TEXTILE ARTICLES NES		2			W 8	9	W 74	236	ART FACONNES MAT TEXTILES
6582	MADE–UP CANVAS GOODS							W 30	96	BACHES,TENTES ETC
65821	MADE–UP COTTN CANVAS GDS							W 30	96	BACHES,TENTES DE COTON
6589	OTH TEXTILE ARTICLES NES		2			W 7	6	W 44	141	AUT ART EN TEXTILES NDA
65899	TXTL ARTCLES NONKNIT NES		2			W 7	6	W 44	141	ART TIS AUT QUE BONNETERIE
67	IRON AND STEEL		3		7		108			FER ET ACIER
674	IRN,STL UNIV,PLATE,SHEET		1		7	W 124	94			LARGES PLATS,TOLES
69	METAL MANUFACTURES NES		174		171		238		405	ART MANUFACT EN METAL NDA
692	METAL TANKS,BOXES,ETC	W 71	138	W 72	145	W 72	158	W 61	135	RECIPIENTS METALLIQUES
6924	MTL TRANSPORT BOXES ETC	W 71	138	W 72	145	W 71	154	W 61	135	FUTS,TAMBOURS,BIDONS
69241	STL TRANSPORT BOXES ETC	W 67	132	W 64	137	W 69	150	W 61	135	FUTS,TAMBOURS,BIDONS FER
695	TOOLS		5		1	W 18	46	W 8	113	OUTILS A MAIN
6953	OTHER HAND TOOLS				1	W 1	16	W 8	113	AUTRES OUTILS A MAIN
69539	HAND TOOLS ETC NES							W 8	113	OUTILLAGE A MAIN NDA
699	BASE METAL MFRS NES	W 10	14	W 1	6	W 22	9	W 158	158	ART MANUFACTURES MET NDA
6997	IRON,STEEL ARTICLES NES							W 137	129	OUV FONTE,FER,ACIER NDA
69979	IRN,STL MANUFACTURES NES							W 137	129	AUT OUVRAGES EN FER NDA
7	MACHINES,TRANSPORT EQUIP		2279		1532		1441		1260	MACHINES MATERIEL TRANSPORT
71	POWER GENERATING EQUIPMT		75		115		245			MACHINES GENERATRICES
713	INTRNL COMBUS PSTN ENGIN	W 7	47	W 2	57		217			MOTEURS EXPL COMB INT, PIECE
7131	AIRCRAFT PSTN ENGINS,PTS		1				202			MOTEURS EXPL P.AVIATION, PIE
71311	AIRCRAFT PISTON ENGINES		1				202			MOTEURS EXPL P.AVIATION
72	MACHS FOR SPCL INDUSTRYS		13		108		26			MAC SPECIALES POUR INDUST
74	GENRL INDUSTRL MACHY NES		293		101		44			MACH APP INDUSTRIE
749	NONELEC MACH PTS,ACC NES	W 95	259	W 10	52		3			PIECES MACH NON ELEC NDA
7499	OTH NONELEC MCHY PTS NES	W 95	259	W 10	50		3			PIECES NON ELECT NDA
74999	MACH PARTS NONELEC NES	W 95	259	W 10	50		3			PIECES MACHINES NDA
75	OFFICE MACHNES,ADP EQUIP		106		64		3			MACH BUREAU TRAIT AUTOM
759	OFFICE,ADP MCH PTS,ACCES	W 1	96	W 1	55					PIECES DU 751 ET 752
7591	OFFICE MACHINE PARTS NES	W 1	96	W 1	55					PIECES DU 7511,7518
76	TELECOMM,SOUND EQUIPMENT		112		93		41		174	EQUIPMENT DE TELECOM
764	TELECOM EQPT,PTS,ACC NES	W 3	107	W 1	79	W 1	34	W 11	174	EQUIP TELECOM,PIECES
7641	LINE TELEPHONE,ETC EQUIP	W 1	95		7		9			APP TELEPHON PAR FIL
7649	PTS NES OF EQUIPMT OF 76	W 3	6		13		2	W 11	174	PIECES DE LA DIV 76
76493	TELECOMM EQUIPMT PTS NES							W 11	174	PIECES 761,762,764.3,8
78	ROAD VEHICLES		658		495		537		585	VEHICULES ROUTIERS
781	PASS MOTOR VEH EXC BUSES	W 48	178	W 49	298	W 63	347	W 75	467	AUTO TRANSPORT PERSONNES
784	MOTOR VEH PRTS,ACCES NES	W 18	465	W 28	162	W 8	156	W 7	118	PIECES 722,781,782,783

Djibouti

5. Special Exports F.O.B. by Commodities according to the S.I.T.C. (Rev. 2) in thousand U.S. Dollars
Exportations Spéciales F.O.B. par Produits d'après la C.T.C.I. (Rév. 2) en milliers de Dollars E.U.

SITC CTCI	COMMODITY	1989		1990		1991		1992		PRODUIT
		WEIGHT POIDS	VALUE VALEUR	WEIGHT POIDS	VALUE VALEUR	WEIGHT POIDS	VALUE VALEUR	WEIGHT POIDS	VALUE VALEUR	
7849	OTHER MOTOR VEHCL PARTS	W 18	465	W 28	162	W 8	156	W 7	118	PIECES 722,781,782,783
79	OTHR TRANSPORT EQUIPMENT		990		497		495		501	AUTRE MATERIEL TRANSPORT
792	AIRCRAFT ETC	W 24	981		427	W 5	333		428	APP NAVIGATION AERIENNE
7929	AIRCRAFT PARTS NES	W 24	981	W 21	410	W 5	333	W 2	422	PIECES DU 792
793	SHIPS AND BOATS ETC			W 7	69	W 13	155		73	NAVIRES BATEAUX,ETC
7932	SHIPS AND BOATS NES			W 4	38	W 13	71		73	NAVIRES ET BATEAUX
79321	YACHTS,SPORTS VESSLS ETC			W 4	38	W 12	69	W 8	62	BATEAUX DE PLAISANCE
7938	TUGS,SPECIAL VESSELS ETC			W 2	11		84			REMORQUEURS,BATEAUX SPEC
79382	SPECL PURPOSE VESSLS ETC						84			BAT–PHARES,–POMPES,DRAGUES
8	MISC MANUFACTURED GOODS		155		116		195		90	ART MANUFACTURES DIVERS
87	PRECISION INSTRUMNTS NES		89		44		94			INSTRUM,APPAR SCIENT NDA
874	MEASURNG,CONTROLNG INSTR	W 1	80		22	W 2	89			INSTRUMENTS DE MESURE
8743	GAS,LIQUID CONTROL INSTR		21		10	W 2	86			APP,INSTR MESURE FLUIDES
89	MISC MANUFCTRD GOODS NES		37		58		41		73	ART MANUFACTURES DIVERS
9	GOODS NOT CLASSD BY KIND		9391		11970		9538		9481	ART TRANSACT NON CLASSES
931	*SPECIAL TRANSACTIONS	W 830	9391	W 801	11845	W 703	9538	W 787	9481	TRANS.SPECIALES
941	*ZOO ANIMALS,PETS ETC			W 305	118					ANIMAUX DE ZOO ETC

1. HISTORICAL SERIES, 1962–1996 GENERAL TRADE, IMPORTS C.I.F., EXPORTS F.O.B.
SERIES HISTORIQUES, 1962–1996 COMMERCE GENERAL, IMPORTATIONS C.A.F., EXPORTATIONS F.O.B

YEAR ANNEE	VALUE IN MILLION E.C. DOLLARS / VALEUR EN MILLION E.C. DOLLARS — MERCHANDISE – MARCHANDISE		GOLD – OR		CONVERSION FACTORS U.S. CENTS PER E.C. DOLLAR / FACTEURS DE CONVERSION CENTS E.U. PAR E.C. DOLLAR		INDEX NUMBERS – INDICES — QUANTUM		UNIT VALUE / VALEUR UNITAIRE	
	IMPORTS	EXPORTS	IMPORTS	EXPORTS	IMPORTS	EXPORTS	IMPORTS	EXPORTS	IMPORTS	EXPORTS
1962	12.80	7.70			58.3340	58.3340				
1963	12.00	7.80			58.3340	58.3340				
1964	15.00	8.60			58.3340	58.3340				
1965	17.20	9.50			58.3340	58.3340				
1966	16.90	10.10			58.3340	58.3340				
1967	17.20	10.80			57.6500	57.6500				
1968	20.10	12.40			50.0000	50.0000				
1969	24.70	14.20			50.0000	50.0000				
1970	31.50	11.80			50.0000	50.0000	31	60	21	16
1971	33.00	12.30			50.7166	50.7166	34	55	25	18
1972	32.90	13.50			52.1216	52.1216	30	54	25	19
1973	32.30	16.70			51.0808	51.0808	38	46	28	30
1974	38.90	20.90			48.7301	48.7301	33	46	34	33
1975	45.00	24.60			46.2878	46.2878	33	42	49	41
1976	49.80	29.10			38.0480	38.0480	34	54	51	41
1977	59.10	32.30			37.0370	37.0370	38	51	55	48
1978	76.80	42.90			37.0370	37.0370	43	63	59	53
1979	60.00	25.40			37.0370	37.0370	32	33	67	59
1980	128.70	26.30			37.0370	37.0370	54	27	89	73
1981	134.10	51.80			37.0370	37.0370	56	53	90	71
1982	128.20	66.00			37.0370	37.0370	47	57	89	76
1983	121.70	74.20			37.0370	37.0370	45	58	88	84
1984	156.10	69.20			37.0370	37.0370	62	59	91	74
1985	149.40	76.80			37.0370	37.0370	21	32		
1986	150.69	117.24			37.0370	37.0370	24	43		
1987	179.22	129.59			37.0370	37.0370	28	49		
1988	236.34	146.41			37.0370	37.0370	30	55		
1989	289.08	121.77			37.0370	37.0370	35	45		
1990	318.39	148.59			37.0370	37.0370	100	100	100	100
1991	295.98	146.62			37.0370	37.0370	90	94	104	105
1992	300.02	150.81			37.0370	37.0370		97		100
1993	253.00	129.00			37.0370	37.0370		95		89
1994	260.00	122.00			37.0370	37.0370		107		97
1995	317.10	122.16			37.0370	37.0370		68		100
1996	350.85	138.11			37.0370	37.0370				

2. IMPORTS BY BROAD ECONOMIC CATEGORY AND EXPORTS BY INDUSTRIAL ORIGIN. (PERCENTAGE OF TOTAL VALUE)
IMPORTATIONS PAR CATEGORIES ECONOMIQUES ET EXPORTATIONS PAR BRANCHE D'ACTIVITE.(EN POURCENTAGE DE LA VALEUR TOTALE)

IMPORTS – IMPORTATIONS

	1990	1991	1992	1993	1994	1995	1996
TOTAL IMPORTS–IMPORTATIONS TOTALES	100.	100.		100.	100.	100.	100.
1 FOOD BEV–ALIMENTATION BOISSONS	20.7	22.9		22.9	24.4	23.1	21.9
11 PRIMARY–PRODUITS DE BASE	4.8	5.0		6.1	7.0	6.5	6.4
111 FOR INDUSTRY–POUR L'INDUSTRIE	0.2	0.3		0.5	0.6	0.6	0.6
112 FOR HOUSEHOLDS–POUR LES MENAGES	4.6	4.7		5.5	6.5	5.9	5.8
12 PROCESSED–PRODUITS ELABORES	15.9	18.0		16.8	17.3	16.5	15.5
121 FOR INDUSTRY–POUR L'INDUSTRIE	3.8	4.1		4.1	3.7	3.5	3.8
122 FOR HOUSEHOLDS–POUR LES MENAGES	12.1	13.9		12.7	13.6	13.0	11.7
2 IND SUPPLIES–APPROV INDUSTRIELS	37.1	35.6		39.0	36.5	36.5	37.9
21 PRIMARY–PRODUITS DE BASE	0.8	0.7		0.6	0.6	0.8	0.4
22 PROCESSED–PRODUITS ELABORES	36.3	34.9		38.5	35.9	35.7	37.5
3 FUELS–COMBUSTIBLES	6.1	7.9		6.1	6.4	5.3	6.3
31 PRIMARY–PRODUITS DE BASE	0.7	1.2		0.8	0.8	0.6	0.8
32 PROCESSED–PRODUITS ELABORES	5.3	6.7		5.3	5.6	4.7	5.5
321 MOTOR SPIRIT–ESSENCE				2.5	2.6	2.1	2.5
322 OTHER–AUTRES	5.3	6.7		2.8	3.0	2.6	3.0
4 MACHINERY–EQUIPEMENT	16.7	13.5		10.3	11.8	16.1	13.3
41 CAPITAL EQUIPMENT–MACHINES	16.7	13.5		9.2	10.8	14.8	12.0
42 PARTS–PIECES ACCESSOIRES				1.1	1.1	1.3	1.3
5 TRANSPORT–TRANSPORT	10.5	9.1		7.9	7.7	6.8	7.9
51 PASSENGER CARS–AUTOMOBILES				2.5	2.0	1.9	2.6
52 OTHER–AUTRES	0.5	0.6		3.0	3.4	2.9	3.1
521 INDUSTRIAL–INDUSTRIELS	0.5	0.6		2.9	3.3	2.8	3.0
522 NON INDUSTRIAL–NON INDUSTRIEL				0.1	0.1	0.0	0.1
53 PARTS–PIECES ACCESSOIRES	10.0	8.5		2.4	2.3	2.1	2.2
6 CONSUM GOODS–BIENS CONSOMMATION	8.9	11.1		13.6	13.1	12.1	12.5
61 DURABLE–DURABLES	1.3	1.9		3.4	3.1	2.6	2.6
62 SEMI DURABLE–SEMI DURABLES	4.9	5.7		5.7	5.6	5.3	5.5
63 NON DURABLE–NON DURABLES	2.7	3.5		4.5	4.4	4.2	4.4
7 GOODS NES–BIENS NDA	0.0	0.0		0.1	0.1	0.1	0.1

EXPORTS – EXPORTATIONS

	1990	1991	1992	1993	1994	1995	1996
TOTAL EXPORTS–EXPORTATIONS TOTALES	100.	100.		100.	100.	100.	100.
1 AGRICULTURE	62.3	64.4		64.5	55.5	47.8	46.3
2 MINING QUARRY–INDUS EXTRACTIVES	0.1	0.4		0.1	0.5	1.3	1.6
3 MANUFACTURING–IND MANUFACTUR	37.6	35.2		35.4	44.0	51.0	52.1
31 FOOD BEV TOBACCO–ALIM BOISS TAB	3.0	2.7		1.6	2.6	2.8	2.2
32 TEXTILES–INDUSTRIES TEXTILES	4.2	1.1		0.6	0.7	0.8	0.3
33 WOOD & PRODUCTS–BOIS & PRODUITS	1.6	2.1		0.0	0.1	0.0	0.4
34 PAPER & PRODUCTS–PAPIER & PRODT	0.1	0.1		2.4	1.6	0.1	0.1
35 CHEMICALS–INDUSTRIES CHIMIQUES	24.2	23.8		28.2	37.0	44.0	47.6
36 NON METAL MIN–MIN NON METAL	0.0	0.0		0.0	0.0	0.0	0.0
37 BASIC METAL–IND METAL BASE				0.0	0.0	0.0	
38 METAL MANUF–MANUF METAL	4.2	4.9		2.4	1.7	3.0	1.4
39 OTH MANUF IND–AUTRES MANUF	0.2	0.4		0.3	0.2	0.1	0.1

3. TRADE BY PRINCIPAL COUNTRIES OF PRODUCTION AND LAST CONSIGNMENT (VALUE IN THOUSAND U.S. DOLLARS)
ECHANGES SELON LES PRINCIPAUX PAYS DE PRODUCTION ET DE DERNIERE CONSIGNATION (VALEUR EN MILLIERS DE DOLLARS EU)

COUNTRIES–PAYS	GENERAL IMPORTS C.I.F. IMPORTATIONS GENERALES C.A.F				
	1992	1993	1994	1995	1996
World	105442	93790	96315	117269	129943
Africa	66	30	249	98	115
Americas	73004	67161	69738	78566	94006
Northern America	38744	37308	36513	41350	55816
LAIA	1773	2041	1551	2128	3020
CACM	777	682	761	1031	1347
Caribbean	30776	26206	29819	32206	32960
Rest of America	934	923	1093	1852	863
As.ex F.USSR	6434	6163	6956	7332	9360
Eur.x F.USSR	24298	20392	19282	31148	26294
EU	22666	18389	17522	29372	24411
EFTA	1533	1321	1182	1251	930
East Europe	98	84	68	134	124
Other Europe				0	598
Former USSR	2	22	43	53	6
Oceania	59	6	8	62	162
USA/Etats–Unis d'Amer	34514	35230	34471	38933	53170
United Kingdom	16970	11817	12164	15829	16906
Trinidad and Tobago	12056	10404	12052	12896	16253
Japan/Japon	4833	3994	4546	5373	7218
Saint Lucia/St. Lucie	3643	3020	4986	5938	3560
Barbados/Barbade	3379	3192	3717	4262	4757
St Vincent & Grenadines	2934	2993	3002	3032	2580
Canada	4229	2074	2042	2416	2647
France,Monac	969	534	910	7673	2372
Jamaica/Jamaïque	1792	1832	1878	1835	2144
Germany/Allemagne	1480	1216	1417	3129	2056
Netherlands/Pays–Bas	1814	1673	1432	1473	1724
Netherlands Antilles	1930	1026	716	984	947
Grenada/Grenade	982	834	637	893	1136
Switz.Liecht	1045	1028	781	863	614
Brazil/Brésil	641	1040	785	810	672
Venezuela	639	566	394	1056	1129
Guyana	627	605	679	1285	449
Guadeloupe	1280	767	715	592	
Antigua and Barbuda	807	770	684	548	543
China/Chine	473	612	718	572	540
Italy/Italie	524	446	706	544	357
Costa Rica	477	422	394	451	816
Saint–Kitts–Nevis	493	357	549	539	534
Martinique	365	798	679	432	
Spain/Espagne	133	1666	78	182	101
Hong Kong	610	544	384	291	324
Dominican Republic	1020	128	147	189	465
Norway,SVD,JM	487	292	401	388	314
Colombia/Colombie	175	129	301	168	1074
Guatemala	293	163	264	580	521
Denmark/Danemark	374	398	387	175	397
Tfyr Macedonia		598	510	391	230
Panama	297	318	289	400	293
Belgium–Luxembourg	45	393	134	105	205
Korea, Republic of	78	174	169	213	208
Singapore/Singapour	221	237	102	132	71
Sweden/Suède	211	91	175	104	144
Malta/Malte					598
Israel/Israël	16	5	282	111	168
Mexico/Mexique	89	167	30	72	105
Belize/Bélize	11		125	167	114
Argentina/Argentine	128	126	34	15	33
Thailand/Thaïlande	20	40	75	107	82
Indonesia/Indonésie	19	58	44	23	104
Zimbabwe	13	18	110	65	39
Ireland/Irlande	46	104	18	28	21
Portugal	20	20	39	55	74
Finland/Finlande	76	14	32	51	28
Honduras		72	82		10

COUNTRIES–PAYS	GENERAL EXPORTS F.O.B. EXPORTATIONS GENERALES F.O.B.				
	1992	1993	1994	1995	1996
Monde	53463	48011	45230	45244	51153
Afrique	1	0	0		
Amériques	20917	21988	23543	27505	28708
Amérique du Nord	2541	2751	3454	3677	3740
ALAI	71	28	42	16	
MCAC		3	3	55	5
Caraïbes	17480	17695	18371	20950	22514
Autre Amérique	826	1511	1673	2807	2449
Asie l'URSS exclus	48	1	114	12	43
Europe l'URSS exclus	31291	25999	21501	17589	22238
UE	31289	25997	21501	17589	22237
AELE			0		1
Europe de l'Est					
Autre de l'Europe	1		0		
Ancienne URSS					
Océanie	233				3
United Kingdom	26100	24400	21483	17297	18205
Jamaica/Jamaïque	5971	4376	4493	5374	10661
USA/Etats–Unis d'Amer	2280	2728	3447	3661	3726
Saint Lucia/St. Lucie	1496	1637	2376	2712	2221
Trinidad and Tobago	1845	1486	1798	2337	2143
Guadeloupe	2176	2267	2080	2772	
Antigua and Barbuda	1753	1459	1473	1871	2573
Guyana	780	1464	1557	2737	2384
Barbados/Barbade	1570	1175	1606	1567	1423
Italy/Italie	5111	1582			
Netherlands Antilles	0	1855	1254	892	671
France,Monac	72	7	1	246	4020
Grenada/Grenade	631	1209	878	676	686
St Vincent & Grenadines	933	694	860	894	617
Saint–Kitts–Nevis	712	600	671	826	1002
Martinique	192	512	447	549	
Montserrat	105	144	74	106	117
British Virgin Islds		39	82	117	129
Bahamas	27	32	58	125	98
Cuba	62	168	110		
Canada	261	24	5	16	14
Belize/Bélize	43	46	90	70	44
Vanuatu	225				
Japan/Japon	32	1	98	12	43
Haiti/Haïti				35	141
Dominican Republic			74	39	8
Venezuela	42	28	29	11	
El Salvador				55	
Germany/Allemagne	3			14	11
Netherlands/Pays–Bas	0	0	16		0
Mexico/Mexique	1		10	5	
Israel/Israël			16		
Portugal	3			13	
Costa Rica		3	3		5
Belgium–Luxembourg		7			
Brazil/Brésil			3		
Tfyr Macedonia		2	0		
Switz.Liecht			0		1
Malta/Malte	1		0		
Korea, Republic of	0				
Ireland/Irlande					0
Panama			0		
China/Chine			0		

(VALUE AS PERCENTAGE OF WORLD TOTAL)(VALEURS EN POURCENTAGE DU TOTAL MONDIAL)

	1987	1988	1989	1990	1991	1992	1993	1994	1995	1996
Africa	0.0	0.0	0.0	0.1	0.0	0.1	0.0	0.3	0.1	0.1
Americas	65.1	62.0	65.2	65.6	68.8	69.2	71.6	72.4	67.0	72.3
Northern America	26.5	28.5	37.8	35.8	35.8	36.7	39.8	37.9	35.3	43.0
LAIA	1.7	1.5	2.6	2.2	2.6	1.7	2.2	1.6	1.8	2.3
CACM	0.6	0.4	0.5	0.7	0.5	0.7	0.7	0.8	0.9	1.0
Caribbean	35.5	30.7	23.6	26.4	29.6	29.2	27.9	31.0	27.5	25.4
Rest of America	0.8	1.0	0.8	0.4	0.3	0.9	1.0	1.1	1.6	0.7
As.ex F.USSR	9.1	11.6	11.1	10.1	8.3	6.1	6.6	7.2	6.3	7.2
Eur.x F.USSR	25.6	25.9	23.5	24.2	22.8	23.0	21.7	20.0	26.6	20.2
EU	24.5	25.3	22.7	22.9	21.3	21.5	19.6	18.2	25.0	18.8
EFTA	1.0	0.6	0.7	1.1	1.2	1.5	1.4	1.2	1.1	0.7
East Europe	0.1	0.1	0.1	0.2	0.3	0.1	0.1	0.1	0.1	0.1
Other Europe	0.0	0.0		0.0	0.0				0.0	0.5
Former USSR	0.1	0.3	0.1	0.0	0.0	0.0	0.0	0.0	0.0	0.0
Oceania	0.0	0.1	0.1	0.1	0.0	0.1	0.0	0.0	0.1	0.1
USA/Etats–Unis d'Amer	23.3	25.3	31.2	33.3	31.4	32.7	37.6	35.8	33.2	40.9
United Kingdom	17.6	18.4	14.4	14.4	13.8	16.1	12.6	12.6	13.5	13.0
Trinidad and Tobago	8.8	8.4	7.2	9.2	10.0	11.4	11.1	12.5	11.0	12.5
Japan/Japon	5.0	5.3	5.8	6.2	5.6	4.6	4.3	4.7	4.6	5.6
Saint Lucia/St. Lucie	10.3	8.1	3.9	4.2	4.2	3.5	3.2	5.2	5.1	2.7
Barbados/Barbade	3.5	3.6	3.2	2.5	3.3	3.2	3.4	3.9	3.6	3.7
St Vincent & Grenadines	2.3	1.8	2.0	2.1	2.5	2.8	3.2	3.1	2.6	2.0
Canada	3.2	3.2	6.6	2.5	4.4	4.0	2.2	2.1	2.1	2.0
France,Monac	1.6	1.3	3.4	1.5	1.3	0.9	0.6	0.9	6.5	1.8
Jamaica/Jamaïque	2.4	1.9	1.7	1.4	1.9	1.7	2.0	2.0	1.6	1.6

	1987	1988	1989	1990	1991	1992	1993	1994	1995	1996
Afrique	0.0					0.0	0.0	0.0		
Amériques	32.3	29.8	42.0	42.9	38.7	39.1	45.8	52.1	60.8	56.1
Amérique du Nord	5.0	5.7	8.6	11.4	5.4	4.8	5.7	7.6	8.1	7.3
ALAI	0.0	0.0	0.0		0.0	0.1	0.1	0.1	0.0	
MCAC							0.0	0.0	0.1	0.0
Caraïbes	25.8	22.7	32.8	30.5	33.1	32.7	36.9	40.6	46.3	44.0
Autre Amérique	1.5	1.4	0.6	1.0	0.2	1.5	3.1	3.7	6.2	4.8
Asie l'URSS exclus	0.0	0.0	0.0	0.0	0.0	0.1	0.0	0.3	0.0	0.1
Europe l'URSS exclus	67.7	70.2	57.9	56.9	61.2	58.5	54.2	47.5	38.9	43.5
UE	67.7	70.2	57.9	56.9	61.2	58.5	54.1	47.5	38.9	43.5
AELE				0.0	0.0			0.0		0.0
Europe de l'Est				0.0	0.0					
Autre de l'Europe						0.0		0.0		
Ancienne URSS				0.2						
Océanie	0.0		0.0	0.0		0.4				0.0
United Kingdom	67.3	60.9	52.1	49.6	53.5	48.8	50.8	47.5	38.2	35.6
Jamaica/Jamaïque	9.0	10.4	13.9	12.3	10.3	11.2	9.1	9.9	11.9	20.8
USA/Etats–Unis d'Amer	4.0	5.3	8.1	11.2	5.2	4.3	5.7	7.6	8.1	7.3
Saint Lucia/St. Lucie	1.7	1.8	3.0	2.0	3.0	2.8	3.4	5.3	6.0	4.3
Trinidad and Tobago	5.9	1.4	2.5	2.6	3.1	3.5	3.1	4.0	5.2	4.2
Guadeloupe	1.9	1.8	2.7	4.3	5.5	4.1	4.7	4.6	6.1	
Antigua and Barbuda	1.3	1.4	1.9	2.1	3.1	3.3	3.0	3.3	4.1	5.0
Guyana	1.5	1.4	0.6	1.0	0.2	1.5	3.0	3.4	6.1	4.7
Barbados/Barbade	1.9	2.1	2.9	2.1	2.2	2.9	2.4	3.6	3.5	2.8
Italy/Italie	0.0	8.8	5.4	7.1	6.0	9.6	3.3			

4. General Imports C.I.F. by Commodities according to the S.I.T.C. (Rev. 2) in thousand U.S. Dollars
Importations Générales C.A.F. par Produits d'après la C.T.C.I. (Rév. 2) en milliers de Dollars E.U.

SITC CTCI	COMMODITY	1993 WEIGHT POIDS	1993 VALUE VALEUR	1994 WEIGHT POIDS	1994 VALUE VALEUR	1995 WEIGHT POIDS	1995 VALUE VALEUR	1996 WEIGHT POIDS	1996 VALUE VALEUR	PRODUIT
	ALL COMMODITIES		93790		96315		117269		129943	TOUS PRODUITS
0	FOOD AND LIVE ANIMALS		17980		19434		22670		24605	ALIMENTS,ANIMAUX VIVANTS
01	MEAT AND PREPARATIONS		3840		4323		4848		5771	VIANDES ET PREPARATIONS
011	MEAT FRESH,CHILLD,FROZEN	W 3055	2831	W 2418	3327	W 2798	3739	W 3154	4483	VIANDES FRAICHES,REF,CONGE
0114	POULTRY FRESH CHLLD,FRZN	W 2733	2353	W 2117	2854	W 2505	3265	W 2818	3913	VOLAILLES MORTES
014	MEAT PREPD,PRSVD,NES ETC	W 458	1007	W 492	990	W 519	1105	W 563	1280	CONSERVES DE VIANDES
0142	SAUSAGES INCLDING TINNED	W 211	477	W 175	422	W 198	438	W 210	529	SAUCISSES,SAUCISSONS
0149	OTH PREPARD,PRESRVD MEAT	W 248	530	W 317	567	W 320	667	W 353	752	AUTRES PREP DE VIANDES
02	DAIRY PRODCTS,BIRDS'EGGS		2891		3051		3706		3993	PRODUITS LAITIERS,OEUFS
022	MILK AND CREAM	W 1478	2281	W 1499	2324	W 1520	2864	W 1668	3121	LAIT ET CREME
0223	MILK AND CREAM FRESH	W 601	737	W 834	1063	W 685	953	W 757	1065	LAIT,CREME FRAIS
0224	MILK,CREAM PRESERVED ETC	W 877	1544	W 665	1261	W 836	1912	W 911	2056	LAIT,CREME CONS,CONC
02242	MILK DRY,1.5% FAT OR LES	W 530	1058	W 330	752	W 326	1017	W 387	1244	LAIT POUDRE INF 1.5%
02243	MILK DRY,OVER 1.5% FAT	W 32	88	W 78	179	W 149	352	W 29	90	LAIT POUDRE SUP 1.5%
02249	MILK(EX DRY) PRSVD,SWEET	W 315	398	W 256	331	W 361	543	W 495	722	LAIT CONS,CONC SUCRE
024	CHEESE AND CURD	W 182	578	W 204	681	W 217	801	W 240	850	FROMAGE ET CAILLEBOTTE
03	FISH AND PREPARATIONS		1143		1349		1350		1678	POISSONS ET PREPARATIONS
035	FISH SALTED,DRIED,SMOKED	W 249	722	W 278	872	W 241	854	W 301	1074	POISSON SECHE,SALE,FUME
03502	COD(NOT IN FILLETS)DRIED	W 165	547	W 168	641	W 108	488	W 138	617	MORUE SECHEE,SALEE
037	FISH ETC PREPD,PRSVD NES	W 123	302	W 148	400	W 340	440	W 210	467	POIS,CRUST,MOL PREPARES
0371	FISH PREPARD,PRESRVD NES	W 123	300	W 148	399	W 339	437	W 210	467	CONSERVES DE POISSONS
04	CEREALS AND PREPARATIONS		4350		4544		5308		5628	CEREALES ET PRODUITS
042	RICE	W 1786	491	W 963	601	W 1776	649	W 1018	730	RIZ
0421	RICE IN HUSK OR HUSKED	W 1688	427	W 845	505	W 1638	532	W 866	572	RIZ SANS AUTRE PREPARATION
04212	RICE HUSKED	W 1688	427	W 844	504	W 1618	528	W 866	572	RIZ CARGO
046	WHEAT ETC MEAL OR FLOUR	W 4167	2252	W 4237	2278	W 4592	2562	W 4392	2543	SEMOULE FARINE,FROMENT
04601	FLOUR OF WHEAT OR MESLIN	W 4046	2157	W 4183	2217	W 4580	2527	W 4380	2507	FARINE DE FROMENT
048	CEREAL ETC PREPARATIONS	W 641	1484	W 799	1501	W 1647	1865	W 1105	2125	PREPTNS A BASE CEREALES
0481	PREPD BREAKFAST FOOD ETC	W 121	337	W 109	339	W 200	451	W 143	440	CEREALES TRAVAILLEES
0484	BAKERY PRODUCTS	W 345	606	W 311	593	W 1168	823	W 439	893	PRODUITS DE BOULANGERIE
04841	BREAD,BISCUIT,COM WAFERS	W 345	606	W 311	593	W 1168	823	W 439	893	PAINS,BISCUITS DE MER
0488	OTH CEREAL PREPS,MALT EX	W 100	396	W 243	399	W 132	377	W 168	438	EXTRAITS DE MALT
05	VEGETABLES AND FRUIT		1617		1694		2322		1825	LEGUMES ET FRUITS
054	VEG ETC FRSH,SMPLY PRSVD	W 1090	781	W 1107	837	W 1358	1374	W 1075	850	LEGUMES FRAIS,CONG,SECS
0542	LEGUMINOUS VEGETBLES DRY	W 372	288	W 291	223	W 395	620	W 269	265	LEGUMES A COSSE SECS
058	FRUIT PRESERVED,PREPARED	W 370	574	W 384	546	W 321	566	W 327	609	CONSERVES DE FRUITS
0585	FRUIT OR VEGETABLE JUICE	W 264	321	W 240	287	W 205	331	W 200	247	JUS DE FRUITS
06	SUGAR AND PREPS,HONEY		1362		1381		1806		1907	SUCRES ET PRODUITS
061	SUGAR AND HONEY	W 2314	1167	W 3150	1112	W 3517	1593	W 3461	1652	SUCRES ET MIEL
0611	RAW BEET AND CANE SUGAR	W 1844	940	W 1500	348	W 1446	625	W 650	278	SUCRES BRUTS
0612	REFINED SUGAR ETC	W 423	185	W 1633	733	W 2036	943	W 2799	1345	SUCRES RAFFINES
07	COFFEE,TEA,COCOA,SPICES		442		547		422		534	CAFE,THE,CACAO,EPICES
081	*FEEDING STUFF FOR ANIML	W 1942	588	W 1959	706	W 2037	727	W 2113	823	NOURRITURE POUR ANIMAUX
0819	FOOD WASTE AND FEED NES	W 1938	587	W 1959	706	W 2037	727	W 2103	807	DECHETS,ALIMENTS NDA
08199	FODDER NES,INCL SWEETNED	W 1938	587	W 1959	706	W 2028	716	W 2103	807	PREPARATIONS FOURRAGERES
09	MISC EDIBLE PRODUCTS		1704		1799		2128		2388	PREP ALIMENTAIRES DIVERSES
091	MARGARINE AND SHORTENING	W 280	433	W 302	516	W 310	532	W 334	598	MARGARINE ET GRAISSES
0914	MARGARINE,EDIBLE FAT NES	W 278	431	W 302	516	W 310	532	W 334	598	MARGARINES,SIMILI SAINDOUX
09141	MARGARINE	W 206	335	W 237	421	W 222	408	W 277	497	MARGARINE
098	EDIBLE PRODCTS,PREPS NES	W 496	1270	W 481	1283	W 649	1596	W 659	1790	PREP ALIMENTAIRES NDA
09804	SAUCES,MIXED SEASONINGS	W 262	451	W 212	419	W 234	444	W 254	522	SAUCES,ASSAISONNEMENTS
09809	MISC FOOD PREPRTIONS NES	W 129	564	W 138	516	W 273	774	W 264	888	PREP ALIMENTAIRES NDA
1	BEVERAGES AND TOBACCO		3944		4380		4847		3198	BOISSONS ET TABACS
11	BEVERAGES		3697		4141		4557		2999	BOISSONS
111	NON-ALCOHL BEVERAGES NES	W 1150	824	W 1138	1063	W 1451	1152	W 1039	1047	BOISSONS NON ALCOOLIQUES
11102	FLAVORED WATERS NON-ALCO	W 1133	817	W 1138	1063	W 1320	1086	W 949	1005	LIMONADES,EAUX GAZEUSES
112	ALCOHOLIC BEVERAGES	W 2705	2872	W 2479	3079	W 3614	3404	W 1132	1952	BOISSONS ALCOOLIQUES
1121	WINE OF FRESH GRAPES ETC	W 327	413	W 320	453	W 375	576	W 266	524	VINS DE RAISINS FRAIS
11212	WINE OF FRESH GRAPES	W 326	410	W 315	443	W 373	571	W 245	476	VINS DE MOUTS DE RAISINS
1123	BEER,ALE,STOUT,PORTER	W 2125	1801	W 1853	1978	W 2582	1970	W 454	570	BIERES
1124	DISTILLED ALCOHOLIC BEVS	W 236	640	W 275	607	W 630	827	W 364	783	ALCOOLS,EAUX-DE-VIE
11249	OTH ALCOHOLC BEVS,CMPNDS	W 137	375	W 171	369	W 483	465	W 195	468	BOISSONS ALCOOLIQUES NDA
2	CRUDE MATERLS,EXCL FUELS		1944		2092		2674		2740	MAT BRUTES NON COMESTIBLES
24	CORK AND WOOD		1456		1756		2159		2271	LIEGE ET BOIS
248	WOOD SHAPED,SLEEPERS	W 2376	1454	W 2814	1664	W 2954	1856	W 5972	2225	BOIS SIMPLEMENT TRAVAILLES
2482	LUMBER SHAPED CONIFER	W 1150	741	W 1387	843	W 1698	1105	W 4053	1248	CONIFERES SCIES,RABOTES
24822	LUMBER PLANED ETC CONIFR	W 1150	741	W 1387	843	W 1698	1105	W 4053	1248	CONIFER RABOTES,RAINES
2483	LUMBER SHAPED NON-CONIFR	W 1226	713	W 1427	821	W 1256	751	W 1919	976	NON CONIFERES SCIES,RABOTES
24831	LUMBER SAWN ETC NON-CON	W 1110	564	W 1311	718	W 1066	641	W 1778	897	SCIES LONGITUDINALEMENT
3	MINERAL FUELS ETC		5980		6344		6611		8526	COMBUSTIBLES MINERAUX LUB
33	PETROLEUM AND PRODUCTS		5262		5529		5909		7475	PETROLE ET DERIVES
334	PETROLEUM PRODUCTS,REFIN	W 26359	5000	W 22830	5361	W 22124	5554	W 17404	7172	PRODUITS RAFFINES
3341	GASOLINE,OTH LIGHT OILS	W 10325	2332	W 11057	2502	W 8989	2490	W 7322	3248	ESSENCES POUR MOTEURS
33411	MOTOR,AVIATION SPIRIT	W 10325	2332	W 11057	2502	W 8961	2482	W 7322	3248	ESSENCES MOTEURS D'AVIONS
3343	GAS OILS	W 11172	1161	W 9291	1756	W 9904	1739	W 7725	2566	GAS OILS
3344	FUEL OILS,NES	W 3410	865	W 1766	558	W 2558	732	W 1553	703	FUEL OILS
3345	LUBS,PETROLEUM OILS NES	W 359	502	W 332	453	W 429	518	W 444	562	HUILES LUBRIFIANTES
33451	LUBS(HIGH PETR CONT) ETC	W 355	484	W 328	435	W 421	489	W 437	536	HUILES LUBRIF,H LOURDES
335	RESIDUAL PETRLM PROD NES	W 457	262	W 107	168	W 720	354	W 362	302	PRODUITS RESIDUELS NDA
341	*GAS,NATURAL AND MANUFCT	W 80318	718	W 202339	813	W 1532	699	W 2108	1050	GAZ NATUREL,GAZ MANUFACT
3413	PETROLM GASES,LIQUEFIED	W 80317	717	W 202339	813	W 1532	699	W 2108	1050	GAZ DE PETROLE LIQUEFIE
34131	LIQUEFIED PROPANE,BUTANE	W 80315	714	W 202334	805	W 1518	680	W 2094	1024	PROPANE,BUTANE LIQUEFIES
4	ANIMAL,VEGETABLE OIL,FAT		3618		3119		3155		8242	HUILES,GRAISSES ANIM,VEG
411	*ANIMAL OILS AND FATS	W 5509	3202	W 4506	2475	W 2733	2643	W 9628	6539	HUILES,GRAISSES ANIMALES
4113	ANIML OIL,FAT,GREASE NES	W 5509	3202	W 4495	2465	W 2733	2643	W 9628	6539	HUILES,GRAISSES ANIMALES NDA
41132	FATS OF BOVINE,SHEEP,ETC	W 5508	3199	W 3395	1975	W 2732	2640	W 9625	6531	SUIFS BRUTS FONDUS
41133	LARD STEARIN AND OIL,ETC			W 1100	490					STEARINE SOLAIRE
42	FIXED VEGETABLE OIL,FAT		115		539		482		1678	HUILES VEGETALES FIXES
423	FIXED VEG OILS,SOFT	W 46	74	W 175	263	W 260	438	W 351	606	HUILES VEGET DOUCES FIXES
4232	SOYA BEAN OIL	W 43	65	W 156	235	W 256	428	W 334	575	HUILE DE SOJA
424	FIXED VEG OIL NONSOFT	W 65	41	W 538	276	W 33	44	W 1649	1071	AUTRES HUILES VEG FIXES
4242	PALM OIL	W 21	10	W 537	269			W 1200	598	HUILE DE PALME
4243	COCONUT (COPRA) OIL					W 17	19	W 436	447	HJUILE DE COPRAH
431	*PROCESD ANML VEG OIL,ET	W 278	301	W 104	105	W 17	30	W 10	25	HUILES,GRAISSES PREPAREES
4312	HYDROGENATED OIL,FAT	W 269	286	W 58	73	W 14	24			HUILES HYDROGENEES
5	CHEMCLS,RELATED PROD NES		12609		12950		15711		16436	PRODUITS CHIMIQUES
51	ORGANIC CHEMICALS		452		492		554		568	PROD CHIMIQ ORGANIQUES
512	ALCOHOLS,PHENOLS ETC	W 232	251	W 285	337	W 309	310	W 284	343	PHENOLS,PHENOLS-ALCOOLS
5121	ACYCLIC ALCOHOLS,DERIVS	W 231	250	W 285	336	W 307	301	W 274	327	ALCOOLS ACYCLIQUES
52	INORGANIC CHEMICALS		956		821		1566		1469	PROD CHIM INORGANIQUES
522	INORG ELEMNTS,OXIDES,ETC	W 1949	810	W 1298	678	W 3064	1325	W 7318	1264	ELEMENTS INORGANIQUES

4. General Imports C.I.F. by Commodities according to the S.I.T.C. (Rev. 2) in thousand U.S. Dollars
Importations Générales C.A.F. par Produits d'après la C.T.C.I. (Rév. 2) en milliers de Dollars E.U.

SITC CTCI	COMMODITY	1993			1994			1995			1996			PRODUIT
		WEIGHT POIDS		VALUE VALEUR	WEIGHT POIDS		VALUE VALEUR	WEIGHT POIDS		VALUE VALEUR	WEIGHT POIDS		VALUE VALEUR	
5225	INORGANIC BASES ETC NES	W	1653	429	W	1050	355	W	2816	830	W	7043	798	AUTRES BASES OXYDES METAL
52252	SODIUM HYDROXIDE, SOLID	W	1482	367	W	517	95	W	300	135	W	60	113	HYDROXYDE DE SODIUM
52253	SODIUM HYDROXIDE, OTHER	W	170	57	W	532	258	W	2514	692	W	6967	659	HYDROXYDE SODIUM AQUEUX
53	DYES,TANNING,COLOUR PROD			1034			955			957			1222	PROD TEINTURE,COLORANTS
533	PIGMENTS,PAINTS,ETC	W	368	916	W	542	903	W	397	944	W	418	1133	PIGMENTS,PEINTURES,VERNIS
5334	VARNISHES,DISTEMPERS ETC	W	191	684	W	210	667	W	215	719	W	257	870	PEINTURES A L'EAU
53342	OTH PAINTS,VARNISHES ETC	W	65	291	W	70	297	W	131	490	W	151	528	AUTRES PEINTURES,VERNIS
541	*MEDICINAL,PHARM PRODUCT	K	87503	1002	K	97799	1111	K	190981	1297	K	116392	1401	PROD MEDICINAUX PHARMACEUT
5417	MEDICAMENTS	K	81758	881	K	93403	982	K	182630	1140	K	105619	1144	MEDICAMENTS
54179	— CONTNG OTH SUBSTANCES	K	78645	855	K	92703	976	K	179283	1111	K	102999	1084	MED CONT AUT SUBSTANCES
55	PERFUME,CLEANING ETC PRD			2704			2930			3405			3574	PROD POUR PARFUM,TOILETTE
551	ESSENTL OILS,PERFUME,ETC	W	114	1027	W	64	1009	W	106	1351	W	95	1291	HUILES ESSENTIELLES
5513	ESSENTL OIL,RESINOID,ETC	W	36	565	W	1	15	W	3	12			7	HUILES ESSENTIELLES,RESIN
5514	MIXED PERFUME SUBSTANCES	W	78	462	W	63	993	W	104	1339	W	94	1283	MELANGES SUBSTAN ODORIFER
553	PERFUMERY,COSMETICS,ETC	W	191	947	W	206	966	W	199	942	W	215	1112	PRODUITS DE PARFUMERIE
554	SOAP,CLEANSING ETC PREPS	W	705	730	W	783	955	W	853	1111	W	1062	1171	SAVONS,PRODUITS DETERSIFS
5542	WASHING PREPARATIONS ETC	W	669	612	W	717	789	W	806	974	W	982	972	PROD ORG TENSIO–ACT NDA
562	*FERTILIZERS,MANUFACTURE	W	7306	2169	W	6263	2078	W	7233	2677	W	6059	1953	ENGRAIS MANUFACTURES
5629	FERTILIZERS NES	W	7285	2144	W	6259	2067	W	7189	2639	W	6035	1922	ENGRAIS NDA
56291	NIT–PHOS–POT FERTLZR NES	W	6983	2071	W	6258	2064	W	7189	2639	W	6034	1919	ENGRAIS CONT N P K
58	PLASTIC MATERIALS ETC			1307			1230			1608			1940	MAT PLAST ARTIFICIELLES
582	PROD OF CONDENSATION ETC	W	286	341	W	386	442	W	407	573	W	455	501	PROD CONDENS,POLYCOND
5825	POLYURETHANES	W	233	242	W	344	355	W	309	390	W	381	367	POLYURETHANES
58251	— IN PRIMARY FORMS	W	233	242	W	344	355	W	309	390	W	381	367	POLYURETHANES PRIMAIRES
583	POLYMERIZATION ETC PRODS	W	528	965	W	421	781	W	561	1028	W	585	1419	PROD POLYMERISATION
5839	OTH POLYMRZTION ETC PROD	W	527	958	W	421	775	W	544	1006	W	585	1418	AUT PROD POLYMER COPOLYM
59	CHEMICAL MATERIALS NES			2951			3327			3629			4227	MAT PROD CHIMIQUES NDA
591	PESTICIDES,DISINFECTANTS	W	333	1901	W	352	2200	W	516	2564	W	585	2676	DESINF,INSECT,FONG,HERB
5911	INSECTICIDES,FOR RETAIL	W	179	780	W	134	697	W	284	1447	W	317	1144	INSECTICIDES VENTE DET
5912	FUNGICIDES,FOR RETAIL	W	18	663	W	47	899	W	14	289	W	50	637	FONGICIDES VENTE AU DET
5913	HERBICIDES,FOR RETAIL	W	115	386	W	154	543	W	192	747	W	185	821	HERBICIDES VENTE AU DET
592	STARCH,INULIN,GLUTEN,ETC	W	302	388	W	132	282	W	60	221	W	248	268	AMIDONS,INUL,GLUT FROM
5922	ALBUMINOID SUBSTAN,GLUES	W	300	387	W	127	272	W	46	192	W	37	196	MAT ALBUMIN,COLLES
598	MISCEL CHEM PRODUCTS NES	W	439	662	W	276	845	W	301	844	W	390	1283	PROD DIV INDUST CHIM NDA
5989	CHEM PRODUCTS,PREPS NES	W	433	643	W	271	831	W	286	773	W	317	1086	PROD PREP CHIMIQUES NDA
59899	OTH CHEM PRODS,PREPS,NES	W	356	510	W	171	664	W	176	575	W	208	864	AUT PRODUITS CHIMIQUES NDA
6	BASIC MANUFACTURES			21215			19907			23720			26206	ART MANUFACTURES
62	RUBBER MANUFACTURES NES			1170			1131			1484			1768	CAOUTCHOUC MANUFACTURE
625	RUBBER TYRES, TUBES ETC	W	315	881	W	337	843	W	502	1004	W	399	1216	PNEUS CAOUTCHOUC VULCANISE
6252	TYRES,NEW,BUS OR LORRY	W	165	511	W	128	483	W	294	540	W	158	600	PNEUS POUR AUTOBUS,CAMIONS
6259	OTH TYRES,TYRE CASES,ETC	W	113	232	W	169	215	W	163	317	W	184	441	AUTRES PNEUS RECHAPES FLAPS
62599	TYRES NES,TYRE CASES,ETC	W	106	203	W	163	187	W	154	271	W	177	406	PNEUS,FLAPS
628	RUBBER ARTICLES NES	W	21	169	W	24	185	W	23	353	W	43	376	OUVRAGES CAOUTCHOUC NDA
63	WOOD,CORK MANUFACTRS NES			1529			1751			1876			2531	OUVRAGES LIEGE ET BOIS
634	VENEERS,PLYWOOD,ETC	W	1341	961	W	1581	1224	W	1662	1050	W	1506	1248	PLACAGES,CONTRE–PLAQUES
6342	PLYWOOD OF WOOD SHEETS	W	1113	843	W	1550	1202	W	1532	980	W	1480	1229	BOIS CONTRE–PLAQUES
635	WOOD MANUFACTURES NES	W	296	562	W	452	521	W	336	824	W	382	1279	ART MANUF EN BOIS NDA
6353	BUILDERS WOODWRK,PREFABS	W	188	423	W	399	405	W	280	720	W	257	968	OUVRAGES DE MENUISERIE
64	PAPER,PAPERBOARD AND MFR			7284			6005			7092			7729	PAPIERS,CARTONS & OUVRAGES
641	PAPER AND PAPERBOARD	W	8899	4763	W	2050	1962	W	658	1479	W	3728	3701	PAPIERS ET CARTONS
6413	KRAFT PAPER,PAPERBOARD	W	4957	1781	W	1116	665	W	61	45	W	146	107	PAPIER ET CARTON KRAFT
64132	SACK KRAFT PAPER IN BULK	W	4957	1781	W	1116	665	W	61	45	W	146	107	PAPIER KRAFT POUR SACS
6415	PAPER,PAPERBRD,BULK,NES	W	3252	1832	W	348	341	W	65	180	W	3026	2010	PAPIERS,CARTONS ROULEAUX
64159	OTHER PAPER ETC,BULK,NES	W	3251	1830	W	347	335	W	63	169	W	3025	1997	AUT PAPIER ROULEAUX FEUILLES
6417	CORRUGATED PAPER ETC,BLK	W	483	426	W	373	272	W	235	256	W	303	275	PAPIERS,CARTONS ONDULES
64174	PAPER ETC CORRUGATED ETC	W	385	370	W	372	271	W	235	254	W	286	261	PAP,CARTONS SIMPL ONDULES
6418	COATED ETC PAPER NES BLK	W	121	522	W	118	464	W	152	660	W	174	1080	PAP,CARTONS COUCHES,ENDUITS
64181	PLASTIC COATED PAPER ETC	W	16	89	W	33	162	W	66	514	W	91	830	PAP,CARTONS ENDUITS,RESINES
64189	COATED PAPER ETC NES	W	105	433	W	84	300	W	85	146	W	83	250	PAPIERS,CARTONS COUCHES
642	PAPER,ETC,PRECUT,ARTS OF	W	1307	2521	W	3423	4042	W	4009	5613	W	2447	4027	PAP,CARTONS DECOUPES
6421	PAPER ETC CONTAINERS	W	910	1109	W	3052	2687	W	3500	4033	W	1994	2320	BOITES,SACS EMBALLAGES
6423	EXERCISE BOOKS ETC	W	59	393	W	64	414	W	76	451	W	61	398	REGISTRES,CAHIERS,CARNETS
6424	PAPER ETC CT TO SIZE NES	W	148	306	W	110	268	W	123	314	W	185	415	PAP,CARTONS DECOUPES
6428	PAPER ETC ARTICLES NES	W	173	613	W	183	598	W	287	700	W	192	793	OUVRAGES EN PATE A PAPIER
64285	PAPER ETC DIAPERS ETC	W	103	430	W	87	393	W	175	386	W	140	542	SERVIETTES HYGIENIQUES
65	TEXTILE YARN,FABRICS,ETC			1543			1757			1386			1369	FILS,TISSUS,ARTICLES TEXTILE
652	COTTON FABRICS,WOVEN	W	21	155	W	51	328	W	45	310	W	35	252	TISSUS DE COTON
653	WOVN MAN–MADE FIB FABRIC	W	76	487	W	62	430	W	57	345	W	42	391	TISSUS FIBRES SYNTH,ARTIF
658	TEXTILE ARTICLES NES	W	42	243	W	62	333	W	31	226	W	36	326	ART FACONNES MAT TEXTILES
66	NONMETAL MINERAL MFS NES			3966			2817			3230			3476	ART MIN NON METALLIQUES
661	LIME,CEMENT,BLDG PRODS	W	8700	1176	W	13589	925	W	22684	1577	W	20217	1280	CHAUX,CIMENTS MAT CONSTR
6612	CEMENT	W	8356	1004	W	13370	796	W	22543	1426	W	20116	1183	CIMENTS HYDRAULIQUES
662	CLAY,REFRACTORY BLDG PRD	W	4048	1976	W	819	575	W	753	596	W	765	628	MAT CONST REFRACTAIRES
6624	BRICKS ETC NONREFRACTORY	W	4048	1976	W	817	571	W	753	594	W	765	627	BRIQUES ETC CERAM NON REFR
66245	GLAZED CERAMIC SETTS ETC	W	3790	1833	W	580	451	W	681	550	W	628	514	AUT CARREAUX CERAMIQUE
664	GLASS	W	79	171	W	185	612	W	147	382	W	96	355	VERRE
6642	OPTICAL GLASS UNWRKD ETC			1	W	95	394	W	13	141	W	22	169	VERRE OPTIQUE,LUNETTERIE
665	GLASSWARE	W	405	433	W	537	538	W	550	542	W	839	913	OUVRAGES EN VERRE
6651	BOTTLES ETC OF GLASS	W	366	291	W	476	392	W	481	387	W	784	733	RECIPIENTS EN VERRE
66511	GLASS BOTTLES ETC NONVAC	W	365	291	W	476	391	W	481	387	W	784	733	BONBONNES,BOUTEILLES,ETC
67	IRON AND STEEL			1851			2362			4085			3153	FER ET ACIER
673	IRON,STEEL SHAPES ETC	W	1700	796	W	2154	1240	W	2380	1157	W	3125	1579	BARRES,PROFIL FER,ACIER
6732	IRON,STEEL BARS ETC	W	1367	610	W	1328	696	W	2277	1067	W	2404	1134	BARRES FER,ACIER
67325	OTH ALLOY STEEL BARS ETC	W	662	306	W	807	374	W	1777	844	W	1783	849	BARRES NON ACIERS ALLIES
67327	IRN, OTH STL BARS FORGED	W	705	304	W	522	322	W	493	214	W	618	280	BARRES FORGEES CREUSES
6733	IRON,STEEL PROFILES ETC	W	48	53	W	638	429	W	28	22	W	440	318	PROFILES,PALPLAN FER,ACIER
67336	IRN,SMPL STL SHEET PILNG	W	4	7	W	614	414	W	8	6	W	228	179	PALPLANCHES EN FER,ACIER
674	IRN,STL UNIV,PLATE,SHEET	W	580	672	W	712	812	W	751	835	W	785	1079	LARGES PLATS,TOLES
6749	OTH IRN,STL PLATES,SHEET	W	505	608	W	683	774	W	746	822	W	713	987	AUTRES TOLES FER,ACIER
67491	— OF IRON OR SIMPLE STL	W	505	608	W	683	767	W	719	809	W	713	986	AUT TOLES AUTRES ACIER FIN
678	IRON,STL TUBES,PIPES,ETC	W	163	341	W	131	306	W	1362	2042	W	230	430	TUBES,TUYAUX EN FONTE,FER
6781	CAST IRON TUBES,PIPES	W	2	9	W	5	14	W	836	1022	W	5	5	TUBES,TUYAUX EN FONTE
6783	IRON,STL TUBES,PIPES NES	W	102	159	W	86	148	W	329	462	W	159	236	AUT TUBES,TUYAUX FER,ACIER
6785	IRON,STEEL TUBE FITTINGS	W	26	126	W	17	115	W	173	488	W	30	142	ACCESSOIRES DE TUYAUTERIE
69	METAL MANUFACTURES NES			3723			3927			4273			5912	ART MANUFACT EN METAL NDA
691	STRUCTURES AND PARTS NES	W	311	1046	W	499	1392	W	515	1488	W	488	2474	CONSTRUCT FER,ACIER,ALU
6911	STRUCTURES,PARTS IRN,STL	W	179	418	W	321	591	W	327	706	W	277	1344	CONSTRUCT FER,ACIER,FONTE
6912	STRUCTURES,PARTS ALUMNM	W	132	627	W	178	801	W	188	782	W	211	1130	CONSTRUCT ALUMINIUM
693	WIRE PRODUCTS NON ELECTR	W	187	252	W	260	328	W	259	387	W	297	442	OUVRAGES FILS METALLIQUES
694	STL,COPPR NAILS,NUTS,ETC	W	128	223	W	184	319	W	203	362	W	181	455	CLOUS,VIS,ECROUS
695	TOOLS	W	79	389	W	47	417	W	49	344	W	72	528	OUTILS A MAIN

4. General Imports C.I.F. by Commodities according to the S.I.T.C. (Rev. 2) in thousand U.S. Dollars
Importations Générales C.A.F. par Produits d'après la C.T.C.I. (Rév. 2) en milliers de Dollars E.U.

SITC CTCI	COMMODITY	1993 WEIGHT POIDS	1993 VALUE VALEUR	1994 WEIGHT POIDS	1994 VALUE VALEUR	1995 WEIGHT POIDS	1995 VALUE VALEUR	1996 WEIGHT POIDS	1996 VALUE VALEUR	PRODUIT
697	BASE MTL HOUSEHOLD EQUIP	W 186	835	W 116	587	W 83	437	W 90	571	ART MENAGE MET COMMUNS
6973	DMSTC HEATG,COOKG APPARA	W 148	647	W 66	333	W 37	236	W 48	310	APPS CHAUF NON ELECTRIQ
69731	IRN,STL DOM COOKG APPARA	W 145	628	W 65	328	W 36	227	W 48	303	APPS CUISSON FER,ACIER
699	BASE METAL MFRS NES	W 130	658	W 162	686	W 192	871	W 223	1018	ART MANUFACTURES MET NDA
6991	LOCKSMITHS WARES,ETC	W 37	233	W 34	235	W 62	394	W 51	301	ARTICLES DE SERRURERIE
7	MACHINES,TRANSPORT EQUIP		17778		19512		27965		28038	MACHINES MATERIEL TRANSPORT
71	POWER GENERATING EQUIPMT		759		1332		819		2687	MACHINES GENERATRICES
713	INTRNL COMBUS PSTN ENGIN	W 17	282	W 16	376	W 15	273	W 17	315	MOTEURS EXPL COMB INT, PIECE
716	ROTATING ELECTRIC PLANT	W 48	449	W 79	941	W 50	521	W 127	2370	APP ELECTR ROTATIFS,PIECES
7161	DC MOTORS AND GENERATORS	W 16	196	W 20	178	W 38	275	W 91	1965	MOTEURS COURANT CONTINU
7162	AC MTRS,GENRTRS,GEN SETS	W 29	193	W 50	515	W 8	80	W 15	144	MOTEURS ELECTRIQUES
71622	AC GENERATORS	W 14	116	W 40	435	W 3	31	W 5	52	GENER COURANT ALTERNATIF
72	MACHS FOR SPCL INDUSTRYS		2232		3222		6621		2761	MAC SPECIALES POUR INDUST
723	CIVIL ENGNEERG EQUIP ETC	W 136	484	W 509	1141	W 460	5457	W 313	1290	APPAREILS DE GENIE CIVIL
7234	CONST,MINING MACHNRY NES	W 135	478	W 470	1054	W 449	5387	W 303	1224	MACH POUR LA CONST, MINES
72342	SLFPRP SHOVELS,EXCAVATRS	W 117	373	W 348	685	W 114	442	W 215	858	PELLES MECANIQUES
72345	PILE DRIVERS,ETC					W 314	4898		2	CHASSE–NEIGE
726	PRINTG,BKBINDG MACHY,PTS	W 4	54	W 14	415	W 10	98	W 5	65	MACHINES POUR IMPRIMERIE
727	FOOD MACHRY NON–DOMESTIC	W 90	506	W 34	264	W 26	86	W 37	364	MACH INDUSTRIES ALIMENT
7272	OTH FOOD PROC MCHY,PARTS	W 90	506	W 34	264	W 26	86	W 37	364	AUT MACH IND ALIMENTAIRE
72722	INDUS FOOD PROC MACH NES	W 89	494	W 32	235	W 25	63	W 16	84	MACHINES BOULANGERIE
728	OTH MACHY FOR SPCL INDUS	W 153	892	W 115	1023	W 27	642	W 113	821	AUT MACH IND PARTICULIERES
7283	OTHR MINERAL WORKG MACHY	W 137	584	W 60	319	W 15	134	W 99	571	MACH TRIER,CRIBLER,BROYER
72832	MINRL CRUSHING ETC MACHY	W 120	435	W 14	143		1	W 15	121	MACH CONCASSER MAT MINER
7284	MACHY FOR SPCL INDUS NES	W 7	204	W 53	683	W 11	451	W 13	215	MACH SPEC IND PARTICUL.
72848	OTH MCHY WITH INDIV FNCT	W 3	130	W 47	615	W 6	241	W 3	18	AUTRES MACHINES NDA
74	GENRL INDUSTRL MACHY NES		2240		2145		4805		3263	MACH APP INDUSTRIE
741	HEATING,COOLING EQUIPMNT	W 59	369	W 89	726	W 722	1611	W 114	728	MACH CHAUFFAGE,PIECES
7414	NONDOM REFRIG EQUIPT,PTS	W 13	100	W 46	255	W 667	962	W 29	186	MAT PRODUCTION DU FROID
74149	PTS NES OF REFRIG EQUIPT		11	W 23	75	W 647	829	W 6	31	PIECES POUR MACH FROID
743	PUMPS NES,CENTRFUGES ETC	W 28	320	W 38	239	W 51	342	W 29	381	POMPES COMPRES,VENT ETC
744	MECHANICAL HANDLING EQU	W 95	473	W 52	330	W 79	404	W 99	522	EQUIP MANUTENTION PIECES
7442	LIFTING,LOADING MACH NES	W 76	281	W 61	148	W 46	188	W 65	167	APP LEVAGE,MANUTENTION
745	NONELEC MACHY,TOOLS NES	W 25	436	W 23	274	W 53	1390	W 65	698	AUT MACH NON ELEC,PIECES
7452	OTH NONELEC MCHS,PTS NES	W 19	307	W 19	229	W 48	1255	W 57	579	AUT MACH NON ELEC,PIECES
74522	PACKAGNG,BOTTLNG,ETC MCH	W 5	142	W 4	81	W 23	875	W 4	77	MACH NETT BOUTEILLES,ETC
749	NONELEC MACH PTS,ACC NES	W 43	462	W 63	468	W 76	898	W 60	707	PIECES MACH NON ELEC NDA
7492	COCKS,VALVES ETC NES	W 33	296	W 49	261	W 64	660	W 47	405	ART ROB,SIM POUR TUYAUX
75	OFFICE MACHNES,ADP EQUIP		1329		1488		1798		2917	MACH BUREAU TRAIT AUTOM
751	OFFICE MACHINES	W 11	242	W 11	301	W 9	249	W 18	323	MACH,APPAREILS DE BUREAU
752	AUTOMTIC DATA PROC EQUIP	W 19	572	W 16	815	W 22	949	W 38	1724	MACH TRAIT INFORMATION
7522	DIGITAL COMPUTERS	W 9	310	W 8	371	W 11	529	W 22	999	MACH DIGITALES COMPLETES
759	OFFICE,ADP MCH PTS,ACCES	W 25	515	W 9	372	W 15	600	W 26	870	PIECES DU 751 ET 752
7599	ACCTG,ETC,ADP MCH PTS,AC	W 19	387	W 7	266	W 10	431	W 21	726	PIECES DU 751 ET 752
76	TELECOMM,SOUND EQUIPMENT		2297		2278		2825		3701	EQUIPMENT DE TELECOM
761	TELEVISION RECEIVERS	W 24	317	W 36	376	W 38	368	W 45	437	RECEPTEURS DE TELEVISION
7611	COLOUR TV RECEIVERS	W 22	293	W 34	361	W 38	366	W 44	432	RECEPTEURS COULEUR
764	TELECOM EQPT,PTS,ACC NES	W 39	1540	W 56	1625	W 56	2120	W 64	2929	EQUIP TELECOM,PIECES
7641	LINE TELEPHONE,ETC EQUIP	W 18	1108	W 19	912	W 14	755	W 19	1007	APP TELEPHON PAR FIL
7649	PTS NES OF EQUIPMT OF 76	W 5	168	W 11	339	W 19	998	W 29	1619	PIECES DE LA DIV 76
76491	PTS NES OF APPAR OF 7641	W 1	67	W 8	289	W 15	926	W 20	1450	PIECES POUR 764.1
77	ELECTRIC MACHNRY NES ETC		2936		2890		4420		4153	MACH APP ELECT NDA
772	SWITCHGEAR ETC,PARTS NES	W 24	360	W 35	490	W 47	966	W 42	843	APP COUPURE,SECT ETC
7721	SWITCHGEAR ETC	W 23	346	W 34	469	W 44	832	W 41	675	APP COUPURE,SECTIONMNT
773	ELECTR DISTRIBUTNG EQUIP	W 370	638	W 117	495	W 251	1079	W 157	879	EQUIPMT DISTRIBUTION ELECT
7731	INSULATED WIRE,CABLE ETC	W 368	619	W 112	462	W 239	1047	W 149	833	FILS,CABLES ISOLES ELECT
775	HOUSEHOLD TYPE EQUIP NES	W 153	928	W 154	948	W 184	1015	W 168	1035	MACH,APP USAGE DOMESTQUE
7752	DOM REFRIGERATRS,FREEZRS	W 99	555	W 82	484	W 104	570	W 94	535	REFRIG,CONGEL MENAGER
77521	DOMESTIC REFRIGERATORS	W 83	465	W 68	387	W 86	483	W 77	435	REFRIGERATEURS
778	ELECTRICAL MACHINERY NES	W 137	786	W 132	732	W 159	964	W 141	942	AUTRES MACH ELECT NDA
7781	BATTERIES,ACCUMULATORS	W 102	311	W 91	262	W 123	418	W 93	338	PILES ET ACCUMULATEURS
78	ROAD VEHICLES		5571		5712		6002		8176	VEHICULES ROUTIERS
781	PASS MOTOR VEH EXC BUSES	W 395	2315	W 386	1914	W 456	2216	W 733	3402	AUTO TRANSPORT PERSONNES
782	LORRIES,SPCL MTR VEH NES	W 264	1475	W 301	1646	W 437	1715	W 454	2286	VEHICULES SPECIAUX,MARCH
7821	LORRIES,TRUCKS	W 264	1475	W 211	1372	W 347	1499	W 434	2198	VEHICULES TRANSP MARCHAND
783	ROAD MOTOR VEHICLES NES	W 105	822	W 146	1146	W 122	1018	W 203	1221	VEHICULES ROUTIERS NDA
7831	BUSES	W 99	807	W 135	1125	W 116	1001	W 148	1120	VOITURES TRANSPORT COMMUN
784	MOTOR VEH PRTS,ACCES NES	W 67	732	W 65	740	W 98	829	W 70	851	PIECES 722,781,782,783
7849	OTHER MOTOR VEHCL PARTS	W 65	729	W 64	736	W 90	814	W 64	841	PIECES 722,781,782,783
79	OTHR TRANSPORT EQUIPMENT		338		367		553		189	AUTRE MATERIEL TRANSPORT
793	SHIPS AND BOATS ETC	W 106	319	W 75	367	W 43	550	W 35	133	NAVIRES BATEAUX,ETC
7932	SHIPS AND BOATS NES	W 105	313	W 43	180	W 37	395	W 34	129	NAVIRES ET BATEAUX
8	MISC MANUFACTURED GOODS		8710		8564		9906		11945	ART MANUFACTURES DIVERS
812	*PLUMBG,HEATNG,LGHTNG EQ	W 85	355	W 134	506	W 103	489	W 110	445	APPAR SANITAIRES CHAUFFAGE
821	*FURNITURE,PARTS THEREOF	W 121	625	W 184	836	W 142	825	W 258	1286	MEUBLES ET PIECES
8219	FURNITURE AND PARTS NES	W 89	407	W 113	483	W 96	555	W 104	802	AUTRES MEUBLES ET PIECES
82191	METAL FURNITURE NES	W 54	254	W 58	236	W 60	325	W 54	532	MEUBLES NDA EN METAL
84	CLOTHING AND ACCESSORIES		1237		1142		1303		1376	VETEMENTS
843	WOMENS OUTERWEAR NONKNIT	W 16	283	W 18	247	W 32	325	W 21	298	VET DESSUS FEMMES MAT TEX
845	OUTERWEAR KNIT NONELASTC	W 36	293	W 12	188	W 18	201	W 23	234	VET DESSOUS,ACCES BONNET
846	UNDER GARMENTS KNITTED	W 48	282	W 21	280	W 22	229	W 35	267	SOUS VETS DE BONNETERIE
851	*FOOTWEAR	W 81	768	W 52	574	W 50	699	W 88	797	CHAUSSURES
85101	FOOTWEAR RUBBER,PLASTIC	W 48	404	W 36	361	W 19	244	W 44	340	CHAUS SEMELLES CAOUTCH
85102	FOOTWEAR LEATHER	W 31	350	W 14	194	W 24	384	W 38	409	CHAUS SEMELLES EN CUIR
87	PRECISION INSTRUMNTS NES		597		527		661		736	INSTRUM,APPAR SCIENT NDA
874	MEASURNG,CONTROLNG INSTR	W 14	244	W 21	228	W 16	362	W 12	333	INSTRUMENTS DE MESURE
88	PHOTO EQU,OPTICL GDS ETC		351		291		397		398	APP,FOURN PHOTO,OP,MONTR
89	MISC MANUFCTRD GOODS NES		4685		4605		5414		6775	ART MANUFACTURES DIVERS
892	PRINTED MATTER	W 135	1774	W 159	1603	W 126	1735	W 186	2307	IMPRIMES
8921	PRINTED BOOKS,GLOBES,ETC	W 76	970	W 76	946	W 80	1074	W 122	1372	LIVRES,BROCHURES,CARTES
89211	PRINTED BOOKS,PAMPHLETS	W 70	930	W 72	932	W 78	1064	W 121	1365	LIVRES,BROCHURES
8928	PRINTED MATTER NES	W 43	629	W 69	500	W 33	478	W 43	719	IMPRIMES NDA
89281	LABELS PAPER,PAPERBOARD	W 22	340	W 28	280	W 21	264	W 22	439	ETIQUETTES TOUS GENRES
893	ARTICLES OF PLASTIC NES		1891	W 894	2091		2587		2967	OUVRAGES EN MAT DIVIS 58
8931	PLSTC PACKG CONTNRS,LIDS	W 194	636	W 189	563	W 221	809	W 344	1105	ART TRANSP EMBALLAGE ETC
8939	MISC PLASTIC ARTICLES	W 436	1227	W 689	1479	W 557	1742	W 547	1818	ART DIVERS EN MAT DIV 58
89399	OTHR PLASTC ARTICLES NES	W 337	1079	W 556	1286	W 479	1622	W 414	1626	AUT OUV MAT DIV 58
894	TOYS,SPORTING GOODS,ETC	W 33	229	W 40	216	W 40	276	W 60	560	VOITURES ENFANTS,JOUETS
899	OTHER MANUFACTURED GOODS		357		309		346		395	AUT ART MANUF DIVERS NDA

5. General Exports F.O.B. by Commodities according to the S.I.T.C. (Rev. 2) in thousand U.S. Dollars
Exportations Générales F.O.B. par Produits d'après la C.T.C.I. (Rév. 2) en milliers de Dollars E.U.

SITC CTCI	COMMODITY	1993 WEIGHT POIDS	1993 VALUE VALEUR	1994 WEIGHT POIDS	1994 VALUE VALEUR	1995 WEIGHT POIDS	1995 VALUE VALEUR	1996 WEIGHT POIDS	1996 VALUE VALEUR	PRODUIT
	ALL COMMODITIES		48011		45230		45244		51153	TOUS PRODUITS
0	FOOD AND LIVE ANIMALS		31563		25855		22449		24311	ALIMENTS,ANIMAUX VIVANTS
04	CEREALS AND PREPARATIONS		73		235		131		140	CEREALES ET PRODUITS
048	CEREAL ETC PREPARATIONS	W 38	73	W 107	227	W 79	131	W 67	140	PREPTNS A BASE CEREALES
0483	MACARONI,SPAGHETTI ETC	W 38	72	W 96	169	W 79	130	W 67	140	PATES ALMENTAIRES
05	VEGETABLES AND FRUIT		30676		24702		21318		23361	LEGUMES ET FRUITS
054	VEG ETC FRSH,SMPLY PRSVD	W 1795	1775	W 1834	1220	W 1803	1715	W 1833	2245	LEGUMES FRAIS,CONG,SECS
0545	OTHER FRESH VEGETABLES	W 255	166	W 392	199	W 418	360	W 557	593	AUTRES LEGUMES FRAIS,REF
05459	FRESH VEGETABLES NES	W 255	166	W 388	197	W 418	360	W 557	593	LEGUMES FRAIS,REFRI NDA
0548	EDIBLE VEG NES FRESH,DRY	W 1538	1608	W 1439	1019	W 1384	1355	W 1274	1651	RACINES,TUBERCULES
05481	ROOTS,TUBERS FRESH,DRY	W 1532	1605	W 1438	1017	W 1384	1354	W 1273	1650	RACINES DE MANIOC ETC
057	FRUIT,NUTS,FRESH,DRIED	W 63218	28669	W 50046	23274	W 37377	19346	W 46988	20875	FRUITS FRAIS OU SECS
0571	ORANGES, MANDARINS ETC	W 508	230	W 572	184	W 583	252	W 503	406	ORANGES,MAND,CLEMENTINES
05711	ORANGES,FRESH OR DRIED	W 486	218	W 549	174	W 567	243	W 475	383	ORANGES FRAICHES,SECHEES
0572	LEMONS,GRAPEFRUIT ETC	W 1576	663	W 1384	433	W 1110	474	W 1008	594	AUTRES AGRUMES FRAIS,SECS
05721	LEMONS,LIMES,FRESH,DRIED	W 113	91	W 160	87	W 152	122	W 153	208	CITRONS ET LIMES
05722	GRAPEFRUITS,FRESH,DRIED	W 1463	572	W 1223	346	W 958	352	W 855	385	PAMPLEMOUSSES,POMELOS
0573	BANANA,PLANTAIN,FRSH,DRY	W 59897	27055	W 46744	22112	W 34844	17894	W 44708	19328	BANANES FRAICHES,SECHEES
0577	NUTS EDIBLE,FRESH,DRIED	W 548	176	W 495	159	W 255	82	W 300	107	FRUITS A COQUES
05771	COCONUTS FRESH OR DRIED	W 543	174	W 491	157	W 253	81	W 297	106	NOIX DE COCO
0579	FRUIT FRESH OR DRIED NES	W 689	545	W 851	385	W 585	643	W 470	439	FRUITS FRAIS,SECS NDA
05797	OTH TROP FRUIT,FRESH,DRY	W 563	486	W 706	326	W 447	571	W 357	380	AVOCATS,MANGUES,GOYAVES
058	FRUIT PRESERVED,PREPARED	W 117	230	W 89	205	W 116	235	W 116	238	CONSERVES DE FRUITS
0585	FRUIT OR VEGETABLE JUICE	W 110	208	W 78	165	W 106	203	W 109	203	JUS DE FRUITS
07	COFFEE,TEA,COCOA,SPICES		371		439		396		384	CAFE,THE,CACAO,EPICES
075	SPICES	W 99	269	W 109	375	W 94	341	W 57	368	EPICES
0752	SPICES,EX PEPPER,PIMENTO	W 91	264	W 103	372	W 81	325	W 48	356	AUTRES EPICES
07521	VANILLA	W 1	68	W 1	153	W 1	169	W 1	205	VANILLE
09	MISC EDIBLE PRODUCTS		415		438		579		410	PREP ALIMENTAIRES DIVERSES
098	EDIBLE PRODCTS,PREPS NES	W 309	412	W 283	436	W 372	574	W 212	410	PREP ALIMENTAIRES NDA
09804	SAUCES,MIXED SEASONINGS	W 305	406	W 279	415	W 368	558	W 209	399	SAUCES,ASSAISONNEMENTS
1	BEVERAGES AND TOBACCO		16		285		296		355	BOISSONS ET TABACS
11	BEVERAGES		11		212		45		96	BOISSONS
111	NON–ALCOHL BEVERAGES NES	W 2	1	W 444	203	W 76	38	W 74	57	BOISSONS NON ALCOOLIQUES
11101	WATERS,ICE AND SNOW			W 440	197	W 73	33	W 53	22	EAU,EAUX MINERALES
12	TOBACCO AND MANUFACTURES		5		73		251		258	TABACS BRUTS FABRIQUES
122	TOBACCO,MANUFACTURED		5	W 2	68	W 8	229	W 7	194	TABACS FABRIQUES
1222	CIGARETTES		3	W 2	66	W 8	221	W 7	193	CIGARETTES
2	CRUDE MATERLS,EXCL FUELS		188		378		702		1148	MAT BRUTES NON COMESTIBLES
24	CORK AND WOOD		4		16		3		184	LIEGE ET BOIS
248	WOOD SHAPED,SLEEPERS	W 1	1		15	W 2	2	W 349	184	BOIS SIMPLEMENT TRAVAILLES
2483	LUMBER SHAPED NON–CONIFR	W 1	1		15	W 2	2	W 349	184	NON CONIFERES SCIES,RABOTES
24831	LUMBER SAWN ETC NON–CON	W 1	1		14			W 345	169	SCIES LONGITUDINALEMENT
27	CRUDE FERTLZR,MINRLS NES		61		224		570		835	ENGRAIS MINERAUX BRUTS
273	STONE,SAND AND GRAVEL	W 8007	46	W 41113	209	W 101479	570	W 136700	835	PIERRES,SABLES,GRAVIERS
2733	SAND,EXCL METAL–BEARING	W 5977	30	W 21000	114	W 15459	83	W 61600	369	SABLES NATURELS
2734	GRAVEL,CRUSHED STONE,ETC	W 2030	15	W 20113	96	W 86020	488	W 75100	466	PIERRES CONCASSEES
5	CHEMCLS,RELATED PROD NES		13084		16153		19306		23676	PRODUITS CHIMIQUES
51	ORGANIC CHEMICALS				139		122		134	PROD CHIMIQ ORGANIQUES
512	ALCOHOLS,PHENOLS ETC			W 290	139	W 202	122	W 201	133	PHENOLS,PHENOLS–ALCOOLS
5121	ACYCLIC ALCOHOLS,DERIVS			W 290	139	W 202	122	W 201	133	ALCOOLS ACYCLIQUES
51218	GLYCEROL,GLYCEROL LYES			W 290	139	W 202	122	W 201	133	GLYCERINE
53	DYES,TANNING,COLOUR PROD		728		914		1511		1680	PROD TEINTURE,COLORANTS
533	PIGMENTS,PAINTS,ETC	W 244	726	W 303	914	W 483	1509	W 689	1680	PIGMENTS,PEINTURES,VERNIS
5334	VARNISHES,DISTEMPERS ETC	W 244	726	W 301	913	W 481	1504	W 689	1680	PEINTURES A L'EAU
53342	OTH PAINTS,VARNISHES ETC	W 244	722	W 299	906	W 463	1454	W 683	1668	AUTRES PEINTURES,VERNIS
55	PERFUME,CLEANING ETC PRD		11786		14618		17019		21223	PROD POUR PARFUM,TOILETTE
551	ESSENTL OILS,PERFUME,ETC	W 22	878	W 11	447	W 13	581	W 19	943	HUILES ESSENTIELLES
5513	ESSENTL OIL,RESINOID,ETC	W 22	878	W 11	447	W 13	581	W 19	940	HUILES ESSENTIELLES,RESIN
553	PERFUMERY,COSMETICS,ETC	W 100	461	W 157	691	W 133	570	W 92	517	PRODUITS DE PARFUMERIE
554	SOAP,CLEANSING ETC PREPS	W 8453	10447	W 11484	13480	W 12023	15868	W 14911	19763	SAVONS,PRODUITS DETERSIFS
5541	SOAPS	W 8085	10020	W 10450	12371	W 11088	14847	W 13826	18500	SAVONS,PROD TENSIO–ACTIFS
5542	WASHING PREPARATIONS ETC	W 368	427	W 1034	1109	W 935	1022	W 1047	1204	PROD ORG TENSIO–ACT NDA
58	PLASTIC MATERIALS ETC		275		288		296		9	MAT PLAST ARTIFICIELLES
583	POLYMERIZATION ETC PRODS	W 128	275	W 117	288	W 98	261	W 3	9	PROD POLYMERISATION
5839	OTH POLYMRZTION ETC PROD	W 128	275	W 117	288	W 98	261	W 3	9	AUT PROD POLYMER COPOLYM
59	CHEMICAL MATERIALS NES		276		185		353		629	MAT PROD CHIMIQUES NDA
591	PESTICIDES,DISINFECTANTS	W 201	271	W 117	183	W 317	350	W 486	620	DESINF,INSECT,FONG,HERB
5914	DISINFECTANTS,ETC,FR RET	W 201	271	W 117	141	W 317	349	W 486	619	DESINFECTANTS VENTE DET
59141	DISINFECTANTS FOR RETAIL	W 197	266	W 117	141	W 317	349	W 486	619	DESINFECTANTS VENTE DET
6	BASIC MANUFACTURES		1384		742		217		117	ART MANUFACTURES
64	PAPER,PAPERBOARD AND MFR		1121		499		12		13	PAPIERS,CARTONS & OUVRAGES
642	PAPER,ETC,PRECUT,ARTS OF	W 1191	1121	W 1180	499		11	W 18	10	PAP,CARTONS DECOUPES
6421	PAPER ETC CONTAINERS	W 1191	1120	W 791	450				2	BOITES,SACS EMBALLAGES
7	MACHINES,TRANSPORT EQUIP		938		517		1219		582	MACHINES MATERIEL TRANSPORT
72	MACHS FOR SPCL INDUSTRYS		297		38		235		44	MAC SPECIALES POUR INDUST
723	CIVIL ENGNEERG EQUIP ETC	W 89	194	W 6	16	W 36	186	W 10	22	APPAREILS DE GENIE CIVIL
7234	CONST,MINING MACHNRY NES	W 89	191	W 5	15	W 18	160	W 10	22	MACH POUR LA CONST, MINES
72342	SLFPRP SHOVELS,EXCAVATRS	W 24	154	W 5	15		20			PELLES MECANIQUES
72343	SLFPRP CONST ETC MCH NES					W 17	139			AUT MACH EXTR,TERRASSEM
74	GENRL INDUSTRL MACHY NES		294		153		370		244	MACH APP INDUSTRIE
741	HEATING,COOLING EQUIPMNT	W 5	70	W 10	137	W 9	143	W 29	92	MACH CHAUFFAGE,PIECES
7416	HEATING,COOLING EQU NES	W 4	39	W 9	122	W 9	143	W 25	83	APP CHANGEMENT TEMP
744	MECHANICAL HANDLING EQU	W 14	186		2	W 23	67	W 20	111	EQUIP MANUTENTION PIECES
7449	PTS NES OF MACHY OF 7442	W 2	178		1	W 1	6	W 1	7	PIECES DU 744.2
78	ROAD VEHICLES		132		191		256		147	VEHICULES ROUTIERS
8	MISC MANUFACTURED GOODS		837		1291		1026		956	ART MANUFACTURES DIVERS
84	CLOTHING AND ACCESSORIES		181		275		256		114	VETEMENTS
847	TEXTILE CLTHNG ACCES NES	W 105	162	W 90	149	W 91	125			ACCES VET MAT TEXT NDA
8472	CLTHNG ACCESRYS ETC KNIT	W 105	162	W 90	149	W 91	124			ACCES VET BONNE NDA
84721	KNIT GLOVES,ETC NONELAST	W 105	162	W 90	149	W 91	124			GANTERIE BONNET NON ELAS
851	*FOOTWEAR	W 21	119	W 36	222	W 50	229	W 32	248	CHAUSSURES
85101	FOOTWEAR RUBBER,PLASTIC	W 21	116	W 35	218	W 50	229	W 32	248	CHAUS SEMELLES CAOUTCH
89	MISC MANUFCTRD GOODS NES		483		688		481		542	ART MANUFACTURES DIVERS
892	PRINTED MATTER	W 1	8		229	W 2	28	W 10	42	IMPRIMES
8928	PRINTED MATTER NES	W 1	4		224	W 1	7		5	IMPRIMES NDA
89283	UNISSUED BANKNOTES ETC				222					TIMBRES–POSTE FISCAUX
893	ARTICLES OF PLASTIC NES	W 105	164	W 74	187	W 48	143	W 85	250	OUVRAGES EN MAT DIVIS 58
8931	PLSTC PACKG CONTNRS,LIDS	W 105	162	W 74	183	W 46	127	W 79	228	ART TRANSP EMBALLAGE ETC
899	OTHER MANUFACTURED GOODS	W 104	223	W 103	239	W 163	288	W 109	212	AUT ART MANUF DIVERS NDA
8993	COMBUSTIBLE PRODUCTS ETC	W 99	184	W 98	191	W 160	248	W 106	186	BOUGIES,ALLUMETTES ETC

5. General Exports F.O.B. by Commodities according to the S.I.T.C. (Rev. 2) in thousand U.S. Dollars
Exportations Générales F.O.B. par Produits d'après la C.T.C.I. (Rév. 2) en milliers de Dollars E.U.

SITC CTCI	COMMODITY	1993			1994			1995			1996			PRODUIT
		WEIGHT POIDS		VALUE VALEUR	WEIGHT POIDS		VALUE VALEUR	WEIGHT POIDS		VALUE VALEUR	WEIGHT POIDS		VALUE VALEUR	
89931	CANDLES,TAPERS,ETC	W	99	184	W	98	191	W	160	248	W	106	186	BOUGIES,CHANDELLES,CIERG

1. HISTORICAL SERIES, 1961–1996 GENERAL TRADE, IMPORTS F.O.B., EXPORTS F.O.B.
SERIES HISTORIQUES, 1961–1996 COMMERCE GENERAL, IMPORTATIONS F.O.B., EXPORTATIONS F.O.B

YEAR ANNEE	VALUE IN MILLION U.S. DOLLARS / VALEUR EN MILLION U.S. DOLLARS — MERCHANDISE –MARCHANDISE		GOLD –OR		CONVERSION FACTORS FACTEURS DE CONVERSION CENTS E.U. PAR		INDEX NUMBERS –INDICES — QUANTUM		UNIT VALUE VALEUR UNITAIRE	
	IMPORTS	EXPORTS	IMPORTS	EXPORTS	IMPORTS	EXPORTS	IMPORTS	EXPORTS	IMPORTS	EXPORTS
1961	69.50	143.10						77		68
1962	129.10	172.40						85		79
1963	160.30	174.10						73		89
1964	192.40	179.40						75		90
1965	86.70	125.50						58		79
1966	160.80	136.70						59		88
1967	174.70	156.20						67		86
1968	196.90	163.50						62		93
1969	217.20	184.10						67		98
1970	278.00	213.60						82		34
1971	309.70	240.70						92		22
1972	337.70	347.60						123		36
1973	421.90	442.20						134		44
1974	673.00	636.80						137		67
1975	772.70	893.80						121		102
1976	763.60	716.40						131		70
1977	847.80	780.50						138		78
1978	860.90	675.50						113		71
1979	1080.40	868.60						132		77
1980	1498.40	961.90						99		92
1981	1450.20	1188.00						109		118
1982	1255.80	767.70						104		76
1983	1279.00	785.20						121		72
1984	1257.10	868.10						122		83
1985	1285.90	738.50						109		71
1986	1432.70	717.61						91		76
1987	1830.20	711.25						111		63
1988	1849.20	889.70						114		90
1989	2258.40	924.39						117		104
1990	2061.70	734.54						100		100
1991	1988.10	658.32						95		95
1992	2500.80	562.40						90		82
1993	2436.20	511.00						93		75
1994	2626.40	633.41						89		87
1995	2976.20	764.63								94
1996	3685.90	815.25								103

2. IMPORTS BY BROAD ECONOMIC CATEGORY AND EXPORTS BY INDUSTRIAL ORIGIN. (PERCENTAGE OF TOTAL VALUE)
IMPORTATIONS PAR CATEGORIES ECONOMIQUES ET EXPORTATIONS PAR BRANCHE D'ACTIVITE.(EN POURCENTAGE DE LA VALEUR TOTALE)

IMPORTS – IMPORTATIONS

	1990	1991	1992	1993	1994	1995	1996
TOTAL IMPORTS–IMPORTATIONS TOTALES							
1 FOOD BEV–ALIMENTATION BOISSONS							
11 PRIMARY–PRODUITS DE BASE							
111 FOR INDUSTRY–POUR L'INDUSTRIE							
112 FOR HOUSEHOLDS–POUR LES MENAGES							
12 PROCESSED–PRODUITS ELABORES							
121 FOR INDUSTRY–POUR L'INDUSTRIE							
122 FOR HOUSEHOLDS–POUR LES MENAGES							
2 IND SUPPLIES–APPROV INDUSTRIELS							
21 PRIMARY–PRODUITS DE BASE							
22 PROCESSED–PRODUITS ELABORES							
3 FUELS–COMBUSTIBLES							
31 PRIMARY–PRODUITS DE BASE							
32 PROCESSED–PRODUITS ELABORES							
321 MOTOR SPIRIT–ESSENCE							
322 OTHER–AUTRES							
4 MACHINERY–EQUIPEMENT							
41 CAPITAL EQUIPMENT–MACHINES							
42 PARTS–PIECES ACCESSOIRES							
5 TRANSPORT–TRANSPORT							
51 PASSENGER CARS–AUTOMOBILES							
52 OTHER–AUTRES							
521 INDUSTRIAL–INDUSTRIELS							
522 NON INDUSTRIAL–NON INDUSTRIEL							
53 PARTS–PIECES ACCESSOIRES							
6 CONSUM GOODS–BIENS CONSOMMATION							
61 DURABLE–DURABLES							
62 SEMI DURABLE–SEMI DURABLES							
63 NON DURABLE–NON DURABLES							
7 GOODS NES–BIENS NDA							

EXPORTS – EXPORTATIONS

	1990	1991	1992	1993	1994	1995	1996
TOTAL EXPORTS–EXPORTATIONS TOTALES			100.	100.	100.		
1 AGRICULTURE			9.0	8.4	9.7		
2 MINING QUARRY–INDUS EXTRACTIVES			0.5	0.3	0.2		
3 MANUFACTURING–IND MANUFACTUR			90.5	91.3	90.1		
31 FOOD BEV TOBACCO–ALIM BOISS TAB			12.8	12.3	10.9		
32 TEXTILES–INDUSTRIES TEXTILES			38.9	40.5	37.1		
33 WOOD & PRODUCTS–BOIS & PRODUITS			0.0	0.0	0.0		
34 PAPER & PRODUCTS–PAPIER & PRODT			0.7	0.7	0.7		
35 CHEMICALS–INDUSTRIES CHIMIQUES			3.9	3.6	3.4		
36 NON METAL MIN–MIN NON METAL			0.3	0.3	0.3		
37 BASIC METAL–IND METAL BASE			8.6	7.7	9.6		
38 METAL MANUF–MANUF METAL			17.9	20.5	21.1		
39 OTH MANUF IND–AUTRES MANUF			7.4	5.7	6.9		

3. TRADE BY PRINCIPAL COUNTRIES OF PROVENANCE AND DESTINATION (VALUE IN THOUSAND U.S. DOLLARS)
ECHANGES SELON LES PRINCIPAUX PAYS DE PROVENANCE ET DE DESTINATION (VALEUR EN MILLIERS DE DOLLARS EU)

COUNTRIES–PAYS	GENERAL IMPORTS C.I.F. IMPORTATIONS GENERALES C.A.F 1991	1992	1993	1994	1995
World					
Africa					
Americas					
Northern America					
LAIA					
CACM					
Caribbean					
Rest of America					
As.ex F.USSR					
Eur.x F.USSR					
EU					
EFTA					
East Europe					
Other Europe					
Former USSR					
Oceania					

COUNTRIES–PAYS	GENERAL EXPORTS F.O.B. # 1 EXPORTATIONS GENERALES F.O.B. 1991	1992	1993	1994	1995
Monde	658323	1715375	1758898	2007775	766700
Afrique	2547	11256	905	2187	2421
Amériques	457625	1566484	1565693	1767042	496952
Amérique du Nord	432614	1530331	1511174	1717573	449175
ALAI	10842	7553	11062	7416	8447
MCAC	2850	9489	7562	10047	4919
Caraïbes	9269	14900	31228	24674	33982
Autre Amérique	2050	4211	4667	7332	429
Asie l'URSS exclus	24000	34446	45674	62068	67559
Europe l'URSS exclus	142045	101828	142504	174852	178884
UE	141888	100351	141561	174166	177465
AELE	157	1477	717	556	1419
Europe de l'Est			114	122	
Autre de l'Europe			112	8	
Ancienne URSS		1045	3373	514	
Océanie		189	684	643	
USA/Etats–Unis d'Amer	419226	1437378	1488828	1698222	414938
Netherlands/Pays–Bas	99152	9279	42432	103683	108333
Canada	13388	92934	22120	18998	33975
Belgium–Luxembourg	20533	39930	44898	21623	28420
Korea, Republic of		23251	22940	37643	35938
Japan/Japon	24000	5322	19485	15532	31621
Spain/Espagne	11071	12065	12415	9422	12245
United Kingdom	2188	16534	17769	12910	1788
Italy/Italie	5457	9503	10278	11298	13191
Haiti/Haïti	3858	285	5863	6954	21804
Germany/Allemagne	2295	6726	5431	4726	7218
Netherlands Antilles	1425	647	13598	4296	3652
Honduras	635	5828	6186	6663	2331
Jamaica/Jamaïque	850	5187	4554	5860	3253
France,Monac	1125	3332	2474	5170	3765
Panama	813	3391	3840	6798	
Portugal	2	2781	5817	4588	8
Brazil/Brésil	6927	2384	1447	1175	207
Guadeloupe	1320	3123	3220	3244	
Thailand/Thaïlande		4805	1419	4276	
Mexico/Mexique	1168	1758	2031	3636	1607
Morocco/Maroc	2003	5581		1103	1337
Costa Rica	2044	2803	783	2450	1892
Venezuela	816	1720	1090	1101	701
Russian Federation		1045	3373	514	
Uruguay	6		4783	5	
Argentina/Argentine		38	14	88	4184
Colombia/Colombie	455	1416	1162	740	530
United States Virg Is	1434				2850
Switz.Liecht	157	1449	715	507	1397
Trinidad and Tobago	382	1065	676	918	1098
Hong Kong		222	407	3306	
Algeria/Algérie		2641	70		1084
Mauritius/Maurice		2977	307		
Martinique		727	1100	880	
Ireland/Irlande				446	2254
Suriname/Suriname	1170	463	317	126	
Ecuador/Equateur	1470	21	94	183	
Barbados/Barbade		315	414	377	628
Guyana	67	341	391	344	427
El Salvador	56	465	302	417	299
British Virgin Islds		1046	46	275	15
Chile/Chili		56	81	12	1218
Guatemala	106	117	236	503	372
Cameroon/Cameroun		50	513	675	
Cuba		1130	55	50	
Saint Lucia/St. Lucie		121	175	518	352
Australia/Australie		101	404	616	
Peru/Pérou		146	352	442	
Antigua and Barbuda		243	475	115	98

(VALUE AS PERCENTAGE OF WORLD TOTAL)(VALEURS EN POURCENTAGE DU TOTAL MONDIAL)

	1986	1987	1988	1989	1990	1991	1992	1993	1994	1995
Africa										
Americas										
Northern America										
LAIA										
CACM										
Caribbean										
Rest of America										
As.ex F.USSR										
Eur.x F.USSR										
EU										
EFTA										
East Europe										
Other Europe										
Former USSR										
Oceania										

	1986	1987	1988	1989	1990	1991	1992	1993	1994	1995
Afrique			0.6	1.3	0.5	0.4	0.7	0.1	0.1	0.3
Amériques			90.2	62.7	71.9	69.5	91.3	89.0	88.0	64.8
Amérique du Nord			89.4	58.8	68.3	65.7	89.2	85.9	85.5	58.6
ALAI			0.3	1.4	1.9	1.6	0.4	0.6	0.4	1.1
MCAC				0.1	0.1	0.4	0.6	0.4	0.5	0.6
Caraïbes			0.5	2.1	1.4	1.4	0.9	1.8	1.2	4.4
Autre Amérique			0.0	0.3	0.2	0.3	0.2	0.3	0.4	0.1
Asie l'URSS exclus			1.1	8.3	2.0	3.6	2.0	2.6	3.1	8.8
Europe l'URSS exclus			8.0	23.6	19.6	21.6	5.9	8.1	8.7	23.3
UE			7.9	22.0	19.6	21.6	5.9	8.0	8.7	23.1
AELE			0.1	0.0	0.0	0.0	0.1	0.0	0.0	0.2
Europe de l'Est								0.0	0.0	
Autre de l'Europe				1.5				0.0	0.0	
Ancienne URSS							0.1	0.2	0.0	
Océanie			0.0	0.0			0.0	0.0	0.0	
USA/Etats–Unis d'Amer			88.0	56.8	66.7	63.7	83.8	84.6	84.6	54.1
Netherlands/Pays–Bas			0.1	17.7	14.6	15.1	0.5	2.4	5.2	14.1
Canada			1.3	1.9	1.6	2.0	5.4	1.3	0.9	4.4
Belgium–Luxembourg			2.0	1.2	1.8	3.1	2.3	2.6	1.1	3.7
Korea, Republic of							1.4	1.3	1.9	4.7
Japan/Japon			1.1	5.8	2.0	3.6	0.3	1.1	0.8	4.1
Spain/Espagne			1.7	1.1	2.2	1.7	0.7	0.7	0.5	1.6
United Kingdom			0.8	0.1	0.2	0.3	1.0	1.0	0.6	0.2
Italy/Italie			0.6	0.5	0.4	0.8	0.6	0.6	0.6	1.7
Haiti/Haïti				0.8	0.6	0.6	0.0	0.3	0.3	2.8

4. General Imports F.O.B. by Commodities according to the S.I.T.C. (Rev. 2) in thousand U.S. Dollars
Importations Générales F.O.B. par Produits d'après la C.T.C.I. (Rév. 2) en milliers de Dollars E.U.

SITC CTCI	COMMODITY	1992		1993		1994		1995		PRODUIT
		WEIGHT POIDS	VALUE VALEUR	WEIGHT POIDS	VALUE VALEUR	WEIGHT POIDS	VALUE VALEUR	WEIGHT POIDS	VALUE VALEUR	
	ALL COMMODITIES		2174600		2118400		2275800		2786400	TOUS PRODUITS
041	WHEAT ETC UNMILLED		41800		40600		39100		50400	FROMENT,EPEAUTRE
061	SUGAR AND HONEY						8600		16000	SUCRES ET MIEL
3	MINERAL FUELS ETC		500800		463300		525800		610100	COMBUSTIBLES MINERAUX LUB
33	PETROLEUM AND PRODUCTS		487800		453000		521700		604900	PETROLE ET DERIVES

5. General Exports F.O.B. by Commodities according to the S.I.T.C. (Rev. 2) in thousand U.S. Dollars
Exportations Générales F.O.B. par Produits d'après la C.T.C.I. (Rév. 2) en milliers de Dollars E.U.

SITC CTCI	COMMODITY	1992 WEIGHT POIDS	1992 VALUE VALEUR	1993 WEIGHT POIDS	1993 VALUE VALEUR	1994 WEIGHT POIDS	1994 VALUE VALEUR	1995 WEIGHT POIDS	1995 VALUE VALEUR	PRODUIT
	ALL COMMODITIES #1		1715375		1758898		2007775		766700	TOUS PRODUITS
0	FOOD AND LIVE ANIMALS		284746		285755		334951			ALIMENTS,ANIMAUX VIVANTS
01	MEAT AND PREPARATIONS		13791		14289		12970			VIANDES ET PREPARATIONS
011	MEAT FRESH,CHILLD,FROZEN	W 5985	12332	W 6533	13416	W 5153	9623			VIANDES FRAICHES,REF,CONGE
0111	BOVINE MEAT FRESH,FROZEN	W 5985	12332	W 6533	13415	W 5091	9540			VIANDES BOVIN FRAI,REF
01111	BOVINE MEAT WITH BONE IN	W 5985	12332	W 6533	13415	W 5091	9540			VIANDES BOVIN NON DESOSS
04	CEREALS AND PREPARATIONS		2139		12752		4856			CEREALES ET PRODUITS
042	RICE			W 29508	11098	W 5827	2157			RIZ
0422	RICE SEMI-MILLED,MILLED			W 29508	11098	W 5827	2157			RIZ POLI,GLACE INCL BRISURES
04222	RICE BROKEN			W 29508	11098	W 5827	2157			BRISURES DE RIZ
05	VEGETABLES AND FRUIT		53867		54096		55347			LEGUMES ET FRUITS
054	VEG ETC FRSH,SMPLY PRSVD	W 37206	10901	W 35738	10411	W 34906	9651			LEGUMES FRAIS,CONG,SECS
0548	EDIBLE VEG NES FRESH,DRY	W 25813	6228	W 22571	5260	W 23477	5320			RACINES,TUBERCULES
05481	ROOTS,TUBERS FRESH,DRY	W 25317	5993	W 22051	4998	W 23061	5132			RACINES DE MANIOC ETC
056	VEGTBLES ETC PRSVD,PREPD	W 13098	5647	W 6847	3522	W 11164	6427			CONSERVES DE LEGUMES
0565	VEGTBLES PRSVD,PREPD NES	W 12467	5529	W 5608	3268	W 10013	6219			LEGUMES PREPARES CONSERVE
05659	OTH VEG PRESVD,PREPD NES	W 12467	5529	W 5608	3268	W 10013	6219			LEGUM PREPAP,CONSERV NDA
057	FRUIT,NUTS,FRESH,DRIED	W 154869	30448	W 175626	31961	W 177523	32571			FRUITS FRAIS OU SECS
0579	FRUIT FRESH OR DRIED NES	W 142849	27287	W 164008	29082	W 165672	29751			FRUITS FRAIS,SECS NDA
05796	DATES,FRESH OR DRIED	W 132331	24988	W 154072	27273	W 152243	27455			DATTES FRAICHES OU SECHES
058	FRUIT PRESERVED,PREPARED	W 11845	6871	W 16918	8202	W 12751	6698			CONSERVES DE FRUITS
06	SUGAR AND PREPS,HONEY		138676		127196		129085			SUCRES ET PRODUITS
061	SUGAR AND HONEY	W 511381	138282	W 530607	126826	W 491399	128672	W 395843	116227	SUCRES ET MIEL
0611	RAW BEET AND CANE SUGAR							W 242377	102278	SUCRES BRUTS
0612	REFINED SUGAR ETC	W 351711	123776	W 316600	109600	W 319735	113345			SUCRES RAFFINES
0615	MOLASSES	W 144044	11481	W 169854	12825	W 148018	10933	W 134194	10414	MELASSES
0619	SUGARS AND SYRUPS NES	W 15323	2811	W 43936	4264	W 23485	4309	W 19272	3535	AUTRES SUCRES SIROPS
07	COFFEE,TEA,COCOA,SPICES		63467		63186		118685			CAFE,THE,CACAO,EPICES
071	COFFEE AND SUBSTITUTES	W 23265	27091	W 20009	25667	W 20364	62919	W 25993	81917	CAFE ET SUCCEDANES
0711	COFFEE GREEN,ROASTED,SUB	W 23265	27091	W 20009	25667	W 20364	62919	W 25993	81917	CAFE TORREFIE OU DECAFEINE
07111	COFFEE GREEN,HUSKS,SKINS	W 23265	27091	W 20009	25667	W 20364	62919			CAFE NON TORREFIE
072	COCOA	W 47275	35256	W 46641	36908	W 52115	55014	W 49783	54325	CACAO
0721	COCOA BEANS,RAW,ROASTED	W 46327	33236	W 45210	33885	W 50780	51380	W 49783	54325	CACAO EN FEVES
073	CHOCOLATE AND PRODUCTS	W 1068	1005	W 526	501	W 561	630	W 2199	5173	CHOCOLAT
09	MISC EDIBLE PRODUCTS		10273		11184		11358			PREP ALIMENTAIRES DIVERSES
098	EDIBLE PRODCTS,PREPS NES	W 12378	10273	W 12407	11184	W 12305	11358			PREP ALIMENTAIRES NDA
09809	MISC FOOD PREPRTIONS NES	W 11400	9577	W 11702	10181	W 11444	10611			PREP ALIMENTAIRES NDA
1	BEVERAGES AND TOBACCO		76852		69476		64111			BOISSONS ET TABACS
12	TOBACCO AND MANUFACTURES		72746		66288		60247			TABACS BRUTS FABRIQUES
121	TOBACCO UNMNFCTRD,REFUSE	W 10950	42224	W 12702	39080	W 6153	29679	W 10195	27331	TABACS BRUTS,DECHETS
1211	TOBACCO,NOT STRIPPED	W 10950	42224	W 12702	39080	W 6153	29679	W 8814	15661	TABACS NON ECOTES
12111	— VIRGI TYPE,FLUE-CURED	W 9819	41317	W 11612	37493	W 5145	28306			VIRGINIE SECHES AIR CHAUD
1212	TOBACCO STRIPPED OR PART							W 1381	11670	TABACS PART ECOTES
122	TOBACCO,MANUFACTURED	W 4004	30522	W 2818	27208	W 2412	30568			TABACS FABRIQUES
1221	CIGARS,CHEROOTS,ETC	W 3614	30173	W 2487	24314	W 2147	26065			CIGARES
2	CRUDE MATERLS,EXCL FUELS		8592		9259		11421			MAT BRUTES NON COMESTIBLES
287	BASE METAL ORES,CONC NES	W 1277	158	W 1096	204	W 981	189	W 79637	242216	MINERAIS METAUX COMMUNS
2872	NICKEL ORES,CONCENTRATES							W 79637	242216	MINERAIS DE NICKEL
28722	NICKEL MATTE,SINTERS,ETC							W 79637	242216	MATTES,SINTERS
29	CRUDE ANIMAL,VEG MAT NES		5256		4259		4917			MATIERES BRUTES ANIM,VEGET
5	CHEMCLS,RELATED PROD NES		46559		50029		51732			PRODUITS CHIMIQUES
51	ORGANIC CHEMICALS		15624		22152		19043			PROD CHIMIQ ORGANIQUES
515	ORG-INORG COMPOUNDS ETC	W 29724	14541	W 36150	16467	W 30977	12417			COMPOSES ORGANO-MINERAUX
5156	HETEROCYCLIC CMPDS ETC	W 29724	14541	W 36150	16467	W 30977	12417			COMPOSES HETEROCYCLIQUES
51569	OTH HETEROCYC CMPDS,ETC	W 29724	14541	W 36150	16467	W 30977	12417	W 34218	15751	AUT COMP HETEROCYCLIQUES
541	*MEDICINAL,PHARM PRODUCT	K 1280100	20757	K 1241023	17101	K 1675687	18516			PROD MEDICINAUX PHARMACEUT
5417	MEDICAMENTS	K 1229673	20067	K 1123268	15691	K 1112086	12555			MEDICAMENTS
54179	— CONTNG OTH SUBSTANCES	K 1055472	17049	K 991065	15115	K 862472	11160			MED CONT AUT SUBSTANCES
58	PLASTIC MATERIALS ETC		4685		5765		6742			MAT PLAST ARTIFICIELLES
585	PLASTIC MATERIAL NES	W 1585	4088	W 2021	5431	W 2457	6553			RESINES ARTIFICIELLES
5851	MODIFIED NATL RESINS ETC	W 1562	4050	W 2020	5430	W 2457	6553			RESINES
6	BASIC MANUFACTURES		314078		316833		400157			ART MANUFACTURES
61	LEATHER,DRESSED FUR,ETC		94806		95874		110292			CUIRS,PELLETERIES
612	LEATHER ETC MANUFACTURES	W 5399	94612	W 4243	94703	W 4421	108495			OUVRAGES EN CUIRS NDA
6123	PREPRD PARTS OF FOOTWEAR	W 5399	94612	W 4242	94615	W 4414	108488			PARTIES DE CHAUSSURES
64	PAPER,PAPERBOARD AND MFR		10118		10054		11164			PAPIERS,CARTONS & OUVRAGES
642	PAPER,ETC,PRECUT,ARTS OF	W 1761	9889	W 1479	9976	W 2851	10851			PAP,CARTONS DECOUPES
6428	PAPER ETC ARTICLES NES	W 1174	8965	W 1213	9637	W 1435	10230			OUVRAGES EN PATE A PAPIER
64289	OTHER ARTICLES OF PAPER	W 1165	8936	W 1213	9637	W 1435	10230			ARTICLES,OUVRAGES EN PAPIER
65	TEXTILE YARN,FABRICS,ETC		41800		52334		64780			FILS,TISSUS,ARTICLES TEXTILE
651	TEXTILE YARN	W 1287	10204	W 1315	10629	W 1380	10784			FILS TEXTILES
6514	SYN FIB YRN,BULK,MONOFIL	W 1281	10148	W 1315	10619	W 1380	10784			FILS CONT 85% FIB TEXT SYNTH
65141	— TEXTRD,CONT POLYAMIDE	W 1254	9864	W 1302	10578	W 1331	10683			FILS TEXT FIB CONT POLYAMID
656	LACE,RIBBONS,TULLE,ETC	W 491	4784	W 488	5856	W 360	3895			TULLES,BRODERIE
657	SPECIAL TXTL FABRC,PRODS	W 708	7595	W 1264	16211	W 1825	26768			TISSUS SPECIAUX
6576	HAT BODIES	W 474	7564	W 1060	16185	W 1592	26744			CLOCHES POUR CHAPEAUX
65761	WOOL,FUR FELT HAT BODIES	W 464	7536	W 1060	16185	W 1592	26744			CLOCHES NON DRESSEES
658	TEXTILE ARTICLES NES	W 2487	12738	W 2832	13289	W 3852	17488			ART FACONNES MAT TEXTILES
6582	MADE-UP CANVAS GOODS	W 2411	11364	W 2795	12982	W 3825	17439			BACHES,TENTES ETC
65829	OTH MADE-UP CANVAS GOODS	W 2411	11364	W 2795	12982	W 3825	17439			BACHES,TENTES EXC COTON
66	NONMETAL MINERAL MFS NES		9296		6447		6455			ART MIN NON METALLIQUES
667	PEARL,PREC-,SEMI-P STONE		6763		3504		2645			PERLES, PIERRES GEMMES
6672	DIAMONDS NONINDUST,UNSET		6763		3504		2643			DIAMANTS BRUTS
66721	— ROUGH,UNSORTED		6763		3504		2643			DIAMANTS BRUTS NON TRIES
67	IRON AND STEEL		144423		133635		190191			FER ET ACIER
671	PIG IRON ETC	W 56020	143930	W 64691	126903	W 83031	182438			FONTE,SPIEGEL,POUDRES
6716	FERRO-ALLOYS	W 56020	143930	W 64691	126903	W 83031	182438			FERRO-ALLIAGES
67169	OTHER FERRO-ALLOYS	W 56020	143930	W 64691	126903	W 83031	182438			AUTRES FERRO-ALLIAGES
674	IRN,STL UNIV,PLATE,SHEET	W 12	209	W 427	6133	W 472	6619			LARGES PLATS,TOLES
6744	IRN,STL HVY PLATE,ROLLED	W 12	209	W 424	6132	W 464	6614			TOLES LAMINEES PLUS 4.75 MM
67441	— OF IRON OR SIMPLE STL	W 12	209	W 424	6132	W 464	6614			TOLES NON ACIER FIN CARB
681	SILVER,PLATINUM,ETC								3450	ARGENT ET PLATINE
6811	SILVER UNWKD,PARTLY WRKD								3450	ARGENT BRUT MI-OUVRE
69	METAL MANUFACTURES NES		12492		16616		16539			ART MANUFACT EN METAL NDA
694	STL,COPPR NAILS,NUTS,ETC	W 2545	8572	W 4587	14330	W 4582	13920			CLOUS,VIS,ECROUS
69401	IRON,STEEL NAILS ETC	W 2534	8558	W 4587	14330	W 4581	13917			CLOUS,POINTES FER,ACIER
7	MACHINES,TRANSPORT EQUIP		171404		190325		232422			MACHINES MATERIEL TRANSPORT
75	OFFICE MACHNES,ADP EQUIP		6175		3276		3346			MACH BUREAU TRAIT AUTOM
759	OFFICE,ADP MCH PTS,ACCES	W 160	6175	W 17	3275	W 77	3344			PIECES DU 751 ET 752
7591	OFFICE MACHINE PARTS NES	W 160	6175	W 17	3275	W 77	3344			PIECES DU 7511,7518
75911	TYPEWRTR PARTS,ACCES NES	W 160	6175	W 17	3275	W 77	3344			PIECES DU 7511

5. General Exports F.O.B. by Commodities according to the S.I.T.C. (Rev. 2) in thousand U.S. Dollars
Exportations Générales F.O.B. par Produits d'après la C.T.C.I. (Rév. 2) en milliers de Dollars E.U.

SITC CTCI	COMMODITY	1992 WEIGHT POIDS	1992 VALUE VALEUR	1993 WEIGHT POIDS	1993 VALUE VALEUR	1994 WEIGHT POIDS	1994 VALUE VALEUR	1995 WEIGHT POIDS	1995 VALUE VALEUR	PRODUIT
76	TELECOMM,SOUND EQUIPMENT		10904		20559		30405			EQUIPMENT DE TELECOM
764	TELECOM EQPT,PTS,ACC NES	W 401	10758	W 687	20558	W 1014	30107			EQUIP TELECOM,PIECES
7643	TV,RADIO TRANSMITTRS ETC	W 179	5604	W 390	12336	W 701	19954			APP EMET TELE RADIO
7649	PTS NES OF EQUIPMT OF 76	W 221	5154	W 296	8215	W 313	10153			PIECES DE LA DIV 76
76493	TELECOMM EQUIPMT PTS NES	W 217	5128	W 292	7939	W 313	10152			PIECES 761,762,764.3,8
77	ELECTRIC MACHNRY NES ETC		152784		163438		192268			MACH APP ELECT NDA
772	SWITCHGEAR ETC,PARTS NES	W 6818	117036	W 6941	103719	W 7244	115995			APP COUPURE,SECT ETC
7721	SWITCHGEAR ETC	W 305	9365	W 852	24865	W 995	33982			APP COUPURE,SECTIONMNT
7722	PRINTED CIRCUITS,PTS NES	W 6513	107671	W 6089	78854	W 6249	82013			CIRCUITS ET PIECES
773	ELECTR DISTRIBUTNG EQUIP	W 80	6708	W 194	8486	W 174	8783			EQUIPMT DISTRIBUTION ELECT
7731	INSULATED WIRE,CABLE ETC	W 80	6708	W 194	8486	W 174	8783			FILS,CABLES ISOLES ELECT
778	ELECTRICAL MACHINERY NES	W 2154	29040	W 2272	51232	W 2428	66994			AUTRES MACH ELECT NDA
7788	OTH ELEC MACHY,EQUIP NES	W 1040	27088	W 1703	50070	W 1905	66068			AUT MACH APP ELEC NDA
77883	ELEC SIGNALLING EQU NES	W 1040	27088	W 1703	50070	W 1870	65904			APP ELECT SIGNAL ACOUS
8	MISC MANUFACTURED GOODS		783485		822362		847584			ART MANUFACTURES DIVERS
821	*FURNITURE,PARTS THEREOF	W 3729	6150	W 3118	5272	W 3070	5718			MEUBLES ET PIECES
831	*TRAVEL GOODS,HANDBAGS	W 4859	30354	W 4883	27829	W 4700	28441			ARTICLES DE VOYAGE ETC
83101	HANDBAGS NES	W 698	5614	W 1137	6913	W 592	3993			SACS A MAIN
83109	OTHER TRAVEL BAGS,CASES	W 4013	23480	W 3597	19921	W 4030	24004			AUT CONTENANTS SIMILAIRES
84	CLOTHING AND ACCESSORIES		486593		526939		509263			VETEMENTS
842	MENS OUTERWEAR NOT KNIT	W 31845	148507	W 35626	160738	W 40128	173671			VET DESSUS POUR HOMMES
8421	— OVERCOATS,OTHER COATS	W 2174	25679	W 1809	22725	W 2011	21718			MANTEAUX HOMMES MAT TEXT
84211	—— OF WOOL,FINE HAIR	W 1598	21294	W 1247	17304	W 1496	18158			MANTEAUX HOMMES DE LAINE
84219	—— OF OTHER FIBRES	W 576	4385	W 562	5421	W 515	3560			MANTEAUX HOMMES AUT FIBR
8422	— SUITS	W 27844	112232	W 30846	120087	W 34826	137637			COMPLETS HOMMES MAT TEXT
84223	—— OF MAN–MADE FIBRES	W 27788	112005	W 30843	120075	W 34815	137605			COMPLETS HOMMES FIB SYNT
8429	— OTHER OUTER GARMENTS	W 1822	10569	W 2936	17827	W 3263	14291			AUT VET DES HOM MAT TEX
84299	—— OF OTHER FIBRES	W 1632	8637	W 2637	14617	W 2975	11016			VET DES HOM NDA AUT FIB
843	WOMENS OUTERWEAR NONKNIT	W 13275	76821	W 17960	104420	W 16397	91497			VET DESSUS FEMMES MAT TEX
8431	— COATS AND JACKETS	W 5398	40362	W 7880	55694	W 7175	47189			MANT,VEST FEM MAT TEXTIL
84311	—— OF WOOL,FINE HAIR	W 3228	25373	W 5069	39258	W 4008	28769			MANT,VEST FEMMES LAINE
84312	—— OF COTTON	W 1119	10194	W 1591	11327	W 1579	11322			MANT,VEST FEMMES COTON
84313	—— OF MAN–MADE FIBRES	W 1051	4795	W 1220	5109	W 1589	7098			MANT,VEST FEM FIBR SYNT
8432	— SUITS AND COSTUMES	W 6961	33181	W 9096	43619	W 8013	38370			COSTUMES–TAIL MAT TEXIL
84321	—— OF WOOL,FINE HAIR	W 1722	9014	W 1558	9044	W 1280	7403			COSTUMES–TAIL LAINE
84322	—— OF COTTON	W 5239	24167	W 7538	34575	W 6733	30967			COSTUMES–TAIL COTON
844	UNDER GARMENTS NOT KNIT	W 23370	153896	W 27574	158299	W 26294	151505			VETEMENT DESSOUS MAT TEX
8441	— MENS SHIRTS	W 15586	112714	W 18085	112330	W 15791	101581			CHEMISES HOMMES MAT TEXT
84411	—— OF COTTON	W 11167	99638	W 10895	88947	W 9138	80417			CHEMISES HOMMES DE COTON
84412	—— OF SYNTHETIC FIBRES	W 449	1391	W 2526	10204	W 1432	4930			CHEMISES HOMMES FIB SYNT
84419	—— OF OTHER FIBRES	W 3969	11685	W 4664	13179	W 5221	16234			CHEMISES HOMMES AUT FIBR
8442	— MENS,OTHR THAN SHIRTS	W 3933	13017	W 5562	18374	W 5496	19303			SOUS–VET HOMMES MAT TEXT
84421	—— OF COTTON	W 3488	9076	W 4726	14057	W 4667	16333			SOUS–VET HOMMES DE COTON
8443	— WOMENS	W 3851	28165	W 3927	27595	W 5007	30621			VET DESSOUS FEM MAT TEXT
84431	— OF COTTON	W 1065	7261	W 842	13052	W 1270	9809			VET DESSOUS FEM DE COTON
84439	— OF OTHER FIBRES	W 2786	20904	W 3085	14543	W 3737	20812			VET DESSOUS FEM AUT FIBR
845	OUTERWEAR KNIT NONELASTC	W 2282	11023	W 5268	21833	W 7715	31250			VET DESSOUS,ACCES BONNET
8451	— JERSEYS,PULLOVERS ETC	W 2282	11023	W 5268	21833	W 7715	31250			CHANDAILS,PULL–OVERS ETC
84519	—— OF OTHER FIBRES	W 2282	11023	W 5268	21833	W 7715	31250			CHANDAILS,PULL AUT FIBR
846	UNDER GARMENTS KNITTED	W 1740	30735	W 1997	21139	W 2461	28525			SOUS VETS DE BONNETERIE
8465	CORSETS,GARTERS,ETC	W 1740	30735	W 1997	21139	W 2461	28525			CORSETS,GAINES ART SIM
84652	CORSETS,BRACES ETC	W 1719	30655	W 1972	20968	W 2385	27887			CORSETS,GAINES,JARRETEL
848	HEADGEAR,NONTXTL CLOTHNG	W 2910	65255	W 2671	59415	W 1578	29661			VET ACCES MAT AUT QUE TEX
8481	LEATHER CLOTHES,ACCESSOR	W 984	23363	W 653	17344	W 314	5898			VET ACCES MAT CUIR ARTIF
8484	HEADGEAR	W 1896	41168	W 2017	42070	W 1264	23763			COIFFURES ET PARTIES NDA
84843	HEADGEAR TEXTILE NONFELT	W 1890	41155	W 2005	42014	W 1259	23750			CHAPEAUX EN BONNETERIE
851	*FOOTWEAR	W 2993	18779	W 2563	14738	W 4919	35298			CHAUSSURES
85101	FOOTWEAR RUBBER,PLASTIC	W 2353	14738	W 1969	7754	W 3182	11276			CHAUS SEMELLES CAOUTCH
85102	FOOTWEAR LEATHER	W 543	3399	W 585	6904	W 1727	23974			CHAUS SEMELLES EN CUIR
87	PRECISION INSTRUMNTS NES		111767		145013		159110			INSTRUM,APPAR SCIENT NDA
872	MEDICAL INSTRUMENTS NES	W 7955	111660	W 8615	144976	W 8961	158999			INSTR,APP MEDIC–CHIR NDA
87202	OTH MEDICAL INSTRUMENTS	W 7955	111660	W 8615	144976	W 8961	158999			INSTRUM,APP MEDECINE
89	MISC MANUFCTRD GOODS NES		127060		99726		107141			ART MANUFACTURES DIVERS
893	ARTICLES OF PLASTIC NES	W 1325	4233	W 1111	4260	W 1778	9688			OUVRAGES EN MAT DIVIS 58
8939	MISC PLASTIC ARTICLES	W 1325	4233	W 1111	4260	W 1778	9688			ART DIVERS EN MAT DIV 58
89399	OTHR PLASTC ARTICLES NES	W 1325	4233	W 1111	4260	W 1778	9688			AUT OUV MAT DIV 58
897	GOLD,SILVER WARE,JEWELRY		113279		85786		87475			BIJOUTERIE,ORFEVRERIE
8972	IMITATION JEWELLERY		707		6018		3836			BIJOUTERIE DE FANTAISIE
8973	PREC JEWLRY,GLD–SILVWARE		84019		60464		71513			BIJOUX OR,ARGENT ORFEVRE
89731	PRECIOUS METAL JEWELLERY		80831		41642		38158			ART BIJOUTERIE,JOAILLER
89732	GOLD,SILVER,ETC WARE		3188		18822		33355			ORFEVRERIE MET PRECIEUX
8974	PREC MTL INDUS,LAB EQUIP		28553		19304		12126			AUT OUV METAUX PRECIEUX
9	GOODS NOT CLASSD BY KIND		28882		12747		61053			ART TRANSACT NON CLASSES
931	*SPECIAL TRANSACTIONS	W 787	3788	W 5630	6858	W 9687	41599			TRANS.SPECIALES
971	*GOLD,NON MONETARY NES	K 7219	24934	K 3184	5835	K 13124	19410		41274	OR NON MONETAIRE
97101	NONMON GLD UNWRT,SEMIMFD	K 7219	24934	K 3184	5835	K 13085	19389			OR,ALLIAGES D'OR BRUTS

FOOT NOTES – NOTES

TABLE 3 –

1 Export data for 1992, 1993 and 1994 include exports from the Industrial Free Zones.

TABLE 5 –

1 Data for 1992, 1993 and 1994 include exports from the Industrial Free Zones.

TABLEAU 3 –

1 En 1992, 1993 et 1994 les exportations incluent les données des zones franches et industrielles.

TABLEAU 5 –

1 Y compris en 1992, 1993 et 1994 les données des zones franches et industrielles.

1. HISTORICAL SERIES, 1961–1996 GENERAL TRADE, IMPORTS C.I.F., EXPORTS F.O.B.
SERIES HISTORIQUES, 1961–1996 COMMERCE GENERAL, IMPORTATIONS C.A.F., EXPORTATIONS F.O.B

YEAR ANNEE	VALUE IN MILLION U.S. DOLLARS VALEUR EN MILLION U.S. DOLLARS MERCHANDISE –MARCHANDISE		GOLD –OR		CONVERSION FACTORS FACTEURS DE CONVERSION CENTS E.U. PAR		INDEX NUMBERS –INDICES QUANTUM		UNIT VALUE VALEUR UNITAIRE	
	IMPORTS	EXPORTS	IMPORTS	EXPORTS	IMPORTS	EXPORTS	IMPORTS	EXPORTS	IMPORTS	EXPORTS
1961	106.40	126.90								
1962	97.10	142.80								
1963	128.00	148.20								
1964	151.90	159.00								
1965	168.90	169.50								
1966	171.90	184.10						47		121
1967	214.20	189.70						51		120
1968	255.50	226.30						70		124
1969	241.80	152.50						54		128
1970	273.80	189.90						49		28
1971	340.20	199.10						49		30
1972	318.60	326.30						64		25
1973	537.10	486.90						91		34
1974	962.50	962.40						66		71
1975	943.00	897.00						60		66
1976	958.80	1257.60						68		74
1977	1189.00	1436.30						53		100
1978	1627.30	1493.80						60		97
1979	1985.60	2067.00						60		136
1980	2253.30	2480.80						58		165
1981	2246.10	2541.60						67		152
1982	2189.00	2340.80						57		164
1983	1465.00	2202.60						76		138
1984	1716.00	2581.30						81		132
1985	1674.40	2779.80						98		128
1986	1810.20	2171.50						105		76
1987	2251.50	1927.80						68		86
1988	1713.50	2192.40						100		72
1989	1854.80	2353.80						98		85
1990	1861.90	2714.30						100		100
1991	2397.40	2851.50						106		88
1992	2500.50	3007.40						108		97
1993	2561.90	2903.70						121		75
1994	3690.30	3819.90						139		83
1995	4193.30	4307.20						150		84
1996	3723.60	4890.00						139		96

2. IMPORTS BY BROAD ECONOMIC CATEGORY AND EXPORTS BY INDUSTRIAL ORIGIN. (PERCENTAGE OF TOTAL VALUE)
IMPORTATIONS PAR CATEGORIES ECONOMIQUES ET EXPORTATIONS PAR BRANCHE D'ACTIVITE.(EN POURCENTAGE DE LA VALEUR TOTALE)

IMPORTS – IMPORTATIONS

	1990	1991	1992	1993	1994	1995	1996
TOTAL IMPORTS–IMPORTATIONS TOTALES	100.	100.	100.	100.	100.	100.	100.
1 FOOD BEV–ALIMENTATION BOISSONS	7.9	6.8	4.2	4.5	5.9	6.6	7.9
11 PRIMARY–PRODUITS DE BASE	4.6	3.5	1.6	2.7	2.6	3.0	3.8
111 FOR INDUSTRY–POUR L'INDUSTRIE	4.5	3.3	1.4	2.3	1.6	2.1	2.6
112 FOR HOUSEHOLDS–POUR LES MENAGES	0.1	0.2	0.2	0.4	0.9	0.9	1.2
12 PROCESSED–PRODUITS ELABORES	3.3	3.3	2.6	1.8	3.4	3.6	4.1
121 FOR INDUSTRY–POUR L'INDUSTRIE	1.1	1.6	1.1	0.4	0.8	0.8	1.1
122 FOR HOUSEHOLDS–POUR LES MENAGES	2.1	1.7	1.5	1.4	2.6	2.8	3.0
2 IND SUPPLIES–APPROV INDUSTRIELS	44.7	41.1	34.9	31.7	32.0	36.1	38.5
21 PRIMARY–PRODUITS DE BASE	2.0	1.6	1.3	1.7	1.4	2.4	2.8
22 PROCESSED–PRODUITS ELABORES	42.7	39.5	33.6	30.1	30.6	33.6	35.7
3 FUELS–COMBUSTIBLES	1.9	0.9	3.9	1.5	2.9	5.8	4.3
31 PRIMARY–PRODUITS DE BASE	0.0	0.0	0.0	0.8	1.5	2.0	3.0
32 PROCESSED–PRODUITS ELABORES	1.9	0.9	3.8	0.7	1.4	3.8	1.3
321 MOTOR SPIRIT–ESSENCE	1.9	0.0	0.0	0.0		0.6	0.1
322 OTHER–AUTRES	0.0	0.9	3.8	0.7	1.4	3.2	1.2
4 MACHINERY–EQUIPEMENT	25.1	26.3	25.7	27.2	20.1	20.2	20.6
41 CAPITAL EQUIPMENT–MACHINES	21.4	22.5	21.6	23.3	17.4	18.2	18.5
42 PARTS–PIECES ACCESSOIRES	3.7	3.8	4.0	3.9	2.6	1.9	2.1
5 TRANSPORT–TRANSPORT	12.9	15.7	19.7	22.4	28.4	19.9	14.6
51 PASSENGER CARS–AUTOMOBILES	2.1	3.2	8.4	10.4	11.6	7.0	5.8
52 OTHER–AUTRES	3.9	6.2	5.7	6.2	11.8	8.5	5.1
521 INDUSTRIAL–INDUSTRIELS	3.8	6.1	5.6	6.1	11.5	8.2	4.9
522 NON INDUSTRIAL–NON INDUSTRIEL	0.1	0.1	0.1	0.2	0.3	0.2	0.1
53 PARTS–PIECES ACCESSOIRES	7.0	6.3	5.6	5.8	5.1	4.4	3.7
6 CONSUM GOODS–BIENS CONSOMMATION	7.1	9.1	11.6	11.9	10.7	11.4	13.8
61 DURABLE–DURABLES	1.0	1.1	1.5	2.0	2.4	2.1	2.6
62 SEMI DURABLE–SEMI DURABLES	1.6	2.4	3.1	3.6	3.5	4.1	4.9
63 NON DURABLE–NON DURABLES	4.5	5.6	7.0	6.4	4.7	5.2	6.3
7 GOODS NES–BIENS NDA	0.4	0.1	0.1	0.7	0.0	0.1	0.2

EXPORTS – EXPORTATIONS

	1990	1991	1992	1993	1994	1995	1996
TOTAL EXPORTS–EXPORTATIONS TOTALES	100.	100.	100.	100.	100.	100.	100.
1 AGRICULTURE	40.2	51.1	46.0	42.8	49.8	47.4	44.1
2 MINING QUARRY–INDUS EXTRACTIVES	46.5	37.2	41.8	38.8	31.4	32.8	32.0
3 MANUFACTURING–IND MANUFACTUR	13.4	11.6	12.2	18.3	18.8	19.8	23.9
31 FOOD BEV TOBACCO–ALIM BOISS TAB	5.0	5.3	5.1	6.9	7.3	8.1	9.9
32 TEXTILES–INDUSTRIES TEXTILES	0.5	0.5	0.9	1.3	1.4	1.3	1.3
33 WOOD & PRODUCTS–BOIS & PRODUITS	0.9	1.0	0.7	1.4	1.2	1.3	1.5
34 PAPER & PRODUCTS–PAPIER & PRODT	0.0	0.0	0.4	0.4	0.3	0.4	0.4
35 CHEMICALS–INDUSTRIES CHIMIQUES	6.0	3.8	3.5	4.5	4.4	4.8	7.3
36 NON METAL MIN–MIN NON METAL	0.2	0.1	0.1	0.3	0.5	0.5	0.5
37 BASIC METAL–IND METAL BASE	0.1	0.1	0.2	0.2	0.3	0.3	0.2
38 METAL MANUF–MANUF METAL	0.6	0.7	1.2	2.9	3.1	2.8	2.5
39 OTH MANUF IND–AUTRES MANUF	0.2	0.2	0.2	0.4	0.3	0.3	0.3

3. TRADE BY PRINCIPAL COUNTRIES OF PROVENANCE AND LAST CONSIGNMENT (VALUE IN THOUSAND U.S. DOLLARS)
ECHANGES SELON LES PRINCIPAUX PAYS DE PROVENANCE ET DE DERNIERE CONSIGNATION (VALEUR EN MILLIERS DE DOLLARS EU)

COUNTRIES–PAYS	GENERAL IMPORTS C.I.F. IMPORTATIONS GENERALES C.A.F				
	1992	1993	1994	1995	1996
World	2501310	2552729	3622019	4195159	3733045
Africa	12914	11180	26965	31882	9129
Americas	1421112	1386252	2111186	2741217	2526217
Northern America	861609	839693	1004136	1374792	1223771
LAIA	488994	435660	1010027	1248190	1164040
CACM	24263	5415	4641	8650	11998
Caribbean	18756	24495	17722	40832	28982
Rest of America	27490	80990	74659	68752	97426
As.ex F.USSR	434233	459112	756933	619038	411272
Eur.x F.USSR	613226	676126	677255	706341	724513
EU	553027	621501	608726	643764	654728
EFTA	48649	36065	41503	43434	40552
East Europe	10717	17754	26527	18655	28460
Other Europe	10	239	210	28	
Former USSR	15079	13905	20279		20011
Oceania	4532	5638	25065	4612	18594
USA/Etats–Unis d'Amer	813586	810162	950327	1289777	1174081
Japan/Japon	326771	344703	515485	361157	209797
Colombia/Colombie	102868	99615	297903	399573	378469
Germany/Allemagne	133501	131237	216983	190451	155491
Brazil/Brésil	119237	99322	226954	187761	142553
Italy/Italie	127972	227380	138191	103157	98066
Venezuela	42979	46887	159982	262568	172623
Mexico/Mexique	57430	59162	150755	158534	197688
Spain/Espagne	131351	119229	82948	93071	170060
Chile/Chili	60516	48430	66620	111501	135185
Panama	27468	80679	73998	68701	97125
Korea, Republic of	19145	43362	102759	102130	60212
Argentina/Argentine	75880	41098	49971	75693	81192
Canada	47344	29439	53624	84679	49534
France,Monac	71853	49317	37531	59293	34594
Switz.Liecht	47088	35547	40191	42080	40015
Belgium–Luxembourg	19764	20254	34475	59241	64479
United Kingdom	25828	37599	35038	51270	45730
Peru/Pérou	27376	34717	52424	39848	40402
Netherlands/Pays–Bas	15113	13777	23973	39685	49769
Hong Kong	6701	9873	10048	19968	30106
Russian Federation	15079	13905	20279		19577
Sweden/Suède	9092	10011	16921	19248	13460
Netherlands Antilles	2241	17996	10741	19596	9520
So. Africa Customs Un	12075	9080	11277	14712	7363
Australia/Australie	4208	3159	24493	1996	17454
Trinidad and Tobago	15445	5759	5726	10264	6726
China/Chine	2820	8946	2510	26551	796
Israel/Israël	6597	5529	7064	8729	13021
Saudi Arabia	17481	0	4613	8115	9733
Poland/Pologne	1349	2811	7277	13393	13064
Korea Dem People's Rp			12566		24864
Turkey/Turquie	620	5103	20507	4891	2061
Guatemala	20019	1142	1393	2614	3519
Uruguay	2020	6183	4635	7230	8173
Romania/Roumanie		3790	6500	4095	12507
Denmark/Danemark	3811	3799	6432	5935	6603
Indonesia/Indonésie	4417	3540	4296	2262	10135
Ireland/Irlande	5315	3965	4851	6142	2943
Austria/Autriche	6050	1900	4637	4431	5555
Costa Rica	3950	4085	2788	4506	5479
Finland/Finlande	2135	2508	5764	5113	3907
Cuba	189	393	553	8519	6392
Algeria/Algérie	0		0	15500	
Singapore/Singapour			10726		4393
Czech Republic		3690	8352		2504
India/Inde	459	572	2782	6619	2714
Portugal	1234	500	891	6559	3831
Angola			12913		39
Hungary/Hongrie	4636	3903	2818	1105	89

COUNTRIES–PAYS	GENERAL EXPORTS F.O.B. EXPORTATIONS GENERALES F.O.B.				
	1992	1993	1994	1995	1996
Monde	3042289	3020002	3843353	4361500	4889834
Afrique	1622	5135	4599	9119	9553
Amériques	1980275	2047372	2499821	2841625	3158192
Amérique du Nord	1425409	1405766	1640798	1871012	1870271
ALAI	404763	517439	717345	761325	854812
MCAC	38965	25851	30140	33213	112339
Caraïbes	12247	9601	9990	14396	108835
Autre Amérique	98890	88714	101549	161679	211934
Asie l'URSS exclus	491845	398204	442792	481970	602138
Europe l'URSS exclus	546747	531223	824680	886114	1009234
UE	500405	493618	759970	843422	942553
AELE	1066	7253	7751	8969	7043
Europe de l'Est	44110	30137	56169	32172	36630
Autre de l'Europe			776	735	28
Ancienne URSS	6728	24239	38366	86423	87299
Océanie	14203	10094	9743	19314	20896
USA/Etats–Unis d'Amer	1421578	1397464	1625100	1853386	1851467
Korea, Republic of	347820	281592	289620	290368	314420
Colombia/Colombie	60884	141356	225982	251889	300481
Chile/Chili	151687	116328	166504	194388	220544
Italy/Italie	93468	120971	155325	173352	195434
Germany/Allemagne	107919	70555	188791	167233	175978
Panama	98769	88093	101366	161606	211731
Spain/Espagne	113223	82155	114575	150088	133171
Peru/Pérou	100760	130334	156813	69243	53269
Japan/Japon	62419	51317	75956	118342	138700
Belgium–Luxembourg	67317	59360	105755	93856	108229
United Kingdom	15236	45673	50417	95677	125127
Argentina/Argentine	30467	53388	71528	89909	84115
France,Monac	33143	45675	63993	79084	82901
Netherlands/Pays–Bas	40296	43338	49332	57307	77389
Mexico/Mexique	33134	42661	76407	54020	57731
Russian Federation	6728	24239	38366	65140	82539
Poland/Pologne	27610	14338	41691	28310	32008
Brazil/Brésil	12820	21026	7513	54050	43864
Venezuela	13297	9718	8012	34102	72443
China/Chine	776	4066	13601	15811	67121
Guatemala	23062	15216	17868	17347	21784
Portugal	2653	11153	18082	16510	19627
El Salvador	5319	745	2820	2134	53450
Canada	3811	8292	15438	17603	18731
New Zealand	12868	8744	8167	17911	15571
Cuba	694	3788	4965	6789	38461
Netherlands Antilles	10440	3969	700	180	35408
Iran (Islamic Rp. of)	3734	18228	12712	10346	62
Nicaragua	214	406	316	8520	28922
Hungary/Hongrie	14972	9997	8079	2169	1051
Finland/Finlande	16427	6676	4963	1957	4902
Costa Rica	9592	8506	7857	2723	3568
Turkey/Turquie	6633	3936	1336	4242	13469
Uruguay	253	235	523	8357	16247
Switz.Liecht	937	6054	4566	7109	6526
Aruba					23937
Israel/Israël	2192	2070	3193	5129	10450
Greece/Grèce	3704	794	156	1596	16666
Saudi Arabia	2795	523	1569	3377	11698
Lithuania/Lituanie				17029	2817
Syrian Arab Republic		71	7778	9518	1030
Ireland/Irlande	5843	4448	5179	195	486
Tunisia/Tunisie		1845	3046	5540	4856
Dominican Republic	502	1340	3932	4129	4335
Hong Kong	535	600	4782	3850	3692
Bolivia/Bolivie	1014	1504	2513	3771	4576
Croatia/Croatie					11869
Honduras	778	977	1279	2489	4615
Korea Dem People's Rp					9835

(VALUE AS PERCENTAGE OF WORLD TOTAL)(VALEURS EN POURCENTAGE DU TOTAL MONDIAL)

	1987	1988	1989	1990	1991	1992	1993	1994	1995	1996
Africa	0.9	1.0	1.9	0.6	1.2	0.5	0.4	0.7	0.8	0.2
Americas	48.0	54.0	59.1	58.2	56.3	56.8	54.3	58.3	65.3	67.7
Northern America	30.8	35.0	36.2	34.8	34.0	34.4	32.9	27.7	32.8	32.8
LAIA	15.2	17.3	20.7	20.7	19.8	19.5	17.1	27.9	29.8	31.2
CACM	0.8	1.0	1.3	1.5	1.0	1.0	0.2	0.1	0.2	0.3
Caribbean	0.2	0.2	0.4	0.7	0.9	0.7	1.0	0.5	1.0	0.8
Rest of America	1.0	0.6	0.4	0.5	0.5	1.1	3.2	2.1	1.6	2.6
As.ex F.USSR	21.0	18.7	11.7	13.0	14.9	17.4	18.0	20.9	14.8	11.0
Eur.x F.USSR	29.2	24.9	26.3	27.7	27.1	24.5	26.5	18.7	16.8	19.4
EU	25.6	21.9	22.2	23.8	23.2	22.1	24.3	16.8	15.3	17.5
EFTA	2.8	2.1	2.6	2.9	2.6	1.9	1.4	1.1	1.0	1.1
East Europe	0.5	0.9	1.4	0.8	1.1	0.4	0.7	0.7	0.4	0.8
Other Europe	0.2	0.1	0.1	0.2	0.2	0.0	0.0	0.0	0.0	
Former USSR	0.1	0.1	0.3	0.2	0.3	0.6	0.5	0.6		0.5
Oceania	0.2	0.6	0.7	0.2	0.1	0.2	0.2	0.7	0.1	0.5
USA/Etats–Unis d'Amer	29.0	33.1	33.9	32.6	31.9	32.5	31.7	26.2	30.7	31.5
Japan/Japon	15.0	13.9	8.2	9.5	10.0	13.1	13.5	14.2	8.6	5.6
Colombia/Colombie	2.3	2.0	2.4	3.2	4.1	4.1	3.9	8.2	9.5	10.1
Germany/Allemagne	9.1	6.2	6.7	7.8	6.1	5.3	5.1	6.0	4.5	4.2
Brazil/Brésil	6.2	6.4	9.3	7.5	5.9	4.8	3.9	6.3	4.5	3.8
Italy/Italie	4.3	3.7	4.5	5.8	6.2	5.1	8.9	3.8	2.5	2.6
Venezuela	0.7	1.3	0.9	1.8	1.8	1.7	1.8	4.4	6.3	4.6
Mexico/Mexique	2.4	3.3	2.9	2.9	1.4	2.3	2.3	4.2	3.8	5.3
Spain/Espagne	3.5	4.0	2.9	2.5	2.3	5.3	4.7	2.3	2.2	4.6
Chile/Chili	1.7	2.0	1.6	1.9	2.7	2.4	1.9	1.8	2.7	3.6

	1987	1988	1989	1990	1991	1992	1993	1994	1995	1996
Afrique	0.2	0.4	0.5	0.5	0.1	0.1	0.2	0.1	0.2	0.2
Amériques	76.0	67.3	79.1	81.9	66.7	65.1	67.8	65.0	65.2	64.6
Amérique du Nord	57.2	46.0	60.7	53.3	49.3	46.9	46.5	42.7	42.9	38.2
ALAI	9.8	12.5	13.3	10.8	12.3	13.3	17.1	18.7	17.5	17.5
MCAC	0.1	0.6	1.9	1.8	0.9	1.3	0.9	0.8	0.8	2.3
Caraïbes	6.7	6.6	0.5	10.9	0.4	0.4	0.3	0.3	0.3	2.2
Autre Amérique	2.2	1.6	2.6	5.0	3.8	3.3	2.9	2.6	3.7	4.3
Asie l'URSS exclus	5.0	5.6	5.4	5.5	15.0	16.2	13.2	11.5	11.1	12.3
Europe l'URSS exclus	8.5	10.4	9.8	11.5	17.6	18.0	17.6	21.5	20.3	20.6
UE	7.5	9.4	9.0	10.2	17.1	16.4	16.3	19.8	19.3	19.3
AELE	0.0	0.0	0.0	0.0	0.0	0.0	0.2	0.2	0.2	0.1
Europe de l'Est	0.9	0.9	0.5	0.9	0.4	1.4	1.0	1.5	0.7	0.7
Autre de l'Europe	0.1	0.1	0.2	0.5	0.2			0.0	0.0	0.0
Ancienne URSS	0.2	0.2	0.2	0.1		0.2	0.8	1.0	2.0	1.8
Océanie	0.5	0.5	0.4	0.5	0.6	0.5	0.3	0.3	0.4	0.4
USA/Etats–Unis d'Amer	57.0	45.9	60.6	53.0	49.2	46.7	46.3	42.3	42.5	37.9
Korea, Republic of	0.0	0.0	0.0	0.9	10.4	11.4	9.3	7.5	6.7	6.4
Colombia/Colombie	1.8	2.0	1.8	1.2	1.1	2.0	4.7	5.9	5.8	6.1
Chile/Chili	1.7	2.7	3.5	2.9	3.7	5.0	3.9	4.3	4.5	4.5
Italy/Italie	0.7	1.3	1.1	1.3	2.1	3.1	4.0	4.0	4.0	4.0
Germany/Allemagne	3.3	4.1	3.3	2.9	4.8	3.5	2.3	4.9	3.8	3.6
Panama	2.2	1.6	2.6	5.0	3.7	3.2	2.9	2.6	3.7	4.3
Spain/Espagne	0.8	1.1	1.7	2.5	4.0	3.7	2.7	3.0	3.4	2.7
Peru/Pérou	2.5	5.9	5.7	5.1	5.8	3.3	4.3	4.1	1.6	1.1
Japan/Japon	2.3	2.5	2.5	1.9	2.2	2.1	1.7	2.0	2.7	2.8

4. General Imports C.I.F. by Commodities according to the S.I.T.C. (Rev. 2) in thousand U.S. Dollars
Importations Générales C.A.F. par Produits d'après la C.T.C.I. (Rév. 2) en milliers de Dollars E.U.

SITC CTCI	COMMODITY	1993		1994		1995		1996		PRODUIT
		WEIGHT POIDS	VALUE VALEUR	WEIGHT POIDS	VALUE VALEUR	WEIGHT POIDS	VALUE VALEUR	WEIGHT POIDS	VALUE VALEUR	
	ALL COMMODITIES		2552729		3622019		4195159		3733045	TOUS PRODUITS
0	FOOD AND LIVE ANIMALS		99960		178919		263196		308713	ALIMENTS,ANIMAUX VIVANTS
02	DAIRY PRODCTS,BIRDS'EGGS		2908		7467		7175		11551	PRODUITS LAITIERS,OEUFS
03	FISH AND PREPARATIONS		581		9744		10951		15803	POISSONS ET PREPARATIONS
034	FISH,FRESH,CHILLED,FROZN	W 373	255	W 11374	9017	W 12704	9863	W 17610	14703	POISSON FRAIS, REFRIG,CONG
0342	FISH FROZEN,EXCL FILLETS	W 363	219	W 11346	8852	W 12674	9734	W 17592	14561	POISSONS CONGELES
04	CEREALS AND PREPARATIONS		59164		70656		113495		134383	CEREALES ET PRODUITS
041	WHEAT ETC UNMILLED	W 216565	45647	W 253428	47169	W 303986	71331	W 351020	85968	FROMENT,EPEAUTRE
0411	DURUM WHEAT UNMILLED	W 216536	45613	W 253428	47169	W 298986	70266	W 334120	81983	FROMENT DUR NON MOULU
044	MAIZE UNMILLED	W 8316	1391	W 11855	2657	W 18348	17256	W 26333	20414	MAIS NON MOULU
048	CEREAL ETC PREPARATIONS	W 2065	3122	W 4626	10752	W 6994	12111	W 8618	16404	PREPTNS A BASE CEREALES
05	VEGETABLES AND FRUIT		9438		19068		29024		32410	LEGUMES ET FRUITS
057	FRUIT,NUTS,FRESH,DRIED	W 5260	4090	W 17027	10883	W 19435	15851	W 22385	17767	FRUITS FRAIS OU SECS
06	SUGAR AND PREPS,HONEY		4645		26251		40572		22892	SUCRES ET PRODUITS
061	SUGAR AND HONEY	W 12194	4205	W 175939	20378	W 75728	33819	W 21824	12863	SUCRES ET MIEL
0612	REFINED SUGAR ETC	W 8624	2441	W 163410	15727	W 63410	27703	W 12151	8280	SUCRES RAFFINES
07	COFFEE,TEA,COCOA,SPICES		4032		12694		14012		12429	CAFE,THE,CACAO,EPICES
081	*FEEDING STUFF FOR ANIML	W 10821	7642	W 8107	6238	W 29127	13812	W 59415	43336	NOURRITURE POUR ANIMAUX
0813	OILCAKE AND OTH RESIDUES		2628	W 16	12	W 19377	6168	W 55383	36713	TOURTEAUX
08131	— OF SOYA BEANS		2628	W 2	3	W 19377	6168	W 55383	36713	TOURTEAUX DE SOJA
09	MISC EDIBLE PRODUCTS		5622		16437		23698		27969	PREP ALIMENTAIRES DIVERSES
098	EDIBLE PRODCTS,PREPS NES	W 1295	5524	W 4081	16397	W 7438	23471	W 5522	27622	PREP ALIMENTAIRES NDA
09809	MISC FOOD PREPRTIONS NES	W 597	4486	W 2943	14232	W 4005	19654	W 4000	24635	PREP ALIMENTAIRES NDA
1	BEVERAGES AND TOBACCO		16219		28675		23640		20560	BOISSONS ET TABACS
11	BEVERAGES		16195		28215		23453		20142	BOISSONS
112	ALCOHOLIC BEVERAGES	W 12624	15821	W 37222	27181	W 21207	22465	W 20528	19761	BOISSONS ALCOOLIQUES
2	CRUDE MATERLS,EXCL FUELS		70569		84342		137884		128022	MAT BRUTES NON COMESTIBLES
23	RUBBER, CRUDE		9320		10985		18454		16131	CAOUTCHOUC BRUT
251	*PULP AND WASTE PAPER	W 7714	4385	W 14298	5317	W 26246	14446	W 28024	7735	PATES A PAPIER,DECHETS
26	TEXTILE FIBRES AND WASTE		33395		37704		56293		53220	FIBRES TEXTILES
263	COTTON	W 13942	13276	W 4350	7416	W 9349	17264	W 7912	16378	COTON
2631	RAW COTTON,EXCL LINTERS	W 13633	13171	W 4147	7347	W 9137	17171	W 7811	16337	COTON EN MASSE
266	SYNTHETIC FIBRES TO SPIN	W 11016	17663	W 17020	27593	W 19094	35821	W 18541	33697	FIBRES SYNTHETIQUES
2665	DISCN SYNTH FIBRE UNCMBD	W 5361	7984	W 8274	12272	W 9698	18165	W 8358	15096	DISCONTINUES EN MASSE
26652	— POLYESTER	W 3970	5707	W 7135	10201	W 8543	15949	W 7192	12713	FIBRES EN POLYESTERS
2666	CONTIN FILAMNT TOW SYNTH	W 4185	6929	W 6780	11383	W 7343	14056	W 8654	15677	CABLES POUR DISCONTINUS
26663	— OF ACRYLIC FIBRES	W 3848	6394	W 6459	10782	W 6901	12966	W 8085	14288	DE FIBRES ACRYLIQUES
27	CRUDE FERTLZR,MINRLS NES		6697		11490		14018		9206	ENGRAIS MINERAUX BRUTS
29	CRUDE ANIMAL,VEG MAT NES		10815		15493		27619		37834	MATIERES BRUTES ANIM,VEGET
292	CRUDE VEG MATERIALS NES	W 1201	9413	W 1572	12386	W 2331	23561	W 2214	33597	MAT BRUTES VEGETALES NDA
2926	LIVE PLANTS,BULBS,ETC	W 457	6258	W 815	8779	W 1356	17833	W 1322	28816	BULBES,TUBERCULES
29269	LIVE PLANTS NES	W 403	5913	W 735	8147	W 1287	17302	W 1137	27356	AUTRES PLANTES VIVANTES
3	MINERAL FUELS ETC		42907		108481		249407		165577	COMBUSTIBLES MINERAUX LUB
33	PETROLEUM AND PRODUCTS		22787		54676		170837		53115	PETROLE ET DERIVES
334	PETROLEUM PRODUCTS,REFIN	W 29547	18295	W 155307	50273	W 724958	158777	W 114099	47833	PRODUITS RAFFINES
3341	GASOLINE,OTH LIGHT OILS	W 1425	1215			W 97292	25826	W 6317	2305	ESSENCES POUR MOTEURS
33411	MOTOR,AVIATION SPIRIT	W 1047	1038			W 96629	25607	W 6284	2294	ESSENCES MOTEURS D'AVIONS
3342	KEROSENE,OTH MEDIUM OILS		1			W 413160	73640	W 55342	15088	PETR LAMPANTS,AUT HUIL
33429	OTH MEDIUM PETROLEUM OIL					W 413160	73640	W 55342	15087	AUTRES HUILES MOYENNES
3343	GAS OILS					W 162592	24408			GAS OILS
3344	FUEL OILS,NES			W 154935	49669	W 20	5			FUEL OILS
3345	LUBS,PETROLEUM OILS NES	W 28122	17078	W 372	604	W 51912	34898	W 52441	30439	HUILES LUBRIFIANTES
33451	LUBS(HIGH PETR CONT) ETC	W 27892	16639			W 50945	32721	W 51812	29035	HUILES LUBRIF,H LOURDES
341	*GAS,NATURAL AND MANUFCT	W 103520	20081	W 142899	53690	W 290884	78342	W 274310	112271	GAZ NATUREL,GAZ MANUFACT
3413	PETROLM GASES,LIQUEFIED	W 103514	20049	W 142898	53685	W 290883	78297	W 274256	111569	GAZ DE PETROLE LIQUEFIE
34131	LIQUEFIED PROPANE,BUTANE	W 103513	20041	W 142874	53107	W 290882	78291	W 261271	70996	PROPANE,BUTANE LIQUEFIES
34139	OTH HYDROCARBON GAS LQFD	W 2	8	W 24	578	W 1	7	W 12985	40572	HYDROCARBURES GAZEUX NDA
4	ANIMAL,VEGETABLE OIL,FAT		10226		21474		26955		40551	HUILES,GRAISSES ANIM,VEG
42	FIXED VEGETABLE OIL,FAT		7338		17885		24229		37230	HUILES VEGETALES FIXES
423	FIXED VEG OILS,SOFT	W 7917	6393	W 29388	17208	W 31151	22749	W 56116	35298	HUILES VEGET DOUCES FIXES
4232	SOYA BEAN OIL	W 7522	5749	W 29052	16353	W 30621	21688	W 54562	33223	HUILE DE SOJA
5	CHEMCLS,RELATED PROD NES		390398		602641		729750		700004	PRODUITS CHIMIQUES
51	ORGANIC CHEMICALS		62699		90297		99882		93977	PROD CHIMIQ ORGANIQUES
512	ALCOHOLS,PHENOLS ETC	W 9186	6246	W 14630	9728	W 25314	12940	W 43806	10178	PHENOLS,PHENOLS–ALCOOLS
513	CARBOXYLIC ACIDS ETC	W 8848	12483	W 14617	21258	W 15540	24432	W 14808	23396	ACIDES CARBOXYLIQUES
5137	MONOACIDS AND DERIVATIVS	W 4785	9353	W 6572	12464	W 10244	15167	W 7057	9239	ACIDES MONOCARBOXYLIQUES
514	NITROGEN–FNCTN COMPOUNDS	W 4703	15854	W 6489	19424	W 6896	23344	W 5532	22946	COMPOSES FONCT AZOTEES
5148	OTH NITROGN–FNCTN CMPNDS	W 3103	8080	W 4840	11936	W 4846	14859	W 3571	12704	AUTRES COMPOSES AZOTES
515	ORG–INORG COMPOUNDS ETC	W 2344	15815	W 3626	25069	W 2744	19364	W 3044	21609	COMPOSES ORGANO–MINERAUX
5155	OTH ORG–INORG COMPOUNDS	W 1267	6612	W 2426	12423	W 1187	6378	W 1376	7688	AUTR COMP ORG–MINERAUX
52	INORGANIC CHEMICALS		31954		39720		48961		44883	PROD CHIM INORGANIQUES
522	INORG ELEMNTS,OXIDES,ETC	W 29877	14891	W 38964	15534	W 37133	18551	W 43085	18007	ELEMENTS INORGANIQUES
523	OTHR INORG CHEMICALS ETC	W 29658	16864	W 54320	24070	W 56102	30331	W 65956	26751	AUT PRODUITS CHIMIQUES INORG
5232	OTH MTL CMPD OF INRG ACD	W 18047	10281	W 36648	14978	W 36017	19027	W 26770	16487	SELS METALLIQUES
53	DYES,TANNING,COLOUR PROD		19479		34149		33962		31700	PROD TEINTURE,COLORANTS
531	SYNT DYE,NAT INDGO,LAKES	W 889	9026	W 1459	13047	W 2997	13059	W 2861	9940	MAT COLOR ORGAN,LAQUES
533	PIGMENTS,PAINTS,ETC	W 3819	9282	W 6229	18695	W 7794	19472	W 15157	20387	PIGMENTS,PEINTURES,VERNIS
541	*MEDICINAL,PHARM PRODUCT	K 6186288	95072		115160		164229	MK 10770	173283	PROD MEDICINAUX PHARMACEUT
5413	ANTIBIOTICS IN BULK	K 111315	9993	K 199455	11829	K 316044	18957	K 251848	13615	ANTIBIOTIQUES NDA
5417	MEDICAMENTS	K 4654707	71857	K 6940291	84209	K 6301873	124814	K 6623306	138026	MEDICAMENTS
54171	— CONTAINNG ANTIBIOTICS	K 1134512	9454	K 961124	12972	K 446405	22175	K 533001	22101	MED CONTN ANTIBIOTIQUES
54172	— CONTAINING HORMONES	K 1183855	11237	K 744304	9425	K 368772	13709	K 464761	18828	MED CONTENANT HORMONES
54179	— CONTNG OTH SUBSTANCES	K 2326216	50453	K 5194590	60832	K 5441159	87638	K 5541310	94514	MED CONT AUT SUBSTANCES
55	PERFUME,CLEANING ETC PRD		19119		32510		36908		40134	PROD POUR PARFUM,TOILETTE
551	ESSENTL OILS,PERFUME,ETC	W 1663	9060	W 1997	11950	W 2834	13482	W 1004	11749	HUILES ESSENTIELLES
5514	MIXED PERFUME SUBSTANCES	W 1566	8223	W 1885	10441	W 2640	11583	W 789	10669	MELANGES SUBSTAN ODORIFER
553	PERFUMERY,COSMETICS,ETC	W 1833	5459	W 3019	8361	W 3994	11374	W 3707	17176	PRODUITS DE PARFUMERIE
554	SOAP,CLEANSING ETC PREPS	W 2505	4600	W 5481	12200	W 6420	12052	W 5855	11209	SAVONS,PRODUITS DETERSIFS
562	*FERTILIZERS,MANUFACTURE	W 100160	20024		52963	W 261263	73500	W 262853	63659	ENGRAIS MANUFACTURES
5621	CHEM NITROGENOUS FERTLZR	W 44977	9907	W 140035	28377	W 133809	39564	W 151290	37665	ENGRAIS AZOTES
56216	UREA	W 43884	9216	W 133340	26230	W 114541	34571	W 122281	30918	UREE
5629	FERTILIZERS NES	W 23363	4356		14902	W 53689	21633	W 37658	14659	ENGRAIS NDA
56292	NITROG–PHOS FERTILZR NES	W 19381	3107		8124	W 33381	14376	W 29101	9895	ENGRAIS NDA CONT N P
58	PLASTIC MATERIALS ETC		62831		140662		139446		120577	MAT PLAST ARTIFICIELLES
582	PROD OF CONDENSATION ETC	W 8690	13695	W 22146	56607	W 17018	28975	W 12151	21772	PROD CONDENS,POLYCOND
5823	ALKYDS,OTHER POLYESTERS	W 2916	4364	W 12465	43568	W 6362	12544	W 4520	7561	ALKYDES ET AUT POLYESTERS
58231	— IN PRIMARY FORMS	W 2850	4098	W 12341	43045	W 6290	12157	W 4438	7207	SOUS FORMES PRIMAIRES
583	POLYMERIZATION ETC PRODS	W 50311	44177	W 87929	79017	W 80919	104563	W 91193	93786	PROD POLYMERISATION
5831	POLYETHYLENE	W 18067	13671	W 27036	20489	W 28104	33594	W 32874	32880	POLYETHYLENE
58311	— IN PRIMARY FORMS	W 17174	12807	W 26175	18983	W 25993	30005	W 30424	27326	POLYETHYLENE PRIMAIRES
5832	POLYPROPYLENE	W 11049	7431	W 19299	15184	W 16295	19688	W 16000	16579	POLYPROPYLENE

4. General Imports C.I.F. by Commodities according to the S.I.T.C. (Rev. 2) in thousand U.S. Dollars
Importations Générales C.A.F. par Produits d'après la C.T.C.I. (Rév. 2) en milliers de Dollars E.U.

SITC CTCI	COMMODITY	1993 WEIGHT POIDS	1993 VALUE VALEUR	1994 WEIGHT POIDS	1994 VALUE VALEUR	1995 WEIGHT POIDS	1995 VALUE VALEUR	1996 WEIGHT POIDS	1996 VALUE VALEUR	PRODUIT
58321	— IN PRIMARY FORMS	W 10791	6756	W 18976	14271	W 15882	18684	W 15689	15844	POLYPROPYLENE PRIMAIRES
5834	POLYVINYL CHLORIDE	W 14012	10997	W 30536	25332	W 25768	27890	W 31010	25067	CHLORURE DE POLYVINYLE
58341	— IN PRIMARY FORMS	W 13612	9911	W 29679	23341	W 24454	24358	W 30001	22576	SOUS FORMES PRIMAIRES
59	CHEMICAL MATERIALS NES		78490		96104		131197		130051	MAT PROD CHIMIQUES NDA
591	PESTICIDES,DISINFECTANTS	W 12758	44932	W 11013	58354	W 15702	86299	W 14059	81510	DESINF,INSECT,FONG,HERB
5911	INSECTICIDES,FOR RETAIL	W 2413	10874	W 2993	13231	W 5311	25519	W 4520	21819	INSECTICIDES VENTE DET
5912	FUNGICIDES,FOR RETAIL	W 7474	21322	W 2970	22889	W 3611	29725	W 2627	28334	FONGICIDES VENTE AU DET
5913	HERBICIDES,FOR RETAIL	W 2190	10670	W 4363	19948	W 6233	29064	W 6381	29859	HERBICIDES VENTE AU DET
598	MISCEL CHEM PRODUCTS NES	W 19934	30977	W 22823	33483	W 25816	39840	W 25912	42413	PROD DIV INDUST CHIM NDA
5989	CHEM PRODUCTS,PREPS NES	W 15227	21805	W 14589	21506	W 16516	24910	W 17659	28925	PROD PREP CHIMIQUES NDA
59899	OTH CHEM PRODS,PREPS,NES	W 9411	14492	W 7349	14892	W 10008	17097	W 11072	21844	AUT PRODUITS CHIMIQUES NDA
6	BASIC MANUFACTURES		445776		576603		788126		738524	ART MANUFACTURES
62	RUBBER MANUFACTURES NES		37327		43443		55627		54463	CAOUTCHOUC MANUFACTURE
625	RUBBER TYRES, TUBES ETC	W 7785	18577	W 12651	30107	W 14636	40076	W 14534	39199	PNEUS CAOUTCHOUC VULCANISE
6251	TYRES NEW FOR MOTOR CARS	W 2272	6043	W 3588	9796	W 3806	11591	W 5797	11611	PNEUS POUR VOITURES
6252	TYRES,NEW,BUS OR LORRY	W 1994	6476	W 4889	12931	W 6285	19712	W 5840	20302	PNEUS POUR AUTOBUS,CAMIONS
628	RUBBER ARTICLES NES	W 2193	11103	W 1514	7970	W 2381	10192	W 1808	10604	OUVRAGES CAOUTCHOUC NDA
64	PAPER,PAPERBOARD AND MFR		49598		103568		144527		124096	PAPIERS,CARTONS & OUVRAGES
641	PAPER AND PAPERBOARD	W 53201	44471	W 97460	91084	W 117818	125776	W 130055	100552	PAPIERS ET CARTONS
6411	NEWSPRINT	W 24514	15288	W 45220	46365	W 47351	43858	W 28988	24160	PAPIER JOURNAL
6412	PRINTG,WRITING PAPER NES	W 6662	5741	W 9889	8359	W 10760	12623	W 9269	9791	PAPIERS POUR L'IMPRESSION
6413	KRAFT PAPER,PAPERBOARD	W 2747	2105	W 4096	2885	W 24859	19735	W 36276	21437	PAPIER ET CARTON KRAFT
64131	KRAFT LINER IN BULK	W 1483	864	W 7	12	W 16332	12657	W 30643	15968	PAP KRAFT POUR COUVERTURES
6415	PAPER,PAPERBRD,BULK,NES	W 17025	12970	W 31811	24282	W 25146	33298	W 36838	30518	PAPIERS,CARTONS ROULEAUX
64159	OTHER PAPER ETC,BULK,NES	W 15436	11938	W 31399	23607	W 24377	32313	W 24708	24085	AUT PAPIER ROULEAUX FEUILLES
642	PAPER,ETC,PRECUT,ARTS OF	W 2513	5126	W 5396	12484	W 8399	18751	W 16083	23544	PAP,CARTONS DECOUPES
6428	PAPER ETC ARTICLES NES	W 497	1993	W 1853	5039	W 2794	8157	W 9960	11798	OUVRAGES EN PATE A PAPIER
65	TEXTILE YARN,FABRICS,ETC		44676		52746		60350		65343	FILS,TISSUS,ARTICLES TEXTILE
651	TEXTILE YARN	W 2680	8258	W 5683	14796	W 6045	18313	W 12980	17227	FILS TEXTILES
6514	SYN FIB YRN,BULK,MONOFIL	W 1896	5404	W 3739	10328	W 4823	12931	W 3899	12719	FILS CONT 85% FIB TEXT SYNTH
652	COTTON FABRICS,WOVEN	W 1358	5002	W 1202	6387	W 1427	4981	W 2626	11215	TISSUS DE COTON
653	WOVN MAN–MADE FIB FABRIC	W 2796	8772	W 1121	6337	W 1017	5114	W 1024	5569	TISSUS FIBRES SYNTH,ARTIF
657	SPECIAL TXTL FABRC,PRODS	W 3057	14231	W 3735	15211	W 3814	19354	W 14079	21346	TISSUS SPECIAUX
6573	COATED ETC TEXTILES NES	W 1868	8528	W 2374	8492	W 2138	9498	W 3171	12902	TISSUS,ART MATIERE TEXT NDA
65733	RUBBERIZED TEXT NOT KNIT	W 1735	8011	W 1998	7332	W 1956	8597	W 2236	10158	TISSUS CAOUTCHOUTES
66	NONMETAL MINERAL MFS NES		35264		66636		86904		82446	ART MIN NON METALLIQUES
661	LIME,CEMENT,BLDG PRODS	W 7699	2105	W 77033	11805	W 180143	18917	W 113038	17742	CHAUX,CIMENTS MAT CONSTR
662	CLAY,REFRACTORY BLDG PRD	W 4721	3642	W 11885	7201	W 20576	13070	W 18362	13560	MAT CONST REFRACTAIRES
663	MINERAL MANUFCTURES NES	W 2762	6078	W 5729	14208	W 4545	8311	W 4298	8251	ART MIN MANUF NDA
664	GLASS	W 19690	12479	W 31648	18826	W 36894	25554	W 35467	23282	VERRE
665	GLASSWARE	W 6808	7450	W 12334	11114	W 16015	15608	W 15851	14226	OUVRAGES EN VERRE
67	IRON AND STEEL		178913		186923		279104		262299	FER ET ACIER
672	IRON,STEEL PRIMARY FORMS	W 136985	63837	W 169945	58633	W 283807	120836		84840	LINGOTS FER,ACIER
6725	IRN,STL BLOOMS,SLABS,ETC	W 98062	49475	W 95884	35435	W 205403	86170	W 191702	58918	BLOOMS,BILLETTES FER ACIER
67251	IRN,SMPLE STL BLOOMS,ETC	W 98049	49394	W 95872	35377	W 205084	85828	W 191648	58823	BLOOMS ETC NON ACIER FIN
6727	IRN,STL COIL FR REROLLNG	W 38869	14321	W 74050	23182	W 77371	34379	W 62794	24859	EBAUCHES POUR TOLES FER
67271	IRON,SIMPLE STEEL COILS	W 38735	14154	W 73689	22933	W 77144	34240	W 60785	23531	EBAUCHES NON EN ACIER
673	IRON,STEEL SHAPES ETC	W 48171	22073	W 94049	35867	W 102273	42088	W 95589	37798	BARRES,PROFIL FER,ACIER
6731	IRON,STEEL WIRE ROD	W 27632	12043	W 45324	19197	W 61072	25052	W 63274	21277	FIL MACHINE FER,ACIER
67311	IRON,SIMPLE STL WIRE ROD	W 26670	11460	W 41935	17891	W 58543	23978	W 63210	21254	FIL MACH AUT ACIER FIN
6732	IRON,STEEL BARS ETC	W 14584	7421	W 30385	10213	W 30965	12279	W 22909	11611	BARRES FER,ACIER
674	IRN,STL UNIV,PLATE,SHEET	W 70072	45188	W 106201	54099	W 111960	73716	W 106056	66907	LARGES PLATS,TOLES
6745	IRN,STL MED PLATE,ROLLED	W 11454	6940	W 14914	5975	W 13577	7967	W 23620	12362	TOLES 3 A 4.75 MM
6746	IRN,STL THIN PLATE,ROLLD	W 31549	18010	W 48605	23598	W 51640	32414	W 36849	23134	TOLES LAM MOINS 3MM
67461	— OF IRON OR SIMPLE STL	W 30133	16049	W 47058	21871	W 49970	28562	W 35792	20595	TOL NON AC FIN MOINS 3 MM
6749	OTH IRN,STL PLATES,SHEET	W 13222	10109	W 27014	16603	W 25120	20113	W 26330	19617	AUTRES TOLES FER,ACIER
67491	— OF IRON OR SIMPLE STL	W 13026	9682	W 26872	16352	W 24805	19281	W 25638	18909	AUT TOLES AUTRES ACIER FIN
678	IRON,STL TUBES,PIPES,ETC	W 32278	44240	W 29098	33149	W 32398	38486	W 52226	67508	TUBES,TUYAUX EN FONTE,FER
6782	IRON,STL SEAMLESS TUBES	W 21461	20754	W 20939	18301	W 28656	29546	W 30986	38557	TUBES,TUYAUX SANS SOUDURE
6783	IRON,STL TUBES,PIPES NES	W 5928	10832	W 3322	5815	W 1877	2592	W 9796	11707	AUT TUBES,TUYAUX FER,ACIER
6785	IRON,STEEL TUBE FITTINGS	W 4428	12087	W 4077	7322	W 1864	6346	W 5840	12635	ACCESSOIRES DE TUYAUTERIE
68	NON–FERROUS METALS		27886		43377		61193		47394	METAUX NON FERREUX
682	COPPER EXC CEMENT COPPER	W 3372	9826	W 5516	15237	W 5573	19850	W 6237	17078	CUIVRE
6822	COPPER,ALLOYS WORKED	W 3213	9465	W 5381	15048	W 5566	19791	W 6223	17020	CUIVRE,ALLIAGES OUVRES
68221	COPPER BARS,WIRE,ETC	W 2510	6409	W 4575	12143	W 4665	15312	W 5525	13965	BARRES,PROFILES ET FILS
684	ALUMINIUM	W 6471	13260	W 12502	23012	W 12557	33903	W 10599	23830	ALUMINIUM
6841	ALUMINIUM,ALLOYS,UNWRGHT	W 4765	7586	W 8106	13055	W 9513	22676	W 6675	13217	ALUMINIUM,ALLIAGES BRUTS
69	METAL MANUFACTURES NES		70809		75366		92159		91372	ART MANUFACT EN METAL NDA
695	TOOLS	W 3885	24798	W 5680	20637	W 4784	20545	W 3707	18941	OUTILS A MAIN
6954	BLADES,TIPS,ETC FR TOOLS	W 1093	16463	W 338	8484	W 395	6538	W 370	8097	OUTILS POUR MACHINE–OUTIL
69541	PARTS TO INSERT IN TOOLS	W 306	9419	W 234	5983	W 213	4820	W 230	6367	OUTILS DE FORAGE
697	BASE MTL HOUSEHOLD EQUIP	W 1957	8421	W 3189	7945	W 2997	9093	W 4068	12035	ART MENAGE MET COMMUNS
699	BASE METAL MFRS NES	W 5611	18211		17382	W 8255	24419	W 9012	25187	ART MANUFACTURES MET NDA
7	MACHINES,TRANSPORT EQUIP		1250702		1737346		1678932		1323251	MACHINES MATERIEL TRANSPORT
71	POWER GENERATING EQUIPMT		105035		99245		141797		133486	MACHINES GENERATRICES
711	STEAM BOILERS & AUX PLNT	W 316	2439	W 566	3326	W 1301	6523	W 2703	25067	GENERATEURS VAPEUR EAU ETC
7111	STEAM BOILERS ETC	W 256	1442	W 527	2890	W 1268	5920	W 2396	20303	GENERATEURS VAPEUR EAU
712	STEAM ENGINES,TURBINES	W 19	592		2269	W 169	1414	W 2871	19848	MACHINES A VAPEUR D'EAU PIEC
7126	STEAM POWR UNITS,ENGINES	W 12	197		86	W 115	400	W 2870	19755	MACHINES A VAPEUR D EAU
713	INTRNL COMBUS PSTN ENGIN	W 10399	67694	W 16683	56408	W 13648	57326	W 4510	34342	MOTEURS EXPL COMB INT, PIECE
7139	PISTON ENGINE PARTS NES	W 4398	52464	W 6726	35028	W 7220	38541	W 2478	25400	PIECES POUR 713.2,3,8
714	ENGINES AND MOTORS NES	W 102	4627	W 118	3355	W 432	18575	W 546	13110	MOTEURS NON ELECTRIQUES
7148	GAS TURBINES NES	W 29	598	W 9	458	W 386	16259	W 512	10617	TURBINES A GAZ
71488	OTHER GAS TURBINES NES	W 17	480	W 6	187	W 380	15558	W 510	10552	AUTRES TURBINES A GAZ
716	ROTATING ELECTRIC PLANT	W 2660	27764	W 3298	32373	W 6233	55228	W 3507	38599	APP ELECTR ROTATIFS,PIECES
7161	DC MOTORS AND GENERATORS	W 513	5041	W 656	14572	W 771	6351	W 696	5975	MOTEURS COURANT CONTINU
7162	AC MTRS,GENRTRS,GEN SETS	W 2000	18847	W 2453	15878	W 5207	47244	W 2747	30539	MOTEURS ELECTRIQUES
71621	AC MTRS,INC UNIVRSL MTRS	W 945	7930	W 1322	6753	W 1647	7281	W 1008	6853	MOT ELEC NON COUR CONTINU
71623	GEN SETS WITH PISTN ENGN	W 461	4463	W 677	6639	W 2800	30456	W 1346	18716	GROUPES MOTEUR EXPLOSION
72	MACHS FOR SPCL INDUSTRYS		212216		184009		201038		167611	MAC SPECIALES POUR INDUST
721	AGRIC MACHY,EXC TRACTORS	W 5307	35046	W 2646	11858	W 3522	17139	W 1901	12686	MACHINES AGRICOLES
7211	CULTIVATING MACHINERY	W 4231	22248	W 1369	3343	W 1625	4664	W 661	2229	MACH PREPARATION DU SOL
72111	PLOUGHS	W 3573	19972	W 89	275	W 89	213	W 60	187	CHARRUES
722	TRACTORS NON–ROAD	W 1477	7646	W 2361	12078	W 2301	13401	W 1524	10282	TRACTEURS
7224	WHEELED TRACTORS NES	W 1049	6460	W 2063	10943	W 1874	10870	W 916	6115	TRACTEURS A ROUES
723	CIVIL ENGNEERG EQUIP ETC	W 7474	40204	W 16032	48710	W 9627	47545		26101	APPAREILS DE GENIE CIVIL
7234	CONST,MINING MACHNRY NES	W 7155	38581	W 15633	46410	W 8767	39439		19319	MACH POUR LA CONST, MINES
72341	SELF–PROPELLD DOZERS,ETC	W 1788	12627	W 2011	12339	W 1975	11230	W 600	4804	BULLDOZERS
72342	SLFPRP SHOVELS,EXCAVATRS	W 4277	20589	W 12947	30044	W 6277	24086	W 1639	11028	PELLES MECANIQUES
724	TEXTILE,LEATHER MACHNRY	W 3678	46064	W 4242	30308	W 3250	22558	W 2521	24020	MACH POUR INDUSTRIE TEXTILE
7244	SPINNING,EXTRDNG,ETC MCH	W 1252	16607	W 1036	9151	W 691	6723	W 708	8665	MACH POUR LE FILAGE

4. General Imports C.I.F. by Commodities according to the S.I.T.C. (Rev. 2) in thousand U.S. Dollars
Importations Générales C.A.F. par Produits d'après la C.T.C.I. (Rév. 2) en milliers de Dollars E.U.

SITC CTCI	COMMODITY	1993 WEIGHT POIDS	1993 VALUE VALEUR	1994 WEIGHT POIDS	1994 VALUE VALEUR	1995 WEIGHT POIDS	1995 VALUE VALEUR	1996 WEIGHT POIDS	1996 VALUE VALEUR	PRODUIT
72449	PTS NES OF MACHS OF 7244	W 681	10620	W 100	1957	W 291	2429	W 92	1886	PIECES DES MACH DU 724.4
7246	AUXIL TXTL MCH,PARTS NES	W 394	13403	W 201	1718	W 154	1831	W 70	2472	MACH PR 724.51,52,53,61
72469	LOOM,KNT MCH ETC PTS NES	W 364	10617	W 187	1487	W 145	1642	W 50	1858	PIECES 724.51,52,53,61
725	PAPER ETC MILL MACHINERY	W 1156	9930	W 443	4760	W 480	5436	W 781	2528	MACHINES FABR PATE PAPIER
726	PRINTG,BKBINDG MACHY,PTS	W 1058	12931	W 1074	18264	W 1735	31946	W 559	9730	MACHINES POUR IMPRIMERIE
7264	PRINTING PRESSES	W 195	2463	W 537	12951	W 1232	24924	W 296	4860	MACHINES A IMPRIMER
72641	ROTARY PRINTING PRESSES	W 195	2463	W 537	12951	W 1232	24924	W 296	4860	MACH IMPRIMER ROTATIVES
727	FOOD MACHRY NON–DOMESTIC	W 1136	13723	W 2992	18484	W 2187	16175	W 2026	14966	MACH INDUSTRIES ALIMENT
7272	OTH FOOD PROC MCHY,PARTS	W 779	11522	W 1142	13634	W 1466	12516	W 1390	11521	AUT MACH IND ALIMENTAIRE
72722	INDUS FOOD PROC MACH NES	W 686	10087	W 961	11535	W 1449	12164	W 1185	11288	MACHINES BOULANGERIE
728	OTH MACHY FOR SPCL INDUS	W 5457	46672	W 4373	39545	W 5312	46838	W 6242	67298	AUT MACH IND PARTICULIERES
7283	OTHR MINERAL WORKG MACHY	W 3368	17931	W 804	4490	W 1271	8244	W 1801	14254	MACH TRIER,CRIBLER,BROYER
72839	PTS NES OF MACHY OF 7283	W 2380	8968	W 340	1464	W 334	2348	W 412	3152	PIECES MACH DU 728.3
7284	MACHY FOR SPCL INDUS NES	W 1757	23689	W 2506	27571	W 3535	34589	W 3896	48662	MACH SPEC IND PARTICUL.
72842	RUBBER,PLASTICS WRKG MCH	W 955	12478	W 843	10683	W 928	13644	W 1352	16121	MACH IND CAOUT MAT PLAST
72848	OTH MCHY WITH INDIV FNCT	W 555	5388	W 901	7675	W 1523	12054	W 1278	13083	AUTRES MACHINES NDA
73	METALWORKING MACHINERY		15684		19642		16999		13129	MACH TRAVAIL DES METAUX
736	METALWORKING MACH–TOOLS	W 1506	11719	W 3173	16245	W 2571	12172	W 1650	8179	MACH–OUTILS TRAVAIL METAUX
74	GENRL INDUSTRL MACHY NES		228705		234959		249159		230954	MACH APP INDUSTRIE
741	HEATING,COOLING EQUIPMNT	W 3912	27320	W 4934	40577	W 5361	36072	W 4759	40942	MACH CHAUFFAGE,PIECES
7414	NONDOM REFRIG EQUIPT,PTS	W 1028	5554	W 1656	15342	W 1907	12714	W 1405	10378	MAT PRODUCTION DU FROID
74141	REFRIG EQUIP NONDOMESTIC	W 540	2799	W 623	11014	W 599	6624	W 697	6519	REFIG INDUSTRIELS
7415	AIR–CONDITIONING MACHNRY	W 947	6083	W 1570	11445	W 1530	7870	W 1181	6753	GROUPES CONDITION AIR
7416	HEATING,COOLING EQU NES	W 619	8032	W 1074	9383	W 1159	8504	W 1217	17834	APP CHANGEMENT TEMP
742	PUMPS FOR LIQUIDS ETC	W 7056	39792	W 6223	50394	W 5107	47253	W 4008	43814	POMPES MOTO–POMPES
7422	CENTRIFUGAL PUMPS NES	W 782	9442	W 721	7116	W 1083	6385	W 831	5891	POMPES CENTRIF NON 742.81
7428	OTHER PUMPS FOR LIQUIDS	W 1980	15658	W 4228	31059	W 2710	26204	W 1936	20791	AUTRES POMPES POUR LIQ
74288	PUMPS FR LIQUIDS NES ETC	W 1956	15390	W 4109	29913	W 2271	17791	W 1749	17247	POMPES POUR LIQUIDES NDA
7429	PTS NES OF PUMPS OF 742	W 4203	13140	W 1160	11065	W 1193	12999	W 1121	15587	PIECES POUR GROUPE 742
743	PUMPS NES,CENTRFUGES ETC	W 4023	28020	W 5399	29721	W 5765	33098	W 5328	40275	POMPES COMPRES,VENT ETC
7431	PUMPS FOR GASES ETC	W 1867	11180	W 2954	14318	W 3051	14967	W 2446	17206	POMPES AIR A VIDE,COMPRES
7436	GAS,LIQUID FILTERS ETC	W 1622	10969	W 1699	10047	W 1866	9924	W 2160	14460	APP POUR FILT DES LIQUIDES
744	MECHANICAL HANDLING EQU	W 3794	23597	W 6805	25881	W 6284	33114	W 3178	20573	EQUIP MANUTENTION PIECES
7442	LIFTING,LOADING MACH NES	W 1931	8108	W 4304	8936	W 2833	18568	W 1624	11066	APP LEVAGE,MANUTENTION
7449	PTS NES OF MACHY OF 7442	W 1239	12023	W 1251	11800	W 1741	7812	W 754	5786	PIECES DU 744.2
745	NONELEC MACHY,TOOLS NES	W 5479	38570	W 4068	37685	W 4587	45967	W 5745	30130	AUT MACH NON ELEC,PIECES
7452	OTH NONELEC MCHS,PTS NES	W 5312	35197	W 3819	33039	W 4315	40217	W 5501	26309	AUT MACH NON ELEC,PIECES
74522	PACKAGNG,BOTTLNG,ETC MCH	W 598	21944	W 1156	19150	W 511	13077	W 514	10580	MACH NETT BOUTEILLES,ETC
74527	SPRAYING MACHINERY	W 4329	8311	W 2265	9470	W 3232	21150	W 4576	10516	APP PROJETER ETC LIQUID
749	NONELEC MACH PTS,ACC NES	W 8691	71405	W 7671	50701	W 6907	53655	W 5153	55221	PIECES MACH NON ELEC NDA
7491	BALL,ROLLER,ETC BEARINGS	W 2956	18409	W 1593	9543	W 1191	10195	W 749	9186	ROULEMENTS BILLES ETC
7492	COCKS,VALVES ETC NES	W 1566	26406	W 2061	19650	W 1991	20610	W 2551	23713	ART ROB,SIM POUR TUYAUX
7493	SHAFT,CRANK,PULLEY ETC	W 3256	14233	W 2245	9704	W 2067	11558	W 936	11712	ARBRES TRANS,VILEBREQUINS
7499	OTH NONELEC MCHY PTS NES	W 913	12357	W 1773	11805	W 1659	11292	W 917	10610	PIECES NON ELECT NDA
75	OFFICE MACHNES,ADP EQUIP		49040		59408		65009		72877	MACH BUREAU TRAIT AUTOM
752	AUTOMTIC DATA PROC EQUIP	W 1184	33772	W 1284	40392	W 1253	45909	W 1238	55484	MACH TRAIT INFORMATION
7522	DIGITAL COMPUTERS	W 385	19910	W 524	21188	W 436	21717	W 222	13506	MACH DIGITALES COMPLETES
7523	DIGITL CENTRL PROCESSORS	W 118	2723	W 216	6316	W 118	8262	W 348	20728	UNITES CENTRALES
7525	ADP PERIPHERAL UNITS	W 67	2328	W 167	4192	W 519	7056	W 421	12225	UNITES PERIPHERIQUES
759	OFFICE,ADP MCH PTS,ACCES	W 948	8530	W 1457	10729	W 1453	8917	W 762	7633	PIECES DU 751 ET 752
76	TELECOMM,SOUND EQUIPMENT		77848		93123		86443		89615	EQUIPMENT DE TELECOM
761	TELEVISION RECEIVERS	W 2619	10194	W 2749	14116	W 2289	9235	W 2902	15813	RECEPTEURS DE TELEVISION
7611	COLOUR TV RECEIVERS	W 1580	8376	W 2257	12641	W 1340	7274	W 2393	14666	RECEPTEURS COULEUR
764	TELECOM EQPT,PTS,ACC NES	W 3184	55765	W 4480	64607	W 2945	64311	W 2441	59238	EQUIP TELECOM,PIECES
7641	LINE TELEPHONE,ETC EQUIP	W 1510	30372	W 1446	17541	W 617	11072	W 948	15091	APP TELEPHON PAR FIL
7643	TV,RADIO TRANSMITTRS ETC	W 251	14850	W 663	24475	W 347	33001	W 329	28119	APP EMET TELE RADIO
7649	PTS NES OF EQUIPMT OF 76	W 985	7874	W 1664	17758	W 1425	16560	W 700	12148	PIECES DE LA DIV 76
76493	TELECOMM EQUIPMT PTS NES	W 539	4429	W 966	13421	W 763	12514	W 396	9465	PIECES 761,762,764.3,8
77	ELECTRIC MACHNRY NES ETC		87470		117094		197093		160029	MACH APP ELECT NDA
771	ELECTRIC POWER MACHY NES	W 1069	7125	W 2224	16036	W 3657	41470	W 2168	15898	MACH PROD,TRANS ELECTR
7711	TRANSFORMERS,ELECTRICAL	W 757	4684	W 1553	10718	W 2478	32424	W 1490	9203	TRANSFO ELECTRIQUES
77118	OTHER ELEC TRANSFORMERS	W 446	3261	W 648	4196	W 1455	23461	W 615	3158	AUTRES TRANSFO ELECTRIQ
772	SWITCHGEAR ETC,PARTS NES		20846	W 4176	22419	W 3433	39731	W 2852	31399	APP COUPURE,SECT ETC
7721	SWITCHGEAR ETC	W 3123	18781	W 4118	21799	W 3396	39104	W 2786	30612	APP COUPURE,SECTIONMNT
773	ELECTR DISTRIBUTNG EQUIP	W 1910	11389	W 2264	9052	W 6449	29295	W 5339	24937	EQUIPMT DISTRIBUTION ELECT
7731	INSULATED WIRE,CABLE ETC	W 1517	10063	W 1483	7384	W 5323	27171	W 4376	22563	FILS,CABLES ISOLES ELECT
775	HOUSEHOLD TYPE EQUIP NES	W 5620	14095	W 7710	28722	W 11521	36157	W 11654	36893	MACH,APP USAGE DOMESTQUE
7752	DOM REFRIGERATRS,FREEZRS	W 1444	4029	W 2998	10816	W 5059	19881	W 5127	17564	REFRIG,CONGEL MENAGER
77521	DOMESTIC REFRIGERATORS	W 1230	3368	W 2783	9989	W 4683	18275	W 4933	16656	REFRIGERATEURS
778	ELECTRICAL MACHINERY NES	W 9678	23931	W 15382	28914	W 16486	37576	W 8560	37142	AUTRES MACH ELECT NDA
7781	BATTERIES,ACCUMULATORS	W 2845	7371	W 4705	9062	W 5582	12641	W 5221	12717	PILES ET ACCUMULATEURS
78	ROAD VEHICLES		468946		915874		694943		440589	VEHICULES ROUTIERS
781	PASS MOTOR VEH EXC BUSES	W 28712	266117	W 55717	418425	W 32976	294203	W 30165	218104	AUTO TRANSPORT PERSONNES
782	LORRIES,SPCL MTR VEH NES	W 56632	130261	W 45621	297564	W 28849	216815	W 14859	120973	VEHICULES SPECIAUX,MARCH
7821	LORRIES,TRUCKS	W 55934	126650	W 41689	287472	W 27028	206136	W 13637	114400	VEHICULES TRANSP MARCHAND
783	ROAD MOTOR VEHICLES NES	W 3656	18565	W 17309	98437	W 14709	99726	W 4567	46147	VEHICULES ROUTIERS NDA
7831	BUSES	W 1714	11086	W 9476	71749	W 9535	74381	W 3505	40345	VOITURES TRANSPORT COMMUN
7832	TRACTORS FOR TR–TRAILERS	W 1942	7479	W 7833	26688	W 5175	25346	W 1062	5802	TRACTEURS ROUTIERS
784	MOTOR VEH PRTS,ACCES NES	W 9247	42821	W 35512	77256	W 15292	65857	W 9296	45000	PIECES 722,781,782,783
7841	MOTOR VEHICLE CHASSIS	W 972	6179	W 14404	35005	W 3653	18666	W 1358	9826	CHASSIS 722,781,782,783
7849	OTHER MOTOR VEHCL PARTS	W 8275	36642	W 21106	42225	W 11583	47110	W 7905	34565	PIECES 722,781,782,783
785	CYCLES,ETC MOTRZD OR NOT	W 5061	8874	W 8753	16438	W 6658	15525	W 2947	8447	MOTOCYCLES SCOOTERS
79	OTHR TRANSPORT EQUIPMENT		5759		13991		26449		14962	AUTRE MATERIEL TRANSPORT
792	AIRCRAFT ETC	W 124	1568	W 180	10661	W 316	21360	W 13	2180	APP NAVIGATION AERIENNE
793	SHIPS AND BOATS ETC	W 4728	4074	W 537	3226	W 2006	4960	W 8858	12644	NAVIRES BATEAUX,ETC
7932	SHIPS AND BOATS NES	W 4614	3578	W 519	2765	W 1992	4088	W 8854	12630	NAVIRES ET BATEAUX
8	MISC MANUFACTURED GOODS		209031		281826		295386		301034	ART MANUFACTURES DIVERS
812	*PLUMBG,HEATNG,LGHTNG EQ	W 1469	3451	W 3552	8389	W 4274	12757	W 3253	11070	APPAR SANITAIRES CHAUFFAGE
821	*FURNITURE,PARTS THEREOF	W 1405	4857	W 4738	16331	W 3412	14070	W 3683	14266	MEUBLES ET PIECES
8219	FURNITURE AND PARTS NES	W 967	2653	W 4124	13126	W 2326	8516	W 2667	8523	AUTRES MEUBLES ET PIECES
84	CLOTHING AND ACCESSORIES		13286		15026		25339		24205	VETEMENTS
851	*FOOTWEAR	W 2086	7472	W 4230	16445	W 3431	15099	W 3177	15851	CHAUSSURES
85102	FOOTWEAR LEATHER	W 1466	5510	W 3008	12107	W 2508	11241	W 2005	11810	CHAUS SEMELLES EN CUIR
87	PRECISION INSTRUMNTS NES		41088		52195		52241		44460	INSTRUM,APPAR SCIENT NDA
872	MEDICAL INSTRUMENTS NES	W 581	6905	W 963	11649	W 825	11323	W 1989	12299	INSTR,APP MEDIC–CHIR NDA
874	MEASURNG,CONTROLNG INSTR	W 1496	30331	W 2153	35882	W 1745	34647	W 1686	25949	INSTRUMENTS DE MESURE
8748	ELEC MEAS,CONTRL EQU NES	W 357	9367	W 556	8534	W 363	7915	W 172	6218	APP ELEC ELECTRO MESURE
87483	OTH ELCTRNC MEAS ETC EQU	W 335	8260	W 450	6948	W 288	6702	W 94	5206	AUT APP ELECTRO DE MESURE
88	PHOTO EQU,OPTICL GDS ETC		17535		15879		20567		22137	APP,FOURN PHOTO,OP,MONTR
882	PHOTO,CINEMA SUPPLIES	W 728	10183	W 1634	9656	W 2170	12795	W 1490	15269	PRODUITS PHOTO,CINEMA
8822	PHOTO FILM EXC DEV CINMA	W 561	8436	W 1273	8480	W 1792	10704	W 1030	12873	PLAQUES,PELLICULES,FILMS

4. General Imports C.I.F. by Commodities according to the S.I.T.C. (Rev. 2) in thousand U.S. Dollars
Importations Générales C.A.F. par Produits d'après la C.T.C.I. (Rév. 2) en milliers de Dollars E.U.

SITC CTCI	COMMODITY	1993 WEIGHT POIDS	1993 VALUE VALEUR	1994 WEIGHT POIDS	1994 VALUE VALEUR	1995 WEIGHT POIDS	1995 VALUE VALEUR	1996 WEIGHT POIDS	1996 VALUE VALEUR	PRODUIT
89	MISC MANUFCTRD GOODS NES		120266		155635		153223		165937	ART MANUFACTURES DIVERS
892	PRINTED MATTER	W 35368	68894	W 18605	72922	W 7314	44861	W 6658	39347	IMPRIMES
8921	PRINTED BOOKS,GLOBES,ETC	W 34048	59122	W 6515	40856	W 5485	35388	W 4858	31091	LIVRES,BROCHURES,CARTES
89211	PRINTED BOOKS,PAMPHLETS	W 34014	59025	W 6469	40738	W 5334	35039	W 4757	30821	LIVRES,BROCHURES
8928	PRINTED MATTER NES	W 693	4522	W 11368	26922	W 669	4695	W 823	3667	IMPRIMES NDA
89281	LABELS PAPER,PAPERBOARD	W 31	197	W 11093	25396	W 245	1378	W 193	1148	ETIQUETTES TOUS GENRES
893	ARTICLES OF PLASTIC NES		18022		31728		43139		49892	OUVRAGES EN MAT DIVIS 58
8931	PLSTC PACKG CONTNRS,LIDS	W 2406	6240	W 2774	9329	W 5122	19177	W 4607	20664	ART TRANSP EMBALLAGE ETC
8939	MISC PLASTIC ARTICLES	W 3250	11258	W 7182	21561	W 7349	22713	W 8643	27887	ART DIVERS EN MAT DIV 58
89399	OTHR PLASTC ARTICLES NES	W 2507	10132	W 5115	19270	W 5753	20507	W 7299	25646	AUT OUV MAT DIV 58
894	TOYS,SPORTING GOODS,ETC	W 5167	18965	W 7675	27591	W 10114	39775	W 21202	41172	VOITURES ENFANTS,JOUETS
8942	TOYS,INDOOR GAMES ETC	W 4462	16409	W 6832	23408	W 8851	34532	W 19535	35586	JOUETS,JEUX ETC
89423	TOYS NES	W 2538	10588	W 3883	14460	W 5139	20982	W 3577	19466	JOUETS,MODELES REDUITS
898	MUSICAL INSTRUMENTS,PTS	W 827	4395	W 1281	8198	W 1498	8478	W 1862	16483	INSTRUMENTS DE MUSIQUE
8983	SOUND RECRDNG TAPE,DISCS	W 672	3604	W 1066	6050	W 1225	6762	W 1628	14859	SUPPORTS SON POUR 763
89832	RECORDED DISCS,TAPES ETC	W 220	2482	W 265	3058	W 367	4404	W 536	12318	DISQUES,PHONO,BANDES
9	GOODS NOT CLASSD BY KIND		16940		1710		1881		6809	ART TRANSACT NON CLASSES
931	*SPECIAL TRANSACTIONS		16316		460		665	W 6467	4816	TRANS.SPECIALES

5. General Exports F.O.B. by Commodities according to the S.I.T.C. (Rev. 2) in thousand U.S. Dollars
Exportations Générales F.O.B. par Produits d'après la C.T.C.I. (Rév. 2) en milliers de Dollars E.U.

SITC CTCI	COMMODITY	1993 WEIGHT POIDS	1993 VALUE VALEUR	1994 WEIGHT POIDS	1994 VALUE VALEUR	1995 WEIGHT POIDS	1995 VALUE VALEUR	1996 WEIGHT POIDS	1996 VALUE VALEUR	PRODUIT
	ALL COMMODITIES		3020002		3843353		4361500		4889834	TOUS PRODUITS
0	FOOD AND LIVE ANIMALS		1407477		2056424		2235874		2415050	ALIMENTS,ANIMAUX VIVANTS
03	FISH AND PREPARATIONS		593809		734859		890220		870958	POISSONS ET PREPARATIONS
034	FISH,FRESH,CHILLED,FROZN	W 24054	53100	W 29253	73063	W 41086	90441	W 41344	87377	POISSON FRAIS, REFRIG,CONG
0341	FISH FRSH,CHLLD,EX FILLT	W 8878	31846	W 10289	44165	W 10474	48126	W 10671	49923	POISSON FRAIS,REFRIGERE
0342	FISH FROZEN,EXCL FILLETS	W 13123	14248	W 15690	16446	W 26562	27078	W 27901	26207	POISSONS CONGELES
036	SHELL FISH FRESH,FROZEN	W 75417	468211	W 78123	557375	W 89629	678649	W 86786	631390	CRUSTACES,MOLLUSQUES
037	FISH ETC PREPD,PRSVD NES	W 35403	71682	W 50529	102789	W 61516	118266	W 75644	150994	POIS,CRUST,MOL PREPARES
0371	FISH PREPARD,PRESRVD NES	W 35303	70783	W 50469	102244	W 61435	117230	W 75592	150309	CONSERVES DE POISSONS
04	CEREALS AND PREPARATIONS		4179		27218		19039		53284	CEREALES ET PRODUITS
042	RICE	W 36	14	W 31700	16602	W 26853	8852	W 92728	33848	RIZ
0422	RICE SEMI–MILLED,MILLED	W 36	14	W 27456	15365	W 24853	8281	W 83453	31745	RIZ POLI,GLACE INCL BRISURES
04221	RICE MILLED UNBROKEN	W 36	14	W 27276	15292	W 24853	8281	W 83393	31719	RIZ POLI,GLACE EXCL BRISURES
044	MAIZE UNMILLED	W 17233	2172	W 45048	7917	W 36530	5976	W 75467	15404	MAIS NON MOULU
05	VEGETABLES AND FRUIT		588240		742576		898442		1054428	LEGUMES ET FRUITS
054	VEG ETC FRSH,SMPLY PRSVD	W 4716	1405	W 6192	4577	W 14240	9493	W 27683	17125	LEGUMES FRAIS,CONG,SECS
057	FRUIT,NUTS,FRESH,DRIED	W 2626786	560732	W 3136503	712355	W 3747173	850247	W 3969399	985057	FRUITS FRAIS OU SECS
0573	BANANA,PLANTAIN,FRSH,DRY	W 2614210	557499	W 3123084	708372	W 3732008	845105	W 3931217	973043	BANANES FRAICHES,SECHEES
058	FRUIT PRESERVED,PREPARED	W 22098	21525	W 20941	19734	W 27819	32944	W 49464	48458	CONSERVES DE FRUITS
0585	FRUIT OR VEGETABLE JUICE	W 7193	10828	W 6454	9373	W 6419	14964	W 9341	24499	JUS DE FRUITS
05857	JUICE OF OTHER FRUIT,VEG	W 2707	3629	W 1613	1882	W 5806	13926	W 8403	23091	JUS AUTRES FRUITS,LEGUMES
0589	FRUIT PREPRD,PRESRVD,NES	W 408	593	W 1567	1818	W 9434	8938	W 28061	15058	FRUITS PREPARES CONSERV
05899	FRUIT,NUTS NES,PRESERVED	W 407	592	W 1559	1808	W 9432	8934	W 28061	15057	FRUITS PREP CONSERV NDA
06	SUGAR AND PREPS,HONEY		11563		15713		27193		42439	SUCRES ET PRODUITS
061	SUGAR AND HONEY	W 16743	7925	W 15721	4446	W 10311	4539	W 57293	22030	SUCRES ET MIEL
0611	RAW BEET AND CANE SUGAR	W 14859	7859	W 6977	2896	W 5880	2593	W 35806	18515	SUCRES BRUTS
062	SUGAR CANDY NON–CHOCLATE	W 1769	3639	W 5551	11267	W 10330	22653	W 8726	20409	SUCRERIES
07	COFFEE,TEA,COCOA,SPICES		190544		517372		378290		324295	CAFE,THE,CACAO,EPICES
071	COFFEE AND SUBSTITUTES	W 84643	107368	W 125067	413819	W 88285	243873	W 77669	159057	CAFE ET SUCCEDANES
0711	COFFEE GREEN,ROASTED,SUB	W 74817	80153	W 114677	368765	W 77702	185719	W 70137	129080	CAFE TORREFIE OU DECAFEINE
07111	COFFEE GREEN,HUSKS,SKINS	W 73718	79242	W 113848	365710	W 77585	185318	W 70093	128985	CAFE NON TORREFIE
0712	COFFEE EXTRACTS,ESSENCES	W 9826	27215	W 10390	45054	W 10583	58154	W 7532	29977	EXTRAITS DE CAFE
072	COCOA	W 71088	78448	W 75910	101033	W 87088	130549	W 100676	157526	CACAO
0721	COCOA BEANS,RAW,ROASTED	W 46310	46287	W 56184	66480	W 63623	81939	W 71100	91036	CACAO EN FEVES
0723	COCOA BUTTER AND PASTE	W 22545	30748	W 16717	32360	W 20777	46626	W 25454	63772	BEURRE ET PATE DE CACAO
07231	COCOA PASTE	W 16033	16415	W 11397	17832	W 13249	20136	W 12827	19126	CACAO EN MASSE
07232	COCOA BUTTER	W 6512	14333	W 5320	14528	W 7528	26490	W 12627	44646	BEURRE DE CACAO
081	*FEEDING STUFF FOR ANIML	W 38727	13260	W 27747	10798	W 30766	13288		55833	NOURRITURE POUR ANIMAUX
0814	MEAT OR FISH MEAL FODDER	W 30082	11885	W 25765	9901	W 25989	11814	W 109953	53454	FARINES DE VIANDES,POISSONS
08142	FISH MEAL FODDER	W 30082	11885	W 25765	9901	W 25989	11814	W 109953	53454	FARINES DE POISSONS
2	CRUDE MATERLS,EXCL FUELS		67207		101341		139341		160807	MAT BRUTES NON COMESTIBLES
24	CORK AND WOOD		16400		22949		33826		30862	LIEGE ET BOIS
247	OTH WOOD ROUGH,SQUARED	W 27276	1159	W 67103	6316	W 84552	14040	W 77914	11529	BOIS BRUTS EQUARRIS
248	WOOD SHAPED,SLEEPERS	W 13335	15241	W 13739	16633	W 18626	19785	W 21482	19333	BOIS SIMPLEMENT TRAVAILLES
2483	LUMBER SHAPED NON--CONIFR	W 9594	12826	W 10205	14326	W 13392	17527	W 14306	16468	NON CONIFERES SCIES,RABOTES
24831	LUMBER SAWN ETC NON–CON	W 9210	12575	W 9877	14047	W 10435	16266	W 11084	14871	SCIES LONGITUDINALEMENT
26	TEXTILE FIBRES AND WASTE		8124		11697		14480		22290	FIBRES TEXTILES
265	VEG FIBRE,EXCL COTN,JUTE	W 11094	8096	W 13576	10701	W 12432	12457	W 14215	14898	FIBRES VEGETALES
2655	MANILA FIBRE,TOW,WASTE	W 10969	8083	W 13521	10665	W 12368	12407	W 14178	14857	ABACA BRUT
29	CRUDE ANIMAL,VEG MAT NES		39301		60793		81361		101266	MATIERES BRUTES ANIM,VEGET
292	CRUDE VEG MATERIALS NES	W 18379	39085	W 26971	60440	W 31546	80374	W 67224	100405	MAT BRUTES VEGETALES NDA
2927	CUT FLOWERS AND FOLIAGE	W 16010	38078	W 22763	59583	W 30400	79434	W 64549	99115	FLEURS,FEUILLAGES COUPES
29271	CUT FLOWERS	W 15995	38036	W 22754	59558	W 30395	79423	W 64544	99091	FLEURS ET BOUTONS
3	MINERAL FUELS ETC		1249878		1304910		1529892		1776073	COMBUSTIBLES MINERAUX LUB
33	PETROLEUM AND PRODUCTS		1249878		1304910		1529892		1776073	PETROLE ET DERIVES
333	CRUDE PETROLEUM		1149022		1185033	MW 11698	1395480	MW 11801	1520815	HUILES BRUTES DE PETROLE
334	PETROLEUM PRODUCTS,REFIN		100842		119853	W 1563477	134392	W 1867104	216523	PRODUITS RAFFINES
3342	KEROSENE,OTH MEDIUM OILS		10701		3058			W 28967	3219	PETR LAMPANTS,AUT HUIL
33429	OTH MEDIUM PETROLEUM OIL		10701		3058					AUTRES HUILES MOYENNES
3343	GAS OILS							W 1810279	185626	GAS OILS
3344	FUEL OILS,NES		90095		116726	W 1563428	134342			FUEL OILS
3345	LUBS,PETROLEUM OILS NES	W 45	46	W 63	69	W 49	50	W 27858	27677	HUILES LUBRIFIANTES
33451	LUBS(HIGH PETR CONT) ETC	W 41	41	W 56	57	W 46	45	W 27845	27658	HUILES LUBRIF,H LOURDES
335	RESIDUAL PETRLM PROD NES	W 25	14	W 33	24	W 36	20	W 281552	38735	PRODUITS RESIDUELS NDA
3352	MINERAL TARS AND PRODCTS			W 8	7			W 281490	38700	GOUDRONS MINERAUX
33525	MINERAL TAR OILS ETC NES			W 8	7			W 281490	38700	AUTRES PRODUITS NDA
4	ANIMAL,VEGETABLE OIL,FAT		7512		12537		15870		15192	HUILES,GRAISSES ANIM,VEG
42	FIXED VEGETABLE OIL,FAT		7390		9553		15245		14455	HUILES VEGETALES FIXES
424	FIXED VEG OIL NONSOFT	W 15374	6944	W 11850	6650	W 22092	14713	W 25632	13811	AUTRES HUILES VEG FIXES
5	CHEMCLS,RELATED PROD NES		32028		39433		54065		62369	PRODUITS CHIMIQUES
541	*MEDICINAL,PHARM PRODUCT	K 562626	8231	K 940056	12292		22281	K 1154529	23055	PROD MEDICINAUX PHARMACEUT
5417	MEDICAMENTS	K 538991	7844	K 528683	9995	K 1074273	21466	K 1131089	22213	MEDICAMENTS
6	BASIC MANUFACTURES		83869		118800		150841		187885	ART MANUFACTURES
62	RUBBER MANUFACTURES NES		72		2438		12723		22608	CAOUTCHOUC MANUFACTURE
625	RUBBER TYRES, TUBES ETC	W 13	35	W 833	2408	W 4264	12701	W 9718	22572	PNEUS CAOUTCHOUC VULCANISE
6252	TYRES,NEW,BUS OR LORRY	W 13	35	W 449	1274	W 2652	7954	W 6638	15559	PNEUS POUR AUTOBUS,CAMIONS
63	WOOD,CORK MANUFACTRS NES		25742		28597		36354		54416	OUVRAGES LIEGE ET BOIS
634	VENEERS,PLYWOOD,ETC	W 45976	22643	W 44395	24158	W 40608	31644	W 57424	49749	PLACAGES,CONTRE–PLAQUES
6341	VENEER SHEETS ETC	W 3296	2577	W 2761	4082	W 2101	6190	W 9922	19500	BOIS SIMPLEMENT SCIES
6342	PLYWOOD OF WOOD SHEETS	W 25557	15912	W 21126	14474	W 30391	22493	W 37516	26550	BOIS CONTRE–PLAQUES
64	PAPER,PAPERBOARD AND MFR		8911		12171		13668		19260	PAPIERS,CARTONS & OUVRAGES
65	TEXTILE YARN,FABRICS,ETC		21203		29908		34884		38387	FILS,TISSUS,ARTICLES TEXTILE
66	NONMETAL MINERAL MFS NES		7175		12448		13991		17636	ART MIN NON METALLIQUES
69	METAL MANUFACTURES NES		13174		19828		24647		22533	ART MANUFACT EN METAL NDA
7	MACHINES,TRANSPORT EQUIP		69979		91434		85979		87478	MACHINES MATERIEL TRANSPORT
78	ROAD VEHICLES		50330		72564		63578		54211	VEHICULES ROUTIERS
781	PASS MOTOR VEH EXC BUSES	W 4465	42816	W 7072	64742	W 5093	48747	W 4185	43465	AUTO TRANSPORT PERSONNES
782	LORRIES,SPCL MTR VEH NES	W 1436	7129	W 1537	7441	W 2945	14214	W 1948	9568	VEHICULES SPECIAUX,MARCH
7821	LORRIES,TRUCKS	W 1385	7103	W 1524	7406	W 2871	14171	W 1941	9538	VEHICULES TRANSP MARCHAND
8	MISC MANUFACTURED GOODS		31401		44167		48210		50790	ART MANUFACTURES DIVERS
84	CLOTHING AND ACCESSORIES		16164		19107		17416		18535	VETEMENTS
89	MISC MANUFCTRD GOODS NES		9652		14618		17669		19458	ART MANUFACTURES DIVERS
9	GOODS NOT CLASSD BY KIND		63029		70231		96183		127499	ART TRANSACT NON CLASSES
971	*GOLD,NON MONETARY NES	K 6384	59384	K 6370	70183	K 7479	95881	K 6402	127422	OR NON MONETAIRE
97101	NONMON GLD UNWRT,SEMIMFD	K 6384	59384	K 6269	70179	K 7479	95881	K 6402	127422	OR,ALLIAGES D'OR BRUTS

1. HISTORICAL SERIES, 1961–1996 SPECIAL TRADE, IMPORTS C.I.F., EXPORTS F.O.B.
SERIES HISTORIQUES, 1961–1996 COMMERCE SPECIAL, IMPORTATIONS C.A.F., EXPORTATIONS F.O.B

YEAR ANNEE	VALUE IN MILLION EGYPTIAN POUNDS VALEUR EN MILLION EGYPTIAN POUNDS MERCHANDISE –MARCHANDISE		GOLD –OR		CONVERSION FACTORS U.S. CENTS PER EGYPTIAN POUND FACTEURS DE CONVERSION CENTS E.U. PAR EGYPTIAN POUND		INDEX NUMBERS –INDICES QUANTUM		UNIT VALUE VALEUR UNITAIRE	
	IMPORTS	EXPORTS	IMPORTS	EXPORTS	IMPORTS	EXPORTS	IMPORTS	EXPORTS	IMPORTS	EXPORTS
1961	238.50	161.20			287.1596	287.1596				
1962	300.90	157.80			245.9099	252.1699				
1963	398.30	225.90			229.9999	229.9999				6
1964	414.30	233.60			229.9999	229.9999				7
1965	405.80	262.50			229.9999	229.9999				7
1966	465.30	262.50			229.9999	229.9999				7
1967	344.30	245.90			229.9999	229.9999				7
1968	289.50	270.30			229.9999	229.9999				8
1969	277.20	323.90			229.9999	229.9999				8
1970	342.00	331.20			230.0011	230.0012				8
1971	399.90	343.20			230.0012	230.0012				8
1972	390.70	358.80			230.0012	230.0012				8
1973	361.10	444.20			254.0006	253.3092				9
1974	920.20	593.30			255.5578	255.5579				16
1975	1539.30	548.60			255.5580	255.5578				11
1976	1489.90	595.50			255.5580	255.5582				14
1977	1884.30	668.50			255.5554	255.5556				12
1978	2632.20	679.80			255.5568	255.5558				13
1979	2686.20	1287.80			142.8567	142.8568				24
1980	3402.00	2132.20			142.8567	142.8567				39
1981	6187.50	2263.00			142.8568	142.8568				41
1982	6354.60	2184.10			142.8582	142.8581				39
1983	7192.00	2250.60			142.8598	142.8598				37
1984	7536.10	2198.00			142.8598	142.8597				37
1985	7772.80	2599.90			70.6999	70.6999				39
1986	8051.40	2053.90			107.8061	107.8054				36
1987	11357.80	3046.00			66.8809	66.8806				40
1988	16308.60	3994.40			53.0843	53.0840				55
1989	16623.70	5734.70			44.7205	44.7207				76
1990	24823.20	6953.80			67.6087	71.2798				100
1991	25216.21	11764.60			32.9540	32.2140				195
1992	27656.10	10173.40			30.1004	30.1080				188
1993	27553.81	7558.80			29.8115	29.7929				203
1994	34598.90	11767.90			29.5339	29.5330				211
1995	39892.00	11703.50			29.4791	29.4755				227
1996	44218.00	12004.10			29.4930	29.4926				234

2. IMPORTS BY BROAD ECONOMIC CATEGORY AND EXPORTS BY INDUSTRIAL ORIGIN. (PERCENTAGE OF TOTAL VALUE)
IMPORTATIONS PAR CATEGORIES ECONOMIQUES ET EXPORTATIONS PAR BRANCHE D'ACTIVITE.(EN POURCENTAGE DE LA VALEUR TOTALE)

IMPORTS – IMPORTATIONS

	1990	1991	1992	1993	1994	1995	1996
TOTAL IMPORTS–IMPORTATIONS TOTALES	100.	100.	100.	100.	100.	100.	100.
1 FOOD BEV–ALIMENTATION BOISSONS	26.1	20.1	23.1	17.0	21.0	22.4	22.5
11 PRIMARY–PRODUITS DE BASE	14.6	12.3	15.3	10.2	14.8	14.1	15.0
111 FOR INDUSTRY–POUR L'INDUSTRIE	9.2	6.9	9.0	5.4	10.0	9.5	11.1
112 FOR HOUSEHOLDS–POUR LES MENAGES	5.4	5.4	6.3	4.8	4.7	4.6	3.9
12 PROCESSED–PRODUITS ELABORES	11.5	7.8	7.8	6.8	6.2	8.3	7.5
121 FOR INDUSTRY–POUR L'INDUSTRIE	4.5	2.3	2.7	3.0	3.3	4.6	4.0
122 FOR HOUSEHOLDS–POUR LES MENAGES	7.0	5.5	5.1	3.8	2.9	3.7	3.5
2 IND SUPPLIES–APPROV INDUSTRIELS	43.4	48.3	43.7	45.7	43.7	46.1	45.7
21 PRIMARY–PRODUITS DE BASE	6.7	7.1	6.9	11.4	6.7	6.8	7.9
22 PROCESSED–PRODUITS ELABORES	36.8	41.1	36.8	34.3	37.0	39.4	37.8
3 FUELS–COMBUSTIBLES	2.7	2.2	1.4	1.7	1.4	1.1	1.3
31 PRIMARY–PRODUITS DE BASE	1.5	1.2	1.0	1.1	1.1	0.9	0.9
32 PROCESSED–PRODUITS ELABORES	1.2	1.0	0.4	0.5	0.3	0.2	0.4
321 MOTOR SPIRIT–ESSENCE	0.0	0.0	0.0		0.0	0.0	
322 OTHER–AUTRES	1.2	1.0	0.4	0.5	0.3	0.2	0.4
4 MACHINERY–EQUIPEMENT	16.9	18.9	20.7	23.5	20.0	18.0	19.3
41 CAPITAL EQUIPMENT–MACHINES	13.7	15.1	16.7	19.4	16.5	15.1	16.2
42 PARTS–PIECES ACCESSOIRES	3.2	3.7	4.0	4.1	3.5	3.0	3.1
5 TRANSPORT–TRANSPORT	7.1	6.2	6.6	7.5	9.2	7.3	6.5
51 PASSENGER CARS–AUTOMOBILES	1.1	1.3	1.4	2.0	2.2	1.8	1.5
52 OTHER–AUTRES	1.3	0.8	1.2	1.2	2.5	1.5	1.4
521 INDUSTRIAL–INDUSTRIELS	1.3	0.8	1.2	1.2	2.5	1.5	1.4
522 NON INDUSTRIAL–NON INDUSTRIEL	0.1	0.0	0.0	0.0	0.0	0.0	0.0
53 PARTS–PIECES ACCESSOIRES	4.6	4.0	4.0	4.3	4.5	3.9	3.6
6 CONSUM GOODS–BIENS CONSOMMATION	3.8	4.4	4.5	4.6	4.7	5.0	4.7
61 DURABLE–DURABLES	1.2	1.3	1.2	1.7	1.5	1.7	1.5
62 SEMI DURABLE–SEMI DURABLES	1.0	0.9	1.0	1.1	1.4	1.4	1.3
63 NON DURABLE–NON DURABLES	1.6	2.1	2.4	1.9	1.8	1.9	1.9
7 GOODS NES–BIENS NDA	0.0	0.0	0.0	0.0	0.0	0.0	0.0

EXPORTS – EXPORTATIONS

	1990	1991	1992	1993	1994	1995	1996
TOTAL EXPORTS–EXPORTATIONS TOTALES	100.	100.	100.	100.	100.	100.	100.
1 AGRICULTURE	16.3	8.1	10.9	9.1	11.3	11.3	8.8
2 MINING QUARRY–INDUS EXTRACTIVES	19.3	50.1	38.8	43.5	24.4	22.9	25.1
3 MANUFACTURING–IND MANUFACTUR	64.4	41.9	50.3	47.4	64.3	65.8	66.1
31 FOOD BEV TOBACCO–ALIM BOISS TAB	2.9	2.8	3.1	3.2	4.8	4.4	5.9
32 TEXTILES–INDUSTRIES TEXTILES	28.1	19.1	19.4	19.4	25.4	24.7	19.5
33 WOOD & PRODUCTS–BOIS & PRODUITS	0.2	0.1	0.1	0.1	0.1	0.2	0.1
34 PAPER & PRODUCTS–PAPIER & PRODT	0.6	0.4	0.4	0.5	0.5	0.6	0.5
35 CHEMICALS–INDUSTRIES CHIMIQUES	15.3	9.0	11.3	10.7	20.3	21.3	29.0
36 NON METAL MIN–MIN NON METAL	0.5	0.8	1.0	1.1	1.1	1.2	1.2
37 BASIC METAL–IND METAL BASE	11.8	6.0	11.0	8.8	8.7	10.5	7.2
38 METAL MANUF–MANUF METAL	4.8	3.6	3.9	3.4	3.2	2.7	2.4
39 OTH MANUF IND–AUTRES MANUF	0.1	0.1	0.1	0.1	0.1	0.2	0.2

3. TRADE BY PRINCIPAL COUNTRIES OF FIRST AND LAST CONSIGNMENT (VALUE IN THOUSAND U.S. DOLLARS)
ECHANGES SELON LES PRINCIPAUX PAYS DE PREMIERE ET DE DERNIERE CONSIGNATION (VALEUR EN MILLIERS DE DOLLARS EU)

COUNTRIES–PAYS	SPECIAL IMPORTS C.I.F. IMPORTATIONS SPECIALES C.A.F					COUNTRIES–PAYS	SPECIAL EXPORTS F.O.B. EXPORTATIONS SPECIALES F.O.B.				
	1992	1993	1994	1995	1996		1992	1993	1994	1995	1996
World	8292967	8175279	9586681	11738964	13019600	Monde	3049953	3105169	3472547	3444140	3534402
Africa	161174	119822	170852	287509	281444	Afrique	190936	164129	170047	179412	170098
Americas	1794664	1472716	2020195	2658530	3261194	Amériques	300140	458237	388585	542919	474908
Northern America	1533619	1275736	1659329	2280902	2706504	Amérique du Nord	292881	436864	374195	530213	464430
LAIA	246289	195332	277553	336062	536844	ALAI	2762	3516	8583	11944	9573
CACM	4568	270	581	738	1092	MCAC	16	0	5187	22	534
Caribbean	8265	1376	82601	40626	16479	Caraïbes	284	431	594	723	364
Rest of America	1924	1	130	201	275	Autre Amérique	4198	17426	27	17	6
As.ex F.USSR	1589009	1572882	1755346	2208990	2404682	Asie l'URSS exclus	1019411	985996	1125423	939387	1084373
Eur.x F.USSR	4092282	4214692	4383119	5325548	5615093	Europe l'URSS exclus	1398622	1382536	1667770	1682562	1735685
EU	3411803	3714017	3834680	4562844	4778056	UE	1210570	1245423	1526400	1577429	1614443
EFTA	307114	229483	223300	324002	360424	AELE	30908	29009	29713	19857	9045
East Europe	265985	206508	258534	315773	402516	Europe de l'Est	120972	68903	69678	57536	59122
Other Europe	1949	6468	12058	64698	1290	Autre de l'Europe	19327	25418	24118	1853	37792
Former USSR	44725	207537	346363	524236	496728	Ancienne URSS	75337	44519	46723	37448	52342
Oceania	291609	232935	430706	152323	432253	Océanie	1512	1392	1283	1609	1776
USA/Etats–Unis d'Amer	1455072	1227687	1615990	2211087	2608752	Italy/Italie	432912	399745	426420	458784	438386
Germany/Allemagne	861207	887786	913383	1044583	1089182	USA/Etats–Unis d'Amer	286415	430389	364446	522077	459936
Italy/Italie	543809	678658	613782	731111	870867	Israel/Israël	290006	229919	188181	173612	343568
France,Monac	414833	542855	592266	685161	577060	Netherlands/Pays–Bas	175076	172115	207047	166688	364771
United Kingdom	361470	335956	349627	379814	441385	Germany/Allemagne	126900	131469	209727	207091	162923
Japan/Japon	357568	366865	400933	313988	344913	Saudi Arabia	202417	196297	154997	113136	122725
Netherlands/Pays–Bas	296540	283603	285547	381439	363489	France,Monac	129279	155431	138193	144254	144676
Australia/Australie	269978	198913	403113	123786	386171	United Kingdom	102215	84934	143935	142417	165721
Switz.Liecht	291247	219994	211455	311916	334112	Singapore/Singapour	144673	128093	146605	92829	90085
Russian Federation	30055	144451	273766	405318	370755	Greece/Grèce	69343	125164	117126	137331	142375
Sweden/Suède	204919	220551	157531	259641	306641	Spain/Espagne	72669	100705	149023	157336	98209
China/Chine	184011	160226	194436	295900	283559	Belgium–Luxembourg	57830	43436	71233	110505	50539
Belgium–Luxembourg	170476	180515	214473	236782	211946	Turkey/Turquie	19649	25816	71461	82651	115263
Saudi Arabia	103777	132597	194051	248931	290533	Korea, Republic of	57147	44540	106238	51620	35580
Brazil/Brésil	134535	118778	158100	189902	265626	Libyan Arab Jamahiriya	58169	62444	44117	52878	51731
Turkey/Turquie	125849	137110	143359	179618	252871	Romania/Roumanie	93218	49882	43375	41263	36874
Spain/Espagne	137775	135670	143068	184494	210811	Japan/Japon	74198	54494	49807	43674	41367
Malaysia/Malaisie	130396	92976	93664	220448	240995	Syrian Arab Republic	36343	49119	57475	56099	55045
Korea, Republic of	91534	125757	107015	227052	192854	Russian Federation	72981	40459	40938	31914	37673
Finland/Finlande	121310	114457	135660	182995	166357	India/Inde	15112	35696	66083	53042	14064
Ireland/Irlande	42504	112879	200141	217897	131730	United Arab Emirates	19550	24799	40772	40999	44408
India/Inde	102582	117818	123821	160703	184382	Lebanon/Liban	21389	26701	35112	43470	33041
Romania/Roumanie	60918	75309	121410	160374	197049	Sudan/Soudan	45799	30002	28945	24460	20999
Argentina/Argentine	83434	71757	93424	115086	237655	Jordan/Jordanie	33564	14472	20964	30912	44627
Denmark/Danemark	90300	88057	96287	94971	94173	Kuwait/ Koweït	36354	35465	26116	16926	19344
Austria/Autriche	76485	62853	74501	82396	125890	Algeria/Algérie	28419	24444	32799	31328	15843
Indonesia/Indonésie	82141	66907	55772	78804	100870	Tunisia/Tunisie	19821	20492	23446	27452	24128
Greece/Grèce	85221	64488	51781	71148	106203	Yemen/Yémen	17105	20746	19103	12457	36530
Ukraine	8442	53759	67261	102850	111995	Switz.Liecht	27926	25374	27682	16708	6603
Canada	78373	48046	43295	69816	97752	Portugal	19740	5595	20609	21479	24022
Libyan Arab Jamahiriya	51045	27543	47939	99597	76777	Sri Lanka	211	15301	29563	18517	11650
Kenya	52050	48155	52665	78672	67061	Cyprus/Chypre	14501	15225	13117	13403	12595
Hong Kong	55481	56302	66817	66896	51641	Denmark/Danemark	11126	10982	20026	14929	4992
Poland/Pologne	77922	42026	47436	48444	67936	Gibraltar	8798	24454	22989	85	2772
Singapore/Singapour	38768	43888	44643	48925	52734	China/Chine	300	30728	10572	6262	7649
Bulgaria/Bulgarie	34395	21297	28700	40757	34664	Morocco/Maroc	6102	10089	12735	15163	8078
Czech Republic		38988	37767	34505	48383	Bulgaria/Bulgarie	11592	12152	15287	1911	8247
Hungary/Hongrie	45366	28290	22691	22032	39100	So. Africa Customs Un	1781	3168	1880	4644	34975
New Zealand	21631	26957	27510	27928	46082	Austria/Autriche	6604	10956	14637	8130	3160
Cuba	8107	1133	82483	40618	16442	Slovenia/Slovénia	1964	7394	9903	12133	6178
Thailand/Thaïlande	26245	19463	31066	33048	38881	Canada	6466	6475	9749	8132	4417
Slovenia/Slovénia	20671	24568	31228	23914	22977	Qatar	9134	8638	5960	5051	5721
Sri Lanka	34015	16730	25705	26260	18322	Croatia/Croatie	3589	4591	5462	9504	6720
Yugoslavia/Yougoslavie	65192	14234	10000	17978	117	Pakistan	7744	3160	6020	4558	8260
Israel/Israël	12340	19077	13025	23272	36649	Malaysia/Malaisie	644	884	6035	12729	8504
Lebanon/Liban	16880	14593	21101	24724	25436	Albania/Albanie	10650	538	483	6079	8656
Pakistan	2216	10879	14539	25004	22945	Bangladesh	1557	636	9747	12315	413
Croatia/Croatie	7617	13989	12341	15923	22687	Ukraine	1232	2810	4610	4268	11269
Syrian Arab Republic	19091	7519	16846	11787	15309	Brazil/Brésil	1993	1385	4901	7993	6988
Norway,SVD,JM	13772	9145	11137	10744	25645	Thailand/Thaïlande	3400	4595	9462	4676	1035

(VALUE AS PERCENTAGE OF WORLD TOTAL)(VALEURS EN POURCENTAGE DU TOTAL MONDIAL)

	1987	1988	1989	1990	1991	1992	1993	1994	1995	1996		1987	1988	1989	1990	1991	1992	1993	1994	1995	1996
Africa	1.0	1.3	1.4	1.4	1.8	1.9	1.5	1.8	2.4	2.2	Afrique	3.7	3.5	2.3	3.7	5.7	6.3	5.3	4.9	5.2	4.8
Americas	15.9	15.4	20.2	17.8	19.3	21.6	18.0	21.1	22.6	25.0	Amériques	8.5	6.7	5.6	9.6	8.6	9.8	14.8	11.2	15.8	13.4
Northern America	14.4	12.7	18.0	14.8	17.1	18.5	15.6	17.3	19.4	20.8	Amérique du Nord	8.4	6.5	5.3	8.8	7.8	9.6	14.1	10.8	15.4	13.1
LAIA	1.2	2.5	1.9	2.3	2.1	3.0	2.4	2.9	2.9	4.1	ALAI	0.1	0.0	0.2	0.0	0.4	0.1	0.1	0.2	0.3	0.3
CACM	0.0	0.0	0.1	0.0	0.0	0.1	0.0	0.0	0.0	0.0	MCAC			0.0	0.7	0.2	0.0	0.0	0.1	0.0	0.0
Caribbean	0.3	0.2	0.2	0.6	0.1	0.1	0.0	0.9	0.3	0.1	Caraïbes	0.0	0.0	0.0		0.0	0.0	0.0	0.0	0.0	0.0
Rest of America	0.0	0.0	0.0	0.0	0.0	0.0	0.0	0.0	0.0	0.0	Autre Amérique		0.3	0.1	0.0	0.2	0.1	0.6	0.0	0.0	0.0
As.ex F.USSR	17.5	16.4	14.7	16.0	17.9	19.2	19.2	18.3	18.8	18.5	Asie l'URSS exclus	19.6	29.3	26.8	24.7	28.9	33.4	31.8	32.4	27.3	30.7
Eur.x F.USSR	57.7	58.1	53.7	52.3	51.1	49.3	51.6	45.7	45.4	43.1	Europe l'URSS exclus	50.6	45.0	49.8	45.2	49.0	45.9	44.5	48.0	48.9	49.1
EU	46.0	45.5	42.7	43.1	42.7	41.1	45.4	40.0	38.9	36.7	UE	39.5	38.1	43.8	38.9	43.1	39.7	40.1	44.0	45.8	45.7
EFTA	2.9	3.2	2.9	2.8	2.6	3.7	2.8	2.3	2.8	2.8	AELE	1.3	1.0	1.3	0.9	0.8	1.0	0.9	0.9	0.6	0.3
East Europe	6.8	6.8	6.4	4.5	4.0	3.2	2.5	2.7	2.7	3.1	Europe de l'Est	8.7	5.6	3.8	4.5	4.6	4.0	2.2	2.0	1.7	1.7
Other Europe	2.1	2.5	1.6	1.9	1.8	0.0	0.1	0.1	0.6	0.0	Autre de l'Europe	1.1	0.3	0.9	0.9	0.4	0.6	0.8	0.7	0.1	1.1
Former USSR	2.7	3.1	3.5	3.0	1.8	0.5	2.5	3.6	4.5	3.8	Ancienne URSS	13.3	12.2	13.3	15.8	6.3	2.5	1.4	1.3	1.1	1.5
Oceania	2.5	2.9	2.8	4.9	3.5	3.5	2.8	4.5	1.3	3.3	Océanie	0.1	0.1	0.0	0.0	0.0	0.0	0.0	0.0	0.0	0.1
USA/Etats–Unis d'Amer	13.7	11.9	17.6	14.1	16.1	17.5	15.0	16.9	18.8	20.0	Italy/Italie	13.7	11.1	13.8	12.2	14.8	14.2	12.9	12.3	13.3	12.4
Germany/Allemagne	11.4	11.1	9.7	10.6	10.4	10.4	10.9	9.5	8.9	8.4	USA/Etats–Unis d'Amer	7.7	6.3	5.2	8.6	7.6	9.4	13.9	10.5	15.2	13.0
Italy/Italie	6.9	7.0	5.8	6.5	6.8	6.6	8.3	6.4	6.2	6.7	Israel/Israël	6.9	6.9	6.4	6.5	10.1	9.5	7.4	5.4	5.0	9.7
France,Monac	7.8	8.4	9.0	9.4	6.9	5.0	6.6	6.2	5.8	4.4	Netherlands/Pays–Bas	5.9	6.9	5.7	6.3	3.8	5.7	5.5	6.0	4.8	10.3
United Kingdom	4.2	4.2	4.2	4.0	4.5	4.4	4.1	3.6	3.2	3.4	Germany/Allemagne	4.2	4.2	5.2	5.6	3.7	4.2	4.2	6.0	6.0	4.6
Japan/Japon	6.4	5.0	3.9	3.7	4.1	4.3	4.5	4.2	2.7	2.6	Saudi Arabia	2.8	3.2	3.0	3.0	3.1	6.6	6.3	4.5	3.3	3.5
Netherlands/Pays–Bas	3.6	3.7	3.2	3.1	3.4	3.6	3.5	3.0	3.2	2.8	France,Monac	4.9	5.8	7.1	4.0	5.9	4.2	5.0	4.0	4.2	4.1
Australia/Australie	2.4	2.5	2.6	4.2	3.4	3.3	2.4	4.2	1.1	3.0	United Kingdom	2.9	2.7	2.6	3.0	2.2	3.4	2.7	4.1	4.1	4.7
Switz.Liecht	2.8	3.1	2.7	2.7	2.4	3.5	2.7	2.2	2.7	2.6	Singapore/Singapour	0.4	5.1	3.6	4.6	6.8	4.7	4.1	4.2	2.7	2.5
Russian Federation						0.4	1.8	2.9	3.5	2.8	Greece/Grèce	1.0	2.3	2.3	1.5	3.8	2.3	4.0	3.4	4.0	4.0

4. Special Imports C.I.F. by Commodities according to the S.I.T.C. (Rev. 2) in thousand U.S. Dollars
Importations Spéciales C.A.F. par Produits d'après la C.T.C.I. (Rév. 2) en milliers de Dollars E.U.

SITC CTCI	COMMODITY	1993		1994		1995		1996		PRODUIT
		WEIGHT POIDS	VALUE VALEUR	WEIGHT POIDS	VALUE VALEUR	WEIGHT POIDS	VALUE VALEUR	WEIGHT POIDS	VALUE VALEUR	
	ALL COMMODITIES		8175279		9586681		11738964		13019600	TOUS PRODUITS
0	FOOD AND LIVE ANIMALS		1603960		2261972		2611772		3058089	ALIMENTS,ANIMAUX VIVANTS
001	*LIVE ANIMALS FOR FOOD	W 54704	60665	W 111411	146763	W 101680	150164	W 48342	79415	ANIMAUX VIVANTS
0011	BOVINE SPECIES,LIVE	W 52822	52369	W 110618	138136	W 101044	140199	W 47351	68026	ESPECE BOVINE
00119	— OTHR THAN FR BREEDING	W 46403	45363	W 102680	125945	W 99220	137558	W 45686	63171	BOVINS NON REPRODUCTEURS
01	MEAT AND PREPARATIONS		170088		181208		214189		175653	VIANDES ET PREPARATIONS
011	MEAT FRESH,CHILLD,FROZEN	W 165948	166954	W 156856	177251	W 140009	207308	W 110859	168435	VIANDES FRAICHES,REF,CONGE
0111	BOVINE MEAT FRESH,FROZEN			W 128827	155468	W 113438	175776	W 90728	145677	VIANDES BOVIN FRAI,REF
01112	BOVINE MEAT BONELESS			W 106761	131326	W 113413	175731	W 88888	142858	VIANDES BOVIN DESOSSEES
0116	EDIBLE OFFAL FRESH,CH,FR	W 165908	166883	W 26675	19320	W 25938	30713	W 19578	21765	ABATS COMESTIBLES
02	DAIRY PRODCTS,BIRDS'EGGS		150541		150968		168947		181289	PRODUITS LAITIERS,OEUFS
022	MILK AND CREAM	W 21321	37197	W 21820	36767	W 27342	54777	W 25330	53622	LAIT ET CREME
0224	MILK,CREAM PRESERVED ETC	W 21209	37128	W 21548	36457	W 27270	54707	W 25220	53351	LAIT,CREME CONS,CONC
023	BUTTER	W 49130	79068	W 52649	75405	W 48816	77223	W 50225	92117	BEURRE
024	CHEESE AND CURD	W 19087	33064	W 21877	38275	W 16623	36846	W 14626	35180	FROMAGE ET CAILLEBOTTE
03	FISH AND PREPARATIONS		46348		72725		74523		109009	POISSONS ET PREPARATIONS
034	FISH,FRESH,CHILLED,FROZN	W 93597	39123	W 132832	56498	W 113437	56855	W 173356	89398	POISSON FRAIS, REFRIG,CONG
0342	FISH FROZEN,EXCL FILLETS			W 131120	54279	W 108918	54444	W 163384	84029	POISSONS CONGELES
04	CEREALS AND PREPARATIONS		724649		1125937		1309716		1720178	CEREALES ET PRODUITS
041	WHEAT ETC UNMILLED	W 2340412	335521	W 6597382	766214	W 5069599	875680	W 5546184	1232024	FROMENT,EPEAUTRE
0411	DURUM WHEAT UNMILLED			W 6363851	738692	W 5069599	875680	W 4958247	1100578	FROMENT DUR NON MOULU
0412	OTHER WHEAT ETC UNMILLED			W 233530	27521			W 587936	131446	AUTRE FROMENT NON MOULU
044	MAIZE UNMILLED	W 1700322	239490	W 2021007	263663	W 2425162	349271	W 2296699	435404	MAIS NON MOULU
046	WHEAT ETC MEAL OR FLOUR	W 694063	144439	W 379858	70735	W 289959	61756	W 56567	14774	SEMOULE FARINE,FROMENT
04601	FLOUR OF WHEAT OR MESLIN	W 673142	139578	W 374051	69517	W 281699	59553	W 43689	12563	FARINE DE FROMENT
05	VEGETABLES AND FRUIT		82997		127899		160442		169402	LEGUMES ET FRUITS
054	VEG ETC FRSH,SMPLY PRSVD	W 166000	66735	W 240816	93380	W 261002	124409	W 271272	130497	LEGUMES FRAIS,CONG,SECS
0541	POTATOES FRSH EXCL SWEET	W 25786	8694	W 34903	18541	W 74108	49946	W 48643	30116	POMMES DE TERRE
0542	LEGUMINOUS VEGETBLES DRY	W 131158	54421	W 200746	71896	W 174271	67290	W 187490	90011	LEGUMES A COSSE SECS
057	FRUIT,NUTS,FRESH,DRIED	W 15002	12203	W 39055	29160	W 38688	29772	W 48791	31518	FRUITS FRAIS OU SECS
06	SUGAR AND PREPS,HONEY		69290		130390		219125		260580	SUCRES ET PRODUITS
061	SUGAR AND HONEY	W 229733	68596	W 439354	129649	W 566539	218403	W 774235	259970	SUCRES ET MIEL
0611	RAW BEET AND CANE SUGAR	W 26000	6828	W 381408	109699	W 392494	143926	W 646186	208625	SUCRES BRUTS
0612	REFINED SUGAR ETC	W 202411	60549	W 53690	16628	W 170051	71077	W 120878	47833	SUCRES RAFFINES
07	COFFEE,TEA,COCOA,SPICES		124056		118057		153493		121536	CAFE,THE,CACAO,EPICES
074	TEA AND MATE	W 65130	106977	W 57230	89903	W 79964	118567	W 65041	86707	THE ET MATE
0741	TEA	W 65130	106977	W 57230	89903	W 79964	118567	W 65041	86707	THE
081	*FEEDING STUFF FOR ANIML	W 469119	143204	W 672006	184170	W 474635	136969	W 696047	211434	NOURRITURE POUR ANIMAUX
0813	OILCAKE AND OTH RESIDUES	W 354570	91514	W 498470	112627	W 309347	65031	W 521878	134460	TOURTEAUX
08131	— OF SOYA BEANS			W 474962	106514	W 305670	64653	W 436905	120209	TOURTEAUX DE SOJA
08139	— OF OTHER OILSEEDS ETC	W 354570	91514	W 23508	6112					TOURTEAUX D'AUTRES OLEAGINEU
0819	FOOD WASTE AND FEED NES	W 71469	34053	W 100177	44237	W 94389	44614	W 101193	46814	DECHETS,ALIMENTS NDA
08199	FODDER NES,INCL SWEETNED	W 71447	34049	W 100102	41753	W 92989	44265	W 90263	43548	PREPARATIONS FOURRAGERES
09	MISC EDIBLE PRODUCTS		32123		23856		24203		29595	PREP ALIMENTAIRES DIVERSES
098	EDIBLE PRODCTS,PREPS NES	W 7414	31897	W 5336	23308	W 7002	23157	W 7524	28042	PREP ALIMENTAIRES NDA
09809	MISC FOOD PREPRTIONS NES	W 6590	30152	W 4585	21830	W 5648	20859	W 6435	26201	PREP ALIMENTAIRES NDA
1	BEVERAGES AND TOBACCO		143899		146506		143236		174455	BOISSONS ET TABACS
12	TOBACCO AND MANUFACTURES		143606		144188		141998		173787	TABACS BRUTS FABRIQUES
121	TOBACCO UNMNFCTRD,REFUSE	W 44129	128024	W 47693	142226	W 48286	134174	W 53084	146305	TABACS BRUTS,DECHETS
1211	TOBACCO,NOT STRIPPED			W 28472	68979	W 26070	60950	W 30382	72874	TABACS NON ECOTES
1212	TOBACCO STRIPPED OR PART			W 18551	72856	W 21376	72739	W 22367	73291	TABACS PART ECOTES
2	CRUDE MATERLS,EXCL FUELS		686140		715847		1059074		1142055	MAT BRUTES NON COMESTIBLES
22	OIL SEEDS,OLEAGINOUS FRT		30348		34340		66761		91635	GRAINES,FRUITS OLEAGINEUX
222	SEEDS FOR'SOFT'FIXED OIL	W 82860	30249	W 95889	31233	W 103963	64404	W 185074	89144	GRAINES HUILES FIXES
2225	SESAME SEEDS	W 18041	12442	W 10679	7067	W 34979	40215	W 39360	44868	GRAINES DE SESAME
23	RUBBER, CRUDE		12307		23517		36925		42717	CAOUTCHOUC BRUT
24	CORK AND WOOD		22911		377180		550953		502165	LIEGE ET BOIS
247	OTH WOOD ROUGH,SQUARED	W 74749	17879	W 118222	30450	W 108118	28581	W 189793	49591	BOIS BRUTS EQUARRIS
248	WOOD SHAPED,SLEEPERS		1502	W 1001438	344625	W 1420120	522266	W 1299151	452452	BOIS SIMPLEMENT TRAVAILLES
2482	LUMBER SHAPED CONIFER		1438	W 791699	256051	W 1246669	445622	W 1061790	346700	CONIFERES SCIES,RABOTES
24821	LUMBER SAWN ETC CONIFER		3	W 791387	255952	W 1246641	445583	W 1061702	346667	CONIFERES SCIES LONGITUD
2483	LUMBER SHAPED NON–CONIFR			W 209447	88453	W 173036	76556	W 236926	105543	NON CONIFERES SCIES,RABOTES
24831	LUMBER SAWN ETC NON–CON			W 204148	86139	W 171236	75319	W 235357	104345	SCIES LONGITUDINALEMENT
251	*PULP AND WASTE PAPER	W 47201	20957	W 58123	30442	W 57194	48659	W 82249	49216	PATES A PAPIER,DECHETS
2512	MECHANICAL WOOD PULP			W 49191	26046	W 48543	43921	W 69390	44071	PATES MECANIQUES DE BOIS
26	TEXTILE FIBRES AND WASTE		89295		88604		159080		163754	FIBRES TEXTILES
263	COTTON	W 10319	15061	W 398	633	W 30710	37695	W 127624	46914	COTON
2631	RAW COTTON,EXCL LINTERS	W 10097	15035			W 30555	37638	W 126966	46144	COTON EN MASSE
266	SYNTHETIC FIBRES TO SPIN	W 27008	50039	W 37158	64851	W 40881	90906	W 43099	78874	FIBRES SYNTHETIQUES
2665	DISCN SYNTH FIBRE UNCMBD	W 19313	33166	W 30403	50693	W 36417	77532	W 38703	68094	DISCONTINUES EN MASSE
26653	— ACRYLIC	W 9299	17205	W 17565	32063	W 19505	42951	W 26307	49797	FIBRES ACRYLIQUES
27	CRUDE FERTLZR,MINRLS NES		24953		34636		41437		72990	ENGRAIS MINERAUX BRUTS
278	OTHER CRUDE MINERALS	W 75326	16844	W 127712	24797	W 105630	25565	W 151342	40528	AUTRES MINERAUX BRUTS
28	METALLIFEROUS ORES,SCRAP		460964		100473		123118		183977	MINERAIS METAL,DECHETS
281	IRON ORE,CONCENTRATES	W 1045732	49572	W 1113675	44658	W 639228	31174	W 881265	50604	MINERAIS DE FER
2815	IRON ORE,CONC,NOT AGGLOM	W 926772	45178	W 599049	24533	W 639228	31174	W 333696	20736	MINERAIS NON AGGLOMERES
287	BASE METAL ORES,CONC NES	W 155397	46267	W 138924	39481	W 244930	76121	W 416628	116515	MINERAIS METAUX COMMUNS
2873	ALUMINIUM ORES,ALUMINA	W 693	446	W 135658	37339	W 242410	74383	W 402268	113004	MINERAIS D'ALUMINIUM
28731	ALUMINIUM ORE,CONCNTRATE			W 134854	36772	W 240687	72843	W 400670	111953	MINERAIS D'ALUMINIUM
2879	OTH NONFER ORE,CONCNTRTE	W 153409	44633	W 2315	1363	W 1417	957	W 1688	1344	MINERAIS D'AUTRES METAUX
28799	OTH BASE MTL ORE,CON NES	W 153409	44633	W 181	99	W 54	80			AUTRES MINERAIS
288	NONFERR METAL SCRAP NES	W 1036740	348241	W 2144	917	W 3370	1089	W 729	295	DECHETS NON FERREUX
2882	OTHER BASE MTL SCRAP NES	W 1036740	348241	W 2144	917	W 3340	1085	W 674	283	AUTRES DECHETS
28821	COPPER WASTE AND SCRAP	W 1033725	345195	W 291	39	W 326	46	W 276	189	DECHETS DE CUIVRE
3	MINERAL FUELS ETC		138927		138948		145412		190422	COMBUSTIBLES MINERAUX LUB
32	COAL,COKE AND BRIQUETTES		93812		106672		99810		124232	HOUILLES,COKES,BRIQUETTES
322	COAL,LIGNITE AND PEAT	W 1522015	92359	W 1863918	106471	W 1559108	99781	W 1884863	123734	HOUILLES,LIGNITES,TOURBE
3222	OTH COAL,NOT AGGLOMERATD	W 1521978	92351	W 1852275	104372	W 1539507	95950	W 1874735	121539	AUTRES HOUILLES
33	PETROLEUM AND PRODUCTS		43739		31588		38969		64760	PETROLE ET DERIVES
334	PETROLEUM PRODUCTS,REFIN	W 162561	40186	W 53527	25232	W 49298	28511	W 182423	51913	PRODUITS RAFFINES
4	ANIMAL,VEGETABLE OIL,FAT		175531		193262		510021		512894	HUILES,GRAISSES ANIM,VEG
42	FIXED VEGETABLE OIL,FAT		156262		172324		466672		481967	HUILES VEGETALES FIXES
423	FIXED VEG OILS,SOFT	W 153378	69528	W 140171	75116	W 349418	235055	W 360265	225124	HUILES VEGET DOUCES FIXES
4232	SOYA BEAN OIL	W 12758	5933	W 64647	37519	W 81168	52271	W 106202	65510	HUILE DE SOJA
4233	COTTON SEED OIL	W 26262	12087	W 1238	715	W 96091	62009	W 21336	13150	HUILE DE COTON
4236	SUNFLOWER SEED OIL	W 113358	51108	W 73805	36196	W 171792	120011	W 232444	145352	HUILE DE TOURNESOL
424	FIXED VEG OIL NONSOFT	W 191795	86734	W 222702	97208	W 379012	231617	W 424243	256843	AUTRES HUILES VEG FIXES
4242	PALM OIL			W 149204	68418	W 248624	163776	W 272250	164361	HUILE DE PALME
4244	PALM KERNEL OIL	W 121995	53543	W 13359	5212	W 30116	15541	W 19677	16090	HUILE DE PALMISTE
4249	FIXED VEGETABLE OILS NES	W 60750	28738	W 35753	15293	W 79980	38458	W 122449	67117	HUILES VEGET FIXES NDA

4. Special Imports C.I.F. by Commodities according to the S.I.T.C. (Rev. 2) in thousand U.S. Dollars
Importations Spéciales C.A.F. par Produits d'après la C.T.C.I. (Rév. 2) en milliers de Dollars E.U.

SITC CTCI	COMMODITY	1993 WEIGHT POIDS	1993 VALUE VALEUR	1994 WEIGHT POIDS	1994 VALUE VALEUR	1995 WEIGHT POIDS	1995 VALUE VALEUR	1996 WEIGHT POIDS	1996 VALUE VALEUR	PRODUIT
5	CHEMCLS,RELATED PROD NES		1064801		1153864		1526341		1596150	PRODUITS CHIMIQUES
51	ORGANIC CHEMICALS		141689		190578		289131		277352	PROD CHIMIQ ORGANIQUES
513	CARBOXYLIC ACIDS ETC	W 30698	30596	W 34354	35091	W 53884	73276	W 54737	68993	ACIDES CARBOXYLIQUES
5138	POLYACIDS AND DERIVATIVS	W 17400	11615	W 17056	13064	W 39494	47001	W 36525	38735	ACIDES POLYCARBOXYLIQUES
514	NITROGEN–FNCTN COMPOUNDS	W 5311	15493	W 10018	42677	W 13249	72359	W 9964	66716	COMPOSES FONCT AZOTEES
5148	OTH NITROGN–FNCTN CMPNDS	W 1570	5071	W 4177	22837	W 7756	40168	W 5638	41578	AUTRES COMPOSES AZOTES
515	ORG–INORG COMPOUNDS ETC	W 7008	53573	W 5705	54259	W 13142	69995	W 6005	79187	COMPOSES ORGANO–MINERAUX
5156	HETEROCYCLIC CMPDS ETC	W 3323	33338	W 2552	25092	W 9180	32186	W 2352	36890	COMPOSES HETEROCYCLIQUES
51569	OTH HETEROCYC CMPDS,ETC	W 2562	31143	W 2167	23839	W 7255	26752	W 1962	35342	AUT COMP HETEROCYCLIQUES
516	OTHER ORGANIC CHEMICALS	W 7806	20179	W 9513	31285	W 12198	31328	W 10816	24790	AUTRES PROD ORGANIQUES
52	INORGANIC CHEMICALS		74322		78926		91706		99047	PROD CHIM INORGANIQUES
523	OTHR INORG CHEMICALS ETC	W 113676	51143	W 103863	53943	W 134422	66317	W 149845	73142	AUT PRODUITS CHIMIQUES INORG
5232	OTH MTL CMPD OF INRG ACD	W 80144	34060	W 72475	39286	W 90765	46340	W 106495	51221	SELS METALLIQUES
53	DYES,TANNING,COLOUR PROD		110202		123974		153097		159163	PROD TEINTURE,COLORANTS
531	SYNT DYE,NAT INDGO,LAKES	W 4037	36653	W 5378	37461	W 8357	38003	W 6374	37472	MAT COLOR ORGAN,LAQUES
5311	SYNTHIC ORGNIC DYESTUFFS	W 3513	34854	W 4432	30277	W 7590	33027	W 5974	33634	MAT COLOR ORGAN SYNTHET
533	PIGMENTS,PAINTS,ETC	W 72424	70124	W 73627	82581	W 99176	110125	W 107140	119138	PIGMENTS,PEINTURES,VERNIS
5331	COLOURING MATERIAL NES	W 42466	28972	W 38124	31492	W 57820	47908	W 50624	46701	AUT MATIERES COLORANTES
5335	GLAZES,DRIERS,PUTTY ETC	W 26041	27544	W 27305	27098	W 31748	31346	W 46416	42401	PREPTNS COLOR UTILISES CERAM
541	*MEDICINAL,PHARM PRODUCT	K 3453177	156493	K 4082009	181307	MK 9501	227564	K 4728952	238441	PROD MEDICINAUX PHARMACEUT
5413	ANTIBIOTICS IN BULK	K 484394	48643	K 572270	36368	K 664107	46336	K 504661	44609	ANTIBIOTIQUES NDA
54139	OTHER ANTIBIOTICS	K 393088	42383	K 301322	24181	K 388297	32886	K 338047	36353	AUTRES ANTIBIOTIQUES
5417	MEDICAMENTS	K 1877485	72347	K 2360571	100734	K 7574920	132074	K 2591894	137369	MEDICAMENTS
54179	— CONTNG OTH SUBSTANCES			K 2178243	91666	K 7394749	114959	K 2377373	115267	MED CONT AUT SUBSTANCES
55	PERFUME,CLEANING ETC PRD		31675		45448		55212		47595	PROD POUR PARFUM,TOILETTE
562	*FERTILIZERS,MANUFACTURE	W 240962	31911	W 67433	13061	W 119391	19659	W 52456	16876	ENGRAIS MANUFACTURES
58	PLASTIC MATERIALS ETC		321041		358139		498452		549309	MAT PLAST ARTIFICIELLES
582	PROD OF CONDENSATION ETC	W 49074	68558	W 38879	62192	W 56384	106811	W 64537	111014	PROD CONDENS,POLYCOND
5823	ALKYDS,OTHER POLYESTERS			W 19151	27533	W 37730	65764	W 41945	62051	ALKYDES ET AUT POLYESTERS
58231	— IN PRIMARY FORMS			W 18593	25873	W 37202	63532	W 41306	60057	SOUS FORMES PRIMAIRES
583	POLYMERIZATION ETC PRODS	W 293735	241695	W 336575	288107	W 311089	381851	W 435325	427702	PROD POLYMERISATION
5831	POLYETHYLENE			W 127584	90208	W 138353	143487	W 184525	162120	POLYETHYLENE
58311	— IN PRIMARY FORMS			W 126775	87696	W 137331	140001	W 183257	159411	POLYETHYLENE PRIMAIRES
5832	POLYPROPYLENE			W 101830	72805	W 72913	88387	W 110615	98626	POLYPROPYLENE
58321	— IN PRIMARY FORMS			W 100709	69835	W 71318	83196	W 109231	95178	POLYPROPYLENE PRIMAIRES
5833	POLYSTYRENE,ITS COPOLYMR			W 32938	31684	W 28383	38841	W 36692	36745	POLYPROPYLENE COPOLYMERES
58331	— IN PRIMARY FORMS			W 32931	31630	W 28210	38428	W 36518	36443	SOUS FORMES PRIMAIRES
5834	POLYVINYL CHLORIDE			W 14680	16412	W 26308	29417	W 48605	41533	CHLORURE DE POLYVINYLE
5839	OTH POLYMRZTION ETC PROD			W 41357	56273	W 26330	52354	W 29254	55696	AUT PROD POLYMER COPOLYM
59	CHEMICAL MATERIALS NES		197127		161941		190976		207309	MAT PROD CHIMIQUES NDA
591	PESTICIDES,DISINFECTANTS	W 9128	67637	W 6952	48238	W 7535	60189	W 10811	77837	DESINF,INSECT,FONG,HERB
5911	INSECTICIDES,FOR RETAIL	W 9128	67637	W 3887	33668	W 4522	42090	W 6155	52525	INSECTICIDES VENTE DET
598	MISCEL CHEM PRODUCTS NES	W 102210	120447	W 54851	102448	W 62932	115933	W 71030	115740	PROD DIV INDUST CHIM NDA
5989	CHEM PRODUCTS,PREPS NES	W 82871	94450	W 36401	78031	W 38303	82799	W 42203	80054	PROD PREP CHIMIQUES NDA
59899	OTH CHEM PRODS,PREPS,NES	W 27428	73717	W 25052	61815	W 24226	63123	W 30387	63616	AUT PRODUITS CHIMIQUES NDA
6	BASIC MANUFACTURES		1517002		1820372		2375400		2602472	ART MANUFACTURES
62	RUBBER MANUFACTURES NES		130255		125627		142949		161097	CAOUTCHOUC MANUFACTURE
621	MATERIALS OF RUBBER	W 8930	34503	W 6742	19305	W 6386	15735	W 7725	17621	PRODUITS EN CAOUTCHOUC
62105	UNHARD VULC RUBBER TUBES	W 3946	24964	W 2437	11686	W 2265	8358	W 3267	9234	TUBES,TUYAUX CAOUT VULC
625	RUBBER TYRES, TUBES ETC	W 25480	70639	W 30707	81469	W 40538	98881	W 38752	115506	PNEUS CAOUTCHOUC VULCANISE
6252	TYRES,NEW,BUS OR LORRY	W 11910	31420	W 9272	27244	W 7836	21280	W 10116	29512	PNEUS POUR AUTOBUS,CAMIONS
6259	OTH TYRES,TYRE CASES,ETC	W 5008	12545	W 14883	35602	W 22425	52781	W 19848	60393	AUTRES PNEUS RECHAPES FLAPS
62599	TYRES NES,TYRE CASES,ETC	W 1907	4769	W 11070	26965	W 15634	41639	W 12721	46381	PNEUS,FLAPS
628	RUBBER ARTICLES NES	W 3808	25112	W 4565	24853	W 3725	28333	W 5468	27970	OUVRAGES CAOUTCHOUC NDA
63	WOOD,CORK MANUFACTRS NES		76315		114750		81233		91480	OUVRAGES LIEGE ET BOIS
634	VENEERS,PLYWOOD,ETC	W 113062	74024	W 226336	111508	W 131086	76135	W 140142	82746	PLACAGES,CONTRE–PLAQUES
6342	PLYWOOD OF WOOD SHEETS	W 91944	54920	W 129174	70137	W 120418	57092	W 124170	64760	BOIS CONTRE–PLAQUES
64	PAPER,PAPERBOARD AND MFR		281950		282445		534717		413671	PAPIERS,CARTONS & OUVRAGES
641	PAPER AND PAPERBOARD	W 439219	264122	W 469846	261637	W 556473	499598	W 485659	365443	PAPIERS ET CARTONS
6411	NEWSPRINT	W 75320	32250	W 69776	30705	W 59654	48806	W 34178	20981	PAPIER JOURNAL
6412	PRINTG,WRITING PAPER NES	W 169980	116314	W 55840	39132	W 26213	30754	W 22988	24926	PAPIERS POUR L'IMPRESSION
64121	— UNCOATED	W 150436	99836	W 33884	18928	W 1706	1432	W 869	841	PAPIERS IMPRES NON COUCHES
6413	KRAFT PAPER,PAPERBOARD			W 47176	21847	W 107885	105811	W 111591	76909	PAPIER ET CARTON KRAFT
64132	SACK KRAFT PAPER IN BULK			W 8415	4901	W 64852	71885	W 43099	42688	PAPIER KRAFT POUR SACS
6415	PAPER,PAPERBRD,BULK,NES	W 127417	65266	W 187746	101665	W 257065	226085	W 204403	157995	PAPIERS,CARTONS ROULEAUX
64159	OTHER PAPER ETC,BULK,NES	W 125325	62571	W 184065	98013	W 254153	221426	W 202511	156086	AUT PAPIER ROULEAUX FEUILLES
6418	COATED ETC PAPER NES BLK	W 66101	49399	W 96708	62506	W 90158	80898	W 91048	76464	PAP,CARTONS COUCHES,ENDUITS
64189	COATED PAPER ETC NES	W 66101	49399	W 93468	54974	W 86310	69922	W 87513	62200	PAPIERS,CARTONS COUCHES
642	PAPER,ETC,PRECUT,ARTS OF	W 12434	17828	W 13556	20808	W 18868	35119	W 26976	48228	PAP,CARTONS DECOUPES
65	TEXTILE YARN,FABRICS,ETC		211409		242177		279658		289639	FILS,TISSUS,ARTICLES TEXTILE
651	TEXTILE YARN	W 56061	114456	W 67403	133383	W 63650	173548	W 81545	198611	FILS TEXTILES
6513	COTTON YARN	W 5883	9601	W 3526	11682	W 8946	35237	W 14983	57291	FILS DE COTON
6514	SYN FIB YRN,BULK,MONOFIL	W 38362	75244	W 50203	89015	W 44263	110261	W 50272	99744	FILS CONT 85% FIB TEXT SYNTH
65142	— NONTXT ETC CONT PAMID			W 35503	58701	W 32565	76347	W 41673	72815	FILS NON TEX FI CON POLYAMID
65146	— OTH NONTXT CONT PESTR	W 33341	60184							AUT NON TEXT POLYESTERS
652	COTTON FABRICS,WOVEN	W 5774	30061	W 6677	34635	W 6394	37266	W 4564	28952	TISSUS DE COTON
6522	WOVEN COTTON BLEACHD,ETC	W 5626	29630	W 6270	32391	W 6227	36370	W 4445	28356	TISSUS COTON BLANCHIS ETC
65224	BLCHED COTTON FABRIC NES	W 5621	29572	W 5419	27789	W 5781	32789	W 3704	23155	AUT TIS PLUS 85% COT BLANCHI
657	SPECIAL TXTL FABRC,PRODS	W 9171	37949	W 10136	39335	W 7575	27017	W 6293	26207	TISSUS SPECIAUX
66	NONMETAL MINERAL MFS NES		87042		106583		160748		234215	ART MIN NON METALLIQUES
661	LIME,CEMENT,BLDG PRODS	W 60283	4460	W 379124	18208	W 1262473	54229	W 2284452	97978	CHAUX,CIMENTS MAT CONSTR
6612	CEMENT	W 54720	1124	W 374135	15282	W 1255673	48616	W 2275746	91083	CIMENTS HYDRAULIQUES
664	GLASS	W 92349	34225	W 76880	30053	W 95834	38202	W 145204	56221	VERRE
67	IRON AND STEEL		424560		545777		782786		1009063	FER ET ACIER
671	PIG IRON ETC	W 140426	28845	W 336935	62445	W 303240	68837	W 296583	84327	FONTE,SPIEGEL,POUDRES
6712	PIG IRN,SPIEGELEISEN ETC	W 112812	13668	W 204495	33623	W 100264	19667	W 152070	31911	FONTES BRUTES
672	IRON,STEEL PRIMARY FORMS	W 256005	63883	W 439461	98403	W 409936	129453	W 834514	234599	LINGOTS FER,ACIER
6725	IRN,STL BLOOMS,SLABS,ETC	W 231239	55640	W 339121	71944	W 282592	68080	W 629646	144631	BLOOMS,BILLETTES FER ACIER
67251	IRN,SMPLE STL BLOOMS,ETC	W 231239	55640	W 338445	71226	W 282518	67887	W 626594	143556	BLOOMS ETC NON ACIER FIN
6727	IRN,STL COIL FR REROLLNG	W 19022	5762	W 27437	13147	W 118988	57726	W 191953	83928	EBAUCHES POUR TOLES FER
67271	IRON,SIMPLE STEEL COILS	W 19022	5762	W 23551	8673	W 115329	49990	W 189837	70585	EBAUCHES NON EN ACIER
673	IRON,STEEL SHAPES ETC	W 354667	89445	W 424112	132161	W 676639	210634	W 971470	274280	BARRES,PROFIL FER,ACIER
6731	IRON,STEEL WIRE ROD		1	W 232628	67343	W 509822	149737	W 448700	126124	FIL MACHINE FER,ACIER
67311	IRON,SIMPLE STL WIRE ROD		1	W 227255	64805	W 479808	139287	W 442197	124132	FIL MACH AUT ACIER FIN
6732	IRON,STEEL BARS ETC	W 319024	79804	W 134509	45558	W 124154	42369	W 479302	130519	BARRES FER,ACIER
67326	IRN,OTH STL BARS HOTROLD			W 98252	26556	W 105010	31586	W 440494	112348	BARRES PLEINES FER,ACIER
67327	IRN, OTH STL BARS FORGED	W 319024	79804	W 25748	13076	W 6293	3042	W 7806	3844	BARRES FORGEES CREUSES
674	IRN,STL UNIV,PLATE,SHEET	W 264522	156378	W 181055	103410	W 369325	244879	W 431695	281947	LARGES PLATS,TOLES
6744	IRN,STL HVY PLATE,ROLLED			W 28252	16542	W 90961	46884	W 96477	50901	TOLES LAMINEES PLUS 4.75 MM
67441	— OF IRON OR SIMPLE STL			W 27250	14603	W 89829	43703	W 94575	44763	TOLES NON ACIER FIN CARB
6746	IRN,STL THIN PLATE,ROLLD			W 16932	14372	W 80581	64808	W 97129	75639	TOLES LAM MOINS 3MM

4. Special Imports C.I.F. by Commodities according to the S.I.T.C. (Rev. 2) in thousand U.S. Dollars
Importations Spéciales C.A.F. par Produits d'après la C.T.C.I. (Rév. 2) en milliers de Dollars E.U.

SITC CTCI	COMMODITY	1993		1994		1995		1996		PRODUIT
		WEIGHT POIDS	VALUE VALEUR	WEIGHT POIDS	VALUE VALEUR	WEIGHT POIDS	VALUE VALEUR	WEIGHT POIDS	VALUE VALEUR	
67461	— OF IRON OR SIMPLE STL			W 12745	5295	W 70946	41704	W 82505	42074	TOL NON AC FIN MOINS 3 MM
6747	TINNED PLATES,SHEETS			W 49999	30359	W 58615	40343	W 70255	54651	TOLES ETAMEES EN ACIER
6749	OTH IRN,STL PLATES,SHEET	W 264521	156367	W 59420	29308	W 111501	74879	W 117425	72362	AUTRES TOLES FER,ACIER
67491	— OF IRON OR SIMPLE STL	W 235503	118384	W 44165	20646	W 103398	63189	W 112401	63936	AUT TOLES AUTRES ACIER FIN
67492	— OF HIGH CARBON STEEL	W 26816	35615							AUT TOL ACIER FIN CARBONE
678	IRON,STL TUBES,PIPES,ETC	W 64851	78359	W 118177	135454	W 102092	112077	W 106365	122639	TUBES,TUYAUX EN FONTE,FER
6782	IRON,STL SEAMLESS TUBES			W 29990	30727	W 25768	22187	W 36417	33744	TUBES,TUYAUX SANS SOUDURE
6783	IRON,STL TUBES,PIPES NES	W 55999	60214	W 76708	75741	W 41923	44973	W 24964	28845	AUT TUBES,TUYAUX FER,ACIER
68	NON–FERROUS METALS		120688		169333		153615		149568	METAUX NON FERREUX
682	COPPER EXC CEMENT COPPER	W 18186	51254	W 16644	51157	W 24961	90702	W 23956	84804	CUIVRE
6822	COPPER,ALLOYS WORKED	W 18185	51238	W 16224	49905	W 24955	90663	W 23862	84627	CUIVRE,ALLIAGES OUVRES
68221	COPPER BARS,WIRE,ETC	W 13054	32295	W 10949	32597	W 18260	62542	W 14881	48148	BARRES,PROFILES ET FILS
684	ALUMINIUM	W 9844	48258	W 73561	102270	W 7241	29172	W 9829	33797	ALUMINIUM
6841	ALUMINIUM,ALLOYS,UNWRGHT	W 5832	31916	W 67693	81591	W 52	82	W 2645	4313	ALUMINIUM,ALLIAGES BRUTS
69	METAL MANUFACTURES NES		182924		230132		236753		249551	ART MANUFACT EN METAL NDA
691	STRUCTURES AND PARTS NES	W 7099	25067	W 23044	34496	W 11553	26695	W 12403	32585	CONSTRUCT FER,ACIER,ALU
6911	STRUCTURES,PARTS IRN,STL	W 6906	23390	W 22936	33851	W 11188	25567	W 11837	30725	CONSTRUCT FER,ACIER,FONTE
693	WIRE PRODUCTS NON ELECTR	W 6495	8960	W 26766	31713	W 11214	20523	W 16907	27006	OUVRAGES FILS METALLIQUES
695	TOOLS	W 11408	32076	W 9640	26618	W 9626	29953	W 11214	32164	OUTILS A MAIN
699	BASE METAL MFRS NES	W 22784	72467	W 26147	91593	W 29541	101723	W 22982	98664	ART MANUFACTURES MET NDA
6997	IRON,STEEL ARTICLES NES	W 10046	33292	W 10848	47878	W 11968	45781	W 5966	45657	OUV FONTE,FER,ACIER NDA
69979	IRN,STL MANUFACTURES NES	W 10028	33237	W 10843	47849	W 11936	45727	W 5919	45539	AUT OUVRAGES EN FER NDA
7	MACHINES,TRANSPORT EQUIP		2531990		2782751		2957654		3300207	MACHINES MATERIEL TRANSPORT
71	POWER GENERATING EQUIPMT		208017		150241		183591		234924	MACHINES GENERATRICES
713	INTRNL COMBUS PSTN ENGIN	W 18860	72434	W 18784	66078	W 19495	85931	W 23548	92301	MOTEURS EXPL COMB INT, PIECE
7132	MOTOR VEHCL PISTN ENGINS	W 10557	26334	W 8739	18322	W 11360	28530	W 13018	31502	MOTEURS EXPL POUR VEHICULES
7139	PISTON ENGINE PARTS NES	W 7960	43615	W 7859	33943	W 6864	43095	W 8297	43774	PIECES POUR 713.2,3,8
716	ROTATING ELECTRIC PLANT	W 10417	81320	W 12402	67270	W 16402	84126	W 16534	96636	APP ELECTR ROTATIFS,PIECES
7161	DC MOTORS AND GENERATORS	W 1271	29716	W 886	5705	W 569	4803	W 644	8437	MOTEURS COURANT CONTINU
7162	AC MTRS,GENRTRS,GEN SETS	W 9146	51604	W 10370	54187	W 14568	65999	W 14274	79296	MOTEURS ELECTRIQUES
71621	AC MTRS,INC UNIVRSL MTRS			W 9478	45118	W 13250	51498	W 11578	51682	MOT ELEC NON COUR CONTINU
718	OTH POWER GENERATG MACHY	W 1471	32928	W 119	1475	W 156	2908	W 370	6926	AUTRES MOTEURS PARTIES
7188	WIND,WATER,ETC ENGINES	W 1469	32852	W 119	1404	W 124	1665	W 370	6926	MOT MACHINES MOTRICES NDA
71889	PARTS NES OF 71881,71882	W 1445	32570	W 66	242			W 19	226	PARTIES DES POS 718.81,82
72	MACHS FOR SPCL INDUSTRYS		527364		438889		475846		608607	MAC SPECIALES POUR INDUST
723	CIVIL ENGNEERG EQUIP ETC	W 15861	68225	W 23873	91911	W 25443	96044	W 34020	118378	APPAREILS DE GENIE CIVIL
7234	CONST,MINING MACHNRY NES	W 13300	46334	W 20576	74701	W 23070	82208	W 31831	102699	MACH POUR LA CONST, MINES
72341	SELF–PROPELLD DOZERS,ETC	W 4805	13558	W 10849	34809	W 10220	30925	W 11349	33643	BULLDOZERS
72343	SLFPRP CONST ETC MCH NES	W 8496	32776	W 2969	12736	W 2929	11723	W 5140	19913	AUT MACH EXTR,TERRASSEM
724	TEXTILE,LEATHER MACHNRY	W 18543	159885	W 13551	124531	W 12315	105851	W 18111	135869	MACH POUR INDUSTRIE TEXTILE
7243	SEWING MACHS,NEEDLES ETC	W 2953	25402	W 1775	17083	W 2176	16672	W 1790	15656	MACHINES A COUDRE,PIECES
7244	SPINNING,EXTRDNG,ETC MCH	W 2928	30988	W 2408	17642	W 1444	17746	W 3661	21852	MACH POUR LE FILAGE
7245	WEAVING,FELT MFG,ETC MCH	W 5874	41336	W 4745	40297	W 4072	34396	W 6078	46092	METIERS A TISSER,PIECES
7247	TEXTILE MACHINERY NES	W 4948	38456	W 3861	38377	W 3899	25348	W 4979	37903	MACH LAVAGE,TEINTURE TEX
72474	OTH TEXTILE MACHNERY NES	W 3729	29449	W 1931	25797	W 1438	11878	W 1981	18691	MACH LAVAGE ETC MAT TEXT
726	PRINTG,BKBINDG MACHY,PTS	W 2228	32495	W 2521	26251	W 1886	21539	W 3590	43297	MACHINES POUR IMPRIMERIE
7264	PRINTING PRESSES	W 1754	26944	W 1097	10107	W 898	9659	W 1501	17629	MACHINES A IMPRIMER
728	OTH MACHY FOR SPCL INDUS	W 24877	218279	W 17172	137734	W 21887	180947	W 28322	212299	AUT MACH IND PARTICULIERES
7284	MACHY FOR SPCL INDUS NES	W 20501	200058	W 11867	113963	W 14757	150695	W 18510	174009	MACH SPEC IND PARTICUL.
72848	OTH MCHY WITH INDIV FNCT	W 16353	160372	W 7553	79189	W 9274	111911	W 10226	109505	AUTRES MACHINES NDA
72849	PTS OF MACHS OF 7284 ETC	W 3951	35913	W 537	8470	W 1595	7471	W 663	15031	PIECES DU 728.4 ETC
73	METALWORKING MACHINERY		54451		55690		54433		82176	MACH TRAVAIL DES METAUX
736	METALWORKING MACH–TOOLS	W 11844	36869	W 16567	42699	W 12765	41049	W 14896	57928	MACH–OUTILS TRAVAIL METAUX
7367	OTH METALWRKG MACH–TOOLS	W 11442	36045	W 1951	6574	W 2046	6775	W 1543	10919	AUT MACH–OUT POUR METAUX
74	GENRL INDUSTRL MACHY NES		509049		657154		785986		845403	MACH APP INDUSTRIE
741	HEATING,COOLING EQUIPMNT	W 9334	58769	W 12364	144508	W 55299	238211	W 17716	154028	MACH CHAUFFAGE,PIECES
7416	HEATING,COOLING EQU NES	W 2690	23735	W 5720	86733	W 9241	176388	W 8006	84216	APP CHANGEMENT TEMP
742	PUMPS FOR LIQUIDS ETC	W 8178	55717	W 8538	61927	W 8438	76566	W 10260	93762	POMPES MOTO–POMPES
7428	OTHER PUMPS FOR LIQUIDS	W 8178	55717	W 6756	41193	W 4830	45059	W 5669	51648	AUTRES POMPES POUR LIQ
74288	PUMPS FR LIQUIDS NES ETC	W 8055	53951	W 6280	34526	W 4486	40900	W 5385	47889	POMPES POUR LIQUIDES NDA
743	PUMPS NES,CENTRFUGES ETC	W 12817	83165	W 24667	121949	W 19466	110842	W 26359	176379	POMPES COMPRES,VENT ETC
7431	PUMPS FOR GASES ETC	W 8284	41850	W 11730	85152	W 12232	63459	W 12928	69717	POMPES AIR A VIDE,COMPRES
7436	GAS,LIQUID FILTERS ETC	W 1571	15235	W 1945	17479	W 2446	20565	W 3726	64440	APP POUR FILT DES LIQUIDES
744	MECHANICAL HANDLING EQU	W 10340	48534	W 13778	56573	W 16280	80579	W 20047	77701	EQUIP MANUTENTION PIECES
7442	LIFTING,LOADING MACH NES	W 5614	31256	W 7277	35019	W 9289	50536	W 9051	41269	APP LEVAGE,MANUTENTION
74428	OTH HANDLING ETC MCH NES	W 5468	30084	W 3262	16492	W 4196	24482	W 4180	18396	AUT APP LEVAGE ETC
745	NONELEC MACHY,TOOLS NES	W 3111	35248	W 2933	33659	W 3483	48362	W 7249	88346	AUT MACH NON ELEC,PIECES
7452	OTH NONELEC MCHS,PTS NES	W 3052	34317	W 2855	32433	W 3407	47148	W 7117	86828	AUT MACH NON ELEC,PIECES
74522	PACKAGNG,BOTTLNG,ETC MCH	W 696	17257	W 757	18557	W 933	26584	W 2286	54752	MACH NETT BOUTEILLES,ETC
749	NONELEC MACH PTS,ACC NES	W 32356	227615	W 29744	238537	W 22930	231427	W 27605	255186	PIECES MACH NON ELEC NDA
7492	COCKS,VALVES ETC NES	W 6824	49705	W 7516	47289	W 8615	60307	W 8875	59086	ART ROB,SIM POUR TUYAUX
7493	SHAFT,CRANK,PULLEY ETC	W 6775	35477	W 6511	45294	W 6080	50145	W 7336	58509	ARBRES TRANS,VILEBREQUINS
7499	OTH NONELEC MCHY PTS NES	W 16441	124182	W 13984	130240	W 5904	102307	W 8036	113548	PIECES NON ELECT NDA
74999	MACH PARTS NONELEC NES	W 14132	102837	W 12101	110627	W 4229	80205	W 6135	91730	PIECES MACHINES NDA
75	OFFICE MACHNES,ADP EQUIP		113914		116513		133101		136211	MACH BUREAU TRAIT AUTOM
752	AUTOMTIC DATA PROC EQUIP	W 731	51414	W 904	50889	W 1255	56998	W 1562	63221	MACH TRAIT INFORMATION
759	OFFICE,ADP MCH PTS,ACCES	W 1225	42258	W 1066	41293	W 1732	50542	W 1712	49521	PIECES DU 751 ET 752
7599	ACCTG,ETC,ADP MCH PTS,AC	W 745	32981	W 559	28292	W 837	35727	W 835	32449	PIECES DU 751 ET 752
76	TELECOMM,SOUND EQUIPMENT		231438		201282		212027		237963	EQUIPMENT DE TELECOM
761	TELEVISION RECEIVERS	W 2733	30907	W 4098	41592	W 7948	78759	W 7358	70612	RECEPTEURS DE TELEVISION
7611	COLOUR TV RECEIVERS	W 2428	29944	W 3136	36782	W 6237	71938	W 5523	62188	RECEPTEURS COULEUR
764	TELECOM EQPT,PTS,ACC NES	W 7028	179661	W 14158	150124	W 5821	118418	W 6302	154461	EQUIP TELECOM,PIECES
7641	LINE TELEPHONE,ETC EQUIP	W 1994	14191	W 1258	29211	W 1290	16397	W 1484	26564	APP TELEPHON PAR FIL
7649	PTS NES OF EQUIPMT OF 76	W 4482	153135	W 12383	101578	W 3939	93520	W 4220	93915	PIECES DE LA DIV 76
76491	PTS NES OF APPAR OF 7641	W 2397	114681	W 10860	78352	W 1551	76348	W 1603	76486	PIECES POUR 764.1
76493	TELECOMM EQUIPMT PTS NES	W 1897	35622	W 1296	18893	W 1850	13960	W 2121	13967	PIECES 761,762,764.3,8
77	ELECTRIC MACHNRY NES ETC		435212		444482		463315		532480	MACH APP ELECT NDA
771	ELECTRIC POWER MACHY NES	W 4924	33041	W 3588	22525	W 4298	27678	W 5595	40876	MACH PROD,TRANS ELECTR
7712	OTH ELEC POWER MACHY NES	W 3864	25842	W 2042	10036	W 1901	10108	W 2208	19721	AUT APP PROD TRANSF ELEC
772	SWITCHGEAR ETC,PARTS NES	W 9076	134560	W 8456	139434	W 10037	133333	W 10090	146512	APP COUPURE,SECT ETC
7721	SWITCHGEAR ETC			W 7036	121821	W 7993	107276	W 9237	134292	APP COUPURE,SECTIONMNT
773	ELECTR DISTRIBUTNG EQUIP	W 28989	138142	W 33267	132111	W 29755	118448	W 44144	129455	EQUIPMT DISTRIBUTION ELECT
7731	INSULATED WIRE,CABLE ETC	W 18348	79571	W 28681	110090	W 23523	91200	W 29719	92259	FILS,CABLES ISOLES ELECT
7732	ELECTRC INSULATING EQUIP	W 10641	58571	W 4585	22021	W 6232	27248	W 14425	37196	EQUIP ISOL ELECTRIQUE
77324	OTHER ELECTRC INSULATORS	W 10531	56827	W 132	2581	W 1109	10823	W 833	5420	ISOLATEURS AUTRES MATIERES
775	HOUSEHOLD TYPE EQUIP NES	W 5349	24910	W 7001	32134	W 7695	34452	W 8376	38659	MACH,APP USAGE DOMESTQUE
776	TRANSISTORS,VALVES,ETC	W 569	11531	W 570	12333	W 2575	23190	W 6380	46146	LAMPES,TUBES,VALVES
778	ELECTRICAL MACHINERY NES	W 16025	79951	W 17493	86255	W 21166	96292	W 20948	97499	AUTRES MACH ELECT NDA
7788	OTH ELEC MACHY,EQUIP NES	W 10076	43626	W 9792	42612	W 10981	46391	W 10124	44476	AUT MACH APP ELEC NDA
78	ROAD VEHICLES		420072		666954		624642		598530	VEHICULES ROUTIERS
781	PASS MOTOR VEH EXC BUSES	W 16097	164683	W 27813	213426	W 32067	216696	W 40887	201235	AUTO TRANSPORT PERSONNES

4. Special Imports C.I.F. by Commodities according to the S.I.T.C. (Rev. 2) in thousand U.S. Dollars
Importations Spéciales C.A.F. par Produits d'après la C.T.C.I. (Rév. 2) en milliers de Dollars E.U.

SITC CTCI	COMMODITY	1993 WEIGHT POIDS	1993 VALUE VALEUR	1994 WEIGHT POIDS	1994 VALUE VALEUR	1995 WEIGHT POIDS	1995 VALUE VALEUR	1996 WEIGHT POIDS	1996 VALUE VALEUR	PRODUIT
782	LORRIES,SPCL MTR VEH NES	W 3239	26670	W 15063	101674	W 5248	44772	W 13081	80301	VEHICULES SPECIAUX,MARCH
7821	LORRIES,TRUCKS	W 2364	18317	W 12770	83761	W 3840	29802	W 10620	61395	VEHICULES TRANSP MARCHAND
783	ROAD MOTOR VEHICLES NES	W 4401	54547	W 9011	97882	W 8888	102653	W 8197	79320	VEHICULES ROUTIERS NDA
7831	BUSES	W 4401	54547	W 8814	96462	W 8487	99323	W 7987	78165	VOITURES TRANSPORT COMMUN
784	MOTOR VEH PRTS,ACCES NES	W 31176	154391	W 48743	227972	W 55558	228370	W 59071	201645	PIECES 722,781,782,783
7849	OTHER MOTOR VEHCL PARTS	W 30976	153670	W 48072	225063	W 54555	223752	W 58364	198546	PIECES 722,781,782,783
79	OTHR TRANSPORT EQUIPMENT		32472		51547		24713		23914	AUTRE MATERIEL TRANSPORT
791	RAILWAY VEHICLES	W 3776	24846	W 1883	20562	W 2419	15947	W 3439	19549	VEHIC MAT CHEMINS DE FER
793	SHIPS AND BOATS ETC	W 878	6934		30800	W 6947	8750	W 704	3874	NAVIRES BATEAUX,ETC
8	MISC MANUFACTURED GOODS		311964		370430		409085		441916	ART MANUFACTURES DIVERS
87	PRECISION INSTRUMNTS NES		126443		134156		137217		168075	INSTRUM,APPAR SCIENT NDA
872	MEDICAL INSTRUMENTS NES	W 1682	54763	W 1742	57404	W 2297	68272	W 2869	89777	INSTR,APP MEDIC–CHIR NDA
87202	OTH MEDICAL INSTRUMENTS	W 1622	51979	W 1462	48403	W 2088	62228	W 2500	80586	INSTRUM,APP MEDECINE
874	MEASURNG,CONTROLNG INSTR	W 2420	62498	W 2412	63933	W 2359	59113	W 3340	65847	INSTRUMENTS DE MESURE
88	PHOTO EQU,OPTICL GDS ETC		61816		64546		72885		68528	APP,FOURN PHOTO,OP,MONTR
882	PHOTO,CINEMA SUPPLIES	W 3164	30177	W 3350	35111	W 3988	37506	W 4189	35394	PRODUITS PHOTO,CINEMA
89	MISC MANUFCTRD GOODS NES		110256		136327		164374		164895	ART MANUFACTURES DIVERS
893	ARTICLES OF PLASTIC NES	W 4389	21354	W 14855	41845	W 25610	56802	W 17241	55400	OUVRAGES EN MAT DIVIS 58
8939	MISC PLASTIC ARTICLES	W 4170	19286	W 13891	37599	W 23814	48872	W 14264	45737	ART DIVERS EN MAT DIV 58
89399	OTHR PLASTC ARTICLES NES	W 4170	19286	W 12778	35939	W 22676	46829	W 13158	43708	AUT OUV MAT DIV 58
894	TOYS,SPORTING GOODS,ETC	W 7650	26869	W 9112	29433	W 12645	38981	W 11934	35169	VOITURES ENFANTS,JOUETS

5. Special Exports F.O.B. by Commodities according to the S.I.T.C. (Rev. 2) in thousand U.S. Dollars
Exportations Spéciales F.O.B. par Produits d'après la C.T.C.I. (Rév. 2) en milliers de Dollars E.U.

SITC CTCI	COMMODITY	1993 WEIGHT POIDS	1993 VALUE VALEUR	1994 WEIGHT POIDS	1994 VALUE VALEUR	1995 WEIGHT POIDS	1995 VALUE VALEUR	1996 WEIGHT POIDS	1996 VALUE VALEUR	PRODUIT
	ALL COMMODITIES		3105169		3472547		3444140		3534402	TOUS PRODUITS
0	FOOD AND LIVE ANIMALS		292141		266148		320907		354931	ALIMENTS,ANIMAUX VIVANTS
001	*LIVE ANIMALS FOR FOOD	W 13080	30600	W 220	1377	W 58	436	W 1654	4375	ANIMAUX VIVANTS
0012	SHEEP AND GOATS,LIVE	W 12785	29354	W 119	266	W 4	9	W 1034	2417	ESPECES OVINE ET CAPRINE
00121	SHEEP,LIVE	W 4729	11172					W 211	486	ESPECE OVINE
00122	GOATS,LIVE	W 8056	18182	W 118	265	W 4	9	W 823	1931	ESPECE CAPRINE
01	MEAT AND PREPARATIONS		14853		8500		3756		2276	VIANDES ET PREPARATIONS
011	MEAT FRESH,CHILLD,FROZEN	W 3567	14532	W 2018	8308	W 1355	3663	W 1022	2129	VIANDES FRAICHES,REF,CONGE
0116	EDIBLE OFFAL FRESH,CH,FR	W 3360	13784	W 52	158	W 28	94	W 177	166	ABATS COMESTIBLES
04	CEREALS AND PREPARATIONS		47615		85988		63159		124090	CEREALES ET PRODUITS
042	RICE	W 142856	39989	W 248193	79111	W 156787	56741	W 328834	117723	RIZ
0421	RICE IN HUSK OR HUSKED	W 136506	38979	W 14023	3984	W 31	13	W 3213	1535	RIZ SANS AUTRE PREPARATION
0422	RICE SEMI–MILLED,MILLED	W 6350	1011	W 234169	75127	W 156756	56728	W 325621	116189	RIZ POLI,GLACE INCL BRISURES
04221	RICE MILLED UNBROKEN			W 229626	74070	W 156756	56728	W 325621	116189	RIZ POLI,GLACE EXCL BRISURES
05	VEGETABLES AND FRUIT		140846		120946		206805		170014	LEGUMES ET FRUITS
054	VEG ETC FRSH,SMPLY PRSVD	W 401320	87620	W 335041	75501	W 609864	152829	W 581057	120973	LEGUMES FRAIS,CONG,SECS
0541	POTATOES FRSH EXCL SWEET	W 175245	32135	W 131865	26599	W 418744	102115	W 411172	79909	POMMES DE TERRE
0545	OTHER FRESH VEGETABLES	W 165093	33627	W 153151	29832	W 139622	25510	W 124855	17876	AUTRES LEGUMES FRAIS,REF
05451	ALLIACEOUS VEGTBLS,FRESH	W 148177	25172	W 137829	23273	W 118483	18466	W 111169	13668	OIGNONS,ECHALOTES,AULX
0546	VEGETABLES SIMPLY PRESVD	W 11477	7935	W 12395	9127	W 12942	10898	W 14532	11204	LEGUMES CONG,CONSER
05461	VEGETABLES FROZEN	W 11296	7800	W 11582	8793	W 12768	10731	W 14480	11189	LEGUMES CONGELES
056	VEGTBLES ETC PRSVD,PREPD	W 9862	14281	W 14079	19084	W 15922	25035	W 13810	19432	CONSERVES DE LEGUMES
0561	VEG DRIED EXC LEGUMINOUS	W 7752	12629	W 11551	17382	W 11411	22427	W 10166	17547	LEGUM DESSECH,DESHYDRAT
057	FRUIT,NUTS,FRESH,DRIED	W 94108	36076	W 65478	23143	W 82124	25315	W 86408	25891	FRUITS FRAIS OU SECS
0571	ORANGES, MANDARINS ETC	W 56872	16996	W 28347	8360	W 42641	13217	W 53669	17358	ORANGES,MAND,CLEMENTINES
05711	ORANGES,FRESH OR DRIED	W 56164	16631	W 27957	8222	W 41969	12985	W 53598	17328	ORANGES FRAICHES,SECHEES
0579	FRUIT FRESH OR DRIED NES	W 23052	12568	W 21593	9319	W 22865	7976	W 18363	5067	FRUITS FRAIS,SECS NDA
06	SUGAR AND PREPS,HONEY		18473		14866		12778		13319	SUCRES ET PRODUITS
062	SUGAR CANDY NON–CHOCLATE	W 7215	11636	W 5038	7642	W 4954	7680	W 2961	5145	SUCRERIES
07	COFFEE,TEA,COCOA,SPICES		6979		11543		10396		14980	CAFE,THE,CACAO,EPICES
081	*FEEDING STUFF FOR ANIML	W 122100	11276	W 58472	5712	W 57763	10154	W 63788	8795	NOURRITURE POUR ANIMAUX
0819	FOOD WASTE AND FEED NES	W 102786	9362	W 54644	5001	W 52669	9171	W 61024	8267	DECHETS,ALIMENTS NDA
09	MISC EDIBLE PRODUCTS		11587		7707		7306		10116	PREP ALIMENTAIRES DIVERSES
098	EDIBLE PRODCTS,PREPS NES	W 3985	10501	W 5075	7518	W 3937	7213	W 4676	9922	PREP ALIMENTAIRES NDA
2	CRUDE MATERLS,EXCL FUELS		95619		305014		240932		180062	MAT BRUTES NON COMESTIBLES
22	OIL SEEDS,OLEAGINOUS FRT		12406		10690		9125		6997	GRAINES,FRUITS OLEAGINEUX
222	SEEDS FOR'SOFT'FIXED OIL	W 16502	11385	W 13480	8807	W 12338	7765	W 9273	5675	GRAINES HUILES FIXES
2221	GROUNDNUTS,GREEN	W 12359	9447	W 7335	6267	W 9718	6795	W 5557	4177	ARACHIDES NON GRILLEES
26	TEXTILE FIBRES AND WASTE		50057		250305		169091		102455	FIBRES TEXTILES
263	COTTON	W 18499	43529	W 116318	237419	W 71607	157831	W 23600	92545	COTON
2631	RAW COTTON,EXCL LINTERS	W 18395	43519	W 113371	233630	W 67417	152217	W 23289	91831	COTON EN MASSE
27	CRUDE FERTLZR,MINRLS NES		9897		14553		19254		21861	ENGRAIS MINERAUX BRUTS
273	STONE,SAND AND GRAVEL	W 65961	3314	W 129530	6919	W 312561	13041	W 715162	14520	PIERRES,SABLES,GRAVIERS
29	CRUDE ANIMAL,VEG MAT NES		19772		23426		32251		44604	MATIERES BRUTES ANIM,VEGET
292	CRUDE VEG MATERIALS NES	W 21426	17940	W 27131	20416	W 28750	28926	W 38192	41076	MAT BRUTES VEGETALES NDA
2924	VEG USED IN PHARMACY ETC	W 9301	9867	W 10547	11366	W 12100	13550	W 13319	16091	PLANTES MEDICINALES
2929	OTH CRUDE VEG MATERIALS	W 1237	790	W 1271	1123	W 2556	6602	W 5733	14679	MATIERES VEGETALES NDA
29291	VEGETABLE SAPS,EXTRACTS	W 1	3	W 122	319	W 1707	5871	W 4570	13480	SUCS,EXTRAITS VEGETAUX
3	MINERAL FUELS ETC		1547916		1360110		1282955		1682100	COMBUSTIBLES MINERAUX LUB
32	COAL,COKE AND BRIQUETTES		24277		34476		48869		47307	HOUILLES,COKES,BRIQUETTES
323	BRIQUETS,COKE,SEMI–COKE	W 253103	22298	W 364236	34361	W 466690	48777	W 394405	47231	BRIQUETTES
3232	COKE,SEMI–COKE,RTRT CRBN	W 243653	21436	W 347412	32861	W 466690	48777	W 394403	47230	COKES ET SEMI–COKES
32321	COKE OF COAL,RETORT CRBN	W 243653	21436							COKES,SEMI–COKES HOUILLE
33	PETROLEUM AND PRODUCTS		1522969		1320407		1231755		1634793	PETROLE ET DERIVES
333	CRUDE PETROLEUM	MW 13006	1314628	W 7867128	792954	W 7242853	719185	W 6684826	816584	HUILES BRUTES DE PETROLE
334	PETROLEUM PRODUCTS,REFIN	W 2518520	198523	W 6072480	503477	W 6077973	496314	W 5964300	810102	PRODUITS RAFFINES
3341	GASOLINE,OTH LIGHT OILS	W 13	2	W 2972	317	W 212555	21759			ESSENCES POUR MOTEURS
33412	SPIRIT TYPE JET FUEL			W 2936	295	W 179506	17850			CARBUREACTEURS
3343	GAS OILS	W 69268	16930	W 97369	15590	W 74121	12370			GAS OILS
3344	FUEL OILS,NES	W 2446040	180677	W 5970689	486330	W 5788043	461504			FUEL OILS
335	RESIDUAL PETRLM PROD NES	W 48297	9817	W 193100	23976	W 39341	16257	W 44892	8108	PRODUITS RESIDUELS NDA
3351	PETRLM JELLY,MINERAL WAX	W 34211	7387	W 23744	3480	W 26980	13415	W 40390	7386	VASELINE,CIRES MINERALES
33512	MINERAL WAXES	W 34211	7387	W 23744	3480	W 26980	13415	W 40390	7386	PARAFFINES,CIRES DE PETROLE
3353	MIN TAR PITCH,PITCH COKE			W 107950	11326					BRAI,COKE DE BRAI
33531	PITCH FROM MINERAL TARS			W 107941	11325					BRAI DE GOUDRON
5	CHEMCLS,RELATED PROD NES		110953		159177		200839		176550	PRODUITS CHIMIQUES
51	ORGANIC CHEMICALS		7040		6951		8413		13823	PROD CHIMIQ ORGANIQUES
52	INORGANIC CHEMICALS		7335		14674		22109		33116	PROD CHIM INORGANIQUES
522	INORG ELEMNTS,OXIDES,ETC	W 25674	5665	W 51196	7684	W 49396	14482	W 60908	18907	ELEMENTS INORGANIQUES
5221	CHEMICAL ELEMENTS	W 40	71	W 1869	899	W 17143	9252	W 22782	13895	ELEMENTS CHIMIQUES
52218	CARBON NES, CARBON BLACK			W 1717	824	W 16874	9189	W 21722	13048	CARBONE NDA
523	OTHR INORG CHEMICALS ETC	W 12594	1245	W 43560	6968	W 57089	7626	W 78751	14209	AUT PRODUITS CHIMIQUES INORG
541	*MEDICINAL,PHARM PRODUCT	K 5992254	26382	K 5065492	28049	K 5462266	35191	K 6525653	41061	PROD MEDICINAUX PHARMACEUT
5417	MEDICAMENTS	K 4416057	22348	K 3559319	22967	K 3309330	28686	K 5339944	36567	MEDICAMENTS
54179	— CONTNG OTH SUBSTANCES			K 3522295	22756	K 3249382	28440	K 5336444	36533	MED CONT AUT SUBSTANCES
55	PERFUME,CLEANING ETC PRD		21531		33813		34622		39153	PROD POUR PARFUM,TOILETTE
553	PERFUMERY,COSMETICS,ETC	W 2092	9544	W 2361	11879	W 1771	9456	W 3430	17284	PRODUITS DE PARFUMERIE
554	SOAP,CLEANSING ETC PREPS	W 5801	4206	W 14371	11912	W 17678	15384	W 12461	12534	SAVONS,PRODUITS DETERSIFS
5542	WASHING PREPARATIONS ETC	W 3317	2740	W 11019	8494	W 11115	10711	W 9225	9440	PROD ORG TENSIO–ACT NDA
562	*FERTILIZERS,MANUFACTURE	W 143189	16412	W 518681	52900	W 481615	65113	W 87286	14724	ENGRAIS MANUFACTURES
5621	CHEM NITROGENOUS FERTLZR	W 137409	15968	W 413644	45495	W 316235	45872	W 36515	6476	ENGRAIS AZOTES
56211	AMMONIUM NITRATE	W 109869	12982	W 197363	19519	W 175818	19462	W 24132	3766	NITRATE D'AMMONIUM
56216	UREA	W 27480	2977	W 113596	13398	W 115528	22444	W 11136	2548	UREE
56219	CHEM NITROG FERTILZR NES			W 97435	12068	W 24889	3966	W 1247	162	ENGRAIS AZOTES NDA
5622	CHEM PHOSPHATIC FERTILZR	W 5600	346	W 104822	7299	W 164787	19154	W 45791	7894	ENGRAIS PHOSPHATES
56222	SUPERPHOSPHATES			W 104822	7299	W 155861	18590	W 45791	7894	SUPERPHOSPHATES
59	CHEMICAL MATERIALS NES		18677		15023		22440		21651	MAT PROD CHIMIQUES NDA
598	MISCEL CHEM PRODUCTS NES	W 28383	14831	W 16690	11269	W 24267	16658	W 24169	16850	PROD DIV INDUST CHIM NDA
5989	CHEM PRODUCTS,PREPS NES	W 28204	14687	W 16381	11048	W 24241	16634	W 24143	16825	PROD PREP CHIMIQUES NDA
59899	OTH CHEM PRODS,PREPS,NES	W 28134	14569	W 16351	10992	W 24193	16528	W 24023	16701	AUT PRODUITS CHIMIQUES NDA
6	BASIC MANUFACTURES		767241		1046801		1035641		788659	ART MANUFACTURES
61	LEATHER,DRESSED FUR,ETC		12547		12269		7211		9491	CUIRS,PELLETERIES
64	PAPER,PAPERBOARD AND MFR		7484		5347		11058		10847	PAPIERS,CARTONS & OUVRAGES
65	TEXTILE YARN,FABRICS,ETC		394663		618851		571210		426426	FILS,TISSUS,ARTICLES TEXTILE
651	TEXTILE YARN	W 68200	221384	W 115555	386865	W 74023	322587	W 47621	204166	FILS TEXTILES
6513	COTTON YARN	W 65906	214100	W 112084	377887	W 69390	305726	W 44612	193485	FILS DE COTON
652	COTTON FABRICS,WOVEN	W 23790	82842	W 31422	121268	W 23823	109209	W 20461	88779	TISSUS DE COTON
6521	GREY WOVEN COTTON FABRIC	W 22090	73604	W 29205	111592	W 23131	105862	W 19492	83813	TISSUS COT ECRUS NON MERCER
65214	GREY WOVEN COTTON NES	W 22085	73555	W 27965	106158	W 19232	88045	W 16603	70474	AUT TISSUS 85% COTON ECRUS
65215	GREY WOVN COTN BLEND NES			W 1240	5434	W 3899	17817	W 2889	13339	AUT TIS MOINS 85% COT ECRUS
658	TEXTILE ARTICLES NES	W 11982	51258	W 13288	64703	W 17038	91844	W 17918	89729	ART FACONNES MAT TEXTILES

5. Special Exports F.O.B. by Commodities according to the S.I.T.C. (Rev. 2) in thousand U.S. Dollars
Exportations Spéciales F.O.B. par Produits d'après la C.T.C.I. (Rév. 2) en milliers de Dollars E.U.

SITC CTCI	COMMODITY	1993 WEIGHT POIDS	1993 VALUE VALEUR	1994 WEIGHT POIDS	1994 VALUE VALEUR	1995 WEIGHT POIDS	1995 VALUE VALEUR	1996 WEIGHT POIDS	1996 VALUE VALEUR	PRODUI"
6584	LINENS ETC	W 10092	46052	W 11835	59206	W 14995	83778	W 13949	78706	LINGE DE MAISON
65841	BED LINEN OF COTTON	W 10025	45838	W 6688	30876	W 7762	41961	W 7178	35235	LINGE DE LIT DE COTON
65845	OTHER LINEN OF COTTON			W 4428	24556	W 6187	35618	W 5556	34282	LINGE DE TOILETTE COTON
659	FLOOR COVERINGS,ETC	W 6342	30628	W 8947	34082	W 7476	33994	W 6457	30745	COUVRE–PARQUETS,TAPIS ETC
6595	MAN–MADE TXTL CARPTS NES	W 45	143	W 5869	21117	W 4905	23785	W 3720	15870	TAPIS MAT TEXT SYNT ARTIF
65951	— TUFTED			W 3708	10883	W 134	405	W 91	323	TAPIS MAT TEXT SYNT TOUFFT
65952	— WOVEN			W 2161	10234	W 4771	23380	W 3629	15546	TAPIS MAT TEXT SYNT TISSES
6596	OTH TXTL CARPETS ETC NES	W 5406	25564	W 1812	5818	W 1578	4922	W 1772	5851	TAPIS AUT MAT TEXT NDA
66	NONMETAL MINERAL MFS NES		23202		28526		27405		27962	ART MIN NON METALLIQUES
665	GLASSWARE	W 5863	8324	W 8088	17130	W 16465	15567	W 15238	12428	OUVRAGES EN VERRE
67	IRON AND STEEL		131448		134771		159973		69005	FER ET ACIER
671	PIG IRON ETC	W 34430	14650	W 31799	16348	W 42120	26916	W 32898	24174	FONTE,SPIEGEL,POUDRES
6716	FERRO–ALLOYS	W 34164	14533	W 31332	16169	W 41937	26845	W 32898	24174	FERRO–ALLIAGES
67162	FERRO–SILICON	W 34164	14533	W 9698	5236	W 41341	26491	W 31745	23430	FERRO–SILICIUM
67169	OTHER FERRO–ALLOYS			W 20834	10893	W 576	348			AUTRES FERRO–ALLIAGES
672	IRON,STEEL PRIMARY FORMS	W 42669	11068	W 5903	1774	W 39498	10768	W 578	181	LINGOTS FER,ACIER
673	IRON,STEEL SHAPES ETC	W 232266	69195	W 229709	68692	W 191085	58490	W 73382	23793	BARRES,PROFIL FER,ACIER
6731	IRON,STEEL WIRE ROD	W 30	2	W 148577	44237	W 35818	10441	W 22957	6625	FIL MACHINE FER,ACIER
67311	IRON,SIMPLE STL WIRE ROD	W 30	2	W 87774	27028	W 35688	10397	W 22957	6625	FIL MACH AUT ACIER FIN
67315	OTHER ALLOY STL WIRE ROD			W 57963	16429					FIL MACH NON ACIERS ALL
6732	IRON,STEEL BARS ETC	W 141198	43802	W 45379	13224	W 87882	25786	W 27823	8177	BARRES FER,ACIER
67326	IRN,OTH STL BARS HOTROLD			W 19382	6165	W 84586	24710	W 27619	8116	BARRES PLEINES FER,ACIER
67327	IRN, OTH STL BARS FORGED	W 141198	43802	W 9826	2838	W 1573	553	W 204	61	BARRES FORGEES CREUSES
6733	IRON,STEEL PROFILES ETC	W 91038	25390	W 35753	11231	W 67385	22263	W 22602	8991	PROFILES,PALPLAN FER,ACIER
67332	LARGE U,I,H SECTIONS ETC			W 12622	4131	W 66412	21619	W 21660	8553	PROFILES PLUS 80MM
67335	OTH IRN,SMPL STL PRFILES	W 91038	25390							AUT PROFILES FER,ACIER
674	IRN,STL UNIV,PLATE,SHEET	W 63501	15551	W 23236	6203	W 37427	10767	W 1854	314	LARGES PLATS,TOLES
6744	IRN,STL HVY PLATE,ROLLED			W 17978	5142	W 36517	10515	W 27	3	TOLES LAMINEES PLUS 4.75 MM
67441	— OF IRON OR SIMPLE STL			W 17978	5142	W 36517	10515	W 27	3	TOLES NON ACIER FIN CARB
6749	OTH IRN,STL PLATES,SHEET	W 63301	15485	W 4790	919	W 905	248	W 113	59	AUTRES TOLES FER,ACIER
67491	— OF IRON OR SIMPLE STL	W 59118	13964	W 264	184	W 905	248	W 38	43	AUT TOLES AUTRES ACIER FIN
677	IRN,STL WIRE(EXCL W ROD)	W 50419	15064	W 102530	29810	W 152342	47808	W 44335	12531	FILS EN FER,ACIER
67701	IRON, SIMPLE STEEL WIRE	W 50419	15064	W 115	39	W 104	44			FILS NON ACIER FIN CARBONE
67702	HIGH CARBON STEEL WIRE			W 72420	20739	W 122575	38314	W 42799	11968	FILS ACIER FIN CARBONE
678	IRON,STL TUBES,PIPES,ETC	W 10283	5696	W 24622	11525	W 7639	5078	W 12294	7856	TUBES,TUYAUX EN FONTE,FER
68	NON–FERROUS METALS		140793		168239		199735		186938	METAUX NON FERREUX
684	ALUMINIUM	W 103355	140558	W 111239	167192	W 93258	197559	W 107368	185073	ALUMINIUM
6841	ALUMINIUM,ALLOYS,UNWRGHT	W 1206	1060	W 15934	27889	W 70282	149727	W 96880	164753	ALUMINIUM,ALLIAGES BRUTS
6842	ALUMINIUM,ALLOYS WORKED	W 102149	139499	W 95305	139303	W 22976	47832	W 10488	20320	ALUMINIUM,ALLIAGES OUVRE
68421	ALUMINIUM BARS,WIRE,ETC	W 92182	120535	W 86788	125519	W 10826	20242	W 7675	14591	BARRES,PROFILES FILS ALU
68422	ALUMNM PLATE,SHEET,STRIP	W 9506	18434	W 4703	8809	W 10303	23647	W 2266	4661	TOLES, PLANCHES EN ALU
69	METAL MANUFACTURES NES		51375		70662		47516		43977	ART MANUFACT EN METAL NDA
693	WIRE PRODUCTS NON ELECTR	W 61267	18844	W 19356	6703	W 2176	3017	W 1972	3213	OUVRAGES FILS METALLIQUES
6932	IRON,STEEL FENCING WIRE	W 59122	17567	W 289	183	W 70	38	W 127	98	RONCES DE FER OU ACIER
696	CUTLERY	W 591	5637	W 966	11118	W 954	11117	W 1053	13314	COUTELLERIE
69603	RAZORS,RAZOR BLADES	W 517	5422	W 945	11016	W 924	11018	W 1043	13266	RASOIRS ET LAMES
697	BASE MTL HOUSEHOLD EQUIP	W 4531	13125	W 4970	13510	W 4445	12441	W 4207	12933	ART MENAGE MET COMMUNS
699	BASE METAL MFRS NES	W 7243	7145	W 78576	31441	W 9717	11434	W 5960	6074	ART MANUFACTURES MET NDA
6997	IRON,STEEL ARTICLES NES	W 4985	2633	W 73153	21951	W 5503	2746	W 4301	2125	OUV FONTE,FER,ACIER NDA
69979	IRN,STL MANUFACTURES NES	W 4968	2602	W 73153	21951	W 5503	2746	W 4301	2125	AUT OUVRAGES EN FER NDA
7	MACHINES,TRANSPORT EQUIP		28817		18693		22120		15551	MACHINES MATERIEL TRANSPORT
8	MISC MANUFACTURED GOODS		253759		305228		329964		323454	ART MANUFACTURES DIVERS
812	*PLUMBG,HEATNG,LGHTNG EQ	W 7475	12396	W 7706	10405	W 9668	15351	W 10559	16365	APPAR SANITAIRES CHAUFFAGE
8122	CERAMIC PLUMBNG FIXTURES	W 6889	8485	W 7572	9383	W 9188	12244	W 10107	13577	EVIERS,LAVABOS,CUVETTES
821	*FURNITURE,PARTS THEREOF	W 7756	19231	W 9004	14955	W 8081	13163	W 9161	13604	MEUBLES ET PIECES
8219	FURNITURE AND PARTS NES	W 7501	18500	W 8966	14792	W 7966	12940	W 9039	13430	AUTRES MEUBLES ET PIECES
82192	WOOD FURNITURE NES	W 7323	17920	W 8741	14077	W 7504	12058	W 8808	13122	MEUBLES NDA EN BOIS
84	CLOTHING AND ACCESSORIES		180692		230561		252536		239323	VETEMENTS
842	MENS OUTERWEAR NOT KNIT	W 8675	79794	W 2654	25801	W 3630	35581	W 5168	46604	VET DESSUS POUR HOMMES
8423	— TROUSERS,BREECHES ETC			W 1669	14250	W 2467	21377	W 3387	29382	PANTALONS HOMMES MAT TEX
8429	— OTHER OUTER GARMENTS	W 8675	79794	W 552	7304	W 887	11525	W 1335	14133	AUT VET DES HOM MAT TEX
84293	—— OF COTTON	W 8472	78134							VET DES HOM NDA COTON
843	WOMENS OUTERWEAR NONKNIT	W 1769	19628	W 7530	66637	W 7530	75024	W 6493	64519	VET DESSUS FEMMES MAT TEX
8435	— BLOUSES			W 1603	15019	W 1903	21040	W 2415	25940	BLOUSES FEM MAT TEXTILES
8439	— OTHER OUTER GARMENTS	W 1769	19628	W 4873	41190	W 4913	46585	W 3543	32720	AUT VET DES FEM MAT TEXT
84399	—— OF OTHER FIBRES	W 1665	15202							VET DES FEM NDA AUT FIBR
844	UNDER GARMENTS NOT KNIT	W 2670	20604	W 6394	52206	W 6972	64716	W 5869	51133	VETEMENT DESSOUS MAT TEX
8441	— MENS SHIRTS			W 4327	34030	W 4476	43985	W 3432	31434	CHEMISES HOMMES MAT TEXT
84411	—— OF COTTON			W 4193	33058	W 4422	43519	W 3339	30640	CHEMISES HOMMES DE COTON
8442	— MENS,OTHR THAN SHIRTS	W 2506	19615	W 1483	13196	W 1863	15112	W 1889	14970	SOUS–VET HOMMES MAT TEXT
84421	—— OF COTTON	W 2375	19288							SOUS–VET HOMMES DE COTON
845	OUTERWEAR KNIT NONELASTC	W 5134	48455	W 1380	10984	W 123	1242	W 251	2472	VET DESSOUS,ACCES BONNET
8459	— OTHER,CLTHG ACCESRYS	W 5134	48455	W 1231	9655	W 99	912	W 162	1832	AUT VET DESSUS DE BONNE
84592	—— OF COTTON	W 5118	48332							AUT VET DESSUS DE COTON
846	UNDER GARMENTS KNITTED	W 1134	9137	W 8010	72934	W 7837	75058	W 7344	73800	SOUS VETS DE BONNETERIE
8462	— OF COTTON NON ELASTIC	W 1100	8870	W 8006	72893	W 7832	74940	W 7195	72368	SOUS–VET BONNET COTON
84629	—— OTHER	W 1100	8870	W 7619	69079	W 7734	74038	W 7195	72368	AUT SOUS–VET BONNET COTON
851	*FOOTWEAR	W 1956	13786	W 1800	10801	W 1940	9520	W 2061	10135	CHAUSSURES
85102	FOOTWEAR LEATHER	W 1488	11528	W 1415	8164	W 1644	6386	W 1579	6045	CHAUS SEMELLES EN CUIR
89	MISC MANUFCTRD GOODS NES		23186		33617		34806		37599	ART MANUFACTURES DIVERS
892	PRINTED MATTER	W 5494	7022	W 9703	10651	W 6615	8321	W 6162	8537	IMPRIMES
893	ARTICLES OF PLASTIC NES	W 5007	10159		17432		19752		20063	OUVRAGES EN MAT DIVIS 58
8932	PLSTC SANITRY,TOILET ART			W 4360	9078	W 4755	13136	W 4813	14453	OBJETS HYGIEN MAT DU 58
8939	MISC PLASTIC ARTICLES	W 5003	10156	W 4839	7971	W 2680	6078	W 2546	5223	ART DIVERS EN MAT DIV 58
89399	OTHR PLASTC ARTICLES NES	W 5003	10156	W 4499	7597	W 2462	5776	W 2266	4955	AUT OUV MAT DIV 58

1. HISTORICAL SERIES, 1961–1996 SPECIAL TRADE, IMPORTS C.I.F., EXPORTS F.O.B.
SERIES HISTORIQUES, 1961–1996 COMMERCE SPECIAL, IMPORTATIONS C.A.F., EXPORTATIONS F.O.B

YEAR ANNEE	VALUE IN MILLION EL SALV. COLONES VALEUR EN MILLION EL SALV. COLONES MERCHANDISE –MARCHANDISE		GOLD –OR		CONVERSION FACTORS U.S. CENTS PER EL SALV. COLON FACTEURS DE CONVERSION CENTS E.U. PAR EL SALV. COLON		INDEX NUMBERS –INDICES QUANTUM		UNIT VALUE VALEUR UNITAIRE	
	IMPORTS	EXPORTS	IMPORTS	EXPORTS	IMPORTS	EXPORTS	IMPORTS	EXPORTS	IMPORTS	EXPORTS
1961	271.80	297.70			40.0000	40.0000				17
1962	312.00	340.80			40.0000	40.0000				16
1963	379.40	384.60			40.0000	40.0000				16
1964	477.80	445.20			40.0000	40.0000				19
1965	501.40	471.80			40.0000	40.0000				20
1966	550.00	472.30			40.0000	40.0000				19
1967	559.80	518.10			40.0000	40.0000				18
1968	533.80	529.30			40.0000	40.0000				17
1969	523.10	505.30			40.0000	40.0000				17
1970	534.00	570.80			40.0000	40.0000				20
1971	618.60	607.90			40.0000	40.0000				20
1972	695.20	754.30			40.0000	40.0000				21
1973	927.60	895.80			40.0000	40.0000				26
1974	1408.50	1156.20			40.0000	40.0000				33
1975	1495.10	1283.40			40.0000	40.0000				34
1976	1794.70	1801.80			40.0000	40.0000				49
1977	2356.10	2431.90			40.0000	40.0000				65
1978	2559.90	1577.40			40.0000	40.0000				54
1979	2529.90	2579.30			40.0000	40.0000				62
1980	2404.30	2684.00			40.0000	40.0000				64
1981	2461.40	1991.80			40.0000	40.0000				59
1982	2141.90	1748.60			40.0000	40.0000				56
1983	2228.70	1838.20			40.0000	40.0000				45
1984	3285.50	1517.80			40.0000	40.0000				
1985	2403.40	1697.40			40.0000	40.0000				
1986	4674.40	3774.60			20.0000	20.0000				
1987	4970.30	2954.70			20.0000	20.0000				
1988	5034.90	3043.80			20.0000	20.0000				
1989	5806.50	2482.50			20.0000	20.0000				
1990	8816.20	3891.68			14.3202	14.9422				100
1991	11359.71	4751.05			12.3762	12.3762				98
1992	14210.10	4983.71			11.9528	11.9891				92
1993	16630.62	6364.73			11.4981	11.4962				99
1994	22491.54	7373.35			11.4452	11.4453				121
1995	24977.29	8736.10			11.4236	11.4239				169
1996	23383.83	8968.66			11.4220	11.4220				154

2. IMPORTS BY BROAD ECONOMIC CATEGORY AND EXPORTS BY INDUSTRIAL ORIGIN. (PERCENTAGE OF TOTAL VALUE)
IMPORTATIONS PAR CATEGORIES ECONOMIQUES ET EXPORTATIONS PAR BRANCHE D'ACTIVITE.(EN POURCENTAGE DE LA VALEUR TOTALE)

IMPORTS – IMPORTATIONS

	1990	1991	1992	1993	1994	1995	1996
TOTAL IMPORTS–IMPORTATIONS TOTALES	100.	100.	100.	100.	100.	100.	100.
1 FOOD BEV–ALIMENTATION BOISSONS	11.3	12.4	11.7	10.0	11.7	11.5	13.0
11 PRIMARY–PRODUITS DE BASE	3.2	5.7	4.3	2.6	3.9	3.1	3.9
111 FOR INDUSTRY–POUR L'INDUSTRIE	1.9	4.4	2.5	1.6	2.6	1.8	2.3
112 FOR HOUSEHOLDS–POUR LES MENAGES	1.3	1.3	1.8	1.0	1.4	1.3	1.6
12 PROCESSED–PRODUITS ELABORES	8.2	6.8	7.5	7.4	7.7	8.5	9.1
121 FOR INDUSTRY–POUR L'INDUSTRIE	2.6	1.7	2.1	2.0	2.2	2.4	2.4
122 FOR HOUSEHOLDS–POUR LES MENAGES	5.6	5.1	5.4	5.4	5.5	6.1	6.7
2 IND SUPPLIES–APPROV INDUSTRIELS	39.2	37.7	34.3	33.0	33.6	33.3	33.8
21 PRIMARY–PRODUITS DE BASE	4.3	4.3	2.8	2.3	3.3	2.7	3.9
22 PROCESSED–PRODUITS ELABORES	34.9	33.4	31.4	30.7	30.3	30.6	29.8
3 FUELS–COMBUSTIBLES	15.3	12.5	13.9	11.2	9.4	9.1	12.1
31 PRIMARY–PRODUITS DE BASE	5.9	10.1	10.2	8.0	5.6	4.2	5.5
32 PROCESSED–PRODUITS ELABORES	9.5	2.4	3.7	3.2	3.8	4.9	6.6
321 MOTOR SPIRIT–ESSENCE	9.4	0.5	1.2	0.4	0.6	0.7	1.5
322 OTHER–AUTRES	0.1	2.0	2.5	2.8	3.2	4.2	5.1
4 MACHINERY–EQUIPEMENT	11.7	14.0	14.1	16.8	16.1	15.1	15.4
41 CAPITAL EQUIPMENT–MACHINES	10.1	12.4	12.6	14.9	14.3	13.0	13.5
42 PARTS–PIECES ACCESSOIRES	1.6	1.6	1.5	1.9	1.8	2.2	1.9
5 TRANSPORT–TRANSPORT	9.9	10.7	12.8	14.6	14.4	14.5	11.0
51 PASSENGER CARS–AUTOMOBILES	2.8	7.0	8.9	5.2	4.3	4.6	3.0
52 OTHER–AUTRES	3.9	0.5	0.6	5.8	6.7	6.7	5.1
521 INDUSTRIAL–INDUSTRIELS	3.6	0.2	0.2	5.5	6.5	6.4	4.8
522 NON INDUSTRIAL–NON INDUSTRIEL	0.2	0.3	0.3	0.3	0.2	0.2	0.2
53 PARTS–PIECES ACCESSOIRES	3.3	3.2	3.4	3.6	3.4	3.2	3.0
6 CONSUM GOODS–BIENS CONSOMMATION	12.4	12.5	13.1	14.4	14.7	16.2	14.5
61 DURABLE–DURABLES	1.8	1.9	2.4	3.2	3.5	3.9	2.9
62 SEMI DURABLE–SEMI DURABLES	3.1	3.5	3.6	4.0	4.3	5.2	4.5
63 NON DURABLE–NON DURABLES	7.5	7.1	7.2	7.2	6.9	7.1	7.1
7 GOODS NES–BIENS NDA	0.2	0.1	0.0	0.0	0.1	0.1	0.2

EXPORTS – EXPORTATIONS

	1990	1991	1992	1993	1994	1995	1996
TOTAL EXPORTS–EXPORTATIONS TOTALES	100.	100.	100.	100.	100.	100.	100.
1 AGRICULTURE	50.5	45.3	33.7	38.6	39.2	46.3	40.3
2 MINING QUARRY–INDUS EXTRACTIVES	0.1	0.1	0.3	0.1	0.1	0.1	0.0
3 MANUFACTURING–IND MANUFACTUR	49.4	54.6	66.0	61.3	60.7	53.6	59.6
31 FOOD BEV TOBACCO–ALIM BOISS TAB	7.3	10.9	15.6	12.4	12.6	11.5	12.7
32 TEXTILES–INDUSTRIES TEXTILES	14.9	17.0	18.0	15.3	15.4	12.0	11.1
33 WOOD & PRODUCTS–BOIS & PRODUITS	0.2	0.1	0.2	0.1	0.1	0.1	0.0
34 PAPER & PRODUCTS–PAPIER & PRODT	5.9	6.0	7.6	8.0	7.6	6.3	6.0
35 CHEMICALS–INDUSTRIES CHIMIQUES	12.1	11.9	14.8	14.4	14.5	13.2	18.9
36 NON METAL MIN–MIN NON METAL	0.2	0.2	0.3	0.5	0.2	0.2	0.2
37 BASIC METAL–IND METAL BASE	3.3	3.1	3.3	3.9	3.6	4.3	4.1
38 METAL MANUF–MANUF METAL	4.9	5.1	5.3	5.9	5.9	5.2	5.8
39 OTH MANUF IND–AUTRES MANUF	0.6	0.4	0.9	0.8	0.9	0.8	0.8

3. TRADE BY PRINCIPAL COUNTRIES OF PROVENANCE AND LAST DESTINATION (VALUE IN THOUSAND U.S. DOLLARS)
ECHANGES SELON LES PRINCIPAUX PAYS DE PROVENANCE ET DE DERNIERE DESTINATION (VALEUR EN MILLIERS DE DOLLARS EU)

COUNTRIES–PAYS	SPECIAL IMPORTS C.I.F. IMPORTATIONS SPECIALES C.A.F					COUNTRIES–PAYS	SPECIAL EXPORTS F.O.B. EXPORTATIONS SPECIALES F.O.B.				
	1992	1993	1994	1995	1996		1992	1993	1994	1995	1996
World	1537506	1860813	2261800	2627670	2670097	Monde	555111	717293	812718	985202	1024266
Africa	1236	1483	1407	6088	1198	Afrique	3152	8198	69	4	2
Americas	1022019	1493830	1767595	2052175	2159858	Amériques	358429	575050	601949	656916	724475
Northern America	627843	805072	950467	1177909	1093909	Amérique du Nord	190576	218898	195900	187652	202887
LAIA	237716	294126	316107	311460	347807	ALAI	21532	25447	38428	26104	26002
CACM	98988	323488	399139	470071	505871	MCAC	125300	306421	343385	415905	455070
Caribbean	1988	4762	21000	29681	36162	Caraïbes	5995	9716	9529	8264	13234
Rest of America	55483	66381	80882	63053	176109	Autre Amérique	15027	14568	14708	18991	27282
As.ex F.USSR	125892	161952	216556	230170	202057	Asie l'URSS exclus	4266	14993	6784	20945	14001
Eur.x F.USSR	180460	184860	260456	263130	271790	Europe l'URSS exclus	58146	118991	203697	307139	285694
EU	161520	166969	239907	244256	257313	UE	57630	118557	203131	304318	285474
EFTA	12761	15678	14665	14395	11027	AELE	360	394	354	2454	110
East Europe	6176	2211	5796	4454	3447	Europe de l'Est	156	39	212	365	110
Other Europe	0		29	25	2	Autre de l'Europe				2	
Former USSR	3531	4228	5576	2944	20606	Ancienne URSS					
Oceania	4587	6409	7837	9029	13541	Océanie	120	61	180	127	67
USA/Etats–Unis d'Amer	614633	790099	938246	1161530	1067570	USA/Etats–Unis d'Amer	186353	212658	183445	172608	197440
Guatemala		205783	242494	284502	279757	Guatemala		157759	178147	204181	210655
Mexico/Mexique	112115	103728	105568	150409	172273	Germany/Allemagne	42986	75273	120824	143176	158950
Japan/Japon	79407	97663	143277	133618	114147	Costa Rica	54954	66040	72259	77470	93277
Venezuela	81527	133651	138422	76565	59587	Honduras	31616	47112	56326	70314	97470
Panama	55454	66364	80855	62749	175860	Nicaragua	38730	35510	36652	63940	53667
Germany/Allemagne	68441	65044	73119	91858	97194	Belgium–Luxembourg	3938	17942	34053	48334	60589
Costa Rica	56248	66325	78919	91122	101715	Netherlands/Pays–Bas	3868	15575	22320	73377	31319
Honduras	28635	34769	46065	59686	70278	Panama	11275	12853	12105	16968	24533
Nicaragua	14105	16612	31661	34760	54110	Mexico/Mexique	12350	17186	21277	8267	12566
Brazil/Brésil	22455	24557	40290	30772	29427	Japan/Japon	3618	14596	6253	14555	10343
Italy/Italie	12456	17399	22837	28942	31162	Canada	4222	6093	12452	15033	5316
Spain/Espagne	12250	16073	28956	31059	24188	Venezuela	5945	5698	11366	10421	5630
United Kingdom	18171	17874	25117	25768	24053	Dominican Republic	4410	6568	7437	6989	8064
Korea, Republic of	9743	19589	20258	28184	22918	France, Monac	684	2288	7280	11531	4662
Netherlands/Pays–Bas	17804	18740	14625	18337	30403	Italy/Italie	2191	3782	4585	5823	7508
Canada	13210	14959	11916	16277	26010	Spain/Espagne	1558	1621	5552	8957	6137
Colombia/Colombie	8283	12115	15174	22534	19047	United Kingdom	1713	1566	2558	4504	9923
Netherlands Antilles	709	563	15769	23165	30348	Belize/Bélize	3752	1702	2602	2013	2696
Switz.Liecht	11053	15069	14534	13714	10722	Colombia/Colombie	203	1439	847	3886	792
France, Monac	7498	8141	14066	17107	16920	Sweden/Suède	262	328	170	2407	3677
Belgium–Luxembourg	7362	9626	16471	12019	11346	Egypt/Egypte	3095	3141			
Hong Kong	8455	8344	8643	13695	12307	Peru/Pérou	141	206	1742	370	3572
Ecuador/Equateur	592	4751	5195	4956	29158	Finland/Finlande	178		583	3792	1290
Argentina/Argentine	6311	5735	3762	8697	19171	Denmark/Danemark	70	25	1977	2324	1335
New Zealand	4527	6369	7775	8823	13268	Netherlands Antilles	501	715	579	715	2749
Finland/Finlande	1878	1523	30784	3083	1686	Ecuador/Equateur	377	179	588	1497	2539
Chile/Chili	4845	5456	5052	14595	7998	Morocco/Maroc		4882			
Russian Federation	3531	4228	5576	2944	20606	Chile/Chili	2151	522	449	905	448
China/Chine	19	217	12387	9228	7895	China/Chine	24		88	3900	285
Sweden/Suède	6160	6067	5620	5008	5745	Portugal	131	33	3136	12	15
Peru/Pérou	1281	4054	2479	2656	10616	Haiti/Haïti	86	1250	614	150	536
Denmark/Danemark	5016	1862	2169	3152	4818	Norway, SVD, JM	122		116	2069	0
Malaysia/Malaisie	1555	1516		6609	6121	Bahamas	441	645	387		471
Singapore/Singapour	1283	2064	1347	3875	4328	Hong Kong	157	154	177	570	807
Austria/Autriche	2635	1650	3139	1975	3394	Bolivia/Bolivie			1597	107	72
Trinidad and Tobago	231	3663	2764	2255	2328	Korea, Republic of	34	149	30	187	1241
Ireland/Irlande	1240	1823	2061	2890	2358	Jamaica/Jamaïque	169	441	281	192	420
So. Africa Customs Un	1056	1257	1087	5096	637	Switz.Liecht	238	394	238	385	110
Portugal	586	975	674	2682	2560	Trinidad and Tobago	339		137	1	320
Indonesia/Indonésie	86	3022	384	912	1148	Brazil/Brésil	0		359	315	70
Czech Republic		1023	1440	1856	1211	Paraguay	84	119	187	234	87
Poland/Pologne	1767	659	1878	528	642	India/Inde			6	399	275
Israel/Israël	236	436	1961	1474	1086	Korea Dem People's Rp					562
Romania/Roumanie	403	429	2366	1457	433	Israel/Israël	412	64	22	2	3
Cuba	0	9	1228	3358	84	Indonesia/Indonésie			0	13	455
Thailand/Thaïlande	247	139	168	484	3061	Australia/Australie	98	40	177	127	5
India/Inde	208	805	748	821	1330	Argentina/Argentine	281	88	12	24	32
Dominican Republic	254	39	229	380	2925	Poland/Pologne	31	13		264	75
Norway, SVD, JM	1461	608	131	642	306	British Virgin Islds	1				378

(VALUE AS PERCENTAGE OF WORLD TOTAL)(VALEURS EN POURCENTAGE DU TOTAL MONDIAL)

	1987	1988	1989	1990	1991	1992	1993	1994	1995	1996		1987	1988	1989	1990	1991	1992	1993	1994	1995	1996
Africa	0.0	0.0	0.0	0.0	0.1	0.1	0.1	0.1	0.2	0.0	Afrique		0.0		0.0	0.0	0.6	1.1	0.0	0.0	0.0
Americas	77.9	79.7	77.0	66.5	78.0	66.5	80.3	78.1	78.1	80.9	Amériques	69.2	70.0	75.7	70.9	74.8	64.6	80.2	74.1	66.7	70.7
Northern America	38.7	37.9	40.1	38.8	42.1	40.8	43.3	42.0	44.8	41.0	Amérique du Nord	46.7	42.9	38.5	35.1	35.7	34.3	30.5	24.1	19.0	19.8
LAIA	17.3	18.8	15.7	10.0	17.7	15.5	15.8	14.0	11.9	13.0	ALAI	0.1	0.3	1.1	1.3	1.9	3.9	3.5	4.7	2.6	2.5
CACM	18.4	19.8	18.2	17.0	17.0	6.4	17.4	17.6	17.9	18.9	MCAC	19.5	24.8	32.8	31.0	33.6	22.6	42.7	42.3	42.2	44.4
Caribbean	0.1	0.1	0.0	0.0	0.2	0.1	0.3	0.9	1.1	1.4	Caraïbes	1.0	0.6	1.8	1.3	1.2	1.1	1.4	1.2	0.8	1.3
Rest of America	3.4	3.2	2.9	0.7	1.0	3.6	3.6	3.6	2.4	6.6	Autre Amérique	1.9	1.4	1.5	2.3	2.4	2.7	2.0	1.8	1.9	2.7
As.ex F.USSR	9.3	7.5	6.7	4.8	7.3	8.2	8.7	9.6	8.8	7.6	Asie l'URSS exclus	4.6	4.7	3.1	1.2	3.1	0.8	2.1	0.8	2.1	1.4
Eur.x F.USSR	12.2	12.3	15.6	11.5	11.9	11.7	9.9	11.5	10.0	10.2	Europe l'URSS exclus	25.7	24.2	21.1	27.7	21.8	10.5	16.6	25.1	31.2	27.9
EU	11.4	11.4	14.2	10.5	11.0	10.5	9.0	10.6	9.3	9.6	UE	25.7	24.2	21.1	27.6	21.5	10.4	16.5	25.0	30.9	27.9
EFTA	0.7	0.8	1.4	1.0	0.8	0.8	0.8	0.6	0.5	0.4	AELE	0.0	0.0	0.0	0.1	0.1	0.1	0.1	0.0	0.2	0.0
East Europe	0.1	0.1	0.0	0.0	0.1	0.4	0.1	0.3	0.2	0.1	Europe de l'Est					0.2	0.0	0.0	0.0	0.0	0.0
Other Europe	0.0	0.0	0.0	0.0	0.0	0.0		0.0	0.0	0.0	Autre de l'Europe									0.0	
Former USSR	0.0	0.0	0.0			0.2	0.2	0.2	0.1	0.8	Ancienne URSS	0.3	1.0								
Oceania	0.4	0.3	0.4	0.4	0.3	0.3	0.3	0.3	0.3	0.5	Océanie	0.0	0.0	0.0	0.1	0.3	0.0	0.0	0.0	0.0	0.0
USA/Etats–Unis d'Amer	37.2	36.9	39.4	37.9	41.1	40.0	42.5	41.5	44.2	40.0	USA/Etats–Unis d'Amer	43.6	39.7	35.9	34.1	34.8	33.6	29.6	22.6	17.5	19.3
Guatemala	13.0	13.4	11.6	11.8	11.6		11.1	10.7	10.8	10.5	Guatemala	11.9	16.3	21.1	17.8	18.4		22.0	21.9	20.7	20.6
Mexico/Mexique	8.4	9.1	7.9	4.9	9.7	7.3	5.6	4.7	5.7	6.5	Germany/Allemagne	21.4	22.3	19.3	25.1	18.0	7.7	10.5	14.9	14.5	15.5
Japan/Japon	6.3	4.7	4.3	3.1	4.8	5.2	5.2	6.3	5.1	4.3	Costa Rica	5.3	5.7	8.2	8.5	7.6	9.9	9.2	8.9	7.9	9.1
Venezuela	6.9	6.6	5.2	3.2	4.1	5.3	7.2	6.1	2.9	2.2	Honduras	1.5	2.2	3.0	3.1	3.7	5.7	6.6	6.9	7.1	9.5
Panama	3.4	3.2	2.9	0.6	1.0	3.6	3.6	3.6	2.4	6.6	Nicaragua	0.9	0.6	0.6	1.6	4.0	7.0	5.0	4.5	6.5	5.2
Germany/Allemagne	5.1	4.1	3.9	3.9	4.3	4.5	3.5	3.2	3.5	3.6	Belgium–Luxembourg	0.9	0.2	0.2	0.7	0.7	0.7	2.5	4.2	4.9	5.9
Costa Rica	3.9	4.8	4.5	3.1	2.9	3.7	3.6	3.5	3.5	3.8	Netherlands/Pays–Bas	0.2	0.2	0.9	0.7	0.9	0.7	2.2	2.7	7.4	3.1
Honduras	1.0	1.4	1.1	1.3	1.3	1.9	1.9	2.0	2.3	2.6	Panama	1.8	1.2	1.1	1.6	1.7	2.0	1.8	1.5	1.7	2.4
Nicaragua	0.4	0.2	1.0	0.8	1.2	0.9	0.9	1.4	1.3	2.0	Mexico/Mexique	0.1	0.2	0.7	0.8	1.4	2.2	2.4	2.6	0.8	1.2

4. Special Imports C.I.F. by Commodities according to the S.I.T.C. (Rev. 2) in thousand U.S. Dollars
Importations Spéciales C.A.F. par Produits d'après la C.T.C.I. (Rév. 2) en milliers de Dollars E.U.

SITC CTCI	COMMODITY	1993 WEIGHT POIDS	1993 VALUE VALEUR	1994 WEIGHT POIDS	1994 VALUE VALEUR	1995 WEIGHT POIDS	1995 VALUE VALEUR	1996 WEIGHT POIDS	1996 VALUE VALEUR	PRODUIT
	ALL COMMODITIES # 1		1860813		2261800		2627670		2670097	TOUS PRODUITS
0	FOOD AND LIVE ANIMALS		178893		257479		290851		358543	ALIMENTS,ANIMAUX VIVANTS
01	MEAT AND PREPARATIONS		8146		12782		19095		27378	VIANDES ET PREPARATIONS
011	MEAT FRESH,CHILLD,FROZEN		6475	W 4157	10797	W 7211	16350	W 12090	23667	VIANDES FRAICHES,REF,CONGE
0111	BOVINE MEAT FRESH,FROZEN	W 2952	6352	W 4086	10688	W 6832	15783	W 11289	22352	VIANDES BOVIN FRAI,REF
02	DAIRY PRODCTS,BIRDS'EGGS		31973		33318		46166		51943	PRODUITS LAITIERS,OEUFS
022	MILK AND CREAM		27685	W 14015	27112	W 16389	37011	W 16979	37660	LAIT ET CREME
0224	MILK,CREAM PRESERVED ETC		27456	W 13271	26620	W 14960	36083	W 14863	36125	LAIT,CREME CONS,CONC
024	CHEESE AND CURD		3519	W 1293	4677	W 2363	7502	W 4801	12963	FROMAGE ET CAILLEBOTTE
04	CEREALS AND PREPARATIONS		53315		100130		99598		128677	CEREALES ET PRODUITS
041	WHEAT ETC UNMILLED	W 105395	21327	W 260294	43121		31383	W 164151	42398	FROMENT,EPEAUTRE
0411	DURUM WHEAT UNMILLED	W 102245	21005	W 232584	40120	W 165809	31382	W 164151	42398	FROMENT DUR NON MOULU
042	RICE		4369	W 27172	8286	W 26519	7298	W 32422	10747	RIZ
044	MAIZE UNMILLED	W 75026	9957	W 146408	22560	W 194655	28740	W 156244	35283	MAIS NON MOULU
048	CEREAL ETC PREPARATIONS		16865	W 16050	20886	W 22141	26859	W 21416	31369	PREPTNS A BASE CEREALES
0484	BAKERY PRODUCTS		4813	W 5273	7345	W 7513	9871	W 8552	11740	PRODUITS DE BOULANGERIE
04842	PASTRY, CAKES ETC		4154	W 4186	5718	W 6198	8216	W 6890	9738	PATISSERIE ETC.
0488	OTH CEREAL PREPS,MALT EX	W 1292	4583	W 1867	6236	W 1678	6896	W 2746	8177	EXTRAITS DE MALT
05	VEGETABLES AND FRUIT		18813		29754		29847		30222	LEGUMES ET FRUITS
054	VEG ETC FRSH,SMPLY PRSVD		6200	W 24339	12881	W 25645	6334	W 16239	5290	LEGUMES FRAIS,CONG,SECS
0542	LEGUMINOUS VEGETBLES DRY	W 4514	2001	W 15608	9263	W 5137	3376	W 3214	2144	LEGUMES A COSSE SECS
057	FRUIT,NUTS,FRESH,DRIED		4497	W 42888	6192		8730	W 36737	11369	FRUITS FRAIS OU SECS
058	FRUIT PRESERVED,PREPARED		5973	W 7480	8112	W 8461	11753	W 11115	10436	CONSERVES DE FRUITS
06	SUGAR AND PREPS,HONEY		6341		7825		10009		10625	SUCRES ET PRODUITS
062	SUGAR CANDY NON–CHOCLATE		4714	W 2634	5421	W 4431	8127	W 4538	8325	SUCRERIES
07	COFFEE,TEA,COCOA,SPICES		4751		5581		8719		9822	CAFE,THE,CACAO,EPICES
081	*FEEDING STUFF FOR ANIML		18777	W 84010	23155		21257	W 113894	39739	NOURRITURE POUR ANIMAUX
0813	OILCAKE AND OTH RESIDUES		13078	W 67546	17193	W 71796	15476	W 95066	31778	TOURTEAUX
08131	— OF SOYA BEANS	W 47911	12960	W 61560	15940	W 71079	15395	W 86978	30320	TOURTEAUX DE SOJA
09	MISC EDIBLE PRODUCTS		31454		36831		46466		49343	PREP ALIMENTAIRES DIVERSES
098	EDIBLE PRODCTS,PREPS NES		29168	W 12758	34397	W 15435	43519	W 17498	45851	PREP ALIMENTAIRES NDA
09804	SAUCES,MIXED SEASONINGS		4785	W 3501	4895	W 5604	7906	W 6586	8843	SAUCES,ASSAISONNEMENTS
09809	MISC FOOD PREPRTIONS NES		17294	W 5378	20675	W 5251	26366	W 5379	26120	PREP ALIMENTAIRES NDA
1	BEVERAGES AND TOBACCO		7595		14231		15100		16471	BOISSONS ET TABACS
11	BEVERAGES		4008		6504		8925		8587	BOISSONS
12	TOBACCO AND MANUFACTURES		3587		7726		6175		7884	TABACS BRUTS FABRIQUES
2	CRUDE MATERLS,EXCL FUELS		52750		81713		67373		95198	MAT BRUTES NON COMESTIBLES
22	OIL SEEDS,OLEAGINOUS FRT		4293		10229		7456		2494	GRAINES,FRUITS OLEAGINEUX
223	SEEDS FOR OTH FIXED OILS	W 13557	3354	W 34155	9151	W 24607	6468	W 1652	611	GRAINES AUTRES HUILES FIXES
2239	OIL SEED FLOUR AND MEAL	W 13354	3248	W 33886	8988	W 24328	6318	W 1448	476	FARINES GRAINES OLEAG
24	CORK AND WOOD		7095		11542		6161		13343	LIEGE ET BOIS
248	WOOD SHAPED,SLEEPERS		6400	W 41238	10669	W 21509	5735	W 42065	12893	BOIS SIMPLEMENT TRAVAILLES
2482	LUMBER SHAPED CONIFER		6057	W 37941	9201	W 17132	3739	W 38444	10897	CONIFERES SCIES,RABOTES
24821	LUMBER SAWN ETC CONIFER		6019	W 35833	8188	W 16105	3291	W 36135	9835	CONIFERES SCIES LONGITUD
251	*PULP AND WASTE PAPER		6446	W 14144	5713	W 16173	10370	W 18400	8125	PATES A PAPIER,DECHETS
26	TEXTILE FIBRES AND WASTE		22154		38191		28929		55175	FIBRES TEXTILES
263	COTTON		11557	W 16448	24540	W 8466	15219	W 21506	41173	COTON
2631	RAW COTTON,EXCL LINTERS	W 8774	11315	W 16111	24427	W 7907	14835	W 21110	40930	COTON EN MASSE
266	SYNTHETIC FIBRES TO SPIN	W 3924	6424	W 4979	7258	W 5286	7133	W 5524	9257	FIBRES SYNTHETIQUES
2665	DISCN SYNTH FIBRE UNCMBD	W 3785	6054	W 4896	7014	W 4872	6547	W 5076	8297	DISCONTINUES EN MASSE
27	CRUDE FERTLZR,MINRLS NES		4082		7268		6598		7717	ENGRAIS MINERAUX BRUTS
3	MINERAL FUELS ETC		210982		215378		243278		325330	COMBUSTIBLES MINERAUX LUB
33	PETROLEUM AND PRODUCTS		199962		201482		226570		299666	PETROLE ET DERIVES
333	CRUDE PETROLEUM	W 938165	138024	W 802905	112014	W 402482	94816	W 720862	121505	HUILES BRUTES DE PETROLE
334	PETROLEUM PRODUCTS,REFIN		59767	W 421886	86799		128553	W 789808	175137	PRODUITS RAFFINES
3341	GASOLINE,OTH LIGHT OILS	W 39768	8287	W 60976	13929	W 38457	19164	W 161900	40512	ESSENCES POUR MOTEURS
3343	GAS OILS	W 131276	38379	W 334925	56592					GAS OILS
3344	FUEL OILS,NES		493	W 2720	381	W 470058	92743	W 599570	113974	FUEL OILS
3345	LUBS,PETROLEUM OILS NES		10756	W 15181	14238	W 13479	15706	W 28319	20633	HUILES LUBRIFIANTES
341	*GAS,NATURAL AND MANUFCT	W 39995	10803	W 57418	13689		16485	W 83198	24936	GAZ NATUREL,GAZ MANUFACT
3413	PETROLM GASES,LIQUEFIED	W 39992	10796	W 57410	13668	W 52475	16483	W 82891	24827	GAZ DE PETROLE LIQUEFIE
4	ANIMAL,VEGETABLE OIL,FAT		41362		59562		74367		76142	HUILES,GRAISSES ANIM,VEG
411	*ANIMAL OILS AND FATS		12412	W 55799	23128	W 45287	27090	W 44991	22846	HUILES,GRAISSES ANIMALES
4113	ANIML OIL,FAT,GREASE NES		12391	W 55778	23085	W 45260	27049	W 42871	21859	HUILES,GRAISSES ANIMALES NDA
41132	FATS OF BOVINE,SHEEP,ETC	W 25881	12370	W 55767	23048	W 45219	26953	W 42825	21776	SUIFS BRUTS FONDUS
42	FIXED VEGETABLE OIL,FAT		26551		32557		44191		47505	HUILES VEGETALES FIXES
423	FIXED VEG OILS,SOFT		20214	W 33347	22506	W 41773	32650	W 44509	32328	HUILES VEGET DOUCES FIXES
4233	COTTON SEED OIL	W 24026	15295	W 29701	19493	W 36941	28146	W 39307	27936	HUILE DE COTON
424	FIXED VEG OIL NONSOFT		6337	W 19643	10050	W 13868	11541	W 22425	15176	AUTRES HUILES VEG FIXES
4242	PALM OIL	W 11968	5355	W 18907	9479	W 12986	10586	W 20871	13607	HUILE DE PALME
5	CHEMCLS,RELATED PROD NES		316950		373017		441416		455390	PRODUITS CHIMIQUES
51	ORGANIC CHEMICALS		30536		32233		41624		42519	PROD CHIMIQ ORGANIQUES
511	HYDROCARBONS NES,DERIVS		3378	W 5318	3427	W 7379	5287	W 8761	8264	HYDROCARBURES NDA
512	ALCOHOLS,PHENOLS ETC		2815	W 13533	6215		6022	W 22995	9187	PHENOLS,PHENOLS–ALCOOLS
5121	ACYCLIC ALCOHOLS,DERIVS		2423	W 13285	5691		5610	W 22630	8585	ALCOOLS ACYCLIQUES
514	NITROGEN–FNCTN COMPOUNDS		4828	W 1466	3966		7128	W 1967	8320	COMPOSES FONCT AZOTEES
515	ORG–INORG COMPOUNDS ETC		9375	W 952	6534	W 1249	9220	W 754	5609	COMPOSES ORGANO–MINERAUX
5156	HETEROCYCLIC CMPDS ETC	W 1083	7020	W 459	4812	W 735	7137	W 181	3357	COMPOSES HETEROCYCLIQUES
52	INORGANIC CHEMICALS		18587		20896		25548		27602	PROD CHIM INORGANIQUES
522	INORG ELEMNTS,OXIDES,ETC		6725	W 22761	7817		9151	W 15954	6958	ELEMENTS INORGANIQUES
523	OTHR INORG CHEMICALS ETC		11847	W 30816	13051	W 33956	16157	W 47074	20573	AUT PRODUITS CHIMIQUES INORG
5232	OTH MTL CMPD OF INRG ACD		7229	W 18495	8055	W 20177	10220	W 26888	13198	SELS METALLIQUES
52322	PHOSPHITES,PHOSPHATES	W 7480	4651	W 8506	5355	W 10609	7586	W 12347	8501	PHOSPHITES,PHOSPHATES
53	DYES,TANNING,COLOUR PROD		19855		23174		24590		27052	PROD TEINTURE,COLORANTS
531	SYNT DYE,NAT INDGO,LAKES		7068	W 1006	9068	W 1454	7969	W 1025	8801	MAT COLOR ORGAN,LAQUES
5311	SYNTHIC ORGNIC DYESTUFFS	W 650	5493	W 617	7327	W 895	6192	W 711	7033	MAT COLOR ORGAN SYNTHET
533	PIGMENTS,PAINTS,ETC		11703	W 5580	13064		15476	W 8589	16518	PIGMENTS,PEINTURES,VERNIS
5334	VARNISHES,DISTEMPERS ETC		4841	W 3551	5714	W 5433	7941	W 6725	9287	PEINTURES A L'EAU
541	*MEDICINAL,PHARM PRODUCT		88787	K 4169557	97022	MK 11865	110796	K 4882220	109695	PROD MEDICINAUX PHARMACEUT
5413	ANTIBIOTICS IN BULK		7061	K 77303	5435	K 126039	8068	K 103636	5975	ANTIBIOTIQUES NDA
5417	MEDICAMENTS		70343	K 3344969	79530	MK 10429	88723	K 3614222	89801	MEDICAMENTS
55	PERFUME,CLEANING ETC PRD		43574		53457		69907		70580	PROD POUR PARFUM,TOILETTE
551	ESSENTL OILS,PERFUME,ETC	W 701	5768	W 673	7142	W 687	8931	W 564	8000	HUILES ESSENTIELLES
5514	MIXED PERFUME SUBSTANCES	W 644	5030	W 581	6093	W 616	7973	W 495	7255	MELANGES SUBSTAN ODORIFER
553	PERFUMERY,COSMETICS,ETC		18492	W 4565	23416	W 9452	30511	W 6007	29481	PRODUITS DE PARFUMERIE
554	SOAP,CLEANSING ETC PREPS		19314	W 25279	22900	W 28904	30464	W 32451	33098	SAVONS,PRODUITS DETERSIFS
5541	SOAPS		11309	W 18672	13882	W 19829	18576	W 25058	22174	SAVONS,PROD TENSIO–ACTIFS
5542	WASHING PREPARATIONS ETC		6671	W 6026	7578	W 8231	9926	W 6663	8991	PROD ORG TENSIO–ACT NDA
562	*FERTILIZERS,MANUFACTURE		26725	W 290072	36576	W 264981	32555	W 276891	51314	ENGRAIS MANUFACTURES
5621	CHEM NITROGENOUS FERTLZR		17371	W 235815	27486	W 188965	26036	W 207994	36001	ENGRAIS AZOTES
56213	AMMONIUM SULPHATE	W 175184	11019	W 191930	21339	W 120835	12977	W 162484	25239	SULFATE D'AMMONIUM

4. Special Imports C.I.F. by Commodities according to the S.I.T.C. (Rev. 2) in thousand U.S. Dollars
Importations Spéciales C.A.F. par Produits d'après la C.T.C.I. (Rév. 2) en milliers de Dollars E.U.

SITC CTCI	COMMODITY	1993 WEIGHT POIDS	1993 VALUE VALEUR	1994 WEIGHT POIDS	1994 VALUE VALEUR	1995 WEIGHT POIDS	1995 VALUE VALEUR	1996 WEIGHT POIDS	1996 VALUE VALEUR	PRODUIT
56216	UREA	W 36264	5117	W 41091	5635	W 58318	11133	W 36748	8807	UREE
5629	FERTILIZERS NES		6778	W 34883	6759	W 54395	2944	W 16321	6151	ENGRAIS NDA
58	PLASTIC MATERIALS ETC		59056		73765		93299		85124	MAT PLAST ARTIFICIELLES
582	PROD OF CONDENSATION ETC		8701	W 4891	8222	W 4152	8630	W 5687	8973	PROD CONDENS,POLYCOND
583	POLYMERIZATION ETC PRODS		46578	W 58604	61605	W 58201	80117	W 59949	71764	PROD POLYMERISATION
5831	POLYETHYLENE		13139	W 25095	19772	W 20842	22581	W 22170	21990	POLYETHYLENE
5832	POLYPROPYLENE	W 5198	6115	W 5354	5569	W 4423	6739	W 5252	6599	POLYPROPYLENE
5834	POLYVINYL CHLORIDE	W 9993	8723	W 11607	11517	W 13269	17311	W 13710	13277	CHLORURE DE POLYVINYLE
5839	OTH POLYMRZTION ETC PROD		13031	W 10758	16421	W 14306	24402	W 13715	21661	AUT PROD POLYMER COPOLYM
59	CHEMICAL MATERIALS NES		29455		35582		42476		40895	MAT PROD CHIMIQUES NDA
591	PESTICIDES,DISINFECTANTS		11893	W 4491	14274	W 8188	17806	W 5907	16933	DESINF,INSECT,FONG,HERB
5911	INSECTICIDES,FOR RETAIL	W 2201	6004	W 3016	7900	W 5362	7853	W 3013	6117	INSECTICIDES VENTE DET
5913	HERBICIDES,FOR RETAIL	W 1160	4282	W 1031	4567	W 1820	7546	W 2237	8637	HERBICIDES VENTE AU DET
598	MISCEL CHEM PRODUCTS NES		13279	W 9151	16473	W 9180	17580	W 10101	18310	PROD DIV INDUST CHIM NDA
5989	CHEM PRODUCTS,PREPS NES		9038	W 7781	11896	W 7905	13129	W 8395	14320	PROD PREP CHIMIQUES NDA
59899	OTH CHEM PRODS,PREPS,NES		6327	W 6042	8997	W 6403	10525	W 6758	11330	AUT PRODUITS CHIMIQUES NDA
6	BASIC MANUFACTURES		345788		399796		487189		435396	ART MANUFACTURES
61	LEATHER,DRESSED FUR,ETC		3658		8887		6212		13795	CUIRS,PELLETERIES
611	LEATHER		2209	W 1016	6807		4556	W 2704	11036	CUIRS,PEAUX PREPARES
62	RUBBER MANUFACTURES NES		31813		31231		39153		37675	CAOUTCHOUC MANUFACTURE
625	RUBBER TYRES, TUBES ETC		25054	W 9690	24808	W 25435	30457	W 12291	30828	PNEUS CAOUTCHOUC VULCANISE
6251	TYRES NEW FOR MOTOR CARS	W 3429	10929	W 2568	8310	W 2079	9070	W 2371	7557	PNEUS POUR VOITURES
6252	TYRES,NEW,BUS OR LORRY		7835	W 2940	9498	W 18803	13143	W 4092	14152	PNEUS POUR AUTOBUS,CAMIONS
6259	OTH TYRES,TYRE CASES,ETC		5715	W 3951	6355	W 4417	7567	W 5605	8384	AUTRES PNEUS RECHAPES FLAPS
63	WOOD,CORK MANUFACTRS NES		9472		8655		9040		9987	OUVRAGES LIEGE ET BOIS
634	VENEERS,PLYWOOD,ETC		7386	W 12136	6670	W 11938	6374	W 12442	7332	PLACAGES,CONTRE--PLAQUES
64	PAPER,PAPERBOARD AND MFR		74740		81585		127458		90293	PAPIERS,CARTONS & OUVRAGES
641	PAPER AND PAPERBOARD		62177	W 82661	67452	W 106133	103546	W 72576	68324	PAPIERS ET CARTONS
6411	NEWSPRINT	W 16774	11570	W 16215	10685	W 19076	19989	W 19854	15691	PAPIER JOURNAL
6412	PRINTG,WRITING PAPER NES		12465	W 15227	15097	W 18371	21453	W 13021	13963	PAPIERS POUR L'IMPRESSION
64122	— COATED,IMPREGNATD ETC	W 9305	8805	W 13904	12484	W 16718	18419	W 10959	10496	PAPIERS IMPRESSION COUCHES
6413	KRAFT PAPER,PAPERBOARD		17701	W 28700	16649	W 47388	31949	W 24092	16462	PAPIER ET CARTON KRAFT
6415	PAPER,PAPERBRD,BULK,NES		8301	W 13068	12491	W 10094	14411	W 7681	9455	PAPIERS,CARTONS ROULEAUX
64159	OTHER PAPER ETC,BULK,NES		7600	W 12700	11660	W 9643	13287	W 7288	8509	AUT PAPIER ROULEAUX FEUILLES
6418	COATED ETC PAPER NES BLK		9139	W 5703	8899	W 8553	12400	W 5644	9954	PAP,CARTONS COUCHES,ENDUITS
642	PAPER,ETC,PRECUT,ARTS OF		12563	W 7586	14133	W 11559	23912	W 11664	21970	PAP,CARTONS DECOUPES
6424	PAPER ETC CT TO SIZE NES		5574	W 2769	5182	W 4339	8258	W 3605	5950	PAP,CARTONS DECOUPES
65	TEXTILE YARN,FABRICS,ETC		45375		54355		59168		45841	FILS,TISSUS,ARTICLES TEXTILE
651	TEXTILE YARN		13380	W 5612	15061		11972	W 3558	10877	FILS TEXTILES
6514	SYN FIB YRN,BULK,MONOFIL		11791	W 5134	13439	W 3459	9210	W 2890	8311	FILS CONT 85% FIB TEXT SYNTH
65142	— NONTXT ETC CONT PAMID		8864	W 3622	8320	W 3087	7561	W 2058	5801	FILS NON TEX FI CON POLYAMID
652	COTTON FABRICS,WOVEN		7092	W 2092	9558		12328	W 1870	9468	TISSUS DE COTON
6522	WOVEN COTTON BLEACHD,ETC		5503	W 1806	8235		11229	W 1653	8450	TISSUS COTON BLANCHIS ETC
65224	BLCHED COTTON FABRIC NES		4433	W 1394	5835	W 1691	8766	W 1236	6305	AUT TIS PLUS 85% COT BLANCHI
653	WOVN MAN–MADE FIB FABRIC		11326	W 2194	11982		13816	W 2072	10849	TISSUS FIBRES SYNTH,ARTIF
657	SPECIAL TXTL FABRC,PRODS		7943	W 2510	10247		10029	W 2047	7447	TISSUS SPECIAUX
66	NONMETAL MINERAL MFS NES		36787		44514		51633		43839	ART MIN NON METALLIQUES
661	LIME,CEMENT,BLDG PRODS		3144	W 49139	6299		10804	W 64991	8217	CHAUX,CIMENTS MAT CONSTR
662	CLAY,REFRACTORY BLDG PRD		6250	W 20259	9015		9448	W 16774	6919	MAT CONST REFRACTAIRES
6624	BRICKS ETC NONREFRACTORY		4378	W 15599	7160		7436	W 14130	5406	BRIQUES ETC CERAM NON REFR
664	GLASS		6730	W 9626	7100	W 10646	8714	W 9788	7765	VERRE
665	GLASSWARE		14877	W 20798	15996	W 18694	15227	W 15672	12761	OUVRAGES EN VERRE
6651	BOTTLES ETC OF GLASS	W 17259	10377	W 18129	11045	W 15957	9865	W 13266	8937	RECIPIENTS EN VERRE
66511	GLASS BOTTLES ETC NONVAC	W 17258	10364	W 18128	11039	W 15946	9848	W 13265	8936	BONBONNES,BOUTEILLES,ETC
67	IRON AND STEEL		67483		81979		80719		98974	FER ET ACIER
672	IRON,STEEL PRIMARY FORMS		6187	W 31975	10375	W 23122	7610	W 57681	17806	LINGOTS FER,ACIER
6724	IRN,STL INGOTS,LUMPS,ETC	W 11291	3027	W 18722	5086	W 15943	4211	W 43635	11929	FER,ACIER LINGOTS,MASSES
67244	OTHER ALLOY STEEL INGOTS	W 11253	2995	W 18069	4670	W 9085	2382	W 29489	8245	LINGOTS AUT ACIERS ALLIES
673	IRON,STEEL SHAPES ETC		22219	W 69631	28102	W 64592	30155	W 54534	22272	BARRES,PROFIL FER,ACIER
6731	IRON,STEEL WIRE ROD		8685	W 31056	10872	W 23862	10675	W 22446	7593	FIL MACHINE FER,ACIER
67311	IRON,SIMPLE STL WIRE ROD		8023	W 30407	10475	W 23688	10035	W 21520	7292	FIL MACH AUT ACIER FIN
6732	IRON,STEEL BARS ETC		8470	W 25852	11116	W 26029	11844	W 17877	7443	BARRES FER,ACIER
67326	IRN,OTH STL BARS HOTROLD	W 17820	7350	W 24226	9743	W 23610	10066	W 16891	6527	BARRES PLEINES FER,ACIER
674	IRN,STL UNIV,PLATE,SHEET		24513	W 41719	25251	W 29266	23802	W 65817	38972	LARGES PLATS,TOLES
6746	IRN,STL THIN PLATE,ROLLD	W 15803	9029	W 16673	8213	W 5606	4308	W 34075	16646	TOLES LAM MOINS 3MM
67461	— OF IRON OR SIMPLE STL	W 14581	8336	W 15541	7566	W 4573	3463	W 33186	16009	TOL NON AC FIN MOINS 3 MM
6749	OTH IRN,STL PLATES,SHEET		10037	W 17332	12953	W 19154	15969	W 18672	16536	AUTRES TOLES FER,ACIER
67491	— OF IRON OR SIMPLE STL		9527	W 17149	12708	W 18837	15466	W 18617	16409	AUT TOLES AUTRES ACIER FIN
678	IRON,STL TUBES,PIPES,ETC		10095	W 15777	12341	W 15540	13416	W 14090	14944	TUBES,TUYAUX EN FONTE,FER
6783	IRON,STL TUBES,PIPES NES		7330	W 11940	8137	W 13311	9433	W 10490	7998	AUT TUBES,TUYAUX FER,ACIER
68	NON–FERROUS METALS		18947		26303		32800		23938	METAUX NON FERREUX
682	COPPER EXC CEMENT COPPER		5236	W 3103	8833	W 2344	8750	W 2229	6799	CUIVRE
6822	COPPER,ALLOYS WORKED		5198	W 3075	8713	W 2292	8512	W 2197	6618	CUIVRE,ALLIAGES OUVRES
68221	COPPER BARS,WIRE,ETC		4202	W 2750	7440	W 2110	7282	W 2061	5889	BARRES,PROFILES ET FILS
684	ALUMINIUM		12083	W 7257	15980	W 7784	23040	W 7832	16265	ALUMINIUM
6842	ALUMINIUM,ALLOYS WORKED		8072	W 4343	10953	W 5103	16204	W 3663	12092	ALUMINIUM,ALLIAGES OUVRE
69	METAL MANUFACTURES NES		57513		62286		81007		71054	ART MANUFACT EN METAL NDA
691	STRUCTURES AND PARTS NES		4805	W 2889	3986	W 5299	6344	W 5732	9947	CONSTRUCT FER,ACIER,ALU
6911	STRUCTURES,PARTS IRN,STL		4450	W 2805	3526	W 5112	5440	W 5519	9177	CONSTRUCT FER,ACIER,FONTE
692	METAL TANKS,BOXES,ETC		10658	W 3495	10134	W 4766	14335	W 4888	14292	RECIPIENTS METALLIQUES
6924	MTL TRANSPORT BOXES ETC		9943	W 3382	9948	W 4601	13435	W 4480	13310	FUTS,TAMBOURS,BIDONS
69242	ALUMNM TRNSPRT BOXES ETC	W 1058	5350	W 993	4505	W 1794	8065	W 1238	6509	FUTS,TAMBOURS,BIDONS ALU
695	TOOLS		6319	W 1283	6933	W 1084	7652	W 1089	6453	OUTILS A MAIN
697	BASE MTL HOUSEHOLD EQUIP		8970	W 2915	10753	W 5264	14258	W 3194	10479	ART MENAGE MET COMMUNS
6973	DMSTC HEATG,COOKG APPARA	W 1747	5855	W 1993	7095	W 2745	8771	W 1829	5780	APPS CHAUF NON ELECTRIQ
699	BASE METAL MFRS NES		14421	W 5730	17095		22609	W 4780	15666	ART MANUFACTURES MET NDA
7	MACHINES,TRANSPORT EQUIP		582529		695697		790051		700060	MACHINES MATERIEL TRANSPORT
71	POWER GENERATING EQUIPMT		48423		55610		34299		58046	MACHINES GENERATRICES
713	INTRNL COMBUS PSTN ENGIN		9262	W 1944	10441	W 2918	12732	W 1789	14090	MOTEURS EXPL COMB INT, PIECE
714	ENGINES AND MOTORS NES		311	W 141	5267	W 119	6384	W 426	19117	MOTEURS NON ELECTRIQUES
716	ROTATING ELECTRIC PLANT		35695	W 903	36977	W 739	8563	W 601	5870	APP ELECTR ROTATIFS,PIECES
72	MACHS FOR SPCL INDUSTRYS		111185		84403		106030		87180	MAC SPECIALES POUR INDUST
723	CIVIL ENGNEERG EQUIP ETC		6879	W 2022	9887	W 2227	11876	W 1288	8607	APPAREILS DE GENIE CIVIL
7234	CONST,MINING MACHNRY NES		6019	W 1771	8233	W 1926	9479	W 1100	6813	MACH POUR LA CONST, MINES
724	TEXTILE,LEATHER MACHNRY		35716	W 3514	34153	W 3539	45402	W 2206	24616	MACH POUR INDUSTRIE TEXTILE
7243	SEWING MACHS,NEEDLES ETC		12146	W 1626	16391	W 1726	20423	W 1107	10737	MACHINES A COUDRE,PIECES
7244	SPINNING,EXTRDNG,ETC MCH		10225	W 893	8134	W 801	9981	W 400	5205	MACH POUR LE FILAGE
726	PRINTG,BKBINDG MACHY,PTS		38063	W 955	11399		13724	W 565	6532	MACHINES POUR IMPRIMERIE
7264	PRINTING PRESSES	W 1545	34599	W 236	4675	W 251	3167	W 211	1840	MACHINES A IMPRIMER
727	FOOD MACHRY NON–DOMESTIC		6612	W 1202	5085	W 813	8187	W 1031	21118	MACH INDUSTRIES ALIMENT
7272	OTH FOOD PROC MCHY,PARTS		5989	W 1141	4569	W 772	7442	W 952	20579	AUT MACH IND ALIMENTAIRE

4. Special Imports C.I.F. by Commodities according to the S.I.T.C. (Rev. 2) in thousand U.S. Dollars
Importations Spéciales C.A.F. par Produits d'après la C.T.C.I. (Rév. 2) en milliers de Dollars E.U.

SITC CTCI	COMMODITY	1993 WEIGHT POIDS	1993 VALUE VALEUR	1994 WEIGHT POIDS	1994 VALUE VALEUR	1995 WEIGHT POIDS	1995 VALUE VALEUR	1996 WEIGHT POIDS	1996 VALUE VALEUR	PRODUIT
72722	INDUS FOOD PROC MACH NES	W 836	5415	W 1080	3301	W 545	6054	W 767	17907	MACHINES BOULANGERIE
728	OTH MACHY FOR SPCL INDUS		11506	W 1761	13303		16492	W 1897	18468	AUT MACH IND PARTICULIERES
7284	MACHY FOR SPCL INDUS NES		6902	W 726	7408		12250	W 1204	13488	MACH SPEC IND PARTICUL.
73	METALWORKING MACHINERY		6260		6916		6729		9902	MACH TRAVAIL DES METAUX
736	METALWORKING MACH–TOOLS		4676	W 1004	4422	W 568	4682	W 1114	8144	MACH–OUTILS TRAVAIL METAUX
74	GENRL INDUSTRL MACHY NES		57997		71168		92378		85130	MACH APP INDUSTRIE
741	HEATING,COOLING EQUIPMNT		13093	W 2577	20109	W 2970	25607	W 3049	20871	MACH CHAUFFAGE,PIECES
7414	NONDOM REFRIG EQUIPT,PTS		5550	W 1266	8575	W 1535	10951	W 1551	9781	MAT PRODUCTION DU FROID
7415	AIR–CONDITIONING MACHNRY		3766	W 930	6884	W 883	6543	W 986	6469	GROUPES CONDITION AIR
742	PUMPS FOR LIQUIDS ETC		5327	W 1006	7376	W 720	9072	W 894	10746	POMPES MOTO–POMPES
743	PUMPS NES,CENTRFUGES ETC		11943	W 2311	13659	W 2812	16170	W 2654	16144	POMPES COMPRES,VENT ETC
7431	PUMPS FOR GASES ETC		5837	W 1371	6818	W 1414	7616	W 1423	6922	POMPES AIR A VIDE,COMPRES
744	MECHANICAL HANDLING EQU		5260	W 1259	7807	W 2035	11128	W 1855	11517	EQUIP MANUTENTION PIECES
745	NONELEC MACHY,TOOLS NES		5360	W 475	6382	W 616	9815	W 733	8875	AUT MACH NON ELEC,PIECES
7452	OTH NONELEC MCHS,PTS NES		4765	W 452	5908	W 594	9213	W 711	8424	AUT MACH NON ELEC,PIECES
749	NONELEC MACH PTS,ACC NES		17013	W 1496	15835	W 1311	20586	W 1396	16977	PIECES MACH NON ELEC NDA
7492	COCKS,VALVES ETC NES		6249	W 636	5346	W 578	6619	W 702	6381	ART ROB,SIM POUR TUYAUX
7499	OTH NONELEC MCHY PTS NES		5238	W 397	5555	W 422	8390	W 342	5189	PIECES NON ELECT NDA
75	OFFICE MACHNES,ADP EQUIP		34311		45378		55157		57605	MACH BUREAU TRAIT AUTOM
751	OFFICE MACHINES		7340	W 456	7232	W 467	9038	W 627	10292	MACH,APPAREILS DE BUREAU
752	AUTOMTIC DATA PROC EQUIP		15645	W 395	19891	W 453	20509	W 341	20358	MACH TRAIT INFORMATION
759	OFFICE,ADP MCH PTS,ACCES		11326	W 465	18254	W 476	25610	W 677	26955	PIECES DU 751 ET 752
7599	ACCTG,ETC,ADP MCH PTS,AC	W 227	8299	W 397	16413	W 427	23639	W 613	24813	PIECES DU 751 ET 752
76	TELECOMM,SOUND EQUIPMENT		36066		68168		73865		68458	EQUIPMENT DE TELECOM
761	TELEVISION RECEIVERS		8056	W 1241	10593	W 1339	15293	W 1463	13051	RECEPTEURS DE TELEVISION
762	RADIO BROADCAST RECEIVRS		6881	W 757	7114	W 932	11760	W 929	8359	RECEPTEURS RADIODIFFUSION
764	TELECOM EQPT,PTS,ACC NES		19441	W 1127	47640	W 1272	43122	W 2142	43513	EQUIP TELECOM,PIECES
7641	LINE TELEPHONE,ETC EQUIP		9199	W 317	18312	W 493	25563	W 1353	17743	APP TELEPHON PAR FIL
7649	PTS NES OF EQUIPMT OF 76		4806	W 450	21997	W 412	9328	W 361	15964	PIECES DE LA DIV 76
76491	PTS NES OF APPAR OF 7641		2498	W 246	19228	W 64	4631	W 182	13627	PIECES POUR 764.1
77	ELECTRIC MACHNRY NES ETC		57623		81942		94295		94091	MACH APP ELECT NDA
771	ELECTRIC POWER MACHY NES		4465	W 1964	8821	W 2656	9087	W 2746	12905	MACH PROD,TRANS ELECTR
7711	TRANSFORMERS,ELECTRICAL		3186	W 1447	6240	W 2305	6779	W 2305	10030	TRANSFO ELECTRIQUES
772	SWITCHGEAR ETC,PARTS NES		9804	W 1008	12017	W 1818	20035	W 1261	14962	APP COUPURE,SECT ETC
7721	SWITCHGEAR ETC		9173	W 1003	11770	W 1813	18486	W 1255	14566	APP COUPURE,SECTIONMNT
773	ELECTR DISTRIBUTNG EQUIP		5334	W 1549	6709	W 1430	7587	W 3010	11493	EQUIPMT DISTRIBUTION ELECT
7731	INSULATED WIRE,CABLE ETC		4877	W 1358	6217	W 1099	6863	W 2568	10606	FILS,CABLES ISOLES ELECT
774	ELECTRO–MEDCL,XRAY EQUIP	W 68	3064	W 257	11162	W 120	4584	W 143	8074	APPAREILS MEDICAUX
7741	ELECTRO–MEDICAL EQUIPMNT	W 31	1131	W 196	7741	W 63	2744	W 80	3313	APP ELECTRICITE MEDICALE
775	HOUSEHOLD TYPE EQUIP NES		12596	W 3574	16538		21055	W 3401	16048	MACH,APP USAGE DOMESTQUE
7752	DOM REFRIGERATRS,FREEZRS		5862	W 1921	8480	W 1834	9047	W 1213	6084	REFRIG,CONGEL MENAGER
778	ELECTRICAL MACHINERY NES		21562	W 6868	25488		30217	W 6909	28542	AUTRES MACH ELECT NDA
7781	BATTERIES,ACCUMULATORS	W 4395	9892	W 4864	10637	W 6500	11597	W 5026	11196	PILES ET ACCUMULATEURS
77811	PRIMARY BATTERIES,CELLS	W 3336	7263	W 3182	7464	W 4007	8018	W 2920	7272	PILES ELECTRIQUES,PIECES
78	ROAD VEHICLES		228829		279463		322818		237122	VEHICULES ROUTIERS
781	PASS MOTOR VEH EXC BUSES	W 23483	97498	W 15580	96376	W 21215	120843	W 18510	78913	AUTO TRANSPORT PERSONNES
782	LORRIES,SPCL MTR VEH NES	W 31440	78907	W 31623	108365	W 36861	122138	W 35648	96309	VEHICULES SPECIAUX,MARCH
7821	LORRIES,TRUCKS	W 30678	75800	W 31064	106218	W 36144	119985	W 34426	88935	VEHICULES TRANSP MARCHAND
783	ROAD MOTOR VEHICLES NES		19577	W 11354	33682	W 16902	39836	W 11621	26433	VEHICULES ROUTIERS NDA
7831	BUSES		14178	W 7667	28082	W 9436	34638	W 8039	21801	VOITURES TRANSPORT COMMUN
784	MOTOR VEH PRTS,ACCES NES		22691	W 3416	29665	W 2396	29120	W 3189	23624	PIECES 722,781,782,783
7849	OTHER MOTOR VEHCL PARTS		22273	W 3194	29078	W 2286	28466	W 2969	22157	PIECES 722,781,782,783
785	CYCLES,ETC MOTRZD OR NOT		7965	W 2256	8987	W 3884	8337	W 1836	8183	MOTOCYCLES SCOOTERS
8	MISC MANUFACTURED GOODS		123264		163486		214729		204714	ART MANUFACTURES DIVERS
812	*PLUMBG,HEATNG,LGHTNG EQ		6195	W 2706	8457	W 4822	9026	W 2822	9387	APPAR SANITAIRES CHAUFFAGE
821	*FURNITURE,PARTS THEREOF		9304	W 9349	14862	W 7050	17061	W 5037	15178	MEUBLES ET PIECES
8219	FURNITURE AND PARTS NES		6707	W 3872	11427	W 5738	12817	W 3618	11286	AUTRES MEUBLES ET PIECES
84	CLOTHING AND ACCESSORIES		12105		19343		30279		24794	VETEMENTS
851	*FOOTWEAR		11769	W 2713	13639	W 3738	19484	W 3840	19617	CHAUSSURES
85101	FOOTWEAR RUBBER,PLASTIC		3761	W 1262	4885	W 1926	7526	W 2087	8212	CHAUS SEMELLES CAOUTCH
85102	FOOTWEAR LEATHER		6407	W 1283	7423	W 1505	10318	W 1419	9118	CHAUS SEMELLES EN CUIR
87	PRECISION INSTRUMNTS NES		14026		22593		24722		25059	INSTRUM,APPAR SCIENT NDA
872	MEDICAL INSTRUMENTS NES		5194	W 532	6826	W 1752	8708	W 597	9016	INSTR,APP MEDIC–CHIR NDA
87202	OTH MEDICAL INSTRUMENTS		4782	W 517	6260	W 986	7227	W 575	8028	INSTRUM,APP MEDECINE
874	MEASURNG,CONTROLNG INSTR		7514	W 528	11251	W 380	12325	W 424	11622	INSTRUMENTS DE MESURE
88	PHOTO EQU,OPTICL GDS ETC		11012		11884		17158		14408	APP,FOURN PHOTO,OP,MONTR
882	PHOTO,CINEMA SUPPLIES		6601	W 549	6647	W 672	9801	W 763	8893	PRODUITS PHOTO,CINEMA
8822	PHOTO FILM EXC DEV CINMA		5773	W 316	5658	W 365	8019	W 336	7503	PLAQUES,PELLICULES,FILMS
89	MISC MANUFCTRD GOODS NES		57541		71279		94139		93998	ART MANUFACTURES DIVERS
892	PRINTED MATTER		9287	W 3179	12519	W 2653	16630	W 3587	22572	IMPRIMES
8921	PRINTED BOOKS,GLOBES,ETC		6820	W 2500	8134	W 1548	10149	W 2193	14988	LIVRES,BROCHURES,CARTES
89211	PRINTED BOOKS,PAMPHLETS		6730	W 2120	7890	W 1502	9962	W 2017	14547	LIVRES,BROCHURES
893	ARTICLES OF PLASTIC NES		19017		24496		30692		30221	OUVRAGES EN MAT DIVIS 58
8931	PLSTC PACKG CONTNRS,LIDS		5966	W 3696	7492	W 4435	10228	W 3463	10937	ART TRANSP EMBALLAGE ETC
8939	MISC PLASTIC ARTICLES		12380	W 5050	16476	W 20359	19646	W 6652	18514	ART DIVERS EN MAT DIV 58
89399	OTHR PLASTC ARTICLES NES		11578	W 4708	15809	W 20210	19109	W 6482	17944	AUT OUV MAT DIV 58
894	TOYS,SPORTING GOODS,ETC		9446	W 2513	10989	W 10447	17537	W 2741	12593	VOITURES ENFANTS,JOUETS
8942	TOYS,INDOOR GAMES ETC		7628	W 2124	8346	W 10067	13171	W 2202	9201	JOUETS,JEUX ETC
89423	TOYS NES		4812	W 1235	4749	W 8898	8132	W 1299	5845	JOUETS,MODELES REDUITS
895	OFFICE SUPPLIES NES		6986	W 2008	6874	W 1240	9518	W 1126	9961	ART PAPET NDA
898	MUSICAL INSTRUMENTS,PTS		4197	W 402	6749		8095	W 677	7688	INSTRUMENTS DE MUSIQUE
899	OTHER MANUFACTURED GOODS		7400		7773		9853		9047	AUT ART MANUF DIVERS NDA

5. Special Exports F.O.B. by Commodities according to the S.I.T.C. (Rev. 2) in thousand U.S. Dollars
Exportations Spéciales F.O.B. par Produits d'après la C.T.C.I. (Rév. 2) en milliers de Dollars E.U.

SITC CTCI	COMMODITY	1993 WEIGHT POIDS	1993 VALUE VALEUR	1994 WEIGHT POIDS	1994 VALUE VALEUR	1995 WEIGHT POIDS	1995 VALUE VALEUR	1996 WEIGHT POIDS	1996 VALUE VALEUR	PRODUIT
	ALL COMMODITIES # 1		717293		812718		985202		1024266	TOUS PRODUITS
0	FOOD AND LIVE ANIMALS		345047		399022		540467		509078	ALIMENTS,ANIMAUX VIVANTS
001	*LIVE ANIMALS FOR FOOD	W 716	2815	W 972	4243	W 864	3679	W 806	3768	ANIMAUX VIVANTS
0014	LIVE POULTRY	W 702	2740	W 928	4169	W 841	3645	W 792	3752	VOLAILLES VIVANTES
00141	LIVE PLTRY 185 GR OR LES	W 416	2450	W 529	3461	W 541	3255	W 614	3508	VOL VIVANTES MOINS 185 GR.
02	DAIRY PRODCTS,BIRDS'EGGS		624		1828		3516		5024	PRODUITS LAITIERS,OEUFS
025	EGGS,BIRDS,FRESH,PRSRVD	W 377	463	W 2202	1788	W 4416	3326	W 5465	4739	OEUFS
0251	— IN SHELL	W 377	463	W 2184	1776	W 4416	3326	W 5465	4739	OEUFS EN COQUILLE
03	FISH AND PREPARATIONS		29550		31257		30233		43603	POISSONS ET PREPARATIONS
034	FISH,FRESH,CHILLED,FROZN		1161	W 1430	4436		1383	W 309	841	POISSON FRAIS, REFRIG,CONG
0341	FISH FRSH,CHLLD,EX FILLT		463	W 1318	3844	W 466	1335	W 279	761	POISSON FRAIS,REFRIGERE
036	SHELL FISH FRESH,FROZEN		25991	W 3725	25014	W 4367	27415	W 5615	40883	CRUSTACES,MOLLUSQUES
04	CEREALS AND PREPARATIONS		13991		17113		34713		19501	CEREALES ET PRODUITS
044	MAIZE UNMILLED		615	W 471	129	W 15678	2969	W 3068	698	MAIS NON MOULU
048	CEREAL ETC PREPARATIONS		12465	W 13993	15772	W 29755	31054	W 14389	17516	PREPTNS A BASE CEREALES
0481	PREPD BREAKFAST FOOD ETC	W 4939	6995	W 6471	9019	W 23084	25047	W 7414	10410	CEREALES TRAVAILLEES
04811	CEREAL FLAKED,ROLLED,ETC	W 262	413	W 23	41	W 16784	16331	W 10	17	GRAINS GERMES DE CEREALES
04812	CEREAL ROASTED, PUFFED	W 4677	6582	W 6448	8978	W 6300	8716	W 7404	10393	PRODTS BASE CEREALES
0484	BAKERY PRODUCTS	W 4101	4234	W 5068	5299	W 4132	4436	W 4822	5699	PRODUITS DE BOULANGERIE
04842	PASTRY, CAKES ETC	W 3037	3727	W 3764	4406	W 2351	3280	W 2656	3869	PATISSERIE ETC.
05	VEGETABLES AND FRUIT		7648		7677		9177		9617	LEGUMES ET FRUITS
054	VEG ETC FRSH,SMPLY PRSVD		2477	W 4480	3339	W 5287	3483	W 7004	4340	LEGUMES FRAIS,CONG,SECS
057	FRUIT,NUTS,FRESH,DRIED		3849	W 7866	3096		3720	W 7695	3271	FRUITS FRAIS OU SECS
0579	FRUIT FRESH OR DRIED NES	W 10014	2638	W 6763	2171		2297	W 6657	2107	FRUITS FRAIS,SECS NDA
05798	OTHER FRESH FRUIT	W 10009	2638	W 6669	2090	W 5086	1750	W 4813	1528	AUTRES FRUITS FRAIS
06	SUGAR AND PREPS,HONEY		46442		44058		49856		53086	SUCRES ET PRODUITS
061	SUGAR AND HONEY		39743	W 162303	35894		43398	W 176532	45671	SUCRES ET MIEL
0611	RAW BEET AND CANE SUGAR	W 99798	29501	W 101911	27690	W 49831	36272	W 81382	31510	SUCRES BRUTS
0612	REFINED SUGAR ETC		5157	W 10073	2861	W 1825	641	W 16241	5123	SUCRES RAFFINES
0615	MOLASSES	W 51137	2855	W 48229	3425	W 42442	3391	W 77140	5798	MELASSES
0616	NATURAL HONEY	W 2162	2216	W 2078	1914	W 2573	3083	W 1756	3231	MIEL NATUREL
062	SUGAR CANDY NON-CHOCLATE	W 5901	6699	W 7506	8164	W 5701	6458	W 6107	7414	SUCRERIES
07	COFFEE,TEA,COCOA,SPICES		224196		268710		396203		341863	CAFE,THE,CACAO,EPICES
071	COFFEE AND SUBSTITUTES	W 171114	223314	W 121095	267767	W 113628	373005	W 138370	339909	CAFE ET SUCCEDANES
0711	COFFEE GREEN,ROASTED,SUB	W 171072	223194	W 119068	263920	W 113393	371763	W 138186	339013	CAFE TORREFIE OU DECAFEINE
0712	COFFEE EXTRACTS,ESSENCES	W 42	120	W 2027	3847	W 235	1242	W 184	896	EXTRAITS DE CAFE
072	COCOA	W 5	9	W 138	110		22330	W 503	605	CACAO
0721	COCOA BEANS,RAW,ROASTED	W 2	3	W 23	16		21930	W 3	9	CACAO EN FEVES
081	*FEEDING STUFF FOR ANIML		3149	W 13200	3570		2337	W 11916	2137	NOURRITURE POUR ANIMAUX
0819	FOOD WASTE AND FEED NES	W 14170	2971	W 12534	2806	W 13657	2329	W 9782	1598	DECHETS,ALIMENTS NDA
08199	FODDER NES,INCL SWEETNED	W 14170	2971	W 12279	2753	W 13294	2276	W 9469	1536	PREPARATIONS FOURRAGERES
09	MISC EDIBLE PRODUCTS		16434		20329		9187		28315	PREP ALIMENTAIRES DIVERSES
098	EDIBLE PRODCTS,PREPS NES		16302	W 17493	19901		7832	W 24728	27620	PREP ALIMENTAIRES NDA
09809	MISC FOOD PREPRTIONS NES	W 14080	13870	W 15227	16478	W 2640	3452	W 22490	23373	PREP ALIMENTAIRES NDA
1	BEVERAGES AND TOBACCO		7439		8391		10480		13918	BOISSONS ET TABACS
11	BEVERAGES		6330		7078		6736		9152	BOISSONS
111	NON-ALCOHL BEVERAGES NES		4735	W 11403	5982		5381	W 16318	7741	BOISSONS NON ALCOOLIQUES
11102	FLAVORED WATERS NON-ALCO		4462	W 11332	5932	W 11871	5380	W 16316	7740	LIMONADES,EAUX GAZEUSES
12	TOBACCO AND MANUFACTURES		1108		1313		3744		4766	TABACS BRUTS FABRIQUES
122	TOBACCO,MANUFACTURED		9	W 119	702	W 599	3118	W 820	4513	TABACS FABRIQUES
1222	CIGARETTES			W 115	673	W 597	3113	W 820	4513	CIGARETTES
2	CRUDE MATERLS,EXCL FUELS		12342		13477		18068		17519	MAT BRUTES NON COMESTIBLES
22	OIL SEEDS,OLEAGINOUS FRT		7330		5574		5245		6599	GRAINES,FRUITS OLEAGINEUX
222	SEEDS FOR'SOFT'FIXED OIL	W 10241	7047	W 5236	5074	W 4476	4939	W 5935	6342	GRAINES HUILES FIXES
2225	SESAME SEEDS	W 8354	5719	W 4372	4747	W 4474	4931	W 5703	6223	GRAINES DE SESAME
26	TEXTILE FIBRES AND WASTE		945		3984		7353		2930	FIBRES TEXTILES
263	COTTON	W 476	841	W 1628	3546	W 3196	7106	W 1151	2416	COTON
2631	RAW COTTON,EXCL LINTERS			W 450	661	W 1365	3106	W 11	22	COTON EN MASSE
2634	COTTON,CARDED OR COMBED	W 226	682	W 986	2744	W 1347	3589	W 741	2024	COTON CARDE OU PEIGNE
29	CRUDE ANIMAL,VEG MAT NES		2734		2708		3553		4356	MATIERES BRUTES ANIM,VEGET
292	CRUDE VEG MATERIALS NES		2661	W 1735	2446		3297	W 2412	4142	MAT BRUTES VEGETALES NDA
3	MINERAL FUELS ETC		1078		4453		613		33122	COMBUSTIBLES MINERAUX LUB
33	PETROLEUM AND PRODUCTS		1078		4436		610		33122	PETROLE ET DERIVES
334	PETROLEUM PRODUCTS,REFIN	W 1346	982	W 17092	4348	W 2357	586	W 157619	33098	PRODUITS RAFFINES
3342	KEROSENE,OTH MEDIUM OILS			W 16468	3854			W 29303	7897	PETR LAMPANTS,AUT HUIL
3344	FUEL OILS,NES					W 1677	121	W 106115	11986	FUEL OILS
3345	LUBS,PETROLEUM OILS NES	W 574	455	W 454	363	W 613	449	W 15429	11226	HUILES LUBRIFIANTES
4	ANIMAL,VEGETABLE OIL,FAT		1343		3338		5324		6414	HUILES,GRAISSES ANIM,VEG
42	FIXED VEGETABLE OIL,FAT		867		1667		4601		5090	HUILES VEGETALES FIXES
423	FIXED VEG OILS,SOFT	W 757	808	W 1316	1314	W 3985	3956	W 4620	4472	HUILES VEGET DOUCES FIXES
4233	COTTON SEED OIL	W 599	574	W 1056	910	W 3336	3082	W 4082	3558	HUILE DE COTON
5	CHEMCLS,RELATED PROD NES		87703		97482		110649		141127	PRODUITS CHIMIQUES
51	ORGANIC CHEMICALS		5911		6362		3191		7633	PROD CHIMIQ ORGANIQUES
512	ALCOHOLS,PHENOLS ETC		5691	W 17928	6104	W 8882	3054	W 20304	7338	PHENOLS,PHENOLS-ALCOOLS
5121	ACYCLIC ALCOHOLS,DERIVS		5688	W 17908	6102	W 8882	3054	W 20276	7316	ALCOOLS ACYCLIQUES
51216	ETHYL ALC,DENATRD SPIRIT	W 18899	5650	W 17842	6057	W 8860	3031	W 20236	7283	ALCOOL ETHYLIQUE NON DENAT
53	DYES,TANNING,COLOUR PROD		5398		5798		7116		9050	PROD TEINTURE,COLORANTS
533	PIGMENTS,PAINTS,ETC		4913	W 4562	5446	W 4681	6808	W 6165	8864	PIGMENTS,PEINTURES,VERNIS
5334	VARNISHES,DISTEMPERS ETC	W 1394	2003	W 1169	2028	W 891	2235	W 5574	7745	PEINTURES A L'EAU
53341	WATER-THINNED PAINTS	W 671	482	W 579	541	W 292	362	W 4566	5149	PEINTURES DILUEES
5335	GLAZES,DRIERS,PUTTY ETC	W 2630	2628	W 3367	3339	W 3673	4059	W 447	459	PREPTNS COLOR UTILISES CERAM
53351	PREPRD PIGMENT,GLAZE ETC	W 2607	2606	W 3360	3327	W 3655	4033	W 230	168	PIGMENTS OPACIFIANTS
541	*MEDICINAL,PHARM PRODUCT		34341	K 3984058	34412		40445	K 6738629	49652	PROD MEDICINAUX PHARMACEUT
5416	GLYCOSIDES,GLANDS,SERA	K 1915497	1831	K 1051291	1401	K 2911903	2407	K 4011456	3509	HETEROSIDES
54164	ANTISERA,MICROB VACCINES	K 1597613	1258	K 1048990	1211	K 2909741	2309	K 3913214	3468	SERUMS,VACCINS
5417	MEDICAMENTS		32116	K 2872061	32568	K 3882900	37439	K 2658460	45649	MEDICAMENTS
55	PERFUME,CLEANING ETC PRD		20592		27919		36546		48392	PROD POUR PARFUM,TOILETTE
553	PERFUMERY,COSMETICS,ETC		4813	W 2435	5794	W 3232	11579	W 3555	14496	PRODUITS DE PARFUMERIE
554	SOAP,CLEANSING ETC PREPS		15732	W 21257	22047		24887	W 33284	33783	SAVONS,PRODUITS DETERSIFS
5541	SOAPS		6730	W 9493	9111	W 13870	12500	W 17596	17326	SAVONS,PROD TENSIO-ACTIFS
5542	WASHING PREPARATIONS ETC	W 7415	8987	W 11763	12935	W 11765	12383	W 15683	16435	PROD ORG TENSIO-ACT NDA
58	PLASTIC MATERIALS ETC		10899		12855		12758		14605	MAT PLAST ARTIFICIELLES
583	POLYMERIZATION ETC PRODS		8162	W 6170	11332	W 5432	11719	W 7008	13338	PROD POLYMERISATION
5834	POLYVINYL CHLORIDE		4196	W 4050	5098	W 3441	5076	W 4491	5514	CHLORURE DE POLYVINYLE
5839	OTH POLYMRZTION ETC PROD	W 1047	3124	W 1671	4593	W 1557	5079	W 2053	5509	AUT PROD POLYMER COPOLYM
59	CHEMICAL MATERIALS NES		8391		7416		7739		9368	MAT PROD CHIMIQUES NDA
591	PESTICIDES,DISINFECTANTS	W 2724	7810	W 2596	6536	W 3384	6913	W 3512	8590	DESINF,INSECT,FONG,HERB
5911	INSECTICIDES,FOR RETAIL	W 1428	5407	W 1122	4448	W 1283	4701	W 1427	5263	INSECTICIDES VENTE DET
6	BASIC MANUFACTURES		166338		171078		189212		188579	ART MANUFACTURES
61	LEATHER,DRESSED FUR,ETC		2215		2510		2695		2287	CUIRS,PELLETERIES
64	PAPER,PAPERBOARD AND MFR		53302		56576		58124		56970	PAPIERS,CARTONS & OUVRAGES

5. Special Exports F.O.B. by Commodities according to the S.I.T.C. (Rev. 2) in thousand U.S. Dollars
Exportations Spéciales F.O.B. par Produits d'après la C.T.C.I. (Rév. 2) en milliers de Dollars E.U.

SITC CTCI	COMMODITY	1993 WEIGHT POIDS	1993 VALUE VALEUR	1994 WEIGHT POIDS	1994 VALUE VALEUR	1995 WEIGHT POIDS	1995 VALUE VALEUR	1996 WEIGHT POIDS	1996 VALUE VALEUR	PRODUIT
641	PAPER AND PAPERBOARD		9984	W 8298	12647	W 8869	15166	W 8239	16386	PAPIERS ET CARTONS
6412	PRINTG,WRITING PAPER NES		2387	W 327	1383	W 564	2288	W 833	2832	PAPIERS POUR L'IMPRESSION
6417	CORRUGATED PAPER ETC,BLK		1653	W 2828	1924	W 3596	2532	W 3412	3164	PAPIERS,CARTONS ONDULES
6418	COATED ETC PAPER NES BLK		4305	W 1607	6518	W 1793	7682	W 1553	7806	PAP,CARTONS COUCHES,ENDUITS
642	PAPER,ETC,PRECUT,ARTS OF		43318	W 30551	43929	W 23511	42958	W 23369	40584	PAP,CARTONS DECOUPES
6421	PAPER ETC CONTAINERS		29485	W 21314	29393	W 14246	25751	W 12923	19795	BOITES,SACS EMBALLAGES
6424	PAPER ETC CT TO SIZE NES		7343	W 5464	6457	W 4682	7078	W 4757	8017	PAP,CARTONS DECOUPES
64243	TOILET PAPER CUT TO SIZE	W 7201	7070	W 5395	6298	W 4633	6995	W 4680	7872	PAPIER HYGIENIQUE
6428	PAPER ETC ARTICLES NES		4580	W 1974	5609	W 2943	7148	W 4334	10437	OUVRAGES EN PATE A PAPIER
64284	PAPER TISSUES,TOWELS ETC	W 952	1742	W 977	2076	W 1251	3002	W 1847	4184	MOUCHOIRS SERVIETTES EN PAP
64285	PAPER ETC DIAPERS ETC	W 583	2305	W 741	3138	W 809	3174	W 969	4762	SERVIETTES HYGIENIQUES
65	TEXTILE YARN,FABRICS,ETC		61090		61638		64285		67255	FILS,TISSUS,ARTICLES TEXTILE
651	TEXTILE YARN		19756	W 7244	21884		18629	W 6361	22069	FILS TEXTILES
6513	COTTON YARN	W 5090	14202	W 4916	13918	W 3920	12963	W 4870	16194	FILS DE COTON
6514	SYN FIB YRN,BULK,MONOFIL		3015	W 483	2270	W 2174	2201	W 404	2146	FILS CONT 85% FIB TEXT SYNTH
6516	DISCON SYN FIB BLEND YRN	W 709	2457	W 1842	5689	W 1182	3449	W 1051	3670	FILS FIBR TEX SYNT DIS MOINS
65166	DISCON SYN FIB–COTTN YRN	W 703	2414	W 1842	5688	W 1178	3431	W 767	2718	FILS TEXT SYNT MELANGE COTON
652	COTTON FABRICS,WOVEN		3757	W 850	3789	W 1507	7713	W 805	4820	TISSUS DE COTON
6521	GREY WOVEN COTTON FABRIC		2595	W 458	2007	W 552	2306	W 171	797	TISSUS COT ECRUS NON MERCER
6522	WOVEN COTTON BLEACHD,ETC		1162	W 392	1782	W 955	5407	W 634	4023	TISSUS COTON BLANCHIS ETC
65224	BLCHED COTTON FABRIC NES		849	W 314	1263	W 728	4125	W 523	3177	AUT TIS PLUS 85% COT BLANCHI
653	WOVN MAN–MADE FIB FABRIC		16679	W 2185	15048		14953	W 2013	14311	TISSUS FIBRES SYNTH,ARTIF
6534	DISC SYN BLEND FABRC NES	W 2084	15581	W 1931	13474	W 1968	13388	W 1861	13296	TISSUS FIBRES SYNTH DISCONT
655	KNITTED,ETC FABRICS		2439	W 156	1376	W 1137	2782	W 396	3211	ETOF BONNETERIE PIECES ETC
6552	OTHER KNIT ETC FAB NONEL		2439	W 156	1376	W 1137	2782	W 396	3211	ETOF BON NON ELAS NON SYNT
657	SPECIAL TXTL FABRC,PRODS		2810	W 473	1611		1616	W 512	1539	TISSUS SPECIAUX
658	TEXTILE ARTICLES NES		14957	W 2682	17286	W 2967	17322	W 2833	20248	ART FACONNES MAT TEXTILES
6584	LINENS ETC		12480	W 2022	14788	W 2486	15002	W 2059	17849	LINGE DE MAISON
66	NONMETAL MINERAL MFS NES		3242		1870		1915		2354	ART MIN NON METALLIQUES
67	IRON AND STEEL		9073		9639		16092		21506	FER ET ACIER
673	IRON,STEEL SHAPES ETC		5224	W 5358	2006	W 6445	2542	W 14502	5402	BARRES,PROFIL FER,ACIER
6732	IRON,STEEL BARS ETC		4383	W 3944	1447	W 6114	2414	W 14216	5261	BARRES FER,ACIER
67326	IRN,OTH STL BARS HOTROLD	W 10983	4263	W 3878	1423	W 6018	2373	W 14027	5161	BARRES PLEINES FER,ACIER
674	IRN,STL UNIV,PLATE,SHEET	W 4420	2011	W 12667	6005	W 22799	11837	W 26832	12845	LARGES PLATS,TOLES
6745	IRN,STL MED PLATE,ROLLED	W 1845	731	W 6652	2650	W 9360	4631	W 12004	5652	TOLES 3 A 4.75 MM
67451	— OF IRON OR SIMPLE STL	W 1845	731	W 6652	2650	W 9360	4631	W 12004	5652	TOLES AUT NON ACIER FIN
6746	IRN,STL THIN PLATE,ROLLD	W 1222	586	W 3166	1929	W 7454	4057	W 7814	3910	TOLES LAM MOINS 3MM
67461	— OF IRON OR SIMPLE STL	W 1221	580	W 3166	1929	W 7435	4049	W 7814	3910	TOL NON AC FIN MOINS 3 MM
68	NON–FERROUS METALS		18547		19306		26709		20933	METAUX NON FERREUX
684	ALUMINIUM		17509	W 3926	18435	W 4335	26316	W 3861	20693	ALUMINIUM
6842	ALUMINIUM,ALLOYS WORKED		17509	W 3921	18408	W 4331	26316	W 3861	20692	ALUMINIUM,ALLIAGES OUVRE
68421	ALUMINIUM BARS,WIRE,ETC	W 1582	5046	W 1688	5429	W 1767	6603	W 1685	6257	BARRES,PROFILES FILS ALU
68423	ALUMINIUM FOIL	W 2070	12246	W 2186	12729	W 2564	19710	W 2170	14408	FEUILLES,BANDES MINCES AL
69	METAL MANUFACTURES NES		16200		18154		17534		15846	ART MANUFACT EN METAL NDA
691	STRUCTURES AND PARTS NES	W 3117	3170	W 6444	4742	W 3655	3689	W 1315	2020	CONSTRUCT FER,ACIER,ALU
6911	STRUCTURES,PARTS IRN,STL	W 2770	1501	W 6025	2784	W 3254	1863	W 1024	685	CONSTRUCT FER,ACIER,FONTE
693	WIRE PRODUCTS NON ELECTR		3010	W 1356	3024		1892	W 601	899	OUVRAGES FILS METALLIQUES
6931	WIRE CABLES, ROPES ETC		2880	W 1051	2768		1646	W 291	675	CORDAGES EN FILS DE FER
69312	COPPER CABLES, ROPES ETC	W 734	2349	W 566	1748	W 54	218	W 41	40	CORDAGES DE CUIVRE
695	TOOLS		4894	W 1648	5415	W 1634	5605	W 1850	5679	OUTILS A MAIN
6951	HAND TOOLS,AGRIC,FOREST		4149	W 1506	4500	W 1530	4500	W 1813	5230	BECHES,PELLES,PIOCHES
699	BASE METAL MFRS NES		2460	W 1348	2318		2779	W 1542	2844	ART MANUFACTURES MET NDA
7	MACHINES,TRANSPORT EQUIP		23483		24781		27504		35292	MACHINES MATERIEL TRANSPORT
74	GENRL INDUSTRL MACHY NES		3198		2491		2988		2596	MACH APP INDUSTRIE
77	ELECTRIC MACHNRY NES ETC		17318		20288		21697		29106	MACH APP ELECT NDA
773	ELECTR DISTRIBUTNG EQUIP	W 2346	8185	W 2373	8465	W 1908	6742	W 2836	10820	EQUIPMT DISTRIBUTION ELECT
7731	INSULATED WIRE,CABLE ETC	W 2346	8183	W 2373	8465	W 1908	6742	W 2836	10820	FILS,CABLES ISOLES ELECT
775	HOUSEHOLD TYPE EQUIP NES	W 1353	5693	W 2053	8211		9651	W 2901	11303	MACH,APP USAGE DOMESTQUE
7752	DOM REFRIGERATRS,FREEZRS	W 1352	5686	W 2051	8204	W 2612	9632	W 2897	11278	REFRIG,CONGEL MENAGER
77521	DOMESTIC REFRIGERATORS	W 1351	5684	W 2051	8204	W 2607	9612	W 2890	11255	REFRIGERATEURS
778	ELECTRICAL MACHINERY NES	W 769	3203	W 1084	3377		5120	W 2598	6715	AUTRES MACH ELECT NDA
7781	BATTERIES,ACCUMULATORS	W 258	430	W 590	1002	W 1123	2043	W 1966	3292	PILES ET ACCUMULATEURS
7782	ELECTRIC LAMPS,BULBS	W 506	2520	W 493	2366	W 533	2995	W 629	3408	LAMPES, TUBES ELECTRIQUES
77821	ELEC FILAMENT LAMPS NES	W 502	2507	W 480	2320	W 528	2972	W 628	3398	LAMPES NON INFRAROUGES
8	MISC MANUFACTURED GOODS		71150		89585		81595		77266	ART MANUFACTURES DIVERS
821	*FURNITURE,PARTS THEREOF		1168	W 1025	1958	W 1597	3316	W 1500	3107	MEUBLES ET PIECES
831	*TRAVEL GOODS,HANDBAGS		4624	W 516	4672	W 494	3599	W 104	853	ARTICLES DE VOYAGE ETC
84	CLOTHING AND ACCESSORIES		29499		37509		33017		27480	VETEMENTS
842	MENS OUTERWEAR NOT KNIT		2170	W 129	1744	W 130	1972	W 118	2468	VET DESSUS POUR HOMMES
843	WOMENS OUTERWEAR NONKNIT		1944	W 155	2792	W 75	1678	W 66	1651	VET DESSUS FEMMES MAT TEX
844	UNDER GARMENTS NOT KNIT		6114	W 508	6197	W 1108	7207	W 347	4579	VETEMENT DESSOUS MAT TEX
8442	— MENS,OTHR THAN SHIRTS		3649	W 384	3644	W 718	5091	W 268	2530	SOUS–VET HOMMES MAT TEXT
845	OUTERWEAR KNIT NONELASTC		6807	W 553	9547	W 328	7668	W 292	5452	VET DESSOUS,ACCES BONNET
846	UNDER GARMENTS KNITTED		10304	W 1455	16054	W 956	12707	W 736	11229	SOUS VETS DE BONNETERIE
8462	— OF COTTON NON ELASTIC		9167	W 1400	15045	W 882	11616	W 670	10305	SOUS–VET BONNET COTON
84621	—— MENS SHIRTS	W 17	594	W 76	1198	W 183	3035	W 88	1382	CHEMISES DE COTON
84629	—— OTHER		8574	W 1324	13848	W 699	8582	W 582	8924	AUT SOUS–VET BONNET COTON
851	*FOOTWEAR		14094	W 3018	17721	W 2476	13059	W 1975	13978	CHAUSSURES
85101	FOOTWEAR RUBBER,PLASTIC	W 773	2339	W 857	2557	W 862	2571	W 764	1748	CHAUS SEMELLES CAOUTCH
85102	FOOTWEAR LEATHER		5842	W 1161	7725	W 894	7064	W 901	8413	CHAUS SEMELLES EN CUIR
85103	SHOES WOOD–,CORK–SOLED	W 136	2134	W 228	3431	W 74	410	W 206	3227	CHAUS SEMELLES BOIS,LIEGE
85104	FOOTWEAR NES	W 518	3779	W 773	4007	W 646	3013	W 103	590	CHAUS SEMELLES AUT MAT
89	MISC MANUFCTRD GOODS NES		20819		25502		27221		28609	ART MANUFACTURES DIVERS
892	PRINTED MATTER		4181	W 697	4826	W 676	3898	W 600	3859	IMPRIMES
8928	PRINTED MATTER NES		2007	W 348	3028	W 320	1962	W 248	1658	IMPRIMES NDA
893	ARTICLES OF PLASTIC NES		9216	W 4839	10376		12755		14253	OUVRAGES EN MAT DIVIS 58
8931	PLSTC PACKG CONTNRS,LIDS	W 2461	5667	W 2378	5688	W 3209	7479	W 2981	7338	ART TRANSP EMBALLAGE ETC
8939	MISC PLASTIC ARTICLES		3448	W 2453	4680	W 2496	5271	W 3003	6905	ART DIVERS EN MAT DIV 58
89399	OTHR PLASTC ARTICLES NES		3297	W 2427	4582	W 2469	5209	W 2941	6745	AUT OUV MAT DIV 58
895	OFFICE SUPPLIES NES		2601	W 609	2794		3403	W 464	2754	ART PAPET NDA
899	OTHER MANUFACTURED GOODS		2872		5452		5613		5815	AUT ART MANUF DIVERS NDA
8998	SMALLWARES,TOILETRYS ETC		1076	W 278	2510		2462	W 230	2479	ART MERCERIE,TOILETTE

FOOT NOTES – NOTES

TABLE 4 –
1 Because of the conversion from SITC Rev.3 to SITC Rev.2, not all data for 1994, 1995 and 1996 are comparable

El Salvador

with those for previous years. For further details see the Introduction.
TABLE 5 –
1 Because of the conversion from SITC Rev.3 to SITC Rev.2, not all data for 1994, 1995 and 1996 are comparable with those for previous years. For further details see the Introduction.
TABLEAU 4 –
1 A cause de la conversion de la CTCI Rev.3 à la CTCI Rev.2, toutes les données pour 1994, 1995 et 1996 ne sont pas comparables à celles des années précédentes. Se référer aux explications supplémentaires dans l'introduction.
TABLEAU 5 –
1 A cause de la conversion de la CTCI Rev.3 à la CTCI Rev.2, toutes les données pour 1994, 1995 et 1996 ne sont pas comparables à celles des années précédentes. Se référer aux explications supplémentaires dans l'introduction.

1. HISTORICAL SERIES, 1958–1995 SPECIAL TRADE, IMPORTS C.I.F., EXPORTS F.O.B.
SERIES HISTORIQUES, 1958–1995 COMMERCE SPECIAL, IMPORTATIONS C.A.F., EXPORTATIONS F.O.B

YEAR ANNEE	VALUE IN MILLION U.S. DOLLARS VALEUR EN MILLION U.S. DOLLARS MERCHANDISE – MARCHANDISE		GOLD – OR		CONVERSION FACTORS FACTEURS DE CONVERSION CENTS E.U. PAR		INDEX NUMBERS – INDICES QUANTUM		UNIT VALUE VALEUR UNITAIRE	
	IMPORTS	EXPORTS	IMPORTS	EXPORTS	IMPORTS	EXPORTS	IMPORTS	EXPORTS	IMPORTS	EXPORTS
1958	11.09	16.15								
1959	11.70	16.17								
1960	13.15	28.71								
1961	13.63	19.85								
1962	16.41	21.76								
1963	13.08	23.84								
1964	17.09	27.85								
1965	18.35	23.34								
1966	18.26	25.96								
1967	20.84	27.03								
1970	23.76	24.83								
1971	27.86	28.35								
1972	26.59	19.22								
1973	26.67	19.09								
1974	15.22	33.90								
1975	19.58	26.46								
1976	4.28	9.88								
1977	9.53	14.33								
1978	9.29	17.32								
1979	19.11	28.72								
1980	28.88	20.06								
1981	40.03	16.51								
1982	45.65	17.28								
1983	25.28	17.69								
1984	25.15	20.27								
1985	26.16	23.38								
1986	51.69	34.94								
1987	57.56	41.93								
1988	61.11	49.35								
1989	51.41	32.70								
1990	60.92	61.73								
1991	67.54	37.45								
1992	56.15	50.50								
1993	60.01	56.65								
1994	36.92	62.26								
1995	49.85	85.60								

2. IMPORTS BY BROAD ECONOMIC CATEGORY AND EXPORTS BY INDUSTRIAL ORIGIN. (PERCENTAGE OF TOTAL VALUE)
IMPORTATIONS PAR CATEGORIES ECONOMIQUES ET EXPORTATIONS PAR BRANCHE D'ACTIVITE. (EN POURCENTAGE DE LA VALEUR TOTALE)

IMPORTS – IMPORTATIONS

	1990	1991	1992	1993	1994	1995	1996
TOTAL IMPORTS–IMPORTATIONS TOTALES							
1 FOOD BEV–ALIMENTATION BOISSONS							
11 PRIMARY–PRODUITS DE BASE							
111 FOR INDUSTRY–POUR L'INDUSTRIE							
112 FOR HOUSEHOLDS–POUR LES MENAGES							
12 PROCESSED–PRODUITS ELABORES							
121 FOR INDUSTRY–POUR L'INDUSTRIE							
122 FOR HOUSEHOLDS–POUR LES MENAGES							
2 IND SUPPLIES–APPROV INDUSTRIELS							
21 PRIMARY–PRODUITS DE BASE							
22 PROCESSED–PRODUITS ELABORES							
3 FUELS–COMBUSTIBLES							
31 PRIMARY–PRODUITS DE BASE							
32 PROCESSED–PRODUITS ELABORES							
321 MOTOR SPIRIT–ESSENCE							
322 OTHER–AUTRES							
4 MACHINERY–EQUIPEMENT							
41 CAPITAL EQUIPMENT–MACHINES							
42 PARTS–PIECES ACCESSOIRES							
5 TRANSPORT–TRANSPORT							
51 PASSENGER CARS–AUTOMOBILES							
52 OTHER–AUTRES							
521 INDUSTRIAL–INDUSTRIELS							
522 NON INDUSTRIAL–NON INDUSTRIEL							
53 PARTS–PIECES ACCESSOIRES							
6 CONSUM GOODS–BIENS CONSOMMATION							
61 DURABLE–DURABLES							
62 SEMI DURABLE–SEMI DURABLES							
63 NON DURABLE–NON DURABLES							
7 GOODS NES–BIENS NDA							

EXPORTS – EXPORTATIONS

	1990	1991	1992	1993	1994	1995	1996
TOTAL EXPORTS–EXPORTATIONS TOTALES							
1 AGRICULTURE							
2 MINING QUARRY–INDUS EXTRACTIVES							
3 MANUFACTURING–IND MANUFACTUR							
31 FOOD BEV TOBACCO–ALIM BOISS TAB							
32 TEXTILES–INDUSTRIES TEXTILES							
33 WOOD & PRODUCTS–BOIS & PRODUITS							
34 PAPER & PRODUCTS–PAPIER & PRODT							
35 CHEMICALS–INDUSTRIES CHIMIQUES							
36 NON METAL MIN–MIN NON METAL							
37 BASIC METAL–IND METAL BASE							
38 METAL MANUF–MANUF METAL							
39 OTH MANUF IND–AUTRES MANUF							

3. TRADE BY PRINCIPAL COUNTRIES OF PRODUCTION AND LAST CONSIGNMENT (VALUE IN THOUSAND U.S. DOLLARS)
ECHANGES SELON LES PRINCIPAUX PAYS DE PRODUCTION ET DE DERNIERE CONSIGNATION (VALEUR EN MILLIERS DE DOLLARS EU)

COUNTRIES–PAYS	SPECIAL IMPORTS C.I.F. IMPORTATIONS SPECIALES C.A.F				
	1987	1988	1989	1990	1991
World	55125	47680	38758	61601	113545
Africa	6955	7563	6471	6657	54197
Americas	1476	5814	741	24604	33565
Northern America	1476	5814	741	24604	33515
LAIA					
CACM					
Caribbean					50
Rest of America					
As.ex F.USSR					1284
Eur.x F.USSR	21603	23545	17248	18843	24069
EU	21603	23545	17248	18843	23413
EFTA					535
East Europe					
Other Europe					
Former USSR					98
Oceania					
USA/Etats–Unis d'Amer	1476	5814	741	24604	33366
Spain/Espagne	12994	9531	8999	10864	11640
Cameroon/Cameroun	4240	4796	3104	3825	29141
France, Monac	6028	11717	7069	5249	5915
Liberia/Libéria					22032
Germany/Allemagne	2582	2297	1180	2731	529
Gabon	2319	1338	774	950	831
Nigeria/Nigéria	384	806	538	1730	537
Italy/Italie					3001
Cote d'Ivoire	12	622	2054	152	
Japan/Japon					868
Togo					799
Belgium–Luxembourg					662
Sweden/Suède					535
United Kingdom					534
Netherlands/Pays–Bas					517
Norway, SVD, JM					483
Mozambique					464
Libyan Arab Jamahiriya					244
Singapore/Singapour					184
Canada					149
Fm Yugoslav					122
China/Chine					119
Thailand/Thaïlande					113
Senegal/Sénégal					113

COUNTRIES–PAYS	SPECIAL EXPORTS F.O.B. EXPORTATIONS SPECIALES F.O.B.				
	1987	1988	1989	1990	1991
Monde	43847	36156	43885	61705	86151
Afrique	5470	5546	11575	31749	60681
Amériques					53
Amérique du Nord					53
ALAI					
MCAC					
Caraïbes					
Autre Amérique					
Asie l'URSS exclus					258
Europe l'URSS exclus	35202	28472	30559	29134	18812
UE	35202	28472	30559	29134	18812
AELE					
Europe de l'Est					
Autre de l'Europe					
Ancienne URSS					
Océanie					
Spain/Espagne	16447	13823	22512	17313	11645
Cameroon/Cameroun	1702	618	925	23085	47212
Nigeria/Nigéria	3627	4501	10182	8433	8955
Netherlands/Pays–Bas	4602	4124	5215	4504	2103
Italy/Italie	6712	4395		3754	1597
France, Monac	2689	3649	2609	1560	1472
Germany/Allemagne	4752	2481	223	2003	1225
Gabon	141	426	468	231	2389
Sao Tome and Principe					1952
Portugal					771
Turkey/Turquie					258
USA/Etats–Unis d'Amer					53

(VALUE AS PERCENTAGE OF WORLD TOTAL)(VALEURS EN POURCENTAGE DU TOTAL MONDIAL)

	1982	1983	1984	1985	1986	1987	1988	1989	1990	1991
Africa					18.9	12.6	15.9	16.7	10.8	47.7
Americas					14.1	2.7	12.2	1.9	39.9	29.6
Northern America					14.1	2.7	12.2	1.9	39.9	29.5
LAIA										
CACM										
Caribbean										0.0
Rest of America										
As.ex F.USSR										1.1
Eur.x F.USSR					43.8	39.2	49.4	44.5	30.6	21.2
EU					43.8	39.2	49.4	44.5	30.6	20.6
EFTA										0.5
East Europe										
Other Europe										
Former USSR										0.1
Oceania										
USA/Etats–Unis d'Amer					14.1	2.7	12.2	1.9	39.9	29.4
Spain/Espagne					32.5	23.6	20.0	23.2	17.6	10.3
Cameroon/Cameroun					7.5	7.7	10.1	8.0	6.2	25.7
France, Monac					8.4	10.9	24.6	18.2	8.5	5.2
Liberia/Libéria										19.4
Germany/Allemagne					2.9	4.7	4.8	3.0	4.4	0.5
Gabon					9.8	4.2	2.8	2.0	1.5	0.7
Nigeria/Nigéria					1.6	0.7	1.7	1.4	2.8	0.5
Italy/Italie										2.6
Cote d'Ivoire						0.0	1.3	5.3	0.2	

	1982	1983	1984	1985	1986	1987	1988	1989	1990	1991
Afrique					1.1	12.5	15.3	26.4	51.5	70.4
Amériques										0.1
Amérique du Nord										0.1
ALAI										
MCAC										
Caraïbes										
Autre Amérique										
Asie l'URSS exclus										0.3
Europe l'URSS exclus					89.1	80.3	78.7	69.6	47.2	21.8
UE					89.1	80.3	78.7	69.6	47.2	21.8
AELE										
Europe de l'Est										
Autre de l'Europe										
Ancienne URSS										
Océanie										
Spain/Espagne					40.0	37.5	38.2	51.3	28.1	13.5
Cameroon/Cameroun					0.1	3.9	1.7	2.1	37.4	54.8
Nigeria/Nigéria					0.5	8.3	12.4	23.2	13.7	10.4
Netherlands/Pays–Bas					33.1	10.5	11.4	11.9	7.3	2.4
Italy/Italie					1.2	15.3	12.2		6.1	1.9
France, Monac					6.0	6.1	10.1	5.9	2.5	1.7
Germany/Allemagne					8.8	10.8	6.9	0.5	3.2	1.4
Gabon					0.4	0.3	1.2	1.1	0.4	2.8
Sao Tome and Principe										2.3
Portugal										0.9

4. Special Imports C.I.F. by Commodities according to the S.I.T.C. (Rev. 2) in thousand U.S. Dollars
Importations Spéciales C.A.F. par Produits d'après la C.T.C.I. (Rév. 2) en milliers de Dollars E.U.

SITC CTCI	COMMODITY	1987 WEIGHT POIDS	1987 VALUE VALEUR	1988 WEIGHT POIDS	1988 VALUE VALEUR	1989 WEIGHT POIDS	1989 VALUE VALEUR	1990 WEIGHT POIDS	1990 VALUE VALEUR	PRODUIT
	ALL COMMODITIES		55125		47680		38758		61601	TOUS PRODUITS
0	FOOD AND LIVE ANIMALS		4524		4663		3080		4340	ALIMENTS,ANIMAUX VIVANTS
01	MEAT AND PREPARATIONS		1066		1404		892		1337	VIANDES ET PREPARATIONS
011	MEAT FRESH,CHILLD,FROZEN	W 811	555	W 1027	586			W 764	279	VIANDES FRAICHES,REF,CONGE
014	MEAT PREPD,PRSVD,NES ETC	W 1630	512	W 903	818	W 889	892	W 755	1058	CONSERVES DE VIANDES
0141	MEAT,FISH EXTRCTS,JUICES	W 1630	512	W 903	818	W 889	892	W 755	1058	EXTRAITS DE VIANDE
02	DAIRY PRODCTS,BIRDS'EGGS		412		624				525	PRODUITS LAITIERS,OEUFS
022	MILK AND CREAM	W 587	412	W 1081	624			W 798	525	LAIT ET CREME
03	FISH AND PREPARATIONS		1131		425				630	POISSONS ET PREPARATIONS
037	FISH ETC PREPD,PRSVD NES	W 1582	1131	W 1205	425			W 3684	630	POIS,CRUST,MOL PREPARES
04	CEREALS AND PREPARATIONS		1221		1599		1443		1400	CEREALES ET PRODUITS
045	CEREALS NES UNMILLED	W 1155	362	W 2611	693	W 1770	412	W 1302	395	AUTRES CEREALES NON MOULUES
047	OTHER CEREAL MEALS,FLOUR	W 2693	758	W 3347	839	W 2952	936	W 3155	896	AUTRES SEMOULES,FARINES
05	VEGETABLES AND FRUIT		364		256		304		156	LEGUMES ET FRUITS
058	FRUIT PRESERVED,PREPARED	W 662	305	W 745	197	W 1096	304	W 464	106	CONSERVES DE FRUITS
0589	FRUIT PREPRD,PRESRVD,NES	W 662	305	W 745	197	W 1096	304	W 464	106	FRUITS PREPARES CONSERV
05899	FRUIT,NUTS NES,PRESERVED	W 662	305	W 745	197	W 1096	304	W 464	106	FRUITS PREP CONSERV NDA
06	SUGAR AND PREPS,HONEY		88		111		151		80	SUCRES ET PRODUITS
061	SUGAR AND HONEY	W 249	88	W 437	111	W 308	151	W 349	80	SUCRES ET MIEL
0612	REFINED SUGAR ETC	W 249	88	W 437	111	W 308	151	W 349	80	SUCRES RAFFINES
081	*FEEDING STUFF FOR ANIML	W 101	72	W 149	97	W 318	165	W 84	59	NOURRITURE POUR ANIMAUX
0819	FOOD WASTE AND FEED NES	W 101	72	W 149	97	W 318	165	W 84	59	DECHETS,ALIMENTS NDA
1	BEVERAGES AND TOBACCO		9010		7938		3934		3198	BOISSONS ET TABACS
11	BEVERAGES		3797		2531		1575		2393	BOISSONS
112	ALCOHOLIC BEVERAGES	W 5601	3797	W 9095	2531	W 5491	1575	W 7629	2393	BOISSONS ALCOOLIQUES
1122	CIDER,PERRY,MEAD ETC	W 5601	3797	W 9095	2531	W 5491	1575	W 7629	2393	CIDRE,POIRE,HYDROMEL
12	TOBACCO AND MANUFACTURES		5213		5407		2359		804	TABACS BRUTS FABRIQUES
121	TOBACCO UNMNFCTRD,REFUSE	W 8	5213	W 393	5407	W 159	2359	W 51	804	TABACS BRUTS,DECHETS
2	CRUDE MATERLS,EXCL FUELS		1732		1678		1460		2589	MAT BRUTES NON COMESTIBLES
26	TEXTILE FIBRES AND WASTE		468		637		266		452	FIBRES TEXTILES
269	WASTE OF TEXTILE FABRICS	W 563	430	W 604	569	W 417	256	W 350	450	FRIPERIE DRILLES,CHIFFONS
26901	BULK TEXT WSTE,OLD CLTHG	W 563	430	W 604	569	W 417	256	W 350	450	ART ET ACCESS D'HABILLEMENT
27	CRUDE FERTLZR,MINRLS NES		1221		1028		1166		2102	ENGRAIS MINERAUX BRUTS
278	OTHER CRUDE MINERALS	W 6272	1221	W 7672	1028	W 7739	1166	W 11211	2102	AUTRES MINERAUX BRUTS
2789	MINERALS CRUDE NES	W 6272	1221	W 7672	1028	W 7739	1166	W 11211	2102	MINERAUX BRUTS NDA
27899	MINERAL SUBSTANCES NES	W 6272	1221	W 7672	1028	W 7739	1166	W 11211	2102	MATIERES MINERALES NDA
3	MINERAL FUELS ETC		5825		3128		4674		4738	COMBUSTIBLES MINERAUX LUB
33	PETROLEUM AND PRODUCTS		5825		3128		4674		4738	PETROLE ET DERIVES
335	RESIDUAL PETRLM PROD NES	W 20387	5825	W 15891	3128	W 18334	4674	W 16990	4738	PRODUITS RESIDUELS NDA
3352	MINERAL TARS AND PRODCTS	W 20387	5825	W 15891	3128	W 18334	4674	W 16990	4738	GOUDRONS MINERAUX
4	ANIMAL,VEGETABLE OIL,FAT		256		174		209		309	HUILES,GRAISSES ANIM,VEG
411	*ANIMAL OILS AND FATS	W 665	256	W 637	174	W 2081	209	W 1211	309	HUILES,GRAISSES ANIMALES
4113	ANIML OIL,FAT,GREASE NES	W 665	256	W 637	174	W 2081	209	W 1211	309	HUILES,GRAISSES ANIMALES NDA
5	CHEMCLS,RELATED PROD NES		3449		2732		5095		2378	PRODUITS CHIMIQUES
52	INORGANIC CHEMICALS		1874		1041		1190		528	PROD CHIM INORGANIQUES
524	RADIOACTIVE ETC MATERIAL	W 1907	1874	W 1654	1041	W 1583	1190	W 669	528	MATIERES RADIOACTIVES
5249	OTH RADIOACTIVE ETC MTLS	W 1907	1874	W 1654	1041	W 1583	1190	W 669	528	AUT MATIERES RADIOACTIVES
52492	OTH CHEMS ASSOC RADIOACT	W 1907	1874	W 1654	1041	W 1583	1190	W 669	528	COMPOSES THORIUM,URANIUM
53	DYES,TANNING,COLOUR PROD		242		239		255		215	PROD TEINTURE,COLORANTS
532	DYES NES,TANNING PROD	W 98	242	W 190	239	W 231	255	W 172	215	EXTRAITS TEINTURE,TANNAGE
5323	SYNTHETC TANNING PRODCTS	W 98	242	W 190	239	W 231	255	W 172	215	PRODUITS TANNANTS
541	*MEDICINAL,PHARM PRODUCT	K 64000	481	K 148000	646	K 2792000	2719	K 84000	816	PROD MEDICINAUX PHARMACEUT
5419	PHARMACEUTICAL GOODS NES	K 64000	481	K 148000	646	K 2792000	2719	K 84000	816	PREP,ART PHARMACEUTIQUES
55	PERFUME,CLEANING ETC PRD		380		244		505		249	PROD POUR PARFUM,TOILETTE
554	SOAP,CLEANSING ETC PREPS	W 613	338	W 594	182	W 586	450	W 721	208	SAVONS,PRODUITS DETERSIFS
5543	POLISHES,CREAMS,ETC	W 613	338	W 594	182	W 586	450	W 721	208	CIRAGES,ENCAUSTIQUES
58	PLASTIC MATERIALS ETC		243		371		259		306	MAT PLAST ARTIFICIELLES
585	PLASTIC MATERIAL NES	W 78	243	W 753	371	W 96	259	W 135	306	RESINES ARTIFICIELLES
5852	OTH ART PLASTIC MTLS NES	W 78	243	W 753	371	W 96	259	W 135	306	AUT MAT PLAST ARTIFICIEL
59	CHEMICAL MATERIALS NES		186		111		101		215	MAT PROD CHIMIQUES NDA
598	MISCEL CHEM PRODUCTS NES	W 30	176	W 55	108	W 30	93	W 95	211	PROD DIV INDUST CHIM NDA
6	BASIC MANUFACTURES		5406		9172		4026		3931	ART MANUFACTURES
62	RUBBER MANUFACTURES NES		796		588		894		837	CAOUTCHOUC MANUFACTURE
621	MATERIALS OF RUBBER	W 143	796	W 214	588	W 1195	894	W 177	837	PRODUITS EN CAOUTCHOUC
63	WOOD,CORK MANUFACTRS NES		600		120		89		360	OUVRAGES LIEGE ET BOIS
635	WOOD MANUFACTURES NES	W 110	600	W 135	120	W 376	89	W 194	354	ART MANUF EN BOIS NDA
6359	OTHER WOOD MANUFACTURES	W 110	600	W 135	120	W 376	89	W 194	354	OUVRAGES EN BOIS NDA
63599	OTHER WOOD ARTICLES NES	W 110	600	W 135	120	W 376	89	W 194	354	AUTRES OUVRAGES EN BOIS NDA
64	PAPER,PAPERBOARD AND MFR		265		284		357		290	PAPIERS,CARTONS & OUVRAGES
642	PAPER,ETC,PRECUT,ARTS OF	W 149	265	W 119	284	W 67	357	W 95	290	PAP,CARTONS DECOUPES
6428	PAPER ETC ARTICLES NES	W 149	265	W 119	284	W 67	357	W 95	290	OUVRAGES EN PATE A PAPIER
64289	OTHER ARTICLES OF PAPER	W 149	265	W 119	284	W 67	357	W 95	290	ARTICLES,OUVRAGES EN PAPIER
65	TEXTILE YARN,FABRICS,ETC		384		301		243		226	FILS,TISSUS,ARTICLES TEXTILE
658	TEXTILE ARTICLES NES	W 251	262	W 268	201	W 68	117	W 14	144	ART FACONNES MAT TEXTILES
6589	OTH TEXTILE ARTICLES NES	W 251	262	W 268	201	W 68	117	W 14	144	AUT ART EN TEXTILES NDA
66	NONMETAL MINERAL MFS NES		392		755		622		524	ART MIN NON METALLIQUES
661	LIME,CEMENT,BLDG PRODS	W 20	50	W 180	110	W 130	156	W 18	59	CHAUX,CIMENTS MAT CONSTR
6613	BUILDING STONE ETC WORKD	W 20	50	W 180	110	W 130	156	W 18	59	PIERRES A BATIR
662	CLAY,REFRACTORY BLDG PRD	W 349	230	W 608	403	W 1056	382	W 427	393	MAT CONST REFRACTAIRES
6624	BRICKS ETC NONREFRACTORY	W 349	230	W 608	403	W 1056	382	W 427	393	BRIQUES ETC CERAM NON REFR
664	GLASS	W 75	112	W 213	243	W 134	85	W 99	72	VERRE
67	IRON AND STEEL		2080		5015		744		958	FER ET ACIER
679	IRN,STL CASTINGS UNWORKD	W 853	2080	W 4114	5015	W 959	744	W 617	958	OUVRAGES EN FONTE,FER,ACIER
68	NON-FERROUS METALS		334		1528		645		415	METAUX NON FERREUX
684	ALUMINIUM	W 279	246	W 461	1387	W 172	531	W 77	267	ALUMINIUM
69	METAL MANUFACTURES NES		517		535		415		249	ART MANUFACT EN METAL NDA
696	CUTLERY	W 97	344	W 114	415	W 99	336	W 64	193	COUTELLERIE
699	BASE METAL MFRS NES	W 39	173	W 51	121	W 55	79	W 6	56	ART MANUFACTURES MET NDA
6996	BASE MTL MISC ARTICLES	W 39	173	W 51	121	W 55	79	W 6	56	ART DIVERS METAUX COMMUNS
7	MACHINES,TRANSPORT EQUIP		22760		15429		13652		35880	MACHINES MATERIEL TRANSPORT
77	ELECTRIC MACHNRY NES ETC		5402		3439		3380		4448	MACH APP ELECT NDA
778	ELECTRICAL MACHINERY NES	W 763	5402	W 702	3439	W 6030	3380	W 637	4448	AUTRES MACH ELECT NDA
78	ROAD VEHICLES		7872		5595		6512		3764	VEHICULES ROUTIERS
783	ROAD MOTOR VEHICLES NES	W 1785	7872	W 1710	5595	W 1364	6512	W 777	3764	VEHICULES ROUTIERS NDA
79	OTHR TRANSPORT EQUIPMENT		4353		100		80		24727	AUTRE MATERIEL TRANSPORT
791	RAILWAY VEHICLES	W 46	726	W 2	1	W 5	14	W 2	11	VEHIC MAT CHEMINS DE FER
7919	RY TRACK FIXT,ETC,PARTS	W 46	726	W 2	1	W 5	14	W 2	11	MATER FIXE VOIES FERREES
793	SHIPS AND BOATS ETC	W 1141	3626	W 8	53	W 8	66	W 93	24715	NAVIRES BATEAUX,ETC
7938	TUGS,SPECIAL VESSELS ETC	W 1141	3626	W 8	53	W 8	66	W 93	24715	REMORQUEURS,BATEAUX SPEC
8	MISC MANUFACTURED GOODS		1951		2329		2462		2725	ART MANUFACTURES DIVERS
821	*FURNITURE,PARTS THEREOF	W 146	912	W 215	887	W 262	878	W 526	1572	MEUBLES ET PIECES

4. Special Imports C.I.F. by Commodities according to the S.I.T.C. (Rev. 2) in thousand U.S. Dollars
Importations Spéciales C.A.F. par Produits d'après la C.T.C.I. (Rév. 2) en milliers de Dollars E.U.

SITC CTCI	COMMODITY	1987 WEIGHT POIDS	1987 VALUE VALEUR	1988 WEIGHT POIDS	1988 VALUE VALEUR	1989 WEIGHT POIDS	1989 VALUE VALEUR	1990 WEIGHT POIDS	1990 VALUE VALEUR	PRODUIT
8219	FURNITURE AND PARTS NES	W 146	912	W 215	887	W 262	878	W 526	1572	AUTRES MEUBLES ET PIECES
82199	OTHR FURN,FURN PARTS NES	W 146	912	W 215	887	W 262	878	W 526	1572	MEUBLES NDA AUTRES MATIERES
84	CLOTHING AND ACCESSORIES		200		136		67		66	VETEMENTS
851	*FOOTWEAR	W 109	221	W 82	170	W 178	578	W 50	143	CHAUSSURES
85105	GAITERS,LEGGINGS,ETC	W 109	221	W 82	170	W 178	578	W 50	143	GUETRES,JAMBIERES ETC
89	MISC MANUFCTRD GOODS NES		230		368		310		455	ART MANUFACTURES DIVERS
892	PRINTED MATTER	W 29	107	W 88	248	W 44	187	W 34	310	IMPRIMES
8928	PRINTED MATTER NES	W 29	107	W 88	248	W 44	187	W 34	310	IMPRIMES NDA
89289	OTHER PRINTED MATTER	W 29	107	W 88	248	W 44	187	W 34	310	GRAVURES,PHOTO AUT IMPR
9	GOODS NOT CLASSD BY KIND		211		421		167		1513	ART TRANSACT NON CLASSES
931	*SPECIAL TRANSACTIONS		209		401				903	TRANS.SPECIALES
961	*COIN NONGOLD,NONCURRENT				2		166		610	MONNAIES NON EMISES

5. Special Exports F.O.B. by Commodities according to the S.I.T.C. (Rev. 2) in thousand U.S. Dollars
Exportations Spéciales F.O.B. par Produits d'après la C.T.C.I. (Rév. 2) en milliers de Dollars E.U.

SITC CTCI	COMMODITY	1987 WEIGHT POIDS	1987 VALUE VALEUR	1988 WEIGHT POIDS	1988 VALUE VALEUR	1989 WEIGHT POIDS	1989 VALUE VALEUR	1990 WEIGHT POIDS	1990 VALUE VALEUR	PRODUIT
	ALL COMMODITIES		43847		36156		43885		61705	TOUS PRODUITS
0	FOOD AND LIVE ANIMALS		12208		9180		8161		6742	ALIMENTS,ANIMAUX VIVANTS
07	COFFEE,TEA,COCOA,SPICES		12078		9029		8135		6688	CAFE,THE,CACAO,EPICES
071	COFFEE AND SUBSTITUTES		252		734	W 301	396		316	CAFE ET SUCCEDANES
072	COCOA	W 7905	11826	W 8432	8295	W 7041	7739	W 5565	6372	CACAO
0721	COCOA BEANS,RAW,ROASTED	W 7905	11826	W 8432	8295	W 7041	7739	W 5565	6372	CACAO EN FEVES
1	BEVERAGES AND TOBACCO		9286		8171		4424		3217	BOISSONS ET TABACS
11	BEVERAGES		1295		3370		1337		896	BOISSONS
112	ALCOHOLIC BEVERAGES	W 639	1295	W 3212	3370	W 2418	1337	W 1373	896	BOISSONS ALCOOLIQUES
1122	CIDER,PERRY,MEAD ETC	W 639	1295	W 3212	3370	W 2418	1337	W 1373	896	CIDRE,POIRE,HYDROMEL
12	TOBACCO AND MANUFACTURES		7991		4801		3086		2321	TABACS BRUTS FABRIQUES
121	TOBACCO UNMNFCTRD,REFUSE	W 199	7991	W 198	4801	W 248	3086	W 94	2321	TABACS BRUTS,DECHETS
2	CRUDE MATERLS,EXCL FUELS		17623		14810		18929		20017	MAT BRUTES NON COMESTIBLES
24	CORK AND WOOD		15882		11611		13285		12839	LIEGE ET BOIS
247	OTH WOOD ROUGH,SQUARED	W 127552	15882	W 108848	11611	W 110773	13285	W 127060	12839	BOIS BRUTS EQUARRIS
2472	SAW–,VENEER–LOGS NON–CON	W 127552	15882	W 108848	11611	W 110773	13285	W 127060	12839	NON CONIFERES SCIAGE,PLAC
24721	— IN THE ROUGH	W 127552	15882	W 108848	11611	W 110773	13285	W 127060	12839	BRUTS ECORCES DEGROSSIS
26	TEXTILE FIBRES AND WASTE		1676		3189		5644		7078	FIBRES TEXTILES
269	WASTE OF TEXTILE FABRICS	W 1770	1636	W 3143	3152	W 3747	5644	W 4427	7028	FRIPERIE DRILLES,CHIFFONS
26901	BULK TEXT WSTE,OLD CLTHG	W 1770	1636	W 3143	3152	W 3747	5644	W 4427	7028	ART ET ACCESS D'HABILLEMENT
5	CHEMCLS,RELATED PROD NES		165		48		9466		61	PRODUITS CHIMIQUES
541	*MEDICINAL,PHARM PRODUCT	K 9000	133	K 1000	5	K 1203000	9434		1	PROD MEDICINAUX PHARMACEUT
6	BASIC MANUFACTURES		457		2045		473		1327	ART MANUFACTURES
65	TEXTILE YARN,FABRICS,ETC		372		38		135		416	FILS,TISSUS,ARTICLES TEXTILE
651	TEXTILE YARN	W 80	369							FILS TEXTILES
6515	YARN OF 6514 FOR RETAIL	W 80	369							FILS CONT 85% FI SYNTHETIQ
65152	— OF DISCONTIN FIBRES	W 80	369							FILS CONT 85% FI TEXT SYNT
655	KNITTED,ETC FABRICS		3					W 113	345	ETOF BONNETERIE PIECES ETC
66	NONMETAL MINERAL MFS NES		9		48		183		818	ART MIN NON METALLIQUES
664	GLASS	W 69	7	W 118	48	W 154	170	W 1267	818	VERRE
67	IRON AND STEEL		35		1839		61		60	FER ET ACIER
679	IRN,STL CASTINGS UNWORKD	W 115	35	W 2226	1839	W 43	61	W 19	60	OUVRAGES EN FONTE,FER,ACIER
68	NON–FERROUS METALS		5		111		11		2	METAUX NON FERREUX
684	ALUMINIUM			W 5	111	W 2	2			ALUMINIUM
7	MACHINES,TRANSPORT EQUIP		4056		1366		1679		24574	MACHINES MATERIEL TRANSPORT
77	ELECTRIC MACHNRY NES ETC		569		112		391		163	MACH APP ELECT NDA
778	ELECTRICAL MACHINERY NES	W 175	569	W 41	112	W 79	391	W 5	163	AUTRES MACH ELECT NDA
78	ROAD VEHICLES		471		266		452		263	VEHICULES ROUTIERS
783	ROAD MOTOR VEHICLES NES	W 75	471	W 76	266	W 161	452	W 34	263	VEHICULES ROUTIERS NDA
79	OTHR TRANSPORT EQUIPMENT		2715		21		13		23852	AUTRE MATERIEL TRANSPORT
793	SHIPS AND BOATS ETC	W 1110	2714	W 2	20	W 2	6	W 6	23852	NAVIRES BATEAUX,ETC
7938	TUGS,SPECIAL VESSELS ETC	W 1110	2714	W 2	20	W 2	6	W 6	23852	REMORQUEURS,BATEAUX SPEC
8	MISC MANUFACTURED GOODS		49		144		506		462	ART MANUFACTURES DIVERS
9	GOODS NOT CLASSD BY KIND				367		216		437	ART TRANSACT NON CLASSES
931	*SPECIAL TRANSACTIONS				366		204		435	TRANS.SPECIALES

1. HISTORICAL SERIES, 1992–1996 GENERAL TRADE, IMPORTS C.I.F., EXPORTS F.O.B.
SERIES HISTORIQUES, 1992–1996 COMMERCE GENERAL, IMPORTATIONS C.A.F., EXPORTATIONS F.O.B

YEAR ANNEE	VALUE IN MILLION KROONS VALEUR EN MILLION KROONS MERCHANDISE –MARCHANDISE IMPORTS	EXPORTS	GOLD –OR IMPORTS	EXPORTS	CONVERSION FACTORS U.S. CENTS PER KROON FACTEURS DE CONVERSION CENTS E.U. PAR KROON IMPORTS	EXPORTS	INDEX NUMBERS –INDICES QUANTUM IMPORTS	EXPORTS	UNIT VALUE VALEUR UNITAIRE IMPORTS	EXPORTS
1992	5128.00	5549.00			8.0319	8.0167				
1993	11848.00	10642.00			7.5670	7.5670				
1994	21561.01	16872.00			7.7140	7.7140				
1995	29101.01	21040.00			8.7449	8.7338				
1996	38367.01	24586.00			8.2926	8.3007				

2. IMPORTS BY BROAD ECONOMIC CATEGORY AND EXPORTS BY INDUSTRIAL ORIGIN. (PERCENTAGE OF TOTAL VALUE)
IMPORTATIONS PAR CATEGORIES ECONOMIQUES ET EXPORTATIONS PAR BRANCHE D'ACTIVITE.(EN POURCENTAGE DE LA VALEUR TOTALE)

IMPORTS – IMPORTATIONS

	1990	1991	1992	1993	1994	1995	1996
TOTAL IMPORTS–IMPORTATIONS TOTALES							100.
1 FOOD BEV–ALIMENTATION BOISSONS							13.6
11 PRIMARY–PRODUITS DE BASE							4.7
111 FOR INDUSTRY–POUR L'INDUSTRIE							2.0
112 FOR HOUSEHOLDS–POUR LES MENAGES							2.8
12 PROCESSED–PRODUITS ELABORES							8.9
121 FOR INDUSTRY–POUR L'INDUSTRIE							1.2
122 FOR HOUSEHOLDS–POUR LES MENAGES							7.7
2 IND SUPPLIES–APPROV INDUSTRIELS							31.5
21 PRIMARY–PRODUITS DE BASE							2.9
22 PROCESSED–PRODUITS ELABORES							28.6
3 FUELS–COMBUSTIBLES							9.3
31 PRIMARY–PRODUITS DE BASE							2.1
32 PROCESSED–PRODUITS ELABORES							7.2
321 MOTOR SPIRIT–ESSENCE							
322 OTHER–AUTRES							7.2
4 MACHINERY–EQUIPEMENT							19.0
41 CAPITAL EQUIPMENT–MACHINES							14.9
42 PARTS–PIECES ACCESSOIRES							4.2
5 TRANSPORT–TRANSPORT							8.4
51 PASSENGER CARS–AUTOMOBILES							3.1
52 OTHER–AUTRES							2.7
521 INDUSTRIAL–INDUSTRIELS							2.6
522 NON INDUSTRIAL–NON INDUSTRIEL							0.1
53 PARTS–PIECES ACCESSOIRES							2.6
6 CONSUM GOODS–BIENS CONSOMMATION							18.1
61 DURABLE–DURABLES							5.5
62 SEMI DURABLE–SEMI DURABLES							7.8
63 NON DURABLE–NON DURABLES							4.7
7 GOODS NES–BIENS NDA							0.0

EXPORTS – EXPORTATIONS

	1990	1991	1992	1993	1994	1995	1996
TOTAL EXPORTS–EXPORTATIONS TOTALES							100.
1 AGRICULTURE							7.3
2 MINING QUARRY–INDUS EXTRACTIVES							1.3
3 MANUFACTURING–IND MANUFACTUR							91.4
31 FOOD BEV TOBACCO–ALIM BOISS TAB							12.5
32 TEXTILES–INDUSTRIES TEXTILES							16.2
33 WOOD & PRODUCTS–BOIS & PRODUITS							7.8
34 PAPER & PRODUCTS–PAPIER & PRODT							2.4
35 CHEMICALS–INDUSTRIES CHIMIQUES							15.4
36 NON METAL MIN–MIN NON METAL							2.3
37 BASIC METAL–IND METAL BASE							1.6
38 METAL MANUF–MANUF METAL							30.6
39 OTH MANUF IND–AUTRES MANUF							2.7

3. TRADE BY PRINCIPAL COUNTRIES OF PRODUCTION AND LAST CONSIGNMENT (VALUE IN THOUSAND U.S. DOLLARS)
ECHANGES SELON LES PRINCIPAUX PAYS DE PRODUCTION ET DE DERNIERE CONSIGNATION (VALEUR EN MILLIERS DE DOLLARS EU)

COUNTRIES–PAYS	GENERAL IMPORTS C.I.F. IMPORTATIONS GENERALES C.A.F					COUNTRIES–PAYS	GENERAL EXPORTS F.O.B. EXPORTATIONS GENERALES F.O.B.				
	1992	1993	1994	1995	1996		1992	1993	1994	1995	1996
World	411844	894000	1660400	2545478	3197033	Monde	444815	803900	1305900	1838816	2074056
Africa		248	4700	3580	22626	Afrique		14402	10200	8090	8048
Americas	20096	31219	55800	86510	102264	Amériques	8345	18600	29800	49704	55947
Northern America	20096	26600	48000	68455	84415	Amérique du Nord	8345	16200	25700	46090	47899
LAIA		4100	6700	13393	13643	ALAI		600	300	479	414
CACM		300	700	1988	1944	MCAC				33	54
Caribbean		117	200	1760	1890	Caraïbes		1700	2800	2618	1221
Rest of America		102	200	914	371	Autre Amérique		100	1000	483	6360
As.ex F.USSR	10931	51800	87000	109921	191596	Asie l'URSS exclus		10500	17200	27569	47427
Eur.x F.USSR	181015	562020	1100500	1773984	2226009	Europe l'URSS exclus	195864	416700	674100	1070236	1153504
EU	181015	540200	1050000	1680850	2070943	UE	185987	388300	624500	995716	1060045
EFTA		9000	20500	42554	69077	AELE	1387	8100	27400	43353	57833
East Europe		12601	28200	48756	83272	Europe de l'Est	8490	19900	20800	30550	30754
Other Europe		19		250	456	Autre de l'Europe			1300	136	3599
Former USSR	177762	242600	406300	570365	650757	Ancienne URSS	188040	343000	574300	683139	808850
Oceania		200	600	1118	3781	Océanie		100	300	77	280
Finland/Finlande	93282	249600	496000	829395	934626	Finland/Finlande	94012	166400	233000	395593	380782
Russian Federation	117017	153600	279100	409981	431466	Russian Federation	92673	182000	301800	322696	340835
Germany/Allemagne	34264	96200	165200	243444	318552	Sweden/Suède	34400	76100	141500	200041	239957
Sweden/Suède	24184	79700	147300	215519	261271	Latvia/Lettonie	47058	69100	107400	137417	171411
Netherlands/Pays–Bas	7285	32400	51000	79088	91186	Germany/Allemagne	17340	64300	89100	132942	146616
Denmark/Danemark	7124	23200	43900	70968	90224	Lithuania/Lituanie	6766	29800	70800	86193	118802
Italy/Italie	1968	18500	40100	66318	103207	Ukraine	30704	28600	40000	69026	104190
USA/Etats–Unis d'Amer	20096	24400	41500	62658	73279	Netherlands/Pays–Bas	22663	32600	41100	85961	61151
United Kingdom	6474	13100	35400	56195	105541	Denmark/Danemark	10622	19100	44300	60476	73516
Japan/Japon	10931	37600	48400	47487	64817	United Kingdom	3728	11200	36400	60384	71889
Lithuania/Lituanie	14923	29600	42700	41137	50004	USA/Etats–Unis d'Amer	8345	14900	23800	43951	45818
Latvia/Lettonie	7028	20200	24100	50533	62036	Belarus/Bélarus	6333	9100	26700	45722	40205
France,Monac	3622	10500	24800	37105	64704	Norway,SVD,JM	1387	4800	19500	34206	31322
Ukraine	13092	14500	27900	26815	51322	Poland/Pologne	8490	8500	8900	21137	24172
Belgium–Luxembourg	2811	9500	23400	39621	45446	Belgium–Luxembourg	1836	5000	14200	16446	25756
Belarus/Bélarus	25702	12900	14000	15719	13834	Italy/Italie	1387	5200	11500	15505	19473
Switz.Liecht		4700	9800	20794	38839	France,Monac		2400	5900	14046	23544
Korea, Republic of		2100	5200	12728	52588	Switz.Liecht		2900	6300	5374	24674
Norway,SVD,JM		4200	10500	21347	29059	Kazakhstan	4505	7400	7100	8861	7681
Poland/Pologne		3600	10000	15060	34799	Japan/Japon		3500	5900	8869	14696
Austria/Autriche		2200	10400	17215	18297	Uzbekistan/Ouzbékistan		2600	5300	5244	8086
Czech Republic		3800	8900	15074	19325	Turkey/Turquie		2100	200	9438	7963
Uzbekistan/Ouzbékistan		1100	7800	10707	25029	Republic of Moldova		2300	2800	3648	9640
Hungary/Hongrie		3800	6400	12962	20565	So. Africa Customs Un		3900	4800	6176	613
China/Chine		3500	8500	11131	16172	Austria/Autriche		2200	1900	5255	4978
Spain/Espagne		2100	4200	10980	17304	Czech Republic		4900	3000	2723	2410
Ireland/Irlande		1500	5200	10676	12807	Portugal		1900	3600	2850	3487
Hong Kong		1400	5500	9248	9059	Korea, Republic of			200	469	10245
Canada		2200	6300	5517	10868	Mauritcnia/Mauritanie		6700	2900	227	638
Cote d'Ivoire			2300	2060	14665	Ireland/Irlande		400	400	4153	5478
Kazakhstan		2000	3100	5033	8651	Hungary/Hongrie		3600	2600	2580	1414
India/Inde		1500	4600	3725	8439	Azerbaijan		3700	3000	1718	1469
Turkmenistan/Turkménistn		2700	3400	2735	4221	Tajikistan/Tadjikistan		3000	3900	1328	1259
Brazil/Brésil		3800	3200	2471	3339	Turkmenistan/Turkménistn		3800	1800	506	2088
Portugal		900	2400	3184	5742	China/Chine		2000	4100	1387	471
Indonesia/Indonésie		400	4000	1974	5473	Iceland/Islande		400	1600	3773	1838
Turkey/Turquie		400	900	2685	6582	Canada		1300	1900	2138	2073
Singapore/Singapour		1300	3100	2603	2976	Bulgaria/Bulgarie		2100	1300	1173	2163
Slovakia		200	1300	3257	4990	Belize/Bélize				44	5775
Malaysia/Malaisie		200	1200	1746	6306	Spain/Espagne		400	1200	1845	2147
Colombia/Colombie		200	1300	3401	4343	Romania/Roumanie		500	3300	1500	35
Republic of Moldova		3600	1500	1910	1756	Egypt/Egypte		2000	1100	5	2011
Tajikistan/Tadjikistan		300	1700	4728	1604	Cyprus/Chypre		100	600	3133	996
Bulgaria/Bulgarie		900	1300	2201	3377	Georgia/Géorgie		500	2800	106	1270
Thailand/Thaïlande		600	1300	2376	3147	Cayman Is/Is Caïmans		1500	1700	1443	1
Israel/Israël		300	700	1789	2317	Malta/Malte			1300	108	2686
Argentina/Argentine			400	1380	3081	Slovakia		300	1700	1436	547
Ecuador/Equateur		100	1500	1797	1433	Philippines				5	2954
Greece/Grèce		800	700	1142	2038	Kyrgyzstan/Kirghizistan		400	100	478	1795
Peru/Pérou			100	3887	207	Hong Kong		200	300	266	1876

(VALUE AS PERCENTAGE OF WORLD TOTAL)(VALEURS EN POURCENTAGE DU TOTAL MONDIAL)

	1987	1988	1989	1990	1991	1992	1993	1994	1995	1996		1987	1988	1989	1990	1991	1992	1993	1994	1995	1996
Africa							0.0	0.3	0.1	0.7	Afrique							1.8	0.8	0.4	0.4
Americas						4.9	3.5	3.4	3.4	3.2	Amériques						1.9	2.3	2.3	2.7	2.7
Northern America						4.9	3.0	2.9	2.7	2.6	Amérique du Nord						1.9	2.0	2.0	2.5	2.3
LAIA							0.5	0.4	0.5	0.4	ALAI							0.1	0.0	0.0	0.0
CACM							0.0	0.0	0.1	0.1	MCAC									0.0	0.0
Caribbean							0.0	0.0	0.1	0.1	Caraïbes							0.2	0.2	0.1	0.1
Rest of America							0.0	0.0	0.0	0.0	Autre Amérique							0.0	0.1	0.0	0.3
As.ex F.USSR						2.7	5.8	5.2	4.3	6.0	Asie l'URSS exclus							1.3	1.3	1.5	2.3
Eur.x F.USSR						44.0	62.9	66.3	69.7	69.6	Europe l'URSS exclus						44.0	51.8	51.6	58.2	55.6
EU						44.0	60.4	63.2	66.0	64.8	UE						41.8	48.3	47.8	54.1	51.1
EFTA							1.0	1.2	1.7	2.2	AELE						0.3	1.0	2.1	2.4	2.8
East Europe							1.4	1.7	1.9	2.6	Europe de l'Est						1.9	2.5	1.6	1.7	1.5
Other Europe							0.0		0.0	0.0	Autre de l'Europe								0.1	0.0	0.2
Former USSR						43.2	27.1	24.5	22.4	20.4	Ancienne URSS						42.3	42.7	44.0	37.2	39.0
Oceania							0.0	0.0	0.0	0.1	Océanie							0.0	0.0	0.0	0.0
Finland/Finlande						22.6	27.9	29.9	32.6	29.2	Finland/Finlande						21.1	20.7	17.8	21.5	18.4
Russian Federation						28.4	17.2	16.8	16.1	13.5	Russian Federation						20.8	22.6	23.1	17.5	16.4
Germany/Allemagne						8.3	10.8	9.9	9.6	10.0	Sweden/Suède						7.7	9.5	10.8	10.9	11.6
Sweden/Suède						5.9	8.9	8.9	8.5	8.2	Latvia/Lettonie						10.6	8.6	8.2	7.5	8.3
Netherlands/Pays–Bas						1.8	3.6	3.1	3.1	2.9	Germany/Allemagne						3.9	8.0	6.8	7.2	7.1
Denmark/Danemark						1.7	2.6	2.6	2.8	2.8	Lithuania/Lituanie						1.5	3.7	5.4	4.7	5.7
Italy/Italie						0.5	2.1	2.4	2.6	3.2	Ukraine						6.9	3.6	3.1	3.8	5.0
USA/Etats–Unis d'Amer						4.9	2.7	2.5	2.5	2.3	Netherlands/Pays–Bas						5.1	4.1	3.1	4.7	2.9
United Kingdom						1.6	1.5	2.1	2.2	3.3	Denmark/Danemark						2.4	2.4	3.4	3.3	3.5
Japan/Japon						2.7	4.2	2.9	1.9	2.0	United Kingdom						0.8	1.4	2.8	3.3	3.5

4. General Imports C.I.F. by Commodities according to the S.I.T.C. (Rev. 2) in thousand U.S. Dollars
Importations Générales C.A.F. par Produits d'après la C.T.C.I. (Rév. 2) en milliers de Dollars E.U.

SITC CTCI	COMMODITY	1993		1994		1995		1996		PRODUIT
		WEIGHT POIDS	VALUE VALEUR	WEIGHT POIDS	VALUE VALEUR	WEIGHT POIDS	VALUE VALEUR	WEIGHT POIDS	VALUE VALEUR	
	ALL COMMODITIES		894000		1660400		2545478		3197033	TOUS PRODUITS
0	FOOD AND LIVE ANIMALS						280586		400032	ALIMENTS,ANIMAUX VIVANTS
01	MEAT AND PREPARATIONS						19271		38946	VIANDES ET PREPARATIONS
011	MEAT FRESH,CHILLD,FROZEN			W 10511	11466	W 90694	14260		32498	VIANDES FRAICHES,REF,CONGE
0113	PIG MEAT FRESH,CHLD,FRZN					W 8313	2836		9638	VIANDE DE PORC
0114	POULTRY FRESH CHLLD,FRZN					W 74193	9279		15109	VOLAILLES MORTES
0141	MEAT,FISH EXTRCTS,JUICES				7086		1		89	EXTRAITS DE VIANDE
02	DAIRY PRODCTS,BIRDS'EGGS						30151		39603	PRODUITS LAITIERS,OEUFS
022	MILK AND CREAM					W 216537	16280		17937	LAIT ET CREME
0224	MILK,CREAM PRESERVED ETC					W 70965	10919		12265	LAIT,CREME CONS,CONC
02242	MILK DRY,1.5% FAT OR LES					W 58381	8411		10991	LAIT POUDRE INF 1.5%
023	BUTTER					W 37692	8312		13962	BEURRE
03	FISH AND PREPARATIONS				11272		14498		21308	POISSONS ET PREPARATIONS
034	FISH,FRESH,CHILLED,FROZN					W 163735	11186		17314	POISSON FRAIS, REFRIG,CONG
0342	FISH FROZEN,EXCL FILLETS					W 113514	7520		12625	POISSONS CONGELES
04	CEREALS AND PREPARATIONS						38133		72268	CEREALES ET PRODUITS
043	BARLEY UNMILLED					W 549299	3992		12334	ORGE NON MONDEE
046	WHEAT ETC MEAL OR FLOUR					W 383081	7705		9948	SEMOULE FARINE,FROMENT
048	CEREAL ETC PREPARATIONS				13365	W 155317	20741		36329	PREPTNS A BASE CEREALES
0484	BAKERY PRODUCTS					W 44008	11370		23660	PRODUITS DE BOULANGERIE
04842	PASTRY, CAKES ETC					W 33290	8187		18139	PATISSERIE ETC.
0488	OTH CEREAL PREPS,MALT EX				13365	W 12350	2183		2151	EXTRAITS DE MALT
05	VEGETABLES AND FRUIT						39368		50443	LEGUMES ET FRUITS
057	FRUIT,NUTS,FRESH,DRIED				12047	W 260519	17312		20740	FRUITS FRAIS OU SECS
058	FRUIT PRESERVED,PREPARED				10729	W 88300	10860		14783	CONSERVES DE FRUITS
06	SUGAR AND PREPS,HONEY				33522		28357		35942	SUCRES ET PRODUITS
061	SUGAR AND HONEY					W 399679	15383		21093	SUCRES ET MIEL
0612	REFINED SUGAR ETC					W 227453	9220		19650	SUCRES RAFFINES
062	SUGAR CANDY NON–CHOCLATE					W 23935	12974		14849	SUCRERIES
07	COFFEE,TEA,COCOA,SPICES				44864		50676		71412	CAFE,THE,CACAO,EPICES
071	COFFEE AND SUBSTITUTES					W 35449	25937		23999	CAFE ET SUCCEDANES
0711	COFFEE GREEN,ROASTED,SUB					W 31993	21794		19918	CAFE TORREFIE OU DECAFEINE
07112	COFFEE ROASTED					W 20649	16012		15604	CAFE TORREFIE
072	COCOA					W 23546	4258		25862	CACAO
0721	COCOA BEANS,RAW,ROASTED					W 21326	3200		20594	CACAO EN FEVES
073	CHOCOLATE AND PRODUCTS					W 33020	16290		16680	CHOCOLAT
081	*FEEDING STUFF FOR ANIML					W 749620	19062		26025	NOURRITURE POUR ANIMAUX
0819	FOOD WASTE AND FEED NES				7892	W 181086	8909		11524	DECHETS,ALIMENTS NDA
08199	FODDER NES,INCL SWEETNED					W 180026	8908		11483	PREPARATIONS FOURRAGERES
09	MISC EDIBLE PRODUCTS				20459		40253		43422	PREP ALIMENTAIRES DIVERSES
091	MARGARINE AND SHORTENING					W 116858	14608		15071	MARGARINE ET GRAISSES
0914	MARGARINE,EDIBLE FAT NES					W 116803	14557		14969	MARGARINES,SIMILI SAINDOUX
09141	MARGARINE					W 113468	13793		14437	MARGARINE
098	EDIBLE PRODCTS,PREPS NES						25646		28351	PREP ALIMENTAIRES NDA
09809	MISC FOOD PREPRTIONS NES					W 55464	16687		18570	PREP ALIMENTAIRES NDA
1	BEVERAGES AND TOBACCO				43740		53865		69929	BOISSONS ET TABACS
11	BEVERAGES				32095		41188		46787	BOISSONS
112	ALCOHOLIC BEVERAGES					W 84226	33795		37864	BOISSONS ALCOOLIQUES
1121	WINE OF FRESH GRAPES ETC					W 40289	10206		12471	VINS DE RAISINS FRAIS
11212	WINE OF FRESH GRAPES					W 36104	8701		10707	VINS DE MOUTS DE RAISINS
1124	DISTILLED ALCOHOLIC BEVS					W 11340	19769		19461	ALCOOLS,EAUX–DE–VIE
11249	OTH ALCOHOLC BEVS,CMPNDS					W 5128	12850		9490	BOISSONS ALCOOLIQUES NDA
12	TOBACCO AND MANUFACTURES				11644		12677		23142	TABACS BRUTS FABRIQUES
122	TOBACCO,MANUFACTURED						10819		22644	TABACS FABRIQUES
1222	CIGARETTES					W 5176	10657		22150	CIGARETTES
2	CRUDE MATERLS,EXCL FUELS						93227		111326	MAT BRUTES NON COMESTIBLES
24	CORK AND WOOD						9424		13224	LIEGE ET BOIS
248	WOOD SHAPED,SLEEPERS						7406		9593	BOIS SIMPLEMENT TRAVAILLES
26	TEXTILE FIBRES AND WASTE						49732		48040	FIBRES TEXTILES
263	COTTON					W 174220	37703		39178	COTON
2631	RAW COTTON,EXCL LINTERS					W 173045	37288		39080	COTON EN MASSE
27	CRUDE FERTLZR,MINRLS NES						11175		13267	ENGRAIS MINERAUX BRUTS
278	OTHER CRUDE MINERALS					W 2321185	4374		9720	AUTRES MINERAUX BRUTS
28	METALLIFEROUS ORES,SCRAP						7343		10278	MINERAIS METAL,DECHETS
29	CRUDE ANIMAL,VEG MAT NES						9004		10133	MATIERES BRUTES ANIM,VEGET
292	CRUDE VEG MATERIALS NES						7902		9076	MAT BRUTES VEGETALES NDA
3	MINERAL FUELS ETC						279799		299565	COMBUSTIBLES MINERAUX LUB
33	PETROLEUM AND PRODUCTS						223803		233151	PETROLE ET DERIVES
334	PETROLEUM PRODUCTS,REFIN					W 5134200	214363		221987	PRODUITS RAFFINES
335	RESIDUAL PETRLM PROD NES					W 767150	9419		11032	PRODUITS RESIDUELS NDA
341	*GAS,NATURAL AND MANUFCT						50882		58745	GAZ NATUREL,GAZ MANUFACT
3414	PETROLEUM GASES, GASEOUS					MV 702276412	49451		57294	GAZ DE PETROLE GAZEUX
4	ANIMAL,VEGETABLE OIL,FAT						16830		15866	HUILES,GRAISSES ANIM,VEG
42	FIXED VEGETABLE OIL,FAT						15215		13935	HUILES VEGETALES FIXES
423	FIXED VEG OILS,SOFT					W 151204	13891		12626	HUILES VEGET DOUCES FIXES
4239	OTH FIXED VEG OILS,SOFT					W 101581	10129		9072	AUTRES HUILES FIXES
42391	RAPE,COLZA,MUSTARD OILS					W 101563	10114		9071	H NAVETTE COLZA MOUTARDE
5	CHEMCLS,RELATED PROD NES						232144		328881	PRODUITS CHIMIQUES
51	ORGANIC CHEMICALS						16938		25194	PROD CHIMIQ ORGANIQUES
52	INORGANIC CHEMICALS						16545		21992	PROD CHIM INORGANIQUES
53	DYES,TANNING,COLOUR PROD						32017		41874	PROD TEINTURE,COLORANTS
533	PIGMENTS,PAINTS,ETC					W 106835	29688		38861	PIGMENTS,PEINTURES,VERNIS
5334	VARNISHES,DISTEMPERS ETC					W 46370	20821		27847	PEINTURES A L'EAU
53342	OTH PAINTS,VARNISHES ETC					W 40574	17568		24178	AUTRES PEINTURES,VERNIS
541	*MEDICINAL,PHARM PRODUCT					MK 18490	51302		58388	PROD MEDICINAUX PHARMACEUT
5417	MEDICAMENTS					MK 12894	45189		51062	MEDICAMENTS
54179	— CONTNG OTH SUBSTANCES					MK 11269	35269		38762	MED CONT AUT SUBSTANCES
55	PERFUME,CLEANING ETC PRD						38407		48785	PROD POUR PARFUM,TOILETTE
553	PERFUMERY,COSMETICS,ETC					W 9648	21658		31650	PRODUITS DE PARFUMERIE
554	SOAP,CLEANSING ETC PREPS					W 71768	15522		16024	SAVONS,PRODUITS DETERSIFS
5542	WASHING PREPARATIONS ETC					W 68545	12296		10837	PROD ORG TENSIO–ACT NDA
562	*FERTILIZERS,MANUFACTURE						8224		34159	ENGRAIS MANUFACTURES
5629	FERTILIZERS NES					W 140544	2674		25225	ENGRAIS NDA
56292	NITROG–PHOS FERTILZR NES					W 22168	423		21220	ENGRAIS NDA CONT N P
572	*EXPLOSIVES,PYROTECH PRO					W 192172	14132		19856	EXPLOSIFS
5721	PREPARED EXPLOSIVES					W 186139	11716		16892	POUDRES,EXPLOSIFS
57212	PREPARED EXPLOSIVES NES					W 186139	11716		16892	EXPLOSIFS PREPARES
58	PLASTIC MATERIALS ETC						37905		46908	MAT PLAST ARTIFICIELLES
582	PROD OF CONDENSATION ETC					W 42296	7016		10624	PROD CONDENS,POLYCOND
583	POLYMERIZATION ETC PRODS					W 97714	29004		34290	PROD POLYMERISATION
5831	POLYETHYLENE					W 50120	9128		9217	POLYETHYLENE

4. General Imports C.I.F. by Commodities according to the S.I.T.C. (Rev. 2) in thousand U.S. Dollars
Importations Générales C.A.F. par Produits d'après la C.T.C.I. (Rév. 2) en milliers de Dollars E.U.

SITC CTCI	COMMODITY	1993		1994		1995		1996		PRODUIT
		WEIGHT POIDS	VALUE VALEUR	WEIGHT POIDS	VALUE VALEUR	WEIGHT POIDS	VALUE VALEUR	WEIGHT POIDS	VALUE VALEUR	
5839	OTH POLYMRZTION ETC PROD					W 10981	9835		12362	AUT PROD POLYMER COPOLYM
59	CHEMICAL MATERIALS NES						16673		31725	MAT PROD CHIMIQUES NDA
598	MISCEL CHEM PRODUCTS NES					W 68514	9986		19653	PROD DIV INDUST CHIM NDA
5989	CHEM PRODUCTS,PREPS NES					W 51005	8643		12230	PROD PREP CHIMIQUES NDA
6	BASIC MANUFACTURES						522913		649442	ART MANUFACTURES
61	LEATHER,DRESSED FUR,ETC						17196		20685	CUIRS,PELLETERIES
611	LEATHER						7418		11362	CUIRS,PEAUX PREPARES
612	LEATHER ETC MANUFACTURES					W 7298	8899		8449	OUVRAGES EN CUIRS NDA
6123	PREPRD PARTS OF FOOTWEAR					W 7254	8454		7989	PARTIES DE CHAUSSURES
62	RUBBER MANUFACTURES NES						25652		30876	CAOUTCHOUC MANUFACTURE
625	RUBBER TYRES, TUBES ETC						16713		21043	PNEUS CAOUTCHOUC VULCANISE
6251	TYRES NEW FOR MOTOR CARS					N 190588	9800		9898	PNEUS POUR VOITURES
63	WOOD,CORK MANUFACTRS NES						30643		33715	OUVRAGES LIEGE ET BOIS
634	VENEERS,PLYWOOD,ETC						20698		23005	PLACAGES,CONTRE–PLAQUES
6342	PLYWOOD OF WOOD SHEETS					V 62145	13772		15989	BOIS CONTRE–PLAQUES
635	WOOD MANUFACTURES NES					W 40035	9775		10523	ART MANUF EN BOIS NDA
6353	BUILDERS WOODWRK,PREFABS		1088		3616	W 24112	8072		8557	OUVRAGES DE MENUISERIE
64	PAPER,PAPERBOARD AND MFR						69825		87213	PAPIERS,CARTONS & OUVRAGES
641	PAPER AND PAPERBOARD						40047		53025	PAPIERS ET CARTONS
6412	PRINTG,WRITING PAPER NES					W 84977	11623		10690	PAPIERS POUR L'IMPRESSION
64122	— COATED,IMPREGNATD ETC					W 73645	9561		8370	PAPIERS IMPRESSION COUCHES
6415	PAPER,PAPERBRD,BULK,NES					W 45295	6417		11219	PAPIERS,CARTONS ROULEAUX
64159	OTHER PAPER ETC,BULK,NES					W 45087	5952		10475	AUT PAPIER ROULEAUX FEUILLES
642	PAPER,ETC,PRECUT,ARTS OF					W 103820	29778		34188	PAP,CARTONS DECOUPES
6421	PAPER ETC CONTAINERS					W 66166	12501		13387	BOITES,SACS EMBALLAGES
6428	PAPER ETC ARTICLES NES					W 13362	9477		10508	OUVRAGES EN PATE A PAPIER
65	TEXTILE YARN,FABRICS,ETC						154155		170537	FILS,TISSUS,ARTICLES TEXTILE
651	TEXTILE YARN					W 10313	11962		15734	FILS TEXTILES
652	COTTON FABRICS,WOVEN						32960		31245	TISSUS DE COTON
6522	WOVEN COTTON BLEACHD,ETC						25326		23916	TISSUS COTON BLANCHIS ETC
65224	BLCHED COTTON FABRIC NES						18551		15851	AUT TIS PLUS 85% COT BLANCHI
653	WOVN MAN–MADE FIB FABRIC						50837		54643	TISSUS FIBRES SYNTH,ARTIF
6531	CONT SYNT WEAVES NONPILE						16534		18356	TISSUS FIBRES SYNTH CONTINUE
65315	CONT SYN TXTL FABRIC NES						15326		17003	TIS PLUS 85% TEXT SYNT CONT
6534	DISC SYN BLEND FABRC NES						16903		16712	TISSUS FIBRES SYNTH DISCONT
65342	DISC SYN FIB–WOOL FABRIC						9021		8681	TISSUS FIB SYNT MEL LAINE
6535	CONT REGN WEAVES NONPILE						9576		9531	TISSUS FIB TEXT ART CONTINU
65355	CONT REGN TXTL FABRC NES						8068		7814	TISSUS 85% TEXT ART CONT
654	OTH WOVEN TEXTILE FABRIC						9224		10322	TISSUS AUT COTON SYNT,ARTIF
655	KNITTED,ETC FABRICS					W 1752	9900		11314	ETOF BONNETERIE PIECES ETC
6552	OTHER KNIT ETC FAB NONEL					W 1752	9900		11314	ETOF BON NON ELAS NON SYNT
657	SPECIAL TXTL FABRC,PRODS						20225		26487	TISSUS SPECIAUX
6573	COATED ETC TEXTILES NES						9344		9013	TISSUS,ART MATIERE TEXT NDA
658	TEXTILE ARTICLES NES						9955		8905	ART FACONNES MAT TEXTILES
66	NONMETAL MINERAL MFS NES						52453		66114	ART MIN NON METALLIQUES
661	LIME,CEMENT,BLDG PRODS						7601		10294	CHAUX,CIMENTS MAT CONSTR
662	CLAY,REFRACTORY BLDG PRD						8678		11523	MAT CONST REFRACTAIRES
663	MINERAL MANUFCTURES NES						12829		14369	ART MIN MANUF NDA
6633	MINRL MFS NES NONCERAMIC						7647		7621	OUVR MAT MINERALE NDA
664	GLASS						15079		20506	VERRE
67	IRON AND STEEL						77999		110345	FER ET ACIER
673	IRON,STEEL SHAPES ETC	W 10330	1689	W 31480	6097	W 187507	9015		15394	BARRES,PROFIL FER,ACIER
674	IRN,STL UNIV,PLATE,SHEET					W 772268	42872		57973	LARGES PLATS,TOLES
6744	IRN,STL HVY PLATE,ROLLED					W 331797	12938		11413	TOLES LAMINEES PLUS 4.75 MM
67441	— OF IRON OR SIMPLE STL					W 267449	9064		9780	TOLES NON ACIER FIN CARB
6747	TINNED PLATES,SHEETS					W 207745	12430		11985	TOLES ETAMEES EN ACIER
6749	OTH IRN,STL PLATES,SHEET					W 113736	10764		19942	AUTRES TOLES FER,ACIER
67491	— OF IRON OR SIMPLE STL					W 106499	9420		19505	AUT TOLES AUTRES ACIER FIN
678	IRON,STL TUBES,PIPES,ETC					W 137153	14097		23930	TUBES,TUYAUX EN FONTE,FER
6782	IRON,STL SEAMLESS TUBES	W 7618	2139	W 5726	6602	W 33993	3349		5046	TUBES,TUYAUX SANS SOUDURE
6783	IRON,STL TUBES,PIPES NES	W 3931	2138	W 7778	4338	W 102630	8422		12130	AUT TUBES,TUYAUX FER,ACIER
68	NON–FERROUS METALS						16084		15881	METAUX NON FERREUX
684	ALUMINIUM					W 20224	11578		10534	ALUMINIUM
6842	ALUMINIUM,ALLOYS WORKED					W 17095	10907		9750	ALUMINIUM,ALLIAGES OUVRE
69	METAL MANUFACTURES NES						78907		114076	ART MANUFACT EN METAL NDA
691	STRUCTURES AND PARTS NES	W 10333	3493	W 8462	7366	W 58522	17182		25857	CONSTRUCT FER,ACIER,ALU
6911	STRUCTURES,PARTS IRN,STL					W 57381	15673		23533	CONSTRUCT FER,ACIER,FONTE
692	METAL TANKS,BOXES,ETC					W 24499	6891		10643	RECIPIENTS METALLIQUES
695	TOOLS					W 2003	8614		10926	OUTILS A MAIN
697	BASE MTL HOUSEHOLD EQUIP						8375		14892	ART MENAGE MET COMMUNS
699	BASE METAL MFRS NES						26561		35083	ART MANUFACTURES MET NDA
6991	LOCKSMITHS WARES,ETC						13688		19053	ARTICLES DE SERRURERIE
69913	BASE MTL DOOR,ETC FITTNG					W 7941	9457		14700	GARNITURES POUR MEUBLES
69979	IRN,STL MANUFACTURES NES	W 1786	1518	W 4060	5169	W 25617	4047		4295	AUT OUVRAGES EN FER NDA
7	MACHINES,TRANSPORT EQUIP						757269		942599	MACHINES MATERIEL TRANSPORT
71	POWER GENERATING EQUIPMT						21553		18246	MACHINES GENERATRICES
711	STEAM BOILERS & AUX PLNT					W 120678	10876		5650	GENERATEURS VAPEUR EAU ETC
72	MACHS FOR SPCL INDUSTRYS						63046		78498	MAC SPECIALES POUR INDUST
721	AGRIC MACHY,EXC TRACTORS						9425		13365	MACHINES AGRICOLES
724	TEXTILE,LEATHER MACHNRY						11050		12662	MACH POUR INDUSTRIE TEXTILE
727	FOOD MACHRY NON–DOMESTIC					W 512	6308		10304	MACH INDUSTRIES ALIMENT
7272	OTH FOOD PROC MCHY,PARTS					W 467	6162		10146	AUT MACH IND ALIMENTAIRE
728	OTH MACHY FOR SPCL INDUS						19617		24609	AUT MACH IND PARTICULIERES
7281	MACH–TOOLS FR SPCL INDUS						11191		7726	MACH–OUTILS SPEC IND PART
72812	MACH–TOOLS TO WORK WOOD					N 18554	9121		5537	MACH–OUT POUR TRAVAIL BOIS
7284	MACHY FOR SPCL INDUS NES					W 633	7156		14168	MACH SPEC IND PARTICUL.
74	GENRL INDUSTRL MACHY NES						83405		111203	MACH APP INDUSTRIE
741	HEATING,COOLING EQUIPMNT						20906		27025	MACH CHAUFFAGE,PIECES
742	PUMPS FOR LIQUIDS ETC						8267		11907	POMPES MOTO–POMPES
743	PUMPS NES,CENTRFUGES ETC						12584		20599	POMPES COMPRES,VENT ETC
7436	GAS,LIQUID FILTERS ETC					W 3471	5677		11727	APP POUR FILT DES LIQUIDES
744	MECHANICAL HANDLING EQU						15291		18335	EQUIP MANUTENTION PIECES
745	NONELEC MACHY,TOOLS NES						11639		13529	AUT MACH NON ELEC,PIECES
7452	OTH NONELEC MCHS,PTS NES						8568		11141	AUT MACH NON ELEC,PIECES
749	NONELEC MACH PTS,ACC NES					W 21917	14718		19809	PIECES MACH NON ELEC NDA
7492	COCKS,VALVES ETC NES					W 19446	9805		14435	ART ROB,SIM POUR TUYAUX
75	OFFICE MACHNES,ADP EQUIP						145384		137251	MACH BUREAU TRAIT AUTOM
751	OFFICE MACHINES						7912		8572	MACH,APPAREILS DE BUREAU
752	AUTOMTIC DATA PROC EQUIP					N 1393852	31573		34324	MACH TRAIT INFORMATION
7525	ADP PERIPHERAL UNITS					N 144194	14014		12229	UNITES PERIPHERIQUES
759	OFFICE,ADP MCH PTS,ACCES					W 12611	105898		94355	PIECES DU 751 ET 752

4. General Imports C.I.F. by Commodities according to the S.I.T.C. (Rev. 2) in thousand U.S. Dollars
Importations Générales C.A.F. par Produits d'après la C.T.C.I. (Rév. 2) en milliers de Dollars E.U.

SITC CTCI	COMMODITY	1993 WEIGHT POIDS	1993 VALUE VALEUR	1994 WEIGHT POIDS	1994 VALUE VALEUR	1995 WEIGHT POIDS	1995 VALUE VALEUR	1996 WEIGHT POIDS	1996 VALUE VALEUR	PRODUIT
7591	OFFICE MACHINE PARTS NES					W 3180	25943		13868	PIECES DU 7511,7518
75915	OTH OFF MCH PTS,ACC NES					W 3083	23654		10698	PIECES DU 751.18,81,88
7599	ACCTG,ETC,ADP MCH PTS,AC					W 9431	79955		80487	PIECES DU 751 ET 752
76	TELECOMM,SOUND EQUIPMENT						118222		186470	EQUIPMENT DE TELECOM
761	TELEVISION RECEIVERS						12250		38168	RECEPTEURS DE TELEVISION
7611	COLOUR TV RECEIVERS						11717		38134	RECEPTEURS COULEUR
764	TELECOM EQPT,PTS,ACC NES						97529		130840	EQUIP TELECOM,PIECES
7641	LINE TELEPHONE,ETC EQUIP					W 229	33424		31046	APP TELEPHON PAR FIL
7643	TV,RADIO TRANSMITTRS ETC						6427		12326	APP EMET TELE RADIO
7649	PTS NES OF EQUIPMT OF 76						54200		79723	PIECES DE LA DIV 76
76491	PTS NES OF APPAR OF 7641					W 55	7772		14413	PIECES POUR 764.1
76493	TELECOMM EQUIPMT PTS NES						44241		55844	PIECES 761,762,764.3,8
77	ELECTRIC MACHNRY NES ETC						122940		168430	MACH APP ELECT NDA
772	SWITCHGEAR ETC,PARTS NES					W 2408	18180		25219	APP COUPURE,SECT ETC
7721	SWITCHGEAR ETC					W 2380	17707		24308	APP COUPURE,SECTIONMNT
773	ELECTR DISTRIBUTNG EQUIP					W 34419	21466		29100	EQUIPMT DISTRIBUTION ELECT
7731	INSULATED WIRE,CABLE ETC					W 33286	21037		28237	FILS,CABLES ISOLES ELECT
774	ELECTRO–MEDCL,XRAY EQUIP						13467		12577	APPAREILS MEDICAUX
7742	X–RAY APPARATUS ETC						7944		5674	APPAREILS A RAYONS X
775	HOUSEHOLD TYPE EQUIP NES						35968		55882	MACH,APP USAGE DOMESTQUE
7751	HOUSEHOLD LDRY EQUIP NES						4937		10455	MACH A LAVER ET SECHOIRS
77511	DOMESTIC WASHING MACHNES						4869		10353	MACH LAVER LINGE MOINS 6 KG
7757	DOMESTIC ELECTRC EQU NES						11167		16168	APP ELECTR DOMEST NDA
7758	ELECTRO–THERMIC APPL NES						14026		21627	APP ELECTROTHERMIQ NDA
77586	ELECTROTHERM DOM APP NES					N 124936	5556		10834	APP ELECTRO THERMIQUES
778	ELECTRICAL MACHINERY NES						27710		30135	AUTRES MACH ELECT NDA
7781	BATTERIES,ACCUMULATORS						7650		9824	PILES ET ACCUMULATEURS
7788	OTH ELEC MACHY,EQUIP NES						9926		10478	AUT MACH APP ELEC NDA
78	ROAD VEHICLES						188550		223117	VEHICULES ROUTIERS
781	PASS MOTOR VEH EXC BUSES		69874		70703	N 45142	96299		98562	AUTO TRANSPORT PERSONNES
782	LORRIES,SPCL MTR VEH NES					N 14443	41636		59544	VEHICULES SPECIAUX,MARCH
7821	LORRIES,TRUCKS		21583		20581	N 13141	32270		48555	VEHICULES TRANSP MARCHAND
7822	SPECIAL MOTOR VEHCLS NES		3348		1849	N 1302	9366		10989	VEHICULES USAGES SPECIAUX
784	MOTOR VEH PRTS,ACCES NES						33973		41322	PIECES 722,781,782,783
7849	OTHER MOTOR VEHCL PARTS					W 19389	33276		38904	PIECES 722,781,782,783
786	TRAILERS,NONMOTR VEH,NES						9235		12681	REMORQUES,CADRES,CONTAIN
79	OTHR TRANSPORT EQUIPMENT						7272		10432	AUTRE MATERIEL TRANSPORT
8	MISC MANUFACTURED GOODS						305738		377757	ART MANUFACTURES DIVERS
812	*PLUMBG,HEATNG,LGHTNG EQ					W 20471	21939		26039	APPAR SANITAIRES CHAUFFAGE
8124	LIGHTING EQUIPMENT NES					W 4154	14046		17379	APPAREILS ECLAIRAGE ETC
81242	LAMPS,FITTINGS BASE METL					W 3700	10775		14221	APPAREILS D'ECLAIRAGE
821	*FURNITURE,PARTS THEREOF					W 53758	38132		42725	MEUBLES ET PIECES
8219	FURNITURE AND PARTS NES					W 49393	27777		28682	AUTRES MEUBLES ET PIECES
82192	WOOD FURNITURE NES		7113		13658	W 28359	15731		16747	MEUBLES NDA EN BOIS
84	CLOTHING AND ACCESSORIES						66110		89595	VETEMENTS
842	MENS OUTERWEAR NOT KNIT						11844		14758	VET DESSUS POUR HOMMES
843	WOMENS OUTERWEAR NONKNIT						15438		19996	VET DESSUS FEMMES MAT TEX
8439	— OTHER OUTER GARMENTS						6561		9972	AUT VET DES FEM MAT TEXT
844	UNDER GARMENTS NOT KNIT						11667		13987	VETEMENT DESSOUS MAT TEX
8441	— MENS SHIRTS						11361		13388	CHEMISES HOMMES MAT TEXT
84412	—— OF SYNTHETIC FIBRES					W 2412	9474		10215	CHEMISES HOMMES FIB SYNT
845	OUTERWEAR KNIT NONELASTC						9417		17222	VET DESSOUS,ACCES BONNET
8459	— OTHER,CLTHG ACCESRYS						5454		12297	AUT VET DESSUS DE BONNE
846	UNDER GARMENTS KNITTED						7687		8945	SOUS VETS DE BONNETERIE
851	*FOOTWEAR					P 2962437	22160		27613	CHAUSSURES
85102	FOOTWEAR LEATHER					P 1283994	15007		19315	CHAUS SEMELLES EN CUIR
87	PRECISION INSTRUMNTS NES						30077		42211	INSTRUM,APPAR SCIENT NDA
872	MEDICAL INSTRUMENTS NES					W 307	10855		14149	INSTR,APP MEDIC–CHIR NDA
87202	OTH MEDICAL INSTRUMENTS					W 280	9596		12492	INSTRUM,APP MEDECINE
874	MEASURNG,CONTROLNG INSTR						15348		21881	INSTRUMENTS DE MESURE
88	PHOTO EQU,OPTICL GDS ETC						15593		18066	APP,FOURN PHOTO,OP,MONTR
882	PHOTO,CINEMA SUPPLIES						7880		8654	PRODUITS PHOTO,CINEMA
89	MISC MANUFCTRD GOODS NES						108103		126554	ART MANUFACTURES DIVERS
892	PRINTED MATTER					W 15615	16114		18207	IMPRIMES
8928	PRINTED MATTER NES					W 5893	10507		9777	IMPRIMES NDA
893	ARTICLES OF PLASTIC NES						50563		59282	OUVRAGES EN MAT DIVIS 58
8931	PLSTC PACKG CONTNRS,LIDS					W 19635	12319		17239	ART TRANSP EMBALLAGE ETC
8939	MISC PLASTIC ARTICLES					W 40176	35528		39442	ART DIVERS EN MAT DIV 58
89399	OTHR PLASTC ARTICLES NES					W 35246	29511		32113	AUT OUV MAT DIV 58
894	TOYS,SPORTING GOODS,ETC						12761		14504	VOITURES ENFANTS,JOUETS
8942	TOYS,INDOOR GAMES ETC						8940		9926	JOUETS,JEUX ETC
899	OTHER MANUFACTURED GOODS						13665		18297	AUT ART MANUF DIVERS NDA

5. General Exports F.O.B. by Commodities according to the S.I.T.C. (Rev. 2) in thousand U.S. Dollars
Exportations Générales F.O.B. par Produits d'après la C.T.C.I. (Rév. 2) en milliers de Dollars E.U.

SITC CTCI	COMMODITY	1993 WEIGHT POIDS	1993 VALUE VALEUR	1994 WEIGHT POIDS	1994 VALUE VALEUR	1995 WEIGHT POIDS	1995 VALUE VALEUR	1996 WEIGHT POIDS	1996 VALUE VALEUR	PRODUIT
	ALL COMMODITIES		803900		1305900		1838816		2074056	TOUS PRODUITS
0	FOOD AND LIVE ANIMALS						272578		290286	ALIMENTS,ANIMAUX VIVANTS
01	MEAT AND PREPARATIONS						16042		8415	VIANDES ET PREPARATIONS
011	MEAT FRESH,CHILLD,FROZEN			W 2416	3435	W 42543	7641		3859	VIANDES FRAICHES,REF,CONGE
014	MEAT PREPD,PRSVD,NES ETC					W 26804	8194		4504	CONSERVES DE VIANDES
0141	MEAT,FISH EXTRCTS,JUICES				69812		4		17	EXTRAITS DE VIANDE
0142	SAUSAGES INCLDING TINNED					W 20229	5550		3037	SAUCISSES,SAUCISSONS
02	DAIRY PRODCTS,BIRDS'EGGS						88199		94752	PRODUITS LAITIERS,OEUFS
022	MILK AND CREAM					W 321705	50193		52551	LAIT ET CREME
0223	MILK AND CREAM FRESH					W 69522	5023		13271	LAIT,CREME FRAIS
0224	MILK,CREAM PRESERVED ETC					W 252184	45170		39280	LAIT,CREME CONS,CONC
02242	MILK DRY,1.5% FAT OR LES					W 233593	41639		37688	LAIT POUDRE INF 1.5%
023	BUTTER					W 124804	26903		28173	BEURRE
024	CHEESE AND CURD					W 40649	10362		13274	FROMAGE ET CAILLEBOTTE
03	FISH AND PREPARATIONS				36453		104589		98943	POISSONS ET PREPARATIONS
034	FISH,FRESH,CHILLED,FROZN					W 477704	38999		25502	POISSON FRAIS, REFRIG,CONG
0342	FISH FROZEN,EXCL FILLETS					W 446621	24101		9859	POISSONS CONGELES
0343	FISH FILLETS,FRESH,CHLLD					W 8231	6913		8748	FILETS FRAIS,REFRIGERES
037	FISH ETC PREPD,PRSVD NES					W 409527	62532		69827	POIS,CRUST,MOL PREPARES
0371	FISH PREPARD,PRESRVD NES					W 409415	61630		69228	CONSERVES DE POISSONS
04	CEREALS AND PREPARATIONS						5886		13143	CEREALES ET PRODUITS
048	CEREAL ETC PREPARATIONS					W 55374	4573		9360	PREPTNS A BASE CEREALES
0484	BAKERY PRODUCTS					W 10465	2676		7896	PRODUITS DE BOULANGERIE
04842	PASTRY, CAKES ETC					W 8373	2224		7265	PATISSERIE ETC.
05	VEGETABLES AND FRUIT						8206		13001	LEGUMES ET FRUITS
057	FRUIT,NUTS,FRESH,DRIED				7452	W 14915	1843		2795	FRUITS FRAIS OU SECS
058	FRUIT PRESERVED,PREPARED				6219	W 37501	3842		7800	CONSERVES DE FRUITS
06	SUGAR AND PREPS,HONEY				18967		9352		12723	SUCRES ET PRODUITS
062	SUGAR CANDY NON–CHOCLATE					W 10467	7188		8576	SUCRERIES
07	COFFEE,TEA,COCOA,SPICES				33584		21953		31168	CAFE,THE,CACAO,EPICES
071	COFFEE AND SUBSTITUTES					W 4613	7037		7258	CAFE ET SUCCEDANES
0711	COFFEE GREEN,ROASTED,SUB					W 4396	5525		5398	CAFE TORREFIE OU DECAFEINE
072	COCOA					W 16531	3307		15152	CACAO
0721	COCOA BEANS,RAW,ROASTED					W 16339	2877		14011	CACAO EN FEVES
073	CHOCOLATE AND PRODUCTS					W 30904	10877		6677	CHOCOLAT
081	*FEEDING STUFF FOR ANIML					W 123340	5989		2617	NOURRITURE POUR ANIMAUX
09	MISC EDIBLE PRODUCTS						10472		14857	PREP ALIMENTAIRES DIVERSES
091	MARGARINE AND SHORTENING					W 38619	5635		5108	MARGARINE ET GRAISSES
0914	MARGARINE,EDIBLE FAT NES					W 38580	5594		5108	MARGARINES,SIMILI SAINDOUX
098	EDIBLE PRODCTS,PREPS NES						4837		9749	PREP ALIMENTAIRES NDA
09809	MISC FOOD PREPRTIONS NES					W 20427	3491		8050	PREP ALIMENTAIRES NDA
1	BEVERAGES AND TOBACCO				26171		15242		21805	BOISSONS ET TABACS
11	BEVERAGES				17455		13658		17186	BOISSONS
111	NON–ALCOHL BEVERAGES NES					W 220935	7510		12592	BOISSONS NON ALCOOLIQUES
11102	FLAVORED WATERS NON–ALCO					W 218611	7308		12379	LIMONADES,EAUX GAZEUSES
112	ALCOHOLIC BEVERAGES					W 11634	6148		4594	BOISSONS ALCOOLIQUES
12	TOBACCO AND MANUFACTURES				8716		1583		4619	TABACS BRUTS FABRIQUES
2	CRUDE MATERLS,EXCL FUELS						219265		210264	MAT BRUTES NON COMESTIBLES
21	HIDES,SKINS,FURS UNDRSSD						11261		9902	CUIRS,PEAUX BRUTS
211	HIDES,SKINS,EXC FURS,RAW						7440		5417	CUIRS ET PEAUX
24	CORK AND WOOD						155391		149875	LIEGE ET BOIS
246	PULPWOOD,CHIPS,WOODWASTE					W 708359	3138		6507	BOIS DE TRITURATION
247	OTH WOOD ROUGH,SQUARED					MW 16262	102579		76214	BOIS BRUTS EQUARRIS
2471	SAW–,VENEER–LOGS CONIFER					W 7919520	59984		49241	CONIFERES POUR SCIAGE,PLACAG
24711	— IN THE ROUGH					W 7919520	59984		49241	ECORCES OU DEGROSSIS
2472	SAW–,VENEER–LOGS NON–CON					W 8342888	42595		26973	NON CONIFERES SCIAGE,PLAC
24721	— IN THE ROUGH					W 8342888	42595		26973	BRUTS ECORCES DEGROSSIS
248	WOOD SHAPED,SLEEPERS						49186		66485	BOIS SIMPLEMENT TRAVAILLES
2482	LUMBER SHAPED CONIFER						46208		61384	CONIFERES SCIES,RABOTES
24821	LUMBER SAWN ETC CONIFER						45040		56750	CONIFERES SCIES LONGITUD
27861	SLAG ETC FRM IRN,STL MFR	W 203070	10759	W 191413	16772				5	SCORIES,LAITIER,BATTIT
28	METALLIFEROUS ORES,SCRAP						37901		36424	MINERAIS METAL,DECHETS
282	IRON AND STEEL SCRAP					W 2544349	21968		22201	– FERRAILLES
28209	— OF OTHR IRON OR STEEL					W 2265732	16697		15776	FERRAILLES DE FER
288	NONFERR METAL SCRAP NES					W 190708	13203		10598	DECHETS NON FERREUX
2882	OTHER BASE MTL SCRAP NES					W 190708	13203		10598	AUTRES DECHETS
28821	COPPER WASTE AND SCRAP					W 51220	6312		4587	DECHETS DE CUIVRE
29	CRUDE ANIMAL,VEG MAT NES						6709		5086	MATIERES BRUTES ANIM,VEGET
292	CRUDE VEG MATERIALS NES						6125		4800	MAT BRUTES VEGETALES NDA
3	MINERAL FUELS ETC						130351		132069	COMBUSTIBLES MINERAUX LUB
32	COAL,COKE AND BRIQUETTES						21283		24076	HOUILLES,COKES,BRIQUETTES
322	COAL,LIGNITE AND PEAT					W 4092600	14291		16131	HOUILLES,LIGNITES,TOURBE
3224	PEAT,NOT AGGLOMERATED					W 3674999	12894		14127	TOURBE
323	BRIQUETS,COKE,SEMI–COKE					W 390216	6991		7944	BRIQUETTES
3232	COKE,SEMI–COKE,RTRT CRBN					W 390215	6990		7944	COKES ET SEMI–COKES
33	PETROLEUM AND PRODUCTS						87597		80677	PETROLE ET DERIVES
334	PETROLEUM PRODUCTS,REFIN					W 3106949	59686		62964	PRODUITS RAFFINES
335	RESIDUAL PETRLM PROD NES					W 2172016	27911		17253	PRODUITS RESIDUELS NDA
3352	MINERAL TARS AND PRODCTS					W 1938277	24090		11421	GOUDRONS MINERAUX
33521	MINERAL TAR					W 1337126	9772		8469	GOUDRONS DE HOUILLE
33522	BENZOLE					W 441355	11172		1761	BENZOLS
351	*ELECTRIC CURRENT					MH 9105	21463		27268	ENERGIE ELECTRIQUE
5	CHEMCLS,RELATED PROD NES						150509		197995	PRODUITS CHIMIQUES
51	ORGANIC CHEMICALS						20533		35552	PROD CHIMIQ ORGANIQUES
511	HYDROCARBONS NES,DERIVS					W 117396	2777		7756	HYDROCARBURES NDA
512	ALCOHOLS,PHENOLS ETC						4108		6234	PHENOLS,PHENOLS–ALCOOLS
513	CARBOXYLIC ACIDS ETC					W 218183	12599		12574	ACIDES CARBOXYLIQUES
5137	MONOACIDS AND DERIVATIVS					W 218073	12388		12384	ACIDES MONOCARBOXYLIQUES
51379	OTH MONOACIDS ETC,DERIVS					W 216884	12017		12123	AUTRES MONOCARBOXYLIQUES
515	ORG–INORG COMPOUNDS ETC					W 1088	423		7531	COMPOSES ORGANO–MINERAUX
5156	HETEROCYCLIC CMPDS ETC								7524	COMPOSES HETEROCYCLIQUES
51561	LACTAMS								7524	LACTAMES .
52	INORGANIC CHEMICALS						35258		37488	PROD CHIM INORGANIQUES
522	INORG ELEMNTS,OXIDES,ETC						21064		23202	ELEMENTS INORGANIQUES
5225	INORGANIC BASES ETC NES					W 1199183	19769		20915	AUTRES BASES OXYDES METAL
52251	AMMONIA,ANHYDROUS ETC					W 1199175	19727		19776	AMMONIAC LIQUEFIE
524	RADIOACTIVE ETC MATERIAL						12750		12021	MATIERES RADIOACTIVES
5249	OTH RADIOACTIVE ETC MTLS						12750		12013	AUT MATIERES RADIOACTIVES
52492	OTH CHEMS ASSOC RADIOACT						12750		12013	COMPOSES THORIUM,URANIUM
53	DYES,TANNING,COLOUR PROD						25842		36765	PROD TEINTURE,COLORANTS
533	PIGMENTS,PAINTS,ETC					W 68447	25285		36291	PIGMENTS,PEINTURES,VERNIS

5. General Exports F.O.B. by Commodities according to the S.I.T.C. (Rev. 2) in thousand U.S. Dollars
Exportations Générales F.O.B. par Produits d'après la C.T.C.I. (Rév. 2) en milliers de Dollars E.U.

SITC CTCI	COMMODITY	1993		1994		1995		1996		PRODUIT
		WEIGHT POIDS	VALUE VALEUR	WEIGHT POIDS	VALUE VALEUR	WEIGHT POIDS	VALUE VALEUR	WEIGHT POIDS	VALUE VALEUR	
5334	VARNISHES,DISTEMPERS ETC					W 41644	18058		24283	PEINTURES A L'EAU
53342	OTH PAINTS,VARNISHES ETC					W 36058	15560		22342	AUTRES PEINTURES,VERNIS
5335	GLAZES,DRIERS,PUTTY ETC					W 26755	6976		11588	PREPTNS COLOR UTILISES CERAM
53354	PUTTY,OTHER FILLINGS ETC					W 26655	6775		11501	MASTICS ENDUITS
541	*MEDICINAL,PHARM PRODUCT					MK 14646	19878		25984	PROD MEDICINAUX PHARMACEUT
5417	MEDICAMENTS					MK 14503	18739		24270	MEDICAMENTS
54179	— CONTNG OTH SUBSTANCES					MK 14403	16647		20611	MED CONT AUT SUBSTANCES
55	PERFUME,CLEANING ETC PRD						10463		8876	PROD POUR PARFUM,TOILETTE
554	SOAP,CLEANSING ETC PREPS					W 32286	6696		4263	SAVONS,PRODUITS DETERSIFS
562	*FERTILIZERS,MANUFACTURE						18661		32570	ENGRAIS MANUFACTURES
5621	CHEM NITROGENOUS FERTLZR						16741		15687	ENGRAIS AZOTES
56216	UREA						14949		13100	UREE
5629	FERTILIZERS NES					W 34333	553		16882	ENGRAIS NDA
56292	NITROG–PHOS FERTILZR NES					W 22210	413		16008	ENGRAIS NDA CONT N P
58	PLASTIC MATERIALS ETC						13060		14730	MAT PLAST ARTIFICIELLES
582	PROD OF CONDENSATION ETC					W 77870	6364		8009	PROD CONDENS,POLYCOND
583	POLYMERIZATION ETC PRODS					W 53093	6396		6615	PROD POLYMERISATION
59	CHEMICAL MATERIALS NES						6805		6009	MAT PROD CHIMIQUES NDA
6	BASIC MANUFACTURES						363719		451370	ART MANUFACTURES
61	LEATHER,DRESSED FUR,ETC						14077		19617	CUIRS,PELLETERIES
612	LEATHER ETC MANUFACTURES					W 3204	8126		8379	OUVRAGES EN CUIRS NDA
6123	PREPRD PARTS OF FOOTWEAR					W 3189	7568		7864	PARTIES DE CHAUSSURES
613	FUR SKINS TANNED,DRESSED					N 32994	1745		7463	PELLETERIES
62	RUBBER MANUFACTURES NES						10729		7096	CAOUTCHOUC MANUFACTURE
625	RUBBER TYRES, TUBES ETC						8465		4065	PNEUS CAOUTCHOUC VULCANISE
63	WOOD,CORK MANUFACTRS NES						76914		92128	OUVRAGES LIEGE ET BOIS
634	VENEERS,PLYWOOD,ETC						40994		45922	PLACAGES,CONTRE–PLAQUES
6342	PLYWOOD OF WOOD SHEETS					V 64460	25450		28416	BOIS CONTRE–PLAQUES
6343	IMPROVED,RECONSTIT WOOD					V 93692	13296		14378	BOIS AMELIORES,RECONST
63432	RECONSTITUTED WOOD		2083		2886	V 92970	13005		14305	BOIS RECONSTITUES
635	WOOD MANUFACTURES NES					W 502529	35911		46177	ART MANUF EN BOIS NDA
6351	BOXES,CASES,CRATES,ETC		1811		4156	W 301067	8481		9966	CAISSES EMBALLAGES BOIS
6353	BUILDERS WOODWRK,PREFABS		4620		9676	W 177477	19505		25980	OUVRAGES DE MENUISERIE
6354	WOOD MFRS DOMESTIC ETC					W 12421	5394		7085	ART MANUF USAGE DOMESTIQUE
64	PAPER,PAPERBOARD AND MFR						23206		45229	PAPIERS,CARTONS & OUVRAGES
641	PAPER AND PAPERBOARD						12990		30970	PAPIERS ET CARTONS
6413	KRAFT PAPER,PAPERBOARD					W 2451	434		9360	PAPIER ET CARTON KRAFT
6416	FIBRE BUILDING BOARD					A 75978	6938		9832	PLAQUES CONSTRUCT EN PATE
64161	HARDBOARD					A 73728	6446		7410	PLAQUES CONSTR COMPRIMES
64162	INSULATING BOARD, ETC		3050		4368	A 2249	492		2422	PLAQUES CONST NON COMPR
642	PAPER,ETC,PRECUT,ARTS OF					W 24119	10215		14259	PAP,CARTONS DECOUPES
65	TEXTILE YARN,FABRICS,ETC						105833		141653	FILS,TISSUS,ARTICLES TEXTILE
651	TEXTILE YARN					W 12901	9132		10853	FILS TEXTILES
6513	COTTON YARN					W 10635	5438		6538	FILS DE COTON
652	COTTON FABRICS,WOVEN						45312		61028	TISSUS DE COTON
6521	GREY WOVEN COTTON FABRIC						15569		29042	TISSUS COT ECRUS NON MERCER
65214	GREY WOVEN COTTON NES						15442		28836	AUT TISSUS 85% COTON ECRUS
6522	WOVEN COTTON BLEACHD,ETC						29744		31986	TISSUS COTON BLANCHIS ETC
65224	BLCHED COTTON FABRIC NES						28122		28878	AUT TIS PLUS 85% COT BLANCHI
657	SPECIAL TXTL FABRC,PRODS						17150		26084	TISSUS SPECIAUX
6577	TEXTILES FOR MACHINERY					W 7248	5283		13046	OUATES,MECHES ART TEXT
65771	TEXTILE WADDING NES ETC					W 7199	5174		12867	OUATES,ARTICLES EN OUATE
658	TEXTILE ARTICLES NES						27283		33603	ART FACONNES MAT TEXTILES
6584	LINENS ETC						21188		24320	LINGE DE MAISON
65841	BED LINEN OF COTTON					W 12456	10513		10679	LINGE DE LIT DE COTON
65845	OTHER LINEN OF COTTON					W 5302	5408		7004	LINGE DE TOILETTE COTON
66	NONMETAL MINERAL MFS NES						42521		46348	ART MIN NON METALLIQUES
661	LIME,CEMENT,BLDG PRODS						15520		16120	CHAUX,CIMENTS MAT CONSTR
6612	CEMENT					W 5151846	14994		15146	CIMENTS HYDRAULIQUES
663	MINERAL MANUFCTURES NES						6895		6471	ART MIN MANUF NDA
6633	MINRL MFS NES NONCERAMIC						6204		5766	OUVR MAT MINERALE NDA
66332	CEMENT,ARTFCL STONE PROD						5683		4901	OUVRAGES EN CIMENT
664	GLASS						10466		10623	VERRE
665	GLASSWARE						7990		11007	OUVRAGES EN VERRE
6651	BOTTLES ETC OF GLASS						6555		9378	RECIPIENTS EN VERRE
66511	GLASS BOTTLES ETC NONVAC						6555		9378	BONBONNES,BOUTEILLES,ETC
67	IRON AND STEEL						23256		21236	FER ET ACIER
674	IRN,STL UNIV,PLATE,SHEET					W 145972	6177		10854	LARGES PLATS,TOLES
68	NON–FERROUS METALS						15596		10611	METAUX NON FERREUX
683	NICKEL					W 13728	7882		2029	NICKEL
6832	NICKEL,ALLOYS WORKED					W 13702	7803		2029	NICKEL,ALLIAGES OUVRES
68322	NICKEL SHEET,POWDER,FOIL					W 13422	7034		1919	TOLES,PLANCHES, FEUILLES NI
69	METAL MANUFACTURES NES						51587		67453	ART MANUFACT EN METAL NDA
691	STRUCTURES AND PARTS NES	W 9260	2739	W 8005	6731	W 98502	15460		35322	CONSTRUCT FER,ACIER,ALU
6911	STRUCTURES,PARTS IRN,STL					W 97425	14852		34279	CONSTRUCT FER,ACIER,FONTE
699	BASE METAL MFRS NES						24507		17771	ART MANUFACTURES MET NDA
6991	LOCKSMITHS WARES,ETC						6119		6846	ARTICLES DE SERRURERIE
6997	IRON,STEEL ARTICLES NES					W 53593	9183		7281	OUV FONTE,FER,ACIER NDA
69979	IRN,STL MANUFACTURES NES	W 2414	1845	W 5710	3860	W 53593	9183		7270	AUT OUVRAGES EN FER NDA
6999	OTHR BASE METAL MFRS ETC					W 1245	6005		892	OUVRAGES EN TUNGST,MOLYB
7	MACHINES,TRANSPORT EQUIP						366646		410510	MACHINES MATERIEL TRANSPORT
71	POWER GENERATING EQUIPMT						12861		14653	MACHINES GENERATRICES
711	STEAM BOILERS & AUX PLNT					W 11356	5823		5216	GENERATEURS VAPEUR EAU ETC
72	MACHS FOR SPCL INDUSTRYS						21763		24272	MAC SPECIALES POUR INDUST
728	OTH MACHY FOR SPCL INDUS						3640		6487	AUT MACH IND PARTICULIERES
74	GENRL INDUSTRL MACHY NES						27443		29625	MACH APP INDUSTRIE
741	HEATING,COOLING EQUIPMNT						12411		11354	MACH CHAUFFAGE,PIECES
7416	HEATING,COOLING EQU NES					W 27610	10318		8364	APP CHANGEMENT TEMP
749	NONELEC MACH PTS,ACC NES					W 6766	5385		6470	PIECES MACH NON ELEC NDA
75	OFFICE MACHNES,ADP EQUIP						89388		71445	MACH BUREAU TRAIT AUTOM
759	OFFICE,ADP MCH PTS,ACCES					W 12225	85466		66020	PIECES DU 751 ET 752
7591	OFFICE MACHINE PARTS NES					W 8092	59295		8902	PIECES DU 7511,7518
75915	OTH OFF MCH PTS,ACC NES					W 8076	58493		8097	PIECES DU 751.18,81,88
7599	ACCTG,ETC,ADP MCH PTS,AC					W 4133	26171		57118	PIECES DU 751 ET 752
76	TELECOMM,SOUND EQUIPMENT						47840		82530	EQUIPMENT DE TELECOM
761	TELEVISION RECEIVERS						3990		9673	RECEPTEURS DE TELEVISION
7611	COLOUR TV RECEIVERS						3949		9670	RECEPTEURS COULEUR
764	TELECOM EQPT,PTS,ACC NES						42718		70695	EQUIP TELECOM,PIECES
7641	LINE TELEPHONE,ETC EQUIP						2692		9244	APP TELEPHON PAR FIL
7649	PTS NES OF EQUIPMT OF 76						36578		55828	PIECES DE LA DIV 76
76493	TELECOMM EQUIPMT PTS NES						34224		48539	PIECES 761,762,764.3,8

5. General Exports F.O.B. by Commodities according to the S.I.T.C. (Rev. 2) in thousand U.S. Dollars
Exportations Générales F.O.B. par Produits d'après la C.T.C.I. (Rév. 2) en milliers de Dollars E.U.

SITC CTCI	COMMODITY	1993		1994		1995		1996		PRODUIT
		WEIGHT POIDS	VALUE VALEUR	WEIGHT POIDS	VALUE VALEUR	WEIGHT POIDS	VALUE VALEUR	WEIGHT POIDS	VALUE VALEUR	
76499	PARTS ETC OF SOUND EQUIP					W 10	1897		6746	PIECES NDA POUR 763
77	ELECTRIC MACHNRY NES ETC						38974		54098	MACH APP ELECT NDA
772	SWITCHGEAR ETC,PARTS NES					W 1332	4358		6988	APP COUPURE,SECT ETC
773	ELECTR DISTRIBUTNG EQUIP					W 12505	13825		21642	EQUIPMT DISTRIBUTION ELECT
7731	INSULATED WIRE,CABLE ETC					W 12479	13769		21318	FILS,CABLES ISOLES ELECT
775	HOUSEHOLD TYPE EQUIP NES						5144		8517	MACH,APP USAGE DOMESTQUE
778	ELECTRICAL MACHINERY NES						10789		10001	AUTRES MACH ELECT NDA
7788	OTH ELEC MACHY,EQUIP NES						8191		3550	AUT MACH APP ELEC NDA
78	ROAD VEHICLES						113714		115845	VEHICULES ROUTIERS
781	PASS MOTOR VEH EXC BUSES		49305		43115	N 9655	59800		59852	AUTO TRANSPORT PERSONNES
782	LORRIES,SPCL MTR VEH NES					N 366	10228		6527	VEHICULES SPECIAUX,MARCH
7822	SPECIAL MOTOR VEHCLS NES		4409		4788	N 186	7599		4233	VEHICULES USAGES SPECIAUX
784	MOTOR VEH PRTS,ACCES NES						37271		40693	PIECES 722,781,782,783
7849	OTHER MOTOR VEHCL PARTS						37159		40597	PIECES 722,781,782,783
79	OTHR TRANSPORT EQUIPMENT						12114		14549	AUTRE MATERIEL TRANSPORT
793	SHIPS AND BOATS ETC						9902		11009	NAVIRES BATEAUX,ETC
7932	SHIPS AND BOATS NES						9355		10527	NAVIRES ET BATEAUX
8	MISC MANUFACTURED GOODS						314591		354669	ART MANUFACTURES DIVERS
812	*PLUMBG,HEATNG,LGHTNG EQ					W 1992	7384		7830	APPAR SANITAIRES CHAUFFAGE
8124	LIGHTING EQUIPMENT NES					W 1563	6108		6204	APPAREILS ECLAIRAGE ETC
821	*FURNITURE,PARTS THEREOF					W 270174	68991		86762	MEUBLES ET PIECES
8211	CHAIRS,SEATS AND PARTS					W 37406	12873		18189	SIEGES ET PIECES
82111	CHAIRS AND OTHER SEATS					W 37109	12047		16717	SIEGES
8212	MED FURN,STUFFD FURNSHGS					W 10541	6318		7256	MOB MEDICO–CHIRUR,PIECES
82122	MATTRESSES ETC					W 10449	5876		6896	SOMMIERS,ARTICLES DE LITERIE
8219	FURNITURE AND PARTS NES					W 222226	49801		61317	AUTRES MEUBLES ET PIECES
82192	WOOD FURNITURE NES		20581		35518	W 176087	39009		43850	MEUBLES NDA EN BOIS
82199	OTHR FURN,FURN PARTS NES					W 41764	9058		15331	MEUBLES NDA AUTRES MATIERES
84	CLOTHING AND ACCESSORIES						145117		158664	VETEMENTS
842	MENS OUTERWEAR NOT KNIT						35256		47093	VET DESSUS POUR HOMMES
8423	— TROUSERS,BREECHES ETC					N 4464248	10642		15216	PANTALONS HOMMES MAT TEX
8424	— JACKETS,BLAZERS ETC						6485		7028	VESTES HOMMES MAT TEXTIL
8429	— OTHER OUTER GARMENTS						10881		15551	AUT VET DES HOM MAT TEX
843	WOMENS OUTERWEAR NONKNIT						58373		55701	VET DESSUS FEMMES MAT TEX
8431	— COATS AND JACKETS						7847		7525	MANT,VEST FEM MAT TEXTIL
8435	— BLOUSES					N 6387614	13846		13166	BLOUSES FEM MAT TEXTILES
8439	— OTHER OUTER GARMENTS						31074		29103	AUT VET DES FEM MAT TEXT
845	OUTERWEAR KNIT NONELASTC						26060		26778	VET DESSOUS,ACCES BONNET
8451	— JERSEYS,PULLOVERS ETC						7826		8954	CHANDAILS,PULL–OVERS ETC
8459	— OTHER,CLTHG ACCESRYS						16185		15896	AUT VET DESSUS DE BONNE
846	UNDER GARMENTS KNITTED						13982		15398	SOUS VETS DE BONNETERIE
8462	— OF COTTON NON ELASTIC						10709		11159	SOUS–VET BONNET COTON
84629	—— OTHER					MN 24297	10361		10727	AUT SOUS–VET BONNET COTON
851	*FOOTWEAR					P 1189939	16138		21773	CHAUSSURES
85101	FOOTWEAR RUBBER,PLASTIC					P 523639	6553		8917	CHAUS SEMELLES CAOUTCH
85102	FOOTWEAR LEATHER					P 418334	7329		11633	CHAUS SEMELLES EN CUIR
87	PRECISION INSTRUMNTS NES						12180		21468	INSTRUM,APPAR SCIENT NDA
874	MEASURNG,CONTROLNG INSTR						6510		12776	INSTRUMENTS DE MESURE
89	MISC MANUFCTRD GOODS NES						61340		53767	ART MANUFACTURES DIVERS
893	ARTICLES OF PLASTIC NES						24820		19487	OUVRAGES EN MAT DIVIS 58
8931	PLSTC PACKG CONTNRS,LIDS					W 30392	14639		7677	ART TRANSP EMBALLAGE ETC
8939	MISC PLASTIC ARTICLES					W 5778	8261		9708	ART DIVERS EN MAT DIV 58
89399	OTHR PLASTC ARTICLES NES					W 3182	5434		6723	AUT OUV MAT DIV 58
894	TOYS,SPORTING GOODS,ETC						16827		14631	VOITURES ENFANTS,JOUETS
8947	OTH SPORT GDS,FAIR AMUSM						14160		11401	AUT ART DE SPORT
89472	OTH OUTDOOR SPORT GOODS						13214		11051	ART POUR JEUX PLEIN AIR
899	OTHER MANUFACTURED GOODS						7526		8458	AUT ART MANUF DIVERS NDA

1. HISTORICAL SERIES, 1961–1996 GENERAL TRADE, IMPORTS C.I.F., EXPORTS F.O.B. # 1
SERIES HISTORIQUES, 1961–1996 COMMERCE GENERAL, IMPORTATIONS C.A.F., EXPORTATIONS F.O.B

YEAR ANNEE	VALUE IN MILLION BIRR # 2 VALEUR EN MILLION BIRR # 2 MERCHANDISE – MARCHANDISE		GOLD – OR		CONVERSION FACTORS U.S. CENTS PER BIRR FACTEURS DE CONVERSION CENTS E.U. PAR BIRR		INDEX NUMBERS – INDICES QUANTUM		UNIT VALUE VALEUR UNITAIRE	
	IMPORTS	EXPORTS	IMPORTS	EXPORTS	IMPORTS	EXPORTS	IMPORTS	EXPORTS	IMPORTS	EXPORTS
1961	228.50	184.20		2.43	40.2500	40.2500		152		49
1962	257.00	199.50			40.2500	40.2500		146		49
1963	276.10	223.40			40.2500	40.2500				
1964	307.70	262.50			40.0000	40.0000				
1965	375.70	289.80			40.0000	40.0000				
1966	404.30	277.00			40.0000	40.0000		113		
1967	357.40	252.70			40.0000	40.0000		113		
1968	432.50	266.00			40.0000	40.0000		119		57
1969	388.30	298.10			40.0000	40.0000		127		57
1970	429.10	305.80			40.0000	40.0000		107		55
1971	469.50	314.10			40.0000	40.0000		123		49
1972	435.60	385.00			43.1050	43.1040		145		51
1973	448.20	503.20			47.9700	47.8390		159		59
1974	586.00	556.20			48.3090	48.3090		132		63
1975	613.10	497.80			48.3090	48.3090		119		57
1976	736.70	603.90			48.3090	48.3090		116		76
1977	810.90	722.00			48.3090	48.3090		85		131
1978	1080.80	640.90			48.3090	48.3090		93		109
1979	1174.60	864.30			48.3090	48.3090		142		140
1980	1494.70	879.10			48.3090	48.3090		104		115
1981	1526.60	805.10			48.3092	48.3092		106		105
1982	1623.40	836.30			48.3508	48.3555		113		110
1983	1813.30	832.80			48.3092	48.3092		122		107
1984	1951.10	863.60			48.3092	48.3092		121		110
1985	2046.40	699.20			48.3092	48.3092		96		110
1986	2278.71	961.33			48.3091	48.3091		111		146
1987	2279.54	765.60			48.3092	48.3092		104		107
1988	2245.90	871.70			48.3092	48.3092		106		111
1989	1972.20	935.00			48.3092	48.3092		115		108
1990	2238.50	615.84			48.3091	48.3092		100		100
1991	976.80	390.48			48.3092	48.3091		57		97
1992	2604.30	448.39			32.9779	37.6683		50		104
1993	3936.70	994.16			20.0000	20.0000		125		157
1994	5658.00	2062.38			18.2554	18.0565				214
1995		2602.91			16.2035	16.2139				215
1996		2650.55				15.7448				226

2. IMPORTS BY BROAD ECONOMIC CATEGORY AND EXPORTS BY INDUSTRIAL ORIGIN. (PERCENTAGE OF TOTAL VALUE)
IMPORTATIONS PAR CATEGORIES ECONOMIQUES ET EXPORTATIONS PAR BRANCHE D'ACTIVITE. (EN POURCENTAGE DE LA VALEUR TOTALE)

IMPORTS – IMPORTATIONS

	1990	1991	1992	1993	1994	1995	1996
TOTAL IMPORTS–IMPORTATIONS TOTALES	100.	100.	100.	100.			
1 FOOD BEV–ALIMENTATION BOISSONS	13.4	5.1	13.4	12.5			
11 PRIMARY–PRODUITS DE BASE	7.9	2.8	11.0	9.0			
111 FOR INDUSTRY–POUR L'INDUSTRIE	7.2	2.4	10.8	8.3			
112 FOR HOUSEHOLDS–POUR LES MENAGES	0.6	0.3	0.2	0.7			
12 PROCESSED–PRODUITS ELABORES	5.5	2.3	2.4	3.5			
121 FOR INDUSTRY–POUR L'INDUSTRIE	2.5	0.3	0.7	1.2			
122 FOR HOUSEHOLDS–POUR LES MENAGES	3.0	2.0	1.8	2.3			
2 IND SUPPLIES–APPROV INDUSTRIELS	24.4	24.0	18.7	26.7			
21 PRIMARY–PRODUITS DE BASE	2.2	1.0	0.9	1.4			
22 PROCESSED–PRODUITS ELABORES	22.3	23.0	17.8	25.3			
3 FUELS–COMBUSTIBLES	11.7	10.5	22.7	21.4			
31 PRIMARY–PRODUITS DE BASE	10.5	6.2	15.3	9.4			
32 PROCESSED–PRODUITS ELABORES	1.2	4.4	7.4	12.0			
321 MOTOR SPIRIT–ESSENCE	0.0	1.5	2.4	0.6			
322 OTHER–AUTRES	1.2	2.9	5.1	11.4			
4 MACHINERY–EQUIPEMENT	23.3	17.1	13.6	11.6			
41 CAPITAL EQUIPMENT–MACHINES	20.9	14.4	11.6	10.0			
42 PARTS–PIECES ACCESSOIRES	2.3	2.7	2.0	1.6			
5 TRANSPORT–TRANSPORT	18.2	29.7	17.2	17.1			
51 PASSENGER CARS–AUTOMOBILES	3.9	5.6	3.2	3.8			
52 OTHER–AUTRES	9.0	18.7	6.3	7.1			
521 INDUSTRIAL–INDUSTRIELS	8.9	18.6	6.1	7.1			
522 NON INDUSTRIAL–NON INDUSTRIEL	0.1	0.1	0.2	0.1			
53 PARTS–PIECES ACCESSOIRES	5.3	5.5	7.7	6.1			
6 CONSUM GOODS–BIENS CONSOMMATION	8.8	13.2	14.3	10.7			
61 DURABLE–DURABLES	1.6	2.4	2.1	1.4			
62 SEMI DURABLE–SEMI DURABLES	3.0	4.0	5.3	2.9			
63 NON DURABLE–NON DURABLES	4.2	6.8	6.9	6.3			
7 GOODS NES–BIENS NDA	0.3	0.3	0.0	0.0			

EXPORTS – EXPORTATIONS

	1990	1991	1992	1993	1994	1995	1996
TOTAL EXPORTS–EXPORTATIONS TOTALES	100.	100.	100.	100.			
1 AGRICULTURE	60.8	77.6	70.7	76.5			
2 MINING QUARRY–INDUS EXTRACTIVES	0.0	0.0					
3 MANUFACTURING–IND MANUFACTUR	39.1	22.4	29.2	23.5			
31 FOOD BEV TOBACCO–ALIM BOISS TAB	27.5	16.8	19.5	18.8			
32 TEXTILES–INDUSTRIES TEXTILES	3.1	2.4	1.1	0.6			
33 WOOD & PRODUCTS–BOIS & PRODUITS			0.0	0.0			
34 PAPER & PRODUCTS–PAPIER & PRODT	0.2	0.1	0.0	0.0			
35 CHEMICALS–INDUSTRIES CHIMIQUES	8.2	2.5	8.6	4.1			
36 NON METAL MIN–MIN NON METAL	0.0		0.0				
37 BASIC METAL–IND METAL BASE		0.0		0.0			
38 METAL MANUF–MANUF METAL	0.0	0.0	0.0	0.0			
39 OTH MANUF IND–AUTRES MANUF	0.0	0.6	0.0	0.0			

3. TRADE BY PRINCIPAL COUNTRIES OF PRODUCTION AND LAST CONSIGNMENT (VALUE IN THOUSAND U.S. DOLLARS)
ECHANGES SELON LES PRINCIPAUX PAYS DE PRODUCTION ET DE DERNIERE CONSIGNATION (VALEUR EN MILLIERS DE DOLLARS EU)

COUNTRIES–PAYS	GENERAL IMPORTS C.I.F. IMPORTATIONS GENERALES C.A.F				
	1989	1990	1991	1992	1993
World	952741	1076106	471810	656601	771584
Africa	36877	38492	45143	71179	64308
Americas	82620	70253	67283	48018	87944
Northern America	75528	67546	67237	47567	87884
LAIA	3429	2173	25	55	53
CACM					
Caribbean	3155	533	19	165	5
Rest of America	509	1	1	231	2
As.ex F.USSR	149438	169380	136502	221892	273085
Eur.x F.USSR	513036	591859	205842	280231	321583
EU	463206	507909	190238	254053	302937
EFTA	19100	26008	6840	23238	13770
East Europe	25353	35601	4620	2486	4540
Other Europe	5377	22341	4143	118	213
Former USSR	129380	139549	4493	1505	864
Oceania	3723	1465	466	445	5882
Italy/Italie	133288	177858	48034	47411	79643
Germany/Allemagne	102759	101409	53771	64766	81643
Saudi Arabia	12211	17144	46773	112891	145226
USA/Etats–Unis d'Amer	53393	57803	61888	34968	73254
Former USSR/Anc. URSS	129380	139549	4493		
United Kingdom	84622	81590	26482	46156	29801
Japan/Japon	62244	70416	45374	34255	31300
Netherlands/Pays–Bas	32731	30413	15684	32522	28345
Djibouti	9057	14159	21822	42855	34464
Kenya	22894	18911	20349	22165	21173
Sweden/Suède	32200	19339	10097	15016	19074
France,Monac	21637	30805	13853	8123	11992
Switz.Liecht	16781	21918	5613	21836	12369
Belgium–Luxembourg	12027	20606	9635	12427	20683
Canada	22134	9743	5349	12600	14629
Jordan/Jordanie	21814	12733	23630	372	146
India/Inde	7790	26440	3330	8461	10877
United Arab Emirates	1415	3022	5862	23854	16242
Yemen/Yémen			1851	22399	23305
Denmark/Danemark	8870	8745	4767	10388	14099
Korea, Republic of	10075	13680	2001	2916	5484
Greece/Grèce	7948	12951	1868	1783	7984
China/Chine	6931	7696	2079	2055	11734
Austria/Autriche	8553	6222	3078	6666	2114
Czechoslovakia	6102	13004	3341	1197	
Finland/Finlande	9085	10526	825	883	1859
Former GDR	8625	13260			
Fm Yugoslav	5106	10652	4124		
Spain/Espagne	4135	4594	1501	5115	4018
Singapore/Singapour	4643	3337	1148	2919	3890
Korea Dem People's Rp	4897	2974	575	3846	3052
Ireland/Irlande	4675	2835	581	2682	1632
Australia/Australie	3723	1269	466	445	5440
Thailand/Thaïlande	46	139	91	2342	8663
Norway,SVD,JM	2217	4060	1174	1340	1349
Egypt/Egypte	2444	1717	1040	1902	2406
Indonesia/Indonésie	2343	1455	172	1839	3472
Hungary/Hongrie	4219	1917	435	540	1893
Israel/Israël	3271	2362	1010	595	1237
Poland/Pologne	3319	1629	387	555	1316
Brazil/Brésil	3385	1822	24	29	53
Sri Lanka	1675	1949	301	564	584
Hong Kong	1039	754	242	631	1482
Zimbabwe	1815	1306	561	275	69
Romania/Roumanie	1168	2498	67	180	96
Turkey/Turquie	899	346	215	266	2177
Cuba	3098	481	17	153	2
Albania/Albanie	141	2508	109	2	787
Bulgaria/Bulgarie	1778	785	281	13	64
Malaysia/Malaisie	1766	553	1	23	458

COUNTRIES–PAYS	GENERAL EXPORTS F.O.B. EXPORTATIONS GENERALES F.O.B.				
	1989	1990	1991	1992	1993
Monde	451706	294163	188609	197171	201706
Afrique	29946	37416	8716	13604	27109
Amériques	68229	40205	10187	8944	20317
Amérique du Nord	66965	32805	10097	8928	20166
ALAI	21	8		15	2
MCAC					
Caraïbes	818	7211			148
Autre Amérique	424	181	90		0
Asie l'URSS exclus	87647	79413	56564	92504	69415
Europe l'URSS exclus	223690	123290	111985	81933	84724
UE	218278	118322	111549	79711	83980
AELE	57	120	393	1128	175
Europe de l'Est	5355	3635	33	1078	569
Autre de l'Europe	0	1213	11	0	0
Ancienne URSS	41846	10511	1022	46	45
Océanie	229	34	134	139	97
Germany/Allemagne	105141	50674	47828	18756	39671
Japan/Japon	48175	43706	38291	40640	38349
Saudi Arabia	29838	29920	14095	45166	19899
USA/Etats–Unis d'Amer	65151	31726	8183	7580	18588
Djibouti	25856	35309	7285	13475	24347
Italy/Italie	29964	22304	11304	12386	15307
United Kingdom	7975	8616	26737	30901	9274
France,Monac	21917	8031	11364	9794	7400
Former USSR/Anc. URSS	41846	10511	1022		
Netherlands/Pays–Bas	25828	7685	3921	2729	4227
Belgium–Luxembourg	14723	8900	8033	2887	6025
Finland/Finlande	8087	3780	1623	1902	1242
Yemen/Yémen			2013	3447	3902
Cuba	818	7211			148
Canada	1814	1079	1914	1349	1579
Greece/Grèce	226	6865	116	78	160
Former GDR	3398	1071			
Former Democratic Yemen	1293	3074			
Sudan/Soudan	1180	262	3		2630
Czechoslovakia	1542	1818		164	
United Arab Emirates	2149	183	1	584	550
Kenya	1688	892	696	36	15
Korea, Republic of	271	586	870	699	865
Spain/Espagne	907	994	519	194	281
Malaysia/Malaisie		50		857	1790
Austria/Autriche	2671	8	7	0	
India/Inde	0	0	0	12	2249
Romania/Roumanie	395	744	0	713	364
Switz.Liecht	55	116	112	1127	175
Singapore/Singapour	93	381	567	316	154
Fm Yugoslav		1135	11		
Former Yemen	1140				
Sweden/Suède	518	220	84	17	217
Tunisia/Tunisie	1011				
Central African Rep.		856			
Israel/Israël	68	405	187	42	129
Korea Dem People's Rp	103	683	10		
Thailand/Thaïlande	0	304	0	207	185
China/Chine			515	69	57
Australia/Australie	229	34	134	139	97
So. Africa Customs Un	19	10	546	1	0
Indonesia/Indonésie				200	355
Turkey/Turquie		116		2	333
Poland/Pologne	20		2	201	205
Denmark/Danemark	252	42	11	68	40
Portugal	69	203		0	136
Hong Kong	1	0		44	235
Iceland/Islande		0	277		
Uganda/Ouganda	140	1	112	8	0
Pakistan	20	5		37	185

(VALUE AS PERCENTAGE OF WORLD TOTAL)(VALEURS EN POURCENTAGE DU TOTAL MONDIAL)

	1984	1985	1986	1987	1988	1989	1990	1991	1992	1993
Africa	1.2	1.4	2.1	2.4	2.3	3.9	3.6	9.6	10.8	8.3
Americas	17.3	19.5	17.7	14.0	13.4	8.7	6.5	14.3	7.3	11.4
Northern America	17.3	19.3	17.6	13.8	13.1	7.9	6.3	14.3	7.2	11.4
LAIA	0.0	0.1	0.1	0.1	0.3	0.4	0.2	0.0	0.0	0.0
CACM					0.0					
Caribbean	0.0	0.1	0.1	0.0	0.0	0.3	0.0	0.0	0.0	0.0
Rest of America	0.0	0.0	0.0	0.0	0.0	0.1	0.0	0.0	0.0	0.0
As.ex F.USSR	12.5	12.8	13.8	17.6	14.3	15.7	15.7	28.9	33.8	35.4
Eur.x F.USSR	45.2	46.7	50.1	52.4	57.0	53.8	55.0	43.6	42.7	41.7
EU	36.7	40.1	44.4	46.9	52.5	48.6	47.2	40.3	38.7	39.3
EFTA	2.3	2.3	1.8	2.2	1.4	2.0	2.4	1.4	3.5	1.8
East Europe	4.0	2.6	2.3	2.3	2.6	2.7	3.3	1.0	0.4	0.6
Other Europe	2.3	1.7	1.7	1.0	0.6	0.6	2.1	0.9	0.0	0.0
Former USSR	23.2	17.4	12.7	12.3	11.0	13.6	13.0	1.0	0.2	0.1
Oceania	0.4	1.6	2.3	0.8	0.3	0.4	0.1	0.1	0.1	0.8
Italy/Italie	9.8	8.0	14.0	18.2	17.3	14.0	16.5	10.2	7.2	10.3
Germany/Allemagne	10.3	10.0	11.8	9.7	10.2	10.8	9.4	11.4	9.9	10.6
Saudi Arabia	0.5	0.9	1.4	1.6	0.8	1.3	1.6	9.9	17.2	18.8
USA/Etats–Unis d'Amer	15.3	16.1	15.0	11.1	10.9	5.6	5.4	13.1	5.3	9.5
Former USSR/Anc. URSS	23.2	17.4	12.7	12.3	11.0	13.6	13.0	1.0		
United Kingdom	6.4	8.7	7.5	6.6	8.1	8.9	7.6	5.6	7.0	3.9
Japan/Japon	6.5	6.0	7.5	9.0	7.9	6.5	6.5	9.6	5.2	4.1
Netherlands/Pays–Bas	1.9	2.8	2.4	2.0	6.0	3.4	2.8	3.3	5.0	3.7
Djibouti	0.2	0.2	0.5	0.9	0.9	1.0	1.3	4.6	6.5	4.5
Kenya	0.5	0.4	0.6	1.0	0.8	2.4	1.8	4.3	3.4	2.7

	1984	1985	1986	1987	1988	1989	1990	1991	1992	1993
Afrique	9.0	6.0	4.4	9.2	5.4	6.6	12.7	4.6	6.9	13.4
Amériques	19.5	10.5	16.6	18.4	10.6	15.1	13.7	5.4	4.5	10.1
Amérique du Nord	19.5	10.5	16.3	18.3	10.1	14.8	11.2	5.4	4.5	10.0
ALAI			0.0	0.0	0.0	0.0	0.0		0.0	0.0
MCAC										
Caraïbes			0.2	0.0	0.5	0.2	2.5			0.1
Autre Amérique		0.0		0.1		0.1	0.1	0.0		0.0
Asie l'URSS exclus	19.2	23.8	14.2	23.9	21.8	19.4	27.0	30.0	46.9	34.4
Europe l'URSS exclus	47.4	54.2	58.2	43.7	55.1	49.5	41.9	59.4	41.6	42.0
UE	43.8	49.9	54.5	39.2	51.1	48.3	40.2	59.1	40.4	41.6
AELE	0.1	0.3	0.6	0.1	0.2	0.0	0.0	0.2	0.6	0.1
Europe de l'Est	3.3	3.4	2.9	4.0	1.3	1.2	1.2	0.0	0.5	0.3
Autre de l'Europe	0.2	0.5	0.2	0.2	2.5	0.0	0.4	0.0	0.0	0.0
Ancienne URSS	4.5	5.3	6.6	4.8	6.8	9.3	3.6	0.5	0.0	0.0
Océanie	0.0	0.1	0.0	0.0	0.1	0.1	0.0	0.1	0.1	0.0
Germany/Allemagne	18.0	18.5	30.8	16.7	23.4	23.3	17.2	25.4	9.5	19.7
Japan/Japon	7.5	10.3	8.0	10.5	12.2	10.7	14.9	20.3	20.6	19.0
Saudi Arabia	4.2	3.7	4.5	7.7	7.0	6.6	10.2	7.5	22.9	9.9
USA/Etats–Unis d'Amer	19.5	10.5	16.2	17.8	9.8	14.4	10.8	4.3	3.8	9.2
Djibouti	6.9	3.6	4.2	8.5	4.8	5.7	12.0	3.9	6.8	12.1
Italy/Italie	7.4	7.7	7.5	8.2	7.1	6.6	7.6	6.0	6.3	7.6
United Kingdom	2.3	3.2	1.5	3.7	1.7	1.8	2.9	14.2	15.7	4.6
France,Monac	5.1	3.8	3.9	3.4	2.9	4.9	2.7	6.0	5.0	3.7
Former USSR/Anc. URSS	4.5	5.3	6.6	4.8	6.8	9.3	3.6	0.5		
Netherlands/Pays–Bas	2.0	13.2	4.1	2.7	5.6	5.7	2.6	2.1	1.4	2.1

4. General Imports C.I.F. by Commodities according to the S.I.T.C. (Rev. 2) in thousand U.S. Dollars
Importations Générales C.A.F. par Produits d'après la C.T.C.I. (Rév. 2) en milliers de Dollars E.U.

SITC CTCI	COMMODITY	1990 WEIGHT POIDS	1990 VALUE VALEUR	1991 WEIGHT POIDS	1991 VALUE VALEUR	1992 WEIGHT POIDS	1992 VALUE VALEUR	1993 WEIGHT POIDS	1993 VALUE VALEUR	PRODUIT
	ALL COMMODITIES		1076106		471810		656601		771584	TOUS PRODUITS
0	FOOD AND LIVE ANIMALS		129824		20151		83418		93928	ALIMENTS,ANIMAUX VIVANTS
02	DAIRY PRODCTS,BIRDS'EGGS		12591		1537		2458		2513	PRODUITS LAITIERS,OEUFS
022	MILK AND CREAM	W 13154	12328	W 629	1309	W 861	2334	W 1811	2400	LAIT ET CREME
0224	MILK,CREAM PRESERVED ETC	W 13146	12325	W 628	1308	W 847	2309	W 1801	2363	LAIT,CREME CONS,CONC
02242	MILK DRY,1.5% FAT OR LES	W 7965	4621	W 418	924	W 390	1382	W 246	387	LAIT POUDRE INF 1.5%
02243	MILK DRY,OVER 1.5% FAT	W 5162	7657	W 210	383	W 452	915	W 1550	1961	LAIT POUDRE SUP 1.5%
04	CEREALS AND PREPARATIONS		102272		14172		76285		78942	CEREALES ET PRODUITS
041	WHEAT ETC UNMILLED	W 289339	76311	W 23810	10059	W 244629	69133	W 233880	62576	FROMENT,EPEAUTRE
0411	DURUM WHEAT UNMILLED					W 4	11	W 722	2951	FROMENT DUR NON MOULU
0412	OTHER WHEAT ETC UNMILLED	W 289339	76311	W 23810	10059	W 244626	69122	W 233158	59625	AUTRE FROMENT NON MOULU
042	RICE	W 948	399	W 1371	1230	W 435	148	W 13170	6167	RIZ
0422	RICE SEMI–MILLED,MILLED	W 754	296	W 191	138	W 63	28	W 13121	6158	RIZ POLI,GLACE INCL BRISURES
046	WHEAT ETC MEAL OR FLOUR	W 28402	12724	W 2630	885	W 8951	1376	W 26114	5127	SEMOULE FARINE,FROMENT
04601	FLOUR OF WHEAT OR MESLIN	W 28370	12697	W 1970	665	W 8951	1376	W 25814	5076	FARINE DE FROMENT
047	OTHER CEREAL MEALS,FLOUR	W 20630	8290		58	W 10030	2032	W 1510	622	AUTRES SEMOULES,FARINES
04701	CEREAL FLOUR(NON–WHEAT)	W 20630	8290		58	W 10030	2032	W 1510	622	FARINES DE CEREALES
048	CEREAL ETC PREPARATIONS	W 1514	3681	W 652	1740	W 3152	2350	W 7517	3796	PREPTNS A BASE CEREALES
0484	BAKERY PRODUCTS	W 1385	3522	W 522	1334	W 2430	1924	W 443	1031	PRODUITS DE BOULANGERIE
05	VEGETABLES AND FRUIT		3552		1207		2025		6617	LEGUMES ET FRUITS
054	VEG ETC FRSH,SMPLY PRSVD	W 4236	3077	W 810	974	W 1325	1657	W 7698	5499	LEGUMES FRAIS,CONG,SECS
0542	LEGUMINOUS VEGETBLES DRY	W 4224	2992	W 790	935	W 1278	1128	W 7609	4817	LEGUMES A COSSE SECS
07	COFFEE,TEA,COCOA,SPICES		3615		340		415		103	CAFE,THE,CACAO,EPICES
074	TEA AND MATE	W 833	3578	W 86	314	W 126	293	W 16	76	THE ET MATE
0741	TEA	W 820	3556	W 86	314	W 118	276	W 16	76	THE
09	MISC EDIBLE PRODUCTS		6086		2278		1858		5607	PREP ALIMENTAIRES DIVERSES
098	EDIBLE PRODCTS,PREPS NES	W 3051	6072	W 950	2267	W 784	1755	W 2044	4256	PREP ALIMENTAIRES NDA
09809	MISC FOOD PREPRTIONS NES	W 2404	4576	W 858	1985	W 161	705	W 1165	3030	PREP ALIMENTAIRES NDA
1	BEVERAGES AND TOBACCO		10211		4620		5833		3857	BOISSONS ET TABACS
11	BEVERAGES		8005		3606		5114		1963	BOISSONS
112	ALCOHOLIC BEVERAGES	W 1798	7991	W 796	3605	W 551	5114	W 239	1962	BOISSONS ALCOOLIQUES
1124	DISTILLED ALCOHOLIC BEVS	W 1343	6773	W 534	3064	W 368	4297	W 198	1809	ALCOOLS,EAUX–DE–VIE
11241	WHISKY	W 1313	6194	W 445	2790	W 341	4210	W 188	1654	WHISKY
2	CRUDE MATERLS,EXCL FUELS		34483		5688		8846		11540	MAT BRUTES NON COMESTIBLES
23	RUBBER, CRUDE		5038		427		918		2147	CAOUTCHOUC BRUT
251	*PULP AND WASTE PAPER	W 5768	5580	W 1721	986	W 1777	789	W 1748	569	PATES A PAPIER,DECHETS
2519	OTHER CELLULOSIC PULPS	W 5768	5580	W 1721	986	W 1777	789	W 1562	530	AUTRES PATES CELLULOSE
25192	PULP OTHR THAN WOOD PULP	W 5768	5580	W 1721	986	W 1777	789	W 1562	530	PATES AUTRES QUE DE BOIS
26	TEXTILE FIBRES AND WASTE		12187		2447		6237		7003	FIBRES TEXTILES
263	COTTON	W 2052	5243	W 172	153	W 156	292	W 127	139	COTON
2631	RAW COTTON,EXCL LINTERS	W 1282	3270							COTON EN MASSE
267	OTHER MAN–MADE FIBRES	W 699	595	W 278	313	W 2491	2423	W 895	653	AUTR FIBR TEXT ARTIF SYNTH
2672	WASTE OF MAN–MADE FIBRES	W 699	595	W 278	313	W 2491	2423	W 895	653	DECHETS FIBR TEXT ARTIF SYNT
26721	— SYNTHETIC	W 699	595	W 278	313	W 2491	2423	W 895	653	DECHETS FIBRES SYNTHETIQUES
269	WASTE OF TEXTILE FABRICS	W 743	3758	W 465	1626	W 1549	3477	W 4823	5829	FRIPERIE DRILLES,CHIFFONS
26901	BULK TEXT WSTE,OLD CLTHG	W 740	3756	W 457	1605	W 1521	3435	W 4817	5813	ART ET ACCESS D'HABILLEMENT
27	CRUDE FERTLZR,MINRLS NES		6425		222		160		915	ENGRAIS MINERAUX BRUTS
271	FERTILIZERS,CRUDE	W 16021	5978		2					ENGRAIS BRUTS
2711	ANIMAL,VEG FERTLZR,CRUDE	W 16000	5957		2					GUANO,ENGRAIS NATURELS
3	MINERAL FUELS ETC		128082		50196		149749		166612	COMBUSTIBLES MINERAUX LUB
33	PETROLEUM AND PRODUCTS		128073		50134		149546		165633	PETROLE ET DERIVES
333	CRUDE PETROLEUM	W 702734	112892	W 193542	29148	W 462345	99993	W 584714	71393	HUILES BRUTES DE PETROLE
334	PETROLEUM PRODUCTS,REFIN	W 30681	13224	W 69660	20543	W 133430	48905	W 340309	92750	PRODUITS RAFFINES
3341	GASOLINE,OTH LIGHT OILS	W 18	7	W 24032	7088	W 46388	15461	W 21600	4429	ESSENCES POUR MOTEURS
33411	MOTOR,AVIATION SPIRIT	W 18	7	W 24032	7088	W 22724	12177	W 21600	4429	ESSENCES MOTEURS D'AVIONS
33419	OTH LIGHT PETROLEUM OILS					W 23664	3284			AUTRES HUILES LEGERES
3342	KEROSENE,OTH MEDIUM OILS	W 15	6	W 22	9	W 332	442	W 95991	33100	PETR LAMPANTS,AUT HUIL
33421	KEROSENE INCL JET FUEL	W 15	6	W 22	9	W 332	442	W 95991	33100	PETROLES LAMPANTS
3343	GAS OILS			W 41587	9347	W 50169	19550	W 185206	37878	GAS OILS
3345	LUBS,PETROLEUM OILS NES	W 12751	11875	W 4020	4100	W 36541	13453	W 37506	17334	HUILES LUBRIFIANTES
33451	LUBS(HIGH PETR CONT) ETC	W 12736	11835	W 4020	4100	W 36540	13442	W 37496	17315	HUILES LUBRIF,H LOURDES
4	ANIMAL,VEGETABLE OIL,FAT		19228		1371		15076		25949	HUILES,GRAISSES ANIM,VEG
42	FIXED VEGETABLE OIL,FAT		19044		583		14024		20774	HUILES VEGETALES FIXES
423	FIXED VEG OILS,SOFT	W 5744	4949	W 88	93	W 33	48	W 736	485	HUILES VEGET DOUCES FIXES
424	FIXED VEG OIL NONSOFT	W 13846	14094	W 408	490	W 15245	13976	W 19609	20289	AUTRES HUILES VEG FIXES
4249	FIXED VEGETABLE OILS NES	W 13846	14094	W 379	479	W 15190	13932	W 19605	20288	HUILES VEGET FIXES NDA
431	*PROCESD ANML VEG OIL,ET	W 25	25	W 349	341	W 2418	968	W 6536	5174	HUILES,GRAISSES PREPAREES
4313	FATTY ACIDS ETC,RESIDUES	W 9	7			W 2418	968	W 6499	5158	ACIDES GRAS INDUST,RESIDUS
43131	FATTY ACIDS,ACID OILS	W 9	7			W 2418	968	W 6499	5158	ACIDES GRAS INDUSTRIELS
5	CHEMCLS,RELATED PROD NES		108810		72735		58256		106125	PRODUITS CHIMIQUES
52	INORGANIC CHEMICALS		20372		6629		8015		20813	PROD CHIM INORGANIQUES
522	INORG ELEMNTS,OXIDES,ETC	W 9798	7834	W 3061	3323	W 5447	4598	W 12314	14993	ELEMENTS INORGANIQUES
5222	INORGANIC ACIDS ETC	W 4918	4556	W 755	1125	W 2500	2509	W 4905	5812	ACIDES INORGANIQUES
52229	OTH INORGANIC ACIDS ETC	W 1888	2648	W 377	894	W 1871	2089	W 3657	5170	AUTRES ACIDES INORGANIQUES
5223	HALGN,SULPHR CMPD NONMET	W 1095	723	W 44	140	W 1263	1364	W 3208	3822	DERIVES HALOGENES
52231	HALOGEN CMPNDS NON–METAL	W 1095	723	W 44	140	W 1263	1364	W 3208	3822	CHLORURES,OXYCHLORURES
5224	ZINC,IRON,LEAD ETC OXIDE	W 36	54	W 3	4		3	W 848	2558	OXYDES METALLIQUES
52247	LEAD OXIDES			W 3	4			W 842	2551	OXYDES DE PLOMB
523	OTHR INORG CHEMICALS ETC	W 10203	12519	W 1604	3290	W 3386	3415	W 4255	5810	AUT PRODUITS CHIMIQUES INORG
5239	INORG CHEM PRODUCTS NES	W 8593	11880	W 1041	2674	W 2843	2560	W 2166	3106	PROD CHIM INORGANIQ NDA
52399	OTH INORG CMPNDS NES ETC	W 8281	11654	W 1036	2671	W 1633	2198	W 1896	2988	AUT COMP INORGANIQUES NDA
53	DYES,TANNING,COLOUR PROD		9905		3469		3206		8712	PROD TEINTURE,COLORANTS
532	DYES NES,TANNING PROD	W 4529	6609	W 924	1909	W 1566	1628	W 2663	3956	EXTRAITS TEINTURE,TANNAGE
5322	DYE,TANN EXTRCTS,TANNINS	W 4448	6454	W 924	1907	W 1425	1435	W 1941	3070	EXT TAN ORIG VEG,TANNINS
53222	DYEING EXTRCTS VEG,ANMAL	W 4388	6402	W 924	1907	W 1425	1435	W 1910	2977	MATI COLOR VEGET ANIMALE
533	PIGMENTS,PAINTS,ETC	W 1035	2702	W 592	1254	W 747	1209	W 2146	3704	PIGMENTS,PEINTURES,VERNIS
541	*MEDICINAL,PHARM PRODUCT	MK 14533	25383	K 1319220	17141	K 2341135	23044	K 2282082	31595	PROD MEDICINAUX PHARMACEUT
5417	MEDICAMENTS	MK 14128	22129	K 1203952	16150	K 2265492	22338	K 2185471	30987	MEDICAMENTS
54172	— CONTAINING HORMONES	K 1499306	9732	K 473393	6662	K 685384	6877	K 661905	6275	MED CONTENANT HORMONES
54173	— CONTAINING ALKALOIDS	MK 12594	12011	K 717595	8942	K 1564536	14898	K 1457730	22554	MED CONTEN ALCALOIDES
55	PERFUME,CLEANING ETC PRD		11456		11546		13979		8527	PROD POUR PARFUM,TOILETTE
551	ESSENTL OILS,PERFUME,ETC	W 24	269	W 462	2123	W 124	435	W 110	1070	HUILES ESSENTIELLES
5513	ESSENTL OIL,RESINOID,ETC	W 19	193	W 462	2121	W 43	325	W 79	1021	HUILES ESSENTIELLES,RESIN
553	PERFUMERY,COSMETICS,ETC	W 247	1217	W 62	611	W 668	2116	W 493	836	PRODUITS DE PARFUMERIE
554	SOAP,CLEANSING ETC PREPS	W 16591	9970	W 15183	8812	W 21875	11429	W 11928	6621	SAVONS,PRODUITS DETERSIFS
5541	SOAPS	W 16155	9007	W 14836	8027	W 21602	11011	W 11592	6172	SAVONS,PROD TENSIO–ACTIFS
562	*FERTILIZERS,MANUFACTURE	W 60137	16115	W 42127	23613	W 159	62	W 88526	18736	ENGRAIS MANUFACTURES
5621	CHEM NITROGENOUS FERTLZR	W 28900	7347	W 20126	5145	W 6	3	W 76657	15052	ENGRAIS AZOTES
56216	UREA	W 6350	1205	W 20126	5145	W 6	3	W 52000	10027	UREE
56219	CHEM NITROG FERTILZR NES	W 22500	5433					W 24657	5024	ENGRAIS AZOTES NDA
5622	CHEM PHOSPHATIC FERTILZR	W 18236	5147							ENGRAIS PHOSPHATES

4. General Imports C.I.F. by Commodities according to the S.I.T.C. (Rev. 2) in thousand U.S. Dollars
Importations Générales C.A.F. par Produits d'après la C.T.C.I. (Rév. 2) en milliers de Dollars E.U.

SITC CTCI	COMMODITY	1990 WEIGHT POIDS	1990 VALUE VALEUR	1991 WEIGHT POIDS	1991 VALUE VALEUR	1992 WEIGHT POIDS	1992 VALUE VALEUR	1993 WEIGHT POIDS	1993 VALUE VALEUR	PRODUIT
56229	CHEM PHOSPH FERTILZR NES	W 18236	5147							ENGRAIS PHOSPHATES NDA
5629	FERTILIZERS NES	W 13000	3621	W 22001	18467	W 153	59	W 11869	3685	ENGRAIS NDA
56292	NITROG–PHOS FERTILZR NES	W 13000	3621			W 88	18	W 10238	2613	ENGRAIS NDA CONT N P
56299	OTHER FERTILIZERS NES			W 22000	18467					AUTRES ENGRAIS NDA
572	*EXPLOSIVES,PYROTECH PRO	W 191	901	W 222	3698	W 9	60	W 276	1040	EXPLOSIFS
5722	FUSES,PRIMERS,DETONATORS			W 222	3698	W 6	46	W 47	119	MECHES,CORDEAUX,AMORCES
58	PLASTIC MATERIALS ETC		4712		1692		1010		5720	MAT PLAST ARTIFICIELLES
583	POLYMERIZATION ETC PRODS	W 2691	4064	W 1261	1542	W 809	853	W 5311	5539	PROD POLYMERISATION
5831	POLYETHYLENE	W 2691	4064	W 1261	1542	W 809	853	W 5311	5539	POLYETHYLENE
58311	— IN PRIMARY FORMS	W 2691	4064	W 1261	1542					POLYETHYLENE PRIMAIRES
59	CHEMICAL MATERIALS NES		19259		4828		8154		10481	MAT PROD CHIMIQUES NDA
591	PESTICIDES,DISINFECTANTS	W 6610	15533	W 475	2971	W 1560	6593	W 1998	5814	DESINF,INSECT,FONG,HERB
5911	INSECTICIDES,FOR RETAIL	W 6277	13538	W 440	2619	W 1411	6144	W 1181	2271	INSECTICIDES VENTE DET
5913	HERBICIDES,FOR RETAIL	W 312	1905	W 35	349	W 112	400	W 283	2739	HERBICIDES VENTE AU DET
598	MISCEL CHEM PRODUCTS NES	W 1250	2553	W 244	945	W 447	904	W 1867	2417	PROD DIV INDUST CHIM NDA
6	BASIC MANUFACTURES		172898		76327		99432		124232	ART MANUFACTURES
62	RUBBER MANUFACTURES NES		17835		9250		15325		17534	CAOUTCHOUC MANUFACTURE
625	RUBBER TYRES, TUBES ETC	W 3215	14212	W 1409	7544	W 4607	14116	W 4516	14006	PNEUS CAOUTCHOUC VULCANISE
6251	TYRES NEW FOR MOTOR CARS	W 595	2823	W 511	2674	W 1636	4815	W 2223	7537	PNEUS POUR VOITURES
6252	TYRES,NEW,BUS OR LORRY	W 1761	7523	W 829	4472	W 2854	7662	W 1912	4999	PNEUS POUR AUTOBUS,CAMIONS
6259	OTH TYRES,TYRE CASES,ETC	W 851	3826	W 60	357	W 115	1635	W 279	1107	AUTRES PNEUS RECHAPES FLAPS
628	RUBBER ARTICLES NES	W 239	1519	W 203	910	W 100	366	W 548	2547	OUVRAGES CAOUTCHOUC NDA
64	PAPER,PAPERBOARD AND MFR		16099		6940		6260		7808	PAPIERS,CARTONS & OUVRAGES
641	PAPER AND PAPERBOARD	W 7278	8130	W 4282	4676	W 4599	4459	W 4552	5201	PAPIERS ET CARTONS
6418	COATED ETC PAPER NES BLK	W 2769	2432	W 1951	1443	W 1386	1228	W 2215	2176	PAP,CARTONS COUCHES,ENDUITS
64189	COATED PAPER ETC NES	W 2769	2432	W 1951	1443	W 1386	1228	W 2215	2176	PAPIERS,CARTONS COUCHES
642	PAPER,ETC,PRECUT,ARTS OF	W 4068	7969	W 1098	2264	W 803	1801	W 1755	2607	PAP,CARTONS DECOUPES
65	TEXTILE YARN,FABRICS,ETC		19529		16192		35976		22589	FILS,TISSUS,ARTICLES TEXTILE
651	TEXTILE YARN	W 1683	7128	W 1263	5394	W 3519	14551	W 2543	9146	FILS TEXTILES
6511	SILK YARN, SILKWORM GUT	W 1526	6479	W 889	4114	W 2557	8484	W 1508	6247	FILS DE SOIE
6513	COTTON YARN	W 15	138	W 263	996	W 911	5904	W 950	2307	FILS DE COTON
65132	— 14 TO 40 KM PER KG	W 7	67	W 250	793	W 691	5355	W 714	1584	FILS COT 14000 A 40000 M KG
653	WOVN MAN–MADE FIB FABRIC	W 289	2485	W 1305	6632	W 5235	13719	W 2001	6865	TISSUS FIBRES SYNTH,ARTIF
6532	DISC SYN TXTL FABRIC NES	W 180	1102	W 333	2072	W 4384	10233	W 1617	5344	TIS DISC MOINS 85% FIBR TEXT
6536	DISC REGN TXTL FABRC NES	W 41	173	W 632	3824	W 448	1973	W 364	1283	TISSUS 85% TEXT ART DISC
657	SPECIAL TXTL FABRC,PRODS	W 454	3072	W 285	497	W 694	2012	W 999	3193	TISSUS SPECIAUX
658	TEXTILE ARTICLES NES	W 1117	5758	W 465	3034	W 556	4352	W 1642	2354	ART FACONNES MAT TEXTILES
6582	MADE–UP CANVAS GOODS	W 645	3201	W 214	1608	W 145	518	W 1170	1211	BACHES,TENTES ETC
6589	OTH TEXTILE ARTICLES NES	W 9	194	W 7	127	W 102	2617	W 24	144	AUT ART EN TEXTILES NDA
65899	TXTL ARTCLES NONKNIT NES	W 8	190	W 7	126	W 98	2598	W 15	126	ART TIS AUT QUE BONNETERIE
66	NONMETAL MINERAL MFS NES		8878		8617		9025		6849	ART MIN NON METALLIQUES
661	LIME,CEMENT,BLDG PRODS	W 3382	1513	W 433	153	W 4485	3278	386	138	CHAUX,CIMENTS MAT CONSTR
6618	MNRL BLDG PRD UNFIRD NES	W 847	492	W 29	74	W 4435	3241	W 13	37	MAT CONST AMIANTE–CIMENT
66183	ASBESTOS–,FIBRE–CMNT PRD	W 689	350	W 26	55	W 4429	3232			OUVRAGES AMIANTE–CIMENT
662	CLAY,REFRACTORY BLDG PRD	W 1596	1174	W 1414	4855	W 834	579	W 1457	1277	MAT CONST REFRACTAIRES
6624	BRICKS ETC NONREFRACTORY	W 692	546	W 999	4509	W 103	82	W 919	938	BRIQUES ETC CERAM NON REFR
66245	GLAZED CERAMIC SETTS ETC	W 189	228	W 976	4497	W 94	72	W 637	655	AUT CARREAUX CERAMIQUE
663	MINERAL MANUFCTURES NES	W 984	2088	W 855	1803	W 2142	2181	W 1744	2894	ART MIN MANUF NDA
6631	GRINDING STONES ETC	W 694	1452	W 558	1110	W 774	1060	W 1609	2509	PIERRES A AIGUISER,MEULES
67	IRON AND STEEL		28121		15559		13913		38552	FER ET ACIER
673	IRON,STEEL SHAPES ETC	W 8393	4914	W 6208	2027	W 4476	1716	W 14556	9249	BARRES,PROFIL FER,ACIER
6731	IRON,STEEL WIRE ROD	W 4538	2732	W 5841	1782	W 1838	584	W 9207	6045	FIL MACHINE FER,ACIER
67311	IRON,SIMPLE STL WIRE ROD	W 4538	2732	W 5841	1782	W 1838	584	W 9207	6045	FIL MACH AUT ACIER FIN
674	IRN,STL UNIV,PLATE,SHEET	W 13539	12229	W 11495	8499	W 12512	9944	W 29863	22491	LARGES PLATS,TOLES
6741	IRON OR STEEL UNIVERSALS	W 1836	1193	W 8684	5858	W 2355	1326	W 3377	1635	LARGES PLATS FER,ACIER
67414	IRN,SMPL STL UNIVERSALS	W 1836	1193	W 8684	5858	W 2355	1326	W 3377	1635	PLATS NON ACIER FIN
6747	TINNED PLATES,SHEETS	W 2889	2457	W 810	730	W 2553	2376	W 11849	10374	TOLES ETAMEES EN ACIER
6749	OTH IRN,STL PLATES,SHEET	W 8814	8580	W 2001	1912	W 7603	6242	W 14637	10482	AUTRES TOLES FER,ACIER
675	IRON,STEEL HOOP,STRIP	W 490	951	W 29	32	W 575	361	W 6913	3635	FEUILLARDS LAMINES
67501	IRN,SMPLE STL HOOP,STRIP	W 490	951	W 29	32	W 575	361	W 6913	3635	FEUILLARDS NON ACIER FIN
678	IRON,STL TUBES,PIPES,ETC	W 6389	8917	W 1221	4470	W 933	1354	W 2262	2219	TUBES,TUYAUX EN FONTE,FER
6782	IRON,STL SEAMLESS TUBES	W 5473	6303	W 1043	3710	W 416	446	W 641	430	TUBES,TUYAUX SANS SOUDURE
68	NON–FERROUS METALS		3752		968		1207		2274	METAUX NON FERREUX
69	METAL MANUFACTURES NES		74581		17163		15697		26226	ART MANUFACT EN METAL NDA
691	STRUCTURES AND PARTS NES	W 8575	20709	W 757	2730	W 2639	3567	W 6435	8952	CONSTRUCT FER,ACIER,ALU
6911	STRUCTURES,PARTS IRN,STL	W 8312	19775	W 697	2116	W 2447	3138	W 6375	8660	CONSTRUCT FER,ACIER,FONTE
692	METAL TANKS,BOXES,ETC	W 6195	14442	W 1035	2338	W 681	1388	W 551	1093	RECIPIENTS METALLIQUES
6924	MTL TRANSPORT BOXES ETC	W 5634	12405	W 994	2080	W 594	1199	W 266	463	FUTS,TAMBOURS,BIDONS
69241	STL TRANSPORT BOXES ETC	W 5400	12056	W 985	1983	W 322	475	W 168	248	FUTS,TAMBOURS,BIDONS FER
693	WIRE PRODUCTS NON ELECTR	W 4826	16011	W 274	627	W 140	315	W 545	996	OUVRAGES FILS METALLIQUES
6931	WIRE CABLES, ROPES ETC	W 4186	14907	W 32	97	W 26	58	W 31	125	CORDAGES EN FILS DE FER
69311	IRN,STEEL CABLE,ROPE ETC	W 3446	13292	W 31	94	W 23	46	W 29	119	CORDAGES FILS FER,ACIER
694	STL,COPPR NAILS,NUTS,ETC	W 2297	5317	W 1554	2097	W 1991	1923	W 1907	2812	CLOUS,VIS,ECROUS
69402	IRN,STL NUTS,BOLTS,ETC	W 385	3239	W 202	649	W 212	309	W 492	567	BOULONS,VIS,ECROUS FER,AC
695	TOOLS	W 1445	7586	W 408	5396	W 309	3064	W 764	3140	OUTILS A MAIN
6954	BLADES,TIPS,ETC FR TOOLS	W 1051	5275	W 224	3957	W 170	2210	W 315	1215	OUTILS POUR MACHINE–OUTIL
69541	PARTS TO INSERT IN TOOLS	W 941	3715	W 210	3762	W 123	902	W 308	1045	OUTILS DE FORAGE
697	BASE MTL HOUSEHOLD EQUIP	W 592	2683	W 449	1369	W 683	1997	W 1055	3371	ART MENAGE MET COMMUNS
699	BASE METAL MFRS NES	W 3857	7166	W 560	2202	W 1325	2483	W 3375	5335	ART MANUFACTURES MET NDA
6991	LOCKSMITHS WARES,ETC	W 462	1343	W 117	634	W 588	855	W 1006	2337	ARTICLES DE SERRURERIE
7	MACHINES,TRANSPORT EQUIP		427253		210482		192831		208897	MACHINES MATERIEL TRANSPORT
71	POWER GENERATING EQUIPMT		12109		5786		2239		3149	MACHINES GENERATRICES
716	ROTATING ELECTRIC PLANT	W 1178	9095	W 443	4808	W 305	1004	W 847	2183	APP ELECTR ROTATIFS,PIECES
7162	AC MTRS,GENRTRS,GEN SETS	W 517	3853	W 117	491	W 270	676	W 293	1074	MOTEURS ELECTRIQUES
7169	PTS NES OF ROT ELEC PLNT	W 638	5123	W 313	4282	W 18	232	W 124	339	PIECES MAC APP ROTATIFS
72	MACHS FOR SPCL INDUSTRYS		115650		28652		43182		34382	MAC SPECIALES POUR INDUST
721	AGRIC MACHY,EXC TRACTORS	W 894	6137		1434	W 318	1776	W 492	1883	MACHINES AGRICOLES
7212	HARVESTING ETC MACHINES	W 655	5162	W 63	714	W 15	409	W 34	504	ENGINS POUR LA RECOLTE
723	CIVIL ENGNEERG EQUIP ETC	W 3679	17643	W 293	2537	W 807	5803	W 1452	9643	APPAREILS DE GENIE CIVIL
7234	CONST,MINING MACHNRY NES	W 880	8443	W 155	1127	W 274	2177	W 657	2845	MACH POUR LA CONST, MINES
72344	BORING,SINKING MACHINERY	W 180	4261	W 1	19			W 1	5	MACHINES DE FORAGE
7239	CONSTR ETC MACHY PTS NES	W 2791	9193	W 130	1404	W 534	3626	W 796	6798	PIECES 723.41–723.46
724	TEXTILE,LEATHER MACHNRY	W 2157	25350	W 1604	6457	W 708	5878	W 2313	9674	MACH POUR INDUSTRIE TEXTILE
7244	SPINNING,EXTRDNG,ETC MCH	W 441	4019	W 14	133	W 41	794	W 3	58	MACH POUR LE FILAGE
7245	WEAVING,FELT MFG,ETC MCH	W 536	6991	W 71	161	W 18	144	W 283	600	METIERS A TISSER,PIECES
72451	WEAVING MACHINES (LOOMS)	W 527	6959	W 70	155	W 9	24	W 274	451	METIERS A TISSER
7246	AUXIL TXTL MCH,PARTS NES	W 840	9861	W 500	1725	W 162	2613	W 1437	4523	MACH PR 724.51,52,53,61
72469	LOOM,KNT MCH ETC PTS NES	W 840	9861	W 500	1725	W 159	2593	W 1437	4523	PIECES 724.51,52,53,61
7248	SKIN,LEATHER WORKNG MACH	W 161	2363	W 986	3906	W 136	944	W 247	3096	MACHINES TRAVAIL DES CUIRS
727	FOOD MACHRY NON–DOMESTIC	W 1558	16763	W 642	7518	W 362	2543	W 816	4862	MACH INDUSTRIES ALIMENT
7271	GRAIN WORKING MCHY,PARTS	W 666	2473	W 143	1190	W 280	1357	W 498	2817	MACH POUR MINOTERIE,PIEC

4. General Imports C.I.F. by Commodities according to the S.I.T.C. (Rev. 2) in thousand U.S. Dollars
Importations Générales C.A.F. par Produits d'après la C.T.C.I. (Rév. 2) en milliers de Dollars E.U.

SITC CTCI	COMMODITY	1990		1991		1992		1993		PRODUIT
		WEIGHT POIDS	VALUE VALEUR	WEIGHT POIDS	VALUE VALEUR	WEIGHT POIDS	VALUE VALEUR	WEIGHT POIDS	VALUE VALEUR	
7272	OTH FOOD PROC MCHY,PARTS	W 892	14290	W 499	6328	W 82	1187	W 318	2045	AUT MACH IND ALIMENTAIRE
72722	INDUS FOOD PROC MACH NES	W 277	5137	W 57	370	W 18	480	W 162	810	MACHINES BOULANGERIE
72729	PTS NES OF MCHY OF 72722	W 615	9153	W 426	5936	W 63	706	W 157	1235	PIECES MACH DU 727.22
728	OTH MACHY FOR SPCL INDUS	W 2674	46434	W 540	9365	W 1334	25731	W 1385	6425	AUT MACH IND PARTICULIERES
7281	MACH–TOOLS FR SPCL INDUS	W 278	2647	W 37	278	W 340	5134	W 145	671	MACH–OUTILS SPEC IND PART
72819	PTS NES OF TOOLS OF 7281	W 48	1221	W 20	171	W 95	4638	W 6	269	PIECES 728.1
7283	OTHR MINERAL WORKG MACHY	W 883	2817	W 241	3222	W 372	1182	W 908	3292	MACH TRIER,CRIBLER,BROYER
72839	PTS NES OF MACHY OF 7283	W 814	2368	W 203	2812					PIECES MACH DU 728.3
7284	MACHY FOR SPCL INDUS NES	W 1513	40970	W 262	5866	W 622	19414	W 332	2462	MACH SPEC IND PARTICUL.
72848	OTH MCHY WITH INDIV FNCT	W 241	6648	W 24	346	W 14	143	W 27	101	AUTRES MACHINES NDA
72849	PTS OF MACHS OF 7284 ETC	W 1242	33326	W 221	5327	W 575	18976	W 287	2210	PIECES DU 728.4 ETC
73	METALWORKING MACHINERY		12999		882		847		1300	MACH TRAVAIL DES METAUX
736	METALWORKING MACH–TOOLS	W 860	9635	W 61	680	W 4	69	W 215	878	MACH–OUTILS TRAVAIL METAUX
7369	PTS NES OF TOOLS OF 736	W 548	7702	W 22	423	W 3	63	W 74	368	PIECES GROUPE 736
737	METALWORKING MACHNRY NES	W 335	3364	W 10	202	W 114	778	W 19	422	MACH TRAV METAUX PIECES
74	GENRL INDUSTRL MACHY NES		40727		13268		7349		14344	MACH APP INDUSTRIE
741	HEATING,COOLING EQUIPMNT	W 353	4801	W 25	713	W 35	836	W 27	198	MACH CHAUFFAGE,PIECES
742	PUMPS FOR LIQUIDS ETC	W 776	6500		5352	W 126	1832	W 344	3755	POMPES MOTO–POMPES
7429	PTS NES OF PUMPS OF 742	W 411	3560		4091	W 54	850	W 189	1858	PIECES POUR GROUPE 742
743	PUMPS NES,CENTRFUGES ETC	W 460	5401	W 76	1822	W 127	1342	W 94	781	POMPES COMPRES,VENT ETC
744	MECHANICAL HANDLING EQU	W 1637	10410	W 390	2041	W 276	1198	W 590	4163	EQUIP MANUTENTION PIECES
7441	FORK LIFT TRCKS,ETC,PTS	W 711	3817	W 45	274	W 35	235	W 418	2835	CHARIOTS POUR USINES ETC
74411	FORK LIFT TRUCKS ETC	W 132	1277	W 33	151	W 30	209	W 336	2413	CHARIOTS POUR LES GARES
7449	PTS NES OF MACHY OF 7442	W 502	4028	W 140	631	W 114	694	W 101	622	PIECES DU 744.2
745	NONELEC MACHY,TOOLS NES	W 595	7242	W 81	746	W 71	387	W 235	1251	AUT MACH NON ELEC,PIECES
7452	OTH NONELEC MCHS,PTS NES	W 478	6921	W 72	723	W 40	230	W 178	1076	AUT MACH NON ELEC,PIECES
74523	PACKING ETC MCHY PTS NES	W 210	3470	W 10	132	W 1	51	W 11	210	PIECES POUR 745.22,775.3
749	NONELEC MACH PTS,ACC NES	W 1180	6373	W 197	2593	W 199	1753	W 573	4195	PIECES MACH NON ELEC NDA
7499	OTH NONELEC MCHY PTS NES	W 473	1750	W 56	535	W 93	887	W 239	2346	PIECES NON ELECT NDA
75	OFFICE MACHNES,ADP EQUIP		5976		6765		6947		6071	MACH BUREAU TRAIT AUTOM
752	AUTOMTIC DATA PROC EQUIP	W 46	1822	W 27	1934	W 54	2981	W 49	2149	MACH TRAIT INFORMATION
759	OFFICE,ADP MCH PTS,ACCES	W 57	1620	W 78	3699	W 62	2568	W 49	2177	PIECES DU 751 ET 752
76	TELECOMM,SOUND EQUIPMENT		23250		13028		17720		8156	EQUIPMENT DE TELECOM
761	TELEVISION RECEIVERS	W 131	2776	W 104	2713	W 166	2896	W 92	1706	RECEPTEURS DE TELEVISION
7611	COLOUR TV RECEIVERS	W 131	2776	W 104	2713	W 166	2896	W 92	1706	RECEPTEURS COULEUR
762	RADIO BROADCAST RECEIVRS	W 33	925	W 45	1311	W 180	2773	W 138	1576	RECEPTEURS RADIODIFFUSION
763	SOUND RECORDRS,PHONOGRPH	W 30	1752	W 19	1445	W 44	1662	W 29	854	PHONO,APP ENREGISTREMENT
7631	ELECTRIC GRAMOPHONES ETC	W 29	1630	W 19	1427	W 43	1605	W 24	720	ELECTROPHON,TOURNE–DISQ
764	TELECOM EQPT,PTS,ACC NES	W 1114	17798	W 236	7559	W 534	10389	W 583	4020	EQUIP TELECOM,PIECES
7641	LINE TELEPHONE,ETC EQUIP	W 4	360	W 4	196	W 105	2354	W 195	766	APP TELEPHON PAR FIL
7648	TELECOMM EQUIPMENT NES	W 44	3330	W 16	2001	W 78	2186	W 6	237	APP TELECOM NDA
76483	RADAR APPARATUS ETC	W 43	3168	W 16	1895	W 76	2045	W 5	167	APP DE RADIOGUIDAGE ETC
7649	PTS NES OF EQUIPMT OF 76	W 1052	13037	W 213	5268	W 340	5681	W 374	2845	PIECES DE LA DIV 76
76491	PTS NES OF APPAR OF 7641	W 1017	11036	W 209	4960	W 315	4567	W 332	1443	PIECES POUR 764.1
77	ELECTRIC MACHNRY NES ETC		38713		9963		16716		25718	MACH APP ELECT NDA
772	SWITCHGEAR ETC,PARTS NES	W 3032	13556	W 160	2426	W 1048	6764	W 935	5404	APP COUPURE,SECT ETC
773	ELECTR DISTRIBUTNG EQUIP	W 3088	9090	W 137	1106	W 468	1719	W 400	1014	EQUIPMT DISTRIBUTION ELECT
7731	INSULATED WIRE,CABLE ETC	W 2869	8479	W 126	1056	W 128	364	W 384	966	FILS,CABLES ISOLES ELECT
774	ELECTRO–MEDCL,XRAY EQUIP	W 6	210	W 1	47	W 3	53	W 146	7576	APPAREILS MEDICAUX
7741	ELECTRO–MEDICAL EQUIPMNT	W 4	108				28	W 143	7523	APP ELECTRICITE MEDICALE
775	HOUSEHOLD TYPE EQUIP NES	W 651	4021	W 294	2274	W 348	2453	W 636	2833	MACH,APP USAGE DOMESTQUE
7752	DOM REFRIGERATRS,FREEZRS	W 343	2247	W 186	1553	W 226	1343	W 253	1110	REFRIG,CONGEL MENAGER
778	ELECTRICAL MACHINERY NES	W 3570	9619	W 2300	3247	W 3028	4300	W 3772	8673	AUTRES MACH ELECT NDA
7781	BATTERIES,ACCUMULATORS	W 2945	5846	W 2231	2550	W 2753	2615	W 2566	4161	PILES ET ACCUMULATEURS
77811	PRIMARY BATTERIES,CELLS	W 1707	2994	W 2086	2089	W 2566	2127	W 1894	2355	PILES ELECTRIQUES,PIECES
7782	ELECTRIC LAMPS,BULBS	W 382	1699	W 22	226	W 201	992	W 958	2621	LAMPES, TUBES ELECTRIQUES
77821	ELEC FILAMENT LAMPS NES	W 381	1691	W 22	224	W 199	977	W 935	2500	LAMPES NON INFRAROUGES
78	ROAD VEHICLES		121752		77506		96703		113440	VEHICULES ROUTIERS
781	PASS MOTOR VEH EXC BUSES	W 7056	42097	W 5778	26561	W 18026	21283	W 4981	29589	AUTO TRANSPORT PERSONNES
782	LORRIES,SPCL MTR VEH NES	W 5706	32889	W 5388	26929	W 8416	35030	W 13879	50587	VEHICULES SPECIAUX,MARCH
7821	LORRIES,TRUCKS	W 5399	30528	W 5221	25906	W 8265	34482	W 13557	48989	VEHICULES TRANSP MARCHAND
783	ROAD MOTOR VEHICLES NES	W 680	4603	W 1088	4654	W 530	2314	W 449	1766	VEHICULES ROUTIERS NDA
7831	BUSES	W 562	3517	W 1019	4330	W 479	1985	W 379	1510	VOITURES TRANSPORT COMMUN
784	MOTOR VEH PRTS,ACCES NES	W 4060	34300	W 1239	16223	W 3763	35154	W 5006	28835	PIECES 722,781,782,783
7849	OTHER MOTOR VEHCL PARTS	W 4023	34212	W 1237	16217	W 3738	35011	W 4999	28795	PIECES 722,781,782,783
786	TRAILERS,NONMOTR VEH,NES		6655	W 830	2645	W 424	1714	W 798	1659	REMORQUES,CADRES,CONTAIN
7861	TRAILERS,TRANSP CONTAINR	W 1268	3875	W 810	2599	W 403	1660	W 740	1370	REMORQUES TOUS VEHICULES
78611	HOUSING,CAMPING TRAILERS	W 1250	3854	W 807	2584	W 403	1660	W 710	1320	REMORQUES POUR CAMPING
79	OTHR TRANSPORT EQUIPMENT		56077		54633		1127		2336	AUTRE MATERIEL TRANSPORT
791	RAILWAY VEHICLES	W 34	1554		1456	W 74	317	W 5	28	VEHIC MAT CHEMINS DE FER
792	AIRCRAFT ETC	W 117	53138	W 257	53056	W 2	630	W 12	1949	APP NAVIGATION AERIENNE
7922	AIRCRFT NES 2000KG OR LS			W 256	52950			W 1	521	AERODYNES MOINS 2000 KG
7928	AIRCRAFT NES,ASSOC EQUIP	W 96	50894		20	W 1	502		36	APP NAVIG AERIENNE NDA
79282	BALLOONS AND AIRSHIPS	W 91	50790			W 1	462			AEROSTATS
8	MISC MANUFACTURED GOODS		45315		30092		43160		30421	ART MANUFACTURES DIVERS
812	*PLUMBG,HEATNG,LGHTNG EQ	W 625	2313	W 355	2252	W 427	1111	W 875	1482	APPAR SANITAIRES CHAUFFAGE
8122	CERAMIC PLUMBNG FIXTURES	W 110	376	W 164	1428	W 226	484	W 508	882	EVIERS,LAVABOS,CUVETTES
821	*FURNITURE,PARTS THEREOF	W 696	3315	W 752	2602	W 642	1617	W 362	1195	MEUBLES ET PIECES
84	CLOTHING AND ACCESSORIES		8087		4503		12991		4246	VETEMENTS
842	MENS OUTERWEAR NOT KNIT	W 277	6496	W 57	1334	W 239	3756	W 95	1029	VET DESSUS POUR HOMMES
8422	— SUITS	W 264	5888	W 2	88	W 33	530	W 7	112	COMPLETS HOMMES MAT TEXT
84222	—— OF COTTON	W 253	5798	W 1	20	W 29	442	W 3	47	COMPLETS HOMMES COTON
843	WOMENS OUTERWEAR NONKNIT	W 34	579	W 27	630	W 131	2269	W 55	592	VET DESSUS FEMMES MAT TEX
847	TEXTILE CLTHNG ACCES NES	W 22	387	W 72	1591	W 269	3868	W 106	1017	ACCES VET MAT TEXT NDA
8471	— NOT KNITTED	W 17	321	W 62	1356	W 204	3123	W 88	849	ACCES VET MAT TEX NON BON
84712	SHAWLS,VEILS ETC,NOT KNT	W 3	65	W 55	1263	W 171	2699	W 76	755	ECHARPES ETC MAT TEXT
851	*FOOTWEAR	W 74	783	W 97	652	W 483	2857	W 306	1257	CHAUSSURES
85101	FOOTWEAR RUBBER,PLASTIC	W 17	121	W 81	395	W 351	2452	W 265	907	CHAUS SEMELLES CAOUTCH
87	PRECISION INSTRUMNTS NES		10065		6789		7039		6377	INSTRUM,APPAR SCIENT NDA
872	MEDICAL INSTRUMENTS NES	W 207	3832	W 259	4672	W 335	3585	W 469	4195	INSTR,APP MEDIC–CHIR NDA
87202	OTH MEDICAL INSTRUMENTS	W 180	3291	W 211	4115	W 224	2629	W 344	2572	INSTRUM,APP MEDECINE
874	MEASURNG,CONTROLNG INSTR	W 171	5431	W 104	2019	W 200	3292	W 133	1937	INSTRUMENTS DE MESURE
88	PHOTO EQU,OPTICL GDS ETC		1910		1470		1766		2810	APP,FOURN PHOTO,OP,MONTR
89	MISC MANUFCTRD GOODS NES		18765		11713		15595		12887	ART MANUFACTURES DIVERS
892	PRINTED MATTER	W 809	5056	W 322	2977	W 631	4641	W 1075	2678	IMPRIMES
8921	PRINTED BOOKS,GLOBES,ETC	W 623	2344	W 229	1535	W 424	3716	W 929	2068	LIVRES,BROCHURES,CARTES
89211	PRINTED BOOKS,PAMPHLETS	W 620	2316	W 228	1531	W 424	3705	W 929	2066	LIVRES,BROCHURES
893	ARTICLES OF PLASTIC NES	W 3417	9645	W 1639	5452	W 4093	6917	W 3415	6314	OUVRAGES EN MAT DIVIS 58
8939	MISC PLASTIC ARTICLES	W 3413	9607	W 1576	5236	W 3662	6014	W 3215	5834	ART DIVERS EN MAT DIV 58
89399	OTHR PLASTC ARTICLES NES	W 3266	9463	W 1572	5223	W 3624	5960	W 3167	5718	AUT OUV MAT DIV 58
895	OFFICE SUPPLIES NES	W 448	2269	W 162	1941	W 190	812	W 284	1728	ART PAPET NDA

4. General Imports C.I.F. by Commodities according to the S.I.T.C. (Rev. 2) in thousand U.S. Dollars
Importations Générales C.A.F. par Produits d'après la C.T.C.I. (Rév. 2) en milliers de Dollars E.U.

SITC CTCI	COMMODITY	1990 WEIGHT POIDS		1990 VALUE VALEUR	1991 WEIGHT POIDS		1991 VALUE VALEUR	1992 WEIGHT POIDS		1992 VALUE VALEUR	1993 WEIGHT POIDS		1993 VALUE VALEUR	PRODUIT
8952	PENS,PENCILS,FOUNTN PENS	W	242	1327	W	116	1490	W	78	443	W	145	876	PLUMES,CRAYONS,STYLOS
89521	FOUNTAIN PENS,ETC	W	143	1001	W	115	1478	W	66	376	W	140	796	PORTE PLUME,STYLO ETC

5. General Exports F.O.B. by Commodities according to the S.I.T.C. (Rev. 2) in thousand U.S. Dollars
Exportations Générales F.O.B. par Produits d'après la C.T.C.I. (Rév. 2) en milliers de Dollars E.U.

SITC CTCI	COMMODITY	1990		1991		1992		1993		PRODUIT
		WEIGHT POIDS	VALUE VALEUR	WEIGHT POIDS	VALUE VALEUR	WEIGHT POIDS	VALUE VALEUR	WEIGHT POIDS	VALUE VALEUR	
	ALL COMMODITIES		294163		188609		197171		201706	TOUS PRODUITS
0	FOOD AND LIVE ANIMALS		182042		126325		113228		138541	ALIMENTS,ANIMAUX VIVANTS
001	*LIVE ANIMALS FOR FOOD	W 4674	4826	W 484	690			W 1048	973	ANIMAUX VIVANTS
0011	BOVINE SPECIES,LIVE	W 3683	4184	W 279	294			W 784	683	ESPECE BOVINE
00111	— PURE BRED FR BREEDING	W 3683	4184	W 279	294			W 784	683	BOVINS REPRODUCTEURS
05	VEGETABLES AND FRUIT		25946		6292		3609		3053	LEGUMES ET FRUITS
054	VEG ETC FRSH,SMPLY PRSVD	W 43519	25321	W 11355	3724	W 9116	3077	W 13621	2807	LEGUMES FRAIS,CONG,SECS
0541	POTATOES FRSH EXCL SWEET	W 2453	569	W 1591	353	W 3506	1419	W 3442	378	POMMES DE TERRE
0542	LEGUMINOUS VEGETBLES DRY	W 30854	21121	W 4286	1756	W 2275	1006	W 3808	1962	LEGUMES A COSSE SECS
0545	OTHER FRESH VEGETABLES	W 9531	3398	W 5212	1542	W 3170	618	W 5650	388	AUTRES LEGUMES FRAIS,REF
05459	FRESH VEGETABLES NES	W 7826	2959	W 4431	1356	W 2404	292	W 3663	210	LEGUMES FRAIS,REFRI NDA
057	FRUIT,NUTS,FRESH,DRIED	W 2716	616	W 3253	2470	W 1401	505	W 2707	246	FRUITS FRAIS OU SECS
0579	FRUIT FRESH OR DRIED NES	W 2714	615	W 3253	2470	W 1363	464	W 2700	245	FRUITS FRAIS,SECS NDA
05798	OTHER FRESH FRUIT	W 2714	615	W 3253	2470	W 1051	154	W 2700	245	AUTRES FRUITS FRAIS
06	SUGAR AND PREPS,HONEY		17653		1773		1622		4883	SUCRES ET PRODUITS
061	SUGAR AND HONEY	W 45607	17653	W 16301	1773	W 13000	1622	W 23632	4883	SUCRES ET MIEL
0612	REFINED SUGAR ETC	W 35595	16773	W 6300	1419	W 13000	1621	W 13631	4633	SUCRES RAFFINES
07	COFFEE,TEA,COCOA,SPICES		132864		117169		107845		129395	CAFE,THE,CACAO,EPICES
071	COFFEE AND SUBSTITUTES	W 64507	131508	W 51316	116233	W 44068	107310	W 70007	129177	CAFE ET SUCCEDANES
0711	COFFEE GREEN,ROASTED,SUB	W 64507	131508	W 51316	116233	W 44048	107301	W 70007	129177	CAFE TORREFIE OU DECAFEINE
075	SPICES	W 1187	1355	W 562	936	W 569	535	W 222	218	EPICES
0752	SPICES,EX PEPPER,PIMENTO	W 1137	1076	W 539	868	W 516	421	W 215	204	AUTRES EPICES
07526	GINGER (EXCPT SWEETENED)	W 731	622	W 394	628	W 370	257	W 93	70	GINGEMBRE
1	BEVERAGES AND TOBACCO		1213		261		52		23	BOISSONS ET TABACS
11	BEVERAGES		1213		6		52		23	BOISSONS
112	ALCOHOLIC BEVERAGES	W 1137	1213	W 7	6	W 31	52	W 51	23	BOISSONS ALCOOLIQUES
2	CRUDE MATERLS,EXCL FUELS		76264		32312		45908		52754	MAT BRUTES NON COMESTIBLES
21	HIDES,SKINS,FURS UNDRSSD		60776		25068		32288		32697	CUIRS,PEAUX BRUTS
211	HIDES,SKINS,EXC FURS,RAW	W 7559	60775		25068	W 4215	32288	W 7577	32697	CUIRS ET PEAUX
2111	BOVINE,EQUINE HIDES,RAW	W 2581	8492	W 1413	3748	W 1059	3384	W 2306	4567	PEAUX DE BOVINS
2114	GOAT AND KID SKINS,RAW	W 2004	11818	W 927	5088	W 1166	4842	W 2275	5413	PEAUX DE CAPRINS
2116	SHEEP SKIN WITH WOOL	W 2952	39980	W 1048	16202	W 1935	23704	W 2839	22517	PEAUX LAINEES D'OVINS
22	OIL SEEDS,OLEAGINOUS FRT		2187		1146		302		283	GRAINES,FRUITS OLEAGINEUX
222	SEEDS FOR'SOFT'FIXED OIL	W 1652	1385	W 430	441	W 29	21	W 372	234	GRAINES HUILES FIXES
2225	SESAME SEEDS	W 1193	1077	W 386	405	W 29	21	W 372	234	GRAINES DE SESAME
223	SEEDS FOR OTH FIXED OILS	W 1285	801	W 1029	705	W 217	281	W 77	49	GRAINES AUTRES HUILES FIXES
2238	OIL SEEDS AND FRUITS NES	W 1255	790	W 1029	705	W 217	281	W 77	49	GRAINES D'OLEAGINEUX NDA
26	TEXTILE FIBRES AND WASTE		481		1374		22			FIBRES TEXTILES
269	WASTE OF TEXTILE FABRICS	W 8	41	W 145	851					FRIPERIE DRILLES,CHIFFONS
26901	BULK TEXT WSTE,OLD CLTHG	W 8	41	W 145	851					ART ET ACCESS D'HABILLEMENT
29	CRUDE ANIMAL,VEG MAT NES		12684		4711		13297		19743	MATIERES BRUTES ANIM,VEGET
291	CRUDE ANIMAL MTRIALS NES	W 43	931	W 42	472	W 33	392	W 8	143	MATIERES BRUTES ANIMALES
292	CRUDE VEG MATERIALS NES	W 3052	11752	W 927	4239	W 1568	12905	W 3001	19600	MAT BRUTES VEGETALES NDA
2924	VEG USED IN PHARMACY ETC	W 1566	8893	W 524	3774	W 970	11770	W 2711	18769	PLANTES MEDICINALES
2927	CUT FLOWERS AND FOLIAGE	W 1096	2020	W 373	400	W 567	895	W 102	330	FLEURS,FEUILLAGES COUPES
29271	CUT FLOWERS	W 1096	2020	W 373	400	W 567	895	W 102	330	FLEURS ET BOUTONS
3	MINERAL FUELS ETC		18130		1836		13162		8020	COMBUSTIBLES MINERAUX LUB
33	PETROLEUM AND PRODUCTS		18130		1836		13162		8020	PETROLE ET DERIVES
334	PETROLEUM PRODUCTS,REFIN	W 187645	18130	W 16044	1836	W 144029	13162	W 148049	8020	PRODUITS RAFFINES
3344	FUEL OILS,NES	W 140662	14371	W 8105	1277	W 144029	13162	W 148049	8020	FUEL OILS
3345	LUBS,PETROLEUM OILS NES	W 46976	3752	W 7938	558					HUILES LUBRIFIANTES
33451	LUBS(HIGH PETR CONT) ETC	W 46976	3752	W 7938	558					HUILES LUBRIF,H LOURDES
4	ANIMAL,VEGETABLE OIL,FAT		704		246		500		869	HUILES,GRAISSES ANIM,VEG
431	*PROCESD ANML VEG OIL,ET	W 215	704	W 70	246	W 130	500	W 246	869	HUILES,GRAISSES PREPAREES
4314	ANIMAL,VEGETABLE WAXES	W 215	704	W 70	246	W 130	500	W 246	869	CIRES ANIMALES,VEGETALES
43144	INSECT WAXES,SPERMACETI	W 215	704	W 70	246	W 130	500	W 246	869	BLANC DE BALEINE
5	CHEMCLS,RELATED PROD NES		5998		2276		2032		175	PRODUITS CHIMIQUES
53	DYES,TANNING,COLOUR PROD		3275		1876		327		71	PROD TEINTURE,COLORANTS
532	DYES NES,TANNING PROD	W 67	3275	W 34	1876	W 10	327	W 2	71	EXTRAITS TEINTURE,TANNAGE
5322	DYE,TANN EXTRCTS,TANNINS	W 67	3275	W 34	1876	W 10	327	W 2	71	EXT TAN ORIG VEG,TANNINS
53222	DYEING EXTRCTS VEG,ANMAL	W 67	3275	W 34	1876	W 10	327	W 2	71	MATI COLOR VEGET ANIMALE
55	PERFUME,CLEANING ETC PRD		2633		285		1695			PROD POUR PARFUM,TOILETTE
551	ESSENTL OILS,PERFUME,ETC	W 54	2633	W 10	285	W 29	1687			HUILES ESSENTIELLES
5513	ESSENTL OIL,RESINOID,ETC	W 54	2633	W 10	285	W 29	1687			HUILES ESSENTIELLES,RESIN
6	BASIC MANUFACTURES		4427		415		63		110	ART MANUFACTURES
65	TEXTILE YARN,FABRICS,ETC		3916		350		55		8	FILS,TISSUS,ARTICLES TEXTILE
652	COTTON FABRICS,WOVEN	W 494	2054	W 78	298	W 11	22			TISSUS DE COTON
6522	WOVEN COTTON BLEACHD,ETC	W 475	1886	W 70	273	W 11	22			TISSUS COTON BLANCHIS ETC
65224	BLCHED COTTON FABRIC NES	W 386	1270			W 11	22			AUT TIS PLUS 85% COT BLANCHI
653	WOVN MAN–MADE FIB FABRIC	W 209	1141							TISSUS FIBRES SYNTH,ARTIF
6532	DISC SYN TXTL FABRIC NES	W 209	1141							TIS DISC MOINS 85% FIBR TEXT
8	MISC MANUFACTURED GOODS		5032		3512		1966		1213	ART MANUFACTURES DIVERS
84	CLOTHING AND ACCESSORIES		3888		2829		1878		1104	VETEMENTS
844	UNDER GARMENTS NOT KNIT	W 214	1647	W 253	1476	W 66	157	W 3	9	VETEMENT DESSOUS MAT TEX
8441	— MENS SHIRTS	W 155	1165	W 248	1443	W 66	157	W 3	9	CHEMISES HOMMES MAT TEXT
84411	—— OF COTTON	W 119	849	W 228	1278	W 66	157	W 3	9	CHEMISES HOMMES DE COTON
845	OUTERWEAR KNIT NONELASTC	W 46	355			W 55	402	W 63	635	VET DESSOUS,ACCES BONNET
8452	— WOMENS DRESSES ETC	W 46	355			W 55	402	W 63	635	ROBES,JUPES BONNETERIE
84529	—— OF OTHER FIBRES		2			W 55	402	W 63	635	ROBES JUPES AUTRES FIBR
848	HEADGEAR,NONTXTL CLOTHNG	W 27	718	W 29	872	W 23	665	W 16	459	VET ACCES MAT AUT QUE TEX
8481	LEATHER CLOTHES,ACCESSOR	W 27	718	W 29	872	W 23	665	W 16	459	VET ACCES MAT CUIR ARTIF
9	GOODS NOT CLASSD BY KIND		326		21415		20251			ART TRANSACT NON CLASSES
971	*GOLD,NON MONETARY NES			K 1849	21348	K 2748	20185			OR NON MONETAIRE
97101	NONMON GLD UNWRT,SEMIMFD					K 2748	20185			OR,ALLIAGES D'OR BRUTS
97102	ROLLED GLD UNWKD,SEMIMFD			K 1849	21348					MET COMMUNS PLAQUES OR

FOOT NOTES – NOTES

TABLE 1 –
1 Prior to 1962, years ending 10 September of years stated.
2 Comparable calendar year figures for merchandise trade, imports: 1960, 207.7; 1961, 224.1; exports: 1960, 192.6; 1961, 188.7.

TABLEAU 1 –
1 Avant 1962, années se terminant le 10 septembre des années indiquées.
2 Les chiffres pour les années calendaires comparables sont, à l'importation : 1960, 207.7; 1961, 224.1; à l'exportation : 1960, 192.6; 1961, 188.7.

1. HISTORICAL SERIES, 1960–1995 GENERAL TRADE, IMPORTS C.I.F., EXPORTS F.O.B.
SERIES HISTORIQUES, 1960–1995 COMMERCE GENERAL, IMPORTATIONS C.A.F., EXPORTATIONS F.O.B

YEAR ANNEE	VALUE IN MILLION KRONER / VALEUR EN MILLION KRONER: MERCHANDISE – MARCHANDISE		GOLD – OR		CONVERSION FACTORS U.S. CENTS PER KRONE / FACTEURS DE CONVERSION CENTS E.U. PAR KRONE		INDEX NUMBERS – INDICES: QUANTUM		UNIT VALUE – VALEUR UNITAIRE	
	IMPORTS	EXPORTS	IMPORTS	EXPORTS	IMPORTS	EXPORTS	IMPORTS	EXPORTS	IMPORTS	EXPORTS
1960	104.00	96.50			14.4778	14.4778				
1961	129.60	97.30			14.4778	14.4778				
1962	135.70	126.30			14.4778	14.4778				
1963	138.40	137.00			14.4778	14.4778				
1964	161.90	135.90			14.4778	14.4778				
1965	182.30	177.80			14.4778	14.4778				
1966	195.30	152.70			14.4778	14.4778				
1967	186.30	177.80			14.3395	14.3360				
1968	211.30	154.10			13.3333	13.3333				
1969	243.80	182.20			13.3333	13.3333				
1970	228.40	251.00			13.3333	13.3333				
1971	301.10	278.70			13.4867	13.4867				
1972	325.70	322.10			14.3368	14.3368				
1973	412.30	471.40			16.5893	16.5893				
1974	606.90	487.20			16.4323	16.4323				
1975	651.20	464.30			17.4028	17.4028				
1976	791.70	632.00			16.5426	16.5500				
1977	910.90	863.70			16.6343	16.6341	89	65	51	57
1978	1008.20	776.30			18.2438	18.2402	91	61	54	56
1979	1075.50	759.10			19.0032	19.0161	93	55	60	57
1980	1235.40	1057.70			17.7333	17.7333	92	62	73	68
1981	1482.70	1140.30			14.0445	14.0445	93	62	84	79
1982	1659.00	1254.90			11.9963	11.9963	99	65	93	86
1983	2222.50	1572.90			10.9313	10.9313	101	79	97	91
1984	2719.50	1640.40			9.6520	9.6520	106	81	105	92
1985	2630.50	1899.00			9.4340	9.4340	112	86	108	97
1986	2664.43	1960.28			12.6216	12.6900	136	86	101	97
1987	3513.10	2359.00			14.6118	14.6118	146	83	116	103
1988	3220.69	2344.66			14.8544	14.8544	146	89	99	100
1989	2530.29	2530.22			13.6807	13.6807	125	102	103	99
1990	2084.21	2578.46			16.2278	16.2278	100	100	100	100
1991	1936.21	2781.37			15.6351	15.6351	100	104	100	110
1992	2008.86	2640.88			16.6050	16.6050				
1993	1421.53	2125.71			15.3971	15.3971				
1994	1539.83	2076.34			15.7208	15.7208				
1995	1767.26	2026.27			17.8508	17.8508				

2. IMPORTS BY BROAD ECONOMIC CATEGORY AND EXPORTS BY INDUSTRIAL ORIGIN. (PERCENTAGE OF TOTAL VALUE)
IMPORTATIONS PAR CATEGORIES ECONOMIQUES ET EXPORTATIONS PAR BRANCHE D'ACTIVITE.(EN POURCENTAGE DE LA VALEUR TOTALE)

IMPORTS – IMPORTATIONS

	1990	1991	1992	1993	1994	1995	1996
TOTAL IMPORTS–IMPORTATIONS TOTALES	100.	100.	100.	100.	100.		
1 FOOD BEV–ALIMENTATION BOISSONS	13.9	17.6	20.7	20.5	20.2		
11 PRIMARY–PRODUITS DE BASE	6.9	10.0	12.2	9.7	10.3		
111 FOR INDUSTRY–POUR L'INDUSTRIE	0.3	0.4	0.4	0.5	0.6		
112 FOR HOUSEHOLDS–POUR LES MENAGES	6.5	9.6	11.8	9.3	9.8		
12 PROCESSED–PRODUITS ELABORES	7.1	7.6	8.5	10.8	9.9		
121 FOR INDUSTRY–POUR L'INDUSTRIE	0.7	0.7	0.7	0.9	0.8		
122 FOR HOUSEHOLDS–POUR LES MENAGES	6.4	7.0	7.8	9.9	9.0		
2 IND SUPPLIES–APPROV INDUSTRIELS	26.9	28.5	31.1	30.6	29.2		
21 PRIMARY–PRODUITS DE BASE	1.5	1.6	2.1	2.5	2.7		
22 PROCESSED–PRODUITS ELABORES	25.4	26.9	29.1	28.1	26.5		
3 FUELS–COMBUSTIBLES	12.0	12.8	12.5	15.4	11.8		
31 PRIMARY–PRODUITS DE BASE	0.0	0.0	0.0	0.0	0.0		
32 PROCESSED–PRODUITS ELABORES	12.0	12.8	12.5	15.4	11.8		
321 MOTOR SPIRIT–ESSENCE	12.0	1.1	0.9	1.2	0.8		
322 OTHER–AUTRES	0.0	11.7	11.6	14.2	11.0		
4 MACHINERY–EQUIPEMENT	10.6	11.1	12.8	11.4	16.6		
41 CAPITAL EQUIPMENT–MACHINES	9.2	9.6	11.7	10.2	15.2		
42 PARTS–PIECES ACCESSOIRES	1.5	1.5	1.1	1.2	1.4		
5 TRANSPORT–TRANSPORT	13.8	6.7	7.9	5.0	4.7		
51 PASSENGER CARS–AUTOMOBILES	0.8	1.1	1.3	0.4	0.7		
52 OTHER–AUTRES	10.8	3.5	4.0	0.7	0.6		
521 INDUSTRIAL–INDUSTRIELS	10.7	3.4	3.9	0.6	0.5		
522 NON INDUSTRIAL–NON INDUSTRIEL	0.1	0.1	0.1	0.1	0.1		
53 PARTS–PIECES ACCESSOIRES	2.2	2.1	2.6	3.9	3.4		
6 CONSUM GOODS–BIENS CONSOMMATION	13.2	13.4	14.4	16.7	17.1		
61 DURABLE–DURABLES	3.2	3.0	3.1	3.0	2.6		
62 SEMI DURABLE–SEMI DURABLES	5.3	5.3	6.5	7.5	8.4		
63 NON DURABLE–NON DURABLES	4.7	5.1	4.8	6.2	6.1		
7 GOODS NES–BIENS NDA	9.5	9.9	0.6	0.3	0.4		

EXPORTS – EXPORTATIONS

	1990	1991	1992	1993	1994	1995	1996
TOTAL EXPORTS–EXPORTATIONS TOTALES	100.	100.	100.	100.	100.		
1 AGRICULTURE	84.0	87.9	81.2	84.8	85.7		
2 MINING QUARRY–INDUS EXTRACTIVES	0.0						
3 MANUFACTURING–IND MANUFACTUR	16.0	12.1	18.8	15.2	14.3		
31 FOOD BEV TOBACCO–ALIM BOISS TAB	9.2	6.6	9.5	11.0	11.1		
32 TEXTILES–INDUSTRIES TEXTILES	0.0	0.0	0.1	0.1	0.2		
33 WOOD & PRODUCTS–BOIS & PRODUITS				0.0	0.1		
34 PAPER & PRODUCTS–PAPIER & PRODT		0.0	0.0	0.0			
35 CHEMICALS–INDUSTRIES CHIMIQUES	0.1	0.1	0.1	0.1	0.1		
36 NON METAL MIN–MIN NON METAL							
37 BASIC METAL–IND METAL BASE							
38 METAL MANUF–MANUF METAL	6.7	5.4	9.1	3.9	2.6		
39 OTH MANUF IND–AUTRES MANUF	0.0	0.0	0.0	0.1	0.2		

3. TRADE BY PRINCIPAL COUNTRIES OF PRODUCTION AND LAST CONSIGNMENT (VALUE IN THOUSAND U.S. DOLLARS)
ECHANGES SELON LES PRINCIPAUX PAYS DE PRODUCTION ET DE DERNIERE CONSIGNATION (VALEUR EN MILLIERS DE DOLLARS EU)

COUNTRIES–PAYS	GENERAL IMPORTS C.I.F. IMPORTATIONS GENERALES C.A.F				
	1991	1992	1993	1994	1995
World	302726	333571	218875	242069	306834
Africa	106	202	160	176	234
Americas	13162	19659	8169	7023	7779
Northern America	12395	18351	7049	4461	5953
LAIA	308	473	417	608	552
CACM	433	289	228	143	144
Caribbean	20	7	52	56	51
Rest of America	6	539	422	1755	1079
As.ex F.USSR	11077	17027	9851	13085	19464
Eur.x F.USSR	274076	286247	194733	213161	267620
EU	200371	212397	145851	163424	207533
EFTA	72723	72166	46979	48646	58537
East Europe	980	1677	1857	1052	1460
Other Europe	2	6	2	4	5
Former USSR	3021	9300	5209	7911	9932
Oceania	1037	949	744	712	636
Denmark/Danemark	137133	118711	80613	85694	105769
Norway,SVD,JM	57358	64374	41805	42184	48377
United Kingdom	14291	19775	15814	26081	24937
Germany/Allemagne	13985	25424	15469	15922	24242
Sweden/Suède	13968	18516	11330	11311	17659
USA/Etats–Unis d'Amer	11562	13127	6471	3361	4651
Iceland/Islande	14069	5859	3447	4912	8162
Japan/Japon	6665	8341	3589	4819	9601
Russian Federation		9296	5134	4439	9803
France,Monac	4282	6608	4827	4737	8211
Netherlands/Pays–Bas	4694	6788	5109	5294	6272
Italy/Italie	2733	3776	2645	3188	4906
Belgium–Luxembourg	2325	3139	2269	3148	4820
Portugal	1758	2787	2136	2441	3026
Finland/Finlande	1999	2790	2041	2006	2158
China/Chine	688	1485	1640	2728	3913
Spain/Espagne	1837	1847	1441	2263	2793
Canada	752	5203	575	1059	1288
Switz.Liecht	1296	1934	1728	1550	1998
Hong Kong	1046	1629	1091	1180	1270
Ireland/Irlande	519	1100	1454	599	1611
Poland/Pologne	341	1006	596	664	959
Lithuania/Lituanie		3	7	3057	4
New Zealand	693	665	566	619	506
Former USSR/Anc. URSS	3021				
Korea, Republic of	476	837	482	479	734
Austria/Autriche	632	709	430	423	603
Falkland Isl (Malvinas)		408	421	903	1047
Indonesia/Indonésie	307	524	437	423	564
India/Inde	225	347	258	586	717
Malaysia/Malaisie	219	479	344	408	558
Greece/Grèce	215	428	273	317	526
Thailand/Thaïlande	211	454	339	320	408
Czech Republic			999	163	275
Costa Rica	396	246	203	120	124
Hungary/Hongrie	421	336	120	78	67
Pakistan	132	192	160	232	261
Belize/Bélize	2			850	27
Singapore/Singapour	160	259	124	167	166
Brazil/Brésil	154	225	159	158	163
Israel/Israël	22	355	86	169	121
Turkey/Turquie	83	100	107	163	278
Bangladesh	50	91	104	232	243
Australia/Australie	340	193	59	35	53
Ecuador/Equateur	15	26	125	171	224
Macau/Macao	83	98	68	89	141
Korea Dem People's Rp	30	79	77	68	185
Czechoslovakia	162	225			
Philippines	68	113	42	56	63
So. Africa Customs Un	31	60	33	65	116

COUNTRIES–PAYS	GENERAL EXPORTS F.O.B. EXPORTATIONS GENERALES F.O.B.				
	1991	1992	1993	1994	1995
Monde	434867	438161	328332	326418	351533
Afrique	469	1022	773		919
Amériques	42735	23723	15774	12143	11993
Amérique du Nord	42735	23723	14047	10495	11896
ALAI			975		
MCAC					
Caraïbes			30	115	
Autre Amérique			721	1532	97
Asie l'URSS exclus	17508	12840	13584	9491	13696
Europe l'URSS exclus	372449	392929	297289	300705	323171
UE	358736	353912	284935	287296	294894
AELE	13223	38985	10979	13376	28235
Europe de l'Est			0	34	43
Autre de l'Europe	489	32	1336		
Ancienne URSS	1707	5057	911	424	667
Océanie		2590		3654	792
Denmark/Danemark	81697	77330	83934	86593	80373
United Kingdom	53565	73867	64104	66653	90156
Germany/Allemagne	78291	65109	45481	37205	35035
France,Monac	39552	39036	36819	36704	29814
Italy/Italie	33220	26636	16326	18621	18068
Spain/Espagne	29901	28609	17498	14952	17447
USA/Etats–Unis d'Amer	30929	22539	8183	9366	7177
Norway,SVD,JM	5584	18315	5426	9693	17304
Japan/Japon	15051	10098	8487	8712	13139
Sweden/Suède	12388	8208	3923	9668	9428
Netherlands/Pays–Bas	6733	10993	8512	6676	6050
Iceland/Islande	5257	17370	707	667	8678
Belgium–Luxembourg	7086	7526	4192	3204	1199
Greece/Grèce	8684	7191	1625	1877	1030
Finland/Finlande	7302	4221	1448	3897	2634
Switz.Liecht	2382	3301	4845	3016	2252
Greenland/Groenland	10298	591	445	821	840
Canada	1507	593	5419	307	3879
Portugal	317	4740	850	1246	3297
Russian Federation		5057	911	424	633
New Zealand		2590		2908	
So. Africa Customs Un		1022	770		547
Panama			721	1258	
Malta/Malte	489	32	1336		
Israel/Israël	246	295	1237		
Former USSR/Anc. URSS	1707				
Australia/Australie				745	792
Cyprus/Chypre			1063		
Ireland/Irlande	1	447	223		362
Chile/Chili			975		
Hong Kong			844	85	33
Malaysia/Malaisie				194	481
Guinea/Guinée	469				
Egypt/Egypte					372
Belize/Bélize				274	97
Dominican Republic			30	115	
Singapore/Singapour			22	73	
Czech Republic				34	43
Estonia/Estonie					33
Korea, Republic of					29
Thailand/Thaïlande					11
Indonesia/Indonésie				0	
Austria/Autriche	0				
Poland/Pologne			0		

(VALUE AS PERCENTAGE OF WORLD TOTAL)(VALEURS EN POURCENTAGE DU TOTAL MONDIAL)

	1986	1987	1988	1989	1990	1991	1992	1993	1994	1995
Africa	0.0	0.0	0.0	0.0	0.0	0.0	0.1	0.1	0.1	0.1
Americas	2.6	1.8	2.0	3.2	2.0	4.3	5.9	3.7	2.9	2.5
Northern America	2.4	1.6	1.7	3.0	1.7	4.1	5.5	3.2	1.8	1.9
LAIA	0.1	0.1	0.1	0.2	0.1	0.1	0.1	0.2	0.3	0.2
CACM	0.1	0.1	0.1	0.1	0.2	0.1	0.1	0.1	0.1	0.0
Caribbean	0.0	0.0	0.0	0.0	0.0	0.0	0.0	0.0	0.0	0.0
Rest of America	0.0	0.0	0.1	0.0	0.0	0.0	0.2	0.2	0.7	0.4
As.ex F.USSR	6.1	5.2	5.0	4.6	3.3	3.7	5.1	4.5	5.4	6.3
Eur.x F.USSR	90.9	92.9	91.1	91.3	93.3	90.5	85.8	89.0	88.1	87.2
EU	74.4	57.7	66.5	68.6	64.0	66.2	63.7	66.6	67.5	67.6
EFTA	15.7	34.5	24.1	22.0	25.9	24.0	21.6	21.5	20.1	19.1
East Europe	0.6	0.7	0.5	0.6	3.3	0.3	0.5	0.8	0.4	0.5
Other Europe	0.3	0.0	0.1	0.0	0.0	0.0	0.0	0.0	0.0	0.0
Former USSR	0.2	0.0	1.7	0.6	1.2	1.0	2.8	2.4	3.3	3.2
Oceania	0.0	0.0	0.1	0.1	0.1	0.3	0.3	0.3	0.3	0.2
Denmark/Danemark	45.5	32.7	39.6	44.4	43.8	45.3	35.6	36.8	35.4	34.5
Norway,SVD,JM	13.1	32.6	21.1	16.3	19.8	18.9	19.3	19.1	17.4	15.8
United Kingdom	4.3	3.3	8.2	3.7	4.8	4.7	5.9	7.2	10.8	8.1
Germany/Allemagne	8.8	7.0	5.8	5.9	4.2	4.6	7.6	7.1	6.6	7.9
Sweden/Suède	7.9	7.3	6.3	5.8	4.9	4.6	5.6	5.2	4.7	5.8
USA/Etats–Unis d'Amer	2.3	1.5	1.6	2.8	1.4	3.8	3.9	3.0	1.4	1.5
Iceland/Islande	2.1	1.4	2.4	4.3	5.5	4.6	1.8	1.6	2.0	2.7
Japan/Japon	4.8	3.9	3.5	3.1	2.0	2.2	2.5	1.6	2.0	3.1
Russian Federation							2.8	2.3	1.8	3.2
France,Monac	1.1	1.3	0.9	2.5	1.2	1.4	2.0	2.2	2.0	2.7

	1986	1987	1988	1989	1990	1991	1992	1993	1994	1995
Afrique						0.1	0.2	0.2		0.3
Amériques	18.8	12.0	13.3	11.9	8.4	9.8	5.4	4.8	3.7	3.4
Amérique du Nord	18.8	11.0	12.8	11.5	8.4	9.8	5.4	4.3	3.2	3.4
ALAI		1.0	0.6	0.3				0.3		
MCAC										
Caraïbes								0.0	0.0	
Autre Amérique	0.1							0.2	0.5	0.0
Asie l'URSS exclus	2.3	2.3	8.3	5.8	3.4	4.0	2.9	4.1	2.9	3.9
Europe l'URSS exclus	78.4	83.6	77.3	79.2	88.1	85.6	89.7	90.5	92.1	91.9
UE	75.3	80.3	68.4	75.2	85.5	82.5	80.8	86.8	88.0	83.9
AELE	3.1	3.0	8.9	4.0	2.3	3.0	8.9	3.3	4.1	8.0
Europe de l'Est		0.2			0.3			0.0	0.0	0.0
Autre de l'Europe						0.1	0.0	0.4		
Ancienne URSS	0.5	0.4	1.0	3.1		0.4	1.2	0.3	0.1	0.2
Océanie		1.7	0.0	0.0	0.1		0.6		1.1	0.2
Denmark/Danemark	17.9	16.2	18.6	16.2	20.8	18.8	17.6	25.6	26.5	22.9
United Kingdom	13.3	7.6	11.5	13.6	14.3	12.3	16.9	19.5	20.4	25.6
Germany/Allemagne	13.5	11.1	9.7	13.4	18.4	18.0	14.9	13.9	11.4	10.0
France,Monac	10.1	8.5	7.6	9.2	11.2	9.1	8.9	11.2	11.2	8.5
Italy/Italie	6.5	7.1	7.2	7.0	4.8	7.6	6.1	5.0	5.7	5.1
Spain/Espagne	2.0	4.5	6.7	7.3	7.9	6.9	6.5	5.3	4.6	5.0
USA/Etats–Unis d'Amer	14.0	10.2	9.1	9.8	4.5	7.1	5.1	2.5	2.9	2.0
Norway,SVD,JM	1.8	2.3	8.0	3.5	1.0	1.3	4.2	1.7	3.0	4.9
Japan/Japon	2.0	2.0	4.9	5.2	3.0	3.5	2.3	2.6	2.7	3.7
Sweden/Suède	2.3	2.0	1.9	3.2	4.0	2.8	1.9	1.2	3.0	2.7

4. General Imports C.I.F. by Commodities according to the S.I.T.C. (Rev. 2) in thousand U.S. Dollars
Importations Générales C.A.F. par Produits d'après la C.T.C.I. (Rév. 2) en milliers de Dollars E.U.

SITC CTCI	COMMODITY	1991		1992		1993		1994		PRODUIT
		WEIGHT POIDS	VALUE VALEUR	WEIGHT POIDS	VALUE VALEUR	WEIGHT POIDS	VALUE VALEUR	WEIGHT POIDS	VALUE VALEUR	
	ALL COMMODITIES		302726		333571		218875		242069	TOUS PRODUITS
0	FOOD AND LIVE ANIMALS		71217		86508		55807		62684	ALIMENTS,ANIMAUX VIVANTS
01	MEAT AND PREPARATIONS		9084		9088		7343		7934	VIANDES ET PREPARATIONS
011	MEAT FRESH,CHILLD,FROZEN	W 2578	6641	W 2394	6280	W 1967	4814	W 1916	5304	VIANDES FRAICHES,REF,CONGE
0111	BOVINE MEAT FRESH,FROZEN	W 669	1838	W 730	1986	W 660	1634	W 645	1644	VIANDES BOVIN FRAI,REF
01112	BOVINE MEAT BONELESS	W 446	1336	W 490	1415	W 517	1288	W 551	1398	VIANDES BOVIN DESOSSEES
0112	MUTTON ETC FRSH,CHLD,FRN	W 738	2145	W 601	1853	W 397	1232	W 510	1653	VIANDE DE MOUTON
0113	PIG MEAT FRESH,CHLD,FRZN	W 391	1242	W 329	1089	W 330	955	W 376	1130	VIANDE DE PORC
0114	POULTRY FRESH CHLLD,FRZN	W 603	1107	W 555	969	W 428	685	W 239	563	VOLAILLES MORTES
014	MEAT PREPD,PRSVD,NES ETC	W 623	2260	W 701	2685	W 682	2361	W 736	2511	CONSERVES DE VIANDES
0142	SAUSAGES INCLDING TINNED	W 288	949	W 315	1139	W 294	973	W 311	1011	SAUCISSES,SAUCISSONS
0149	OTH PREPARD,PRESRVD MEAT	W 335	1311	W 384	1531	W 387	1376	W 425	1500	AUTRES PREP DE VIANDES
02	DAIRY PRODCTS,BIRDS'EGGS		4251		4396		3466		3229	PRODUITS LAITIERS,OEUFS
022	MILK AND CREAM	W 1384	1348	W 1246	1243	W 876	831	W 670	722	LAIT ET CREME
0223	MILK AND CREAM FRESH	W 1313	1202	W 1188	1082	W 823	691	W 606	560	LAIT,CREME FRAIS
024	CHEESE AND CURD	W 475	1780	W 483	1855	W 463	1626	W 434	1545	FROMAGE ET CAILLEBOTTE
025	EGGS,BIRDS,FRESH,PRSRVD	W 509	660	W 616	803	W 538	668	W 487	627	OEUFS
0251	— IN SHELL	W 507	655	W 613	793	W 536	660	W 485	620	OEUFS EN COQUILLE
03	FISH AND PREPARATIONS		16949		26752		10675		13334	POISSONS ET PREPARATIONS
034	FISH,FRESH,CHILLED,FROZN	W 7224	12293	W 14046	23397	W 7243	7468	W 9221	9408	POISSON FRAIS, REFRIG,CONG
0341	FISH FRSH,CHLLD,EX FILLT	W 1609	1305	W 4690	6991	W 2430	1739	W 2083	974	POISSON FRAIS,REFRIGERE
0342	FISH FROZEN,EXCL FILLETS	W 4774	8718	W 9272	16070	W 4233	4577	W 6707	7556	POISSONS CONGELES
0343	FISH FILLETS,FRESH,CHLLD	W 273	843		1	W 505	1015	W 37	76	FILETS FRAIS,REFRIGERES
0344	FISH FILLETS,FROZEN	W 568	1427	W 84	336	W 75	137	W 394	802	FILETS CONGELES
035	FISH SALTED,DRIED,SMOKED	W 20	45	W 15	39	W 7	19	W 591	934	POISSON SECHE,SALE,FUME
03503	FISH(EX COD)DRIED,SALTED		1	W 14	31	W 5	9	W 436	884	POISSONS SECHES,SALES
036	SHELL FISH FRESH,FROZEN	W 3377	4343	W 2569	2875	W 2007	2741	W 1811	2548	CRUSTACES,MOLLUSQUES
04	CEREALS AND PREPARATIONS		4228		4902		4762		4893	CEREALES ET PRODUITS
046	WHEAT ETC MEAL OR FLOUR	W 2293	895	W 1995	795	W 1886	674	W 2092	744	SEMOULE FARINE,FROMENT
04601	FLOUR OF WHEAT OR MESLIN	W 2255	884	W 1975	783	W 1879	670	W 2086	741	FARINE DE FROMENT
048	CEREAL ETC PREPARATIONS	W 1554	2816	W 2059	3683	W 2260	3736	W 2461	3804	PREPTNS A BASE CEREALES
0484	BAKERY PRODUCTS	W 603	1677	W 760	2262	W 954	2415	W 1101	2581	PRODUITS DE BOULANGERIE
04841	BREAD,BISCUIT,COM WAFERS	W 293	626	W 435	926	W 553	1042	W 693	1153	PAINS,BISCUITS DE MER
04842	PASTRY, CAKES ETC	W 310	1051	W 325	1336	W 401	1372	W 408	1428	PATISSERIE ETC.
05	VEGETABLES AND FRUIT		6175		7946		6426		6709	LEGUMES ET FRUITS
054	VEG ETC FRSH,SMPLY PRSVD	W 3390	1970	W 4825	2878	W 4630	2349	W 4236	2626	LEGUMES FRAIS,CONG,SECS
0541	POTATOES FRSH EXCL SWEET	W 2567	877	W 3130	875	W 3058	665	W 2820	1024	POMMES DE TERRE
0545	OTHER FRESH VEGETABLES	W 469	497	W 934	977	W 924	867	W 828	869	AUTRES LEGUMES FRAIS,REF
05459	FRESH VEGETABLES NES	W 347	411	W 718	800	W 705	703	W 612	675	LEGUMES FRAIS,REFRI NDA
056	VEGTBLES ETC PRSVD,PREPD	W 331	805	W 427	1126	W 395	925	W 393	945	CONSERVES DE LEGUMES
0565	VEGTBLES PRSVD,PREPD NES	W 319	786	W 416	1104	W 382	900	W 382	924	LEGUMES PREPARES CONSERVE
05659	OTH VEG PRESVD,PREPD NES	W 143	524	W 244	839	W 206	664	W 223	705	LEGUM PREPAP,CONSERV NDA
057	FRUIT,NUTS,FRESH,DRIED	W 1363	1855	W 1763	2256	W 1621	1791	W 1520	1817	FRUITS FRAIS OU SECS
058	FRUIT PRESERVED,PREPARED	W 1534	1545	W 1298	1686	W 1291	1361	W 1198	1322	CONSERVES DE FRUITS
06	SUGAR AND PREPS,HONEY		2266		2502		1928		2147	SUCRES ET PRODUITS
062	SUGAR CANDY NON-CHOCLATE	W 299	1520	W 325	1832	W 259	1339	W 286	1441	SUCRERIES
07	COFFEE,TEA,COCOA,SPICES		3223		3697		2793		3323	CAFE,THE,CACAO,EPICES
071	COFFEE AND SUBSTITUTES	W 209	864	W 272	1203	W 226	889	W 256	1246	CAFE ET SUCCEDANES
0711	COFFEE GREEN,ROASTED,SUB	W 206	835	W 267	1153	W 223	868	W 254	1224	CAFE TORREFIE OU DECAFEINE
07112	COFFEE ROASTED	W 206	835	W 264	1136	W 214	835	W 250	1200	CAFE TORREFIE
073	CHOCOLATE AND PRODUCTS	W 277	1621	W 252	1593	W 221	1255	W 268	1445	CHOCOLAT
081	*FEEDING STUFF FOR ANIML	W 27094	22244	W 27712	22934	W 19414	14330	W 19948	16919	NOURRITURE POUR ANIMAUX
0819	FOOD WASTE AND FEED NES	W 26209	21909	W 26545	22360	W 18649	13981	W 19125	16597	DECHETS,ALIMENTS NDA
08199	FODDER NES,INCL SWEETNED	W 26209	21909	W 26545	22360	W 18643	13978	W 19124	16595	PREPARATIONS FOURRAGERES
09	MISC EDIBLE PRODUCTS		2752		4256		4071		4165	PREP ALIMENTAIRES DIVERSES
091	MARGARINE AND SHORTENING	W 338	355	W 823	901	W 781	801	W 733	776	MARGARINE ET GRAISSES
0914	MARGARINE,EDIBLE FAT NES	W 335	351	W 821	898	W 780	799	W 732	774	MARGARINES,SIMILI SAINDOUX
09141	MARGARINE	W 277	286	W 742	796	W 715	719	W 672	693	MARGARINE
098	EDIBLE PRODCTS,PREPS NES	W 585	2397	W 953	3355	W 930	3270	W 844	3389	PREP ALIMENTAIRES NDA
09809	MISC FOOD PREPRTIONS NES	W 329	1331	W 557	1948	W 528	2007	W 440	2077	PREP ALIMENTAIRES NDA
1	BEVERAGES AND TOBACCO		5858		7149		4842		4381	BOISSONS ET TABACS
11	BEVERAGES		4098		5216		3158		2738	BOISSONS
111	NON-ALCOHL BEVERAGES NES	W 747	819	W 1079	1034	W 1172	1007	W 862	801	BOISSONS NON ALCOOLIQUES
11102	FLAVORED WATERS NON-ALCO	W 723	787	W 994	963	W 1101	939	W 768	720	LIMONADES,EAUX GAZEUSES
112	ALCOHOLIC BEVERAGES	W 758	3279	W 1316	4182	W 1369	2152	W 1482	1936	BOISSONS ALCOOLIQUES
1121	WINE OF FRESH GRAPES ETC	W 225	868	W 464	1264	W 216	433	W 241	438	VINS DE RAISINS FRAIS
11212	WINE OF FRESH GRAPES	W 218	832	W 448	1174	W 201	402	W 230	417	VINS DE MOUTS DE RAISINS
1124	DISTILLED ALCOHOLIC BEVS	W 272	2043	W 389	2427	W 447	1317	W 395	1086	ALCOOLS,EAUX-DE-VIE
11249	OTH ALCOHOLC BEVS,CMPNDS	W 252	1802	W 381	2365	W 409	1139	W 357	934	BOISSONS ALCOOLIQUES NDA
12	TOBACCO AND MANUFACTURES		1760		1933		1684		1643	TABACS BRUTS FABRIQUES
122	TOBACCO,MANUFACTURED	W 88	1759	W 90	1933	W 86	1684	W 79	1643	TABACS FABRIQUES
1222	CIGARETTES	W 53	1287	W 57	1421	W 49	1126	W 45	1062	CIGARETTES
2	CRUDE MATERLS,EXCL FUELS		8795		11879		6937		8510	MAT BRUTES NON COMESTIBLES
24	CORK AND WOOD		4328		5512		1628		1430	LIEGE ET BOIS
248	WOOD SHAPED,SLEEPERS	W 5205	3761	W 6674	4614	W 2647	1334	W 1757	1110	BOIS SIMPLEMENT TRAVAILLES
2482	LUMBER SHAPED CONIFER	W 5097	3606	W 6519	4375	W 2544	1188	W 1679	957	CONIFERES SCIES,RABOTES
24821	LUMBER SAWN ETC CONIFER	W 4892	3164	W 5073	3286	W 2116	917	W 1196	617	CONIFERES SCIES LONGITUD
24822	LUMBER PLANED ETC CONIFR	W 205	442	W 1446	1089	W 428	271	W 483	340	CONIFER RABOTES,RAINES
26	TEXTILE FIBRES AND WASTE		164		472		189		952	FIBRES TEXTILES
266	SYNTHETIC FIBRES TO SPIN	W 8	30	W 76	293	W 11	39	W 109	804	FIBRES SYNTHETIQUES
2666	CONTIN FILAMNT TOW SYNTH	W 8	30	W 76	291	W 11	39	W 109	804	CABLES POUR DISCONTINUS
26669	— OF OTH SYNTHTC FIBRES	W 5	17		15	W 8	29	W 87	738	D'AUTRES FIBRES TEXT SYNT
27	CRUDE FERTLZR,MINRLS NES		2068		2158		1331		1541	ENGRAIS MINERAUX BRUTS
278	OTHER CRUDE MINERALS	W 25516	1575	W 22080	1778	W 16767	1197	W 19049	1459	AUTRES MINERAUX BRUTS
2783	COMMON SALT,ETC	W 20234	1061	W 16680	1104	W 10644	635	W 17756	1263	SEL
29	CRUDE ANIMAL,VEG MAT NES		2092		3589		3725		4509	MATIERES BRUTES ANIM,VEGET
291	CRUDE ANIMAL MTRIALS NES	W 11413	1337	W 25148	2541	W 29203	2825	W 39574	3657	MATIERES BRUTES ANIMALES
2919	OTH ANIMAL MATERIALS NES	W 11411	1336	W 25148	2540	W 29203	2825	W 39574	3643	MAT ORIGINE ANIMALE NDA
29194	FISH WASTE	W 11228	1165	W 25127	2481	W 29100	2741	W 39466	3538	DECHETS DE POISSONS
292	CRUDE VEG MATERIALS NES	W 362	755	W 256	1049	W 230	899	W 195	852	MAT BRUTES VEGETALES NDA
3	MINERAL FUELS ETC		38939		41805		33889		28719	COMBUSTIBLES MINERAUX LUB
33	PETROLEUM AND PRODUCTS		38833		41665		33787		28630	PETROLE ET DERIVES
334	PETROLEUM PRODUCTS,REFIN	W 188734	38735	W 196099	41585	W 189938	33726	W 169248	28568	PRODUITS RAFFINES
3341	GASOLINE,OTH LIGHT OILS	W 14455	3202	W 12976	3046	W 12690	2612	W 10406	2001	ESSENCES POUR MOTEURS
33411	MOTOR,AVIATION SPIRIT	W 14324	3106	W 8	14	W 8	13	W 13	20	ESSENCES MOTEURS D'AVIONS
33419	OTH LIGHT PETROLEUM OILS	W 131	96	W 12968	3032	W 12682	2599	W 10392	1981	AUTRES HUILES LEGERES
3343	GAS OILS	W 147521	29665	W 175445	33473	W 138387	25013	W 133354	21696	GAS OILS
3344	FUEL OILS,NES	W 21283	2760	W 10	3	W 35756	3655	W 22494	2196	FUEL OILS
3345	LUBS,PETROLEUM OILS NES	W 3814	2732	W 6076	4722	W 1517	2109	W 1646	2418	HUILES LUBRIFIANTES
33451	LUBS(HIGH PETR CONT) ETC	W 3812	2720	W 6069	4663	W 1489	2042	W 1625	2348	HUILES LUBRIF,H LOURDES
5	CHEMCLS,RELATED PROD NES		21680		27343		20181		20107	PRODUITS CHIMIQUES

4. General Imports C.I.F. by Commodities according to the S.I.T.C. (Rev. 2) in thousand U.S. Dollars
Importations Générales C.A.F. par Produits d'après la C.T.C.I. (Rév. 2) en milliers de Dollars E.U.

SITC CTCI	COMMODITY	1991			1992			1993			1994			PRODUIT
		WEIGHT POIDS		VALUE VALEUR	WEIGHT POIDS		VALUE VALEUR	WEIGHT POIDS		VALUE VALEUR	WEIGHT POIDS		VALUE VALEUR	
51	ORGANIC CHEMICALS			731			1246			556			522	PROD CHIMIQ ORGANIQUES
52	INORGANIC CHEMICALS			444			2088			1356			1063	PROD CHIM INORGANIQUES
522	INORG ELEMNTS,OXIDES,ETC	W	302	272	W	441	690	W	451	786	W	468	823	ELEMENTS INORGANIQUES
523	OTHR INORG CHEMICALS ETC	W	131	90	W	1078	1353	W	247	565	W	155	234	AUT PRODUITS CHIMIQUES INORG
5239	INORG CHEM PRODUCTS NES	W	2	3	W	930	1223	W	72	430	W	15	90	PROD CHIM INORGANIQ NDA
52391	HYDROGEN PEROXIDE				W	929	1207	W	71	426	W	14	86	PEROXYDE D'HYDROGENE
53	DYES,TANNING,COLOUR PROD			4157			4466			3908			3352	PROD TEINTURE,COLORANTS
531	SYNT DYE,NAT INDGO,LAKES	W	7	1169	W	15	1568	W	18	1774	W	10	1238	MAT COLOR ORGAN,LAQUES
5311	SYNTHIC ORGNIC DYESTUFFS	W	7	1169	W	8	1558	W	10	1765	W	7	1235	MAT COLOR ORGAN SYNTHET
533	PIGMENTS,PAINTS,ETC	W	667	2854	W	704	2877	W	602	2115	W	539	2078	PIGMENTS,PEINTURES,VERNIS
5334	VARNISHES,DISTEMPERS ETC	W	535	2356	W	566	2281	W	518	1705	W	463	1728	PEINTURES A L'EAU
53342	OTH PAINTS,VARNISHES ETC	W	347	1711	W	330	1362	W	306	1105	W	299	1139	AUTRES PEINTURES,VERNIS
541	*MEDICINAL,PHARM PRODUCT	K	115272	6766	K	180931	9517	K	91647	6634	K	91581	7302	PROD MEDICINAUX PHARMACEUT
5416	GLYCOSIDES,GLANDS,SERA	K	834	357	K	31691	2654	K	6187	785	K	11171	1561	HETEROSIDES
54164	ANTISERA,MICROB VACCINES	K	446	315	K	9046	1702	K	1623	285	K	6832	1097	SERUMS,VACCINS
5417	MEDICAMENTS	K	89666	5647	K	123529	5948	K	53193	5042	K	60167	5002	MEDICAMENTS
54179	— CONTNG OTH SUBSTANCES	K	81874	5517	K	115507	5071	K	50006	4408	K	56251	4409	MED CONT AUT SUBSTANCES
55	PERFUME,CLEANING ETC PRD			2929			4093			3488			3574	PROD POUR PARFUM,TOILETTE
553	PERFUMERY,COSMETICS,ETC	W	99	1206	W	162	1840	W	158	1574	W	158	1660	PRODUITS DE PARFUMERIE
554	SOAP,CLEANSING ETC PREPS	W	820	1634	W	947	2124	W	915	1813	W	884	1707	SAVONS,PRODUITS DETERSIFS
5542	WASHING PREPARATIONS ETC	W	619	1153	W	858	1725	W	840	1527	W	772	1380	PROD ORG TENSIO-ACT NDA
572	*EXPLOSIVES,PYROTECH PRO	W	300	1033	W	196	749	W	65	243	W	82	269	EXPLOSIFS
58	PLASTIC MATERIALS ETC			3525			3521			2500			2351	MAT PLAST ARTIFICIELLES
583	POLYMERIZATION ETC PRODS	W	1725	3218	W	1594	3147	W	1390	2366	W	1316	2162	PROD POLYMERISATION
5831	POLYETHYLENE	W	906	1162	W	606	718	W	487	640	W	478	539	POLYETHYLENE
58311	— IN PRIMARY FORMS	W	850	1027	W	550	568	W	429	508	W	434	434	POLYETHYLENE PRIMAIRES
5833	POLYSTYRENE,ITS COPOLYMR	W	573	1171	W	771	1432	W	774	1124	W	667	980	POLYPROPYLENE COPOLYMERES
58331	— IN PRIMARY FORMS	W	572	1166	W	770	1430	W	774	1124	W	666	977	SOUS FORMES PRIMAIRES
59	CHEMICAL MATERIALS NES			1445			1152			1064			1159	MAT PROD CHIMIQUES NDA
6	BASIC MANUFACTURES			42837			53021			35111			35442	ART MANUFACTURES
62	RUBBER MANUFACTURES NES			1963			2456			1632			1975	CAOUTCHOUC MANUFACTURE
625	RUBBER TYRES, TUBES ETC	W	265	1321	W	272	1601	W	216	1108	W	280	1356	PNEUS CAOUTCHOUC VULCANISE
6251	TYRES NEW FOR MOTOR CARS	W	131	793	W	155	993	W	113	623	W	141	793	PNEUS POUR VOITURES
63	WOOD,CORK MANUFACTRS NES			5482			6206			3218			2082	OUVRAGES LIEGE ET BOIS
634	VENEERS,PLYWOOD,ETC	W	3147	3088	W	3136	3301	W	1517	1435	W	995	977	PLACAGES,CONTRE-PLAQUES
6342	PLYWOOD OF WOOD SHEETS	W	2274	2009	W	2125	1999	W	930	844	W	515	552	BOIS CONTRE-PLAQUES
635	WOOD MANUFACTURES NES	W	1622	2358	W	1725	2875	W	1012	1771	W	509	1081	ART MANUF EN BOIS NDA
6353	BUILDERS WOODWRK,PREFABS	W	626	1625	W	442	2014	W	275	1300	W	153	720	OUVRAGES DE MENUISERIE
64	PAPER,PAPERBOARD AND MFR			10505			12580			9468			9980	PAPIERS,CARTONS & OUVRAGES
641	PAPER AND PAPERBOARD	W	2194	3008	W	3892	5169	W	2056	2874	W	1539	2668	PAPIERS ET CARTONS
6418	COATED ETC PAPER NES BLK	W	480	1105	W	664	1304	W	349	843	W	267	829	PAP,CARTONS COUCHES,ENDUITS
64189	COATED PAPER ETC NES	W	253	834	W	269	867	W	216	698	W	183	732	PAPIERS,CARTONS COUCHES
642	PAPER,ETC,PRECUT,ARTS OF	W	3378	7497	W	2681	7411	W	2759	6594	W	3229	7311	PAP,CARTONS DECOUPES
6421	PAPER ETC CONTAINERS	W	2876	5364	W	1966	4183	W	1976	3580	W	2349	4146	BOITES,SACS EMBALLAGES
6428	PAPER ETC ARTICLES NES	W	328	1183	W	438	1956	W	435	1685	W	441	1834	OUVRAGES EN PATE A PAPIER
64285	PAPER ETC DIAPERS ETC	W	140	577	W	259	1086	W	262	1078	W	249	1152	SERVIETTES HYGIENIQUES
65	TEXTILE YARN,FABRICS,ETC			4949			8502			6840			7112	FILS,TISSUS,ARTICLES TEXTILE
654	OTH WOVEN TEXTILE FABRIC	W	30	117	W	137	4039	W	276	3546	W	124	3497	TISSUS AUT COTON SYNT,ARTIF
6549	WOVEN FABRICS NES				W	127	3955	W	259	3456	W	116	3455	TISSUS NDA
65499	PILE,CHENILLE FABRIC NES				W	127	3953	W	258	3451	W	116	3453	VELOURS NDA
657	SPECIAL TXTL FABRC,PRODS	W	522	3226	W	430	2625	W	328	1817	W	293	1802	TISSUS SPECIAUX
6575	CORDAGE AND MANUFACTURES	W	496	3011	W	396	2315	W	309	1637	W	271	1593	FICELLES,CORDES,CORDAGES
65751	CORDAGE,CABLE,ROPE,TWINE	W	243	1006	W	227	1024	W	114	450	W	76	284	CORDAGES TRESSES OU NON
65752	NETTING OF ROPE,TWINE	W	251	1991	W	168	1281	W	192	1168	W	190	1281	FILETS MAT DU 657.51
66	NONMETAL MINERAL MFS NES			4459			5517			3299			2622	ART MIN NON METALLIQUES
661	LIME,CEMENT,BLDG PRODS	W	14354	1889	W	12081	1814	W	7112	1012	W	4807	767	CHAUX,CIMENTS MAT CONSTR
6612	CEMENT	W	13899	1524	W	11346	1195	W	6790	685	W	4517	460	CIMENTS HYDRAULIQUES
663	MINERAL MANUFCTURES NES	W	3315	1193	W	3053	1632	W	1775	777	W	804	516	ART MIN MANUF NDA
664	GLASS	W	363	574	W	573	985	W	298	736	W	217	424	VERRE
67	IRON AND STEEL			3780			3680			1972			2193	FER ET ACIER
674	IRN,STL UNIV,PLATE,SHEET	W	998	1150	W	720	1086	W	364	378	W	396	467	LARGES PLATS,TOLES
678	IRON,STL TUBES,PIPES,ETC	W	482	1177	W	389	999	W	169	451	W	195	529	TUBES,TUYAUX EN FONTE,FER
68	NON-FERROUS METALS			1772			1827			1033			990	METAUX NON FERREUX
684	ALUMINIUM	W	232	1190	W	216	1280	W	121	694	W	134	656	ALUMINIUM
6842	ALUMINIUM,ALLOYS WORKED	W	232	1190	W	216	1280	W	121	692	W	132	647	ALUMINIUM,ALLIAGES OUVRE
69	METAL MANUFACTURES NES			9901			12195			7514			8344	ART MANUFACT EN METAL NDA
691	STRUCTURES AND PARTS NES	W	612	2150	W	562	1969	W	286	1153	W	233	959	CONSTRUCT FER,ACIER,ALU
6911	STRUCTURES,PARTS IRN,STL	W	574	1720	W	483	1252	W	267	971	W	215	805	CONSTRUCT FER,ACIER,FONTE
693	WIRE PRODUCTS NON ELECTR	W	922	1521	W	1538	2778	W	974	1571	W	1045	1789	OUVRAGES FILS METALLIQUES
6931	WIRE CABLES, ROPES ETC	W	579	1174	W	1198	2383	W	683	1254	W	882	1576	CORDAGES EN FILS DE FER
69311	IRN,STEEL CABLE,ROPE ETC	W	575	1135	W	1169	2221	W	659	1171	W	846	1437	CORDAGES FILS FER,ACIER
699	BASE METAL MFRS NES	W	763	3704	W	685	3986	W	418	2567	W	532	3127	ART MANUFACTURES MET NDA
6991	LOCKSMITHS WARES,ETC	W	91	862	W	106	1013	W	53	618	W	47	503	ARTICLES DE SERRURERIE
6997	IRON,STEEL ARTICLES NES	W	333	1291	W	263	1605	W	132	959	W	261	1595	OUV FONTE,FER,ACIER NDA
69979	IRN,STL MANUFACTURES NES	W	298	1229	W	222	1463	W	124	925	W	246	1554	AUT OUVRAGES EN FER NDA
7	MACHINES,TRANSPORT EQUIP			53744			67922			33132			47821	MACHINES MATERIEL TRANSPORT
71	POWER GENERATING EQUIPMT			3621			3224			4585			3789	MACHINES GENERATRICES
713	INTRNL COMBUS PSTN ENGIN	W	131	2557	W	64	2123	W	64	4013	W	121	3212	MOTEURS EXPL COMB INT, PIECE
7131	AIRCRAFT PSTN ENGINS,PTS			1				W	2	2033			33	MOTEURS EXPL P.AVIATION, PIE
71311	AIRCRAFT PISTON ENGINES							W	1	960			1	MOTEURS EXPL P.AVIATION
71319	PTS NES OF ENGN OF 71311			1				W	1	1073			32	PIECES POUR 713.11
7133	MARINE PISTON ENGINES	W	81	1338	W	26	345	W	21	202	W	31	556	MOTEURS EXPL POUR BATEAUX
71332	—— OTHER THAN OUTBOARD	W	79	1282	W	24	284	W	21	194	W	30	538	MOT BATEAUX AUT HORSBORD
7139	PISTON ENGINE PARTS NES	W	39	1099	W	27	1616	W	36	1712	W	39	2167	PIECES POUR 713.2,3,8
72	MACHS FOR SPCL INDUSTRYS			5255			7368			3670			5240	MAC SPECIALES POUR INDUST
727	FOOD MACHRY NON-DOMESTIC	W	46	1769	W	84	2652	W	28	607	W	68	1762	MACH INDUSTRIES ALIMENT
7272	OTH FOOD PROC MCHY,PARTS	W	41	1723	W	80	2551	W	27	580	W	66	1745	AUT MACH IND ALIMENTAIRE
72722	INDUS FOOD PROC MACH NES	W	41	1723	W	80	2551	W	27	580	W	66	1745	MACHINES BOULANGERIE
728	OTH MACHY FOR SPCL INDUS	W	67	1970	W	96	2800	W	191	2510	W	85	2693	AUT MACH IND PARTICULIERES
7284	MACHY FOR SPCL INDUS NES	W	45	1664	W	61	2351	W	175	2264	W	78	2581	MACH SPEC IND PARTICUL.
72848	OTH MCHY WITH INDIV FNCT	W	26	621	W	54	2088	W	167	2159	W	65	2385	AUTRES MACHINES NDA
72849	PTS OF MACHS OF 7284 ETC	W	18	1026	W	4	159	W	2	81	W	3	124	PIECES DU 728.4 ETC
74	GENRL INDUSTRL MACHY NES			9555			10415			5423			7390	MACH APP INDUSTRIE
741	HEATING,COOLING EQUIPMNT	W	195	2957	W	156	2540	W	43	879	W	63	1193	MACH CHAUFFAGE,PIECES
7414	NONDOM REFRIG EQUIPT,PTS	W	96	1104	W	100	1551	W	20	231	W	38	569	MAT PRODUCTION DU FROID
74141	REFRIG EQUIP NONDOMESTIC	W	50	572	W	94	1371	W	18	134	W	27	395	REFIG INDUSTRIELS
7416	HEATING,COOLING EQU NES	W	64	1189	W	31	493	W	6	159	W	8	175	APP CHANGEMENT TEMP
742	PUMPS FOR LIQUIDS ETC	W	32	816	W	32	1205	W	28	821	W	25	768	POMPES MOTO-POMPES
743	PUMPS NES,CENTRFUGES ETC	W	69	1200	W	73	1442	W	36	759	W	46	1198	POMPES COMPRES,VENT ETC
744	MECHANICAL HANDLING EQU	W	203	2361	W	249	2494	W	75	1494	W	303	2326	EQUIP MANUTENTION PIECES
7442	LIFTING,LOADING MACH NES	W	73	843	W	112	1017	W	28	397	W	94	934	APP LEVAGE,MANUTENTION

4. General Imports C.I.F. by Commodities according to the S.I.T.C. (Rev. 2) in thousand U.S. Dollars
Importations Générales C.A.F. par Produits d'après la C.T.C.I. (Rév. 2) en milliers de Dollars E.U.

SITC CTCI	COMMODITY	1991 WEIGHT POIDS	1991 VALUE VALEUR	1992 WEIGHT POIDS	1992 VALUE VALEUR	1993 WEIGHT POIDS	1993 VALUE VALEUR	1994 WEIGHT POIDS	1994 VALUE VALEUR	PRODUIT
7449	PTS NES OF MACHY OF 7442	W 74	1134	W 38	823	W 42	1090	W 30	788	PIECES DU 744.2
745	NONELEC MACHY,TOOLS NES	W 43	997	W 40	1059	W 19	568	W 27	927	AUT MACH NON ELEC,PIECES
7452	OTH NONELEC MCHS,PTS NES	W 42	959	W 38	1029	W 19	552	W 26	909	AUT MACH NON ELEC,PIECES
749	NONELEC MACH PTS,ACC NES	W 46	1224	W 59	1674	W 28	901	W 27	979	PIECES MACH NON ELEC NDA
75	OFFICE MACHNES,ADP EQUIP		6118		8062		4727		5990	MACH BUREAU TRAIT AUTOM
751	OFFICE MACHINES	W 30	1168	W 21	761	W 15	580	W 19	809	MACH,APPAREILS DE BUREAU
7518	OFFICE MACHINES NES	W 27	1009	W 17	606	W 12	403	W 17	664	MACH,APP DE BUREAU NDA
752	AUTOMTIC DATA PROC EQUIP	W 13	1835	W 57	5848	W 37	2873	W 37	3143	MACH TRAIT INFORMATION
7522	DIGITAL COMPUTERS	W 1	169	W 14	1581	W 10	786	W 7	732	MACH DIGITALES COMPLETES
7523	DIGITL CENTRL PROCESSORS	W 5	703	W 9	1092	W 4	333	W 3	279	UNITES CENTRALES
7525	ADP PERIPHERAL UNITS	W 4	275	W 16	1395	W 11	875	W 15	1136	UNITES PERIPHERIQUES
759	OFFICE,ADP MCH PTS,ACCES	W 28	3114	W 19	1453	W 14	1274	W 21	2038	PIECES DU 751 ET 752
7599	ACCTG,ETC,ADP MCH PTS,AC	W 19	2592	W 8	1059	W 10	988	W 16	1696	PIECES DU 751 ET 752
76	TELECOMM,SOUND EQUIPMENT		5731		7639		3676		13107	EQUIPMENT DE TELECOM
764	TELECOM EQPT,PTS,ACC NES	W 50	4287	W 70	5913	W 42	2932	W 59	12291	EQUIP TELECOM,PIECES
7641	LINE TELEPHONE,ETC EQUIP	W 9	760	W 7	1044	W 7	645	W 7	1725	APP TELEPHON PAR FIL
7643	TV,RADIO TRANSMITTRS ETC	W 3	456	W 6	1247	W 2	483	W 3	503	APP EMET TELE RADIO
7648	TELECOMM EQUIPMENT NES	W 4	1051	W 3	450	W 2	210	W 16	2562	APP TELECOM NDA
76483	RADAR APPARATUS ETC	W 3	954	W 2	372	W 2	183	W 15	2448	APP DE RADIOGUIDAGE ETC
7649	PTS NES OF EQUIPMT OF 76	W 27	1850	W 40	2848	W 24	1444	W 42	7232	PIECES DE LA DIV 76
76491	PTS NES OF APPAR OF 7641	W 8	621	W 7	1159	W 3	339	W 26	5835	PIECES POUR 764.1
76493	TELECOMM EQUIPMT PTS NES	W 19	1200	W 32	1622	W 21	1087	W 15	1360	PIECES 761,762,764.3,8
77	ELECTRIC MACHNRY NES ETC		6856		8809		5635		5840	MACH APP ELECT NDA
772	SWITCHGEAR ETC,PARTS NES		1464	W 85	1933	W 49	1124	W 51	1339	APP COUPURE,SECT ETC
7721	SWITCHGEAR ETC	W 57	1457	W 85	1871	W 48	1110	W 51	1322	APP COUPURE,SECTIONMNT
773	ELECTR DISTRIBUTNG EQUIP	W 218	1261	W 179	1190	W 106	604	W 93	545	EQUIPMT DISTRIBUTION ELECT
7731	INSULATED WIRE,CABLE ETC	W 216	1156	W 161	950	W 104	501	W 86	443	FILS,CABLES ISOLES ELECT
775	HOUSEHOLD TYPE EQUIP NES	W 227	2054	W 246	2367	W 186	1526	W 188	1536	MACH,APP USAGE DOMESTQUE
778	ELECTRICAL MACHINERY NES	W 164	1670	W 156	2044	W 146	1750	W 180	1928	AUTRES MACH ELECT NDA
7781	BATTERIES,ACCUMULATORS	W 123	680	W 115	760	W 112	598	W 136	732	PILES ET ACCUMULATEURS
78	ROAD VEHICLES		7342		9790		4544		5557	VEHICULES ROUTIERS
781	PASS MOTOR VEH EXC BUSES	W 388	3360	W 513	4221	W 119	913	W 177	1611	AUTO TRANSPORT PERSONNES
782	LORRIES,SPCL MTR VEH NES	W 244	1776	W 180	1960	W 64	884	W 83	878	VEHICULES SPECIAUX,MARCH
7821	LORRIES,TRUCKS	W 196	1569	W 106	1015	W 19	206	W 52	193	VEHICULES TRANSP MARCHAND
7822	SPECIAL MOTOR VEHCLS NES	W 47	207	W 75	945	W 45	678	W 31	685	VEHICULES USAGES SPECIAUX
784	MOTOR VEH PRTS,ACCES NES	W 160	1632	W 211	2843	W 155	2157	W 160	2340	PIECES 722,781,782,783
7849	OTHER MOTOR VEHCL PARTS	W 156	1590	W 208	2831	W 154	2154	W 156	2330	PIECES 722,781,782,783
79	OTHR TRANSPORT EQUIPMENT		9066		12234		761		726	AUTRE MATERIEL TRANSPORT
792	AIRCRAFT ETC		13	W 5	1215	W 3	658	W 6	405	APP NAVIGATION AERIENNE
7929	AIRCRAFT PARTS NES		13	W 4	1189	W 2	639	W 6	405	PIECES DU 792
793	SHIPS AND BOATS ETC	W 1553	9050	W 2027	11017	W 10	93	W 21	299	NAVIRES BATEAUX,ETC
7932	SHIPS AND BOATS NES	W 1393	8228	W 1990	10649		2		1	NAVIRES ET BATEAUX
79323	OTHER CARGO VESSELS	W 336	4339	W 6	186					AUT BATEAUX TRANS MARCH
79324	FISHING VESSELS ETC	W 1036	3742	W 1984	10460					BATEAUX DE PECHE
8	MISC MANUFACTURED GOODS		29513		36114		28095		33356	ART MANUFACTURES DIVERS
812	*PLUMBG,HEATNG,LGHTNG EQ	W 236	1574	W 293	2235	W 169	1246	W 119	1082	APPAR SANITAIRES CHAUFFAGE
8124	LIGHTING EQUIPMENT NES	W 40	775	W 60	1177	W 48	794	W 51	797	APPAREILS ECLAIRAGE ETC
81242	LAMPS,FITTINGS BASE METL	W 35	601	W 50	1010	W 44	696	W 47	724	APPAREILS D'ECLAIRAGE
821	*FURNITURE,PARTS THEREOF	W 920	4774	W 958	5563	W 677	3518	W 610	3340	MEUBLES ET PIECES
8211	CHAIRS,SEATS AND PARTS	W 101	934	W 147	1329	W 96	730	W 106	879	SIEGES ET PIECES
82111	CHAIRS AND OTHER SEATS	W 101	932	W 145	1314	W 96	727	W 105	861	SIEGES
8219	FURNITURE AND PARTS NES	W 741	3158	W 752	3541	W 524	2210	W 430	1758	AUTRES MEUBLES ET PIECES
82192	WOOD FURNITURE NES	W 594	2429	W 618	2671	W 410	1599	W 337	1343	MEUBLES NDA EN BOIS
84	CLOTHING AND ACCESSORIES		5493		7343		6362		8533	VETEMENTS
842	MENS OUTERWEAR NOT KNIT	W 33	1197	W 28	1092	W 28	905	W 47	1333	VET DESSUS POUR HOMMES
8423	— TROUSERS,BREECHES ETC	W 21	664	W 17	602	W 19	555	W 31	785	PANTALONS HOMMES MAT TEX
843	WOMENS OUTERWEAR NONKNIT	W 29	1300	W 40	1873	W 33	1308	W 46	1886	VET DESSUS FEMMES MAT TEX
8439	— OTHER OUTER GARMENTS	W 19	666	W 25	932	W 18	601	W 27	941	AUT VET DES FEM MAT TEXT
845	OUTERWEAR KNIT NONELASTC	W 32	1363	W 49	2147	W 47	1899	W 60	2333	VET DESSOUS,ACCES BONNET
8451	— JERSEYS,PULLOVERS ETC	W 16	640	W 15	711	W 21	865	W 27	1036	CHANDAILS,PULL–OVERS ETC
8459	— OTHER,CLTHG ACCESRYS	W 14	585	W 30	1209	W 21	783	W 28	1045	AUT VET DESSUS DE BONNE
846	UNDER GARMENTS KNITTED	W 15	576	W 23	941	W 24	729	W 35	934	SOUS VETS DE BONNETERIE
848	HEADGEAR,NONTXTL CLOTHNG	W 21	441	W 27	534	W 54	1007	W 78	1347	VET ACCES MAT AUT QUE TEX
8484	HEADGEAR	W 1	33	W 3	97	W 35	715	W 47	882	COIFFURES ET PARTIES NDA
84843	HEADGEAR TEXTILE NONFELT	W 1	26	W 2	53	W 35	701	W 44	808	CHAPEAUX EN BONNETERIE
851	*FOOTWEAR	W 57	1481	W 91	2256	W 56	1209	W 64	1351	CHAUSSURES
85102	FOOTWEAR LEATHER	W 41	1241	W 68	1733	W 29	823	W 39	951	CHAUS SEMELLES EN CUIR
87	PRECISION INSTRUMNTS NES		2185		2875		3485		4499	INSTRUM,APPAR SCIENT NDA
872	MEDICAL INSTRUMENTS NES	W 10	404	W 5	419	W 8	829	W 11	808	INSTR,APP MEDIC–CHIR NDA
87202	OTH MEDICAL INSTRUMENTS	W 9	310	W 4	342	W 7	585	W 10	763	INSTRUM,APP MEDECINE
874	MEASURNG,CONTROLNG INSTR	W 16	1593	W 23	2211	W 24	2390	W 43	3463	INSTRUMENTS DE MESURE
8741	SURVEYING INSTRUMENTS	W 4	692	W 4	596	W 2	308	W 5	911	INST GEODESIE,TOPO ETC
8745	MEAS,CONTRL,SCI INST NES	W 1	50	W 9	747	W 13	963	W 29	1016	APP SCIENT MESURE NDA
87453	MECHANCL TESTING APPARAT			W 8	697	W 11	855	W 27	820	MACH NON ELEC ESSAIS MEC
8748	ELEC MEAS,CONTRL EQU NES	W 1	246	W 1	176	W 3	609	W 2	975	APP ELEC ELECTRO MESURE
87483	OTH ELCTRNC MEAS ETC EQU	W 1	214	W 1	168	W 2	597	W 2	960	AUT APP ELECTRO DE MESURE
88	PHOTO EQU,OPTICL GDS ETC		1029		1465		915		1031	APP,FOURN PHOTO,OP,MONTR
89	MISC MANUFCTRD GOODS NES		12851		14051		11201		13363	ART MANUFACTURES DIVERS
892	PRINTED MATTER	W 507	4684	W 281	3345	W 281	2767	W 404	3852	IMPRIMES
8921	PRINTED BOOKS,GLOBES,ETC	W 235	2284	W 79	1316	W 70	948	W 63	1019	LIVRES,BROCHURES,CARTES
89211	PRINTED BOOKS,PAMPHLETS	W 92	1416	W 77	1277	W 68	919	W 58	947	LIVRES,BROCHURES
8922	NEWSPAPERS,PERIODICALS	W 151	928	W 57	390	W 78	563	W 201	1522	JOURNAUX ET PERIODIQUES
8928	PRINTED MATTER NES	W 112	1330	W 137	1544	W 130	1206	W 136	1245	IMPRIMES NDA
893	ARTICLES OF PLASTIC NES	W 943	3922		5058	W 692	3588		3774	OUVRAGES EN MAT DIVIS 58
8931	PLSTC PACKG CONTNRS,LIDS	W 222	997	W 388	1692	W 283	1248	W 382	1553	ART TRANSP EMBALLAGE ETC
8939	MISC PLASTIC ARTICLES	W 716	2849	W 523	3246	W 404	2286	W 361	2152	ART DIVERS EN MAT DIV 58
89399	OTHR PLASTC ARTICLES NES	W 618	2356	W 410	2687	W 284	1818	W 266	1731	AUT OUV MAT DIV 58
894	TOYS,SPORTING GOODS,ETC	W 147	1835	W 154	2022	W 108	1314	W 178	1881	VOITURES ENFANTS,JOUETS
8942	TOYS,INDOOR GAMES ETC	W 64	766	W 79	1093	W 68	848	W 99	1050	JOUETS,JEUX ETC
898	MUSICAL INSTRUMENTS,PTS	W 27	1018	W 37	1032	W 30	1440	W 34	1460	INSTRUMENTS DE MUSIQUE
8983	SOUND RECRDNG TAPE,DISCS	W 15	599	W 30	826	W 24	1048	W 29	1299	SUPPORTS SON POUR 763
89832	RECORDED DISCS,TAPES ETC	W 6	447	W 13	538	W 7	460	W 10	919	DISQUES,PHONO,BANDES
899	OTHER MANUFACTURED GOODS		928		1394		1059		1340	AUT ART MANUF DIVERS NDA
9	GOODS NOT CLASSD BY KIND		29729		1477		586		722	ART TRANSACT NON CLASSES
931	*SPECIAL TRANSACTIONS	W 5291	29724	W 238	1469	W 39	571	W 30	714	TRANS.SPECIALES

5. General Exports F.O.B. by Commodities according to the S.I.T.C. (Rev. 2) in thousand U.S. Dollars
Exportations Générales F.O.B. par Produits d'après la C.T.C.I. (Rév. 2) en milliers de Dollars E.U.

SITC CTCI	COMMODITY	1991		1992		1993		1994		PRODUIT
		WEIGHT POIDS	VALUE VALEUR	WEIGHT POIDS	VALUE VALEUR	WEIGHT POIDS	VALUE VALEUR	WEIGHT POIDS	VALUE VALEUR	
	ALL COMMODITIES		434867		438161		328332		326418	TOUS PRODUITS
0	FOOD AND LIVE ANIMALS		406650		389757		306819		310110	ALIMENTS,ANIMAUX VIVANTS
03	FISH AND PREPARATIONS		400044		379614		296592		297446	POISSONS ET PREPARATIONS
034	FISH,FRESH,CHILLED,FROZN	W 99521	283690	W 88013	275454	W 85319	217547	W 74079	202561	POISSON FRAIS, REFRIG,CONG
0341	FISH FRSH,CHLLD,EX FILLT	W 45625	89404	W 39850	100421	W 41851	92854	W 33165	77018	POISSON FRAIS,REFRIGERE
0342	FISH FROZEN,EXCL FILLETS	W 11820	42283	W 9099	34812	W 10704	23594	W 5583	13752	POISSONS CONGELES
0343	FISH FILLETS,FRESH,CHLLD	W 3390	13100	W 6319	26451	W 5210	19043	W 5863	23331	FILETS FRAIS,REFRIGERES
0344	FISH FILLETS,FROZEN	W 38687	138904	W 32744	113769	W 27554	82057	W 29468	88459	FILETS CONGELES
035	FISH SALTED,DRIED,SMOKED	W 13278	65116	W 12284	61254	W 7516	30373	W 10371	42667	POISSON SECHE,SALE,FUME
03503	FISH(EX COD)DRIED,SALTED	W 13071	63155	W 11922	57645	W 7118	26797	W 9664	35783	POISSONS SECHES,SALES
03504	FISH SMOKED	W 197	1942	W 343	3398	W 398	3574	W 660	6733	POISSONS FUMES
036	SHELL FISH FRESH,FROZEN	W 6768	33291	W 2929	19269	W 5643	30463	W 8971	34642	CRUSTACES,MOLLUSQUES
037	FISH ETC PREPD,PRSVD NES	W 3273	17947	W 4287	23637	W 3870	18209	W 3908	17577	POIS,CRUST,MOL PREPARES
0371	FISH PREPARD,PRESRVD NES	W 1054	2410	W 1839	6021	W 2062	6839	W 2287	6538	CONSERVES DE POISSONS
0372	SHELL FISH PREPRD,PRESVD	W 2218	15537	W 2448	17616	W 1808	11370	W 1621	11039	CRUSTACES,COQUIL PREPARES
081	*FEEDING STUFF FOR ANIML	W 12751	6607	W 19016	10142	W 22328	10222	W 23829	11898	NOURRITURE POUR ANIMAUX
0814	MEAT OR FISH MEAL FODDER	W 12716	6582	W 19015	10140	W 22325	10210	W 22416	10726	FARINES DE VIANDES,POISSONS
08142	FISH MEAL FODDER	W 12716	6582	W 19015	10140	W 22325	10210	W 22416	10726	FARINES DE POISSONS
0819	FOOD WASTE AND FEED NES	W 35	24		2		12	W 1413	1172	DECHETS,ALIMENTS NDA
08199	FODDER NES,INCL SWEETNED	W 35	24		2		12	W 1413	1172	PREPARATIONS FOURRAGERES
2	CRUDE MATERLS,EXCL FUELS		3305		4368		2149		3058	MAT BRUTES NON COMESTIBLES
29	CRUDE ANIMAL,VEG MAT NES		3180		4198		1976		2575	MATIERES BRUTES ANIM,VEGET
291	CRUDE ANIMAL MTRIALS NES	W 42753	3180	W 45697	4198	W 27126	1976	W 29311	2575	MATIERES BRUTES ANIMALES
2919	OTH ANIMAL MATERIALS NES	W 42753	3180	W 45697	4198	W 27126	1976	W 29311	2575	MAT ORIGINE ANIMALE NDA
29194	FISH WASTE	W 42738	3168	W 45697	4198	W 27126	1976	W 29311	2575	DECHETS DE POISSONS
4	ANIMAL,VEGETABLE OIL,FAT		780		3306		5430		2965	HUILES,GRAISSES ANIM,VEG
411	*ANIMAL OILS AND FATS	W 2835	780	W 9463	3306	W 16487	5430	W 10278	2965	HUILES,GRAISSES ANIMALES
4111	OILS OF FISH,WHALES ETC	W 2835	780	W 9463	3306	W 16487	5430	W 10278	2965	GRAISSES,HUILES DE POISSONS
41112	OTHER FISH OILS AND FATS	W 2835	780	W 9463	3306	W 16487	5430	W 10278	2965	AUTRES HUILES ET GRAISSES
6	BASIC MANUFACTURES		147		292		366		1024	ART MANUFACTURES
7	MACHINES,TRANSPORT EQUIP		23480		39924		12830		8026	MACHINES MATERIEL TRANSPORT
79	OTHR TRANSPORT EQUIPMENT		23434		39924		12338		7916	AUTRE MATERIEL TRANSPORT
793	SHIPS AND BOATS ETC	W 4744	23434	W 6996	39924	W 7962	12338	W 4286	7916	NAVIRES BATEAUX,ETC
7932	SHIPS AND BOATS NES	W 4744	23434	W 6706	39642	W 7962	12338	W 4286	7916	NAVIRES ET BATEAUX
79323	OTHER CARGO VESSELS	W 1100	3339	W 964	4301	W 3158	3243	W 2128	2783	AUT BATEAUX TRANS MARCH
79324	FISHING VESSELS ETC	W 3143	19452	W 5742	35341	W 4722	9019	W 2156	5125	BATEAUX DE PECHE

1. HISTORICAL SERIES, 1961–1996 GENERAL TRADE, IMPORTS C.I.F., EXPORTS F.O.B.
SERIES HISTORIQUES, 1961–1996 COMMERCE GENERAL, IMPORTATIONS C.A.F., EXPORTATIONS F.O.B

YEAR ANNEE	VALUE IN MILLION FIJI DOLLARS VALEUR EN MILLION FIJI DOLLARS MERCHANDISE –MARCHANDISE IMPORTS	EXPORTS	GOLD –OR IMPORTS	EXPORTS	CONVERSION FACTORS U.S. CENTS PER FIJI DOLLAR FACTEURS DE CONVERSION CENTS E.U. PAR FIJI DOLLAR IMPORTS	EXPORTS	INDEX NUMBERS –INDICES QUANTUM IMPORTS	EXPORTS	UNIT VALUE VALEUR UNITAIRE IMPORTS	EXPORTS
1961	34.40	23.90	0.01	2.40	126.1250	126.1250				
1962	34.80	29.10	0.01	2.30	126.1250	126.1250				
1963	40.40	41.20		3.10	126.1250	126.1250				
1964	55.20	49.50	0.01	2.70	126.1250	126.1250				
1965	58.20	39.40		3.00	126.1250	126.1250				
1966	50.50	35.90	0.01	3.00	126.1250	126.1250				
1967	56.30	39.50	0.01	3.10	125.0600	125.0150				
1968	68.40	45.70	0.01	3.40	114.8320	114.8320				
1969	77.90	49.90	0.01	3.30	114.8320	114.8320				
1970	90.50	59.00	0.01	3.30	114.8320	114.8320				
1971	111.50	59.00	0.02	2.60	116.7380	117.2200				
1972	131.50	61.60	0.02	3.90	121.2040	119.5080				
1973	174.70	74.40	0.02	6.10	126.0050	127.0040				
1974	219.30	123.70	0.04	8.60	124.5230	124.8030				
1975	221.80	142.30	0.12	8.50	121.0680	119.1930				
1976	238.00	122.50	0.16	7.20	110.4230	110.0350				
1977	281.00	164.30	0.14	6.50	109.1210	109.8100				
1978	300.00	166.50	0.21	4.90	118.3640	119.2430				
1979	392.90	215.00	0.35	6.40	119.6580	119.5820				
1980	458.80	305.60	0.23	12.00	122.5530	123.3810				
1981	539.90	269.00	0.48	11.60	117.0591	115.7757				
1982	475.60	267.60			108.2365	106.8719				
1983	493.20	244.90			98.1908	97.8534				
1984	487.10	279.40			92.3739	91.4452				
1985	508.00	271.40			86.9212	87.1189				
1986	493.60	383.02			88.1690	87.5722				
1987	465.11	483.12			81.4973	78.9356				
1988	658.82	531.19			70.0407	70.0158				
1989	860.44	658.62			67.5036	67.3683				
1990	1112.90	731.86			67.7531	68.0514				
1991	961.77	664.60			67.7923	67.8170				
1992	947.11	666.98			66.5841	66.4621				
1993	1109.81	692.40			64.8944	64.9260				
1994	1209.85	800.49			68.5257	68.7404				
1995	1218.93	869.94			71.1090	71.1100				
1996	1359.48	1013.01			71.2862	71.2050				

2. IMPORTS BY BROAD ECONOMIC CATEGORY AND EXPORTS BY INDUSTRIAL ORIGIN. (PERCENTAGE OF TOTAL VALUE)
IMPORTATIONS PAR CATEGORIES ECONOMIQUES ET EXPORTATIONS PAR BRANCHE D'ACTIVITE.(EN POURCENTAGE DE LA VALEUR TOTALE)

IMPORTS – IMPORTATIONS

	1990	1991	1992	1993	1994	1995	1996
TOTAL IMPORTS–IMPORTATIONS TOTALES	100.	100.	100.	100.	100.		
1 FOOD BEV–ALIMENTATION BOISSONS	13.8	16.1	15.5	17.0	14.8		
11 PRIMARY–PRODUITS DE BASE	8.6	9.9	7.9	9.4	8.6		
111 FOR INDUSTRY–POUR L'INDUSTRIE	2.5	2.9	2.9	2.7	2.7		
112 FOR HOUSEHOLDS–POUR LES MENAGES	6.1	7.0	5.1	6.6	5.9		
12 PROCESSED–PRODUITS ELABORES	5.2	6.2	7.5	7.7	6.2		
121 FOR INDUSTRY–POUR L'INDUSTRIE	1.4	1.6	2.4	1.7	1.4		
122 FOR HOUSEHOLDS–POUR LES MENAGES	3.9	4.7	5.1	6.0	4.8		
2 IND SUPPLIES–APPROV INDUSTRIELS	27.1	30.4	31.0	27.5	28.1		
21 PRIMARY–PRODUITS DE BASE	0.8	1.0	1.1	0.8	0.6		
22 PROCESSED–PRODUITS ELABORES	26.3	29.5	29.8	26.7	27.4		
3 FUELS–COMBUSTIBLES	14.1	15.0	14.0	13.6	11.2		
31 PRIMARY–PRODUITS DE BASE	0.4	0.7	0.6	0.7	0.6		
32 PROCESSED–PRODUITS ELABORES	13.7	14.3	13.4	12.9	10.6		
321 MOTOR SPIRIT–ESSENCE							
322 OTHER–AUTRES	13.7	14.3	13.4	12.9	10.6		
4 MACHINERY–EQUIPEMENT	13.0	12.9	11.2	14.6	12.3		
41 CAPITAL EQUIPMENT–MACHINES	11.2	10.5	9.3	12.5	10.5		
42 PARTS–PIECES ACCESSOIRES	1.8	2.5	1.9	2.1	1.7		
5 TRANSPORT–TRANSPORT	16.9	8.9	12.9	9.9	18.6		
51 PASSENGER CARS–AUTOMOBILES	2.1	1.9	2.4	2.5	1.9		
52 OTHER–AUTRES	11.0	3.5	7.5	4.0	12.7		
521 INDUSTRIAL–INDUSTRIELS	10.9	3.4	7.5	3.9	12.6		
522 NON INDUSTRIAL–NON INDUSTRIEL	0.1	0.1	0.1	0.1	0.1		
53 PARTS–PIECES ACCESSOIRES	3.8	3.5	2.9	3.4	4.0		
6 CONSUM GOODS–BIENS CONSOMMATION	14.0	15.6	14.5	16.2	13.9		
61 DURABLE–DURABLES	5.1	5.2	4.6	5.0	4.1		
62 SEMI DURABLE–SEMI DURABLES	5.7	6.9	6.2	7.4	6.1		
63 NON DURABLE–NON DURABLES	3.2	3.5	3.7	3.7	3.6		
7 GOODS NES–BIENS NDA	1.1	1.0	1.0	1.2	1.1		

EXPORTS – EXPORTATIONS

	1990	1991	1992	1993	1994	1995	1996
TOTAL EXPORTS–EXPORTATIONS TOTALES	100.	100.	100.	100.	100.		
1 AGRICULTURE	4.9	3.4	3.7	3.0	4.3		
2 MINING QUARRY–INDUS EXTRACTIVES	0.0	0.0	0.0	0.0	0.0		
3 MANUFACTURING–IND MANUFACTUR	95.1	96.6	96.3	97.0	95.7		
31 FOOD BEV TOBACCO–ALIM BOISS TAB	45.0	51.7	47.7	46.0	45.1		
32 TEXTILES–INDUSTRIES TEXTILES	20.1	22.1	22.1	27.6	22.9		
33 WOOD & PRODUCTS–BOIS & PRODUITS	5.5	4.5	5.8	3.6	4.8		
34 PAPER & PRODUCTS–PAPIER & PRODT	0.7	1.0	1.0	1.3	0.8		
35 CHEMICALS–INDUSTRIES CHIMIQUES	13.5	11.5	10.9	12.9	10.1		
36 NON METAL MIN–MIN NON METAL	0.7	0.4	0.2	0.2	0.1		
37 BASIC METAL–IND METAL BASE	1.0	0.4	0.8	0.6	0.7		
38 METAL MANUF–MANUF METAL	7.5	4.1	6.7	3.7	9.8		
39 OTH MANUF IND–AUTRES MANUF	1.1	1.0	1.0	1.2	1.3		

3. TRADE BY PRINCIPAL COUNTRIES OF PROVENANCE AND LAST DESTINATION (VALUE IN THOUSAND U.S. DOLLARS)
ECHANGES SELON LES PRINCIPAUX PAYS DE PROVENANCE ET DE DERNIERE DESTINATION (VALEUR EN MILLIERS DE DOLLARS EU)

COUNTRIES–PAYS	GENERAL IMPORTS C.I.F. IMPORTATIONS GENERALES C.A.F				
	1992	1993	1994	1995	1996
World	630736	526623	837793	866778	984018
Africa	708	777	974		
Americas	58654	26553	129071	65684	98600
Northern America	57181	24934	126672	65684	98600
LAIA	1004	861	1844		
CACM	16	28	36		
Caribbean	393	684	499		
Rest of America	60	46	21		
As.ex F.USSR	210168	181136	247449	207867	185892
Eur.x F.USSR	48587	33733	34579	32310	32236
EU	45288	31080	32698	32310	32236
EFTA	1923	1337	1374		
East Europe	1369	1315	507		
Other Europe	1	1	0		
Former USSR	359	47	76		
Oceania	309947	282609	421688	474477	582552
Australia/Australie	202187	172872	275946	336594	437093
New Zealand	106128	108292	141009	137883	145460
USA/Etats–Unis d'Amer	55127	22455	123715	61542	91818
Japan/Japon	64970	63447	66876	62342	51596
Singapore/Singapour	40374	28378	62188	61869	49663
China/Chine	21315	18960	26492	24975	24693
Hong Kong	20239	16800	17674	23964	16984
United Kingdom	19941	15787	14500	17979	17626
Thailand/Thaïlande	11531	11607	12856	12354	17857
Korea, Republic of	11425	7664	9408	12560	12733
Malaysia/Malaisie	5712	5284	8293	9803	12367
Germany/Allemagne	9634	5328	6478	9795	8875
France,Monac	8480	3255	3050	4451	5672
India/Inde	6963	7382	9955		
Indonesia/Indonésie	7073	6966	9624		
Canada	2054	2477	2938	4141	6782
Belgium–Luxembourg	2944	2215	3054		
Italy/Italie	1705	1256	1879		
Netherlands/Pays–Bas	1390	1383	1954		
Papua New Guinea	877	1080	2669		
Switz.Liecht	1699	1269	1177		
Sri Lanka	1422	1206	1309		
Brazil/Brésil	805	661	1257		
Pakistan	1087	826	757		
Philippines	543	566	926		
Sweden/Suède	563	748	630		
Czech Republic		1195	404		
Solomon Isls	369	180	901		
Dominica/Dominique	347	316	460		
Spain/Espagne	175	367	347		
Kiribati	1	7	848		
So. Africa Customs Un	202	159	492		
Poland/Pologne	717	19	34		
Mali	277	230	127		
Finland/Finlande	76	321	174		
Czechoslovakia	493				
Mexico/Mexique	148	122	204		
Korea Dem People's Rp	195	168	85		
Denmark/Danemark	65	200	164		
Austria/Autriche	39	144	230		
Norway,SVD,JM	218	66	122		
Malawi	66	139	188		
Guadeloupe	2	362	25		
Tonga	238	32	97		
Ukraine	326	16	8		
Chile/Chili	38	32	279		
Iran (Islamic Rp. of)	90	129	104		
Viet Nam		8	277		
Portugal	40	40	54	85	63
Ireland/Irlande	11	34	186		

COUNTRIES–PAYS	GENERAL EXPORTS F.O.B. EXPORTATIONS GENERALES F.O.B.				
	1992	1993	1994	1995	1996
Monde	428049	297683	550337	618619	725047
Afrique	196	102	738		
Amériques	71726	47839	124403	90541	77394
Amérique du Nord	71488	47809	124283	90541	77394
ALAI	13	8	68		
MCAC	24	2	36		
Caraïbes	201	20	17		
Autre Amérique	0				
Asie l'URSS exclus	58927	23702	81354	82278	98253
Europe l'URSS exclus	136354	85847	111742	137716	131080
UE	136346	85806	111466	137716	131080
AELE	7	41	277		
Europe de l'Est	1				
Autre de l'Europe					
Ancienne URSS	6	15	68		
Océanie	145838	122031	207736	181083	292190
Australia/Australie	61659	63030	118617	148171	202010
United Kingdom	132479	81820	106851	124873	104275
USA/Etats–Unis d'Amer	59721	34046	98638	71180	61306
New Zealand	24815	17256	29285	32912	90180
Japan/Japon	22516	14838	37575	36143	48404
Malaysia/Malaisie	27133	3392	26209	29398	21578
Canada	11764	13760	25645	19361	16088
Tonga	13697	9255	15233		
Portugal		3		9609	24757
American Samoa	9001	5371	7758		
Samoa	8237	5341	7188		
China/Chine	3548	10	1222	6032	9537
Hong Kong	3960	1841	2436	5382	5407
Korea, Republic of	158	634	7207	4284	6642
Kiribati	5514	4305	4989		
Vanuatu	4018	3446	4468		
Cook Islands/Iles Cook	4601	2910	3443		
Singapore/Singapour	1028	1949	644	775	6524
Germany/Allemagne	3305	1615	1280	2687	1593
Tuvalu	3468	2501	2990		
French Polynesia	2273	1794	2528		
Papua New Guinea	1082	939	4331		
New Caledonia	2020	1392	2107		
Norfolk Island	1405	1445	1712		
Solomon Isls	1354	1412	1329		
Netherlands/Pays–Bas	204	2011	1431		
Nauru	911	679	801		
Wallis and Futuna Is	1268	414	509		
France,Monac	176	178	702	547	455
Indonesia/Indonésie	62	556	790		
Niue/Nioué	334	451	309		
Italy/Italie	76	140	851		
Thailand/Thaïlande	101	168	172	264	162
Cote d'Ivoire	74	27	512		
Sri Lanka	12	21	383		
Spain/Espagne	71	2	164		
Switz.Liecht	1	25	180		
Dominica/Dominique	184		2		
Philippines	7	4	121		
Denmark/Danemark	7	12	95		
India/Inde	20	10	73		
Turkey/Turquie	6	24	48		
Belgium–Luxembourg	22	22	25		
Ukraine	5	15	49		
Mexico/Mexique			62		
Pakistan			42		
Nicaragua	23	2	16		
So. Africa Customs Un	5	4	30		
Viet Nam		12	23		
Sweden/Suède	1	0	33		

(VALUE AS PERCENTAGE OF WORLD TOTAL)(VALEURS EN POURCENTAGE DU TOTAL MONDIAL)

	1987	1988	1989	1990	1991	1992	1993	1994	1995	1996
Africa	0.1	0.1	0.1	0.1	0.1	0.1	0.1	0.1		
Americas	6.1	5.4	5.8	13.6	5.2	9.3	5.0	15.4	7.6	10.0
Northern America	5.9	5.3	5.6	13.5	4.9	9.1	4.7	15.1	7.6	10.0
LAIA	0.2	0.1	0.2	0.1	0.2	0.2	0.2	0.2		
CACM	0.0		0.0	0.0	0.0	0.0	0.0	0.0		
Caribbean	0.0	0.0	0.0	0.0	0.0	0.1	0.1	0.1		
Rest of America	0.0	0.0	0.0	0.0	0.0	0.0	0.0	0.0		
As.ex F.USSR	37.9	33.0	39.0	33.2	36.8	33.3	34.4	29.5	24.0	18.9
Eur.x F.USSR	9.4	12.0	7.4	7.8	6.6	7.7	6.4	4.1	3.7	3.3
EU	8.7	11.4	6.7	7.2	6.0	7.2	5.9	3.9	3.7	3.3
EFTA	0.4	0.3	0.3	0.3	0.3	0.3	0.3	0.2		
East Europe	0.2	0.2	0.3	0.2	0.3	0.2	0.2	0.1		
Other Europe	0.0	0.0	0.0	0.0	0.0	0.0	0.0	0.0		
Former USSR	0.0	0.0	0.0	0.0	0.0	0.1	0.0	0.0		
Oceania	46.4	49.6	47.6	45.1	51.0	49.1	53.7	50.3	54.7	59.2
Australia/Australie	28.7	29.4	30.2	27.8	31.6	32.1	32.8	32.9	38.8	44.4
New Zealand	16.9	18.9	16.5	16.3	18.2	16.8	20.6	16.8	15.9	14.8
USA/Etats–Unis d'Amer	5.3	4.9	5.3	13.0	4.4	8.7	4.3	14.8	7.1	9.3
Japan/Japon	12.1	10.2	13.6	11.1	11.3	10.3	12.0	8.0	7.2	5.2
Singapore/Singapour	11.4	4.2	5.4	5.8	6.1	6.4	5.4	7.4	7.1	5.0
China/Chine	2.5	2.7	3.3	2.8	2.9	3.4	3.6	3.2	2.9	2.5
Hong Kong	2.0	3.3	3.3	2.9	3.6	3.2	3.2	2.1	2.8	1.7
United Kingdom	4.4	3.7	3.0	3.1	3.0	3.2	3.0	1.7	2.1	1.8
Thailand/Thaïlande	1.1	1.2	1.6	1.7	2.3	1.8	2.2	1.5	1.4	1.8
Korea, Republic of	1.8	3.5	4.3	2.1	1.8	1.8	1.5	1.1	1.4	1.3

	1987	1988	1989	1990	1991	1992	1993	1994	1995	1996
Afrique	0.0	0.0	0.0	0.0	0.0	0.0	0.0	0.1		
Amériques	7.1	6.7	8.1	10.9	13.4	16.8	16.1	22.6	14.6	10.7
Amérique du Nord	6.8	6.7	8.1	10.9	13.3	16.7	16.1	22.6	14.6	10.7
ALAI	0.2	0.0	0.0		0.0	0.0	0.0	0.0		
MCAC			0.0	0.0		0.0	0.0	0.0		
Caraïbes	0.0	0.0	0.0		0.0	0.0	0.0	0.0		
Autre Amérique		0.0				0.0				
Asie l'URSS exclus	17.4	15.6	15.5	16.2	13.5	13.8	8.0	14.8	13.3	13.6
Europe l'URSS exclus	35.1	29.3	25.3	23.9	33.4	31.9	28.8	20.3	22.3	18.1
UE	35.0	29.3	25.3	23.9	33.4	31.9	28.8	20.3	22.3	18.1
AELE	0.0	0.0	0.0	0.0	0.0	0.0	0.0	0.1		
Europe de l'Est	0.1	0.0	0.0	0.0		0.0				
Autre de l'Europe				0.0	0.0					
Ancienne URSS			0.0			0.0	0.0	0.0		
Océanie	34.5	40.9	45.6	43.0	34.7	34.1	41.0	37.7	29.3	40.3
Australia/Australie	17.8	22.2	20.4	17.7	14.2	14.4	21.2	21.6	24.0	27.9
United Kingdom	34.0	28.6	24.5	23.1	32.6	30.9	27.5	19.4	20.2	14.4
USA/Etats–Unis d'Amer	5.5	3.0	5.6	8.5	10.3	14.0	11.4	17.9	11.5	8.5
New Zealand	5.7	7.4	14.1	11.8	8.4	5.8	5.8	5.3	5.3	12.4
Japan/Japon	3.0	4.9	6.1	5.9	5.2	5.3	5.0	6.8	5.8	6.7
Malaysia/Malaisie	7.4	4.1	5.9	4.9	4.0	6.3	1.1	4.8	4.8	3.0
Canada	1.4	3.7	2.5	2.3	3.0	2.7	4.6	4.7	3.1	2.2
Tonga	2.9	2.7	2.7	2.9	2.9	3.2	3.1	2.8		
Portugal	0.0			0.0			0.0		1.6	3.4
American Samoa	1.7	1.6	1.5	2.0	1.3	2.1	1.8	1.4		

4. General Imports C.I.F. by Commodities according to the S.I.T.C. (Rev. 2) in thousand U.S. Dollars
Importations Générales C.A.F. par Produits d'après la C.T.C.I. (Rév. 2) en milliers de Dollars E.U.

SITC CTCI	COMMODITY	1993 WEIGHT POIDS	1993 VALUE VALEUR	1994 WEIGHT POIDS	1994 VALUE VALEUR	1995 WEIGHT POIDS	1995 VALUE VALEUR	1996 WEIGHT POIDS	1996 VALUE VALEUR	PRODUIT
	ALL COMMODITIES		526623		837793		866778		984018	TOUS PRODUITS
0	FOOD AND LIVE ANIMALS		83939		115162		129643		138903	ALIMENTS,ANIMAUX VIVANTS
01	MEAT AND PREPARATIONS		14180		15694					VIANDES ET PREPARATIONS
011	MEAT FRESH,CHILLD,FROZEN	W 11918	13638	W 12427	14855					VIANDES FRAICHES,REF,CONGE
0112	MUTTON ETC FRSH,CHLD,FRN	W 8956	9124	W 10916	12101					VIANDE DE MOUTON
0114	POULTRY FRESH CHLLD,FRZN	W 1740	2930	W 446	880					VOLAILLES MORTES
02	DAIRY PRODCTS,BIRDS'EGGS		9797		12143					PRODUITS LAITIERS,OEUFS
022	MILK AND CREAM	W 3174	5731	W 3452	6197					LAIT ET CREME
0224	MILK,CREAM PRESERVED ETC	W 2603	5616	W 3121	5805					LAIT,CREME CONS,CONC
02243	MILK DRY,OVER 1.5% FAT	W 2183	5056	W 2416	4949					LAIT POUDRE SUP 1.5%
023	BUTTER	W 1750	3026	W 2248	4020					BEURRE
03	FISH AND PREPARATIONS		8492		18007					POISSONS ET PREPARATIONS
034	FISH,FRESH,CHILLED,FROZN		5230	W 12400	14201					POISSON FRAIS, REFRIG,CONG
0341	FISH FRSH,CHLLD,EX FILLT		2447	W 5125	5002					POISSON FRAIS,REFRIGERE
0342	FISH FROZEN,EXCL FILLETS		2486	W 6898	8671					POISSONS CONGELES
037	FISH ETC PREPD,PRSVD NES	W 2003	2420	W 1654	2621					POIS,CRUST,MOL PREPARES
0371	FISH PREPARD,PRESRVD NES	W 2001	2412	W 1653	2616					CONSERVES DE POISSONS
04	CEREALS AND PREPARATIONS		22427		31030					CEREALES ET PRODUITS
041	WHEAT ETC UNMILLED		7523	W 78504	14843					FROMENT,EPEAUTRE
0412	OTHER WHEAT ETC UNMILLED		7523	W 78504	14843					AUTRE FROMENT NON MOULU
042	RICE		7296		7938					RIZ
0421	RICE IN HUSK OR HUSKED	W 12086	4056	W 56973	5026					RIZ SANS AUTRE PREPARATION
04212	RICE HUSKED	W 12086	4056	W 56542	4884					RIZ CARGO
0422	RICE SEMI–MILLED,MILLED		3240		2912					RIZ POLI,GLACE INCL BRISURES
04221	RICE MILLED UNBROKEN	W 9511	2652		2382					RIZ POLI,GLACE EXCL BRISURES
046	WHEAT ETC MEAL OR FLOUR	W 8915	2154	W 9500	1854					SEMOULE FARINE,FROMENT
048	CEREAL ETC PREPARATIONS	W 3246	3537	W 3925	4752					PREPTNS A BASE CEREALES
05	VEGETABLES AND FRUIT		15669		19754					LEGUMES ET FRUITS
054	VEG ETC FRSH,SMPLY PRSVD	W 27962	10547		13076					LEGUMES FRAIS,CONG,SECS
0541	POTATOES FRSH EXCL SWEET	W 14424	3316	W 15950	4329					POMMES DE TERRE
0542	LEGUMINOUS VEGETBLES DRY	W 5425	1840	W 6802	2441					LEGUMES A COSSE SECS
0545	OTHER FRESH VEGETABLES	W 7284	4473	W 8372	5198					AUTRES LEGUMES FRAIS,REF
05451	ALLIACEOUS VEGTBLS,FRESH	W 5771	3483	W 6415	3822					OIGNONS,ECHALOTES,AULX
057	FRUIT,NUTS,FRESH,DRIED	W 2548	2605	W 3117	3334					FRUITS FRAIS OU SECS
058	FRUIT PRESERVED,PREPARED	W 1205	1969	W 1998	2609					CONSERVES DE FRUITS
07	COFFEE,TEA,COCOA,SPICES		3927		5099					CAFE,THE,CACAO,EPICES
081	*FEEDING STUFF FOR ANIML		2406		3911					NOURRITURE POUR ANIMAUX
09	MISC EDIBLE PRODUCTS		4365		6210					PREP ALIMENTAIRES DIVERSES
098	EDIBLE PRODCTS,PREPS NES		3022		4609					PREP ALIMENTAIRES NDA
1	BEVERAGES AND TOBACCO		4729		7196		9374		9390	BOISSONS ET TABACS
11	BEVERAGES		3985		5454					BOISSONS
112	ALCOHOLIC BEVERAGES		3225		4128					BOISSONS ALCOOLIQUES
1124	DISTILLED ALCOHOLIC BEVS		1625		1816					ALCOOLS,EAUX–DE–VIE
2	CRUDE MATERLS,EXCL FUELS		3323		4837		6473		6297	MAT BRUTES NON COMESTIBLES
3	MINERAL FUELS ETC		71746		94252		97754		131763	COMBUSTIBLES MINERAUX LUB
33	PETROLEUM AND PRODUCTS		68093		89381					PETROLE ET DERIVES
334	PETROLEUM PRODUCTS,REFIN	W 332360	67723	W 479797	88871					PRODUITS RAFFINES
341	*GAS,NATURAL AND MANUFCT	W 7390	2646	W 9716	3455					GAZ NATUREL,GAZ MANUFACT
3413	PETROLM GASES,LIQUEFIED	W 7390	2646	W 9716	3455					GAZ DE PETROLE LIQUEFIE
34139	OTH HYDROCARBON GAS LQFD	W 7390	2645	W 9716	3452					HYDROCARBURES GAZEUX NDA
4	ANIMAL,VEGETABLE OIL,FAT		6041		8711		11724		10580	HUILES,GRAISSES ANIM,VEG
42	FIXED VEGETABLE OIL,FAT		4709		6899					HUILES VEGETALES FIXES
423	FIXED VEG OILS,SOFT		3781		5700					HUILES VEGET DOUCES FIXES
4232	SOYA BEAN OIL		3365	W 7065	5260					HUILE DE SOJA
5	CHEMCLS,RELATED PROD NES		38097		58680		66015		73261	PRODUITS CHIMIQUES
52	INORGANIC CHEMICALS		4248		4645					PROD CHIM INORGANIQUES
522	INORG ELEMNTS,OXIDES,ETC		2202		2333					ELEMENTS INORGANIQUES
523	OTHR INORG CHEMICALS ETC	W 3160	2044	W 3353	2301					AUT PRODUITS CHIMIQUES INORG
53	DYES,TANNING,COLOUR PROD		2209		3265					PROD TEINTURE,COLORANTS
533	PIGMENTS,PAINTS,ETC		1988		2932					PIGMENTS,PEINTURES,VERNIS
541	*MEDICINAL,PHARM PRODUCT		7049		11200					PROD MEDICINAUX PHARMACEUT
5417	MEDICAMENTS		5455		8825					MEDICAMENTS
54171	— CONTAINNG ANTIBIOTICS		5455		8825					MED CONTN ANTIBIOTIQUES
55	PERFUME,CLEANING ETC PRD		7338		11322					PROD POUR PARFUM,TOILETTE
553	PERFUMERY,COSMETICS,ETC		4244		6913					PRODUITS DE PARFUMERIE
554	SOAP,CLEANSING ETC PREPS		1999		3204					SAVONS,PRODUITS DETERSIFS
562	*FERTILIZERS,MANUFACTURE	W 22517	3479	W 55319	8196					ENGRAIS MANUFACTURES
5621	CHEM NITROGENOUS FERTLZR	W 7463	917	W 30592	3757					ENGRAIS AZOTES
56213	AMMONIUM SULPHATE	W 7011	774	W 28438	3476					SULFATE D'AMMONIUM
58	PLASTIC MATERIALS ETC		6392		10206					MAT PLAST ARTIFICIELLES
583	POLYMERIZATION ETC PRODS		4892		8275					PROD POLYMERISATION
5831	POLYETHYLENE		1604		2118					POLYETHYLENE
5839	OTH POLYMRZTION ETC PROD		1501		2923					AUT PROD POLYMER COPOLYM
59	CHEMICAL MATERIALS NES		4754		5832					MAT PROD CHIMIQUES NDA
591	PESTICIDES,DISINFECTANTS		1686		2053					DESINF,INSECT,FONG,HERB
6	BASIC MANUFACTURES		120859		198691		239611		254926	ART MANUFACTURES
61	LEATHER,DRESSED FUR,ETC		1158		3838					CUIRS,PELLETERIES
62	RUBBER MANUFACTURES NES		8310		13449					CAOUTCHOUC MANUFACTURE
625	RUBBER TYRES, TUBES ETC	N 205963	4798	N 370819	8252					PNEUS CAOUTCHOUC VULCANISE
6252	TYRES,NEW,BUS OR LORRY	N 19096	2123	N 38845	3857					PNEUS POUR AUTOBUS,CAMIONS
628	RUBBER ARTICLES NES		2022		2955					OUVRAGES CAOUTCHOUC NDA
64	PAPER,PAPERBOARD AND MFR		17468		25539					PAPIERS,CARTONS & OUVRAGES
641	PAPER AND PAPERBOARD		13082		19614					PAPIERS ET CARTONS
6412	PRINTG,WRITING PAPER NES		3854	W 5109	5610					PAPIERS POUR L'IMPRESSION
64121	— UNCOATED		3854	W 5109	5610					PAPIERS IMPRES NON COUCHES
6417	CORRUGATED PAPER ETC,BLK	W 4912	4279	W 5427	6201					PAPIERS,CARTONS ONDULES
64171	KRAFT PAPER CREPED ETC	W 4912	4279	W 5427	6201					PAPIER KRAFT CREPE ROULEAU
642	PAPER,ETC,PRECUT,ARTS OF		4386		5925					PAP,CARTONS DECOUPES
6421	PAPER ETC CONTAINERS		2017		2303					BOITES,SACS EMBALLAGES
65	TEXTILE YARN,FABRICS,ETC		44567		86080					FILS,TISSUS,ARTICLES TEXTILE
651	TEXTILE YARN		2710		3531					FILS TEXTILES
652	COTTON FABRICS,WOVEN		12247		20720					TISSUS DE COTON
6521	GREY WOVEN COTTON FABRIC	A 6609	5826	A 8627	8768					TISSUS COT ECRUS NON MERCER
65214	GREY WOVEN COTTON NES	A 6269	5602	A 7487	7616					AUT TISSUS 85% COTON ECRUS
6522	WOVEN COTTON BLEACHD,ETC		6420		11952					TISSUS COTON BLANCHIS ETC
65225	BLCHD COTN BLEND FAB NES	A 19903	6417	A 22292	11869					AUT TIS MOINS 85% COT BLANCH
653	WOVN MAN–MADE FIB FABRIC		15813		26233					TISSUS FIBRES SYNTH,ARTIF
6531	CONT SYNT WEAVES NONPILE	A 4274	7085	A 4847	6628					TISSUS FIBRES SYNTH CONTINUE
65315	CONT SYN TXTL FABRIC NES	A 4274	7085	A 4847	6628					TIS PLUS 85% TEXT SYNT CONT
6532	DISC SYN TXTL FABRIC NES	A 2296	3328	A 2763	5864					TIS DISC MOINS 85% FIBR TEXT
6534	DISC SYN BLEND FABRC NES		5255		11008					TISSUS FIBRES SYNTH DISCONT

4. General Imports C.I.F. by Commodities according to the S.I.T.C. (Rev. 2) in thousand U.S. Dollars
Importations Générales C.A.F. par Produits d'après la C.T.C.I. (Rév. 2) en milliers de Dollars E.U.

SITC CTCI	COMMODITY	1993 WEIGHT POIDS	1993 VALUE VALEUR	1994 WEIGHT POIDS	1994 VALUE VALEUR	1995 WEIGHT POIDS	1995 VALUE VALEUR	1996 WEIGHT POIDS	1996 VALUE VALEUR	PRODUIT
65341	DISC SYN FIB–COTTN FABRC	A 669	960	A 1696	3105					TISSUS FIB SYNT DIS MEL COTO
65342	DISC SYN FIB–WOOL FABRIC		4295		7904					TISSUS FIB SYNT MEL LAINE
655	KNITTED,ETC FABRICS		7923		26009					ETOF BONNETERIE PIECES ETC
6552	OTHER KNIT ETC FAB NONEL		7923		26009					ETOF BON NON ELAS NON SYNT
656	LACE,RIBBONS,TULLE,ETC		1069		2738					TULLES,BRODERIE
657	SPECIAL TXTL FABRC,PRODS		1579		2843					TISSUS SPECIAUX
658	TEXTILE ARTICLES NES		1678		2000					ART FACONNES MAT TEXTILES
66	NONMETAL MINERAL MFS NES		8335		10532					ART MIN NON METALLIQUES
662	CLAY,REFRACTORY BLDG PRD		1866		2448					MAT CONST REFRACTAIRES
664	GLASS		1774		2072					VERRE
665	GLASSWARE		2552		2854					OUVRAGES EN VERRE
6651	BOTTLES ETC OF GLASS		1799		1975					RECIPIENTS EN VERRE
66511	GLASS BOTTLES ETC NONVAC		1799		1973					BONBONNES,BOUTEILLES,ETC
67	IRON AND STEEL		15890		21894					FER ET ACIER
672	IRON,STEEL PRIMARY FORMS	W 4349	1604	W 8598	2951					LINGOTS FER,ACIER
6724	IRN,STL INGOTS,LUMPS,ETC	W 3995	1318	W 8149	2613					FER,ACIER LINGOTS,MASSES
67241	IRON,SIMPLE STEEL INGOTS	W 3967	1299	W 8149	2613					LINGOTS EN FER ET ACIER
673	IRON,STEEL SHAPES ETC	W 5663	2805	W 8467	4019					BARRES,PROFIL FER,ACIER
674	IRN,STL UNIV,PLATE,SHEET		6365	W 10544	8976					LARGES PLATS,TOLES
6747	TINNED PLATES,SHEETS	W 2011	1689	W 2150	2048					TOLES ETAMEES EN ACIER
6749	OTH IRN,STL PLATES,SHEET		4515	W 7840	6519					AUTRES TOLES FER,ACIER
67491	— OF IRON OR SIMPLE STL		4436	W 7835	6507					AUT TOLES AUTRES ACIER FIN
678	IRON,STL TUBES,PIPES,ETC		2959		4180					TUBES,TUYAUX EN FONTE,FER
6782	IRON,STL SEAMLESS TUBES	W 1354	1921	W 3093	2626					TUBES,TUYAUX SANS SOUDURE
68	NON–FERROUS METALS		5962		8233					METAUX NON FERREUX
687	TIN	W 2243	3448	W 2794	3623					ETAIN
6872	TIN,ALLOYS WORKED	W 2243	3448	W 2793	3622					ETAIN ET ALLIAGES OUVRES
68722	TIN SHEET,PLATE,STRIP	W 2243	3448	W 2790	3601					TABLES,PLANCHES ETAIN
69	METAL MANUFACTURES NES		18458		26652					ART MANUFACT EN METAL NDA
691	STRUCTURES AND PARTS NES		1824		3003					CONSTRUCT FER,ACIER,ALU
6911	STRUCTURES,PARTS IRN,STL		1495		2721					CONSTRUCT FER,ACIER,FONTE
692	METAL TANKS,BOXES,ETC		2766		3898					RECIPIENTS METALLIQUES
6924	MTL TRANSPORT BOXES ETC		2567		3612					FUTS,TAMBOURS,BIDONS
69241	STL TRANSPORT BOXES ETC	MN 13422	1611	MN 18953	2254					FUTS,TAMBOURS,BIDONS FER
694	STL,COPPR NAILS,NUTS,ETC		2024		2658					CLOUS,VIS,ECROUS
69402	IRN,STL NUTS,BOLTS,ETC		1740		2397					BOULONS,VIS,ECROUS FER,AC
695	TOOLS		2437		3824					OUTILS A MAIN
697	BASE MTL HOUSEHOLD EQUIP		2767		3726					ART MENAGE MET COMMUNS
699	BASE METAL MFRS NES		4614		7113					ART MANUFACTURES MET NDA
7	MACHINES,TRANSPORT EQUIP		129165		258900		197530		234392	MACHINES MATERIEL TRANSPORT
71	POWER GENERATING EQUIPMT		7691		11165					MACHINES GENERATRICES
713	INTRNL COMBUS PSTN ENGIN		4157		5279					MOTEURS EXPL COMB INT, PIECE
7139	PISTON ENGINE PARTS NES		1729		2112					PIECES POUR 713.2,3,8
716	ROTATING ELECTRIC PLANT		1900		4368					APP ELECTR ROTATIFS,PIECES
7162	AC MTRS,GENRTRS,GEN SETS	N 772	940	N 547	3032					MOTEURS ELECTRIQUES
71623	GEN SETS WITH PISTN ENGN	N 719	923	N 522	3019					GROUPES MOTEUR EXPLOSION
72	MACHS FOR SPCL INDUSTRYS		14296		18892					MAC SPECIALES POUR INDUST
723	CIVIL ENGNEERG EQUIP ETC		5714		4736					APPAREILS DE GENIE CIVIL
7234	CONST,MINING MACHNRY NES		4864		3677					MACH POUR LA CONST, MINES
72341	SELF–PROPELLD DOZERS,ETC	N 39	1678	N 21	948					BULLDOZERS
72342	SLFPRP SHOVELS,EXCAVATRS	N 101	2533	N 65	1719					PELLES MECANIQUES
724	TEXTILE,LEATHER MACHNRY		1934		4442					MACH POUR INDUSTRIE TEXTILE
7243	SEWING MACHS,NEEDLES ETC		988		2813					MACHINES A COUDRE,PIECES
727	FOOD MACHRY NON–DOMESTIC		1291		3567					MACH INDUSTRIES ALIMENT
7272	OTH FOOD PROC MCHY,PARTS		1249		3386					AUT MACH IND ALIMENTAIRE
72722	INDUS FOOD PROC MACH NES		1249		3386					MACHINES BOULANGERIE
728	OTH MACHY FOR SPCL INDUS		2847		3126					AUT MACH IND PARTICULIERES
73	METALWORKING MACHINERY		2371		4766					MACH TRAVAIL DES METAUX
736	METALWORKING MACH–TOOLS		1933		4172					MACH–OUTILS TRAVAIL METAUX
7361	METAL CUTTING MACH–TOOLS		1343		2797					MACH–OUT ENLEVEMENT METAL
74	GENRL INDUSTRL MACHY NES		18472		31464					MACH APP INDUSTRIE
741	HEATING,COOLING EQUIPMNT		2973		7048					MACH CHAUFFAGE,PIECES
742	PUMPS FOR LIQUIDS ETC		2115		3194					POMPES MOTO–POMPES
743	PUMPS NES,CENTRFUGES ETC		2422		3685					POMPES COMPRES,VENT ETC
744	MECHANICAL HANDLING EQU		2036		5128					EQUIP MANUTENTION PIECES
7442	LIFTING,LOADING MACH NES		1214		3018					APP LEVAGE,MANUTENTION
745	NONELEC MACHY,TOOLS NES		2849		4479					AUT MACH NON ELEC,PIECES
7452	OTH NONELEC MCHS,PTS NES		1623		2458					AUT MACH NON ELEC,PIECES
749	NONELEC MACH PTS,ACC NES		6076		7930					PIECES MACH NON ELEC NDA
7492	COCKS,VALVES ETC NES		2047		2603					ART ROB,SIM POUR TUYAUX
75	OFFICE MACHNES,ADP EQUIP		8089		11923					MACH BUREAU TRAIT AUTOM
751	OFFICE MACHINES		1715		2429					MACH,APPAREILS DE BUREAU
752	AUTOMTIC DATA PROC EQUIP		3919		6144					MACH TRAIT INFORMATION
7522	DIGITAL COMPUTERS		2886		3468					MACH DIGITALES COMPLETES
7528	OFF–LINE DATA PROC EQUIP		936		2545					MACH AUXIL TRAIT INFORM
759	OFFICE,ADP MCH PTS,ACCES		2455		3350					PIECES DU 751 ET 752
7599	ACCTG,ETC,ADP MCH PTS,AC		2416		3270					PIECES DU 751 ET 752
76	TELECOMM,SOUND EQUIPMENT		19576		17623					EQUIPMENT DE TELECOM
761	TELEVISION RECEIVERS	N 12973	2877	N 7030	2230					RECEPTEURS DE TELEVISION
7611	COLOUR TV RECEIVERS	N 12973	2877	N 7030	2230					RECEPTEURS COULEUR
762	RADIO BROADCAST RECEIVRS	N 69648	2878	N 41444	1904					RECEPTEURS RADIODIFFUSION
7622	PORTABLE RADIO RECEIVERS	N 66162	2722	N 33931	1513					RECEPT PORTATIFS RADIO
763	SOUND RECORDRS,PHONOGRPH		2987		3597					PHONO,APP ENREGISTREMENT
7638	OTHR SOUND APPARATUS ETC		2547		3225					AUT APP D'ENREGIS,REPROD
76381	TV IMAGE,SND RECRDRS ETC		1735		1468					APP ENREG,REPRO IMAG,SON
764	TELECOM EQPT,PTS,ACC NES		10834		9891					EQUIP TELECOM,PIECES
7641	LINE TELEPHONE,ETC EQUIP		5991		5504					APP TELEPHON PAR FIL
7649	PTS NES OF EQUIPMT OF 76		3131		1729					PIECES DE LA DIV 76
76491	PTS NES OF APPAR OF 7641		2074		874					PIECES POUR 764.1
77	ELECTRIC MACHNRY NES ETC		16793		22613					MACH APP ELECT NDA
772	SWITCHGEAR ETC,PARTS NES		3319		6255					APP COUPURE,SECT ETC
7721	SWITCHGEAR ETC		3241		6189					APP COUPURE,SECTIONMNT
773	ELECTR DISTRIBUTNG EQUIP		2250		2054					EQUIPMT DISTRIBUTION ELECT
7731	INSULATED WIRE,CABLE ETC		2111		1874					FILS,CABLES ISOLES ELECT
775	HOUSEHOLD TYPE EQUIP NES		5263		6257					MACH,APP USAGE DOMESTQUE
7752	DOM REFRIGERATRS,FREEZRS	N 9487	2651	N 10096	3053					REFRIG,CONGEL MENAGER
77521	DOMESTIC REFRIGERATORS	N 7806	2055	N 9374	2724					REFRIGERATEURS
778	ELECTRICAL MACHINERY NES		4832		6565					AUTRES MACH ELECT NDA
7781	BATTERIES,ACCUMULATORS		2034		2513					PILES ET ACCUMULATEURS
78	ROAD VEHICLES		35223		43854					VEHICULES ROUTIERS
781	PASS MOTOR VEH EXC BUSES	N 1541	13313	N 1891	15808					AUTO TRANSPORT PERSONNES

4. General Imports C.I.F. by Commodities according to the S.I.T.C. (Rev. 2) in thousand U.S. Dollars
Importations Générales C.A.F. par Produits d'après la C.T.C.I. (Rév. 2) en milliers de Dollars E.U.

SITC CTCI	COMMODITY	1993 WEIGHT POIDS	1993 VALUE VALEUR	1994 WEIGHT POIDS	1994 VALUE VALEUR	1995 WEIGHT POIDS	1995 VALUE VALEUR	1996 WEIGHT POIDS	1996 VALUE VALEUR	PRODUIT
782	LORRIES,SPCL MTR VEH NES	N 1368	14571	N 1487	18548					VEHICULES SPECIAUX,MARCH
7821	LORRIES,TRUCKS	N 1355	14146	N 1427	17927					VEHICULES TRANSP MARCHAND
784	MOTOR VEH PRTS,ACCES NES	N 304322	4944	N 472898	6857					PIECES 722,781,782,783
7849	OTHER MOTOR VEHCL PARTS	N 303929	4252	N 472581	6006					PIECES 722,781,782,783
79	OTHR TRANSPORT EQUIPMENT		6655		96600					AUTRE MATERIEL TRANSPORT
792	AIRCRAFT ETC		1863		93254					APP NAVIGATION AERIENNE
7924	AIRCRFT NES OVER 15000KG			N 1	80983					AERODYNES PLUS 15000 KG
7929	AIRCRAFT PARTS NES		1810		10539					PIECES DU 792
793	SHIPS AND BOATS ETC	N 5615	4602	N 5897	2671					NAVIRES BATEAUX,ETC
7932	SHIPS AND BOATS NES	N 452	4249	N 1046	2199					NAVIRES ET BATEAUX
79323	OTHER CARGO VESSELS	N 103	3532	N 63	1053					AUT BATEAUX TRANS MARCH
8	MISC MANUFACTURED GOODS		61874		81165		99079		114633	ART MANUFACTURES DIVERS
812	*PLUMBG,HEATNG,LGHTNG EQ		2067		2763					APPAR SANITAIRES CHAUFFAGE
821	*FURNITURE,PARTS THEREOF		2633		2453					MEUBLES ET PIECES
831	*TRAVEL GOODS,HANDBAGS		1776		2350					ARTICLES DE VOYAGE ETC
84	CLOTHING AND ACCESSORIES		10480		15101					VETEMENTS
843	WOMENS OUTERWEAR NONKNIT		2860		3700					VET DESSUS FEMMES MAT TEX
844	UNDER GARMENTS NOT KNIT		1292		2603					VETEMENT DESSOUS MAT TEX
845	OUTERWEAR KNIT NONELASTC		2090	N 1140350	2596					VET DESSOUS,ACCES BONNET
846	UNDER GARMENTS KNITTED		1707		3031					SOUS VETS DE BONNETERIE
8462	— OF COTTON NON ELASTIC	N 1642764	1324	N 2547156	2520					SOUS–VET BONNET COTON
84629	—— OTHER	N 1642764	1324	N 2547156	2520					AUT SOUS–VET BONNET COTON
851	*FOOTWEAR	P 1431481	5623	P 1687996	6362					CHAUSSURES
85101	FOOTWEAR RUBBER,PLASTIC	P 853545	2445	P 742202	2345					CHAUS SEMELLES CAOUTCH
85102	FOOTWEAR LEATHER	P 563420	3119	P 928655	3971					CHAUS SEMELLES EN CUIR
87	PRECISION INSTRUMNTS NES		7853		5759					INSTRUM,APPAR SCIENT NDA
872	MEDICAL INSTRUMENTS NES		5268		1455					INSTR,APP MEDIC–CHIR NDA
87202	OTH MEDICAL INSTRUMENTS		5086		1077					INSTRUM,APP MEDECINE
874	MEASURNG,CONTROLNG INSTR		2072		3516					INSTRUMENTS DE MESURE
88	PHOTO EQU,OPTICL GDS ETC		4956		8566					APP,FOURN PHOTO,OP,MONTR
882	PHOTO,CINEMA SUPPLIES		1668		2793					PRODUITS PHOTO,CINEMA
885	WATCHES AND CLOCKS		1930		3496					HORLOGERIE
8851	WATCHES,MOVEMENTS,CASES		1734		3252					MONTRES,MOUVEMENTS,BOITES
88511	WATCHES		1649		3163					MONTRES POCHE,BRACELET
89	MISC MANUFCTRD GOODS NES		26486		37810					ART MANUFACTURES DIVERS
892	PRINTED MATTER		3277		5676					IMPRIMES
8921	PRINTED BOOKS,GLOBES,ETC		2240		3379					LIVRES,BROCHURES,CARTES
89211	PRINTED BOOKS,PAMPHLETS		2199		3321					LIVRES,BROCHURES
893	ARTICLES OF PLASTIC NES		8967		11863					OUVRAGES EN MAT DIVIS 58
8931	PLSTC PACKG CONTNRS,LIDS		2600		3651					ART TRANSP EMBALLAGE ETC
8939	MISC PLASTIC ARTICLES		6180		7873					ART DIVERS EN MAT DIV 58
89399	OTHR PLASTC ARTICLES NES		5383		6523					AUT OUV MAT DIV 58
894	TOYS,SPORTING GOODS,ETC		2551		3056					VOITURES ENFANTS,JOUETS
897	GOLD,SILVER WARE,JEWELRY		6519		9413					BIJOUTERIE,ORFEVRERIE
8973	PREC JEWLRY,GLD–SILVWARE		5636		8165					BIJOUX OR,ARGENT ORFEVRE
89731	PRECIOUS METAL JEWELLERY		5503		8060					ART BIJOUTERIE,JOAILLER
898	MUSICAL INSTRUMENTS,PTS		1749		2628					INSTRUMENTS DE MUSIQUE
899	OTHER MANUFACTURED GOODS		2129		3059					AUT ART MANUF DIVERS NDA
9	GOODS NOT CLASSD BY KIND		6849		10199		9573		9873	ART TRANSACT NON CLASSES
931	*SPECIAL TRANSACTIONS		6445		8585					TRANS.SPECIALES

5. General Exports F.O.B. by Commodities according to the S.I.T.C. (Rev. 2) in thousand U.S. Dollars
Exportations Générales F.O.B. par Produits d'après la C.T.C.I. (Rév. 2) en milliers de Dollars E.U.

SITC CTCI	COMMODITY	1993 WEIGHT POIDS	1993 VALUE VALEUR	1994 WEIGHT POIDS	1994 VALUE VALEUR	1995 WEIGHT POIDS	1995 VALUE VALEUR	1996 WEIGHT POIDS	1996 VALUE VALEUR	PRODUIT
	ALL COMMODITIES		297683		550337		618619		725047	TOUS PRODUITS
0	FOOD AND LIVE ANIMALS		130298		242985		282805		282555	ALIMENTS,ANIMAUX VIVANTS
01	MEAT AND PREPARATIONS		1085		1430					VIANDES ET PREPARATIONS
014	MEAT PREPD,PRSVD,NES ETC	W 876	954	W 489	1138					CONSERVES DE VIANDES
0149	OTH PREPARD,PRESRVD MEAT	W 867	928	W 485	1129					AUTRES PREP DE VIANDES
03	FISH AND PREPARATIONS		22594		38898					POISSONS ET PREPARATIONS
034	FISH,FRESH,CHILLED,FROZN		3201	W 3356	8970		15735			POISSON FRAIS, REFRIG,CONG
0341	FISH FRSH,CHLLD,EX FILLT		459	W 2870	7135					POISSON FRAIS,REFRIGERE
0343	FISH FILLETS,FRESH,CHLLD	W 693	2279	W 222	814					FILETS FRAIS,REFRIGERES
036	SHELL FISH FRESH,FROZEN	W 272	1395	W 465	2355					CRUSTACES,MOLLUSQUES
037	FISH ETC PREPD,PRSVD NES	W 14501	17509	W 9918	27343					POIS,CRUST,MOL PREPARES
0371	FISH PREPARD,PRESRVD NES	W 14495	17501	W 9901	27325					CONSERVES DE POISSONS
04	CEREALS AND PREPARATIONS		5998		7735					CEREALES ET PRODUITS
048	CEREAL ETC PREPARATIONS	W 4936	5483	W 5877	7028					PREPTNS A BASE CEREALES
0481	PREPD BREAKFAST FOOD ETC	W 400	1268	W 644	2541					CEREALES TRAVAILLEES
04812	CEREAL ROASTED, PUFFED	W 400	1268	W 644	2541					PRODTS BASE CEREALES
0483	MACARONI,SPAGHETTI ETC	W 3278	2872	W 4133	3205					PATES ALMENTAIRES
0484	BAKERY PRODUCTS	W 1216	1207	W 1099	1275					PRODUITS DE BOULANGERIE
04842	PASTRY, CAKES ETC	W 1121	1023	W 965	1048					PATISSERIE ETC.
05	VEGETABLES AND FRUIT		2504		7296					LEGUMES ET FRUITS
054	VEG ETC FRSH,SMPLY PRSVD	W 777	629	W 4302	4559					LEGUMES FRAIS,CONG,SECS
0548	EDIBLE VEG NES FRESH,DRY	W 392	305	W 3747	4036					RACINES,TUBERCULES
05488	VEG PRODTS NES FRESH,DRY	W 319	250	W 3578	3923					PROD VEGET ALIM HUMAINE
058	FRUIT PRESERVED,PREPARED	W 854	1621	W 1346	2226					CONSERVES DE FRUITS
0582	FRUIT PRESERVED BY SUGAR	W 518	1302	W 391	1179					FRUITS CONFITS AU SUCRE
06	SUGAR AND PREPS,HONEY		95676		185436					SUCRES ET PRODUITS
061	SUGAR AND HONEY	W 254482	94986		182740		196344			SUCRES ET MIEL
0611	RAW BEET AND CANE SUGAR	W 201585	91735	W 460353	173352					SUCRES BRUTS
0615	MOLASSES	W 44546	2450	W 140316	9350		15147			MELASSES
062	SUGAR CANDY NON–CHOCLATE	W 1140	690	W 1310	2696					SUCRERIES
07	COFFEE,TEA,COCOA,SPICES		1362		1640					CAFE,THE,CACAO,EPICES
075	SPICES	W 923	950	W 1122	1262					EPICES
0752	SPICES,EX PEPPER,PIMENTO	W 915	938	W 1110	1232					AUTRES EPICES
2	CRUDE MATERLS,EXCL FUELS		9911		25552		36639		30534	MAT BRUTES NON COMESTIBLES
24	CORK AND WOOD		7443		21547		32090			LIEGE ET BOIS
246	PULPWOOD,CHIPS,WOODWASTE		3232		11731					BOIS DE TRITURATION
24602	PULPWOOD CHIPS,PARTICLES		3232		10879					EN FORME DE PLAQUETTES
248	WOOD SHAPED,SLEEPERS		4028		8835					BOIS SIMPLEMENT TRAVAILLES
2481	RAILWAY SLEEPERS,TIES	W 93451	3376		7515					TRAVERSES VOIES FERREES
28	METALLIFEROUS ORES,SCRAP		927		794					MINERAIS METAL,DECHETS
29	CRUDE ANIMAL,VEG MAT NES		1257		2660					MATIERES BRUTES ANIM,VEGET
292	CRUDE VEG MATERIALS NES		917		1815					MAT BRUTES VEGETALES NDA
2924	VEG USED IN PHARMACY ETC	W 186	895	W 340	1794					PLANTES MEDICINALES
3	MINERAL FUELS ETC		30166		40667		46301		58878	COMBUSTIBLES MINERAUX LUB
33	PETROLEUM AND PRODUCTS		30151		40632					PETROLE ET DERIVES
334	PETROLEUM PRODUCTS,REFIN	W 125441	30149	W 189572	40628					PRODUITS RAFFINES
4	ANIMAL,VEGETABLE OIL,FAT		2427		2819		3111		4395	HUILES,GRAISSES ANIM,VEG
42	FIXED VEGETABLE OIL,FAT		2408		2784					HUILES VEGETALES FIXES
424	FIXED VEG OIL NONSOFT		2266		2645					AUTRES HUILES VEG FIXES
4243	COCONUT (COPRA) OIL		2256	W 4169	2624		2773			HJUILE DE COPRAH
5	CHEMCLS,RELATED PROD NES		3522		5195		5264		6147	PRODUITS CHIMIQUES
53	DYES,TANNING,COLOUR PROD		946		959					PROD TEINTURE,COLORANTS
533	PIGMENTS,PAINTS,ETC		946		958					PIGMENTS,PEINTURES,VERNIS
55	PERFUME,CLEANING ETC PRD		1799		3118					PROD POUR PARFUM,TOILETTE
553	PERFUMERY,COSMETICS,ETC		918		1601					PRODUITS DE PARFUMERIE
6	BASIC MANUFACTURES		18093		27216		31050		40670	ART MANUFACTURES
61	LEATHER,DRESSED FUR,ETC		1385		2102					CUIRS,PELLETERIES
612	LEATHER ETC MANUFACTURES		1213		2007					OUVRAGES EN CUIRS NDA
6123	PREPRD PARTS OF FOOTWEAR		1173		1521					PARTIES DE CHAUSSURES
63	WOOD,CORK MANUFACTRS NES		2740		4791					OUVRAGES LIEGE ET BOIS
634	VENEERS,PLYWOOD,ETC		2622		4613					PLACAGES,CONTRE–PLAQUES
6341	VENEER SHEETS ETC		1	V 687	2		2824			BOIS SIMPLEMENT SCIES
6342	PLYWOOD OF WOOD SHEETS		2608		4595		1739			BOIS CONTRE–PLAQUES
64	PAPER,PAPERBOARD AND MFR		3231		3701					PAPIERS,CARTONS & OUVRAGES
642	PAPER,ETC,PRECUT,ARTS OF		3005		3364					PAP,CARTONS DECOUPES
6421	PAPER ETC CONTAINERS		2739		3080					BOITES,SACS EMBALLAGES
65	TEXTILE YARN,FABRICS,ETC		7113		9723					FILS,TISSUS,ARTICLES TEXTILE
652	COTTON FABRICS,WOVEN		2598		2687					TISSUS DE COTON
6521	GREY WOVEN COTTON FABRIC	A 1000	981	A 769	709					TISSUS COT ECRUS NON MERCER
65214	GREY WOVEN COTTON NES	A 990	959	A 762	694					AUT TISSUS 85% COTON ECRUS
6522	WOVEN COTTON BLEACHD,ETC		1617		1978					TISSUS COTON BLANCHIS ETC
65225	BLCHD COTN BLEND FAB NES	A 1962	1617	A 2735	1977					AUT TIS MOINS 85% COT BLANCH
658	TEXTILE ARTICLES NES		2909		4917					ART FACONNES MAT TEXTILES
6584	LINENS ETC		1074		4179					LINGE DE MAISON
65842	BED LINEN OF OTHR FIBRES		684		3579					LINGE DE LIT AUT FIBRES
6589	OTH TEXTILE ARTICLES NES		963		654					AUT ART EN TEXTILES NDA
65898	KNITTED ETC ARTICLES NES		963		315					ART BONNET NON ELASTIQUE
67	IRON AND STEEL		1409		2724					FER ET ACIER
674	IRN,STL UNIV,PLATE,SHEET		956		1735					LARGES PLATS,TOLES
6749	OTH IRN,STL PLATES,SHEET		895		1610					AUTRES TOLES FER,ACIER
67491	— OF IRON OR SIMPLE STL		894		1608					AUT TOLES AUTRES ACIER FIN
69	METAL MANUFACTURES NES		1452		2298					ART MANUFACT EN METAL NDA
7	MACHINES,TRANSPORT EQUIP		6158		43841		13096		83066	MACHINES MATERIEL TRANSPORT
77	ELECTRIC MACHNRY NES ETC		1615		2145					MACH APP ELECT NDA
79	OTHR TRANSPORT EQUIPMENT		621		36881					AUTRE MATERIEL TRANSPORT
792	AIRCRAFT ETC		397		36596					APP NAVIGATION AERIENNE
7923	AIRCRFT NES2000–15000KG		8		34370					AERODYNES 2000 A 15000 KG
7929	AIRCRAFT PARTS NES		389		2225					PIECES DU 792
8	MISC MANUFACTURED GOODS		71633		114825		153429		154943	ART MANUFACTURES DIVERS
821	*FURNITURE,PARTS THEREOF		1079		1640					MEUBLES ET PIECES
8219	FURNITURE AND PARTS NES		1030		1593					AUTRES MEUBLES ET PIECES
84	CLOTHING AND ACCESSORIES		62926		98792					VETEMENTS
842	MENS OUTERWEAR NOT KNIT		18947		40887					VET DESSUS POUR HOMMES
8421	— OVERCOATS,OTHER COATS	N 69540	1481	N 545458	1189					MANTEAUX HOMMES MAT TEXT
84211	—— OF WOOL,FINE HAIR	N 69540	1481	N 545458	1189					MANTEAUX HOMMES DE LAINE
8422	— SUITS	N 139944	1601	N 115730	3382					COMPLETS HOMMES MAT TEXT
84221	—— OF WOOL,FINE HAIR	N 139944	1601	N 115730	3382					COMPLETS HOMMES LAINE
8423	— TROUSERS,BREECHES ETC	N 1668468	12918	MN 11452	27695					PANTALONS HOMMES MAT TEX
8429	— OTHER OUTER GARMENTS		2947		8620					AUT VET DES HOM MAT TEX
843	WOMENS OUTERWEAR NONKNIT		13395		22441					VET DESSUS FEMMES MAT TEX
8432	— SUITS AND COSTUMES	N 279360	1163	N 235800	1073					COSTUMES–TAIL MAT TEXIL

5. General Exports F.O.B. by Commodities according to the S.I.T.C. (Rev. 2) in thousand U.S. Dollars
Exportations Générales F.O.B. par Produits d'après la C.T.C.I. (Rév. 2) en milliers de Dollars E.U.

SITC CTCI	COMMODITY	1993		1994		1995		1996		PRODUIT
		WEIGHT POIDS	VALUE VALEUR	WEIGHT POIDS	VALUE VALEUR	WEIGHT POIDS	VALUE VALEUR	WEIGHT POIDS	VALUE VALEUR	
8434	— SKIRTS	N 287796	1659	N 948120	2398					JUPES EN MAT TEXTILES
8435	— BLOUSES	N 753504	2425	N 3138324	4342					BLOUSES FEM MAT TEXTILES
8439	— OTHER OUTER GARMENTS		7876		13377					AUT VET DES FEM MAT TEXT
844	UNDER GARMENTS NOT KNIT		11087		9110					VETEMENT DESSOUS MAT TEX
8441	— MENS SHIRTS		8079		6422					CHEMISES HOMMES MAT TEXT
84411	—— OF COTTON	MN 13965	8017	N 2787936	6254					CHEMISES HOMMES DE COTON
8442	— MENS,OTHR THAN SHIRTS	N 752412	2480	N 619620	1582					SOUS–VET HOMMES MAT TEXT
845	OUTERWEAR KNIT NONELASTC	N 2499660	7979	N 4324213	13254					VET DESSOUS,ACCES BONNET
8451	— JERSEYS,PULLOVERS ETC	N 451392	1258	N 339336	998					CHANDAILS,PULL–OVERS ETC
8459	— OTHER,CLTHG ACCESRYS	N 1981332	6213	N 3874438	11666					AUT VET DESSUS DE BONNE
846	UNDER GARMENTS KNITTED		11446		12778					SOUS VETS DE BONNETERIE
8462	— OF COTTON NON ELASTIC	N 3055344	9432	N 4145688	6415					SOUS–VET BONNET COTON
84629	—— OTHER	N 3055344	9432	N 4145688	6415					AUT SOUS–VET BONNET COTON
8463	— OF SYNTH FBR NONELAST	N 346932	1984		6324					SOUS–VET BONNET FIB SYNT
84632	—— MENS SHIRTS	N 346932	1984	N 1359156	6322					CHEMISES DE BON FIB SYNMT
851	*FOOTWEAR	P 592908	4469	P 958578	8877					CHAUSSURES
85101	FOOTWEAR RUBBER,PLASTIC	P 208421	573	P 503580	3891					CHAUS SEMELLES CAOUTCH
85102	FOOTWEAR LEATHER	P 253585	2704	P 300366	4019					CHAUS SEMELLES EN CUIR
85103	SHOES WOOD–,CORK–SOLED	P 129872	1180	P 154243	967					CHAUS SEMELLES BOIS,LIEGE
89	MISC MANUFCTRD GOODS NES		2079		3230					ART MANUFACTURES DIVERS
9	GOODS NOT CLASSD BY KIND		25112		46638		46309		63435	ART TRANSACT NON CLASSES
931	*SPECIAL TRANSACTIONS		2208		4912					TRANS.SPECIALES
971	*GOLD,NON MONETARY NES	K 1927	22897	K 3924	41726					OR NON MONETAIRE
97101	NONMON GLD UNWRT,SEMIMFD	K 1927	22897	K 3924	41726					OR,ALLIAGES D'OR BRUTS

1. HISTORICAL SERIES, 1961–1996 GENERAL TRADE, IMPORTS C.I.F., EXPORTS F.O.B.
SERIES HISTORIQUES, 1961–1996 COMMERCE GENERAL, IMPORTATIONS C.A.F., EXPORTATIONS F.O.B

YEAR ANNEE	VALUE IN MILLION NEW MARKKAA / VALEUR EN MILLION NEW MARKKAA — MERCHANDISE–MARCHANDISE IMPORTS	EXPORTS	GOLD # 1–OR IMPORTS	EXPORTS	CONVERSION FACTORS U.S. CENTS PER NEW MARKKA / FACTEURS DE CONVERSION CENTS E.U. PAR NEW MARKKA IMPORTS	EXPORTS	INDEX NUMBERS –INDICES — QUANTUM IMPORTS	EXPORTS	UNIT VALUE / VALEUR UNITAIRE IMPORTS	EXPORTS
1961	3690.20	3374.10	0.01		31.2500	31.2500	25	26	14	13
1962	3928.70	3533.10	0.01		31.2500	31.2500	27	28	14	13
1963	3866.90	3678.00	0.01		31.2500	31.2500	26	28	14	13
1964	4816.50	4131.90	0.37		31.2500	31.2500	32	30	15	14
1965	5265.10	4566.00	0.68		31.2500	31.2500	35	32	15	14
1966	5524.40	4816.90	0.50	0.01	31.2500	31.2500	36	34	15	14
1967	5794.40	5231.20	10.18	0.11	29.3000	29.3400	36	36	16	14
1968	6710.90	6874.20	5.45		23.8100	23.8100	25	40	19	17
1969	8504.80	8344.70	8.43	0.02	23.8100	23.8100	43	46	19	18
1970	11071.40	9686.70	7.41		23.8100	23.8100	52	49	21	19
1971	11734.40	9897.20	8.60	0.45	23.8100	23.8100	51	48	22	20
1972	13106.70	12082.00	12.20		24.1136	24.1129	53	54	24	22
1973	16599.00	14605.20	16.64		26.2331	26.2650	60	59	27	24
1974	25666.30	20686.40	13.57		26.5351	26.5368	65	58	39	36
1975	28002.00	20247.40			27.2324	27.1769	65	48	42	41
1976	28555.10	24504.60			25.8863	25.8788	62	57	45	42
1977	30707.80	30931.40			24.7733	24.7804	57	63	52	49
1978	32337.70	35206.20			24.3313	24.3484	54	67	58	52
1979	44222.10	43430.00			25.7787	25.7322	64	73	67	58
1980	58250.40	52794.60			26.8519	26.8076	73	80	78	65
1981	61269.40	60308.00			23.1795	23.2386	68	82	88	72
1982	64751.40	63026.00			20.6752	20.8364	69	80	91	77
1983	71527.90	69692.30			17.9731	17.9636	71	83	98	82
1984	74681.60	80904.10			16.6608	16.6927	71	91	102	87
1985	81520.20	84027.90			16.2333	16.2049	75	92	105	90
1986	77600.99	82578.99			19.7586	19.7824	80	93	95	88
1987	82806.99	85516.00			22.8509	22.8730	86	94	93	89
1988	92118.00	92902.00			23.7120	23.8430	94	97	95	94
1989	105518.70	99781.84			23.3260	23.3211	104	97	98	101
1990	103066.00	101380.00			26.1994	26.2107	100	100	100	100
1991	87821.01	93088.00			24.8318	24.7924	83	91	102	100
1992	94984.00	107471.00			22.3029	22.2893	81	99	113	106
1993	103162.00	133962.00			17.4801	17.5028	78	117	129	113
1994	119897.00	153690.00			19.3617	19.2972	93	133	125	113
1995	122428.00	172380.00			22.9636	22.9571	100	139	123	121
1996	134422.00	176592.00			21.7753	21.7690			125	121

2. IMPORTS BY BROAD ECONOMIC CATEGORY AND EXPORTS BY INDUSTRIAL ORIGIN. (PERCENTAGE OF TOTAL VALUE)
IMPORTATIONS PAR CATEGORIES ECONOMIQUES ET EXPORTATIONS PAR BRANCHE D'ACTIVITE.(EN POURCENTAGE DE LA VALEUR TOTALE)

IMPORTS – IMPORTATIONS

	1990	1991	1992	1993	1994	1995	1996
TOTAL IMPORTS–IMPORTATIONS TOTALES	100.	100.	100.	100.	100.	100.	100.
1 FOOD BEV–ALIMENTATION BOISSONS	4.3	5.3	5.5	5.9	6.2	5.4	6.0
11 PRIMARY–PRODUITS DE BASE	2.1	2.6	2.6	2.9	3.3	2.5	2.8
111 FOR INDUSTRY–POUR L'INDUSTRIE	0.7	0.8	0.8	1.1	1.3	1.0	1.1
112 FOR HOUSEHOLDS–POUR LES MENAGES	1.4	1.7	1.8	1.8	1.9	1.5	1.7
12 PROCESSED–PRODUITS ELABORES	2.2	2.7	2.9	3.0	2.9	2.9	3.2
121 FOR INDUSTRY–POUR L'INDUSTRIE	0.3	0.4	0.4	0.6	0.6	0.5	0.5
122 FOR HOUSEHOLDS–POUR LES MENAGES	1.8	2.3	2.4	2.4	2.3	2.5	2.7
2 IND SUPPLIES–APPROV INDUSTRIELS	28.6	28.7	30.7	31.5	31.5	32.0	28.3
21 PRIMARY–PRODUITS DE BASE	4.6	4.9	6.1	6.1	5.6	6.1	5.9
22 PROCESSED–PRODUITS ELABORES	24.0	23.8	24.5	25.5	25.8	25.9	22.4
3 FUELS–COMBUSTIBLES	11.7	13.3	12.8	12.7	11.5	8.7	10.5
31 PRIMARY–PRODUITS DE BASE	8.2	9.6	8.5	8.6	8.1	6.3	7.3
32 PROCESSED–PRODUITS ELABORES	3.4	3.7	4.3	4.0	3.4	2.4	3.2
321 MOTOR SPIRIT–ESSENCE	0.2	0.4	0.6	0.6	0.2	0.2	0.2
322 OTHER–AUTRES	3.3	3.3	3.8	3.4	3.2	2.3	3.0
4 MACHINERY–EQUIPEMENT	25.3	23.4	23.5	24.8	27.0	29.0	27.8
41 CAPITAL EQUIPMENT–MACHINES	20.8	19.0	18.2	17.7	18.9	20.0	20.3
42 PARTS–PIECES ACCESSOIRES	4.6	4.4	5.3	7.0	8.1	9.1	7.5
5 TRANSPORT–TRANSPORT	13.9	11.7	10.4	9.9	9.6	10.3	11.7
51 PASSENGER CARS–AUTOMOBILES	4.3	3.4	2.6	2.2	2.8	3.0	3.5
52 OTHER–AUTRES	4.5	3.3	2.4	3.6	2.1	2.7	2.9
521 INDUSTRIAL–INDUSTRIELS	4.3	3.1	2.3	3.4	1.9	2.6	2.7
522 NON INDUSTRIAL–NON INDUSTRIEL	0.2	0.2	0.2	0.1	0.1	0.1	0.2
53 PARTS–PIECES ACCESSOIRES	5.0	5.0	5.4	4.1	4.7	4.6	5.3
6 CONSUM GOODS–BIENS CONSOMMATION	15.3	16.7	15.4	14.1	13.6	12.6	13.6
61 DURABLE–DURABLES	3.9	3.9	3.3	2.8	2.8	2.7	3.1
62 SEMI DURABLE–SEMI DURABLES	8.1	8.9	8.0	7.4	7.0	6.5	6.8
63 NON DURABLE–NON DURABLES	3.2	3.9	4.1	4.0	3.7	3.4	3.8
7 GOODS NES–BIENS NDA	0.9	0.9	1.8	1.0	0.8	1.9	2.1

EXPORTS – EXPORTATIONS

	1990	1991	1992	1993	1994	1995	1996
TOTAL EXPORTS–EXPORTATIONS TOTALES	100.	100.	100.	100.	100.	100.	100.
1 AGRICULTURE	1.0	1.2	1.2	1.5	2.2	1.4	1.7
2 MINING QUARRY–INDUS EXTRACTIVES	0.4	0.5	0.4	0.4	0.4	0.3	0.3
3 MANUFACTURING–IND MANUFACTUR	98.6	98.3	98.4	98.1	97.4	98.3	98.0
31 FOOD BEV TOBACCO–ALIM BOISS TAB	2.2	2.0	2.1	2.5	2.4	2.1	2.4
32 TEXTILES–INDUSTRIES TEXTILES	3.4	2.9	2.7	2.3	2.3	2.0	2.1
33 WOOD & PRODUCTS–BOIS & PRODUITS	7.5	7.0	6.8	7.5	8.3	7.0	6.2
34 PAPER & PRODUCTS–PAPIER & PRODT	31.3	32.0	30.3	27.9	26.8	27.7	23.9
35 CHEMICALS–INDUSTRIES CHIMIQUES	9.4	11.4	11.3	10.6	10.2	9.0	9.9
36 NON METAL MIN–MIN NON METAL	1.1	1.2	1.3	1.4	1.3	1.2	1.2
37 BASIC METAL–IND METAL BASE	8.1	9.4	9.7	8.9	8.4	8.0	7.7
38 METAL MANUF–MANUF METAL	35.1	31.8	33.6	36.3	37.0	40.0	43.0
39 OTH MANUF IND–AUTRES MANUF	0.6	0.7	0.6	0.6	0.7	1.4	1.6

3. TRADE BY PRINCIPAL COUNTRIES OF PRODUCTION AND LAST CONSIGNMENT (VALUE IN THOUSAND U.S. DOLLARS)
ECHANGES SELON LES PRINCIPAUX PAYS DE PRODUCTION ET DE DERNIERE CONSIGNATION (VALEUR EN MILLIERS DE DOLLARS EU)

COUNTRIES–PAYS	GENERAL IMPORTS C.I.F. IMPORTATIONS GENERALES C.A.F					COUNTRIES–PAYS	GENERAL EXPORTS F.O.B. EXPORTATIONS GENERALES F.O.B.				
	1992	1993	1994	1995	1996		1992	1993	1994	1995	1996
World	21176034	18032786	23358225	29519876	30859641	Monde	23952181	23473423	29764899	40408551	40561537
Africa	208305	149326	149914	143594	204038	Afrique	411310	425667	501883	624799	544107
Americas	1970942	1825668	2533571	2872138	3039225	Amériques	1904562	2406743	2733215	3919977	4048029
Northern America	1426697	1439568	1943358	2320697	2441307	Amérique du Nord	1568137	2014675	2294036	2932982	3416343
LAIA	372252	284830	414806	401729	441568	ALAI	261740	290602	371466	541365	553370
CACM	36565	37507	78641	80664	94087	MCAC	21459	11911	39084	39726	10016
Caribbean	112430	31807	53411	47457	32658	Caraïbes	44279	80644	25059	252071	54967
Rest of America	22998	31955	43356	21591	29605	Autre Amérique	8947	8911	3570	153832	13333
As.ex F.USSR	2614322	2220361	3139881	3680650	3445818	Asie l'URSS exclus	2180413	2969972	3525877	5516838	6019773
Eur.x F.USSR	14225176	11917917	14857133	19353251	20441490	Europe l'URSS exclus	17574026	15473048	19310184	25179869	24219092
EU	12472342	10282355	12782268	17015447	18089795	UE	15684257	13672692	16894787	22417282	21383432
EFTA	1260040	1231014	1532541	1726242	1776325	AELE	1275828	1115863	1376436	1725221	1609416
East Europe	455387	379306	510537	571612	541356	Europe de l'Est	560243	639716	972907	978876	1129554
Other Europe	7558	3741	6484	10117	4588	Autre de l'Europe	8616	6779	10764	5024	5610
Former USSR						Ancienne URSS					
Oceania	156355	108592	168169	239796	317284	Océanie	286820	325167	414566	593959	536763
Germany/Allemagne	3521050	2938891	3425432	4584685	4634259	Germany/Allemagne	3642007	2993197	3883221	5306755	4795969
Sweden/Suède	2407543	1838908	2435277	3415158	3680805	Sweden/Suède	3017470	2699562	3177506	4036366	4264137
United Kingdom	1829339	1590329	1924589	2420736	2728799	United Kingdom	2497896	2391459	2996887	4110291	4052556
Russian Federation	1548838	1482517	1968257	2121391	2137192	USA/Etats–Unis d'Amer	1407623	1831721	2101188	2658230	3189837
USA/Etats–Unis d'Amer	1289122	1312826	1780495	2127769	2257742	Russian Federation	861506	1372804	1530740	1917409	2439705
Japan/Japon	1160324	1042923	1517885	1876171	1591902	France, Monac	1561712	1206720	1450009	1770889	1666694
Norway,SVD,JM	835315	862557	1108783	1216100	1226801	Netherlands/Pays–Bas	1210461	1147681	1475825	1661521	1558975
France, Monac	875125	708277	924121	1192576	1381729	Denmark/Danemark	845936	771184	1005683	1271037	1215671
Italy/Italie	763774	666566	907288	1173969	1254336	Norway,SVD,JM	828491	734687	917181	1181484	1130328
Netherlands/Pays–Bas	751687	649193	801120	1091119	1103762	Italy/Italie	926120	731666	858104	1169379	1007894
Denmark/Danemark	711958	565170	710315	947582	1080943	Belgium–Luxembourg	584260	486654	625531	1138728	981605
Belgium–Luxembourg	598982	527989	637187	862092	902664	Spain/Espagne	620513	605663	662484	996456	855109
Switz.Liecht	409148	356651	405826	500930	530480	Japan/Japon	301055	378252	609110	1022709	1044116
China/Chine	242224	256489	354242	393323	454497	Estonia/Estonie			647181	939126	1099463
Spain/Espagne	266210	231203	307316	390675	434596	Poland/Pologne	361503	353317	483440	506853	577347
Austria/Autriche	257743	206296	261184	368355	330504	Switz.Liecht	420031	359152	435617	513081	447045
Poland/Pologne	280994	241709	299966	315535	284096	China/Chine	272247	256475	435306	596087	587813
Portugal	266355	190615	211407	241739	225429	Korea, Republic of	184467	245961	403529	514712	587622
Ireland/Irlande	152605	120442	173580	248170	251990	Hong Kong	157766	206786	351205	557926	659262
Estonia/Estonie			218265	358550	364105	Australia/Australie	254770	289076	374919	530402	440729
Korea, Republic of	201704	127156	177417	227613	172428	Austria/Autriche	301229	246696	306307	346464	347066
Australia/Australie	119616	71910	134364	213744	269689	Thailand/Thaïlande	147281	280161	208305	373740	375880
Canada	137257	126526	162457	191219	183016	Singapore/Singapour	121598	184079	276737	328544	368210
Hong Kong	122168	112269	162631	164038	150936	Indonesia/Indonésie	71506	220624	101918	360085	302370
Malaysia/Malaisie	77695	115046	176007	197560	127106	Canada	160256	181065	192240	273408	226098
Brazil/Brésil	133355	103212	175717	121237	126648	Greece/Grèce	163065	126212	169394	213846	206376
Singapore/Singapour	140989	101978	122110	132646	118333	Portugal	168051	146365	147387	191023	193245
Colombia/Colombie	76456	84192	119085	114188	118104	Ireland/Irlande	145538	119635	136448	204526	238134
Thailand/Thaïlande	79976	72295	99875	114508	125254	United Arab Emirates	27894	37290	43439	238435	477539
Hungary/Hongrie	76004	55386	79431	77715	88680	Hungary/Hongrie	95547	131983	218336	177216	178143
Czech Republic		58423	84850	106274	109084	Malaysia/Malaisie	79423	109052	156318	225249	178839
Greece/Grèce	69972	48478	63454	78592	79978	India/Inde	89902	71421	135735	192760	207895
Chile/Chili	70352	39510	38025	73763	107776	Latvia/Lettonie	44462	43711	151846	220893	230602
India/Inde	47718	45895	48224	56374	68529	Turkey/Turquie	86468	133225	105221	153523	209304
Indonesia/Indonésie	26492	23879	42508	50420	113969	Czech Republic		77633	163604	177663	246184
Kazakhstan	9590	22472	18881	42224	125798	Egypt/Egypte	104450	113019	116748	167146	138189
Philippines	22162	29778	58772	53390	53486	So. Africa Customs Un	71094	61731	158242	188688	158308
So. Africa Customs Un	45760	29659	48173	42989	41068	Saudi Arabia	100852	120349	111976	151219	134968
Turkey/Turquie	30676	26415	40454	48987	57923	Brazil/Brésil	71106	71388	106208	182679	176016
Israel/Israël	35567	27158	38046	43887	56580	Philippines	56307	178287	81003	99121	146433
Saudi Arabia	155730	7912	12168	5412	6205	Israel/Israël	74894	82984	98188	174486	122852
Costa Rica	14449	19097	46527	42228	50214	Iran (Islamic Rp. of)	95565	60442	93248	59834	121745
Argentina/Argentine	56224	25198	22684	38279	24873	Lithuania/Lituanie	27529	55835	77974	114826	151298
Latvia/Lettonie	17069	23073	31408	54084	35886	Argentina/Argentine	41918	51000	77537	99758	83814
Morocco/Maroc	32625	25408	30600	27752	32952	Bahamas	34477	68358	93	228361	7302
Panama	22993	31890	43095	21366	18062	Chile/Chili	39030	66540	55712	76655	99506
Slovakia		9987	25550	45889	38632	Ukraine	35516	40482	53501	85623	100283
Lithuania/Lituanie	9754	13879	24663	32061	34308	Mexico/Mexique	40025	41527	54738	49647	72112
Nigeria/Nigéria	78394	33159	7	8	62	Pakistan	20219	22677	22481	67687	109453
Bahamas	76747	2	16183	15870	54	New Zealand	31050	32305	38390	61010	68177

(VALUE AS PERCENTAGE OF WORLD TOTAL)(VALEURS EN POURCENTAGE DU TOTAL MONDIAL)

	1987	1988	1989	1990	1991	1992	1993	1994	1995	1996		1987	1988	1989	1990	1991	1992	1993	1994	1995	1996
Africa	0.6	0.5	0.5	0.4	0.7	1.0	0.8	0.6	0.5	0.7	Afrique	1.8	1.5	1.6	1.8	1.5	1.7	1.8	1.7	1.5	1.3
Americas	7.8	9.4	9.2	9.3	9.4	9.3	10.1	10.8	9.7	9.8	Amériques	7.5	8.9	8.8	8.4	8.6	8.0	10.3	9.2	9.7	10.0
Northern America	5.8	7.1	7.2	7.6	7.4	6.7	8.0	8.3	7.9	7.9	Amérique du Nord	6.3	8.1	7.7	6.9	6.8	6.5	8.6	7.7	7.3	8.4
LAIA	1.4	1.8	1.5	1.3	1.5	1.8	1.6	1.8	1.4	1.4	ALAI	0.8	0.7	0.9	1.3	1.3	1.1	1.2	1.2	1.3	1.4
CACM	0.4	0.3	0.3	0.2	0.2	0.2	0.2	0.3	0.3	0.3	MCAC	0.1	0.1	0.1	0.1	0.1	0.1	0.1	0.1	0.1	0.0
Caribbean	0.1	0.2	0.3	0.2	0.2	0.5	0.2	0.2	0.2	0.1	Caraïbes	0.3	0.1	0.1	0.1	0.4	0.2	0.3	0.1	0.6	0.1
Rest of America	0.1	0.1	0.0	0.1	0.1	0.1	0.2	0.2	0.1	0.1	Autre Amérique	0.0	0.0	0.0	0.0	0.0	0.0	0.0	0.0	0.4	0.0
As.ex F.USSR	11.2	12.0	11.9	11.8	12.6	12.3	12.3	13.4	12.5	11.2	Asie l'URSS exclus	7.0	6.7	7.3	7.2	9.4	9.1	12.7	11.8	13.7	14.8
Eur.x F.USSR	65.3	65.1	66.0	67.7	67.4	67.2	66.1	63.6	65.6	66.2	Europe l'URSS exclus	66.0	65.0	64.5	66.7	72.1	73.4	65.9	64.9	62.3	59.7
EU	58.3	57.8	59.0	60.1	58.8	58.9	57.0	54.7	57.6	58.6	UE	57.5	58.1	58.1	60.2	64.7	65.5	58.2	56.8	55.5	52.7
EFTA	4.2	4.2	4.0	5.1	6.3	6.0	6.8	6.6	5.8	5.8	AELE	6.6	5.2	4.7	4.8	5.3	5.3	4.8	4.6	4.3	4.0
East Europe	2.6	2.6	2.5	2.4	2.2	2.2	2.1	2.2	1.9	1.8	Europe de l'Est	1.5	1.4	1.6	1.4	1.8	2.3	2.7	3.3	2.4	2.8
Other Europe	0.0	0.0	0.0	0.0	0.0	0.0	0.0	0.0	0.0	0.0	Autre de l'Europe	0.0	0.0	0.0	0.1	0.1	0.0	0.0	0.0	0.0	0.0
Former USSR	13.9	11.5	11.1	9.5	8.5						Ancienne URSS	15.3	14.7	14.3	12.5	4.8					
Oceania	0.3	0.6	0.4	0.5	0.6	0.7	0.6	0.7	0.8	1.0	Océanie	1.1	1.2	1.3	1.0	1.1	1.2	1.4	1.4	1.5	1.3
Germany/Allemagne	17.4	16.8	17.3	17.0	16.9	16.6	16.3	14.7	15.5	15.0	Germany/Allemagne	10.8	10.5	10.5	12.0	15.0	15.2	12.8	13.0	13.1	11.8
Sweden/Suède	12.8	13.3	13.6	12.9	12.0	11.4	10.2	10.4	11.6	11.9	Sweden/Suède	14.8	14.0	14.1	14.0	13.6	12.6	11.5	10.7	10.0	10.5
United Kingdom	7.1	6.7	6.5	7.6	7.6	8.6	8.8	8.2	8.2	8.8	United Kingdom	11.3	12.9	11.8	10.4	10.1	10.4	10.2	10.1	10.2	10.0
Russian Federation						7.3	8.2	8.4	7.2	6.9	USA/Etats–Unis d'Amer	5.1	5.7	6.4	5.8	6.1	5.9	7.8	7.1	6.6	7.9
USA/Etats–Unis d'Amer	5.2	6.3	6.3	6.8	6.8	6.1	7.3	7.6	7.2	7.3	Russian Federation						3.6	5.8	5.1	4.7	6.0
Japan/Japon	7.1	7.4	7.3	6.4	6.0	5.5	5.8	6.5	6.4	5.2	France, Monac	5.2	5.2	5.3	6.0	5.7	6.5	5.1	4.9	4.4	4.1
Norway,SVD,JM	2.1	2.2	2.2	3.3	4.5	3.9	4.8	4.7	4.1	4.0	Netherlands/Pays–Bas	3.5	3.6	3.9	4.2	4.8	5.1	4.9	5.0	4.1	3.8
France, Monac	4.2	4.0	4.1	4.2	4.0	4.1	3.9	4.0	4.0	4.5	Denmark/Danemark	3.9	3.5	3.2	3.5	3.7	3.5	3.3	3.4	3.1	3.0
Italy/Italie	4.4	4.4	4.6	4.6	4.2	3.6	3.7	3.9	4.0	4.1	Norway, SVD, JM	4.7	3.4	2.9	3.0	3.3	3.5	3.1	3.1	2.9	2.8
Netherlands/Pays–Bas	3.1	3.2	3.2	3.2	3.4	3.5	3.6	3.4	3.7	3.6	Italy/Italie	2.5	2.6	2.9	3.1	3.4	3.9	3.1	2.9	2.9	2.5

4. General Imports C.I.F. by Commodities according to the S.I.T.C. (Rev. 2) in thousand U.S. Dollars
Importations Générales C.A.F. par Produits d'après la C.T.C.I. (Rév. 2) en milliers de Dollars E.U.

SITC CTCI	COMMODITY	1993 WEIGHT POIDS	1993 VALUE VALEUR	1994 WEIGHT POIDS	1994 VALUE VALEUR	1995 WEIGHT POIDS	1995 VALUE VALEUR	1996 WEIGHT POIDS	1996 VALUE VALEUR	PRODUIT
	ALL COMMODITIES		18032786		23358225		29519876		30859641	TOUS PRODUITS
0	FOOD AND LIVE ANIMALS		1017238		1400086		1441324		1719251	ALIMENTS,ANIMAUX VIVANTS
01	MEAT AND PREPARATIONS		4688		15157		93639		109401	VIANDES ET PREPARATIONS
03	FISH AND PREPARATIONS		83218		116388		92013		111724	POISSONS ET PREPARATIONS
04	CEREALS AND PREPARATIONS		87046		87427		147296		209018	CEREALES ET PRODUITS
048	CEREAL ETC PREPARATIONS	W 22649	53755	W 22310	50072	W 39141	95392	W 61657	126751	PREPTNS A BASE CEREALES
05	VEGETABLES AND FRUIT		406215		555297		438753		543426	LEGUMES ET FRUITS
054	VEG ETC FRSH,SMPLY PRSVD	W 109071	98892	W 128013	119491	W 95916	109561	W 116289	136627	LEGUMES FRAIS,CONG,SECS
0545	OTHER FRESH VEGETABLES	W 49583	56240	W 63470	64177	W 44441	56190	W 58356	71044	AUTRES LEGUMES FRAIS,REF
057	FRUIT,NUTS,FRESH,DRIED	W 300890	203204	W 411689	295023	W 227974	213449		263714	FRUITS FRAIS OU SECS
0573	BANANA,PLANTAIN,FRSH,DRY	W 96346	54770	W 168552	95455	W 66194	44091	W 58489	53360	BANANES FRAICHES,SECHEES
058	FRUIT PRESERVED,PREPARED	W 73933	90273	W 96291	125879	W 58323	96112	W 77366	121580	CONSERVES DE FRUITS
06	SUGAR AND PREPS,HONEY		58080		61340		82961		98569	SUCRES ET PRODUITS
07	COFFEE,TEA,COCOA,SPICES		204027		319004		281418		291046	CAFE,THE,CACAO,EPICES
071	COFFEE AND SUBSTITUTES	W 77367	133266	W 80870	238769	W 49709	185190	W 66980	194544	CAFE ET SUCCEDANES
0711	COFFEE GREEN,ROASTED,SUB	W 77019	129628	W 80480	233978	W 49389	180350	W 66586	189744	CAFE TORREFIE OU DECAFEINE
07111	COFFEE GREEN,HUSKS,SKINS	W 76084	127425	W 78921	227154	W 47613	169669	W 64081	176236	CAFE NON TORREFIE
081	*FEEDING STUFF FOR ANIML	W 128621	70901	W 186340	101641	W 156290	103203	W 184872	123757	NOURRITURE POUR ANIMAUX
09	MISC EDIBLE PRODUCTS		84084		120048		139899		144551	PREP ALIMENTAIRES DIVERSES
098	EDIBLE PRODCTS,PREPS NES	W 26997	83513	W 42633	118307	W 36400	130288	W 35105	134901	PREP ALIMENTAIRES NDA
09809	MISC FOOD PREPRTIONS NES	W 14253	47487	W 30072	80624	W 22359	84859	W 18958	84510	PREP ALIMENTAIRES NDA
1	BEVERAGES AND TOBACCO		114104		144862		193167		206419	BOISSONS ET TABACS
11	BEVERAGES		62788		76270		144594		141269	BOISSONS
112	ALCOHOLIC BEVERAGES	W 35580	57145	W 37804	70652	W 48423	139164	W 50122	135099	BOISSONS ALCOOLIQUES
2	CRUDE MATERLS,EXCL FUELS		1267288		1544289		2173126		2081441	MAT BRUTES NON COMESTIBLES
21	HIDES,SKINS,FURS UNDRSSD		25673		32206		96054		109969	CUIRS,PEAUX BRUTS
212	FURSKINS,RAW	W 124	14323	W 141	16151	W 533	82134	W 471	100396	PELLETERIES BRUTES
24	CORK AND WOOD		248102		329881		581195		392436	LIEGE ET BOIS
246	PULPWOOD,CHIPS,WOODWASTE	W 416571	12559	W 4687052	194865	W 506676	21204	W 574115	22393	BOIS DE TRITURATION
24601	PULPWOOD ROUGH OR SPLIT			W 4209022	175758					EN RONDINS REFENDUS
247	OTH WOOD ROUGH,SQUARED	W 4648886	192315	W 1547894	76058	W 8796076	492115	W 6032356	311934	BOIS BRUTS EQUARRIS
2471	SAW–,VENEER–LOGS CONIFER	W 874998	35543	W 1547894	76039	W 2133041	123913	W 2452392	128875	CONIFERES POUR SCIAGE,PLACAG
24711	— IN THE ROUGH	W 874998	35543	W 1547894	76039	W 2133041	123913	W 2452392	128875	ECORCES OU DEGROSSIS
2472	SAW–,VENEER–LOGS NON–CON	W 3773888	156772		19	W 6663036	368202	W 3579965	183059	NON CONIFERES SCIAGE,PLAC
24721	— IN THE ROUGH	W 3773888	156772		19	W 6663036	368202	W 3579965	183059	BRUTS ECORCES DEGROSSIS
251	*PULP AND WASTE PAPER		73848		94647		157697		67960	PATES A PAPIER,DECHETS
27	CRUDE FERTLZR,MINRLS NES		233255		269370		295257		258701	ENGRAIS MINERAUX BRUTS
278	OTHER CRUDE MINERALS	W 2005565	207223	W 2219630	237617	W 2229213	256855	W 1939041	222341	AUTRES MINERAUX BRUTS
2782	REFRACTORY MINERALS NES	W 1257000	163710	W 1426197	188786	W 1458938	205684	W 1284504	177463	ARGILE MINERAUX REFRACTAIRES
27821	CLAY ETC	W 1221315	159438	W 1385071	183722	W 1418272	200178	W 1237922	170869	ARGILES
28	METALLIFEROUS ORES,SCRAP		479678		572765		747130		961508	MINERAIS METAL,DECHETS
281	IRON ORE,CONCENTRATES	W 3360692	84979	W 3617586	90366	W 2964994	81225	W 3305776	103428	MINERAIS DE FER
2815	IRON ORE,CONC,NOT AGGLOM	W 2667641	68810	W 2753445	70930	W 2359725	65788	W 2647692	86591	MINERAIS NON AGGLOMERES
282	IRON AND STEEL SCRAP	W 139680	19307	W 335731	53330	W 294589	61984	W 226197	92793	FERRAILLES
287	BASE METAL ORES,CONC NES		236829		304653		423975		574593	MINERAIS METAUX COMMUNS
2871	CPR ORE ETC,CEMENT COPPR	W 324385	119155	W 292801	128381	W 293680	178099	W 494218	267361	MINERAIS DE CUIVRE,MATTES
28711	COPPER ORES,EXCL MATTE	W 324385	119155	W 292791	128357	W 293676	178062	W 494217	267360	MINERAIS DE CUIVRE
2872	NICKEL ORES,CONCENTRATES	W 85723	26201	W 114022	54155	W 138918	121207	W 210452	193347	MINERAIS DE NICKEL
28721	NICKEL ORES,EXCL MATTE	W 85362	24986	W 111084	43291	W 134831	100365	W 200610	151397	MINERAIS DE NICKEL
2875	ZINC ORES,CONCENTRATES	W 274978	65895	W 337393	88858	W 211074	61364	W 288603	77067	MINERAIS DE ZINC
288	NONFERR METAL SCRAP NES	W 168194	138442	W 197637	124364	W 88341	179905	W 118886	190528	DECHETS NON FERREUX
2881	METALIFEROUS NONFER WSTE	W 70407	55293	W 116950	69218	W 15647	102882	W 36208	119600	CENDRES ET RESIDUS
2882	OTHER BASE MTL SCRAP NES	W 97787	83150	W 80687	55146	W 72693	77022	W 82678	70929	AUTRES DECHETS
29	CRUDE ANIMAL,VEG MAT NES		96593		112039		114789		120938	MATIERES BRUTES ANIM,VEGET
292	CRUDE VEG MATERIALS NES	W 17912	82604	W 18627	90851	W 15437	93690	W 17504	95691	MAT BRUTES VEGETALES NDA
3	MINERAL FUELS ETC		2310826		2709501		2609010		3272628	COMBUSTIBLES MINERAUX LUB
32	COAL,COKE AND BRIQUETTES		261744		347534		325118		329569	HOUILLES,COKES,BRIQUETTES
322	COAL,LIGNITE AND PEAT	W 5992482	219943	W 8114981	305170	W 5891598	289765	W 6253644	290077	HOUILLES,LIGNITES,TOURBE
3222	OTH COAL,NOT AGGLOMERATD	W 5948331	218995	W 8087168	304074	W 5887173	289093	W 6250334	289695	AUTRES HOUILLES
33	PETROLEUM AND PRODUCTS		1631716		1881153		1734708		2309209	PETROLE ET DERIVES
333	CRUDE PETROLEUM	W 8217915	1080477	MW 9837	1267229	W 8394853	1209053	MW 9498	1569333	HUILES BRUTES DE PETROLE
334	PETROLEUM PRODUCTS,REFIN	W 3344664	520909	W 4446042	577797	W 3366834	490082	W 4248363	706573	PRODUITS RAFFINES
3341	GASOLINE,OTH LIGHT OILS	W 553661	111379	W 228385	40209	W 220605	47372	W 317222	72567	ESSENCES POUR MOTEURS
33411	MOTOR,AVIATION SPIRIT	W 324746	72960	W 76003	16857	W 137090	31660	W 144912	35416	ESSENCES MOTEURS D'AVIONS
3343	GAS OILS	W 1363698	236214	W 1329366	203526	W 723268	75859	W 1043368	153887	GAS OILS
3344	FUEL OILS,NES	W 954847	85217	W 2090613	198517	W 2300222	289792	W 2727918	393265	FUEL OILS
3345	LUBS,PETROLEUM OILS NES	W 439645	81692	W 649246	113779	W 118370	74437	W 142990	82426	HUILES LUBRIFIANTES
33451	LUBS(HIGH PETR CONT) ETC	W 435578	70489	W 644519	99694	W 113142	57462	W 135993	62258	HUILES LUBRIF,H LOURDES
341	*GAS,NATURAL AND MANUFCT		252386		312056		357279		393146	GAZ NATUREL,GAZ MANUFACT
3414	PETROLEUM GASES, GASEOUS		202108		250244		313808		335115	GAZ DE PETROLE GAZEUX
351	*ELECTRIC CURRENT	H 8013831	164980	H 7170561	168758		191905		240704	ENERGIE ELECTRIQUE
5	CHEMCLS,RELATED PROD NES		2332410		2895000		3511358		3399052	PRODUITS CHIMIQUES
51	ORGANIC CHEMICALS		408556		550347		629898		528618	PROD CHIMIQ ORGANIQUES
511	HYDROCARBONS NES,DERIVS		118500		159906		191585		143250	HYDROCARBURES NDA
5112	CYCLIC HYDROCARBONS	W 135672	57844	W 137935	82892	W 105908	100021	W 112451	66821	HYDROCARBURES CYCLIQUES
51125	STYRENE	W 80840	43044	W 106244	74181	W 94408	95356	W 97447	61011	STYRENE
512	ALCOHOLS,PHENOLS ETC		44475		84114		107509		85805	PHENOLS,PHENOLS–ALCOOLS
5121	ACYCLIC ALCOHOLS,DERIVS		40278		73427		88976		66459	ALCOOLS ACYCLIQUES
513	CARBOXYLIC ACIDS ETC		64599		85705		122767		99148	ACIDES CARBOXYLIQUES
514	NITROGEN–FNCTN COMPOUNDS		56650		71683		84049		81620	COMPOSES FONCT AZOTEES
516	OTHER ORGANIC CHEMICALS		94810		113418		89891		79231	AUTRES PROD ORGANIQUES
52	INORGANIC CHEMICALS		224772		293381		402708		341119	PROD CHIM INORGANIQUES
522	INORG ELEMNTS,OXIDES,ETC		126070		173335		265759		211523	ELEMENTS INORGANIQUES
5225	INORGANIC BASES ETC NES		88836		115930		203887		154231	AUTRES BASES OXYDES METAL
52253	SODIUM HYDROXIDE, OTHER	W 537750	35047	W 634118	43218	W 656430	115698	W 622159	79483	HYDROXYDE SODIUM AQUEUX
523	OTHR INORG CHEMICALS ETC		93922		115368		131214		124341	AUT PRODUITS CHIMIQUES INORG
53	DYES,TANNING,COLOUR PROD		172625		214985		259173		263315	PROD TEINTURE,COLORANTS
531	SYNT DYE,NAT INDGO,LAKES	W 14193	64075	W 17722	74816	W 17873	92862	W 19181	83731	MAT COLOR ORGAN,LAQUES
533	PIGMENTS,PAINTS,ETC	W 38579	104820	W 49012	135968	W 47653	162262	W 55393	175479	PIGMENTS,PEINTURES,VERNIS
5334	VARNISHES,DISTEMPERS ETC	W 15296	54409	W 19019	69472	W 20575	84233	W 24053	93205	PEINTURES A L'EAU
541	*MEDICINAL,PHARM PRODUCT		411205	MK 11393	482470		591290		630581	PROD MEDICINAUX PHARMACEUT
5417	MEDICAMENTS	K 8437418	335370	MK 9542	396343	MK 9536	496786	MK 10780	532416	MEDICAMENTS
54179	— CONTNG OTH SUBSTANCES	K 7694791	252218	K 8855203	306784	K 8578677	378394	MK 9827	412686	MED CONT AUT SUBSTANCES
55	PERFUME,CLEANING ETC PRD		186273		211900		248299		327021	PROD POUR PARFUM,TOILETTE
553	PERFUMERY,COSMETICS,ETC	W 11057	86030	W 13468	101891	W 14305	126501	W 29005	197456	PRODUITS DE PARFUMERIE
554	SOAP,CLEANSING ETC PREPS	W 54813	83911	W 52170	90218	W 54093	101549	W 55903	102723	SAVONS,PRODUITS DETERSIFS
5542	WASHING PREPARATIONS ETC	W 49998	71376	W 47339	77155	W 48739	85644	W 51130	87443	PROD ORG TENSIO–ACT NDA
58	PLASTIC MATERIALS ETC		548791		680237		845067		770089	MAT PLAST ARTIFICIELLES
582	PROD OF CONDENSATION ETC	W 59661	144690	W 71665	180775	W 67940	215786	W 70024	211955	PROD CONDENS,POLYCOND
583	POLYMERIZATION ETC PRODS	W 332132	391631	W 369371	484783	W 366106	614133	W 366723	540353	PROD POLYMERISATION
5831	POLYETHYLENE	W 146857	121446	W 158970	145828	W 138582	181006	W 135656	152122	POLYETHYLENE

4. General Imports C.I.F. by Commodities according to the S.I.T.C. (Rev. 2) in thousand U.S. Dollars
Importations Générales C.A.F. par Produits d'après la C.T.C.I. (Rév. 2) en milliers de Dollars E.U.

SITC CTCI	COMMODITY	1993 WEIGHT POIDS	1993 VALUE VALEUR	1994 WEIGHT POIDS	1994 VALUE VALEUR	1995 WEIGHT POIDS	1995 VALUE VALEUR	1996 WEIGHT POIDS	1996 VALUE VALEUR	PRODUIT
58311	— IN PRIMARY FORMS	W 136590	101678	W 146784	120707	W 127866	153200	W 122002	124500	POLYETHYLENE PRIMAIRES
5836	ACRYLIC POLYMERS,ETC	W 43781	61459	W 49045	71187	W 49840	85872	W 52738	83853	POLYM ACRYLIQ METHACRYLI
58361	— IN PRIMARY FORMS	W 42081	56122	W 47004	64645	W 48422	79452	W 50928	76547	SOUS FORMES PRIMAIRES
5839	OTH POLYMRZTION ETC PROD	W 34898	91476	W 39547	115537	W 46069	145340	W 47450	129252	AUT PROD POLYMER COPOLYM
59	CHEMICAL MATERIALS NES		335755		396994		480284		476261	MAT PROD CHIMIQUES NDA
592	STARCH,INULIN,GLUTEN,ETC	W 130431	82660	W 158473	111251	W 130747	133199	W 140129	142243	AMIDONS,INUL,GLUT FROM
5922	ALBUMINOID SUBSTAN,GLUES	W 116663	77853	W 126914	100179	W 108777	118721	W 119191	128465	MAT ALBUMIN,COLLES
598	MISCEL CHEM PRODUCTS NES		213960		243304		297185		284213	PROD DIV INDUST CHIM NDA
5989	CHEM PRODUCTS,PREPS NES	W 103603	159076	W 122944	178989		229738	W 158722	219534	PROD PREP CHIMIQUES NDA
59899	OTH CHEM PRODS,PREPS,NES	W 74601	97779	W 86696	119955		161951	W 131524	153512	AUT PRODUITS CHIMIQUES NDA
6	BASIC MANUFACTURES		2578116		3472446		4556735		4144857	ART MANUFACTURES
62	RUBBER MANUFACTURES NES		152462		208704		261695		258366	CAOUTCHOUC MANUFACTURE
625	RUBBER TYRES, TUBES ETC	W 22186	75471	W 29956	107048	W 34056	143778	W 35193	144666	PNEUS CAOUTCHOUC VULCANISE
64	PAPER,PAPERBOARD AND MFR		298295		373085		517085		498598	PAPIERS,CARTONS & OUVRAGES
641	PAPER AND PAPERBOARD	W 201397	184910	W 243714	237938	W 253080	322052	W 298155	327545	PAPIERS ET CARTONS
6418	COATED ETC PAPER NES BLK	W 31971	75757	W 40070	95142	W 46474	125235	W 40243	111021	PAP,CARTONS COUCHES,ENDUITS
642	PAPER,ETC,PRECUT,ARTS OF	W 39350	113384	W 44543	135147	W 45882	195032	W 52289	171052	PAP,CARTONS DECOUPES
6428	PAPER ETC ARTICLES NES	W 24188	68911	W 26181	80307	W 27814	130057	W 31763	103612	OUVRAGES EN PATE A PAPIER
64285	PAPER ETC DIAPERS ETC	W 13974	46541	W 13887	52666	W 15465	92930	W 17199	63371	SERVIETTES HYGIENIQUES
65	TEXTILE YARN,FABRICS,ETC		462400		575937		605584		610144	FILS,TISSUS,ARTICLES TEXTILE
651	TEXTILE YARN	W 19479	96698	W 23805	124375		124947		113395	FILS TEXTILES
653	WOVN MAN–MADE FIB FABRIC	W 4900	76125	W 6058	89748	W 5414	91160	W 5602	90396	TISSUS FIBRES SYNTH,ARTIF
657	SPECIAL TXTL FABRC,PRODS	W 13581	121685	W 16456	152441	W 15887	163979	W 17774	175070	TISSUS SPECIAUX
6577	TEXTILES FOR MACHINERY	W 1826	56493	W 2082	69177	W 2155	72681	W 2092	77661	OUATES,MECHES ART TEXT
66	NONMETAL MINERAL MFS NES		240871		296846		348657		355064	ART MIN NON METALLIQUES
662	CLAY,REFRACTORY BLDG PRD	W 94042	54647	W 105625	66866		80155	W 109618	76022	MAT CONST REFRACTAIRES
663	MINERAL MANUFCTURES NES	W 108506	69989	W 78316	81598	W 75397	91922	W 79592	85728	ART MIN MANUF NDA
67	IRON AND STEEL		658574		895314		1362113		1153634	FER ET ACIER
671	PIG IRON ETC	W 134331	131391	W 164336	183507	W 208361	257632	W 191152	218115	FONTE,SPIEGEL,POUDRES
6716	FERRO–ALLOYS	W 111330	126861	W 130247	176061	W 128660	243213	W 117137	204263	FERRO–ALLIAGES
67169	OTHER FERRO–ALLOYS	W 90373	114048	W 98032	156373	W 104430	221800	W 90725	181691	AUTRES FERRO–ALLIAGES
672	IRON,STEEL PRIMARY FORMS	W 223411	78059	W 349829	94386	W 653756	201353	W 576604	152608	LINGOTS FER,ACIER
6725	IRN,STL BLOOMS,SLABS,ETC	W 129518	29427	W 227805	52468	W 561386	161016	W 461729	110085	BLOOMS,BILLETTES FER ACIER
67251	IRN,SMPLE STL BLOOMS,ETC	W 123445	23204	W 222807	48349	W 556053	152371	W 459717	106982	BLOOMS ETC NON ACIER FIN
673	IRON,STEEL SHAPES ETC	W 163444	89104	W 217823	126931	W 261973	189004	W 255370	164574	BARRES,PROFIL FER,ACIER
6732	IRON,STEEL BARS ETC	W 71892	49334	W 104841	73105	W 119254	114067	W 126283	101352	BARRES FER,ACIER
674	IRN,STL UNIV,PLATE,SHEET	W 241651	191700	W 306517	258500	W 335055	373504	W 304058	314392	LARGES PLATS,TOLES
6744	IRN,STL HVY PLATE,ROLLED	W 53734	49799	W 82508	72364	W 81662	123624	W 68761	95200	TOLES LAMINEES PLUS 4.75 MM
67443	— OF STAINLESS ETC STL	W 15840	33383	W 19179	44723	W 25095	90337	W 20921	68928	TOLES ACIER INOXYDABLE
6749	OTH IRN,STL PLATES,SHEET	W 80116	55941	W 86214	72555	W 97554	102262	W 87538	80595	AUTRES TOLES FER,ACIER
67491	— OF IRON OR SIMPLE STL	W 78452	51292	W 84174	65652	W 95244	92020	W 85530	73764	AUT TOLES AUTRES ACIER FIN
678	IRON,STL TUBES,PIPES,ETC	W 92357	123357	W 121011	173273	W 139376	260197	W 127782	219839	TUBES,TUYAUX EN FONTE,FER
6782	IRON,STL SEAMLESS TUBES	W 31517	49584	W 40747	64123	W 50331	96806	W 41472	75898	TUBES,TUYAUX SANS SOUDURE
6783	IRON,STL TUBES,PIPES NES	W 53638	40862	W 70130	59804	W 78264	98204	W 75194	79132	AUT TUBES,TUYAUX FER,ACIER
68	NON–FERROUS METALS		280749		465331		633216		461900	METAUX NON FERREUX
682	COPPER EXC CEMENT COPPER	W 45917	114262	W 72253	198865	W 80855	291212	W 67352	198083	CUIVRE
6821	COPPER NES,ALLOYS,UNWRT	W 21463	40167	W 38383	86178	W 43801	132814	W 24882	57111	CUIVRE BRUT
68212	COPPER REFINED,UNWROUGHT	W 20573	38412	W 37460	84589	W 43141	130303	W 24547	55801	CUIVRE AFFINE BRUT
6822	COPPER,ALLOYS WORKED	W 24454	74094	W 33870	112687	W 37054	158398	W 42470	140972	CUIVRE,ALLIAGES OUVRES
683	NICKEL	W 6679	33841	W 7797	51266	W 12170	103685	W 7808	59849	NICKEL
684	ALUMINIUM	W 54777	117119	W 79063	190508	W 63773	213997	W 66187	170830	ALUMINIUM
6842	ALUMINIUM,ALLOYS WORKED	W 29074	86876	W 40305	130988	W 40750	165457	W 33149	115371	ALUMINIUM,ALLIAGES OUVRE
69	METAL MANUFACTURES NES		398060		528021		692320		670184	ART MANUFACT EN METAL NDA
694	STL,COPPR NAILS,NUTS,ETC	W 14666	46329	W 20142	67099	W 25006	93205	W 25651	90173	CLOUS,VIS,ECROUS
695	TOOLS	W 5803	79699	W 7420	108292	W 9614	144747	W 8789	143545	OUTILS A MAIN
699	BASE METAL MFRS NES	W 32183	152264	W 39975	201731		257808		240947	ART MANUFACTURES MET NDA
7	MACHINES,TRANSPORT EQUIP		6112121		8379902		11414764		12065604	MACHINES MATERIEL TRANSPORT
71	POWER GENERATING EQUIPMT		344815		502443		548857		782374	MACHINES GENERATRICES
712	STEAM ENGINES,TURBINES	W 460	16392	W 1045	12538	W 1065	22225	W 4004	171163	MACHINES A VAPEUR D'EAU PIEC
7129	STM ENGINE ETC PARTS NES	W 179	7963	W 197	5461	W 159	6726	W 3100	143449	PARTIES,PIECES DU 712.6
713	INTRNL COMBUS PSTN ENGIN	W 13091	140883	W 17450	183509	W 25233	242512	W 19246	224948	MOTEURS EXPL COMB INT, PIECE
7139	PISTON ENGINE PARTS NES	W 8478	81273	W 10736	99422	W 17232	134178	W 11707	123683	PIECES POUR 713.2,3,8
714	ENGINES AND MOTORS NES	W 434	21630	W 926	97420	W 575	53418	W 853	122908	MOTEURS NON ELECTRIQUES
716	ROTATING ELECTRIC PLANT	W 8780	89290	W 11026	125541	W 10443	120339	W 12219	131493	APP ELECTR ROTATIFS,PIECES
7162	AC MTRS,GENRTRS,GEN SETS	W 6333	63395	W 7411	73542	W 8164	87323	W 8922	91692	MOTEURS ELECTRIQUES
718	OTH POWER GENERATG MACHY	W 991	69654	W 2287	71979	W 1865	87695	W 2049	114080	AUTRES MOTEURS PARTIES
72	MACHS FOR SPCL INDUSTRYS		481159		650666		936392		987811	MAC SPECIALES POUR INDUST
721	AGRIC MACHY,EXC TRACTORS	W 8703	35853	W 9198	48642	W 12583	94563	W 15296	100741	MACHINES AGRICOLES
722	TRACTORS NON–ROAD	W 7278	43394	W 9188	69481	W 13708	99073	W 15331	118110	TRACTEURS
7224	WHEELED TRACTORS NES	W 7266	43390	W 9151	69393	W 13603	98560	W 15302	117814	TRACTEURS A ROUES
723	CIVIL ENGNEERG EQUIP ETC	W 4622	22969	W 11818	59943	W 17052	106779	W 16439	95552	APPAREILS DE GENIE CIVIL
7234	CONST,MINING MACHNRY NES	W 4092	19630	W 11105	55058	W 15902	98037	W 15330	86479	MACH POUR LA CONST, MINES
725	PAPER ETC MILL MACHINERY	W 3754	53548	W 5693	76944	W 8193	118676	W 11491	182127	MACHINES FABR PATE PAPIER
7259	PTS NES OF MACHS OF 725	W 3015	39649	W 3938	44254	W 6469	78412	W 8834	113286	PIECES GROUPE 725
72591	PTS NES OF MACHS OF 7251	W 2892	35131	W 3824	39869	W 6169	69730	W 8482	102290	PIECES DU 725.1
726	PRINTG,BKBINDG MACHY,PTS	W 3230	90075	W 1508	44771	W 2380	75871	W 2129	78073	MACHINES POUR IMPRIMERIE
7264	PRINTING PRESSES	W 2676	69158	W 748	15184	W 1183	33758	W 1191	39696	MACHINES A IMPRIMER
72641	ROTARY PRINTING PRESSES	W 2676	69158	W 748	15184	W 1183	33758	W 1191	39696	MACH IMPRIMER ROTATIVES
728	OTH MACHY FOR SPCL INDUS	W 10332	174815	W 16055	291739	W 15908	348382	W 17943	326868	AUT MACH IND PARTICULIERES
7284	MACHY FOR SPCL INDUS NES	W 6257	142530	W 10357	245212	W 8881	274023	W 10240	250278	MACH SPEC IND PARTICUL.
72848	OTH MCHY WITH INDIV FNCT	W 3795	85169	W 6358	149038	W 5160	168247	W 4852	121134	AUTRES MACHINES NDA
73	METALWORKING MACHINERY		82765		142361		233091		207553	MACH TRAVAIL DES METAUX
736	METALWORKING MACH–TOOLS	W 4609	54020	W 7563	98941	W 10094	159865	W 12154	156537	MACH–OUTILS TRAVAIL METAUX
74	GENRL INDUSTRL MACHY NES		902716		1157157		1458130		1538310	MACH APP INDUSTRIE
741	HEATING,COOLING EQUIPMNT	W 9555	127182	W 11850	176528	W 15457	222782	W 17690	232021	MACH CHAUFFAGE,PIECES
7416	HEATING,COOLING EQU NES	W 3934	61133	W 4538	77712	W 4947	88306	W 4414	88103	APP CHANGEMENT TEMP
742	PUMPS FOR LIQUIDS ETC	W 4170	83519	W 5083	109261	W 6042	133206	W 6438	138196	POMPES MOTO–POMPES
743	PUMPS NES,CENTRFUGES ETC	W 12770	173104	W 14790	191515	W 14135	200476	W 15249	226967	POMPES COMPRES,VENT ETC
7431	PUMPS FOR GASES ETC	W 4396	55998	W 5084	58551	W 4744	58005	W 5393	72044	POMPES AIR A VIDE,COMPRES
7436	GAS,LIQUID FILTERS ETC	W 4314	61156	W 5042	64918	W 4692	68108	W 3932	65782	APP POUR FILT DES LIQUIDES
744	MECHANICAL HANDLING EQU	W 18965	125583	W 22930	155680	W 28354	217133	W 31043	230704	EQUIP MANUTENTION PIECES
7442	LIFTING,LOADING MACH NES	W 5475	46502	W 6682	55879	W 9847	78574	W 11613	94213	APP LEVAGE,MANUTENTION
7449	PTS NES OF MACHY OF 7442	W 11071	68440	W 12508	78939	W 13894	107669	W 14733	103642	PIECES DU 744.2
745	NONELEC MACHY,TOOLS NES	W 4911	107070	W 6637	147258	W 8984	169360	W 10671	197970	AUT MACH NON ELEC,PIECES
7452	OTH NONELEC MCHS,PTS NES	W 4239	91000	W 5745	120975	W 7990	134132	W 9393	161525	AUT MACH NON ELEC,PIECES
749	NONELEC MACH PTS,ACC NES	W 19814	286257	W 25282	376915	W 32025	515173	W 33210	512453	PIECES MACH NON ELEC NDA
7492	COCKS,VALVES ETC NES	W 5561	112010	W 7001	151026	W 8439	205079	W 9139	202580	ART ROB,SIM POUR TUYAUX
7493	SHAFT,CRANK,PULLEY ETC	W 9149	98680	W 12172	123210	W 16272	170142	W 16710	166622	ARBRES TRANS,VILEBREQUINS
75	OFFICE MACHNES,ADP EQUIP		837030		1195939		1597866		1486506	MACH BUREAU TRAIT AUTOM
751	OFFICE MACHINES	W 1685	49222	W 2403	81160	W 2513	84401	W 2552	81672	MACH,APPAREILS DE BUREAU
752	AUTOMTIC DATA PROC EQUIP	W 6297	511258	W 9123	671630	W 10865	885388	W 12288	948516	MACH TRAIT INFORMATION

4. General Imports C.I.F. by Commodities according to the S.I.T.C. (Rev. 2) in thousand U.S. Dollars
Importations Générales C.A.F. par Produits d'après la C.T.C.I. (Rév. 2) en milliers de Dollars E.U.

SITC CTCI	COMMODITY	1993 WEIGHT POIDS	1993 VALUE VALEUR	1994 WEIGHT POIDS	1994 VALUE VALEUR	1995 WEIGHT POIDS	1995 VALUE VALEUR	1996 WEIGHT POIDS	1996 VALUE VALEUR	PRODUIT
7522	DIGITAL COMPUTERS	W 361	44786	W 519	72105	W 420	93489	W 976	137166	MACH DIGITALES COMPLETES
7523	DIGITL CENTRL PROCESSORS	W 1521	169900	W 2205	206647	W 2299	275303	W 2195	259706	UNITES CENTRALES
7524	DIGITL CENTRL STOR UNITS	W 592	120715	W 840	151307	W 1093	170819	W 1000	176657	UNITES MEMOIRE CENTRALES
7525	ADP PERIPHERAL UNITS	W 3530	136771	W 5086	186250	W 6361	279677	W 7240	293627	UNITES PERIPHERIQUES
759	OFFICE,ADP MCH PTS,ACCES	W 3320	276549	W 4020	443149	W 5814	628078	W 6785	456317	PIECES DU 751 ET 752
7599	ACCTG,ETC,ADP MCH PTS,AC	W 2822	251141	W 3419	409843	W 5069	589386	W 6110	422178	PIECES DU 751 ET 752
76	TELECOMM,SOUND EQUIPMENT		450661		684463		912782		1042625	EQUIPMENT DE TELECOM
764	TELECOM EQPT,PTS,ACC NES	W 5065	331230	W 6349	515736	W 7799	699260	W 8667	790571	EQUIP TELECOM,PIECES
7641	LINE TELEPHONE,ETC EQUIP	W 692	53282	W 948	94017	W 1068	119941	W 1188	137441	APP TELEPHON PAR FIL
7643	TV,RADIO TRANSMITTRS ETC	W 190	42874	W 335	103233	W 323	122874	W 430	190307	APP EMET TELE RADIO
7649	PTS NES OF EQUIPMT OF 76	W 2517	170789	W 3048	261214	W 3542	378988	W 3705	393003	PIECES DE LA DIV 76
76491	PTS NES OF APPAR OF 7641	W 533	61031	W 1240	86249	W 1453	117758	W 1176	119791	PIECES POUR 764.1
76493	TELECOMM EQUIPMT PTS NES	W 1653	105657	W 1517	170271	W 1969	255424	W 2397	259562	PIECES 761,762,764.3,8
77	ELECTRIC MACHNRY NES ETC		1548819		2317589		3325247		3121930	MACH APP ELECT NDA
771	ELECTRIC POWER MACHY NES	W 5812	101689	W 7343	148232	W 8605	229064	W 8149	206486	MACH PROD,TRANS ELECTR
7712	OTH ELEC POWER MACHY NES	W 3976	79809	W 4608	112984	W 5918	187505	W 5807	170043	AUT APP PROD TRANSF ELEC
77121	STATIC CONVERTERS ETC	W 1345	49039	W 1675	66457	W 2134	99575	W 1937	96174	CONVERTISSEURS STATIQUES
772	SWITCHGEAR ETC,PARTS NES	W 7062	273842	W 8923	389892	W 11410	580364	W 11368	544609	APP COUPURE,SECT ETC
7721	SWITCHGEAR ETC	W 6527	218113	W 8068	291095	W 9717	400767	W 10159	398015	APP COUPURE,SECTIONMNT
7722	PRINTED CIRCUITS,PTS NES	W 285	35558	W 574	69334	W 1015	132986	W 785	110559	CIRCUITS ET PIECES
773	ELECTR DISTRIBUTNG EQUIP	W 17637	101113	W 21933	150157	W 25637	204507	W 24282	209276	EQUIPMT DISTRIBUTION ELECT
7731	INSULATED WIRE,CABLE ETC	W 16218	90178	W 20603	137124	W 24437	192559	W 23054	194644	FILS,CABLES ISOLES ELECT
775	HOUSEHOLD TYPE EQUIP NES	W 23640	157180	W 29369	207758	W 31671	246557	W 42315	333602	MACH,APP USAGE DOMESTQUE
7758	ELECTRO–THERMIC APPL NES	W 6821	58009	W 9219	83367	W 8952	89554	W 12544	124065	APP ELECTROTHERMIQ NDA
776	TRANSISTORS,VALVES,ETC	W 13173	568624	W 15225	889735	W 16794	1316808	W 13708	1105224	LAMPES,TUBES,VALVES
7762	OTH ELECTRONIC TUBES ETC	W 4998	106396	W 6402	137897	W 8271	205191	W 7649	184316	AUT LAMPES ELECTRONIQUES
7763	DIODES,TRANSISTORS,ETC	W 266	75806	W 455	122968	W 633	189573	W 521	147148	DIODES,TRANSISTORS
7764	ELECTRONIC MICROCIRCUITS	W 345	327850	W 471	562094	W 740	826870	W 586	706598	MICROSTRUCTURES ELECTRON
778	ELECTRICAL MACHINERY NES	W 22725	304107	W 30508	482803	W 31094	692042	W 33782	652732	AUTRES MACH ELECT NDA
7781	BATTERIES,ACCUMULATORS	W 12779	78835	W 17682	161567	W 17307	223725	W 20050	210900	PILES ET ACCUMULATEURS
77812	ELECTRIC ACCUMULATORS	W 10127	62255	W 14902	142758	W 14372	197948	W 16942	190052	ACCUMULATEURS ELECTRIQ
7788	OTH ELEC MACHY,EQUIP NES	W 4470	132138	W 5845	193512	W 5762	316483	W 5128	291664	AUT MACH APP ELEC NDA
77883	ELEC SIGNALLING EQU NES	W 315	28344	W 439	56365	W 524	93153	W 484	97268	APP ELECT SIGNAL ACOUS
77884	ELECTRICAL CONDENSERS	W 673	48621	W 908	72762	W 1290	114776	W 995	91311	CONDENSATEURS ELECTRIQUES
78	ROAD VEHICLES		899838		1424899		1928400		2142320	VEHICULES ROUTIERS
781	PASS MOTOR VEH EXC BUSES	W 61331	404323	W 84746	649691	W 96034	878228	W 120033	1077582	AUTO TRANSPORT PERSONNES
782	LORRIES,SPCL MTR VEH NES	W 13587	104166	W 22556	199972	W 37312	395922	W 39529	406090	VEHICULES SPECIAUX,MARCH
7821	LORRIES,TRUCKS	W 13191	101531	W 21949	193930	W 36307	388473	W 38739	396284	VEHICULES TRANSP MARCHAND
784	MOTOR VEH PRTS,ACCES NES	W 36471	323683	W 53848	474121	W 59003	528914	W 58115	512072	PIECES 722,781,782,783
7841	MOTOR VEHICLE CHASSIS	W 4456	51498	W 6212	76536	W 3219	46347	W 2959	44275	CHASSIS 722,781,782,783
7849	OTHER MOTOR VEHCL PARTS	W 31795	271121	W 47425	396893	W 55706	481886	W 54993	466941	PIECES 722,781,782,783
79	OTHR TRANSPORT EQUIPMENT		564319		304385		474000		756176	AUTRE MATERIEL TRANSPORT
792	AIRCRAFT ETC		184118	W 447	217177	W 619	299902	W 956	572876	APP NAVIGATION AERIENNE
7923	AIRCRFT NES2000–15000KG	W 16	22756	W 36	53473	W 63	130642	W 52	102588	AERODYNES 2000 A 15000 KG
7924	AIRCRFT NES OVER 15000KG	W 127	102626	W 153	82917	W 89	42641	W 162	83848	AERODYNES PLUS 15000 KG
7929	AIRCRAFT PARTS NES	W 220	55627	W 207	68994	W 394	109849	W 721	377499	PIECES DU 792
793	SHIPS AND BOATS ETC		361469		40779		120742	W 24106	137463	NAVIRES BATEAUX,ETC
7932	SHIPS AND BOATS NES		355055	W 34043	34966	W 31801	100281	W 22000	120441	NAVIRES ET BATEAUX
79323	OTHER CARGO VESSELS	W 109614	347246	W 28073	25797	W 31077	92961	W 21286	110441	AUT BATEAUX TRANS MARCH
8	MISC MANUFACTURED GOODS		2082353		2590905		3017362		3267064	ART MANUFACTURES DIVERS
812	*PLUMBG,HEATNG,LGHTNG EQ	W 8203	59336	W 10810	77637	W 11463	101355	W 13474	113265	APPAR SANITAIRES CHAUFFAGE
821	*FURNITURE,PARTS THEREOF	W 31850	114119	W 36330	162107	W 37118	199329	W 43882	238259	MEUBLES ET PIECES
8219	FURNITURE AND PARTS NES	W 17610	45829	W 20011	62087	W 21436	81127	W 26220	104902	AUTRES MEUBLES ET PIECES
84	CLOTHING AND ACCESSORIES		569630		703948		796686		878706	VETEMENTS
842	MENS OUTERWEAR NOT KNIT	W 4056	87032	W 5218	115675	W 5120	138662	W 5353	153218	VET DESSUS POUR HOMMES
843	WOMENS OUTERWEAR NONKNIT	W 5099	147868	W 5932	179153	W 6569	208294	W 6436	223542	VET DESSUS FEMMES MAT TEX
8439	— OTHER OUTER GARMENTS	W 3258	77019	W 3846	96747	W 3870	101617	W 3719	103929	AUT VET DES FEM MAT TEXT
845	OUTERWEAR KNIT NONELASTC	W 6137	139272	W 7322	163241	W 7064	180191	W 7867	193901	VET DESSOUS,ACCES BONNET
8451	— JERSEYS,PULLOVERS ETC	W 3226	75615	W 3857	89258	W 3564	93612	W 3736	97469	CHANDAILS,PULL–OVERS ETC
8459	— OTHER,CLTHG ACCESRYS	W 2704	56475	W 3208	65810	W 3121	73824	W 3786	85194	AUT VET DESSUS DE BONNE
846	UNDER GARMENTS KNITTED	W 4435	85977	W 5264	102197	W 4963	117411	W 5558	135130	SOUS VETS DE BONNETERIE
8462	— OF COTTON NON ELASTIC	W 3314	59371	W 4368	75705	W 4125	86025	W 4486	93280	SOUS–VET BONNET COTON
84629	—— OTHER	W 3314	59371	W 4208	72823	W 4125	86025	W 4486	93280	AUT SOUS–VET BONNET COTON
851	*FOOTWEAR	W 8695	115646	W 11697	157788	W 8458	147574	W 9425	177172	CHAUSSURES
85102	FOOTWEAR LEATHER	W 5311	85416	W 7586	122079	W 5602	115400	W 6359	138927	CHAUS SEMELLES EN CUIR
87	PRECISION INSTRUMNTS NES		337786		412533		532754		544885	INSTRUM,APPAR SCIENT NDA
872	MEDICAL INSTRUMENTS NES	W 1443	64934	W 1637	81756	W 3306	96212	W 1882	104852	INSTR,APP MEDIC–CHIR NDA
87202	OTH MEDICAL INSTRUMENTS	W 1210	57421	W 1462	73959	W 3052	84366	W 1622	90160	INSTRUM,APP MEDECINE
874	MEASURNG,CONTROLNG INSTR	W 2884	228968	W 3418	285955	W 3674	365607	W 4185	379140	INSTRUMENTS DE MESURE
8743	GAS,LIQUID CONTROL INSTR	W 1003	74831	W 1221	94257	W 1237	113424	W 1650	131464	APP,INSTR MESURE FLUIDES
8748	ELEC MEAS,CONTRL EQU NES	W 496	60630	W 497	76094	W 610	112022	W 649	100819	APP ELEC ELECTRO MESURE
87483	OTH ELCTRNC MEAS ETC EQU	W 430	54935	W 413	68632	W 521	102431	W 567	90023	AUT APP ELECTRO DE MESURE
88	PHOTO EQU,OPTICL GDS ETC		160861		202166		227216		229391	APP,FOURN PHOTO,OP,MONTR
882	PHOTO,CINEMA SUPPLIES	W 7886	82656	W 8506	101814	W 8018	112288	W 8190	113764	PRODUITS PHOTO,CINEMA
8822	PHOTO FILM EXC DEV CINMA	W 4698	64339	W 5048	78469	W 5046	87359	W 5094	89491	PLAQUES,PELLICULES,FILMS
89	MISC MANUFCTRD GOODS NES		705211		851287		980020		1044831	ART MANUFACTURES DIVERS
892	PRINTED MATTER	W 14473	117090	W 16267	132469	W 13045	124230	W 14863	139942	IMPRIMES
893	ARTICLES OF PLASTIC NES		220910		273848		317226		344447	OUVRAGES EN MAT DIVIS 58
8931	PLSTC PACKG CONTNRS,LIDS	W 12362	54704	W 13458	60603	W 16597	70834	W 19647	84925	ART TRANSP EMBALLAGE ETC
8939	MISC PLASTIC ARTICLES	W 31547	161970	W 37623	207971	W 38975	242216	W 42152	254187	ART DIVERS EN MAT DIV 58
89399	OTHR PLASTC ARTICLES NES	W 22548	135352	W 27742	175703	W 28138	201709	W 32597	219996	AUT OUV MAT DIV 58
894	TOYS,SPORTING GOODS,ETC	W 14545	123551	W 14646	135331	W 14820	160608	W 16686	175154	VOITURES ENFANTS,JOUETS
8942	TOYS,INDOOR GAMES ETC	W 9743	75379	W 9433	80616	W 9807	98030	W 10576	99626	JOUETS,JEUX ETC
898	MUSICAL INSTRUMENTS,PTS	W 4522	107195	W 5156	138454	W 5366	201159	W 5509	190878	INSTRUMENTS DE MUSIQUE
8983	SOUND RECRDNG TAPE,DISCS	W 3859	94478	W 4450	122642	W 4686	185546	W 4847	175488	SUPPORTS SON POUR 763
89832	RECORDED DISCS,TAPES ETC	W 1608	64969	W 2015	91295	W 2184	157617	W 2236	143875	DISQUES,PHONO,BANDES
899	OTHER MANUFACTURED GOODS		75346		94763		96573		107412	AUT ART MANUF DIVERS NDA
9	GOODS NOT CLASSD BY KIND		188257		179952		547239		644461	ART TRANSACT NON CLASSES
931	*SPECIAL TRANSACTIONS						484346		506065	TRANS.SPECIALES
951	*WAR FIREARMS,AMMUNITION		179765		168400		51195		130493	VEHIC BLINDES ARMES
95106	AMMUNITION NES		141245		110561		10097		103535	PROJECTILES,MUNITIONS

5. General Exports F.O.B. by Commodities according to the S.I.T.C. (Rev. 2) in thousand U.S. Dollars
Exportations Générales F.O.B. par Produits d'après la C.T.C.I. (Rév. 2) en milliers de Dollars E.U.

SITC CTCI	COMMODITY	1993		1994		1995		1996		PRODUIT
		WEIGHT POIDS	VALUE VALEUR	WEIGHT POIDS	VALUE VALEUR	WEIGHT POIDS	VALUE VALEUR	WEIGHT POIDS	VALUE VALEUR	
	ALL COMMODITIES		23473423		29764899		40408551		40561537	TOUS PRODUITS
0	FOOD AND LIVE ANIMALS		628565		870340		800222		947710	ALIMENTS,ANIMAUX VIVANTS
02	DAIRY PRODCTS,BIRDS'EGGS		123733		150597		205347		228755	PRODUITS LAITIERS,OEUFS
024	CHEESE AND CURD	W 25550	73920	W 27521	84768	W 29415	107067	W 29113	109605	FROMAGE ET CAILLEBOTTE
04	CEREALS AND PREPARATIONS		151077		144645		143973		206970	CEREALES ET PRODUITS
05	VEGETABLES AND FRUIT		61302		188510		66671		70544	LEGUMES ET FRUITS
057	FRUIT,NUTS,FRESH,DRIED	W 43719	31636	W 150119	124637	W 21676	19038	W 12307	12818	FRUITS FRAIS OU SECS
07	COFFEE,TEA,COCOA,SPICES		116308		149727		144160		155782	CAFE,THE,CACAO,EPICES
073	CHOCOLATE AND PRODUCTS	W 30019	89678	W 30394	102106	W 24587	104528	W 25407	106081	CHOCOLAT
09	MISC EDIBLE PRODUCTS		61256		105029		108960		124118	PREP ALIMENTAIRES DIVERSES
1	BEVERAGES AND TOBACCO		80674		111328		115565		151718	BOISSONS ET TABACS
11	BEVERAGES		67023		92436		91668		113879	BOISSONS
2	CRUDE MATERLS,EXCL FUELS		2051031		2945219		3608427		3099984	MAT BRUTES NON COMESTIBLES
21	HIDES,SKINS,FURS UNDRSSD		122165		234972		325638		450032	CUIRS,PEAUX BRUTS
212	FURSKINS,RAW	W 1110	104077	W 1232	209821	W 1762	301054	W 1827	428411	PELLETERIES BRUTES
21201	MINK SKINS,RAW	W 161	20763	W 180	41419	W 391	69445	W 457	146810	PEAUX DE VISON BRUTES
21209	OTHER FURSKINS,RAW	W 949	83314	W 1051	168403	W 1371	231610	W 1370	281601	AUTRES PELLETERIES BRUTES
24	CORK AND WOOD		1173001		1705287		1896832		1567206	LIEGE ET BOIS
247	OTH WOOD ROUGH,SQUARED	W 682026	80837	W 1130272	129999	W 797090	108594	W 491345	79776	BOIS BRUTS EQUARRIS
2471	SAW–,VENEER–LOGS CONIFER	W 672729	78463	W 1130272	129999	W 749327	100103	W 479710	76061	CONIFERES POUR SCIAGE,PLACAG
24711	— IN THE ROUGH	W 672729	78463	W 1130272	129999	W 749327	100103	W 479710	76061	ECORCES OU DEGROSSIS
248	WOOD SHAPED,SLEEPERS	W 3432506	1085120	W 3974439	1565659	W 3842438	1777463	W 3614750	1474850	BOIS SIMPLEMENT TRAVAILLES
2482	LUMBER SHAPED CONIFER	W 3409946	1075233	W 3939331	1546132	W 3818023	1761153	W 3593658	1460823	CONIFERES SCIES,RABOTES
24821	LUMBER SAWN ETC CONIFER	W 3341474	1041122	W 3851729	1484818	W 3761967	1710851	W 3535199	1415144	CONIFERES SCIES LONGITUD
251	*PULP AND WASTE PAPER	W 1489662	515039		723858	W 1346886	1043176	W 1585882	761543	PATES A PAPIER,DECHETS
2517	SODA,SULPHATE WOOD PULP	W 1371180	480075	W 1418851	688952	W 1231911	985124	W 1472017	723159	PATES CHIMIQUES AU SULFATE
25172	— BLEACHED,NONDISSOLVNG	W 1327413	459601	W 1382683	667708	W 1200671	959027	W 1442475	704479	PATES BLANCHIES
26	TEXTILE FIBRES AND WASTE		90618		97807		103284		80116	FIBRES TEXTILES
267	OTHER MAN–MADE FIBRES		88408		95118		98998		76688	AUTR FIBR TEXT ARTIF SYNTH
2671	REGENERATD FIBRE TO SPIN		81809		87554		91848		68105	FIBRES TEXT ARTIFIC
26711	DISCN REGEN FIBRE UNCMBD		81803		87554		91787		68105	FIBRES TEX ARTIF DISCONT
27	CRUDE FERTLZR,MINRLS NES		78239		93218		98954		97604	ENGRAIS MINERAUX BRUTS
28	METALLIFEROUS ORES,SCRAP		65187		81158		130105		131379	MINERAIS METAL,DECHETS
3	MINERAL FUELS ETC		641180		673287		768495		1250020	COMBUSTIBLES MINERAUX LUB
33	PETROLEUM AND PRODUCTS		624886		644982		750635		1050716	PETROLE ET DERIVES
334	PETROLEUM PRODUCTS,REFIN	W 3307451	618942	W 3571649	635948	W 3889325	738348	W 4688942	1035508	PRODUITS RAFFINES
3341	GASOLINE,OTH LIGHT OILS	W 1964533	375577	W 2356323	419116	W 2356163	440773	W 2897592	620356	ESSENCES POUR MOTEURS
33411	MOTOR,AVIATION SPIRIT	W 1862465	356981	W 2134974	381438	W 887651	169976	W 1451904	309884	ESSENCES MOTEURS D'AVIONS
33419	OTH LIGHT PETROLEUM OILS	W 102068	18596	W 221349	37678	W 1468259	270593	W 1445555	310287	AUTRES HUILES LEGERES
3343	GAS OILS	W 1196727	209073	W 1165089	184877	W 36796	5987	W 134	124	GAS OILS
3344	FUEL OILS,NES	W 63952	3994	W 207	35	W 1055624	177718	W 1458727	292223	FUEL OILS
351	*ELECTRIC CURRENT	H 429345	4869	H 630177	13847		6525		184033	ENERGIE ELECTRIQUE
5	CHEMCLS,RELATED PROD NES		1460091		1894387		2332897		2431021	PRODUITS CHIMIQUES
51	ORGANIC CHEMICALS		227003		337359		382366		366736	PROD CHIMIQ ORGANIQUES
512	ALCOHOLS,PHENOLS ETC		73147		102759		106858		84870	PHENOLS,PHENOLS–ALCOOLS
516	OTHER ORGANIC CHEMICALS		75103		105852		124402		143665	AUTRES PROD ORGANIQUES
52	INORGANIC CHEMICALS		158802		224701		321779		359096	PROD CHIM INORGANIQUES
522	INORG ELEMNTS,OXIDES,ETC		78423		102290		134137		154595	ELEMENTS INORGANIQUES
523	OTHR INORG CHEMICALS ETC		77089		119246		184258		201260	AUT PRODUITS CHIMIQUES INORG
53	DYES,TANNING,COLOUR PROD		206430		262034		317495		332327	PROD TEINTURE,COLORANTS
533	PIGMENTS,PAINTS,ETC		197249		249794		298278		309886	PIGMENTS,PEINTURES,VERNIS
5331	COLOURING MATERIAL NES		140861		157444		184410		160619	AUT MATIERES COLORANTES
541	*MEDICINAL,PHARM PRODUCT		155444		192109		214391		204950	PROD MEDICINAUX PHARMACEUT
5417	MEDICAMENTS	K 763395	93859	K 1218642	128163	K 1618014	159155	K 908164	143701	MEDICAMENTS
54179	— CONTNG OTH SUBSTANCES	K 627193	84260	K 1048651	118242	K 1566832	152363	K 859751	134210	MED CONT AUT SUBSTANCES
562	*FERTILIZERS,MANUFACTURE		73563		83856		96678		109562	ENGRAIS MANUFACTURES
58	PLASTIC MATERIALS ETC		444085		566202		699292		698246	MAT PLAST ARTIFICIELLES
583	POLYMERIZATION ETC PRODS		380513		471187		579400		570956	PROD POLYMERISATION
5831	POLYETHYLENE		83858		84523		100479		116944	POLYETHYLENE
5839	OTH POLYMRZTION ETC PROD	W 83422	144872		194998		224817	W 131362	248620	AUT PROD POLYMER COPOLYM
59	CHEMICAL MATERIALS NES		137757		162383		224346		237424	MAT PROD CHIMIQUES NDA
598	MISCEL CHEM PRODUCTS NES		116264		132238		172680		183196	PROD DIV INDUST CHIM NDA
5989	CHEM PRODUCTS,PREPS NES	W 44490	69754	W 36052	82984	W 56413	113011	W 171057	124479	PROD PREP CHIMIQUES NDA
6	BASIC MANUFACTURES		9664041		11726395		15729993		14473143	ART MANUFACTURES
62	RUBBER MANUFACTURES NES		94493		125883		176472		181509	CAOUTCHOUC MANUFACTURE
625	RUBBER TYRES, TUBES ETC	W 19893	69405	W 25230	92050	W 28832	128796	W 28950	138416	PNEUS CAOUTCHOUC VULCANISE
63	WOOD,CORK MANUFACTRS NES		671350		888251		1021398		1009502	OUVRAGES LIEGE ET BOIS
634	VENEERS,PLYWOOD,ETC	W 533264	420431	W 613425	528905	W 570479	642309	W 621888	615845	PLACAGES,CONTRE–PLAQUES
6342	PLYWOOD OF WOOD SHEETS	W 376380	371847	W 431536	458911	W 387782	545094	W 436605	529688	BOIS CONTRE–PLAQUES
635	WOOD MANUFACTURES NES		250675		359043	W 147548	378791	W 172803	393299	ART MANUF EN BOIS NDA
6353	BUILDERS WOODWRK,PREFABS	W 121691	242248	W 161254	347592	W 140210	366508	W 163981	381612	OUVRAGES DE MENUISERIE
64	PAPER,PAPERBOARD AND MFR		5851817		6996964		9772898		8554499	PAPIERS,CARTONS & OUVRAGES
641	PAPER AND PAPERBOARD	W 8971697	5622402	MW 9930	6689108	MW 9771	9313057	MW 9231	8070503	PAPIERS ET CARTONS
6411	NEWSPRINT	W 1249782	520478	W 1252541	559811	W 1098951	727877	W 1050550	733936	PAPIER JOURNAL
6412	PRINTG,WRITING PAPER NES	W 2746653	1874598	W 3256025	2371731	W 3425718	3585687	W 3209289	2943348	PAPIERS POUR L'IMPRESSION
64121	— UNCOATED	W 333841	196079	W 377638	277539	W 411937	466243	W 464244	402791	PAPIERS IMPRES NON COUCHES
64122	— COATED,IMPREGNATD ETC	W 2412812	1678520	W 2878387	2094192	W 3013781	3119444	W 2745045	2540557	PAPIERS IMPRESSION COUCHES
6413	KRAFT PAPER,PAPERBOARD	W 703948	449308	W 797034	554292	W 744027	693428	W 655594	542907	PAPIER ET CARTON KRAFT
64131	KRAFT LINER IN BULK	W 192013	94405	W 196979	109563	W 187997	149831	W 193218	124235	PAP KRAFT POUR COUVERTURES
64139	KRAFT PAPER PAPERBD,NES	W 420950	300881	W 479026	370180	W 446531	448867	W 370930	338672	PAPIER,CARTON KRAFT NDA
6415	PAPER,PAPERBRD,BULK,NES	W 3083088	1659384	W 3289967	1903266	W 3216617	2703085	W 2936749	2263798	PAPIERS,CARTONS ROULEAUX
64151	SEMI–CHEM FLUTING PAPER	W 406065	114282	W 416730	133680	W 403394	209119	W 383778	145073	PAPIER FLUTING
64159	OTHER PAPER ETC,BULK,NES	W 2636417	1485639	W 2826595	1698236	W 2774375	2419286	W 2504992	2036204	AUT PAPIER ROULEAUX FEUILLES
6417	CORRUGATED PAPER ETC,BLK	W 81855	77300	W 77741	77152	W 68530	95479	W 67531	87913	PAPIERS,CARTONS ONDULES
64172	CREPED HSHOLD PAPER ETC	W 77696	71221	W 70057	67557	W 59887	79842	W 57858	73387	PAPIER NON KRAFT CREPE
6418	COATED ETC PAPER NES BLK	W 1020443	992684	W 1159051	1166186	W 1129630	1437254	W 1226770	1437065	PAP,CARTONS COUCHES,ENDUITS
64181	PLASTIC COATED PAPER ETC	W 295448	289362	W 334290	351317	W 248981	348499	W 260839	338857	PAP,CARTONS ENDUITS,RESINES
64189	COATED PAPER ETC NES	W 711178	690448	W 809182	797652	W 870066	1073567	W 957140	1087349	PAPIERS,CARTONS COUCHES
642	PAPER,ETC,PRECUT,ARTS OF	W 208681	229415	W 250941	307855	W 263469	459841	W 299026	483996	PAP,CARTONS DECOUPES
6421	PAPER ETC CONTAINERS	W 28555	47700	W 37878	68502	W 48584	112052	W 58138	129663	BOITES,SACS EMBALLAGES
6428	PAPER ETC ARTICLES NES	W 141966	120443	W 169019	166331	W 162345	242658	W 190096	252266	OUVRAGES EN PATE A PAPIER
65	TEXTILE YARN,FABRICS,ETC		219729		289959		365120		375680	FILS,TISSUS,ARTICLES TEXTILE
657	SPECIAL TXTL FABRC,PRODS	W 21176	106407	W 30259	143386	W 31180	187540	W 36837	201402	TISSUS SPECIAUX
66	NONMETAL MINERAL MFS NES		303870		362927		457056		463545	ART MIN NON METALLIQUES
663	MINERAL MANUFCTURES NES		73048		92474		117035		115846	ART MIN MANUF NDA
664	GLASS		173149		191155		243254		252809	VERRE
6647	SAFETY GLASS CUT OR NOT	W 24592	100140	W 27555	110874	W 27225	126356	W 26785	120897	GLACES DE SECURITE
67	IRON AND STEEL		1403736		1707813		2224012		2085840	FER ET ACIER
672	IRON,STEEL PRIMARY FORMS		244561		231570		265559		259867	LINGOTS FER,ACIER
6727	IRN,STL COIL FR REROLLNG		212880		186631		209318		185405	EBAUCHES POUR TOLES FER
67271	IRON,SIMPLE STEEL COILS		95421		79279		60842		82648	EBAUCHES NON EN ACIER

5. General Exports F.O.B. by Commodities according to the S.I.T.C. (Rev. 2) in thousand U.S. Dollars
Exportations Générales F.O.B. par Produits d'après la C.T.C.I. (Rév. 2) en milliers de Dollars E.U.

SITC CTCI	COMMODITY	1993 WEIGHT POIDS	1993 VALUE VALEUR	1994 WEIGHT POIDS	1994 VALUE VALEUR	1995 WEIGHT POIDS	1995 VALUE VALEUR	1996 WEIGHT POIDS	1996 VALUE VALEUR	PRODUIT
67274	STNLESS STEEL ETC COILS	W 75132	113107	W 66450	100670	W 52951	143503	W 54477	99621	EBAUCHES ACIER INOXYDBLE
673	IRON,STEEL SHAPES ETC	W 364273	137399	W 386441	166776	W 409836	227399	W 416080	221321	BARRES,PROFIL FER,ACIER
6732	IRON,STEEL BARS ETC	W 161556	70457	W 165808	82228	W 197856	131111	W 162505	105788	BARRES FER,ACIER
674	IRN,STL UNIV,PLATE,SHEET		768222		989456		1287533		1219939	LARGES PLATS,TOLES
6744	IRN,STL HVY PLATE,ROLLED		163849		175689		213297		250801	TOLES LAMINEES PLUS 4.75 MM
67441	— OF IRON OR SIMPLE STL		127536		135887		127391		175887	TOLES NON ACIER FIN CARB
6745	IRN,STL MED PLATE,ROLLED		96482		102122		159560		133213	TOLES 3 A 4.75 MM
67453	— OF STAINLESS ETC STL	W 36241	65365	W 43533	78381	W 43320	123810	W 42101	90106	TOLES ACIER INOXYDABLE
6746	IRN,STL THIN PLATE,ROLLD		328429		479652		616475		543130	TOLES LAM MOINS 3MM
67463	— OF STAINLESS ETC STL	W 151639	257639	W 216890	373342	W 195766	509013	W 198801	411823	TOL ACIER INOX MOINS 3 MM
6749	OTH IRN,STL PLATES,SHEET		179410		231870		297848	W 366901	292548	AUTRES TOLES FER,ACIER
67491	— OF IRON OR SIMPLE STL		152316		198195		242464	W 334162	249706	AUT TOLES AUTRES ACIER FIN
678	IRON,STL TUBES,PIPES,ETC		183909		232999		322615		292533	TUBES,TUYAUX EN FONTE,FER
6783	IRON,STL TUBES,PIPES NES		153072		192731		268980		242103	AUT TUBES,TUYAUX FER,ACIER
68	NON-FERROUS METALS		680593		791891		1008472		1029507	METAUX NON FERREUX
682	COPPER EXC CEMENT COPPER	W 132162	350166	W 128454	392536	W 123928	509822	W 153622	479924	CUIVRE
6821	COPPER NES,ALLOYS,UNWRT	W 54966	109701	W 48235	115209	W 39010	120395	W 76765	181108	CUIVRE BRUT
6822	COPPER,ALLOYS WORKED	W 77195	240464	W 80219	277327	W 84918	389427	W 76857	298815	CUIVRE,ALLIAGES OUVRES
68222	COPPER PLATE,SHEET,STRIP	W 31882	92606	W 30763	104348	W 33382	146996	W 42368	155619	TOLES DE PLUS 0.15 MM
68225	COPPER TUBES,PIPES,ETC	W 29846	97002	W 29573	105543	W 31598	149262	W 19832	81888	TUBES,TUYAUX EN CUIVRE
683	NICKEL	W 12917	67536	W 12617	77109	W 13103	108859	W 22092	169673	NICKEL
6831	NICKEL,ALLOYS UNWROUGHT	W 12849	67212	W 12532	76420	W 12847	106615	W 21475	164883	NICKEL ET ALLIAGES BRUTS
684	ALUMINIUM	W 48191	81893	W 47259	104528	W 46491	138576	W 47789	112594	ALUMINIUM
686	ZINC	W 141257	136371	W 142234	137862		137278		146481	ZINC
6861	ZINC,ALLOYS UNWROUGHT	W 141113	136032	W 141693	136567	W 130308	135620	W 140236	143851	ZINC ET ALLIAGES BRUTS
69	METAL MANUFACTURES NES		383261		494101		632591		668583	ART MANUFACT EN METAL NDA
691	STRUCTURES AND PARTS NES	W 91582	175729	W 99176	195723	W 124153	289210	W 137015	296161	CONSTRUCT FER,ACIER,ALU
6911	STRUCTURES,PARTS IRN,STL	W 89692	164606	W 95868	172957	W 120780	257176	W 133749	268529	CONSTRUCT FER,ACIER,FONTE
699	BASE METAL MFRS NES		96268	W 41062	150807		170675		176191	ART MANUFACTURES MET NDA
7	MACHINES,TRANSPORT EQUIP		7359785		9474754		14263963		15532595	MACHINES MATERIEL TRANSPORT
71	POWER GENERATING EQUIPMT		776237		832633		1079352		1214951	MACHINES GENERATRICES
711	STEAM BOILERS & AUX PLNT	W 17559	107570	W 10737	100438	W 14806	123412	W 16544	122941	GENERATEURS VAPEUR EAU ETC
713	INTRNL COMBUS PSTN ENGIN	W 15675	214014	W 11980	197507	W 15602	214936	W 16451	235111	MOTEURS EXPL COMB INT, PIECE
7133	MARINE PISTON ENGINES	W 6028	89647	W 2581	39606	W 3065	48778	W 6442	96889	MOTEURS EXPL POUR BATEAUX
71332	—— OTHER THAN OUTBOARD	W 6016	89289	W 2563	39071	W 3056	48447	W 6419	96129	MOT BATEAUX AUT HORSBORD
7139	PISTON ENGINE PARTS NES	W 6090	109243	W 5964	130351	W 8677	118964	W 6106	97398	PIECES POUR 713.2,3,8
716	ROTATING ELECTRIC PLANT	W 36807	431899	W 47073	507414	W 59217	692766	W 68801	797535	APP ELECTR ROTATIFS,PIECES
7162	AC MTRS,GENRTRS,GEN SETS	W 33059	383206	W 43419	457272	W 53329	619714	W 60362	692014	MOTEURS ELECTRIQUES
71621	AC MTRS,INC UNIVRSL MTRS	W 15199	107168	W 21825	158342	W 25094	187193	W 28472	225228	MOT ELEC NON COUR CONTINU
71623	GEN SETS WITH PSTN ENGN	W 17267	266765	W 20305	279936	W 24874	408613	W 28188	430785	GROUPES MOTEUR EXPLOSION
72	MACHS FOR SPCL INDUSTRYS		1254973		1557369		2252416		2292170	MAC SPECIALES POUR INDUST
722	TRACTORS NON-ROAD	W 13107	89581	W 19730	142200	W 24738	238739	W 26626	263655	TRACTEURS
7224	WHEELED TRACTORS NES	W 12969	88981	W 19583	140751	W 24738	238739	W 26589	263548	TRACTEURS A ROUES
723	CIVIL ENGNEERG EQUIP ETC	W 25913	195214	W 21043	215680	W 19741	295720	W 21342	306065	APPAREILS DE GENIE CIVIL
7234	CONST,MINING MACHNRY NES	W 24675	161480	W 19851	181235	W 18088	248549	W 19553	255326	MACH POUR LA CONST, MINES
725	PAPER ETC MILL MACHINERY	W 47457	487396	W 40611	526736	W 76637	921257	W 55005	884512	MACHINES FABR PATE PAPIER
7251	PAPER,PULP MAKING MACHRY	W 31228	270417	W 24483	305013	W 50421	491090	W 35540	501452	MACHINES FABR PATE CARTON
72511	CELLULOSE PULP MFG MACHY	W 19407	158230	W 10846	147439	W 31011	258853	W 14970	220942	MACH FABR PATE CELLULOSE
72512	PAPER ETC MAKING ETC MCH	W 11821	112186	W 13637	157574	W 19409	232237	W 20570	280510	MACH FABR FINITION DU PAP
7259	PTS NES OF MACHS OF 725	W 14251	193761	W 13423	187565	W 22538	375912	W 16064	320111	PIECES GROUPE 725
72591	PTS NES OF MACHS OF 7251	W 13810	186526	W 12585	173581	W 21655	355720	W 15517	306027	PIECES DU 725.1
728	OTH MACHY FOR SPCL INDUS	W 35909	389787	W 44725	560558	W 45589	684696	W 43989	710795	AUT MACH IND PARTICULIERES
7281	MACH-TOOLS FR SPCL INDUS	W 5885	59103	W 8740	97746	W 5163	78232	W 4977	65068	MACH-OUTILS SPEC IND PART
7283	OTHR MINERAL WORKG MACHY	W 12536	73215	W 15245	92869	W 18095	137219	W 15917	123334	MACH TRIER,CRIBLER,BROYER
7284	MACHY FOR SPCL INDUS NES	W 17488	257469	W 20739	369943	W 22331	469245	W 23094	522393	MACH SPEC IND PARTICUL.
72848	OTH MCHY WITH INDIV FNCT	W 8600	166248	W 11299	240107	W 10510	268036	W 12369	325831	AUTRES MACHINES NDA
73	METALWORKING MACHINERY		95453		153071		209097		232144	MACH TRAVAIL DES METAUX
736	METALWORKING MACH-TOOLS	W 5321	56641	W 6229	86145	W 7686	134583	W 8753	161145	MACH-OUTILS TRAVAIL METAUX
74	GENRL INDUSTRL MACHY NES		1059009		1322481		1765372		1778501	MACH APP INDUSTRIE
741	HEATING,COOLING EQUIPMNT	W 20498	183295	W 21165	199753	W 22872	255805	W 23110	264662	MACH CHAUFFAGE,PIECES
7416	HEATING,COOLING EQU NES	W 7870	92609	W 6503	79682	W 7983	105603	W 6811	105239	APP CHANGEMENT TEMP
742	PUMPS FOR LIQUIDS ETC	W 4596	60176	W 4829	74182	W 6038	101256	W 6428	123162	POMPES MOTO-POMPES
743	PUMPS NES,CENTRFUGES ETC	W 6898	95453	W 8193	128442	W 8416	153581	W 8720	176570	POMPES COMPRES,VENT ETC
744	MECHANICAL HANDLING EQU	W 65470	467098	W 73804	588364	W 85421	782231	W 77794	729504	EQUIP MANUTENTION PIECES
7441	FORK LIFT TRCKS,ETC,PTS	W 11888	78412	W 12435	85860	W 19424	157584	W 20818	181575	CHARIOTS POUR USINES ETC
74411	FORK LIFT TRUCKS ETC	W 11867	78238	W 12416	85613	W 19393	157273	W 20737	180726	CHARIOTS POUR LES GARES
7442	LIFTING,LOADING MACH NES	W 36701	230464	W 40531	282604	W 41648	345470	W 36575	316054	APP LEVAGE,MANUTENTION
74428	OTH HANDLING ETC MCH NES	W 16553	123738	W 22048	172197	W 23206	218313	W 20886	204499	AUT APP LEVAGE ETC
7449	PTS NES OF MACHY OF 7442	W 16881	158223	W 20838	219900	W 24348	279178	W 20402	231875	PIECES DU 744.2
745	NONELEC MACHY,TOOLS NES	W 3900	60443	W 4518	71763	W 7009	126674	W 6385	110748	AUT MACH NON ELEC,PIECES
749	NONELEC MACH PTS,ACC NES	W 12297	192544	W 14541	259977	W 17555	345823	W 18701	373854	PIECES MACH NON ELEC NDA
7492	COCKS,VALVES ETC NES	W 6854	131107	W 8477	173338	W 8978	222157	W 9444	232355	ART ROB,SIM POUR TUYAUX
75	OFFICE MACHNES,ADP EQUIP		636708		868659		1070140		997979	MACH BUREAU TRAIT AUTOM
752	AUTOMTIC DATA PROC EQUIP	W 13205	550352	W 16581	721637	W 23396	918497	W 22590	884421	MACH TRAIT INFORMATION
7522	DIGITAL COMPUTERS	W 122	16754	W 81	10526	W 5986	404260	W 315	49560	MACH DIGITALES COMPLETES
7523	DIGITL CENTRL PROCESSORS	W 3176	260903	W 3531	335301	W 287	23841	W 3404	307331	UNITES CENTRALES
7525	ADP PERIPHERAL UNITS	W 9628	242001	W 12683	329895	W 16874	463466	W 18515	487241	UNITES PERIPHERIQUES
759	OFFICE,ADP MCH PTS,ACCES	W 717	72649	W 1261	128075	W 1530	137150	W 1919	99991	PIECES DU 751 ET 752
7599	ACCTG,ETC,ADP MCH PTS,AC	W 622	69555	W 1102	122959	W 1409	133674	W 1670	94831	PIECES DU 751 ET 752
76	TELECOMM,SOUND EQUIPMENT		1217265		1980509		3482419		4103601	EQUIPMENT DE TELECOM
761	TELEVISION RECEIVERS	W 10208	139418	W 10804	159329	W 10444	190810	W 6674	129564	RECEPTEURS DE TELEVISION
7611	COLOUR TV RECEIVERS	W 10204	139117	W 10794	158914	W 10441	190553	W 6666	128464	RECEPTEURS COULEUR
764	TELECOM EQPT,PTS,ACC NES	W 6048	1055270	W 9246	1796916	W 12281	3277884	W 14448	3946133	EQUIP TELECOM,PIECES
7641	LINE TELEPHONE,ETC EQUIP	W 1341	321879	W 1631	422034	W 2171	853697	W 2429	1092770	APP TELEPHON PAR FIL
7643	TV,RADIO TRANSMITTRS ETC	W 1671	463519	W 3395	873913	W 4571	1689741	W 4895	2017323	APP EMET TELE RADIO
7649	PTS NES OF EQUIPMT OF 76	W 2458	260172	W 3340	486791	W 4088	701713	W 5396	797826	PIECES DE LA DIV 76
76491	PTS NES OF APPAR OF 7641	W 592	112438	W 713	209888	W 737	192296	W 933	260478	PIECES POUR 764.1
76493	TELECOMM EQUIPMT PTS NES	W 1834	146234	W 2561	272821	W 3324	505675	W 3996	524619	PIECES 761,762,764.3,8
77	ELECTRIC MACHNRY NES ETC		936452		1282250		1810299		1980926	MACH APP ELECT NDA
771	ELECTRIC POWER MACHY NES	W 25664	257040	W 30787	357690	W 37455	577495	W 34580	625372	MACH PROD,TRANS ELECTR
7712	OTH ELEC POWER MACHY NES	W 19393	216832	W 22617	306729	W 29294	494457	W 26827	542351	AUT APP PROD TRANSF ELEC
77121	STATIC CONVERTERS ETC	W 3210	146716	W 4631	216465	W 11354	371413	W 7417	420288	CONVERTISSEURS STATIQUES
772	SWITCHGEAR ETC,PARTS NES	W 7031	163053	W 8483	226073	W 8805	271246	W 9380	291207	APP COUPURE,SECT ETC
7721	SWITCHGEAR ETC	W 6913	150747	W 8052	198640	W 8511	245308	W 9075	266232	APP COUPURE,SECTIONMNT
773	ELECTR DISTRIBUTNG EQUIP	W 22503	104630	W 29450	140463	W 28233	175835	W 35780	204934	EQUIPMT DISTRIBUTION ELECT
7731	INSULATED WIRE,CABLE ETC	W 22148	101956	W 29156	137717	W 27997	172772	W 35493	200709	FILS,CABLES ISOLES ELECT
774	ELECTRO-MEDCL,XRAY EQUIP	W 1048	145114	W 1377	182162	W 1433	215330	W 1885	250518	APPAREILS MEDICAUX
7741	ELECTRO-MEDICAL EQUIPMNT	W 273	75151	W 422	99608	W 551	123072	W 928	157107	APP ELECTRICITE MEDICALE
775	HOUSEHOLD TYPE EQUIP NES	W 10423	67136	W 12173	85037	W 13001	111697	W 19037	194507	MACH,APP USAGE DOMESTQUE
776	TRANSISTORS,VALVES,ETC	W 211	56357	W 238	87500	W 673	119673	W 922	121840	LAMPES,TUBES,VALVES
778	ELECTRICAL MACHINERY NES	W 6662	143122	W 7974	203325	W 7670	339024	W 6998	292548	AUTRES MACH ELECT NDA

5. General Exports F.O.B. by Commodities according to the S.I.T.C. (Rev. 2) in thousand U.S. Dollars
Exportations Générales F.O.B. par Produits d'après la C.T.C.I. (Rév. 2) en milliers de Dollars E.U.

SITC CTCI	COMMODITY	1993 WEIGHT POIDS	1993 VALUE VALEUR	1994 WEIGHT POIDS	1994 VALUE VALEUR	1995 WEIGHT POIDS	1995 VALUE VALEUR	1996 WEIGHT POIDS	1996 VALUE VALEUR	PRODUIT
7781	BATTERIES,ACCUMULATORS	W 3018	30472	W 4375	75036	W 3758	187108	W 2943	140956	PILES ET ACCUMULATEURS
77812	ELECTRIC ACCUMULATORS	W 2864	29648	W 4118	73627	W 3464	182484	W 2359	136665	ACCUMULATEURS ELECTRIQ
7788	OTH ELEC MACHY,EQUIP NES	W 2529	92640	W 2020	95493	W 2225	113269	W 2135	111649	AUT MACH APP ELEC NDA
78	ROAD VEHICLES		616614		901220		1166656		1197009	VEHICULES ROUTIERS
781	PASS MOTOR VEH EXC BUSES	W 46785	244997	W 43246	372145	W 46206	559434	W 49366	609247	AUTO TRANSPORT PERSONNES
782	LORRIES,SPCL MTR VEH NES	W 33744	139065	W 32532	191260	W 23595	198401	W 19018	177448	VEHICULES SPECIAUX,MARCH
7821	LORRIES,TRUCKS	W 25886	81023	W 27015	127922	W 18444	119220	W 15056	117854	VEHICULES TRANSP MARCHAND
783	ROAD MOTOR VEHICLES NES	W 8928	71208	W 7137	88222	W 5427	78780	W 4981	78442	VEHICULES ROUTIERS NDA
7831	BUSES	W 8864	70923	W 7123	88186	W 5375	78696	W 4902	77910	VOITURES TRANSPORT COMMUN
784	MOTOR VEH PRTS,ACCES NES	W 21187	101832	W 31470	159780	W 37964	222722	W 32927	223902	PIECES 722,781,782,783
7849	OTHER MOTOR VEHCL PARTS	W 20139	92726	W 30172	146450	W 37076	210180	W 31197	203879	PIECES 722,781,782,783
79	OTHR TRANSPORT EQUIPMENT		767073		576562		1428212		1735315	AUTRE MATERIEL TRANSPORT
793	SHIPS AND BOATS ETC		728047		519600		1292831		1645543	NAVIRES BATEAUX,ETC
7932	SHIPS AND BOATS NES	W 186405	694327	W 248945	431229	W 169415	1199197	W 171313	1514918	NAVIRES ET BATEAUX
79322	TANKERS OF ALL KINDS			W 52811	36100	W 48610	221838	W 70000	402057	BATEAUX–CITERNES
79323	OTHER CARGO VESSELS	W 181934	627094	W 72068	315910	W 118342	913693	W 98204	1040844	AUT BATEAUX TRANS MARCH
7938	TUGS,SPECIAL VESSELS ETC		18526		4078	W 329	2662	W 36418	124839	REMORQUEURS,BATEAUX SPEC
79382	SPECL PURPOSE VESSLS ETC	N 11	7333	N 9	2271	W 125	1690	W 36110	123558	BAT–PHARES,–POMPES,DRAGUES
8	MISC MANUFACTURED GOODS		1554638		2028478		2339151		2345479	ART MANUFACTURES DIVERS
812	*PLUMBG,HEATNG,LGHTNG EQ		157811		220260		210183		223175	APPAR SANITAIRES CHAUFFAGE
8121	CENTRAL HEATING EQUIPMNT	W 30337	81049	W 36847	110019	W 30906	87092	W 34302	94816	CHAUDIERES,RADIATEURS
821	*FURNITURE,PARTS THEREOF	W 53987	216909	W 72982	328046	W 63340	366868	W 60310	326786	MEUBLES ET PIECES
8219	FURNITURE AND PARTS NES	W 44651	131159	W 62734	214565	W 54738	230978	W 51956	212919	AUTRES MEUBLES ET PIECES
82192	WOOD FURNITURE NES	W 30253	90564	W 41366	153768	W 33974	156331	W 31934	141126	MEUBLES NDA EN BOIS
84	CLOTHING AND ACCESSORIES		216316		251731		273101		261573	VETEMENTS
843	WOMENS OUTERWEAR NONKNIT	W 1283	71045	W 1409	75948	W 1242	80323	W 1223	74350	VET DESSUS FEMMES MAT TEX
87	PRECISION INSTRUMNTS NES		298052		369202		493545		496527	INSTRUM,APPAR SCIENT NDA
874	MEASURNG,CONTROLNG INSTR	W 1719	243333	W 2178	298203	W 3345	412188	W 2587	384474	INSTRUMENTS DE MESURE
8743	GAS,LIQUID CONTROL INSTR	W 609	72758	W 838	104247	W 1326	143950	W 1119	127216	APP,INSTR MESURE FLUIDES
89	MISC MANUFCTRD GOODS NES		587110		747710		869136		896931	ART MANUFACTURES DIVERS
892	PRINTED MATTER	W 80706	185157	W 101867	243244	W 127612	360612	W 132831	377238	IMPRIMES
8922	NEWSPAPERS,PERIODICALS	W 26291	55783	W 40564	83739	W 68073	152855	W 79136	172939	JOURNAUX ET PERIODIQUES
8928	PRINTED MATTER NES	W 42467	94415	W 47238	112599	W 45559	138505	W 41206	140094	IMPRIMES NDA
89286	TRADE ADV MATRL,CATALOGS	W 39644	75103	W 43417	87663	W 41625	100299	W 38226	97484	IMPRIMES PUBLICITAIRES
893	ARTICLES OF PLASTIC NES		213414		261634		253523		263811	OUVRAGES EN MAT DIVIS 58
8939	MISC PLASTIC ARTICLES	W 32168	147467	W 37538	187756	W 30069	176162	W 32494	182688	ART DIVERS EN MAT DIV 58
89399	OTHR PLASTC ARTICLES NES	W 28374	137507	W 32452	172164	W 26121	159582	W 28513	166997	AUT OUV MAT DIV 58
894	TOYS,SPORTING GOODS,ETC	W 10392	96839	W 12998	124785	W 10861	135331	W 11703	133364	VOITURES ENFANTS,JOUETS
9	GOODS NOT CLASSD BY KIND		18902		22154		418722		296923	ART TRANSACT NON CLASSES
931	*SPECIAL TRANSACTIONS						357223		240799	TRANS.SPECIALES

FOOT NOTES – NOTES

TABLE 1 –

1 The gold trade excludes partly–worked gold, which is included in merchandise trade.

TABLEAU 1 –

1 Le commerce de l'or exclut l'or partiellement travaillé qui est compris dans le commerce de marchandises.

1. HISTORICAL SERIES, 1961–1996 SPECIAL TRADE, IMPORTS C.I.F., EXPORTS F.O.B. SERIES HISTORIQUES, 1961–1996 COMMERCE SPECIAL, IMPORTATIONS C.A.F., EXPORTATIONS F.O.B

YEAR ANNEE	VALUE IN MILLION FRENCH FRANCS VALEUR EN MILLION FRENCH FRANCS MERCHANDISE –MARCHANDISE IMPORTS	EXPORTS	GOLD # 1 –OR IMPORTS	EXPORTS	CONVERSION FACTORS U.S. CENTS PER FRENCH FRANC FACTEURS DE CONVERSION CENTS E.U. PAR FRENCH FRANC IMPORTS	EXPORTS	INDEX NUMBERS –INDICES QUANTUM IMPORTS	EXPORTS	UNIT VALUE VALEUR UNITAIRE IMPORTS	EXPORTS
1961	32960.00	35587.00	1126.00	192.00	20.2550	20.2550	13	16	21	20
1962	37101.00	36333.00	449.00	115.00	20.2550	20.2550	15	17	21	20
1963	43073.00	39890.00	1688.00	135.00	20.2550	20.2550	17	18	21	21
1964	49700.00	44386.00			20.2550	20.2550	19	19	22	22
1965	51029.00	49609.00			20.2550	20.2550	20	21	22	22
1966	58453.00	53782.00			20.2550	20.2550	22	22	22	22
1967	61251.00	56198.00			20.2550	20.2550	23	24	22	22
1968	69029.00	62723.00			20.2550	20.2550	27	26	22	22
1969	90023.00	77759.00			19.3200	19.3200	33	30	23	24
1970	106190.00	99641.00			18.0000	18.0000	35	35	26	26
1971	117997.00	113970.00			18.0700	18.0700	38	38	27	27
1972	135606.00	131497.00			19.8269	19.8315	43	43	27	28
1973	166123.00	159714.00			22.5579	22.5660	48	48	29	31
1974	254651.00	220213.00			20.8098	20.8216	50	53	43	39
1975	231269.00	223362.00			23.3459	23.3824	47	50	42	41
1976	308012.00	266228.00			20.9027	20.9217	55	55	46	45
1977	346207.00	311550.00			20.3537	20.3616	57	59	52	49
1978	368401.00	344594.00			22.1937	22.2006	60	62	52	51
1979	457128.00	414677.00			23.5355	23.5297	67	68	58	56
1980	570778.00	469694.00			23.6663	23.6566	71	70	68	63
1981	654239.00	549500.00			18.4753	18.4478	68	72	82	70
1982	757595.00	606094.00			15.2647	15.2829	69	70	92	80
1983	799754.00	694659.00			13.1784	13.1332	67	72	100	87
1984	905421.00	813003.00			11.4744	11.4655	69	76	110	95
1985	962746.00	870812.00			11.1984	11.2117	72	79	111	98
1986	895891.90	863539.90			14.4476	14.4594	77	78	93	94
1987	949817.00	888912.90			16.6873	16.6948	82	81	92	93
1988	1053798.00	997648.90			16.8237	16.8208	90	88	95	96
1989	1216839.00	1102501.00			15.6933	15.6982	95	95	101	102
1990	1266788.00	1142182.00			18.4093	18.4007	100	100	100	100
1991	1297131.00	1200488.00			17.7956	17.7795	102	105	99	100
1992	1263933.00	1227504.00			18.8993	18.8930	104	109	95	97
1993	1135291.00	1166648.00			17.6827	17.6773	107	111	91	94
1994	1276609.00	1306033.00			18.0665	18.0755	117	120	94	100
1995	1381278.00	1432334.00			20.0525	20.0605	123	129	96	102
1996	1429356.00	1473888.00			19.5460	19.5434			96	102

2. IMPORTS BY BROAD ECONOMIC CATEGORY AND EXPORTS BY INDUSTRIAL ORIGIN. (PERCENTAGE OF TOTAL VALUE) IMPORTATIONS PAR CATEGORIES ECONOMIQUES ET EXPORTATIONS PAR BRANCHE D'ACTIVITE.(EN POURCENTAGE DE LA VALEUR TOTALE)

IMPORTS – IMPORTATIONS

	1990	1991	1992	1993	1994	1995	1996
TOTAL IMPORTS–IMPORTATIONS TOTALES	100.	100.	100.	100.	100.	100.	100.
1 FOOD BEV–ALIMENTATION BOISSONS	8.6	9.1	9.3	9.7	9.7	9.4	9.0
11 PRIMARY–PRODUITS DE BASE	4.8	5.0	5.0	5.1	5.2	4.8	4.4
111 FOR INDUSTRY–POUR L'INDUSTRIE	0.7	0.8	0.7	0.8	1.0	0.9	0.8
112 FOR HOUSEHOLDS–POUR LES MENAGES	4.1	4.3	4.2	4.3	4.2	3.9	3.6
12 PROCESSED–PRODUITS ELABORES	3.8	4.0	4.3	4.6	4.6	4.6	4.6
121 FOR INDUSTRY–POUR L'INDUSTRIE	0.5	0.6	0.6	0.6	0.6	0.6	0.6
122 FOR HOUSEHOLDS–POUR LES MENAGES	3.2	3.5	3.7	4.0	3.9	4.0	4.0
2 IND SUPPLIES–APPROV INDUSTRIELS	31.3	29.2	29.4	28.7	30.0	31.3	29.0
21 PRIMARY–PRODUITS DE BASE	2.7	2.5	2.4	2.3	2.4	2.4	2.1
22 PROCESSED–PRODUITS ELABORES	28.5	26.7	27.0	26.4	27.6	28.9	27.0
3 FUELS–COMBUSTIBLES	9.4	9.6	8.5	8.6	7.6	6.7	8.2
31 PRIMARY–PRODUITS DE BASE	7.0	7.1	6.2	6.5	5.6	5.2	6.4
32 PROCESSED–PRODUITS ELABORES	2.5	2.5	2.3	2.1	1.9	1.5	1.8
321 MOTOR SPIRIT–ESSENCE						0.4	0.4
322 OTHER–AUTRES	2.5	2.5	2.3	2.1	1.9	1.1	1.3
4 MACHINERY–EQUIPEMENT	20.4	20.4	20.2	19.8	20.1	21.0	21.5
41 CAPITAL EQUIPMENT–MACHINES	16.3	16.2	16.0	15.3	15.3	15.7	16.2
42 PARTS–PIECES ACCESSOIRES	4.1	4.2	4.2	4.4	4.8	5.3	5.3
5 TRANSPORT–TRANSPORT	13.9	14.6	15.2	15.0	15.5	14.7	15.1
51 PASSENGER CARS–AUTOMOBILES	5.4	5.0	5.7	5.8	5.6	5.4	5.9
52 OTHER–AUTRES	3.0	3.2	2.8	2.5	3.0	3.2	2.9
521 INDUSTRIAL–INDUSTRIELS	2.7	2.9	2.5	2.2	2.7	3.0	2.6
522 NON INDUSTRIAL–NON INDUSTRIEL	0.3	0.3	0.3	0.4	0.3	0.3	0.3
53 PARTS–PIECES ACCESSOIRES	5.6	6.3	6.7	6.6	6.9	6.1	6.3
6 CONSUM GOODS–BIENS CONSOMMATION	16.2	16.9	17.3	18.1	17.0	16.9	17.1
61 DURABLE–DURABLES	4.8	4.6	4.4	4.5	4.2	4.0	4.0
62 SEMI DURABLE–SEMI DURABLES	8.5	9.2	9.6	10.0	9.2	9.0	9.2
63 NON DURABLE–NON DURABLES	2.9	3.1	3.3	3.6	3.6	3.8	3.9
7 GOODS NES–BIENS NDA	0.1	0.2	0.1	0.1	0.1	0.1	0.1

EXPORTS – EXPORTATIONS

	1990	1991	1992	1993	1994	1995	1996
TOTAL EXPORTS–EXPORTATIONS TOTALES	100.	100.	100.	100.	100.	100.	100.
1 AGRICULTURE	6.3	5.8	5.7	5.7	4.7	4.4	4.5
2 MINING QUARRY–INDUS EXTRACTIVES	0.6	0.6	0.6	0.5	0.5	0.5	0.5
3 MANUFACTURING–IND MANUFACTUR	93.1	93.6	93.7	93.8	94.8	95.1	95.1
31 FOOD BEV TOBACCO–ALIM BOISS TAB	10.3	10.3	10.5	11.0	10.9	10.4	10.3
32 TEXTILES–INDUSTRIES TEXTILES	6.3	6.1	6.1	6.0	5.9	5.7	5.6
33 WOOD & PRODUCTS–BOIS & PRODUITS	0.6	0.6	0.6	0.6	0.6	0.6	0.6
34 PAPER & PRODUCTS–PAPIER & PRODT	2.9	2.9	2.9	2.8	2.9	3.1	2.8
35 CHEMICALS–INDUSTRIES CHIMIQUES	17.9	18.0	17.8	18.8	18.8	16.8	18.8
36 NON METAL MIN–MIN NON METAL	2.0	1.9	1.9	2.0	2.0	1.9	1.9
37 BASIC METAL–IND METAL BASE	6.4	5.9	5.5	5.3	5.5	5.4	5.3
38 METAL MANUF–MANUF METAL	43.7	45.2	45.7	44.5	45.5	45.8	46.8
39 OTH MANUF IND–AUTRES MANUF	2.8	2.6	2.6	2.8	2.7	5.4	3.0

3. TRADE BY PRINCIPAL COUNTRIES OF PRODUCTION AND LAST CONSIGNMENT (VALUE IN THOUSAND U.S. DOLLARS)
ECHANGES SELON LES PRINCIPAUX PAYS DE PRODUCTION ET DE DERNIERE CONSIGNATION (VALEUR EN MILLIERS DE DOLLARS EU)

COUNTRIES–PAYS	SPECIAL IMPORTS C.I.F. IMPORTATIONS SPECIALES C.A.F				
	1992	1993	1994	1995	1996
World	238907562	200796666	228281602	273387396	274913790
Africa	11202866	9401987	10397245	11397399	12021378
Americas	26623148	22830550	25978736	29051052	29513536
Northern America	21698033	18769751	21106183	23432300	24208058
LAIA	4147260	3418377	4053177	4567202	4354847
CACM	92075	108989	178487	216906	208271
Caribbean	525425	445453	573200	615254	542736
Rest of America	160355	87980	67688	219389	199624
As.ex F.USSR	30166253	27997441	29431275	34398357	35768106
Eur.x F.USSR	161588391	133792818	154808672	189622896	190928004
EU	149926788	123304531	142619497	174572710	174586873
EFTA	8638818	7792183	8991547	11018467	11622301
East Europe	1942480	1814752	2179106	2865282	3465067
Other Europe	191233	161011	194074	214444	262923
Former USSR	3586259	3113208	3336818	4025599	4621989
Oceania	1266710	856866	1045932	1242146	1169684
Germany/Allemagne	44622183	35379476	40657371	50549379	48265901
Italy/Italie	25418899	19828631	22999672	27283567	28125112
Belgium–Luxembourg	20585787	17845735	20791094	24506229	23345367
USA/Etats–Unis d'Amer	20115734	17565223	19476218	21320206	22420887
United Kingdom	18413445	16153169	18219304	21897694	23128864
Spain/Espagne	12913907	10923920	13929196	17811860	19176778
Netherlands/Pays–Bas	12130534	10264281	11331816	14493581	14419300
Japan/Japon	9772362	8274143	8507363	9589316	8967039
Switz.Liecht	5390088	4982885	5752157	7096232	6872292
China/Chine	3503387	3751730	4105535	5142225	6028271
Sweden/Suède	3544349	2884940	3101275	4060814	3928806
Norway,SVD,JM	3084999	2679350	3109535	3794822	4621841
Russian Federation	3191190	2620284	2811567	3486013	3975776
Ireland/Irlande	2680430	2446842	2731186	3487783	3810896
Portugal	2695535	2168813	2615404	3090944	3196512
Saudi Arabia	2797676	2679545	2781874	2554641	2907875
Morocco/Maroc	1993325	1920897	2143081	2595863	2568728
Denmark/Danemark	2256876	1782448	2032041	2439819	2437162
Austria/Autriche	2065761	1812261	2055925	2264118	2249716
Finland/Finlande	1943741	1342518	1650190	2076307	1918748
Brazil/Brésil	1664967	1483042	1891875	1997477	1839938
Canada	1542377	1192209	1602056	2094448	1778859
Singapore/Singapour	1286962	1223179	1548824	1899093	2249594
Algeria/Algérie	1877434	1376531	1496581	1509213	1720523
Korea, Republic of	1351439	1248663	1335596	1899018	1659753
Tunisia/Tunisie	1115627	1078298	1206326	1452431	1513447
Iran (Islamic Rp. of)	1090955	1434622	1034149	1374109	1289389
Thailand/Thaïlande	1017276	1017213	1163438	1357506	1505672
Malaysia/Malaisie	906611	916662	1080962	1479852	1510376
Turkey/Turquie	939502	818059	936081	1147666	1187314
Nigeria/Nigéria	730095	765476	1087875	781934	1389206
India/Inde	721428	762426	904415	1107268	1143514
Poland/Pologne	658131	663659	814294	1026109	1298392
Indonesia/Indonésie	805809	807949	807737	909389	1023446
Australia/Australie	950205	595217	755713	887729	766968
Israel/Israël	692403	663621	692613	869781	832217
Cote d'Ivoire	526274	581885	653026	915196	813961
So. Africa Customs Un	756748	504434	595790	703376	830666
Hong Kong	739743	623175	584444	639873	636843
Slovenia/Slovénia	327626	518260	653534	770910	826584
Chile/Chili	602947	523405	553401	739379	580589
Greece/Grèce	655341	471498	505023	610614	583711
Mexico/Mexique	700862	481032	543193	510984	506566
Hungary/Hongrie	421262	357976	402614	529217	683050
Libyan Arab Jamahiriya	686557	428549	421833	314616	452278
Cameroon/Cameroun	516892	377207	429273	526164	405508
Argentina/Argentine	481546	353191	363473	479218	492891
Gabon	701837	446641	408819	306457	250313
Syrian Arab Republic	515739	306002	364880	420125	430710
Romania/Roumanie	274505	283465	330366	458003	514350

COUNTRIES–PAYS	SPECIAL EXPORTS F.O.B. EXPORTATIONS SPECIALES F.O.B.				
	1992	1993	1994	1995	1996
Monde	231940677	206275044	233307296	284045721	283901301
Afrique	15219802	13599939	14256211	17770304	16192140
Amériques	25466163	24180824	26762847	29087337	25273951
Amérique du Nord	17410824	16343111	18188191	18724539	19263924
ALAI	3884336	3706170	4789384	4830227	5058926
MCAC	140490	172101	109546	191949	145711
Caraïbes	2697086	2581501	2565626	3092149	573679
Autre Amérique	1333427	1377940	1110100	2248472	231711
Asie l'URSS exclus	23035282	24057188	26886894	34257138	33705358
Europe l'URSS exclus	163928667	140536707	161586072	198115156	200533160
UE	150780408	128030445	147630865	180281311	181001485
AELE	9092865	8789561	9809180	12264256	12348884
Europe de l'Est	2690244	2503564	2788091	3979610	5136155
Autre de l'Europe	620354	533091	532144	614743	757797
Ancienne URSS	2120093	1977418	1711475	2278405	2853527
Océanie	2072933	1688282	1890167	2335363	2439939
Germany/Allemagne	40722926	35741864	39975009	50152203	49120360
Italy/Italie	25289267	19370329	21926765	27405314	26420892
United Kingdom	21389495	19369617	23112421	26292883	26853056
Belgium–Luxembourg	21337086	17673240	20431054	24258149	24147433
Spain/Espagne	16774615	13775976	16691729	20880124	22712240
USA/Etats–Unis d'Amer	15120996	14787251	16423031	16763648	17311931
Netherlands/Pays–Bas	11310107	9885330	10813350	13118488	13028831
Switz.Liecht	8074687	7858986	8799254	11044584	11084380
Japan/Japon	4182635	4074770	4583161	5590063	5353922
Portugal	3853960	3158418	3473662	3973200	3897665
Sweden/Suède	2346221	2125652	2682769	3656243	4050383
Hong Kong	1587690	1989135	2339999	3783314	3516151
Austria/Autriche	2137954	2098051	2547973	3270658	3143247
Algeria/Algérie	2224747	2104219	2414038	2855569	2460495
Morocco/Maroc	2130437	2014280	2175408	2590320	2394423
Denmark/Danemark	1942403	1663989	2041379	2538566	2577438
China/Chine	1394774	1602028	2168007	2640218	2422594
Greece/Grèce	1888743	1610230	1678409	2162501	2272609
Canada	2244613	1507090	1636537	1878751	1918260
Turkey/Turquie	1361811	1894032	1383314	1834625	2553835
Tunisia/Tunisie	1711884	1610687	1779731	1968571	1868970
Singapore/Singapour	1265002	1574876	1445301	1800849	2513018
Russian Federation	1877259	1474615	1213829	1674702	2002376
Korea, Republic of	1237793	1281837	1700335	1968199	1974159
Saudi Arabia	1805104	1397185	1320305	1329661	1411807
Ireland/Irlande	1013821	921501	1439396	1449762	1451265
Poland/Pologne	820544	823318	961372	1408490	2055775
Reunion/Réunion	1488166	1223608	1459443	1668034	
Malaysia/Malaisie	362452	553776	1066967	2385525	1337741
Australia/Australie	963877	862853	1049080	1259238	1400318
French Guiana	1198999	1205825	998269	2112054	
Egypt/Egypte	840020	1034078	861265	1188587	1423419
Brazil/Brésil	632665	755419	966109	1410695	1511264
Thailand/Thaïlande	854669	783015	902090	1712210	978564
Mexico/Mexique	1285474	828584	1360415	897925	857794
Norway,SVD,JM	973979	894516	973138	1161551	1209661
United Arab Emirates	1065159	855700	859282	1285752	1064819
Indonesia/Indonésie	1251391	803650	755992	1037521	1273068
Argentina/Argentine	703646	817754	1082344	1024543	1258273
Israel/Israël	787061	769679	1011768	1130292	1150782
Finland/Finlande	773811	636249	816950	1123220	1326066
Guadeloupe	1076024	1014613	1122704	1321114	
Martinique	1067324	979615	1051931	1276595	
India/Inde	673045	763271	809811	1055091	1072833
So. Africa Customs Un	761906	633350	865486	1061756	926711
Cote d'Ivoire	793026	621277	534633	937414	801414
Iran (Islamic Rp. of)	744691	730349	818134	566016	672461
Czech Republic		475442	683336	969997	1254976
Slovenia/Slovénia	261125	501145	634941	734696	892647
Nigeria/Nigéria	791385	560083	457010	420255	506489

(VALUE AS PERCENTAGE OF WORLD TOTAL)(VALEURS EN POURCENTAGE DU TOTAL MONDIAL)

	1987	1988	1989	1990	1991	1992	1993	1994	1995	1996
Africa	5.5	5.1	4.9	5.2	5.1	4.7	4.7	4.6	4.2	4.4
Americas	10.1	10.9	10.8	11.0	12.5	11.1	11.4	11.4	10.6	10.7
Northern America	7.9	8.5	8.5	8.8	10.4	9.1	9.3	9.2	8.6	8.8
LAIA	1.9	2.0	2.0	1.9	1.8	1.7	1.7	1.8	1.7	1.6
CACM	0.1	0.0	0.0	0.0	0.0	0.0	0.1	0.1	0.1	0.1
Caribbean	0.3	0.3	0.2	0.2	0.2	0.2	0.2	0.3	0.2	0.2
Rest of America	0.0	0.0	0.0	0.0	0.0	0.1	0.0	0.0	0.1	0.1
As.ex F.USSR	11.1	11.3	11.9	11.8	12.8	12.6	13.9	12.9	12.6	13.0
Eur.x F.USSR	69.5	68.8	68.6	68.2	66.1	67.6	66.6	67.8	69.4	69.5
EU	64.3	63.7	63.2	62.9	61.1	62.8	61.4	62.5	63.9	63.5
EFTA	3.7	3.7	3.9	3.9	3.7	3.6	3.9	3.9	4.0	4.2
East Europe	1.2	1.1	1.1	1.0	0.8	0.8	0.9	1.0	1.0	1.3
Other Europe	0.4	0.4	0.4	0.5	0.4	0.1	0.1	0.1	0.1	0.1
Former USSR	1.6	1.6	1.4	1.4	1.3	1.5	1.6	1.5	1.5	1.7
Oceania	0.8	0.8	0.8	0.5	0.5	0.5	0.4	0.5	0.5	0.4
Germany/Allemagne	19.8	19.7	19.3	18.8	17.8	18.7	17.6	17.8	18.5	17.6
Italy/Italie	11.7	11.6	11.5	11.6	10.9	10.6	9.9	10.1	10.0	10.2
Belgium–Luxembourg	9.4	9.1	9.2	8.8	8.4	8.6	8.9	9.1	9.0	8.5
USA/Etats–Unis d'Amer	7.2	7.7	7.7	8.1	9.6	8.4	8.7	8.5	7.8	8.2
United Kingdom	7.1	7.3	7.1	7.3	7.5	7.7	8.0	8.0	8.0	8.4
Spain/Espagne	4.4	4.2	4.4	4.7	5.1	5.4	5.4	6.1	6.5	7.0
Netherlands/Pays–Bas	5.6	5.3	5.2	5.1	5.2	5.1	5.1	5.0	5.3	5.2
Japan/Japon	3.8	4.2	4.1	4.0	4.1	4.1	4.1	3.7	3.5	3.3
Switz.Liecht	2.5	2.5	2.5	2.5	2.3	2.3	2.5	2.5	2.6	2.5
China/Chine	0.7	0.8	0.9	0.9	1.3	1.5	1.9	1.8	1.9	2.2

	1987	1988	1989	1990	1991	1992	1993	1994	1995	1996
Afrique	7.8	7.3	7.4	7.3	6.9	6.6	6.6	6.1	6.3	5.7
Amériques	11.7	11.7	10.5	10.0	10.8	11.0	11.7	11.5	10.2	8.9
Amérique du Nord	8.3	8.6	7.6	7.1	7.5	7.5	7.9	7.8	6.6	6.8
ALAI	1.7	1.5	1.4	1.3	1.5	1.7	1.8	2.1	1.7	1.8
MCAC	0.1	0.1	0.1	0.0	0.1	0.1	0.1	0.0	0.1	0.1
Caraïbes	1.2	1.2	1.2	1.2	1.1	1.2	1.3	1.1	1.1	0.2
Autre Amérique	0.4	0.2	0.3	0.4	0.6	0.6	0.7	0.5	0.8	0.1
Asie l'URSS exclus	8.7	8.5	9.7	9.4	9.6	9.9	11.7	11.5	12.1	11.9
Europe l'URSS exclus	69.7	70.4	70.3	71.6	71.1	70.7	68.1	69.3	69.7	70.6
UE	63.1	64.3	64.0	65.3	65.3	65.0	62.1	63.3	63.5	63.8
AELE	4.9	4.6	4.6	4.7	4.2	3.9	4.3	4.2	4.3	4.3
Europe de l'Est	0.9	0.9	1.0	0.8	1.0	1.2	1.2	1.2	1.4	1.8
Autre de l'Europe	0.6	0.6	0.7	0.8	0.6	0.3	0.3	0.2	0.2	0.3
Ancienne URSS	1.2	1.2	1.0	0.7	0.7	0.9	1.0	0.7	0.8	1.0
Océanie	0.8	0.9	1.0	0.9	0.9	0.9	0.8	0.8	0.8	0.9
Germany/Allemagne	16.6	16.4	16.0	17.2	18.6	17.6	17.3	17.1	17.7	17.3
Italy/Italie	12.1	12.2	12.1	11.4	11.0	10.9	9.4	9.4	9.6	9.3
United Kingdom	8.8	9.8	9.6	9.4	8.9	9.2	9.4	9.9	9.3	9.5
Belgium–Luxembourg	9.3	9.0	8.9	9.4	9.0	9.2	8.6	8.8	8.5	8.5
Spain/Espagne	5.4	5.5	5.8	6.4	6.9	7.2	6.7	7.2	7.4	8.0
USA/Etats–Unis d'Amer	7.3	7.3	6.6	6.1	6.4	6.5	7.2	7.0	5.9	6.1
Netherlands/Pays–Bas	5.1	5.6	5.7	5.6	4.9	4.9	4.8	4.6	4.6	4.6
Switz.Liecht	4.3	4.2	4.2	4.2	3.7	3.5	3.8	3.8	3.9	3.9
Japan/Japon	1.5	1.7	1.9	1.9	2.0	1.8	2.0	2.0	2.0	1.9
Portugal	1.1	1.2	1.4	1.3	1.5	1.7	1.5	1.5	1.4	1.4

4. Special Imports C.I.F. by Commodities according to the S.I.T.C. (Rev. 2) in thousand U.S. Dollars
Importations Spéciales C.A.F. par Produits d'après la C.T.C.I. (Rév. 2) en milliers de Dollars E.U.

SITC CTCI	COMMODITY	1993		1994		1995		1996		PRODUIT
		WEIGHT POIDS	VALUE VALEUR	WEIGHT POIDS	VALUE VALEUR	WEIGHT POIDS	VALUE VALEUR	WEIGHT POIDS	VALUE VALEUR	
	ALL COMMODITIES		200796666		228281602		273387396		274913790	TOUS PRODUITS
0	FOOD AND LIVE ANIMALS		19023867		21435416		24605767		23611100	ALIMENTS,ANIMAUX VIVANTS
01	MEAT AND PREPARATIONS		3623109		3922317		4214074		3652543	VIANDES ET PREPARATIONS
011	MEAT FRESH,CHILLD,FROZEN	W 1039426	3217686	W 1084577	3503181	W 1085730	3716765	W 973532	3134038	VIANDES FRAICHES,REF,CONGE
0111	BOVINE MEAT FRESH,FROZEN	W 393257	1512320	W 426454	1661195	W 394097	1652992	W 265474	982285	VIANDES BOVIN FRAI,REF
01111	BOVINE MEAT WITH BONE IN	W 331243	1161737	W 352617	1255294	W 306741	1167689	W 194906	644656	VIANDES BOVIN NON DESOSS
02	DAIRY PRODCTS,BIRDS'EGGS		1658375		1759404		2179217		2013078	PRODUITS LAITIERS,OEUFS
022	MILK AND CREAM	W 655188	607502	W 833613	670908	W 955263	818114	W 874273	743682	LAIT ET CREME
03	FISH AND PREPARATIONS		2479343		2705782		3159086		3206148	POISSONS ET PREPARATIONS
034	FISH,FRESH,CHILLED,FROZN	W 466333	1155318	W 395450	1208425	W 403990	1347648	W 455778	1415484	POISSON FRAIS, REFRIG,CONG
036	SHELL FISH FRESH,FROZEN	W 186327	693458	W 148684	790712	W 156826	917572	W 168604	890714	CRUSTACES,MOLLUSQUES
04	CEREALS AND PREPARATIONS		1661324		1785488		2001064		2196088	CEREALES ET PRODUITS
048	CEREAL ETC PREPARATIONS	W 577870	1175559	W 646852	1273344	W 711755	1496878	W 798385	1609547	PREPTNS A BASE CEREALES
0484	BAKERY PRODUCTS	W 243874	680333	W 266880	731580	W 287734	860215	W 322005	915440	PRODUITS DE BOULANGERIE
05	VEGETABLES AND FRUIT		4824411		5431234		6318509		6062918	LEGUMES ET FRUITS
054	VEG ETC FRSH,SMPLY PRSVD	W 2486446	1428635	W 2645440	1596917		1943858		1849786	LEGUMES FRAIS,CONG,SECS
057	FRUIT,NUTS,FRESH,DRIED	W 2637931	2125135	W 2641139	2374863	W 2660950	2648195	W 2455972	2512129	FRUITS FRAIS OU SECS
0579	FRUIT FRESH OR DRIED NES	W 634521	683398	W 655330	745287	W 675251	874155	W 698706	847748	FRUITS FRAIS,SECS NDA
058	FRUIT PRESERVED,PREPARED	W 804133	895349	W 990975	1038011	W 1040630	1217759	W 971702	1189853	CONSERVES DE FRUITS
06	SUGAR AND PREPS,HONEY		608786		639905		800261		691513	SUCRES ET PRODUITS
07	COFFEE,TEA,COCOA,SPICES		1621801		2331041		2981220		2728834	CAFE,THE,CACAO,EPICES
071	COFFEE AND SUBSTITUTES	W 381966	639678	W 376837	1051897	W 357580	1377049	W 380165	1110140	CAFE ET SUCCEDANES
0711	COFFEE GREEN,ROASTED,SUB	W 364658	540009	W 364551	937785	W 345128	1238389	W 367550	970997	CAFE TORREFIE OU DECAFEINE
07111	COFFEE GREEN,HUSKS,SKINS	W 318022	406595	W 317530	748891	W 293944	965397	W 315509	748446	CAFE NON TORREFIE
073	CHOCOLATE AND PRODUCTS	W 168059	568569	W 219917	770803	W 243435	980287	W 254276	961522	CHOCOLAT
081	*FEEDING STUFF FOR ANIML	W 5532261	1414523	W 6142762	1531472	W 5850902	1491681		1701668	NOURRITURE POUR ANIMAUX
0813	OILCAKE AND OTH RESIDUES	W 4088027	892275	W 4776944	998593	W 4548361	910341	W 4467280	1134075	TOURTEAUX
08131	— OF SOYA BEANS	W 3281884	753733	W 3943069	863001	W 3635689	766912	W 3386625	934768	TOURTEAUX DE SOJA
09	MISC EDIBLE PRODUCTS		679204		791959		906239		918721	PREP ALIMENTAIRES DIVERSES
1	BEVERAGES AND TOBACCO		2427553		2711657		3234369		3388001	BOISSONS ET TABACS
11	BEVERAGES		1132216		1282673		1568107		1651464	BOISSONS
112	ALCOHOLIC BEVERAGES	W 1015422	985416	W 1206808	1096355	W 1167729	1304234	W 1156950	1372816	BOISSONS ALCOOLIQUES
12	TOBACCO AND MANUFACTURES		1295337		1428984		1666262		1736537	TABACS BRUTS FABRIQUES
122	TOBACCO,MANUFACTURED	W 72972	1181888	W 68258	1296839	W 63961	1544792	W 65746	1620879	TABACS FABRIQUES
1222	CIGARETTES	W 67848	1031195	W 62585	1124629	W 58296	1341991	W 58055	1382496	CIGARETTES
2	CRUDE MATERLS,EXCL FUELS		6361441		8067626		10009724		8697267	MAT BRUTES NON COMESTIBLES
23	RUBBER, CRUDE		503587		602252		826173		809440	CAOUTCHOUC BRUT
24	CORK AND WOOD		850782		1151580		1310735		1112407	LIEGE ET BOIS
248	WOOD SHAPED,SLEEPERS	W 1079906	573939	W 1237900	747939	W 1231042	824326	W 1356488	764143	BOIS SIMPLEMENT TRAVAILLES
251	*PULP AND WASTE PAPER	W 3002686	835469	W 3331097	1170192	W 3220411	1831267	W 3129831	1176124	PATES A PAPIER,DECHETS
2517	SODA,SULPHATE WOOD PULP	W 1806610	702252	W 1884609	935344	W 1768928	1425072	W 1880661	992602	PATES CHIMIQUES AU SULFATE
25172	— BLEACHED,NONDISSOLVNG	W 1788997	695172	W 1868784	928285	W 1757944	1416888	W 1868591	986402	PATES BLANCHIES
26	TEXTILE FIBRES AND WASTE		769895		1024562		1163871		945843	FIBRES TEXTILES
27	CRUDE FERTLZR,MINRLS NES		612566		686814		763032		761522	ENGRAIS MINERAUX BRUTS
28	METALLIFEROUS ORES,SCRAP		1262406		1549164		1969035		1688381	MINERAIS METAL,DECHETS
29	CRUDE ANIMAL,VEG MAT NES		1179091		1300814		1594603		1621586	MATIERES BRUTES ANIM,VEGET
292	CRUDE VEG MATERIALS NES	W 297094	931236	W 278001	1011569	W 303520	1251607	W 334733	1285598	MAT BRUTES VEGETALES NDA
3	MINERAL FUELS ETC		17922507		17592445		18633517		22857552	COMBUSTIBLES MINERAUX LUB
32	COAL,COKE AND BRIQUETTES		929108		931484		965631		1068567	HOUILLES,COKES,BRIQUETTES
322	COAL,LIGNITE AND PEAT	MW 14483	805444	MW 13044	772522	MW 13656	836775	MW 16224	943658	HOUILLES,LIGNITES,TOURBE
3222	OTH COAL,NOT AGGLOMERATD	MW 12053	612616	MW 10585	580292	MW 11506	661420	MW 14366	781582	AUTRES HOUILLES
33	PETROLEUM AND PRODUCTS		13495418		13166438		13814056		17691269	PETROLE ET DERIVES
333	CRUDE PETROLEUM	MW 75094	8949245	MW 75360	8784054	MW 75743	9614572	MW 83131	12746387	HUILES BRUTES DE PETROLE
334	PETROLEUM PRODUCTS,REFIN	MW 24789	4266857	MW 25136	4064311	MW 21956	3811943	MW 22054	4545460	PRODUITS RAFFINES
3341	GASOLINE,OTH LIGHT OILS					W 6156672	1154657	W 6792303	1453909	ESSENCES POUR MOTEURS
3343	GAS OILS					MW 11352	1856058	W 67703	17398	GAS OILS
3344	FUEL OILS,NES					W 3685300	441668	MW 14291	2642051	FUEL OILS
341	*GAS,NATURAL AND MANUFCT	MW 24874	3248890	MW 26629	3301797	MW 25930	3626885	MW 27492	3884566	GAZ NATUREL,GAZ MANUFACT
3413	PETROLM GASES,LIQUEFIED	W 8673667	1241817	W 8665397	1173719	W 7168311	1126644	W 6611738	1151714	GAZ DE PETROLE LIQUEFIE
34139	OTH HYDROCARBON GAS LQFD	W 6790649	909357	W 6474479	818965	W 5433249	766776	W 4980505	739086	HYDROCARBURES GAZEUX NDA
3414	PETROLEUM GASES, GASEOUS	MW 16201	2004500	MW 17964	2126320	MW 18761	2498479	MW 20880	2731414	GAZ DE PETROLE GAZEUX
4	ANIMAL,VEGETABLE OIL,FAT		693410		849412		1125758		1076729	HUILES,GRAISSES ANIM,VEG
5	CHEMCLS,RELATED PROD NES		22503776		26758201		33559124		32862654	PRODUITS CHIMIQUES
51	ORGANIC CHEMICALS		5026785		6235301		7571064		7431859	PROD CHIMIQ ORGANIQUES
511	HYDROCARBONS NES,DERIVS	W 1377240	665661	W 1506536	830616	W 1585121	1100513	W 1503904	898860	HYDROCARBURES NDA
512	ALCOHOLS,PHENOLS ETC	W 1248976	502828	W 1308740	768808	W 1284922	885433	W 1395056	811305	PHENOLS,PHENOLS–ALCOOLS
513	CARBOXYLIC ACIDS ETC	W 450597	672654	W 603024	897587	W 599884	1158122	W 574380	1011340	ACIDES CARBOXYLIQUES
514	NITROGEN–FNCTN COMPOUNDS	W 286435	1552524	W 324721	1760890	W 353605	2134390	W 370945	2083336	COMPOSES FONCT AZOTEES
5148	OTH NITROGN–FNCTN CMPNDS	W 106195	763569	W 124808	912712	W 127170	1153557	W 130368	1102343	AUTRES COMPOSES AZOTES
51482	IMIDE–,IMIDE–FNCT CMPNDS	W 28860	534077	W 34930	640217	W 40200	836931	W 38212	774176	COMPOSES A FONCTION IMIDE
515	ORG–INORG COMPOUNDS ETC	W 88779	1112942	W 102829	1404780	W 116026	1599823	W 121107	1989755	COMPOSES ORGANO–MINERAUX
5156	HETEROCYCLIC CMPDS ETC	W 32935	746950	W 45260	890826	W 52853	1140712	W 48154	1421606	COMPOSES HETEROCYCLIQUES
51569	OTH HETEROCYC CMPDS,ETC	W 28634	727138	W 39811	869065	W 46263	1108431	W 42140	1391499	AUT COMP HETEROCYCLIQUES
52	INORGANIC CHEMICALS		2081363		2194054		2657161		2600082	PROD CHIM INORGANIQUES
522	INORG ELEMNTS,OXIDES,ETC	W 2435722	701096	W 2711748	812350	W 3006139	1030108	W 2792533	1010953	ELEMENTS INORGANIQUES
523	OTHR INORG CHEMICALS ETC	W 1421944	694782	W 1760352	774597	W 1733553	890449	W 1759473	848338	AUT PRODUITS CHIMIQUES INORG
524	RADIOACTIVE ETC MATERIAL		685484		607108		736604		740791	MATIERES RADIOACTIVES
5241	RADIOACTIVE ELEMENTS ETC		668232		581268		700768		688067	RADIOELEMENTS,ISOTOPES
53	DYES,TANNING,COLOUR PROD		1419301		1639585		2035999		2014386	PROD TEINTURE,COLORANTS
533	PIGMENTS,PAINTS,ETC	W 323228	855797	W 353497	1008629	W 366481	1211252	W 406314	1247041	PIGMENTS,PEINTURES,VERNIS
541	*MEDICINAL,PHARM PRODUCT	MK 75636	3587518		4203481	MK 103452	5626218		5722980	PROD MEDICINAUX PHARMACEUT
5417	MEDICAMENTS	MK 38750	1985804	MK 43963	2203519	MK 55623	3210670	MK 58509	3418662	MEDICAMENTS
54179	— CONTNG OTH SUBSTANCES	MK 32924	1400770	MK 37233	1615471	MK 47216	2349010	MK 46572	2507607	MED CONT AUT SUBSTANCES
55	PERFUME,CLEANING ETC PRD		1646052		2097444		2418545		2399156	PROD POUR PARFUM,TOILETTE
553	PERFUMERY,COSMETICS,ETC	W 128953	704554	W 149844	966573	W 154830	1007778	W 163537	989181	PRODUITS DE PARFUMERIE
554	SOAP,CLEANSING ETC PREPS	W 528205	617523	W 627597	733810	W 673288	854389	W 686904	825286	SAVONS,PRODUITS DETERSIFS
562	*FERTILIZERS,MANUFACTURE	W 6272810	723845	W 7011316	911720	W 7817956	1252862	W 8168639	1305595	ENGRAIS MANUFACTURES
58	PLASTIC MATERIALS ETC		4955216		5882242		7499231		6938503	MAT PLAST ARTIFICIELLES
582	PROD OF CONDENSATION ETC	W 732614	1392614	W 810136	1616206	W 879271	2151887	W 901092	1982911	PROD CONDENS,POLYCOND
5823	ALKYDS,OTHER POLYESTERS	W 244144	575774	W 275385	659445	W 318610	957847	W 340188	853941	ALKYDES ET AUT POLYESTERS
583	POLYMERIZATION ETC PRODS	W 2437600	3394431	W 2851570	4070702	W 2822789	5133136	W 2992092	4750749	PROD POLYMERISATION
5831	POLYETHYLENE	W 839108	821696	W 930288	913467	W 876152	1146259	W 922569	1018350	POLYETHYLENE
5839	OTH POLYMRZTION ETC PROD	W 427877	967344	W 548885	1202479	W 569698	1555641	W 652793	1577801	AUT PROD POLYMER COPOLYM
59	CHEMICAL MATERIALS NES		3028375		3560882		4455725		4408206	MAT PROD CHIMIQUES NDA
591	PESTICIDES,DISINFECTANTS	W 148077	940249	W 155949	1132796	W 174450	1480472	W 183323	1484446	DESINF,INSECT,FONG,HERB
598	MISCEL CHEM PRODUCTS NES	W 2689027	1707335	W 2666889	1980702	W 2686313	2464935	W 1829023	2430876	PROD DIV INDUST CHIM NDA
5989	CHEM PRODUCTS,PREPS NES	W 2365448	1324647	W 2329484	1544923	W 2346104	1940474	W 1525923	1926588	PROD PREP CHIMIQUES NDA
59899	OTH CHEM PRODS,PREPS,NES	W 2076870	985929	W 2093390	1169654	W 1938831	1479549	W 1260533	1493137	AUT PRODUITS CHIMIQUES NDA
6	BASIC MANUFACTURES		31591563		37072163		46502563		42980615	ART MANUFACTURES
61	LEATHER,DRESSED FUR,ETC		687734		797443		868159		827252	CUIRS,PELLETERIES
62	RUBBER MANUFACTURES NES		1579677		1847185		2181174		2245405	CAOUTCHOUC MANUFACTURE

4. Special Imports C.I.F. by Commodities according to the S.I.T.C. (Rev. 2) in thousand U.S. Dollars
Importations Spéciales C.A.F. par Produits d'après la C.T.C.I. (Rév. 2) en milliers de Dollars E.U.

SITC CTCI	COMMODITY	1993 WEIGHT POIDS	1993 VALUE VALEUR	1994 WEIGHT POIDS	1994 VALUE VALEUR	1995 WEIGHT POIDS	1995 VALUE VALEUR	1996 WEIGHT POIDS	1996 VALUE VALEUR	PRODUIT
625	RUBBER TYRES, TUBES ETC	W 247100	937598	W 274154	1076872	W 303546	1263006	W 342178	1343048	PNEUS CAOUTCHOUC VULCANISE
63	WOOD,CORK MANUFACTRS NES		971563		1080097		1318258		1308691	OUVRAGES LIEGE ET BOIS
64	PAPER,PAPERBOARD AND MFR		4787423		5573820		7317001		6789955	PAPIERS,CARTONS & OUVRAGES
641	PAPER AND PAPERBOARD	W 4242363	3519356	W 4917626	4124178	W 4786928	5452040	W 4931701	4894336	PAPIERS ET CARTONS
6412	PRINTG,WRITING PAPER NES	W 1038643	950138	W 1276252	1171548	W 1382741	1700227	W 1444595	1505197	PAPIERS POUR L'IMPRESSION
64122	— COATED,IMPREGNATD ETC	W 907297	840688	W 1125314	1038492	W 1195893	1451796	W 1249380	1301651	PAPIERS IMPRESSION COUCHES
6415	PAPER,PAPERBRD,BULK,NES	W 1512025	911792	W 1712631	1095568	W 1567704	1466983	W 1609654	1250179	PAPIERS,CARTONS ROULEAUX
64159	OTHER PAPER ETC,BULK,NES	W 1421591	846385	W 1601229	1011592	W 1477282	1363066	W 1506857	1152618	AUT PAPIER ROULEAUX FEUILLES
6418	COATED ETC PAPER NES BLK	W 619420	820590	W 666856	885253	W 636516	1049947	W 651575	959334	PAP,CARTONS COUCHES,ENDUITS
64189	COATED PAPER ETC NES	W 506369	605496	W 545745	663417	W 481058	756448	W 469892	649371	PAPIERS,CARTONS COUCHES
642	PAPER,ETC,PRECUT,ARTS OF	W 583350	1268067	W 698321	1449642	W 733872	1864961	W 841031	1895620	PAP,CARTONS DECOUPES
65	TEXTILE YARN,FABRICS,ETC		6003841		6621151		7542836		7083500	FILS,TISSUS,ARTICLES TEXTILE
651	TEXTILE YARN	W 400911	1711094	W 427242	1874383	W 411562	2146676	W 405526	2035036	FILS TEXTILES
6514	SYN FIB YRN,BULK,MONOFIL	W 161801	679319	W 165854	747558	W 162221	885520	W 169309	861700	FILS CONT 85% FIB TEXT SYNTH
652	COTTON FABRICS,WOVEN	W 109405	664580	W 109833	761906	W 101643	825386	W 96831	788536	TISSUS DE COTON
653	WOVN MAN–MADE FIB FABRIC	W 78296	824491	W 90879	954337	W 97961	1139525	W 88327	1005792	TISSUS FIBRES SYNTH,ARTIF
657	SPECIAL TXTL FABRC,PRODS	W 174128	817793	W 171555	863704	W 173018	1057463	W 174215	1001238	TISSUS SPECIAUX
658	TEXTILE ARTICLES NES	W 85727	612841	W 91701	693136	W 98472	820163	W 92864	819903	ART FACONNES MAT TEXTILES
66	NONMETAL MINERAL MFS NES		3703947		4027459		4695329		4553181	ART MIN NON METALLIQUES
662	CLAY,REFRACTORY BLDG PRD	W 1103939	669378	W 1225414	752586	W 1248739	852460	W 1347017	866093	MAT CONST REFRACTAIRES
664	GLASS	W 645741	768592	W 756295	835828	W 786829	1004362	W 833573	983593	VERRE
665	GLASSWARE	W 917531	646632	W 984933	708950	W 1005390	871751	W 931336	818225	OUVRAGES EN VERRE
67	IRON AND STEEL		5414644		7001894		9370464		8010317	FER ET ACIER
672	IRON,STEEL PRIMARY FORMS	W 2405100	907388	W 3249843	1303998	W 3634878	1760429	W 3345005	1459928	LINGOTS FER,ACIER
6727	IRN,STL COIL FR REROLLNG	W 1841196	722606	W 2316077	993273	W 2579349	1336704	W 2541874	1154350	EBAUCHES POUR TOLES FER
67271	IRON,SIMPLE STEEL COILS	W 1693315	565204	W 2111249	769527	W 2384467	1074854	W 2327110	878793	EBAUCHES NON EN ACIER
673	IRON,STEEL SHAPES ETC	W 2339097	1068151	W 2614601	1296360	W 2955378	1822386	W 2808422	1526516	BARRES,PROFIL FER,ACIER
6732	IRON,STEEL BARS ETC	W 792855	436261	W 1003927	572015	W 1174366	857154	W 1000498	682391	BARRES FER,ACIER
674	IRN,STL UNIV,PLATE,SHEET	W 3321148	2026532	W 3977608	2624478	W 4042165	3377997	W 3794205	2742431	LARGES PLATS,TOLES
6746	IRN,STL THIN PLATE,ROLLD	W 1072022	673277	W 1174227	816749	W 1234225	1143857	W 1071939	794924	TOLES LAM MOINS 3MM
6749	OTH IRN,STL PLATES,SHEET	W 973969	602366	W 1241836	809051	W 1275157	1007881	W 1306540	941219	AUTRES TOLES FER,ACIER
67491	— OF IRON OR SIMPLE STL	W 955871	573367	W 1227419	781769	W 1256083	970042	W 1292272	908907	AUT TOLES AUTRES ACIER FIN
678	IRON,STL TUBES,PIPES,ETC	W 702225	701413	W 812220	853258	W 855107	1130558	W 941389	1119224	TUBES,TUYAUX EN FONTE,FER
68	NON–FERROUS METALS		3916175		4934442		6787015		5766623	METAUX NON FERREUX
682	COPPER EXC CEMENT COPPER	W 663008	1522755	W 744209	1879637	W 779684	2598992	W 707474	1963035	CUIVRE
6821	COPPER NES,ALLOYS,UNWRT	W 456920	896162	W 480209	1032701	W 516014	1519937	W 477146	1094470	CUIVRE BRUT
68212	COPPER REFINED,UNWROUGHT	W 440793	864563	W 467631	1005253	W 499550	1479039	W 456320	1052558	CUIVRE AFFINE BRUT
6822	COPPER,ALLOYS WORKED	W 206088	626593	W 264000	846936	W 263671	1079055	W 230328	868566	CUIVRE,ALLIAGES OUVRES
684	ALUMINIUM	W 713278	1530772	W 849735	1920578	W 881416	2610654	W 904513	2351431	ALUMINIUM
6841	ALUMINIUM,ALLOYS,UNWRGHT	W 372245	490337	W 444828	674448	W 469305	964215	W 491124	861806	ALUMINIUM,ALLIAGES BRUTS
6842	ALUMINIUM,ALLOYS WORKED	W 341033	1040435	W 404907	1246129	W 412111	1646440	W 413389	1489626	ALUMINIUM,ALLIAGES OUVRE
69	METAL MANUFACTURES NES		4526558		5188673		6422328		6395690	ART MANUFACT EN METAL NDA
695	TOOLS	W 59118	655287	W 65058	754179	W 68143	920224	W 72288	898471	OUTILS A MAIN
699	BASE METAL MFRS NES	W 537883	1734426	W 482040	2021872	W 513433	2532128	W 509947	2570738	ART MANUFACTURES MET NDA
7	MACHINES,TRANSPORT EQUIP		69120061		80445191		96726098		99648399	MACHINES MATERIEL TRANSPORT
71	POWER GENERATING EQUIPMT		6080264		7053696		6821557		6713363	MACHINES GENERATRICES
713	INTRNL COMBUS PSTN ENGIN	W 180960	1772281	W 222768	2151698		2664518	W 235573	2623725	MOTEURS EXPL COMB INT, PIECE
7132	MOTOR VEHCL PISTN ENGINS	W 64554	663345	W 80843	887053	W 85607	1092998	W 89515	1118593	MOTEURS EXPL POUR VEHICULES
7139	PISTON ENGINE PARTS NES	W 90821	788378	W 111310	859594	W 114423	1122634	W 114301	1068646	PIECES POUR 713.2,3,8
714	ENGINES AND MOTORS NES	W 7298	3109193	W 6980	3412787	W 24526	2560229	W 8018	2618205	MOTEURS NON ELECTRIQUES
7144	REACTION ENGINES	W 1055	1274635	W 1294	1622270	W 531	767379	W 499	646633	PROPULSEURS A REACTION
7149	ENGINE & MOTOR PARTS NES	W 5564	1663616	W 5471	1656640	W 23625	1630421	W 6990	1800019	PIECES 714 ET 718.88
71491	PARTS NES OF 7144,71481	W 1684	1407605	W 1638	1337326	W 1662	1287774	W 2229	1383843	PIECES DES PROPULSEURS
716	ROTATING ELECTRIC PLANT	W 74764	671817	W 62786	760614	W 78070	944001	W 81604	1034147	APP ELECTR ROTATIFS,PIECES
72	MACHS FOR SPCL INDUSTRYS		4587852		5440060		7132763		7501284	MAC SPECIALES POUR INDUST
721	AGRIC MACHY,EXC TRACTORS	W 126208	792276	W 163464	1010020	W 170129	1217064	W 180111	1310075	MACHINES AGRICOLES
7212	HARVESTING ETC MACHINES	W 88027	588980	W 99237	723721	W 107123	840836	W 115415	923307	ENGINS POUR LA RECOLTE
722	TRACTORS NON–ROAD	W 67620	417673	W 88184	596145	W 120793	922173	W 139469	1122727	TRACTEURS
7224	WHEELED TRACTORS NES	W 67237	415918	W 87989	594732	W 120468	919300	W 139177	1118634	TRACTEURS A ROUES
723	CIVIL ENGNEERG EQUIP ETC	W 72641	501416	W 97528	628469	W 126174	902706	W 107117	784099	APPAREILS DE GENIE CIVIL
728	OTH MACHY FOR SPCL INDUS	W 98303	1458746	W 105867	1633874	W 125087	2134138	W 123709	2221476	AUT MACH IND PARTICULIERES
7284	MACHY FOR SPCL INDUS NES	W 64086	1151364	W 67639	1281091	W 77548	1663645	W 74535	1749415	MACH SPEC IND PARTICUL.
73	METALWORKING MACHINERY		1110946		1282562		1742390		1925720	MACH TRAVAIL DES METAUX
736	METALWORKING MACH–TOOLS	W 55568	864210	W 62826	1011817	W 71296	1390022	W 78059	1564318	MACH–OUTILS TRAVAIL METAUX
74	GENRL INDUSTRL MACHY NES		7800483		9018114		11412323		11801163	MACH APP INDUSTRIE
741	HEATING,COOLING EQUIPMNT	W 89407	1082620	W 96521	1222464	W 117547	1568782	W 132710	1751743	MACH CHAUFFAGE,PIECES
742	PUMPS FOR LIQUIDS ETC	W 50231	956767	W 58089	1139383		1448737	W 66579	1471450	POMPES MOTO–POMPES
743	PUMPS NES,CENTRFUGES ETC	W 112061	1240437	W 129689	1417548	W 167107	1678313	W 153429	1797281	POMPES COMPRES,VENT ETC
744	MECHANICAL HANDLING EQU	W 206154	1201446	W 213623	1432651	W 276427	2000075	W 278153	2059584	EQUIP MANUTENTION PIECES
7449	PTS NES OF MACHY OF 7442	W 118004	538353	W 108412	663124	W 147859	972463	W 139275	987847	PIECES DU 744.2
745	NONELEC MACHY,TOOLS NES	W 63992	1177920	W 69040	1237831	W 81707	1517011	W 82337	1518429	AUT MACH NON ELEC,PIECES
7452	OTH NONELEC MCHS,PTS NES	W 56613	977664	W 61563	1029980	W 73697	1266815	W 73868	1285817	AUT MACH NON ELEC,PIECES
749	NONELEC MACH PTS,ACC NES	W 218018	2141293	W 241016	2568237	W 267947	3199406	W 275049	3202676	PIECES MACH NON ELEC NDA
7492	COCKS,VALVES ETC NES	W 57647	855819	W 63757	991588	W 69515	1189631	W 72847	1194035	ART ROB,SIM POUR TUYAUX
75	OFFICE MACHNES,ADP EQUIP		9257654		10796264		13215012		13342470	MACH BUREAU TRAIT AUTOM
751	OFFICE MACHINES	W 25612	807572	W 26294	843757	W 27193	955350	W 26364	818073	MACH,APPAREILS DE BUREAU
7518	OFFICE MACHINES NES	W 20535	636647	W 21722	688715	W 23023	778480	W 22537	674532	MACH,APP DE BUREAU NDA
752	AUTOMTIC DATA PROC EQUIP	W 76289	5742422	W 92868	6416085	W 106022	7566189	W 135604	7936015	MACH TRAIT INFORMATION
7522	DIGITAL COMPUTERS	W 5570	892501	W 5224	789252	W 5443	844311	W 6183	992360	MACH DIGITALES COMPLETES
7523	DIGITL CENTRL PROCESSORS	W 12151	1656343	W 10747	1824242	W 11420	1762390	W 13763	1548468	UNITES CENTRALES
7524	DIGITL CENTRL STOR UNITS	W 5990	1047199	W 12767	1145009	W 10003	1433400	W 11064	1449797	UNITES MEMOIRE CENTRALES
7525	ADP PERIPHERAL UNITS	W 46959	1694558	W 58074	2150323	W 70961	2761929	W 90110	3022745	UNITES PERIPHERIQUES
759	OFFICE,ADP MCH PTS,ACCES	W 38263	2707659	W 42521	3536422	W 49153	4693473	W 56699	4588382	PIECES DU 751 ET 752
7599	ACCTG,ETC,ADP MCH PTS,AC	W 19901	2124495	W 22312	2874404	W 26400	3881679	W 32273	3814361	PIECES DU 751 ET 752
76	TELECOMM,SOUND EQUIPMENT		4671287		5282233		6422256		6686519	EQUIPMENT DE TELECOM
761	TELEVISION RECEIVERS	W 56517	815678	W 55411	831635	W 69324	1062321	W 64756	1057349	RECEPTEURS DE TELEVISION
7611	COLOUR TV RECEIVERS	W 55931	799424	W 54879	817332	W 68630	1040472	W 64107	1038380	RECEPTEURS COULEUR
762	RADIO BROADCAST RECEIVRS	W 35897	723930	W 34481	809333	W 39334	904762	W 32628	749905	RECEPTEURS RADIODIFFUSION
763	SOUND RECORDRS,PHONOGRPH	W 19712	795811	W 19699	836151	W 21289	872043	W 20597	970245	PHONO,APP ENREGISTREMENT
7638	OTHR SOUND APPARATUS ETC	W 19007	785454	W 19201	828494	W 20815	863084	W 20072	961271	AUT APP D'ENREGIS,REPROD
764	TELECOM EQPT,PTS,ACC NES	W 59641	2335868	W 66597	2805114	W 82834	3583131	W 83337	3909021	EQUIP TELECOM,PIECES
7641	LINE TELEPHONE,ETC EQUIP	W 5307	351552	W 7377	454148	W 8095	674846	W 10356	950397	APP TELEPHON PAR FIL
7649	PTS NES OF EQUIPMT OF 76	W 29084	1006980	W 33370	1186071	W 42953	1437628	W 41176	1743092	PIECES DE LA DIV 76
76493	TELECOMM EQUIPMT PTS NES	W 18904	593400	W 22197	660382	W 30210	772597	W 27574	960047	PIECES 761,762,764.3,8
77	ELECTRIC MACHNRY NES ETC		11901272		13544356		17221235		17339119	MACH APP ELECT NDA
771	ELECTRIC POWER MACHY NES	W 48762	625027	W 52841	731003	W 71762	1002485	W 75860	1053283	MACH PROD,TRANS ELECTR
7712	OTH ELEC POWER MACHY NES	W 31897	457645	W 34865	542794	W 42886	766306	W 54526	844648	AUT APP PROD TRANSF ELEC
772	SWITCHGEAR ETC,PARTS NES	W 62440	2082439	W 71411	2164888	W 84535	2527431	W 88700	2586226	APP COUPURE,SECT ETC
7721	SWITCHGEAR ETC	W 57105	1400147	W 62907	1634709	W 75023	2026695	W 77407	2084461	APP COUPURE,SECTIONMNT
773	ELECTR DISTRIBUTNG EQUIP	W 109630	893342	W 137430	1071929	W 158403	1375299	W 161914	1388286	EQUIPMT DISTRIBUTION ELECT
7731	INSULATED WIRE,CABLE ETC	W 100822	808523	W 128494	955635	W 147762	1232464	W 150296	1247663	FILS,CABLES ISOLES ELECT

4. Special Imports C.I.F. by Commodities according to the S.I.T.C. (Rev. 2) in thousand U.S. Dollars
Importations Spéciales C.A.F. par Produits d'après la C.T.C.I. (Rév. 2) en milliers de Dollars E.U.

SITC CTCI	COMMODITY	1993		1994		1995		1996		PRODUIT
		WEIGHT POIDS	VALUE VALEUR	WEIGHT POIDS	VALUE VALEUR	WEIGHT POIDS	VALUE VALEUR	WEIGHT POIDS	VALUE VALEUR	
775	HOUSEHOLD TYPE EQUIP NES	W 336235	1941894	W 348816	2072545	W 401641	2438899	W 374989	2413639	MACH,APP USAGE DOMESTQUE
776	TRANSISTORS,VALVES,ETC	W 56554	3158752	W 62233	3762129	W 74330	5195423	W 72441	5292195	LAMPES,TUBES,VALVES
7763	DIODES,TRANSISTORS,ETC	W 4098	532362	W 3747	637818	W 5828	850945	W 5735	835845	DIODES,TRANSISTORS
7764	ELECTRONIC MICROCIRCUITS	W 6004	2115453	W 8430	2540546	W 8934	3616384	W 8907	3754707	MICROSTRUCTURES ELECTRON
778	ELECTRICAL MACHINERY NES	W 301505	2667390	W 272320	3114561	W 276134	3960945	W 347215	3881152	AUTRES MACH ELECT NDA
7788	OTH ELEC MACHY,EQUIP NES	W 50054	1055910	W 54965	1236746	W 64047	1662192	W 64339	1613829	AUT MACH APP ELEC NDA
78	ROAD VEHICLES		18894097		22030943		27490356		28485767	VEHICULES ROUTIERS
781	PASS MOTOR VEH EXC BUSES	W 1125546	11595918	W 1204083	12638071	W 1234561	14589788	W 1454558	16043703	AUTO TRANSPORT PERSONNES
782	LORRIES,SPCL MTR VEH NES	W 181747	1444060	W 272767	2409253	W 284441	3033269	W 311260	3094341	VEHICULES SPECIAUX,MARCH
7821	LORRIES,TRUCKS	W 175204	1380216	W 263905	2324090	W 273473	2920109	W 299305	2975822	VEHICULES TRANSP MARCHAND
783	ROAD MOTOR VEHICLES NES	W 58670	626798	W 84276	1001888	W 170789	2443186	W 142184	1997193	VEHICULES ROUTIERS NDA
7832	TRACTORS FOR TR–TRAILERS	W 45264	422945	W 67671	767535	W 152495	2177548	W 125324	1758493	TRACTEURS ROUTIERS
784	MOTOR VEH PRTS,ACCES NES	W 581698	3841517	W 716999	4587074	W 785303	5731165	W 787689	5617906	PIECES 722,781,782,783
7849	OTHER MOTOR VEHCL PARTS	W 565758	3734243	W 694255	4405885	W 761470	5461770	W 768012	5348096	PIECES 722,781,782,783
785	CYCLES,ETC MOTRZD OR NOT	W 90563	1048513	W 82452	1006095	W 96991	1201999	W 137977	1283632	MOTOCYCLES SCOOTERS
79	OTHR TRANSPORT EQUIPMENT		4816207		5996964		5268205		5852993	AUTRE MATERIEL TRANSPORT
791	RAILWAY VEHICLES	W 45404	518948	W 71215	1278201	W 41475	357017		129999	VEHIC MAT CHEMINS DE FER
7915	FRT,MAINT CARS NOT POWRD	W 14979	291773	W 39124	876215	W 9604	226469	W 1315	19863	WAGONS DE SERVICE
79152	RAILWAY FREIGHT CARS NES	W 13620	274495	W 38440	863739	W 9032	217946	W 525	3078	WAGONS MARCHANDISES
792	AIRCRAFT ETC	W 10408	3729757	W 11090	4398329	W 10525	4289604	W 11201	5021757	APP NAVIGATION AERIENNE
7924	AIRCRFT NES OVER 15000KG	W 1273	853085	W 1470	782302	W 1960	991264	W 1942	740740	AERODYNES PLUS 15000 KG
7929	AIRCRAFT PARTS NES	W 8587	2723294	W 9043	3461026	W 7984	3051520	W 8714	4017309	PIECES DU 792
8	MISC MANUFACTURED GOODS		30570471		32574939		38089945		38828230	ART MANUFACTURES DIVERS
812	*PLUMBG,HEATNG,LGHTNG EQ	W 143113	695379	W 159335	773090	W 163005	905958	W 180677	1029412	APPAR SANITAIRES CHAUFFAGE
821	*FURNITURE,PARTS THEREOF	W 629336	2474347	W 687987	2737516	W 754699	3205729	W 783992	3377804	MEUBLES ET PIECES
8211	CHAIRS,SEATS AND PARTS	W 153536	902541	W 162792	974463	W 176595	1115753	W 176987	1193661	SIEGES ET PIECES
82111	CHAIRS AND OTHER SEATS	W 129099	784760	W 135085	813980	W 144110	911367	W 148469	973030	SIEGES
8219	FURNITURE AND PARTS NES	W 442938	1317275	W 496082	1487378	W 547795	1775447	W 566617	1821176	AUTRES MEUBLES ET PIECES
82192	WOOD FURNITURE NES	W 286954	835283	W 320484	917302	W 345546	1094151	W 360184	1130622	MEUBLES NDA EN BOIS
831	*TRAVEL GOODS,HANDBAGS	W 54735	599926	W 61290	677871	W 72630	827593	W 78129	858119	ARTICLES DE VOYAGE ETC
84	CLOTHING AND ACCESSORIES		8634573		9128415		10292179		10897829	VETEMENTS
842	MENS OUTERWEAR NOT KNIT	W 82109	1655395	W 81730	1691509	W 80248	1889380	W 81804	1983778	VET DESSUS POUR HOMMES
8423	— TROUSERS,BREECHES ETC	W 50217	840759	W 49056	833861	W 46626	926706	W 49682	1014925	PANTALONS HOMMES MAT TEX
843	WOMENS OUTERWEAR NONKNIT	W 71525	1819211	W 67912	1923678	W 72597	2288229	W 81440	2498773	VET DESSUS FEMMES MAT TEX
8439	— OTHER OUTER GARMENTS	W 46514	854463	W 41218	919196	W 43254	1062160	W 47993	1185684	AUT VET DES FEM MAT TEXT
844	UNDER GARMENTS NOT KNIT	W 27671	628303	W 28416	613200	W 29279	676899	W 27657	666174	VETEMENT DESSOUS MAT TEX
845	OUTERWEAR KNIT NONELASTC	W 103312	2228355	W 108999	2337752	W 99034	2541058	W 104979	2653803	VET DESSOUS,ACCES BONNET
8451	— JERSEYS,PULLOVERS ETC	W 58151	1269730	W 57956	1260168	W 49295	1311685	W 52505	1388110	CHANDAILS,PULL–OVERS ETC
8459	— OTHER,CLTHG ACCESRYS	W 39655	811108	W 44834	927209	W 45147	1073878	W 46483	1123252	AUT VET DESSUS DE BONNE
846	UNDER GARMENTS KNITTED	W 65747	1388624	W 70114	1558183	W 74140	1792900	W 82290	1956028	SOUS VETS DE BONNETERIE
8462	— OF COTTON NON ELASTIC	W 49252	906721	W 52368	986538	W 56159	1168518	W 63644	1282554	SOUS–VET BONNET COTON
84629	—— OTHER	W 49252	906721	W 52368	986538	W 56159	1168518	W 63644	1282554	AUT SOUS–VET BONNET COTON
851	*FOOTWEAR	W 134443	1998785	W 142978	2153695	W 147500	2427453	W 145144	2452213	CHAUSSURES
85102	FOOTWEAR LEATHER	W 107119	1747901	W 112544	1865103	W 110861	2043477	W 105506	2010587	CHAUS SEMELLES EN CUIR
87	PRECISION INSTRUMNTS NES		3744539		3956772		4732509		4853544	INSTRUM,APPAR SCIENT NDA
872	MEDICAL INSTRUMENTS NES	W 22885	951214	W 20264	986673	W 23334	1214293	W 23579	1294906	INSTR,APP MEDIC–CHIR NDA
87202	OTH MEDICAL INSTRUMENTS	W 21057	877824	W 18186	909040	W 20880	1121460	W 20576	1194391	INSTRUM,APP MEDECINE
874	MEASURNG,CONTROLNG INSTR	W 40282	2487622	W 35538	2656418	W 37946	3076094	W 41483	3090391	INSTRUMENTS DE MESURE
8748	ELEC MEAS,CONTRL EQU NES	W 4827	623516	W 4589	696711	W 5725	835367	W 5131	828814	APP ELEC ELECTRO MESURE
88	PHOTO EQU,OPTICL GDS ETC		2479111		2651578		3025109		2869019	APP,FOURN PHOTO,OP,MONTR
882	PHOTO,CINEMA SUPPLIES	W 85493	1062417	W 94296	1137272	W 99000	1307287	W 97039	1240739	PRODUITS PHOTO,CINEMA
8822	PHOTO FILM EXC DEV CINMA	W 55682	884078	W 62720	921340	W 67703	1060513	W 64026	999298	PLAQUES,PELLICULES,FILMS
89	MISC MANUFCTRD GOODS NES		9943810		10496002		12673414		12490289	ART MANUFACTURES DIVERS
892	PRINTED MATTER	W 368370	1477709	W 420685	1683547	W 481119	2131291	W 485194	1965367	IMPRIMES
8928	PRINTED MATTER NES	W 187310	596385	W 220852	708536	W 232998	866579	W 231776	846805	IMPRIMES NDA
893	ARTICLES OF PLASTIC NES		2668677		3026225		3831341		3847622	OUVRAGES EN MAT DIVIS 58
8931	PLSTC PACKG CONTNRS,LIDS	W 296707	837104	W 328075	929328	W 338273	1212727	W 360951	1197922	ART TRANSP EMBALLAGE ETC
8939	MISC PLASTIC ARTICLES	W 411023	1753401	W 472698	2014254	W 474466	2508934	W 531227	2524063	ART DIVERS EN MAT DIV 58
89399	OTHR PLASTC ARTICLES NES	W 314387	1536508	W 370615	1795082	W 377247	2262997	W 426634	2267566	AUT OUV MAT DIV 58
894	TOYS,SPORTING GOODS,ETC	W 218743	1985693	W 206344	1856644	W 220159	2105403	W 215413	2143594	VOITURES ENFANTS,JOUETS
8942	TOYS,INDOOR GAMES ETC	W 170771	1550907	W 157023	1378223	W 164742	1530386	W 154480	1527044	JOUETS,JEUX ETC
89423	TOYS NES	W 103336	716997	W 87495	675334	W 84128	799053	W 77489	757040	JOUETS,MODELES REDUITS
89424	INDOOR GAME EQUIPMENT	W 40149	605184	W 39874	461118	W 42414	408375	W 39899	452520	ART,JEUX DE SOCIETE
897	GOLD,SILVER WARE,JEWELRY		646826		676427		732056		697896	BIJOUTERIE,ORFEVRERIE
898	MUSICAL INSTRUMENTS,PTS	W 92880	1611053	W 88252	1579952	W 111100	1957784	W 105888	1935062	INSTRUMENTS DE MUSIQUE
8983	SOUND RECRDNG TAPE,DISCS	W 80437	1430805	W 77763	1391378	W 100021	1763877	W 95855	1740693	SUPPORTS SON POUR 763
89832	RECORDED DISCS,TAPES ETC	W 30219	894347	W 27309	870941	W 34552	1180298	W 35596	1210612	DISQUES,PHONO,BANDES
899	OTHER MANUFACTURED GOODS		904019		997881		1182176		1199634	AUT ART MANUF DIVERS NDA
9	GOODS NOT CLASSD BY KIND		582017		774553		900532		963244	ART TRANSACT NON CLASSES
971	*GOLD,NON MONETARY NES	K 684800	497816	K 645600	670063	K 870297	791843	K 267067	825292	OR NON MONETAIRE

5. Special Exports F.O.B. by Commodities according to the S.I.T.C. (Rev. 2) in thousand U.S. Dollars
Exportations Spéciales F.O.B. par Produits d'après la C.T.C.I. (Rév. 2) en milliers de Dollars E.U.

SITC CTCI	COMMODITY	1993 WEIGHT POIDS	1993 VALUE VALEUR	1994 WEIGHT POIDS	1994 VALUE VALEUR	1995 WEIGHT POIDS	1995 VALUE VALEUR	1996 WEIGHT POIDS	1996 VALUE VALEUR	PRODUIT
	ALL COMMODITIES		206275044		233307296		284045721		283901301	TOUS PRODUITS
0	FOOD AND LIVE ANIMALS		25301208		26054305		30460585		29974735	ALIMENTS,ANIMAUX VIVANTS
001	*LIVE ANIMALS FOR FOOD	W 566689	1672811	W 562907	1812595	W 597829	1912354	W 630760	1706668	ANIMAUX VIVANTS
0011	BOVINE SPECIES,LIVE	W 471035	1442612	W 466658	1558789	W 494778	1620360	W 533414	1408474	ESPECE BOVINE
00119	— OTHR THAN FR BREEDING	W 455530	1402271	W 446875	1502872	W 470040	1546401	W 505909	1336393	BOVINS NON REPRODUCTEURS
01	MEAT AND PREPARATIONS		3745314		4090099		4613128		4321534	VIANDES ET PREPARATIONS
011	MEAT FRESH,CHILLD,FROZEN	W 1469532	3308876	W 1563020	3551484	W 1543992	3926076	W 1471271	3664572	VIANDES FRAICHES,REF,CONGE
0111	BOVINE MEAT FRESH,FROZEN	W 534756	1546122	W 518663	1531277	W 431532	1574397	W 351863	1117015	VIANDES BOVIN FRAI,REF
01111	BOVINE MEAT WITH BONE IN	W 347108	1023792	W 339864	1024722	W 271502	1072973	W 206595	741994	VIANDES BOVIN NON DESOSS
0114	POULTRY FRESH CHLLD,FRZN	W 649605	1140150	W 684287	1264090	W 737476	1408734	W 752235	1564870	VOLAILLES MORTES
02	DAIRY PRODCTS,BIRDS'EGGS		3626773		4010325		4717252		4345924	PRODUITS LAITIERS,OEUFS
022	MILK AND CREAM	W 1531055	1420536	W 1824319	1678427	W 1738573	2035548	W 1618105	1726022	LAIT ET CREME
0224	MILK,CREAM PRESERVED ETC	W 618717	900080	W 667583	1049537	W 685941	1328228	W 668207	1087240	LAIT,CREME CONS,CONC
024	CHEESE AND CURD	W 420850	1845287	W 438383	1972499	W 457975	2243448	W 464881	2238111	FROMAGE ET CAILLEBOTTE
03	FISH AND PREPARATIONS		806296		884493		973325		980619	POISSONS ET PREPARATIONS
04	CEREALS AND PREPARATIONS		7430218		6128919		7483732		7600211	CEREALES ET PRODUITS
041	WHEAT ETC UNMILLED	MW 18087	3060843	MW 12600	1998974	MW 16333	2964355	MW 14733	2882962	FROMENT,EPEAUTRE
0412	OTHER WHEAT ETC UNMILLED	MW 17323	2859709	MW 12226	1918646	MW 15572	2770380	MW 14064	2725461	AUTRE FROMENT NON MOULU
043	BARLEY UNMILLED	W 5132673	758988	W 3338460	533363	W 2922413	572696	W 3225053	631216	ORGE NON MONDEE
044	MAIZE UNMILLED	W 7636777	1740816	W 8009015	1655010	W 6474232	1641719	W 6601528	1616870	MAIS NON MOULU
048	CEREAL ETC PREPARATIONS	W 1585153	1285113	W 1625982	1382364	W 1655810	1663929	W 1654796	1733297	PREPTNS A BASE CEREALES
05	VEGETABLES AND FRUIT		2883928		3145311		3632895		3701472	LEGUMES ET FRUITS
054	VEG ETC FRSH,SMPLY PRSVD	W 2725082	1190521	W 2432797	1149266	W 2526627	1328550	W 2562467	1304884	LEGUMES FRAIS,CONG,SECS
057	FRUIT,NUTS,FRESH,DRIED	W 1202445	940122	W 1292611	1189976	W 1373583	1348295		1487002	FRUITS FRAIS OU SECS
06	SUGAR AND PREPS,HONEY		1601831		1823046		2026560		2076952	SUCRES ET PRODUITS
061	SUGAR AND HONEY	W 3381313	1453936	W 3135688	1653360	W 2929236	1849877	W 3422340	1913078	SUCRES ET MIEL
0612	REFINED SUGAR ETC	W 2717800	1162253	W 2469110	1346479	W 2770802	1782951	W 2615531	1491678	SUCRES RAFFINES
07	COFFEE,TEA,COCOA,SPICES		804054		1305602		1682452		1731703	CAFE,THE,CACAO,EPICES
073	CHOCOLATE AND PRODUCTS	W 152217	514083	W 199421	734098	W 235107	1123385	W 242912	1028100	CHOCOLAT
081	*FEEDING STUFF FOR ANIML	W 3040508	1171668	W 2886109	1175790	W 2898381	1377858	W 2949321	1365006	NOURRITURE POUR ANIMAUX
0819	FOOD WASTE AND FEED NES	W 1654935	984184	W 1744489	1014822	W 1722520	1196395	W 1833620	1180489	DECHETS,ALIMENTS NDA
08199	FODDER NES,INCL SWEETNED	W 1036963	895110	W 1039174	913400	W 1131697	1098928	W 1174950	1077444	PREPARATIONS FOURRAGERES
09	MISC EDIBLE PRODUCTS		1558316		1678125		2041029		2144646	PREP ALIMENTAIRES DIVERSES
098	EDIBLE PRODCTS,PREPS NES	W 434510	1521597	W 388722	1617320	W 412612	1977987	W 413926	2092487	PREP ALIMENTAIRES NDA
09809	MISC FOOD PREPRTIONS NES	W 250655	1250774	W 286526	1434974	W 306441	1761124	W 303020	1864801	PREP ALIMENTAIRES NDA
1	BEVERAGES AND TOBACCO		6669729		7365636		8332905		8378666	BOISSONS ET TABACS
11	BEVERAGES		6471774		7145232		8064600		8086943	BOISSONS
111	NON–ALCOHL BEVERAGES NES	W 4718350	648203	W 5035485	747130	W 4724930	870971	W 3897877	758525	BOISSONS NON ALCOOLIQUES
112	ALCOHOLIC BEVERAGES	W 1717996	5823572	W 1795687	6398102	W 1825259	7193629	W 1969299	7328418	BOISSONS ALCOOLIQUES
1121	WINE OF FRESH GRAPES ETC	W 1241960	3646927	W 1275567	3973928	W 1258469	4606604	W 1383242	4814783	VINS DE RAISINS FRAIS
11212	WINE OF FRESH GRAPES	W 1219880	3610349	W 1248626	3936964	W 1226920	4565175	W 1365205	4785319	VINS DE MOUTS DE RAISINS
1124	DISTILLED ALCOHOLIC BEVS	W 346554	2062563	W 374049	2294342	W 389690	2417677	W 383298	2316617	ALCOOLS,EAUX–DE–VIE
11242	DISTILLD WINE,GRAPE MARC	W 197557	1703604	W 226169	1902561	W 224477	1941606	W 222337	1829814	EAUX–DE–VIE NATURELLES
2	CRUDE MATERLS,EXCL FUELS		4669256		5564631		6305483		6081818	MAT BRUTES NON COMESTIBLES
24	CORK AND WOOD		635950		749507		871058		787900	LIEGE ET BOIS
28	METALLIFEROUS ORES,SCRAP		968834		1162390		1378464		1137163	MINERAIS METAL,DECHETS
3	MINERAL FUELS ETC		5665549		5784038		6854298		7429341	COMBUSTIBLES MINERAUX LUB
33	PETROLEUM AND PRODUCTS		2534750		2546263		2589380		3314386	PETROLE ET DERIVES
334	PETROLEUM PRODUCTS,REFIN	MW 13884	2314500	MW 13145	2328367	MW 11442	2351996	MW 14087	3073480	PRODUITS RAFFINES
3341	GASOLINE,OTH LIGHT OILS					W 4375031	798903	W 5111258	1059806	ESSENCES POUR MOTEURS
33411	MOTOR,AVIATION SPIRIT					W 3565643	634741	W 4260064	871508	ESSENCES MOTEURS D'AVIONS
3344	FUEL OILS,NES					W 2814772	270324	W 6276249	947974	FUEL OILS
351	*ELECTRIC CURRENT		2711526		2881227		3839000		3671130	ENERGIE ELECTRIQUE
5	CHEMCLS,RELATED PROD NES		28997281		33269373		35793963		40217499	PRODUITS CHIMIQUES
51	ORGANIC CHEMICALS		5668779		7004862		5770023		8732127	PROD CHIMIQ ORGANIQUES
511	HYDROCARBONS NES,DERIVS	W 1318454	664355	W 3103550	3074532	W 1219641	868156	W 3360099	3659801	HYDROCARBURES NDA
5112	CYCLIC HYDROCARBONS	W 541600	216189	W 2383297	2666127	W 479579	337290	W 2558652	3202539	HYDROCARBURES CYCLIQUES
51129	OTH CYCLIC HYDROCARBONS	W 11832	16514	W 9327	14444	W 16947	24034	W 2184267	3042600	AUT HYDROCARBURES CYCLIQUES
512	ALCOHOLS,PHENOLS ETC	W 930415	710047	W 605198	499191	W 577304	601208	W 634097	581716	PHENOLS,PHENOLS–ALCOOLS
513	CARBOXYLIC ACIDS ETC	W 738877	870832	W 271373	534291	W 252299	650258	W 266452	644636	ACIDES CARBOXYLIQUES
514	NITROGEN–FNCTN COMPOUNDS		1657197	W 257720	1177211	W 252450	1398197	W 203658	1433803	COMPOSES FONCT AZOTEES
5148	OTH NITROGN–FNCTN CMPNDS		723360	W 199988	661328	W 177779	787449	W 127021	818981	AUTRES COMPOSES AZOTES
515	ORG–INORG COMPOUNDS ETC	W 172662	1094218	W 123525	1157061	W 132249	1555543	W 136391	1683667	COMPOSES ORGANO–MINERAUX
5156	HETEROCYCLIC CMPDS ETC	W 21072	660789	W 22661	793746	W 33608	1046433	W 25701	1153092	COMPOSES HETEROCYCLIQUES
51569	OTH HETEROCYC CMPDS,ETC	W 14521	637341	W 17052	766278	W 29430	1020059	W 21059	1124640	AUT COMP HETEROCYCLIQUES
516	OTHER ORGANIC CHEMICALS	W 851464	672130	W 665677	562576		696660	W 641871	728505	AUTRES PROD ORGANIQUES
52	INORGANIC CHEMICALS		2529707		2508222		2209069		2053670	PROD CHIM INORGANIQUES
522	INORG ELEMNTS,OXIDES,ETC		687821	W 3450638	1099993		561721		510364	ELEMENTS INORGANIQUES
524	RADIOACTIVE ETC MATERIAL		1283501		1058829		1217386		1125810	MATIERES RADIOACTIVES
5241	RADIOACTIVE ELEMENTS ETC		1190589		989351		1142587		1093656	RADIOELEMENTS,ISOTOPES
53	DYES,TANNING,COLOUR PROD		1418071		1626772		1894208		2021837	PROD TEINTURE,COLORANTS
533	PIGMENTS,PAINTS,ETC	W 375441	870755	W 406397	972301	W 427035	1229673	W 424750	1149512	PIGMENTS,PEINTURES,VERNIS
541	*MEDICINAL,PHARM PRODUCT		4964743	MK 153106	5415370	MK 178057	6864380		7244716	PROD MEDICINAUX PHARMACEUT
5417	MEDICAMENTS	MK 117827	3430931	MK 121855	3911982	MK 143051	5065037	MK 137654	5324862	MEDICAMENTS
54179	— CONTNG OTH SUBSTANCES	MK 106332	2731428	MK 106697	3118819	MK 129209	4086747	MK 124725	4261038	MED CONT AUT SUBSTANCES
55	PERFUME,CLEANING ETC PRD		5427290		6287004		7557314		7636737	PROD POUR PARFUM,TOILETTE
553	PERFUMERY,COSMETICS,ETC	W 299511	4125366	W 294817	4836678	W 334703	5782173	W 377853	5877261	PRODUITS DE PARFUMERIE
554	SOAP,CLEANSING ETC PREPS	W 541603	787929	W 628933	875892	W 679426	1057955	W 693309	1016069	SAVONS,PRODUITS DETERSIFS
5542	WASHING PREPARATIONS ETC	W 452808	594903	W 544298	691367	W 597808	856946	W 613445	824169	PROD ORG TENSIO–ACT NDA
58	PLASTIC MATERIALS ETC		4729483		5642399		6113596		6883021	MAT PLAST ARTIFICIELLES
582	PROD OF CONDENSATION ETC	W 394190	887044	W 285598	473649	W 331909	655466	W 317975	613732	PROD CONDENS,POLYCOND
583	POLYMERIZATION ETC PRODS	W 3680603	3659505	W 4212098	5106008	W 3783974	5389572	W 4461610	6208574	PROD POLYMERISATION
5831	POLYETHYLENE	W 1052114	808937	W 1050107	814849	W 970644	1083359	W 955763	957418	POLYETHYLENE
58311	— IN PRIMARY FORMS	W 972761	627827	W 959868	667262	W 882981	924280	W 861259	801842	POLYETHYLENE PRIMAIRES
5834	POLYVINYL CHLORIDE	W 719109	621732	W 722400	738995	W 692795	966730	W 832668	858787	CHLORURE DE POLYVINYLE
5839	OTH POLYMRZTION ETC PROD	W 532429	796657	W 924224	1968241	W 662491	1247181	W 1143366	2528890	AUT PROD POLYMER COPOLYM
59	CHEMICAL MATERIALS NES		3906321		4442368		5035160		5283216	MAT PROD CHIMIQUES NDA
591	PESTICIDES,DISINFECTANTS	W 164469	1074134	W 188681	1336458	W 179100	1517989	W 199918	1665055	DESINF,INSECT,FONG,HERB
592	STARCH,INULIN,GLUTEN,ETC	W 701864	687757	W 696373	743991	W 536316	818573	W 745699	952454	AMIDONS,INUL,GLUT FROM
598	MISCEL CHEM PRODUCTS NES	W 1624761	2144430	W 1597991	2361919	W 1517888	2698598	W 1491100	2665707	PROD DIV INDUST CHIM NDA
5982	ANTI–KNOCK PREPARTNS ETC	W 475921	823831	W 474969	809849	W 515686	928336	W 519764	871224	PREPARAT ANTIDETONANTES
5989	CHEM PRODUCTS,PREPS NES	W 1023238	1213692	W 879390	1292568	W 927422	1626304	W 894759	1656941	PROD PREP CHIMIQUES NDA
59899	OTH CHEM PRODS,PREPS,NES	W 823256	850160	W 693987	866430	W 744577	1158252	W 714854	1233945	AUT PRODUITS CHIMIQUES NDA
6	BASIC MANUFACTURES		33192818		38359893		46603804		45742071	ART MANUFACTURES
62	RUBBER MANUFACTURES NES		2985716		3389155		3879359		4076419	CAOUTCHOUC MANUFACTURE
625	RUBBER TYRES, TUBES ETC	W 517898	2158742	W 556082	2365843	W 569684	2639256	W 614298	2759945	PNEUS CAOUTCHOUC VULCANISE
6251	TYRES NEW FOR MOTOR CARS	W 246418	1191475	W 266929	1339810	W 283749	1541743	W 303242	1623049	PNEUS POUR VOITURES
63	WOOD,CORK MANUFACTRS NES		857901		1027085		1305836		1316382	OUVRAGES LIEGE ET BOIS
64	PAPER,PAPERBOARD AND MFR		4080109		4897085		6368689		5924699	PAPIERS,CARTONS & OUVRAGES
641	PAPER AND PAPERBOARD	W 3407523	2833555	W 3970478	3555985	W 3885962	4711124	W 4199997	4324858	PAPIERS ET CARTONS
6412	PRINTG,WRITING PAPER NES	W 987946	885330	W 1122423	1070255	W 1109985	1449103	W 1195015	1236350	PAPIERS POUR L'IMPRESSION

5. Special Exports F.O.B. by Commodities according to the S.I.T.C. (Rev. 2) in thousand U.S. Dollars
Exportations Spéciales F.O.B. par Produits d'après la C.T.C.I. (Rév. 2) en milliers de Dollars E.U.

SITC CTCI	COMMODITY	1993 WEIGHT POIDS	1993 VALUE VALEUR	1994 WEIGHT POIDS	1994 VALUE VALEUR	1995 WEIGHT POIDS	1995 VALUE VALEUR	1996 WEIGHT POIDS	1996 VALUE VALEUR	PRODUIT
64122	— COATED,IMPREGNATD ETC	W 851544	757406	W 965803	908610	W 962974	1233853	W 1034194	1042643	PAPIERS IMPRESSION COUCHES
6415	PAPER,PAPERBRD,BULK,NES	W 936176	665021	W 1074324	850386	W 1016618	1117477	W 1205309	1020902	PAPIERS,CARTONS ROULEAUX
64159	OTHER PAPER ETC,BULK,NES	W 794861	568804	W 924189	721191	W 868383	942841	W 1055253	863166	AUT PAPIER ROULEAUX FEUILLES
6418	COATED ETC PAPER NES BLK	W 326722	573359	W 436223	760909	W 421530	931549	W 459485	940805	PAP,CARTONS COUCHES,ENDUITS
642	PAPER,ETC,PRECUT,ARTS OF	W 581622	1246554	W 703193	1341100		1657564	W 654306	1599841	PAP,CARTONS DECOUPES
65	TEXTILE YARN,FABRICS,ETC		5690683		6541645		7911835		7644672	FILS,TISSUS,ARTICLES TEXTILE
651	TEXTILE YARN	W 246962	1264360	W 293067	1551496	W 316048	1844950	W 323924	1679396	FILS TEXTILES
652	COTTON FABRICS,WOVEN	W 85168	910550	W 90538	1054613		1192073	W 92243	1185647	TISSUS DE COTON
6522	WOVEN COTTON BLEACHD,ETC	W 67329	805858	W 72301	937423	W 75779	1064639	W 72173	1050164	TISSUS COTON BLANCHIS ETC
653	WOVN MAN-MADE FIB FABRIC	W 150933	1076212	W 98096	1250465	W 94980	1581114	W 97467	1579565	TISSUS FIBRES SYNTH,ARTIF
657	SPECIAL TXTL FABRC,PRODS	W 96681	718743	W 97127	726092	W 110977	910412	W 115653	907173	TISSUS SPECIAUX
66	NONMETAL MINERAL MFS NES		4048961		4468613		5208036		5251500	ART MIN NON METALLIQUES
664	GLASS	W 679411	773090	W 728149	817649	W 831659	1039784	W 829800	1047868	VERRE
665	GLASSWARE	W 739359	1394457	W 815480	1542795	W 807662	1727922	W 840742	1734027	OUVRAGES EN VERRE
6652	HOUSEHLD,HOTEL ETC GLASS	W 346885	905915	W 345884	999100	W 364728	1104401	W 377673	1106130	OBJETS VERRE TABLE,CUISINE
67	IRON AND STEEL		7601795		8800896		10575540		10343340	FER ET ACIER
672	IRON,STEEL PRIMARY FORMS	W 4167446	1380240	W 4144926	1507931	W 3783397	1790841		1599934	LINGOTS FER,ACIER
6727	IRN,STL COIL FR REROLLNG	W 2593493	817060	W 2580193	904746	W 2496446	1076667	W 2848115	986774	EBAUCHES POUR TOLES FER
67271	IRON,SIMPLE STEEL COILS	W 2511145	742959	W 2485018	834135	W 2409745	990057	W 2755758	927083	EBAUCHES NON EN ACIER
673	IRON,STEEL SHAPES ETC	W 2992652	1355641	W 2966371	1531380	W 2859689	1976316	W 2823957	1695197	BARRES,PROFIL FER,ACIER
6732	IRON,STEEL BARS ETC	W 1066768	552366	W 1192906	692715	W 1168843	961690	W 1156964	867464	BARRES FER,ACIER
674	IRN,STL UNIV,PLATE,SHEET	W 3801882	2706780	W 4322690	3192855	W 4827314	4235424	W 4648888	3767918	LARGES PLATS,TOLES
6746	IRN,STL THIN PLATE,ROLLD	W 1256624	986456	W 1432482	1098085	W 1335427	1407526	W 1284993	1193350	TOLES LAM MOINS 3MM
6749	OTH IRN,STL PLATES,SHEET	W 1449743	938922	W 1623373	1112228	W 1812880	1450584	W 1799561	1285599	AUTRES TOLES FER,ACIER
67491	— OF IRON OR SIMPLE STL	W 1401510	822560	W 1546100	976682	W 1740629	1277842	W 1656827	1087051	AUT TOLES AUTRES ACIER FIN
678	IRON,STL TUBES,PIPES,ETC	W 1140380	1282691	W 1375592	1550228	W 1018728	1542641	W 1452241	1894313	TUBES,TUYAUX EN FONTE,FER
68	NON-FERROUS METALS		3180324		3861411		4698169		4626281	METAUX NON FERREUX
682	COPPER EXC CEMENT COPPER		1013559	W 473904	1311645	W 474012	1729056	W 462112	1455056	CUIVRE
6822	COPPER,ALLOYS WORKED		948358	W 443446	1254426	W 447496	1669478	W 435946	1401876	CUIVRE,ALLIAGES OUVRES
68221	COPPER BARS,WIRE,ETC	W 274731	630398	W 344255	861447	W 355328	1151004	W 349512	977312	BARRES,PROFILES ET FILS
684	ALUMINIUM	W 662863	1480223	W 671438	1683078	W 661007	2185534	W 701751	1990687	ALUMINIUM
6842	ALUMINIUM,ALLOYS WORKED	W 425280	1165649	W 459459	1343093	W 456442	1727700	W 419261	1483021	ALUMINIUM,ALLIAGES OUVRE
68422	ALUMNM PLATE,SHEET,STRIP	W 310464	772022	W 340729	905330	W 336614	1163368	W 309687	997555	TOLES, PLANCHES EN ALU
69	METAL MANUFACTURES NES		4322969		4882143		6108895		5990126	ART MANUFACT EN METAL NDA
691	STRUCTURES AND PARTS NES	W 264971	622207	W 274038	693421	W 288723	795743	W 349373	717003	CONSTRUCT FER,ACIER,ALU
699	BASE METAL MFRS NES	W 298479	1678234	W 320305	1835678		2380172		2392720	ART MANUFACTURES MET NDA
7	MACHINES,TRANSPORT EQUIP		78965117		91760632		112491996		115326805	MACHINES MATERIEL TRANSPORT
71	POWER GENERATING EQUIPMT		7714284		8724665		9207611		9098022	MACHINES GENERATRICES
713	INTRNL COMBUS PSTN ENGIN	W 276578	2705815	W 306468	3283465		3639024	W 346263	3944374	MOTEURS EXPL COMB INT, PIECE
7132	MOTOR VEHCL PSTN ENGINS	W 136560	1407044	W 156360	1724141	W 155394	2103055	W 218509	2474380	MOTEURS EXPL POUR VEHICULES
7139	PISTON ENGINE PARTS NES	W 121333	1008766	W 126442	1202760	W 113196	1283388	W 109023	1250490	PIECES POUR 713.2,3,8
714	ENGINES AND MOTORS NES	W 14671	3087186	W 19703	3324884	W 22300	3141773	W 19623	2958262	MOTEURS NON ELECTRIQUES
7144	REACTION ENGINES	W 1039	1313444	W 968	1311523	W 477	730308	W 451	687516	PROPULSEURS A REACTION
7149	ENGINE & MOTOR PARTS NES	W 10954	1530474	W 13480	1613465	W 16418	1836555	W 15421	1941766	PIECES 714 ET 718.88
71491	PARTS NES OF 7144,71481	W 999	1114081	W 1099	1188055	W 1203	1206019	W 1224	1317155	PIECES DES PROPULSEURS
716	ROTATING ELECTRIC PLANT	W 122726	1235359	W 132457	1396100	W 144573	1605637	W 157261	1546515	APP ELECTR ROTATIFS,PIECES
7162	AC MTRS,GENRTRS,GEN SETS	W 72198	770732	W 78426	823178	W 88229	1018045	W 95803	1013921	MOTEURS ELECTRIQUES
72	MACHS FOR SPCL INDUSTRYS		5021931		6007508		7279712		7497404	MAC SPECIALES POUR INDUST
723	CIVIL ENGNEERG EQUIP ETC	W 163414	1005221	W 190168	1270632	W 208300	1435419	W 206637	1320471	APPAREILS DE GENIE CIVIL
7234	CONST,MINING MACHNRY NES	W 136989	811907	W 163005	1066731	W 172674	1183003	W 170798	1069730	MACH POUR LA CONST, MINES
72342	SLFPRP SHOVELS,EXCAVATRS	W 96564	575581	W 122858	740905	W 131808	825094	W 129922	739702	PELLES MECANIQUES
724	TEXTILE,LEATHER MACHNRY	W 46274	748132	W 49457	863273	W 49065	979680	W 53145	1006614	MACH POUR INDUSTRIE TEXTILE
728	OTH MACHY FOR SPCL INDUS	W 128747	1619520	W 110523	1903480	W 118141	2366269	W 140889	2503306	AUT MACH IND PARTICULIERES
7284	MACHY FOR SPCL INDUS NES	W 78770	1211150	W 58726	1449441	W 69154	1947430	W 75928	1902817	MACH SPEC IND PARTICUL.
73	METALWORKING MACHINERY		968573		951243		1367523		1322796	MACH TRAVAIL DES METAUX
736	METALWORKING MACH-TOOLS	W 41564	508949	W 42601	590928		880242	W 58032	777199	MACH-OUTILS TRAVAIL METAUX
74	GENRL INDUSTRL MACHY NES		8642477		10009907		12597041		13292737	MACH APP INDUSTRIE
741	HEATING,COOLING EQUIPMNT	W 140894	1692991	W 174770	2014120	W 223867	2551043	W 220369	2644270	MACH CHAUFFAGE,PIECES
7416	HEATING,COOLING EQU NES	W 57014	668177	W 77257	823523	W 67597	886812	W 77661	914540	APP CHANGEMENT TEMP
742	PUMPS FOR LIQUIDS ETC	W 42367	863996	W 44219	1064211	W 57989	1268648	W 60035	1437760	POMPES MOTO-POMPES
743	PUMPS NES,CENTRFUGES ETC		1342487	W 108907	1609297	W 123773	2030174	W 141942	2179068	POMPES COMPRES,VENT ETC
744	MECHANICAL HANDLING EQU	W 331992	1526969	W 281766	1711096	W 333858	2259727	W 342100	2303645	EQUIP MANUTENTION PIECES
7442	LIFTING,LOADING MACH NES	W 194785	690766	W 107529	684905	W 110961	838967	W 120182	869418	APP LEVAGE,MANUTENTION
7449	PTS NES OF MACHY OF 7442	W 97251	604895	W 121448	730945	W 155649	986549	W 145730	975542	PIECES DU 744.2
745	NONELEC MACHY,TOOLS NES	W 46422	622685	W 34407	647420	W 37460	766085	W 37726	848776	AUT MACH NON ELEC,PIECES
749	NONELEC MACH PTS,ACC NES	W 209098	2593349	W 217353	2963763	W 237727	3721364	W 247618	3879218	PIECES MACH NON ELEC NDA
7491	BALL,ROLLER,ETC BEARINGS	W 47740	566742	W 59280	761603	W 64050	972466	W 67913	1043599	ROULEMENTS BILLES ETC
7492	COCKS,VALVES ETC NES	W 56367	1052435	W 56905	1116339	W 63778	1331656	W 68021	1416757	ART ROB,SIM POUR TUYAUX
75	OFFICE MACHNES,ADP EQUIP		5864095		6766088		8964070		9815396	MACH BUREAU TRAIT AUTOM
752	AUTOMTIC DATA PROC EQUIP	W 33518	3335460	W 42612	3882883	W 59759	5714220	W 91567	6496893	MACH TRAIT INFORMATION
7523	DIGITL CENTRL PROCESSORS	W 11952	1921069	W 13749	2011454	W 22319	2804123	W 22018	2911588	UNITES CENTRALES
7525	ADP PERIPHERAL UNITS	W 15802	654517	W 22716	980883	W 28296	1584110	W 58009	1997738	UNITES PERIPHERIQUES
759	OFFICE,ADP MCH PTS,ACCES	W 20934	1967556	W 29429	2255714	W 24588	2474869	W 32575	2617860	PIECES DU 751 ET 752
7599	ACCTG,ETC,ADP MCH PTS,AC	W 9723	1686780	W 19103	1968248	W 13218	2115955	W 20623	2242197	PIECES DU 751 ET 752
76	TELECOMM,SOUND EQUIPMENT		3981578		4682563		6327822		6797218	EQUIPMENT DE TELECOM
761	TELEVISION RECEIVERS	W 52193	732798	W 50257	690250	W 61043	898571	W 65850	899549	RECEPTEURS DE TELEVISION
7611	COLOUR TV RECEIVERS	W 52096	728816	W 50148	685861	W 60860	892251	W 65781	896893	RECEPTEURS COULEUR
764	TELECOM EQPT,PTS,ACC NES	W 46644	2690277	W 37913	3329047	W 44356	4588689	W 52093	5081477	EQUIP TELECOM,PIECES
7641	LINE TELEPHONE,ETC EQUIP	W 9677	903247	W 12357	1217469	W 11702	1503538	W 11772	1529983	APP TELEPHON PAR FIL
7643	TV,RADIO TRANSMITTRS ETC	W 1580	344982	W 1701	458340	W 3199	901637	W 5224	1307270	APP EMET TELE RADIO
7649	PTS NES OF EQUIPMT OF 76	W 15463	1104747	W 16988	1225440	W 20872	1718424	W 27362	1796995	PIECES DE LA DIV 76
76493	TELECOMM EQUIPMT PTS NES	W 7598	488028	W 9574	622178	W 13375	925898	W 20157	1022859	PIECES 761,762,764.3,8
77	ELECTRIC MACHNRY NES ETC		12701899		14935296		19400910		20307340	MACH APP ELECT NDA
771	ELECTRIC POWER MACHY NES	W 65158	766702	W 67214	845913	W 70108	985591	W 82068	1061793	MACH PROD,TRANS ELECTR
772	SWITCHGEAR ETC,PARTS NES	W 123988	3307361	W 133079	3907257	W 143995	4715508	W 147305	4700396	APP COUPURE,SECT ETC
7721	SWITCHGEAR ETC	W 122471	3174333	W 131427	3748243	W 141960	4485680	W 144531	4436273	APP COUPURE,SECTIONMNT
773	ELECTR DISTRIBUTNG EQUIP	W 172819	893976	W 202156	990054	W 212487	1315031	W 207487	1385016	EQUIPMT DISTRIBUTION ELECT
7731	INSULATED WIRE,CABLE ETC	W 149071	756578	W 178805	853712	W 184740	1121021	W 186744	1233100	FILS,CABLES ISOLES ELECT
774	ELECTRO-MEDCL,XRAY EQUIP	W 4690	586750	W 6046	725670	W 5883	768832	W 6136	790111	APPAREILS MEDICAUX
775	HOUSEHOLD TYPE EQUIP NES	W 194371	1681913	W 214358	1850129	W 224615	2204201	W 233067	2349430	MACH,APP USAGE DOMESTQUE
7758	ELECTRO-THERMIC APPL NES	W 94364	887602	W 99267	974759	W 110065	1176482	W 118333	1305397	APP ELECTROTHERMIQ NDA
77586	ELECTROTHERM DOM APP NES	W 69307	609531	W 71393	647702	W 78444	770720	W 84704	874089	APP ELECTRO THERMIQUES
776	TRANSISTORS,VALVES,ETC	W 37961	2974165	W 45955	3738918	W 53158	5641682	W 59321	6113809	LAMPES,TUBES,VALVES
7763	DIODES,TRANSISTORS,ETC	W 3217	519979	W 3467	704278	W 3556	923370	W 5283	909698	DIODES,TRANSISTORS
7764	ELECTRONIC MICROCIRCUITS	W 6140	2004189	W 5255	2465550	W 6357	4035070	W 8197	4492708	MICROSTRUCTURES ELECTRON
778	ELECTRICAL MACHINERY NES	W 346683	2491033	W 388742	2877355	W 392807	3770064	W 409286	3906784	AUTRES MACH ELECT NDA
7783	AUTOMOTIVE ELECTR EQUIP	W 57483	828486	W 60720	913907	W 72498	1112861	W 75218	1160797	EQUIP ELECT MOTEURS EXPL
7788	OTH ELEC MACHY,EQUIP NES	W 87835	846457	W 87679	1005427	W 105188	1402962	W 99287	1414380	AUT MACH APP ELEC NDA
78	ROAD VEHICLES		22773021		26647873		31377022		31618599	VEHICULES ROUTIERS
781	PASS MOTOR VEH EXC BUSES	W 1318765	12299040	W 1447587	13789468	W 1357653	15212202	W 1449977	15803789	AUTO TRANSPORT PERSONNES
782	LORRIES,SPCL MTR VEH NES	W 194275	1309250	W 232062	1790433	W 289709	2434330	W 286414	2456959	VEHICULES SPECIAUX,MARCH

5. Special Exports F.O.B. by Commodities according to the S.I.T.C. (Rev. 2) in thousand U.S. Dollars
Exportations Spéciales F.O.B. par Produits d'après la C.T.C.I. (Rév. 2) en milliers de Dollars E.U.

SITC CTCI	COMMODITY	1993 WEIGHT POIDS	1993 VALUE VALEUR	1994 WEIGHT POIDS	1994 VALUE VALEUR	1995 WEIGHT POIDS	1995 VALUE VALEUR	1996 WEIGHT POIDS	1996 VALUE VALEUR	PRODUIT
7821	LORRIES,TRUCKS	W 179183	1149751	W 217180	1641399	W 272017	2226150	W 266822	2237835	VEHICULES TRANSP MARCHAND
783	ROAD MOTOR VEHICLES NES	W 80274	416609	W 115951	839516	W 208421	2240058	W 192728	1907951	VEHICULES ROUTIERS NDA
7832	TRACTORS FOR TR–TRAILERS	W 68970	300507	W 103637	714254	W 192214	2073056	W 174515	1763253	TRACTEURS ROUTIERS
784	MOTOR VEH PRTS,ACCES NES	W 1416740	7929908	W 1214006	9294264	W 1265663	10323632	W 1339267	10346541	PIECES 722,781,782,783
7849	OTHER MOTOR VEHCL PARTS	W 1399426	7778846	W 1190619	9098043	W 1234343	10021198	W 1309146	10069874	PIECES 722,781,782,783
79	OTHR TRANSPORT EQUIPMENT		11295350		13035490		15970285		15577293	AUTRE MATERIEL TRANSPORT
791	RAILWAY VEHICLES	W 57090	553150	W 85189	1233325	W 70359	644238	W 79851	489847	VEHIC MAT CHEMINS DE FER
792	AIRCRAFT ETC	W 13979	9819492	W 16094	11080119	W 16656	13548371	W 45070	13223888	APP NAVIGATION AERIENNE
7923	AIRCRFT NES2000–15000KG	W 941	807511	W 1156	1216135	W 1178	1180926	W 1048	1161319	AERODYNES 2000 A 15000 KG
7924	AIRCRFT NES OVER 15000KG	W 9496	7378872	W 10836	7865368	W 11132	10058932	W 11462	7679595	AERODYNES PLUS 15000 KG
7928	AIRCRAFT NES,ASSOC EQUIP	W 217	47669	W 76	6996	W 235	20083	W 20551	1214984	APP NAVIG AERIENNE NDA
79283	AIRCRAFT LAUNCHERS ETC	W 200	43728	W 55	5495	W 211	19167	W 20500	1212466	CATAPULTES
7929	AIRCRAFT PARTS NES	W 2968	1376511	W 3658	1800365	W 3724	2057605	W 11693	2899642	PIECES DU 792
793	SHIPS AND BOATS ETC	W 415763	922707	W 292991	722046	W 795429	1777676	W 226241	1863558	NAVIRES BATEAUX,ETC
7932	SHIPS AND BOATS NES	W 378125	826172	W 248219	648269	W 761211	1414175	W 196924	1054496	NAVIRES ET BATEAUX
8	MISC MANUFACTURED GOODS		21780987		23918714		28166613		28201187	ART MANUFACTURES DIVERS
812	*PLUMBG,HEATNG,LGHTNG EQ	W 139827	858626	W 162480	988064	W 166151	1143213	W 181461	1162157	APPAR SANITAIRES CHAUFFAGE
821	*FURNITURE,PARTS THEREOF	W 292056	1648593	W 363036	1807876	W 340201	2080240	W 372888	2197506	MEUBLES ET PIECES
8219	FURNITURE AND PARTS NES	W 184324	862061	W 234419	948833	W 212340	1076868	W 239453	1136876	AUTRES MEUBLES ET PIECES
831	*TRAVEL GOODS,HANDBAGS	W 17797	771203	W 20749	972426	W 22977	1206797	W 22035	1232511	ARTICLES DE VOYAGE ETC
84	CLOTHING AND ACCESSORIES		4561996		4975405		5622420		5529808	VETEMENTS
843	WOMENS OUTERWEAR NONKNIT	W 37389	1720271	W 29395	1910364	W 28492	2116202	W 27178	2038336	VET DESSUS FEMMES MAT TEX
8439	— OTHER OUTER GARMENTS	W 23553	1070870	W 19264	1208960	W 17615	1321589	W 17453	1276714	AUT VET DES FEM MAT TEXT
845	OUTERWEAR KNIT NONELASTC		1010087	W 23416	1039622	W 21199	1141496	W 22176	1166416	VET DESSOUS,ACCES BONNET
846	UNDER GARMENTS KNITTED	W 15428	716820	W 14703	798935	W 15551	970182	W 18890	978393	SOUS VETS DE BONNETERIE
851	*FOOTWEAR	W 46682	954233	W 44298	958672	W 41724	1038561	W 39137	952345	CHAUSSURES
85102	FOOTWEAR LEATHER	W 33335	744196	W 31477	756777	W 29348	823956	W 27285	762418	CHAUS SEMELLES EN CUIR
87	PRECISION INSTRUMNTS NES		3183954		3462960		4307759		4365524	INSTRUM,APPAR SCIENT NDA
874	MEASURNG,CONTROLNG INSTR		2368232	W 38011	2515502	W 36405	3038461	W 36410	3038954	INSTRUMENTS DE MESURE
88	PHOTO EQU,OPTICL GDS ETC		1933787		2067961		2244725		2278323	APP,FOURN PHOTO,OP,MONTR
882	PHOTO,CINEMA SUPPLIES	W 66452	856863	W 73394	904389	W 76186	981594	W 75023	1050723	PRODUITS PHOTO,CINEMA
8822	PHOTO FILM EXC DEV CINMA	W 41239	781157	W 44832	825316	W 46856	891661	W 46075	950589	PLAQUES,PELLICULES,FILMS
89	MISC MANUFCTRD GOODS NES		7868595		8685350		10522900		10483015	ART MANUFACTURES DIVERS
892	PRINTED MATTER	W 279049	1474828	W 268853	1601646	W 314690	2004252	W 331892	1904874	IMPRIMES
893	ARTICLES OF PLASTIC NES		2421403		2698508		3458248		3452081	OUVRAGES EN MAT DIVIS 58
8931	PLSTC PACKG CONTNRS,LIDS	W 159586	748135	W 230321	812580	W 203947	965775	W 201526	938945	ART TRANSP EMBALLAGE ETC
8939	MISC PLASTIC ARTICLES	W 337496	1578705	W 365395	1788625	W 446930	2377444	W 406543	2398402	ART DIVERS EN MAT DIV 58
89399	OTHR PLASTC ARTICLES NES	W 279457	1410142	W 304919	1609499	W 382090	2155473	W 342958	2180966	AUT OUV MAT DIV 58
894	TOYS,SPORTING GOODS,ETC	W 88010	969741	W 90842	1061560	W 94410	1175150	W 90206	1107235	VOITURES ENFANTS,JOUETS
897	GOLD,SILVER WARE,JEWELRY		712312		785273		802255		844011	BIJOUTERIE,ORFEVRERIE
898	MUSICAL INSTRUMENTS,PTS	W 48121	770741	W 53576	848474		1163888		1157444	INSTRUMENTS DE MUSIQUE
8983	SOUND RECRDNG TAPE,DISCS	W 45001	684010	W 52572	756371	W 65483	1058643	W 63275	1050878	SUPPORTS SON POUR 763
899	OTHER MANUFACTURED GOODS		751456		814255		970247		988840	AUT ART MANUF DIVERS NDA
9	GOODS NOT CLASSD BY KIND		596755		653862		8257534		1887918	ART TRANSACT NON CLASSES
931	*SPECIAL TRANSACTIONS	W 22	176	W 14207	38405	W 8664404	7684213		1174779	TRANS.SPECIALES

FOOT NOTES – NOTES

TABLE 1 –

1 The gold trade includes crude gold, gold specie and partly–worked gold.

TABLEAU 1 –

1 Le commerce d'or comprend l'or brut, les monnaies en or et l'or partiellement travaillé.

1. HISTORICAL SERIES, 1960–1995 SPECIAL TRADE, IMPORTS C.I.F., EXPORTS F.O.B.
SERIES HISTORIQUES, 1960–1995 COMMERCE SPECIAL, IMPORTATIONS C.A.F., EXPORTATIONS F.O.B

YEAR ANNEE	VALUE IN MILLION FRANCS VALEUR EN MILLION FRANCS MERCHANDISE –MARCHANDISE		GOLD –OR		CONVERSION FACTORS U.S. CENTS PER FRANC FACTEURS DE CONVERSION CENTS E.U. PAR FRANC		INDEX NUMBERS –INDICES QUANTUM		UNIT VALUE VALEUR UNITAIRE	
	IMPORTS	EXPORTS	IMPORTS	EXPORTS	IMPORTS	EXPORTS	IMPORTS	EXPORTS	IMPORTS	EXPORTS
1960	37.20	2.30			20.2600	20.2600				
1961	37.50	2.30			20.2600	20.2600				
1962	52.20	2.30			20.2600	20.2600				
1963	55.80	4.50			20.2600	20.2600				
1964	78.80	3.40			20.2600	20.2600				
1965	99.10	14.30			20.5500	20.5500				
1966	137.30	20.90			20.5500	20.5500				
1967	207.90	28.20			20.5500	20.5500				
1968	257.00	28.10			20.5500	20.5500				
1969	258.70	28.00			19.4794	18.9550				
1970	252.00	23.80			18.0044	18.0044				
1971	217.40	14.80			18.0720	18.0749				
1972	228.10	23.30			19.8329	19.8782				
1973	250.30	23.20			22.5918	22.7260				
1974	271.20	7.00			20.9748	20.7176				
1975	307.20	10.60			23.3586	23.4130				
1976	412.40	19.00			20.8235	20.9980				
1977	705.70	35.60			20.4012	20.4254				
1978	860.90	33.30			22.2232	22.2432				
1979	1067.10	70.50			23.5240	23.6498				
1980	1077.80	105.40			23.6571	23.7253				
1981	1355.40	192.10			18.4377	18.4342				
1982	1643.00	211.90			15.2234	15.4922				
1983	2136.60	294.10			13.0384	12.9147				
1984	2156.10	326.70			11.5171	11.4456				
1985	2287.10	330.90			11.2527	11.1439				
1986	2056.56	225.53			14.3237	14.3113				
1987	2371.92	323.73			16.6224	16.6294				
1988	3038.44	305.88			16.6942	16.7439				
1989	3618.04	362.54			15.7016	15.6627				
1990	4278.28	505.72			18.3502	18.3170				
1991	4336.33	392.86			17.7452	17.7931				
1992	3554.31	508.11			18.8360	18.8420				
1993	2977.76	543.08			17.5816	17.4952				
1994	3746.11	757.20			18.0367	17.9947				
1995	3750.00	653.63			20.0647	19.9815				

2. IMPORTS BY BROAD ECONOMIC CATEGORY AND EXPORTS BY INDUSTRIAL ORIGIN. (PERCENTAGE OF TOTAL VALUE)
IMPORTATIONS PAR CATEGORIES ECONOMIQUES ET EXPORTATIONS PAR BRANCHE D'ACTIVITE.(EN POURCENTAGE DE LA VALEUR TOTALE)

IMPORTS – IMPORTATIONS

	1990	1991	1992	1993	1994	1995	1996
TOTAL IMPORTS–IMPORTATIONS TOTALES	100.	100.	100.	100.	100.	100.	
1 FOOD BEV–ALIMENTATION BOISSONS	14.1	13.9	16.6	17.8	16.7	17.3	
11 PRIMARY–PRODUITS DE BASE	4.2	4.1	4.8	5.2	4.6	4.7	
111 FOR INDUSTRY–POUR L'INDUSTRIE	0.2	0.2	0.2	0.3	0.2	0.3	
112 FOR HOUSEHOLDS–POUR LES MENAGES	4.0	3.8	4.6	4.9	4.4	4.4	
12 PROCESSED–PRODUITS ELABORES	9.9	9.8	11.7	12.6	12.0	12.6	
121 FOR INDUSTRY–POUR L'INDUSTRIE	0.7	0.7	0.8	0.9	0.7	0.7	
122 FOR HOUSEHOLDS–POUR LES MENAGES	9.2	9.1	11.0	11.8	11.3	11.9	
2 IND SUPPLIES–APPROV INDUSTRIELS	22.7	20.6	19.9	15.8	16.9	15.8	
21 PRIMARY–PRODUITS DE BASE	0.4	0.3	0.3	0.3	0.3	0.2	
22 PROCESSED–PRODUITS ELABORES	22.3	20.3	19.6	15.5	16.6	15.5	
3 FUELS–COMBUSTIBLES	7.6	8.2	8.6	2.7	6.8	5.3	
31 PRIMARY–PRODUITS DE BASE	0.3	0.2	0.2	0.1	0.1	0.2	
32 PROCESSED–PRODUITS ELABORES	7.4	8.0	8.4	2.6	6.7	5.1	
321 MOTOR SPIRIT–ESSENCE	7.3	8.0	8.4	2.5		0.2	
322 OTHER–AUTRES	0.0	0.0	0.0	0.0	6.7	4.9	
4 MACHINERY–EQUIPEMENT	26.4	24.2	19.1	25.1	18.3	15.3	
41 CAPITAL EQUIPMENT–MACHINES	24.8	22.2	16.9	23.1	16.1	13.2	
42 PARTS–PIECES ACCESSOIRES	1.5	2.0	2.1	2.0	2.2	2.2	
5 TRANSPORT–TRANSPORT	13.1	14.3	14.7	15.5	20.4	25.5	
51 PASSENGER CARS–AUTOMOBILES	4.2	4.5	3.0	4.3	4.7	5.3	
52 OTHER–AUTRES	5.3	5.4	6.7	4.6	4.7	5.5	
521 INDUSTRIAL–INDUSTRIELS	4.8	4.9	6.1	4.0	4.1	4.9	
522 NON INDUSTRIAL–NON INDUSTRIEL	0.5	0.6	0.6	0.5	0.6	0.6	
53 PARTS–PIECES ACCESSOIRES	3.6	4.3	5.0	6.6	11.1	14.8	
6 CONSUM GOODS–BIENS CONSOMMATION	14.6	15.6	17.7	17.1	16.4	17.8	
61 DURABLE–DURABLES	4.6	4.8	5.6	4.3	4.1	5.1	
62 SEMI DURABLE–SEMI DURABLES	6.1	6.6	7.1	7.1	7.2	7.5	
63 NON DURABLE–NON DURABLES	3.9	4.2	5.0	5.7	5.1	5.2	
7 GOODS NES–BIENS NDA	1.6	3.3	3.4	5.9	4.6	3.0	

EXPORTS – EXPORTATIONS

	1990	1991	1992	1993	1994	1995	1996
TOTAL EXPORTS–EXPORTATIONS TOTALES	100.	100.	100.	100.	100.	100.	
1 AGRICULTURE	65.3	64.7	53.1	42.0	32.1	37.5	
2 MINING QUARRY–INDUS EXTRACTIVES	0.1	0.1	0.0	0.0	0.0		
3 MANUFACTURING–IND MANUFACTUR	34.6	35.2	46.9	58.0	67.9	62.5	
31 FOOD BEV TOBACCO–ALIM BOISS TAB	2.5	3.4	4.2	1.7	1.2	1.4	
32 TEXTILES–INDUSTRIES TEXTILES	0.2	0.5	0.3	0.4	7.6	0.4	
33 WOOD & PRODUCTS–BOIS & PRODUITS	4.8	2.7	1.5	0.7	1.7	1.1	
34 PAPER & PRODUCTS–PAPIER & PRODT	0.1	1.2	0.4	0.2	0.2	0.1	
35 CHEMICALS–INDUSTRIES CHIMIQUES	2.4	2.2	0.3	0.6	1.0	1.9	
36 NON METAL MIN–MIN NON METAL	0.0	0.1	0.0	0.1	0.1	0.0	
37 BASIC METAL–IND METAL BASE	0.2	0.2	0.3	0.2	0.3	0.3	
38 METAL MANUF–MANUF METAL	23.9	24.6	39.5	53.8	55.7	57.2	
39 OTH MANUF IND–AUTRES MANUF	0.4	0.3	0.4	0.4	0.1	0.1	

3. TRADE BY PRINCIPAL COUNTRIES OF PRODUCTION AND LAST CONSIGNMENT (VALUE IN THOUSAND U.S. DOLLARS)
ECHANGES SELON LES PRINCIPAUX PAYS DE PRODUCTION ET DE DERNIERE CONSIGNATION (VALEUR EN MILLIERS DE DOLLARS EU)

COUNTRIES–PAYS	SPECIAL IMPORTS C.I.F. IMPORTATIONS SPECIALES C.A.F				
	1991	1992	1993	1994	1995
World	772962	717940	546287	675635	783251
Africa	1371	1226	810	2812	1953
Americas	106846	110269	51033	85191	95283
Northern America	20083	21644	14623	19532	28697
LAIA	10224	15056	11828	11132	14885
CACM	10	16	3	4	182
Caribbean	76407	73229	24446	54095	50937
Rest of America	122	324	134	428	582
As.ex F.USSR	37104	33569	23470	26467	29166
Eur.x F.USSR	618976	563873	452969	528239	606779
EU	614592	561181	451267	526418	602152
EFTA	2572	1673	1185	1376	3766
East Europe	814	632	324	193	401
Other Europe	999	39	14	45	27
Former USSR	296	184	42	63	3276
Oceania	710	1098	898	914	1025
France,Monac	474642	468991	376100	410134	475809
Trinidad and Tobago	59425	60245	14621	44712	40226
Italy/Italie	40755	22113	18018	39921	38060
Germany/Allemagne	53265	15040	14848	26347	21343
USA/Etats–Unis d'Amer	19720	21433	14446	19264	26197
Belgium–Luxembourg	11052	11081	17198	22035	32480
Japan/Japon	22090	18411	12607	11585	11329
Netherlands/Pays–Bas	19420	17166	10257	11077	16680
Brazil/Brésil	7256	8178	8709	7810	8441
Martinique	12703	9203	6060	5313	6797
United Kingdom		10819	7528	7932	7849
Spain/Espagne	9691	6621	3300	3691	5676
China/Chine	4320	4571	3260	4275	4976
Venezuela	2144	4592	2640	2963	5835
Guadeloupe	2761	3322	3585	3129	3056
Korea, Republic of	1593	1678	1968	4609	5844
Denmark/Danemark	1699	1904	1520	1705	1945
Sweden/Suède	1772	1133	1217	2276	787
Thailand/Thaïlande	1860	1492	1315	881	1360
Portugal	637	4684	564	391	571
Hong Kong	1672	1479	923	952	1091
Switz.Liecht	1627	1066	726	922	1103
Norway,SVD,JM	917	568	459	454	2655
Singapore/Singapour	1255	1620	507	557	767
New Zealand	619	1013	858	857	1007
Morocco/Maroc	475	427	280	2076	875
Malaysia/Malaisie	520	913	695	871	653
Russian Federation		182	38	63	3273
Canada	350	212	177	267	2500
Austria/Autriche	530	467	303	550	701
Indonesia/Indonésie	196	417	241	506	914
Netherlands Antilles	1042	23		510	516
Chile/Chili	169	1646	101	39	47
Ireland/Irlande	714	418	357	245	151
Turkey/Turquie	804	154	135	298	332
Suriname/Suriname	116	253	129	386	542
India/Inde	236	250	159	461	247
Finland/Finlande	287	663	34	88	71
Tunisia/Tunisie	129	171	89	347	402
Argentina/Argentine	341	315	169	17	248
Fm Yugoslav	985				
Slovenia/Slovénia		2	179	206	432
Israel/Israël	128	268	77	97	216
Jamaica/Jamaïque	259	174	18	195	73
Czechoslovakia	389	244			
Reunion/Réunion	23	148	150	176	135
So. Africa Customs Un	165	241	92	1	123
Romania/Roumanie	206	79	84	49	102
Poland/Pologne	120	135	107	48	90
Philippines	142	88	92	69	89

COUNTRIES–PAYS	SPECIAL EXPORTS F.O.B. EXPORTATIONS SPECIALES F.O.B.				
	1991	1992	1993	1994	1995
Monde	69974	102109	102139	148861	158168
Afrique	17	88	7	5	436
Amériques	14418	17836	17196	28208	26097
Amérique du Nord	372	1796	2209	7469	1660
ALAI	330	787	339	2851	2721
MCAC			17	25	
Caraïbes	13666	15218	14543	17839	21048
Autre Amérique	49	35	89	24	669
Asie l'URSS exclus	120		40		
Europe l'URSS exclus	55420	84153	84856	120596	131635
UE	54574	81484	80236	115064	122752
AELE	846	2669	4620	5532	8883
Europe de l'Est					
Autre de l'Europe					
Ancienne URSS					
Océanie		32	26	25	
France,Monac	41822	71496	72768	106648	109145
Guadeloupe	7801	9367	9772	10207	13363
Martinique	5758	5686	4669	7619	7676
Switz.Liecht	845	2664	4620	5532	8867
Italy/Italie	4701	699	2320	2836	4180
USA/Etats–Unis d'Amer	309	1726	1944	7467	1658
Belgium–Luxembourg	484	1082	2172	467	5019
Brazil/Brésil	326	766	339	2848	2721
United Kingdom		5009	409	1357	97
Germany/Allemagne	5033	403	36	271	965
Netherlands/Pays–Bas	1436	1814	735	1654	566
Spain/Espagne	679	437	692	1031	2623
Portugal	356	346	1006		
Suriname/Suriname	46	21	83	24	617
Denmark/Danemark	62	139	92	314	158
Gabon	17	63	6		303
Austria/Autriche				376	
Canada	4	70	227	3	2
Haiti/Haïti	60	103	102		
Japan/Japon	120				
Sweden/Suède			6	112	
So. Africa Customs Un					82
Bermuda/Bermudes	34		38		
Panama	4	14	6		46
Finland/Finlande		61			
Tunisia/Tunisie					40
Hong Kong			30		
Venezuela	4	22		3	
Norway,SVD,JM	1	5			16
Reunion/Réunion		6			10
Jamaica/Jamaïque				13	
Trinidad and Tobago	9				3
India/Inde			10		
Netherlands Antilles	5	2			
Guyana					6
Dominican Republic					5
Madagascar			1		1

(VALUE AS PERCENTAGE OF WORLD TOTAL)(VALEURS EN POURCENTAGE DU TOTAL MONDIAL)

	1986	1987	1988	1989	1990	1991	1992	1993	1994	1995
Africa	0.3	0.3	0.2	0.2	0.3	0.2	0.2	0.1	0.4	0.2
Americas	18.0	17.6	14.1	15.9	13.3	13.8	15.4	9.3	12.6	12.2
Northern America	6.0	4.5	3.3	4.5	3.6	2.6	3.0	2.7	2.9	3.7
LAIA	1.3	1.0	1.3	1.2	1.1	1.3	2.1	2.2	1.6	1.9
CACM	0.0	0.0	0.0	0.0	0.0	0.0	0.0	0.0	0.0	0.0
Caribbean	10.2	11.7	9.3	10.0	8.6	9.9	10.2	4.5	8.0	6.5
Rest of America	0.4	0.4	0.2	0.1	0.0	0.0	0.0	0.0	0.1	0.1
As.ex F.USSR	5.5	5.0	5.3	4.6	3.9	4.8	4.7	4.3	3.9	3.7
Eur.x F.USSR	75.5	76.1	79.6	78.3	81.5	80.1	78.5	82.9	78.2	77.5
EU	74.9	75.4	78.8	77.5	81.0	79.5	78.2	82.6	77.9	76.9
EFTA	0.3	0.3	0.3	0.3	0.2	0.3	0.2	0.2	0.2	0.5
East Europe	0.3	0.3	0.3	0.3	0.1	0.1	0.1	0.1	0.0	0.1
Other Europe	0.1	0.1	0.2	0.1	0.1	0.1	0.0	0.0	0.0	0.0
Former USSR	0.1	0.1	0.1	0.1	0.0	0.0	0.0	0.0	0.0	0.4
Oceania	0.1	0.1	0.1	0.2	0.1	0.1	0.2	0.2	0.1	0.1
France,Monac	63.0	62.1	64.5	62.3	61.6	61.4	65.3	68.8	60.7	60.7
Trinidad and Tobago	7.7	9.3	6.7	7.3	6.6	7.7	8.4	2.7	6.6	5.1
Italy/Italie	2.9	3.2	3.6	3.6	4.3	5.3	3.1	3.3	5.9	4.9
Germany/Allemagne	3.4	3.4	3.0	3.4	5.9	6.9	2.1	2.7	3.9	2.7
USA/Etats–Unis d'Amer	4.5	4.3	3.3	4.5	3.6	2.6	3.0	2.6	2.9	3.3
Belgium–Luxembourg	1.3	1.2	1.9	2.1	2.8	1.4	1.5	3.1	3.3	4.1
Japan/Japon	4.2	3.2	3.3	2.9	2.3	2.9	2.6	2.3	1.7	1.4
Netherlands/Pays–Bas	2.0	2.0	1.5	1.8	1.4	2.5	2.4	1.9	1.6	2.1
Brazil/Brésil	0.7	0.6	1.0	1.0	0.7	0.9	1.1	1.6	1.2	1.1
Martinique	1.8	1.4	1.4	1.1	1.1	1.6	1.3	1.1	0.8	0.9

	1986	1987	1988	1989	1990	1991	1992	1993	1994	1995
Afrique	0.0	0.9	0.2	0.1	0.6	0.0	0.1	0.0	0.0	0.3
Amériques	59.5	47.2	38.2	29.7	21.8	20.6	17.5	16.8	18.9	16.5
Amérique du Nord	35.8	22.0	16.1	13.9	3.1	0.5	1.8	2.2	5.0	1.0
ALAI	0.5	0.2	0.1	0.1	1.8	0.5	0.8	0.3	1.9	1.7
MCAC								0.0	0.0	
Caraïbes	22.3	24.6	21.4	13.8	15.8	19.5	14.9	14.2	12.0	13.3
Autre Amérique	0.8	0.3	0.6	1.9	1.2	0.1	0.0	0.1	0.0	0.4
Asie l'URSS exclus	15.6	10.7	7.2	1.6	0.6	0.2		0.0		
Europe l'URSS exclus	24.8	41.2	54.4	67.4	76.9	79.2	82.4	83.1	81.0	83.2
UE	23.6	40.9	52.9	67.3	75.9	78.0	79.8	78.6	77.3	77.6
AELE	1.2	0.3	1.5	0.0	1.1	1.2	2.6	4.5	3.7	5.6
Europe de l'Est										
Autre de l'Europe										
Ancienne URSS										
Océanie				0.0	0.0		0.0	0.0	0.0	
France,Monac	22.6	38.4	42.3	48.4	49.3	59.8	70.0	71.2	71.6	69.0
Guadeloupe	13.0	14.3	14.5	10.1	11.0	11.1	9.2	9.6	6.9	8.4
Martinique	9.1	10.3	5.6	3.5	4.2	8.2	5.6	4.6	5.1	4.9
Switz.Liecht	1.2	0.3	1.5	0.0	1.1	1.2	2.6	4.5	3.7	5.6
Italy/Italie	0.0		0.6	3.7	3.3	6.7	0.7	2.3	1.9	2.6
USA/Etats–Unis d'Amer	35.8	21.9	16.0	13.7	3.0	0.4	1.7	1.9	5.0	1.0
Belgium–Luxembourg	0.1	0.0	0.2	0.2	0.1	0.7	1.1	2.1	0.3	3.2
Brazil/Brésil	0.5	0.2	0.1	0.1	1.8	0.5	0.7	0.3	1.9	1.7
United Kingdom	0.3	1.5	2.3	2.4	4.5		4.9	0.4	0.9	0.1
Germany/Allemagne	0.1	0.2	1.3	0.5	0.7	7.2	0.4	0.0	0.2	0.6

4. Special Imports C.I.F. by Commodities according to the S.I.T.C. (Rev. 2) in thousand U.S. Dollars
Importations Spéciales C.A.F. par Produits d'après la C.T.C.I. (Rév. 2) en milliers de Dollars E.U.

SITC CTCI	COMMODITY	1992 WEIGHT POIDS	1992 VALUE VALEUR	1993 WEIGHT POIDS	1993 VALUE VALEUR	1994 WEIGHT POIDS	1994 VALUE VALEUR	1995 WEIGHT POIDS	1995 VALUE VALEUR	PRODUIT
	ALL COMMODITIES		717940		546287		675635		783251	TOUS PRODUITS
0	FOOD AND LIVE ANIMALS		90939		76340		89508		104342	ALIMENTS,ANIMAUX VIVANTS
01	MEAT AND PREPARATIONS		26894		22440		25172		29605	VIANDES ET PREPARATIONS
011	MEAT FRESH,CHILLD,FROZEN	W 6369	19966	W 5796	16303	W 6391	17478	W 6950	20707	VIANDES FRAICHES,REF,CONGE
0111	BOVINE MEAT FRESH,FROZEN	W 1021	6923	W 916	5562	W 1193	6221	W 1160	6973	VIANDES BOVIN FRAI,REF
01112	BOVINE MEAT BONELESS	W 824	5128	W 776	4476	W 1034	5087	W 1040	6186	VIANDES BOVIN DESOSSEES
0113	PIG MEAT FRESH,CHLD,FRZN	W 566	2425	W 555	2038	W 684	2015	W 906	3254	VIANDE DE PORC
0114	POULTRY FRESH CHLLD,FRZN	W 4173	8409	W 3801	7006	W 4064	7822	W 4409	8896	VOLAILLES MORTES
014	MEAT PREPD,PRSVD,NES ETC	W 1416	5823	W 1457	5496	W 1846	6950	W 1772	7828	CONSERVES DE VIANDES
0149	OTH PREPARD,PRESRVD MEAT	W 1093	4417	W 1190	4345	W 1361	4938	W 1349	6036	AUTRES PREP DE VIANDES
02	DAIRY PRODCTS,BIRDS'EGGS		13207		11449		13672		15624	PRODUITS LAITIERS,OEUFS
022	MILK AND CREAM	W 5172	7699	W 4931	6547	W 5568	7278	W 5890	8257	LAIT ET CREME
0223	MILK AND CREAM FRESH	W 3874	3596	W 3723	3108	W 4192	3331	W 4478	3757	LAIT,CREME FRAIS
0224	MILK,CREAM PRESERVED ETC	W 1298	4104	W 1208	3439	W 1377	3947	W 1412	4500	LAIT,CREME CONS,CONC
024	CHEESE AND CURD	W 471	3211	W 495	3534	W 718	4770	W 821	5779	FROMAGE ET CAILLEBOTTE
03	FISH AND PREPARATIONS		5101		3858		4484		5118	POISSONS ET PREPARATIONS
034	FISH,FRESH,CHILLED,FROZN	W 943	2131	W 1079	1819	W 1254	2365	W 1204	2350	POISSON FRAIS, REFRIG,CONG
0341	FISH FRSH,CHLLD,EX FILLT	W 870	1927	W 1008	1649	W 1170	2046	W 1149	2159	POISSON FRAIS,REFRIGERE
04	CEREALS AND PREPARATIONS		12192		11481		13249		14668	CEREALES ET PRODUITS
046	WHEAT ETC MEAL OR FLOUR	W 5368	3087	W 5278	2705	W 5184	2809	W 5464	3067	SEMOULE FARINE,FROMENT
04601	FLOUR OF WHEAT OR MESLIN	W 5367	3086	W 5278	2703	W 5179	2804	W 5459	3062	FARINE DE FROMENT
048	CEREAL ETC PREPARATIONS	W 2239	7564	W 2166	7197	W 2925	9029	W 3278	10018	PREPTNS A BASE CEREALES
0484	BAKERY PRODUCTS	W 939	4053	W 945	3909	W 1211	4681	W 1405	5004	PRODUITS DE BOULANGERIE
04841	BREAD,BISCUIT,COM WAFERS	W 724	3070	W 644	2628	W 812	3242	W 974	3637	PAINS,BISCUITS DE MER
0488	OTH CEREAL PREPS,MALT EX	W 315	1792	W 453	1903	W 732	2772	W 852	3278	EXTRAITS DE MALT
05	VEGETABLES AND FRUIT		13478		9640		12575		14798	LEGUMES ET FRUITS
054	VEG ETC FRSH,SMPLY PRSVD	W 4302	4129	W 3521	3293	W 4495	4428	W 4357	5022	LEGUMES FRAIS,CONG,SECS
056	VEGTBLES ETC PRSVD,PREPD	W 1802	3369	W 1133	2009	W 1547	2804	W 1954	3973	CONSERVES DE LEGUMES
0565	VEGTBLES PRSVD,PREPD NES	W 1658	3085	W 1011	1795	W 1452	2665	W 1818	3810	LEGUMES PREPARES CONSERVE
05659	OTH VEG PRESVD,PREPD NES	W 1577	2896	W 958	1666	W 1350	2441	W 1713	3602	LEGUM PREPAP,CONSERV NDA
058	FRUIT PRESERVED,PREPARED	W 2029	3914	W 1589	2792	W 2048	3451	W 2527	3959	CONSERVES DE FRUITS
06	SUGAR AND PREPS,HONEY		4359		3265		3868		4665	SUCRES ET PRODUITS
061	SUGAR AND HONEY	W 2851	3330	W 2181	2358	W 2709	2847	W 2699	3362	SUCRES ET MIEL
0612	REFINED SUGAR ETC	W 2093	2461	W 1454	1567	W 1915	2163	W 2064	2541	SUCRES RAFFINES
07	COFFEE,TEA,COCOA,SPICES		3353		3430		4012		4653	CAFE,THE,CACAO,EPICES
073	CHOCOLATE AND PRODUCTS	W 276	1584	W 327	1837	W 399	2130	W 415	2445	CHOCOLAT
081	*FEEDING STUFF FOR ANIML	W 7494	4774	W 7657	4211	W 8052	4656	W 7716	4951	NOURRITURE POUR ANIMAUX
0819	FOOD WASTE AND FEED NES	W 7256	4671	W 7080	3972	W 7485	4411	W 7066	4648	DECHETS,ALIMENTS NDA
08199	FODDER NES,INCL SWEETNED	W 7256	4671	W 7080	3972	W 7485	4411	W 7066	4648	PREPARATIONS FOURRAGERES
09	MISC EDIBLE PRODUCTS		7279		6023		7334		9135	PREP ALIMENTAIRES DIVERSES
098	EDIBLE PRODCTS,PREPS NES	W 1833	6485	W 1654	5334	W 2247	6544	W 2652	8299	PREP ALIMENTAIRES NDA
09809	MISC FOOD PREPRTIONS NES	W 985	3800	W 876	3249	W 1328	4304	W 1562	5227	PREP ALIMENTAIRES NDA
1	BEVERAGES AND TOBACCO		35252		28199		30502		39030	BOISSONS ET TABACS
11	BEVERAGES		31194		24464		26237		34335	BOISSONS
111	NON-ALCOHL BEVERAGES NES	W 13848	9701	W 13732	8560	W 15007	9927	W 18290	12682	BOISSONS NON ALCOOLIQUES
11101	WATERS,ICE AND SNOW	W 8097	3701	W 8239	3202	W 8190	3261	W 9665	4235	EAU,EAUX MINERALES
11102	FLAVORED WATERS NON-ALCO	W 5751	6001	W 5493	5358	W 6817	6666	W 8625	8447	LIMONADES,EAUX GAZEUSES
112	ALCOHOLIC BEVERAGES	W 11955	21493	W 8863	15904	W 8814	16311	W 11638	21653	BOISSONS ALCOOLIQUES
1121	WINE OF FRESH GRAPES ETC	W 2536	7546	W 2005	5451	W 2304	6159	W 2757	8409	VINS DE RAISINS FRAIS
11212	WINE OF FRESH GRAPES	W 2385	7116	W 1920	5184	W 2180	5848	W 2671	8073	VINS DE MOUTS DE RAISINS
1123	BEER,ALE,STOUT,PORTER	W 7961	9282	W 5913	7279	W 5486	6910	W 7496	8979	BIERES
1124	DISTILLED ALCOHOLIC BEVS	W 1367	4555	W 890	3085	W 942	3133	W 1303	4152	ALCOOLS,EAUX-DE-VIE
11249	OTH ALCOHOLC BEVS,CMPNDS	W 1089	2943	W 699	1998	W 763	2092	W 1093	2761	BOISSONS ALCOOLIQUES NDA
12	TOBACCO AND MANUFACTURES		4058		3735		4265		4695	TABACS BRUTS FABRIQUES
122	TOBACCO,MANUFACTURED	W 172	4009	W 164	3678	W 162	4212	W 160	4617	TABACS FABRIQUES
1222	CIGARETTES	W 169	3911	W 160	3580	W 157	4107	W 159	4545	CIGARETTES
2	CRUDE MATERLS,EXCL FUELS		2998		1455		2040		1807	MAT BRUTES NON COMESTIBLES
3	MINERAL FUELS ETC		62191		15210		45986		41934	COMBUSTIBLES MINERAUX LUB
33	PETROLEUM AND PRODUCTS		61094		14421		44984		40525	PETROLE ET DERIVES
334	PETROLEUM PRODUCTS,REFIN	W 224411	60473	W 61139	14009	W 201225	43865	W 164139	39930	PRODUITS RAFFINES
3341	GASOLINE,OTH LIGHT OILS	W 224365	60347	W 61121	13916			W 3461	1237	ESSENCES POUR MOTEURS
33419	OTH LIGHT PETROLEUM OILS	W 224365	60347	W 61121	13916			W 64	72	AUTRES HUILES LEGERES
3342	KEROSENE,OTH MEDIUM OILS							W 23193	6088	PETR LAMPANTS,AUT HUIL
33421	KEROSENE INCL JET FUEL							W 23193	6088	PETROLES LAMPANTS
3343	GAS OILS							W 102738	24046	GAS OILS
3344	FUEL OILS,NES							W 32626	5361	FUEL OILS
3345	LUBS,PETROLEUM OILS NES	W 46	126	W 18	93			W 2122	3197	HUILES LUBRIFIANTES
33451	LUBS(HIGH PETR CONT) ETC							W 2081	3056	HUILES LUBRIF,H LOURDES
4	ANIMAL,VEGETABLE OIL,FAT		2363		1891		2483		2838	HUILES,GRAISSES ANIM,VEG
42	FIXED VEGETABLE OIL,FAT		2327		1880		2451		2766	HUILES VEGETALES FIXES
5	CHEMCLS,RELATED PROD NES		45041		36481		46966		57950	PRODUITS CHIMIQUES
51	ORGANIC CHEMICALS		2402		550		2257		3005	PROD CHIMIQ ORGANIQUES
52	INORGANIC CHEMICALS		2234		1995		6318		7271	PROD CHIM INORGANIQUES
522	INORG ELEMNTS,OXIDES,ETC	W 213	1203	W 279	1180	W 528	2762	W 650	3981	ELEMENTS INORGANIQUES
5221	CHEMICAL ELEMENTS	W 91	957	W 216	1043	W 434	2620	W 526	3744	ELEMENTS CHIMIQUES
52211	GASES,EXCL HALOGENS	W 67	863	W 167	885	W 405	2487	W 480	3387	OXYGENE,AZOTE,HYDROGENE
523	OTHR INORG CHEMICALS ETC	W 950	1027	W 923	811	W 1442	3545	W 1852	3281	AUT PRODUITS CHIMIQUES INORG
5231	METAL CMPD OF INORG ACID	W 748	771	W 681	519	W 1255	3367	W 1671	3082	SELS METALLIQUES
53	DYES,TANNING,COLOUR PROD		4960		3592		3795		4423	PROD TEINTURE,COLORANTS
533	PIGMENTS,PAINTS,ETC	W 2431	4840	W 1766	3524	W 2331	3725	W 2261	4370	PIGMENTS,PEINTURES,VERNIS
5334	VARNISHES,DISTEMPERS ETC	W 1338	3637	W 987	2718	W 1135	2793	W 1051	3208	PEINTURES A L'EAU
541	*MEDICINAL,PHARM PRODUCT	K 424637	10545	K 420974	10363	K 523864	12963	K 567005	17203	PROD MEDICINAUX PHARMACEUT
5417	MEDICAMENTS	K 384784	9205	K 374421	9048	K 484141	11008	K 528595	14308	MEDICAMENTS
54179	— CONTNG OTH SUBSTANCES	K 349603	8082	K 360988	8179	K 474238	10604	K 519216	14070	MED CONT AUT SUBSTANCES
55	PERFUME,CLEANING ETC PRD		13079		12928		11838		14314	PROD POUR PARFUM,TOILETTE
553	PERFUMERY,COSMETICS,ETC	W 655	6483	W 666	5989	W 627	5699	W 725	6948	PRODUITS DE PARFUMERIE
554	SOAP,CLEANSING ETC PREPS	W 2480	6190	W 2752	6578	W 3046	5896	W 3420	7071	SAVONS,PRODUITS DETERSIFS
5542	WASHING PREPARATIONS ETC	W 1802	4452	W 1944	4264	W 2209	4369	W 2679	5237	PROD ORG TENSIO-ACT NDA
59	CHEMICAL MATERIALS NES		6729		4687		6076		7129	MAT PROD CHIMIQUES NDA
591	PESTICIDES,DISINFECTANTS	W 552	3196	W 431	2410	W 587	2828	W 531	3325	DESINF,INSECT,FONG,HERB
5911	INSECTICIDES,FOR RETAIL	W 368	2200	W 255	1572	W 427	1931	W 342	2320	INSECTICIDES VENTE DET
598	MISCEL CHEM PRODUCTS NES	W 960	2998	W 521	1998	W 696	2797	W 885	3460	PROD DIV INDUST CHIM NDA
5989	CHEM PRODUCTS,PREPS NES	W 910	2847	W 493	1944	W 650	2653	W 836	3270	PROD PREP CHIMIQUES NDA
59899	OTH CHEM PRODS,PREPS,NES	W 687	2191	W 277	1376	W 452	2075	W 602	2825	AUT PRODUITS CHIMIQUES NDA
6	BASIC MANUFACTURES		113919		64907		85032		92464	ART MANUFACTURES
62	RUBBER MANUFACTURES NES		5104		3784		4025		5841	CAOUTCHOUC MANUFACTURE
625	RUBBER TYRES, TUBES ETC	W 723	4263	W 563	3175	W 659	3557	W 806	5020	PNEUS CAOUTCHOUC VULCANISE
6251	TYRES NEW FOR MOTOR CARS	W 277	1640	W 273	1538	W 354	1885	W 441	2769	PNEUS POUR VOITURES
63	WOOD,CORK MANUFACTRS NES		6413		3148		4567		4308	OUVRAGES LIEGE ET BOIS
634	VENEERS,PLYWOOD,ETC	W 2119	2178	W 1287	1029	W 1658	1399	W 1499	1522	PLACAGES,CONTRE-PLAQUES
635	WOOD MANUFACTURES NES	W 1567	4227	W 1498	2111	W 1506	3159	W 926	2774	ART MANUF EN BOIS NDA

4. Special Imports C.I.F. by Commodities according to the S.I.T.C. (Rev. 2) in thousand U.S. Dollars
Importations Spéciales C.A.F. par Produits d'après la C.T.C.I. (Rév. 2) en milliers de Dollars E.U.

SITC CTCI	COMMODITY	1992 WEIGHT POIDS	1992 VALUE VALEUR	1993 WEIGHT POIDS	1993 VALUE VALEUR	1994 WEIGHT POIDS	1994 VALUE VALEUR	1995 WEIGHT POIDS	1995 VALUE VALEUR	PRODUIT
6353	BUILDERS WOODWRK,PREFABS	W 1382	3601	W 1383	1629	W 1364	2676	W 785	2177	OUVRAGES DE MENUISERIE
64	PAPER,PAPERBOARD AND MFR		10795		9020		10023		12640	PAPIERS,CARTONS & OUVRAGES
641	PAPER AND PAPERBOARD	W 772	1865	W 655	1459	W 841	1737	W 1145	2725	PAPIERS ET CARTONS
642	PAPER,ETC,PRECUT,ARTS OF	W 2010	8930	W 2007	7562	W 2236	8286	W 2452	9915	PAP,CARTONS DECOUPES
6423	EXERCISE BOOKS ETC	W 450	2777	W 443	2145	W 535	2649	W 463	2982	REGISTRES,CAHIERS,CARNETS
6428	PAPER ETC ARTICLES NES	W 861	3880	W 817	3522	W 843	3480	W 960	4216	OUVRAGES EN PATE A PAPIER
64285	PAPER ETC DIAPERS ETC	W 523	2547	W 478	2371	W 501	2530	W 618	3029	SERVIETTES HYGIENIQUES
65	TEXTILE YARN,FABRICS,ETC		6337		4632		5744		9263	FILS,TISSUS,ARTICLES TEXTILE
658	TEXTILE ARTICLES NES	W 335	3039	W 233	2570	W 298	3278	W 448	5930	ART FACONNES MAT TEXTILES
6582	MADE–UP CANVAS GOODS	W 77	628	W 48	271	W 57	400	W 194	2488	BACHES,TENTES ETC
6584	LINENS ETC	W 157	1740	W 112	1801	W 172	2443	W 182	2786	LINGE DE MAISON
66	NONMETAL MINERAL MFS NES		26798		9838		11094		13419	ART MIN NON METALLIQUES
661	LIME,CEMENT,BLDG PRODS	W 155674	18034	W 41100	4124	W 61482	4584	W 59019	4445	CHAUX,CIMENTS MAT CONSTR
6612	CEMENT	W 154825	17011	W 40641	3703	W 61101	4148	W 58394	3900	CIMENTS HYDRAULIQUES
662	CLAY,REFRACTORY BLDG PRD	W 6061	3924	W 3987	2379	W 4415	2530	W 5855	3619	MAT CONST REFRACTAIRES
6624	BRICKS ETC NONREFRACTORY	W 5682	3701	W 3889	2306	W 4298	2449	W 5809	3595	BRIQUES ETC CERAM NON REFR
66245	GLAZED CERAMIC SETTS ETC	W 4749	3009	W 3136	1924	W 3584	2061	W 5106	3114	AUT CARREAUX CERAMIQUE
67	IRON AND STEEL		11342		5474		9156		10736	FER ET ACIER
672	IRON,STEEL PRIMARY FORMS	W 3246	2938	W 802	631	W 2401	2140	W 76	90	LINGOTS FER,ACIER
6727	IRN,STL COIL FR REROLLNG	W 3246	2938	W 802	631	W 2355	2085	W 76	88	EBAUCHES POUR TOLES FER
67271	IRON,SIMPLE STEEL COILS	W 3183	2897	W 789	622	W 2355	2085	W 76	88	EBAUCHES NON EN ACIER
673	IRON,STEEL SHAPES ETC	W 7081	3766	W 3306	1890	W 3364	2092	W 3684	2867	BARRES,PROFIL FER,ACIER
6732	IRON,STEEL BARS ETC	W 5454	2868	W 2273	994	W 1944	939	W 2500	1426	BARRES FER,ACIER
67326	IRN,OTH STL BARS HOTROLD	W 4946	2511	W 1704	723	W 1181	521	W 957	527	BARRES PLEINES FER,ACIER
674	IRN,STL UNIV,PLATE,SHEET	W 1387	1389	W 1231	896	W 1600	1290	W 3361	3467	LARGES PLATS,TOLES
6749	OTH IRN,STL PLATES,SHEET	W 1117	1218	W 862	659	W 1254	1045	W 3266	3339	AUTRES TOLES FER,ACIER
67491	— OF IRON OR SIMPLE STL	W 1114	1206	W 848	644	W 1225	1025	W 3262	3328	AUT TOLES AUTRES ACIER FIN
678	IRON,STL TUBES,PIPES,ETC	W 1595	2628	W 795	1672	W 1542	3104	W 1713	3376	TUBES,TUYAUX EN FONTE,FER
69	METAL MANUFACTURES NES		45811		28262		39095		34333	ART MANUFACT EN METAL NDA
691	STRUCTURES AND PARTS NES	W 6630	25967	W 4031	13337	W 6857	23165	W 4741	14353	CONSTRUCT FER,ACIER,ALU
6911	STRUCTURES,PARTS IRN,STL	W 6142	21801	W 3806	11623	W 6261	19410	W 4202	11498	CONSTRUCT FER,ACIER,FONTE
6912	STRUCTURES,PARTS ALUMNM	W 488	4166	W 224	1715	W 597	3754	W 539	2855	CONSTRUCT ALUMINIUM
693	WIRE PRODUCTS NON ELECTR	W 1332	2320	W 1172	1392	W 1070	1488	W 1773	2342	OUVRAGES FILS METALLIQUES
695	TOOLS	W 308	5101	W 258	3142	W 280	5083	W 449	5365	OUTILS A MAIN
6953	OTHER HAND TOOLS	W 224	3259	W 214	2769	W 207	3666	W 345	3665	AUTRES OUTILS A MAIN
69539	HAND TOOLS ETC NES	W 185	2673	W 189	2241	W 190	2994	W 320	3315	OUTILLAGE A MAIN NDA
697	BASE MTL HOUSEHOLD EQUIP	W 362	2723	W 283	1843	W 389	2387	W 368	2447	ART MENAGE MET COMMUNS
699	BASE METAL MFRS NES	W 1109	6422	W 727	5760	W 685	4684	W 881	7001	ART MANUFACTURES MET NDA
6991	LOCKSMITHS WARES,ETC	W 272	2288	W 159	1489	W 185	1513	W 223	2022	ARTICLES DE SERRURERIE
6996	BASE MTL MISC ARTICLES	W 147	1223	W 106	2196	W 76	794	W 89	1949	ART DIVERS METAUX COMMUNS
7	MACHINES,TRANSPORT EQUIP		250041		243146		280409		329784	MACHINES MATERIEL TRANSPORT
71	POWER GENERATING EQUIPMT		14138		43883		22487		27021	MACHINES GENERATRICES
713	INTRNL COMBUS PSTN ENGIN	W 190	6006	W 159	5464	W 193	5534	W 401	6684	MOTEURS EXPL COMB INT, PIECE
7139	PISTON ENGINE PARTS NES	W 76	3787	W 62	3865	W 69	3420	W 88	3512	PIECES POUR 713.2,3,8
714	ENGINES AND MOTORS NES	W 521	2697	W 836	19206	W 201	10139	W 252	16463	MOTEURS NON ELECTRIQUES
7148	GAS TURBINES NES	W 434	1234	W 88	3510		8			TURBINES A GAZ
71488	OTHER GAS TURBINES NES	W 434	980	W 88	3510		8			AUTRES TURBINES A GAZ
7149	ENGINE & MOTOR PARTS NES	W 87	1463	W 749	15695	W 201	10131	W 252	15972	PIECES 714 ET 718.88
71491	PARTS NES OF 7144,71481		1	W 34	3752	W 9	2979	W 250	15798	PIECES DES PROPULSEURS
71499	PARTS NES,OF 71488,71888	W 87	1462	W 715	11942	W 192	7152	W 2	174	PIECES 714.88 ET 718.88
716	ROTATING ELECTRIC PLANT	W 149	2810	W 219	4736	W 143	1484	W 206	3154	APP ELECTR ROTATIFS,PIECES
7162	AC MTRS,GENRTRS,GEN SETS	W 108	1648	W 167	3198	W 123	1172	W 187	2831	MOTEURS ELECTRIQUES
71622	AC GENERATORS	W 5	133	W 78	1692	W 6	104	W 11	128	GENER COURANT ALTERNATIF
718	OTH POWER GENERATG MACHY	W 253	2419	W 643	14169	W 176	5167	W 5	247	AUTRES MOTEURS PARTIES
7188	WIND,WATER,ETC ENGINES	W 253	2419	W 643	14169	W 176	5167	W 5	247	MOT MACHINES MOTRICES NDA
71889	PARTS NES OF 71881,71882	W 248	2288	W 641	14107	W 175	5152	W 3	205	PARTIES DES POS 718.81,82
72	MACHS FOR SPCL INDUSTRYS		18474		9644		8612		11197	MAC SPECIALES POUR INDUST
723	CIVIL ENGNEERG EQUIP ETC	W 1356	8777	W 743	4023	W 667	3172	W 842	4221	APPAREILS DE GENIE CIVIL
7234	CONST,MINING MACHNRY NES	W 1121	6318	W 682	3463	W 587	2627	W 683	3277	MACH POUR LA CONST, MINES
72342	SLFPRP SHOVELS,EXCAVATRS	W 697	4015	W 434	1958	W 362	1663	W 437	1820	PELLES MECANIQUES
728	OTH MACHY FOR SPCL INDUS	W 707	5976	W 363	3305	W 360	2652	W 353	2225	AUT MACH IND PARTICULIERES
7283	OTHR MINERAL WORKG MACHY	W 510	2818	W 230	1282	W 204	1066	W 150	731	MACH TRIER,CRIBLER,BROYER
74	GENRL INDUSTRL MACHY NES		32468		26154		26766		28037	MACH APP INDUSTRIE
741	HEATING,COOLING EQUIPMNT	W 631	9179	W 524	8189	W 609	7258	W 486	7506	MACH CHAUFFAGE,PIECES
7414	NONDOM REFRIG EQUIPT,PTS	W 200	2122	W 160	1889	W 92	1090	W 165	2072	MAT PRODUCTION DU FROID
74141	REFRIG EQUIP NONDOMESTIC	W 166	1721	W 138	1689	W 78	870	W 131	1613	REFIG INDUSTRIELS
7415	AIR–CONDITIONING MACHNRY	W 336	4703	W 307	3695	W 476	5123	W 271	4385	GROUPES CONDITION AIR
742	PUMPS FOR LIQUIDS ETC	W 180	2382	W 198	1921	W 208	2266	W 239	2251	POMPES MOTO–POMPES
743	PUMPS NES,CENTRFUGES ETC	W 164	3563	W 188	3165	W 143	2821	W 224	4527	POMPES COMPRES,VENT ETC
744	MECHANICAL HANDLING EQU	W 1076	9280	W 840	8320	W 804	8701	W 682	7329	EQUIP MANUTENTION PIECES
7441	FORK LIFT TRCKS,ETC,PTS	W 426	2462	W 192	1201	W 160	746	W 99	781	CHARIOTS POUR USINES ETC
74411	FORK LIFT TRUCKS ETC	W 425	2402	W 191	1199	W 134	688	W 99	781	CHARIOTS POUR LES GARES
7442	LIFTING,LOADING MACH NES	W 434	3799	W 448	3788	W 440	5304	W 210	2220	APP LEVAGE,MANUTENTION
74428	OTH HANDLING ETC MCH NES	W 265	2077	W 190	1776	W 125	2632	W 171	1736	AUT APP LEVAGE ETC
7449	PTS NES OF MACHY OF 7442	W 216	3019	W 200	3330	W 204	2651	W 373	4328	PIECES DU 744.2
745	NONELEC MACHY,TOOLS NES	W 140	3231	W 94	1654	W 127	2375	W 109	2541	AUT MACH NON ELEC,PIECES
7452	OTH NONELEC MCHS,PTS NES	W 107	2310	W 76	1137	W 102	1633	W 81	1553	AUT MACH NON ELEC,PIECES
749	NONELEC MACH PTS,ACC NES	W 278	4833	W 214	2905	W 160	3346	W 252	3883	PIECES MACH NON ELEC NDA
7492	COCKS,VALVES ETC NES	W 197	3537	W 167	2087	W 112	2715	W 168	2708	ART ROB,SIM POUR TUYAUX
75	OFFICE MACHNES,ADP EQUIP		17635		16812		24914		22188	MACH BUREAU TRAIT AUTOM
751	OFFICE MACHINES	W 51	2128	W 53	1708	W 49	1870	W 59	2525	MACH,APPAREILS DE BUREAU
752	AUTOMTIC DATA PROC EQUIP	W 83	8985	W 59	7841	W 105	14723	W 104	9252	MACH TRAIT INFORMATION
7521	ANALOG,HYBRID COMPUTERS	W 1	134	W 4	942	W 16	6315	W 1	91	MACH POUR TRAIT INFORMAT
7522	DIGITAL COMPUTERS	W 21	2621	W 19	3807	W 28	2841	W 25	3172	MACH DIGITALES COMPLETES
7523	DIGITL CENTRL PROCESSORS	W 22	2248	W 8	944	W 16	1876	W 12	1092	UNITES CENTRALES
759	OFFICE,ADP MCH PTS,ACCES	W 44	6522	W 44	7263	W 55	8321	W 47	10410	PIECES DU 751 ET 752
7599	ACCTG,ETC,ADP MCH PTS,AC	W 32	5909	W 32	6655	W 42	7517	W 33	8407	PIECES DU 751 ET 752
76	TELECOMM,SOUND EQUIPMENT		23965		25036		20403		27630	EQUIPMENT DE TELECOM
761	TELEVISION RECEIVERS	W 207	4165	W 90	1883	W 150	2476	W 163	3417	RECEPTEURS DE TELEVISION
7611	COLOUR TV RECEIVERS	W 204	4110	W 89	1829	W 149	2398	W 162	3382	RECEPTEURS COULEUR
762	RADIO BROADCAST RECEIVRS	W 101	2046	W 62	1098	W 125	2360	W 175	3571	RECEPTEURS RADIODIFFUSION
763	SOUND RECORDRS,PHONOGRPH	W 57	2759	W 26	1081	W 31	1678	W 56	3941	PHONO,APP ENREGISTREMENT
7638	OTHR SOUND APPARATUS ETC	W 55	2711	W 25	1040	W 31	1658	W 56	3929	AUT APP D'ENREGIS,REPROD
76381	TV IMAGE,SND RECRDRS ETC	W 33	1983	W 15	707	W 19	1186	W 46	3422	APP ENREG,REPRO IMAG,SON
764	TELECOM EQPT,PTS,ACC NES	W 245	14995	W 548	20974	W 240	13888	W 300	16700	EQUIP TELECOM,PIECES
7641	LINE TELEPHONE,ETC EQUIP	W 49	4903	W 40	4584	W 71	6721	W 97	7102	APP TELEPHON PAR FIL
7643	TV,RADIO TRANSMITTRS ETC	W 10	2409	W 39	4594	W 4	784	W 5	1844	APP EMET TELE RADIO
7649	PTS NES OF EQUIPMT OF 76	W 129	5023	W 441	10775	W 131	5187	W 150	5508	PIECES DE LA DIV 76
76491	PTS NES OF APPAR OF 7641	W 89	2863	W 105	3199	W 83	3240	W 76	2161	PIECES POUR 764.1
76493	TELECOMM EQUIPMT PTS NES	W 39	1990	W 333	7527	W 44	1875	W 64	2629	PIECES 761,762,764.3,8
77	ELECTRIC MACHNRY NES ETC		42196		30796		35529		35916	MACH APP ELECT NDA

4. Special Imports C.I.F. by Commodities according to the S.I.T.C. (Rev. 2) in thousand U.S. Dollars
Importations Spéciales C.A.F. par Produits d'après la C.T.C.I. (Rév. 2) en milliers de Dollars E.U.

SITC CTCI	COMMODITY	1992		1993		1994		1995		PRODUIT
		WEIGHT POIDS	VALUE VALEUR	WEIGHT POIDS	VALUE VALEUR	WEIGHT POIDS	VALUE VALEUR	WEIGHT POIDS	VALUE VALEUR	
771	ELECTRIC POWER MACHY NES	W 225	2934	W 234	2998	W 305	2788	W 99	2053	MACH PROD,TRANS ELECTR
7711	TRANSFORMERS,ELECTRICAL	W 179	1828	W 195	1689	W 270	1985	W 66	644	TRANSFO ELECTRIQUES
772	SWITCHGEAR ETC,PARTS NES	W 518	15451	W 438	11599	W 466	12664	W 377	11584	APP COUPURE,SECT ETC
7721	SWITCHGEAR ETC	W 516	15065	W 438	11543	W 464	12613	W 376	11465	APP COUPURE,SECTIONMNT
773	ELECTR DISTRIBUTNG EQUIP	W 1225	5680	W 960	5607	W 977	4428	W 758	3966	EQUIPMT DISTRIBUTION ELECT
7731	INSULATED WIRE,CABLE ETC	W 1211	5527	W 954	5518	W 973	4292	W 748	3876	FILS,CABLES ISOLES ELECT
775	HOUSEHOLD TYPE EQUIP NES	W 1840	9052	W 873	4807	W 1221	6951	W 1626	9647	MACH,APP USAGE DOMESTQUE
7752	DOM REFRIGERATRS,FREEZRS	W 1040	3874	W 410	1882	W 527	2721	W 653	3903	REFRIG,CONGEL MENAGER
77521	DOMESTIC REFRIGERATORS	W 652	2364	W 310	1351	W 378	1868	W 440	2566	REFRIGERATEURS
7758	ELECTRO–THERMIC APPL NES	W 255	2080	W 132	1096	W 200	1516	W 309	2356	APP ELECTROTHERMIQ NDA
778	ELECTRICAL MACHINERY NES	W 478	6041	W 476	4841	W 568	7419	W 633	7424	AUTRES MACH ELECT NDA
7781	BATTERIES,ACCUMULATORS	W 342	1805	W 365	1663	W 430	1952	W 510	2637	PILES ET ACCUMULATEURS
7788	OTH ELEC MACHY,EQUIP NES	W 37	2372	W 23	1614	W 41	2813	W 35	2726	AUT MACH APP ELEC NDA
78	ROAD VEHICLES		66598		56350		81048		88606	VEHICULES ROUTIERS
781	PASS MOTOR VEH EXC BUSES	W 1912	21676	W 2161	23720	W 2844	31537	W 3444	41275	AUTO TRANSPORT PERSONNES
782	LORRIES,SPCL MTR VEH NES	W 2224	21392	W 1345	13178	W 1375	15728	W 1634	17300	VEHICULES SPECIAUX,MARCH
7821	LORRIES,TRUCKS	W 1743	16481	W 1173	11136	W 1201	12899	W 1480	16552	VEHICULES TRANSP MARCHAND
7822	SPECIAL MOTOR VEHCLS NES	W 481	4911	W 172	2043	W 175	2829	W 154	748	VEHICULES USAGES SPECIAUX
783	ROAD MOTOR VEHICLES NES	W 220	2462	W 52	540	W 153	1636	W 123	1577	VEHICULES ROUTIERS NDA
784	MOTOR VEH PRTS,ACCES NES	W 682	13174	W 631	11969	W 682	20102	W 768	13821	PIECES 722,781,782,783
7849	OTHER MOTOR VEHCL PARTS	W 677	13082	W 626	11927	W 680	20067	W 765	13786	PIECES 722,781,782,783
785	CYCLES,ETC MOTRZD OR NOT	W 365	5328	W 283	3726	W 325	4754	W 379	5901	MOTOCYCLES SCOOTERS
7851	MOTORCYCLES ETC	W 191	2949	W 132	2051	W 143	2465	W 153	3178	MOTO VELO MOTEUR AUXIL
786	TRAILERS,NONMOTR VEH,NES	W 456	2567	W 427	3217	W 781	7291	W 1131	8731	REMORQUES,CADRES,CONTAIN
7861	TRAILERS,TRANSP CONTAINR	W 320	1783	W 351	2857	W 665	6759	W 998	8000	REMORQUES TOUS VEHICULES
78613	CONTAINERS INC ROAD–RAIL	W 160	1069	W 222	2119	W 608	6508	W 852	7129	CADRES ET CONTAINERS
79	OTHR TRANSPORT EQUIPMENT		33410		33744		60082		88566	AUTRE MATERIEL TRANSPORT
792	AIRCRAFT ETC	W 335	20001	W 384	29950	W 733	59358	W 870	83914	APP NAVIGATION AERIENNE
7921	HELICOPTERS	W 6	3942	W 7	997	W 10	2556	W 6	2782	HELICOPTERES
7923	AIRCRFT NES2000–15000KG	W 3	2582							AERODYNES 2000 A 15000 KG
7924	AIRCRFT NES OVER 15000KG		26	W 1	141			W 23	3139	AERODYNES PLUS 15000 KG
7928	AIRCRAFT NES,ASSOC EQUIP	W 42	2923	W 156	19447	W 156	16523	W 92	7206	APP NAVIG AERIENNE NDA
79283	AIRCRAFT LAUNCHERS ETC	W 42	2923	W 155	19438	W 156	16522	W 92	7206	CATAPULTES
7929	AIRCRAFT PARTS NES	W 273	9092	W 217	9082	W 566	40250	W 745	70606	PIECES DU 792
793	SHIPS AND BOATS ETC	W 649	13338	W 164	3788	W 58	702	W 345	4600	NAVIRES BATEAUX,ETC
7931	WARSHIPS	W 62	3390		1					NAVIRES DE GUERRE
7932	SHIPS AND BOATS NES	W 347	9338	W 158	3708	W 27	377	W 314	4416	NAVIRES ET BATEAUX
79321	YACHTS,SPORTS VESSLS ETC	W 73	952	W 47	1881	W 27	377	W 29	496	BATEAUX DE PLAISANCE
79323	OTHER CARGO VESSELS	W 70	5060							AUT BATEAUX TRANS MARCH
79324	FISHING VESSELS ETC	W 204	3326	W 111	1826			W 285	3920	BATEAUX DE PECHE
8	MISC MANUFACTURED GOODS		96101		66060		78546		96966	ART MANUFACTURES DIVERS
812	*PLUMBG,HEATNG,LGHTNG EQ	W 575	3541	W 290	1753	W 357	2393	W 428	2618	APPAR SANITAIRES CHAUFFAGE
8124	LIGHTING EQUIF MENT NES	W 200	2375	W 124	1272	W 148	1869	W 152	1819	APPAREILS ECLAIRAGE ETC
821	*FURNITURE,PARTS THEREOF	W 4196	18380	W 3466	11844	W 2928	11889	W 4071	16877	MEUBLES ET PIECES
8211	CHAIRS,SEATS AND PARTS	W 751	3953	W 631	2043	W 544	2324	W 656	2950	SIEGES ET PIECES
82111	CHAIRS AND OTHER SEATS	W 750	3943	W 626	2006	W 539	2300	W 653	2929	SIEGES
8219	FURNITURE AND PARTS NES	W 3244	13357	W 2660	8846	W 2097	7908	W 3113	12257	AUTRES MEUBLES ET PIECES
82191	METAL FURNITURE NES	W 671	4764	W 353	1993	W 330	1968	W 566	3148	MEUBLES NDA EN METAL
82192	WOOD FURNITURE NES	W 2432	7534	W 2105	6200	W 1564	4795	W 2297	7956	MEUBLES NDA EN BOIS
84	CLOTHING AND ACCESSORIES		12743		10428		12211		14839	VETEMENTS
842	MENS OUTERWEAR NOT KNIT	W 99	3204	W 85	2026	W 146	3565	W 171	4730	VET DESSUS POUR HOMMES
8423	— TROUSERS,BREECHES ETC	W 56	1437	W 50	1012	W 118	2556	W 123	3456	PANTALONS HOMMES MAT TEX
843	WOMENS OUTERWEAR NONKNIT	W 113	3595	W 104	2737	W 122	2959	W 174	4163	VET DESSUS FEMMES MAT TEX
8439	— OTHER OUTER GARMENTS	W 64	2460	W 65	2184	W 89	2532	W 147	3538	AUT VET DES FEM MAT TEXT
845	OUTERWEAR KNIT NONELASTC	W 43	1730	W 64	2188	W 70	2513	W 61	2412	VET DESSOUS,ACCES BONNET
8459	— OTHER,CLTHG ACCESRYS	W 34	1392	W 60	2115	W 65	2432	W 57	2256	AUT VET DESSUS DE BONNE
846	UNDER GARMENTS KNITTED	W 95	2493	W 103	2303	W 102	1647	W 117	1995	SOUS VETS DE BONNETERIE
851	*FOOTWEAR	W 347	5571	W 277	4461	W 299	4899	W 391	7409	CHAUSSURES
85102	FOOTWEAR LEATHER	W 161	3968	W 132	3477	W 201	3844	W 247	5646	CHAUS SEMELLES EN CUIR
87	PRECISION INSTRUMNTS NES		15051		8240		11164		15552	INSTRUM,APPAR SCIENT NDA
872	MEDICAL INSTRUMENTS NES	W 48	2175	W 24	1557	W 61	3566	W 43	2666	INSTR,APP MEDIC–CHIR NDA
87202	OTH MEDICAL INSTRUMENTS	W 38	1772	W 21	1339	W 57	2697	W 40	2400	INSTRUM,APP MEDECINE
874	MEASURNG,CONTROLNG INSTR	W 94	12244	W 60	6249	W 63	6704	W 65	12318	INSTRUMENTS DE MESURE
8741	SURVEYING INSTRUMENTS	W 6	2555	W 3	1427	W 8	1030	W 4	709	INST GEODESIE,TOPO ETC
87412	SURVEY INSTR ETC NONELEC	W 6	2525	W 2	310	W 8	547	W 4	490	INSTR GEODESIE,TOPO ETC
8742	MEASUR,DRAW ETC INST,PTS	W 58	3526	W 23	2232	W 27	1312	W 22	6278	INST DESSIN,TRACAGE,PCS
87421	MEASURNG,DRAWNG ETC INST	W 19	1052	W 23	2222	W 26	1234	W 20	6001	INSTRUM DESSIN,TRACAGE
87429	PTS NES OF INST OF 87421	W 39	2474		10	W 1	78	W 2	277	PIECES DU 874.21
8748	ELEC MEAS,CONTRL EQU NES	W 15	3871	W 10	1686	W 10	2225	W 14	2907	APP ELEC ELECTRO MESURE
87483	OTH ELCTRNC MEAS ETC EQU	W 15	3712	W 9	1429	W 9	1773	W 12	2467	AUT APP ELECTRO DE MESURE
88	PHOTO EQU,OPTICL GDS ETC		4239		3338		3559		4268	APP,FOURN PHOTO,OP,MONTR
89	MISC MANUFCTRD GOODS NES		35173		24801		31202		33842	ART MANUFACTURES DIVERS
892	PRINTED MATTER	W 714	9031	W 543	5985	W 582	6297	W 639	7328	IMPRIMES
8921	PRINTED BOOKS,GLOBES,ETC	W 205	3611	W 203	2989	W 186	3022	W 189	3657	LIVRES,BROCHURES,CARTES
89211	PRINTED BOOKS,PAMPHLETS	W 202	3580	W 201	2939	W 183	2975	W 187	3582	LIVRES,BROCHURES
8922	NEWSPAPERS,PERIODICALS	W 233	2860	W 98	959	W 114	1073	W 148	1316	JOURNAUX ET PERIODIQUES
8928	PRINTED MATTER NES	W 267	2458	W 236	1942	W 273	2111	W 291	2199	IMPRIMES NDA
893	ARTICLES OF PLASTIC NES		12904		8721		12136		13433	OUVRAGES EN MAT DIVIS 58
8931	PLSTC PACKG CONTNRS,LIDS	W 607	2458	W 499	1767	W 556	2044	W 754	3044	ART TRANSP EMBALLAGE ETC
8939	MISC PLASTIC ARTICLES	W 2434	10076	W 1914	6619	W 2407	9866	W 2343	10116	ART DIVERS EN MAT DIV 58
89399	OTHR PLASTC ARTICLES NES	W 2212	9051	W 1724	5964	W 2246	9196	W 2042	9011	AUT OUV MAT DIV 58
894	TOYS,SPORTING GOODS,ETC	W 387	4590	W 409	4480	W 491	5982	W 516	5782	VOITURES ENFANTS,JOUETS
8942	TOYS,INDOOR GAMES ETC	W 220	2940	W 268	3137	W 291	3043	W 339	3814	JOUETS,JEUX ETC
89423	TOYS NES	W 115	1455	W 168	1701	W 185	1746	W 227	2472	JOUETS,MODELES REDUITS
898	MUSICAL INSTRUMENTS,PTS	W 134	3787	W 70	1707	W 92	2357	W 92	2133	INSTRUMENTS DE MUSIQUE
8983	SOUND RECRDNG TAPE,DISCS	W 83	2952	W 64	1580	W 77	2147	W 71	1856	SUPPORTS SON POUR 763
899	OTHER MANUFACTURED GOODS		2326		2137		2258		2743	AUT ART MANUF DIVERS NDA
9	GOODS NOT CLASSD BY KIND		19094		12599		14163		16138	ART TRANSACT NON CLASSES
911	*MAIL NOT CLASSED BY KIN		14699		12028					COLIS POSTAUX
931	*SPECIAL TRANSACTIONS						12537		13303	TRANS.SPECIALES
951	*WAR FIREARMS,AMMUNITION	W 34	4331	W 16	539	W 40	1559	W 52	2799	VEHIC BLINDES ARMES
95106	AMMUNITION NES	W 33	4318	W 16	524	W 40	1524	W 51	2731	PROJECTILES,MUNITIONS

5. Special Exports F.O.B. by Commodities according to the S.I.T.C. (Rev. 2) in thousand U.S. Dollars
Exportations Spéciales F.O.B. par Produits d'après la C.T.C.I. (Rév. 2) en milliers de Dollars E.U.

SITC CTCI	COMMODITY	1992		1993		1994		1995		PRODUIT
		WEIGHT POIDS	VALUE VALEUR	WEIGHT POIDS	VALUE VALEUR	WEIGHT POIDS	VALUE VALEUR	WEIGHT POIDS	VALUE VALEUR	
	ALL COMMODITIES		102109		102139		148861		158168	TOUS PRODUITS
0	FOOD AND LIVE ANIMALS		52359		39763		43679		50848	ALIMENTS,ANIMAUX VIVANTS
03	FISH AND PREPARATIONS		42006		30190		36148		40350	POISSONS ET PREPARATIONS
034	FISH,FRESH,CHILLED,FROZN	W 784	3931	W 1075	4032	W 1160	4879	W 1161	5451	POISSON FRAIS, REFRIG,CONG
0341	FISH FRSH,CHLLD,EX FILLT			W 224	804	W 61	313	W 72	369	POISSON FRAIS,REFRIGERE
0342	FISH FROZEN,EXCL FILLETS	W 718	3619	W 835	3172	W 1093	4524	W 1089	5079	POISSONS CONGELES
0344	FISH FILLETS,FROZEN	W 66	311	W 14	51	W 6	35			FILETS CONGELES
036	SHELL FISH FRESH,FROZEN	W 3801	38075	W 3038	26111	W 3837	31178	W 3677	34877	CRUSTACES,MOLLUSQUES
04	CEREALS AND PREPARATIONS		10145		9426		7161		10206	CEREALES ET PRODUITS
042	RICE	W 19451	10144	W 16843	9424	W 10868	7161	W 13619	10206	RIZ
0421	RICE IN HUSK OR HUSKED	W 13187	6315	W 14123	7923	W 8663	5625	W 11411	8346	RIZ SANS AUTRE PREPARATION
04211	RICE IN THE HUSK	W 6420	2229	W 4297	1416	W 540	217	W 1136	395	RIZ PADDY
04212	RICE HUSKED	W 6767	4087	W 9826	6507	W 8123	5408	W 10275	7951	RIZ CARGO
0422	RICE SEMI–MILLED,MILLED	W 6264	3829	W 2721	1501	W 2204	1536	W 2208	1860	RIZ POLI,GLACE INCL BRISURES
04221	RICE MILLED UNBROKEN	W 2854	2766	W 1239	1158	W 1382	1310	W 1614	1639	RIZ POLI,GLACE EXCL BRISURES
04222	RICE BROKEN	W 3410	1063	W 1481	343	W 822	226	W 594	221	BRISURES DE RIZ
2	CRUDE MATERLS,EXCL FUELS		1683		905		2821		2492	MAT BRUTES NON COMESTIBLES
24	CORK AND WOOD		1588		879		2778		2330	LIEGE ET BOIS
247	OTH WOOD ROUGH,SQUARED	W 1780	392	W 1575	334	W 2129	557	W 2502	965	BOIS BRUTS EQUARRIS
2472	SAW–,VENEER–LOGS NON–CON	W 1266	281	W 1575	334	W 2129	557	W 2502	965	NON CONIFERES SCIAGE,PLAC
24721	— IN THE ROUGH	W 1266	281	W 1575	334	W 2129	557	W 2502	965	BRUTS ECORCES DEGROSSIS
248	WOOD SHAPED,SLEEPERS	W 3313	1195	W 1214	545	W 4625	2208	W 2219	1362	BOIS SIMPLEMENT TRAVAILLES
2483	LUMBER SHAPED NON–CONIFR	W 2748	1042	W 1141	521	W 4569	2180	W 2160	1329	NON CONIFERES SCIES,RABOTES
24831	LUMBER SAWN ETC NON–CON	W 2748	1042	W 1100	514	W 4319	1990	W 1691	968	SCIES LONGITUDINALEMENT
5	CHEMCLS,RELATED PROD NES		226		407		1287		2171	PRODUITS CHIMIQUES
52	INORGANIC CHEMICALS		85		18		789		1461	PROD CHIM INORGANIQUES
523	OTHR INORG CHEMICALS ETC				1	W 121	761	W 215	1411	AUT PRODUITS CHIMIQUES INORG
5231	METAL CMPD OF INORG ACID				1	W 120	687	W 214	1313	SELS METALLIQUES
52314	CHLORATES, BROMATES ETC				1	W 120	687	W 214	1313	CHLORATES,PERCHLORATES
572	*EXPLOSIVES,PYROTECH PRO		26		92	W 2	230	W 1	533	EXPLOSIFS
5722	FUSES,PRIMERS,DETONATORS		19		70	W 1	221		527	MECHES,CORDEAUX,AMORCES
6	BASIC MANUFACTURES		3458		22840		35607		15291	ART MANUFACTURES
65	TEXTILE YARN,FABRICS,ETC		2		4		1900		89	FILS,TISSUS,ARTICLES TEXTILE
657	SPECIAL TXTL FABRC,PRODS		1			W 1001	1894	W 1	4	TISSUS SPECIAUX
6571	FELT AND ARTICLES NES					W 1000	1891			FEUTRES,ART EN FEUTRE
69	METAL MANUFACTURES NES		2766		22323		32958		14608	ART MANUFACT EN METAL NDA
691	STRUCTURES AND PARTS NES	W 179	459	W 123	203	W 76	149	W 252	691	CONSTRUCT FER,ACIER,ALU
6911	STRUCTURES,PARTS IRN,STL	W 179	442	W 122	201	W 66	142	W 252	691	CONSTRUCT FER,ACIER,FONTE
695	TOOLS	W 63	1997	W 510	21764	W 485	32148	W 246	13641	OUTILS A MAIN
6953	OTHER HAND TOOLS	W 63	1995	W 507	21751	W 215	1408	W 207	3975	AUTRES OUTILS A MAIN
69531	HAND SAWS AND SAW BLADES				17	W 1	519	W 1	1	SCIES A MAIN,LAMES
69539	HAND TOOLS ETC NES	W 63	1989	W 506	21734	W 214	878	W 206	3972	OUTILLAGE A MAIN NDA
6954	BLADES,TIPS,ETC FR TOOLS		1		13	W 270	30740	W 39	9665	OUTILS POUR MACHINE–OUTIL
69541	PARTS TO INSERT IN TOOLS		1		13	W 270	30740	W 39	9665	OUTILS DE FORAGE
696	CUTLERY				1		462			COUTELLERIE
69606	BASE METAL TABLEWARE NES						462			CUILLERS,FOURCHETTES
7	MACHINES,TRANSPORT EQUIP		22752		22325		37707		52126	MACHINES MATERIEL TRANSPORT
71	POWER GENERATING EQUIPMT		587		1148		2421		2423	MACHINES GENERATRICES
712	STEAM ENGINES,TURBINES					W 4	747			MACHINES A VAPEUR D'EAU PIEC
7126	STEAM POWR UNITS,ENGINES					W 4	747			MACHINES A VAPEUR D EAU
713	INTRNL COMBUS PSTN ENGIN	W 4	64	W 10	426	W 15	483	W 60	1462	MOTEURS EXPL COMB INT, PIECE
7138	PISTON ENGINES NES					W 2	6	W 56	1332	MOTEURS A PISTONS NDA
7139	PISTON ENGINE PARTS NES	W 2	55	W 7	408	W 3	360	W 1	35	PIECES POUR 713.2,3,8
714	ENGINES AND MOTORS NES			W 14	471	W 65	1115	W 8	610	MOTEURS NON ELECTRIQUES
7148	GAS TURBINES NES					W 45	531		340	TURBINES A GAZ
71488	OTHER GAS TURBINES NES					W 45	531			AUTRES TURBINES A GAZ
7149	ENGINE & MOTOR PARTS NES			W 14	471	W 20	584	W 8	269	PIECES 714 ET 718.88
71499	PARTS NES,OF 71488,71888			W 14	471	W 20	572	W 8	269	PIECES 714.88 ET 718.88
716	ROTATING ELECTRIC PLANT	W 45	480	W 20	246	W 3	76	W 26	344	APP ELECTR ROTATIFS,PIECES
7162	AC MTRS,GENRTRS,GEN SETS	W 37	437	W 20	173	W 2	60	W 16	274	MOTEURS ELECTRIQUES
71623	GEN SETS WITH PISTN ENGN	W 34	328	W 19	104	W 1	4	W 13	153	GROUPES MOTEUR EXPLOSION
72	MACHS FOR SPCL INDUSTRYS		714		2809		638		814	MAC SPECIALES POUR INDUST
723	CIVIL ENGNEERG EQUIP ETC	W 85	206	W 685	1823	W 67	73	W 145	559	APPAREILS DE GENIE CIVIL
7234	CONST,MINING MACHNRY NES	W 85	192	W 599	1710	W 67	73	W 72	313	MACH POUR LA CONST, MINES
72341	SELF–PROPELLD DOZERS,ETC	W 14	21	W 116	521	W 26	52			BULLDOZERS
72342	SLFPRP SHOVELS,EXCAVATRS	W 35	123	W 371	676	W 31	13	W 26	28	PELLES MECANIQUES
728	OTH MACHY FOR SPCL INDUS	W 66	392	W 441	955	W 201	546	W 192	223	AUT MACH IND PARTICULIERES
7283	OTHR MINERAL WORKG MACHY	W 24	91	W 398	857	W 169	368	W 160	140	MACH TRIER,CRIBLER,BROYER
72833	MNRL MIXING,KNEADING MCH	W 24	89	W 155	615					MACH MELANGER MAT MINER
74	GENRL INDUSTRL MACHY NES		1306		1702		925		1431	MACH APP INDUSTRIE
744	MECHANICAL HANDLING EQU	W 415	985	W 291	1321	W 169	458	W 257	687	EQUIP MANUTENTION PIECES
7441	FORK LIFT TRCKS,ETC,PTS	W 207	401	W 198	185			W 116	311	CHARIOTS POUR USINES ETC
74411	FORK LIFT TRUCKS ETC	W 207	401	W 57	173			W 116	311	CHARIOTS POUR LES GARES
7442	LIFTING,LOADING MACH NES	W 183	547	W 187	1104	W 103	233	W 134	349	APP LEVAGE,MANUTENTION
74424	LIFTS AND SKIP HOISTS	W 27	387				17			ASCENSEURS,MONTE–CHARGE
74428	OTH HANDLING ETC MCH NES	W 49	60	W 164	1001	W 70	185	W 44	330	AUT APP LEVAGE ETC
75	OFFICE MACHNES,ADP EQUIP		2644		1954		1939		2580	MACH BUREAU TRAIT AUTOM
752	AUTOMTIC DATA PROC EQUIP	W 5	1098	W 11	844	W 4	522	W 4	670	MACH TRAIT INFORMATION
7522	DIGITAL COMPUTERS	W 2	195	W 10	779	W 2	258	W 3	285	MACH DIGITALES COMPLETES
7528	OFF–LINE DATA PROC EQUIP	W 1	412		17		69	W 1	369	MACH AUXIL TRAIT INFORM
759	OFFICE,ADP MCH PTS,ACCES	W 2	1389	W 3	1068	W 5	1409	W 5	1881	PIECES DU 751 ET 752
7599	ACCTG,ETC,ADP MCH PTS,AC	W 2	1382	W 3	1068	W 5	1407	W 5	1881	PIECES DU 751 ET 752
76	TELECOMM,SOUND EQUIPMENT		1230		1343		934		3155	EQUIPMENT DE TELECOM
764	TELECOM EQPT,PTS,ACC NES	W 6	1019	W 11	1332	W 3	788	W 11	3024	EQUIP TELECOM,PIECES
7641	LINE TELEPHONE,ETC EQUIP	W 4	471	W 5	754	W 1	375	W 2	259	APP TELEPHON PAR FIL
7648	TELECOMM EQUIPMENT NES	W 1	246	W 1	176		95		876	APP TELECOM NDA
76482	TELEVISION CAMERAS			W 1	49		1		610	APP PRISE DE VUES TELE
7649	PTS NES OF EQUIPMT OF 76		45		210		63	W 8	1793	PIECES DE LA DIV 76
76491	PTS NES OF APPAR OF 7641		39		24		23	W 7	1699	PIECES POUR 764.1
77	ELECTRIC MACHNRY NES ETC		925		750		1292		1016	MACH APP ELECT NDA
772	SWITCHGEAR ETC,PARTS NES	W 2	163	W 6	376	W 30	625	W 8	764	APP COUPURE,SECT ETC
7721	SWITCHGEAR ETC	W 2	163	W 6	356	W 30	625	W 8	764	APP COUPURE,SECTIONMNT
776	TRANSISTORS,VALVES,ETC		367		87		30		18	LAMPES,TUBES,VALVES
7764	ELECTRONIC MICROCIRCUITS		367		34		30		10	MICROSTRUCTURES ELECTRON
78	ROAD VEHICLES		1845		2253		7826		9533	VEHICULES ROUTIERS
782	LORRIES,SPCL MTR VEH NES	W 100	308	W 313	1064	W 59	107	W 33	68	VEHICULES SPECIAUX,MARCH
7821	LORRIES,TRUCKS	W 16	99	W 282	944	W 21	78	W 33	68	VEHICULES TRANSP MARCHAND
783	ROAD MOTOR VEHICLES NES				4			W 106	2105	VEHICULES ROUTIERS NDA
7831	BUSES							W 106	2105	VOITURES TRANSPORT COMMUN
784	MOTOR VEH PRTS,ACCES NES	W 3	27	W 9	62	W 9	25	W 830	4899	PIECES 722,781,782,783
7841	MOTOR VEHICLE CHASSIS							W 600	2641	CHASSIS 722,781,782,783

5. Special Exports F.O.B. by Commodities according to the S.I.T.C. (Rev. 2) in thousand U.S. Dollars
Exportations Spéciales F.O.B. par Produits d'après la C.T.C.I. (Rév. 2) en milliers de Dollars E.U.

SITC CTCI	COMMODITY	1992		1993		1994		1995		PRODUIT
		WEIGHT POIDS	VALUE VALEUR	WEIGHT POIDS	VALUE VALEUR	WEIGHT POIDS	VALUE VALEUR	WEIGHT POIDS	VALUE VALEUR	
7849	OTHER MOTOR VEHCL PARTS	W 3	27	W 9	62	W 9	25	W 230	2257	PIECES 722,781,782,783
786	TRAILERS,NONMOTR VEH,NES	W 89	1430	W 87	1044	W 635	7554	W 544	2407	REMORQUES,CADRES,CONTAIN
7861	TRAILERS,TRANSP CONTAINR	W 89	1430	W 84	1041	W 634	7552	W 533	2384	REMORQUES TOUS VEHICULES
78613	CONTAINERS INC ROAD–RAIL	W 87	1426	W 74	901	W 632	7541	W 527	2382	CADRES ET CONTAINERS
79	OTHR TRANSPORT EQUIPMENT		13467		10340		21571		31113	AUTRE MATERIEL TRANSPORT
791	RAILWAY VEHICLES			W 17	353					VEHIC MAT CHEMINS DE FER
7915	FRT,MAINT CARS NOT POWRD			W 17	353					WAGONS DE SERVICE
79152	RAILWAY FREIGHT CARS NES			W 17	353					WAGONS MARCHANDISES
792	AIRCRAFT ETC	W 38	13116	W 93	9876	W 228	21535	W 370	29393	APP NAVIGATION AERIENNE
7921	HELICOPTERS					W 8	14229	W 6	17404	HELICOPTERES
7924	AIRCRFT NES OVER 15000KG				875	W 1	454			AERODYNES PLUS 15000 KG
7928	AIRCRAFT NES,ASSOC EQUIP			W 64	5907	W 214	6069	W 177	1853	APP NAVIG AERIENNE NDA
79283	AIRCRAFT LAUNCHERS ETC			W 64	5907	W 214	6069	W 177	1853	CATAPULTES
7929	AIRCRAFT PARTS NES	W 38	13116	W 25	3060	W 5	782	W 184	10109	PIECES DU 792
793	SHIPS AND BOATS ETC	W 100	351	W 23	111	W 3	36	W 206	1720	NAVIRES BATEAUX,ETC
7932	SHIPS AND BOATS NES	W 100	322	W 23	88	W 3	36	W 69	1195	NAVIRES ET BATEAUX
79324	FISHING VESSELS ETC	W 100	322	W 22	70			W 63	1059	BATEAUX DE PECHE
8	MISC MANUFACTURED GOODS		11654		5477		12116		9751	ART MANUFACTURES DIVERS
84	CLOTHING AND ACCESSORIES		202		322		7854		461	VETEMENTS
842	MENS OUTERWEAR NOT KNIT	W 1	68		14	W 68	7620	W 4	229	VET DESSUS POUR HOMMES
8423	— TROUSERS,BREECHES ETC				14	W 68	7620	W 4	222	PANTALONS HOMMES MAT TEX
87	PRECISION INSTRUMNTS NES		10406		2411		3137		5046	INSTRUM,APPAR SCIENT NDA
874	MEASURNG,CONTROLNG INSTR	W 42	10341	W 4	2310	W 14	2929	W 41	4867	INSTRUMENTS DE MESURE
8741	SURVEYING INSTRUMENTS	W 3	642		1126	W 2	882	W 3	633	INST GEODESIE,TOPO ETC
87411	NAVIG INSTR NONELEC ETC		540		1059		384		492	INSTR NAVIGATION
87412	SURVEY INSTR ETC NONELEC	W 3	102		67	W 2	498	W 3	142	INSTR GEODESIE,TOPO ETC
8742	MEASUR,DRAW ETC INST,PTS	W 11	6476	W 3	902	W 9	1359	W 36	3219	INST DESSIN,TRACAGE,PCS
87421	MEASURNG,DRAWNG ETC INST	W 11	6475	W 3	901	W 9	1341	W 35	2608	INSTRUM DESSIN,TRACAGE
87429	PTS NES OF INST OF 87421		1		1		18	W 1	611	PIECES DU 874.21
8748	ELEC MEAS,CONTRL EQU NES	W 28	3010	W 1	256	W 1	367	W 1	481	APP ELEC ELECTRO MESURE
87483	OTH ELCTRNC MEAS ETC EQU	W 28	2992	W 1	251	W 1	232	W 1	327	AUT APP ELECTRO DE MESURE
88	PHOTO EQU,OPTICL GDS ETC		489		264		325		664	APP,FOURN PHOTO,OP,MONTR
881	PHOTO APPARAT,EQUIPT NES		117		82		260	W 1	642	APP,EQUIP PHOTO NDA
8812	CINEMA CAMERAS,PROJ,ETC		105		30		260		629	APPAREILS CINEMA,PIECES
88121	— FOR FILM UNDER 16MM		105		30		248		609	APP CINEMA MOINS 16 MM
89	MISC MANUFCTRD GOODS NES		464		2378		398		3541	ART MANUFACTURES DIVERS
894	TOYS,SPORTING GOODS,ETC		18	W 26	2058		3	W 22	3369	VOITURES ENFANTS,JOUETS
8946	NON–MILITARY ARMS,AMMO			W 24	2030			W 20	3332	ARMES NON MILITAIRES
89461	NON–MILITARY FIREARMS							W 20	3332	ARMES A FEU
89462	AIRGUNS,TRUNCHEONS,ETC			W 24	2030					AUT ARMES AIR COMPRIME
9	GOODS NOT CLASSD BY KIND		9970		10415		15634		25172	ART TRANSACT NON CLASSES
971	*GOLD,NON MONETARY NES	K 953	9970	K 1834	10318	K 1451	15623	K 2253	25111	OR NON MONETAIRE
97101	NONMON GLD UNWRT,SEMIMFD	K 953	9970	K 1834	10318	K 1451	15623	K 2253	25111	OR,ALLIAGES D'OR BRUTS

1. HISTORICAL SERIES, 1960–1995 GENERAL TRADE, IMPORTS C.I.F., EXPORTS F.O.B. # 1
SERIES HISTORIQUES, 1960–1995 COMMERCE GENERAL, IMPORTATIONS C.A.F., EXPORTATIONS F.O.B

YEAR ANNEE	VALUE IN MILLION C.F.P. FRANCS VALEUR EN MILLION C.F.P. FRANCS MERCHANDISE –MARCHANDISE		GOLD –OR		CONVERSION FACTORS U.S. CENTS PER C.F.P. FRANC FACTEURS DE CONVERSION CENTS E.U. PAR C.F.P. FRANC		INDEX NUMBERS –INDICES QUANTUM		UNIT VALUE VALEUR UNITAIRE	
	IMPORTS	EXPORTS	IMPORTS	EXPORTS	IMPORTS	EXPORTS	IMPORTS	EXPORTS	IMPORTS	EXPORTS
1960	1644.00	1125.00			1.1140	1.1140				
1961	2097.00	1035.00			1.1140	1.1140				
1962	2226.00	972.00			1.1140	1.1140				
1963	2894.00	919.00			1.1140	1.1140				
1964	6391.00	997.00			1.1140	1.1140				
1965	9637.00	920.00			1.1140	1.1140				
1966	14946.00	1560.00			1.1140	1.1140				
1967	10227.00	1167.00			1.1140	1.1140				
1968	15617.00	1039.00			1.1140	1.1140				
1969	10368.00	1303.00			1.0523	1.0821				
1970	13642.00	1840.00			0.9902	0.9902				
1971	14073.00	1749.00			0.9902	0.9902				
1972	14271.00	1341.00			1.0915	1.0934				
1973	16898.00	1497.00			1.2512	1.2638				
1974	25151.00	2775.00			1.1442	1.1530				
1975	22322.00	1969.00			1.2855	1.2859				
1976	25700.00	1911.00			1.1480	1.1481				
1977	29187.00	1464.00			1.1207	1.1188				
1978	33070.00	2978.00			1.2193	1.2288				
1979	36705.00	2215.00			1.2975	1.3011				
1980	42030.00	2340.00			1.3025	1.2899				
1981	53877.00	2861.00			1.0143	1.0098				
1982	62307.00	3349.00			0.8342	0.8339				
1983	74242.10	4820.00			0.7183	0.7147				
1984	85622.80	5083.10			0.6293	0.6211				
1985	88940.00	6564.40			0.6169	0.6193				
1986	92666.99	5112.00			0.7941	0.7941				
1987	90586.98	9095.00			0.9132	0.9143				
1988	87486.72	8111.99			0.9240	0.9212				
1989	91664.00	10308.00			0.8632	0.8616				
1990	91926.00	11011.18			1.0105	1.0048				
1991	93865.33	13148.00			0.9744	0.9686				
1992	86046.00	10184.00			1.0392	1.0494				
1993	86904.99	15183.00			0.9806	0.9766				
1994	87866.00	22286.99			1.0023	1.0147				
1995	91382.98	17548.00			1.1152	1.1186				

2. IMPORTS BY BROAD ECONOMIC CATEGORY AND EXPORTS BY INDUSTRIAL ORIGIN. (PERCENTAGE OF TOTAL VALUE)
IMPORTATIONS PAR CATEGORIES ECONOMIQUES ET EXPORTATIONS PAR BRANCHE D'ACTIVITE.(EN POURCENTAGE DE LA VALEUR TOTALE)

IMPORTS – IMPORTATIONS

	1990	1991	1992	1993	1994	1995	1996
TOTAL IMPORTS–IMPORTATIONS TOTALES							
1 FOOD BEV–ALIMENTATION BOISSONS							
11 PRIMARY–PRODUITS DE BASE							
111 FOR INDUSTRY–POUR L'INDUSTRIE							
112 FOR HOUSEHOLDS–POUR LES MENAGES							
12 PROCESSED–PRODUITS ELABORES							
121 FOR INDUSTRY–POUR L'INDUSTRIE							
122 FOR HOUSEHOLDS–POUR LES MENAGES							
2 IND SUPPLIES–APPROV INDUSTRIELS							
21 PRIMARY–PRODUITS DE BASE							
22 PROCESSED–PRODUITS ELABORES							
3 FUELS–COMBUSTIBLES							
31 PRIMARY–PRODUITS DE BASE							
32 PROCESSED–PRODUITS ELABORES							
321 MOTOR SPIRIT–ESSENCE							
322 OTHER–AUTRES							
4 MACHINERY–EQUIPEMENT							
41 CAPITAL EQUIPMENT–MACHINES							
42 PARTS–PIECES ACCESSOIRES							
5 TRANSPORT–TRANSPORT							
51 PASSENGER CARS–AUTOMOBILES							
52 OTHER–AUTRES							
521 INDUSTRIAL–INDUSTRIELS							
522 NON INDUSTRIAL–NON INDUSTRIEL							
53 PARTS–PIECES ACCESSOIRES							
6 CONSUM GOODS–BIENS CONSOMMATION							
61 DURABLE–DURABLES							
62 SEMI DURABLE–SEMI DURABLES							
63 NON DURABLE–NON DURABLES							
7 GOODS NES–BIENS NDA							

EXPORTS – EXPORTATIONS

	1990	1991	1992	1993	1994	1995	1996
TOTAL EXPORTS–EXPORTATIONS TOTALES							
1 AGRICULTURE							
2 MINING QUARRY–INDUS EXTRACTIVES							
3 MANUFACTURING–IND MANUFACTUR							
31 FOOD BEV TOBACCO–ALIM BOISS TAB							
32 TEXTILES–INDUSTRIES TEXTILES							
33 WOOD & PRODUCTS–BOIS & PRODUITS							
34 PAPER & PRODUCTS–PAPIER & PRODT							
35 CHEMICALS–INDUSTRIES CHIMIQUES							
36 NON METAL MIN–MIN NON METAL							
37 BASIC METAL–IND METAL BASE							
38 METAL MANUF–MANUF METAL							
39 OTH MANUF IND–AUTRES MANUF							

3. TRADE BY PRINCIPAL COUNTRIES OF ORIGIN AND LAST CONSIGNMENT (VALUE IN THOUSAND U.S. DOLLARS)
ECHANGES SELON LES PRINCIPAUX PAYS D'ORIGINE ET DE DERNIERE CONSIGNATION (VALEUR EN MILLIERS DE DOLLARS EU)

COUNTRIES–PAYS	GENERAL IMPORTS C.I.F. IMPORTATIONS GENERALES C.A.F				
	1990	1991	1992	1993	1994
World	929382	913894	893758	852190	880691
Africa					
Americas	101393	112020	121147	117015	122822
Northern America	101393	112020	121147	117015	122822
LAIA					
CACM					
Caribbean					
Rest of America					
As.ex F.USSR	53189	60992	53644	41146	35501
Eur.x F.USSR	479163	433878	406405	393123	394225
EU	479163	433878	406405	393123	394225
EFTA					
East Europe					
Other Europe					
Former USSR					
Oceania	102627	113578	113812	108445	125488
France, Monac	479163	433878	406405	393123	394225
USA/Etats–Unis d'Amer	101393	112020	121147	117015	122822
Australia/Australie	59083	63826	61904	45980	60118
New Zealand	43544	49752	51908	62464	65370
Israel/Israël	42240	46703	44407		
Japan/Japon				41146	35501
Singapore/Singapour	10949	14289	9237		

COUNTRIES–PAYS	GENERAL EXPORTS F.O.B. EXPORTATIONS GENERALES F.O.B.				
	1990	1991	1992	1993	1994
Monde	110661	127239	106767	148951	226156
Afrique					
Amériques	11125	13363	11497	11807	19026
Amérique du Nord	11125	13363	11497	11807	19026
ALAI					
MCAC					
Caraïbes					
Autre Amérique					
Asie l'URSS exclus				62971	103530
Europe l'URSS exclus	32703	61376	36274	51047	73992
UE	32703	61376	36274	51047	73992
AELE					
Europe de l'Est					
Autre de l'Europe					
Ancienne URSS					
Océanie	3437	3983	4154	2832	2760
France, Monac	32703	61376	36274	51047	73992
Japan/Japon				62971	103530
USA/Etats–Unis d'Amer	11125	13363	11497	11807	19026
New Caledonia	3437	3983	4154	2832	2760

(VALUE AS PERCENTAGE OF WORLD TOTAL)(VALEURS EN POURCENTAGE DU TOTAL MONDIAL)

	1985	1986	1987	1988	1989	1990	1991	1992	1993	1994
Africa	0.4	0.3	0.3	0.5						
Americas	11.8	14.6	0.7	12.5	12.5	10.9	12.3	13.6	13.7	13.9
Northern America	8.3	13.8	0.2	11.5	12.5	10.9	12.3	13.6	13.7	13.9
LAIA	0.2	0.4	0.4	1.0						
CACM				0.0						
Caribbean	3.3	0.5	0.0	0.0						
Rest of America	0.0	0.0	0.0							
As.ex F.USSR	15.6	9.9	14.8	9.5	4.0	5.7	6.7	6.0	4.8	4.0
Eur.x F.USSR	60.2	64.6	64.4	65.9	63.3	51.6	47.5	45.5	46.1	44.8
EU	59.8	64.3	64.2	65.4	63.3	51.6	47.5	45.5	46.1	44.8
EFTA	0.4	0.3	0.1	0.3						
East Europe				0.1						
Other Europe				0.0						
Former USSR	2.7			0.0						
Oceania	8.8	8.9	13.8	11.6	10.7	11.0	12.4	12.7	12.7	14.2
France, Monac	46.0	50.1	51.4	53.4	52.3	51.6	47.5	45.5	46.1	44.8
USA/Etats–Unis d'Amer	8.2	13.6		11.3	12.5	10.9	12.3	13.6	13.7	13.9
Australia/Australie	1.7	4.3	7.6	6.3	5.9	6.4	7.0	6.9	5.4	6.8
New Zealand	6.3	4.4	6.0	5.1	4.8	4.7	5.4	5.8	7.3	7.4
Israel/Israël				0.0		4.5	5.1	5.0		
Japan/Japon	4.8	5.1	4.8	4.4	4.0				4.8	4.0
Singapore/Singapour		2.4	2.3	1.0		1.2	1.6	1.0		

	1985	1986	1987	1988	1989	1990	1991	1992	1993	1994
Afrique			0.0	0.0						
Amériques	10.5	11.6	9.7	23.7	13.9	10.1	10.5	10.8	7.9	8.4
Amérique du Nord	10.4	11.6	9.4	23.6	13.9	10.1	10.5	10.8	7.9	8.4
ALAI	0.1		0.1	0.1						
MCAC										
Caraïbes	0.1		0.2	0.0						
Autre Amérique	0.0									
Asie l'URSS exclus	26.8	18.6	38.5	23.1					42.3	45.8
Europe l'URSS exclus	54.3	53.6	46.6	42.5	35.5	29.6	48.2	34.0	34.3	32.7
UE	54.3	53.5	45.8	40.0	35.5	29.6	48.2	34.0	34.3	32.7
AELE	0.0	0.1	0.9	2.5						
Europe de l'Est										
Autre de l'Europe										
Ancienne URSS	0.1									
Océanie	7.6	14.9	3.9	10.6	3.6	3.1	3.1	3.9	1.9	1.2
France, Monac	26.9	52.1	38.5	37.4	35.5	29.6	48.2	34.0	34.3	32.7
Japan/Japon	26.7	18.2	38.5	22.5					42.3	45.8
USA/Etats–Unis d'Amer	10.4	11.6	9.4	18.9	13.9	10.1	10.5	10.8	7.9	8.4
New Caledonia	6.4	14.3	2.9	9.7	3.6	3.1	3.1	3.9	1.9	1.2

4. General Imports C.I.F. by Commodities according to the S.I.T.C. (Rev. 2) in thousand U.S. Dollars
Importations Générales C.A.F. par Produits d'après la C.T.C.I. (Rév. 2) en milliers de Dollars E.U.

SITC CTCI	COMMODITY	1992		1993		1994		1995		PRODUIT
		WEIGHT POIDS	VALUE VALEUR	WEIGHT POIDS	VALUE VALEUR	WEIGHT POIDS	VALUE VALEUR	WEIGHT POIDS	VALUE VALEUR	
	ALL COMMODITIES		893758		852190		880691		1019103	TOUS PRODUITS
0	FOOD AND LIVE ANIMALS				39351		42157			ALIMENTS,ANIMAUX VIVANTS
01	MEAT AND PREPARATIONS				39351		42157			VIANDES ET PREPARATIONS
011	MEAT FRESH,CHILLD,FROZEN		39887		39351		42157		49013	VIANDES FRAICHES,REF,CONGE
1	BEVERAGES AND TOBACCO				19749		19936			BOISSONS ET TABACS
11	BEVERAGES		16302		16258		16327		20442	BOISSONS
12	TOBACCO AND MANUFACTURES		3595		3491		3608		4149	TABACS BRUTS FABRIQUES
5	CHEMCLS,RELATED PROD NES				21367		22482			PRODUITS CHIMIQUES
541	*MEDICINAL,PHARM PRODUCT		21102		21367		22482		29307	PROD MEDICINAUX PHARMACEUT
6	BASIC MANUFACTURES				28349		25849			ART MANUFACTURES
67	IRON AND STEEL		31409		28349		25849		30668	FER ET ACIER
7	MACHINES,TRANSPORT EQUIP		174126		159740		170892		184989	MACHINES MATERIEL TRANSPORT

5. General Exports F.O.B. by Commodities according to the S.I.T.C. (Rev. 2) in thousand U.S. Dollars
Exportations Générales F.O.B. par Produits d'après la C.T.C.I. (Rév. 2) en milliers de Dollars E.U.

SITC CTCI	COMMODITY	1992		1993		1994		1995		PRODUIT
		WEIGHT POIDS	VALUE VALEUR	WEIGHT POIDS	VALUE VALEUR	WEIGHT POIDS	VALUE VALEUR	WEIGHT POIDS	VALUE VALEUR	
	ALL COMMODITIES		106767		148951		226156		196292	TOUS PRODUITS
0	FOOD AND LIVE ANIMALS				1143		883			ALIMENTS,ANIMAUX VIVANTS
07	COFFEE,TEA,COCOA,SPICES				1133		873			CAFE,THE,CACAO,EPICES
07521	VANILLA		489	W 15	1133	W 10	873		1425	VANILLE
2	CRUDE MATERLS,EXCL FUELS				1973		2577			MAT BRUTES NON COMESTIBLES
29	CRUDE ANIMAL,VEG MAT NES				1973		2577			MATIERES BRUTES ANIM,VEGET
4	ANIMAL,VEGETABLE OIL,FAT				1738		3805			HUILES,GRAISSES ANIM,VEG
42	FIXED VEGETABLE OIL,FAT				1738		3805			HUILES VEGETALES FIXES
4243	COCONUT (COPRA) OIL		2155	W 5050	1738	W 7744	3805		2979	HJUILE DE COPRAH
5	CHEMCLS,RELATED PROD NES				1143		1684			PRODUITS CHIMIQUES
55	PERFUME,CLEANING ETC PRD				1143		1684			PROD POUR PARFUM,TOILETTE
553	PERFUMERY,COSMETICS,ETC		955		1143	W 264	1684		1902	PRODUITS DE PARFUMERIE
6	BASIC MANUFACTURES				75901		120830			ART MANUFACTURES
66	NONMETAL MINERAL MFS NES				75901		120830			ART MIN NON METALLIQUES
6671	PEARLS UNSET,UNSTRUNG		44683		75901		120830		10799	PERLES FINES NON SERTIES
8	MISC MANUFACTURED GOODS				1973		2577			ART MANUFACTURES DIVERS
89	MISC MANUFCTRD GOODS NES				1973		2577			ART MANUFACTURES DIVERS
89911	GOODS OF ANML CARVNG MTL		1427	W 181	1973	W 541	2577		2056	ECAILLE,NACRE,IVOIRE ETC
9	GOODS NOT CLASSD BY KIND				2354		2100			ART TRANSACT NON CLASSES
931	*SPECIAL TRANSACTIONS			W 1191	2354	W 892	2100			TRANS.SPECIALES

FOOT NOTES – NOTES

TABLE 1 –
1 Prior to 1983, special trade.
TABLEAU 1 –
1 Avant 1983, commerce spécial.

1. HISTORICAL SERIES, 1961–1996 SPECIAL TRADE, IMPORTS C.I.F., EXPORTS F.O.B.
SERIES HISTORIQUES, 1961–1996 COMMERCE SPECIAL, IMPORTATIONS C.A.F., EXPORTATIONS F.O.B

YEAR ANNEE	VALUE IN MILLION C.F.A. FRANCS VALEUR EN MILLION C.F.A. FRANCS MERCHANDISE –MARCHANDISE IMPORTS	EXPORTS	GOLD –OR IMPORTS	EXPORTS	CONVERSION FACTORS U.S. CENTS PER C.F.A. FRANC FACTEURS DE CONVERSION CENTS E.U. PAR C.F.A. FRANC IMPORTS	EXPORTS	INDEX NUMBERS –INDICES QUANTUM IMPORTS	EXPORTS	UNIT VALUE VALEUR UNITAIRE IMPORTS	EXPORTS
1961	8831.00	13767.00	0.10	97.80	0.4051	0.4051				
1962	10061.00	14535.00	0.30	92.60	0.4051	0.4051				
1963	11874.00	17859.00		266.00	0.4051	0.4051				
1964	13742.00	22253.00		287.60	0.4051	0.4051				
1965	15425.00	23686.00		253.00	0.4051	0.4051				
1966	16209.00	24669.00		212.70	0.4051	0.4051				
1967	16585.00	29516.00		163.00	0.4051	0.4051				
1968	15875.00	30714.00		89.40	0.4051	0.4051				
1969	20127.00	36663.00		56.10	0.3853	0.3853				
1970	22232.00	33662.00		53.90	0.3601	0.3601				
1971	25309.00	49428.00			0.3616	0.3610				
1972	35001.00	50279.00			0.3970	0.3970				
1973	36978.00	63926.00		26.60	0.4641	0.4529				
1974	110626.00	204227.00			0.4175	0.4167				
1975	100559.00	201921.00			0.4681	0.4665				
1976	120238.00	271447.00			0.4163	0.4186				
1977	176000.00	329840.00			0.4071	0.4071				
1978	139174.00	249850.00			0.4277	0.4277				
1979	113108.00	393186.00			0.4704	0.4704				
1980	142310.00	459060.00			0.4733	0.4733				
1981	228600.00	597900.00			0.3680	0.3680				
1982	237500.00	709900.00			0.3043	0.3043				
1983	324900.00	752700.00			0.2624	0.2624				
1984	387950.00	881700.00			0.2289	0.2289				
1985	438400.00	876700.00			0.2226	0.2226				
1986	300000.00	440000.00			0.2888	0.2888				
1987	219900.00	386599.90			0.3327	0.3327				
1988	235700.00	356100.10			0.3357	0.3357				
1989	244600.00	509600.00			0.3137	0.3137				
1990	250000.00	600000.00			0.3688	0.3688				
1991	235400.00	632699.90			0.3545	0.3545				
1992	185200.00	551099.90			0.3778	0.3778				
1993	239300.00	649799.90			0.3832	0.3540				
1994	420000.00	1304900.00			0.1806	0.1800				
1995	440199.90	1354400.00			0.2002	0.2002				
1996	459482.80	1609523.00			0.1955	0.1954				

2. IMPORTS BY BROAD ECONOMIC CATEGORY AND EXPORTS BY INDUSTRIAL ORIGIN. (PERCENTAGE OF TOTAL VALUE)
IMPORTATIONS PAR CATEGORIES ECONOMIQUES ET EXPORTATIONS PAR BRANCHE D'ACTIVITE. (EN POURCENTAGE DE LA VALEUR TOTALE)

IMPORTS – IMPORTATIONS

	1990	1991	1992	1993	1994	1995	1996
TOTAL IMPORTS–IMPORTATIONS TOTALES				100.	100.		100.
1 FOOD BEV–ALIMENTATION BOISSONS				18.3	16.5		18.2
11 PRIMARY–PRODUITS DE BASE				7.0	6.6		6.6
111 FOR INDUSTRY–POUR L'INDUSTRIE				1.2	1.3		1.4
112 FOR HOUSEHOLDS–POUR LES MENAGES				5.7	5.3		5.2
12 PROCESSED–PRODUITS ELABORES				11.3	9.9		11.7
121 FOR INDUSTRY–POUR L'INDUSTRIE				1.7	1.6		2.0
122 FOR HOUSEHOLDS–POUR LES MENAGES				9.6	8.3		9.6
2 IND SUPPLIES–APPROV INDUSTRIELS				22.5	22.0		21.8
21 PRIMARY–PRODUITS DE BASE				1.1	1.1		1.0
22 PROCESSED–PRODUITS ELABORES				21.4	20.9		20.7
3 FUELS–COMBUSTIBLES				1.9	2.4		3.4
31 PRIMARY–PRODUITS DE BASE				0.0	0.0		0.4
32 PROCESSED–PRODUITS ELABORES				1.8	2.4		3.1
321 MOTOR SPIRIT–ESSENCE							0.1
322 OTHER–AUTRES				1.8	2.4		3.0
4 MACHINERY–EQUIPEMENT				28.8	32.6		28.6
41 CAPITAL EQUIPMENT–MACHINES				23.9	26.5		23.1
42 PARTS–PIECES ACCESSOIRES				4.9	6.1		5.5
5 TRANSPORT–TRANSPORT				13.7	14.1		14.1
51 PASSENGER CARS–AUTOMOBILES				4.0	2.6		3.3
52 OTHER–AUTRES				6.0	6.7		5.3
521 INDUSTRIAL–INDUSTRIELS				5.9	6.6		5.2
522 NON INDUSTRIAL–NON INDUSTRIEL				0.0	0.1		0.1
53 PARTS–PIECES ACCESSOIRES				3.8	4.8		5.5
6 CONSUM GOODS–BIENS CONSOMMATION				14.7	12.3		13.5
61 DURABLE–DURABLES				3.1	2.6		2.6
62 SEMI DURABLE–SEMI DURABLES				4.4	4.1		4.3
63 NON DURABLE–NON DURABLES				7.2	5.5		6.6
7 GOODS NES–BIENS NDA				0.1	0.2		0.3

EXPORTS – EXPORTATIONS

	1990	1991	1992	1993	1994	1995	1996
TOTAL EXPORTS–EXPORTATIONS TOTALES				100.	100.		100.
1 AGRICULTURE				3.1	8.9		13.0
2 MINING QUARRY–INDUS EXTRACTIVES				94.3	89.1		83.3
3 MANUFACTURING–IND MANUFACTUR				2.6	2.0		3.6
31 FOOD BEV TOBACCO–ALIM BOISS TAB				0.1	0.0		0.1
32 TEXTILES–INDUSTRIES TEXTILES				0.1	0.1		0.1
33 WOOD & PRODUCTS–BOIS & PRODUITS				0.1	0.1		0.8
34 PAPER & PRODUCTS–PAPIER & PRODT				0.0	0.0		0.0
35 CHEMICALS–INDUSTRIES CHIMIQUES				1.7	1.3		1.9
36 NON METAL MIN–MIN NON METAL				0.0	0.0		0.0
37 BASIC METAL–IND METAL BASE				0.0	0.0		0.0
38 METAL MANUF–MANUF METAL				0.6	0.4		0.6
39 OTH MANUF IND–AUTRES MANUF				0.0	0.0		0.0

3. TRADE BY PRINCIPAL COUNTRIES OF PRODUCTION AND LAST CONSIGNMENT (VALUE IN THOUSAND U.S. DOLLARS)
ECHANGES SELON LES PRINCIPAUX PAYS DE PRODUCTION ET DE DERNIERE CONSIGNATION (VALEUR EN MILLIERS DE DOLLARS EU)

COUNTRIES–PAYS	SPECIAL IMPORTS C.I.F. IMPORTATIONS SPECIALES C.A.F				
	1992	1993	1994	1995	1996
World		774913	707515		898128
Africa		43176	41551		60625
Americas		91381	107689		112971
Northern America		77212	89534		101220
LAIA		14131	6838		7268
CACM		4	7		226
Caribbean		6	50		4222
Rest of America		29	11260		36
As.ex F.USSR		29450	24654		100456
Eur.x F.USSR		539039	482189		617893
EU		533265	478439		611216
EFTA		5186	3130		4433
East Europe		507	572		2226
Other Europe		19	4		2
Former USSR		3255	1238		569
Oceania		1046	2481		1409
France, Monac		370395	281364		384768
USA/Etats–Unis d'Amer		70991	83528		93400
United Kingdom		29405	45138		42836
Netherlands/Pays–Bas		36031	35085		40849
Germany/Allemagne		27821	39691		41093
Italy/Italie		24273	29646		31312
Belgium–Luxembourg		22519	24545		37095
Japan/Japon					53764
Spain/Espagne		11198	11423		21019
Cameroon/Cameroun		6348	12039		12094
Cote d'Ivoire		6301	7588		13706
Thailand/Thaïlande		4341	3335		15316
Morocco/Maroc		10117	4502		6611
Canada		6221	6006		7819
So. Africa Customs Un		3521	4493		9254
Senegal/Sénégal		4395	4612		7624
Nigeria/Nigéria		5820	3006		6440
Ireland/Irlande		4342	4965		5665
Hong Kong		5528	3825		4783
Brazil/Brésil		7317	3738		2868
Viet Nam		4124	5949		1950
Panama		29	11260		36
Korea, Republic of		3826	2678		4673
Argentina/Argentine		5294	2271		3304
China/Chine		4324	2358		3993
Sweden/Suède		3982	2922		2619
Switz.Liecht		2193	2200		2904
Norway,SVD,JM		2950	919		1491
Russian Federation		3255	1238		290
Singapore/Singapour		1113	875		2697
Aruba					4221
Portugal		808	2053		1059
Congo		1015	1343		1243
Denmark/Danemark		1215	704		1375
Turkey/Turquie		688	802		1643
Lebanon/Liban		713	842		1457
Indonesia/Indonésie		839	819		1307
Pakistan		24	14		2837
Tunisia/Tunisie		646	1229		805
India/Inde		359	176		2088
New Zealand		976	1263		362
Togo		850	771		740
Afghanistan		1174	1015		1
Zimbabwe		1575	529		
Finland/Finlande		872	271		688
Mexico/Mexique		533	334		560
Benin/Bénin		736	456		230
Poland/Pologne		93	149		1177
Uruguay		767	330		223
Angola		934	14		370

COUNTRIES–PAYS	SPECIAL EXPORTS F.O.B. EXPORTATIONS SPECIALES F.O.B.				
	1992	1993	1994	1995	1996
Monde		2637019	2391038		3145603
Afrique		59542	99900		72350
Amériques		1549478	1220792		2173376
Amérique du Nord		1440462	1193025		2015306
ALAI		108911	26756		19023
MCAC					
Caraïbes		17	27		139046
Autre Amérique		88	984		
Asie l'URSS exclus		102025	179816		335559
Europe l'URSS exclus		682482	783548		401035
UE		651302	721931		361818
AELE		13780	19655		36957
Europe de l'Est		183	0		2260
Autre de l'Europe		17216	41961		
Ancienne URSS					130
Océanie		21488			11569
USA/Etats–Unis d'Amer		1388198	1192938		2015264
France, Monac		505554	361561		239809
China/Chine		29382	54465		136241
United Kingdom		93106	61834		7310
Spain/Espagne		32886	92466		36767
Netherlands/Pays–Bas		2913	89032		30721
Chile/Chili		81620	22564		17502
Netherlands Antilles					121405
Morocco/Maroc		14474	76187		16825
Portugal		1908	91224		6254
Korea, Republic of		16065	35393		24186
Japan/Japon					66125
Israel/Israël		9892	19846		34512
Singapore/Singapour		17100	40567		1967
Gibraltar		17215	41961		
Switz.Liecht		10821	9821		34681
Canada		52264	87		43
Philippines		1885	12128		30514
Turkey/Turquie		7561	5707		22952
Australia/Australie		21487			11569
Greece/Grèce		4189	9699		18759
Guinea/Guinée		5540	4110		22749
Argentina/Argentine		25371	105		27
Italy/Italie		3639	10492		11242
Dem. Rep. of the Congo		9583	5648		6432
Senegal/Sénégal		15039	350		3073
Korea Dem People's Rp		16187	47		880
Norway,SVD,JM		2960	9834		2276
Belgium–Luxembourg		5766	1667		6212
Trinidad and Tobago					12183
Germany/Allemagne		1257	3923		4534
India/Inde		272	5052		2634
Thailand/Thaïlande		599	369		6412
Togo		1932	2894		1681
Algeria/Algérie		304	2316		3625
Congo		41	158		5471
Aruba					5436
So. Africa Customs Un		21	746		4120
Mozambique		4272			
Angola		687	2065		840
Mexico/Mexique		1327	806		1450
Benin/Bénin		944	1385		1120
Hong Kong		0	695		2732
Colombia/Colombie		535	2793		
Cameroon/Cameroun		1136	623		1308
Cyprus/Chypre		35	1859		612
Cote d'Ivoire		1482	249		601
Gambia/Gambie		287	810		902
Tunisia/Tunisie		99	356		1238
Nigeria/Nigéria		912	89		144

(VALUE AS PERCENTAGE OF WORLD TOTAL)(VALEURS EN POURCENTAGE DU TOTAL MONDIAL)

	1987	1988	1989	1990	1991	1992	1993	1994	1995	1996
Africa							5.6	5.9		6.8
Americas							11.8	15.2		12.6
Northern America							10.0	12.7		11.3
LAIA							1.8	1.0		0.8
CACM							0.0	0.0		0.0
Caribbean							0.0	0.0		0.5
Rest of America							0.0	1.6		0.0
As.ex F.USSR							3.8	3.5		11.2
Eur.x F.USSR							69.6	68.2		68.8
EU							68.8	67.6		68.1
EFTA							0.7	0.4		0.5
East Europe							0.1	0.1		0.2
Other Europe							0.0	0.0		0.0
Former USSR							0.4	0.2		0.1
Oceania							0.1	0.4		0.2
France, Monac							47.8	39.8		42.8
USA/Etats–Unis d'Amer							9.2	11.8		10.4
United Kingdom							3.8	6.4		4.8
Netherlands/Pays–Bas							4.6	5.0		4.5
Germany/Allemagne							3.6	5.6		4.6
Italy/Italie							3.1	4.2		3.5
Belgium–Luxembourg							2.9	3.5		4.1
Japan/Japon										6.0
Spain/Espagne							1.4	1.6		2.3
Cameroon/Cameroun							0.8	1.7		1.3

	1987	1988	1989	1990	1991	1992	1993	1994	1995	1996
Afrique							2.3	4.2		2.3
Amériques							58.8	51.1		69.1
Amérique du Nord							54.6	49.9		64.1
ALAI							4.1	1.1		0.6
MCAC										
Caraïbes							0.0	0.0		4.4
Autre Amérique							0.0	0.0		
Asie l'URSS exclus							3.9	7.5		10.7
Europe l'URSS exclus							25.9	32.8		12.7
UE							24.7	30.2		11.5
AELE							0.5	0.8		1.2
Europe de l'Est							0.0	0.0		0.1
Autre de l'Europe							0.7	1.8		
Ancienne URSS										0.0
Océanie							0.8			0.4
USA/Etats–Unis d'Amer							52.6	49.9		64.1
France, Monac							19.2	15.1		7.6
China/Chine							1.1	2.3		4.3
United Kingdom							3.5	2.6		0.2
Spain/Espagne							1.2	3.9		1.2
Netherlands/Pays–Bas							0.1	3.7		1.0
Chile/Chili							3.1	0.9		0.6
Netherlands Antilles										3.9
Morocco/Maroc							0.5	3.2		0.5
Portugal							0.1	3.8		0.2

4. Special Imports C.I.F. by Commodities according to the S.I.T.C. (Rev. 2) in thousand U.S. Dollars
Importations Spéciales C.A.F. par Produits d'après la C.T.C.I. (Rév. 2) en milliers de Dollars E.U.

SITC CTCI	COMMODITY	1993 WEIGHT POIDS	1993 VALUE VALEUR	1994 WEIGHT POIDS	1994 VALUE VALEUR	1995 WEIGHT POIDS	1995 VALUE VALEUR	1996 WEIGHT POIDS	1996 VALUE VALEUR	PRODUIT
	ALL COMMODITIES		774913		707515				898128	TOUS PRODUITS
0	FOOD AND LIVE ANIMALS		131504		105820				145697	ALIMENTS,ANIMAUX VIVANTS
01	MEAT AND PREPARATIONS		34821		32048				37822	VIANDES ET PREPARATIONS
011	MEAT FRESH,CHILLD,FROZEN	W 26742	31482	W 26952	28923			W 22270	32807	VIANDES FRAICHES,REF,CONGE
0111	BOVINE MEAT FRESH,FROZEN	W 14595	16717	W 12804	13145			W 6738	10120	VIANDES BOVIN FRAI,REF
01111	BOVINE MEAT WITH BONE IN	W 1852	2855	W 1126	1552			W 850	1719	VIANDES BOVIN NON DESOSS
01112	BOVINE MEAT BONELESS	W 12743	13862	W 11678	11592			W 5887	8401	VIANDES BOVIN DESOSSEES
0113	PIG MEAT FRESH,CHLD,FRZN	W 2470	2550	W 2960	2772			W 2848	3087	VIANDE DE PORC
0114	POULTRY FRESH CHLLD,FRZN	W 4015	4086	W 7582	8297			W 10020	15652	VOLAILLES MORTES
0116	EDIBLE OFFAL FRESH,CH,FR	W 4816	6318	W 2767	3123			W 2255	2720	ABATS COMESTIBLES
014	MEAT PREPD,PRSVD,NES ETC	W 1281	3187	W 1063	2812			W 1483	4736	CONSERVES DE VIANDES
0149	OTH PREPARD,PRESRVD MEAT	W 1075	2458	W 733	1929			W 1081	3497	AUTRES PREP DE VIANDES
02	DAIRY PRODCTS,BIRDS'EGGS		16051		10729				15498	PRODUITS LAITIERS,OEUFS
022	MILK AND CREAM	W 8099	12019	W 5190	7698			W 7297	11617	LAIT ET CREME
0224	MILK,CREAM PRESERVED ETC	W 7342	11230	W 4487	7057			W 5694	9947	LAIT,CREME CONS,CONC
02243	MILK DRY,OVER 1.5% FAT	W 1225	3155	W 838	1768			W 1079	3221	LAIT POUDRE SUP 1.5%
02249	MILK(EX DRY) PRSVD,SWEET	W 5841	7473	W 3295	4228			W 4342	6059	LAIT CONS,CONC SUCRE
024	CHEESE AND CURD	W 524	2384	W 457	1701			W 561	2430	FROMAGE ET CAILLEBOTTE
03	FISH AND PREPARATIONS		15442		8689				13582	POISSONS ET PREPARATIONS
034	FISH,FRESH,CHILLED,FROZN	W 4106	4255	W 5207	4028			W 8577	7111	POISSON FRAIS, REFRIG,CONG
0342	FISH FROZEN,EXCL FILLETS	W 4102	4230	W 5202	4005			W 8173	6826	POISSONS CONGELES
037	FISH ETC PREPD,PRSVD NES	W 5196	8720	W 2607	3982			W 3208	5435	POIS,CRUST,MOL PREPARES
0371	FISH PREPARD,PRESRVD NES	W 5177	8664	W 2595	3949			W 3203	5410	CONSERVES DE POISSONS
04	CEREALS AND PREPARATIONS		35456		32277				48422	CEREALES ET PRODUITS
041	WHEAT ETC UNMILLED	W 40296	7989	W 42602	7947			W 39283	10823	FROMENT,EPEAUTRE
0412	OTHER WHEAT ETC UNMILLED	W 40202	7954	W 42602	7947			W 39283	10823	AUTRE FROMENT NON MOULU
042	RICE	W 27934	7689	W 31068	8570			W 43444	16239	RIZ
0422	RICE SEMI--MILLED,MILLED	W 27932	7681	W 31066	8563			W 43443	16237	RIZ POLI,GLACE INCL BRISURES
04221	RICE MILLED UNBROKEN	W 27932	7681	W 30777	8459			W 43188	16126	RIZ POLI,GLACE EXCL BRISURES
047	OTHER CEREAL MEALS,FLOUR	W 4475	2185	W 4084	2114			W 5402	3572	AUTRES SEMOULES,FARINES
04702	MEAL OR GROATS NON–WHEAT	W 4450	2171	W 4081	2110			W 5391	3559	GRUAUX,SEMOULES DE CEREALES
048	CEREAL ETC PREPARATIONS	W 14715	15487	W 28837	12608			W 13660	15198	PREPTNS A BASE CEREALES
0482	MALT INCLUDING FLOUR	W 10584	6219	W 25550	6107			W 9600	7773	MALT MEME TORREFIE
0488	OTH CEREAL PREPS,MALT EX	W 1408	6150	W 819	3427			W 674	3356	EXTRAITS DE MALT
05	VEGETABLES AND FRUIT		12763		9979				13308	LEGUMES ET FRUITS
054	VEG ETC FRSH,SMPLY PRSVD	W 9584	7304	W 7038	5665			W 8573	7813	LEGUMES FRAIS,CONG,SECS
0546	VEGETABLES SIMPLY PRESVD	W 4056	3243	W 3746	3284			W 4760	4667	LEGUMES CONG,CONSER
05461	VEGETABLES FROZEN	W 4053	3239	W 3745	3283			W 4759	4666	LEGUMES CONGELES
07	COFFEE,TEA,COCOA,SPICES		2959		1727				2506	CAFE,THE,CACAO,EPICES
081	*FEEDING STUFF FOR ANIML	W 5871	3736	W 2669	1569			W 3335	1872	NOURRITURE POUR ANIMAUX
0819	FOOD WASTE AND FEED NES	W 4575	2840	W 2175	1341			W 1759	1311	DECHETS,ALIMENTS NDA
08199	FODDER NES,INCL SWEETNED	W 4575	2840	W 2175	1341			W 1759	1310	PREPARATIONS FOURRAGERES
09	MISC EDIBLE PRODUCTS		9446		7983				11662	PREP ALIMENTAIRES DIVERSES
098	EDIBLE PRODCTS,PREPS NES	W 2855	7818	W 2379	6179			W 3173	9263	PREP ALIMENTAIRES NDA
09809	MISC FOOD PREPRTIONS NES	W 1239	4371	W 847	2784			W 1204	4762	PREP ALIMENTAIRES NDA
1	BEVERAGES AND TOBACCO		17677		15544				23110	BOISSONS ET TABACS
11	BEVERAGES		13085		11522				17024	BOISSONS
112	ALCOHOLIC BEVERAGES	W 12192	11700	W 10087	10196			W 13811	15587	BOISSONS ALCOOLIQUES
1121	WINE OF FRESH GRAPES ETC	W 9961	5451	W 8039	5437			W 10426	9322	VINS DE RAISINS FRAIS
11212	WINE OF FRESH GRAPES	W 9873	5157	W 7988	5268			W 10382	9151	VINS DE MOUTS DE RAISINS
1124	DISTILLED ALCOHOLIC BEVS	W 758	4657	W 812	3375			W 1682	4067	ALCOOLS,EAUX–DE–VIE
11249	OTH ALCOHOLC BEVS,CMPNDS	W 420	2368	W 444	1698			W 1200	2390	BOISSONS ALCOOLIQUES NDA
12	TOBACCO AND MANUFACTURES		4592		4022				6086	TABACS BRUTS FABRIQUES
122	TOBACCO,MANUFACTURED	W 331	4279	W 301	4022			W 350	5813	TABACS FABRIQUES
1223	OTH MANUFACTURED TOBACCO	W 294	3634	W 253	3226			W 301	4509	TABACS FUMER,CHIQUER,PRISER
2	CRUDE MATERLS,EXCL FUELS		8179		8102				9595	MAT BRUTES NON COMESTIBLES
26	TEXTILE FIBRES AND WASTE		3005		2790				4468	FIBRES TEXTILES
269	WASTE OF TEXTILE FABRICS	W 1310	2958	W 2200	2701			W 3431	4384	FRIPERIE DRILLES,CHIFFONS
26901	BULK TEXT WSTE,OLD CLTHG	W 1209	2811	W 2090	2513			W 3312	4228	ART ET ACCESS D'HABILLEMENT
27	CRUDE FERTLZR,MINRLS NES		3706		3797				3387	ENGRAIS MINERAUX BRUTS
278	OTHER CRUDE MINERALS	W 9418	2460	W 10982	3279			W 8044	2490	AUTRES MINERAUX BRUTS
3	MINERAL FUELS ETC		14511		17103				31590	COMBUSTIBLES MINERAUX LUB
33	PETROLEUM AND PRODUCTS		14305		16918				28297	PETROLE ET DERIVES
334	PETROLEUM PRODUCTS,REFIN	W 56669	14191	W 54782	16769			W 108944	27433	PRODUITS RAFFINES
3342	KEROSENE,OTH MEDIUM OILS							W 23021	5221	PETR LAMPANTS,AUT HUIL
33421	KEROSENE INCL JET FUEL							W 22266	4689	PETROLES LAMPANTS
3343	GAS OILS							W 76823	15341	GAS OILS
3345	LUBS,PETROLEUM OILS NES	W 195	717	W 165	499			W 8227	6347	HUILES LUBRIFIANTES
33451	LUBS(HIGH PETR CONT) ETC							W 7976	5660	HUILES LUBRIF,H LOURDES
341	*GAS,NATURAL AND MANUFCT	W 77	193	W 80	175			W 1001	3276	GAZ NATUREL,GAZ MANUFACT
3413	PETROLM GASES,LIQUEFIED	W 76	184	W 80	171			W 991	3234	GAZ DE PETROLE LIQUEFIE
34131	LIQUEFIED PROPANE,BUTANE	W 76	183	W 80	171			W 990	3226	PROPANE,BUTANE LIQUEFIES
4	ANIMAL,VEGETABLE OIL,FAT		1078		1113				2889	HUILES,GRAISSES ANIM,VEG
42	FIXED VEGETABLE OIL,FAT		1048		1078				2870	HUILES VEGETALES FIXES
5	CHEMCLS,RELATED PROD NES		83554		70061				93047	PRODUITS CHIMIQUES
51	ORGANIC CHEMICALS		3882		3229				4438	PROD CHIMIQ ORGANIQUES
52	INORGANIC CHEMICALS		5408		5009				4801	PROD CHIM INORGANIQUES
522	INORG ELEMNTS,OXIDES,ETC	W 2075	2311	W 2347	2587			W 1945	2175	ELEMENTS INORGANIQUES
523	OTHR INORG CHEMICALS ETC	W 4773	2549	W 2952	2155			W 3694	2505	AUT PRODUITS CHIMIQUES INORG
53	DYES,TANNING,COLOUR PROD		2919		2061				3935	PROD TEINTURE,COLORANTS
533	PIGMENTS,PAINTS,ETC	W 1266	2658	W 982	1900			W 1950	3594	PIGMENTS,PEINTURES,VERNIS
541	*MEDICINAL,PHARM PRODUCT	K 1328736	30701	K 883575	18411			K 1482824	33356	PROD MEDICINAUX PHARMACEUT
5417	MEDICAMENTS	K 1237687	28272	K 820185	16669			K 1368240	30696	MEDICAMENTS
54171	— CONTAINNG ANTIBIOTICS	K 81222	3073	K 34599	931			K 74046	1691	MED CONTN ANTIBIOTIQUES
54179	— CONTNG OTH SUBSTANCES	K 1093543	23549	K 769115	15071			K 1266601	27853	MED CONT AUT SUBSTANCES
55	PERFUME,CLEANING ETC PRD		12542		12315				13523	PROD POUR PARFUM,TOILETTE
551	ESSENTL OILS,PERFUME,ETC	W 147	2296	W 155	3528			W 208	4357	HUILES ESSENTIELLES
5514	MIXED PERFUME SUBSTANCES	W 138	2242	W 143	3449			W 202	4269	MELANGES SUBSTAN ODORIFER
553	PERFUMERY,COSMETICS,ETC	W 1061	2795	W 1022	2802			W 1281	2839	PRODUITS DE PARFUMERIE
554	SOAP,CLEANSING ETC PREPS	W 4034	7451	W 3414	5986			W 3505	6327	SAVONS,PRODUITS DETERSIFS
5542	WASHING PREPARATIONS ETC	W 3273	6087	W 2662	4805			W 2676	4989	PROD ORG TENSIO–ACT NDA
58	PLASTIC MATERIALS ETC		7222		9814				9935	MAT PLAST ARTIFICIELLES
582	PROD OF CONDENSATION ETC	W 1415	2242	W 2074	2966			W 2364	3710	PROD CONDENS,POLYCOND
583	POLYMERIZATION ETC PRODS	W 2218	3658	W 2548	4217			W 2328	4554	PROD POLYMERISATION
59	CHEMICAL MATERIALS NES		18228		16204				19821	MAT PROD CHIMIQUES NDA
591	PESTICIDES,DISINFECTANTS	W 776	3093	W 944	2685			W 1107	3922	DESINF,INSECT,FONG,HERB
598	MISCEL CHEM PRODUCTS NES	W 4659	13253	W 4568	12330			W 3979	13872	PROD DIV INDUST CHIM NDA
5982	ANTI–KNOCK PREPARTNS ETC	W 934	2708	W 1440	4364			W 1337	4980	PREPARAT ANTIDETONANTES
5989	CHEM PRODUCTS,PREPS NES	W 3672	10322	W 3051	7823			W 2620	8832	PROD PREP CHIMIQUES NDA
59899	OTH CHEM PRODS,PREPS,NES	W 3290	9298	W 2625	6798			W 2218	7783	AUT PRODUITS CHIMIQUES NDA
6	BASIC MANUFACTURES		123787		112114				150246	ART MANUFACTURES

4. Special Imports C.I.F. by Commodities according to the S.I.T.C. (Rev. 2) in thousand U.S. Dollars
Importations Spéciales C.A.F. par Produits d'après la C.T.C.I. (Rév. 2) en milliers de Dollars E.U.

SITC CTCI	COMMODITY	1993 WEIGHT POIDS	1993 VALUE VALEUR	1994 WEIGHT POIDS	1994 VALUE VALEUR	1995 WEIGHT POIDS	1995 VALUE VALEUR	1996 WEIGHT POIDS	1996 VALUE VALEUR	PRODUIT
62	RUBBER MANUFACTURES NES		9942		12223				17011	CAOUTCHOUC MANUFACTURE
621	MATERIALS OF RUBBER	W 237	2398	W 229	2948			W 155	2164	PRODUITS EN CAOUTCHOUC
62105	UNHARD VULC RUBBER TUBES	W 160	1949	W 188	2590			W 108	1825	TUBES,TUYAUX CAOUT VULC
625	RUBBER TYRES, TUBES ETC	W 1592	5528	W 1936	7031			W 2580	11499	PNEUS CAOUTCHOUC VULCANISE
6252	TYRES,NEW,BUS OR LORRY	W 654	2909	W 790	3438			W 1144	6338	PNEUS POUR AUTOBUS,CAMIONS
6259	OTH TYRES,TYRE CASES,ETC	W 672	1381	W 906	2448			W 1246	4037	AUTRES PNEUS RECHAPES FLAPS
62599	TYRES NES,TYRE CASES,ETC	W 558	995	W 793	2010			W 1032	2980	PNEUS,FLAPS
628	RUBBER ARTICLES NES	W 176	2016	W 155	2244			W 239	3348	OUVRAGES CAOUTCHOUC NDA
64	PAPER,PAPERBOARD AND MFR		19409		14063				16776	PAPIERS,CARTONS & OUVRAGES
641	PAPER AND PAPERBOARD		8068	W 2424	5171			W 2928	6815	PAPIERS ET CARTONS
6415	PAPER,PAPERBRD,BULK,NES	W 1172	2888	W 482	1185			W 908	2144	PAPIERS,CARTONS ROULEAUX
64159	OTHER PAPER ETC,BULK,NES	W 1155	2793	W 467	1108			W 893	2026	AUT PAPIER ROULEAUX FEUILLES
642	PAPER,ETC,PRECUT,ARTS OF	W 4384	11341	W 3378	8892			W 3619	9961	PAP,CARTONS DECOUPES
6421	PAPER ETC CONTAINERS	W 2656	5194	W 1606	3153			W 1957	4359	BOITES,SACS EMBALLAGES
6423	EXERCISE BOOKS ETC	W 850	2580	W 899	2776			W 724	2376	REGISTRES,CAHIERS,CARNETS
6428	PAPER ETC ARTICLES NES	W 636	2658	W 635	2073			W 589	1958	OUVRAGES EN PATE A PAPIER
65	TEXTILE YARN,FABRICS,ETC		10004		6868				10362	FILS,TISSUS,ARTICLES TEXTILE
652	COTTON FABRICS,WOVEN		3011	W 528	1556			W 302	1665	TISSUS DE COTON
6522	WOVEN COTTON BLEACHD,ETC	W 674	2931	W 526	1542			W 299	1645	TISSUS COTON BLANCHIS ETC
658	TEXTILE ARTICLES NES	W 832	2747	W 592	2060			W 797	4017	ART FACONNES MAT TEXTILES
66	NONMETAL MINERAL MFS NES		11962		13196				18198	ART MIN NON METALLIQUES
661	LIME,CEMENT,BLDG PRODS	W 7573	2669	W 8783	1981			W 11939	3590	CHAUX,CIMENTS MAT CONSTR
662	CLAY,REFRACTORY BLDG PRD	W 5879	3344	W 5372	2719			W 8769	4462	MAT CONST REFRACTAIRES
6624	BRICKS ETC NONREFRACTORY	W 5635	3135	W 5071	2533			W 8237	3935	BRIQUES ETC CERAM NON REFR
66245	GLAZED CERAMIC SETTS ETC	W 4911	2616	W 4539	2292			W 7783	3727	AUT CARREAUX CERAMIQUE
665	GLASSWARE	W 1052	2088	W 3792	3376			W 5621	4346	OUVRAGES EN VERRE
6651	BOTTLES ETC OF GLASS	W 72	141	W 3175	1962			W 4932	2881	RECIPIENTS EN VERRE
66511	GLASS BOTTLES ETC NONVAC	W 71	140	W 3175	1961			W 4932	2881	BONBONNES,BOUTEILLES,ETC
67	IRON AND STEEL		30858		27255				37304	FER ET ACIER
673	IRON,STEEL SHAPES ETC	W 7878	3442	W 8388	3967			W 14764	8042	BARRES,PROFIL FER,ACIER
6732	IRON,STEEL BARS ETC	W 5443	2195	W 6510	2835			W 10627	4474	BARRES FER,ACIER
67326	IRN,OTH STL BARS HOTROLD	W 3193	1193	W 4840	1991			W 9471	3835	BARRES PLEINES FER,ACIER
6733	IRON,STEEL PROFILES ETC	W 1817	1003	W 1545	949			W 4065	3516	PROFILES,PALPLAN FER,ACIER
67332	LARGE U,I,H SECTIONS ETC	W 1148	611	W 1048	648			W 3083	2774	PROFILES PLUS 80MM
674	IRN,STL UNIV,PLATE,SHEET	W 3696	2761	W 3204	2393			W 3875	2939	LARGES PLATS,TOLES
678	IRON,STL TUBES,PIPES,ETC	W 12345	23718	W 7058	19713			W 13618	24294	TUBES,TUYAUX EN FONTE,FER
6782	IRON,STL SEAMLESS TUBES	W 9740	13654	W 5729	10267			W 11335	17549	TUBES,TUYAUX SANS SOUDURE
6783	IRON,STL TUBES,PIPES NES	W 1284	2566	W 666	804			W 1319	1430	AUT TUBES,TUYAUX FER,ACIER
6785	IRON,STEEL TUBE FITTINGS	W 535	6822	W 511	8517			W 431	4549	ACCESSOIRES DE TUYAUTERIE
68	NON–FERROUS METALS		7211		6498				6756	METAUX NON FERREUX
684	ALUMINIUM	W 2273	6742	W 2817	5917			W 1976	5859	ALUMINIUM
6842	ALUMINIUM,ALLOYS WORKED	W 2273	6742	W 2817	5917			W 1975	5851	ALUMINIUM,ALLIAGES OUVRE
68422	ALUMNM PLATE,SHEET,STRIP	W 2103	5629	W 2639	4911			W 1739	4219	TOLES, PLANCHES EN ALU
69	METAL MANUFACTURES NES		32580		30991				42247	ART MANUFACT EN METAL NDA
691	STRUCTURES AND PARTS NES	W 1462	3694	W 756	2318			W 574	1455	CONSTRUCT FER,ACIER,ALU
6911	STRUCTURES,PARTS IRN,STL	W 1361	3180	W 719	1879			W 541	1278	CONSTRUCT FER,ACIER,FONTE
692	METAL TANKS,BOXES,ETC	W 781	2450	W 885	2299			W 1233	5276	RECIPIENTS METALLIQUES
6924	MTL TRANSPORT BOXES ETC	W 658	1801	W 715	1905			W 845	3317	FUTS,TAMBOURS,BIDONS
693	WIRE PRODUCTS NON ELECTR	W 1199	3071	W 1475	3615			W 1940	4800	OUVRAGES FILS METALLIQUES
6931	WIRE CABLES, ROPES ETC	W 839	2419	W 1067	2743			W 1444	4043	CORDAGES EN FILS DE FER
69311	IRN,STEEL CABLE,ROPE ETC	W 824	2351	W 1055	2678			W 1276	3491	CORDAGES FILS FER,ACIER
694	STL,COPPR NAILS,NUTS,ETC	W 860	2844	W 755	3424			W 1012	3506	CLOUS,VIS,ECROUS
69402	IRN,STL NUTS,BOLTS,ETC	W 415	2456	W 359	3041			W 464	2982	BOULONS,VIS,ECROUS FER,AC
695	TOOLS	W 390	4909	W 385	6576			W 669	9147	OUTILS A MAIN
6953	OTHER HAND TOOLS	W 213	2206	W 160	2209			W 311	3369	AUTRES OUTILS A MAIN
6954	BLADES,TIPS,ETC FR TOOLS	W 118	2491	W 162	4116			W 237	5311	OUTILS POUR MACHINE–OUTIL
69541	PARTS TO INSERT IN TOOLS	W 112	2383	W 154	3928			W 231	5111	OUTILS DE FORAGE
697	BASE MTL HOUSEHOLD EQUIP	W 1025	4414	W 602	2888			W 738	2960	ART MENAGE MET COMMUNS
699	BASE METAL MFRS NES	W 2252	10035	W 1966	9039			W 3090	13944	ART MANUFACTURES MET NDA
6996	BASE MTL MISC ARTICLES	W 682	2963	W 775	2585			W 821	3287	ART DIVERS METAUX COMMUNS
6997	IRON,STEEL ARTICLES NES	W 555	1921	W 395	1964			W 1396	5217	OUV FONTE,FER,ACIER NDA
69979	IRN,STL MANUFACTURES NES	W 471	1860	W 395	1955			W 1393	5205	AUT OUVRAGES EN FER NDA
7	MACHINES,TRANSPORT EQUIP		316400		314250				351936	MACHINES MATERIEL TRANSPORT
71	POWER GENERATING EQUIPMT		26878		25895				26279	MACHINES GENERATRICES
713	INTRNL COMBUS PSTN ENGIN	W 370	8818	W 357	8461			W 563	14764	MOTEURS EXPL COMB INT, PIECE
7131	AIRCRAFT PSTN ENGINS,PTS	W 10	1518	W 4	820			W 16	3170	MOTEURS EXPL P.AVIATION, PIE
7133	MARINE PISTON ENGINES	W 131	2445	W 80	1518			W 129	2414	MOTEURS EXPL POUR BATEAUX
7139	PISTON ENGINE PARTS NES	W 163	4289	W 198	5502			W 253	8030	PIECES POUR 713.2,3,8
714	ENGINES AND MOTORS NES	W 160	9508	W 18	1926			W 54	5662	MOTEURS NON ELECTRIQUES
7148	GAS TURBINES NES	W 134	8556	W 7	987			W 38	3894	TURBINES A GAZ
71488	OTHER GAS TURBINES NES	W 134	8555	W 7	987			W 37	3647	AUTRES TURBINES A GAZ
716	ROTATING ELECTRIC PLANT	W 416	5852	W 491	14323			W 321	4740	APP ELECTR ROTATIFS,PIECES
7161	DC MOTORS AND GENERATORS	W 134	2634	W 44	625			W 53	619	MOTEURS COURANT CONTINU
7162	AC MTRS,GENRTRS,GEN SETS	W 270	2906	W 433	13169			W 257	3663	MOTEURS ELECTRIQUES
71622	AC GENERATORS	W 18	141	W 243	10923			W 18	401	GENER COURANT ALTERNATIF
72	MACHS FOR SPCL INDUSTRYS		21048		46390				36896	MAC SPECIALES POUR INDUST
722	TRACTORS NON–ROAD	W 215	1170	W 833	6255			W 610	4004	TRACTEURS
7224	WHEELED TRACTORS NES	W 132	1140	W 664	6045			W 527	3993	TRACTEURS A ROUES
723	CIVIL ENGNEERG EQUIP ETC	W 1979	12054	W 5680	30872			W 3397	23226	APPAREILS DE GENIE CIVIL
7234	CONST,MINING MACHNRY NES	W 1440	8375	W 3669	22360			W 2425	15386	MACH POUR LA CONST, MINES
72341	SELF–PROPELLD DOZERS,ETC	W 800	5164	W 2182	14881			W 1079	7006	BULLDOZERS
72342	SLFPRP SHOVELS,EXCAVATRS	W 423	2239	W 1294	6878			W 1122	7086	PELLES MECANIQUES
7239	CONSTR ETC MACHY PTS NES	W 403	3256	W 1862	8045			W 771	7162	PIECES 723.41–723.46
728	OTH MACHY FOR SPCL INDUS	W 730	3221	W 996	6421			W 833	6521	AUT MACH IND PARTICULIERES
7281	MACH–TOOLS FR SPCL INDUS	W 41	403	W 490	3167			W 186	1622	MACH–OUTILS SPEC IND PART
72812	MACH–TOOLS TO WORK WOOD	W 34	350	W 386	2415			W 158	1239	MACH–OUT POUR TRAVAIL BOIS
74	GENRL INDUSTRL MACHY NES		67014		82159				105886	MACH APP INDUSTRIE
741	HEATING,COOLING EQUIPMNT	W 484	5726	W 657	5003			W 780	7921	MACH CHAUFFAGE,PIECES
7415	AIR–CONDITIONING MACHNRY	W 106	1173	W 159	1610			W 340	3629	GROUPES CONDITION AIR
7416	HEATING,COOLING EQU NES	W 260	3363	W 235	1242			W 140	1497	APP CHANGEMENT TEMP
742	PUMPS FOR LIQUIDS ETC	W 436	10731	W 627	14092			W 752	10011	POMPES MOTO–POMPES
7428	OTHER PUMPS FOR LIQUIDS	W 189	3977	W 342	6641			W 633	5277	AUTRES POMPES POUR LIQ
74288	PUMPS FR LIQUIDS NES ETC	W 176	3655	W 331	6327			W 622	4945	POMPES POUR LIQUIDES NDA
7429	PTS NES OF PUMPS OF 742	W 105	3581	W 251	6434			W 71	3471	PIECES POUR GROUPE 742
743	PUMPS NES,CENTRFUGES ETC	W 985	14581		18524			W 1533	35849	POMPES COMPRES,VENT ETC
7431	PUMPS FOR GASES ETC	W 327	3344	W 383	4011			W 1076	27200	POMPES AIR A VIDE,COMPRES
7436	GAS,LIQUID FILTERS ETC	W 565	7430	W 265	2958			W 376	5008	APP POUR FILT DES LIQUIDES
7439	PTS NES OF APP OF 7435,6	W 71	3435	W 463	11267			W 47	3300	PIECES 743.5 ET 743.6
744	MECHANICAL HANDLING EQU	W 1184	4868	W 1715	9188			W 1916	10596	EQUIP MANUTENTION PIECES
7442	LIFTING,LOADING MACH NES	W 505	2103	W 903	4702			W 775	4311	APP LEVAGE,MANUTENTION
74428	OTH HANDLING ETC MCH NES	W 137	875	W 274	2349			W 429	2766	AUT APP LEVAGE ETC

4. Special Imports C.I.F. by Commodities according to the S.I.T.C. (Rev. 2) in thousand U.S. Dollars
Importations Spéciales C.A.F. par Produits d'après la C.T.C.I. (Rév. 2) en milliers de Dollars E.U.

SITC CTCI	COMMODITY	1993 WEIGHT POIDS	1993 VALUE VALEUR	1994 WEIGHT POIDS	1994 VALUE VALEUR	1995 WEIGHT POIDS	1995 VALUE VALEUR	1996 WEIGHT POIDS	1996 VALUE VALEUR	PRODUIT
7449	PTS NES OF MACHY OF 7442	W 186	1682	W 382	3744			W 463	4525	PIECES DU 744.2
745	NONELEC MACHY,TOOLS NES	W 154	2738	W 141	3034			W 398	7937	AUT MACH NON ELEC,PIECES
7452	OTH NONELEC MCHS,PTS NES	W 98	1599	W 91	1777			W 340	6005	AUT MACH NON ELEC,PIECES
74522	PACKAGNG,BOTTLNG,ETC MCH	W 23	303	W 24	420			W 194	2965	MACH NETT BOUTEILLES,ETC
749	NONELEC MACH PTS,ACC NES	W 1287	28370	W 2161	32318			W 1344	33572	PIECES MACH NON ELEC NDA
7491	BALL,ROLLER,ETC BEARINGS	W 131	2315	W 295	3251			W 251	4061	ROULEMENTS BILLES ETC
7492	COCKS,VALVES ETC NES	W 758	17554	W 1200	17589			W 659	15820	ART ROB,SIM POUR TUYAUX
7493	SHAFT,CRANK,PULLEY ETC	W 197	4266	W 526	6369			W 204	7213	ARBRES TRANS,VILEBREQUINS
7499	OTH NONELEC MCHY PTS NES	W 201	4235	W 139	5110			W 230	6478	PIECES NON ELECT NDA
74992	METAL–PLASTIC GASKETS	W 154	3767	W 117	4326			W 186	6112	JOINTS METALLOPLASTIQUES
75	OFFICE MACHNES,ADP EQUIP		15190		12254				19672	MACH BUREAU TRAIT AUTOM
751	OFFICE MACHINES	W 103	2376	W 71	1797			W 89	2320	MACH,APPAREILS DE BUREAU
752	AUTOMTIC DATA PROC EQUIP	W 113	8950	W 93	7970			W 180	13863	MACH TRAIT INFORMATION
7522	DIGITAL COMPUTERS	W 37	2836	W 43	4583			W 93	6920	MACH DIGITALES COMPLETES
7523	DIGITL CENTRL PROCESSORS	W 30	3511	W 5	327			W 9	746	UNITES CENTRALES
7525	ADP PERIPHERAL UNITS	W 18	1365	W 20	1636			W 51	3792	UNITES PERIPHERIQUES
759	OFFICE,ADP MCH PTS,ACCES	W 30	3864	W 22	2486			W 36	3490	PIECES DU 751 ET 752
7599	ACCTG,ETC,ADP MCH PTS,AC	W 20	3339	W 14	2001			W 26	2841	PIECES DU 751 ET 752
76	TELECOMM,SOUND EQUIPMENT		18983		16551				22843	EQUIPMENT DE TELECOM
761	TELEVISION RECEIVERS	W 353	2664	W 234	1975			W 476	3168	RECEPTEURS DE TELEVISION
7611	COLOUR TV RECEIVERS	W 275	2390	W 229	1952			W 442	2893	RECEPTEURS COULEUR
764	TELECOM EQPT,PTS,ACC NES	W 210	13338	W 202	12342			W 188	17042	EQUIP TELECOM,PIECES
7641	LINE TELEPHONE,ETC EQUIP	W 33	3746	W 26	2011			W 26	2502	APP TELEPHON PAR FIL
7643	TV,RADIO TRANSMITTRS ETC	W 25	3404	W 16	2024			W 35	6268	APP EMET TELE RADIO
7648	TELECOMM EQUIPMENT NES	W 6	419	W 63	4342			W 16	2072	APP TELECOM NDA
76483	RADAR APPARATUS ETC	W 2	356	W 56	4123			W 10	1641	APP DE RADIOGUIDAGE ETC
7649	PTS NES OF EQUIPMT OF 76	W 118	5199	W 69	3631			W 93	5416	PIECES DE LA DIV 76
76491	PTS NES OF APPAR OF 7641	W 16	2560	W 5	1161			W 13	3941	PIECES POUR 764.1
76493	TELECOMM EQUIPMT PTS NES	W 87	2011	W 64	2319			W 75	1363	PIECES 761,762,764.3,8
77	ELECTRIC MACHNRY NES ETC		40040		29772				42796	MACH APP ELECT NDA
771	ELECTRIC POWER MACHY NES	W 153	2200	W 202	2603			W 392	4233	MACH PROD,TRANS ELECTR
772	SWITCHGEAR ETC,PARTS NES	W 550	15270	W 350	9105			W 426	11934	APP COUPURE,SECT ETC
7721	SWITCHGEAR ETC	W 548	15149	W 348	8925			W 422	11546	APP COUPURE,SECTIONMNT
773	ELECTR DISTRIBUTNG EQUIP	W 1424	6614	W 1511	5853			W 1409	8009	EQUIPMT DISTRIBUTION ELECT
7731	INSULATED WIRE,CABLE ETC	W 1405	6453	W 1506	5790			W 1315	7532	FILS,CABLES ISOLES ELECT
775	HOUSEHOLD TYPE EQUIP NES	W 1298	6712		4500			W 1319	7050	MACH,APP USAGE DOMESTQUE
7752	DOM REFRIGERATRS,FREEZRS	W 914	4718	W 484	2647			W 791	4330	REFRIG,CONGEL MENAGER
77522	DOMESTIC DEEP–FREEZERS	W 515	2636	W 287	1570			W 422	2482	MEUBLES CONGELATEURS
778	ELECTRICAL MACHINERY NES	W 921	6586	W 936	6642			W 1104	9392	AUTRES MACH ELECT NDA
7781	BATTERIES,ACCUMULATORS	W 657	2270	W 691	2537			W 755	3958	PILES ET ACCUMULATEURS
77812	ELECTRIC ACCUMULATORS	W 518	1744	W 524	1862			W 527	3108	ACCUMULATEURS ELECTRIQ
78	ROAD VEHICLES		68744		57639				84189	VEHICULES ROUTIERS
781	PASS MOTOR VEH EXC BUSES	W 3883	30788	W 2333	18649			W 4604	29394	AUTO TRANSPORT PERSONNES
782	LORRIES,SPCL MTR VEH NES	W 3190	18806	W 2637	14105			W 3924	23337	VEHICULES SPECIAUX,MARCH
7821	LORRIES,TRUCKS	W 2933	17721	W 2437	13245			W 3328	19758	VEHICULES TRANSP MARCHAND
7822	SPECIAL MOTOR VEHCLS NES	W 257	1085	W 200	860			W 596	3579	VEHICULES USAGES SPECIAUX
783	ROAD MOTOR VEHICLES NES	W 1194	8086	W 1645	11937			W 2502	16588	VEHICULES ROUTIERS NDA
7831	BUSES	W 753	5433	W 563	4304			W 1468	9780	VOITURES TRANSPORT COMMUN
7832	TRACTORS FOR TR–TRAILERS	W 441	2652	W 1082	7633			W 1034	6808	TRACTEURS ROUTIERS
784	MOTOR VEH PRTS,ACCES NES	W 683	9437	W 821	11030			W 748	11628	PIECES 722,781,782,783
7849	OTHER MOTOR VEHCL PARTS	W 654	9216	W 815	10900			W 740	11493	PIECES 722,781,782,783
79	OTHR TRANSPORT EQUIPMENT		57752		42798				12313	AUTRE MATERIEL TRANSPORT
791	RAILWAY VEHICLES	W 1645	4895	W 580	1560			W 140	932	VEHIC MAT CHEMINS DE FER
7915	FRT,MAINT CARS NOT POWRD	W 1524	3903							WAGONS DE SERVICE
79152	RAILWAY FREIGHT CARS NES	W 1506	3488							WAGONS MARCHANDISES
792	AIRCRAFT ETC	W 22	2010	W 32	3354			W 41	7293	APP NAVIGATION AERIENNE
7929	AIRCRAFT PARTS NES	W 17	1678	W 21	2237			W 27	5288	PIECES DU 792
793	SHIPS AND BOATS ETC	W 24344	50846	W 21863	37883			W 5162	4088	NAVIRES BATEAUX,ETC
7932	SHIPS AND BOATS NES	W 3197	13243	W 8648	18328			W 1298	1294	NAVIRES ET BATEAUX
79323	OTHER CARGO VESSELS	W 2328	12144	W 8581	17975			W 1277	939	AUT BATEAUX TRANS MARCH
7938	TUGS,SPECIAL VESSELS ETC	W 21137	37559	W 13212	19553			W 995	1357	REMORQUEURS,BATEAUX SPEC
79382	SPECL PURPOSE VESSLS ETC	W 20990	37213	W 13002	19215			W 99	86	BAT–PHARES,–POMPES,DRAGUES
8	MISC MANUFACTURED GOODS		77888		62295				89123	ART MANUFACTURES DIVERS
812	*PLUMBG,HEATNG,LGHTNG EQ	W 552	3024	W 476	2526			W 707	3678	APPAR SANITAIRES CHAUFFAGE
8124	LIGHTING EQUIPMENT NES	W 268	2248	W 211	1933			W 333	2732	APPAREILS ECLAIRAGE ETC
821	*FURNITURE,PARTS THEREOF	W 1483	9387	W 1382	7866			W 1430	9132	MEUBLES ET PIECES
8219	FURNITURE AND PARTS NES	W 1044	5925	W 1070	5733			W 914	4445	AUTRES MEUBLES ET PIECES
82192	WOOD FURNITURE NES	W 318	1869	W 394	2539			W 382	2300	MEUBLES NDA EN BOIS
82199	OTHR FURN,FURN PARTS NES	W 639	3496	W 550	2351			W 362	1110	MEUBLES NDA AUTRES MATIERES
84	CLOTHING AND ACCESSORIES		6298		5200				7266	VETEMENTS
851	*FOOTWEAR		3606	W 1386	2716			W 1445	3752	CHAUSSURES
87	PRECISION INSTRUMNTS NES		21328		16942				29787	INSTRUM,APPAR SCIENT NDA
872	MEDICAL INSTRUMENTS NES	W 110	3533	W 92	1840			W 153	3858	INSTR,APP MEDIC–CHIR NDA
87202	OTH MEDICAL INSTRUMENTS	W 105	3300	W 78	1620			W 96	3295	INSTRUM,APP MEDECINE
874	MEASURNG,CONTROLNG INSTR	W 440	15306	W 759	14342			W 594	24231	INSTRUMENTS DE MESURE
8741	SURVEYING INSTRUMENTS	W 27	1098	W 10	1053			W 14	3448	INST GEODESIE,TOPO ETC
8742	MEASUR,DRAW ETC INST,PTS	W 215	4865	W 540	5576			W 262	7885	INST DESSIN,TRACAGE,PCS
87421	MEASURNG,DRAWNG ETC INST	W 209	4610	W 530	5226			W 255	7547	INSTRUM DESSIN,TRACAGE
8743	GAS,LIQUID CONTROL INSTR	W 98	4146	W 30	1727			W 49	2811	APP,INSTR MESURE FLUIDES
8748	ELEC MEAS,CONTRL EQU NES	W 70	3938	W 145	4422			W 218	6252	APP ELEC ELECTRO MESURE
87483	OTH ELCTRNC MEAS ETC EQU	W 60	2989	W 108	3490			W 165	4508	AUT APP ELECTRO DE MESURE
8749	INSTR PTS NES,ACCESSORYS	W 14	702	W 20	953			W 43	3327	PIECES 873,874.3,54,874.8
88	PHOTO EQU,OPTICL GDS ETC		3113		2084				3012	APP,FOURN PHOTO,OP,MONTR
89	MISC MANUFCTRD GOODS NES		29808		23885				30945	ART MANUFACTURES DIVERS
892	PRINTED MATTER		13591	W 805	9117			W 829	11525	IMPRIMES
8921	PRINTED BOOKS,GLOBES,ETC	W 398	7732	W 422	5418			W 372	6045	LIVRES,BROCHURES,CARTES
89211	PRINTED BOOKS,PAMPHLETS	W 386	7578	W 416	5388			W 366	5995	LIVRES,BROCHURES
8922	NEWSPAPERS,PERIODICALS		4081	W 267	2486			W 303	3439	JOURNAUX ET PERIODIQUES
893	ARTICLES OF PLASTIC NES		7287		6820				8892	OUVRAGES EN MAT DIVIS 58
8931	PLSTC PACKG CONTNRS,LIDS	W 534	2094	W 851	2010			W 1110	2870	ART TRANSP EMBALLAGE ETC
8939	MISC PLASTIC ARTICLES	W 1415	4900	W 2041	4606			W 1770	5781	ART DIVERS EN MAT DIV 58
89399	OTHR PLASTC ARTICLES NES	W 1139	4354	W 1761	4198			W 1391	5107	AUT OUV MAT DIV 58
894	TOYS,SPORTING GOODS,ETC	W 362	2124	W 310	2240			W 484	3189	VOITURES ENFANTS,JOUETS
895	OFFICE SUPPLIES NES	W 188	2398	W 174	2045			W 224	2971	ART PAPET NDA

Gabon

5. Special Exports F.O.B. by Commodities according to the S.I.T.C. (Rev. 2) in thousand U.S. Dollars
Exportations Spéciales F.O.B. par Produits d'après la C.T.C.I. (Rév. 2) en milliers de Dollars E.U.

SITC CTCI	COMMODITY	1993		1994		1995		1996		PRODUIT
		WEIGHT POIDS	VALUE VALEUR	WEIGHT POIDS	VALUE VALEUR	WEIGHT POIDS	VALUE VALEUR	WEIGHT POIDS	VALUE VALEUR	
	ALL COMMODITIES		2637019		2391038				3145603	TOUS PRODUITS
2	CRUDE MATERLS,EXCL FUELS		240062		292734				475915	MAT BRUTES NON COMESTIBLES
23	RUBBER, CRUDE		1051		2874				9643	CAOUTCHOUC BRUT
232	NATURAL RUBBER,GUMS	W 1391	1051	W 2964	2853			W 8254	9634	LATEX CAOUTCHOUC NATUREL
23202	OTHER NATURAL RUBBER	W 1391	1051	W 2601	2563			W 8254	9634	CAOUTCHOUC NATUREL
24	CORK AND WOOD		77290		208037				402225	LIEGE ET BOIS
247	OTH WOOD ROUGH,SQUARED	W 429167	77280	W 533963	207844			W 1713213	398623	BOIS BRUTS EQUARRIS
2472	SAW–,VENEER–LOGS NON–CON	W 429167	77280	W 533963	207844			W 1713213	398623	NON CONIFERES SCIAGE,PLAC
24721	— IN THE ROUGH	W 429167	77280	W 533963	207844			W 1713213	398623	BRUTS ECORCES DEGROSSIS
28	METALLIFEROUS ORES,SCRAP		161070		81381				63529	MINERAIS METAL,DECHETS
287	BASE METAL ORES,CONC NES	W 2688583	161002	W 3095671	81288			W 2119146	63309	MINERAIS METAUX COMMUNS
2877	MANGANESE ORE,CONCENTRTE	W 2688583	161002	W 3095671	81288			W 2119146	63309	MINERAIS DE MANGANESE
3	MINERAL FUELS ETC		2355388		2070659				2602629	COMBUSTIBLES MINERAUX LUB
33	PETROLEUM AND PRODUCTS		2355380		2070659				2602571	PETROLE ET DERIVES
333	CRUDE PETROLEUM	MW 14258	2326009	MW 15834	2048177			MW 18571	2557418	HUILES BRUTES DE PETROLE
334	PETROLEUM PRODUCTS,REFIN	W 258772	29371	W 258953	22482			W 315783	45153	PRODUITS RAFFINES
3344	FUEL OILS,NES							W 210180	23703	FUEL OILS
5	CHEMCLS,RELATED PROD NES		15659		8895				13314	PRODUITS CHIMIQUES
52	INORGANIC CHEMICALS		15120		8365				11685	PROD CHIM INORGANIQUES
524	RADIOACTIVE ETC MATERIAL		12594		7556				10865	MATIERES RADIOACTIVES
5241	RADIOACTIVE ELEMENTS ETC		12594		7556				10865	RADIOELEMENTS,ISOTOPES
6	BASIC MANUFACTURES		5642		6302				25983	ART MANUFACTURES
63	WOOD,CORK MANUFACTRS NES		3219		3080				21453	OUVRAGES LIEGE ET BOIS
634	VENEERS,PLYWOOD,ETC	W 14675	3077	W 13637	3063			W 19591	21252	PLACAGES,CONTRE–PLAQUES
6342	PLYWOOD OF WOOD SHEETS	W 13290	2852	W 12640	2872			W 17000	19612	BOIS CONTRE–PLAQUES
7	MACHINES,TRANSPORT EQUIP		6537		5080				12283	MACHINES MATERIEL TRANSPORT
8	MISC MANUFACTURED GOODS		9176		4899				9702	ART MANUFACTURES DIVERS

1. HISTORICAL SERIES, 1960–1995 GENERAL TRADE, IMPORTS C.I.F., EXPORTS F.O.B.
SERIES HISTORIQUES, 1960–1995 COMMERCE GENERAL, IMPORTATIONS C.A.F., EXPORTATIONS F.O.B

YEAR ANNEE	VALUE IN MILLION DALASIS VALEUR EN MILLION DALASIS MERCHANDISE –MARCHANDISE		GOLD –OR		CONVERSION FACTORS U.S. CENTS PER DALASI FACTEURS DE CONVERSION CENTS E.U. PAR DALASI		INDEX NUMBERS –INDICES QUANTUM		UNIT VALUE VALEUR UNITAIRE	
	IMPORTS	EXPORTS	IMPORTS	EXPORTS	IMPORTS	EXPORTS	IMPORTS	EXPORTS	IMPORTS	EXPORTS
1960	16.11	15.24			56.0000	56.0000				
1961	22.86	17.58			56.0000	56.0000				
1962	22.41	18.29			56.0000	56.0000				
1963	21.15	16.04			56.0000	56.0000				
1964	21.68	17.10			56.0000	56.0000				
1965	28.97	25.06			56.0000	56.0000				
1966	32.29	29.85			56.0000	56.0000				
1967	34.97	32.17			51.1120	51.1120				
1968	43.90	27.85			48.0000	48.0000				
1969	40.65	35.16			48.0000	48.0000				
1970	37.42	35.34			48.0000	48.0000				
1971	44.75	28.03			48.1962	48.1617				
1972	49.53	38.53			50.0036	51.4010				
1973	53.69	36.92			58.1678	61.4582				
1974	76.06	80.49			58.4883	59.4121				
1975	108.72	85.66			55.1795	57.7407				
1976	165.51	82.12			45.1182	46.4692				
1977	177.72	116.66			44.0684	43.5635				
1978	209.78	86.89			47.8669	47.2971				
1979	265.51	120.91			53.0001	52.9652				
1980	280.46	69.07			57.9783	57.4819				
1981	238.89	65.13			51.2267	52.9547				
1982	227.90	145.97			43.8131	44.7099				
1983	304.25	190.20			37.8920	38.2103				
1984	354.16	230.81			27.8110	28.8198				
1985	362.25	267.26			25.7522	24.9827				
1986	733.39	235.73			14.2578	14.7828				
1987	897.24	281.39			14.1748	14.1098				
1988	919.36	388.72			14.9054	14.9054				
1989	1221.01	198.05			13.2014	13.5615				
1990	1482.11	244.80			12.6777	12.5770				
1991	1759.38	333.45			11.4934	11.4258				
1992	1944.94	510.52			11.1802	11.1753				
1993	2372.27	604.73			10.9751	11.0312				
1994	2002.89	337.80			10.3691	10.3691				
1995	1339.84	155.23			10.4696	10.5203				

2. IMPORTS BY BROAD ECONOMIC CATEGORY AND EXPORTS BY INDUSTRIAL ORIGIN. (PERCENTAGE OF TOTAL VALUE)
IMPORTATIONS PAR CATEGORIES ECONOMIQUES ET EXPORTATIONS PAR BRANCHE D'ACTIVITE.(EN POURCENTAGE DE LA VALEUR TOTALE)

IMPORTS – IMPORTATIONS

	1990	1991	1992	1993	1994	1995	1996
TOTAL IMPORTS–IMPORTATIONS TOTALES							
1 FOOD BEV–ALIMENTATION BOISSONS							
11 PRIMARY–PRODUITS DE BASE							
111 FOR INDUSTRY–POUR L'INDUSTRIE							
112 FOR HOUSEHOLDS–POUR LES MENAGES							
12 PROCESSED–PRODUITS ELABORES							
121 FOR INDUSTRY–POUR L'INDUSTRIE							
122 FOR HOUSEHOLDS–POUR LES MENAGES							
2 IND SUPPLIES–APPROV INDUSTRIELS							
21 PRIMARY–PRODUITS DE BASE							
22 PROCESSED–PRODUITS ELABORES							
3 FUELS–COMBUSTIBLES							
31 PRIMARY–PRODUITS DE BASE							
32 PROCESSED–PRODUITS ELABORES							
321 MOTOR SPIRIT–ESSENCE							
322 OTHER–AUTRES							
4 MACHINERY–EQUIPEMENT							
41 CAPITAL EQUIPMENT–MACHINES							
42 PARTS–PIECES ACCESSOIRES							
5 TRANSPORT–TRANSPORT							
51 PASSENGER CARS–AUTOMOBILES							
52 OTHER–AUTRES							
521 INDUSTRIAL–INDUSTRIELS							
522 NON INDUSTRIAL–NON INDUSTRIEL							
53 PARTS–PIECES ACCESSOIRES							
6 CONSUM GOODS–BIENS CONSOMMATION							
61 DURABLE–DURABLES							
62 SEMI DURABLE–SEMI DURABLES							
63 NON DURABLE–NON DURABLES							
7 GOODS NES–BIENS NDA							

EXPORTS – EXPORTATIONS

	1990	1991	1992	1993	1994	1995	1996
TOTAL EXPORTS–EXPORTATIONS TOTALES							
1 AGRICULTURE							
2 MINING QUARRY–INDUS EXTRACTIVES							
3 MANUFACTURING–IND MANUFACTUR							
31 FOOD BEV TOBACCO–ALIM BOISS TAB							
32 TEXTILES–INDUSTRIES TEXTILES							
33 WOOD & PRODUCTS–BOIS & PRODUITS							
34 PAPER & PRODUCTS–PAPIER & PRODT							
35 CHEMICALS–INDUSTRIES CHIMIQUES							
36 NON METAL MIN–MIN NON METAL							
37 BASIC METAL–IND METAL BASE							
38 METAL MANUF–MANUF METAL							
39 OTH MANUF IND–AUTRES MANUF							

3. TRADE BY PRINCIPAL COUNTRIES OF FIRST AND LAST CONSIGNMENT (VALUE IN THOUSAND U.S. DOLLARS)
ECHANGES SELON LES PRINCIPAUX PAYS DE PREMIERE ET DE DERNIERE CONSIGNATION (VALEUR EN MILLIERS DE DOLLARS EU)

COUNTRIES–PAYS	GENERAL IMPORTS C.I.F. IMPORTATIONS GENERALES C.A.F				
	1991	1992	1993	1994	1995
World	202208		260000	226640	140315
Africa	11229		19000	46145	27303
Americas	6804			10535	10814
Northern America	6804			7101	7489
LAIA				3419	3183
CACM					0
Caribbean				14	2
Rest of America					140
As.ex F.USSR	58384		2000	52548	33633
Eur.x F.USSR	98667			114962	67462
EU	95380			113202	66303
EFTA	1345			1193	820
East Europe	1942			567	308
Other Europe					16
Former USSR				1886	628
Oceania				83	54
United Kingdom	26572			24448	19895
France, Monac	16814			32805	11110
Cote d'Ivoire	3333			35625	19029
China/Chine	29537			11792	8808
Netherlands/Pays–Bas	21331			13473	7055
Germany/Allemagne	12573			13173	8878
Belgium–Luxembourg	8551			14083	10166
Hong Kong	13136			10071	5136
Senegal/Sénégal	5229		16000	2654	4051
Japan/Japon	8103			8731	4949
USA/Etats–Unis d'Amer	6804			6919	7333
Thailand/Thaïlande	6137			6535	4862
Pakistan			1000	10178	761
Spain/Espagne	1747			5509	4490
Italy/Italie	5367			2961	2530
Denmark/Danemark	977			4354	1508
Malawi	2666			2125	2044
Brazil/Brésil				3404	2068
India/Inde				1290	3782
Sweden/Suède	1448			2190	536
Viet Nam				1239	2547
Cameroon/Cameroun				2694	106
Russian Federation				1885	628
Norway,SVD,JM	919			853	429
Nigeria/Nigéria			1000	468	378
Indonesia/Indonésie			1000	252	294
Gabon				1013	475
Brunei Darussalam				569	760
Guinea/Guinée			1000	197	16
Myanmar	1149				
Syrian Arab Republic				604	542
Switz.Liecht	425			327	391
Morocco/Maroc			1000	48	13
Former GDR	1046				
Argentina/Argentine					1020
Poland/Pologne	345			444	214
Singapore/Singapour	322			388	181
Czechoslovakia	552			96	73
Korea, Republic of				234	284
Sierra Leone				247	212
Mauritania/Mauritanie				342	115
Ethiopia/Ethiopie				15	428
Israel/Israël				33	275
Canada				182	96
So. Africa Customs Un				70	178
Turkey/Turquie				69	149
Lebanon/Liban				180	32
Ghana				127	49
Panama					140
Greece/Grèce				49	66

COUNTRIES–PAYS	GENERAL EXPORTS F.O.B. EXPORTATIONS GENERALES F.O.B.				
	1991	1992	1993	1994	1995
Monde	39770		67000		
Afrique	10123		12000		
Amériques	69				
Amérique du Nord	69				
ALAI					
MCAC					
Caraïbes					
Autre Amérique					
Asie l'URSS exclus	1085		2000		
Europe l'URSS exclus	15195				
UE	14281				
AELE	914				
Europe de l'Est					
Autre de l'Europe					
Ancienne URSS					
Océanie					
Guinea/Guinée	754		10000		
Guinea–Bissau	6866				
United Kingdom	5827				
Netherlands/Pays–Bas	3062				
France, Monac	2982				
Senegal/Sénégal	948		2000		
Malaysia/Malaisie			2000		
Belgium–Luxembourg	1782				
Mali	1234				
Switz.Liecht	914				
China/Chine	880				
Germany/Allemagne	400				
Ghana	320				
Italy/Italie	228				
Hong Kong	206				
USA/Etats–Unis d'Amer	69				

(VALUE AS PERCENTAGE OF WORLD TOTAL)(VALEURS EN POURCENTAGE DU TOTAL MONDIAL)

	1986	1987	1988	1989	1990	1991	1992	1993	1994	1995
Africa						5.6		7.3	20.4	19.5
Americas						3.4			4.6	7.7
Northern America						3.4			3.1	5.3
LAIA									1.5	2.3
CACM										0.0
Caribbean									0.0	0.0
Rest of America										0.1
As.ex F.USSR						28.9		0.8	23.2	24.0
Eur.x F.USSR						48.8			50.7	48.1
EU						47.2			49.9	47.3
EFTA						0.7			0.5	0.6
East Europe						1.0			0.3	0.2
Other Europe										0.0
Former USSR									0.8	0.4
Oceania									0.0	0.0
United Kingdom						13.1			10.8	14.2
France, Monac						8.3			14.5	7.9
Cote d'Ivoire						1.6			15.7	13.6
China/Chine						14.6			5.2	6.3
Netherlands/Pays–Bas						10.5			5.9	5.0
Germany/Allemagne						6.2			5.8	6.3
Belgium–Luxembourg						4.2			6.2	7.2
Hong Kong						6.5			4.4	3.7
Senegal/Sénégal						2.6		6.2	1.2	2.9
Japan/Japon						4.0			3.9	3.5

	1986	1987	1988	1989	1990	1991	1992	1993	1994	1995
Afrique	0.3	0.1	0.1			25.5		17.9		
Amériques	2.0	0.7	0.5			0.2				
Amérique du Nord	2.0	0.6	0.5			0.2				
ALAI	0.1	0.1	0.1							
MCAC										
Caraïbes										
Autre Amérique										
Asie l'URSS exclus	31.4	22.5	25.3			2.7		3.0		
Europe l'URSS exclus	66.3	76.7	74.1			38.2				
UE	50.2	65.8	63.6			35.9				
AELE	16.1	10.9	10.5			2.3				
Europe de l'Est										
Autre de l'Europe										
Ancienne URSS										
Océanie	0.0	0.0								
Guinea/Guinée						1.9		14.9		
Guinea–Bissau						17.3				
United Kingdom	10.5	7.9	7.7			14.7				
Netherlands/Pays–Bas	0.0	0.0	0.0			7.7				
France, Monac	13.9	4.4	4.2			7.5				
Senegal/Sénégal	0.1	0.1	0.1			2.4		3.0		
Malaysia/Malaisie								3.0		
Belgium–Luxembourg	17.7	35.4	34.2			4.5				
Mali						3.1				
Switz.Liecht	16.1	10.9	10.5			2.3				

4. General Imports C.I.F. by Commodities according to the S.I.T.C. (Rev. 2) in thousand U.S. Dollars
Importations Générales C.A.F. par Produits d'après la C.T.C.I. (Rév. 2) en milliers de Dollars E.U.

SITC CTCI	COMMODITY	1992		1993		1994		1995		PRODUIT
		WEIGHT POIDS	VALUE VALEUR	WEIGHT POIDS	VALUE VALEUR	WEIGHT POIDS	VALUE VALEUR	WEIGHT POIDS	VALUE VALEUR	
	ALL COMMODITIES						226640		140315	TOUS PRODUITS
0	FOOD AND LIVE ANIMALS						61194		37327	ALIMENTS,ANIMAUX VIVANTS
001	*LIVE ANIMALS FOR FOOD						1010		43	ANIMAUX VIVANTS
0011	BOVINE SPECIES,LIVE						965		1	ESPECE BOVINE
01	MEAT AND PREPARATIONS						1664		415	VIANDES ET PREPARATIONS
011	MEAT FRESH,CHILLD,FROZEN						799		374	VIANDES FRAICHES,REF,CONGE
014	MEAT PREPD,PRSVD,NES ETC						858		36	CONSERVES DE VIANDES
0149	OTH PREPARD,PRESRVD MEAT						824		6	AUTRES PREP DE VIANDES
02	DAIRY PRODCTS,BIRDS'EGGS						5799		3947	PRODUITS LAITIERS,OEUFS
022	MILK AND CREAM						3434		3486	LAIT ET CREME
0223	MILK AND CREAM FRESH						1748		1090	LAIT,CREME FRAIS
0224	MILK,CREAM PRESERVED ETC						1631		2343	LAIT,CREME CONS,CONC
025	EGGS,BIRDS,FRESH,PRSRVD						1921		269	OEUFS
0251	— IN SHELL						1882		242	OEUFS EN COQUILLE
03	FISH AND PREPARATIONS						953		350	POISSONS ET PREPARATIONS
04	CEREALS AND PREPARATIONS						22915		16063	CEREALES ET PRODUITS
041	WHEAT ETC UNMILLED						3319		14	FROMENT,EPEAUTRE
0411	DURUM WHEAT UNMILLED						3319		14	FROMENT DUR NON MOULU
042	RICE						14517		11273	RIZ
046	WHEAT ETC MEAL OR FLOUR						26		501	SEMOULE FARINE,FROMENT
04602	MEAL,GROATS OF WHEAT ETC						26		501	GRUAUX,SEMOULES FROMENT
047	OTHER CEREAL MEALS,FLOUR						4331		3229	AUTRES SEMOULES,FARINES
04701	CEREAL FLOUR(NON–WHEAT)						4331		3229	FARINES DE CEREALES
048	CEREAL ETC PREPARATIONS						718		1045	PREPTNS A BASE CEREALES
0488	OTH CEREAL PREPS,MALT EX						54		501	EXTRAITS DE MALT
05	VEGETABLES AND FRUIT						8634		4603	LEGUMES ET FRUITS
054	VEG ETC FRSH,SMPLY PRSVD						3739		1216	LEGUMES FRAIS,CONG,SECS
0545	OTHER FRESH VEGETABLES						3269		726	AUTRES LEGUMES FRAIS,REF
05451	ALLIACEOUS VEGTBLS,FRESH						3235		699	OIGNONS,ECHALOTES,AULX
056	VEGTBLES ETC PRSVD,PREPD						2699		1853	CONSERVES DE LEGUMES
0564	FLOUR ETC OF FRUIT,VEGET						724		25	FARINES,SEMOULES,FLOCONS
05643	POTATO FLOUR,MEAL,FLAKES						709		21	FLOCONS DE POMMES DE TERRE
0565	VEGTBLES PRSVD,PREPD NES						1897		1785	LEGUMES PREPARES CONSERVE
05659	OTH VEG PRESVD,PREPD NES						1849		1726	LEGUM PREPAP,CONSERV NDA
057	FRUIT,NUTS,FRESH,DRIED						1797		1121	FRUITS FRAIS OU SECS
0577	NUTS EDIBLE,FRESH,DRIED						1268		1082	FRUITS A COQUES
06	SUGAR AND PREPS,HONEY						14326		8689	SUCRES ET PRODUITS
061	SUGAR AND HONEY						14202		8462	SUCRES ET MIEL
0611	RAW BEET AND CANE SUGAR						14027		8456	SUCRES BRUTS
07	COFFEE,TEA,COCOA,SPICES						2099		1381	CAFE,THE,CACAO,EPICES
074	TEA AND MATE						1566		1164	THE ET MATE
0741	TEA						1564		1163	THE
09	MISC EDIBLE PRODUCTS						3344		1672	PREP ALIMENTAIRES DIVERSES
091	MARGARINE AND SHORTENING						1673		571	MARGARINE ET GRAISSES
0914	MARGARINE,EDIBLE FAT NES						1672		571	MARGARINES,SIMILI SAINDOUX
09141	MARGARINE						1672		571	MARGARINE
098	EDIBLE PRODCTS,PREPS NES						1671		1101	PREP ALIMENTAIRES NDA
09809	MISC FOOD PREPRTIONS NES						953		576	PREP ALIMENTAIRES NDA
1	BEVERAGES AND TOBACCO						20531		6478	BOISSONS ET TABACS
11	BEVERAGES						1760		795	BOISSONS
111	NON–ALCOHL BEVERAGES NES						901		474	BOISSONS NON ALCOOLIQUES
112	ALCOHOLIC BEVERAGES						859		321	BOISSONS ALCOOLIQUES
12	TOBACCO AND MANUFACTURES						18771		5683	TABACS BRUTS FABRIQUES
121	TOBACCO UNMNFCTRD,REFUSE						2357		2044	TABACS BRUTS,DECHETS
1211	TOBACCO,NOT STRIPPED						2357		2044	TABACS NON ECOTES
122	TOBACCO,MANUFACTURED						16414		3638	TABACS FABRIQUES
1222	CIGARETTES						16409		3593	CIGARETTES
2	CRUDE MATERLS,EXCL FUELS						2046		1822	MAT BRUTES NON COMESTIBLES
26	TEXTILE FIBRES AND WASTE						891		955	FIBRES TEXTILES
269	WASTE OF TEXTILE FABRICS						826		902	FRIPERIE DRILLES,CHIFFONS
26901	BULK TEXT WSTE,OLD CLTHG						825		901	ART ET ACCESS D'HABILLEMENT
3	MINERAL FUELS ETC						36871		20206	COMBUSTIBLES MINERAUX LUB
32	COAL,COKE AND BRIQUETTES						805			HOUILLES,COKES,BRIQUETTES
322	COAL,LIGNITE AND PEAT						805			HOUILLES,LIGNITES,TOURBE
3221	ANTHRACITE,NOT AGGLOMRTD						805			ANTHRACITE
33	PETROLEUM AND PRODUCTS						29484		19765	PETROLE ET DERIVES
334	PETROLEUM PRODUCTS,REFIN						28733		19334	PRODUITS RAFFINES
341	*GAS,NATURAL AND MANUFCT						6582		438	GAZ NATUREL,GAZ MANUFACT
4	ANIMAL,VEGETABLE OIL,FAT						3699		3865	HUILES,GRAISSES ANIM,VEG
42	FIXED VEGETABLE OIL,FAT						2644		3292	HUILES VEGETALES FIXES
423	FIXED VEG OILS,SOFT						798		1990	HUILES VEGET DOUCES FIXES
4234	GROUNDNUT(PEANUT) OIL						332		764	HUILE D'ARACHIDE
4239	OTH FIXED VEG OILS,SOFT						101		870	AUTRES HUILES FIXES
42391	RAPE,COLZA,MUSTARD OILS						101		870	H NAVETTE COLZA MOUTARDE
424	FIXED VEG OIL NONSOFT						1846		1302	AUTRES HUILES VEG FIXES
431	*PROCESD ANML VEG OIL,ET						1044		547	HUILES,GRAISSES PREPAREES
4312	HYDROGENATED OIL,FAT						1044		547	HUILES HYDROGENEES
5	CHEMCLS,RELATED PROD NES						12284		7816	PRODUITS CHIMIQUES
52	INORGANIC CHEMICALS						1070		1895	PROD CHIM INORGANIQUES
522	INORG ELEMNTS,OXIDES,ETC						645		1743	ELEMENTS INORGANIQUES
5222	INORGANIC ACIDS ETC						374		1331	ACIDES INORGANIQUES
52223	NITRIC,SULPHONITRIC ACID						305		1250	ACIDE NITRIQUE
53	DYES,TANNING,COLOUR PROD						751		714	PROD TEINTURE,COLORANTS
533	PIGMENTS,PAINTS,ETC						725		667	PIGMENTS,PEINTURES,VERNIS
5334	VARNISHES,DISTEMPERS ETC						639		537	PEINTURES A L'EAU
541	*MEDICINAL,PHARM PRODUCT						3540		2965	PROD MEDICINAUX PHARMACEUT
5417	MEDICAMENTS						3205		2563	MEDICAMENTS
55	PERFUME,CLEANING ETC PRD						1519		758	PROD POUR PARFUM,TOILETTE
553	PERFUMERY,COSMETICS,ETC						854		198	PRODUITS DE PARFUMERIE
562	*FERTILIZERS,MANUFACTURE						1789		43	ENGRAIS MANUFACTURES
5621	CHEM NITROGENOUS FERTLZR						1612			ENGRAIS AZOTES
56216	UREA						1612			UREE
59	CHEMICAL MATERIALS NES						2724		912	MAT PROD CHIMIQUES NDA
591	PESTICIDES,DISINFECTANTS						1504		796	DESINF,INSECT,FONG,HERB
5911	INSECTICIDES,FOR RETAIL						1504		796	INSECTICIDES VENTE DET
598	MISCEL CHEM PRODUCTS NES						1120		79	PROD DIV INDUST CHIM NDA
5989	CHEM PRODUCTS,PREPS NES						1001		61	PROD PREP CHIMIQUES NDA
59893	CULTURE MEDIA,PREPARED						924			MILIEUX DE CULTURE
6	BASIC MANUFACTURES						32664		20959	ART MANUFACTURES
62	RUBBER MANUFACTURES NES						1059		1472	CAOUTCHOUC MANUFACTURE
621	MATERIALS OF RUBBER						50		651	PRODUITS EN CAOUTCHOUC

4. General Imports C.I.F. by Commodities according to the S.I.T.C. (Rev. 2) in thousand U.S. Dollars
Importations Générales C.A.F. par Produits d'après la C.T.C.I. (Rév. 2) en milliers de Dollars E.U.

SITC CTCI	COMMODITY	1992		1993		1994		1995		PRODUIT
		WEIGHT POIDS	VALUE VALEUR	WEIGHT POIDS	VALUE VALEUR	WEIGHT POIDS	VALUE VALEUR	WEIGHT POIDS	VALUE VALEUR	
62105	UNHARD VULC RUBBER TUBES						38		641	TUBES,TUYAUX CAOUT VULC
625	RUBBER TYRES, TUBES ETC						906		803	PNEUS CAOUTCHOUC VULCANISE
6251	TYRES NEW FOR MOTOR CARS						758		678	PNEUS POUR VOITURES
63	WOOD,CORK MANUFACTRS NES						745		309	OUVRAGES LIEGE ET BOIS
64	PAPER,PAPERBOARD AND MFR						2061		1610	PAPIERS,CARTONS & OUVRAGES
641	PAPER AND PAPERBOARD						740		474	PAPIERS ET CARTONS
642	PAPER,ETC,PRECUT,ARTS OF						1320		1136	PAP,CARTONS DECOUPES
6421	PAPER ETC CONTAINERS						504		461	BOITES,SACS EMBALLAGES
65	TEXTILE YARN,FABRICS,ETC						14742		8616	FILS,TISSUS,ARTICLES TEXTILE
651	TEXTILE YARN						1056		236	FILS TEXTILES
6513	COTTON YARN						904		123	FILS DE COTON
65135	— PUT UP FOR RETAIL						793		15	FILS CONDS VENTE DETAIL
652	COTTON FABRICS,WOVEN						8809		6147	TISSUS DE COTON
6522	WOVEN COTTON BLEACHD,ETC						8175		6059	TISSUS COTON BLANCHIS ETC
65224	BLCHED COTTON FABRIC NES						7822		5758	AUT TIS PLUS 85% COT BLANCHI
653	WOVN MAN-MADE FIB FABRIC						3039		1793	TISSUS FIBRES SYNTH,ARTIF
6535	CONT REGN WEAVES NONPILE						625		722	TISSUS FIB TEXT ART CONTINU
654	OTH WOVEN TEXTILE FABRIC						681		81	TISSUS AUT COTON SYNT,ARTIF
658	TEXTILE ARTICLES NES						797		156	ART FACONNES MAT TEXTILES
66	NONMETAL MINERAL MFS NES						4723		3361	ART MIN NON METALLIQUES
661	LIME,CEMENT,BLDG PRODS						3061		2371	CHAUX,CIMENTS MAT CONSTR
6612	CEMENT						2942		2189	CIMENTS HYDRAULIQUES
662	CLAY,REFRACTORY BLDG PRD						908		583	MAT CONST REFRACTAIRES
6624	BRICKS ETC NONREFRACTORY						327		441	BRIQUES ETC CERAM NON REFR
67	IRON AND STEEL						2884		2703	FER ET ACIER
673	IRON,STEEL SHAPES ETC						1023		1650	BARRES,PROFIL FER,ACIER
6732	IRON,STEEL BARS ETC						466		687	BARRES FER,ACIER
67326	IRN,OTH STL BARS HOTROLD						345		608	BARRES PLEINES FER,ACIER
6733	IRON,STEEL PROFILES ETC						551		740	PROFILES,PALPLAN FER,ACIER
67336	IRN,SMPL STL SHEET PILNG						535		686	PALPLANCHES EN FER,ACIER
674	IRN,STL UNIV,PLATE,SHEET						878		826	LARGES PLATS,TOLES
678	IRON,STL TUBES,PIPES,ETC						799		135	TUBES,TUYAUX EN FONTE,FER
68	NON-FERROUS METALS						1671		678	METAUX NON FERREUX
684	ALUMINIUM						820		505	ALUMINIUM
6842	ALUMINIUM,ALLOYS WORKED						368		505	ALUMINIUM,ALLIAGES OUVRE
687	TIN						767			ETAIN
6872	TIN,ALLOYS WORKED						767			ETAIN ET ALLIAGES OUVRES
68724	TIN TUBES,FITTINGS,ETC						765			TUBES,TUYAUX EN ETAIN
69	METAL MANUFACTURES NES						4752		2198	ART MANUFACT EN METAL NDA
691	STRUCTURES AND PARTS NES						776		78	CONSTRUCT FER,ACIER,ALU
692	METAL TANKS,BOXES,ETC						734		183	RECIPIENTS METALLIQUES
697	BASE MTL HOUSEHOLD EQUIP						466		503	ART MENAGE MET COMMUNS
699	BASE METAL MFRS NES						2041		415	ART MANUFACTURES MET NDA
6991	LOCKSMITHS WARES,ETC						959		173	ARTICLES DE SERRURERIE
6998	MFRS NES OF CPR,NIKL,ETC						779		142	OUVRAGES EN CU,NI,AL,PB,ZN
69985	ZINC MANUFACTURES NES						737		118	OUVRAGES EN ZINC
7	MACHINES,TRANSPORT EQUIP						39922		28447	MACHINES MATERIEL TRANSPORT
71	POWER GENERATING EQUIPMT						2189		1157	MACHINES GENERATRICES
716	ROTATING ELECTRIC PLANT						1206		790	APP ELECTR ROTATIFS,PIECES
7169	PTS NES OF ROT ELEC PLNT						703		273	PIECES MAC APP ROTATIFS
72	MACHS FOR SPCL INDUSTRYS						2224		2198	MAC SPECIALES POUR INDUST
721	AGRIC MACHY,EXC TRACTORS						513		595	MACHINES AGRICOLES
723	CIVIL ENGNEERG EQUIP ETC						563		757	APPAREILS DE GENIE CIVIL
74	GENRL INDUSTRL MACHY NES						3545		3039	MACH APP INDUSTRIE
741	HEATING,COOLING EQUIPMNT						723		334	MACH CHAUFFAGE,PIECES
742	PUMPS FOR LIQUIDS ETC						758		1365	POMPES MOTO-POMPES
7428	OTHER PUMPS FOR LIQUIDS						758		1365	AUTRES POMPES POUR LIQ
74281	GARAGE-TYPE FUEL PUMPS						758		1365	POMPES DISTRIB CARBURNTS
743	PUMPS NES,CENTRFUGES ETC						721		197	POMPES COMPRES,VENT ETC
744	MECHANICAL HANDLING EQU						620		561	EQUIP MANUTENTION PIECES
75	OFFICE MACHNES,ADP EQUIP						1957		1460	MACH BUREAU TRAIT AUTOM
752	AUTOMTIC DATA PROC EQUIP						1357		974	MACH TRAIT INFORMATION
7521	ANALOG,HYBRID COMPUTERS						1357		974	MACH POUR TRAIT INFORMAT
76	TELECOMM,SOUND EQUIPMENT						4919		4288	EQUIPMENT DE TELECOM
763	SOUND RECORDRS,PHONOGRPH						790		495	PHONO,APP ENREGISTREMENT
7638	OTHR SOUND APPARATUS ETC						747		453	AUT APP D'ENREGIS,REPROD
764	TELECOM EQPT,PTS,ACC NES						3200		3452	EQUIP TELECOM,PIECES
7641	LINE TELEPHONE,ETC EQUIP						2794		1775	APP TELEPHON PAR FIL
7643	TV,RADIO TRANSMITTRS ETC						84		427	APP EMET TELE RADIO
7649	PTS NES OF EQUIPMT OF 76						181		1205	PIECES DE LA DIV 76
76493	TELECOMM EQUIPMT PTS NES						165		1169	PIECES 761,762,764.3,8
77	ELECTRIC MACHNRY NES ETC						6187		4205	MACH APP ELECT NDA
772	SWITCHGEAR ETC,PARTS NES						689		447	APP COUPURE,SECT ETC
7721	SWITCHGEAR ETC						688		432	APP COUPURE,SECTIONMNT
774	ELECTRO-MEDCL,XRAY EQUIP						460		1004	APPAREILS MEDICAUX
7741	ELECTRO-MEDICAL EQUIPMNT						444		994	APP ELECTRICITE MEDICALE
775	HOUSEHOLD TYPE EQUIP NES						802		796	MACH,APP USAGE DOMESTQUE
7752	DOM REFRIGERATRS,FREEZRS						639		611	REFRIG,CONGEL MENAGER
77521	DOMESTIC REFRIGERATORS						639		611	REFRIGERATEURS
776	TRANSISTORS,VALVES,ETC						703		74	LAMPES,TUBES,VALVES
7763	DIODES,TRANSISTORS,ETC						696		59	DIODES,TRANSISTORS
778	ELECTRICAL MACHINERY NES						2876		1657	AUTRES MACH ELECT NDA
7781	BATTERIES,ACCUMULATORS						1591		1480	PILES ET ACCUMULATEURS
77811	PRIMARY BATTERIES,CELLS						1376		1330	PILES ELECTRIQUES,PIECES
7788	OTH ELEC MACHY,EQUIP NES						862		45	AUT MACH APP ELEC NDA
77881	ELECTRO-MAGNETS ETC						763		2	ELECTRO-AIMANTS
78	ROAD VEHICLES						18335		11428	VEHICULES ROUTIERS
781	PASS MOTOR VEH EXC BUSES						9104		8099	AUTO TRANSPORT PERSONNES
782	LORRIES,SPCL MTR VEH NES						1503		625	VEHICULES SPECIAUX,MARCH
7821	LORRIES,TRUCKS						977		307	VEHICULES TRANSP MARCHAND
783	ROAD MOTOR VEHICLES NES						1609		219	VEHICULES ROUTIERS NDA
7831	BUSES						1609		219	VOITURES TRANSPORT COMMUN
784	MOTOR VEH PRTS,ACCES NES						2054		1556	PIECES 722,781,782,783
7849	OTHER MOTOR VEHCL PARTS						2046		1544	PIECES 722,781,782,783
785	CYCLES,ETC MOTRZD OR NOT						3798		886	MOTOCYCLES SCOOTERS
7851	MOTORCYCLES ETC						3373		586	MOTO VELO MOTEUR AUXIL
79	OTHR TRANSPORT EQUIPMENT						504		581	AUTRE MATERIEL TRANSPORT
793	SHIPS AND BOATS ETC						324		430	NAVIRES BATEAUX,ETC
8	MISC MANUFACTURED GOODS						15597		11113	ART MANUFACTURES DIVERS
821	*FURNITURE,PARTS THEREOF						1356		628	MEUBLES ET PIECES
8219	FURNITURE AND PARTS NES						828		456	AUTRES MEUBLES ET PIECES

4. General Imports C.I.F. by Commodities according to the S.I.T.C. (Rev. 2) in thousand U.S. Dollars
Importations Générales C.A.F. par Produits d'après la C.T.C.I. (Rév. 2) en milliers de Dollars E.U.

SITC CTCI	COMMODITY	1992		1993		1994		1995		PRODUIT
		WEIGHT POIDS	VALUE VALEUR	WEIGHT POIDS	VALUE VALEUR	WEIGHT POIDS	VALUE VALEUR	WEIGHT POIDS	VALUE VALEUR	
82191	METAL FURNITURE NES						828		456	MEUBLES NDA EN METAL
84	CLOTHING AND ACCESSORIES						1650		995	VETEMENTS
851	*FOOTWEAR						2359		1686	CHAUSSURES
85101	FOOTWEAR RUBBER,PLASTIC						1294		899	CHAUS SEMELLES CAOUTCH
85102	FOOTWEAR LEATHER						1065		788	CHAUS SEMELLES EN CUIR
88	PHOTO EQU,OPTICL GDS ETC						609		513	APP,FOURN PHOTO,OP,MONTR
89	MISC MANUFCTRD GOODS NES						8280		6317	ART MANUFACTURES DIVERS
892	PRINTED MATTER						3094		2262	IMPRIMES
8921	PRINTED BOOKS,GLOBES,ETC						316		947	LIVRES,BROCHURES,CARTES
89211	PRINTED BOOKS,PAMPHLETS						261		912	LIVRES,BROCHURES
8922	NEWSPAPERS,PERIODICALS						1610		679	JOURNAUX ET PERIODIQUES
8928	PRINTED MATTER NES						1154		621	IMPRIMES NDA
89286	TRADE ADV MATRL,CATALOGS						374		543	IMPRIMES PUBLICITAIRES
893	ARTICLES OF PLASTIC NES						1508		1266	OUVRAGES EN MAT DIVIS 58
8939	MISC PLASTIC ARTICLES						940		1026	ART DIVERS EN MAT DIV 58
89399	OTHR PLASTC ARTICLES NES						773		857	AUT OUV MAT DIV 58
894	TOYS,SPORTING GOODS,ETC						721		107	VOITURES ENFANTS,JOUETS
899	OTHER MANUFACTURED GOODS						2453		2056	AUT ART MANUF DIVERS NDA
8993	COMBUSTIBLE PRODUCTS ETC						2285		1818	BOUGIES,ALLUMETTES ETC
89931	CANDLES,TAPERS,ETC						1464		1271	BOUGIES,CHANDELLES,CIERG
89932	MATCHES						707		544	ALLUMETTES
9	GOODS NOT CLASSD BY KIND								2281	ART TRANSACT NON CLASSES
931	*SPECIAL TRANSACTIONS						1650		2243	TRANS.SPECIALES

5. General Exports F.O.B. by Commodities according to the S.I.T.C. (Rev. 2) in thousand U.S. Dollars
Exportations Générales F.O.B. par Produits d'après la C.T.C.I. (Rév. 2) en milliers de Dollars E.U.

SITC CTCI	COMMODITY	1992		1993		1994		1995		PRODUIT
		WEIGHT POIDS	VALUE VALEUR	WEIGHT POIDS	VALUE VALEUR	WEIGHT POIDS	VALUE VALEUR	WEIGHT POIDS	VALUE VALEUR	
	ALL COMMODITIES						38407		27794	TOUS PRODUITS
0	FOOD AND LIVE ANIMALS						6095		4797	ALIMENTS,ANIMAUX VIVANTS
02	DAIRY PRODCTS,BIRDS'EGGS						251		55	PRODUITS LAITIERS,OEUFS
022	MILK AND CREAM						249		55	LAIT ET CREME
0223	MILK AND CREAM FRESH						249		55	LAIT,CREME FRAIS
03	FISH AND PREPARATIONS						2711		2525	POISSONS ET PREPARATIONS
034	FISH,FRESH,CHILLED,FROZN						283		87	POISSON FRAIS, REFRIG,CONG
0342	FISH FROZEN,EXCL FILLETS						244		82	POISSONS CONGELES
035	FISH SALTED,DRIED,SMOKED						335		367	POISSON SECHE,SALE,FUME
03503	FISH(EX COD)DRIED,SALTED						332		364	POISSONS SECHES,SALES
036	SHELL FISH FRESH,FROZEN						2086		2066	CRUSTACES,MOLLUSQUES
04	CEREALS AND PREPARATIONS						337		66	CEREALES ET PRODUITS
048	CEREAL ETC PREPARATIONS						324		34	PREPTNS A BASE CEREALES
0484	BAKERY PRODUCTS						324		34	PRODUITS DE BOULANGERIE
04842	PASTRY, CAKES ETC						324		34	PATISSERIE ETC.
05	VEGETABLES AND FRUIT						1594		1839	LEGUMES ET FRUITS
054	VEG ETC FRSH,SMPLY PRSVD						737		1347	LEGUMES FRAIS,CONG,SECS
0542	LEGUMINOUS VEGETBLES DRY						224		926	LEGUMES A COSSE SECS
0545	OTHER FRESH VEGETABLES						438		405	AUTRES LEGUMES FRAIS,REF
05459	FRESH VEGETABLES NES						438		402	LEGUMES FRAIS,REFRI NDA
056	VEGTBLES ETC PRSVD,PREPD						152		12	CONSERVES DE LEGUMES
0565	VEGTBLES PRSVD,PREPD NES						152		12	LEGUMES PREPARES CONSERVE
05659	OTH VEG PRESVD,PREPD NES						144		12	LEGUM PREPAP,CONSERV NDA
057	FRUIT,NUTS,FRESH,DRIED						705		480	FRUITS FRAIS OU SECS
0577	NUTS EDIBLE,FRESH,DRIED						243		179	FRUITS A COQUES
05773	CASHEW NUTS,FRESH,DRIED						232		179	NOIX DE CAJOU
0579	FRUIT FRESH OR DRIED NES						452		291	FRUITS FRAIS,SECS NDA
05797	OTH TROP FRUIT,FRESH,DRY						384		263	AVOCATS,MANGUES,GOYAVES
06	SUGAR AND PREPS,HONEY						1099		297	SUCRES ET PRODUITS
061	SUGAR AND HONEY						477		51	SUCRES ET MIEL
0619	SUGARS AND SYRUPS NES						377			AUTRES SUCRES SIROPS
062	SUGAR CANDY NON–CHOCLATE						622		245	SUCRERIES
1	BEVERAGES AND TOBACCO						240		165	BOISSONS ET TABACS
12	TOBACCO AND MANUFACTURES						200		165	TABACS BRUTS FABRIQUES
121	TOBACCO UNMNFCTRD,REFUSE						196		87	TABACS BRUTS,DECHETS
1211	TOBACCO,NOT STRIPPED						196		49	TABACS NON ECOTES
2	CRUDE MATERLS,EXCL FUELS						14368		11855	MAT BRUTES NON COMESTIBLES
21	HIDES,SKINS,FURS UNDRSSD						79		90	CUIRS,PEAUX BRUTS
211	HIDES,SKINS,EXC FURS,RAW						79		90	CUIRS ET PEAUX
2112	CALF AND KIP SKINS,RAW						71		85	PEAUX DE VEAUX
22	OIL SEEDS,OLEAGINOUS FRT						8440		10013	GRAINES,FRUITS OLEAGINEUX
222	SEEDS FOR'SOFT'FIXED OIL						8440		10013	GRAINES HUILES FIXES
2221	GROUNDNUTS,GREEN						8143		9982	ARACHIDES NON GRILLEES
2223	COTTON SEEDS						297		15	GRAINES DE COTON
26	TEXTILE FIBRES AND WASTE						5520		1738	FIBRES TEXTILES
263	COTTON						5517		1728	COTON
2631	RAW COTTON,EXCL LINTERS						3566			COTON EN MASSE
2632	COTTON LINTERS						1951		1728	LINTERS DE COTON
29	CRUDE ANIMAL,VEG MAT NES						329			MATIERES BRUTES ANIM,VEGET
292	CRUDE VEG MATERIALS NES						325			MAT BRUTES VEGETALES NDA
2927	CUT FLOWERS AND FOLIAGE						255			FLEURS,FEUILLAGES COUPES
29271	CUT FLOWERS						255			FLEURS ET BOUTONS
5	CHEMCLS,RELATED PROD NES						754		335	PRODUITS CHIMIQUES
562	*FERTILIZERS,MANUFACTURE								299	ENGRAIS MANUFACTURES
5621	CHEM NITROGENOUS FERTLZR								109	ENGRAIS AZOTES
56216	UREA								109	UREE
5629	FERTILIZERS NES								190	ENGRAIS NDA
56291	NIT–PHOS–POT FERTLZR NES								190	ENGRAIS CONT N P K
572	*EXPLOSIVES,PYROTECH PRO						233			EXPLOSIFS
5723	PYROTECHNIC ARTICLES						233			ARTICLES DE PYROTECHNIE
59	CHEMICAL MATERIALS NES						516		12	MAT PROD CHIMIQUES NDA
591	PESTICIDES,DISINFECTANTS						503		12	DESINF,INSECT,FONG,HERB
5914	DISINFECTANTS,ETC,FR RET						503		3	DESINFECTANTS VENTE DET
59149	RAT POISONS ETC FR RTAIL						503		3	ANTIPARASITES VENTE DET
6	BASIC MANUFACTURES						2667		1390	ART MANUFACTURES
65	TEXTILE YARN,FABRICS,ETC						2516		1260	FILS,TISSUS,ARTICLES TEXTILE
652	COTTON FABRICS,WOVEN						387		288	TISSUS DE COTON
6521	GREY WOVEN COTTON FABRIC						66		190	TISSUS COT ECRUS NON MERCER
65215	GREY WOVN COTN BLEND NES						23		127	AUT TIS MOINS 85% COT ECRUS
6522	WOVEN COTTON BLEACHD,ETC						321		98	TISSUS COTON BLANCHIS ETC
65225	BLCHD COTN BLEND FAB NES						312		28	AUT TIS MOINS 85% COT BLANCH
653	WOVN MAN–MADE FIB FABRIC						1625		595	TISSUS FIBRES SYNTH,ARTIF
6535	CONT REGN WEAVES NONPILE						1554		350	TISSUS FIB TEXT ART CONTINU
65356	CONT REG BLEND FABRC NES						1481		350	TIS MOINS 85% TEXT ART CONT
6538	DISC REG BLEND FABRC NES						71		230	TIS MOINS 85% TEXT ART DISC
65389	OTH DISC REG BLEND FABRC						58		230	TISSUS TEX ART CONT MEL AUT
654	OTH WOVEN TEXTILE FABRIC						491		290	TISSUS AUT COTON SYNT,ARTIF
6542	WOVEN WOOL,HAIR NONPILE						491		290	TIS PLUS 85% LAINE,POILS
65422	WOVN COMB WOOL,FINE HAIR						491		290	TISSUS 85% LAINE,PLS PEIG
69	METAL MANUFACTURES NES						45		102	ART MANUFACT EN METAL NDA
7	MACHINES,TRANSPORT EQUIP						845		529	MACHINES MATERIEL TRANSPORT
71	POWER GENERATING EQUIPMT						266		2	MACHINES GENERATRICES
716	ROTATING ELECTRIC PLANT						260			APP ELECTR ROTATIFS,PIECES
7169	PTS NES OF ROT ELEC PLNT						260			PIECES MAC APP ROTATIFS
72	MACHS FOR SPCL INDUSTRYS						240			MAC SPECIALES POUR INDUST
723	CIVIL ENGNEERG EQUIP ETC						240			APPAREILS DE GENIE CIVIL
7234	CONST,MINING MACHNRY NES						240			MACH POUR LA CONST, MINES
72341	SELF–PROPELLD DOZERS,ETC						232			BULLDOZERS
77	ELECTRIC MACHNRY NES ETC						167		281	MACH APP ELECT NDA
778	ELECTRICAL MACHINERY NES						167		273	AUTRES MACH ELECT NDA
7781	BATTERIES,ACCUMULATORS						167		272	PILES ET ACCUMULATEURS
77811	PRIMARY BATTERIES,CELLS						167		272	PILES ELECTRIQUES,PIECES
78	ROAD VEHICLES						34		191	VEHICULES ROUTIERS
781	PASS MOTOR VEH EXC BUSES						32		158	AUTO TRANSPORT PERSONNES
8	MISC MANUFACTURED GOODS						5249		2026	ART MANUFACTURES DIVERS
87	PRECISION INSTRUMNTS NES						108		115	INSTRUM,APPAR SCIENT NDA
874	MEASURNG,CONTROLNG INSTR						108		115	INSTRUMENTS DE MESURE
8741	SURVEYING INSTRUMENTS								110	INST GEODESIE,TOPO ETC
87412	SURVEY INSTR ETC NONELEC								110	INSTR GEODESIE,TOPO ETC
89	MISC MANUFCTRD GOODS NES						5062		1860	ART MANUFACTURES DIVERS
892	PRINTED MATTER						3413			IMPRIMES

5. General Exports F.O.B. by Commodities according to the S.I.T.C. (Rev. 2) in thousand U.S. Dollars
Exportations Générales F.O.B. par Produits d'après la C.T.C.I. (Rév. 2) en milliers de Dollars E.U.

SITC CTCI	COMMODITY	1992		1993		1994		1995		PRODUIT
		WEIGHT POIDS	VALUE VALEUR	WEIGHT POIDS	VALUE VALEUR	WEIGHT POIDS	VALUE VALEUR	WEIGHT POIDS	VALUE VALEUR	
8928	PRINTED MATTER NES						3361			IMPRIMES NDA
89283	UNISSUED BANKNOTES ETC						3361			TIMBRES–POSTE FISCAUX
899	OTHER MANUFACTURED GOODS						1614		1801	AUT ART MANUF DIVERS NDA
8993	COMBUSTIBLE PRODUCTS ETC						1614		1794	BOUGIES,ALLUMETTES ETC
89931	CANDLES,TAPERS,ETC						1614		1789	BOUGIES,CHANDELLES,CIERG
9	GOODS NOT CLASSD BY KIND						8189		6659	ART TRANSACT NON CLASSES
931	*SPECIAL TRANSACTIONS						8104		6629	TRANS.SPECIALES

1. HISTORICAL SERIES, 1992–1995 GENERAL TRADE, IMPORTS C.I.F., EXPORTS F.O.B.
SERIES HISTORIQUES, 1992–1995 COMMERCE GENERAL, IMPORTATIONS C.A.F., EXPORTATIONS F.O.B

YEAR ANNEE	VALUE IN MILLION U.S. DOLLARS / VALEUR EN MILLION U.S. DOLLARS — MERCHANDISE – MARCHANDISE		GOLD – OR		CONVERSION FACTORS FACTEURS DE CONVERSION CENTS E.U. PAR		INDEX NUMBERS – INDICES — QUANTUM		UNIT VALUE VALEUR UNITAIRE	
	IMPORTS	EXPORTS	IMPORTS	EXPORTS	IMPORTS	EXPORTS	IMPORTS	EXPORTS	IMPORTS	EXPORTS
1992	227.00	68.00								
1993	167.00	69.00								
1994	471.00	70.00								
1995	250.00	140.00								

2. IMPORTS BY BROAD ECONOMIC CATEGORY AND EXPORTS BY INDUSTRIAL ORIGIN. (PERCENTAGE OF TOTAL VALUE)
IMPORTATIONS PAR CATEGORIES ECONOMIQUES ET EXPORTATIONS PAR BRANCHE D'ACTIVITE. (EN POURCENTAGE DE LA VALEUR TOTALE)

IMPORTS – IMPORTATIONS

	1990	1991	1992	1993	1994	1995	1996
TOTAL IMPORTS–IMPORTATIONS TOTALES							
1 FOOD BEV–ALIMENTATION BOISSONS							
11 PRIMARY–PRODUITS DE BASE							
111 FOR INDUSTRY–POUR L'INDUSTRIE							
112 FOR HOUSEHOLDS–POUR LES MENAGES							
12 PROCESSED–PRODUITS ELABORES							
121 FOR INDUSTRY–POUR L'INDUSTRIE							
122 FOR HOUSEHOLDS–POUR LES MENAGES							
2 IND SUPPLIES–APPROV INDUSTRIELS							
21 PRIMARY–PRODUITS DE BASE							
22 PROCESSED–PRODUITS ELABORES							
3 FUELS–COMBUSTIBLES							
31 PRIMARY–PRODUITS DE BASE							
32 PROCESSED–PRODUITS ELABORES							
321 MOTOR SPIRIT–ESSENCE							
322 OTHER–AUTRES							
4 MACHINERY–EQUIPEMENT							
41 CAPITAL EQUIPMENT–MACHINES							
42 PARTS–PIECES ACCESSOIRES							
5 TRANSPORT–TRANSPORT							
51 PASSENGER CARS–AUTOMOBILES							
52 OTHER–AUTRES							
521 INDUSTRIAL–INDUSTRIELS							
522 NON INDUSTRIAL–NON INDUSTRIEL							
53 PARTS–PIECES ACCESSOIRES							
6 CONSUM GOODS–BIENS CONSOMMATION							
61 DURABLE–DURABLES							
62 SEMI DURABLE–SEMI DURABLES							
63 NON DURABLE–NON DURABLES							
7 GOODS NES–BIENS NDA							

EXPORTS – EXPORTATIONS

	1990	1991	1992	1993	1994	1995	1996
TOTAL EXPORTS–EXPORTATIONS TOTALES							
1 AGRICULTURE							
2 MINING QUARRY–INDUS EXTRACTIVES							
3 MANUFACTURING–IND MANUFACTUR							
31 FOOD BEV TOBACCO–ALIM BOISS TAB							
32 TEXTILES–INDUSTRIES TEXTILES							
33 WOOD & PRODUCTS–BOIS & PRODUITS							
34 PAPER & PRODUCTS–PAPIER & PRODT							
35 CHEMICALS–INDUSTRIES CHIMIQUES							
36 NON METAL MIN–MIN NON METAL							
37 BASIC METAL–IND METAL BASE							
38 METAL MANUF–MANUF METAL							
39 OTH MANUF IND–AUTRES MANUF							

3. TRADE BY PRINCIPAL COUNTRIES OF ORIGIN AND DESTINATION (VALUE IN THOUSAND U.S. DOLLARS)
ECHANGES SELON LES PRINCIPAUX PAYS D'ORIGINE ET DE DESTINATION (VALEUR EN MILLIERS DE DOLLARS EU)

COUNTRIES–PAYS	GENERAL IMPORTS C.I.F. IMPORTATIONS GENERALES C.A.F					COUNTRIES–PAYS	GENERAL EXPORTS F.O.B. EXPORTATIONS GENERALES F.O.B.				
	1990	1991	1992	1993	1994		1990	1991	1992	1993	1994
World					329516	Monde					209050
Africa					1152	Afrique					
Americas					5222	Amériques					3962
Northern America					5222	Amérique du Nord					3731
LAIA						ALAI					231
CACM						MCAC					
Caribbean						Caraïbes					
Rest of America						Autre Amérique					
As.ex F.USSR					43397	Asie l'URSS exclus					33172
Eur.x F.USSR					15749	Europe l'URSS exclus					5224
EU					11521	UE					1034
EFTA					105	AELE					27
East Europe					4123	Europe de l'Est					4163
Other Europe						Autre de l'Europe					
Former USSR					263922	Ancienne URSS					166598
Oceania						Océanie					
Turkmenistan/Turkménistn					215473	Azerbaijan					52717
Turkey/Turquie					40935	Russian Federation					47902
Azerbaijan					22327	Armenia/Arménie					31423
Russian Federation					20535	Turkey/Turquie					27413
USA/Etats–Unis d'Amer					4954	Turkmenistan/Turkménistn					14625
Germany/Allemagne					4672	Kazakhstan					9004
Ukraine					3514	Ukraine					4835
Italy/Italie					2676	Iran (Islamic Rp. of)					4783
Czech Republic					1855	USA/Etats–Unis d'Amer					3731
Greece/Grèce					1805	Belarus/Bélarus					3031
Romania/Roumanie					1682	Czech Republic					2746
Cameroon/Cameroun					1152	Uzbekistan/Ouzbékistan					2345
Armenia/Arménie					1013	Hungary/Hongrie					1139
Cyprus/Chypre					961	China/Chine					970
Netherlands/Pays–Bas					737	Italy/Italie					461
Austria/Autriche					645	Tajikistan/Tadjikistan					300
Singapore/Singapour					595	Argentina/Argentine					231
Kazakhstan					453	France,Monac					177
United Kingdom					442	Republic of Moldova					155
Iran (Islamic Rp. of)					418	Denmark/Danemark					128
Belarus/Bélarus					332	Kyrgyzstan/Kirghizistan					108
Bulgaria/Bulgarie					306	Greece/Grèce					99
France,Monac					284	Germany/Allemagne					90
Canada					268	Romania/Roumanie					76
Denmark/Danemark					215	Poland/Pologne					76
Poland/Pologne					162	Bulgaria/Bulgarie					41
China/Chine					152	Netherlands/Pays–Bas					22
Uzbekistan/Ouzbékistan					131	United Kingdom					13
Japan/Japon					121	Israel/Israël					6
Hungary/Hongrie					114						
Israel/Israël					109						
Hong Kong					106						
Tajikistan/Tadjikistan					52						
Republic of Moldova					26						
Kyrgyzstan/Kirghizistan					7						

(VALUE AS PERCENTAGE OF WORLD TOTAL)(VALEURS EN POURCENTAGE DU TOTAL MONDIAL)

	1985	1986	1987	1988	1989	1990	1991	1992	1993	1994		1985	1986	1987	1988	1989	1990	1991	1992	1993	1994
Africa										0.3	Afrique										
Americas										1.6	Amériques										1.9
Northern America										1.6	Amérique du Nord										1.8
LAIA											ALAI										0.1
CACM											MCAC										
Caribbean											Caraïbes										
Rest of America											Autre Amérique										
As.ex F.USSR										13.2	Asie l'URSS exclus										15.9
Eur.x F.USSR										4.8	Europe l'URSS exclus										2.5
EU										3.5	UE										0.5
EFTA										0.0	AELE										0.0
East Europe										1.3	Europe de l'Est										2.0
Other Europe											Autre de l'Europe										
Former USSR										80.1	Ancienne URSS										79.7
Oceania											Océanie										
Turkmenistan/Turkménistn										65.4	Azerbaijan										25.2
Turkey/Turquie										12.4	Russian Federation										22.9
Azerbaijan										6.8	Armenia/Arménie										15.0
Russian Federation										6.2	Turkey/Turquie										13.1
USA/Etats–Unis d'Amer										1.5	Turkmenistan/Turkménistn										7.0
Germany/Allemagne										1.4	Kazakhstan										4.3
Ukraine										1.1	Ukraine										2.3
Italy/Italie										0.8	Iran (Islamic Rp. of)										2.3
Czech Republic										0.6	USA/Etats–Unis d'Amer										1.8
Greece/Grèce										0.5	Belarus/Bélarus										1.4

4. General Imports C.I.F. by Commodities according to the S.I.T.C. (Rev. 2) in thousand U.S. Dollars
Importations Générales C.A.F. par Produits d'après la C.T.C.I. (Rév. 2) en milliers de Dollars E.U.

SITC CTCI	COMMODITY	1991		1992		1993		1994		PRODUIT
		WEIGHT POIDS	VALUE VALEUR	WEIGHT POIDS	VALUE VALEUR	WEIGHT POIDS	VALUE VALEUR	WEIGHT POIDS	VALUE VALEUR	
	ALL COMMODITIES								329516	TOUS PRODUITS

5. General Exports F.O.B. by Commodities according to the S.I.T.C. (Rev. 2) in thousand U.S. Dollars
Exportations Générales F.O.B. par Produits d'après la C.T.C.I. (Rév. 2) en milliers de Dollars E.U.

SITC CTCI	COMMODITY	1991		1992		1993		1994		PRODUIT
		WEIGHT POIDS	VALUE VALEUR	WEIGHT POIDS	VALUE VALEUR	WEIGHT POIDS	VALUE VALEUR	WEIGHT POIDS	VALUE VALEUR	
	ALL COMMODITIES								209050	TOUS PRODUITS

1. HISTORICAL SERIES, 1961–1996 SPECIAL TRADE, IMPORTS C.I.F., EXPORTS F.O.B.
SERIES HISTORIQUES, 1961–1996 COMMERCE SPECIAL, IMPORTATIONS C.A.F., EXPORTATIONS F.O.B

YEAR ANNEE	VALUE IN MILLION DEUTSCHE MARK / VALEUR EN MILLION DEUTSCHE MARK: MERCHANDISE–MARCHANDISE		GOLD–OR		CONVERSION FACTORS U.S. CENTS PER DEUTSCHE MARK / FACTEURS DE CONVERSION CENTS E.U. PAR DEUTSCHE MARK		INDEX NUMBERS–INDICES: QUANTUM		UNIT VALUE / VALEUR UNITAIRE	
	IMPORTS	EXPORTS	IMPORTS	EXPORTS	IMPORTS	EXPORTS	IMPORTS	EXPORTS	IMPORTS	EXPORTS
1961	44127.90	51171.25	368.40	28.80	24.7936	24.7936	24	26	105	86
1962	49118.00	53054.39	446.40	37.76	25.0000	25.0000	27	27	103	87
1963	52075.18	58462.39	301.00	49.36	25.0000	25.0000	29	29	102	87
1964	58453.58	64860.00	383.40	57.76	25.0000	25.0000	33	33	102	87
1965	69888.77	71569.54	555.60	78.16	25.0000	25.0000	38	35	104	88
1966	72089.98	80536.38	576.40	88.16	25.0000	25.0000	40	41	103	86
1967	69402.37	86942.72	777.20	98.56	25.0000	25.0000	39	44	103	86
1968	80600.00	99369.98	575.60	178.60	25.0000	25.0000	46	51	101	86
1969	99704.00	116207.60	661.40	208.00	25.6126	25.6295	54	56	103	88
1970	109606.00	125275.90	476.20	132.50	27.3220	27.3220	45	43	69	62
1971	120119.00	136011.00	492.60	97.48	28.7074	28.7241	41	37	54	57
1972	128743.90	149023.00	597.80	107.80	31.0297	31.0296	43	40	54	58
1973	145417.00	178395.90	904.80	169.00	37.7102	37.8357	46	45	58	61
1974	179733.00	230577.90	1763.00	514.00	38.7794	38.7561	44	50	75	72
1975	184313.00	221589.00			40.6570	40.6952	44	45	77	77
1976	222173.00	256641.90			39.8003	39.8088	52	53	79	76
1977	235177.90	273614.00			43.1384	43.1521	53	55	81	78
1978	243707.00	284907.00			49.9580	50.0002	56	57	79	78
1979	292039.90	314469.10			54.6562	54.6314	61	59	88	82
1980	341380.30	350327.80			55.0707	55.0712	64	65	97	64
1981	369178.80	396898.00			44.4051	44.3547	61	69	110	90
1982	376463.80	427740.90			41.4000	41.2465	62	71	111	94
1983	390192.10	432281.00			39.1855	39.1931	64	71	111	95
1984	434256.80	488222.90			34.8287	34.7759	67	77	117	98
1985	463811.00	537164.20			34.1839	34.2557	70	82	120	102
1986	413744.30	526363.10			46.1281	46.2234	75	83	101	99
1987	409641.20	527376.60			55.7077	55.7562	79	86	95	96
1988	439609.30	567653.80			56.9695	56.9497	84	92	96	96
1989	547607.00	682146.00			53.5223	53.5119	90	99	103	101
1990	556580.10	661880.00			62.0472	62.0472	100	100	100	100
1991	645410.00	666170.10			60.4923	60.4923	113	100	102	99
1992	628189.90	658469.80			64.1952	64.1952	115	102	99	99
1993	571909.80	632219.90			60.5218	60.5218	104	98	93	94
1994	622919.90	694690.00			61.7649	61.7649	114	112	95	93
1995	635889.90	727300.10			69.9105	69.9020	115	116	98	95
1996	685740.00	784329.90			66.4546	66.4436	125	128	98	94

2. IMPORTS BY BROAD ECONOMIC CATEGORY AND EXPORTS BY INDUSTRIAL ORIGIN. (PERCENTAGE OF TOTAL VALUE)
IMPORTATIONS PAR CATEGORIES ECONOMIQUES ET EXPORTATIONS PAR BRANCHE D'ACTIVITE.(EN POURCENTAGE DE LA VALEUR TOTALE)

IMPORTS – IMPORTATIONS

	1990	1991	1992	1993	1994	1995	1996
TOTAL IMPORTS–IMPORTATIONS TOTALES	100.	100.	100.	100.	100.	100.	100.
1 FOOD BEV–ALIMENTATION BOISSONS	9.1	9.0	9.3	8.7	9.3	9.0	8.8
11 PRIMARY–PRODUITS DE BASE	5.0	4.9	5.0	4.6	5.0	4.9	4.8
111 FOR INDUSTRY–POUR L'INDUSTRIE	1.4	1.1	1.1	0.9	1.3	1.3	1.2
112 FOR HOUSEHOLDS–POUR LES MENAGES	3.6	3.8	3.9	3.7	3.7	3.6	3.6
12 PROCESSED–PRODUITS ELABORES	4.1	4.1	4.3	4.2	4.3	4.1	4.0
121 FOR INDUSTRY–POUR L'INDUSTRIE	0.5	0.5	0.5	0.5	0.5	0.5	0.5
122 FOR HOUSEHOLDS–POUR LES MENAGES	3.6	3.6	3.8	3.7	3.8	3.6	3.5
2 IND SUPPLIES–APPROV INDUSTRIELS	30.2	27.3	27.6	25.4	27.5	28.8	25.6
21 PRIMARY–PRODUITS DE BASE	3.3	2.9	3.0	2.7	2.9	2.9	2.5
22 PROCESSED–PRODUITS ELABORES	26.9	24.4	24.7	22.7	24.6	25.9	23.1
3 FUELS–COMBUSTIBLES	8.2	8.2	7.3	7.9	6.9	6.3	7.8
31 PRIMARY–PRODUITS DE BASE	5.3	5.4	5.1	5.6	5.1	4.7	5.8
32 PROCESSED–PRODUITS ELABORES	2.8	2.8	2.3	2.3	1.8	1.6	2.0
321 MOTOR SPIRIT–ESSENCE	1.1	0.9	0.8	0.7	0.6	0.5	0.5
322 OTHER–AUTRES	1.8	1.9	1.5	1.6	1.3	1.1	1.5
4 MACHINERY–EQUIPEMENT	18.6	18.9	19.2	18.8	19.7	20.4	19.7
41 CAPITAL EQUIPMENT–MACHINES	14.1	14.5	14.7	14.2	14.4	14.5	14.2
42 PARTS–PIECES ACCESSOIRES	4.5	4.4	4.4	4.6	5.3	5.9	5.5
5 TRANSPORT–TRANSPORT	13.6	16.2	15.6	14.3	14.2	14.2	14.8
51 PASSENGER CARS–AUTOMOBILES	5.0	6.2	5.8	5.1	4.8	5.2	5.4
52 OTHER–AUTRES	3.4	4.6	4.0	3.3	3.0	2.7	2.7
521 INDUSTRIAL–INDUSTRIELS	3.2	4.3	3.7	2.9	2.6	2.3	2.4
522 NON INDUSTRIAL–NON INDUSTRIEL	0.2	0.3	0.3	0.4	0.4	0.4	0.4
53 PARTS–PIECES ACCESSOIRES	5.3	5.4	5.8	5.9	6.4	6.3	6.6
6 CONSUM GOODS–BIENS CONSOMMATION	18.1	19.0	19.0	19.7	19.1	17.8	17.8
61 DURABLE–DURABLES	5.0	5.0	5.0	5.1	4.9	4.6	4.6
62 SEMI DURABLE–SEMI DURABLES	10.8	11.5	11.5	12.0	11.4	10.5	10.5
63 NON DURABLE–NON DURABLES	2.3	2.5	2.6	2.6	2.8	2.7	2.7
7 GOODS NES–BIENS NDA	2.0	1.5	1.9	4.8	3.2	3.6	5.5

EXPORTS – EXPORTATIONS

	1990	1991	1992	1993	1994	1995	1996
TOTAL EXPORTS–EXPORTATIONS TOTALES	100.	100.	100.	100.	100.	100.	100.
1 AGRICULTURE	1.1	1.2	1.3	1.1	1.2	1.1	1.2
2 MINING QUARRY–INDUS EXTRACTIVES	0.7	0.7	0.6	0.5	0.5	0.5	0.7
3 MANUFACTURING–IND MANUFACTUR	98.2	981	981	984 9	8.3 9	8.4 9	8.1
31 FOOD BEV TOBACCO–ALIM BOISS TAB	4.2	4.6	4.6	4.8	4.6	4.3	4.3
32 TEXTILES–INDUSTRIES TEXTILES	5.7	5.8	5.8	5.4	5.2	4.8	4.6
33 WOOD & PRODUCTS–BOIS & PRODUITS	0.5	0.5	0.5	0.4	0.5	0.5	0.4
34 PAPER & PRODUCTS–PAPIER & PRODT	3.0	3.0	3.0	2.9	3.1	3.3	3.1
35 CHEMICALS–INDUSTRIES CHIMIQUES	16.2	16.3	16.2	16.3	17.0	16.8	16.6
36 NON METAL MIN–MIN NON METAL	1.7	1.6	1.6	1.5	1.5	1.5	1.5
37 BASIC METAL–IND METAL BASE	5.8	5.4	5.0	5.0	5.0	5.4	4.8
38 METAL MANUF–MANUF METAL	58.2	57.8	58.5	56.9	57.6	58.0	58.0
39 OTH MANUF IND–AUTRES MANUF	2.7	31	30	4.8	3.1	3.4	4.8

3. TRADE BY PRINCIPAL COUNTRIES OF PRODUCTION AND LAST CONSIGNMENT (VALUE IN THOUSAND U.S. DOLLARS)
ECHANGES SELON LES PRINCIPAUX PAYS DE PRODUCTION ET DE DERNIERE CONSIGNATION (VALEUR EN MILLIERS DE DOLLARS EU)

COUNTRIES–PAYS	SPECIAL IMPORTS C.I.F. IMPORTATIONS SPECIALES C.A.F				
	1992	1993	1994	1995	1996
World	408307127	342558712	381538916	464145333	444395999
Africa	10538459	8638717	8800639	9550626	9704160
Americas	39201096	34342706	39181710	45852392	45100332
Northern America	29797895	26782505	30292688	35357611	35832860
LAIA	8421796	6605877	7653946	8881068	7804680
CACM	500043	541771	818990	956892	806144
Caribbean	242043	249849	222278	295028	324381
Rest of America	239319	162704	193808	361793	332267
As.ex F.USSR	63989255	60359521	64691386	75180197	72886685
Eur.x F.USSR	284164181	229687088	257012626	319208528	302050287
EU	243630007	192239873	212496933	262159684	245143565
EFTA	22316262	20317643	23112247	27715597	27710172
East Europe	14179885	13927296	17884426	25204164	25232499
Other Europe	318682	244137	248524	288718	252527
Former USSR	8301213	7885178	9941145	11843012	12356169
Oceania	1942085	1515811	1784921	2068906	1824319
France, Monac	48878364	39636740	42243255	51076667	47228708
Netherlands/Pays–Bas	39176821	30217688	31929212	40669217	38168168
Italy/Italie	37439065	29132392	32085835	39734834	36550866
USA/Etats–Unis d'Amer	27079081	24395456	27591665	31616521	32540644
United Kingdom	27942690	21448745	23918749	30452998	30284376
Belgium–Luxembourg	28688982	20598281	23532808	30734679	27988728
Japan/Japon	24366078	20636750	21116091	24758938	22674960
Austria/Autriche	17954056	15961677	18194150	18195119	16787504
Switz.Liecht	16254410	14566493	16472754	19898659	18448983
Spain/Espagne	11011394	8994452	10794770	14661798	14625020
China/Chine	7483266	8344413	9501712	11155796	11911128
Sweden/Suède	9024354	7591566	8690834	9745089	9215833
Russian Federation	7436516	6483879	8164253	9499884	10218355
Denmark/Danemark	9213878	6381079	7124491	8929270	7955518
Norway,SVD,JM	5825283	5563967	6396518	7552005	9020384
Poland/Pologne	5326242	5219094	6279449	8681804	8090613
Czech Republic		3889904	5270921	7406427	7554869
Turkey/Turquie	4386568	4025605	4478652	5558356	5612769
Ireland/Irlande	3948493	3601783	4252348	5904233	4956206
Finland/Finlande	4195263	3416561	4339193	4997722	4167393
Korea, Republic of	3448362	3440315	4216115	5284216	4297632
Portugal	3791584	3236038	3446425	4895054	5263836
Hungary/Hongrie	2970042	2734392	3359820	4831537	5260014
Brazil/Brésil	3453150	2670424	3193149	3495101	3239701
Canada	2708880	2382910	2696436	3736794	3285958
Singapore/Singapour	2373814	2448138	2964024	2974707	2869434
Malaysia/Malaisie	2232763	2063715	2460322	3161839	3106658
Hong Kong	3038012	2631142	2412024	2553966	2319771
India/Inde	1722502	1956751	2150625	2516241	2632899
Greece/Grèce	2365063	2022871	1944863	2163004	1951409
Thailand/Thaïlande	1876566	1897493	2087139	2267906	2174196
Slovenia/Slovénia	1245802	1813012	2069231	2540861	2421664
So. Africa Customs Un	2065053	1621224	1660144	2027117	2058656
Indonesia/Indonésie	1394091	1618225	1857739	1995693	2189134
Libyan Arab Jamahiriya	1890425	1587859	1521285	1518183	1989155
Slovakia		899384	1363198	2196430	2274373
Algeria/Algérie	1575154	1406282	1047668	955518	1014671
Romania/Roumanie	805891	827178	1134939	1505347	1499681
Australia/Australie	1321466	949011	1094131	1185199	1026051
Saudi Arabia	1272435	1186124	949388	876611	931737
Argentina/Argentine	1174528	956497	1040802	1035985	895836
Israel/Israël	864053	877986	967360	1142913	1148437
Philippines	753822	780715	934247	1057421	1250932
Czechoslovakia	4672682				
Nigeria/Nigéria	1454540	869145	951100	689028	706843
Colombia/Colombie	811322	707128	869225	1162382	788629
Tunisia/Tunisie	771547	741171	830787	954897	973998
Chile/Chili	795818	621527	760187	1083054	928931
Croatia/Croatie	528402	832491	866613	945908	854610
Iran (Islamic Rp. of)	725629	795708	828084	814545	723421

COUNTRIES–PAYS	SPECIAL EXPORTS F.O.B. EXPORTATIONS SPECIALES F.O.B.				
	1992	1993	1994	1995	1996
Monde	430276307	380074808	427100056	523696751	512693598
Afrique	9859464	8651474	9077469	11084474	10257974
Amériques	39302227	39828186	46710361	54148984	55077403
Amérique du Nord	30131779	30673789	36247766	41050176	42731567
ALAI	8188631	8262221	9505457	11646541	11526906
MCAC	270360	286606	313386	350247	333386
Caraïbes	392949	340022	319591	446864	387654
Autre Amérique	318508	265548	324161	655156	97890
Asie l'URSS exclus	50839665	52237324	58895927	72369328	73836722
Europe l'URSS exclus	317907875	265920648	298023426	368750543	355761102
UE	272621795	222923902	247842517	304762725	290054148
AELE	26622044	23676087	26774937	32404040	29995075
Europe de l'Est	15048825	16129483	19557816	26977241	30730259
Autre de l'Europe	340539	322714	344494	327336	302301
Ancienne URSS	8887504	9632009	10235987	11390177	12183931
Océanie	2866492	2854273	3435095	4596783	4086279
France, Monac	55776923	46819124	51329397	61364328	56317158
United Kingdom	33330313	30423231	34258224	43299137	40960794
Italy/Italie	39948201	28756095	32416090	39747800	38084513
Netherlands/Pays–Bas	35747352	29246646	32617958	39894319	38085359
USA/Etats–Unis d'Amer	27429000	28243637	33512334	38170340	39920348
Belgium–Luxembourg	31712572	25908872	28927074	34324291	31951616
Austria/Autriche	25613568	22537523	24570748	29110654	28737595
Switz.Liecht	22817035	20422538	22941728	27952023	25372542
Spain/Espagne	17857388	12642725	13741036	18262318	18534592
Japan/Japon	9423855	9521370	11118509	13163483	14088504
Sweden/Suède	9383650	7667335	9500248	12841484	12254876
Denmark/Danemark	8335648	6839265	7988589	10026361	9257374
Poland/Pologne	5293680	5864288	6418862	8877864	10861774
Russian Federation	7409480	6875760	6643522	7197108	7603719
China/Chine	3694865	5795730	6350809	7538505	7224248
Czech Republic		4623234	5975700	8264709	9200151
Turkey/Turquie	4230099	5086154	3875902	6359165	7574024
Korea, Republic of	3085237	3452376	4581285	6116750	6557881
Portugal	4566890	3740121	3651927	4737307	5236193
Hungary/Hongrie	3007233	3116916	3951284	4911602	5540984
Greece/Grèce	4835413	3848749	3554471	3882604	3562417
Finland/Finlande	3624757	2816057	3336319	4824567	4871280
Norway,SVD,JM	3628987	3107971	3695918	4281403	4419075
Hong Kong	2729952	3009211	3586038	4038329	4239884
Brazil/Brésil	1869198	2556660	3148699	5057591	4798964
So. Africa Customs Un	2827383	2636860	3150690	4101924	3706535
Australia/Australie	2476527	2466331	2924031	3674149	3488226
Singapore/Singapour	2069255	2252996	2809494	3669723	3860225
Thailand/Thaïlande	1743290	2036534	2791667	3758774	3513757
Canada	2693977	2388264	2716169	2869731	2798538
Mexico/Mexique	2796694	2602381	2783593	2388514	2560922
Saudi Arabia	2712354	2177883	2558503	2472589	2553162
Iran (Islamic Rp. of)	5102110	2487588	1579155	1646633	1477699
India/Inde	1814939	1816575	2074560	3194361	3116265
Indonesia/Indonésie	1994013	1897036	2189263	2747741	2657012
Israel/Israël	2060487	1890176	2232850	2482648	2549572
Malaysia/Malaisie	1366289	1440209	2096902	2862429	2809489
Ireland/Irlande	1889120	1678159	1950436	2447555	2200381
Slovenia/Slovénia	903780	1489211	1735724	2194244	2057826
United Arab Emirates	1114475	1332657	1640203	1610532	1441227
Egypt/Egypte	1231482	1294744	1286660	1514575	1695042
Romania/Roumanie	853132	1090209	1246287	1794330	1924980
Slovakia		846914	1265496	2158132	2443253
Croatia/Croatie	627203	1069493	1346922	1555606	1646442
Argentina/Argentine	1033012	938789	1263527	1285190	1517758
Czechoslovakia	5304022				
Ukraine	632620	929923	1098461	1256389	1289248
Philippines	626151	645622	844233	973944	1310448
Tunisia/Tunisie	862304	788335	797986	928397	933367
Morocco/Maroc	679555	630621	763561	766669	692948

(VALUE AS PERCENTAGE OF WORLD TOTAL)(VALEURS EN POURCENTAGE DU TOTAL MONDIAL)

	1987	1988	1989	1990	1991	1992	1993	1994	1995	1996
Africa	3.3	3.2	3.0	3.0	2.7	2.6	2.5	2.3	2.1	2.2
Americas	9.8	10.5	11.4	10.2	9.7	9.6	10.0	10.3	9.9	10.1
Northern America	7.0	7.4	8.4	7.5	7.3	7.3	7.8	7.9	7.6	8.1
LAIA	2.4	2.6	2.7	2.4	2.2	2.1	1.9	2.0	1.9	1.8
CACM	0.2	0.2	0.2	0.2	0.2	0.1	0.2	0.2	0.2	0.2
Caribbean	0.1	0.1	0.1	0.1	0.1	0.1	0.1	0.1	0.1	0.1
Rest of America	0.1	0.1	0.1	0.1	0.1	0.1	0.0	0.1	0.1	0.1
As.ex F.USSR	14.5	15.0	15.1	15.1	15.9	15.7	17.6	17.0	16.2	16.4
Eur.x F.USSR	69.9	69.0	68.0	69.3	69.0	69.6	67.1	67.4	68.8	68.0
EU	60.4	59.6	58.8	59.9	59.5	59.7	56.1	55.7	56.5	55.2
EFTA	6.1	5.9	5.7	5.7	5.3	5.5	5.9	6.1	6.0	6.2
East Europe	2.1	2.1	2.1	2.3	2.9	3.5	4.1	4.7	5.4	5.7
Other Europe	1.3	1.3	1.3	1.4	1.3	0.1	0.1	0.1	0.1	0.1
Former USSR	1.8	1.6	1.7	1.7	2.2	2.0	2.3	2.6	2.6	2.8
Oceania	0.7	0.7	0.7	0.6	0.5	0.5	0.4	0.5	0.4	0.4
France, Monac	11.6	12.1	11.9	11.8	12.3	12.0	11.6	11.1	11.0	10.6
Netherlands/Pays–Bas	11.0	10.3	10.3	10.2	9.8	9.6	8.8	8.4	8.8	8.6
Italy/Italie	9.6	9.2	8.9	9.4	9.3	9.2	8.5	8.4	8.6	8.2
USA/Etats–Unis d'Amer	6.2	6.6	7.5	6.7	6.5	6.6	7.1	7.2	6.8	7.3
United Kingdom	7.2	6.9	6.9	6.7	6.6	6.8	6.3	6.3	6.6	6.8
Belgium–Luxembourg	7.1	7.1	6.9	7.2	7.1	7.0	6.0	6.2	6.6	6.3
Japan/Japon	6.2	6.4	6.4	6.0	6.1	6.0	6.0	5.5	5.3	5.1
Austria/Autriche	4.2	4.3	4.1	4.3	4.2	4.4	4.7	4.8	3.9	3.8
Switz.Liecht	4.6	4.5	4.2	4.2	3.9	4.0	4.3	4.3	4.3	4.2
Spain/Espagne	2.0	2.0	2.1	2.4	2.7	2.7	2.6	2.8	3.2	3.3

	1987	1988	1989	1990	1991	1992	1993	1994	1995	1996
Afrique	2.7	2.8	2.7	2.5	2.4	2.3	2.3	2.1	2.1	2.0
Amériques	12.5	10.6	9.9	9.9	9.0	9.1	10.5	10.9	10.3	10.7
Amérique du Nord	10.4	8.9	8.1	8.0	7.0	7.0	8.1	8.5	7.8	8.3
ALAI	1.8	1.5	1.5	1.6	1.8	1.9	2.2	2.2	2.2	2.2
MCAC	0.1	0.1	0.1	0.1	0.1	0.1	0.1	0.1	0.1	0.1
Caraïbes	0.2	0.1	0.1	0.2	0.1	0.1	0.1	0.1	0.1	0.1
Autre Amérique	0.1	0.0	0.1	0.1	0.1	0.1	0.1	0.1	0.1	0.0
Asie l'URSS exclus	9.9	9.9	9.9	10.8	11.4	11.8	13.7	13.8	13.8	14.4
Europe l'URSS exclus	72.6	74.1	74.7	74.3	73.8	73.9	70.0	69.8	70.4	69.4
UE	62.3	64.1	64.7	64.0	63.2	63.4	58.7	58.0	58.2	56.6
AELE	7.2	7.0	6.8	6.9	6.5	6.2	6.2	6.3	6.2	5.9
Europe de l'Est	1.9	1.8	2.0	2.0	3.0	3.5	4.2	4.6	5.2	6.0
Autre de l'Europe	1.2	1.2	1.2	1.3	1.1	0.1	0.1	0.1	0.1	0.1
Ancienne URSS	1.5	1.7	1.8	1.6	2.7	2.1	2.5	2.4	2.2	2.4
Océanie	0.8	0.7	0.8	0.7	0.6	0.7	0.8	0.8	0.9	0.8
France, Monac	12.1	12.6	13.2	13.1	13.2	13.0	12.3	12.0	11.7	11.0
United Kingdom	8.8	9.3	9.3	8.5	7.6	7.7	8.0	8.0	8.3	8.0
Italy/Italie	8.7	9.1	9.3	9.3	9.2	9.3	7.6	7.6	7.6	7.4
Netherlands/Pays–Bas	8.7	8.7	8.5	8.5	8.4	8.3	7.7	7.6	7.6	7.4
USA/Etats–Unis d'Amer	9.5	8.0	7.3	7.3	6.3	6.4	7.4	7.8	7.3	7.8
Belgium–Luxembourg	7.4	7.4	7.2	7.4	7.3	7.4	6.8	6.8	6.6	6.2
Austria/Autriche	5.4	5.6	5.5	5.7	5.9	6.0	5.9	5.8	5.6	5.6
Switz.Liecht	6.1	6.1	5.9	6.0	5.6	5.3	5.4	5.4	5.3	4.9
Spain/Espagne	2.9	3.2	3.5	3.6	4.1	4.2	3.3	3.2	3.5	3.6
Japan/Japon	2.0	2.3	2.4	2.7	2.5	2.2	2.5	2.6	2.5	2.7

4. Special Imports C.I.F. by Commodities according to the S.I.T.C. (Rev. 2) in thousand U.S. Dollars
Importations Spéciales C.A.F. par Produits d'après la C.T.C.I. (Rév. 2) en milliers de Dollars E.U.

SITC CTCI	COMMODITY	1993 WEIGHT POIDS	1993 VALUE VALEUR	1994 WEIGHT POIDS	1994 VALUE VALEUR	1995 WEIGHT POIDS	1995 VALUE VALEUR	1996 WEIGHT POIDS	1996 VALUE VALEUR	PRODUIT
	ALL COMMODITIES		342558712		381538916		464145333		444395999	TOUS PRODUITS
0	FOOD AND LIVE ANIMALS		28242902		32400169		38093038		35801063	ALIMENTS,ANIMAUX VIVANTS
01	MEAT AND PREPARATIONS		4885388		5260030		5836294		5442600	VIANDES ET PREPARATIONS
011	MEAT FRESH,CHILLD,FROZEN	W 1550103	4196564		4460720		4984120		4659657	VIANDES FRAICHES,REF,CONGE
0111	BOVINE MEAT FRESH,FROZEN	W 295421	1323892	W 266891	1239665	W 241499	1213602	W 205790	883724	VIANDES BOVIN FRAI,REF
0113	PIG MEAT FRESH,CHLD,FRZN	W 791240	1608800	W 838653	1770443	W 836259	2141770	W 770078	2100488	VIANDE DE PORC
02	DAIRY PRODCTS,BIRDS'EGGS		2905904		3319566		4183576		3775487	PRODUITS LAITIERS,OEUFS
024	CHEESE AND CURD	W 376629	1834460	W 432767	2085594	W 478849	2588816	W 458442	2315697	FROMAGE ET CAILLEBOTTE
03	FISH AND PREPARATIONS		1768441		2186874		2362164		2365832	POISSONS ET PREPARATIONS
034	FISH,FRESH,CHILLED,FROZN	W 436534	1057888	W 498038	1277821	W 491102	1374909	W 506093	1365528	POISSON FRAIS, REFRIG,CONG
04	CEREALS AND PREPARATIONS		2224195		2339210		2744612		2623877	CEREALES ET PRODUITS
048	CEREAL ETC PREPARATIONS	W 969917	1245000	W 1085209	1430315	W 1174669	1676627	W 1108813	1557917	PREPTNS A BASE CEREALES
05	VEGETABLES AND FRUIT		9688068		11014465		12924826		12428183	LEGUMES ET FRUITS
054	VEG ETC FRSH,SMPLY PRSVD	W 5356398	3349426	W 5282463	3668860	W 5248102	4393653	W 4836588	4065393	LEGUMES FRAIS,CONG,SECS
0545	OTHER FRESH VEGETABLES	W 1874280	1763771	W 2049128	1834945	W 2155141	2198956	W 2092429	2125357	AUTRES LEGUMES FRAIS,REF
05459	FRESH VEGETABLES NES	W 1539789	1614572	W 1698108	1662044	W 1765630	1987076	W 1714388	1959040	LEGUMES FRAIS,REFRI NDA
057	FRUIT,NUTS,FRESH,DRIED	W 4834255	3899597	W 5029235	4703393	W 5475042	5521826	W 5200092	5386923	FRUITS FRAIS OU SECS
0579	FRUIT FRESH OR DRIED NES	W 1184960	1186526	W 1282745	1354154	W 1308796	1533125	W 1314579	1432188	FRUITS FRAIS,SECS NDA
058	FRUIT PRESERVED,PREPARED	W 1523350	1570030	W 1624570	1690155	W 1573102	1968346	W 1635582	2035702	CONSERVES DE FRUITS
07	COFFEE,TEA,COCOA,SPICES		2777603		3854162		4791736		4018906	CAFE,THE,CACAO,EPICES
071	COFFEE AND SUBSTITUTES	W 833073	1365631	W 800043	2039274	W 756921	2858860	W 790101	2129018	CAFE ET SUCCEDANES
0711	COFFEE GREEN,ROASTED,SUB	W 817612	1271335	W 782715	1912403	W 742602	2725094	W 772678	1986506	CAFE TORREFIE OU DECAFEINE
07111	COFFEE GREEN,HUSKS,SKINS	W 810291	1236886	W 775506	1875360	W 736556	2680971	W 764223	1938318	CAFE NON TORREFIE
081	*FEEDING STUFF FOR ANIML	W 7420211	1557405	W 6887115	1599799	W 6856945	1793974	W 6214567	1802307	NOURRITURE POUR ANIMAUX
09	MISC EDIBLE PRODUCTS		1384598		1570139		1924151		1737004	PREP ALIMENTAIRES DIVERSES
098	EDIBLE PRODCTS,PREPS NES	W 361418	1339227		1522286		1855042		1669612	PREP ALIMENTAIRES NDA
09809	MISC FOOD PREPRTIONS NES	W 209624	1101670	W 240498	1250450	W 253744	1494861	W 245699	1355546	PREP ALIMENTAIRES NDA
1	BEVERAGES AND TOBACCO		3619059		3994906		4415604		4245172	BOISSONS ET TABACS
11	BEVERAGES		2520812		2752803		3021133		2947599	BOISSONS
112	ALCOHOLIC BEVERAGES	W 1478925	2228389	W 1603904	2322399	W 1571937	2654742	W 1610835	2711828	BOISSONS ALCOOLIQUES
1121	WINE OF FRESH GRAPES ETC	W 1009271	1344348	W 1129601	1447022	W 1064934	1726723	W 1129821	1854582	VINS DE RAISINS FRAIS
11212	WINE OF FRESH GRAPES	W 929962	1300991	W 1012474	1392214	W 987553	1680133	W 1071925	1821599	VINS DE MOUTS DE RAISINS
12	TOBACCO AND MANUFACTURES		1098247		1242103		1394471		1297573	TABACS BRUTS FABRIQUES
2	CRUDE MATERLS,EXCL FUELS		13816750		16962783		20290141		17113771	MAT BRUTES NON COMESTIBLES
22	OIL SEEDS,OLEAGINOUS FRT		1292533		1467388		1476609		1522566	GRAINES,FRUITS OLEAGINEUX
222	SEEDS FOR'SOFT'FIXED OIL	W 4429289	1187791	W 4507237	1333227		1315851	W 4405313	1379868	GRAINES HUILES FIXES
24	CORK AND WOOD		1873572		2295832		2276390		1788293	LIEGE ET BOIS
248	WOOD SHAPED,SLEEPERS	W 3523244	1598359	W 3939435	1979819	W 3517694	1904827	W 3257955	1526693	BOIS SIMPLEMENT TRAVAILLES
2482	LUMBER SHAPED CONIFER	W 2947219	1164479	W 3357932	1500166	W 2930313	1397159	W 2783769	1130301	CONIFERES SCIES,RABOTES
24821	LUMBER SAWN ETC CONIFER	W 2763070	1039278	W 3146128	1339647	W 2803850	1283911	W 2660280	1038287	CONIFERES SCIES LONGITUD
251	*PULP AND WASTE PAPER	W 4210025	1679247	W 5190434	2343259	W 5152310	3594644	W 4788146	2362809	PATES A PAPIER,DECHETS
2517	SODA,SULPHATE WOOD PULP	W 3001891	1262829	W 3635334	1804552	W 3365602	2738085	W 3254046	1827600	PATES CHIMIQUES AU SULFATE
25172	— BLEACHED,NONDISSOLVNG	W 2923278	1229264	W 3545026	1763429	W 3314294	2700048	W 3204227	1800515	PATES BLANCHIES
26	TEXTILE FIBRES AND WASTE		1014650		1381566		1546147		1245073	FIBRES TEXTILES
27	CRUDE FERTLZR,MINRLS NES		1192352		1370826		1527640		1321086	ENGRAIS MINERAUX BRUTS
28	METALLIFEROUS ORES,SCRAP		3449300		4179691		5156500		4557928	MINERAIS METAL,DECHETS
281	IRON ORE,CONCENTRATES	MW 35505	1018646	MW 42773	1250147	MW 43316	1410015	MW 39375	1208329	MINERAIS DE FER
288	NONFERR METAL SCRAP NES	W 900135	959043		1203679		1578612		1223821	DECHETS NON FERREUX
29	CRUDE ANIMAL,VEG MAT NES		2502910		2928873		3457200		3209104	MATIERES BRUTES ANIM,VEGET
292	CRUDE VEG MATERIALS NES	W 680096	1982502		2352719		2791053		2584683	MAT BRUTES VEGETALES NDA
2927	CUT FLOWERS AND FOLIAGE	W 221373	1037270	W 248696	1197721	W 249838	1359554	W 243350	1231467	FLEURS,FEUILLAGES COUPES
3	MINERAL FUELS ETC		27225612		26754345		28875076		35158157	COMBUSTIBLES MINERAUX LUB
33	PETROLEUM AND PRODUCTS		19984654		19331817		19929241		24275962	PETROLE ET DERIVES
333	CRUDE PETROLEUM	MW 99998	12673848	MW 107579	12878107	MW 100549	13054221	MW 103542	16008444	HUILES BRUTES DE PETROLE
334	PETROLEUM PRODUCTS,REFIN	MW 39770	6844527	MW 37097	5914710	MW 37095	6288485	MW 38374	7634750	PRODUITS RAFFINES
3341	GASOLINE,OTH LIGHT OILS	MW 13087	2387976	MW 12793	2124341	MW 12790	2271226	MW 11650	2370151	ESSENCES POUR MOTEURS
33411	MOTOR,AVIATION SPIRIT	W 7281938	1363998	W 6978491	1172327	W 6880952	1228129	W 6540796	1362210	ESSENCES MOTEURS D'AVIONS
3343	GAS OILS	MW 18429	3135077	MW 16309	2508525	MW 17271	2740960	MW 19913	3867227	GAS OILS
341	*GAS,NATURAL AND MANUFCT	MW 45918	5576332	MW 47886	5542266	MW 52744	6834562	MW 68138	8793500	GAZ NATUREL,GAZ MANUFACT
3414	PETROLEUM GASES, GASEOUS	MW 44827	5377758	MW 46774	5360665	MW 51820	6639390	MW 66932	8503915	GAZ DE PETROLE GAZEUX
4	ANIMAL,VEGETABLE OIL,FAT		911630		1159232		1336739		1289248	HUILES,GRAISSES ANIM,VEG
5	CHEMCLS,RELATED PROD NES		27532506		33051975		41256577		38323589	PRODUITS CHIMIQUES
51	ORGANIC CHEMICALS		6581647		8030761		9885568		9014460	PROD CHIMIQ ORGANIQUES
511	HYDROCARBONS NES,DERIVS	W 2237494	942040	W 2453065	1150138	W 2498323	1595091	W 2481005	1217367	HYDROCARBURES NDA
513	CARBOXYLIC ACIDS ETC	W 798761	950388	W 855354	1128770		1565430	W 931281	1371552	ACIDES CARBOXYLIQUES
514	NITROGEN–FNCTN COMPOUNDS	W 622923	2151606		2895829		3369092		3187196	COMPOSES FONCT AZOTEES
5148	OTH NITROGN–FNCTN CMPNDS	W 246918	788586	W 286635	1248132	W 249142	1547133	W 261750	1434459	AUTRES COMPOSES AZOTES
515	ORG–INORG COMPOUNDS ETC	W 174111	960464		1128703		1343090		1474745	COMPOSES ORGANO–MINERAUX
52	INORGANIC CHEMICALS		1981967		2454741		2617046		2555551	PROD CHIM INORGANIQUES
53	DYES,TANNING,COLOUR PROD		1554856		1746539		2115543		1942534	PROD TEINTURE,COLORANTS
533	PIGMENTS,PAINTS,ETC	W 480092	1023962		1164978		1395361		1207671	PIGMENTS,PEINTURES,VERNIS
541	*MEDICINAL,PHARM PRODUCT	MK 102827	4221727	MK 118737	5349120		6663155		6942189	PROD MEDICINAUX PHARMACEUT
5417	MEDICAMENTS	MK 61852	2505198	MK 73045	3321531	MK 81053	4046265	MK 77461	4029161	MEDICAMENTS
54179	— CONTNG OTH SUBSTANCES	MK 54024	1885398	MK 65195	2499781	MK 73213	2971262	MK 69808	2931341	MED CONT AUT SUBSTANCES
55	PERFUME,CLEANING ETC PRD		2042619		2553663		3160695		3042113	PROD POUR PARFUM,TOILETTE
553	PERFUMERY,COSMETICS,ETC	W 107334	1146652	W 142761	1398575	W 168758	1743523	W 188786	1624049	PRODUITS DE PARFUMERIE
58	PLASTIC MATERIALS ETC		7177996		8517898		10990904		9353364	MAT PLAST ARTIFICIELLES
582	PROD OF CONDENSATION ETC	W 1132216	2222478	W 1294103	2524910	W 1352096	3282383	W 1282146	2977991	PROD CONDENS,POLYCOND
583	POLYMERIZATION ETC PRODS	W 4048109	4723145	W 4658632	5707921	W 4478189	7351607	W 4309089	6042426	PROD POLYMERISATION
5831	POLYETHYLENE	W 1425162	1157337	W 1599147	1396114	W 1479018	1810768	W 1366228	1427544	POLYETHYLENE
58311	— IN PRIMARY FORMS	W 1287004	931426	W 1428392	1111338	W 1311196	1446376	W 1220775	1145272	POLYETHYLENE PRIMAIRES
5839	OTH POLYMRZTION ETC PROD	W 609247	1331525	W 763715	1614465	W 782961	2075888	W 746373	1847784	AUT PROD POLYMER COPOLYM
59	CHEMICAL MATERIALS NES		3035078		3537523		4535943		4449261	MAT PROD CHIMIQUES NDA
598	MISCEL CHEM PRODUCTS NES	W 1633242	2047420		2418426		2992454		2958260	PROD DIV INDUST CHIM NDA
5989	CHEM PRODUCTS,PREPS NES	W 1183145	1593544	W 1391086	1934335	W 1557084	2420876	W 1584833	2427243	PROD PREP CHIMIQUES NDA
59899	OTH CHEM PRODS,PREPS,NES	W 870967	1128421	W 1016830	1390780	W 1228875	1801694	W 1287668	1818098	AUT PRODUITS CHIMIQUES NDA
6	BASIC MANUFACTURES		53216577		63351058		79868605		67757470	ART MANUFACTURES
61	LEATHER,DRESSED FUR,ETC		1237384		1350631		1481709		1386477	CUIRS,PELLETERIES
62	RUBBER MANUFACTURES NES		3217559		3613317		4385609		4105554	CAOUTCHOUC MANUFACTURE
625	RUBBER TYRES, TUBES ETC	W 494062	1966983	W 551516	2182054	W 617492	2660534	W 577824	2444856	PNEUS CAOUTCHOUC VULCANISE
6251	TYRES NEW FOR MOTOR CARS	W 231780	1167422	W 258270	1286045	W 287298	1556324	W 266368	1418609	PNEUS POUR VOITURES
63	WOOD,CORK MANUFACTRS NES		3153065		3898194		4425378		3806923	OUVRAGES LIEGE ET BOIS
634	VENEERS,PLYWOOD,ETC	W 1810365	1125403	W 1899514	1290295	W 1958612	1592780	W 1679091	1262222	PLACAGES,CONTRE–PLAQUES
635	WOOD MANUFACTURES NES	W 1530198	1897129	W 1937897	2493504	W 1909708	2697484	W 1830790	2430607	ART MANUF EN BOIS NDA
6353	BUILDERS WOODWRK,PREFABS	W 670210	1301115	W 858211	1763694	W 755826	1815206	W 732358	1590164	OUVRAGES DE MENUISERIE
64	PAPER,PAPERBOARD AND MFR		6559620		7539758		10042552		8605324	PAPIERS,CARTONS & OUVRAGES
641	PAPER AND PAPERBOARD	W 7274958	5299825		6100347	W 7949300	8252022		6883570	PAPIERS ET CARTONS
6412	PRINTG,WRITING PAPER NES	W 1408794	1258787	W 1709409	1554169	W 1719519	2136436	W 1703168	1756514	PAPIERS POUR L'IMPRESSION
64122	— COATED,IMPREGNATD ETC	W 1197174	1072547	W 1454781	1317335	W 1436568	1752724	W 1404095	1432878	PAPIERS IMPRESSION COUCHES
6415	PAPER,PAPERBRD,BULK,NES	W 2319246	1425524	W 2529527	1664348	W 2467850	2334701	W 2300519	1814727	PAPIERS,CARTONS ROULEAUX
64159	OTHER PAPER ETC,BULK,NES	W 2106506	1305820	W 2314386	1532643	W 2265491	2150562	W 2110778	1687451	AUT PAPIER ROULEAUX FEUILLES

4. Special Imports C.I.F. by Commodities according to the S.I.T.C. (Rev. 2) in thousand U.S. Dollars
Importations Spéciales C.A.F. par Produits d'après la C.T.C.I. (Rév. 2) en milliers de Dollars E.U.

SITC CTCI	COMMODITY	1993 WEIGHT POIDS	1993 VALUE VALEUR	1994 WEIGHT POIDS	1994 VALUE VALEUR	1995 WEIGHT POIDS	1995 VALUE VALEUR	1996 WEIGHT POIDS	1996 VALUE VALEUR	PRODUIT
6418	COATED ETC PAPER NES BLK	W 778412	1036470	W 830928	1080162	W 831734	1358631	W 715758	1109498	PAP,CARTONS COUCHES,ENDUITS
642	PAPER,ETC,PRECUT,ARTS OF	W 652329	1259795	W 738029	1439411	W 743043	1790530	W 751541	1721754	PAP,CARTONS DECOUPES
65	TEXTILE YARN,FABRICS,ETC		10153386		11113229		12654473		11554656	FILS,TISSUS,ARTICLES TEXTILE
651	TEXTILE YARN	W 420148	1941602		2168374		2569401		2307846	FILS TEXTILES
653	WOVN MAN–MADE FIB FABRIC	W 118843	1444077	W 118874	1553853	W 118695	1857242	W 111043	1559544	TISSUS FIBRES SYNTH,ARTIF
654	OTH WOVEN TEXTILE FABRIC	W 59744	1066447	W 71805	1172802	W 70155	1220320	W 62023	1014303	TISSUS AUT COTON SYNT,ARTIF
657	SPECIAL TXTL FABRC,PRODS	W 158646	1024097	W 183272	1179451	W 186339	1416917	W 187026	1302763	TISSUS SPECIAUX
658	TEXTILE ARTICLES NES	W 153665	1335349	W 172199	1462185	W 179709	1675270	W 196377	1688821	ART FACONNES MAT TEXTILES
659	FLOOR COVERINGS,ETC	W 289983	1785340		1833042		2023154		1869200	COUVRE–PARQUETS,TAPIS ETC
66	NONMETAL MINERAL MFS NES		5865119		6834194		8088173		7081798	ART MIN NON METALLIQUES
661	LIME,CEMENT,BLDG PRODS	MW 9852	1080566	MW 11502	1223231		1400216		1189761	CHAUX,CIMENTS MAT CONSTR
662	CLAY,REFRACTORY BLDG PRD	W 3015383	1183924	W 3896348	1475696	W 3755192	1712732		1358757	MAT CONST REFRACTAIRES
6624	BRICKS ETC NONREFRACTORY	W 2774992	1021341	W 3636988	1285387	W 3495454	1497134	W 2822978	1151743	BRIQUES ETC CERAM NON REFR
663	MINERAL MANUFCTURES NES	W 2216523	1063441		1306326		1613226		1440209	ART MIN MANUF NDA
664	GLASS	W 825033	966694	W 1023176	1143686	W 1071655	1442886	W 959666	1334300	VERRE
67	IRON AND STEEL		8835012		11342148		16103588		12085628	FER ET ACIER
671	PIG IRON ETC	W 1072792	615599		955032		1411800		1068397	FONTE,SPIEGEL,POUDRES
672	IRON,STEEL PRIMARY FORMS	W 2316246	980436	W 3053207	1377415	W 3681187	2137425	W 2532595	1438402	LINGOTS FER,ACIER
673	IRON,STEEL SHAPES ETC	W 5262270	2191183	W 5993709	2651229	W 6646442	3753690	W 4789949	2414963	BARRES,PROFIL FER,ACIER
6732	IRON,STEEL BARS ETC	W 2328896	1022575	W 2681985	1264516	W 2978964	1907147	W 2158660	1265763	BARRES FER,ACIER
674	IRN,STL UNIV,PLATE,SHEET	W 5022937	3054830	W 6256114	3912950	W 6890273	5601817	W 5889830	4397844	LARGES PLATS,TOLES
6746	IRN,STL THIN PLATE,ROLLD	W 1411912	981135	W 1668224	1221137	W 1798628	1837542	W 1659262	1511406	TOLES LAM MOINS 3MM
6749	OTH IRN,STL PLATES,SHEET	W 1445496	932035	W 1850800	1196131	W 2098960	1606062	W 1848466	1301284	AUTRES TOLES FER,ACIER
67491	— OF IRON OR SIMPLE STL	W 1431822	883516	W 1840640	1153594	W 2087336	1544828	W 1835462	1233558	AUT TOLES AUTRES ACIER FIN
678	IRON,STL TUBES,PIPES,ETC	W 1465926	1375163		1649689		2169806		1877364	TUBES,TUYAUX EN FONTE,FER
68	NON–FERROUS METALS		6327906		8661766		11767801		9073647	METAUX NON FERREUX
682	COPPER EXC CEMENT COPPER	W 907470	2105924		2888744		3695197		2719580	CUIVRE
6821	COPPER NES,ALLOYS,UNWRT	W 598664	1154539	W 652222	1421043	W 656442	1898299	W 574194	1373148	CUIVRE BRUT
68212	COPPER REFINED,UNWROUGHT	W 527969	1012267	W 563161	1217716	W 602323	1730227	W 486849	1144642	CUIVRE AFFINE BRUT
6822	COPPER,ALLOYS WORKED	W 308810	951385	W 473264	1467701	W 443420	1796898	W 373954	1346432	CUIVRE,ALLIAGES OUVRES
684	ALUMINIUM	W 1389322	2683612	W 1890170	3814795	W 2057119	5466523	W 1748859	4133189	ALUMINIUM
6841	ALUMINIUM,ALLOYS,UNWRGHT	W 864845	1167329	W 1203073	1820097	W 1340855	2758073	W 1108756	1920550	ALUMINIUM,ALLIAGES BRUTS
6842	ALUMINIUM,ALLOYS WORKED	W 524477	1516283	W 687097	1994698	W 716264	2708450	W 640103	2212639	ALUMINIUM,ALLIAGES OUVRE
69	METAL MANUFACTURES NES		7867526		8997821		10919322		10057463	ART MANUFACT EN METAL NDA
691	STRUCTURES AND PARTS NES	W 752346	1419451	W 805049	1545284	W 868662	1794731	W 773983	1558612	CONSTRUCT FER,ACIER,ALU
6911	STRUCTURES,PARTS IRN,STL	W 706435	1071915	W 759964	1172244	W 819158	1390013	W 727296	1196127	CONSTRUCT FER,ACIER,FONTE
695	TOOLS	W 95425	1256876	W 113207	1503297	W 118773	1851276	W 111131	1724911	OUTILS A MAIN
699	BASE METAL MFRS NES	W 564396	2474276		2920431		3606419		3426698	ART MANUFACTURES MET NDA
7	MACHINES,TRANSPORT EQUIP		113398628		129136037		155439071		152562391	MACHINES MATERIEL TRANSPORT
71	POWER GENERATING EQUIPMT		6635927		8092638		9850469		10896326	MACHINES GENERATRICES
713	INTRNL COMBUS PSTN ENGIN	W 264595	2991477	W 310816	3622694	W 350185	4357537	W 418839	4735622	MOTEURS EXPL COMB INT, PIECE
7132	MOTOR VEHCL PISTN ENGINS	W 169255	1948071	W 197112	2309078	W 222342	2718326	W 260612	3000784	MOTEURS EXPL POUR VEHICULES
7139	PISTON ENGINE PARTS NES	W 71132	772938	W 81985	960839	W 95425	1242388	W 131794	1401865	PIECES POUR 713.2,3,8
714	ENGINES AND MOTORS NES	W 12242	1775962	W 12677	2372031	W 15851	2969519	W 20025	3521923	MOTEURS NON ELECTRIQUES
7144	REACTION ENGINES	W 523	454515	W 1253	933443	W 1091	1182423	W 1575	1530639	PROPULSEURS A REACTION
7149	ENGINE & MOTOR PARTS NES	W 10996	1071954	W 10687	1125590	W 13765	1366471	W 16954	1626942	PIECES 714 ET 718.88
716	ROTATING ELECTRIC PLANT	W 153016	1325180	W 198198	1664268	W 236078	2027372	W 231968	1997519	APP ELECTR ROTATIFS,PIECES
72	MACHS FOR SPCL INDUSTRYS		6260899		6841001		8031536		7221364	MAC SPECIALES POUR INDUST
728	OTH MACHY FOR SPCL INDUS	W 174924	2228451	W 199135	2452090	W 212042	2934436	W 189026	2737758	AUT MACH IND PARTICULIERES
7284	MACHY FOR SPCL INDUS NES	W 79130	1559004	W 92278	1707883	W 102769	2133555	W 100411	2034679	MACH SPEC IND PARTICUL.
73	METALWORKING MACHINERY		1711784		1812426		2489169		2620962	MACH TRAVAIL DES METAUX
736	METALWORKING MACH–TOOLS	W 97601	1313930	W 106606	1408181	W 128679	1982753	W 126843	2108414	MACH–OUTILS TRAVAIL METAUX
74	GENRL INDUSTRL MACHY NES		11233391		12583627		15535267		15113768	MACH APP INDUSTRIE
741	HEATING,COOLING EQUIPMNT	W 153504	1750686	W 165760	1830298	W 181431	2291457	W 191689	2418232	MACH CHAUFFAGE,PIECES
742	PUMPS FOR LIQUIDS ETC	W 73450	994486	W 85976	1148118	W 97233	1471576	W 107667	1601065	POMPES MOTO–POMPES
743	PUMPS NES,CENTRFUGES ETC	W 157447	1854915	W 175305	1976751	W 191632	2422968	W 197604	2488671	POMPES COMPRES,VENT ETC
744	MECHANICAL HANDLING EQU	W 378894	1921276	W 441326	2088373	W 478280	2489057	W 444976	2144608	EQUIP MANUTENTION PIECES
745	NONELEC MACHY,TOOLS NES	W 57891	1110277		1276513		1444787		1342348	AUT MACH NON ELEC,PIECES
749	NONELEC MACH PTS,ACC NES	W 293022	3601751	W 349386	4263574	W 439563	5415422	W 441561	5118844	PIECES MACH NON ELEC NDA
7491	BALL,ROLLER,ETC BEARINGS	W 63910	798650	W 83510	980841	W 111937	1436785	W 112408	1387832	ROULEMENTS BILLES ETC
7492	COCKS,VALVES ETC NES	W 91484	1416350	W 99445	1633165	W 105309	1925569	W 103138	1826893	ART ROB,SIM POUR TUYAUX
75	OFFICE MACHNES,ADP EQUIP		16131075		18105731		22120678		20238445	MACH BUREAU TRAIT AUTOM
751	OFFICE MACHINES	W 39028	1182539	W 39518	1273729	W 45005	1541708	W 41869	1319170	MACH,APPAREILS DE BUREAU
752	AUTOMTIC DATA PROC EQUIP	W 125214	10249967	W 143902	11113838	W 177881	13362585	W 169666	12160360	MACH TRAIT INFORMATION
7523	DIGITL CENTRL PROCESSORS	W 22024	2997845	W 16588	2830069	W 20987	3237804	W 20551	3083248	UNITES CENTRALES
7524	DIGITL CENTRL STOR UNITS	W 11769	2166108	W 14007	2546781	W 18142	3354321	W 13690	2891439	UNITES MEMOIRE CENTRALES
7525	ADP PERIPHERAL UNITS	W 83267	3868390	W 104713	4255363	W 129687	5264536	W 127782	4590292	UNITES PERIPHERIQUES
759	OFFICE,ADP MCH PTS,ACCES	W 76004	4698569	W 78798	5718164	W 91510	7216385	W 94879	6758915	PIECES DU 751 ET 752
7599	ACCTG,ETC,ADP MCH PTS,AC	W 52603	3927436	W 55709	4871441	W 66086	6215971	W 74149	6010535	PIECES DU 751 ET 752
76	TELECOMM,SOUND EQUIPMENT		9955120		11122224		12238772		11651751	EQUIPMENT DE TELECOM
761	TELEVISION RECEIVERS	W 124749	1774238	W 114945	1684116	W 118692	1904934	W 114003	1732993	RECEPTEURS DE TELEVISION
7611	COLOUR TV RECEIVERS	W 123836	1753779	W 114106	1661802	W 117859	1878493	W 113304	1712761	RECEPTEURS COULEUR
762	RADIO BROADCAST RECEIVRS	W 62781	1447377	W 62820	1494894	W 61802	1710591	W 65999	1588485	RECEPTEURS RADIODIFFUSION
763	SOUND RECORDRS,PHONOGRPH	W 39666	1468198	W 37627	1495010	W 33732	1411261	W 37762	1742089	PHONO,APP ENREGISTREMENT
7638	OTHR SOUND APPARATUS ETC	W 38367	1448333	W 36556	1478384	W 32923	1397828	W 37032	1730560	AUT APP D'ENREGIS,REPROD
764	TELECOM EQPT,PTS,ACC NES	W 114123	5265307	W 130137	6448204	W 124766	7211986	W 127331	6588184	EQUIP TELECOM,PIECES
7641	LINE TELEPHONE,ETC EQUIP	W 16359	1166920	W 18754	1261276	W 21912	1969803	W 22847	1948558	APP TELEPHON PAR FIL
7649	PTS NES OF EQUIPMT OF 76	W 48825	2212090	W 57947	3114067	W 46705	2744047	W 45012	2487368	PIECES DE LA DIV 76
76491	PTS NES OF APPAR OF 7641	W 6225	928754	W 7088	1294685	W 4769	923190	W 4581	809254	PIECES POUR 764.1
77	ELECTRIC MACHNRY NES ETC		19747830		25414499		32699286		30660192	MACH APP ELECT NDA
771	ELECTRIC POWER MACHY NES	W 63766	1028723	W 79456	1251925	W 82335	1624517	W 85964	1707739	MACH PROD,TRANS ELECTR
7712	OTH ELEC POWER MACHY NES	W 40062	755054	W 51924	926688	W 52626	1220848	W 57474	1340706	AUT APP PROD TRANSF ELEC
772	SWITCHGEAR ETC,PARTS NES	W 92333	3269044	W 95483	3869918	W 112342	4868082	W 117671	4783126	APP COUPURE,SECT ETC
7721	SWITCHGEAR ETC	W 71166	2608101	W 85456	3039294	W 101624	3869904	W 107300	3874901	APP COUPURE,SECTIONMNT
773	ELECTR DISTRIBUTNG EQUIP	W 311401	1971823	W 354262	2435270	W 373694	2996618	W 363524	3088999	EQUIPMT DISTRIBUTION ELECT
7731	INSULATED WIRE,CABLE ETC	W 301457	1861379	W 343272	2305406	W 361778	2851883	W 350575	2924791	FILS,CABLES ISOLES ELECT
775	HOUSEHOLD TYPE EQUIP NES	W 389439	2747819		3180094		3651724		3516491	MACH,APP USAGE DOMESTQUE
7758	ELECTRO–THERMIC APPL NES	W 163172	1317965	W 172879	1419559	W 177549	1565129	W 183839	1547880	APP ELECTROTHERMIQ NDA
776	TRANSISTORS,VALVES,ETC	W 34089	5017292	W 71841	7245466	W 72840	9792988	W 73356	9117033	LAMPES,TUBES,VALVES
7764	ELECTRONIC MICROCIRCUITS	W 4929	3901114	W 5978	5593324	W 8903	7694792	W 17171	7200917	MICROSTRUCTURES ELECTRON
778	ELECTRICAL MACHINERY NES	W 300670	4986290		6646149		8785506		7462756	AUTRES MACH ELECT NDA
7788	OTH ELEC MACHY,EQUIP NES	W 95444	2709791	W 90756	3818314	W 100426	5270507	W 81245	4214511	AUT MACH APP ELEC NDA
77889	ELEC PARTS OF MACHY NES	W 1004	843803	W 934	1503862	W 1102	2231795	W 1162	1312480	PIECES ELEC DE MACH NDA
78	ROAD VEHICLES		30483624		34760124		44171846		45408435	VEHICULES ROUTIERS
781	PASS MOTOR VEH EXC BUSES	W 1687053	17299003	W 1720333	18274213	W 1862018	23255150	W 2069484	24127286	AUTO TRANSPORT PERSONNES
782	LORRIES,SPCL MTR VEH NES	W 253262	2158217	W 298714	2677461	W 319815	3416745	W 366819	3838776	VEHICULES SPECIAUX,MARCH
7821	LORRIES,TRUCKS	W 234016	2002879	W 279903	2515124	W 307373	3285806	W 354421	3724456	VEHICULES TRANSP MARCHAND
783	ROAD MOTOR VEHICLES NES	W 33251	420894	W 47784	681211	W 85400	1592387	W 80607	1389580	VEHICULES ROUTIERS NDA
7832	TRACTORS FOR TR–TRAILERS	W 20334	237482	W 36382	502980	W 76813	1452837	W 70302	1252192	TRACTEURS ROUTIERS
784	MOTOR VEH PRTS,ACCES NES	W 1056190	8233266	W 1309233	10738334	W 1578333	12926326	W 1566428	13183776	PIECES 722,781,782,783
7849	OTHER MOTOR VEHCL PARTS	W 1032173	8045186	W 1272953	10416917	W 1549336	12616654	W 1539210	12920051	PIECES 722,781,782,783

4. Special imports C.I.F. by Commodities according to the S.I.T.C. (Rev. 2) in thousand U.S. Dollars
Importations Spéciales C.A.F. par Produits d'après la C.T.C.I. (Rév. 2) en milliers de Dollars E.U.

SITC CTCI	COMMODITY	1993		1994		1995		1996		PRODUIT
		WEIGHT POIDS	VALUE VALEUR	WEIGHT POIDS	VALUE VALEUR	WEIGHT POIDS	VALUE VALEUR	WEIGHT POIDS	VALUE VALEUR	
785	CYCLES,ETC MOTRZD OR NOT	W 136384	1874047	W 132290	1834842	W 141108	2250613	W 141145	2145384	MOTOCYCLES SCOOTERS
79	OTHR TRANSPORT EQUIPMENT		11238978		10403767		8302048		8751148	AUTRE MATERIEL TRANSPORT
792	AIRCRAFT ETC	W 23131	10159371	W 20257	9431897	W 17749	7514724	W 15787	8118116	APP NAVIGATION AERIENNE
7924	AIRCRFT NES OVER 15000KG	W 7544	5806541	W 6926	5404886	W 4809	3693814	W 4844	3835760	AERODYNES PLUS 15000 KG
7929	AIRCRAFT PARTS NES	W 14602	4032403	W 12557	3837517	W 12144	3458890	W 10194	3915525	PIECES DU 792
8	MISC MANUFACTURED GOODS		56770918		61155672		67971180		66276363	ART MANUFACTURES DIVERS
812	*PLUMBG,HEATNG,LGHTNG EQ	W 413512	1780647	W 482688	2056866	W 474014	2300154	W 434293	2033584	APPAR SANITAIRES CHAUFFAGE
821	*FURNITURE,PARTS THEREOF	W 1393530	5006546	W 1578200	5714848	W 1715075	6910720	W 1743668	6845829	MEUBLES ET PIECES
8211	CHAIRS,SEATS AND PARTS	W 397695	1765228	W 455880	2057736	W 524895	2648167	W 542218	2743013	SIEGES ET PIECES
82111	CHAIRS AND OTHER SEATS	W 334489	1313774	W 374546	1422143	W 422827	1671674	W 431217	1643665	SIEGES
8219	FURNITURE AND PARTS NES	W 944153	2787655	W 1059016	3139207	W 1126326	3697817	W 1137594	3545785	AUTRES MEUBLES ET PIECES
82192	WOOD FURNITURE NES	W 627625	1848439	W 706360	2085886	W 728087	2387647	W 740187	2260874	MEUBLES NDA EN BOIS
831	*TRAVEL GOODS,HANDBAGS	W 96327	1035072	W 102626	1077536	W 110507	1241295	W 106082	1182296	ARTICLES DE VOYAGE ETC
84	CLOTHING AND ACCESSORIES		22200584		22717176		24553654		24105095	VETEMENTS
842	MENS OUTERWEAR NOT KNIT	W 147802	3620862	W 155061	3861687	W 146684	4032541	W 153077	4081735	VET DESSUS POUR HOMMES
8423	— TROUSERS,BREECHES ETC	W 84346	1733641	W 87321	1852430	W 84813	1975989	W 92154	2068916	PANTALONS HOMMES MAT TEX
843	WOMENS OUTERWEAR NONKNIT	W 189189	6336630	W 198999	6641511	W 196280	7222937	W 204450	6898736	VET DESSUS FEMMES MAT TEX
8431	— COATS AND JACKETS	W 31476	1289562	W 32076	1299509	W 30064	1335170	W 29614	1221048	MANT,VEST FEM MAT TEXTIL
8435	— BLOUSES	W 31719	1354427	W 33753	1432094	W 32916	1503928	W 33057	1295970	BLOUSES FEM MAT TEXTILES
8439	— OTHER OUTER GARMENTS	W 99284	2618222	W 105872	2822102	W 99959	2933161	W 108903	3073060	AUT VET DES FEM MAT TEXT
844	UNDER GARMENTS NOT KNIT	W 61529	1354279	W 62764	1379972	W 64490	1526380	W 58799	1334305	VETEMENT DESSOUS MAT TEX
8441	— MENS SHIRTS	W 56438	1238887	W 56765	1242366	W 58950	1372531	W 53062	1188104	CHEMISES HOMMES MAT TEXT
845	OUTERWEAR KNIT NONELASTC	W 200923	5367276	W 191597	5154081	W 186632	5524400	W 211728	5588234	VET DESSOUS,ACCES BONNET
8451	— JERSEYS,PULLOVERS ETC	W 108518	3144492	W 110114	3139480	W 104395	3155519	W 121137	3310580	CHANDAILS,PULL–OVERS ETC
8459	— OTHER,CLTHG ACCESRYS	W 76868	1808760	W 69622	1669967	W 68150	1868392	W 73605	1879070	AUT VET DESSUS DE BONNE
846	UNDER GARMENTS KNITTED	W 147371	3088601	W 142952	3076386	W 148560	3569940	W 156319	3561755	SOUS VETS DE BONNETERIE
8462	— OF COTTON NON ELASTIC	W 117125	2209827	W 112327	2165698	W 117444	2523018	W 125693	2545945	SOUS–VET BONNET COTON
84629	—— OTHER	W 117125	2209827	W 112327	2165698	W 117444	2523018	W 125693	2545945	AUT SOUS–VET BONNET COTON
848	HEADGEAR,NONTXTL CLOTHNG	W 73215	1619551	W 80254	1710208	W 80171	1690200	W 80597	1630274	VET ACCES MAT AUT QUE TEX
8481	LEATHER CLOTHES,ACCESSOR	W 36287	1104399	W 40024	1167509	W 37114	1123295	W 33864	1021382	VET ACCES MAT CUIR ARTIF
851	*FOOTWEAR	W 235295	4192139	W 253470	4473123	W 231101	4460745	W 238692	4570237	CHAUSSURES
85102	FOOTWEAR LEATHER	W 186453	3638710	W 198820	3869851	W 180379	3890523	W 183394	3938199	CHAUS SEMELLES EN CUIR
87	PRECISION INSTRUMNTS NES		5271941		5937832		6946370		7242506	INSTRUM,APPAR SCIENT NDA
872	MEDICAL INSTRUMENTS NES	W 24778	1320149	W 32219	1450483	W 35548	1767798	W 37084	1768289	INSTR,APP MEDIC–CHIR NDA
87202	OTH MEDICAL INSTRUMENTS	W 20829	1197621	W 26861	1311246	W 29452	1600695	W 30345	1604800	INSTRUM,APP MEDECINE
874	MEASURNG,CONTROLNG INSTR	W 43320	3322462	W 51516	3761443	W 54881	4309811	W 57074	4499374	INSTRUMENTS DE MESURE
88	PHOTO EQU,OPTICL GDS ETC		3875759		4259621		4812422		4624852	APP,FOURN PHOTO,OP,MONTR
882	PHOTO,CINEMA SUPPLIES	W 89866	1415903	W 114932	1587169	W 116552	1804130	W 107746	1641090	PRODUITS PHOTO,CINEMA
8822	PHOTO FILM EXC DEV CINMA	W 56500	1111771	W 73552	1237497	W 79192	1413605	W 66593	1229904	PLAQUES,PELLICULES,FILMS
885	WATCHES AND CLOCKS		1029806		1136177		1242594		1107736	HORLOGERIE
89	MISC MANUFCTRD GOODS NES		13408230		14918670		16745820		15671964	ART MANUFACTURES DIVERS
892	PRINTED MATTER	W 275529	1292925	W 381178	1467753	W 279484	1525746	W 266376	1389411	IMPRIMES
893	ARTICLES OF PLASTIC NES		3724483		4357497		5264507		4957230	OUVRAGES EN MAT DIVIS 58
8939	MISC PLASTIC ARTICLES	W 527801	2774443	W 622489	3231370	W 691288	3942951	W 656091	3741422	ART DIVERS EN MAT DIV 58
89399	OTHR PLASTC ARTICLES NES	W 453207	2528698	W 544560	2977925	W 600857	3625527	W 559910	3424025	AUT OUV MAT DIV 58
894	TOYS,SPORTING GOODS,ETC	W 282185	2694186	W 301106	2863414	W 316326	3219824	W 330389	3199584	VOITURES ENFANTS,JOUETS
8942	TOYS,INDOOR GAMES ETC	W 226462	2106886	W 237263	2203057	W 242835	2450878	W 242953	2272300	JOUETS,JEUX ETC
89423	TOYS NES	W 115188	1064184	W 110653	1045329	W 108696	1124273	W 107632	1049212	JOUETS,MODELES REDUITS
898	MUSICAL INSTRUMENTS,PTS	W 112145	2591892	W 129267	2918902	W 133614	3093466	W 130797	2647620	INSTRUMENTS DE MUSIQUE
8983	SOUND RECRDNG TAPE,DISCS	W 99707	2311226	W 115103	2617648	W 118916	2755410	W 115930	2328012	SUPPORTS SON POUR 763
89832	RECORDED DISCS,TAPES ETC	W 36227	1417328	W 40804	1651950	W 38599	1745958	W 34829	1390746	DISQUES,PHONO,BANDES
899	OTHER MANUFACTURED GOODS		1510004		1632598		1882480		1806145	AUT ART MANUF DIVERS NDA
9	GOODS NOT CLASSD BY KIND		17824130		13572739		26599302		25868775	ART TRANSACT NON CLASSES
931	*SPECIAL TRANSACTIONS	W 750778	16239831	W 644086	12139712	W 448091	25066370	W 498960	24378866	TRANS.SPECIALES
971	*GOLD,NON MONETARY NES	K 257754	1428406	K 303369	1263964	K 223940	1377015	K 277014	1353465	OR NON MONETAIRE
97101	NONMON GLD UNWRT,SEMIMFD	K 117864	1361413	K 95612	1182642	K 100377	1260438	K 94890	1192470	OR,ALLIAGES D'OR BRUTS

5. Special Exports F.O.B. by Commodities according to the S.I.T.C. (Rev. 2) in thousand U.S. Dollars
Exportations Spéciales F.O.B. par Produits d'après la C.T.C.I. (Rév. 2) en milliers de Dollars E.U.

SITC CTCI	COMMODITY	1993		1994		1995		1996		PRODUIT
		WEIGHT POIDS	VALUE VALEUR	WEIGHT POIDS	VALUE VALEUR	WEIGHT POIDS	VALUE VALEUR	WEIGHT POIDS	VALUE VALEUR	
	ALL COMMODITIES		380074808		427100056		523696751		512693598	TOUS PRODUITS
0	FOOD AND LIVE ANIMALS		16799641		18147157		21178061		20907747	ALIMENTS,ANIMAUX VIVANTS
01	MEAT AND PREPARATIONS		2138689		2027594		2196345		2010816	VIANDES ET PREPARATIONS
011	MEAT FRESH,CHILLD,FROZEN	W 748155	1742254	W 667075	1642782	W 637062	1738401	W 607766	1537129	VIANDES FRAICHES,REF,CONGE
0111	BOVINE MEAT FRESH,FROZEN	W 507488	1330034	W 407235	1183002	W 361102	1145273	W 357975	959433	VIANDES BOVIN FRAI,REF
02	DAIRY PRODCTS,BIRDS'EGGS		4309906		4105484		5063460		4956811	PRODUITS LAITIERS,OEUFS
022	MILK AND CREAM	W 3187747	2688985	W 3328515	2461215	W 3577986	3137563	W 3611493	2931578	LAIT ET CREME
0224	MILK,CREAM PRESERVED ETC	W 1109544	1561078	W 1176360	1301348	W 1154378	1677873	W 1331202	1560922	LAIT,CREME CONS,CONC
024	CHEESE AND CURD	W 357570	1344755	W 386940	1413347	W 406632	1611413	W 466979	1738824	FROMAGE ET CAILLEBOTTE
04	CEREALS AND PREPARATIONS		2725109		3069801		3667871		3828674	CEREALES ET PRODUITS
048	CEREAL ETC PREPARATIONS	W 873539	1460854	W 1058192	1618502	W 1170945	1807815	W 1126502	1814108	PREPTNS A BASE CEREALES
05	VEGETABLES AND FRUIT		1498413		1801542		2103953		2166691	LEGUMES ET FRUITS
07	COFFEE,TEA,COCOA,SPICES		1617916		2294049		2612663		2595396	CAFE,THE,CACAO,EPICES
081	*FEEDING STUFF FOR ANIML	W 4314954	1357607	W 4319251	1343363	W 4501174	1446536	W 4358323	1449212	NOURRITURE POUR ANIMAUX
1	BEVERAGES AND TOBACCO		2725770		3280185		3478231		3519241	BOISSONS ET TABACS
11	BEVERAGES		1484882		1860098		2027454		1881952	BOISSONS
112	ALCOHOLIC BEVERAGES	W 1218517	1258357	W 1410227	1609321	W 1354068	1760545	W 1305417	1631565	BOISSONS ALCOOLIQUES
12	TOBACCO AND MANUFACTURES		1240888		1420087		1450777		1637289	TABACS BRUTS FABRIQUES
122	TOBACCO,MANUFACTURED	W 90241	1177251	W 100703	1325476	W 93539	1341151	W 107328	1497837	TABACS FABRIQUES
2	CRUDE MATERLS,EXCL FUELS		6390736		7814061		9736852		8194156	MAT BRUTES NON COMESTIBLES
26	TEXTILE FIBRES AND WASTE		1211993		1417806		1651306		1538386	FIBRES TEXTILES
28	METALLIFEROUS ORES,SCRAP		1676246		2137782		2734157		2076005	MINERAIS METAL,DECHETS
3	MINERAL FUELS ETC		4847002		5219532		5502551		6980008	COMBUSTIBLES MINERAUX LUB
33	PETROLEUM AND PRODUCTS		3409238		3685440		3752645		4129219	PETROLE ET DERIVES
334	PETROLEUM PRODUCTS,REFIN	MW 14981	2998638	MW 15695	3133510		3148917	MW 13836	3501708	PRODUITS RAFFINES
341	*GAS,NATURAL AND MANUFCT	W 2124542	378006	W 2293277	403682	W 5289548	741239	MW 14601	1685799	GAZ NATUREL,GAZ MANUFACT
3414	PETROLEUM GASES, GASEOUS	W 1473600	263568	W 1533355	278923	W 4593295	600963	MW 13964	1549433	GAZ DE PETROLE GAZEUX
5	CHEMCLS,RELATED PROD NES		47354418		55584542		67211613		65176521	PRODUITS CHIMIQUES
51	ORGANIC CHEMICALS		9856355		11753139		14533946		13467616	PROD CHIMIQ ORGANIQUES
512	ALCOHOLS,PHENOLS ETC	W 1600019	1296625		1757652		2299919		1975074	PHENOLS,PHENOLS–ALCOOLS
5121	ACYCLIC ALCOHOLS,DERIVS	W 1323229	997581	W 1604298	1395263	W 1518281	1841603	W 1748320	1585778	ALCOOLS ACYCLIQUES
513	CARBOXYLIC ACIDS ETC	W 1227499	1400671		1746305		2289947		2020895	ACIDES CARBOXYLIQUES
514	NITROGEN–FNCTN COMPOUNDS	W 839232	3211909		3739611		4497182		4394168	COMPOSES FONCT AZOTEES
5148	OTH NITROGN–FNCTN CMPNDS	W 400770	1699027	W 502926	2014030	W 562066	2528085	W 566499	2612886	AUTRES COMPOSES AZOTES
51482	IMIDE–,IMIDE–FNCT CMPNDS	W 118989	1052151	W 156639	1244269	W 187584	1515104	W 163140	1596514	COMPOSES A FONCTION IMIDE
515	ORG–INORG COMPOUNDS ETC	W 150099	1674883		1950433		2140275		2182654	COMPOSES ORGANO–MINERAUX
516	OTHER ORGANIC CHEMICALS	W 963965	1221278	W 1097149	1444619		1802512	W 1157452	1724848	AUTRES PROD ORGANIQUES
52	INORGANIC CHEMICALS		4089835		3306648		3871414		3759762	PROD CHIM INORGANIQUES
522	INORG ELEMNTS,OXIDES,ETC	W 3627126	1408043		1661087		2081977		1980847	ELEMENTS INORGANIQUES
523	OTHR INORG CHEMICALS ETC	W 4086344	2483328		1471316		1655387		1629985	AUT PRODUITS CHIMIQUES INORG
53	DYES,TANNING,COLOUR PROD		5070752		5687853		6412300		6320788	PROD TEINTURE,COLORANTS
531	SYNT DYE,NAT INDGO,LAKES	W 172589	2173858	W 194155	2337827	W 197041	2483780	W 214271	2415593	MAT COLOR ORGAN,LAQUES
5311	SYNTHIC ORGNIC DYESTUFFS	W 121311	1956145	W 135090	2109207	W 133091	2228849	W 138513	2127362	MAT COLOR ORGAN SYNTHET
533	PIGMENTS,PAINTS,ETC	W 1059473	2760420	W 1185664	3196992	W 1192213	3761991		3724553	PIGMENTS,PEINTURES,VERNIS
5334	VARNISHES,DISTEMPERS ETC	W 268133	1178255	W 318452	1417298	W 339554	1708000	W 360000	1705252	PEINTURES A L'EAU
541	*MEDICINAL,PHARM PRODUCT	MK 159950	7599870		8739135		10268294		10555397	PROD MEDICINAUX PHARMACEUT
5417	MEDICAMENTS	MK 106296	4539513	MK 122871	5218549	MK 122573	6305154	MK 122326	6569065	MEDICAMENTS
54179	— CONTNG OTH SUBSTANCES	MK 98659	3800139	MK 113978	4347976	MK 113483	5187077	MK 114026	5399647	MED CONT AUT SUBSTANCES
55	PERFUME,CLEANING ETC PRD		3279566		3791183		4542530		4469032	PROD POUR PARFUM,TOILETTE
553	PERFUMERY,COSMETICS,ETC	W 175479	1365727	W 221467	1674292	W 256320	2047783	W 256182	2002386	PRODUITS DE PARFUMERIE
554	SOAP,CLEANSING ETC PREPS	W 914481	1466609	W 988556	1598124	W 1016974	1887798	W 1092068	1852723	SAVONS,PRODUITS DETERSIFS
5542	WASHING PREPARATIONS ETC	W 815986	1227755	W 885304	1343848	W 904236	1577552	W 959971	1521052	PROD ORG TENSIO–ACT NDA
58	PLASTIC MATERIALS ETC		11227883		13609753		17018412		16065253	MAT PLAST ARTIFICIELLES
582	PROD OF CONDENSATION ETC	W 1517542	3480731	W 1859489	4243416	W 1939487	5448333	W 1943999	5221743	PROD CONDENS,POLYCOND
5823	ALKYDS,OTHER POLYESTERS	W 421679	1027643	W 539945	1290585	W 607520	1841395	W 609435	1713775	ALKYDES ET AUT POLYESTERS
583	POLYMERIZATION ETC PRODS	W 7504108	7375792	W 5722340	8942875	W 5747217	11086002	W 5928099	10378505	PROD POLYMERISATION
5831	POLYETHYLENE	W 1185122	1172989	W 1392354	1386042	W 1485371	1867750	W 1503899	1771397	POLYETHYLENE
5834	POLYVINYL CHLORIDE	W 835737	1385637	W 990245	1630374	W 1002276	2096613	W 1031591	1893273	CHLORURE DE POLYVINYLE
5839	OTH POLYMRZTION ETC PROD	W 876509	2280087	W 1144819	2775720	W 1102048	3282127	W 1154014	3179579	AUT PROD POLYMER COPOLYM
59	CHEMICAL MATERIALS NES		6616150		7576271		9286213		9237423	MAT PROD CHIMIQUES NDA
591	PESTICIDES,DISINFECTANTS	W 156183	1279344	W 191159	1571424	W 198979	1861026	W 202481	1808987	DESINF,INSECT,FONG,HERB
598	MISCEL CHEM PRODUCTS NES	W 2828819	4510815		5088362		6297419		6329780	PROD DIV INDUST CHIM NDA
5989	CHEM PRODUCTS,PREPS NES	W 2536207	3992790	W 2760916	4468637	W 2923744	5600564	W 2826011	5632392	PROD PREP CHIMIQUES NDA
59899	OTH CHEM PRODS,PREPS,NES	W 2076533	2876555	W 2241691	3244843	W 2367419	4160762	W 2313535	4243667	AUT PRODUITS CHIMIQUES NDA
6	BASIC MANUFACTURES		61401097		69572725		86887844		80066398	ART MANUFACTURES
62	RUBBER MANUFACTURES NES		3386831		3771908		4566429		4588267	CAOUTCHOUC MANUFACTURE
625	RUBBER TYRES, TUBES ETC	W 386636	1610579	W 424755	1767158	W 437724	2022182	W 465173	2095036	PNEUS CAOUTCHOUC VULCANISE
63	WOOD,CORK MANUFACTRS NES		1281440		1435718		1801182		1701580	OUVRAGES LIEGE ET BOIS
64	PAPER,PAPERBOARD AND MFR		7886379		9506922		12817852		11516417	PAPIERS,CARTONS & OUVRAGES
641	PAPER AND PAPERBOARD	W 5196254	4796142	W 6684919	6173702	W 7115270	8790226	W 7332072	7810419	PAPIERS ET CARTONS
6412	PRINTG,WRITING PAPER NES	W 1562797	1412994	W 1996194	1856000	W 2298662	2877828	W 2251840	2408286	PAPIERS POUR L'IMPRESSION
64122	— COATED,IMPREGNATD ETC	W 1450967	1305025	W 1866735	1718134	W 2145137	2649352	W 2102862	2221924	PAPIERS IMPRESSION COUCHES
6415	PAPER,PAPERBRD,BULK,NES	W 2167075	1463913	W 2796757	1906357	W 2709416	2626690	W 2722705	2141075	PAPIERS,CARTONS ROULEAUX
64159	OTHER PAPER ETC,BULK,NES	W 2100594	1366804	W 2722267	1799589	W 2642986	2505711	W 2654145	2028440	AUT PAPIER ROULEAUX FEUILLES
6418	COATED ETC PAPER NES BLK	W 665383	1200845	W 857088	1513928	W 879234	1928415	W 949702	1841573	PAP,CARTONS COUCHES,ENDUITS
642	PAPER,ETC,PRECUT,ARTS OF	W 1258863	3090237	W 1390517	3333220	W 1388377	4027626	W 1367427	3705998	PAP,CARTONS DECOUPES
6428	PAPER ETC ARTICLES NES	W 496512	1475760	W 516228	1543824	W 546687	1895613	W 543507	1717766	OUVRAGES EN PATE A PAPIER
65	TEXTILE YARN,FABRICS,ETC		11784660		12863730		14647845		13806370	FILS,TISSUS,ARTICLES TEXTILE
651	TEXTILE YARN	W 542245	2800030	W 623069	3249953	W 585988	3676670		3521240	FILS TEXTILES
6514	SYN FIB YRN,BULK,MONOFIL	W 307502	1475849	W 358019	1673828	W 338857	1918592	W 366219	1894677	FILS CONT 85% FIB TEXT SYNTH
652	COTTON FABRICS,WOVEN	W 124188	1396930	W 127211	1528419	W 116226	1637628	W 119671	1589960	TISSUS DE COTON
6522	WOVEN COTTON BLEACHD,ETC	W 87369	1222111	W 88211	1334079	W 82637	1430405	W 85774	1399591	TISSUS COTON BLANCHIS ETC
653	WOVN MAN–MADE FIB FABRIC	W 192452	2781554	W 161950	2782313	W 158540	3152509	W 152533	2741696	TISSUS FIBRES SYNTH,ARTIF
657	SPECIAL TXTL FABRC,PRODS	W 227538	1838337	W 260590	2050830	W 273319	2473670	W 281013	2393198	TISSUS SPECIAUX
66	NONMETAL MINERAL MFS NES		5866581		6457844		7740764		7329901	ART MIN NON METALLIQUES
663	MINERAL MANUFCTURES NES	W 1579118	1530398		1711098		2084773	W 1816885	2030554	ART MIN MANUF NDA
664	GLASS	W 945910	1312752	W 1078726	1546266	W 1098870	1915915		1961062	VERRE
67	IRON AND STEEL		11987805		13955153		18123985		15588435	FER ET ACIER
672	IRON,STEEL PRIMARY FORMS	W 5154399	2198209	W 4564887	2325719	W 4650303	2970036	W 5087637	2277845	LINGOTS FER,ACIER
6727	IRN,STL COIL FR REROLLNG	W 3223903	1638580	W 2885267	1738653	W 2788317	2155466	W 2823139	1494935	EBAUCHES POUR TOLES FER
673	IRON,STEEL SHAPES ETC	W 3805179	1859951	W 4144746	2195472	W 4602963	2935876	W 4300989	2460274	BARRES,PROFIL FER,ACIER
674	IRN,STL UNIV,PLATE,SHEET	W 7690496	4792627	W 8398589	5637931	W 8771547	7461391	W 8363423	6332411	LARGES PLATS,TOLES
6746	IRN,STL THIN PLATE,ROLLD	W 2896323	1895995	W 2928875	2047053	W 2832049	2715233	W 2744889	2307833	TOLES LAM MOINS 3MM
6749	OTH IRN,STL PLATES,SHEET	W 1908648	1227415	W 2507855	1677486	W 2741567	2170366	W 2685091	1870391	AUTRES TOLES FER,ACIER
67491	— OF IRON OR SIMPLE STL	W 1886400	1175395	W 2469666	1605991	W 2721396	2083857	W 2670254	1800942	AUT TOLES AUTRES ACIER FIN
678	IRON,STL TUBES,PIPES,ETC	W 1902154	2284794		2882694		3601474		3465751	TUBES,TUYAUX EN FONTE,FER
68	NON–FERROUS METALS		6641442		7197848		9704655		8602164	METAUX NON FERREUX
682	COPPER EXC CEMENT COPPER	W 814623	2726158		2742847		3654038		3316993	CUIVRE
6822	COPPER,ALLOYS WORKED	W 705864	2505546	W 626770	2330490	W 688449	3192088	W 648784	2647362	CUIVRE,ALLIAGES OUVRES
684	ALUMINIUM	W 932522	2751257		3175176	W 1223155	4462816	W 1172064	3939554	ALUMINIUM
6842	ALUMINIUM,ALLOYS WORKED	W 685099	2395873	W 794284	2726518	W 923767	3787510	W 911731	3467250	ALUMINIUM,ALLIAGES OUVRE

5. Special Exports F.O.B. by Commodities according to the S.I.T.C. (Rev. 2) in thousand U.S. Dollars
Exportations Spéciales F.O.B. par Produits d'après la C.T.C.I. (Rév. 2) en milliers de Dollars E.U.

SITC CTCI	COMMODITY	1993 WEIGHT POIDS	1993 VALUE VALEUR	1994 WEIGHT POIDS	1994 VALUE VALEUR	1995 WEIGHT POIDS	1995 VALUE VALEUR	1996 WEIGHT POIDS	1996 VALUE VALEUR	PRODUIT
68422	ALUMNM PLATE,SHEET,STRIP	W 373192	1052996	W 458405	1273067	W 588443	1978020	W 577211	1786147	TOLES, PLANCHES EN ALU
69	METAL MANUFACTURES NES		11207671		12846494		15631929		15345750	ART MANUFACT EN METAL NDA
691	STRUCTURES AND PARTS NES	W 506516	1459306	W 554079	1537101	W 598546	1894910	W 626245	1942219	CONSTRUCT FER,ACIER,ALU
695	TOOLS	W 92488	2146977	W 107105	2546067	W 109061	3071740	W 111310	3042968	OUTILS A MAIN
6954	BLADES,TIPS,ETC FR TOOLS	W 35459	1321354	W 47212	1640107	W 46144	1961801	W 46475	1937366	OUTILS POUR MACHINE-OUTIL
699	BASE METAL MFRS NES	W 622327	4346985	W 730317	5029338		6207312		6181410	ART MANUFACTURES MET NDA
6991	LOCKSMITHS WARES,ETC	W 187901	1939892	W 229460	2292828	W 244940	2757747	W 262617	2779338	ARTICLES DE SERRURERIE
69913	BASE MTL DOOR,ETC FITTNG	W 157848	1451152	W 194228	1695675	W 206896	2010294	W 222305	2022203	GARNITURES POUR MEUBLES
7	MACHINES,TRANSPORT EQUIP		183339108		209185690		255995788		254120676	MACHINES MATERIEL TRANSPORT
71	POWER GENERATING EQUIPMT		10806156		12344209		14398351		15900224	MACHINES GENERATRICES
713	INTRNL COMBUS PSTN ENGIN	W 459567	5201905	W 545101	5974714	W 608489	7360651	W 644122	8057079	MOTEURS EXPL COMB INT, PIECE
7132	MOTOR VEHCL PSTN ENGINS	W 166104	1983161	W 195380	2044492	W 206782	2544676	W 227747	2806313	MOTEURS EXPL POUR VEHICULES
7139	PISTON ENGINE PARTS NES	W 235462	2444535	W 275863	2895825	W 320595	3577588	W 333949	3877860	PIECES POUR 713.2,3,8
714	ENGINES AND MOTORS NES	W 20362	1757298	W 20648	2257885	W 16493	2218190	W 25632	2993205	MOTEURS NON ELECTRIQUES
7149	ENGINE & MOTOR PARTS NES	W 15997	1072183	W 17531	1127492	W 14983	1225187	W 21522	1622705	PIECES 714 ET 718.88
716	ROTATING ELECTRIC PLANT	W 170194	2348448	W 199020	2675588	W 223417	3180869	W 232861	3186141	APP ELECTR ROTATIFS,PIECES
7162	AC MTRS,GENRTRS,GEN SETS	W 114657	1523890	W 132213	1749835	W 145232	2020085	W 154643	2057148	MOTEURS ELECTRIQUES
71621	AC MTRS,INC UNIVRSL MTRS	W 93309	1171447	W 105096	1315939	W 127411	1720644	W 132800	1756284	MOT ELEC NON COUR CONTINU
72	MACHS FOR SPCL INDUSTRYS		22502888		24306974		30020029		30361328	MAC SPECIALES POUR INDUST
721	AGRIC MACHY,EXC TRACTORS	W 177132	1347011	W 203258	1547995	W 210333	1869969	W 234214	1964538	MACHINES AGRICOLES
722	TRACTORS NON-ROAD	W 140005	967881	W 172405	1278642	W 199070	1662958	W 211635	1672560	TRACTEURS
7224	WHEELED TRACTORS NES	W 139962	967249	W 172360	1278341	W 199035	1662746	W 211603	1672407	TRACTEURS A ROUES
723	CIVIL ENGNEERG EQUIP ETC	W 186545	1474712	W 222000	1677735	W 253694	2161067	W 256884	2026219	APPAREILS DE GENIE CIVIL
7234	CONST,MINING MACHNRY NES	W 151829	1187137	W 178552	1342924	W 205342	1737784	W 209797	1632571	MACH POUR LA CONST, MINES
724	TEXTILE,LEATHER MACHNRY	W 268588	5811178	W 259615	5677600	W 266914	6459795	W 253665	5963784	MACH POUR INDUSTRIE TEXTILE
7244	SPINNING,EXTRDNG,ETC MCH	W 117160	2455029	W 110863	2258836	W 120165	2655266	W 105550	2249851	MACH POUR LE FILAGE
7245	WEAVING,FELT MFG,ETC MCH	W 63966	1169302	W 64556	1264354	W 64043	1385167	W 60310	1322495	METIERS A TISSER,PIECES
725	PAPER ETC MILL MACHINERY	W 49379	1118230	W 62488	1302439	W 72403	1712619	W 80255	1978274	MACHINES FABR PATE PAPIER
726	PRINTG,BKBINDG MACHY,PTS	W 130246	3375500	W 129852	3440380	W 148879	4447030	W 166899	4698030	MACHINES POUR IMPRIMERIE
7264	PRINTING PRESSES	W 89041	2237756	W 85723	2196334	W 100515	2969134	W 117727	3282398	MACHINES A IMPRIMER
72641	ROTARY PRINTING PRESSES	W 89041	2237756	W 85723	2196334	W 100515	2969134	W 117727	3282398	MACH IMPRIMER ROTATIVES
728	OTH MACHY FOR SPCL INDUS	W 384248	7424743		8304822		10461201		10665329	AUT MACH IND PARTICULIERES
7284	MACHY FOR SPCL INDUS NES	W 233366	5504726	W 272275	6128833	W 320387	7919367	W 324781	8177078	MACH SPEC IND PARTICUL.
72842	RUBBER,PLASTICS WRKG MCH	W 85935	1818524	W 90413	1911616	W 105295	2421298	W 110595	2465582	MACH IND CAOUT MAT PLAST
72848	OTH MCHY WITH INDIV FNCT	W 80626	1945628	W 101040	2181382	W 104259	2671317	W 111535	2883975	AUTRES MACHINES NDA
72849	PTS OF MACHS OF 7284 ETC	W 38782	1144827	W 39259	1173500	W 48609	1550802	W 48841	1544896	PIECES DU 728.4 ETC
73	METALWORKING MACHINERY		5289789		5522194		7004211		7355514	MACH TRAVAIL DES METAUX
736	METALWORKING MACH-TOOLS	W 210706	4095140	W 242341	4291421	W 259658	5383237	W 265537	5742690	MACH-OUTILS TRAVAIL METAUX
7361	METAL CUTTING MACH-TOOLS	W 76338	1387514	W 100902	1601524	W 101543	2040200	W 98651	2053576	MACH-OUT ENLEVEMENT METAL
737	METALWORKING MACHNRY NES	W 110867	1194649	W 118042	1230773	W 117253	1620974	W 120326	1612824	MACH TRAV METAUX PIECES
74	GENRL INDUSTRL MACHY NES		27010593		29931791		37251765		37373040	MACH APP INDUSTRIE
741	HEATING,COOLING EQUIPMNT	W 212062	3336573	W 220396	3673279	W 238759	4452545	W 292791	4830754	MACH CHAUFFAGE,PIECES
7416	HEATING,COOLING EQU NES	W 95565	1646571	W 101083	1867741	W 109008	2192235	W 133875	2427275	APP CHANGEMENT TEMP
742	PUMPS FOR LIQUIDS ETC	W 108649	3171015	W 126457	3727886	W 138601	4573246	W 142493	4557695	POMPES MOTO-POMPES
7428	OTHER PUMPS FOR LIQUIDS	W 24366	1081169	W 30003	1371226	W 31117	1670488	W 31050	1598288	AUTRES POMPES POUR LIQ
74288	PUMPS FR LIQUIDS NES ETC	W 22424	1036699	W 27677	1314426	W 28980	1609867	W 29384	1556661	POMPES POUR LIQUIDES NDA
743	PUMPS NES,CENTRFUGES ETC	W 211078	3824210	W 238363	4318706	W 279881	5446823	W 291914	5475192	POMPES COMPRES,VENT ETC
7431	PUMPS FOR GASES ETC	W 63510	1038084	W 76121	1232998	W 94888	1578878	W 94413	1519579	POMPES AIR A VIDE,COMPRES
7436	GAS,LIQUID FILTERS ETC	W 66122	1145754	W 74650	1295507	W 82266	1620876	W 88585	1629081	APP POUR FILT DES LIQUIDES
744	MECHANICAL HANDLING EQU	W 448072	3865201	W 517159	4232639	W 601845	5476383	W 621296	5449337	EQUIP MANUTENTION PIECES
7442	LIFTING,LOADING MACH NES	W 170386	1709430	W 171451	1724766	W 205889	2265167	W 213541	2226951	APP LEVAGE,MANUTENTION
7449	PTS NES OF MACHY OF 7442	W 187549	1541696	W 215473	1659590	W 242982	2103615	W 246405	2115561	PIECES DU 744.2
745	NONELEC MACHY,TOOLS NES	W 149726	4327168	W 171340	4835054	W 181934	5619282	W 178237	5660322	AUT MACH NON ELEC,PIECES
7452	OTH NONELEC MCHS,PTS NES	W 141237	3978016	W 161625	4426190	W 172302	5172418	W 168512	5224728	AUT MACH NON ELEC,PIECES
74522	PACKAGNG,BOTTLNG,ETC MCH	W 45517	1923476	W 56416	2190274	W 56631	2519427	W 56550	2630171	MACH NETT BOUTEILLES,ETC
749	NONELEC MACH PTS,ACC NES	W 541365	8486426	W 610857	9144227	W 675347	11683486	W 658621	11399740	PIECES MACH NON ELEC NDA
7491	BALL,ROLLER,ETC BEARINGS	W 87461	1344052	W 107679	1585931	W 134062	2208020	W 127739	2062566	ROULEMENTS BILLES ETC
7492	COCKS,VALVES ETC NES	W 119253	2825858	W 122047	3038444	W 128932	3767721	W 131414	3642945	ART ROB,SIM POUR TUYAUX
7493	SHAFT,CRANK,PULLEY ETC	W 225140	2316297	W 283924	2625934	W 327156	3420095	W 295162	3364972	ARBRES TRANS,VILEBREQUINS
7499	OTH NONELEC MCHY PTS NES	W 109511	2000219	W 97207	1893918	W 85198	2287648	W 104307	2329257	PIECES NON ELECT NDA
75	OFFICE MACHNES,ADP EQUIP		8744412		9920875		12951644		12068128	MACH BUREAU TRAIT AUTOM
752	AUTOMTIC DATA PROC EQUIP	W 48422	5196381	W 57331	5722112		7390083	W 71597	6901486	MACH TRAIT INFORMATION
7523	DIGITL CENTRL PROCESSORS	W 12437	1881498	W 11582	1771099	W 17531	2344932	W 17399	2120945	UNITES CENTRALES
7524	DIGITL CENTRL STOR UNITS	W 7305	1141465	W 6458	1151360	W 9753	1635233	W 7678	1395682	UNITES MEMOIRE CENTRALES
7525	ADP PERIPHERAL UNITS	W 23224	1477152	W 33322	1731063	W 40024	2155110	W 40775	2027836	UNITES PERIPHERIQUES
759	OFFICE,ADP MCH PTS,ACCES	W 29937	2596246	W 34078	3157249	W 40954	4206336	W 41892	3949968	PIECES DU 751 ET 752
7599	ACCTG,ETC,ADP MCH PTS,AC	W 15541	2124473	W 16889	2670615	W 24541	3656289	W 26577	3497769	PIECES DU 751 ET 752
76	TELECOMM,SOUND EQUIPMENT		7308823		9182328		11168974		11587688	EQUIPMENT DE TELECOM
764	TELECOM EQPT,PTS,ACC NES	W 73198	5297519	W 79562	6924381	W 76913	8636833	W 88392	9062230	EQUIP TELECOM,PIECES
7641	LINE TELEPHONE,ETC EQUIP	W 14562	1499328	W 18096	1853407	W 19668	2386171	W 22355	2497132	APP TELEPHON PAR FIL
7643	TV,RADIO TRANSMITTRS ETC	W 4905	569826	W 4507	1441278	W 5793	2550243	W 7465	2993190	APP EMET TELE RADIO
7649	PTS NES OF EQUIPMT OF 76	W 40248	2687213	W 42597	3075757	W 35558	3052327	W 38925	2887111	PIECES DE LA DIV 76
76491	PTS NES OF APPAR OF 7641	W 13608	1508773	W 14675	1796617	W 10565	1615964	W 9561	1421769	PIECES POUR 764.1
77	ELECTRIC MACHNRY NES ETC		27782711		33045980		42573334		40488944	MACH APP ELECT NDA
771	ELECTRIC POWER MACHY NES	W 108230	1485592	W 109763	1743635	W 114345	2333457	W 129539	2497959	MACH PROD,TRANS ELECTR
7712	OTH ELEC POWER MACHY NES	W 69173	1062488	W 71294	1298408	W 77654	1831164	W 84521	1961124	AUT APP PROD TRANSF ELEC
772	SWITCHGEAR ETC,PARTS NES	W 199039	7581280	W 223108	8625552	W 254018	10838237	W 269777	10858767	APP COUPURE,SECT ETC
7721	SWITCHGEAR ETC	W 192888	6599495	W 215421	7795018	W 245264	10005264	W 261701	10096779	APP COUPURE,SECTIONMNT
773	ELECTR DISTRIBUTNG EQUIP	W 232513	1796808	W 255829	2067702	W 297808	2784908	W 312629	2886700	EQUIPMT DISTRIBUTION ELECT
7731	INSULATED WIRE,CABLE ETC	W 204945	1498255	W 230244	1709051	W 268041	2273911	W 283057	2369136	FILS,CABLES ISOLES ELECT
774	ELECTRO-MEDCL,XRAY EQUIP	W 15838	2059382	W 16100	2228421	W 17273	2666033	W 18825	2694170	APPAREILS MEDICAUX
7742	X-RAY APPARATUS ETC	W 11945	1506329	W 11995	1589124	W 12547	1876721	W 13328	1893306	APPAREILS A RAYONS X
775	HOUSEHOLD TYPE EQUIP NES	W 409447	3860677	W 433563	4122513	W 439029	4755332	W 455705	4561641	MACH,APP USAGE DOMESTQUE
7758	ELECTRO-THERMIC APPL NES	W 100816	1190246	W 105575	1277699	W 103816	1408859	W 97400	1323001	APP ELECTROTHERMIQ NDA
776	TRANSISTORS,VALVES,ETC	W 65500	4092180	W 93042	5943023	W 93788	8003380	W 100037	7147474	LAMPES,TUBES,VALVES
7764	ELECTRONIC MICROCIRCUITS	W 3553	2839429	W 3972	4312452	W 4724	5798146	W 4229	5108934	MICROSTRUCTURES ELECTRON
778	ELECTRICAL MACHINERY NES	W 451193	6906792	W 496896	8315134	W 547544	11191987	W 559224	9842233	AUTRES MACH ELECT NDA
7783	AUTOMOTIVE ELECTR EQUIP	W 100071	1564240	W 106946	1817537	W 127346	2349018	W 129834	2431479	EQUIP ELECT MOTEURS EXPL
7788	OTH ELEC MACHY,EQUIP NES	W 153501	3016260	W 164641	3738473	W 179417	5550722	W 164552	4152650	AUT MACH APP ELEC NDA
77889	ELEC PARTS OF MACHY NES	W 3268	842632	W 2226	1309676	W 2567	2316306	W 2909	1040863	PIECES ELEC DE MACH NDA
78	ROAD VEHICLES		58633377		68802667		83140479		84369230	VEHICULES ROUTIERS
781	PASS MOTOR VEH EXC BUSES	W 2543270	35458589	W 2955382	42225571	W 3163109	48602065	W 3554211	51624055	AUTO TRANSPORT PERSONNES
782	LORRIES,SPCL MTR VEH NES	W 472682	3619405	W 621650	4661386	W 670602	6110973	W 786962	6470581	VEHICULES SPECIAUX,MARCH
7821	LORRIES,TRUCKS	W 399197	2898182	W 536936	3922799	W 567905	5152345	W 659774	5389250	VEHICULES TRANSP MARCHAND
783	ROAD MOTOR VEHICLES NES	W 179963	1695159	W 236702	2286209	W 326722	4171928	W 304015	3366610	VEHICULES ROUTIERS NDA
7832	TRACTORS FOR TR-TRAILERS	W 126926	1137536	W 169887	1586358	W 268978	3536364	W 237203	2646737	TRACTEURS ROUTIERS
784	MOTOR VEH PRTS,ACCES NES	W 1961065	16195065	W 2129405	17778368	W 2323321	21931557	W 2131318	20554208	PIECES 722,781,782,783
7849	OTHER MOTOR VEHCL PARTS	W 1924008	15770535	W 2090944	17334656	W 2270403	21316963	W 2079123	19967052	PIECES 722,781,782,783
786	TRAILERS,NONMOTR VEH,NES	W 257194	1258181	W 302816	1415563	W 321770	1775701	W 334938	1684854	REMORQUES,CADRES,CONTAIN
79	OTHR TRANSPORT EQUIPMENT		12370680		12298292		12868310		10347612	AUTRE MATERIEL TRANSPORT
791	RAILWAY VEHICLES	W 141691	1525326	W 172300	2091421	W 98679	1261531	W 90651	912181	VEHIC MAT CHEMINS DE FER

5. Special Exports F.O.B. by Commodities according to the S.I.T.C. (Rev. 2) in thousand U.S. Dollars
Exportations Spéciales F.O.B. par Produits d'après la C.T.C.I. (Rév. 2) en milliers de Dollars E.U.

SITC CTCI	COMMODITY	1993		1994		1995		1996		PRODUIT
		WEIGHT POIDS	VALUE VALEUR	WEIGHT POIDS	VALUE VALEUR	WEIGHT POIDS	VALUE VALEUR	WEIGHT POIDS	VALUE VALEUR	
792	AIRCRAFT ETC	W 17546	8563975	W 16302	8441248	W 16580	9015187	W 14524	7957395	APP NAVIGATION AERIENNE
7924	AIRCRFT NES OVER 15000KG	W 7252	4738731	W 6394	4747662	W 6657	4994795	W 5210	4174161	AERODYNES PLUS 15000 KG
7929	AIRCRAFT PARTS NES	W 9875	3694114	W 9146	3461974	W 8888	3556257	W 8373	3372046	PIECES DU 792
793	SHIPS AND BOATS ETC	W 1219777	2281379	W 827053	1765623	W 344297	2591592	W 202783	1478036	NAVIRES BATEAUX,ETC
7932	SHIPS AND BOATS NES	W 701005	2074128	W 331726	1498552	W 310125	2531247	W 189266	1427846	NAVIRES ET BATEAUX
79323	OTHER CARGO VESSELS	W 627864	1767161	W 292840	1164640	W 270736	2188922	W 185074	1352439	AUT BATEAUX TRANS MARCH
8	MISC MANUFACTURED GOODS		42246184		45746479		52985997		52402580	ART MANUFACTURES DIVERS
812	*PLUMBG,HEATNG,LGHTNG EQ	W 174765	1611587	W 189888	1782489	W 192183	2014739	W 214924	2092735	APPAR SANITAIRES CHAUFFAGE
821	*FURNITURE,PARTS THEREOF	W 732278	4090292	W 778625	4356490	W 808935	4983245	W 799759	4784044	MEUBLES ET PIECES
8211	CHAIRS,SEATS AND PARTS	W 138169	1185682	W 156632	1300308	W 165947	1547920	W 161452	1497044	SIEGES ET PIECES
8219	FURNITURE AND PARTS NES	W 565220	2265661	W 591722	2383613	W 611025	2774186	W 606602	2678294	AUTRES MEUBLES ET PIECES
82192	WOOD FURNITURE NES	W 400351	1508943	W 424509	1626150	W 426219	1850352	W 417682	1804634	MEUBLES NDA EN BOIS
84	CLOTHING AND ACCESSORIES		6612269		6671750		7502794		7368634	VETEMENTS
842	MENS OUTERWEAR NOT KNIT	W 20509	1172848	W 20623	1185805	W 22706	1352581	W 22999	1361895	VET DESSUS POUR HOMMES
843	WOMENS OUTERWEAR NONKNIT	W 33085	2646181	W 32127	2654987	W 32289	2963680	W 33818	2861802	VET DESSUS FEMMES MAT TEX
87	PRECISION INSTRUMNTS NES		9561608		10318839		12385940		12754438	INSTRUM,APPAR SCIENT NDA
872	MEDICAL INSTRUMENTS NES	W 23619	1812209	W 25403	1839756	W 27982	2258113	W 30010	2293429	INSTR,APP MEDIC–CHIR NDA
87202	OTH MEDICAL INSTRUMENTS	W 19986	1566337	W 21460	1606197	W 23174	1919983	W 24900	1937419	INSTRUM,APP MEDECINE
874	MEASURNG,CONTROLNG INSTR	W 64180	6601496		7192393		8583191		8914694	INSTRUMENTS DE MESURE
8742	MEASUR,DRAW ETC INST,PTS	W 19931	1632952	W 22068	1742252	W 23542	2089607	W 24489	2177508	INST DESSIN,TRACAGE,PCS
87421	MEASURNG,DRAWNG ETC INST	W 17770	1423352	W 19055	1500852	W 20481	1797711	W 21346	1833307	INSTRUM DESSIN,TRACAGE
8743	GAS,LIQUID CONTROL INSTR	W 18420	1664817	W 19717	1858189	W 21502	2237863	W 22397	2258862	APP,INSTR MESURE FLUIDES
8748	ELEC MEAS,CONTRL EQU NES	W 7743	1609286	W 8144	1770468	W 9242	2174240	W 9915	2260526	APP ELEC ELECTRO MESURE
87483	OTH ELCTRNC MEAS ETC EQU	W 6652	1478619	W 6867	1606683	W 7616	1963240	W 8022	2042771	AUT APP ELECTRO DE MESURE
88	PHOTO EQU,OPTICL GDS ETC		3880766		4298422		4862218		4770657	APP,FOURN PHOTO,OP,MONTR
882	PHOTO,CINEMA SUPPLIES	W 169883	1716667		2000832		2178096		2220498	PRODUITS PHOTO,CINEMA
8822	PHOTO FILM EXC DEV CINMA	W 122618	1476747	W 141221	1681738	W 144792	1815520	W 129021	1796549	PLAQUES,PELLICULES,FILMS
89	MISC MANUFCTRD GOODS NES		15006136		16694501		19400304		18967396	ART MANUFACTURES DIVERS
892	PRINTED MATTER	W 603792	3081214	W 740606	3385793	W 739767	3837775	W 728027	3781272	IMPRIMES
8928	PRINTED MATTER NES	W 282166	1170254	W 410613	1352018	W 403761	1604269	W 431695	1644451	IMPRIMES NDA
893	ARTICLES OF PLASTIC NES		5217653		5876778		7196305		6991162	OUVRAGES EN MAT DIVIS 58
8931	PLSTC PACKG CONTNRS,LIDS	W 338692	1386873	W 381594	1519427	W 387203	1798481	W 391950	1677749	ART TRANSP EMBALLAGE ETC
8939	MISC PLASTIC ARTICLES	W 552484	3645138	W 634232	4166047	W 667462	5180409	W 700751	5080441	ART DIVERS EN MAT DIV 58
89399	OTHR PLASTC ARTICLES NES	W 485883	3350178	W 556996	3848617	W 587641	4805158	W 616201	4719975	AUT OUV MAT DIV 58
894	TOYS,SPORTING GOODS,ETC	W 110952	1411437	W 116735	1512164	W 124744	1778944	W 122886	1683026	VOITURES ENFANTS,JOUETS
898	MUSICAL INSTRUMENTS,PTS	W 103370	2136402	W 126249	2375181	W 129411	2474878	W 138567	2740438	INSTRUMENTS DE MUSIQUE
8983	SOUND RECRDNG TAPE,DISCS	W 97677	1888566	W 119553	2093643	W 122372	2146200	W 131626	2410274	SUPPORTS SON POUR 763
89832	RECORDED DISCS,TAPES ETC	W 33958	1140911	W 41238	1240982	W 37737	1155382	W 37615	1305244	DISQUES,PHONO,BANDES
899	OTHER MANUFACTURED GOODS		1282676		1404674		1639465		1580997	AUT ART MANUF DIVERS NDA
9	GOODS NOT CLASSD BY KIND		14056613		11399856		19248195		20123140	ART TRANSACT NON CLASSES
931	*SPECIAL TRANSACTIONS	W 644643	13073221	W 680480	10190121	W 548019	17705623	W 529315	18614613	TRANS.SPECIALES

Ghana

1. HISTORICAL SERIES, 1957–1994 GENERAL TRADE, IMPORTS C.I.F., EXPORTS F.O.B.
SERIES HISTORIQUES, 1957–1994 COMMERCE GENERAL, IMPORTATIONS C.A.F., EXPORTATIONS F.O.B

YEAR ANNEE	VALUE IN MILLION CEDIS NEW CEDIS MERCHANDISE –MARCHANDISE		GOLD –OR		CONVERSION FACTORS U.S. CENTS PER CEDI NEW CEDI FACTEURS DE CONVERSION CENTS E.U. PAR CEDI		INDEX NUMBERS –INDICES QUANTUM		UNIT VALUE VALEUR UNITAIRE	
	IMPORTS	EXPORTS	IMPORTS	EXPORTS	IMPORTS	EXPORTS	IMPORTS	EXPORTS	IMPORTS	EXPORTS
1957	232.00	196.30		23.51	116.6700	116.6700				
1958	203.00	225.50		25.44	116.6700	116.6700				
1959	271.30	245.20		26.88	116.6700	116.6700				
1960	311.10	251.70	0.02	26.61	116.6700	116.6700				
1961	337.90	250.50	4.92	25.80	116.6700	116.6700				
1962	285.80	249.10	0.05	27.01	116.6700	116.6700				
1963	312.80	234.20	0.25	27.09	116.6700	116.6700				
1964	291.60	250.40	0.24	24.74	116.6700	116.6700				
1965	381.80	249.40	0.10	22.86	116.6700	116.6700				
1966	301.50	209.20		20.47	116.6700	116.6700				
1967	261.50	224.20	0.02	20.97	118.4000	124.0700				
1968	313.90	313.00	0.10	25.79	98.0000	98.0000				
1969	354.40	307.60		25.67	98.0000	98.0000				
1970	419.10	467.40		25.70	98.0000	98.0000				
1971	443.10	357.50	0.65	28.50	98.0000	98.0000				
1972	393.30	564.40	0.46	50.40	74.4442	75.9734				
1973	526.00	730.40	0.30	35.50	86.2113	86.2881				
1974	943.70	840.90			86.9569	86.9569				
1975	909.30	928.30			86.9572	86.9571				
1976	991.70	932.60			86.9569	86.9569				
1977	1315.20	1166.10			86.9568	86.9569				
1978	1682.00	1580.00			60.0485	68.1463				
1979	2344.20	2737.10			36.3640	36.3640				
1980	3103.60	3157.80			36.3640	36.3640				
1981	3041.00	2924.00			36.3640	36.3640				
1982	1939.00	2402.00			36.3640	36.3640				
1983	11021.80	10225.10			4.9200	4.9200				
1984	20871.00	20161.00			2.7772	2.7863				
1985	39826.00	33185.00			1.8367	1.8599				
1986	93358.00	78180.00			1.1200	1.1200				
1987	174780.00	143304.00			0.6673	0.6678				
1988	185605.00	205705.00			0.4871	0.4901				
1989	346982.90	275290.10			0.3680	0.3706				
1991	388132.10				0.2714					
1992	950553.00	547237.80			0.2288	0.2288				
1994	2029173.00				0.1043					

2. IMPORTS BY BROAD ECONOMIC CATEGORY AND EXPORTS BY INDUSTRIAL ORIGIN. (PERCENTAGE OF TOTAL VALUE)
IMPORTATIONS PAR CATEGORIES ECONOMIQUES ET EXPORTATIONS PAR BRANCHE D'ACTIVITE.(EN POURCENTAGE DE LA VALEUR TOTALE)

IMPORTS – IMPORTATIONS

	1990	1991	1992	1993	1994	1995	1996
TOTAL IMPORTS–IMPORTATIONS TOTALES		100.	100.				
1 FOOD BEV–ALIMENTATION BOISSONS		4.6	10.6				
11 PRIMARY–PRODUITS DE BASE		2.2	3.6				
111 FOR INDUSTRY–POUR L'INDUSTRIE		1.4	1.3				
112 FOR HOUSEHOLDS–POUR LES MENAGES		0.8	2.3				
12 PROCESSED–PRODUITS ELABORES		2.4	7.0				
121 FOR INDUSTRY–POUR L'INDUSTRIE		0.7	1.1				
122 FOR HOUSEHOLDS–POUR LES MENAGES		1.7	5.9				
2 IND SUPPLIES–APPROV INDUSTRIELS		18.7	29.0				
21 PRIMARY–PRODUITS DE BASE		1.2	1.6				
22 PROCESSED–PRODUITS ELABORES		17.5	27.4				
3 FUELS–COMBUSTIBLES		8.3	16.3				
31 PRIMARY–PRODUITS DE BASE		7.9	13.9				
32 PROCESSED–PRODUITS ELABORES		0.3	2.3				
321 MOTOR SPIRIT–ESSENCE		0.3	2.3				
322 OTHER–AUTRES		0.0	0.0				
4 MACHINERY–EQUIPEMENT		54.8	18.7				
41 CAPITAL EQUIPMENT–MACHINES		53.6	17.0				
42 PARTS–PIECES ACCESSOIRES		1.2	1.7				
5 TRANSPORT–TRANSPORT		8.5	14.6				
51 PASSENGER CARS–AUTOMOBILES		1.3	3.8				
52 OTHER–AUTRES		4.7	7.0				
521 INDUSTRIAL–INDUSTRIELS		4.3	6.5				
522 NON INDUSTRIAL–NON INDUSTRIEL		0.4	0.5				
53 PARTS–PIECES ACCESSOIRES		2.6	3.8				
6 CONSUM GOODS–BIENS CONSOMMATION		4.1	8.7				
61 DURABLE–DURABLES		0.8	1.9				
62 SEMI DURABLE–SEMI DURABLES		1.7	4.1				
63 NON DURABLE–NON DURABLES		1.6	2.7				
7 GOODS NES–BIENS NDA		1.0	2.2				

EXPORTS – EXPORTATIONS

	1990	1991	1992	1993	1994	1995	1996
TOTAL EXPORTS–EXPORTATIONS TOTALES		100.	100.				
1 AGRICULTURE		68.2	51.1				
2 MINING QUARRY–INDUS EXTRACTIVES		4.4	10.7				
3 MANUFACTURING–IND MANUFACTUR		27.4	38.2				
31 FOOD BEV TOBACCO–ALIM BOISS TAB		1.9	4.7				
32 TEXTILES–INDUSTRIES TEXTILES		0.2	0.2				
33 WOOD & PRODUCTS–BOIS & PRODUITS		6.3	12.8				
34 PAPER & PRODUCTS–PAPIER & PRODT		0.0	0.0				
35 CHEMICALS–INDUSTRIES CHIMIQUES		1.5	3.6				
36 NON METAL MIN–MIN NON METAL		0.0	0.0				
37 BASIC METAL–IND METAL BASE		14.5	7.2				
38 METAL MANUF–MANUF METAL		0.9	3.4				
39 OTH MANUF IND–AUTRES MANUF		2.1	6.1				

3. TRADE BY PRINCIPAL COUNTRIES OF PRODUCTION AND LAST CONSIGNMENT (VALUE IN THOUSAND U.S. DOLLARS)
ECHANGES SELON LES PRINCIPAUX PAYS DE PRODUCTION ET DE DERNIERE CONSIGNATION (VALEUR EN MILLIERS DE DOLLARS EU)

COUNTRIES–PAYS	GENERAL IMPORTS C.I.F. IMPORTATIONS GENERALES C.A.F				
	1988	1989	1990	1991	1992
World					2145400
Africa					405432
Americas					315707
Northern America					239891
LAIA					28294
CACM					54
Caribbean					47190
Rest of America					279
As.ex F.USSR					384510
Eur.x F.USSR					999246
EU					931503
EFTA					46449
East Europe					19947
Other Europe					261
Former USSR					10159
Oceania					22566
United Kingdom					368479
Nigeria/Nigéria					304889
USA/Etats–Unis d'Amer					218514
Germany/Allemagne					191571
Japan/Japon					142349
Italy/Italie					125520
Netherlands/Pays–Bas					69238
France,Monac					66767
China/Chine					56448
Tunisia/Tunisie					47235
Jamaica/Jamaïque					42307
Belgium–Luxembourg					41893
Switz.Liecht					32077
Korea, Republic of					27531
Cote d'Ivoire					23031
Australia/Australie					22008
Brazil/Brésil					21446
Canada					21377
Thailand/Thaïlande					20314
Sweden/Suède					19499
India/Inde					18593
Hong Kong					17515
Pakistan					16861
Denmark/Danemark					16089
Viet Nam					15209
Singapore/Singapour					14234
Norway,SVD,JM					14150
Syrian Arab Republic					13072
Spain/Espagne					10843
Russian Federation					10155
Indonesia/Indonésie					9817
Romania/Roumanie					9753
Zimbabwe					8143
Greece/Grèce					7848
Cameroon/Cameroun					7620
Malaysia/Malaisie					6508
Togo					6082
Austria/Autriche					5134
Poland/Pologne					5050
Saudi Arabia					4745
Cuba					4573
Israel/Israël					4163
Ireland/Irlande					4108
Venezuela					3433
Czechoslovakia					3339
Finland/Finlande					3106
Korea Dem People's Rp					2767
Turkey/Turquie					2221
Argentina/Argentine					2168
Bangladesh					1697

COUNTRIES–PAYS	GENERAL EXPORTS F.O.B. EXPORTATIONS GENERALES F.O.B.				
	1988	1989	1990	1991	1992
Monde					1234427
Afrique					207412
Amériques					41540
Amérique du Nord					36520
ALAI					1064
MCAC					4
Caraïbes					3874
Autre Amérique					78
Asie l'URSS exclus					32629
Europe l'URSS exclus					909393
UE					374631
AELE					522918
Europe de l'Est					8461
Autre de l'Europe					29
Ancienne URSS					3926
Océanie					162
Switz.Liecht					513417
United Kingdom					119393
Togo					90028
Germany/Allemagne					80492
Cote d'Ivoire					67453
Netherlands/Pays–Bas					59390
Nigeria/Nigéria					42053
USA/Etats–Unis d'Amer					32302
Belgium–Luxembourg					27315
Ireland/Irlande					24060
Japan/Japon					22387
France,Monac					20406
Italy/Italie					17638
Spain/Espagne					17476
Norway,SVD,JM					9501
Romania/Roumanie					5155
Angola					4855
Saudi Arabia					4502
Canada					4218
Russian Federation					3925
Cuba					3849
Finland/Finlande					3499
Yugoslavia/Yougoslavie					3354
Poland/Pologne					3243
Denmark/Danemark					2563
Greece/Grèce					1269
Morocco/Maroc					1131
Hong Kong					1091
India/Inde					1054
Chile/Chili					965
Portugal					918
Singapore/Singapour					824
Israel/Israël					736
Lebanon/Liban					676
Philippines					489
Ethiopia/Ethiopie					488
Zimbabwe					306
Egypt/Egypte					274
Turkey/Turquie					260
Sweden/Suède					192
Korea, Republic of					184
Tunisia/Tunisie					182
Gabon					132
Libyan Arab Jamahiriya					101
Brazil/Brésil					93
United Arab Emirates					84
Kenya					72
Benin/Bénin					58
Australia/Australie					55
Burkina Faso					55

(VALUE AS PERCENTAGE OF WORLD TOTAL)(VALEURS EN POURCENTAGE DU TOTAL MONDIAL)

	1983	1984	1985	1986	1987	1988	1989	1990	1991	1992
Africa	7.0	5.8	18.2	18.6	8.8					18.9
Americas	34.3	26.4	12.9	14.5	15.3					14.7
Northern America	24.1	14.5	9.4	13.6	14.3					11.2
LAIA	4.1	4.4	1.5	0.1	1.0					1.3
CACM										0.0
Caribbean	0.0		1.9	0.8	0.0					2.2
Rest of America	6.1	7.5								0.0
As.ex F.USSR	7.8	11.6	10.1	9.3	9.6					17.9
Eur.x F.USSR	47.8	55.8	53.4	53.2	63.2					46.6
EU	44.0	50.3	50.9	50.0	61.0					43.4
EFTA	2.8	2.9	1.9	2.6	1.7					2.2
East Europe	0.5	0.8	0.2	0.3	0.3					0.9
Other Europe	0.4	1.9	0.3	0.4	0.3					0.0
Former USSR	3.1	0.3	0.0	0.1	0.0					0.5
Oceania	0.0	0.0		0.0	0.1					1.1
United Kingdom	21.5	23.5	26.7	20.8	34.6					17.2
Nigeria/Nigéria			14.3	7.1	6.7					14.2
USA/Etats–Unis d'Amer	20.9	9.9	7.6	11.2	12.5					10.2
Germany/Allemagne	8.2	9.8	11.9	13.0	11.6					8.9
Japan/Japon	3.0	6.5	6.9	4.5	5.5					6.6
Italy/Italie	5.0	5.5	3.9	3.6	3.3					5.9
Netherlands/Pays–Bas	3.0	3.9	3.1	4.1	3.3					3.2
France,Monac	1.9	1.9	2.5	4.2	4.1					3.1
China/Chine			0.6	0.5	0.5					2.6
Tunisia/Tunisie		0.0	0.0	0.0	0.1					2.2

	1983	1984	1985	1986	1987	1988	1989	1990	1991	1992
Afrique	2.6	2.1	3.6	2.6	1.8					16.8
Amériques	25.3	12.3	12.7	21.5	21.8					3.4
Amérique du Nord	25.2	12.3	12.7	21.2	21.6					3.0
ALAI	0.0	0.0	0.0	0.0	0.0					0.1
MCAC										0.0
Caraïbes	0.0	0.0	0.0	0.3	0.2					0.3
Autre Amérique				0.0						0.0
Asie l'URSS exclus	19.4	21.8	15.8	13.4	11.4					2.6
Europe l'URSS exclus	50.7	61.0	49.3	52.1	47.9					73.7
UE	44.7	52.6	45.1	40.3	44.4					30.3
AELE	5.5	6.1	2.4	9.9	1.7					42.4
Europe de l'Est			0.7	0.2	0.3					0.7
Autre de l'Europe	0.5	2.3	0.6	1.5	1.5					0.0
Ancienne URSS	0.9	0.4	3.5	4.6	3.3					0.3
Océanie	1.2	2.4	1.0	0.5	0.1					0.0
Switz.Liecht	3.1	2.4	1.1	9.1	1.0					41.6
United Kingdom	16.7	19.4	22.1	16.8	20.0					9.7
Togo	0.6		2.3	1.5	1.1					7.3
Germany/Allemagne	11.9	11.0	7.9	9.8	10.4					6.5
Cote d'Ivoire	0.1	0.1	0.8	0.6	0.5					5.5
Netherlands/Pays–Bas	3.7	4.2	8.4	6.3	5.7					4.8
Nigeria/Nigéria			0.0	0.1	0.1					3.4
USA/Etats–Unis d'Amer	24.7	12.1	12.7	21.2	21.2					2.6
Belgium–Luxembourg			0.2	2.2	0.9					2.2
Ireland/Irlande	1.2	1.3	0.8	1.0	1.5					1.9

4. General Imports C.I.F. by Commodities according to the S.I.T.C. (Rev. 2) in thousand U.S. Dollars
Importations Générales C.A.F. par Produits d'après la C.T.C.I. (Rév. 2) en milliers de Dollars E.U.

SITC CTCI	COMMODITY	1989 WEIGHT POIDS	1989 VALUE VALEUR	1990 WEIGHT POIDS	1990 VALUE VALEUR	1991 WEIGHT POIDS	1991 VALUE VALEUR	1992 WEIGHT POIDS	1992 VALUE VALEUR	PRODUIT
	ALL COMMODITIES						511475		2145400	TOUS PRODUITS
0	FOOD AND LIVE ANIMALS						22826		222692	ALIMENTS,ANIMAUX VIVANTS
01	MEAT AND PREPARATIONS						2080		22165	VIANDES ET PREPARATIONS
011	MEAT FRESH,CHILLD,FROZEN					W 4069	1774	W 105686	18429	VIANDES FRAICHES,REF,CONGE
0111	BOVINE MEAT FRESH,FROZEN					W 2677	1005	W 95939	13576	VIANDES BOVIN FRAI,REF
01112	BOVINE MEAT BONELESS					W 2677	999	W 95743	13442	VIANDES BOVIN DESOSSEES
02	DAIRY PRODCTS,BIRDS'EGGS						1538		14648	PRODUITS LAITIERS,OEUFS
022	MILK AND CREAM					W 859	1307	W 9215	12827	LAIT ET CREME
0224	MILK,CREAM PRESERVED ETC					W 857	1304	W 8412	12397	LAIT,CREME CONS,CONC
02242	MILK DRY,1.5% FAT OR LES					W 732	1131	W 4818	8586	LAIT POUDRE INF 1.5%
03	FISH AND PREPARATIONS						3873		33287	POISSONS ET PREPARATIONS
034	FISH,FRESH,CHILLED,FROZN					W 2207	2382	W 25773	29272	POISSON FRAIS, REFRIG,CONG
0342	FISH FROZEN,EXCL FILLETS					W 695	1558	W 17256	23722	POISSONS CONGELES
04	CEREALS AND PREPARATIONS						12513		114240	CEREALES ET PRODUITS
041	WHEAT ETC UNMILLED					W 23471	5110	W 26224	24300	FROMENT,EPEAUTRE
0412	OTHER WHEAT ETC UNMILLED					W 23471	5110	W 26224	24300	AUTRE FROMENT NON MOULU
042	RICE					W 4435	3364	W 271841	73352	RIZ
0422	RICE SEMI-MILLED,MILLED					W 4399	3355	W 271224	72452	RIZ POLI,GLACE INCL BRISURES
04221	RICE MILLED UNBROKEN					W 2687	2813	W 223357	64401	RIZ POLI,GLACE EXCL BRISURES
04222	RICE BROKEN					W 1711	543	W 47867	8051	BRISURES DE RIZ
045	CEREALS NES UNMILLED					W 12137	2024	W 4069	1269	AUTRES CEREALES NON MOULUES
0459	OTHER CEREALS UNMILLED					W 12137	2024	W 4064	1265	SARRASIN,MILLET,SORGHO
04599	OTH CEREALS UNMILLED NES					W 11819	1927	W 3	1	AUTRES CEREALES NDA
048	CEREAL ETC PREPARATIONS					W 6695	1330	W 30350	8929	PREPTNS A BASE CEREALES
06	SUGAR AND PREPS,HONEY						2146		26013	SUCRES ET PRODUITS
061	SUGAR AND HONEY					W 11928	2125	W 60266	25460	SUCRES ET MIEL
0611	RAW BEET AND CANE SUGAR					W 2990	1094	W 15516	8957	SUCRES BRUTS
0612	REFINED SUGAR ETC					W 8437	866	W 44259	16300	SUCRES RAFFINES
1	BEVERAGES AND TOBACCO						1238		9516	BOISSONS ET TABACS
2	CRUDE MATERLS,EXCL FUELS						34658		94826	MAT BRUTES NON COMESTIBLES
26	TEXTILE FIBRES AND WASTE						4072		20572	FIBRES TEXTILES
263	COTTON					W 1461	2191	W 1836	2689	COTON
2631	RAW COTTON,EXCL LINTERS					W 1456	2187	W 1747	2549	COTON EN MASSE
269	WASTE OF TEXTILE FABRICS					W 2463	1578	W 21699	16635	FRIPERIE DRILLES,CHIFFONS
26901	BULK TEXT WSTE,OLD CLTHG					W 2462	1567	W 21619	16622	ART ET ACCESS D'HABILLEMENT
27	CRUDE FERTLZR,MINRLS NES						1610		3538	ENGRAIS MINERAUX BRUTS
28	METALLIFEROUS ORES,SCRAP						28299		66961	MINERAIS METAL,DECHETS
287	BASE METAL ORES,CONC NES					W 108696	28299	W 287431	66744	MINERAIS METAUX COMMUNS
2873	ALUMINIUM ORES,ALUMINA					W 108696	28298	W 287422	66698	MINERAIS D'ALUMINIUM
28732	ALUMINA(ALUMINIUM OXIDE)					W 108696	28298	W 287381	66595	ALUMINE (OXYDE ALUMINIUM)
3	MINERAL FUELS ETC						45299		374344	COMBUSTIBLES MINERAUX LUB
33	PETROLEUM AND PRODUCTS						45297		374083	PETROLE ET DERIVES
333	CRUDE PETROLEUM					W 265855	40544	W 1966563	298726	HUILES BRUTES DE PETROLE
334	PETROLEUM PRODUCTS,REFIN					W 1177	1654	W 223360	49760	PRODUITS RAFFINES
3341	GASOLINE,OTH LIGHT OILS					W 1147	1642	W 223207	49333	ESSENCES POUR MOTEURS
33419	OTH LIGHT PETROLEUM OILS					W 1147	1642	W 223207	49333	AUTRES HUILES LEGERES
335	RESIDUAL PETRLM PROD NES					W 14301	3099	W 62118	25597	PRODUITS RESIDUELS NDA
3354	PETROLM BITUMEN,COKE ETC					W 8000	1798	W 40339	19624	BITUME,COKE DE PETROLE
33541	PETROLEUM BITUMEN, ETC							W 10236	11818	BITUME DE PETROLE
33542	PETROLEUM COKE					W 8000	1798	W 30006	7648	COKE DE PETROLE
4	ANIMAL,VEGETABLE OIL,FAT						441		7701	HUILES,GRAISSES ANIM,VEG
42	FIXED VEGETABLE OIL,FAT						437		7516	HUILES VEGETALES FIXES
5	CHEMCLS,RELATED PROD NES						22323		238782	PRODUITS CHIMIQUES
51	ORGANIC CHEMICALS						1462		13578	PROD CHIMIQ ORGANIQUES
52	INORGANIC CHEMICALS						3115		19954	PROD CHIM INORGANIQUES
523	OTHR INORG CHEMICALS ETC					W 2710	2006	W 22618	13675	AUT PRODUITS CHIMIQUES INORG
5231	METAL CMPD OF INORG ACID					W 1369	788	W 13320	7062	SELS METALLIQUES
53	DYES,TANNING,COLOUR PROD						1762		20854	PROD TEINTURE,COLORANTS
533	PIGMENTS,PAINTS,ETC					W 653	950	W 10079	14605	PIGMENTS,PEINTURES,VERNIS
5334	VARNISHES,DISTEMPERS ETC					W 442	587	W 9005	11692	PEINTURES A L'EAU
53342	OTH PAINTS,VARNISHES ETC					W 318	416	W 6595	7782	AUTRES PEINTURES,VERNIS
541	*MEDICINAL,PHARM PRODUCT					K 422896	4820	K 7319604	45846	PROD MEDICINAUX PHARMACEUT
5417	MEDICAMENTS					K 275974	3285	K 3475829	21664	MEDICAMENTS
54179	— CONTNG OTH SUBSTANCES					K 201550	2076	K 2402266	14786	MED CONT AUT SUBSTANCES
5419	PHARMACEUTICAL GOODS NES					K 93931	1041	K 3744116	22111	PREP,ART PHARMACEUTIQUES
54199	OTH PHARMACEUTICAL GOODS					K 68693	880	K 3394239	21037	AUT PREP PHARMACEUTIQUES
55	PERFUME,CLEANING ETC PRD						2060		12872	PROD POUR PARFUM,TOILETTE
562	*FERTILIZERS,MANUFACTURE					W 518	276	W 20914	7961	ENGRAIS MANUFACTURES
572	*EXPLOSIVES,PYROTECH PRO					W 444	1798	W 2824	5096	EXPLOSIFS
5721	PREPARED EXPLOSIVES					W 441	1777	W 2564	3721	POUDRES,EXPLOSIFS
57212	PREPARED EXPLOSIVES NES					W 422	1734	W 2546	3679	EXPLOSIFS PREPARES
58	PLASTIC MATERIALS ETC						3274		15797	MAT PLAST ARTIFICIELLES
583	POLYMERIZATION ETC PRODS					W 1478	2534	W 10411	12226	PROD POLYMERISATION
5831	POLYETHYLENE					W 867	1330	W 6841	6559	POLYETHYLENE
58311	— IN PRIMARY FORMS					W 720	961	W 6820	6513	POLYETHYLENE PRIMAIRES
59	CHEMICAL MATERIALS NES						3755		96825	MAT PROD CHIMIQUES NDA
591	PESTICIDES,DISINFECTANTS					W 193	634	W 2589	15910	DESINF,INSECT,FONG,HERB
5911	INSECTICIDES,FOR RETAIL					W 174	509	W 1573	7809	INSECTICIDES VENTE DET
598	MISCEL CHEM PRODUCTS NES					W 534	2465	W 26656	79164	PROD DIV INDUST CHIM NDA
5989	CHEM PRODUCTS,PREPS NES					W 391	2162	W 24286	73962	PROD PREP CHIMIQUES NDA
59899	OTH CHEM PRODS,PREPS,NES					W 255	1961	W 22295	70747	AUT PRODUITS CHIMIQUES NDA
6	BASIC MANUFACTURES						45756		297705	ART MANUFACTURES
62	RUBBER MANUFACTURES NES						3699		28368	CAOUTCHOUC MANUFACTURE
625	RUBBER TYRES, TUBES ETC					W 1510	2462	W 26128	24922	PNEUS CAOUTCHOUC VULCANISE
6252	TYRES,NEW,BUS OR LORRY					W 517	1318	W 5042	14606	PNEUS POUR AUTOBUS,CAMIONS
6259	OTH TYRES,TYRE CASES,ETC					W 832	927	W 13400	6972	AUTRES PNEUS RECHAPES FLAPS
64	PAPER,PAPERBOARD AND MFR						5882		30228	PAPIERS,CARTONS & OUVRAGES
641	PAPER AND PAPERBOARD					W 5684	5460	W 36892	24518	PAPIERS ET CARTONS
6413	KRAFT PAPER,PAPERBOARD					W 2952	2693	W 9928	8037	PAPIER ET CARTON KRAFT
64131	KRAFT LINER IN BULK					W 2578	2445	W 4389	3475	PAP KRAFT POUR COUVERTURES
6415	PAPER,PAPERBRD,BULK,NES					W 464	640	W 15444	8024	PAPIERS,CARTONS ROULEAUX
64159	OTHER PAPER ETC,BULK,NES					W 360	389	W 14132	7370	AUT PAPIER ROULEAUX FEUILLES
65	TEXTILE YARN,FABRICS,ETC						5293		33829	FILS,TISSUS,ARTICLES TEXTILE
652	COTTON FABRICS,WOVEN					W 165	917	W 4357	9061	TISSUS DE COTON
6522	WOVEN COTTON BLEACHD,ETC					W 160	864	W 4093	7894	TISSUS COTON BLANCHIS ETC
653	WOVN MAN-MADE FIB FABRIC					W 165	652	W 2811	7408	TISSUS FIBRES SYNTH,ARTIF
657	SPECIAL TXTL FABRC,PRODS					W 852	1382	W 2364	7537	TISSUS SPECIAUX
658	TEXTILE ARTICLES NES					W 3307	1906	W 6932	5107	ART FACONNES MAT TEXTILES
6581	BAGS,SACKS OF TEXTILES					W 3258	1658	W 5920	3002	SACS EMBALLAGE TEXTILES
66	NONMETAL MINERAL MFS NES						10605		91169	ART MIN NON METALLIQUES
661	LIME,CEMENT,BLDG PRODS					W 131096	7419	W 535066	86767	CHAUX,CIMENTS MAT CONSTR

4. General Imports C.I.F. by Commodities according to the S.I.T.C. (Rev. 2) in thousand U.S. Dollars
Importations Générales C.A.F. par Produits d'après la C.T.C.I. (Rév. 2) en milliers de Dollars E.U.

SITC CTCI	COMMODITY	1989		1990		1991		1992		PRODUIT
		WEIGHT POIDS	VALUE VALEUR	WEIGHT POIDS	VALUE VALEUR	WEIGHT POIDS	VALUE VALEUR	WEIGHT POIDS	VALUE VALEUR	
6612	CEMENT					W 127426	6654	W 513012	77329	CIMENTS HYDRAULIQUES
665	GLASSWARE					W 1191	1545	W 225	114	OUVRAGES EN VERRE
67	IRON AND STEEL						7467		45929	FER ET ACIER
673	IRON,STEEL SHAPES ETC					W 1895	1879	W 14640	10181	BARRES,PROFIL FER,ACIER
674	IRN,STL UNIV,PLATE,SHEET					W 1221	1476	W 21635	13408	LARGES PLATS,TOLES
678	IRON,STL TUBES,PIPES,ETC					W 385	768	W 6928	17308	TUBES,TUYAUX EN FONTE,FER
6783	IRON,STL TUBES,PIPES NES					W 137	258	W 4512	9971	AUT TUBES,TUYAUX FER,ACIER
679	IRN,STL CASTINGS UNWORKD					W 2517	2220	W 3142	3020	OUVRAGES EN FONTE,FER,ACIER
6793	IRON,STL FORGINGS ROUGH					W 2297	2030	W 2987	2666	OUVRAGES FORGES,ESTAMPES
69	METAL MANUFACTURES NES						10690		59303	ART MANUFACT EN METAL NDA
691	STRUCTURES AND PARTS NES					W 671	2890	W 5312	15352	CONSTRUCT FER,ACIER,ALU
6911	STRUCTURES,PARTS IRN,STL					W 634	2513	W 4757	12791	CONSTRUCT FER,ACIER,FONTE
692	METAL TANKS,BOXES,ETC					W 150	602	W 1848	8679	RECIPIENTS METALLIQUES
6924	MTL TRANSPORT BOXES ETC					W 102	347	W 1571	7514	FUTS,TAMBOURS,BIDONS
693	WIRE PRODUCTS NON ELECTR					W 668	1889	W 1499	3347	OUVRAGES FILS METALLIQUES
6931	WIRE CABLES, ROPES ETC					W 386	1739	W 1030	2538	CORDAGES EN FILS DE FER
695	TOOLS					W 1168	2179	W 6444	11100	OUTILS A MAIN
699	BASE METAL MFRS NES					W 507	1365	W 5155	10598	ART MANUFACTURES MET NDA
7	MACHINES,TRANSPORT EQUIP						321815		721832	MACHINES MATERIEL TRANSPORT
71	POWER GENERATING EQUIPMT						3345		26744	MACHINES GENERATRICES
713	INTRNL COMBUS PSTN ENGIN					W 1571	1675	W 10331	10253	MOTEURS EXPL COMB INT, PIECE
716	ROTATING ELECTRIC PLANT					W 142	1177	W 821	7380	APP ELECTR ROTATIFS,PIECES
72	MACHS FOR SPCL INDUSTRYS						242940		85218	MAC SPECIALES POUR INDUST
723	CIVIL ENGNEERG EQUIP ETC					W 1302	6218	W 4318	26502	APPAREILS DE GENIE CIVIL
7234	CONST,MINING MACHNRY NES					W 1234	4975	W 3460	18342	MACH POUR LA CONST, MINES
72341	SELF-PROPELLD DOZERS,ETC					W 465	1790	W 1773	9125	BULLDOZERS
72342	SLFPRP SHOVELS,EXCAVATRS					W 733	2832	W 1015	4694	PELLES MECANIQUES
724	TEXTILE,LEATHER MACHNRY					W 154	633	W 2900	10388	MACH POUR INDUSTRIE TEXTILE
727	FOOD MACHRY NON-DOMESTIC					W 549	1544	W 1686	6367	MACH INDUSTRIES ALIMENT
728	OTH MACHY FOR SPCL INDUS					W 100318	233739	W 3555	31644	AUT MACH IND PARTICULIERES
7281	MACH-TOOLS FR SPCL INDUS					W 110	1325	W 750	7291	MACH-OUTILS SPEC IND PART
7283	OTHR MINERAL WORKG MACHY					W 100163	231338	W 1537	10636	MACH TRIER,CRIBLER,BROYER
72839	PTS NES OF MACHY OF 7283					W 100116	230856	W 872	4741	PIECES MACH DU 728.3
7284	MACHY FOR SPCL INDUS NES					W 45	1077	W 1268	13717	MACH SPEC IND PARTICUL.
73	METALWORKING MACHINERY						1774		10188	MACH TRAVAIL DES METAUX
736	METALWORKING MACH-TOOLS					W 128	1660	W 739	7317	MACH-OUTILS TRAVAIL METAUX
74	GENRL INDUSTRL MACHY NES						15134		160689	MACH APP INDUSTRIE
741	HEATING,COOLING EQUIPMNT					W 346	2013	W 2146	14258	MACH CHAUFFAGE,PIECES
742	PUMPS FOR LIQUIDS ETC					W 101	2148	W 732	7770	POMPES MOTO-POMPES
743	PUMPS NES,CENTRFUGES ETC					W 218	1263	W 1834	7484	POMPES COMPRES,VENT ETC
744	MECHANICAL HANDLING EQU						6222	W 7356	103690	EQUIP MANUTENTION PIECES
7442	LIFTING,LOADING MACH NES						1240	W 1222	7667	APP LEVAGE,MANUTENTION
7449	PTS NES OF MACHY OF 7442					W 864	4362	W 5834	94707	PIECES DU 744.2
745	NONELEC MACHY,TOOLS NES					W 141	1342	W 807	11077	AUT MACH NON ELEC,PIECES
7452	OTH NONELEC MCHS,PTS NES					W 94	762	W 580	7751	AUT MACH NON ELEC,PIECES
749	NONELEC MACH PTS,ACC NES					W 361	2147	W 1313	16410	PIECES MACH NON ELEC NDA
7499	OTH NONELEC MCHY PTS NES					W 98	728	W 699	12049	PIECES NON ELECT NDA
74999	MACH PARTS NONELEC NES					W 82	666	W 533	7775	PIECES MACHINES NDA
75	OFFICE MACHNES,ADP EQUIP						3568		25819	MACH BUREAU TRAIT AUTOM
752	AUTOMTIC DATA PROC EQUIP					W 30	1634	W 268	14780	MACH TRAIT INFORMATION
7522	DIGITAL COMPUTERS					W 10	743	W 87	7389	MACH DIGITALES COMPLETES
759	OFFICE,ADP MCH PTS,ACCES					W 40	848	W 148	7135	PIECES DU 751 ET 752
76	TELECOMM,SOUND EQUIPMENT						2227		27723	EQUIPMENT DE TELECOM
761	TELEVISION RECEIVERS					W 109	479	W 3881	12177	RECEPTEURS DE TELEVISION
7611	COLOUR TV RECEIVERS					W 49	245	W 3118	8566	RECEPTEURS COULEUR
764	TELECOM EQPT,PTS,ACC NES					W 64	1355	W 1192	11939	EQUIP TELECOM,PIECES
77	ELECTRIC MACHNRY NES ETC						12270		107999	MACH APP ELECT NDA
771	ELECTRIC POWER MACHY NES					W 164	982	W 917	9291	MACH PROD,TRANS ELECTR
772	SWITCHGEAR ETC,PARTS NES					W 439	3930	W 3261	22229	APP COUPURE,SECT ETC
7721	SWITCHGEAR ETC					W 438	3889	W 3254	21922	APP COUPURE,SECTIONMNT
773	ELECTR DISTRIBUTNG EQUIP					W 285	1489	W 7536	31434	EQUIPMT DISTRIBUTION ELECT
7731	INSULATED WIRE,CABLE ETC					W 270	1453	W 6613	27179	FILS,CABLES ISOLES ELECT
774	ELECTRO-MEDCL,XRAY EQUIP					W 32	547	W 274	8119	APPAREILS MEDICAUX
7741	ELECTRO-MEDICAL EQUIPMNT					W 30	533	W 222	7358	APP ELECTRICITE MEDICALE
775	HOUSEHOLD TYPE EQUIP NES					W 989	1838	W 9750	13965	MACH,APP USAGE DOMESTQUE
7752	DOM REFRIGERATRS,FREEZRS					W 559	1252	W 7137	10213	REFRIG,CONGEL MENAGER
77521	DOMESTIC REFRIGERATORS					W 389	818	W 6005	7435	REFRIGERATEURS
778	ELECTRICAL MACHINERY NES					W 2034	3482	W 11959	22615	AUTRES MACH ELECT NDA
7781	BATTERIES,ACCUMULATORS					W 1230	2430	W 9349	11919	PILES ET ACCUMULATEURS
77811	PRIMARY BATTERIES,CELLS					W 915	866	W 7145	7740	PILES ELECTRIQUES,PIECES
77812	ELECTRIC ACCUMULATORS					W 315	1553	W 2147	4014	ACCUMULATEURS ELECTRIQ
78	ROAD VEHICLES						27906		259343	VEHICULES ROUTIERS
781	PASS MOTOR VEH EXC BUSES					W 1565	6486	W 17317	81804	AUTO TRANSPORT PERSONNES
782	LORRIES,SPCL MTR VEH NES					W 2479	11270	W 19940	101628	VEHICULES SPECIAUX,MARCH
7821	LORRIES,TRUCKS					W 2210	9534	W 19402	95794	VEHICULES TRANSP MARCHAND
7822	SPECIAL MOTOR VEHCLS NES					W 269	1736	W 538	5834	VEHICULES USAGES SPECIAUX
783	ROAD MOTOR VEHICLES NES					W 610	3926	W 7118	26819	VEHICULES ROUTIERS NDA
7831	BUSES					W 544	3537	W 6583	23190	VOITURES TRANSPORT COMMUN
784	MOTOR VEH PRTS,ACCES NES					W 2992	3989	W 14555	35926	PIECES 722,781,782,783
7849	OTHER MOTOR VEHCL PARTS					W 2926	3660	W 14273	35190	PIECES 722,781,782,783
785	CYCLES,ETC MOTRZD OR NOT					W 730	1871	W 3940	10654	MOTOCYCLES SCOOTERS
7852	CYCLES, ETC NON-MOTOR					W 607	1274	W 2710	7026	VELOCIPEDES SANS MOTEUR
79	OTHR TRANSPORT EQUIPMENT						12650		18110	AUTRE MATERIEL TRANSPORT
791	RAILWAY VEHICLES						11725	W 159	4369	VEHIC MAT CHEMINS DE FER
7914	RY COACHES NES NOT POWRD						5778			VOITURES A VOYAGEURS
7919	RY TRACK FIXT,ETC,PARTS					W 767	5269	W 159	4365	MATER FIXE VOIES FERREES
79191	RY TRACK FIXTURES ETC					W 92	2903	W 46	3460	APP DE SIGNALISATION
79199	PARTS NES OF 7911-7915					W 674	2366	W 113	905	PIECES 791.1 ET 5
792	AIRCRAFT ETC					W 6	861	W 34	10601	APP NAVIGATION AERIENNE
7923	AIRCRFT NES2000-15000KG							W 5	7377	AERODYNES 2000 A 15000 KG
8	MISC MANUFACTURED GOODS						17012		173392	ART MANUFACTURES DIVERS
812	*PLUMBG,HEATNG,LGHTNG EQ					W 269	406	W 1312	6522	APPAR SANITAIRES CHAUFFAGE
84	CLOTHING AND ACCESSORIES						1629		10915	VETEMENTS
851	*FOOTWEAR					W 589	2739	W 2337	8848	CHAUSSURES
87	PRECISION INSTRUMNTS NES						1869		23687	INSTRUM,APPAR SCIENT NDA
872	MEDICAL INSTRUMENTS NES					W 39	527	W 535	8425	INSTR,APP MEDIC-CHIR NDA
87202	OTH MEDICAL INSTRUMENTS					W 38	512	W 501	8117	INSTRUM,APP MEDECINE
874	MEASURNG,CONTROLNG INSTR						1175	W 680	12534	INSTRUMENTS DE MESURE
89	MISC MANUFCTRD GOODS NES						8778		112233	ART MANUFACTURES DIVERS
892	PRINTED MATTER					W 165	6559	W 2486	53346	IMPRIMES
8921	PRINTED BOOKS,GLOBES,ETC					W 116	1238	W 1283	8199	LIVRES,BROCHURES,CARTES

4. General Imports C.I.F. by Commodities according to the S.I.T.C. (Rev. 2) in thousand U.S. Dollars
Importations Générales C.A.F. par Produits d'après la C.T.C.I. (Rév. 2) en milliers de Dollars E.U.

SITC CTCI	COMMODITY	1989 WEIGHT POIDS	1989 VALUE VALEUR	1990 WEIGHT POIDS	1990 VALUE VALEUR	1991 WEIGHT POIDS	1991 VALUE VALEUR	1992 WEIGHT POIDS	1992 VALUE VALEUR	PRODUIT
89211	PRINTED BOOKS,PAMPHLETS					W 114	1229	W 1110	6671	LIVRES,BROCHURES
8928	PRINTED MATTER NES					W 37	5294	W 1091	44818	IMPRIMES NDA
89283	UNISSUED BANKNOTES ETC						5106	W 635	43299	TIMBRES-POSTE FISCAUX
893	ARTICLES OF PLASTIC NES						1175		19381	OUVRAGES EN MAT DIVIS 58
8939	MISC PLASTIC ARTICLES					W 927	955	W 12768	12502	ART DIVERS EN MAT DIV 58
89399	OTHR PLASTC ARTICLES NES					W 409	580	W 9504	9869	AUT OUV MAT DIV 58
894	TOYS,SPORTING GOODS,ETC					W 159	349	W 10413	32930	VOITURES ENFANTS,JOUETS
8942	TOYS,INDOOR GAMES ETC					W 11	88	W 9315	30291	JOUETS,JEUX ETC
89421	LARGE SIZE WHEELED TOYS							W 9080	29946	VOITURES AMUSEM ENFANTS

5. General Exports F.O.B. by Commodities according to the S.I.T.C. (Rev. 2) in thousand U.S. Dollars
Exportations Générales F.O.B. par Produits d'après la C.T.C.I. (Rév. 2) en milliers de Dollars E.U.

SITC CTCI	COMMODITY	1989 WEIGHT POIDS	1989 VALUE VALEUR	1990 WEIGHT POIDS	1990 VALUE VALEUR	1991 WEIGHT POIDS	1991 VALUE VALEUR	1992 WEIGHT POIDS	1992 VALUE VALEUR	PRODUIT
	ALL COMMODITIES						617368		1234427	TOUS PRODUITS
0	FOOD AND LIVE ANIMALS						191029		354740	ALIMENTS,ANIMAUX VIVANTS
03	FISH AND PREPARATIONS						2065		16767	POISSONS ET PREPARATIONS
034	FISH,FRESH,CHILLED,FROZN					W 927	1813	W 17566	13651	POISSON FRAIS, REFRIG,CONG
0342	FISH FROZEN,EXCL FILLETS					W 456	801	W 13792	8120	POISSONS CONGELES
0343	FISH FILLETS,FRESH,CHLLD					W 469	1011	W 3285	5122	FILETS FRAIS,REFRIGERES
05	VEGETABLES AND FRUIT						6705		24688	LEGUMES ET FRUITS
054	VEG ETC FRSH,SMPLY PRSVD					W 86	61	W 5188	15735	LEGUMES FRAIS,CONG,SECS
0545	OTHER FRESH VEGETABLES					W 13	13	W 1267	4701	AUTRES LEGUMES FRAIS,REF
05459	FRESH VEGETABLES NES					W 13	13	W 1263	4700	LEGUMES FRAIS,REFRI NDA
0548	EDIBLE VEG NES FRESH,DRY					W 63	35	W 3859	10980	RACINES,TUBERCULES
05481	ROOTS,TUBERS FRESH,DRY					W 63	35	W 3859	10980	RACINES DE MANIOC ETC
057	FRUIT,NUTS,FRESH,DRIED					W 5186	6551	W 17759	8891	FRUITS FRAIS OU SECS
0579	FRUIT FRESH OR DRIED NES					W 4843	6247	W 17457	8567	FRUITS FRAIS,SECS NDA
05795	PINEAPPLES,FRESH,DRIED					W 4756	6226	W 17210	8330	ANANAS FRAIS OU SECS
07	COFFEE,TEA,COCOA,SPICES						182099		311884	CAFE,THE,CACAO,EPICES
072	COCOA					W 88728	180096	W 213018	300564	CACAO
0721	COCOA BEANS,RAW,ROASTED					W 86879	173362	W 206841	283358	CACAO EN FEVES
0723	COCOA BUTTER AND PASTE					W 1850	6734	W 6125	17182	BEURRE ET PATE DE CACAO
07232	COCOA BUTTER					W 1850	6734	W 6125	17182	BEURRE DE CACAO
073	CHOCOLATE AND PRODUCTS					W 2480	1780	W 12768	9823	CHOCOLAT
2	CRUDE MATERLS,EXCL FUELS						189194		183785	MAT BRUTES NON COMESTIBLES
23	RUBBER, CRUDE						1754		4546	CAOUTCHOUC BRUT
232	NATURAL RUBBER,GUMS					W 2303	1754	W 6924	4545	LATEX CAOUTCHOUC NATUREL
23201	NATURAL RUBBER LATEX					W 2218	1699	W 6307	4151	LATEX NATUREL
24	CORK AND WOOD						164899		99539	LIEGE ET BOIS
247	OTH WOOD ROUGH,SQUARED						138273	W 149858	28534	BOIS BRUTS EQUARRIS
2472	SAW-,VENEER-LOGS NON-CON					W 403932	138266	W 147426	27899	NON CONIFERES SCIAGE,PLAC
24721	— IN THE ROUGH					W 403932	138266	W 147426	27899	BRUTS ECORCES DEGROSSIS
248	WOOD SHAPED,SLEEPERS					W 55317	26594	W 159870	70983	BOIS SIMPLEMENT TRAVAILLES
2483	LUMBER SHAPED NON-CONIFR					W 55295	26586	W 159870	70983	NON CONIFERES SCIES,RABOTES
24831	LUMBER SAWN ETC NON-CON					W 55288	26578	W 159870	70983	SCIES LONGITUDINALEMENT
27	CRUDE FERTLZR,MINRLS NES						6766		24275	ENGRAIS MINERAUX BRUTS
277	NATURAL ABRASIVES NES						6655		24272	ABRASIFS NATURELS NDA
2771	INDUSTRIAL DIAMONDS						6655		24271	DIAMANTS INDUSTRIELS
28	METALLIFEROUS ORES,SCRAP						14790		52630	MINERAIS METAL,DECHETS
287	BASE METAL ORES,CONC NES					W 121727	14401	W 656699	51084	MINERAIS METAUX COMMUNS
2873	ALUMINIUM ORES,ALUMINA					W 72284	6510	W 399525	17065	MINERAIS D'ALUMINIUM
28731	ALUMINIUM ORE,CONCNTRATE					W 72284	6510	W 399525	17065	MINERAIS D'ALUMINIUM
2877	MANGANESE ORE,CONCENTRTE					W 49437	7597	W 257128	33887	MINERAIS DE MANGANESE
3	MINERAL FUELS ETC						13978		66607	COMBUSTIBLES MINERAUX LUB
33	PETROLEUM AND PRODUCTS						4604		23210	PETROLE ET DERIVES
334	PETROLEUM PRODUCTS,REFIN					W 22919	4604	W 114724	23210	PRODUITS RAFFINES
3341	GASOLINE,OTH LIGHT OILS					W 22919	4604	W 114724	23210	ESSENCES POUR MOTEURS
33419	OTH LIGHT PETROLEUM OILS					W 22919	4604	W 114724	23210	AUTRES HUILES LEGERES
351	*ELECTRIC CURRENT						9357		42977	ENERGIE ELECTRIQUE
5	CHEMCLS,RELATED PROD NES						2538		2343	PRODUITS CHIMIQUES
52	INORGANIC CHEMICALS						2488		742	PROD CHIM INORGANIQUES
523	OTHR INORG CHEMICALS ETC						2012	W 191	150	AUT PRODUITS CHIMIQUES INORG
5233	METALLIC ACID SALTS ETC						2012			SELS ACIDES D'OXYDES METAL E
52332	PRECIOUS METAL CMPDS ETC						2012			METAUX PRECIEUX ETAT COLLOID
6	BASIC MANUFACTURES						76521		76370	ART MANUFACTURES
63	WOOD,CORK MANUFACTRS NES						3537		20067	OUVRAGES LIEGE ET BOIS
634	VENEERS,PLYWOOD,ETC					W 4449	3103	W 16760	17958	PLACAGES,CONTRE-PLAQUES
6341	VENEER SHEETS ETC					W 4347	2988	W 13800	14616	BOIS SIMPLEMENT SCIES
66	NONMETAL MINERAL MFS NES						1934		2009	ART MIN NON METALLIQUES
667	PEARL,PREC-,SEMI-P STONE						1932		1997	PERLES, PIERRES GEMMES
6671	PEARLS UNSET,UNSTRUNG						1932		1997	PERLES FINES NON SERTIES
67	IRON AND STEEL								6152	FER ET ACIER
678	IRON,STL TUBES,PIPES,ETC							W 1006	6126	TUBES,TUYAUX EN FONTE,FER
6783	IRON,STL TUBES,PIPES NES							W 984	5133	AUT TUBES,TUYAUX FER,ACIER
68	NON-FERROUS METALS						69230		45136	METAUX NON FERREUX
681	SILVER,PLATINUM,ETC						3475			ARGENT ET PLATINE
6812	METALS OF PLATINUM GROUP						3475			PLATINE
68122	ROLLED PLATINUM ETC						3475			PLAQUE PLATINE BRUT MI-OU
684	ALUMINIUM					W 71	65722	W 79	45050	ALUMINIUM
6841	ALUMINIUM,ALLOYS,UNWRGHT					W 71	65722	W 60	40789	ALUMINIUM,ALLIAGES BRUTS
6842	ALUMINIUM,ALLOYS WORKED							W 19	4261	ALUMINIUM,ALLIAGES OUVRE
68422	ALUMNM PLATE,SHEET,STRIP							W 19	4261	TOLES, PLANCHES EN ALU
7	MACHINES,TRANSPORT EQUIP						2411		14868	MACHINES MATERIEL TRANSPORT
78	ROAD VEHICLES						1423		10715	VEHICULES ROUTIERS
786	TRAILERS,NONMOTR VEH,NES					W 8989	1320	W 88838	9310	REMORQUES,CADRES,CONTAIN
7861	TRAILERS,TRANSP CONTAINR					W 8989	1320	W 88838	9310	REMORQUES TOUS VEHICULES
78613	CONTAINERS INC ROAD-RAIL					W 8989	1320	W 88838	9310	CADRES ET CONTAINERS
8	MISC MANUFACTURED GOODS						1395		6440	ART MANUFACTURES DIVERS
9	GOODS NOT CLASSD BY KIND						140209		525363	ART TRANSACT NON CLASSES
971	*GOLD,NON MONETARY NES					K 16254	140114		525199	OR NON MONETAIRE
97101	NONMON GLD UNWRT,SEMIMFD					K 16185	139804		525199	OR,ALLIAGES D'OR BRUTS

1. HISTORICAL SERIES, 1960–1995 SPECIAL TRADE, IMPORTS C.I.F., EXPORTS F.O.B.
SERIES HISTORIQUES, 1960–1995 COMMERCE SPECIAL, IMPORTATIONS C.A.F., EXPORTATIONS F.O.B

YEAR ANNEE	VALUE IN MILLION DRACHMAS VALEUR EN MILLION DRACHMAS MERCHANDISE –MARCHANDISE		GOLD –OR		CONVERSION FACTORS U.S. CENTS PER DRACHMA FACTEURS DE CONVERSION CENTS E.U. PAR DRACHMA		INDEX NUMBERS –INDICES QUANTUM		UNIT VALUE VALEUR UNITAIRE	
	IMPORTS	EXPORTS	IMPORTS	EXPORTS	IMPORTS	EXPORTS	IMPORTS	EXPORTS	IMPORTS	EXPORTS
1960	21061.00	6096.00			3.3330	3.3330	11	9	5	6
1961	21422.00	6700.00			3.3330	3.3330	13	10	5	6
1962	21038.00	7503.00			3.3330	3.3330	14	11	5	6
1963	24129.00	8703.00			3.3330	3.3330	16	11	5	6
1964	26553.00	9257.00			3.3330	3.3330	18	12	5	6
1965	34012.00	9833.00			3.3330	3.3330	22	13	5	6
1966	36686.00	12180.00			3.3330	3.3330	23	15	5	6
1967	35589.00	14856.00			3.3330	3.3330	24	19	5	6
1968	41831.00	14047.00			3.3330	3.3330	26	19	5	6
1969	47825.00	16609.00			3.3330	3.3330	29	22	5	6
1970	58750.00	19276.00			3.3330	3.3330	31	25	5	6
1971	62943.00	19874.00			3.3330	3.3330	33	25	5	6
1972	70374.00	26126.00			3.3333	3.3333	38	32	6	7
1973	102979.00	42812.00			3.3836	3.4012	48	40	7	9
1974	132181.00	60891.00			3.3333	3.3333	43	44	10	11
1975	172041.00	74441.00			3.0936	3.0716	42	48	12	13
1976	223160.00	93812.00			2.7108	2.7108	46	56	13	14
1977	253231.00	101331.00			2.6880	2.6880	49	55	14	15
1978	287729.00	123727.00			2.7285	2.7280	51	63	16	16
1979	356820.00	144239.00			2.6727	2.6727	55	67	19	18
1980	452881.00	221109.00			2.3254	2.3254	51	74	25	25
1981	493765.00	237928.50			1.7817	1.7848	51	65	29	29
1982	665920.00	286281.00			1.5051	1.5010	57	62	36	36
1983	848294.00	392652.00			1.1220	1.1237	59	74	44	41
1984	1083940.00	542665.70			0.8704	0.8865	61	83	53	51
1985	1412797.00	629188.10			0.7177	0.7219	71	86	61	57
1986	1587399.00	790000.10			0.7152	0.7151	72	101	69	62
1987	1773400.00	880999.90			0.7423	0.7414	81	103	68	67
1988	1758000.00	776400.10			0.7010	0.6994	66	77	82	80
1989	2629400.00	1231000.00			0.6142	0.6128	89	105	92	92
1990	3137900.00	1280999.00			0.6304	0.6328	100	100	100	100
1991	3921900.00	1584600.00			0.5503	0.5475	113	115	109	109
1992	4442300.00	1880800.00			0.5230	0.5231	130	147	110	106
1993	5051600.00	1934200.00			0.4356	0.4538	143	143	112	109
1994	5207601.00	2276600.00			0.4127	0.4125	150	149	110	121
1995	6007149.00	2539356.00			0.4316	0.4314			124	126

2. IMPORTS BY BROAD ECONOMIC CATEGORY AND EXPORTS BY INDUSTRIAL ORIGIN. (PERCENTAGE OF TOTAL VALUE)
IMPORTATIONS PAR CATEGORIES ECONOMIQUES ET EXPORTATIONS PAR BRANCHE D'ACTIVITE.(EN POURCENTAGE DE LA VALEUR TOTALE)

IMPORTS – IMPORTATIONS

	1990	1991	1992	1993	1994	1995	1996
TOTAL IMPORTS–IMPORTATIONS TOTALES	100.	100.	100.	100.	100.	100.	
1 FOOD BEV–ALIMENTATION BOISSONS	13.9	12.4	12.8	12.2	13.9	13.9	
11 PRIMARY–PRODUITS DE BASE	7.5	6.0	6.6	5.9	6.8	7.0	
111 FOR INDUSTRY–POUR L'INDUSTRIE	1.8	1.7	1.3	1.3	1.5	1.7	
112 FOR HOUSEHOLDS–POUR LES MENAGES	5.7	4.3	5.3	4.6	5.3	5.3	
12 PROCESSED–PRODUITS ELABORES	6.4	6.4	6.2	6.3	7.1	6.9	
121 FOR INDUSTRY–POUR L'INDUSTRIE	0.3	0.3	0.3	0.3	0.4	0.4	
122 FOR HOUSEHOLDS–POUR LES MENAGES	6.0	6.1	5.8	6.0	6.7	6.5	
2 IND SUPPLIES–APPROV INDUSTRIELS	34.3	31.8	28.5	26.8	29.9	31.9	
21 PRIMARY–PRODUITS DE BASE	2.9	2.9	2.1	2.0	2.1	2.3	
22 PROCESSED–PRODUITS ELABORES	31.4	28.9	26.4	24.8	27.9	29.6	
3 FUELS–COMBUSTIBLES	7.6	9.5	9.7	10.6	9.8	7.2	
31 PRIMARY–PRODUITS DE BASE	5.3	6.7	7.6	7.9	7.1	5.4	
32 PROCESSED–PRODUITS ELABORES	2.3	2.8	2.1	2.7	2.7	1.8	
321 MOTOR SPIRIT–ESSENCE	0.1	2.7	1.9	2.6	0.3	0.3	
322 OTHER–AUTRES	2.1	0.2	0.2	0.2	2.3	1.5	
4 MACHINERY–EQUIPEMENT	15.2	14.0	14.8	14.4	14.8	14.5	
41 CAPITAL EQUIPMENT–MACHINES	13.2	12.1	12.8	12.5	12.8	12.6	
42 PARTS–PIECES ACCESSOIRES	2.0	1.9	2.0	1.9	2.0	2.0	
5 TRANSPORT–TRANSPORT	15.7	18.9	19.5	20.2	13.1	12.8	
51 PASSENGER CARS–AUTOMOBILES	5.4	7.1	8.7	7.0	4.6	4.9	
52 OTHER–AUTRES	5.7	7.9	6.6	9.3	4.5	3.7	
521 INDUSTRIAL–INDUSTRIELS	5.3	7.5	6.2	8.9	4.1	3.2	
522 NON INDUSTRIAL–NON INDUSTRIEL	0.5	0.4	0.4	0.4	0.4	0.4	
53 PARTS–PIECES ACCESSOIRES	4.5	3.9	4.2	3.9	3.9	4.2	
6 CONSUM GOODS–BIENS CONSOMMATION	13.3	13.1	14.2	15.3	17.7	19.1	
61 DURABLE–DURABLES	4.1	3.7	3.8	4.2	4.6	4.3	
62 SEMI DURABLE–SEMI DURABLES	6.3	6.4	6.7	6.8	8.0	8.0	
63 NON DURABLE–NON DURABLES	2.9	3.0	3.7	4.3	5.1	6.8	
7 GOODS NES–BIENS NDA	0.1	0.1	0.5	0.4	0.7	0.5	

EXPORTS – EXPORTATIONS

	1990	1991	1992	1993	1994	1995	1996
TOTAL EXPORTS–EXPORTATIONS TOTALES	100.	100.	100.	100.	100.	100.	
1 AGRICULTURE	15.5	18.5	16.6	15.6	16.4	15.1	
2 MINING QUARRY–INDUS EXTRACTIVES	3.0	2.6	2.0	2.5	1.8	2.1	
3 MANUFACTURING–IND MANUFACTUR	81.4	78.8	81.4	81.9	81.7	82.8	
31 FOOD BEV TOBACCO–ALIM BOISS TAB	16.1	14.2	18.5	16.8	16.3	18.2	
32 TEXTILES–INDUSTRIES TEXTILES	29.5	28.0	28.8	27.5	23.7	22.9	
33 WOOD & PRODUCTS–BOIS & PRODUITS	0.4	0.5	0.5	0.7	0.6	0.5	
34 PAPER & PRODUCTS–PAPIER & PRODT	0.9	0.9	0.8	0.9	0.9	1.5	
35 CHEMICALS–INDUSTRIES CHIMIQUES	12.2	13.3	9.8	13.3	16.0	12.7	
36 NON METAL MIN–MIN NON METAL	4.2	3.9	4.3	4.3	4.8	4.0	
37 BASIC METAL–IND METAL BASE	11.1	8.9	8.3	6.8	7.5	8.7	
38 METAL MANUF–MANUF METAL	6.5	6.4	6.8	9.0	9.2	11.4	
39 OTH MANUF IND–AUTRES MANUF	0.5	2.8	3.5	2.5	2.7	2.9	

3. TRADE BY PRINCIPAL COUNTRIES OF FIRST AND LAST CONSIGNMENT (VALUE IN THOUSAND U.S. DOLLARS)
ECHANGES SELON LES PRINCIPAUX PAYS DE PREMIERE ET DE DERNIERE CONSIGNATION (VALEUR EN MILLIERS DE DOLLARS EU)

COUNTRIES–PAYS	SPECIAL IMPORTS C.I.F. IMPORTATIONS SPECIALES C.A.F				
	1991	1992	1993	1994	1995
World	21580137	23451579	22004476	21491557	25926782
Africa	960655	1131235	975439	1059297	805727
Americas	1467183	1211515	1180618	1051730	1408739
Northern America	994498	902367	884496	747788	935708
LAIA	345409	241357	210636	269225	390284
CACM	8736	29283	6461	4984	3145
Caribbean	50365	13221	55215	10762	3100
Rest of America	68175	25286	23810	18971	76502
As.ex F.USSR	3635412	3891713	4218416	2870151	3228391
Eur.x F.USSR	15056625	16654590	15003372	15740656	19608966
EU	13785416	15562680	13846899	14584224	18126244
EFTA	455528	491544	511046	464835	506027
East Europe	578057	506994	471634	638131	911222
Other Europe	237624	11089	110658	11609	4442
Former USSR	399455	434100	548799	725202	830013
Oceania	53505	56869	42728	40966	39008
Germany/Allemagne	4183486	4782993	3722093	3522040	4289712
Italy/Italie	3066124	3353880	3081719	3576040	4848993
France,Monac	1676049	1850090	1735881	1731855	2106275
Netherlands/Pays–Bas	1288744	1614562	1458934	1603199	1796789
United Kingdom	1155091	1292028	1337456	1335772	1683346
Japan/Japon	1434360	1493212	1497403	821414	682245
USA/Etats–Unis d'Amer	926282	846711	819330	687974	840358
Belgium–Luxembourg	741415	827051	740394	819753	938254
Spain/Espagne	465694	521811	590271	675643	876355
Iran (Islamic Rp. of)	622678	661299	737337	524675	467988
Russian Federation		387330	509285	548400	703047
Switz.Liecht	350967	417814	419798	397347	439802
Libyan Arab Jamahiriya	530555	493344	350496	281727	157777
Sweden/Suède	354441	294304	278208	346507	379722
Egypt/Egypte	69784	284436	438475	470703	323312
Denmark/Danemark	233847	319196	299369	311555	374783
Korea, Republic of	166001	279828	445149	188303	343080
Saudi Arabia	290505	304056	290567	190466	268891
China/Chine	193951	237914	291030	280738	336996
Austria/Autriche	273814	333894	232379	223918	268500
Bulgaria/Bulgarie	156263	160586	197995	318064	483756
Ireland/Irlande	124022	143004	163394	183842	265982
Turkey/Turquie	168280	143725	138398	170845	209679
Finland/Finlande	155072	141559	138113	178446	207520
Brazil/Brésil	201051	117576	78872	117571	193453
Israel/Israël	124660	98112	82034	86894	129147
Romania/Roumanie	92436	67782	65640	93330	134219
Former USSR/Anc. URSS	399455				
Portugal	67615	88308	68686	75653	90012
Cyprus/Chypre	44845	43958	171199	51431	75072
Argentina/Argentine	68895	63124	65936	72769	80988
Singapore/Singapour	80701	76982	63482	67346	60388
Canada	68083	55612	61903	58753	95328
Hungary/Hongrie	105651	70691	47703	47452	66967
Norway,SVD,JM	90078	57221	78095	54838	57281
Poland/Pologne	93494	52104	46501	47756	66329
India/Inde	53760	45729	49980	55818	87438
Hong Kong	69103	60523	52569	48385	52975
So. Africa Customs Un	74947	65150	30543	39258	64785
Ukraine		486	33957	151423	88093
Indonesia/Indonésie	29188	37553	47881	64268	83619
Thailand/Thaïlande	44558	49760	45728	51735	65731
Czechoslovakia	118300	137792			
Malaysia/Malaisie	38911	47939	56886	46249	62327
Czech Republic			76284	74651	92097
Fm Yugoslav	226961				
Panama	68171	25283	23659	18896	76473
Tunisia/Tunisie	33169	77039	12374	45949	36741
Cote d'Ivoire	64471	51006	12286	15618	56136
Liberia/Libéria	1691	46465	37518	81125	6864

COUNTRIES–PAYS	SPECIAL EXPORTS F.O.B. EXPORTATIONS SPECIALES F.O.B.				
	1991	1992	1993	1994	1995
Monde	8647160	9838273	8783720	9398984	10954635
Afrique	321493	354374	292042	348839	282444
Amériques	646510	540148	617763	708450	569987
Amérique du Nord	536798	433173	434634	509499	392127
ALAI	20301	47018	86190	76684	93565
MCAC	6204	6235	7299	13282	7161
Caraïbes	27611	22165	44271	61259	35828
Autre Amérique	55597	31557	45368	47727	41306
Asie l'URSS exclus	957205	1106775	1200802	1317554	1406974
Europe l'URSS exclus	6521333	7584354	6294931	6581116	8174705
UE	5809531	6762112	5175675	5356162	6645073
AELE	156239	181170	156472	140700	180094
Europe de l'Est	341498	483823	687814	876601	1083631
Autre de l'Europe	214064	66984	94400	176157	148902
Ancienne URSS	87795	124368	239320	352238	433858
Océanie	44714	46829	44528	43983	53303
Germany/Allemagne	2062969	2329391	2082971	1983110	2421845
Italy/Italie	1441803	1809928	1161653	1299067	1543978
France,Monac	650086	711412	546278	501674	597391
United Kingdom	590149	691687	500544	550657	667513
USA/Etats–Unis d'Amer	494003	381756	392406	455366	343738
Cyprus/Chypre	251930	322358	274141	305654	322405
Bulgaria/Bulgarie	87573	166767	315599	413418	447010
Netherlands/Pays–Bas	294357	272573	219425	233678	297221
Spain/Espagne	147731	244046	152259	216595	378808
Belgium–Luxembourg	196841	249670	133949	152703	212273
Russian Federation		112043	193099	243285	269834
Turkey/Turquie	105054	133024	154425	138187	220978
Austria/Autriche	134908	147859	126689	132489	149295
Albania/Albanie	12182	41164	131410	213363	261008
Lebanon/Liban	97290	87183	106336	172153	183803
Switz.Liecht	119575	135290	124933	106285	146084
Saudi Arabia	103309	126063	145213	142135	83756
Romania/Roumanie	84605	107125	92901	93440	180245
Sweden/Suède	117366	123615	85421	88554	127907
Israel/Israël	53199	76740	93643	109443	120632
Egypt/Egypte	64281	119834	76896	105816	81008
Malta/Malte	54160	59799	93915	123735	101815
Japan/Japon	85475	89696	77927	93989	84374
Denmark/Danemark	72026	68654	65914	77479	86021
Poland/Pologne	74722	70981	57175	69763	85343
Finland/Finlande	65040	57526	46077	53275	62754
Libyan Arab Jamahiriya	68491	62091	64875	49840	35192
Canada	41525	50994	41839	44393	42839
Panama	55595	31513	45121	47538	40872
Ukraine		2712	32962	81474	103174
Australia/Australie	41681	43128	40143	39265	48492
Tunisia/Tunisie	35868	36623	33640	48589	51066
United Arab Emirates	33822	36706	39743	50429	40676
Hungary/Hongrie	36466	35500	37931	40794	47047
Portugal	24814	33800	36316	36696	64918
Tfyr Macedonia			145269	14173	36644
Syrian Arab Republic	33678	29086	37826	37909	40690
Norway,SVD,JM	36070	44983	30635	33270	33418
Fm Yugoslav	159530				
Brazil/Brésil	4727	12092	47827	32203	61959
Algeria/Algérie	36825	14596	17151	61368	22754
Czech Republic			34367	36230	53336
China/Chine	25477	18656	43980	17304	16543
Ireland/Irlande	11441	21949	18178	30185	35147
Bahamas	17777	13561	31040	35533	17607
Hong Kong	10778	13160	24800	32269	33476
Czechoslovakia	45950	62286			
Gibraltar	127	6720	271	52197	46960
Indonesia/Indonésie	4230	5906	10237	32779	52437
Yugoslavia/Yougoslavie		82749		0	21791

(VALUE AS PERCENTAGE OF WORLD TOTAL)(VALEURS EN POURCENTAGE DU TOTAL MONDIAL)

	1986	1987	1988	1989	1990	1991	1992	1993	1994	1995
Africa	7.1	5.7	4.0	3.9	3.6	4.5	4.8	4.4	4.9	3.1
Americas	4.9	4.5	6.5	5.8	5.8	6.8	5.2	5.4	4.9	5.4
Northern America	3.4	3.1	4.3	3.9	4.0	4.6	3.8	4.0	3.5	3.6
LAIA	1.4	1.2	1.8	1.6	1.6	1.6	1.0	1.0	1.3	1.5
CACM	0.0	0.0	0.0	0.0	0.0	0.0	0.1	0.0	0.0	0.0
Caribbean	0.1	0.1	0.1	0.1	0.0	0.2	0.1	0.3	0.1	0.0
Rest of America	0.0	0.1	0.3	0.2	0.0	0.3	0.1	0.1	0.1	0.3
As.ex F.USSR	17.3	15.7	13.7	15.5	14.6	16.8	16.6	19.2	13.4	12.5
Eur.x F.USSR	67.4	71.1	73.1	73.0	73.9	69.8	71.0	68.2	73.2	75.6
EU	61.5	64.4	66.2	66.4	67.7	63.9	66.4	62.9	67.9	69.9
EFTA	2.2	2.4	2.5	2.2	2.3	2.1	2.1	2.3	2.2	2.0
East Europe	2.4	2.7	3.2	2.8	2.4	2.7	2.2	2.1	3.0	3.5
Other Europe	1.3	1.6	1.3	1.5	1.4	1.1	0.0	0.5	0.1	0.0
Former USSR	2.5	2.5	2.1	1.5	1.8	1.9	1.9	2.5	3.4	3.2
Oceania	0.8	0.4	0.6	0.4	0.3	0.2	0.2	0.2	0.2	0.2
Germany/Allemagne	21.2	22.2	20.3	19.9	20.6	19.4	20.4	16.9	16.4	16.5
Italy/Italie	11.6	12.3	14.5	14.9	15.4	14.2	14.3	14.0	16.6	18.7
France,Monac	8.1	7.8	8.0	6.9	8.1	7.8	7.9	7.9	8.1	8.1
Netherlands/Pays–Bas	6.7	7.0	6.9	6.9	6.7	6.0	6.9	6.6	7.5	6.9
United Kingdom	4.2	4.9	5.0	5.8	5.3	5.4	5.5	6.1	6.2	6.5
Japan/Japon	6.1	4.2	5.7	6.6	5.9	6.6	6.4	6.8	3.8	2.6
USA/Etats–Unis d'Amer	3.0	2.8	3.8	3.4	3.7	4.3	3.6	3.7	3.2	3.2
Belgium–Luxembourg	3.4	3.4	3.7	3.9	3.7	3.4	3.5	3.4	3.8	3.6
Spain/Espagne	1.3	1.4	2.1	1.9	2.0	2.2	2.2	2.7	3.1	3.4
Iran (Islamic Rp. of)	0.4	0.2	0.1	1.9	1.9	2.9	2.8	3.4	2.4	1.8

	1986	1987	1988	1989	1990	1991	1992	1993	1994	1995
Afrique	5.4	3.9	4.2	3.7	3.8	3.7	3.6	3.3	3.7	2.6
Amériques	8.3	7.6	7.7	7.3	7.2	7.5	5.5	7.0	7.5	5.2
Amérique du Nord	7.8	7.5	6.8	6.4	6.2	6.2	4.4	4.9	5.4	3.6
ALAI	0.1	0.1	0.4	0.1	0.1	0.2	0.5	1.0	0.8	0.9
MCAC	0.0	0.0	0.0	0.1	0.1	0.1	0.1	0.1	0.1	0.1
Caraïbes	0.3	0.0	0.2	0.3	0.3	0.3	0.2	0.5	0.7	0.3
Autre Amérique	0.1	0.0	0.3	0.4	0.5	0.6	0.3	0.5	0.5	0.4
Asie l'URSS exclus	11.3	9.7	11.8	10.2	10.4	11.1	11.2	13.7	14.0	12.8
Europe l'URSS exclus	72.7	76.5	73.8	75.8	75.3	75.4	77.1	71.7	70.0	74.6
UE	65.9	70.4	67.9	68.8	67.7	67.2	68.7	58.9	57.0	60.7
AELE	1.7	1.7	1.7	1.7	1.8	1.8	1.8	1.8	1.5	1.6
Europe de l'Est	3.6	3.1	2.7	3.4	3.1	3.9	4.9	7.8	9.3	9.9
Autre de l'Europe	1.5	1.2	1.5	1.9	2.7	2.5	0.7	1.1	1.9	1.4
Ancienne URSS	1.4	1.2	1.6	1.8	1.6	1.0	1.3	2.7	3.7	4.0
Océanie	0.4	0.6	0.4	0.6	0.9	0.5	0.5	0.5	0.5	0.5
Germany/Allemagne	23.7	24.5	25.1	20.8	21.8	23.9	23.7	23.7	21.1	22.1
Italy/Italie	13.5	16.3	14.2	20.3	17.1	16.7	18.4	13.2	13.8	14.1
France,Monac	9.5	8.7	8.6	8.8	9.6	7.5	7.2	6.2	5.3	5.5
United Kingdom	6.8	8.3	7.7	7.4	7.3	6.8	7.0	5.7	5.9	6.1
USA/Etats–Unis d'Amer	7.1	6.8	6.3	5.7	5.6	5.7	3.9	4.5	4.8	3.1
Cyprus/Chypre	1.5	1.5	2.6	2.3	2.5	2.9	3.3	3.1	3.3	2.9
Bulgaria/Bulgarie	1.0	0.6	0.6	0.9	0.7	1.0	1.7	3.6	4.4	4.1
Netherlands/Pays–Bas	5.0	3.8	3.4	3.2	3.5	3.4	2.8	2.5	2.5	2.7
Spain/Espagne	0.9	1.4	1.4	1.3	1.5	1.7	2.5	1.7	2.3	3.5
Belgium–Luxembourg	2.8	2.8	2.5	2.1	2.0	2.3	2.5	1.5	1.6	1.9

4. Special Imports C.I.F. by Commodities according to the S.I.T.C. (Rev. 2) in thousand U.S. Dollars
Importations Spéciales C.A.F. par Produits d'après la C.T.C.I. (Rév. 2) en milliers de Dollars E.U.

SITC CTCI	COMMODITY	1992			1993			1994			1995			PRODUIT
			WEIGHT POIDS	VALUE VALEUR		WEIGHT POIDS	VALUE VALEUR		WEIGHT POIDS	VALUE VALEUR		WEIGHT POIDS	VALUE VALEUR	
	ALL COMMODITIES			23451579			22004476			21491557			25926782	TOUS PRODUITS
0	FOOD AND LIVE ANIMALS			2764141			2471436			2758203			3398989	ALIMENTS,ANIMAUX VIVANTS
001	*LIVE ANIMALS FOR FOOD	W	32765	71164	W	27951	55633	W	27252	54703	W	26965	58521	ANIMAUX VIVANTS
01	MEAT AND PREPARATIONS			971688			776086			824154			946411	VIANDES ET PREPARATIONS
011	MEAT FRESH,CHILLD,FROZEN	W	274148	919527	W	254923	731583	W	294661	780626	W	308265	896488	VIANDES FRAICHES,REF,CONGE
0111	BOVINE MEAT FRESH,FROZEN	W	147315	594668	W	131313	481136	W	149489	474572	W	145377	524716	VIANDES BOVIN FRAI,REF
01111	BOVINE MEAT WITH BONE IN	W	114014	470627	W	94116	354570	W	93476	343995	W	108818	390514	VIANDES BOVIN NON DESOSS
01112	BOVINE MEAT BONELESS	W	33301	124041	W	37197	126566	W	56013	130577	W	36559	134202	VIANDES BOVIN DESOSSEES
0113	PIG MEAT FRESH,CHLD,FRZN	W	77595	219068	W	70789	149399	W	85939	179911	W	107827	250010	VIANDE DE PORC
02	DAIRY PRODCTS,BIRDS'EGGS			536506			535754			593150			615864	PRODUITS LAITIERS,OEUFS
022	MILK AND CREAM	W	156805	271429	W	155638	250790	W	166580	277860	W	158050	286363	LAIT ET CREME
0224	MILK,CREAM PRESERVED ETC	W	132695	235354	W	123296	206670	W	132113	226632	W	129080	238414	LAIT,CREME CONS,CONC
02249	MILK(EX DRY) PRSVD,SWEET	W	117064	193628	W	105490	166050	W	115148	186469	W	112835	193623	LAIT CONS,CONC SUCRE
024	CHEESE AND CURD	W	49226	230986	W	56399	252470	W	64676	278255	W	62011	285949	FROMAGE ET CAILLEBOTTE
03	FISH AND PREPARATIONS			164587			145260			153666			202068	POISSONS ET PREPARATIONS
04	CEREALS AND PREPARATIONS			317729			289410			309649			485772	CEREALES ET PRODUITS
041	WHEAT ETC UNMILLED	W	265685	76709	W	273678	58756	W	382630	79081	W	744296	173396	FROMENT,EPEAUTRE
0412	OTHER WHEAT ETC UNMILLED	W	256181	73174	W	262788	55529	W	381696	78569	W	647881	145831	AUTRE FROMENT NON MOULU
044	MAIZE UNMILLED	W	218854	72414	W	217903	59340	W	153244	44372	W	304658	90607	MAIS NON MOULU
048	CEREAL ETC PREPARATIONS	W	59784	137428	W	89662	133943	W	124169	151412	W	100129	178023	PREPTNS A BASE CEREALES
05	VEGETABLES AND FRUIT			258887			227333			313907			389192	LEGUMES ET FRUITS
054	VEG ETC FRSH,SMPLY PRSVD	W	181771	101539	W	169420	86519	W	248035	123770	W	228202	154746	LEGUMES FRAIS,CONG,SECS
057	FRUIT,NUTS,FRESH,DRIED	W	82325	82406	W	86299	71563	W	116085	118659	W	130105	149653	FRUITS FRAIS OU SECS
06	SUGAR AND PREPS,HONEY			46126			42392			38410			115851	SUCRES ET PRODUITS
061	SUGAR AND HONEY	W	27944	24249	W	36421	27031	W	16781	12157	W	94403	85237	SUCRES ET MIEL
07	COFFEE,TEA,COCOA,SPICES			148294			118620			163995			233881	CAFE,THE,CACAO,EPICES
071	COFFEE AND SUBSTITUTES	W	11494	68287	W	15835	52472	W	18259	93570	W	20607	131896	CAFE ET SUCCEDANES
081	*FEEDING STUFF FOR ANIML	W	251873	138443	W	407023	156531	W	402324	161732	W	378050	170910	NOURRITURE POUR ANIMAUX
0819	FOOD WASTE AND FEED NES	W	84910	89487	W	89572	79168	W	96986	83703	W	105216	96267	DECHETS,ALIMENTS NDA
08199	FODDER NES,INCL SWEETNED	W	83418	89210	W	88615	79020	W	88247	82526	W	98269	95102	PREPARATIONS FOURRAGERES
09	MISC EDIBLE PRODUCTS			110716			124417			144838			180520	PREP ALIMENTAIRES DIVERSES
098	EDIBLE PRODCTS,PREPS NES	W	26099	100670	W	34258	115660	W	38421	133100	W	42213	164604	PREP ALIMENTAIRES NDA
09809	MISC FOOD PREPRTIONS NES	W	13662	79340	W	19700	95175	W	22498	112562	W	25242	139319	PREP ALIMENTAIRES NDA
1	BEVERAGES AND TOBACCO			464386			476127			452188			532577	BOISSONS ET TABACS
11	BEVERAGES			271711			278131			250093			285599	BOISSONS
112	ALCOHOLIC BEVERAGES	W	85425	246093	W	79023	256464	W	68077	227975	W	78359	264528	BOISSONS ALCOOLIQUES
1124	DISTILLED ALCOHOLIC BEVS	W	47608	199836	W	47950	219778	W	38548	192076	W	43758	221251	ALCOOLS,EAUX–DE–VIE
11241	WHISKY	W	32552	146608	W	35972	174319	W	25669	142256	W	29674	162233	WHISKY
12	TOBACCO AND MANUFACTURES			192675			197996			202096			246978	TABACS BRUTS FABRIQUES
121	TOBACCO UNMNFCTRD,REFUSE	W	20301	102918	W	15274	83169	W	18016	77046	W	19846	98079	TABACS BRUTS,DECHETS
122	TOBACCO,MANUFACTURED	W	8719	89757	W	10538	114827	W	11905	125050	W	13495	148899	TABACS FABRIQUES
1222	CIGARETTES	W	7176	78637	W	9226	104054	W	10967	113942	W	11747	132747	CIGARETTES
2	CRUDE MATERLS,EXCL FUELS			728739			626390			718917			903116	MAT BRUTES NON COMESTIBLES
22	OIL SEEDS,OLEAGINOUS FRT			115143			111651			121186			116404	GRAINES,FRUITS OLEAGINEUX
222	SEEDS FOR'SOFT'FIXED OIL	W	393150	113599	W	360246	109959	W	370039	119621	W	289530	114972	GRAINES HUILES FIXES
2222	SOYA BEANS	W	330312	82324	W	309611	80993	W	275471	76289	W	219483	59784	FEVES DE SOJA
24	CORK AND WOOD			197411			157115			199753			218584	LIEGE ET BOIS
248	WOOD SHAPED,SLEEPERS	W	307075	150070	W	261388	114261	W	308409	145724	W	335883	171071	BOIS SIMPLEMENT TRAVAILLES
2482	LUMBER SHAPED CONIFER	W	258776	121859	W	203661	82579	W	244160	109342	W	269507	129138	CONIFERES SCIES,RABOTES
24821	LUMBER SAWN ETC CONIFER	W	251183	116632	W	194634	77032	W	233272	102481	W	261654	122209	CONIFERES SCIES LONGITUD
251	*PULP AND WASTE PAPER	W	112218	55294	W	91895	38836	W	108862	58873	W	155895	127053	PATES A PAPIER,DECHETS
2517	SODA,SULPHATE WOOD PULP	W	66950	34696	W	65925	28378	W	79967	44561	W	109430	97286	PATES CHIMIQUES AU SULFATE
25172	— BLEACHED,NONDISSOLVNG	W	66903	34665	W	64927	27968	W	79069	44076	W	108974	96997	PATES BLANCHIES
26	TEXTILE FIBRES AND WASTE			111361			73814			75916			89360	FIBRES TEXTILES
28	METALLIFEROUS ORES,SCRAP			37639			63723			51124			80645	MINERAIS METAL,DECHETS
29	CRUDE ANIMAL,VEG MAT NES			77637			69155			76633			90945	MATIERES BRUTES ANIM,VEGET
292	CRUDE VEG MATERIALS NES	W	20500	69263	W	21239	62020	W	23073	66260	W	26533	80347	MAT BRUTES VEGETALES NDA
3	MINERAL FUELS ETC			2302597			2345572			2115876			1890774	COMBUSTIBLES MINERAUX LUB
33	PETROLEUM AND PRODUCTS			2210313			2262848			2035626			1796982	PETROLE ET DERIVES
333	CRUDE PETROLEUM	MW	13215	1719272	MW	12687	1672311	MW	13375	1468809	MW	11356	1329863	HUILES BRUTES DE PETROLE
334	PETROLEUM PRODUCTS,REFIN	W	2774299	461537	W	4165591	574417	W	4194946	549443	W	2831412	438779	PRODUITS RAFFINES
3341	GASOLINE,OTH LIGHT OILS	W	2769431	448699	W	4160300	562263	W	399745	67665	W	420255	71567	ESSENCES POUR MOTEURS
33419	OTH LIGHT PETROLEUM OILS	W	2769431	448699	W	4160300	562263	W	370242	61831	W	420155	71549	AUTRES HUILES LEGERES
3343	GAS OILS							W	1147616	173985	W	684197	107794	GAS OILS
3344	FUEL OILS,NES							W	2440152	214319	W	1536432	161668	FUEL OILS
3345	LUBS,PETROLEUM OILS NES	W	4868	12838	W	5290	12155	W	158097	84664	W	147587	92020	HUILES LUBRIFIANTES
33451	LUBS(HIGH PETR CONT) ETC							W	151793	70361	W	141770	77350	HUILES LUBRIF,H LOURDES
4	ANIMAL,VEGETABLE OIL,FAT			73173			53130			87702			89595	HUILES,GRAISSES ANIM,VEG
42	FIXED VEGETABLE OIL,FAT			59795			41854			74524			73441	HUILES VEGETALES FIXES
5	CHEMCLS,RELATED PROD NES			2429688			2380656			2667886			3344558	PRODUITS CHIMIQUES
51	ORGANIC CHEMICALS			329931			338921			385815			471036	PROD CHIMIQ ORGANIQUES
511	HYDROCARBONS NES,DERIVS	W	130117	59870	W	163716	72424	W	133096	74491	W	104125	77209	HYDROCARBURES NDA
513	CARBOXYLIC ACIDS ETC	W	49395	54132	W	50434	48579	W	47916	55787	W	51044	80552	ACIDES CARBOXYLIQUES
514	NITROGEN–FNCTN COMPOUNDS	W	8836	98846	W	10965	90079	W	13163	99940	W	13013	113670	COMPOSES FONCT AZOTEES
515	ORG–INORG COMPOUNDS ETC	W	3495	66812	W	3976	78397	W	4113	93762	W	4678	114942	COMPOSES ORGANO–MINERAUX
5156	HETEROCYCLIC CMPDS ETC	W	662	42807	W	561	51798	W	1022	64921	W	1339	80800	COMPOSES HETEROCYCLIQUES
52	INORGANIC CHEMICALS			131955			139848			142694			187319	PROD CHIM INORGANIQUES
522	INORG ELEMNTS,OXIDES,ETC	W	320791	56799	W	384023	68629	W	379858	72601	W	417707	101530	ELEMENTS INORGANIQUES
5225	INORGANIC BASES ETC NES	W	304701	40445	W	358158	51973	W	305486	52599	W	353172	77929	AUTRES BASES OXYDES METAL
523	OTHR INORG CHEMICALS ETC	W	148700	73060	W	155898	65341	W	157328	63474	W	178772	78473	AUT PRODUITS CHIMIQUES INORG
53	DYES,TANNING,COLOUR PROD			224929			193526			202721			239849	PROD TEINTURE,COLORANTS
533	PIGMENTS,PAINTS,ETC	W	58885	166751	W	62047	141807	W	69913	153797	W	76299	183008	PIGMENTS,PEINTURES,VERNIS
5334	VARNISHES,DISTEMPERS ETC	W	15756	68635	W	20112	65526	W	21249	65353	W	25778	78554	PEINTURES A L'EAU
541	*MEDICINAL,PHARM PRODUCT	K	7175753	511315	K	8690291	567477	MK	12021	664690	MK	10869	823993	PROD MEDICINAUX PHARMACEUT
5417	MEDICAMENTS	K	4763634	387395	K	6415952	427778	K	8652374	505568	K	7626087	646545	MEDICAMENTS
54171	— CONTAINNG ANTIBIOTICS	K	538269	61857	K	672900	67147	K	1115089	74607	K	1129871	78659	MED CONTN ANTIBIOTIQUES
54179	— CONTNG OTH SUBSTANCES	K	4050262	288418	K	5429986	320411	K	7117435	377228	K	5930482	500373	MED CONT AUT SUBSTANCES
55	PERFUME,CLEANING ETC PRD			273558			258469			308107			358998	PROD POUR PARFUM,TOILETTE
553	PERFUMERY,COSMETICS,ETC	W	14757	134783	W	15820	143424	W	20361	177829	W	25672	205611	PRODUITS DE PARFUMERIE
554	SOAP,CLEANSING ETC PREPS	W	67331	108449	W	61432	87085	W	73365	98543	W	81619	114663	SAVONS,PRODUITS DETERSIFS
5542	WASHING PREPARATIONS ETC	W	60122	90891	W	52369	69019	W	63952	81500	W	68377	92592	PROD ORG TENSIO–ACT NDA
562	*FERTILIZERS,MANUFACTURE	W	615542	77689	W	662998	77488	W	719509	102980	W	722943	122829	ENGRAIS MANUFACTURES
58	PLASTIC MATERIALS ETC			544313			472232			525814			729908	MAT PLAST ARTIFICIELLES
582	PROD OF CONDENSATION ETC	W	57970	97079	W	68608	98169	W	81501	98243	W	106516	143624	PROD CONDENS,POLYCOND
5823	ALKYDS,OTHER POLYESTERS	W	23244	47032	W	28707	47801	W	41442	45915	W	68884	77959	ALKYDES ET AUT POLYESTERS
583	POLYMERIZATION ETC PRODS	W	360923	433103	W	362761	361257	W	399628	414397	W	427127	569189	PROD POLYMERISATION
5831	POLYETHYLENE	W	183719	160183	W	183481	138472	W	196181	152379	W	189584	217774	POLYETHYLENE
58311	— IN PRIMARY FORMS	W	171604	149060	W	171863	127463	W	181332	136078	W	174041	194545	POLYETHYLENE PRIMAIRES
5832	POLYPROPYLENE	W	50751	54426	W	52032	45086	W	56842	54284	W	89977	77987	POLYPROPYLENE
5834	POLYVINYL CHLORIDE	W	68437	72576	W	62723	59038	W	63933	69773	W	64907	97211	CHLORURE DE POLYVINYLE
5839	OTH POLYMRZTION ETC PROD	W	26306	95129	W	27156	70051	W	37983	77685	W	38984	104996	AUT PROD POLYMER COPOLYM

4. Special Imports C.I.F. by Commodities according to the S.I.T.C. (Rev. 2) in thousand U.S. Dollars
Importations Spéciales C.A.F. par Produits d'après la C.T.C.I. (Rév. 2) en milliers de Dollars E.U.

SITC CTCI	COMMODITY	1992 WEIGHT POIDS	1992 VALUE VALEUR	1993 WEIGHT POIDS	1993 VALUE VALEUR	1994 WEIGHT POIDS	1994 VALUE VALEUR	1995 WEIGHT POIDS	1995 VALUE VALEUR	PRODUIT
59	CHEMICAL MATERIALS NES		330822		325276		329760		402557	MAT PROD CHIMIQUES NDA
591	PESTICIDES,DISINFECTANTS	W 18195	108661	W 17302	104306	W 17562	113304	W 26553	137639	DESINF,INSECT,FONG,HERB
598	MISCEL CHEM PRODUCTS NES	W 75157	179769	W 103192	181667	W 80894	169978	W 96301	210882	PROD DIV INDUST CHIM NDA
5989	CHEM PRODUCTS,PREPS NES	W 64576	154768	W 77007	135414	W 60239	132162	W 70160	163802	PROD PREP CHIMIQUES NDA
59899	OTH CHEM PRODS,PREPS,NES	W 46842	124895	W 45694	107096	W 43433	104907	W 50064	129061	AUT PRODUITS CHIMIQUES NDA
6	BASIC MANUFACTURES		4224483		3614634		3929030		5093240	ART MANUFACTURES
61	LEATHER,DRESSED FUR,ETC		258596		177270		215699		208673	CUIRS,PELLETERIES
613	FUR SKINS TANNED,DRESSED	W 2156	207334	W 2050	129355	W 1886	152914	W 1778	136700	PELLETERIES
62	RUBBER MANUFACTURES NES		162176		170923		175832		240889	CAOUTCHOUC MANUFACTURE
625	RUBBER TYRES, TUBES ETC	W 28375	117579	W 32301	129557	W 33003	134540	W 40089	184853	PNEUS CAOUTCHOUC VULCANISE
6251	TYRES NEW FOR MOTOR CARS	W 6802	39868	W 10282	52138	W 12149	62263	W 15029	88917	PNEUS POUR VOITURES
63	WOOD,CORK MANUFACTRS NES		99301		69910		75134		93150	OUVRAGES LIEGE ET BOIS
64	PAPER,PAPERBOARD AND MFR		505252		510921		579260		859027	PAPIERS,CARTONS & OUVRAGES
641	PAPER AND PAPERBOARD	W 468092	387025	W 523383	364320	W 566261	425509	W 666892	673730	PAPIERS ET CARTONS
6411	NEWSPRINT	W 78127	46264	W 90761	44382	W 101363	54805	W 90069	77926	PAPIER JOURNAL
6412	PRINTG,WRITING PAPER NES	W 96749	107027	W 115429	98171	W 127349	115315	W 128973	178417	PAPIERS POUR L'IMPRESSION
64122	— COATED,IMPREGNATD ETC	W 84131	94014	W 101243	85454	W 111891	101214	W 112698	155972	PAPIERS IMPRESSION COUCHES
6415	PAPER,PAPERBRD,BULK,NES	W 85160	65535	W 101352	58248	W 91976	65043	W 125900	117637	PAPIERS,CARTONS ROULEAUX
6418	COATED ETC PAPER NES BLK	W 43512	82011	W 49730	84067	W 52516	89616	W 58736	128430	PAP,CARTONS COUCHES,ENDUITS
642	PAPER,ETC,PRECUT,ARTS OF	W 45648	118227	W 61457	146601	W 65763	153751	W 68776	185296	PAP,CARTONS DECOUPES
6428	PAPER ETC ARTICLES NES	W 16985	43434	W 33239	78995	W 30115	73971	W 32144	90605	OUVRAGES EN PATE A PAPIER
65	TEXTILE YARN,FABRICS,ETC		1340197		980680		1051981		1168480	FILS,TISSUS,ARTICLES TEXTILE
651	TEXTILE YARN	W 50561	287002	W 38657	191025	W 47049	212101	W 44325	243432	FILS TEXTILES
6513	COTTON YARN	W 20401	89592	W 10717	46207	W 13761	56958	W 10579	54247	FILS DE COTON
6514	SYN FIB YRN,BULK,MONOFIL	W 10288	72591	W 10280	58051	W 9941	57331	W 11310	70586	FILS CONT 85% FIB TEXT SYNTH
652	COTTON FABRICS,WOVEN	W 11298	134468	W 11066	111301	W 12427	118812	W 11867	131031	TISSUS DE COTON
6522	WOVEN COTTON BLEACHD,ETC	W 10681	129235	W 10022	102032	W 10854	106684	W 10675	120645	TISSUS COTON BLANCHIS ETC
65224	BLCHED COTTON FABRIC NES	W 8893	97971	W 8247	77948	W 9180	82207	W 8631	89753	AUT TIS PLUS 85% COT BLANCHI
653	WOVN MAN-MADE FIB FABRIC	W 23710	442426	W 20704	303842	W 22328	308698	W 23632	336271	TISSUS FIBRES SYNTH,ARTIF
6531	CONT SYNT WEAVES NONPILE	W 6793	125876	W 6947	100121	W 8011	103650	W 8819	121691	TISSUS FIBRES SYNTH CONTINUE
65315	CONT SYN TXTL FABRIC NES	W 6013	114992	W 6344	92526	W 6754	92357	W 7135	104684	TIS PLUS 85% TEXT SYNT CONT
6534	DISC SYN BLEND FABRC NES	W 6224	90853	W 5406	61048	W 6229	60503	W 6326	68482	TISSUS FIBRES SYNTH DISCONT
6538	DISC REG BLEND FABRC NES	W 3941	78484	W 2829	46695	W 2756	49324	W 2257	43520	TIS MOINS 85% TEXT ART DISC
654	OTH WOVEN TEXTILE FABRIC	W 4573	107221	W 3921	74660	W 4166	81562	W 3975	72504	TISSUS AUT COTON SYNT,ARTIF
655	KNITTED,ETC FABRICS	W 5030	76258	W 3741	48729	W 7324	59918	W 5467	79974	ETOF BONNETERIE PIECES ETC
6552	OTHER KNIT ETC FAB NONEL	W 5030	76258	W 3741	48729	W 7324	59918	W 5467	79974	ETOF BON NON ELAS NON SYNT
657	SPECIAL TXTL FABRC,PRODS	W 12699	102636	W 12900	83048	W 14669	95365	W 14637	96783	TISSUS SPECIAUX
658	TEXTILE ARTICLES NES	W 9614	70567	W 10847	72728	W 14348	74762	W 12015	86243	ART FACONNES MAT TEXTILES
659	FLOOR COVERINGS,ETC	W 16931	79888	W 16292	68826	W 16477	71660	W 18736	89413	COUVRE-PARQUETS,TAPIS ETC
66	NONMETAL MINERAL MFS NES		424262		377404		396205		477360	ART MIN NON METALLIQUES
662	CLAY,REFRACTORY BLDG PRD	W 355143	169766	W 343128	139858	W 375056	150720	W 424113	177381	MAT CONST REFRACTAIRES
6624	BRICKS ETC NONREFRACTORY	W 329833	153230	W 308441	121596	W 351576	136085	W 399016	160649	BRIQUES ETC CERAM NON REFR
66245	GLAZED CERAMIC SETTS ETC	W 324248	151112	W 303681	119706	W 341557	132442	W 390495	156425	AUT CARREAUX CERAMIQUE
664	GLASS	W 104158	76485	W 108112	64003	W 105559	60788	W 124282	81037	VERRE
665	GLASSWARE	W 87560	91361	W 82753	85780	W 86691	88989	W 105409	101510	OUVRAGES EN VERRE
67	IRON AND STEEL		637239		581221		601883		894660	FER ET ACIER
672	IRON,STEEL PRIMARY FORMS	W 971239	228703	W 576717	137221	W 667639	165340	W 847130	267287	LINGOTS FER,ACIER
6725	IRN,STL BLOOMS,SLABS,ETC	W 837242	185037	W 387276	80907	W 549834	127844	W 626425	178899	BLOOMS,BILLETTES FER,ACIER
67251	IRN,SMPLE STL BLOOMS,ETC	W 837214	184993	W 387070	80682	W 549421	127559	W 624496	178002	BLOOMS ETC NON ACIER FIN
6727	IRN,STL COIL FR REROLLNG	W 115465	38856	W 160877	48208	W 113210	36768	W 220120	88232	EBAUCHES POUR TOLES FER
67271	IRON,SIMPLE STEEL COILS	W 115395	38660	W 160284	47556	W 112581	36111	W 219730	87549	EBAUCHES NON EN ACIER
673	IRON,STEEL SHAPES ETC	W 311012	114157	W 454468	155358	W 435554	150481	W 572106	225332	BARRES,PROFIL FER,ACIER
6732	IRON,STEEL BARS ETC	W 152723	57221	W 278649	95558	W 289585	97382	W 384343	148277	BARRES FER,ACIER
67326	IRN,OTH STL BARS HOTROLD	W 141858	45796	W 261336	82776	W 279101	86306	W 362281	128251	BARRES PLEINES FER,ACIER
674	IRN,STL UNIV,PLATE,SHEET	W 185648	130100	W 279543	177033	W 298349	187984	W 348209	267361	LARGES PLATS,TOLES
6746	IRN,STL THIN PLATE,ROLLD	W 55184	39096	W 56242	42977	W 67020	49170	W 86049	83650	TOLES LAM MOINS 3MM
6749	OTH IRN,STL PLATES,SHEET	W 52231	43379	W 106881	65734	W 95399	59146	W 100766	80532	AUTRES TOLES FER,ACIER
678	IRON,STL TUBES,PIPES,ETC	W 134154	119306	W 74435	69309	W 56881	56647	W 54861	66083	TUBES,TUYAUX EN FONTE,FER
6783	IRON,STL TUBES,PIPES NES	W 115194	89126	W 45045	33891	W 31580	26117	W 20769	22769	AUT TUBES,TUYAUX FER,ACIER
68	NON-FERROUS METALS		301206		316041		387979		613448	METAUX NON FERREUX
682	COPPER EXC CEMENT COPPER	W 63983	143442	W 89752	185961	W 79093	193531	W 103371	315861	CUIVRE
6821	COPPER NES,ALLOYS,UNWRT	W 48981	91603	W 68152	127918	W 62332	141153	W 79959	237423	CUIVRE BRUT
68212	COPPER REFINED,UNWROUGHT	W 48889	91343	W 68043	127650	W 62193	140783	W 79677	236569	CUIVRE AFFINE BRUT
6822	COPPER,ALLOYS WORKED	W 15002	51839	W 21600	58043	W 16761	52378	W 23412	78438	CUIVRE,ALLIAGES OUVRES
684	ALUMINIUM	W 64484	117514	W 49556	88029	W 87391	146439	W 109230	240248	ALUMINIUM
6841	ALUMINIUM,ALLOYS,UNWRGHT	W 47400	59860	W 19321	21619	W 56689	80946	W 79667	148400	ALUMINIUM,ALLIAGES BRUTS
6842	ALUMINIUM,ALLOYS WORKED	W 17084	57654	W 30236	66410	W 30702	65493	W 29563	91847	ALUMINIUM,ALLIAGES OUVRE
69	METAL MANUFACTURES NES		496254		430264		445057		537553	ART MANUFACT EN METAL NDA
697	BASE MTL HOUSEHOLD EQUIP	W 14424	82241	W 16353	75005	W 17710	73385	W 24617	85455	ART MENAGE MET COMMUNS
699	BASE METAL MFRS NES	W 28785	166120	W 33674	149322	W 35155	151589	W 45932	190038	ART MANUFACTURES MET NDA
6991	LOCKSMITHS WARES,ETC	W 10065	82841	W 12382	72958	W 12890	74810	W 14069	91106	ARTICLES DE SERRURERIE
7	MACHINES,TRANSPORT EQUIP		7969178		7729170		6120568		7111040	MACHINES MATERIEL TRANSPORT
71	POWER GENERATING EQUIPMT		342472		314307		321425		412857	MACHINES GENERATRICES
713	INTRNL COMBUS PSTN ENGIN	W 13785	121475	W 10198	105007	W 10275	88674	W 27826	213445	MOTEURS EXPL COMB INT, PIECE
7139	PISTON ENGINE PARTS NES	W 2200	51187	W 2652	46262	W 4362	44984	W 22471	170619	PIECES POUR 713.2,3,8
714	ENGINES AND MOTORS NES	W 346	133067	W 302	99837	W 325	113591	W 223	78942	MOTEURS NON ELECTRIQUES
7144	REACTION ENGINES	W 230	99546	W 152	74593	W 121	76088	W 105	59913	PROPULSEURS A REACTION
716	ROTATING ELECTRIC PLANT	W 8499	77282	W 9390	88971	W 7497	54410	W 7394	60176	APP ELECTR ROTATIFS,PIECES
72	MACHS FOR SPCL INDUSTRYS		843698		630565		572019		734126	MAC SPECIALES POUR INDUST
721	AGRIC MACHY,EXC TRACTORS	W 12352	88678	W 9535	62030	W 9701	57047	W 11033	67488	MACHINES AGRICOLES
722	TRACTORS NON-ROAD	W 22671	99245	W 10829	34348	W 9475	32893	W 12204	55309	TRACTEURS
7224	WHEELED TRACTORS NES	W 22641	99074	W 10790	34177	W 9426	32799	W 12133	55006	TRACTEURS A ROUES
723	CIVIL ENGNEERG EQUIP ETC	W 43579	137625	W 37632	104630	W 25760	69373	W 30960	89988	APPAREILS DE GENIE CIVIL
7234	CONST,MINING MACHNRY NES	W 40144	117818	W 33635	86868	W 22644	55740	W 27079	75154	MACH POUR LA CONST, MINES
724	TEXTILE,LEATHER MACHNRY	W 8458	183942	W 6613	130772	W 7486	130484	W 13834	200594	MACH POUR INDUSTRIE TEXTILE
7244	SPINNING,EXTRDNG,ETC MCH	W 3678	51808	W 2180	40319	W 2752	34723	W 5585	78033	MACH POUR LE FILAGE
727	FOOD MACHRY NON-DOMESTIC	W 3375	77140	W 3535	61301	W 3520	63948	W 3077	65392	MACH INDUSTRIES ALIMENT
7272	OTH FOOD PROC MCHY,PARTS	W 2880	72854	W 2637	51557	W 3170	58775	W 2827	60607	AUT MACH IND ALIMENTAIRE
728	OTH MACHY FOR SPCL INDUS	W 15390	185825	W 15306	154080	W 13740	144787	W 17207	181294	AUT MACH IND PARTICULIERES
7284	MACHY FOR SPCL INDUS NES	W 6091	99962	W 7150	99324	W 6848	98122	W 8980	125200	MACH SPEC IND PARTICUL.
73	METALWORKING MACHINERY		98488		70261		63665		81143	MACH TRAVAIL DES METAUX
74	GENRL INDUSTRL MACHY NES		906375		786324		793315		1006853	MACH APP INDUSTRIE
741	HEATING,COOLING EQUIPMNT	W 21042	250287	W 21119	244771	W 22467	261037	W 28846	351535	MACH CHAUFFAGE,PIECES
7415	AIR-CONDITIONING MACHNRY	W 7412	112555	W 8876	123000	W 10819	145742	W 14037	192011	GROUPES CONDITION AIR
743	PUMPS NES,CENTRFUGES ETC	W 13726	133153	W 11634	113635	W 12116	109281	W 14528	140760	POMPES COMPRES,VENT ETC
744	MECHANICAL HANDLING EQU	W 22755	117458	W 21085	86782	W 20244	76819	W 20510	106010	EQUIP MANUTENTION PIECES
745	NONELEC MACHY,TOOLS NES	W 6215	139862	W 6154	119179	W 9487	125944	W 9012	140805	AUT MACH NON ELEC,PIECES
7452	OTH NONELEC MCHS,PTS NES	W 5485	120364	W 5481	104403	W 8794	111804	W 8251	123270	AUT MACH NON ELEC,PIECES
749	NONELEC MACH PTS,ACC NES	W 14768	199734	W 15449	163871	W 14939	163915	W 18763	194438	PIECES MACH NON ELEC NDA
7492	COCKS,VALVES ETC NES	W 9679	120796	W 10282	96940	W 9506	94324	W 12918	111170	ART ROB,SIM POUR TUYAUX
75	OFFICE MACHNES,ADP EQUIP		368703		345547		364774		451640	MACH BUREAU TRAIT AUTOM

4. Special Imports C.I.F. by Commodities according to the S.I.T.C. (Rev. 2) in thousand U.S. Dollars
Importations Spéciales C.A.F. par Produits d'après la C.T.C.I. (Rév. 2) en milliers de Dollars E.U.

SITC CTCI	COMMODITY	1992 WEIGHT POIDS	1992 VALUE VALEUR	1993 WEIGHT POIDS	1993 VALUE VALEUR	1994 WEIGHT POIDS	1994 VALUE VALEUR	1995 WEIGHT POIDS	1995 VALUE VALEUR	PRODUIT
752	AUTOMTIC DATA PROC EQUIP	W 3651	187749	W 3245	167937	W 3338	191314	W 4576	233397	MACH TRAIT INFORMATION
7528	OFF–LINE DATA PROC EQUIP	W 1177	86606	W 1182	63975	W 954	62655	W 984	58547	MACH AUXIL TRAIT INFORM
759	OFFICE,ADP MCH PTS,ACCES	W 1968	123765	W 2537	129252	W 2731	121762	W 3049	156877	PIECES DU 751 ET 752
7599	ACCTG,ETC,ADP MCH PTS,AC	W 1391	101463	W 1963	110646	W 2033	106661	W 2479	136927	PIECES DU 751 ET 752
76	TELECOMM,SOUND EQUIPMENT		437444		707154		716639		695590	EQUIPMENT DE TELECOM
761	TELEVISION RECEIVERS	W 8511	112133	W 11143	144093	W 10249	144429	W 9969	121731	RECEPTEURS DE TELEVISION
7611	COLOUR TV RECEIVERS	W 7944	106942	W 10876	140736	W 10013	141192	W 9864	118793	RECEPTEURS COULEUR
764	TELECOM EQPT,PTS,ACC NES	W 4929	261406	W 7744	457933	W 9221	463973	W 10134	456846	EQUIP TELECOM,PIECES
7641	LINE TELEPHONE,ETC EQUIP	W 1255	53730	W 1685	66983	W 1601	55464	W 2412	68574	APP TELEPHON PAR FIL
7643	TV,RADIO TRANSMITTRS ETC	W 97	15970	W 283	39542	W 376	71380	W 847	97967	APP EMET TELE RADIO
7649	PTS NES OF EQUIPMT OF 76	W 1703	136088	W 3092	279641	W 4655	282898	W 3937	226776	PIECES DE LA DIV 76
76491	PTS NES OF APPAR OF 7641	W 927	82719	W 1988	225504	W 1469	184803	W 1806	150316	PIECES POUR 764.1
76493	TELECOMM EQUIPMT PTS NES	W 698	50714	W 954	49667	W 3056	91557	W 1967	71087	PIECES 761,762,764.3,8
77	ELECTRIC MACHNRY NES ETC		857095		819383		845080		950012	MACH APP ELECT NDA
772	SWITCHGEAR ETC,PARTS NES	W 5893	130995	W 5738	112149	W 5931	118541	W 6179	124545	APP COUPURE,SECT ETC
7721	SWITCHGEAR ETC	W 5786	118173	W 5618	106216	W 5838	113708	W 6071	119231	APP COUPURE,SECTIONMNT
773	ELECTR DISTRIBUTNG EQUIP	W 7422	35254	W 10173	77372	W 8249	40606	W 6018	32089	EQUIPMT DISTRIBUTION ELECT
7731	INSULATED WIRE,CABLE ETC	W 5614	30465	W 8539	69595	W 5815	32232	W 4324	25871	FILS,CABLES ISOLES ELECT
775	HOUSEHOLD TYPE EQUIP NES	W 46010	327483	W 51062	314836	W 58537	352566	W 71737	401642	MACH,APP USAGE DOMESTQUE
7751	HOUSEHOLD LDRY EQUIP NES	W 12421	61352	W 15106	61715	W 18590	74529	W 19467	78291	MACH A LAVER ET SECHOIRS
77511	DOMESTIC WASHING MACHNES	W 12331	60642	W 14991	60711	W 18456	73626	W 19368	77467	MACH LAVER LINGE MOINS 6 KG
7752	DOM REFRIGERATRS,FREEZRS	W 17033	98339	W 17724	88056	W 19075	94202	W 28047	111219	REFRIG,CONGEL MENAGER
77521	DOMESTIC REFRIGERATORS	W 15710	88207	W 15370	76439	W 16531	81737	W 24245	94272	REFRIGERATEURS
7758	ELECTRO–THERMIC APPL NES	W 10419	99305	W 10775	92113	W 12088	103969	W 13513	121434	APP ELECTROTHERMIQ NDA
77586	ELECTROTHERM DOM APP NES	W 5338	55259	W 5549	54516	W 7022	65312	W 8050	74981	APP ELECTRO THERMIQUES
778	ELECTRICAL MACHINERY NES	W 27983	241407	W 29109	211011	W 35806	221735	W 38628	252958	AUTRES MACH ELECT NDA
7788	OTH ELEC MACHY,EQUIP NES	W 8319	83302	W 9810	75012	W 12323	72342	W 10958	70776	AUT MACH APP ELEC NDA
78	ROAD VEHICLES		3113815		2351945		1704580		2216232	VEHICULES ROUTIERS
781	PASS MOTOR VEH EXC BUSES	W 191508	2031103	W 152553	1544185	W 102238	992297	W 121221	1278975	AUTO TRANSPORT PERSONNES
782	LORRIES,SPCL MTR VEH NES	W 121988	450679	W 76914	249113	W 52555	164503	W 65399	250081	VEHICULES SPECIAUX,MARCH
7821	LORRIES,TRUCKS	W 108651	395405	W 66770	208534	W 47631	146895	W 57372	225150	VEHICULES TRANSP MARCHAND
783	ROAD MOTOR VEHICLES NES	W 21217	96630	W 11979	42346	W 9829	34046	W 12308	57769	VEHICULES ROUTIERS NDA
784	MOTOR VEH PRTS,ACCES NES	W 61505	379042	W 55548	377520	W 56986	376600	W 70347	461568	PIECES 722,781,782,783
7849	OTHER MOTOR VEHCL PARTS	W 59642	368424	W 54455	367494	W 55132	363030	W 67424	451829	PIECES 722,781,782,783
785	CYCLES,ETC MOTRZD OR NOT	W 17339	121245	W 16318	114708	W 15792	115981	W 16366	141302	MOTOCYCLES SCOOTERS
7851	MOTORCYCLES ETC	W 12389	87324	W 11023	79781	W 9812	78000	W 9894	96366	MOTO VELO MOTEUR AUXIL
79	OTHR TRANSPORT EQUIPMENT		1001089		1703684		739072		562588	AUTRE MATERIEL TRANSPORT
792	AIRCRAFT ETC	W 757	165833	W 684	257414	W 445	119597	W 506	101159	APP NAVIGATION AERIENNE
7924	AIRCRFT NES OVER 15000KG	W 55	5324	W 239	151454	W 76	28967	W 33	32067	AERODYNES PLUS 15000 KG
7929	AIRCRAFT PARTS NES	W 599	127448	W 319	68796	W 245	60823	W 251	53848	PIECES DU 792
793	SHIPS AND BOATS ETC	W 26642	820141		1433942	W 9076	603750	W 4647	429646	NAVIRES BATEAUX,ETC
7932	SHIPS AND BOATS NES	W 15327	811995	W 16841	1429126	W 4597	599680	W 3607	425212	NAVIRES ET BATEAUX
79322	TANKERS OF ALL KINDS	W 6876	280267	W 9518	484076	W 557	193637	W 125	90925	BATEAUX–CITERNES
79323	OTHER CARGO VESSELS	W 5501	484652	W 3893	896865	W 2210	376578	W 1544	303573	AUT BATEAUX TRANS MARCH
8	MISC MANUFACTURED GOODS		2337113		2168536		2452601		3384875	ART MANUFACTURES DIVERS
812	*PLUMBG,HEATNG,LGHTNG EQ	W 29492	100905	W 30285	90188	W 31478	98146	W 44584	120534	APPAR SANITAIRES CHAUFFAGE
821	*FURNITURE,PARTS THEREOF	W 24678	146293	W 27232	127508	W 30144	140279	W 55057	196440	MEUBLES ET PIECES
8219	FURNITURE AND PARTS NES	W 17349	93601	W 19122	79219	W 20218	86174	W 44608	125686	AUTRES MEUBLES ET PIECES
82192	WOOD FURNITURE NES	W 10551	58405	W 11744	49513	W 13385	59450	W 27105	82235	MEUBLES NDA EN BOIS
84	CLOTHING AND ACCESSORIES		567002		533699		615774		794061	VETEMENTS
842	MENS OUTERWEAR NOT KNIT	W 2274	102732	W 3229	103941	W 4175	107070	W 4328	130454	VET DESSUS POUR HOMMES
843	WOMENS OUTERWEAR NONKNIT	W 3295	144327	W 3140	122130	W 3866	137137	W 4600	174129	VET DESSUS FEMMES MAT TEX
845	OUTERWEAR KNIT NONELASTC	W 3117	107833	W 3823	107373	W 3844	121333	W 5600	164545	VET DESSOUS,ACCES BONNET
8459	— OTHER,CLTHG ACCESRYS	W 2172	66409	W 2514	57950	W 2434	68955	W 3509	97549	AUT VET DESSUS DE BONNE
846	UNDER GARMENTS KNITTED	W 3712	95865	W 3356	76878	W 4210	95542	W 4466	121730	SOUS VETS DE BONNETERIE
848	HEADGEAR,NONTXTL CLOTHNG	W 2908	51468	W 3635	53838	W 4087	72848	W 4625	98039	VET ACCES MAT AUT QUE TEX
851	*FOOTWEAR	W 10188	144464	W 10896	138510	W 13592	161985	W 13292	198413	CHAUSSURES
85102	FOOTWEAR LEATHER	W 7182	117906	W 8014	112142	W 10553	129579	W 9824	159300	CHAUS SEMELLES EN CUIR
87	PRECISION INSTRUMNTS NES		332591		278517		282785		336738	INSTRUM,APPAR SCIENT NDA
872	MEDICAL INSTRUMENTS NES	W 2866	124200	W 2866	115484	W 6897	119876	W 4756	146907	INSTR,APP MEDIC–CHIR NDA
87202	OTH MEDICAL INSTRUMENTS	W 2654	115036	W 2639	107767	W 6635	111462	W 4431	136621	INSTRUM,APP MEDECINE
874	MEASURNG,CONTROLNG INSTR	W 3141	181504	W 3078	142461	W 3806	145441		170195	INSTRUMENTS DE MESURE
88	PHOTO EQU,OPTICL GDS ETC		218272		201558		215908		684347	APP,FOURN PHOTO,OP,MONTR
882	PHOTO,CINEMA SUPPLIES	W 6997	77208	W 7168	75136	W 7369	80273		533112	PRODUITS PHOTO,CINEMA
8822	PHOTO FILM EXC DEV CINMA	W 4411	67068	W 4367	64483	W 4468	69071		519456	PLAQUES,PELLICULES,FILMS
88222	PHOTO FILM ROLL UNEXPOSD	W 362	18258	W 514	21162	W 612	24480		451249	PEL SENSIB PERF OU NON
885	WATCHES AND CLOCKS		64310		56616		64966		72589	HORLOGERIE
89	MISC MANUFCTRD GOODS NES		793695		769233		903803		1013474	ART MANUFACTURES DIVERS
892	PRINTED MATTER	W 9596	92547	W 12129	96545	W 14296	113541	W 14160	122302	IMPRIMES
893	ARTICLES OF PLASTIC NES		228217		190350		217974		280051	OUVRAGES EN MAT DIVIS 58
8939	MISC PLASTIC ARTICLES	W 29515	168061	W 30247	136845	W 33759	144492	W 84801	193259	ART DIVERS EN MAT DIV 58
89399	OTHR PLASTC ARTICLES NES	W 21564	147614	W 23033	120457	W 26728	126882	W 76580	173456	AUT OUV MAT DIV 58
894	TOYS,SPORTING GOODS,ETC	W 17180	161458	W 19508	176227	W 24224	232027	W 27334	236213	VOITURES ENFANTS,JOUETS
8942	TOYS,INDOOR GAMES ETC	W 13785	123816	W 15296	137471	W 20258	194416	W 22924	192836	JOUETS,JEUX ETC
89424	INDOOR GAME EQUIPMENT	W 4280	42383	W 4225	49155	W 7953	112017	W 7762	91496	ART,JEUX DE SOCIETE
898	MUSICAL INSTRUMENTS,PTS	W 3822	90082	W 4467	102062	W 6776	111418	W 9972	123355	INSTRUMENTS DE MUSIQUE
8983	SOUND RECRDNG TAPE,DISCS	W 3056	75586	W 3604	88142	W 5843	99313	W 7421	106934	SUPPORTS SON POUR 763
89832	RECORDED DISCS,TAPES ETC	W 873	48840	W 991	60366	W 2976	70288	W 2411	77459	DISQUES,PHONO,BANDES
899	OTHER MANUFACTURED GOODS		143334		125225		130465		137798	AUT ART MANUF DIVERS NDA
9	GOODS NOT CLASSD BY KIND		158080		138825		188586		178018	ART TRANSACT NON CLASSES
911	*MAIL NOT CLASSED BY KIN		124580		94122					COLIS POSTAUX
931	*SPECIAL TRANSACTIONS						143548	W 246498	127887	TRANS.SPECIALES

5. Special Exports F.O.B. by Commodities according to the S.I.T.C. (Rev. 2) in thousand U.S. Dollars
Exportations Spéciales F.O.B. par Produits d'après la C.T.C.I. (Rév. 2) en milliers de Dollars E.U.

SITC CTCI	COMMODITY	1992 WEIGHT POIDS	1992 VALUE VALEUR	1993 WEIGHT POIDS	1993 VALUE VALEUR	1994 WEIGHT POIDS	1994 VALUE VALEUR	1995 WEIGHT POIDS	1995 VALUE VALEUR	PRODUIT
	ALL COMMODITIES		9838273		8783720		9398984		10954635	TOUS PRODUITS
0	FOOD AND LIVE ANIMALS		2084459		1736704		1887954		1985244	ALIMENTS,ANIMAUX VIVANTS
01	MEAT AND PREPARATIONS		31077		33515		56138		51145	VIANDES ET PREPARATIONS
014	MEAT PREPD,PRSVD,NES ETC	W 3109	21304	W 4982	16660	W 6561	31545	W 7915	27258	CONSERVES DE VIANDES
02	DAIRY PRODCTS,BIRDS'EGGS		82162		78587		96543		112740	PRODUITS LAITIERS,OEUFS
024	CHEESE AND CURD	W 12889	63995	W 12540	62835	W 13757	78949	W 16078	92869	FROMAGE ET CAILLEBOTTE
03	FISH AND PREPARATIONS		115940		134743		152888		174919	POISSONS ET PREPARATIONS
034	FISH,FRESH,CHILLED,FROZN	W 5682	53841	W 9690	75680	W 14647	105119	W 15693	117325	POISSON FRAIS, REFRIG,CONG
0341	FISH FRSH,CHLLD,EX FILLT	W 4839	51143	W 8742	71636	W 13063	96565	W 13744	105570	POISSON FRAIS,REFRIGERE
037	FISH ETC PREPD,PRSVD NES	W 3561	26762	W 3699	27051	W 3905	24087	W 4166	27021	POIS,CRUST,MOL PREPARES
04	CEREALS AND PREPARATIONS		480276		282944		325980		215263	CEREALES ET PRODUITS
041	WHEAT ETC UNMILLED	W 992488	268525	W 647713	160008	W 952736	172270	W 334765	88969	FROMENT,EPEAUTRE
0411	DURUM WHEAT UNMILLED	W 988869	267496	W 623417	154892	W 929765	168086	W 334713	88943	FROMENT DUR NON MOULU
042	RICE	W 19495	8136	W 52592	24400	W 83712	38438	W 117383	58965	RIZ
0421	RICE IN HUSK OR HUSKED	W 12188	5753	W 46843	22381	W 76590	35775	W 108659	54515	RIZ SANS AUTRE PREPARATION
04211	RICE IN THE HUSK	W 12101	5672	W 46373	22160	W 76162	35625	W 108622	54471	RIZ PADDY
044	MAIZE UNMILLED	W 667458	156275	W 141149	21659	W 285606	41050	W 16002	2838	MAIS NON MOULU
048	CEREAL ETC PREPARATIONS	W 22373	38298	W 107916	60451	W 80700	56333	W 45772	55831	PREPTNS A BASE CEREALES
0484	BAKERY PRODUCTS	W 9567	27634	W 9522	28277	W 11608	32860	W 12383	32298	PRODUITS DE BOULANGERIE
05	VEGETABLES AND FRUIT		1251304		1049282		1125065		1275140	LEGUMES ET FRUITS
054	VEG ETC FRSH,SMPLY PRSVD	W 291368	220029	W 281546	197833	W 256048	218212	W 254006	260301	LEGUMES FRAIS,CONG,SECS
0545	OTHER FRESH VEGETABLES	W 75744	61964	W 56396	55022	W 64770	74294	W 56304	100533	AUTRES LEGUMES FRAIS,REF
05459	FRESH VEGETABLES NES	W 75086	61063	W 55177	53746	W 60277	72536	W 52698	99652	LEGUMES FRAIS,REFRI NDA
0546	VEGETABLES SIMPLY PRESVD	W 168318	140686	W 191741	131145	W 168661	131260	W 147403	137903	LEGUMES CONG,CONSER
05461	VEGETABLES FROZEN	W 167191	139592	W 190350	129823	W 167931	130265	W 146802	136791	LEGUMES CONGELES
056	VEGTBLES ETC PRSVD,PREPD	W 89413	147330	W 84054	120921	W 95051	128567	W 82797	132553	CONSERVES DE LEGUMES
0565	VEGTBLES PRSVD,PREPD NES	W 87984	144350	W 83656	120292	W 94275	127263	W 81009	130363	LEGUMES PREPARES CONSERVE
05659	OTH VEG PRESVD,PREPD NES	W 61303	118550	W 60334	97876	W 64947	100983	W 56471	106276	LEGUM PREPAP,CONSERV NDA
057	FRUIT,NUTS,FRESH,DRIED	W 887359	488601	W 888705	388772	W 1106738	461681	'W 848027	482553	FRUITS FRAIS OU SECS
0571	ORANGES, MANDARINS ETC	W 404948	117116	W 438376	102375	W 572836	135473	W 281555	86074	ORANGES,MAND,CLEMENTINES
05711	ORANGES,FRESH OR DRIED	W 389279	110253	W 420949	96058	W 555155	128570	W 263072	74889	ORANGES FRAICHES,SECHEES
0575	GRAPES FRESH OR DRIED	W 201375	214698	W 144535	131874	W 167655	151387	W 172882	194688	RAISINS FRAIS OU SECS
05751	GRAPES FRESH	W 128082	80695	W 74142	48647	W 102784	78979	W 111916	108059	RAISINS FRAIS
05752	GRAPES DRIED(RAISINS)	W 73293	134004	W 70393	83227	W 64872	72408	W 60966	86628	RAISINS SECS
0579	FRUIT FRESH OR DRIED NES	W 238348	107877	W 200702	96404	W 244533	112815	W 293422	135032	FRUITS FRAIS,SECS NDA
05793	STONE FRUIT FRESH NES	W 80846	58577	W 73646	55417	W 83322	63139	W 92382	83614	FRUITS A NOYAU NDA FRAIS
05798	OTHER FRESH FRUIT	W 156709	48461	W 126650	40451	W 160191	48749	W 199601	50114	AUTRES FRUITS FRAIS
058	FRUIT PRESERVED,PREPARED	W 479671	395345	W 460897	341757	W 459976	316604	W 480606	399733	CONSERVES DE FRUITS
0589	FRUIT PREPRD,PRESRVD,NES	W 409574	337011	W 404511	292765	W 410523	274829	W 413111	333408	FRUITS PREPARES CONSERV
05899	FRUIT,NUTS NES,PRESERVED	W 407353	332155	W 401947	287815	W 406944	267457	W 407274	320975	FRUITS PREP CONSERV NDA
07	COFFEE,TEA,COCOA,SPICES		21806		46644		54710		62450	CAFE,THE,CACAO,EPICES
081	*FEEDING STUFF FOR ANIML	W 210742	38568	W 226067	53462	W 85214	15211	W 91985	18537	NOURRITURE POUR ANIMAUX
0819	FOOD WASTE AND FEED NES	W 135774	24475	W 132251	27670	W 38967	5699	W 19215	5351	DECHETS,ALIMENTS NDA
08199	FODDER NES,INCL SWEETNED	W 77167	16096	W 124986	27024	W 18693	4933	W 9025	3826	PREPARATIONS FOURRAGERES
09	MISC EDIBLE PRODUCTS		38153		38620		41994		54035	PREP ALIMENTAIRES DIVERSES
098	EDIBLE PRODCTS,PREPS NES	W 16298	37243	W 17495	36884	W 18221	40457	W 20032	47218	PREP ALIMENTAIRES NDA
09809	MISC FOOD PREPRTIONS NES	W 14766	35359	W 15335	34449	W 14837	37578	W 14372	42708	PREP ALIMENTAIRES NDA
1	BEVERAGES AND TOBACCO		650564		550161		516682		615378	BOISSONS ET TABACS
11	BEVERAGES		141209		144029		174507		210475	BOISSONS
111	NON-ALCOHL BEVERAGES NES	W 64927	10674	W 90821	29813	W 131831	36162	W 95967	19702	BOISSONS NON ALCOOLIQUES
11102	FLAVORED WATERS NON-ALCO	W 17302	8624	W 50009	28652	W 63252	33860	W 29912	16944	LIMONADES,EAUX GAZEUSES
112	ALCOHOLIC BEVERAGES	W 102077	130535	W 105822	114216	W 141778	138345	W 152349	190773	BOISSONS ALCOOLIQUES
1121	WINE OF FRESH GRAPES ETC	W 68096	78073	W 55237	60909	W 65920	62179	W 66237	80577	VINS DE RAISINS FRAIS
11212	WINE OF FRESH GRAPES	W 67011	77728	W 53010	60378	W 54694	58836	W 60580	78071	VINS DE MOUTS DE RAISINS
1124	DISTILLED ALCOHOLIC BEVS	W 25947	46822	W 25967	38619	W 31753	52907	W 58594	87207	ALCOOLS,EAUX-DE-VIE
11242	DISTILLD WINE,GRAPE MARC	W 8431	22214	W 6019	13426	W 11091	25584	W 19504	34575	EAUX-DE-VIE NATURELLES
11249	OTH ALCOHOLC BEVS,CMPNDS	W 17320	23659	W 19451	23653	W 19957	24381	W 38684	49440	BOISSONS ALCOOLIQUES NDA
12	TOBACCO AND MANUFACTURES		509355		406132		342175		404903	TABACS BRUTS FABRIQUES
121	TOBACCO UNMNFCTRD,REFUSE	W 118693	394002	W 119062	349609	W 106195	292489	W 121408	308832	TABACS BRUTS,DECHETS
1211	TOBACCO,NOT STRIPPED	W 84805	323829	W 101513	317054	W 68103	235700	W 88952	263931	TABACS NON ECOTES
1212	TOBACCO STRIPPED OR PART	W 28597	67778	W 13171	30555	W 31239	53462	W 26202	42118	TABACS PART ECOTES
122	TOBACCO,MANUFACTURED	W 17824	115353	W 8012	56523	W 7046	49686	W 13420	96071	TABACS FABRIQUES
1222	CIGARETTES	W 17815	115271	W 8001	56413	W 7044	49666	W 13399	95914	CIGARETTES
2	CRUDE MATERLS,EXCL FUELS		425197		506245		601227		777566	MAT BRUTES NON COMESTIBLES
21	HIDES,SKINS,FURS UNDRSSD		29260		20788		28912		37466	CUIRS,PEAUX BRUTS
211	HIDES,SKINS,EXC FURS,RAW	W 8786	28901	W 6676	20542	W 6831	28465	W 6716	35728	CUIRS ET PEAUX
24	CORK AND WOOD		27322		33722		23496		16934	LIEGE ET BOIS
26	TEXTILE FIBRES AND WASTE		123026		215563		295839		408631	FIBRES TEXTILES
263	COTTON	W 96049	110664	W 199816	204868	W 209325	283243	W 211894	394798	COTON
2631	RAW COTTON,EXCL LINTERS	W 71916	92909	W 176602	190944	W 187534	264142	W 191246	370659	COTON EN MASSE
27	CRUDE FERTLZR,MINRLS NES		93275		95944		107178		128619	ENGRAIS MINERAUX BRUTS
273	STONE,SAND AND GRAVEL	W 136565	25700	W 167303	27860	W 163185	27408	W 130482	26842	PIERRES,SABLES,GRAVIERS
278	OTHER CRUDE MINERALS	W 752747	57935	W 672936	58770	W 743080	70902	W 971075	92189	AUTRES MINERAUX BRUTS
2782	REFRACTORY MINERALS NES	W 331118	34482	W 219436	24861	W 284230	31737	W 350892	38150	ARGILE MINERAUX REFRACTAIRES
27824	MAGNESITE, ETC	W 194730	31860	W 155932	23280	W 196140	28733	W 205972	32364	CARBONATE DE MAGNESIUM
28	METALLIFEROUS ORES,SCRAP		119992		107251		107362		136424	MINERAIS METAL,DECHETS
287	BASE METAL ORES,CONC NES	W 1377206	104033	W 1202421	92933	W 1058984	72384	W 1170197	106205	MINERAIS METAUX COMMUNS
2873	ALUMINIUM ORES,ALUMINA	W 1299323	84612	W 1102182	70469	W 1031282	65883	W 1122330	97142	MINERAIS D'ALUMINIUM
28731	ALUMINIUM ORE,CONCNTRATE	W 965679	27028	W 861487	27132	W 740851	23037	W 777455	25629	MINERAIS D'ALUMINIUM
28732	ALUMINA(ALUMINIUM OXIDE)	W 333644	57584	W 240695	43336	W 290431	42846	W 344875	71512	ALUMINE (OXYDE ALUMINIUM)
3	MINERAL FUELS ETC		518656		688469		972070		713490	COMBUSTIBLES MINERAUX LUB
33	PETROLEUM AND PRODUCTS		508077		673812		962304		700218	PETROLE ET DERIVES
333	CRUDE PETROLEUM	W 533213	53082	W 536142	59077	W 269997	26505	W 517877	50125	HUILES BRUTES DE PETROLE
334	PETROLEUM PRODUCTS,REFIN	W 2856393	453353	W 4341086	610639	W 7037736	932868	W 4386648	648571	PRODUITS RAFFINES
3341	GASOLINE,OTH LIGHT OILS	W 2856073	452928	W 4340873	610371	W 1798674	284184	W 1297558	210075	ESSENCES POUR MOTEURS
33411	MOTOR,AVIATION SPIRIT					W 577017	103731	W 370937	62172	ESSENCES MOTEURS D'AVIONS
33419	OTH LIGHT PETROLEUM OILS	W 2856073	452928	W 4340873	610371	W 1221656	180452	W 926601	147884	AUTRES HUILES LEGERES
3342	KEROSENE,OTH MEDIUM OILS					W 746201	117894	W 477715	78227	PETR LAMPANTS,AUT HUIL
33421	KEROSENE INCL JET FUEL					W 745892	117667	W 476338	76845	PETROLES LAMPANTS
3343	GAS OILS					W 1139179	186226	W 719434	113136	GAS OILS
3344	FUEL OILS,NES					W 3124539	254377	W 1734834	169742	FUEL OILS
3345	LUBS,PETROLEUM OILS NES	W 320	425	W 213	268	W 229144	90187	W 157107	77391	HUILES LUBRIFIANTES
33451	LUBS(HIGH PETR CONT) ETC					W 228982	89989	W 156960	76965	HUILES LUBRIF,H LOURDES
4	ANIMAL,VEGETABLE OIL,FAT		550527		314171		345017		605487	HUILES,GRAISSES ANIM,VEG
42	FIXED VEGETABLE OIL,FAT		548663		313426		344247		604071	HUILES VEGETALES FIXES
423	FIXED VEG OILS,SOFT	W 223763	548546	W 159333	312745	W 145462	343902	W 214200	598445	HUILES VEGET DOUCES FIXES
4235	OLIVE OIL	W 209296	538950	W 125962	291761	W 123168	327814	W 183750	574419	HUILE D'OLIVE
5	CHEMCLS,RELATED PROD NES		336653		378170		366067		481848	PRODUITS CHIMIQUES
51	ORGANIC CHEMICALS		28205		48311		50143		32074	PROD CHIMIQ ORGANIQUES
511	HYDROCARBONS NES,DERIVS	W 43563	20472	W 83290	39032	W 70517	29553	W 25036	19766	HYDROCARBURES NDA
5113	HALOG DERIV OF HYDROCARB	W 43525	20429	W 83155	38886	W 70350	29421	W 24521	19513	DERIVES HALOGENES HYDROCAR

5. Special Exports F.O.B. by Commodities according to the S.I.T.C. (Rev. 2) in thousand U.S. Dollars
Exportations Spéciales F.O.B. par Produits d'après la C.T.C.I. (Rév. 2) en milliers de Dollars E.U.

SITC CTCI	COMMODITY	1992 WEIGHT POIDS	1992 VALUE VALEUR	1993 WEIGHT POIDS	1993 VALUE VALEUR	1994 WEIGHT POIDS	1994 VALUE VALEUR	1995 WEIGHT POIDS	1995 VALUE VALEUR	PRODUIT
51139	OTH HALOG HYDRCARB DERIV	W 43525	20429	W 83155	38886	W 70343	29415	W 24489	19486	AUTRE DERIVES HALOGENES
52	INORGANIC CHEMICALS		9932		29674		12035		20489	PROD CHIM INORGANIQUES
53	DYES,TANNING,COLOUR PROD		50907		43346		45395		56387	PROD TEINTURE,COLORANTS
541	*MEDICINAL,PHARM PRODUCT	K 1373330	40111	K 1690079	73671	K 2037372	73679	K 2191430	77803	PROD MEDICINAUX PHARMACEUT
5417	MEDICAMENTS	K 1053531	37039	K 1279367	68152	K 1931476	71935	K 1971443	68558	MEDICAMENTS
55	PERFUME,CLEANING ETC PRD		39151		50746		50577		65101	PROD POUR PARFUM,TOILETTE
553	PERFUMERY,COSMETICS,ETC	W 8093	23404	W 9495	25761	W 7794	23805	W 9090	35444	PRODUITS DE PARFUMERIE
562	*FERTILIZERS,MANUFACTURE	W 358551	44363	W 277637	33505	W 153046	17611	W 421577	68251	ENGRAIS MANUFACTURES
5629	FERTILIZERS NES	W 142158	23701	W 155427	24124	W 91799	12410	W 198775	36649	ENGRAIS NDA
58	PLASTIC MATERIALS ETC		75724		51458		61630		82263	MAT PLAST ARTIFICIELLES
583	POLYMERIZATION ETC PRODS	W 44718	70577	W 37890	43978	W 42321	52385	W 43174	69247	PROD POLYMERISATION
5834	POLYVINYL CHLORIDE	W 25449	39872	W 18555	12479	W 18568	14685	W 18028	18015	CHLORURE DE POLYVINYLE
58341	— IN PRIMARY FORMS	W 22959	34898	W 17136	9750	W 17572	13910	W 17431	16553	SOUS FORMES PRIMAIRES
59	CHEMICAL MATERIALS NES		47312		45417		52914		78628	MAT PROD CHIMIQUES NDA
598	MISCEL CHEM PRODUCTS NES	W 563603	39576	W 512765	35391	W 514199	40200	W 702397	58770	PROD DIV INDUST CHIM NDA
5989	CHEM PRODUCTS,PREPS NES	W 559028	35059	W 508942	31176	W 510436	35559	W 698773	53713	PROD PREP CHIMIQUES NDA
59892	ACTIVTED NAT MINRL PROD	W 554197	29189	W 504186	26484	W 502268	27135	W 690060	41452	CHARBONS ACTIVES
6	BASIC MANUFACTURES		2098457		1739401		1917522		2325493	ART MANUFACTURES
61	LEATHER,DRESSED FUR,ETC		103789		62272		59963		55262	CUIRS,PELLETERIES
613	FUR SKINS TANNED,DRESSED	W 751	74128	W 362	33478	W 346	33096	W 389	29006	PELLETERIES
62	RUBBER MANUFACTURES NES		30640		33788		42050		57370	CAOUTCHOUC MANUFACTURE
63	WOOD,CORK MANUFACTRS NES		35150		36519		39231		46507	OUVRAGES LIEGE ET BOIS
634	VENEERS,PLYWOOD,ETC	W 33484	31249	W 35872	31631	W 41127	32324	W 52428	41542	PLACAGES,CONTRE–PLAQUES
64	PAPER,PAPERBOARD AND MFR		62091		56919		60291		92651	PAPIERS,CARTONS & OUVRAGES
641	PAPER AND PAPERBOARD	W 47873	38507	W 41273	32581	W 51405	34014	W 59046	49689	PAPIERS ET CARTONS
642	PAPER,ETC,PRECUT,ARTS OF	W 10842	23584	W 10293	24338	W 12295	26277	W 16778	42961	PAP,CARTONS DECOUPES
65	TEXTILE YARN,FABRICS,ETC		520027		446036		430671		520782	FILS,TISSUS,ARTICLES TEXTILE
651	TEXTILE YARN	W 58900	274315	W 55629	221893	W 50566	210837	W 52188	265103	FILS TEXTILES
6513	COTTON YARN	W 47014	208951	W 40337	153892	W 35334	145900	W 38522	182185	FILS DE COTON
6517	REGEN FIBRE YARN,MONOFIL	W 5569	33021	W 4758	31814	W 4132	25847	W 4611	38446	FILS TEXT ART NON VENTE DT
65171	CONT VISCOSE RAYON YARN	W 5555	32930	W 4739	31738	W 4082	25633	W 4604	38391	FILS RAY,VIS NON VENTE DET
652	COTTON FABRICS,WOVEN	W 12463	67658	W 10824	56405	W 13820	69750	W 13801	76611	TISSUS DE COTON
6522	WOVEN COTTON BLEACHD,ETC	W 9737	55643	W 8816	47397	W 10510	53244	W 9884	55323	TISSUS COTON BLANCHIS ETC
65224	BLCHED COTTON FABRIC NES	W 8609	47788	W 8736	46496	W 10430	52402	W 9776	53974	AUT TIS PLUS 85% COT BLANCHI
655	KNITTED,ETC FABRICS	W 3857	33223	W 3574	25721	W 3344	26588	W 4136	36326	ETOF BONNETERIE PIECES ETC
6552	OTHER KNIT ETC FAB NONEL	W 3857	33223	W 3574	25721	W 3344	26588	W 4136	36326	ETOF BON NON ELAS NON SYNT
658	TEXTILE ARTICLES NES	W 9958	81291	W 9922	77491	W 7923	57565	W 8480	71969	ART FACONNES MAT TEXTILES
6589	OTH TEXTILE ARTICLES NES	W 6406	58991	W 6204	54012	W 4535	36200	W 4826	45641	AUT ART EN TEXTILES NDA
65898	KNITTED ETC ARTICLES NES	W 6396	58780	W 6121	53700	W 4517	36073	W 4811	45497	ART BONNET NON ELASTIQUE
659	FLOOR COVERINGS,ETC	W 6646	32310	W 6808	31424	W 6658	28711	W 5904	28388	COUVRE–PARQUETS,TAPIS ETC
66	NONMETAL MINERAL MFS NES		414235		372221		442198		423068	ART MIN NON METALLIQUES
661	LIME,CEMENT,BLDG PRODS	W 7203627	352315	W 6420649	319559	W 7933680	373185	W 6850244	336680	CHAUX,CIMENTS MAT CONSTR
6612	CEMENT	W 7001714	235743	W 6211757	205558	W 7713873	268941	W 6647568	232836	CIMENTS HYDRAULIQUES
6613	BUILDING STONE ETC WORKD	W 196078	113139	W 200813	110050	W 208283	99543	W 188189	97856	PIERRES A BATIR
66132	BUILDING STONE WORKED	W 195696	113061	W 200406	109963	W 207616	99360	W 187571	97696	OUVR EN PIERRES DE TAILLE
67	IRON AND STEEL		402534		225973		282666		353637	FER ET ACIER
672	IRON,STEEL PRIMARY FORMS	W 288583	98044	W 243634	63356	W 243133	75540	W 225883	82204	LINGOTS FER,ACIER
6727	IRN,STL COIL FR REROLLNG	W 264359	93212	W 178223	48189	W 228352	72219	W 205869	77408	EBAUCHES POUR TOLES FER
67271	IRON,SIMPLE STEEL COILS	W 264358	93209	W 178221	48187	W 228339	72184	W 205866	77407	EBAUCHES NON EN ACIER
673	IRON,STEEL SHAPES ETC	W 56923	15388	W 90701	38955	W 52198	14810	W 56183	18777	BARRES,PROFIL FER,ACIER
6732	IRON,STEEL BARS ETC	W 55541	14507	W 70561	33115	W 50098	13793	W 52465	16830	BARRES FER,ACIER
67326	IRN,OTH STL BARS HOTROLD	W 55461	14387	W 70488	33035	W 49180	13375	W 47674	14970	BARRES PLEINES FER,ACIER
674	IRN,STL UNIV,PLATE,SHEET	W 413024	226635		83329	W 282888	150441	W 329068	209281	LARGES PLATS,TOLES
6746	IRN,STL THIN PLATE,ROLLD	W 143841	59399	W 61489	23713	W 125811	59443	W 112647	62775	TOLES LAM MOINS 3MM
67461	— OF IRON OR SIMPLE STL	W 143805	59329	W 61290	23339	W 125575	58998	W 112574	62634	TOL NON AC FIN MOINS 3 MM
6747	TINNED PLATES,SHEETS	W 96826	63514	W 17278	11363	W 49502	29547	W 90087	64230	TOLES ETAMEES EN ACIER
6749	OTH IRN,STL PLATES,SHEET	W 168801	101947	W 59500	35079	W 103651	59801	W 101299	72369	AUTRES TOLES FER,ACIER
67491	— OF IRON OR SIMPLE STL	W 168688	101553	W 59119	34777	W 103537	59558	W 100817	71654	AUT TOLES AUTRES ACIER FIN
678	IRON,STL TUBES,PIPES,ETC	W 90335	44668	W 56133	27895	W 27771	17233	W 43951	29480	TUBES,TUYAUX EN FONTE,FER
6783	IRON,STL TUBES,PIPES NES	W 89484	42719	W 54262	24422	W 26383	13748	W 38296	22756	AUT TUBES,TUYAUX FER,ACIER
68	NON–FERROUS METALS		406517		367758		419285		598281	METAUX NON FERREUX
682	COPPER EXC CEMENT COPPER	W 30640	93720	W 38152	94475	W 33003	95857	W 43981	159069	CUIVRE
6822	COPPER,ALLOYS WORKED	W 29124	90136	W 38130	94432	W 32811	95470	W 43637	158479	CUIVRE,ALLIAGES OUVRES
68221	COPPER BARS,WIRE,ETC	W 9067	22370	W 20980	44250	W 8989	20121	W 13583	39727	BARRES,PROFILES ET FILS
68222	COPPER PLATE,SHEET,STRIP	W 6395	19453	W 6480	16382	W 9847	29429	W 12667	47006	TOLES DE PLUS 0.15 MM
68225	COPPER TUBES,PIPES,ETC	W 13327	45741	W 10468	32426	W 13793	44767	W 17260	70836	TUBES,TUYAUX EN CUIVRE
684	ALUMINIUM	W 154691	311814	W 148409	269490	W 159189	322747	W 155802	436283	ALUMINIUM
6841	ALUMINIUM,ALLOYS,UNWRGHT	W 69813	107958	W 72851	100089	W 52975	78675	W 49311	103444	ALUMINIUM,ALLIAGES BRUTS
6842	ALUMINIUM,ALLOYS WORKED	W 84878	203856	W 75558	169402	W 106214	244072	W 106490	332839	ALUMINIUM,ALLIAGES OUVRE
68421	ALUMINIUM BARS,WIRE,ETC	W 21723	54036	W 19730	49885	W 24850	65716	W 25756	95272	BARRES,PROFILES FILS ALU
68422	ALUMNM PLATE,SHEET,STRIP	W 32447	69508	W 32352	64415	W 52110	108942	W 52671	146527	TOLES, PLANCHES EN ALU
68423	ALUMINIUM FOIL	W 23603	63647	W 20160	47664	W 22856	54049	W 24425	77513	FEUILLES,BANDES MINCES AL
69	METAL MANUFACTURES NES		123473		137916		141168		177935	ART MANUFACT EN METAL NDA
692	METAL TANKS,BOXES,ETC	W 8560	30305	W 7323	25412	W 9096	27714	W 10393	43140	RECIPIENTS METALLIQUES
6924	MTL TRANSPORT BOXES ETC	W 8122	28896	W 5103	24784	W 8340	27125	W 9508	41449	FUTS,TAMBOURS,BIDONS
697	BASE MTL HOUSEHOLD EQUIP	W 4111	31946	W 4287	29923	W 4890	35412	W 3919	31163	ART MENAGE MET COMMUNS
699	BASE METAL MFRS NES	W 7243	28502	W 8399	31216	W 8707	34569	W 9056	40866	ART MANUFACTURES MET NDA
7	MACHINES,TRANSPORT EQUIP		471981		548136		577295		877982	MACHINES MATERIEL TRANSPORT
71	POWER GENERATING EQUIPMT		53328		36904		56944		140911	MACHINES GENERATRICES
713	INTRNL COMBUS PSTN ENGIN	W 4036	35169	W 4014	27756	W 4873	42205	W 6301	55505	MOTEURS EXPL COMB INT, PIECE
7139	PISTON ENGINE PARTS NES	W 3865	33527	W 3820	24552	W 4711	38165	W 6083	52213	PIECES POUR 713.2,3,8
714	ENGINES AND MOTORS NES	W 138	9072	W 45	5790	W 23	7768	W 766	80199	MOTEURS NON ELECTRIQUES
7144	REACTION ENGINES	W 119	3668	W 19	1173	W 11	511	W 748	53034	PROPULSEURS A REACTION
72	MACHS FOR SPCL INDUSTRYS		39355		57469		61798		68108	MAC SPECIALES POUR INDUST
74	GENRL INDUSTRL MACHY NES		57448		58042		66366		104652	MACH APP INDUSTRIE
741	HEATING,COOLING EQUIPMNT	W 2260	17816	W 2871	20531	W 3248	25468	W 5174	48522	MACH CHAUFFAGE,PIECES
76	TELECOMM,SOUND EQUIPMENT		42947		76601		60833		70205	EQUIPMENT DE TELECOM
764	TELECOM EQPT,PTS,ACC NES	W 334	41378		71737	W 573	56457	W 578	65691	EQUIP TELECOM,PIECES
7649	PTS NES OF EQUIPMT OF 76	W 273	36683		68608	W 488	50373	W 499	30783	PIECES DE LA DIV 76
76491	PTS NES OF APPAR OF 7641	W 134	26234	W 235	58574	W 400	46041	W 399	26365	PIECES POUR 764.1
77	ELECTRIC MACHNRY NES ETC		175747		179332		215214		300530	MACH APP ELECT NDA
772	SWITCHGEAR ETC,PARTS NES	W 1377	25018	W 1587	29387	W 2057	31413	W 2993	46469	APP COUPURE,SECT ETC
7721	SWITCHGEAR ETC	W 1368	24515	W 1561	28109	W 2027	29999	W 2954	44316	APP COUPURE,SECTIONMNT
773	ELECTR DISTRIBUTNG EQUIP	W 37462	91979	W 34858	74660	W 42137	91950	W 45848	132084	EQUIPMT DISTRIBUTION ELECT
7731	INSULATED WIRE,CABLE ETC	W 37448	91539	W 34839	73845	W 42096	90305	W 45758	129950	FILS,CABLES ISOLES ELECT
775	HOUSEHOLD TYPE EQUIP NES	W 4406	26512	W 7523	41973	W 11439	60854	W 14575	84422	MACH,APP USAGE DOMESTQUE
7752	DOM REFRIGERATRS,FREEZRS	W 2315	11066	W 3953	19462	W 6762	32455	W 7975	40907	REFRIG,CONGEL MENAGER
78	ROAD VEHICLES		25502		49751		42681		61625	VEHICULES ROUTIERS
79	OTHR TRANSPORT EQUIPMENT		50581		59938		48278		100357	AUTRE MATERIEL TRANSPORT
792	AIRCRAFT ETC		13565		14910	W 71	17308	W 156	69100	APP NAVIGATION AERIENNE
7924	AIRCRFT NES OVER 15000KG		1845		681			W 60	35502	AERODYNES PLUS 15000 KG

5. Special Exports F.O.B. by Commodities according to the S.I.T.C. (Rev. 2) in thousand U.S. Dollars
Exportations Spéciales F.O.B. par Produits d'après la C.T.C.I. (Rév. 2) en milliers de Dollars E.U.

SITC CTCI	COMMODITY	1992 WEIGHT POIDS	1992 VALUE VALEUR	1993 WEIGHT POIDS	1993 VALUE VALEUR	1994 WEIGHT POIDS	1994 VALUE VALEUR	1995 WEIGHT POIDS	1995 VALUE VALEUR	PRODUIT
793	SHIPS AND BOATS ETC	W 12070	36463	W 13617	43596	W 4281	29246	W 9723	30458	NAVIRES BATEAUX,ETC
7932	SHIPS AND BOATS NES	W 11066	33112	W 8187	41099	W 4153	25335	W 9514	26823	NAVIRES ET BATEAUX
79323	OTHER CARGO VESSELS	W 7605	21074	W 6000	31500	W 3650	16371	W 9156	19163	AUT BATEAUX TRANS MARCH
8	MISC MANUFACTURED GOODS		2395058		2146802		1995085		2284836	ART MANUFACTURES DIVERS
821	*FURNITURE,PARTS THEREOF	W 4788	16018	W 9488	29326	W 10641	31131	W 8604	35779	MEUBLES ET PIECES
84	CLOTHING AND ACCESSORIES		2145189		1844001		1670226		1844737	VETEMENTS
842	MENS OUTERWEAR NOT KNIT	W 4762	116820	W 3635	95903	W 3762	93235	W 3044	80975	VET DESSUS POUR HOMMES
8423	— TROUSERS,BREECHES ETC	W 2408	48264	W 2073	39616	W 2287	42910	W 1684	36624	PANTALONS HOMMES MAT TEX
843	WOMENS OUTERWEAR NONKNIT	W 14236	445965	W 10886	373743	W 8717	298944	W 9526	281439	VET DESSUS FEMMES MAT TEX
8431	— COATS AND JACKETS	W 1951	73607	W 1347	58621	W 988	40422	W 783	36043	MANT,VEST FEM MAT TEXTIL
8434	— SKIRTS	W 4261	113166	W 2691	83717	W 2347	65445	W 2065	68123	JUPES EN MAT TEXTILES
8435	— BLOUSES	W 3510	137941	W 2993	124634	W 2467	100610	W 4148	90410	BLOUSES FEM MAT TEXTILES
8439	— OTHER OUTER GARMENTS	W 3874	97093	W 3206	80292	W 2274	67313	W 1905	62387	AUT VET DES FEM MAT TEXT
845	OUTERWEAR KNIT NONELASTC	W 27841	697631	W 23248	591686	W 23368	581214	W 27140	686958	VET DESSOUS,ACCES BONNET
8451	— JERSEYS,PULLOVERS ETC	W 3885	99632	W 5005	117053	W 5273	124107	W 5314	133804	CHANDAILS,PULL–OVERS ETC
8452	— WOMENS DRESSES ETC	W 2751	72590	W 1941	58279	W 2076	58358	W 2389	78729	ROBES,JUPES BONNETERIE
8459	— OTHER,CLTHG ACCESRYS	W 21206	525409	W 16303	416353	W 16020	398749	W 19437	474425	AUT VET DESSUS DE BONNE
846	UNDER GARMENTS KNITTED	W 28190	587818	W 23474	531164	W 20174	480952	W 23154	596882	SOUS VETS DE BONNETERIE
8462	— OF COTTON NON ELASTIC	W 26869	552068	W 21835	482304	W 18836	443035	W 22092	552691	SOUS–VET BONNET COTON
84629	—— OTHER	W 26869	552068	W 21835	482304	W 18836	443035	W 22092	552691	AUT SOUS–VET BONNET COTON
8463	— OF SYNTH FBR NONELAST	W 1269	31178	W 1513	38517	W 1218	27457	W 850	23262	SOUS–VET BONNET FIB SYNT
84631	—— PANTY HOSE (TIGHTS)	W 1074	25717	W 1363	34428	W 953	20414	W 667	17950	COLLANTS BON FIBR SYNT
848	HEADGEAR,NONTXTL CLOTHNG	W 1030	290381	W 947	240356	W 934	199426	W 970	181171	VET ACCES MAT AUT QUE TEX
8483	FUR ETC,CLOTHES,PRODUCTS	W 880	285434	W 806	235377	W 740	193909	W 621	173248	VETEMENTS DE FOURRURE
84831	ARTICLES OF FURSKIN,NES	W 880	285431	W 802	235242	W 737	193756	W 615	173030	PELLETERIES OUVREES NDA
851	*FOOTWEAR	W 2569	41143	W 2768	49627	W 1987	34839	W 1753	38423	CHAUSSURES
85102	FOOTWEAR LEATHER	W 1721	31174	W 1569	32791	W 989	23124	W 1076	27412	CHAUS SEMELLES EN CUIR
87	PRECISION INSTRUMNTS NES		24857		24526		33890		48675	INSTRUM,APPAR SCIENT NDA
89	MISC MANUFCTRD GOODS NES		149357		171857		191717		274955	ART MANUFACTURES DIVERS
892	PRINTED MATTER	W 3283	20229	W 3633	22495	W 3368	22938		65272	IMPRIMES
8928	PRINTED MATTER NES	W 629	4437	W 597	4833	W 583	5102		44772	IMPRIMES NDA
89283	UNISSUED BANKNOTES ETC	W 5	325	W 22	389	W 8	669		39555	TIMBRES–POSTE FISCAUX
893	ARTICLES OF PLASTIC NES		78522		83723		95335		121551	OUVRAGES EN MAT DIVIS 58
8939	MISC PLASTIC ARTICLES	W 19937	68322	W 21750	64710	W 24231	71247	W 28912	100166	ART DIVERS EN MAT DIV 58
89399	OTHR PLASTC ARTICLES NES	W 19787	67488	W 21116	62369	W 23660	68607	W 28256	97012	AUT OUV MAT DIV 58
9	GOODS NOT CLASSD BY KIND		306723		175461		220064		287312	ART TRANSACT NON CLASSES
911	*MAIL NOT CLASSED BY KIN		304374		163185					COLIS POSTAUX
931	*SPECIAL TRANSACTIONS						199640		260026	TRANS.SPECIALES

1. HISTORICAL SERIES, 1961–1996 GENERAL TRADE, IMPORTS C.I.F., EXPORTS F.O.B.
SERIES HISTORIQUES, 1961–1996 COMMERCE GENERAL, IMPORTATIONS C.A.F., EXPORTATIONS F.O.B

YEAR ANNEE	VALUE IN MILLION DANISH KRONER VALEUR EN MILLION DANISH KRONER MERCHANDISE –MARCHANDISE		GOLD –OR		CONVERSION FACTORS U.S. CENTS PER DANISH KRONE FACTEURS DE CONVERSION CENTS E.U. PAR DANISH KRONE		INDEX NUMBERS –INDICES QUANTUM		UNIT VALUE VALEUR UNITAIRE	
	IMPORTS	EXPORTS	IMPORTS	EXPORTS	IMPORTS	EXPORTS	IMPORTS	EXPORTS	IMPORTS	EXPORTS
1961	118.70	58.20			14.4800	14.4800				
1962	153.90	61.80			14.4800	14.4800				
1963	174.10	75.60			14.4800	14.4800				
1964	197.00	72.50			14.4800	14.4800				
1965	234.80	89.80			14.4800	14.4800				
1966	269.00	103.00			14.4800	14.4800				
1967	320.90	91.30			14.3360	14.3360				
1968	360.00	90.00			13.3300	13.3300				
1969	375.00	88.00			13.3300	13.3300				
1970	397.50	105.00			13.3300	13.3300				
1971	452.80	139.00			13.4800	13.4800				
1972	502.70	152.60			14.3330	14.3330				
1973	565.70	191.10			16.5300	16.5300				
1974	633.70	551.10			16.7900	16.7900				
1975	741.90	509.40			17.3900	17.3900				
1976	777.90	516.50			16.5800	16.6500				
1977	964.60	555.20			16.6100	16.5600				
1978	980.30	559.30			18.2730	18.3530				
1979	1447.60	921.20			18.9730	18.9540				
1980	1846.20	1167.60			17.7280	17.7110				
1981	2101.80	1442.20			14.0445	14.0445				
1982	2286.50	1422.30			11.9963	11.9963				
1983	2421.00	1644.70			10.9313	10.9313				
1984	2836.30	1750.60			9.6520	9.6520				
1985	3140.20	1841.80			9.4340	9.4340				
1986	2911.83	2078.46			12.3541	12.3541				
1987	3470.68	2369.48			14.6118	14.6118				
1988	3494.66	2630.63			14.8544	14.8544				
1989	2914.96	3055.94			13.6807	13.6807				
1990	2755.68	2794.69			16.2278	16.2278				
1991	2609.04	2179.20			15.6351	15.6351				
1992	2754.17	2008.60			16.5861	16.5861				
1993	2243.61	2029.66			15.4242	15.4242				
1994	2311.78	1810.72			16.9403	16.9403				
1995	2357.37	2035.42			17.8635	17.8657				
1996	2705.22	2140.93			17.2398	17.2413				

2. IMPORTS BY BROAD ECONOMIC CATEGORY AND EXPORTS BY INDUSTRIAL ORIGIN. (PERCENTAGE OF TOTAL VALUE)
IMPORTATIONS PAR CATEGORIES ECONOMIQUES ET EXPORTATIONS PAR BRANCHE D'ACTIVITE.(EN POURCENTAGE DE LA VALEUR TOTALE)

IMPORTS – IMPORTATIONS

	1990	1991	1992	1993	1994	1995	1996
TOTAL IMPORTS–IMPORTATIONS TOTALES	100.	100.	100.	100.	100.	100.	100.
1 FOOD BEV–ALIMENTATION BOISSONS	15.5	18.4	18.1	15.2	14.2	13.2	13.9
11 PRIMARY–PRODUITS DE BASE	4.8	6.3	7.2	5.5	5.2	4.7	4.2
111 FOR INDUSTRY–POUR L'INDUSTRIE	0.4	0.5	0.4	0.1	0.2	0.2	0.2
112 FOR HOUSEHOLDS–POUR LES MENAGES	4.4	5.8	6.8	5.3	5.0	4.5	3.9
12 PROCESSED–PRODUITS ELABORES	10.8	12.1	11.0	9.7	9.0	8.5	9.7
121 FOR INDUSTRY–POUR L'INDUSTRIE	0.4	0.6	0.5	0.4	0.4	0.3	0.4
122 FOR HOUSEHOLDS–POUR LES MENAGES	10.3	11.5	10.4	9.3	8.6	8.2	9.3
2 IND SUPPLIES–APPROV INDUSTRIELS	19.1	21.2	18.1	21.2	18.5	21.5	18.0
21 PRIMARY–PRODUITS DE BASE	0.7	0.5	0.4	0.4	0.4	0.4	0.4
22 PROCESSED–PRODUITS ELABORES	18.4	20.7	17.7	20.8	18.1	21.1	17.5
3 FUELS–COMBUSTIBLES	11.9	11.9	9.8	11.1	9.8	5.8	9.9
31 PRIMARY–PRODUITS DE BASE	0.1	0.1	0.1	0.2	0.1	0.1	0.1
32 PROCESSED–PRODUITS ELABORES	11.8	11.8	9.7	10.9	9.7	5.7	9.8
321 MOTOR SPIRIT–ESSENCE	11.7	11.8	9.7	10.9			
322 OTHER–AUTRES	0.0	0.0	0.0	0.0	9.7	5.7	9.8
4 MACHINERY–EQUIPEMENT	14.9	13.7	15.5	15.1	15.7	14.1	14.0
41 CAPITAL EQUIPMENT–MACHINES	12.5	11.7	13.8	13.1	13.6	12.1	11.9
42 PARTS–PIECES ACCESSOIRES	2.3	2.0	1.7	2.0	2.2	2.0	2.1
5 TRANSPORT–TRANSPORT	9.4	6.5	12.9	7.0	7.3	10.2	15.5
51 PASSENGER CARS–AUTOMOBILES	0.8	0.7	0.5	0.4	0.4	0.6	0.7
52 OTHER–AUTRES	4.6	2.0	9.0	3.3	3.3	6.3	10.5
521 INDUSTRIAL–INDUSTRIELS	4.5	1.9	8.9	3.2	3.1	6.2	10.4
522 NON INDUSTRIAL–NON INDUSTRIEL	0.1	0.1	0.1	0.1	0.2	0.1	0.1
53 PARTS–PIECES ACCESSOIRES	4.1	3.8	3.5	3.4	3.6	3.3	4.3
6 CONSUM GOODS–BIENS CONSOMMATION	15.8	15.1	14.1	16.5	16.6	16.1	13.5
61 DURABLE–DURABLES	4.4	4.1	3.7	4.5	4.0	4.5	3.7
62 SEMI DURABLE–SEMI DURABLES	7.2	6.6	6.1	7.5	7.9	7.2	6.2
63 NON DURABLE–NON DURABLES	4.1	4.4	4.2	4.5	4.7	4.4	3.7
7 GOODS NES–BIENS NDA	13.4	13.2	11.5	13.9	17.9	19.2	15.3

EXPORTS – EXPORTATIONS

	1990	1991	1992	1993	1994	1995	1996
TOTAL EXPORTS–EXPORTATIONS TOTALES	100.	100.	100.	100.	100.	100.	100.
1 AGRICULTURE	65.8	68.6	63.2	59.7	63.5	62.4	59.9
2 MINING QUARRY–INDUS EXTRACTIVES	0.0	0.0	0.0				
3 MANUFACTURING–IND MANUFACTUR	34.2	31.4	36.8	40.3	36.5	37.6	40.1
31 FOOD BEV TOBACCO–ALIM BOISS TAB	30.4	26.9	31.6	33.0	30.5	33.3	32.6
32 TEXTILES–INDUSTRIES TEXTILES	0.2	0.1	0.2	0.2	0.3	0.2	0.3
33 WOOD & PRODUCTS–BOIS & PRODUITS	0.0			0.0	0.0	0.0	
34 PAPER & PRODUCTS–PAPIER & PRODT	0.0	0.1	0.0	0.0	0.0	0.0	0.0
35 CHEMICALS–INDUSTRIES CHIMIQUES	0.9	0.9	1.0	1.2	1.1	0.8	1.2
36 NON METAL MIN–MIN NON METAL	0.0	0.0	0.0	0.0	0.0	0.0	0.0
37 BASIC METAL–IND METAL BASE	0.0	0.0	0.0	0.0	0.0	0.0	0.0
38 METAL MANUF–MANUF METAL	0.6	1.4	1.8	1.7	0.5	0.4	2.4
39 OTH MANUF IND–AUTRES MANUF	2.1	2.1	2.1	4.1	4.1	2.8	3.6

3. TRADE BY PRINCIPAL COUNTRIES OF PRODUCTION AND LAST CONSIGNMENT (VALUE IN THOUSAND U.S. DOLLARS)
ECHANGES SELON LES PRINCIPAUX PAYS DE PRODUCTION ET DE DERNIERE CONSIGNATION (VALEUR EN MILLIERS DE DOLLARS EU)

COUNTRIES–PAYS	GENERAL IMPORTS C.I.F. IMPORTATIONS GENERALES C.A.F				
	1992	1993	1994	1995	1996
World	453100	346059	391623	421109	466375
Africa	340	139	103	239	237
Americas	14951	17205	22338	15265	31323
Northern America	13945	16558	21406	14332	30202
LAIA	658	460	848	888	770
CACM	308	158	47	16	314
Caribbean	39	27	38	22	33
Rest of America	1	2	0	7	5
As.ex F.USSR	21591	18969	19474	21929	20629
Eur.x F.USSR	412405	306371	346804	381508	411817
EU	379558	290502	332446	350269	355616
EFTA	32104	15216	13147	29678	55113
East Europe	646	401	382	378	811
Other Europe	20	168	557	1005	113
Former USSR	2619	2134	1440	361	332
Oceania	846	778	544	828	855
Denmark/Danemark	332254	258740	299507	314920	309803
Norway,SVD,JM	29752	14046	11498	13050	53938
Japan/Japon	14494	12379	12792	14072	11422
USA/Etats–Unis d'Amer	11163	13885	12858	10206	16767
Germany/Allemagne	12981	8413	8698	9893	10313
Sweden/Suède	7800	4960	6019	7498	7738
Canada	2781	2673	8538	4125	13435
United Kingdom	7231	5884	4657	5024	5678
Iceland/Islande	1482	820	1012	15934	786
France,Monac	4593	2899	2724	2659	7103
Netherlands/Pays–Bas	3694	2618	3547	3211	4526
Italy/Italie	3167	2339	2534	2554	4611
Korea, Republic of	1988	2154	1753	1745	1608
Finland/Finlande	3177	1452	1418	1290	1712
China/Chine	1476	1189	1830	1809	2478
Russian Federation	2503	2109	1387	312	243
Portugal	1496	1250	1155	1110	1101
Belgium–Luxembourg	1377	937	1021	1015	1088
Hong Kong	1299	1400	809	818	1004
Switz.Liecht	870	350	637	694	388
Spain/Espagne	926	344	328	361	912
New Zealand	576	514	421	457	798
Austria/Autriche	449	410	349	216	426
Faeroe Islds/Is Féroé	20	139	556	984	109
Ireland/Irlande	256	158	431	364	416
India/Inde	126	190	273	346	584
Indonesia/Indonésie	179	212	218	221	521
Chile/Chili	326	129	306	296	238
Ecuador/Equateur	8	202	367	373	294
Malaysia/Malaisie	217	159	211	260	316
Thailand/Thaïlande	214	183	209	291	238
Australia/Australie	270	255	107	366	55
Poland/Pologne	181	109	126	154	313
Hungary/Hongrie	329	152	66	26	180
Singapore/Singapour	143	59	115	187	198
Costa Rica	304	157	45	13	177
Slovenia/Slovénia	20	62	264	174	163
Greece/Grèce	157	99	57	152	190
Turkey/Turquie	171	90	108	134	145
Brazil/Brésil	169	90	103	123	127
Czech Republic		87	108	115	218
So. Africa Customs Un	98	91	30	56	161
Pakistan	70	109	115	85	51
Israel/Israël	210	12	13	15	174
Bangladesh	43	72	80	68	128
Macau/Macao	29	30	35	76	85
Philippines	52	37	49	32	57
Viet Nam	1	12	23	26	136
Sri Lanka	83	21	15	18	37
Bulgaria/Bulgarie	52	16	33	18	23

COUNTRIES–PAYS	GENERAL EXPORTS F.O.B. EXPORTATIONS GENERALES F.O.B.				
	1992	1993	1994	1995	1996
Monde	332755	313059	306742	363643	369125
Afrique					
Amériques	9769	8117	2964	2207	1021
Amérique du Nord	9769	8117	2964	2207	1021
ALAI					
MCAC					
Caraïbes					
Autre Amérique					
Asie l'URSS exclus	12169	40913	18197	17764	17199
Europe l'URSS exclus	301801	253630	280696	340786	343064
UE	300714	253173	280504	339458	333686
AELE	1086	458	193	1328	9378
Europe de l'Est					
Autre de l'Europe	1				
Ancienne URSS	3251				
Océanie		3933			
Denmark/Danemark	293529	236861	262161	322544	318295
Japan/Japon	12166	40913	18188	16878	16298
United Kingdom	7177	14242	17722	16913	14958
USA/Etats–Unis d'Amer	7584	6037	2953	2155	503
Iceland/Islande	1019	450	138	443	5743
Canada	2185	2080	11	52	518
Norway,SVD,JM	67	7	54	885	3636
New Zealand		3933			
Russian Federation	3251				
Germany/Allemagne	3	2066	618	1	
Thailand/Thaïlande					304
Sweden/Suède			3		245
France,Monac		2			132
Ireland/Irlande					56
Hong Kong		0	9		
Belgium–Luxembourg	2	2	0		
Korea, Republic of	2		0		
Finland/Finlande	2	1			
Faeroe Islds/Is Féroé	1				
Austria/Autriche					0
Netherlands/Pays–Bas	0				
Switz.Liecht		0			
Italy/Italie		0			

(VALUE AS PERCENTAGE OF WORLD TOTAL)(VALEURS EN POURCENTAGE DU TOTAL MONDIAL)

	1987	1988	1989	1990	1991	1992	1993	1994	1995	1996
Africa	0.0	0.1	0.1	0.1	0.1	0.1	0.0	0.0	0.1	0.1
Americas	4.2	4.7	4.6	5.4	3.9	3.3	5.0	5.7	3.6	6.7
Northern America	4.0	4.4	4.3	5.1	3.6	3.1	4.8	5.5	3.4	6.5
LAIA	0.1	0.1	0.2	0.2	0.2	0.1	0.1	0.2	0.2	0.2
CACM	0.0	0.1	0.1	0.1	0.1	0.1	0.0	0.0	0.0	0.1
Caribbean	0.0	0.0	0.0	0.0	0.0	0.0	0.0	0.0	0.0	0.0
Rest of America	0.0	0.0	0.0	0.0	0.0	0.0	0.0	0.0	0.0	0.0
As.ex F.USSR	6.3	5.8	5.3	5.3	5.6	4.8	5.5	5.0	5.2	4.4
Eur.x F.USSR	89.0	89.1	89.5	88.9	90.0	91.0	88.5	88.6	90.6	88.3
EU	83.4	82.2	84.6	79.0	78.7	83.8	83.9	84.9	83.2	76.3
EFTA	4.8	6.6	4.6	9.7	11.0	7.1	4.4	3.4	7.0	11.8
East Europe	0.2	0.2	0.3	0.2	0.2	0.1	0.1	0.1	0.1	0.2
Other Europe	0.6	0.1	0.1	0.0	0.0	0.0	0.0	0.1	0.2	0.0
Former USSR	0.0	0.1	0.1	0.0	0.1	0.6	0.6	0.4	0.1	0.1
Oceania	0.2	0.1	0.2	0.1	0.2	0.2	0.2	0.1	0.2	0.2
Denmark/Danemark	67.0	66.0	69.2	65.6	66.8	73.3	74.8	76.5	74.8	66.4
Norway,SVD,JM	4.1	5.2	3.8	8.8	10.3	6.6	4.1	2.9	3.1	11.6
Japan/Japon	4.4	3.8	3.5	3.9	4.0	3.2	3.6	3.3	3.3	2.4
USA/Etats–Unis d'Amer	3.7	2.8	3.7	4.6	2.7	2.5	4.0	3.3	2.4	3.6
Germany/Allemagne	4.2	4.0	4.4	3.8	3.2	2.9	2.4	2.2	2.3	2.2
Sweden/Suède	4.0	3.6	3.0	2.5	2.2	1.7	1.4	1.5	1.8	1.7
Canada	0.3	1.7	0.6	0.5	1.0	0.6	0.8	2.2	1.0	2.9
United Kingdom	1.7	1.6	2.2	1.8	1.5	1.6	1.7	1.2	1.2	1.2
Iceland/Islande	0.5	1.1	0.5	0.6	0.4	0.3	0.2	0.3	3.8	0.2
France,Monac	1.2	1.2	1.2	1.4	1.5	1.0	0.8	0.7	0.6	1.5

	1987	1988	1989	1990	1991	1992	1993	1994	1995	1996
Afrique										
Amériques	2.7	0.0	0.0	0.0	0.0	2.9	2.6	1.0	0.6	0.3
Amérique du Nord	2.7	0.0	0.0	0.0	0.0	2.9	2.6	1.0	0.6	0.3
ALAI										
MCAC										
Caraïbes										
Autre Amérique										
Asie l'URSS exclus		0.0	0.4	0.9	0.9	3.7	13.1	5.9	4.9	4.7
Europe l'URSS exclus	96.4	98.6	98.7	97.6	97.5	90.7	81.0	91.5	93.7	92.9
UE	95.6	96.2	97.5	97.5	96.8	90.4	80.9	91.4	93.3	90.4
AELE	0.8	2.4	1.3	0.1	0.7	0.3	0.1	0.1	0.4	2.5
Europe de l'Est										
Autre de l'Europe			0.0			0.0				
Ancienne URSS						1.0				
Océanie					0.0		1.3			
Denmark/Danemark	84.8	76.8	73.8	91.1	93.5	88.2	75.7	85.5	88.7	86.2
Japan/Japon		0.0	0.4	0.9	0.9	3.7	13.1	5.9	4.6	4.4
United Kingdom	0.0	1.4	2.1	4.1	2.7	2.2	4.5	5.8	4.7	4.1
USA/Etats–Unis d'Amer					0.0	2.3	1.9	1.0	0.6	0.1
Iceland/Islande		0.0	0.0	0.0	0.7	0.3	0.1	0.0	0.1	1.6
Canada	2.7	0.0	0.0	0.0		0.7	0.7	0.0	0.0	0.1
Norway,SVD,JM	0.8	2.4	1.2	0.1	0.0	0.0	0.0	0.0	0.2	1.0
New Zealand					0.0		1.3			
Russian Federation						1.0				
Germany/Allemagne	4.0	7.2	11.2	1.5	0.1	0.0	0.7	0.2	0.0	

4. General Imports C.I.F. by Commodities according to the S.I.T.C. (Rev. 2) in thousand U.S. Dollars
Importations Générales C.A.F. par Produits d'après la C.T.C.I. (Rév. 2) en milliers de Dollars E.U.

SITC CTCI	COMMODITY	1993 WEIGHT POIDS	1993 VALUE VALEUR	1994 WEIGHT POIDS	1994 VALUE VALEUR	1995 WEIGHT POIDS	1995 VALUE VALEUR	1996 WEIGHT POIDS	1996 VALUE VALEUR	PRODUIT
	ALL COMMODITIES		346059		391623		421109		466375	TOUS PRODUITS
0	FOOD AND LIVE ANIMALS		42861		44587		44433		54809	ALIMENTS,ANIMAUX VIVANTS
01	MEAT AND PREPARATIONS		13245		14512		14647		16201	VIANDES ET PREPARATIONS
011	MEAT FRESH,CHILLD,FROZEN	W 2234	8303	W 2286	9230	W 2098	9318	W 2278	10139	VIANDES FRAICHES,REF,CONGE
0111	BOVINE MEAT FRESH,FROZEN	W 531	2867	W 490	2928	W 522	3222	W 630	3823	VIANDES BOVIN FRAI,REF
01112	BOVINE MEAT BONELESS	W 477	2526	W 451	2651	W 430	2837	W 570	3353	VIANDES BOVIN DESOSSEES
0113	PIG MEAT FRESH,CHLD,FRZN	W 1081	3866	W 1125	4380	W 1054	4432	W 944	4235	VIANDE DE PORC
014	MEAT PREPD,PRSVD,NES ETC	W 1022	4276	W 993	4589	W 918	4631	W 1075	5447	CONSERVES DE VIANDES
0142	SAUSAGES INCLDING TINNED	W 531	2043	W 557	2342	W 510	2358	W 577	2752	SAUCISSES,SAUCISSONS
0149	OTH PREPARD,PRESRVD MEAT	W 491	2233	W 435	2247	W 409	2272	W 498	2695	AUTRES PREP DE VIANDES
02	DAIRY PRODCTS,BIRDS'EGGS		7359		7718		7641		8752	PRODUITS LAITIERS,OEUFS
022	MILK AND CREAM	W 3239	3673	W 3109	3809	W 2687	3606	W 3058	4222	LAIT ET CREME
0223	MILK AND CREAM FRESH	W 3149	3289	W 3017	3442	W 2590	3159	W 2964	3737	LAIT,CREME FRAIS
024	CHEESE AND CURD	W 464	2124	W 450	2368	W 412	2489	W 419	2759	FROMAGE ET CAILLEBOTTE
025	EGGS,BIRDS,FRESH,PRSRVD	W 524	1053	W 449	1055	W 408	1024	W 439	1275	OEUFS
03	FISH AND PREPARATIONS		4266		3876		4099		6264	POISSONS ET PREPARATIONS
034	FISH,FRESH,CHILLED,FROZN	W 2539	3586	W 741	1487	W 1574	2513	W 28	205	POISSON FRAIS, REFRIG,CONG
0342	FISH FROZEN,EXCL FILLETS	W 2533	3539	W 734	1446	W 1568	2476	W 22	155	POISSONS CONGELES
036	SHELL FISH FRESH,FROZEN	W 334	387	W 1446	1820	W 376	759	W 523	893	CRUSTACES,MOLLUSQUES
037	FISH ETC PREPD,PRSVD NES	W 53	217	W 53	225	W 73	393	W 430	4916	POIS,CRUST,MOL PREPARES
0372	SHELL FISH PREPRD,PRESVD	W 2	22	W 4	32	W 7	84	W 347	4571	CRUSTACES,COQUIL PREPARES
04	CEREALS AND PREPARATIONS		4670		3860		4153		6275	CEREALES ET PRODUITS
048	CEREAL ETC PREPARATIONS	W 1753	3345	W 868	2585	W 869	3137	W 1319	4677	PREPTNS A BASE CEREALES
0484	BAKERY PRODUCTS	W 647	1855	W 584	1790	W 506	1793	W 622	2264	PRODUITS DE BOULANGERIE
04841	BREAD,BISCUIT,COM WAFERS	W 544	1366	W 500	1353	W 410	1230	W 497	1604	PAINS,BISCUITS DE MER
05	VEGETABLES AND FRUIT		5179		5626		5163		5220	LEGUMES ET FRUITS
057	FRUIT,NUTS,FRESH,DRIED	W 1015	1349	W 1205	1923	W 771	1282	W 899	1541	FRUITS FRAIS OU SECS
058	FRUIT PRESERVED,PREPARED	W 1729	2107	W 1467	1880	W 1302	1881	W 955	1593	CONSERVES DE FRUITS
0585	FRUIT OR VEGETABLE JUICE	W 1492	1675	W 1349	1596	W 1197	1593	W 781	1110	JUS DE FRUITS
05858	MIXTURES OF DIFF JUICES	W 1053	1167	W 959	1109	W 763	952	W 530	720	MELANGES JUS FRUITS,LEGUMES
06	SUGAR AND PREPS,HONEY		2447		2890		2606		3288	SUCRES ET PRODUITS
061	SUGAR AND HONEY	W 1306	1009	W 1359	1298	W 1205	1251	W 1529	1457	SUCRES ET MIEL
0612	REFINED SUGAR ETC	W 1295	966	W 1345	1185	W 1194	1142	W 1521	1432	SUCRES RAFFINES
062	SUGAR CANDY NON–CHOCLATE	W 237	1438	W 219	1592	W 191	1355	W 270	1831	SUCRERIES
07	COFFEE,TEA,COCOA,SPICES		1247		1682		1758		2262	CAFE,THE,CACAO,EPICES
09	MISC EDIBLE PRODUCTS		3920		3870		3885		5359	PREP ALIMENTAIRES DIVERSES
098	EDIBLE PRODCTS,PREPS NES	W 766	3102	W 614	2887	W 634	2934	W 1038	4484	PREP ALIMENTAIRES NDA
09809	MISC FOOD PREPRTIONS NES	W 647	2713	W 500	2430	W 508	2452	W 850	3814	PREP ALIMENTAIRES NDA
1	BEVERAGES AND TOBACCO		14361		16078		15222		15834	BOISSONS ET TABACS
11	BEVERAGES		10176		11446		11467		10932	BOISSONS
111	NON–ALCOHL BEVERAGES NES	W 1661	1971	W 1900	2462	W 1192	1727	W 1284	1855	BOISSONS NON ALCOOLIQUES
11102	FLAVORED WATERS NON–ALCO	W 1649	1955	W 1883	2440	W 1174	1703	W 1243	1805	LIMONADES,EAUX GAZEUSES
112	ALCOHOLIC BEVERAGES	W 8970	8205	W 8767	8984	W 7674	9740	W 6802	9077	BOISSONS ALCOOLIQUES
1123	BEER,ALE,STOUT,PORTER	W 8657	6904	W 8542	7770	W 7435	8240	W 6458	7022	BIERES
12	TOBACCO AND MANUFACTURES		4185		4631		3755		4902	TABACS BRUTS FABRIQUES
122	TOBACCO,MANUFACTURED	W 164	4185	W 165	4631	W 128	3755	W 168	4902	TABACS FABRIQUES
1222	CIGARETTES	W 147	3786	W 148	4193	W 116	3434	W 153	4519	CIGARETTES
2	CRUDE MATERLS,EXCL FUELS		4785		5723		6366		6472	MAT BRUTES NON COMESTIBLES
24	CORK AND WOOD		3382		3982		4540		4648	LIEGE ET BOIS
248	WOOD SHAPED,SLEEPERS	W 3349	3362	W 3865	3859	W 3783	4299	W 3713	4083	BOIS SIMPLEMENT TRAVAILLES
2482	LUMBER SHAPED CONIFER	W 2962	2838	W 3327	3327	W 3474	3976	W 3094	3505	CONIFERES SCIES,RABOTES
24821	LUMBER SAWN ETC CONIFER	W 2697	2411	W 3252	3159	W 3367	3773	W 3051	3350	CONIFERES SCIES LONGITUD
27	CRUDE FERTLZR,MINRLS NES		1120		1194		1205		1123	ENGRAIS MINERAUX BRUTS
278	OTHER CRUDE MINERALS	W 2964	1054	W 2795	1116	W 2735	1154	W 2486	1019	AUTRES MINERAUX BRUTS
3	MINERAL FUELS ETC		38922		38217		24367		46629	COMBUSTIBLES MINERAUX LUB
33	PETROLEUM AND PRODUCTS		38101		37820		23968		46270	PETROLE ET DERIVES
334	PETROLEUM PRODUCTS,REFIN	W 171215	37664	W 163141	37292	W 105682	23372	W 185073	45747	PRODUITS RAFFINES
3341	GASOLINE,OTH LIGHT OILS	W 171180	37568							ESSENCES POUR MOTEURS
33419	OTH LIGHT PETROLEUM OILS	W 171180	37568							AUTRES HUILES LEGERES
5	CHEMCLS,RELATED PROD NES		14090		15637		16994		15228	PRODUITS CHIMIQUES
53	DYES,TANNING,COLOUR PROD		2630		2972		3820		3215	PROD TEINTURE,COLORANTS
532	DYES NES,TANNING PROD	W 42	780	W 112	1073	W 74	1393	W 65	564	EXTRAITS TEINTURE,TANNAGE
5322	DYE,TANN EXTRCTS,TANNINS	W 40	775	W 109	1069	W 74	1393	W 65	564	EXT TAN ORIG VEG,TANNINS
53222	DYEING EXTRCTS VEG,ANMAL	W 40	775	W 109	1069	W 74	1393	W 65	564	MATI COLOR VEGET ANIMALE
533	PIGMENTS,PAINTS,ETC	W 404	1838	W 368	1893	W 449	2416	W 553	2648	PIGMENTS,PEINTURES,VERNIS
5334	VARNISHES,DISTEMPERS ETC	W 332	1576	W 323	1686	W 417	2144	W 522	2420	PEINTURES A L'EAU
53341	WATER–THINNED PAINTS	W 257	1120	W 187	902	W 207	1036	W 165	816	PEINTURES DILUEES
53342	OTH PAINTS,VARNISHES ETC	W 73	449	W 136	780	W 209	1093	W 356	1594	AUTRES PEINTURES,VERNIS
541	*MEDICINAL,PHARM PRODUCT	K 86373	5250	K 89360	5839	K 79614	6139	K 77387	5369	PROD MEDICINAUX PHARMACEUT
5417	MEDICAMENTS	K 69827	4681	K 74699	5155	K 71955	5566	K 69549	4871	MEDICAMENTS
54179	— CONTNG OTH SUBSTANCES	K 69827	4681	K 74699	5155	K 71954	5566	K 69501	4862	MED CONT AUT SUBSTANCES
55	PERFUME,CLEANING ETC PRD		2192		3019		2928		2311	PROD POUR PARFUM,TOILETTE
553	PERFUMERY,COSMETICS,ETC	W 48	885	W 58	1339	W 50	1263	W 37	907	PRODUITS DE PARFUMERIE
554	SOAP,CLEANSING ETC PREPS	W 538	1193	W 667	1671	W 650	1647	W 537	1404	SAVONS,PRODUITS DETERSIFS
5542	WASHING PREPARATIONS ETC	W 475	1008	W 601	1464	W 593	1477	W 488	1217	PROD ORG TENSIO–ACT NDA
58	PLASTIC MATERIALS ETC		1484		1564		1604		1381	MAT PLAST ARTIFICIELLES
583	POLYMERIZATION ETC PRODS	W 300	1116	W 284	1111	W 226	1117	W 311	972	PROD POLYMERISATION
6	BASIC MANUFACTURES		62196		61266		77026		70394	ART MANUFACTURES
62	RUBBER MANUFACTURES NES		1000		1060		1270		1487	CAOUTCHOUC MANUFACTURE
63	WOOD,CORK MANUFACTRS NES		15888		11222		13364		9994	OUVRAGES LIEGE ET BOIS
634	VENEERS,PLYWOOD,ETC	W 3655	4712	W 3459	4911	W 2503	4147	W 2649	3339	PLACAGES,CONTRE–PLAQUES
6342	PLYWOOD OF WOOD SHEETS	W 3215	4057	W 3146	4419	W 2168	3576	W 2403	2893	BOIS CONTRE–PLAQUES
635	WOOD MANUFACTURES NES	W 3528	11135	W 1491	6291	W 2014	9202	W 1695	6625	ART MANUF EN BOIS NDA
6353	BUILDERS WOODWRK,PREFABS	W 3254	10777	W 1107	5840	W 1583	8647	W 1053	5883	OUVRAGES DE MENUISERIE
64	PAPER,PAPERBOARD AND MFR		10573		9481		8648		9292	PAPIERS,CARTONS & OUVRAGES
641	PAPER AND PAPERBOARD	W 1100	2028	W 851	1671	W 747	1575	W 940	1867	PAPIERS ET CARTONS
642	PAPER,ETC,PRECUT,ARTS OF	W 4315	8544	W 3682	7811	W 2999	7074	W 3491	7425	PAP,CARTONS DECOUPES
6421	PAPER ETC CONTAINERS	W 3884	6951	W 3195	6068	W 2495	5232	W 2952	5486	BOITES,SACS EMBALLAGES
65	TEXTILE YARN,FABRICS,ETC		5232		5918		5651		4856	FILS,TISSUS,ARTICLES TEXTILE
657	SPECIAL TXTL FABRC,PRODS	W 369	2650	W 358	3087	W 291	2239	W 277	2053	TISSUS SPECIAUX
6575	CORDAGE AND MANUFACTURES	W 333	2424	W 338	2803	W 273	2109	W 256	1945	FICELLES,CORDES,CORDAGES
65752	NETTING OF ROPE,TWINE	W 212	1688	W 189	1729	W 168	1407	W 155	1342	FILETS MAT DU 657.51
659	FLOOR COVERINGS,ETC	W 259	1266	W 224	1239	W 233	1447	W 255	1515	COUVRE–PARQUETS,TAPIS ETC
66	NONMETAL MINERAL MFS NES		9318		13837		24544		23407	ART MIN NON METALLIQUES
661	LIME,CEMENT,BLDG PRODS	W 4349	1395	W 3785	1361	W 5112	1868	W 8046	2659	CHAUX,CIMENTS MAT CONSTR
6612	CEMENT	W 4255	1246	W 3737	1252	W 5065	1761	W 7958	2506	CIMENTS HYDRAULIQUES
663	MINERAL MANUFCTURES NES	W 3396	4606	W 4182	9197	W 34616	18786	W 31920	16736	ART MIN MANUF NDA
6633	MINRL MFS NES NONCERAMIC	W 3170	3484	W 4110	8746	W 34537	18321	W 31870	16405	OUVR MAT MINERALE NDA
66331	ARTICLES OF PLASTER	W 1957	1000	W 1491	757	W 3186	1756	W 574	772	OUVRAGES EN PLATRE
66332	CEMENT,ARTFCL STONE PROD	W 1208	2469	W 2617	7987	W 31350	16563	W 31296	15632	OUVRAGES EN CIMENT
6635	MINRL INSULATNG PROD NES	W 213	1049	W 61	396	W 60	383	W 37	269	LAINES DE LAITIER

4. General Imports C.I.F. by Commodities according to the S.I.T.C. (Rev. 2) in thousand U.S. Dollars
Importations Générales C.A.F. par Produits d'après la C.T.C.I. (Rév. 2) en milliers de Dollars E.U.

SITC CTCI	COMMODITY	1993 WEIGHT POIDS	1993 VALUE VALEUR	1994 WEIGHT POIDS	1994 VALUE VALEUR	1995 WEIGHT POIDS	1995 VALUE VALEUR	1996 WEIGHT POIDS	1996 VALUE VALEUR	PRODUIT
664	GLASS	W 447	2220	W 425	2221	W 512	2781	W 515	2706	VERRE
6649	GLASS NES	W 370	2051	W 367	2069	W 440	2621	W 456	2575	VERRE NDA
66494	GLASS FIBRE AND PROD NES	W 351	2000	W 316	1941	W 364	2408	W 387	2436	LAINE DE VERRE,FIBRES
67	IRON AND STEEL		4118		3310		4695		3989	FER ET ACIER
673	IRON,STEEL SHAPES ETC	W 1368	1632	W 420	628	W 601	1248	W 459	658	BARRES,PROFIL FER,ACIER
6733	IRON,STEEL PROFILES ETC	W 1075	1381	W 294	490	W 368	1016	W 247	467	PROFILES,PALPLAN FER,ACIER
678	IRON,STL TUBES,PIPES,ETC	W 644	1776	W 331	1629	W 383	2448	W 514	2528	TUBES,TUYAUX EN FONTE,FER
69	METAL MANUFACTURES NES		15442		15712		18127		16581	ART MANUFACT EN METAL NDA
691	STRUCTURES AND PARTS NES	W 1407	5063	W 772	3145	W 1294	3696	W 721	2654	CONSTRUCT FER,ACIER,ALU
6911	STRUCTURES,PARTS IRN,STL	W 1380	4762	W 752	2881	W 1263	3382	W 688	2232	CONSTRUCT FER,ACIER,FONTE
692	METAL TANKS,BOXES,ETC	W 361	1422	W 503	1710	W 298	1341	W 323	1306	RECIPIENTS METALLIQUES
6924	MTL TRANSPORT BOXES ETC	W 274	900	W 427	1300	W 282	1149	W 308	1180	FUTS,TAMBOURS,BIDONS
693	WIRE PRODUCTS NON ELECTR	W 649	1679	W 636	1676	W 564	1641	W 546	1380	OUVRAGES FILS METALLIQUES
6931	WIRE CABLES, ROPES ETC	W 627	1613	W 591	1543	W 530	1512	W 536	1345	CORDAGES EN FILS DE FER
69311	IRN,STEEL CABLE,ROPE ETC	W 611	1549	W 591	1540	W 526	1473	W 536	1345	CORDAGES FILS FER,ACIER
695	TOOLS	W 42	900	W 48	1070	W 90	1637	W 75	1909	OUTILS A MAIN
6953	OTHER HAND TOOLS	W 34	682	W 43	957	W 77	1476	W 67	1633	AUTRES OUTILS A MAIN
69539	HAND TOOLS ETC NES	W 26	537	W 38	860	W 66	1303	W 61	1506	OUTILLAGE A MAIN NDA
697	BASE MTL HOUSEHOLD EQUIP	W 81	890	W 126	1484	W 122	1600	W 115	1192	ART MENAGE MET COMMUNS
699	BASE METAL MFRS NES	W 867	4527	W 1028	5757	W 1104	6901	W 1159	7096	ART MANUFACTURES MET NDA
6997	IRON,STEEL ARTICLES NES	W 513	2191	W 695	3163	W 719	3508	W 703	3338	OUV FONTE,FER,ACIER NDA
69979	IRN,STL MANUFACTURES NES	W 512	2182	W 694	3158	W 718	3502	W 701	3328	AUT OUVRAGES EN FER NDA
6998	MFRS NES OF CPR,NIKL,ETC	W 108	865	W 71	919	W 103	1539	W 129	1720	OUVRAGES EN CU,NI,AL,PB,ZN
69983	ALUMINIUM MANUFACTS NES	W 83	763	W 44	822	W 82	1447	W 106	1633	OUVRAGES EN ALUMINIUM
7	MACHINES,TRANSPORT EQUIP		77788		91050		103648		137451	MACHINES MATERIEL TRANSPORT
71	POWER GENERATING EQUIPMT		7957		10308		8584		10333	MACHINES GENERATRICES
713	INTRNL COMBUS PSTN ENGIN	W 150	5474	W 180	6602	W 167	6318	W 197	6902	MOTEURS EXPL COMB INT, PIECE
7133	MARINE PISTON ENGINES	W 58	1820	W 89	2724	W 77	2609	W 72	2238	MOTEURS EXPL POUR BATEAUX
71331	—— OUTBOARD	W 40	1342	W 57	1978	W 52	1920	W 49	1618	MOTEURS BATEAUX HORSBORD
7139	PISTON ENGINE PARTS NES	W 74	3283	W 61	3294	W 67	3062	W 100	3568	PIECES POUR 713.2,3,8
716	ROTATING ELECTRIC PLANT	W 123	1730	W 98	2480	W 78	1926	W 145	2874	APP ELECTR ROTATIFS,PIECES
7162	AC MTRS,GENRTRS,GEN SETS	W 112	1438	W 71	1668	W 70	1718	W 54	1154	MOTEURS ELECTRIQUES
71623	GEN SETS WITH PISTN ENGN	W 91	947	W 59	1500	W 61	1441	W 46	1027	GROUPES MOTEUR EXPLOSION
72	MACHS FOR SPCL INDUSTRYS		7629		8087		7543		11530	MAC SPECIALES POUR INDUST
723	CIVIL ENGNEERG EQUIP ETC	W 64	573	W 128	1019	W 257	2342	W 292	2488	APPAREILS DE GENIE CIVIL
7234	CONST,MINING MACHNRY NES	W 45	394	W 114	878	W 215	2078	W 247	2035	MACH POUR LA CONST, MINES
72342	SLFPRP SHOVELS,EXCAVATRS	W 42	316	W 102	606	W 206	1959	W 225	1795	PELLES MECANIQUES
727	FOOD MACHRY NON–DOMESTIC	W 152	2966	W 150	4573	W 132	2914	W 178	7186	MACH INDUSTRIES ALIMENT
7272	OTH FOOD PROC MCHY,PARTS	W 152	2951	W 149	4564	W 111	2748	W 178	7183	AUT MACH IND ALIMENTAIRE
72722	INDUS FOOD PROC MACH NES	W 152	2951	W 149	4564	W 111	2748	W 178	7183	MACHINES BOULANGERIE
728	OTH MACHY FOR SPCL INDUS	W 103	2945	W 43	1008	W 56	1169	W 36	779	AUT MACH IND PARTICULIERES
7284	MACHY FOR SPCL INDUS NES	W 79	2633	W 17	450	W 34	803	W 16	505	MACH SPEC IND PARTICUL.
72849	PTS OF MACHS OF 7284 ETC	W 55	2276	W 4	101	W 1	40	W 6	152	PIECES DU 728.4 ETC
74	GENRL INDUSTRL MACHY NES		8177		12357		13460		11463	MACH APP INDUSTRIE
741	HEATING,COOLING EQUIPMNT	W 129	2219	W 319	5578	W 352	5907	W 277	3575	MACH CHAUFFAGE,PIECES
7414	NONDOM REFRIG EQUIPT,PTS	W 86	1304	W 182	3787	W 185	3714	W 61	1328	MAT PRODUCTION DU FROID
74141	REFRIG EQUIP NONDOMESTIC	W 59	671	W 158	3079	W 146	2581	W 21	374	REFIG INDUSTRIELS
7416	HEATING,COOLING EQU NES	W 16	352	W 34	937	W 64	1203	W 127	1431	APP CHANGEMENT TEMP
743	PUMPS NES,CENTRFUGES ETC	W 50	956	W 57	1044	W 63	1457	W 78	1259	POMPES COMPRES,VENT ETC
744	MECHANICAL HANDLING EQU	W 189	2281	W 155	2601	W 166	2642	W 232	3148	EQUIP MANUTENTION PIECES
7449	PTS NES OF MACHY OF 7442	W 68	1313	W 53	1491	W 51	1648	W 84	1914	PIECES DU 744.2
745	NONELEC MACHY,TOOLS NES	W 58	961	W 46	1275	W 60	1894	W 51	1392	AUT MACH NON ELEC,PIECES
7452	OTH NONELEC MCHS,PTS NES	W 51	787	W 37	1068	W 49	1692	W 43	1154	AUT MACH NON ELEC,PIECES
749	NONELEC MACH PTS,ACC NES	W 52	1078	W 26	1004	W 22	869	W 19	1259	PIECES MACH NON ELEC NDA
75	OFFICE MACHNES,ADP EQUIP		11913		13426		11202		10786	MACH BUREAU TRAIT AUTOM
751	OFFICE MACHINES	W 30	1690	W 26	2697	W 20	1214	W 18	901	MACH,APPAREILS DE BUREAU
7512	CALCULATNG,ACCTG,ETC MCH	W 3	214	W 8	1734	W 2	162	W 2	121	MACHINE A CALCULER ETC
75123	CASH REGISTERS	W 1	120	W 5	1306	W 1	109	W 1	82	CAISSES ENREGISTREUSES
7518	OFFICE MACHINES NES	W 27	1435	W 17	919	W 17	1011	W 16	770	MACH,APP DE BUREAU NDA
75182	PHOTO,THERMOCOPY APPARAT	W 19	1092	W 13	718	W 16	921	W 14	649	APPAREILS DE PHOTOCOPIE
752	AUTOMTIC DATA PROC EQUIP	W 33	4645	W 24	3397	W 26	2750	W 20	1953	MACH TRAIT INFORMATION
7522	DIGITAL COMPUTERS	W 14	1041	W 7	906	W 10	978	W 5	449	MACH DIGITALES COMPLETES
7523	DIGITL CENTRL PROCESSORS	W 7	1883	W 6	1332	W 5	899	W 3	420	UNITES CENTRALES
759	OFFICE,ADP MCH PTS,ACCES	W 47	5578	W 61	7331	W 57	7238	W 71	7932	PIECES DU 751 ET 752
7591	OFFICE MACHINE PARTS NES	W 11	576	W 18	1332	W 10	735	W 5	450	PIECES DU 7511,7518
7599	ACCTG,ETC,ADP MCH PTS,AC	W 36	5001	W 44	5999	W 47	6503	W 66	7483	PIECES DU 751 ET 752
76	TELECOMM,SOUND EQUIPMENT		11091		12945		11458		14592	EQUIPMENT DE TELECOM
761	TELEVISION RECEIVERS	W 71	1407	W 48	946	W 66	1605	W 62	1307	RECEPTEURS DE TELEVISION
7611	COLOUR TV RECEIVERS	W 71	1402	W 48	939	W 66	1591	W 61	1297	RECEPTEURS COULEUR
763	SOUND RECORDRS,PHONOGRPH	W 37	1335	W 13	707	W 15	875	W 13	644	PHONO,APP ENREGISTREMENT
7638	OTHR SOUND APPARATUS ETC	W 36	1329	W 13	700	W 14	864	W 13	640	AUT APP D'ENREGIS,REPROD
764	TELECOM EQPT,PTS,ACC NES	W 71	7656	W 132	10671	W 118	8479	W 135	11952	EQUIP TELECOM,PIECES
7641	LINE TELEPHONE,ETC EQUIP	W 11	1428	W 16	3625	W 10	1955	W 11	1686	APP TELEPHON PAR FIL
7643	TV,RADIO TRANSMITTRS ETC	W 5	1103	W 3	814	W 2	744	W 4	664	APP EMET TELE RADIO
7648	TELECOMM EQUIPMENT NES	W 11	900	W 62	2185	W 50	1402	W 11	696	APP TELECOM NDA
76482	TELEVISION CAMERAS	W 8	349	W 60	1565	W 48	950	W 10	327	APP PRISE DE VUES TELE
7649	PTS NES OF EQUIPMT OF 76	W 29	3942	W 28	3619	W 45	4104	W 91	8563	PIECES DE LA DIV 76
76491	PTS NES OF APPAR OF 7641	W 16	2620	W 12	2521	W 10	767	W 17	2293	PIECES POUR 764.1
76493	TELECOMM EQUIPMT PTS NES	W 12	1135	W 15	1044	W 35	3281	W 73	6185	PIECES 761,762,764.3,8
77	ELECTRIC MACHNRY NES ETC		13062		12969		15687		14557	MACH APP ELECT NDA
772	SWITCHGEAR ETC,PARTS NES	W 166	4465	W 141	3586	W 188	5609	W 164	5523	APP COUPURE,SECT ETC
7721	SWITCHGEAR ETC	W 166	4448	W 141	3579	W 188	5563	W 164	5490	APP COUPURE,SECTIONMNT
773	ELECTR DISTRIBUTNG EQUIP	W 257	1721	W 212	1645	W 324	2353	W 216	1718	EQUIPMT DISTRIBUTION ELECT
7731	INSULATED WIRE,CABLE ETC	W 256	1701	W 212	1642	W 240	2216	W 215	1703	FILS,CABLES ISOLES ELECT
775	HOUSEHOLD TYPE EQUIP NES	W 258	2831	W 305	3278	W 275	3298	W 276	2901	MACH,APP USAGE DOMESTQUE
7758	ELECTRO–THERMIC APPL NES	W 92	1138	W 88	1094	W 90	1282	W 79	917	APP ELECTROTHERMIQ NDA
778	ELECTRICAL MACHINERY NES	W 130	2730	W 165	3466	W 147	3368	W 170	3235	AUTRES MACH ELECT NDA
7788	OTH ELEC MACHY,EQUIP NES	W 15	1138	W 19	1523	W 11	1022	W 10	860	AUT MACH APP ELEC NDA
78	ROAD VEHICLES		8481		10608		12095		12357	VEHICULES ROUTIERS
781	PASS MOTOR VEH EXC BUSES	W 97	1281	W 114	1664	W 157	2357	W 230	3403	AUTO TRANSPORT PERSONNES
782	LORRIES,SPCL MTR VEH NES	W 311	4218	W 349	5192	W 377	5527	W 332	4746	VEHICULES SPECIAUX,MARCH
7821	LORRIES,TRUCKS	W 266	3394	W 305	4182	W 356	5038	W 289	4298	VEHICULES TRANSP MARCHAND
784	MOTOR VEH PRTS,ACCES NES	W 90	2099	W 104	2489	W 120	2864	W 113	2556	PIECES 722,781,782,783
7849	OTHER MOTOR VEHCL PARTS	W 89	2087	W 104	2480	W 120	2857	W 111	2538	PIECES 722,781,782,783
79	OTHR TRANSPORT EQUIPMENT		9221		10051		23260		51357	AUTRE MATERIEL TRANSPORT
792	AIRCRAFT ETC	W 20	6586	W 25	8225	W 25	6936	W 51	21092	APP NAVIGATION AERIENNE
7921	HELICOPTERS	W 6	2607			W 14	3791	W 22	12500	HELICOPTERES
7923	AIRCRFT NES2000–15000KG	W 2	1021	W 15	5131					AERODYNES 2000 A 15000 KG
7929	AIRCRAFT PARTS NES	W 9	2879	W 10	3066	W 12	3143	W 25	8402	PIECES DU 792
793	SHIPS AND BOATS ETC	W 224	2633	W 242	1825	W 2325	16309	W 3552	30265	NAVIRES BATEAUX,ETC
7932	SHIPS AND BOATS NES	W 221	2544	W 233	1518	W 2319	16045	W 3548	30142	NAVIRES ET BATEAUX

4. General Imports C.I.F. by Commodities according to the S.I.T.C. (Rev. 2) in thousand U.S. Dollars
Importations Générales C.A.F. par Produits d'après la C.T.C.I. (Rév. 2) en milliers de Dollars E.U.

SITC CTCI	COMMODITY	1993		1994		1995		1996		PRODUIT
		WEIGHT POIDS	VALUE VALEUR	WEIGHT POIDS	VALUE VALEUR	WEIGHT POIDS	VALUE VALEUR	WEIGHT POIDS	VALUE VALEUR	
79321	YACHTS,SPORTS VESSLS ETC	W 31	618	W 51	1078	W 38	941	W 62	1598	BATEAUX DE PLAISANCE
79324	FISHING VESSELS ETC	W 190	1926	W 182	440	W 2281	15104	W 3486	28543	BATEAUX DE PECHE
8	MISC MANUFACTURED GOODS		42867		48806		52230		48263	ART MANUFACTURES DIVERS
812	*PLUMBG,HEATNG,LGHTNG EQ	W 234	2760	W 184	2132	W 255	2929	W 131	2243	APPAR SANITAIRES CHAUFFAGE
8121	CENTRAL HEATING EQUIPMNT	W 163	1289	W 123	760	W 173	1102	W 84	812	CHAUDIERES,RADIATEURS
8124	LIGHTING EQUIPMENT NES	W 53	1348	W 46	1271	W 44	1695	W 40	1366	APPAREILS ECLAIRAGE ETC
81242	LAMPS,FITTINGS BASE METL	W 50	1263	W 41	1164	W 41	1610	W 37	1259	APPAREILS D'ECLAIRAGE
821	*FURNITURE,PARTS THEREOF	W 1044	6858	W 928	7286	W 1282	10184	W 1252	9130	MEUBLES ET PIECES
8211	CHAIRS,SEATS AND PARTS	W 165	1604	W 219	2248	W 165	2307	W 222	2420	SIEGES ET PIECES
82111	CHAIRS AND OTHER SEATS	W 164	1575	W 219	2230	W 164	2278	W 221	2404	SIEGES
8219	FURNITURE AND PARTS NES	W 812	4477	W 669	4388	W 1051	6882	W 981	5669	AUTRES MEUBLES ET PIECES
82192	WOOD FURNITURE NES	W 675	3519	W 550	3290	W 923	5639	W 807	4214	MEUBLES NDA EN BOIS
84	CLOTHING AND ACCESSORIES		9548		11841		10183		10481	VETEMENTS
842	MENS OUTERWEAR NOT KNIT	W 55	2156	W 60	2835	W 47	2456	W 51	2248	VET DESSUS POUR HOMMES
8429	— OTHER OUTER GARMENTS	W 21	1042	W 20	1165	W 21	1234	W 20	1076	AUT VET DES HOM MAT TEX
843	WOMENS OUTERWEAR NONKNIT	W 59	1877	W 54	2135	W 48	2205	W 64	2610	VET DESSUS FEMMES MAT TEX
8439	— OTHER OUTER GARMENTS	W 45	1360	W 40	1510	W 39	1568	W 53	1973	AUT VET DES FEM MAT TEXT
845	OUTERWEAR KNIT NONELASTC	W 94	3141	W 97	3423	W 51	2726	W 65	2927	VET DESSOUS,ACCES BONNET
8451	— JERSEYS,PULLOVERS ETC	W 46	1730	W 38	1489	W 24	1348	W 35	1601	CHANDAILS,PULL–OVERS ETC
8459	— OTHER,CLTHG ACCESRYS	W 47	1361	W 57	1846	W 25	1278	W 29	1258	AUT VET DESSUS DE BONNE
848	HEADGEAR,NONTXTL CLOTHNG	W 39	771	W 52	1186	W 42	950	W 47	963	VET ACCES MAT AUT QUE TEX
851	*FOOTWEAR	W 88	2466	W 105	3109	W 84	2773	W 105	3036	CHAUSSURES
85102	FOOTWEAR LEATHER	W 57	1850	W 54	1987	W 52	1895	W 78	2479	CHAUS SEMELLES EN CUIR
87	PRECISION INSTRUMNTS NES		3692		3382		3520		3479	INSTRUM,APPAR SCIENT NDA
872	MEDICAL INSTRUMENTS NES	W 16	1574	W 13	1081	W 9	807	W 36	876	INSTR,APP MEDIC–CHIR NDA
87202	OTH MEDICAL INSTRUMENTS	W 15	1449	W 12	884	W 8	746	W 31	762	INSTRUM,APP MEDECINE
874	MEASURNG,CONTROLNG INSTR	W 14	1855	W 22	1891	W 23	2322	W 16	1958	INSTRUMENTS DE MESURE
88	PHOTO EQU,OPTICL GDS ETC		1569		1693		1981		1792	APP,FOURN PHOTO,OP,MONTR
89	MISC MANUFCTRD GOODS NES		15737		19054		20402		17854	ART MANUFACTURES DIVERS
892	PRINTED MATTER	W 224	2845	W 187	3099	W 222	3531	W 288	3408	IMPRIMES
8921	PRINTED BOOKS,GLOBES,ETC	W 102	1598	W 105	1881	W 73	1794	W 77	1706	LIVRES,BROCHURES,CARTES
89211	PRINTED BOOKS,PAMPHLETS	W 101	1580	W 105	1851	W 72	1767	W 75	1632	LIVRES,BROCHURES
8928	PRINTED MATTER NES	W 116	1097	W 80	1170	W 135	1585	W 209	1650	IMPRIMES NDA
893	ARTICLES OF PLASTIC NES		4263		4981		6061	W 1052	4739	OUVRAGES EN MAT DIVIS 58
8931	PLSTC PACKG CONTNRS,LIDS	W 518	1482	W 760	2235	W 786	2783	W 613	2011	ART TRANSP EMBALLAGE ETC
8939	MISC PLASTIC ARTICLES	W 417	2632	W 325	2685	W 392	3224	W 434	2650	ART DIVERS EN MAT DIV 58
89399	OTHR PLASTC ARTICLES NES	W 309	2071	W 223	1928	W 282	2381	W 227	1715	AUT OUV MAT DIV 58
894	TOYS,SPORTING GOODS,ETC	W 220	3692	W 293	4821	W 289	4889	W 334	4424	VOITURES ENFANTS,JOUETS
8942	TOYS,INDOOR GAMES ETC	W 88	1546	W 115	1860	W 137	2049	W 182	2346	JOUETS,JEUX ETC
89423	TOYS NES	W 44	695	W 64	1016	W 69	886	W 120	1437	JOUETS,MODELES REDUITS
8946	NON–MILITARY ARMS,AMMO	W 84	1349	W 139	1948	W 112	2021	W 86	1322	ARMES NON MILITAIRES
89463	HUNTNG,SPORTNG AMMUNTION	W 79	964	W 132	1382	W 107	1604	W 81	920	MUNITIONS
898	MUSICAL INSTRUMENTS,PTS	W 45	2479	W 38	2974	W 40	3056	W 50	2716	INSTRUMENTS DE MUSIQUE
8983	SOUND RECRDNG TAPE,DISCS	W 40	2259	W 35	2789	W 37	2870	W 47	2578	SUPPORTS SON POUR 763
89832	RECORDED DISCS,TAPES ETC	W 27	1961	W 28	2640	W 25	2622	W 27	2305	DISQUES,PHONO,BANDES
899	OTHER MANUFACTURED GOODS		1646		2175		1826		1467	AUT ART MANUF DIVERS NDA
8996	HEARING,ORTHOPAEDIC AIDS		815		1177		950		696	APPAREILS D'ORTHOPEDIE
9	GOODS NOT CLASSD BY KIND		48114		70094		80686		71185	ART TRANSACT NON CLASSES
931	*SPECIAL TRANSACTIONS	W 7803	48049	W 33523	70005	W 20459	80658	W 20672	71093	TRANS.SPECIALES

5. General Exports F.O.B. by Commodities according to the S.I.T.C. (Rev. 2) in thousand U.S. Dollars
Exportations Générales F.O.B. par Produits d'après la C.T.C.I. (Rév. 2) en milliers de Dollars E.U.

SITC CTCI	COMMODITY	1993		1994		1995		1996		PRODUIT
		WEIGHT POIDS	VALUE VALEUR	WEIGHT POIDS	VALUE VALEUR	WEIGHT POIDS	VALUE VALEUR	WEIGHT POIDS	VALUE VALEUR	
	ALL COMMODITIES		313059		306742		363643		369125	TOUS PRODUITS
0	FOOD AND LIVE ANIMALS		289664		287265		345697		336112	ALIMENTS,ANIMAUX VIVANTS
03	FISH AND PREPARATIONS		289589		287155		344786		334882	POISSONS ET PREPARATIONS
034	FISH,FRESH,CHILLED,FROZN	W 11513	43148	W 11047	49379	W 13534	64716	W 16946	60538	POISSON FRAIS, REFRIG,CONG
0342	FISH FROZEN,EXCL FILLETS	W 2672	7725	W 2393	8586	W 4738	18531	W 5869	19374	POISSONS CONGELES
0344	FISH FILLETS,FROZEN	W 8694	35257	W 8635	40766	W 8672	45819	W 7824	40213	FILETS CONGELES
036	SHELL FISH FRESH,FROZEN	W 32563	142739	W 34826	144092	W 33948	160660	W 35330	158677	CRUSTACES,MOLLUSQUES
037	FISH ETC PREPD,PRSVD NES	W 13446	103064	W 12729	92984	W 14229	118631	W 13001	114672	POIS,CRUST,MOL PREPARES
0372	SHELL FISH PREPRD,PRESVD	W 13446	103064	W 12729	92984	W 14229	118631	W 13001	114671	CRUSTACES,COQUIL PREPARES
081	*FEEDING STUFF FOR ANIML			W 74	68	W 790	846	W 1135	1159	NOURRITURE POUR ANIMAUX
0814	MEAT OR FISH MEAL FODDER			W 74	68	W 790	846	W 1135	1159	FARINES DE VIANDES,POISSONS
08142	FISH MEAL FODDER			W 74	68	W 790	846	W 1135	1159	FARINES DE POISSONS
2	CRUDE MATERLS,EXCL FUELS		450		976		2404		5244	MAT BRUTES NON COMESTIBLES
21	HIDES,SKINS,FURS UNDRSSD		401		578		1097		1200	CUIRS,PEAUX BRUTS
29	CRUDE ANIMAL,VEG MAT NES		13		310		1245		4021	MATIERES BRUTES ANIM,VEGET
291	CRUDE ANIMAL MTRIALS NES	W 4	13	W 55	310	W 220	1245	W 334	4021	MATIERES BRUTES ANIMALES
2919	OTH ANIMAL MATERIALS NES	W 4	7	W 54	252	W 220	1240	W 334	3987	MAT ORIGINE ANIMALE NDA
29199	ANIMAL PRODUCTS,NES			W 52	251	W 81	1226	W 333	3976	PROD ORIGINE ANIMALE NDA
3	MINERAL FUELS ETC		3812		3316		2885		4242	COMBUSTIBLES MINERAUX LUB
33	PETROLEUM AND PRODUCTS		3812		3316		2885		4242	PETROLE ET DERIVES
334	PETROLEUM PRODUCTS,REFIN	W 8059	3812	W 6308	3316	W 5755	2885	W 6933	4242	PRODUITS RAFFINES
3341	GASOLINE,OTH LIGHT OILS	W 8059	3812							ESSENCES POUR MOTEURS
33419	OTH LIGHT PETROLEUM OILS	W 8059	3812							AUTRES HUILES LEGERES
7	MACHINES,TRANSPORT EQUIP		5076		1187		984		8483	MACHINES MATERIEL TRANSPORT
79	OTHR TRANSPORT EQUIPMENT		3960		20		43		6454	AUTRE MATERIEL TRANSPORT
792	AIRCRAFT ETC		23		19		14	W 4	1114	APP NAVIGATION AERIENNE
793	SHIPS AND BOATS ETC	W 1159	3937		1	W 16	29	W 1246	5340	NAVIRES BATEAUX,ETC
7932	SHIPS AND BOATS NES	W 1159	3936		1	W 16	29	W 1246	5340	NAVIRES ET BATEAUX
79324	FISHING VESSELS ETC	W 1158	3933					W 1246	5338	BATEAUX DE PECHE
8	MISC MANUFACTURED GOODS		4265		3587		4315		5768	ART MANUFACTURES DIVERS
84	CLOTHING AND ACCESSORIES		551		971		778		999	VETEMENTS
848	HEADGEAR,NONTXTL CLOTHNG	W 2	517	W 4	953	W 4	746	W 4	980	VET ACCES MAT AUT QUE TEX
8483	FUR ETC,CLOTHES,PRODUCTS	W 2	514	W 4	947	W 3	741	W 4	978	VETEMENTS DE FOURRURE
84831	ARTICLES OF FURSKIN,NES	W 2	514	W 4	947	W 3	741	W 4	978	PELLETERIES OUVREES NDA
89	MISC MANUFCTRD GOODS NES		3552		2424		3348		4624	ART MANUFACTURES DIVERS
896	WORKS OF ART ETC		3382		2200		3140		4387	OBJETS D'ART
89604	STAMPS FOR PHILATELY		3345		2141		3101		4343	TIMBRES–POSTE
9	GOODS NOT CLASSD BY KIND		9583		10169		7144		8862	ART TRANSACT NON CLASSES
931	*SPECIAL TRANSACTIONS	W 1078	9580	W 803	10167	W 656	7137	W 746	8862	TRANS.SPECIALES

1. HISTORICAL SERIES, 1971–1992 GENERAL TRADE, IMPORTS C.I.F., EXPORTS F.O.B.
SERIES HISTORIQUES, 1971–1992 COMMERCE GENERAL, IMPORTATIONS C.A.F., EXPORTATIONS F.O.B

YEAR ANNEE	VALUE IN MILLION E.C. DOLLARS VALEUR EN MILLION E.C. DOLLARS MERCHANDISE –MARCHANDISE IMPORTS	EXPORTS	GOLD –OR IMPORTS	EXPORTS	CONVERSION FACTORS U.S. CENTS PER E.C. DOLLAR FACTEURS DE CONVERSION CENTS E.U. PAR E.C. DOLLAR IMPORTS	EXPORTS	INDEX NUMBERS –INDICES QUANTUM IMPORTS	EXPORTS	UNIT VALUE VALEUR UNITAIRE IMPORTS	EXPORTS
1971	46.10	10.20			50.0000	50.0000				
1972	42.80	10.50			52.1387	52.1387				
1973	42.50	14.50			51.0808	51.0808				
1974	38.10	19.30			48.7301	48.7301				
1975	52.80	26.90			46.2878	46.2878				
1976	66.30	33.80			38.0480	38.0480				
1977	84.80	38.80			37.0370	37.0370				
1978	96.50	45.60			37.0370	37.0370				
1979	118.00	57.80			37.0370	37.0370				
1980	135.60	46.90			37.0370	37.0370				
1981	146.70	51.40			37.0370	37.0370				
1982	152.40	50.10			37.0370	37.0370				
1983	154.50	51.80			37.0370	37.0370				
1984	151.10	49.10			37.0370	37.0370				
1985	187.00	60.30			37.0370	37.0370				
1986	225.72	84.36			37.0370	37.0370				
1987	239.17	86.10			37.0370	37.0370				
1988	248.80	88.50			37.0370	37.0370				
1989	267.90	75.40			37.0370	37.0370				
1990	283.80	71.60			37.0370	37.0370				
1991	327.00	61.50			37.0370	37.0370				
1992	287.80	53.90			37.0370	37.0370				

2. IMPORTS BY BROAD ECONOMIC CATEGORY AND EXPORTS BY INDUSTRIAL ORIGIN. (PERCENTAGE OF TOTAL VALUE)
IMPORTATIONS PAR CATEGORIES ECONOMIQUES ET EXPORTATIONS PAR BRANCHE D'ACTIVITE. (EN POURCENTAGE DE LA VALEUR TOTALE)

IMPORTS – IMPORTATIONS

	1990	1991	1992	1993	1994	1995	1996
TOTAL IMPORTS–IMPORTATIONS TOTALES	100.	100.					
1 FOOD BEV–ALIMENTATION BOISSONS	27.0	25.1					
11 PRIMARY–PRODUITS DE BASE	9.1	8.2					
111 FOR INDUSTRY–POUR L'INDUSTRIE	2.9	2.2					
112 FOR HOUSEHOLDS–POUR LES MENAGES	6.2	6.0					
12 PROCESSED–PRODUITS ELABORES	17.9	16.9					
121 FOR INDUSTRY–POUR L'INDUSTRIE	2.0	2.1					
122 FOR HOUSEHOLDS–POUR LES MENAGES	15.9	14.8					
2 IND SUPPLIES–APPROV INDUSTRIELS	28.1	27.8					
21 PRIMARY–PRODUITS DE BASE	0.9	0.6					
22 PROCESSED–PRODUITS ELABORES	27.2	27.1					
3 FUELS–COMBUSTIBLES	6.5	6.9					
31 PRIMARY–PRODUITS DE BASE	1.2	1.2					
32 PROCESSED–PRODUITS ELABORES	5.3	5.7					
321 MOTOR SPIRIT–ESSENCE	2.9	2.6					
322 OTHER–AUTRES	2.4	3.1					
4 MACHINERY–EQUIPEMENT	11.5	14.7					
41 CAPITAL EQUIPMENT–MACHINES	10.4	13.6					
42 PARTS–PIECES ACCESSOIRES	1.1	1.1					
5 TRANSPORT–TRANSPORT	9.7	9.3					
51 PASSENGER CARS–AUTOMOBILES	3.0	2.1					
52 OTHER–AUTRES	4.0	4.6					
521 INDUSTRIAL–INDUSTRIELS	3.9	4.5					
522 NON INDUSTRIAL–NON INDUSTRIEL	0.1	0.1					
53 PARTS–PIECES ACCESSOIRES	2.8	2.6					
6 CONSUM GOODS–BIENS CONSOMMATION	17.0	16.1					
61 DURABLE–DURABLES	3.7	2.6					
62 SEMI DURABLE–SEMI DURABLES	7.6	7.7					
63 NON DURABLE–NON DURABLES	5.8	5.8					
7 GOODS NES–BIENS NDA	0.1	0.1					

EXPORTS – EXPORTATIONS

	1990	1991	1992	1993	1994	1995	1996
TOTAL EXPORTS–EXPORTATIONS TOTALES	100.	100.					
1 AGRICULTURE	61.4	59.7					
2 MINING QUARRY–INDUS EXTRACTIVES							
3 MANUFACTURING–IND MANUFACTUR	38.5	40.2					
31 FOOD BEV TOBACCO–ALIM BOISS TAB	4.7	7.8					
32 TEXTILES–INDUSTRIES TEXTILES	14.8	11.8					
33 WOOD & PRODUCTS–BOIS & PRODUITS	0.4	0.6					
34 PAPER & PRODUCTS–PAPIER & PRODT	4.7	4.1					
35 CHEMICALS–INDUSTRIES CHIMIQUES	4.4	4.9					
36 NON METAL MIN–MIN NON METAL	0.2	0.0					
37 BASIC METAL–IND METAL BASE	0.5	0.1					
38 METAL MANUF–MANUF METAL	8.5	10.7					
39 OTH MANUF IND–AUTRES MANUF	0.4	0.2					

3. TRADE BY PRINCIPAL COUNTRIES OF PRODUCTION AND LAST CONSIGNMENT (VALUE IN THOUSAND U.S. DOLLARS)
ECHANGES SELON LES PRINCIPAUX PAYS DE PRODUCTION ET DE DERNIERE CONSIGNATION (VALEUR EN MILLIERS DE DOLLARS EU)

COUNTRIES–PAYS	GENERAL IMPORTS C.I.F. IMPORTATIONS GENERALES C.A.F				
	1987	1988	1989	1990	1991
World	88600	92161	100859	108944	117231
Africa	211	11	122	44	14
Americas	52953	55996	62688	69717	79047
Northern America	29651	28489	34124	38472	43926
LAIA	2558	3933	2985	3947	4428
CACM	1191	2319	516	187	974
Caribbean	18796	20768	24446	26799	29426
Rest of America	758	487	616	312	292
As.ex F.USSR	11245	10614	11487	12643	11913
Eur.x F.USSR	23072	24084	25786	24211	24762
EU	22179	23253	24884	23175	23758
EFTA	507	545	555	608	706
East Europe	267	159	267	291	105
Other Europe	120	127	80	137	193
Former USSR	2	19	24	10	32
Oceania	1101	1426	745	2293	1464
USA/Etats–Unis d'Amer	23822	23464	30154	33319	37796
United Kingdom	14936	15094	17234	15873	16194
Trinidad and Tobago	10574	11467	13290	17120	18640
Japan/Japon	6381	5433	6423	7758	8318
Canada	5821	5008	3966	5151	6127
Barbados/Barbade	2817	3678	4006	3641	4099
Netherlands/Pays–Bas	1873	2182	2076	2702	2304
Jamaica/Jamaïque	1594	1387	1701	1554	1455
Saint Lucia/St. Lucie	1231	1423	1648	1686	1346
Venezuela	834	1586	1408	1146	2307
Germany/Allemagne	1587	1646	1293	1185	1444
New Zealand	1015	1349	689	2251	1430
Denmark/Danemark	947	917	1362	940	1005
Brazil/Brésil	662	1115	1023	1295	941
Dominican Republic	925	1111	1398	762	501
Italy/Italie	774	1445	749	524	502
France, Monac	819	738	726	861	620
Thailand/Thaïlande	591	1338	779	645	194
Korea, Republic of	595	862	799	718	437
Hong Kong	719	512	804	835	539
St Vincent & Grenadines	722	347	821	582	853
Honduras	999	1928	313		
China/Chine	434	472	644	735	753
Netherlands Antilles	62	620	777	486	1083
Colombia/Colombie	565	163	109	1067	667
Dominica/Dominique	547	487	511	459	556
Norway, SVD, JM	428	449	431	430	602
Argentina/Argentine	423	732	303	402	384
Ireland/Irlande	298	412	301	442	583
Guyana	289	258	383	282	253
Belgium–Luxembourg	232	174	291	181	377
Guatemala	98	146	155	134	665
Sweden/Suède	159	148	179	235	461
Finland/Finlande	223	241	253	81	89
Saint–Kitts–Nevis	106	132	117	226	303
Costa Rica	95	244	47	52	308
Antigua and Barbuda	159	96	82	188	172
Fm Yugoslav	119	120	43	136	190
Singapore/Singapour	95	116	81	195	107
Suriname/Suriname	431	28	113		0
Spain/Espagne	152	147	142	57	59
Mexico/Mexique	30	312	48	28	74
Switz.Liecht	78	96	119	106	83
Former GDR	120	102	141	93	
India/Inde	52	30	60	95	201
Portugal	134	62	72	64	65
Panama	38	155	111	30	29
Bangladesh	101	120	9	34	45
Israel/Israël	96	161	8	14	12
Aruba		1	1	11	264

COUNTRIES–PAYS	GENERAL EXPORTS F.O.B. EXPORTATIONS GENERALES F.O.B.				
	1987	1988	1989	1990	1991
Monde	31568	32929	27988	26211	23194
Afrique					0
Amériques	9598	13607	12364	13198	13684
Amérique du Nord	2982	5286	5182	4791	4490
ALAI	1787	1263	1046	1425	841
MCAC					0
Caraïbes	4660	6950	6039	6802	8345
Autre Amérique	168	109	97	180	9
Asie l'URSS exclus	795	351	455	797	524
Europe l'URSS exclus	21175	18971	15115	12217	8986
UE	21119	18365	15105	11859	8984
AELE	0			4	2
Europe de l'Est	55	605	10	353	
Autre de l'Europe					
Ancienne URSS					
Océanie				0	
United Kingdom	7284	7643	5762	5322	4684
Netherlands/Pays–Bas	7404	6676	7056	5138	1907
USA/Etats–Unis d'Amer	1925	4324	4146	4265	4169
Trinidad and Tobago	3020	4271	3483	2881	2924
Germany/Allemagne	5351	3927	2242	1296	2184
Saint Lucia/St. Lucie	212	366	937	1268	1824
Canada	1057	962	1035	526	320
Barbados/Barbade	507	572	553	935	1036
Argentina/Argentine	1251	907	306	483	377
Dominica/Dominique	557	607	340	424	463
St Vincent & Grenadines	193	234	342	638	939
Japan/Japon	693	143	292	675	524
Venezuela	103	147	292	914	332
Antigua and Barbuda	45	111	51	126	742
Former GDR	55	605		353	
Jamaica/Jamaïque	2	413	137	301	114
Belgium–Luxembourg	848	3			14
Brazil/Brésil	433	1	351	2	0
Saint–Kitts–Nevis	73	68	160	173	203
Guyana	156	99	97	180	2
Jordan/Jordanie	89	148	115	110	
France, Monac		77	22	85	159
Colombia/Colombie		196	96		
Martinique	5	214	2	9	18
Italy/Italie	173	9	2		3
Uruguay				25	131
Netherlands Antilles	2	60	21	12	15
Israel/Israël		60	44		
Sweden/Suède	36	16	2	8	10
Denmark/Danemark	9	14	16	6	21
Dominican Republic	34	4			
Spain/Espagne	13	0		1	2
Mexico/Mexique		12			
Singapore/Singapour				11	
Poland/Pologne			10		
Panama					7
Switz.Liecht				4	2
Austria/Autriche	1	1	2	1	
Aruba		2		2	0
Cuba					4
Suriname/Suriname	2				
Finland/Finlande				1	
Hong Kong	1			0	
Norway, SVD, JM	0				
Korea, Republic of	0				
Korea Dem People's Rp					0

(VALUE AS PERCENTAGE OF WORLD TOTAL)(VALEURS EN POURCENTAGE DU TOTAL MONDIAL)

	1982	1983	1984	1985	1986	1987	1988	1989	1990	1991
Africa			0.1	0.0	0.1	0.2	0.0	0.1	0.0	0.0
Americas			62.7	61.0	61.4	59.8	60.8	62.2	64.0	67.4
Northern America			29.6	30.4	33.4	33.5	30.9	33.8	35.3	37.5
LAIA			2.1	2.2	2.6	2.9	4.3	3.0	3.6	3.8
CACM			0.9	1.0	1.7	1.3	2.5	0.5	0.2	0.8
Caribbean			28.2	25.5	22.9	21.2	22.5	24.2	24.6	25.1
Rest of America			1.9	1.9	0.8	0.9	0.5	0.6	0.3	0.2
As.ex F.USSR			10.4	12.3	11.7	12.7	11.5	11.4	11.6	10.2
Eur.x F.USSR			25.8	25.5	25.2	26.0	26.1	25.6	22.2	21.1
EU			25.3	25.1	24.6	25.0	25.2	24.7	21.3	20.3
EFTA			0.2	0.2	0.2	0.6	0.6	0.6	0.6	0.6
East Europe			0.3	0.2	0.3	0.3	0.2	0.3	0.3	0.1
Other Europe			0.0	0.0	0.1	0.1	0.1	0.1	0.1	0.2
Former USSR			0.1	0.1	0.0	0.0	0.0	0.0	0.0	0.0
Oceania			0.9	1.0	1.5	1.2	1.5	0.7	2.1	1.2
USA/Etats–Unis d'Amer			25.1	24.7	25.5	26.9	25.5	29.9	30.6	32.2
United Kingdom			18.3	17.6	16.9	16.9	16.4	17.1	14.6	13.8
Trinidad and Tobago			14.9	13.2	13.4	11.9	12.4	13.2	15.7	15.9
Japan/Japon			6.9	8.1	7.0	7.2	5.9	6.4	7.1	7.1
Canada			4.4	5.7	7.8	6.6	5.4	3.9	4.7	5.2
Barbados/Barbade			3.8	4.3	3.5	3.2	4.0	4.0	3.3	3.5
Netherlands/Pays–Bas			1.8	1.7	2.2	2.1	2.4	2.1	2.5	2.0
Jamaica/Jamaïque			1.9	1.8	1.7	1.8	1.5	1.7	1.4	1.2
Saint Lucia/St. Lucie			1.7	1.1	1.2	1.4	1.5	1.6	1.5	1.1
Venezuela			0.4	0.2	1.0	0.9	1.7	1.4	1.1	2.0

	1982	1983	1984	1985	1986	1987	1988	1989	1990	1991
Afrique										0.0
Amériques			45.2	41.9	36.7	30.4	41.3	44.2	50.4	59.0
Amérique du Nord			8.5	5.0	11.2	9.4	16.1	18.5	18.3	19.4
ALAI			0.9	1.1	1.4	5.7	3.8	3.7	5.4	3.6
MCAC										0.0
Caraïbes			35.7	35.6	24.0	14.8	21.1	21.6	25.9	36.0
Autre Amérique			0.0	0.2	0.1	0.5	0.3	0.3	0.7	0.0
Asie l'URSS exclus			0.2	0.4	0.6	2.5	1.1	1.6	3.0	2.3
Europe l'URSS exclus			54.6	57.6	62.8	67.1	57.6	54.0	46.6	38.7
UE			53.4	55.8	61.5	66.9	55.8	54.0	45.2	38.7
AELE			0.0	0.0		0.0			0.0	0.0
Europe de l'Est			1.3	1.8	1.3	0.2	1.8	0.0	1.3	
Autre de l'Europe										
Ancienne URSS										
Océanie									0.0	
United Kingdom			29.4	26.5	27.0	23.1	23.2	20.6	20.3	20.2
Netherlands/Pays–Bas			10.4	17.6	16.9	23.5	20.3	25.2	19.6	8.2
USA/Etats–Unis d'Amer			5.6	3.3	4.6	6.1	13.1	14.8	16.3	18.0
Trinidad and Tobago			33.7	32.9	21.6	9.6	13.0	12.4	11.0	12.6
Germany/Allemagne			10.7	10.2	14.4	17.0	11.9	8.0	4.9	9.4
Saint Lucia/St. Lucie			0.0	0.0	0.1	0.7	1.1	3.3	4.8	7.9
Canada			3.0	1.7	6.6	3.3	2.9	3.7	2.0	1.4
Barbados/Barbade			0.8	1.1	1.0	1.6	1.7	2.0	3.6	4.5
Argentina/Argentine			0.9	1.1	0.2	4.0	2.8	1.1	1.8	1.6
Dominica/Dominique			0.2	0.9	0.3	1.8	1.8	1.2	1.6	2.0

4. General Imports C.I.F. by Commodities according to the S.I.T.C. (Rev. 2) in thousand U.S. Dollars
Importations Générales C.A.F. par Produits d'après la C.T.C.I. (Rév. 2) en milliers de Dollars E.U.

SITC CTCI	COMMODITY	1988		1989		1990		1991		PRODUIT
		WEIGHT POIDS	VALUE VALEUR	WEIGHT POIDS	VALUE VALEUR	WEIGHT POIDS	VALUE VALEUR	WEIGHT POIDS	VALUE VALEUR	
	ALL COMMODITIES		92161		100859		108944		117231	TOUS PRODUITS
0	FOOD AND LIVE ANIMALS		22115		25676		27632		27978	ALIMENTS,ANIMAUX VIVANTS
01	MEAT AND PREPARATIONS		5005		5629		5701		6134	VIANDES ET PREPARATIONS
011	MEAT FRESH,CHILLD,FROZEN	W 3188	3287	W 3544	3897	W 3404	3825	W 3720	3985	VIANDES FRAICHES,REF,CONGE
0111	BOVINE MEAT FRESH,FROZEN	W 93	297	W 92	286	W 75	249	W 61	219	VIANDES BOVIN FRAI,REF
0114	POULTRY FRESH CHLLD,FRZN	W 2948	2799	W 3295	3373	W 3198	3411	W 3484	3505	VOLAILLES MORTES
012	MEAT DRIED,SALTED,SMOKED	W 325	750	W 258	641	W 312	810	W 322	764	VIANDE,ABATS SALES,SECHES
0121	PIG MEAT DRIED,SLTD,SMKD	W 214	455	W 187	432	W 234	582	W 242	544	LARD,JAMBONS
0129	MEAT NES DRIED,SLTD,SMKD	W 111	295	W 71	209	W 78	227	W 81	220	VIANDE NDA SALEE,SAUMURE
014	MEAT PREPD,PRSVD,NES ETC	W 432	968		1091	W 415	1066	W 507	1385	CONSERVES DE VIANDES
0142	SAUSAGES INCLDING TINNED	W 175	407	W 186	454	W 150	349	W 171	404	SAUCISSES,SAUCISSONS
0149	OTH PREPARD,PRESRVD MEAT	W 257	561		637	W 266	717	W 336	981	AUTRES PREP DE VIANDES
02	DAIRY PRODCTS,BIRDS'EGGS		4353		4753		4838		4797	PRODUITS LAITIERS,OEUFS
022	MILK AND CREAM	W 2348	3435	W 2234	3834	W 2194	3677	W 2148	3482	LAIT ET CREME
0224	MILK,CREAM PRESERVED ETC	W 2337	3424	W 2231	3829	W 2193	3676	W 2067	3360	LAIT,CREME CONS,CONC
02242	MILK DRY,1.5% FAT OR LES	W 156	363	W 5	16	W 70	154	W 52	104	LAIT POUDRE INF 1.5%
02243	MILK DRY,OVER 1.5% FAT	W 1085	1965	W 981	2436	W 825	1978	W 673	1605	LAIT POUDRE SUP 1.5%
02249	MILK(EX DRY) PRSVD,SWEET	W 1096	1096	W 1242	1375	W 1298	1544	W 1294	1586	LAIT CONS,CONC SUCRE
024	CHEESE AND CURD	W 360	823	W 257	812	W 367	1077	W 432	1193	FROMAGE ET CAILLEBOTTE
03	FISH AND PREPARATIONS		1253		1509		1627		2008	POISSONS ET PREPARATIONS
035	FISH SALTED,DRIED,SMOKED	W 319	850	W 424	1169	W 365	1162	W 422	1578	POISSON SECHE,SALE,FUME
03502	COD(NOT IN FILLETS)DRIED	W 121	372	W 195	626	W 187	692	W 160	709	MORUE SECHEE,SALEE
03503	FISH(EX COD)DRIED,SALTED	W 142	364	W 163	419	W 133	380	W 198	707	POISSONS SECHES,SALES
037	FISH ETC PREPD,PRSVD NES	W 202	346	W 131	284	W 170	418	W 168	382	POIS,CRUST,MOL PREPARES
0371	FISH PREPARD,PRESRVD NES	W 202	344	W 130	281	W 169	414	W 166	374	CONSERVES DE POISSONS
04	CEREALS AND PREPARATIONS		4576		5700		5767		5942	CEREALES ET PRODUITS
041	WHEAT ETC UNMILLED	W 7575	1332	W 10048	2025	W 9863	2027	W 11323	1974	FROMENT,EPEAUTRE
0412	OTHER WHEAT ETC UNMILLED	W 7575	1332	W 10048	2025	W 9863	2027	W 10123	1774	AUTRE FROMENT NON MOULU
042	RICE	W 2465	1279		1345	W 1991	1094		925	RIZ
0421	RICE IN HUSK OR HUSKED	W 2360	1208	W 3230	1291	W 1896	1028	W 870	464	RIZ SANS AUTRE PREPARATION
04212	RICE HUSKED	W 2360	1208	W 3230	1291	W 1830	988	W 870	464	RIZ CARGO
0422	RICE SEMI–MILLED,MILLED	W 105	70		54	W 95	66		462	RIZ POLI,GLACE INCL BRISURES
04221	RICE MILLED UNBROKEN	W 87	65	W 71	54	W 95	66	W 695	461	RIZ POLI,GLACE EXCL BRISURES
046	WHEAT ETC MEAL OR FLOUR	W 40	48	W 50	70	W 45	73	W 1797	544	SEMOULE FARINE,FROMENT
04601	FLOUR OF WHEAT OR MESLIN	W 14	6	W 22	15	W 21	10	W 1775	495	FARINE DE FROMENT
048	CEREAL ETC PREPARATIONS	W 1014	1698	W 1211	2013	W 1325	2221	W 1354	2141	PREPTNS A BASE CEREALES
0481	PREPD BREAKFAST FOOD ETC	W 117	372	W 183	527	W 173	557	W 162	524	CEREALES TRAVAILLEES
04812	CEREAL ROASTED, PUFFED	W 107	350	W 174	500	W 162	528	W 162	524	PRODTS BASE CEREALES
0484	BAKERY PRODUCTS	W 357	750	W 414	864	W 547	1077	W 509	998	PRODUITS DE BOULANGERIE
04842	PASTRY, CAKES ETC	W 356	748	W 411	856	W 543	1065	W 501	982	PATISSERIE ETC.
0488	OTH CEREAL PREPS,MALT EX	W 83	299	W 91	334	W 83	295	W 74	265	EXTRAITS DE MALT
05	VEGETABLES AND FRUIT		1789		2247		2739		2302	LEGUMES ET FRUITS
054	VEG ETC FRSH,SMPLY PRSVD	W 1647	931	W 1803	1119	W 2176	1472	W 1610	1066	LEGUMES FRAIS,CONG,SECS
0541	POTATOES FRSH EXCL SWEET	W 943	439	W 962	462	W 1108	624	W 872	455	POMMES DE TERRE
0545	OTHER FRESH VEGETABLES	W 485	309	W 491	349	W 729	519	W 498	373	AUTRES LEGUMES FRAIS,REF
05451	ALLIACEOUS VEGTBLS,FRESH	W 400	243	W 425	287	W 497	350	W 409	271	OIGNONS,ECHALOTES,AULX
058	FRUIT PRESERVED,PREPARED	W 452	592	W 569	741	W 699	893	W 654	888	CONSERVES DE FRUITS
0585	FRUIT OR VEGETABLE JUICE	W 391	427	W 480	504	W 624	684	W 561	625	JUS DE FRUITS
05851	ORANGE JUICE	W 218	239	W 257	265	W 383	429	W 317	352	JUS D'ORANGE
06	SUGAR AND PREPS,HONEY		1950		2235		2869		2400	SUCRES ET PRODUITS
061	SUGAR AND HONEY		1775		2017		2661		2237	SUCRES ET MIEL
0611	RAW BEET AND CANE SUGAR	W 2725	853	W 495647	1033	W 602323	1372	W 1720	1098	SUCRES BRUTS
0612	REFINED SUGAR ETC	W 2090	849	W 2048	947	W 2244	1235	W 2144	1122	SUCRES RAFFINES
07	COFFEE,TEA,COCOA,SPICES		414		474		529		467	CAFE,THE,CACAO,EPICES
081	*FEEDING STUFF FOR ANIML		194		286		410		422	NOURRITURE POUR ANIMAUX
09	MISC EDIBLE PRODUCTS		2576		2834		3116		3435	PREP ALIMENTAIRES DIVERSES
091	MARGARINE AND SHORTENING	W 688	1045	W 684	1033	W 738	1106	W 722	1070	MARGARINE ET GRAISSES
0914	MARGARINE,EDIBLE FAT NES	W 688	1045	W 684	1033	W 738	1106	W 722	1070	MARGARINES,SIMILI SAINDOUX
09141	MARGARINE	W 432	661	W 465	697	W 492	741	W 490	773	MARGARINE
09149	OTH PREPARED EDIBLE FATS	W 256	383	W 220	336	W 246	365	W 231	297	SIMILI–SAINDOUX
098	EDIBLE PRODCTS,PREPS NES		1532		1801		2010		2366	PREP ALIMENTAIRES NDA
09804	SAUCES,MIXED SEASONINGS	W 267	431	W 302	458	W 313	521	W 367	540	SAUCES,ASSAISONNEMENTS
09809	MISC FOOD PREPRTIONS NES	W 427	778	W 505	981	W 647	1141	W 751	1422	PREP ALIMENTAIRES NDA
1	BEVERAGES AND TOBACCO		2292		2220		2431		2091	BOISSONS ET TABACS
11	BEVERAGES		2092		2058		2270		1919	BOISSONS
111	NON–ALCOHL BEVERAGES NES		785		849		1023		896	BOISSONS NON ALCOOLIQUES
11102	FLAVORED WATERS NON–ALCO	W 749	771	W 766	831	W 936	1004	W 818	867	LIMONADES,EAUX GAZEUSES
112	ALCOHOLIC BEVERAGES	W 708	1307	W 622	1208	W 610	1247	W 501	1023	BOISSONS ALCOOLIQUES
1123	BEER,ALE,STOUT,PORTER	W 405	556	W 359	467	W 336	490	W 268	345	BIERES
1124	DISTILLED ALCOHOLIC BEVS	W 172	481	W 154	466	W 141	420	W 135	402	ALCOOLS,EAUX–DE–VIE
2	CRUDE MATERLS,EXCL FUELS		5090		3628		3973		3012	MAT BRUTES NON COMESTIBLES
24	CORK AND WOOD		4422		3125		3667		2622	LIEGE ET BOIS
247	OTH WOOD ROUGH,SQUARED	W 691	259		66	W 707	374	W 56	29	BOIS BRUTS EQUARRIS
2479	PTPROPS,POLES,PILING,ETC	W 2	1	W 146	64	W 707	374	W 44	23	POTEAUX DE MINES
248	WOOD SHAPED,SLEEPERS	W 14471	4163	W 7509	3059	W 6537	3293	W 7047	2592	BOIS SIMPLEMENT TRAVAILLES
2482	LUMBER SHAPED CONIFER	W 2689	1260	W 2075	839	W 2057	1129	W 2735	1049	CONIFERES SCIES,RABOTES
24821	LUMBER SAWN ETC CONIFER	W 905	345	W 672	237	W 683	334	W 749	301	CONIFERES SCIES LONGITUD
24822	LUMBER PLANED ETC CONIFR	W 1784	915	W 1403	602	W 1375	794	W 1986	748	CONIFER RABOTES,RAINES
2483	LUMBER SHAPED NON–CONIFR	W 11782	2903	W 5435	2220	W 4480	2165	W 4309	1539	NON CONIFERES SCIES,RABOTES
24831	LUMBER SAWN ETC NON–CON	W 1058	722	W 1609	586	W 1028	517	W 1000	396	SCIES LONGITUDINALEMENT
24832	LUMBER PLANED ETC NONCON	W 10723	2181	W 3826	1634	W 3452	1648	W 3308	1143	RABOTES,RAINES,LANGUETES
27	CRUDE FERTLZR,MINRLS NES		560		351		147		178	ENGRAIS MINERAUX BRUTS
278	OTHER CRUDE MINERALS	W 1215	507		324		122		127	AUTRES MINERAUX BRUTS
2789	MINERALS CRUDE NES	W 778	414		237		9		17	MINERAUX BRUTS NDA
27896	NATURAL ASPHALT,BITUMEN	W 713	389	W 674	229		7	W 75	15	BITUMES,ASPHALTES NATURELS
3	MINERAL FUELS ETC		5070		5874		7450		8644	COMBUSTIBLES MINERAUX LUB
33	PETROLEUM AND PRODUCTS		4207		4899		6138		7229	PETROLE ET DERIVES
334	PETROLEUM PRODUCTS,REFIN		3776		4562		5791		6675	PRODUITS RAFFINES
3341	GASOLINE,OTH LIGHT OILS		2261		2738	W 15009	3195	W 10763	3039	ESSENCES POUR MOTEURS
33411	MOTOR,AVIATION SPIRIT	W 10361	2261	W 11280	2738	W 15009	3195	W 10057	2856	ESSENCES MOTEURS D'AVIONS
3343	GAS OILS	W 4786	828	W 6318	1064	W 22841	1836	W 9986	2654	GAS OILS
3345	LUBS,PETROLEUM OILS NES		482		543		555		453	HUILES LUBRIFIANTES
33451	LUBS(HIGH PETR CONT) ETC		472		536		551		445	HUILES LUBRIF,H LOURDES
335	RESIDUAL PETRLM PROD NES		431		338	W 639	347		554	PRODUITS RESIDUELS NDA
3354	PETROLM BITUMEN,COKE ETC		384		316	W 629	307	W 2766	461	BITUME,COKE DE PETROLE
33543	BITUMINOUS MIXTURES ETC	W 1427	371	W 1411	316	W 629	307	W 1122	253	MELANGES BITUMINEUX
341	*GAS,NATURAL AND MANUFCT	W 2405	861	W 2203	959	W 2565	1297	W 2878	1412	GAZ NATUREL,GAZ MANUFACT
3413	PETROLM GASES,LIQUEFIED	W 2405	860	W 2202	958	W 2565	1297	W 2877	1411	GAZ DE PETROLE LIQUEFIE
34131	LIQUEFIED PROPANE,BUTANE	W 2404	857	W 2202	958	W 2564	1296	W 2651	1320	PROPANE,BUTANE LIQUEFIES
4	ANIMAL,VEGETABLE OIL,FAT		433		424		406		422	HUILES,GRAISSES ANIM,VEG
42	FIXED VEGETABLE OIL,FAT		415		405		388		373	HUILES VEGETALES FIXES

4. General Imports C.I.F. by Commodities according to the S.I.T.C. (Rev. 2) in thousand U.S. Dollars
Importations Générales C.A.F. par Produits d'après la C.T.C.I. (Rév. 2) en milliers de Dollars E.U.

SITC CTCI	COMMODITY	1988		1989		1990		1991		PRODUIT
		WEIGHT POIDS	VALUE VALEUR	WEIGHT POIDS	VALUE VALEUR	WEIGHT POIDS	VALUE VALEUR	WEIGHT POIDS	VALUE VALEUR	
5	CHEMCLS,RELATED PROD NES		8446		9602		9818		9995	PRODUITS CHIMIQUES
52	INORGANIC CHEMICALS		308		415		349		307	PROD CHIM INORGANIQUES
522	INORG ELEMNTS,OXIDES,ETC	W 159	239	W 193	353	W 145	273		234	ELEMENTS INORGANIQUES
53	DYES,TANNING,COLOUR PROD		988		1020		1195		1393	PROD TEINTURE,COLORANTS
531	SYNT DYE,NAT INDGO,LAKES		317	W 102	269	W 186	396	W 233	443	MAT COLOR ORGAN,LAQUES
5312	SYNTH LUMIN,INDIGO,LAKES	W 141	236	W 81	229	W 180	386	W 97	286	LUMINOPHORES ORGAN SYNTH
53121	SYN ORG LUMIN ETC,INDIGO	W 141	236	W 81	229	W 180	386	W 97	286	PROD ORGANIQ SYNTH LUMIN
533	PIGMENTS,PAINTS,ETC		662		749		796		912	PIGMENTS,PEINTURES,VERNIS
5334	VARNISHES,DISTEMPERS ETC		506		534		594		679	PEINTURES A L'EAU
53342	OTH PAINTS,VARNISHES ETC	V 108	428	V 107	373	V 107	475	V 86	418	AUTRES PEINTURES,VERNIS
541	*MEDICINAL,PHARM PRODUCT	K 126996	1530	K 228334	1909	K 197341	2117	K 156946	1971	PROD MEDICINAUX PHARMACEUT
5417	MEDICAMENTS	K 116869	1372	K 216226	1739	K 187498	1989	K 141246	1754	MEDICAMENTS
54179	— CONTNG OTH SUBSTANCES	K 116648	1364	K 216049	1735	K 186466	1981	K 141222	1753	MED CONT AUT SUBSTANCES
55	PERFUME,CLEANING ETC PRD		2477		2700		2945		3113	PROD POUR PARFUM,TOILETTE
553	PERFUMERY,COSMETICS,ETC		853		988		1038		1104	PRODUITS DE PARFUMERIE
554	SOAP,CLEANSING ETC PREPS	W 1268	1617	W 1598	1703	W 1492	1901	W 1389	1986	SAVONS,PRODUITS DETERSIFS
5541	SOAPS	W 508	667	W 604	589	W 610	629	W 462	660	SAVONS,PROD TENSIO–ACTIFS
5542	WASHING PREPARATIONS ETC	W 741	890	W 970	1044	W 845	1183	W 904	1256	PROD ORG TENSIO–ACT NDA
562	*FERTILIZERS,MANUFACTURE	W 2590	573	W 4047	595	W 2538	779		694	ENGRAIS MANUFACTURES
5621	CHEM NITROGENOUS FERTLZR	W 1988	451	W 2079	453	W 1624	398	W 1558	400	ENGRAIS AZOTES
56219	CHEM NITROG FERTILZR NES	W 1950	435	W 1917	434	W 1578	379	W 1375	361	ENGRAIS AZOTES NDA
5629	FERTILIZERS NES	W 452	92	W 742	142	W 912	381	W 1146	292	ENGRAIS NDA
56291	NIT–PHOS–POT FERTLZR NES	W 312	71	W 134	11	W 790	351	W 357	90	ENGRAIS CONT N P K
58	PLASTIC MATERIALS ETC		1185		1347		1077		965	MAT PLAST ARTIFICIELLES
583	POLYMERIZATION ETC PRODS	W 313	831	W 353	1030	W 243	678	W 166	480	PROD POLYMERISATION
5839	OTH POLYMRZTION ETC PROD	W 313	831	W 353	1030	W 243	678	W 166	480	AUT PROD POLYMER COPOLYM
585	PLASTIC MATERIAL NES	W 132	252	W 117	260	W 189	320	W 132	407	RESINES ARTIFICIELLES
59	CHEMICAL MATERIALS NES		1254		1479		1231		1393	MAT PROD CHIMIQUES NDA
591	PESTICIDES,DISINFECTANTS	W 281	717	W 380	825	W 407	738	W 394	792	DESINF,INSECT,FONG,HERB
5911	INSECTICIDES,FOR RETAIL	W 111	378	W 266	429	W 152	344	W 178	414	INSECTICIDES VENTE DET
598	MISCEL CHEM PRODUCTS NES		387		447		284		379	PROD DIV INDUST CHIM NDA
5989	CHEM PRODUCTS,PREPS NES	W 116	359	W 120	383	W 81	275	W 101	361	PROD PREP CHIMIQUES NDA
6	BASIC MANUFACTURES		18039		21775		20482		23694	ART MANUFACTURES
62	RUBBER MANUFACTURES NES		1410		1398		1416		1548	CAOUTCHOUC MANUFACTURE
625	RUBBER TYRES, TUBES ETC	N 41463	1140	N 48549	970	N 112791	1103		1239	PNEUS CAOUTCHOUC VULCANISE
6252	TYRES,NEW,BUS OR LORRY	N 5446	313	N 2063	147	N 2856	208	N 2235	171	PNEUS POUR AUTOBUS,CAMIONS
6259	OTH TYRES,TYRE CASES,ETC	N 28102	581	N 38235	612	N 102420	678		736	AUTRES PNEUS RECHAPES FLAPS
62599	TYRES NES,TYRE CASES,ETC			N 30513	572					PNEUS,FLAPS
63	WOOD,CORK MANUFACTRS NES		1425		1424		1665		2071	OUVRAGES LIEGE ET BOIS
634	VENEERS,PLYWOOD,ETC		1089		1070		1195		1431	PLACAGES,CONTRE–PLAQUES
6342	PLYWOOD OF WOOD SHEETS	V 2424	896	V 3211	939	V 2504	1124	V 2055	763	BOIS CONTRE–PLAQUES
6344	WOOD–BASED PANELS NES	V 105	47	V 231	53	V 98	41	V 1803	520	PANNEAUX SUPPORT BOIS NDA
63442	INLAID WOOD,MARQUETRY	V 76	26	V 113	29	V 69	25	V 1703	480	BOIS MARQUETES,INCRUSTES
635	WOOD MANUFACTURES NES		329		349		467		636	ART MANUF EN BOIS NDA
6353	BUILDERS WOODWRK,PREFABS	W 1087	170		211	W 226	250	W 444	364	OUVRAGES DE MENUISERIE
64	PAPER,PAPERBOARD AND MFR		2719		3881		3671		3868	PAPIERS,CARTONS & OUVRAGES
641	PAPER AND PAPERBOARD	W 530	619	W 827	1514	W 725	1034	W 497	771	PAPIERS ET CARTONS
6415	PAPER,PAPERBRD,BULK,NES	W 315	334	W 386	815	W 61	155	W 227	314	PAPIERS,CARTONS ROULEAUX
64159	OTHER PAPER ETC,BULK,NES	W 304	314	W 370	783	W 52	135	W 204	261	AUT PAPIER ROULEAUX FEUILLES
6418	COATED ETC PAPER NES BLK	W 110	154	W 145	268	W 573	694	W 125	237	PAP,CARTONS COUCHES,ENDUITS
64189	COATED PAPER ETC NES	W 19	37	W 24	61	W 503	601	W 125	236	PAPIERS,CARTONS COUCHES
642	PAPER,ETC,PRECUT,ARTS OF	W 1231	2099	W 1302	2367	W 1625	2637	W 1603	3097	PAP,CARTONS DECOUPES
6421	PAPER ETC CONTAINERS	W 936	948	W 954	1093	W 1126	1039	W 891	1044	BOITES,SACS EMBALLAGES
6423	EXERCISE BOOKS ETC	W 67	472	W 69	442	W 90	537	W 105	594	REGISTRES,CAHIERS,CARNETS
6424	PAPER ETC CT TO SIZE NES	W 90	277	W 138	362	W 181	510	W 403	777	PAP,CARTONS DECOUPES
64243	TOILET PAPER CUT TO SIZE	W 5	9	W 3	23	W 21	79	W 315	425	PAPIER HYGIENIQUE
64249	OTH PAPER CT TO SIZE NES	W 67	192	W 123	263	W 146	342	W 78	257	AUT PAP CARTON DECOUP NDA
6428	PAPER ETC ARTICLES NES	W 120	311	W 121	361	W 209	445	W 184	569	OUVRAGES EN PATE A PAPIER
65	TEXTILE YARN,FABRICS,ETC		1814		2570		2590		2479	FILS,TISSUS,ARTICLES TEXTILE
653	WOVN MAN–MADE FIB FABRIC	A 394	586	A 677	1069	A 582	920	A 1056	757	TISSUS FIBRES SYNTH,ARTIF
6532	DISC SYN TXTL FABRIC NES	A 316	504	A 590	934	A 502	754	A 410	638	TIS DISC MOINS 85% FIBR TEXT
655	KNITTED,ETC FABRICS	A 6	13	A 59	92	A 98	246	A 220	431	ETOF BONNETERIE PIECES ETC
657	SPECIAL TXTL FABRC,PRODS		187		252		334		264	TISSUS SPECIAUX
658	TEXTILE ARTICLES NES		449		397		465		388	ART FACONNES MAT TEXTILES
66	NONMETAL MINERAL MFS NES		3392		4105		3824		5444	ART MIN NON METALLIQUES
661	LIME,CEMENT,BLDG PRODS	W 29301	1947		2158	W 29291	2114	W 33496	2377	CHAUX,CIMENTS MAT CONSTR
6612	CEMENT	W 28799	1803	W 31477	2070	W 28857	1950	W 33306	2256	CIMENTS HYDRAULIQUES
662	CLAY,REFRACTORY BLDG PRD		261		455		349		456	MAT CONST REFRACTAIRES
6624	BRICKS ETC NONREFRACTORY		256		447		347		419	BRIQUES ETC CERAM NON REFR
663	MINERAL MANUFCTURES NES	W 25	68	W 358	414	W 346	322	W 363	220	ART MIN MANUF NDA
664	GLASS		328		346		335		560	VERRE
665	GLASSWARE		705		622		595		1679	OUVRAGES EN VERRE
6651	BOTTLES ETC OF GLASS		542		477		465		1502	RECIPIENTS EN VERRE
66511	GLASS BOTTLES ETC NONVAC		542		476		464		1499	BONBONNES,BOUTEILLES,ETC
67	IRON AND STEEL		2129		2564		1896		1952	FER ET ACIER
672	IRON,STEEL PRIMARY FORMS	W 1434	850	W 979	708		477		288	LINGOTS FER,ACIER
6727	IRN,STL COIL FR REROLLNG	W 1272	847	W 869	707		475	W 344	280	EBAUCHES POUR TOLES FER
67271	IRON,SIMPLE STEEL COILS	W 1272	847	W 869	707	W 501	474	W 197	166	EBAUCHES NON EN ACIER
673	IRON,STEEL SHAPES ETC		547	W 3791	795	W 1856	769	W 1668	702	BARRES,PROFIL FER,ACIER
6731	IRON,STEEL WIRE ROD	W 454	175	W 697	248	W 961	352	W 478	176	FIL MACHINE FER,ACIER
67311	IRON,SIMPLE STL WIRE ROD	W 454	175	W 697	248	W 961	352	W 464	167	FIL MACH AUT ACIER FIN
6732	IRON,STEEL BARS ETC		326	W 963	450	W 809	341	W 1155	495	BARRES FER,ACIER
67326	IRN,OTH STL BARS HOTROLD	W 785	307			W 780	327	W 321	215	BARRES PLEINES FER,ACIER
674	IRN,STL UNIV,PLATE,SHEET		252		475	W 153	168		136	LARGES PLATS,TOLES
6749	OTH IRN,STL PLATES,SHEET	W 420	214	W 381	386	W 92	96		130	AUTRES TOLES FER,ACIER
67491	— OF IRON OR SIMPLE STL	W 420	214	W 381	386	W 92	96	W 120	129	AUT TOLES AUTRES ACIER FIN
678	IRON,STL TUBES,PIPES,ETC	W 521	414		531		372	W 281	494	TUBES,TUYAUX EN FONTE,FER
69	METAL MANUFACTURES NES		4984		5685		5205		6095	ART MANUFACT EN METAL NDA
691	STRUCTURES AND PARTS NES	W 551	1431	W 467	1402	W 461	1377	W 537	1246	CONSTRUCT FER,ACIER,ALU
6911	STRUCTURES,PARTS IRN,STL	W 398	846	W 353	784	W 356	714	W 391	566	CONSTRUCT FER,ACIER,FONTE
6912	STRUCTURES,PARTS ALUMNM	W 153	584	W 114	618	W 105	663	W 146	680	CONSTRUCT ALUMINIUM
692	METAL TANKS,BOXES,ETC	W 133	273	W 251	683	W 143	327	W 240	803	RECIPIENTS METALLIQUES
6921	METAL STORAGE TANKS ETC	W 34	64	W 55	365	W 13	48	W 47	532	CUVES EN FONTE,FER,ALU
69211	STEEL STORAGE TANKS ETC	W 34	64	W 55	365	W 13	41	W 46	531	CUVES EN FONTE FER OU ACIER
6924	MTL TRANSPORT BOXES ETC	W 99	209	W 195	318	W 129	279	W 193	271	FUTS,TAMBOURS,BIDONS
693	WIRE PRODUCTS NON ELECTR	W 290	333	W 373	614	W 294	389	W 313	577	OUVRAGES FILS METALLIQUES
6931	WIRE CABLES, ROPES ETC	W 47	119	W 108	314	W 29	75	W 36	273	CORDAGES EN FILS DE FER
694	STL,COPPR NAILS,NUTS,ETC	W 191	346	W 188	431	W 188	436	W 164	385	CLOUS,VIS,ECROUS
695	TOOLS		406		449		496		547	OUTILS A MAIN
6953	OTHER HAND TOOLS		251		258		279		353	AUTRES OUTILS A MAIN
697	BASE MTL HOUSEHOLD EQUIP		1088		667		814		908	ART MENAGE MET COMMUNS

4. General Imports C.I.F. by Commodities according to the S.I.T.C. (Rev. 2) in thousand U.S. Dollars
Importations Générales C.A.F. par Produits d'après la C.T.C.I. (Rév. 2) en milliers de Dollars E.U.

SITC CTCI	COMMODITY	1988 WEIGHT POIDS	1988 VALUE VALEUR	1989 WEIGHT POIDS	1989 VALUE VALEUR	1990 WEIGHT POIDS	1990 VALUE VALEUR	1991 WEIGHT POIDS	1991 VALUE VALEUR	PRODUIT
6973	DMSTC HEATG,COOKG APPARA		812		351		496		526	APPS CHAUF NON ELECTRIQ
69731	IRN,STL DOM COOKG APPARA	N 2318	509	N 1158	199	N 1940	307	N 2605	281	APPS CUISSON FER,ACIER
699	BASE METAL MFRS NES	W 268	1041	W 321	1359	W 265	1264	W 626	1548	ART MANUFACTURES MET NDA
6991	LOCKSMITHS WARES,ETC	W 68	377	W 55	312	W 61	498	W 59	394	ARTICLES DE SERRURERIE
6997	IRON,STEEL ARTICLES NES	W 67	346	W 171	665	W 102	380	W 206	535	OUV FONTE,FER,ACIER NDA
69979	IRN,STL MANUFACTURES NES	W 66	318	W 170	661	W 102	377	W 206	534	AUT OUVRAGES EN FER NDA
7	MACHINES,TRANSPORT EQUIP		20840		20594		24421		28379	MACHINES MATERIEL TRANSPORT
71	POWER GENERATING EQUIPMT		1250		1263		1071		1923	MACHINES GENERATRICES
711	STEAM BOILERS & AUX PLNT		71		81		6		1028	GENERATEURS VAPEUR EAU ETC
7112	AUXILIARY BOILER PLANT							W 16	713	APPAREILS AUXIL DU 711.1
713	INTRNL COMBUS PSTN ENGIN		755		951		607		572	MOTEURS EXPL COMB INT, PIECE
7139	PISTON ENGINE PARTS NES	W 19	563	W 32	778	W 13	403	W 17	349	PIECES POUR 713.2,3,8
716	ROTATING ELECTRIC PLANT		419		215		457		267	APP ELECTR ROTATIFS,PIECES
72	MACHS FOR SPCL INDUSTRYS		2946		1688		1721		1963	MAC SPECIALES POUR INDUST
722	TRACTORS NON–ROAD	N 6	313	N 5	95	N 3	57	N 3	151	TRACTEURS
723	CIVIL ENGNEERG EQUIP ETC	W 49	257	W 73	478	W 405	535	W 175	574	APPAREILS DE GENIE CIVIL
7234	CONST,MINING MACHNRY NES	W 46	199	W 54	302	W 399	474	W 145	339	MACH POUR LA CONST, MINES
72348	PUBLIC WORKS MACHNRY NES	W 46	199			W 399	474	W 145	339	MACHINES TRAVAUX PUBLICS
726	PRINTG,BKBINDG MACHY,PTS	W 16	309	W 6	75	W 12	101	W 2	42	MACHINES POUR IMPRIMERIE
727	FOOD MACHRY NON–DOMESTIC	W 38	728	W 12	108	W 22	415	W 13	174	MACH INDUSTRIES ALIMENT
7271	GRAIN WORKING MCHY,PARTS	W 16	423	W 3	36	W 7	70	W 2	18	MACH POUR MINOTERIE,PIEC
72711	GRAIN MILLING ETC MACHRY	W 12	403	W 2	22			W 1	5	MACHINES POUR MINOTERIE
7272	OTH FOOD PROC MCHY,PARTS	W 22	305	W 9	72	W 16	345	W 11	156	AUT MACH IND ALIMENTAIRE
72722	INDUS FOOD PROC MACH NES	W 21	292	W 8	58	W 15	332	W 11	148	MACHINES BOULANGERIE
728	OTH MACHY FOR SPCL INDUS	W 157	1105	W 96	409	W 29	289	W 74	574	AUT MACH IND PARTICULIERES
7283	OTHR MINERAL WORKG MACHY	W 143	952	W 67	223	W 12	101	W 31	118	MACH TRIER,CRIBLER,BROYER
7284	MACHY FOR SPCL INDUS NES	W 8	111	W 27	127	W 10	90	W 31	428	MACH SPEC IND PARTICUL.
73	METALWORKING MACHINERY		70		348		155		259	MACH TRAVAIL DES METAUX
736	METALWORKING MACH–TOOLS	W 17	51	W 42	307	W 3	115	W 12	114	MACH–OUTILS TRAVAIL METAUX
74	GENRL INDUSTRL MACHY NES		3197		2710		2644		5111	MACH APP INDUSTRIE
741	HEATING,COOLING EQUIPMNT		653		642		852		1591	MACH CHAUFFAGE,PIECES
7414	NONDOM REFRIG EQUIPT,PTS		394		312		452		940	MAT PRODUCTION DU FROID
74141	REFRIG EQUIP NONDOMESTIC		280		178		301		880	REFIG INDUSTRIELS
7415	AIR–CONDITIONING MACHNRY		189		279		360		632	GROUPES CONDITION AIR
742	PUMPS FOR LIQUIDS ETC		215		260		230		1397	POMPES MOTO–POMPES
743	PUMPS NES,CENTRFUGES ETC		472		355		359		567	POMPES COMPRES,VENT ETC
744	MECHANICAL HANDLING EQU		470		669		282		379	EQUIP MANUTENTION PIECES
7442	LIFTING,LOADING MACH NES	W 23	382	W 69	407	W 14	122	W 28	269	APP LEVAGE,MANUTENTION
74428	OTH HANDLING ETC MCH NES	W 23	382	W 69	407	W 14	122	W 28	269	AUT APP LEVAGE ETC
745	NONELEC MACHY,TOOLS NES	W 78	904	W 19	276	W 28	394	W 72	589	AUT MACH NON ELEC,PIECES
7452	OTH NONELEC MCHS,PTS NES	W 75	882	W 14	212	W 23	317	W 69	535	AUT MACH NON ELEC,PIECES
74522	PACKAGNG,BOTTLNG,ETC MCH	W 63	724	W 3	41	W 4	126	W 57	311	MACH NETT BOUTEILLES,ETC
749	NONELEC MACH PTS,ACC NES	W 120	483	W 40	508	W 41	528	W 45	588	PIECES MACH NON ELEC NDA
75	OFFICE MACHNES,ADP EQUIP		1057		879		2282		1696	MACH BUREAU TRAIT AUTOM
751	OFFICE MACHINES	N 2767	231	N 5957	224	N 3758	308	N 5437	441	MACH,APPAREILS DE BUREAU
752	AUTOMTIC DATA PROC EQUIP	N 200	552	N 228	442	N 536	1455	N 367	733	MACH TRAIT INFORMATION
759	OFFICE,ADP MCH PTS,ACCES	W 7	274	W 5	213	W 13	518	W 14	521	PIECES DU 751 ET 752
7591	OFFICE MACHINE PARTS NES	W 5	242	W 4	154	W 12	494	W 12	504	PIECES DU 7511,7518
76	TELECOMM,SOUND EQUIPMENT		2220		2230		3339		4461	EQUIPMENT DE TELECOM
761	TELEVISION RECEIVERS	N 973	172	N 1766	314	N 1532	306	N 1312	262	RECEPTEURS DE TELEVISION
764	TELECOM EQPT,PTS,ACC NES		1735		1616		2762		3873	EQUIP TELECOM,PIECES
7641	LINE TELEPHONE,ETC EQUIP	W 20	1527	W 35	1305	W 34	2318	W 45	2167	APP TELEPHON PAR FIL
7649	PTS NES OF EQUIPMT OF 76	W 7	89	W 6	153	W 14	196	W 26	1150	PIECES DE LA DIV 76
76491	PTS NES OF APPAR OF 7641	W 1	24	W 1	62	W 1	93	W 16	1005	PIECES POUR 764.1
77	ELECTRIC MACHNRY NES ETC		3961		4178		4654		4259	MACH APP ELECT NDA
771	ELECTRIC POWER MACHY NES		325		312		261		341	MACH PROD,TRANS ELECTR
7711	TRANSFORMERS,ELECTRICAL	N 2701	297	N 1539	209	N 4444	235	N 2671	181	TRANSFO ELECTRIQUES
772	SWITCHGEAR ETC,PARTS NES	W 30	602	W 56	1040	W 46	766	W 31	747	APP COUPURE,SECT ETC
7721	SWITCHGEAR ETC	W 26	496	W 50	824	W 43	709	W 26	573	APP COUPURE,SECTIONMNT
773	ELECTR DISTRIBUTNG EQUIP	W 403	1116	W 227	1045	W 725	1687	W 367	1575	EQUIPMT DISTRIBUTION ELECT
7731	INSULATED WIRE,CABLE ETC	W 392	1067	W 205	968	W 723	1668	W 365	1545	FILS,CABLES ISOLES ELECT
775	HOUSEHOLD TYPE EQUIP NES		1097		781		967		554	MACH,APP USAGE DOMESTQUE
7752	DOM REFRIGERATRS,FREEZRS	N 2782	799	N 1417	461	N 1822	619	N 840	231	REFRIG,CONGEL MENAGER
77521	DOMESTIC REFRIGERATORS	N 2383	697	N 1271	412	N 1653	554	N 781	211	REFRIGERATEURS
778	ELECTRICAL MACHINERY NES		725		970		948		994	AUTRES MACH ELECT NDA
7781	BATTERIES,ACCUMULATORS		460		461		491		467	PILES ET ACCUMULATEURS
77811	PRIMARY BATTERIES,CELLS	N 1180822	281	N 1012758	307	N 801967	314	N 421026	160	PILES ELECTRIQUES,PIECES
78	ROAD VEHICLES		6059		7124		8460		7468	VEHICULES ROUTIERS
781	PASS MOTOR VEH EXC BUSES	N 348	2065	N 453	2555	N 510	3227	N 376	2520	AUTO TRANSPORT PERSONNES
782	LORRIES,SPCL MTR VEH NES	N 243	2062	N 371	2673	N 312	2836	N 305	2711	VEHICULES SPECIAUX,MARCH
7821	LORRIES,TRUCKS	N 237	1942	N 292	2649	N 309	2749	N 301	2516	VEHICULES TRANSP MARCHAND
783	ROAD MOTOR VEHICLES NES		990	N 84	786	N 126	1175	N 115	1297	VEHICULES ROUTIERS NDA
7831	BUSES	N 80	990	N 84	786	N 126	1175	N 115	1297	VOITURES TRANSPORT COMMUN
784	MOTOR VEH PRTS,ACCES NES		723		774		956	W 76	793	PIECES 722,781,782,783
7849	OTHER MOTOR VEHCL PARTS	W 87	706	W 165	765	W 94	943	W 71	763	PIECES 722,781,782,783
79	OTHR TRANSPORT EQUIPMENT		80		172		93		1240	AUTRE MATERIEL TRANSPORT
793	SHIPS AND BOATS ETC	N 28	80	N 140	171	N 63	84	N 1130	1240	NAVIRES BATEAUX,ETC
7932	SHIPS AND BOATS NES	N 20	75	N 54	110	N 22	83	N 814	1227	NAVIRES ET BATEAUX
79328	OTHER SHIPS AND BOATS	N 8	48	N 26	36	N 13	17	N 810	1206	NAVIRES ET BATEAUX NDA
8	MISC MANUFACTURED GOODS		9748		10967		12209		12978	ART MANUFACTURES DIVERS
812	*PLUMBG,HEATNG,LGHTNG EQ		434		496		600		418	APPAR SANITAIRES CHAUFFAGE
821	*FURNITURE,PARTS THEREOF		881		734		1466		942	MEUBLES ET PIECES
8211	CHAIRS,SEATS AND PARTS		213		252		432		213	SIEGES ET PIECES
82111	CHAIRS AND OTHER SEATS	N 3516	207	N 7103	248	N 6508	426	N 3450	213	SIEGES
8219	FURNITURE AND PARTS NES	W 128	537	W 88	385	W 239	883	W 117	617	AUTRES MEUBLES ET PIECES
82191	METAL FURNITURE NES	W 39	120	W 40	172	W 156	418	W 51	267	MEUBLES NDA EN METAL
84	CLOTHING AND ACCESSORIES		2150		2315		2446		2267	VETEMENTS
842	MENS OUTERWEAR NOT KNIT	N 92876	297		370	N 92188	361	N 54107	321	VET DESSUS POUR HOMMES
843	WOMENS OUTERWEAR NONKNIT	N 83447	278	N 215487	321	N 109794	471	N 109371	492	VET DESSUS FEMMES MAT TEX
844	UNDER GARMENTS NOT KNIT		327		326		344		235	VETEMENT DESSOUS MAT TEX
848	HEADGEAR,NONTXTL CLOTHNG		938		885		820		832	VET ACCES MAT AUT QUE TEX
8484	HEADGEAR	MN 20772	887	MN 14846	783	MN 16459	732	MN 16091	728	COIFFURES ET PARTIES NDA
84843	HEADGEAR TEXTILE NONFELT	MN 20762	849	MN 14832	756	MN 16446	682	MN 16073	680	CHAPEAUX EN BONNETERIE
851	*FOOTWEAR		1230		1288		1363		1235	CHAUSSURES
85101	FOOTWEAR RUBBER,PLASTIC	P 117159	379	P 126048	409	P 163894	520	P 65149	182	CHAUS SEMELLES CAOUTCH
85102	FOOTWEAR LEATHER	P 161685	848	P 130144	872	P 153359	833	P 154534	906	CHAUS SEMELLES EN CUIR
87	PRECISION INSTRUMNTS NES		613		476		732		755	INSTRUM,APPAR SCIENT NDA
874	MEASURNG,CONTROLNG INSTR	W 7	246	W 10	156	W 11	381	W 15	463	INSTRUMENTS DE MESURE
88	PHOTO EQU,OPTICL GDS ETC		270		383		438		373	APP,FOURN PHOTO,OP,MONTR
89	MISC MANUFCTRD GOODS NES		4004		5129		5015		6856	ART MANUFACTURES DIVERS
892	PRINTED MATTER	W 105	1197	W 136	1284	W 124	1402	W 172	2171	IMPRIMES

4. General Imports C.I.F. by Commodities according to the S.I.T.C. (Rev. 2) in thousand U.S. Dollars
Importations Générales C.A.F. par Produits d'après la C.T.C.I. (Rév. 2) en milliers de Dollars E.U.

SITC CTCI	COMMODITY	1988 WEIGHT POIDS	1988 VALUE VALEUR	1989 WEIGHT POIDS	1989 VALUE VALEUR	1990 WEIGHT POIDS	1990 VALUE VALEUR	1991 WEIGHT POIDS	1991 VALUE VALEUR	PRODUIT
8921	PRINTED BOOKS,GLOBES,ETC	W 70	827	W 92	892	W 85	931	W 115	1536	LIVRES,BROCHURES,CARTES
89211	PRINTED BOOKS,PAMPHLETS	W 69	817	W 88	878	W 82	919	W 103	1489	LIVRES,BROCHURES
8928	PRINTED MATTER NES	W 26	300	W 34	329	W 27	383	W 34	454	IMPRIMES NDA
893	ARTICLES OF PLASTIC NES	W 448	1862	W 640	2772	W 583	2506	W 1072	3419	OUVRAGES EN MAT DIVIS 58
8931	PLSTC PACKG CONTNRS,LIDS	W 59	313	W 122	556	W 140	587	W 225	692	ART TRANSP EMBALLAGE ETC
8939	MISC PLASTIC ARTICLES	W 368	1432	W 488	2095	W 420	1754	W 836	2663	ART DIVERS EN MAT DIV 58
89399	OTHR PLASTC ARTICLES NES	W 359	1378	W 456	2022	W 396	1661	W 825	2615	AUT OUV MAT DIV 58
899	OTHER MANUFACTURED GOODS		408		452		465		497	AUT ART MANUF DIVERS NDA

5. General Exports F.O.B. by Commodities according to the S.I.T.C. (Rev. 2) in thousand U.S. Dollars
Exportations Générales F.O.B. par Produits d'après la C.T.C.I. (Rév. 2) en milliers de Dollars E.U.

SITC CTCI	COMMODITY	1988 WEIGHT POIDS	1988 VALUE VALEUR	1989 WEIGHT POIDS	1989 VALUE VALEUR	1990 WEIGHT POIDS	1990 VALUE VALEUR	1991 WEIGHT POIDS	1991 VALUE VALEUR	PRODUIT
	ALL COMMODITIES		32929		27988		26211		23194	TOUS PRODUITS
0	FOOD AND LIVE ANIMALS		26326		21665		17266		15544	ALIMENTS,ANIMAUX VIVANTS
03	FISH AND PREPARATIONS		277		160		61		164	POISSONS ET PREPARATIONS
034	FISH,FRESH,CHILLED,FROZN		206		104		40		117	POISSON FRAIS, REFRIG,CONG
0341	FISH FRSH,CHLLD,EX FILLT		200		104		40		16	POISSON FRAIS,REFRIGERE
0342	FISH FROZEN,EXCL FILLETS		6				1	W 56	101	POISSONS CONGELES
04	CEREALS AND PREPARATIONS		695		751		805		1366	CEREALES ET PRODUITS
046	WHEAT ETC MEAL OR FLOUR		661		731		755		1322	SEMOULE FARINE,FROMENT
04601	FLOUR OF WHEAT OR MESLIN		661		731		755		1322	FARINE DE FROMENT
05	VEGETABLES AND FRUIT		7433		5669		5312		5950	LEGUMES ET FRUITS
054	VEG ETC FRSH,SMPLY PRSVD		23		22		35		71	LEGUMES FRAIS,CONG,SECS
057	FRUIT,NUTS,FRESH,DRIED		7407		5646		5246		5877	FRUITS FRAIS OU SECS
0573	BANANA,PLANTAIN,FRSH,DRY		5949		4530		4277		4051	BANANES FRAICHES,SECHEES
0579	FRUIT FRESH OR DRIED NES		1444		1107		906		1769	FRUITS FRAIS,SECS NDA
05798	OTHER FRESH FRUIT		1399		1105		842		1737	AUTRES FRUITS FRAIS
07	COFFEE,TEA,COCOA,SPICES		17725		14862		10688		7711	CAFE,THE,CACAO,EPICES
072	COCOA		3284		2496		2621		3065	CACAO
0721	COCOA BEANS,RAW,ROASTED		3283		2495		2620		3062	CACAO EN FEVES
075	SPICES		14441		12332		8052		4633	EPICES
0752	SPICES,EX PEPPER,PIMENTO		14437		12331		8047		4633	AUTRES EPICES
07524	NUTMEG,MACE,CARDAMOMS		14311		12212		7859		4522	NOIX MUSCADES
07528	THYME ETC, OTHER SPICES		35		31		106		50	THYM,SAFRAN,LAURIER
081	*FEEDING STUFF FOR ANIML		91		124		193		205	NOURRITURE POUR ANIMAUX
0812	BRAN,POLLARD,SHARPS,ETC		90		59		63		81	SONS
08122	BRAN,ETC OF OTHR CEREALS		90		59		63		81	SONS D'AUTRES CEREALES
0819	FOOD WASTE AND FEED NES				41		118		111	DECHETS,ALIMENTS NDA
09	MISC EDIBLE PRODUCTS		53		31		99		91	PREP ALIMENTAIRES DIVERSES
098	EDIBLE PRODCTS,PREPS NES		53		31		88		91	PREP ALIMENTAIRES NDA
09809	MISC FOOD PREPRTIONS NES		51		31		84		82	PREP ALIMENTAIRES NDA
2	CRUDE MATERLS,EXCL FUELS		75		57		100		155	MAT BRUTES NON COMESTIBLES
24	CORK AND WOOD		1		20		73		111	LIEGE ET BOIS
248	WOOD SHAPED,SLEEPERS	W 2	1		20	W 104	73	W 225	111	BOIS SIMPLEMENT TRAVAILLES
2483	LUMBER SHAPED NON--CONIFR	W 2	1		20	W 104	73	W 225	111	NON CONIFERES SCIES,RABOTES
24832	LUMBER PLANED ETC NONCON			W 32	20	W 104	73	W 193	110	RABOTES,RAINES,LANGUETES
5	CHEMCLS,RELATED PROD NES		547		915		948		951	PRODUITS CHIMIQUES
53	DYES,TANNING,COLOUR PROD		301		376		527		853	PROD TEINTURE,COLORANTS
533	PIGMENTS,PAINTS,ETC		294		376		512		853	PIGMENTS,PEINTURES,VERNIS
5334	VARNISHES,DISTEMPERS ETC		294		373		499		816	PEINTURES A L'EAU
53341	WATER--THINNED PAINTS	V 55	103	V 36	106	V 59	152	V 112	269	PEINTURES DILUEES
53342	OTH PAINTS,VARNISHES ETC	V 83	190		267	V 121	342	V 183	547	AUTRES PEINTURES,VERNIS
55	PERFUME,CLEANING ETC PRD		173		495		303		6	PROD POUR PARFUM,TOILETTE
553	PERFUMERY,COSMETICS,ETC		169		495		301		6	PRODUITS DE PARFUMERIE
58	PLASTIC MATERIALS ETC		4		4		107		39	MAT PLAST ARTIFICIELLES
583	POLYMERIZATION ETC PRODS				4		107		17	PROD POLYMERISATION
5839	OTH POLYMRZTION ETC PROD				4		107		17	AUT PROD POLYMER COPOLYM
6	BASIC MANUFACTURES		1088		1531		2415		2123	ART MANUFACTURES
62	RUBBER MANUFACTURES NES		8		2		92		124	CAOUTCHOUC MANUFACTURE
621	MATERIALS OF RUBBER						80		42	PRODUITS EN CAOUTCHOUC
62101	SHEETS ETC UNVULC RUBBER						80		42	PLAQUES,FEUILLES CAOUT
628	RUBBER ARTICLES NES				1		8		80	OUVRAGES CAOUTCHOUC NDA
64	PAPER,PAPERBOARD AND MFR		377		854		1189		935	PAPIERS,CARTONS & OUVRAGES
642	PAPER,ETC,PRECUT,ARTS OF		377		849		1189		920	PAP,CARTONS DECOUPES
6424	PAPER ETC CT TO SIZE NES		345		836		1140		875	PAP,CARTONS DECOUPES
64243	TOILET PAPER CUT TO SIZE		344		804		1083		831	PAPIER HYGIENIQUE
65	TEXTILE YARN,FABRICS,ETC		46		170		175		249	FILS,TISSUS,ARTICLES TEXTILE
658	TEXTILE ARTICLES NES		35		160		125		224	ART FACONNES MAT TEXTILES
6584	LINENS ETC				3		117		193	LINGE DE MAISON
65842	BED LINEN OF OTHR FIBRES						101		136	LINGE DE LIT AUT FIBRES
6589	OTH TEXTILE ARTICLES NES		29		155		1		2	AUT ART EN TEXTILES NDA
65898	KNITTED ETC ARTICLES NES		26		155				1	ART BONNET NON ELASTIQUE
67	IRON AND STEEL		264		19		130		21	FER ET ACIER
672	IRON,STEEL PRIMARY FORMS						117			LINGOTS FER,ACIER
6727	IRN,STL COIL FR REROLLNG					N 122	117			EBAUCHES POUR TOLES FER
67271	IRON,SIMPLE STEEL COILS					N 122	117			EBAUCHES NON EN ACIER
674	IRN,STL UNIV,PLATE,SHEET		244				9	N 16	10	LARGES PLATS,TOLES
6749	OTH IRN,STL PLATES,SHEET		244					N 16	10	AUTRES TOLES FER,ACIER
67491	— OF IRON OR SIMPLE STL		244					N 16	10	AUT TOLES AUTRES ACIER FIN
69	METAL MANUFACTURES NES		285		435		751		720	ART MANUFACT EN METAL NDA
696	CUTLERY		147		364		623		426	COUTELLERIE
69605	CLIPPERS,CLEAVERS,ETC		147		364		622		426	AUT ART DE COUTELLERIE
697	BASE MTL HOUSEHOLD EQUIP		76		16		98		213	ART MENAGE MET COMMUNS
6973	DMSTC HEATG,COOKG APPARA		76		16		88		212	APPS CHAUF NON ELECTRIQ
69731	IRN,STL DOM COOKG APPARA	N 278	58	N 61	12	N 567	85	N 1585	209	APPS CUISSON FER,ACIER
7	MACHINES,TRANSPORT EQUIP		2394		1102		1449		1713	MACHINES MATERIEL TRANSPORT
71	POWER GENERATING EQUIPMT		122		339		202		218	MACHINES GENERATRICES
713	INTRNL COMBUS PSTN ENGIN		93		306		153		134	MOTEURS EXPL COMB INT, PIECE
7131	AIRCRAFT PSTN ENGINS,PTS	N 1	1		253	N 1	5			MOTEURS EXPL P.AVIATION, PIE
71311	AIRCRAFT PISTON ENGINES	N 1	1	N 200	219	N 1	5			MOTEURS EXPL P.AVIATION
7139	PISTON ENGINE PARTS NES		40		39		130		71	PIECES POUR 713.2,3,8
716	ROTATING ELECTRIC PLANT		28		29		26		76	APP ELECTR ROTATIFS,PIECES
72	MACHS FOR SPCL INDUSTRYS		1040		79		260		80	MAC SPECIALES POUR INDUST
723	CIVIL ENGNEERG EQUIP ETC		746		3				2	APPAREILS DE GENIE CIVIL
7234	CONST,MINING MACHNRY NES		746		1				2	MACH POUR LA CONST, MINES
72348	PUBLIC WORKS MACHNRY NES		746						2	MACHINES TRAVAUX PUBLICS
724	TEXTILE,LEATHER MACHNRY	N 1	1				113		16	MACH POUR INDUSTRIE TEXTILE
7243	SEWING MACHS,NEEDLES ETC						113		14	MACHINES A COUDRE,PIECES
72431	SEWING MACHINES					N 214	113	N 44	14	MACHINES A COUDRE
728	OTH MACHY FOR SPCL INDUS		285		8		136			AUT MACH IND PARTICULIERES
7283	OTHR MINERAL WORKG MACHY		285				2			MACH TRIER,CRIBLER,BROYER
7284	MACHY FOR SPCL INDUS NES				8		134			MACH SPEC IND PARTICUL.
72842	RUBBER,PLASTICS WRKG MCH						121			MACH IND CAOUT MAT PLAST
74	GENRL INDUSTRL MACHY NES		467		102		171		242	MACH APP INDUSTRIE
741	HEATING,COOLING EQUIPMNT		37		3		74		78	MACH CHAUFFAGE,PIECES
744	MECHANICAL HANDLING EQU		360		8		2		11	EQUIP MANUTENTION PIECES
7442	LIFTING,LOADING MACH NES		356		8		2		9	APP LEVAGE,MANUTENTION
74428	OTH HANDLING ETC MCH NES		356		8		2		9	AUT APP LEVAGE ETC
76	TELECOMM,SOUND EQUIPMENT		98		136		95		102	EQUIPMENT DE TELECOM
764	TELECOM EQPT,PTS,ACC NES		33		128		90		83	EQUIP TELECOM,PIECES
7641	LINE TELEPHONE,ETC EQUIP		13		85		51		45	APP TELEPHON PAR FIL
77	ELECTRIC MACHNRY NES ETC		52		259		568		528	MACH APP ELECT NDA
771	ELECTRIC POWER MACHY NES		19	N 224	78	N 756	205		49	MACH PROD,TRANS ELECTR

5. General Exports F.O.B. by Commodities according to the S.I.T.C. (Rev. 2) in thousand U.S. Dollars
Exportations Générales F.O.B. par Produits d'après la C.T.C.I. (Rév. 2) en milliers de Dollars E.U.

SITC CTCI	COMMODITY	1988 WEIGHT POIDS	1988 VALUE VALEUR	1989 WEIGHT POIDS	1989 VALUE VALEUR	1990 WEIGHT POIDS	1990 VALUE VALEUR	1991 WEIGHT POIDS	1991 VALUE VALEUR	PRODUIT
7711	TRANSFORMERS,ELECTRICAL	N 33	14	N 222	76	N 751	201	N 184	45	TRANSFO ELECTRIQUES
772	SWITCHGEAR ETC,PARTS NES		19		114		179		304	APP COUPURE,SECT ETC
7721	SWITCHGEAR ETC		8		114		179		275	APP COUPURE,SECTIONMNT
773	ELECTR DISTRIBUTNG EQUIP				10		163		4	EQUIPMT DISTRIBUTION ELECT
7731	INSULATED WIRE,CABLE ETC				10		163		4	FILS,CABLES ISOLES ELECT
775	HOUSEHOLD TYPE EQUIP NES	N 16	1		22	N 28	8		139	MACH,APP USAGE DOMESTQUE
7752	DOM REFRIGERATRS,FREEZRS			N 34	17	N 4	2	N 248	121	REFRIG,CONGEL MENAGER
77521	DOMESTIC REFRIGERATORS			N 31	15	N 4	2	N 238	118	REFRIGERATEURS
78	ROAD VEHICLES		571		156		83		493	VEHICULES ROUTIERS
781	PASS MOTOR VEH EXC BUSES	N 6	47	N 7	65	N 6	67	N 18	393	AUTO TRANSPORT PERSONNES
782	LORRIES,SPCL MTR VEH NES	N 17	428	N 4	37	N 1	4		34	VEHICULES SPECIAUX,MARCH
7821	LORRIES,TRUCKS	N 16	384	N 4	37	N 1	4		34	VEHICULES TRANSP MARCHAND
8	MISC MANUFACTURED GOODS		2487		2711		3978		2629	ART MANUFACTURES DIVERS
831	*TRAVEL GOODS,HANDBAGS	N 658744	728	N 985760	552	N 419361	906	N 25994	157	ARTICLES DE VOYAGE ETC
83101	HANDBAGS NES	N 586774	576	N 960826	422	N 394087	738	N 13288	89	SACS A MAIN
83109	OTHER TRAVEL BAGS,CASES	N 71970	151	N 24934	130	N 25274	168	N 10506	67	AUT CONTENANTS SIMILAIRES
84	CLOTHING AND ACCESSORIES		1254		1495		2357		2182	VETEMENTS
842	MENS OUTERWEAR NOT KNIT	N 23593	47	N 6923	70	N 20273	162	N 15848	155	VET DESSUS POUR HOMMES
8423	— TROUSERS,BREECHES ETC	N 23593	47	N 6324	63	N 18979	151	N 10743	142	PANTALONS HOMMES MAT TEX
84239	—— OF OTHER FIBRES	N 2660	17	N 1108	27	N 10709	140	N 9526	120	PANTALONS HOMMES AUT FIB
843	WOMENS OUTERWEAR NONKNIT	N 51840	92	N 6255	72	N 37825	129	N 9116	57	VET DESSUS FEMMES MAT TEX
8439	— OTHER OUTER GARMENTS	N 31976	53	N 2476	8	N 28731	88	N 4296	30	AUT VET DES FEM MAT TEXT
84399	—— OF OTHER FIBRES	N 31976	53	N 2476	8	N 22749	79	N 3958	29	VET DES FEM NDA AUT FIBR
844	UNDER GARMENTS NOT KNIT	N 2995	12	N 25166	47	N 400343	778	N 93543	189	VETEMENT DESSOUS MAT TEX
8441	— MENS SHIRTS	N 1663	6	N 8285	21	N 47445	103	N 24396	75	CHEMISES HOMMES MAT TEXT
84419	—— OF OTHER FIBRES			N 2765	11	N 46245	102	N 21762	66	CHEMISES HOMMES AUT FIBR
8442	— MENS,OTHR THAN SHIRTS	N 1332	6			N 58695	82	N 17586	28	SOUS–VET HOMMES MAT TEXT
8443	— WOMENS			N 16809	25	N 294203	593	N 51561	87	VET DESSOUS FEM MAT TEXT
84431	— OF COTTON					N 57654	171	N 17766	15	VET DESSOUS FEM DE COTON
84432	— OF SYNTHETIC FIBRES					N 197765	400	N 18644	36	VET DESSOUS FEM FIB SYNT
845	OUTERWEAR KNIT NONELASTC	N 72160	210	N 71833	416	N 51838	185	N 70921	178	VET DESSOUS,ACCES BONNET
8451	— JERSEYS,PULLOVERS ETC	N 54651	161	N 39763	279	N 42525	154	N 68761	168	CHANDAILS,PULL–OVERS ETC
84519	—— OF OTHER FIBRES	N 26688	82	N 39763	279	N 35720	135	N 16472	42	CHANDAILS,PULL AUT FIBR
8452	— WOMENS DRESSES ETC			N 23840	88			N 1711	8	ROBES,JUPES BONNETERIE
84522	—— OF COTTON			N 23840	88			N 1675	8	ROBES,JUPES DE COTON
846	UNDER GARMENTS KNITTED	N 178440	244	N 151294	262	N 205131	270		372	SOUS VETS DE BONNETERIE
8462	— OF COTTON NON ELASTIC	N 2085	10			N 21210	46	N 132245	203	SOUS–VET BONNET COTON
84629	—— OTHER	N 2061	10			N 21210	46	N 124157	182	AUT SOUS–VET BONNET COTON
8464	— OF OTH FIBRE NONELAST	N 176355	234	N 142180	242	N 175969	212	N 78558	105	SOUS–VET BON AUT FIBRES
84649	—— OF FIBRES NES	N 176355	234	N 142180	242	N 175969	212	N 77898	105	SOUS–VET BON AUT FIBRES
847	TEXTILE CLTHNG ACCES NES						56		163	ACCES VET MAT TEXT NDA
8471	— NOT KNITTED						23		111	ACCES VET MAT TEX NON BON
84714	GLOVES,SOCKS ETC,NOT KNT					P 5760	21	P 86381	109	BAS,CHAUSSETTES MAT TEXT
848	HEADGEAR,NONTXTL CLOTHNG		648		629		777		1067	VET ACCES MAT AUT QUE TEX
8484	HEADGEAR	MN 10414	648	MN 11137	629	MN 9533	776	MN 13081	1067	COIFFURES ET PARTIES NDA
84843	HEADGEAR TEXTILE NONFELT	MN 10414	648	MN 11137	628	MN 9532	776	MN 12537	1026	CHAPEAUX EN BONNETERIE
851	*FOOTWEAR	P 24091	137	P 46526	342	P 15975	442		119	CHAUSSURES
85102	FOOTWEAR LEATHER	P 22341	126	P 45806	334	P 15830	441	P 7015	117	CHAUS SEMELLES EN CUIR
87	PRECISION INSTRUMNTS NES		255		64		22		14	INSTRUM,APPAR SCIENT NDA
872	MEDICAL INSTRUMENTS NES		212		1		2			INSTR,APP MEDIC–CHIR NDA
87202	OTH MEDICAL INSTRUMENTS		212		1		2			INSTRUM,APP MEDECINE
89	MISC MANUFCTRD GOODS NES		96		188		236		122	ART MANUFACTURES DIVERS
893	ARTICLES OF PLASTIC NES		19		106		96		62	OUVRAGES EN MAT DIVIS 58
8931	PLSTC PACKG CONTNRS,LIDS		1		93		74		18	ART TRANSP EMBALLAGE ETC

1. HISTORICAL SERIES, 1960–1995 SPECIAL TRADE, IMPORTS C.I.F., EXPORTS F.O.B.
SERIES HISTORIQUES, 1960–1995 COMMERCE SPECIAL, IMPORTATIONS C.A.F., EXPORTATIONS F.O.B

YEAR ANNEE	VALUE IN MILLION FRANCS VALEUR EN MILLION FRANCS MERCHANDISE – MARCHANDISE IMPORTS	EXPORTS	GOLD – OR IMPORTS	EXPORTS	CONVERSION FACTORS U.S. CENTS PER FRANC FACTEURS DE CONVERSION CENTS E.U. PAR FRANC IMPORTS	EXPORTS	INDEX NUMBERS – INDICES QUANTUM IMPORTS	EXPORTS	UNIT VALUE VALEUR UNITAIRE IMPORTS	EXPORTS
1960	238.30	171.50			20.2600	20.2600				
1961	258.60	178.10			20.2600	20.2600				
1962	283.70	173.60			20.2600	20.2600				
1963	342.20	188.40			20.2600	20.2600				
1964	391.90	171.70			20.2600	20.2600				
1965	420.70	186.90			20.2600	20.2600				
1966	448.40	182.90			20.2600	20.2600				
1967	491.60	160.10			20.2600	20.2600				
1968	504.10	187.90			20.2600	20.2600				
1969	546.40	175.60			19.3800	19.7600				
1970	709.20	209.00			18.0000	18.0000				
1971	692.50	231.00			18.0700	18.0400				
1972	747.30	201.10			19.8220	19.8750				
1973	895.70	284.80			22.5972	22.7315				
1974	1104.20	277.70			20.7943	20.8333				
1975	1315.00	352.60			23.3254	23.8056				
1976	1514.70	429.40			20.9870	20.9591				
1977	1843.70	387.50			20.3673	20.3752				
1978	1909.70	498.90			22.2049	22.4083				
1979	2539.70	647.90			23.5514	23.4323				
1980	3073.60	446.10			23.6774	23.9628				
1981	3534.00	509.30			18.4377	18.1148				
1982	4116.90	548.40			15.1589	15.1503				
1983	5038.60	626.70			13.0918	13.2666				
1984	5230.80	750.80			11.4420	11.4666				
1985	5745.00	669.20			11.2539	11.1786				
1986	5457.50	747.65			13.9551	13.9614				
1987	6228.74	564.08			16.6717	16.5392				
1988	7169.08	909.22			17.3387	17.3930				
1989	7888.11	707.13			15.8639	15.8532				
1990	8937.01	648.79			18.4580	18.2163				
1991	9217.90	830.20			17.8315	17.6829				
1992	8021.03	689.91			18.8182	18.7879				
1993	7902.97	725.95			17.6282	17.6361				
1994	8540.26	845.33			18.0240	17.9740				
1995	9401.24	787.97			20.1025	20.1443				

2. IMPORTS BY BROAD ECONOMIC CATEGORY AND EXPORTS BY INDUSTRIAL ORIGIN. (PERCENTAGE OF TOTAL VALUE)
IMPORTATIONS PAR CATEGORIES ECONOMIQUES ET EXPORTATIONS PAR BRANCHE D'ACTIVITE.(EN POURCENTAGE DE LA VALEUR TOTALE)

IMPORTS – IMPORTATIONS

	1990	1991	1992	1993	1994	1995	1996
TOTAL IMPORTS–IMPORTATIONS TOTALES	100.	100.	100.	100.	100.	100.	
1 FOOD BEV–ALIMENTATION BOISSONS	18.2	18.2	20.0	21.9	21.4	20.0	
11 PRIMARY–PRODUITS DE BASE	6.8	6.7	8.0	8.2	8.2	7.6	
111 FOR INDUSTRY–POUR L'INDUSTRIE	1.2	1.1	1.7	1.5	1.5	1.4	
112 FOR HOUSEHOLDS–POUR LES MENAGES	5.6	5.6	6.3	6.7	6.7	6.2	
12 PROCESSED–PRODUITS ELABORES	11.4	11.5	12.0	13.7	13.2	12.3	
121 FOR INDUSTRY–POUR L'INDUSTRIE	0.4	0.4	0.4	0.5	0.3	0.2	
122 FOR HOUSEHOLDS–POUR LES MENAGES	11.0	11.1	11.6	13.2	12.9	12.1	
2 IND SUPPLIES–APPROV INDUSTRIELS	22.5	19.2	20.7	19.9	20.6	19.4	
21 PRIMARY–PRODUITS DE BASE	0.7	0.6	0.7	0.7	0.7	0.7	
22 PROCESSED–PRODUITS ELABORES	21.8	18.7	20.0	19.2	19.9	18.8	
3 FUELS–COMBUSTIBLES	5.3	4.5	5.5	2.0	1.7	5.7	
31 PRIMARY–PRODUITS DE BASE	0.2	0.2	0.2	0.1	0.1	3.0	
32 PROCESSED–PRODUITS ELABORES	5.1	4.4	5.3	1.9	1.6	2.7	
321 MOTOR SPIRIT–ESSENCE	5.1	4.3	5.3	1.9		0.5	
322 OTHER–AUTRES	0.0	0.0	0.0	0.0	1.6	2.1	
4 MACHINERY–EQUIPEMENT	12.0	11.5	11.7	12.6	12.6	12.0	
41 CAPITAL EQUIPMENT–MACHINES	11.1	10.7	10.8	11.6	11.5	10.9	
42 PARTS–PIECES ACCESSOIRES	0.9	0.9	0.8	1.0	1.0	1.1	
5 TRANSPORT–TRANSPORT	18.3	23.2	16.0	16.4	16.9	18.4	
51 PASSENGER CARS–AUTOMOBILES	4.5	4.5	3.7	6.2	7.2	6.8	
52 OTHER–AUTRES	10.4	14.6	9.0	5.8	5.8	8.2	
521 INDUSTRIAL–INDUSTRIELS	10.1	14.3	8.7	5.5	5.4	7.9	
522 NON INDUSTRIAL–NON INDUSTRIEL	0.3	0.3	0.3	0.3	0.4	0.3	
53 PARTS–PIECES ACCESSOIRES	3.4	4.0	3.4	4.3	4.0	3.4	
6 CONSUM GOODS–BIENS CONSOMMATION	21.4	21.3	23.6	24.3	24.4	22.7	
61 DURABLE–DURABLES	6.2	5.7	6.1	5.6	5.8	5.5	
62 SEMI DURABLE–SEMI DURABLES	8.5	8.6	9.0	9.7	9.6	9.0	
63 NON DURABLE–NON DURABLES	6.7	7.0	8.5	8.9	9.0	8.2	
7 GOODS NES–BIENS NDA	2.4	2.0	2.5	3.0	2.3	1.8	

EXPORTS – EXPORTATIONS

	1990	1991	1992	1993	1994	1995	1996
TOTAL EXPORTS–EXPORTATIONS TOTALES	100.	100.	100.	100.	100.	100.	
1 AGRICULTURE	34.5	39.2	43.1	32.1	26.4	28.7	
2 MINING QUARRY–INDUS EXTRACTIVES	0.0	0.0	0.1	0.0	0.2	0.1	
3 MANUFACTURING–IND MANUFACTUR	65.4	60.8	56.9	67.9	73.4	71.3	
31 FOOD BEV TOBACCO–ALIM BOISS TAB	42.9	32.8	33.5	42.5	35.0	23.6	
32 TEXTILES–INDUSTRIES TEXTILES	0.4	0.4	0.7	0.6	0.6	0.9	
33 WOOD & PRODUCTS–BOIS & PRODUITS	0.0	0.3	0.1	0.1	0.2	0.2	
34 PAPER & PRODUCTS–PAPIER & PRODT	1.4	1.1	1.6	1.7	1.7	2.0	
35 CHEMICALS–INDUSTRIES CHIMIQUES	4.1	2.8	3.3	1.8	1.9	2.0	
36 NON METAL MIN–MIN NON METAL	0.3	0.4	0.4	0.6	0.2	0.1	
37 BASIC METAL–IND METAL BASE	0.2	0.2	0.1	0.2	0.2	0.3	
38 METAL MANUF–MANUF METAL	16.0	22.8	17.1	20.1	33.6	41.5	
39 OTH MANUF IND–AUTRES MANUF	0.2	0.2	0.1	0.2	0.1	0.7	

3. TRADE BY PRINCIPAL COUNTRIES OF PRODUCTION AND LAST CONSIGNMENT (VALUE IN THOUSAND U.S. DOLLARS)
ECHANGES SELON LES PRINCIPAUX PAYS DE PRODUCTION ET DE DERNIERE CONSIGNATION (VALEUR EN MILLIERS DE DOLLARS EU)

COUNTRIES–PAYS	SPECIAL IMPORTS C.I.F. IMPORTATIONS SPECIALES C.A.F				
	1991	1992	1993	1994	1995
World	1649142	1549293	1418015	1539214	1901312
Africa	5996	6972	6225	6408	8059
Americas	302728	240626	166867	171548	277159
Northern America	141379	65031	49438	57236	67334
LAIA	39634	40896	35784	42039	47488
CACM	2661	3765	3821	3802	4833
Caribbean	111031	122290	69055	58436	145430
Rest of America	8023	8644	8768	10035	12074
As.ex F.USSR	86648	94106	81788	88713	108804
Eur.x F.USSR	1246611	1201180	1153788	1264898	1495512
EU	1234264	1187177	1141991	1253027	1479293
EFTA	8267	10841	8512	8063	9801
East Europe	2281	2398	2672	3491	4572
Other Europe	1799	34	54	18	1228
Former USSR	415	443	203	105	198
Oceania	6625	5704	8642	5927	6271
France, Monac	991895	948281	933438	1027240	1213891
USA/Etats–Unis d'Amer	137803	61244	46554	48248	62418
Italy/Italie	74697	57831	46585	55431	64987
Germany/Allemagne	53957	54878	61678	55316	60766
Martinique	32664	62719	46483	39622	45920
Japan/Japon	40223	40663	35870	36361	41642
Netherlands Antilles	63447	49695	10099	2886	16500
Spain/Espagne	30686	31791	16892	22758	35048
Belgium–Luxembourg	20963	23673	23092	29238	31255
Brazil/Brésil	18759	18603	21090	25161	27360
Netherlands/Pays–Bas	18468	19741	19332	23584	24937
United Kingdom	18666	17372	18723	21114	26068
Trinidad and Tobago	7907	4048	5629	7673	70341
Venezuela	16484	17405	10258	11347	13498
China/Chine	7404	9769	10263	13358	15624
Korea, Republic of	5521	6691	10200	12431	14449
French Guiana	7776	6717	7887	8249	10698
Sweden/Suède	8074	15240	9527	2447	3303
New Zealand	5765	5058	5230	5384	5897
Denmark/Danemark	3381	5513	5047	5661	7549
Canada	3548	3707	2873	8958	4752
Finland/Finlande	7553	7349	1549	2908	3346
Thailand/Thaïlande	3728	4084	3490	3802	4452
Singapore/Singapour	3548	3973	1662	1455	8165
Norway,SVD,JM	3224	5304	3591	2842	3611
Portugal	3761	2844	3775	3317	4312
Malaysia/Malaisie	1362	4519	3891	3172	4585
Honduras	2116	3389	3557	3295	4166
Switz.Liecht	3347	3019	3282	2954	3731
Dominican Republic	2415	2535	3423	3507	4311
Indonesia/Indonésie	1295	1719	2591	3292	4311
Iceland/Islande	1695	2518	1640	2267	2459
Colombia/Colombie	1390	2207	1998	2562	2373
Hong Kong	2664	2355	1571	1303	1367
Morocco/Maroc	1841	2396	1343	1620	1949
Tunisia/Tunisie	684	1172	2088	2098	2003
Austria/Autriche	973	1364	1272	1992	1931
India/Inde	1291	1273	1427	1892	1426
Czech Republic			1772	2467	3049
Turkey/Turquie	2053	1186	1102	1240	1315
Dominica/Dominique	1248	404	961	1408	2355
Israel/Israël	1161	775	390	869	2497
Jamaica/Jamaïque	552	561	565	1195	1956
Ireland/Irlande	761	811	682	1411	1140
Argentina/Argentine	842	1049	601	749	1013
Madagascar	450	596	764	1012	1292
Suriname/Suriname	159	1007	528	1166	1208
Chile/Chili	1381	647	848	399	572
So. Africa Customs Un	985	1254	517	131	703
Philippines	1035	727	628	563	488

COUNTRIES–PAYS	SPECIAL EXPORTS F.O.B. EXPORTATIONS SPECIALES F.O.B.				
	1991	1992	1993	1994	1995
Monde	146993	136763	129688	152259	161974
Afrique	605	31	141	122	848
Amériques	39131	28883	25052	30268	35947
Amérique du Nord	9283	1269	2079	3976	6227
ALAI	118	1292	250	406	553
MCAC		4			5
Caraïbes	25945	22219	19099	22198	25698
Autre Amérique	3785	4098	3625	3688	3463
Asie l'URSS exclus	21	2048	368		16
Europe l'URSS exclus	107036	105795	103754	121813	125127
UE	106900	105793	103084	121653	124714
AELE	12	2	9	68	411
Europe de l'Est			26		
Autre de l'Europe	124		635	91	
Ancienne URSS					
Océanie	18		283	17	5
France, Monac	103349	88400	101177	114910	106561
Martinique	24987	21376	18345	20346	17050
USA/Etats–Unis d'Amer	9272	1257	2039	3465	5518
French Guiana	3522	3900	3625	3686	3463
Portugal	1	9424			
Italy/Italie	712	80	14	221	7405
Belgium–Luxembourg	256	278	482	2695	4366
Sweden/Suède	2299	5046	56	23	4
Bahamas					7051
United Kingdom		103	685	2202	3598
Germany/Allemagne	272	1303	645	1326	489
China/Chine		2036	1		
Colombia/Colombie	2	1031		267	185
Canada	11	13	34	511	709
Netherlands/Pays–Bas	3	1027	11	162	5
Saint Lucia/St. Lucie	242	50	63	791	48
Dominica/Dominique	213	284	86	220	310
Haiti/Haïti	91	48	394	185	302
Austria/Autriche					882
Malta/Malte			635	91	
Guinea/Guinée				14	705
Finland/Finlande					624
Ireland/Irlande					564
Comoros/Comores	530				
Venezuela	96	157	113	80	72
Switz.Liecht	12	1	9	68	409
Panama	263	182		2	
Spain/Espagne	9	130	13	115	154
Antigua and Barbuda	34	279	7	11	72
Trinidad and Tobago	250	4	80	23	31
Netherlands Antilles	86		17	102	176
Japan/Japon			368		
Cuba			2	6	345
Brazil/Brésil	20	105	132	58	34
Anguilla				185	158
French Polynesia	15		283	2	
Reunion/Réunion	75	30	131	26	37
Mexico/Mexique					263
Dominican Republic	21	76	27	54	41
British Virgin Islds	5	2		174	
Mauritius/Maurice				47	79
Fm Yugoslav	124				
St Vincent & Grenadines		1	11	6	91
Saint–Kitts–Nevis	6	58	10	15	16
Barbados/Barbade	1	2	46	36	3
Greece/Grèce					60
Jamaica/Jamaïque		34			2
Grenada/Grenade	1	5	12	12	
Czech Republic			26		
Madagascar		1		22	

(VALUE AS PERCENTAGE OF WORLD TOTAL)(VALEURS EN POURCENTAGE DU TOTAL MONDIAL)

	1986	1987	1988	1989	1990	1991	1992	1993	1994	1995
Africa	0.6	0.6	0.9	0.7	0.8	0.4	0.4	0.4	0.4	0.4
Americas	13.6	11.9	11.9	12.8	14.2	18.4	15.5	11.8	11.1	14.6
Northern America	2.4	3.4	3.1	3.0	4.2	8.6	4.2	3.5	3.7	3.5
LAIA	1.1	1.2	1.5	1.7	2.4	2.4	2.6	2.5	2.7	2.5
CACM	0.5	0.4	0.4	0.6	0.4	0.2	0.2	0.3	0.2	0.3
Caribbean	8.6	5.9	6.0	6.7	6.5	6.7	7.9	4.9	3.8	7.6
Rest of America	0.9	1.0	0.9	0.7	0.6	0.5	0.6	0.6	0.7	0.6
As.ex F.USSR	3.9	4.4	4.7	4.8	4.4	5.3	6.1	5.8	5.8	5.7
Eur.x F.USSR	81.3	81.9	81.8	81.2	80.2	75.6	77.5	81.4	82.2	78.7
EU	80.3	80.9	80.9	80.3	79.4	74.8	76.6	80.5	81.4	77.8
EFTA	0.7	0.7	0.6	0.5	0.5	0.5	0.7	0.6	0.5	0.5
East Europe	0.2	0.3	0.3	0.3	0.2	0.1	0.2	0.2	0.2	0.2
Other Europe	0.1	0.1	0.1	0.1	0.1	0.1	0.0	0.0	0.0	0.1
Former USSR	0.1	0.1	0.1	0.0	0.0	0.0	0.0	0.0	0.0	0.0
Oceania	0.4	0.4	0.4	0.4	0.4	0.4	0.4	0.6	0.4	0.3
France, Monac	65.4	64.5	64.7	64.4	65.6	60.1	61.2	65.8	66.7	63.8
USA/Etats–Unis d'Amer	2.3	3.3	2.9	3.0	4.1	8.4	4.0	3.3	3.1	3.3
Italy/Italie	4.4	4.4	4.0	4.0	3.5	4.5	3.7	3.3	3.6	3.4
Germany/Allemagne	3.1	3.7	3.9	4.4	3.3	3.3	3.5	4.3	3.6	3.2
Martinique	5.7	2.9	2.2	1.9	2.0	2.0	4.0	3.3	2.6	2.4
Japan/Japon	2.5	2.7	2.4	2.8	2.2	2.4	2.6	2.5	2.4	2.2
Netherlands Antilles	1.8	1.8	2.6	3.6	3.1	3.8	3.2	0.7	0.2	0.9
Spain/Espagne	1.7	2.0	2.0	1.9	1.9	1.9	2.1	1.2	1.5	1.8
Belgium–Luxembourg	1.8	1.6	1.5	1.4	1.3	1.3	1.5	1.6	1.9	1.6
Brazil/Brésil	0.3	0.5	0.8	0.9	1.2	1.1	1.2	1.5	1.6	1.4

	1986	1987	1988	1989	1990	1991	1992	1993	1994	1995
Afrique	0.0	3.0	0.1	0.0	0.1	0.4	0.0	0.1	0.1	0.5
Amériques	20.9	28.3	17.0	23.6	18.6	26.6	21.1	19.3	19.9	22.2
Amérique du Nord	2.5	0.5	0.3	1.1	0.2	6.3	0.9	1.6	2.6	3.8
ALAI	0.1	0.2	0.1	0.2	0.1	0.1	0.9	0.2	0.3	0.3
MCAC		0.0	0.0	0.0			0.0			0.0
Caraïbes	16.1	24.5	14.2	19.3	14.6	17.7	16.2	14.7	14.6	15.9
Autre Amérique	2.2	3.1	2.3	3.0	3.7	2.6	3.0	2.8	2.4	2.1
Asie l'URSS exclus		0.0	0.0	0.0		0.0	1.5	0.3		0.0
Europe l'URSS exclus	78.9	68.7	82.9	76.3	81.4	72.8	77.4	80.0	80.0	77.3
UE	78.9	68.7	82.9	76.3	81.2	72.7	77.4	79.5	79.9	77.0
AELE	0.0	0.0	0.1	0.0	0.1	0.0	0.0	0.0	0.0	0.3
Europe de l'Est					0.0			0.0		
Autre de l'Europe						0.1		0.5	0.1	
Ancienne URSS										
Océanie	0.0	0.0	0.0	0.1	0.0	0.0		0.2	0.0	0.0
France, Monac	72.4	67.9	67.4	69.8	75.9	70.3	64.6	78.0	75.5	65.8
Martinique	13.9	22.3	13.5	18.4	14.0	17.0	15.6	14.1	13.4	10.5
USA/Etats–Unis d'Amer	2.5	0.4	0.3	0.9	0.2	6.3	0.9	1.6	2.3	3.4
French Guiana	2.1	3.1	2.3	3.0	3.6	2.4	2.9	2.8	2.4	2.1
Portugal	5.6		14.6	5.4	4.1	0.0	6.9			
Italy/Italie	0.0	0.1	0.3	0.1	0.1	0.5	0.1	0.0	0.1	4.6
Belgium–Luxembourg	0.0	0.0	0.1	0.5	0.0	0.2	0.2	0.4	1.8	2.7
Sweden/Suède			0.0	0.0	0.0	1.6	3.7	0.0	0.0	0.0
Bahamas	0.0	0.0	0.0							4.4
United Kingdom	0.0	0.0	0.2	0.1	0.4		0.1	0.5	1.4	2.2

4. Special Imports C.I.F. by Commodities according to the S.I.T.C. (Rev. 2) in thousand U.S. Dollars
Importations Spéciales C.A.F. par Produits d'après la C.T.C.I. (Rév. 2) en milliers de Dollars E.U.

SITC CTCI	COMMODITY	1992 WEIGHT POIDS	1992 VALUE VALEUR	1993 WEIGHT POIDS	1993 VALUE VALEUR	1994 WEIGHT POIDS	1994 VALUE VALEUR	1995 WEIGHT POIDS	1995 VALUE VALEUR	PRODUIT
	ALL COMMODITIES		1549293		1418015		1539214		1901312	TOUS PRODUITS
0	FOOD AND LIVE ANIMALS		253368		253259		268836		302835	ALIMENTS,ANIMAUX VIVANTS
01	MEAT AND PREPARATIONS		64927		65319		69141		74688	VIANDES ET PREPARATIONS
011	MEAT FRESH,CHILLD,FROZEN	W 16851	44784	W 17786	44557	W 18823	46226	W 18923	49266	VIANDES FRAICHES,REF,CONGE
0111	BOVINE MEAT FRESH,FROZEN	W 2126	14347	W 2367	14184	W 2283	14299	W 2446	16397	VIANDES BOVIN FRAI,REF
01111	BOVINE MEAT WITH BONE IN	W 436	3217	W 711	5276	W 556	3902	W 471	3595	VIANDES BOVIN NON DESOSS
01112	BOVINE MEAT BONELESS	W 1690	11131	W 1656	8908	W 1726	10396	W 1975	12802	VIANDES BOVIN DESOSSEES
0112	MUTTON ETC FRSH,CHLD,FRN	W 2063	5313	W 2342	6296	W 2419	5977	W 2546	6499	VIANDE DE MOUTON
0113	PIG MEAT FRESH,CHLD,FRZN	W 1158	4231	W 1617	4721	W 1540	4208	W 1677	5412	VIANDE DE PORC
0114	POULTRY FRESH CHLLD,FRZN	W 10401	18587	W 10285	16914	W 11437	19402	W 11087	18330	VOLAILLES MORTES
012	MEAT DRIED,SALTED,SMOKED	W 1357	4233	W 1574	4649	W 1581	4637	W 1419	4870	VIANDE,ABATS SALES,SECHES
014	MEAT PREPD,PRSVD,NES ETC	W 3643	15910	W 4223	16112	W 4495	18278	W 4756	20551	CONSERVES DE VIANDES
0142	SAUSAGES INCLDING TINNED	W 718	3242	W 1287	4998	W 831	5911	W 1606	6505	SAUCISSES,SAUCISSONS
0149	OTH PREPARD,PRESRVD MEAT	W 2922	12644	W 2935	11112	W 3664	12366	W 3148	14042	AUTRES PREP DE VIANDES
02	DAIRY PRODCTS,BIRDS'EGGS		39527		41606		44159		51932	PRODUITS LAITIERS,OEUFS
022	MILK AND CREAM	W 18976	23892	W 20619	21723	W 22616	24131	W 23841	28769	LAIT ET CREME
0223	MILK AND CREAM FRESH	W 15603	10924	W 17402	11274	W 18651	12434	W 20355	15320	LAIT,CREME FRAIS
0224	MILK,CREAM PRESERVED ETC	W 3373	12968	W 3217	10450	W 3965	11697	W 3485	13449	LAIT,CREME CONS,CONC
02243	MILK DRY,OVER 1.5% FAT	W 1552	8004	W 1667	6833	W 2241	7658	W 1897	9047	LAIT POUDRE SUP 1.5%
024	CHEESE AND CURD	W 1696	10345	W 2568	15074	W 2565	15348	W 2833	18012	FROMAGE ET CAILLEBOTTE
03	FISH AND PREPARATIONS		24023		21093		25162		30523	POISSONS ET PREPARATIONS
034	FISH,FRESH,CHILLED,FROZN	W 2024	6397	W 1880	5659	W 2116	7660	W 2027	8042	POISSON FRAIS, REFRIG,CONG
0342	FISH FROZEN,EXCL FILLETS	W 1496	4907	W 1474	4426	W 1657	5963	W 1497	5927	POISSONS CONGELES
035	FISH SALTED,DRIED,SMOKED	W 1535	8669	W 1402	6684	W 1546	6697	W 1628	8690	POISSON SECHE,SALE,FUME
03503	FISH(EX COD)DRIED,SALTED	W 1425	8100	W 1121	5192	W 1300	5454	W 1460	7569	POISSONS SECHES,SALES
036	SHELL FISH FRESH,FROZEN	W 803	5416	W 970	5421	W 887	6819	W 1272	9281	CRUSTACES,MOLLUSQUES
04	CEREALS AND PREPARATIONS		51961		50379		51277		55637	CEREALES ET PRODUITS
041	WHEAT ETC UNMILLED	W 61474	17825	W 51012	13385	W 55498	13620	W 56712	15034	FROMENT,EPEAUTRE
0412	OTHER WHEAT ETC UNMILLED	W 61472	17824	W 51012	13385	W 55492	13616	W 56712	15033	AUTRE FROMENT NON MOULU
042	RICE	W 14227	11401	W 13005	10847	W 12221	10946	W 13122	13254	RIZ
0421	RICE IN HUSK OR HUSKED	W 9439	5850	W 8393	5611	W 7823	5696	W 8312	7098	RIZ SANS AUTRE PREPARATION
04212	RICE HUSKED	W 9433	5839	W 8387	5600	W 7809	5674	W 8304	7081	RIZ CARGO
0422	RICE SEMI–MILLED,MILLED	W 4788	5550	W 4612	5236	W 4399	5249	W 4810	6155	RIZ POLI,GLACE INCL BRISURES
04221	RICE MILLED UNBROKEN	W 4534	5412	W 4495	5162	W 4333	5212	W 4806	6151	RIZ POLI,GLACE EXCL BRISURES
048	CEREAL ETC PREPARATIONS	W 8052	19567	W 11172	22886	W 11306	23058	W 9549	23688	PREPTNS A BASE CEREALES
0484	BAKERY PRODUCTS	W 3159	11866	W 3809	13562	W 5507	14085	W 4629	14920	PRODUITS DE BOULANGERIE
04841	BREAD,BISCUIT,COM WAFERS	W 2268	7914	W 2381	8082	W 3377	6786	W 2909	9461	PAINS,BISCUITS DE MER
04842	PASTRY, CAKES ETC	W 891	3952	W 1428	5480	W 2130	7299	W 1720	5459	PATISSERIE ETC.
05	VEGETABLES AND FRUIT		38191		37353		43192		51366	LEGUMES ET FRUITS
054	VEG ETC FRSH,SMPLY PRSVD	W 20209	13799	W 18271	14194	W 18987	15478	W 20531	19882	LEGUMES FRAIS,CONG,SECS
0545	OTHER FRESH VEGETABLES	W 5776	5667	W 6069	6005	W 6471	6187	W 7368	7854	AUTRES LEGUMES FRAIS,REF
056	VEGTBLES ETC PRSVD,PREPD	W 2992	5639	W 3358	5420	W 4212	6317	W 4429	6976	CONSERVES DE LEGUMES
0565	VEGTBLES PRSVD,PREPD NES	W 2807	5017	W 3185	5022	W 4042	5848	W 4256	6557	LEGUMES PREPARES CONSERVE
05659	OTH VEG PRESVD,PREPD NES	W 2495	4391	W 2837	4476	W 3647	5194	W 4149	6286	LEGUM PREPAP,CONSERV NDA
057	FRUIT,NUTS,FRESH,DRIED	W 8118	8866	W 9750	9115	W 10500	10321	W 10766	11040	FRUITS FRAIS OU SECS
058	FRUIT PRESERVED,PREPARED	W 4906	9888	W 4948	8623	W 6983	11075	W 8822	13468	CONSERVES DE FRUITS
0585	FRUIT OR VEGETABLE JUICE	W 3274	4892	W 3075	3930	W 4600	4967	W 6374	7101	JUS DE FRUITS
06	SUGAR AND PREPS,HONEY		6360		10221		7145		7162	SUCRES ET PRODUITS
061	SUGAR AND HONEY	W 3520	3950		7224	W 3363	3828	W 2749	3467	SUCRES ET MIEL
07	COFFEE,TEA,COCOA,SPICES		7865		7489		8676		10250	CAFE,THE,CACAO,EPICES
073	CHOCOLATE AND PRODUCTS	W 773	4609	W 1064	5000	W 1283	5326	W 1208	5555	CHOCOLAT
081	*FEEDING STUFF FOR ANIML	W 7167	5441	W 8628	5893	W 9350	6246	W 9229	6435	NOURRITURE POUR ANIMAUX
0819	FOOD WASTE AND FEED NES	W 4542	4620	W 5274	4871	W 5889	5209	W 5504	5303	DECHETS,ALIMENTS NDA
08199	FODDER NES,INCL SWEETNED	W 4542	4620	W 5274	4871	W 5889	5209	W 5504	5303	PREPARATIONS FOURRAGERES
09	MISC EDIBLE PRODUCTS		14591		13441		12989		14108	PREP ALIMENTAIRES DIVERSES
098	EDIBLE PRODCTS,PREPS NES	W 4228	12177	W 4502	11114	W 4230	10663	W 4428	11333	PREP ALIMENTAIRES NDA
09809	MISC FOOD PREPRTIONS NES	W 2878	7453	W 3028	7154	W 2374	6220	W 2521	6614	PREP ALIMENTAIRES NDA
1	BEVERAGES AND TOBACCO		65296		66770		70996		88052	BOISSONS ET TABACS
11	BEVERAGES		58329		60010		62902		78763	BOISSONS
111	NON–ALCOHL BEVERAGES NES	W 23945	24101	W 25606	23111	W 31680	26082	W 40221	32557	BOISSONS NON ALCOOLIQUES
11102	FLAVORED WATERS NON–ALCO	W 20651	21295	W 21123	20166	W 25600	22593	W 30529	27420	LIMONADES,EAUX GAZEUSES
112	ALCOHOLIC BEVERAGES	W 13115	34227	W 14994	36900	W 16521	36820	W 16433	46205	BOISSONS ALCOOLIQUES
1121	WINE OF FRESH GRAPES ETC	W 7648	24350	W 9141	26297	W 9194	25536	W 8778	32630	VINS DE RAISINS FRAIS
11212	WINE OF FRESH GRAPES	W 7387	23619	W 8872	25536	W 8986	24963	W 8570	31926	VINS DE MOUTS DE RAISINS
1123	BEER,ALE,STOUT,PORTER	W 4551	6131	W 4772	6318	W 6320	7879	W 6753	9478	BIERES
12	TOBACCO AND MANUFACTURES		6968		6760		8094		9290	TABACS BRUTS FABRIQUES
122	TOBACCO,MANUFACTURED	W 296	6968	W 298	6760	W 343	8093	W 346	9290	TABACS FABRIQUES
1222	CIGARETTES	W 291	6737	W 288	6465	W 331	7770	W 337	8824	CIGARETTES
2	CRUDE MATERLS,EXCL FUELS		27240		25376		28606		36195	MAT BRUTES NON COMESTIBLES
24	CORK AND WOOD		20245		19796		21761		27118	LIEGE ET BOIS
248	WOOD SHAPED,SLEEPERS	W 36631	17613	W 35833	17218	W 39832	20086	W 45339	25399	BOIS SIMPLEMENT TRAVAILLES
2482	LUMBER SHAPED CONIFER	W 25980	12060	W 29111	13396	W 28646	13254	W 22015	11003	CONIFERES SCIES,RABOTES
24821	LUMBER SAWN ETC CONIFER	W 24203	10775	W 25508	10865	W 24951	10860	W 19884	9138	CONIFERES SCIES LONGITUD
2483	LUMBER SHAPED NON–CONIFR	W 10651	5553	W 6722	3823	W 11186	6829	W 23324	14396	NON CONIFERES SCIES,RABOTES
24831	LUMBER SAWN ETC NON–CON	W 10163	5038	W 6413	3543	W 8911	5076	W 19558	11072	SCIES LONGITUDINALEMENT
3	MINERAL FUELS ETC		87160		29081		26793		110668	COMBUSTIBLES MINERAUX LUB
33	PETROLEUM AND PRODUCTS		83623		28129		24834		52528	PETROLE ET DERIVES
334	PETROLEUM PRODUCTS,REFIN	W 399100	81934	W 185156	27298	W 159764	23578	W 280603	50771	PRODUITS RAFFINES
3341	GASOLINE,OTH LIGHT OILS	W 398978	81629	W 185076	27104			W 39866	10028	ESSENCES POUR MOTEURS
33411	MOTOR,AVIATION SPIRIT							W 39581	9793	ESSENCES MOTEURS D'AVIONS
33419	OTH LIGHT PETROLEUM OILS	W 398978	81629	W 185076	27104			W 285	235	AUTRES HUILES LEGERES
3342	KEROSENE,OTH MEDIUM OILS							W 42669	8555	PETR LAMPANTS,AUT HUIL
33421	KEROSENE INCL JET FUEL							W 42669	8555	PETROLES LAMPANTS
3343	GAS OILS							W 37968	8132	GAS OILS
3344	FUEL OILS,NES							W 153814	15751	FUEL OILS
3345	LUBS,PETROLEUM OILS NES	W 122	305	W 80	194			W 6285	8305	HUILES LUBRIFIANTES
33451	LUBS(HIGH PETR CONT) ETC							W 6146	7932	HUILES LUBRIF,H LOURDES
341	*GAS,NATURAL AND MANUFCT	W 12413	3495	W 3283	815	W 8499	1837	W 118282	57962	GAZ NATUREL,GAZ MANUFACT
3413	PETROLM GASES,LIQUEFIED	W 12413	3495	W 3283	815	W 7618	1755	W 118262	57960	GAZ DE PETROLE LIQUEFIE
34131	LIQUEFIED PROPANE,BUTANE	W 12413	3495	W 3282	809	W 7617	1752	W 118262	57960	PROPANE,BUTANE LIQUEFIES
4	ANIMAL,VEGETABLE OIL,FAT		7243		6817		8460		8156	HUILES,GRAISSES ANIM,VEG
42	FIXED VEGETABLE OIL,FAT		7087		6666		8279		8002	HUILES VEGETALES FIXES
423	FIXED VEG OILS,SOFT	W 4687	5699	W 4889	5739	W 5503	7135	W 4976	6925	HUILES VEGET DOUCES FIXES
4236	SUNFLOWER SEED OIL	W 3537	4277	W 4068	4648	W 4737	5966	W 4398	5957	HUILE DE TOURNESOL
5	CHEMCLS,RELATED PROD NES		142021		137990		150308		172816	PRODUITS CHIMIQUES
53	DYES,TANNING,COLOUR PROD		10459		9874		11269		11540	PROD TEINTURE,COLORANTS
533	PIGMENTS,PAINTS,ETC	W 5220	10238	W 5473	9675	W 6023	11130	W 5712	11346	PIGMENTS,PEINTURES,VERNIS
5334	VARNISHES,DISTEMPERS ETC	W 2051	6894	W 2106	6719	W 2230	7309	W 1842	7160	PEINTURES A L'EAU
541	*MEDICINAL,PHARM PRODUCT	K 1924359	56672	K 1847441	57251	K 2041515	65220	K 2103848	78090	PROD MEDICINAUX PHARMACEUT
5416	GLYCOSIDES,GLANDS,SERA	K 9044	2602	K 11257	3334	K 10154	3913	K 14067	5948	HETEROSIDES
54164	ANTISERA,MICROB VACCINES	K 7130	2371	K 8209	2729	K 7842	3361	K 11887	5840	SERUMS,VACCINS

4. Special Imports C.I.F. by Commodities according to the S.I.T.C. (Rev. 2) in thousand U.S. Dollars
Importations Spéciales C.A.F. par Produits d'après la C.T.C.I. (Rév. 2) en milliers de Dollars E.U.

SITC CTCI	COMMODITY	1992		1993		1994		1995		PRODUIT
		WEIGHT POIDS	VALUE VALEUR	WEIGHT POIDS	VALUE VALEUR	WEIGHT POIDS	VALUE VALEUR	WEIGHT POIDS	VALUE VALEUR	
5417	MEDICAMENTS	K 1828715	52128	K 1744546	52110	K 1919237	58722	K 1989586	69612	MEDICAMENTS
54179	— CONTNG OTH SUBSTANCES	K 1823432	51911	K 1740194	51932	K 1908383	58345	K 1981694	69196	MED CONT AUT SUBSTANCES
55	PERFUME,CLEANING ETC PRD		34782		32857		34686		35579	PROD POUR PARFUM,TOILETTE
553	PERFUMERY,COSMETICS,ETC	W 1963	18305	W 2143	17341	W 2379	18648	W 2398	19855	PRODUITS DE PARFUMERIE
554	SOAP,CLEANSING ETC PREPS	W 7382	15610	W 7934	14703	W 9482	14995	W 8311	14814	SAVONS,PRODUITS DETERSIFS
5542	WASHING PREPARATIONS ETC	W 5579	11456	W 6335	11294	W 7802	11615	W 6853	11079	PROD ORG TENSIO–ACT NDA
562	*FERTILIZERS,MANUFACTURE	W 17521	6071	W 18652	5968	W 14929	4516	W 11309	4119	ENGRAIS MANUFACTURES
5629	FERTILIZERS NES	W 15385	5519	W 16207	5384	W 12128	3850	W 8851	3421	ENGRAIS NDA
56291	NIT–PHOS–POT FERTLZR NES	W 15242	5380	W 15863	5168	W 11816	3671	W 8234	2982	ENGRAIS CONT N P K
58	PLASTIC MATERIALS ETC		8965		7716		7370		10902	MAT PLAST ARTIFICIELLES
583	POLYMERIZATION ETC PRODS	W 4405	7689	W 4674	6919	W 3908	6181	W 4835	9331	PROD POLYMERISATION
59	CHEMICAL MATERIALS NES		20932		20314		22386		27478	MAT PROD CHIMIQUES NDA
591	PESTICIDES,DISINFECTANTS	W 2126	12161	W 2107	11476	W 1998	11814	W 2545	15225	DESINF,INSECT,FONG,HERB
5911	INSECTICIDES,FOR RETAIL	W 1343	6991	W 1287	6740	W 1368	7554	W 1801	9711	INSECTICIDES VENTE DET
598	MISCEL CHEM PRODUCTS NES	W 2099	7090	W 2290	7410	W 2767	8876	W 2837	10404	PROD DIV INDUST CHIM NDA
5989	CHEM PRODUCTS,PREPS NES	W 2054	6859	W 2245	7168	W 2727	8645	W 2804	10181	PROD PREP CHIMIQUES NDA
59899	OTH CHEM PRODS,PREPS,NES	W 1274	5063	W 1534	5629	W 2025	7130	W 2122	8739	AUT PRODUITS CHIMIQUES NDA
6	BASIC MANUFACTURES		237002		205109		236236		259528	ART MANUFACTURES
62	RUBBER MANUFACTURES NES		11858		12315		12678		16507	CAOUTCHOUC MANUFACTURE
625	RUBBER TYRES, TUBES ETC	W 2232	10295	W 2498	10849	W 2635	11061	W 3019	14418	PNEUS CAOUTCHOUC VULCANISE
6251	TYRES NEW FOR MOTOR CARS	W 854	4681	W 1045	5443	W 1018	5363	W 1294	7673	PNEUS POUR VOITURES
63	WOOD,CORK MANUFACTRS NES		19551		19542		19358		22010	OUVRAGES LIEGE ET BOIS
634	VENEERS,PLYWOOD,ETC	W 7198	6017	W 7235	6487	W 7883	7011	W 8511	7762	PLACAGES,CONTRE–PLAQUES
6342	PLYWOOD OF WOOD SHEETS	W 5959	5028	W 6462	5822	W 7288	6434	W 7544	6816	BOIS CONTRE–PLAQUES
635	WOOD MANUFACTURES NES	W 6601	13511	W 5498	13029	W 4861	12314	W 5004	14230	ART MANUF EN BOIS NDA
6353	BUILDERS WOODWRK,PREFABS	W 5603	11373	W 4758	10807	W 4153	10024	W 4248	11352	OUVRAGES DE MENUISERIE
64	PAPER,PAPERBOARD AND MFR		36591		31956		34630		39289	PAPIERS,CARTONS & OUVRAGES
641	PAPER AND PAPERBOARD	W 11735	11668	W 9713	8956	W 10608	10616	W 9813	14298	PAPIERS ET CARTONS
642	PAPER,ETC,PRECUT,ARTS OF	W 6429	24922	W 6869	23001	W 7185	24014	W 6397	24991	PAP,CARTONS DECOUPES
6421	PAPER ETC CONTAINERS	W 2040	5021	W 2456	4665	W 2267	4924	W 1929	5014	BOITES,SACS EMBALLAGES
6423	EXERCISE BOOKS ETC	W 1187	6056	W 1079	5099	W 1307	5882	W 1204	6630	REGISTRES,CAHIERS,CARNETS
6428	PAPER ETC ARTICLES NES	W 2381	11284	W 2514	10907	W 2535	10291	W 2425	10740	OUVRAGES EN PATE A PAPIER
64285	PAPER ETC DIAPERS ETC	W 1274	7175	W 1321	7190	W 1223	6532	W 1269	6766	SERVIETTES HYGIENIQUES
65	TEXTILE YARN,FABRICS,ETC		19346		17284		20406		21973	FILS,TISSUS,ARTICLES TEXTILE
658	TEXTILE ARTICLES NES	W 728	7511	W 711	7519	W 850	8237	W 818	9717	ART FACONNES MAT TEXTILES
6584	LINENS ETC	W 293	4546	W 452	5444	W 456	5682	W 463	5706	LINGE DE MAISON
66	NONMETAL MINERAL MFS NES		45497		34901		42289		48205	ART MIN NON METALLIQUES
661	LIME,CEMENT,BLDG PRODS	W 187119	15780	W 159079	11725	W 229799	17526	W 196320	17343	CHAUX,CIMENTS MAT CONSTR
6612	CEMENT	W 184866	14015	W 156334	9730	W 226517	15234	W 193269	14687	CIMENTS HYDRAULIQUES
662	CLAY,REFRACTORY BLDG PRD	W 25218	15407	W 19560	10824	W 20621	11076	W 25386	14723	MAT CONST REFRACTAIRES
6624	BRICKS ETC NONREFRACTORY	W 24213	14919	W 18915	10593	W 20334	10901	W 24855	14474	BRIQUES ETC CERAM NON REFR
66245	GLAZED CERAMIC SETTS ETC	W 20879	12698	W 17165	9502	W 19293	10224	W 22818	13387	AUT CARREAUX CERAMIQUE
665	GLASSWARE	W 4333	5145	W 5352	5077	W 4292	4975	W 3537	4806	OUVRAGES EN VERRE
67	IRON AND STEEL		34911		28799		36426		36260	FER ET ACIER
673	IRON,STEEL SHAPES ETC	W 17088	7337	W 22735	9162	W 25715	11383	W 23378	11196	BARRES,PROFIL FER,ACIER
6732	IRON,STEEL BARS ETC	W 8187	3515	W 9912	4141	W 11179	4829	W 7310	4093	BARRES FER,ACIER
674	IRN,STL UNIV,PLATE,SHEET	W 9523	10651	W 8956	8252	W 11434	10485	W 12622	14394	LARGES PLATS,TOLES
6749	OTH IRN,STL PLATES,SHEET	W 8812	10132	W 8140	7610	W 10833	10001	W 11799	13593	AUTRES TOLES FER,ACIER
67491	— OF IRON OR SIMPLE STL	W 8800	10117	W 8133	7584	W 10830	9989	W 11771	13564	AUT TOLES AUTRES ACIER FIN
678	IRON,STL TUBES,PIPES,ETC	W 9396	14908	W 8001	9931	W 9530	12504	W 5598	8410	TUBES,TUYAUX EN FONTE,FER
6781	CAST IRON TUBES,PIPES	W 5903	9466	W 1351	1935	W 5086	5955	W 2049	2609	TUBES,TUYAUX EN FONTE
68	NON–FERROUS METALS		5718		4491		7346		9932	METAUX NON FERREUX
684	ALUMINIUM	W 714	4658	W 623	3332	W 1044	5880	W 1357	8085	ALUMINIUM
6842	ALUMINIUM,ALLOYS WORKED	W 714	4658	W 623	3332	W 1043	5879	W 1357	8085	ALUMINIUM,ALLIAGES OUVRE
68421	ALUMINIUM BARS,WIRE,ETC	W 518	3576	W 471	2522	W 811	4510	W 1069	6366	BARRES,PROFILES FILS ALU
69	METAL MANUFACTURES NES		63209		55531		62699		64970	ART MANUFACT EN METAL NDA
691	STRUCTURES AND PARTS NES	W 7024	20031	W 7033	18105	W 8278	20832	W 6057	19383	CONSTRUCT FER,ACIER,ALU
6911	STRUCTURES,PARTS IRN,STL	W 6332	14386	W 6447	14473	W 7837	17689	W 5863	17947	CONSTRUCT FER,ACIER,FONTE
6912	STRUCTURES,PARTS ALUMNM	W 691	5646	W 586	3632	W 442	3143	W 194	1437	CONSTRUCT ALUMINIUM
692	METAL TANKS,BOXES,ETC	W 2084	6494	W 1317	4050	W 929	3096	W 579	2050	RECIPIENTS METALLIQUES
695	TOOLS	W 391	4861	W 583	5386	W 737	6047	W 744	6514	OUTILS A MAIN
6953	OTHER HAND TOOLS	W 308	3982	W 471	4441	W 646	5210	W 646	5565	AUTRES OUTILS A MAIN
69539	HAND TOOLS ETC NES	W 285	3542	W 450	4152	W 622	4827	W 629	5225	OUTILLAGE A MAIN NDA
697	BASE MTL HOUSEHOLD EQUIP	W 1415	10082	W 1316	8447		10353	W 1594	10329	ART MENAGE MET COMMUNS
699	BASE METAL MFRS NES	W 1951	12619	W 2034	11357	W 2439	13107	W 2756	16037	ART MANUFACTURES MET NDA
6991	LOCKSMITHS WARES,ETC	W 757	5611	W 707	5051	W 748	5583	W 957	7534	ARTICLES DE SERRURERIE
7	MACHINES,TRANSPORT EQUIP		453231		425941		469920		607010	MACHINES MATERIEL TRANSPORT
71	POWER GENERATING EQUIPMT		19141		36225		28718		21563	MACHINES GENERATRICES
713	INTRNL COMBUS PSTN ENGIN	W 379	11845	W 956	19508	W 845	19475	W 402	12774	MOTEURS EXPL COMB INT, PIECE
7138	PISTON ENGINES NES	W 7	176	W 634	9658	W 511	9840	W 14	285	MOTEURS A PISTONS NDA
7139	PISTON ENGINE PARTS NES	W 216	9274	W 158	6037	W 192	6949	W 221	9393	PIECES POUR 713.2,3,8
714	ENGINES AND MOTORS NES	W 7	620	W 212	7575	W 8	1180	W 3	249	MOTEURS NON ELECTRIQUES
7149	ENGINE & MOTOR PARTS NES	W 7	424	W 210	6186	W 7	895	W 3	229	PIECES 714 ET 718.88
71499	PARTS NES,OF 71488,71888	W 7	384	W 210	6160	W 7	892	W 2	196	PIECES 714.88 ET 718.88
716	ROTATING ELECTRIC PLANT	W 286	4249	W 386	6769	W 367	5428	W 444	7052	APP ELECTR ROTATIFS,PIECES
7162	AC MTRS,GENRTRS,GEN SETS	W 234	3219	W 341	5398	W 277	3803	W 362	5525	MOTEURS ELECTRIQUES
72	MACHS FOR SPCL INDUSTRYS		26692		21067		28692		29552	MAC SPECIALES POUR INDUST
723	CIVIL ENGNEERG EQUIP ETC	W 983	6138	W 769	3532	W 895	5318	W 1089	7121	APPAREILS DE GENIE CIVIL
7234	CONST,MINING MACHNRY NES	W 814	4887	W 597	2563	W 725	4460	W 903	6142	MACH POUR LA CONST, MINES
728	OTH MACHY FOR SPCL INDUS	W 1343	10546		8111	W 839	8987	W 966	9249	AUT MACH IND PARTICULIERES
7283	OTHR MINERAL WORKG MACHY	W 1008	5789	W 619	2793	W 543	3412	W 658	3550	MACH TRIER,CRIBLER,BROYER
74	GENRL INDUSTRL MACHY NES		46344		48566		46730		58642	MACH APP INDUSTRIE
741	HEATING,COOLING EQUIPMNT	W 1302	15347	W 1326	14481	W 1367	14252	W 1530	18674	MACH CHAUFFAGE,PIECES
7414	NONDOM REFRIG EQUIPT,PTS	W 336	3613	W 371	3582	W 433	4079	W 600	6899	MAT PRODUCTION DU FROID
74141	REFRIG EQUIP NONDOMESTIC	W 254	2795	W 274	2693	W 331	3094	W 498	5758	REFIG INDUSTRIELS
7415	AIR–CONDITIONING MACHNRY	W 683	7711	W 592	6664	W 619	6648	W 653	7690	GROUPES CONDITION AIR
743	PUMPS NES,CENTRFUGES ETC	W 348	5140	W 384	5281	W 412	6407	W 377	5737	POMPES COMPRES,VENT ETC
744	MECHANICAL HANDLING EQU	W 1090	8409	W 1439	7812	W 1132	8324	W 1388	10661	EQUIP MANUTENTION PIECES
745	NONELEC MACHY,TOOLS NES	W 433	6793	W 698	9191	W 451	6008	W 778	10324	AUT MACH NON ELEC,PIECES
7452	OTH NONELEC MCHS,PTS NES	W 387	5509	W 641	8258	W 420	5332	W 699	9046	AUT MACH NON ELEC,PIECES
749	NONELEC MACH PTS,ACC NES	W 810	7644	W 824	8338	W 658	8688	W 628	9599	PIECES MACH NON ELEC NDA
7492	COCKS,VALVES ETC NES	W 462	5071	W 410	5159	W 468	5905	W 462	5961	ART ROB,SIM POUR TUYAUX
75	OFFICE MACHNES,ADP EQUIP		26662		27640		31028		40658	MACH BUREAU TRAIT AUTOM
751	OFFICE MACHINES	W 107	4259	116	4844	W 119	4921	W 150	6806	MACH,APPAREILS DE BUREAU
752	AUTOMTIC DATA PROC EQUIP	W 208	18167	W 234	17482	W 265	20259	W 301	25575	MACH TRAIT INFORMATION
7522	DIGITAL COMPUTERS	W 75	6619	W 99	7532	W 131	10317	W 142	12365	MACH DIGITALES COMPLETES
7525	ADP PERIPHERAL UNITS	W 56	4335	W 82	4928	W 80	4913	W 89	6284	UNITES PERIPHERIQUES
759	OFFICE,ADP MCH PTS,ACCES	W 53	4236	W 62	5314	W 70	5848	W 90	8276	PIECES DU 751 ET 752
7599	ACCTG,ETC,ADP MCH PTS,AC	W 25	2923	W 35	3856	W 43	4365	W 57	6575	PIECES DU 751 ET 752
76	TELECOMM,SOUND EQUIPMENT		36087		34520		39848		42973	EQUIPMENT DE TELECOM
761	TELEVISION RECEIVERS	W 422	7473	W 417	6409	W 429	6921	W 460	7954	RECEPTEURS DE TELEVISION

4. Special Imports C.I.F. by Commodities according to the S.I.T.C. (Rev. 2) in thousand U.S. Dollars
Importations Spéciales C.A.F. par Produits d'après la C.T.C.I. (Rév. 2) en milliers de Dollars E.U.

SITC CTCI	COMMODITY	1992 WEIGHT POIDS	1992 VALUE VALEUR	1993 WEIGHT POIDS	1993 VALUE VALEUR	1994 WEIGHT POIDS	1994 VALUE VALEUR	1995 WEIGHT POIDS	1995 VALUE VALEUR	PRODUIT
7611	COLOUR TV RECEIVERS	W 418	7393	W 412	6318	W 427	6848	W 459	7874	RECEPTEURS COULEUR
762	RADIO BROADCAST RECEIVRS	W 174	4052	W 186	4183	W 295	5715	W 291	6762	RECEPTEURS RADIODIFFUSION
764	TELECOM EQPT,PTS,ACC NES	W 499	19964	W 548	20863	W 510	22990	W 574	23837	EQUIP TELECOM,PIECES
7641	LINE TELEPHONE,ETC EQUIP	W 122	6845	W 104	6009	W 109	9490	W 123	8782	APP TELEPHON PAR FIL
7649	PTS NES OF EQUIPMT OF 76	W 244	7668	W 284	7386	W 256	7372	W 281	8455	PIECES DE LA DIV 76
76491	PTS NES OF APPAR OF 7641	W 181	6247	W 220	5871	W 180	4455	W 185	6514	PIECES POUR 764.1
77	ELECTRIC MACHNRY NES ETC		71468		59431		67451		93874	MACH APP ELECT NDA
771	ELECTRIC POWER MACHY NES	W 938	4695	W 437	3924	W 463	4294	W 521	6557	MACH PROD,TRANS ELECTR
772	SWITCHGEAR ETC,PARTS NES	W 670	16604	W 765	13949	W 734	17359	W 854	21720	APP COUPURE,SECT ETC
7721	SWITCHGEAR ETC	W 670	16580	W 764	13923	W 733	17237	W 853	21675	APP COUPURE,SECTIONMNT
773	ELECTR DISTRIBUTNG EQUIP	W 3142	13488	W 2442	9161	W 2297	8579	W 3475	20425	EQUIPMT DISTRIBUTION ELECT
7731	INSULATED WIRE,CABLE ETC	W 3050	12998	W 2413	8971	W 2261	8320	W 3457	20185	FILS,CABLES ISOLES ELECT
775	HOUSEHOLD TYPE EQUIP NES	W 3455	20257	W 3052	18015	W 3501	20089	W 4249	25181	MACH,APP USAGE DOMESTQUE
7751	HOUSEHOLD LDRY EQUIP NES	W 993	4242	W 825	3720	W 1035	4187	W 1374	5743	MACH A LAVER ET SECHOIRS
7752	DOM REFRIGERATRS,FREEZRS	W 1538	8556	W 1276	7044	W 1505	8102	W 1765	9540	REFRIG,CONGEL MENAGER
77521	DOMESTIC REFRIGERATORS	W 1134	6135	W 931	5188	W 1164	6188	W 1234	6567	REFRIGERATEURS
7758	ELECTRO–THERMIC APPL NES	W 517	4478	W 577	4384	W 609	4971	W 665	5869	APP ELECTROTHERMIQ NDA
778	ELECTRICAL MACHINERY NES	W 1026	13877	W 1255	12938	W 1544	14205	W 1507	15443	AUTRES MACH ELECT NDA
7782	ELECTRIC LAMPS,BULBS	W 140	5347	W 72	1274	W 119	1404	W 105	1486	LAMPES, TUBES ELECTRIQUES
78	ROAD VEHICLES		127506		152552		184497		217696	VEHICULES ROUTIERS
781	PASS MOTOR VEH EXC BUSES	W 5206	56601	W 8493	88106	W 10219	110341	W 10894	129783	AUTO TRANSPORT PERSONNES
782	LORRIES,SPCL MTR VEH NES	W 3529	33025	W 3216	28261	W 3493	33549	W 4117	40957	VEHICULES SPECIAUX,MARCH
7821	LORRIES,TRUCKS	W 3240	30081	W 2837	24738	W 3284	31289	W 3783	39023	VEHICULES TRANSP MARCHAND
783	ROAD MOTOR VEHICLES NES	W 515	6855	W 485	5942	W 509	5484	W 751	7085	VEHICULES ROUTIERS NDA
7831	BUSES	W 443	6359	W 424	5600	W 434	4884	W 605	6351	VOITURES TRANSPORT COMMUN
784	MOTOR VEH PRTS,ACCES NES	W 1359	21518	W 1489	21496	W 1481	23127	W 1575	28515	PIECES 722,781,782,783
7849	OTHER MOTOR VEHCL PARTS	W 1339	21290	W 1440	21042	W 1439	22909	W 1558	28259	PIECES 722,781,782,783
785	CYCLES,ETC MOTRZD OR NOT	W 451	6892	W 580	6808	W 600	8124	W 578	8097	MOTOCYCLES SCOOTERS
79	OTHR TRANSPORT EQUIPMENT		97312		44054		41038		99990	AUTRE MATERIEL TRANSPORT
792	AIRCRAFT ETC	W 28	10991	W 18	3702	W 19	1561	W 28	7927	APP NAVIGATION AERIENNE
7923	AIRCRFT NES2000–15000KG	W 7	5280					W 16	6782	AERODYNES 2000 A 15000 KG
793	SHIPS AND BOATS ETC	W 2497	86316	W 1194	40350	W 1016	39464	W 2186	92063	NAVIRES BATEAUX,ETC
7932	SHIPS AND BOATS NES	W 2383	84085	W 1173	39971	W 1008	39289	W 2174	91706	NAVIRES ET BATEAUX
79321	YACHTS,SPORTS VESSLS ETC	W 1862	61298	W 783	21062	W 999	39078	W 1382	65589	BATEAUX DE PLAISANCE
79323	OTHER CARGO VESSELS	W 510	22744	W 381	18851			W 644	23821	AUT BATEAUX TRANS MARCH
8	MISC MANUFACTURED GOODS		239886		225354		243504		282556	ART MANUFACTURES DIVERS
812	*PLUMBG,HEATNG,LGHTNG EQ	W 1651	9660	W 1370	7380	W 1465	7211	W 1762	11527	APPAR SANITAIRES CHAUFFAGE
8124	LIGHTING EQUIPMENT NES	W 541	5610	W 486	4848	W 439	4185	W 554	7437	APPAREILS ECLAIRAGE ETC
821	*FURNITURE,PARTS THEREOF	W 11105	46732	W 10376	38342	W 11479	41125	W 12189	47180	MEUBLES ET PIECES
8211	CHAIRS,SEATS AND PARTS	W 1857	11172	W 1867	9099	W 2125	10069	W 2231	11551	SIEGES ET PIECES
82111	CHAIRS AND OTHER SEATS	W 1833	11074	W 1857	9029	W 2113	9963	W 2225	11502	SIEGES
8219	FURNITURE AND PARTS NES	W 8605	32345	W 7979	26417	W 8751	27677	W 9263	31742	AUTRES MEUBLES ET PIECES
82191	METAL FURNITURE NES	W 1053	6327	W 841	4662	W 962	4635	W 972	4914	MEUBLES NDA EN METAL
82192	WOOD FURNITURE NES	W 6895	22364	W 6440	18704	W 6904	19444	W 7320	22728	MEUBLES NDA EN BOIS
84	CLOTHING AND ACCESSORIES		40359		42000		47776		52595	VETEMENTS
842	MENS OUTERWEAR NOT KNIT	W 256	8748	W 337	9169	W 388	9361	W 380	10362	VET DESSUS POUR HOMMES
8423	— TROUSERS,BREECHES ETC	W 208	6318	W 252	6164	W 280	6369	W 287	6898	PANTALONS HOMMES MAT TEX
843	WOMENS OUTERWEAR NONKNIT	W 224	11178	W 366	13000	W 462	15369	W 467	16969	VET DESSUS FEMMES MAT TEX
8439	— OTHER OUTER GARMENTS	W 129	6429	W 212	8041	W 271	9194	W 287	10362	AUT VET DES FEM MAT TEXT
844	UNDER GARMENTS NOT KNIT	W 117	4911	W 154	5116	W 205	6086	W 165	5497	VETEMENT DESSOUS MAT TEX
8441	— MENS SHIRTS	W 91	4172	W 125	4524	W 153	5159	W 125	4670	CHEMISES HOMMES MAT TEXT
845	OUTERWEAR KNIT NONELASTC	W 143	4814	W 188	3855	W 198	4640	W 184	6086	VET DESSOUS,ACCES BONNET
846	UNDER GARMENTS KNITTED	W 374	8073	W 367	7907	W 486	9290	W 456	10156	SOUS VETS DE BONNETERIE
8462	— OF COTTON NON ELASTIC	W 341	6111	W 325	6077	W 431	7227	W 394	7806	SOUS–VET BONNET COTON
84629	—— OTHER	W 341	6111	W 325	6077	W 431	7227	W 394	7806	AUT SOUS–VET BONNET COTON
851	*FOOTWEAR	W 940	22518	W 1086	22184	W 1143	21752	W 1109	25341	CHAUSSURES
85102	FOOTWEAR LEATHER	W 604	17791	W 724	17799	W 807	17778	W 734	19668	CHAUS SEMELLES EN CUIR
87	PRECISION INSTRUMNTS NES		14485		12105		15970		18939	INSTRUM,APPAR SCIENT NDA
872	MEDICAL INSTRUMENTS NES	W 132	6187	W 132	5620	W 200	8373	W 231	9189	INSTR,APP MEDIC–CHIR NDA
87202	OTH MEDICAL INSTRUMENTS	W 122	5302	W 121	5139	W 189	7818	W 218	8372	INSTRUM,APP MEDECINE
874	MEASURNG,CONTROLNG INSTR	W 99	5420	W 103	5029	W 109	5622	W 124	6709	INSTRUMENTS DE MESURE
88	PHOTO EQU,OPTICL GDS ETC		6368		7008		7558		8379	APP,FOURN PHOTO,OP,MONTR
89	MISC MANUFCTRD GOODS NES		95472		92449		98415		113957	ART MANUFACTURES DIVERS
892	PRINTED MATTER	W 3382	34573	W 4003	34759	W 4468	36734	W 4675	39457	IMPRIMES
8921	PRINTED BOOKS,GLOBES,ETC	W 690	12254	W 906	12689	W 1108	15117	W 1085	16710	LIVRES,BROCHURES,CARTES
89211	PRINTED BOOKS,PAMPHLETS	W 681	12156	W 902	12630	W 1074	14900	W 1071	16551	LIVRES,BROCHURES
8922	NEWSPAPERS,PERIODICALS	W 2006	16834	W 2266	16434	W 2179	15185	W 2543	15272	JOURNAUX ET PERIODIQUES
8928	PRINTED MATTER NES	W 660	5118	W 789	5290	W 1152	6035	W 1014	7025	IMPRIMES NDA
893	ARTICLES OF PLASTIC NES		24607		22767		24507		29127	OUVRAGES EN MAT DIVIS 58
8931	PLSTC PACKG CONTNRS,LIDS	W 1288	6081	W 1363	5514	W 1624	6077	W 1832	8127	ART TRANSP EMBALLAGE ETC
8939	MISC PLASTIC ARTICLES	W 3970	17566	W 4196	16122	W 4524	17238	W 4203	19578	ART DIVERS EN MAT DIV 58
89399	OTHR PLASTC ARTICLES NES	W 3450	15677	W 3638	14497	W 4096	15784	W 3718	17988	AUT OUV MAT DIV 58
894	TOYS,SPORTING GOODS,ETC	W 849	10802	W 963	11108	W 1111	11297	W 1315	13523	VOITURES ENFANTS,JOUETS
8942	TOYS,INDOOR GAMES ETC	W 492	7346	W 652	8020	W 671	7416	W 800	9225	JOUETS,JEUX ETC
897	GOLD,SILVER WARE,JEWELRY		5419		3436		4090		5196	BIJOUTERIE,ORFEVRERIE
898	MUSICAL INSTRUMENTS,PTS	W 191	7576	W 261	8604	W 246	8731	W 255	11226	INSTRUMENTS DE MUSIQUE
8983	SOUND RECRDNG TAPE,DISCS	W 146	6901	W 196	7833	W 180	7887	W 193	10364	SUPPORTS SON POUR 763
89832	RECORDED DISCS,TAPES ETC	W 92	5654	W 123	6592	W 111	6649	W 127	9147	DISQUES,PHONO,BANDES
899	OTHER MANUFACTURED GOODS		8484		7823		8464		10810	AUT ART MANUF DIVERS NDA
9	GOODS NOT CLASSD BY KIND		36846		42317		35556		33496	ART TRANSACT NON CLASSES
911	*MAIL NOT CLASSED BY KIN		36489		41850					COLIS POSTAUX
931	*SPECIAL TRANSACTIONS						35364		33205	TRANS.SPECIALES

5. Special Exports F.O.B. by Commodities according to the S.I.T.C. (Rev. 2) in thousand U.S. Dollars
Exportations Spéciales F.O.B. par Produits d'après la C.T.C.I. (Rév. 2) en milliers de Dollars E.U.

SITC CTCI	COMMODITY	1992 WEIGHT POIDS	1992 VALUE VALEUR	1993 WEIGHT POIDS	1993 VALUE VALEUR	1994 WEIGHT POIDS	1994 VALUE VALEUR	1995 WEIGHT POIDS	1995 VALUE VALEUR	PRODUIT
	ALL COMMODITIES		136763		129688		152259		161974	TOUS PRODUITS
0	FOOD AND LIVE ANIMALS		93747		86817		84749		74487	ALIMENTS,ANIMAUX VIVANTS
01	MEAT AND PREPARATIONS		83		188		650		440	VIANDES ET PREPARATIONS
014	MEAT PREPD,PRSVD,NES ETC	W 8	75	W 23	188	W 81	586	W 50	440	CONSERVES DE VIANDES
0149	OTH PREPARD,PRESRVD MEAT	W 8	75	W 21	165	W 81	586	W 49	435	AUTRES PREP DE VIANDES
02	DAIRY PRODCTS,BIRDS'EGGS		768		720		667		450	PRODUITS LAITIERS,OEUFS
022	MILK AND CREAM	W 366	652	W 272	525	W 312	646	W 155	450	LAIT ET CREME
0223	MILK AND CREAM FRESH	W 354	609	W 260	502	W 276	552	W 153	429	LAIT,CREME FRAIS
04	CEREALS AND PREPARATIONS		9702		9760		10331		7758	CEREALES ET PRODUITS
042	RICE	W 1486	852	W 1966	1162	W 397	277	W 344	155	RIZ
0422	RICE SEMI–MILLED,MILLED	W 1486	852	W 1816	1136	W 397	277	W 344	155	RIZ POLI,GLACE INCL BRISURES
04221	RICE MILLED UNBROKEN	W 866	583	W 1075	858	W 245	228	W 17	24	RIZ POLI,GLACE EXCL BRISURES
046	WHEAT ETC MEAL OR FLOUR	W 19192	8778	W 18816	8223	W 24231	9865	W 16968	7467	SEMOULE FARINE,FROMENT
04601	FLOUR OF WHEAT OR MESLIN	W 19192	8778	W 18816	8223	W 24231	9865	W 16968	7467	FARINE DE FROMENT
05	VEGETABLES AND FRUIT		59148		40960		39793		46151	LEGUMES ET FRUITS
057	FRUIT,NUTS,FRESH,DRIED	W 103204	58408	W 102447	40449	W 89932	39463	W 67079	45857	FRUITS FRAIS OU SECS
0573	BANANA,PLANTAIN,FRSH,DRY	W 101155	52547	W 99830	33295	W 87809	33227	W 65980	41051	BANANES FRAICHES,SECHEES
0579	FRUIT FRESH OR DRIED NES	W 2046	5841	W 2612	7125	W 2098	6197	W 1079	4757	FRUITS FRAIS,SECS NDA
05798	OTHER FRESH FRUIT	W 2025	5771	W 2592	7065	W 2071	6110	W 1071	4720	AUTRES FRUITS FRAIS
058	FRUIT PRESERVED,PREPARED	W 415	634	W 199	320	W 81	170	W 93	234	CONSERVES DE FRUITS
0585	FRUIT OR VEGETABLE JUICE	W 385	553	W 135	172	W 18	23	W 10	10	JUS DE FRUITS
06	SUGAR AND PREPS,HONEY		22884		33979		31989		18744	SUCRES ET PRODUITS
061	SUGAR AND HONEY	W 39077	22884	W 57577	33979	W 57454	31984	W 26216	18654	SUCRES ET MIEL
0611	RAW BEET AND CANE SUGAR	W 39033	22843	W 56024	33849	W 51152	31395	W 26203	18621	SUCRES BRUTS
081	*FEEDING STUFF FOR ANIML	W 6888	693		551	W 3522	384	W 1851	218	NOURRITURE POUR ANIMAUX
0812	BRAN,POLLARD,SHARPS,ETC	W 6516	567	W 3236	285	W 2983	231	W 1613	139	SONS
08122	BRAN,ETC OF OTHR CEREALS	W 6516	567	W 3236	285	W 2983	231	W 1613	139	SONS D'AUTRES CEREALES
09	MISC EDIBLE PRODUCTS		308		301		510		328	PREP ALIMENTAIRES DIVERSES
098	EDIBLE PRODCTS,PREPS NES	W 207	305	W 124	293	W 230	501	W 154	327	PREP ALIMENTAIRES NDA
1	BEVERAGES AND TOBACCO		10771		9823		8586		10009	BOISSONS ET TABACS
11	BEVERAGES		10748		9806		8578		10009	BOISSONS
111	NON–ALCOHL BEVERAGES NES	W 3500	2250	W 3229	1923	W 2987	1644	W 3094	1686	BOISSONS NON ALCOOLIQUES
11101	WATERS,ICE AND SNOW	W 2364	722	W 2081	595	W 2115	590	W 2517	848	EAU,EAUX MINERALES
11102	FLAVORED WATERS NON–ALCO	W 1136	1528	W 1148	1328	W 871	1054	W 577	838	LIMONADES,EAUX GAZEUSES
112	ALCOHOLIC BEVERAGES	W 5478	8498	W 5441	7883	W 4425	6933	W 4054	8323	BOISSONS ALCOOLIQUES
1121	WINE OF FRESH GRAPES ETC	W 11	16	W 22	31	W 4	16	W 37	636	VINS DE RAISINS FRAIS
11212	WINE OF FRESH GRAPES	W 11	16	W 22	31	W 4	16	W 37	636	VINS DE MOUTS DE RAISINS
1123	BEER,ALE,STOUT,PORTER	W 687	1001	W 584	784	W 221	309	W 17	29	BIERES
1124	DISTILLED ALCOHOLIC BEVS	W 4780	7481	W 4836	7069	W 4200	6608	W 4000	7656	ALCOOLS,EAUX–DE–VIE
11249	OTH ALCOHOLC BEVS,CMPNDS	W 4780	7481	W 4835	7068	W 4200	6608	W 3985	7586	BOISSONS ALCOOLIQUES NDA
2	CRUDE MATERLS,EXCL FUELS		1027		740		1089		1180	MAT BRUTES NON COMESTIBLES
28	METALLIFEROUS ORES,SCRAP		748		493		703		872	MINERAIS METAL,DECHETS
288	NONFERR METAL SCRAP NES	W 610	748	W 432	493	W 583	703	W 557	872	DECHETS NON FERREUX
2882	OTHER BASE MTL SCRAP NES	W 562	747	W 432	493	W 583	703	W 557	872	AUTRES DECHETS
28823	ALUMINIUM WSTE AND SCRAP	W 562	747	W 432	493	W 529	680	W 557	872	DECHETS D'ALUMINIUM
5	CHEMCLS,RELATED PROD NES		3664		1410		1569		1852	PRODUITS CHIMIQUES
53	DYES,TANNING,COLOUR PROD		1312		71		102		212	PROD TEINTURE,COLORANTS
533	PIGMENTS,PAINTS,ETC	W 475	1286	W 31	71	W 32	102	W 50	212	PIGMENTS,PEINTURES,VERNIS
5334	VARNISHES,DISTEMPERS ETC	W 474	1282	W 18	52	W 32	101	W 39	194	PEINTURES A L'EAU
53341	WATER–THINNED PAINTS	W 457	1252	W 11	38	W 21	66	W 23	88	PEINTURES DILUEES
55	PERFUME,CLEANING ETC PRD		487		231		534		868	PROD POUR PARFUM,TOILETTE
553	PERFUMERY,COSMETICS,ETC	W 33	459	W 14	175	W 48	391	W 48	673	PRODUITS DE PARFUMERIE
58	PLASTIC MATERIALS ETC		371		472		414		213	MAT PLAST ARTIFICIELLES
583	POLYMERIZATION ETC PRODS	W 160	365	W 338	456	W 167	414	W 113	211	PROD POLYMERISATION
59	CHEMICAL MATERIALS NES		1050		240		119		135	MAT PROD CHIMIQUES NDA
591	PESTICIDES,DISINFECTANTS	W 221	1017	W 24	166	W 9	71	W 20	118	DESINF,INSECT,FONG,HERB
5911	INSECTICIDES,FOR RETAIL	W 221	1010	W 14	115	W 8	67	W 17	97	INSECTICIDES VENTE DET
6	BASIC MANUFACTURES		2867		3124		5450		7227	ART MANUFACTURES
64	PAPER,PAPERBOARD AND MFR		649		552		913		676	PAPIERS,CARTONS & OUVRAGES
641	PAPER AND PAPERBOARD	W 58	384	W 57	421	W 57	423	W 32	322	PAPIERS ET CARTONS
642	PAPER,ETC,PRECUT,ARTS OF	W 57	266	W 31	131	W 60	490	W 70	354	PAP,CARTONS DECOUPES
66	NONMETAL MINERAL MFS NES		584		640		312		114	ART MIN NON METALLIQUES
661	LIME,CEMENT,BLDG PRODS	W 5009	428	W 7572	524	W 1600	186			CHAUX,CIMENTS MAT CONSTR
6612	CEMENT	W 5006	423	W 7572	524	W 1600	185			CIMENTS HYDRAULIQUES
69	METAL MANUFACTURES NES		1188		1189		3650		5469	ART MANUFACT EN METAL NDA
691	STRUCTURES AND PARTS NES	W 89	219	W 49	204	W 125	462	W 76	281	CONSTRUCT FER,ACIER,ALU
692	METAL TANKS,BOXES,ETC	W 266	258	W 105	555	W 822	2646	W 1318	4185	RECIPIENTS METALLIQUES
6924	MTL TRANSPORT BOXES ETC	W 266	258	W 105	555	W 821	2642	W 1318	4184	FUTS,TAMBOURS,BIDONS
69241	STL TRANSPORT BOXES ETC	W 96	122	W 63	393	W 783	2543	W 1278	4027	FUTS,TAMBOURS,BIDONS FER
7	MACHINES,TRANSPORT EQUIP		20252		23028		45601		59082	MACHINES MATERIEL TRANSPORT
71	POWER GENERATING EQUIPMT		3739		2318		3128		2286	MACHINES GENERATRICES
712	STEAM ENGINES,TURBINES	W 1	121	W 20	582	W 15	1062	W 13	607	MACHINES A VAPEUR D'EAU PIEC
7129	STM ENGINE ETC PARTS NES	W 1	121	W 20	582	W 14	945	W 12	473	PARTIES,PIECES DU 712.6
713	INTRNL COMBUS PSTN ENGIN	W 773	2838	W 75	1100	W 81	1061	W 55	740	MOTEURS EXPL COMB INT, PIECE
7138	PISTON ENGINES NES	W 740	2060	W 9	51	W 7	47	W 7	37	MOTEURS A PISTONS NDA
7139	PISTON ENGINE PARTS NES	W 19	670	W 60	891	W 66	653	W 34	524	PIECES POUR 713.2,3,8
714	ENGINES AND MOTORS NES	W 1	676	W 2	457	W 3	792	W 2	635	MOTEURS NON ELECTRIQUES
7144	REACTION ENGINES			W 1	240	W 3	605	W 1	504	PROPULSEURS A REACTION
7148	GAS TURBINES NES	W 1	564	W 1	176		180			TURBINES A GAZ
71481	TURBO–PROPELLERS	W 1	564	W 1	176		180			TURBO–PROPULSEURS
72	MACHS FOR SPCL INDUSTRYS		1770		1817		1387		791	MAC SPECIALES POUR INDUST
727	FOOD MACHRY NON–DOMESTIC	W 236	1151	W 23	168	W 61	296	W 20	153	MACH INDUSTRIES ALIMENT
7272	OTH FOOD PROC MCHY,PARTS	W 236	1151	W 21	149	W 61	296	W 11	71	AUT MACH IND ALIMENTAIRE
72722	INDUS FOOD PROC MACH NES	W 236	1151	W 16	132	W 61	296	W 11	71	MACHINES BOULANGERIE
728	OTH MACHY FOR SPCL INDUS	W 27	463	W 345	922	W 59	456	W 36	138	AUT MACH IND PARTICULIERES
7281	MACH–TOOLS FR SPCL INDUS	W 22	433	W 29	222	W 6	109	W 8	41	MACH–OUTILS SPEC IND PART
72812	MACH–TOOLS TO WORK WOOD	W 22	426	W 26	196	W 3	27	W 8	40	MACH–OUT POUR TRAVAIL BOIS
7283	OTHR MINERAL WORKG MACHY	W 3	3	W 245	647	W 9	17	W 15	10	MACH TRIER,CRIBLER,BROYER
72832	MINRL CRUSHING ETC MACHY			W 243	638	W 1	2			MACH CONCASSER MAT MINER
74	GENRL INDUSTRL MACHY NES		760		663		1229		1622	MACH APP INDUSTRIE
744	MECHANICAL HANDLING EQU	W 145	355	W 71	186	W 300	645	W 49	125	EQUIP MANUTENTION PIECES
745	NONELEC MACHY,TOOLS NES	W 28	111	W 30	48	W 13	100	W 143	1143	AUT MACH NON ELEC,PIECES
7452	OTH NONELEC MCHS,PTS NES	W 27	105	W 15	34	W 11	91	W 143	1138	AUT MACH NON ELEC,PIECES
74522	PACKAGNG,BOTTLNG,ETC MCH	W 24	74	W 2	4	W 5	45	W 141	1092	MACH NETT BOUTEILLES,ETC
75	OFFICE MACHNES,ADP EQUIP		419		619		878		996	MACH BUREAU TRAIT AUTOM
759	OFFICE,ADP MCH PTS,ACCES	W 2	128	W 4	256	W 4	249	W 7	514	PIECES DU 751 ET 752
76	TELECOMM,SOUND EQUIPMENT		463		1118		812		1161	EQUIPMENT DE TELECOM
764	TELECOM EQPT,PTS,ACC NES	W 6	422	W 19	1031	W 8	684	W 10	1142	EQUIP TELECOM,PIECES
77	ELECTRIC MACHNRY NES ETC		1068		810		711		567	MACH APP ELECT NDA
78	ROAD VEHICLES		2443		2568		2802		3497	VEHICULES ROUTIERS
781	PASS MOTOR VEH EXC BUSES	W 120	1308	W 185	1791	W 261	1723	W 305	2353	AUTO TRANSPORT PERSONNES

5. Special Exports F.O.B. by Commodities according to the S.I.T.C. (Rev. 2) in thousand U.S. Dollars
Exportations Spéciales F.O.B. par Produits d'après la C.T.C.I. (Rév. 2) en milliers de Dollars E.U.

SITC CTCI	COMMODITY	1992 WEIGHT POIDS	1992 VALUE VALEUR	1993 WEIGHT POIDS	1993 VALUE VALEUR	1994 WEIGHT POIDS	1994 VALUE VALEUR	1995 WEIGHT POIDS	1995 VALUE VALEUR	PRODUIT
782	LORRIES,SPCL MTR VEH NES	W 90	508	W 91	467	W 75	246	W 130	310	VEHICULES SPECIAUX,MARCH
7821	LORRIES,TRUCKS	W 61	274	W 91	467	W 75	246	W 101	199	VEHICULES TRANSP MARCHAND
79	OTHR TRANSPORT EQUIPMENT		9479		13069		34634		48103	AUTRE MATERIEL TRANSPORT
792	AIRCRAFT ETC	W 1	399	W 9	846	W 14	5884	W 17	5434	APP NAVIGATION AERIENNE
7921	HELICOPTERS			W 2	353	W 3	141	W 3	906	HELICOPTERES
7929	AIRCRAFT PARTS NES	W 1	399	W 3	436	W 11	5743	W 14	4528	PIECES DU 792
793	SHIPS AND BOATS ETC	W 364	9080	W 656	12223	W 1326	28750	W 1352	42669	NAVIRES BATEAUX,ETC
7932	SHIPS AND BOATS NES	W 364	9080	W 648	12041	W 1326	28744	W 1352	42655	NAVIRES ET BATEAUX
79321	YACHTS,SPORTS VESSLS ETC	W 245	4062	W 646	12027	W 1309	27386	W 1056	27788	BATEAUX DE PLAISANCE
79323	OTHER CARGO VESSELS	W 119	5018			W 17	1358	W 296	14866	AUT BATEAUX TRANS MARCH
8	MISC MANUFACTURED GOODS		4063		4687		5124		7964	ART MANUFACTURES DIVERS
84	CLOTHING AND ACCESSORIES		646		451		553		906	VETEMENTS
843	WOMENS OUTERWEAR NONKNIT	W 3	163	W 2	115	W 14	172	W 10	536	VET DESSUS FEMMES MAT TEX
8439	— OTHER OUTER GARMENTS	W 2	125	W 2	88	W 2	134	W 9	511	AUT VET DES FEM MAT TEXT
87	PRECISION INSTRUMNTS NES		480		574		716		1265	INSTRUM,APPAR SCIENT NDA
874	MEASURNG,CONTROLNG INSTR	W 1	276	W 1	417	W 3	393	W 5	954	INSTRUMENTS DE MESURE
88	PHOTO EQU,OPTICL GDS ETC		398		451		81		116	APP,FOURN PHOTO,OP,MONTR
89	MISC MANUFCTRD GOODS NES		2270		2685		3089		4963	ART MANUFACTURES DIVERS
892	PRINTED MATTER	W 52	1398	W 59	1559	W 59	1571	W 106	2438	IMPRIMES
8921	PRINTED BOOKS,GLOBES,ETC	W 32	638	W 23	500	W 23	460	W 20	412	LIVRES,BROCHURES,CARTES
89211	PRINTED BOOKS,PAMPHLETS	W 32	638	W 23	500	W 23	460	W 19	393	LIVRES,BROCHURES
8922	NEWSPAPERS,PERIODICALS	W 8	568	W 15	816	W 13	904	W 71	1879	JOURNAUX ET PERIODIQUES
893	ARTICLES OF PLASTIC NES		630	W 344	871	W 764	1187	W 505	1229	OUVRAGES EN MAT DIVIS 58
8931	PLSTC PACKG CONTNRS,LIDS	W 122	413	W 269	618	W 345	951	W 424	909	ART TRANSP EMBALLAGE ETC
897	GOLD,SILVER WARE,JEWELRY		30		26		28		908	BIJOUTERIE,ORFEVRERIE
8973	PREC JEWLRY,GLD–SILVWARE		18		21		22		898	BIJOUX OR,ARGENT ORFEVRE
89731	PRECIOUS METAL JEWELLERY		18		21		22		898	ART BIJOUTERIE,JOAILLER

1. HISTORICAL SERIES, 1961–1996 SPECIAL TRADE, IMPORTS C.I.F., EXPORTS F.O.B.
SERIES HISTORIQUES, 1961–1996 COMMERCE SPECIAL, IMPORTATIONS C.A.F., EXPORTATIONS F.O.B

YEAR ANNEE	VALUE IN MILLION U.S. DOLLARS VALEUR EN MILLION U.S. DOLLARS MERCHANDISE –MARCHANDISE		GOLD –OR		CONVERSION FACTORS U.S. CENTS PER QUETZAL FACTEURS DE CONVERSION CENTS E.U. PAR QUETZAL		INDEX NUMBERS –INDICES QUANTUM		UNIT VALUE VALEUR UNITAIRE	
	IMPORTS	EXPORTS	IMPORTS	EXPORTS	IMPORTS	EXPORTS	IMPORTS	EXPORTS	IMPORTS	EXPORTS
1961	133.60	112.70								
1962	136.00	117.80								
1963	171.10	154.00								
1964	202.10	164.50								
1965	228.30	187.90								
1966	207.60	228.70								
1967	247.10	202.20								
1968	249.40	226.70								
1969	250.20	258.60								
1970	284.30	290.20								
1971	303.30	283.20								
1972	324.00	327.50								
1973	431.00	436.20								
1974	700.50	572.10					65	63	63	76
1975	732.70	623.50					62	58	69	90
1976	838.90	760.40					71	76	69	84
1977	1052.50	1160.20					53	130	77	113
1978	1309.60	1092.40					91	71	85	132
1979	1503.90	1241.40					91	70	100	151
1980	1598.20	1519.80					89	92	109	142
1981	1673.50	1226.10					87	88	116	120
1982	1388.00	1119.80					70	95	120	101
1983	1135.00	1158.80					62	98	111	102
1984	1278.50	1122.30					48	122	138	92
1985	1174.90	1020.60					70	81	101	109
1986	958.50	1043.80					57	113	101	81
1987	1447.20	987.30					88	90	100	94
1988	1557.00	1021.70					62	91	128	96
1989	1653.80	1108.00					92	101	117	106
1990	1648.80	1163.00					100	100	100	100
1991	1851.30	1202.20					117	125	96	79
1992	2531.50	1295.30					125	145	123	77
1993	2599.30	1340.40					133	136	119	85
1994	2604.20	1521.50					148	147	109	88
1995	3292.50	2155.50								98
1996	3146.10	2030.80								87

2. IMPORTS BY BROAD ECONOMIC CATEGORY AND EXPORTS BY INDUSTRIAL ORIGIN. (PERCENTAGE OF TOTAL VALUE)
IMPORTATIONS PAR CATEGORIES ECONOMIQUES ET EXPORTATIONS PAR BRANCHE D'ACTIVITE.(EN POURCENTAGE DE LA VALEUR TOTALE)

IMPORTS – IMPORTATIONS

	1990	1991	1992	1993	1994	1995	1996
TOTAL IMPORTS–IMPORTATIONS TOTALES	100.	100.	100.	100.	100.	100.	100.
1 FOOD BEV–ALIMENTATION BOISSONS	7.7	9.0	9.0	9.0	10.9	9.5	10.9
11 PRIMARY–PRODUITS DE BASE	2.2	2.5	2.7	2.9	3.2	2.6	4.0
111 FOR INDUSTRY–POUR L'INDUSTRIE	1.9	2.0	1.9	2.1	2.5	1.9	3.4
112 FOR HOUSEHOLDS–POUR LES MENAGES	0.3	0.5	0.8	0.7	0.6	0.7	0.7
12 PROCESSED–PRODUITS ELABORES	5.5	6.5	6.3	6.2	7.7	6.9	6.9
121 FOR INDUSTRY–POUR L'INDUSTRIE	1.5	1.7	1.2	1.1	1.5	1.0	1.1
122 FOR HOUSEHOLDS–POUR LES MENAGES	4.0	4.8	5.1	5.1	6.2	5.9	5.8
2 IND SUPPLIES–APPROV INDUSTRIELS	39.8	39.2	35.5	33.1	34.5	34.7	32.8
21 PRIMARY–PRODUITS DE BASE	2.5	2.6	1.7	2.1	1.9	2.1	2.8
22 PROCESSED–PRODUITS ELABORES	37.3	36.6	33.8	30.9	32.7	32.6	30.0
3 FUELS–COMBUSTIBLES	16.5	16.4	13.5	11.7	11.3	12.2	14.6
31 PRIMARY–PRODUITS DE BASE	7.3	7.3	6.1	4.7	5.1	4.5	5.4
32 PROCESSED–PRODUITS ELABORES	9.1	9.1	7.5	6.9	6.1	7.7	9.2
321 MOTOR SPIRIT–ESSENCE	3.2	3.0	2.3	3.0	2.5	2.6	3.9
322 OTHER–AUTRES	6.0	6.0	5.2	3.9	3.7	5.0	5.3
4 MACHINERY–EQUIPEMENT	17.8	16.6	19.1	18.5	14.4	14.6	15.4
41 CAPITAL EQUIPMENT–MACHINES	15.5	14.5	17.0	16.5	12.2	12.4	13.0
42 PARTS–PIECES ACCESSOIRES	2.2	2.1	2.1	2.0	2.2	2.2	2.4
5 TRANSPORT–TRANSPORT	9.6	10.5	13.6	17.4	16.4	16.6	14.1
51 PASSENGER CARS–AUTOMOBILES	5.6	6.1	9.4	7.1	6.4	6.1	5.0
52 OTHER–AUTRES	0.5	0.7	0.7	6.8	6.7	6.9	5.8
521 INDUSTRIAL–INDUSTRIELS	0.3	0.4	0.4	6.5	6.4	6.6	5.5
522 NON INDUSTRIAL–NON INDUSTRIEL	0.2	0.2	0.3	0.3	0.3	0.3	0.3
53 PARTS–PIECES ACCESSOIRES	3.6	3.7	3.5	3.4	3.2	3.6	3.4
6 CONSUM GOODS–BIENS CONSOMMATION	8.0	8.3	9.0	10.2	12.4	12.3	12.0
61 DURABLE–DURABLES	1.7	1.4	1.7	2.4	2.9	3.1	2.6
62 SEMI DURABLE–SEMI DURABLES	2.7	3.1	3.5	3.9	4.6	4.6	4.4
63 NON DURABLE–NON DURABLES	3.6	3.8	3.8	3.9	4.8	4.6	5.0
7 GOODS NES–BIENS NDA	0.6	0.1	0.3	0.2	0.1	0.1	0.1

EXPORTS – EXPORTATIONS

	1990	1991	1992	1993	1994	1995	1996
TOTAL EXPORTS–EXPORTATIONS TOTALES	100.	100.	100.	100.	100.	100.	100.
1 AGRICULTURE	52.1	46.5	44.2	43.9	43.7	47.2	45.0
2 MINING QUARRY–INDUS EXTRACTIVES	2.1	1.9	1.8	2.0	1.9	2.1	3.4
3 MANUFACTURING–IND MANUFACTUR	45.9	51.6	54.0	54.1	54.5	50.7	51.6
31 FOOD BEV TOBACCO–ALIM BOISS TAB	20.3	22.4	22.8	22.3	22.1	21.6	20.1
32 TEXTILES–INDUSTRIES TEXTILES	6.1	6.3	6.1	6.1	5.6	4.4	4.9
33 WOOD & PRODUCTS–BOIS & PRODUITS	1.1	1.2	1.4	1.2	1.1	0.8	0.9
34 PAPER & PRODUCTS–PAPIER & PRODT	0.9	1.3	1.3	1.5	1.5	1.5	2.2
35 CHEMICALS–INDUSTRIES CHIMIQUES	12.4	13.8	14.0	14.0	14.4	13.3	14.2
36 NON METAL MIN–MIN NON METAL	1.1	1.5	2.1	2.6	2.8	2.3	2.2
37 BASIC METAL–IND METAL BASE	1.2	1.5	2.4	2.4	2.6	2.7	3.0
38 METAL MANUF–MANUF METAL	2.4	3.1	3.1	3.4	3.8	3.5	3.7
39 OTH MANUF IND–AUTRES MANUF	0.5	0.4	0.5	0.5	0.6	0.5	0.6

3. TRADE BY PRINCIPAL COUNTRIES OF PRODUCTION AND LAST DESTINATION (VALUE IN THOUSAND U.S. DOLLARS)
ECHANGES SELON LES PRINCIPAUX PAYS DE PRODUCTION ET DE DERNIERE DESTINATION (VALEUR EN MILLIERS DE DOLLARS EU)

COUNTRIES–PAYS	SPECIAL IMPORTS C.I.F. IMPORTATIONS SPECIALES C.A.F				
	1992	1993	1994	1995	1996
World	2462757	2668116	2647192	3292459	3146216
Africa	5391	7529	5053	2891	2357
Americas	1865525	2075521	2058265	2631293	2541765
Northern America	1141109	1345537	1197935	1528816	1465803
LAIA	425017	430128	444272	615724	636954
CACM	241146	235223	292333	291462	242977
Caribbean	24540	14917	55419	107824	115693
Rest of America	33712	49716	68306	87468	80338
As.ex F.USSR	241466	239429	202990	252076	212345
Eur.x F.USSR	344172	331194	342672	371871	365362
EU	305928	298317	313016	343907	337329
EFTA	31923	29539	21249	19864	23920
East Europe	6279	3043	8122	7842	4098
Other Europe	2	141	285	36	7
Former USSR	3292	9830	27170	24710	10543
Oceania	2911	4613	8011	9618	11904
USA/Etats–Unis d'Amer	1117133	1313250	1169003	1478469	1409442
Mexico/Mexique	143050	168522	185892	308218	322510
El Salvador	140955	138881	165033	161241	128755
Venezuela	101292	130894	137235	151740	165345
Japan/Japon	146653	137973	100618	121157	99320
Germany/Allemagne	113301	102157	104839	116101	99610
Costa Rica	73214	65045	83784	69289	62022
Panama	33612	49510	68051	86434	79813
Brazil/Brésil	61202	56740	48359	50828	42812
Aruba	15802	8640	2010	101951	106952
Italy/Italie	48825	46187	39489	36872	38492
Canada	23931	32230	28880	50308	56208
Honduras	22654	27616	37567	53252	44019
United Kingdom	33943	37171	34585	39510	31487
Netherlands/Pays–Bas	22917	24648	29006	30220	46543
Spain/Espagne	23787	23723	26109	32230	40852
Colombia/Colombie	28020	25928	24397	32109	31411
Argentina/Argentine	49114	19273	12471	21471	28520
Korea, Republic of	17561	20197	22539	34830	27829
Ecuador/Equateur	25336	16405	20959	29860	28881
Belgium–Luxembourg	15873	17444	18995	32445	31441
France, Monac	22778	19131	24074	21266	17404
Hong Kong	16759	21209	19493	22921	20071
Switz.Liecht	25991	24638	14561	15232	18563
Russian Federation	3292	9830	27170	24710	10543
Netherlands Antilles	292	10	47316	990	2629
Chile/Chili	12270	7488	8758	11018	11326
Sweden/Suède	8949	7227	9055	11150	8743
Ireland/Irlande	5091	8074	11401	9425	8158
New Zealand	1400	3878	7441	8942	11358
Nicaragua	4323	3681	5949	7680	8181
Israel/Israël	7347	4303	6525	5202	5783
Peru/Pérou	4337	4562	5368	9222	5314
Norway, SVD, JM	5928	4897	6682	4632	5357
Denmark/Danemark	4116	4604	3923	8364	4503
Finland/Finlande	1729	3574	8366	1894	5170
So. Africa Customs Un	5207	6018	3471	2627	2119
Austria/Autriche	3973	3671	2313	3689	3712
China/Chine	2242	2042	4073	3588	4898
Trinidad and Tobago	2964	4026	4200	1244	2603
Singapore/Singapour	2225	3308	1801	2694	1878
India/Inde	842	2404	2132	2991	3188
Korea Dem People's Rp	2138	3379	3666	887	716
Poland/Pologne	2436	1987	4420	1086	747
Romania/Roumanie	1826	285	2574	4122	878
Malaysia/Malaisie	2801	1165	1423	1891	524
Indonesia/Indonésie	573	1453	1437	2023	1824
Thailand/Thaïlande	369	1017	817	943	1992
Turkey/Turquie	2073	161	382	793	1210
Cuba	0	534	617	1011	2316

COUNTRIES–PAYS	SPECIAL EXPORTS F.O.B. EXPORTATIONS SPECIALES F.O.B.				
	1992	1993	1994	1995	1996
Monde	1295291	1338222	1502445	1935516	2030734
Afrique	47839	21423	19241	13229	8518
Amériques	1009571	1078671	1176737	1404701	1616740
Amérique du Nord	472927	523169	498340	628929	787800
ALAI	82093	78219	141635	139763	150011
MCAC	395376	418218	474936	565759	577981
Caraïbes	24813	23656	23891	28959	47380
Autre Amérique	34362	35408	37935	41292	53567
Asie l'URSS exclus	61916	62561	111764	195276	91285
Europe l'URSS exclus	157944	170755	187062	315071	293302
UE	152708	163525	182355	303792	271571
AELE	4352	3855	3797	6310	13203
Europe de l'Est	884	3371	910	4952	8434
Autre de l'Europe		4		17	94
Ancienne URSS	4974	3858	3229	5566	19588
Océanie	13047	953	3650	1673	1088
USA/Etats–Unis d'Amer	459093	510562	483405	605835	746733
El Salvador	182544	191162	228972	268893	258045
Honduras	61050	77013	87024	124849	140238
Costa Rica	89612	95465	97607	101015	99787
Germany/Allemagne	44306	59281	65264	112526	102601
Nicaragua	62169	54578	61333	71002	79911
Mexico/Mexique	58745	47619	67168	45003	79984
Japan/Japon	21928	23254	38800	53514	42093
Panama	26845	28520	32678	37012	46333
Netherlands/Pays–Bas	22217	20752	27940	38351	29392
Belgium–Luxembourg	18885	15142	16599	32709	27308
Canada	13833	12605	14894	22193	37741
Italy/Italie	23006	14548	18409	23338	21239
Saudi Arabia	21156	18598	19765	19792	18847
Peru/Pérou	1217	16444	17887	28606	29488
Venezuela	472	4068	29528	37808	12518
France, Monac	9092	15372	14982	21546	21563
United Kingdom	10159	15848	11243	13193	18311
Sweden/Suède	5598	5396	10286	25562	21494
Dominican Republic	6367	11972	14819	16789	14151
Finland/Finlande	7552	7528	7256	16055	13831
Chile/Chili	4555	282	11261	19037	13492
Sri Lanka	5987	1159	23629	12433	92
Russian Federation	4974	3858	3229	5566	19588
Spain/Espagne	6434	4886	6436	11930	7490
China/Chine			1	34048	82
Haiti/Haïti	6018	4508	5068	5114	12838
Morocco/Maroc	15401	4827	146	4895	4881
Colombia/Colombie	3353	4411	4587	6562	9625
Belize/Bélize	4012	6159	5136	3925	6308
Ecuador/Equateur	13428	2006	5900	895	1544
United Arab Emirates	3301	4301	4794	4930	2939
Algeria/Algérie	2355	5028	8771	3047	
Egypt/Egypte	16716	334	526	924	534
Switz.Liecht	3488	2893	3304	4414	4513
Jamaica/Jamaïque	6954	873	819	1964	6828
Singapore/Singapour	2258	4197	2630	4145	4162
Portugal	3369	2801	2308	4669	4088
Fiji/Fidji	12326		2737		
So. Africa Customs Un	364	6794	468	4257	3074
Barbados/Barbade	2877	3436	1677	2167	3263
Norway, SVD, JM	864	963	493	1895	8690
Nigeria/Nigéria		2883	9266	18	15
Tunisia/Tunisie	9672	1557			
Brazil/Brésil	63	2980	5035	948	1893
Syrian Arab Republic	602	1456	2600	2631	2752
Poland/Pologne	347	408	846	3512	4506
Kuwait/ Koweït	1528	1860	2166	2227	1775
Israel/Israël	997	1543	1644	2532	2731
Trinidad and Tobago	682	1181	300	668	5861

(VALUE AS PERCENTAGE OF WORLD TOTAL)(VALEURS EN POURCENTAGE DU TOTAL MONDIAL)

	1987	1988	1989	1990	1991	1992	1993	1994	1995	1996
Africa	0.2	0.3	0.5	0.5	0.3	0.2	0.3	0.2	0.1	0.1
Americas	66.5	62.7	64.9	71.7	73.4	75.7	77.8	77.8	79.9	80.8
Northern America	38.7	39.0	40.7	41.8	43.7	46.3	50.4	45.3	46.4	46.6
LAIA	17.9	13.1	12.8	18.2	17.9	17.3	16.1	16.8	18.7	20.2
CACM	9.3	9.8	10.2	8.2	8.5	9.8	8.8	11.0	8.9	7.7
Caribbean	0.2	0.3	0.2	2.7	2.5	1.0	0.6	2.1	3.3	3.7
Rest of America	0.4	0.5	1.0	0.8	0.8	1.4	1.9	2.6	2.7	2.6
As.ex F.USSR	11.0	12.7	12.0	9.8	10.6	9.8	9.0	7.7	7.7	6.7
Eur.x F.USSR	21.2	23.5	21.9	17.7	15.5	14.0	12.4	12.9	11.3	11.6
EU	18.3	20.5	18.5	15.3	13.6	12.4	11.2	11.8	10.4	10.7
EFTA	1.8	1.7	2.1	1.8	1.6	1.3	1.1	0.8	0.6	0.8
East Europe	0.7	1.3	1.2	0.6	0.3	0.3	0.1	0.3	0.2	0.1
Other Europe	0.4	0.0	0.0	0.0	0.0	0.0	0.0	0.0	0.0	0.0
Former USSR	0.6	0.0	0.2	0.2	0.0	0.1	0.4	1.0	0.8	0.3
Oceania	0.1	0.2	0.2	0.1	0.2	0.1	0.2	0.3	0.3	0.4
USA/Etats–Unis d'Amer	36.9	37.3	38.7	40.3	42.6	45.4	49.2	44.2	44.9	44.8
Mexico/Mexique	9.0	6.2	5.9	6.7	6.6	5.8	6.3	7.0	9.4	10.3
El Salvador	5.1	5.4	5.6	4.9	5.3	5.7	5.2	6.2	4.9	4.1
Venezuela	6.2	1.4	2.1	7.2	4.5	4.1	4.9	5.2	4.6	5.3
Japan/Japon	6.3	7.3	6.0	6.0	6.6	6.0	5.2	3.8	3.7	3.2
Germany/Allemagne	6.5	6.8	6.5	5.6	4.7	4.6	3.8	4.0	3.5	3.2
Costa Rica	3.1	3.3	3.2	2.3	2.3	3.0	2.4	3.2	2.1	2.0
Panama	0.4	0.5	1.0	0.7	0.8	1.4	1.9	2.6	2.6	2.5
Brazil/Brésil	1.5	3.8	2.6	1.5	1.9	2.5	2.1	1.8	1.5	1.4
Aruba				2.6	1.8	0.6	0.3	0.1	3.1	3.4

	1987	1988	1989	1990	1991	1992	1993	1994	1995	1996
Afrique	0.0	1.3	0.9	2.0	2.2	3.7	1.6	1.3	0.7	0.4
Amériques	71.6	61.1	71.1	76.0	78.0	77.9	80.6	78.3	72.6	79.6
Amérique du Nord	39.1	28.2	36.4	41.2	39.1	36.5	39.1	33.2	32.5	38.8
ALAI	2.2	3.7	7.1	4.7	6.8	6.3	5.8	9.4	7.2	7.4
MCAC	25.8	23.5	23.6	24.8	27.0	30.5	31.3	31.6	29.2	28.5
Caraïbes	1.8	3.1	1.4	2.3	2.1	1.9	1.8	1.6	1.5	2.3
Autre Amérique	2.6	2.6	2.5	3.0	3.1	2.7	2.6	2.5	2.1	2.6
Asie l'URSS exclus	8.4	10.4	6.7	7.5	7.2	4.8	4.7	7.4	10.1	4.5
Europe l'URSS exclus	19.4	22.9	18.5	13.9	12.5	12.2	12.8	12.5	16.3	14.4
UE	18.3	17.6	16.6	13.6	12.2	11.8	12.2	12.1	15.7	13.4
AELE	0.4	0.3	0.4	0.3	0.3	0.3	0.3	0.3	0.3	0.7
Europe de l'Est	0.7	4.9	1.4	0.0	0.0	0.1	0.3	0.1	0.3	0.4
Autre de l'Europe	0.0	0.0	0.0	0.0	0.0		0.0		0.0	0.0
Ancienne URSS	0.3	4.1	2.5	0.6		0.4	0.3	0.2	0.3	1.0
Océanie	0.0	0.0	0.0	0.0	0.0	1.0	0.1	0.2	0.1	0.1
USA/Etats–Unis d'Amer	38.4	27.3	34.8	39.8	37.8	35.4	38.2	32.2	31.3	36.8
El Salvador	15.1	12.8	12.0	12.4	12.9	14.1	14.3	15.2	13.9	12.7
Honduras	2.8	3.1	3.3	3.3	3.6	4.7	5.8	5.8	6.5	6.9
Costa Rica	6.6	6.5	6.9	6.3	6.3	6.9	7.1	6.5	5.2	4.9
Germany/Allemagne	6.7	7.7	7.0	5.5	3.8	3.4	4.4	4.3	5.8	5.1
Nicaragua	1.3	1.2	1.5	2.8	4.2	4.8	4.1	4.1	3.7	3.9
Mexico/Mexique	1.1	2.2	5.0	3.1	5.2	4.5	3.6	4.5	2.3	3.9
Japan/Japon	1.8	2.1	2.5	3.0	2.8	1.7	1.7	2.6	2.8	2.1
Panama	2.5	2.4	2.1	2.4	2.3	2.1	2.1	2.2	1.9	2.3
Netherlands/Pays–Bas	2.9	2.5	2.2	2.0	2.3	1.7	1.6	1.9	2.0	1.4

4. Special Imports C.I.F. by Commodities according to the S.I.T.C. (Rev. 2) in thousand U.S. Dollars
Importations Spéciales C.A.F. par Produits d'après la C.T.C.I. (Rév. 2) en milliers de Dollars E.U.

SITC CTCI	COMMODITY	1993 WEIGHT POIDS	1993 VALUE VALEUR	1994 WEIGHT POIDS	1994 VALUE VALEUR	1995 WEIGHT POIDS	1995 VALUE VALEUR	1996 WEIGHT POIDS	1996 VALUE VALEUR	PRODUIT
	ALL COMMODITIES		2668116		2647192		3292459		3146216	TOUS PRODUITS
0	FOOD AND LIVE ANIMALS		235402		284477		308482		369526	ALIMENTS,ANIMAUX VIVANTS
01	MEAT AND PREPARATIONS		7294		6101		9905		10068	VIANDES ET PREPARATIONS
02	DAIRY PRODCTS,BIRDS'EGGS		32798		36858		34673		40238	PRODUITS LAITIERS,OEUFS
022	MILK AND CREAM	W 19030	29791	W 20154	33365	W 17755	29881	W 17168	34106	LAIT ET CREME
0224	MILK,CREAM PRESERVED ETC	W 11898	23792	W 14715	29480	W 12296	25327	W 13924	30967	LAIT,CREME CONS,CONC
02243	MILK DRY,OVER 1.5% FAT	W 9026	20264	W 11962	25971	W 9149	20888	W 11028	27406	LAIT POUDRE SUP 1.5%
04	CEREALS AND PREPARATIONS		104835		123846		123686		176783	CEREALES ET PRODUITS
041	WHEAT ETC UNMILLED	W 217866	39306	W 356259	55833	W 232804	48439	W 354069	84794	FROMENT,EPEAUTRE
0411	DURUM WHEAT UNMILLED	W 192074	34496	W 340430	53991	W 232804	48438	W 335637	80868	FROMENT DUR NON MOULU
042	RICE	W 26286	11032	W 16535	6476	W 33532	10239	W 25016	7071	RIZ
0421	RICE IN HUSK OR HUSKED	W 20070	9820	W 9529	2997	W 21018	5839	W 24353	6776	RIZ SANS AUTRE PREPARATION
04211	RICE IN THE HUSK	W 19860	9725	W 8724	2607	W 20870	5788	W 24311	6755	RIZ PADDY
044	MAIZE UNMILLED	W 146752	23991	W 151161	22933	W 174254	24980	W 216852	43728	MAIS NON MOULU
048	CEREAL ETC PREPARATIONS	W 24849	24941	W 26277	29951	W 44068	36703	W 39025	38085	PREPTNS A BASE CEREALES
0481	PREPD BREAKFAST FOOD ETC	W 4977	7305	W 6250	9118	W 9429	10226	W 10910	10666	CEREALES TRAVAILLEES
04812	CEREAL ROASTED, PUFFED	W 4340	6106	W 5437	8285	W 5178	7761	W 4328	6930	PRODTS BASE CEREALES
0484	BAKERY PRODUCTS	W 7495	9000	W 9100	12560	W 8165	11518	W 7599	10937	PRODUITS DE BOULANGERIE
04842	PASTRY, CAKES ETC	W 5415	7050	W 5979	8485	W 5014	7297	W 4189	6359	PATISSERIE ETC.
05	VEGETABLES AND FRUIT		13548		18493		25512		28943	LEGUMES ET FRUITS
06	SUGAR AND PREPS,HONEY		7297		9817		9637		9330	SUCRES ET PRODUITS
081	*FEEDING STUFF FOR ANIML	W 47507	13535	W 77333	22761	W 98614	28869	W 107941	38063	NOURRITURE POUR ANIMAUX
0813	OILCAKE AND OTH RESIDUES	W 38644	9617	W 64785	16335	W 84310	20273	W 97231	30998	TOURTEAUX
08131	— OF SOYA BEANS	W 38643	9615	W 64679	16305	W 84284	20268	W 96764	30823	TOURTEAUX DE SOJA
09	MISC EDIBLE PRODUCTS		45143		52848		60873		52163	PREP ALIMENTAIRES DIVERSES
098	EDIBLE PRODCTS,PREPS NES	W 17461	44842	W 21046	52522	W 22259	59592	W 21309	51294	PREP ALIMENTAIRES NDA
09809	MISC FOOD PREPRTIONS NES	W 13727	38868	W 16272	45836	W 16850	51102	W 15249	43147	PREP ALIMENTAIRES NDA
1	BEVERAGES AND TOBACCO		12158		14409		19725		20429	BOISSONS ET TABACS
11	BEVERAGES		11882		13278		16145		16320	BOISSONS
112	ALCOHOLIC BEVERAGES	W 3980	7844	W 5928	9270	W 6184	11379	W 4938	11528	BOISSONS ALCOOLIQUES
2	CRUDE MATERLS,EXCL FUELS		52959		41792		64457		63252	MAT BRUTES NON COMESTIBLES
22	OIL SEEDS,OLEAGINOUS FRT		4388		4571		5150		9668	GRAINES,FRUITS OLEAGINEUX
26	TEXTILE FIBRES AND WASTE		21975		16800		30257		28435	FIBRES TEXTILES
263	COTTON	W 4986	5885	W 3634	4481	W 7678	11904	W 8827	13114	COTON
2631	RAW COTTON,EXCL LINTERS	W 4203	5477	W 3419	4337	W 6704	11389	W 7313	12270	COTON EN MASSE
266	SYNTHETIC FIBRES TO SPIN	W 5481	8751	W 3852	6179	W 4443	8650	W 3461	6096	FIBRES SYNTHETIQUES
29	CRUDE ANIMAL,VEG MAT NES		8695		7663		8181		8079	MATIERES BRUTES ANIM,VEGET
292	CRUDE VEG MATERIALS NES	W 3004	8349	W 1594	7228	W 1461	7780	W 2072	7527	MAT BRUTES VEGETALES NDA
3	MINERAL FUELS ETC		322518		305159		410402		466671	COMBUSTIBLES MINERAUX LUB
33	PETROLEUM AND PRODUCTS		294123		274981		374337		423363	PETROLE ET DERIVES
333	CRUDE PETROLEUM	W 694897	98222	W 788478	106183	W 781135	114004	W 738980	128030	HUILES BRUTES DE PETROLE
334	PETROLEUM PRODUCTS,REFIN	W 794210	184885	W 831898	162080	W 1205421	251599	W 1129647	288862	PRODUITS RAFFINES
3341	GASOLINE,OTH LIGHT OILS	W 327169	80410	W 308187	65103	W 367059	86188	W 379252	123614	ESSENCES POUR MOTEURS
33419	OTH LIGHT PETROLEUM OILS					W 367059	86188	W 379252	123614	AUTRES HUILES LEGERES
3342	KEROSENE,OTH MEDIUM OILS	W 5527	1257	W 1601	370	W 59839	11883	W 68474	16083	PETR LAMPANTS,AUT HUIL
33429	OTH MEDIUM PETROLEUM OIL					W 59839	11883	W 68474	16083	AUTRES HUILES MOYENNES
3343	GAS OILS	W 89517	17935	W 1898	347					GAS OILS
3344	FUEL OILS,NES	W 358322	74484	W 503600	83545	W 753521	136006	W 658703	132392	FUEL OILS
3345	LUBS,PETROLEUM OILS NES	W 13675	10799	W 16612	12715	W 25002	17521	W 23219	16773	HUILES LUBRIFIANTES
33451	LUBS(HIGH PETR CONT) ETC	W 13369	10385	W 16314	12183	W 24623	16928	W 22523	15735	HUILES LUBRIF,H LOURDES
335	RESIDUAL PETRLM PROD NES	W 14794	11016	W 9925	6718	W 12999	8733	W 11606	6472	PRODUITS RESIDUELS NDA
341	*GAS,NATURAL AND MANUFCT	W 107520	28156	W 117569	29889	W 134099	35473	W 144303	42774	GAZ NATUREL,GAZ MANUFACT
3413	PETROLM GASES,LIQUEFIED	W 107413	28088	W 117484	29821	W 134064	35443	W 144240	42717	GAZ DE PETROLE LIQUEFIE
34131	LIQUEFIED PROPANE,BUTANE	W 90558	23723	W 117431	29771	W 133950	35349	W 144173	42663	PROPANE,BUTANE LIQUEFIES
4	ANIMAL,VEGETABLE OIL,FAT		44054		48513		56925		49629	HUILES,GRAISSES ANIM,VEG
411	*ANIMAL OILS AND FATS	W 33098	14163	W 30363	13387	W 43004	17670	W 29635	16727	HUILES,GRAISSES ANIMALES
4113	ANIML OIL,FAT,GREASE NES	W 32674	13880	W 29948	13119	W 42412	17295	W 29334	16540	HUILES,GRAISSES ANIMALES NDA
41132	FATS OF BOVINE,SHEEP,ETC	W 32517	13552	W 29769	12806	W 41900	16650	W 28100	15289	SUIFS BRUTS FONDUS
42	FIXED VEGETABLE OIL,FAT		27322		32890		37445		31533	HUILES VEGETALES FIXES
423	FIXED VEG OILS,SOFT	W 35146	22259	W 36498	24662	W 37129	29299	W 37580	25975	HUILES VEGET DOUCES FIXES
4232	SOYA BEAN OIL	W 14060	11037	W 13687	9070	W 7386	5217	W 5747	3790	HUILE DE SOJA
4233	COTTON SEED OIL	W 1899	1119	W 10982	7809	W 4113	3083	W 13272	10409	HUILE DE COTON
4236	SUNFLOWER SEED OIL	W 18503	9376	W 11667	7443	W 25249	20132	W 18173	10538	HUILE DE TOURNESOL
424	FIXED VEG OIL NONSOFT	W 8796	5063	W 14992	8228	W 10529	8146	W 7476	5558	AUTRES HUILES VEG FIXES
5	CHEMCLS,RELATED PROD NES		414862		459367		558827		528204	PRODUITS CHIMIQUES
51	ORGANIC CHEMICALS		53577		49047		61704		56173	PROD CHIMIQ ORGANIQUES
513	CARBOXYLIC ACIDS ETC	W 6620	11066	W 6454	9710	W 7610	12393	W 8130	10721	ACIDES CARBOXYLIQUES
514	NITROGEN–FNCTN COMPOUNDS	W 3047	9556	W 3055	10040	W 3900	15094	W 3444	14438	COMPOSES FONCT AZOTEES
5148	OTH NITROGN–FNCTN CMPNDS	W 1161	4900	W 1108	5144	W 1916	10104	W 1850	10014	AUTRES COMPOSES AZOTES
515	ORG–INORG COMPOUNDS ETC	W 2224	14533	W 2116	10330	W 1692	10605	W 1751	11002	COMPOSES ORGANO–MINERAUX
5156	HETEROCYCLIC CMPDS ETC	W 1249	8992	W 1166	5924	W 403	4303	W 404	3720	COMPOSES HETEROCYCLIQUES
51569	OTH HETEROCYC CMPDS,ETC	W 1247	8905	W 1166	5876	W 403	4116	W 404	3679	AUT COMP HETEROCYCLIQUES
516	OTHER ORGANIC CHEMICALS	W 4050	8349	W 4808	8032	W 1604846	10110	W 3752	7603	AUTRES PROD ORGANIQUES
52	INORGANIC CHEMICALS		33111		33683		38223		36514	PROD CHIM INORGANIQUES
522	INORG ELEMNTS,OXIDES,ETC		12822	W 42515	12281	W 51764	17828	W 45426	14884	ELEMENTS INORGANIQUES
523	OTHR INORG CHEMICALS ETC	W 54464	20147	W 56410	21294	W 56819	20353	W 63185	21570	AUT PRODUITS CHIMIQUES INORG
5232	OTH MTL CMPD OF INRG ACD	W 36836	13441	W 27766	13497	W 32094	12438	W 39974	13651	SELS METALLIQUES
52322	PHOSPHITES,PHOSPHATES	W 8421	6739	W 13225	8152	W 11745	6987	W 14684	7713	PHOSPHITES,PHOSPHATES
53	DYES,TANNING,COLOUR PROD		28012		29772		33385		30805	PROD TEINTURE,COLORANTS
531	SYNT DYE,NAT INDGO,LAKES	W 3305	8169	W 1539	10355	W 2853	10635	W 2321	9744	MAT COLOR ORGAN,LAQUES
533	PIGMENTS,PAINTS,ETC	W 6951	15112	W 8504	16544	W 9597	19727	W 9938	18634	PIGMENTS,PEINTURES,VERNIS
541	*MEDICINAL,PHARM PRODUCT	K 5887484	79876	K 5727455	90727	K 7123817	106028	K 6489352	107381	PROD MEDICINAUX PHARMACEUT
5417	MEDICAMENTS	K 3007861	57897	K 3423864	68920	K 4839679	81398	K 5457295	86280	MEDICAMENTS
54171	— CONTAINNG ANTIBIOTICS	K 531032	11437	K 733652	16934	K 544149	17678	K 543407	14698	MED CONTN ANTIBIOTIQUES
54179	— CONTNG OTH SUBSTANCES	K 2377137	40882	K 2502335	46936	K 4058570	57764	K 4476935	64409	MED CONT AUT SUBSTANCES
55	PERFUME,CLEANING ETC PRD		37857		46580		53646		53020	PROD POUR PARFUM,TOILETTE
551	ESSENTL OILS,PERFUME,ETC	W 1515	17124	W 1380	15425	W 1237	17776	W 1306	17831	HUILES ESSENTIELLES
5514	MIXED PERFUME SUBSTANCES	W 953	13374	W 1200	13190	W 1071	15322	W 1068	15662	MELANGES SUBSTAN ODORIFER
553	PERFUMERY,COSMETICS,ETC	W 2196	8389	W 3994	14250	W 4301	16132	W 5082	15789	PRODUITS DE PARFUMERIE
554	SOAP,CLEANSING ETC PREPS	W 12298	12344	W 17569	16905	W 21565	19738	W 19943	19401	SAVONS,PRODUITS DETERSIFS
5542	WASHING PREPARATIONS ETC	W 4872	6689	W 7127	8889	W 7588	9717	W 8310	9479	PROD ORG TENSIO–ACT NDA
562	*FERTILIZERS,MANUFACTURE	W 315536	38687	W 473611	66512	W 438065	74823	W 382738	67195	ENGRAIS MANUFACTURES
5621	CHEM NITROGENOUS FERTLZR	W 246089	29049	W 379655	49525	W 285493	46176	W 263065	43533	ENGRAIS AZOTES
56213	AMMONIUM SULPHATE	W 57875	4532	W 142683	13394	W 114542	12884	W 125708	13713	SULFATE D'AMMONIUM
56216	UREA	W 132013	17677	W 126881	20738	W 93418	18975	W 92922	19922	UREE
56219	CHEM NITROG FERTILZR NES	W 33911	3643	W 76057	9304	W 29543	5722	W 23334	4989	ENGRAIS AZOTES NDA
5623	CHEM POTASSIC FERTILIZER	W 37723	4841	W 46548	7943	W 55071	7696	W 54753	8717	ENGRAIS POTASSIQUES
5629	FERTILIZERS NES	W 15770	3302	W 20589	4003	W 62834	13295	W 30494	7350	ENGRAIS NDA
58	PLASTIC MATERIALS ETC		82538		78467		111945		99395	MAT PLAST ARTIFICIELLES
582	PROD OF CONDENSATION ETC	W 9019	11881	W 6049	9411	W 8773	13698	W 8004	12446	PROD CONDENS,POLYCOND
583	POLYMERIZATION ETC PRODS	W 77032	66159	W 67682	64735	W 74523	93809	W 81239	82668	PROD POLYMERISATION

4. Special Imports C.I.F. by Commodities according to the S.I.T.C. (Rev. 2) in thousand U.S. Dollars
Importations Spéciales C.A.F. par Produits d'après la C.T.C.I. (Rév. 2) en milliers de Dollars E.U.

SITC CTCI	COMMODITY	1993 WEIGHT POIDS	1993 VALUE VALEUR	1994 WEIGHT POIDS	1994 VALUE VALEUR	1995 WEIGHT POIDS	1995 VALUE VALEUR	1996 WEIGHT POIDS	1996 VALUE VALEUR	PRODUIT
5831	POLYETHYLENE	W 38447	29407	W 27270	21133	W 32352	36966	W 31654	30596	POLYETHYLENE
58311	— IN PRIMARY FORMS	W 37680	27614	W 26931	20239	W 31825	35216	W 31252	28926	POLYETHYLENE PRIMAIRES
5832	POLYPROPYLENE	W 9513	8328	W 10161	10178	W 10206	14909	W 10819	12467	POLYPROPYLENE
5834	POLYVINYL CHLORIDE	W 12579	9884	W 14208	13600	W 12998	14476	W 18268	15149	CHLORURE DE POLYVINYLE
58341	— IN PRIMARY FORMS	W 11923	8600	W 13173	11441	W 12058	12239	W 17096	12643	SOUS FORMES PRIMAIRES
5839	OTH POLYMRZTION ETC PROD	W 12849	14234	W 10853	13471	W 13500	19313	W 14650	17294	AUT PROD POLYMER COPOLYM
59	CHEMICAL MATERIALS NES		60550		63970		78297		76959	MAT PROD CHIMIQUES NDA
591	PESTICIDES,DISINFECTANTS	W 7610	37153	W 8897	40734	W 10797	50136	W 9063	47598	DESINF,INSECT,FONG,HERB
5911	INSECTICIDES,FOR RETAIL	W 1757	12524	W 1805	12203	W 1884	13084	W 1693	12582	INSECTICIDES VENTE DET
5912	FUNGICIDES,FOR RETAIL	W 1849	10381	W 2252	12050	W 3414	17503	W 2447	15584	FONGICIDES VENTE AU DET
5913	HERBICIDES,FOR RETAIL	W 3283	13057	W 3913	14863	W 4488	17483	W 4146	17902	HERBICIDES VENTE AU DET
598	MISCEL CHEM PRODUCTS NES	W 13325	18299	W 11687	18056	W 12764	22089	W 12975	22156	PROD DIV INDUST CHIM NDA
5989	CHEM PRODUCTS,PREPS NES	W 9596	12116	W 8063	11758	W 8694	14898	W 9593	15681	PROD PREP CHIMIQUES NDA
59899	OTH CHEM PRODS,PREPS,NES	W 5778	8648	W 4777	8456	W 4761	10734	W 5455	11408	AUT PRODUITS CHIMIQUES NDA
6	BASIC MANUFACTURES		461418		479209		605358		500767	ART MANUFACTURES
62	RUBBER MANUFACTURES NES		33279		32963		47004		42572	CAOUTCHOUC MANUFACTURE
625	RUBBER TYRES, TUBES ETC	W 9145	22019	W 8702	22426	W 12401	34297	W 16196	31017	PNEUS CAOUTCHOUC VULCANISE
6252	TYRES,NEW,BUS OR LORRY	W 3141	7885	W 2797	7982	W 4534	14523	W 4947	15020	PNEUS POUR AUTOBUS,CAMIONS
6259	OTH TYRES,TYRE CASES,ETC	W 4076	8202	W 3581	6800	W 4615	8845	W 5321	7320	AUTRES PNEUS RECHAPES FLAPS
64	PAPER,PAPERBOARD AND MFR		110859		115539		166273		117133	PAPIERS,CARTONS & OUVRAGES
641	PAPER AND PAPERBOARD	W 130427	81507	W 120755	79861	W 132950	126309	W 99486	84158	PAPIERS ET CARTONS
6411	NEWSPRINT	W 25078	16402	W 21202	13044	W 20495	18199	W 18314	16568	PAPIER JOURNAL
6412	PRINTG,WRITING PAPER NES	W 11364	10715	W 10371	9069	W 13256	15343	W 12700	10659	PAPIERS POUR L'IMPRESSION
64122	— COATED,IMPREGNATD ETC	W 10383	9838	W 10052	8400	W 12815	14036	W 12196	9621	PAPIERS IMPRESSION COUCHES
6413	KRAFT PAPER,PAPERBOARD	W 65742	26395	W 57301	27674	W 62317	45399	W 30639	19461	PAPIER ET CARTON KRAFT
64131	KRAFT LINER IN BULK	W 31803	11001	W 23757	11155	W 33992	23834	W 20267	10692	PAP KRAFT POUR COUVERTURES
64139	KRAFT PAPER PAPERBD,NES	W 28792	11671	W 28173	13138	W 22563	15937	W 5329	4064	PAPIER,CARTON KRAFT NDA
6415	PAPER,PAPERBRD,BULK,NES	W 17918	14403	W 22443	17674	W 28110	31170	W 28567	24548	PAPIERS,CARTONS ROULEAUX
64159	OTHER PAPER ETC,BULK,NES	W 14073	11642	W 18059	14650	W 18556	24103	W 19832	19344	AUT PAPIER ROULEAUX FEUILLES
6418	COATED ETC PAPER NES BLK	W 6271	9772	W 8411	11150	W 6841	14455	W 6741	10706	PAP,CARTONS COUCHES,ENDUITS
64189	COATED PAPER ETC NES	W 4837	7272	W 6915	7978	W 5038	9506	W 4997	7534	PAPIERS,CARTONS COUCHES
642	PAPER,ETC,PRECUT,ARTS OF	W 20440	29352	W 24973	35678	W 27264	39964	W 22493	32975	PAP,CARTONS DECOUPES
6421	PAPER ETC CONTAINERS	W 9448	14102	W 13873	17109	W 15797	18637	W 10619	12642	BOITES,SACS EMBALLAGES
6428	PAPER ETC ARTICLES NES	W 2611	5432	W 3278	7550	W 4874	9945	W 5179	9889	OUVRAGES EN PATE A PAPIER
65	TEXTILE YARN,FABRICS,ETC		50544		48767		51986		42931	FILS,TISSUS,ARTICLES TEXTILE
651	TEXTILE YARN	W 8339	17730	W 4264	13757	W 4218	13933	W 3910	10325	FILS TEXTILES
6514	SYN FIB YRN,BULK,MONOFIL	W 5633	11664	W 2302	7045	W 2527	7677	W 1973	6481	FILS CONT 85% FIB TEXT SYNTH
653	WOVN MAN-MADE FIB FABRIC	W 3062	9456	W 2138	10043	W 2249	11866	W 1579	7302	TISSUS FIBRES SYNTH,ARTIF
657	SPECIAL TXTL FABRC,PRODS	W 3412	10767	W 2832	9312	W 2812	9848	W 2794	9894	TISSUS SPECIAUX
66	NONMETAL MINERAL MFS NES		43122		53729		59938		60236	ART MIN NON METALLIQUES
661	LIME,CEMENT,BLDG PRODS	W 116503	6530	W 196371	16001	W 228085	14938	W 278981	19319	CHAUX,CIMENTS MAT CONSTR
6612	CEMENT	W 115634	6142	W 195334	15381	W 226682	14234	W 276518	18336	CIMENTS HYDRAULIQUES
664	GLASS	W 17138	8892	W 16824	8162	W 28171	13078	W 25123	11857	VERRE
665	GLASSWARE	W 14533	13577	W 15951	12258	W 11019	10980	W 8268	8866	OUVRAGES EN VERRE
67	IRON AND STEEL		117156		112157		142448		116814	FER ET ACIER
672	IRON,STEEL PRIMARY FORMS	W 127752	41254	W 81876	30650	W 48527	19997	W 57310	21131	LINGOTS FER,ACIER
6724	IRN,STL INGOTS,LUMPS,ETC	W 65305	21177	W 53939	19547	W 26442	10837	W 32760	11833	FER,ACIER LINGOTS,MASSES
67241	IRON,SIMPLE STEEL INGOTS	W 52690	18110	W 53617	19488	W 25256	10443	W 32608	11776	LINGOTS EN FER ET ACIER
6725	IRN,STL BLOOMS,SLABS,ETC	W 40234	10922	W 17538	6995	W 10896	2875	W 8007	2273	BLOOMS,BILLETTES FER ACIER
67251	IRN,SMPLE STL BLOOMS,ETC	W 40146	10744	W 17469	6861	W 10883	2826	W 7998	2253	BLOOMS ETC NON ACIER FIN
6727	IRN,STL COIL FR REROLLNG	W 22214	9155	W 10399	4108	W 11189	6285	W 16543	7024	EBAUCHES POUR TOLES FER
67271	IRON,SIMPLE STEEL COILS	W 22053	9078	W 9877	3857	W 10411	5776	W 15174	6285	EBAUCHES NON EN ACIER
673	IRON,STEEL SHAPES ETC	W 62493	23829	W 41298	15195	W 62951	26784	W 54384	22447	BARRES,PROFIL FER,ACIER
6731	IRON,STEEL WIRE ROD	W 28775	11620	W 21169	8533	W 26164	14496	W 24429	10408	FIL MACHINE FER,ACIER
67311	IRON,SIMPLE STL WIRE ROD	W 23369	9812	W 10715	3898	W 15738	5808	W 10972	4244	FIL MACH AUT ACIER FIN
674	IRN,STL UNIV,PLATE,SHEET	W 70602	36337	W 161698	53532	W 129634	81783	W 88727	55651	LARGES PLATS,TOLES
6746	IRN,STL THIN PLATE,ROLLD	W 30695	15313	W 113289	32617	W 69188	46258	W 51539	32722	TOLES LAM MOINS 3MM
67461	— OF IRON OR SIMPLE STL	W 29691	14369	W 111620	31660	W 66471	44565	W 50225	31586	TOL NON AC FIN MOINS 3 MM
6749	OTH IRN,STL PLATES,SHEET	W 13106	6902	W 14052	9585	W 27189	18795	W 19236	14097	AUTRES TOLES FER,ACIER
67491	— OF IRON OR SIMPLE STL	W 9377	5371	W 9104	6591	W 24663	16593	W 17302	12228	AUT TOLES AUTRES ACIER FIN
678	IRON,STL TUBES,PIPES,ETC	W 14683	13121	W 8887	8571	W 7903	8781	W 10726	13852	TUBES,TUYAUX EN FONTE,FER
68	NON-FERROUS METALS		22285		25493		29470		24269	METAUX NON FERREUX
684	ALUMINIUM	W 4362	13687	W 4398	16085	W 15049	17792	W 4990	13690	ALUMINIUM
6842	ALUMINIUM,ALLOYS WORKED	W 3422	12321	W 3941	15292	W 14639	17589	W 4510	13440	ALUMINIUM,ALLIAGES OUVRE
68423	ALUMINIUM FOIL	W 1386	6473	W 1769	9445	W 1663	9676	W 1091	6501	FEUILLES,BANDES MINCES AL
69	METAL MANUFACTURES NES		75990		81499		99071		88747	ART MANUFACT EN METAL NDA
692	METAL TANKS,BOXES,ETC	W 4092	8943	W 3487	9477	W 4732	16103	W 4668	13222	RECIPIENTS METALLIQUES
6924	MTL TRANSPORT BOXES ETC	W 3478	7991	W 3284	8925	W 3992	14234	W 4192	11965	FUTS,TAMBOURS,BIDONS
69242	ALUMNM TRNSPRT BOXES ETC	W 1313	4896	W 1563	5586	W 2574	10667	W 2724	7758	FUTS,TAMBOURS,BIDONS ALU
695	TOOLS	W 3446	15291	W 4056	15538	W 3755	15858	W 3508	16240	OUTILS A MAIN
6953	OTHER HAND TOOLS	W 1853	9987	W 2547	10283	W 2157	10181	W 2109	9778	AUTRES OUTILS A MAIN
697	BASE MTL HOUSEHOLD EQUIP	W 5742	11619	W 5125	13082	W 6779	14624	W 5273	11876	ART MENAGE MET COMMUNS
699	BASE METAL MFRS NES	W 7606	20659	W 6938	20392	W 9644	30121	W 9069	26278	ART MANUFACTURES MET NDA
7	MACHINES,TRANSPORT EQUIP		965284		826498		1033218		921229	MACHINES MATERIEL TRANSPORT
71	POWER GENERATING EQUIPMT		100518		34848		58668		46782	MACHINES GENERATRICES
713	INTRNL COMBUS PSTN ENGIN	W 4590	18596	W 2757	19123	W 2980	22825	W 3514	22338	MOTEURS EXPL COMB INT, PIECE
7139	PISTON ENGINE PARTS NES	W 2552	10283	W 1207	13369	W 1228	16475	W 2000	17444	PIECES POUR 713.2,3,8
716	ROTATING ELECTRIC PLANT	W 8911	74944	W 1708	12182	W 3229	29121	W 2095	17075	APP ELECTR ROTATIFS,PIECES
7161	DC MOTORS AND GENERATORS	W 228	2209	W 404	3383	W 1340	14276	W 484	2840	MOTEURS COURANT CONTINU
7162	AC MTRS,GENRTRS,GEN SETS	W 1238	6774	W 1157	6293	W 1652	12263	W 1302	7018	MOTEURS ELECTRIQUES
7169	PTS NES OF ROT ELEC PLNT	W 7412	65813	W 144	2474	W 230	2496	W 303	7149	PIECES MAC APP ROTATIFS
72	MACHS FOR SPCL INDUSTRYS		124595		88467		104066		112991	MAC SPECIALES POUR INDUST
721	AGRIC MACHY,EXC TRACTORS	W 1998	8289	W 1787	8276	W 2127	7982	W 1449	7709	MACHINES AGRICOLES
722	TRACTORS NON-ROAD	W 2560	8455	W 2156	10730	W 2101	10315	W 1469	6834	TRACTEURS
7224	WHEELED TRACTORS NES	W 2342	7831	W 1765	9111	W 1837	9146	W 1165	5937	TRACTEURS A ROUES
723	CIVIL ENGNEERG EQUIP ETC	W 2079	8196	W 2147	10774	W 3886	17856	W 6353	24839	APPAREILS DE GENIE CIVIL
7234	CONST,MINING MACHNRY NES	W 1842	7386	W 2000	9929	W 3562	16741	W 5918	22701	MACH POUR LA CONST, MINES
72342	SLFPRP SHOVELS,EXCAVATRS	W 947	3422	W 1167	5717	W 1778	8575	W 3590	10779	PELLES MECANIQUES
724	TEXTILE,LEATHER MACHNRY	W 2997	18642	W 2235	14523	W 2210	14667	W 2006	17602	MACH POUR INDUSTRIE TEXTILE
726	PRINTG,BKBINDG MACHY,PTS	W 1063	14838	W 655	5436	W 1005	8624	W 804	10039	MACHINES POUR IMPRIMERIE
727	FOOD MACHRY NON-DOMESTIC	W 2802	32855	W 2309	16498	W 1996	15512	W 3229	15193	MACH INDUSTRIES ALIMENT
7272	OTH FOOD PROC MCHY,PARTS	W 2492	31683	W 2198	15265	W 1683	11307	W 2367	10791	AUT MACH IND ALIMENTAIRE
72722	INDUS FOOD PROC MACH NES	W 1909	29681	W 1141	9881	W 1296	7804	W 1909	5989	MACHINES BOULANGERIE
728	OTH MACHY FOR SPCL INDUS	W 3012	26770	W 2574	20763	W 3956	27811	W 5350	26742	AUT MACH IND PARTICULIERES
7283	OTHR MINERAL WORKG MACHY	W 801	10307	W 791	4224	W 754	4760	W 1168	6021	MACH TRIER,CRIBLER,BROYER
7284	MACHY FOR SPCL INDUS NES	W 1547	12498	W 883	11677	W 2345	18101	W 1384	16448	MACH SPEC IND PARTICUL.
72842	RUBBER,PLASTICS WRKG MCH	W 708	5444	W 269	3053	W 1676	11295	W 677	5617	MACH IND CAOUT MAT PLAST
73	METALWORKING MACHINERY		8337		7262		8346		7418	MACH TRAVAIL DES METAUX
74	GENRL INDUSTRL MACHY NES		103721		107941		128214		123707	MACH APP INDUSTRIE
741	HEATING,COOLING EQUIPMNT	W 2692	15893	W 2104	13301	W 2814	16333	W 3138	14489	MACH CHAUFFAGE,PIECES
742	PUMPS FOR LIQUIDS ETC	W 1506	10703	W 1363	14458	W 1472	15657	W 2133	18796	POMPES MOTO-POMPES

4. Special Imports C.I.F. by Commodities according to the S.I.T.C. (Rev. 2) in thousand U.S. Dollars
Importations Spéciales C.A.F. par Produits d'après la C.T.C.I. (Rév. 2) en milliers de Dollars E.U.

SITC CTCI	COMMODITY	1993		1994		1995		1996		PRODUIT
		WEIGHT POIDS	VALUE VALEUR	WEIGHT POIDS	VALUE VALEUR	WEIGHT POIDS	VALUE VALEUR	WEIGHT POIDS	VALUE VALEUR	
7428	OTHER PUMPS FOR LIQUIDS	W 918	7998	W 1118	10817	W 1176	11027	W 1714	14070	AUTRES POMPES POUR LIQ
74288	PUMPS FR LIQUIDS NES ETC	W 734	6020	W 1026	9065	W 1094	9740	W 1564	11614	POMPES POUR LIQUIDES NDA
743	PUMPS NES,CENTRFUGES ETC	W 2054	12501	W 2042	14050	W 3005	17225	W 3030	19269	POMPES COMPRES,VENT ETC
744	MECHANICAL HANDLING EQU	W 4103	18102	W 4163	17830	W 4405	19384	W 3499	20395	EQUIP MANUTENTION PIECES
7442	LIFTING,LOADING MACH NES	W 2495	9393	W 2156	8450	W 2090	8891	W 1378	6668	APP LEVAGE,MANUTENTION
745	NONELEC MACHY,TOOLS NES	W 1641	20192	W 1795	21428	W 1858	26586	W 1607	19922	AUT MACH NON ELEC,PIECES
7452	OTH NONELEC MCHS,PTS NES	W 1545	18609	W 1489	19339	W 1675	24559	W 1395	17839	AUT MACH NON ELEC,PIECES
74522	PACKAGNG,BOTTLNG,ETC MCH	W 613	10466	W 543	10806	W 641	13388	W 425	7733	MACH NETT BOUTEILLES,ETC
749	NONELEC MACH PTS,ACC NES	W 2852	26330	W 2758	26874	W 3845	33030	W 3219	30836	PIECES MACH NON ELEC NDA
7492	COCKS,VALVES ETC NES	W 1143	9931	W 1136	9877	W 1327	11276	W 1698	11894	ART ROB,SIM POUR TUYAUX
75	OFFICE MACHNES,ADP EQUIP		45289		52879		61806		71134	MACH BUREAU TRAIT AUTOM
751	OFFICE MACHINES	W 867	10255	W 888	12791	W 1103	13165	W 896	13191	MACH,APPAREILS DE BUREAU
752	AUTOMTIC DATA PROC EQUIP	W 799	18625	W 711	21674	W 551	23533	W 557	27710	MACH TRAIT INFORMATION
7522	DIGITAL COMPUTERS	W 467	11793	W 394	16063	W 383	18558	W 405	19235	MACH DIGITALES COMPLETES
759	OFFICE,ADP MCH PTS,ACCES	W 709	16409	W 1105	18414	W 1408	25108	W 1914	30233	PIECES DU 751 ET 752
7599	ACCTG,ETC,ADP MCH PTS,AC	W 542	12799	W 1029	16654	W 1303	22546	W 1705	27318	PIECES DU 751 ET 752
76	TELECOMM,SOUND EQUIPMENT		86162		67933		94861		85273	EQUIPMENT DE TELECOM
761	TELEVISION RECEIVERS	W 1339	6608	W 1806	10849	W 2273	16046	W 1505	11262	RECEPTEURS DE TELEVISION
7611	COLOUR TV RECEIVERS	W 1113	6148	W 1550	10251	W 2067	15353	W 1318	10668	RECEPTEURS COULEUR
762	RADIO BROADCAST RECEIVRS	W 1334	7255	W 1438	9491	W 1848	16225	W 1060	8404	RECEPTEURS RADIODIFFUSION
7622	PORTABLE RADIO RECEIVERS	W 927	5615	W 963	6823	W 1429	12660	W 549	3142	RECEPT PORTATIFS RADIO
764	TELECOM EQPT,PTS,ACC NES	W 3315	68043	W 2497	43727	W 2668	56843	W 2440	62603	EQUIP TELECOM,PIECES
7641	LINE TELEPHONE,ETC EQUIP	W 1581	56455	W 617	29741	W 759	37216	W 925	42067	APP TELEPHON PAR FIL
7649	PTS NES OF EQUIPMT OF 76	W 898	5780	W 593	4922	W 847	10251	W 885	11296	PIECES DE LA DIV 76
77	ELECTRIC MACHNRY NES ETC		84850		86468		101913		95938	MACH APP ELECT NDA
772	SWITCHGEAR ETC,PARTS NES	W 1144	11511	W 1159	11597	W 1271	11469	W 1978	12817	APP COUPURE,SECT ETC
7721	SWITCHGEAR ETC	W 1090	10948	W 1148	11313	W 1265	11271	W 1964	12608	APP COUPURE,SECTIONMNT
773	ELECTR DISTRIBUTNG EQUIP	W 4630	16811	W 4318	12447	W 4242	13477	W 7496	12927	EQUIPMT DISTRIBUTION ELECT
7731	INSULATED WIRE,CABLE ETC	W 4275	15989	W 4114	11906	W 3969	12625	W 7035	11890	FILS,CABLES ISOLES ELECT
775	HOUSEHOLD TYPE EQUIP NES	W 6456	20286	W 6934	23901	W 7638	28297	W 5577	22481	MACH,APP USAGE DOMESTQUE
7752	DOM REFRIGERATRS,FREEZRS	W 3213	10309	W 3626	12664	W 3798	13655	W 2480	9753	REFRIG,CONGEL MENAGER
77521	DOMESTIC REFRIGERATORS	W 3054	9682	W 3459	11955	W 3548	12609	W 2267	8889	REFRIGERATEURS
778	ELECTRICAL MACHINERY NES	W 5144	23861	W 5945	27414	W 6907	33875	W 9262	33728	AUTRES MACH ELECT NDA
7783	AUTOMOTIVE ELECTR EQUIP	W 799	7582	W 697	7974	W 1126	11302	W 2379	9427	EQUIP ELECT MOTEURS EXPL
78	ROAD VEHICLES		404704		372462		468919		371494	VEHICULES ROUTIERS
781	PASS MOTOR VEH EXC BUSES	W 37693	189987	W 37061	170595	W 40309	201072	W 44142	157037	AUTO TRANSPORT PERSONNES
782	LORRIES,SPCL MTR VEH NES	W 36486	133639	W 34792	131091	W 46632	163354	W 49574	126093	VEHICULES SPECIAUX,MARCH
7821	LORRIES,TRUCKS	W 36004	131746	W 34498	130407	W 45994	161595	W 49440	125694	VEHICULES TRANSP MARCHAND
783	ROAD MOTOR VEHICLES NES	W 9033	29286	W 9541	26327	W 14857	44343	W 13755	37960	VEHICULES ROUTIERS NDA
7831	BUSES	W 4162	18754	W 4798	15400	W 6815	22617	W 5499	16957	VOITURES TRANSPORT COMMUN
7832	TRACTORS FOR TR–TRAILERS	W 4871	10532	W 4743	10927	W 8042	21726	W 8256	21003	TRACTEURS ROUTIERS
784	MOTOR VEH PRTS,ACCES NES	W 5325	28653	W 4618	24650	W 6868	32130	W 5168	29946	PIECES 722,781,782,783
7849	OTHER MOTOR VEHCL PARTS	W 3985	21354	W 4470	24098	W 6583	30882	W 4738	28828	PIECES 722,781,782,783
785	CYCLES,ETC MOTRZD OR NOT	W 4961	19778	W 4062	15297	W 5949	22630	W 3830	16490	MOTOCYCLES SCOOTERS
7853	INVAL CARR, PTS OF 785	W 3074	10644	W 2478	7641	W 4070	12736	W 2375	8292	FAUTEUILS INVALIDES,PIECES
78539	PARTS,ACCES NES OF 785	W 3050	10541	W 2466	7575	W 4045	12628	W 2346	8211	PIECES DU 785
79	OTHR TRANSPORT EQUIPMENT		7108		8238		6424		6491	AUTRE MATERIEL TRANSPORT
8	MISC MANUFACTURED GOODS		157596		184714		231217		222243	ART MANUFACTURES DIVERS
821	*FURNITURE,PARTS THEREOF	W 3834	9607	W 5429	12700	W 8098	18636	W 8907	17394	MEUBLES ET PIECES
8219	FURNITURE AND PARTS NES	W 2794	6910	W 3910	9414	W 5958	13861	W 5955	13894	AUTRES MEUBLES ET PIECES
84	CLOTHING AND ACCESSORIES		19693		22269		24773		27262	VETEMENTS
851	*FOOTWEAR	W 3143	8784	W 3794	12126	W 2903	12778	W 2615	9522	CHAUSSURES
87	PRECISION INSTRUMNTS NES		16793		19144		22512		21241	INSTRUM,APPAR SCIENT NDA
874	MEASURNG,CONTROLNG INSTR	W 663	10345	W 929	11183	W 833	12007	W 1050	12031	INSTRUMENTS DE MESURE
88	PHOTO EQU,OPTICL GDS ETC		15683		16994		20461		19802	APP,FOURN PHOTO,OP,MONTR
882	PHOTO,CINEMA SUPPLIES	W 808	10096	W 844	10570	W 1072	12537	W 923	12607	PRODUITS PHOTO,CINEMA
8822	PHOTO FILM EXC DEV CINMA	W 529	8239	W 478	8296	W 645	9743	W 602	9715	PLAQUES,PELLICULES,FILMS
89	MISC MANUFCTRD GOODS NES		78608		92487		121015		115759	ART MANUFACTURES DIVERS
892	PRINTED MATTER	W 2567	15183	W 3058	16464	W 3558	20982	W 3633	21316	IMPRIMES
8921	PRINTED BOOKS,GLOBES,ETC	W 1551	9718	W 1791	10062	W 2329	14125	W 2051	13584	LIVRES,BROCHURES,CARTES
89211	PRINTED BOOKS,PAMPHLETS	W 1434	8977	W 1715	9763	W 2195	13538	W 1936	12994	LIVRES,BROCHURES
893	ARTICLES OF PLASTIC NES		25024		29649		40176		36224	OUVRAGES EN MAT DIVIS 58
8931	PLSTC PACKG CONTNRS,LIDS	W 3065	9818	W 3787	11868	W 4728	17294	W 5714	14509	ART TRANSP EMBALLAGE ETC
8939	MISC PLASTIC ARTICLES	W 5490	14571	W 5763	17057	W 6410	21700	W 7364	20839	ART DIVERS EN MAT DIV 58
89399	OTHR PLASTC ARTICLES NES	W 4956	13019	W 5334	16239	W 5742	20311	W 6572	19761	AUT OUV MAT DIV 58
894	TOYS,SPORTING GOODS,ETC	W 4039	13574	W 5273	16452	W 6213	22940	W 5533	22651	VOITURES ENFANTS,JOUETS
8942	TOYS,INDOOR GAMES ETC	W 3342	10908	W 4252	10970	W 4922	15685	W 4147	15663	JOUETS,JEUX ETC
895	OFFICE SUPPLIES NES	W 1326	7510	W 1435	8756	W 1771	10461	W 1945	9876	ART PAPET NDA
898	MUSICAL INSTRUMENTS,PTS	W 901	6607	W 1085	9105	W 1222	13668	W 1425	11866	INSTRUMENTS DE MUSIQUE
8983	SOUND RECRDNG TAPE,DISCS	W 667	4803	W 824	7472	W 918	11427	W 1071	9894	SUPPORTS SON POUR 763
899	OTHER MANUFACTURED GOODS		8517		8760		9621		9650	AUT ART MANUF DIVERS NDA

5. Special Exports F.O.B. by Commodities according to the S.I.T.C. (Rev. 2) in thousand U.S. Dollars
Exportations Spéciales F.O.B. par Produits d'après la C.T.C.I. (Rév. 2) en milliers de Dollars E.U.

SITC CTCI	COMMODITY	1993		1994		1995		1996		PRODUIT
		WEIGHT POIDS	VALUE VALEUR	WEIGHT POIDS	VALUE VALEUR	WEIGHT POIDS	VALUE VALEUR	WEIGHT POIDS	VALUE VALEUR	
	ALL COMMODITIES		1338222		1502445		1935516		2030734	TOUS PRODUITS
0	FOOD AND LIVE ANIMALS		763304		859818		1191227		1139134	ALIMENTS,ANIMAUX VIVANTS
01	MEAT AND PREPARATIONS		23210		9953		7762		4672	VIANDES ET PREPARATIONS
011	MEAT FRESH,CHILLD,FROZEN	W 13593	18374	W 6258	8881	W 4613	6421	W 2202	3041	VIANDES FRAICHES,REF,CONGE
0111	BOVINE MEAT FRESH,FROZEN	W 12645	17298	W 5687	8247	W 3984	5802	W 1590	2530	VIANDES BOVIN FRAI,REF
01112	BOVINE MEAT BONELESS	W 10064	14820	W 5532	8076	W 3679	5357	W 1590	2530	VIANDES BOVIN DESOSSEES
014	MEAT PREPD,PRSVD,NES ETC	W 1895	4798	W 395	1072	W 338	1341	W 434	1628	CONSERVES DE VIANDES
0149	OTH PREPARD,PRESRVD MEAT	W 1842	4587	W 345	912	W 269	1121	W 346	1362	AUTRES PREP DE VIANDES
03	FISH AND PREPARATIONS		27125		31365		23236		27519	POISSONS ET PREPARATIONS
036	SHELL FISH FRESH,FROZEN	W 5929	25834	W 6401	29833	W 4219	22595	W 5090	26707	CRUSTACES,MOLLUSQUES
04	CEREALS AND PREPARATIONS		26654		32234		45644		53102	CEREALES ET PRODUITS
044	MAIZE UNMILLED	W 519	337	W 1816	839	W 49718	7957	W 15473	4474	MAIS NON MOULU
047	OTHER CERE/ ᆢ MEALS,FLOUR	W 1491	839	W 1032	1109	W 5115	2952	W 11652	6438	AUTRES SEMOULES,FARINES
048	CEREAL ETC PREPARATIONS	W 9440	22593	W 14147	27564	W 19568	31861	W 24873	39636	PREPTNS A BASE CEREALES
0481	PREPD BREAKFAST FOOD ETC	W 5805	16750	W 6617	17840	W 8328	19176	W 8679	21913	CEREALES TRAVAILLEES
04812	CEREAL ROASTED, PUFFED	W 4826	15414	W 5319	16116	W 5533	16641	W 6522	18777	PRODTS BASE CEREALES
0484	BAKERY PRODUCTS	W 1805	2208	W 4680	4936	W 7505	7609	W 10663	10381	PRODUITS DE BOULANGERIE
04842	PASTRY, CAKES ETC	W 1294	1593	W 3108	3356	W 4321	4789	W 5905	6550	PATISSERIE ETC.
05	VEGETABLES AND FRUIT		169753		189960		215750		251728	LEGUMES ET FRUITS
054	VEG ETC FRSH,SMPLY PRSVD	W 101022	40606	W 113223	43524	W 132174	44398	W 169888	53952	LEGUMES FRAIS,CONG,SECS
0545	OTHER FRESH VEGETABLES	W 48236	16468	W 49048	13200	W 65170	15782	W 93341	22870	AUTRES LEGUMES FRAIS,REF
05451	ALLIACEOUS VEGTBLS,FRESH	W 15318	4030	W 8766	1425	W 11019	1435	W 13269	1802	OIGNONS,ECHALOTES,AULX
05459	FRESH VEGETABLES NES	W 32918	12439	W 40282	11775	W 54151	14347	W 80071	21068	LEGUMES FRAIS,REFRI NDA
0546	VEGETABLES SIMPLY PRESVD	W 36099	22594	W 45732	28966	W 41755	27159	W 43846	29009	LEGUMES CONG,CONSER
05461	VEGETABLES FROZEN	W 35753	22452	W 44915	28664	W 41282	27032	W 43630	28940	LEGUMES CONGELES
057	FRUIT,NUTS,FRESH,DRIED	W 555251	118487	W 648880	135004	W 745834	159857	W 786197	185431	FRUITS FRAIS OU SECS
0573	BANANA,PLANTAIN,FRSH,DRY	W 399158	83087	W 577463	114316	W 665426	139222	W 669686	156284	BANANES FRAICHES,SECHEES
0577	NUTS EDIBLE,FRESH,DRIED	W 93999	17658	W 2426	1595	W 10633	1547	W 7470	740	FRUITS A COQUES
05771	COCONUTS FRESH OR DRIED	W 93599	16616	W 1465	244	W 10309	185	W 6970	132	NOIX DE COCO
0579	FRUIT FRESH OR DRIED NES	W 59196	17194	W 66441	18658	W 65775	18658	W 105140	27870	FRUITS FRAIS,SECS NDA
05798	OTHER FRESH FRUIT	W 52096	14118	W 55512	14373	W 49341	12730	W 84324	19826	AUTRES FRUITS FRAIS
058	FRUIT PRESERVED,PREPARED	W 8339	6715	W 8981	7423	W 9551	6744	W 9967	6537	CONSERVES DE FRUITS
0585	FRUIT OR VEGETABLE JUICE	W 4556	4201	W 5301	5035	W 4467	4459	W 4292	3953	JUS DE FRUITS
06	SUGAR AND PREPS,HONEY		164648		181551		261646		228851	SUCRES ET PRODUITS
061	SUGAR AND HONEY	W 907611	154271	W 913872	169970	W 1173716	250875	W 1109470	221901	SUCRES ET MIEL
0611	RAW BEET AND CANE SUGAR	W 673076	145409	W 692793	161469	W 866937	238171	W 796195	202035	SUCRES BRUTS
0615	MOLASSES	W 231740	7089	W 218330	6672	W 305443	11474	W 311259	16999	MELASSES
062	SUGAR CANDY NON-CHOCLATE	W 5274	10377	W 6123	11581	W 5796	10772	W 4967	6950	SUCRERIES
07	COFFEE,TEA,COCOA,SPICES		308967		362661		582910		514798	CAFE,THE,CACAO,EPICES
071	COFFEE AND SUBSTITUTES	W 220852	267802	W 179455	318556	W 206963	539748	W 241604	473021	CAFE ET SUCCEDANES
0711	COFFEE GREEN,ROASTED,SUB	W 220817	267763	W 179454	318551	W 206963	539747	W 241573	472970	CAFE TORREFIE OU DECAFEINE
07111	COFFEE GREEN,HUSKS,SKINS	W 220610	267490	W 179363	318278	W 206791	539288	W 241295	472433	CAFE NON TORREFIE
075	SPICES	W 14994	39799	W 14002	42734	W 14624	41163	W 22509	40003	EPICES
0752	SPICES,EX PEPPER,PIMENTO	W 14708	39506	W 13826	42550	W 14252	40851	W 22088	39604	AUTRES EPICES
07524	NUTMEG,MACE,CARDAMOMS	W 14444	39361	W 13293	42367	W 13923	40744	W 21556	39385	NOIX MUSCADES
09	MISC EDIBLE PRODUCTS		33382		44159		47167		51213	PREP ALIMENTAIRES DIVERSES
098	EDIBLE PRODCTS,PREPS NES	W 14996	30278	W 19776	40647	W 21328	42170	W 23347	45951	PREP ALIMENTAIRES NDA
09805	SOUPS AND BROTHS	W 7771	19462	W 11696	27367	W 12717	28944	W 13843	31644	SOUPES,POTAGES,BOUILLONS
09809	MISC FOOD PREPRTIONS NES	W 2874	'6123	W 3485	7621	W 3298	6688	W 3108	6693	PREP ALIMENTAIRES NDA
1	BEVERAGES AND TOBACCO		46390		34297		ı28441		38123	BOISSONS ET TABACS
11	BEVERAGES		3088		4883		6109		6609	BOISSONS
12	TOBACCO AND MANUFACTURES		43302		29414		22331		31514	TABACS BRUTS FABRIQUES
121	TOBACCO UNMNFCTRD,REFUSE	W 16550	39375	W 9832	24525	W 5439	17951	W 10038	27193	TABACS BRUTS,DECHETS
1211	TOBACCO,NOT STRIPPED	W 8570	18697	W 5139	12081	W 2150	7377	W 4358	12169	TABACS NON ECOTES
1212	TOBACCO STRIPPED OR PART	W 6347	20283	W 4091	12284	W 2976	10508	W 5072	14717	TABACS PART ECOTES
122	TOBACCO,MANUFACTURED	W 864	3927	W 813	4889	W 618	4381	W 580	4321	TABACS FABRIQUES
1222	CIGARETTES	W 546	2194	W 807	4873	W 611	4378	W 580	4321	CIGARETTES
2	CRUDE MATERLS,EXCL FUELS		82837		99518		122154		145913	MAT BRUTES NON COMESTIBLES
22	OIL SEEDS,OLEAGINOUS FRT		24762		28235		33695		36453	GRAINES,FRUITS OLEAGINEUX
222	SEEDS FOR'SOFT'FIXED OIL	W 28745	18589	W 33087	23693	W 35042	30639	W 32969	32435	GRAINES HUILES FIXES
2225	SESAME SEEDS	W 24879	15979	W 32170	23060	W 34519	30313	W 32169	31469	GRAINES DE SESAME
223	SEEDS FOR OTH FIXED OILS	W 12474	6173	W 8243	4542	W 3106	3056	W 1691	4017	GRAINES AUTRES HUILES FIXES
23	RUBBER, CRUDE		19647		27330		36112		48621	CAOUTCHOUC BRUT
232	NATURAL RUBBER,GUMS	W 20685	19559	W 39145	27245	W 29772	36050	W 40060	48566	LATEX CAOUTCHOUC NATUREL
23201	NATURAL RUBBER LATEX	W 14913	13083	W 19363	15903	W 20945	21761	W 28001	30788	LATEX NATUREL
23202	OTHER NATURAL RUBBER	W 5126	4846	W 19153	9240	W 8547	13432	W 11900	17303	CAOUTCHOUC NATUREL
24	CORK AND WOOD		7789		8571		9315		8885	LIEGE ET BOIS
248	WOOD SHAPED,SLEEPERS	W 25289	7663	W 28820	8438	W 35363	9086	W 32091	8315	BOIS SIMPLEMENT TRAVAILLES
2483	LUMBER SHAPED NON-CONIFR	W 10137	4356	W 11534	4950	W 9496	4081	W 7953	3466	NON CONIFERES SCIES,RABOTES
24831	LUMBER SAWN ETC NON-CON	W 9599	4276	W 11346	4822	W 9051	3701	W 7519	3038	SCIES LONGITUDINALEMENT
26	TEXTILE FIBRES AND WASTE		5361		1679		1243		1104	FIBRES TEXTILES
263	COTTON	W 5403	4628	W 2518	1068	W 1096	606	W 454	742	COTON
2631	RAW COTTON,EXCL LINTERS	W 3719	4139	W 942	735	W 102	125	W 283	573	COTON EN MASSE
27	CRUDE FERTLZR,MINRLS NES		4976		4826		6145		6195	ENGRAIS MINERAUX BRUTS
29	CRUDE ANIMAL,VEG MAT NES		18551		25165		30094		38256	MATIERES BRUTES ANIM,VEGET
292	CRUDE VEG MATERIALS NES	W 19920	18482	W 19416	24814	W 22378	29993	W 27594	38165	MAT BRUTES VEGETALES NDA
2925	SEEDS,ETC FOR PLANTING	W 190	5107	W 248	5988	W 354	7047	W 144	6551	SEMENCES NDA
2926	LIVE PLANTS,BULBS,ETC	W 12021	5740	W 9202	5664	W 11781	7406	W 13857	9971	BULBES,TUBERCULES
29269	LIVE PLANTS NES	W 11968	5712	W 9173	5658	W 11658	7362	W 13727	9941	AUTRES PLANTES VIVANTES
2927	CUT FLOWERS AND FOLIAGE	W 5989	6538	W 8445	12143	W 8891	13927	W 11915	19482	FLEURS,FEUILLAGES COUPES
29271	CUT FLOWERS	W 2093	3843	W 3465	7839	W 3320	8897	W 3815	10759	FLEURS ET BOUTONS
29272	CUT FOLIAGE	W 3896	2695	W 4981	4304	W 5570	5030	W 8100	8723	FEUILLAGES,RAMEAUX ETC
3	MINERAL FUELS ETC		27421		27794		39689		65799	COMBUSTIBLES MINERAUX LUB
33	PETROLEUM AND PRODUCTS		27409		27793		39687		65751	PETROLE ET DERIVES
333	CRUDE PETROLEUM	W 200727	22291	W 185592	22200	W 126816	32834	W 530434	60443	HUILES BRUTES DE PETROLE
334	PETROLEUM PRODUCTS,REFIN	W 5299	5080	W 6133	5531	W 7294	6832	W 6884	5213	PRODUITS RAFFINES
3345	LUBS,PETROLEUM OILS NES	W 4804	4829	W 5925	5437	W 7294	6831	W 4679	4583	HUILES LUBRIFIANTES
33451	LUBS(HIGH PETR CONT) ETC	W 4535	4491	W 5223	4799	W 6524	6109	W 4047	3963	HUILES LUBRIF,H LOURDES
4	ANIMAL,VEGETABLE OIL,FAT		6081		9678		8127		15912	HUILES,GRAISSES ANIM,VEG
42	FIXED VEGETABLE OIL,FAT		4799		7179		5901		10555	HUILES VEGETALES FIXES
423	FIXED VEG OILS,SOFT	W 4738	3937	W 6018	5199	W 4176	4232	W 5734	5481	HUILES VEGET DOUCES FIXES
5	CHEMCLS,RELATED PROD NES		148784		173422		207264		236664	PRODUITS CHIMIQUES
51	ORGANIC CHEMICALS		4032		6967		10962		19487	PROD CHIMIQ ORGANIQUES
512	ALCOHOLS,PHENOLS ETC	W 10113	2175	W 10794	4992	W 13566	7214	W 21270	11584	PHENOLS,PHENOLS-ALCOOLS
5121	ACYCLIC ALCOHOLS,DERIVS	W 10110	2171	W 10779	4974	W 13565	7210	W 21158	11552	ALCOOLS ACYCLIQUES
51216	ETHYL ALC,DENATRD SPIRIT	W 9907	1970	W 10485	4605	W 13166	6604	W 20331	10364	ALCOOL ETHYLIQUE NON DENAT
53	DYES,TANNING,COLOUR PROD		6650		6892		7795		8084	PROD TEINTURE,COLORANTS
533	PIGMENTS,PAINTS,ETC	W 5046	6165	W 5959	6369	W 6488	6832	W 7152	7673	PIGMENTS,PEINTURES,VERNIS
5334	VARNISHES,DISTEMPERS ETC	W 4927	5951	W 5829	6200	W 6394	6602	W 7009	7351	PEINTURES A L'EAU
53342	OTH PAINTS,VARNISHES ETC	W 3803	4379	W 5105	5125	W 5610	5430	W 6335	6296	AUTRES PEINTURES,VERNIS
541	*MEDICINAL,PHARM PRODUCT	K 5628117	59258	K 6618386	64685	K 5785152	74942	K 6788963	74370	PROD MEDICINAUX PHARMACEUT

5. Special Exports F.O.B. by Commodities according to the S.I.T.C. (Rev. 2) in thousand U.S. Dollars
Exportations Spéciales F.O.B. par Produits d'après la C.T.C.I. (Rév. 2) en milliers de Dollars E.U.

SITC CTCI	COMMODITY	1993 WEIGHT POIDS	1993 VALUE VALEUR	1994 WEIGHT POIDS	1994 VALUE VALEUR	1995 WEIGHT POIDS	1995 VALUE VALEUR	1996 WEIGHT POIDS	1996 VALUE VALEUR	PRODUIT
5417	MEDICAMENTS	K 4569753	55757	K 5610561	60648	K 4799453	70670	K 5929850	70274	MEDICAMENTS
54171	— CONTAINNG ANTIBIOTICS	K 216545	3968	K 342084	4826	K 197727	10371	K 265217	10621	MED CONTN ANTIBIOTIQUES
54172	— CONTAINING HORMONES	K 258909	7368	K 1013881	10622	K 786425	10063	K 226335	4925	MED CONTENANT HORMONES
54179	— CONTNG OTH SUBSTANCES	K 4089335	44265	K 4249952	44982	K 3802822	49811	K 5421733	54362	MED CONT AUT SUBSTANCES
55	PERFUME,CLEANING ETC PRD		46886		52804		57960		69302	PROD POUR PARFUM,TOILETTE
551	ESSENTL OILS,PERFUME,ETC	W 1380	5126	W 321	1913	W 453	2559	W 277	1783	HUILES ESSENTIELLES
5513	ESSENTL OIL,RESINOID,ETC	W 1104	4171	W 131	1114	W 244	1363	W 148	1091	HUILES ESSENTIELLES,RESIN
553	PERFUMERY,COSMETICS,ETC	W 4957	19463	W 6963	25574	W 7402	28906	W 18492	31614	PRODUITS DE PARFUMERIE
554	SOAP,CLEANSING ETC PREPS	W 22210	22297	W 24423	25317	W 24391	26495	W 65317	35904	SAVONS,PRODUITS DETERSIFS
5541	SOAPS	W 17361	17326	W 16853	18311	W 14932	17376	W 57289	28047	SAVONS,PROD TENSIO–ACTIFS
5542	WASHING PREPARATIONS ETC	W 4349	4245	W 6569	6047	W 7437	7200	W 7125	6795	PROD ORG TENSIO–ACT NDA
58	PLASTIC MATERIALS ETC		7728		11111		11948		12138	MAT PLAST ARTIFICIELLES
583	POLYMERIZATION ETC PRODS	W 5294	6798	W 8273	10056	W 7498	10539	W 7612	10761	PROD POLYMERISATION
59	CHEMICAL MATERIALS NES		20134		25147		37702		45986	MAT PROD CHIMIQUES NDA
591	PESTICIDES,DISINFECTANTS	W 5191	12739	W 6631	17159	W 9420	28566	W 11100	38333	DESINF,INSECT,FONG,HERB
5911	INSECTICIDES,FOR RETAIL	W 3060	6251	W 4022	9440	W 4469	10700	W 4973	12205	INSECTICIDES VENTE DET
5912	FUNGICIDES,FOR RETAIL	W 161	1098	W 63	457	W 350	5326	W 710	10496	FONGICIDES VENTE AU DET
5913	HERBICIDES,FOR RETAIL	W 1743	4936	W 2215	6849	W 4171	11995	W 4977	15085	HERBICIDES VENTE AU DET
6	BASIC MANUFACTURES		158142		180650		202160		232841	ART MANUFACTURES
62	RUBBER MANUFACTURES NES		14534		15405		19478		18413	CAOUTCHOUC MANUFACTURE
625	RUBBER TYRES, TUBES ETC	W 4013	12162	W 5118	13428	W 5770	17272	W 5262	16372	PNEUS CAOUTCHOUC VULCANISE
6251	TYRES NEW FOR MOTOR CARS	W 1458	4592	W 1784	4763	W 1507	4871	W 1490	4976	PNEUS POUR VOITURES
6252	TYRES,NEW,BUS OR LORRY	W 2030	6515	W 2156	6218	W 2562	8280	W 2365	7898	PNEUS POUR AUTOBUS,CAMIONS
63	WOOD,CORK MANUFACTRS NES		8739		8293		6570		8976	OUVRAGES LIEGE ET BOIS
635	WOOD MANUFACTURES NES	W 2945	4833	W 2270	4953	W 2485	4500	W 19953	5730	ART MANUF EN BOIS NDA
64	PAPER,PAPERBOARD AND MFR		16641		18012		24607		38373	PAPIERS,CARTONS & OUVRAGES
642	PAPER,ETC,PRECUT,ARTS OF	W 11750	13357	W 13438	14401	W 17871	20756	W 39337	33315	PAP,CARTONS DECOUPES
6421	PAPER ETC CONTAINERS	W 8372	8478	W 8667	8814	W 12210	13193	W 33691	25526	BOITES,SACS EMBALLAGES
65	TEXTILE YARN,FABRICS,ETC		39299		44475		40344		50230	FILS,TISSUS,ARTICLES TEXTILE
652	COTTON FABRICS,WOVEN	W 2750	10522	W 3843	16254	W 2959	12924	W 5011	21834	TISSUS DE COTON
6522	WOVEN COTTON BLEACHD,ETC	W 2071	8005	W 3572	15455	W 2776	12361	W 4585	20753	TISSUS COTON BLANCHIS ETC
65224	BLCHED COTTON FABRIC NES	W 1228	4220	W 1924	7272	W 1411	5823	W 1969	7128	AUT TIS PLUS 85% COT BLANCHI
65225	BLCHD COTN BLEND FAB NES	W 751	3390	W 1547	7643	W 1197	5893	W 2468	13068	AUT TIS MOINS 85% COT BLANCH
653	WOVN MAN–MADE FIB FABRIC	W 2640	15635	W 4198	17263	W 2982	14272	W 4079	16937	TISSUS FIBRES SYNTH,ARTIF
6531	CONT SYNT WEAVES NONPILE	W 1065	6960	W 1879	5371	W 1235	5848	W 2634	9611	TISSUS FIBRES SYNTH CONTINUE
65315	CONT SYN TXTL FABRIC NES	W 982	6281	W 1876	5355	W 1235	5848	W 2610	9552	TIS PLUS 85% TEXT SYNT CONT
6534	DISC SYN BLEND FABRC NES	W 975	4964	W 1252	6196	W 1062	4241	W 801	2937	TISSUS FIBRES SYNTH DISCONT
65341	DISC SYN FIB–COTTN FABRC	W 833	4240	W 1128	5504	W 1025	4078	W 800	2926	TISSUS FIB SYNT DIS MEL COTO
66	NONMETAL MINERAL MFS NES		28622		34347		36260		34092	ART MIN NON METALLIQUES
665	GLASSWARE	W 40816	22422	W 53138	26641	W 61900	29546	W 55064	26898	OUVRAGES EN VERRE
6651	BOTTLES ETC OF GLASS	W 37007	19866	W 48882	23808	W 59708	27786	W 52237	24551	RECIPIENTS EN VERRE
66511	GLASS BOTTLES ETC NONVAC	W 37007	19866	W 48882	23806	W 59708	27786	W 52237	24551	BONBONNES,BOUTEILLES,ETC
67	IRON AND STEEL		31372		39082		52114		58173	FER ET ACIER
673	IRON,STEEL SHAPES ETC	W 29980	12490	W 41827	16902	W 46277	19130	W 52385	15833	BARRES,PROFIL FER,ACIER
6732	IRON,STEEL BARS ETC	W 21602	8262	W 32406	12040	W 36342	14406	W 31103	10979	BARRES FER,ACIER
67326	IRN,OTH STL BARS HOTROLD	W 21228	8109	W 32376	12024	W 36192	14344	W 30786	10819	BARRES PLEINES FER,ACIER
6733	IRON,STEEL PROFILES ETC	W 8312	4202	W 9420	4861	W 9903	4703	W 21205	4705	PROFILES,PALPLAN FER,ACIER
674	IRN,STL UNIV,PLATE,SHEET	W 12604	9905	W 17625	13198	W 47038	19418	W 30051	24791	LARGES PLATS,TOLES
6749	OTH IRN,STL PLATES,SHEET	W 11762	9382	W 16340	12516	W 44609	18066	W 28325	23872	AUTRES TOLES FER,ACIER
67491	— OF IRON OR SIMPLE STL	W 11762	9382	W 16340	12516	W 44588	18047	W 28302	23861	AUT TOLES AUTRES ACIER FIN
678	IRON,STL TUBES,PIPES,ETC	W 11351	7119	W 12174	7308	W 17643	11792	W 18511	11274	TUBES,TUYAUX EN FONTE,FER
6783	IRON,STL TUBES,PIPES NES	W 11231	6972	W 11738	7058	W 17400	11554	W 18342	11047	AUT TUBES,TUYAUX FER,ACIER
69	METAL MANUFACTURES NES		16842		18627		19718		20102	ART MANUFACT EN METAL NDA
692	METAL TANKS,BOXES,ETC	W 2071	3718	W 2645	5136	W 4399	7116	W 4898	8886	RECIPIENTS METALLIQUES
6924	MTL TRANSPORT BOXES ETC	W 1788	3291	W 2635	5117	W 4290	6991	W 4828	8824	FUTS,TAMBOURS,BIDONS
7	MACHINES,TRANSPORT EQUIP		19715		27590		35520		37336	MACHINES MATERIEL TRANSPORT
74	GENRL INDUSTRL MACHY NES		3718		5547		10319		10051	MACH APP INDUSTRIE
741	HEATING,COOLING EQUIPMNT	W 599	2751	W 796	4508	W 1609	9287	W 1433	7729	MACH CHAUFFAGE,PIECES
7414	NONDOM REFRIG EQUIPT,PTS	W 514	2596	W 783	4418	W 1595	9084	W 1400	7433	MAT PRODUCTION DU FROID
74141	REFRIG EQUIP NONDOMESTIC	W 423	2345	W 667	4083	W 1462	8692	W 1266	6912	REFIG INDUSTRIELS
77	ELECTRIC MACHNRY NES ETC		11911		12447		14943		15543	MACH APP ELECT NDA
775	HOUSEHOLD TYPE EQUIP NES	W 556	2812	W 598	3135	W 1028	5956	W 1186	6209	MACH,APP USAGE DOMESTQUE
778	ELECTRICAL MACHINERY NES	W 3656	8586	W 4105	9110	W 3805	8439	W 3576	9060	AUTRES MACH ELECT NDA
7781	BATTERIES,ACCUMULATORS	W 3652	8565	W 4098	9086	W 3791	8364	W 3533	8604	PILES ET ACCUMULATEURS
77811	PRIMARY BATTERIES,CELLS	W 3464	8542	W 3802	9030	W 3429	8184	W 3354	8565	PILES ELECTRIQUES,PIECES
78	ROAD VEHICLES		2060		6432		6902		8312	VEHICULES ROUTIERS
8	MISC MANUFACTURED GOODS		85049		89614		100877		118808	ART MANUFACTURES DIVERS
812	*PLUMBG,HEATNG,LGHTNG EQ	W 3486	5898	W 5223	8016	W 6068	8788	W 8580	11126	APPAR SANITAIRES CHAUFFAGE
8122	CERAMIC PLUMBNG FIXTURES	W 3478	5870	W 5173	7913	W 6032	8723	W 8574	11078	EVIERS,LAVABOS,CUVETTES
821	*FURNITURE,PARTS THEREOF	W 2568	6130	W 3264	7535	W 4156	8636	W 5410	13108	MEUBLES ET PIECES
8219	FURNITURE AND PARTS NES	W 1392	3356	W 1954	4931	W 2308	5220	W 3241	8094	AUTRES MEUBLES ET PIECES
82192	WOOD FURNITURE NES	W 768	1823	W 1211	3148	W 1456	3352	W 2316	6242	MEUBLES NDA EN BOIS
84	CLOTHING AND ACCESSORIES		32531		30527		35569		38670	VETEMENTS
843	WOMENS OUTERWEAR NONKNIT	W 912	6435	W 477	6974	W 470	6424	W 1180	7195	VET DESSUS FEMMES MAT TEX
845	OUTERWEAR KNIT NONELASTC	W 560	7160	W 276	3977	W 351	5426	W 450	6177	VET DESSOUS,ACCES BONNET
8459	— OTHER,CLTHG ACCESRYS	W 406	5071	W 144	2077	W 232	3259	W 344	4151	AUT VET DESSUS DE BONNE
846	UNDER GARMENTS KNITTED	W 744	8464	W 675	9140	W 948	11042	W 938	10516	SOUS VETS DE BONNETERIE
8463	— OF SYNTH FBR NONELAST	W 348	4424	W 392	4977	W 309	4743	W 348	4710	SOUS–VET BONNET FIB SYNT
848	HEADGEAR,NONTXTL CLOTHNG	W 842	4517	W 890	5688	W 677	5476	W 1055	9325	VET ACCES MAT AUT QUE TEX
851	*FOOTWEAR	W 1548	8154	W 1167	6949	W 1228	7894	W 1463	8981	CHAUSSURES
85102	FOOTWEAR LEATHER	W 753	4734	W 528	3986	W 601	5239	W 646	5741	CHAUS SEMELLES EN CUIR
89	MISC MANUFCTRD GOODS NES		30218		34769		38292		44800	ART MANUFACTURES DIVERS
893	ARTICLES OF PLASTIC NES		18792	W 13131	21143		23583		25400	OUVRAGES EN MAT DIVIS 58
8931	PLSTC PACKG CONTNRS,LIDS	W 4887	9007	W 7347	9207	W 6875	12995	W 8002	14124	ART TRANSP EMBALLAGE ETC
8939	MISC PLASTIC ARTICLES	W 6560	9180	W 5712	11790	W 4152	10131	W 4854	10550	ART DIVERS EN MAT DIV 58
89399	OTHR PLASTC ARTICLES NES	W 6380	8758	W 5632	11517	W 4126	10046	W 4808	10408	AUT OUV MAT DIV 58

1. HISTORICAL SERIES, 1961–1996 GENERAL TRADE, IMPORTS C.I.F., EXPORTS F.O.B.
SERIES HISTORIQUES, 1961–1996 COMMERCE GENERAL, IMPORTATIONS C.A.F., EXPORTATIONS F.O.B

YEAR ANNEE	VALUE IN MILLION GOURDES VALEUR EN MILLION GOURDES MERCHANDISE –MARCHANDISE		GOLD –OR		CONVERSION FACTORS U.S. CENTS PER GOURDE FACTEURS DE CONVERSION CENTS E.U. PAR GOURDE		INDEX NUMBERS –INDICES QUANTUM		UNIT VALUE VALEUR UNITAIRE	
	IMPORTS	EXPORTS	IMPORTS	EXPORTS	IMPORTS	EXPORTS	IMPORTS	EXPORTS	IMPORTS	EXPORTS
1961	164.40	151.70			20.0000	20.0000				
1962	185.90	204.20			20.0000	20.0000				
1963	180.10	216.10			20.0000	20.0000				
1964	179.50	189.80			20.0000	20.0000				
1965	185.60	188.90			20.0000	20.0000				
1966	180.00	191.90			20.0000	20.0000				
1967	189.60	161.70			20.0000	20.0000				
1968	183.00	178.70			20.0000	20.0000				
1969	218.00	186.30			20.0000	20.0000				
1970	259.70	202.60			20.0000	20.0000				
1971	297.70	236.30			20.0000	20.0000				
1972	299.70	210.40			20.0000	20.0000				
1973	369.70	261.40			20.0000	20.0000				
1974	556.60	356.70			20.0000	20.0000				
1975	712.60	405.90			20.0000	20.0000				
1976	1005.30	587.70			20.0000	20.0000				
1977	1041.20	716.50			20.0000	20.0000				
1978	1103.40	794.70			20.0000	20.0000				
1979	1330.80	741.90			20.0000	20.0000				
1980	1770.20	1130.70			20.0000	20.0000				
1981	2239.80	756.80			20.0000	20.0000				
1982	1936.40	812.70			20.0000	20.0000				
1983	2201.50	768.50			20.0000	20.0000				
1984	2360.40	893.20			20.0000	20.0000				
1985	2207.80	871.20			20.0000	20.0000				
1986	1799.90	922.20			20.0000	20.0000				
1987	1995.90	1067.70			20.0000	20.0000				
1988	1721.30	896.40			20.0000	20.0000				
1989	1455.00	720.30			20.0000	20.0000				
1990	1661.10	801.30			20.0000	20.0000				
1991	2414.20	1005.20			19.2081	18.9140				
1992	2727.90	719.40			10.1964	10.0375				
1993	4555.70	1029.30			7.8713	7.7508				
1994	3783.60	1236.70			6.8560	7.0397				
1995	9866.20	1666.50			6.6249	6.6982				
1996	10448.20	1413.90			6.3717	6.3812				

2. IMPORTS BY BROAD ECONOMIC CATEGORY AND EXPORTS BY INDUSTRIAL ORIGIN. (PERCENTAGE OF TOTAL VALUE)
IMPORTATIONS PAR CATEGORIES ECONOMIQUES ET EXPORTATIONS PAR BRANCHE D'ACTIVITE.(EN POURCENTAGE DE LA VALEUR TOTALE)

IMPORTS – IMPORTATIONS

	1990	1991	1992	1993	1994	1995	1996
TOTAL IMPORTS–IMPORTATIONS TOTALES							
1 FOOD BEV–ALIMENTATION BOISSONS							
11 PRIMARY–PRODUITS DE BASE							
111 FOR INDUSTRY–POUR L'INDUSTRIE							
112 FOR HOUSEHOLDS–POUR LES MENAGES							
12 PROCESSED–PRODUITS ELABORES							
121 FOR INDUSTRY–POUR L'INDUSTRIE							
122 FOR HOUSEHOLDS–POUR LES MENAGES							
2 IND SUPPLIES–APPROV INDUSTRIELS							
21 PRIMARY–PRODUITS DE BASE							
22 PROCESSED–PRODUITS ELABORES							
3 FUELS–COMBUSTIBLES							
31 PRIMARY–PRODUITS DE BASE							
32 PROCESSED–PRODUITS ELABORES							
321 MOTOR SPIRIT–ESSENCE							
322 OTHER–AUTRES							
4 MACHINERY–EQUIPEMENT							
41 CAPITAL EQUIPMENT–MACHINES							
42 PARTS–PIECES ACCESSOIRES							
5 TRANSPORT–TRANSPORT							
51 PASSENGER CARS–AUTOMOBILES							
52 OTHER–AUTRES							
521 INDUSTRIAL–INDUSTRIELS							
522 NON INDUSTRIAL–NON INDUSTRIEL							
53 PARTS–PIECES ACCESSOIRES							
6 CONSUM GOODS–BIENS CONSOMMATION							
61 DURABLE–DURABLES							
62 SEMI DURABLE–SEMI DURABLES							
63 NON DURABLE–NON DURABLES							
7 GOODS NES–BIENS NDA							

EXPORTS – EXPORTATIONS

	1990	1991	1992	1993	1994	1995	1996
TOTAL EXPORTS–EXPORTATIONS TOTALES							
1 AGRICULTURE							
2 MINING QUARRY–INDUS EXTRACTIVES							
3 MANUFACTURING–IND MANUFACTUR							
31 FOOD BEV TOBACCO–ALIM BOISS TAB							
32 TEXTILES–INDUSTRIES TEXTILES							
33 WOOD & PRODUCTS–BOIS & PRODUITS							
34 PAPER & PRODUCTS–PAPIER & PRODT							
35 CHEMICALS–INDUSTRIES CHIMIQUES							
36 NON METAL MIN–MIN NON METAL							
37 BASIC METAL–IND METAL BASE							
38 METAL MANUF–MANUF METAL							
39 OTH MANUF IND–AUTRES MANUF							

3. TRADE BY PRINCIPAL COUNTRIES OF PRODUCTION AND LAST CONSIGNMENT (VALUE IN THOUSAND U.S. DOLLARS)
ECHANGES SELON LES PRINCIPAUX PAYS DE PRODUCTION ET DE DERNIERE CONSIGNATION (VALEUR EN MILLIERS DE DOLLARS EU)

COUNTRIES–PAYS	SPECIAL IMPORTS C.I.F. IMPORTATIONS SPECIALES C.A.F				
	1987	1988	1989	1990	1991
World					
Africa					
Americas					
Northern America					
LAIA					
CACM					
Caribbean					
Rest of America					
As.ex F.USSR					
Eur.x F.USSR					
EU					
EFTA					
East Europe					
Other Europe					
Former USSR					
Oceania					

COUNTRIES–PAYS	GENERAL EXPORTS F.O.B. EXPORTATIONS GENERALES F.O.B.				
	1987	1988	1989	1990	1991
Monde		180059	152118	171112	187638
Afrique		9	17	6	1
Amériques		138916	113115	147677	162600
Amérique du Nord		137854	111519	146500	161443
ALAI		219	487	484	486
MCAC		83	335	130	30
Caraïbes		710	745	563	572
Autre Amérique		50	29		69
Asie l'URSS exclus		1660	3232	2043	1135
Europe l'URSS exclus		39469	35673	21385	23860
UE		37963	35273	21373	23678
AELE		1506	401	0	183
Europe de l'Est				8	
Autre de l'Europe				4	
Ancienne URSS					
Océanie		5	80		42
USA/Etats–Unis d'Amer		135452	108128	142288	158707
Italy/Italie		14030	13537	6783	9748
Belgium–Luxembourg		7315	8543	5052	4575
France, Monac		8695	6061	4635	3774
Germany/Allemagne		4848	4103	3275	3270
Canada		2402	3391	4211	2737
Japan/Japon		1495	3226	2038	1081
Netherlands/Pays–Bas		2234	1200	650	870
United Kingdom		220	845	607	719
Switz.Liecht		1502	400	0	183
Spain/Espagne		577	685	138	440
Dominican Republic		456	267	305	276
Mexico/Mexique		139	375	422	312
Denmark/Danemark		17	166	114	153
Netherlands Antilles		9	234	95	74
Sweden/Suède		26	126	119	86
Guatemala		65	99	128	28
Costa Rica		15	162		

(VALUE AS PERCENTAGE OF WORLD TOTAL)(VALEURS EN POURCENTAGE DU TOTAL MONDIAL)

	1982	1983	1984	1985	1986	1987	1988	1989	1990	1991
Africa										
Americas										
Northern America										
LAIA										
CACM										
Caribbean										
Rest of America										
As.ex F.USSR										
Eur.x F.USSR										
EU										
EFTA										
East Europe										
Other Europe										
Former USSR										
Oceania										

	1982	1983	1984	1985	1986	1987	1988	1989	1990	1991
Afrique							0.0	0.0	0.0	0.0
Amériques							77.2	74.4	86.3	86.7
Amérique du Nord							76.6	73.3	85.6	86.0
ALAI							0.1	0.3	0.3	0.3
MCAC							0.0	0.2	0.1	0.0
Caraïbes							0.4	0.5	0.3	0.3
Autre Amérique							0.0	0.0		0.0
Asie l'URSS exclus							0.9	2.1	1.2	0.6
Europe l'URSS exclus							21.9	23.5	12.5	12.7
UE							21.1	23.2	12.5	12.6
AELE							0.8	0.3	0.0	0.1
Europe de l'Est									0.0	
Autre de l'Europe									0.0	
Ancienne URSS										
Océanie							0.0	0.1		0.0
USA/Etats–Unis d'Amer							75.2	71.1	83.2	84.6
Italy/Italie							7.8	8.9	4.0	5.2
Belgium–Luxembourg							4.1	5.6	3.0	2.4
France, Monac							4.8	4.0	2.7	2.0
Germany/Allemagne							2.7	2.7	1.9	1.7
Canada							1.3	2.2	2.5	1.5
Japan/Japon							0.8	2.1	1.2	0.6
Netherlands/Pays–Bas							1.2	0.8	0.4	0.5
United Kingdom							0.1	0.6	0.4	0.4
Switz.Liecht							0.8	0.3	0.0	0.1

4. General Imports C.I.F. by Commodities according to the S.I.T.C. (Rév. 2) in thousand U.S. Dollars
Importations Générales C.A.F. par Produits d'après la C.T.C.I. (Rév. 2) en milliers de Dollars E.U.

SITC CTCI	COMMODITY	1989		1990		1991		1992		PRODUIT
		WEIGHT POIDS	VALUE VALEUR	WEIGHT POIDS	VALUE VALEUR	WEIGHT POIDS	VALUE VALEUR	WEIGHT POIDS	VALUE VALEUR	
	ALL COMMODITIES		313740		332220		400080		278030	TOUS PRODUITS
0	FOOD AND LIVE ANIMALS		64980		63240		72980		79230	ALIMENTS,ANIMAUX VIVANTS
1	BEVERAGES AND TOBACCO		3800		4860		10760		4260	BOISSONS ET TABACS
2	CRUDE MATERLS,EXCL FUELS		6820		8020		5560		1730	MAT BRUTES NON COMESTIBLES
3	MINERAL FUELS ETC		55520		70820		58020		61210	COMBUSTIBLES MINERAUX LUB
4	ANIMAL,VEGETABLE OIL,FAT		26520		31200		51020		47830	HUILES,GRAISSES ANIM,VEG
5	CHEMCLS,RELATED PROD NES		28940		37120		43590		22180	PRODUITS CHIMIQUES
6	BASIC MANUFACTURES		44020		51000		70700		36630	ART MANUFACTURES
7	MACHINES,TRANSPORT EQUIP		53460		48600		63500		18220	MACHINES MATERIEL TRANSPORT
8	MISC MANUFACTURED GOODS		26520		15420		22280		5710	ART MANUFACTURES DIVERS
9	GOODS NOT CLASSD BY KIND		3160		1940		1030		1030	ART TRANSACT NON CLASSES

5. General Exports F.O.B. by Commodities according to the S.I.T.C. (Rev. 2) in thousand U.S. Dollars
Exportations Générales F.O.B. par Produits d'après la C.T.C.I. (Rév. 2) en milliers de Dollars E.U.

SITC CTCI	COMMODITY	1989 WEIGHT POIDS	1989 VALUE VALEUR	1990 WEIGHT POIDS	1990 VALUE VALEUR	1991 WEIGHT POIDS	1991 VALUE VALEUR	1992 WEIGHT POIDS	1992 VALUE VALEUR	PRODUIT
	ALL COMMODITIES		152118		171112		187638		77730	TOUS PRODUITS
0	FOOD AND LIVE ANIMALS		40718		23101		26661		9620	ALIMENTS,ANIMAUX VIVANTS
06	SUGAR AND PREPS,HONEY		535		182		3081			SUCRES ET PRODUITS
061	SUGAR AND HONEY		535		182		3081			SUCRES ET MIEL
0615	MOLASSES		48							MELASSES
07	COFFEE,TEA,COCOA,SPICES		36125		19198		18440		9620	CAFE,THE,CACAO,EPICES
071	COFFEE AND SUBSTITUTES		34148		16723		17284		9090	CAFE ET SUCCEDANES
0711	COFFEE GREEN,ROASTED,SUB		34148		16723		17284		9090	CAFE TORREFIE OU DECAFEINE
072	COCOA		1926		2455		1093		530	CACAO
0721	COCOA BEANS,RAW,ROASTED								530	CACAO EN FEVES
5	CHEMCLS,RELATED PROD NES		647		768		1596		3970	PRODUITS CHIMIQUES
55	PERFUME,CLEANING ETC PRD		647		692		1558		3970	PROD POUR PARFUM,TOILETTE
5513	ESSENTL OIL,RESINOID,ETC		647		692		1557		3970	HUILES ESSENTIELLES,RESIN
6	BASIC MANUFACTURES		23542		23998		27611		50130	ART MANUFACTURES
65	TEXTILE YARN,FABRICS,ETC		10598		6230		8928		1680	FILS,TISSUS,ARTICLES TEXTILE
65761	WOOL,FUR FELT HAT BODIES		6283						1680	CLOCHES NON DRESSEES

Honduras

1. HISTORICAL SERIES, 1961–1996 SPECIAL TRADE, IMPORTS C.I.F., EXPORTS F.O.B.
SERIES HISTORIQUES, 1961–1996 COMMERCE SPECIAL, IMPORTATIONS C.A.F., EXPORTATIONS F.O.B

YEAR ANNEE	VALUE IN MILLION U.S. DOLLARS / VALEUR EN MILLION U.S. DOLLARS — MERCHANDISE –MARCHANDISE		GOLD –OR		CONVERSION FACTORS FACTEURS DE CONVERSION CENTS E.U. PAR		INDEX NUMBERS –INDICES — QUANTUM		UNIT VALUE / VALEUR UNITAIRE	
	IMPORTS	EXPORTS	IMPORTS	EXPORTS	IMPORTS	EXPORTS	IMPORTS	EXPORTS	IMPORTS	EXPORTS
1961	72.00	73.00		0.18				139		139
1962	79.80	81.45		0.21				144		149
1963	95.10	83.30		0.23				150		146
1964	101.65	93.80		0.20				158		156
1965	121.95	126.60		0.27				222		152
1966	149.05	145.50		0.23				258		147
1967	164.75	158.05		0.29				273		153
1968	184.70	178.95		0.08				308		156
1969	184.25	165.85								
1970	220.67	179.04		0.32				78		78
1971	193.39	188.78						93		104
1972	192.79	204.04						94		
1973	262.25	261.35						97		
1974	380.10	294.25						75		
1975	404.28	303.20						77		53
1976	453.08	397.21						89		74
1977	579.41	518.57						101		121
1978	699.21	612.77						104		104
1979	825.78	733.62						121		94
1980	1008.70	829.50						118		112
1981	949.10	760.70						115		95
1982	700.50	659.50						113		93
1983	802.60	671.80						108		87
1984	893.40	725.30						105		96
1985	888.10	780.00						115		98
1986	875.00	854.20						107		127
1987	827.40	791.40						123		100
1988	940.10	841.90						109		108
1989	968.60	858.50						99		105
1990	934.80	831.00						100		100
1991	955.10	792.40						88		98
1992	1036.60	801.50						102		77
1993	1130.00	814.00						90		78
1994	1055.90	842.50						79		89
1995	1218.60	1060.70								124
1996	1693.50	1106.10								110

2. IMPORTS BY BROAD ECONOMIC CATEGORY AND EXPORTS BY INDUSTRIAL ORIGIN. (PERCENTAGE OF TOTAL VALUE)
IMPORTATIONS PAR CATEGORIES ECONOMIQUES ET EXPORTATIONS PAR BRANCHE D'ACTIVITE.(EN POURCENTAGE DE LA VALEUR TOTALE)

IMPORTS – IMPORTATIONS

	1990	1991	1992	1993	1994	1995	1996
TOTAL IMPORTS–IMPORTATIONS TOTALES	100.	100.	100.	100.	100.	100.	
1 FOOD BEV–ALIMENTATION BOISSONS	7.9	9.2	8.5	10.3	12.4	10.1	
11 PRIMARY–PRODUITS DE BASE	2.6	3.1	3.3	4.0	4.0	3.0	
111 FOR INDUSTRY–POUR L'INDUSTRIE	2.3	2.7	2.7	3.1	3.3	2.1	
112 FOR HOUSEHOLDS–POUR LES MENAGES	0.3	0.4	0.6	0.9	0.7	0.9	
12 PROCESSED–PRODUITS ELABORES	5.3	6.0	5.2	6.3	8.4	7.1	
121 FOR INDUSTRY–POUR L'INDUSTRIE	0.5	0.5	0.6	0.8	1.9	1.2	
122 FOR HOUSEHOLDS–POUR LES MENAGES	4.8	5.5	4.6	5.6	6.5	5.9	
2 IND SUPPLIES–APPROV INDUSTRIELS	36.9	39.0	37.3	34.2	32.3	34.1	
21 PRIMARY–PRODUITS DE BASE	2.4	3.4	2.8	2.0	1.6	2.1	
22 PROCESSED–PRODUITS ELABORES	34.5	35.6	34.5	32.3	30.7	32.1	
3 FUELS–COMBUSTIBLES	16.0	15.3	12.9	13.5	12.6	11.4	
31 PRIMARY–PRODUITS DE BASE	7.8	6.6	3.8	0.5	1.0	0.3	
32 PROCESSED–PRODUITS ELABORES	8.3	8.7	9.1	13.1	11.6	11.0	
321 MOTOR SPIRIT–ESSENCE	0.9	0.6	0.6	5.2	3.7	2.0	
322 OTHER–AUTRES	7.4	8.0	8.4	7.8	7.9	9.1	
4 MACHINERY–EQUIPEMENT	13.7	13.2	15.3	14.9	17.7	19.6	
41 CAPITAL EQUIPMENT–MACHINES	12.4	11.8	13.7	13.3	16.0	18.1	
42 PARTS–PIECES ACCESSOIRES	1.4	1.4	1.5	1.7	1.7	1.5	
5 TRANSPORT–TRANSPORT	11.5	9.8	12.2	12.4	11.6	9.7	
51 PASSENGER CARS–AUTOMOBILES	6.6	5.5	7.6	2.6	2.4	1.3	
52 OTHER–AUTRES	0.8	0.5	0.7	6.1	5.7	5.3	
521 INDUSTRIAL–INDUSTRIELS	0.5	0.2	0.3	5.8	5.4	5.0	
522 NON INDUSTRIAL–NON INDUSTRIEL	0.3	0.3	0.4	0.3	0.3	0.3	
53 PARTS–PIECES ACCESSOIRES	4.2	3.8	3.9	3.8	3.5	3.1	
6 CONSUM GOODS–BIENS CONSOMMATION	13.5	12.8	13.8	14.4	13.3	15.0	
61 DURABLE–DURABLES	1.7	1.2	1.6	1.9	1.8	2.5	
62 SEMI DURABLE–SEMI DURABLES	5.3	5.3	6.0	5.9	5.7	6.8	
63 NON DURABLE–NON DURABLES	6.5	6.3	6.2	6.6	5.8	5.7	
7 GOODS NES–BIENS NDA	0.4	0.8	0.1	0.2	0.0	0.1	

EXPORTS – EXPORTATIONS

	1990	1991	1992	1993	1994	1995	1996
TOTAL EXPORTS–EXPORTATIONS TOTALES	100.	100.	100.	100.	100.	100.	
1 AGRICULTURE	75.0	75.2	74.7	72.3	71.6	83.7	
2 MINING QUARRY–INDUS EXTRACTIVES	0.0	0.4	2.6	1.1	1.0	0.0	
3 MANUFACTURING–IND MANUFACTUR	25.0	24.3	22.7	26.6	27.4	16.3	
31 FOOD BEV TOBACCO–ALIM BOISS TAB	10.0	11.0	8.7	12.2	11.5	5.7	
32 TEXTILES–INDUSTRIES TEXTILES	2.7	3.2	3.4	2.0	2.4	1.2	
33 WOOD & PRODUCTS–BOIS & PRODUITS	2.6	2.0	2.2	3.8	4.2	2.6	
34 PAPER & PRODUCTS–PAPIER & PRODT	0.7	1.8	1.7	1.9	2.2	1.2	
35 CHEMICALS–INDUSTRIES CHIMIQUES	2.7	3.1	3.1	2.3	2.6	2.1	
36 NON METAL MIN–MIN NON METAL	0.9	0.5	0.5	0.3	0.3	0.3	
37 BASIC METAL–IND METAL BASE	4.1	1.1	0.3	0.2	0.3	0.3	
38 METAL MANUF–MANUF METAL	1.1	1.4	2.1	3.7	3.9	2.8	
39 OTH MANUF IND–AUTRES MANUF	0.1	0.1	0.6	0.1	0.1	0.1	

3. TRADE BY PRINCIPAL COUNTRIES OF PRODUCTION AND LAST DESTINATION (VALUE IN THOUSAND U.S. DOLLARS)
ECHANGES SELON LES PRINCIPAUX PAYS DE PRODUCTION ET DE DERNIERE DESTINATION (VALEUR EN MILLIERS DE DOLLARS EU)

COUNTRIES–PAYS	SPECIAL IMPORTS C.I.F. IMPORTATIONS SPECIALES C.A.F				
	1991	1992	1993	1994	1995
World	963456	1056728	1304410	1334602	1727523
Africa	312	497	670	3321	2127
Americas	727234	868706	1054823	1026992	1319404
Northern America	477631	571502	678947	645198	815972
LAIA	138809	130298	96250	100637	152276
CACM	92679	114480	165361	156060	244076
Caribbean	2052	22274	80662	96045	63645
Rest of America	16064	30152	33603	29052	43435
As.ex F.USSR	87651	87677	111700	109420	107715
Eur.x F.USSR	103064	90688	125047	170176	265967
EU	91348	79580	112715	155809	251093
EFTA	9015	8758	10304	10561	12180
East Europe	2553	2312	1897	3798	2614
Other Europe	148	0	132	7	81
Former USSR	329	819	6553	3589	4982
Oceania	2177	646	1365	2106	4137
USA/Etats–Unis d'Amer	469615	564701	666125	633431	804734
Guatemala	42850	48792	76663	83129	118229
Japan/Japon	57807	52976	70327	55705	59168
Mexico/Mexique	52685	66473	34837	40429	72215
El Salvador	20298	30682	44085	46425	68300
Netherlands Antilles	0	13517	62105	79188	48655
Netherlands/Pays–Bas	16532	5126	11742	21253	129793
Germany/Allemagne	27701	23446	37270	47381	42338
Costa Rica	20624	26799	37624	21765	44841
Panama	15547	29168	33511	28921	43319
Brazil/Brésil	17971	26227	24580	24566	26329
Venezuela	50288	15269	11603	11457	21736
Spain/Espagne	8188	16910	6929	27536	26970
Colombia/Colombie	8104	10331	15171	15186	18707
Belgium–Luxembourg	3814	5096	9640	19313	14775
Switz.Liecht	8823	8663	10188	10458	11996
Canada	7561	6759	12586	11651	10912
Italy/Italie	5348	5990	14248	8510	12016
United Kingdom	9091	8984	10355	9745	7301
Hong Kong	8998	11436	9727	7708	4845
Nicaragua	8907	8207	6990	4741	12705
France,Monac	6592	6326	8829	8581	5153
China/Chine	3551	3908	6748	6813	7954
Korea Dem People's Rp	176	4438	7690	5847	8372
Aruba		1866	6086	9357	6434
Sweden/Suède	3009	1893	3139	4104	3940
Russian Federation		819	6553	3589	4982
Chile/Chili	3482	1914	2579	2973	4935
Argentina/Argentine	3021	4170	3609	1842	2499
Denmark/Danemark	4653	1607	3949	1768	3115
Ireland/Irlande	948	1914	2798	5232	3851
Korea, Republic of	2929	551	1331	4532	4396
Peru/Pérou	2389	2635	2393	2534	1643
Trinidad and Tobago	90	3151	4094	2702	1540
Viet Nam				10384	2
Dominican Republic	1406	946	1229	1370	4769
Ecuador/Equateur	743	2104	964	1520	3897
New Zealand	1960	527	1333	2064	3314
Finland/Finlande	4193	1124	2414	863	494
British Virgin Islds			4235	3205	
Israel/Israël	500	651	2214	1743	2248
Bahamas	28	1987	2174	88	1771
Poland/Pologne	1170	620	702	1483	1321
India/Inde	988	1011	782	825	1487
Austria/Autriche	951	720	309	666	776
Portugal	328	376	1093	857	541
Romania/Roumanie	351	758	209	1076	707
Thailand/Thaïlande	142	427	449	649	993
Czech Republic			681	1118	497
Libyan Arab Jamahiriya				2085	

COUNTRIES–PAYS	SPECIAL EXPORTS F.O.B. EXPORTATIONS SPECIALES F.O.B.				
	1991	1992	1993	1994	1995
Monde	616652	737396	664759	614049	656012
Afrique	39	384	177	272	373
Amériques	384923	457354	454082	396022	342423
Amérique du Nord	335350	395863	382317	335496	288018
ALAI	8082	4096	5924	3964	4933
MCAC	32201	48048	51318	40081	36843
Caraïbes	5414	5242	11070	11579	9975
Autre Amérique	3876	4104	3454	4903	2654
Asie l'URSS exclus	55773	43726	28936	38830	67545
Europe l'URSS exclus	170157	228770	179422	173360	242234
UE	160355	223410	177519	170916	238389
AELE	3606	3361	1698	2354	1202
Europe de l'Est	4241	1982	205	90	2564
Autre de l'Europe	1955	17			78
Ancienne URSS		1396		172	60
Océanie	121	44	208	201	0
USA/Etats–Unis d'Amer	332264	390795	381018	331021	279949
Germany/Allemagne	43292	97567	93095	76021	126700
Belgium–Luxembourg	37335	34639	29959	18622	23165
Japan/Japon	35250	18634	19242	24893	44198
Italy/Italie	24807	34459	5659	9581	15446
Spain/Espagne	11113	10844	13706	22099	25305
El Salvador	16415	23218	18199	13953	9038
United Kingdom	11223	14556	10556	12669	10804
Nicaragua	4265	8855	13453	10642	18423
Netherlands/Pays–Bas	13596	6843	8810	12896	10923
Guatemala	8920	11917	13645	6847	4297
Korea Dem People's Rp	1664	5848	7992	11941	18107
France,Monac	1282	2351	5084	9838	11821
Portugal	6202	6805	7834	3449	4042
Sweden/Suède	11174	14639	1178	576	50
Costa Rica	2600	4057	6020	8639	5086
Korea, Republic of	14382	3329	227	297	4027
Canada	3087	5014	1111	4472	8069
Mexico/Mexique	3485	2313	4197	1881	2074
Iran (Islamic Rp. of)	539	12302	910		
Finland/Finlande		154	1272	3967	7395
Panama	1981	2323	2706	3421	2303
Switz.Liecht	3606	3349	1653	2214	1202
Guadeloupe	998	909	2247	2124	1473
Colombia/Colombie	1092	779	1359	1561	1951
Trinidad and Tobago	98	223	1440	2361	2367
Saint Lucia/St. Lucie	869	854	914	1711	1296
Belize/Bélize	931	1532	748	1472	351
Martinique	1263	473	1131	853	1080
Dominican Republic	628	663	524	1000	1065
Saudi Arabia	2869	775	162		
Barbados/Barbade	461	205	1089	773	754
Israel/Israël	819	587	181	752	909
Grenada/Grenade		819	592	921	904
Ecuador/Equateur	2811	17	0	58	48
Czechoslovakia	1218	1545			
Jamaica/Jamaïque	118	572	1117	783	106
Hungary/Hongrie	1658	349	93	30	395
Poland/Pologne	574	89	31	49	1608
Venezuela	668	953	215	101	254
St Vincent & Grenadines	417	219	612	480	401
Mongolia/Mongolie		2035			7
Fm Yugoslav	1907				
Denmark/Danemark	77	93	28	616	966
Russian Federation		1396		172	60
Austria/Autriche	48	66	122	315	1038
Ireland/Irlande	206	389	210	267	512
Aruba		18	672	340	272
Suriname/Suriname	737	229			
Peru/Pérou	22	14	2	166	595

(VALUE AS PERCENTAGE OF WORLD TOTAL)(VALEURS EN POURCENTAGE DU TOTAL MONDIAL)

	1986	1987	1988	1989	1990	1991	1992	1993	1994	1995
Africa	0.1	0.0	0.1	0.0	0.0	0.0	0.0	0.1	0.2	0.1
Americas	68.9	70.6	69.1	72.0	72.7	75.5	82.2	80.9	77.0	76.4
Northern America	38.2	39.8	42.5	44.6	43.7	49.6	54.1	52.1	48.3	47.2
LAIA	19.2	18.7	17.4	16.0	16.6	14.4	12.3	7.4	7.5	8.8
CACM	7.7	6.0	6.6	8.4	8.1	9.6	10.8	12.7	11.7	14.1
Caribbean	1.0	2.8	0.1	0.2	0.2	0.2	2.1	6.2	7.2	3.7
Rest of America	2.7	3.3	2.5	2.7	4.1	1.7	2.9	2.6	2.2	2.5
As.ex F.USSR	13.4	13.8	12.6	11.6	10.5	9.1	8.3	8.6	8.2	6.2
Eur.x F.USSR	16.6	14.4	13.9	11.8	11.5	10.7	8.6	9.6	12.8	15.4
EU	15.5	12.7	12.2	10.1	10.1	9.5	7.5	8.6	11.7	14.5
EFTA	0.8	1.1	1.0	1.3	1.2	0.9	0.8	0.8	0.8	0.7
East Europe	0.3	0.5	0.8	0.4	0.2	0.3	0.2	0.1	0.3	0.2
Other Europe	0.0	0.0	0.0	0.0	0.0	0.0	0.0	0.0	0.0	0.0
Former USSR	0.0	0.0	0.0	0.1	0.0	0.0	0.1	0.5	0.3	0.3
Oceania	0.1	0.1	0.1	0.1	0.1	0.2	0.1	0.1	0.2	0.2
USA/Etats–Unis d'Amer	37.4	38.9	41.6	43.5	43.3	48.7	53.4	51.1	47.5	46.6
Guatemala	3.2	2.7	3.6	4.9	3.7	4.4	4.6	5.9	6.2	6.8
Japan/Japon	10.0	9.8	9.2	8.2	7.0	6.0	5.0	5.4	4.2	3.4
Mexico/Mexique	5.4	6.2	7.2	6.4	4.8	5.5	6.3	2.7	3.0	4.2
El Salvador	1.1	1.1	1.4	1.5	1.7	2.1	2.9	3.4	3.5	4.0
Netherlands Antilles	0.9	2.6				0.0	1.3	4.8	5.9	2.8
Netherlands/Pays–Bas	1.8	2.6	2.1	1.3	1.3	1.7	0.5	0.9	1.6	7.5
Germany/Allemagne	4.1	2.9	3.5	3.3	4.0	2.9	2.2	2.9	3.6	2.5
Costa Rica	3.2	2.0	1.4	1.6	1.6	2.1	2.5	2.9	1.6	2.6
Panama	2.7	3.3	2.5	2.7	4.1	1.6	2.8	2.6	2.2	2.5

	1986	1987	1988	1989	1990	1991	1992	1993	1994	1995
Afrique	0.3	0.7	0.9	0.4	0.0	0.0	0.1	0.0	0.0	0.1
Amériques	56.3	64.0	52.9	52.3	59.7	62.4	62.0	68.3	64.5	52.2
Amérique du Nord	50.7	56.6	44.6	44.7	52.1	54.4	53.7	57.5	54.6	43.9
ALAI	0.3	0.9	1.2	0.4	0.9	1.3	0.6	0.9	0.6	0.8
MCAC	2.4	3.4	3.9	4.8	4.4	5.2	6.5	7.7	6.5	5.6
Caraïbes	2.4	2.5	2.7	2.3	1.9	0.9	0.7	1.7	1.9	1.5
Autre Amérique	0.5	0.6	0.6	0.2	0.5	0.6	0.6	0.5	0.8	0.4
Asie l'URSS exclus	11.6	6.4	8.4	10.6	7.3	9.0	5.9	4.4	6.3	10.3
Europe l'URSS exclus	31.6	28.4	36.6	35.5	29.8	27.6	31.0	27.0	28.2	36.9
UE	30.2	26.2	27.8	26.7	28.1	26.0	30.3	26.7	27.8	36.3
AELE	0.3	0.9	0.1	0.4	0.6	0.6	0.5	0.3	0.4	0.2
Europe de l'Est	0.8	1.2	8.8	8.2	1.0	0.7	0.3	0.0	0.0	0.4
Autre de l'Europe	0.3	0.1	0.0	0.2	0.1	0.3	0.0			0.0
Ancienne URSS	0.1	0.5	1.0	0.3	2.3		0.2		0.0	0.0
Océanie	0.0	0.0	0.1	0.8	0.6	0.0	0.0	0.0	0.0	0.0
USA/Etats–Unis d'Amer	50.6	56.4	44.1	44.3	51.6	53.9	53.0	57.3	53.9	42.7
Germany/Allemagne	12.0	10.8	8.7	9.4	9.9	7.0	13.2	14.0	12.4	19.3
Belgium–Luxembourg	4.5	3.3	6.9	6.1	5.9	6.1	4.7	4.5	3.0	3.5
Japan/Japon	9.9	4.9	5.9	7.6	5.1	5.7	2.5	2.9	4.1	6.7
Italy/Italie	6.9	6.0	3.7	2.4	3.3	4.0	4.7	0.9	1.6	2.4
Spain/Espagne	1.9	1.7	2.3	1.6	1.7	1.8	1.5	2.1	3.6	3.9
El Salvador	0.8	1.4	1.8	1.8	1.8	2.7	3.1	2.7	2.3	1.4
United Kingdom	0.8	0.6	2.4	3.3	2.1	1.8	2.0	1.6	2.1	1.6
Nicaragua	0.3	0.2	0.2	0.4	0.3	0.7	1.2	2.0	1.7	2.8
Netherlands/Pays–Bas	2.5	1.8	2.0	1.8	1.1	2.2	0.9	1.3	2.1	1.7

4. Special Imports C.I.F. by Commodities according to the S.I.T.C. (Rev. 2) in thousand U.S. Dollars
Importations Spéciales C.A.F. par Produits d'après la C.T.C.I. (Rév. 2) en milliers de Dollars E.U.

SITC CTCI	COMMODITY	1992 WEIGHT POIDS	1992 VALUE VALEUR	1993 WEIGHT POIDS	1993 VALUE VALEUR	1994 WEIGHT POIDS	1994 VALUE VALEUR	1995 WEIGHT POIDS	1995 VALUE VALEUR	PRODUIT
	ALL COMMODITIES # 1		1056728		1304410		1334602		1727523	TOUS PRODUITS
0	FOOD AND LIVE ANIMALS		99823		145662		178035		183900	ALIMENTS,ANIMAUX VIVANTS
01	MEAT AND PREPARATIONS		1306		3761		2495		5467	VIANDES ET PREPARATIONS
02	DAIRY PRODCTS,BIRDS'EGGS		10833		20556		20233		22462	PRODUITS LAITIERS,OEUFS
022	MILK AND CREAM	W 5222	9157	W 10748	18254	W 7306	15105	W 8185	16775	LAIT ET CREME
0224	MILK,CREAM PRESERVED ETC	W 4470	8800	W 10545	18081	W 7245	15024	W 7923	16505	LAIT,CREME CONS,CONC
02243	MILK DRY,OVER 1.5% FAT							W 6720	14287	LAIT POUDRE SUP 1.5%
03	FISH AND PREPARATIONS		2438		4910		3109		5827	POISSONS ET PREPARATIONS
04	CEREALS AND PREPARATIONS		31667		49135		72852		68233	CEREALES ET PRODUITS
041	WHEAT ETC UNMILLED	W 95161	21234	W 178034	32983	W 225002	37903	W 99556	24531	FROMENT,EPEAUTRE
0411	DURUM WHEAT UNMILLED			W 26734	7028	W 30588	3621	W 16301	4602	FROMENT DUR NON MOULU
0412	OTHER WHEAT ETC UNMILLED			W 151300	25955	W 194415	34282	W 83256	19930	AUTRE FROMENT NON MOULU
042	RICE	W 1782	636	W 3914	1116	W 9459	6257	W 21060	7874	RIZ
0421	RICE IN HUSK OR HUSKED	W 365	110	W 760	267	W 4563	1429	W 17130	6603	RIZ SANS AUTRE PREPARATION
04211	RICE IN THE HUSK							W 16816	6529	RIZ PADDY
0422	RICE SEMI-MILLED,MILLED	W 1417	525	W 3154	849	W 4895	4828	W 3930	1271	RIZ POLI,GLACE INCL BRISURES
044	MAIZE UNMILLED	W 18575	2777	W 13540	2450	W 33977	5083	W 17383	9572	MAIS NON MOULU
047	OTHER CEREAL MEALS,FLOUR	W 208	135	W 3367	1016	W 25644	9165	W 697	430	AUTRES SEMOULES,FARINES
04702	MEAL OR GROATS NON-WHEAT			W 261	92	W 13045	6455	W 49	19	GRUAUX,SEMOULES DE CEREALES
048	CEREAL ETC PREPARATIONS	W 10287	6557	W 14232	10945	W 18366	14083	W 29924	24730	PREPTNS A BASE CEREALES
0481	PREPD BREAKFAST FOOD ETC	W 2216	2605	W 4451	3779	W 4903	5120	W 9887	8655	CEREALES TRAVAILLEES
0484	BAKERY PRODUCTS	W 921	1018	W 1568	1491	W 1705	2284	W 5151	6035	PRODUITS DE BOULANGERIE
05	VEGETABLES AND FRUIT		6147		7810		8345		12843	LEGUMES ET FRUITS
054	VEG ETC FRSH,SMPLY PRSVD	W 2050	1154	W 4833	2728	W 5227	3584	W 8114	5974	LEGUMES FRAIS,CONG,SECS
06	SUGAR AND PREPS,HONEY		2668		6634		10313		6768	SUCRES ET PRODUITS
061	SUGAR AND HONEY	W 6935	2040	W 16586	4440	W 21469	7317	W 6981	2815	SUCRES ET MIEL
0611	RAW BEET AND CANE SUGAR	W 6722	1856	W 15611	3999	W 19626	6466	W 3547	1334	SUCRES BRUTS
081	*FEEDING STUFF FOR ANIML	W 45791	13884	W 45739	16714	W 55381	16428	W 70689	18000	NOURRITURE POUR ANIMAUX
0813	OILCAKE AND OTH RESIDUES	W 31358	7758	W 23132	10430	W 30642	9305	W 31379	8185	TOURTEAUX
08131	— OF SOYA BEANS	W 30826	7667	W 23043	10411	W 30641	9304	W 31160	8132	TOURTEAUX DE SOJA
0819	FOOD WASTE AND FEED NES	W 10381	4234	W 19922	5018	W 17894	5035	W 21248	6256	DECHETS,ALIMENTS NDA
08199	FODDER NES,INCL SWEETNED	W 10381	4234	W 17882	4799	W 17878	5031	W 21174	6214	PREPARATIONS FOURRAGERES
09	MISC EDIBLE PRODUCTS		26883		32362		39932		39235	PREP ALIMENTAIRES DIVERSES
098	EDIBLE PRODCTS,PREPS NES	W 6032	26848	W 7112	31770	W 9226	39202	W 10189	38470	PREP ALIMENTAIRES NDA
09805	SOUPS AND BROTHS	W 938	1952	W 1051	2479	W 2192	5480	W 2204	5488	SOUPES,POTAGES,BOUILLONS
09809	MISC FOOD PREPRTIONS NES	W 3122	22787	W 3101	25889	W 4363	30611	W 4587	28912	PREP ALIMENTAIRES NDA
1	BEVERAGES AND TOBACCO		6441		7332		6704		11707	BOISSONS ET TABACS
11	BEVERAGES		2382		3067		3090		5864	BOISSONS
12	TOBACCO AND MANUFACTURES		4059		4265		3614		5843	TABACS BRUTS FABRIQUES
121	TOBACCO UNMNFCTRD,REFUSE	W 1088	4059	W 1310	3893	W 1260	3331	W 1249	5623	TABACS BRUTS,DECHETS
1211	TOBACCO,NOT STRIPPED	W 1007	3417	W 919	2675	W 946	2579	W 837	3795	TABACS NON ECOTES
2	CRUDE MATERLS,EXCL FUELS		30531		27536		19589		28759	MAT BRUTES NON COMESTIBLES
22	OIL SEEDS,OLEAGINOUS FRT		4116		4141		3361		6406	GRAINES,FRUITS OLEAGINEUX
222	SEEDS FOR'SOFT'FIXED OIL	W 9497	3736	W 11139	3215	W 1515	518	W 2608	805	GRAINES HUILES FIXES
2223	COTTON SEEDS	W 9454	3702				1	W 19	34	GRAINES DE COTON
223	SEEDS FOR OTH FIXED OILS	W 201	380	W 390	925		2843	W 11186	5601	GRAINES AUTRES HUILES FIXES
26	TEXTILE FIBRES AND WASTE		6107		5349		4710		8381	FIBRES TEXTILES
27	CRUDE FERTLZR,MINRLS NES		10951		4551		2076		3357	ENGRAIS MINERAUX BRUTS
271	FERTILIZERS,CRUDE	W 23201	6102	W 641	414	W 337	158	W 716	402	ENGRAIS BRUTS
2712	NATURAL SODIUM NITRATE	W 21569	5256	W 6	3		1	W 140	46	NITRATE SODIUM NATUREL
278	OTHER CRUDE MINERALS	W 28012	4241	W 27316	3670	W 6212	1377	W 8548	2309	AUTRES MINERAUX BRUTS
2789	MINERALS CRUDE NES	W 26037	3396	W 19684	2262	W 3657	555	W 4033	1012	MINERAUX BRUTS NDA
29	CRUDE ANIMAL,VEG MAT NES		5321		8444		6123		4562	MATIERES BRUTES ANIM,VEGET
291	CRUDE ANIMAL MTRIALS NES	W 1222	2375	W 2654	4784		2720	W 159	597	MATIERES BRUTES ANIMALES
2919	OTH ANIMAL MATERIALS NES	W 1222	2375	W 2652	4783		2719	W 159	597	MAT ORIGINE ANIMALE NDA
29194	FISH WASTE	W 24	47	W 2550	4506		2350	W 23	170	DECHETS DE POISSONS
3	MINERAL FUELS ETC		138275		180227		173180		199138	COMBUSTIBLES MINERAUX LUB
33	PETROLEUM AND PRODUCTS		134730		174117		159329		193186	PETROLE ET DERIVES
333	CRUDE PETROLEUM	W 270278	37067	W 14	7	W 5	3	W 16	5	HUILES BRUTES DE PETROLE
334	PETROLEUM PRODUCTS,REFIN	W 311597	95576	W 615689	169995	W 654151	154562	W 827491	190372	PRODUITS RAFFINES
3341	GASOLINE,OTH LIGHT OILS	W 7348	6836	W 227782	68149	W 183066	49715	W 146598	33934	ESSENCES POUR MOTEURS
33411	MOTOR,AVIATION SPIRIT	W 7283	6715							ESSENCES MOTEURS D'AVIONS
33419	OTH LIGHT PETROLEUM OILS							W 146598	33934	AUTRES HUILES LEGERES
3342	KEROSENE,OTH MEDIUM OILS	W 58282	21401	W 69226	20328	W 60337	17276	W 41407	8343	PETR LAMPANTS,AUT HUIL
33429	OTH MEDIUM PETROLEUM OIL	W 58282	21401					W 41407	8343	AUTRES HUILES MOYENNES
3343	GAS OILS	W 180926	47996	W 306116	71804	W 400813	79479			GAS OILS
3344	FUEL OILS,NES	W 5933	1990	W 149	124	W 93	66	W 623436	137666	FUEL OILS
3345	LUBS,PETROLEUM OILS NES	W 59108	17352	W 12416	9590	W 9841	8026	W 16051	10429	HUILES LUBRIFIANTES
33451	LUBS(HIGH PETR CONT) ETC	W 59062	17251					W 15989	10281	HUILES LUBRIF,H LOURDES
335	RESIDUAL PETRLM PROD NES	W 2410	2088	W 33785	4116	W 19343	4764	W 11178	2809	PRODUITS RESIDUELS NDA
341	*GAS,NATURAL AND MANUFCT	W 9484	3345	W 21588	5854	W 72807	13585	W 21022	5690	GAZ NATUREL,GAZ MANUFACT
3413	PETROLM GASES,LIQUEFIED	W 9484	3345	W 20458	5506	W 54651	10255	W 21018	5680	GAZ DE PETROLE LIQUEFIE
34131	LIQUEFIED PROPANE,BUTANE							W 21018	5678	PROPANE,BUTANE LIQUEFIES
4	ANIMAL,VEGETABLE OIL,FAT		5851		6367		5214		16114	HUILES,GRAISSES ANIM,VEG
411	*ANIMAL OILS AND FATS	W 10982	4493	W 8493	4494	W 4757	2314	W 15153	8980	HUILES,GRAISSES ANIMALES
4113	ANIML OIL,FAT,GREASE NES	W 10870	4418	W 8306	4378	W 4455	2143	W 14809	8788	HUILES,GRAISSES ANIMALES NDA
41132	FATS OF BOVINE,SHEEP,ETC	W 10790	4345	W 7978	4218	W 4440	2122	W 14792	8763	SUIFS BRUTS FONDUS
42	FIXED VEGETABLE OIL,FAT		750		1253		1907		5413	HUILES VEGETALES FIXES
5	CHEMCLS,RELATED PROD NES		206488		235960		224361		292738	PRODUITS CHIMIQUES
51	ORGANIC CHEMICALS		10439		11734		11695		19906	PROD CHIMIQ ORGANIQUES
511	HYDROCARBONS NES,DERIVS	W 4311	4275	W 6678	5875	W 6055	4826	W 9741	9835	HYDROCARBURES NDA
5111	ACYCLIC HYDROCARBONS	W 3332	3272	W 158	93	W 100	111	W 88	102	HYDROCARBURES ACYCLIQUES
5112	CYCLIC HYDROCARBONS			W 5433	4658	W 5307	3881	W 6492	5640	HYDROCARBURES CYCLIQUES
52	INORGANIC CHEMICALS		12394		13078		14671		19585	PROD CHIM INORGANIQUES
522	INORG ELEMNTS,OXIDES,ETC	W 15898	5744	W 16851	5811	W 18416	6044	W 14481	9573	ELEMENTS INORGANIQUES
523	OTHR INORG CHEMICALS ETC	W 10502	6628	W 13851	7187	W 17822	8616	W 22539	9983	AUT PRODUITS CHIMIQUES INORG
5232	OTH MTL CMPD OF INRG ACD	W 5478	3171	W 6676	3613	W 9483	4900	W 11653	5694	SELS METALLIQUES
53	DYES,TANNING,COLOUR PROD		9983		11304		10460		14141	PROD TEINTURE,COLORANTS
533	PIGMENTS,PAINTS,ETC	W 4212	6692	W 3860	7644	W 3368	6186	W 4811	9340	PIGMENTS,PEINTURES,VERNIS
5334	VARNISHES,DISTEMPERS ETC	W 3500	4021	W 3144	4843	W 2543	3989	W 3505	5944	PEINTURES A L'EAU
541	*MEDICINAL,PHARM PRODUCT	K 5907927	51205	MK 16964	64340	K 7917774	58515	MK 12017	74773	PROD MEDICINAUX PHARMACEUT
5417	MEDICAMENTS	K 5224110	46659	MK 15874	57838	K 6989161	51853	MK 11047	65761	MEDICAMENTS
54171	— CONTAINNG ANTIBIOTICS							K 1613278	9539	MED CONTN ANTIBIOTIQUES
54172	— CONTAINING HORMONES							K 3408420	11011	MED CONTENANT HORMONES
54179	— CONTNG OTH SUBSTANCES							K 5403850	44919	MED CONT AUT SUBSTANCES
55	PERFUME,CLEANING ETC PRD		11054		14943		15181		22864	PROD POUR PARFUM,TOILETTE
551	ESSENTL OILS,PERFUME,ETC	W 631	3698	W 1149	4233	W 648	3875	W 1038	6518	HUILES ESSENTIELLES
5514	MIXED PERFUME SUBSTANCES	W 611	3641	W 731	2770	W 436	1980	W 414	2244	MELANGES SUBSTAN ODORIFER
553	PERFUMERY,COSMETICS,ETC	W 1488	4823	W 1993	7256	W 2073	7256	W 3040	9880	PRODUITS DE PARFUMERIE
554	SOAP,CLEANSING ETC PREPS	W 2821	2533	W 3285	3454	W 4291	4050	W 5737	6465	SAVONS,PRODUITS DETERSIFS
562	*FERTILIZERS,MANUFACTURE	W 89831	21692	W 177902	28008	W 135763	26453	W 124782	27871	ENGRAIS MANUFACTURES

4. Special Imports C.I.F. by Commodities according to the S.I.T.C. (Rev. 2) in thousand U.S. Dollars
Importations Spéciales C.A.F. par Produits d'après la C.T.C.I. (Rév. 2) en milliers de Dollars E.U.

SITC CTCI	COMMODITY	1992		1993		1994		1995		PRODUIT
		WEIGHT POIDS	VALUE VALEUR	WEIGHT POIDS	VALUE VALEUR	WEIGHT POIDS	VALUE VALEUR	WEIGHT POIDS	VALUE VALEUR	
5621	CHEM NITROGENOUS FERTLZR	W 43275	9590	W 90245	11422	W 55777	9419	W 60002	12297	ENGRAIS AZOTES
56216	UREA			W 63824	7564	W 35047	6342	W 27534	6940	UREE
56219	CHEM NITROG FERTILZR NES	W 37804	7624	W 9393	1458	W 6718	948	W 3526	714	ENGRAIS AZOTES NDA
5623	CHEM POTASSIC FERTILIZER	W 27661	6376	W 38873	6856	W 28442	5400	W 18156	3305	ENGRAIS POTASSIQUES
56239	CHEM POTASS FERTILZR NES	W 27661	6376	W 25805	4988	W 10182	2717	W 13635	2154	ENGRAIS POTASSIQUES NDA
5629	FERTILIZERS NES	W 5012	2706	W 35012	7221	W 48854	10569	W 45872	11763	ENGRAIS NDA
56291	NIT–PHOS–POT FERTLZR NES			W 9535	2575	W 27375	5504	W 28477	6311	ENGRAIS CONT N P K
56292	NITROG–PHOS FERTILZR NES			W 10405	1722	W 19204	4170	W 15817	4734	ENGRAIS NDA CONT N P
58	PLASTIC MATERIALS ETC		43232		40191		41533		60646	MAT PLAST ARTIFICIELLES
582	PROD OF CONDENSATION ETC	W 1528	2961	W 4572	5236	W 4605	5166	W 4895	7317	PROD CONDENS,POLYCOND
583	POLYMERIZATION ETC PRODS	W 33445	32807	W 55397	31547	W 35465	33445	W 38965	50020	PROD POLYMERISATION
5831	POLYETHYLENE	W 32474	31645	W 8832	6880	W 11631	9802	W 13715	16864	POLYETHYLENE
58311	— IN PRIMARY FORMS							W 13049	15509	POLYETHYLENE PRIMAIRES
5832	POLYPROPYLENE			W 3075	3129	W 4476	4519	W 4714	7484	POLYPROPYLENE
58321	— IN PRIMARY FORMS			W 2725	1835	W 4020	3238	W 4152	5306	POLYPROPYLENE PRIMAIRES
5834	POLYVINYL CHLORIDE			W 30820	8020	W 10992	9058	W 10248	11163	CHLORURE DE POLYVINYLE
58341	— IN PRIMARY FORMS							W 9982	10372	SOUS FORMES PRIMAIRES
5839	OTH POLYMRZTION ETC PROD	W 414	138	W 9845	9749	W 6109	7244	W 7253	9945	AUT PROD POLYMER COPOLYM
585	PLASTIC MATERIAL NES	W 4540	4548	W 45	63	W 50	117	W 12	47	RESINES ARTIFICIELLES
59	CHEMICAL MATERIALS NES		46022		51313		44923		52094	MAT PROD CHIMIQUES NDA
591	PESTICIDES,DISINFECTANTS	W 12798	37134	W 14284	40898	W 9894	33924	W 13295	39453	DESINF,INSECT,FONG,HERB
5911	INSECTICIDES,FOR RETAIL	W 2023	6636	W 1736	7554	W 1264	5849	W 2073	7371	INSECTICIDES VENTE DET
5912	FUNGICIDES,FOR RETAIL	W 7874	20979	W 8232	22379	W 5918	17349	W 7479	19558	FONGICIDES VENTE AU DET
5913	HERBICIDES,FOR RETAIL	W 1730	6875	W 3412	8022	W 1984	8220	W 2529	8941	HERBICIDES VENTE AU DET
598	MISCEL CHEM PRODUCTS NES	W 4710	7599	W 5245	8084	W 4664	8302	W 5352	9316	PROD DIV INDUST CHIM NDA
5989	CHEM PRODUCTS,PREPS NES	W 3746	5885	W 3292	5451	W 3538	6352	W 4572	7334	PROD PREP CHIMIQUES NDA
59899	OTH CHEM PRODS,PREPS,NES	W 1839	3860	W 1701	3329	W 1893	4392	W 2820	4728	AUT PRODUITS CHIMIQUES NDA
6	BASIC MANUFACTURES		211786		255034		242701		341449	ART MANUFACTURES
62	RUBBER MANUFACTURES NES		19605		27668		20410		25240	CAOUTCHOUC MANUFACTURE
625	RUBBER TYRES, TUBES ETC	W 7347	15981	W 11191	21925	W 8208	16738	W 10646	20374	PNEUS CAOUTCHOUC VULCANISE
6251	TYRES NEW FOR MOTOR CARS	W 5537	12208	W 1876	4117	W 1456	3690	W 1851	4802	PNEUS POUR VOITURES
6252	TYRES,NEW,BUS OR LORRY			W 3170	8830	W 2908	7526	W 3505	8580	PNEUS POUR AUTOBUS,CAMIONS
6259	OTH TYRES,TYRE CASES,ETC	W 1212	2997	W 5923	8332	W 3617	4838	W 5057	6287	AUTRES PNEUS RECHAPES FLAPS
62599	TYRES NES,TYRE CASES,ETC	W 962	2298	W 5472	7229	W 3291	3961	W 4483	5216	PNEUS,FLAPS
64	PAPER,PAPERBOARD AND MFR		59737		71440		62048		97831	PAPIERS,CARTONS & OUVRAGES
641	PAPER AND PAPERBOARD	W 78578	45420	W 95354	53200	W 81319	45064	W 93581	73560	PAPIERS ET CARTONS
6411	NEWSPRINT	W 120	273	W 7071	4701	W 6687	4458	W 7582	6126	PAPIER JOURNAL
6412	PRINTG,WRITING PAPER NES	W 50992	25779	W 2262	2219	W 3129	2762	W 3948	4732	PAPIERS POUR L'IMPRESSION
64121	— UNCOATED	W 50992	25779	W 838	702	W 152	209	W 504	1157	PAPIERS IMPRES NON COUCHES
6413	KRAFT PAPER,PAPERBOARD	W 3	4	W 50980	23980	W 53132	24255	W 52212	36124	PAPIER ET CARTON KRAFT
64131	KRAFT LINER IN BULK							W 44667	29531	PAP KRAFT POUR COUVERTURES
6415	PAPER,PAPERBRD,BULK,NES	W 21966	12897	W 15429	10814	W 10362	7614	W 18664	17450	PAPIERS,CARTONS ROULEAUX
64159	OTHER PAPER ETC,BULK,NES	W 21952	12860	W 13143	9526	W 8644	6553	W 11732	11894	AUT PAPIER ROULEAUX FEUILLES
6418	COATED ETC PAPER NES BLK	W 3332	4144	W 13509	7948	W 2746	2876	W 1792	2965	PAP,CARTONS COUCHES,ENDUITS
642	PAPER,ETC,PRECUT,ARTS OF	W 11674	14316	W 15221	18239	W 12533	16984	W 15954	24271	PAP,CARTONS DECOUPES
6421	PAPER ETC CONTAINERS	W 9539	11055	W 12212	12460	W 9231	11166	W 11174	15271	BOITES,SACS EMBALLAGES
6428	PAPER ETC ARTICLES NES	W 670	795	W 1265	2606	W 1813	3170	W 3274	5760	OUVRAGES EN PATE A PAPIER
65	TEXTILE YARN,FABRICS,ETC		32187		31131		30928		45738	FILS,TISSUS,ARTICLES TEXTILE
651	TEXTILE YARN	W 3268	9435		6367	W 1993	5317	W 1873	6394	FILS TEXTILES
6513	COTTON YARN	W 1428	4675	W 663	1998	W 540	1520	W 291	1084	FILS DE COTON
65131	— 14 KM PER KG OR LESS	W 1401	4537							FILS COT MOINS 14000 M KG
652	COTTON FABRICS,WOVEN	W 1917	7782	W 2205	7010	W 2628	8749	W 3402	10427	TISSUS DE COTON
6521	GREY WOVEN COTTON FABRIC	W 1444	6218	W 729	2904	W 215	830	W 62	333	TISSUS COT ECRUS NON MERCER
65215	GREY WOVN COTN BLEND NES	W 1261	4851	W 172	763	W 22	68	W 3	10	AUT TIS MOINS 85% COT ECRUS
6522	WOVEN COTTON BLEACHD,ETC	W 474	1564	W 1475	4106	W 2413	7919	W 3339	10094	TISSUS COTON BLANCHIS ETC
65224	BLCHED COTTON FABRIC NES	W 474	1564	W 950	2303	W 1986	6257	W 2719	7656	AUT TIS PLUS 85% COT BLANCHI
653	WOVN MAN–MADE FIB FABRIC	W 1346	4678	W 1634	5822	W 2333	7168	W 3106	11504	TISSUS FIBRES SYNTH,ARTIF
6534	DISC SYN BLEND FABRC NES	W 573	1592	W 837	3334	W 1421	4582	W 1681	7297	TISSUS FIBRES SYNTH DISCONT
65341	DISC SYN FIB–COTTN FABRC							W 1320	5452	TISSUS FIB SYNT DIS MEL COTO
657	SPECIAL TXTL FABRC,PRODS	W 2869	4978	W 1682	6023	W 1169	4282	W 1721	6415	TISSUS SPECIAUX
66	NONMETAL MINERAL MFS NES		19338		26496		23209		37143	ART MIN NON METALLIQUES
662	CLAY,REFRACTORY BLDG PRD	W 3991	2215	W 7823	4294	W 8272	3949	W 10919	5012	MAT CONST REFRACTAIRES
665	GLASSWARE	W 19938	10906	W 22651	14096	W 18236	10869	W 37484	20950	OUVRAGES EN VERRE
6651	BOTTLES ETC OF GLASS	W 18231	8748	W 21095	11813	W 16656	8607	W 35754	18213	RECIPIENTS EN VERRE
66511	GLASS BOTTLES ETC NONVAC	W 18227	8738	W 21094	11812	W 16650	8580	W 35754	18213	BONBONNES,BOUTEILLES,ETC
67	IRON AND STEEL		37472		40553		50035		61291	FER ET ACIER
672	IRON,STEEL PRIMARY FORMS	W 3774	1470	W 15813	5432	W 7566	3982	W 10843	2961	LINGOTS FER,ACIER
673	IRON,STEEL SHAPES ETC	W 37740	15876	W 27558	10865	W 54214	19049	W 48702	20187	BARRES,PROFIL FER,ACIER
6731	IRON,STEEL WIRE ROD	W 29484	12171	W 14755	5351	W 37532	12210	W 21028	7863	FIL MACHINE FER,ACIER
67311	IRON,SIMPLE STL WIRE ROD	W 28153	10855	W 11262	4174	W 33542	10850	W 19160	7102	FIL MACH AUT ACIER FIN
6732	IRON,STEEL BARS ETC	W 3849	1668	W 7028	3030	W 8009	3335	W 16677	7014	BARRES FER,ACIER
67326	IRN,OTH STL BARS HOTROLD	W 3849	1668	W 4677	1897	W 6853	2696	W 16030	6449	BARRES PLEINES FER,ACIER
6733	IRON,STEEL PROFILES ETC	W 4407	2037	W 5775	2484	W 8673	3504	W 10996	5309	PROFILES,PALPLAN FER,ACIER
674	IRN,STL UNIV,PLATE,SHEET	W 23320	14049		14516	W 33849	19458	W 37516	24072	LARGES PLATS,TOLES
6746	IRN,STL THIN PLATE,ROLLD			W 11820	4985	W 14576	6965	W 8451	5013	TOLES LAM MOINS 3MM
67461	— OF IRON OR SIMPLE STL			W 7982	3294	W 11037	5212	W 7623	4549	TOL NON AC FIN MOINS 3 MM
6749	OTH IRN,STL PLATES,SHEET	W 19556	12221		6524	W 13527	9149	W 13981	10990	AUTRES TOLES FER,ACIER
67491	— OF IRON OR SIMPLE STL	W 19556	12221	W 7952	5923	W 13484	9086	W 13750	10706	AUT TOLES AUTRES ACIER FIN
678	IRON,STL TUBES,PIPES,ETC	W 8331	3406	W 7619	6430	W 4142	3940	W 8261	10718	TUBES,TUYAUX EN FONTE,FER
6783	IRON,STL TUBES,PIPES NES	W 6309	1496	W 3616	2276	W 3011	2083	W 6612	6255	AUT TUBES,TUYAUX FER,ACIER
68	NON–FERROUS METALS		9083		13909		15070		17275	METAUX NON FERREUX
684	ALUMINIUM		4286	W 3279	8124	W 2669	8312	W 2986	11870	ALUMINIUM
6842	ALUMINIUM,ALLOYS WORKED		4275	W 3275	8120	W 2667	8306	W 2974	11740	ALUMINIUM,ALLIAGES OUVRE
68423	ALUMINIUM FOIL		2153	W 1149	4167	W 1116	4550	W 1214	6326	FEUILLES,BANDES MINCES AL
69	METAL MANUFACTURES NES		32003		40433		37934		52768	ART MANUFACT EN METAL NDA
691	STRUCTURES AND PARTS NES		3577	W 1535	1400	W 815	1271	W 1703	6054	CONSTRUCT FER,ACIER,ALU
6911	STRUCTURES,PARTS IRN,STL		3492	W 1433	1142	W 677	931	W 1589	5592	CONSTRUCT FER,ACIER,FONTE
692	METAL TANKS,BOXES,ETC	W 2449	5669	W 3006	6860	W 2485	8275	W 3787	11191	RECIPIENTS METALLIQUES
6924	MTL TRANSPORT BOXES ETC	W 2367	5376	W 2920	6489	W 1947	5408	W 3099	8990	FUTS,TAMBOURS,BIDONS
69241	STL TRANSPORT BOXES ETC	W 1839	3221	W 1181	2491	W 826	1440	W 1623	2712	FUTS,TAMBOURS,BIDONS FER
69242	ALUMNM TRNSPRT BOXES ETC	W 394	1861	W 757	3175	W 671	2952	W 1045	5461	FUTS,TAMBOURS,BIDONS ALU
693	WIRE PRODUCTS NON ELECTR	W 1177	1589	W 7667	4741	W 2531	3329	W 2312	3052	OUVRAGES FILS METALLIQUES
695	TOOLS	W 1522	5730	W 1378	7092	W 1451	5459	W 1975	8107	OUTILS A MAIN
6953	OTHER HAND TOOLS	W 668	3382	W 639	4602	W 721	3294	W 1001	5156	AUTRES OUTILS A MAIN
697	BASE MTL HOUSEHOLD EQUIP	W 1456	3130	W 1710	4220	W 1597	4460	W 1949	4870	ART MENAGE MET COMMUNS
699	BASE METAL MFRS NES	W 2376	7316		10312	W 5645	9744	W 5655	13119	ART MANUFACTURES MET NDA
6991	LOCKSMITHS WARES,ETC	W 1008	3514	W 1359	4327	W 1108	3779	W 1860	4909	ARTICLES DE SERRURERIE
7	MACHINES,TRANSPORT EQUIP		273760		342528		386348		502714	MACHINES MATERIEL TRANSPORT
71	POWER GENERATING EQUIPMT		28166		16226		55445		130786	MACHINES GENERATRICES
713	INTRNL COMBUS PSTN ENGIN	W 1389	8183	W 1429	6845	W 1958	6022	W 1348	7507	MOTEURS EXPL COMB INT, PIECE
716	ROTATING ELECTRIC PLANT	W 2166	14637	W 807	5967	W 5845	45375	W 6513	113386	APP ELECTR ROTATIFS,PIECES

4. Special Imports C.I.F. by Commodities according to the S.I.T.C. (Rev. 2) in thousand U.S. Dollars
Importations Spéciales C.A.F. par Produits d'après la C.T.C.I. (Rév. 2) en milliers de Dollars E.U.

SITC CTCI	COMMODITY	1992 WEIGHT POIDS	1992 VALUE VALEUR	1993 WEIGHT POIDS	1993 VALUE VALEUR	1994 WEIGHT POIDS	1994 VALUE VALEUR	1995 WEIGHT POIDS	1995 VALUE VALEUR	PRODUIT
7161	DC MOTORS AND GENERATORS							W 949	15666	MOTEURS COURANT CONTINU
7169	PTS NES OF ROT ELEC PLNT							W 4819	93001	PIECES MAC APP ROTATIFS
718	OTH POWER GENERATG MACHY	W 208	4139	W 80	1220		469	W 86	6228	AUTRES MOTEURS PARTIES
7188	WIND,WATER,ETC ENGINES	W 208	4139	W 67	1121		456	W 86	6218	MOT MACHINES MOTRICES NDA
71882	OTH HYDRAULIC ENGNS,MTRS	W 208	4139	W 31	719		19	W 64	5516	MACH MOTRICES HYDRAULQUES
72	MACHS FOR SPCL INDUSTRYS		41899		50609		44234		57440	MAC SPECIALES POUR INDUST
721	AGRIC MACHY,EXC TRACTORS	W 1232	4855	W 1637	6387	W 1573	6215	W 1930	7893	MACHINES AGRICOLES
722	TRACTORS NON–ROAD	W 1753	6414	W 2006	6868	W 1373	5005	W 1261	4565	TRACTEURS
723	CIVIL ENGNEERG EQUIP ETC	W 2004	7436	W 3288	11516	W 1446	5455	W 1791	7208	APPAREILS DE GENIE CIVIL
7234	CONST,MINING MACHNRY NES	W 1990	7285	W 3110	10805	W 1318	4767	W 1509	5779	MACH POUR LA CONST, MINES
724	TEXTILE,LEATHER MACHNRY	W 1163	6824	W 1382	6481	W 1756	9942	W 1430	11311	MACH POUR INDUSTRIE TEXTILE
7243	SEWING MACHS,NEEDLES ETC	W 493	3344	W 776	3316	W 862	3865	W 891	5610	MACHINES A COUDRE,PIECES
726	PRINTG,BKBINDG MACHY,PTS	W 240	2507	W 537	3993	W 245	3360	W 478	3127	MACHINES POUR IMPRIMERIE
727	FOOD MACHRY NON–DOMESTIC	W 472	3613	W 534	3176	W 671	4528	W 1164	7505	MACH INDUSTRIES ALIMENT
7272	OTH FOOD PROC MCHY,PARTS	W 434	2766	W 481	2840	W 602	3875	W 1119	6828	AUT MACH IND ALIMENTAIRE
72722	INDUS FOOD PROC MACH NES	W 434	2766	W 363	2012	W 292	1615	W 1106	6386	MACHINES BOULANGERIE
728	OTH MACHY FOR SPCL INDUS	W 1652	8824	W 1710	10925	W 1224	8482	W 3680	14178	AUT MACH IND PARTICULIERES
7284	MACHY FOR SPCL INDUS NES	W 608	4737	W 381	5194	W 368	3626	W 521	6121	MACH SPEC IND PARTICUL.
72848	OTH MCHY WITH INDIV FNCT	W 607	4735	W 125	2104	W 88	663	W 140	1150	AUTRES MACHINES NDA
74	GENRL INDUSTRL MACHY NES		46784		55489		55182		70743	MACH APP INDUSTRIE
741	HEATING,COOLING EQUIPMNT	W 3442	14037	W 2666	9916	W 1674	8962	W 3267	17469	MACH CHAUFFAGE,PIECES
7414	NONDOM REFRIG EQUIPT,PTS	W 2165	7962	W 1294	2618	W 540	2547	W 1573	10613	MAT PRODUCTION DU FROID
74141	REFRIG EQUIP NONDOMESTIC							W 1335	9426	REFIG INDUSTRIELS
7415	AIR–CONDITIONING MACHNRY	W 701	2547	W 793	4034	W 706	3575	W 1074	3883	GROUPES CONDITION AIR
742	PUMPS FOR LIQUIDS ETC	W 927	6523	W 900	6686	W 779	6169	W 2195	8376	POMPES MOTO–POMPES
7428	OTHER PUMPS FOR LIQUIDS							W 1926	5991	AUTRES POMPES POUR LIQ
743	PUMPS NES,CENTRFUGES ETC	W 1163	7411	W 1272	7455	W 1335	6198	W 1477	9835	POMPES COMPRES,VENT ETC
7431	PUMPS FOR GASES ETC	W 630	3959	W 532	3038	W 461	2591	W 544	2990	POMPES AIR A VIDE,COMPRES
7436	GAS,LIQUID FILTERS ETC	W 522	3244	W 491	2923	W 724	2611	W 712	4320	APP POUR FILT DES LIQUIDES
744	MECHANICAL HANDLING EQU	W 731	3370	W 1840	10097	W 2100	15425	W 1354	6819	EQUIP MANUTENTION PIECES
7442	LIFTING,LOADING MACH NES	W 504	2449	W 789	3443	W 1310	10280	W 600	2062	APP LEVAGE,MANUTENTION
745	NONELEC MACHY,TOOLS NES	W 769	6901	W 1304	10538	W 1040	8620	W 1854	17174	AUT MACH NON ELEC,PIECES
7452	OTH NONELEC MCHS,PTS NES	W 723	6123	W 1263	9806	W 1005	7797	W 1776	15976	AUT MACH NON ELEC,PIECES
74522	PACKAGNG,BOTTLNG,ETC MCH	W 166	2879	W 415	4537	W 113	1845	W 754	9025	MACH NETT BOUTEILLES,ETC
749	NONELEC MACH PTS,ACC NES	W 1563	8541	W 1913	10796	W 1301	9809	W 1287	11070	PIECES MACH NON ELEC NDA
75	OFFICE MACHNES,ADP EQUIP		15354		22059		21818		26674	MACH BUREAU TRAIT AUTOM
752	AUTOMTIC DATA PROC EQUIP	W 309	11069	W 429	13618	W 326	10932	W 575	14798	MACH TRAIT INFORMATION
7521	ANALOG,HYBRID COMPUTERS							W 193	8287	MACH POUR TRAIT INFORMAT
759	OFFICE,ADP MCH PTS,ACCES	W 121	2663	W 248	5841	W 281	8262	W 331	8084	PIECES DU 751 ET 752
7599	ACCTG,ETC,ADP MCH PTS,AC			W 206	4929	W 246	7415	W 241	6718	PIECES DU 751 ET 752
76	TELECOMM,SOUND EQUIPMENT		16975		26904		38178		23613	EQUIPMENT DE TELECOM
764	TELECOM EQPT,PTS,ACC NES	W 563	11713	W 907	22826	W 844	34715	W 745	14145	EQUIP TELECOM,PIECES
7641	LINE TELEPHONE,ETC EQUIP	W 408	9991	W 338	8751	W 206	14099	W 263	4181	APP TELEPHON PAR FIL
7648	TELECOMM EQUIPMENT NES	W 5	596	W 42	5490	W 47	6701	W 20	434	APP TELECOM NDA
7649	PTS NES OF EQUIPMT OF 76	W 65	539	W 198	7550	W 505	12205	W 268	6291	PIECES DE LA DIV 76
76491	PTS NES OF APPAR OF 7641			W 102	5697	W 428	10651	W 101	2879	PIECES POUR 764.1
77	ELECTRIC MACHNRY NES ETC		20559		39519		42351		55322	MACH APP ELECT NDA
771	ELECTRIC POWER MACHY NES			W 1257	4161	W 1006	3244	W 1332	7440	MACH PROD,TRANS ELECTR
7711	TRANSFORMERS,ELECTRICAL			W 934	2599	W 703	2197	W 1014	5908	TRANSFO ELECTRIQUES
77118	OTHER ELEC TRANSFORMERS			W 518	1491	W 395	1215	W 859	5303	AUTRES TRANSFO ELECTRIQ
772	SWITCHGEAR ETC,PARTS NES	W 440	3790	W 742	4984	W 815	6640	W 987	7601	APP COUPURE,SECT ETC
7721	SWITCHGEAR ETC	W 420	2509	W 728	4846	W 807	6515	W 964	7441	APP COUPURE,SECTIONMNT
773	ELECTR DISTRIBUTNG EQUIP	W 669	2416	W 1259	4545	W 2092	9340	W 1385	5250	EQUIPMT DISTRIBUTION ELECT
7731	INSULATED WIRE,CABLE ETC	W 487	1576	W 1044	4066	W 1626	8473	W 1133	4480	FILS,CABLES ISOLES ELECT
775	HOUSEHOLD TYPE EQUIP NES	W 2038	4109	W 3999	11199	W 3617	10615	W 5513	18687	MACH,APP USAGE DOMESTQUE
7752	DOM REFRIGERATRS,FREEZRS			W 2135	6297	W 1971	5974	W 3355	12251	REFRIG,CONGEL MENAGER
77521	DOMESTIC REFRIGERATORS			W 1749	4852	W 1499	4196	W 2066	6215	REFRIGERATEURS
77522	DOMESTIC DEEP–FREEZERS			W 386	1445	W 472	1778	W 1289	6037	MEUBLES CONGELATEURS
778	ELECTRICAL MACHINERY NES	W 2697	9779	W 3239	12112	W 3081	10436	W 3673	14812	AUTRES MACH ELECT NDA
78	ROAD VEHICLES		99442		126366		119952		132500	VEHICULES ROUTIERS
781	PASS MOTOR VEH EXC BUSES	W 29339	80554	W 12862	33341	W 7386	31663	W 4343	22461	AUTO TRANSPORT PERSONNES
782	LORRIES,SPCL MTR VEH NES	W 51	365	W 23271	64984	W 15449	50489	W 17490	64587	VEHICULES SPECIAUX,MARCH
7821	LORRIES,TRUCKS			W 21963	59786	W 14745	48807	W 16118	59804	VEHICULES TRANSP MARCHAND
7822	SPECIAL MOTOR VEHCLS NES	W 51	365	W 1308	5198	W 704	1682	W 1372	4784	VEHICULES USAGES SPECIAUX
783	ROAD MOTOR VEHICLES NES			W 3392	7118	W 4310	14376	W 5042	17532	VEHICULES ROUTIERS NDA
7831	BUSES			W 2844	6086	W 3193	13316	W 3630	14592	VOITURES TRANSPORT COMMUN
784	MOTOR VEH PRTS,ACCES NES	W 2741	10406	W 3375	13027	W 2640	15206	W 4220	18131	PIECES 722,781,782,783
7849	OTHER MOTOR VEHCL PARTS	W 2679	10241	W 2685	10293	W 2346	14513	W 4093	17872	PIECES 722,781,782,783
785	CYCLES,ETC MOTRZD OR NOT	W 1947	5938	W 2093	6156	W 2786	6919	W 9200	7716	MOTOCYCLES SCOOTERS
79	OTHR TRANSPORT EQUIPMENT		1413		1857		6622		1715	AUTRE MATERIEL TRANSPORT
793	SHIPS AND BOATS ETC	W 62	307	W 146	656	W 1462	5575	W 117	528	NAVIRES BATEAUX,ETC
8	MISC MANUFACTURED GOODS		83184		102742		98149		150227	ART MANUFACTURES DIVERS
812	*PLUMBG,HEATNG,LGHTNG EQ	W 1534	2425	W 2699	3942	W 2253	3874	W 3127	6193	APPAR SANITAIRES CHAUFFAGE
821	*FURNITURE,PARTS THEREOF	W 1102	2378	W 1278	3128	W 1158	3295	W 7692	5749	MEUBLES ET PIECES
84	CLOTHING AND ACCESSORIES		34441		37616		37540		61611	VETEMENTS
842	MENS OUTERWEAR NOT KNIT	W 1933	11125	W 591	4298	W 166	1366	W 898	5197	VET DESSUS POUR HOMMES
843	WOMENS OUTERWEAR NONKNIT	W 630	4121	W 361	1996	W 332	2758	W 1125	5109	VET DESSUS FEMMES MAT TEX
844	UNDER GARMENTS NOT KNIT	W 1898	17121	W 2075	13275	W 1265	7760	W 2786	21615	VETEMENT DESSOUS MAT TEX
8441	— MENS SHIRTS			W 1987	12496	W 1205	7535	W 2665	20853	CHEMISES HOMMES MAT TEXT
84411	—— OF COTTON			W 473	4036	W 145	1119	W 1311	9793	CHEMISES HOMMES DE COTON
84412	—— OF SYNTHETIC FIBRES			W 1514	8460	W 1061	6415	W 1354	11059	CHEMISES HOMMES FIB SYNT
8442	— MENS,OTHR THAN SHIRTS	W 1821	16771	W 77	734	W 53	206	W 97	663	SOUS–VET HOMMES MAT TEXT
845	OUTERWEAR KNIT NONELASTC	W 15	99	W 1137	7347	W 1187	10145	W 1409	11699	VET DESSOUS,ACCES BONNET
8459	— OTHER,CLTHG ACCESRYS							W 1227	10961	AUT VET DESSUS DE BONNE
846	UNDER GARMENTS KNITTED	W 141	853	W 914	6662		5673	W 1628	11052	SOUS VETS DE BONNETERIE
8462	— OF COTTON NON ELASTIC			W 781	5742		5082	W 685	4951	SOUS–VET BONNET COTON
84621	—— MENS SHIRTS			W 420	3814	W 386	4027			CHEMISES DE COTON
8463	— OF SYNTH FBR NONELAST			W 120	729	W 66	420	W 833	5797	SOUS–VET BONNET FIB SYNT
84632	—— MENS SHIRTS			W 54	263	W 28	111	W 760	5371	CHEMISES DE BON FIB SYNMT
847	TEXTILE CLTHNG ACCES NES	W 129	600	W 361	3039	W 918	8728	W 721	5697	ACCES VET MAT TEXT NDA
8471	— NOT KNITTED	W 28	112	W 135	974	W 844	8142	W 582	5220	ACCES VET MAT TEX NON BON
84713	TIES,CRAVATS ETC,NOT KNT	W 1	28	W 14	170	W 824	8050	W 530	4825	CRAVATES MAT TEX NON BON
87	PRECISION INSTRUMNTS NES		9105		9607		7215		8980	INSTRUM,APPAR SCIENT NDA
872	MEDICAL INSTRUMENTS NES	W 342	4231	W 312	3591	W 293	1970	W 274	2255	INSTR,APP MEDIC–CHIR NDA
87202	OTH MEDICAL INSTRUMENTS	W 329	4062	W 296	3401	W 266	1830	W 248	2045	INSTRUM,APP MEDECINE
874	MEASURNG,CONTROLNG INSTR	W 340	4032	W 507	5041	W 320	3284	W 472	4634	INSTRUMENTS DE MESURE
88	PHOTO EQU,OPTICL GDS ETC		4616		4722		4784		5695	APP,FOURN PHOTO,OP,MONTR
89	MISC MANUFCTRD GOODS NES		27660		40794		38633		56297	ART MANUFACTURES DIVERS
892	PRINTED MATTER	W 1510	4862	W 2004	8398	W 1465	6443	W 2051	8584	IMPRIMES
8921	PRINTED BOOKS,GLOBES,ETC	W 1024	3159	W 947	4397	W 753	3624	W 680	4216	LIVRES,BROCHURES,CARTES
89211	PRINTED BOOKS,PAMPHLETS	W 997	3123	W 923	4277	W 732	3537	W 619	3925	LIVRES,BROCHURES

Honduras

4. Special Imports C.I.F. by Commodities according to the S.I.T.C. (Rev. 2) in thousand U.S. Dollars
Importations Spéciales C.A.F. par Produits d'après la C.T.C.I. (Rév. 2) en milliers de Dollars E.U.

SITC CTCI	COMMODITY	1992		1993		1994		1995		PRODUIT
		WEIGHT POIDS	VALUE VALEUR	WEIGHT POIDS	VALUE VALEUR	WEIGHT POIDS	VALUE VALEUR	WEIGHT POIDS	VALUE VALEUR	
893	ARTICLES OF PLASTIC NES	W 4984	11956		18401		17906		27296	OUVRAGES EN MAT DIVIS 58
8931	PLSTC PACKG CONTNRS,LIDS	W 2762	5741	W 2562	8135	W 3019	8885	W 4404	13826	ART TRANSP EMBALLAGE ETC
8939	MISC PLASTIC ARTICLES	W 1857	5159	W 2463	9857	W 2915	8686	W 12553	12912	ART DIVERS EN MAT DIV 58
89399	OTHR PLASTC ARTICLES NES	W 1013	3965	W 1820	9251	W 2696	8044	W 12002	11532	AUT OUV MAT DIV 58
894	TOYS,SPORTING GOODS,ETC	W 1123	3494	W 1238	4509	W 1810	4975	W 2146	7437	VOITURES ENFANTS,JOUETS
8942	TOYS,INDOOR GAMES ETC	W 871	2596	W 1029	3754	W 1182	3687	W 1656	5902	JOUETS,JEUX ETC
895	OFFICE SUPPLIES NES	W 534	3053	W 710	3632	W 530	3440	W 879	5474	ART PAPET NDA

5. Special Exports F.O.B. by Commodities according to the S.I.T.C. (Rev. 2) in thousand U.S. Dollars
Exportations Spéciales F.O.B. par Produits d'après la C.T.C.I. (Rév. 2) en milliers de Dollars E.U.

SITC CTCI	COMMODITY	1992 WEIGHT POIDS	1992 VALUE VALEUR	1993 WEIGHT POIDS	1993 VALUE VALEUR	1994 WEIGHT POIDS	1994 VALUE VALEUR	1995 WEIGHT POIDS	1995 VALUE VALEUR	PRODUIT
	ALL COMMODITIES # 1		737396		664759		614049		656012	TOUS PRODUITS
0	FOOD AND LIVE ANIMALS		576071		516055		473190		561154	ALIMENTS,ANIMAUX VIVANTS
001	*LIVE ANIMALS FOR FOOD	W 5545	3712	W 54	41	W 45	39	W 67	25	ANIMAUX VIVANTS
0011	BOVINE SPECIES,LIVE	W 5491	3677	W 5	6	W 27	7	W 9	8	ESPECE BOVINE
00119	— OTHR THAN FR BREEDING	W 4280	3040	W 5	6	W 25	5	W 4	2	BOVINS NON REPRODUCTEURS
01	MEAT AND PREPARATIONS		37278		43013		39477		14270	VIANDES ET PREPARATIONS
011	MEAT FRESH,CHILLD,FROZEN	W 16821	37275	W 18870	42898	W 17004	39466	W 6391	14254	VIANDES FRAICHES,REF,CONGE
0111	BOVINE MEAT FRESH,FROZEN	W 16509	37048	W 16886	39607	W 16087	37751	W 5925	13160	VIANDES BOVIN FRAI,REF
01112	BOVINE MEAT BONELESS							W 5925	13160	VIANDES BOVIN DESOSSEES
03	FISH AND PREPARATIONS		42500		55869		74889		37704	POISSONS ET PREPARATIONS
036	SHELL FISH FRESH,FROZEN	W 8054	41335	W 10294	54830	W 11851	73191	W 5741	35807	CRUSTACES,MOLLUSQUES
05	VEGETABLES AND FRUIT		341616		273865		153799		158427	LEGUMES ET FRUITS
054	VEG ETC FRSH,SMPLY PRSVD	W 19868	3981	W 38562	4873		3654	W 23604	4207	LEGUMES FRAIS,CONG,SECS
0545	OTHER FRESH VEGETABLES	W 2508	412	W 11649	1754	W 2876	645	W 10000	2019	AUTRES LEGUMES FRAIS,REF
05459	FRESH VEGETABLES NES			W 11598	1748	W 2517	617	W 9965	2019	LEGUMES FRAIS,REFRI NDA
0546	VEGETABLES SIMPLY PRESVD	W 1004	274	W 12484	2569		2588	W 4784	936	LEGUMES CONG,CONSER
05462	VEG PRSVD UNFRZN UNTINND	W 689	215	W 11325	2371	W 13525	2394	W 4646	822	LEGUMES CONSER PROVISOIR
057	FRUIT,NUTS,FRESH,DRIED	W 1305805	329871	W 1062677	263334	W 640042	145367	W 683366	150205	FRUITS FRAIS OU SECS
0572	LEMONS,GRAPEFRUIT ETC	W 15007	3172	W 18904	3914	W 6752	1708	W 10148	2077	AUTRES AGRUMES FRAIS,SECS
05722	GRAPEFRUITS,FRESH,DRIED							W 9817	2053	PAMPLEMOUSSES,POMELOS
0573	BANANA,PLANTAIN,FRSH,DRY	W 1155444	292828	W 863169	217780	W 475274	112370	W 530893	120935	BANANES FRAICHES,SECHEES
0577	NUTS EDIBLE,FRESH,DRIED	W 66476	20769	W 2370	718	W 1663	397	W 835	353	FRUITS A COQUES
05773	CASHEW NUTS,FRESH,DRIED	W 49945	19868	W 512	210	W 752	200	W 150	95	NOIX DE CAJOU
0579	FRUIT FRESH OR DRIED NES	W 57922	12821	W 157685	40149	W 141981	30448	W 124221	26055	FRUITS FRAIS,SECS NDA
05795	PINEAPPLES,FRESH,DRIED	W 96	34	W 54339	18531	W 42915	9481	W 44228	11750	ANANAS FRAIS OU SECS
05798	OTHER FRESH FRUIT	W 54060	11972	W 102896	21465	W 98470	20855	W 79691	14211	AUTRES FRUITS FRAIS
058	FRUIT PRESERVED,PREPARED	W 14247	7121	W 7966	5039	W 7262	4273	W 6903	3916	CONSERVES DE FRUITS
0583	FRUIT JAMS,JELLIES ETC	W 10168	4670	W 3324	1703	W 2800	1286	W 2632	1057	PATES DE FRUITS CONFITURES
0585	FRUIT OR VEGETABLE JUICE	W 3484	2110	W 4358	3178	W 2825	1840	W 3296	2093	JUS DE FRUITS
06	SUGAR AND PREPS,HONEY		6977		6679		6409		8452	SUCRES ET PRODUITS
061	SUGAR AND HONEY	W 29395	6825	W 29255	5941	W 28431	6051	W 34473	7719	SUCRES ET MIEL
0611	RAW BEET AND CANE SUGAR	W 12829	5371	W 11627	4842	W 8978	3662	W 11529	5143	SUCRES BRUTS
0615	MOLASSES	W 16550	1433	W 17626	1099	W 17989	1745	W 22944	2575	MELASSES
07	COFFEE,TEA,COCOA,SPICES		138911		132361		194852		337548	CAFE,THE,CACAO,EPICES
071	COFFEE AND SUBSTITUTES	W 108353	135801	W 102484	128917	W 102657	192119	W 106557	335641	CAFE ET SUCCEDANES
0711	COFFEE GREEN,ROASTED,SUB	W 108353	135801	W 102484	128917	W 102654	192110	W 106557	335641	CAFE TORREFIE OU DECAFEINE
07111	COFFEE GREEN,HUSKS,SKINS							W 106557	335641	CAFE NON TORREFIE
072	COCOA	W 2542	2070	W 2453	2041	W 1306	1379	W 1127	1271	CACAO
0721	COCOA BEANS,RAW,ROASTED	W 2541	2069	W 2453	2039	W 1306	1379	W 1127	1271	CACAO EN FEVES
09	MISC EDIBLE PRODUCTS		2697		2708		637		1592	PREP ALIMENTAIRES DIVERSES
098	EDIBLE PRODCTS,PREPS NES	W 2680	2677	W 2316	2640	W 555	616	W 1596	1592	PREP ALIMENTAIRES NDA
09804	SAUCES,MIXED SEASONINGS	W 2300	2426	W 2163	2502	W 469	508	W 1325	1356	SAUCES,ASSAISONNEMENTS
1	BEVERAGES AND TOBACCO		12155		17971		9967		3323	BOISSONS ET TABACS
12	TOBACCO AND MANUFACTURES		12124		17819		9753		3142	TABACS BRUTS FABRIQUES
121	TOBACCO UNMNFCTRD,REFUSE	W 3952	12124	W 2858	6347	W 1374	2856	W 590	1180	TABACS BRUTS,DECHETS
1211	TOBACCO,NOT STRIPPED	W 1868	4045	W 2837	6335	W 1341	2846	W 575	1164	TABACS NON ECOTES
1212	TOBACCO STRIPPED OR PART	W 2083	8079	W 12	3	W 11	3	W 9	11	TABACS PART ECOTES
122	TOBACCO,MANUFACTURED			W 2897	11473	W 1998	6897		1962	TABACS FABRIQUES
1221	CIGARS,CHEROOTS,ETC			W 663	3702	W 1711	6350	W 457	1907	CIGARES
1222	CIGARETTES			W 845	2943	W 31	142	W 1	5	CIGARETTES
1223	OTH MANUFACTURED TOBACCO			W 1390	4827	W 256	404		50	TABACS FUMER,CHIQUER,PRISER
2	CRUDE MATERLS,EXCL FUELS		41235		35203		35178		26009	MAT BRUTES NON COMESTIBLES
24	CORK AND WOOD		16455		22691		22451		17709	LIEGE ET BOIS
247	OTH WOOD ROUGH,SQUARED	W 52223	14525	W 53297	13102	W 48845	12543	W 47156	12980	BOIS BRUTS EQUARRIS
2471	SAW–,VENEER–LOGS CONIFER	W 93	16	W 53286	13097	W 48160	12381	W 44977	12127	CONIFERES POUR SCIAGE,PLACAG
24711	— IN THE ROUGH			W 53286	13097	W 48160	12381	W 44977	12127	ECORCES OU DEGROSSIS
2479	PTPROPS,POLES,PILING,ETC	W 52130	14509							POTEAUX DE MINES
248	WOOD SHAPED,SLEEPERS	W 8565	1895	W 29959	9488	W 31181	9648	W 14574	4551	BOIS SIMPLEMENT TRAVAILLES
2482	LUMBER SHAPED CONIFER	W 8532	1881	W 29660	9325	W 28441	8996	W 13681	4311	CONIFERES SCIES,RABOTES
24821	LUMBER SAWN ETC CONIFER	W 7388	1072	W 26151	8629	W 26556	8498	W 13030	4157	CONIFERES SCIES LONGITUD
28	METALLIFEROUS ORES,SCRAP		19063		7101		6363		2283	MINERAIS METAL,DECHETS
287	BASE METAL ORES,CONC NES	W 42611	17332		5961		4596	W 183	48	MINERAIS METAUX COMMUNS
2875	ZINC ORES,CONCENTRATES				5191		4259	W 163	38	MINERAIS DE ZINC
288	NONFERR METAL SCRAP NES			W 422	99	W 793	162	W 6215	2156	DECHETS NON FERREUX
2882	OTHER BASE MTL SCRAP NES			W 422	99	W 793	162	W 6155	2111	AUTRES DECHETS
29	CRUDE ANIMAL,VEG MAT NES		2632		2057		2902		2147	MATIERES BRUTES ANIM,VEGET
292	CRUDE VEG MATERIALS NES	W 3593	2621	W 2555	2042	W 3574	2778	W 2011	2074	MAT BRUTES VEGETALES NDA
3	MINERAL FUELS ETC		3503		70		322		138	COMBUSTIBLES MINERAUX LUB
33	PETROLEUM AND PRODUCTS		3503		70		310		68	PETROLE ET DERIVES
334	PETROLEUM PRODUCTS,REFIN	W 44661	3480		46	W 1031	121	W 203	68	PRODUITS RAFFINES
3341	GASOLINE,OTH LIGHT OILS	W 44661	3480			W 123	15	W 73	18	ESSENCES POUR MOTEURS
33419	OTH LIGHT PETROLEUM OILS	W 44661	3480					W 73	18	AUTRES HUILES LEGERES
4	ANIMAL,VEGETABLE OIL,FAT		5027		8185		6614		3672	HUILES,GRAISSES ANIM,VEG
42	FIXED VEGETABLE OIL,FAT		4770		6652		6190		3287	HUILES VEGETALES FIXES
424	FIXED VEG OIL NONSOFT	W 10647	4770	W 15082	6384	W 9724	4612	W 4271	3143	AUTRES HUILES VEG FIXES
4242	PALM OIL			W 14424	6191	W 8686	4320	W 4075	3080	HUILE DE PALME
4249	FIXED VEGETABLE OILS NES	W 10647	4770	W 119	49					HUILES VEGET FIXES NDA
5	CHEMCLS,RELATED PROD NES		15835		12129		13359		10949	PRODUITS CHIMIQUES
55	PERFUME,CLEANING ETC PRD		8576		3934		3923		4601	PROD POUR PARFUM,TOILETTE
554	SOAP,CLEANSING ETC PREPS	W 11291	7936	W 5777	3641	W 5472	3809	W 6529	4424	SAVONS,PRODUITS DETERSIFS
5541	SOAPS	W 7784	4696	W 4530	2342	W 4400	2647	W 5197	3221	SAVONS,PROD TENSIO–ACTIFS
5542	WASHING PREPARATIONS ETC	W 3441	3022	W 1135	1007	W 948	797	W 1216	922	PROD ORG TENSIO–ACT NDA
562	*FERTILIZERS,MANUFACTURE	W 3	7	W 2184	438	W 14920	2844	W 3791	941	ENGRAIS MANUFACTURES
5623	CHEM POTASSIC FERTILIZER			W 160	21	W 9490	2009	W 2063	502	ENGRAIS POTASSIQUES
56239	CHEM POTASS FERTILZR NES			W 160	21	W 9490	2009	W 2063	502	ENGRAIS POTASSIQUES NDA
59	CHEMICAL MATERIALS NES		4458		4525		4080		1983	MAT PROD CHIMIQUES NDA
598	MISCEL CHEM PRODUCTS NES	W 3848	2673	W 5280	3023	W 4413	2415	W 2329	1448	PROD DIV INDUST CHIM NDA
5981	CHEMCLS FROM WOOD,RESIN	W 3697	2481	W 5232	2969	W 4169	2303	W 2096	1309	PROD CHIM BASE BOIS RESIN
59814	ROSIN,RESIN ACIDS,ETC	W 3333	2190	W 4802	2654	W 3731	2011	W 1925	1187	COLOPHANES RESINIQUES
6	BASIC MANUFACTURES		36256		35775		37847		28895	ART MANUFACTURES
63	WOOD,CORK MANUFACTRS NES		14575		15890		16059		12236	OUVRAGES LIEGE ET BOIS
634	VENEERS,PLYWOOD,ETC	W 10996	3117	W 36828	7031	W 26234	5468	W 17751	4084	PLACAGES,CONTRE–PLAQUES
6349	WOOD SIMPLY SHAPED NES	W 7612	1309	W 33686	5181	W 23618	3906	W 15685	2719	BOIS SIMPL TRAVAILLES NDA
63491	HOOPWOOD,SPLIT POLES ETC	W 7591	1298	W 33686	5181	W 23618	3906	W 15685	2719	BOIS ETC
635	WOOD MANUFACTURES NES	W 43944	11458	W 21431	8859	W 25972	10591	W 18524	8152	ART MANUF EN BOIS NDA
6359	OTHER WOOD MANUFACTURES	W 42184	10333	W 17671	6941	W 23227	8608	W 15350	6017	OUVRAGES EN BOIS NDA
63591	TOOLS,HANDLES ETC WOOD	W 28047	6510	W 12169	4038	W 12734	3769	W 9138	2872	OUTILS MANCHES D'OUTILS
63599	OTHER WOOD ARTICLES NES	W 13857	3663	W 5501	2903	W 10493	4839	W 6212	3145	AUTRES OUVRAGES EN BOIS NDA
64	PAPER,PAPERBOARD AND MFR		1538		3717		9515		6389	PAPIERS,CARTONS & OUVRAGES
642	PAPER,ETC,PRECUT,ARTS OF	W 1742	1312	W 3252	2908	W 14234	8532	W 7976	5351	PAP,CARTONS DECOUPES
6421	PAPER ETC CONTAINERS	W 1239	705	W 2068	1472	W 13478	7776	W 7122	4622	BOITES,SACS EMBALLAGES

5. Special Exports F.O.B. by Commodities according to the S.I.T.C. (Rev. 2) in thousand U.S. Dollars
Exportations Spéciales F.O.B. par Produits d'après la C.T.C.I. (Rév. 2) en milliers de Dollars E.U.

SITC CTCI	COMMODITY	1992 WEIGHT POIDS	1992 VALUE VALEUR	1993 WEIGHT POIDS	1993 VALUE VALEUR	1994 WEIGHT POIDS	1994 VALUE VALEUR	1995 WEIGHT POIDS	1995 VALUE VALEUR	PRODUIT
65	TEXTILE YARN,FABRICS,ETC		8726		5740		4822		3835	FILS,TISSUS,ARTICLES TEXTILE
652	COTTON FABRICS,WOVEN	W 1279	4686	W 213	875	W 247	978	W 140	632	TISSUS DE COTON
6522	WOVEN COTTON BLEACHD,ETC	W 1238	4466	W 148	673	W 60	321	W 58	284	TISSUS COTON BLANCHIS ETC
65224	BLCHED COTTON FABRIC NES	W 1238	4466	W 84	295	W 6	22	W 42	171	AUT TIS PLUS 85% COT BLANCHI
66	NONMETAL MINERAL MFS NES		3673		2252		1669		1914	ART MIN NON METALLIQUES
661	LIME,CEMENT,BLDG PRODS	W 35260	3551	W 4010	1138	W 11406	1078	W 5745	713	CHAUX,CIMENTS MAT CONSTR
67	IRON AND STEEL		1560		1306		1869		983	FER ET ACIER
69	METAL MANUFACTURES NES		3269		5458		3320		2503	ART MANUFACT EN METAL NDA
7	MACHINES,TRANSPORT EQUIP		3216		3574		3165		4565	MACHINES MATERIEL TRANSPORT
77	ELECTRIC MACHNRY NES ETC		1179		2677		1648		1848	MACH APP ELECT NDA
8	MISC MANUFACTURED GOODS		39489		34068		33191		16238	ART MANUFACTURES DIVERS
821	*FURNITURE,PARTS THEREOF	W 2805	8585	W 4547	15127	W 5383	16786	W 2866	9168	MEUBLES ET PIECES
8219	FURNITURE AND PARTS NES	W 2516	7566	W 4154	13896	W 4738	15429	W 2545	8454	AUTRES MEUBLES ET PIECES
82192	WOOD FURNITURE NES							W 1984	6734	MEUBLES NDA EN BOIS
84	CLOTHING AND ACCESSORIES		16041		6791		9542		3916	VETEMENTS
842	MENS OUTERWEAR NOT KNIT	W 1862	4975	W 363	620	W 324	598	W 70	172	VET DESSUS POUR HOMMES
844	UNDER GARMENTS NOT KNIT	W 1502	6970	W 300	996	W 90	506	W 156	476	VETEMENT DESSOUS MAT TEX
8442	— MENS,OTHR THAN SHIRTS	W 1461	5997	W 85	257	W 15	30	W 104	192	SOUS--VET HOMMES MAT TEXT
845	OUTERWEAR KNIT NONELASTC	W 210	1266	W 1323	2542	W 1797	3539	W 263	1105	VET DESSOUS,ACCES BONNET
846	UNDER GARMENTS KNITTED	W 39	618	W 535	1920	W 900	3120	W 326	1434	SOUS VETS DE BONNETERIE
8462	— OF COTTON NON ELASTIC			W 260	738	W 839	2594	W 45	339	SOUS--VET BONNET COTON
89	MISC MANUFCTRD GOODS NES		14236		11432		6232		2648	ART MANUFACTURES DIVERS
892	PRINTED MATTER	W 58	10465	W 55	8649	W 53	3654		76	IMPRIMES
8928	PRINTED MATTER NES	W 40	10362	W 50	8627	W 50	3630		69	IMPRIMES NDA
89283	UNISSUED BANKNOTES ETC	W 1	10153		8544	W 1	3500			TIMBRES--POSTE FISCAUX
893	ARTICLES OF PLASTIC NES	W 1480	2389	W 1165	1953		2139	W 1613	2356	OUVRAGES EN MAT DIVIS 58
8939	MISC PLASTIC ARTICLES	W 1480	2389	W 319	537	W 525	948	W 489	778	ART DIVERS EN MAT DIV 58
89399	OTHR PLASTC ARTICLES NES	W 1480	2389	W 314	520	W 525	948	W 489	778	AUT OUV MAT DIV 58
9	GOODS NOT CLASSD BY KIND		4609		1729		1216		1068	ART TRANSACT NON CLASSES
961	*COIN NONGOLD,NONCURRENT		3650							MONNAIES NON EMISES

FOOT NOTES – NOTES

TABLE 4 –

1 Because of the conversion from SITC Rev.3 to SITC Rev.2, not all data for 1993, 1994 and 1995 are comparable with those for previous years. For further details see the Introduction.

TABLE 5 –

1 Because of the conversion from SITC Rev.3 to SITC Rev.2, not all data for 1993, 1994 and 1995 are comparable with those for previous years. For further details see the Introduction.

TABLEAU 4 –

1 A cause de la conversion de la CTCI Rev.3 à la CTCI Rev.2, toutes les données pour 1993, 1994 et 1995 ne sont pas comparables à celles des années précédentes. Se référer aux explications supplémentaires dans l'introduction.

TABLEAU 5 –

1 A cause de la conversion de la CTCI Rev.3 à la CTCI Rev.2, toutes les données pour 1993, 1994 et 1995 ne sont pas comparables à celles des années précédentes. Se référer aux explications supplémentaires dans l'introduction.

1. HISTORICAL SERIES, 1961–1996 GENERAL TRADE, IMPORTS C.I.F., EXPORTS F.O.B.
SERIES HISTORIQUES, 1961–1996 COMMERCE GENERAL, IMPORTATIONS C.A.F., EXPORTATIONS F.O.B

YEAR ANNEE	VALUE IN MILLION HONGKONG DOLLARS VALEUR EN MILLION HONGKONG DOLLARS MERCHANDISE –MARCHANDISE		GOLD –OR		CONVERSION FACTORS U.S. CENTS PER HONG KONG DOLLAR FACTEURS DE CONVERSION CENTS E.U. PAR HONG KONG DOLLAR		INDEX NUMBERS –INDICES QUANTUM		UNIT VALUE VALEUR UNITAIRE	
	IMPORTS	EXPORTS	IMPORTS	EXPORTS	IMPORTS	EXPORTS	IMPORTS	EXPORTS	IMPORTS	EXPORTS
1961	5970.00	3930.00	206.50	219.90	17.5000	17.5000				
1962	6657.00	4387.00	227.80	205.50	17.5000	17.5000				
1963	7412.00	4991.00	245.10	244.60	17.5000	17.5000				
1964	8551.00	5784.00	156.10	156.80	17.5000	17.5000				
1965	8965.00	6530.00	308.90	298.80	17.5000	17.5000				
1966	10097.00	7563.00	285.10	293.00	17.5000	17.5000				
1967	10449.00	8781.00	385.70	358.10	17.3600	17.3600				
1968	12472.00	10570.00	254.70	164.40	16.5000	16.5000	33	30	65	64
1969	14893.00	13197.00	448.40	183.70	16.5000	16.5000	38	35	69	68
1970	17607.00	15238.00	306.70	192.40	16.5000	16.5000	11	12	25	25
1971	20256.00	17164.00	373.20	249.00	16.7406	16.7497	12	12	26	27
1972	21764.00	19400.00	207.20	175.00	17.7797	17.7739	13	13	27	28
1973	29005.00	25999.00	428.10	205.00	19.4929	19.5030	14	14	32	33
1974	34120.00	30036.00	389.10	240.00	19.8345	19.8399	13	14	41	40
1975	33472.00	29832.00			20.1870	20.1755	13	15	39	39
1976	43292.00	41557.00			20.5157	20.5169	17	18	41	43
1977	48701.00	44833.00			21.4726	21.4712	18	19	43	44
1978	63056.00	53908.00			21.3328	21.3305	22	21	46	46
1979	85837.00	75934.00			19.9650	19.9585	25	25	54	53
1980	111651.00	98242.00			20.0746	20.0733	30	26	58	59
1981	138374.80	122162.70			17.8357	17.7939	33	30	65	64
1982	142892.60	127384.70			16.4839	16.4734	33	29	68	68
1983	175442.40	160699.40			13.6848	13.6594	36	34	76	75
1984	223370.20	221440.80			12.7909	12.7908	41	41	85	85
1985	231419.70	235152.30			12.8351	12.8355	44	43	83	85
1986	275966.80	276527.80			12.8157	12.8158	49	50	87	87
1987	377933.00	378020.40			12.8237	12.8237	65	66	90	90
1988	498774.40	493054.20			12.8106	12.8106	82	84	94	93
1989	562793.10	570512.40			12.8209	12.8201	90	92	98	98
1990	642354.10	639873.90			12.8393	12.8400	100	100	100	100
1991	778979.20	765882.60			12.8700	12.8710	119	117	102	103
1992	955297.90	924954.20			12.9206	12.9208	145	140	102	104
1993	1072603.00	1046242.00			12.9272	12.9271	164	160	102	103
1994	1250299.00	1170055.00			12.9391	12.9392	187	176	104	105
1995	1491271.00	1344150.00			12.9268	12.9267	213	197	109	108
1996	1535728.00	1397941.00			12.9294	12.9294	222	207	108	108

2. IMPORTS BY BROAD ECONOMIC CATEGORY AND EXPORTS BY INDUSTRIAL ORIGIN. (PERCENTAGE OF TOTAL VALUE)
IMPORTATIONS PAR CATEGORIES ECONOMIQUES ET EXPORTATIONS PAR BRANCHE D'ACTIVITE.(EN POURCENTAGE DE LA VALEUR TOTALE)

IMPORTS – IMPORTATIONS

	1990	1991	1992	1993	1994	1995	1996
TOTAL IMPORTS–IMPORTATIONS TOTALES	100.	100.	100.	100.	100.	100.	100.
1 FOOD BEV–ALIMENTATION BOISSONS	6.2	5.8	5.2	4.6	4.8	4.6	4.7
11 PRIMARY–PRODUITS DE BASE	3.5	3.2	2.9	2.6	2.6	2.5	2.5
111 FOR INDUSTRY–POUR L'INDUSTRIE	0.6	0.5	0.5	0.4	0.3	0.3	0.2
112 FOR HOUSEHOLDS–POUR LES MENAGES	2.9	2.7	2.4	2.2	2.2	2.2	2.3
12 PROCESSED–PRODUITS ELABORES	2.7	2.6	2.3	2.1	2.2	2.2	2.2
121 FOR INDUSTRY–POUR L'INDUSTRIE	0.3	0.2	0.2	0.2	0.3	0.3	0.4
122 FOR HOUSEHOLDS–POUR LES MENAGES	2.5	2.4	2.1	1.9	1.9	1.8	1.9
2 IND SUPPLIES–APPROV INDUSTRIELS	36.4	35.3	32.5	30.2	31.1	31.5	30.2
21 PRIMARY–PRODUITS DE BASE	4.5	3.9	3.6	3.3	3.4	3.4	3.1
22 PROCESSED–PRODUITS ELABORES	31.9	31.4	28.9	26.9	27.6	28.1	27.1
3 FUELS–COMBUSTIBLES	2.4	2.1	2.0	1.8	1.9	1.9	2.2
31 PRIMARY–PRODUITS DE BASE	0.5	0.4	0.4	0.3	0.2	0.2	0.2
32 PROCESSED–PRODUITS ELABORES	1.9	1.6	1.6	1.5	1.7	1.7	2.0
321 MOTOR SPIRIT–ESSENCE	0.1	0.1	0.1	0.1	0.1	0.1	0.1
322 OTHER–AUTRES	1.8	1.6	1.5	1.3	1.6	1.6	1.9
4 MACHINERY–EQUIPEMENT	18.3	19.0	20.7	22.4	22.8	25.4	26.5
41 CAPITAL EQUIPMENT–MACHINES	11.8	12.2	13.8	14.9	14.7	15.8	17.0
42 PARTS–PIECES ACCESSOIRES	6.5	6.7	6.9	7.5	8.1	9.6	9.5
5 TRANSPORT–TRANSPORT	3.1	3.5	4.9	6.2	5.3	5.1	4.6
51 PASSENGER CARS–AUTOMOBILES	0.6	0.8	1.7	2.7	1.9	1.4	1.1
52 OTHER–AUTRES	1.3	1.5	1.7	2.0	1.9	2.1	1.7
521 INDUSTRIAL–INDUSTRIELS	1.1	1.0	1.1	1.2	1.1	1.4	1.2
522 NON INDUSTRIAL–NON INDUSTRIEL	0.3	0.4	0.6	0.8	0.8	0.7	0.5
53 PARTS–PIECES ACCESSOIRES	1.2	1.3	1.5	1.5	1.6	1.6	1.8
6 CONSUM GOODS–BIENS CONSOMMATION	33.2	33.9	34.3	34.4	33.7	31.0	31.2
61 DURABLE–DURABLES	10.1	9.7	9.9	9.6	10.0	9.3	8.9
62 SEMI DURABLE–SEMI DURABLES	19.9	20.9	21.1	21.8	20.7	18.9	19.5
63 NON DURABLE–NON DURABLES	3.2	3.3	3.3	3.0	2.9	2.8	2.9
7 GOODS NES–BIENS NDA	0.5	0.4	0.5	0.4	0.4	0.4	0.5

EXPORTS – EXPORTATIONS

	1990	1991	1992	1993	1994	1995	1996
TOTAL EXPORTS–EXPORTATIONS TOTALES	100.	100.	100.	100.	100.	100.	100.
1 AGRICULTURE	1.9	1.7	1.5	1.2	1.3	1.1	1.1
2 MINING QUARRY–INDUS EXTRACTIVES	1.5	1.2	0.9	0.9	0.9	0.9	0.8
3 MANUFACTURING–IND MANUFACTUR	96.5	97.1	97.6	97.9	97.9	98.0	98.1
31 FOOD BEV TOBACCO–ALIM BOISS TAB	3.2	3.2	2.9	2.6	2.7	2.5	2.6
32 TEXTILES–INDUSTRIES TEXTILES	33.8	34.0	31.8	30.2	28.9	26.6	26.6
33 WOOD & PRODUCTS–BOIS & PRODUITS	0.5	0.4	0.4	0.4	0.5	0.5	0.5
34 PAPER & PRODUCTS–PAPIER & PRODT	1.7	1.7	1.7	1.6	1.6	1.7	1.8
35 CHEMICALS–INDUSTRIES CHIMIQUES	8.9	9.9	10.2	10.0	10.7	11.7	11.6
36 NON METAL MIN–MIN NON METAL	0.7	0.7	0.9	1.0	1.0	1.0	0.9
37 BASIC METAL–IND METAL BASE	1.4	1.6	2.0	2.1	2.0	2.5	2.7
38 METAL MANUF–MANUF METAL	35.3	34.8	36.2	39.4	39.9	41.3	41.2
39 OTH MANUF IND–AUTRES MANUF	11.1	10.8	11.5	10.7	10.5	10.2	10.2

3. TRADE BY PRINCIPAL COUNTRIES OF FIRST AND LAST CONSIGNMENT (VALUE IN THOUSAND U.S. DOLLARS)
ECHANGES SELON LES PRINCIPAUX PAYS DE PREMIERE ET DE DERNIERE CONSIGNATION (VALEUR EN MILLIERS DE DOLLARS EU)

COUNTRIES–PAYS	GENERAL IMPORTS C.I.F. IMPORTATIONS GENERALES C.A.F				
	1992	1993	1994	1995	1996
World	127340143	141307580	165877554	196071781	201285554
Africa	1133754	1327002	1462394	1552921	1173420
Americas	11511925	12201039	14597554	18102387	18356908
Northern America	10646535	11335814	13669946	16880693	16990984
LAIA	839081	843411	897432	1182787	1314948
CACM	3648	4596	7575	11409	14383
Caribbean	5682	4315	11176	6773	5365
Rest of America	16978	12904	11425	20725	31227
As.ex F.USSR	97066895	108667544	127267940	149541177	153388992
Eur.x F.USSR	15652384	16910722	20092571	23915651	24937317
EU	12946801	14500061	17146459	20935996	22472633
EFTA	2586671	2210487	2750390	2836685	2244546
East Europe	102027	184122	186027	132390	189789
Other Europe	6052	6886	5220	5180	20387
Former USSR	77195	109844	327933	507654	680477
Oceania	1872109	2073961	2111247	2434363	2731203
China/Chine	45797915	52003569	60937325	69742573	73776020
Japan/Japon	21485936	23031831	25289017	28718475	26982508
USA/Etats–Unis d'Amer	9799159	10636180	12519389	15428564	15785669
Korea, Republic of	5783840	6341433	7655177	10147438	10844338
Singapore/Singapour	5054002	6189748	8026836	10101696	10574219
United Kingdom	3012652	3026472	3736746	4133876	4699646
Germany/Allemagne	2837977	3248537	3719858	4147081	4391654
Italy/Italie	1915513	2311345	2947206	3572571	4117945
Malaysia/Malaisie	1657036	2049603	2606744	3724393	4398935
France,Monac	1439050	1913712	1991646	3739779	3320149
Switz.Liecht	2534599	2137734	2676445	2702676	2124328
Thailand/Thaïlande	1525994	1682457	2225002	2728855	3070629
Australia/Australie	1593634	1754329	1711303	1931678	2185922
Netherlands/Pays–Bas	1254870	1344943	1535988	1811638	1863537
India/Inde	753478	1221654	1463813	1876922	1968227
Belgium–Luxembourg	1328446	1273610	1480243	1354165	1248849
Indonesia/Indonésie	879973	943281	1288880	1633434	1631080
So. Africa Customs Un	1053744	1242847	1333430	1398897	1001471
Canada	847277	699257	1150088	1450860	1204206
Philippines	704850	583662	609087	863179	951737
Israel/Israël	617349	642104	718251	777506	772443
Pakistan	547587	360062	574414	626519	828772
Sweden/Suède	281350	339196	388063	484355	793348
Brazil/Brésil	407397	398831	443770	420363	509464
Spain/Espagne	268290	343713	424738	478866	602236
United Arab Emirates	176215	396489	562332	404936	270327
New Zealand	245355	276622	348789	431676	481649
Finland/Finlande	150180	167878	298010	470726	608925
Russian Federation	77195	91386	281659	460783	652273
Denmark/Danemark	199607	223487	274801	299627	386859
Saudi Arabia	133651	117640	227715	364020	250251
Austria/Autriche	184181	183809	212073	263039	239261
Macau/Macao	239390	231778	216665	204687	183014
Argentina/Argentine	98939	139238	186913	295755	251096
Viet Nam	148614	138844	147950	173624	196370
Turkey/Turquie	25125	114123	223524	237729	202801
Mexico/Mexique	95336	90154	95952	216620	224153
Oman	78243	114464	213528	77399	92581
Chile/Chili	107113	99273	68027	106871	157982
Norway,SVD,JM	51697	70375	72359	130996	116733
Ireland/Irlande	38533	52371	72965	88159	98713
Bangladesh	36192	53816	70539	99685	90164
Poland/Pologne	55637	86462	77007	50153	79933
Bahrain/Bahreïn	18715	63235	69042	77043	116227
Myanmar	49065	61632	55002	64201	64715
Czech Republic		65317	74234	55837	87532
Uruguay	47985	48236	39288	55241	81450
Korea Dem People's Rp	58456	69671	36286	35146	51048
Greece/Grèce	17295	45681	28166	41559	53681
Peru/Pérou	42779	29976	30708	33422	46439

COUNTRIES–PAYS	GENERAL EXPORTS F.O.B. EXPORTATIONS GENERALES F.O.B.				
	1992	1993	1994	1995	1996
Monde	119586447	135384625	151465165	173870820	180915781
Afrique	2236737	2040472	1982518	2454779	2322469
Amériques	32672942	36940427	41836316	45431089	45523076
Amérique du Nord	29688383	33431466	37574941	40504734	40879402
ALAI	1618620	2048090	2651758	3357815	3211831
MCAC	118702	141046	153322	144970	142383
Caraïbes	187949	192024	182746	196127	189652
Autre Amérique	1059288	1127801	1273548	1227445	1099809
Asie l'URSS exclus	60263101	70185277	79764896	94434528	100279347
Europe l'URSS exclus	21959182	23557795	24812900	28092179	29125147
UE	20403202	21853298	23035463	26083301	26967314
AELE	1249288	1313855	1359346	1458118	1486825
Europe de l'Est	259219	341977	376025	502283	593036
Autre de l'Europe	27145	25986	22092	26034	29508
Ancienne URSS	245018	333425	329216	352000	536420
Océanie	2095428	2223274	2646182	2983245	3053015
China/Chine	35426909	43694178	49674036	57870274	61999439
USA/Etats–Unis d'Amer	27580974	31160456	35177058	37851769	38368268
Japan/Japon	6261725	6959529	8437344	10594915	11838575
Germany/Allemagne	6339339	7083140	7054033	7500292	7587558
United Kingdom	4282156	4592962	4870673	5588835	6029624
Singapore/Singapour	3130933	3683098	4215754	4945323	4965952
Korea, Republic of	1953241	2298167	2418587	2821100	2980346
Netherlands/Pays–Bas	1894080	2132728	2370016	2825061	2965408
Canada	2082732	2248082	2377097	2633597	2491739
France,Monac	1835072	2012904	2133156	2666539	2814802
Australia/Australie	1660801	1779860	2127386	2375686	2438357
Philippines	1109869	1339123	1870667	2009304	2150212
Italy/Italie	1676379	1478976	1601632	1805102	1772023
Macau/Macao	1291201	1411704	1560357	1684425	1842510
Thailand/Thaïlande	1059791	1021280	1292678	1624200	1810774
Malaysia/Malaisie	832488	901290	1155595	1572228	1703273
Panama	1047240	1118488	1266672	1220079	1091650
Spain/Espagne	944637	995670	1121406	1330644	1305703
Belgium–Luxembourg	941558	1047911	1051242	1126991	1157129
United Arab Emirates	704903	884411	971443	1196291	1278887
Switz.Liecht	925032	975946	979449	1037375	1057460
Indonesia/Indonésie	734391	844797	920621	1061922	1006220
Sweden/Suède	715512	716914	824292	731894	816955
Austria/Autriche	590124	656127	745056	828792	779292
So. Africa Customs Un	569378	633854	696982	855469	797035
Brazil/Brésil	93976	306036	548611	1204066	1146735
Viet Nam	940277	510064	523737	636930	601413
India/Inde	329691	385105	522274	802533	769078
Saudi Arabia	516410	541827	511422	520377	528654
Denmark/Danemark	492240	412491	477194	572848	643561
Mexico/Mexique	586594	512761	559718	391929	351371
Chile/Chili	246871	316368	453329	616603	603813
Bangladesh	307574	358921	433519	500344	448346
Argentina/Argentine	312897	420497	502217	360946	433125
Norway,SVD,JM	315755	332016	373361	413812	422285
Israel/Israël	256122	333539	374777	426879	423726
Russian Federation	245018	315592	303358	315483	493741
Sri Lanka	279556	337242	317697	363541	352624
Turkey/Turquie	224279	318947	199203	408634	485896
Finland/Finlande	206143	203216	292513	344836	402801
New Zealand	218277	241963	282015	328061	318504
Egypt/Egypte	220000	229962	272913	331286	326816
Paraguay	122122	177516	308573	420185	308071
Nigeria/Nigéria	397728	291580	177301	238105	220214
Greece/Grèce	214580	232772	219417	286519	288664
Poland/Pologne	138062	171394	171272	242812	309657
Portugal	156244	177481	147117	226339	177167
Ireland/Irlande	115139	110005	127717	248607	226629
American Samoa	119399	114120	151915	197251	214042
Venezuela	165335	177463	88135	116631	94524

(VALUE AS PERCENTAGE OF WORLD TOTAL)(VALEURS EN POURCENTAGE DU TOTAL MONDIAL)

	1987	1988	1989	1990	1991	1992	1993	1994	1995	1996
Africa	0.8	0.8	0.8	0.6	0.8	0.9	0.9	0.9	0.8	0.6
Americas	9.8	10.1	9.8	9.8	9.8	9.0	8.6	8.8	9.2	9.1
Northern America	9.1	9.0	8.8	9.1	9.0	8.4	8.0	8.2	8.6	8.4
LAIA	0.8	1.0	1.0	0.7	0.7	0.7	0.6	0.5	0.6	0.7
CACM	0.0	0.0	0.0	0.0	0.0	0.0	0.0	0.0	0.0	0.0
Caribbean	0.0	0.0	0.0	0.0	0.0	0.0	0.0	0.0	0.0	0.0
Rest of America	0.0	0.0	0.0	0.0	0.0	0.0	0.0	0.0	0.0	0.0
As.ex F.USSR	73.5	74.5	75.4	74.6	75.8	76.2	76.9	76.7	76.3	76.2
Eur.x F.USSR	14.0	12.9	12.6	13.4	12.1	12.3	12.0	12.1	12.2	12.4
EU	11.8	11.0	10.6	10.5	9.7	10.2	10.3	10.3	10.7	11.2
EFTA	2.0	1.6	1.8	2.9	2.3	2.0	1.6	1.7	1.4	1.1
East Europe	0.2	0.2	0.1	0.1	0.1	0.1	0.1	0.1	0.1	0.1
Other Europe	0.0	0.1	0.0	0.0	0.0	0.0	0.0	0.0	0.0	0.0
Former USSR	0.2	0.2	0.1	0.1	0.1	0.1	0.1	0.2	0.3	0.3
Oceania	1.5	1.4	1.2	1.3	1.6	1.5	1.5	1.3	1.2	1.4
China/Chine	31.0	31.1	35.0	35.8	36.4	36.0	36.8	36.7	35.6	36.7
Japan/Japon	19.0	18.8	16.4	15.7	15.8	16.9	16.3	15.2	14.6	13.4
USA/Etats–Unis d'Amer	8.5	8.5	8.3	8.4	8.3	7.7	7.5	7.5	7.9	7.8
Korea, Republic of	4.5	5.3	4.5	4.3	4.5	4.5	4.5	4.6	5.2	5.4
Singapore/Singapour	3.8	3.7	4.0	4.0	3.9	4.0	4.4	4.8	5.2	5.3
United Kingdom	3.1	2.6	2.3	2.5	2.3	2.4	2.1	2.3	2.1	2.3
Germany/Allemagne	2.7	2.6	2.4	2.3	2.1	2.2	2.3	2.2	2.1	2.2
Italy/Italie	1.6	1.6	1.8	1.6	1.5	1.5	1.6	1.8	1.8	2.0
Malaysia/Malaisie	1.0	1.2	1.2	1.2	1.2	1.3	1.5	1.6	1.9	2.2
France,Monac	1.4	1.4	1.4	1.3	1.1	1.1	1.4	1.2	1.9	1.6

	1987	1988	1989	1990	1991	1992	1993	1994	1995	1996
Afrique	1.8	1.7	1.5	1.7	1.7	1.9	1.5	1.3	1.4	1.3
Amériques	31.4	27.9	29.0	27.8	26.8	27.3	27.3	27.6	26.1	25.2
Amérique du Nord	30.0	26.7	27.4	25.9	24.5	24.8	24.7	24.8	23.3	22.6
ALAI	0.5	0.4	0.6	0.9	1.2	1.4	1.5	1.8	1.9	1.8
MCAC	0.1	0.1	0.1	0.1	0.1	0.1	0.1	0.1	0.1	0.1
Caraïbes	0.3	0.2	0.2	0.2	0.2	0.2	0.1	0.1	0.1	0.1
Autre Amérique	0.6	0.5	0.7	0.7	0.9	0.9	0.8	0.8	0.7	0.6
Asie l'URSS exclus	45.1	49.2	48.7	48.1	48.9	50.4	51.8	52.7	54.3	55.4
Europe l'URSS exclus	19.1	18.6	18.3	20.3	20.5	18.4	17.4	16.4	16.2	16.1
UE	17.4	17.1	16.8	18.7	19.0	17.1	16.1	15.2	15.0	14.9
AELE	1.4	1.2	1.2	1.2	1.2	1.0	1.0	0.9	0.8	0.8
Europe de l'Est	0.2	0.2	0.3	0.2	0.3	0.2	0.3	0.2	0.3	0.3
Autre de l'Europe	0.1	0.1	0.1	0.2	0.1	0.0	0.0	0.0	0.0	0.0
Ancienne URSS	0.1	0.1	0.1	0.1	0.2	0.2	0.2	0.2	0.2	0.3
Océanie	2.3	2.3	2.2	1.9	1.8	1.8	1.6	1.7	1.7	1.7
China/Chine	23.3	26.9	25.7	24.7	27.1	29.6	32.3	32.8	33.3	34.3
USA/Etats–Unis d'Amer	27.9	24.8	25.3	24.1	22.7	23.1	23.0	23.2	21.8	21.2
Japan/Japon	5.1	5.9	6.2	5.7	5.4	5.2	5.1	5.6	6.1	6.5
Germany/Allemagne	5.4	5.0	5.0	6.5	6.7	5.3	5.2	4.7	4.3	4.2
United Kingdom	4.6	4.5	4.1	4.0	3.7	3.6	3.4	3.2	3.2	3.3
Singapore/Singapour	2.7	2.8	3.0	3.2	2.7	2.6	2.7	2.8	2.8	2.7
Korea, Republic of	2.6	2.6	2.6	2.3	2.2	1.6	1.7	1.6	1.6	1.6
Netherlands/Pays–Bas	1.5	1.7	1.5	1.7	1.6	1.6	1.6	1.6	1.6	1.6
Canada	2.2	2.0	2.1	1.9	1.8	1.7	1.7	1.6	1.5	1.4
France,Monac	1.5	1.5	1.4	1.6	1.7	1.5	1.5	1.4	1.5	1.6

4. General Imports C.I.F. by Commodities according to the S.I.T.C. (Rev. 2) in thousand U.S. Dollars
Importations Générales C.A.F. par Produits d'après la C.T.C.I. (Rév. 2) en milliers de Dollars E.U.

SITC CTCI	COMMODITY	1993 WEIGHT POIDS	1993 VALUE VALEUR	1994 WEIGHT POIDS	1994 VALUE VALEUR	1995 WEIGHT POIDS	1995 VALUE VALEUR	1996 WEIGHT POIDS	1996 VALUE VALEUR	PRODUIT
	ALL COMMODITIES		141307580		165877554		196071781		201285554	TOUS PRODUITS
0	FOOD AND LIVE ANIMALS		5575519		6552093		7497101		7986702	ALIMENTS,ANIMAUX VIVANTS
01	MEAT AND PREPARATIONS		736180		1003693		1380747		1507377	VIANDES ET PREPARATIONS
011	MEAT FRESH,CHILLD,FROZEN	W 468724	601557	W 669084	840690	W 931530	1194208	W 1039598	1285896	VIANDES FRAICHES,REF,CONGE
0114	POULTRY FRESH CHLLD,FRZN	W 356864	341311	W 490146	500741	W 688381	746496	W 789243	832307	VOLAILLES MORTES
03	FISH AND PREPARATIONS		1369912		1637981		1821141		1914462	POISSONS ET PREPARATIONS
036	SHELL FISH FRESH,FROZEN	W 106965	641371	W 110148	799313	W 111330	884679	W 104051	869318	CRUSTACES,MOLLUSQUES
05	VEGETABLES AND FRUIT		1416340		1531264		1621732		1649977	LEGUMES ET FRUITS
057	FRUIT,NUTS,FRESH,DRIED	W 739714	745210	W 787349	812214	W 831496	916454	W 879541	999488	FRUITS FRAIS OU SECS
09	MISC EDIBLE PRODUCTS		405099		484201		588408		688124	PREP ALIMENTAIRES DIVERSES
098	EDIBLE PRODCTS,PREPS NES	W 160495	383956	W 184213	456644	W 202839	530129	W 218853	633678	PREP ALIMENTAIRES NDA
1	BEVERAGES AND TOBACCO		2340929		2481364		2455419		2436380	BOISSONS ET TABACS
11	BEVERAGES		810599		952383		1053340		996381	BOISSONS
112	ALCOHOLIC BEVERAGES	W 142388	564839	W 212923	648864	W 269850	710818	W 248399	632752	BOISSONS ALCOOLIQUES
1124	DISTILLED ALCOHOLIC BEVS	W 26410	431635	W 28407	462318	W 28624	474403	W 23714	356388	ALCOOLS,EAUX–DE–VIE
12	TOBACCO AND MANUFACTURES		1530330		1528981		1402080		1439998	TABACS BRUTS FABRIQUES
122	TOBACCO,MANUFACTURED	W 60322	1428414	W 65501	1432632	W 60116	1295338		1344462	TABACS FABRIQUES
1222	CIGARETTES	W 59900	1423077	W 64702	1424999	W 59015	1285307		1332537	CIGARETTES
2	CRUDE MATERLS,EXCL FUELS		2362643		3034363		4101354		3986742	MAT BRUTES NON COMESTIBLES
21	HIDES,SKINS,FURS UNDRSSD		294894		437034		529256		615767	CUIRS,PEAUX BRUTS
26	TEXTILE FIBRES AND WASTE		646894		1007101		1256778		1112170	FIBRES TEXTILES
28	METALLIFEROUS ORES,SCRAP		236309		241776		705585		646034	MINERAIS METAL,DECHETS
288	NONFERR METAL SCRAP NES	W 252120	139206	W 304279	166580	W 634801	607687	W 542877	545254	DECHETS NON FERREUX
2882	OTHER BASE MTL SCRAP NES	W 202988	136892	W 258463	162970	W 576919	600130	W 511850	539695	AUTRES DECHETS
29	CRUDE ANIMAL,VEG MAT NES		569887		566601		588458		559739	MATIERES BRUTES ANIM,VEGET
292	CRUDE VEG MATERIALS NES		440971		437964		459872		434483	MAT BRUTES VEGETALES NDA
3	MINERAL FUELS ETC		2529170		3166464		3720246		4497736	COMBUSTIBLES MINERAUX LUB
32	COAL,COKE AND BRIQUETTES		432775		304619		339855		254758	HOUILLES,COKES,BRIQUETTES
322	COAL,LIGNITE AND PEAT	MW 11830	432110	W 8450951	304161	MW 9109	339653	W 6769969	254417	HOUILLES,LIGNITES,TOURBE
3222	OTH COAL,NOT AGGLOMERATD	MW 11827	431595	W 8449060	303728	MW 9107	339342	W 6767758	253873	AUTRES HOUILLES
33	PETROLEUM AND PRODUCTS		2052489		2371155		2877814		3569975	PETROLE ET DERIVES
334	PETROLEUM PRODUCTS,REFIN	MW 11765	2017858	MW 14012	2343060	MW 16516	2841581		3531892	PRODUITS RAFFINES
3342	KEROSENE,OTH MEDIUM OILS	W 2266162	466089	W 2827154	526663	W 2815298	525858	W 3018046	687860	PETR LAMPANTS,AUT HUIL
33421	KEROSENE INCL JET FUEL	W 2259136	464113	W 2804088	520875	W 2808657	523820	W 3016360	687230	PETROLES LAMPANTS
3343	GAS OILS	W 4989771	945430	W 6425876	1082264	W 8631872	1474238	W 9091896	1906190	GAS OILS
5	CHEMCLS,RELATED PROD NES		8535255		10767490		14308693		13477631	PRODUITS CHIMIQUES
51	ORGANIC CHEMICALS		867840		1265991		1908170		1741422	PROD CHIMIQ ORGANIQUES
52	INORGANIC CHEMICALS		476754		567144		625234		580166	PROD CHIM INORGANIQUES
53	DYES,TANNING,COLOUR PROD		984895		1062336		1127545		1237051	PROD TEINTURE,COLORANTS
531	SYNT DYE,NAT INDGO,LAKES	W 56963	519301	W 56287	498372	W 61714	478514	W 64193	503963	MAT COLOR ORGAN,LAQUES
5311	SYNTHIC ORGNIC DYESTUFFS	W 55999	501821	W 55345	479517	W 59491	452198	W 62493	480536	MAT COLOR ORGAN SYNTHET
533	PIGMENTS,PAINTS,ETC		417511		512634		590577		663866	PIGMENTS,PEINTURES,VERNIS
541	*MEDICINAL,PHARM PRODUCT		862358		1021727		1178042		1216409	PROD MEDICINAUX PHARMACEUT
5417	MEDICAMENTS		442325		521776		621501		680772	MEDICAMENTS
55	PERFUME,CLEANING ETC PRD		731511		904761		1103954		1195099	PROD POUR PARFUM,TOILETTE
553	PERFUMERY,COSMETICS,ETC		415099		538835		652242		711511	PRODUITS DE PARFUMERIE
58	PLASTIC MATERIALS ETC		3689249		4889458		7068985		6287588	MAT PLAST ARTIFICIELLES
582	PROD OF CONDENSATION ETC	W 317382	637880	W 430337	832772	W 584378	1342565	W 611705	1266759	PROD CONDENS,POLYCOND
5823	ALKYDS,OTHER POLYESTERS	W 181902	319696	W 272150	451666	W 395391	827813	W 387980	686907	ALKYDES ET AUT POLYESTERS
58231	— IN PRIMARY FORMS	W 162560	255493	W 249775	368916	W 368641	719964	W 359941	565313	SOUS FORMES PRIMAIRES
583	POLYMERIZATION ETC PRODS	W 3343082	3002330	W 4293074	4007735	W 5256560	5664870	W 5211697	4960592	PROD POLYMERISATION
5831	POLYETHYLENE	W 629877	390346	W 904952	547192	W 1144790	877705	W 1146092	809480	POLYETHYLENE
58311	— IN PRIMARY FORMS	W 397352	270749	W 591407	397931	W 797390	705046	W 824307	652582	POLYETHYLENE PRIMAIRES
5832	POLYPROPYLENE	W 306989	246052	W 424742	383279	W 609100	672303	W 595326	601716	POLYPROPYLENE
5833	POLYSTYRENE,ITS COPOLYMR	W 1220397	1003814	W 1521017	1412065	W 1728335	2054491	W 1752935	1591468	POLYPROPYLENE COPOLYMERES
58331	— IN PRIMARY FORMS	W 1034836	926884	W 1284467	1299225	W 1487043	1908527	W 1530370	1488705	SOUS FORMES PRIMAIRES
5834	POLYVINYL CHLORIDE	W 645470	755269	W 734987	899989	W 829517	1073759	W 886762	1023626	CHLORURE DE POLYVINYLE
58343	— PLATES,STRIP,ETC NES	W 261842	500674	W 299794	573795	W 305014	630873	W 313086	604733	SOUS FORME DE PLAQUES
5839	OTH POLYMRZTION ETC PROD	W 481441	509536	W 633710	646030	W 874156	848281	W 756482	796047	AUT PROD POLYMER COPOLYM
59	CHEMICAL MATERIALS NES		811846		958002		1220576		1165893	MAT PROD CHIMIQUES NDA
598	MISCEL CHEM PRODUCTS NES		578320		699183		845052		805292	PROD DIV INDUST CHIM NDA
5989	CHEM PRODUCTS,PREPS NES		449892		576504		707344		694216	PROD PREP CHIMIQUES NDA
6	BASIC MANUFACTURES		29033475		34068487		40059372		40536919	ART MANUFACTURES
61	LEATHER,DRESSED FUR,ETC		2037114		2309586		2773720		3049776	CUIRS,PELLETERIES
611	LEATHER		1483097		1786272		2245754		2373505	CUIRS,PEAUX PREPARES
6114	LEATHR BOVINE NES,EQUINE		898145		914364	A 72408	1371825		1525445	CUIRS DE BOVINS
612	LEATHER ETC MANUFACTURES		426548		384313		393412		490284	OUVRAGES EN CUIRS NDA
63	WOOD,CORK MANUFACTRS NES		624423		806511		896274		904966	OUVRAGES LIEGE ET BOIS
634	VENEERS,PLYWOOD,ETC		406875		538950		580908		563263	PLACAGES,CONTRE–PLAQUES
64	PAPER,PAPERBOARD AND MFR		2134225		2613199		3313797		3325471	PAPIERS,CARTONS & OUVRAGES
641	PAPER AND PAPERBOARD		1592576		1997447		2533810		2485674	PAPIERS ET CARTONS
6418	COATED ETC PAPER NES BLK	W 540134	442646	W 737644	584755	W 799406	739209	W 901952	705314	PAP,CARTONS COUCHES,ENDUITS
64189	COATED PAPER ETC NES	W 490716	374804	W 676559	503473	W 759639	668853	W 853142	629965	PAPIERS,CARTONS COUCHES
642	PAPER,ETC,PRECUT,ARTS OF		541649		615752		779987		839797	PAP,CARTONS DECOUPES
65	TEXTILE YARN,FABRICS,ETC		12876591		15349794		16953574		16597079	FILS,TISSUS,ARTICLES TEXTILE
651	TEXTILE YARN	W 759561	2454748	W 913149	3124760	W 1025891	3835632	W 1103864	3870028	FILS TEXTILES
6512	WOOL,HAIR YARN,INCL TOPS	W 57341	529681	W 55239	558928	W 53640	583305	W 57933	578925	FILS DE LAINE,DE POILS
6513	COTTON YARN	W 228902	578038	W 292868	891491	W 310770	1088261	W 392477	1340350	FILS DE COTON
6514	SYN FIB YRN,BULK,MONOFIL	W 296880	687567	W 384175	870146	W 495394	1337860	W 489170	1164513	FILS CONT 85% FIB TEXT SYNTH
65144	— TEXTRD,CONT POLYESTER	W 196905	321731	W 232222	426190	W 311581	730750	W 345774	663056	FILS TEX FI CONT POLYESTERS
652	COTTON FABRICS,WOVEN	A 2500995	1934569	A 2431199	2272728	A 2395198	2612974	A 2233525	2681066	TISSUS DE COTON
6522	WOVEN COTTON BLEACHD,ETC	A 1751585	1598002	A 1717447	1831620	A 1824235	2199388	A 1645479	2210396	TISSUS COTON BLANCHIS ETC
65224	BLCHED COTTON FABRIC NES	A 1579577	1391154	A 1543566	1590024	A 1625922	1899151	A 1415454	1845735	AUT TIS PLUS 85% COT BLANCHI
653	WOVN MAN–MADE FIB FABRIC	A 4509892	3773857	A 4971345	4429900	A 4965019	4908451	A 4895258	4657862	TISSUS FIBRES SYNTH,ARTIF
6531	CONT SYNT WEAVES NONPILE	A 2533403	2298674	A 3024290	2817722	A 3172170	3157046	A 3279304	3014628	TISSUS FIBRES SYNTH CONTINUE
65315	CONT SYN TXTL FABRIC NES	A 2335817	2096832	A 2814443	2592532	A 2955909	2919906	A 3112573	2814412	TIS PLUS 85% TEXT SYNT CONT
6534	DISC SYN BLEND FABRC NES	A 1069157	605394	A 985155	632058	A 946653	680239	A 897843	639625	TISSUS FIBRES SYNTH DISCONT
65341	DISC SYN FIB–COTTN FABRC	A 902236	437784	A 790593	449101	A 741222	460428	A 695810	423154	TISSUS FIB SYNT DIS MEL COTO
654	OTH WOVEN TEXTILE FABRIC		966772		1095833		971343		837736	TISSUS AUT COTON SYNT,ARTIF
655	KNITTED,ETC FABRICS	W 307357	1648214	W 366574	2106868	W 359292	2087923	W 362741	2020223	ETOF BONNETERIE PIECES ETC
6552	OTHER KNIT ETC FAB NONEL	W 307357	1648214	W 366574	2106868	W 359292	2087923	W 362741	2020223	ETOF BON NON ELAS NON SYNT
657	SPECIAL TXTL FABRC,PRODS		1061592		1156161		1291531		1312896	TISSUS SPECIAUX
6573	COATED ETC TEXTILES NES	W 192500	738835	W 220841	850664	W 229709	960698	W 250060	988763	TISSUS,ART MATIERE TEXT NDA
65732	PLASTIC COATED TEXTILES	W 185588	695586	W 213574	807311	W 221147	910645	W 242192	941354	TISSUS IMPREGNES
658	TEXTILE ARTICLES NES	MN 1114549	563527	MN 1241257	608810	MN 1177809	637676	MN 1028795	608755	ART FACONNES MAT TEXTILES
66	NONMETAL MINERAL MFS NES		4331213		5160371		5701109		5632795	ART MIN NON METALLIQUES
666	POTTERY		440623		473963		505259		478696	POTERIE
667	PEARL,PREC–,SEMI–P STONE		2767129		3338242		3624121		3362308	PERLES, PIERRES GEMMES
6672	DIAMONDS NONINDUST,UNSET		2416057		2915069		3078190		2958404	DIAMANTS BRUTS
66729	— CUT ETC NOT SET		2347996		2834507		2968880		2818479	DIAMANTS TAILLES
67	IRON AND STEEL		2757837		2873812		3739862		4081738	FER ET ACIER

4. General Imports C.I.F. by Commodities according to the S.I.T.C. (Rev. 2) in thousand U.S. Dollars
Importations Générales C.A.F. par Produits d'après la C.T.C.I. (Rév. 2) en milliers de Dollars E.U.

SITC CTCI	COMMODITY	1993 WEIGHT POIDS	1993 VALUE VALEUR	1994 WEIGHT POIDS	1994 VALUE VALEUR	1995 WEIGHT POIDS	1995 VALUE VALEUR	1996 WEIGHT POIDS	1996 VALUE VALEUR	PRODUIT
673	IRON,STEEL SHAPES ETC	W 2524884	891651	W 2683613	913374	W 2123103	784169	W 2233623	820300	BARRES,PROFIL FER,ACIER
6732	IRON,STEEL BARS ETC	W 1763970	611075	W 1771316	587702	W 1450023	502539	W 1553162	537625	BARRES FER,ACIER
67326	IRN,OTH STL BARS HOTROLD	W 1705618	545096	W 1702363	508023	W 1343756	402330	W 1483660	446491	BARRES PLEINES FER,ACIER
674	IRN,STL UNIV,PLATE,SHEET	W 1888229	1355726	W 2014779	1474672	W 2504396	2372930	W 2962219	2587819	LARGES PLATS,TOLES
6746	IRN,STL THIN PLATE,ROLLD	W 820382	760361	W 1027136	941119	W 1200973	1471391	W 1575736	1625287	TOLES LAM MOINS 3MM
67463	— OF STAINLESS ETC STL	W 275905	518659	W 378558	652408	W 432779	1067521	W 601352	1140957	TOL ACIER INOX MOINS 3 MM
68	NON–FERROUS METALS		1744885		1934250		3133097		3297784	METAUX NON FERREUX
682	COPPER EXC CEMENT COPPER	W 287217	867569	W 298247	926525	W 371681	1392018	W 435267	1424426	CUIVRE
6822	COPPER,ALLOYS WORKED	W 232171	749485	W 274980	875275	W 320418	1243394	W 343721	1212462	CUIVRE,ALLIAGES OUVRES
684	ALUMINIUM	W 207563	388786	W 250134	519460	W 478398	1099025	W 586841	1189795	ALUMINIUM
6841	ALUMINIUM,ALLOYS,UNWRGHT	W 129099	159688	W 147913	223948	W 362053	683381	W 465610	742325	ALUMINIUM,ALLIAGES BRUTS
69	METAL MANUFACTURES NES		2201929		2610780		3033036		3074660	ART MANUFACT EN METAL NDA
697	BASE MTL HOUSEHOLD EQUIP		407323		457645		614330		621424	ART MENAGE MET COMMUNS
699	BASE METAL MFRS NES		859609		962398		1094108		1074106	ART MANUFACTURES MET NDA
7	MACHINES,TRANSPORT EQUIP		48751767		57344722		71541933		73492293	MACHINES MATERIEL TRANSPORT
71	POWER GENERATING EQUIPMT		1560341		2318564		2884374		2796515	MACHINES GENERATRICES
713	INTRNL COMBUS PSTN ENGIN		411514		659495		910313		953250	MOTEURS EXPL COMB INT, PIECE
716	ROTATING ELECTRIC PLANT		1012538		1269743		1557705		1427741	APP ELECTR ROTATIFS,PIECES
7162	AC MTRS,GENRTRS,GEN SETS	MN 851329	743258	MN 1114290	932793	MN 1215903	1059240	MN 1143511	1040632	MOTEURS ELECTRIQUES
71621	AC MTRS,INC UNIVRSL MTRS	MN 851265	515416	MN 1114236	659648	MN 1215861	799203	MN 1143465	751037	MOT ELEC NON COUR CONTINU
72	MACHS FOR SPCL INDUSTRYS		2963073		2480883		2725281		3064295	MAC SPECIALES POUR INDUST
723	CIVIL ENGNEERG EQUIP ETC		424915		277153		367923		291963	APPAREILS DE GENIE CIVIL
724	TEXTILE,LEATHER MACHNRY		1145868		893347		841373		992462	MACH POUR INDUSTRIE TEXTILE
7243	SEWING MACHS,NEEDLES ETC		520650		420367		387093		377172	MACHINES A COUDRE,PIECES
72431	SEWING MACHINES	N 1564229	456478	N 1364827	359220	N 1080360	321458	N 992365	308528	MACHINES A COUDRE
728	OTH MACHY FOR SPCL INDUS		924783		844316		1006852		1192101	AUT MACH IND PARTICULIERES
7284	MACHY FOR SPCL INDUS NES		733640		706196		819463		984093	MACH SPEC IND PARTICUL.
73	METALWORKING MACHINERY		585187		549923		609070		686399	MACH TRAVAIL DES METAUX
736	METALWORKING MACH–TOOLS		432552		414110		425130		501716	MACH–OUTILS TRAVAIL METAUX
74	GENRL INDUSTRL MACHY NES		3800089		4403252		4931496		5154803	MACH APP INDUSTRIE
741	HEATING,COOLING EQUIPMNT		1445436		1721542		1794421		1677627	MACH CHAUFFAGE,PIECES
7415	AIR–CONDITIONING MACHNRY		1198767		1458849		1498169		1352487	GROUPES CONDITION AIR
743	PUMPS NES,CENTRFUGES ETC		644144		706092		862917		981202	POMPES COMPRES,VENT ETC
744	MECHANICAL HANDLING EQU		673477		812364		904958		965236	EQUIP MANUTENTION PIECES
749	NONELEC MACH PTS,ACC NES		667186		749513		900673		992084	PIECES MACH NON ELEC NDA
75	OFFICE MACHNES,ADP EQUIP		4772081		6271151		8885450		10522267	MACH BUREAU TRAIT AUTOM
751	OFFICE MACHINES	MN 177724	652158	MN 214862	781716	MN 271209	1064116	MN 270112	1070541	MACH,APPAREILS DE BUREAU
752	AUTOMTIC DATA PROC EQUIP	MN 20885	1636721	MN 24730	2089007	MN 34110	2699537	MN 70876	4461364	MACH TRAIT INFORMATION
7523	DIGITL CENTRL PROCESSORS	N 482007	570880	N 549046	761936	N 658011	904666	N 950319	1260019	UNITES CENTRALES
7524	DIGITL CENTRL STOR UNITS	N 4824390	390272	N 8753766	559840	MN 19184	885626	MN 18051	933066	UNITES MEMOIRE CENTRALES
7525	ADP PERIPHERAL UNITS	MN 15431	582446	MN 14914	624557	MN 13718	723952	MN 50198	1789516	UNITES PERIPHERIQUES
759	OFFICE,ADP MCH PTS,ACCES		2483202		3400428		5121798		4990362	PIECES DU 751 ET 752
7599	ACCTG,ETC,ADP MCH PTS,AC		2238466		3003869		4612910		4424285	PIECES DU 751 ET 752
76	TELECOMM,SOUND EQUIPMENT		12067107		15606937		18869995		18234845	EQUIPMENT DE TELECOM
761	TELEVISION RECEIVERS	MN 10758	1903982	MN 12313	2467623	MN 12743	2678068	N 8769685	2188338	RECEPTEURS DE TELEVISION
7611	COLOUR TV RECEIVERS	N 8005624	1783506	MN 9155	2343254	MN 9714	2553028	N 7334202	2137013	RECEPTEURS COULEUR
762	RADIO BROADCAST RECEIVRS	MN 178161	2470910	MN 214135	3329863	MN 225463	3480110	MN 220346	3053853	RECEPTEURS RADIODIFFUSION
7622	PORTABLE RADIO RECEIVERS	MN 142750	1401200	MN 171895	1875336	MN 184364	1934977	MN 179309	1643797	RECEPT PORTATIFS RADIO
7628	OTHER RADIO RECEIVERS	MN 23628	899652	MN 26551	1237684	MN 27002	1281065	MN 26023	1081880	AUTRES RECEPT RADIO
763	SOUND RECORDRS,PHONOGRPH	MN 49371	1538930	MN 51777	2193665	MN 57317	2388219	MN 51975	2572452	PHONO,APP ENREGISTREMENT
7638	OTHR SOUND APPARATUS ETC	MN 49085	1526143	MN 51674	2180225	MN 57019	2374649	MN 51400	2546571	AUT APP D'ENREGIS,REPROD
76381	TV IMAGE,SND RECRDRS ETC	N 8737012	923301	N 7881348	1484110	N 8390477	1622298	N 8334782	1836851	APP ENREG,REPRO IMAG,SON
76388	DICTATING MACHINES ETC	MN 40348	602843	MN 43793	696115	MN 48629	752350	MN 43066	709720	MACHINES A DICTER
764	TELECOM EQPT,PTS,ACC NES		6153285		7615786		10323598		10420202	EQUIP TELECOM,PIECES
7641	LINE TELEPHONE,ETC EQUIP		899828		1040668		1510220		2006058	APP TELEPHON PAR FIL
7642	MICROPH,LOUDSPKR,AMPLIFR	MN 534436	464735	MN 628228	657804	MN 735088	857339	MN 606914	798468	MICRO,HAUT–PARLEUR,AMPLI
7643	TV,RADIO TRANSMITTRS ETC	MN 22072	961367	MN 25152	1227881	MN 30913	2226915	MN 20582	2299467	APP EMET TELE RADIO
7648	TELECOMM EQUIPMENT NES	MN 31775	1105035	MN 30304	1084239	MN 34241	1526500	MN 43091	947563	APP TELECOM NDA
76481	RADIOTELEPHONE ETC RCVRS	N 7472396	785652	N 7003845	730667	MN 9781	1016588	N 7663481	752161	RECEP RADIOTELEPHONIE
7649	PTS NES OF EQUIPMT OF 76		2722321		3605193		4202624		4368647	PIECES DE LA DIV 76
76491	PTS NES OF APPAR OF 7641		305341		358409		464724		706336	PIECES POUR 764.1
76493	TELECOMM EQUIPMT PTS NES		1171210		1453466		1922369		1995201	PIECES 761,762,764.3,8
76499	PARTS ETC OF SOUND EQUIP		1123878		1634935		1582086		1491969	PIECES NDA POUR 763
77	ELECTRIC MACHNRY NES ETC		15436916		18403428		24575680		25897846	MACH APP ELECT NDA
771	ELECTRIC POWER MACHY NES		1258082		1545889		2199934		2403133	MACH PROD,TRANS ELECTR
7712	OTH ELEC POWER MACHY NES		954757		1175940		1706584		1869209	AUT APP PROD TRANSF ELEC
77121	STATIC CONVERTERS ETC	MN 1221296	379013	MN 1539010	468665	MN 2089637	614386	MN 1786445	767536	CONVERTISSEURS STATIQUES
77129	PTS NES OF MACHY OF 771		414352		512047		817067		771343	PIECES MACH DU 771
772	SWITCHGEAR ETC,PARTS NES		1686014		2010416		2592001		2693713	APP COUPURE,SECT ETC
7721	SWITCHGEAR ETC		1193532		1430483		1856472		1895068	APP COUPURE,SECTIONMNT
773	ELECTR DISTRIBUTNG EQUIP		799560		901485		1117201		1207881	EQUIPMT DISTRIBUTION ELECT
7731	INSULATED WIRE,CABLE ETC		784827		884190		1089606		1181163	FILS,CABLES ISOLES ELECT
775	HOUSEHOLD TYPE EQUIP NES		1984689		2224271		2707188		3008017	MACH,APP USAGE DOMESTQUE
7757	DOMESTIC ELECTRC EQU NES		776271		858624		1029767		1137743	APP ELECTR DOMEST NDA
7758	ELECTRO–THERMIC APPL NES		1021227		1121776		1397336		1567196	APP ELECTROTHERMIQ NDA
77586	ELECTROTHERM DOM APP NES	MN 41304	461038	MN 44764	523106	MN 56443	711919	MN 70033	821967	APP ELECTRO THERMIQUES
776	TRANSISTORS,VALVES,ETC		7153644		8862169		12458749		12831386	LAMPES,TUBES,VALVES
7761	TV PICTURE TUBES	N 4949752	302298	N 5982260	407363	N 7806492	560397	MN 10911	943860	TUBES CATHODIQUES
7763	DIODES,TRANSISTORS,ETC	MN 21518650	741878	MN 25706416	906290	MN 30345215	1196548	MN 31675362	1394649	DIODES,TRANSISTORS
7764	ELECTRONIC MICROCIRCUITS	MN 16106391	5664475	MN 10274441	6992874	MN 10330070	9957227	MN 10573904	9004387	MICROSTRUCTURES ELECTRON
7768	ELCTRNC COMP PTS,CRYSTLS		442550		551534		740305		1478935	CRIST PIEZO–ELEC,PCS 776
77689	ELECTRNIC COMPON PTS NES		308786		393256		517741		1291144	PIECES DU GROUPE 776
778	ELECTRICAL MACHINERY NES		2353919		2666944		3292791		3489285	AUTRES MACH ELECT NDA
7781	BATTERIES,ACCUMULATORS		593894		678659		927552		978352	PILES ET ACCUMULATEURS
7788	OTH ELEC MACHY,EQUIP NES		1178175		1344341		1605089		1694418	AUT MACH APP ELEC NDA
77884	ELECTRICAL CONDENSERS	MN 34908550	594008	MN 42169660	699349	MN 241093384	866544	MN 361906091	857752	CONDENSATEURS ELECTRIQUES
78	ROAD VEHICLES		6523921		6652976		5967403		5169619	VEHICULES ROUTIERS
781	PASS MOTOR VEH EXC BUSES	N 195691	3714455	N 156653	3043969	N 132048	2702180	N 134838	2247861	AUTO TRANSPORT PERSONNES
782	LORRIES,SPCL MTR VEH NES	N 26595	439154	N 32499	549064	N 7185	178322	N 7959	200067	VEHICULES SPECIAUX,MARCH
7821	LORRIES,TRUCKS	N 26338	419366	N 32311	535742	N 6873	153246	N 7685	172619	VEHICULES TRANSP MARCHAND
783	ROAD MOTOR VEHICLES NES	N 11767	271524	N 22366	549386	N 10186	337799	N 13505	377397	VEHICULES ROUTIERS NDA
784	MOTOR VEH PRTS,ACCES NES		539279		719338		785082		843228	PIECES 722,781,782,783
7849	OTHER MOTOR VEHCL PARTS		490014		639898		707656		715894	PIECES 722,781,782,783
785	CYCLES,ETC MOTRZD OR NOT		1440637		1633902		1798030		1362404	MOTOCYCLES SCOOTERS
7851	MOTORCYCLES ETC	N 703724	881021	N 868607	1044552	N 966677	1158761	N 709055	768609	MOTO VELO MOTEUR AUXIL
79	OTHR TRANSPORT EQUIPMENT		1043051		657609		2093184		1965705	AUTRE MATERIEL TRANSPORT
792	AIRCRAFT ETC		789522		472886		1933221		1843730	APP NAVIGATION AERIENNE
7924	AIRCRFT NES OVER 15000KG	N 9	711701	N 4	325116	N 16	1811000	N 16	1675814	AERODYNES PLUS 15000 KG
8	MISC MANUFACTURED GOODS		38840893		43393277		47853402		50665602	ART MANUFACTURES DIVERS
812	*PLUMBG,HEATNG,LGHTNG EQ		811592		893298		990679		1115839	APPAR SANITAIRES CHAUFFAGE
8124	LIGHTING EQUIPMENT NES		755341		823864		920954		1035890	APPAREILS ECLAIRAGE ETC

4. General Imports C.I.F. by Commodities according to the S.I.T.C. (Rev. 2) in thousand U.S. Dollars
Importations Générales C.A.F. par Produits d'après la C.T.C.I. (Rév. 2) en milliers de Dollars E.U.

SITC CTCI	COMMODITY	1993 WEIGHT POIDS	1993 VALUE VALEUR	1994 WEIGHT POIDS	1994 VALUE VALEUR	1995 WEIGHT POIDS	1995 VALUE VALEUR	1996 WEIGHT POIDS	1996 VALUE VALEUR	PRODUIT
81242	LAMPS,FITTINGS BASE METL		442126		518565		592670		677968	APPAREILS D'ECLAIRAGE
821	*FURNITURE,PARTS THEREOF		790979		966708		996677		1054784	MEUBLES ET PIECES
8219	FURNITURE AND PARTS NES		449198		591542		614208		625851	AUTRES MEUBLES ET PIECES
831	*TRAVEL GOODS,HANDBAGS	MN 1538803	2710526	MN 1723680	3209652	MN 1922519	3607901	MN 1933532	3876957	ARTICLES DE VOYAGE ETC
83101	HANDBAGS NES	MN 273983	1048429	MN 300039	1208642	MN 310159	1292660	MN 309844	1405509	SACS A MAIN
83109	OTHER TRAVEL BAGS,CASES	MN 1165218	1388168	MN 1305778	1685687	MN 1486786	1967370	MN 1505923	2085833	AUT CONTENANTS SIMILAIRES
84	CLOTHING AND ACCESSORIES		11819230		12475620		12675973		13657703	VETEMENTS
842	MENS OUTERWEAR NOT KNIT	MN 392721	1856276	MN 393968	1883293	MN 357776	1868643	MN 358125	2020571	VET DESSUS POUR HOMMES
8423	— TROUSERS,BREECHES ETC	MN 219471	694441	MN 225126	768479	MN 221405	852791	MN 226972	965508	PANTALONS HOMMES MAT TEX
8429	— OTHER OUTER GARMENTS	MN 131802	661731	MN 137628	710447	MN 107175	631867	MN 100455	634402	AUT VET DES HOM MAT TEX
843	WOMENS OUTERWEAR NONKNIT	MN 579288	3345086	MN 573237	3358443	MN 571426	3229453	MN 586632	3421136	VET DESSUS FEMMES MAT TEX
8431	— COATS AND JACKETS	MN 30563	491405	MN 28187	468263	MN 29445	492710	MN 34329	549676	MANT,VEST FEM MAT TEXTIL
8435	— BLOUSES	MN 162239	1003018	MN 140631	848801	MN 116744	698230	MN 118353	678388	BLOUSES FEM MAT TEXTILES
8439	— OTHER OUTER GARMENTS	MN 321399	1263400	MN 330915	1374419	MN 341055	1344657	MN 347639	1477703	AUT VET DES FEM MAT TEXT
844	UNDER GARMENTS NOT KNIT	MN 292748	952960	MN 299676	896500		830589		913961	VETEMENT DESSOUS MAT TEX
8441	— MENS SHIRTS	MN 207533	731938	MN 221020	669580		627916		715182	CHEMISES HOMMES MAT TEXT
84412	—— OF SYNTHETIC FIBRES	MN 116938	441377	MN 118397	326170		261824		323580	CHEMISES HOMMES FIB SYNT
845	OUTERWEAR KNIT NONELASTC	MN 621889	2820357	MN 662984	3067237	MN 708668	3149964	MN 778228	3540517	VET DESSOUS,ACCES BONNET
8451	— JERSEYS,PULLOVERS ETC	MN 305169	1829368	MN 324568	1962582	MN 314198	1922236	MN 341793	2095665	CHANDAILS,PULL–OVERS ETC
8459	— OTHER,CLTHG ACCESRYS	MN 302029	873599	MN 322677	966853	MN 374236	1087799	MN 413352	1289350	AUT VET DESSUS DE BONNE
846	UNDER GARMENTS KNITTED		1556260		1757812		2054020		2210232	SOUS VETS DE BONNETERIE
8462	— OF COTTON NON ELASTIC	MN 1763191	1194459	MN 1822576	1330885	MN 1806639	1596720	MN 1721725	1714457	SOUS–VET BONNET COTON
84629	—— OTHER	MN 1727241	1040477	MN 1782376	1151748	MN 1761434	1370916	MN 1674287	1458380	AUT SOUS–VET BONNET COTON
848	HEADGEAR,NONTXTL CLOTHNG		925892		1080474		1104770		1062388	VET ACCES MAT AUT QUE TEX
8481	LEATHER CLOTHES,ACCESSOR		492283		635589		633336		568128	VET ACCES MAT CUIR ARTIF
851	*FOOTWEAR	MP 1348279	4974275	MP 1439760	5734672	MP 1473855	6439032	MP 1407827	6865990	CHAUSSURES
85101	FOOTWEAR RUBBER,PLASTIC	MP 759898	2078297	MP 821402	2360414	MP 862123	2626941	MP 853256	2771813	CHAUS SEMELLES CAOUTCH
85102	FOOTWEAR LEATHER	MP 543354	2852150	MP 581215	3341720	MP 576768	3780342	MP 521011	4064778	CHAUS SEMELLES EN CUIR
87	PRECISION INSTRUMNTS NES		1148254		1311820		1605990		2042040	INSTRUM,APPAR SCIENT NDA
874	MEASURNG,CONTROLNG INSTR		658516		690561		818181		1096590	INSTRUMENTS DE MESURE
88	PHOTO EQU,OPTICL GDS ETC		6100537		6821707		7836986		7808393	APP,FOURN PHOTO,OP,MONTR
881	PHOTO APPARAT,EQUIPT NES		961480		1062993		1332105		1442045	APP,EQUIP PHOTO NDA
8811	CAMERAS STILL,FLASH APP		868701		981606		1230753		1314826	APPAREILS PHOTO,PIECES
88111	STILL CAMERAS	MN 54645	534794	MN 58194	617828	MN 79344	711040	MN 86570	777632	APPAREILS PHOTOGRAPHIQ
882	PHOTO,CINEMA SUPPLIES		491679		658846		850064		880368	PRODUITS PHOTO,CINEMA
8822	PHOTO FILM EXC DEV CINMA		460060		609977		754895		776177	PLAQUES,PELLICULES,FILMS
885	WATCHES AND CLOCKS		4305019		4714612		5205055		4976516	HORLOGERIE
8851	WATCHES,MOVEMENTS,CASES		3436133		3751084		4034395		3785752	MONTRES,MOUVEMENTS,BOITES
88511	WATCHES		2128739		2348988		2597491		2526473	MONTRES POCHE,BRACELET
88513	WATCH MOVEMENTS ASSEMBLD		1147131		1221671		1243312		1085591	MOUVEMENTS TERMINES
8852	CLOCKS,CLOCK,WATCH PARTS		868886		963528		1170660		1190764	HORLOGES,MOUV,PARTIES
88529	CLOCK,WATCH PARTS NES		647239		699227		838793		834916	FOURNIT D HORLOG NDA
89	MISC MANUFCTRD GOODS NES		10485500		11979800		13700166		14243896	ART MANUFACTURES DIVERS
893	ARTICLES OF PLASTIC NES		1748111		2099928		2422845		2598003	OUVRAGES EN MAT DIVIS 58
8931	PLSTC PACKG CONTNRS,LIDS		310043		458584		764940		810563	ART TRANSP EMBALLAGE ETC
8939	MISC PLASTIC ARTICLES		1422025		1626860		1639615		1764497	ART DIVERS EN MAT DIV 58
89399	OTHR PLASTC ARTICLES NES		1330854		1493217		1501090		1625201	AUT OUV MAT DIV 58
894	TOYS,SPORTING GOODS,ETC		4582377		5366659		6149443		6559985	VOITURES ENFANTS,JOUETS
8942	TOYS,INDOOR GAMES ETC		4161787		4790602		5400368		5744193	JOUETS,JEUX ETC
89422	DOLLS		485330		520579	MN 554403	579321	MN 546744	522660	POUPEES
89423	TOYS NES		2361362		2737768		2965678		3212493	JOUETS,MODELES REDUITS
89424	INDOOR GAME EQUIPMENT		753313		853747		958412		1045801	ART,JEUX DE SOCIETE
89425	XMAS DECORATIONS ETC		549859		656320		869257		938328	ART DIVERTIS,FETES
8947	OTH SPORT GDS,FAIR AMUSM		361067		483443		651721		707472	AUT ART DE SPORT
89472	OTH OUTDOOR SPORT GOODS		317625		432516		578096		640203	ART POUR JEUX PLEIN AIR
897	GOLD,SILVER WARE,JEWELRY		832390		885885		1042897		1015704	BIJOUTERIE,ORFEVRERIE
8973	PREC JEWLRY,GLD–SILVWARE		685162		733191		877189		845123	BIJOUX OR,ARGENT ORFEVRE
89731	PRECIOUS METAL JEWELLERY		617800		653176		793249		770244	ART BIJOUTERIE,JOAILLER
898	MUSICAL INSTRUMENTS,PTS		868259		886686		1016869		958565	INSTRUMENTS DE MUSIQUE
8983	SOUND RECRDNG TAPE,DISCS		778917		777325		871110		803167	SUPPORTS SON POUR 763
89831	PREPD SND RECORDNG MEDIA		574383		531157		569548	MN 1201430	542417	SUPPORTS PREPARES
899	OTHER MANUFACTURED GOODS		1760511		1930122		2116349		2100035	AUT ART MANUF DIVERS NDA
8994	UMBRELLAS,CANES ETC		457698		539266		522933		487740	PARAPLUIES,CANNES ETC
8999	OTHER MANUF GOODS NES		479200		553476		650979		621305	OUVRAGES DIVERS NDA
9	GOODS NOT CLASSD BY KIND		3180526		4684800		3990814		3639346	ART TRANSACT NON CLASSES
931	*SPECIAL TRANSACTIONS		509668		607352		636064		856146	TRANS.SPECIALES
971	*GOLD,NON MONETARY NES		2649700		4050875		3317554	K 220236	2742491	OR NON MONETAIRE
97101	NONMON GLD UNWRT,SEMIMFD	K 234056	2643602	K 326104	4041143	K 265657	3288638	K 217535	2715693	OR,ALLIAGES D'OR BRUTS

5. General Exports F.O.B. by Commodities according to the S.I.T.C. (Rev. 2) in thousand U.S. Dollars
Exportations Générales F.O.B. par Produits d'après la C.T.C.I. (Rév. 2) en milliers de Dollars E.U.

SITC CTCI	COMMODITY	1993		1994		1995		1996		PRODUIT
		WEIGHT POIDS	VALUE VALEUR	WEIGHT POIDS	VALUE VALEUR	WEIGHT POIDS	VALUE VALEUR	WEIGHT POIDS	VALUE VALEUR	
	ALL COMMODITIES		135384625		151465165		173870820		180915781	TOUS PRODUITS
0	FOOD AND LIVE ANIMALS		2024423		2434836		2741060		3152112	ALIMENTS,ANIMAUX VIVANTS
01	MEAT AND PREPARATIONS		188120		240064		409954		710793	VIANDES ET PREPARATIONS
011	MEAT FRESH,CHILLD,FROZEN	W 179206	166570	W 217820	211344	W 360819	373838	W 654585	676472	VIANDES FRAICHES,REF,CONGE
0114	POULTRY FRESH CHLLD,FRZN	W 169183	143299	W 204235	184690	W 333554	332583	W 567843	560378	VOLAILLES MORTES
03	FISH AND PREPARATIONS		500497		615246		577860		583279	POISSONS ET PREPARATIONS
05	VEGETABLES AND FRUIT		562873		592554		618371		672412	LEGUMES ET FRUITS
1	BEVERAGES AND TOBACCO		2003237		2225744		2075042		2174760	BOISSONS ET TABACS
11	BEVERAGES		504810		633143		615611		520624	BOISSONS
112	ALCOHOLIC BEVERAGES	W 72188	396014	W 124580	511607	W 167688	511672	W 133971	430826	BOISSONS ALCOOLIQUES
12	TOBACCO AND MANUFACTURES		1498426		1592601		1459430		1654136	TABACS BRUTS FABRIQUES
122	TOBACCO,MANUFACTURED	W 81248	1491787	W 85133	1584857	W 75393	1453801		1623103	TABACS FABRIQUES
1222	CIGARETTES	W 80964	1488886	W 84470	1579829	W 74335	1446805		1616831	CIGARETTES
2	CRUDE MATERLS,EXCL FUELS		1846714		2236472		3066898		2839006	MAT BRUTES NON COMESTIBLES
26	TEXTILE FIBRES AND WASTE		492946		667552		854174		778989	FIBRES TEXTILES
28	METALLIFEROUS ORES,SCRAP		302436		339487		641893		590054	MINERAIS METAL,DECHETS
29	CRUDE ANIMAL,VEG MAT NES		493170		449093		437514		433386	MATIERES BRUTES ANIM,VEGET
3	MINERAL FUELS ETC		1232104		1211547		1684306		2013273	COMBUSTIBLES MINERAUX LUB
33	PETROLEUM AND PRODUCTS		957963		1086431		1578330		1964671	PETROLE ET DERIVES
334	PETROLEUM PRODUCTS,REFIN	W 4929353	935782	W 5384305	1070309	W 8133412	1561053		1946404	PRODUITS RAFFINES
3343	GAS OILS	W 2387871	484780	W 2962677	557447	W 5342492	955721	W 6055791	1324745	GAS OILS
5	CHEMCLS,RELATED PROD NES		6807509		8369689		10743249		10622857	PRODUITS CHIMIQUES
51	ORGANIC CHEMICALS		624718		900969		1372167		1378177	PROD CHIMIQ ORGANIQUES
53	DYES,TANNING,COLOUR PROD		787249		845051		895492		977447	PROD TEINTURE,COLORANTS
531	SYNT DYE,NAT INDGO,LAKES	W 48522	444708	W 49449	430843	W 53432	405093	W 55919	452741	MAT COLOR ORGAN,LAQUES
5311	SYNTHIC ORGNIC DYESTUFFS	W 47812	431403	W 47699	413781	W 50244	385313	W 53516	428057	MAT COLOR ORGAN SYNTHET
541	*MEDICINAL,PHARM PRODUCT		738260		832934		975281		1020097	PROD MEDICINAUX PHARMACEUT
5417	MEDICAMENTS		334025		404625		477617		542854	MEDICAMENTS
55	PERFUME,CLEANING ETC PRD		434551		511496		571835		622276	PROD POUR PARFUM,TOILETTE
58	PLASTIC MATERIALS ETC		3172117		4069159		5522583		5256018	MAT PLAST ARTIFICIELLES
582	PROD OF CONDENSATION ETC	W 223091	370751	W 310644	507689	W 402796	831458	W 424621	763309	PROD CONDENS,POLYCOND
5823	ALKYDS,OTHER POLYESTERS	W 131716	196254	W 204239	286739	W 276682	538395	W 270186	416348	ALKYDES ET AUT POLYESTERS
583	POLYMERIZATION ETC PRODS	W 3096507	2771199	W 3969293	3534887	W 4658915	4656249	W 4650347	4455436	PROD POLYMERISATION
5831	POLYETHYLENE	W 493990	311057	W 682114	429825	W 828557	633833	W 871698	658658	POLYETHYLENE
58311	— IN PRIMARY FORMS	W 290297	219533	W 440419	326568	W 572559	509173	W 677781	556113	POLYETHYLENE PRIMAIRES
5833	POLYSTYRENE,ITS COPOLYMR	W 1307791	1062649	W 1653006	1411616	W 1777254	1810255	W 1816747	1622048	POLYPROPYLENE COPOLYMERES
58331	— IN PRIMARY FORMS	W 1109606	991684	W 1416034	1317555	W 1513875	1680985	W 1574141	1516581	SOUS FORMES PRIMAIRES
5834	POLYVINYL CHLORIDE	W 671295	770218	W 748333	854822	W 869290	1029065	W 907012	1047062	CHLORURE DE POLYVINYLE
58343	— PLATES,STRIP,ETC NES	W 230020	451822	W 250837	476363	W 268612	515354	W 252511	520207	SOUS FORME DE PLAQUES
5839	OTH POLYMRZTION ETC PROD	W 352693	375413	W 514820	483607	W 676792	614300	W 527317	558716	AUT PROD POLYMER COPOLYM
59	CHEMICAL MATERIALS NES		694398		806670		974572		973001	MAT PROD CHIMIQUES NDA
598	MISCEL CHEM PRODUCTS NES		516641		590061		688307		702286	PROD DIV INDUST CHIM NDA
5989	CHEM PRODUCTS,PREPS NES		403889		493284		575654		613247	PROD PREP CHIMIQUES NDA
6	BASIC MANUFACTURES		22643981		25318094		29298667		30733419	ART MANUFACTURES
61	LEATHER,DRESSED FUR,ETC		1565344		1737924		1977508		2229557	CUIRS,PELLETERIES
611	LEATHER		1041364		1231314		1450316		1557605	CUIRS,PEAUX PREPARES
6114	LEATHR BOVINE NES,EQUINE		700289		740421	A 58072	973438		1080353	CUIRS DE BOVINS
63	WOOD,CORK MANUFACTRS NES		474822		657822		712265		662182	OUVRAGES LIEGE ET BOIS
64	PAPER,PAPERBOARD AND MFR		1354496		1616822		1970055		2241282	PAPIERS,CARTONS & OUVRAGES
641	PAPER AND PAPERBOARD		817751		1003994		1269242		1472687	PAPIERS ET CARTONS
642	PAPER,ETC,PRECUT,ARTS OF		536745		612827		700814		768595	PAP,CARTONS DECOUPES
65	TEXTILE YARN,FABRICS,ETC		11290088		12615939		13892042		14213648	FILS,TISSUS,ARTICLES TEXTILE
651	TEXTILE YARN	W 590946	1959071	W 732883	2369995	W 809941	2893089	W 927977	3135600	FILS TEXTILES
6513	COTTON YARN	W 108783	334535	W 172245	537236	W 198235	668630	W 271751	927159	FILS DE COTON
6514	SYN FIB YRN,BULK,MONOFIL	W 286682	631536	W 365314	784752	W 419116	1119556	W 461923	1089877	FILS CONT 85% FIB TEXT SYNTH
65144	— TEXTRD,CONT POLYESTER	W 211788	328237	W 248525	417854	W 250664	560538	W 355079	668283	FILS TEX FI CONT POLYESTERS
652	COTTON FABRICS,WOVEN	A 2463524	2429379	A 2309326	2617333	A 2336521	2898006	A 2227947	3010225	TISSUS DE COTON
6522	WOVEN COTTON BLEACHD,ETC	A 1978553	2230097	A 1826539	2323419	A 1910830	2599970	A 1776941	2665530	TISSUS COTON BLANCHIS ETC
65224	BLCHED COTTON FABRIC NES	A 1844453	2048071	A 1690950	2117878	A 1769312	2348185	A 1599785	2343060	AUT TIS PLUS 85% COT BLANCHI
653	WOVN MAN–MADE FIB FABRIC	A 3358790	2512004	A 3577803	2815386	A 3507599	3077132	A 3399281	3048891	TISSUS FIBRES SYNTH,ARTIF
6531	CONT SYNT WEAVES NONPILE	A 1662842	1356077	A 2048395	1621196	A 2114545	1827890	A 2213415	1892749	TISSUS FIBRES SYNTH CONTINUE
65315	CONT SYN TXTL FABRIC NES	A 1530311	1222001	A 1909454	1469507	A 1956394	1661539	A 2065974	1727872	TIS PLUS 85% TEXT SYNT CONT
6534	DISC SYN BLEND FABRC NES	A 1035815	587653	A 812753	551495	A 787479	582304	A 721246	534713	TISSUS FIBRES SYNTH DISCONT
65341	DISC SYN FIB–COTTN FABRC	A 914447	463171	A 706526	435864	A 660493	441203	A 602876	400251	TISSUS FIB SYNT DIS MEL COTO
654	OTH WOVEN TEXTILE FABRIC		880677		929337		812959		708628	TISSUS AUT COTON SYNT,ARTIF
6541	SILK FABRICS WOVEN	A 131149	484159	A 136705	463038	A 115839	381176	A 86209	308959	TISSUS DE SOIE
655	KNITTED,ETC FABRICS	W 306777	1551877	W 343782	1781641	W 344594	1920025	W 354694	2036196	ETOF BONNETERIE PIECES ETC
6552	OTHER KNIT ETC FAB NONEL	W 306777	1551877	W 343782	1781641	W 344594	1920025	W 354694	2036196	ETOF BON NON ELAS NON SYNT
657	SPECIAL TXTL FABRC,PRODS		903624		972758		1074684		1084474	TISSUS SPECIAUX
6573	COATED ETC TEXTILES NES	W 151350	620998	W 175196	695269	W 180406	786994	W 193361	811516	TISSUS,ART MATIERE TEXT NDA
65732	PLASTIC COATED TEXTILES	W 146440	591832	W 170197	668744	W 175168	756776	W 187765	779164	TISSUS IMPREGNES
658	TEXTILE ARTICLES NES	MN 1012372	623034	MN 1033661	647384	MN 1043152	670159	MN 900120	612662	ART FACONNES MAT TEXTILES
6584	LINENS ETC	MN 547044	413182	MN 511219	388394	MN 455408	371761	MN 410301	348903	LINGE DE MAISON
66	NONMETAL MINERAL MFS NES		2269920		2612112		2908963		2950443	ART MIN NON METALLIQUES
666	POTTERY		528588		557204		599268		558246	POTERIE
667	PEARL,PREC–,SEMI–P STONE		1167106		1350227		1415426		1440899	PERLES, PIERRES GEMMES
6672	DIAMONDS NONINDUST,UNSET		777324		906165		975380		1009609	DIAMANTS BRUTS
66729	— CUT ETC NOT SET		723886		807656		835460		806090	DIAMANTS TAILLES
67	IRON AND STEEL		1742327		1771353		2262340		2642582	FER ET ACIER
673	IRON,STEEL SHAPES ETC	W 1231069	437448	W 1157391	398317	W 549819	216200	W 412057	171592	BARRES,PROFIL FER,ACIER
674	IRN,STL UNIV,PLATE,SHEET	W 1411622	1072171	W 1604645	1167636	W 2014461	1790304	W 2453382	2165266	LARGES PLATS,TOLES
6746	IRN,STL THIN PLATE,ROLLD	W 749206	662489	W 906158	775390	W 1058665	1112137	W 1414985	1400070	TOLES LAM MOINS 3MM
67463	— OF STAINLESS ETC STL	W 210339	417528	W 279006	495400	W 298553	720016	W 492698	928996	TOL ACIER INOX MOINS 3 MM
68	NON–FERROUS METALS		1146962		1286035		2075364		2236134	METAUX NON FERREUX
682	COPPER EXC CEMENT COPPER	W 194831	526528	W 213861	585559	W 271495	890297	W 327373	996242	CUIVRE
6822	COPPER,ALLOYS WORKED	W 153836	439930	W 193825	539009	W 238708	794039	W 272775	864804	CUIVRE,ALLIAGES OUVRES
684	ALUMINIUM	W 134321	255246	W 169994	348917	W 334879	754898	W 408747	853495	ALUMINIUM
69	METAL MANUFACTURES NES		2635817		2819484		3238836		3247180	ART MANUFACT EN METAL NDA
696	CUTLERY	MN 1915053	391617	MN 2151132	430201		535293	MN 20456247	524648	COUTELLERIE
697	BASE MTL HOUSEHOLD EQUIP		672846		730047		873094		854343	ART MENAGE MET COMMUNS
6974	BASE MTL DMSTC ARTIC NES	W 101163	434197	W 108404	483165	W 140153	560819	W 135004	547622	ARTICLES NDA FONTE,FER,ETC
699	BASE METAL MFRS NES		989031		1066112		1192495		1219604	ART MANUFACTURES MET NDA
7	MACHINES,TRANSPORT EQUIP		41349072		47437925		56217218		58194630	MACHINES MATERIEL TRANSPORT
71	POWER GENERATING EQUIPMT		1328061		1638240		2000576		1940952	MACHINES GENERATRICES
716	ROTATING ELECTRIC PLANT		957011		1117090		1409218		1316425	APP ELECTR ROTATIFS,PIECES
7162	AC MTRS,GENRTRS,GEN SETS	MN 557099	661167	MN 717354	827317	MN 848377	997735	MN 796026	965711	MOTEURS ELECTRIQUES
71621	AC MTRS,INC UNIVRSL MTRS	MN 557049	460628	MN 717309	590385	MN 848337	759760	MN 795984	693898	MOT ELEC NON COUR CONTINU
72	MACHS FOR SPCL INDUSTRYS		2924699		2352917		2330538		2723280	MAC SPECIALES POUR INDUST
724	TEXTILE,LEATHER MACHNRY		1221442		967444		887890		932932	MACH POUR INDUSTRIE TEXTILE
7243	SEWING MACHS,NEEDLES ETC		464307		438722		400572		348773	MACHINES A COUDRE,PIECES
72431	SEWING MACHINES	N 1464367	430211	N 1506703	408526	N 1219154	362361	N 1039123	313972	MACHINES A COUDRE

5. General Exports F.O.B. by Commodities according to the S.I.T.C. (Rev. 2) in thousand U.S. Dollars
Exportations Générales F.O.B. par Produits d'après la C.T.C.I. (Rév. 2) en milliers de Dollars E.U.

SITC CTCI	COMMODITY	1993 WEIGHT POIDS	1993 VALUE VALEUR	1994 WEIGHT POIDS	1994 VALUE VALEUR	1995 WEIGHT POIDS	1995 VALUE VALEUR	1996 WEIGHT POIDS	1996 VALUE VALEUR	PRODUIT
728	OTH MACHY FOR SPCL INDUS		1012845		860778		901204		1077888	AUT MACH IND PARTICULIERES
7284	MACHY FOR SPCL INDUS NES		834445		731400		762160		907565	MACH SPEC IND PARTICUL.
72842	RUBBER,PLASTICS WRKG MCH	N 30042	446484	N 26537	406977	N 22575	358021	N 26326	437470	MACH IND CAOUT MAT PLAST
73	METALWORKING MACHINERY		610367		577641		570243		637121	MACH TRAVAIL DES METAUX
736	METALWORKING MACH-TOOLS		430800		405013		382875		460908	MACH-OUTILS TRAVAIL METAUX
74	GENRL INDUSTRL MACHY NES		2565928		2920892		3111040		3349927	MACH APP INDUSTRIE
741	HEATING,COOLING EQUIPMNT		958113		1085381		1075243		1030067	MACH CHAUFFAGE,PIECES
7415	AIR-CONDITIONING MACHNRY		750763		881654		872448		805265	GROUPES CONDITION AIR
743	PUMPS NES,CENTRFUGES ETC		463139		496373		548379		630462	POMPES COMPRES,VENT ETC
749	NONELEC MACH PTS,ACC NES		565243		611647		655795		702814	PIECES MACH NON ELEC NDA
75	OFFICE MACHNES,ADP EQUIP		5946791		7073984		9722646		10840989	MACH BUREAU TRAIT AUTOM
751	OFFICE MACHINES	MN 189477	893990	MN 232767	1200884	MN 282721	1446862	MN 286249	1369624	MACH,APPAREILS DE BUREAU
7512	CALCULATNG,ACCTG,ETC MCH	MN 153719	383365	MN 194413	507110	MN 242108	609688	MN 245287	711323	MACHINE A CALCULER ETC
75121	CALCULATING MACHINES	MN 153638	361290	MN 194288	478297	MN 241908	567058	MN 245084	675779	MACHINES A CALCULER
7518	OFFICE MACHINES NES	MN 35505	487330	MN 37995	665802	MN 40122	804722	MN 40309	596748	MACH,APP DE BUREAU NDA
75182	PHOTO,THERMOCOPY APPARAT	N 363390	351922	N 590361	503475	N 762216	607287	N 564228	457244	APPAREILS DE PHOTOCOPIE
752	AUTOMTIC DATA PROC EQUIP	MN 21074	1176379	MN 24331	1323337	MN 35061	1745654	MN 65928	2926437	MACH TRAIT INFORMATION
7523	DIGITL CENTRL PROCESSORS	N 383941	438098	N 356588	505995	N 602923	682492	N 513603	821728	UNITES CENTRALES
7525	ADP PERIPHERAL UNITS	MN 17930	456039	MN 16778	447222	MN 18159	525507	MN 50403	1481366	UNITES PERIPHERIQUES
759	OFFICE,ADP MCH PTS,ACCES		3876422		4549763		6530130		6544928	PIECES DU 751 ET 752
7599	ACCTG,ETC,ADP MCH PTS,AC		3701242		4262875		6114141		6002404	PIECES DU 751 ET 752
76	TELECOMM,SOUND EQUIPMENT		11293223		14384760		16752615		16102989	EQUIPMENT DE TELECOM
761	TELEVISION RECEIVERS	MN 9750	1240169	MN 10402	1553599	MN 10428	1512441	N 6719602	1025847	RECEPTEURS DE TELEVISION
7611	COLOUR TV RECEIVERS	N 6412281	1084955	N 7071059	1406074	N 7186168	1369762	N 5196603	970052	RECEPTEURS COULEUR
762	RADIO BROADCAST RECEIVRS	MN 191408	3110418	MN 230396	4041337	MN 258211	4540127	MN 242661	3827682	RECEPTEURS RADIODIFFUSION
7622	PORTABLE RADIO RECEIVERS	MN 150965	1947137	MN 185207	2524449	MN 208918	2833711	MN 195023	2293169	RECEPT PORTATIFS RADIO
7628	OTHER RADIO RECEIVERS	MN 29119	951227	MN 30534	1246527	MN 34888	1353393	MN 32801	1081991	AUTRES RECEPT RADIO
763	SOUND RECORDRS,PHONOGRPH	MN 49439	972526		1357717	MN 58777	1637396	MN 57000	1855463	PHONO,APP ENREGISTREMENT
7638	OTHR SOUND APPARATUS ETC	MN 49121	970624	MN 54586	1357008	MN 58538	1631392	MN 56683	1847801	AUT APP D'ENREGIS,REPROD
76381	TV IMAGE,SND RECRDRS ETC	N 1287958	317198	N 2640498	380795	N 2880120	547311	N 4766446	757431	APP ENREG,REPRO IMAG,SON
76388	DICTATING MACHINES ETC	MN 47833	653425	MN 51945	976213	MN 55658	1084081	MN 51917	1090370	MACHINES A DICTER
764	TELECOM EQPT,PTS,ACC NES		5970110		7432107		9062650		9393997	EQUIP TELECOM,PIECES
7641	LINE TELEPHONE,ETC EQUIP		881464		1019475		1443398	MN 306291	2319308	APP TELEPHON PAR FIL
7642	MICROPH,LOUDSPKR,AMPLIFR	MN 231176	363214	MN 324353	574179	MN 407531	867669	MN 380628	926029	MICRO,HAUT-PARLEUR,AMPLI
7643	TV,RADIO TRANSMITTRS ETC	MN 20207	789857	MN 25912	1135123	MN 29395	1464072	MN 18594	700273	APP EMET TELE RADIO
7649	PTS NES OF EQUIPMT OF 76		3599830		4397621		4950287		5201474	PIECES DE LA DIV 76
76491	PTS NES OF APPAR OF 7641		379426		393334		489934		841417	PIECES POUR 764.1
76493	TELECOMM EQUIPMT PTS NES		2156280		2457263		2746603		2568051	PIECES 761,762,764.3,8
76499	PARTS ETC OF SOUND EQUIP		958366		1422947		1527156		1621198	PIECES NDA POUR 763
77	ELECTRIC MACHNRY NES ETC		12323202		14551799		19594346		20624979	MACH APP ELECT NDA
771	ELECTRIC POWER MACHY NES		1432444		1765505		2466776		2610352	MACH PROD,TRANS ELECTR
7712	OTH ELEC POWER MACHY NES		1179494		1449842		2045013		2168628	AUT APP PROD TRANSF ELEC
77121	STATIC CONVERTERS ETC	MN 771466	544658	MN 1102874	647582	MN 1297640	876669	MN 1068295	987091	CONVERTISSEURS STATIQUES
77129	PTS NES OF MACHY OF 771		375488		465305		702147		704491	PIECES MACH DU 771
772	SWITCHGEAR ETC,PARTS NES		1458571		1759929		2301950		2461939	APP COUPURE,SECT ETC
7721	SWITCHGEAR ETC		911003		1055486		1350435		1439141	APP COUPURE,SECTIONMNT
7722	PRINTED CIRCUITS,PTS NES		453548		592851		800514		877313	CIRCUITS ET PIECES
773	ELECTR DISTRIBUTNG EQUIP		619760		753082		993770		1071707	EQUIPMT DISTRIBUTION ELECT
7731	INSULATED WIRE,CABLE ETC		606766		742693		980199		1058268	FILS,CABLES ISOLES ELECT
775	HOUSEHOLD TYPE EQUIP NES		2464353		2696675		3281536		3619044	MACH,APP USAGE DOMESTQUE
7757	DOMESTIC ELECTRC EQU NES		1030142		1094878		1282199		1416011	APP ELECTR DOMEST NDA
77572	DOM ELEC ROOM FANS ETC	MN 32455	457851	MN 37654	509260	MN 50541	657925	MN 52462	709227	HOTTES ASPIRANTES,VENTIL
7758	ELECTRO-THERMIC APPL NES		1347110		1480185		1796719		1982817	APP ELECTROTHERMIQ NDA
77583	ELEC HAIR DRESSING APPAR	MN 84022	433433	MN 91877	438161	MN 91799	474365	MN 92856	483823	APP ELECT POUR COIFFURE
77586	ELECTROTHERM DOM APP NES	MN 42470	524223	MN 46013	610210	MN 58711	818219	MN 69144	961789	APP ELECTRO THERMIQUES
776	TRANSISTORS,VALVES,ETC		4105819		5175641		7576045		7649687	LAMPES,TUBES,VALVES
7761	TV PICTURE TUBES	N 5288623	346516	N 6510277	450165	N 7757718	592705	MN 10789	934799	TUBES CATHODIQUES
7763	DIODES,TRANSISTORS,ETC	MN 14998827	590393	MN 23372812	733094	MN 34616229	1037214	MN 113340793	1080583	DIODES,TRANSISTORS
7764	ELECTRONIC MICROCIRCUITS	MN 7112241	2898107	MN 52112744	3690392	MN 9087141	5493961	MN 11883538	5139569	MICROSTRUCTURES ELECTRON
778	ELECTRICAL MACHINERY NES		2088867		2271793		2838025		3062831	AUTRES MACH ELECT NDA
7781	BATTERIES,ACCUMULATORS		528717		626535		873199		959480	PILES ET ACCUMULATEURS
7788	OTH ELEC MACHY,EQUIP NES		971662		1053661		1306819		1325397	AUT MACH APP ELEC NDA
78	ROAD VEHICLES		4236143		3830812		2000994		1827923	VEHICULES ROUTIERS
781	PASS MOTOR VEH EXC BUSES	N 71489	1871222	N 45378	1092202	N 15774	303991	N 24212	314174	AUTO TRANSPORT PERSONNES
782	LORRIES,SPCL MTR VEH NES	N 21919	388142	N 29689	559949	N 2837	70533	N 2793	55727	VEHICULES SPECIAUX,MARCH
7821	LORRIES,TRUCKS	N 21671	368067	N 29388	540022	N 2523	45274	N 2573	38137	VEHICULES TRANSP MARCHAND
784	MOTOR VEH PRTS,ACCES NES		621570		553321		497980		516696	PIECES 722,781,782,783
7849	OTHER MOTOR VEHCL PARTS		431259		334573		361639		420040	PIECES 722,781,782,783
785	CYCLES,ETC MOTRZD OR NOT		1211170		1223126		1071881		869396	MOTOCYCLES SCOOTERS
7851	MOTORCYCLES ETC	N 520620	679395	N 404114	583857	N 162208	215267	N 101418	135137	MOTO VELO MOTEUR AUXIL
7853	INVAL CARR, PTS OF 785		285474		341219		588478		509671	FAUTEUILS INVALIDES,PIECES
78539	PARTS,ACCES NES OF 785		285019		341000		587709		507561	PIECES DU 785
8	MISC MANUFACTURED GOODS		56405498		61001407		66636065		69611761	ART MANUFACTURES DIVERS
812	*PLUMBG,HEATNG,LGHTNG EQ		1025302		1098160		1289001		1424416	APPAR SANITAIRES CHAUFFAGE
8124	LIGHTING EQUIPMENT NES		981651		1056795		1235529		1376769	APPAREILS ECLAIRAGE ETC
81242	LAMPS,FITTINGS BASE METL		545515		621465		725464		823552	APPAREILS D'ECLAIRAGE
821	*FURNITURE,PARTS THEREOF		569198		709378		770254		789084	MEUBLES ET PIECES
831	*TRAVEL GOODS,HANDBAGS	MN 1619140	3562049	MN 1770872	4071682	MN 2027468	4630253	MN 2088968	4835748	ARTICLES DE VOYAGE ETC
83101	HANDBAGS NES	MN 243827	1252845	MN 263354	1391061	MN 265008	1448917	MN 270079	1531267	SACS A MAIN
83109	OTHER TRAVEL BAGS,CASES	MN 1233958	1936110	MN 1338622	2261021	MN 1594642	2731048	MN 1650408	2813328	AUT CONTENANTS SIMILAIRES
84	CLOTHING AND ACCESSORIES		21013058		21428858		21327152		22009265	VETEMENTS
842	MENS OUTERWEAR NOT KNIT	MN 430165	3072667	MN 431468	3066101	MN 391379	3004382	MN 386497	3141023	VET DESSUS POUR HOMMES
8423	— TROUSERS,BREECHES ETC	MN 252759	1320516	MN 255994	1355289	MN 247655	1434495	MN 257176	1593924	PANTALONS HOMMES MAT TEX
8424	— JACKETS,BLAZERS ETC	MN 46983	646057	MN 39538	554101	MN 38533	517736	MN 37602	518001	VESTES HOMMES MAT TEXTIL
8429	— OTHER OUTER GARMENTS	MN 125138	983326	MN 131747	1052033	MN 101029	953316	MN 88122	936919	AUT VET DES HOM MAT TEX
843	WOMENS OUTERWEAR NONKNIT	MN 694358	5896216	MN 670136	5764497	MN 679921	5668010	MN 697085	5936186	VET DESSUS FEMMES MAT TEX
8431	— COATS AND JACKETS	MN 38656	835577	MN 36384	765297	MN 34637	761402	MN 37782	810592	MANT,VEST FEM MAT TEXTIL
8435	— BLOUSES	MN 199292	1813007	MN 178490	1609405	MN 156300	1422973	MN 148688	1328043	BLOUSES FEM MAT TEXTILES
8439	— OTHER OUTER GARMENTS	MN 390843	2371288	MN 383216	2429094	MN 405814	2462936	MN 421914	2737700	AUT VET DES FEM MAT TEXT
844	UNDER GARMENTS NOT KNIT		1906510		1796424	MN 321221	1699808		1603940	VETEMENT DESSOUS MAT TEX
8441	— MENS SHIRTS		1545528		1444651	MN 245976	1389398		1303493	CHEMISES HOMMES MAT TEXT
84411	—— OF COTTON	MN 139635	930995	MN 146941	955490	MN 143436	985748	MN 139675	986651	CHEMISES HOMMES DE COTON
84412	—— OF SYNTHETIC FIBRES		614533		489161	MN 102540	403650		316842	CHEMISES HOMMES FIB SYNT
845	OUTERWEAR KNIT NONELASTC	MN 787266	5865968	MN 832560	6152644	MN 847619	5914379	MN 867672	6123311	VET DESSOUS,ACCES BONNET
8451	— JERSEYS,PULLOVERS ETC	MN 346588	3707703	MN 366864	3860372	MN 340342	3551935	MN 356324	3680309	CHANDAILS,PULL-OVERS ETC
8459	— OTHER,CLTHG ACCESRYS	MN 415412	1901994	MN 443977	2063172	MN 483086	2101749	MN 486849	2174839	AUT VET DESSUS DE BONNE
846	UNDER GARMENTS KNITTED		2445441		2658997		2989633		3039388	SOUS VETS DE BONNETERIE
8462	— OF COTTON NON ELASTIC	MN 1811800	1898777	MN 1793581	2056054	MN 1737039	2310727	MN 1606817	2384465	SOUS-VET BONNET COTON
84621	—— MENS SHIRTS	MN 59039	425578	MN 65226	488722	MN 62963	517948	MN 59677	496558	CHEMISES DE COTON
84629	—— OTHER	MN 1752762	1473198	MN 1728355	1567332	MN 1674076	1792779	MN 1547140	1887907	AUT SOUS-VET BONNET COTON
8465	CORSETS,GARTERS,ETC	MN 279703	437106	MN 317621	483487	MN 322557	539268	MN 304656	515811	CORSETS,GAINES ART SIM

5. General Exports F.O.B. by Commodities according to the S.I.T.C. (Rev. 2) in thousand U.S. Dollars
Exportations Générales F.O.B. par Produits d'après la C.T.C.I. (Rév. 2) en milliers de Dollars E.U.

SITC CTCI	COMMODITY	1993		1994		1995		1996		PRODUIT
		WEIGHT POIDS	VALUE VALEUR	WEIGHT POIDS	VALUE VALEUR	WEIGHT POIDS	VALUE VALEUR	WEIGHT POIDS	VALUE VALEUR	
847	TEXTILE CLTHNG ACCES NES		411827		466723		534596		579046	ACCES VET MAT TEXT NDA
848	HEADGEAR,NONTXTL CLOTHNG		1414429		1523471		1516345		1586371	VET ACCES MAT AUT QUE TEX
8481	LEATHER CLOTHES,ACCESSOR		685949		809465		793509		741893	VET ACCES MAT CUIR ARTIF
851	*FOOTWEAR	MP 1328864	5767781	MP 1405618	6554206	MP 1446541	7401059	MP 1389228	7954634	CHAUSSURES
85101	FOOTWEAR RUBBER,PLASTIC	MP 718505	2445167	MP 769695	2694455	MP 836413	3111590	MP 831405	3284133	CHAUS SEMELLES CAOUTCH
85102	FOOTWEAR LEATHER	MP 560606	3248380	MP 597439	3804493	MP 579570	4246661	MP 529032	4628461	CHAUS SEMELLES EN CUIR
87	PRECISION INSTRUMNTS NES		1070279		1226587		1554045		1877835	INSTRUM,APPAR SCIENT NDA
871	OPTICAL INSTRUMENTS		266550		369944		579499		711838	APPAR,INSTRUM D'OPTIQUE
87109	OPTICAL INSTRUMENTS NES		197566		282757		467204		590137	APP,INSTRUM OPTIQUE NDA
874	MEASURNG,CONTROLNG INSTR		568743		583295		661343		784573	INSTRUMENTS DE MESURE
88	PHOTO EQU,OPTICL GDS ETC		6485554		7187928		8379724		8696714	APP,FOURN PHOTO,OP,MONTR
881	PHOTO APPARAT,EQUIPT NES		1028095		1121911		1482009		1627370	APP,EQUIP PHOTO NDA
8811	CAMERAS STILL,FLASH APP		952392		1070201		1423157		1549880	APPAREILS PHOTO,PIECES
88111	STILL CAMERAS	MN 62346	583880	MN 58962	621880	MN 77350	814779	MN 83973	893752	APPAREILS PHOTOGRAPHIQ
88119	PTS NES OF APPAR OF 8811		345312		423699		567201		616966	PIECES POUR 881.1
882	PHOTO,CINEMA SUPPLIES		323034		412145		524498		512320	PRODUITS PHOTO,CINEMA
884	OPTICAL GOODS NES		393414		446484		570501		669555	ELEMENTS OPTIQ,ART LUNET
8842	SPECTACLES AND FRAMES		335290		390582		507866		585428	LUNETTES ET MONTURES
885	WATCHES AND CLOCKS		4722663		5193429		5789699		5879243	HORLOGERIE
8851	WATCHES,MOVEMENTS,CASES		3680723		3970939		4398806		4476580	MONTRES,MOUVEMENTS,BOITES
88511	WATCHES		3066268		3294036		3663917		3822057	MONTRES POCHE,BRACELET
8852	CLOCKS,CLOCK,WATCH PARTS		1041940		1222489		1390893		1402663	HORLOGES,MOUV,PARTIES
88529	CLOCK,WATCH PARTS NES		685064		758619		810114		768991	FOURNIT D HORLOG NDA
89	MISC MANUFCTRD GOODS NES		16912278		18724607		21284577		22024066	ART MANUFACTURES DIVERS
892	PRINTED MATTER		740478		772628		888710		901529	IMPRIMES
8921	PRINTED BOOKS,GLOBES,ETC		434662		443522		517623		536317	LIVRES,BROCHURES,CARTES
89211	PRINTED BOOKS,PAMPHLETS		406302		404177		459228		474245	LIVRES,BROCHURES
893	ARTICLES OF PLASTIC NES		2332764		2742170		3219866		3354906	OUVRAGES EN MAT DIVIS 58
8931	PLSTC PACKG CONTNRS,LIDS		410766		629036		1107050		1032165	ART TRANSP EMBALLAGE ETC
8939	MISC PLASTIC ARTICLES		1911665		2102978		2096610		2296069	ART DIVERS EN MAT DIV 58
89399	OTHR PLASTC ARTICLES NES		1786967		1952539		1937324		2128712	AUT OUV MAT DIV 58
894	TOYS,SPORTING GOODS,ETC		8649705		9702033		11055482		11624152	VOITURES ENFANTS,JOUETS
8942	TOYS,INDOOR GAMES ETC		8122387		9002967		10127065		10608486	JOUETS,JEUX ETC
89422	DOLLS		675803		705049		797210		856298	POUPEES
89423	TOYS NES		5267067		5855072		6277976		6528588	JOUETS,MODELES REDUITS
89424	INDOOR GAME EQUIPMENT		966524		1076961		1262366		1392916	ART,JEUX DE SOCIETE
89425	XMAS DECORATIONS ETC		1200222		1339197		1755027		1792203	ART DIVERTIS,FETES
8947	OTH SPORT GDS,FAIR AMUSM		470441		602981		825630		897475	AUT ART DE SPORT
89472	OTH OUTDOOR SPORT GOODS		397811		523706		713918		785267	ART POUR JEUX PLEIN AIR
897	GOLD,SILVER WARE,JEWELRY		1406686		1484543		1660590		1690280	BIJOUTERIE,ORFEVRERIE
8973	PREC JEWLRY,GLD–SILVWARE		1045001		1112978		1289351		1335809	BIJOUX OR,ARGENT ORFEVRE
89731	PRECIOUS METAL JEWELLERY		926464		963651		1129622		1194134	ART BIJOUTERIE,JOAILLER
898	MUSICAL INSTRUMENTS,PTS		871102		783070		915509		901744	INSTRUMENTS DE MUSIQUE
8983	SOUND RECRDNG TAPE,DISCS		799960		692145		796317		771156	SUPPORTS SON POUR 763
89831	PREPD SND RECORDNG MEDIA		680172		576589		629639	MN 1245580	599386	SUPPORTS PREPARES
899	OTHER MANUFACTURED GOODS		2552170		2818833		3079081		3071031	AUT ART MANUF DIVERS NDA
8994	UMBRELLAS,CANES ETC		546816		630060		617667		578999	PARAPLUIES,CANNES ETC
89941	UMBRELLAS,SUNSHADES	MN 262308	454007	MN 300263	524053	MN 281717	523793	MN 266155	509662	PARAPLUIES,PARASOLS ETC
8998	SMALLWARES,TOILETRYS ETC		438838		456939		525334		618937	ART MERCERIE,TOILETTE
8999	OTHER MANUF GOODS NES		978229		1104570		1201829		1129540	OUVRAGES DIVERS NDA
89993	ARTIFICIAL FLOWERS ETC		864264		997075		1075273		1010798	FLEURS ARTIFICIELLES
9	GOODS NOT CLASSD BY KIND		990533		974006		1088365		1275341	ART TRANSACT NON CLASSES
931	*SPECIAL TRANSACTIONS		846860		884823		957048		1096572	TRANS.SPECIALES

1. HISTORICAL SERIES, 1961–1996 GENERAL TRADE, IMPORTS C.I.F., EXPORTS F.O.B.
SERIES HISTORIQUES, 1961–1996 COMMERCE GENERAL, IMPORTATIONS C.A.F., EXPORTATIONS F.O.B

YEAR ANNEE	VALUE IN MILLION EXCHANGE FORINT / VALEUR EN MILLION EXCHANGE FORINT — MERCHANDISE # 1 – MARCHANDISE IMPORTS	EXPORTS	GOLD – OR IMPORTS	EXPORTS	CONVERSION FACTORS U.S. CENTS PER EXCHANGE FORINT / FACTEURS DE CONVERSION CENTS E.U. PAR EXCHANGE FORINT IMPORTS	EXPORTS	INDEX NUMBERS – INDICES: QUANTUM IMPORTS	QUANTUM EXPORTS	UNIT VALUE / VALEUR UNITAIRE IMPORTS	UNIT VALUE EXPORTS
1961	12040.00	12080.00			8.5200	8.5200	22	15	38	48
1962	13485.00	12906.00			8.5200	8.5200	25	16	37	47
1963	15327.00	14156.00			8.5200	8.5200	29	18	37	48
1964	17546.00	15870.00			8.5200	8.5200	32	19	38	48
1965	17849.00	17721.00			8.5200	8.5200	32	22	38	49
1966	18379.00	18705.00			8.5200	8.5200	33	24	37	47
1967	20841.00	19971.00			8.5200	8.5200	39	26	36	46
1968	21163.00	21004.00			8.5200	8.5200	40	27	35	46
1969	22631.00	24462.00			8.5200	8.5200	42	31	36	47
1970	29410.00	27197.00			8.5200	8.5200	54	33	37	48
1971	35098.00	29355.00			8.5200	8.5200	63	36	37	48
1972	34093.00	35583.00			9.2507	9.2507	60	43	38	49
1973	37299.00	42039.00			10.5063	10.5460	62	48	41	52
1974	51010.00	46927.00			10.9315	10.9315	72	50	47	56
1975	61537.00	52170.00			11.6611	11.6759	76	52	54	59
1976	230056.00	204833.00			2.4030	2.4080	79	57	50	56
1977	267309.00	238590.00			2.4401	2.4443	86	64	54	58
1978	300933.00	240707.00			2.6258	2.6359	97	65	54	58
1979	308905.00	282129.00			2.8079	2.8135	94	73	57	60
1980	299899.00	281012.00			3.0793	3.0877	93	74	56	60
1981	314284.30	299405.30			2.9044	2.9099	94	77	59	62
1982	324818.70	324486.10			2.7134	2.7018	91	80	61	62
1983	364963.10	374107.90			2.3298	2.3244	92	86	66	66
1984	390511.10	413956.90			2.0720	2.0685	92	92	70	69
1985	410127.60	424600.60			2.0062	2.0118	99	96	73	71
1986	425005.00	406203.90			2.1864	2.1849	102	94	77	72
1987	443955.90	432609.00			2.1286	2.1277	104	97	78	74
1988	460893.90	492325.80			1.9822	1.9782	104	104	81	79
1989	523506.90	571322.80			1.6816	1.6775	105	104	91	91
1990	544900.10	603600.10			1.5912	1.5900	100	100	100	100
1991	855600.10	764300.00			1.3343	1.3345	105	95	146	131
1992	878599.90	843600.10			1.2640	1.2656	98	96	161	143
1993	1158099.00	819899.90			1.0811	1.0841	119	84	176	160
1994	1518299.00	1128699.00			0.9473	0.9470	136	97	203	189
1995	1894400.00	1576100.00			0.7942	0.7889	131	106	269	254
1996	2426400.00	1936400.00			0.6534	0.6531				

2. IMPORTS BY BROAD ECONOMIC CATEGORY AND EXPORTS BY INDUSTRIAL ORIGIN. (PERCENTAGE OF TOTAL VALUE)
IMPORTATIONS PAR CATEGORIES ECONOMIQUES ET EXPORTATIONS PAR BRANCHE D'ACTIVITE.(EN POURCENTAGE DE LA VALEUR TOTALE)

IMPORTS – IMPORTATIONS

	1990	1991	1992	1993	1994	1995	1996
TOTAL IMPORTS–IMPORTATIONS TOTALES						100.	100.
1 FOOD BEV–ALIMENTATION BOISSONS						3.9	3.4
11 PRIMARY–PRODUITS DE BASE						2.0	1.6
111 FOR INDUSTRY–POUR L'INDUSTRIE						0.8	0.7
112 FOR HOUSEHOLDS–POUR LES MENAGES						1.2	0.9
12 PROCESSED–PRODUITS ELABORES						1.9	1.8
121 FOR INDUSTRY–POUR L'INDUSTRIE						0.3	0.4
122 FOR HOUSEHOLDS–POUR LES MENAGES						1.6	1.4
2 IND SUPPLIES–APPROV INDUSTRIELS						39.7	39.0
21 PRIMARY–PRODUITS DE BASE						2.4	2.4
22 PROCESSED–PRODUITS ELABORES						37.3	36.7
3 FUELS–COMBUSTIBLES						11.7	13.6
31 PRIMARY–PRODUITS DE BASE						8.9	10.8
32 PROCESSED–PRODUITS ELABORES						2.8	2.8
321 MOTOR SPIRIT–ESSENCE							
322 OTHER–AUTRES						2.8	2.8
4 MACHINERY–EQUIPEMENT						21.2	21.6
41 CAPITAL EQUIPMENT–MACHINES						17.8	18.2
42 PARTS–PIECES ACCESSOIRES						3.4	3.4
5 TRANSPORT–TRANSPORT						8.0	7.9
51 PASSENGER CARS–AUTOMOBILES						2.7	2.8
52 OTHER–AUTRES						2.8	2.6
521 INDUSTRIAL–INDUSTRIELS						2.7	2.5
522 NON INDUSTRIAL–NON INDUSTRIEL						0.1	0.0
53 PARTS–PIECES ACCESSOIRES						2.5	2.5
6 CONSUM GOODS–BIENS CONSOMMATION						13.6	13.5
61 DURABLE–DURABLES						3.0	2.8
62 SEMI DURABLE–SEMI DURABLES						6.3	6.5
63 NON DURABLE–NON DURABLES						4.3	4.2
7 GOODS NES–BIENS NDA						1.8	1.0

EXPORTS – EXPORTATIONS

	1990	1991	1992	1993	1994	1995	1996
TOTAL EXPORTS–EXPORTATIONS TOTALES						100.	100.
1 AGRICULTURE						8.1	5.6
2 MINING QUARRY–INDUS EXTRACTIVES						0.3	0.5
3 MANUFACTURING–IND MANUFACTUR						91.6	93.9
31 FOOD BEV TOBACCO–ALIM BOISS TAB						14.2	15.3
32 TEXTILES–INDUSTRIES TEXTILES						12.9	13.7
33 WOOD & PRODUCTS–BOIS & PRODUITS						1.6	1.7
34 PAPER & PRODUCTS–PAPIER & PRODT						1.6	2.0
35 CHEMICALS–INDUSTRIES CHIMIQUES						16.5	15.8
36 NON METAL MIN–MIN NON METAL						1.9	2.2
37 BASIC METAL–IND METAL BASE						6.3	5.5
38 METAL MANUF–MANUF METAL						32.9	33.1
39 OTH MANUF IND–AUTRES MANUF						3.7	4.5

3. TRADE BY PRINCIPAL COUNTRIES OF PURCHASE AND SALE (VALUE IN THOUSAND U.S. DOLLARS)
ECHANGES SELON LES PRINCIPAUX PAYS D'ACHAT ET DE VENTE (VALEUR EN MILLIERS DE DOLLARS EU)

COUNTRIES–PAYS	GENERAL IMPORTS C.I.F. IMPORTATIONS GENERALES C.A.F				
	1992	1993	1994	1995	1996
World	11078877	12530286	14553612	15466222	16208896
Africa	47443	58764	90190	154206	147252
Americas	540091	701357	685524	751034	863776
Northern America	361452	522424	485727	523765	616066
LAIA	164997	165164	187692	218429	235763
CACM	8621	9835	8331	7424	6851
Caribbean	764	564	424	850	2199
Rest of America	4257	3370	3350	566	2897
As.ex F.USSR	626148	802530	960692	1050433	1207904
Eur.x F.USSR	7902451	8087118	10484841	11218681	11569302
EU	6648352	6816244	8888486	9514933	9684512
EFTA	368807	377924	413727	407387	377235
East Europe	744832	758005	1038908	1134633	1334214
Other Europe	500	670	1042	1368	1519
Former USSR	1867500	2780145	2192626	2284168	2405501
Oceania	7596	5848	5549	7419	15003
Germany/Allemagne	2608726	2704291	3402866	3628234	3819833
Russian Federation	1867500	2446756	1745839	1839785	2020500
Austria/Autriche	1592717	1455844	1748270	1663721	1535645
Italy/Italie	698603	750265	1017550	1220388	1312582
France,Monac	342351	416671	497164	610747	686647
USA/Etats–Unis d'Amer	323257	489422	451717	481734	568888
United Kingdom	320618	319151	571116	476470	528764
Netherlands/Pays–Bas	329492	337464	443170	483651	513253
Switz.Liecht	347375	360325	392603	384026	352205
Japan/Japon	264042	343460	392939	339239	361495
Belgium–Luxembourg	222244	248508	321745	391457	411951
Czech Republic		263967	347433	363995	487353
Slovakia		237992	355589	369703	382155
Sweden/Suède	205226	191957	303288	311422	281346
Ukraine		142838	297078	346824	292102
Poland/Pologne	179353	148239	193337	248452	298397
Finland/Finlande	113160	142156	236527	214597	191239
Spain/Espagne	68465	106139	144592	220606	162838
Brazil/Brésil	113440	123165	139019	140745	173656
Romania/Roumanie	70159	85074	118961	130166	146538
China/Chine	40093	71553	99175	126316	192236
Korea, Republic of	54016	67227	98742	146391	148998
Denmark/Danemark	67766	75739	105327	117026	117683
Czechoslovakia	475859				
Slovenia/Slovénia		62219	80428	92793	88751
Ireland/Irlande	40659	26347	39160	89159	46406
Croatia/Croatie		56901	51785	57054	48402
Greece/Grèce	31336	34369	40309	53967	52651
Turkey/Turquie	25868	23930	47919	46104	56912
Singapore/Singapour	34365	44683	42118	35000	39214
Canada	38068	32920	34002	42022	47146
Israel/Israël	30970	29826	33362	47443	50910
Yugoslavia/Yougoslavie	139960	2809	818	965	28969
Lithuania/Lituanie		108456	43893	10136	8319
India/Inde	30288	33395	25536	32517	45852
Hong Kong	10031	21631	27246	46646	58483
Malaysia/Malaisie	10004	16272	24108	33691	52318
Uganda/Ouganda	2849	8253	27114	49774	39854
Indonesia/Indonésie	19965	18795	24121	26559	38404
Belarus/Bélarus		15903	42545	32916	35882
Thailand/Thaïlande	15356	20644	22476	27336	23915
Norway,SVD,JM	19765	17211	20711	22450	23276
Bulgaria/Bulgarie	17762	20958	22962	21760	19187
Portugal	6989	7343	17402	33488	23674
Kazakhstan		28624	30624	12401	12130
Uzbekistan/Ouzbékistan		16568	17761	21181	24594
Peru/Pérou	10316	7746	12831	23582	24350
Viet Nam	9262	10168	14558	10813	14204
So. Africa Customs Un	8427	8189	2960	15442	21379
Argentina/Argentine	4674	5147	7897	25140	11781

COUNTRIES–PAYS	GENERAL EXPORTS F.O.B. EXPORTATIONS GENERALES F.O.B.				
	1992	1993	1994	1995	1996
Monde	10704720	8906242	10699843	12865482	13144047
Afrique	96828	79196	77564	125164	105331
Amériques	447863	450472	531329	498577	555680
Amérique du Nord	393380	401736	466089	435457	487226
ALAI	41774	40424	49969	58289	61441
MCAC	2047	2195	1638	882	1647
Caraïbes	10190	5226	5805	3632	4907
Autre Amérique	472	891	7828	317	459
Asie l'URSS exclus	762115	650109	511644	540015	553247
Europe l'URSS exclus	7959911	6293092	8215795	9968771	10376230
UE	6673690	5178762	6817962	8079403	8249955
AELE	228369	188070	186627	200981	203213
Europe de l'Est	674405	673278	796696	1158959	1250885
Autre de l'Europe	4286	3365	3446	3338	2450
Ancienne URSS	1406988	1360535	1241362	1416047	1240008
Océanie	20845	20203	22292	22854	23340
Germany/Allemagne	2967807	2370265	3017454	3686764	3814760
Austria/Autriche	1143533	897452	1163883	1303271	1394715
Italy/Italie	1020758	713359	906052	1096275	1054963
Russian Federation	1406988	952812	807038	822791	776631
France,Monac	342991	307301	379665	517854	486513
USA/Etats–Unis d'Amer	344454	376166	430467	413540	464310
United Kingdom	213618	203171	464736	391497	383800
Netherlands/Pays–Bas	239242	210365	270706	374897	351729
Poland/Pologne	143064	163364	221981	337140	387767
Romania/Roumanie	189522	183833	197248	357451	277558
Belgium–Luxembourg	240862	162972	210308	273388	284831
Ukraine		159956	229765	317694	219836
Switz.Liecht	206916	173222	168734	178238	176947
Czech Republic		170087	197716	207387	289703
Slovenia/Slovénia		139886	195843	255214	219983
Slovakia		128137	143633	213151	251031
Sweden/Suède	130962	91212	124889	125708	137825
Yugoslavia/Yougoslavie	379161	14646	27260	29760	145741
Croatia/Croatie		78691	144714	172150	190179
Spain/Espagne	126583	65626	94943	122267	141591
Japan/Japon	98436	85876	91917	76809	101308
Turkey/Turquie	135408	95244	32396	52467	56911
Finland/Finlande	71131	49315	72833	56997	62865
Czechoslovakia	290582				
Greece/Grèce	78403	57771	42156	48709	59998
Lithuania/Lituanie		107870	52668	39822	60563
Denmark/Danemark	55998	39007	51359	57931	53811
Iran (Islamic Rp. of)	114985	57750	26503	33430	23307
Israel/Israël	39700	32041	66674	49956	40431
Belarus/Bélarus		37790	39345	78957	43036
Uzbekistan/Ouzbékistan		27673	50357	71415	19814
Bulgaria/Bulgarie	39261	23293	32145	38348	32492
Egypt/Egypte	39703	31765	26021	24978	40910
Bosnia and Herzegovina		2833	18182	40038	97554
Canada	48432	24822	35136	21588	22627
Saudi Arabia	25698	29949	26365	29140	33902
Lebanon/Liban	29997	23696	23418	33597	21172
Syrian Arab Republic	31171	33170	22214	18405	26177
India/Inde	23962	39115	26280	23218	16260
China/Chine	15902	50957	11720	22359	16931
Kazakhstan		37252	24208	23529	32226
Pakistan	23261	22711	19442	23049	20864
Kuwait/ Koweït	20257	21562	21957	12530	27423
Australia/Australie	19301	18906	20941	21299	20943
Norway,SVD,JM	20958	14550	17148	22195	25521
Brazil/Brésil	16414	12004	15973	27689	27010
Tfyr Macedonia		13561	25065	28928	16270
Cyprus/Chypre	25120	8859	9143	16423	22289
Hong Kong	9006	13502	14729	20037	19639
Algeria/Algérie	7376	7133	8277	44463	7747

(VALUE AS PERCENTAGE OF WORLD TOTAL)(VALEURS EN POURCENTAGE DU TOTAL MONDIAL)

	1987	1988	1989	1990	1991	1992	1993	1994	1995	1996
Africa	1.0	1.4	0.9	3.6	2.6	0.4	0.5	0.6	1.0	0.9
Americas	5.1	5.6	5.2	5.4	4.6	4.9	5.6	4.7	4.9	5.3
Northern America	2.7	2.3	2.6	2.8	2.8	3.3	4.2	3.3	3.4	3.8
LAIA	2.1	2.9	2.3	2.4	1.6	1.5	1.3	1.3	1.4	1.5
CACM	0.1	0.2	0.1	0.2	0.2	0.1	0.1	0.1	0.0	0.0
Caribbean	0.2	0.2	0.1	0.0	0.0	0.0	0.0	0.0	0.0	0.0
Rest of America	0.0	0.0	0.0	0.0	0.0	0.0	0.0	0.0	0.0	0.0
As.ex F.USSR	7.7	6.9	6.3	7.2	7.4	5.7	6.4	6.6	6.8	7.5
Eur.x F.USSR	57.6	60.9	65.4	64.6	68.5	71.3	64.5	72.0	72.5	71.4
EU	32.7	34.9	39.7	43.2	56.9	60.0	54.4	61.1	61.5	59.7
EFTA	2.7	2.7	3.1	3.2	3.6	3.3	3.0	2.8	2.6	2.3
East Europe	19.0	18.8	17.2	14.7	7.0	6.7	6.0	7.1	7.3	8.2
Other Europe	3.2	4.4	5.4	3.5	1.1	0.0	0.0	0.0	0.0	0.0
Former USSR	28.5	25.0	22.1	19.1	15.4	16.9	22.2	15.1	14.8	14.8
Oceania	0.1	0.2	0.1	0.1	0.1	0.1	0.0	0.0	0.0	0.1
Germany/Allemagne	13.9	13.9	16.1	17.4	21.5	23.5	21.6	23.4	23.5	23.6
Russian Federation						16.9	19.5	12.0	11.9	12.5
Austria/Autriche	6.4	7.2	8.6	10.0	13.4	14.4	11.6	12.0	10.8	9.5
Italy/Italie	2.7	3.1	3.4	4.1	7.3	6.3	6.0	7.0	7.9	8.1
France,Monac	1.9	2.0	2.2	2.1	2.7	3.1	3.3	3.4	3.9	4.2
USA/Etats--Unis d'Amer	2.5	2.2	2.5	2.6	2.6	2.9	3.9	3.1	3.1	3.5
United Kingdom	1.7	1.8	2.2	2.1	2.5	2.9	2.5	3.9	3.1	3.3
Netherlands/Pays–Bas	1.5	1.8	2.1	2.1	2.7	3.0	2.7	3.0	3.1	3.2
Switz.Liecht	2.6	2.6	2.9	3.1	3.4	3.1	2.9	2.7	2.5	2.2
Japan/Japon	1.5	1.5	1.6	2.1	2.7	2.4	2.7	2.7	2.2	2.2

	1987	1988	1989	1990	1991	1992	1993	1994	1995	1996
Afrique	2.7	2.5	2.0	2.1	1.4	0.9	0.9	0.7	1.0	0.8
Amériques	4.7	4.5	5.0	4.7	4.5	4.2	5.1	5.0	3.9	4.2
Amérique du Nord	3.4	3.4	3.7	3.8	3.5	3.7	4.5	4.4	3.4	3.7
ALAI	0.7	0.5	0.7	0.5	0.8	0.4	0.5	0.5	0.5	0.5
MCAC	0.0	0.0	0.0	0.0	0.0	0.0	0.0	0.0	0.0	0.0
Caraïbes	0.5	0.6	0.5	0.3	0.3	0.1	0.1	0.1	0.0	0.0
Autre Amérique	0.0	0.1	0.1	0.0	0.0	0.0	0.0	0.1	0.0	0.0
Asie l'URSS exclus	8.4	10.5	9.7	9.4	9.9	7.1	7.3	4.8	4.2	4.2
Europe l'URSS exclus	51.4	54.5	57.9	63.4	70.5	74.4	70.7	76.8	77.5	78.9
UE	27.1	30.5	33.8	42.3	58.7	62.3	58.1	63.7	62.8	62.8
AELE	2.0	2.1	1.8	2.1	2.1	2.1	2.1	1.7	1.6	1.5
Europe de l'Est	17.4	17.1	15.9	11.2	6.1	6.3	7.6	7.4	9.0	9.5
Autre de l'Europe	4.9	4.8	6.3	7.8	3.7	0.0	0.0	0.0	0.0	0.0
Ancienne URSS	32.7	27.6	25.1	20.2	13.4	13.1	15.3	11.6	11.0	9.4
Océanie	0.1	0.3	0.2	0.2	0.2	0.2	0.2	0.2	0.2	0.2
Germany/Allemagne	9.9	11.0	12.0	17.1	26.9	27.7	26.6	28.2	28.7	29.0
Austria/Autriche	5.5	5.7	6.5	7.5	10.8	10.7	10.1	10.9	10.1	10.6
Italy/Italie	3.6	4.2	4.7	5.9	7.6	9.5	8.0	8.5	8.5	8.0
Russian Federation						13.1	10.7	7.5	6.4	5.9
France,Monac	1.9	2.0	2.4	2.7	2.9	3.2	3.5	3.5	4.0	3.7
USA/Etats–Unis d'Amer	3.0	2.9	3.3	3.5	3.2	3.2	4.2	4.0	3.2	3.5
United Kingdom	1.5	1.9	1.8	2.0	2.0	2.0	2.3	4.3	3.0	2.9
Netherlands/Pays–Bas	1.1	1.2	1.3	1.5	2.1	2.2	2.4	2.5	2.9	2.7
Poland/Pologne	3.4	3.3	3.2	1.7	2.1	1.3	1.8	2.1	2.6	3.0
Romania/Roumanie	1.8	1.7	1.5	1.8	1.3	1.8	2.1	1.8	2.8	2.1

4. General Imports C.I.F. by Commodities according to the S.I.T.C. (Rev. 2) in thousand U.S. Dollars
Importations Générales C.A.F. par Produits d'après la C.T.C.I. (Rév. 2) en milliers de Dollars E.U.

SITC CTCI	COMMODITY	1993 WEIGHT POIDS	1993 VALUE VALEUR	1994 WEIGHT POIDS	1994 VALUE VALEUR	1995 WEIGHT POIDS	1995 VALUE VALEUR	1996 WEIGHT POIDS	1996 VALUE VALEUR	PRODUIT
	ALL COMMODITIES		12530321		14553612		15466222		16208896	TOUS PRODUITS
0	FOOD AND LIVE ANIMALS		629959		809752		714605		688868	ALIMENTS,ANIMAUX VIVANTS
01	MEAT AND PREPARATIONS		49275		109595		70154		37075	VIANDES ET PREPARATIONS
011	MEAT FRESH,CHILLD,FROZEN			W 85171	107547	W 50802	69103	W 27527	36704	VIANDES FRAICHES,REF,CONGE
0113	PIG MEAT FRESH,CHLD,FRZN			W 40079	51721	W 30993	43610	W 11824	17775	VIANDE DE PORC
02	DAIRY PRODCTS,BIRDS'EGGS		47934		41053		21691		21403	PRODUITS LAITIERS,OEUFS
04	CEREALS AND PREPARATIONS		47146		87483		50462		62268	CEREALES ET PRODUITS
05	VEGETABLES AND FRUIT		95834		125439		138915		126614	LEGUMES ET FRUITS
057	FRUIT,NUTS,FRESH,DRIED			W 177378	58822	W 201765	60829	W 170268	59836	FRUITS FRAIS OU SECS
06	SUGAR AND PREPS,HONEY		42859		21899		19664		13162	SUCRES ET PRODUITS
07	COFFEE,TEA,COCOA,SPICES		93269		143692		156846		152444	CAFE,THE,CACAO,EPICES
071	COFFEE AND SUBSTITUTES			W 42911	86037	W 29315	99251	W 33032	81824	CAFE ET SUCCEDANES
0711	COFFEE GREEN,ROASTED,SUB			W 40415	71347	W 27268	86774	W 30374	65794	CAFE TORREFIE OU DECAFEINE
07111	COFFEE GREEN,HUSKS,SKINS			W 40318	71097	W 27151	86306	W 30272	65350	CAFE NON TORREFIE
081	*FEEDING STUFF FOR ANIML			W 573381	166139	W 679313	186708	W 662133	217535	NOURRITURE POUR ANIMAUX
0813	OILCAKE AND OTH RESIDUES			W 495239	119414	W 588901	131578	W 576129	164621	TOURTEAUX
08131	— OF SOYA BEANS			W 452900	114298	W 539112	126440	W 515065	157700	TOURTEAUX DE SOJA
09	MISC EDIBLE PRODUCTS		74956		86139		44368		34282	PREP ALIMENTAIRES DIVERSES
098	EDIBLE PRODCTS,PREPS NES			W 23579	78581	W 15775	41455	W 14922	31477	PREP ALIMENTAIRES NDA
09809	MISC FOOD PREPRTIONS NES			W 15779	66539	W 8313	29405	W 7423	21198	PREP ALIMENTAIRES NDA
1	BEVERAGES AND TOBACCO		70881		92201		79010		99643	BOISSONS ET TABACS
12	TOBACCO AND MANUFACTURES		44373		59644		48934		71285	TABACS BRUTS FABRIQUES
121	TOBACCO UNMNFCTRD,REFUSE			W 16138	55961	W 13030	44357	W 19431	58451	TABACS BRUTS,DECHETS
1212	TOBACCO STRIPPED OR PART			W 10614	44000	W 9928	38791	W 14666	51019	TABACS PART ECOTES
2	CRUDE MATERLS,EXCL FUELS		384355		526716		612490		574569	MAT BRUTES NON COMESTIBLES
23	RUBBER, CRUDE		27002		35134		52821		51987	CAOUTCHOUC BRUT
24	CORK AND WOOD		93322		111633		138506		112078	LIEGE ET BOIS
248	WOOD SHAPED,SLEEPERS			W 470536	98845	W 525831	120701	W 444181	96119	BOIS SIMPLEMENT TRAVAILLES
2482	LUMBER SHAPED CONIFER			W 423726	90961	W 478600	111439	W 416691	87066	CONIFERES SCIES,RABOTES
24821	LUMBER SAWN ETC CONIFER			W 418417	86463	W 472628	106337	W 410453	81760	CONIFERES SCIES LONGITUD
251	*PULP AND WASTE PAPER			W 178139	57021	W 150347	82438	W 208198	75786	PATES A PAPIER,DECHETS
26	TEXTILE FIBRES AND WASTE		65927		82951		87588		90544	FIBRES TEXTILES
27	CRUDE FERTLZR,MINRLS NES		47514		50763		54638		63645	ENGRAIS MINERAUX BRUTS
28	METALLIFEROUS ORES,SCRAP		24737		61819		74018		70079	MINERAIS METAL,DECHETS
281	IRON ORE,CONCENTRATES			W 2179368	56698	W 2090676	58917	W 1471522	53011	MINERAIS DE FER
2816	IRON ORE AGGLOMERATES			W 677243	16052	W 1165957	40520	W 1471522	53011	MINERAIS AGGLOMERES
29	CRUDE ANIMAL,VEG MAT NES		57754		68366		64769		61644	MATIERES BRUTES ANIM,VEGET
292	CRUDE VEG MATERIALS NES			W 14885	49796	W 10098	47829	W 9096	42397	MAT BRUTES VEGETALES NDA
3	MINERAL FUELS ETC		1670408		1724260		1812385		2207680	COMBUSTIBLES MINERAUX LUB
32	COAL,COKE AND BRIQUETTES		153001		206479		202259		216891	HOUILLES,COKES,BRIQUETTES
322	COAL,LIGNITE AND PEAT			W 2586644	111393	W 2150592	103486	W 2448340	125173	HOUILLES,LIGNITES,TOURBE
3222	OTH COAL,NOT AGGLOMERATD			W 1934751	90882	W 1760751	91067	W 1892707	106239	AUTRES HOUILLES
323	BRIQUETS,COKE,SEMI–COKE			W 1013833	95086	W 928951	98773	W 995523	91718	BRIQUETTES
3232	COKE,SEMI–COKE,RTRT CRBN			W 959288	90688	W 902172	96350	W 976675	89853	COKES ET SEMI–COKES
33	PETROLEUM AND PRODUCTS		975726		976609		951313		1048767	PETROLE ET DERIVES
333	CRUDE PETROLEUM			W 5821385	590623	W 5872242	678748	W 5512325	766637	HUILES BRUTES DE PETROLE
334	PETROLEUM PRODUCTS,REFIN			W 2487845	381606	W 1675978	267943	W 1651584	271210	PRODUITS RAFFINES
341	*GAS,NATURAL AND MANUFCT			W 5628942	492211	W 6105983	597680	W 8254489	851774	GAZ NATUREL,GAZ MANUFACT
3414	PETROLEUM GASES, GASEOUS			W 5619001	491083	W 6082451	592959	W 8170895	834740	GAZ DE PETROLE GAZEUX
351	*ELECTRIC CURRENT				48961		61133		90248	ENERGIE ELECTRIQUE
5	CHEMCLS,RELATED PROD NES		1490901		1768163		2112765		2148595	PRODUITS CHIMIQUES
51	ORGANIC CHEMICALS		309846		355541		490051		400595	PROD CHIMIQ ORGANIQUES
511	HYDROCARBONS NES,DERIVS			W 224145	114943	W 234646	178652	W 147721	101025	HYDROCARBURES NDA
5111	ACYCLIC HYDROCARBONS			W 85029	37298	W 100245	63467	W 54824	31966	HYDROCARBURES ACYCLIQUES
51111	ETHYLENE			W 73729	31810	W 92359	57113	W 50009	27659	ETHYLENE
5112	CYCLIC HYDROCARBONS			W 81259	49091	W 88124	80078	W 80134	54766	HYDROCARBURES CYCLIQUES
51125	STYRENE			W 74419	45954	W 80925	75066	W 75345	51697	STYRENE
512	ALCOHOLS,PHENOLS ETC			W 66474	28402	W 88922	55197	W 84154	39997	PHENOLS,PHENOLS–ALCOOLS
5121	ACYCLIC ALCOHOLS,DERIVS			W 62660	23703	W 86405	47151	W 80882	31439	ALCOOLS ACYCLIQUES
513	CARBOXYLIC ACIDS ETC			W 38169	49372	W 36666	67440	W 39434	61091	ACIDES CARBOXYLIQUES
514	NITROGEN–FNCTN COMPOUNDS			W 53407	89364	W 50317	108425	W 61496	120019	COMPOSES FONCT AZOTEES
5148	OTH NITROGN–FNCTN CMPNDS			W 25750	48678	W 20529	54832	W 30735	56984	AUTRES COMPOSES AZOTES
515	ORG–INORG COMPOUNDS ETC			W 8595	42895	W 9036	47550	W 9395	44220	COMPOSES ORGANO–MINERAUX
52	INORGANIC CHEMICALS		91856		103918		112798		119021	PROD CHIM INORGANIQUES
523	OTHR INORG CHEMICALS ETC				55762		66615		69602	AUT PRODUITS CHIMIQUES INORG
53	DYES,TANNING,COLOUR PROD		104720		124731		143616		151474	PROD TEINTURE,COLORANTS
533	PIGMENTS,PAINTS,ETC			W 32707	93478	W 31624	111204	W 36461	117275	PIGMENTS,PEINTURES,VERNIS
541	*MEDICINAL,PHARM PRODUCT				446255		441712		464890	PROD MEDICINAUX PHARMACEUT
5417	MEDICAMENTS			K 6050285	365151	K 7742044	352389	MK 9615	362524	MEDICAMENTS
54171	— CONTAINING ANTIBIOTICS			K 705033	53985	K 883067	43253	K 1272706	67048	MED CONTN ANTIBIOTIQUES
54179	— CONTNG OTH SUBSTANCES			K 5198791	289343	K 6600343	290502	K 7942325	252813	MED CONT AUT SUBSTANCES
55	PERFUME,CLEANING ETC PRD		140447		174737		200019		221967	PROD POUR PARFUM,TOILETTE
551	ESSENTL OILS,PERFUME,ETC			W 1907	21544	W 3660	41929	W 4506	51686	HUILES ESSENTIELLES
5514	MIXED PERFUME SUBSTANCES			W 1806	20747	W 3527	40789	W 4404	50585	MELANGES SUBSTAN ODORIFER
553	PERFUMERY,COSMETICS,ETC			W 23547	87042	W 21522	83971	W 23280	92258	PRODUITS DE PARFUMERIE
554	SOAP,CLEANSING ETC PREPS			W 64289	66151	W 65547	74119	W 72305	78023	SAVONS,PRODUITS DETERSIFS
5542	WASHING PREPARATIONS ETC			W 56571	55026	W 57181	59246	W 63829	64805	PROD ORG TENSIO–ACT NDA
562	*FERTILIZERS,MANUFACTURE			W 518806	44689	W 436998	43999	W 592113	76489	ENGRAIS MANUFACTURES
58	PLASTIC MATERIALS ETC		264218		271186		375867		392422	MAT PLAST ARTIFICIELLES
582	PROD OF CONDENSATION ETC			W 53659	81341	W 57004	112554	W 62732	112759	PROD CONDENS,POLYCOND
5823	ALKYDS,OTHER POLYESTERS			W 16819	35101	W 19513	53258	W 25151	51320	ALKYDES ET AUT POLYESTERS
583	POLYMERIZATION ETC PRODS			W 132110	181983	W 134313	255221	W 166568	272135	PROD POLYMERISATION
5831	POLYETHYLENE			W 50305	44759	W 47377	63664	W 54334	58226	POLYETHYLENE
5839	OTH POLYMRZTION ETC PROD			W 15243	52367	W 16045	67563	W 17687	71916	AUT PROD POLYMER COPOLYM
59	CHEMICAL MATERIALS NES		231674		246954		304524		320536	MAT PROD CHIMIQUES NDA
591	PESTICIDES,DISINFECTANTS			W 18318	86972	W 21838	103197	W 20962	118691	DESINF,INSECT,FONG,HERB
5913	HERBICIDES,FOR RETAIL			W 5438	42435	W 5968	49579	W 6235	58130	HERBICIDES VENTE AU DET
598	MISCEL CHEM PRODUCTS NES			W 71032	124465	W 85767	155866	W 94305	156421	PROD DIV INDUST CHIM NDA
5989	CHEM PRODUCTS,PREPS NES			W 41351	98283	W 48928	119991	W 50974	121605	PROD PREP CHIMIQUES NDA
59899	OTH CHEM PRODS,PREPS,NES			W 27654	65567	W 35143	80970	W 31881	82483	AUT PRODUITS CHIMIQUES NDA
6	BASIC MANUFACTURES		2285858		2959780		3628261		3705581	ART MANUFACTURES
61	LEATHER,DRESSED FUR,ETC		119471		207007		250207		297183	CUIRS,PELLETERIES
611	LEATHER			W 7182	133322	W 7187	168863	W 7695	200618	CUIRS,PEAUX PREPARES
6114	LEATHR BOVINE NES,EQUINE			W 4345	93468	W 4927	124140	W 5765	152627	CUIRS DE BOVINS
612	LEATHER ETC MANUFACTURES				65250	W 6769	72617	W 8226	84460	OUVRAGES EN CUIRS NDA
6123	PREPRD PARTS OF FOOTWEAR			W 6447	62271	W 6531	68020	W 8095	82133	PARTIES DE CHAUSSURES
62	RUBBER MANUFACTURES NES		105811		135539		143805		154361	CAOUTCHOUC MANUFACTURE
625	RUBBER TYRES, TUBES ETC			W 26937	66957	W 23359	66834	W 21599	70509	PNEUS CAOUTCHOUC VULCANISE
628	RUBBER ARTICLES NES			W 5040	50791	W 4818	57304	W 4902	58145	OUVRAGES CAOUTCHOUC NDA
63	WOOD,CORK MANUFACTRS NES		37856		53267		59397		69543	OUVRAGES LIEGE ET BOIS
64	PAPER,PAPERBOARD AND MFR		320806		421309		514368		517435	PAPIERS,CARTONS & OUVRAGES

4. General Imports C.I.F. by Commodities according to the S.I.T.C. (Rev. 2) in thousand U.S. Dollars
Importations Générales C.A.F. par Produits d'après la C.T.C.I. (Rév. 2) en milliers de Dollars E.U.

SITC CTCI	COMMODITY	1993		1994		1995		1996		PRODUIT
		WEIGHT POIDS	VALUE VALEUR	WEIGHT POIDS	VALUE VALEUR	WEIGHT POIDS	VALUE VALEUR	WEIGHT POIDS	VALUE VALEUR	
641	PAPER AND PAPERBOARD			W 317781	251919	W 294476	311958	W 320927	310356	PAPIERS ET CARTONS
6411	NEWSPRINT			W 106432	53693	W 91589	69455	W 84525	68291	PAPIER JOURNAL
6412	PRINTG,WRITING PAPER NES			W 67164	66046	W 70573	85274	W 79486	86223	PAPIERS POUR L'IMPRESSION
64122	— COATED,IMPREGNATD ETC			W 65472	63005	W 66347	78214	W 72177	75631	PAPIERS IMPRESSION COUCHES
6415	PAPER,PAPERBRD,BULK,NES			W 83181	60528	W 80568	76708	W 76768	55647	PAPIERS,CARTONS ROULEAUX
64159	OTHER PAPER ETC,BULK,NES			W 60260	47467	W 72054	69382	W 69869	50324	AUT PAPIER ROULEAUX FEUILLES
6418	COATED ETC PAPER NES BLK			W 21202	39136	W 19414	46947	W 33851	61526	PAP,CARTONS COUCHES,ENDUITS
642	PAPER,ETC,PRECUT,ARTS OF			W 105823	169390	W 105034	202410	W 113184	207079	PAP,CARTONS DECOUPES
6421	PAPER ETC CONTAINERS			W 64952	90700	W 63282	103827	W 66533	106171	BOITES,SACS EMBALLAGES
6428	PAPER ETC ARTICLES NES			W 23832	46484	W 27439	63623	W 28237	63622	OUVRAGES EN PATE A PAPIER
65	TEXTILE YARN,FABRICS,ETC		651820		753938		882103		917385	FILS,TISSUS,ARTICLES TEXTILE
651	TEXTILE YARN				104456		136464	W 32537	136617	FILS TEXTILES
6514	SYN FIB YRN,BULK,MONOFIL			W 8300	43651	W 10036	53756	W 10675	55562	FILS CONT 85% FIB TEXT SYNTH
652	COTTON FABRICS,WOVEN			W 12823	96741	W 13767	114724	W 15682	127293	TISSUS DE COTON
6522	WOVEN COTTON BLEACHD,ETC			W 9168	78004	W 10642	97935	W 11997	110710	TISSUS COTON BLANCHIS ETC
65224	BLCHED COTTON FABRIC NES			W 7307	58847	W 8413	70372	W 9487	82258	AUT TIS PLUS 85% COT BLANCHI
653	WOVN MAN–MADE FIB FABRIC			W 16841	212493	W 16175	223506	W 16456	222179	TISSUS FIBRES SYNTH,ARTIF
6534	DISC SYN BLEND FABRC NES			W 4572	55702	W 4370	57266	W 4534	61657	TISSUS FIBRES SYNTH DISCONT
654	OTH WOVEN TEXTILE FABRIC			W 4078	103281	W 4394	118018	W 4195	119546	TISSUS AUT COTON SYNT,ARTIF
6542	WOVEN WOOL,HAIR NONPILE			W 2060	61189	W 1997	68194	W 1893	64580	TIS PLUS 85% LAINE,POILS
65422	WOVN COMB WOOL,FINE HAIR			W 1429	43634	W 1304	48227	W 1258	45764	TISSUS 85% LAINE,PLS PEIG
655	KNITTED,ETC FABRICS			W 4352	57428	W 4854	72264	W 5970	82608	ETOF BONNETERIE PIECES ETC
6552	OTHER KNIT ETC FAB NONEL			W 4352	57428	W 4854	72264	W 5970	82608	ETOF BON NON ELAS NON SYNT
656	LACE,RIBBONS,TULLE,ETC			W 10077	45835	W 2228	59301	W 2336	63664	TULLES,BRODERIE
657	SPECIAL TXTL FABRC,PRODS			W 11314	82688	W 12416	103998	W 11851	110422	TISSUS SPECIAUX
6573	COATED ETC TEXTILES NES			W 4319	39042	W 5665	54700	W 5301	57423	TISSUS,ART MATIERE TEXT NDA
66	NONMETAL MINERAL MFS NES		178608		257719		278154		295775	ART MIN NON METALLIQUES
662	CLAY,REFRACTORY BLDG PRD			W 152266	68018	W 143638	68811	W 137718	69294	MAT CONST REFRACTAIRES
6624	BRICKS ETC NONREFRACTORY			W 134365	52932	W 121560	50855	W 120019	50905	BRIQUES ETC CERAM NON REFR
663	MINERAL MANUFCTURES NES			W 51222	51178	W 56938	56254	W 70408	60125	ART MIN MANUF NDA
664	GLASS			W 31974	60333	W 38824	67634	W 36671	79177	VERRE
67	IRON AND STEEL		285034		335429		496586		454431	FER ET ACIER
672	IRON,STEEL PRIMARY FORMS			W 165172	40162	W 355938	95808	W 189258	53430	LINGOTS FER,ACIER
6725	IRN,STL BLOOMS,SLABS,ETC			W 139515	31912	W 311737	78604	W 168049	44164	BLOOMS,BILLETTES FER ACIER
67251	IRN,SMPLE STL BLOOMS,ETC			W 137019	29725	W 311457	77548	W 166405	42151	BLOOMS ETC NON ACIER FIN
673	IRON,STEEL SHAPES ETC			W 113381	51190	W 132819	75516	W 144926	86283	BARRES,PROFIL FER,ACIER
674	IRN,STL UNIV,PLATE,SHEET			W 166539	118202	W 180771	172614	W 175393	162245	LARGES PLATS,TOLES
6746	IRN,STL THIN PLATE,ROLLD			W 23751	27718	W 30560	48998	W 21145	32571	TOLES LAM MOINS 3MM
6749	OTH IRN,STL PLATES,SHEET			W 38738	28799	W 46614	38075	W 57104	49288	AUTRES TOLES FER,ACIER
678	IRON,STL TUBES,PIPES,ETC			W 66155	77508	W 63916	89832	W 62390	85934	TUBES,TUYAUX EN FONTE,FER
68	NON–FERROUS METALS		259716		372923		521267		508446	METAUX NON FERREUX
682	COPPER EXC CEMENT COPPER			W 30878	87185	W 34796	123858	W 45555	138768	CUIVRE
6822	COPPER,ALLOYS WORKED			W 13673	51329	W 20357	85652	W 33124	109678	CUIVRE,ALLIAGES OUVRES
68221	COPPER BARS,WIRE,ETC			W 6371	16248	W 12283	38237	W 25678	66483	BARRES,PROFILES ET FILS
684	ALUMINIUM			W 151420	246247	W 160364	353158	W 168127	319190	ALUMINIUM
6841	ALUMINIUM,ALLOYS,UNWRGHT			W 130669	179845	W 134309	256715	W 142687	229191	ALUMINIUM,ALLIAGES BRUTS
6842	ALUMINIUM,ALLOYS WORKED			W 20750	66402	W 26054	96443	W 25441	89999	ALUMINIUM,ALLIAGES OUVRE
69	METAL MANUFACTURES NES		326736		422649		482374		491022	ART MANUFACT EN METAL NDA
691	STRUCTURES AND PARTS NES			W 35974	75912	W 36370	84411	W 37364	82684	CONSTRUCT FER,ACIER,ALU
6911	STRUCTURES,PARTS IRN,STL			W 33367	59455	W 33194	65654	W 34502	64619	CONSTRUCT FER,ACIER,FONTE
692	METAL TANKS,BOXES,ETC			W 18769	43633	W 18563	48430	W 20591	55547	RECIPIENTS METALLIQUES
695	TOOLS			W 4849	57186	W 4017	62849	W 4233	67392	OUTILS A MAIN
697	BASE MTL HOUSEHOLD EQUIP			W 12108	54865	W 11729	52303	W 13001	45841	ART MENAGE MET COMMUNS
699	BASE METAL MFRS NES				130645		160805		172113	ART MANUFACTURES MET NDA
6991	LOCKSMITHS WARES,ETC			W 6986	48775	W 8234	56401	W 9383	61120	ARTICLES DE SERRURERIE
7	MACHINES,TRANSPORT EQUIP		4584177		4488285		4553889		4874039	MACHINES MATERIEL TRANSPORT
71	POWER GENERATING EQUIPMT		205821		158026		149182		136832	MACHINES GENERATRICES
713	INTRNL COMBUS PSTN ENGIN				88645		63978	W 3921	39297	MOTEURS EXPL COMB INT, PIECE
7132	MOTOR VEHCL PISTN ENGINS			W 4377	61954	W 2577	36420	W 1541	8946	MOTEURS EXPL POUR VEHICULES
716	ROTATING ELECTRIC PLANT			W 6000	46278	W 5160	57140	W 5248	52843	APP ELECTR ROTATIFS,PIECES
72	MACHS FOR SPCL INDUSTRYS		442177		546050		510206		544163	MAC SPECIALES POUR INDUST
721	AGRIC MACHY,EXC TRACTORS			W 35159	85531	W 25310	97660	W 23118	120090	MACHINES AGRICOLES
7212	HARVESTING ETC MACHINES			W 13629	46324	W 15995	62752	W 14373	81055	ENGINS POUR LA RECOLTE
72122	COMBINE HARVESTR–THRESHR			W 5932	18738	W 9835	34399	W 8468	50800	MOISSONNEUSES–BATTEUSES
722	TRACTORS NON–ROAD			W 43603	64727	W 16307	32440	W 15675	48823	TRACTEURS
7224	WHEELED TRACTORS NES			W 42831	63807	W 15950	32039	W 15388	48442	TRACTEURS A ROUES
723	CIVIL ENGNEERG EQUIP ETC			W 16903	66937	W 11920	48889	W 10892	41403	APPAREILS DE GENIE CIVIL
7234	CONST,MINING MACHNRY NES			W 14669	56964	W 9890	39608	W 9707	36491	MACH POUR LA CONST, MINES
724	TEXTILE,LEATHER MACHNRY			W 4888	49842	W 3600	47247		50780	MACH POUR INDUSTRIE TEXTILE
727	FOOD MACHRY NON–DOMESTIC			W 4052	69630	W 3178	46463	W 2651	38190	MACH INDUSTRIES ALIMENT
7272	OTH FOOD PROC MCHY,PARTS			W 3653	67718	W 3039	45042	W 2324	35556	AUT MACH IND ALIMENTAIRE
72722	INDUS FOOD PROC MACH NES			W 3440	63534	W 2876	44423	W 2308	35477	MACHINES BOULANGERIE
728	OTH MACHY FOR SPCL INDUS			W 11950	140134	W 13404	174952	W 18320	178940	AUT MACH IND PARTICULIERES
7284	MACHY FOR SPCL INDUS NES			W 6451	105914	W 7655	137098	W 12705	136187	MACH SPEC IND PARTICUL.
72842	RUBBER,PLASTICS WRKG MCH			W 2203	22293	W 3378	47285	W 4821	38166	MACH IND CAOUT MAT PLAST
73	METALWORKING MACHINERY		51487		66049		83024		99055	MACH TRAVAIL DES METAUX
736	METALWORKING MACH–TOOLS			W 5905	45590	W 6479	58081	W 10098	71648	MACH–OUTILS TRAVAIL METAUX
74	GENRL INDUSTRL MACHY NES		556052		720852		775096		758988	MACH APP INDUSTRIE
741	HEATING,COOLING EQUIPMNT			W 15521	134707	W 16209	153368	W 17898	166797	MACH CHAUFFAGE,PIECES
7414	NONDOM REFRIG EQUIPT,PTS			W 6167	41700	W 6997	46761	W 7182	51120	MAT PRODUCTION DU FROID
7415	AIR–CONDITIONING MACHNRY			W 3268	38733	W 3101	43132	W 3807	49439	GROUPES CONDITION AIR
742	PUMPS FOR LIQUIDS ETC			W 3885	73804	W 4001	74957	W 3185	63939	POMPES MOTO–POMPES
743	PUMPS NES,CENTRFUGES ETC			W 11126	113407	W 11994	127457	W 11903	114365	POMPES COMPRES,VENT ETC
7436	GAS,LIQUID FILTERS ETC			W 2828	44568	W 2868	44500	W 2387	37258	APP POUR FILT DES LIQUIDES
744	MECHANICAL HANDLING EQU			W 13046	82058	W 14905	88607	W 14777	90489	EQUIP MANUTENTION PIECES
745	NONELEC MACHY,TOOLS NES			W 10390	147970	W 9783	136998	W 7201	123917	AUT MACH NON ELEC,PIECES
7452	OTH NONELEC MCHS,PTS NES			W 10080	139557	W 9476	128008	W 6942	115157	AUT MACH NON ELEC,PIECES
74522	PACKAGNG,BOTTLNG,ETC MCH			W 3589	79841	W 3117	65943	W 1992	57673	MACH NETT BOUTEILLES,ETC
749	NONELEC MACH PTS,ACC NES			W 11923	168906	W 13067	193709	W 12921	199481	PIECES MACH NON ELEC NDA
7492	COCKS,VALVES ETC NES			W 4669	77288	W 5056	86456	W 5022	85328	ART ROB,SIM POUR TUYAUX
75	OFFICE MACHNES,ADP EQUIP		427994		454492		425481		402653	MACH BUREAU TRAIT AUTOM
751	OFFICE MACHINES				63364		63404	W 2147	56890	MACH,APPAREILS DE BUREAU
752	AUTOMTIC DATA PROC EQUIP			W 5050	284215	W 4759	250233	W 5080	249826	MACH TRAIT INFORMATION
7522	DIGITAL COMPUTERS			W 522	58352	W 387	48095	W 510	51977	MACH DIGITALES COMPLETES
7523	DIGITL CENTRL PROCESSORS			W 728	69078	W 559	55621	W 320	46489	UNITES CENTRALES
7525	ADP PERIPHERAL UNITS			W 3006	96378	W 3117	98988	W 2374	68623	UNITES PERIPHERIQUES
759	OFFICE,ADP MCH PTS,ACCES			W 1790	106913	W 2073	111844		95937	PIECES DU 751 ET 752
7599	ACCTG,ETC,ADP MCH PTS,AC			W 1350	88061	W 1664	90502	W 1743	72896	PIECES DU 751 ET 752
76	TELECOMM,SOUND EQUIPMENT		373642		520935		470589		613819	EQUIPMENT DE TELECOM
764	TELECOM EQPT,PTS,ACC NES			W 7489	437526	W 7457	391506	W 8369	527811	EQUIP TELECOM,PIECES
7641	LINE TELEPHONE,ETC EQUIP			W 942	92734	W 967	76364	W 1054	112842	APP TELEPHON PAR FIL

4. General Imports C.I.F. by Commodities according to the S.I.T.C. (Rev. 2) in thousand U.S. Dollars
Importations Générales C.A.F. par Produits d'après la C.T.C.I. (Rév. 2) en milliers de Dollars E.U.

SITC CTCI	COMMODITY	1993 WEIGHT POIDS	1993 VALUE VALEUR	1994 WEIGHT POIDS	1994 VALUE VALEUR	1995 WEIGHT POIDS	1995 VALUE VALEUR	1996 WEIGHT POIDS	1996 VALUE VALEUR	PRODUIT
7643	TV,RADIO TRANSMITTRS ETC			W 482	104905	W 357	81539	W 1314	178792	APP EMET TELE RADIO
7649	PTS NES OF EQUIPMT OF 76			W 4367	215714	W 4714	208261	W 4436	208819	PIECES DE LA DIV 76
76491	PTS NES OF APPAR OF 7641			W 640	79769	W 605	78281	W 334	57820	PIECES POUR 764.1
76493	TELECOMM EQUIPMT PTS NES			W 2019	70476	W 2428	74932	W 2202	65669	PIECES 761,762,764.3,8
76499	PARTS ETC OF SOUND EQUIP			W 1647	65092	W 1602	54249	W 1763	83184	PIECES NDA POUR 763
77	ELECTRIC MACHNRY NES ETC		653919		897000		1098182		1218472	MACH APP ELECT NDA
771	ELECTRIC POWER MACHY NES			W 2740	43800	W 3411	57740	W 4104	61266	MACH PROD,TRANS ELECTR
772	SWITCHGEAR ETC,PARTS NES			W 6885	225009	W 9121	308688	W 10023	333646	APP COUPURE,SECT ETC
7721	SWITCHGEAR ETC			W 5865	164563	W 7648	227062	W 8364	250733	APP COUPURE,SECTIONMNT
7722	PRINTED CIRCUITS,PTS NES			W 600	43623	W 1022	60593	W 1284	60479	CIRCUITS ET PIECES
773	ELECTR DISTRIBUTNG EQUIP			W 25047	166454	W 29518	208792	W 30842	267560	EQUIPMT DISTRIBUTION ELECT
7731	INSULATED WIRE,CABLE ETC			W 22996	138068	W 26772	162758	W 26775	186757	FILS,CABLES ISOLES ELECT
7732	ELECTRC INSULATING EQUIP			W 2051	28386	W 2747	46034	W 4067	80803	EQUIP ISOL ELECTRIQUE
77327	OTH ELEC INSUL FITTG NES			W 992	22852	W 1596	37757	W 2377	63976	PIECES ISOL EN AUT MATIERES
775	HOUSEHOLD TYPE EQUIP NES			W 22330	118959	W 27177	132675	W 23428	119353	MACH,APP USAGE DOMESTQUE
7758	ELECTRO–THERMIC APPL NES			W 6757	45329	W 8551	49739	W 7919	49774	APP ELECTROTHERMIQ NDA
776	TRANSISTORS,VALVES,ETC				103959	W 4655	122978	W 4603	155998	LAMPES,TUBES,VALVES
7764	ELECTRONIC MICROCIRCUITS			W 309	54952	W 229	54566	W 342	79408	MICROSTRUCTURES ELECTRON
778	ELECTRICAL MACHINERY NES			W 17154	198922		236881	W 16764	251250	AUTRES MACH ELECT NDA
7788	OTH ELEC MACHY,EQUIP NES			W 3788	83142		118947	W 3798	129815	AUT MACH APP ELEC NDA
77884	ELECTRICAL CONDENSERS			W 640	32753	W 662	67527	W 760	81370	CONDENSATEURS ELECTRIQUES
78	ROAD VEHICLES		869393		1086248		909992		991096	VEHICULES ROUTIERS
781	PASS MOTOR VEH EXC BUSES			W 177233	511518	W 99327	417810	W 82661	456736	AUTO TRANSPORT PERSONNES
782	LORRIES,SPCL MTR VEH NES			W 68757	239246	W 64858	215519	W 59737	214026	VEHICULES SPECIAUX,MARCH
7821	LORRIES,TRUCKS			W 65964	220976	W 62299	198908	W 56339	200177	VEHICULES TRANSP MARCHAND
783	ROAD MOTOR VEHICLES NES			W 11975	42258	W 10904	42434	W 15405	83785	VEHICULES ROUTIERS NDA
7832	TRACTORS FOR TR–TRAILERS			W 6652	28088	W 5824	33113	W 9553	71912	TRACTEURS ROUTIERS
784	MOTOR VEH PRTS,ACCES NES			W 34607	214550	W 23809	159914	W 23381	162851	PIECES 722,781,782,783
7849	OTHER MOTOR VEHCL PARTS			W 32828	206793	W 21865	153330	W 22003	157684	PIECES 722,781,782,783
786	TRAILERS,NONMOTR VEH,NES			W 28803	49476	W 19704	48641	W 17137	49000	REMORQUES,CADRES,CONTAIN
79	OTHR TRANSPORT EQUIPMENT		1003693		38633		132137		108961	AUTRE MATERIEL TRANSPORT
791	RAILWAY VEHICLES			W 10680	13593	W 26099	127097	W 14383	52690	VEHIC MAT CHEMINS DE FER
7914	RY COACHES NES NOT POWRD					W 4278	98151	W 301	7189	VOITURES A VOYAGEURS
792	AIRCRAFT ETC			W 409	23031	W 48	3644	W 387	53467	APP NAVIGATION AERIENNE
8	MISC MANUFACTURED GOODS		1389909		1577637		1630116		1697594	ART MANUFACTURES DIVERS
812	*PLUMBG,HEATNG,LGHTNG EQ			W 13373	71643	W 14679	76607	W 16672	84279	APPAR SANITAIRES CHAUFFAGE
8124	LIGHTING EQUIPMENT NES			W 5093	44044	W 5324	45532	W 6114	49558	APPAREILS ECLAIRAGE ETC
821	*FURNITURE,PARTS THEREOF			W 55117	170211	W 42748	155457	W 40754	154132	MEUBLES ET PIECES
8211	CHAIRS,SEATS AND PARTS			W 13594	51989	W 12161	59860	W 11449	65262	SIEGES ET PIECES
8219	FURNITURE AND PARTS NES			W 40494	106602	W 29559	86198	W 28119	80085	AUTRES MEUBLES ET PIECES
82192	WOOD FURNITURE NES			W 26002	61276	W 18392	48474	W 16536	43229	MEUBLES NDA EN BOIS
84	CLOTHING AND ACCESSORIES		320860		339223		376376		393453	VETEMENTS
843	WOMENS OUTERWEAR NONKNIT			W 6454	66208	W 4187	61757	W 3975	62886	VET DESSUS FEMMES MAT TEX
844	UNDER GARMENTS NOT KNIT			W 8685	33007	W 11146	47232	W 5591	43479	VETEMENT DESSOUS MAT TEX
845	OUTERWEAR KNIT NONELASTC			W 6886	47312	W 3812	55422	W 3587	57644	VET DESSOUS,ACCES BONNET
846	UNDER GARMENTS KNITTED			W 17570	113906	W 10134	125993	W 9471	135537	SOUS VETS DE BONNETERIE
8462	— OF COTTON NON ELASTIC			W 15251	69971	W 8198	75362	W 7384	83903	SOUS–VET BONNET COTON
84629	—— OTHER			W 15251	69971	W 8198	75362	W 7384	83903	AUT SOUS–VET BONNET COTON
851	*FOOTWEAR			W 31209	95826	W 18425	85080	W 18254	100010	CHAUSSURES
85102	FOOTWEAR LEATHER			W 20328	80839	W 14700	74391	W 11912	74416	CHAUS SEMELLES EN CUIR
87	PRECISION INSTRUMNTS NES		229737		272688		265763		264427	INSTRUM,APPAR SCIENT NDA
872	MEDICAL INSTRUMENTS NES			W 1843	98984	W 1898	79753	W 1807	70571	INSTR,APP MEDIC–CHIR NDA
87202	OTH MEDICAL INSTRUMENTS			W 1565	86846	W 1697	71373	W 1538	61098	INSTRUM,APP MEDECINE
874	MEASURNG,CONTROLNG INSTR				150762	W 3566	161823		161296	INSTRUMENTS DE MESURE
8748	ELEC MEAS,CONTRL EQU NES			W 365	51925	W 389	49611	W 313	51181	APP ELEC ELECTRO MESURE
87483	OTH ELCTRNC MEAS ETC EQU			W 309	47228	W 283	45674	W 240	45614	AUT APP ELECTRO DE MESURE
88	PHOTO EQU,OPTICL GDS ETC		82126		88072		84354		83590	APP,FOURN PHOTO,OP,MONTR
89	MISC MANUFCTRD GOODS NES		428364		518674		568210		597592	ART MANUFACTURES DIVERS
892	PRINTED MATTER				102783	W 18755	102164	W 15930	90272	IMPRIMES
8928	PRINTED MATTER NES				52602	W 7930	52429	W 7262	53589	IMPRIMES NDA
893	ARTICLES OF PLASTIC NES				179164		231223		264416	OUVRAGES EN MAT DIVIS 58
8931	PLSTC PACKG CONTNRS,LIDS			W 13760	40072	W 14602	48796	W 20834	64932	ART TRANSP EMBALLAGE ETC
8939	MISC PLASTIC ARTICLES			W 24174	134906	W 23182	176993	W 25409	191171	ART DIVERS EN MAT DIV 58
89399	OTHR PLASTC ARTICLES NES			W 20309	125741	W 19563	167542	W 22281	183321	AUT OUV MAT DIV 58
894	TOYS,SPORTING GOODS,ETC			W 13847	71223	W 11447	62016	W 10695	67271	VOITURES ENFANTS,JOUETS
8942	TOYS,INDOOR GAMES ETC			W 10727	51739	W 8869	43926	W 8132	44939	JOUETS,JEUX ETC
898	MUSICAL INSTRUMENTS,PTS			W 4768	48675		57256	W 4096	54834	INSTRUMENTS DE MUSIQUE
8983	SOUND RECRDNG TAPE,DISCS			W 4216	43116	W 5179	52801	W 3910	50484	SUPPORTS SON POUR 763
899	OTHER MANUFACTURED GOODS				68492		71963		79590	AUT ART MANUF DIVERS NDA
9	GOODS NOT CLASSD BY KIND		713		588943		281570		169465	ART TRANSACT NON CLASSES
931	*SPECIAL TRANSACTIONS				587541		280661		166252	TRANS.SPECIALES

5. General Exports F.O.B. by Commodities according to the S.I.T.C. (Rev. 2) in thousand U.S. Dollars
Exportations Générales F.O.B. par Produits d'après la C.T.C.I. (Rév. 2) en milliers de Dollars E.U.

SITC CTCI	COMMODITY	1993		1994		1995		1996		PRODUIT
		WEIGHT POIDS	VALUE VALEUR	WEIGHT POIDS	VALUE VALEUR	WEIGHT POIDS	VALUE VALEUR	WEIGHT POIDS	VALUE VALEUR	
	ALL COMMODITIES		8906888		10699843		12865482		13144047	TOUS PRODUITS
0	FOOD AND LIVE ANIMALS		1494021		1728732		2254183		2049925	ALIMENTS,ANIMAUX VIVANTS
001	*LIVE ANIMALS FOR FOOD			W 61295	125701	W 54806	121966	W 67080	135816	ANIMAUX VIVANTS
0011	BOVINE SPECIES,LIVE			W 31963	52828	W 27850	49482	W 33873	51020	ESPECE BOVINE
00119	— OTHR THAN FR BREEDING			W 27528	43631	W 25471	43189	W 32760	49051	BOVINS NON REPRODUCTEURS
0012	SHEEP AND GOATS,LIVE			W 20393	51195	W 19306	50463	W 18683	52205	ESPECES OVINE ET CAPRINE
00121	SHEEP,LIVE			W 20368	51142	W 19269	50334	W 18645	52086	ESPECE OVINE
01	MEAT AND PREPARATIONS		564437		594765		687401		787578	VIANDES ET PREPARATIONS
011	MEAT FRESH,CHILLD,FROZEN			W 149982	457549	W 184589	543066	W 237814	618020	VIANDES FRAICHES,REF,CONGE
0111	BOVINE MEAT FRESH,FROZEN			W 13447	32981	W 8207	23212	W 10506	28141	VIANDES BOVIN FRAI,REF
0113	PIG MEAT FRESH,CHLD,FRZN			W 41647	90560	W 54052	124420	W 103046	228624	VIANDE DE PORC
0114	POULTRY FRESH CHLLD,FRZN			W 76354	228199	W 105530	295191	W 107312	283807	VOLAILLES MORTES
0118	MEAT NES FRESH,CHLD,FRZN			W 12927	100045	W 13553	96839	W 11886	72339	AUTRES VIANDES,ABATS
01181	POULTRY LIVER FRESH,ETC			W 2282	60300	W 2168	47840	W 1372	35349	FOIES DE VOLAILLES
01189	OTHER MEAT NES FRESH,ETC			W 10645	39745	W 11385	48999	W 10514	36990	VIANDE,ABATS COMESTIBLES
014	MEAT PREPD,PRSVD,NES ETC			W 36034	133943	W 32963	143909	W 45633	158550	CONSERVES DE VIANDES
0142	SAUSAGES INCLDING TINNED			W 8189	60658	W 9312	72410	W 15324	92349	SAUCISSES,SAUCISSONS
0149	OTH PREPARD,PRESRVD MEAT			W 27845	73285	W 23651	71499	W 30309	66201	AUTRES PREP DE VIANDES
02	DAIRY PRODCTS,BIRDS'EGGS		65616		40007		51214		60744	PRODUITS LAITIERS,OEUFS
04	CEREALS AND PREPARATIONS		117849		204481		594688		206503	CEREALES ET PRODUITS
041	WHEAT ETC UNMILLED			W 759001	81208	W 2764835	333467	W 299463	54496	FROMENT,EPEAUTRE
0411	DURUM WHEAT UNMILLED			W 137863	14472	W 647703	74846	W 32537	6297	FROMENT DUR NON MOULU
0412	OTHER WHEAT ETC UNMILLED			W 621138	66736	W 2117132	258621	W 266925	48199	AUTRE FROMENT NON MOULU
044	MAIZE UNMILLED			W 180607	74704	W 601031	109333	W 129157	42135	MAIS NON MOULU
046	WHEAT ETC MEAL OR FLOUR			W 57582	11117	W 370315	75901	W 66965	19745	SEMOULE FARINE,FROMENT
04601	FLOUR OF WHEAT OR MESLIN			W 57079	10938	W 367949	75498	W 57984	16927	FARINE DE FROMENT
048	CEREAL ETC PREPARATIONS			W 37117	24897	W 82274	42540	W 91466	56318	PREPTNS A BASE CEREALES
05	VEGETABLES AND FRUIT		442067		534730		511021		522404	LEGUMES ET FRUITS
054	VEG ETC FRSH,SMPLY PRSVD			W 290312	120905	W 232318	127689	W 419299	140602	LEGUMES FRAIS,CONG,SECS
0545	OTHER FRESH VEGETABLES			W 99416	59607	W 118177	69094	W 124687	64528	AUTRES LEGUMES FRAIS,REF
05459	FRESH VEGETABLES NES			W 58425	45092	W 66440	52393	W 61897	51253	LEGUMES FRAIS,REFRI NDA
0546	VEGETABLES SIMPLY PRESVD			W 58198	40825	W 57814	41988	W 82593	54846	LEGUMES CONG,CONSER
05461	VEGETABLES FROZEN			W 55700	39280	W 57331	41727	W 82479	54812	LEGUMES CONGELES
056	VEGTBLES ETC PRSVD,PREPD			W 131810	123726	W 144789	144231	W 138401	114432	CONSERVES DE LEGUMES
0565	VEGTBLES PRSVD,PREPD NES			W 124648	103130	W 138009	120578	W 130811	91315	LEGUMES PREPARES CONSERVE
05651	VEGTBLS,FRUIT IN VINEGAR			W 79252	62236	W 92768	80984	W 71501	47453	LEGUM CONSERV AU VINAIGRE
05659	OTH VEG PRESVD,PREPD NES			W 45396	40894	W 45241	39594	W 59310	43862	LEGUM PREPAP,CONSERV NDA
057	FRUIT,NUTS,FRESH,DRIED			W 189552	75567	W 123241	48636	W 201830	69569	FRUITS FRAIS OU SECS
0579	FRUIT FRESH OR DRIED NES			W 89057	41268	W 86866	33266	W 144566	49175	FRUITS FRAIS,SECS NDA
058	FRUIT PRESERVED,PREPARED			W 264324	214532	W 289931	190465	W 270299	197801	CONSERVES DE FRUITS
0585	FRUIT OR VEGETABLE JUICE			W 192432	144814	W 231706	128575	W 212016	137136	JUS DE FRUITS
05857	JUICE OF OTHER FRUIT,VEG			W 136397	111968	W 144303	85010	W 146950	109156	JUS AUTRES FRUITS,LEGUMES
06	SUGAR AND PREPS,HONEY		30035		26831		54191		57027	SUCRES ET PRODUITS
061	SUGAR AND HONEY			W 20081	19480	W 72456	45961	W 68720	41297	SUCRES ET MIEL
07	COFFEE,TEA,COCOA,SPICES		50920		71959		78086		82993	CAFE,THE,CACAO,EPICES
073	CHOCOLATE AND PRODUCTS			W 13487	38795	W 12675	38403	W 15225	46185	CHOCOLAT
081	*FEEDING STUFF FOR ANIML			W 132017	30357	W 213197	44432	W 286604	70211	NOURRITURE POUR ANIMAUX
0819	FOOD WASTE AND FEED NES			W 92938	23452	W 92669	27808	W 148817	51006	DECHETS,ALIMENTS NDA
09	MISC EDIBLE PRODUCTS		52723		92059		103118		118488	PREP ALIMENTAIRES DIVERSES
098	EDIBLE PRODCTS,PREPS NES			W 71174	84099	W 71314	97622	W 97936	111533	PREP ALIMENTAIRES NDA
09809	MISC FOOD PREPRTIONS NES			W 55845	63201	W 54369	71492	W 80422	87392	PREP ALIMENTAIRES NDA
1	BEVERAGES AND TOBACCO		204065		192029		258749		323622	BOISSONS ET TABACS
11	BEVERAGES		180822		178047		257526		235179	BOISSONS
111	NON-ALCOHL BEVERAGES NES			W 27485	14014	W 35908	15197	W 189138	72548	BOISSONS NON ALCOOLIQUES
11102	FLAVORED WATERS NON-ALCO			W 26676	13730	W 34501	14860	W 185592	71435	LIMONADES,EAUX GAZEUSES
112	ALCOHOLIC BEVERAGES			W 223219	164033	W 312009	242329	W 216660	162631	BOISSONS ALCOOLIQUES
1121	WINE OF FRESH GRAPES ETC			W 104267	93543	W 127413	124363	W 108778	96052	VINS DE RAISINS FRAIS
11212	WINE OF FRESH GRAPES			W 102201	92507	W 126893	124197	W 106178	93988	VINS DE MOUTS DE RAISINS
1124	DISTILLED ALCOHOLIC BEVS			W 93349	61633	W 168623	113041	W 97450	61735	ALCOOLS,EAUX-DE-VIE
11249	OTH ALCOHOLC BEVS,CMPNDS			W 93122	61437	W 168236	112756	W 97386	61667	BOISSONS ALCOOLIQUES NDA
12	TOBACCO AND MANUFACTURES		23242		13982		1223		88443	TABACS BRUTS FABRIQUES
122	TOBACCO,MANUFACTURED			W 1786	11100			W 13147	83298	TABACS FABRIQUES
1222	CIGARETTES			W 1786	11100			W 7374	56754	CIGARETTES
2	CRUDE MATERLS,EXCL FUELS		510329		523155		595809		573213	MAT BRUTES NON COMESTIBLES
22	OIL SEEDS,OLEAGINOUS FRT		91182		99001		101506		121217	GRAINES,FRUITS OLEAGINEUX
222	SEEDS FOR'SOFT'FIXED OIL			W 304447	90700	W 311750	92532	W 344629	103069	GRAINES HUILES FIXES
2224	SUNFLOWER SEEDS			W 271384	82253	W 249486	77037	W 219900	70070	GRAINES DE TOURNESOL
24	CORK AND WOOD		103485		115615		130116		122821	LIEGE ET BOIS
247	OTH WOOD ROUGH,SQUARED			W 914758	53229	W 928673	61325	W 802481	52559	BOIS BRUTS EQUARRIS
2472	SAW-,VENEER-LOGS NON-CON			W 771341	46566	W 928673	61325	W 645902	43966	NON CONIFERES SCIAGE,PLAC
24721	— IN THE ROUGH			W 771341	46566	W 928673	61325	W 645902	43966	BRUTS ECORCES DEGROSSIS
248	WOOD SHAPED,SLEEPERS			W 138431	52016	W 141753	57526	W 140891	56489	BOIS SIMPLEMENT TRAVAILLES
2483	LUMBER SHAPED NON-CONIFR			W 131508	49049	W 133114	53746	W 128920	52402	NON CONIFERES SCIES,RABOTES
24831	LUMBER SAWN ETC NON-CON			W 116672	37619	W 120209	41594	W 116194	40692	SCIES LONGITUDINALEMENT
26	TEXTILE FIBRES AND WASTE		33494		30173		36495		30735	FIBRES TEXTILES
28	METALLIFEROUS ORES,SCRAP		152172		129351		195279		153580	MINERAIS METAL,DECHETS
282	IRON AND STEEL SCRAP			W 637401	66344	W 751557	90046	W 611508	63937	FERRAILLES
28209	— OF OTHR IRON OR STEEL			W 611020	61036	W 734242	84284	W 590921	57823	FERRAILLES DE FER
287	BASE METAL ORES,CONC NES			W 76930	17000	W 160817	36403	W 176057	49204	MINERAIS METAUX COMMUNS
2873	ALUMINIUM ORES,ALUMINA			W 76930	17000	W 160789	36379	W 176057	49204	MINERAIS D'ALUMINIUM
28732	ALUMINA(ALUMINIUM OXIDE)			W 76930	17000	W 141275	35775	W 176057	49204	ALUMINE (OXYDE ALUMINIUM)
288	NONFERR METAL SCRAP NES			W 55562	46007	W 64000	68830	W 50768	40422	DECHETS NON FERREUX
2882	OTHER BASE MTL SCRAP NES			W 53360	45064	W 61640	67838	W 48826	40026	AUTRES DECHETS
28821	COPPER WASTE AND SCRAP			W 17833	25915	W 22125	43618	W 13233	20567	DECHETS DE CUIVRE
29	CRUDE ANIMAL,VEG MAT NES		101564		124900		109265		118864	MATIERES BRUTES ANIM,VEGET
291	CRUDE ANIMAL MTRIALS NES				97065		70105	W 12186	77924	MATIERES BRUTES ANIMALES
2919	OTH ANIMAL MATERIALS NES				76026		49002	W 8245	60178	MAT ORIGINE ANIMALE NDA
29196	BIRDS SKINS,FEATHERS,ETC			W 5403	69443	W 3496	42498	W 3963	53553	PLUMES,DUVETS BRUTS
292	CRUDE VEG MATERIALS NES			W 28379	27835	W 32820	39160	W 34712	40940	MAT BRUTES VEGETALES NDA
3	MINERAL FUELS ETC		360880		367688		384104		427454	COMBUSTIBLES MINERAUX LUB
33	PETROLEUM AND PRODUCTS		335621		340672		353410		372292	PETROLE ET DERIVES
334	PETROLEUM PRODUCTS,REFIN			W 1654608	302808	W 1665610	316591	W 1530032	340159	PRODUITS RAFFINES
335	RESIDUAL PETRLM PROD NES			W 139980	37864	W 93791	36819	W 58108	32133	PRODUITS RESIDUELS NDA
4	ANIMAL,VEGETABLE OIL,FAT		88454		85096		48223		49327	HUILES,GRAISSES ANIM,VEG
42	FIXED VEGETABLE OIL,FAT		73433		77184		42596		41256	HUILES VEGETALES FIXES
423	FIXED VEG OILS,SOFT			W 111461	76796	W 39870	42297	W 45737	41019	HUILES VEGET DOUCES FIXES
4236	SUNFLOWER SEED OIL			W 111461	76796	W 39870	42296	W 45737	41019	HUILE DE TOURNESOL
5	CHEMCLS,RELATED PROD NES		1080261		1037913		1420593		1296372	PRODUITS CHIMIQUES
51	ORGANIC CHEMICALS		297961		199113		265133		210383	PROD CHIMIQ ORGANIQUES
511	HYDROCARBONS NES,DERIVS			W 194940	49523	W 226553	93611	W 115675	30249	HYDROCARBURES NDA
5112	CYCLIC HYDROCARBONS			W 105902	26393	W 140937	54417	W 96608	25220	HYDROCARBURES CYCLIQUES

5. General Exports F.O.B. by Commodities according to the S.I.T.C. (Rev. 2) in thousand U.S. Dollars
Exportations Générales F.O.B. par Produits d'après la C.T.C.I. (Rév. 2) en milliers de Dollars E.U.

SITC CTCI	COMMODITY	1993 WEIGHT POIDS	1993 VALUE VALEUR	1994 WEIGHT POIDS	1994 VALUE VALEUR	1995 WEIGHT POIDS	1995 VALUE VALEUR	1996 WEIGHT POIDS	1996 VALUE VALEUR	PRODUIT
513	CARBOXYLIC ACIDS ETC			W 23183	20050	W 35685	44950		22692	ACIDES CARBOXYLIQUES
514	NITROGEN–FNCTN COMPOUNDS				82443		79978		80153	COMPOSES FONCT AZOTEES
5146	OXYGEN–FNCT AMINO–CMPNDS			W 8248	44691	W 7079	36504	W 6361	29155	COMP AMINES FONCT OXYGEN
515	ORG–INORG COMPOUNDS ETC				35000	W 794	37434	W 2655	65904	COMPOSES ORGANO–MINERAUX
5156	HETEROCYCLIC CMPDS ETC				32787	W 702	33853	W 1067	50156	COMPOSES HETEROCYCLIQUES
51569	OTH HETEROCYC CMPDS,ETC				32787	W 702	33853	W 1067	50156	AUT COMP HETEROCYCLIQUES
52	INORGANIC CHEMICALS		71129		62011		105683		91144	PROD CHIM INORGANIQUES
522	INORG ELEMNTS,OXIDES,ETC				61096	W 392922	92193	W 333156	80406	ELEMENTS INORGANIQUES
5225	INORGANIC BASES ETC NES			W 230782	44407	W 278159	64442	W 206701	49860	AUTRES BASES OXYDES METAL
541	*MEDICINAL,PHARM PRODUCT			K 7993742	249449		276603		281358	PROD MEDICINAUX PHARMACEUT
5417	MEDICAMENTS			K 6561245	216128	K 7836984	230025	K 8152475	243518	MEDICAMENTS
54173	— CONTAINING ALKALOIDS			K 244124	24077	K 542917	39361	K 347944	32952	MED CONTEN ALCALOIDES
54179	— CONTNG OTH SUBSTANCES			K 5483393	164309	K 5672191	154588	K 7328840	189703	MED CONT AUT SUBSTANCES
55	PERFUME,CLEANING ETC PRD		14570		17355		24538		52004	PROD POUR PARFUM,TOILETTE
58	PLASTIC MATERIALS ETC		328676		397701		563729		459465	MAT PLAST ARTIFICIELLES
583	POLYMERIZATION ETC PRODS			W 510983	388448	W 516430	548895	W 495684	446211	PROD POLYMERISATION
5831	POLYETHYLENE			W 178268	116175	W 193402	179000	W 166161	134568	POLYETHYLENE
58311	— IN PRIMARY FORMS			W 167364	104455	W 181976	161341	W 157807	122607	POLYETHYLENE PRIMAIRES
5832	POLYPROPYLENE			W 101285	65401	W 87729	83551	W 81633	66619	POLYPROPYLENE
58321	— IN PRIMARY FORMS			W 94971	55178	W 82716	68664	W 76619	54210	POLYPROPYLENE PRIMAIRES
5833	POLYSTYRENE,ITS COPOLYMR			W 69589	66783	W 73818	100736	W 75870	78871	POLYPROPYLENE COPOLYMERES
58331	— IN PRIMARY FORMS			W 69280	66075	W 73652	100335	W 75236	77668	SOUS FORMES PRIMAIRES
5834	POLYVINYL CHLORIDE			W 148998	114530	W 148981	147096	W 154329	115875	CHLORURE DE POLYVINYLE
58341	— IN PRIMARY FORMS			W 138428	97241	W 137256	124536	W 139710	89133	SOUS FORMES PRIMAIRES
5839	OTH POLYMRZTION ETC PROD			W 10543	19943	W 8991	29735	W 12812	39582	AUT PROD POLYMER COPOLYM
59	CHEMICAL MATERIALS NES		92023		83369		141557		150153	MAT PROD CHIMIQUES NDA
591	PESTICIDES,DISINFECTANTS			W 10059	49636	W 9567	68443	W 13614	62173	DESINF,INSECT,FONG,HERB
598	MISCEL CHEM PRODUCTS NES				13360		61716		66265	PROD DIV INDUST CHIM NDA
5989	CHEM PRODUCTS,PREPS NES			W 11134	11146		58944	W 36911	64868	PROD PREP CHIMIQUES NDA
59899	OTH CHEM PRODS,PREPS,NES			W 7278	6762	W 27281	53622	W 33146	59820	AUT PRODUITS CHIMIQUES NDA
6	BASIC MANUFACTURES		1436669		1724000		2275024		2405274	ART MANUFACTURES
61	LEATHER,DRESSED FUR,ETC		33607		150338		154116		168951	CUIRS,PELLETERIES
611	LEATHER				36797		40697	W 6796	44584	CUIRS,PEAUX PREPARES
612	LEATHER ETC MANUFACTURES			W 3908	110463	W 4109	109625	W 4261	119932	OUVRAGES EN CUIRS NDA
6123	PREPRD PARTS OF FOOTWEAR			W 3783	109200	W 3875	105718	W 4135	118560	PARTIES DE CHAUSSURES
62	RUBBER MANUFACTURES NES		81729		107089		139160		158651	CAOUTCHOUC MANUFACTURE
625	RUBBER TYRES, TUBES ETC			W 25512	65391	W 32995	84402	W 32952	91166	PNEUS CAOUTCHOUC VULCANISE
6252	TYRES,NEW,BUS OR LORRY			W 11871	29629	W 14926	40842	W 14829	42899	PNEUS POUR AUTOBUS,CAMIONS
6259	OTH TYRES,TYRE CASES,ETC			W 13518	35352	W 17761	42777	W 17916	47459	AUTRES PNEUS RECHAPES FLAPS
62599	TYRES NES,TYRE CASES,ETC			W 12896	34033	W 16877	40470	W 17130	45097	PNEUS,FLAPS
628	RUBBER ARTICLES NES			W 5828	29906	W 7897	41077	W 8842	44122	OUVRAGES CAOUTCHOUC NDA
63	WOOD,CORK MANUFACTRS NES		69966		111128		146211		168293	OUVRAGES LIEGE ET BOIS
634	VENEERS,PLYWOOD,ETC			W 85877	30479	W 82355	36263	W 106536	43999	PLACAGES,CONTRE–PLAQUES
635	WOOD MANUFACTURES NES			W 129730	80627	W 194069	109930	W 194344	124199	ART MANUF EN BOIS NDA
6353	BUILDERS WOODWRK,PREFABS			W 25207	51982	W 30701	68820	W 35523	78488	OUVRAGES DE MENUISERIE
64	PAPER,PAPERBOARD AND MFR		68576		120030		162844		228803	PAPIERS,CARTONS & OUVRAGES
641	PAPER AND PAPERBOARD			W 106516	54055	W 120484	72845	W 171884	117608	PAPIERS ET CARTONS
6415	PAPER,PAPERBRD,BULK,NES			W 55051	23431	W 53132	27814	W 104559	67320	PAPIERS,CARTONS ROULEAUX
64159	OTHER PAPER ETC,BULK,NES			W 9644	7873	W 12983	14548	W 103040	65535	AUT PAPIER ROULEAUX FEUILLES
642	PAPER,ETC,PRECUT,ARTS OF			W 35431	65975	W 42512	89999	W 52674	111195	PAP,CARTONS DECOUPES
6428	PAPER ETC ARTICLES NES			W 15332	38097	W 18520	51801	W 22381	68292	OUVRAGES EN PATE A PAPIER
64285	PAPER ETC DIAPERS ETC			W 9534	33120	W 11447	45017	W 14568	59727	SERVIETTES HYGIENIQUES
65	TEXTILE YARN,FABRICS,ETC		200322		234904		273079		280059	FILS,TISSUS,ARTICLES TEXTILE
651	TEXTILE YARN			W 10489	49634	W 11919	49729	W 9630	48811	FILS TEXTILES
658	TEXTILE ARTICLES NES				68030		89851	W 12149	90932	ART FACONNES MAT TEXTILES
6584	LINENS ETC			W 2655	31591	W 3665	48183	W 4019	51361	LINGE DE MAISON
66	NONMETAL MINERAL MFS NES		208649		204982		230595		265352	ART MIN NON METALLIQUES
662	CLAY,REFRACTORY BLDG PRD			W 58594	27122	W 60065	35217	W 119838	39612	MAT CONST REFRACTAIRES
663	MINERAL MANUFCTURES NES				29743		42615		58108	ART MIN MANUF NDA
664	GLASS			W 146180	66397	W 132956	72564	W 139757	69020	VERRE
6644	GLASS SURFACE–GROUND ETC			W 108350	37227	W 99036	41390	W 107709	38023	VERRE COULE,LAMINE
665	GLASSWARE			W 5154	33020	W 6013	34511	W 22694	46145	OUVRAGES EN VERRE
67	IRON AND STEEL		314163		268853		385742		373744	FER ET ACIER
672	IRON,STEEL PRIMARY FORMS			W 116912	36116	W 218654	84087	W 355089	103468	LINGOTS FER,ACIER
6727	IRN,STL COIL FR REROLLNG			W 101224	29324	W 193276	68791	W 315180	89403	EBAUCHES POUR TOLES FER
67271	IRON,SIMPLE STEEL COILS			W 101159	29300	W 193140	68730	W 315180	89403	EBAUCHES NON EN ACIER
673	IRON,STEEL SHAPES ETC			W 161694	49247	W 141378	54044	W 91507	35565	BARRES,PROFIL FER,ACIER
6733	IRON,STEEL PROFILES ETC			W 126496	34755	W 70293	23832	W 52606	17305	PROFILES,PALPLAN FER,ACIER
674	IRN,STL UNIV,PLATE,SHEET				119301	W 354887	166596	W 397004	158399	LARGES PLATS,TOLES
6744	IRN,STL HVY PLATE,ROLLED			W 142271	44378	W 151277	62204	W 92393	31037	TOLES LAMINEES PLUS 4.75 MM
67441	— OF IRON OR SIMPLE STL			W 142227	44284	W 151065	61686	W 92299	30781	TOLES NON ACIER FIN CARB
6745	IRN,STL MED PLATE,ROLLED			W 49473	18844	W 95061	39258	W 166675	58514	TOLES 3 A 4.75 MM
67451	— OF IRON OR SIMPLE STL			W 46676	17170	W 89714	34801	W 161215	54295	TOLES AUT NON ACIER FIN
6746	IRN,STL THIN PLATE,ROLLD			W 135086	55540	W 107319	63697	W 132919	63074	TOLES LAM MOINS 3MM
67461	— OF IRON OR SIMPLE STL			W 132073	49750	W 101898	50419	W 129794	56448	TOL NON AC FIN MOINS 3 MM
678	IRON,STL TUBES,PIPES,ETC			W 91888	49668	W 95971	65086	W 87259	58021	TUBES,TUYAUX EN FONTE,FER
68	NON–FERROUS METALS		190444		261912		416894		347865	METAUX NON FERREUX
682	COPPER EXC CEMENT COPPER			W 13271	31451	W 21591	62158	W 14252	38283	CUIVRE
6822	COPPER,ALLOYS WORKED			W 13072	31163	W 21139	61074	W 14252	38283	CUIVRE,ALLIAGES OUVRES
684	ALUMINIUM			W 124529	227465	W 142555	353654	W 143359	309381	ALUMINIUM
6841	ALUMINIUM,ALLOYS,UNWRGHT			W 32369	47021	W 48617	99673	W 20416	35997	ALUMINIUM,ALLIAGES BRUTS
6842	ALUMINIUM,ALLOYS WORKED			W 92160	180444	W 93939	253981	W 122943	273384	ALUMINIUM,ALLIAGES OUVRE
68421	ALUMINIUM BARS,WIRE,ETC			W 28207	50890	W 38099	96024	W 63446	132890	BARRES,PROFILES FILS ALU
68422	ALUMNM PLATE,SHEET,STRIP			W 57701	113833	W 49937	139098	W 56570	130226	TOLES, PLANCHES EN ALU
69	METAL MANUFACTURES NES		269213		264764		366383		413556	ART MANUFACT EN METAL NDA
691	STRUCTURES AND PARTS NES			W 43919	82278	W 52911	115547	W 61995	125260	CONSTRUCT FER,ACIER,ALU
6911	STRUCTURES,PARTS IRN,STL			W 39230	54635	W 46462	77562	W 55907	89712	CONSTRUCT FER,ACIER,FONTE
692	METAL TANKS,BOXES,ETC			W 19360	41621	W 15903	42055	W 16475	48420	RECIPIENTS METALLIQUES
697	BASE MTL HOUSEHOLD EQUIP			W 14229	42804	W 16856	54078	W 19865	61445	ART MENAGE MET COMMUNS
6973	DMSTC HEATG,COOKG APPARA			W 10766	29291	W 12867	36623	W 15506	42255	APPS CHAUF NON ELECTRIQ
699	BASE METAL MFRS NES				64657		103495		132447	ART MANUFACTURES MET NDA
6991	LOCKSMITHS WARES,ETC			W 6382	27098	W 8203	34584	W 9443	41487	ARTICLES DE SERRURERIE
6998	MFRS NES OF CPR,NIKL,ETC				11935	W 4576	23373	W 8812	41269	OUVRAGES EN CU,NI,AL,PB,ZN
7	MACHINES,TRANSPORT EQUIP		2143641		2433074		3245787		3284088	MACHINES MATERIEL TRANSPORT
71	POWER GENERATING EQUIPMT		120788		94371		106471		135541	MACHINES GENERATRICES
716	ROTATING ELECTRIC PLANT				53498	W 10896	52774	W 13853	64911	APP ELECTR ROTATIFS,PIECES
72	MACHS FOR SPCL INDUSTRYS		181401		192904		242098		239908	MAC SPECIALES POUR INDUST
721	AGRIC MACHY,EXC TRACTORS			W 18136	64358		72798	W 20091	77200	MACHINES AGRICOLES
7212	HARVESTING ETC MACHINES			W 12099	47824	W 12159	50333	W 12892	56673	ENGINS POUR LA RECOLTE
72129	PTS NES OF MACHY OF 7212			W 4974	15974	W 5955	19601	W 9398	40494	PIECES POUR MACH 721.2
723	CIVIL ENGNEERG EQUIP ETC			W 15728	35799	W 17767	45720	W 14206	36654	APPAREILS DE GENIE CIVIL

5. General Exports F.O.B. by Commodities according to the S.I.T.C. (Rev. 2) in thousand U.S. Dollars
Exportations Générales F.O.B. par Produits d'après la C.T.C.I. (Rév. 2) en milliers de Dollars E.U.

SITC CTCI	COMMODITY	1993 WEIGHT POIDS	1993 VALUE VALEUR	1994 WEIGHT POIDS	1994 VALUE VALEUR	1995 WEIGHT POIDS	1995 VALUE VALEUR	1996 WEIGHT POIDS	1996 VALUE VALEUR	PRODUIT
7239	CONSTR ETC MACHY PTS NES			W 14610	31215	W 16043	40851	W 12372	30634	PIECES 723.41–723.46
728	OTH MACHY FOR SPCL INDUS			W 8601	45580	W 8484	71970	W 11512	68568	AUT MACH IND PARTICULIERES
7284	MACHY FOR SPCL INDUS NES			W 4115	33593	W 3971	56058	W 6156	50520	MACH SPEC IND PARTICUL.
73	METALWORKING MACHINERY		43406		36623		49501		55624	MACH TRAVAIL DES METAUX
74	GENRL INDUSTRL MACHY NES		228441		311612		399158		411327	MACH APP INDUSTRIE
741	HEATING,COOLING EQUIPMNT			W 8015	45122	W 8982	58619	W 12893	76641	MACH CHAUFFAGE,PIECES
742	PUMPS FOR LIQUIDS ETC			W 2798	39049	W 3280	59333	W 2759	33768	POMPES MOTO–POMPES
7428	OTHER PUMPS FOR LIQUIDS			W 665	29187	W 1151	45295	W 697	19220	AUTRES POMPES POUR LIQ
74288	PUMPS FR LIQUIDS NES ETC			W 635	28837	W 1133	45064	W 654	18748	POMPES POUR LIQUIDES NDA
743	PUMPS NES,CENTRFUGES ETC			W 5032	41563	W 5550	50890	W 6120	57138	POMPES COMPRES,VENT ETC
744	MECHANICAL HANDLING EQU				50927	W 27743	64069		62410	EQUIP MANUTENTION PIECES
7449	PTS NES OF MACHY OF 7442			W 25298	39753	W 22845	48473	W 20470	44596	PIECES DU 744.2
749	NONELEC MACH PTS,ACC NES			W 13642	118940	W 15658	142945	W 14172	142407	PIECES MACH NON ELEC NDA
7492	COCKS,VALVES ETC NES			W 5638	55527	W 5436	60846	W 4580	58272	ART ROB,SIM POUR TUYAUX
7499	OTH NONELEC MCHY PTS NES			W 2101	28918	W 2207	32027	W 3284	42083	PIECES NON ELECT NDA
75	OFFICE MACHNES,ADP EQUIP		23327		29277		70840		47891	MACH BUREAU TRAIT AUTOM
759	OFFICE,ADP MCH PTS,ACCES			W 1351	18682	W 1213	52581	W 1159	29058	PIECES DU 751 ET 752
7599	ACCTG,ETC,ADP MCH PTS,AC			W 972	16370	W 929	50239	W 843	23217	PIECES DU 751 ET 752
76	TELECOMM,SOUND EQUIPMENT		240969		357166		436155		309457	EQUIPMENT DE TELECOM
761	TELEVISION RECEIVERS			W 2162	29157	W 5844	84453		31072	RECEPTEURS DE TELEVISION
7611	COLOUR TV RECEIVERS			W 2138	29095	W 5837	84383	W 2868	31053	RECEPTEURS COULEUR
763	SOUND RECORDRS,PHONOGRPH			W 322	10088		49885		6200	PHONO,APP ENREGISTREMENT
7638	OTHR SOUND APPARATUS ETC			W 322	10085	W 1925	49869		6196	AUT APP D'ENREGIS,REPROD
76381	TV IMAGE,SND RECRDRS ETC			W 6	411	W 1771	44217		439	APP ENREG,REPRO IMAG,SON
764	TELECOM EQPT,PTS,ACC NES				290534		281493		241988	EQUIP TELECOM,PIECES
7649	PTS NES OF EQUIPMT OF 76			W 10992	264258	W 9204	264261	W 9380	221136	PIECES DE LA DIV 76
76493	TELECOMM EQUIPMT PTS NES			W 3069	72867	W 2955	86491	W 4033	82444	PIECES 761,762,764.3,8
76499	PARTS ETC OF SOUND EQUIP			W 6738	183167	W 5215	165427	W 4265	129129	PIECES NDA POUR 763
77	ELECTRIC MACHNRY NES ETC		606454		839777		1246684		1491106	MACH APP ELECT NDA
771	ELECTRIC POWER MACHY NES			W 3140	32237	W 2643	46095	W 6608	73515	MACH PROD,TRANS ELECTR
7711	TRANSFORMERS,ELECTRICAL			W 1530	11314	W 1150	15045	W 4263	40159	TRANSFO ELECTRIQUES
77118	OTHER ELEC TRANSFORMERS			W 1264	9942	W 974	14145	W 4256	40113	AUTRES TRANSFO ELECTRIQ
772	SWITCHGEAR ETC,PARTS NES			W 7200	151916	W 10440	286574	W 12525	294281	APP COUPURE,SECT ETC
7721	SWITCHGEAR ETC			W 6290	102072	W 9193	206230	W 10231	198619	APP COUPURE,SECTIONMNT
7722	PRINTED CIRCUITS,PTS NES			W 802	43699	W 1073	72116	W 2224	90567	CIRCUITS ET PIECES
773	ELECTR DISTRIBUTNG EQUIP			W 15496	160966		250644	W 46140	350543	EQUIPMT DISTRIBUTION ELECT
7731	INSULATED WIRE,CABLE ETC			W 13823	151156	W 20602	237218	W 43980	339894	FILS,CABLES ISOLES ELECT
775	HOUSEHOLD TYPE EQUIP NES				103228	W 36108	154087	W 41425	185445	MACH,APP USAGE DOMESTQUE
7752	DOM REFRIGERATRS,FREEZRS			W 21794	77192	W 28894	114825	W 32571	135659	REFRIG,CONGEL MENAGER
77521	DOMESTIC REFRIGERATORS			W 17337	62069	W 21516	86434	W 22695	96351	REFRIGERATEURS
778	ELECTRICAL MACHINERY NES			W 35305	362741	W 40199	453908	W 43462	530604	AUTRES MACH ELECT NDA
7782	ELECTRIC LAMPS,BULBS			W 25983	265697	W 29900	302419	W 32244	369344	LAMPES, TUBES ELECTRIQUES
77821	ELEC FILAMENT LAMPS NES			W 14921	144936	W 16841	163579	W 17830	189522	LAMPES NON INFRAROUGES
77822	ELEC DISCHARGE LAMPS NES			W 9274	107652	W 10733	119987	W 11570	148748	LAMPES NON ULTRA–VIOLETS
7783	AUTOMOTIVE ELECTR EQUIP			W 4549	63256	W 5554	79419	W 4580	65472	EQUIP ELECT MOTEURS EXPL
77831	IGNITION,STARTING EQUIP			W 2984	37405	W 3928	50388	W 2905	35649	APP ELEC ALLUM,DEMARRAGE
7788	OTH ELEC MACHY,EQUIP NES			W 677	25915	W 1106	63668	W 975	82331	AUT MACH APP ELEC NDA
77884	ELECTRICAL CONDENSERS			W 41	13568	W 172	45217	W 346	67436	CONDENSATEURS ELECTRIQUES
78	ROAD VEHICLES		564371		542061		681727		557078	VEHICULES ROUTIERS
781	PASS MOTOR VEH EXC BUSES			W 65714	130089	W 97632	186255	W 26695	52502	AUTO TRANSPORT PERSONNES
783	ROAD MOTOR VEHICLES NES			W 17461	110769	W 21459	114839	W 18142	113453	VEHICULES ROUTIERS NDA
7831	BUSES			W 17115	110019	W 20701	111894	W 17034	107935	VOITURES TRANSPORT COMMUN
784	MOTOR VEH PRTS,ACCES NES			W 54423	219123	W 58188	249541	W 63079	256372	PIECES 722,781,782,783
7849	OTHER MOTOR VEHCL PARTS			W 53424	212425	W 57398	244845	W 62407	253416	PIECES 722,781,782,783
786	TRAILERS,NONMOTR VEH,NES			W 23450	63815	W 37491	104062	W 40667	101955	REMORQUES,CADRES,CONTAIN
7868	OTH NONMOTR VEHICLES ETC			W 17855	46864	W 28284	81432	W 31034	73129	AUT VEHIC NON AUTO,PIECES
78689	PTS NES OF TRAILERS ETC			W 17182	44729	W 27021	76744	W 29539	67570	PIECES 786.11,12,786.81
79	OTHR TRANSPORT EQUIPMENT		134485		29283		13153		36156	AUTRE MATERIEL TRANSPORT
8	MISC MANUFACTURED GOODS		1582267		1772179		1959271		2210194	ART MANUFACTURES DIVERS
812	*PLUMBG,HEATNG,LGHTNG EQ			W 14684	60275		74610		83838	APPAR SANITAIRES CHAUFFAGE
8124	LIGHTING EQUIPMENT NES			W 8953	49175		58667		64634	APPAREILS ECLAIRAGE ETC
81242	LAMPS,FITTINGS BASE METL			W 8330	43637	W 9736	52316	W 10722	56239	APPAREILS D'ECLAIRAGE
821	*FURNITURE,PARTS THEREOF			W 44796	161245	W 49117	232874	W 56674	283482	MEUBLES ET PIECES
8211	CHAIRS,SEATS AND PARTS			W 17184	78907	W 21977	143747	W 25622	182786	SIEGES ET PIECES
82111	CHAIRS AND OTHER SEATS			W 13300	63109	W 15452	78782	W 19416	87576	SIEGES
82119	PTS NES OF CHAIRS ETC			W 3884	15798	W 6525	64965	W 6206	95210	PIECES DU 821.11
8219	FURNITURE AND PARTS NES			W 25783	63952	W 24552	66736	W 27899	74448	AUTRES MEUBLES ET PIECES
82192	WOOD FURNITURE NES			W 17200	42883	W 17808	45298	W 17276	42607	MEUBLES NDA EN BOIS
831	*TRAVEL GOODS,HANDBAGS			W 3104	30454	W 3462	29201	W 4046	43786	ARTICLES DE VOYAGE ETC
84	CLOTHING AND ACCESSORIES		804698		993736		1034620		1108996	VETEMENTS
842	MENS OUTERWEAR NOT KNIT			W 7553	220359	W 7977	232280	W 8758	252098	VET DESSUS POUR HOMMES
8422	— SUITS			W 923	38952	W 989	43155	W 1056	46317	COMPLETS HOMMES MAT TEXT
8423	— TROUSERS,BREECHES ETC			W 3671	78904	W 4011	85981	W 4689	99348	PANTALONS HOMMES MAT TEX
8424	— JACKETS,BLAZERS ETC			W 1477	58559	W 1308	53218	W 1437	55695	VESTES HOMMES MAT TEXTIL
843	WOMENS OUTERWEAR NONKNIT			W 8518	369427	W 8113	347783	W 8396	356438	VET DESSUS FEMMES MAT TEX
8431	— COATS AND JACKETS			W 2598	120599	W 2377	102630	W 2170	99827	MANT,VEST FEM MAT TEXTIL
8433	— DRESSES			W 778	39202	W 972	46217	W 1028	46908	ROBES EN MAT–TEXTILES
8434	— SKIRTS			W 1096	43402	W 1013	40968	W 964	36822	JUPES EN MAT TEXTILES
8435	— BLOUSES			W 1185	58439	W 953	46621	W 915	43622	BLOUSES FEM MAT TEXTILES
8439	— OTHER OUTER GARMENTS			W 2350	83085	W 2145	82051	W 2616	97777	AUT VET DES FEM MAT TEXT
845	OUTERWEAR KNIT NONELASTC			W 4847	118840	W 5458	133159	W 5741	139943	VET DESSOUS,ACCES BONNET
8451	— JERSEYS,PULLOVERS ETC			W 2195	48208	W 2641	55428	W 3001	61599	CHANDAILS,PULL–OVERS ETC
8459	— OTHER,CLTHG ACCESRYS			W 2396	61304	W 2514	66455	W 2427	67000	AUT VET DESSUS DE BONNE
846	UNDER GARMENTS KNITTED			W 7147	185899	W 8785	216795	W 9490	243154	SOUS VETS DE BONNETERIE
8462	— OF COTTON NON ELASTIC			W 5698	111848	W 7215	136504	W 7711	152893	SOUS–VET BONNET COTON
84629	—— OTHER			W 5698	111848	W 7215	136504	W 7711	152893	AUT SOUS–VET BONNET COTON
8465	CORSETS,GARTERS,ETC			W 853	63888	W 1007	73783	W 1100	81835	CORSETS,GAINES ART SIM
84651	BRASSIERES			W 696	55778	W 732	62686	W 813	68576	SOUTIENS–GORGE,BUSTIERS
847	TEXTILE CLTHNG ACCES NES			W 1346	32101	W 1432	32527		34132	ACCES VET MAT TEXT NDA
848	HEADGEAR,NONTXTL CLOTHNG				36154		36267		44509	VET ACCES MAT AUT QUE TEX
851	*FOOTWEAR			W 9067	168120	W 8607	160763	W 9733	198673	CHAUSSURES
85102	FOOTWEAR LEATHER			W 8569	165715	W 7985	157396	W 8663	180134	CHAUS SEMELLES EN CUIR
87	PRECISION INSTRUMNTS NES		89185		100668		131149		138858	INSTRUM,APPAR SCIENT NDA
872	MEDICAL INSTRUMENTS NES			W 1748	26080	W 2778	38868		46942	INSTR,APP MEDIC–CHIR NDA
87202	OTH MEDICAL INSTRUMENTS			W 1585	24253	W 2593	36691	W 3727	45569	INSTRUM,APP MEDECINE
874	MEASURNG,CONTROLNG INSTR				58897		72411		69243	INSTRUMENTS DE MESURE
89	MISC MANUFCTRD GOODS NES		193340		225779		268044		314879	ART MANUFACTURES DIVERS
892	PRINTED MATTER				33450	W 15826	41474		41898	IMPRIMES
893	ARTICLES OF PLASTIC NES				87511		129608		158264	OUVRAGES EN MAT DIVIS 58
8931	PLSTC PACKG CONTNRS,LIDS			W 16022	29675	W 17569	45093	W 21848	62642	ART TRANSP EMBALLAGE ETC
8939	MISC PLASTIC ARTICLES			W 18365	56421	W 23237	82610	W 28368	93442	ART DIVERS EN MAT DIV 58

5. General Exports F.O.B. by Commodities according to the S.I.T.C. (Rev. 2) in thousand U.S. Dollars
Exportations Générales F.O.B. par Produits d'après la C.T.C.I. (Rév. 2) en milliers de Dollars E.U.

SITC CTCI	COMMODITY	1993		1994		1995		1996		PRODUIT
		WEIGHT POIDS	VALUE VALEUR	WEIGHT POIDS	VALUE VALEUR	WEIGHT POIDS	VALUE VALEUR	WEIGHT POIDS	VALUE VALEUR	
89399	OTHR PLASTC ARTICLES NES			W 13310	46026	W 15473	63678	W 20700	74897	AUT OUV MAT DIV 58
894	TOYS,SPORTING GOODS,ETC			W 7688	48396	W 5993	38625	W 7919	48697	VOITURES ENFANTS,JOUETS
8942	TOYS,INDOOR GAMES ETC			W 7081	43677	W 4976	31784	W 5926	37890	JOUETS,JEUX ETC
9	GOODS NOT CLASSD BY KIND		6302		835977		423739		524578	ART TRANSACT NON CLASSES
931	*SPECIAL TRANSACTIONS				824430		413459		511253	TRANS.SPECIALES

FOOT NOTES – NOTES

TABLE 1 –

1 Beginning 1 January, 1976, data are expressed in 'forints' and are not comparable with the earlier data, which are in 'exchange forints'.

TABLEAU 1 –

1 A partir du 1er janvier 1976 les données sont exprimées en 'forints', et ne sont pas comparables aux données précédentes qui étaient exprimées en 'forints convertibles'.

1. HISTORICAL SERIES, 1961–1996 SPECIAL TRADE, IMPORTS C.I.F., EXPORTS F.O.B.
SERIES HISTORIQUES, 1961–1996 COMMERCE SPECIAL, IMPORTATIONS C.A.F., EXPORTATIONS F.O.B

YEAR ANNEE	VALUE IN MILLION ICELANDIC KRONUR VALEUR EN MILLION ICELANDIC KRONUR MERCHANDISE # 1 –MARCHANDISE		GOLD –OR		CONVERSION FACTORS U.S. CENTS PER ICELANDIC KRONA FACTEURS DE CONVERSION CENTS E.U. PAR ICELANDIC KRONA		INDEX NUMBERS –INDICES QUANTUM		UNIT VALUE VALEUR UNITAIRE	
	IMPORTS	EXPORTS	IMPORTS	EXPORTS	IMPORTS	EXPORTS	IMPORTS	EXPORTS	IMPORTS	EXPORTS
1961	3228.40	3074.70			2.3256	2.3256	23	28		
1962	3836.70	3628.00			2.3256	2.3256	27	33		
1963	4717.10	4042.80			2.3256	2.3256	32	36		
1964	5636.00	4776.00			2.3256	2.3256	33	38		
1965	5901.60	5563.20			2.3256	2.3256	37	39		
1966	6852.70	6041.50			2.3256	2.3256	43	42		
1967	7116.20	4303.10			2.2789	2.2575	44	33		
1968	8246.20	5097.70			1.6783	1.6125	40	31		
1969	10855.90	9466.40			1.1364	1.1364	36	37		
1970	13644.60	12915.00			1.1364	1.1364	44	43		
1971	18931.50	13177.90			1.1401	1.1393	54	36		
1972	20043.40	16701.00			1.1382	1.1404	58	44		
1973	31811.00	26020.00			1.1267	1.1163	68	48		1
1974	52555.00	32880.00			0.9858	1.0062	73	44	1	1
1975	75064.00	47435.00			0.6504	0.6482	62	47	1	1
1976	85667.00	73498.00			0.5485	0.5497	63	54	1	1
1977	120916.00	101880.00			0.5018	0.5031	71	59	2	2
1978	184332.00	176286.00			0.3655	0.3636	77	69	2	3
1979	292133.00	278450.00			0.2786	0.2802	78	75	4	4
1980	480162.00	445953.00			0.2083	0.2088	83	81	6	6
1981	7484.70	6536.20			13.0873	13.1488	88	81	9	9
1982	11644.80	8478.80			8.0856	8.0817	85	67	14	14
1983	20606.00	18633.00			3.9590	4.0208	76	76	27	27
1984	26780.30	23557.00			3.1337	3.1421	81	78	34	33
1985	37600.30	33749.60			2.4044	2.4114	88	86	44	42
1986	45910.00	45093.01			2.4295	2.4366	95	95	49	51
1987	61237.01	53053.01			2.5960	2.5902	118	99	53	58
1988	68996.00	61674.00			2.3159	2.3087	112	98	63	68
1989	80284.00	79131.01			1.7460	1.7520	100	101	83	85
1990	97559.01	92624.00			1.7215	1.7177	100	100	100	100
1991	104129.00	91560.00			1.6910	1.6918	105	92	103	108
1992	96895.01	87833.01			1.7384	1.7400	97	91	104	104
1993	90775.01	94710.00			1.4779	1.4783	84	96	113	107
1994	102499.00	113279.00			1.4361	1.4327	90	108	118	113
1995	113388.00	116613.00			1.5478	1.5463	96	105	123	120
1996	145165.00	108977.00			1.4984	1.5025			116	116

2. IMPORTS BY BROAD ECONOMIC CATEGORY AND EXPORTS BY INDUSTRIAL ORIGIN. (PERCENTAGE OF TOTAL VALUE)
IMPORTATIONS PAR CATEGORIES ECONOMIQUES ET EXPORTATIONS PAR BRANCHE D'ACTIVITE.(EN POURCENTAGE DE LA VALEUR TOTALE)

IMPORTS – IMPORTATIONS

	1990	1991	1992	1993	1994	1995	1996
TOTAL IMPORTS–IMPORTATIONS TOTALES	100.	100.	100.	100.	100.	100.	100.
1 FOOD BEV–ALIMENTATION BOISSONS	8.1	8.1	8.5	10.3	10.2	10.4	9.5
11 PRIMARY–PRODUITS DE BASE	2.8	2.6	2.6	3.8	3.8	4.4	4.0
111 FOR INDUSTRY–POUR L'INDUSTRIE	0.6	0.6	0.6	0.7	0.8	0.9	0.8
112 FOR HOUSEHOLDS–POUR LES MENAGES	2.2	2.1	2.0	3.1	3.0	3.5	3.2
12 PROCESSED–PRODUITS ELABORES	5.3	5.5	5.9	6.5	6.4	6.1	5.5
121 FOR INDUSTRY–POUR L'INDUSTRIE	0.8	0.7	0.7	0.9	0.9	0.8	0.7
122 FOR HOUSEHOLDS–POUR LES MENAGES	4.6	4.8	5.2	5.6	5.5	5.2	4.8
2 IND SUPPLIES–APPROV INDUSTRIELS	26.1	27.0	25.9	27.1	26.2	27.4	26.0
21 PRIMARY–PRODUITS DE BASE	1.3	1.1	1.1	1.2	1.2	1.2	1.2
22 PROCESSED–PRODUITS ELABORES	24.8	25.9	24.8	25.9	25.0	26.2	24.8
3 FUELS–COMBUSTIBLES	9.8	8.3	8.2	9.0	8.2	7.1	7.7
31 PRIMARY–PRODUITS DE BASE	0.4	0.4	0.3	0.4	0.4	0.4	0.3
32 PROCESSED–PRODUITS ELABORES	9.3	7.9	7.9	8.7	7.8	6.7	7.4
321 MOTOR SPIRIT–ESSENCE			1.9	1.8	1.8	1.4	1.6
322 OTHER–AUTRES	9.3	7.9	6.0	6.9	6.0	5.3	5.8
4 MACHINERY–EQUIPEMENT	17.8	19.4	18.2	18.7	19.5	20.5	21.7
41 CAPITAL EQUIPMENT–MACHINES	13.9	15.7	14.3	14.8	15.5	16.5	17.6
42 PARTS–PIECES ACCESSOIRES	3.9	3.7	3.9	3.9	4.1	4.0	4.1
5 TRANSPORT–TRANSPORT	17.7	14.6	16.1	10.6	12.2	12.0	14.2
51 PASSENGER CARS–AUTOMOBILES	3.4	4.8	3.8	3.8	3.5	4.3	5.2
52 OTHER–AUTRES	11.2	6.7	9.4	3.7	5.5	4.9	6.6
521 INDUSTRIAL–INDUSTRIELS	11.0	6.5	9.2	3.5	5.4	4.7	6.4
522 NON INDUSTRIAL–NON INDUSTRIEL	0.2	0.2	0.2	0.2	0.1	0.2	0.1
53 PARTS–PIECES ACCESSOIRES	3.1	3.1	2.9	3.1	3.2	2.8	2.5
6 CONSUM GOODS–BIENS CONSOMMATION	20.4	22.3	22.9	24.0	23.2	22.4	20.6
61 DURABLE–DURABLES	4.4	5.0	4.9	4.8	4.7	4.6	4.5
62 SEMI DURABLE–SEMI DURABLES	11.1	12.1	12.2	12.7	12.3	11.9	10.6
63 NON DURABLE–NON DURABLES	4.9	5.2	5.8	6.5	6.2	6.0	5.5
7 GOODS NES–BIENS NDA	0.2	0.2	0.2	0.3	0.4	0.2	0.3

EXPORTS – EXPORTATIONS

	1990	1991	1992	1993	1994	1995	1996
TOTAL EXPORTS–EXPORTATIONS TOTALES	100.	100.	100.	100.	100.	100.	100.
1 AGRICULTURE	71.6	78.4	73.8	64.9	61.4	55.3	54.0
2 MINING QUARRY–INDUS EXTRACTIVES	0.6	0.6	0.6	0.6	0.9	1.1	0.8
3 MANUFACTURING–IND MANUFACTUR	27.7	21.1	25.7	34.5	37.7	43.6	45.2
31 FOOD BEV TOBACCO–ALIM BOISS TAB	8.6	5.6	9.6	17.6	18.2	20.7	22.8
32 TEXTILES–INDUSTRIES TEXTILES	2.3	2.0	1.7	1.4	1.4	1.7	1.7
33 WOOD & PRODUCTS–BOIS & PRODUITS	0.0	0.0	0.0	0.0	0.2	0.1	0.0
34 PAPER & PRODUCTS–PAPIER & PRODT	0.1	0.1	0.1	0.2	0.2	0.2	0.2
35 CHEMICALS–INDUSTRIES CHIMIQUES	0.3	0.3	0.4	0.4	0.4	0.9	0.9
36 NON METAL MIN–MIN NON METAL	0.1	0.1	0.1	0.1	0.1	0.1	0.1
37 BASIC METAL–IND METAL BASE	13.0	10.9	11.1	11.2	12.0	13.4	12.7
38 METAL MANUF–MANUF METAL	2.7	1.6	2.1	3.2	5.0	6.1	5.8
39 OTH MANUF IND–AUTRES MANUF	0.7	0.5	0.6	0.5	0.3	0.4	1.0

3. TRADE BY PRINCIPAL COUNTRIES OF CONSIGNMENT (VALUE IN THOUSAND U.S. DOLLARS)
ECHANGES SELON LES PRINCIPAUX PAYS DE CONSIGNATION (VALEUR EN MILLIERS DE DOLLARS EU)

COUNTRIES–PAYS	SPECIAL IMPORTS C.I.F. IMPORTATIONS SPECIALES C.A.F				
	1992	1993	1994	1995	1996
World	1679966	1349420	1472390	1751354	2041549
Africa	4170	3816	4267	4103	4247
Americas	167487	149563	157306	181388	224836
Northern America	156549	138315	146847	169253	212625
LAIA	7230	7179	7219	7336	6317
CACM	963	1901	1629	1991	2374
Caribbean	71	50	321	1021	1831
Rest of America	2675	2119	1290	1787	1688
As.ex F.USSR	168241	139233	138318	172758	189049
Eur.x F.USSR	1269322	987204	1102276	1285230	1513037
EU	970450	782224	858490	1047352	1150684
EFTA	266119	190231	228935	199276	306190
East Europe	13498	12502	13015	32758	51874
Other Europe	17943	1502	980	4937	2972
Former USSR	26495	36064	36166	52148	58620
Oceania	44251	33539	33081	55727	51760
Norway,SVD,JM	244705	166983	210683	178274	276166
Germany/Allemagne	208033	160804	165253	200000	222200
United Kingdom	142941	120993	145336	168776	208281
Denmark/Danemark	148250	126562	132574	164833	170504
USA/Etats–Unis d'Amer	138979	125956	131151	147130	192781
Sweden/Suède	114682	91431	103313	122338	137092
Netherlands/Pays–Bas	125157	80936	92345	119789	121847
Japan/Japon	96730	74778	59215	76931	81898
France,Monac	54724	45940	50890	74367	66919
Italy/Italie	59365	47122	47419	57237	65663
Australia/Australie	42795	32551	32150	54361	50502
Russian Federation	26461	34133	32784	40899	50632
Belgium–Luxembourg	30941	26113	29597	35319	39996
Finland/Finlande	28484	26623	27943	32251	33637
Spain/Espagne	14591	18733	20438	28239	35375
Switz.Liecht	21414	23248	18252	21002	30025
China/Chine	11743	13761	19497	23609	26635
Korea, Republic of	12640	11255	15374	20629	22730
Portugal	19934	13720	17657	15271	14714
Poland/Pologne	6562	6467	5398	22500	39941
Canada	17082	8384	15355	16807	18615
Ireland/Irlande	10018	10254	14238	17327	20769
Austria/Autriche	11267	11051	9940	10041	12558
Hong Kong	10786	7777	7673	9384	10382
Faeroe Islds/Is Féroé	17875	1433	936	4861	2871
Thailand/Thaïlande	3466	4373	5513	4941	5226
Czech Republic		4420	4774	6210	7262
India/Inde	1789	2731	4038	5171	5634
Brazil/Brésil	4086	4149	3574	3560	2776
Singapore/Singapour	2506	2354	3132	4027	3946
Malaysia/Malaisie	1555	1840	2863	3775	4398
Indonesia/Indonésie	1511	1903	2301	2907	3050
Greenland/Groenland	443	3931	289	5231	1023
Estonia/Estonie		1429	2052	4491	2853
Israel/Israël	6265	895	1133	854	1533
Turkey/Turquie	1497	1199	1414	1986	3097
Greece/Grèce	2062	1943	1545	1564	1129
Tunisia/Tunisie	2182	2058	1962	1332	600
Panama	2354	1409	1131	1319	1043
Latvia/Lettonie	10	250	721	2841	3280
So. Africa Customs Un	424	1000	1472	1834	2332
Costa Rica	770	1458	1327	1293	1992
Hungary/Hongrie	979	763	1221	1419	2033
New Zealand	1455	988	930	1355	1249
Colombia/Colombie	759	737	1925	1443	1089
Lithuania/Lituanie	1	33	175	3755	1734
Pakistan	930	1040	1176	997	933
Czechoslovakia	5071				
Mexico/Mexique	908	1062	689	1063	1167
Philippines	1033	731	891	914	855

COUNTRIES–PAYS	SPECIAL EXPORTS F.O.B. EXPORTATIONS SPECIALES F.O.B.				
	1992	1993	1994	1995	1996
Monde	1527076	1399324	1626668	1802507	1897083
Afrique	13053	18732	12168	11571	11411
Amériques	187922	237197	263600	280209	327498
Amérique du Nord	181252	230758	258920	271094	257225
ALAI	3410	5330	4530	8902	13678
MCAC	1	3	0	0	7
Caraïbes	3259	1106	0	5	56288
Autre Amérique			150	208	300
Asie l'URSS exclus	150316	166988	255944	248075	232102
Europe l'URSS exclus	1169860	968310	1082427	1241848	1302260
UE	1087528	864577	1001557	1129964	1177989
AELE	72566	98334	73756	98891	107848
Europe de l'Est	1668	1551	2289	3709	6264
Autre de l'Europe	7682	3662	4397	8738	7962
Ancienne URSS	4792	5733	10769	12195	22070
Océanie	1133	2267	1761	8609	1741
United Kingdom	382870	302573	330965	347416	359714
USA/Etats–Unis d'Amer	174537	222196	235784	223397	234035
Germany/Allemagne	190212	154485	208823	246142	243763
Japan/Japon	115236	129751	229199	204551	185791
France,Monac	150677	115242	117659	122368	126811
Denmark/Danemark	85941	78728	103964	141268	136593
Spain/Espagne	78286	68262	75532	65971	73319
Norway,SVD,JM	34018	47118	45395	59027	70398
Netherlands/Pays–Bas	30851	30791	26412	53259	67925
Switz.Liecht	38548	51215	28361	39864	37449
Italy/Italie	42706	28599	37765	36886	36088
Portugal	44006	22901	20401	32764	48628
Belgium–Luxembourg	23677	22360	29444	32038	25675
Sweden/Suède	23946	16317	16904	23489	24341
Canada	5246	7384	21590	30342	21961
Greece/Grèce	17596	11539	13484	14302	12616
Finland/Finlande	14673	9946	15269	8929	18124
Nigeria/Nigéria	11925	12616	9844	8068	8675
Russian Federation	4659	5480	9839	10461	19304
Cayman Is/Is Caïmans	768	626			38127
Faeroe Islds/Is Féroé	7682	3662	4384	8738	7952
Brazil/Brésil	2277	2720	2733	7228	10137
Greenland/Groenland	1469	1164	1546	17356	1229
Korea, Republic of	1549	3336	2540	7362	7080
Antigua and Barbuda	2426				18144
Ireland/Irlande	1386	1437	2739	2991	2519
New Zealand	90	1620	838	7353	743
Poland/Pologne	443	571	1288	1734	4557
Cyprus/Chypre	5108	2369	299	398	404
Austria/Autriche	702	1398	2196	2141	1873
So. Africa Customs Un	73	353	1703	3167	1842
Israel/Israël	1122	1888	619	530	1207
Chile/Chili	481	1542	386	660	1770
Australia/Australie	1041	645	878	1256	998
Liberia/Libéria		4646			
China/Chine	105	128	398	2541	1037
Turkey/Turquie	22	201	181	1179	2053
Hong Kong	205	738	1051	405	1229
Lithuania/Lituanie	12	168	421	1118	1215
Czech Republic		278	844	663	1116
Colombia/Colombie	194	854	975	183	208
Slovenia/Slovénia			257	502	1599
India/Inde	65	194	466	805	827
Thailand/Thaïlande	154	354	393	314	1067
Malawi	869	909		32	
Mexico/Mexique	306	0	310	130	1025
Romania/Roumanie	92	494	106	898	15
Estonia/Estonie	2	53	297	498	678
Singapore/Singapour	323	229	280	471	166
Malaysia/Malaisie	24	39	98	58	1074

(VALUE AS PERCENTAGE OF WORLD TOTAL)(VALEURS EN POURCENTAGE DU TOTAL MONDIAL)

	1987	1988	1989	1990	1991	1992	1993	1994	1995	1996
Africa	0.2	0.2	0.3	0.3	0.2	0.2	0.3	0.3	0.2	0.2
Americas	8.5	8.7	12.3	15.7	11.8	10.0	11.1	10.7	10.4	11.0
Northern America	7.6	8.0	11.5	15.0	11.1	9.3	10.2	10.0	9.7	10.4
LAIA	0.6	0.5	0.5	0.4	0.5	0.4	0.5	0.5	0.4	0.3
CACM	0.1	0.1	0.1	0.1	0.1	0.1	0.1	0.1	0.1	0.1
Caribbean	0.0	0.0	0.0	0.0	0.0	0.0	0.0	0.0	0.1	0.1
Rest of America	0.1	0.1	0.2	0.2	0.1	0.2	0.2	0.1	0.1	0.1
As.ex F.USSR	10.8	9.7	7.8	8.5	11.0	10.0	10.3	9.4	9.9	9.3
Eur.x F.USSR	74.6	75.8	72.6	67.9	70.7	75l6	73.2	74.9	73.4	74.1
EU	63.4	63.5	62.1	59.8	62.5	57.8	58.0	58.3	59.8	56.4
EFTA	9.3	10.1	8.0	6.3	6.9	15.8	14.1	15.5	11.4	15.0
East Europe	1.6	2.0	2.3	1.7	0.9	0.8	0.9	0.9	1.9	2.5
Other Europe	0.2	0.1	0.1	0.2	0.4	1.1	0.1	0.1	0.3	0.1
Former USSR	4.2	3.5	4.2	5.0	3.3	1.6	2.7	2.5	3.0	2.9
Oceania	1.8	2.1	2.7	2.6	3.0	2.6	2.5	2.2	3.2	2.5
Norway,SVD,JM	8.3	9.0	6.6	5.0	5.5	14.6	12.4	14.3	10.2	13.5
Germany/Allemagne	15.2	14.2	13.1	12.4	13.0	12.4	11.9	11.2	11.4	10.9
United Kingdom	8.2	8.2	8.1	8.1	8.2	8.5	9.0	9.9	9.6	10.2
Denmark/Danemark	9.2	9.2	9.1	8.6	8.6	8.8	9.4	9.0	9.4	8.4
USA/Etats–Unis d'Amer	7.1	7.5	11.0	14.4	10.4	8.3	9.3	8.9	8.4	9.4
Sweden/Suède	8.2	8.8	8.2	7.6	7.6	6.8	6.8	7.0	7.0	6.7
Netherlands/Pays–Bas	8.1	8.2	10.4	10.4	10.0	7.4	6.0	6.3	6.8	6.0
Japan/Japon	8.2	6.9	4.9	5.6	7.4	5.8	5.5	4.0	4.4	4.0
France,Monac	3.4	3.1	3.1	3.0	3.6	3.3	3.4	3.5	4.2	3.3
Italy/Italie	3.1	4.4	3.1	3.1	3.3	3.5	3.5	3.2	3.3	3.2

	1987	1988	1989	1990	1991	1992	1993	1994	1995	1996
Afrique	1.6	1.2	0.7	0.7	0.8	0.9	1.3	0.7	0.6	0.6
Amériques	19.0	14.6	16.1	10.8	13.4	12.3	17.0	16.2	15.5	17.3
Amérique du Nord	18.9	14.3	14.8	10.4	13.0	11.9	16.5	15.9	15.0	13.6
ALAI	0.1	0.1	0.5	0.2	0.3	0.2	0.4	0.3	0.5	0.7
MCAC	0.0	0.0	0.0	0.0	0.0	0.0	0.0	0.0	0.0	0.0
Caraïbes	0.0	0.1	0.8	0.2	0.0	0.2	0.1	0.0	0.0	3.0
Autre Amérique	0.0	0.1						0.0	0.0	0.0
Asie l'URSS exclus	8.3	8.7	9.2	7.4	9.7	9.8	11.9	15.7	13.8	12.2
Europe l'URSS exclus	67.3	71.8	70.7	78.4	75.6	76.6	69.2	66.5	68.9	68.6
UE	61.1	62.0	59.8	70.7	68.9	71.2	61.8	61.6	62.7	62.1
AELE	4.5	6.9	7.7	5.6	5.6	4.8	7.0	4.5	5.5	5.7
Europe de l'Est	1.1	1.9	1.8	0.4	0.3	0.1	0.1	0.1	0.2	0.3
Autre de l'Europe	0.7	1.0	1.4	1.7	0.9	0.5	0.3	0.3	0.5	0.4
Ancienne URSS	3.6	3.6	3.1	2.5	0.5	0.3	0.4	0.7	0.7	1.2
Océanie	0.1	0.1	0.2	0.1	0.1	0.1	0.2	0.1	0.5	0.1
United Kingdom	19.4	23.3	20.8	25.3	23.4	25.1	21.6	20.3	19.3	19.0
USA/Etats–Unis d'Amer	18.3	13.6	14.3	9.9	12.6	11.4	15.9	14.5	12.4	12.3
Germany/Allemagne	10.0	10.3	11.9	12.7	12.1	12.5	11.0	12.8	13.7	12.8
Japan/Japon	7.8	7.6	7.1	6.0	7.9	7.5	9.3	14.1	11.3	9.8
France,Monac	5.4	4.8	5.7	9.0	10.1	9.9	8.2	7.2	6.8	6.7
Denmark/Danemark	3.9	3.3	3.7	5.0	4.2	5.6	5.6	6.4	7.8	7.2
Spain/Espagne	3.0	3.4	3.4	5.0	4.8	5.1	4.9	4.6	3.7	3.9
Norway,SVD,JM	1.8	2.4	2.2	1.5	1.6	2.2	3.4	2.8	3.3	3.7
Netherlands/Pays–Bas	0.9	1.1	1.7	2.1	1.7	2.0	2.2	1.6	3.0	3.6
Switz.Liecht	2.7	4.5	5.5	4.2	4.0	2.5	3.7	1.7	2.2	2.0

4. Special Imports C.I.F. by Commodities according to the S.I.T.C. (Rev. 2) in thousand U.S. Dollars
Importations Spéciales C.A.F. par Produits d'après la C.T.C.I. (Rév. 2) en milliers de Dollars E.U.

SITC CTCI	COMMODITY	1993 WEIGHT POIDS	1993 VALUE VALEUR	1994 WEIGHT POIDS	1994 VALUE VALEUR	1995 WEIGHT POIDS	1995 VALUE VALEUR	1996 WEIGHT POIDS	1996 VALUE VALEUR	PRODUIT
	ALL COMMODITIES		1349420		1472390		1751354		2041549	TOUS PRODUITS
0	FOOD AND LIVE ANIMALS		126860		137690		168162		177852	ALIMENTS,ANIMAUX VIVANTS
03	FISH AND PREPARATIONS		23024		24486		39554		42055	POISSONS ET PREPARATIONS
034	FISH,FRESH,CHILLED,FROZN	W 9582	11878	W 15918	18152	W 19739	24146	W 19824	28374	POISSON FRAIS, REFRIG,CONG
0341	FISH FRSH,CHLLD,EX FILLT	W 1248	1295	W 5145	3947	W 7680	6219	W 2516	2912	POISSON FRAIS,REFRIGERE
0342	FISH FROZEN,EXCL FILLETS	W 8110	10226	W 10430	13532	W 11905	17358	W 16222	22980	POISSONS CONGELES
036	SHELL FISH FRESH,FROZEN	W 8830	9416	W 4156	4775	W 6307	13007	W 5469	8046	CRUSTACES,MOLLUSQUES
04	CEREALS AND PREPARATIONS		25719		27900		32497		35747	CEREALES ET PRODUITS
048	CEREAL ETC PREPARATIONS	W 21028	19355	W 19085	19789	W 17977	21553	W 8958	22146	PREPTNS A BASE CEREALES
0481	PREPD BREAKFAST FOOD ETC	W 15883	8639	W 13576	8519	W 12521	8936	W 2935	7573	CEREALES TRAVAILLEES
04812	CEREAL ROASTED, PUFFED	W 1752	5659	W 1867	6422	W 1895	6388	W 2013	6681	PRODTS BASE CEREALES
0484	BAKERY PRODUCTS	W 2606	7289	W 2581	7181	W 2680	8191	W 2933	9293	PRODUITS DE BOULANGERIE
04842	PASTRY, CAKES ETC	W 1489	4310	W 1447	4158	W 1508	4499	W 1621	4962	PATISSERIE ETC.
05	VEGETABLES AND FRUIT		32586		34333		37223		40219	LEGUMES ET FRUITS
054	VEG ETC FRSH,SMPLY PRSVD	W 10548	7781	W 10640	8722	W 7641	8178	W 8865	9414	LEGUMES FRAIS,CONG,SECS
057	FRUIT,NUTS,FRESH,DRIED	W 12387	14185	W 12408	14491	W 12822	16606	W 12455	17873	FRUITS FRAIS OU SECS
058	FRUIT PRESERVED,PREPARED	W 4553	7101	W 4571	7507	W 4162	8010	W 4227	8248	CONSERVES DE FRUITS
06	SUGAR AND PREPS,HONEY		8494		10096		10975		11030	SUCRES ET PRODUITS
061	SUGAR AND HONEY	W 11830	5509	W 13270	6992	W 12420	7482	W 13103	7229	SUCRES ET MIEL
0612	REFINED SUGAR ETC	W 11282	4885	W 12696	6356	W 11821	6772	W 12469	6471	SUCRES RAFFINES
07	COFFEE,TEA,COCOA,SPICES		14674		16858		21559		20059	CAFE,THE,CACAO,EPICES
071	COFFEE AND SUBSTITUTES	W 2271	6735	W 2024	8463	W 2067	11612	W 2152	10255	CAFE ET SUCCEDANES
0711	COFFEE GREEN,ROASTED,SUB	W 2217	6015	W 1977	7686	W 2017	10675	W 2078	9148	CAFE TORREFIE OU DECAFEINE
07112	COFFEE ROASTED	W 1302	4311	W 1244	5302	W 1210	7376	W 1399	7095	CAFE TORREFIE
073	CHOCOLATE AND PRODUCTS	W 1146	5168	W 1210	5470	W 1279	6204	W 1301	6426	CHOCOLAT
081	*FEEDING STUFF FOR ANIMAL	W 14837	5375	W 9839	5675	W 8199	6820	W 8581	6512	NOURRITURE POUR ANIMAUX
0819	FOOD WASTE AND FEED NES	W 3275	3215	W 3662	4141	W 3686	5579	W 5200	5307	DECHETS,ALIMENTS NDA
08199	FODDER NES,INCL SWEETNED	W 3275	3215	W 3608	4106	W 3624	5533	W 3825	5024	PREPARATIONS FOURRAGERES
09	MISC EDIBLE PRODUCTS		16629		17847		18714		20717	PREP ALIMENTAIRES DIVERSES
098	EDIBLE PRODCTS,PREPS NES	W 3728	16517	W 3641	17743	W 3846	18554	W 4110	20500	PREP ALIMENTAIRES NDA
09809	MISC FOOD PREPRTIONS NES	W 1573	10002	W 1295	10771	W 1366	10345	W 1533	11994	PREP ALIMENTAIRES NDA
1	BEVERAGES AND TOBACCO		26114		27306		31870		34047	BOISSONS ET TABACS
11	BEVERAGES		13346		14082		17897		19235	BOISSONS
112	ALCOHOLIC BEVERAGES	W 7685	13151	W 7977	13810	W 9259	17366	W 10089	18714	BOISSONS ALCOOLIQUES
1121	WINE OF FRESH GRAPES ETC	W 1836	4629	W 2051	5323	W 2166	6082	W 2174	6541	VINS DE RAISINS FRAIS
11212	WINE OF FRESH GRAPES	W 1670	4137	W 1865	4773	W 2043	5698	W 2096	6334	VINS DE MOUTS DE RAISINS
1124	DISTILLED ALCOHOLIC BEVS	W 1367	5035	W 1275	5241	W 1575	6678	W 1475	6713	ALCOOLS,EAUX-DE-VIE
12	TOBACCO AND MANUFACTURES		12767		13224		13973		14812	TABACS BRUTS FABRIQUES
122	TOBACCO,MANUFACTURED	W 527	12767	W 551	13217	W 541	13973	W 554	14812	TABACS FABRIQUES
1222	CIGARETTES	W 462	11060	W 469	11377	W 470	11944	W 497	12835	CIGARETTES
2	CRUDE MATERLS,EXCL FUELS		65396		66447		93325		92414	MAT BRUTES NON COMESTIBLES
24	CORK AND WOOD		17856		17327		20550		21475	LIEGE ET BOIS
248	WOOD SHAPED,SLEEPERS	W 48652	17132	W 37983	16374	W 45748	19732	W 44980	20312	BOIS SIMPLEMENT TRAVAILLES
2482	LUMBER SHAPED CONIFER	W 46991	14654	W 36299	13746	W 43892	16540	W 42819	16380	CONIFERES SCIES,RABOTES
24821	LUMBER SAWN ETC CONIFER	W 46662	14110	W 35932	13179	W 43757	16168	W 42640	16116	CONIFERES SCIES LONGITUD
27	CRUDE FERTLZR,MINRLS NES		8974		11133		11618		13508	ENGRAIS MINERAUX BRUTS
278	OTHER CRUDE MINERALS	W 175629	7632		9844	W 209292	10471	W 223336	11189	AUTRES MINERAUX BRUTS
2783	COMMON SALT,ETC	W 57010	3827	W 89068	5273	W 95194	5868	W 90996	5734	SEL
28	METALLIFEROUS ORES,SCRAP		33037		32379		53626		50278	MINERAIS METAL,DECHETS
287	BASE METAL ORES,CONC NES	W 158329	32029	W 169692	31559	W 229470	52564	W 203152	48958	MINERAIS METAUX COMMUNS
2873	ALUMINIUM ORES,ALUMINA	W 158224	31997	W 169580	31533	W 229470	52564	W 203152	48956	MINERAIS D'ALUMINIUM
28732	ALUMINA(ALUMINIUM OXIDE)	W 158224	31997	W 169580	31533	W 229470	52564	W 203152	48956	ALUMINE (OXYDE ALUMINIUM)
3	MINERAL FUELS ETC		124836		122843		127580		161266	COMBUSTIBLES MINERAUX LUB
32	COAL,COKE AND BRIQUETTES		6042		9012		7777		9302	HOUILLES,COKES,BRIQUETTES
322	COAL,LIGNITE AND PEAT	W 54456	4362	W 71395	5571	W 65369	5766	W 66069	5871	HOUILLES,LIGNITES,TOURBE
3221	ANTHRACITE,NOT AGGLOMRTD	W 47470	3874	W 52763	4502	W 58106	5259	W 59543	5333	ANTHRACITE
33	PETROLEUM AND PRODUCTS		118297		113385		119252		151463	PETROLE ET DERIVES
334	PETROLEUM PRODUCTS,REFIN	W 655875	114998	W 660476	110397	W 676053	115239	W 726238	146917	PRODUITS RAFFINES
3341	GASOLINE,OTH LIGHT OILS	W 122086	24343	W 144781	25971	W 134428	24949	W 153162	32008	ESSENCES POUR MOTEURS
33411	MOTOR,AVIATION SPIRIT	W 120218	23747	W 142385	25284	W 132191	24220	W 151165	31298	ESSENCES MOTEURS D'AVIONS
3342	KEROSENE,OTH MEDIUM OILS	W 113745	20119	W 102337	17066	W 72293	12641	W 96873	20467	PETR LAMPANTS,AUT HUIL
33421	KEROSENE INCL JET FUEL	W 64388	12182	W 73833	12808	W 72283	12638	W 96693	20439	PETROLES LAMPANTS
33429	OTH MEDIUM PETROLEUM OIL	W 49357	7937	W 28503	4259	W 10	3	W 180	29	AUTRES HUILES MOYENNES
3343	GAS OILS	W 283007	48445	W 289483	46168	W 296042	47050	W 355160	68745	GAS OILS
3344	FUEL OILS,NES	W 129786	13034	W 116642	11827	W 165227	19724	W 113211	14876	FUEL OILS
3345	LUBS,PETROLEUM OILS NES	W 7251	9056	W 7234	9364	W 8063	10876	W 7830	10820	HUILES LUBRIFIANTES
33451	LUBS(HIGH PETR CONT) ETC	W 7046	8449	W 6926	8451	W 7688	9812	W 7479	9651	HUILES LUBRIF,H LOURDES
4	ANIMAL,VEGETABLE OIL,FAT		4125		4812		5423		5732	HUILES,GRAISSES ANIM,VEG
5	CHEMCLS,RELATED PROD NES		118244		128862		155686		166431	PRODUITS CHIMIQUES
51	ORGANIC CHEMICALS		5008		6556		8508		9333	PROD CHIMIQ ORGANIQUES
52	INORGANIC CHEMICALS		6805		7165		9070		10141	PROD CHIM INORGANIQUES
53	DYES,TANNING,COLOUR PROD		11403		11655		13259		14928	PROD TEINTURE,COLORANTS
533	PIGMENTS,PAINTS,ETC	W 4193	10183	W 3772	10026	W 3710	11435	W 4018	12955	PIGMENTS,PEINTURES,VERNIS
5334	VARNISHES,DISTEMPERS ETC	W 1081	4282	W 1065	4027	W 1128	4969	W 1224	5446	PEINTURES A L'EAU
5335	GLAZES,DRIERS,PUTTY ETC	W 2724	4065	W 2272	3668	W 2210	3786	W 2327	4192	PREPTNS COLOR UTILISES CERAM
541	*MEDICINAL,PHARM PRODUCT		34737		37025	K 465327	44879		49428	PROD MEDICINAUX PHARMACEUT
5417	MEDICAMENTS	K 333034	29075	K 342694	31059	K 345367	37458	K 372708	41930	MEDICAMENTS
54172	— CONTAINING HORMONES	K 19336	4352	K 20117	4668	K 23298	5877	K 29274	7093	MED CONTENANT HORMONES
54179	— CONTNG OTH SUBSTANCES	K 283324	21749	K 293886	23497	K 294492	28664	K 315373	31838	MED CONT AUT SUBSTANCES
55	PERFUME,CLEANING ETC PRD		21420		21889		24084		26134	PROD POUR PARFUM,TOILETTE
553	PERFUMERY,COSMETICS,ETC	W 1339	12341	W 1312	12627	W 1358	14448	W 1416	15400	PRODUITS DE PARFUMERIE
554	SOAP,CLEANSING ETC PREPS	W 3564	8342	W 3586	8454	W 3253	8711	W 3780	9663	SAVONS,PRODUITS DETERSIFS
5542	WASHING PREPARATIONS ETC	W 2945	6064	W 2975	6302	W 2617	6352	W 2932	6901	PROD ORG TENSIO-ACT NDA
562	*FERTILIZERS,MANUFACTURE	W 19797	2799	W 19038	3322	W 23391	5422	W 21608	4342	ENGRAIS MANUFACTURES
58	PLASTIC MATERIALS ETC		22058		26403		34294		33520	MAT PLAST ARTIFICIELLES
582	PROD OF CONDENSATION ETC	W 1968	4229	W 2282	5664	W 2433	6698	W 2462	6658	PROD CONDENS,POLYCOND
583	POLYMERIZATION ETC PRODS	W 11092	17428	W 13024	20073	W 12870	26916	W 15227	26325	PROD POLYMERISATION
5831	POLYETHYLENE	W 6342	7093	W 7910	9042	W 7397	12272	W 9039	11362	POLYETHYLENE
58311	— IN PRIMARY FORMS	W 5752	5581	W 7055	7066	W 6666	9453	W 8220	9023	POLYETHYLENE PRIMAIRES
5839	OTH POLYMRZTION ETC PROD	W 907	3790	W 952	3770	W 1288	5460	W 1422	5816	AUT PROD POLYMER COPOLYM
59	CHEMICAL MATERIALS NES		12200		13150		14934		16324	MAT PROD CHIMIQUES NDA
598	MISCEL CHEM PRODUCTS NES	W 7243	8963	W 7044	9687	W 6429	10860	W 7927	12046	PROD DIV INDUST CHIM NDA
5989	CHEM PRODUCTS,PREPS NES	W 1790	6141	W 1969	6500	W 2117	7979	W 2592	8514	PROD PREP CHIMIQUES NDA
59899	OTH CHEM PRODS,PREPS,NES	W 1466	5137	W 1613	5479	W 1808	6853	W 2227	7297	AUT PRODUITS CHIMIQUES NDA
6	BASIC MANUFACTURES		242816		256183		303724		350479	ART MANUFACTURES
62	RUBBER MANUFACTURES NES		15778		16236		19455		20458	CAOUTCHOUC MANUFACTURE
625	RUBBER TYRES, TUBES ETC	W 2601	8094	W 2730	8468	W 2803	10587	W 2735	10970	PNEUS CAOUTCHOUC VULCANISE
6251	TYRES NEW FOR MOTOR CARS	W 977	4432	W 1128	4694	W 1219	5926	W 1352	6381	PNEUS POUR VOITURES
628	RUBBER ARTICLES NES	W 862	4548	W 793	4503	W 726	5239	W 774	5476	OUVRAGES CAOUTCHOUC NDA
63	WOOD,CORK MANUFACTRS NES		19992		20786		24756		27617	OUVRAGES LIEGE ET BOIS
634	VENEERS,PLYWOOD,ETC	W 14007	8755	W 12440	8458	W 13306	10453	W 13155	9962	PLACAGES,CONTRE-PLAQUES

4. Special Imports C.I.F. by Commodities according to the S.I.T.C. (Rev. 2) in thousand U.S. Dollars
Importations Spéciales C.A.F. par Produits d'après la C.T.C.I. (Rév. 2) en milliers de Dollars E.U.

SITC CTCI	COMMODITY	1993 WEIGHT POIDS	1993 VALUE VALEUR	1994 WEIGHT POIDS	1994 VALUE VALEUR	1995 WEIGHT POIDS	1995 VALUE VALEUR	1996 WEIGHT POIDS	1996 VALUE VALEUR	PRODUIT
6343	IMPROVED,RECONSTIT WOOD	W 11046	4516	W 9657	4038	W 10338	5262	W 10299	4943	BOIS AMELIORES,RECONST
63432	RECONSTITUTED WOOD	W 11015	4403	W 9649	4012	W 10325	5161	W 10280	4834	BOIS RECONSTITUES
635	WOOD MANUFACTURES NES	W 4423	10996	W 4377	12147	W 4476	14080	W 6099	17406	ART MANUF EN BOIS NDA
6353	BUILDERS WOODWRK,PREFABS	W 3652	9150	W 3748	9978	W 3905	11608	W 5213	14200	OUVRAGES DE MENUISERIE
64	PAPER,PAPERBOARD AND MFR		54551		59236		70356		72129	PAPIERS,CARTONS & OUVRAGES
641	PAPER AND PAPERBOARD	W 29051	29125	W 33172	32121	W 31748	39137	W 33181	39769	PAPIERS ET CARTONS
6412	PRINTG,WRITING PAPER NES	W 5377	6184	W 5373	6334	W 5909	8845	W 6085	8615	PAPIERS POUR L'IMPRESSION
64122	— COATED,IMPREGNATD ETC	W 4413	5005	W 4423	5057	W 4700	6655	W 4794	6601	PAPIERS IMPRESSION COUCHES
6415	PAPER,PAPERBRD,BULK,NES	W 5857	4974	W 6294	5239	W 5858	6560	W 5482	5680	PAPIERS,CARTONS ROULEAUX
64159	OTHER PAPER ETC,BULK,NES	W 4012	4053	W 3861	3974	W 3493	4715	W 3236	4046	AUT PAPIER ROULEAUX FEUILLES
6418	COATED ETC PAPER NES BLK	W 3866	8381	W 3924	8870	W 3882	9910	W 3989	10174	PAP,CARTONS COUCHES,ENDUITS
64181	PLASTIC COATED PAPER ETC	W 2802	5416	W 2895	5405	W 2645	5988	W 2769	6073	PAP,CARTONS ENDUITS,RESINES
642	PAPER,ETC,PRECUT,ARTS OF	W 10056	25426	W 10816	27115	W 10671	31220	W 12244	32359	PAP,CARTONS DECOUPES
6421	PAPER ETC CONTAINERS	W 5181	9041	W 6193	10893	W 6241	12658	W 7821	13732	BOITES,SACS EMBALLAGES
6428	PAPER ETC ARTICLES NES	W 3164	10858	W 2938	11008	W 2800	12660	W 2960	13181	OUVRAGES EN PATE A PAPIER
64285	PAPER ETC DIAPERS ETC	W 1400	6202	W 1229	6340	W 1136	7074	W 1098	6602	SERVIETTES HYGIENIQUES
65	TEXTILE YARN,FABRICS,ETC		37427		39465		45490		53616	FILS,TISSUS,ARTICLES TEXTILE
657	SPECIAL TXTL FABRC,PRODS	W 2196	14327		15375	W 2573	18433		24677	TISSUS SPECIAUX
6575	CORDAGE AND MANUFACTURES	W 1848	11549	W 2091	12340	W 2143	14623	W 2729	20696	FICELLES,CORDES,CORDAGES
65751	CORDAGE,CABLE,ROPE,TWINE	W 1190	5366	W 1207	5050	W 1401	6899	W 1489	7232	CORDAGES TRESSES OU NON
65752	NETTING OF ROPE,TWINE	W 636	5964	W 835	6882	W 712	7482	W 1188	13091	FILETS MAT DU 657.51
658	TEXTILE ARTICLES NES	W 643	5991	W 704	6480	W 815	7587	W 881	7921	ART FACONNES MAT TEXTILES
659	FLOOR COVERINGS,ETC	W 967	4186	W 984	4389	W 941	4556	W 1167	5510	COUVRE–PARQUETS,TAPIS ETC
66	NONMETAL MINERAL MFS NES		22579		22641		24601		26698	ART MIN NON METALLIQUES
664	GLASS	W 3629	5315	W 3468	5178	W 3509	5891	W 3479	6085	VERRE
665	GLASSWARE	W 3002	5211	W 3142	5472	W 2425	5201	W 2483	5193	OUVRAGES EN VERRE
67	IRON AND STEEL		25154		26309		34011		42805	FER ET ACIER
673	IRON,STEEL SHAPES ETC	W 16164	7817	W 14414	7589	W 13158	8177	W 22550	13112	BARRES,PROFIL FER,ACIER
674	IRN,STL UNIV,PLATE,SHEET	W 9696	8497	W 9918	9281	W 11288	12658	W 13192	13903	LARGES PLATS,TOLES
6749	OTH IRN,STL PLATES,SHEET	W 5116	4530	W 4459	4057	W 4634	5011	W 6251	6397	AUTRES TOLES FER,ACIER
67491	— OF IRON OR SIMPLE STL	W 4749	4200	W 4241	3828	W 4479	4759	W 6101	6151	AUT TOLES AUTRES ACIER FIN
678	IRON,STL TUBES,PIPES,ETC	W 5924	7526	W 6025	8191	W 6082	11090	W 7279	12508	TUBES,TUYAUX EN FONTE,FER
68	NON–FERROUS METALS		8863		10101		14768		18290	METAUX NON FERREUX
684	ALUMINIUM	W 1709	6408		7375	W 2510	11049	W 4094	13749	ALUMINIUM
6842	ALUMINIUM,ALLOYS WORKED	W 1115	5364	W 1165	6126	W 1331	7987	W 1977	10218	ALUMINIUM,ALLIAGES OUVRE
69	METAL MANUFACTURES NES		57285		60036		68666		87114	ART MANUFACT EN METAL NDA
691	STRUCTURES AND PARTS NES	W 3049	8290	W 3147	7478	W 2851	8245	W 7825	19470	CONSTRUCT FER,ACIER,ALU
6911	STRUCTURES,PARTS IRN,STL	W 2884	6849	W 2857	5505	W 2592	6113	W 7545	17185	CONSTRUCT FER,ACIER,FONTE
692	METAL TANKS,BOXES,ETC	W 923	4881	W 1162	6151	W 1167	5972	W 1522	7363	RECIPIENTS METALLIQUES
6924	MTL TRANSPORT BOXES ETC	W 849	4572	W 1110	5847	W 1034	5426	W 1254	6153	FUTS,TAMBOURS,BIDONS
693	WIRE PRODUCTS NON ELECTR	W 4004	7506	W 4226	8353	W 4561	9758	W 4664	10074	OUVRAGES FILS METALLIQUES
6931	WIRE CABLES, ROPES ETC	W 3362	6605	W 3641	7542	W 4095	9052	W 3981	8962	CORDAGES EN FILS DE FER
69311	IRN,STEEL CABLE,ROPE ETC	W 3313	6444	W 3576	7336	W 3995	8612	W 3838	8453	CORDAGES FILS FER,ACIER
694	STL,COPPR NAILS,NUTS,ETC	W 969	5029	W 900	4973	W 1011	6019	W 1218	7268	CLOUS,VIS,ECROUS
695	TOOLS	W 424	6576	W 395	6583	W 410	7460	W 454	8853	OUTILS A MAIN
697	BASE MTL HOUSEHOLD EQUIP	W 562	4127	W 597	4323	W 640	4942	W 606	4985	ART MENAGE MET COMMUNS
699	BASE METAL MFRS NES		19119	W 3266	20108	W 3585	23780		26404	ART MANUFACTURES MET NDA
6991	LOCKSMITHS WARES,ETC	W 559	6012	W 566	6020	W 730	7093	W 669	7568	ARTICLES DE SERRURERIE
69913	BASE MTL DOOR,ETC FITTNG	W 465	4491	W 488	4522	W 643	5295	W 560	5688	GARNITURES POUR MEUBLES
6997	IRON,STEEL ARTICLES NES	W 1015	5542	W 1054	5917	W 1122	6735	W 1618	8565	OUV FONTE,FER,ACIER NDA
69979	IRN,STL MANUFACTURES NES	W 1008	5508	W 1047	5878	W 1118	6709	W 1615	8539	AUT OUVRAGES EN FER NDA
7	MACHINES,TRANSPORT EQUIP		391082		462842		564289		729151	MACHINES MATERIEL TRANSPORT
71	POWER GENERATING EQUIPMT		21537		20397		17723		21352	MACHINES GENERATRICES
713	INTRNL COMBUS PSTN ENGIN	W 295	6877	W 265	6645	W 287	7959	W 332	9308	MOTEURS EXPL COMB INT, PIECE
7139	PISTON ENGINE PARTS NES	W 119	4182	W 95	4184	W 107	4493	W 119	5373	PIECES POUR 713.2,3,8
714	ENGINES AND MOTORS NES	W 18	4896	W 38	8634	W 26	3867	W 48	3662	MOTEURS NON ELECTRIQUES
7144	REACTION ENGINES	W 5	3946	W 27	7238	W 11	2203	W 26	2115	PROPULSEURS A REACTION
716	ROTATING ELECTRIC PLANT	W 472	7885	W 245	3628	W 280	4094	W 302	5371	APP ELECTR ROTATIFS,PIECES
7169	PTS NES OF ROT ELEC PLNT	W 242	4675	W 11	227	W 11	304	W 11	338	PIECES MAC APP ROTATIFS
72	MACHS FOR SPCL INDUSTRYS		39220		37384		53175		65626	MAC SPECIALES POUR INDUST
721	AGRIC MACHY,EXC TRACTORS	W 637	4684	W 719	5437	W 874	7187	W 1006	7737	MACHINES AGRICOLES
722	TRACTORS NON–ROAD	W 743	4365	W 587	3694	W 790	5948	W 1011	7795	TRACTEURS
7224	WHEELED TRACTORS NES	W 743	4365	W 587	3694	W 790	5948	W 1011	7795	TRACTEURS A ROUES
723	CIVIL ENGNEERG EQUIP ETC	W 1869	9948	W 1455	7889	W 1403	8958	W 2484	14200	APPAREILS DE GENIE CIVIL
7234	CONST,MINING MACHNRY NES	W 1708	8999	W 1280	7046	W 1248	7815	W 2116	11842	MACH POUR LA CONST, MINES
72342	SLFPRP SHOVELS,EXCAVATRS	W 1130	5144	W 767	4102	W 817	4606	W 1425	7507	PELLES MECANIQUES
727	FOOD MACHRY NON–DOMESTIC	W 198	6972	W 347	8052	W 476	15018	W 650	13444	MACH INDUSTRIES ALIMENT
7272	OTH FOOD PROC MCHY,PARTS	W 185	6805	W 341	7928	W 471	14903	W 643	13243	AUT MACH IND ALIMENTAIRE
72722	INDUS FOOD PROC MACH NES	W 184	6777	W 340	7921	W 470	14859	W 642	13238	MACHINES BOULANGERIE
728	OTH MACHY FOR SPCL INDUS	W 663	9106	W 925	7890	W 639	8179	W 1064	15624	AUT MACH IND PARTICULIERES
7284	MACHY FOR SPCL INDUS NES	W 254	5537	W 307	4428	W 296	5008	W 588	10299	MACH SPEC IND PARTICUL.
73	METALWORKING MACHINERY		2358		4131		6693		9153	MACH TRAVAIL DES METAUX
74	GENRL INDUSTRL MACHY NES		56129		64740		82395		124102	MACH APP INDUSTRIE
741	HEATING,COOLING EQUIPMNT	W 667	9284	W 1183	12694	W 1495	14727	W 2531	31033	MACH CHAUFFAGE,PIECES
7414	NONDOM REFRIG EQUIPT,PTS	W 206	2652	W 397	4105	W 497	6762	W 902	10476	MAT PRODUCTION DU FROID
74141	REFRIG EQUIP NONDOMESTIC	W 159	1872	W 313	3169	W 386	4843	W 687	7957	REFIG INDUSTRIELS
7416	HEATING,COOLING EQU NES	W 208	3495	W 652	7424	W 893	6498	W 1520	18879	APP CHANGEMENT TEMP
742	PUMPS FOR LIQUIDS ETC	W 215	5235	W 307	7002	W 338	8457	W 448	11109	POMPES MOTO–POMPES
743	PUMPS NES,CENTRFUGES ETC	W 433	6980	W 519	7983	W 607	10593	W 1377	17703	POMPES COMPRES,VENT ETC
744	MECHANICAL HANDLING EQU	W 1621	12315	W 1714	12187	W 2189	18431	W 3449	29078	EQUIP MANUTENTION PIECES
7441	FORK LIFT TRCKS,ETC,PTS	W 604	3584	W 767	3416	W 1014	6191	W 1791	12497	CHARIOTS POUR USINES ETC
74411	FORK LIFT TRUCKS ETC	W 601	3547	W 766	3391	W 1013	6152	W 1788	12462	CHARIOTS POUR LES GARES
7442	LIFTING,LOADING MACH NES	W 719	6008	W 585	5543	W 840	8257	W 1278	11957	APP LEVAGE,MANUTENTION
74428	OTH HANDLING ETC MCH NES	W 385	3349	W 319	2972	W 440	4113	W 563	6181	AUT APP LEVAGE ETC
745	NONELEC MACHY,TOOLS NES	W 302	6562	W 335	7357	W 383	10072	W 381	9961	AUT MACH NON ELEC,PIECES
7452	OTH NONELEC MCHS,PTS NES	W 270	5912	W 312	6851	W 356	9411	W 348	9196	AUT MACH NON ELEC,PIECES
749	NONELEC MACH PTS,ACC NES	W 606	15753	W 681	17518	W 722	20116	W 923	25218	PIECES MACH NON ELEC NDA
7492	COCKS,VALVES ETC NES	W 290	6128	W 320	7284	W 324	8669	W 421	10377	ART ROB,SIM POUR TUYAUX
7493	SHAFT,CRANK,PULLEY ETC	W 135	3869	W 163	4470	W 210	5450	W 284	8246	ARBRES TRANS,VILEBREQUINS
75	OFFICE MACHNES,ADP EQUIP		37349		49137		59699		71695	MACH BUREAU TRAIT AUTOM
752	AUTOMTIC DATA PROC EQUIP	W 308	25271	W 422	36334	W 480	44601	W 572	55308	MACH TRAIT INFORMATION
7522	DIGITAL COMPUTERS	W 89	7423	W 163	14014	W 170	13945	W 180	18165	MACH DIGITALES COMPLETES
7523	DIGITL CENTRL PROCESSORS	W 58	4172	W 50	3790	W 26	3263	W 49	7503	UNITES CENTRALES
7524	DIGITL CENTRL STOR UNITS	W 26	2248	W 40	3577	W 59	6934	W 39	8059	UNITES MEMOIRE CENTRALES
7525	ADP PERIPHERAL UNITS	W 87	7767	W 116	11131	W 148	14093	W 159	11971	UNITES PERIPHERIQUES
759	OFFICE,ADP MCH PTS,ACCES	W 73	8771	W 77	9220	W 100	11502	W 117	11894	PIECES DU 751 ET 752
7599	ACCTG,ETC,ADP MCH PTS,AC	W 56	7982	W 58	8216	W 78	10075	W 90	10421	PIECES DU 751 ET 752
76	TELECOMM,SOUND EQUIPMENT		37320		53335		60315		63947	EQUIPMENT DE TELECOM
761	TELEVISION RECEIVERS	W 306	7293	W 422	9716	W 434	11129	W 650	14603	RECEPTEURS DE TELEVISION
7611	COLOUR TV RECEIVERS	W 302	7077	W 419	9626	W 430	10988	W 647	14465	RECEPTEURS COULEUR
764	TELECOM EQPT,PTS,ACC NES	W 297	24118	W 372	37085	W 398	40440	W 418	40609	EQUIP TELECOM,PIECES

4. Special Imports C.I.F. by Commodities according to the S.I.T.C. (Rev. 2) in thousand U.S. Dollars
Importations Spéciales C.A.F. par Produits d'après la C.T.C.I. (Rév. 2) en milliers de Dollars E.U.

SITC CTCI	COMMODITY	1993 WEIGHT POIDS	1993 VALUE VALEUR	1994 WEIGHT POIDS	1994 VALUE VALEUR	1995 WEIGHT POIDS	1995 VALUE VALEUR	1996 WEIGHT POIDS	1996 VALUE VALEUR	PRODUIT
7641	LINE TELEPHONE,ETC EQUIP	W 59	4089	W 70	4737	W 90	7650	W 95	8408	APP TELEPHON PAR FIL
7643	TV,RADIO TRANSMITTRS ETC	W 30	3552	W 35	6140	W 56	10960	W 86	13579	APP EMET TELE RADIO
7648	TELECOMM EQUIPMENT NES	W 26	4096	W 20	3897	W 30	5100	W 24	3608	APP TELECOM NDA
7649	PTS NES OF EQUIPMT OF 76	W 106	10860	W 173	20830	W 135	14896	W 106	12958	PIECES DE LA DIV 76
76491	PTS NES OF APPAR OF 7641	W 49	8330	W 64	14206	W 38	8805	W 29	8682	PIECES POUR 764.1
76493	TELECOMM EQUIPMT PTS NES	W 55	2348	W 107	6374	W 95	5813	W 75	4017	PIECES 761,762,764.3,8
77	ELECTRIC MACHNRY NES ETC		78109		82615		97823		112450	MACH APP ELECT NDA
771	ELECTRIC POWER MACHY NES	W 362	3421	W 475	4821	W 424	5141	W 654	7401	MACH PROD,TRANS ELECTR
772	SWITCHGEAR ETC,PARTS NES	W 525	13653	W 438	11016	W 560	15529	W 571	15472	APP COUPURE,SECT ETC
7721	SWITCHGEAR ETC	W 520	13194	W 433	10478	W 555	15020	W 564	14776	APP COUPURE,SECTIONMNT
773	ELECTR DISTRIBUTNG EQUIP	W 1839	7568	W 1995	8165	W 1886	9743	W 2675	12954	EQUIPMT DISTRIBUTION ELECT
7731	INSULATED WIRE,CABLE ETC	W 1782	7108	W 1952	7760	W 1846	9210	W 2611	12151	FILS,CABLES ISOLES ELECT
775	HOUSEHOLD TYPE EQUIP NES	W 1560	13444	W 1555	14286	W 1584	16069	W 1822	18546	MACH,APP USAGE DOMESTQUE
7758	ELECTRO–THERMIC APPL NES	W 459	5160	W 489	5264	W 493	5824	W 559	6388	APP ELECTROTHERMIQ NDA
778	ELECTRICAL MACHINERY NES	W 47679	35397	W 54644	39976	W 54141	45513	W 52731	52142	AUTRES MACH ELECT NDA
7788	OTH ELEC MACHY,EQUIP NES	W 46590	24418	W 53436	28189	W 52885	31995	W 51305	37158	AUT MACH APP ELEC NDA
77887	ELECTRICAL CARBONS	W 46509	21112	W 53355	24594	W 52800	28156	W 51212	32923	PIECES CHARBON,GRAPHITE
78	ROAD VEHICLES		85866		83265		118861		157796	VEHICULES ROUTIERS
781	PASS MOTOR VEH EXC BUSES	W 6261	51481	W 6307	51635	W 8213	75865	W 12031	105467	AUTO TRANSPORT PERSONNES
782	LORRIES,SPCL MTR VEH NES	W 2355	14799	W 1846	12207	W 2512	20749	W 3087	24482	VEHICULES SPECIAUX,MARCH
7821	LORRIES,TRUCKS	W 2210	13763	W 1711	12013	W 2271	18739	W 2995	23839	VEHICULES TRANSP MARCHAND
784	MOTOR VEH PRTS,ACCES NES	W 990	11253	W 1002	10889	W 1174	13591	W 1190	13942	PIECES 722,781,782,783
7849	OTHER MOTOR VEHCL PARTS	W 950	10957	W 936	10287	W 1117	13199	W 1132	13572	PIECES 722,781,782,783
79	OTHR TRANSPORT EQUIPMENT		33196		67839		67605		103030	AUTRE MATERIEL TRANSPORT
792	AIRCRAFT ETC	W 72	7471	W 36	9186	W 202	20360	W 48	7556	APP NAVIGATION AERIENNE
7921	HELICOPTERS		17			W 10	12112			HELICOPTERES
7929	AIRCRAFT PARTS NES	W 18	4877	W 19	6648	W 23	6816	W 33	5864	PIECES DU 792
793	SHIPS AND BOATS ETC	W 6215	25706	W 10045	58640	W 19788	47171	W 23905	95432	NAVIRES BATEAUX,ETC
7932	SHIPS AND BOATS NES	W 5860	24505	W 9656	57552	W 13208	43514	W 23774	95072	NAVIRES ET BATEAUX
79323	OTHER CARGO VESSELS	W 9	60			W 398	479	W 9850	24658	AUT BATEAUX TRANS MARCH
79324	FISHING VESSELS ETC	W 5821	23967	W 9516	57011	W 12793	42651	W 13881	69708	BATEAUX DE PECHE
8	MISC MANUFACTURED GOODS		246824		259572		297379		318368	ART MANUFACTURES DIVERS
812	*PLUMBG,HEATNG,LGHTNG EQ	W 1498	10046	W 1516	9578	W 1649	11071	W 1749	12410	APPAR SANITAIRES CHAUFFAGE
8124	LIGHTING EQUIPMENT NES	W 607	7395	W 626	7107	W 694	8265	W 742	9063	APPAREILS ECLAIRAGE ETC
81242	LAMPS,FITTINGS BASE METL	W 548	6501	W 577	6539	W 639	7449	W 688	8279	APPAREILS D'ECLAIRAGE
821	*FURNITURE,PARTS THEREOF	W 5999	28843	W 6212	30667	W 6417	35031	W 6772	39308	MEUBLES ET PIECES
8211	CHAIRS,SEATS AND PARTS	W 1068	9084	W 1152	10238	W 1325	11578	W 1438	12865	SIEGES ET PIECES
82111	CHAIRS AND OTHER SEATS	W 1016	8608	W 1068	9516	W 1246	10769	W 1364	12130	SIEGES
8212	MED FURN,STUFFD FURNSHGS	W 543	4633	W 682	5312	W 728	6164	W 894	6487	MOB MEDICO–CHIRUR,PIECES
8219	FURNITURE AND PARTS NES	W 4388	15125	W 4378	15118	W 4364	17289	W 4439	19955	AUTRES MEUBLES ET PIECES
82192	WOOD FURNITURE NES	W 2515	8651	W 2564	9025	W 2516	9799	W 2761	12349	MEUBLES NDA EN BOIS
84	CLOTHING AND ACCESSORIES		67952		70373		79065		80153	VETEMENTS
842	MENS OUTERWEAR NOT KNIT	W 278	11082	W 309	11512	W 412	14839	W 384	14989	VET DESSUS POUR HOMMES
843	WOMENS OUTERWEAR NONKNIT	W 426	20568	W 477	21738	W 482	23152	W 488	23532	VET DESSUS FEMMES MAT TEX
8431	— COATS AND JACKETS	W 70	4173	W 74	4145	W 74	4679	W 93	5382	MANT,VEST FEM MAT TEXTIL
8439	— OTHER OUTER GARMENTS	W 270	10582	W 285	10631	W 298	11545	W 283	11617	AUT VET DES FEM MAT TEXT
845	OUTERWEAR KNIT NONELASTC	W 346	13864	W 375	14310	W 418	15735	W 430	16091	VET DESSOUS,ACCES BONNET
8451	— JERSEYS,PULLOVERS ETC	W 214	8634	W 241	9177	W 249	9278	W 252	9682	CHANDAILS,PULL–OVERS ETC
8459	— OTHER,CLTHG ACCESRYS	W 120	4635	W 117	4451	W 154	5688	W 166	5797	AUT VET DESSUS DE BONNE
846	UNDER GARMENTS KNITTED	W 274	9571	W 310	9672	W 296	11268	W 299	11667	SOUS VETS DE BONNETERIE
8462	— OF COTTON NON ELASTIC	W 216	6668	W 244	6385	W 211	7010	W 229	7516	SOUS–VET BONNET COTON
84629	—— OTHER	W 216	6668	W 244	6385	W 211	7010	W 229	7516	AUT SOUS–VET BONNET COTON
848	HEADGEAR,NONTXTL CLOTHNG	W 249	5441	W 252	5041	W 283	5289	W 302	5363	VET ACCES MAT AUT QUE TEX
851	*FOOTWEAR	W 585	13696	W 609	15170	W 636	17671	W 595	17201	CHAUSSURES
85102	FOOTWEAR LEATHER	W 398	10759	W 429	11984	W 462	14200	W 425	13882	CHAUS SEMELLES EN CUIR
87	PRECISION INSTRUMNTS NES		21816		24722		29811		35056	INSTRUM,APPAR SCIENT NDA
872	MEDICAL INSTRUMENTS NES	W 75	6390	W 81	5632	W 111	7593	W 122	6516	INSTR,APP MEDIC–CHIR NDA
87202	OTH MEDICAL INSTRUMENTS	W 62	5536	W 66	4681	W 100	6695	W 103	5253	INSTRUM,APP MEDECINE
874	MEASURNG,CONTROLNG INSTR	W 147	13836	W 165	17632	W 241	19872	W 217	25948	INSTRUMENTS DE MESURE
8741	SURVEYING INSTRUMENTS	W 19	3941	W 20	4844	W 34	4855	W 31	8216	INST GEODESIE,TOPO ETC
88	PHOTO EQU,OPTICL GDS ETC		14003		14866		16904		18346	APP,FOURN PHOTO,OP,MONTR
882	PHOTO,CINEMA SUPPLIES	W 506	6746	W 537	7582	W 511	8233	W 521	8351	PRODUITS PHOTO,CINEMA
8822	PHOTO FILM EXC DEV CINMA	W 352	4877	W 368	5408	W 359	5684	W 363	5614	PLAQUES,PELLICULES,FILMS
89	MISC MANUFCTRD GOODS NES		87300		91162		104057		111823	ART MANUFACTURES DIVERS
892	PRINTED MATTER	W 1289	14390	W 1258	14127	W 1213	14855	W 1176	15128	IMPRIMES
8921	PRINTED BOOKS,GLOBES,ETC	W 538	5956	W 536	6041	W 450	6239	W 521	6770	LIVRES,BROCHURES,CARTES
89211	PRINTED BOOKS,PAMPHLETS	W 516	5763	W 515	5850	W 414	5870	W 502	6543	LIVRES,BROCHURES
8928	PRINTED MATTER NES	W 400	5105	W 379	4873	W 369	4459	W 343	4563	IMPRIMES NDA
893	ARTICLES OF PLASTIC NES		30562		34053		39833		43425	OUVRAGES EN MAT DIVIS 58
8931	PLSTC PACKG CONTNRS,LIDS	W 3045	11297	W 3988	13373	W 3927	16043	W 4141	16966	ART TRANSP EMBALLAGE ETC
8939	MISC PLASTIC ARTICLES	W 2610	18704	W 2752	20169	W 2959	23222	W 3085	25709	ART DIVERS EN MAT DIV 58
89399	OTHR PLASTC ARTICLES NES	W 1987	15923	W 2200	17685	W 2390	20293	W 2461	22502	AUT OUV MAT DIV 58
894	TOYS,SPORTING GOODS,ETC	W 1152	14534	W 1227	13976	W 1240	15201	W 1410	17458	VOITURES ENFANTS,JOUETS
8942	TOYS,INDOOR GAMES ETC	W 678	9654	W 721	8638	W 768	9618	W 892	11216	JOUETS,JEUX ETC
89424	INDOOR GAME EQUIPMENT	W 194	4133	W 172	2539	W 150	2702	W 252	3745	ART,JEUX DE SOCIETE
8947	OTH SPORT GDS,FAIR AMUSM	W 370	4002	W 379	4446	W 327	4557	W 379	5091	AUT ART DE SPORT
898	MUSICAL INSTRUMENTS,PTS	W 377	14508	W 378	14981	W 393	18030	W 408	18996	INSTRUMENTS DE MUSIQUE
8983	SOUND RECRDNG TAPE,DISCS	W 279	12013	W 300	13312	W 314	15790	W 327	16487	SUPPORTS SON POUR 763
89832	RECORDED DISCS,TAPES ETC	W 159	9890	W 155	11050	W 167	13129	W 194	13855	DISQUES,PHONO,BANDES
899	OTHER MANUFACTURED GOODS		6993		7591		9137		9817	AUT ART MANUF DIVERS NDA
9	GOODS NOT CLASSD BY KIND		3124		5834		3916		5809	ART TRANSACT NON CLASSES
931	*SPECIAL TRANSACTIONS		2802		5000		3114	W 956	4921	TRANS.SPECIALES

5. Special Exports F.O.B. by Commodities according to the S.I.T.C. (Rev. 2) in thousand U.S. Dollars
Exportations Spéciales F.O.B. par Produits d'après la C.T.C.I. (Rév. 2) en milliers de Dollars E.U.

SITC CTCI	COMMODITY	1993 WEIGHT POIDS	1993 VALUE VALEUR	1994 WEIGHT POIDS	1994 VALUE VALEUR	1995 WEIGHT POIDS	1995 VALUE VALEUR	1996 WEIGHT POIDS	1996 VALUE VALEUR	PRODUIT
	ALL COMMODITIES		1399324		1626668		1802507		1897083	TOUS PRODUITS
0	FOOD AND LIVE ANIMALS		1103388		1246744		1320324		1385286	ALIMENTS,ANIMAUX VIVANTS
01	MEAT AND PREPARATIONS		3180		5140		5142		8146	VIANDES ET PREPARATIONS
011	MEAT FRESH,CHILLD,FROZEN	W 1158	3140	W 1571	5081	W 1462	5056	W 3261	7923	VIANDES FRAICHES,REF,CONGE
0112	MUTTON ETC FRSH,CHLD,FRN	W 1044	2365	W 1324	3913	W 1140	3395	W 3024	7041	VIANDE DE MOUTON
03	FISH AND PREPARATIONS		1017134		1157628		1210474		1217591	POISSONS ET PREPARATIONS
034	FISH,FRESH,CHILLED,FROZN	W 250482	662334	W 275270	717406	W 242864	691612	W 276678	670835	POISSON FRAIS, REFRIG,CONG
0341	FISH FRSH,CHLLD,EX FILLT	W 67943	100593	W 58195	91582	W 42795	78602	W 39618	69188	POISSON FRAIS,REFRIGERE
0342	FISH FROZEN,EXCL FILLETS	W 62971	132402	W 92394	188730	W 85100	189177	W 128074	215680	POISSONS CONGELES
0343	FISH FILLETS,FRESH,CHLLD	W 4196	20134	W 5620	28103	W 6984	36199	W 8497	42222	FILETS FRAIS,REFRIGERES
0344	FISH FILLETS,FROZEN	W 115372	409204	W 119061	408992	W 107985	387634	W 100488	343745	FILETS CONGELES
035	FISH SALTED,DRIED,SMOKED	W 57227	176919	W 67312	207355	W 66741	231016	W 74859	261721	POISSON SECHE,SALE,FUME
03502	COD(NOT IN FILLETS)DRIED	W 8853	20311	W 8086	19129	W 8046	21203	W 7956	22777	MORUE SECHEE,SALEE
03503	FISH(EX COD)DRIED,SALTED	W 48203	155040	W 58943	186029	W 58605	208803	W 66703	236460	POISSONS SECHES,SALES
036	SHELL FISH FRESH,FROZEN	W 9766	63076	W 12166	64302	W 11365	64858	W 17291	80590	CRUSTACES,MOLLUSQUES
037	FISH ETC PREPD,PRSVD NES	W 17534	114804	W 24735	168565	W 24612	222988	W 26617	204445	POIS,CRUST,MOL PREPARES
0371	FISH PREPARD,PRESRVD NES	W 1697	13788	W 1826	16025	W 2225	20536	W 2471	18650	CONSERVES DE POISSONS
0372	SHELL FISH PREPRD,PRESVD	W 15837	101016	W 22909	152540	W 22388	202452	W 24146	185795	CRUSTACES,COQUIL PREPARES
081	*FEEDING STUFF FOR ANIML	W 189361	79893	W 180871	79628	W 185099	99055	W 253565	154027	NOURRITURE POUR ANIMAUX
0814	MEAT OR FISH MEAL FODDER	W 184383	77719	W 175800	77554	W 173752	90847	W 248505	151460	FARINES DE VIANDES,POISSONS
08142	FISH MEAL FODDER	W 184383	77719	W 175800	77554	W 173752	90847	W 248505	151460	FARINES DE POISSONS
0819	FOOD WASTE AND FEED NES	W 3813	1900	W 4228	1902	W 10210	7908	W 4195	2420	DECHETS,ALIMENTS NDA
08199	FODDER NES,INCL SWEETNED	W 3813	1900	W 4228	1902	W 10210	7908	W 4195	2420	PREPARATIONS FOURRAGERES
1	BEVERAGES AND TOBACCO		3709		7518		3466		2578	BOISSONS ET TABACS
11	BEVERAGES		3709		7518		3466		2578	BOISSONS
111	NON-ALCOHL BEVERAGES NES	W 6184	3411	W 12190	6946	W 5977	2829	W 6103	2521	BOISSONS NON ALCOOLIQUES
2	CRUDE MATERLS,EXCL FUELS		17181		30391		36535		32728	MAT BRUTES NON COMESTIBLES
21	HIDES,SKINS,FURS UNDRSSD		3880		6752		4900		6768	CUIRS,PEAUX BRUTS
212	FURSKINS,RAW	W 17	2576	W 34	5639	W 20	4092	W 25	6061	PELLETERIES BRUTES
27	CRUDE FERTLZR,MINRLS NES		7812		15151		20068		14683	ENGRAIS MINERAUX BRUTS
277	NATURAL ABRASIVES NES	W 36592	1342	W 230458	6926	W 303852	9972	W 165033	5253	ABRASIFS NATURELS NDA
2772	OTHER NATURAL ABRASIVES	W 36592	1342	W 230458	6926	W 303852	9972	W 165033	5253	AUTR ABRASIFS NATURELS NDA
27722	OTHER NAT ABRASIVES NES	W 36592	1342	W 230458	6926	W 303852	9972	W 165033	5253	PIERRE PONCE,EMERI
278	OTHER CRUDE MINERALS	W 20382	6309	W 25365	7962	W 28264	9921	W 30353	9338	AUTRES MINERAUX BRUTS
2789	MINERALS CRUDE NES	W 19563	6125	W 24572	7746	W 27740	9849	W 26368	8959	MINERAUX BRUTS NDA
27895	SILICEOUS EARTHS	W 19555	6122	W 24560	7745	W 27740	9849	W 26358	8954	FARINES SILICEUSES FOSSILES
28	METALLIFEROUS ORES,SCRAP		2759		5179		6646		5332	MINERAIS METAL,DECHETS
4	ANIMAL,VEGETABLE OIL,FAT		41488		31651		37565		58699	HUILES,GRAISSES ANIM,VEG
411	*ANIMAL OILS AND FATS	W 113426	41488	W 89559	31651	W 91359	37565	W 139156	58698	HUILES,GRAISSES ANIMALES
4111	OILS OF FISH,WHALES ETC	W 113423	41485	W 89557	31650	W 91357	37562	W 139156	58698	GRAISSES,HUILES DE POISSONS
41111	FISH LIVER OIL	W 1837	4675	W 1076	3939	W 1364	4049	W 1799	4922	HUILES DE FOIES
41112	OTHER FISH OILS AND FATS	W 111586	36810	W 88481	27711	W 89993	33513	W 137357	53776	AUTRES HUILES ET GRAISSES
5	CHEMCLS,RELATED PROD NES		1585		1854		11978		9727	PRODUITS CHIMIQUES
541	*MEDICINAL,PHARM PRODUCT	K 8457	727	K 5376	570	K 104515	9430		7025	PROD MEDICINAUX PHARMACEUT
5417	MEDICAMENTS	K 8068	656	K 5312	449	K 104393	9395	K 60282	6777	MEDICAMENTS
54179	— CONTNG OTH SUBSTANCES	K 1416	195	K 2942	237	K 100126	8967	K 59857	6726	MED CONT AUT SUBSTANCES
6	BASIC MANUFACTURES		180590		222635		278788		281267	ART MANUFACTURES
61	LEATHER,DRESSED FUR,ETC		9758		12078		15418		18432	CUIRS,PELLETERIES
613	FUR SKINS TANNED,DRESSED	W 315	9205	W 307	12009	W 315	15107	W 399	17942	PELLETERIES
65	TEXTILE YARN,FABRICS,ETC		4459		5220		9930		9977	FILS,TISSUS,ARTICLES TEXTILE
657	SPECIAL TXTL FABRC,PRODS	W 299	2656	W 311	2999	W 605	7323	W 806	7037	TISSUS SPECIAUX
6575	CORDAGE AND MANUFACTURES	W 299	2656	W 311	2999	W 605	7322	W 806	7037	FICELLES,CORDES,CORDAGES
65752	NETTING OF ROPE,TWINE	W 190	2181	W 209	2477	W 418	6372	W 578	5955	FILETS MAT DU 657.51
67	IRON AND STEEL		34923		38550		49900		57647	FER ET ACIER
671	PIG IRON ETC	W 64457	34895	W 70798	38525	W 71518	49662	W 68199	57279	FONTE,SPIEGEL,POUDRES
6716	FERRO-ALLOYS	W 64457	34895	W 70798	38525	W 71518	49662	W 68199	57279	FERRO-ALLIAGES
67162	FERRO-SILICON	W 64457	34895	W 70798	38525	W 71453	49644	W 68192	57277	FERRO-SILICIUM
68	NON-FERROUS METALS		122139		155231		190241		181873	METAUX NON FERREUX
684	ALUMINIUM	W 91806	122105	W 100570	155192	W 99663	190212	W 101126	181851	ALUMINIUM
6841	ALUMINIUM,ALLOYS,UNWRGHT	W 91801	122089	W 100567	155183	W 99657	190180	W 101125	181804	ALUMINIUM,ALLIAGES BRUTS
69	METAL MANUFACTURES NES		6712		6040		7929		7407	ART MANUFACT EN METAL NDA
697	BASE MTL HOUSEHOLD EQUIP	W 500	4854	W 455	4197	W 416	4987	W 347	4184	ART MENAGE MET COMMUNS
6974	BASE MTL DMSTC ARTIC NES	W 500	4851	W 455	4197	W 415	4986	W 347	4183	ARTICLES NDA FONTE,FER,ETC
69743	— OF ALUMINIUM	W 499	4844	W 453	4183	W 414	4961	W 346	4174	ARTICLES NDA EN ALUMINIUM
7	MACHINES,TRANSPORT EQUIP		31993		66148		92332		93883	MACHINES MATERIEL TRANSPORT
72	MACHS FOR SPCL INDUSTRYS		4497		6021		10349		6558	MAC SPECIALES POUR INDUST
725	PAPER ETC MILL MACHINERY	W 27	1132	W 86	2273	W 146	5738	W 98	2262	MACHINES FABR PATE PAPIER
74	GENRL INDUSTRL MACHY NES		6424		10179		15216		22258	MACH APP INDUSTRIE
745	NONELEC MACHY,TOOLS NES	W 83	5702	W 104	9308	W 162	14345	W 248	20829	AUT MACH NON ELEC,PIECES
7452	OTH NONELEC MCHS,PTS NES	W 83	5702	W 104	9308	W 162	14345	W 247	20824	AUT MACH NON ELEC,PIECES
74525	WEIGHING MACHINERY	W 65	5093	W 90	8361	W 144	12900	W 233	19586	APP INSTRUMENTS PESAGE
79	OTHR TRANSPORT EQUIPMENT		19346		48401		63842		62641	AUTRE MATERIEL TRANSPORT
792	AIRCRAFT ETC	W 2	42	W 67	26537	W 67	29441	W 68	38237	APP NAVIGATION AERIENNE
7924	AIRCRFT NES OVER 15000KG			W 67	26537	W 67	29438	W 65	38127	AERODYNES PLUS 15000 KG
793	SHIPS AND BOATS ETC	W 16586	19305	W 5173	21864	W 7650	34401	W 16188	24404	NAVIRES BATEAUX,ETC
7932	SHIPS AND BOATS NES	W 16586	19305	W 5173	21864	W 7642	34383	W 16140	24093	NAVIRES ET BATEAUX
79323	OTHER CARGO VESSELS	W 12745	12295			W 5	38	W 13607	18144	AUT BATEAUX TRANS MARCH
79324	FISHING VESSELS ETC	W 3840	7009	W 5173	21864	W 7637	34343	W 2523	5926	BATEAUX DE PECHE
8	MISC MANUFACTURED GOODS		12892		14580		15826		15116	ART MANUFACTURES DIVERS
84	CLOTHING AND ACCESSORIES		4341		4046		3708		3319	VETEMENTS
89	MISC MANUFCTRD GOODS NES		8303		10162		10797		10602	ART MANUFACTURES DIVERS
9	GOODS NOT CLASSD BY KIND		5781		3945		4833		16644	ART TRANSACT NON CLASSES
931	*SPECIAL TRANSACTIONS		5781		3942		4830	W 1011	7394	TRANS.SPECIALES
961	*COIN NONGOLD,NONCURRENT				2		3		9249	MONNAIES NON EMISES

FOOT NOTES – NOTES

TABLE 1 –

1 Beginning 1 January, 1981, the new krona was introduced with a value of 100 old kronur.

TABLEAU 1 –

1 A partir du 1er janvier, 1981, la nouvelle króna a la valeur de 100 anciennes krónur.

1. HISTORICAL SERIES, 1961–1996 GENERAL TRADE, IMPORTS C.I.F., EXPORTS F.O.B.
SERIES HISTORIQUES, 1961–1996 COMMERCE GENERAL, IMPORTATIONS C.A.F., EXPORTATIONS F.O.B

YEAR ANNEE	VALUE IN MILLION INDIAN RUPEES VALEUR EN MILLION INDIAN RUPEES MERCHANDISE – MARCHANDISE IMPORTS	EXPORTS	GOLD – OR IMPORTS	EXPORTS	CONVERSION FACTORS U.S. CENTS PER INDIAN RUPEE FACTEURS DE CONVERSION CENTS E.U. PAR INDIAN RUPEE IMPORTS	EXPORTS	INDEX NUMBERS – INDICES QUANTUM IMPORTS	QUANTUM EXPORTS	UNIT VALUE VALEUR UNITAIRE IMPORTS	UNIT VALUE EXPORTS
1961	10845.00	6601.00	10.40		21.0000	21.0000	26	29	10	10
1962	11241.00	6682.00			21.0000	21.0000	28	30	9	9
1963	11795.00	7741.00	13.90		21.0000	21.0000	27	34	10	9
1964	13429.00	8128.00	7.60		21.0000	21.0000	29	37	10	9
1965	13809.00	8030.00	4.20		21.0000	21.0000	35	34	10	10
1966	20190.00	11552.00	4.70		15.4560	15.8970	34	32	15	15
1967	20950.00	12097.00	3.60		13.3330	13.3330	35	34	15	15
1968	19280.00	13207.00	6.80		13.3330	13.3330	34	38	15	14
1969	16630.00	13763.00	3.50		13.3330	13.3330	28	37	15	15
1970	15933.00	15198.00	9.00		13.3330	13.3330	30	40	15	15
1971	18155.00	15256.00	265.30		13.3330	13.3330	35	41	14	16
1972	16792.00	18227.00	10.60		13.2010	13.1730	32	44	15	17
1973	24164.00	22730.00	8.30		12.9117	12.9036	35	44	19	21
1974	40787.00	31786.00			12.3503	12.3527	37	49	31	26
1975	53389.00	36412.00			11.9599	11.9606	38	52	38	26
1976	50736.00	49698.00			11.1651	11.1641	30	61	40	30
1977	57592.00	55516.00			11.4622	11.4470	36	55	37	34
1978	64301.00	54443.00			12.2150	12.2138	43	52	38	34
1979	82373.00	63801.00			12.3120	12.3036	42	64	44	35
1980	110755.00	65908.00			12.7221	12.7117	46	76	52	34
1981	135441.50	72423.10			11.5581	11.5619	53	44	55	41
1982	135615.50	83091.00			10.5923	10.5988	56	48	55	44
1983	135682.30	88096.40			9.9013	9.8898	67	49	48	49
1984	175384.10	112077.90			8.8602	8.8096	57	54	61	57
1985	190780.80	107342.30			8.1688	8.1513	65	52	65	60
1986	194502.00	118524.00			7.9243	7.9232	85	59	54	58
1987	216134.00	146417.00			7.7166	7.7171	90	71	60	65
1988	266059.00	184099.00			7.1801	7.1889	96	74	69	78
1989	334010.80	257553.00			6.1525	6.1626	97	91	86	93
1990	413565.90	314394.10			5.7023	5.7159	100	100	100	100
1991	459379.90	401230.00			4.4505	4.4182	91	114	122	111
1992	611130.10	508709.80			3.8606	3.8609	120	116	125	142
1993	694459.90	656890.10			3.2816	3.2840	138	140	117	155
1994	842170.10	785029.80			3.1873	3.1874	168	154	122	168
1995	1121469.00	994909.90			3.0785	3.0796	261	189	110	167
1996	1323980.00	1170119.00			2.8231	2.8251				172

2. IMPORTS BY BROAD ECONOMIC CATEGORY AND EXPORTS BY INDUSTRIAL ORIGIN. (PERCENTAGE OF TOTAL VALUE)
IMPORTATIONS PAR CATEGORIES ECONOMIQUES ET EXPORTATIONS PAR BRANCHE D'ACTIVITE.(EN POURCENTAGE DE LA VALEUR TOTALE)

IMPORTS – IMPORTATIONS

	1990	1991	1992	1993	1994	1995	1996
TOTAL IMPORTS–IMPORTATIONS TOTALES	100.	100.	100.	100.	100.	100.	
1 FOOD BEV–ALIMENTATION BOISSONS	3.2	2.5	3.6	2.8	5.7	4.0	
11 PRIMARY–PRODUITS DE BASE	1.8	1.4	2.6	1.9	1.8	1.5	
111 FOR INDUSTRY–POUR L'INDUSTRIE	0.1	0.0	1.2	0.2	0.0	0.1	
112 FOR HOUSEHOLDS–POUR LES MENAGES	1.7	1.3	1.4	1.7	1.7	1.5	
12 PROCESSED–PRODUITS ELABORES	1.4	1.2	1.0	0.9	3.9	2.5	
121 FOR INDUSTRY–POUR L'INDUSTRIE	0.9	0.7	0.4	0.4	1.1	1.9	
122 FOR HOUSEHOLDS–POUR LES MENAGES	0.5	0.5	0.6	0.5	2.8	0.6	
2 IND SUPPLIES–APPROV INDUSTRIELS	42.3	42.9	43.0	40.9	41.4	41.1	
21 PRIMARY–PRODUITS DE BASE	16.6	16.6	18.5	16.6	12.6	11.8	
22 PROCESSED–PRODUITS ELABORES	25.7	26.3	24.5	24.3	28.8	29.3	
3 FUELS–COMBUSTIBLES	27.3	29.9	29.8	27.3	23.9	23.8	
31 PRIMARY–PRODUITS DE BASE	16.1	18.4	19.2	17.0	14.3	12.1	
32 PROCESSED–PRODUITS ELABORES	11.2	11.5	10.7	10.3	9.6	11.7	
321 MOTOR SPIRIT–ESSENCE							
322 OTHER–AUTRES	11.2	11.5	10.7	10.3	9.6	11.7	
4 MACHINERY–EQUIPEMENT	15.5	12.9	13.3	14.3	16.0	18.1	
41 CAPITAL EQUIPMENT–MACHINES	10.8	8.7	9.4	10.6	12.3	14.0	
42 PARTS–PIECES ACCESSOIRES	4.7	4.2	3.9	3.7	3.6	4.1	
5 TRANSPORT–TRANSPORT	3.6	2.1	2.4	5.7	4.3	3.5	
51 PASSENGER CARS–AUTOMOBILES	0.0	0.0	0.0	0.0	0.1	0.1	
52 OTHER–AUTRES	1.2	0.2	0.6	3.8	1.6	0.8	
521 INDUSTRIAL–INDUSTRIELS	1.2	0.2	0.6	3.8	1.6	0.8	
522 NON INDUSTRIAL–NON INDUSTRIEL		0.0	0.0	0.0	0.0	0.0	
53 PARTS–PIECES ACCESSOIRES	2.3	1.8	1.8	1.8	2.6	2.5	
6 CONSUM GOODS–BIENS CONSOMMATION	1.9	1.7	1.6	1.7	1.9	2.3	
61 DURABLE–DURABLES	0.3	0.2	0.3	0.4	0.4	0.4	
62 SEMI DURABLE–SEMI DURABLES	0.4	0.4	0.4	0.4	0.6	1.1	
63 NON DURABLE–NON DURABLES	1.3	1.1	0.9	0.9	0.9	0.9	
7 GOODS NES–BIENS NDA	6.2	8.0	6.2	7.4	6.8	7.1	

EXPORTS – EXPORTATIONS

	1990	1991	1992	1993	1994	1995	1996
TOTAL EXPORTS–EXPORTATIONS TOTALES	100.	100.	100.	100.	100.	100.	
1 AGRICULTURE	14.3	12.7	10.5	11.4	10.9	10.2	
2 MINING QUARRY–INDUS EXTRACTIVES	19.6	18.3	18.5	20.0	18.5	17.9	
3 MANUFACTURING–IND MANUFACTUR	66.1	69.0	71.0	68.7	70.6	71.9	
31 FOOD BEV TOBACCO–ALIM BOISS TAB	5.0	5.9	7.1	7.3	5.7	9.6	
32 TEXTILES–INDUSTRIES TEXTILES	32.8	33.9	34.3	31.1	33.5	31.1	
33 WOOD & PRODUCTS–BOIS & PRODUITS	0.1	0.1	0.1	0.2	0.1	0.1	
34 PAPER & PRODUCTS–PAPIER & PRODT	0.2	0.2	0.3	0.3	0.4	0.5	
35 CHEMICALS–INDUSTRIES CHIMIQUES	12.1	12.1	11.3	11.2	12.0	11.7	
36 NON METAL MIN–MIN NON METAL	0.5	0.7	0.9	1.2	1.3	1.2	
37 BASIC METAL–IND METAL BASE	2.1	2.7	3.6	4.2	3.6	3.8	
38 METAL MANUF–MANUF METAL	9.9	9.9	9.9	9.6	9.9	10.2	
39 OTH MANUF IND–AUTRES MANUF	3.4	3.5	3.6	3.6	4.0	3.8	

3. TRADE BY PRINCIPAL COUNTRIES OF FIRST AND LAST CONSIGNMENT (VALUE IN THOUSAND U.S. DOLLARS)
ECHANGES SELON LES PRINCIPAUX PAYS DE PREMIERE ET DE DERNIERE CONSIGNATION (VALEUR EN MILLIERS DE DOLLARS EU)

COUNTRIES–PAYS	GENERAL IMPORTS C.I.F. IMPORTATIONS GENERALES C.A.F				
	1991	1992	1993	1994	1995
World	19509430	24452423	23304090	28654756	36592082
Africa	976619	1529112	1437143	1487380	1983776
Americas	2509604	3081855	3192357	3928857	4800942
Northern America	2166253	2772857	2917185	3157105	4210054
LAIA	329757	302667	266413	759529	579254
CACM	652	1116	855	5663	5164
Caribbean	12925	4806	7591	6514	5540
Rest of America	17	410	312	47	931
As.ex F.USSR	6501607	7982997	7456742	10506673	12384954
Eur.x F.USSR	6262749	8114598	7752930	8589821	11391366
EU	5825061	7377598	7048853	7500853	9981066
EFTA	178465	462749	542605	870678	1036420
East Europe	200979	246453	145362	180306	332815
Other Europe	58244	57	2114	5	650
Former USSR	519676	284470	380130	749225	1188494
Oceania	636669	1005510	739214	997230	1090359
USA/Etats–Unis d'Amer	1891189	2325546	2682751	2891644	3829701
Germany/Allemagne	1551338	1837207	1773243	2185200	3137398
Japan/Japon	1364304	1587558	1513109	2036537	2462000
Belgium–Luxembourg	1394561	2042160	1873467	1205565	1690817
United Kingdom	1185528	1564611	1508309	1556264	1901850
Saudi Arabia	1109345	1374631	1221600	1273075	1367218
United Arab Emirates	993778	1021743	841418	1304260	1247193
Australia/Australie	560839	931650	657083	915059	1019590
France,Monac	579787	589960	582066	608024	770785
Switz.Liecht	151816	422613	506300	824304	996707
Kuwait/ Koweït	214990	621646	555572	670306	813251
Italy/Italie	403677	396434	425947	698888	905545
Nigeria/Nigéria	125175	646519	827319	423835	768007
Korea, Republic of	313676	396862	563013	629519	813352
Singapore/Singapour	311141	366737	413505	707663	853370
Iran (Islamic Rp. of)	584989	444412	378732	534417	582073
Malaysia/Malaisie	391092	439529	248093	488646	896837
China/Chine	20966	140817	299443	757279	810147
Netherlands/Pays–Bas	260801	398109	352631	373319	551690
Russian Federation		284470	257004	504413	822825
Canada	275061	447307	234407	265461	380352
Morocco/Maroc	360501	293146	157988	275310	300364
Brazil/Brésil	194498	192370	121958	540444	260477
Hong Kong	106723	190367	188592	286329	387077
Sweden/Suède	162616	181511	160661	298541	243571
Indonesia/Indonésie	67258	67009	119642	316590	460097
Jordan/Jordanie	145288	158722	110907	153478	191458
Denmark/Danemark	57717	83353	99641	184769	269465
Israel/Israël	64946	123819	145738	151318	205660
Ukraine			106924	199926	332264
Spain/Espagne	65792	83538	102135	172884	176452
Myanmar	51221	129574	121272	126766	161989
Former USSR/Anc. URSS	519676				
Egypt/Egypte	67046	98577	63475	222984	67170
Thailand/Thaïlande	48747	65164	57204	171618	169312
Qatar	35780	111879	132129	114622	107473
Finland/Finlande	73390	65074	66838	108117	170393
So. Africa Customs Un	4438	1864	37292	152554	244621
Tunisia/Tunisie	86363	107669	55925	90552	85708
Austria/Autriche	68852	103001	49038	57818	114855
Poland/Pologne	79123	90982	45403	44836	129982
New Zealand	68345	67973	74051	75937	62159
Pakistan	57607	144887	43566	52746	45016
Bahrain/Bahreïn	48545	48076	54665	103524	60469
Argentina/Argentine	36829	25057	38283	73009	130836
Zambia/Zambie	49381	77731	50515	54697	59815
Un. Rep. of Tanzania	34559	40993	60733	54340	96049
Mexico/Mexique	63213	54394	55941	40022	64540
Turkey/Turquie	59456	50395	33679	79814	51128
Senegal/Sénégal	101288	102637	17738	12782	26277

COUNTRIES–PAYS	GENERAL EXPORTS F.O.B. EXPORTATIONS GENERALES F.O.B.				
	1991	1992	1993	1994	1995
Monde	17899912	20711318	22236949	26330037	31649957
Afrique	554210	795426	819048	985537	1659551
Amériques	3238642	4324478	4468111	5648481	6167734
Amérique du Nord	3116014	4142761	4227068	5289762	5805471
ALAI	88976	141407	202638	295823	302152
MCAC	2692	5150	5194	6953	7163
Caraïbes	9179	10490	13842	20008	21264
Autre Amérique	21782	24670	19370	35935	31685
Asie l'URSS exclus	6174019	7450473	8957505	10154025	12554266
Europe l'URSS exclus	5644674	6644036	6518678	7816769	9233298
UE	5061786	6125238	6032696	7336684	8684444
AELE	264104	276738	270960	315775	344647
Europe de l'Est	282419	222142	198894	144427	179447
Autre de l'Europe	36365	10335	7427	8315	8947
Ancienne URSS	1643139	678459	793924	901199	1141243
Océanie	229746	286344	281875	407140	441499
USA/Etats–Unis d'Amer	2926784	3928943	3999051	5022525	5501786
Japan/Japon	1654620	1604969	1740833	2026533	2207587
Germany/Allemagne	1272340	1594397	1539117	1747681	1967235
United Kingdom	1140550	1356182	1379477	1690889	1998140
Hong Kong	615490	854779	1249485	1517344	1814819
United Arab Emirates	739876	909841	1157869	1265841	1422160
Belgium–Luxembourg	669098	764438	843892	992464	1113466
Italy/Italie	581075	695048	604072	857921	1010812
Singapore/Singapour	389560	657569	751945	770280	889543
Russian Federation		677497	649277	807143	1041832
Bangladesh	324583	396970	430164	644645	1045818
France,Monac	426265	526821	504323	582131	741336
Netherlands/Pays–Bas	373336	463911	511193	585492	765208
Saudi Arabia	352000	455247	510771	435678	480485
Thailand/Thaïlande	198995	283386	357236	406587	471246
Former USSR/Anc. URSS	1643139				
Sri Lanka	174535	277098	287953	366597	398049
Indonesia/Indonésie	147009	154740	234923	277685	660390
Korea, Republic of	241305	195383	206417	332437	446882
Australia/Australie	202915	249384	245242	346442	374363
Spain/Espagne	216966	247193	207509	287472	414871
Malaysia/Malaisie	202799	212100	247299	286545	391748
Canada	189003	213556	227832	266819	303310
Switz.Liecht	219529	222464	221022	247412	279230
China/Chine	48271	157850	279057	254224	331695
Iran (Islamic Rp. of)	122763	127857	159709	156749	154579
Israel/Israël	64179	95084	131867	150257	215611
Nigeria/Nigéria	103883	161588	119262	109127	150435
Egypt/Egypte	81195	127631	121013	119808	163755
Sweden/Suède	92581	112272	107422	146939	145708
So. Africa Customs Un	5937	11097	37377	160794	337819
Kuwait/ Koweït	52387	121043	105975	133911	135083
Turkey/Turquie	53182	115979	112218	95258	171444
Kenya	41829	64412	70826	122696	244278
Denmark/Danemark	78698	96606	89638	129412	145161
Nepal/Népal	77282	80958	98140	120075	159564
Mauritius/Maurice	53473	66608	85985	113871	135603
Oman	74072	83357	83724	88406	109181
Philippines	64374	61060	58244	99535	143770
Austria/Autriche	61492	79734	84981	95380	90310
Poland/Pologne	80586	71841	52211	67197	87244
Jordan/Jordanie	102045	49545	71635	53927	79595
Un. Rep. of Tanzania	48131	78227	63665	65822	81141
Portugal	44900	57741	54185	68122	91392
Greece/Grèce	29975	56998	54061	73502	98401
Pakistan	40165	56739	64066	57233	76590
Bahrain/Bahreïn	49365	55799	62383	59055	59140
Norway,SVD,JM	44168	53526	49498	66595	63909
Mexico/Mexique	27982	48198	56811	78264	54656
Brazil/Brésil	17320	18577	58862	82794	85547

(VALUE AS PERCENTAGE OF WORLD TOTAL)(VALEURS EN POURCENTAGE DU TOTAL MONDIAL)

	1986	1987	1988	1989	1990	1991	1992	1993	1994	1995
Africa	4.4	3.0	3.6	2.6	2.5	5.0	6.3	6.2	5.2	5.4
Americas	13.3	12.7	15.0	15.3	14.1	12.9	12.6	13.7	13.7	13.1
Northern America	11.2	10.3	12.9	13.3	12.0	11.1	11.3	12.5	11.0	11.5
LAIA	2.0	2.2	2.0	2.0	2.1	1.7	1.2	1.1	2.7	1.6
CACM	0.0	0.0	0.0	0.0	0.0	0.0	0.0	0.0	0.0	0.0
Caribbean	0.1	0.2	0.0	0.1	0.1	0.1	0.0	0.0	0.0	0.0
Rest of America	0.0	0.0	0.0	0.0	0.0	0.0	0.0	0.0	0.0	0.0
As.ex F.USSR	33.3	33.1	33.7	30.6	32.3	33.3	32.6	32.0	36.7	33.8
Eur.x F.USSR	39.6	39.1	36.6	37.8	33.0	32.1	33.2	33.3	30.0	31.1
EU	34.9	35.3	24.7	26.6	21.9	29.9	30.2	30.2	26.2	27.3
EFTA	2.0	1.5	1.3	1.2	1.3	0.9	1.9	2.3	3.0	2.8
East Europe	2.1	1.6	10.1	9.5	9.5	1.0	1.0	0.6	0.6	0.9
Other Europe	0.5	0.8	0.5	0.5	0.4	0.3	0.0	0.0	0.0	0.0
Former USSR	3.9	5.2	3.0	4.6	3.9	2.7	1.2	1.6	2.6	3.2
Oceania	2.3	2.5	2.8	2.7	3.5	3.3	4.1	3.2	3.5	3.0
USA/Etats–Unis d'Amer	9.3	9.0	11.4	12.0	10.7	9.7	9.5	11.5	10.1	10.5
Germany/Allemagne	9.5	9.7				8.0	7.5	7.6	7.6	8.6
Japan/Japon	12.8	9.5	9.3	8.0	7.5	7.0	6.5	6.5	7.1	6.7
Belgium–Luxembourg	5.5	6.2	7.3	7.6	6.3	7.1	8.4	8.0	4.2	4.6
United Kingdom	8.2	8.2	8.5	8.3	6.4	6.1	6.4	6.5	5.4	5.2
Saudi Arabia	4.2	3.3	6.3	3.7	5.8	5.7	5.6	5.2	4.4	3.7
United Arab Emirates	1.7	3.4	3.0	3.3	3.2	5.1	4.2	3.6	4.6	3.4
Australia/Australie	2.0	2.2	2.5	2.5	3.1	2.9	3.8	2.8	3.2	2.8
France,Monac	3.4	3.6	2.8	4.5	2.8	3.0	2.4	2.5	2.1	2.1
Switz.Liecht	1.7	1.1	1.0	1.0	1.1	0.8	1.7	2.2	2.9	2.7

	1986	1987	1988	1989	1990	1991	1992	1993	1994	1995
Afrique	2.7	2.4	2.3	2.3	2.5	3.1	3.8	3.7	3.7	5.2
Amériques	20.1	19.9	20.0	17.5	16.1	18.1	20.9	20.1	21.5	19.5
Amérique du Nord	19.8	19.7	19.4	17.1	15.6	17.4	20.0	19.0	20.1	18.3
ALAI	0.2	0.1	0.4	0.2	0.3	0.5	0.7	0.9	1.1	1.0
MCAC	0.0	0.0	0.0	0.0	0.0	0.0	0.0	0.0	0.0	0.0
Caraïbes	0.1	0.1	0.1	0.1	0.1	0.1	0.1	0.1	0.1	0.1
Autre Amérique	0.0	0.0	0.0	0.0	0.1	0.1	0.1	0.1	0.1	0.1
Asie l'URSS exclus	29.1	28.2	30.4	29.6	29.2	34.5	36.0	40.3	38.6	39.7
Europe l'URSS exclus	28.4	31.5	29.5	29.8	32.1	31.5	32.1	29.3	29.7	29.2
UE	22.8	26.1	19.1	19.5	21.0	28.3	29.6	27.1	27.9	27.4
AELE	1.4	1.5	1.5	1.5	1.4	1.5	1.3	1.2	1.2	1.1
Europe de l'Est	3.6	3.7	8.5	8.5	9.4	1.6	1.1	0.9	0.5	0.6
Autre de l'Europe	0.6	0.4	0.4	0.3	0.3	0.2	0.0	0.0	0.0	0.0
Ancienne URSS	15.0	12.5	13.8	16.9	16.1	9.2	3.3	3.6	3.4	3.6
Océanie	1.4	1.3	1.5	1.4	1.1	1.3	1.4	1.3	1.5	1.4
USA/Etats–Unis d'Amer	18.7	18.6	18.4	16.2	14.7	16.4	19.0	18.0	19.1	17.4
Japan/Japon	10.7	10.3	10.6	9.9	9.3	9.2	7.7	7.8	7.7	7.0
Germany/Allemagne	5.9	6.8				7.1	7.7	6.9	6.6	6.2
United Kingdom	5.6	6.5	5.7	5.8	6.5	6.4	6.5	6.2	6.4	6.3
Hong Kong	3.3	2.8	4.0	3.2	3.3	3.4	4.1	5.6	5.8	5.7
United Arab Emirates	2.3	2.0	2.1	2.6	2.4	4.1	4.4	5.2	4.8	4.5
Belgium–Luxembourg	2.8	3.1	4.4	4.4	3.9	3.7	3.7	3.8	3.8	3.5
Italy/Italie	2.5	3.2	2.7	2.7	3.1	3.2	3.4	2.7	3.3	3.2
Singapore/Singapour	1.7	1.7	1.6	1.7	2.1	2.2	3.2	3.4	2.9	2.8
Russian Federation							3.3	2.9	3.1	3.3

4. General Imports C.I.F. by Commodities according to the S.I.T.C. (Rev. 2) in thousand U.S. Dollars
Importations Générales C.A.F. par Produits d'après la C.T.C.I. (Rév. 2) en milliers de Dollars E.U.

SITC CTCI	COMMODITY	1992		1993		1994		1995		PRODUIT
		WEIGHT POIDS	VALUE VALEUR	WEIGHT POIDS	VALUE VALEUR	WEIGHT POIDS	VALUE VALEUR	WEIGHT POIDS	VALUE VALEUR	
	ALL COMMODITIES		24452423		23304090		28654756		36592082	TOUS PRODUITS
0	FOOD AND LIVE ANIMALS		806712		607511		1423748		768878	ALIMENTS,ANIMAUX VIVANTS
04	CEREALS AND PREPARATIONS		372659		92602		29409		24036	CEREALES ET PRODUITS
041	WHEAT ETC UNMILLED	W 1363695	273971	W 241695	40056	W 540	122	W 8240	3100	FROMENT,EPEAUTRE
0412	OTHER WHEAT ETC UNMILLED	W 1342695	269545	W 229897	38134	W 540	122	W 8240	3100	AUTRE FROMENT NON MOULU
05	VEGETABLES AND FRUIT		351788		414101		520204		538504	LEGUMES ET FRUITS
054	VEG ETC FRSH,SMPLY PRSVD	W 396277	133677	W 667466	190744	W 583063	199928	W 502833	212120	LEGUMES FRAIS,CONG,SECS
0542	LEGUMINOUS VEGETBLES DRY	W 388593	130929	W 652983	186336	W 582124	198738	W 502234	211585	LEGUMES A COSSE SECS
057	FRUIT,NUTS,FRESH,DRIED	W 72072	218096	W 92238	223338	W 131390	319936	W 129475	325475	FRUITS FRAIS OU SECS
0577	NUTS EDIBLE,FRESH,DRIED	W 17007	192205	W 15425	192928	W 21505	275751	W 23197	288735	FRUITS A COQUES
05773	CASHEW NUTS,FRESH,DRIED	W 135	145204	W 191	153882	W 228	220056	W 223	226717	NOIX DE CAJOU
06	SUGAR AND PREPS,HONEY		5423		6020		731959		69734	SUCRES ET PRODUITS
061	SUGAR AND HONEY	W 9128	5412	W 22011	5970	W 1787959	731767	W 156324	69096	SUCRES ET MIEL
0612	REFINED SUGAR ETC			W 284	116	W 1669494	682290	W 150632	64397	SUCRES RAFFINES
2	CRUDE MATERLS,EXCL FUELS		2058237		1513476		2391735		2709406	MAT BRUTES NON COMESTIBLES
23	RUBBER, CRUDE		100574		109016		118330		214586	CAOUTCHOUC BRUT
233	RUBBER,SYNTHTIC,RECLAIMD	W 49234	82538	W 66886	91514	W 76370	109590	W 74742	131456	LATEX CAOUTCH SYNTH REGEN
2331	SYNTHETIC RUBBER ETC	W 49205	82505	W 66870	91456	W 75904	109229	W 74578	131360	LATEX CAOUTCH SYNTHETIQUE
24	CORK AND WOOD		216318		139534		212553		232690	LIEGE ET BOIS
247	OTH WOOD ROUGH,SQUARED	W 567709	206836	W 335639	134425	W 467966	204134	W 515279	225357	BOIS BRUTS EQUARRIS
2472	SAW–,VENEER–LOGS NON–CON	W 562160	205786	W 335622	134421	W 465840	203499	W 512828	224695	NON CONIFERES SCIAGE,PLAC
24721	— IN THE ROUGH	W 562160	205786	W 335622	134421	W 465840	203499	W 512828	224695	BRUTS ECORCES DEGROSSIS
251	*PULP AND WASTE PAPER	W 436836	157817	W 626139	158544	W 596527	202352	W 549777	274665	PATES A PAPIER,DECHETS
26	TEXTILE FIBRES AND WASTE		373446		314301		614749		616484	FIBRES TEXTILES
261	SILK	W 2863	86789	W 5004	86277	W 6095	107408	W 4289	91999	SOIE
2613	RAW SILK NOT THROWN	W 2769	86156	W 4892	85643	W 5403	103963	W 4150	90315	SOIE GREGE
263	COTTON	W 52727	84282	W 4070	5905	W 80870	161580	W 69620	155502	COTON
2631	RAW COTTON,EXCL LINTERS	W 52606	84215	W 3822	5863	W 80503	161381	W 69452	155407	COTON EN MASSE
266	SYNTHETIC FIBRES TO SPIN	W 13573	24365	W 25923	35652	W 60888	100387	W 55901	110389	FIBRES SYNTHETIQUES
268	WOOL(EXC TOPS),ANML HAIR	W 44594	128790	W 64710	128441	W 44229	127375	W 52481	159725	LAINES ET POILS
27	CRUDE FERTLZR,MINRLS NES		411183		281056		402994		441159	ENGRAIS MINERAUX BRUTS
271	FERTILIZERS,CRUDE	W 2231028	176989	W 1922803	121992		152617	W 2443828	156431	ENGRAIS BRUTS
2713	NAT CALCM PHOSPHATES ETC	W 2230859	176864	W 1922739	121963	W 2540138	149142	W 2443753	156383	PHOSPHATES DE CALCIUM
27131	— UNGROUND	W 1018279	80430	W 983401	62357	W 1316653	74266	W 1401026	87821	PHOSPHATES NON MOULUS
27132	— GROUND	W 1212580	96434	W 939338	59606	W 1223485	74876	W 1042727	68562	PHOSPHATES MOULUS
274	SULPHUR,UNRSTD IRN PYRTE	W 1398401	135066	W 1264374	72183	W 1600599	135838	W 1543021	144097	SOUFRE ET PYRITES
2741	SULPHUR,EX SULP IN 52215	W 1398379	135042	W 1264367	72175	W 1600570	135811	W 1543002	144079	SOUFRE
278	OTHER CRUDE MINERALS	W 211949	83336	W 235922	71887	W 296875	93841	W 320754	107486	AUTRES MINERAUX BRUTS
28	METALLIFEROUS ORES,SCRAP		741634		442337		748169		820708	MINERAIS METAL,DECHETS
282	IRON AND STEEL SCRAP	W 2768154	517629	W 1096284	223901	W 2171672	428406	W 1948520	395297	FERRAILLES
28209	— OF OTHR IRON OR STEEL	W 2742563	511744	W 1046293	214696	W 1993553	393881	W 1858493	360802	FERRAILLES DE FER
288	NONFERR METAL SCRAP NES	W 129090	148603	W 220338	164356	W 263900	176007	W 289850	280493	DECHETS NON FERREUX
2882	OTHER BASE MTL SCRAP NES	W 60443	101723	W 148019	127285	W 159089	123856	W 183925	212415	AUTRES DECHETS
28821	COPPER WASTE AND SCRAP	W 51470	97770	W 97784	109618	W 85071	95250	W 110931	169206	DECHETS DE CUIVRE
3	MINERAL FUELS ETC		7228326		6338758		6832734		8677775	COMBUSTIBLES MINERAUX LUB
32	COAL,COKE AND BRIQUETTES		533659		466501		708390		923459	HOUILLES,COKES,BRIQUETTES
322	COAL,LIGNITE AND PEAT	W 6493849	505262	W 7331163	451287	MW 10740	648350	MW 12512	802660	HOUILLES,LIGNITES,TOURBE
3222	OTH COAL,NOT AGGLOMERATD	W 6492398	504501	W 7329928	450729	MW 10732	646894	MW 12510	801803	AUTRES HOUILLES
323	BRIQUETS,COKE,SEMI–COKE		28397		15214		60040		120799	BRIQUETTES
3232	COKE,SEMI–COKE,RTRT CRBN		28397		15214		60040		120799	COKES ET SEMI–COKES
33	PETROLEUM AND PRODUCTS		6644146		5816607		6037008		7618900	PETROLE ET DERIVES
333	CRUDE PETROLEUM	MW 29380	4080417	MW 30822	3407425	MW 27349	3285560	MW 27357	3442075	HUILES BRUTES DE PETROLE
334	PETROLEUM PRODUCTS,REFIN		2544801		2359158		2656556		4083419	PRODUITS RAFFINES
335	RESIDUAL PETRLM PROD NES	W 66768	18928	W 285671	50024	W 513176	94892	W 531103	93406	PRODUITS RESIDUELS NDA
3352	MINERAL TARS AND PRODCTS	W 50981	12892	W 280427	47877	W 505946	91927	W 522916	89470	GOUDRONS MINERAUX
33525	MINERAL TAR OILS ETC NES	W 50346	11915	W 274690	46115	W 495414	88436	W 516810	87831	AUTRES PRODUITS NDA
341	*GAS,NATURAL AND MANUFCT		50521		55651		87337		135416	GAZ NATUREL,GAZ MANUFACT
3413	PETROLM GASES,LIQUEFIED		50485		55584		87303		132009	GAZ DE PETROLE LIQUEFIE
34131	LIQUEFIED PROPANE,BUTANE		50469		55351		84960		118100	PROPANE,BUTANE LIQUEFIES
4	ANIMAL,VEGETABLE OIL,FAT		107470		104515		264430		756934	HUILES,GRAISSES ANIM,VEG
42	FIXED VEGETABLE OIL,FAT		75186		57206		207593		698423	HUILES VEGETALES FIXES
423	FIXED VEG OILS,SOFT	W 62577	44616	W 30677	21554	W 51871	39602	W 226013	152758	HUILES VEGET DOUCES FIXES
424	FIXED VEG OIL NONSOFT	W 50700	30570	W 88000	35651	W 304032	167991	W 866920	545665	AUTRES HUILES VEG FIXES
4242	PALM OIL	W 35155	16501	W 73268	26966	W 287498	155005	W 850397	531996	HUILE DE PALME
5	CHEMCLS,RELATED PROD NES		3448694		2979387		4185491		5582004	PRODUITS CHIMIQUES
51	ORGANIC CHEMICALS		722068		883065		1382055		1699710	PROD CHIMIQ ORGANIQUES
511	HYDROCARBONS NES,DERIVS	W 350752	177869	W 867338	341016	W 1136916	587776	W 1312903	705191	HYDROCARBURES NDA
5111	ACYCLIC HYDROCARBONS	W 63554	35272	W 231566	74585	W 272735	131525	W 355324	147369	HYDROCARBURES ACYCLIQUES
51111	ETHYLENE	W 41072	18327	W 215546	66408	W 245641	117435	W 326511	129489	ETHYLENE
5112	CYCLIC HYDROCARBONS	W 157803	81131	W 381581	150975	W 550539	309065	W 644959	415577	HYDROCARBURES CYCLIQUES
51124	XYLENES,CHEMICALLY PURE	W 45904	24759	W 158295	61675	W 251241	145366	W 245805	195784	XYLENES PURS
51125	STYRENE	W 27174	16441	W 72396	35715	W 99521	80391	W 139986	113799	STYRENE
5113	HALOG DERIV OF HYDROCARB	W 126343	55538	W 250423	109448	W 306826	137887	W 305756	133380	DERIVES HALOGENES HYDROCAR
51139	OTH HALOG HYDRCARB DERIV	W 118357	51214	W 204005	83932	W 283191	121952	W 295791	127324	AUTRE DERIVES HALOGENES
512	ALCOHOLS,PHENOLS ETC	W 56406	62275	W 74874	67538	W 114410	123648	W 149834	157837	PHENOLS,PHENOLS–ALCOOLS
5121	ACYCLIC ALCOHOLS,DERIVS	W 43505	39530	W 51878	42057	W 91994	86783	W 111141	101383	ALCOOLS ACYCLIQUES
513	CARBOXYLIC ACIDS ETC	W 49208	72371	W 127252	109462	W 197095	197180	W 188568	281147	ACIDES CARBOXYLIQUES
5138	POLYACIDS AND DERIVATIVS	W 26329	27930	W 85927	57611	W 134373	122042	W 137612	189484	ACIDES POLYCARBOXYLIQUES
51389	OTH POLYACIDS ETC,DERIVS	W 22619	24602	W 52624	38572	W 74784	74102	W 105659	153727	ACIDES POLYCARBOXYLIQUES
514	NITROGEN–FNCTN COMPOUNDS	W 65950	138944	W 65200	116920	W 107401	186824	W 105072	225329	COMPOSES FONCT AZOTEES
5148	OTH NITROGN–FNCTN CMPNDS	W 41531	62730	W 37065	55642	W 63940	90399	W 70773	124074	AUTRES COMPOSES AZOTES
515	ORG–INORG COMPOUNDS ETC	W 40595	105014	W 31205	78905	W 34950	106765	W 21703	99377	COMPOSES ORGANO–MINERAUX
5156	HETEROCYCLIC CMPDS ETC	W 35070	85043	W 24341	56519	W 24067	70631	W 11350	56518	COMPOSES HETEROCYCLIQUES
516	OTHER ORGANIC CHEMICALS	W 32718	165595	W 35114	169224	W 41576	179861	W 62828	230828	AUTRES PROD ORGANIQUES
5169	ORGANIC CHEMICALS,NES	W 7825	115816	W 11695	124044	W 9796	119961	W 11550	142105	PROD CHIM ORGANIQUES NDA
51699	OTHER ORGANIC COMPOUNDS	W 7291	105712	W 11193	116208	W 8968	110113	W 10926	132460	AUTRES COMPOS ORGANIQUES
52	INORGANIC CHEMICALS		873349		487785		755518		860172	PROD CHIM INORGANIQUES
522	INORG ELEMNTS,OXIDES,ETC		841960		451449		703960		790507	ELEMENTS INORGANIQUES
5222	INORGANIC ACIDS ETC	W 2685846	652335	W 1536142	282537	W 2089995	453560	W 2074581	499928	ACIDES INORGANIQUES
52224	PHOSPHORIC ACIDS ETC	W 2683367	646676	W 1533646	277608	W 2083974	446040	W 2071052	493753	ACIDES PHOSPHORIQUES
5225	INORGANIC BASES ETC NES	W 847580	142952	W 677144	106751	W 869286	189351	W 873982	219980	AUTRES BASES OXYDES METAL
52251	AMMONIA,ANHYDROUS ETC	W 778021	116966	W 550059	77633	W 753325	157795	W 799190	183069	AMMONIAC LIQUEFIE
53	DYES,TANNING,COLOUR PROD		71701		87708		134091		143930	PROD TEINTURE,COLORANTS
541	*MEDICINAL,PHARM PRODUCT		313791		257839		298471		405053	PROD MEDICINAUX PHARMACEUT
5413	ANTIBIOTICS IN BULK	K 2932986	188943	K 3149265	155833	K 4454485	192427	K 6126668	249342	ANTIBIOTIQUES NDA
54131	PENICILLINS AND DERIVTVS	K 1791686	80724	K 2229394	80544	K 3435050	114421	K 5167422	162337	PENICILLINES ET DERIVES
54139	OTHER ANTIBIOTICS	K 897370	101238	K 648789	70462	K 805770	71904	K 780581	81446	AUTRES ANTIBIOTIQUES
562	*FERTILIZERS,MANUFACTURE		780497	W 4634979	631687	W 4630075	763928	W 6595445	1378352	ENGRAIS MANUFACTURES
5621	CHEM NITROGENOUS FERTLZR		280026	W 2400234	300711	W 2196209	409038	W 3134929	768875	ENGRAIS AZOTES
56216	UREA	W 1472240	279882	W 2343136	293218	W 2135672	399029	W 3134822	768785	UREE
5623	CHEM POTASSIC FERTILIZER	W 1264938	222026	W 1117624	144819	W 1717276	205499	W 2026659	257535	ENGRAIS POTASSIQUES

4. General Imports C.I.F. by Commodities according to the S.I.T.C. (Rev. 2) in thousand U.S. Dollars
Importations Générales C.A.F. par Produits d'après la C.T.C.I. (Rév. 2) en milliers de Dollars E.U.

SITC CTCI	COMMODITY	1992			1993			1994			1995			PRODUIT
			WEIGHT POIDS	VALUE VALEUR		WEIGHT POIDS	VALUE VALEUR		WEIGHT POIDS	VALUE VALEUR		WEIGHT POIDS	VALUE VALEUR	
56231	POTASSIUM CHLORIDE	W	1225097	214455	W	1086248	139790	W	1703423	202471	W	1885667	238161	CHLORURE DE POTASSIUM
5629	FERTILIZERS NES	W	1180596	278374	W	1117121	186157	W	716590	149391	W	1433857	351942	ENGRAIS NDA
56292	NITROG–PHOS FERTILZR NES	W	1084227	253715	W	1112497	185561	W	697822	147235	W	1310406	322628	ENGRAIS NDA CONT N P
58	PLASTIC MATERIALS ETC			460165			424239			590147			779738	MAT PLAST ARTIFICIELLES
582	PROD OF CONDENSATION ETC	W	13393	48716	W	20211	55243	W	56743	119963	W	53376	144177	PROD CONDENS,POLYCOND
583	POLYMERIZATION ETC PRODS	W	475481	402225	W	557918	360825	W	579139	456709	W	659047	622947	PROD POLYMERISATION
5831	POLYETHYLENE	W	219388	177254	W	230237	134862	W	231638	150956	W	290002	236767	POLYETHYLENE
58311	— IN PRIMARY FORMS	W	217778	176119	W	216734	131603	W	221956	147258	W	277012	230867	POLYETHYLENE PRIMAIRES
5832	POLYPROPYLENE	W	93906	78615	W	165625	96334	W	181958	129879	W	212435	191798	POLYPROPYLENE
58321	— IN PRIMARY FORMS	W	93401	75208	W	165071	92704	W	180817	123880	W	211107	184932	POLYPROPYLENE PRIMAIRES
59	CHEMICAL MATERIALS NES			191401			168904			205217			248967	MAT PROD CHIMIQUES NDA
598	MISCEL CHEM PRODUCTS NES			170441			146191			167346			198252	PROD DIV INDUST CHIM NDA
5989	CHEM PRODUCTS,PREPS NES			102564			86409			109721			133359	PROD PREP CHIMIQUES NDA
6	BASIC MANUFACTURES			4823653			4798066			4868846			6297243	ART MANUFACTURES
61	LEATHER,DRESSED FUR,ETC			84943			104965			99025			113568	CUIRS,PELLETERIES
611	LEATHER	A	2211	67700	A	3070	81394	A	2475	71859	A	3000	83706	CUIRS,PEAUX PREPARES
64	PAPER,PAPERBOARD AND MFR			196129			219639			242980			467323	PAPIERS,CARTONS & OUVRAGES
641	PAPER AND PAPERBOARD	W	264777	179981	W	345612	204515	W	348465	218388	W	420117	434106	PAPIERS ET CARTONS
6411	NEWSPRINT	W	243119	137867	W	315918	148174	W	298375	155033	W	347908	302357	PAPIER JOURNAL
65	TEXTILE YARN,FABRICS,ETC			165933			228043			330834			358326	FILS,TISSUS,ARTICLES TEXTILE
651	TEXTILE YARN			69110			104977			159670			143100	FILS TEXTILES
6514	SYN FIB YRN,BULK,MONOFIL	W	9203	37603	W	30541	68663	W	50210	108871	W	30175	85905	FILS CONT 85% FIB TEXT SYNTH
65142	— NONTXT ETC CONT PAMID	W	8171	30683	W	27267	58237	W	42254	87524	W	25546	67644	FILS NON TEX FI CON POLYAMID
66	NONMETAL MINERAL MFS NES			2834053			2723730			1770944			2265737	ART MIN NON METALLIQUES
667	PEARL,PREC–,SEMI–P STONE			2732814			2635784			1633441			2109932	PERLES, PIERRES GEMMES
6672	DIAMONDS NONINDUST,UNSET			2659541			2582704			1579626			2050355	DIAMANTS BRUTS
66722	— SRTD,ROUGH,SIMPLY WKD			2632092			2531915			1500669			1951850	DIAMANTS TRIES BRUTS
67	IRON AND STEEL			871638			796950			1165423			1444363	FER ET ACIER
671	PIG IRON ETC	W	121724	75070	W	26389	39690	W	92338	81410	W	91269	106335	FONTE,SPIEGEL,POUDRES
672	IRON,STEEL PRIMARY FORMS	W	711902	242186	W	630129	209806	W	886174	311162	W	598340	277129	LINGOTS FER,ACIER
6727	IRN,STL COIL FR REROLLNG	W	419273	185658	W	413156	155843	W	608102	237515	W	258113	164042	EBAUCHES POUR TOLES FER
67271	IRON,SIMPLE STEEL COILS	W	376288	142477	W	380379	122957	W	544001	179794	W	222974	95098	EBAUCHES NON EN ACIER
673	IRON,STEEL SHAPES ETC	W	59445	54421	W	64960	51201	W	134778	96043	W	164695	120141	BARRES,PROFIL FER,ACIER
674	IRN,STL UNIV,PLATE,SHEET	W	393198	294273	W	395601	240479	W	825024	456096	W	1157000	701408	LARGES PLATS,TOLES
6744	IRN,STL HVY PLATE,ROLLED	W	123453	71442	W	119132	50589	W	390368	162159	W	621431	287395	TOLES LAMINEES PLUS 4.75 MM
67441	— OF IRON OR SIMPLE STL	W	119001	64784	W	115362	44807	W	382758	152380	W	612973	270900	TOLES NON ACIER FIN CARB
6745	IRN,STL MED PLATE,ROLLED	W	78342	79866	W	97289	76894	W	154094	109270	W	182246	139976	TOLES 3 A 4.75 MM
6749	OTH IRN,STL PLATES,SHEET	W	55247	43605	W	70963	48313	W	102829	80036	W	141074	131714	AUTRES TOLES FER,ACIER
678	IRON,STL TUBES,PIPES,ETC	W	100193	151746	W	248477	221149	W	195000	184259	W	141627	190029	TUBES,TUYAUX EN FONTE,FER
6782	IRON,STL SEAMLESS TUBES	W	86019	119490	W	180157	154404	W	176320	154399	W	115042	146553	TUBES,TUYAUX SANS SOUDURE
68	NON–FERROUS METALS			447517			485376			974343			1240955	METAUX NON FERREUX
681	SILVER,PLATINUM,ETC			7491			10918			246204			333812	ARGENT ET PLATINE
6811	SILVER UNWKD,PARTLY WRKD			6878			9533			243894			331254	ARGENT BRUT MI–OUVRE
68113	SILVER UNWROUGHT			5987			8226			223083			307467	ARGENT ET ALLIAGES BRUTS
682	COPPER EXC CEMENT COPPER	W	91548	286472	W	135065	280858	W	148260	373506	W	138007	447590	CUIVRE
6821	COPPER NES,ALLOYS,UNWRT	W	52431	150367	W	88960	167114	W	84758	193451	W	83664	249628	CUIVRE BRUT
68212	COPPER REFINED,UNWROUGHT	W	51132	146638	W	87144	163663	W	79995	181925	W	82895	247322	CUIVRE AFFINE BRUT
6822	COPPER,ALLOYS WORKED	W	39117	136106	W	46104	113743	W	63502	180055	W	54343	197962	CUIVRE,ALLIAGES OUVRES
68221	COPPER BARS,WIRE,ETC	W	36307	111240	W	42604	92444	W	58295	150138	W	46783	149895	BARRES,PROFILES ET FILS
684	ALUMINIUM	W	8515	29985	W	50830	76633	W	88425	171101	W	102065	219040	ALUMINIUM
6841	ALUMINIUM,ALLOYS,UNWRGHT	W	3748	5746	W	43823	52316	W	78903	136676	W	92460	176030	ALUMINIUM,ALLIAGES BRUTS
69	METAL MANUFACTURES NES			161036			175289			204101			271847	ART MANUFACT EN METAL NDA
699	BASE METAL MFRS NES	W	6508	79158	W	6522	72091	W	8337	85372	W	12879	120344	ART MANUFACTURES MET NDA
7	MACHINES,TRANSPORT EQUIP			3451928			4332315			5435884			7366710	MACHINES MATERIEL TRANSPORT
71	POWER GENERATING EQUIPMT			265777			325159			537597			784981	MACHINES GENERATRICES
713	INTRNL COMBUS PSTN ENGIN			86903			81120			121692			178588	MOTEURS EXPL COMB INT, PIECE
7139	PISTON ENGINE PARTS NES	W	3531	75004	W	3212	57461	W	4518	80598	W	6035	107725	PIECES POUR 713.2,3,8
714	ENGINES AND MOTORS NES			31576			132536			142822			112742	MOTEURS NON ELECTRIQUES
7149	ENGINE & MOTOR PARTS NES	W	753	25679	W	2573	125813	W	4272	139689	W	1527	74713	PIECES 714 ET 718.88
71499	PARTS NES,OF 71488,71888	W	737	24989	W	2524	124399	W	4207	138365	W	1466	72829	PIECES 714.88 ET 718.88
716	ROTATING ELECTRIC PLANT			64149			71761			220514			418502	APP ELECTR ROTATIFS,PIECES
7169	PTS NES OF ROT ELEC PLNT	W	1168	26313	W	1753	31646	W	6900	127215	W	12861	234835	PIECES MAC APP ROTATIFS
72	MACHS FOR SPCL INDUSTRYS			683391			843635			1235113			1720526	MAC SPECIALES POUR INDUST
724	TEXTILE,LEATHER MACHNRY			357068			460996			670864			795715	MACH POUR INDUSTRIE TEXTILE
7244	SPINNING,EXTRDNG,ETC MCH			145089			208530			284175			337242	MACH POUR LE FILAGE
72443	SPINNING,REELING,ETC MCH	N	314	49300	N	858	69236	N	1220	127516	N	1170	163216	MACH POUR LA FILATURE
72449	PTS NES OF MACHS OF 7244	W	2503	62276	W	3780	71066	W	3113	73149	W	4090	89045	PIECES DES MACH DU 724.4
7245	WEAVING,FELT MFG,ETC MCH			98967			109988			182124			250446	METIERS A TISSER,PIECES
72453	GIMPING,WARPING ETC MCHS	N	397	27874	N	722	36746	N	1249	90235	N	1347	83522	METIERS A TULLE ETC
726	PRINTG,BKBINDG MACHY,PTS			29068			48081			84647			155488	MACHINES POUR IMPRIMERIE
728	OTH MACHY FOR SPCL INDUS			206321			237271			335026			555631	AUT MACH IND PARTICULIERES
7284	MACHY FOR SPCL INDUS NES			135789			157246			278807			470269	MACH SPEC IND PARTICUL.
72842	RUBBER,PLASTICS WRKG MCH	N	267	15979	N	581	27570	N	3032	70907	N	2727	155884	MACH IND CAOUT MAT PLAST
72848	OTH MCHY WITH INDIV FNCT	N	7419	46502	N	6382	62006	N	9371	111504	N	15849	194097	AUTRES MACHINES NDA
73	METALWORKING MACHINERY			211594			164374			248862			416240	MACH TRAVAIL DES METAUX
736	METALWORKING MACH–TOOLS			155149			119369			182756			319843	MACH–OUTILS TRAVAIL METAUX
7361	METAL CUTTING MACH–TOOLS	N	1129	91354	N	1058	59364	N	3646	75780	N	4169	144938	MACH–OUT ENLEVEMENT METAL
74	GENRL INDUSTRL MACHY NES			694428			710643			923848			1377733	MACH APP INDUSTRIE
741	HEATING,COOLING EQUIPMNT			85039			81414			116159			232351	MACH CHAUFFAGE,PIECES
743	PUMPS NES,CENTRFUGES ETC			88102			98711			122243			197157	POMPES COMPRES,VENT ETC
744	MECHANICAL HANDLING EQU			115314			131260			163209			222256	EQUIP MANUTENTION PIECES
7449	PTS NES OF MACHY OF 7442	W	5768	90837	W	6844	106318	W	5172	112545	W	7140	118179	PIECES DU 744.2
749	NONELEC MACH PTS,ACC NES			325707			298068			383906			523925	PIECES MACH NON ELEC NDA
7491	BALL,ROLLER,ETC BEARINGS	MN	11548	87703	MN	12217	74077	MN	12480	90331	MN	27553	140832	ROULEMENTS BILLES ETC
7493	SHAFT,CRANK,PULLEY ETC			120633	N	1037118	104361	N	2419902	126021	N	3816260	161058	ARBRES TRANS,VILEBREQUINS
7499	OTH NONELEC MCHY PTS NES	W	2025	54920	W	2308	54939	W	3395	88165	W	5435	112772	PIECES NON ELECT NDA
75	OFFICE MACHNES,ADP EQUIP			182124			199731			286189			406398	MACH BUREAU TRAIT AUTOM
752	AUTOMTIC DATA PROC EQUIP	N	104861	72092	N	133336	84282	N	331213	127159	N	479994	194027	MACH TRAIT INFORMATION
759	OFFICE,ADP MCH PTS,ACCES	W	1687	105128	W	1707	111165	W	2704	143327	W	3570	185748	PIECES DU 751 ET 752
7599	ACCTG,ETC,ADP MCH PTS,AC	W	1348	96595	W	1425	102899	W	2231	131707	W	3135	175340	PIECES DU 751 ET 752
76	TELECOMM,SOUND EQUIPMENT			179563			173363			260852			352164	EQUIPMENT DE TELECOM
764	TELECOM EQPT,PTS,ACC NES			167625			169019			249920			326954	EQUIP TELECOM,PIECES
7649	PTS NES OF EQUIPMT OF 76	W	3407	113377	W	2317	74159	W	4626	133925	W	7196	190293	PIECES DE LA DIV 76
77	ELECTRIC MACHNRY NES ETC			723671			646200			830819			1213928	MACH APP ELECT NDA
772	SWITCHGEAR ETC,PARTS NES			158848			131142			172386			224804	APP COUPURE,SECT ETC
7721	SWITCHGEAR ETC	MN	108079	123475	MN	105898	99604			123720	MN	176863	164899	APP COUPURE,SECTIONMNT
774	ELECTRO–MEDCL,XRAY EQUIP			78220			58223			94429			106452	APPAREILS MEDICAUX
776	TRANSISTORS,VALVES,ETC			240684			211621			269270			440084	LAMPES,TUBES,VALVES
7764	ELECTRONIC MICROCIRCUITS	MN	101772	115495	MN	100091	99258	MN	221567	120182	MN	180966	214653	MICROSTRUCTURES ELECTRON
778	ELECTRICAL MACHINERY NES			164738			165127			190015			259443	AUTRES MACH ELECT NDA
7788	OTH ELEC MACHY,EQUIP NES			139217			133380			147222			190227	AUT MACH APP ELEC NDA

4. General Imports C.I.F. by Commodities according to the S.I.T.C. (Rev. 2) in thousand U.S. Dollars
Importations Générales C.A.F. par Produits d'après la C.T.C.I. (Rév. 2) en milliers de Dollars E.U.

SITC CTCI	COMMODITY	1992 WEIGHT POIDS	1992 VALUE VALEUR	1993 WEIGHT POIDS	1993 VALUE VALEUR	1994 WEIGHT POIDS	1994 VALUE VALEUR	1995 WEIGHT POIDS	1995 VALUE VALEUR	PRODUIT
78	ROAD VEHICLES		216983		222432		292257		456334	VEHICULES ROUTIERS
784	MOTOR VEH PRTS,ACCES NES		185886		183468		244108		382191	PIECES 722,781,782,783
7849	OTHER MOTOR VEHCL PARTS	W 21069	183679	W 20889	181877	W 29951	239323	W 37188	371175	PIECES 722,781,782,783
79	OTHR TRANSPORT EQUIPMENT		294398		1046779		820347		638405	AUTRE MATERIEL TRANSPORT
792	AIRCRAFT ETC		137861		935137		732674		486677	APP NAVIGATION AERIENNE
7924	AIRCRFT NES OVER 15000KG		24907	N 25	787326	N 9	318383	N 6	132878	AERODYNES PLUS 15000 KG
7929	AIRCRAFT PARTS NES	W 522	71651	W 554	90346	W 801	306262	W 840	269923	PIECES DU 792
793	SHIPS AND BOATS ETC	N 195	109469		81153	N 280	72011	N 371	103586	NAVIRES BATEAUX,ETC
7932	SHIPS AND BOATS NES	N 176	93390	N 86	23227	N 102	23667	N 47	26844	NAVIRES ET BATEAUX
79324	FISHING VESSELS ETC	N 170	90553	N 1	46	N 9	14265	N 22	24829	BATEAUX DE PECHE
8	MISC MANUFACTURED GOODS		786279		689683		866679		1310096	ART MANUFACTURES DIVERS
87	PRECISION INSTRUMNTS NES		427523		348235		372202		544918	INSTRUM,APPAR SCIENT NDA
874	MEASURNG,CONTROLNG INSTR		346232		280196		278968		406474	INSTRUMENTS DE MESURE
8748	ELEC MEAS,CONTRL EQU NES	N 26532	76140	N 36028	62005	N 57703	68595	N 98315	96251	APP ELEC ELECTRO MESURE
8749	INSTR PTS NES,ACCESSORYS	W 1507	124525	W 1325	88421	W 2489	70239	W 2044	104926	PIECES 873,874.3,54,874.8
88	PHOTO EQU,OPTICL GDS ETC		148575		141353		180238		217107	APP,FOURN PHOTO,OP,MONTR
882	PHOTO,CINEMA SUPPLIES		115331		109390		140619		158055	PRODUITS PHOTO,CINEMA
8822	PHOTO FILM EXC DEV CINMA		111720		105221		134295		150240	PLAQUES,PELLICULES,FILMS
89	MISC MANUFCTRD GOODS NES		200029		191428		302415		523375	ART MANUFACTURES DIVERS
892	PRINTED MATTER		83616		68774		71013		95724	IMPRIMES
893	ARTICLES OF PLASTIC NES		32888		36613		84369	W 10864	167515	OUVRAGES EN MAT DIVIS 58
8939	MISC PLASTIC ARTICLES	W 2438	26679	W 3243	30087	W 4641	74896	W 9030	156257	ART DIVERS EN MAT DIV 58
89399	OTHR PLASTC ARTICLES NES	W 2408	26465	W 3202	29833	W 4593	74375	W 8991	155862	AUT OUV MAT DIV 58
898	MUSICAL INSTRUMENTS,PTS		29121		32559		60841		162377	INSTRUMENTS DE MUSIQUE
8983	SOUND RECRDNG TAPE,DISCS	N 632010	28464	N 1197022	31498	N 2252418	59682	N 6294220	160016	SUPPORTS SON POUR 763
89832	RECORDED DISCS,TAPES ETC	N 130135	24729	N 155430	28004	N 439949	54721	N 859167	147165	DISQUES,PHONO,BANDES
9	GOODS NOT CLASSD BY KIND		1736870		1935202		2376416		3107509	ART TRANSACT NON CLASSES
931	*SPECIAL TRANSACTIONS		1487540		1687924		1905405		2553355	TRANS.SPECIALES
971	*GOLD,NON MONETARY NES	K 18504	246378	K 19710	245820	K 39055	470039	K 45677	539529	OR NON MONETAIRE
97101	NONMON GLD UNWRT,SEMIMFD	K 18356	246172	K 19669	245783	K 39038	470021	K 45677	539527	OR,ALLIAGES D'OR BRUTS

5. General Exports F.O.B. by Commodities according to the S.I.T.C. (Rev. 2) in thousand U.S. Dollars
Exportations Générales F.O.B. par Produits d'après la C.T.C.I. (Rév. 2) en milliers de Dollars E.U.

SITC CTCI	COMMODITY	1992		1993		1994		1995		PRODUIT
		WEIGHT POIDS	VALUE VALEUR	WEIGHT POIDS	VALUE VALEUR	WEIGHT POIDS	VALUE VALEUR	WEIGHT POIDS	VALUE VALEUR	
	ALL COMMODITIES		20711318		22236949		26330037		31698602	TOUS PRODUITS
0	FOOD AND LIVE ANIMALS		3046254		3384189		3752875		5351154	ALIMENTS,ANIMAUX VIVANTS
01	MEAT AND PREPARATIONS		99781		110040		126131		184890	VIANDES ET PREPARATIONS
011	MEAT FRESH,CHILLD,FROZEN	W 89476	98794	W 112861	109494	W 127875	125396	W 169352	183186	VIANDES FRAICHES,REF,CONGE
0111	BOVINE MEAT FRESH,FROZEN	W 81614	82719	W 101666	89505	W 116138	103306	W 159704	165419	VIANDES BOVIN FRAI,REF
01112	BOVINE MEAT BONELESS	W 76365	77807	W 82170	73373	W 93590	86415	W 131840	137656	VIANDES BOVIN DESOSSEES
03	FISH AND PREPARATIONS		665665		807073		1119550		1000282	POISSONS ET PREPARATIONS
034	FISH,FRESH,CHILLED,FROZN	W 75993	92540	W 96490	102543	W 144183	172685	W 141405	196019	POISSON FRAIS, REFRIG,CONG
0342	FISH FROZEN,EXCL FILLETS	W 70657	79508	W 89107	85942	W 133480	144652	W 119092	143357	POISSONS CONGELES
036	SHELL FISH FRESH,FROZEN	W 130402	570710	W 154387	700258	W 168914	938703	W 158032	797611	CRUSTACES,MOLLUSQUES
04	CEREALS AND PREPARATIONS		400523		441887		429616		1603212	CEREALES ET PRODUITS
041	WHEAT ETC UNMILLED	W 36749	3939	W 390	66	W 86628	13484	W 632468	109313	FROMENT,EPEAUTRE
0412	OTHER WHEAT ETC UNMILLED	W 36749	3939	W 350	59	W 86546	13471	W 593176	102141	AUTRE FROMENT NON MOULU
042	RICE	W 580410	376358	W 767687	410207	W 890613	384019	W 4914011	1361515	RIZ
0422	RICE SEMI–MILLED,MILLED	W 580334	376337	W 767671	410203	W 890528	384001	W 4911441	1360930	RIZ POLI,GLACE INCL BRISURES
04221	RICE MILLED UNBROKEN	W 579840	376123	W 767660	410198	W 890268	383927	W 4893966	1357309	RIZ POLI,GLACE EXCL BRISURES
046	WHEAT ETC MEAL OR FLOUR	W 986	192	W 3790	793	W 5545	1213	W 460859	97602	SEMOULE FARINE,FROMENT
04601	FLOUR OF WHEAT OR MESLIN	W 986	192	W 3478	746	W 5543	1212	W 459099	97215	FARINE DE FROMENT
05	VEGETABLES AND FRUIT		487702		545608		649025		681795	LEGUMES ET FRUITS
054	VEG ETC FRSH,SMPLY PRSVD	W 352086	83232	W 442306	95272	W 524459	118016	W 536670	153883	LEGUMES FRAIS,CONG,SECS
057	FRUIT,NUTS,FRESH,DRIED	W 85559	345337	W 88817	393537	W 100637	459223	W 116035	441601	FRUITS FRAIS OU SECS
0577	NUTS EDIBLE,FRESH,DRIED	W 5571	306107	W 7113	356070	W 7519	417661	W 7844	394556	FRUITS A COQUES
05773	CASHEW NUTS,FRESH,DRIED	W 58	287341	W 70	333248	W 77	396395	W 70	368302	NOIX DE CAJOU
06	SUGAR AND PREPS,HONEY		139172		58877		22842		159469	SUCRES ET PRODUITS
061	SUGAR AND HONEY	W 486605	138371	W 206348	57992	W 54197	21679	W 740578	155510	SUCRES ET MIEL
0612	REFINED SUGAR ETC	W 364764	122185	W 118992	35543	W 39368	15579	W 169621	75597	SUCRES RAFFINES
07	COFFEE,TEA,COCOA,SPICES		624690		647566		793906		976346	CAFE,THE,CACAO,EPICES
071	COFFEE AND SUBSTITUTES	W 115318	145602	W 120123	174054	W 130090	335496	W 157330	448536	CAFE ET SUCCEDANES
0711	COFFEE GREEN,ROASTED,SUB	W 110642	119387	W 114023	141489	W 123923	289441	W 148866	366143	CAFE TORREFIE OU DECAFEINE
07111	COFFEE GREEN,HUSKS,SKINS	W 108739	113099	W 112680	137326	W 122122	282740	W 144944	355672	CAFE NON TORREFIE
074	TEA AND MATE	W 166359	366414	W 153159	330604	W 150874	306934	W 158333	345214	THE ET MATE
0741	TEA	W 166359	366414	W 153159	330604	W 150874	306934	W 158333	345213	THE
075	SPICES	W 104554	112241	W 163468	142095	W 137623	149167	W 176847	179940	EPICES
0751	PEPPER AND PIMENTO	W 37854	52423	W 78161	81799	W 56516	92854	W 81134	115674	POIVRE,PIMENTS
081	*FEEDING STUFF FOR ANIML	W 3690596	597594	W 4905737	748185	W 3955107	582380	W 4327302	706300	NOURRITURE POUR ANIMAUX
0813	OILCAKE AND OTH RESIDUES	W 3314911	565929	W 4302178	711404	W 3576682	551473	W 4020286	677686	TOURTEAUX
08131	— OF SOYA BEANS	W 1862867	429112	W 2755837	551538	W 1929742	386682	W 2591803	545318	TOURTEAUX DE SOJA
08136	— OF RAPE OR COLZA SEED	W 853398	65456	W 778192	69079	W 1040514	93141	W 971707	74594	TOURTEAUX DE NAVETTE,COLZA
1	BEVERAGES AND TOBACCO		193350		159428		95911		145378	BOISSONS ET TABACS
12	TOBACCO AND MANUFACTURES		182870		147032		81134		133175	TABACS BRUTS FABRIQUES
121	TOBACCO UNMNFCTRD,REFUSE	W 70607	137169	W 90493	117401	W 42930	58641	W 77678	112869	TABACS BRUTS,DECHETS
1212	TOBACCO STRIPPED OR PART	W 34423	93109	W 41820	69676	W 17543	32619	W 13337	27249	TABACS PART ECOTES
2	CRUDE MATERLS,EXCL FUELS		1111433		1298665		1208214		1544102	MAT BRUTES NON COMESTIBLES
22	OIL SEEDS,OLEAGINOUS FRT		48874		84575		83089		157617	GRAINES,FRUITS OLEAGINEUX
222	SEEDS FOR'SOFT'FIXED OIL	W 56577	36814	W 265058	72159	W 103723	73795	W 197156	140849	GRAINES HUILES FIXES
26	TEXTILE FIBRES AND WASTE		101416		224691		78191		89143	FIBRES TEXTILES
263	COTTON	W 63735	70126	W 193663	208365	W 34801	44515	W 36369	61982	COTON
2631	RAW COTTON,EXCL LINTERS	W 63455	69928	W 192197	206288	W 29350	37237	W 26676	48998	COTON EN MASSE
27	CRUDE FERTLZR,MINRLS NES		185299		194707		249275		278363	ENGRAIS MINERAUX BRUTS
273	STONE,SAND AND GRAVEL	W 1543028	148469	W 1378784	154244	W 1787520	197210	W 2391998	213980	PIERRES,SABLES,GRAVIERS
2731	BLDG,DIMENSION STONE	W 1264212	146444	W 967680	149437	W 1176458	189433	W 1568326	202217	PIERRES DE TAILLE
27313	GRANITE,SANDSTONE,ETC	W 1191591	130861	W 881780	134378	W 1076643	168512	W 1442220	182717	GYPSE,BASALTE,GRES
28	METALLIFEROUS ORES,SCRAP		549033		582371		562989		698960	MINERAIS METAL,DECHETS
281	IRON ORE,CONCENTRATES	MW 22167	425923	MW 26857	437932	MW 26058	413270	MW 31720	512952	MINERAIS DE FER
2815	IRON ORE,CONC,NOT AGGLOM	MW 20927	388220	MW 25630	406929	MW 24788	379253	MW 29243	446400	MINERAIS NON AGGLOMERES
287	BASE METAL ORES,CONC NES		121518	W 1541920	143584	W 1564150	148630	W 1404981	183888	MINERAIS METAUX COMMUNS
2873	ALUMINIUM ORES,ALUMINA	W 585490	72234	W 772370	89653	W 576779	74656	W 597956	98447	MINERAIS D'ALUMINIUM
28732	ALUMINA(ALUMINIUM OXIDE)	W 338252	62486	W 539947	86842	W 479569	73693	W 447988	97068	ALUMINE (OXYDE ALUMINIUM)
29	CRUDE ANIMAL,VEG MAT NES		217530		207499		224621		309690	MATIERES BRUTES ANIM,VEGET
292	CRUDE VEG MATERIALS NES		176090		168896		186096		267783	MAT BRUTES VEGETALES NDA
2929	OTH CRUDE VEG MATERIALS	W 78124	66480	W 91798	67542	W 86762	73944	W 104268	109964	MATIERES VEGETALES NDA
3	MINERAL FUELS ETC		586729		496191		514151		526908	COMBUSTIBLES MINERAUX LUB
33	PETROLEUM AND PRODUCTS		538224		399703		424779		465691	PETROLE ET DERIVES
334	PETROLEUM PRODUCTS,REFIN		532755		398684		418415		454601	PRODUITS RAFFINES
341	*GAS,NATURAL AND MANUFCT		29032		75189		55591		31716	GAZ NATUREL,GAZ MANUFACT
3413	PETROLM GASES,LIQUEFIED		17947		74566		52419		27053	GAZ DE PETROLE LIQUEFIE
34139	OTH HYDROCARBON GAS LQFD		17947		74566		52419		26991	HYDROCARBURES GAZEUX NDA
4	ANIMAL,VEGETABLE OIL,FAT		57422		101131		153279		257941	HUILES,GRAISSES ANIM,VEG
42	FIXED VEGETABLE OIL,FAT		46180		89806		126424		216154	HUILES VEGETALES FIXES
424	FIXED VEG OIL NONSOFT	W 67544	46018	W 135806	89100	W 165673	125903	W 271737	203290	AUTRES HUILES VEG FIXES
4245	CASTOR OIL	W 59637	38557	W 131351	85812	W 159169	120007	W 269892	200303	HUILE DE RICIN
5	CHEMCLS,RELATED PROD NES		1383498		1533704		2133992		2563535	PRODUITS CHIMIQUES
51	ORGANIC CHEMICALS		320086		363958		557408		719815	PROD CHIMIQ ORGANIQUES
511	HYDROCARBONS NES,DERIVS	W 19255	27717	W 23397	37206	W 34332	61950	W 57012	98283	HYDROCARBURES NDA
513	CARBOXYLIC ACIDS ETC	W 28150	28964	W 62004	43986	W 79474	83312	W 89932	117068	ACIDES CARBOXYLIQUES
514	NITROGEN–FNCTN COMPOUNDS	W 28770	124399	W 35746	133269	W 47729	188991	W 44282	205044	COMPOSES FONCT AZOTEES
5146	OXYGEN–FNCT AMINO–CMPNDS	W 16265	71317	W 16238	62156	W 22444	97707	W 19634	108728	COMP AMINES FONCT OXYGEN
516	OTHER ORGANIC CHEMICALS	W 10217	75395	W 11964	73771	W 15569	103724	W 23647	161007	AUTRES PROD ORGANIQUES
5169	ORGANIC CHEMICALS,NES	W 3796	53413	W 4178	57746	W 4488	82175	W 4105	116267	PROD CHIM ORGANIQUES NDA
51699	OTHER ORGANIC COMPOUNDS	W 3561	53094	W 3751	56717	W 4042	80004	W 3725	114272	AUTRES COMPOS ORGANIQUES
52	INORGANIC CHEMICALS		73780		66332		86345		109398	PROD CHIM INORGANIQUES
53	DYES,TANNING,COLOUR PROD		299349		308537		381132		360425	PROD TEINTURE,COLORANTS
531	SYNT DYE,NAT INDGO,LAKES	W 35377	279070	W 43575	289770	W 51444	352128	W 49017	336436	MAT COLOR ORGAN,LAQUES
5311	SYNTHIC ORGNIC DYESTUFFS	W 31429	254262	W 39236	267679	W 46991	330206	W 44720	312989	MAT COLOR ORGAN SYNTHET
541	*MEDICINAL,PHARM PRODUCT		431241		482878		585763		724155	PROD MEDICINAUX PHARMACEUT
5417	MEDICAMENTS		371491		409829		484204		582915	MEDICAMENTS
54171	— CONTAINNG ANTIBIOTICS		75741		85414		118482		164945	MED CONTN ANTIBIOTIQUES
54179	— CONTNG OTH SUBSTANCES		288465		310037		340265		395291	MED CONT AUT SUBSTANCES
55	PERFUME,CLEANING ETC PRD		105393		151450		186158		169267	PROD POUR PARFUM,TOILETTE
553	PERFUMERY,COSMETICS,ETC	W 15373	57399	W 21655	68637	W 26917	89084	W 24421	81912	PRODUITS DE PARFUMERIE
58	PLASTIC MATERIALS ETC		44956		57861		163587		224856	MAT PLAST ARTIFICIELLES
582	PROD OF CONDENSATION ETC	W 6521	18351	W 11237	27175	W 38047	70702	W 53530	137264	PROD CONDENS,POLYCOND
5823	ALKYDS,OTHER POLYESTERS	W 5562	17032	W 9305	24915	W 32734	63607	W 50588	132341	ALKYDES ET AUT POLYESTERS
58232	— PLATES,FILM,STRIP ETC	W 5061	16101	W 7037	23500	W 31187	61313	W 48271	127853	SOUS FORME PLAQUES,FEUIL
583	POLYMERIZATION ETC PRODS	W 15488	23483	W 19240	27682	W 79873	88148	W 65594	80861	PROD POLYMERISATION
59	CHEMICAL MATERIALS NES		104053		94941		147110		223778	MAT PROD CHIMIQUES NDA
591	PESTICIDES,DISINFECTANTS	W 8684	69045	W 9683	58738	W 12553	84162	W 21994	155948	DESINF,INSECT,FONG,HERB
5911	INSECTICIDES,FOR RETAIL	W 6533	53348	W 7729	48502	W 10350	71158	W 19856	142142	INSECTICIDES VENTE DET
6	BASIC MANUFACTURES		8362718		9098707		10737239		12382462	ART MANUFACTURES
61	LEATHER,DRESSED FUR,ETC		623140		540797		684386		716360	CUIRS,PELLETERIES
611	LEATHER	A 21669	311498	A 21635	269396	A 27722	382399	A 26303	369970	CUIRS,PEAUX PREPARES

5. General Exports F.O.B. by Commodities according to the S.I.T.C. (Rev. 2) in thousand U.S. Dollars
Exportations Générales F.O.B. par Produits d'après la C.T.C.I. (Rév. 2) en milliers de Dollars E.U.

SITC CTCI	COMMODITY	1992 WEIGHT POIDS	1992 VALUE VALEUR	1993 WEIGHT POIDS	1993 VALUE VALEUR	1994 WEIGHT POIDS	1994 VALUE VALEUR	1995 WEIGHT POIDS	1995 VALUE VALEUR	PRODUIT
6114	LEATHR BOVINE NES,EQUINE	A 5460	73771	A 5870	70801	A 8409	112591	A 8210	113479	CUIRS DE BOVINS
6116	LEATHER OF OTH HIDE,SKIN	A 10856	154831	A 9516	117602	A 11752	157816	A 12198	170766	PEAUX PREP D'AUTRES ANIMAUX
61161	LEATHER FROM GOAT,KID	A 10851	154745	A 9496	117391	A 11736	157601	A 12177	170436	PEAUX DE CAPRINS PREPAREES
612	LEATHER ETC MANUFACTURES		311643		271401		301987		346390	OUVRAGES EN CUIRS NDA
6123	PREPRD PARTS OF FOOTWEAR	W 7140	239746	W 7071	217873	W 6146	217787	W 7141	247155	PARTIES DE CHAUSSURES
62	RUBBER MANUFACTURES NES		234267		242192		273675		289412	CAOUTCHOUC MANUFACTURE
625	RUBBER TYRES, TUBES ETC	MN 35498	202692	MN 32601	204591	MN 29256	237559	MN 26093	235858	PNEUS CAOUTCHOUC VULCANISE
6252	TYRES,NEW,BUS OR LORRY	N 1514304	152071	N 1924322	160541	N 2380385	176715	N 1806897	177867	PNEUS POUR AUTOBUS,CAMIONS
64	PAPER,PAPERBOARD AND MFR		29980		34577		73031		113056	PAPIERS,CARTONS & OUVRAGES
65	TEXTILE YARN,FABRICS,ETC		2933394		2917852		3829886		4358587	FILS,TISSUS,ARTICLES TEXTILE
651	TEXTILE YARN		651337		655611		1051163		1349480	FILS TEXTILES
6513	COTTON YARN	W 150820	432857	W 161102	462180	W 211635	755141	W 260530	974204	FILS DE COTON
6516	DISCON SYN FIB BLEND YRN	W 18493	58638	W 11772	34938	W 15256	48744	W 28745	98708	FILS FIBR TEX SYNT DIS MOINS
6517	REGEN FIBRE YARN,MONOFIL	W 14966	52287	W 15645	46944	W 24387	77219	W 28863	104928	FILS TEXT ART NON VENTE DT
652	COTTON FABRICS,WOVEN	A 779593	688974	A 854392	683279	A 1018958	913253	A 944519	959775	TISSUS DE COTON
6521	GREY WOVEN COTTON FABRIC	A 439750	377081	A 482457	355628	A 555124	449513	A 473918	430676	TISSUS COT ECRUS NON MERCER
65214	GREY WOVEN COTTON NES	A 418349	363417	A 460272	343498	A 511014	430590	A 448039	413501	AUT TISSUS 85% COTON ECRUS
6522	WOVEN COTTON BLEACHD,ETC	A 339843	311893	A 371935	327651	A 463834	463740	A 470601	529099	TISSUS COTON BLANCHIS ETC
65224	BLCHED COTTON FABRIC NES	A 241030	223808	A 285072	250285	A 360711	353372	A 349369	376253	AUT TIS PLUS 85% COT BLANCHI
65225	BLCHD COTN BLEND FAB NES	A 95669	85324	A 81562	72309	A 97338	104170	A 115672	146035	AUT TIS MOINS 85% COT BLANCH
653	WOVN MAN–MADE FIB FABRIC		221700		252041		354566		420194	TISSUS FIBRES SYNTH,ARTIF
6531	CONT SYNT WEAVES NONPILE	A 85149	122447	A 103874	144632	A 155492	230999	A 169962	236118	TISSUS FIBRES SYNTH CONTINUE
65315	CONT SYN TXTL FABRIC NES	A 66419	90841	A 83447	114968	A 131714	195365	A 138140	191107	TIS PLUS 85% TEXT SYNT CONT
6534	DISC SYN BLEND FABRC NES	A 21318	34386	A 41612	59219	A 42813	66029	A 77212	124875	TISSUS FIBRES SYNTH DISCONT
654	OTH WOVEN TEXTILE FABRIC		203845		170967		203507		202675	TISSUS AUT COTON SYNT,ARTIF
6541	SILK FABRICS WOVEN	L 79677	137059	L 24122	112477	L 22825	121988	L 22029	121580	TISSUS DE SOIE
655	KNITTED,ETC FABRICS	W 11425	62231	W 11088	50019	W 14992	72924	W 13929	68817	ETOF BONNETERIE PIECES ETC
6552	OTHER KNIT ETC FAB NONEL	W 11425	62231	W 11088	50019	W 14992	72924	W 13929	68817	ETOF BON NON ELAS NON SYNT
658	TEXTILE ARTICLES NES		405505		424500		543239		646096	ART FACONNES MAT TEXTILES
6584	LINENS ETC	A 31336	31696	A 32124	30147	A 40599	42030	A 183272	187202	LINGE DE MAISON
65849	OTH FURN ART OF OTH FIBR	A 24405	25551	A 26144	25199	A 33799	35519	A 172763	177183	AUT ART AMEUBLEMENT AUT FIBR
6589	OTH TEXTILE ARTICLES NES		298646		313709		418081		351527	AUT ART EN TEXTILES NDA
65898	KNITTED ETC ARTICLES NES	A 265653	253912	A 312384	277666	A 399441	382572	A 323515	309365	ART BONNET NON ELASTIQUE
659	FLOOR COVERINGS,ETC		630202		604498		610866		624814	COUVRE–PARQUETS,TAPIS ETC
6592	CARPETS ETC KNOTTED	A 3282	173190	A 3028	152080	A 2502	136667	A 2869	159514	TAPIS POINTS NOUES,ENROULES
65921	— OF WOOL OR FINE HAIR	A 2814	154568	A 2710	144962	A 2288	133252	A 2650	155653	TAP NOUES,ENROULES LAINE
6594	WOOL CARPETS ETC NES	A 10280	252933	A 8480	208452	A 8359	205817	A 7629	186430	TAPIS DE LAINE
65942	— WOVEN	A 9900	244055	A 8073	198377	A 7929	194768	A 6930	167636	TAPIS DE LAINE TISSES
6596	OTH TXTL CARPETS ETC NES		196452		238340		264380		272415	TAPIS AUT MAT TEXT NDA
65962	— OTHR THAN KNOTTED ETC		194489		237282		260167		268533	TAPIS AUT QUE NOUES TOUF
66	NONMETAL MINERAL MFS NES		3293674		3907417		4389664		5104886	ART MIN NON METALLIQUES
661	LIME,CEMENT,BLDG PRODS	W 817165	111269	W 1884860	172032	W 1940277	230450	W 1156610	225487	CHAUX,CIMENTS MAT CONSTR
6612	CEMENT	W 731428	33968	W 1759508	72309	W 1762251	77397	W 943401	44554	CIMENTS HYDRAULIQUES
6613	BUILDING STONE ETC WORKD	W 80169	76351	W 100809	96141	W 154632	149504	W 185030	176695	PIERRES A BATIR
66132	BUILDING STONE WORKED	W 71025	73858	W 94901	94461	W 148298	147385	W 176822	173821	OUVR EN PIERRES DE TAILLE
667	PEARL,PREC–,SEMI–P STONE		3119648		3667587		4061873		4752563	PERLES, PIERRES GEMMES
6672	DIAMONDS NONINDUST,UNSET		3005757		3573652		3936920		4588928	DIAMANTS BRUTS
66729	— CUT ETC NOT SET		3003230		3573201		3935528		4582793	DIAMANTS TAILLES
6673	PREC–,SEMI–PR STONES NES		107264		86079		116279		153163	AUTRES PIERRES NON SERTIES
67	IRON AND STEEL		531543		804452		775303		1026903	FER ET ACIER
671	PIG IRON ETC	W 187697	99931	W 869454	171226	W 874883	188646	W 909400	245988	FONTE,SPIEGEL,POUDRES
6712	PIG IRN,SPIEGELEISEN ETC	W 17151	2845	W 689435	90546	W 608651	84271	W 511849	76524	FONTES BRUTES
6716	FERRO–ALLOYS	W 170149	96950	W 178906	80265	W 199761	95719	W 222518	144036	FERRO–ALLIAGES
67169	OTHER FERRO–ALLOYS	W 158857	91163	W 176784	79357	W 189105	91292	W 217759	141950	AUTRES FERRO–ALLIAGES
672	IRON,STEEL PRIMARY FORMS	W 145803	61641	W 511278	125192	W 235397	81420	W 315038	107078	LINGOTS FER,ACIER
6725	IRN,STL BLOOMS,SLABS,ETC	W 50190	18806	W 414882	98836	W 141791	50084	W 225260	69874	BLOOMS,BILLETTES FER ACIER
67255	OTH ALLOY STL BLOOMS ETC	W 32751	8348	W 367663	82934	W 104900	25571	W 105446	27443	BLOOMS ETC AUT AC ALLIES
673	IRON,STEEL SHAPES ETC	W 568867	201133	W 624322	202874	W 418811	167374	W 420559	217095	BARRES,PROFIL FER,ACIER
6732	IRON,STEEL BARS ETC	W 455231	155734	W 349683	117392	W 247744	106713	W 272298	146185	BARRES FER,ACIER
67322	HIGH CARBON STL BARS ETC	W 211450	63093	W 92561	26279	W 43303	12614	W 41619	12691	BARRES ACIER FIN CARBONE
674	IRN,STL UNIV,PLATE,SHEET	W 103374	56765	W 396501	165695	W 338542	147638	W 340151	202395	LARGES PLATS,TOLES
6747	TINNED PLATES,SHEETS	W 25106	16858	W 180681	71474	W 112098	57895	W 69222	40404	TOLES ETAMEES EN ACIER
678	IRON,STL TUBES,PIPES,ETC	W 72268	48630	W 119597	71559	W 114974	77406	W 165576	95008	TUBES,TUYAUX EN FONTE,FER
68	NON–FERROUS METALS		209974		131564		175537		159032	METAUX NON FERREUX
684	ALUMINIUM	W 119095	184966	W 83118	115354	W 88739	144169	W 62584	127184	ALUMINIUM
6841	ALUMINIUM,ALLOYS,UNWRGHT	W 102441	146367	W 64487	75645	W 66900	92736	W 41298	68201	ALUMINIUM,ALLIAGES BRUTS
69	METAL MANUFACTURES NES		492481		473033		497268		579776	ART MANUFACT EN METAL NDA
695	TOOLS		91295		91314		90469		119010	OUTILS A MAIN
6953	OTHER HAND TOOLS		69773		75654		69167		93188	AUTRES OUTILS A MAIN
697	BASE MTL HOUSEHOLD EQUIP		72993		78582		98661		118167	ART MENAGE MET COMMUNS
6974	BASE MTL DMSTC ARTIC NES		63884		71416		89501		109141	ARTICLES NDA FONTE,FER,ETC
699	BASE METAL MFRS NES	W 238239	181726	W 127232	147230	W 90928	148038	W 69981	180048	ART MANUFACTURES MET NDA
6997	IRON,STEEL ARTICLES NES	W 201504	93290	W 81422	51734	W 47470	38235	W 25516	43776	OUV FONTE,FER,ACIER NDA
69979	IRN,STL MANUFACTURES NES	W 200840	92654	W 81005	51392	W 47070	37724	W 20039	41529	AUT OUVRAGES EN FER NDA
7	MACHINES,TRANSPORT EQUIP		1449879		1508958		1882839		2370817	MACHINES MATERIEL TRANSPORT
71	POWER GENERATING EQUIPMT		156046		171721		149698		172920	MACHINES GENERATRICES
713	INTRNL COMBUS PSTN ENGIN		103624		112686		106958		117869	MOTEURS EXPL COMB INT, PIECE
72	MACHS FOR SPCL INDUSTRYS		176643		155739		212407		240907	MAC SPECIALES POUR INDUST
724	TEXTILE,LEATHER MACHNRY		65693		58266		73526		70806	MACH POUR INDUSTRIE TEXTILE
74	GENRL INDUSTRL MACHY NES		149291		157656		186578		209798	MACH APP INDUSTRIE
75	OFFICE MACHNES,ADP EQUIP		76454		115625		156683		224426	MACH BUREAU TRAIT AUTOM
752	AUTOMTIC DATA PROC EQUIP	N 453704	33798	N 1077336	59497		83412		94179	MACH TRAIT INFORMATION
759	OFFICE,ADP MCH PTS,ACCES	W 440	35634	W 447	52931	W 477	67312	W 967	122884	PIECES DU 751 ET 752
7599	ACCTG,ETC,ADP MCH PTS,AC	W 297	33863	W 357	52122	W 391	66355	W 823	121258	PIECES DU 751 ET 752
76	TELECOMM,SOUND EQUIPMENT		43032		48241		69698		137898	EQUIPMENT DE TELECOM
77	ELECTRIC MACHNRY NES ETC		209440		228403		299186		430403	MACH APP ELECT NDA
776	TRANSISTORS,VALVES,ETC		23393		25287		34469		102433	LAMPES,TUBES,VALVES
778	ELECTRICAL MACHINERY NES		60737		72589		88815		106192	AUTRES MACH ELECT NDA
78	ROAD VEHICLES		572000		568008		717330		876845	VEHICULES ROUTIERS
781	PASS MOTOR VEH EXC BUSES	N 19537	84502		89684	N 26776	144703	N 32255	181373	AUTO TRANSPORT PERSONNES
784	MOTOR VEH PRTS,ACCES NES		157361		185162		251370		276676	PIECES 722,781,782,783
7841	MOTOR VEHICLE CHASSIS	N 3056	31674	N 7588	66854	N 11747	119507	N 12384	108333	CHASSIS 722,781,782,783
7849	OTHER MOTOR VEHCL PARTS	W 40528	118806	W 43505	114279	W 41807	127173	W 47877	162765	PIECES 722,781,782,783
785	CYCLES,ETC MOTRZD OR NOT		211077		227831		229373		322949	MOTOCYCLES SCOOTERS
7853	INVAL CARR, PTS OF 785		139751	W 90804	128606	W 71331	111538		189061	FAUTEUILS INVALIDES,PIECES
78539	PARTS,ACCES NES OF 785	W 90093	139742	W 90804	128606	W 71331	111538	W 98060	189038	PIECES DU 785
8	MISC MANUFACTURED GOODS		4164004		4293361		5406239		6045125	ART MANUFACTURES DIVERS
831	*TRAVEL GOODS,HANDBAGS	MN 61327	215181	MN 72194	198710	MN 81384	253659	MN 86914	309235	ARTICLES DE VOYAGE ETC
83101	HANDBAGS NES	MN 27972	116768	MN 42501	115401	MN 41387	142397	MN 42151	156421	SACS A MAIN
83109	OTHER TRAVEL BAGS,CASES	MN 32402	86112	MN 28890	71484	MN 39075	98370	MN 43861	133849	AUT CONTENANTS SIMILAIRES
84	CLOTHING AND ACCESSORIES		3105919		2976916		3711939		4124071	VETEMENTS

5. General Exports F.O.B. by Commodities according to the S.I.T.C. (Rev. 2) in thousand U.S. Dollars
Exportations Générales F.O.B. par Produits d'après la C.T.C.I. (Rév. 2) en milliers de Dollars E.U.

SITC CTCI	COMMODITY	1992		1993		1994		1995		PRODUIT
		WEIGHT POIDS	VALUE VALEUR	WEIGHT POIDS	VALUE VALEUR	WEIGHT POIDS	VALUE VALEUR	WEIGHT POIDS	VALUE VALEUR	
842	MENS OUTERWEAR NOT KNIT	MN 16478	94860	MN 19644	103593	MN 27629	156827	MN 33824	163062	VET DESSUS POUR HOMMES
843	WOMENS OUTERWEAR NONKNIT	MN 225288	1217425	MN 217389	1076736	MN 252102	1409207	MN 306286	1568750	VET DESSUS FEMMES MAT TEX
8433	— DRESSES	MN 24617	207958	MN 26628	199836	MN 31850	285974	MN 42433	374012	ROBES EN MAT–TEXTILES
8434	— SKIRTS	MN 19436	112332	MN 24093	123190	MN 35323	193900	MN 42479	202378	JUPES EN MAT TEXTILES
8435	— BLOUSES	MN 130741	623324	MN 110820	491898	MN 126334	617666	MN 151846	661166	BLOUSES FEM MAT TEXTILES
8439	— OTHER OUTER GARMENTS	MN 41145	187810	MN 47356	188173	MN 49726	214612	MN 61023	241902	AUT VET DES FEM MAT TEXT
844	UNDER GARMENTS NOT KNIT	MN 113403	523428	MN 123560	522863	MN 155846	724586	MN 170387	827727	VETEMENT DESSOUS MAT TEX
8441	— MENS SHIRTS	MN 100292	481123	MN 105115	464291	MN 134461	658966	MN 145663	755020	CHEMISES HOMMES MAT TEXT
84411	—— OF COTTON	MN 80293	404682	MN 88271	414697	MN 113029	604491	MN 130243	714125	CHEMISES HOMMES DE COTON
84412	—— OF SYNTHETIC FIBRES	MN 19999	76442	MN 16844	49594	MN 21433	54475	MN 15420	40895	CHEMISES HOMMES FIB SYNT
845	OUTERWEAR KNIT NONELASTC	MN 87582	312774	MN 103639	325304	MN 98344	338536	MN 106807	348717	VET DESSOUS,ACCES BONNET
8451	— JERSEYS,PULLOVERS ETC	MN 26061	109766	MN 27023	111265	MN 25071	116011	MN 26247	118842	CHANDAILS,PULL–OVERS ETC
8459	— OTHER,CLTHG ACCESRYS	MN 52502	153230	MN 66850	163486	MN 65205	175627	MN 73086	185435	AUT VET DESSUS DE BONNE
846	UNDER GARMENTS KNITTED	MN 1165117	408709	MN 197268	417084	MN 183614	480265	MN 218878	608245	SOUS VETS DE BONNETERIE
8462	— OF COTTON NON ELASTIC	MN 1055317	131923	MN 78996	149327	MN 78179	167190	MN 92832	213682	SOUS–VET BONNET COTON
84629	—— OTHER	MN 1055317	131923	MN 78996	149327	MN 78179	167190	MN 92832	213682	AUT SOUS–VET BONNET COTON
8463	— OF SYNTH FBR NONELAST	MN 108804	275438	MN 117486	266929	MN 104308	312082	MN 124460	393179	SOUS–VET BONNET FIB SYNT
84632	—— MENS SHIRTS	MN 104286	273115	MN 114457	265258	MN 101362	310431	MN 118424	389823	CHEMISES DE BON FIB SYNMT
847	TEXTILE CLTHNG ACCES NES		116534		140507		172649		148116	ACCES VET MAT TEXT NDA
8471	— NOT KNITTED		112398		135095		165267		139712	ACCES VET MAT TEX NON BON
84712	SHAWLS,VEILS ETC,NOT KNT	MN 62047	101817	MN 86406	125049	MN 105428	154009	MN 88735	126908	ECHARPES ETC MAT TEXT
848	HEADGEAR,NONTXTL CLOTHNG		432190		390829		429870		459453	VET ACCES MAT AUT QUE TEX
8481	LEATHER CLOTHES,ACCESSOR	MN 13992	415669	MN 16892	369139	MN 15191	407312	MN 17217	435206	VET ACCES MAT CUIR ARTIF
851	*FOOTWEAR	MP 28244	232700	MP 37688	279999	MP 39773	345729	MP 38285	345059	CHAUSSURES
85102	FOOTWEAR LEATHER	MP 26114	224277	MP 35346	272924	MP 36688	336467	MP 34689	339158	CHAUS SEMELLES EN CUIR
89	MISC MANUFCTRD GOODS NES		524642		736934		971493		1126950	ART MANUFACTURES DIVERS
893	ARTICLES OF PLASTIC NES		72394		192266		217301		238375	OUVRAGES EN MAT DIVIS 58
8931	PLSTC PACKG CONTNRS,LIDS	W 6759	14458	W 19998	82407	W 18942	55921	W 23147	46724	ART TRANSP EMBALLAGE ETC
8939	MISC PLASTIC ARTICLES	W 18769	57135	W 27355	108612	W 36736	160639	W 35603	190630	ART DIVERS EN MAT DIV 58
89399	OTHR PLASTC ARTICLES NES	W 15236	49640	W 20419	95864	W 29107	143287	W 26785	173331	AUT OUV MAT DIV 58
897	GOLD,SILVER WARE,JEWELRY		315478		336220		446640		510547	BIJOUTERIE,ORFEVRERIE
8973	PREC JEWLRY,GLD–SILVWARE		305849		320519		431640		495412	BIJOUX OR,ARGENT ORFEVRE
89731	PRECIOUS METAL JEWELLERY		303463		317804		429880		493518	ART BIJOUTERIE,JOAILLER
898	MUSICAL INSTRUMENTS,PTS		40163		75944		128686		164234	INSTRUMENTS DE MUSIQUE
8983	SOUND RECRDNG TAPE,DISCS	MN 12979	34777	MN 35035	69566	MN 47157	120378		154899	SUPPORTS SON POUR 763
89832	RECORDED DISCS,TAPES ETC	N 5609564	22340	MN 13786	47432	MN 20320	87890		126449	DISQUES,PHONO,BANDES
9	GOODS NOT CLASSD BY KIND		356032		362615		445298		511180	ART TRANSACT NON CLASSES
931	*SPECIAL TRANSACTIONS		355882		362221		444998		510925	TRANS.SPECIALES

1. HISTORICAL SERIES, 1961–1996 SPECIAL TRADE, IMPORTS C.I.F., EXPORTS F.O.B.
SERIES HISTORIQUES, 1961–1996 COMMERCE SPECIAL, IMPORTATIONS C.A.F., EXPORTATIONS F.O.B

YEAR ANNEE	VALUE IN MILLION U.S. DOLLARS VALEUR EN MILLION U.S. DOLLARS MERCHANDISE –MARCHANDISE IMPORTS	EXPORTS	GOLD –OR IMPORTS	EXPORTS	CONVERSION FACTORS FACTEURS DE CONVERSION CENTS E.U. PAR IMPORTS	EXPORTS	INDEX NUMBERS –INDICES QUANTUM IMPORTS	EXPORTS	UNIT VALUE VALEUR UNITAIRE IMPORTS	EXPORTS
1961	796.20	788.20								
1962	647.00	663.70								
1963	521.40	697.90								
1964	679.90	724.20								
1965	694.70	707.70								
1966	526.70	678.70								
1967	649.20	665.40								
1968	715.80	730.70						33		8
1969	780.70	853.70						31		10
1970	1001.50	1108.10						39		16
1971	1102.80	1233.60						47		16
1972	1561.70	1777.70						56		19
1973	2729.10	3210.80						68		28
1974	3841.90	7426.30						70		61
1975	4769.80	7102.50						73		64
1976	5673.10	8546.50						83		67
1977	6230.30	10852.60						95		75
1978	6690.40	11643.20						100		77
1979	7202.30	15590.10						97		107
1980	10834.40	23950.40						92		157
1981	13272.20	25164.50						75		157
1982	16859.90	22328.30						72		153
1983	16351.80	21145.90						87		136
1984	13882.10	21887.90						81		133
1985	10259.10	18586.70						91		125
1986	10718.40	16075.00						98		87
1987	12890.70	17135.01						94		88
1988	13248.50	19465.01						93		82
1989	16360.00	22159.50						102		82
1990	21837.01	25673.90						100		100
1991	25868.80	29142.00						128		88
1992	27279.60	33966.90						141		84
1993	28327.81	36823.01						148		77
1994	31983.01	40055.01						163		97
1995	40630.00	45417.01						171		111
1996	42929.01	49814.00						179		117

2. IMPORTS BY BROAD ECONOMIC CATEGORY AND EXPORTS BY INDUSTRIAL ORIGIN. (PERCENTAGE OF TOTAL VALUE)
IMPORTATIONS PAR CATEGORIES ECONOMIQUES ET EXPORTATIONS PAR BRANCHE D'ACTIVITE.(EN POURCENTAGE DE LA VALEUR TOTALE)

IMPORTS – IMPORTATIONS

	1990	1991	1992	1993	1994	1995	1996
TOTAL IMPORTS–IMPORTATIONS TOTALES	100.	100.	100.	100.	100.	100.	100.
1 FOOD BEV–ALIMENTATION BOISSONS	3.9	4.1	5.2	4.7	5.5	6.9	8.6
11 PRIMARY–PRODUITS DE BASE	2.5	2.7	2.9	3.2	3.8	3.7	4.6
111 FOR INDUSTRY–POUR L'INDUSTRIE	2.2	2.3	2.4	2.6	3.1	3.0	3.9
112 FOR HOUSEHOLDS–POUR LES MENAGES	0.4	0.3	0.5	0.6	0.7	0.7	0.7
12 PROCESSED–PRODUITS ELABORES	1.4	1.5	2.4	1.5	1.8	3.2	4.0
121 FOR INDUSTRY–POUR L'INDUSTRIE	0.8	0.4	1.0	0.6	0.4	0.7	0.8
122 FOR HOUSEHOLDS–POUR LES MENAGES	0.6	1.1	1.3	0.9	1.3	2.5	3.3
2 IND SUPPLIES–APPROV INDUSTRIELS	41.4	38.9	40.9	41.9	41.9	42.4	39.0
21 PRIMARY–PRODUITS DE BASE	5.8	5.8	5.7	5.5	5.6	6.0	5.4
22 PROCESSED–PRODUITS ELABORES	35.6	33.1	35.2	36.4	36.3	36.4	33.6
3 FUELS–COMBUSTIBLES	8.6	8.7	7.5	7.5	7.5	7.3	8.5
31 PRIMARY–PRODUITS DE BASE	5.5	4.6	3.9	3.3	3.4	3.3	3.6
32 PROCESSED–PRODUITS ELABORES	3.1	4.1	3.6	4.1	4.1	4.0	4.9
321 MOTOR SPIRIT–ESSENCE	3.0	4.0	3.4	0.1	0.0	0.2	0.1
322 OTHER–AUTRES	0.1	0.1	0.2	4.0	4.0	3.8	4.8
4 MACHINERY–EQUIPEMENT	32.5	36.0	36.6	35.1	30.8	29.6	32.0
41 CAPITAL EQUIPMENT–MACHINES	29.2	32.8	33.1	31.4	27.1	26.4	28.8
42 PARTS–PIECES ACCESSOIRES	3.2	3.2	3.5	3.7	3.7	3.2	3.1
5 TRANSPORT–TRANSPORT	11.1	10.0	7.1	8.4	11.9	11.1	9.6
51 PASSENGER CARS–AUTOMOBILES	1.6	0.9	0.6	0.7	0.3	0.4	0.5
52 OTHER–AUTRES	2.9	3.2	1.9	1.8	2.5	1.8	1.5
521 INDUSTRIAL–INDUSTRIELS	2.9	3.2	1.9	1.8	2.5	1.8	1.5
522 NON INDUSTRIAL–NON INDUSTRIEL	0.0	0.0	0.0	0.0	0.0	0.0	0.0
53 PARTS–PIECES ACCESSOIRES	6.5	5.9	4.6	5.9	9.1	8.9	7.6
6 CONSUM GOODS–BIENS CONSOMMATION	2.2	2.0	2.0	2.1	2.1	2.3	2.1
61 DURABLE–DURABLES	1.0	0.7	0.7	0.6	0.6	0.7	0.6
62 SEMI DURABLE–SEMI DURABLES	0.7	0.7	0.8	0.9	0.8	0.8	0.8
63 NON DURABLE–NON DURABLES	0.5	0.5	0.6	0.7	0.7	0.7	0.7
7 GOODS NES–BIENS NDA	0.3	0.3	0.5	0.4	0.3	0.4	0.2

EXPORTS – EXPORTATIONS

	1990	1991	1992	1993	1994	1995	1996
TOTAL EXPORTS–EXPORTATIONS TOTALES	100.	100.	100.	100.	100.	100.	100.
1 AGRICULTURE	11.6	11.1	9.6	9.7	11.1	11.3	10.3
2 MINING QUARRY–INDUS EXTRACTIVES	41.2	37.2	32.3	28.2	26.6	26.3	26.7
3 MANUFACTURING–IND MANUFACTUR	47.2	51.7	58.1	62.1	62.3	62.5	63.1
31 FOOD BEV TOBACCO–ALIM BOISS TAB	3.3	3.9	4.1	4.2	5.2	4.8	5.1
32 TEXTILES–INDUSTRIES TEXTILES	13.5	17.1	21.5	20.9	18.6	17.5	16.7
33 WOOD & PRODUCTS–BOIS & PRODUITS	13.0	12.6	12.4	15.0	13.0	11.0	10.3
34 PAPER & PRODUCTS–PAPIER & PRODT	0.9	1.1	1.2	1.5	1.8	3.2	2.8
35 CHEMICALS–INDUSTRIES CHIMIQUES	8.1	7.7	7.5	6.5	6.7	8.3	8.9
36 NON METAL MIN–MIN NON METAL	0.9	0.8	1.0	0.9	0.8	0.8	0.8
37 BASIC METAL–IND METAL BASE	3.4	3.1	2.5	2.1	2.4	3.0	2.5
38 METAL MANUF–MANUF METAL	3.3	4.6	6.9	9.5	11.2	11.9	13.5
39 OTH MANUF IND–AUTRES MANUF	0.6	0.8	1.1	1.7	2.7	2.0	2.5

3. TRADE BY PRINCIPAL COUNTRIES OF PRODUCTION AND CONSUMPTION (VALUE IN THOUSAND U.S. DOLLARS)
ECHANGES SELON LES PRINCIPAUX PAYS DE PRODUCTION ET DE COMSOMMATION (VALEUR EN MILLIERS DE DOLLARS EU)

COUNTRIES–PAYS	SPECIAL IMPORTS C.I.F. IMPORTATIONS SPECIALES C.A.F				
	1992	1993	1994	1995	1996
World	27279623	28327766	31983499	40628732	42928495
Africa	213274	140467	331471	607863	642931
Americas	4769693	4289867	4839542	6654363	6934503
Northern America	4281771	3664512	4084626	5566572	5845429
LAIA	478876	609791	714951	1071730	1061889
CACM	427	4625	18838	1914	2785
Caribbean	4221	3018	1940	738	526
Rest of America	4399	7921	19187	13408	23873
As.ex F.USSR	14273273	14997856	17725718	21761798	22239914
Eur.x F.USSR	6369338	7169029	7091260	8885577	9879771
EU	5977487	6650672	6612071	8175231	9233561
EFTA	287742	411459	340004	488956	477461
East Europe	83115	100792	132620	207843	142498
Other Europe	9494	4445	4340	11810	19820
Former USSR	46608	96495	220303	438111	378439
Oceania	1552327	1575425	1732766	2225046	2782627
Japan/Japon	6013748	6248429	7740111	9216822	8504005
USA/Etats–Unis d'Amer	3822440	3254516	3587850	4755908	5059812
Germany/Allemagne	2141053	2072406	2472725	2819188	3001390
Korea, Republic of	1894104	2103064	2165933	2451303	2411397
Singapore/Singapour	1670684	1793268	1877053	2367471	2875267
Australia/Australie	1412962	1399374	1541965	2015539	2535081
China/Chine	751517	935983	1369028	1495223	1597560
France, Monac	816266	853385	788272	1063570	1005985
United Kingdom	719364	782014	710107	902497	1117796
Italy/Italie	558177	523225	667823	790960	1212111
Saudi Arabia	852036	351122	680210	943289	664594
Malaysia/Malaisie	524574	517405	578772	766964	823731
Netherlands/Pays–Bas	506461	626036	563735	842098	492986
Canada	459331	409996	496776	810664	785617
Thailand/Thaïlande	344658	235347	406186	737108	1095408
India/Inde	215549	335400	318275	478847	866163
Sweden/Suède	267610	455506	356111	354075	718664
Belgium–Luxembourg	324288	339772	291966	401120	393616
Switz.Liecht	253015	333362	266164	380625	370152
Brazil/Brésil	174609	288287	313457	413727	412759
Iran (Islamic Rp. of)	124751	502983	248702	257027	453562
Austria/Autriche	203575	277675	186835	315276	303798
Hong Kong	228963	247150	240534	274555	262334
Finland/Finlande	105842	265526	241274	252002	330823
Russian Federation	46608	96495	220303	438111	378439
Spain/Espagne	178031	261822	174081	219288	345337
Chile/Chili	112799	134658	197586	291261	260175
New Zealand	135919	161041	156230	205663	244528
Argentina/Argentine	128142	107062	110802	224762	213907
Denmark/Danemark	123993	158441	105878	105148	190983
Kuwait/ Koweït	389	70136	176750	195940	201959
Viet Nam	33159	39067	78841	156825	204366
Pakistan	99948	59295	32338	102630	188984
Norway, SVD, JM	34726	78098	73839	108331	107309
Mexico/Mexique	56099	58222	41625	92453	113936
Nigeria/Nigéria	610	709	26247	172936	149303
Philippines	52158	57145	65260	81250	89560
Jordan/Jordanie	59802	35408	30451	54570	66418
Turkey/Turquie	19841	17161	73722	47128	71947
Poland/Pologne	28867	25279	44848	50821	56690
Myanmar	10981	15187	37174	104972	32625
Greece/Grèce	7482	12257	26355	61381	76143
United Arab Emirates	9661	9172	53436	56421	40478
So. Africa Customs Un					153930
Libyan Arab Jamahiriya	222	14739	54510	47542	36173
Czech Republic		47901	38392	27629	34782
Ireland/Irlande	23340	21107	22475	40631	39301
Peru/Pérou	776	15330	40486	33133	41088
Korea Dem People's Rp	23395	16750	24834	27336	30774
Cote d'Ivoire	10415	17025	17306	36412	37302

COUNTRIES–PAYS	SPECIAL EXPORTS F.O.B. EXPORTATIONS SPECIALES F.O.B.				
	1992	1993	1994	1995	1996
Monde	33966997	36822772	40053434	45417982	49814716
Afrique	418879	460813	582897	621322	639227
Amériques	5036264	6002138	6710898	7439952	7939228
Amérique du Nord	4708138	5533976	6150256	6680713	7162740
ALAI	148219	270182	363414	524587	564419
MCAC	3648	7931	5558	7648	8704
Caraïbes	50358	37312	33747	21565	21971
Autre Amérique	125902	152738	157923	205439	181395
Asie l'URSS exclus	22533825	23772833	25630092	29060952	31685109
Europe l'URSS exclus	5074130	5585389	6241013	7067058	8069639
UE	4929116	5392082	5949393	6760271	7723270
AELE	54001	73560	84131	86779	94549
Europe de l'Est	83240	106128	173331	190988	211964
Autre de l'Europe	4330	4445	21670	18193	30354
Ancienne URSS	69874	125230	90691	134180	133964
Océanie	831037	875379	796294	1094312	1347512
Japan/Japon	10760524	11171991	10929041	12288297	12885234
USA/Etats–Unis d'Amer	4419105	5229797	5828564	6321714	6794657
Singapore/Singapour	3313543	3371977	4149658	3766716	4564605
Korea, Republic of	2083284	2220458	2592972	2916749	3281014
China/Chine	1396437	1249494	1321675	1741718	2057472
Netherlands/Pays–Bas	1100287	1086425	1323452	1452361	1666577
Hong Kong	881102	900361	1321494	1657059	1624832
Germany/Allemagne	977797	1178175	1263444	1381587	1488977
United Kingdom	843811	1004889	1038150	1128649	1192939
Australia/Australie	746125	773672	705368	915231	1201525
Malaysia/Malaisie	487535	585989	738495	986567	1109734
Italy/Italie	582846	614846	660672	783730	743573
Thailand/Thaïlande	352799	467656	401344	702880	822636
Saudi Arabia	583055	556345	413122	448180	515614
United Arab Emirates	376901	490292	522567	519056	601210
France, Monac	494700	499854	426141	519776	564111
Belgium–Luxembourg	401219	365740	409275	538694	681646
Spain/Espagne	254577	332722	453907	534604	812663
Philippines	181307	285029	365060	590256	688407
Canada	289032	304179	321691	358999	368083
India/Inde	69591	99926	277747	381024	530974
Viet Nam	190665	206777	245972	287585	364073
Egypt/Egypte	164132	175200	141114	195075	180932
Panama	113191	130729	140978	183751	152251
Pakistan	80808	122570	142396	119322	124798
Mexico/Mexique	87323	140354	144310	88412	127766
Russian Federation	69874	125230	90691	134180	133964
Denmark/Danemark	96790	97728	109678	111328	125821
Brazil/Brésil	9977	40961	75805	201455	210359
Bangladesh	88626	100976	85657	90303	117067
Sri Lanka	60432	85108	80825	102959	107002
Turkey/Turquie	45621	77375	64730	126504	113570
Poland/Pologne	39671	60756	98733	105440	117139
Algeria/Algérie	41631	64585	186394	83157	27836
New Zealand	37416	61313	51649	129811	100742
Sweden/Suède	45107	46270	47905	50317	158575
Iran (Islamic Rp. of)	54981	14721	30870	132216	98891
Kuwait/ Koweït	45242	55857	64229	64834	73317
Greece/Grèce	28935	45448	63131	78942	85633
Chile/Chili	20900	32440	47745	104390	88159
Switz.Liecht	39530	52017	58202	56841	63037
Democratic Kampuchea	23005	39647	44202	79983	60369
Nigeria/Nigéria	47858	53896	33142	50459	54939
Jordan/Jordanie	25111	44631	37703	73077	53644
Yemen/Yémen	46575	61633	34719	49537	40343
Myanmar	14208	39750	35224	60419	78018
So. Africa Customs Un	5095		23712	85662	107807
Ireland/Irlande	46276	40529	37459	36724	37554
Argentina/Argentine	11593	28396	45231	47933	65142
Austria/Autriche	24005	32123	45826	52626	37775

(VALUE AS PERCENTAGE OF WORLD TOTAL)(VALEURS EN POURCENTAGE DU TOTAL MONDIAL)

	1987	1988	1989	1990	1991	1992	1993	1994	1995	1996
Africa	1.2	1.5	1.2	0.8	0.8	0.8	0.5	1.0	1.5	1.5
Americas	15.6	16.9	18.2	15.8	16.8	17.5	15.1	15.1	16.4	16.2
Northern America	13.9	15.2	15.5	13.4	14.5	15.7	12.9	12.8	13.7	13.6
LAIA	1.6	1.6	2.6	2.3	2.2	1.8	2.2	2.2	2.6	2.5
CACM	0.0	0.0	0.0	0.1	0.0	0.0	0.0	0.1	0.0	0.0
Caribbean	0.0	0.1	0.1	0.0	0.0	0.0	0.0	0.0	0.0	0.0
Rest of America	0.0	0.0	0.0	0.0	0.0	0.0	0.0	0.1	0.0	0.1
As.ex F.USSR	55.3	53.2	53.7	54.8	54.6	52.3	52.9	55.4	53.6	51.8
Eur.x F.USSR	23.1	22.7	19.5	22.1	21.7	23.3	25.3	22.2	21.9	23.0
EU	21.3	20.5	17.6	20.1	20.0	21.9	23.5	20.7	20.1	21.5
EFTA	1.1	1.6	1.1	1.3	1.2	1.1	1.5	1.1	1.2	1.1
East Europe	0.6	0.5	0.7	0.5	0.4	0.3	0.4	0.4	0.5	0.3
Other Europe	0.1	0.1	0.1	0.1	0.1	0.0	0.0	0.0	0.0	0.0
Former USSR	0.1	0.3	0.3	0.2	0.2	0.2	0.3	0.7	1.1	0.9
Oceania	4.4	5.1	6.3	6.0	5.8	5.7	5.6	5.4	5.5	6.5
Japan/Japon	29.1	25.6	23.0	24.3	24.5	22.0	22.1	24.2	22.7	19.8
USA/Etats–Unis d'Amer	11.4	13.1	13.6	11.5	13.1	14.0	11.5	11.2	11.7	11.8
Germany/Allemagne	6.8	6.7	5.6	6.9	8.0	7.8	7.3	7.7	6.9	7.0
Korea, Republic of	2.2	2.8	3.4	4.5	5.6	6.9	7.4	6.8	6.0	5.6
Singapore/Singapour	7.7	6.8	6.9	5.8	6.6	6.1	6.3	5.9	5.8	6.7
Australia/Australie	3.7	4.4	5.7	5.4	5.3	5.2	4.9	4.8	5.0	5.9
China/Chine	3.3	3.3	3.2	3.0	3.2	2.8	3.3	4.3	3.7	3.7
France, Monac	3.2	3.5	2.5	2.9	2.1	3.0	3.0	2.5	2.6	2.3
United Kingdom	2.6	2.6	2.2	2.0	2.3	2.6	2.8	2.2	2.2	2.6
Italy/Italie	1.9	1.9	2.1	1.9	2.1	2.0	1.8	2.1	1.9	2.8

	1987	1988	1989	1990	1991	1992	1993	1994	1995	1996
Afrique	0.9	1.4	1.0	0.8	1.4	1.2	1.3	1.5	1.4	1.3
Amériques	20.4	16.8	16.5	14.0	13.3	14.8	16.3	16.8	16.4	15.9
Amérique du Nord	20.1	16.5	16.2	13.6	12.6	13.9	15.0	15.4	14.7	14.4
ALAI	0.1	0.1	0.2	0.3	0.3	0.4	0.7	0.9	1.2	1.1
MCAC	0.0	0.0	0.0	0.0	0.0	0.0	0.0	0.0	0.0	0.0
Caraïbes	0.1	0.0	0.0	0.0	0.1	0.1	0.1	0.1	0.0	0.0
Autre Amérique	0.0	0.1	0.1	0.1	0.3	0.4	0.4	0.4	0.5	0.4
Asie l'URSS exclus	66.4	67.9	68.6	70.4	69.3	66.3	64.6	64.0	64.0	63.6
Europe l'URSS exclus	9.8	11.9	11.3	12.5	13.6	14.9	15.2	15.6	15.6	16.2
UE	9.2	11.4	10.7	12.0	13.1	14.5	14.6	14.9	14.9	15.5
AELE	0.1	0.1	0.1	0.2	0.2	0.2	0.2	0.2	0.2	0.2
Europe de l'Est	0.5	0.4	0.4	0.3	0.3	0.2	0.3	0.4	0.4	0.4
Autre de l'Europe	0.1	0.0	0.1	0.1	0.1	0.0	0.0	0.1	0.0	0.1
Ancienne URSS	0.5	0.2	0.5	0.3	0.1	0.2	0.3	0.2	0.3	0.3
Océanie	2.1	1.7	2.0	1.9	2.3	2.4	2.4	2.0	2.4	2.7
Japan/Japon	43.1	41.7	42.2	42.5	36.9	31.7	30.3	27.3	27.1	25.9
USA/Etats–Unis d'Amer	19.5	16.0	15.8	13.1	12.0	13.0	14.2	14.6	13.9	13.6
Singapore/Singapour	8.5	8.6	8.1	7.4	8.3	9.8	9.2	10.4	8.3	9.2
Korea, Republic of	3.9	4.4	4.2	5.3	6.7	6.1	6.0	6.5	6.4	6.6
China/Chine	2.0	2.6	2.6	3.2	4.1	4.1	3.4	3.3	3.8	4.1
Netherlands/Pays–Bas	2.9	3.4	3.1	2.8	2.9	3.2	3.0	3.3	3.2	3.3
Hong Kong	2.4	2.9	2.5	2.4	2.4	2.6	2.4	3.3	3.6	3.3
Germany/Allemagne	2.1	2.4	2.2	2.9	3.1	2.9	3.2	3.2	3.0	3.0
United Kingdom	1.2	1.8	1.7	2.0	2.2	2.5	2.7	2.6	2.5	2.4
Australia/Australie	1.8	1.5	1.7	1.6	2.2	2.2	2.1	1.8	2.0	2.4

4. Special Imports C.I.F. by Commodities according to the S.I.T.C. (Rev. 2) in thousand U.S. Dollars
Importations Spéciales C.A.F. par Produits d'après la C.T.C.I. (Rév. 2) en milliers de Dollars E.U.

SITC CTCI	COMMODITY	1993 WEIGHT POIDS	1993 VALUE VALEUR	1994 WEIGHT POIDS	1994 VALUE VALEUR	1995 WEIGHT POIDS	1995 VALUE VALEUR	1996 WEIGHT POIDS	1996 VALUE VALEUR	PRODUIT
	ALL COMMODITIES		28327766		31983499		40628732		42928495	TOUS PRODUITS
0	FOOD AND LIVE ANIMALS		1340431		1895605		3020020		3926518	ALIMENTS,ANIMAUX VIVANTS
001	*LIVE ANIMALS FOR FOOD	W 14360	27617	W 21709	56037	W 78012	126521	W 122770	204463	ANIMAUX VIVANTS
0011	BOVINE SPECIES,LIVE	W 14183	20532	W 21507	45181	W 76346	112313	W 122394	190420	ESPECE BOVINE
00119	— OTHR THAN FR BREEDING	W 11942	17113	W 21070	43568	W 75042	109146	W 121060	187405	BOVINS NON REPRODUCTEURS
02	DAIRY PRODCTS,BIRDS'EGGS		123628		122891		223335		191823	PRODUITS LAITIERS,OEUFS
022	MILK AND CREAM	W 53829	96517	W 63425	97014	W 91290	178855	W 75041	150312	LAIT ET CREME
0224	MILK,CREAM PRESERVED ETC	W 44760	82527	W 54360	84419	W 77323	153843	W 63011	127588	LAIT,CREME CONS,CONC
02242	MILK DRY,1.5% FAT OR LES	W 36637	70277	W 44060	74200	W 60692	136161	W 45916	104769	LAIT POUDRE INF 1.5%
04	CEREALS AND PREPARATIONS		546002		926567		1551466		2002460	CEREALES ET PRODUITS
041	WHEAT ETC UNMILLED	W 2525520	442005	W 3297139	579681	W 4054202	803409	W 4116261	1050364	FROMENT,EPEAUTRE
0412	OTHER WHEAT ETC UNMILLED	W 2525520	442005	W 3295022	579060	W 4054202	803409	W 4111842	1048931	AUTRE FROMENT NON MOULU
042	RICE	W 24317	7196	W 633048	157322	W 1807875	514476	W 2149758	766316	RIZ
0422	RICE SEMI–MILLED,MILLED	W 18909	4856	W 622426	153294	W 1778967	504410	W 2130032	759580	RIZ POLI,GLACE INCL BRISURES
04221	RICE MILLED UNBROKEN	W 4743	1836	W 271802	69792	W 1309510	375172	W 2040203	731055	RIZ POLI,GLACE EXCL BRISURES
04222	RICE BROKEN	W 14166	3020	W 350624	83503	W 469457	129238	W 89828	28525	BRISURES DE RIZ
044	MAIZE UNMILLED	W 494470	68037	W 1118284	153510	W 973968	154115	W 617348	132887	MAIS NON MOULU
05	VEGETABLES AND FRUIT		131917		197750		240485		249637	LEGUMES ET FRUITS
054	VEG ETC FRSH,SMPLY PRSVD	W 122732	60100	W 239221	102166	W 242869	125172	W 198928	123004	LEGUMES FRAIS,CONG,SECS
06	SUGAR AND PREPS,HONEY		85163		61997		279834		513392	SUCRES ET PRODUITS
061	SUGAR AND HONEY	W 248881	81361	W 151497	55984	W 611775	272047	W 1311381	505419	SUCRES ET MIEL
0611	RAW BEET AND CANE SUGAR	W 146231	44439	W 15207	5869	W 231051	104848	W 422400	179958	SUCRES BRUTS
0612	REFINED SUGAR ETC	W 80172	26833	W 103633	37494	W 323403	145640	W 685338	288407	SUCRES RAFFINES
081	*FEEDING STUFF FOR ANIML	W 1127177	334011	W 1408968	416584	W 1557601	460373	W 1763145	603227	NOURRITURE POUR ANIMAUX
0813	OILCAKE AND OTH RESIDUES	W 699947	148330	W 806674	172349	W 988840	209566	W 1215572	320086	TOURTEAUX
08131	— OF SOYA BEANS	W 361065	91702	W 498592	121107	W 681875	163722	W 942292	265934	TOURTEAUX DE SOJA
0814	MEAT OR FISH MEAL FODDER	W 292016	127168	W 437293	166659	W 324526	140943	W 175935	110643	FARINES DE VIANDES,POISSONS
08142	FISH MEAL FODDER	W 155064	81872	W 247918	102689	W 136752	77897	W 133612	92288	FARINES DE POISSONS
0819	FOOD WASTE AND FEED NES	W 121513	56140	W 153993	75464	W 228375	107499	W 357836	169093	DECHETS,ALIMENTS NDA
08199	FODDER NES,INCL SWEETNED	W 87215	42288	W 93864	50479	W 162395	83387	W 307820	145825	PREPARATIONS FOURRAGERES
1	BEVERAGES AND TOBACCO		119184		141716		178054		220142	BOISSONS ET TABACS
12	TOBACCO AND MANUFACTURES		99544		125300		156128		181418	TABACS BRUTS FABRIQUES
121	TOBACCO UNMNFCTRD,REFUSE	W 30226	76997	W 40322	100216	W 47953	115474	W 45060	134153	TABACS BRUTS,DECHETS
2	CRUDE MATERLS,EXCL FUELS		2423604		2723692		3624022		3441227	MAT BRUTES NON COMESTIBLES
22	OIL SEEDS,OLEAGINOUS FRT		271125		339559		287005		383400	GRAINES,FRUITS OLEAGINEUX
222	SEEDS FOR'SOFT'FIXED OIL	W 878643	269672	W 958586	336273	W 759157	282281	W 916456	373643	GRAINES HUILES FIXES
2222	SOYA BEANS	W 723864	197120	W 800461	243734	W 607393	180590	W 746329	251656	FEVES DE SOJA
23	RUBBER, CRUDE		115133		137650		215467		203010	CAOUTCHOUC BRUT
233	RUBBER,SYNTHTIC,RECLAIMD	W 99436	114446	W 115677	134707	W 139803	204029	W 133777	195882	LATEX CAOUTCH SYNTH REGEN
2331	SYNTHETIC RUBBER ETC	W 98928	113790	W 115167	134413	W 138699	203474	W 130925	191089	LATEX CAOUTCH SYNTHETIQUE
251	*PULP AND WASTE PAPER	W 1712430	479007	W 1853578	614179	W 1738800	882257	W 2134901	704542	PATES A PAPIER,DECHETS
2511	WASTE PAPER,PPRBOARD ETC	W 872369	128392	W 1009510	176122	W 1054154	309851	W 1296954	234134	DECHETS DE PAPIER
2516	CHEM WOOD PULP DISSOLVNG	W 135274	78997	W 158145	111210	W 172430	182780	W 193435	157583	PATES CHIMIQUES DE BOIS
2517	SODA,SULPHATE WOOD PULP	W 548857	208369	W 566504	271031	W 357534	280986	W 441929	224745	PATES CHIMIQUES AU SULFATE
25172	— BLEACHED,NONDISSOLVNG	W 526293	200490	W 483236	231666	W 290098	230092	W 391798	202797	PATES BLANCHIES
26	TEXTILE FIBRES AND WASTE		797730		948249		1244729		1261281	FIBRES TEXTILES
263	COTTON	W 416663	556975	W 441630	701332	W 459570	923158	W 492783	980576	COTON
2631	RAW COTTON,EXCL LINTERS	W 415717	556424	W 440726	700629	W 458440	922280	W 492166	980057	COTON EN MASSE
266	SYNTHETIC FIBRES TO SPIN	W 114273	177387	W 123286	197700	W 133347	279012	W 119090	206919	FIBRES SYNTHETIQUES
2665	DISCN SYNTH FIBRE UNCMBD	W 76364	113962	W 83428	133799	W 90379	189310	W 75621	134735	DISCONTINUES EN MASSE
27	CRUDE FERTLZR,MINRLS NES		177018		242263		303531		343932	ENGRAIS MINERAUX BRUTS
278	OTHER CRUDE MINERALS	W 942307	111345	W 1115340	127027	W 1254699	171936	W 1362123	177423	AUTRES MINERAUX BRUTS
28	METALLIFEROUS ORES,SCRAP		503583		344616		541308		395776	MINERAIS METAL,DECHETS
281	IRON ORE,CONCENTRATES	W 2124109	111551	W 1606401	84818	W 2507146	142090	W 2512637	148406	MINERAIS DE FER
282	IRON AND STEEL SCRAP	W 1886822	292153	W 1023999	175255	W 1462330	268940	W 788479	132726	FERRAILLES
28209	— OF OTHR IRON OR STEEL	W 1423786	221755	W 759884	131907	W 1180290	219329	W 744035	125341	FERRAILLES DE FER
287	BASE METAL ORES,CONC NES	W 388710	86220	W 385037	73788	W 631533	123931	W 377891	108662	MINERAIS METAUX COMMUNS
3	MINERAL FUELS ETC		2202412		2487589		3094914		3774946	COMBUSTIBLES MINERAUX LUB
33	PETROLEUM AND PRODUCTS		2170234		2461839		3045102		3746169	PETROLE ET DERIVES
333	CRUDE PETROLEUM	W 6402697	917241	MW 9473	1073171	MW 9261	1317622	MW 9350	1518924	HUILES BRUTES DE PETROLE
334	PETROLEUM PRODUCTS,REFIN	W 5733530	1163677	W 6408555	1290525	W 7857043	1604760	MW 9821	2086147	PRODUITS RAFFINES
3341	GASOLINE,OTH LIGHT OILS	W 1146908	230970	W 1462778	276603	W 365012	70679	W 197132	45068	ESSENCES POUR MOTEURS
33412	SPIRIT TYPE JET FUEL	W 959022	191248	W 1420089	268594					CARBUREACTEURS
3342	KEROSENE,OTH MEDIUM OILS	W 1258279	133075	W 175001	41539	W 1568905	270078	W 1868810	429277	PETR LAMPANTS,AUT HUIL
33421	KEROSENE INCL JET FUEL	W 16	2	W 117728	21632	W 1568905	270078	W 1868810	429277	PETROLES LAMPANTS
33429	OTH MEDIUM PETROLEUM OIL	W 1258263	133073	W 57273	19906					AUTRES HUILES MOYENNES
3343	GAS OILS	W 2927505	579363	W 3498028	582883	W 4515668	783594	W 4738525	963566	GAS OILS
3344	FUEL OILS,NES			W 773483	82197	W 918194	119829	W 2581382	337471	FUEL OILS
3345	LUBS,PETROLEUM OILS NES	W 400838	220269	W 499265	307302	W 489264	360580	W 434815	310766	HUILES LUBRIFIANTES
33451	LUBS(HIGH PETR CONT) ETC	W 373439	172807	W 468961	244676	W 437563	272993	W 379311	205629	HUILES LUBRIF,H LOURDES
335	RESIDUAL PETRLM PROD NES	W 385577	89315	W 419192	98144	W 506882	122719	W 575770	141097	PRODUITS RESIDUELS NDA
4	ANIMAL,VEGETABLE OIL,FAT		100492		104234		104327		101067	HUILES,GRAISSES ANIM,VEG
42	FIXED VEGETABLE OIL,FAT		87168		84737		78073		82330	HUILES VEGETALES FIXES
5	CHEMCLS,RELATED PROD NES		3961549		4757270		6130197		5876867	PRODUITS CHIMIQUES
51	ORGANIC CHEMICALS		1207440		1609726		2327938		2226744	PROD CHIMIQ ORGANIQUES
511	HYDROCARBONS NES,DERIVS	W 610343	252565	W 889028	455218	W 1000285	636802	W 1016870	544484	HYDROCARBURES NDA
5111	ACYCLIC HYDROCARBONS	W 259966	90442	W 361324	163718	W 402037	207586	W 319279	159875	HYDROCARBURES ACYCLIQUES
51111	ETHYLENE	W 228869	72413	W 308098	132515	W 354809	175563	W 198430	85774	ETHYLENE
5112	CYCLIC HYDROCARBONS	W 199829	72109	W 369779	168413	W 462438	310240	W 511892	264950	HYDROCARBURES CYCLIQUES
51124	XYLENES,CHEMICALLY PURE	W 20259	8692	W 144184	72999	W 216642	187761	W 268581	174837	XYLENES PURS
5113	HALOG DERIV OF HYDROCARB	W 148591	86369	W 156160	120139	W 133842	115267	W 183397	115648	DERIVES HALOGENES HYDROCAR
512	ALCOHOLS,PHENOLS ETC		150525		223971	W 562063	366590	W 603145	332330	PHENOLS,PHENOLS–ALCOOLS
5121	ACYCLIC ALCOHOLS,DERIVS		126974		164937	W 534308	325999	W 571355	288665	ALCOOLS ACYCLIQUES
51215	ETHYLENE GLYCOL	W 122929	54522	W 143225	64595	W 226014	155345	W 252301	161446	ETHYLENE–GLYCOL
513	CARBOXYLIC ACIDS ETC	W 401279	326774	W 360927	350037	W 445407	563424	W 488566	538251	ACIDES CARBOXYLIQUES
5137	MONOACIDS AND DERIVATIVS	W 100634	112656	W 107634	138011	W 151158	210253	W 130353	196898	ACIDES MONOCARBOXYLIQUES
5138	POLYACIDS AND DERIVATIVS	W 294899	198515	W 241239	187916	W 286236	331994	W 351031	318382	ACIDES POLYCARBOXYLIQUES
51389	OTH POLYACIDS ETC,DERIVS	W 281956	189806	W 220124	169993	W 262389	299710	W 324912	296196	ACIDES POLYCARBOXYLIQUES
514	NITROGEN–FNCTN COMPOUNDS	W 86590	211647	W 93782	245062	W 99473	301101	W 101869	296527	COMPOSES FONCT AZOTEES
5148	OTH NITROGN–FNCTN CMPNDS	W 58491	116914	W 62531	137970	W 59561	157930	W 66065	174399	AUTRES COMPOSES AZOTES
515	ORG–INORG COMPOUNDS ETC	W 29595	149376	W 55127	208079	W 69604	296565	W 77993	350991	COMPOSES ORGANO–MINERAUX
5156	HETEROCYCLIC CMPDS ETC	W 14656	79658	W 36364	110335	W 45709	160889	W 48018	163963	COMPOSES HETEROCYCLIQUES
516	OTHER ORGANIC CHEMICALS		116553	W 116203	127360		163456	W 152207	164162	AUTRES PROD ORGANIQUES
52	INORGANIC CHEMICALS		388606		446956		522469		526603	PROD CHIM INORGANIQUES
522	INORG ELEMNTS,OXIDES,ETC	W 357537	184986	W 746420	235575	W 646945	263797	W 376637	235083	ELEMENTS INORGANIQUES
523	OTHR INORG CHEMICALS ETC		202909	W 724203	210547	W 835318	257765	W 933998	289973	AUT PRODUITS CHIMIQUES INORG
5232	OTH MTL CMPD OF INRG ACD		144985	W 588722	153342	W 693785	189985	W 801650	218197	SELS METALLIQUES
53	DYES,TANNING,COLOUR PROD		394786		430737		504725		505174	PROD TEINTURE,COLORANTS
531	SYNT DYE,NAT INDGO,LAKES	W 26341	210946	W 30545	213470	W 31918	238328	W 32235	245276	MAT COLOR ORGAN,LAQUES
5311	SYNTHIC ORGNIC DYESTUFFS	W 23352	184806	W 27464	188721	W 28091	211928	W 26613	204829	MAT COLOR ORGAN SYNTHET
533	PIGMENTS,PAINTS,ETC	W 91707	166901	W 113680	201955	W 135175	251191	W 137670	248694	PIGMENTS,PEINTURES,VERNIS

4. Special Imports C.I.F. by Commodities according to the S.I.T.C. (Rev. 2) in thousand U.S. Dollars
Importations Spéciales C.A.F. par Produits d'après la C.T.C.I. (Rév. 2) en milliers de Dollars E.U.

SITC CTCI	COMMODITY	1993 WEIGHT POIDS	1993 VALUE VALEUR	1994 WEIGHT POIDS	1994 VALUE VALEUR	1995 WEIGHT POIDS	1995 VALUE VALEUR	1996 WEIGHT POIDS	1996 VALUE VALEUR	PRODUIT
541	*MEDICINAL,PHARM PRODUCT	K 7139858	187942	MK 11081	190606		249650	MK 11271	265142	PROD MEDICINAUX PHARMACEUT
55	PERFUME,CLEANING ETC PRD		166466		220871		242766		259113	PROD POUR PARFUM,TOILETTE
551	ESSENTL OILS,PERFUME,ETC	W 10090	100065	W 13410	130420	W 29073	148372	W 13655	165237	HUILES ESSENTIELLES
5514	MIXED PERFUME SUBSTANCES	W 9442	95396	W 12722	124152	W 28338	140507	W 12941	156458	MELANGES SUBSTAN ODORIFER
562	*FERTILIZERS,MANUFACTURE	W 660574	99937	W 485798	75111	W 764162	133743	W 1111433	214886	ENGRAIS MANUFACTURES
58	PLASTIC MATERIALS ETC		981316		1145261		1390689		1166362	MAT PLAST ARTIFICIELLES
582	PROD OF CONDENSATION ETC	W 153140	264184	W 187153	325628	W 193999	429067	W 181407	362266	PROD CONDENS,POLYCOND
5823	ALKYDS,OTHER POLYESTERS	W 60578	90527	W 88747	128521	W 93005	201387	W 83567	140056	ALKYDES ET AUT POLYESTERS
58231	— IN PRIMARY FORMS	W 54452	74176	W 82152	112126	W 86305	182132	W 79023	124970	SOUS FORMES PRIMAIRES
583	POLYMERIZATION ETC PRODS	W 685600	648019	W 725043	754156	W 665160	893468	W 614361	740799	PROD POLYMERISATION
5831	POLYETHYLENE	W 314680	223159	W 278570	221283	W 212261	241547	W 203053	206280	POLYETHYLENE
58311	— IN PRIMARY FORMS	W 305716	210674	W 269638	205935	W 200199	219223	W 183764	174749	POLYETHYLENE PRIMAIRES
5832	POLYPROPYLENE	W 154659	129476	W 156099	134802	W 143228	172048	W 125333	127530	POLYPROPYLENE
58321	— IN PRIMARY FORMS	W 151857	124625	W 151808	128308	W 136123	158430	W 116261	108777	POLYPROPYLENE PRIMAIRES
5839	OTH POLYMRZTION ETC PROD	W 135229	183817	W 173674	237821	W 177641	272902	W 164708	236661	AUT PROD POLYMER COPOLYM
59	CHEMICAL MATERIALS NES		522328		623545		740635		698818	MAT PROD CHIMIQUES NDA
592	STARCH,INULIN,GLUTEN,ETC	W 72452	78759	W 207678	120035	W 291146	192777	W 107551	122078	AMIDONS,INUL,GLUT FROM
598	MISCEL CHEM PRODUCTS NES		425979	W 216684	482555	W 237830	523609	W 224168	540975	PROD DIV INDUST CHIM NDA
5982	ANTI-KNOCK PREPARTNS ETC	W 44081	124490	W 41944	113164	W 50341	137269	W 30130	85991	PREPARAT ANTIDETONANTES
5989	CHEM PRODUCTS,PREPS NES		265099	W 150531	333973	W 159053	343302	W 171458	420725	PROD PREP CHIMIQUES NDA
59899	OTH CHEM PRODS,PREPS,NES	W 75130	152655	W 86612	171393	W 98359	200396	W 114340	265524	AUT PRODUITS CHIMIQUES NDA
6	BASIC MANUFACTURES		5007721		5386703		6855150		6844613	ART MANUFACTURES
61	LEATHER,DRESSED FUR,ETC		427637		468408		442742		415259	CUIRS,PELLETERIES
611	LEATHER	W 25852	318355	W 27783	346449	W 27044	320521	W 32077	286458	CUIRS,PEAUX PREPARES
6114	LEATHR BOVINE NES,EQUINE	W 24177	293097	W 25648	319721	W 24126	291191	W 25907	248108	CUIRS DE BOVINS
612	LEATHER ETC MANUFACTURES	W 19802	108936	W 20926	121683	W 19160	121752	W 20577	128046	OUVRAGES EN CUIRS NDA
6123	PREPRD PARTS OF FOOTWEAR	W 19734	106830	W 20708	118840	W 18991	117811	W 19697	122440	PARTIES DE CHAUSSURES
62	RUBBER MANUFACTURES NES		90080		116991		155312		193787	CAOUTCHOUC MANUFACTURE
64	PAPER,PAPERBOARD AND MFR		228524		253822		326124		299631	PAPIERS,CARTONS & OUVRAGES
641	PAPER AND PAPERBOARD	W 117146	168310	W 186831	194169	W 157024	244225	W 210320	212914	PAPIERS ET CARTONS
65	TEXTILE YARN,FABRICS,ETC		1129119		1175261		1327143		1288310	FILS,TISSUS,ARTICLES TEXTILE
651	TEXTILE YARN	W 79951	280109	W 81841	279608	W 87758	319922	W 71098	297166	FILS TEXTILES
6514	SYN FIB YRN,BULK,MONOFIL	W 44267	147896	W 42914	133399	W 40002	144572	W 35084	138845	FILS CONT 85% FIB TEXT SYNTH
65142	— NONTXT ETC CONT PAMID	W 30754	100288	W 29057	81573	W 28265	94540	W 25285	98554	FILS NON TEX FI CON POLYAMID
6517	REGEN FIBRE YARN,MONOFIL	W 22427	91624	W 25055	97480	W 28595	115731	W 22898	97621	FILS TEXT ART NON VENTE DT
65171	CONT VISCOSE RAYON YARN	W 21680	89292	W 23403	92058	W 27536	111748	W 22254	94914	FILS RAY,VIS NON VENTE DET
652	COTTON FABRICS,WOVEN	W 17340	121759	W 14158	110918	W 19924	139437	W 16159	141641	TISSUS DE COTON
6522	WOVEN COTTON BLEACHD,ETC	W 14217	111749	W 12417	104236	W 18808	134102	W 14974	136874	TISSUS COTON BLANCHIS ETC
65224	BLCHED COTTON FABRIC NES	W 12441	90710	W 10938	89169	W 17044	116510	W 12827	115160	AUT TIS PLUS 85% COT BLANCHI
653	WOVN MAN-MADE FIB FABRIC	W 30199	223201	W 36423	237752	W 35653	231612	W 29559	186703	TISSUS FIBRES SYNTH,ARTIF
6531	CONT SYNT WEAVES NONPILE	W 13972	115518	W 18353	135969	W 20177	142488	W 18158	116842	TISSUS FIBRES SYNTH CONTINUE
65315	CONT SYN TXTL FABRIC NES	W 13711	113365	W 18226	134645	W 19955	139435	W 17886	113664	TIS PLUS 85% TEXT SYNT CONT
655	KNITTED,ETC FABRICS	W 21545	156308	W 19972	160803	W 23867	210487	W 22224	194013	ETOF BONNETERIE PIECES ETC
6552	OTHER KNIT ETC FAB NONEL	W 21545	156308	W 19972	160803	W 23867	210487	W 22224	194013	ETOF BON NON ELAS NON SYNT
657	SPECIAL TXTL FABRC,PRODS	W 43296	253261	W 44677	290356	W 47496	325272	W 51449	356731	TISSUS SPECIAUX
6573	COATED ETC TEXTILES NES	W 24404	130024	W 23085	138669	W 24447	152781	W 27142	160080	TISSUS,ART MATIERE TEXT NDA
65732	PLASTIC COATED TEXTILES	W 18781	102609	W 16442	109721	W 16631	119698	W 17266	113079	TISSUS IMPREGNES
66	NONMETAL MINERAL MFS NES		274643		340695		478476		521338	ART MIN NON METALLIQUES
661	LIME,CEMENT,BLDG PRODS	W 251350	11857	W 927997	59732	W 1852069	118738	W 2065438	133410	CHAUX,CIMENTS MAT CONSTR
662	CLAY,REFRACTORY BLDG PRD	W 110976	94521	W 114261	102631	W 164119	146131	W 168041	144429	MAT CONST REFRACTAIRES
6623	REFRACTORY BUILDING PROD	W 88477	85137	W 91843	94900	W 112753	126871	W 108899	121382	BRIQUES REFRACTAIRES
67	IRON AND STEEL		1669175		1684088		2451001		2370733	FER ET ACIER
671	PIG IRON ETC	W 512769	102425	W 599841	115142	W 1132090	218080	W 633392	143898	FONTE,SPIEGEL,POUDRES
672	IRON,STEEL PRIMARY FORMS	W 1226124	372358	W 1241317	382747	W 1953028	670493	W 1774657	568287	LINGOTS FER,ACIER
6725	IRN,STL BLOOMS,SLABS,ETC	W 770178	203535	W 924911	238193	W 1388143	391577	W 1376311	395686	BLOOMS,BILLETTES FER ACIER
67251	IRN,SMPLE STL BLOOMS,ETC	W 770119	203455	W 924511	236061	W 1387769	391243	W 1375831	395222	BLOOMS ETC NON ACIER FIN
6727	IRN,STL COIL FR REROLLNG	W 435164	165637	W 315904	144375	W 564421	278497	W 398163	172438	EBAUCHES POUR TOLES FER
67271	IRON,SIMPLE STEEL COILS	W 385701	136876	W 242483	104795	W 481236	223827	W 356689	149662	EBAUCHES NON EN ACIER
673	IRON,STEEL SHAPES ETC	W 286579	158651	W 356039	205140	W 469798	278169	W 465753	265681	BARRES,PROFIL FER,ACIER
674	IRN,STL UNIV,PLATE,SHEET	W 770411	532073	W 850030	586746	W 979927	796227	W 928128	746750	LARGES PLATS,TOLES
6744	IRN,STL HVY PLATE,ROLLED	W 84551	64728	W 132313	91661	W 173198	126814	W 134822	115737	TOLES LAMINEES PLUS 4.75 MM
6746	IRN,STL THIN PLATE,ROLLD	W 503797	321538	W 485631	323115	W 553620	448296	W 533685	412844	TOLES LAM MOINS 3MM
67461	— OF IRON OR SIMPLE STL	W 459753	249715	W 442471	250009	W 475936	304861	W 469988	306044	TOL NON AC FIN MOINS 3 MM
67463	— OF STAINLESS ETC STL	W 35354	64611	W 36347	66950	W 51911	124596	W 43068	91217	TOL ACIER INOX MOINS 3 MM
678	IRON,STL TUBES,PIPES,ETC	W 257091	386322	W 190844	317392	W 218832	379513	W 330195	545411	TUBES,TUYAUX EN FONTE,FER
6782	IRON,STL SEAMLESS TUBES	W 120148	194558	W 110056	142523	W 136851	167441	W 195285	275275	TUBES,TUYAUX SANS SOUDURE
6783	IRON,STL TUBES,PIPES NES	W 116032	102427	W 54771	79029	W 56616	126524	W 107019	158800	AUT TUBES,TUYAUX FER,ACIER
6785	IRON,STEEL TUBE FITTINGS	W 18206	85264	W 19575	88655	W 21911	81467	W 25654	106305	ACCESSOIRES DE TUYAUTERIE
68	NON-FERROUS METALS		519374		643601		1018746		905386	METAUX NON FERREUX
682	COPPER EXC CEMENT COPPER	W 70525	191645	W 90636	234610	W 122308	392449	W 129989	358776	CUIVRE
6821	COPPER NES,ALLOYS,UNWRT	W 50279	117920	W 66341	154152	W 94906	276761	W 107396	269928	CUIVRE BRUT
68212	COPPER REFINED,UNWROUGHT	W 50225	117814	W 66246	153809	W 94842	276550	W 107372	269853	CUIVRE AFFINE BRUT
684	ALUMINIUM	W 103087	198347	W 131656	254284	W 176497	432327	W 152573	336984	ALUMINIUM
6841	ALUMINIUM,ALLOYS,UNWRGHT	W 67770	97245	W 100618	158653	W 138381	301342	W 118499	210271	ALUMINIUM,ALLIAGES BRUTS
6842	ALUMINIUM,ALLOYS WORKED	W 35316	101102	W 31038	95631	W 38116	130985	W 34074	126714	ALUMINIUM,ALLIAGES OUVRE
686	ZINC	W 79340	90586	W 93776	105119	W 105905	129174	W 96634	121742	ZINC
6861	ZINC,ALLOYS UNWROUGHT	W 77609	87337	W 91557	101381	W 102488	123993	W 94201	117488	ZINC ET ALLIAGES BRUTS
69	METAL MANUFACTURES NES		635560		662196		611649		813214	ART MANUFACT EN METAL NDA
691	STRUCTURES AND PARTS NES	W 57859	207485	W 77834	189093	W 46121	103210	W 57866	256315	CONSTRUCT FER,ACIER,ALU
6911	STRUCTURES,PARTS IRN,STL	W 57303	205429	W 77153	185297	W 45535	99076	W 56800	252634	CONSTRUCT FER,ACIER,FONTE
695	TOOLS	W 11701	87381	W 15874	105303	W 19494	98031	W 21918	143278	OUTILS A MAIN
699	BASE METAL MFRS NES	W 37264	143523	W 39738	173772	W 63063	196714	W 48986	211101	ART MANUFACTURES MET NDA
7	MACHINES,TRANSPORT EQUIP		12116388		13426297		16257140		17458566	MACHINES MATERIEL TRANSPORT
71	POWER GENERATING EQUIPMT		1616805		1752011		1827610		1968590	MACHINES GENERATRICES
711	STEAM BOILERS & AUX PLNT	W 20631	174919	W 24593	173358	W 19213	122485	W 48707	241279	GENERATEURS VAPEUR EAU ETC
7111	STEAM BOILERS ETC	W 12293	86045	W 15776	84070	W 8887	40098	W 15828	107635	GENERATEURS VAPEUR EAU
712	STEAM ENGINES,TURBINES	W 12552	342815	W 14074	334311	W 9371	244450	W 10157	188773	MACHINES A VAPEUR D'EAU PIEC
7126	STEAM POWR UNITS,ENGINES	W 7968	210466	W 10345	255752	W 7958	197029	W 2344	67821	MACHINES A VAPEUR D EAU
7129	STM ENGINE ETC PARTS NES	W 4584	132349	W 3729	78559	W 1413	47421	W 7813	120952	PARTIES,PIECES DU 712.6
713	INTRNL COMBUS PSTN ENGIN	W 44273	439069	W 77391	717805	W 92259	855630	W 88662	727414	MOTEURS EXPL COMB INT, PIECE
7132	MOTOR VEHCL PISTN ENGINS	W 21086	220254	W 50359	548225	W 52357	641906	W 48053	517187	MOTEURS EXPL POUR VEHICULES
7139	PISTON ENGINE PARTS NES	W 15364	133024	W 19017	109312	W 28526	127511	W 28162	134756	PIECES POUR 713.2,3,8
714	ENGINES AND MOTORS NES	W 5750	263229	W 2790	138810	W 1966	95690	W 6067	311404	MOTEURS NON ELECTRIQUES
7148	GAS TURBINES NES	W 4009	195601	W 2122	90830	W 1384	38766	W 2729	144923	TURBINES A GAZ
71488	OTHER GAS TURBINES NES	W 3961	177480	W 2099	86141	W 1302	33919	W 2669	140651	AUTRES TURBINES A GAZ
7149	ENGINE & MOTOR PARTS NES	W 1728	61363	W 563	40654	W 519	49718	W 3219	152614	PIECES 714 ET 718.88
716	ROTATING ELECTRIC PLANT	W 29991	370342	W 35105	367745	W 42200	487254	W 41133	459614	APP ELECTR ROTATIFS,PIECES
7162	AC MTRS,GENRTRS,GEN SETS	W 22440	267370	W 25790	263319	W 31672	335603	W 26429	312883	MOTEURS ELECTRIQUES
71623	GEN SETS WITH PISTN ENGN	W 11660	151271	W 13540	165198	W 17844	222541	W 11945	173903	GROUPES MOTEUR EXPLOSION
72	MACHS FOR SPCL INDUSTRYS		2773864		3014710		3891394		4118326	MAC SPECIALES POUR INDUST
723	CIVIL ENGINEERG EQUIP ETC	W 64327	410201	W 88739	520883	W 79156	492139	W 86886	483174	APPAREILS DE GENIE CIVIL

4. Special Imports C.I.F. by Commodities according to the S.I.T.C. (Rev. 2) in thousand U.S. Dollars
Importations Spéciales C.A.F. par Produits d'après la C.T.C.I. (Rév. 2) en milliers de Dollars E.U.

SITC CTCI	COMMODITY	1993			1994			1995			1996			PRODUIT
			WEIGHT POIDS	VALUE VALEUR		WEIGHT POIDS	VALUE VALEUR		WEIGHT POIDS	VALUE VALEUR		WEIGHT POIDS	VALUE VALEUR	
7234	CONST,MINING MACHNRY NES	W	47773	261594	W	74480	412898	W	64209	379157	W	72882	374068	MACH POUR LA CONST, MINES
72341	SELF–PROPELLD DOZERS,ETC	W	16446	98413	W	23184	146729	W	19296	126872	W	14387	82248	BULLDOZERS
72342	SLFPRP SHOVELS,EXCAVATRS	W	25364	131589	W	45188	234001	W	37406	202385	W	47411	237432	PELLES MECANIQUES
7239	CONSTR ETC MACHY PTS NES	W	12948	134676	W	8872	87960	W	8726	83543	W	10039	91970	PIECES 723.41–723.46
724	TEXTILE,LEATHER MACHNRY	W	67449	815077	W	83821	836924	W	103354	1051335	W	63843	740379	MACH POUR INDUSTRIE TEXTILE
7244	SPINNING,EXTRDNG,ETC MCH	W	28908	416475	W	32409	370861	W	54054	593692	W	27149	382635	MACH POUR LE FILAGE
72441	TEXTILE EXTRUDING MACHS	W	5077	108600	W	4697	62254	W	8186	152889	W	3043	92615	MACH FILAGE TEXT SYNTH
72443	SPINNING,REELING,ETC MCH	W	14454	171041	W	19644	196594	W	22579	213795	W	14348	179297	MACH POUR LA FILATURE
7245	WEAVING,FELT MFG,ETC MCH	W	18491	183862	W	26881	234453	W	24036	221855	W	16746	173105	METIERS A TISSER,PIECES
72451	WEAVING MACHINES (LOOMS)	W	11603	95282	W	19261	145557	W	14485	133996	W	10810	97440	METIERS A TISSER
7247	TEXTILE MACHINERY NES	W	7471	106629	W	12593	135446	W	11361	122793	W	8515	94568	MACH LAVAGE,TEINTURE TEX
72474	OTH TEXTILE MACHNERY NES	W	5691	87514	W	10118	115292	W	7437	100256	W	5021	69549	MACH LAVAGE ETC MAT TEXT
725	PAPER ETC MILL MACHINERY	W	54963	537263	W	25581	387518	W	55117	672973	W	65792	806777	MACHINES FABR PATE PAPIER
7251	PAPER,PULP MAKING MACHRY	W	46291	447653	W	17093	297136	W	25396	305115	W	33595	406239	MACHINES FABR PATE CARTON
72511	CELLULOSE PULP MFG MACHY	W	42269	426476	W	13035	264447	W	9993	97850	W	17504	178382	MACH FABR PATE CELLULOSE
72512	PAPER ETC MAKING ETC MCH	W	4022	21177	W	4058	32689	W	15402	207266	W	16091	227857	MACH FABR FINITION DU PAP
7259	PTS NES OF MACHS OF 725	W	4242	53901	W	3758	49342	W	23298	307761	W	25570	313836	PIECES GROUPE 725
72591	PTS NES OF MACHS OF 7251	W	3879	47963	W	3541	47529	W	23059	304240	W	24899	302040	PIECES DU 725.1
726	PRINTG,BKBINDG MACHY,PTS	W	6439	139593	W	8501	156859	W	8171	193872	W	8076	168131	MACHINES POUR IMPRIMERIE
7264	PRINTING PRESSES	W	3517	98540	W	3831	79642	W	4051	124182	W	5033	111509	MACHINES A IMPRIMER
72641	ROTARY PRINTING PRESSES	W	3517	98540	W	3831	79642	W	4051	124182	W	5033	111509	MACH IMPRIMER ROTATIVES
727	FOOD MACHRY NON–DOMESTIC	W	10122	95020	W	13731	103435	W	14009	124456	W	19015	165753	MACH INDUSTRIES ALIMENT
7272	OTH FOOD PROC MCHY,PARTS	W	8133	83363	W	12145	96271	W	12328	102614	W	15481	146973	AUT MACH IND ALIMENTAIRE
728	OTH MACHY FOR SPCL INDUS	W	61870	726698	W	89994	952700	W	111532	1268703	W	135948	1641125	AUT MACH IND PARTICULIERES
7281	MACH–TOOLS FR SPCL INDUS	W	17157	124188	W	24826	194836	W	19059	166621	W	18057	166318	MACH–OUTILS SPEC IND PART
72812	MACH–TOOLS TO WORK WOOD	W	14919	99856	W	19697	146050	W	14871	114645	W	12781	108122	MACH–OUT POUR TRAVAIL BOIS
7283	OTHR MINERAL WORKG MACHY	W	16024	166860	W	18288	123228	W	37490	225725	W	51543	454974	MACH TRIER,CRIBLER,BROYER
72839	PTS NES OF MACHY OF 7283	W	4027	31506	W	6977	41433	W	14929	85712	W	22511	208340	PIECES MACH DU 728.3
7284	MACHY FOR SPCL INDUS NES	W	28689	435650	W	46879	634636	W	54983	876357	W	66348	1019833	MACH SPEC IND PARTICUL.
72842	RUBBER,PLASTICS WRKG MCH	W	12846	147853	W	23774	292134	W	24879	380048	W	28053	311602	MACH IND CAOUT MAT PLAST
72848	OTH MCHY WITH INDIV FNCT	W	8968	161070	W	13738	194323	W	19198	248999	W	23818	409846	AUTRES MACHINES NDA
73	METALWORKING MACHINERY			366222			436653			596238			595785	MACH TRAVAIL DES METAUX
736	METALWORKING MACH–TOOLS	W	29923	244776	W	51700	319007	W	65619	453255	W	58484	454038	MACH–OUTILS TRAVAIL METAUX
7361	METAL CUTTING MACH–TOOLS	W	11541	111513	W	21134	130435	W	25502	178478	W	21035	166511	MACH–OUT ENLEVEMENT METAL
7362	METAL FORMING MACH–TOOLS	W	11730	57649	W	19677	102534	W	26841	162048	W	21019	146825	MACH–OUTILS DEFORM METAL
737	METALWORKING MACHNRY NES	W	16643	121446	W	23470	117646	W	41851	142983	W	24794	141747	MACH TRAV METAUX PIECES
74	GENRL INDUSTRL MACHY NES			2348027			2392957			3059169			3629132	MACH APP INDUSTRIE
741	HEATING,COOLING EQUIPMNT	W	66800	655961	W	67315	643078	W	81782	838104	W	98840	944005	MACH CHAUFFAGE,PIECES
7413	INDUS FURNACES ETC,PARTS	W	6907	74085	W	13432	92364	W	13865	126453	W	20502	215717	FOURS IND,LABOR,PIECES
74132	INDUST FURNACES NONELECT	W	5037	34915	W	10395	72066	W	11746	107675	W	16541	173446	FOURS NON ELECTRIQUES
7415	AIR–CONDITIONING MACHNRY	W	10967	122150	W	10777	134348	W	12587	143605	W	11986	111368	GROUPES CONDITION AIR
7416	HEATING,COOLING EQU NES	W	34601	358370	W	29957	313848	W	37717	423661	W	45693	471508	APP CHANGEMENT TEMP
742	PUMPS FOR LIQUIDS ETC	W	16671	216123	W	19103	210402	W	25560	250322	W	26492	300047	POMPES MOTO–POMPES
743	PUMPS NES,CENTRFUGES ETC	W	30016	393437	W	36039	375879	W	49185	429279	W	50361	528165	POMPES COMPRES,VENT ETC
7431	PUMPS FOR GASES ETC	W	13592	185110	W	19086	144825	W	19587	184985	W	22838	223847	POMPES AIR A VIDE,COMPRES
7436	GAS,LIQUID FILTERS ETC	W	8176	98009	W	8507	104968	W	10676	102363	W	14076	160571	APP POUR FILT DES LIQUIDES
744	MECHANICAL HANDLING EQU	W	87527	495256	W	87575	498696	W	130342	796003	W	146195	909758	EQUIP MANUTENTION PIECES
7442	LIFTING,LOADING MACH NES	W	30531	193697	W	33034	191798	W	54134	304333	W	64378	391705	APP LEVAGE,MANUTENTION
74428	OTH HANDLING ETC MCH NES	W	15312	99430	W	12362	87995	W	23556	140535	W	34929	217865	AUT APP LEVAGE ETC
7449	PTS NES OF MACHY OF 7442	W	47360	251960	W	42209	236424	W	63210	409796	W	64438	436008	PIECES DU 744.2
745	NONELEC MACHY,TOOLS NES	W	7791	144859	W	11549	162908	W	12056	223999	W	14946	324072	AUT MACH NON ELEC,PIECES
7452	OTH NONELEC MCHS,PTS NES	W	5784	126473	W	9032	138284	W	9888	202074	W	12182	293168	AUT MACH NON ELEC,PIECES
74522	PACKAGNG,BOTTLNG,ETC MCH	W	1974	71279	W	2830	73586	W	4402	134612	W	5029	203002	MACH NETT BOUTEILLES,ETC
749	NONELEC MACH PTS,ACC NES	W	44146	442390	W	46569	501996	W	54538	521461	W	59313	623085	PIECES MACH NON ELEC NDA
7492	COCKS,VALVES ETC NES	W	14864	204503	W	16718	247841	W	17595	199246	W	20899	260377	ART ROB,SIM POUR TUYAUX
7493	SHAFT,CRANK,PULLEY ETC	W	13728	97058	W	16212	101072	W	17051	116740	W	17875	121481	ARBRES TRANS,VILEBREQUINS
7499	OTH NONELEC MCHY PTS NES	W	11474	111130	W	9578	125250	W	14247	169747	W	15033	197516	PIECES NON ELECT NDA
74991	FOUNDRY MOULDS ETC NES	W	7709	78661	W	6288	92465	W	9538	128576	W	10315	157324	MOULES POUR METAUX
75	OFFICE MACHNES,ADP EQUIP			200727			176470			241110			304830	MACH BUREAU TRAIT AUTOM
752	AUTOMTIC DATA PROC EQUIP	W	1703	115856	W	2116	94171	W	2533	121699	W	5931	195537	MACH TRAIT INFORMATION
76	TELECOMM,SOUND EQUIPMENT			999079			759457			1086151			1766273	EQUIPMENT DE TELECOM
764	TELECOM EQPT,PTS,ACC NES	W	32526	979476	W	30446	741157	W	35644	1060970	W	32646	1724262	EQUIP TELECOM,PIECES
7641	LINE TELEPHONE,ETC EQUIP	W	2034	272525	W	4531	300129	W	4700	401332	W	4599	454670	APP TELEPHON PAR FIL
7643	TV,RADIO TRANSMITTRS ETC	W	1565	134200	W	693	75275	W	939	95747	W	1956	367359	APP EMET TELE RADIO
7648	TELECOMM EQUIPMENT NES	W	392	111245	W	260	30423	W	396	57066	W	760	102063	APP TELECOM NDA
76483	RADAR APPARATUS ETC	W	358	107097	W	211	24047	W	286	31921	W	216	49946	APP DE RADIOGUIDAGE ETC
7649	PTS NES OF EQUIPMT OF 76	W	25369	446322	W	22499	324224	W	26093	492216	W	21621	786687	PIECES DE LA DIV 76
76491	PTS NES OF APPAR OF 7641	W	2041	134161	W	1883	101410	W	2613	171333	W	4177	355931	PIECES POUR 764.1
76493	TELECOMM EQUIPMT PTS NES	W	12194	151692	W	12021	154484	W	14664	275140	W	11431	404873	PIECES 761,762,764.3,8
76499	PARTS ETC OF SOUND EQUIP	W	8204	147709	W	5011	54352	W	3332	27853	W	2325	15941	PIECES NDA POUR 763
77	ELECTRIC MACHNRY NES ETC			1709503			1758172			1965631			1868313	MACH APP ELECT NDA
771	ELECTRIC POWER MACHY NES	W	21604	240239	W	20824	218504	W	20466	206255	W	26756	241853	MACH PROD,TRANS ELECTR
7711	TRANSFORMERS,ELECTRICAL	W	15485	169168	W	13662	160449	W	13071	132094	W	18951	173980	TRANSFO ELECTRIQUES
77118	OTHER ELEC TRANSFORMERS	W	9335	112362	W	6967	73724	W	8199	90397	W	11815	105937	AUTRES TRANSFO ELECTRIQ
772	SWITCHGEAR ETC,PARTS NES	W	26432	571241	W	27708	557170	W	31727	559295	W	27398	476510	APP COUPURE,SECT ETC
7721	SWITCHGEAR ETC	W	23783	516334	W	24836	502406	W	29365	515485	W	25388	439572	APP COUPURE,SECTIONMNT
773	ELECTR DISTRIBUTNG EQUIP	W	34900	185483	W	41474	220501	W	56729	237873	W	55193	270520	EQUIPMT DISTRIBUTION ELECT
7731	INSULATED WIRE,CABLE ETC	W	21042	132298	W	20764	167045	W	32659	181932	W	46059	235114	FILS,CABLES ISOLES ELECT
776	TRANSISTORS,VALVES,ETC	W	27174	300507	W	33886	327900	W	41011	398058	W	37435	333697	LAMPES,TUBES,VALVES
7761	TV PICTURE TUBES	W	23143	171440	W	28738	201387	W	34911	250764	W	30798	210151	TUBES CATHODIQUES
778	ELECTRICAL MACHINERY NES	W	49441	347332	W	54904	373675	W	66049	436819	W	57884	439113	AUTRES MACH ELECT NDA
7788	OTH ELEC MACHY,EQUIP NES	W	33166	217144	W	36090	227593	W	43316	255812	W	32608	185522	AUT MACH APP ELEC NDA
78	ROAD VEHICLES			1324123			2335224			2983730			2673454	VEHICULES ROUTIERS
781	PASS MOTOR VEH EXC BUSES	W	23656	190652	W	10469	85736	W	17325	159214	W	26679	226903	AUTO TRANSPORT PERSONNES
782	LORRIES,SPCL MTR VEH NES	W	15738	128134	W	34278	239126	W	42630	303667	W	51091	369018	VEHICULES SPECIAUX,MARCH
7821	LORRIES,TRUCKS	W	11526	88473	W	27832	209460	W	36094	268391	W	40687	297469	VEHICULES TRANSP MARCHAND
784	MOTOR VEH PRTS,ACCES NES	W	87458	701969	W	171194	1532541	W	201365	1843233	W	163265	1359471	PIECES 722,781,782,783
7849	OTHER MOTOR VEHCL PARTS	W	87243	700017	W	170949	1530555	W	200798	1835741	W	162810	1354444	PIECES 722,781,782,783
785	CYCLES,ETC MOTRZD OR NOT	W	38823	270297	W	40008	403476	W	47223	557789	W	52245	639812	MOTOCYCLES SCOOTERS
7853	INVAL CARR, PTS OF 785	W	38039	268608	W	39667	401973	W	46367	556250	W	51093	638067	FAUTEUILS INVALIDES,PIECES
78539	PARTS,ACCES NES OF 785	W	37964	268366	W	39370	401424	W	46227	555726	W	50977	637653	PIECES DU 785
79	OTHR TRANSPORT EQUIPMENT			778037			800644			606106			533864	AUTRE MATERIEL TRANSPORT
791	RAILWAY VEHICLES	W	5543	118863	W	6178	56055	W	8273	99056	W	4062	55590	VEHIC MAT CHEMINS DE FER
792	AIRCRAFT ETC	W	1345	332523	W	708	230192	W	688	228656	W	708	234587	APP NAVIGATION AERIENNE
7924	AIRCRFT NES OVER 15000KG	W	657	139025	W	269	131735	W	215	115938	W	57	15075	AERODYNES PLUS 15000 KG
7929	AIRCRAFT PARTS NES	W	399	106390	W	302	68763	W	346	100394	W	553	180024	PIECES DU 792
793	SHIPS AND BOATS ETC	W	145350	326652	W	205760	514398	W	94428	278395	W	194799	243686	NAVIRES BATEAUX,ETC
7932	SHIPS AND BOATS NES	W	47985	63428	W	116027	314129	W	64845	127877	W	108078	124325	NAVIRES ET BATEAUX
79323	OTHER CARGO VESSELS	W	45770	54003	W	109206	295384	W	61125	117417	W	10506	41456	AUT BATEAUX TRANS MARCH
7938	TUGS,SPECIAL VESSELS ETC	W	97156	262466	W	88455	197777	W	26971	95819	W	86350	111467	REMORQUEURS,BATEAUX SPEC
79382	SPECL PURPOSE VESSLS ETC	W	92010	235199	W	83832	177586	W	19510	79308	W	68690	84457	BAT–PHARES,–POMPES,DRAGUES

4. Special Imports C.I.F. by Commodities according to the S.I.T.C. (Rev. 2) in thousand U.S. Dollars
Importations Spéciales C.A.F. par Produits d'après la C.T.C.I. (Rév. 2) en milliers de Dollars E.U.

SITC CTCI	COMMODITY	1993 WEIGHT POIDS		1993 VALUE VALEUR	1994 WEIGHT POIDS		1994 VALUE VALEUR	1995 WEIGHT POIDS		1995 VALUE VALEUR	1996 WEIGHT POIDS		1996 VALUE VALEUR	PRODUIT
8	MISC MANUFACTURED GOODS			967774			1003609			1282566			1214993	ART MANUFACTURES DIVERS
87	PRECISION INSTRUMNTS NES			420168			369579			441386			482736	INSTRUM,APPAR SCIENT NDA
874	MEASURNG,CONTROLNG INSTR	W	10088	351971	W	10605	322721	W	11785	376940	W	11650	432985	INSTRUMENTS DE MESURE
8743	GAS,LIQUID CONTROL INSTR	W	3409	98208	W	3422	85501	W	3593	95562	W	4011	147734	APP,INSTR MESURE FLUIDES
88	PHOTO EQU,OPTICL GDS ETC			186039			222112			263653			193948	APP,FOURN PHOTO,OP,MONTR
882	PHOTO,CINEMA SUPPLIES	W	10989	105630	W	18590	131132	W	13741	134683	W	13151	122751	PRODUITS PHOTO,CINEMA
8822	PHOTO FILM EXC DEV CINMA	W	6736	89339	W	8535	111078	W	8288	115483	W	8202	103831	PLAQUES,PELLICULES,FILMS
89	MISC MANUFCTRD GOODS NES			305003			318598			422530			419311	ART MANUFACTURES DIVERS
893	ARTICLES OF PLASTIC NES			95356			101486			119938			122865	OUVRAGES EN MAT DIVIS 58
9	GOODS NOT CLASSD BY KIND			88211			56785			82343			69555	ART TRANSACT NON CLASSES

5. Special Exports F.O.B. by Commodities according to the S.I.T.C. (Rev. 2) in thousand U.S. Dollars
Exportations Spéciales F.O.B. par Produits d'après la C.T.C.I. (Rév. 2) en milliers de Dollars E.U.

SITC CTCI	COMMODITY	1993 WEIGHT POIDS	1993 VALUE VALEUR	1994 WEIGHT POIDS	1994 VALUE VALEUR	1995 WEIGHT POIDS	1995 VALUE VALEUR	1996 WEIGHT POIDS	1996 VALUE VALEUR	PRODUIT
	ALL COMMODITIES		36822772		40053434		45417982		49814716	TOUS PRODUITS
0	FOOD AND LIVE ANIMALS		2921166		3550746		3579875		3764409	ALIMENTS,ANIMAUX VIVANTS
03	FISH AND PREPARATIONS		1416136		1581520		1665290		1676848	POISSONS ET PREPARATIONS
034	FISH,FRESH,CHILLED,FROZN	W 319675	391619	W 313169	369378	W 333513	417867	W 351675	424755	POISSON FRAIS, REFRIG,CONG
0341	FISH FRSH,CHLLD,EX FILLT	W 142911	248663	W 114562	202546	W 121846	222709	W 121909	202100	POISSON FRAIS,REFRIGERE
0342	FISH FROZEN,EXCL FILLETS	W 170200	123273	W 189299	135433	W 201011	160583	W 217516	183611	POISSONS CONGELES
036	SHELL FISH FRESH,FROZEN	W 114327	906843	W 116991	1050850	W 109959	1080776	W 115110	1063599	CRUSTACES,MOLLUSQUES
05	VEGETABLES AND FRUIT		296268		303869		299488		376082	LEGUMES ET FRUITS
054	VEG ETC FRSH,SMPLY PRSVD	W 1172164	140241	W 885527	111372	W 679670	111918	W 562852	88077	LEGUMES FRAIS,CONG,SECS
07	COFFEE,TEA,COCOA,SPICES		858297		1296918		1250460		1275712	CAFE,THE,CACAO,EPICES
071	COFFEE AND SUBSTITUTES	W 352272	351861	W 291152	753634	W 231478	613979	W 368626	605948	CAFE ET SUCCEDANES
0711	COFFEE GREEN,ROASTED,SUB	W 349916	344211	W 289304	745804	W 230199	606370	W 366603	595268	CAFE TORREFIE OU DECAFEINE
07111	COFFEE GREEN,HUSKS,SKINS	W 348998	341043	W 288974	744741	W 230099	605742	W 366472	594912	CAFE NON TORREFIE
072	COCOA	W 226023	204755	W 228679	273166	W 230063	301046	W 318704	365311	CACAO
0721	COCOA BEANS,RAW,ROASTED	W 200112	165679	W 200299	213113	W 196443	224488	W 274119	262847	CACAO EN FEVES
074	TEA AND MATE	W 123926	155696	W 84916	96181	W 79227	87719	W 101551	112401	THE ET MATE
0741	TEA	W 123926	155696	W 84916	96181	W 79227	87719	W 101532	112343	THE
075	SPICES	W 126680	139800	W 108792	167092	W 126279	240448	W 110096	183437	EPICES
0751	PEPPER AND PIMENTO	W 27905	46249	W 36364	79150	W 58373	156948	W 37520	101775	POIVRE,PIMENTS
081	*FEEDING STUFF FOR ANIML	W 1217333	126060	W 1495075	157223	W 1388460	141919	W 1557957	207085	NOURRITURE POUR ANIMAUX
1	BEVERAGES AND TOBACCO		192519		138166		195416		229349	BOISSONS ET TABACS
12	TOBACCO AND MANUFACTURES		176652		126422		186769		219499	TABACS BRUTS FABRIQUES
2	CRUDE MATERLS,EXCL FUELS		2553682		3235403		5033641		5081164	MAT BRUTES NON COMESTIBLES
23	RUBBER, CRUDE		980273		1274641		1965431		1922845	CAOUTCHOUC BRUT
232	NATURAL RUBBER,GUMS	W 1215762	979086	W 1245537	1273081	W 1324169	1963895	W 1435365	1920055	LATEX CAOUTCHOUC NATUREL
23202	OTHER NATURAL RUBBER	W 1170148	931860	W 1207547	1228349	W 1296320	1919301	W 1408098	1872882	CAOUTCHOUC NATUREL
24	CORK AND WOOD		400067		388812		363151		325987	LIEGE ET BOIS
248	WOOD SHAPED,SLEEPERS	W 447922	358299	W 354668	346125	W 292870	314962	W 294269	279740	BOIS SIMPLEMENT TRAVAILLES
2483	LUMBER SHAPED NON–CONIFR	W 436678	345419	W 346700	335568	W 284350	304197	W 266140	269202	NON CONIFERES SCIES,RABOTES
24831	LUMBER SAWN ETC NON–CON	W 146288	122250	W 166151	162468	W 153974	161102	W 143829	136165	SCIES LONGITUDINALEMENT
24832	LUMBER PLANED ETC NONCON	W 290390	223169	W 180548	173099	W 130375	143095	W 122311	133037	RABOTES,RAINES,LANGUETES
251	*PULP AND WASTE PAPER	W 131566	42396	W 236015	137715	W 681802	513312	W 1128457	431786	PATES A PAPIER,DECHETS
2517	SODA,SULPHATE WOOD PULP	W 99375	34201	W 107047	63046	W 574980	437885	W 1126025	431232	PATES CHIMIQUES AU SULFATE
25172	— BLEACHED,NONDISSOLVNG	W 86552	30061	W 102456	61214	W 562899	430662	W 1124024	430591	PATES BLANCHIES
28	METALLIFEROUS ORES,SCRAP		899194		1148215		1883540		2034263	MINERAIS METAL,DECHETS
287	BASE METAL ORES,CONC NES	W 3728351	892428	W 3675552	1133225	W 4002487	1870202	W 4422937	2019005	MINERAIS METAUX COMMUNS
2871	CPR ORE ETC,CEMENT COPPR	W 922508	694625	W 1075634	857646	W 1412139	1537532	W 1860097	1747668	MINERAIS DE CUIVRE,MATTES
28711	COPPER ORES,EXCL MATTE	W 922508	694625	W 1075634	857646	W 1412057	1537413	W 1860070	1747629	MINERAIS DE CUIVRE
2872	NICKEL ORES,CONCENTRATES	W 1592171	180776	W 1559626	251902	W 1787978	321752	W 1836563	260174	MINERAIS DE NICKEL
28722	NICKEL MATTE,SINTERS,ETC	W 46609	149877	W 61766	224609	W 54824	280988	W 45373	217231	MATTES,SINTERS
3	MINERAL FUELS ETC		10390885		10523467		11508596		12860837	COMBUSTIBLES MINERAUX LUB
32	COAL,COKE AND BRIQUETTES		645075		829648		1043722		1123665	HOUILLES,COKES,BRIQUETTES
322	COAL,LIGNITE AND PEAT	MW 18717	642141	MW 25366	819264	MW 31572	1033195	MW 31957	1120948	HOUILLES,LIGNITES,TOURBE
3222	OTH COAL,NOT AGGLOMERATD	MW 17569	601131	MW 24221	779835	MW 29745	972986	MW 30586	1072747	AUTRES HOUILLES
33	PETROLEUM AND PRODUCTS		5693081		6004695		6442899		7243257	PETROLE ET DERIVES
333	CRUDE PETROLEUM	MW 36178	4778357	MW 43677	5071565	MW 40674	5145704	MW 38255	5711811	HUILES BRUTES DE PETROLE
334	PETROLEUM PRODUCTS,REFIN	W 7612870	905533	W 8625439	923317	MW 10722	1276434	MW 10385	1502098	PRODUITS RAFFINES
3341	GASOLINE,OTH LIGHT OILS	W 917291	130278	W 896974	133847	W 1482395	322835	W 1417719	336887	ESSENCES POUR MOTEURS
33411	MOTOR,AVIATION SPIRIT	W 872475	121724	W 867878	127954	W 1142780	182241	W 1128358	211800	ESSENCES MOTEURS D'AVIONS
33419	OTH LIGHT PETROLEUM OILS					W 339615	140594	W 289361	125088	AUTRES HUILES LEGERES
3342	KEROSENE,OTH MEDIUM OILS	W 6685175	772665	W 877539	137999					PETR LAMPANTS,AUT HUIL
33429	OTH MEDIUM PETROLEUM OIL	W 6685175	772665	W 877539	137999					AUTRES HUILES MOYENNES
3344	FUEL OILS,NES			W 6760790	638648	W 7948732	826874	W 7893929	1021727	FUEL OILS
341	*GAS,NATURAL AND MANUFCT	MW 27123	4052729	MW 29344	3689124	MW 28190	4021971	MW 29344	4493915	GAZ NATUREL,GAZ MANUFACT
3413	PETROLM GASES,LIQUEFIED	MW 27123	4052690	MW 29344	3689124	MW 28190	4021971	MW 29344	4493915	GAZ DE PETROLE LIQUEFIE
34131	LIQUEFIED PROPANE,BUTANE	W 2531007	376913	W 2514541	305752	W 2384200	406901	W 2568849	467898	PROPANE,BUTANE LIQUEFIES
34139	OTH HYDROCARBON GAS LQFD	MW 24592	3675776	MW 26829	3383372	MW 25805	3615070	MW 26775	4026018	HYDROCARBURES GAZEUX NDA
4	ANIMAL,VEGETABLE OIL,FAT		848121		1374441		1383592		1567769	HUILES,GRAISSES ANIM,VEG
42	FIXED VEGETABLE OIL,FAT		708444		1132361		1040826		1343669	HUILES VEGETALES FIXES
424	FIXED VEG OIL NONSOFT	W 1908227	690429	W 2370637	1115354	W 1728526	1034709	W 2410601	1338392	AUTRES HUILES VEG FIXES
4242	PALM OIL	W 1372081	472441	W 1631203	717811	W 1265024	747414	W 1671956	825415	HUILE DE PALME
4243	COCONUT (COPRA) OIL	W 258353	103636	W 392872	213167	W 148280	93571	W 378819	266474	HJUILE DE COPRAH
4244	PALM KERNEL OIL	W 275225	110187	W 340504	177583	W 311399	187267	W 341319	235168	HUILE DE PALMISTE
431	*PROCESD ANML VEG OIL,ET	W 384265	136550	W 585543	240291	W 572641	341773	W 467705	223015	HUILES,GRAISSES PREPAREES
4313	FATTY ACIDS ETC,RESIDUES	W 381012	132090	W 570670	229863	W 549629	324884	W 335525	161557	ACIDES GRAS INDUST,RESIDUS
43131	FATTY ACIDS,ACID OILS	W 381012	132090	W 570270	229415	W 548462	324728	W 335525	161557	ACIDES GRAS INDUSTRIELS
5	CHEMCLS,RELATED PROD NES		823692		1001177		1510139		1723568	PRODUITS CHIMIQUES
51	ORGANIC CHEMICALS		243569		334596		488905		514116	PROD CHIMIQ ORGANIQUES
512	ALCOHOLS,PHENOLS ETC		44364		78817	W 88853	99167	W 213010	164259	PHENOLS,PHENOLS–ALCOOLS
5121	ACYCLIC ALCOHOLS,DERIVS		43458		75947	W 88350	96242	W 212439	161153	ALCOOLS ACYCLIQUES
513	CARBOXYLIC ACIDS ETC	W 56999	35783	W 130672	72358	W 171291	154639	W 202490	121450	ACIDES CARBOXYLIQUES
514	NITROGEN–FNCTN COMPOUNDS	W 97652	134432	W 109465	138930	W 110405	154832	W 110121	173094	COMPOSES FONCT AZOTEES
5146	OXYGEN–FNCT AMINO–CMPNDS	W 92206	120863	W 98640	122920	W 94527	128515	W 96111	144219	COMP AMINES FONCT OXYGEN
55	PERFUME,CLEANING ETC PRD		132666		152398		187893		198169	PROD POUR PARFUM,TOILETTE
562	*FERTILIZERS,MANUFACTURE	W 1332283	151831	W 1372921	178286	W 1329277	275705	W 1260320	269572	ENGRAIS MANUFACTURES
5621	CHEM NITROGENOUS FERTLZR	W 1248232	140177	W 1187458	152049	W 1052972	220605	W 1260051	269469	ENGRAIS AZOTES
56216	UREA	W 1248232	140177	W 1187371	152005	W 1052962	220594	W 1260002	269213	UREE
58	PLASTIC MATERIALS ETC		111828		122464		305775		387256	MAT PLAST ARTIFICIELLES
582	PROD OF CONDENSATION ETC	W 32929	39729	W 25234	26316	W 89120	138929	W 179201	186828	PROD CONDENS,POLYCOND
5823	ALKYDS,OTHER POLYESTERS	W 11973	22082	W 9707	15564	W 66132	121852	W 151793	162118	ALKYDES ET AUT POLYESTERS
58231	— IN PRIMARY FORMS	W 11155	18652	W 9133	12742	W 65394	118067	W 148625	152416	SOUS FORMES PRIMAIRES
583	POLYMERIZATION ETC PRODS	W 68873	71752	W 83329	95864	W 129004	166123	W 198131	199657	PROD POLYMERISATION
6	BASIC MANUFACTURES		9722963		9534881		10527155		10887881	ART MANUFACTURES
62	RUBBER MANUFACTURES NES		106139		134940		235113		299441	CAOUTCHOUC MANUFACTURE
625	RUBBER TYRES, TUBES ETC	W 45196	82511	W 49990	103435	W 78735	181943	W 105565	247197	PNEUS CAOUTCHOUC VULCANISE
63	WOOD,CORK MANUFACTRS NES		5129691		4832378		4662458		4839797	OUVRAGES LIEGE ET BOIS
634	VENEERS,PLYWOOD,ETC	W 6488305	4585381	W 6189650	4123920	W 5736792	3825472	W 5606114	3985823	PLACAGES,CONTRE–PLAQUES
6342	PLYWOOD OF WOOD SHEETS	W 5774021	4220971	W 5338355	3716437	W 4909803	3461987	W 4855086	3595387	BOIS CONTRE–PLAQUES
6343	IMPROVED,RECONSTIT WOOD	W 409391	327472	W 469781	387834	W 471725	343048	W 432036	371105	BOIS AMELIORES,RECONST
63431	IMPROVED WOOD	W 253343	289714	W 261734	339785	W 241533	286156	W 248245	329102	BOIS AMELIORES
635	WOOD MANUFACTURES NES	W 513407	544244	W 703622	708405	W 638973	836880	W 635175	853824	ART MANUF EN BOIS NDA
6353	BUILDERS WOODWRK,PREFABS	W 400068	386860	W 480032	534012	W 527087	643897	W 523958	663272	OUVRAGES DE MENUISERIE
64	PAPER,PAPERBOARD AND MFR		494517		595174		933146		947320	PAPIERS,CARTONS & OUVRAGES
641	PAPER AND PAPERBOARD	W 666427	404229	W 761950	486173	W 909214	781723	W 1997124	793913	PAPIERS ET CARTONS
6412	PRINTG,WRITING PAPER NES	W 76201	60153	W 139313	120039	W 183161	202199	W 1110480	305536	PAPIERS POUR L'IMPRESSION
64122	— COATED,IMPREGNATD ETC	W 75665	59217	W 130707	112477	W 144216	150941	W 1010361	210415	PAPIERS IMPRESSION COUCHES
6415	PAPER,PAPERBRD,BULK,NES	W 350389	223218	W 300341	200636	W 400827	376406	W 521188	288121	PAPIERS,CARTONS ROULEAUX
64159	OTHER PAPER ETC,BULK,NES	W 318487	214811	W 262771	188912	W 345784	352803	W 356901	266621	AUT PAPIER ROULEAUX FEUILLES
642	PAPER,ETC,PRECUT,ARTS OF	W 72983	90288	W 93082	109001	W 104696	151423	W 108181	153407	PAP,CARTONS DECOUPES
65	TEXTILE YARN,FABRICS,ETC		2656234		2515871		2738142		2856830	FILS,TISSUS,ARTICLES TEXTILE
651	TEXTILE YARN	W 159259	389953	W 228580	678760	W 254494	813171	W 312882	912586	FILS TEXTILES

5. Special Exports F.O.B. by Commodities according to the S.I.T.C. (Rev. 2) in thousand U.S. Dollars
Exportations Spéciales F.O.B. par Produits d'après la C.T.C.I. (Rév. 2) en milliers de Dollars E.U.

SITC CTCI	COMMODITY	1993 WEIGHT POIDS	1993 VALUE VALEUR	1994 WEIGHT POIDS	1994 VALUE VALEUR	1995 WEIGHT POIDS	1995 VALUE VALEUR	1996 WEIGHT POIDS	1996 VALUE VALEUR	PRODUIT
6513	COTTON YARN	W 41926	112209	W 60375	258087	W 62725	244381	W 78109	287570	FILS DE COTON
6514	SYN FIB YRN,BULK,MONOFIL	W 54365	89120	W 70439	133552	W 84962	216879	W 93825	193735	FILS CONT 85% FIB TEXT SYNTH
65144	— TEXTRD,CONT POLYESTER	W 35548	47511	W 48243	78850	W 60741	143187	W 61423	109950	FILS TEX FI CONT POLYESTERS
6516	DISCON SYN FIB BLEND YRN	W 49494	146463	W 78441	228800	W 77492	247426	W 102659	316974	FILS FIBR TEX SYNT DIS MOINS
65168	OTH DISC SYN BLEND YARN	W 27155	79012	W 48029	137071	W 43477	134147	W 50654	165787	FILS TEXT SYNT MELANGE AUT F
652	COTTON FABRICS,WOVEN	W 52473	342414	W 64175	318415	W 56305	323777	W 65768	347768	TISSUS DE COTON
6521	GREY WOVEN COTTON FABRIC	W 34085	140773	W 42714	183983	W 36255	173769	W 40163	180789	TISSUS COT ECRUS NON MERCER
65214	GREY WOVEN COTTON NES	W 24599	98881	W 31411	139943	W 27189	135053	W 31640	148451	AUT TISSUS 85% COTON ECRUS
6522	WOVEN COTTON BLEACHD,ETC	W 18388	201641	W 21461	134432	W 20050	150008	W 25606	166979	TISSUS COTON BLANCHIS ETC
65224	BLCHED COTTON FABRIC NES	W 13745	165061	W 16100	90974	W 14969	104727	W 20514	126175	AUT TIS PLUS 85% COT BLANCHI
653	WOVN MAN–MADE FIB FABRIC	W 146186	1205276	W 147476	1115689	W 145942	1179944	W 162839	1150697	TISSUS FIBRES SYNTH,ARTIF
6531	CONT SYNT WEAVES NONPILE	W 62732	717367	W 68494	703599	W 71396	763457	W 80871	717427	TISSUS FIBRES SYNTH CONTINUE
65315	CONT SYN TXTL FABRIC NES	W 59202	692630	W 64829	688120	W 69036	750986	W 78209	703511	TIS PLUS 85% TEXT SYNT CONT
6534	DISC SYN BLEND FABRC NES	W 47620	263404	W 43605	227021	W 42334	248927	W 49721	272977	TISSUS FIBRES SYNTH DISCONT
65341	DISC SYN FIB–COTTN FABRC	W 34332	186650	W 35143	176309	W 31403	185027	W 37637	206678	TISSUS FIB SYNT DIS MEL COTO
6536	DISC REGN TXTL FABRC NES	W 26655	114325	W 26661	131528	W 20714	97025	W 21816	94781	TISSUS 85% TEXT ART DISC
656	LACE,RIBBONS,TULLE,ETC	W 9565	331309	W 4442	60126	W 3815	49539	W 3659	45429	TULLES,BRODERIE
65606	EMBROIDERY	W 5934	226561	W 2535	35463	W 1889	27501	W 2000	27323	BRODERIES PIECES,BANDES
658	TEXTILE ARTICLES NES	W 40074	206313	W 35758	175062	W 43842	176810	W 46082	194833	ART FACONNES MAT TEXTILES
6584	LINENS ETC	W 15830	157613	W 10208	110352	W 8339	82710	W 9610	94476	LINGE DE MAISON
66	NONMETAL MINERAL MFS NES		333359		322444		343672		409758	ART MIN NON METALLIQUES
665	GLASSWARE	W 183060	112587	W 171086	101309	W 179835	103389	W 225455	133775	OUVRAGES EN VERRE
67	IRON AND STEEL		310489		311105		379521		338253	FER ET ACIER
672	IRON,STEEL PRIMARY FORMS	W 272970	78539	W 411000	128582	W 387974	155143	W 203053	67064	LINGOTS FER,ACIER
6727	IRN,STL COIL FR REROLLNG	W 154618	48720	W 390759	123005	W 364716	147393	W 199503	65029	EBAUCHES POUR TOLES FER
67271	IRON,SIMPLE STEEL COILS	W 147282	46457	W 373796	117687	W 362458	146614	W 199502	65025	EBAUCHES NON EN ACIER
673	IRON,STEEL SHAPES ETC	W 430727	140674	W 190852	60291	W 94722	40086	W 108076	52647	BARRES,PROFIL FER,ACIER
68	NON–FERROUS METALS		295316		405011		710102		665071	METAUX NON FERREUX
684	ALUMINIUM	W 503748	170732	W 177761	235770	W 238460	369298	W 204721	302155	ALUMINIUM
6841	ALUMINIUM,ALLOYS,UNWRGHT	W 132348	145168	W 148452	204855	W 187985	332693	W 180331	263641	ALUMINIUM,ALLIAGES BRUTS
687	TIN	W 17945	90571	W 22404	118366	W 39712	239378	W 46384	276055	ETAIN
6871	TIN,ALLOYS UNWROUGHT	W 17875	90208	W 22328	118142	W 39667	239223	W 46312	275812	ETAIN ET ALLIAGES BRUTS
69	METAL MANUFACTURES NES		318717		330613		422938		434421	ART MANUFACT EN METAL NDA
697	BASE MTL HOUSEHOLD EQUIP	W 46668	136191	W 36159	125874	W 38551	143367	W 39085	152324	ART MENAGE MET COMMUNS
6974	BASE MTL DMSTC ARTIC NES	W 43356	123678	W 32060	109922	W 32429	123534	W 35508	139575	ARTICLES NDA FONTE,FER,ETC
7	MACHINES,TRANSPORT EQUIP		2204988		3044667		3823503		4994018	MACHINES MATERIEL TRANSPORT
72	MACHS FOR SPCL INDUSTRYS		31662		33836		160807		126350	MAC SPECIALES POUR INDUST
74	GENRL INDUSTRL MACHY NES		91605		125094		144498		192248	MACH APP INDUSTRIE
75	OFFICE MACHNES,ADP EQUIP		156655		299885		501433		799997	MACH BUREAU TRAIT AUTOM
752	AUTOMTIC DATA PROC EQUIP	W 3200	89017	W 2799	96213	W 9373	169942	W 21904	423531	MACH TRAIT INFORMATION
7525	ADP PERIPHERAL UNITS	W 2069	31008	W 1565	25982	W 7953	124344	W 7954	172729	UNITES PERIPHERIQUES
7528	OFF–LINE DATA PROC EQUIP	W 45	3472	W 218	16774	W 626	27790	W 12530	221934	MACH AUXIL TRAIT INFORM
759	OFFICE,ADP MCH PTS,ACCES	W 3959	47084	W 12705	136209	W 4777	252879	W 2065	338600	PIECES DU 751 ET 752
7599	ACCTG,ETC,ADP MCH PTS,AC	W 1017	13811	W 2013	96460	W 2874	220256	W 1540	275244	PIECES DU 751 ET 752
76	TELECOMM,SOUND EQUIPMENT		963576		1472453		1634280		2068162	EQUIPMENT DE TELECOM
761	TELEVISION RECEIVERS	W 7148	114217	W 7300	183166	W 2401	33154	W 3245	45148	RECEPTEURS DE TELEVISION
7611	COLOUR TV RECEIVERS	W 7116	114028	W 7212	181340	W 1998	23409	W 3179	43426	RECEPTEURS COULEUR
762	RADIO BROADCAST RECEIVRS	W 14886	238670	W 22124	268880	W 34268	519467	W 25245	460753	RECEPTEURS RADIODIFFUSION
7628	OTHER RADIO RECEIVERS	W 8048	99826	W 14245	131490	W 26006	354606	W 18008	222762	AUTRES RECEPT RADIO
763	SOUND RECORDRS,PHONOGRPH	W 13183	353199	W 21332	620398	W 23554	692611	W 30047	838216	PHONO,APP ENREGISTREMENT
7638	OTHR SOUND APPARATUS ETC	W 13120	352484	W 21292	619542	W 23299	686186	W 29911	831319	AUT APP D'ENREGIS,REPROD
76381	TV IMAGE,SND RECRDRS ETC	W 11604	327678	W 17758	510432	W 17411	527285	W 21689	648789	APP ENREG,REPRO IMAG,SON
76388	DICTATING MACHINES ETC	W 1516	24806	W 3534	109110	W 5888	158901	W 8222	182531	MACHINES A DICTER
764	TELECOM EQPT,PTS,ACC NES	W 21621	257491	W 32009	400009	W 34441	389048	W 42660	724044	EQUIP TELECOM,PIECES
7641	LINE TELEPHONE,ETC EQUIP	W 3010	53746	W 3604	80464	W 3777	64190	W 2984	230971	APP TELEPHON PAR FIL
7649	PTS NES OF EQUIPMT OF 76	W 7861	138094	W 13526	233946	W 14646	229761	W 17744	365819	PIECES DE LA DIV 76
76493	TELECOMM EQUIPMT PTS NES	W 4425	73131	W 9339	147980	W 12458	149645	W 12861	231252	PIECES 761,762,764.3,8
77	ELECTRIC MACHNRY NES ETC		439701		613645		808485		1085528	MACH APP ELECT NDA
776	TRANSISTORS,VALVES,ETC	W 1705	48985	W 2421	107321	W 2769	145344	W 8082	220395	LAMPES,TUBES,VALVES
778	ELECTRICAL MACHINERY NES	W 82662	225973	W 87891	317844	W 101189	386754	W 119246	466436	AUTRES MACH ELECT NDA
7781	BATTERIES,ACCUMULATORS	W 67144	145706	W 72225	182342	W 81400	225579	W 96574	279756	PILES ET ACCUMULATEURS
77811	PRIMARY BATTERIES,CELLS	W 38868	88357	W 45775	127708	W 54346	151709	W 51463	161668	PILES ELECTRIQUES,PIECES
78	ROAD VEHICLES		334173		314167		372173		348226	VEHICULES ROUTIERS
785	CYCLES,ETC MOTRZD OR NOT	W 37122	252350	W 39598	243229	W 40745	246867	W 31535	183576	MOTOCYCLES SCOOTERS
7851	MOTORCYCLES ETC	W 9733	114041	W 6070	71651	W 4930	57910	W 4090	48705	MOTO VELO MOTEUR AUXIL
7853	INVAL CARR, PTS OF 785	W 21287	107106	W 26950	139685	W 29387	157725	W 24094	120155	FAUTEUILS INVALIDES,PIECES
78539	PARTS,ACCES NES OF 785	W 21287	107105	W 26950	139683	W 29370	157616	W 24094	120155	PIECES DU 785
79	OTHR TRANSPORT EQUIPMENT		153449		133854		107911		223573	AUTRE MATERIEL TRANSPORT
793	SHIPS AND BOATS ETC	W 11580	98768	W 34549	68386	W 38982	91011	W 64584	192698	NAVIRES BATEAUX,ETC
8	MISC MANUFACTURED GOODS		6982345		7499869		7806113		8613700	ART MANUFACTURES DIVERS
821	*FURNITURE,PARTS THEREOF	W 280602	676146	W 325814	784440	W 355761	865840	W 381786	952615	MEUBLES ET PIECES
8211	CHAIRS,SEATS AND PARTS	W 103163	292113	W 118627	322514	W 125941	357265	W 134911	404878	SIEGES ET PIECES
82111	CHAIRS AND OTHER SEATS	W 93188	273751	W 105458	303725	W 112378	337159	W 119234	383184	SIEGES
8219	FURNITURE AND PARTS NES	W 176073	375198	W 205625	457115	W 227622	501274	W 245653	541936	AUTRES MEUBLES ET PIECES
82192	WOOD FURNITURE NES	W 106831	204522	W 128976	264933	W 152967	311166	W 162904	354089	MEUBLES NDA EN BOIS
82199	OTHR FURN,FURN PARTS NES	W 67701	165668	W 74939	188249	W 73643	187822	W 81020	183748	MEUBLES NDA AUTRES MATIERES
84	CLOTHING AND ACCESSORIES		3558912		3272855		3451810		3654682	VETEMENTS
842	MENS OUTERWEAR NOT KNIT	W 48594	841309	W 46046	823611	W 49697	727923	W 54788	834501	VET DESSUS POUR HOMMES
8421	— OVERCOATS,OTHER COATS	W 6742	106148	W 6043	122991	W 6715	115990	W 5823	115042	MANTEAUX HOMMES MAT TEXT
8423	— TROUSERS,BREECHES ETC	W 16418	233900	W 17958	225516	W 21370	263776	W 24743	326946	PANTALONS HOMMES MAT TEX
8429	— OTHER OUTER GARMENTS	W 20321	429271	W 17659	401885	W 17281	285989	W 20119	330012	AUT VET DES HOM MAT TEX
843	WOMENS OUTERWEAR NONKNIT	W 56611	1002452	W 54048	860637	W 55560	887727	W 60556	964926	VET DESSUS FEMMES MAT TEX
8433	— DRESSES	W 10683	203872	W 9758	148188	W 10532	173658	W 12716	213652	ROBES EN MAT–TEXTILES
8435	— BLOUSES	W 11727	227711	W 11511	209757	W 9324	180636	W 10841	194254	BLOUSES FEM MAT TEXTILES
8439	— OTHER OUTER GARMENTS	W 21083	329770	W 22145	324899	W 23185	336266	W 24903	373947	AUT VET DES FEM MAT TEXT
844	UNDER GARMENTS NOT KNIT	W 18929	312039	W 20439	313906	W 27253	434342	W 25746	408490	VETEMENT DESSOUS MAT TEX
8441	— MENS SHIRTS	W 13635	234130	W 15554	247524	W 20593	330252	W 19343	314537	CHEMISES HOMMES MAT TEXT
84411	—— OF COTTON	W 7643	139204	W 8805	147515	W 11534	198748	W 11539	203588	CHEMISES HOMMES DE COTON
845	OUTERWEAR KNIT NONELASTC	W 54733	694793	W 42968	577983	W 44028	620958	W 46280	654749	VET DESSOUS,ACCES BONNET
8451	— JERSEYS,PULLOVERS ETC	W 26371	281598	W 19329	243372	W 20046	258220	W 21543	290725	CHANDAILS,PULL–OVERS ETC
8459	— OTHER,CLTHG ACCESRYS	W 21528	308893	W 17528	252729	W 18850	283639	W 20053	296134	AUT VET DESSUS DE BONNE
846	UNDER GARMENTS KNITTED	W 29345	468642	W 29693	425924	W 31843	489686	W 33875	505661	SOUS VETS DE BONNETERIE
8462	— OF COTTON NON ELASTIC	W 17359	249949	W 18342	223053	W 19292	245975	W 20826	251165	SOUS–VET BONNET COTON
84629	—— OTHER	W 17359	249949	W 18342	223053	W 19292	245975	W 20826	251165	AUT SOUS–VET BONNET COTON
8463	— OF SYNTH FBR NONELAST	W 9925	155815	W 8850	135523	W 9448	156898	W 10180	169170	SOUS–VET BONNET FIB SYNT
84632	—— MENS SHIRTS	W 9825	154237	W 8770	134798	W 9322	155236	W 9943	166030	CHEMISES DE BON FIB SYNMT
848	HEADGEAR,NONTXTL CLOTHNG	W 14507	168217	W 16562	194546	W 17187	210184	W 22160	200721	VET ACCES MAT AUT QUE TEX
8481	LEATHER CLOTHES,ACCESSOR	W 4379	119565	W 3696	147993	W 3472	146447	W 3557	121852	VET ACCES MAT CUIR ARTIF
851	*FOOTWEAR	W 159075	1628016	W 170935	1848348	W 177373	1998140	W 168460	2134972	CHAUSSURES
85101	FOOTWEAR RUBBER,PLASTIC	W 36262	308754	W 41024	318698	W 46267	375681	W 52546	459608	CHAUS SEMELLES CAOUTCH
85102	FOOTWEAR LEATHER	W 120750	1305816	W 127094	1511450	W 128764	1601937	W 114341	1662304	CHAUS SEMELLES EN CUIR

5. Special Exports F.O.B. by Commodities according to the S.I.T.C. (Rev. 2) in thousand U.S. Dollars
Exportations Spéciales F.O.B. par Produits d'après la C.T.C.I. (Rév. 2) en milliers de Dollars E.U.

SITC CTCI	COMMODITY	1993 WEIGHT POIDS	1993 VALUE VALEUR	1994 WEIGHT POIDS	1994 VALUE VALEUR	1995 WEIGHT POIDS	1995 VALUE VALEUR	1996 WEIGHT POIDS	1996 VALUE VALEUR	PRODUIT
88	PHOTO EQU,OPTICL GDS ETC		199374		172810		200042		233341	APP,FOURN PHOTO,OP,MONTR
881	PHOTO APPARAT,EQUIPT NES	W 1490	155018	W 1336	117653	W 1499	123572	W 1874	122967	APP,EQUIP PHOTO NDA
8811	CAMERAS STILL,FLASH APP	W 1085	148086	W 979	115945	W 986	122838	W 1218	122387	APPAREILS PHOTO,PIECES
88111	STILL CAMERAS	W 1040	143437	W 945	112103	W 891	121074	W 1181	118971	APPAREILS PHOTOGRAPHIQ
89	MISC MANUFCTRD GOODS NES		794676		1282623		1142509		1478424	ART MANUFACTURES DIVERS
893	ARTICLES OF PLASTIC NES		130561		141498		185184		203737	OUVRAGES EN MAT DIVIS 58
894	TOYS,SPORTING GOODS,ETC	W 28337	219307	W 25839	181337	W 34635	344935	W 35079	405093	VOITURES ENFANTS,JOUETS
8942	TOYS,INDOOR GAMES ETC	W 23940	190795	W 21593	153833	W 30661	310765	W 31390	371990	JOUETS,JEUX ETC
89423	TOYS NES	W 19297	147624	W 17673	120727	W 21224	138748	W 17731	140067	JOUETS,MODELES REDUITS
89424	INDOOR GAME EQUIPMENT	W 297	5437	W 274	4879	W 4765	130862	W 6235	167213	ART,JEUX DE SOCIETE
897	GOLD,SILVER WARE,JEWELRY		240389		726267		334825		528173	BIJOUTERIE,ORFEVRERIE
8973	PREC JEWLRY,GLD-SILVWARE		235154		721744		331099		524707	BIJOUX OR,ARGENT ORFEVRE
89731	PRECIOUS METAL JEWELLERY		213813		698532		303343		490710	ART BIJOUTERIE,JOAILLER
9	GOODS NOT CLASSD BY KIND		182412		150617		49954		92021	ART TRANSACT NON CLASSES
971	*GOLD,NON MONETARY NES	K 26185	180238	K 11821	146315	K 3916	45407	K 8737	87962	OR NON MONETAIRE
97101	NONMON GLD UNWRT,SEMIMFD	K 16179	180184	K 11607	146300	K 3738	45389	K 7689	87959	OR,ALLIAGES D'OR BRUTS

1. HISTORICAL SERIES, 1959–1994 GENERAL TRADE, IMPORTS C.I.F., EXPORTS F.O.B.
SERIES HISTORIQUES, 1959–1994 COMMERCE GENERAL, IMPORTATIONS C.A.F., EXPORTATIONS F.O.B

YEAR ANNEE	VALUE IN MILLION IRANIAN RIALS # 1 VALEUR EN MILLION IRANIAN RIALS # 1 MERCHANDISE – MARCHANDISE		GOLD – OR		CONVERSION FACTORS U.S. CENTS PER IRANIAN RIAL FACTEURS DE CONVERSION CENTS E.U. PAR IRANIAN RIAL		INDEX NUMBERS – INDICES QUANTUM		UNIT VALUE VALEUR UNITAIRE	
	IMPORTS	EXPORTS	IMPORTS	EXPORTS	IMPORTS	EXPORTS	IMPORTS	EXPORTS	IMPORTS	EXPORTS
1959	47.34	58.33			1.3201	1.3201				
1960	49.24	61.74			1.3201	1.3201				
1961	51.51	51.20			1.3201	1.3201				
1962	40.14	74.24			1.3201	1.3201				
1963	39.22	69.46			1.3201	1.3201				
1964	50.67	94.95			1.3201	1.3201				
1965	65.15	98.71			1.3201	1.3201				
1966	70.32	99.18			1.3201	1.3201				
1967	85.24	146.20			1.3201	1.3201				
1968	104.80	142.50			1.3201	1.3201				
1969	115.70	159.10			1.3201	1.3201				
1970	125.90	198.71			1.3201	1.3201				
1971	141.90	289.80			1.3201	1.3201				
1972	182.50	306.00			1.3201	1.3201				
1973	233.02	425.80			1.4560	1.4571				
1974	367.40	1458.80			1.4787	1.4787				
1975	700.30	1367.10			1.4770	1.4784				
1976	905.20	1651.60			1.4245	1.4231				
1977	1034.00	1713.10			1.4161	1.4161				
1978	954.90	1557.60			1.4189	1.4189				
1979	686.30	1407.80			1.4189	1.4189				
1980	863.30	994.39			1.4185	1.4219				
1981	985.30	980.79			1.2722	1.2840				
1982	1002.30	936.71			1.1961	1.1836				
1983	1582.70	1684.69			1.1568	1.1580				
1984	1332.67	1127.79			1.1145	1.1107				
1985	1058.34	1218.62			1.0997	1.1037				
1986	720.69	521.88			1.2654	1.2722				
1987	658.85	734.86			1.3992	1.4056				
1988	567.92	594.17			1.4577	1.4538				
1989	927.30	939.95			1.3910	1.3887				
1990	1261.70	1205.70			1.4756	1.4858				
1992	2009.95	1299.58			1.5262	1.5288				
1993	24457.35	14409.04			0.0973	0.0885				
1994	60349.65	30620.63			0.0572	0.0572				

2. IMPORTS BY BROAD ECONOMIC CATEGORY AND EXPORTS BY INDUSTRIAL ORIGIN. (PERCENTAGE OF TOTAL VALUE)
IMPORTATIONS PAR CATEGORIES ECONOMIQUES ET EXPORTATIONS PAR BRANCHE D'ACTIVITE.(EN POURCENTAGE DE LA VALEUR TOTALE)

IMPORTS – IMPORTATIONS

	1990	1991	1992	1993	1994	1995	1996
TOTAL IMPORTS–IMPORTATIONS TOTALES							
1 FOOD BEV–ALIMENTATION BOISSONS							
11 PRIMARY–PRODUITS DE BASE							
111 FOR INDUSTRY–POUR L'INDUSTRIE							
112 FOR HOUSEHOLDS–POUR LES MENAGES							
12 PROCESSED–PRODUITS ELABORES							
121 FOR INDUSTRY–POUR L'INDUSTRIE							
122 FOR HOUSEHOLDS–POUR LES MENAGES							
2 IND SUPPLIES–APPROV INDUSTRIELS							
21 PRIMARY–PRODUITS DE BASE							
22 PROCESSED–PRODUITS ELABORES							
3 FUELS–COMBUSTIBLES							
31 PRIMARY–PRODUITS DE BASE							
32 PROCESSED–PRODUITS ELABORES							
321 MOTOR SPIRIT–ESSENCE							
322 OTHER–AUTRES							
4 MACHINERY–EQUIPEMENT							
41 CAPITAL EQUIPMENT–MACHINES							
42 PARTS–PIECES ACCESSOIRES							
5 TRANSPORT–TRANSPORT							
51 PASSENGER CARS–AUTOMOBILES							
52 OTHER–AUTRES							
521 INDUSTRIAL–INDUSTRIELS							
522 NON INDUSTRIAL–NON INDUSTRIEL							
53 PARTS–PIECES ACCESSOIRES							
6 CONSUM GOODS–BIENS CONSOMMATION							
61 DURABLE–DURABLES							
62 SEMI DURABLE–SEMI DURABLES							
63 NON DURABLE–NON DURABLES							
7 GOODS NES–BIENS NDA							

EXPORTS – EXPORTATIONS

	1990	1991	1992	1993	1994	1995	1996
TOTAL EXPORTS–EXPORTATIONS TOTALES							
1 AGRICULTURE							
2 MINING QUARRY–INDUS EXTRACTIVES							
3 MANUFACTURING–IND MANUFACTUR							
31 FOOD BEV TOBACCO–ALIM BOISS TAB							
32 TEXTILES–INDUSTRIES TEXTILES							
33 WOOD & PRODUCTS–BOIS & PRODUITS							
34 PAPER & PRODUCTS–PAPIER & PRODT							
35 CHEMICALS–INDUSTRIES CHIMIQUES							
36 NON METAL MIN–MIN NON METAL							
37 BASIC METAL–IND METAL BASE							
38 METAL MANUF–MANUF METAL							
39 OTH MANUF IND–AUTRES MANUF							

3. TRADE BY PRINCIPAL COUNTRIES OF PURCHASE AND FIRST CONSIGNMENT (VALUE IN THOUSAND U.S. DOLLARS)
ECHANGES SELON LES PRINCIPAUX PAYS D'ACHAT ET DE PREMIERE CONSIGNATION (VALEUR EN MILLIERS DE DOLLARS EU)

COUNTRIES–PAYS	GENERAL IMPORTS C.I.F. IMPORTATIONS GENERALES C.A.F				
	1990	1991	1992	1993	1994
World	18722000		30712066	23797000	34520000
Africa			176800	106000	113000
Americas	1604000		2441391		
Northern America	414000		1427789		
LAIA	1190000		972770		
CACM			13797		
Caribbean			26072		
Rest of America			963		
As.ex F.USSR	4636000		8812684	2057000	2012000
Eur.x F.USSR	9861000		18114855		
EU	9105000		16521863		
EFTA	546000		834938		
East Europe			604255		
Other Europe			424		
Former USSR	305000		553484		241000
Oceania	684000		371526		
Germany/Allemagne	3430000		7524108		
Japan/Japon	1933000		3679790		
United Arab Emirates	971000		1520199	1101000	1069000
Italy/Italie	1499000		2901302		
United Kingdom	1015000		1677171		
Turkey/Turquie	726000		668291	318000	294000
Belgium–Luxembourg	797000		1065731		
Switz.Liecht	546000		769005		
France,Monac	489000		823379		
Korea, Republic of	635000		676464		
Netherlands/Pays–Bas	576000		673320		
Brazil/Brésil	645000		404281		
Canada	414000		607186		
Austria/Autriche	450000		564244		
Argentina/Argentine	545000		437386		
Australia/Australie	684000		237243		
USA/Etats–Unis d'Amer			820604		
Sweden/Suède	281000		518513		
Saudi Arabia			80103	272000	264000
Spain/Espagne	287000		317456		
China/Chine	172000		338098		
Azerbaijan			205128		241000
Thailand/Thaïlande	199000		244574		
Iraq			418976		
Oman			1532	202000	196000
Denmark/Danemark	147000		239589		
Russian Federation			331751		
Former USSR/Anc. URSS	305000				
Finland/Finlande	134000		137517		
India/Inde			244461		
Indonesia/Indonésie			200659	16000	16000
Fm Yugoslav	210000				
Singapore/Singapour			179577		
Malaysia/Malaisie			41054	65000	68000
Czechoslovakia			168064		
Senegal/Sénégal			108431	24000	26000
Bangladesh			80756	32000	42000
Yugoslavia/Yougoslavie			153375		
Pakistan			102106	20000	29000
Romania/Roumanie			140498		
Morocco/Maroc			12270	61000	66000
New Zealand			134169		
Hungary/Hongrie			124385		
Poland/Pologne			104412		
Sri Lanka			88177		
Bulgaria/Bulgarie			66808		
Norway,SVD,JM			65890		
Peru/Pérou			62236		
Kuwait/ Koweït			61390		
Tunisia/Tunisie			42760	8000	7000

COUNTRIES–PAYS	GENERAL EXPORTS F.O.B. # 1 EXPORTATIONS GENERALES F.O.B.				
	1990	1991	1992	1993	1994
Monde	17926900		19868000	12752000	17515000
Afrique	5200		53349	204000	205000
Amériques	13200		73401		
Amérique du Nord	13200		64919		
ALAI			8462		
MCAC			10		
Caraïbes			6		
Autre Amérique			4		
Asie l'URSS exclus	396300		1168060	1704000	1763000
Europe l'URSS exclus	820200		1452402		
UE	714100		1273125		
AELE	106100		164647		
Europe de l'Est			12185		
Autre de l'Europe					
Ancienne URSS	26900		192944	253000	125000
Océanie			6449		
Turkey/Turquie	106100		356634	692000	689000
Germany/Allemagne	399800		747567		
United Arab Emirates	152500		335354	225000	219000
Indonesia/Indonésie			1412	457000	444000
Italy/Italie	159000		221710		
Morocco/Maroc	5200		45	156000	160000
Azerbaijan			28047	211000	61000
Pakistan	7000		36079	135000	118000
Switz.Liecht	106100		160901		
China/Chine			147063		
Belarus/Bélarus			138970		
Japan/Japon	52100		82245		
Kuwait/ Koweït			51015		80000
Turkmenistan/Turkménistn			20841	42000	63000
United Kingdom	50100		74081		
France,Monac	36100		85882		
Sudan/Soudan			37382	41000	42000
Saudi Arabia			4247	32000	65000
Malaysia/Malaisie			2468	56000	39000
Lebanon/Liban			27612	30000	31000
Bahrain/Bahreïn			22450	25000	25000
Canada	13200		50608		
Austria/Autriche	17700		37688		
Qatar			18145	17000	17000
Belgium–Luxembourg	18900		28799		
Syrian Arab Republic			9855	17000	18000
India/Inde	24400		17376		
Korea, Republic of	25700		14212		
Netherlands/Pays–Bas	7400		24267		
Spain/Espagne	10900		16567		
Former USSR/Anc. URSS	26900				
Jordan/Jordanie			3455	10000	10000
Sweden/Suède	9200		13638		
Singapore/Singapour	15000		6928		
Bangladesh	4400		94	6000	6000
USA/Etats–Unis d'Amer			14311		
Tunisia/Tunisie			3902	7000	3000
Afghanistan			13359		
Finland/Finlande			9735		
Korea Dem People's Rp	9100		2		
Denmark/Danemark	5000		3877		
Hong Kong			8137		
Greece/Grèce			7212		
Oman			1810	2000	2000
Libyan Arab Jamahiriya			5639		
Australia/Australie			5508		
Cyprus/Chypre			5146		
Romania/Roumanie			4560		
Norway,SVD,JM			3746		
Venezuela			3477		

(VALUE AS PERCENTAGE OF WORLD TOTAL)(VALEURS EN POURCENTAGE DU TOTAL MONDIAL)

	1985	1986	1987	1988	1989	1990	1991	1992	1993	1994
Africa				0.1	0.4			0.6	0.4	0.3
Americas				8.1	9.6	8.6		7.9		
Northern America				1.8	2.4	2.2		4.6		
LAIA				6.3	7.2	6.4		3.2		
CACM								0.0		
Caribbean								0.1		
Rest of America								0.0		
As.ex F.USSR				24.6	27.9	24.8		28.7	8.6	5.8
Eur.x F.USSR				54.0	49.0	52.7		59.0		
EU				49.3	44.5	48.6		53.8		
EFTA				2.9	2.7	2.9		2.7		
East Europe				0.4	0.5			2.0		
Other Europe				0.6	0.6			0.0		
Former USSR				1.4	0.9	1.6		1.8		0.7
Oceania				3.9	4.2	3.7		1.2		
Germany/Allemagne				19.2	17.3	18.3		24.5		
Japan/Japon				12.3	10.4	10.3		12.0		
United Arab Emirates				1.8	4.0	5.2		4.9	4.6	3.1
Italy/Italie				6.1	6.5	8.0		9.4		
United Kingdom				6.9	5.4	5.4		5.5		
Turkey/Turquie				6.4	6.2	3.9		2.2	1.3	0.9
Belgium–Luxembourg				3.6	3.0	4.3		3.5		
Switz.Liecht				2.9	2.6	2.9		2.5		
France,Monac				2.8	2.2	2.6		2.7		
Korea, Republic of				0.8	2.0	3.4		2.2		

	1985	1986	1987	1988	1989	1990	1991	1992	1993	1994
Afrique				0.1	0.3	0.0		0.3	1.6	1.2
Amériques				7.2	2.2	0.1		0.4		
Amérique du Nord				3.5	1.0	0.1		0.3		
ALAI				3.8	1.3			0.0		
MCAC					0.0			0.0		
Caraïbes				0.0	0.0			0.0		
Autre Amérique				0.0	0.0			0.0		
Asie l'URSS exclus				32.1	29.9	2.2		5.9	13.4	10.1
Europe l'URSS exclus				54.5	51.8	4.6		7.3		
UE				49.2	49.5	4.0		6.4		
AELE				0.8	1.3	0.6		0.8		
Europe de l'Est				2.8	0.2			0.1		
Autre de l'Europe				0.9	0.9					
Ancienne URSS				0.4	0.1	0.2		1.0	2.0	0.7
Océanie				0.0	0.0			0.0		
Turkey/Turquie				6.8	4.4	0.6		1.8	5.4	3.9
Germany/Allemagne				5.8	5.1	2.2		3.8		
United Arab Emirates				0.8	0.6	0.9		1.7	1.8	1.3
Indonesia/Indonésie				0.2	0.2			0.0	3.6	2.5
Italy/Italie				9.2	9.2	0.9		1.1		
Morocco/Maroc				0.0	0.0	0.0		0.0	1.2	0.9
Azerbaijan								0.1	1.7	0.3
Pakistan				0.8	0.7	0.0		0.2	1.1	0.7
Switz.Liecht				0.7	1.2	0.6		0.8		
China/Chine					0.3			0.7		

4. General Imports C.I.F. by Commodities according to the S.I.T.C. (Rev. 2) in thousand U.S. Dollars
Importations Générales C.A.F. par Produits d'après la C.T.C.I. (Rév. 2) en milliers de Dollars E.U.

SITC CTCI	COMMODITY	1987		1988		1989		1990		PRODUIT
		WEIGHT POIDS	VALUE VALEUR	WEIGHT POIDS	VALUE VALEUR	WEIGHT POIDS	VALUE VALEUR	WEIGHT POIDS	VALUE VALEUR	
	ALL COMMODITIES						12807000		18722000	TOUS PRODUITS
0	FOOD AND LIVE ANIMALS						2779000		2138000	ALIMENTS,ANIMAUX VIVANTS
02	DAIRY PRODCTS,BIRDS'EGGS						265000		150000	PRODUITS LAITIERS,OEUFS
04	CEREALS AND PREPARATIONS						1856000		1240000	CEREALES ET PRODUITS
06	SUGAR AND PREPS,HONEY						221000		351000	SUCRES ET PRODUITS
07	COFFEE,TEA,COCOA,SPICES						43000		133000	CAFE,THE,CACAO,EPICES
09	MISC EDIBLE PRODUCTS						386000		237000	PREP ALIMENTAIRES DIVERSES
1	BEVERAGES AND TOBACCO						77000		47000	BOISSONS ET TABACS
2	CRUDE MATERLS,EXCL FUELS						392000		753000	MAT BRUTES NON COMESTIBLES
23	RUBBER, CRUDE						72000		102000	CAOUTCHOUC BRUT
232	NATURAL RUBBER,GUMS						72000		102000	LATEX CAOUTCHOUC NATUREL
26	TEXTILE FIBRES AND WASTE						137000		180000	FIBRES TEXTILES
27	CRUDE FERTLZR,MINRLS NES						63000		108000	ENGRAIS MINERAUX BRUTS
29	CRUDE ANIMAL,VEG MAT NES						120000		363000	MATIERES BRUTES ANIM,VEGET
3	MINERAL FUELS ETC						319000		422000	COMBUSTIBLES MINERAUX LUB
4	ANIMAL,VEGETABLE OIL,FAT						359000		323000	HUILES,GRAISSES ANIM,VEG
431	*PROCESD ANML VEG OIL,ET						316000		279000	HUILES,GRAISSES PREPAREES
5	CHEMCLS,RELATED PROD NES						2048000		2876000	PRODUITS CHIMIQUES
53	DYES,TANNING,COLOUR PROD						74000		166000	PROD TEINTURE,COLORANTS
541	*MEDICINAL,PHARM PRODUCT						254000		386000	PROD MEDICINAUX PHARMACEUT
58	PLASTIC MATERIALS ETC						368000		790000	MAT PLAST ARTIFICIELLES
59	CHEMICAL MATERIALS NES						479000		559000	MAT PROD CHIMIQUES NDA
6	BASIC MANUFACTURES						2553000		5153000	ART MANUFACTURES
64	PAPER,PAPERBOARD AND MFR						326000		404000	PAPIERS,CARTONS & OUVRAGES
65	TEXTILE YARN,FABRICS,ETC						423000		460000	FILS,TISSUS,ARTICLES TEXTILE
66	NONMETAL MINERAL MFS NES						104000		247000	ART MIN NON METALLIQUES
67	IRON AND STEEL						1059000		2927000	FER ET ACIER
7	MACHINES,TRANSPORT EQUIP						3842000		6264000	MACHINES MATERIEL TRANSPORT
71	POWER GENERATING EQUIPMT						2051000		3886000	MACHINES GENERATRICES
77	ELECTRIC MACHNRY NES ETC						715000		1344000	MACH APP ELECT NDA
8	MISC MANUFACTURED GOODS						381000		683000	ART MANUFACTURES DIVERS
87	PRECISION INSTRUMNTS NES						267000		498000	INSTRUM,APPAR SCIENT NDA
89	MISC MANUFCTRD GOODS NES						95000		155000	ART MANUFACTURES DIVERS
9	GOODS NOT CLASSD BY KIND						57000		63000	ART TRANSACT NON CLASSES
931	*SPECIAL TRANSACTIONS						57000		63000	TRANS.SPECIALES

5. General Exports F.O.B. by Commodities according to the S.I.T.C. (Rev. 2) in thousand U.S. Dollars
Exportations Générales F.O.B. par Produits d'après la C.T.C.I. (Rév. 2) en milliers de Dollars E.U.

SITC CTCI	COMMODITY	1989 WEIGHT POIDS	1989 VALUE VALEUR	1990 WEIGHT POIDS	1990 VALUE VALEUR	1991 WEIGHT POIDS	1991 VALUE VALEUR	1992 WEIGHT POIDS	1992 VALUE VALEUR	PRODUIT
	ALL COMMODITIES		13037100		17926900		18661000		19868000	TOUS PRODUITS
0	FOOD AND LIVE ANIMALS		366800		396000					ALIMENTS,ANIMAUX VIVANTS
05	VEGETABLES AND FRUIT		319100		333000					LEGUMES ET FRUITS
057	FRUIT,NUTS,FRESH,DRIED		319100		333000		477896		503498	FRUITS FRAIS OU SECS
05779	NUTS EDIBLE,FRSH,DRY,NES		272900		258000		338857		363933	FRUITS A COQUES NDA
2	CRUDE MATERLS,EXCL FUELS		123100		92700					MAT BRUTES NON COMESTIBLES
21	HIDES,SKINS,FURS UNDRSSD		94200		56800					CUIRS,PEAUX BRUTS
3	MINERAL FUELS ETC		11993200		16614700					COMBUSTIBLES MINERAUX LUB
33	PETROLEUM AND PRODUCTS		11993200		16614700					PETROLE ET DERIVES
333	CRUDE PETROLEUM	MW 101049	11899022							HUILES BRUTES DE PETROLE
52	INORGANIC CHEMICALS						47188		69088	PROD CHIM INORGANIQUES
6	BASIC MANUFACTURES		367900		590600					ART MANUFACTURES
65	TEXTILE YARN,FABRICS,ETC		344700		509100					FILS,TISSUS,ARTICLES TEXTILE
659	FLOOR COVERINGS,ETC		344700		509100		1125268		1133303	COUVRE-PARQUETS,TAPIS ETC
68	NON-FERROUS METALS		17000		77300					METAUX NON FERREUX
6822	COPPER,ALLOYS WORKED		17000		77300					CUIVRE,ALLIAGES OUVRES
68221	COPPER BARS,WIRE,ETC						62784		157097	BARRES,PROFILES ET FILS
9	GOODS NOT CLASSD BY KIND		140600		198800					ART TRANSACT NON CLASSES
931	*SPECIAL TRANSACTIONS		140600		198800					TRANS.SPECIALES

FOOT NOTES – NOTES

TABLE 1 –
1 Values are in thousand million rials.
TABLE 3 –
1 In 1990, 1991 and 1992 exports of petroleum products are included at the World total level only.
TABLEAU 1 –
1 Les évaluations sont exprimées en milliards de rials.
TABLEAU 3 –
1 En 1990, 1991, 1992 et 1993 les exportations des produits pétroliers sont comprises seulement au niveau du monde.

1. HISTORICAL SERIES, 1956–1990 SPECIAL TRADE, IMPORTS C.I.F., EXPORTS F.O.B.
SERIES HISTORIQUES, 1956–1990 COMMERCE SPECIAL, IMPORTATIONS C.A.F., EXPORTATIONS F.O.B

YEAR ANNEE	VALUE IN MILLION IRAQI DINARS VALEUR EN MILLION IRAQI DINARS MERCHANDISE –MARCHANDISE		GOLD –OR		CONVERSION FACTORS U.S. CENTS PER IRAQI DINAR FACTEURS DE CONVERSION CENTS E.U. PAR IRAQI DINAR		INDEX NUMBERS –INDICES QUANTUM		UNIT VALUE VALEUR UNITAIRE	
	IMPORTS	EXPORTS	IMPORTS	EXPORTS	IMPORTS	EXPORTS	IMPORTS	EXPORTS	IMPORTS	EXPORTS
1956	113.32	170.57	1260.00		280.0000	280.0000				152
1957	121.79	128.39	6420.00		280.0000	280.0000				159
1958	109.80	202.24	1764.00		280.0000	280.0000				158
1959	116.48	216.28	18999.00		280.0000	280.0000				148
1960	138.92	233.62	33.04		280.0000	280.0000				145
1961	145.67	236.34			280.0000	280.0000				141
1962	128.76	247.15	5270.00		280.0000	280.0000				142
1963	113.99	278.85	1419.00		280.0000	280.0000				142
1964	147.45	299.94	1211.00		280.0000	280.0000				141
1965	162.61	314.95			280.0000	280.0000				141
1966	176.09	333.51	405.00		280.0000	280.0000				141
1967	151.24	297.40	912.00		280.0000	280.0000				142
1968	144.16	371.72	204.00		280.0000	280.0000				
1969	157.17	372.12	341.00		280.0000	280.0000				
1970	181.65	392.79			280.0000	280.0000				
1971	247.87	500.03			283.0523	283.0523				
1972	234.68	371.31			300.6572	300.3425				
1973	270.32	587.80			330.8950	332.3700				
1974	700.09	1949.40			338.6228	338.6230				
1975	1244.77	2450.17			338.6229	338.6229				
1976	1150.90	2738.10			338.6227	338.6227				
1977	1323.15	2849.60			338.6230	338.6227				
1978	1244.05	3266.40			338.6230	338.6227				
1979	2143.05	6329.00			338.6229	338.6228				
1980	2571.18	7760.30			338.6229	338.6228				
1981	3350.08	3109.70			338.6230	338.6228				
1982	3168.65	3055.70			334.2239	335.4560				
1983	2062.77	3041.80			321.6900	321.6907				
1984	2080.73				321.6900					
1985	2368.33				321.6900					
1986	1977.20	2032.54			321.6900	321.6899				
1987	1198.00	2587.60			321.6900	321.6873				
1988	1852.68	3192.00			321.6900	321.6898				
1989	2162.39	4538.53			321.6900	321.6900				
1990	1502.65				321.6908					

2. IMPORTS BY BROAD ECONOMIC CATEGORY AND EXPORTS BY INDUSTRIAL ORIGIN. (PERCENTAGE OF TOTAL VALUE)
IMPORTATIONS PAR CATEGORIES ECONOMIQUES ET EXPORTATIONS PAR BRANCHE D'ACTIVITE.(EN POURCENTAGE DE LA VALEUR TOTALE)

IMPORTS – IMPORTATIONS

	1990	1991	1992	1993	1994	1995	1996
TOTAL IMPORTS–IMPORTATIONS TOTALES							
1 FOOD BEV–ALIMENTATION BOISSONS							
11 PRIMARY–PRODUITS DE BASE							
111 FOR INDUSTRY–POUR L'INDUSTRIE							
112 FOR HOUSEHOLDS–POUR LES MENAGES							
12 PROCESSED–PRODUITS ELABORES							
121 FOR INDUSTRY–POUR L'INDUSTRIE							
122 FOR HOUSEHOLDS–POUR LES MENAGES							
2 IND SUPPLIES–APPROV INDUSTRIELS							
21 PRIMARY–PRODUITS DE BASE							
22 PROCESSED–PRODUITS ELABORES							
3 FUELS–COMBUSTIBLES							
31 PRIMARY–PRODUITS DE BASE							
32 PROCESSED–PRODUITS ELABORES							
321 MOTOR SPIRIT–ESSENCE							
322 OTHER–AUTRES							
4 MACHINERY–EQUIPEMENT							
41 CAPITAL EQUIPMENT–MACHINES							
42 PARTS–PIECES ACCESSOIRES							
5 TRANSPORT–TRANSPORT							
51 PASSENGER CARS–AUTOMOBILES							
52 OTHER–AUTRES							
521 INDUSTRIAL–INDUSTRIELS							
522 NON INDUSTRIAL–NON INDUSTRIEL							
53 PARTS–PIECES ACCESSOIRES							
6 CONSUM GOODS–BIENS CONSOMMATION							
61 DURABLE–DURABLES							
62 SEMI DURABLE–SEMI DURABLES							
63 NON DURABLE–NON DURABLES							
7 GOODS NES–BIENS NDA							

EXPORTS – EXPORTATIONS

	1990	1991	1992	1993	1994	1995	1996
TOTAL EXPORTS–EXPORTATIONS TOTALES							
1 AGRICULTURE							
2 MINING QUARRY–INDUS EXTRACTIVES							
3 MANUFACTURING–IND MANUFACTUR							
31 FOOD BEV TOBACCO–ALIM BOISS TAB							
32 TEXTILES–INDUSTRIES TEXTILES							
33 WOOD & PRODUCTS–BOIS & PRODUITS							
34 PAPER & PRODUCTS–PAPIER & PRODT							
35 CHEMICALS–INDUSTRIES CHIMIQUES							
36 NON METAL MIN–MIN NON METAL							
37 BASIC METAL–IND METAL BASE							
38 METAL MANUF–MANUF METAL							
39 OTH MANUF IND–AUTRES MANUF							

3. TRADE BY PRINCIPAL COUNTRIES OF PURCHASE AND DESTINATION (VALUE IN THOUSAND U.S. DOLLARS)
ECHANGES SELON LES PRINCIPAUX PAYS D'ACHAT ET DE DESTINATION (VALEUR EN MILLIERS DE DOLLARS EU)

COUNTRIES–PAYS	SPECIAL IMPORTS C.I.F. IMPORTATIONS SPECIALES C.A.F				
	1986	1987	1988	1989	1990
World	6360451	3853840	5959877	6956189	4833865
Africa	70714	31085	49515	124713	69369
Americas	938984	859469	1533554	1684903	968686
Northern America	388840	478829	1149244	1226823	808857
LAIA	540668	376194	365015	444495	158805
CACM			32	145	814
Caribbean	9474	4446	19263	13440	209
Rest of America	3				
As.ex F.USSR	2570921	1438974	2009874	2048721	1588029
Eur.x F.USSR	2673347	1434435	2005203	2633010	1947521
EU	2226957	1133163	1578311	2139509	1602859
EFTA	85795	59545	70974	95256	129818
East Europe	192486	146260	201433	215092	89404
Other Europe	277			1184	2348
Former USSR	26633	19597	70662	75674	77907
Oceania	59069	61919	165709	203015	127090
USA/Etats–Unis d'Amer	363735	467683	979331	1001685	658438
Japan/Japon	1296018	318554	532995	621113	397213
Turkey/Turquie	557971	672982	824726	408919	196025
Germany/Allemagne	492308	260218	322259	459608	389403
United Kingdom	479553	250355	394579	448507	322082
Brazil/Brésil	537467	371381	346013	416421	139549
France,Monac	291390	156293	277995	410412	278265
Italy/Italie	439306	217327	129551	285111	193992
Jordan/Jordanie	118700	138693	164265	209957	220319
Fm Yugoslav	167832	95468	154485	181970	123091
China/Chine	188687	79338	99216	148039	157866
Korea, Republic of	188481	48363	98521	123909	149396
Canada	25105	11147	169913	225138	150419
Australia/Australie	48270	55334	153382	196218	108693
Netherlands/Pays–Bas	104459	57100	111591	102577	93802
Switz.Liecht	80352	58882	65718	94358	126604
Ireland/Irlande	17169	20385	150358	144905	31587
Romania/Roumanie	46680	78698	113331	91099	30062
Sweden/Suède	81828	63209	63026	40636	64779
Indonesia/Indonésie	13340	7714	38873	122744	104855
Spain/Espagne	60716	8084	43431	129004	40520
Belgium–Luxembourg	57441	21026	57550	68150	68343
Former USSR/Anc. URSS	26633	19597	70662	75674	77907
Austria/Autriche	130030	56058		1107	50882
Sri Lanka	34244	51589	50084	33453	52310
Saudi Arabia	4616	11629	37194	96491	62540
India/Inde	30522	7325	32320	65168	57467
Thailand/Thaïlande	9368	10001	22290	59223	68935
Egypt/Egypte	17487	20070	29956	67532	31230
Former GDR	31004	13717	20617	39536	20926
Bulgaria/Bulgarie	35682	26932	40909	15361	4584
Denmark/Danemark	33260	7881	16274	27421	33855
Malaysia/Malaisie	22669	16538	27273	27688	15094
Kuwait/ Koweït	17114	22589	17600	26906	23995
Lebanon/Liban	16532	13817	16689	19456	27566
Czechoslovakia	38834	11433	13579	17384	8522
Poland/Pologne	19208	2310	10056	38989	18430
Tunisia/Tunisie	16738	5523	12089	33864	18800
Morocco/Maroc	36383	3005	3233	18655	15927
Greece/Grèce	18735	10510	3699	11060	20791
Singapore/Singapour	25719	3809	9451	12848	5031
Hungary/Hongrie	21077	13170	2940	12710	6881
New Zealand	10799	6585	12311	6791	18397
Hong Kong	14051	7798	13765	8914	6675
Finland/Finlande	18044	4050	4433	7595	13109
Cuba	9474	4446	19263	13440	209
Uruguay		4430	18253	10638	10024
Cyprus/Chypre	9133	4909	5790	6437	5739
Bangladesh	3548	8789	2709	9200	3127
Bahrain/Bahreïn	48	360	122	17802	8589

COUNTRIES–PAYS	SPECIAL EXPORTS F.O.B. # 1 EXPORTATIONS SPECIALES F.O.B.				
	1986	1987	1988	1989	1990
Monde	6538470	8323989	10268338	12333722	392015
Afrique	2863	396	1306	3442	21843
Amériques	1284745	1430029	2468537	3561361	270
Amérique du Nord	355078	340094	1465462	2362625	270
ALAI	929667	1089935	1002840	1197240	
MCAC			235	1496	
Caraïbes					
Autre Amérique					
Asie l'URSS exclus	1552639	1412263	2167221	3120720	304872
Europe l'URSS exclus	2996071	3400931	3029490	3469212	55601
UE	2416489	3025876	2603281	3090453	18874
AELE	331	357	109	34932	16
Europe de l'Est	67934	34260	672	1824	26263
Autre de l'Europe					
Ancienne URSS	304447	943026	836813	1333366	8898
Océanie	97	16		35	16
USA/Etats–Unis d'Amer	354103	291311	1458940	2290825	158
Brazil/Brésil	929667	1089935	1002840	1197240	
Turkey/Turquie	647849	834686	1052595	1330964	83466
Former USSR/Anc. URSS	304447	943026	835700	1331703	8898
Japan/Japon	775022	504226	712100	1170609	106
Italy/Italie	377145	644631	687101	549757	10642
France,Monac	454106	635841	517360	623884	817
Spain/Espagne	604249	384327	369994	575749	669
Fm Yugoslav	511317	340438	425428	342003	10448
United Kingdom	325887	399265	293066	167024	4404
Netherlands/Pays–Bas	301032	161352	152898	532262	225
India/Inde	77966	409	293029	438841	14737
Belgium–Luxembourg	109106	226984	147505	249629	
Greece/Grèce	59545	254851	192548	189382	273
Germany/Allemagne	71179	215890	121967	76913	1744
Portugal	114192	89432	120842	125819	
Jordan/Jordanie	22364	12321	28373	25201	101567
Kuwait/ Koweït	11182	18468	46217	44245	25304
Canada	975	48783	6522	71801	113
United Arab Emirates	10236	31233	21492	30905	24696
Saudi Arabia	2718	6424	7145	17732	25816
Former GDR	53782	418	1113	1663	293
Thailand/Thaïlande				38421	3825
Switz.Liecht	331	357	109	34932	16
Bulgaria/Bulgarie		32169		261	
Romania/Roumanie					25005
Egypt/Egypte	1737	51	1065	421	11710
Sweden/Suède		13236		35	87
Pakistan	518	881	1541	3844	6527
Poland/Pologne	12965				10
Indonesia/Indonésie				4555	8300
Tunisia/Tunisie			35	35	7032
Bangladesh			48	1982	4825
Czechoslovakia	936	1673	634	1563	955
Former Yemen	39		659	3513	1226
Sri Lanka	3	39	93	4214	1074
Lebanon/Liban	364	1499	354	1084	521
China/Chine	3014	733			
Singapore/Singapour	682	631	367	862	582
Cyprus/Chypre	100	437	2557		
Hong Kong	409	170	196	2088	
Sudan/Soudan	778	119	3	196	1403
Somalia/Somalie				1830	
Morocco/Maroc	347	225	203	959	
Guatemala			235	1496	
Bahrain/Bahreïn	3	97	212	454	232
Mauritius/Maurice					968
Malaysia/Malaisie					782
Qatar	51	10	125	412	170
Korea, Republic of			71	206	380

(VALUE AS PERCENTAGE OF WORLD TOTAL)(VALEURS EN POURCENTAGE DU TOTAL MONDIAL)

	1981	1982	1983	1984	1985	1986	1987	1988	1989	1990
Africa						1.1	0.8	0.8	1.8	1.4
Americas						14.8	22.3	25.7	24.2	20.0
Northern America						6.1	12.4	19.3	17.6	16.7
LAIA						8.5	9.8	6.1	6.4	3.3
CACM								0.0	0.0	0.0
Caribbean						0.1	0.1	0.3	0.2	0.0
Rest of America						0.0				
As.ex F.USSR						40.4	37.3	33.7	29.5	32.9
Eur.x F.USSR						42.0	37.2	33.6	37.9	40.3
EU						35.0	29.4	26.5	30.8	33.2
EFTA						1.3	1.5	1.2	1.4	2.7
East Europe						3.0	3.8	3.4	3.1	1.8
Other Europe						0.0			0.0	0.0
Former USSR						0.4	0.5	1.2	1.1	1.6
Oceania						0.9	1.6	2.8	2.9	2.6
USA/Etats–Unis d'Amer						5.7	12.1	16.4	14.4	13.6
Japan/Japon						20.4	8.3	8.9	8.9	8.2
Turkey/Turquie						8.8	17.5	13.8	5.9	4.1
Germany/Allemagne						7.7	6.8	5.4	6.6	8.1
United Kingdom						7.5	6.5	6.6	6.4	6.7
Brazil/Brésil						8.5	9.6	5.8	6.0	2.9
France,Monac						4.6	4.1	4.7	5.9	5.8
Italy/Italie						6.9	5.6	2.2	4.1	4.0
Jordan/Jordanie						1.9	3.6	2.8	3.0	4.6
Fm Yugoslav						2.6	2.5	2.6	2.6	2.5

	1981	1982	1983	1984	1985	1986	1987	1988	1989	1990
Afrique						0.0	0.0	0.0	0.0	5.6
Amériques						19.6	17.2	24.0	28.9	0.1
Amérique du Nord						5.4	4.1	14.3	19.2	0.1
ALAI						14.2	13.1	9.8	9.7	
MCAC								0.0	0.0	
Caraïbes										
Autre Amérique										
Asie l'URSS exclus						23.7	17.0	21.1	25.3	77.8
Europe l'URSS exclus						45.8	40.9	29.5	28.1	14.2
UE						37.0	36.4	25.4	25.1	4.8
AELE						0.0	0.0	0.0	0.3	0.0
Europe de l'Est						1.0	0.4	0.0	0.0	6.7
Autre de l'Europe										
Ancienne URSS						4.7	11.3	8.1	10.8	2.3
Océanie						0.0	0.0		0.0	0.0
USA/Etats–Unis d'Amer						5.4	3.5	14.2	18.6	0.0
Brazil/Brésil						14.2	13.1	9.8	9.7	
Turkey/Turquie						9.9	10.0	10.3	10.8	21.3
Former USSR/Anc. URSS						4.7	11.3	8.1	10.8	2.3
Japan/Japon						11.9	6.1	6.9	9.5	0.0
Italy/Italie						5.8	7.7	6.7	4.5	2.7
France,Monac						6.9	7.6	5.0	5.1	0.2
Spain/Espagne						9.2	4.6	3.6	4.7	0.2
Fm Yugoslav						7.8	4.1	4.1	2.8	2.7
United Kingdom						5.0	4.8	2.9	1.4	1.1

4. Special Imports C.I.F. by Commodities according to the S.I.T.C. (Rev. 2) in thousand U.S. Dollars
Importations Spéciales C.A.F. par Produits d'après la C.T.C.I. (Rév. 2) en milliers de Dollars E.U.

SITC CTCI	COMMODITY	1987		1988		1989		1990		PRODUIT
		WEIGHT POIDS	VALUE VALEUR	WEIGHT POIDS	VALUE VALEUR	WEIGHT POIDS	VALUE VALEUR	WEIGHT POIDS	VALUE VALEUR	
	ALL COMMODITIES		3853840		5959877		6956189		4833865	TOUS PRODUITS
0	FOOD AND LIVE ANIMALS		1020121				1668140		1347045	ALIMENTS,ANIMAUX VIVANTS
01	MEAT AND PREPARATIONS		241280						116156	VIANDES ET PREPARATIONS
02	DAIRY PRODCTS,BIRDS'EGGS		172149						271696	PRODUITS LAITIERS,OEUFS
04	CEREALS AND PREPARATIONS		185634						486061	CEREALES ET PRODUITS
05	VEGETABLES AND FRUIT		68845						72901	LEGUMES ET FRUITS
06	SUGAR AND PREPS,HONEY		173549						234412	SUCRES ET PRODUITS
07	COFFEE,TEA,COCOA,SPICES		80741						90977	CAFE,THE,CACAO,EPICES
081	*FEEDING STUFF FOR ANIML		53787						53664	NOURRITURE POUR ANIMAUX
09	MISC EDIBLE PRODUCTS		36139						20675	PREP ALIMENTAIRES DIVERSES
1	BEVERAGES AND TOBACCO		50586				126463		91109	BOISSONS ET TABACS
11	BEVERAGES		32						39809	BOISSONS
12	TOBACCO AND MANUFACTURES		50550						51300	TABACS BRUTS FABRIQUES
2	CRUDE MATERLS,EXCL FUELS		64364				271198		77431	MAT BRUTES NON COMESTIBLES
24	CORK AND WOOD		16545						26758	LIEGE ET BOIS
26	TEXTILE FIBRES AND WASTE		13791						499	FIBRES TEXTILES
27	CRUDE FERTLZR,MINRLS NES		12118						11677	ENGRAIS MINERAUX BRUTS
29	CRUDE ANIMAL,VEG MAT NES		11755						5581	MATIERES BRUTES ANIM,VEGET
3	MINERAL FUELS ETC		11394				28868		20781	COMBUSTIBLES MINERAUX LUB
33	PETROLEUM AND PRODUCTS		11246						20398	PETROLE ET DERIVES
4	ANIMAL,VEGETABLE OIL,FAT		27588				9857		7447	HUILES,GRAISSES ANIM,VEG
42	FIXED VEGETABLE OIL,FAT		15515						6865	HUILES VEGETALES FIXES
5	CHEMCLS,RELATED PROD NES		402055				660021		427677	PRODUITS CHIMIQUES
51	ORGANIC CHEMICALS		41427						62334	PROD CHIMIQ ORGANIQUES
53	DYES,TANNING,COLOUR PROD		18922						31896	PROD TEINTURE,COLORANTS
541	*MEDICINAL,PHARM PRODUCT		117121						116754	PROD MEDICINAUX PHARMACEUT
55	PERFUME,CLEANING ETC PRD		21920						41189	PROD POUR PARFUM,TOILETTE
562	*FERTILIZERS,MANUFACTURE		13363						48	ENGRAIS MANUFACTURES
58	PLASTIC MATERIALS ETC		124369						87516	MAT PLAST ARTIFICIELLES
59	CHEMICAL MATERIALS NES		6312						82983	MAT PROD CHIMIQUES NDA
6	BASIC MANUFACTURES		902820				2004881		1121582	ART MANUFACTURES
61	LEATHER,DRESSED FUR,ETC		10159						22817	CUIRS,PELLETERIES
62	RUBBER MANUFACTURES NES		85434						61986	CAOUTCHOUC MANUFACTURE
63	WOOD,CORK MANUFACTRS NES		19871						59249	OUVRAGES LIEGE ET BOIS
64	PAPER,PAPERBOARD AND MFR		71866						103922	PAPIERS,CARTONS & OUVRAGES
65	TEXTILE YARN,FABRICS,ETC		232823						240322	FILS,TISSUS,ARTICLES TEXTILE
66	NONMETAL MINERAL MFS NES		40604						38197	ART MIN NON METALLIQUES
67	IRON AND STEEL		240840						369213	FER ET ACIER
68	NON–FERROUS METALS		37799						43740	METAUX NON FERREUX
69	METAL MANUFACTURES NES		163425						182134	ART MANUFACT EN METAL NDA
7	MACHINES,TRANSPORT EQUIP		1153159				1741636		1463866	MACHINES MATERIEL TRANSPORT
71	POWER GENERATING EQUIPMT								751822	MACHINES GENERATRICES
72	MACHS FOR SPCL INDUSTRYS								362699	MAC SPECIALES POUR INDUST
73	METALWORKING MACHINERY								349346	MACH TRAVAIL DES METAUX
77	ELECTRIC MACHNRY NES ETC		278641							MACH APP ELECT NDA
8	MISC MANUFACTURED GOODS		213512				438280		273298	ART MANUFACTURES DIVERS
812	*PLUMBG,HEATNG,LGHTNG EQ		16718						35058	APPAR SANITAIRES CHAUFFAGE
821	*FURNITURE,PARTS THEREOF		19234						8763	MEUBLES ET PIECES
84	CLOTHING AND ACCESSORIES		38268						96266	VETEMENTS
89	MISC MANUFCTRD GOODS NES		45937						44680	ART MANUFACTURES DIVERS

 Iraq

5. Special Exports F.O.B. by Commodities according to the S.I.T.C. (Rev. 2) in thousand U.S. Dollars
Exportations Spéciales F.O.B. par Produits d'après la C.T.C.I. (Rév. 2) en milliers de Dollars E.U.

SITC CTCI	COMMODITY	1987 WEIGHT POIDS	1987 VALUE VALEUR	1988 WEIGHT POIDS	1988 VALUE VALEUR	1989 WEIGHT POIDS	1989 VALUE VALEUR	1990 WEIGHT POIDS	1990 VALUE VALEUR	PRODUIT
	ALL COMMODITIES # 1		8323989		10268338		12333722		392015	TOUS PRODUITS
0	FOOD AND LIVE ANIMALS		64836				105476		77871	ALIMENTS,ANIMAUX VIVANTS
04	CEREALS AND PREPARATIONS		3410						19716	CEREALES ET PRODUITS
05	VEGETABLES AND FRUIT		56546						55643	LEGUMES ET FRUITS
1	BEVERAGES AND TOBACCO		32285				28203		15390	BOISSONS ET TABACS
12	TOBACCO AND MANUFACTURES		32169						15004	TABACS BRUTS FABRIQUES
2	CRUDE MATERLS,EXCL FUELS		27340				38345		156779	MAT BRUTES NON COMESTIBLES
21	HIDES,SKINS,FURS UNDRSSD		12687						18452	CUIRS,PEAUX BRUTS
22	OIL SEEDS,OLEAGINOUS FRT		61						20231	GRAINES,FRUITS OLEAGINEUX
26	TEXTILE FIBRES AND WASTE		8367						24027	FIBRES TEXTILES
27	CRUDE FERTLZR,MINRLS NES		132						82279	ENGRAIS MINERAUX BRUTS
28	METALLIFEROUS ORES,SCRAP		914						2471	MINERAIS METAL,DECHETS
29	CRUDE ANIMAL,VEG MAT NES		4835						9300	MATIERES BRUTES ANIM,VEGET
3	MINERAL FUELS ETC		8179091				12068180		1911	COMBUSTIBLES MINERAUX LUB
32	COAL,COKE AND BRIQUETTES		45673							HOUILLES,COKES,BRIQUETTES
33	PETROLEUM AND PRODUCTS		8133418						1911	PETROLE ET DERIVES
333	CRUDE PETROLEUM	MW 83450	8129429	MW 102729	9002973	MW 110820	12061920			HUILES BRUTES DE PETROLE
4	ANIMAL,VEGETABLE OIL,FAT								1525	HUILES,GRAISSES ANIM,VEG
42	FIXED VEGETABLE OIL,FAT								1525	HUILES VEGETALES FIXES
5	CHEMCLS,RELATED PROD NES		4677				43312		89394	PRODUITS CHIMIQUES
51	ORGANIC CHEMICALS		4169						47452	PROD CHIMIQ ORGANIQUES
541	*MEDICINAL,PHARM PRODUCT		103						4179	PROD MEDICINAUX PHARMACEUT
562	*FERTILIZERS,MANUFACTURE								25362	ENGRAIS MANUFACTURES
58	PLASTIC MATERIALS ETC		109						8943	MAT PLAST ARTIFICIELLES
59	CHEMICAL MATERIALS NES		238						2081	MAT PROD CHIMIQUES NDA
6	BASIC MANUFACTURES		14952				26115		33427	ART MANUFACTURES
65	TEXTILE YARN,FABRICS,ETC		1425						4977	FILS,TISSUS,ARTICLES TEXTILE
66	NONMETAL MINERAL MFS NES		12636						24252	ART MIN NON METALLIQUES
68	NON–FERROUS METALS		840						2496	METAUX NON FERREUX
7	MACHINES,TRANSPORT EQUIP		730				12440		3564	MACHINES MATERIEL TRANSPORT
72	MACHS FOR SPCL INDUSTRYS								3014	MAC SPECIALES POUR INDUST
8	MISC MANUFACTURED GOODS		77				5311		12150	ART MANUFACTURES DIVERS
821	*FURNITURE,PARTS THEREOF		35						2204	MEUBLES ET PIECES
84	CLOTHING AND ACCESSORIES		42						1239	VETEMENTS
851	*FOOTWEAR								5861	CHAUSSURES

FOOT NOTES – NOTES

TABLE 3 –
1 In 1990 exports of most petroleum products are excluded.
TABLE 5 –
1 In 1990 most petroleum products are excluded.
TABLEAU 3 –
1 La plupart des exportations des produits pétroliers est exclue en 1990.
TABLEAU 5 –
1 La plupart des produits pétroliers est exclue en 1990.

1. HISTORICAL SERIES, 1961–1996 GENERAL TRADE, IMPORTS C.I.F., EXPORTS F.O.B.
SERIES HISTORIQUES, 1961–1996 COMMERCE GENERAL, IMPORTATIONS C.A.F., EXPORTATIONS F.O.B

YEAR ANNEE	VALUE IN MILLION IRISH POUNDS VALEUR EN MILLION IRISH POUNDS MERCHANDISE –MARCHANDISE		GOLD –OR		CONVERSION FACTORS U.S. CENTS PER IRISH POUND FACTEURS DE CONVERSION CENTS E.U. PAR IRISH POUND		INDEX NUMBERS –INDICES QUANTUM		UNIT VALUE VALEUR UNITAIRE	
	IMPORTS	EXPORTS	IMPORTS	EXPORTS	IMPORTS	EXPORTS	IMPORTS	EXPORTS	IMPORTS	EXPORTS
1961	261.40	180.50			280.0000	280.0000	17	11	13	13
1962	273.70	174.40			280.0000	280.0000	18	11	13	13
1963	307.90	197.20			280.0000	280.0000	20	12	13	13
1964	349.60	222.60			280.0000	280.0000	22	13	13	14
1965	372.00	221.30			280.0000	280.0000	23	12	13	14
1966	373.30	244.80			280.0000	280.0000	23	14	13	14
1967	392.40	285.80			275.1700	275.3200	25	16	13	14
1968	496.60	333.40			240.0000	240.0000	29	17	15	15
1969	590.30	371.90			240.0000	240.0000	33	18	15	16
1970	655.50	433.10			240.0000	240.0000	34	19	16	17
1971	754.90	538.70			243.0450	243.3800	36	21	17	18
1972	838.10	647.50			249.4580	249.1080	38	22	18	21
1973	1137.20	869.20			245.3610	245.2030	46	24	20	25
1974	1626.80	1134.40			234.5720	234.3970	45	26	29	31
1975	1704.10	1447.40			221.7360	220.5620	39	28	36	37
1976	2337.90	1859.10			179.4800	178.3210	45	29	42	46
1977	3090.90	2578.20			174.5100	174.8230	50	34	50	53
1978	3713.10	2963.20			191.7710	192.0230	58	37	52	56
1979	4827.90	3496.10			204.7030	205.1310	66	40	58	61
1980	5420.70	4082.00			205.7530	205.7460	63	44	70	67
1981	6577.50	4776.70			161.2575	160.6862	64	44	83	77
1982	6890.20	6379.80			141.1912	140.2556	62	47	89	86
1983	7366.80	6943.80			124.7355	124.1352	64	53	93	94
1984	8912.90	8897.60			108.4137	108.2176	71	63	102	101
1985	9432.70	9743.20			106.2652	106.3493	72	65	104	104
1986	8621.00	9374.00			134.0769	134.2688	75	69	93	97
1987	9155.00	10723.00			148.9809	149.1719	80	79	93	97
1988	10215.00	12305.00			152.6120	152.6120	83	83	99	104
1989	12284.00	14597.00			141.8980	141.8980	94	92	105	110
1990	12469.00	14337.00			165.8646	165.6368	100	100	100	100
1991	12851.00	15019.00			161.5127	161.2822	101	106	102	99
1992	13195.00	16744.00			170.3880	170.3989	106	121	100	97
1993	14885.00	19830.00			146.4145	146.3525	113	133	105	104
1994	17283.01	22753.01			149.9185	150.1117	128	153	108	104
1995	20619.01	27825.01			160.3755	160.4223	146	184	113	106
1996	22352.00	30102.00			160.0416	160.0589	160	200	111	105

2. IMPORTS BY BROAD ECONOMIC CATEGORY AND EXPORTS BY INDUSTRIAL ORIGIN. (PERCENTAGE OF TOTAL VALUE)
IMPORTATIONS PAR CATEGORIES ECONOMIQUES ET EXPORTATIONS PAR BRANCHE D'ACTIVITE.(EN POURCENTAGE DE LA VALEUR TOTALE)

IMPORTS – IMPORTATIONS

	1990	1991	1992	1993	1994	1995	1996
TOTAL IMPORTS–IMPORTATIONS TOTALES	100.	100.	100.	100.	100.	100.	100.
1 FOOD BEV–ALIMENTATION BOISSONS	8.1	8.9	9.1	7.7	7.5	6.6	6.6
11 PRIMARY–PRODUITS DE BASE	2.5	2.7	2.6	2.1	2.2	2.1	2.0
111 FOR INDUSTRY–POUR L'INDUSTRIE	0.6	0.7	0.6	0.5	0.5	0.4	0.4
112 FOR HOUSEHOLDS–POUR LES MENAGES	1.9	2.0	1.9	1.6	1.7	1.7	1.6
12 PROCESSED–PRODUITS ELABORES	5.7	6.2	6.6	5.7	5.4	4.6	4.7
121 FOR INDUSTRY–POUR L'INDUSTRIE	0.8	0.8	0.9	0.8	0.8	0.7	0.7
122 FOR HOUSEHOLDS–POUR LES MENAGES	4.9	5.4	5.7	4.9	4.6	3.8	4.0
2 IND SUPPLIES–APPROV INDUSTRIELS	28.8	28.8	27.9	24.8	25.2	24.5	23.2
21 PRIMARY–PRODUITS DE BASE	2.5	2.5	2.2	2.3	2.3	1.9	1.6
22 PROCESSED–PRODUITS ELABORES	26.3	26.3	25.7	22.5	22.9	22.6	21.6
3 FUELS–COMBUSTIBLES	6.3	5.7	5.1	4.7	3.8	3.2	3.6
31 PRIMARY–PRODUITS DE BASE	3.1	2.6	2.4	2.1	1.8	1.5	1.5
32 PROCESSED–PRODUITS ELABORES	3.3	3.1	2.7	2.6	2.0	1.7	2.1
321 MOTOR SPIRIT–ESSENCE	0.8	0.7	0.6	0.5	0.4	0.4	0.4
322 OTHER–AUTRES	2.5	2.4	2.0	2.1	1.6	1.4	1.6
4 MACHINERY–EQUIPEMENT	26.7	26.7	28.5	30.6	31.6	35.6	34.5
41 CAPITAL EQUIPMENT–MACHINES	16.6	16.4	17.0	18.1	19.1	20.3	22.2
42 PARTS–PIECES ACCESSOIRES	10.0	10.3	11.5	12.6	12.5	15.3	12.4
5 TRANSPORT–TRANSPORT	9.6	8.3	7.7	7.1	7.8	7.3	7.8
51 PASSENGER CARS–AUTOMOBILES	3.4	2.8	3.0	2.8	3.1	2.8	3.6
52 OTHER–AUTRES	3.1	2.7	1.9	1.6	1.6	1.8	1.6
521 INDUSTRIAL–INDUSTRIELS	3.0	2.6	1.8	1.4	1.5	1.7	1.6
522 NON INDUSTRIAL–NON INDUSTRIEL	0.1	0.1	0.1	0.1	0.1	0.1	0.1
53 PARTS–PIECES ACCESSOIRES	3.1	2.8	2.8	2.7	3.1	2.7	2.6
6 CONSUM GOODS–BIENS CONSOMMATION	17.2	18.4	18.5	15.9	15.0	13.4	15.7
61 DURABLE–DURABLES	3.4	3.6	3.2	2.4	2.3	2.2	3.0
62 SEMI DURABLE–SEMI DURABLES	9.9	10.4	10.8	9.8	9.0	7.7	9.4
63 NON DURABLE–NON DURABLES	4.0	4.3	4.4	3.7	3.7	3.4	3.3
7 GOODS NES–BIENS NDA	3.2	3.2	3.1	9.0	9.0	9.4	8.5

EXPORTS – EXPORTATIONS

	1990	1991	1992	1993	1994	1995	1996
TOTAL EXPORTS–EXPORTATIONS TOTALES	100.	100.	100.	100.	100.	100.	100.
1 AGRICULTURE	3.7	3.2	2.9	2.3	2.5	1.9	1.9
2 MINING QUARRY–INDUS EXTRACTIVES	0.9	0.8	0.8	0.7	0.6	0.5	0.4
3 MANUFACTURING–IND MANUFACTUR	95.3	95.9	96.3	97.0	96.9	97.7	97.7
31 FOOD BEV TOBACCO–ALIM BOISS TAB	19.6	20.4	22.5	20.3	21.4	18.1	15.1
32 TEXTILES–INDUSTRIES TEXTILES	4.5	4.7	4.3	3.5	3.7	2.8	2.8
33 WOOD & PRODUCTS–BOIS & PRODUITS	0.3	0.3	0.3	0.2	0.2	0.2	0.2
34 PAPER & PRODUCTS–PAPIER & PRODT	1.3	1.4	1.3	0.9	1.1	0.9	0.9
35 CHEMICALS–INDUSTRIES CHIMIQUES	19.4	21.3	22.7	22.3	26.5	20.9	25.9
36 NON METAL MIN–MIN NON METAL	1.2	1.1	1.0	0.8	0.8	0.6	0.7
37 BASIC METAL–IND METAL BASE	1.0	0.8	0.7	0.7	0.6	0.5	0.5
38 METAL MANUF–MANUF METAL	42.4	41.1	39.2	40.1	42.4	45.9	50.7
39 OTH MANUF IND–AUTRES MANUF	5.5	4.8	4.2	8.0	0.2	7.7	0.8

3. TRADE BY PRINCIPAL COUNTRIES OF ORIGIN AND LAST DESTINATION (VALUE IN THOUSAND U.S. DOLLARS)
ECHANGES SELON LES PRINCIPAUX PAYS D'ORIGINE ET DE DERNIERE DESTINATION (VALEUR EN MILLIERS DE DOLLARS EU)

COUNTRIES–PAYS	GENERAL IMPORTS C.I.F. IMPORTATIONS GENERALES C.A.F				
	1992	1993	1994	1995	1996
World	22482714	21663012	25763835	32321039	35764674
Africa	277460	260674	335821	394555	396017
Americas	3450251	3986950	5042938	6181558	6089402
Northern America	3291238	3828692	4868168	5949744	5786859
LAIA	142138	140258	148443	186080	253180
CACM	5896	9743	8809	18729	16845
Caribbean	10263	7773	11726	18873	24498
Rest of America	717	483	5792	8132	8019
As.ex F.USSR	2255747	3193965	3362600	5313199	6202061
Eur.x F.USSR	16262381	13330884	15740958	18985128	21086982
EU	15542080	12680357	14958289	18141058	20197754
EFTA	573997	532431	637081	666186	683137
East Europe	122373	98998	125121	145313	180308
Other Europe	3857	3104	4583	8211	6065
Former USSR	52775	53683	41209	58817	81945
Oceania	32524	35321	41099	64648	65774
United Kingdom	9544738	7846242	9347762	11498328	12430291
USA/Etats–Unis d'Amer	3186944	3709927	4709908	5717229	5537317
Germany/Allemagne	1880529	1568616	1816644	2256245	2452196
Japan/Japon	1125327	1416192	1233577	1705841	1929937
France,Monac	1000270	845815	980963	1200332	1395600
Netherlands/Pays–Bas	990500	680876	727298	871299	1048308
Singapore/Singapour	188444	475656	540574	1292682	1580271
Italy/Italie	534421	440820	567975	637658	750391
Belgium–Luxembourg	465747	326516	343480	405733	466760
Norway,SVD,JM	363796	327762	374171	446950	441052
Sweden/Suède	334053	300013	370114	346100	481640
Malaysia/Malaisie	62590	164666	293760	530392	538475
China/Chine	147308	306723	307210	346699	407115
Spain/Espagne	209073	194142	258472	313524	447435
Switz.Liecht	205981	201965	258567	215690	235519
Denmark/Danemark	216606	166060	186700	227213	261634
Korea, Republic of	114141	130640	126801	268888	392635
Hong Kong	147240	170967	170532	230231	189650
Finland/Finlande	163519	134434	150260	200562	233317
Canada	104069	118734	158178	232147	249305
Thailand/Thaïlande	47793	39231	65172	116217	254966
Portugal	91213	69827	88223	92170	121293
Austria/Autriche	91603	90379	97558	70957	83796
Brazil/Brésil	73355	84994	91123	92175	75692
Guinea/Guinée	78611	75866	75637	85581	100870
Poland/Pologne	89517	74874	79992	72521	81081
India/Inde	39369	37886	54127	89668	107866
Indonesia/Indonésie	42561	57796	57802	57569	61071
Israel/Israël	47116	37231	43712	44673	82356
So. Africa Customs Un	25234	34006	64818	69560	54484
Turkey/Turquie	36081	35731	41117	60516	72009
Morocco/Maroc	39698	28217	43688	66052	51784
Mexico/Mexique	12371	11556	12357	54567	103140
Russian Federation	46026	37681	22347	29994	45789
Ghana	29897	28034	38437	40874	44053
Philippines	18662	16749	32615	47131	62372
Cote d'Ivoire	13817	10119	20015	50706	63828
Australia/Australie	18306	20626	23478	37482	37938
Czech Republic		13035	24513	32973	42446
Greece/Grèce	19808	16616	22840	20938	25094
New Zealand	12833	13908	15665	24672	24977
Tunisia/Tunisie	12382	13308	14001	22356	24045
Pakistan	15031	16355	20477	19292	12426
Mali	23423	27782	27382	1458	643
Argentina/Argentine	14168	11029	10890	7614	30143
Hungary/Hongrie	6477	6847	10563	20183	29178
Kenya	15534	13265	13247	12973	14985
Colombia/Colombie	13871	10865	10793	9546	20126
Sri Lanka	8872	8707	11403	14223	19809
Cyprus/Chypre	13360	14056	12075	9755	9236

COUNTRIES–PAYS	GENERAL EXPORTS F.O.B. EXPORTATIONS GENERALES F.O.B.				
	1992	1993	1994	1995	1996
Monde	28334545	28856521	34395136	43789356	45565370
Afrique	377904	482991	602184	695689	738547
Amériques	2961615	3280953	3547111	4426969	5203412
Amérique du Nord	2630868	2927877	3179068	3979708	4683924
ALAI	265050	246478	277825	379159	445823
MCAC	21760	27510	25236	23136	25667
Caraïbes	34312	70157	55317	32903	32187
Autre Amérique	9625	8931	9666	12063	15811
Asie l'URSS exclus	1759063	2281692	2647060	3452026	4247625
Europe l'URSS exclus	22651624	21452863	26167339	33355943	33764499
UE	21855679	20520215	24901631	31649154	31797862
AELE	687342	784721	1052454	1285184	1458947
Europe de l'Est	73376	115013	174691	365751	429667
Autre de l'Europe	25086	23586	22076	30141	36349
Ancienne URSS	195217	102260	240512	407959	448776
Océanie	190287	200362	228905	268209	335448
United Kingdom	8915160	8204000	9615392	11140145	11428295
Germany/Allemagne	3616294	3832459	4836993	6328624	5844822
France,Monac	2731599	2640151	3138665	4143416	3904669
USA/Etats–Unis d'Amer	2332264	2621713	2858189	3641814	4302731
Netherlands/Pays–Bas	1977471	1672351	1900593	3063628	3234796
Belgium–Luxembourg	1379810	1165623	1336970	1908551	2226879
Italy/Italie	1158846	1044474	1334110	1658289	1645271
Japan/Japon	817975	1063444	1074085	1307430	1376277
Spain/Espagne	705961	636026	841780	1073628	1092257
Sweden/Suède	496726	499847	757417	809534	857457
Switz.Liecht	465397	515092	666785	795379	895045
Denmark/Danemark	287269	262969	329201	546394	609819
Norway,SVD,JM	214088	259792	372103	472270	536251
Canada	295758	303926	319038	335666	378166
Russian Federation	192279	87510	208170	351086	358158
Malaysia/Malaisie	48112	45430	174761	348199	559864
Austria/Autriche	153071	162933	251210	263517	229717
Australia/Australie	162276	172820	194403	229564	293503
Finland/Finlande	145848	118460	237017	279398	262143
Saudi Arabia	162968	202867	187560	241459	234830
Greece/Grèce	146884	159972	173661	263375	269069
Singapore/Singapour	89344	137871	202266	267656	283846
Hong Kong	101251	144761	160852	163867	224773
Egypt/Egypte	68173	136689	214843	195262	160346
Portugal	140741	120949	148623	170656	192668
So. Africa Customs Un	69020	87434	143375	166249	246046
Korea, Republic of	40431	54920	124872	158826	328623
Mexico/Mexique	147822	113605	92521	127779	161305
Israel/Israël	55788	58555	96492	144718	159660
Poland/Pologne	30455	48848	62501	137412	169127
Philippines	37215	31238	39643	82316	231566
Brazil/Brésil	34972	63486	77840	88982	110826
Turkey/Turquie	30208	58504	48258	98823	124335
United Arab Emirates	38599	56111	67129	84787	91116
Czech Republic		34771	56926	108591	130365
Thailand/Thaïlande	34960	27171	43546	66665	109730
Nigeria/Nigéria	56185	49895	47600	67384	60046
Hungary/Hongrie	16143	24378	41178	71028	80139
Iran (Islamic Rp. of)	20346	29779	53341	58944	31369
Argentina/Argentine	18757	16329	30289	51799	58562
China/Chine	15938	29249	33444	37905	49309
Algeria/Algérie	12612	24775	36459	30006	52845
Chile/Chili	22887	23108	32744	35916	41218
India/Inde	17852	39805	26144	29721	37235
Libyan Arab Jamahiriya	18522	30288	14312	59368	28016
Kuwait/ Koweït	21731	25123	30331	30130	36243
New Zealand	23442	23159	28685	29249	34826
Cyprus/Chypre	22587	22568	23873	28071	26945
Pakistan	22171	18536	15048	32898	26304
Malta/Malte	20370	20479	18571	25477	28663

(VALUE AS PERCENTAGE OF WORLD TOTAL)(VALEURS EN POURCENTAGE DU TOTAL MONDIAL)

	1987	1988	1989	1990	1991	1992	1993	1994	1995	1996
Africa	1.3	1.2	1.3	1.3	1.2	1.2	1.2	1.3	1.2	1.1
Americas	18.9	17.8	17.9	16.3	16.7	15.3	18.4	19.6	19.1	17.0
Northern America	18.2	17.1	17.1	15.6	16.0	14.6	17.7	18.9	18.4	16.2
LAIA	0.6	0.7	0.7	0.7	0.7	0.6	0.6	0.6	0.6	0.7
CACM	0.0	0.0	0.1	0.0	0.0	0.0	0.0	0.0	0.1	0.0
Caribbean	0.2	0.0	0.0	0.0	0.0	0.0	0.0	0.0	0.1	0.1
Rest of America	0.0	0.0	0.0	0.0	0.0	0.0	0.0	0.0	0.0	0.0
As.ex F.USSR	8.0	8.8	9.4	9.6	9.8	10.0	14.7	13.1	16.4	17.3
Eur.x F.USSR	70.9	71.1	70.1	71.8	71.3	72.3	61.5	61.1	58.7	59.0
EU	68.4	69.1	68.3	69.4	68.3	69.1	58.5	58.1	56.1	56.5
EFTA	1.4	1.1	1.0	1.5	2.3	2.6	2.5	2.5	2.1	1.9
East Europe	1.0	0.8	0.7	0.7	0.6	0.5	0.5	0.5	0.4	0.5
Other Europe	0.1	0.1	0.1	0.1	0.1	0.0	0.0	0.0	0.0	0.0
Former USSR	0.4	0.3	0.4	0.3	0.4	0.2	0.2	0.2	0.2	0.2
Oceania	0.2	0.2	0.3	0.2	0.1	0.1	0.2	0.2	0.2	0.2
United Kingdom	41.7	42.1	40.9	42.2	41.4	42.5	36.2	36.3	35.6	34.8
USA/Etats–Unis d'Amer	17.0	15.9	16.1	14.6	15.0	14.2	17.1	18.3	17.7	15.5
Germany/Allemagne	8.4	8.6	8.7	8.3	8.2	8.4	7.2	7.1	7.0	6.9
Japan/Japon	4.3	4.9	5.9	5.6	5.0	5.0	6.5	4.8	5.3	5.4
France,Monac	4.4	4.1	4.1	4.6	4.4	4.4	3.9	3.8	3.7	3.9
Netherlands/Pays–Bas	3.7	4.0	4.1	4.1	4.4	4.4	3.1	2.8	2.7	2.9
Singapore/Singapour	0.2	0.4	0.3	0.5	0.7	0.8	2.2	2.1	4.0	4.4
Italy/Italie	2.5	2.5	2.6	2.6	2.5	2.4	2.0	2.2	2.0	2.1
Belgium–Luxembourg	2.2	2.1	2.2	2.2	2.1	2.1	1.5	1.3	1.3	1.3
Norway,SVD,JM	0.6	0.4	0.4	0.8	1.5	1.6	1.5	1.5	1.4	1.2

	1987	1988	1989	1990	1991	1992	1993	1994	1995	1996
Afrique	2.4	2.4	1.9	1.5	1.5	1.3	1.7	1.8	1.6	1.6
Amériques	10.4	10.1	10.1	10.4	11.1	10.5	11.4	10.3	10.1	11.4
Amérique du Nord	9.2	9.1	9.0	9.4	10.1	9.3	10.1	9.2	9.1	10.3
ALAI	1.0	0.8	1.0	0.8	0.7	0.9	0.9	0.8	0.9	1.0
MCAC	0.1	0.0	0.0	0.0	0.1	0.1	0.1	0.1	0.1	0.1
Caraïbes	0.2	0.1	0.1	0.2	0.2	0.1	0.2	0.2	0.1	0.1
Autre Amérique	0.0	0.0	0.0	0.0	0.0	0.0	0.0	0.0	0.0	0.0
Asie l'URSS exclus	5.4	5.8	5.9	5.2	5.4	6.2	7.9	7.7	7.9	9.3
Europe l'URSS exclus	80.1	80.2	80.5	81.0	80.4	79.9	74.3	76.1	76.2	74.1
UE	76.7	77.1	77.3	78.0	77.4	77.1	71.1	72.4	72.3	69.8
AELE	2.8	2.5	2.6	2.5	2.5	2.4	2.7	3.1	2.9	3.2
Europe de l'Est	0.4	0.4	0.3	0.3	0.3	0.3	0.4	0.5	0.8	0.9
Autre de l'Europe	0.3	0.1	0.3	0.1	0.2	0.1	0.1	0.1	0.1	0.1
Ancienne URSS	0.2	0.1	0.3	0.6	0.5	0.7	0.4	0.7	0.9	1.0
Océanie	1.0	0.9	0.8	0.7	0.7	0.7	0.7	0.7	0.6	0.7
United Kingdom	34.2	35.4	33.5	33.7	31.9	31.5	28.4	28.0	25.4	25.1
Germany/Allemagne	11.2	11.1	11.0	11.7	12.7	12.8	13.3	14.1	14.5	12.8
France,Monac	9.3	9.1	10.0	10.5	9.5	9.6	9.1	9.1	9.5	8.6
USA/Etats–Unis d'Amer	7.8	7.7	7.9	8.2	8.7	8.2	9.1	8.3	8.3	9.4
Netherlands/Pays–Bas	7.3	7.0	7.1	5.8	6.6	7.0	5.8	5.5	7.0	7.1
Belgium–Luxembourg	4.8	4.4	4.5	4.4	4.9	4.9	4.0	3.9	4.4	4.9
Italy/Italie	3.7	3.8	4.4	4.4	4.3	4.1	3.6	3.9	3.8	3.6
Japan/Japon	1.7	1.9	2.2	1.8	2.3	2.9	3.7	3.1	3.0	3.0
Spain/Espagne	1.7	1.9	2.1	2.3	2.5	2.5	2.2	2.4	2.5	2.4
Sweden/Suède	1.9	1.9	1.8	1.9	1.7	1.8	1.7	2.2	1.8	1.9

4. General Imports C.I.F. by Commodities according to the S.I.T.C. (Rev. 2) in thousand U.S. Dollars
Importations Générales C.A.F. par Produits d'après la C.T.C.I. (Rév. 2) en milliers de Dollars E.U.

SITC CTCI	COMMODITY	1993 WEIGHT POIDS	1993 VALUE VALEUR	1994 WEIGHT POIDS	1994 VALUE VALEUR	1995 WEIGHT POIDS	1995 VALUE VALEUR	1996 WEIGHT POIDS	1996 VALUE VALEUR	PRODUIT
	ALL COMMODITIES		21663012		25763835		32321039		35764674	TOUS PRODUITS
0	FOOD AND LIVE ANIMALS		1791108		2094610		2298665		2456973	ALIMENTS,ANIMAUX VIVANTS
01	MEAT AND PREPARATIONS		117151		169480		221697		225901	VIANDES ET PREPARATIONS
011	MEAT FRESH,CHILLD,FROZEN	W 25287	51969	W 43387	85173	W 53325	117607	W 47890	105750	VIANDES FRAICHES,REF,CONGE
02	DAIRY PRODCTS,BIRDS'EGGS		110456		140179		193447		216130	PRODUITS LAITIERS,OEUFS
022	MILK AND CREAM	W 104213	60316	W 110832	79471	W 197521	128057	W 197064	128206	LAIT ET CREME
0223	MILK AND CREAM FRESH	W 93164	40649	W 98280	54464	W 185741	107313	W 183978	108456	LAIT,CREME FRAIS
04	CEREALS AND PREPARATIONS		341665		385143		415144		424832	CEREALES ET PRODUITS
048	CEREAL ETC PREPARATIONS	W 120412	243633	W 125572	264746	W 133937	277089	W 144226	296377	PREPTNS A BASE CEREALES
0481	PREPD BREAKFAST FOOD ETC	W 32610	67630	W 32637	76356	W 33884	74499	W 38826	78665	CEREALES TRAVAILLEES
0484	BAKERY PRODUCTS	W 62312	134380	W 64474	144865	W 69888	156899	W 74565	170231	PRODUITS DE BOULANGERIE
04842	PASTRY, CAKES ETC	W 31677	79709	W 32334	86380	W 28352	83235	W 28671	83860	PATISSERIE ETC.
05	VEGETABLES AND FRUIT		360302		402271		436481		489272	LEGUMES ET FRUITS
054	VEG ETC FRSH,SMPLY PRSVD	W 263043	145052	W 289224	171533	W 222840	187531	W 266883	208824	LEGUMES FRAIS,CONG,SECS
057	FRUIT,NUTS,FRESH,DRIED	W 173699	123919	W 164866	139129	W 159371	146832	W 165516	161394	FRUITS FRAIS OU SECS
058	FRUIT PRESERVED,PREPARED	W 47455	67491	W 44344	67654	W 48110	78028	W 62639	86546	CONSERVES DE FRUITS
06	SUGAR AND PREPS,HONEY		117005		119257		136648		150607	SUCRES ET PRODUITS
07	COFFEE,TEA,COCOA,SPICES		160240		195592		202370		210866	CAFE,THE,CACAO,EPICES
073	CHOCOLATE AND PRODUCTS	W 26232	95404	W 29310	114845	W 28722	119568	W 28950	120697	CHOCOLAT
081	*FEEDING STUFF FOR ANIML	W 2017324	363463	W 2465725	442453	W 2160838	422505	W 2049294	421281	NOURRITURE POUR ANIMAUX
0813	OILCAKE AND OTH RESIDUES	W 733726	130932	W 836275	146431	W 685705	120325	W 669749	143720	TOURTEAUX
08131	— OF SOYA BEANS	W 295920	71082	W 284541	66536	W 282975	65731	W 273906	79182	TOURTEAUX DE SOJA
0819	FOOD WASTE AND FEED NES	W 924472	177999	W 1204948	224919	W 1073504	226634	W 986839	203881	DECHETS,ALIMENTS NDA
08193	BEET-PULP,BAGASSE,ETC	W 775015	113490	W 1002580	145649	W 885539	136837	W 485581	81927	PULPES,AUTRES DECHETS
08199	FODDER NES,INCL SWEETNED	W 149337	64299	W 202366	79265	W 187965	89796	W 501253	121952	PREPARATIONS FOURRAGERES
09	MISC EDIBLE PRODUCTS		108915		121391		119637		145747	PREP ALIMENTAIRES DIVERSES
098	EDIBLE PRODCTS,PREPS NES	W 83878	96391	W 55809	111966	W 55222	109022	W 109676	127597	PREP ALIMENTAIRES NDA
1	BEVERAGES AND TOBACCO		277344		312678		303491		372312	BOISSONS ET TABACS
11	BEVERAGES		213750		248594		234295		296159	BOISSONS
112	ALCOHOLIC BEVERAGES	W 106559	162098	W 116567	185949	W 94436	180663	W 115387	215929	BOISSONS ALCOOLIQUES
2	CRUDE MATERLS,EXCL FUELS		470105		582085		617123		630780	MAT BRUTES NON COMESTIBLES
24	CORK AND WOOD		98197		154208		144674		160490	LIEGE ET BOIS
248	WOOD SHAPED,SLEEPERS	W 188402	86990	W 253311	139040	W 185615	128325	W 214707	141941	BOIS SIMPLEMENT TRAVAILLES
2482	LUMBER SHAPED CONIFER	W 138508	50872	W 186526	82738	W 130770	67074	W 154096	77650	CONIFERES SCIES,RABOTES
24821	LUMBER SAWN ETC CONIFER	W 137338	48376	W 184972	79675	W 128748	63271	W 149116	70066	CONIFERES SCIES LONGITUD
26	TEXTILE FIBRES AND WASTE		70281		80579		94850		89193	FIBRES TEXTILES
27	CRUDE FERTLZR,MINRLS NES		61936		104206		89786		82882	ENGRAIS MINERAUX BRUTS
28	METALLIFEROUS ORES,SCRAP		136036		117360		134880		128120	MINERAIS METAL,DECHETS
287	BASE METAL ORES,CONC NES	W 2224199	81025	W 2401105	80484		93043	W 2922533	107020	MINERAIS METAUX COMMUNS
2873	ALUMINIUM ORES,ALUMINA	W 2184997	76360	W 2369329	76935	W 2721121	88644	W 2882380	101453	MINERAIS D'ALUMINIUM
28731	ALUMINIUM ORE,CONCNTRATE	W 2184776	75904	W 2369136	76571	W 2720864	87956	W 2882167	100878	MINERAIS D'ALUMINIUM
3	MINERAL FUELS ETC		1040868		999247		1071138		1326502	COMBUSTIBLES MINERAUX LUB
32	COAL,COKE AND BRIQUETTES		200059		176218		177203		161854	HOUILLES,COKES,BRIQUETTES
322	COAL,LIGNITE AND PEAT	W 2885253	194624	W 4832345	170973	W 2611269	172802	W 2606239	156738	HOUILLES,LIGNITES,TOURBE
3222	OTH COAL,NOT AGGLOMERATD	W 2746132	179779	W 4733364	158820	W 2538343	164060	W 2487249	144546	AUTRES HOUILLES
33	PETROLEUM AND PRODUCTS		821489		804518		871683		1099959	PETROLE ET DERIVES
333	CRUDE PETROLEUM	W 1861189	241513	W 2305205	270600	W 1983871	277602	W 2076881	325993	HUILES BRUTES DE PETROLE
334	PETROLEUM PRODUCTS,REFIN	W 3550048	556364	W 3086852	506847	W 3456398	560969	W 3871962	734982	PRODUITS RAFFINES
3341	GASOLINE,OTH LIGHT OILS	W 470219	97650	W 551471	102900	W 630222	122912	W 720130	159959	ESSENCES POUR MOTEURS
33411	MOTOR,AVIATION SPIRIT	W 434544	85636	W 539004	99113	W 618050	115882	W 693222	150587	ESSENCES MOTEURS D'AVIONS
3342	KEROSENE,OTH MEDIUM OILS	W 479452	92310	W 448843	80141	W 384339	72833	W 505565	109188	PETR LAMPANTS,AUT HUIL
33421	KEROSENE INCL JET FUEL	W 471444	90578	W 439091	78148	W 376270	71291	W 451612	100482	PETROLES LAMPANTS
3343	GAS OILS	W 1300473	227296	W 1198114	199865	W 1162387	204137	W 1570481	313441	GAS OILS
3344	FUEL OILS,NES	W 1258241	110411	W 846395	88625	W 1239102	127917	W 1024391	114441	FUEL OILS
4	ANIMAL,VEGETABLE OIL,FAT		77742		97354		122683		125447	HUILES,GRAISSES ANIM,VEG
5	CHEMCLS,RELATED PROD NES		2620124		3255011		4040182		4255110	PRODUITS CHIMIQUES
51	ORGANIC CHEMICALS		594678		772128		1076896		1034635	PROD CHIMIQ ORGANIQUES
513	CARBOXYLIC ACIDS ETC	W 60498	119692	W 65603	130216	W 80642	368366	W 80110	211001	ACIDES CARBOXYLIQUES
5139	OXY-FNCT ACIDS,DERIVATVS	W 5624	71424	W 7484	58099	W 11616	260132	W 8542	117303	ACIDES CARBOXYLIQUES
514	NITROGEN-FNCTN COMPOUNDS	W 45354	185643	W 24484	257302	W 30646	327507	W 29241	300628	COMPOSES FONCT AZOTEES
5147	AMIDE-FNCT CMPD,EXC UREA	W 8851	82578	W 7538	159656	W 5088	146568	W 5175	143761	COMPOSES CARBOXYAMIDE
5148	OTH NITROGN-FNCTN CMPNDS	W 28105	69246	W 7340	66908	W 9685	127453	W 10373	110421	AUTRES COMPOSES AZOTES
51482	IMIDE-,IMIDE-FNCT CMPNDS	W 1604	38990	W 2408	50206	W 3517	105348	W 3098	80394	COMPOSES A FONCTION IMIDE
515	ORG-INORG COMPOUNDS ETC	W 7802	182504	W 10452	205909	W 16795	214056	W 20800	334446	COMPOSES ORGANO-MINERAUX
5156	HETEROCYCLIC CMPDS ETC	W 4033	116914	W 7227	141356	W 12466	178692	W 15590	292224	COMPOSES HETEROCYCLIQUES
51569	OTH HETEROCYC CMPDS,ETC	W 3769	115459	W 7079	140647	W 11759	172818	W 15483	291128	AUT COMP HETEROCYCLIQUES
516	OTHER ORGANIC CHEMICALS	W 19012	57730	W 23137	113820	W 21829	90540	W 24490	115498	AUTRES PROD ORGANIQUES
52	INORGANIC CHEMICALS		139444		140354		181908		209477	PROD CHIM INORGANIQUES
522	INORG ELEMNTS,OXIDES,ETC	W 322578	87727	W 268525	80984	W 340662	104930	W 335947	109969	ELEMENTS INORGANIQUES
53	DYES,TANNING,COLOUR PROD		101379		118573		136462		155170	PROD TEINTURE,COLORANTS
533	PIGMENTS,PAINTS,ETC	W 30671	80498	W 33647	95221	W 35258	106167	W 37307	120072	PIGMENTS,PEINTURES,VERNIS
541	*MEDICINAL,PHARM PRODUCT	MK 18143	441844	MK 22096	586504	MK 26872	724132	MK 26690	738935	PROD MEDICINAUX PHARMACEUT
5417	MEDICAMENTS	MK 11595	284661	MK 15312	381020	MK 19435	464540	MK 15626	459055	MEDICAMENTS
54171	— CONTAINNG ANTIBIOTICS	K 1187372	31394	K 2907911	56314	K 3823848	89276	K 2010308	138398	MED CONTN ANTIBIOTIQUES
54179	— CONTNG OTH SUBSTANCES	MK 9940	234804	MK 11697	295737	MK 14763	338572	MK 12132	278531	MED CONT AUT SUBSTANCES
55	PERFUME,CLEANING ETC PRD		308575		371959		412260		472725	PROD POUR PARFUM,TOILETTE
551	ESSENTL OILS,PERFUME,ETC	W 6282	62831	W 7011	80262	W 7690	96089	W 13682	112681	HUILES ESSENTIELLES
553	PERFUMERY,COSMETICS,ETC	W 21119	133501	W 26805	167180	W 24075	175960	W 26947	202114	PRODUITS DE PARFUMERIE
554	SOAP,CLEANSING ETC PREPS	W 62151	112243	W 73366	124517	W 67843	140212	W 91596	157929	SAVONS,PRODUITS DETERSIFS
5542	WASHING PREPARATIONS ETC	W 51464	95329	W 61257	103528	W 54851	116382	W 77733	134466	PROD ORG TENSIO-ACT NDA
562	*FERTILIZERS,MANUFACTURE	W 1275941	178695	W 1295747	195392	W 1646150	289696	W 1506265	273175	ENGRAIS MANUFACTURES
5629	FERTILIZERS NES	W 572566	94408	W 588966	106606	W 822823	164063	W 656205	138617	ENGRAIS NDA
56291	NIT-PHOS-POT FERTLZR NES	W 350782	58476	W 341357	61044	W 499412	97111	W 421640	82744	ENGRAIS CONT N P K
58	PLASTIC MATERIALS ETC		457358		563960		740266		710439	MAT PLAST ARTIFICIELLES
582	PROD OF CONDENSATION ETC	W 61861	114332	W 72184	137437	W 78389	198070	W 105595	170367	PROD CONDENS,POLYCOND
5823	ALKYDS,OTHER POLYESTERS	W 29906	63951	W 35215	72528	W 39463	113447	W 27637	78745	ALKYDES ET AUT POLYESTERS
583	POLYMERIZATION ETC PRODS	W 273188	314674	W 313591	401211	W 414575	514882	W 343731	513083	PROD POLYMERISATION
5831	POLYETHYLENE	W 63380	66426	W 78679	88802	W 75573	95798	W 85365	99501	POLYETHYLENE
5833	POLYSTYRENE,ITS COPOLYMR	W 67988	53520	W 58858	75795	W 148900	107769	W 56891	92949	POLYPROPYLENE COPOLYMERES
5839	OTH POLYMRZTION ETC PROD	W 63329	80588	W 79535	102222	W 89034	136260	W 89817	140261	AUT PROD POLYMER COPOLYM
59	CHEMICAL MATERIALS NES		395747		503873		476231		658298	MAT PROD CHIMIQUES NDA
592	STARCH,INULIN,GLUTEN,ETC	W 36523	129538	W 40941	122155	W 33148	100430	W 97717	233423	AMIDONS,INUL,GLUT FROM
5922	ALBUMINOID SUBSTAN,GLUES	W 20641	114971	W 28078	112078	W 21650	91647	W 85355	224781	MAT ALBUMIN,COLLES
59224	PROTEIN AND DERIVATS,ETC	W 8640	88079	W 11180	75223	W 6479	47638	W 26580	161294	PEPTONES
598	MISCEL CHEM PRODUCTS NES	W 138539	209567	W 140695	314754	W 170133	301118	W 170895	344180	PROD DIV INDUST CHIM NDA
5989	CHEM PRODUCTS,PREPS NES	W 116767	188931	W 116626	284687	W 145595	273431	W 153591	320736	PROD PREP CHIMIQUES NDA
59899	OTH CHEM PRODS,PREPS,NES	W 109836	166068	W 109333	262299	W 138480	248288	W 146497	288241	AUT PRODUITS CHIMIQUES NDA
6	BASIC MANUFACTURES		2548536		2996414		3682584		3897465	ART MANUFACTURES
62	RUBBER MANUFACTURES NES		137992		158422		177384		207875	CAOUTCHOUC MANUFACTURE
625	RUBBER TYRES, TUBES ETC	W 20834	65997	W 23784	78607	W 24667	88934	W 29228	109309	PNEUS CAOUTCHOUC VULCANISE
63	WOOD,CORK MANUFACTRS NES		78303		98841		112148		138900	OUVRAGES LIEGE ET BOIS

4. General Imports C.I.F. by Commodities according to the S.I.T.C. (Rev. 2) in thousand U.S. Dollars
Importations Générales C.A.F. par Produits d'après la C.T.C.I. (Rév. 2) en milliers de Dollars E.U.

SITC CTCI	COMMODITY	1993 WEIGHT POIDS	1993 VALUE VALEUR	1994 WEIGHT POIDS	1994 VALUE VALEUR	1995 WEIGHT POIDS	1995 VALUE VALEUR	1996 WEIGHT POIDS	1996 VALUE VALEUR	PRODUIT
64	PAPER,PAPERBOARD AND MFR		573229		647336		852728		833979	PAPIERS,CARTONS & OUVRAGES
641	PAPER AND PAPERBOARD	W 415669	347809	W 463043	400991	W 459970	527998	W 428595	484726	PAPIERS ET CARTONS
6415	PAPER,PAPERBRD,BULK,NES	W 101494	75620	W 110839	83629	W 128743	138364	W 105423	97719	PAPIERS,CARTONS ROULEAUX
64159	OTHER PAPER ETC,BULK,NES	W 77988	66229	W 85607	71835	W 108632	122353	W 80454	86859	AUT PAPIER ROULEAUX FEUILLES
6418	COATED ETC PAPER NES BLK	W 51798	82207	W 55509	92299	W 66643	129418	W 65497	127308	PAP,CARTONS COUCHES,ENDUITS
64189	COATED PAPER ETC NES	W 44843	69186	W 43863	72834	W 54175	99315	W 52503	95461	PAPIERS,CARTONS COUCHES
642	PAPER,ETC,PRECUT,ARTS OF	W 97851	225421	W 115263	246345	W 138254	324730	W 301019	349253	PAP,CARTONS DECOUPES
6421	PAPER ETC CONTAINERS	W 43718	85963	W 58676	100809	W 64320	129613	W 225471	152506	BOITES,SACS EMBALLAGES
6428	PAPER ETC ARTICLES NES	W 23088	74519	W 28872	80511	W 37303	104534	W 38861	106619	OUVRAGES EN PATE A PAPIER
65	TEXTILE YARN,FABRICS,ETC		511258		556815		610693		657939	FILS,TISSUS,ARTICLES TEXTILE
651	TEXTILE YARN	W 42965	159302	W 47912	171800	W 50142	188519	W 53566	198496	FILS TEXTILES
653	WOVN MAN–MADE FIB FABRIC	W 7794	75073	W 8275	79955	W 7930	82152	W 7865	84604	TISSUS FIBRES SYNTH,ARTIF
66	NONMETAL MINERAL MFS NES		255874		309857		350903		421913	ART MIN NON METALLIQUES
663	MINERAL MANUFCTURES NES	W 184723	59686	W 194108	81379	W 212187	86624	W 303900	94881	ART MIN MANUF NDA
67	IRON AND STEEL		283602		362260		497953		517949	FER ET ACIER
673	IRON,STEEL SHAPES ETC	W 131315	59686	W 188996	85735	W 213506	113581	W 273069	130836	BARRES,PROFIL FER,ACIER
674	IRN,STL UNIV,PLATE,SHEET	W 161192	109715	W 179418	140057	W 202373	191690	W 235643	205585	LARGES PLATS,TOLES
6749	OTH IRN,STL PLATES,SHEET	W 79944	61861	W 81933	81279	W 92674	100341	W 113132	113186	AUTRES TOLES FER,ACIER
67491	— OF IRON OR SIMPLE STL	W 76113	55372	W 76194	70354	W. 90719	94541	W 111483	108552	AUT TOLES AUTRES ACIER FIN
678	IRON,STL TUBES,PIPES,ETC	W 51945	57507	W 65425	70637	W 93441	104617	W 86429	94545	TUBES,TUYAUX EN FONTE,FER
68	NON–FERROUS METALS		250920		336080		459919		427145	METAUX NON FERREUX
682	COPPER EXC CEMENT COPPER	W 30720	77179	W 35095	96834	W 38747	140030	W 37928	131390	CUIVRE
6822	COPPER,ALLOYS WORKED	W 30158	76058	W 34861	96031	W 38495	139122	W 37509	129599	CUIVRE,ALLIAGES OUVRES
684	ALUMINIUM	W 54423	142085	W 68970	173587	W 67905	206063	W 89843	196868	ALUMINIUM
6842	ALUMINIUM,ALLOYS WORKED	W 44084	126385	W 58734	155908	W 62544	192875	W 82573	183565	ALUMINIUM,ALLIAGES OUVRE
68422	ALUMNM PLATE,SHEET,STRIP	W 25965	69334	W 41023	89479	W 44064	104827	W 44772	90860	TOLES, PLANCHES EN ALU
69	METAL MANUFACTURES NES		443557		511965		598706		674925	ART MANUFACT EN METAL NDA
695	TOOLS	W 5753	65130	W 6565	76057	W 6185	79140	W 7000	86560	OUTILS A MAIN
699	BASE METAL MFRS NES	W 37812	158706	W 37832	183286	W 36649	194891	W 40096	213118	ART MANUFACTURES MET NDA
7	MACHINES,TRANSPORT EQUIP		7990197		9923880		13649211		15045710	MACHINES MATERIEL TRANSPORT
71	POWER GENERATING EQUIPMT		353683		410794		420389		416267	MACHINES GENERATRICES
713	INTRNL COMBUS PSTN ENGIN	W 4537	63766	W 7535	85097	W 5558	115807	W 5413	121292	MOTEURS EXPL COMB INT, PIECE
714	ENGINES AND MOTORS NES	W 1536	212294	W 2315	217577	W 2368	214253	W 1625	175690	MOTEURS NON ELECTRIQUES
7144	REACTION ENGINES	W 512	80235	W 616	84630	W 397	70472	W 279	55205	PROPULSEURS A REACTION
7149	ENGINE & MOTOR PARTS NES	W 737	98207	W 1439	94187	W 1696	78526	W 1246	100400	PIECES 714 ET 718.88
71491	PARTS NES OF 7144,71481	W 113	77426	W 86	68735	W 73	67866	W 91	86739	PIECES DES PROPULSEURS
72	MACHS FOR SPCL INDUSTRYS		569500		688255		763547		980856	MAC SPECIALES POUR INDUST
721	AGRIC MACHY,EXC TRACTORS	W 14122	88877	W 16211	111792	W 17529	138104	W 18941	148665	MACHINES AGRICOLES
728	OTH MACHY FOR SPCL INDUS	W 11936	249970	W 13087	258498	W 16032	269439	W 16425	425012	AUT MACH IND PARTICULIERES
7284	MACHY FOR SPCL INDUS NES	W 4965	176610	W 6852	196899	W 7237	208502	W 8749	350542	MACH SPEC IND PARTICUL.
72848	OTH MCHY WITH INDIV FNCT	W 1911	93298	W 1340	81051	W 1714	60313	W 2614	74214	AUTRES MACHINES NDA
72849	PTS OF MACHS OF 7284 ETC	W 1761	54470	W 2383	76599	W 3908	110474	W 3487	184997	PIECES DU 728.4 ETC
73	METALWORKING MACHINERY		82813		88638		86972		102990	MACH TRAVAIL DES METAUX
736	METALWORKING MACH–TOOLS	W 3372	69720	W 3323	74868	W 3289	64593	W 4646	81224	MACH–OUTILS TRAVAIL METAUX
74	GENRL INDUSTRL MACHY NES		586234		639295		749274		900098	MACH APP INDUSTRIE
741	HEATING,COOLING EQUIPMNT	W 11644	153165	W 14625	155396	W 19288	207725	W 19305	236332	MACH CHAUFFAGE,PIECES
743	PUMPS NES,CENTRFUGES ETC	W 8846	92445	W 6974	98264	W 6690	98501	W 7675	113060	POMPES COMPRES,VENT ETC
744	MECHANICAL HANDLING EQU	W 9861	66971	W 11569	88898	W 14067	118185	W 19306	167718	EQUIP MANUTENTION PIECES
745	NONELEC MACHY,TOOLS NES	W 4934	75248	W 4957	84908	W 3603	76507	W 4387	117588	AUT MACH NON ELEC,PIECES
7452	OTH NONELEC MCHS,PTS NES	W 4638	67916	W 4661	76714	W 3301	67864	W 4003	104239	AUT MACH NON ELEC,PIECES
749	NONELEC MACH PTS,ACC NES	W 7958	147577	W 7977	152833	W 9282	174116	W 12125	184918	PIECES MACH NON ELEC NDA
7492	COCKS,VALVES ETC NES	W 3979	74473	W 3743	70488	W 3992	81365	W 4754	86727	ART ROB,SIM POUR TUYAUX
75	OFFICE MACHNES,ADP EQUIP		2612426		3329707		5595653		6113540	MACH BUREAU TRAIT AUTOM
752	AUTOMTIC DATA PROC EQUIP	W 14344	1061971	W 17941	1703939	W 33608	2769615	W 53309	3492317	MACH TRAIT INFORMATION
7522	DIGITAL COMPUTERS	W 410	64878	W 2311	284582	W 2273	286926	W 5449	473428	MACH DIGITALES COMPLETES
7523	DIGITL CENTRL PROCESSORS	W 636	134616	W 1044	89561	W 2070	147873	W 2541	198805	UNITES CENTRALES
7524	DIGITL CENTRL STOR UNITS	W 2631	478221	W 6140	1105187	W 8519	1835549	W 10472	2114601	UNITES MEMOIRE CENTRALES
7525	ADP PERIPHERAL UNITS	W 6247	123714	W 5375	122190	W 14515	311654	W 29613	567514	UNITES PERIPHERIQUES
7528	OFF–LINE DATA PROC EQUIP	W 4325	252964	W 3016	96343	W 6183	181145	W 5040	124528	MACH AUXIL TRAIT INFORM
759	OFFICE,ADP MCH PTS,ACCES	W 18139	1528461	W 19874	1600652	W 27279	2794595	W 28906	2580464	PIECES DU 751 ET 752
7599	ACCTG,ETC,ADP MCH PTS,AC	W 17449	1500160	W 19077	1573967	W 26243	2749008	W 26619	2532620	PIECES DU 751 ET 752
76	TELECOMM,SOUND EQUIPMENT		465447		537733		638483		939368	EQUIPMENT DE TELECOM
763	SOUND RECORDRS,PHONOGRPH	W 1339	36490	W 1501	42277	W 1753	79815	W 4034	244853	PHONO,APP ENREGISTREMENT
7638	OTHR SOUND APPARATUS ETC	W 1063	32518	W 1209	35609	W 1667	77299	W 3978	243168	AUT APP D'ENREGIS,REPROD
76381	TV IMAGE,SND RECRDRS ETC	W 751	24371	W 703	25301	W 1065	61448	W 3087	222488	APP ENREG,REPRO IMAG,SON
764	TELECOM EQPT,PTS,ACC NES	W 7333	347873	W 6647	407856	W 8710	466217	W 9009	579301	EQUIP TELECOM,PIECES
7641	LINE TELEPHONE,ETC EQUIP	W 525	38607	W 611	95761	W 917	67561	W 1238	108557	APP TELEPHON PAR FIL
7649	PTS NES OF EQUIPMT OF 76	W 5821	263080	W 4454	238268	W 4670	288753	W 4457	349916	PIECES DE LA DIV 76
76491	PTS NES OF APPAR OF 7641	W 1492	156045	W 1498	124274	W 1736	142099	W 1890	179888	PIECES POUR 764.1
76493	TELECOMM EQUIPMT PTS NES	W 1048	84733	W 944	79568	W 1234	109466	W 1532	141218	PIECES 761,762,764.3,8
77	ELECTRIC MACHNRY NES ETC		2123810		2691827		3541641		3265255	MACH APP ELECT NDA
771	ELECTRIC POWER MACHY NES	W 3136	78491	W 3920	113423	W 6776	161796	W 10786	269148	MACH PROD,TRANS ELECTR
7712	OTH ELEC POWER MACHY NES	W 1429	44889	W 2070	72669	W 2810	103269	W 6635	200649	AUT APP PROD TRANSF ELEC
77121	STATIC CONVERTERS ETC	W 486	23605	W 719	35654	W 1063	49744	W 4360	126962	CONVERTISSEURS STATIQUES
772	SWITCHGEAR ETC,PARTS NES	W 16667	510217	W 14698	591844	W 14956	665487	W 17083	678389	APP COUPURE,SECT ETC
7721	SWITCHGEAR ETC	W 11499	300576	W 12651	348808	W 11933	346809	W 13080	326657	APP COUPURE,SECTIONMNT
7722	PRINTED CIRCUITS,PTS NES	W 4904	184635	W 1697	213892	W 2676	274481	W 3692	314537	CIRCUITS ET PIECES
773	ELECTR DISTRIBUTNG EQUIP	W 14551	109758	W 17094	109433	W 22140	150811	W 22902	154626	EQUIPMT DISTRIBUTION ELECT
7731	INSULATED WIRE,CABLE ETC	W 12975	95888	W 14490	94060	W 18225	131425	W 18546	134034	FILS,CABLES ISOLES ELECT
775	HOUSEHOLD TYPE EQUIP NES	W 26592	178274	W 26102	188965	W 31404	225598		257305	MACH,APP USAGE DOMESTQUE
7758	ELECTRO–THERMIC APPL NES	W 10653	86214	W 10794	89960	W 11397	103450		104195	APP ELECTROTHERMIQ NDA
776	TRANSISTORS,VALVES,ETC	W 1303	927507		1317149	W 2965	1774010	W 2819	1400397	LAMPES,TUBES,VALVES
7764	ELECTRONIC MICROCIRCUITS	W 795	877455		1260251	W 2443	1690124	W 1660	1205702	MICROSTRUCTURES ELECTRON
7768	ELCTRNC COMP PTS,CRYSTLS	W 208	21154	W 151	25455	W 180	36980	W 667	146230	CRIST PIEZO–ELEC,PCS 776
77689	ELECTRNIC COMPON PTS NES	W 166	9494	W 115	9734	W 129	14027	W 628	121792	PIECES DU GROUPE 776
778	ELECTRICAL MACHINERY NES	W 13452	309487	W 15221	358991	W 21491	550268	W 21584	483136	AUTRES MACH ELECT NDA
7781	BATTERIES,ACCUMULATORS	W 6645	61164	W 8313	133480	W 12889	171869	W 12504	117553	PILES ET ACCUMULATEURS
77812	ELECTRIC ACCUMULATORS	W 4370	43424	W 6370	114645	W 7797	106175	W 9963	78855	ACCUMULATEURS ELECTRIQ
7788	OTH ELEC MACHY,EQUIP NES	W 3100	195892	W 2412	153049	W 3277	298812	W 3879	281366	AUT MACH APP ELEC NDA
77883	ELEC SIGNALLING EQU NES	W 925	105728	W 849	61955	W 1016	100507	W 1556	85693	APP ELECT SIGNAL ACOUS
78	ROAD VEHICLES		939296		1271139		1449413		1932834	VEHICULES ROUTIERS
781	PASS MOTOR VEH EXC BUSES	W 84840	614893	W 93317	790321	W 92674	907077	W 140064	1286482	AUTO TRANSPORT PERSONNES
782	LORRIES,SPCL MTR VEH NES	W 23362	125832	W 33330	205504	W 30270	246830	W 36831	319797	VEHICULES SPECIAUX,MARCH
7821	LORRIES,TRUCKS	W 22448	123291	W 32572	202622	W 29781	244518	W 36212	316048	VEHICULES TRANSP MARCHAND
784	MOTOR VEH PRTS,ACCES NES	W 16938	128230	W 20545	169413	W 19031	181080	W 21549	198618	PIECES 722,781,782,783
7849	OTHER MOTOR VEHCL PARTS	W 15958	120856	W 19416	161628	W 18093	174926	W 20279	186164	PIECES 722,781,782,783
79	OTHR TRANSPORT EQUIPMENT		256989		266492		403838		394500	AUTRE MATERIEL TRANSPORT
792	AIRCRAFT ETC	W 808	241450	W 538	187800	W 735	260696	W 1353	338046	APP NAVIGATION AERIENNE
7924	AIRCRFT NES OVER 15000KG	W 148	130851	W 31	28053	W 111	80806	W 131	29679	AERODYNES PLUS 15000 KG
7929	AIRCRAFT PARTS NES	W 469	102362	W 495	159401	W 606	179522	W 780	235832	PIECES DU 792
8	MISC MANUFACTURED GOODS		2922195		3222654		3570209		4676140	ART MANUFACTURES DIVERS

4. General Imports C.I.F. by Commodities according to the S.I.T.C. (Rev. 2) in thousand U.S. Dollars
Importations Générales C.A.F. par Produits d'après la C.T.C.I. (Rév. 2) en milliers de Dollars E.U.

SITC CTCI	COMMODITY	1993		1994		1995		1996		PRODUIT
		WEIGHT POIDS	VALUE VALEUR	WEIGHT POIDS	VALUE VALEUR	WEIGHT POIDS	VALUE VALEUR	WEIGHT POIDS	VALUE VALEUR	
812	*PLUMBG,HEATNG,LGHTNG EQ	W 14146	67697	W 18161	74709	W 20374	88215	W 23161	115568	APPAR SANITAIRES CHAUFFAGE
821	*FURNITURE,PARTS THEREOF	W 24807	102744	W 24381	115176	W 26662	139691	W 35145	183937	MEUBLES ET PIECES
8219	FURNITURE AND PARTS NES	W 18425	67396	W 17630	73748	W 18106	80970	W 25124	117040	AUTRES MEUBLES ET PIECES
84	CLOTHING AND ACCESSORIES		719460		783108		842612		1019860	VETEMENTS
842	MENS OUTERWEAR NOT KNIT	W 4317	105948	W 5002	123088	W 5245	133659	W 6184	162197	VET DESSUS POUR HOMMES
843	WOMENS OUTERWEAR NONKNIT	W 5172	183097	W 4965	192415	W 5152	216778	W 6518	265313	VET DESSUS FEMMES MAT TEX
8439	— OTHER OUTER GARMENTS	W 2640	71952	W 2527	75277	W 2566	85796	W 3031	98810	AUT VET DES FEM MAT TEXT
845	OUTERWEAR KNIT NONELASTC	W 7790	206463	W 7751	214273	W 8102	217378	W 9952	262216	VET DESSOUS,ACCES BONNET
8451	— JERSEYS,PULLOVERS ETC	W 4067	111545	W 3787	114291	W 3909	116368	W 5158	145918	CHANDAILS,PULL–OVERS ETC
8459	— OTHER,CLTHG ACCESRYS	W 3172	78211	W 3514	83994	W 3595	80347	W 4263	95655	AUT VET DESSUS DE BONNE
846	UNDER GARMENTS KNITTED	W 6605	115132	W 9827	129019	W 6855	145307	W 6675	158874	SOUS VETS DE BONNETERIE
8462	— OF COTTON NON ELASTIC	W 4143	66290	W 7528	73096	W 4680	87621	W 4294	90598	SOUS–VET BONNET COTON
84629	—— OTHER	W 4143	66290	W 7528	73096	W 4680	87621	W 4294	90598	AUT SOUS–VET BONNET COTON
851	*FOOTWEAR	W 27397	300027	W 19203	281248	W 12926	245920	W 14808	266109	CHAUSSURES
85102	FOOTWEAR LEATHER	W 21121	234678	W 13896	220290	W 9737	201456	W 10909	213702	CHAUS SEMELLES EN CUIR
87	PRECISION INSTRUMNTS NES		373588		397868		551762		614522	INSTRUM,APPAR SCIENT NDA
872	MEDICAL INSTRUMENTS NES	W 5679	158252	W 5125	169774	W 5780	220290	W 7020	281104	INSTR,APP MEDIC–CHIR NDA
87202	OTH MEDICAL INSTRUMENTS	W 5159	145971	W 4579	156001	W 5002	199841	W 6388	263937	INSTRUM,APP MEDECINE
874	MEASURNG,CONTROLNG INSTR	W 2551	185306	W 2419	194146	W 5483	285720	W 5842	291644	INSTRUMENTS DE MESURE
8748	ELEC MEAS,CONTRL EQU NES	W 587	62287	W 416	60967	W 727	109696	W 799	94354	APP ELEC ELECTRO MESURE
87483	OTH ELCTRNC MEAS ETC EQU	W 557	58602	W 367	56263	W 681	105719	W 733	87360	AUT APP ELECTRO DE MESURE
88	PHOTO EQU,OPTICL GDS ETC		193661		208908		205989		229042	APP,FOURN PHOTO,OP,MONTR
884	OPTICAL GOODS NES	W 650	74556	W 617	78376	W 692	87518	W 852	107208	ELEMENTS OPTIQ,ART LUNET
89	MISC MANUFCTRD GOODS NES		1139284		1329359		1461660		2205246	ART MANUFACTURES DIVERS
892	PRINTED MATTER	W 27077	199812	W 31636	227410	W 25009	240919	W 36400	277643	IMPRIMES
8921	PRINTED BOOKS,GLOBES,ETC	W 7214	77292	W 5908	80605	W 5276	90501	W 13347	123062	LIVRES,BROCHURES,CARTES
89211	PRINTED BOOKS,PAMPHLETS	W 6457	74248	W 5555	78222	W 5020	88213	W 13029	120127	LIVRES,BROCHURES
8922	NEWSPAPERS,PERIODICALS	W 12185	62582	W 16112	77938	W 8723	78194	W 9498	69606	JOURNAUX ET PERIODIQUES
893	ARTICLES OF PLASTIC NES		368038		419734		487823		590216	OUVRAGES EN MAT DIVIS 58
8931	PLSTC PACKG CONTNRS,LIDS	W 75394	170368	W 82346	195003	W 106698	238539	W 151628	251324	ART TRANSP EMBALLAGE ETC
8939	MISC PLASTIC ARTICLES	W 49079	189593	W 51352	215380	W 50446	239626	W 77674	326815	ART DIVERS EN MAT DIV 58
89399	OTHR PLASTC ARTICLES NES	W 42966	169439	W 45230	197054	W 43633	217730	W 70511	302747	AUT OUV MAT DIV 58
894	TOYS,SPORTING GOODS,ETC	W 16928	149795	W 21284	152615	W 20265	170880	W 22741	207499	VOITURES ENFANTS,JOUETS
8942	TOYS,INDOOR GAMES ETC	W 14269	119153	W 17908	125042	W 16509	134385	W 18263	156045	JOUETS,JEUX ETC
898	MUSICAL INSTRUMENTS,PTS	W 13353	312602	W 15254	392486	W 12771	396359	W 13691	870078	INSTRUMENTS DE MUSIQUE
8983	SOUND RECRDNG TAPE,DISCS	W 13099	307441	W 14988	386378	W 12503	389747	W 13337	861523	SUPPORTS SON POUR 763
89831	PREPD SND RECORDNG MEDIA	W 8750	179333	W 7342	185659	W 8038	173333	W 8153	207598	SUPPORTS PREPARES
89832	RECORDED DISCS,TAPES ETC	W 4349	128108	W 7646	200719	W 4465	216414	W 5184	653926	DISQUES,PHONO,BANDES
899	OTHER MANUFACTURED GOODS		58881		75555		96400		168495	AUT ART MANUF DIVERS NDA
8996	HEARING,ORTHOPAEDIC AIDS		22246		34132		52361		112895	APPAREILS D'ORTHOPEDIE
89962	ORTHOPAEDIC ETC GOODS		21346		32893		50359		111100	APPAREILS D'ORTHOPEDIE
9	GOODS NOT CLASSD BY KIND		1924795		2279903		2965754		2978235	ART TRANSACT NON CLASSES
931	*SPECIAL TRANSACTIONS		1911857		2267229		2950142		2963288	TRANS.SPECIALES

5. General Exports F.O.B. by Commodities according to the S.I.T.C. (Rev. 2) in thousand U.S. Dollars
Exportations Générales F.O.B. par Produits d'après la C.T.C.I. (Rév. 2) en milliers de Dollars E.U.

SITC CTCI	COMMODITY	1993 WEIGHT POIDS	1993 VALUE VALEUR	1994 WEIGHT POIDS	1994 VALUE VALEUR	1995 WEIGHT POIDS	1995 VALUE VALEUR	1996 WEIGHT POIDS	1996 VALUE VALEUR	PRODUIT
	ALL COMMODITIES		28856521		34395136		43789356		45565370	TOUS PRODUITS
0	FOOD AND LIVE ANIMALS		5655653		6365784		7704845		6625718	ALIMENTS,ANIMAUX VIVANTS
001	*LIVE ANIMALS FOR FOOD	W 166402	226433	W 182908	277788	W 172552	257628	W 114597	224829	ANIMAUX VIVANTS
0011	BOVINE SPECIES,LIVE	W 152138	142544	W 171152	176595	W 161657	175850	W 86979	89777	ESPECE BOVINE
00119	— OTHR THAN FR BREEDING	W 150592	139099	W 169981	174015	W 159221	170611	W 86647	89063	BOVINS NON REPRODUCTEURS
01	MEAT AND PREPARATIONS		1659320		1805802		1930010		1737427	VIANDES ET PREPARATIONS
011	MEAT FRESH,CHILLD,FROZEN	W 528035	1500623	W 593388	1598124	W 595403	1695229	W 552878	1481680	VIANDES FRAICHES,REF,CONGE
0111	BOVINE MEAT FRESH,FROZEN	W 341785	1069253	W 409449	1152912	W 420311	1236097	W 336717	914784	VIANDES BOVIN FRAI,REF
01111	BOVINE MEAT WITH BONE IN	W 78645	280631	W 74472	256282	W 61725	235560	W 49070	158429	VIANDES BOVIN NON DESOSS
01112	BOVINE MEAT BONELESS	W 263140	788622	W 334977	896631	W 358587	1000537	W 287648	756355	VIANDES BOVIN DESOSSEES
0112	MUTTON ETC FRSH,CHLD,FRN	W 63973	188043	W 64599	196499	W 48711	153089	W 61753	220934	VIANDE DE MOUTON
0113	PIG MEAT FRESH,CHLD,FRZN	W 64841	147895	W 69079	151089	W 71765	191491	W 93563	217284	VIANDE DE PORC
014	MEAT PREPD,PRSVD,NES ETC	W 38163	126654	W 51128	173712	W 61388	204106	W 59858	226994	CONSERVES DE VIANDES
0149	OTH PREPARD,PRESRVD MEAT	W 35922	121321	W 48827	166630	W 59130	196645	W 57601	218897	AUTRES PREP DE VIANDES
02	DAIRY PRODCTS,BIRDS'EGGS		1111638		1131916		1571341		1207760	PRODUITS LAITIERS,OEUFS
022	MILK AND CREAM	W 277731	442162	W 297040	408381	W 404661	674315	W 305944	383635	LAIT ET CREME
0224	MILK,CREAM PRESERVED ETC	W 207812	396584	W 165533	336924	W 240242	568918	W 139478	296966	LAIT,CREME CONS,CONC
02242	MILK DRY,1.5% FAT OR LES	W 118225	250103	W 79957	185505	W 144806	380068	W 58753	145903	LAIT POUDRE INF 1.5%
02243	MILK DRY,OVER 1.5% FAT	W 40601	106137	W 45608	112504	W 40170	128876	W 35716	103148	LAIT POUDRE SUP 1.5%
023	BUTTER	W 108728	398365	W 110324	393757	W 137980	583589	W 118716	439301	BEURRE
024	CHEESE AND CURD	W 117251	271055	W 89358	329485	W 76953	312923	W 94727	384308	FROMAGE ET CAILLEBOTTE
03	FISH AND PREPARATIONS		246948		274012		327062		385167	POISSONS ET PREPARATIONS
034	FISH,FRESH,CHILLED,FROZN	W 184842	165755	W 208315	183287	W 241241	220508	W 231148	260851	POISSON FRAIS, REFRIG,CONG
0341	FISH FRSH,CHLLD,EX FILLT	W 76731	103441	W 67548	99698	W 56250	94112	W 36759	91901	POISSON FRAIS,REFRIGERE
04	CEREALS AND PREPARATIONS		396878		494444		605911		637018	CEREALES ET PRODUITS
048	CEREAL ETC PREPARATIONS	W 164424	356319	W 183802	468960	W 223865	586745	W 231405	609817	PREPTNS A BASE CEREALES
0484	BAKERY PRODUCTS	W 19617	53398	W 40681	112393	W 51340	152839	W 63824	178494	PRODUITS DE BOULANGERIE
0488	OTH CEREAL PREPS,MALT EX	W 76925	274256	W 83544	333448	W 105470	405966	W 103783	398353	EXTRAITS DE MALT
05	VEGETABLES AND FRUIT		114810		136168		158272		165949	LEGUMES ET FRUITS
06	SUGAR AND PREPS,HONEY		95661		95343		130459		139053	SUCRES ET PRODUITS
07	COFFEE,TEA,COCOA,SPICES		184156		222010		210576		220356	CAFE,THE,CACAO,EPICES
073	CHOCOLATE AND PRODUCTS	W 78605	181740	W 76165	218588	W 69665	206716	W 75843	214250	CHOCOLAT
09	MISC EDIBLE PRODUCTS		1545418		1832139		2395057		1780628	PREP ALIMENTAIRES DIVERSES
098	EDIBLE PRODCTS,PREPS NES	W 98579	1526318	W 114675	1808699	W 135393	2368172	W 101641	1744548	PREP ALIMENTAIRES NDA
09809	MISC FOOD PREPRTIONS NES	W 90046	1513585	W 107974	1776231	W 128440	2348061	W 94177	1720697	PREP ALIMENTAIRES NDA
1	BEVERAGES AND TOBACCO		638518		678918		746969		824324	BOISSONS ET TABACS
11	BEVERAGES		576373		606270		662788		735220	BOISSONS
112	ALCOHOLIC BEVERAGES	W 338965	549017	W 342827	568944	W 395723	611459	W 412245	681063	BOISSONS ALCOOLIQUES
1123	BEER,ALE,STOUT,PORTER	W 253794	125126	W 267630	141179	W 308718	182961	W 328566	197897	BIERES
1124	DISTILLED ALCOHOLIC BEVS	W 77064	415531	W 71400	421443	W 84441	422245	W 79957	477586	ALCOOLS,EAUX–DE–VIE
11249	OTH ALCOHOLC BEVS,CMPNDS	W 62717	370097	W 58618	369790	W 66894	364451	W 61185	407854	BOISSONS ALCOOLIQUES NDA
2	CRUDE MATERLS,EXCL FUELS		747095		794896		891628		892580	MAT BRUTES NON COMESTIBLES
21	HIDES,SKINS,FURS UNDRSSD		90114		110188		112713		106014	CUIRS,PEAUX BRUTS
211	HIDES,SKINS,EXC FURS,RAW	W 56367	88103	W 51466	107975	W 48514	110988	W 48413	103286	CUIRS ET PEAUX
26	TEXTILE FIBRES AND WASTE		151911		151190		192096		162750	FIBRES TEXTILES
266	SYNTHETIC FIBRES TO SPIN	W 81336	121208	W 70230	113643	W 78691	147471	W 54174	114944	FIBRES SYNTHETIQUES
2665	DISCN SYNTH FIBRE UNCMBD	W 60525	91119	W 70174	113091	W 78629	146391	W 54051	113391	DISCONTINUES EN MASSE
26652	— POLYESTER	W 54328	78261	W 65238	101235	W 74444	134965	W 50794	104122	FIBRES EN POLYESTERS
28	METALLIFEROUS ORES,SCRAP		298437		341075		373276		370704	MINERAIS METAL,DECHETS
287	BASE METAL ORES,CONC NES	W 1492534	267192	W 1718139	299262	W 1670863	328901	W 1702765	331785	MINERAIS METAUX COMMUNS
2873	ALUMINIUM ORES,ALUMINA	W 1035569	175459	W 1227534	198341	W 1251925	219470	W 1346339	234677	MINERAIS D'ALUMINIUM
28732	ALUMINA(ALUMINIUM OXIDE)	W 923197	157255	W 1213876	195826	W 1197651	207792	W 1346339	234676	ALUMINE (OXYDE ALUMINIUM)
2875	ZINC ORES,CONCENTRATES	W 408052	87689	W 340281	86727	W 325529	92071	W 282567	77431	MINERAIS DE ZINC
3	MINERAL FUELS ETC		172827		167296		194016		190167	COMBUSTIBLES MINERAUX LUB
33	PETROLEUM AND PRODUCTS		110557		119943		127881		127230	PETROLE ET DERIVES
334	PETROLEUM PRODUCTS,REFIN	W 949102	109345	W 970844	118243	W 964551	124783	W 884765	123042	PRODUITS RAFFINES
5	CHEMCLS,RELATED PROD NES		5537345		7051370		8042357		10679052	PRODUITS CHIMIQUES
51	ORGANIC CHEMICALS		2730084		3634463		4014712		5043571	PROD CHIMIQ ORGANIQUES
513	CARBOXYLIC ACIDS ETC	W 39264	169184	W 20192	174934	W 36572	155558	W 52535	189827	ACIDES CARBOXYLIQUES
5139	OXY–FNCT ACIDS,DERIVATVS	W 36319	104251	W 17478	72166	W 13980	80539	W 17067	76494	ACIDES CARBOXYLIQUES
514	NITROGEN–FNCTN COMPOUNDS	W 20791	1065461	W 19734	1415524	W 22728	1651681	W 37728	1861178	COMPOSES FONCT AZOTEES
5146	OXYGEN–FNCT AMINO–CMPNDS	W 2220	148294	W 2190	222996	W 6394	291677	W 18880	353831	COMP AMINES FONCT OXYGEN
5147	AMIDE–FNCT CMPD,EXC UREA	W 11712	234569	W 12806	229409	W 12098	225810	W 12022	207695	COMPOSES CARBOXYAMIDE
5148	OTH NITROGN–FNCTN CMPNDS	W 1772	648685	W 1635	885630	W 3822	1035839	W 5466	1166807	AUTRES COMPOSES AZOTES
51482	IMIDE–,IMIDE–FNCT CMPNDS	W 1172	642654	W 1277	872975	W 3329	1027833	W 5124	1164474	COMPOSES A FONCTION IMIDE
515	ORG–INORG COMPOUNDS ETC	W 29496	1433391	W 39588	1974210	W 38028	2120726	W 55931	2897690	COMPOSES ORGANO–MINERAUX
5156	HETEROCYCLIC CMPDS ETC	W 27831	1360784	W 39288	1936027	W 27304	2021257	W 31871	2811301	COMPOSES HETEROCYCLIQUES
51569	OTH HETEROCYC CMPDS,ETC	W 27830	1359739	W 39275	1934700	W 27254	2016631	W 31871	2811279	AUT COMP HETEROCYCLIQUES
52	INORGANIC CHEMICALS		46824		43052		127275		151784	PROD CHIM INORGANIQUES
541	*MEDICINAL,PHARM PRODUCT	MK 66532	1391217	MK 71176	1847554	MK 73762	2105843	MK 94486	2782846	PROD MEDICINAUX PHARMACEUT
5413	ANTIBIOTICS IN BULK	K 288931	160537	K 243943	98355	K 364100	170676	K 491627	243864	ANTIBIOTIQUES NDA
54139	OTHER ANTIBIOTICS	K 113893	99415	K 47491	56592	K 118259	130304	K 226470	207037	AUTRES ANTIBIOTIQUES
5417	MEDICAMENTS	MK 53106	1040364	MK 66712	1510377	MK 69928	1646301	MK 88197	2150371	MEDICAMENTS
54171	— CONTAINNG ANTIBIOTICS	K 2522018	88217	K 3949354	136869	K 4108027	178292	K 5552334	260723	MED CONTN ANTIBIOTIQUES
54172	— CONTAINING HORMONES	K 531596	34537	K 2947294	99698	K 1436424	208397	K 1561600	208909	MED CONTENANT HORMONES
54173	— CONTAINING ALKALOIDS	K 387048	42312	K 865799	122567	K 831053	133843	K 66628	6556	MED CONTEN ALCALOIDES
54179	— CONTNG OTH SUBSTANCES	MK 49665	875298	MK 58950	1151242	MK 63553	1125769	MK 81017	1674182	MED CONT AUT SUBSTANCES
5419	PHARMACEUTICAL GOODS NES	K 1832979	100350	K 1617278	141824	K 2154715	183453	K 3103279	209684	PREP,ART PHARMACEUTIQUES
54199	OTH PHARMACEUTICAL GOODS	K 950164	86581	K 641032	127906	K 787065	159677	K 1906619	184843	AUT PREP PHARMACEUTIQUES
55	PERFUME,CLEANING ETC PRD		710416		794692		908510		1362559	PROD POUR PARFUM,TOILETTE
551	ESSENTL OILS,PERFUME,ETC	W 10724	301640	W 12630	325069	W 16756	416513	W 30725	803058	HUILES ESSENTIELLES
5514	MIXED PERFUME SUBSTANCES	W 10462	296921	W 11802	309161	W 16033	400409	W 29952	787011	MELANGES SUBSTAN ODORIFER
553	PERFUMERY,COSMETICS,ETC	W 39132	371711	W 44458	430063	W 49322	448498	W 57134	517126	PRODUITS DE PARFUMERIE
58	PLASTIC MATERIALS ETC		167866		205700		231554		239859	MAT PLAST ARTIFICIELLES
583	POLYMERIZATION ETC PRODS	W 26705	104865	W 29887	123177	W 59485	138321	W 90860	142202	PROD POLYMERISATION
59	CHEMICAL MATERIALS NES		413091		431482		545337		991986	MAT PROD CHIMIQUES NDA
592	STARCH,INULIN,GLUTEN,ETC	W 37226	269398	W 39025	248275	W 68266	337328	W 54402	288087	AMIDONS,INUL,GLUT FROM
5922	ALBUMINOID SUBSTAN,GLUES	W 35614	268668	W 34888	246050	W 66415	336981	W 54111	287939	MAT ALBUMIN,COLLES
59221	CASEIN AND DERIVATVS,ETC	W 30273	133755	W 30598	134471	W 42155	219951	W 32579	176257	CASEINES,CASEINATES
598	MISCEL CHEM PRODUCTS NES	W 23333	129429	W 26527	157268	W 28200	175443	W 33630	665426	PROD DIV INDUST CHIM NDA
5989	CHEM PRODUCTS,PREPS NES	W 10915	98730	W 11333	123629	W 14310	138034	W 26082	646883	PROD PREP CHIMIQUES NDA
59899	OTH CHEM PRODS,PREPS,NES	W 7600	85402	W 7905	108079	W 8716	120132	W 21014	631839	AUT PRODUITS CHIMIQUES NDA
6	BASIC MANUFACTURES		1678648		1888114		2105710		2198899	ART MANUFACTURES
62	RUBBER MANUFACTURES NES		179287		201867		215358		198483	CAOUTCHOUC MANUFACTURE
625	RUBBER TYRES, TUBES ETC	W 20542	94077	W 21322	105124	W 21640	102291	W 17880	85477	PNEUS CAOUTCHOUC VULCANISE
6251	TYRES NEW FOR MOTOR CARS	W 19799	92020	W 21017	103894	W 21039	99991	W 16287	78305	PNEUS POUR VOITURES
64	PAPER,PAPERBOARD AND MFR		143433		161475		215835		229756	PAPIERS,CARTONS & OUVRAGES
641	PAPER AND PAPERBOARD	W 152223	90004	W 158230	101979	W 203203	140210	W 217348	121776	PAPIERS ET CARTONS
65	TEXTILE YARN,FABRICS,ETC		466809		522792		586598		598593	FILS,TISSUS,ARTICLES TEXTILE
651	TEXTILE YARN	W 41042	143739	W 43128	167273	W 54399	238153	W 62963	267684	FILS TEXTILES
6514	SYN FIB YRN,BULK,MONOFIL	W 29125	82567	W 28441	83302	W 38890	130944	W 48478	164660	FILS CONT 85% FIB TEXT SYNTH

5. General Exports F.O.B. by Commodities according to the S.I.T.C. (Rev. 2) in thousand U.S. Dollars
Exportations Générales F.O.B. par Produits d'après la C.T.C.I. (Rév. 2) en milliers de Dollars E.U.

SITC CTCI	COMMODITY	1993 WEIGHT POIDS	1993 VALUE VALEUR	1994 WEIGHT POIDS	1994 VALUE VALEUR	1995 WEIGHT POIDS	1995 VALUE VALEUR	1996 WEIGHT POIDS	1996 VALUE VALEUR	PRODUIT
65144	— TEXTRD,CONT POLYESTER	W 27127	72328	W 27313	76313	W 35402	114395	W 46385	146571	FILS TEX FI CONT POLYESTERS
66	NONMETAL MINERAL MFS NES		287079		326011		312116		370485	ART MIN NON METALLIQUES
67	IRON AND STEEL		134506		128282		152205		149621	FER ET ACIER
673	IRON,STEEL SHAPES ETC	W 331389	112905	W 253842	108585	W 275987	124522	W 291723	117668	BARRES,PROFIL FER,ACIER
6733	IRON,STEEL PROFILES ETC	W 323965	108744	W 245614	104513	W 270167	120935	W 284037	113309	PROFILES,PALPLAN FER,ACIER
67332	LARGE U,I,H SECTIONS ETC	W 318400	99831	W 240654	89940	W 264997	102892	W 276877	88910	PROFILES PLUS 80MM
69	METAL MANUFACTURES NES		348566		414022		452150		464171	ART MANUFACT EN METAL NDA
699	BASE METAL MFRS NES	W 29854	153723	W 38034	181351	W 29550	187201	W 28591	191346	ART MANUFACTURES MET NDA
6998	MFRS NES OF CPR,NIKL,ETC	W 20974	114628	W 26602	138682	W 20250	138802	W 19014	129746	OUVRAGES EN CU,NI,AL,PB,ZN
69983	ALUMINIUM MANUFACTS NES	W 20512	104988	W 26142	128586	W 20054	130288	W 18862	122184	OUVRAGES EN ALUMINIUM
7	MACHINES,TRANSPORT EQUIP		8319782		10293786		15126718		16749058	MACHINES MATERIEL TRANSPORT
71	POWER GENERATING EQUIPMT		188108		222563		300988		365732	MACHINES GENERATRICES
714	ENGINES AND MOTORS NES	W 471	98297	W 489	112605	W 755	178433	W 801	181977	MOTEURS NON ELECTRIQUES
72	MACHS FOR SPCL INDUSTRYS		165650		237071		239223		266109	MAC SPECIALES POUR INDUST
728	OTH MACHY FOR SPCL INDUS	W 5110	57600	W 6090	115484	W 8509	110394	W 6857	120208	AUT MACH IND PARTICULIERES
74	GENRL INDUSTRL MACHY NES		509640		611342		767940		835127	MACH APP INDUSTRIE
741	HEATING,COOLING EQUIPMNT	W 14025	210534	W 16901	242808	W 24318	346555	W 24032	350466	MACH CHAUFFAGE,PIECES
7414	NONDOM REFRIG EQUIPT,PTS	W 9918	170306	W 9637	205845	W 16431	302168	W 16087	288424	MAT PRODUCTION DU FROID
74141	REFRIG EQUIP NONDOMESTIC	W 7763	154243	W 7945	182891	W 14999	283899	W 14421	266247	REFIG INDUSTRIELS
75	OFFICE MACHNES,ADP EQUIP		5276210		6080059		9346745		10213733	MACH BUREAU TRAIT AUTOM
752	AUTOMTIC DATA PROC EQUIP	W 23685	2612742	W 28581	3677921	W 48703	5719794	W 75895	6177022	MACH TRAIT INFORMATION
7522	DIGITAL COMPUTERS	W 955	302993	W 2218	310291	W 2270	525689	W 16050	1615652	MACH DIGITALES COMPLETES
7523	DIGITL CENTRL PROCESSORS	W 10125	1382627	W 10531	1585245	W 22702	2885055	W 25762	1569549	UNITES CENTRALES
7524	DIGITL CENTRL STOR UNITS	W 1149	262541	W 3647	1036911	W 4601	1447851	W 8906	2151183	UNITES MEMOIRE CENTRALES
7525	ADP PERIPHERAL UNITS	W 10532	579624	W 8623	486393	W 3932	135687	W 12900	451656	UNITES PERIPHERIQUES
7528	OFF–LINE DATA PROC EQUIP	W 799	66902	W 3493	253740	W 15144	718743	W 11517	293948	MACH AUXIL TRAIT INFORM
759	OFFICE,ADP MCH PTS,ACCES	W 20300	2659719	W 20962	2396934	W 23838	3620059	W 29173	4007311	PIECES DU 751 ET 752
7591	OFFICE MACHINE PARTS NES	W 1534	233594	W 1809	230880	W 2650	449299	W 3091	515008	PIECES DU 7511,7518
75915	OTH OFF MCH PTS,ACC NES	W 1137	192929	W 1190	191251	W 1997	432576	W 2401	490833	PIECES DU 751.18,81,88
7599	ACCTG,ETC,ADP MCH PTS,AC	W 18767	2426125	W 19153	2166053	W 21187	3170760	W 26082	3492303	PIECES DU 751 ET 752
76	TELECOMM,SOUND EQUIPMENT		451924		735009		851269		999403	EQUIPMENT DE TELECOM
764	TELECOM EQPT,PTS,ACC NES	W 8228	446601	W 11607	729645	W 10069	832979	W 9936	972419	EQUIP TELECOM,PIECES
7641	LINE TELEPHONE,ETC EQUIP	W 808	72110	W 1302	100295	W 1101	163450	W 1858	260833	APP TELEPHON PAR FIL
7643	TV,RADIO TRANSMITTRS ETC	W 218	44778	W 636	112167	W 595	176291	W 596	183958	APP EMET TELE RADIO
7648	TELECOMM EQUIPMENT NES	W 101	22176	W 869	95003	W 1011	137070	W 540	184998	APP TELECOM NDA
7649	PTS NES OF EQUIPMT OF 76	W 3807	260401	W 5442	369174	W 4309	300519	W 4716	305237	PIECES DE LA DIV 76
76491	PTS NES OF APPAR OF 7641	W 1426	172375	W 1535	235319	W 1276	206832	W 1096	243582	PIECES POUR 764.1
77	ELECTRIC MACHNRY NES ETC		1460125		2092516		3261203		3634850	MACH APP ELECT NDA
771	ELECTRIC POWER MACHY NES	W 4439	75532	W 5151	106404	W 5523	121142	W 6538	144467	MACH PROD,TRANS ELECTR
772	SWITCHGEAR ETC,PARTS NES	W 5882	325415	W 8047	375946	W 9917	485900	W 11730	650517	APP COUPURE,SECT ETC
7721	SWITCHGEAR ETC	W 5239	261753	W 7490	311055	W 9311	369366	W 10112	446679	APP COUPURE,SECTIONMNT
773	ELECTR DISTRIBUTNG EQUIP	W 34531	213417	W 32557	196474	W 40474	243648	W 65946	309121	EQUIPMT DISTRIBUTION ELECT
7731	INSULATED WIRE,CABLE ETC	W 34496	213113	W 32499	195315	W 40257	241573	W 65617	305663	FILS,CABLES ISOLES ELECT
775	HOUSEHOLD TYPE EQUIP NES	W 20668	231499	W 21093	278906	W 23938	335739	W 22552	316526	MACH,APP USAGE DOMESTQUE
7758	ELECTRO–THERMIC APPL NES	W 9452	110561	W 9099	127486	W 8864	147717	W 8628	129444	APP ELECTROTHERMIQ NDA
776	TRANSISTORS,VALVES,ETC	W 808	394836	W 1284	750254	W 2271	1509727	W 1765	1780386	LAMPES,TUBES,VALVES
7764	ELECTRONIC MICROCIRCUITS	W 377	335795	W 1003	677975	W 2008	1393351	W 1097	1532648	MICROSTRUCTURES ELECTRON
7768	ELCTRNC COMP PTS,CRYSTLS	W 315	16905	W 94	24209	W 86	49312	W 410	148355	CRIST PIEZO–ELEC,PCS 776
77689	ELECTRNIC COMPON PTS NES	W 314	16849	W 90	22212	W 85	49110	W 393	146806	PIECES DU GROUPE 776
778	ELECTRICAL MACHINERY NES	W 3724	213023	W 7076	371435	W 7647	548921	W 7362	418555	AUTRES MACH ELECT NDA
7781	BATTERIES,ACCUMULATORS	W 511	34554	W 2001	143844	W 1720	116156	W 678	20743	PILES ET ACCUMULATEURS
77812	ELECTRIC ACCUMULATORS	W 445	30872	W 1841	133863	W 1371	111165	W 260	11949	ACCUMULATEURS ELECTRIQ
7788	OTH ELEC MACHY,EQUIP NES	W 1154	126704	W 2611	160512	W 3292	365478	W 4026	330546	AUT MACH APP ELEC NDA
77889	ELEC PARTS OF MACHY NES	W 241	77476	W 119	93623	W 76	185320	W 101	117531	PIECES ELEC DE MACH NDA
78	ROAD VEHICLES		126991		166539		190571		197204	VEHICULES ROUTIERS
79	OTHR TRANSPORT EQUIPMENT		118360		109461		128060		183875	AUTRE MATERIEL TRANSPORT
792	AIRCRAFT ETC	W 490	98462	W 418	90610		103378	W 1002	160087	APP NAVIGATION AERIENNE
8	MISC MANUFACTURED GOODS		4040812		5058003		5928816		7360974	ART MANUFACTURES DIVERS
84	CLOTHING AND ACCESSORIES		456830		475205		504928		532158	VETEMENTS
845	OUTERWEAR KNIT NONELASTC	W 5794	96209	W 8082	115382	W 7568	122122	W 8527	131703	VET DESSOUS,ACCES BONNET
846	UNDER GARMENTS KNITTED	W 12422	171154	W 12524	168864	W 12019	176472	W 8216	146006	SOUS VETS DE BONNETERIE
8462	— OF COTTON NON ELASTIC	W 10779	124664	W 11083	132833	W 11155	151770	W 7828	122534	SOUS–VET BONNET COTON
84629	—— OTHER	W 10779	124664	W 11083	132833	W 11155	151770	W 7828	122534	AUT SOUS–VET BONNET COTON
87	PRECISION INSTRUMNTS NES		753030		770134		947275		1299755	INSTRUM,APPAR SCIENT NDA
872	MEDICAL INSTRUMENTS NES	W 14474	491517	W 16065	514121	W 15658	632676	W 18090	918918	INSTR,APP MEDIC–CHIR NDA
87202	OTH MEDICAL INSTRUMENTS	W 13762	453682	W 14975	457129	W 14421	552191	W 16368	779343	INSTRUM,APP MEDECINE
87203	MECHANO–THERAPY APPARAT	W 710	37802	W 1089	56983	W 1235	80272	W 1722	139574	APP DE MECANOTHERAPIE
874	MEASURNG,CONTROLNG INSTR	W 1359	202725	W 5419	182937	W 7597	215849	W 8527	264702	INSTRUMENTS DE MESURE
88	PHOTO EQU,OPTICL GDS ETC		280919		239795		261365		274796	APP,FOURN PHOTO,OP,MONTR
884	OPTICAL GOODS NES	W 1091	228728	W 1059	192464	W 1029	205640	W 1536	231354	ELEMENTS OPTIQ,ART LUNET
8841	OPTICAL ELEMENTS	W 558	89640	W 570	76921	W 526	73436	W 956	97873	LENTILLES,PRISMES,MIROIR
88411	OPTICAL ELMNTS UNMOUNTED	W 545	89145	W 560	76267	W 500	72439	W 946	97070	LENTIL,MIROIRS NON MONT
8842	SPECTACLES AND FRAMES	W 532	139088	W 489	115543	W 503	132205	W 580	133480	LUNETTES ET MONTURES
88422	SPECTACLES ETC	W 475	129812	W 311	90654	W 404	120905	W 512	119603	LUNETTES
89	MISC MANUFCTRD GOODS NES		2362343		3339228		3997933		5001629	ART MANUFACTURES DIVERS
892	PRINTED MATTER	W 16453	111016	W 15518	157520	W 13570	172009	W 15240	194365	'PRIMES
893	ARTICLES OF PLASTIC NES		241147		285661		324286	W 85247	345385	OUVRAGES EN MA . DIVIS 58
8939	MISC PLASTIC ARTICLES	W 48309	176798	W 54027	214325	W 54609	237552	W 59462	250837	ART DIVERS EN MAT DIV 58
89399	OTHR PLASTC ARTICLES NES	W 20503	109169	W 24918	132391	W 28543	154336	W 30214	164337	AUT OUV MAT DIV 58
894	TOYS,SPORTING GOODS,ETC	W 20643	137554	W 26390	166807	W 25971	200144	W 24633	200494	VOITURES ENFANTS,JOUETS
8942	TOYS,INDOOR GAMES ETC	W 16874	88620	W 22720	115578	W 22211	141319	W 21102	133704	JOUETS,JEUX ETC
898	MUSICAL INSTRUMENTS,PTS	W 54514	1669334	W 45444	2508604	W 38275	3009619	W 55437	3921483	INSTRUMENTS DE MUSIQUE
8983	SOUND RECRDNG TAPE,DISCS	W 54493	1668302	W 45399	2508132	W 38238	3008378	W 55376	3919679	SUPPORTS SON POUR 763
89831	PREPD SND RECORDNG MEDIA	W 22338	242399	W 21182	228335	W 22090	260448	W 22703	270280	SUPPORTS PREPARES
89832	RECORDED DISCS,TAPES ETC	W 32155	1425903	W 24218	2279797	W 16148	2747930	W 32673	3649399	DISQUES,PHONO,BANDES
899	OTHER MANUFACTURED GOODS		114443		124526		181364		226732	AUT ART MANUF DIVERS NDA
8996	HEARING,ORTHOPAEDIC AIDS		70513		72317		120903		158429	APPAREILS D'ORTHOPEDIE
89962	ORTHOPAEDIC ETC GOODS		70513		71574		111551		140771	APPAREILS D'ORTHOPEDIE
9	GOODS NOT CLASSD BY KIND		2040201		2067662		3010772		588	ART TRANSACT NON CLASSES
931	*SPECIAL TRANSACTIONS	W 45882	2039505	W 164119	2066290		3010433			TRANS.SPECIALES

1. HISTORICAL SERIES, 1961–1996 SPECIAL TRADE, IMPORTS C.I.F., EXPORTS F.O.B.
SERIES HISTORIQUES, 1961–1996 COMMERCE SPECIAL, IMPORTATIONS C.A.F., EXPORTATIONS F.O.B

YEAR ANNEE	VALUE IN MILLION U.S. DOLLARS VALEUR EN MILLION U.S. DOLLARS MERCHANDISE –MARCHANDISE		GOLD –OR		CONVERSION FACTORS FACTEURS DE CONVERSION CENTS E.U. PAR		INDEX NUMBERS –INDICES QUANTUM		UNIT VALUE VALEUR UNITAIRE	
	IMPORTS	EXPORTS	IMPORTS	EXPORTS	IMPORTS	EXPORTS	IMPORTS	EXPORTS	IMPORTS	EXPORTS
1961	583.50	239.10					32	24	23	25
1962	625.80	271.40					35	28	23	24
1963	660.30	338.30					36	33	23	25
1964	814.90	351.80					44	35	23	25
1965	814.30	406.10					24	17	23	24
1966	816.10	476.90					23	18	24	25
1967	756.30	517.30					22	21	24	25
1968	1092.90	602.10					32	24	23	25
1969	1302.10	688.70					36	26	24	26
1970	1422.50	733.60					39	28	25	26
1971	1780.00	915.10					47	33	25	27
1972	1948.00	1099.80					48	37	27	29
1973	2968.60	1391.80					57	39	34	35
1974	4176.50	1737.40					58	41	47	42
1975	4108.70	1834.60					55	41	49	44
1976	4076.60	2305.80					56	51	48	44
1977	4759.90	2963.10					60	55	52	52
1978	5631.00	3716.10					62	55	61	66
1979	7396.50	4313.40					65	57	75	75
1980	7878.30	5291.90					58	62	90	83
1981	7847.00	5328.90					59	66	87	80
1982	7960.40	4990.60					66	65	79	76
1983	8370.00	4893.80					72	66	76	73
1984	8072.10	5622.40					71	75	76	72
1985	8020.90	6084.40					73	82	74	72
1986	10813.40	7154.00					86	91	74	74
1987	14359.20	8454.00					96	101	81	78
1988	15018.30	8198.00					97	96	87	89
1989	14347.10	10738.00					92	100	93	92
1990	16793.70	11576.00					100	100	100	100
1991	18621.37	11911.16					116	98	95	100
1992	20194.38	13074.99					130	107	95	101
1993	22610.14	14805.77					146	121	92	102
1994	25232.23	16881.38					166	140	94	100
1995	29567.99	19038.10					182	150	102	105
1996	31137.90	20474.43					193	162	101	105

2. IMPORTS BY BROAD ECONOMIC CATEGORY AND EXPORTS BY INDUSTRIAL ORIGIN. (PERCENTAGE OF TOTAL VALUE)
IMPORTATIONS PAR CATEGORIES ECONOMIQUES ET EXPORTATIONS PAR BRANCHE D'ACTIVITE.(EN POURCENTAGE DE LA VALEUR TOTALE)

IMPORTS – IMPORTATIONS

	1990	1991	1992	1993	1994	1995	1996
TOTAL IMPORTS–IMPORTATIONS TOTALES	100.	100.	100.	100.	100.	100.	100.
1 FOOD BEV–ALIMENTATION BOISSONS	6.7	6.5	6.1	5.7	5.9	5.6	5.7
11 PRIMARY–PRODUITS DE BASE	3.9	3.9	3.4	3.2	3.3	2.9	3.0
111 FOR INDUSTRY–POUR L'INDUSTRIE	2.6	2.2	2.1	2.0	1.9	1.8	1.9
112 FOR HOUSEHOLDS–POUR LES MENAGES	1.3	1.7	1.3	1.2	1.3	1.1	1.1
12 PROCESSED–PRODUITS ELABORES	2.9	2.6	2.7	2.5	2.6	2.6	2.7
121 FOR INDUSTRY–POUR L'INDUSTRIE	0.5	0.4	0.5	0.4	0.4	0.4	0.3
122 FOR HOUSEHOLDS–POUR LES MENAGES	2.3	2.2	2.2	2.1	2.2	2.2	2.4
2 IND SUPPLIES–APPROV INDUSTRIELS	47.3	44.0	42.8	42.0	41.2	42.1	40.0
21 PRIMARY–PRODUITS DE BASE	22.5	18.0	18.3	19.0	18.8	18.0	18.5
22 PROCESSED–PRODUITS ELABORES	24.7	26.0	24.4	23.0	22.4	24.1	21.6
3 FUELS–COMBUSTIBLES	8.8	7.6	7.8	7.4	6.0	6.0	6.1
31 PRIMARY–PRODUITS DE BASE	7.1	6.2	7.1	6.6	5.3	4.8	5.0
32 PROCESSED–PRODUITS ELABORES	1.7	1.3	0.7	0.8	0.8	1.2	1.1
321 MOTOR SPIRIT–ESSENCE	1.6	1.3	0.6	0.7	0.7		
322 OTHER–AUTRES	0.1	0.0	0.1	0.0	0.0	1.2	1.1
4 MACHINERY–EQUIPEMENT	18.5	21.1	20.7	22.1	23.0	23.1	24.7
41 CAPITAL EQUIPMENT–MACHINES	14.7	17.0	16.6	17.6	18.3	18.2	19.2
42 PARTS–PIECES ACCESSOIRES	3.7	4.1	4.1	4.5	4.7	5.0	5.6
5 TRANSPORT–TRANSPORT	8.8	11.0	11.7	11.5	12.5	11.6	11.3
51 PASSENGER CARS–AUTOMOBILES	3.3	4.1	5.6	4.9	5.3	5.1	4.7
52 OTHER–AUTRES	2.8	4.1	3.2	3.6	4.6	3.7	3.4
521 INDUSTRIAL–INDUSTRIELS	2.7	4.0	3.1	3.4	4.4	3.6	3.3
522 NON INDUSTRIAL–NON INDUSTRIEL	0.1	0.1	0.1	0.1	0.2	0.1	0.1
53 PARTS–PIECES ACCESSOIRES	2.7	2.9	2.9	3.0	2.5	2.8	3.1
6 CONSUM GOODS–BIENS CONSOMMATION	8.6	8.5	9.3	9.9	10.1	10.0	10.7
61 DURABLE–DURABLES	3.1	3.1	3.3	3.4	3.4	3.3	3.4
62 SEMI DURABLE–SEMI DURABLES	3.3	3.3	3.7	4.1	4.2	4.4	4.7
63 NON DURABLE–NON DURABLES	2.2	2.1	2.3	2.4	2.4	2.4	2.6
7 GOODS NES–BIENS NDA	1.4	1.3	1.6	1.3	1.3	1.5	1.5

EXPORTS – EXPORTATIONS

	1990	1991	1992	1993	1994	1995	1996
TOTAL EXPORTS–EXPORTATIONS TOTALES	100.	100.	100.	100.	100.	100.	100.
1 AGRICULTURE	5.6	5.8	4.4	3.9	3.7	4.1	4.2
2 MINING QUARRY–INDUS EXTRACTIVES	31.1	30.0	29.8	29.0	30.4	30.7	31.2
3 MANUFACTURING–IND MANUFACTUR	63.3	64.3	65.8	67.1	65.9	65.2	64.7
31 FOOD BEV TOBACCO–ALIM BOISS TAB	5.2	4.3	4.0	3.4	3.1	2.8	2.7
32 TEXTILES–INDUSTRIES TEXTILES	6.3	6.9	7.2	6.1	5.9	5.7	5.2
33 WOOD & PRODUCTS–BOIS & PRODUITS	0.2	0.1	0.1	0.1	0.1	0.1	0.0
34 PAPER & PRODUCTS–PAPIER & PRODT	0.5	0.6	0.6	0.5	0.5	0.5	0.5
35 CHEMICALS–INDUSTRIES CHIMIQUES	16.2	16.6	16.4	16.7	16.6	17.2	16.8
36 NON METAL MIN–MIN NON METAL	0.2	0.3	0.2	0.2	0.3	0.4	0.4
37 BASIC METAL–IND METAL BASE	1.0	0.9	0.8	0.6	0.7	0.9	0.9
38 METAL MANUF–MANUF METAL	30.8	31.2	32.9	36.0	35.7	32.5	35.4
39 OTH MANUF IND–AUTRES MANUF	2.9	3.4	3.7	3.4	3.0	5.1	2.8

3. TRADE BY PRINCIPAL COUNTRIES OF PURCHASE AND LAST CONSIGNMENT (VALUE IN THOUSAND U.S. DOLLARS)
ECHANGES SELON LES PRINCIPAUX PAYS D'ACHAT ET DE DERNIERE CONSIGNATION (VALEUR EN MILLIERS DE DOLLARS EU)

COUNTRIES–PAYS	SPECIAL IMPORTS C.I.F. IMPORTATIONS SPECIALES C.A.F				
	1992	1993	1994	1995	1996
World	18813602	20517692	23778852	28344295	29948534
Africa	332534	326024	329563	413620	389502
Americas	3566619	3977517	4696470	5764418	6447859
Northern America	3348615	3751204	4426593	5491024	6149511
LAIA	208115	206571	253379	245140	262559
CACM	2726	5171	3947	3454	4137
Caribbean	330	484	346	1186	525
Rest of America	6833	14088	12205	23614	31127
As.ex F.USSR	1867876	2162134	2483340	3128665	3338641
Eur.x F.USSR	11396734	12319085	14591791	16877691	17489302
EU	9832290	10548454	12719036	14687409	15356956
EFTA	1408126	1576725	1587426	1758279	1738384
East Europe	139139	172043	211788	263891	212564
Other Europe	7676	9411	55028	155317	164102
Former USSR	22947	75272	119046	276645	237348
Oceania	56160	55556	62997	78166	91167
USA/Etats–Unis d'Amer	3234361	3643213	4271080	5263609	5965658
Belgium–Luxembourg	2391561	2504902	3049950	3433427	3637900
Germany/Allemagne	2246938	2132744	2467528	2745723	2801194
United Kingdom	1509442	1773646	2056748	2324751	2632926
Italy/Italie	1308683	1496257	1849083	2193860	2258074
Switz.Liecht	1353048	1533846	1530262	1680492	1648562
France,Monac	844845	857676	1058249	1158331	1165426
Japan/Japon	998231	1047692	963613	931387	1097080
Netherlands/Pays–Bas	615692	700551	789165	949074	943907
Spain/Espagne	203834	208496	398002	520864	619981
Sweden/Suède	206409	286223	326718	380375	362367
Hong Kong	183483	248808	281105	365126	412648
So. Africa Customs Un	267378	253877	236739	295126	300899
Korea, Republic of	102570	137854	282381	385257	352444
Turkey/Turquie	79594	91995	162111	256341	246157
India/Inde	74682	128932	151726	186744	246307
Canada	113446	107991	155512	227415	183815
Singapore/Singapour	92050	84631	124784	275126	189284
Finland/Finlande	90317	104289	123952	233485	211381
Denmark/Danemark	139707	139336	140162	167123	152975
Austria/Autriche	84950	115140	128741	155121	148165
Thailand/Thaïlande	77407	99461	118459	159067	173807
Ireland/Irlande	55756	71317	105581	159072	171601
Greece/Grèce	73417	84490	115909	150928	136853
Russian Federation	20913	55601	70169	212762	180544
Portugal	60741	73387	109247	115275	114206
China/Chine	4979	32652	80092	128830	160887
Romania/Roumanie	36645	64381	89599	105842	99855
Norway,SVD,JM	53964	41333	56620	76842	87618
Brazil/Brésil	59709	74291	80283	36238	48238
Australia/Australie	54994	52678	60321	73201	47243
Uruguay	54019	48789	54836	58469	66636
Argentina/Argentine	41498	31823	44772	58094	58885
Colombia/Colombie	31352	37484	40440	56444	52543
Hungary/Hongrie	35340	34715	24453	40045	39856
Czech Republic		36292	51664	44909	24772
Cyprus/Chypre	22813	29618	31635	32628	38447
Gabon	36609	40488	37742	13599	8014
Ukraine	1020	8846	23519	43690	43360
Bulgaria/Bulgarie	12109	9750	18106	45191	29933
Egypt/Egypte	7282	10930	27658	45670	23332
Poland/Pologne	18423	23498	20976	18710	13264
Kenya	14793	12445	11816	13146	17947
Zimbabwe		2	8325	19510	19296
Philippines	5756	6969	12593	10814	10454
Panama	6833	14088	12205	2951	8985
Republic of Moldova	241	7503	11452	15693	9631
Chile/Chili	2888	3641	6125	10688	13305
Czechoslovakia	36622				
Slovenia/Slovénia	979	5349	12713	5803	7648

COUNTRIES–PAYS	SPECIAL EXPORTS F.O.B. EXPORTATIONS SPECIALES F.O.B.				
	1992	1993	1994	1995	1996
Monde	13082257	14825325	16933986	19047421	20510239
Afrique	228818	264218	285075	353986	387503
Amériques	4396000	5121996	5897867	6410023	7026557
Amérique du Nord	4081047	4724651	5368613	5850131	6405670
ALAI	275116	355729	478520	494575	556445
MCAC	28413	25168	28239	34216	40571
Caraïbes	5687	7769	8383	15954	15278
Autre Amérique	5738	8679	14113	15147	8593
Asie l'URSS exclus	2188602	2638560	3320394	4030828	4349854
Europe l'URSS exclus	5078478	5182204	5566159	6871845	7324899
UE	4659614	4538010	4961306	6150146	6588344
AELE	260637	297154	376072	376753	340620
Europe de l'Est	129571	318495	192038	294331	318038
Autre de l'Europe	1088	5286	4018	17625	14533
Ancienne URSS	77996	203992	300994	386684	412006
Océanie	143427	158779	214664	247620	237195
USA/Etats–Unis d'Amer	3995816	4621673	5262378	5735233	6281245
United Kingdom	1004872	816112	848977	1160130	1364813
Japan/Japon	689085	768951	989371	1322487	1216312
Belgium–Luxembourg	650394	797470	910381	1019787	1122896
Germany/Allemagne	762654	786603	850252	1039191	1037070
Hong Kong	666427	722522	843779	967723	1066143
Netherlands/Pays–Bas	553787	554030	633130	808044	890366
France,Monac	620504	576059	584031	704908	670596
Italy/Italie	459604	437341	505203	567392	553096
Switz.Liecht	231149	271952	346899	344125	300817
India/Inde	127544	228290	361899	314499	315743
Spain/Espagne	242810	199241	236314	313788	352321
Thailand/Thaïlande	91062	146701	248904	275346	334345
Korea, Republic of	89374	138210	147820	301874	364362
Russian Federation	67217	118518	192525	259171	258740
Philippines	109927	187091	207897	174277	198191
Australia/Australie	115600	134672	180418	218034	214189
Turkey/Turquie	114531	135065	130981	184025	196964
Singapore/Singapour	120729	118134	151093	170549	200374
So. Africa Customs Un	125514	122639	128607	173941	179739
Greece/Grèce	109102	114660	108736	204404	165900
Brazil/Brésil	66485	80449	128281	131956	186650
Canada	85135	102937	106168	114802	124213
Romania/Roumanie	48769	92787	74508	132323	112197
Sweden/Suède	57052	52458	74287	91296	118179
Austria/Autriche	69040	67070	79814	81076	75511
Chile/Chili	31005	73679	78874	111686	50372
Argentina/Argentine	41700	59234	76809	71006	94862
China/Chine	54455	54697	59502	84546	82715
Poland/Pologne	24103	39679	39083	63848	80236
Cyprus/Chypre	28296	33964	41748	61479	74781
Mexico/Mexique	33683	36480	76595	33257	54503
Denmark/Danemark	40950	41575	38328	53592	55955
Czech Republic		135455	21866	27668	44950
Portugal	42787	51285	41348	44891	46330
Colombia/Colombie	22796	25305	40388	65648	56704
Hungary/Hongrie	29845	35285	33648	46080	59516
Ireland/Irlande	27039	22161	28140	29562	83635
Ukraine	5435	22448	36071	56770	68439
Norway,SVD,JM	25103	24871	28833	32224	39107
Finland/Finlande	19020	21945	22365	32085	51676
Peru/Pérou	23926	13562	22192	24579	46551
Egypt/Egypte	6667	9556	20668	31017	57544
Kenya	16725	27180	25533	23790	30802
Ecuador/Equateur	17732	25255	12484	28368	34618
Sri Lanka	7969	11453	14279	33027	48350
Nigeria/Nigéria	26535	26432	21436	20672	19885
New Zealand	19538	17107	22675	23368	21623
Slovenia/Slovénia	1791	13309	19625	17708	47978
Venezuela	27304	25681	25053	10736	7867

(VALUE AS PERCENTAGE OF WORLD TOTAL)(VALEURS EN POURCENTAGE DU TOTAL MONDIAL)

	1987	1988	1989	1990	1991	1992	1993	1994	1995	1996
Africa	2.2	1.9	1.9	1.8	1.8	1.8	1.6	1.4	1.5	1.3
Americas	18.1	18.5	19.8	19.8	21.5	19.0	19.4	19.8	20.3	21.5
Northern America	17.2	17.3	18.5	18.6	20.1	17.8	18.3	18.6	19.4	20.5
LAIA	0.8	1.1	1.2	1.1	1.2	1.1	1.0	1.1	0.9	0.9
CACM	0.0	0.0	0.0	0.0	0.0	0.0	0.0	0.0	0.0	0.0
Caribbean	0.0	0.0	0.0	0.0	0.0	0.0	0.0	0.0	0.0	0.0
Rest of America	0.1	0.1	0.1	0.1	0.1	0.0	0.1	0.1	0.1	0.1
As.ex F.USSR	6.4	7.2	6.1	7.2	8.6	9.9	10.5	10.4	11.0	11.1
Eur.x F.USSR	63.9	64.1	62.6	61.6	59.5	60.6	60.0	61.4	59.5	58.4
EU	55.8	54.3	52.5	51.3	49.8	52.3	51.4	53.5	51.8	51.3
EFTA	7.6	9.2	9.5	9.4	8.8	7.5	7.7	6.7	6.2	5.8
East Europe	0.4	0.5	0.5	0.7	0.8	0.7	0.8	0.9	0.9	0.7
Other Europe	0.1	0.1	0.1	0.1	0.1	0.0	0.0	0.2	0.5	0.5
Former USSR	0.0	0.0	0.0	0.1	0.3	0.1	0.4	0.5	1.0	0.8
Oceania	0.4	0.7	0.4	0.2	0.3	0.3	0.3	0.3	0.3	0.3
USA/Etats–Unis d'Amer	16.2	16.6	17.9	17.8	19.3	17.2	17.8	18.0	18.6	19.9
Belgium–Luxembourg	14.2	15.2	15.2	13.2	11.1	12.7	12.2	12.8	12.1	12.1
Germany/Allemagne	12.9	11.3	10.8	11.7	11.9	11.9	10.4	10.4	9.7	9.4
United Kingdom	9.4	9.3	8.8	8.6	8.3	8.0	8.6	8.6	8.2	8.8
Italy/Italie	6.3	6.1	5.8	6.1	6.5	7.0	7.3	7.8	7.7	7.5
Switz.Liecht	7.4	9.0	9.3	9.2	8.5	7.2	7.5	6.4	5.9	5.5
France,Monac	4.6	4.2	4.1	3.9	4.2	4.5	4.2	4.5	4.1	3.9
Japan/Japon	3.4	3.7	2.7	3.6	4.3	5.3	5.1	4.1	3.3	3.7
Netherlands/Pays–Bas	3.2	3.5	3.5	3.5	3.4	3.3	3.4	3.3	3.3	3.2
Spain/Espagne	1.1	1.0	1.1	1.0	1.0	1.1	1.0	1.7	1.8	2.1

	1987	1988	1989	1990	1991	1992	1993	1994	1995	1996
Afrique	1.9	1.9	1.7	1.4	1.6	1.7	1.8	1.7	1.9	1.9
Amériques	36.0	34.1	34.1	32.3	33.5	33.6	34.5	34.8	33.7	34.3
Amérique du Nord	33.0	31.6	31.9	29.7	31.0	31.2	31.9	31.7	30.7	31.2
ALAI	2.4	2.1	1.8	2.5	2.2	2.1	2.4	2.8	2.6	2.7
MCAC	0.1	0.1	0.1	0.1	0.1	0.2	0.2	0.2	0.2	0.2
Caraïbes	0.3	0.1	0.3	0.1	0.1	0.0	0.1	0.0	0.1	0.1
Autre Amérique	0.1	0.1	0.0	0.0	0.1	0.0	0.1	0.1	0.1	0.0
Asie l'URSS exclus	13.0	15.7	16.2	17.2	15.8	16.7	17.8	19.6	21.2	21.2
Europe l'URSS exclus	37.0	37.8	36.7	40.3	40.9	38.8	35.0	32.9	36.1	35.7
UE	33.8	34.4	32.9	36.6	37.2	35.6	30.6	29.3	32.3	32.1
AELE	2.6	2.8	2.9	2.7	2.5	2.0	2.0	2.2	2.0	1.7
Europe de l'Est	0.3	0.4	0.6	0.6	0.8	1.0	2.1	1.1	1.5	1.6
Autre de l'Europe	0.3	0.2	0.3	0.4	0.3	0.0	0.0	0.0	0.1	0.1
Ancienne URSS	0.0	0.0	0.1	0.0	0.1	0.6	1.4	1.8	2.0	2.0
Océanie	1.0	1.2	1.2	0.9	1.0	1.1	1.1	1.3	1.3	1.2
USA/Etats–Unis d'Amer	32.0	30.7	30.9	28.8	30.2	30.5	31.2	31.1	30.1	30.6
United Kingdom	7.8	7.9	6.8	7.0	6.7	7.7	5.5	5.0	6.1	6.7
Japan/Japon	5.8	6.7	7.0	7.2	6.1	5.3	5.2	5.8	6.9	5.9
Belgium–Luxembourg	3.2	3.9	4.0	5.7	5.8	5.0	5.4	5.4	5.4	5.5
Germany/Allemagne	5.6	5.3	4.9	5.9	6.7	5.8	5.3	5.0	5.5	5.1
Hong Kong	4.5	5.3	4.8	4.4	4.6	5.1	4.9	5.0	5.1	5.2
Netherlands/Pays–Bas	4.6	4.7	4.6	4.5	4.5	4.2	3.7	3.7	4.2	4.3
France,Monac	4.6	3.9	4.1	4.8	4.8	4.7	3.9	3.4	3.7	3.3
Italy/Italie	3.6	3.9	3.9	4.2	3.9	3.5	2.9	3.0	3.0	2.7
Switz.Liecht	2.3	2.4	2.4	2.4	2.3	1.8	1.8	2.0	1.8	1.5

4. Special Imports C.I.F. by Commodities according to the S.I.T.C. (Rev. 2) in thousand U.S. Dollars
Importations Spéciales C.A.F. par Produits d'après la C.T.C.I. (Rév. 2) en milliers de Dollars E.U.

SITC CTCI	COMMODITY	1993 WEIGHT POIDS	1993 VALUE VALEUR	1994 WEIGHT POIDS	1994 VALUE VALEUR	1995 WEIGHT POIDS	1995 VALUE VALEUR	1996 WEIGHT POIDS	1996 VALUE VALEUR	PRODUIT
	ALL COMMODITIES		20517692		23778852		28344295		29948534	TOUS PRODUITS
0	FOOD AND LIVE ANIMALS		1086030		1299212		1503163		1686108	ALIMENTS,ANIMAUX VIVANTS
01	MEAT AND PREPARATIONS		100827		146817		109299		120746	VIANDES ET PREPARATIONS
011	MEAT FRESH,CHILLD,FROZEN		100822		146609		109259		120229	VIANDES FRAICHES,REF,CONGE
0111	BOVINE MEAT FRESH,FROZEN		94764		135648		100668		111316	VIANDES BOVIN FRAI,REF
01111	BOVINE MEAT WITH BONE IN		90561		19048		563		1343	VIANDES BOVIN NON DESOSS
01112	BOVINE MEAT BONELESS		4202		116601		100105	W 48057	109973	VIANDES BOVIN DESOSSEES
03	FISH AND PREPARATIONS		86198		88309		114836		112855	POISSONS ET PREPARATIONS
034	FISH,FRESH,CHILLED,FROZN		67348		68140		91158		87918	POISSON FRAIS, REFRIG,CONG
04	CEREALS AND PREPARATIONS		386547		420277		492659		607911	CEREALES ET PRODUITS
041	WHEAT ETC UNMILLED		144574		173345		145491	W 852144	189682	FROMENT,EPEAUTRE
0412	OTHER WHEAT ETC UNMILLED		93954		132244		112577	W 674243	148667	AUTRE FROMENT NON MOULU
043	BARLEY UNMILLED		52098		71713		66086	W 416987	72883	ORGE NON MONDEE
044	MAIZE UNMILLED		66555		51605		104697	W 679286	120449	MAIS NON MOULU
048	CEREAL ETC PREPARATIONS		59167		68929		83842		90336	PREPTNS A BASE CEREALES
05	VEGETABLES AND FRUIT		152042		181624		216022		217745	LEGUMES ET FRUITS
06	SUGAR AND PREPS,HONEY		146522		165365		206547		212028	SUCRES ET PRODUITS
061	SUGAR AND HONEY		124990		134770		172022		172116	SUCRES ET MIEL
0612	REFINED SUGAR ETC		116870		126945		162483	W 408476	162780	SUCRES RAFFINES
07	COFFEE,TEA,COCOA,SPICES		84346		125206		164650		153263	CAFE,THE,CACAO,EPICES
071	COFFEE AND SUBSTITUTES		40973		64621		101398		84051	CAFE ET SUCCEDANES
09	MISC EDIBLE PRODUCTS		60234		82197		110457		156714	PREP ALIMENTAIRES DIVERSES
098	EDIBLE PRODCTS,PREPS NES		59990		81839		103125		153411	PREP ALIMENTAIRES NDA
09809	MISC FOOD PREPRTIONS NES		50834		70586		90380		134389	PREP ALIMENTAIRES NDA
1	BEVERAGES AND TOBACCO		92268		104740		110863		114454	BOISSONS ET TABACS
12	TOBACCO AND MANUFACTURES		76396		84834		89926		91372	TABACS BRUTS FABRIQUES
2	CRUDE MATERLS,EXCL FUELS		552907		599337		714485		661934	MAT BRUTES NON COMESTIBLES
22	OIL SEEDS,OLEAGINOUS FRT		149408		133891		161292		179915	GRAINES,FRUITS OLEAGINEUX
222	SEEDS FOR'SOFT'FIXED OIL		148367		132541		160161		179174	GRAINES HUILES FIXES
2222	SOYA BEANS		125934		102731		126775	W 447182	139393	FEVES DE SOJA
24	CORK AND WOOD		142957		178038		179765		159531	LIEGE ET BOIS
248	WOOD SHAPED,SLEEPERS		100648		125583		140764		132173	BOIS SIMPLEMENT TRAVAILLES
2482	LUMBER SHAPED CONIFER		95041		121463		103828		94642	CONIFERES SCIES,RABOTES
24821	LUMBER SAWN ETC CONIFER		94692		121072		103773		94294	CONIFERES SCIES LONGITUD
251	*PULP AND WASTE PAPER		52577		55580		92414		54923	PATES A PAPIER,DECHETS
26	TEXTILE FIBRES AND WASTE		66562		71078		70403		68889	FIBRES TEXTILES
27	CRUDE FERTLZR,MINRLS NES		72415		81782		110752		100711	ENGRAIS MINERAUX BRUTS
3	MINERAL FUELS ETC		1521530		1439064		1686169		1846101	COMBUSTIBLES MINERAUX LUB
33	PETROLEUM AND PRODUCTS		1517470		1434475		1681533		1836646	PETROLE ET DERIVES
333	CRUDE PETROLEUM		1349332		1242030		1349088	MW 10257	1490309	HUILES BRUTES DE PETROLE
334	PETROLEUM PRODUCTS,REFIN		155624		179079		318282		307186	PRODUITS RAFFINES
3341	GASOLINE,OTH LIGHT OILS		147556		169830					ESSENCES POUR MOTEURS
33419	OTH LIGHT PETROLEUM OILS		147556		169830					AUTRES HUILES LEGERES
4	ANIMAL,VEGETABLE OIL,FAT		60066		86891		88839		68745	HUILES,GRAISSES ANIM,VEG
5	CHEMCLS,RELATED PROD NES		1848647		2056441		2565518		2620704	PRODUITS CHIMIQUES
51	ORGANIC CHEMICALS		442910		496260		603509		636344	PROD CHIMIQ ORGANIQUES
511	HYDROCARBONS NES,DERIVS		72833		91441		102605		95655	HYDROCARBURES NDA
513	CARBOXYLIC ACIDS ETC		65599		76594		104232		103045	ACIDES CARBOXYLIQUES
514	NITROGEN–FNCTN COMPOUNDS		143211		149433		188764		207204	COMPOSES FONCT AZOTEES
5148	OTH NITROGN–FNCTN CMPNDS		88506		91419		117249		130690	AUTRES COMPOSES AZOTES
515	ORG–INORG COMPOUNDS ETC		64167		66022		79364		84107	COMPOSES ORGANO–MINERAUX
52	INORGANIC CHEMICALS		114890		131462		147937		142341	PROD CHIM INORGANIQUES
53	DYES,TANNING,COLOUR PROD		126613		141017		165280		168265	PROD TEINTURE,COLORANTS
533	PIGMENTS,PAINTS,ETC		89005		102280		124569		132495	PIGMENTS,PEINTURES,VERNIS
541	*MEDICINAL,PHARM PRODUCT		315723		347039		419134		477041	PROD MEDICINAUX PHARMACEUT
5417	MEDICAMENTS		218830		251887		319540		367658	MEDICAMENTS
54179	— CONTNG OTH SUBSTANCES		197151		228687		296198		343363	MED CONT AUT SUBSTANCES
55	PERFUME,CLEANING ETC PRD		128859		160188		196888		219424	PROD POUR PARFUM,TOILETTE
553	PERFUMERY,COSMETICS,ETC		44082		63115		86191		99046	PRODUITS DE PARFUMERIE
58	PLASTIC MATERIALS ETC		442738		477734		650951		574279	MAT PLAST ARTIFICIELLES
582	PROD OF CONDENSATION ETC		131446		148118		224955		181507	PROD CONDENS,POLYCOND
5823	ALKYDS,OTHER POLYESTERS		82010		92159		158765		115752	ALKYDES ET AUT POLYESTERS
58231	— IN PRIMARY FORMS		71494		80957		142811		102477	SOUS FORMES PRIMAIRES
583	POLYMERIZATION ETC PRODS		297722		314914		410054		377197	PROD POLYMERISATION
5831	POLYETHYLENE		82368		95744		128697		116442	POLYETHYLENE
58311	— IN PRIMARY FORMS		73665		83494		115666		104872	POLYETHYLENE PRIMAIRES
5839	OTH POLYMRZTION ETC PROD		72668		81243		82641		82524	AUT PROD POLYMER COPOLYM
59	CHEMICAL MATERIALS NES		263663		289958		360532		385244	MAT PROD CHIMIQUES NDA
598	MISCEL CHEM PRODUCTS NES		197298		215340		268173		289264	PROD DIV INDUST CHIM NDA
5989	CHEM PRODUCTS,PREPS NES		172913		187021		238097		260051	PROD PREP CHIMIQUES NDA
59899	OTH CHEM PRODS,PREPS,NES		132886		149186		195643		208846	AUT PRODUITS CHIMIQUES NDA
6	BASIC MANUFACTURES		6555745		7544705		9104436		9224049	ART MANUFACTURES
62	RUBBER MANUFACTURES NES		130011		128503		152844		163445	CAOUTCHOUC MANUFACTURE
625	RUBBER TYRES, TUBES ETC		68328		63213		77139		82961	PNEUS CAOUTCHOUC VULCANISE
63	WOOD,CORK MANUFACTRS NES		50525		80620		110740		126771	OUVRAGES LIEGE ET BOIS
64	PAPER,PAPERBOARD AND MFR		353813		448874		637177		521504	PAPIERS,CARTONS & OUVRAGES
641	PAPER AND PAPERBOARD		306936		384622		556193		439317	PAPIERS ET CARTONS
6411	NEWSPRINT		55954		67305		126272	W 128314	103085	PAPIER JOURNAL
6413	KRAFT PAPER,PAPERBOARD		67747		86629		128866		88768	PAPIER ET CARTON KRAFT
6415	PAPER,PAPERBRD,BULK,NES		52620		64672		94188		65165	PAPIERS,CARTONS ROULEAUX
64159	OTHER PAPER ETC,BULK,NES		46718		58734		86314		56568	AUT PAPIER ROULEAUX FEUILLES
65	TEXTILE YARN,FABRICS,ETC		692178		744153		827588		767368	FILS,TISSUS,ARTICLES TEXTILE
651	TEXTILE YARN		237973		246219		270620		228263	FILS TEXTILES
6513	COTTON YARN		95895		109348		121100		94945	FILS DE COTON
6514	SYN FIB YRN,BULK,MONOFIL		71909		72218		81018		73906	FILS CONT 85% FIB TEXT SYNTH
652	COTTON FABRICS,WOVEN		67101		74842		88281		74967	TISSUS DE COTON
653	WOVN MAN–MADE FIB FABRIC		146378		156542		172135		158169	TISSUS FIBRES SYNTH,ARTIF
655	KNITTED,ETC FABRICS		69804		80305		90047		91252	ETOF BONNETERIE PIECES ETC
6552	OTHER KNIT ETC FAB NONEL		69804		80305		90047		91252	ETOF BON NON ELAS NON SYNT
657	SPECIAL TXTL FABRC,PRODS		66259		73720		95268		103571	TISSUS SPECIAUX
66	NONMETAL MINERAL MFS NES		3952376		4602713		5261513		5696471	ART MIN NON METALLIQUES
661	LIME,CEMENT,BLDG PRODS		121739		154379		200549		173918	CHAUX,CIMENTS MAT CONSTR
6612	CEMENT		77966		98333		128659		95337	CIMENTS HYDRAULIQUES
662	CLAY,REFRACTORY BLDG PRD		72273		85191		117942		133216	MAT CONST REFRACTAIRES
6624	BRICKS ETC NONREFRACTORY		55949		74238		102429		119649	BRIQUES ETC CERAM NON REFR
665	GLASSWARE		51926		73511		85419		96103	OUVRAGES EN VERRE
667	PEARL,PREC–,SEMI–P STONE		3578259		4152397		4695039		5122268	PERLES, PIERRES GEMMES
6672	DIAMONDS NONINDUST,UNSET		3541588		4124746		4656340		5078268	DIAMANTS BRUTS
66722	— SRTD,ROUGH,SIMPLY WKD		2997374		3485054		3932760		4230521	DIAMANTS TRIES BRUTS
66729	— CUT ETC NOT SET		544214		639691		723580		847747	DIAMANTS TAILLES
67	IRON AND STEEL		580824		607403		930058		751089	FER ET ACIER

4. Special Imports C.I.F. by Commodities according to the S.I.T.C. (Rev. 2) in thousand U.S. Dollars
Importations Spéciales C.A.F. par Produits d'après la C.T.C.I. (Rév. 2) en milliers de Dollars E.U.

SITC CTCI	COMMODITY	1993 WEIGHT POIDS	1993 VALUE VALEUR	1994 WEIGHT POIDS	1994 VALUE VALEUR	1995 WEIGHT POIDS	1995 VALUE VALEUR	1996 WEIGHT POIDS	1996 VALUE VALEUR	PRODUIT
672	IRON,STEEL PRIMARY FORMS		120746		129666		190474		134695	LINGOTS FER,ACIER
6727	IRN,STL COIL FR REROLLNG		84524		74351		115392		76197	EBAUCHES POUR TOLES FER
67271	IRON,SIMPLE STEEL COILS		83849		73380		114095		74303	EBAUCHES NON EN ACIER
673	IRON,STEEL SHAPES ETC		152828		184598		280726		241116	BARRES,PROFIL FER,ACIER
6732	IRON,STEEL BARS ETC		75274		79583		146642		126165	BARRES FER,ACIER
67326	IRN,OTH STL BARS HOTROLD		53643		54578		109934	W 282829	85390	BARRES PLEINES FER,ACIER
674	IRN,STL UNIV,PLATE,SHEET		212640		194230		314268		238526	LARGES PLATS,TOLES
6749	OTH IRN,STL PLATES,SHEET		104325		95656		161145		120130	AUTRES TOLES FER,ACIER
67491	— OF IRON OR SIMPLE STL		86522		74388		135879		100602	AUT TOLES AUTRES ACIER FIN
678	IRON,STL TUBES,PIPES,ETC		61534		65978		90649		97310	TUBES,TUYAUX EN FONTE,FER
68	NON-FERROUS METALS		305431		367605		510072		459832	METAUX NON FERREUX
682	COPPER EXC CEMENT COPPER		124659		141704		198352		170129	CUIVRE
6822	COPPER,ALLOYS WORKED		123549		140813		195810		167672	CUIVRE,ALLIAGES OUVRES
68221	COPPER BARS,WIRE,ETC		80857		95378		124635	W 36592	99139	BARRES,PROFILES ET FILS
684	ALUMINIUM		129942		164163		230627		216143	ALUMINIUM
6841	ALUMINIUM,ALLOYS,UNWRGHT		47019		65911		95237	W 42302	78440	ALUMINIUM,ALLIAGES BRUTS
6842	ALUMINIUM,ALLOYS WORKED		82923		98252		135390		137703	ALUMINIUM,ALLIAGES OUVRE
69	METAL MANUFACTURES NES		444499		521152		630330		696475	ART MANUFACT EN METAL NDA
695	TOOLS		68596		76263		99159		105307	OUTILS A MAIN
699	BASE METAL MFRS NES		175953		230479		252349		261153	ART MANUFACTURES MET NDA
6997	IRON,STEEL ARTICLES NES		65410		101633		94796		84477	OUV FONTE,FER,ACIER NDA
69979	IRN,STL MANUFACTURES NES		65398		101172		94735		84278	AUT OUVRAGES EN FER NDA
7	MACHINES,TRANSPORT EQUIP		6706919		8228258		9610929		10445554	MACHINES MATERIEL TRANSPORT
71	POWER GENERATING EQUIPMT		301498		301929		371459		421497	MACHINES GENERATRICES
714	ENGINES AND MOTORS NES		115747		108941		200131		206603	MOTEURS NON ELECTRIQUES
7149	ENGINE & MOTOR PARTS NES		49155		49695		121170		121934	PIECES 714 ET 718.88
71491	PARTS NES OF 7144,71481		41494		45979		77118		110635	PIECES DES PROPULSEURS
716	ROTATING ELECTRIC PLANT		64234		114255		100731		109060	APP ELECTR ROTATIFS,PIECES
7162	AC MTRS,GENRTRS,GEN SETS		49806		84399		81229		84198	MOTEURS ELECTRIQUES
72	MACHS FOR SPCL INDUSTRYS		779936		893760		910158		823796	MAC SPECIALES POUR INDUST
723	CIVIL ENGNEERG EQUIP ETC		153934		171516		138485		106947	APPAREILS DE GENIE CIVIL
7234	CONST,MINING MACHNRY NES		130176		133117		118890		95613	MACH POUR LA CONST, MINES
72342	SLFPRP SHOVELS,EXCAVATRS		108717		106879		90996		71676	PELLES MECANIQUES
724	TEXTILE,LEATHER MACHNRY		122066		115144		100551		97493	MACH POUR INDUSTRIE TEXTILE
726	PRINTG,BKBINDG MACHY,PTS		59951		105001		120396		72770	MACHINES POUR IMPRIMERIE
728	OTH MACHY FOR SPCL INDUS		340343		364473		407444		387083	AUT MACH IND PARTICULIERES
7284	MACHY FOR SPCL INDUS NES		246097		246734		297550		302956	MACH SPEC IND PARTICUL.
72842	RUBBER,PLASTICS WRKG MCH		68699		69912		70101		80360	MACH IND CAOUT MAT PLAST
72848	OTH MCHY WITH INDIV FNCT		133552		130508		174227		169435	AUTRES MACHINES NDA
73	METALWORKING MACHINERY		105479		141465		144930		163144	MACH TRAVAIL DES METAUX
736	METALWORKING MACH-TOOLS		85768		113051		119752		132006	MACH-OUTILS TRAVAIL METAUX
74	GENRL INDUSTRL MACHY NES		837956		994278		1265230		1374397	MACH APP INDUSTRIE
741	HEATING,COOLING EQUIPMNT		156134		192953		234885		302225	MACH CHAUFFAGE,PIECES
7415	AIR-CONDITIONING MACHNRY		28404		39300		64677		95161	GROUPES CONDITION AIR
7416	HEATING,COOLING EQU NES		48401		78132		72416		76692	APP CHANGEMENT TEMP
742	PUMPS FOR LIQUIDS ETC		69329		71799		88587		99783	POMPES MOTO-POMPES
743	PUMPS NES,CENTRFUGES ETC		169420		200287		259011		259790	POMPES COMPRES,VENT ETC
7431	PUMPS FOR GASES ETC		79233		88196		115592		114741	POMPES AIR A VIDE,COMPRES
744	MECHANICAL HANDLING EQU		141686		181859		277067		254102	EQUIP MANUTENTION PIECES
7441	FORK LIFT TRCKS,ETC,PTS		37096		45472		85540		58949	CHARIOTS POUR USINES ETC
74411	FORK LIFT TRUCKS ETC		36804		45047		85257		58503	CHARIOTS POUR LES GARES
7442	LIFTING,LOADING MACH NES		67426		93310		132103		124659	APP LEVAGE,MANUTENTION
745	NONELEC MACHY,TOOLS NES		83270		112965		113563		128491	AUT MACH NON ELEC,PIECES
7452	OTH NONELEC MCHS,PTS NES		75627		105339		104962		118554	AUT MACH NON ELEC,PIECES
749	NONELEC MACH PTS,ACC NES		218117		234414		292117		330006	PIECES MACH NON ELEC NDA
7492	COCKS,VALVES ETC NES		84706		89135		105860		123481	ART ROB,SIM POUR TUYAUX
7499	OTH NONELEC MCHY PTS NES		70511		78834		98549		112217	PIECES NON ELECT NDA
75	OFFICE MACHNES,ADP EQUIP		620893		743650		941545		1129447	MACH BUREAU TRAIT AUTOM
752	AUTOMTIC DATA PROC EQUIP		376638		420074		506275		616515	MACH TRAIT INFORMATION
7528	OFF-LINE DATA PROC EQUIP		276671		315370		399281		464744	MACH AUXIL TRAIT INFORM
759	OFFICE,ADP MCH PTS,ACCES		206920		275988		379224		458445	PIECES DU 751 ET 752
7599	ACCTG,ETC,ADP MCH PTS,AC		194096		259766		361017		441306	PIECES DU 751 ET 752
76	TELECOMM,SOUND EQUIPMENT		531744		680846		1008506		1203555	EQUIPMENT DE TELECOM
761	TELEVISION RECEIVERS		81627		86021		88664		97958	RECEPTEURS DE TELEVISION
7611	COLOUR TV RECEIVERS		80074		84654		87587	N 345607	95476	RECEPTEURS COULEUR
762	RADIO BROADCAST RECEIVRS		59047		76085		69206		65582	RECEPTEURS RADIODIFFUSION
764	TELECOM EQPT,PTS,ACC NES		357686		482984		809780		992836	EQUIP TELECOM,PIECES
7641	LINE TELEPHONE,ETC EQUIP		66608		81738		104630		141722	APP TELEPHON PAR FIL
7643	TV,RADIO TRANSMITTRS ETC		107375		182836		366682		473352	APP EMET TELE RADIO
7648	TELECOMM EQUIPMENT NES		28177		30020		87893		52449	APP TELECOM NDA
7649	PTS NES OF EQUIPMT OF 76		140865		169299		218661		288411	PIECES DE LA DIV 76
76491	PTS NES OF APPAR OF 7641		67197		82369		104376		147185	PIECES POUR 764.1
76493	TELECOMM EQUIPMT PTS NES		68447		81730		109117		134756	PIECES 761,762,764.3,8
77	ELECTRIC MACHNRY NES ETC		1406113		1762556		2038245		2428562	MACH APP ELECT NDA
771	ELECTRIC POWER MACHY NES		79005		114303		132659		166278	MACH PROD,TRANS ELECTR
7712	OTH ELEC POWER MACHY NES		56947		75562		95037		117039	AUT APP PROD TRANSF ELEC
772	SWITCHGEAR ETC,PARTS NES		395171		513723		504065		621339	APP COUPURE,SECT ETC
7721	SWITCHGEAR ETC		327055		422567		400021		498044	APP COUPURE,SECTIONMNT
773	ELECTR DISTRIBUTNG EQUIP		69706		78783		119583		117122	EQUIPMT DISTRIBUTION ELECT
7731	INSULATED WIRE,CABLE ETC		58821		64966		94042		95841	FILS,CABLES ISOLES ELECT
775	HOUSEHOLD TYPE EQUIP NES		182129		198434		237677		252324	MACH,APP USAGE DOMESTQUE
7758	ELECTRO-THERMIC APPL NES		67589		68928		80449		84759	APP ELECTROTHERMIQ NDA
776	TRANSISTORS,VALVES,ETC		392419		502010		606349		721827	LAMPES,TUBES,VALVES
7763	DIODES,TRANSISTORS,ETC		53450		61418		76539		90099	DIODES,TRANSISTORS
7764	ELECTRONIC MICROCIRCUITS		302972		403018		485591		583089	MICROSTRUCTURES ELECTRON
778	ELECTRICAL MACHINERY NES		248790		298139		382742		480017	AUTRES MACH ELECT NDA
7788	OTH ELEC MACHY,EQUIP NES		125499		149970		217374		276122	AUT MACH APP ELEC NDA
77884	ELECTRICAL CONDENSERS		35493		56614		86928		105411	CONDENSATEURS ELECTRIQUES
77886	OTH ELEC MACHINERY NES		73714		74414		83038		119050	AUT MACH APP ELECTRIQUES
78	ROAD VEHICLES		1753160		2177093		2328035		2332098	VEHICULES ROUTIERS
781	PASS MOTOR VEH EXC BUSES		1003857		1257751		1439567	N 148895	1410043	AUTO TRANSPORT PERSONNES
782	LORRIES,SPCL MTR VEH NES		454025		588359		538445		583529	VEHICULES SPECIAUX,MARCH
7821	LORRIES,TRUCKS		432043		532269		469120		526466	VEHICULES TRANSP MARCHAND
783	ROAD MOTOR VEHICLES NES		50033		77139		47467	N 278	33562	VEHICULES ROUTIERS NDA
7831	BUSES		47871		75139		45824	N 258	31897	VOITURES TRANSPORT COMMUN
784	MOTOR VEH PRTS,ACCES NES		181649		172450		214683		211396	PIECES 722,781,782,783
7841	MOTOR VEHICLE CHASSIS		71705		53278		56616		52448	CHASSIS 722,781,782,783
7849	OTHER MOTOR VEHCL PARTS		108756		118498		156783		156960	PIECES 722,781,782,783
79	OTHR TRANSPORT EQUIPMENT		370139		532680		602821		569058	AUTRE MATERIEL TRANSPORT
792	AIRCRAFT ETC		296859		503836		504800		294061	APP NAVIGATION AERIENNE
7924	AIRCRFT NES OVER 15000KG		93928		311300		278300		18259	AERODYNES PLUS 15000 KG

4. Special Imports C.I.F. by Commodities according to the S.I.T.C. (Rev. 2) in thousand U.S. Dollars
Importations Spéciales C.A.F. par Produits d'après la C.T.C.I. (Rév. 2) en milliers de Dollars E.U.

SITC CTCI	COMMODITY	1993 WEIGHT POIDS	1993 VALUE VALEUR	1994 WEIGHT POIDS	1994 VALUE VALEUR	1995 WEIGHT POIDS	1995 VALUE VALEUR	1996 WEIGHT POIDS	1996 VALUE VALEUR	PRODUIT
7929	AIRCRAFT PARTS NES		192831		182957		212026		245577	PIECES DU 792
793	SHIPS AND BOATS ETC		34874		14098		62817		230750	NAVIRES BATEAUX,ETC
7932	SHIPS AND BOATS NES		32522		11431		60171		227000	NAVIRES ET BATEAUX
79323	OTHER CARGO VESSELS		29965		7829		117		220189	AUT BATEAUX TRANS MARCH
8	MISC MANUFACTURED GOODS		1661627		1948193		2376276		2694969	ART MANUFACTURES DIVERS
821	*FURNITURE,PARTS THEREOF		131324		193018		235905		273784	MEUBLES ET PIECES
8219	FURNITURE AND PARTS NES		82835		131224		159760		183925	AUTRES MEUBLES ET PIECES
82192	WOOD FURNITURE NES		59187		100638		121863		137506	MEUBLES NDA EN BOIS
84	CLOTHING AND ACCESSORIES		181405		211361		269568		331725	VETEMENTS
843	WOMENS OUTERWEAR NONKNIT		57722		75704		103164		131608	VET DESSUS FEMMES MAT TEX
851	*FOOTWEAR		68505		96950		122511		146226	CHAUSSURES
85102	FOOTWEAR LEATHER		62847		91222		111614		125620	CHAUS SEMELLES EN CUIR
87	PRECISION INSTRUMNTS NES		396959		443241		525473		629237	INSTRUM,APPAR SCIENT NDA
872	MEDICAL INSTRUMENTS NES		96784		105717		117422		136257	INSTR,APP MEDIC–CHIR NDA
87202	OTH MEDICAL INSTRUMENTS		82673		90105		99588		116082	INSTRUM,APP MEDECINE
874	MEASURNG,CONTROLNG INSTR		249767		267944		330439		392328	INSTRUMENTS DE MESURE
8748	ELEC MEAS,CONTRL EQU NES		97536		106812		116628		133846	APP ELEC ELECTRO MESURE
87483	OTH ELCTRNC MEAS ETC EQU		94692		103516		112447		129918	AUT APP ELECTRO DE MESURE
88	PHOTO EQU,OPTICL GDS ETC		170306		197879		249483		251323	APP,FOURN PHOTO,OP,MONTR
882	PHOTO,CINEMA SUPPLIES		70899		75777		91516		88101	PRODUITS PHOTO,CINEMA
89	MISC MANUFCTRD GOODS NES		660586		744577		875855		951690	ART MANUFACTURES DIVERS
893	ARTICLES OF PLASTIC NES		175748		198972		262056		263480	OUVRAGES EN MAT DIVIS 58
8939	MISC PLASTIC ARTICLES		136452		151954		185335		193236	ART DIVERS EN MAT DIV 58
89399	OTHR PLASTC ARTICLES NES		128098		143442		175683		183494	AUT OUV MAT DIV 58
894	TOYS,SPORTING GOODS,ETC		91929		110022		108015		102169	VOITURES ENFANTS,JOUETS
8942	TOYS,INDOOR GAMES ETC		73857		86937		75503		74771	JOUETS,JEUX ETC
897	GOLD,SILVER WARE,JEWELRY		101123		113034		136226		153870	BIJOUTERIE,ORFEVRERIE
8973	PREC JEWLRY,GLD–SILVWARE		89511		98915		121798		137250	BIJOUX OR,ARGENT ORFEVRE
89731	PRECIOUS METAL JEWELLERY		85599		94555		117124		133237	ART BIJOUTERIE,JOAILLER
898	MUSICAL INSTRUMENTS,PTS		125963		139229		164984		198428	INSTRUMENTS DE MUSIQUE
8983	SOUND RECRDNG TAPE,DISCS		114016		127208		153385		187075	SUPPORTS SON POUR 763
89832	RECORDED DISCS,TAPES ETC		85914		96741		123079		153014	DISQUES,PHONO,BANDES
899	OTHER MANUFACTURED GOODS		73705		77276		85959		92731	AUT ART MANUF DIVERS NDA
9	GOODS NOT CLASSD BY KIND		431951		472011		583617		585916	ART TRANSACT NON CLASSES
931	*SPECIAL TRANSACTIONS		253282		301916		426749		430831	TRANS.SPECIALES
971	*GOLD,NON MONETARY NES		167761		167299		155073		153012	OR NON MONETAIRE
97101	NONMON GLD UNWRT,SEMIMFD		160970		166108		154080		152092	OR,ALLIAGES D'OR BRUTS

5. Special Exports F.O.B. by Commodities according to the S.I.T.C. (Rev. 2) in thousand U.S. Dollars
Exportations Spéciales F.O.B. par Produits d'après la C.T.C.I. (Rév. 2) en milliers de Dollars E.U.

SITC CTCI	COMMODITY	1993 WEIGHT POIDS	1993 VALUE VALEUR	1994 WEIGHT POIDS	1994 VALUE VALEUR	1995 WEIGHT POIDS	1995 VALUE VALEUR	1996 WEIGHT POIDS	1996 VALUE VALEUR	PRODUIT
	ALL COMMODITIES		14825325		16933986		19047421		20510239	TOUS PRODUITS
0	FOOD AND LIVE ANIMALS		792157		809926		936050		979867	ALIMENTS,ANIMAUX VIVANTS
05	VEGETABLES AND FRUIT		516579		516169		674387		631769	LEGUMES ET FRUITS
054	VEG ETC FRSH,SMPLY PRSVD		82560		85501		116355		131363	LEGUMES FRAIS,CONG,SECS
057	FRUIT,NUTS,FRESH,DRIED		216968		214842		311916		298392	FRUITS FRAIS OU SECS
0571	ORANGES, MANDARINS ETC	W 145313	63545	W 156327	69156		114847		104710	ORANGES,MAND,CLEMENTINES
05711	ORANGES,FRESH OR DRIED	W 113708	44833	W 134289	56879		89935	W 1710977	79973	ORANGES FRAICHES,SECHEES
0572	LEMONS,GRAPEFRUIT ETC		57100		57358		86416		75838	AUTRES AGRUMES FRAIS,SECS
05722	GRAPEFRUITS,FRESH,DRIED	W 109297	54046	W 98673	54487		82987	W 1224740	70027	PAMPLEMOUSSES,POMELOS
0579	FRUIT FRESH OR DRIED NES		78583		74410		90124		96820	FRUITS FRAIS,SECS NDA
058	FRUIT PRESERVED,PREPARED		197929		195519		222952		170041	CONSERVES DE FRUITS
0585	FRUIT OR VEGETABLE JUICE		114690		107016		109197		96558	JUS DE FRUITS
05851	ORANGE JUICE		58570		52132		47473		39739	JUS D'ORANGE
0589	FRUIT PREPRD,PRESRVD,NES		66332		70065		88054		45589	FRUITS PREPARES CONSERV
05899	FRUIT,NUTS NES,PRESERVED		65360		69525		87729		45325	FRUITS PREP CONSERV NDA
07	COFFEE,TEA,COCOA,SPICES		56390		51903		58206		50066	CAFE,THE,CACAO,EPICES
09	MISC EDIBLE PRODUCTS		95651		115365		88939		182843	PREP ALIMENTAIRES DIVERSES
098	EDIBLE PRODCTS,PREPS NES		95313		115089		88410		182557	PREP ALIMENTAIRES NDA
09809	MISC FOOD PREPRTIONS NES		68446		94533		67969		165457	PREP ALIMENTAIRES NDA
2	CRUDE MATERLS,EXCL FUELS		403113		469325		506659		549248	MAT BRUTES NON COMESTIBLES
26	TEXTILE FIBRES AND WASTE		40682		71721		50850		61224	FIBRES TEXTILES
263	COTTON		27539		53661		39505		58381	COTON
2631	RAW COTTON,EXCL LINTERS		27532		53627		39431	W 269885	58300	COTON EN MASSE
27	CRUDE FERTLZR,MINRLS NES		105293		102396		99279		104403	ENGRAIS MINERAUX BRUTS
271	FERTILIZERS,CRUDE		79287		73557		70581		80017	ENGRAIS BRUTS
2713	NAT CALCM PHOSPHATES ETC		69574		69067		61126	MW 19350	72779	PHOSPHATES DE CALCIUM
27131	— UNGROUND		69574		69067		61126	MW 19350	72779	PHOSPHATES NON MOULUS
29	CRUDE ANIMAL,VEG MAT NES		213123		230186		274283		307020	MATIERES BRUTES ANIM,VEGET
292	CRUDE VEG MATERIALS NES		213007		229380		273615		306980	MAT BRUTES VEGETALES NDA
2927	CUT FLOWERS AND FOLIAGE	MN 1031226	135182		137587		173950	MN 15651292	194762	FLEURS,FEUILLAGES COUPES
29271	CUT FLOWERS	MN 913106	126804	MN 946451	129518		163769	MN 13650036	183840	FLEURS ET BOUTONS
3	MINERAL FUELS ETC		89393		92214		4614		105118	COMBUSTIBLES MINERAUX LUB
33	PETROLEUM AND PRODUCTS		88706		91641		4068		104459	PETROLE ET DERIVES
333	CRUDE PETROLEUM		84147		85337		191		398	HUILES BRUTES DE PETROLE
334	PETROLEUM PRODUCTS,REFIN		1820		4421		2103	MW 5441761	102737	PRODUITS RAFFINES
5	CHEMCLS,RELATED PROD NES		2079334		2316915		2626529		2650927	PRODUITS CHIMIQUES
51	ORGANIC CHEMICALS		566817		625739		737485		729982	PROD CHIMIQ ORGANIQUES
511	HYDROCARBONS NES,DERIVS		96412		128299		172038		149260	HYDROCARBURES NDA
5112	CYCLIC HYDROCARBONS		34526		59196		94127		54119	HYDROCARBURES CYCLIQUES
51124	XYLENES,CHEMICALLY PURE		21488		38149		77420	W 718114	36582	XYLENES PURS
5113	HALOG DERIV OF HYDROCARB		57061		64291		74461		89845	DERIVES HALOGENES HYDROCAR
51139	OTH HALOG HYDRCARB DERIV		57005		64170		74267		89845	AUTRE DERIVES HALOGENES
512	ALCOHOLS,PHENOLS ETC		99068		104580		114939		121105	PHENOLS,PHENOLS–ALCOOLS
5123	PHENOLS,PHEN ALCS,DERIVS		96040		96220		109416		114638	PHENOLS,PHENOLS–ALCOOLS
51237	DERIVATVS OF PHENOL ETC		92315		94030		107620	W 444984	110911	DERIVES HALOGENES
513	CARBOXYLIC ACIDS ETC		54278		70559		91696		82785	ACIDES CARBOXYLIQUES
5139	OXY–FNCT ACIDS,DERIVATVS		37823		49466		57291		57976	ACIDES CARBOXYLIQUES
514	NITROGEN–FNCTN COMPOUNDS		106499		109580		134440		140296	COMPOSES FONCT AZOTEES
5148	OTH NITROGN–FNCTN CMPNDS		54770		56218		76645		67521	AUTRES COMPOSES AZOTES
51482	IMIDE–,IMIDE–FNCT CMPNDS		43350		46031		66735	W 110736	59906	COMPOSES A FONCTION IMIDE
515	ORG–INORG COMPOUNDS ETC		154912		150594		158558		160461	COMPOSES ORGANO–MINERAUX
5154	ORGANO–SULPHUR CMPNDS		61140		61817		62560		69225	THIOCOMPOSES ORGANIQUES
5156	HETEROCYCLIC CMPDS ETC		70593		66737		79539		74508	COMPOSES HETEROCYCLIQUES
51569	OTH HETEROCYC CMPDS,ETC		70593		66706		79447		74426	AUT COMP HETEROCYCLIQUES
516	OTHER ORGANIC CHEMICALS		55647		62127		65814		76075	AUTRES PROD ORGANIQUES
52	INORGANIC CHEMICALS		290393		281688		377359		394689	PROD CHIM INORGANIQUES
522	INORG ELEMNTS,OXIDES,ETC		106586		114884		151538		169284	ELEMENTS INORGANIQUES
5222	INORGANIC ACIDS ETC		55283		52126		64643		89138	ACIDES INORGANIQUES
52224	PHOSPHORIC ACIDS ETC		55230		51607		64367	W 1990790	88970	ACIDES PHOSPHORIQUES
523	OTHR INORG CHEMICALS ETC		182978		165126		224214		224071	AUT PRODUITS CHIMIQUES INORG
5231	METAL CMPD OF INORG ACID		56189		58656		60229		65810	SELS METALLIQUES
5232	OTH MTL CMPD OF INRG ACD		106179		92080		137762		132245	SELS METALLIQUES
52321	NITRITES AND NITRATES		67331		57341		102244		101225	NITRITES ET NITRATES
541	*MEDICINAL,PHARM PRODUCT		187910		276378		255348		334291	PROD MEDICINAUX PHARMACEUT
5417	MEDICAMENTS		156555		239217		217643		289035	MEDICAMENTS
54172	— CONTAINING HORMONES		52445		60597		55450		46981	MED CONTENANT HORMONES
54179	— CONTNG OTH SUBSTANCES		103770		176530		160521		242022	MED CONT AUT SUBSTANCES
55	PERFUME,CLEANING ETC PRD		55558		73529		100999		106013	PROD POUR PARFUM,TOILETTE
562	*FERTILIZERS,MANUFACTURE		238124		288120		341319		324497	ENGRAIS MANUFACTURES
5622	CHEM PHOSPHATIC FERTILZR		51608		74601		94798		95172	ENGRAIS PHOSPHATES
56222	SUPERPHOSPHATES		42937		56687		72068		66976	SUPERPHOSPHATES
5629	FERTILIZERS NES		178677		208744		242468		224867	ENGRAIS NDA
56299	OTHER FERTILIZERS NES		162536		190452		222682	MW 15333	198521	AUTRES ENGRAIS NDA
58	PLASTIC MATERIALS ETC		225730		274949		406379		332048	MAT PLAST ARTIFICIELLES
582	PROD OF CONDENSATION ETC		45547		56328		86213		83085	PROD CONDENS,POLYCOND
5823	ALKYDS,OTHER POLYESTERS		36578		43040		61631		62869	ALKYDES ET AUT POLYESTERS
58232	— PLATES,FILM,STRIP ETC		35735		42526		61009	W 107416	61938	SOUS FORME PLAQUES,FEUIL
583	POLYMERIZATION ETC PRODS		179759		218448		319656		248747	PROD POLYMERISATION
5831	POLYETHYLENE		47099		43072		56520		46902	POLYETHYLENE
5832	POLYPROPYLENE		9465		31494		59462		36378	POLYPROPYLENE
5834	POLYVINYL CHLORIDE		36190		47490		61131		35549	CHLORURE DE POLYVINYLE
5839	OTH POLYMRZTION ETC PROD		75317		79955		103022		106865	AUT PROD POLYMER COPOLYM
59	CHEMICAL MATERIALS NES		506070		486331		384801		402383	MAT PROD CHIMIQUES NDA
591	PESTICIDES,DISINFECTANTS		52485		68252		108554	W 210710	105612	DESINF,INSECT,FONG,HERB
5914	DISINFECTANTS,ETC,FR RET		52485		68252		108554	W 210710	105612	DESINFECTANTS VENTE DET
59149	RAT POISONS ETC FR RTAIL		52485		68252		108554	W 210710	105612	ANTIPARASITES VENTE DET
598	MISCEL CHEM PRODUCTS NES		450729		416092		272329		292642	PROD DIV INDUST CHIM NDA
5989	CHEM PRODUCTS,PREPS NES		449397		415341		271096		291739	PROD PREP CHIMIQUES NDA
59899	OTH CHEM PRODS,PREPS,NES		434584		399103		248281		276175	AUT PRODUITS CHIMIQUES NDA
6	BASIC MANUFACTURES		5036717		6046428		7061286		7660639	ART MANUFACTURES
62	RUBBER MANUFACTURES NES		88835		103158		121000		117946	CAOUTCHOUC MANUFACTURE
625	RUBBER TYRES, TUBES ETC		68766		79862		94090		90451	PNEUS CAOUTCHOUC VULCANISE
6259	OTH TYRES,TYRE CASES,ETC		68340		77973		91790		88889	AUTRES PNEUS RECHAPES FLAPS
62599	TYRES NES,TYRE CASES,ETC		68267		77903		91647		88676	PNEUS,FLAPS
65	TEXTILE YARN,FABRICS,ETC		326725		350393		402209		396933	FILS,TISSUS,ARTICLES TEXTILE
651	TEXTILE YARN		69475		72680		91193		96167	FILS TEXTILES
6514	SYN FIB YRN,BULK,MONOFIL		64163		67084		83693		92265	FILS CONT 85% FIB TEXT SYNTH
657	SPECIAL TXTL FABRC,PRODS		67813		72573		75157		80524	TISSUS SPECIAUX
658	TEXTILE ARTICLES NES		74696		89659		99314		87892	ART FACONNES MAT TEXTILES
6584	LINENS ETC		63812		76540		91725		77788	LINGE DE MAISON
66	NONMETAL MINERAL MFS NES		4142653		5019004		5821256		6354181	ART MIN NON METALLIQUES

5. Special Exports F.O.B. by Commodities according to the S.I.T.C. (Rev. 2) in thousand U.S. Dollars
Exportations Spéciales F.O.B. par Produits d'après la C.T.C.I. (Rév. 2) en milliers de Dollars E.U.

SITC CTCI	COMMODITY	1993		1994		1995		1996		PRODUIT
		WEIGHT POIDS	VALUE VALEUR	WEIGHT POIDS	VALUE VALEUR	WEIGHT POIDS	VALUE VALEUR	WEIGHT POIDS	VALUE VALEUR	
667	PEARL,PREC–,SEMI–P STONE		4113847		4967557		5744255		6284417	PERLES, PIERRES GEMMES
6672	DIAMONDS NONINDUST,UNSET		4040134		4892210		5666184		6202472	DIAMANTS BRUTS
66722	— SRTD,ROUGH,SIMPLY WKD		398174		524610		755000		949457	DIAMANTS TRIES BRUTS
66729	— CUT ETC NOT SET		3641959		4367163		4911184		5253015	DIAMANTS TAILLES
6673	PREC–,SEMI–PR STONES NES		73465		75317		78015		81893	AUTRES PIERRES NON SERTIES
68	NON–FERROUS METALS		60182		81625		125783		114250	METAUX NON FERREUX
684	ALUMINIUM		51867		71894		108563		100076	ALUMINIUM
6842	ALUMINIUM,ALLOYS WORKED		50004		69655		103652		93453	ALUMINIUM,ALLIAGES OUVRE
69	METAL MANUFACTURES NES		343928		407399		480533		546498	ART MANUFACT EN METAL NDA
695	TOOLS		179726		215535		268495		316108	OUTILS A MAIN
6954	BLADES,TIPS,ETC FR TOOLS		160020		193085		244574		294227	OUTILS POUR MACHINE–OUTIL
69543	CARBIDE TOOL TIPS ETC		119354		148098		189491		231156	PLAQUETTES,POINTES D'OUTILS
699	BASE METAL MFRS NES		91184		100828		101427		104913	ART MANUFACTURES MET NDA
7	MACHINES,TRANSPORT EQUIP		4603417		5182715		5107027		5980129	MACHINES MATERIEL TRANSPORT
71	POWER GENERATING EQUIPMT		117704		97675		155147		179918	MACHINES GENERATRICES
714	ENGINES AND MOTORS NES		55066		70542		111310		121524	MOTEURS NON ELECTRIQUES
7144	REACTION ENGINES		17466		30078		66495		72552	PROPULSEURS A REACTION
716	ROTATING ELECTRIC PLANT		49338		12156		22664		25036	APP ELECTR ROTATIFS,PIECES
72	MACHS FOR SPCL INDUSTRYS		1305725		1382314		709835		538990	MAC SPECIALES POUR INDUST
726	PRINTG,BKBINDG MACHY,PTS		376315		411297		479805		338148	MACHINES POUR IMPRIMERIE
7263	TYPESET ETC MCH,TYPE ETC		319362		260162		228785		173101	MACH COMPOSER,CLICHER
72631	TYPE SET,FOUND ETC MACHY		319361		260142		228785		173101	MACH COMPOSER CARACTERES
7267	OTH PRINTG & ANCILL MACH		10652		53028		116660		103616	AUT MACH IMPRIMERIE,PIEC
72671	PRINTING MACHINERY NES		10573		52995		116648		103567	AUT MACH IMPRIMERIE
7269	PTS OF 72631, 7264, 7267		45939		95582		120944		59572	PIECES 726.31 726.4 726.7
72691	PTS NES OF MCHS OF 72631		45910		62312		55870		57245	PIECES 726.31
72699	PTS NES OF MCH OF 7264,7		30		33270		65074		2327	PIECES 726.4 ET 726.7
728	OTH MACHY FOR SPCL INDUS		877819		899927		156080		127802	AUT MACH IND PARTICULIERES
7284	MACHY FOR SPCL INDUS NES		869405		887984		141727		112954	MACH SPEC IND PARTICUL.
72848	OTH MCHY WITH INDIV FNCT		861488		879455		133207		103243	AUTRES MACHINES NDA
74	GENRL INDUSTRL MACHY NES		460965		549774		551820		724304	MACH APP INDUSTRIE
741	HEATING,COOLING EQUIPMNT		104879		140888		199720		247139	MACH CHAUFFAGE,PIECES
7415	AIR–CONDITIONING MACHNRY		59179		86548		146044		181086	GROUPES CONDITION AIR
743	PUMPS NES,CENTRFUGES ETC		51979		58423		61312		76686	POMPES COMPRES,VENT ETC
745	NONELEC MACHY,TOOLS NES		52260		54721		82990		135767	AUT MACH NON ELEC,PIECES
7452	OTH NONELEC MCHS,PTS NES		51974		54320		82579		135053	AUT MACH NON ELEC,PIECES
74527	SPRAYING MACHINERY		47797		48554		76680		126330	APP PROJETER ETC LIQUID
749	NONELEC MACH PTS,ACC NES		249768		291778		203179		259892	PIECES MACH NON ELEC NDA
7499	OTH NONELEC MCHY PTS NES		208818		242120		147158		200636	PIECES NON ELECT NDA
74999	MACH PARTS NONELEC NES		203594		238570		144170		197461	PIECES MACHINES NDA
75	OFFICE MACHNES,ADP EQUIP		590668		525195		343748		850482	MACH BUREAU TRAIT AUTOM
752	AUTOMTIC DATA PROC EQUIP		349112		336882		147000		602642	MACH TRAIT INFORMATION
7528	OFF–LINE DATA PROC EQUIP		342081		319023		131974		598928	MACH AUXIL TRAIT INFORM
759	OFFICE,ADP MCH PTS,ACCES		240252		186511		193602		245348	PIECES DU 751 ET 752
7591	OFFICE MACHINE PARTS NES		168948		99016		53615		68414	PIECES DU 7511,7518
75915	OTH OFF MCH PTS,ACC NES		168914		98886		53396		67023	PIECES DU 751.18,81,88
7599	ACCTG,ETC,ADP MCH PTS,AC		71304		87495		139987		176934	PIECES DU 751 ET 752
76	TELECOMM,SOUND EQUIPMENT		906279		1197858		1570232		1802997	EQUIPEMENT DE TELECOM
762	RADIO BROADCAST RECEIVRS		165433		148792		260320		130622	RECEPTEURS RADIODIFFUSION
7622	PORTABLE RADIO RECEIVERS		131301		123219		259721		129839	RECEPT PORTATIFS RADIO
764	TELECOM EQPT,PTS,ACC NES		718738		1005145		1281186		1653569	EQUIP TELECOM,PIECES
7641	LINE TELEPHONE,ETC EQUIP		148316		237365		226338		297910	APP TELEPHON PAR FIL
7643	TV,RADIO TRANSMITTRS ETC		169162		216506		308081		325767	APP EMET TELE RADIO
7649	PTS NES OF EQUIPMT OF 76		395041		543362		699503		988532	PIECES DE LA DIV 76
76491	PTS NES OF APPAR OF 7641		298193		437530		600696		916612	PIECES POUR 764.1
76493	TELECOMM EQUIPMT PTS NES		95539		104727		98068		68618	PIECES 761,762,764.3,8
77	ELECTRIC MACHNRY NES ETC		807592		965270		1197837		1313411	MACH APP ELECT NDA
772	SWITCHGEAR ETC,PARTS NES		115010		189862		259379		304108	APP COUPURE,SECT ETC
7721	SWITCHGEAR ETC		35083		51764		55409		86074	APP COUPURE,SECTIONMNT
7723	FIXED,VARIABLE RESISTORS		69148		124496		183200		195016	POTENTIOMETRES PIECES
774	ELECTRO–MEDCL,XRAY EQUIP		134900		157365		188622		217741	APPAREILS MEDICAUX
7742	X–RAY APPARATUS ETC		127720		134296		160207		181619	APPAREILS A RAYONS X
776	TRANSISTORS,VALVES,ETC		385467		407271		454870		411190	LAMPES,TUBES,VALVES
7764	ELECTRONIC MICROCIRCUITS		366500		397570		441536		398244	MICROSTRUCTURES ELECTRON
778	ELECTRICAL MACHINERY NES		106546		128250		198166		262186	AUTRES MACH ELECT NDA
7784	ELECTRO–MECH HAND TOOLS		53506		64955		316		241	OUTILS ELECTROMEC,PIECES
7788	OTH ELEC MACHY,EQUIP NES		31417		34916		164199		234467	AUT MACH APP ELEC NDA
77883	ELEC SIGNALLING EQU NES		1040		4519		79614		75503	APP ELECT SIGNAL ACOUS
77886	OTH ELEC MACHINERY NES		15607		10078		28454		83851	AUT MACH APP ELECTRIQUES
79	OTHR TRANSPORT EQUIPMENT		358696		374161		485986		462331	AUTRE MATERIEL TRANSPORT
792	AIRCRAFT ETC		340870		355902		465894		422858	APP NAVIGATION AERIENNE
7929	AIRCRAFT PARTS NES		286024		311655		362638		391950	PIECES DU 792
8	MISC MANUFACTURED GOODS		1772489		1961437		2309180		2509332	ART MANUFACTURES DIVERS
821	*FURNITURE,PARTS THEREOF		48080		38448		49632		33470	MEUBLES ET PIECES
84	CLOTHING AND ACCESSORIES		571006		627370		663225		643600	VETEMENTS
842	MENS OUTERWEAR NOT KNIT		85380		95964		85101		85189	VET DESSUS POUR HOMMES
843	WOMENS OUTERWEAR NONKNIT		88204		105221		104343		101188	VET DESSUS FEMMES MAT TEX
8439	— OTHER OUTER GARMENTS		56205		71577		67195		70635	AUT VET DES FEM MAT TEXT
845	OUTERWEAR KNIT NONELASTC		184780		188957		201618		170577	VET DESSOUS,ACCES BONNET
8459	— OTHER,CLTHG ACCESRYS		154442		160256		175490	MN 117121	145254	AUT VET DESSUS DE BONNE
846	UNDER GARMENTS KNITTED		148179		165086		186962		196610	SOUS VETS DE BONNETERIE
8462	— OF COTTON NON ELASTIC		129665		148202		172341		176248	SOUS–VET BONNET COTON
84629	—— OTHER		129665		148202		169940		171528	AUT SOUS–VET BONNET COTON
847	TEXTILE CLTHNG ACCES NES		54249		63565		76235		80006	ACCES VET MAT TEXT NDA
8472	CLTHNG ACCESRYS ETC KNIT		53085		62559		74846		78703	ACCES VET BONNE NDA
84722	KNIT SOCKS,ETC NONELASTC		53066		62541		74800		78687	CHAUSSETTES BON. NON ELAS
87	PRECISION INSTRUMNTS NES		278332		321886		439550		574084	INSTRUM,APPAR SCIENT NDA
871	OPTICAL INSTRUMENTS		34394		21785		59046		68926	APPAR,INSTRUM D'OPTIQUE
87109	OPTICAL INSTRUMENTS NES		31710		16525		54485		62903	APP,INSTRUM OPTIQUE NDA
872	MEDICAL INSTRUMENTS NES		92957		108514		129471		176155	INSTR,APP MEDIC–CHIR NDA
87202	OTH MEDICAL INSTRUMENTS		78485		100632		124585		169353	INSTRUM,APP MEDECINE
874	MEASURNG,CONTROLNG INSTR		144988		181904		240795		317238	INSTRUMENTS DE MESURE
8742	MEASUR,DRAW ETC INST,PTS		67215		86049		109596		157806	INST DESSIN,TRACAGE,PCS
87421	MEASURNG,DRAWNG ETC INST		45492		62313		81505		133071	INSTRUM DESSIN,TRACAGE
8748	ELEC MEAS,CONTRL EQU NES		30247		44795		60847		56987	APP ELEC ELECTRO MESURE
88	PHOTO EQU,OPTICL GDS ETC		48750		58975		60900		71862	APP,FOURN PHOTO,OP,MONTR
89	MISC MANUFCTRD GOODS NES		797050		882154		1065178		1148885	ART MANUFACTURES DIVERS
893	ARTICLES OF PLASTIC NES		274712		334695		456315		525935	OUVRAGES EN MAT DIVIS 58
8931	PLSTC PACKG CONTNRS,LIDS		49719		71220		107589		75517	ART TRANSP EMBALLAGE ETC
8939	MISC PLASTIC ARTICLES		221343		257961		340179		444974	ART DIVERS EN MAT DIV 58
89399	OTHR PLASTC ARTICLES NES		216950		253544		334554		440354	AUT OUV MAT DIV 58

5. Special Exports F.O.B. by Commodities according to the S.I.T.C. (Rev. 2) in thousand U.S. Dollars
Exportations Spéciales F.O.B. par Produits d'après la C.T.C.I. (Rév. 2) en milliers de Dollars E.U.

SITC CTCI	COMMODITY	1993		1994		1995		1996		PRODUIT
		WEIGHT POIDS	VALUE VALEUR	WEIGHT POIDS	VALUE VALEUR	WEIGHT POIDS	VALUE VALEUR	WEIGHT POIDS	VALUE VALEUR	
897	GOLD,SILVER WARE,JEWELRY		419292		413183		459477		485048	BIJOUTERIE,ORFEVRERIE
8973	PREC JEWLRY,GLD–SILVWARE		417228		408217		453122		474579	BIJOUX OR,ARGENT ORFEVRE
89731	PRECIOUS METAL JEWELLERY		399969		379651		430387		466837	ART BIJOUTERIE,JOAILLER
9	GOODS NOT CLASSD BY KIND		25193		25055		456367		43834	ART TRANSACT NON CLASSES
931	*SPECIAL TRANSACTIONS		23272		23326		453070		34724	TRANS.SPECIALES

1. HISTORICAL SERIES, 1961–1996 SPECIAL TRADE, IMPORTS C.I.F., EXPORTS F.O.B. SERIES HISTORIQUES, 1961–1996 COMMERCE SPECIAL, IMPORTATIONS C.A.F., EXPORTATIONS F.O.B

YEAR ANNEE	VALUE IN MILLION LIRE # 1 VALEUR EN MILLION LIRE # 1 MERCHANDISE –MARCHANDISE IMPORTS	EXPORTS	GOLD –OR IMPORTS	EXPORTS	CONVERSION FACTORS U.S. CENTS PER LIRA FACTEURS DE CONVERSION CENTS E.U. PAR LIRA IMPORTS	EXPORTS	INDEX NUMBERS –INDICES QUANTUM IMPORTS	EXPORTS	UNIT VALUE VALEUR UNITAIRE IMPORTS	EXPORTS
1961	3264.50	2614.30	32.70	1.20	0.1600	0.1600	17	13	9	10
1962	3797.10	2918.40	83.30		0.1600	0.1600	20	14	9	10
1963	4744.70	3159.00	59.40		0.1600	0.1600	24	15	9	11
1964	4532.80	3724.00	29.60		0.1600	0.1600	23	17	9	11
1965	4611.40	4499.80	36.00		0.1600	0.1600	23	21	9	11
1966	5367.90	5024.00	31.10	0.60	0.1600	0.1600	26	24	9	10
1967	6141.60	5440.90	37.20	1.40	0.1600	0.1600	30	26	10	10
1968	6428.70	6366.00	193.00	1.60	0.1600	0.1600	31	30	10	10
1969	7791.80	7330.50	43.00	2.10	0.1600	0.1600	37	34	10	11
1970	9355.90	8253.90	87.80	0.30	0.1600	0.1600	43	36	10	11
1971	9901.30	9361.70	156.70	0.90	0.1614	0.1615	43	39	11	12
1972	11243.60	10849.40	0.40	0.90	0.1715	0.1715	48	44	11	12
1973	16343.40	12989.30	0.20	1.30	0.1713	0.1713	53	44	14	14
1974	26715.00	19826.00	0.20	2.50	0.1538	0.1537	50	47	24	21
1975	25199.60	22866.40			0.1529	0.1530	45	49	26	23
1976	36730.60	31166.70			0.1196	0.1196	52	55	33	28
1977	42429.10	39967.60			0.1134	0.1134	52	59	38	33
1978	47857.90	47505.30			0.1180	0.1180	56	66	40	36
1979	64597.20	59926.30			0.1206	0.1206	63	71	47	42
1980	85564.30	66719.40			0.1164	0.1164	65	65	61	50
1981	103675.00	86040.00			0.0878	0.0874	60	68	79	62
1982	116212.00	99231.00			0.0742	0.0740	60	68	88	72
1983	122002.00	110537.00			0.0659	0.0658	60	71	93	77
1984	148162.00	129015.00			0.0568	0.0568	66	75	103	84
1985	172876.00	149701.00			0.0526	0.0527	72	81	111	91
1986	148195.90	145014.80			0.0671	0.0673	75	82	91	87
1987	162352.90	150440.90			0.0774	0.0774	83	84	90	88
1988	180013.90	166379.90			0.0770	0.0769	88	89	94	92
1989	209909.90	192887.90			0.0729	0.0729	96	97	101	98
1990	217703.90	203597.90			0.0836	0.0837	100	100	100	100
1991	225747.90	209738.90			0.0810	0.0808	105	100	99	103
1992	232110.90	219440.90			0.0812	0.0812	108	104	99	104
1993	232990.90	263966.90			0.0637	0.0635	96	112	110	115
1994	272381.90	305757.90			0.0621	0.0622	108	125	115	120
1995	335660.90	376164.90			0.0614	0.0614	119	141	129	131
1996	319396.90	387197.90			0.0648	0.0648	114	139	129	137

2. IMPORTS BY BROAD ECONOMIC CATEGORY AND EXPORTS BY INDUSTRIAL ORIGIN. (PERCENTAGE OF TOTAL VALUE) IMPORTATIONS PAR CATEGORIES ECONOMIQUES ET EXPORTATIONS PAR BRANCHE D'ACTIVITE.(EN POURCENTAGE DE LA VALEUR TOTALE)

IMPORTS – IMPORTATIONS

	1990	1991	1992	1993	1994	1995	1996
TOTAL IMPORTS–IMPORTATIONS TOTALES	100.	100.	100.	100.	100.	100.	100.
1 FOOD BEV–ALIMENTATION BOISSONS	10.6	11.6	11.2	11.8	11.1	10.1	10.1
11 PRIMARY–PRODUITS DE BASE	7.0	7.7	7.5	7.7	7.1	6.5	6.3
111 FOR INDUSTRY–POUR L'INDUSTRIE	2.4	2.6	2.5	2.6	2.3	2.3	2.2
112 FOR HOUSEHOLDS–POUR LES MENAGES	4.6	5.0	5.0	5.0	4.8	4.2	4.1
12 PROCESSED–PRODUITS ELABORES	3.6	3.9	3.7	4.1	4.0	3.7	3.8
121 FOR INDUSTRY–POUR L'INDUSTRIE	0.3	0.3	0.3	0.4	0.4	0.4	0.4
122 FOR HOUSEHOLDS–POUR LES MENAGES	3.2	3.6	3.3	3.7	3.6	3.2	3.4
2 IND SUPPLIES–APPROV INDUSTRIELS	34.6	32.2	31.9	33.0	35.9	37.6	34.7
21 PRIMARY–PRODUITS DE BASE	5.4	4.8	4.4	4.8	5.3	5.1	4.6
22 PROCESSED–PRODUITS ELABORES	29.2	27.3	27.5	28.2	30.6	32.5	30.1
3 FUELS–COMBUSTIBLES	10.5	9.4	8.5	9.4	8.3	7.3	8.5
31 PRIMARY–PRODUITS DE BASE	7.7	7.0	6.3	6.9	5.9	5.3	6.3
32 PROCESSED–PRODUITS ELABORES	2.8	2.5	2.3	2.5	2.3	2.0	2.2
321 MOTOR SPIRIT–ESSENCE	0.4	0.4	0.3	0.4		0.3	0.3
322 OTHER–AUTRES	2.4	2.1	2.0	2.0	2.3	1.8	1.9
4 MACHINERY–EQUIPEMENT	17.8	18.0	17.8	17.5	17.8	18.9	19.2
41 CAPITAL EQUIPMENT–MACHINES	13.6	13.6	13.3	12.7	12.7	13.6	14.0
42 PARTS–PIECES ACCESSOIRES	4.3	4.3	4.5	4.8	5.1	5.3	5.2
5 TRANSPORT–TRANSPORT	13.7	14.6	15.8	12.8	12.2	12.3	12.9
51 PASSENGER CARS–AUTOMOBILES	7.1	7.6	9.1	6.9	6.5	6.7	7.1
52 OTHER–AUTRES	3.0	3.4	3.1	2.3	2.2	2.0	2.2
521 INDUSTRIAL–INDUSTRIELS	2.8	3.1	2.8	2.0	1.9	1.7	2.0
522 NON INDUSTRIAL–NON INDUSTRIEL	0.2	0.3	0.3	0.3	0.3	0.2	0.3
53 PARTS–PIECES ACCESSOIRES	3.5	3.6	3.6	3.5	3.5	3.6	3.6
6 CONSUM GOODS–BIENS CONSOMMATION	10.2	11.4	12.1	12.4	11.9	11.2	11.8
61 DURABLE–DURABLES	3.2	3.4	3.2	3.0	2.8	2.5	2.5
62 SEMI DURABLE–SEMI DURABLES	4.5	5.4	5.9	6.2	6.0	5.7	6.0
63 NON DURABLE–NON DURABLES	2.6	2.7	3.0	3.2	3.2	3.0	3.3
7 GOODS NES–BIENS NDA	2.6	2.9	2.6	3.2	2.7	2.7	2.9

EXPORTS – EXPORTATIONS

	1990	1991	1992	1993	1994	1995	1996
TOTAL EXPORTS–EXPORTATIONS TOTALES	100.	100.	100.	100.	100.	100.	100.
1 AGRICULTURE	2.1	2.3	2.1	2.1	2.2	2.0	1.9
2 MINING QUARRY–INDUS EXTRACTIVES	0.3	0.3	0.3	0.3	0.3	0.3	0.3
3 MANUFACTURING–IND MANUFACTUR	97.5	97.4	97.6	97.6	97.5	97.7	97.8
31 FOOD BEV TOBACCO–ALIM BOISS TAB	4.5	4.9	5.3	5.1	4.9	4.9	5.0
32 TEXTILES–INDUSTRIES TEXTILES	18.4	17.7	17.6	17.5	17.8	16.9	17.1
33 WOOD & PRODUCTS–BOIS & PRODUITS	0.5	0.5	0.5	0.5	0.5	0.5	0.5
34 PAPER & PRODUCTS–PAPIER & PRODT	2.0	2.0	2.0	2.1	2.1	2.4	2.2
35 CHEMICALS–INDUSTRIES CHIMIQUES	11.6	11.9	12.5	12.4	12.0	12.1	11.9
36 NON METAL MIN–MIN NON METAL	4.0	3.9	4.0	4.0	4.1	4.0	3.8
37 BASIC METAL–IND METAL BASE	4.6	4.4	4.3	4.6	4.6	4.8	4.2
38 METAL MANUF–MANUF METAL	47.1	47.4	46.9	46.9	47.1	47.9	48.9
39 OTH MANUF IND–AUTRES MANUF	4.7	4.6	4.5	4.4	4.3	4.3	4.3

3. TRADE BY PRINCIPAL COUNTRIES OF PRODUCTION AND LAST CONSIGNMENT (VALUE IN THOUSAND U.S. DOLLARS)
ECHANGES SELON LES PRINCIPAUX PAYS DE PRODUCTION ET DE DERNIERE CONSIGNATION (VALEUR EN MILLIERS DE DOLLARS EU)

COUNTRIES–PAYS	SPECIAL IMPORTS C.I.F. IMPORTATIONS SPECIALES C.A.F				
	1992	1993	1994	1995	1996
World	188705919	147817494	167975069	204099177	206965491
Africa	13038231	10843858	11661426	13875503	15161203
Americas	15884983	12590263	13487656	17026120	17108531
Northern America	11362405	9089952	9269312	11694911	12046107
LAIA	3931007	3176548	3841120	4838381	4584129
CACM	225812	129334	167276	163685	173109
Caribbean	233840	113409	144912	251052	241864
Rest of America	131919	81020	65036	78091	63322
As.ex F.USSR	19712729	17074209	18105546	22442014	22557523
Eur.x F.USSR	134041562	101293374	117253941	142187176	144353475
EU	118710164	87886387	101418705	123448501	125935075
EFTA	9350027	8375706	9015780	9894183	9773114
East Europe	3283556	3024918	4246757	5866981	6081344
Other Europe	607332	437890	608430	568868	216337
Former USSR	4450555	4766437	5926901	6855174	5951960
Oceania	1053693	916846	1121670	1350865	1447852
Germany/Allemagne	40687974	28627166	32310903	38962190	38243042
France,Monac	27276549	20142047	22781147	28317344	28007387
United Kingdom	10799816	8616478	10265811	12390718	13630877
Netherlands/Pays–Bas	11148902	8417031	9591507	11229233	12369634
USA/Etats–Unis d'Amer	9874567	7861939	7803265	9890872	10172855
Belgium–Luxembourg	9137293	6885628	7970035	9761760	9892754
Switz.Liecht	8490961	7591525	8254950	9100240	8855334
Spain/Espagne	6345226	4953531	6517790	8018501	8559353
Russian Federation	3984312	3878171	4801637	5306835	4697790
Austria/Autriche	4121393	3272212	3761814	4751322	4743918
Japan/Japon	4410546	3811362	3960551	4491328	3976170
Libyan Arab Jamahiriya	3870172	3338939	3362164	3742624	4527777
China/Chine	2778902	2593678	3128268	3920356	4033765
So. Africa Customs Un	2587599	2099720	2206252	2838085	2455239
Sweden/Suède	2415242	1812738	2114422	2778301	2866556
Algeria/Algérie	2466805	1935547	1627021	2289282	2718596
Brazil/Brésil	1848865	1528253	1847777	2039605	1890174
Denmark/Danemark	1899884	1522572	1660766	1869939	1907401
Saudi Arabia	2105082	1720328	1481472	1581786	1889094
Ireland/Irlande	1350846	1162178	1569539	1884777	2081406
Canada	1473295	1219800	1457237	1803844	1857319
Iran (Islamic Rp. of)	1648437	1382538	1023191	1753718	1938861
Greece/Grèce	1627393	1120355	1322755	1468740	1524056
Turkey/Turquie	973245	799075	1122407	1539744	1574560
Egypt/Egypte	1162483	918007	1206859	1096487	1156383
Finland/Finlande	1208435	886575	966366	1195142	1106697
India/Inde	767723	815537	1008724	1341263	1330921
Hungary/Hongrie	963983	766446	967816	1271645	1252310
Poland/Pologne	891719	829776	921710	1227582	1349269
Australia/Australie	882522	752483	913993	1113162	1180663
Korea, Republic of	977274	693913	817055	1086501	1020487
Romania/Roumanie	363747	462691	907364	1370496	1432670
Tunisia/Tunisie	641623	607379	872289	1032484	1174009
Slovenia/Slovénia	410105	681157	914130	1168977	1090168
Indonesia/Indonésie	689350	722146	811292	976548	930093
Norway,SVD,JM	836931	769094	747016	781693	908246
Croatia/Croatie	399184	726170	824933	971626	828724
Portugal	691210	467876	585850	820535	1001992
Argentina/Argentine	607106	534209	696630	862462	850663
Thailand/Thaïlande	632949	552817	566006	676117	694449
Malaysia/Malaisie	494504	501102	542719	692671	747523
Czech Republic		516394	670818	820064	786047
Syrian Arab Republic	437687	429589	480851	611052	785713
Ukraine	296855	506283	593206	798597	539930
Singapore/Singapour	564396	506542	512021	614264	488397
Israel/Israël	462803	421197	483897	541513	561796
Chile/Chili	471856	379075	392636	625264	569210
Malta/Malte	601109	422352	606134	567227	214336
Morocco/Maroc	370658	307760	374119	426005	445351
Bulgaria/Bulgarie	233663	191011	325100	504955	517365

COUNTRIES–PAYS	SPECIAL EXPORTS F.O.B. EXPORTATIONS SPECIALES F.O.B.				
	1992	1993	1994	1995	1996
Monde	178401639	168511226	190004650	231346424	250830252
Afrique	7293616	7031093	6943166	8081051	8296227
Amériques	18752394	20319649	23633543	27309846	30074491
Amérique du Nord	13816227	14453517	16518362	19066931	20295629
ALAI	4010327	4318729	5759037	7042275	7740667
MCAC	145172	191644	180959	186748	220668
Caraïbes	369470	960586	758488	550050	887994
Autre Amérique	411198	395174	416698	463842	929532
Asie l'URSS exclus	23267123	25539389	27502653	34731825	39107206
Europe l'URSS exclus	124384928	111199515	126677330	154574927	165230309
UE	109902703	96047612	108717554	131604512	139229521
AELE	7821219	7408312	7977011	9769277	10563832
Europe de l'Est	3670604	4468805	5594038	7790595	9889645
Autre de l'Europe	1077793	1102435	1267022	1365710	1047963
Ancienne URSS	2911430	2335164	2838767	3672938	4774897
Océanie	1158328	1248365	1584453	1896005	2186549
Germany/Allemagne	36310675	32819782	36119190	43248452	43691524
France,Monac	26064433	22135592	24851637	30018906	31778234
USA/Etats–Unis d'Amer	12433774	13036822	14744629	16902402	18452056
United Kingdom	11700492	10779273	12337421	14292760	16196698
Spain/Espagne	9324551	7376970	8920799	11314270	12526209
Switz.Liecht	7086994	6621919	7169346	8771190	9268666
Belgium–Luxembourg	5917852	5019751	5667413	6637630	6907746
Netherlands/Pays–Bas	5592825	4740994	5440628	6824020	7366323
Austria/Autriche	4408259	4201313	4670325	5487438	5903063
Japan/Japon	3424236	3202262	4055063	5347488	5583622
Greece/Grèce	3233081	2989101	3404733	4356103	4713313
Hong Kong	2079321	2509152	3139440	3905386	4388668
Portugal	2923445	2255252	2560720	3211503	3327218
Turkey/Turquie	2012615	2657979	1911560	3233599	4283963
Russian Federation	2682640	1717763	2172928	2869483	3717765
China/Chine	1497167	2468567	2285558	2695458	2868512
Poland/Pologne	1146980	1501092	1769295	2514444	3427383
Brazil/Brésil	865120	1080853	1845951	3170586	3113099
Sweden/Suède	1706843	1431139	1731168	2227795	2503965
Korea, Republic of	1166644	1282851	1780347	2301059	2829404
Israel/Israël	1331418	1512157	1790934	2191657	2226901
Saudi Arabia	2012758	2024821	1556316	1524286	1855130
Canada	1297640	1394030	1741544	2151783	1821322
Denmark/Danemark	1395539	1218814	1592126	2004420	2111826
Singapore/Singapour	1156421	1121485	1423759	1747431	2075366
Slovenia/Slovénia	536569	1162594	1423027	1922609	1955827
United Arab Emirates	856870	974236	1462735	1636464	1580672
Australia/Australie	894809	940948	1306544	1543568	1771748
Egypt/Egypte	1060942	1209881	1348355	1204579	1430149
Argentina/Argentine	854898	974981	1405412	1335352	1622724
Hungary/Hongrie	816960	997739	1181007	1414845	1522652
Croatia/Croatie	314770	792366	1372373	1675568	1667815
Tunisia/Tunisie	1132029	1036876	965173	1196519	1419365
Iran (Islamic Rp. of)	2051676	1295216	721537	518564	719013
Malta/Malte	1003829	957508	1057264	1234788	867364
Romania/Roumanie	505523	636776	877267	1283443	1670375
Libyan Arab Jamahiriya	1074238	1122250	754481	956544	1016073
So. Africa Customs Un	631831	700981	866402	1172623	1243764
Czech Republic		629279	859105	1328113	1740715
Thailand/Thaïlande	558519	731092	754115	1163581	1291192
Norway,SVD,JM	691653	750606	778347	960983	1243053
Algeria/Algérie	1065569	843023	934305	789627	734446
Finland/Finlande	758121	562197	758608	1050731	1202659
India/Inde	484981	529986	709450	1095038	1214512
Mexico/Mexique	879313	770714	926132	616464	830034
Lebanon/Liban	522613	632370	773628	894467	1049862
Ireland/Irlande	566586	517434	662785	930483	1000742
Malaysia/Malaisie	394674	515188	568692	917793	1007383
Indonesia/Indonésie	435609	474363	643329	748710	1098101
Morocco/Maroc	550653	529050	601542	626009	691380

(VALUE AS PERCENTAGE OF WORLD TOTAL)(VALEURS EN POURCENTAGE DU TOTAL MONDIAL)

	1987	1988	1989	1990	1991	1992	1993	1994	1995	1996
Africa	7.7	7.1	7.9	8.4	7.8	6.9	7.3	6.9	6.8	7.3
Americas	8.6	9.1	9.1	8.4	8.9	8.4	8.5	8.0	8.3	8.3
Northern America	6.0	6.3	6.2	5.9	6.4	6.0	6.1	5.5	5.7	5.8
LAIA	2.3	2.4	2.6	2.3	2.2	2.1	2.1	2.3	2.4	2.2
CACM	0.1	0.2	0.1	0.1	0.1	0.1	0.1	0.1	0.1	0.1
Caribbean	0.1	0.1	0.1	0.1	0.2	0.1	0.1	0.1	0.1	0.1
Rest of America	0.1	0.1	0.1	0.1	0.1	0.1	0.1	0.0	0.0	0.0
As.ex F.USSR	11.3	10.4	10.2	10.0	10.3	10.4	11.6	10.8	11.0	10.9
Eur.x F.USSR	69.3	70.1	69.4	70.1	69.7	71.0	68.5	69.8	69.7	69.7
EU	60.7	61.8	61.1	61.8	61.8	62.9	59.5	60.4	60.5	60.8
EFTA	5.2	4.8	4.7	5.0	4.8	5.0	5.7	5.4	4.8	4.7
East Europe	1.8	1.8	1.8	1.5	1.4	1.7	2.0	2.5	2.9	2.9
Other Europe	1.5	1.7	1.9	1.9	1.7	0.3	0.3	0.4	0.3	0.1
Former USSR	2.3	2.3	2.4	2.3	2.5	2.4	3.2	3.5	3.4	2.9
Oceania	0.7	0.9	0.8	0.7	0.6	0.6	0.6	0.7	0.7	0.7
Germany/Allemagne	21.1	21.8	21.2	21.2	20.9	21.6	19.4	19.2	19.1	18.5
France,Monac	14.6	14.8	14.7	14.2	14.2	14.5	13.6	13.6	13.9	13.5
United Kingdom	5.3	5.1	4.8	5.2	5.7	5.7	5.8	6.1	6.1	6.6
Netherlands/Pays–Bas	5.6	5.7	5.5	5.7	5.7	5.9	5.7	5.7	5.5	6.0
USA/Etats–Unis d'Amer	5.3	5.6	5.5	5.1	5.6	5.2	5.3	4.6	4.8	4.9
Belgium–Luxembourg	5.0	4.9	5.0	5.1	4.9	4.8	4.7	4.7	4.8	4.8
Switz.Liecht	4.8	4.5	4.3	4.6	4.4	4.5	5.1	4.9	4.5	4.3
Spain/Espagne	2.2	2.4	2.4	3.0	3.5	3.4	3.4	3.9	3.9	4.1
Russian Federation						2.1	2.6	2.9	2.6	2.3
Austria/Autriche	2.3	2.4	2.3	2.3	2.2	2.2	2.2	2.2	2.3	2.3

	1987	1988	1989	1990	1991	1992	1993	1994	1995	1996
Afrique	4.9	4.8	4.8	4.5	4.4	4.1	4.2	3.7	3.5	3.3
Amériques	12.9	12.1	12.0	10.6	10.1	10.5	12.1	12.4	11.8	12.0
Amérique du Nord	10.8	10.0	9.7	8.5	7.7	7.7	8.6	8.7	8.2	8.1
ALAI	1.6	1.6	1.7	1.6	1.9	2.2	2.6	3.0	3.0	3.1
MCAC	0.1	0.1	0.1	0.1	0.1	0.1	0.1	0.1	0.1	0.1
Caraïbes	0.3	0.3	0.3	0.3	0.3	0.2	0.6	0.4	0.2	0.4
Autre Amérique	0.1	0.1	0.1	0.1	0.2	0.2	0.2	0.2	0.2	0.4
Asie l'URSS exclus	10.2	10.5	11.1	10.9	11.8	13.0	15.2	14.5	15.0	15.6
Europe l'URSS exclus	68.7	69.6	69.0	71.3	71.1	69.7	66.0	66.7	66.8	65.9
UE	60.6	61.7	61.0	62.6	63.2	61.6	57.0	57.2	56.9	55.5
AELE	5.4	5.2	4.9	5.0	4.6	4.4	4.4	4.2	4.2	4.2
Europe de l'Est	1.2	1.2	1.3	1.4	1.5	2.1	2.7	2.9	3.4	3.9
Autre de l'Europe	1.5	1.6	1.8	2.2	1.8	0.6	0.7	0.7	0.6	0.4
Ancienne URSS	1.9	1.6	1.8	1.6	1.4	1.6	1.4	1.5	1.6	1.9
Océanie	0.9	0.9	1.0	0.8	0.7	0.6	0.7	0.8	0.8	0.9
Germany/Allemagne	18.6	18.1	17.0	19.0	21.0	20.4	19.5	19.0	18.7	17.4
France,Monac	16.3	16.6	16.3	16.4	15.2	14.6	13.1	13.1	13.0	12.7
USA/Etats–Unis d'Amer	9.6	8.9	8.6	7.6	6.9	7.0	7.7	7.8	7.3	7.4
United Kingdom	7.4	8.0	7.9	7.1	6.7	6.6	6.4	6.5	6.2	6.5
Spain/Espagne	3.6	4.2	4.9	5.1	5.2	5.2	4.4	4.7	4.9	5.0
Switz.Liecht	4.7	4.7	4.5	4.5	4.2	4.0	3.9	3.8	3.8	3.7
Belgium–Luxembourg	3.4	3.4	3.3	3.4	3.4	3.3	3.0	3.0	2.9	2.8
Netherlands/Pays–Bas	3.1	3.1	3.1	3.1	3.2	3.1	2.8	2.9	2.9	2.9
Austria/Autriche	2.5	2.5	2.4	2.4	2.5	2.5	2.5	2.5	2.4	2.4
Japan/Japon	1.6	1.9	2.3	2.3	2.2	1.9	1.9	2.1	2.3	2.2

4. Special Imports C.I.F. by Commodities according to the S.I.T.C. (Rev. 2) in thousand U.S. Dollars
Importations Spéciales C.A.F. par Produits d'après la C.T.C.I. (Rév. 2) en milliers de Dollars E.U.

SITC CTCI	COMMODITY	1993		1994		1995		1996		PRODUIT
		WEIGHT POIDS	VALUE VALEUR	WEIGHT POIDS	VALUE VALEUR	WEIGHT POIDS	VALUE VALEUR	WEIGHT POIDS	VALUE VALEUR	
	ALL COMMODITIES		147817494		167975069		204099177		206965491	TOUS PRODUITS
0	FOOD AND LIVE ANIMALS		16277935		17220081		19380246		19571345	ALIMENTS,ANIMAUX VIVANTS
001	*LIVE ANIMALS FOR FOOD	W 646721	1573254	W 587002	1512644	W 557948	1523692	W 579388	1424664	ANIMAUX VIVANTS
0011	BOVINE SPECIES,LIVE	W 391116	1115392	W 373899	1103401	W 360541	1117679	W 368556	967951	ESPECE BOVINE
00119	— OTHR THAN FR BREEDING	W 374631	1072671	W 359634	1065986	W 351522	1092619	W 355476	935276	BOVINS NON REPRODUCTEURS
01	MEAT AND PREPARATIONS		3478176		3551650		3691557		3607313	VIANDES ET PREPARATIONS
011	MEAT FRESH,CHILLD,FROZEN	W 1097658	3325280	W 1080047	3389405	W 1055341	3518080	W 1061124	3451837	VIANDES FRAICHES,REF,CONGE
0111	BOVINE MEAT FRESH,FROZEN	W 403342	1766182	W 395098	1749103	W 355851	1716679	W 300225	1340718	VIANDES BOVIN FRAI,REF
01111	BOVINE MEAT WITH BONE IN	W 374756	1621618	W 345380	1540769	W 312293	1483876	W 258199	1126472	VIANDES BOVIN NON DESOSS
0113	PIG MEAT FRESH,CHLD,FRZN	W 579834	1190119	W 572052	1272054	W 602100	1468005	W 662779	1764419	VIANDE DE PORC
02	DAIRY PRODCTS,BIRDS'EGGS		2656247		2793922		3065077		2984356	PRODUITS LAITIERS,OEUFS
022	MILK AND CREAM	W 1955189	1248912	W 2178524	1336194	W 2182682	1480433	W 2189583	1425547	LAIT ET CREME
0223	MILK AND CREAM FRESH	W 1709250	822990	W 1923711	919872	W 1951936	1031995	W 1962555	1002388	LAIT,CREME FRAIS
024	CHEESE AND CURD	W 284284	1233803	W 294453	1273154	W 291507	1391182	W 296433	1334933	FROMAGE ET CAILLEBOTTE
03	FISH AND PREPARATIONS		2078240		2182230		2374710		2515562	POISSONS ET PREPARATIONS
034	FISH,FRESH,CHILLED,FROZN	W 277481	898813	W 264542	884441	W 266227	941368	W 268238	1024634	POISSON FRAIS, REFRIG,CONG
036	SHELL FISH FRESH,FROZEN	W 183579	591610	W 191906	671995	W 207100	771598	W 214965	801764	CRUSTACES,MOLLUSQUES
04	CEREALS AND PREPARATIONS		1861638		1665611		2165284		2381588	CEREALES ET PRODUITS
041	WHEAT ETC UNMILLED	W 5022934	1142626	W 4880480	962340	W 5554036	1234135	W 6262027	1395691	FROMENT,EPEAUTRE
0412	OTHER WHEAT ETC UNMILLED	W 4092527	884023	W 4022046	789323	W 4523037	971564	W 5048667	1087006	AUTRE FROMENT NON MOULU
05	VEGETABLES AND FRUIT		2065888		2428334		2762475		2795914	LEGUMES ET FRUITS
054	VEG ETC FRSH,SMPLY PRSVD	W 1637857	746231	W 1639263	848558	W 1639468	1005477	W 1461976	901949	LEGUMES FRAIS,CONG,SECS
057	FRUIT,NUTS,FRESH,DRIED	W 1041266	856978	W 1138381	1090099	W 1168058	1164785	W 1220373	1265164	FRUITS FRAIS OU SECS
07	COFFEE,TEA,COCOA,SPICES		798721		1132675		1554688		1319569	CAFE,THE,CACAO,EPICES
071	COFFEE AND SUBSTITUTES	W 331889	467940	W 326601	744587	W 319067	1105644	W 330938	876698	CAFE ET SUCCEDANES
0711	COFFEE GREEN,ROASTED,SUB	W 329403	447118	W 322399	709902	W 316561	1073451	W 328087	847487	CAFE TORREFIE OU DECAFEINE
07111	COFFEE GREEN,HUSKS,SKINS	W 328202	442994	W 320028	700155	W 312905	1053063	W 320542	812065	CAFE NON TORREFIE
081	*FEEDING STUFF FOR ANIML	W 3500736	1078117	W 3604979	1124705	W 3982654	1242859	W 3844123	1403286	NOURRITURE POUR ANIMAUX
0819	FOOD WASTE AND FEED NES	W 971792	574170	W 980681	597216	W 1148776	701344	W 1024373	702600	DECHETS,ALIMENTS NDA
08199	FODDER NES,INCL SWEETNED	W 454299	498109	W 471917	522475	W 497068	603471	W 640890	634843	PREPARATIONS FOURRAGERES
1	BEVERAGES AND TOBACCO		1526718		1803624		1917894		2117716	BOISSONS ET TABACS
11	BEVERAGES		632819		697041		757030		792510	BOISSONS
112	ALCOHOLIC BEVERAGES	W 398027	592081	W 422598	661487	W 418160	716888	W 420913	734917	BOISSONS ALCOOLIQUES
12	TOBACCO AND MANUFACTURES		893899		1106582		1160864		1325206	TABACS BRUTS FABRIQUES
122	TOBACCO,MANUFACTURED	W 39020	777957	W 43643	994591	W 41898	1022878	W 42830	1190564	TABACS FABRIQUES
1222	CIGARETTES	W 37842	752752	W 41625	968402	W 38566	984818	W 39353	1148045	CIGARETTES
2	CRUDE MATERLS,EXCL FUELS		10313168		12909301		15551999		13492505	MAT BRUTES NON COMESTIBLES
21	HIDES,SKINS,FURS UNDRSSD		1050672		1462745		1627739		1543081	CUIRS,PEAUX BRUTS
211	HIDES,SKINS,EXC FURS,RAW	W 462720	983439	W 562270	1385652	W 585806	1545376	W 564745	1415324	CUIRS ET PEAUX
2111	BOVINE,EQUINE HIDES,RAW	W 364693	614357	W 456215	900200	W 488769	1013105	W 476305	931396	PEAUX DE BOVINS
22	OIL SEEDS,OLEAGINOUS FRT		455755		438090		437665		401142	GRAINES,FRUITS OLEAGINEUX
222	SEEDS FOR'SOFT'FIXED OIL	W 1758900	450459	W 1541641	432026	W 1557675	429935	W 1209553	394213	GRAINES HUILES FIXES
23	RUBBER, CRUDE		373393		465730		652969		628061	CAOUTCHOUC BRUT
24	CORK AND WOOD		2070356		2491519		2845163		2464964	LIEGE ET BOIS
247	OTH WOOD ROUGH,SQUARED	W 3585539	500779	W 4239106	633668	W 4411891	741233	W 3871668	619998	BOIS BRUTS EQUARRIS
248	WOOD SHAPED,SLEEPERS	W 3530897	1512637	W 4001518	1785796	W 3990067	2027314	W 3921153	1770804	BOIS SIMPLEMENT TRAVAILLES
2482	LUMBER SHAPED CONIFER	W 2383862	882297	W 2668572	1016066	W 2590244	1132353	W 2652448	1031012	CONIFERES SCIES,RABOTES
24821	LUMBER SAWN ETC CONIFER	W 2347845	853869	W 2625840	982562	W 2549369	1094884	W 2603513	991733	CONIFERES SCIES LONGITUD
2483	LUMBER SHAPED NON–CONIFR	W 1143127	629478	W 1323935	767849	W 1386425	891261	W 1234921	730939	NON CONIFERES SCIES,RABOTES
24831	LUMBER SAWN ETC NON–CON	W 1052762	513499	W 1241122	650917	W 1309196	769440	W 1164235	628297	SCIES LONGITUDINALEMENT
251	*PULP AND WASTE PAPER	W 3371381	1040625	W 3847980	1460215	W 3882912	2466537	W 3947413	1588353	PATES A PAPIER,DECHETS
2517	SODA,SULPHATE WOOD PULP	W 2079541	786306	W 2209850	1062265	W 2270028	1819541	W 2362166	1200360	PATES CHIMIQUES AU SULFATE
25172	— BLEACHED,NONDISSOLVNG	W 2046916	774152	W 2174511	1046181	W 2229829	1790435	W 2345156	1191763	PATES BLANCHIES
26	TEXTILE FIBRES AND WASTE		1688158		2363266		2612011		2399351	FIBRES TEXTILES
263	COTTON	W 381273	482449	W 412013	615928	W 407448	812389	W 403523	786089	COTON
2631	RAW COTTON,EXCL LINTERS	W 329335	443549	W 348290	560753	W 345466	734601	W 345711	721149	COTON EN MASSE
268	WOOL(EXC TOPS),ANML HAIR	W 159759	582548	W 190351	903738	W 163256	908199	W 161528	813086	LAINES ET POILS
27	CRUDE FERTLZR,MINRLS NES		928042		1029266		1185364		1176966	ENGRAIS MINERAUX BRUTS
28	METALLIFEROUS ORES,SCRAP		1934132		2404194		2896208		2423695	MINERAIS METAL,DECHETS
282	IRON AND STEEL SCRAP	W 5903910	714214	W 6264261	908690	W 6315489	1091282	W 4927595	719210	FERRAILLES
28209	–- OF OTHR IRON OR STEEL	W 5502567	644034	W 5905078	819783	W 5937211	960688	W 4599307	605206	FERRAILLES DE FER
288	NONFERR METAL SCRAP NES	W 551537	468446	W 643579	700314	W 650139	813215	W 690245	723300	DECHETS NON FERREUX
2882	OTHER BASE MTL SCRAP NES	W 405901	394708	W 502660	615697	W 468495	718358	W 524730	645679	AUTRES DECHETS
29	CRUDE ANIMAL,VEG MAT NES		772035		794275		828344		866892	MATIERES BRUTES ANIM,VEGET
292	CRUDE VEG MATERIALS NES	W 197374	647676	W 207930	652668	W 193011	659682	W 238197	691739	MAT BRUTES VEGETALES NDA
3	MINERAL FUELS ETC		13810835		13730234		15060550		17521905	COMBUSTIBLES MINERAUX LUB
32	COAL,COKE AND BRIQUETTES		831973		892786		1194349		1042437	HOUILLES,COKES,BRIQUETTES
322	COAL,LIGNITE AND PEAT	MW 14282	762944	MW 16198	839741	MW 19038	1063064	MW 17125	964019	HOUILLES,LIGNITES,TOURBE
3222	OTH COAL,NOT AGGLOMERATD	MW 13264	684399	MW 15308	762686	MW 18267	984286	MW 16332	886261	AUTRES HOUILLES
33	PETROLEUM AND PRODUCTS		12634517		12515818		13436139		15991213	PETROLE ET DERIVES
333	CRUDE PETROLEUM	MW 75566	8872737	MW 75626	8584436	MW 73062	9103250	MW 74542	11264048	HUILES BRUTES DE PETROLE
334	PETROLEUM PRODUCTS,REFIN	MW 29317	3481999	MW 31862	3618160	MW 31302	3947083	MW 30433	4379626	PRODUITS RAFFINES
3341	GASOLINE,OTH LIGHT OILS	W 3292370	642558			W 3192958	568213	W 3288909	672612	ESSENCES POUR MOTEURS
3343	GAS OILS	W 3019731	532463			W 2022142	331044	W 1813731	381689	GAS OILS
3344	FUEL OILS,NES	MW 22811	2158476			MW 25922	2844678	MW 25104	3089459	FUEL OILS
4	ANIMAL,VEGETABLE OIL,FAT		1065864		1388305		1382691		1750094	HUILES,GRAISSES ANIM,VEG
42	FIXED VEGETABLE OIL,FAT		981875		1231552		1237633		1602978	HUILES VEGETALES FIXES
423	FIXED VEG OILS,SOFT	W 516536	798963	W 526036	1005790	W 452255	955919	W 448091	1309199	HUILES VEGET DOUCES FIXES
4235	OLIVE OIL	W 298327	678685	W 332661	862159	W 248405	804742	W 253404	1176696	HUILE D'OLIVE
5	CHEMCLS,RELATED PROD NES		18081022		21041228		25993861		26367220	PRODUITS CHIMIQUES
51	ORGANIC CHEMICALS		4532464		5454294		6799906		6743677	PROD CHIMIQ ORGANIQUES
511	HYDROCARBONS NES,DERIVS	W 994906	434751	W 1034786	517847	W 870009	610166	W 973714	543263	HYDROCARBURES NDA
512	ALCOHOLS,PHENOLS ETC	W 1156361	471310		653364	W 1266153	909706	W 1282878	764931	PHENOLS,PHENOLS–ALCOOLS
5121	ACYCLIC ALCOHOLS,DERIVS	W 1100019	356941		533507	W 1187063	749346	W 1209911	588409	ALCOOLS ACYCLIQUES
513	CARBOXYLIC ACIDS ETC	W 627656	664198	W 795261	858814	W 846100	1244563	W 828180	1112883	ACIDES CARBOXYLIQUES
514	NITROGEN–FNCTN COMPOUNDS	W 317980	1370540	W 422172	1692538	W 455587	2060262	W 453564	2105592	COMPOSES FONCT AZOTEES
5148	OTH NITROGN–FNCTN CMPNDS	W 162503	875748	W 228711	1127290	W 247410	1399560	W 249003	1411365	AUTRES COMPOSES AZOTES
51482	IMIDE–,IMIDE–FNCT CMPNDS	W 36778	651310	W 41012	840098	W 47606	970093	W 48590	989030	COMPOSES A FONCTION IMIDE
515	ORG–INORG COMPOUNDS ETC	W 138644	1158468	W 175365	1220426	W 178637	1349535	W 180259	1618834	COMPOSES ORGANO–MINERAUX
5156	HETEROCYCLIC CMPDS ETC	W 99241	909911	W 127148	944764	W 130280	1039621	W 126637	1202163	COMPOSES HETEROCYCLIQUES
51569	OTH HETEROCYC CMPDS,ETC	W 20794	792151	W 21702	808469	W 25820	849937	W 34821	1023806	AUT COMP HETEROCYCLIQUES
516	OTHER ORGANIC CHEMICALS	W 522147	433196	W 583638	511306	W 540812	625673	W 507897	598175	AUTRES PROD ORGANIQUES
52	INORGANIC CHEMICALS		873608		1043851		1224179		1271281	PROD CHIM INORGANIQUES
522	INORG ELEMNTS,OXIDES,ETC	W 1275030	444749	W 1297740	521026	W 1313322	658660	W 1338026	666186	ELEMENTS INORGANIQUES
53	DYES,TANNING,COLOUR PROD		1277674		1502487		1636112		1686039	PROD TEINTURE,COLORANTS
531	SYNT DYE,NAT INDGO,LAKES	W 58349	571577	W 69791	663406	W 69915	684102	W 75696	713552	MAT COLOR ORGAN,LAQUES
5311	SYNTHIC ORGNIC DYESTUFFS	W 51679	538489	W 63007	628248	W 62430	646784	W 66246	669636	MAT COLOR ORGAN SYNTHET
533	PIGMENTS,PAINTS,ETC	W 256438	632762	W 300498	749822	W 296181	863541	W 295869	877131	PIGMENTS,PEINTURES,VERNIS
541	*MEDICINAL,PHARM PRODUCT		3227656		3262451	MK 59793	3902450	MK 64548	4616832	PROD MEDICINAUX PHARMACEUT
5413	ANTIBIOTICS IN BULK	K 3130981	584102		539555	K 3668437	683012	K 4634394	746299	ANTIBIOTIQUES NDA
54139	OTHER ANTIBIOTICS	K 960640	468603	K 1108575	415464	K 1268933	549535	K 1516803	601984	AUTRES ANTIBIOTIQUES

4. Special Imports C.I.F. by Commodities according to the S.I.T.C. (Rev. 2) in thousand U.S. Dollars
Importations Spéciales C.A.F. par Produits d'après la C.T.C.I. (Rév. 2) en milliers de Dollars E.U.

SITC CTCI	COMMODITY	1993 WEIGHT POIDS	1993 VALUE VALEUR	1994 WEIGHT POIDS	1994 VALUE VALEUR	1995 WEIGHT POIDS	1995 VALUE VALEUR	1996 WEIGHT POIDS	1996 VALUE VALEUR	PRODUIT
5417	MEDICAMENTS		1598323		1730106	MK 36680	2063369	MK 39867	2586801	MEDICAMENTS
54179	— CONTNG OTH SUBSTANCES	MK 17024	1070157	MK 25323	1234100	MK 32140	1573081	MK 35763	1991296	MED CONT AUT SUBSTANCES
55	PERFUME,CLEANING ETC PRD		1275108		1418372		1593792		1622444	PROD POUR PARFUM,TOILETTE
553	PERFUMERY,COSMETICS,ETC	W 82535	709831	W 91466	801552	W 95792	909366	W 98516	898363	PRODUITS DE PARFUMERIE
562	*FERTILIZERS,MANUFACTURE	W 2641228	360331	W 3359673	543729	W 3374589	657201	W 3009164	634842	ENGRAIS MANUFACTURES
58	PLASTIC MATERIALS ETC		4279041		5330744		7256123		6722645	MAT PLAST ARTIFICIELLES
582	PROD OF CONDENSATION ETC	W 560087	1134625	W 666160	1388347	W 782632	1964203	W 755260	1879521	PROD CONDENS,POLYCOND
5823	ALKYDS,OTHER POLYESTERS	W 227129	435353	W 261242	518769	W 332961	827202	W 335118	735900	ALKYDES ET AUT POLYESTERS
58231	— IN PRIMARY FORMS	W 205061	350447	W 232931	409073	W 300822	674815	W 303606	588019	SOUS FORMES PRIMAIRES
583	POLYMERIZATION ETC PRODS	W 3176413	2985984		3759106	W 3701898	5071893	W 3867806	4615653	PROD POLYMERISATION
5831	POLYETHYLENE	W 948112	667914	W 991099	739908	W 952572	1023878	W 1029287	950604	POLYETHYLENE
58311	— IN PRIMARY FORMS	W 880540	585078	W 908771	644288	W 878554	911380	W 952027	840458	POLYETHYLENE PRIMAIRES
5832	POLYPROPYLENE	W 626158	450192	W 765515	607613	W 701739	836511	W 751443	733240	POLYPROPYLENE
58321	— IN PRIMARY FORMS	W 582960	342461	W 713571	475501	W 646890	655441	W 691753	563701	POLYPROPYLENE PRIMAIRES
5833	POLYSTYRENE,ITS COPOLYMR	W 505755	461438	W 589376	606278	W 598555	845248	W 619611	720794	POLYPROPYLENE COPOLYMERES
58331	— IN PRIMARY FORMS	W 490759	439070	W 569654	576533	W 578652	810312	W 600079	689639	SOUS FORMES PRIMAIRES
5834	POLYVINYL CHLORIDE	W 443895	355862	W 493828	475952	W 519875	639057	W 555125	518235	CHLORURE DE POLYVINYLE
5839	OTH POLYMRZTION ETC PROD	W 460617	720360		941486	W 692218	1257666	W 663311	1199328	AUT PROD POLYMER COPOLYM
59	CHEMICAL MATERIALS NES		2218164		2450725		2867288		2998879	MAT PROD CHIMIQUES NDA
598	MISCEL CHEM PRODUCTS NES	W 703417	1545829		1715946	W 810800	2037393	W 826139	2108783	PROD DIV INDUST CHIM NDA
5989	CHEM PRODUCTS,PREPS NES	W 538676	1300402		1449596	W 624830	1710530	W 638397	1767502	PROD PREP CHIMIQUES NDA
59899	OTH CHEM PRODS,PREPS,NES	W 410524	969331		1100362	W 460514	1312469	W 445574	1337679	AUT PRODUITS CHIMIQUES NDA
6	BASIC MANUFACTURES		22162615		28412336		37232248		34568090	ART MANUFACTURES
61	LEATHER,DRESSED FUR,ETC		1414682		2213707		2495160		2712661	CUIRS,PELLETERIES
611	LEATHER	W 225702	974912	W 335648	1616881	W 335649	1784055	W 367174	1853958	CUIRS,PEAUX PREPARES
6114	LEATHR BOVINE NES,EQUINE	W 162025	516479	W 243088	913553	W 253182	1015351	W 269782	1002183	CUIRS DE BOVINS
612	LEATHER ETC MANUFACTURES	W 20682	355956	W 28319	490802	W 30479	588208	W 33967	717963	OUVRAGES EN CUIRS NDA
6123	PREPRD PARTS OF FOOTWEAR	W 19696	341325	W 27077	473345	W 29180	569079	W 32724	698546	PARTIES DE CHAUSSURES
62	RUBBER MANUFACTURES NES		1265081		1485752		1796296		1921538	CAOUTCHOUC MANUFACTURE
625	RUBBER TYRES, TUBES ETC	W 231597	900756	W 270614	1071067	W 303688	1252295	W 305111	1325105	PNEUS CAOUTCHOUC VULCANISE
6251	TYRES NEW FOR MOTOR CARS	W 90478	431421	W 115715	547445	W 126339	616341	W 129925	658339	PNEUS POUR VOITURES
63	WOOD,CORK MANUFACTRS NES		588060		699964		882672		908191	OUVRAGES LIEGE ET BOIS
64	PAPER,PAPERBOARD AND MFR		2328715		2971310		4045061		3462729	PAPIERS,CARTONS & OUVRAGES
641	PAPER AND PAPERBOARD	W 3257581	2021074	W 3813891	2624314	W 3674959	3577820	W 3497679	2998234	PAPIERS ET CARTONS
6412	PRINTG,WRITING PAPER NES	W 456249	360520	W 563956	481964	W 568212	660337	W 542536	541442	PAPIERS POUR L'IMPRESSION
6413	KRAFT PAPER,PAPERBOARD	W 795208	380254	W 949322	508162	W 863656	717864	W 895431	610463	PAPIER ET CARTON KRAFT
6415	PAPER,PAPERBRD,BULK,NES	W 980257	517181	W 1164032	689752	W 1124398	1010843	W 1014860	738636	PAPIERS,CARTONS ROULEAUX
64159	OTHER PAPER ETC,BULK,NES	W 752334	424553	W 874099	556063	W 858385	814594	W 770383	599577	AUT PAPIER ROULEAUX FEUILLES
6418	COATED ETC PAPER NES BLK	W 349198	441420	W 423997	588318	W 400678	680933	W 381775	621264	PAP,CARTONS COUCHES,ENDUITS
65	TEXTILE YARN,FABRICS,ETC		4653030		6004394		6861053		6506167	FILS,TISSUS,ARTICLES TEXTILE
651	TEXTILE YARN	W 413500	1822235	W 557140	2567103	W 546674	3029507	W 511788	2846538	FILS TEXTILES
6512	WOOL,HAIR YARN,INCL TOPS	W 67295	415582	W 84976	580917	W 83025	708493	W 72872	612093	FILS DE LAINE,DE POILS
6514	SYN FIB YRN,BULK,MONOFIL	W 127422	592970	W 169524	740287	W 175747	941261	W 184622	1053514	FILS CONT 85% FIB TEXT SYNTH
65142	— NONTXT ETC CONT PAMID	W 90837	408655	W 117698	485133	W 119461	619835	W 122254	696378	FILS NON TEX FI CON POLYAMID
652	COTTON FABRICS,WOVEN	W 108552	624065	W 144947	832250	W 140582	942405	W 128798	871088	TISSUS DE COTON
653	WOVN MAN–MADE FIB FABRIC	W 76819	560127	W 92157	691110	W 97549	815394	W 94267	789683	TISSUS FIBRES SYNTH,ARTIF
657	SPECIAL TXTL FABRC,PRODS	W 64075	434619	W 69398	504606	W 72307	594866	W 78788	611898	TISSUS SPECIAUX
66	NONMETAL MINERAL MFS NES		2057384		2238151		2582634		2658904	ART MIN NON METALLIQUES
664	GLASS	W 726674	506751	W 729483	581070	W 787799	728255	W 703837	732381	VERRE
67	IRON AND STEEL		4577251		6205295		9558463		8088455	FER ET ACIER
671	PIG IRON ETC	W 1398331	459071	W 1971550	678334	W 2399738	965400	W 1944474	807601	FONTE,SPIEGEL,POUDRES
672	IRON,STEEL PRIMARY FORMS	W 3605310	1189203	W 4773979	1684255	W 5990102	2611487	W 4903012	1959193	LINGOTS FER,ACIER
6725	IRN,STL BLOOMS,SLABS,ETC	W 668902	208922	W 1251982	381859	W 1982898	713620	W 1102234	416951	BLOOMS,BILLETTES FER ACIER
6727	IRN,STL COIL FR REROLLNG	W 2900255	960667	W 3442285	1268674	W 3931568	1864226	W 3739975	1504842	EBAUCHES POUR TOLES FER
67271	IRON,SIMPLE STEEL COILS	W 2783044	813722	W 3322873	1113364	W 3769321	1559892	W 3589836	1274328	EBAUCHES NON EN ACIER
673	IRON,STEEL SHAPES ETC	W 1206873	647455	W 1401059	795348	W 1727012	1207375	W 1297339	976146	BARRES,PROFIL FER,ACIER
674	IRN,STL UNIV,PLATE,SHEET	W 2859995	1638919	W 3685487	2302025	W 4606614	3577625	W 4150222	3097003	LARGES PLATS,TOLES
6746	IRN,STL THIN PLATE,ROLLD	W 1319348	804509	W 1626716	1109922	W 2071994	1772972	W 1863374	1439258	TOLES LAM MOINS 3MM
67461	— OF IRON OR SIMPLE STL	W 1074143	427162	W 1289331	577525	W 1666925	905968	W 1429172	691679	TOL NON AC FIN MOINS 3 MM
67463	— OF STAINLESS ETC STL	W 190986	330889	W 262410	469442	W 297443	763899	W 306391	628336	TOL ACIER INOX MOINS 3 MM
6749	OTH IRN,STL PLATES,SHEET	W 755378	385160	W 973289	548510	W 1171304	825201	W 1092904	716560	AUTRES TOLES FER,ACIER
67491	— OF IRON OR SIMPLE STL	W 743981	361378	W 961340	522001	W 1154879	783006	W 1047863	663065	AUT TOLES AUTRES ACIER FIN
678	IRON,STL TUBES,PIPES,ETC	W 426313	437643		502600	W 672346	828044	W 666346	856840	TUBES,TUYAUX EN FONTE,FER
68	NON–FERROUS METALS		3259402		4304246		6122855		5264968	METAUX NON FERREUX
682	COPPER EXC CEMENT COPPER	W 626722	1405630	W 697959	1758275	W 736427	2453217	W 776163	2188511	CUIVRE
6821	COPPER NES,ALLOYS,UNWRT	W 423972	822786	W 429066	941886	W 451613	1321391	W 489828	1188499	CUIVRE BRUT
68212	COPPER REFINED,UNWROUGHT	W 419397	812409	W 420520	918034	W 435321	1269808	W 463245	1131191	CUIVRE AFFINE BRUT
6822	COPPER,ALLOYS WORKED	W 202750	582844	W 268893	816389	W 284813	1131826	W 286335	1000012	CUIVRE,ALLIAGES OUVRES
684	ALUMINIUM	W 716772	1224599		1723886	W 946883	2413789	W 837689	1950562	ALUMINIUM
6841	ALUMINIUM,ALLOYS,UNWRGHT	W 435789	566901	W 577593	898337	W 574477	1203569	W 484899	865960	ALUMINIUM,ALLIAGES BRUTS
6842	ALUMINIUM,ALLOYS WORKED	W 280983	657697		825548	W 372406	1210220	W 352790	1084603	ALUMINIUM,ALLIAGES OUVRE
68422	ALUMNM PLATE,SHEET,STRIP	W 195101	421347	W 232295	524483	W 256203	771281	W 228361	643026	TOLES, PLANCHES EN ALU
69	METAL MANUFACTURES NES		2019010		2289517		2888054		3044476	ART MANUFACT EN METAL NDA
695	TOOLS	W 32137	505536		597309	W 39006	748249	W 39527	805581	OUTILS A MAIN
699	BASE METAL MFRS NES	W 143563	766079		874155	W 198861	1119510	W 192115	1112554	ART MANUFACTURES MET NDA
7	MACHINES,TRANSPORT EQUIP		41980589		47332215		59736745		62336673	MACHINES MATERIEL TRANSPORT
71	POWER GENERATING EQUIPMT		2024284		2243263		3054666		3105521	MACHINES GENERATRICES
713	INTRNL COMBUS PSTN ENGIN	W 60831	925529	W 77156	1050011	W 100583	1434958	W 90744	1432898	MOTEURS EXPL COMB INT, PIECE
7139	PISTON ENGINE PARTS NES	W 19960	422909	W 31310	477103	W 47467	668863	W 36821	640628	PIECES POUR 713.2,3,8
714	ENGINES AND MOTORS NES	W 2826	462458		493976	W 4386	653163	W 5834	750474	MOTEURS NON ELECTRIQUES
716	ROTATING ELECTRIC PLANT	W 67734	531496	W 75022	585766	W 95122	816640	W 89051	735549	APP ELECTR ROTATIFS,PIECES
7162	AC MTRS,GENRTRS,GEN SETS	W 53837	395500	W 59623	432258	W 78420	624971	W 75279	578994	MOTEURS ELECTRIQUES
72	MACHS FOR SPCL INDUSTRYS		2897735		3170146		4459229		4615006	MAC SPECIALES POUR INDUST
724	TEXTILE,LEATHER MACHNRY	W 33882	709010		926960	W 55077	1223273	W 52756	1125311	MACH POUR INDUSTRIE TEXTILE
728	OTH MACHY FOR SPCL INDUS	W 45636	942044		947837	W 55962	1345388	W 57258	1359713	AUT MACH IND PARTICULIERES
7284	MACHY FOR SPCL INDUS NES	W 29400	782540	W 26089	770435	W 36028	1111637	W 37063	1113031	MACH SPEC IND PARTICUL.
73	METALWORKING MACHINERY		899474		1074078		1620502		1708747	MACH TRAVAIL DES METAUX
736	METALWORKING MACH–TOOLS	W 47621	741128		892447	W 84085	1350688	W 94296	1436004	MACH–OUTILS TRAVAIL METAUX
7361	METAL CUTTING MACH–TOOLS	W 18948	240008		385911	W 35276	614899	W 41113	655311	MACH–OUT ENLEVEMENT METAL
74	GENRL INDUSTRL MACHY NES		4598034		5373440		7191936		7481870	MACH APP INDUSTRIE
741	HEATING,COOLING EQUIPMNT	W 51940	670693	W 51401	720632	W 74024	1098470	W 81348	1172295	MACH CHAUFFAGE,PIECES
742	PUMPS FOR LIQUIDS ETC	W 25147	562021	W 29716	700536	W 31618	863957	W 32846	853900	POMPES MOTO–POMPES
743	PUMPS NES,CENTRFUGES ETC	W 71180	780165		912412	W 105255	1255951	W 102950	1225107	POMPES COMPRES,VENT ETC
744	MECHANICAL HANDLING EQU	W 84194	548304	W 100589	600286	W 138104	854554	W 149452	910950	EQUIP MANUTENTION PIECES
745	NONELEC MACHY,TOOLS NES	W 23120	536426		581468	W 31293	677484	W 31230	711397	AUT MACH NON ELEC,PIECES
749	NONELEC MACH PTS,ACC NES	W 100675	1500426		1858106	W 158298	2441521	W 160896	2608221	PIECES MACH NON ELEC NDA
7491	BALL,ROLLER,ETC BEARINGS	W 30520	412432		558486	W 58664	838275	W 59661	887243	ROULEMENTS BILLES ETC
7492	COCKS,VALVES ETC NES	W 31766	515629		607716	W 39585	753084	W 40793	807221	ART ROB,SIM POUR TUYAUX
75	OFFICE MACHNES,ADP EQUIP		5089763		5373912		6743501		7464465	MACH BUREAU TRAIT AUTOM
751	OFFICE MACHINES	W 17057	474444		489863	W 17589	544195	W 14006	442334	MACH,APPAREILS DE BUREAU
752	AUTOMTIC DATA PROC EQUIP		2728532		2912919	W 53194	3601418	W 57595	4077754	MACH TRAIT INFORMATION

4. Special Imports C.I.F. by Commodities according to the S.I.T.C. (Rev. 2) in thousand U.S. Dollars
Importations Spéciales C.A.F. par Produits d'après la C.T.C.I. (Rév. 2) en milliers de Dollars E.U.

SITC CTCI	COMMODITY	1993		1994		1995		1996		PRODUIT
		WEIGHT POIDS	VALUE VALEUR	WEIGHT POIDS	VALUE VALEUR	WEIGHT POIDS	VALUE VALEUR	WEIGHT POIDS	VALUE VALEUR	
7523	DIGITL CENTRL PROCESSORS	W 6500	623030	W 6703	651564	W 8476	910987	W 9327	1174372	UNITES CENTRALES
7524	DIGITL CENTRL STOR UNITS		688623	W 3279	689024	W 3857	792713	W 4281	956384	UNITES MEMOIRE CENTRALES
7525	ADP PERIPHERAL UNITS	W 21154	680715	W 27806	795876	W 33155	1038052	W 37719	1089212	UNITES PERIPHERIQUES
7528	OFF–LINE DATA PROC EQUIP	W 5176	500814		501244	W 5862	544135	W 4839	667472	MACH AUXIL TRAIT INFORM
759	OFFICE,ADP MCH PTS,ACCES	W 20193	1886788		1971130	W 27092	2597889	W 35565	2944377	PIECES DU 751 ET 752
7599	ACCTG,ETC,ADP MCH PTS,AC	W 15332	1681206		1749030	W 21572	2341275	W 26058	2620199	PIECES DU 751 ET 752
76	TELECOMM,SOUND EQUIPMENT		2983097		3571284		4246115		4517205	EQUIPMENT DE TELECOM
761	TELEVISION RECEIVERS	W 39317	588087	W 39113	594118	W 41621	641329	W 38404	644091	RECEPTEURS DE TELEVISION
7611	COLOUR TV RECEIVERS	W 38833	575927	W 38586	579644	W 41062	625144	W 38006	635732	RECEPTEURS COULEUR
763	SOUND RECORDRS,PHONOGRPH	W 13274	473235	W 12518	481227	W 10356	417114	W 9872	509895	PHONO,APP ENREGISTREMENT
7638	OTHR SOUND APPARATUS ETC	W 12879	466701	W 12122	474061	W 10001	410932	W 9621	505099	AUT APP D'ENREGIS,REPROD
764	TELECOM EQPT,PTS,ACC NES	W 27769	1536288		2024393	W 36651	2676817	W 35082	2843816	EQUIP TELECOM,PIECES
7641	LINE TELEPHONE,ETC EQUIP	W 4688	310026		379334	W 7298	567589	W 7783	660121	APP TELEPHON PAR FIL
7643	TV,RADIO TRANSMITTRS ETC	W 1678	307062		584305	W 3923	932090	W 3629	1033322	APP EMET TELE RADIO
7649	PTS NES OF EQUIPMT OF 76	W 9288	558390		626195	W 10654	706191	W 9287	832178	PIECES DE LA DIV 76
77	ELECTRIC MACHNRY NES ETC		7642711		9491629		11689248		11087473	MACH APP ELECT NDA
771	ELECTRIC POWER MACHY NES	W 21579	324261	W 29239	428556	W 34575	579503	W 37693	662593	MACH PROD,TRANS ELECTR
772	SWITCHGEAR ETC,PARTS NES	W 43632	1627808		1937278	W 61753	2528146	W 60334	2478217	APP COUPURE,SECT ETC
7721	SWITCHGEAR ETC	W 40591	1358295		1648785	W 57118	2151146	W 56263	2137334	APP COUPURE,SECTIONMNT
775	HOUSEHOLD TYPE EQUIP NES	W 82627	677424	W 92314	736731	W 103903	869044	W 100047	853883	MACH,APP USAGE DOMESTQUE
776	TRANSISTORS,VALVES,ETC	W 39507	2763830		3681988	W 47391	4390254	W 51560	3873142	LAMPES,TUBES,VALVES
7764	ELECTRONIC MICROCIRCUITS	W 2286	2109128		2940364	W 3084	3441798	W 3171	2906277	MICROSTRUCTURES ELECTRON
778	ELECTRICAL MACHINERY NES	W 141969	1693587		2100985	W 190906	2579264	W 183703	2371581	AUTRES MACH ELECT NDA
7788	OTH ELEC MACHY,EQUIP NES	W 30578	665634		838663	W 40649	1070614	W 42471	928624	AUT MACH APP ELEC NDA
78	ROAD VEHICLES		13572531		14908865		18825463		20389128	VEHICULES ROUTIERS
781	PASS MOTOR VEH EXC BUSES	W 1086385	9977561	W 1178456	10728267	W 1317465	13299202	W 1312307	14431228	AUTO TRANSPORT PERSONNES
782	LORRIES,SPCL MTR VEH NES	W 120292	820712	W 157718	1081844	W 190663	1456681	W 209492	1744687	VEHICULES SPECIAUX,MARCH
7821	LORRIES,TRUCKS	W 115726	778202	W 152524	1035137	W 185610	1405848	W 199992	1647747	VEHICULES TRANSP MARCHAND
783	ROAD MOTOR VEHICLES NES	W 25800	233914	W 34993	322831	W 67739	666289	W 69287	749660	VEHICULES ROUTIERS NDA
784	MOTOR VEH PRTS,ACCES NES	W 209399	1750589	W 231735	1994892	W 287162	2491730	W 315117	2530141	PIECES 722,781,782,783
7849	OTHER MOTOR VEHCL PARTS	W 206266	1717078	W 228342	1963073	W 282124	2433461	W 310796	2473517	PIECES 722,781,782,783
785	CYCLES,ETC MOTRZD OR NOT	W 48863	698987	W 49251	676265	W 53812	772821	W 52667	776039	MOTOCYCLES SCOOTERS
79	OTHR TRANSPORT EQUIPMENT		2272959		2125598		1906085		1967259	AUTRE MATERIEL TRANSPORT
792	AIRCRAFT ETC	W 4933	1863483		1974120	W 4286	1673450	W 4017	1546348	APP NAVIGATION AERIENNE
7924	AIRCRFT NES OVER 15000KG	W 2858	960979	W 3742	1275315	W 2531	843180	W 2438	847314	AERODYNES PLUS 15000 KG
7929	AIRCRAFT PARTS NES	W 1499	484614		443052	W 1339	615516	W 1279	524257	PIECES DU 792
8	MISC MANUFACTURED GOODS		14286368		15661865		18335527		19416868	ART MANUFACTURES DIVERS
821	*FURNITURE,PARTS THEREOF	W 127896	537306	W 141070	582299	W 157231	698845	W 169400	739816	MEUBLES ET PIECES
84	CLOTHING AND ACCESSORIES		3587727		3972851		4658994		4999002	VETEMENTS
842	MENS OUTERWEAR NOT KNIT	W 43697	964074	W 54907	1126090	W 55934	1240939	W 56664	1363067	VET DESSUS POUR HOMMES
843	WOMENS OUTERWEAR NONKNIT	W 23826	753946		813914	W 31579	936390	W 32909	999569	VET DESSUS FEMMES MAT TEX
845	OUTERWEAR KNIT NONELASTC	W 28478	638520	W 33236	692668	W 35895	798910	W 39594	935684	VET DESSOUS,ACCES BONNET
846	UNDER GARMENTS KNITTED	W 26615	502051		508333	W 36081	652256	W 35195	669179	SOUS VETS DE BONNETERIE
851	*FOOTWEAR	W 62887	773090	W 82648	987528	W 85472	1111011	W 84398	1187064	CHAUSSURES
85102	FOOTWEAR LEATHER	W 49872	667439	W 66624	853086	W 67456	935291	W 63687	979090	CHAUS SEMELLES EN CUIR
87	PRECISION INSTRUMNTS NES		2643982		2882690		3440049		3630901	INSTRUM,APPAR SCIENT NDA
872	MEDICAL INSTRUMENTS NES	W 12661	687393		719491	W 15922	806547	W 16498	910264	INSTR,APP MEDIC–CHIR NDA
87202	OTH MEDICAL INSTRUMENTS	W 11392	628788		664268	W 14356	744573	W 15000	835588	INSTRUM,APP MEDECINE
874	MEASURNG,CONTROLNG INSTR	W 17714	1768760		1942574	W 23111	2327390	W 23714	2426706	INSTRUMENTS DE MESURE
8742	MEASUR,DRAW ETC INST,PTS	W 5494	518524		571756	W 6944	717205	W 6840	717161	INST DESSIN,TRACAGE,PCS
8748	ELEC MEAS,CONTRL EQU NES	W 2484	434165		470448	W 2859	568751	W 3541	629603	APP ELEC ELECTRO MESURE
88	PHOTO EQU,OPTICL GDS ETC		1854218		1943752		2146411		2167433	APP,FOURN PHOTO,OP,MONTR
882	PHOTO,CINEMA SUPPLIES	W 53615	661497		698949	W 61124	745907	W 56092	787905	PRODUITS PHOTO,CINEMA
8822	PHOTO FILM EXC DEV CINMA	W 34155	522906		525595	W 41277	567849	W 36757	607861	PLAQUES,PELLICULES,FILMS
885	WATCHES AND CLOCKS		745941		769629		845451		781067	HORLOGERIE
8851	WATCHES,MOVEMENTS,CASES		617439		633783		691920		637966	MONTRES,MOUVEMENTS,BOITES
88511	WATCHES		567879		588680		643062		595702	MONTRES POCHE,BRACELET
89	MISC MANUFCTRD GOODS NES		4239494		4556264		5431554		5772727	ART MANUFACTURES DIVERS
893	ARTICLES OF PLASTIC NES		1032825		1170031		1409171		1410610	OUVRAGES EN MAT DIVIS 58
8939	MISC PLASTIC ARTICLES	W 130322	751715	W 151610	839608	W 156845	1004814	W 154692	1013307	ART DIVERS EN MAT DIV 58
89399	OTHR PLASTC ARTICLES NES	W 108243	692649	W 127076	774907	W 133068	930389	W 131129	935410	AUT OUV MAT DIV 58
894	TOYS,SPORTING GOODS,ETC	W 108875	1026540	W 122620	1027447	W 133135	1157608	W 134879	1290355	VOITURES ENFANTS,JOUETS
8942	TOYS,INDOOR GAMES ETC	W 89577	792696	W 96430	747835	W 102410	813129	W 100015	892311	JOUETS,JEUX ETC
89423	TOYS NES	W 57707	447921	W 61817	431027	W 61298	431291	W 58369	423519	JOUETS,MODELES REDUITS
898	MUSICAL INSTRUMENTS,PTS	W 38423	687985		725227	W 43377	975357	W 43807	1063000	INSTRUMENTS DE MUSIQUE
8983	SOUND RECRDNG TAPE,DISCS	W 33191	591834		625157	W 37198	863311	W 37991	953303	SUPPORTS SON POUR 763
89832	RECORDED DISCS,TAPES ETC	W 9521	324970		361829	W 14699	596986	W 14935	672365	DISQUES,PHONO,BANDES
899	OTHER MANUFACTURED GOODS		586861		655168		738148		793190	AUT ART MANUF DIVERS NDA
9	GOODS NOT CLASSD BY KIND		8312381		8475881		9507416		9823074	ART TRANSACT NON CLASSES
931	*SPECIAL TRANSACTIONS	MW 23744	4391806	MW 21947	4256127	MW 25860	5123066	MW 27625	5685722	TRANS.SPECIALES
971	*GOLD,NON MONETARY NES	K 355264	3862685		4173449	K 352873	4317692	K 336070	4057083	OR NON MONETAIRE
97101	NONMON GLD UNWRT,SEMIMFD	K 351703	3860729		4170504	K 346071	4313866	K 331746	4054993	OR,ALLIAGES D'OR BRUTS

5. Special Exports F.O.B. by Commodities according to the S.I.T.C. (Rev. 2) in thousand U.S. Dollars
Exportations Spéciales F.O.B. par Produits d'après la C.T.C.I. (Rév. 2) en milliers de Dollars E.U.

SITC CTCI	COMMODITY	1993 WEIGHT POIDS	1993 VALUE VALEUR	1994 WEIGHT POIDS	1994 VALUE VALEUR	1995 WEIGHT POIDS	1995 VALUE VALEUR	1996 WEIGHT POIDS	1996 VALUE VALEUR	PRODUIT
	ALL COMMODITIES		168511226		190004650		231346424		250830252	TOUS PRODUITS
0	FOOD AND LIVE ANIMALS		8940977		9691744		11226253		11995105	ALIMENTS,ANIMAUX VIVANTS
01	MEAT AND PREPARATIONS		811041		833883		919139		1090314	VIANDES ET PREPARATIONS
02	DAIRY PRODCTS,BIRDS'EGGS		680769		742292		864956		945396	PRODUITS LAITIERS,OEUFS
024	CHEESE AND CURD	W 110767	589702	W 113954	644572	W 121096	762492	W 136015	845626	FROMAGE ET CAILLEBOTTE
04	CEREALS AND PREPARATIONS		2066177		2229276		2445712		2834607	CEREALES ET PRODUITS
048	CEREAL ETC PREPARATIONS	W 1105445	1279026	W 1169697	1429514	W 1272460	1737263	W 1457863	1998483	PREPTNS A BASE CEREALES
0483	MACARONI,SPAGHETTI ETC	W 964949	825871	W 996570	876405	W 1064197	1012724	W 1234537	1204404	PATES ALMENTAIRES
0484	BAKERY PRODUCTS	W 121613	413442	W 149362	506794	W 183762	675313	W 202515	755033	PRODUITS DE BOULANGERIE
05	VEGETABLES AND FRUIT		3746889		4195439		4835721		4828177	LEGUMES ET FRUITS
054	VEG ETC FRSH,SMPLY PRSVD	W 2018627	1332202		1394988	W 2348943	1730844	W 2218528	1692831	LEGUMES FRAIS,CONG,SECS
0546	VEGETABLES SIMPLY PRESVD	W 1112871	702896	W 1040265	688668	W 1110305	804356	W 1072453	796196	LEGUMES CONG,CONSER
05461	VEGETABLES FROZEN	W 1108660	697680	W 1036301	684102	W 1107287	800180	W 1070224	791378	LEGUMES CONGELES
057	FRUIT,NUTS,FRESH,DRIED	W 2391700	1702206	W 2634500	2026296	W 2385570	2132181	W 2518425	2081559	FRUITS FRAIS OU SECS
0579	FRUIT FRESH OR DRIED NES	W 1018705	825961	W 1213725	996065	W 992927	1019324	W 1154546	978616	FRUITS FRAIS,SECS NDA
058	FRUIT PRESERVED,PREPARED	W 593402	572638	W 639907	614958	W 668997	774314	W 670801	829938	CONSERVES DE FRUITS
07	COFFEE,TEA,COCOA,SPICES		521550		558101		789029		829618	CAFE,THE,CACAO,EPICES
1	BEVERAGES AND TOBACCO		2062401		2449007		2935755		3135007	BOISSONS ET TABACS
11	BEVERAGES		1884927		2286811		2739662		2875135	BOISSONS
112	ALCOHOLIC BEVERAGES	W 1608041	1789559	W 2055891	2156880	W 2175674	2598448	W 1761557	2733920	BOISSONS ALCOOLIQUES
1121	WINE OF FRESH GRAPES ETC	W 1461768	1477492	W 1890729	1808551	W 1970602	2184159	W 1586523	2360987	VINS DE RAISINS FRAIS
11212	WINE OF FRESH GRAPES	W 1292498	1310747	W 1698313	1635649	W 1762699	1973841	W 1391274	2128692	VINS DE MOUTS DE RAISINS
2	CRUDE MATERLS,EXCL FUELS		1558176		1810298		2267335		2323558	MAT BRUTES NON COMESTIBLES
3	MINERAL FUELS ETC		3697043		3052098		2932597		3146336	COMBUSTIBLES MINERAUX LUB
33	PETROLEUM AND PRODUCTS		3616134		2981111		2851679		3076184	PETROLE ET DERIVES
334	PETROLEUM PRODUCTS,REFIN		3511312	MW 19477	2872043	MW 17156	2755193	MW 15894	2967339	PRODUITS RAFFINES
3341	GASOLINE,OTH LIGHT OILS		1090626			W 3708276	649022	W 3393310	678262	ESSENCES POUR MOTEURS
33411	MOTOR,AVIATION SPIRIT	W 3398345	610194			W 2892669	500937	W 2810850	562391	ESSENCES MOTEURS D'AVIONS
3343	GAS OILS	W 7248302	1188053			W 7092280	1085868	W 7137241	1345153	GAS OILS
4	ANIMAL,VEGETABLE OIL,FAT		577560		643682		973313		1195793	HUILES,GRAISSES ANIM,VEG
42	FIXED VEGETABLE OIL,FAT		503501		554271		851056		1060639	HUILES VEGETALES FIXES
423	FIXED VEG OILS,SOFT	W 250913	445410	W 251076	499403	W 272177	775598	W 241720	974810	HUILES VEGET DOUCES FIXES
4235	OLIVE OIL	W 158674	383398	W 157358	424419	W 187607	706449	W 173314	921034	HUILE D'OLIVE
5	CHEMCLS,RELATED PROD NES		11817427		13649490		17430845		18649787	PRODUITS CHIMIQUES
51	ORGANIC CHEMICALS		2406713		2637951		3340162		3406199	PROD CHIMIQ ORGANIQUES
514	NITROGEN–FNCTN COMPOUNDS	W 145668	954664		1043376	W 175101	1204118	W 193064	1311913	COMPOSES FONCT AZOTEES
53	DYES,TANNING,COLOUR PROD		762423		897036		1136366		1291811	PROD TEINTURE,COLORANTS
533	PIGMENTS,PAINTS,ETC	W 279435	543839		642841	W 399891	845418	W 452577	961795	PIGMENTS,PEINTURES,VERNIS
541	*MEDICINAL,PHARM PRODUCT	MK 53739	2491494		2759299	MK 80770	3629990	MK 78040	4281314	PROD MEDICINAUX PHARMACEUT
5413	ANTIBIOTICS IN BULK	K 4652989	757989		792203	K 6096858	993134	K 6036585	1057063	ANTIBIOTIQUES NDA
54139	OTHER ANTIBIOTICS	K 2580665	588835	K 2440721	640194	K 3198343	789032	K 3289367	858868	AUTRES ANTIBIOTIQUES
5417	MEDICAMENTS	MK 41027	1358235	MK 48472	1549580	MK 66033	2171082	MK 63427	2709986	MEDICAMENTS
54171	— CONTAINNG ANTIBIOTICS	K 8054697	525023	K 6763074	523660	K 7820028	679080	K 6932777	836387	MED CONTN ANTIBIOTIQUES
54179	— CONTNG OTH SUBSTANCES	MK 30481	761316	MK 38947	935012	MK 55049	1373561	MK 51945	1689014	MED CONT AUT SUBSTANCES
55	PERFUME,CLEANING ETC PRD		965226		1233745		1505296		1783918	PROD POUR PARFUM,TOILETTE
553	PERFUMERY,COSMETICS,ETC	W 68963	501504	W 93182	643283	W 112601	848568	W 132972	1003978	PRODUITS DE PARFUMERIE
58	PLASTIC MATERIALS ETC		3222423		3915930		5271944		5093878	MAT PLAST ARTIFICIELLES
582	PROD OF CONDENSATION ETC	W 599857	879478	W 700741	1071729	W 766273	1519213	W 794023	1463100	PROD CONDENS,POLYCOND
583	POLYMERIZATION ETC PRODS	W 1588307	2233369	W 1845227	2746608	W 1848832	3633365	W 2030742	3502196	PROD POLYMERISATION
5831	POLYETHYLENE	W 485702	395547	W 544271	491951	W 548678	721445	W 561451	637658	POLYETHYLENE
5834	POLYVINYL CHLORIDE	W 351300	469869	W 409979	585756	W 376799	725081	W 413777	676957	CHLORURE DE POLYVINYLE
5839	OTH POLYMRZTION ETC PROD	W 316246	713200	W 382517	882405	W 384994	1100814	W 453552	1161193	AUT PROD POLYMER COPOLYM
59	CHEMICAL MATERIALS NES		1513777		1738240		1965624		2152913	MAT PROD CHIMIQUES NDA
598	MISCEL CHEM PRODUCTS NES	W 774817	1198833	W 818935	1339956	W 664427	1495037	W 672751	1594069	PROD DIV INDUST CHIM NDA
5989	CHEM PRODUCTS,PREPS NES	W 635743	1013892	W 644330	1110951	W 480413	1227570	W 481883	1316881	PROD PREP CHIMIQUES NDA
59899	OTH CHEM PRODS,PREPS,NES	W 472890	791116	W 522366	869612	W 399056	920806	W 386699	970677	AUT PRODUITS CHIMIQUES NDA
6	BASIC MANUFACTURES		37691746		43399564		52881452		54582448	ART MANUFACTURES
61	LEATHER,DRESSED FUR,ETC		2747318		3446201		3989774		4523218	CUIRS,PELLETERIES
611	LEATHER	W 141370	2107575	W 174322	2661775	W 192076	3065967	W 222921	3416914	CUIRS,PEAUX PREPARES
6114	LEATHR BOVINE NES,EQUINE	W 95708	1278858	W 123360	1595747	W 143704	1930969	W 163765	2139557	CUIRS DE BOVINS
612	LEATHER ETC MANUFACTURES	W 72259	597388	W 87998	731362	W 93806	849092	W 106290	948950	OUVRAGES EN CUIRS NDA
6123	PREPRD PARTS OF FOOTWEAR	W 70899	554301	W 86559	682933	W 92304	794670	W 104765	891815	PARTIES DE CHAUSSURES
62	RUBBER MANUFACTURES NES		1745749		1992107		2447811		2633461	CAOUTCHOUC MANUFACTURE
625	RUBBER TYRES, TUBES ETC	W 206693	863099	W 234892	988030	W 270347	1202564	W 273384	1219915	PNEUS CAOUTCHOUC VULCANISE
6251	TYRES NEW FOR MOTOR CARS	W 111220	522976	W 131649	630852	W 141937	733934	W 136525	711621	PNEUS POUR VOITURES
63	WOOD,CORK MANUFACTRS NES		666622		804657		951073		999218	OUVRAGES LIEGE ET BOIS
64	PAPER,PAPERBOARD AND MFR		2454046		2817363		3906324		3972136	PAPIERS,CARTONS & OUVRAGES
641	PAPER AND PAPERBOARD	W 1710235	1586135		1815031	W 1964908	2543302	W 2057137	2379501	PAPIERS ET CARTONS
6412	PRINTG,WRITING PAPER NES	W 633548	569965	W 730514	674794	W 755402	936356	W 763625	804265	PAPIERS POUR L'IMPRESSION
64122	— COATED,IMPREGNATD ETC	W 628732	558794	W 724701	661010	W 746737	914207	W 745428	772677	PAPIERS IMPRESSION COUCHES
6418	COATED ETC PAPER NES BLK	W 431436	482062	W 456875	523012	W 465181	744076	W 497979	762344	PAP,CARTONS COUCHES,ENDUITS
642	PAPER,ETC,PRECUT,ARTS OF	W 482682	867912		1002332	W 603168	1363023	W 708839	1592634	PAP,CARTONS DECOUPES
65	TEXTILE YARN,FABRICS,ETC		9481211		10874800		12809166		13185246	FILS,TISSUS,ARTICLES TEXTILE
651	TEXTILE YARN	W 359878	2008129	W 367546	2222872	W 394832	2602014	W 436910	2731923	FILS TEXTILES
6514	SYN FIB YRN,BULK,MONOFIL	W 152640	628758	W 158074	665723	W 168286	803805	W 171606	807356	FILS CONT 85% FIB TEXT SYNTH
652	COTTON FABRICS,WOVEN	W 90519	1044161		1278420	W 115939	1591178	W 118966	1709186	TISSUS DE COTON
6522	WOVEN COTTON BLEACHD,ETC	W 78313	941145		1160012	W 106534	1476118	W 110695	1596447	TISSUS COTON BLANCHIS ETC
65224	BLCHED COTTON FABRIC NES	W 60657	687224		820432	W 82491	1058413	W 86082	1179374	AUT TIS PLUS 85% COT BLANCHI
653	WOVN MAN–MADE FIB FABRIC	W 122800	1962107		2260590	W 131268	2643298	W 130350	2535274	TISSUS FIBRES SYNTH,ARTIF
6531	CONT SYNT WEAVES NONPILE	W 31093	523313	W 33705	583714	W 35339	659822	W 34713	634802	TISSUS FIBRES SYNTH CONTINUE
6534	DISC SYN BLEND FABRC NES	W 48287	534714		571679	W 39443	555287	W 40557	564777	TISSUS FIBRES SYNTH DISCONT
654	OTH WOVEN TEXTILE FABRIC	W 92836	2467694	W 93191	2775257	W 94105	3072144	W 92045	2999025	TISSUS AUT COTON SYNT,ARTIF
6542	WOVEN WOOL,HAIR NONPILE	W 30640	924122	W 29642	1140559	W 29151	1305958	W 32594	1375025	TIS PLUS 85% LAINE,POILS
65422	WOVN COMB WOOL,FINE HAIR	W 22818	689131	W 20213	833582	W 19856	971924	W 22009	1020236	TISSUS 85% LAINE,PLS PEIG
6543	WOVEN WOOL ETC FABRC NES	W 44586	796675	W 42632	767742	W 44836	921596	W 45701	924421	TISSUS LAINE,POILS FINS NDA
65432	WOOL–DISC SYN FIBR FABRC	W 40470	677537	W 38911	643513	W 39696	747636	W 41840	786581	TISSUS LAINE MEL SYNT DISC
655	KNITTED,ETC FABRICS	W 38778	571556	W 43526	652544	W 45735	763845	W 49358	853435	ETOF BONNETERIE PIECES ETC
6552	OTHER KNIT ETC FAB NONEL	W 38778	571556	W 43526	652544	W 45735	763845	W 49358	853435	ETOF BON NON ELAS NON SYNT
657	SPECIAL TXTL FABRC,PRODS	W 147081	930961	W 167040	1074950	W 189582	1362659	W 207720	1497575	TISSUS SPECIAUX
66	NONMETAL MINERAL MFS NES		6455721		7485930		8744575		8974538	ART MIN NON METALLIQUES
661	LIME,CEMENT,BLDG PRODS	W 2872540	1693103	W 3512502	1910711	W 4315553	2201275	W 4697436	2329629	CHAUX,CIMENTS MAT CONSTR
6613	BUILDING STONE ETC WORKD	W 2295369	1526233	W 2522787	1709230	W 2629778	1923969	W 2638436	2017328	PIERRES A BATIR
66132	BUILDING STONE WORKED	W 2030773	1447444	W 2224988	1601333	W 2360250	1821161	W 2383685	1929493	OUVR EN PIERRES DE TAILLE
662	CLAY,REFRACTORY BLDG PRD	W 4717539	2694108	W 5477135	3130967	W 5997553	3562958	W 6090648	3625413	MAT CONST REFRACTAIRES
6624	BRICKS ETC NONREFRACTORY	W 4572231	2582246	W 5325927	3006963	W 5812348	3399368	W 5892608	3442413	BRIQUES ETC CERAM NON REFR
66245	GLAZED CERAMIC SETTS ETC	W 3959919	2274096	W 4556106	2629378	W 4730920	2874276	W 4544459	2778921	AUT CARREAUX CERAMIQUE
663	MINERAL MANUFCTURES NES	W 498544	494924	W 700675	623239	W 857577	776663	W 966829	860020	ART MIN MANUF NDA
664	GLASS	W 476476	649123	W 450783	739088	W 416831	901586	W 389233	780663	VERRE
665	GLASSWARE	W 450408	597814	W 473250	691503	W 548202	836697	W 527953	897470	OUVRAGES EN VERRE
67	IRON AND STEEL		6207424		6753906		8496266		8010781	FER ET ACIER
672	IRON,STEEL PRIMARY FORMS	W 2855191	855307	W 1774286	662406	W 1798823	943131	W 2552611	1029033	LINGOTS FER,ACIER

5. Special Exports F.O.B. by Commodities according to the S.I.T.C. (Rev. 2) in thousand U.S. Dollars
Exportations Spéciales F.O.B. par Produits d'après la C.T.C.I. (Rév. 2) en milliers de Dollars E.U.

SITC CTCI	COMMODITY	1993 WEIGHT POIDS	1993 VALUE VALEUR	1994 WEIGHT POIDS	1994 VALUE VALEUR	1995 WEIGHT POIDS	1995 VALUE VALEUR	1996 WEIGHT POIDS	1996 VALUE VALEUR	PRODUIT
6727	IRN,STL COIL FR REROLLNG	W 1470657	500351	W 1140022	438263	W 973444	577368	W 1895587	785421	EBAUCHES POUR TOLES FER
673	IRON,STEEL SHAPES ETC	W 4593122	1743689	W 4093247	1816087	W 3711660	2209350	W 3714904	1882023	BARRES,PROFIL FER,ACIER
6732	IRON,STEEL BARS ETC	W 2995215	1108334	W 2606144	1148105	W 2333076	1412150	W 2181108	1153913	BARRES FER,ACIER
67326	IRN,OTH STL BARS HOTROLD	W 2522864	744916	W 2048965	660658	W 1719037	670035	W 1630859	532991	BARRES PLEINES FER,ACIER
674	IRN,STL UNIV,PLATE,SHEET	W 2175252	1271420	W 2420597	1553150	W 2167343	1904086	W 1996158	1605437	LARGES PLATS,TOLES
6746	IRN,STL THIN PLATE,ROLLD	W 593288	412423	W 715277	512155	W 682898	748661	W 646769	572351	TOLES LAM MOINS 3MM
678	IRON,STL TUBES,PIPES,ETC	W 1832378	1779363	W 2073844	2091127	W 1962837	2631641	W 2204083	2770288	TUBES,TUYAUX EN FONTE,FER
6783	IRON,STL TUBES,PIPES NES	W 1152203	836833	W 1368576	1056320	W 1228267	1327487	W 1444424	1292894	AUT TUBES,TUYAUX FER,ACIER
68	NON–FERROUS METALS		1519749		1928267		2536951		2449019	METAUX NON FERREUX
682	COPPER EXC CEMENT COPPER	W 185378	600283	W 245575	857018	W 235634	978615	W 239142	893580	CUIVRE
6822	COPPER,ALLOYS WORKED	W 175670	579048	W 229592	816036	W 212865	912339	W 220125	845249	CUIVRE,ALLIAGES OUVRES
684	ALUMINIUM	W 286918	789055	W 298863	910690	W 328406	1329317	W 340223	1265074	ALUMINIUM
6842	ALUMINIUM,ALLOYS WORKED	W 252551	745522	W 274072	872254	W 291776	1254013	W 300861	1200900	ALUMINIUM,ALLIAGES OUVRE
69	METAL MANUFACTURES NES		6413905		7296334		8999512		9834832	ART MANUFACT EN METAL NDA
691	STRUCTURES AND PARTS NES	W 305097	693225	W 361420	744794	W 443462	1012940	W 401945	1060407	CONSTRUCT FER,ACIER,ALU
6911	STRUCTURES,PARTS IRN,STL	W 280631	521885	W 333488	558021	W 405488	731157	W 365801	769385	CONSTRUCT FER,ACIER,FONTE
694	STL,COPPR NAILS,NUTS,ETC	W 299642	515304	W 248556	599793	W 263500	765003	W 233599	714679	CLOUS,VIS,ECROUS
69402	IRN,STL NUTS,BOLTS,ETC	W 285369	480722	W 233712	563187	W 248072	721285	W 217554	666209	BOULONS,VIS,ECROUS FER,AC
695	TOOLS	W 81284	564053	W 96350	637307	W 122764	886188	W 115675	972942	OUTILS A MAIN
697	BASE MTL HOUSEHOLD EQUIP	W 213885	1142897	W 243414	1313453	W 256847	1503172	W 267780	1719705	ART MENAGE MET COMMUNS
6974	BASE MTL DMSTC ARTIC NES	W 82812	488837	W 99197	581388	W 105672	685742	W 115826	809235	ARTICLES NDA FONTE,FER,ETC
699	BASE METAL MFRS NES	W 621466	2650076		3092028	W 798042	3743035	W 849226	4174296	ART MANUFACTURES MET NDA
6991	LOCKSMITHS WARES,ETC	W 139521	888460	W 168942	1018329	W 183485	1221834	W 197257	1385947	ARTICLES DE SERRURERIE
69913	BASE MTL DOOR,ETC FITTNG	W 115725	672752	W 142377	783696	W 153561	939393	W 165523	1074843	GARNITURES POUR MEUBLES
6997	IRON,STEEL ARTICLES NES	W 241865	661407	W 280339	747759	W 306312	907492	W 312057	984617	OUV FONTE,FER,ACIER NDA
69979	IRN,STL MANUFACTURES NES	W 241551	660650	W 280092	747051	W 306035	906413	W 311636	982868	AUT OUVRAGES EN FER NDA
6998	MFRS NES OF CPR,NIKL,ETC	W 94357	504410	W 111648	613798	W 116402	754013	W 128143	823440	OUVRAGES EN CU,NI,AL,PB,ZN
7	MACHINES,TRANSPORT EQUIP		61763109		69730633		86706221		96042995	MACHINES MATERIEL TRANSPORT
71	POWER GENERATING EQUIPMT		3330164		3613845		4616720		5327406	MACHINES GENERATRICES
713	INTRNL COMBUS PSTN ENGIN	W 114876	1337151	W 144599	1602597	W 186508	2101642	W 169386	2057161	MOTEURS EXPL COMB INT, PIECE
7132	MOTOR VEHCL PISTN ENGINS	W 42838	478153	W 54464	609316	W 77540	905102	W 56066	714938	MOTEURS EXPL POUR VEHICULES
7139	PISTON ENGINE PARTS NES	W 53547	652093	W 66520	728259	W 82426	880200	W 83911	972955	PIECES POUR 713.2,3,8
714	ENGINES AND MOTORS NES	W 14446	810263		853301	W 18089	1025951	W 28014	1502098	MOTEURS NON ELECTRIQUES
7149	ENGINE & MOTOR PARTS NES	W 10072	506723		466591	W 13804	604354	W 22083	1014830	PIECES 714 ET 718.88
716	ROTATING ELECTRIC PLANT	W 102326	791461	W 122220	905569	W 138325	1100098	W 161650	1291822	APP ELECTR ROTATIFS,PIECES
7162	AC MTRS,GENRTRS,GEN SETS	W 73617	560409	W 90366	683009	W 100052	815873	W 114693	986226	MOTEURS ELECTRIQUES
72	MACHS FOR SPCL INDUSTRYS		12167458		13353756		16140481		17935774	MAC SPECIALES POUR INDUST
721	AGRIC MACHY,EXC TRACTORS	W 146947	762805		910112	W 202201	1097038	W 210674	1290607	MACHINES AGRICOLES
722	TRACTORS NON–ROAD	W 111635	668770	W 123448	725100	W 151171	974163	W 171787	1215811	TRACTEURS
7224	WHEELED TRACTORS NES	W 110112	661922	W 120958	714693	W 148593	963017	W 168415	1198840	TRACTEURS A ROUES
723	CIVIL ENGNEERG EQUIP ETC	W 140065	685301	W 179885	809831	W 197669	987793	W 196284	1076029	APPAREILS DE GENIE CIVIL
7234	CONST,MINING MACHNRY NES	W 118810	571438	W 153064	698905	W 171264	865424	W 165857	930927	MACH POUR LA CONST, MINES
724	TEXTILE,LEATHER MACHNRY	W 189146	2546449	W 185540	2522174	W 206736	2964843	W 222245	3393652	MACH POUR INDUSTRIE TEXTILE
7244	SPINNING,EXTRDNG,ETC MCH	W 42311	650179	W 42401	573877	W 47739	713691	W 47762	750576	MACH POUR LE FILAGE
7245	WEAVING,FELT MFG,ETC MCH	W 53335	702864	W 43841	649324	W 53302	805893	W 63132	1052561	METIERS A TISSER,PIECES
7247	TEXTILE MACHINERY NES	W 47959	553586	W 50603	606173	W 54472	693059	W 57792	748645	MACH LAVAGE,TEINTURE TEX
726	PRINTG,BKBINDG MACHY,PTS	W 29015	531183	W 34641	604933	W 38117	718468	W 41670	844297	MACHINES POUR IMPRIMERIE
727	FOOD MACHRY NON–DOMESTIC	W 45202	779663	W 49151	855139	W 54559	969882	W 57604	1043005	MACH INDUSTRIES ALIMENT
7272	OTH FOOD PROC MCHY,PARTS	W 38809	703992	W 41945	775305	W 44328	855226	W 46929	931130	AUT MACH IND ALIMENTAIRE
72722	INDUS FOOD PROC MACH NES	W 35627	657460	W 36707	701304	W 41484	818825	W 43649	883906	MACHINES BOULANGERIE
728	OTH MACHY FOR SPCL INDUS	W 498027	5737252	W 551993	6445730	W 644180	7799665	W 627614	8327888	AUT MACH IND PARTICULIERES
7281	MACH–TOOLS FR SPCL INDUS	W 168872	1560648	W 175526	1779173	W 193991	2060540	W 184302	2087567	MACH–OUTILS SPEC IND PART
72811	MACH–TOOLS TO WRK MINRLS	W 82815	588905	W 73561	621249	W 79203	684590	W 77588	720617	MACH POUR TRAVAIL PIERRE
72812	MACH–TOOLS TO WORK WOOD	W 72737	795347	W 88861	967085	W 100788	1174125	W 89310	1100965	MACH–OUT POUR TRAVAIL BOIS
7283	OTHR MINERAL WORKG MACHY	W 85489	647975	W 92876	619796	W 106857	728856	W 103098	799149	MACH TRIER,CRIBLER,BROYER
7284	MACHY FOR SPCL INDUS NES	W 243666	3528629	W 283591	4046760	W 343332	5010269	W 340214	5441172	MACH SPEC IND PARTICUL.
72842	RUBBER,PLASTICS WRKG MCH	W 53162	768066	W 59225	930996	W 70483	1085605	W 82417	1356613	MACH IND CAOUT MAT PLAST
72848	OTH MCHY WITH INDIV FNCT	W 115365	1475336	W 140698	1662991	W 169334	2176581	W 135181	2023339	AUTRES MACHINES NDA
72849	PTS OF MACHS OF 7284 ETC	W 59947	1028263	W 67543	1144878	W 80943	1342709	W 98503	1585256	PIECES DU 728.4 ETC
73	METALWORKING MACHINERY		2342795		2446313		3212208		3889812	MACH TRAVAIL DES METAUX
736	METALWORKING MACH–TOOLS	W 120814	1689098	W 124471	1689205	W 148102	2169562	W 171803	2638630	MACH–OUTILS TRAVAIL METAUX
7361	METAL CUTTING MACH–TOOLS	W 34886	520706	W 36494	517430	W 42870	713316	W 45307	809588	MACH–OUT ENLEVEMENT METAL
737	METALWORKING MACHNRY NES	W 69967	653698	W 85164	757108	W 111178	1042646	W 122429	1251183	MACH TRAV METAUX PIECES
74	GENRL INDUSTRL MACHY NES		13336252		15049900		18659055		21978116	MACH APP INDUSTRIE
741	HEATING,COOLING EQUIPMNT	W 313664	2843533	W 351213	3089095	W 417490	3980499	W 468383	4757296	MACH CHAUFFAGE,PIECES
7414	NONDOM REFRIG EQUIPT,PTS	W 95538	734964	W 113050	850546	W 135354	1106549	W 137890	1252592	MAT PRODUCTION DU FROID
74141	REFRIG EQUIP NONDOMESTIC	W 58194	527410	W 67429	608986	W 87953	807347	W 90104	928644	REFIG INDUSTRIELS
7415	AIR–CONDITIONING MACHNRY	W 29705	372486	W 34653	436155	W 46972	667927	W 57980	847902	GROUPES CONDITION AIR
7416	HEATING,COOLING EQU NES	W 111448	1118581	W 121056	1161615	W 136776	1420331	W 153227	1689258	APP CHANGEMENT TEMP
742	PUMPS FOR LIQUIDS ETC	W 97189	998730	W 109039	1118759	W 127953	1374051	W 134881	1568712	POMPES MOTO–POMPES
7428	OTHER PUMPS FOR LIQUIDS	W 68365	643841	W 73217	692888	W 87190	841789	W 90853	932289	AUTRES POMPES POUR LIQ
74288	PUMPS FR LIQUIDS NES ETC	W 67985	639614	W 72676	686088	W 86265	828166	W 89192	902553	POMPES POUR LIQUIDES NDA
743	PUMPS NES,CENTRFUGES ETC	W 248709	1871908	W 286827	2077883	W 335563	2597773	W 371487	3040562	POMPES COMPRES,VENT ETC
7431	PUMPS FOR GASES ETC	W 108384	660714	W 129271	812166	W 147607	975927	W 157926	1099467	POMPES AIR A VIDE,COMPRES
744	MECHANICAL HANDLING EQU	W 238156	1312480	W 301326	1604275	W 379664	2127671	W 383774	2409473	EQUIP MANUTENTION PIECES
7442	LIFTING,LOADING MACH NES	W 102114	655672	W 134635	798043	W 167519	1040893	W 168150	1181264	APP LEVAGE,MANUTENTION
7449	PTS NES OF MACHY OF 7442	W 105604	479891	W 129337	588735	W 160402	774946	W 164125	900433	PIECES DU 744.2
745	NONELEC MACHY,TOOLS NES	W 115784	2423736		2785722	W 163867	3378732	W 192048	4079570	AUT MACH NON ELEC,PIECES
7452	OTH NONELEC MCHS,PTS NES	W 109297	2299065		2636251	W 154807	3209414	W 183538	3896936	AUT MACH NON ELEC,PIECES
74522	PACKAGNG,BOTTLNG,ETC MCH	W 43520	1453528		1652607	W 55949	1925263	W 65022	2273367	MACH NETT BOUTEILLES,ETC
74527	SPRAYING MACHINERY	W 42196	368703	W 53201	464558	W 68675	618368	W 84122	803678	APP PROJETER ETC LIQUID
749	NONELEC MACH PTS,ACC NES	W 334969	3885864		4374167	W 425253	5200330	W 471448	6122504	PIECES MACH NON ELEC NDA
7491	BALL,ROLLER,ETC BEARINGS	W 36158	426486	W 48539	511929	W 60157	765469	W 61714	787983	ROULEMENTS BILLES ETC
7492	COCKS,VALVES ETC NES	W 197859	2174767	W 217783	2411000	W 233944	2704027	W 263405	3185760	ART ROB,SIM POUR TUYAUX
7493	SHAFT,CRANK,PULLEY ETC	W 66767	610488		688320	W 94291	861719	W 99700	994800	ARBRES TRANS,VILEBREQUINS
7499	OTH NONELEC MCHY PTS NES	W 34185	674124		762917	W 36861	869114	W 46629	1153962	PIECES NON ELECT NDA
74991	FOUNDRY MOULDS ETC NES	W 17502	396141	W 20797	459717	W 21756	559784	W 31063	829510	MOULES POUR METAUX
75	OFFICE MACHNES,ADP EQUIP		4174935		4365258		5285895		4783114	MACH BUREAU TRAIT AUTOM
752	AUTOMTIC DATA PROC EQUIP	W 29366	2087385		2169741	W 31491	2312965	W 25164	2147397	MACH TRAIT INFORMATION
7523	DIGITL CENTRL PROCESSORS	W 8768	1109110	W 9313	1108220	W 10513	1173531	W 9154	1135844	UNITES CENTRALES
7525	ADP PERIPHERAL UNITS	W 17542	500282	W 17930	603933	W 18107	649999	W 11385	400579	UNITES PERIPHERIQUES
759	OFFICE,ADP MCH PTS,ACCES	W 10116	1759623	W 10308	1898416	W 12800	2568354	W 12566	2330100	PIECES DU 751 ET 752
7599	ACCTG,ETC,ADP MCH PTS,AC	W 7377	1707266	W 7382	1836186	W 10203	2510064	W 9357	2258033	PIECES DU 751 ET 752
76	TELECOMM,SOUND EQUIPMENT		1845841		1950875		2662321		2997602	EQUIPMENT DE TELECOM
764	TELECOM EQPT,PTS,ACC NES	W 28539	1369104		1447935	W 45262	2082208	W 48631	2424563	EQUIP TELECOM,PIECES
7649	PTS NES OF EQUIPMT OF 76	W 14287	622985		722582	W 26456	1058771	W 29748	1328703	PIECES DE LA DIV 76
77	ELECTRIC MACHNRY NES ETC		9840564		11593453		14039184		15012405	MACH APP ELECT NDA
771	ELECTRIC POWER MACHY NES	W 55923	380567		536609	W 80896	683706	W 92436	761922	MACH PROD,TRANS ELECTR
772	SWITCHGEAR ETC,PARTS NES	W 57255	1330684		1496157	W 77222	1866320	W 91192	2160372	APP COUPURE,SECT ETC
7721	SWITCHGEAR ETC	W 54197	1155652		1293564	W 73504	1592645	W 87144	1895887	APP COUPURE,SECTIONMNT
773	ELECTR DISTRIBUTNG EQUIP	W 209530	803337	W 201760	770460	W 207613	969500	W 228676	1037079	EQUIPMT DISTRIBUTION ELECT

5. Special Exports F.O.B. by Commodities according to the S.I.T.C. (Rev. 2) in thousand U.S. Dollars
Exportations Spéciales F.O.B. par Produits d'après la C.T.C.I. (Rév. 2) en milliers de Dollars E.U.

SITC CTCI	COMMODITY	1993		1994		1995		1996		PRODUIT
		WEIGHT POIDS	VALUE VALEUR	WEIGHT POIDS	VALUE VALEUR	WEIGHT POIDS	VALUE VALEUR	WEIGHT POIDS	VALUE VALEUR	
7731	INSULATED WIRE,CABLE ETC	W 200662	763888	W 189770	717491	W 193135	910102	W 215076	971366	FILS,CABLES ISOLES ELECT
775	HOUSEHOLD TYPE EQUIP NES	W 677868	3624484	W 881298	4296865	W 1007996	5131088	W 1051682	5499527	MACH,APP USAGE DOMESTQUE
7751	HOUSEHOLD LDRY EQUIP NES	W 278717	1097005	W 366881	1304080	W 421545	1583083	W 460202	1810768	MACH A LAVER ET SECHOIRS
77511	DOMESTIC WASHING MACHNES	W 261978	1001873	W 346141	1191843	W 398759	1453501	W 437729	1677268	MACH LAVER LINGE MOINS 6 KG
7752	DOM REFRIGERATRS,FREEZRS	W 193025	1094696	W 252759	1202978	W 291152	1471472	W 284850	1449077	REFRIG,CONGEL MENAGER
77521	DOMESTIC REFRIGERATORS	W 141037	806538	W 187102	893347	W 216473	1094708	W 204529	1036417	REFRIGERATEURS
7758	ELECTRO–THERMIC APPL NES	W 144945	982804	W 181042	1212497	W 200918	1355535	W 208162	1448352	APP ELECTROTHERMIQ NDA
77586	ELECTROTHERM DOM APP NES	W 57312	510923	W 86655	678980	W 97003	761963	W 97001	783450	APP ELECTRO THERMIQUES
776	TRANSISTORS,VALVES,ETC		1781140		2221851	W 93010	2678642	W 103138	2718840	LAMPES,TUBES,VALVES
7764	ELECTRONIC MICROCIRCUITS		1239912		1568292	W 676	1860014	W 765	1815395	MICROSTRUCTURES ELECTRON
778	ELECTRICAL MACHINERY NES	W 252989	1730516		2040667	W 274652	2453539	W 283200	2551556	AUTRES MACH ELECT NDA
7788	OTH ELEC MACHY,EQUIP NES	W 123334	783380		953623	W 97783	1077744	W 95128	1045923	AUT MACH APP ELEC NDA
78	ROAD VEHICLES		11587883		14339384		19058347		20055924	VEHICULES ROUTIERS
781	PASS MOTOR VEH EXC BUSES	W 623822	4627711	W 739747	5897328	W 878280	8017018	W 827086	7825911	AUTO TRANSPORT PERSONNES
782	LORRIES,SPCL MTR VEH NES	W 233587	1440211	W 302367	2030404	W 357448	2645942	W 362910	2779383	VEHICULES SPECIAUX,MARCH
7821	LORRIES,TRUCKS	W 197325	1182847	W 254707	1674138	W 309407	2241545	W 313317	2369467	VEHICULES TRANSP MARCHAND
784	MOTOR VEH PRTS,ACCES NES	W 759333	3878585	W 915391	4429020	W 1139154	6053014	W 1207216	6953431	PIECES 722,781,782,783
7849	OTHER MOTOR VEHCL PARTS	W 738860	3708250	W 884053	4245784	W 1113623	5814499	W 1182594	6706838	PIECES 722,781,782,783
785	CYCLES,ETC MOTRZD OR NOT	W 130474	1234931	W 154498	1553455	W 156420	1847596	W 153457	2006333	MOTOCYCLES SCOOTERS
7851	MOTORCYCLES ETC	W 23378	427848	W 35113	646938	W 38860	810360	W 47650	981890	MOTO VELO MOTEUR AUXIL
79	OTHR TRANSPORT EQUIPMENT		3137216		3017848		3032010		4062843	AUTRE MATERIEL TRANSPORT
792	AIRCRAFT ETC	W 3908	1855235		1999988	W 3687	1600207	W 4295	1942099	APP NAVIGATION AERIENNE
7923	AIRCRFT NES2000–15000KG	W 976	574484	W 368	195236	W 276	155457	W 213	176954	AERODYNES 2000 A 15000 KG
7924	AIRCRFT NES OVER 15000KG	W 1665	658382	W 4149	1167856	W 1806	700152	W 2237	840930	AERODYNES PLUS 15000 KG
7929	AIRCRAFT PARTS NES	W 1179	533887		525229	W 1473	623825	W 1714	828182	PIECES DU 792
793	SHIPS AND BOATS ETC	W 889621	903195	W 360001	722358	W 378028	1237371	W 539669	1771858	NAVIRES BATEAUX,ETC
7932	SHIPS AND BOATS NES	W 769431	862093	W 352225	696496	W 251797	875785	W 433775	1582914	NAVIRES ET BATEAUX
79323	OTHER CARGO VESSELS	W 693636	629074	W 305123	361144	W 207270	503681	W 217849	977398	AUT BATEAUX TRANS MARCH
8	MISC MANUFACTURED GOODS		38748303		43632283		51839051		57515172	ART MANUFACTURES DIVERS
812	*PLUMBG,HEATNG,LGHTNG EQ	W 340441	1651658	W 380381	1921770	W 399139	2213793	W 420595	2464495	APPAR SANITAIRES CHAUFFAGE
8121	CENTRAL HEATING EQUIPMNT	W 173934	489030	W 196187	589434	W 201216	704134	W 215847	805979	CHAUDIERES,RADIATEURS
8124	LIGHTING EQUIPMENT NES	W 111208	1004580	W 125046	1142452	W 137767	1299229	W 137384	1421444	APPAREILS ECLAIRAGE ETC
81242	LAMPS,FITTINGS BASE METL	W 81174	837577	W 93063	961908	W 100641	1082476	W 93158	1160456	APPAREILS D'ECLAIRAGE
821	*FURNITURE,PARTS THEREOF	W 1185154	5797352	W 1411908	6735357	W 1571245	8365513	W 1623754	9038148	MEUBLES ET PIECES
8211	CHAIRS,SEATS AND PARTS	W 377812	2322909	W 404354	2515303	W 445622	3167781	W 447357	3376258	SIEGES ET PIECES
82111	CHAIRS AND OTHER SEATS	W 344592	2191460	W 361842	2349321	W 391749	2936841	W 386784	3105682	SIEGES
8219	FURNITURE AND PARTS NES	W 790087	3299576	W 987288	4018314	W 1097942	4934225	W 1145473	5362022	AUTRES MEUBLES ET PIECES
82192	WOOD FURNITURE NES	W 433700	2056404	W 540930	2490185	W 616752	3088434	W 634763	3354218	MEUBLES NDA EN BOIS
82199	OTHR FURN,FURN PARTS NES	W 257920	886618	W 324224	1093002	W 346292	1320587	W 371811	1432601	MEUBLES NDA AUTRES MATIERES
831	*TRAVEL GOODS,HANDBAGS	W 20394	936388	W 25617	1243545	W 28031	1566689	W 27118	1855691	ARTICLES DE VOYAGE ETC
83101	HANDBAGS NES	W 11170	651185	W 14080	852045	W 15456	1065242	W 14252	1268010	SACS A MAIN
84	CLOTHING AND ACCESSORIES		11163344		12528151		14178399		16074771	VETEMENTS
842	MENS OUTERWEAR NOT KNIT	W 45529	1893142	W 49185	2144197	W 50483	2513922	W 51712	2798173	VET DESSUS POUR HOMMES
8423	— TROUSERS,BREECHES ETC	W 30439	854340	W 31396	895383	W 31416	977143	W 32277	1075587	PANTALONS HOMMES MAT TEX
8429	— OTHER OUTER GARMENTS	W 8019	467347	W 10069	604401	W 10786	768764	W 11089	872943	AUT VET DES HOM MAT TEX
843	WOMENS OUTERWEAR NONKNIT	W 38984	2570499	W 45455	3078186	W 47815	3593024	W 51687	4132997	VET DESSUS FEMMES MAT TEX
8439	— OTHER OUTER GARMENTS	W 27417	1543998	W 32148	1946813	W 32927	2129610	W 36972	2555643	AUT VET DES FEM MAT TEXT
845	OUTERWEAR KNIT NONELASTC	W 81012	3585141	W 83283	3740803	W 76653	3969210	W 80082	4344274	VET DESSOUS,ACCES BONNET
8451	— JERSEYS,PULLOVERS ETC	W 62488	2761519	W 63716	2787961	W 57186	2908605	W 57201	3097431	CHANDAILS,PULL–OVERS ETC
8459	— OTHER,CLTHG ACCESRYS	W 16299	657464	W 17081	771380	W 16661	833116	W 20032	1020469	AUT VET DESSUS DE BONNE
846	UNDER GARMENTS KNITTED	W 36099	1055465	W 40278	1181876	W 45030	1390622	W 48335	1678607	SOUS VETS DE BONNETERIE
8463	— OF SYNTH FBR NONELAST	W 22641	557649	W 24954	581280	W 27597	667295	W 29319	872553	SOUS–VET BONNET FIB SYNT
84631	—— PANTY HOSE (TIGHTS)	W 21652	506458	W 23833	518680	W 26161	582103	W 27440	762292	COLLANTS BON FIBR SYNT
847	TEXTILE CLTHNG ACCES NES	W 33377	1040052	W 34897	1188918	W 32465	1306822	W 36389	1508036	ACCES VET MAT TEXT NDA
8471	— NOT KNITTED	W 9153	699679	W 9529	819845	W 9932	933512	W 10620	1047262	ACCES VET MAT TEX NON BON
848	HEADGEAR,NONTXTL CLOTHNG	W 14080	626124	W 15435	743846	W 15548	828865	W 16736	945833	VET ACCES MAT AUT QUE TEX
851	*FOOTWEAR	W 266345	5743107	W 290725	6465382	W 295826	7304452	W 294334	7967861	CHAUSSURES
85101	FOOTWEAR RUBBER,PLASTIC	W 64782	703971	W 68103	733373	W 67887	801380	W 61774	783310	CHAUS SEMELLES CAOUTCH
85102	FOOTWEAR LEATHER	W 194740	4944226	W 215362	5620787	W 220981	6392181	W 225838	7060814	CHAUS SEMELLES EN CUIR
87	PRECISION INSTRUMNTS NES		1881095		2035699		2442341		2787453	INSTRUM,APPAR SCIENT NDA
874	MEASURNG,CONTROLNG INSTR	W 32330	1385733		1491087	W 35305	1762745	W 40422	1999420	INSTRUMENTS DE MESURE
88	PHOTO EQU,OPTICL GDS ETC		1397609		1568314		2004763		2372237	APP,FOURN PHOTO,OP,MONTR
884	OPTICAL GOODS NES	W 3019	676419		782730	W 4190	1047765	W 4716	1265136	ELEMENTS OPTIQ,ART LUNET
8842	SPECTACLES AND FRAMES	W 2594	647171	W 2897	753117	W 3837	1015072	W 4381	1232205	LUNETTES ET MONTURES
88421	SPECTACLE FRAMES	W 1825	528441	W 1961	581425	W 2406	702724	W 2390	769979	MONTURES DE LUNETTES
89	MISC MANUFCTRD GOODS NES		10177751		11134066		13763102		14954515	ART MANUFACTURES DIVERS
892	PRINTED MATTER	W 314007	1067321	W 354251	1208130	W 391952	1521782	W 409469	1591815	IMPRIMES
893	ARTICLES OF PLASTIC NES		2483176		2856373		3612873		3861337	OUVRAGES EN MAT DIVIS 58
8939	MISC PLASTIC ARTICLES	W 526934	1928533	W 583909	2216122	W 594484	2769784	W 646862	2928484	ART DIVERS EN MAT DIV 58
89399	OTHR PLASTC ARTICLES NES	W 521747	1907245	W 577517	2194272	W 587886	2742067	W 637594	2880131	AUT OUV MAT DIV 58
894	TOYS,SPORTING GOODS,ETC	W 151376	1203756	W 182269	1454280	W 202911	1805526	W 200589	1927785	VOITURES ENFANTS,JOUETS
8942	TOYS,INDOOR GAMES ETC	W 90860	623665	W 105243	724969	W 116677	845618	W 109556	840949	JOUETS,JEUX ETC
896	WORKS OF ART ETC		118401		48461		609114		1090936	OBJETS D'ART
89603	ORIGINAL SCULPTURE ETC		44424		17117		578266		1033243	PROD ORIG STATUAIRE
897	GOLD,SILVER WARE,JEWELRY		4207312		4297512		4745683		4937452	BIJOUTERIE,ORFEVRERIE
8973	PREC JEWLRY,GLD–SILVWARE		4100346		4200542		4644191		4834483	BIJOUX OR,ARGENT ORFEVRE
89731	PRECIOUS METAL JEWELLERY		4035248		4114856		4541945		4727315	ART BIJOUTERIE,JOAILLER
899	OTHER MANUFACTURED GOODS		574082		648571		739740		818418	AUT ART MANUF DIVERS NDA
9	GOODS NOT CLASSD BY KIND		1654483		1945851		2153602		2244050	ART TRANSACT NON CLASSES
931	*SPECIAL TRANSACTIONS	W 1006938	1383333	W 1754092	1727008	W 1267509	1961339	W 1380635	2034985	TRANS.SPECIALES

FOOT NOTES – NOTES

TABLE 1 –

1 Values are in thousand million lire.

TABLEAU 1 –

1 Les évaluations sont exprimées en milliards de lires.

1. HISTORICAL SERIES, 1961–1996 GENERAL TRADE, IMPORTS C.I.F., EXPORTS F.O.B.
SERIES HISTORIQUES, 1961–1996 COMMERCE GENERAL, IMPORTATIONS C.A.F., EXPORTATIONS F.O.B

YEAR ANNEE	VALUE IN MILLION JAMAICAN DOLLARS VALEUR EN MILLION JAMAICAN DOLLARS MERCHANDISE–MARCHANDISE		GOLD–OR		CONVERSION FACTORS U.S. CENTS PER JAMAICAN DOLLAR FACTEURS DE CONVERSION CENTS E.U. PAR JAMAICAN DOLLAR		INDEX NUMBERS –INDICES QUANTUM		UNIT VALUE VALEUR UNITAIRE	
	IMPORTS	EXPORTS	IMPORTS	EXPORTS	IMPORTS	EXPORTS	IMPORTS	EXPORTS	IMPORTS	EXPORTS
1961	150.80	127.30			140.0000	140.0000				
1962	159.20	129.70			140.0000	140.0000				
1963	161.10	144.20			140.0000	140.0000				
1964	206.70	154.50			140.0000	140.0000				
1965	206.50	153.10			140.0000	140.0000				
1966	233.70	162.90			140.0000	140.0000				
1967	252.60	163.30			138.1300	138.5750				
1968	320.40	183.00			120.0000	120.0000				
1969	363.30	211.80			120.0000	120.0000				
1970	437.80	284.80			120.0000	120.0000				
1971	459.80	282.70			120.0000	120.0000				
1972	489.30	300.20			125.7570	126.0920				
1973	615.10	354.60			110.6420	110.6420				
1974	850.80	549.10			110.0000	110.0000				
1975	1021.40	690.20			110.0000	110.0000				
1976	829.80	572.80			110.0000	110.0000				
1977	781.60	698.60			110.0000	110.0000				
1978	1260.00	1142.50			69.8794	68.9586				
1979	1754.40	1445.80			56.5432	56.5310				
1980	2086.60	1715.00			56.1349	56.1350				
1981	2623.40	1735.10			56.1349	56.1350				
1982	2460.30	1367.00			56.1350	56.1350				
1983	2841.00	1392.10			53.8694	52.6045				
1984	4509.50	2732.50			25.4151	25.7863				
1985	6146.70	3128.30			18.0641	18.0379				
1986	5322.40	3225.90			18.2520	18.2528				
1987	6790.50	3873.60			18.2241	18.2244				
1988	7983.20	4830.30			18.2197	18.2210				
1989	10668.30	5746.60			17.3702	17.3618				
1990	13923.00	8305.00			13.8168	13.9464				
1991	20830.00	13079.00			8.6926	8.3885				
1992	38267.01	24099.01			4.3765	4.3478				
1993	52847.01	26361.01			3.9684	4.0548				
1994	71654.00	39461.01			3.0159	3.0175				
1995	97563.01	48510.00			2.8245	2.8454				
1996	108096.00	50701.01			2.6967	2.6762				

2. IMPORTS BY BROAD ECONOMIC CATEGORY AND EXPORTS BY INDUSTRIAL ORIGIN. (PERCENTAGE OF TOTAL VALUE)
IMPORTATIONS PAR CATEGORIES ECONOMIQUES ET EXPORTATIONS PAR BRANCHE D'ACTIVITE.(EN POURCENTAGE DE LA VALEUR TOTALE)

IMPORTS – IMPORTATIONS

	1990	1991	1992	1993	1994	1995	1996
TOTAL IMPORTS–IMPORTATIONS TOTALES	100.	100.			100.	100.	
1 FOOD BEV–ALIMENTATION BOISSONS	12.9	12.4			11.8	11.9	
11 PRIMARY–PRODUITS DE BASE	5.8	5.5			5.2	4.4	
111 FOR INDUSTRY–POUR L'INDUSTRIE	2.7	2.6			2.3	1.5	
112 FOR HOUSEHOLDS–POUR LES MENAGES	3.1	2.9			3.0	2.9	
12 PROCESSED–PRODUITS ELABORES	7.1	6.9			6.5	7.5	
121 FOR INDUSTRY–POUR L'INDUSTRIE	1.6	1.6			1.0	1.3	
122 FOR HOUSEHOLDS–POUR LES MENAGES	5.5	5.3			5.6	6.2	
2 IND SUPPLIES–APPROV INDUSTRIELS	28.3	30.2			26.8	27.6	
21 PRIMARY–PRODUITS DE BASE	2.2	1.6			2.2	1.8	
22 PROCESSED–PRODUITS ELABORES	26.1	28.6			24.7	25.7	
3 FUELS–COMBUSTIBLES	19.7	19.0			14.8	12.6	
31 PRIMARY–PRODUITS DE BASE	1.0	8.1			4.7	3.8	
32 PROCESSED–PRODUITS ELABORES	18.8	10.9			10.0	8.8	
321 MOTOR SPIRIT–ESSENCE	1.4	10.7			9.9	8.6	
322 OTHER–AUTRES	17.4	0.2			0.1	0.2	
4 MACHINERY–EQUIPEMENT	15.2	13.7			14.3	15.0	
41 CAPITAL EQUIPMENT–MACHINES	12.9	11.1			12.0	13.1	
42 PARTS–PIECES ACCESSOIRES	2.3	2.7			2.3	1.9	
5 TRANSPORT–TRANSPORT	10.3	10.2			10.2	11.7	
51 PASSENGER CARS–AUTOMOBILES	2.2	4.0			4.6	5.5	
52 OTHER–AUTRES	5.8	3.6			3.0	3.4	
521 INDUSTRIAL–INDUSTRIELS	5.7	3.5			2.9	3.3	
522 NON INDUSTRIAL–NON INDUSTRIEL	0.2	0.1			0.1	0.1	
53 PARTS–PIECES ACCESSOIRES	2.3	2.6			2.6	2.8	
6 CONSUM GOODS–BIENS CONSOMMATION	11.9	13.1			19.9	18.2	
61 DURABLE–DURABLES	2.1	2.4			4.0	4.0	
62 SEMI DURABLE–SEMI DURABLES	6.4	7.6			12.5	10.9	
63 NON DURABLE–NON DURABLES	3.4	3.2			3.3	3.3	
7 GOODS NES–BIENS NDA	1.7	1.3			2.2	3.0	

EXPORTS – EXPORTATIONS

	1990	1991	1992	1993	1994	1995	1996
TOTAL EXPORTS–EXPORTATIONS TOTALES	100.	100.			100.	100.	
1 AGRICULTURE	7.0	7.8			9.6	9.4	
2 MINING QUARRY–INDUS EXTRACTIVES	9.2	10.7			6.2	5.3	
3 MANUFACTURING–IND MANUFACTUR	83.8	81.6			84.3	85.3	
31 FOOD BEV TOBACCO–ALIM BOISS TAB	12.2	14.1			11.6	12.4	
32 TEXTILES–INDUSTRIES TEXTILES	7.7	8.5			20.8	20.4	
33 WOOD & PRODUCTS–BOIS & PRODUITS	0.0	0.0			0.0	0.0	
34 PAPER & PRODUCTS–PAPIER & PRODT	0.2	0.2			0.2	0.2	
35 CHEMICALS–INDUSTRIES CHIMIQUES	59.1	54.7			47.5	47.8	
36 NON METAL MIN–MIN NON METAL	0.3	0.3			0.3	0.3	
37 BASIC METAL–IND METAL BASE	0.2	0.1			0.1	0.1	
38 METAL MANUF–MANUF METAL	4.0	3.6			3.4	3.9	
39 OTH MANUF IND–AUTRES MANUF	0.1	0.1			0.3	0.2	

3. TRADE BY PRINCIPAL COUNTRIES OF ORIGIN AND LAST CONSIGNMENT (VALUE IN THOUSAND U.S. DOLLARS)
ECHANGES SELON LES PRINCIPAUX PAYS D'ORIGINE ET DE DERNIERE CONSIGNATION (VALEUR EN MILLIERS DE DOLLARS EU)

COUNTRIES–PAYS	GENERAL IMPORTS C.I.F. IMPORTATIONS GENERALES C.A.F				
	1992	1993	1994	1995	1996
World	1775393	2189243	2221397	2772872	2916358
Africa	693		1232	1736	1950
Americas	1299058	115414	1669966	1990381	2167323
Northern America	961585		1277029	1505637	1614328
LAIA	212058		187335	195027	207878
CACM	7251		12197	14147	25457
Caribbean	92008	104377	178078	256643	293480
Rest of America	26156	11037	15327	18927	26180
As.ex F.USSR	143362		230570	325119	257853
Eur.x F.USSR	188903		241511	332761	359572
EU	170562		211892	296741	326459
EFTA	16652		22483	25506	24629
East Europe	1597		7097	10453	7920
Other Europe	8		3	31	427
Former USSR	1684		3691	4655	6536
Oceania	13482		14380	20334	20118
USA/Etats–Unis d'Amer	891613		1195824	1406467	1526392
Trinidad and Tobago	31993	79678	121932	203378	242807
Japan/Japon	84752		132718	184835	163777
United Kingdom	84298		96534	112459	116068
Canada	69969		81190	99153	87915
Mexico/Mexique	114367		63003	71686	74580
Venezuela	69990		70771	56689	66802
Brazil/Brésil	21647		35756	42503	51175
France,Monac	13158		20180	34338	63387
Germany/Allemagne	22581		25304	37684	34112
Netherlands Antilles	39911		29027	18756	8899
Netherlands/Pays–Bas	10911		19185	20305	34488
Italy/Italie	14686		16366	23702	18573
Turkey/Turquie	10480		8845	35532	16904
Barbados/Barbade	5925	14844	11915	15436	19529
China/Chine	9668		16798	18415	22367
New Zealand	12741		11210	15708	16712
Switz.Liecht	10717		12355	16604	16582
Spain/Espagne	7721		6999	16554	19258
Hong Kong	10425		15252	14573	10156
Korea, Republic of	11424		15921	22502	
Belgium–Luxembourg	6142		8207	13958	16751
Guyana	16944	7950	5651	6713	7464
Panama	7356		7248	9930	14191
Dominica/Dominique	6741	6390	4519	5554	10944
Costa Rica	4237		8911	9254	10845
Norway,SVD,JM	5930		10031	8830	7367
Thailand/Thaïlande	6352		6488	9610	6753
Colombia/Colombie	3862		7360	8312	9240
Sweden/Suède	4199		7047	9113	5741
Guatemala	1223		1770	4083	13851
Indonesia/Indonésie	2438		6354	5429	6696
Finland/Finlande	670		4571	10421	3841
Ireland/Irlande	3069		2754	4864	7324
Austria/Autriche	1230		1398	10916	2076
Dominican Republic	2868		3513	3497	5665
Malaysia/Malaisie	1905		2954	4976	5409
Argentina/Argentine	1182		2665	6580	3029
Ecuador/Equateur	171		5961	6869	111
Poland/Pologne	576		3199	5957	3071
Australia/Australie	700		3038	4495	3371
Belize/Bélize	1397	3087	2356	2237	1693
Russian Federation			2177	2853	4169
India/Inde	988		1825	2947	3157
Bahamas	69		3287	4066	1190
Denmark/Danemark	1330		1694	2196	3279
Czech Republic			1633	2919	3071
Saint Lucia/St. Lucie	1117	2090	2093	1122	386
Korea Dem People's Rp	1300		2391	1593	1512
Israel/Israël	841		1526	2184	1972

COUNTRIES–PAYS	GENERAL EXPORTS F.O.B. EXPORTATIONS GENERALES F.O.B.				
	1992	1993	1994	1995	1996
Monde	1053592	1075376	1210651	1423784	1386876
Afrique	49744		45011	49764	43811
Amériques	592095	59848	696013	778856	758107
Amérique du Nord	511365		588180	679436	678416
ALAI	8942		35413	23192	10164
MCAC	729		408	909	1090
Caraïbes	59012	50068	59850	61167	54646
Autre Amérique	12047	9780	12162	14152	13791
Asie l'URSS exclus	15774		17165	36573	32461
Europe l'URSS exclus	386269		404515	517650	523965
UE	271887		302783	408933	432665
AELE	114221		101393	107938	90846
Europe de l'Est	143		340	542	450
Autre de l'Europe	18				
Ancienne URSS	4238		42431	37533	25658
Océanie	2649		2436	2681	2596
USA/Etats–Unis d'Amer	390580		440909	525527	514458
United Kingdom	180161		162026	191771	183613
Canada	119758		146628	153138	163516
Norway,SVD,JM	113697		101312	107752	90683
Netherlands/Pays–Bas	55844		48868	107783	123586
France,Monac	3335		62856	85106	79971
Ghana	49624		42049	49573	43531
Trinidad and Tobago	26336	21861	20434	21155	17035
Russian Federation			42399	37368	25563
Japan/Japon	15079		15575	27308	31268
Barbados/Barbade	12524	13311	12735	12223	12016
Sweden/Suède	5651		19203	15996	16285
Brazil/Brésil	7429		29663	16632	3119
Guyana	4882	5972	6879	6776	5827
Finland/Finlande	20375		96	505	3475
Germany/Allemagne	4531		6426	5802	5845
Belize/Bélize	3869	3808	3670	5031	3912
Saint Lucia/St. Lucie	3468	4248	4232	3699	3102
Portugal	21				18199
Antigua and Barbuda	2839	3432	2781	2442	2520
Cayman Is/Is Caïmans	2477		2972	3689	3721
Dominican Republic	2488		2154	2727	3716
Mexico/Mexique	1049		3226	3483	3196
New Zealand	2333		2208	2067	2394
St Vincent & Grenadines	1534	1895	1724	2008	1580
Dominica/Dominique	1585	1669	1755	1578	1771
Saint–Kitts–Nevis	1378	1587	1614	1525	1712
Suriname/Suriname	2566		1080	1205	2373
Bahamas	1007		2023	1373	2094
Bangladesh			184	4656	638
Grenada/Grenade		1753	1481	1099	1067
Belgium–Luxembourg	1217		2335	964	543
Martinique	241		2005	2415	
Netherlands Antilles	622		1127	1234	1476
Former USSR/Anc. URSS	4238				
Colombia/Colombie	158		1566	1451	988
Haiti/Haïti	62		971	1562	1205
Panama	546		421	1101	1678
China/Chine			32	3546	18
Gambia/Gambie			2947		
Bermuda/Bermudes	1027		643	772	438
Guadeloupe	207		915	1664	
Peru/Pérou	233		300	614	1183
Italy/Italie	213		854	514	346
Cuba	244		245	276	919
Chile/Chili			147	636	804
Montserrat	289	312	324	232	294
Honduras	448		171	305	516
Jamaica/Jamaïque	1313				
Poland/Pologne	84		306	441	433

(VALUE AS PERCENTAGE OF WORLD TOTAL)(VALEURS EN POURCENTAGE DU TOTAL MONDIAL)

	1987	1988	1989	1990	1991	1992	1993	1994	1995	1996
Africa	0.6	0.0	0.0	0.0	0.1	0.0		0.1	0.1	0.1
Americas	72.7	71.9	74.0	76.4	75.6	73.2	5.3	75.2	71.8	74.3
Northern America	55.0	56.1	56.6	55.4	56.8	54.2		57.5	54.3	55.4
LAIA	11.9	10.5	10.5	14.6	10.6	11.9		8.4	7.0	7.1
CACM	0.6	0.5	0.5	0.3	0.4	0.4		0.5	0.5	0.9
Caribbean	4.4	4.1	5.5	5.4	7.0	5.2	4.8	8.0	9.3	10.1
Rest of America	0.8	0.6	0.9	0.7	0.8	1.5	0.5	0.7	0.7	0.9
As.ex F.USSR	8.3	8.0	7.8	7.6	10.2	8.1		10.4	11.7	8.8
Eur.x F.USSR	15.0	16.9	14.2	12.7	12.1	10.6		10.9	12.0	12.3
EU	14.1	15.8	12.9	11.3	10.9	9.6		9.5	10.7	11.2
EFTA	0.6	0.7	0.8	1.3	0.8	0.9		1.0	0.9	0.8
East Europe	0.2	0.4	0.5	0.2	0.3	0.1		0.3	0.4	0.3
Other Europe	0.0	0.0	0.0	0.0	0.1	0.0		0.0	0.0	0.0
Former USSR	0.6	0.4	0.5	0.3	0.1	0.1		0.2	0.2	0.2
Oceania	0.8	1.0	1.2	0.9	0.7	0.8		0.6	0.7	0.7
USA/Etats–Unis d'Amer	49.4	48.8	50.9	49.1	52.4	50.2		53.8	50.7	52.3
Trinidad and Tobago	3.1	2.4	3.2	2.8	2.6	1.8	3.6	5.5	7.3	8.3
Japan/Japon	4.1	3.4	4.0	4.8	7.4	4.8		6.0	6.7	5.6
United Kingdom	6.9	6.9	6.2	5.3	5.9	4.7		4.3	4.1	4.0
Canada	5.6	7.3	5.7	6.3	4.4	3.9		3.7	3.6	3.0
Mexico/Mexique	4.6	3.6	2.1	5.0	3.9	6.4		2.8	2.6	2.6
Venezuela	4.0	4.3	5.5	5.1	5.4	3.9		3.2	2.0	2.3
Brazil/Brésil	1.8	2.2	1.9	3.8	0.9	1.2		1.6	1.5	1.8
France,Monac	0.7	2.8	0.9	0.9	0.8	0.7		0.9	1.2	2.2
Germany/Allemagne	2.0	1.6	1.9	1.4	1.3	1.3		1.1	1.4	1.2

	1987	1988	1989	1990	1991	1992	1993	1994	1995	1996
Afrique	0.0	0.5	2.6	4.6	3.9	4.7		3.7	3.5	3.2
Amériques	60.4	60.6	49.5	50.0	52.4	56.2	5.6	57.5	54.7	54.7
Amérique du Nord	51.1	51.4	39.9	41.2	43.2	48.5		48.6	47.7	48.9
ALAI	1.0	0.5	1.6	1.7	1.8	0.8		2.9	1.6	0.7
MCAC	0.4	0.4	0.2	0.0	0.1	0.1		0.0	0.1	0.1
Caraïbes	6.7	6.7	6.4	5.7	6.4	5.6	4.7	4.9	4.3	3.9
Autre Amérique	1.3	1.5	1.3	1.4	0.9	1.1	0.9	1.0	1.0	1.0
Asie l'URSS exclus	1.2	1.2	0.9	0.8	1.0	1.5		1.4	2.6	2.3
Europe l'URSS exclus	33.5	33.3	35.0	39.6	39.1	36.7		33.4	36.4	37.8
UE	30.4	32.2	30.3	28.1	31.4	25.8		25.0	28.7	31.2
AELE	3.1	1.0	4.6	11.5	7.7	10.8		8.4	7.6	6.6
Europe de l'Est	0.1	0.2	0.0	0.0		0.0		0.0	0.0	0.0
Autre de l'Europe	0.0	0.0	0.2	0.0	0.0	0.0				
Ancienne URSS	4.1	3.8	11.3	4.3	2.6	0.4		3.5	2.6	1.9
Océanie	0.2	0.3	0.3	0.2	0.9	0.3		0.2	0.2	0.2
USA/Etats–Unis d'Amer	37.3	36.8	26.2	29.8	32.1	37.1		36.4	36.9	37.1
United Kingdom	17.5	19.0	15.2	15.2	16.8	17.1		13.4	13.5	13.2
Canada	13.7	14.5	13.6	11.3	11.1	11.4		12.1	10.8	11.8
Norway,SVD,JM	3.0	0.9	4.5	11.5	7.7	10.8		8.4	7.6	6.5
Netherlands/Pays–Bas	11.6	10.7	11.7	9.6	9.5	5.3		4.0	7.6	8.9
France,Monac	0.1	0.2	2.5	0.5	0.3	0.3		5.2	6.0	5.8
Ghana		0.5	2.6	4.6	3.9	4.7		3.5	3.5	3.1
Trinidad and Tobago	2.5	3.0	3.1	2.8	2.8	2.5	2.0	1.7	1.5	1.2
Russian Federation								3.5	2.6	1.8
Japan/Japon	1.2	1.0	0.9	0.7	0.8	1.4		1.3	1.9	2.3

4. General Imports C.I.F. by Commodities according to the S.I.T.C. (Rev. 2) in thousand U.S. Dollars
Importations Générales C.A.F. par Produits d'après la C.T.C.I. (Rév. 2) en milliers de Dollars E.U.

SITC CTCI	COMMODITY	1993 WEIGHT POIDS	1993 VALUE VALEUR	1994 WEIGHT POIDS	1994 VALUE VALEUR	1995 WEIGHT POIDS	1995 VALUE VALEUR	1996 WEIGHT POIDS	1996 VALUE VALEUR	PRODUIT
	ALL COMMODITIES		2189243		2221397		2772872		2916358	TOUS PRODUITS
0	FOOD AND LIVE ANIMALS		259718		248678		336646		365603	ALIMENTS,ANIMAUX VIVANTS
01	MEAT AND PREPARATIONS				43935		56561		52717	VIANDES ET PREPARATIONS
011	MEAT FRESH,CHILLD,FROZEN			W 48092	33161	W 52337	39718	W 54031	41917	VIANDES FRAICHES,REF,CONGE
0114	POULTRY FRESH CHLLD,FRZN			W 38115	21616	W 40784	25023	W 42662	26832	VOLAILLES MORTES
0116	EDIBLE OFFAL FRESH,CH,FR			W 7174	6888	W 7904	8589	W 7805	8966	ABATS COMESTIBLES
014	MEAT PREPD,PRSVD,NES ETC			W 4063	9928	W 4915	15720	W 3477	9583	CONSERVES DE VIANDES
0149	OTH PREPARD,PRESRVD MEAT			W 3694	8846	W 4425	14437	W 2770	8017	AUTRES PREP DE VIANDES
02	DAIRY PRODCTS,BIRDS'EGGS				31831		44954		44533	PRODUITS LAITIERS,OEUFS
022	MILK AND CREAM			W 8583	13230	W 10086	20428	W 9093	19891	LAIT ET CREME
0224	MILK,CREAM PRESERVED ETC			W 8431	12977	W 9827	19847	W 8789	19206	LAIT,CREME CONS,CONC
02243	MILK DRY,OVER 1.5% FAT			W 6683	10464	W 7892	16706	W 7169	16402	LAIT POUDRE SUP 1.5%
024	CHEESE AND CURD			W 3071	7825	W 4699	12355	W 3803	11304	FROMAGE ET CAILLEBOTTE
025	EGGS,BIRDS,FRESH,PRSRVD			W 2559	7333	W 2614	7430	W 3029	8681	OEUFS
0251	— IN SHELL			W 2558	7329	W 2602	7394	W 3013	8637	OEUFS EN COQUILLE
03	FISH AND PREPARATIONS				28524		37165		39055	POISSONS ET PREPARATIONS
034	FISH,FRESH,CHILLED,FROZN			W 5692	5521	W 6318	7715	W 7659	10914	POISSON FRAIS, REFRIG,CONG
0342	FISH FROZEN,EXCL FILLETS			W 5620	5340	W 6035	7108	W 7336	10077	POISSONS CONGELES
035	FISH SALTED,DRIED,SMOKED			W 3524	10452	W 3755	12929	W 4314	15231	POISSON SECHE,SALE,FUME
03503	FISH(EX COD)DRIED,SALTED			W 2404	7779	W 2382	8824	W 2845	10879	POISSONS SECHES,SALES
037	FISH ETC PREPD,PRSVD NES			W 5782	10694	W 8094	13186	W 5674	10421	POIS,CRUST,MOL PREPARES
0371	FISH PREPARD,PRESRVD NES			W 5777	10664	W 8084	13145	W 5661	10362	CONSERVES DE POISSONS
04	CEREALS AND PREPARATIONS				81749		104331		114715	CEREALES ET PRODUITS
041	WHEAT ETC UNMILLED			W 79930	11571	W 88370	16989	W 43192	13728	FROMENT,EPEAUTRE
0412	OTHER WHEAT ETC UNMILLED			W 49930	7416	W 88370	16989	W 43191	13727	AUTRE FROMENT NON MOULU
042	RICE			W 82221	24295	W 121981	23294	W 78705	29852	RIZ
0421	RICE IN HUSK OR HUSKED			W 67332	19549	W 105912	18794	W 53165	20682	RIZ SANS AUTRE PREPARATION
04212	RICE HUSKED			W 67319	19546	W 105909	18790	W 53164	20679	RIZ CARGO
0422	RICE SEMI–MILLED,MILLED			W 14889	4746	W 16069	4499	W 25540	9171	RIZ POLI,GLACE INCL BRISURES
04221	RICE MILLED UNBROKEN			W 11891	3929	W 16069	4499	W 25539	9169	RIZ POLI,GLACE EXCL BRISURES
044	MAIZE UNMILLED			W 200534	25396	W 177668	27074	W 157966	30454	MAIS NON MOULU
048	CEREAL ETC PREPARATIONS			W 16100	17794	W 21690	29084	W 24253	37841	PREPTNS A BASE CEREALES
0484	BAKERY PRODUCTS			W 1410	3256	W 2566	6523	W 3288	8986	PRODUITS DE BOULANGERIE
0488	OTH CEREAL PREPS,MALT EX			W 2363	6361	W 3922	10385	W 6095	14652	EXTRAITS DE MALT
05	VEGETABLES AND FRUIT				14761		19214		23004	LEGUMES ET FRUITS
054	VEG ETC FRSH,SMPLY PRSVD			W 9471	7053	W 12631	8453	W 18482	9614	LEGUMES FRAIS,CONG,SECS
06	SUGAR AND PREPS,HONEY				18631		27092		38281	SUCRES ET PRODUITS
061	SUGAR AND HONEY			W 45245	16636	W 90560	23885	W 290931	35183	SUCRES ET MIEL
0612	REFINED SUGAR ETC			W 39926	13847	W 30909	14259	W 282274	31094	SUCRES RAFFINES
081	*FEEDING STUFF FOR ANIML			W 20650	8787	W 61842	23106	W 65903	22014	NOURRITURE POUR ANIMAUX
0813	OILCAKE AND OTH RESIDUES			W 16056	4035	W 52406	12033	W 51483	15651	TOURTEAUX
08131	— OF SOYA BEANS			W 15263	3854	W 52206	11985	W 51483	15651	TOURTEAUX DE SOJA
0819	FOOD WASTE AND FEED NES			W 2674	3830	W 6094	9899	W 4751	3509	DECHETS,ALIMENTS NDA
08199	FODDER NES,INCL SWEETNED			W 2674	3830	W 6094	9898	W 4751	3509	PREPARATIONS FOURRAGERES
09	MISC EDIBLE PRODUCTS				13718		16433		21455	PREP ALIMENTAIRES DIVERSES
098	EDIBLE PRODCTS,PREPS NES			W 4059	9691	W 4047	11201	W 5667	15507	PREP ALIMENTAIRES NDA
09809	MISC FOOD PREPRTIONS NES			W 3051	7554	W 2622	8239	W 4165	12285	PREP ALIMENTAIRES NDA
1	BEVERAGES AND TOBACCO		16713		26706		36186		35803	BOISSONS ET TABACS
11	BEVERAGES				19433		29221		26129	BOISSONS
111	NON–ALCOHL BEVERAGES NES			W 8969	5921	W 38719	22178	W 42026	20046	BOISSONS NON ALCOOLIQUES
11102	FLAVORED WATERS NON–ALCO			W 8542	5637	W 38196	21806	W 41298	19570	LIMONADES,EAUX GAZEUSES
112	ALCOHOLIC BEVERAGES			W 16666	13512	W 6994	7043	W 3038	6082	BOISSONS ALCOOLIQUES
1123	BEER,ALE,STOUT,PORTER			W 15353	9498	W 5376	2397	W 1117	683	BIERES
12	TOBACCO AND MANUFACTURES				7273		6966		9675	TABACS BRUTS FABRIQUES
121	TOBACCO UNMNFCTRD,REFUSE			W 1218	6955	W 886	6732	W 1226	9167	TABACS BRUTS,DECHETS
1212	TOBACCO STRIPPED OR PART			W 1199	6829	W 819	6287	W 1219	9094	TABACS PART ECOTES
2	CRUDE MATERLS,EXCL FUELS		63214		64840		52995		51305	MAT BRUTES NON COMESTIBLES
22	OIL SEEDS,OLEAGINOUS FRT				17452		4781		1701	GRAINES,FRUITS OLEAGINEUX
222	SEEDS FOR'SOFT'FIXED OIL			W 63581	17384	W 17697	4732	W 180	218	GRAINES HUILES FIXES
2222	SOYA BEANS			W 63417	17156	W 17593	4589	W 23	15	FEVES DE SOJA
24	CORK AND WOOD				34655		35296		34820	LIEGE ET BOIS
248	WOOD SHAPED,SLEEPERS			W 59904	29913	W 61888	30841	W 60921	30860	BOIS SIMPLEMENT TRAVAILLES
2482	LUMBER SHAPED CONIFER			W 55688	26484	W 56705	27185	W 56421	27231	CONIFERES SCIES,RABOTES
24821	LUMBER SAWN ETC CONIFER			W 53371	25103	W 54477	25458	W 53832	25752	CONIFERES SCIES LONGITUD
3	MINERAL FUELS ETC		343869		330042		351234		444657	COMBUSTIBLES MINERAUX LUB
33	PETROLEUM AND PRODUCTS				316414		334110		425040	PETROLE ET DERIVES
333	CRUDE PETROLEUM			W 832290	95111	W 747315	93464	W 622616	89631	HUILES BRUTES DE PETROLE
334	PETROLEUM PRODUCTS,REFIN			W 1685675	219516	W 1654248	238972	W 1493687	333782	PRODUITS RAFFINES
3341	GASOLINE,OTH LIGHT OILS							W 345006	72571	ESSENCES POUR MOTEURS
33411	MOTOR,AVIATION SPIRIT							W 343429	69478	ESSENCES MOTEURS D'AVIONS
3342	KEROSENE,OTH MEDIUM OILS							W 170738	33332	PETR LAMPANTS,AUT HUIL
33421	KEROSENE INCL JET FUEL							W 166855	32401	PETROLES LAMPANTS
3343	GAS OILS							W 279242	54034	GAS OILS
3344	FUEL OILS,NES							W 610667	157323	FUEL OILS
3345	LUBS,PETROLEUM OILS NES							W 88034	16522	HUILES LUBRIFIANTES
33451	LUBS(HIGH PETR CONT) ETC							W 87869	16119	HUILES LUBRIF,H LOURDES
341	*GAS,NATURAL AND MANUFCT			W 72752	10347	W 83587	12678	W 87334	16041	GAZ NATUREL,GAZ MANUFACT
3413	PETROLM GASES,LIQUEFIED			W 72748	10330	W 83583	12673	W 87332	16030	GAZ DE PETROLE LIQUEFIE
34131	LIQUEFIED PROPANE,BUTANE			W 71654	10157	W 83583	12673	W 87331	16020	PROPANE,BUTANE LIQUEFIES
4	ANIMAL,VEGETABLE OIL,FAT		11575		18129		19983		23334	HUILES,GRAISSES ANIM,VEG
42	FIXED VEGETABLE OIL,FAT				11100		11726		15708	HUILES VEGETALES FIXES
423	FIXED VEG OILS,SOFT			W 9593	7416	W 7906	8149	W 15604	12341	HUILES VEGET DOUCES FIXES
4232	SOYA BEAN OIL			W 6437	5859	W 7790	7849	W 15517	12042	HUILE DE SOJA
5	CHEMCLS,RELATED PROD NES		205068		212361		264531		286599	PRODUITS CHIMIQUES
51	ORGANIC CHEMICALS				19673		24946		22437	PROD CHIMIQ ORGANIQUES
512	ALCOHOLS,PHENOLS ETC			W 32196	6285	W 37886	10039	W 22617	8429	PHENOLS,PHENOLS–ALCOOLS
5121	ACYCLIC ALCOHOLS,DERIVS			W 32138	6001	W 37813	9787	W 22520	8001	ALCOOLS ACYCLIQUES
52	INORGANIC CHEMICALS				46537		65794		72082	PROD CHIM INORGANIQUES
522	INORG ELEMNTS,OXIDES,ETC			W 487096	26122		48887	W 340863	57744	ELEMENTS INORGANIQUES
5225	INORGANIC BASES ETC NES			W 477768	18843	W 305267	40142	W 335238	49819	AUTRES BASES OXYDES METAL
52253	SODIUM HYDROXIDE, OTHER			W 476979	18204	W 304371	39444	W 324450	47925	HYDROXYDE SODIUM AQUEUX
523	OTHR INORG CHEMICALS ETC			W 30965	19914	W 38824	16798	W 29271	13783	AUT PRODUITS CHIMIQUES INORG
5239	INORG CHEM PRODUCTS NES			W 4895	9941	W 3416	6844	W 2378	4563	PROD CHIM INORGANIQ NDA
52399	OTH INORG CMPNDS NES ETC			W 4138	9456	W 2335	6212	W 1324	3905	AUT COMP INORGANIQUES NDA
53	DYES,TANNING,COLOUR PROD				8637		11365		12701	PROD TEINTURE,COLORANTS
533	PIGMENTS,PAINTS,ETC			W 5380	7759	W 7806	10167	W 9896	11250	PIGMENTS,PEINTURES,VERNIS
541	*MEDICINAL,PHARM PRODUCT				32135	K 1663573	40316	K 1482893	44788	PROD MEDICINAUX PHARMACEUT
5417	MEDICAMENTS			K 1007293	28308	K 1381350	35465	K 1288830	40613	MEDICAMENTS
54179	— CONTNG OTH SUBSTANCES			K 901263	22340	K 1275125	28649	K 1179632	33619	MED CONT AUT SUBSTANCES
55	PERFUME,CLEANING ETC PRD				26641		31515		41802	PROD POUR PARFUM,TOILETTE
553	PERFUMERY,COSMETICS,ETC			W 893	7324	W 1706	10343	W 1711	10900	PRODUITS DE PARFUMERIE

4. General Imports C.I.F. by Commodities according to the S.I.T.C. (Rev. 2) in thousand U.S. Dollars
Importations Générales C.A.F. par Produits d'après la C.T.C.I. (Rév. 2) en milliers de Dollars E.U.

SITC CTCI	COMMODITY	1993		1994		1995		1996		PRODUIT
		WEIGHT POIDS	VALUE VALEUR	WEIGHT POIDS	VALUE VALEUR	WEIGHT POIDS	VALUE VALEUR	WEIGHT POIDS	VALUE VALEUR	
554	SOAP,CLEANSING ETC PREPS			W 11726	16728	W 13469	18150	W 22685	28151	SAVONS,PRODUITS DETERSIFS
5541	SOAPS			W 6375	9282	W 5974	8869	W 9630	13868	SAVONS,PROD TENSIO–ACTIFS
5542	WASHING PREPARATIONS ETC			W 5115	6867	W 7252	8653	W 12368	12464	PROD ORG TENSIO–ACT NDA
562	*FERTILIZERS,MANUFACTURE			W 61650	9621	W 55653	13763	W 58567	11724	ENGRAIS MANUFACTURES
58	PLASTIC MATERIALS ETC				38863		43845		41059	MAT PLAST ARTIFICIELLES
583	POLYMERIZATION ETC PRODS			W 23885	33293	W 22002	35918	W 19789	32446	PROD POLYMERISATION
5833	POLYSTYRENE,ITS COPOLYMR			W 8591	7849	W 8735	10529	W 781	796	POLYPROPYLENE COPOLYMERES
58331	— IN PRIMARY FORMS			W 8591	7849	W 8735	10529	W 781	796	SOUS FORMES PRIMAIRES
5839	OTH POLYMRZTION ETC PROD			W 8085	15101	W 7284	15361	W 18520	30847	AUT PROD POLYMER COPOLYM
59	CHEMICAL MATERIALS NES				29778		32633		39426	MAT PROD CHIMIQUES NDA
591	PESTICIDES,DISINFECTANTS			W 2778	8566	W 2942	10045	W 3590	11836	DESINF,INSECT,FONG,HERB
598	MISCEL CHEM PRODUCTS NES			W 21117	18532	W 21386	20203	W 24581	24622	PROD DIV INDUST CHIM NDA
5982	ANTI–KNOCK PREPARTNS ETC			W 18156	12205	W 18341	12272	W 19751	13134	PREPARAT ANTIDETONANTES
5989	CHEM PRODUCTS,PREPS NES			W 2508	5418	W 2642	7046	W 4400	10692	PROD PREP CHIMIQUES NDA
6	BASIC MANUFACTURES		358238		355687		463485		413533	ART MANUFACTURES
62	RUBBER MANUFACTURES NES				24760		36758		38125	CAOUTCHOUC MANUFACTURE
625	RUBBER TYRES, TUBES ETC			W 3478	12664	W 6571	24841	W 5914	22716	PNEUS CAOUTCHOUC VULCANISE
6251	TYRES NEW FOR MOTOR CARS			W 906	3368	W 2799	10779	W 2544	9423	PNEUS POUR VOITURES
628	RUBBER ARTICLES NES			W 864	8502	W 961	8637	W 1100	11040	OUVRAGES CAOUTCHOUC NDA
63	WOOD,CORK MANUFACTRS NES				15664		18130		21914	OUVRAGES LIEGE ET BOIS
634	VENEERS,PLYWOOD,ETC			W 25008	9503	W 15086	10485	W 14511	10216	PLACAGES,CONTRE–PLAQUES
6342	PLYWOOD OF WOOD SHEETS			W 21767	7338	W 12195	8525	W 11861	8245	BOIS CONTRE–PLAQUES
635	WOOD MANUFACTURES NES			W 3598	6146	W 3646	7546	W 5724	11680	ART MANUF EN BOIS NDA
64	PAPER,PAPERBOARD AND MFR				71642		94314		87861	PAPIERS,CARTONS & OUVRAGES
641	PAPER AND PAPERBOARD			W 61730	49232	W 66526	67854	W 61434	56821	PAPIERS ET CARTONS
6411	NEWSPRINT			W 7462	3953	W 11226	8402	W 8886	7428	PAPIER JOURNAL
6413	KRAFT PAPER,PAPERBOARD			W 16929	11205	W 15992	12915	W 15056	10054	PAPIER ET CARTON KRAFT
64131	KRAFT LINER IN BULK			W 16929	11205	W 15992	12915			PAP KRAFT POUR COUVERTURES
64139	KRAFT PAPER PAPERBD,NES							W 15056	10054	PAPIER,CARTON KRAFT NDA
6415	PAPER,PAPERBRD,BULK,NES			W 7176	7337	W 8609	11999	W 8682	9712	PAPIERS,CARTONS ROULEAUX
64159	OTHER PAPER ETC,BULK,NES			W 7048	6928	W 8481	11610	W 7019	7559	AUT PAPIER ROULEAUX FEUILLES
6417	CORRUGATED PAPER ETC,BLK			W 13990	10145	W 14449	13861	W 11638	10395	PAPIERS,CARTONS ONDULES
6418	COATED ETC PAPER NES BLK			W 9216	10888	W 10515	14981	W 11498	14991	PAP,CARTONS COUCHES,ENDUITS
642	PAPER,ETC,PRECUT,ARTS OF			W 8750	22411	W 9076	26461	W 10467	31040	PAP,CARTONS DECOUPES
6421	PAPER ETC CONTAINERS			W 3785	7111	W 3938	8711	W 5216	11289	BOITES,SACS EMBALLAGES
6428	PAPER ETC ARTICLES NES			W 2549	9000	W 2833	11176	W 3228	13598	OUVRAGES EN PATE A PAPIER
64285	PAPER ETC DIAPERS ETC			W 1412	5422	W 1778	7583	W 2202	9481	SERVIETTES HYGIENIQUES
65	TEXTILE YARN,FABRICS,ETC				78808		74314		69350	FILS,TISSUS,ARTICLES TEXTILE
651	TEXTILE YARN			W 1151	7335	W 658	4752	W 662	4094	FILS TEXTILES
652	COTTON FABRICS,WOVEN			W 3075	17635	W 2622	14102	W 1898	10504	TISSUS DE COTON
6522	WOVEN COTTON BLEACHD,ETC			W 2055	12763	W 2423	13078	W 1746	9846	TISSUS COTON BLANCHIS ETC
65225	BLCHD COTN BLEND FAB NES			W 865	6877	W 908	5099	W 852	4664	AUT TIS MOINS 85% COT BLANCH
653	WOVN MAN–MADE FIB FABRIC			W 3664	20339	W 3798	21205	W 3854	22048	TISSUS FIBRES SYNTH,ARTIF
6534	DISC SYN BLEND FABRC NES			W 1959	9871	W 2095	10073	W 1771	8627	TISSUS FIBRES SYNTH DISCONT
65341	DISC SYN FIB–COTTN FABRC			W 1699	7474	W 1803	7809	W 1478	7419	TISSUS FIB SYNT DIS MEL COTO
656	LACE,RIBBONS,TULLE,ETC			W 568	7830	W 728	7160	W 592	5688	TULLES,BRODERIE
657	SPECIAL TXTL FABRC,PRODS			W 1588	12210	W 1847	11899	W 1576	10818	TISSUS SPECIAUX
6573	COATED ETC TEXTILES NES			W 1058	9373	W 1030	7942	W 896	6597	TISSUS,ART MATIERE TEXT NDA
65733	RUBBERIZED TEXT NOT KNIT			W 752	7900	W 726	6451	W 688	5119	TISSUS CAOUTCHOUTES
66	NONMETAL MINERAL MFS NES				37244		47551		46048	ART MIN NON METALLIQUES
661	LIME,CEMENT,BLDG PRODS			W 44531	6684	W 124386	10632	W 61304	8551	CHAUX,CIMENTS MAT CONSTR
662	CLAY,REFRACTORY BLDG PRD			W 18407	10324	W 26991	14948	W 30601	15721	MAT CONST REFRACTAIRES
6624	BRICKS ETC NONREFRACTORY			W 15350	8194	W 24894	12923	W 26755	12841	BRIQUES ETC CERAM NON REFR
66245	GLAZED CERAMIC SETTS ETC			W 11234	6015	W 17800	9235	W 20079	9361	AUT CARREAUX CERAMIQUE
665	GLASSWARE			W 11224	9782	W 7882	8658	W 4675	7076	OUVRAGES EN VERRE
6651	BOTTLES ETC OF GLASS			W 10233	7456	W 6376	5177	W 3238	3659	RECIPIENTS EN VERRE
66511	GLASS BOTTLES ETC NONVAC			W 10233	7444	W 6376	5176	W 3238	3657	BONBONNES,BOUTEILLES,ETC
67	IRON AND STEEL				43560		87714		50253	FER ET ACIER
673	IRON,STEEL SHAPES ETC			W 52978	19536	W 90770	38241	W 49054	17828	BARRES,PROFIL FER,ACIER
6732	IRON,STEEL BARS ETC			W 45264	14873	W 74851	25832	W 43305	14329	BARRES FER,ACIER
67325	OTH ALLOY STEEL BARS ETC			W 34278	11367	W 74066	25270	W 41825	13792	BARRES NON ACIERS ALLIES
6733	IRON,STEEL PROFILES ETC			W 5644	3801	W 13329	11128	W 4455	2930	PROFILES,PALPLAN FER,ACIER
674	IRN,STL UNIV,PLATE,SHEET			W 13388	9737	W 20235	14876	W 18135	13878	LARGES PLATS,TOLES
678	IRON,STL TUBES,PIPES,ETC			W 3127	8051	W 10506	24878	W 7449	11790	TUBES,TUYAUX EN FONTE,FER
6783	IRON,STL TUBES,PIPES NES			W 1874	2884	W 7001	15184	W 5361	5821	AUT TUBES,TUYAUX FER,ACIER
68	NON–FERROUS METALS				14988		20671		17638	METAUX NON FERREUX
684	ALUMINIUM			W 2083	6205	W 2811	10265	W 2729	9075	ALUMINIUM
69	METAL MANUFACTURES NES				67767		82377		81011	ART MANUFACT EN METAL NDA
691	STRUCTURES AND PARTS NES			W 3935	7640	W 5078	10581	W 5258	11067	CONSTRUCT FER,ACIER,ALU
6911	STRUCTURES,PARTS IRN,STL			W 3746	6545	W 4807	9376	W 4925	9430	CONSTRUCT FER,ACIER,FONTE
692	METAL TANKS,BOXES,ETC			W 4185	11632	W 3982	10659	W 3772	10549	RECIPIENTS METALLIQUES
6924	MTL TRANSPORT BOXES ETC			W 4042	10897	W 3587	9407	W 3500	9321	FUTS,TAMBOURS,BIDONS
693	WIRE PRODUCTS NON ELECTR			W 5515	8686	W 5050	9584	W 3860	6971	OUVRAGES FILS METALLIQUES
697	BASE MTL HOUSEHOLD EQUIP			W 2350	8340	W 2629	10273	W 2766	11016	ART MENAGE MET COMMUNS
699	BASE METAL MFRS NES				18672	W 6076	24961		24696	ART MANUFACTURES MET NDA
7	MACHINES,TRANSPORT EQUIP		564442		547407		759078		776158	MACHINES MATERIEL TRANSPORT
71	POWER GENERATING EQUIPMT				42093		52444		58516	MACHINES GENERATRICES
712	STEAM ENGINES,TURBINES			W 260	12464	W 83	8694	W 109	10434	MACHINES A VAPEUR D'EAU PIEC
7129	STM ENGINE ETC PARTS NES			W 212	10623	W 62	4248	W 74	4188	PARTIES,PIECES DU 712.6
713	INTRNL COMBUS PSTN ENGIN			W 1763	13658	W 1825	19473	W 1822	20154	MOTEURS EXPL COMB INT, PIECE
7139	PISTON ENGINE PARTS NES			W 259	4574	W 343	5849	W 447	9587	PIECES POUR 713.2,3,8
716	ROTATING ELECTRIC PLANT			W 865	12419	W 800	14092	W 1636	22968	APP ELECTR ROTATIFS,PIECES
7161	DC MOTORS AND GENERATORS			W 243	5593	W 150	4900	W 884	12951	MOTEURS COURANT CONTINU
72	MACHS FOR SPCL INDUSTRYS				42380		46851		57142	MAC SPECIALES POUR INDUST
723	CIVIL ENGNEERG EQUIP ETC			W 2111	5615	W 3524	11890	W 4801	23812	APPAREILS DE GENIE CIVIL
7234	CONST,MINING MACHNRY NES			W 1914	5212	W 3200	11462	W 4399	22521	MACH POUR LA CONST, MINES
72342	SLFPRP SHOVELS,EXCAVATRS			W 1410	4015	W 2207	8827	W 2198	8685	PELLES MECANIQUES
724	TEXTILE,LEATHER MACHNRY			W 774	9636	W 1163	6362		6277	MACH POUR INDUSTRIE TEXTILE
726	PRINTG,BKBINDG MACHY,PTS			W 356	7173	W 174	4155	W 112	2381	MACHINES POUR IMPRIMERIE
728	OTH MACHY FOR SPCL INDUS			W 1129	8784	W 1071	8646	W 1108	12386	AUT MACH IND PARTICULIERES
74	GENRL INDUSTRL MACHY NES				95109		105796		144185	MACH APP INDUSTRIE
741	HEATING,COOLING EQUIPMNT			W 1734	16713	W 2080	21135	W 2424	22716	MACH CHAUFFAGE,PIECES
7414	NONDOM REFRIG EQUIPT,PTS			W 649	5964	W 882	8350	W 1224	9690	MAT PRODUCTION DU FROID
742	PUMPS FOR LIQUIDS ETC			W 600	10751	W 512	10707	W 1440	14705	POMPES MOTO–POMPES
743	PUMPS NES,CENTRFUGES ETC			W 1017	11808	W 1138	13680	W 1232	19292	POMPES COMPRES,VENT ETC
7431	PUMPS FOR GASES ETC			W 342	3277	W 480	4167	W 493	9011	POMPES AIR A VIDE,COMPRES
744	MECHANICAL HANDLING EQU			W 1713	14392	W 2763	18845	W 10656	36892	EQUIP MANUTENTION PIECES
7442	LIFTING,LOADING MACH NES			W 755	4641	W 1277	5891	W 9165	23526	APP LEVAGE,MANUTENTION
74422	SHIP DERRICKS,CRANES ETC			W 164	504	W 421	707	W 8373	17343	GRUES,PONTS ROULANTS
7449	PTS NES OF MACHY OF 7442			W 474	5845	W 603	5978	W 831	10463	PIECES DU 744.2
745	NONELEC MACHY,TOOLS NES			W 578	10352	W 657	9479	W 1175	12797	AUT MACH NON ELEC,PIECES

4. General Imports C.I.F. by Commodities according to the S.I.T.C. (Rev. 2) in thousand U.S. Dollars
Importations Générales C.A.F. par Produits d'après la C.T.C.I. (Rév. 2) en milliers de Dollars E.U.

SITC CTCI	COMMODITY	1993		1994		1995		1996		PRODUIT
		WEIGHT POIDS	VALUE VALEUR	WEIGHT POIDS	VALUE VALEUR	WEIGHT POIDS	VALUE VALEUR	WEIGHT POIDS	VALUE VALEUR	
7452	OTH NONELEC MCHS,PTS NES			W 557	9945	W 634	9038	W 1144	12254	AUT MACH NON ELEC,PIECES
749	NONELEC MACH PTS,ACC NES			W 1821	31093	W 1830	31950	W 2168	37784	PIECES MACH NON ELEC NDA
7492	COCKS,VALVES ETC NES			W 841	12823	W 867	14258	W 890	16109	ART ROB,SIM POUR TUYAUX
7493	SHAFT,CRANK,PULLEY ETC			W 448	7564	W 476	8440	W 763	10651	ARBRES TRANS,VILEBREQUINS
75	OFFICE MACHNES,ADP EQUIP				33240		46047		54673	MACH BUREAU TRAIT AUTOM
752	AUTOMTIC DATA PROC EQUIP			W 280	16621	W 412	25345	W 445	32846	MACH TRAIT INFORMATION
7522	DIGITAL COMPUTERS			W 136	9615	W 193	14007	W 189	18425	MACH DIGITALES COMPLETES
759	OFFICE,ADP MCH PTS,ACCES			W 202	12707	W 214	14297	W 222	16693	PIECES DU 751 ET 752
7599	ACCTG,ETC,ADP MCH PTS,AC			W 160	11300	W 151	11705	W 184	14829	PIECES DU 751 ET 752
76	TELECOMM,SOUND EQUIPMENT				51551		67109		69424	EQUIPMENT DE TELECOM
761	TELEVISION RECEIVERS			W 554	5639	W 993	9360	W 1019	9589	RECEPTEURS DE TELEVISION
7611	COLOUR TV RECEIVERS			W 527	5412	W 949	9176	W 978	9341	RECEPTEURS COULEUR
764	TELECOM EQPT,PTS,ACC NES			W 873	41155	W 959	51294	W 860	51918	EQUIP TELECOM,PIECES
7641	LINE TELEPHONE,ETC EQUIP			W 369	22098	W 520	27754	W 319	23470	APP TELEPHON PAR FIL
7643	TV,RADIO TRANSMITTRS ETC			W 42	4036	W 80	8880	W 76	9944	APP EMET TELE RADIO
7649	PTS NES OF EQUIPMT OF 76			W 340	12979	W 255	12175	W 375	15891	PIECES DE LA DIV 76
76491	PTS NES OF APPAR OF 7641			W 117	7774	W 114	9723	W 55	9478	PIECES POUR 764.1
77	ELECTRIC MACHNRY NES ETC				89589		110548		97710	MACH APP ELECT NDA
771	ELECTRIC POWER MACHY NES			W 2991	15237	W 1380	9140	W 1408	12861	MACH PROD,TRANS ELECTR
7711	TRANSFORMERS,ELECTRICAL			W 2381	10608	W 1150	4556	W 1147	8203	TRANSFO ELECTRIQUES
77118	OTHER ELEC TRANSFORMERS			W 2165	10122	W 762	3299	W 821	6007	AUTRES TRANSFO ELECTRIQ
772	SWITCHGEAR ETC,PARTS NES			W 1064	21959	W 1362	23477	W 1111	19727	APP COUPURE,SECT ETC
7721	SWITCHGEAR ETC			W 1051	19864	W 1356	22102	W 1107	18975	APP COUPURE,SECTIONMNT
773	ELECTR DISTRIBUTNG EQUIP			W 3117	18330	W 5234	32249	W 3043	17320	EQUIPMT DISTRIBUTION ELECT
7731	INSULATED WIRE,CABLE ETC			W 2800	17286	W 4647	30453	W 2784	16197	FILS,CABLES ISOLES ELECT
775	HOUSEHOLD TYPE EQUIP NES			W 3439	15409	W 4698	22547	W 4587	23362	MACH,APP USAGE DOMESTQUE
7752	DOM REFRIGERATRS,FREEZRS			W 2432	9911	W 3407	15090	W 3076	14661	REFRIG,CONGEL MENAGER
77521	DOMESTIC REFRIGERATORS			W 1899	7381	W 2809	12198	W 2527	11949	REFRIGERATEURS
778	ELECTRICAL MACHINERY NES			W 2380	16181	W 3294	18510	W 3077	20834	AUTRES MACH ELECT NDA
78	ROAD VEHICLES				183675		265391		238385	VEHICULES ROUTIERS
781	PASS MOTOR VEH EXC BUSES			W 15031	101347	W 27233	151738	W 29099	135972	AUTO TRANSPORT PERSONNES
782	LORRIES,SPCL MTR VEH NES			W 12307	49206	W 14591	65122	W 14317	58372	VEHICULES SPECIAUX,MARCH
7821	LORRIES,TRUCKS			W 11959	47933	W 13876	52651	W 13653	55392	VEHICULES TRANSP MARCHAND
7822	SPECIAL MOTOR VEHCLS NES			W 347	1273	W 716	12472	W 664	2980	VEHICULES USAGES SPECIAUX
783	ROAD MOTOR VEHICLES NES			W 3073	10024	W 4671	19790	W 4804	12747	VEHICULES ROUTIERS NDA
7831	BUSES			W 1032	7092	W 1799	15474	W 1176	7474	VOITURES TRANSPORT COMMUN
784	MOTOR VEH PRTS,ACCES NES			W 2537	16635	W 3651	19636	W 3289	21781	PIECES 722,781,782,783
7849	OTHER MOTOR VEHCL PARTS			W 2251	16091	W 3155	18926	W 3012	21012	PIECES 722,781,782,783
79	OTHR TRANSPORT EQUIPMENT				7140		62737		53468	AUTRE MATERIEL TRANSPORT
792	AIRCRAFT ETC			W 126	4689	W 19	1213	W 101	50418	APP NAVIGATION AERIENNE
7924	AIRCRFT NES OVER 15000KG							W 60	45002	AERODYNES PLUS 15000 KG
793	SHIPS AND BOATS ETC			W 446	1649	W 20604	60552	W 300	1865	NAVIRES BATEAUX,ETC
7938	TUGS,SPECIAL VESSELS ETC			W 293	301	W 20409	59137	W 10	250	REMORQUEURS,BATEAUX SPEC
79383	FLOATING STRUCTURES NES			W 2	33	W 20403	59071	W 2	24	ENGINS FLOTTANTS DIVERS
8	MISC MANUFACTURED GOODS		313030		369083		406931		438974	ART MANUFACTURES DIVERS
812	*PLUMBG,HEATNG,LGHTNG EQ			W 1785	6363	W 2571	8412	W 2279	8835	APPAR SANITAIRES CHAUFFAGE
821	*FURNITURE,PARTS THEREOF			W 3912	13971	W 5191	19249	W 6146	22716	MEUBLES ET PIECES
8219	FURNITURE AND PARTS NES			W 2161	7641	W 3646	12245	W 4156	14672	AUTRES MEUBLES ET PIECES
82192	WOOD FURNITURE NES			W 1244	4585	W 2468	7794	W 3039	8999	MEUBLES NDA EN BOIS
84	CLOTHING AND ACCESSORIES				223860		226979		238828	VETEMENTS
844	UNDER GARMENTS NOT KNIT			W 11604	111354	W 16655	118531	W 21242	145847	VETEMENT DESSOUS MAT TEX
8441	— MENS SHIRTS			W 11542	110838	W 16577	117851	W 21149	145049	CHEMISES HOMMES MAT TEXT
84412	—— OF SYNTHETIC FIBRES			W 11508	110368	W 16537	117238	W 21098	144080	CHEMISES HOMMES FIB SYNT
846	UNDER GARMENTS KNITTED			W 3356	105090	W 3594	96966	W 3167	78442	SOUS VETS DE BONNETERIE
8463	— OF SYNTH FBR NONELAST			W 2348	90285	W 2607	85114	W 2188	66510	SOUS–VET BONNET FIB SYNT
84631	—— PANTY HOSE (TIGHTS)			W 2339	90125	W 2572	84329	W 2163	66062	COLLANTS BON FIBR SYNT
8465	CORSETS,GARTERS,ETC			W 555	12005	W 325	7015	W 328	7113	CORSETS,GAINES ART SIM
84651	BRASSIERES			W 335	6790	W 208	3823	W 120	1939	SOUTIENS–GORGE,BUSTIERS
851	*FOOTWEAR			W 576	5482	W 961	8389	W 1319	10800	CHAUSSURES
87	PRECISION INSTRUMNTS NES				16133		16595		21698	INSTRUM,APPAR SCIENT NDA
874	MEASURNG,CONTROLNG INSTR			W 239	10430	W 262	11147	W 354	15146	INSTRUMENTS DE MESURE
88	PHOTO EQU,OPTICL GDS ETC				16525		20326		21382	APP,FOURN PHOTO,OP,MONTR
885	WATCHES AND CLOCKS				10104		12070		12559	HORLOGERIE
8851	WATCHES,MOVEMENTS,CASES				9551		11413		11954	MONTRES,MOUVEMENTS,BOITES
88511	WATCHES				9501		11378		11917	MONTRES POCHE,BRACELET
89	MISC MANUFCTRD GOODS NES				85067		104747		111925	ART MANUFACTURES DIVERS
892	PRINTED MATTER			W 2503	19911	W 3181	24566	W 3798	29299	IMPRIMES
8921	PRINTED BOOKS,GLOBES,ETC			W 1659	13353	W 2325	17410	W 2640	17658	LIVRES,BROCHURES,CARTES
89211	PRINTED BOOKS,PAMPHLETS			W 1643	13210	W 2295	17254	W 2597	17481	LIVRES,BROCHURES
893	ARTICLES OF PLASTIC NES				23868		32761		32692	OUVRAGES EN MAT DIVIS 58
8931	PLSTC PACKG CONTNRS,LIDS			W 2699	10454	W 3574	12711	W 4168	13330	ART TRANSP EMBALLAGE ETC
8939	MISC PLASTIC ARTICLES			W 3067	12903	W 5011	19266	W 4670	18647	ART DIVERS EN MAT DIV 58
89399	OTHR PLASTC ARTICLES NES			W 2703	12167	W 4190	17995	W 4108	17620	AUT OUV MAT DIV 58
897	GOLD,SILVER WARE,JEWELRY				26943		29936		30603	BIJOUTERIE,ORFEVRERIE
8973	PREC JEWLRY,GLD–SILVWARE				26764		29701		30235	BIJOUX OR,ARGENT ORFEVRE
89731	PRECIOUS METAL JEWELLERY				26321		29195		29586	ART BIJOUTERIE,JOAILLER
9	GOODS NOT CLASSD BY KIND		53376		48463		81802		80392	ART TRANSACT NON CLASSES
931	*SPECIAL TRANSACTIONS				47453		80981		79673	TRANS.SPECIALES

5. General Exports F.O.B. by Commodities according to the S.I.T.C. (Rev. 2) in thousand U.S. Dollars
Exportations Générales F.O.B. par Produits d'après la C.T.C.I. (Rév. 2) en milliers de Dollars E.U.

SITC CTCI	COMMODITY	1993		1994		1995		1996		PRODUIT
		WEIGHT POIDS	VALUE VALEUR	WEIGHT POIDS	VALUE VALEUR	WEIGHT POIDS	VALUE VALEUR	WEIGHT POIDS	VALUE VALEUR	
	ALL COMMODITIES		1075376		1210651		1423784		1386876	TOUS PRODUITS
0	FOOD AND LIVE ANIMALS		226809		210255		263927		277988	ALIMENTS,ANIMAUX VIVANTS
02	DAIRY PRODCTS,BIRDS'EGGS				3533		4662		3990	PRODUITS LAITIERS,OEUFS
03	FISH AND PREPARATIONS				13975		18003		19566	POISSONS ET PREPARATIONS
036	SHELL FISH FRESH,FROZEN			W 2248	12490	W 2411	15533	W 3016	16143	CRUSTACES,MOLLUSQUES
04	CEREALS AND PREPARATIONS				8616		7921		8433	CEREALES ET PRODUITS
048	CEREAL ETC PREPARATIONS			W 3114	6946	W 3538	7809	W 3710	8425	PREPTNS A BASE CEREALES
0484	BAKERY PRODUCTS			W 2263	3989	W 2593	4846	W 2642	4850	PRODUITS DE BOULANGERIE
04841	BREAD,BISCUIT,COM WAFERS			W 2263	3989	W 2593	4846	W 1725	2842	PAINS,BISCUITS DE MER
05	VEGETABLES AND FRUIT				77339		85230		81949	LEGUMES ET FRUITS
054	VEG ETC FRSH,SMPLY PRSVD			W 18834	16019	W 18825	18325	W 18379	16269	LEGUMES FRAIS,CONG,SECS
0548	EDIBLE VEG NES FRESH,DRY			W 14755	13476	W 14958	15622	W 15123	13990	RACINES,TUBERCULES
05481	ROOTS,TUBERS FRESH,DRY			W 14636	13421	W 14858	15562	W 15032	13940	RACINES DE MANIOC ETC
057	FRUIT,NUTS,FRESH,DRIED			W 90666	55877	W 100268	58907	W 103499	59331	FRUITS FRAIS OU SECS
0571	ORANGES, MANDARINS ETC			W 7669	2658	W 9027	3772	W 10149	4803	ORANGES,MAND,CLEMENTINES
0573	BANANA,PLANTAIN,FRSH,DRY			W 75680	45917	W 83018	45794	W 85746	45220	BANANES FRAICHES,SECHEES
0579	FRUIT FRESH OR DRIED NES			W 5949	6319	W 7109	8623	W 6246	8321	FRUITS FRAIS,SECS NDA
05798	OTHER FRESH FRUIT			W 4981	5450	W 5721	7309	W 5306	7246	AUTRES FRUITS FRAIS
058	FRUIT PRESERVED,PREPARED			W 2869	5047	W 4252	7451	W 2508	5661	CONSERVES DE FRUITS
06	SUGAR AND PREPS,HONEY				68124		96135		109313	SUCRES ET PRODUITS
061	SUGAR AND HONEY			W 126224	67949	W 145004	96012	W 181488	109246	SUCRES ET MIEL
0611	RAW BEET AND CANE SUGAR			W 126106	67925	W 144986	96003	W 181473	109229	SUCRES BRUTS
07	COFFEE,TEA,COCOA,SPICES				27019		38741		40561	CAFE,THE,CACAO,EPICES
071	COFFEE AND SUBSTITUTES			W 982	16699	W 1549	28256	W 1660	32262	CAFE ET SUCCEDANES
0711	COFFEE GREEN,ROASTED,SUB			W 972	16563	W 1544	28160	W 1651	32098	CAFE TORREFIE OU DECAFEINE
07111	COFFEE GREEN,HUSKS,SKINS			W 948	16029	W 1525	27638	W 1631	31487	CAFE NON TORREFIE
072	COCOA			W 2874	4190	W 2286	3900	W 1607	2661	CACAO
075	SPICES			W 2412	4683	W 2330	5264	W 2013	4793	EPICES
0751	PEPPER AND PIMENTO			W 2143	3802	W 2065	4387	W 1731	3804	POIVRE,PIMENTS
09	MISC EDIBLE PRODUCTS				9339		10901		11747	PREP ALIMENTAIRES DIVERSES
098	EDIBLE PRODCTS,PREPS NES			W 3875	9339	W 4362	10901	W 4617	11747	PREP ALIMENTAIRES NDA
09804	SAUCES,MIXED SEASONINGS			W 1324	3562	W 1371	4465	W 1187	3942	SAUCES,ASSAISONNEMENTS
09809	MISC FOOD PREPRTIONS NES			W 2010	4288	W 2392	4729	W 2864	5778	PREP ALIMENTAIRES NDA
1	BEVERAGES AND TOBACCO		40647		40181		43455		47523	BOISSONS ET TABACS
11	BEVERAGES				33700		34797		37309	BOISSONS
112	ALCOHOLIC BEVERAGES			W 26297	32732	W 25921	33745	W 17037	36307	BOISSONS ALCOOLIQUES
1123	BEER,ALE,STOUT,PORTER			W 8685	7572	W 9326	8009	W 8848	7855	BIERES
1124	DISTILLED ALCOHOLIC BEVS			W 17079	23985	W 16048	24494	W 7477	26872	ALCOOLS,EAUX-DE-VIE
11249	OTH ALCOHOLC BEVS,CMPNDS			W 17073	23960	W 16041	24471	W 7469	26842	BOISSONS ALCOOLIQUES NDA
12	TOBACCO AND MANUFACTURES				6480		8658		10214	TABACS BRUTS FABRIQUES
122	TOBACCO,MANUFACTURED			W 145	6229	W 175	8399	W 186	9837	TABACS FABRIQUES
1221	CIGARS,CHEROOTS,ETC			W 133	5991	W 161	8138	W 170	9534	CIGARES
2	CRUDE MATERLS,EXCL FUELS		531991		615203		706429		692600	MAT BRUTES NON COMESTIBLES
28	METALLIFEROUS ORES,SCRAP				608712		699801		687020	MINERAIS METAL,DECHETS
287	BASE METAL ORES,CONC NES			W 3939046	606429	W 3593957	697801	W 7139451	685363	MINERAIS METAUX COMMUNS
2873	ALUMINIUM ORES,ALUMINA			W 3939046	606429	W 3593907	697757	W 7139451	685363	MINERAIS D'ALUMINIUM
28731	ALUMINIUM ORE,CONCNTRATE			W 649419	72944	W 609095	72182	W 3917478	78350	MINERAIS D'ALUMINIUM
28732	ALUMINA(ALUMINIUM OXIDE)			W 3289627	533485	W 2984812	625575	W 3221973	607013	ALUMINE (OXYDE ALUMINIUM)
29	CRUDE ANIMAL,VEG MAT NES				4087		2986		2523	MATIERES BRUTES ANIM,VEGET
292	CRUDE VEG MATERIALS NES			W 46334	4087	W 11695	2979		2523	MAT BRUTES VEGETALES NDA
3	MINERAL FUELS ETC		6558		5978		7632		5977	COMBUSTIBLES MINERAUX LUB
33	PETROLEUM AND PRODUCTS				5978		7632		5977	PETROLE ET DERIVES
334	PETROLEUM PRODUCTS,REFIN			W 14525	5971	W 17706	7610	W 12886	5962	PRODUITS RAFFINES
5	CHEMCLS,RELATED PROD NES		25441		24574		37456		46591	PRODUITS CHIMIQUES
51	ORGANIC CHEMICALS				648		9240		18584	PROD CHIMIQ ORGANIQUES
512	ALCOHOLS,PHENOLS ETC			W 103	62	W 25907	9086	W 31151	13704	PHENOLS,PHENOLS–ALCOOLS
5121	ACYCLIC ALCOHOLS,DERIVS			W 103	62	W 25907	9086	W 31151	13704	ALCOOLS ACYCLIQUES
51216	ETHYL ALC,DENATRD SPIRIT					W 25752	9000	W 30694	12106	ALCOOL ETHYLIQUE NON DENAT
516	OTHER ORGANIC CHEMICALS			W 30	33	W 19	20	W 10979	4216	AUTRES PROD ORGANIQUES
5161	ETHERS,EPOXIDES,ACETALS			W 1	4	W 11	11	W 10976	4212	ETHERS–OXYDES,ALCOOLS
51611	ETHERS,ETHER–ALCOHOL,ETC			W 1	3	W 11	11	W 10976	4212	ETHERS–OXYDES
52	INORGANIC CHEMICALS				7247		11070		10219	PROD CHIM INORGANIQUES
522	INORG ELEMNTS,OXIDES,ETC			W 60242	5928	W 79124	9885	W 53000	8902	ELEMENTS INORGANIQUES
5225	INORGANIC BASES ETC NES			W 59425	5704	W 76834	8894	W 49009	6586	AUTRES BASES OXYDES METAL
52256	ALUMINIUM HYDROXIDE			W 59406	5671	W 76834	8894	W 49009	6586	HYDROXYDE D'ALUMINIUM
55	PERFUME,CLEANING ETC PRD				12374		13203		12241	PROD POUR PARFUM,TOILETTE
551	ESSENTL OILS,PERFUME,ETC			W 759	3361	W 773	3611	W 2190	5143	HUILES ESSENTIELLES
553	PERFUMERY,COSMETICS,ETC			W 1149	5993	W 1157	6167	W 1043	5229	PRODUITS DE PARFUMERIE
6	BASIC MANUFACTURES		16064		21304		19372		19417	ART MANUFACTURES
62	RUBBER MANUFACTURES NES				7127		5166		5592	CAOUTCHOUC MANUFACTURE
625	RUBBER TYRES, TUBES ETC			W 2205	7112		5143	W 1541	5525	PNEUS CAOUTCHOUC VULCANISE
66	NONMETAL MINERAL MFS NES				3948		4007		1902	ART MIN NON METALLIQUES
69	METAL MANUFACTURES NES				5329		4782		4328	ART MANUFACT EN METAL NDA
7	MACHINES,TRANSPORT EQUIP		14311		27788		43630		31591	MACHINES MATERIEL TRANSPORT
71	POWER GENERATING EQUIPMT				11041		15431		6235	MACHINES GENERATRICES
713	INTRNL COMBUS PSTN ENGIN			W 32	10906	W 53	15349	W 44	5953	MOTEURS EXPL COMB INT, PIECE
7131	AIRCRAFT PSTN ENGINS,PTS			W 28	10886	W 49	15308	W 32	5613	MOTEURS EXPL P.AVIATION, PIE
71311	AIRCRAFT PISTON ENGINES			W 28	10870	W 47	14764	W 31	5531	MOTEURS EXPL P.AVIATION
72	MACHS FOR SPCL INDUSTRYS				876		4946		2336	MAC SPECIALES POUR INDUST
724	TEXTILE,LEATHER MACHNRY			W 41	530	W 243	4668	W 105	1219	MACH POUR INDUSTRIE TEXTILE
7245	WEAVING,FELT MFG,ETC MCH					W 185	4487		3	METIERS A TISSER,PIECES
72453	GIMPING,WARPING ETC MCHS					W 185	4487		3	METIERS A TULLE ETC
77	ELECTRIC MACHNRY NES ETC				2566		5079		3986	MACH APP ELECT NDA
79	OTHR TRANSPORT EQUIPMENT				8961		11116		13089	AUTRE MATERIEL TRANSPORT
792	AIRCRAFT ETC			W 56	8901	W 71	11100	W 47	12646	APP NAVIGATION AERIENNE
7929	AIRCRAFT PARTS NES			W 56	8901	W 56	11090	W 47	12646	PIECES DU 792
8	MISC MANUFACTURED GOODS		211925		263826		301002		265162	ART MANUFACTURES DIVERS
821	*FURNITURE,PARTS THEREOF			W 755	4497	W 561	3483	W 433	3367	MEUBLES ET PIECES
84	CLOTHING AND ACCESSORIES				249080		287334		250309	VETEMENTS
842	MENS OUTERWEAR NOT KNIT			W 410	5993	W 456	6472	W 520	7600	VET DESSUS POUR HOMMES
8423	— TROUSERS,BREECHES ETC			W 341	4648	W 394	5401	W 429	5887	PANTALONS HOMMES MAT TEX
843	WOMENS OUTERWEAR NONKNIT			W 998	15073	W 844	13724	W 760	13996	VET DESSUS FEMMES MAT TEX
8439	— OTHER OUTER GARMENTS			W 894	12591	W 788	11652	W 751	13783	AUT VET DES FEM MAT TEXT
844	UNDER GARMENTS NOT KNIT			W 665	9135	W 578	10731	W 410	8745	VETEMENT DESSOUS MAT TEX
8441	— MENS SHIRTS			W 293	6450	W 404	8157	W 318	7475	CHEMISES HOMMES MAT TEXT
84412	—— OF SYNTHETIC FIBRES			W 229	5268	W 372	7728	W 316	7398	CHEMISES HOMMES FIB SYNT
845	OUTERWEAR KNIT NONELASTC			W 688	10049	W 515	8467	W 227	3807	VET DESSOUS,ACCES BONNET
8459	— OTHER,CLTHG ACCESRYS			W 548	7873	W 384	6824	W 217	3665	AUT VET DESSUS DE BONNE
846	UNDER GARMENTS KNITTED			W 10500	206762	W 14601	245205	W 13902	214847	SOUS VETS DE BONNETERIE
8462	— OF COTTON NON ELASTIC			W 7576	74022	W 11819	110822	W 12098	127906	SOUS–VET BONNET COTON
84629	—— OTHER			W 7576	74022	W 11819	110822	W 12098	127906	AUT SOUS–VET BONNET COTON

5. General Exports F.O.B. by Commodities according to the S.I.T.C. (Rev. 2) in thousand U.S. Dollars
Exportations Générales F.O.B. par Produits d'après la C.T.C.I. (Rév. 2) en milliers de Dollars E.U.

SITC CTCI	COMMODITY	1993 WEIGHT POIDS	1993 VALUE VALEUR	1994 WEIGHT POIDS	1994 VALUE VALEUR	1995 WEIGHT POIDS	1995 VALUE VALEUR	1996 WEIGHT POIDS	1996 VALUE VALEUR	PRODUIT
8463	— OF SYNTH FBR NONELAST			W 2220	113943	W 2214	117745	W 1369	74609	SOUS–VET BONNET FIB SYNT
84631	—— PANTY HOSE (TIGHTS)			W 2176	113275	W 2097	116039	W 1366	74579	COLLANTS BON FIBR SYNT
8465	CORSETS,GARTERS,ETC			W 704	18796	W 567	16638	W 435	12332	CORSETS,GAINES ART SIM
84651	BRASSIERES			W 322	11972	W 275	10501	W 141	5521	SOUTIENS–GORGE,BUSTIERS
84652	CORSETS,BRACES ETC			W 382	6824	W 292	6138	W 294	6811	CORSETS,GAINES,JARRETEL
89	MISC MANUFCTRD GOODS NES				8074		7458		7987	ART MANUFACTURES DIVERS

1. HISTORICAL SERIES, 1961–1996 GENERAL TRADE, IMPORTS C.I.F., EXPORTS F.O.B.
SERIES HISTORIQUES, 1961–1996 COMMERCE GENERAL, IMPORTATIONS C.A.F., EXPORTATIONS F.O.B

YEAR ANNEE	VALUE IN MILLION YEN VALEUR EN MILLION YEN MERCHANDISE – MARCHANDISE		GOLD – OR		CONVERSION FACTORS U.S. CENTS PER YEN FACTEURS DE CONVERSION CENTS E.U. PAR YEN		INDEX NUMBERS – INDICES QUANTUM		UNIT VALUE VALEUR UNITAIRE	
	IMPORTS	EXPORTS	IMPORTS	EXPORTS	IMPORTS	EXPORTS	IMPORTS	EXPORTS	IMPORTS	EXPORTS
1961	2091433.00	1524838.00	230.40	554.40	0.2778	0.2778	46	41	140	123
1962	2029158.00	1769618.00	50.40	842.30	0.2778	0.2778	46	49	138	120
1963	2424766.00	1962563.00	86.39	878.30	0.2778	0.2778	54	55	139	119
1964	2857451.00	2402088.00	50.40	914.30	0.2778	0.2778	62	68	143	118
1965	2940605.00	3042477.00	50.40	806.30	0.2778	0.2778	63	88	146	116
1966	3428006.00	3519078.00		1526.00	0.2778	0.2778	73	101	147	116
1967	4198711.00	3758966.00	50.40	1418.00	0.2778	0.2778	89	105	146	120
1968	4675407.00	4669796.00	4082.00	986.30	0.2778	0.2778	101	130	144	120
1969	5408473.00	5756403.00	18877.00	1706.00	0.2778	0.2778	117	154	144	125
1970	6797221.00	6954369.00	30360.00	1166.00	0.2778	0.2778	35	25	57	69
1971	6909956.00	8392769.00	31209.00	782.70	0.2853	0.2862	35	29	58	70
1972	7228977.00	8806072.00	27114.00	628.30	0.3247	0.3247	40	31	53	69
1973	10404356.00	10031427.00	95600.00	1641.00	0.3682	0.3681	53	33	59	73
1974	18076381.00	16207880.00			0.3436	0.3426	50	40	106	98
1975	17170026.00	16545312.00			0.3371	0.3375	44	40	115	101
1976	19229167.00	19934617.00			0.3370	0.3372	48	48	117	101
1977	19131781.00	21648068.00			0.3700	0.3718	49	52	114	101
1978	16727625.00	20555841.00			0.4743	0.4745	52	52	94	96
1979	24245350.00	22531538.00			0.4565	0.4573	59	53	121	104
1980	31994998.00	29382000.00			0.4392	0.4418	57	62	164	115
1981	31464001.00	33469001.00			0.4554	0.4542	56	68	164	119
1982	32655998.00	34432999.00			0.4029	0.4021	56	67	171	125
1983	30015000.00	34909999.00			0.4213	0.4210	57	72	156	117
1984	32319999.00	40325001.00			0.4214	0.4208	63	84	152	117
1985	31075999.00	41958998.00			0.4200	0.4223	63	88	146	116
1986	21551001.00	35291000.00			0.5920	0.5974	69	87	92	98
1987	21738999.00	33315999.00			0.6950	0.6944	75	87	85	92
1988	24007000.00	33927999.00			0.7807	0.7808	87	91	81	90
1989	28980998.00	37823000.00			0.7238	0.7244	94	95	90	97
1990	33854001.00	41457000.00			0.6954	0.6938	100	100	100	100
1991	31900000.00	42359001.00			0.7439	0.7440	104	103	91	100
1992	29526999.00	43010998.00			0.7900	0.7903	104	104	84	100
1993	26823999.00	40199999.00			0.9009	0.9012	107	102	75	96
1994	28051001.00	40469999.00			0.9813	0.9811	121	103	69	95
1995	31533998.00	41531998.00			1.0655	1.0673	136	107	68	94
1996	37992001.00	44728999.00			0.9191	0.9187	141	107	80	101

2. IMPORTS BY BROAD ECONOMIC CATEGORY AND EXPORTS BY INDUSTRIAL ORIGIN. (PERCENTAGE OF TOTAL VALUE)
IMPORTATIONS PAR CATEGORIES ECONOMIQUES ET EXPORTATIONS PAR BRANCHE D'ACTIVITE.(EN POURCENTAGE DE LA VALEUR TOTALE)

IMPORTS – IMPORTATIONS

	1990	1991	1992	1993	1994	1995	1996
TOTAL IMPORTS–IMPORTATIONS TOTALES	100.	100.	100.	100.	100.	100.	100.
1 FOOD BEV–ALIMENTATION BOISSONS	12.4	13.2	14.5	14.8	15.6	13.8	13.2
11 PRIMARY–PRODUITS DE BASE	9.3	9.8	10.7	11.1	11.5	10.1	9.5
111 FOR INDUSTRY–POUR L'INDUSTRIE	2.1	2.0	2.1	2.1	2.5	1.8	2.0
112 FOR HOUSEHOLDS–POUR LES MENAGES	7.2	7.8	8.6	9.0	9.0	8.3	7.5
12 PROCESSED–PRODUITS ELABORES	3.1	3.4	3.7	3.8	4.1	3.7	3.6
121 FOR INDUSTRY–POUR L'INDUSTRIE	0.6	0.6	0.7	0.6	0.6	0.6	0.5
122 FOR HOUSEHOLDS–POUR LES MENAGES	2.5	2.8	3.1	3.2	3.5	3.2	3.1
2 IND SUPPLIES–APPROV INDUSTRIELS	32.2	32.5	30.1	30.2	29.1	29.0	26.3
21 PRIMARY–PRODUITS DE BASE	11.9	11.1	10.5	10.2	9.3	8.5	7.7
22 PROCESSED–PRODUITS ELABORES	20.4	21.4	19.6	20.0	19.8	20.5	18.6
3 FUELS–COMBUSTIBLES	24.4	23.3	22.7	20.5	17.5	16.0	17.3
31 PRIMARY–PRODUITS DE BASE	20.1	19.9	19.9	18.2	15.6	14.2	15.0
32 PROCESSED–PRODUITS ELABORES	4.3	3.4	2.9	2.3	1.9	1.8	2.3
321 MOTOR SPIRIT–ESSENCE			1.5	1.2	1.0	1.1	1.2
322 OTHER–AUTRES	4.3	3.4	1.3	1.1	0.9	0.7	1.1
4 MACHINERY–EQUIPEMENT	10.9	11.7	11.7	12.6	14.1	17.4	19.5
41 CAPITAL EQUIPMENT–MACHINES	7.8	8.1	8.0	8.5	9.4	11.4	13.1
42 PARTS–PIECES ACCESSOIRES	3.2	3.5	3.7	4.1	4.7	6.0	6.5
5 TRANSPORT–TRANSPORT	5.6	5.2	5.2	5.1	5.6	5.4	5.3
51 PASSENGER CARS–AUTOMOBILES	2.7	2.2	2.2	2.1	2.6	3.0	2.9
52 OTHER–AUTRES	1.5	1.6	1.5	1.4	1.6	1.0	0.9
521 INDUSTRIAL–INDUSTRIELS	1.4	1.5	1.4	1.3	1.5	0.8	0.8
522 NON INDUSTRIAL–NON INDUSTRIEL	0.1	0.1	0.1	0.1	0.1	0.1	0.1
53 PARTS–PIECES ACCESSOIRES	1.5	1.4	1.5	1.5	1.4	1.4	1.5
6 CONSUM GOODS–BIENS CONSOMMATION	13.2	12.8	14.3	15.4	16.7	17.0	16.9
61 DURABLE–DURABLES	4.2	3.1	3.0	3.2	3.7	3.9	3.9
62 SEMI DURABLE–SEMI DURABLES	7.3	7.8	9.1	9.9	10.6	10.8	10.8
63 NON DURABLE–NON DURABLES	1.8	1.9	2.2	2.3	2.4	2.4	2.2
7 GOODS NES–BIENS NDA	1.2	1.4	1.5	1.4	1.5	1.4	1.4

EXPORTS – EXPORTATIONS

	1990	1991	1992	1993	1994	1995	1996
TOTAL EXPORTS–EXPORTATIONS TOTALES	100.	100.	100.	100.	100.	100.	100.
1 AGRICULTURE	0.3	0.3	0.3	0.2	0.2	0.2	0.3
2 MINING QUARRY–INDUS EXTRACTIVES	0.1	0.1	0.1	0.1	0.1	0.1	0.1
3 MANUFACTURING–IND MANUFACTUR	99.6	99.6	99.6	99.6	99.6	99.7	99.6
31 FOOD BEV TOBACCO–ALIM BOISS TAB	0.5	0.4	0.4	0.4	0.4	0.4	0.4
32 TEXTILES–INDUSTRIES TEXTILES	2.3	2.4	2.4	2.1	1.9	1.8	1.9
33 WOOD & PRODUCTS–BOIS & PRODUITS	0.0	0.0	0.0	0.0	0.0	0.0	0.0
34 PAPER & PRODUCTS–PAPIER & PRODT	0.9	0.8	0.8	0.7	0.7	0.7	0.6
35 CHEMICALS–INDUSTRIES CHIMIQUES	8.8	8.7	8.8	8.8	9.3	10.2	10.4
36 NON METAL MIN–MIN NON METAL	1.1	1.1	1.1	1.1	1.2	1.3	1.3
37 BASIC METAL–IND METAL BASE	5.2	5.1	4.7	4.8	4.6	5.0	4.7
38 METAL MANUF–MANUF METAL	77.6	77.8	78.2	78.6	78.5	77.0	76.6
39 OTH MANUF IND–AUTRES MANUF	3.2	3.2	3.2	3.1	3.1	3.3	3.7

3. TRADE BY PRINCIPAL COUNTRIES OF PRODUCTION AND LAST CONSIGNMENT (VALUE IN THOUSAND U.S. DOLLARS)
ECHANGES SELON LES PRINCIPAUX PAYS DE PRODUCTION ET DE DERNIERE CONSIGNATION (VALEUR EN MILLIERS DE DOLLARS EU)

COUNTRIES–PAYS	GENERAL IMPORTS C.I.F. IMPORTATIONS GENERALES C.A.F				
	1992	1993	1994	1995	1996
World	233021535	240670207	274741972	336094207	349186135
Africa	3535409	3781357	4017749	4624511	4968843
Americas	68772200	71866174	81395207	98142919	101048332
Northern America	60496163	63981191	72304549	86784408	90003390
LAIA	7688257	7368558	8532376	10714281	10422272
CACM	175976	143093	226472	282432	263540
Caribbean	243082	201623	177873	219012	208592
Rest of America	168722	171709	153937	142786	150538
As.ex F.USSR	104860746	109693728	125111841	155076470	166166206
Eur.x F.USSR	38341626	37195397	43413131	54647612	54748391
EU	33700904	32913148	38839887	48871892	49381779
EFTA	4040558	3802524	4147784	5281885	4828746
East Europe	546037	423043	377390	443245	479582
Other Europe	4744	8501	5754	10491	17186
Former USSR	2538609	3027217	3730896	5109081	4337506
Oceania	14970393	15103088	17068383	18491518	17912922
USA/Etats–Unis d'Amer	52716566	55764485	63288200	75900478	79771031
China/Chine	16925933	20437099	27483606	36017105	40436102
Korea, Republic of	11568277	11638808	13488876	17281350	15948887
Australia/Australie	12445488	12216770	13641649	14558428	14229450
Indonesia/Indonésie	12228974	12499510	12923617	14225667	15193831
Germany/Allemagne	10750514	9787554	11120991	13725596	14161664
United Arab Emirates	9733276	9005007	9143999	10203251	11516119
Saudi Arabia	10181161	8937503	8387118	9730278	10664668
Canada	7680306	8091287	8917408	10777654	10114660
Malaysia/Malaisie	6572264	7639694	8228439	10564382	11750420
Thailand/Thaïlande	5945138	6488264	8192092	10119957	10212284
United Kingdom	4894935	4945298	5907798	7133666	7168249
France, Monac	5405232	5127418	5668088	6679188	6264968
Italy/Italie	4156072	3824145	4932142	6362026	6759409
Singapore/Singapour	3092063	3600592	4645129	6864280	7322606
Russian Federation	2404420	2756027	3473665	4738302	3936973
Switz.Liecht	3185055	2839190	3068706	4053719	3563416
Brazil/Brésil	2844640	2841474	3245698	3942095	3754119
Philippines	2336656	2373662	2651964	3476127	4522051
Iran (Islamic Rp. of)	2604509	2439276	2758886	2823677	3279875
India/Inde	2043307	2283264	2665381	2924138	2842786
Chile/Chili	1886323	1820741	2163752	3166318	2762662
So. Africa Customs Un	1934355	1920362	2220828	2567473	2852903
Hong Kong	2044368	1986453	2144184	2738346	2574304
Qatar	2175510	2121460	1972527	2177227	2466972
Kuwait/ Koweït	1188910	1676678	2093002	2779114	3174968
New Zealand	1724032	1750572	2067863	2542171	2458068
Sweden/Suède	1206912	1538381	1832363	2584946	2798438
Belgium–Luxembourg	1294031	1393283	1840650	2393554	2358031
Oman	1962415	1558950	1858006	1869442	1955398
Netherlands/Pays–Bas	1314431	1334472	1602551	2186746	2102989
Denmark/Danemark	1436184	1555697	1637872	1922531	1702742
Ireland/Irlande	1076221	1301734	1415285	1978596	2104722
Mexico/Mexique	1247265	1074063	1341693	1495523	1889632
Viet Nam	868164	1064532	1348065	1720353	2017803
Brunei Darussalam	1359639	1416206	1204777	1356296	1392391
Spain/Espagne	770873	727457	1134744	1510108	1552183
Israel/Israël	694620	776255	980122	1296186	1231620
Norway,SVD,JM	712599	803450	864271	994942	1004919
Austria/Autriche	744924	685654	790323	910177	965676
Finland/Finlande	354238	424108	657574	1156939	1162730
Papua New Guinea	411978	675662	755181	728853	595206
Pakistan	530067	500878	549118	593851	574770
Argentina/Argentine	511636	488951	434334	427622	521669
Peru/Pérou	346487	340127	425002	536607	427073
Venezuela	446868	363621	344369	468052	285625
Bahrain/Bahreïn	304092	381656	393838	370477	431617
Colombia/Colombie	228130	272119	389010	414077	396229
Morocco/Maroc	249044	266605	285412	377786	409810
Korea Dem People's Rp	257866	250686	319949	342051	291370

COUNTRIES–PAYS	GENERAL EXPORTS F.O.B. # 1 EXPORTATIONS GENERALES F.O.B.				
	1992	1993	1994	1995	1996
Monde	339650782	360911139	395599981	442937421	410947003
Afrique	6404799	7295713	6869856	7381717	5700111
Amériques	118631225	128595375	142270174	146365770	134836018
Amérique du Nord	103847813	112712954	124651858	127886613	118138214
ALAI	8936189	9604775	10159515	10109521	9147067
MCAC	519834	536222	443885	479493	353466
Caraïbes	989994	1083370	1072206	648173	1217922
Autre Amérique	4337395	4658053	5942710	7241970	5979349
Asie l'URSS exclus	132207504	148788814	168455699	202745634	191806212
Europe l'URSS exclus	72345349	64776311	65733050	74668323	67346724
UE	67128902	60222034	61384121	70515648	63136881
AELE	4311129	3771964	3658146	3284544	3173161
Europe de l'Est	715612	622293	561793	734408	867836
Autre de l'Europe	143777	122643	92100	74304	101309
Ancienne URSS	1195854	1675851	1381389	1339381	1270968
Océanie	8866045	9778533	10889409	10436424	9986971
USA/Etats–Unis d'Amer	96489127	106353276	118706206	122024092	112990836
Hong Kong	20734103	22666747	25712897	27725068	25355852
Korea, Republic of	17793394	19066775	24317738	31225960	29327997
Germany/Allemagne	20337584	18146887	17812843	20348944	18198350
Singapore/Singapour	12962035	16557309	19596314	23011419	20758839
China/Chine	11926404	17158371	18694013	21991318	21886794
Thailand/Thaïlande	10359859	12256756	14676847	19729984	18263487
United Kingdom	12304740	12047943	12747629	14113496	12476350
Malaysia/Malaisie	8115365	9603208	12333104	16776983	15327789
Netherlands/Pays–Bas	8110578	7450458	8379287	9941654	9251182
Australia/Australie	7043546	7702228	8693885	8099173	7404944
Indonesia/Indonésie	5576062	5986107	7652715	9968202	9058516
Canada	7089578	6328062	5913459	5819557	5120754
Philippines	3514995	4812315	5896748	7118085	8403662
France, Monac	6325185	5488657	5261680	6083874	5500014
Panama	4293272	4607972	5887430	7179026	5910197
Belgium–Luxembourg	4861443	4274295	4108508	4879398	4318866
Mexico/Mexique	3809120	3960104	4198841	3575697	3653031
Italy/Italie	3906606	3242101	3355904	4081803	3383886
Saudi Arabia	4850008	4102339	3261547	2712069	3011437
Spain/Espagne	3242409	2209416	2109766	2394701	2186311
United Arab Emirates	2727619	2551740	2261964	2110629	2309838
Switz.Liecht	2803454	2151713	2267547	2337074	2027484
So. Africa Customs Un	1757055	2032354	2054607	2469558	2075158
India/Inde	1486491	1521214	2041211	2538341	2431606
Brazil/Brésil	1139086	1613282	1875556	2584489	2217561
Ireland/Irlande	1164639	1486210	1685729	2089583	1911385
Liberia/Libéria	1490646	2157110	2046240	1806416	808995
Sweden/Suède	1697667	1292834	1483997	1698639	1438183
New Zealand	1114239	1272277	1535171	1623857	1676111
Austria/Autriche	1790448	1331850	1249670	1197684	967422
Iran (Islamic Rp. of)	2658408	1459679	929145	660597	716247
Norway,SVD,JM	1444033	1580255	1359510	900691	1094601
Russian Federation	1073795	1496628	1174387	1153516	1023002
Pakistan	1295478	1375349	853185	1230774	1155820
Israel/Israël	1002744	989837	871871	1012148	1108388
Finland/Finlande	689122	687720	985067	1387683	1149335
Turkey/Turquie	846525	1286808	621792	912718	1113687
Colombia/Colombie	643881	929783	1031831	1091305	887927
Chile/Chili	957391	802339	938260	914437	838876
Denmark/Danemark	916997	790939	856878	913911	807681
Greece/Grèce	966321	983505	609884	657988	792229
Kuwait/ Koweït	765670	974522	680346	634170	858693
Portugal	815163	789220	737278	726292	755687
Viet Nam	450180	634431	643673	921897	1138864
Egypt/Egypte	583239	745576	708994	817511	793953
Oman	794023	796394	703052	690166	655038
Argentina/Argentine	708993	710657	671813	466292	469640
Venezuela	832721	744309	423555	500499	354007
Bahamas	416135	483690	570404	96458	718282

(VALUE AS PERCENTAGE OF WORLD TOTAL)(VALEURS EN POURCENTAGE DU TOTAL MONDIAL)

	1987	1988	1989	1990	1991	1992	1993	1994	1995	1996
Africa	2.6	2.2	2.0	1.6	1.6	1.5	1.6	1.5	1.4	1.4
Americas	29.4	31.4	31.3	30.1	30.0	29.5	29.9	29.6	29.2	28.9
Northern America	25.3	27.1	27.2	26.1	26.0	26.0	26.6	26.3	25.8	25.8
LAIA	3.7	4.0	3.8	3.8	3.7	3.3	3.1	3.1	3.2	3.0
CACM	0.1	0.1	0.1	0.1	0.1	0.1	0.1	0.1	0.1	0.1
Caribbean	0.2	0.2	0.1	0.1	0.1	0.1	0.1	0.1	0.1	0.1
Rest of America	0.1	0.1	0.1	0.1	0.1	0.1	0.1	0.1	0.0	0.0
As.ex F.USSR	44.5	41.5	41.6	42.1	43.7	45.0	45.6	45.5	46.1	47.6
Eur.x F.USSR	15.5	16.6	17.0	18.4	16.8	16.5	15.5	15.8	16.3	15.7
EU	12.8	13.9	14.4	16.0	14.5	14.5	13.7	14.1	14.5	14.1
EFTA	2.4	2.2	2.2	2.0	1.9	1.7	1.6	1.5	1.6	1.4
East Europe	0.3	0.4	0.4	0.3	0.3	0.2	0.2	0.1	0.1	0.1
Other Europe	0.0	0.1	0.0	0.0	0.0	0.0	0.0	0.0	0.0	0.0
Former USSR	1.6	1.5	1.4	1.4	1.4	1.1	1.3	1.4	1.5	1.2
Oceania	6.4	6.8	6.7	6.3	6.6	6.4	6.3	6.2	5.5	5.1
USA/Etats–Unis d'Amer	21.2	22.6	23.0	22.5	22.7	22.6	23.2	23.0	22.6	22.8
China/Chine	5.0	5.3	5.3	5.1	6.0	7.3	8.5	10.0	10.7	11.6
Korea, Republic of	5.4	6.3	6.2	5.0	5.2	5.0	4.8	4.9	5.1	4.6
Australia/Australie	5.3	5.5	5.5	5.3	5.5	5.3	5.1	5.0	4.3	4.1
Indonesia/Indonésie	5.6	5.1	5.2	5.4	5.4	5.2	5.2	4.7	4.2	4.4
Germany/Allemagne	4.1	4.3	4.3	4.9	4.5	4.6	4.1	4.0	4.1	4.1
United Arab Emirates	3.6	2.8	2.9	3.9	4.4	4.2	3.7	3.3	3.0	3.3
Saudi Arabia	4.9	3.4	3.3	4.5	4.3	4.4	3.7	3.1	2.9	3.1
Canada	4.1	4.4	4.1	3.6	3.3	3.3	3.4	3.2	3.2	2.9
Malaysia/Malaisie	3.2	2.5	2.4	2.3	2.7	2.8	3.2	3.0	3.1	3.4

	1987	1988	1989	1990	1991	1992	1993	1994	1995	1996
Afrique	2.4	2.2	1.9	1.9	1.8	1.9	2.0	1.7	1.7	1.4
Amériques	42.7	39.8	39.7	37.4	35.5	34.9	35.6	36.0	33.0	32.8
Amérique du Nord	39.2	36.5	36.6	34.1	31.7	30.6	31.2	31.5	28.9	28.7
ALAI	2.0	1.9	1.9	1.9	2.2	2.6	2.7	2.6	2.3	2.2
MCAC	0.1	0.1	0.1	0.1	0.1	0.2	0.1	0.1	0.1	0.1
Caraïbes	0.3	0.3	0.3	0.3	0.3	0.3	0.3	0.3	0.1	0.3
Autre Amérique	1.1	1.0	0.9	1.0	1.3	1.3	1.3	1.5	1.6	1.5
Asie l'URSS exclus	30.7	32.3	32.9	34.6	37.4	38.9	41.2	42.6	45.8	46.7
Europe l'URSS exclus	20.0	21.4	20.7	22.1	22.0	21.3	17.9	16.6	16.9	16.4
UE	18.3	19.7	19.2	20.4	20.4	19.8	16.7	15.5	15.9	15.4
AELE	1.4	1.3	1.2	1.3	1.3	1.3	1.0	0.9	0.7	0.8
Europe de l'Est	0.3	0.3	0.2	0.3	0.2	0.2	0.2	0.1	0.2	0.2
Autre de l'Europe	0.1	0.1	0.1	0.1	0.1	0.0	0.0	0.0	0.0	0.0
Ancienne URSS	1.1	1.2	1.1	0.9	0.7	0.4	0.5	0.3	0.3	0.3
Océanie	3.0	3.2	3.6	3.1	2.7	2.6	2.7	2.8	2.4	2.4
USA/Etats–Unis d'Amer	36.8	34.1	34.1	31.7	29.3	28.4	29.5	30.0	27.5	27.5
Hong Kong	3.9	4.4	4.2	4.6	5.2	6.1	6.3	6.5	6.3	6.2
Korea, Republic of	5.8	5.8	6.0	6.1	6.4	5.2	5.3	6.1	7.0	7.1
Germany/Allemagne	5.6	6.0	5.8	6.2	6.6	6.0	5.0	4.5	4.6	4.4
Singapore/Singapour	2.6	3.1	3.4	3.7	3.9	3.8	4.6	5.0	5.2	5.1
China/Chine	3.6	3.6	3.1	2.1	2.7	3.5	4.8	4.7	5.0	5.3
Thailand/Thaïlande	1.3	1.9	2.5	3.2	3.0	3.1	3.4	3.7	4.5	4.4
United Kingdom	3.7	4.0	3.9	3.8	3.5	3.6	3.3	3.2	3.2	3.0
Malaysia/Malaisie	0.9	1.2	1.5	1.9	2.4	2.4	2.7	3.1	3.8	3.7
Netherlands/Pays–Bas	1.8	1.9	1.9	2.1	2.3	2.4	2.1	2.1	2.2	2.3

4. General Imports C.I.F. by Commodities according to the S.I.T.C. (Rev. 2) in thousand U.S. Dollars
Importations Générales C.A.F. par Produits d'après la C.T.C.I. (Rév. 2) en milliers de Dollars E.U.

SITC CTCI	COMMODITY	1993 WEIGHT POIDS	1993 VALUE VALEUR	1994 WEIGHT POIDS	1994 VALUE VALEUR	1995 WEIGHT POIDS	1995 VALUE VALEUR	1996 WEIGHT POIDS	1996 VALUE VALEUR	PRODUIT
	ALL COMMODITIES # 1		240670207		274741972		336094207		349186135	TOUS PRODUITS
0	FOOD AND LIVE ANIMALS		35222975		41700939		45748126		46101221	ALIMENTS,ANIMAUX VIVANTS
01	MEAT AND PREPARATIONS		6800131		7764258		9652748		9372962	VIANDES ET PREPARATIONS
011	MEAT FRESH,CHILLD,FROZEN	W 1572596	6477220	W 1727115	7381660	W 1984455	9114808	W 2035349	8688926	VIANDES FRAICHES,REF,CONGE
0111	BOVINE MEAT FRESH,FROZEN	W 511553	2443138	W 588609	2855269	W 648739	3246712	W 629639	2715862	VIANDES BOVIN FRAI,REF
01112	BOVINE MEAT BONELESS	W 500836	2392163	W 575095	2795095	W 636108	3175974	W 614419	2644602	VIANDES BOVIN DESOSSEES
0113	PIG MEAT FRESH,CHLD,FRZN	W 457236	2556980	W 493903	2920638	W 580675	3723785	W 653293	3827018	VIANDE DE PORC
0114	POULTRY FRESH CHLLD,FRZN	W 401279	747401	W 454727	986960	W 549252	1305697	W 560643	1287863	VOLAILLES MORTES
03	FISH AND PREPARATIONS		13917093		15866727		17378117		16666419	POISSONS ET PREPARATIONS
034	FISH,FRESH,CHILLED,FROZN	W 1696500	6074412	W 1716601	6746101	W 1755951	7242315	W 1757164	7116834	POISSON FRAIS, REFRIG,CONG
0341	FISH FRSH,CHLLD,EX FILLT	W 145134	1312922	W 159386	1605085	W 166716	1719625	W 167600	1513453	POISSON FRAIS,REFRIGERE
0342	FISH FROZEN,EXCL FILLETS	W 1432114	3909761	W 1427056	4206616	W 1420084	4224989	W 1417770	4424266	POISSONS CONGELES
0344	FISH FILLETS,FROZEN	W 115056	812362	W 124760	878989	W 162993	1231648	W 165717	1117613	FILETS CONGELES
036	SHELL FISH FRESH,FROZEN	W 827786	5782817	W 830948	6773075	W 798573	7363197	W 821450	6686413	CRUSTACES,MOLLUSQUES
037	FISH ETC PREPD,PRSVD NES	W 160950	1679506	W 190954	1960355	W 220956	2336193	W 243784	2418788	POIS,CRUST,MOL PREPARES
0371	FISH PREPARD,PRESRVD NES	W 97797	1147375	W 113366	1318444	W 128739	1534284	W 148385	1616996	CONSERVES DE POISSONS
04	CEREALS AND PREPARATIONS		4648177		6525347		5435668		6907134	CEREALES ET PRODUITS
041	WHEAT ETC UNMILLED	W 5813656	1136399	W 6352435	1352460	W 5965296	1342412	W 5927749	1560696	FROMENT,EPEAUTRE
0412	OTHER WHEAT ETC UNMILLED	W 5665486	1109368	W 6179028	1304546	W 5792466	1293199	W 5728434	1502021	AUTRE FROMENT NON MOULU
042	RICE	W 107861	41138	W 2536319	1436640	W 28971	22256	W 444992	266955	RIZ
0421	RICE IN HUSK OR HUSKED	W 5	7	W 1741365	993886	W 22831	18300	W 300924	200936	RIZ SANS AUTRE PREPARATION
04212	RICE HUSKED	W 5	7	W 1741365	993886	W 22831	18300	W 300924	200936	RIZ CARGO
044	MAIZE UNMILLED	MW 16863	2132765	MW 15930	2261863	MW 16584	2395351	MW 16004	3048386	MAIS NON MOULU
048	CEREAL ETC PREPARATIONS	W 1063323	653739	W 1174268	772703	W 1215973	950823	W 1292145	1115615	PREPTNS A BASE CEREALES
05	VEGETABLES AND FRUIT		4847069		5775171		6277545		6093705	LEGUMES ET FRUITS
054	VEG ETC FRSH,SMPLY PRSVD	W 1385718	1587931	W 1703801	2015514	W 1696152	2159869	W 1716564	2157012	LEGUMES FRAIS,CONG,SECS
0545	OTHER FRESH VEGETABLES	W 346370	607773	W 581498	866018	W 632952	984667	W 562966	840229	AUTRES LEGUMES FRAIS,REF
057	FRUIT,NUTS,FRESH,DRIED	W 1778666	1727377	W 1877888	1844164	W 1815376	1946265	W 1695885	1862361	FRUITS FRAIS OU SECS
058	FRUIT PRESERVED,PREPARED	W 556635	931900	W 739090	1223696	W 837268	1407408	W 766160	1295510	CONSERVES DE FRUITS
07	COFFEE,TEA,COCOA,SPICES		1256768		1752319		2084851		2051342	CAFE,THE,CACAO,EPICES
071	COFFEE AND SUBSTITUTES	W 341078	624388	W 371590	1064805	W 326110	1264651	W 355404	1073461	CAFE ET SUCCEDANES
0711	COFFEE GREEN,ROASTED,SUB	W 315212	528044	W 347622	958637	W 302720	1114953	W 330307	932472	CAFE TORREFIE OU DECAFEINE
07111	COFFEE GREEN,HUSKS,SKINS	W 312524	510473	W 345280	941730	W 300563	1092054	W 326914	900279	CAFE NON TORREFIE
081	*FEEDING STUFF FOR ANIML	W 6109931	1817974	W 5955199	1851672	W 6311549	2208562	W 6249320	2287167	NOURRITURE POUR ANIMAUX
1	BEVERAGES AND TOBACCO		3917017		4790914		5027721		4482963	BOISSONS ET TABACS
11	BEVERAGES		1804808		2192968		2271801		1971973	BOISSONS
112	ALCOHOLIC BEVERAGES	W 306025	1672177	W 550290	1948213	W 534132	1955886	W 455041	1748459	BOISSONS ALCOOLIQUES
1124	DISTILLED ALCOHOLIC BEVS	W 111640	1240607	W 121744	1251241	W 118782	1173061	W 123264	1016142	ALCOOLS,EAUX–DE–VIE
12	TOBACCO AND MANUFACTURES		2112209		2597946		2755920		2510990	TABACS BRUTS FABRIQUES
122	TOBACCO,MANUFACTURED	W 58891	1504832	W 67217	1912077	W 72296	2173692	W 77450	2037161	TABACS FABRIQUES
1222	CIGARETTES	W 58699	1500575	W 66908	1906499	W 71912	2167955	W 77192	2032127	CIGARETTES
2	CRUDE MATERLS,EXCL FUELS		28255174		29659410		34267819		31611778	MAT BRUTES NON COMESTIBLES
22	OIL SEEDS,OLEAGINOUS FRT		2127730		2282553		2297162		2629017	GRAINES,FRUITS OLEAGINEUX
222	SEEDS FOR'SOFT'FIXED OIL	W 7205223	2057486	W 7011717	2211812	W 7061468	2224487	W 7157237	2561366	GRAINES HUILES FIXES
2222	SOYA BEANS	W 5031147	1375403	W 4731319	1405205	W 4813489	1372395	W 4870324	1652704	FEVES DE SOJA
23	RUBBER, CRUDE		748799		869412		1316906		1245774	CAOUTCHOUC BRUT
232	NATURAL RUBBER,GUMS	W 644249	571952	W 654067	666687	W 703967	1096004	W 732835	1063884	LATEX CAOUTCHOUC NATUREL
24	CORK AND WOOD		11601130		11401699		12247219		11654813	LIEGE ET BOIS
246	PULPWOOD,CHIPS,WOODWASTE	MW 11266	1629802	MW 11973	1795580	MW 13684	2337441	MW 13693	2225004	BOIS DE TRITURATION
24602	PULPWOOD CHIPS,PARTICLES	MW 11262	1627691	MW 11968	1793006	MW 13679	2334555	MW 13687	2222108	EN FORME DE PLAQUETTES
247	OTH WOOD ROUGH,SQUARED	MW 16842	5652293	MW 16068	4990606	MW 15713	4740695	MW 25270	4435813	BOIS BRUTS EQUARRIS
2471	SAW–,VENEER–LOGS CONIFER	MW 10315	3216846	MW 10107	3025908	MW 10431	3161064	MW 10256	2962753	CONIFERES POUR SCIAGE,PLACAG
24711	— IN THE ROUGH	MW 10315	3216846	MW 10107	3025908	MW 10431	3161064	MW 10256	2962753	ECORCES OU DEGROSSIS
2472	SAW–,VENEER–LOGS NON–CON	W 6527593	2435447	W 5960920	1964698	W 5281714	1579630	W 5013986	1473060	NON CONIFERES SCIAGE,PLAC
24721	— IN THE ROUGH	W 6527593	2435447	W 5960920	1964698	W 5281714	1579630	W 5013986	1473060	BRUTS ECORCES DEGROSSIS
248	WOOD SHAPED,SLEEPERS	W 6571970	4279951	W 6641851	4573938	W 7283370	5122363		4941856	BOIS SIMPLEMENT TRAVAILLES
2482	LUMBER SHAPED CONIFER	W 5324033	3174284	W 5450747	3412459	W 6008962	3790038		3725291	CONIFERES SCIES,RABOTES
24821	LUMBER SAWN ETC CONIFER	W 5230359	3116504	W 5348250	3340453	W 5889195	3703305	W 6068674	3628200	CONIFERES SCIES LONGITUD
2483	LUMBER SHAPED NON–CONIFR	W 1210505	1088658	W 1158959	1144126	W 1241002	1312641		1198429	NON CONIFERES SCIES,RABOTES
24831	LUMBER SAWN ETC NON–CON	W 1067085	927333	W 1021175	955966	W 1078383	1078327	W 989363	949928	SCIES LONGITUDINALEMENT
251	*PULP AND WASTE PAPER	W 3704800	1572670	W 4117268	1963231	W 4061440	2984118	W 3850644	2009955	PATES A PAPIER,DECHETS
2517	SODA,SULPHATE WOOD PULP	W 2588764	1110312	W 2977404	1487412	W 2803730	2280476	W 2658478	1459041	PATES CHIMIQUES AU SULFATE
25172	— BLEACHED,NONDISSOLVNG	W 2477031	1062646	W 2857310	1431998	W 2669369	2179912	W 2537938	1395968	PATES BLANCHIES
26	TEXTILE FIBRES AND WASTE		1405373		1663290		1594797		1500633	FIBRES TEXTILES
27	CRUDE FERTLZR,MINRLS NES		1726988		1797567		1912828		1843008	ENGRAIS MINERAUX BRUTS
278	OTHER CRUDE MINERALS	MW 13792	1016988	MW 14109	1057656	MW 15599	1205333	MW 15255	1208375	AUTRES MINERAUX BRUTS
28	METALLIFEROUS ORES,SCRAP		7003768		7491735		9418892		8299428	MINERAIS METAL,DECHETS
281	IRON ORE,CONCENTRATES	MW 114484	3033994	MW 116090	2904132	MW 120435	3126937	MW 119205	3117797	MINERAIS DE FER
2815	IRON ORE,CONC,NOT AGGLOM	MW 104942	2654912	MW 106360	2523562	MW 111247	2740744	MW 110426	2751693	MINERAIS NON AGGLOMERES
287	BASE METAL ORES,CONC NES	MW 12816	2929350	MW 11992	3417835	MW 13428	4805683	MW 13680	3965200	MINERAIS METAUX COMMUNS
2871	CPR ORE ETC,CEMENT COPPR	W 3741284	1833748	W 3459011	2247747	W 3828506	3092996	W 3848021	2476297	MINERAIS DE CUIVRE,MATTES
28711	COPPER ORES,EXCL MATTE	W 3740883	1833352	W 3457066	2245814	W 3825212	3088095	W 3840935	2466900	MINERAIS DE CUIVRE
288	NONFERR METAL SCRAP NES	W 407121	691353	W 456370	825535	W 423410	1011694		723237	DECHETS NON FERREUX
29	CRUDE ANIMAL,VEG MAT NES		1596069		1745457		1987067		2026405	MATIERES BRUTES ANIM,VEGET
292	CRUDE VEG MATERIALS NES		986830		1126748		1284161		1287181	MAT BRUTES VEGETALES NDA
3	MINERAL FUELS ETC		49384157		48195763		53976342		60931227	COMBUSTIBLES MINERAUX LUB
32	COAL,COKE AND BRIQUETTES		5993722		5795246		6704591		7023978	HOUILLES,COKES,BRIQUETTES
322	COAL,LIGNITE AND PEAT	MW 114024	5965043	MW 117273	5752136	MW 126319	6636857	MW 129605	6947012	HOUILLES,LIGNITES,TOURBE
3222	OTH COAL,NOT AGGLOMERATD	MW 111418	5811679	MW 114689	5606287	MW 123398	6462328	MW 126183	6749117	AUTRES HOUILLES
33	PETROLEUM AND PRODUCTS		33624323		32982848		36249615		41697563	PETROLE ET DERIVES
333	CRUDE PETROLEUM	MW 213575	27771439	MW 226364	27233288	MW 223793	29627157	MW 219943	33089229	HUILES BRUTES DE PETROLE
334	PETROLEUM PRODUCTS,REFIN	MW 31517	5330811	MW 33440	5125802	MW 35237	5864719	MW 39689	7903280	PRODUITS RAFFINES
3341	GASOLINE,OTH LIGHT OILS	MW 16493	2771412	MW 18623	2806684	MW 21866	3645346	MW 21885	4259124	ESSENCES POUR MOTEURS
33419	OTH LIGHT PETROLEUM OILS	MW 16432	2755582	MW 18534	2789045	MW 21827	3637876	MW 21757	4229755	AUTRES HUILES LEGERES
3342	KEROSENE,OTH MEDIUM OILS	W 4441966	977910	W 4598839	893438	W 4089084	841250	W 7269123	1801856	PETR LAMPANTS,AUT HUIL
3344	FUEL OILS,NES	W 6161735	821573	W 5207615	636404	W 4718959	602220	W 6088987	916059	FUEL OILS
341	*GAS,NATURAL AND MANUFCT		9766112		9417669		11022136		12209686	GAZ NATUREL,GAZ MANUFACT
3413	PETROLM GASES,LIQUEFIED	MW 54591	9766108	MW 56945	9417634	MW 57894	11022097	MW 61288	12209665	GAZ DE PETROLE LIQUEFIE
34131	LIQUEFIED PROPANE,BUTANE	MW 15283	2602286	MW 14828	2477320	MW 14971	3342949	MW 15403	3566683	PROPANE,BUTANE LIQUEFIES
34139	OTH HYDROCARBON GAS LQFD	MW 39308	7163822	MW 42117	6940314	MW 42923	7679147	MW 45886	8642982	HYDROCARBURES GAZEUX NDA
5	CHEMCLS,RELATED PROD NES		17522688		19606275		23862394		22570330	PRODUITS CHIMIQUES
51	ORGANIC CHEMICALS		5093909		5830315		7633376		6799407	PROD CHIMIQ ORGANIQUES
512	ALCOHOLS,PHENOLS ETC		821233		1112040		1483681		1093047	PHENOLS,PHENOLS–ALCOOLS
5121	ACYCLIC ALCOHOLS,DERIVS		662445		937084		1257313		883467	ALCOOLS ACYCLIQUES
514	NITROGEN–FNCTN COMPOUNDS	W 296819	1568532	W 350792	1797409	W 397042	2335547	W 420723	1999743	COMPOSES FONCT AZOTEES
5148	OTH NITROGN–FNCTN CMPNDS	W 146396	796421	W 170947	861831	W 179674	1169456	W 197591	911664	AUTRES COMPOSES AZOTES
515	ORG–INORG COMPOUNDS ETC	W 71715	1417765	W 76408	1543252	W 97756	2036530	W 100687	2037938	COMPOSES ORGANO–MINERAUX
5156	HETEROCYCLIC CMPDS ETC	W 46799	1128416	W 46503	1196051	W 57614	1552301	W 56482	1564477	COMPOSES HETEROCYCLIQUES
51569	OTH HETEROCYC CMPDS,ETC	W 43489	1097438	W 43196	1158951	W 54136	1511282	W 51637	1518809	AUT COMP HETEROCYCLIQUES
52	INORGANIC CHEMICALS		2633083		2889842		3423933		3175561	PROD CHIM INORGANIQUES
522	INORG ELEMNTS,OXIDES,ETC	W 651919	790123	W 673447	902352	W 880731	1259190	W 903771	1310863	ELEMENTS INORGANIQUES

4. General Imports C.I.F. by Commodities according to the S.I.T.C. (Rev. 2) in thousand U.S. Dollars
Importations Générales C.A.F. par Produits d'après la C.T.C.I. (Rév. 2) en milliers de Dollars E.U.

SITC CTCI	COMMODITY	1993 WEIGHT POIDS	1993 VALUE VALEUR	1994 WEIGHT POIDS	1994 VALUE VALEUR	1995 WEIGHT POIDS	1995 VALUE VALEUR	1996 WEIGHT POIDS	1996 VALUE VALEUR	PRODUIT
524	RADIOACTIVE ETC MATERIAL		1386810		1446857		1505591		1214267	MATIERES RADIOACTIVES
5241	RADIOACTIVE ELEMENTS ETC		1323435		1349557		1366724	K 2398	1057709	RADIOELEMENTS,ISOTOPES
541	*MEDICINAL,PHARM PRODUCT	MK 30480	3930433	MK 34828	4221960	MK 39561	4916670		4501813	PROD MEDICINAUX PHARMACEUT
5417	MEDICAMENTS	MK 13762	1859227	MK 15765	2050639	MK 18691	2496198	MK 21760	2186602	MEDICAMENTS
54179	— CONTNG OTH SUBSTANCES	MK 11540	1077956	MK 13432	1169361	MK 16229	1459440	MK 19441	1291601	MED CONT AUT SUBSTANCES
55	PERFUME,CLEANING ETC PRD		965111		1186932		1502420		1574373	PROD POUR PARFUM,TOILETTE
58	PLASTIC MATERIALS ETC		1534717		1725632		2028097		2034244	MAT PLAST ARTIFICIELLES
583	POLYMERIZATION ETC PRODS	W 369294	777715	W 447743	926649	W 418746	1098949	W 453339	1112446	PROD POLYMERISATION
59	CHEMICAL MATERIALS NES		2191554		2445695		2884002		3029192	MAT PROD CHIMIQUES NDA
598	MISCEL CHEM PRODUCTS NES	W 647203	1511343	W 703068	1676529	W 776773	1983165	W 856904	2093617	PROD DIV INDUST CHIM NDA
5989	CHEM PRODUCTS,PREPS NES	W 268708	1095348	W 316163	1247844	W 353259	1483300	W 417218	1587102	PROD PREP CHIMIQUES NDA
59899	OTH CHEM PRODS,PREPS,NES	W 188674	752989	W 222149	851945	W 258461	1031515	W 306424	1128007	AUT PRODUITS CHIMIQUES NDA
6	BASIC MANUFACTURES		27005179		31294387		39846600		38048739	ART MANUFACTURES
62	RUBBER MANUFACTURES NES		827073		906299		1030491		983632	CAOUTCHOUC MANUFACTURE
63	WOOD,CORK MANUFACTRS NES		2932665		3089850		3688828		4472032	OUVRAGES LIEGE ET BOIS
634	VENEERS,PLYWOOD,ETC		2242323		2217165		2415282		2954642	PLACAGES,CONTRE–PLAQUES
6342	PLYWOOD OF WOOD SHEETS	A 585294	1973091	A 517756	1921928	A 623395	2103579	V 5380471	2601417	BOIS CONTRE–PLAQUES
635	WOOD MANUFACTURES NES		672573		851880		1249281	W 686149	1494942	ART MANUF EN BOIS NDA
64	PAPER,PAPERBOARD AND MFR		1478555		1734956		2214907		2434268	PAPIERS,CARTONS & OUVRAGES
641	PAPER AND PAPERBOARD	W 1531752	1308960	W 1742664	1515264	W 1868720	1924770	W 2239417	2136058	PAPIERS ET CARTONS
65	TEXTILE YARN,FABRICS,ETC		4182871		5519395		6350672		6531534	FILS,TISSUS,ARTICLES TEXTILE
651	TEXTILE YARN	W 332021	1103087	W 376191	1486090	W 361460	1619805	W 399875	1718048	FILS TEXTILES
658	TEXTILE ARTICLES NES	W 122708	721425	W 170425	1102326	W 200636	1423254	W 200552	1414858	ART FACONNES MAT TEXTILES
66	NONMETAL MINERAL MFS NES		4403932		5207446		6177023		5953727	ART MIN NON METALLIQUES
667	PEARL,PREC–,SEMI–P STONE		2635735		3058062		3364797		2986076	PERLES, PIERRES GEMMES
6672	DIAMONDS NONINDUST,UNSET		1934826		2201521		2576954		2191852	DIAMANTS BRUTS
66729	— CUT ETC NOT SET		1919834		2181280		2560809		2171144	DIAMANTS TAILLES
67	IRON AND STEEL		4094958		4100896		5907848		4543143	FER ET ACIER
671	PIG IRON ETC	W 3073999	1198614	W 3285052	1258936	W 4646015	2030596	W 2632418	1594539	FONTE,SPIEGEL,POUDRES
6716	FERRO–ALLOYS	W 1437664	922082	W 1474386	926372	W 1869476	1486211	W 1677432	1372487	FERRO–ALLIAGES
67169	OTHER FERRO–ALLOYS	W 840178	585285	W 904092	602697	W 1188404	1027994	W 1048897	889640	AUTRES FERRO–ALLIAGES
672	IRON,STEEL PRIMARY FORMS	W 2703792	1034460		894547	W 3112259	1326524	W 2702474	924850	LINGOTS FER,ACIER
6727	IRN,STL COIL FR REROLLNG	W 2381255	927740		794420	W 2540376	1106154	W 2402383	835427	EBAUCHES POUR TOLES FER
67271	IRON,SIMPLE STEEL COILS	W 2372724	915819	W 2015008	779971	W 2531025	1089226	W 2392109	820198	EBAUCHES NON EN ACIER
674	IRN,STL UNIV,PLATE,SHEET	W 2349639	1146839	W 2462890	1218881	W 2854307	1574342	W 2411117	1152739	LARGES PLATS,TOLES
68	NON–FERROUS METALS		6624212		7771383		10662568		9080562	METAUX NON FERREUX
681	SILVER,PLATINUM,ETC		1236901		1554784		1716662	K 1569659	1457723	ARGENT ET PLATINE
6812	METALS OF PLATINUM GROUP		1148652		1386930		1519428	K 76137	1274355	PLATINE
68123	PLATINUM,ALLOYS UNWRGHT		744411		902910		918486	K 68023	870535	PLATINE,ALLIAGES BRUTS
682	COPPER EXC CEMENT COPPER	W 453594	1044151	W 462720	1108335	W 477189	1549216	W 427834	1203179	CUIVRE
6821	COPPER NES,ALLOYS,UNWRT	W 416491	876140	W 412398	871881	W 419829	1229911	W 372151	925084	CUIVRE BRUT
68212	COPPER REFINED,UNWROUGHT	W 376401	802490	W 363860	761602	W 397575	1158996	W 365302	907883	CUIVRE AFFINE BRUT
684	ALUMINIUM	W 2665168	3451450	W 2712102	3937797	W 2901878	5620062	W 2862265	4820490	ALUMINIUM
6841	ALUMINIUM,ALLOYS,UNWRGHT	W 2604601	3249354	W 2639423	3691679	W 2802785	5217466	W 2758858	4375879	ALUMINIUM,ALLIAGES BRUTS
69	METAL MANUFACTURES NES		2097828		2530695		3282498		3487340	ART MANUFACT EN METAL NDA
699	BASE METAL MFRS NES	W 120360	737039	W 149120	867381	W 200808	1157192	W 239836	1281850	ART MANUFACTURES MET NDA
7	MACHINES,TRANSPORT EQUIP		40858898		52581979		75721894		85058395	MACHINES MATERIEL TRANSPORT
71	POWER GENERATING EQUIPMT		2439786		2794526		3585571		3694842	MACHINES GENERATRICES
714	ENGINES AND MOTORS NES	W 4162	1159492	W 4261	1162586	W 5903	1486959	W 5994	1575594	MOTEURS NON ELECTRIQUES
716	ROTATING ELECTRIC PLANT	W 40963	670446	W 55765	870347	W 77040	1180816	W 91990	1290669	APP ELECTR ROTATIFS,PIECES
7162	AC MTRS,GENRTRS,GEN SETS	W 31547	583810	W 41716	740059	W 55956	995013	W 66213	1066478	MOTEURS ELECTRIQUES
72	MACHS FOR SPCL INDUSTRYS		2435045		2641184		3447077		4181763	MAC SPECIALES POUR INDUST
728	OTH MACHY FOR SPCL INDUS	W 37940	1129138	W 47209	1257571	W 65041	1708959		2233894	AUT MACH IND PARTICULIERES
7284	MACHY FOR SPCL INDUS NES	W 27833	1015400	W 33971	1106915	W 45924	1515164		2004500	MACH SPEC IND PARTICUL.
72848	OTH MCHY WITH INDIV FNCT	W 17548	581211	W 21152	644388	W 26865	861229	W 33123	1203456	AUTRES MACHINES NDA
73	METALWORKING MACHINERY		583564		609767		911979		1168315	MACH TRAVAIL DES METAUX
74	GENRL INDUSTRL MACHY NES		3525763		3907192		5246742		6075531	MACH APP INDUSTRIE
741	HEATING,COOLING EQUIPMNT		810919		846968		1183753		1299263	MACH CHAUFFAGE,PIECES
743	PUMPS NES,CENTRFUGES ETC	W 40118	693214	W 41359	754955	W 68596	1026461	W 79970	1213656	POMPES COMPRES,VENT ETC
749	NONELEC MACH PTS,ACC NES	W 63595	1075855	W 76103	1191755	W 101488	1553045	W 121202	1787816	PIECES MACH NON ELEC NDA
75	OFFICE MACHNES,ADP EQUIP		6985023		9358443		16273438		19479198	MACH BUREAU TRAIT AUTOM
752	AUTOMTIC DATA PROC EQUIP	W 24660	3972418	W 40101	5472042	W 96086	10429045	MN 48723	12405611	MACH TRAIT INFORMATION
7522	DIGITAL COMPUTERS	W 2165	393687	W 2715	470577	W 7638	1233545	N 1229621	1023071	MACH DIGITALES COMPLETES
7523	DIGITL CENTRL PROCESSORS	W 8359	1927448	W 11554	2554412	W 23396	4308729	N 2269429	4845703	UNITES CENTRALES
7524	DIGITL CENTRL STOR UNITS	W 3472	961805	W 5184	1339152	W 9679	2716465	MN 21351	3571023	UNITES MEMOIRE CENTRALES
7525	ADP PERIPHERAL UNITS	W 9397	403233	W 18263	653151	W 50536	1461551	MN 21959	1949241	UNITES PERIPHERIQUES
759	OFFICE,ADP MCH PTS,ACCES	W 22672	2799046	W 32906	3570636	W 49460	5305219	W 64425	6439116	PIECES DU 751 ET 752
7599	ACCTG,ETC,ADP MCH PTS,AC	W 13070	2665379	W 17691	3329621	W 29556	4969287	W 41049	5996205	PIECES DU 751 ET 752
76	TELECOMM,SOUND EQUIPMENT		4230617		6213001		9144070		10633958	EQUIPMENT DE TELECOM
761	TELEVISION RECEIVERS	W 47497	631922	W 76669	1007871	W 102978	1390856	N 7699822	1484297	RECEPTEURS DE TELEVISION
7611	COLOUR TV RECEIVERS	W 47053	620624	W 76363	999539	W 102679	1382624	N 7610085	1471888	RECEPTEURS COULEUR
763	SOUND RECORDRS,PHONOGRPH	W 9723	321071	W 15306	530912	W 24949	936420		1141352	PHONO,APP ENREGISTREMENT
7638	OTHR SOUND APPARATUS ETC	W 9244	315294	W 15017	526008	W 24586	928005		1130753	AUT APP D'ENREGIS,REPROD
764	TELECOM EQPT,PTS,ACC NES	W 69594	2820203	W 95043	4019057	W 109468	5813914		7097514	EQUIP TELECOM,PIECES
7641	LINE TELEPHONE,ETC EQUIP	W 5256	650130	W 7636	673952	W 11829	1189708	MN 10739	1826264	APP TELEPHON PAR FIL
7643	TV,RADIO TRANSMITTRS ETC	W 1035	207746	W 1911	582386	W 2765	1215983	W 2251	1126097	APP EMET TELE RADIO
7649	PTS NES OF EQUIPMT OF 76	W 32068	1464027	W 49247	2125455	W 49401	2613028	W 52168	3265622	PIECES DE LA DIV 76
76493	TELECOMM EQUIPMT PTS NES	W 10674	566310	W 14656	816304	W 15506	1010030	W 20530	1526363	PIECES 761,762,764.3,8
77	ELECTRIC MACHNRY NES ETC		10417434		13877478		21476284		23902329	MACH APP ELECT NDA
771	ELECTRIC POWER MACHY NES	W 44819	788220	W 56902	1008970	W 73302	1426369	W 86443	1692946	MACH PROD,TRANS ELECTR
7712	OTH ELEC POWER MACHY NES	W 22945	478476	W 27879	638568	W 35525	971110	W 46187	1257555	AUT APP PROD TRANSF ELEC
772	SWITCHGEAR ETC,PARTS NES	W 18893	1139593	W 21830	1219596	W 30160	1738602	W 39212	2012763	APP COUPURE,SECT ETC
7721	SWITCHGEAR ETC	W 16000	917002	W 18756	1049693	W 25808	1472226	W 33875	1670315	APP COUPURE,SECTIONMNT
773	ELECTR DISTRIBUTNG EQUIP	W 38050	568568	W 44071	680197	W 60257	987422	W 89754	1324390	EQUIPMT DISTRIBUTION ELECT
7731	INSULATED WIRE,CABLE ETC	W 35460	549062	W 42987	659698	W 57966	958903	W 86273	1290637	FILS,CABLES ISOLES ELECT
775	HOUSEHOLD TYPE EQUIP NES	W 54857	608143	W 76997	828206	W 121734	1268723	W 150096	1353820	MACH,APP USAGE DOMESTQUE
776	TRANSISTORS,VALVES,ETC		5286400		7306195		12260390		13239663	LAMPES,TUBES,VALVES
7764	ELECTRONIC MICROCIRCUITS	MN 3700960	4223425	MN 4148359	6067284	MN 5570746	10843736	MN 5387991	11726772	MICROSTRUCTURES ELECTRON
778	ELECTRICAL MACHINERY NES	W 63809	1510339	W 83140	2186802	W 110998	2986929		3320646	AUTRES MACH ELECT NDA
7788	OTH ELEC MACHY,EQUIP NES	W 24095	1070639	W 32081	1630882	W 45910	2234764		2455747	AUT MACH APP ELEC NDA
77886	OTH ELEC MACHINERY NES	W 4794	726972	W 6421	1199535	W 9048	1682343	MN 74239	1742390	AUT MACH APP ELECTRIQUES
78	ROAD VEHICLES		6733073		8967527		12540712		13019888	VEHICULES ROUTIERS
781	PASS MOTOR VEH EXC BUSES	N 207319	5052065	N 295476	6951325	N 401836	9992524	N 439638	10245219	AUTO TRANSPORT PERSONNES
784	MOTOR VEH PRTS,ACCES NES	W 133688	1046475	W 140229	1136821	W 161502	1454482	W 181973	1633201	PIECES 722,781,782,783
7849	OTHER MOTOR VEHCL PARTS	W 133176	1040494	W 139856	1130672	W 160979	1444586	W 181253	1624333	PIECES 722,781,782,783
79	OTHR TRANSPORT EQUIPMENT		3508593		4212859		3096021		2902569	AUTRE MATERIEL TRANSPORT
792	AIRCRAFT ETC	W 4387	3209000	W 4844	3891304	W 3839	2768035	W 3737	2528343	APP NAVIGATION AERIENNE
7924	AIRCRFT NES OVER 15000KG	W 2607	2464437	W 3209	3142812	W 1825	1846094	W 1542	1531507	AERODYNES PLUS 15000 KG
8	MISC MANUFACTURED GOODS		32941925		39978016		49364646		53215143	ART MANUFACTURES DIVERS
821	*FURNITURE,PARTS THEREOF	W 374924	1933460	W 519747	2676587	W 624003	3155427	W 709990	3453047	MEUBLES ET PIECES
8211	CHAIRS,SEATS AND PARTS	W 109526	712581	W 152830	949215	W 171953	1071677	W 185148	1166600	SIEGES ET PIECES

4. General Imports C.I.F. by Commodities according to the S.I.T.C. (Rev. 2) in thousand U.S. Dollars
Importations Générales C.A.F. par Produits d'après la C.T.C.I. (Rév. 2) en milliers de Dollars E.U.

SITC CTCI	COMMODITY	1993			1994			1995			1996			PRODUIT
			WEIGHT POIDS	VALUE VALEUR		WEIGHT POIDS	VALUE VALEUR		WEIGHT POIDS	VALUE VALEUR		WEIGHT POIDS	VALUE VALEUR	
8219	FURNITURE AND PARTS NES	W	233239	820358	W	312880	1113836	W	392550	1414393	W	467007	1631577	AUTRES MEUBLES ET PIECES
831	*TRAVEL GOODS,HANDBAGS	W	62845	1901015	W	83043	2373212	W	106831	2953044	W	108502	3023252	ARTICLES DE VOYAGE ETC
83109	OTHER TRAVEL BAGS,CASES	W	47650	1194250	W	63121	1514261	W	83640	2069909	W	83492	2107215	AUT CONTENANTS SIMILAIRES
84	CLOTHING AND ACCESSORIES			12622698			15294532			18787384			19699962	VETEMENTS
842	MENS OUTERWEAR NOT KNIT	W	96746	2305879	W	108730	2624027	W	117722	3244602	W	136659	3736031	VET DESSUS POUR HOMMES
8423	— TROUSERS,BREECHES ETC	W	35205	637134	W	40116	751070	W	50135	1068473	W	56703	1161893	PANTALONS HOMMES MAT TEX
8429	— OTHER OUTER GARMENTS	W	41388	918043	W	43426	968588	W	44310	1157442	W	57815	1535602	AUT VET DES HOM MAT TEX
843	WOMENS OUTERWEAR NONKNIT	W	100038	2955426	W	114085	3526011	W	129726	4555929	W	141958	4971861	VET DESSUS FEMMES MAT TEX
8431	— COATS AND JACKETS	W	15642	705162	W	18559	892297	W	21866	1137054	W	26826	1326635	MANT,VEST FEM MAT TEXTIL
8439	— OTHER OUTER GARMENTS	W	55758	1168728	W	60310	1300941	W	66058	1679666	W	73595	1922541	AUT VET DES FEM MAT TEXT
844	UNDER GARMENTS NOT KNIT	W	49118	852899	W	62857	1112959	W	61814	1287289	W	59183	1267629	VETEMENT DESSOUS MAT TEX
845	OUTERWEAR KNIT NONELASTC	W	149962	3196905	W	181593	4241304	W	191271	5053236	W	193468	5069042	VET DESSOUS,ACCES BONNET
8451	— JERSEYS,PULLOVERS ETC	W	95503	2284872	W	112023	2964576	W	114820	3438455	W	117029	3390889	CHANDAILS,PULL–OVERS ETC
8459	— OTHER,CLTHG ACCESRYS	W	51301	802757	W	64781	1112985	W	69482	1357400	W	69769	1420495	AUT VET DESSUS DE BONNE
846	UNDER GARMENTS KNITTED	W	81343	1545806	W	91127	1847940	W	111866	2511906	W	112140	2585925	SOUS VETS DE BONNETERIE
8462	— OF COTTON NON ELASTIC	W	58319	902270	W	67836	1124513	W	87986	1615001	W	85954	1631278	SOUS–VET BONNET COTON
84629	—— OTHER	W	58319	902270	W	67836	1124513	W	87986	1615001	W	85954	1631278	AUT SOUS–VET BONNET COTON
847	TEXTILE CLTHNG ACCES NES	W	25748	652887	W	35908	864399	W	43239	1003289	W	47032	992665	ACCES VET MAT TEXT NDA
848	HEADGEAR,NONTXTL CLOTHNG	W	44663	1112896	W	47960	1077893	W	50669	1131134	W	54665	1076809	VET ACCES MAT AUT QUE TEX
851	*FOOTWEAR	W	150371	1901031	W	178221	2190943	W	200053	2746868	W	213325	3117967	CHAUSSURES
85101	FOOTWEAR RUBBER,PLASTIC	W	67068	800010	W	80953	889845	W	92083	1145948	W	100216	1296874	CHAUS SEMELLES CAOUTCH
85102	FOOTWEAR LEATHER	W	80800	1082248	W	94622	1276346	W	106599	1586584	W	111553	1805155	CHAUS SEMELLES EN CUIR
87	PRECISION INSTRUMNTS NES			3737317			4506570			5666056			6822648	INSTRUM,APPAR SCIENT NDA
872	MEDICAL INSTRUMENTS NES	W	12886	1047617	W	13971	1280377	W	16946	1734445	W	22442	1961030	INSTR,APP MEDIC–CHIR NDA
87202	OTH MEDICAL INSTRUMENTS	W	11706	974382	W	12557	1196513	W	14116	1597842	W	17488	1780514	INSTRUM,APP MEDECINE
874	MEASURNG,CONTROLNG INSTR	W	12011	2394126	W	14854	2822753	W	20060	3391024			4042067	INSTRUMENTS DE MESURE
8742	MEASUR,DRAW ETC INST,PTS	W	3753	659468	W	4286	690474	W	6383	863619			1125930	INST DESSIN,TRACAGE,PCS
8748	ELEC MEAS,CONTRL EQU NES	W	2444	723558	W	3004	939487	W	3520	1163612	W	4179	1362304	APP ELEC ELECTRO MESURE
87483	OTH ELCTRNC MEAS ETC EQU	W	2361	706421	W	2919	920619	W	3411	1138954	W	4009	1329054	AUT APP ELECTRO DE MESURE
88	PHOTO EQU,OPTICL GDS ETC			2635156			3169690			3887752			4146078	APP,FOURN PHOTO,OP,MONTR
885	WATCHES AND CLOCKS			1191711			1438751			1762122			1782004	HORLOGERIE
8851	WATCHES,MOVEMENTS,CASES			1016951			1194719			1444157			1445999	MONTRES,MOUVEMENTS,BOITES
88511	WATCHES			919412			1113554			1365143	MN	54154	1354470	MONTRES POCHE,BRACELET
89	MISC MANUFCTRD GOODS NES			8020286			9521576			11785432			12520505	ART MANUFACTURES DIVERS
893	ARTICLES OF PLASTIC NES			1020592			1277867			1740454	W	461276	1980025	OUVRAGES EN MAT DIVIS 58
8939	MISC PLASTIC ARTICLES	W	115922	706950	W	148165	871548	W	195040	1192000	W	226846	1370570	ART DIVERS EN MAT DIV 58
89399	OTHR PLASTC ARTICLES NES	W	97604	635192	W	127298	786538	W	166196	1071095	W	191291	1240880	AUT OUV MAT DIV 58
894	TOYS,SPORTING GOODS,ETC	W	157233	2420095	W	175169	2605587	W	225648	3509634	W	246092	3744099	VOITURES ENFANTS,JOUETS
8942	TOYS,INDOOR GAMES ETC	W	104316	965214	W	117966	1019297	W	157595	1404602	W	181764	1668813	JOUETS,JEUX ETC
8947	OTH SPORT GDS,FAIR AMUSM	W	49721	1421790	W	53105	1545364	W	62527	2049593	W	59008	2003781	AUT ART DE SPORT
89472	OTH OUTDOOR SPORT GOODS	W	37842	1148765	W	44438	1276720	W	48828	1652687	W	43960	1488333	ART POUR JEUX PLEIN AIR
897	GOLD,SILVER WARE,JEWELRY			987860			1274535			1414621	W	2367	1308171	BIJOUTERIE,ORFEVRERIE
8973	PREC JEWLRY,GLD–SILVWARE			838414			1056877			1203371	W	1306	1142155	BIJOUX OR,ARGENT ORFEVRE
89731	PRECIOUS METAL JEWELLERY			771848			997368			1141134	W	462	1093263	ART BIJOUTERIE,JOAILLER
898	MUSICAL INSTRUMENTS,PTS			1041811			1422226			1837300			2033505	INSTRUMENTS DE MUSIQUE
8983	SOUND RECRDNG TAPE,DISCS			795706			1111438			1488223			1667864	SUPPORTS SON POUR 763
89832	RECORDED DISCS,TAPES ETC			528404			765331			1048294	MN	134949	1086622	DISQUES,PHONO,BANDES
899	OTHER MANUFACTURED GOODS			1237644			1436270			1609346			1700348	AUT ART MANUF DIVERS NDA
9	GOODS NOT CLASSD BY KIND			5092123			6370105			7518233			6395880	ART TRANSACT NON CLASSES
931	*SPECIAL TRANSACTIONS	W	142289	2969722	W	227234	3507782	W	213762	3902100			4452084	TRANS.SPECIALES
971	*GOLD,NON MONETARY NES	K	179578	1953860	K	201164	2434133	K	278144	3250334	K	272918	1690590	OR NON MONETAIRE
97101	NONMON GLD UNWRT,SEMIMFD	K	176351	1932702	K	197349	2402951	K	271332	3201605	K	135667	1631379	OR,ALLIAGES D'OR BRUTS

5. General Exports F.O.B. by Commodities according to the S.I.T.C. (Rev. 2) in thousand U.S. Dollars
Exportations Générales F.O.B. par Produits d'après la C.T.C.I. (Rév. 2) en milliers de Dollars E.U.

SITC CTCI	COMMODITY	1993 WEIGHT POIDS	1993 VALUE VALEUR	1994 WEIGHT POIDS	1994 VALUE VALEUR	1995 WEIGHT POIDS	1995 VALUE VALEUR	1996 WEIGHT POIDS	1996 VALUE VALEUR	PRODUIT
	ALL COMMODITIES # 1		360911139		395599981		442937421		410947003	TOUS PRODUITS
0	FOOD AND LIVE ANIMALS		1643460		1644174		1611697		1558074	ALIMENTS,ANIMAUX VIVANTS
2	CRUDE MATERLS,EXCL FUELS		2236936		2567511		3085655		3033127	MAT BRUTES NON COMESTIBLES
3	MINERAL FUELS ETC		2149490		2517838		2735785		2197042	COMBUSTIBLES MINERAUX LUB
33	PETROLEUM AND PRODUCTS		1878709		2212596		2387738		1900153	PETROLE ET DERIVES
334	PETROLEUM PRODUCTS,REFIN	W 6587900	1749864	W 7561858	2066404	MW 9072	2200183	W 8160078	1695044	PRODUITS RAFFINES
5	CHEMCLS,RELATED PROD NES		19534305		22863198		29253562		27922226	PRODUITS CHIMIQUES
51	ORGANIC CHEMICALS		6795436		8040410		11133025		10290375	PROD CHIMIQ ORGANIQUES
511	HYDROCARBONS NES,DERIVS	W 2154130	1088411	W 2474343	1482034	W 3527642	2735044	W 3427432	1982341	HYDROCARBURES NDA
5112	CYCLIC HYDROCARBONS	W 1780838	747605	W 1995075	1072444	W 2571311	2064077	W 2434968	1349262	HYDROCARBURES CYCLIQUES
513	CARBOXYLIC ACIDS ETC	W 1229325	1473836	W 1382635	1797370	W 1442272	2559490	W 1484518	2476253	ACIDES CARBOXYLIQUES
514	NITROGEN–FNCTN COMPOUNDS	W 484799	1691430	W 534117	1922451	W 567798	2342721	W 592474	2237919	COMPOSES FONCT AZOTEES
5148	OTH NITROGN–FNCTN CMPNDS	W 297267	889745	W 317017	1038668	W 375593	1425417	W 389973	1368727	AUTRES COMPOSES AZOTES
515	ORG–INORG COMPOUNDS ETC	W 264881	1409595	W 300060	1508961	W 328448	1806109	W 355249	1946343	COMPOSES ORGANO–MINERAUX
5156	HETEROCYCLIC CMPDS ETC	W 207440	1065055	W 229343	1108897	W 260227	1357954	W 276175	1372958	COMPOSES HETEROCYCLIQUES
52	INORGANIC CHEMICALS		1244376		1390280		1676740		1656797	PROD CHIM INORGANIQUES
53	DYES,TANNING,COLOUR PROD		1602652		1792818		1934214		1913620	PROD TEINTURE,COLORANTS
533	PIGMENTS,PAINTS,ETC	W 153457	934286	W 166384	1113834	W 163273	1263058	W 173763	1300724	PIGMENTS,PEINTURES,VERNIS
541	*MEDICINAL,PHARM PRODUCT		1472559		1547862		1843700		1889361	PROD MEDICINAUX PHARMACEUT
58	PLASTIC MATERIALS ETC		5150974		6135250		7975090		7434041	MAT PLAST ARTIFICIELLES
582	PROD OF CONDENSATION ETC	W 513477	1678812	W 640214	2041343	W 759939	2824461	W 722676	2609233	PROD CONDENS,POLYCOND
583	POLYMERIZATION ETC PRODS	W 1991622	3295163	W 2349102	3912890	W 2722629	4952427	W 2949574	4606873	PROD POLYMERISATION
5839	OTH POLYMRZTION ETC PROD	W 456037	1367152	W 535024	1628894	W 591426	1993906	W 670013	1915193	AUT PROD POLYMER COPOLYM
59	CHEMICAL MATERIALS NES		2406995		3020062		3672575		3729868	MAT PROD CHIMIQUES NDA
598	MISCEL CHEM PRODUCTS NES	W 427213	1906276	W 480252	2479813	W 478795	3085305	W 419622	3219421	PROD DIV INDUST CHIM NDA
5989	CHEM PRODUCTS,PREPS NES	W 389266	1779699	W 434895	2328303	W 435696	2919275	W 370394	3034023	PROD PREP CHIMIQUES NDA
59899	OTH CHEM PRODS,PREPS,NES	W 294050	1305113	W 325068	1742518	W 334756	2229049	W 273176	2387077	AUT PRODUITS CHIMIQUES NDA
6	BASIC MANUFACTURES		40141715		42851312		49847503		45733366	ART MANUFACTURES
62	RUBBER MANUFACTURES NES		4003783		4452019		5283261		5273204	CAOUTCHOUC MANUFACTURE
625	RUBBER TYRES, TUBES ETC	W 849021	2423615	W 891214	2602032	W 1016385	3184019	W 1083846	3377633	PNEUS CAOUTCHOUC VULCANISE
6252	TYRES,NEW,BUS OR LORRY	W 330127	917315	W 334647	935246	W 406123	1189062	W 442367	1295529	PNEUS POUR AUTOBUS,CAMIONS
628	RUBBER ARTICLES NES	W 56203	1080063	W 60741	1284783	W 60552	1463727	W 59802	1336690	OUVRAGES CAOUTCHOUC NDA
64	PAPER,PAPERBOARD AND MFR		2007894		2145644		2404953		1943912	PAPIERS,CARTONS & OUVRAGES
641	PAPER AND PAPERBOARD	W 918327	1333943	W 1032739	1470867	W 1058948	1729080	W 861459	1414765	PAPIERS ET CARTONS
65	TEXTILE YARN,FABRICS,ETC		6712545		6777526		7174074		6927006	FILS,TISSUS,ARTICLES TEXTILE
651	TEXTILE YARN	W 172660	1093893	W 188261	1126965	W 172368	1145631	W 158782	1019871	FILS TEXTILES
653	WOVN MAN–MADE FIB FABRIC	W 135837	2696225	W 136393	2621859	W 131066	2731259	W 143204	2686199	TISSUS FIBRES SYNTH,ARTIF
6531	CONT SYNT WEAVES NONPILE	W 75997	1576829	W 79710	1542667	W 78506	1623034	W 89887	1649735	TISSUS FIBRES SYNTH CONTINUE
65315	CONT SYN TXTL FABRIC NES	W 73855	1527539	W 77087	1485789	W 74622	1536214	W 84597	1547843	TIS PLUS 85% TEXT SYNT CONT
66	NONMETAL MINERAL MFS NES		4122534		4834160		5868328		5748588	ART MIN NON METALLIQUES
663	MINERAL MANUFCTURES NES	W 124785	1300298	W 123582	1519184	W 134958	1885536	W 131533	1862763	ART MIN MANUF NDA
664	GLASS	W 441361	1280784	W 584090	1755454	W 652893	2387149	W 562875	2125733	VERRE
6649	GLASS NES	W 327644	786631	W 426768	1131569	W 466949	1425464	W 445647	1384286	VERRE NDA
67	IRON AND STEEL		14543931		14915371		17607953		15284058	FER ET ACIER
672	IRON,STEEL PRIMARY FORMS		1477003	W 4196914	1553225	W 3974816	2184482	W 2718737	1368440	LINGOTS FER,ACIER
6727	IRN,STL COIL FR REROLLNG	W 3752638	1352347	W 2637222	1150269	W 3340933	1939696	W 2290434	1210186	EBAUCHES POUR TOLES FER
673	IRON,STEEL SHAPES ETC	W 4012980	2042995	W 3288876	1807568	W 2788033	1899715	W 2783640	1705131	BARRES,PROFIL FER,ACIER
674	IRN,STL UNIV,PLATE,SHEET	MW 41045	7144740	MW 11359	7598273	MW 12410	9670656	MW 11072	8403192	LARGES PLATS,TOLES
6744	IRN,STL HVY PLATE,ROLLED	W 2051874	1041429	W 1994682	1104167	W 2188862	1437837	W 1997575	1235332	TOLES LAMINEES PLUS 4.75 MM
6746	IRN,STL THIN PLATE,ROLLD	W 4178092	2777673	W 4406711	3076835	W 4931705	3998603	W 4336683	3458398	TOLES LAM MOINS 3MM
67461	— OF IRON OR SIMPLE STL	W 3604966	1788709	W 3767677	1945127	W 4266496	2505558	W 3693498	2232751	TOL NON AC FIN MOINS 3 MM
67463	— OF STAINLESS ETC STL	W 410222	858399	W 508566	1018024	W 524650	1346734	W 493569	1085334	TOL ACIER INOX MOINS 3 MM
6749	OTH IRN,STL PLATES,SHEET	W 3175848	2064255	W 3535911	2309968	W 3742330	2887135	W 3367210	2487091	AUTRES TOLES FER,ACIER
67491	— OF IRON OR SIMPLE STL	W 2652137	1637396	W 2855927	1790505	W 2987546	2230389	W 2728526	1942427	AUT TOLES AUTRES ACIER FIN
678	IRON,STL TUBES,PIPES,ETC	W 3418096	3312569	W 3216595	3152719	W 2589350	3023079	W 2372349	2989146	TUBES,TUYAUX EN FONTE,FER
6782	IRON,STL SEAMLESS TUBES	W 1841245	1784916	W 1726879	1734136	W 1448730	1738419	W 1267700	1760112	TUBES,TUYAUX SANS SOUDURE
6783	IRON,STL TUBES,PIPES NES	W 1420376	1109916	W 1372972	1057161	W 1053270	892156	W 1006662	873692	AUT TUBES,TUYAUX FER,ACIER
68	NON–FERROUS METALS		2546216		2925079		4042115		3732741	METAUX NON FERREUX
682	COPPER EXC CEMENT COPPER	W 426429	1498492		1632838	W 485747	2310724	W 1277114	2004985	CUIVRE
6822	COPPER,ALLOYS WORKED	W 255025	1138650	W 300588	1352315	W 314903	1793834	W 310555	1573268	CUIVRE,ALLIAGES OUVRES
69	METAL MANUFACTURES NES		5842773		6430886		7145078		6527775	ART MANUFACT EN METAL NDA
695	TOOLS		1683681		1867332		2215130	W 77513	1969476	OUTILS A MAIN
6954	BLADES,TIPS,ETC FR TOOLS	W 51957	1331095	W 57056	1516990	W 66130	1832594	W 58178	1639546	OUTILS POUR MACHINE–OUTIL
69541	PARTS TO INSERT IN TOOLS	W 45745	1099522	W 51202	1257874	W 60065	1501082	W 51924	1331592	OUTILS DE FORAGE
699	BASE METAL MFRS NES		1916867		2128139		2376996	W 223657	2161146	ART MANUFACTURES MET NDA
7	MACHINES,TRANSPORT EQUIP		259582561		284160213		310708263		285090096	MACHINES MATERIEL TRANSPORT
71	POWER GENERATING EQUIPMT		14363830		17348604		19145245		17285251	MACHINES GENERATRICES
713	INTRNL COMBUS PSTN ENGIN	W 1008165	9557057	W 1127761	11657153	W 1129811	13119205	W 1065134	11748640	MOTEURS EXPL COMB INT, PIECE
7132	MOTOR VEHCL PISTN ENGINS	W 632998	4413690	W 704648	5523476	W 672749	5988815	W 621330	5127790	MOTEURS EXPL POUR VEHICULES
7138	PISTON ENGINES NES	W 97342	1078995	W 113014	1351458	W 124459	1596858	W 112892	1298112	MOTEURS A PISTONS NDA
7139	PISTON ENGINE PARTS NES	W 231142	3286517	W 267022	3982164	W 276786	4573865	W 280313	4491347	PIECES POUR 713.2,3,8
716	ROTATING ELECTRIC PLANT	W 157170	2935863	W 155910	3335095	W 156526	3678318	W 152684	3198664	APP ELECTR ROTATIFS,PIECES
7162	AC MTRS,GENRTRS,GEN SETS	W 107671	2038653	W 101496	2208641	W 105181	2446734	W 106702	2146480	MOTEURS ELECTRIQUES
71621	AC MTRS,INC UNIVRSL MTRS	W 44080	1340743	W 48824	1557726	W 50842	1754964	W 51974	1529802	MOT ELEC NON COUR CONTINU
72	MACHS FOR SPCL INDUSTRYS		17532976		19666194		23355920		22069976	MAC SPECIALES POUR INDUST
723	CIVIL ENGNEERG EQUIP ETC	W 864070	3219792	W 888909	3534168	W 940403	3845132	W 1039331	3707544	APPAREILS DE GENIE CIVIL
7234	CONST,MINING MACHNRY NES	W 836745	3110655	W 858310	3416901	W 912274	3722202	W 1011440	3595532	MACH POUR LA CONST, MINES
72342	SLFPRP SHOVELS,EXCAVATRS	W 708277	2408534	W 724842	2648416	W 775464	2933414	W 857815	2815764	PELLES MECANIQUES
724	TEXTILE,LEATHER MACHNRY		4891706		4510556		4685400		3919118	MACH POUR INDUSTRIE TEXTILE
7243	SEWING MACHS,NEEDLES ETC	W 48014	1354099	W 37170	1209013	W 35927	1250895	W 31788	1015829	MACHINES A COUDRE,PIECES
72431	SEWING MACHINES	W 46339	1166990	W 35548	1021874	W 34230	1050991	W 29910	837836	MACHINES A COUDRE
7244	SPINNING,EXTRDNG,ETC MCH	W 69247	1451289	W 67246	1268611	W 81502	1424379	W 63969	1062662	MACH POUR LE FILAGE
7245	WEAVING,FELT MFG,ETC MCH	W 79821	1544612	W 78967	1491101	W 72385	1467211	W 71485	1381700	METIERS A TISSER,PIECES
726	PRINTG,BKBINDG MACHY,PTS	W 54823	1231219	W 61189	1402263	W 66652	1709692	W 72797	1664773	MACHINES POUR IMPRIMERIE
728	OTH MACHY FOR SPCL INDUS	W 242703	6710850	W 281396	8527624	W 313964	11259813		10933354	AUT MACH IND PARTICULIERES
7284	MACHY FOR SPCL INDUS NES	W 188180	5940290	W 225610	7659874	W 256710	10177440		9840291	MACH SPEC IND PARTICUL.
72842	RUBBER,PLASTICS WRKG MCH	W 101436	1331736	W 115463	1519531	W 123158	1711406	W 138302	1810894	MACH IND CAOUT MAT PLAST
72848	OTH MCHY WITH INDIV FNCT	W 69913	3606109	W 87299	4849266	W 105240	6760974	W 111935	6357652	AUTRES MACHINES NDA
73	METALWORKING MACHINERY		5084642		6142894		8977999		9410033	MACH TRAVAIL DES METAUX
736	METALWORKING MACH–TOOLS	W 207038	4056200	W 245747	4707231	W 331391	7103711	W 390175	7523418	MACH–OUTILS TRAVAIL METAUX
7361	METAL CUTTING MACH–TOOLS	W 74210	1803470	W 88950	2137112	W 124272	3499635	W 137339	3597920	MACH–OUT ENLEVEMENT METAL
73613	LATHES,METALWORKING	W 31621	643522	W 40363	801283	W 61633	1380953	W 64707	1311502	TOURS A METAUX
7362	METAL FORMING MACH–TOOLS	W 74080	851434	W 85744	948644	W 109298	1270688	W 131495	1331467	MACH–OUTILS DEFORM METAL
7367	OTH METALWRKG MACH–TOOLS	W 46289	994139	W 55844	1100900	W 79727	1621365	W 95556	1839356	AUT MACH–OUT POUR METAUX
737	METALWORKING MACHNRY NES	W 60945	1028442	W 80622	1435663	W 94919	1874288	W 136102	1886616	MACH TRAV METAUX PIECES
74	GENRL INDUSTRL MACHY NES		22019672		24870882		29444653		27893457	MACH APP INDUSTRIE
741	HEATING,COOLING EQUIPMNT		4372827		4668831		5618344		5386739	MACH CHAUFFAGE,PIECES
7415	AIR–CONDITIONING MACHNRY	N 3304563	1989698		2052661		1996552		1728140	GROUPES CONDITION AIR
7416	HEATING,COOLING EQU NES	W 52501	1132104	W 66259	1478101	W 105796	2131806	W 86211	2209053	APP CHANGEMENT TEMP
742	PUMPS FOR LIQUIDS ETC	W 75970	1968776	W 78233	2146058	W 87146	2411776	W 90185	2157373	POMPES MOTO–POMPES
743	PUMPS NES,CENTRFUGES ETC	W 236020	3786377	W 246593	4230798	W 254828	4866524	W 247370	4479323	POMPES COMPRES,VENT ETC

5. General Exports F.O.B. by Commodities according to the S.I.T.C. (Rev. 2) in thousand U.S. Dollars
Exportations Générales F.O.B. par Produits d'après la C.T.C.I. (Rév. 2) en milliers de Dollars E.U.

SITC CTCI	COMMODITY	1993 WEIGHT POIDS	1993 VALUE VALEUR	1994 WEIGHT POIDS	1994 VALUE VALEUR	1995 WEIGHT POIDS	1995 VALUE VALEUR	1996 WEIGHT POIDS	1996 VALUE VALEUR	PRODUIT
7431	PUMPS FOR GASES ETC	W 146598	1972689	W 150951	2199329	W 157016	2589848	W 149285	2422593	POMPES AIR A VIDE,COMPRES
744	MECHANICAL HANDLING EQU	W 522084	3480223	W 584331	4167346	W 645259	4850386	W 685784	4799924	EQUIP MANUTENTION PIECES
7441	FORK LIFT TRCKS,ETC,PTS	W 254038	996258	W 294779	1197120	W 325046	1369198	W 361496	1374238	CHARIOTS POUR USINES ETC
74411	FORK LIFT TRUCKS ETC	W 254008	995269	W 294651	1196201	W 325001	1368176	W 361376	1372296	CHARIOTS POUR LES GARES
7442	LIFTING,LOADING MACH NES	W 136878	1575566	W 145732	1832598	W 163744	2146742	W 190281	2284900	APP LEVAGE,MANUTENTION
7449	PTS NES OF MACHY OF 7442	W 131169	908399	W 143821	1137628	W 156469	1334446	W 134008	1140786	PIECES DU 744.2
745	NONELEC MACHY,TOOLS NES	W 43529	1504215	W 40445	1501019	W 44717	1718291	W 45475	1622444	AUT MACH NON ELEC,PIECES
749	NONELEC MACH PTS,ACC NES	W 405667	6907254	W 445673	8156829	W 497182	9979332	W 494192	9447653	PIECES MACH NON ELEC NDA
7491	BALL,ROLLER,ETC BEARINGS	W 126536	1610297	W 139522	1898105	W 164611	2510764	W 163539	2360223	ROULEMENTS BILLES ETC
7492	COCKS,VALVES ETC NES	W 62690	1602761	W 59553	1757141	W 66450	2110298	W 65530	1975818	ART ROB,SIM POUR TUYAUX
7493	SHAFT,CRANK,PULLEY ETC	W 181822	2131302	W 204466	2539629	W 217918	3025635	W 213719	2832872	ARBRES TRANS,VILEBREQUINS
7499	OTH NONELEC MCHY PTS NES	W 34617	1562894	W 42133	1961954	W 48202	2332635	W 51404	2278740	PIECES NON ELECT NDA
74991	FOUNDRY MOULDS ETC NES	W 21430	1080265	W 27462	1373208	W 31384	1614899	W 33879	1592534	MOULES POUR METAUX
75	OFFICE MACHNES,ADP EQUIP		33112966		35170183		37452361		35053992	MACH BUREAU TRAIT AUTOM
751	OFFICE MACHINES		3830429		3908797		3940400		3432634	MACH,APPAREILS DE BUREAU
7518	OFFICE MACHINES NES	W 112507	3200062	W 109980	3420465	W 103990	3565214	W 97389	3136904	MACH,APP DE BUREAU NDA
75182	PHOTO,THERMOCOPY APPARAT	W 104682	2838604	W 102049	3027497	W 96287	3165318	W 90693	2812872	APPAREILS DE PHOTOCOPIE
752	AUTOMTIC DATA PROC EQUIP	W 263714	16860334	W 227492	15975296	W 237365	17162525	MN 65665	15848707	MACH TRAIT INFORMATION
7522	DIGITAL COMPUTERS	W 28245	3018809	W 7298	1593599	W 7576	2015252	N 2254211	2228187	MACH DIGITALES COMPLETES
7524	DIGITL CENTRL STOR UNITS	W 32754	5105761	W 22177	4843349	W 24913	5137711	MN 38176	5298682	UNITES MEMOIRE CENTRALES
7525	ADP PERIPHERAL UNITS	W 192281	7291909	W 187409	7868671	W 189873	7920576	MN 18408	6678747	UNITES PERIPHERIQUES
759	OFFICE,ADP MCH PTS,ACCES	W 180884	12422203	W 191818	15286091	W 197943	16349435	W 211387	15772652	PIECES DU 751 ET 752
7591	OFFICE MACHINE PARTS NES	W 87914	2846750	W 92895	3211130	W 97881	3693775	W 94750	3407980	PIECES DU 7511,7518
75919	COPY MACH PRTS,ACCES NES	W 84438	2711616	W 89348	3042248	W 94872	3473205	W 89731	2948257	PIECES DU 751.82
7599	ACCTG,ETC,ADP MCH PTS,AC	W 92970	9575453	W 98923	12074961	W 100062	12655660	W 116637	12364672	PIECES DU 751 ET 752
76	TELECOMM,SOUND EQUIPMENT		29496216		30083286		28311306		23221836	EQUIPMENT DE TELECOM
761	TELEVISION RECEIVERS	N 5929960	2239626	N 5121991	2449809	N 4182319	2256098	N 3653027	2031576	RECEPTEURS DE TELEVISION
7611	COLOUR TV RECEIVERS	N 5667239	2196724	N 4870588	2410062	N 3981210	2218129	N 3438892	2002861	RECEPTEURS COULEUR
762	RADIO BROADCAST RECEIVRS	MN 19317	2718124	MN 14771	2327153	MN 13860	2283912	MN 9866	1518825	RECEPTEURS RADIODIFFUSION
7621	MTR VEHC RADIO RECEIVERS	N 8906573	1353625	N 8345024	1252635	MN 9049	1386651	N 6314167	962489	RECEPTEURS RADIO AUTO
763	SOUND RECORDRS,PHONOGRPH		6737320		6482543		5558841		4730846	PHONO,APP ENREGISTREMENT
7638	OTHR SOUND APPARATUS ETC		6688694		6444287		5511426		4697056	AUT APP D'ENREGIS,REPROD
76381	TV IMAGE,SND RECRDRS ETC	W 81628	4122773	W 80134	4140298	W 58326	3323848	W 46382	2826193	APP ENREG,REPRO IMAG,SON
76388	DICTATING MACHINES ETC	MN 29778	2565920	MN 25190	2303990	MN 21874	2187578		1870863	MACHINES A DICTER
764	TELECOM EQPT,PTS,ACC NES		17801146		18823780		18212455		14940589	EQUIP TELECOM,PIECES
7641	LINE TELEPHONE,ETC EQUIP	W 53996	3743557	W 55176	3922736	W 42552	2945746	N 8115128	2430370	APP TELEPHON PAR FIL
7642	MICROPH,LOUDSPKR,AMPLIFR		1229651		1178174		1030787		673301	MICRO,HAUT–PARLEUR,AMPLI
7643	TV,RADIO TRANSMITTRS ETC	W 13531	2233237	W 13550	2330466	W 9949	1643718		903378	APP EMET TELE RADIO
7648	TELECOMM EQUIPMENT NES		5149997		4942252		5432168		4666516	APP TELECOM NDA
76482	TELEVISION CAMERAS	W 13640	4250692	W 12939	4171225	W 14130	4692462	W 12723	4078154	APP PRISE DE VUES TELE
7649	PTS NES OF EQUIPMT OF 76	W 104025	5444703	W 114591	6450151	W 104281	7160036	W 90954	6267024	PIECES DE LA DIV 76
76491	PTS NES OF APPAR OF 7641	W 9682	1266483	W 13483	1547692	W 17074	2024069	W 16689	2003993	PIECES POUR 764.1
76493	TELECOMM EQUIPMT PTS NES	W 28132	1784952	W 27887	2035266	W 26027	2258429	W 21554	2104113	PIECES 761,762,764.3,8
76499	PARTS ETC OF SOUND EQUIP	W 56902	2280115	W 64126	2744697	W 51915	2745398	W 43409	2037027	PIECES NDA POUR 763
77	ELECTRIC MACHNRY NES ETC		47086353		58101342		74160486		66229538	MACH APP ELECT NDA
771	ELECTRIC POWER MACHY NES	W 69607	2016714	W 67893	2203091	W 71117	2532283	W 74620	2320442	MACH PROD,TRANS ELECTR
7712	OTH ELEC POWER MACHY NES	W 41362	1518247	W 41019	1717164	W 43600	2002069	W 45214	1891963	AUT APP PROD TRANSF ELEC
772	SWITCHGEAR ETC,PARTS NES	W 136658	8010940	W 148966	9729235	W 155244	11434943	W 170279	10422741	APP COUPURE,SECT ETC
7721	SWITCHGEAR ETC	W 112798	6224768	W 121326	7449883	W 127289	8620440	W 144720	7930174	APP COUPURE,SECTIONMNT
7722	PRINTED CIRCUITS,PTS NES	W 11251	827806	W 14031	1100372	W 13827	1434061	W 12909	1368425	CIRCUITS ET PIECES
7723	FIXED,VARIABLE RESISTORS	W 12610	958367	W 13610	1178980	W 14129	1380442	W 12650	1124142	POTENTIOMETRES PIECES
773	ELECTR DISTRIBUTNG EQUIP	W 158496	1834152	W 144299	1878678	W 151712	2086389	W 170427	2011273	EQUIPMT DISTRIBUTION ELECT
7731	INSULATED WIRE,CABLE ETC	W 106096	1309128	W 99784	1291529	W 100528	1418731	W 107510	1358341	FILS,CABLES ISOLES ELECT
774	ELECTRO–MEDCL,XRAY EQUIP	W 14748	1744399	W 12955	1688580	W 13124	1809495		1778786	APPAREILS MEDICAUX
775	HOUSEHOLD TYPE EQUIP NES		1340306		1153029		1019782		883440	MACH,APP USAGE DOMESTQUE
776	TRANSISTORS,VALVES,ETC		21956377		29263503		40846952		35656515	LAMPES,TUBES,VALVES
7762	OTH ELECTRONIC TUBES ETC	W 133815	2576861	W 137990	2751224	W 173909	3901938	MN 34458	3704408	AUT LAMPES ELECTRONIQUES
7763	DIODES,TRANSISTORS,ETC	MN 60627385	2273387	MN 72702997	2928327	MN 91252086	3883862	MN 84234930	3753958	DIODES,TRANSISTORS
7764	ELECTRONIC MICROCIRCUITS	MN 10959364	13184915	MN 13438717	18460335	MN 15805403	26470342	MN 642261249	22283336	MICROSTRUCTURES ELECTRON
7768	ELCTRNC COMP PTS,CRYSTLS		3183066		4287423		5661440		5428439	CRIST PIEZO–ELEC,PCS 776
77681	PIEZO–ELEC CRYSTALS,MNTD	MN 3499318	793755	MN 4595677	1152415	MN 4817019	1353076	MN 5804700	1095353	CRISTAUX PIEZO–ELECTRIQ
77689	ELECTRNIC COMPON PTS NES	W 59712	2389311	W 54551	3135008	W 51403	4308364	W 46448	4333087	PIECES DU GROUPE 776
778	ELECTRICAL MACHINERY NES		10183463		12185226		14430642		13156342	AUTRES MACH ELECT NDA
7781	BATTERIES,ACCUMULATORS	W 113647	1704252	W 93478	2283535	W 91243	2690740		2630539	PILES ET ACCUMULATEURS
77812	ELECTRIC ACCUMULATORS	W 79468	1262448	W 62504	1786964	W 60568	2156028	W 57218	2152966	ACCUMULATEURS ELECTRIQ
7783	AUTOMOTIVE ELECTR EQUIP	W 132654	2086465	W 142607	2368994	W 142218	2612948	W 138535	2344532	EQUIP ELECT MOTEURS EXPL
77831	IGNITION,STARTING EQUIP	W 102282	1379385	W 111206	1573694	W 113378	1826479	W 111659	1663699	APP ELEC ALLUM,DEMARRAGE
7788	OTH ELEC MACHY,EQUIP NES		5319386		6411806		7951129		7163403	AUT MACH APP ELEC NDA
77884	ELECTRICAL CONDENSERS	MN 59049356	1903443	MN 82631148	2489208	MN 138097091	3221583	W 37287	2764676	CONDENSATEURS ELECTRIQUES
77886	OTH ELEC MACHINERY NES	W 15059	1980711	W 13735	2127682	W 16981	2509222	MN 301986	2374582	AUT MACH APP ELECTRIQUES
78	ROAD VEHICLES		79908322		80294223		78071354		73258681	VEHICULES ROUTIERS
781	PASS MOTOR VEH EXC BUSES	N 3927686	47129690	N 3385363	44920662	N 2981754	41673773	N 3232330	39973644	AUTO TRANSPORT PERSONNES
782	LORRIES,SPCL MTR VEH NES		9664115		9976244		9615997		8989691	VEHICULES SPECIAUX,MARCH
7821	LORRIES,TRUCKS		9385692		9717994		9273037	N 901775	8613028	VEHICULES TRANSP MARCHAND
783	ROAD MOTOR VEHICLES NES		1536922		1563667		1161549		1151965	VEHICULES ROUTIERS NDA
7831	BUSES	N 85133	1294757	N 81281	1391078	N 57132	1005658	N 61847	1006616	VOITURES TRANSPORT COMMUN
784	MOTOR VEH PRTS,ACCES NES		15326026		18118393		19656346		17445977	PIECES 722,781,782,783
7849	OTHER MOTOR VEHCL PARTS	W 1702393	14720844	W 1868465	17377766	W 1829420	18745098	W 1735388	16629671	PIECES 722,781,782,783
785	CYCLES,ETC MOTRZD OR NOT		6056872		5509562		5803854		5591134	MOTOCYCLES SCOOTERS
7851	MOTORCYCLES ETC	N 2371379	4240917	N 2028153	3867384		3947575	N 2158714	4004470	MOTO VELO MOTEUR AUXIL
7853	INVAL CARR, PTS OF 785		1788955		1622397		1839307	W 93595	1576870	FAUTEUILS INVALIDES,PIECES
78539	PARTS,ACCES NES OF 785		1783976		1618222		1835934	W 93497	1573934	PIECES DU 785
79	OTHR TRANSPORT EQUIPMENT		10977584		12482606		11788940		10667333	AUTRE MATERIEL TRANSPORT
793	SHIPS AND BOATS ETC	W 8842867	10187698	W 8886267	11615332	MW 9343	10932151		9612350	NAVIRES BATEAUX,ETC
7932	SHIPS AND BOATS NES	W 8742284	10083852	W 8802479	11204496	MW 9288	10865083		9309490	NAVIRES ET BATEAUX
79322	TANKERS OF ALL KINDS	W 4852781	5432042	W 2551188	3393905	W 2705738	2975554		3045976	BATEAUX–CITERNES
79323	OTHER CARGO VESSELS	W 3850550	4487773	W 6208723	7559544	W 6541424	7633301		6057162	AUT BATEAUX TRANS MARCH
8	MISC MANUFACTURED GOODS		29079911		30892228		35660941		34562542	ART MANUFACTURES DIVERS
87	PRECISION INSTRUMNTS NES		7938776		9341785		11503348		11357988	INSTRUM,APPAR SCIENT NDA
871	OPTICAL INSTRUMENTS	W 10123	1361886	W 11037	1763087	W 11167	2150137	W 13004	2225201	APPAR,INSTRUM D'OPTIQUE
87109	OPTICAL INSTRUMENTS NES	W 5957	950657	W 7184	1295348	W 7656	1540385	W 8683	1604992	APP,INSTRUM OPTIQUE NDA
872	MEDICAL INSTRUMENTS NES	W 23775	1338328	W 23089	1352480	W 22396	1417287	W 22383	1307614	INSTR,APP MEDIC–CHIR NDA
87202	OTH MEDICAL INSTRUMENTS	W 19738	1202250	W 18502	1187559	W 18016	1258473	W 18845	1204614	INSTRUM,APP MEDECINE
874	MEASURNG,CONTROLNG INSTR	W 42493	4960461	W 46029	5939437	W 52419	7628623	W 57167	7563800	INSTRUMENTS DE MESURE
8742	MEASUR,DRAW ETC INST,PTS	W 12290	1067130	W 12139	1192560	W 15271	1603518	W 18524	1705876	INST DESSIN,TRACAGE,PCS
87421	MEASURNG,DRAWNG ETC INST	W 11219	942661	W 11078	1060225	W 13688	1413783	W 17124	1498787	INSTRUM DESSIN,TRACAGE
8743	GAS,LIQUID CONTROL INSTR	W 14090	1470270	W 15921	1830059	W 16296	2062095	W 16522	1891890	APP,INSTR MESURE FLUIDES
8748	ELEC MEAS,CONTRL EQU NES	W 6253	1264029	W 7142	1596320	W 8951	2286472	W 9121	2196910	APP ELEC ELECTRO MESURE
87483	OTH ELCTRNC MEAS ETC EQU	W 6178	1252908	W 7053	1584070	W 8865	2272976	W 9021	2179473	AUT APP ELECTRO DE MESURE
88	PHOTO EQU,OPTICL GDS ETC		10085084		10785789		12290252		11750810	APP,FOURN PHOTO,OP,MONTR
881	PHOTO APPARAT,EQUIPT NES		3063378		3592489		4421322		4481259	APP,EQUIP PHOTO NDA

5. General Exports F.O.B. by Commodities according to the S.I.T.C. (Rev. 2) in thousand U.S. Dollars
Exportations Générales F.O.B. par Produits d'après la C.T.C.I. (Rév. 2) en milliers de Dollars E.U.

SITC CTCI	COMMODITY	1993		1994		1995		1996		PRODUIT
		WEIGHT POIDS	VALUE VALEUR	WEIGHT POIDS	VALUE VALEUR	WEIGHT POIDS	VALUE VALEUR	WEIGHT POIDS	VALUE VALEUR	
8811	CAMERAS STILL,FLASH APP		1751516		1791360		1817904		1714355	APPAREILS PHOTO,PIECES
88111	STILL CAMERAS	MN 38341	1319308	MN 39310	1241232	MN 44854	1180523	MN 36690	1128276	APPAREILS PHOTOGRAPHIQ
8813	OTH PHOTO,CINE EQUIP NES	W 15475	1303068	W 16333	1794887	W 17531	2598390		2762836	APP,MAT PHOTO,CINEMA
88139	PHOTO,CINE LAB EQUIP NES	W 11915	1156161	W 13132	1649164	W 14579	2451898	N 177088	2637877	APP TYPES UTIL LABOR
882	PHOTO,CINEMA SUPPLIES		3328296		3673920		4188105		4024764	PRODUITS PHOTO,CINEMA
8821	CHEM PHOTO GOODS,RETAIL	W 59900	1236565	W 61941	1446852	W 68492	1768001	W 71003	1653577	PROD CHIMIQ USAGES PHOTO
8822	PHOTO FILM EXC DEV CINMA	A 449648	2091731	A 452601	2227068	A 471065	2420104		2371187	PLAQUES,PELLICULES,FILMS
884	OPTICAL GOODS NES		1285101		1319746		1482409		1403668	ELEMENTS OPTIQ,ART LUNET
885	WATCHES AND CLOCKS		2403859		2195794		2195682		1837545	HORLOGERIE
8851	WATCHES,MOVEMENTS,CASES		1862187		1686778		1659561		1414445	MONTRES,MOUVEMENTS,BOITES
89	MISC MANUFCTRD GOODS NES		9507657		9296612		10507363		10177996	ART MANUFACTURES DIVERS
893	ARTICLES OF PLASTIC NES		1298646		1493281		1756678	W 117052	1649900	OUVRAGES EN MAT DIVIS 58
8939	MISC PLASTIC ARTICLES	W 81474	1049826	W 81151	1201584	W 81823	1391103	W 87751	1294735	ART DIVERS EN MAT DIV 58
89399	OTHR PLASTC ARTICLES NES	W 65369	996542	W 65844	1148215	W 68656	1340803	W 73001	1244352	AUT OUV MAT DIV 58
894	TOYS,SPORTING GOODS,ETC		1916447		1583863		2096515		2280570	VOITURES ENFANTS,JOUETS
8942	TOYS,INDOOR GAMES ETC	W 24994	1499716	W 22188	1150627	W 26719	1623696	W 35395	1784358	JOUETS,JEUX ETC
89424	INDOOR GAME EQUIPMENT	W 17833	1315269	W 16118	976612	W 21830	1466288	W 30704	1640844	ART,JEUX DE SOCIETE
898	MUSICAL INSTRUMENTS,PTS		3642280		3501814	W 122985	3696803		3792740	INSTRUMENTS DE MUSIQUE
8983	SOUND RECRDNG TAPE,DISCS	W 114306	2551188	W 97391	2458782	W 85784	2680087		2926285	SUPPORTS SON POUR 763
89831	PREPD SND RECORDNG MEDIA	W 110136	2243668	W 92996	2160227	W 81650	2357530	W 81047	2599485	SUPPORTS PREPARES
9	GOODS NOT CLASSD BY KIND		6155476		7674968		9476724		10389358	ART TRANSACT NON CLASSES
931	*SPECIAL TRANSACTIONS	W 329885	5905301	W 383411	7316320	W 642197	9066261	W 545995	9884803	TRANS.SPECIALES

FOOT NOTES – NOTES

TABLE 3 –
1 Exports to Liberia consist principally of ships for Liberian registry.
TABLE 4 –
1 Includes re–imports.
TABLE 5 –
1 Includes re–exports.
TABLEAU 3 –
1 Les exportations vers le Libéria consistent surtout de navires enregistrés sous pavillon libérien.
TABLEAU 4 –
1 Y compris les réimportations.
TABLEAU 5 –
1 Y compris les réexportations.

1. HISTORICAL SERIES, 1961–1996 GENERAL TRADE, IMPORTS C.I.F., EXPORTS F.O.B. #1
SERIES HISTORIQUES, 1961–1996 COMMERCE GENERAL, IMPORTATIONS C.A.F., EXPORTATIONS F.O.B

YEAR ANNEE	VALUE IN MILLION JORDANIAN DINARS / VALEUR EN MILLION JORDANIAN DINARS — MERCHANDISE – MARCHANDISE		GOLD – OR		CONVERSION FACTORS U.S. CENTS PER JORDANIAN DINAR / FACTEURS DE CONVERSION CENTS E.U. PAR JORDANIAN DINAR		INDEX NUMBERS – INDICES — QUANTUM		UNIT VALUE / VALEUR UNITAIRE	
	IMPORTS	EXPORTS	IMPORTS	EXPORTS	IMPORTS	EXPORTS	IMPORTS	EXPORTS	IMPORTS	EXPORTS
1961	41.90	5.30			280.0000	280.0000	11	6	14	19
1962	45.60	5.90			280.0000	280.0000	10	8	14	19
1963	50.90	6.60			280.0000	280.0000	11	11	14	19
1964	53.60	8.70			280.0000	280.0000	17	10	14	19
1965	56.00	9.90			280.0000	280.0000	17	11	15	19
1966	68.20	10.40			280.0000	280.0000	21	13	14	19
1967	55.10	11.30			280.0000	280.0000	23	10	16	20
1968	57.50	14.30			280.0000	280.0000	28	9	18	20
1969	67.80	14.80			280.0000	280.0000	24	11	18	21
1970	65.90	12.20			280.0000	280.0000	23	6	18	20
1971	76.60	11.40			280.0000	280.0000	27	8	16	21
1972	95.30	17.00			280.0000	280.0000	29	8	18	21
1973	107.80	19.00			305.7830	305.5860	26	13	26	20
1974	155.70	49.80			311.9310	312.1340	29	19	33	41
1975	232.90	48.90			312.3910	313.0160	10	6	18	23
1976	338.70	68.70			301.0650	301.1060	15	7	17	22
1977	454.40	82.10			303.9140	303.6550	18	8	17	22
1978	458.80	90.90			326.6470	326.3450	20	9	17	21
1979	589.50	120.90			332.7870	332.7430	86	32	47	42
1980	716.00	171.60			334.4050	334.2840	85	40	59	49
1981	1047.50	242.60			300.6278	301.5760	81	21	50	39
1982	1142.50	264.50			283.6940	284.5715	89	22	51	43
1983	1103.30	210.60			274.6308	274.8350	90	22	46	39
1984	1071.30	290.70			259.8862	258.7057	84	31	49	43
1985	1074.40	310.90			254.2936	254.1612	101	72	62	58
1986	850.20	256.00			286.0511	286.1834	106	74	47	50
1987	915.50	315.70			295.2200	295.2200	110	88	48	46
1988	1022.50	381.50			264.5387	262.1128	116	102	51	53
1989	1230.00	637.60			172.8350	173.6358	96	104	74	84
1990	1725.80	706.10			150.8096	150.5477	100	100	100	100
1991	1710.50	770.70			146.6166	146.5649	99	88	100	111
1992	2214.00	829.30			147.0031	147.0345	136	97	95	107
1993	2453.60	864.70			144.2223	144.0789	148	104	96	108
1994	2362.60	995.20			143.1500	143.1154	144	112	94	114
1995	2590.40	1241.10			142.7040	142.5193	152	137	99	117
1996	3139.10	1288.10			141.0439	141.0439	170	135	110	126

2. IMPORTS BY BROAD ECONOMIC CATEGORY AND EXPORTS BY INDUSTRIAL ORIGIN. (PERCENTAGE OF TOTAL VALUE)
IMPORTATIONS PAR CATEGORIES ECONOMIQUES ET EXPORTATIONS PAR BRANCHE D'ACTIVITE. (EN POURCENTAGE DE LA VALEUR TOTALE)

IMPORTS – IMPORTATIONS

	1990	1991	1992	1993	1994	1995	1996
TOTAL IMPORTS–IMPORTATIONS TOTALES	100.	100.	100.	100.	100.	100.	
1 FOOD BEV–ALIMENTATION BOISSONS	21.4	22.8	16.7	17.0	18.1	17.2	
11 PRIMARY–PRODUITS DE BASE	13.4	15.1	10.6	11.0	9.0	8.4	
111 FOR INDUSTRY–POUR L'INDUSTRIE	9.2	9.1	6.1	6.9	5.3	5.0	
112 FOR HOUSEHOLDS–POUR LES MENAGES	4.2	6.0	4.5	4.1	3.6	3.4	
12 PROCESSED–PRODUITS ELABORES	8.0	7.7	6.1	6.1	9.1	8.8	
121 FOR INDUSTRY–POUR L'INDUSTRIE	1.0	1.6	1.4	1.9	3.0	3.7	
122 FOR HOUSEHOLDS–POUR LES MENAGES	7.1	6.1	4.8	4.2	6.1	5.1	
2 IND SUPPLIES–APPROV INDUSTRIELS	30.5	34.5	32.2	31.0	32.0	33.4	
21 PRIMARY–PRODUITS DE BASE	4.3	4.6	4.2	3.2	3.3	3.4	
22 PROCESSED–PRODUITS ELABORES	26.2	29.9	28.0	27.8	28.7	30.0	
3 FUELS–COMBUSTIBLES	18.1	14.5	13.7	12.8	12.6	13.0	
31 PRIMARY–PRODUITS DE BASE	13.9	12.0	10.6	9.9	10.2	10.3	
32 PROCESSED–PRODUITS ELABORES	4.2	2.5	3.1	2.9	2.5	2.7	
321 MOTOR SPIRIT–ESSENCE	0.0	0.3	0.8	0.7	2.4	2.7	
322 OTHER–AUTRES	4.2	2.2	2.3	2.3	0.0	0.0	
4 MACHINERY–EQUIPEMENT	9.6	9.4	13.4	16.1	15.7	14.0	
41 CAPITAL EQUIPMENT–MACHINES	7.5	6.9	11.0	13.4	13.6	12.3	
42 PARTS–PIECES ACCESSOIRES	2.1	2.4	2.4	2.6	2.1	1.8	
5 TRANSPORT–TRANSPORT	11.4	10.2	13.5	12.8	11.6	12.1	
51 PASSENGER CARS–AUTOMOBILES	0.9	1.0	1.5	1.5	1.6	2.0	
52 OTHER–AUTRES	2.5	1.8	4.2	4.1	3.5	4.0	
521 INDUSTRIAL–INDUSTRIELS	2.4	1.8	4.2	4.0	3.5	4.0	
522 NON INDUSTRIAL–NON INDUSTRIEL	0.0	0.0	0.0	0.0	0.0	0.0	
53 PARTS–PIECES ACCESSOIRES	8.0	7.3	7.9	7.3	6.5	6.0	
6 CONSUM GOODS–BIENS CONSOMMATION	7.9	8.1	9.7	9.1	9.5	9.7	
61 DURABLE–DURABLES	1.8	1.6	2.0	2.0	2.0	1.9	
62 SEMI DURABLE–SEMI DURABLES	3.2	3.4	4.2	3.8	3.9	3.9	
63 NON DURABLE–NON DURABLES	2.9	3.1	3.6	3.3	3.5	3.9	
7 GOODS NES–BIENS NDA	1.1	0.7	0.6	1.1	0.5	0.6	

EXPORTS – EXPORTATIONS

	1990	1991	1992	1993	1994	1995	1996
TOTAL EXPORTS–EXPORTATIONS TOTALES	100.	100.	100.	100.	100.	100.	
1 AGRICULTURE	8.3	10.2	9.9	10.2	8.9	7.5	
2 MINING QUARRY–INDUS EXTRACTIVES	32.4	29.2	26.4	22.0	19.7	18.4	
3 MANUFACTURING–IND MANUFACTUR	59.2	60.7	63.7	67.8	71.4	74.1	
31 FOOD BEV TOBACCO–ALIM BOISS TAB	2.1	8.1	6.3	9.0	9.5	16.4	
32 TEXTILES–INDUSTRIES TEXTILES	4.4	4.8	4.4	5.0	4.4	4.7	
33 WOOD & PRODUCTS–BOIS & PRODUITS	0.8	0.0	0.1	0.1	0.2	0.0	
34 PAPER & PRODUCTS–PAPIER & PRODT	1.3	1.4	2.2	3.6	2.0	2.2	
35 CHEMICALS–INDUSTRIES CHIMIQUES	28.5	28.2	30.4	27.8	30.4	28.6	
36 NON METAL MIN–MIN NON METAL	4.2	4.2	3.5	2.8	3.5	3.5	
37 BASIC METAL–IND METAL BASE	0.7	0.7	1.2	1.2	0.6	0.9	
38 METAL MANUF–MANUF METAL	15.2	12.5	14.7	17.5	19.9	16.0	
39 OTH MANUF IND–AUTRES MANUF	2.1	0.8	0.9	0.7	0.9	1.7	

3. TRADE BY PRINCIPAL COUNTRIES OF PRODUCTION AND DESTINATION (VALUE IN THOUSAND U.S. DOLLARS)
ECHANGES SELON LES PRINCIPAUX PAYS DE PRODUCTION ET DE DESTINATION (VALEUR EN MILLIERS DE DOLLARS EU)

COUNTRIES–PAYS	GENERAL IMPORTS C.I.F. IMPORTATIONS GENERALES C.A.F				
	1991	1992	1993	1994	1995
World	2512047	3254652	3538674	3382314	3696391
Africa	103079	139302	115782	98947	103403
Americas	337043	435224	535589	408201	461995
Northern America	284889	377102	460560	348481	354719
LAIA	45065	56227	72961	56749	104820
CACM	1632	1271	1898	2769	2249
Caribbean	5457	623	170	198	206
Rest of America				4	
As.ex F.USSR	993118	1367578	1374987	1381659	1603733
Eur.x F.USSR	937781	1204070	1328157	1336375	1362891
EU	811488	1027136	1174476	1199886	1226199
EFTA	27755	38809	30531	36103	59479
East Europe	83550	128694	111793	93891	71214
Other Europe	14988	242	165	396	382
Former USSR	27417	52993	96068	97248	101382
Oceania	72397	43480	81868	48501	53099
Iraq	275789	434301	442772	417096	451323
USA/Etats–Unis d'Amer	261648	361852	449241	332920	343220
Germany/Allemagne	195596	274521	292474	263920	311594
Italy/Italie	108135	163065	194564	199209	197985
United Kingdom	113923	159366	184487	172871	177712
Japan/Japon	89755	194328	178285	134020	130491
France,Monac	108094	114798	142110	159034	169974
Turkey/Turquie	83918	143193	84295	89974	126991
Netherlands/Pays–Bas	84757	77305	90283	128954	102066
Saudi Arabia	40632	57803	70151	102387	130440
Belgium–Luxembourg	65356	72875	84052	100589	74184
Korea, Republic of	36380	68684	88429	83369	109621
China/Chine	42810	76658	72955	89504	84176
India/Inde	78543	45874	62702	55683	69481
Malaysia/Malaisie	16376	29010	57745	94782	107841
Syrian Arab Republic	57295	31409	47072	69073	78431
Spain/Espagne	26507	53668	44051	54441	58130
Egypt/Egypte	33632	55153	41266	42986	46247
Brazil/Brésil	25669	32202	58316	37746	52610
Thailand/Thaïlande	38684	60448	44735	22351	26778
Romania/Roumanie	32770	46807	40941	39353	30681
Switz.Liecht	22811	37275	28963	34771	57687
Ukraine		8782	45024	71223	55396
Australia/Australie	37224	22465	49992	29798	40133
Lebanon/Liban	30987	44571	34901	25769	42493
Indonesia/Indonésie	15443	22708	31912	35186	54830
Russian Federation		43861	47642	24346	43925
Sweden/Suède	26673	30932	36348	30375	34306
Austria/Autriche	25724	33417	35292	23996	23857
Bulgaria/Bulgarie	14244	40331	30891	27025	16011
Zimbabwe	44433	46345	26452	7587	1173
New Zealand	35172	21015	31876	18703	12966
Argentina/Argentine	11809	21666	11765	16083	48030
Denmark/Danemark	18560	17253	20557	28330	22331
Bahrain/Bahreïn	15823	4367	16510	22325	40363
Libyan Arab Jamahiriya	9949	13186	29767	22321	17037
Greece/Grèce	23424	13790	21938	13438	11656
Canada	23240	15250	11310	15537	11481
Singapore/Singapour	19132	13225	13591	8566	14222
Sri Lanka	14135	12086	11255	12933	12157
Finland/Finlande	6827	7136	15685	7733	16446
Ireland/Irlande	6736	7487	10090	11694	14605
United Arab Emirates	3481	8757	8701	11905	15973
Hungary/Hongrie	8051	14994	14176	5855	5521
Iran (Islamic Rp. of)	11349	6514	11062	7311	8561
Poland/Pologne	9283	7700	7646	11180	6546
Yemen/Yémen	24598	1653	3644	4785	3633
Czechoslovakia	19202	18653			
Tunisia/Tunisie	5411	8951	5898	14943	588
Qatar	9524	7434	4719	5435	7685

COUNTRIES–PAYS	GENERAL EXPORTS F.O.B. EXPORTATIONS GENERALES F.O.B.				
	1991	1992	1993	1994	1995
Monde	1131558	1219361	1245795	1424330	1768853
Afrique	64661	77147	43103	79197	93206
Amériques	16498	26292	46282	57757	77483
Amérique du Nord	13053	19222	39197	48006	70165
ALAI	3422	6797	6411	9455	6799
MCAC	22		25	13	329
Caraïbes				1	190
Autre Amérique		273	649	282	
Asie l'URSS exclus	699424	711050	723602	797198	1065525
Europe l'URSS exclus	87480	135563	124508	136068	158028
UE	51915	60992	108911	123841	142026
AELE	18816	52106	1272	908	506
Europe de l'Est	8861	13092	10476	7689	12253
Autre de l'Europe	7889	36	56	60	87
Ancienne URSS	24873	2330	37529	10127	14926
Océanie	1447	6711	13939	25813	13943
Iraq	131943	102439	139052	164962	301682
India/Inde	161772	142105	95076	126549	162919
Saudi Arabia	18089	110200	123682	110536	108210
United Arab Emirates	43734	41363	48134	68782	67174
Indonesia/Indonésie	35627	43492	54369	40034	39220
Syrian Arab Republic	16654	22627	36100	49805	63193
USA/Etats–Unis d'Amer	12832	19053	38301	47468	68251
Lebanon/Liban	19276	17965	27667	29150	38952
Iran (Islamic Rp. of)	49249	29199	14387	6371	27947
China/Chine	47819	20593	24148	12008	19502
France,Monac	16086	12268	21167	35530	30263
Turkey/Turquie	20827	24246	20343	15749	30374
United Kingdom	5088	8095	43992	27123	20622
Bahrain/Bahreïn	17258	11837	20604	23011	21458
Japan/Japon	15853	17839	14236	18290	19147
Netherlands/Pays–Bas	9974	11731	16434	19073	25854
Korea, Republic of	14912	17775	10883	20797	18645
Malaysia/Malaisie	11119	13621	16169	18858	21210
Libyan Arab Jamahiriya	21501	15229	11278	14031	16999
Yemen/Yémen	12689	17713	17178	11088	15767
Switz.Liecht	18813	51972	1238	879	405
Qatar	15737	12796	14705	13346	14655
Italy/Italie	6026	7078	10604	16371	28918
Ethiopia/Ethiopie	14170	29108	2513	5544	17038
Sudan/Soudan	9099	12603	8949	15050	18357
Pakistan	6867	8789	5858	24019	16042
Egypt/Egypte	7537	8337	8618	16192	16997
Russian Federation		2017	37056	8756	8156
Germany/Allemagne	7496	15143	5719	8691	8795
Australia/Australie	1160	4615	8074	18043	11073
Thailand/Thaïlande	16220	13137	5807	1967	5789
Philippines	4775	5718	4581	5648	21543
Algeria/Algérie	1024	2305	861	15223	10923
Tunisia/Tunisie	6571	4839	5736	6130	6093
Brazil/Brésil	3419	6792	6344	5913	6307
Greece/Grèce	3497	2738	5288	6716	9793
Romania/Roumanie	2902	5538	6041	4059	7550
Former USSR/Anc. URSS	24873				
Singapore/Singapour	5877	3750	2409	9364	3425
Spain/Espagne	1490	1271	2289	4532	11632
Nepal/Népal	2221	4239	3796	2066	7412
Bangladesh	6909	5033	2201	2124	2694
New Zealand	287	2096	5864	7770	2835
Yugoslavia/Yougoslavie		9337	3372	3125	2794
Oman	1238	2451	3457	2869	4398
Bulgaria/Bulgarie	1363	2786	3252	3098	3771
Sri Lanka	5344	5012	1217	1173	372
Mauritius/Maurice	1076	1215	2903	2933	1531
Belgium–Luxembourg	1426	1230	1333	4096	1393
Poland/Pologne	4040	4182	51	138	81

(VALUE AS PERCENTAGE OF WORLD TOTAL)(VALEURS EN POURCENTAGE DU TOTAL MONDIAL)

	1986	1987	1988	1989	1990	1991	1992	1993	1994	1995
Africa	2.9	2.4	2.4	3.6	2.9	4.1	4.3	3.3	2.9	2.8
Americas	10.6	12.0	14.9	16.0	19.1	13.4	13.4	15.1	12.1	12.5
Northern America	9.2	10.5	13.3	14.5	17.6	11.3	11.6	13.0	10.3	9.6
LAIA	1.2	1.3	1.4	1.3	1.2	1.8	1.7	2.1	1.7	2.8
CACM	0.1	0.1	0.2	0.1	0.1	0.1	0.0	0.1	0.1	0.1
Caribbean	0.0	0.0	0.0	0.0	0.2	0.2	0.0	0.0	0.0	0.0
Rest of America	0.0	0.0	0.0	0.0					0.0	
As.ex F.USSR	41.5	44.0	41.5	40.3	39.0	39.5	42.0	38.9	40.8	43.4
Eur.x F.USSR	43.7	40.9	39.9	38.7	35.7	37.3	37.0	37.5	39.5	36.9
EU	37.4	33.9	31.8	32.3	29.9	32.3	31.6	33.2	35.5	33.2
EFTA	1.4	1.1	2.1	1.9	1.3	1.1	1.2	0.9	1.1	1.6
East Europe	4.5	4.9	5.5	3.8	3.7	3.3	4.0	3.2	2.8	1.9
Other Europe	0.5	0.8	0.6	0.8	0.7	0.6	0.0	0.0	0.0	0.0
Former USSR	0.7	0.4	0.4	0.4	0.7	1.1	1.6	2.7	2.9	2.7
Oceania	0.6	0.4	0.9	0.7	1.4	2.9	1.3	2.3	1.4	1.4
Iraq	9.5	11.0	11.5	17.3	15.8	11.0	13.3	12.5	12.3	12.2
USA/Etats–Unis d'Amer	8.8	10.2	12.6	13.8	17.0	10.4	11.1	12.7	9.8	9.3
Germany/Allemagne	7.6	7.7	6.5	6.3	5.5	7.8	8.4	8.3	7.8	8.4
Italy/Italie	5.9	5.1	4.5	4.2	3.9	4.3	5.0	5.5	5.9	5.4
United Kingdom	8.0	6.4	6.3	6.0	4.8	4.5	4.9	5.2	5.1	4.8
Japan/Japon	7.8	6.1	5.3	3.7	3.1	3.6	6.0	5.0	4.0	3.5
France,Monac	3.9	3.7	3.9	5.9	5.7	4.3	3.5	4.0	4.7	4.6
Turkey/Turquie	3.2	3.8	2.9	2.3	2.7	3.3	4.4	2.4	2.7	3.4
Netherlands/Pays–Bas	3.2	3.0	3.2	2.8	2.8	3.4	2.4	2.6	3.8	2.8
Saudi Arabia	7.4	8.9	7.5	2.8	4.6	1.6	1.8	2.0	3.0	3.5

	1986	1987	1988	1989	1990	1991	1992	1993	1994	1995
Afrique	4.3	5.7	6.1	5.1	7.5	5.7	6.3	3.5	5.6	5.3
Amériques	2.3	3.1	1.3	2.5	4.7	1.5	2.2	3.7	4.1	4.4
Amérique du Nord	0.8	1.9	1.1	2.4	4.6	1.2	1.6	3.1	3.4	4.0
ALAI	1.5	0.9	0.1	0.0	0.1	0.3	0.6	0.5	0.7	0.4
MCAC		0.3	0.2	0.1		0.0		0.0	0.0	0.0
Caraïbes									0.0	0.0
Autre Amérique							0.0	0.1	0.0	
Asie l'URSS exclus	69.8	64.1	70.8	73.2	77.4	61.8	58.3	58.1	56.0	60.2
Europe l'URSS exclus	23.2	19.9	21.8	18.8	8.2	7.7	11.1	10.0	9.6	8.9
UE	11.7	8.4	9.9	10.4	5.9	4.6	5.0	8.7	8.7	8.0
AELE	1.2	3.8	5.5	1.3	0.1	1.7	4.3	0.1	0.1	0.0
Europe de l'Est	6.0	5.5	3.8	5.2	1.0	0.8	1.1	0.8	0.5	0.7
Autre de l'Europe	4.3	2.2	2.6	1.9	1.2	0.7	0.0	0.0	0.0	0.0
Ancienne URSS	0.0	0.0	0.0	0.0	1.4	2.2	0.2	3.0	0.7	0.8
Océanie	0.4	7.2	0.0	0.3	0.0	0.1	0.6	1.1	1.8	0.8
Iraq	17.7	19.7	18.4	20.9	18.6	11.7	8.4	11.2	11.6	17.1
India/Inde	13.4	7.1	14.6	15.0	18.3	14.3	11.7	7.6	8.9	9.2
Saudi Arabia	11.4	9.4	9.4	8.5	7.1	1.6	9.0	9.9	7.8	6.1
United Arab Emirates	2.0	1.6	2.2	2.5	3.5	3.9	3.4	3.9	4.8	3.8
Indonesia/Indonésie	3.0	2.5	2.9	4.3	4.3	3.1	3.6	4.4	2.8	2.2
Syrian Arab Republic	2.2	2.8	1.5	2.6	1.5	1.5	1.9	2.9	3.5	3.6
USA/Etats–Unis d'Amer	0.6	1.9	1.0	2.2	4.6	1.1	1.6	3.1	3.3	3.9
Lebanon/Liban	0.6	0.7	0.6	0.7	1.5	1.7	1.5	2.2	2.0	2.2
Iran (Islamic Rp. of)	0.0		0.0		0.3	4.4	2.4	1.2	0.4	1.6
China/Chine	3.0	3.2	4.2	1.7	2.6	4.2	1.7	1.9	0.8	1.1

4. General Imports C.I.F. by Commodities according to the S.I.T.C. (Rev. 2) in thousand U.S. Dollars
Importations Générales C.A.F. par Produits d'après la C.T.C.I. (Rév. 2) en milliers de Dollars E.U.

SITC CTCI	COMMODITY	1992		1993		1994		1995		PRODUIT
		WEIGHT POIDS	VALUE VALEUR	WEIGHT POIDS	VALUE VALEUR	WEIGHT POIDS	VALUE VALEUR	WEIGHT POIDS	VALUE VALEUR	
	ALL COMMODITIES		3254652		3538674		3382314		3696391	TOUS PRODUITS
0	FOOD AND LIVE ANIMALS		615510		631742		585935		598072	ALIMENTS,ANIMAUX VIVANTS
001	*LIVE ANIMALS FOR FOOD		38047		39833	W 630	43798	W 580	42407	ANIMAUX VIVANTS
0011	BOVINE SPECIES,LIVE	N 21015	13705	N 13602	9105	W 24	16376	W 23	14474	ESPECE BOVINE
00119	— OTHR THAN FR BREEDING	N 21015	13705	N 13602	9105	W 24	16376	W 23	13744	BOVINS NON REPRODUCTEURS
0012	SHEEP AND GOATS,LIVE	N 515159	21186	N 675548	28898	W 567	25072	W 522	25325	ESPECES OVINE ET CAPRINE
00121	SHEEP,LIVE	N 497814	19974	N 633580	27160	W 504	22420	W 522	25219	ESPECE OVINE
01	MEAT AND PREPARATIONS		74500		84572		67550		49979	VIANDES ET PREPARATIONS
011	MEAT FRESH,CHILLD,FROZEN	W 45333	73883	W 53262	84375	W 38391	61846	W 25098	41997	VIANDES FRAICHES,REF,CONGE
0111	BOVINE MEAT FRESH,FROZEN	W 18851	24353	W 23289	31118	W 19035	25951	W 14189	23056	VIANDES BOVIN FRAI,REF
01111	BOVINE MEAT WITH BONE IN	W 18851	24353	W 23289	31118	W 13581	21170	W 10483	17660	VIANDES BOVIN NON DESOSS
0112	MUTTON ETC FRSH,CHLD,FRN	W 17670	38517	W 19782	40934	W 13402	29605	W 8808	16199	VIANDE DE MOUTON
0114	POULTRY FRESH CHLLD,FRZN	W 7628	9092	W 9569	11471	W 5211	5086	W 1677	2083	VOLAILLES MORTES
02	DAIRY PRODCTS,BIRDS'EGGS		50885		59661		44022		55820	PRODUITS LAITIERS,OEUFS
022	MILK AND CREAM	W 15410	34436	W 19072	42319	W 12291	24601	W 15064	33588	LAIT ET CREME
0224	MILK,CREAM PRESERVED ETC	W 15167	33942	W 18691	41479	W 9172	21454	W 11914	30176	LAIT,CREME CONS,CONC
02242	MILK DRY,1.5% FAT OR LES	W 12663	31045	W 15462	38318	W 7369	17184	W 10652	26506	LAIT POUDRE INF 1.5%
024	CHEESE AND CURD	W 4854	12260	W 4748	12041	W 5712	14713	W 5559	15513	FROMAGE ET CAILLEBOTTE
03	FISH AND PREPARATIONS		16377		19682		19316		23766	POISSONS ET PREPARATIONS
034	FISH,FRESH,CHILLED,FROZN	W 7661	9282	W 8932	10891	W 7714	9106	W 9575	12090	POISSON FRAIS, REFRIG,CONG
0342	FISH FROZEN,EXCL FILLETS	W 7656	9208	W 8927	10825	W 5920	5505	W 8749	8883	POISSONS CONGELES
04	CEREALS AND PREPARATIONS		228439		248587		187823		201086	CEREALES ET PRODUITS
041	WHEAT ETC UNMILLED					W 508126	74236	W 335435	56869	FROMENT,EPEAUTRE
0411	DURUM WHEAT UNMILLED					W 248424	38571	W 335435	56869	FROMENT DUR NON MOULU
0412	OTHER WHEAT ETC UNMILLED					W 259702	35665			AUTRE FROMENT NON MOULU
042	RICE	W 81725	30780	W 84535	29555	W 62064	22852	W 76283	30997	RIZ
0421	RICE IN HUSK OR HUSKED	W 81725	30780	W 84535	29555					RIZ SANS AUTRE PREPARATION
04212	RICE HUSKED	W 81725	30780	W 84535	29555					RIZ CARGO
0422	RICE SEMI–MILLED,MILLED					W 62064	22852	W 76283	30997	RIZ POLI,GLACE INCL BRISURES
04221	RICE MILLED UNBROKEN					W 62064	22852	W 76283	30997	RIZ POLI,GLACE EXCL BRISURES
043	BARLEY UNMILLED	W 293481	33057	W 482996	51339	W 471864	43750	W 487930	53907	ORGE NON MONDEE
044	MAIZE UNMILLED	W 1129677	156960	W 1017086	159845	W 298905	40795	W 348308	50609	MAIS NON MOULU
05	VEGETABLES AND FRUIT		64491		41657		40657		61496	LEGUMES ET FRUITS
054	VEG ETC FRSH,SMPLY PRSVD	W 54268	25549	W 44437	20161	W 54576	23410	W 57054	29786	LEGUMES FRAIS,CONG,SECS
0542	LEGUMINOUS VEGETBLES DRY	W 28187	14162	W 20488	8935	W 24997	10589	W 26677	14387	LEGUMES A COSSE SECS
057	FRUIT,NUTS,FRESH,DRIED	W 71572	31492	W 19072	14550	W 13040	10632	W 36269	24779	FRUITS FRAIS OU SECS
0571	ORANGES, MANDARINS ETC	W 34510	9892	W 117	14	W 844	85	W 11407	4581	ORANGES,MAND,CLEMENTINES
05711	ORANGES,FRESH OR DRIED	W 34510	9892	W 117	14	W 844	85	W 11407	4581	ORANGES FRAICHES,SECHEES
0579	FRUIT FRESH OR DRIED NES	W 27846	11407	W 8796	4170	W 6068	3760	W 5279	3420	FRUITS FRAIS,SECS NDA
06	SUGAR AND PREPS,HONEY		46947		52897		85433		49163	SUCRES ET PRODUITS
061	SUGAR AND HONEY	W 139453	44904	W 162011	51074	W 214563	83446	W 100783	46556	SUCRES ET MIEL
0612	REFINED SUGAR ETC	W 135422	42365	W 156660	47714	W 212050	80500	W 94581	42331	SUCRES RAFFINES
07	COFFEE,TEA,COCOA,SPICES		26080		21269		28808		34986	CAFE,THE,CACAO,EPICES
071	COFFEE AND SUBSTITUTES	W 6231	8268	W 2654	4265	W 2635	7510	W 4440	14900	CAFE ET SUCCEDANES
0711	COFFEE GREEN,ROASTED,SUB	W 6163	7553	W 2548	3357	W 2523	6442	W 4289	13381	CAFE TORREFIE OU DECAFEINE
07111	COFFEE GREEN,HUSKS,SKINS	W 6023	7254	W 2520	3179	W 2432	6150	W 4288	13380	CAFE NON TORREFIE
074	TEA AND MATE	W 4618	11737	W 4520	11104	W 5626	13787	W 5153	12054	THE ET MATE
0741	TEA	W 4618	11737	W 4520	11104	W 5624	13786	W 5153	12054	THE
081	*FEEDING STUFF FOR ANIML	W 161940	50622		44974	W 169928	50836	W 204494	57701	NOURRITURE POUR ANIMAUX
0813	OILCAKE AND OTH RESIDUES	W 116430	30652	W 89477	22711	W 116971	28464	W 140437	32107	TOURTEAUX
08131	— OF SOYA BEANS					W 116971	28464	W 139910	32038	TOURTEAUX DE SOJA
08139	— OF OTHER OILSEEDS ETC	W 116430	30652	W 89477	22711					TOURTEAUX D'AUTRES OLEAGINEU
0819	FOOD WASTE AND FEED NES	W 37685	18321	W 44497	20714	W 38908	19476	W 38321	20537	DECHETS,ALIMENTS NDA
08199	FODDER NES,INCL SWEETNED	W 37685	18321	W 44497	20714	W 37608	19331	W 38321	20537	PREPARATIONS FOURRAGERES
09	MISC EDIBLE PRODUCTS		19122		18612		17692		21669	PREP ALIMENTAIRES DIVERSES
098	EDIBLE PRODCTS,PREPS NES	W 7151	19062	W 7090	18568	W 3949	17659	W 4615	21304	PREP ALIMENTAIRES NDA
09809	MISC FOOD PREPRTIONS NES	W 6112	16494	W 4864	15253	W 2481	14095	W 2958	17798	PREP ALIMENTAIRES NDA
1	BEVERAGES AND TOBACCO		13706		13920		19869		14170	BOISSONS ET TABACS
12	TOBACCO AND MANUFACTURES		10492		10296		17719		11673	TABACS BRUTS FABRIQUES
122	TOBACCO,MANUFACTURED	W 146	4502	W 358	7052	W 1447	10466	W 1323	9967	TABACS FABRIQUES
2	CRUDE MATERLS,EXCL FUELS		94349		111228		101763		130034	MAT BRUTES NON COMESTIBLES
22	OIL SEEDS,OLEAGINOUS FRT		10085		10703		8019		13576	GRAINES,FRUITS OLEAGINEUX
222	SEEDS FOR'SOFT'FIXED OIL	W 12926	10084	W 17598	10653	W 12476	7932	W 15661	13546	GRAINES HUILES FIXES
24	CORK AND WOOD		31736		29917		24302		27402	LIEGE ET BOIS
248	WOOD SHAPED,SLEEPERS	MW 77698	29038	MW 79937	28657	W 6999	21765	W 6450	26791	BOIS SIMPLEMENT TRAVAILLES
2483	LUMBER SHAPED NON–CONIFR	MW 57027	20431	MW 53323	18522	W 4750	20725	W 4204	26009	NON CONIFERES SCIES,RABOTES
24831	LUMBER SAWN ETC NON–CON	MW 57027	20431	MW 53323	18508	W 4725	20717	W 4186	25950	SCIES LONGITUDINALEMENT
251	*PULP AND WASTE PAPER	W 7578	4833	W 14911	7756	W 13915	7796	W 16899	14593	PATES A PAPIER,DECHETS
26	TEXTILE FIBRES AND WASTE		15750		20635		20244		23768	FIBRES TEXTILES
269	WASTE OF TEXTILE FABRICS	W 8491	11208	W 10411	12848	W 9600	12111	W 10768	13776	FRIPERIE DRILLES,CHIFFONS
26901	BULK TEXT WSTE,OLD CLTHG	W 8431	11152	W 10374	12805	W 9535	12059	W 10480	13574	ART ET ACCESS D'HABILLEMENT
27	CRUDE FERTLZR,MINRLS NES		11095		16527		27336		36479	ENGRAIS MINERAUX BRUTS
274	SULPHUR,UNRSTD IRN PYRTE	W 65080	4742	W 183275	9769	W 305911	20477	W 301549	27705	SOUFRE ET PYRITES
2741	SULPHUR,EX SULP IN 52215	W 64811	4662	W 182153	9565	W 305911	20477	W 301508	27691	SOUFRE
28	METALLIFEROUS ORES,SCRAP		7808		14685		2330		2445	MINERAIS METAL,DECHETS
288	NONFERR METAL SCRAP NES	W 4399	6011	W 9046	11754	W 1982	1947	W 1676	2169	DECHETS NON FERREUX
2882	OTHER BASE MTL SCRAP NES	W 4399	6011	W 9046	11754	W 1982	1947	W 1666	2155	AUTRES DECHETS
29	CRUDE ANIMAL,VEG MAT NES		10235		8952		8920		8774	MATIERES BRUTES ANIM,VEGET
3	MINERAL FUELS ETC		446045		453984		426284		477531	COMBUSTIBLES MINERAUX LUB
33	PETROLEUM AND PRODUCTS		437602		445849		415815		454686	PETROLE ET DERIVES
333	CRUDE PETROLEUM	W 2974858	336409	W 2899533	341525	W 2977092	332602	W 3162859	355776	HUILES BRUTES DE PETROLE
334	PETROLEUM PRODUCTS,REFIN	W 842298	100251	W 885730	103705	W 893537	82195	W 942344	98358	PRODUITS RAFFINES
3342	KEROSENE,OTH MEDIUM OILS	W 800892	78868	W 862786	89104					PETR LAMPANTS,AUT HUIL
33421	KEROSENE INCL JET FUEL	W 159564	27580	W 157742	27001					PETROLES LAMPANTS
33429	OTH MEDIUM PETROLEUM OIL	W 641328	51288	W 705044	62103					AUTRES HUILES MOYENNES
3345	LUBS,PETROLEUM OILS NES	W 41406	21383	W 22945	14601					HUILES LUBRIFIANTES
33451	LUBS(HIGH PETR CONT) ETC	W 41068	21025	W 22425	14158					HUILES LUBRIF,H LOURDES
341	*GAS,NATURAL AND MANUFCT	W 34168	7144	W 42280	6915	W 52399	9431	W 82103	21813	GAZ NATUREL,GAZ MANUFACT
3413	PETROLM GASES,LIQUEFIED	W 34168	7144	W 42280	6915	W 52399	9431	W 82102	21808	GAZ DE PETROLE LIQUEFIE
34139	OTH HYDROCARBON GAS LQFD	W 34168	7144	W 42280	6915	W 52399	9431	W 82102	21808	HYDROCARBURES GAZEUX NDA
4	ANIMAL,VEGETABLE OIL,FAT		55315		61515		118112		135136	HUILES,GRAISSES ANIM,VEG
42	FIXED VEGETABLE OIL,FAT		52721		58920		111678		124998	HUILES VEGETALES FIXES
423	FIXED VEG OILS,SOFT	W 18707	26140	W 17328	10697	W 17346	19736	W 15376	11813	HUILES VEGET DOUCES FIXES
4232	SOYA BEAN OIL	W 9969	5826	W 16135	8614	W 9555	6578	W 14959	11343	HUILE DE SOJA
4235	OLIVE OIL	W 8285	19838	W 1112	2000	W 6996	12281	W 88	50	HUILE D'OLIVE
424	FIXED VEG OIL NONSOFT	W 57589	26581	W 111257	48223	W 185705	91942	W 166532	113185	AUTRES HUILES VEG FIXES
4242	PALM OIL	W 50758	21157	W 103931	43785	W 173487	82241	W 156062	104839	HUILE DE PALME
5	CHEMCLS,RELATED PROD NES		357094		354953		401574		443692	PRODUITS CHIMIQUES
51	ORGANIC CHEMICALS		47238		37366		44496		51265	PROD CHIMIQ ORGANIQUES
513	CARBOXYLIC ACIDS ETC	W 8995	8610	W 8381	7671	W 8869	9383	W 9543	14022	ACIDES CARBOXYLIQUES

4. General Imports C.I.F. by Commodities according to the S.I.T.C. (Rev. 2) in thousand U.S. Dollars
Importations Générales C.A.F. par Produits d'après la C.T.C.I. (Rév. 2) en milliers de Dollars E.U.

SITC CTCI	COMMODITY	1992			1993			1994			1995			PRODUIT
		WEIGHT POIDS		VALUE VALEUR	WEIGHT POIDS		VALUE VALEUR	WEIGHT POIDS		VALUE VALEUR	WEIGHT POIDS		VALUE VALEUR	
516	OTHER ORGANIC CHEMICALS	W	2792	19527			8512	W	3709	16941	W	3422	14994	AUTRES PROD ORGANIQUES
5169	ORGANIC CHEMICALS,NES	W	458	15238			6708	W	839	14183	W	571	11385	PROD CHIM ORGANIQUES NDA
51699	OTHER ORGANIC COMPOUNDS	W	426	14864	W	608	6482	W	770	13756	W	522	10984	AUTRES COMPOS ORGANIQUES
52	INORGANIC CHEMICALS			41153			42670			65900			67753	PROD CHIM INORGANIQUES
522	INORG ELEMNTS,OXIDES,ETC	W	158722	28964	W	145159	26159	W	203262	43221	W	197966	50767	ELEMENTS INORGANIQUES
5225	INORGANIC BASES ETC NES	W	88474	15703	W	137002	19127	W	194572	33943	W	189174	42061	AUTRES BASES OXYDES METAL
52251	AMMONIA,ANHYDROUS ETC	W	57711	7152	W	119014	13527	W	177463	30948	W	160045	36679	AMMONIAC LIQUEFIE
523	OTHR INORG CHEMICALS ETC	W	30499	11821	W	41749	16027	W	55426	22308	W	42984	16576	AUT PRODUITS CHIMIQUES INORG
5232	OTH MTL CMPD OF INRG ACD	W	16417	7666	W	21453	10120	W	33755	17722	W	25764	12767	SELS METALLIQUES
52322	PHOSPHITES,PHOSPHATES	W	6901	4769	W	12493	7525	W	27270	15522	W	17932	9780	PHOSPHITES,PHOSPHATES
53	DYES,TANNING,COLOUR PROD			12240			12221			15251			15862	PROD TEINTURE,COLORANTS
533	PIGMENTS,PAINTS,ETC	W	5737	9796	W	6370	9784	W	7077	12607	W	7772	13569	PIGMENTS,PEINTURES,VERNIS
541	*MEDICINAL,PHARM PRODUCT	K	4831789	86714	K	5299586	99570	K	5087046	101399	K	5979880	128021	PROD MEDICINAUX PHARMACEUT
5413	ANTIBIOTICS IN BULK	K	967169	16311	K	1329213	31092	K	556245	21224	K	859338	21107	ANTIBIOTIQUES NDA
54139	OTHER ANTIBIOTICS	K	967167	16310	K	1329213	31092	K	482502	19167	K	807756	18324	AUTRES ANTIBIOTIQUES
5417	MEDICAMENTS	K	3285655	62140	K	3542291	60684	K	3790690	68057	K	4489677	92918	MEDICAMENTS
54171	— CONTAINNG ANTIBIOTICS	K	2690952	53929	K	2784320	52228	K	860466	14167	K	488648	14626	MED CONTN ANTIBIOTIQUES
54179	— CONTNG OTH SUBSTANCES							K	2592649	48555	K	3687939	74911	MED CONT AUT SUBSTANCES
55	PERFUME,CLEANING ETC PRD			25190			30222			22018			25334	PROD POUR PARFUM,TOILETTE
554	SOAP,CLEANSING ETC PREPS	W	15508	14107	W	23979	18643	W	11063	10825	W	9893	11858	SAVONS,PRODUITS DETERSIFS
5541	SOAPS	W	7334	5491	W	17984	11563	W	7605	5486	W	6922	6436	SAVONS,PROD TENSIO–ACTIFS
562	*FERTILIZERS,MANUFACTURE	W	81364	17941	W	48871	10978	W	31690	8738	W	42718	11490	ENGRAIS MANUFACTURES
5621	CHEM NITROGENOUS FERTLZR	W	75209	13412	W	44364	8114	W	25767	4932	W	32828	6114	ENGRAIS AZOTES
56211	AMMONIUM NITRATE	W	72862	12066	W	16363	3632	W	5368	1154	W	6968	1547	NITRATE D'AMMONIUM
58	PLASTIC MATERIALS ETC			89998			89447			100475			102884	MAT PLAST ARTIFICIELLES
582	PROD OF CONDENSATION ETC	W	4770	8848	W	6756	11347	W	7288	12201	W	5266	10655	PROD CONDENS,POLYCOND
583	POLYMERIZATION ETC PRODS	W	79438	78107	W	85538	76025	W	97607	85306	W	73281	88967	PROD POLYMERISATION
5831	POLYETHYLENE	W	77250	75226	W	82927	72995	W	41262	31065	W	33514	35192	POLYETHYLENE
58311	— IN PRIMARY FORMS	W	68184	57289	W	74048	55653	W	40165	29154	W	32364	32731	POLYETHYLENE PRIMAIRES
58313	— PLATES,FILM,STRIP,ETC	W	8528	17115	W	8675	16210	W	1052	1770	W	1108	2333	POLYETHYLENE PLAQUES
5832	POLYPROPYLENE	W	90	77	W	292	296	W	17666	14811	W	14982	19928	POLYPROPYLENE
58321	— IN PRIMARY FORMS	W	90	77	W	292	296	W	15493	11023	W	12338	13221	POLYPROPYLENE PRIMAIRES
5833	POLYSTYRENE,ITS COPOLYMR							W	10572	10547	W	5838	7863	POLYPROPYLENE COPOLYMERES
58331	— IN PRIMARY FORMS							W	10500	10376	W	5744	7624	SOUS FORMES PRIMAIRES
5834	POLYVINYL CHLORIDE							W	17350	13758	W	10755	11508	CHLORURE DE POLYVINYLE
58341	— IN PRIMARY FORMS							W	16833	12774	W	9923	10064	SOUS FORMES PRIMAIRES
5839	OTH POLYMRZTION ETC PROD							W	7734	11188	W	6313	11372	AUT PROD POLYMER COPOLYM
59	CHEMICAL MATERIALS NES			34926			31596			42309			40946	MAT PROD CHIMIQUES NDA
591	PESTICIDES,DISINFECTANTS	W	2298	11510	W	1739	8730	W	1969	9568	W	1778	9478	DESINF,INSECT,FONG,HERB
5912	FUNGICIDES,FOR RETAIL	W	2286	11486	W	1725	8701	W	458	1867	W	605	3003	FONGICIDES VENTE AU DET
598	MISCEL CHEM PRODUCTS NES	W	8293	18972	W	9287	17323	W	24810	28177	W	21909	27315	PROD DIV INDUST CHIM NDA
5989	CHEM PRODUCTS,PREPS NES	W	7433	17257	W	8555	15971	W	21149	21705	W	20307	23589	PROD PREP CHIMIQUES NDA
59899	OTH CHEM PRODS,PREPS,NES	W	6258	15409	W	6692	14025	W	18620	18896	W	19003	21051	AUT PRODUITS CHIMIQUES NDA
6	BASIC MANUFACTURES			622855			695587			620516			720022	ART MANUFACTURES
62	RUBBER MANUFACTURES NES			45840			44528			38122			44820	CAOUTCHOUC MANUFACTURE
625	RUBBER TYRES, TUBES ETC	W	15050	37296	W	16428	36007	W	13738	30011	W	16249	37197	PNEUS CAOUTCHOUC VULCANISE
6251	TYRES NEW FOR MOTOR CARS							W	8330	20711	W	12435	30405	PNEUS POUR VOITURES
6252	TYRES,NEW,BUS OR LORRY	W	14919	36996	W	16233	35566	W	1369	3340	W	1578	4376	PNEUS POUR AUTOBUS,CAMIONS
63	WOOD,CORK MANUFACTRS NES			28576			34401			33148			27382	OUVRAGES LIEGE ET BOIS
634	VENEERS,PLYWOOD,ETC			21990			27274	W	53059	25847	W	30825	22776	PLACAGES,CONTRE–PLAQUES
6342	PLYWOOD OF WOOD SHEETS	MV	22459	7760	MV	22315	7073	W	41682	22881	W	22604	19908	BOIS CONTRE–PLAQUES
6344	WOOD–BASED PANELS NES	W	30648	13794	W	35619	19712							PANNEAUX SUPPORT BOIS NDA
63441	BLOCKBOARD,LAMINBRD, ETC	W	30648	13794	W	35619	19712							BOIS CONTRE–PLAQUES
64	PAPER,PAPERBOARD AND MFR			74660			84130			68912			107594	PAPIERS,CARTONS & OUVRAGES
641	PAPER AND PAPERBOARD	W	83624	60382	W	111915	72744	W	85376	58192	W	96351	92421	PAPIERS ET CARTONS
6412	PRINTG,WRITING PAPER NES	W	23777	19159	W	36953	26698	W	2029	2059	W	1864	2544	PAPIERS POUR L'IMPRESSION
64121	— UNCOATED	W	21546	16240	W	33954	23301	W	113	189	W	67	186	PAPIERS IMPRES NON COUCHES
6413	KRAFT PAPER,PAPERBOARD	W	21574	12471	W	24903	13512	W	19731	10498	W	24239	19483	PAPIER ET CARTON KRAFT
64131	KRAFT LINER IN BULK	W	21574	12471	W	24903	13512	W	7052	2727	W	8534	5714	PAP KRAFT POUR COUVERTURES
6415	PAPER,PAPERBRD,BULK,NES	W	4630	7218	W	6310	6600	W	22145	16795	W	29010	34547	PAPIERS,CARTONS ROULEAUX
64159	OTHER PAPER ETC,BULK,NES	W	931	2660	W	776	1262	W	20666	15675	W	28901	34310	AUT PAPIER ROULEAUX FEUILLES
6418	COATED ETC PAPER NES BLK	W	17664	14666	W	20301	16383	W	13690	13200	W	14595	17038	PAP,CARTONS COUCHES,ENDUITS
64189	COATED PAPER ETC NES	W	3005	5192	W	3826	6101	W	13330	12543	W	14210	16395	PAPIERS,CARTONS COUCHES
642	PAPER,ETC,PRECUT,ARTS OF	W	6467	14279	W	5591	11385	W	5370	10720	W	8198	15173	PAP,CARTONS DECOUPES
65	TEXTILE YARN,FABRICS,ETC			139365			137580			125473			127496	FILS,TISSUS,ARTICLES TEXTILE
651	TEXTILE YARN	W	12201	44981			44225	W	9638	34836	W	9378	37121	FILS TEXTILES
6512	WOOL,HAIR YARN,INCL TOPS	W	71	869	W	92	909	W	1572	10096	W	1205	13762	FILS DE LAINE,DE POILS
6514	SYN FIB YRN,BULK,MONOFIL	W	8944	33970	W	10104	32473	W	3040	9665	W	3304	9818	FILS CONT 85% FIB TEXT SYNTH
65141	— TEXTRD,CONT POLYAMIDE	W	3025	10607	W	3585	11796	W	496	1892	W	531	1784	FILS TEXT FIB CONT POLYAMID
65142	— NONTXT ETC CONT PAMID	W	5715	21454	W	6386	19943	W	1217	3885	W	1538	4364	FILS NON TEX FI CON POLYAMID
653	WOVN MAN–MADE FIB FABRIC	W	10056	59653	W	10779	61291	W	9628	56294	W	9157	56768	TISSUS FIBRES SYNTH,ARTIF
6531	CONT SYNT WEAVES NONPILE	W	10011	59488	W	10745	61101	W	8236	48253	W	7933	49210	TISSUS FIBRES SYNTH CONTINUE
65314	CONT SYN TYRE CORD FABRC	W	8656	52042	W	9252	54191	W	792	3702	W	516	2172	TIS ARMATURE PNEUMATIQUES
65315	CONT SYN TXTL FABRIC NES	W	1356	7447	W	1493	6911	W	7444	44551	W	7417	47038	TIS PLUS 85% TEXT SYNT CONT
657	SPECIAL TXTL FABRC,PRODS	W	4193	9491	W	4197	9922	W	4551	10740	W	4082	11667	TISSUS SPECIAUX
66	NONMETAL MINERAL MFS NES			40479			43686			47477			48598	ART MIN NON METALLIQUES
662	CLAY,REFRACTORY BLDG PRD	W	23107	8185			10942	W	25223	8560	W	25720	10186	MAT CONST REFRACTAIRES
665	GLASSWARE	W	20173	17022	W	16251	14535	W	27290	20054	W	23625	18618	OUVRAGES EN VERRE
6651	BOTTLES ETC OF GLASS	W	14777	8780	W	10074	6599	W	21238	11194	W	16702	9692	RECIPIENTS EN VERRE
66511	GLASS BOTTLES ETC NONVAC	W	14777	8778	W	10069	6590	W	21226	11164	W	16698	9682	BONBONNES,BOUTEILLES,ETC
67	IRON AND STEEL			196367			227863			190014			210890	FER ET ACIER
672	IRON,STEEL PRIMARY FORMS	W	292041	76686	W	211349	61703	W	217558	58878	W	257277	77058	LINGOTS FER,ACIER
6725	IRN,STL BLOOMS,SLABS,ETC	W	256801	62063	W	164140	42187	W	158309	37596	W	210726	57222	BLOOMS,BILLETTES FER ACIER
67251	IRN,SMPLE STL BLOOMS,ETC	W	256801	62063	W	164140	42187	W	157783	37096	W	210291	56783	BLOOMS ETC NON ACIER FIN
6727	IRN,STL COIL FR REROLLNG	W	32088	11200	W	42697	15532	W	46381	18270	W	46486	19742	EBAUCHES POUR TOLES FER
67271	IRON,SIMPLE STEEL COILS	W	32088	11200	W	42697	15532	W	39392	14034	W	38346	15341	EBAUCHES NON EN ACIER
673	IRON,STEEL SHAPES ETC	W	156499	51075	W	268423	77868	W	196195	58326	W	195263	59846	BARRES,PROFIL FER,ACIER
6731	IRON,STEEL WIRE ROD	W	13937	4385	W	947	441	W	115026	31598	W	67687	19107	FIL MACHINE FER,ACIER
67311	IRON,SIMPLE STL WIRE ROD	W	13937	4385	W	947	441	W	103699	28414	W	53775	15012	FIL MACH AUT ACIER FIN
6732	IRON,STEEL BARS ETC	W	109679	34803	W	219837	58869	W	44720	12616	W	95789	27873	BARRES FER,ACIER
67325	OTH ALLOY STEEL BARS ETC							W	12680	3512	W	41746	12100	BARRES NON ACIERS ALLIES
67327	IRN, OTH STL BARS FORGED	W	97131	30781	W	207550	55813	W	10475	3151	W	10769	2869	BARRES FORGEES CREUSES
6733	IRON,STEEL PROFILES ETC	W	32883	11887	W	47640	18558	W	36449	14112	W	31787	12865	PROFILES,PALPLAN FER,ACIER
67331	SMALL U,I,H SECTIONS ETC	W	32883	11887	W	47640	18558	W	15634	5601	W	11222	4122	PROFILES MOINS 80MM
674	IRN,STL UNIV,PLATE,SHEET	W	66267	35039	W	113321	57313	W	80157	44389	W	77271	45902	LARGES PLATS,TOLES
6744	IRN,STL HVY PLATE,ROLLED	W	12936	10080	W	17780	13356	W	15954	7973	W	9117	4189	TOLES LAMINEES PLUS 4.75 MM
67441	— OF IRON OR SIMPLE STL	W	12936	10080	W	17780	13356	W	15571	7801	W	9089	4160	TOLES NON ACIER FIN CARB
6745	IRN,STL MED PLATE,ROLLED	W	45340	21303	W	81314	37985	W	14227	7304	W	10769	6504	TOLES 3 A 4.75 MM
67451	— OF IRON OR SIMPLE STL	W	45340	21303	W	81314	37985	W	13832	7097	W	10607	6357	TOLES AUT NON ACIER FIN
6746	IRN,STL THIN PLATE,ROLLD							W	15140	7771	W	24979	12965	TOLES LAM MOINS 3MM
67461	— OF IRON OR SIMPLE STL							W	14804	7290	W	24234	12131	TOL NON AC FIN MOINS 3 MM

4. General Imports C.I.F. by Commodities according to the S.I.T.C. (Rev. 2) in thousand U.S. Dollars
Importations Générales C.A.F. par Produits d'après la C.T.C.I. (Rév. 2) en milliers de Dollars E.U.

SITC CTCI	COMMODITY	1992 WEIGHT POIDS	1992 VALUE VALEUR	1993 WEIGHT POIDS	1993 VALUE VALEUR	1994 WEIGHT POIDS	1994 VALUE VALEUR	1995 WEIGHT POIDS	1995 VALUE VALEUR	PRODUIT
6749	OTH IRN,STL PLATES,SHEET					W 25677	15232	W 18700	11955	AUTRES TOLES FER,ACIER
67491	— OF IRON OR SIMPLE STL					W 25040	14210	W 17949	10893	AUT TOLES AUTRES ACIER FIN
678	IRON,STL TUBES,PIPES,ETC	W 33385	26271	W 23261	25038	W 25058	21208	W 24317	22445	TUBES,TUYAUX EN FONTE,FER
6782	IRON,STL SEAMLESS TUBES	W 26163	17811	W 19652	17145	W 2940	2140	W 5535	4221	TUBES,TUYAUX SANS SOUDURE
6783	IRON,STL TUBES,PIPES NES	W 1447	934	W 225	151	W 18664	13616	W 15790	13144	AUT TUBES,TUYAUX FER,ACIER
68	NON–FERROUS METALS		23148		26568		35561		53409	METAUX NON FERREUX
682	COPPER EXC CEMENT COPPER		11092		13929	W 4721	12860	W 6681	22766	CUIVRE
6822	COPPER,ALLOYS WORKED		10249		13652	W 4482	12458	W 6499	22306	CUIVRE,ALLIAGES OUVRES
68221	COPPER BARS,WIRE,ETC	W 2212	5824	W 4076	8872	W 3469	8459	W 5505	17156	BARRES,PROFILES ET FILS
684	ALUMINIUM	W 4530	11310	W 5310	11439	W 10201	19322	W 10189	25925	ALUMINIUM
6841	ALUMINIUM,ALLOYS,UNWRGHT	W 1118	990	W 1043	921	W 7086	10252	W 6250	13350	ALUMINIUM,ALLIAGES BRUTS
6842	ALUMINIUM,ALLOYS WORKED	W 3413	10321	W 4267	10518	W 3114	9070	W 3939	12575	ALUMINIUM,ALLIAGES OUVRE
69	METAL MANUFACTURES NES		73403		95488		80982		98501	ART MANUFACT EN METAL NDA
691	STRUCTURES AND PARTS NES	W 1517	4470	W 10252	14985	W 10854	9724	W 9700	27046	CONSTRUCT FER,ACIER,ALU
6911	STRUCTURES,PARTS IRN,STL	W 1445	4323	W 10166	14552	W 10656	8876	W 9627	26728	CONSTRUCT FER,ACIER,FONTE
692	METAL TANKS,BOXES,ETC	W 2444	7985	W 4223	14571	W 5413	15093	W 4339	12766	RECIPIENTS METALLIQUES
6924	MTL TRANSPORT BOXES ETC	W 2177	7260	W 3356	12296	W 4391	13984	W 3628	12144	FUTS,TAMBOURS,BIDONS
69242	ALUMNM TRNSPRT BOXES ETC	W 540	4647	W 1447	9774	W 2310	11244	W 1547	8709	FUTS,TAMBOURS,BIDONS ALU
697	BASE MTL HOUSEHOLD EQUIP		21782		22529	W 5229	19357	W 5049	19374	ART MENAGE MET COMMUNS
6973	DMSTC HEATG,COOKG APPARA		8660		12517	W 2304	9448	W 2245	8769	APPS CHAUF NON ELECTRIQ
69734	COPPER DOMSTC STOVES,ETC	W 1685	7619	W 2534	10921	W 105	307	W 68	305	APP NON ELEC CUISSON CUIVRE
699	BASE METAL MFRS NES	W 7602	20573		22599	W 6745	18417	W 7722	18753	ART MANUFACTURES MET NDA
6991	LOCKSMITHS WARES,ETC	W 2754	10110	W 3086	11109	W 2991	10358	W 2510	8502	ARTICLES DE SERRURERIE
7	MACHINES,TRANSPORT EQUIP		802345		957095		858820		905487	MACHINES MATERIEL TRANSPORT
71	POWER GENERATING EQUIPMT		56246		87125		58865		33029	MACHINES GENERATRICES
714	ENGINES AND MOTORS NES		19	W 2	25	W 663	13140	W 324	13587	MOTEURS NON ELECTRIQUES
7144	REACTION ENGINES		1	W 1	16	W 603	11848	W 305	12280	PROPULSEURS A REACTION
716	ROTATING ELECTRIC PLANT	W 3611	14704	W 4637	20605	W 3674	38533	W 2735	11261	APP ELECTR ROTATIFS,PIECES
7162	AC MTRS,GENRTRS,GEN SETS	W 3048	12117	W 4429	19646	W 3129	36172	W 2559	9768	MOTEURS ELECTRIQUES
71621	AC MTRS,INC UNIVRSL MTRS	W 3048	12117	W 4429	19646	W 2660	34078	W 2377	8148	MOT ELEC NON COUR CONTINU
718	OTH POWER GENERATG MACHY	W 3969	38613	W 5498	63678	W 139	1529	W 55	688	AUTRES MOTEURS PARTIES
7187	NUCLEAR REACTORS,PTS NES	W 3967	38574	W 5492	63493		7	W 17	43	REACTEURS NUCLEAIRES
72	MACHS FOR SPCL INDUSTRYS		98706		132049		141428		127864	MAC SPECIALES POUR INDUST
723	CIVIL ENGNEERG EQUIP ETC		32441		55955	W 289	20983	W 124	23699	APPAREILS DE GENIE CIVIL
7234	CONST,MINING MACHNRY NES		31461		54007	W 135	19350	W 53	22344	MACH POUR LA CONST, MINES
72341	SELF–PROPELLD DOZERS,ETC	N 423	25622	N 600	42975		14430		13437	BULLDOZERS
724	TEXTILE,LEATHER MACHNRY		24451		24497	W 2020	20339	W 1275	14111	MACH POUR INDUSTRIE TEXTILE
726	PRINTG,BKBINDG MACHY,PTS	W 716	13790	W 1117	15254	W 854	9427	W 544	7924	MACHINES POUR IMPRIMERIE
727	FOOD MACHRY NON–DOMESTIC	W 359	4505	W 1170	8683	W 1425	13653	W 1430	16580	MACH INDUSTRIES ALIMENT
7272	OTH FOOD PROC MCHY,PARTS	W 321	3760	W 1150	8364	W 1338	12936	W 1157	14478	AUT MACH IND ALIMENTAIRE
72722	INDUS FOOD PROC MACH NES	W 308	3679	W 1099	7678	W 1227	11266	W 1051	14008	MACHINES BOULANGERIE
728	OTH MACHY FOR SPCL INDUS	W 2131	9518	W 2228	13139	W 7609	61828	W 5125	51173	AUT MACH IND PARTICULIERES
7284	MACHY FOR SPCL INDUS NES	W 1	5	W 1	22	W 4964	48890	W 3508	44285	MACH SPEC IND PARTICUL.
72845	MTL ETC TREATNG MACH NES					W 1122	11766	W 333	6197	MACH TRAITEMENT METAUX
72848	OTH MCHY WITH INDIV FNCT					W 2394	23562	W 1574	21610	AUTRES MACHINES NDA
73	METALWORKING MACHINERY		15841		22270		25129		26320	MACH TRAVAIL DES METAUX
736	METALWORKING MACH–TOOLS	W 4986	14734	W 6989	21124	W 6189	20257	W 5843	22982	MACH–OUTILS TRAVAIL METAUX
7361	METAL CUTTING MACH–TOOLS	W 4964	14271	W 6760	20219	W 2468	5403	W 1689	4913	MACH–OUT ENLEVEMENT METAL
73611	ULTRASNC ETC MTLWKG MCHS	W 4964	14271	W 6760	20219	W 25	106	W 3	53	MACH–OUT ELECTRO–EROSION
7367	OTH METALWRKG MACH–TOOLS					W 2099	10779	W 2738	12682	AUT MACH–OUT POUR METAUX
74	GENRL INDUSTRL MACHY NES		118367		152842		129577		134459	MACH APP INDUSTRIE
741	HEATING,COOLING EQUIPMNT		19549		24674	W 2653	25707	W 3539	28218	MACH CHAUFFAGE,PIECES
7414	NONDOM REFRIG EQUIPT,PTS		5183		7785	W 1077	11689	W 1326	7694	MAT PRODUCTION DU FROID
742	PUMPS FOR LIQUIDS ETC	W 1606	16113	W 1549	15390	W 1770	12782	W 1425	14152	POMPES MOTO–POMPES
7422	CENTRIFUGAL PUMPS NES	W 1050	10628	W 989	9272	W 80	378	W 38	437	POMPES CENTRIF NON 742.81
7428	OTHER PUMPS FOR LIQUIDS	W 556	5485	W 560	6118	W 1562	10513	W 1140	10119	AUTRES POMPES POUR LIQ
74288	PUMPS FR LIQUIDS NES ETC					W 1538	10432	W 1138	10086	POMPES POUR LIQUIDES NDA
743	PUMPS NES,CENTRFUGES ETC	W 1539	11069	W 3314	19042	W 2334	14349	W 1849	15294	POMPES COMPRES,VENT ETC
744	MECHANICAL HANDLING EQU		5411		9990	W 1796	9814	W 1809	11740	EQUIP MANUTENTION PIECES
745	NONELEC MACHY,TOOLS NES	W 785	9984	W 1307	14035	W 1221	15931	W 1682	20495	AUT MACH NON ELEC,PIECES
7452	OTH NONELEC MCHS,PTS NES	W 709	9081	W 1255	13621	W 1145	15234	W 1627	20071	AUT MACH NON ELEC,PIECES
749	NONELEC MACH PTS,ACC NES	W 4004	56242	W 6347	69712	W 5164	50994	W 3393	44562	PIECES MACH NON ELEC NDA
7492	COCKS,VALVES ETC NES	W 1396	13388	W 2313	18415	W 1925	14662	W 1398	14411	ART ROB,SIM POUR TUYAUX
7493	SHAFT,CRANK,PULLEY ETC	W 1727	31767	W 2994	39576	W 1771	22367	W 1027	17557	ARBRES TRANS,VILEBREQUINS
7499	OTH NONELEC MCHY PTS NES	W 562	8466	W 760	9713	W 1113	10460	W 539	9446	PIECES NON ELECT NDA
75	OFFICE MACHNES,ADP EQUIP		34509		35382		37499		36137	MACH BUREAU TRAIT AUTOM
752	AUTOMTIC DATA PROC EQUIP	N 15864	18641	N 18840	20269	W 21	22973	W 21	19206	MACH TRAIT INFORMATION
7521	ANALOG,HYBRID COMPUTERS	N 15864	18641	N 18840	20269	W 3	3611	W 4	4571	MACH POUR TRAIT INFORMAT
7522	DIGITAL COMPUTERS					W 14	15921	W 10	10442	MACH DIGITALES COMPLETES
76	TELECOMM,SOUND EQUIPMENT		32432		40166		36638		68109	EQUIPMENT DE TELECOM
761	TELEVISION RECEIVERS		16931		19956	W 121	5991	W 153	6205	RECEPTEURS DE TELEVISION
7611	COLOUR TV RECEIVERS		12063		14016	W 94	5422	W 134	5582	RECEPTEURS COULEUR
764	TELECOM EQPT,PTS,ACC NES	W 233	11699	W 332	15939	W 1264	26591	W 1994	57730	EQUIP TELECOM,PIECES
7641	LINE TELEPHONE,ETC EQUIP	W 159	10768	W 248	15195	W 151	6568	W 385	29311	APP TELEPHON PAR FIL
7649	PTS NES OF EQUIPMT OF 76	W 13	571	W 11	285	W 1034	16328	W 1539	26820	PIECES DE LA DIV 76
76493	TELECOMM EQUIPMT PTS NES					W 915	11016	W 1329	16086	PIECES 761,762,764.3,8
77	ELECTRIC MACHNRY NES ETC		50505		75634		87509		91202	MACH APP ELECT NDA
772	SWITCHGEAR ETC,PARTS NES	W 942	11800	W 2190	20257	W 1639	14660	W 1259	16185	APP COUPURE,SECT ETC
7721	SWITCHGEAR ETC	W 109	1913	W 219	1929	W 1592	13991	W 1244	16006	APP COUPURE,SECTIONMNT
7722	PRINTED CIRCUITS,PTS NES	W 833	9887	W 1971	18329		10		22	CIRCUITS ET PIECES
773	ELECTR DISTRIBUTNG EQUIP	W 2417	7168	W 6892	18169	W 4913	13825	W 6149	18804	EQUIPMT DISTRIBUTION ELECT
7731	INSULATED WIRE,CABLE ETC	W 2267	6707	W 5735	15468	W 4775	13260	W 5467	14975	FILS,CABLES ISOLES ELECT
774	ELECTRO–MEDCL,XRAY EQUIP	W 63	2763	W 67	3770	W 154	12702	W 143	8862	APPAREILS MEDICAUX
775	HOUSEHOLD TYPE EQUIP NES		12345		15572	W 1405	21521	W 1671	22462	MACH,APP USAGE DOMESTQUE
778	ELECTRICAL MACHINERY NES	W 3560	14169	W 3319	15869	W 3654	17936	W 3724	16927	AUTRES MACH ELECT NDA
78	ROAD VEHICLES		259227		282322		249271		300296	VEHICULES ROUTIERS
781	PASS MOTOR VEH EXC BUSES	N 7481	61540	N 7367	63750	W 6	52842	W 8	74389	AUTO TRANSPORT PERSONNES
782	LORRIES,SPCL MTR VEH NES	N 5707	72527	N 6136	91060	W 7	93894	W 7	109731	VEHICULES SPECIAUX,MARCH
7821	LORRIES,TRUCKS	N 5514	61810	N 5928	80456	W 7	87455	W 6	101890	VEHICULES TRANSP MARCHAND
7822	SPECIAL MOTOR VEHCLS NES	N 193	10716	N 208	10603		6439		7841	VEHICULES USAGES SPECIAUX
783	ROAD MOTOR VEHICLES NES	N 961	19919	N 1036	25634	W 1	15454	W 1	32357	VEHICULES ROUTIERS NDA
7831	BUSES	N 958	19568	N 1035	25541	W 1	15437	W 1	32071	VOITURES TRANSPORT COMMUN
784	MOTOR VEH PRTS,ACCES NES		96808		91821	W 15147	77778	W 15416	79300	PIECES 722,781,782,783
7849	OTHER MOTOR VEHCL PARTS	W 17080	93048	W 17290	89056	W 15146	70757	W 15415	70655	PIECES 722,781,782,783
79	OTHR TRANSPORT EQUIPMENT		136512		129304		92903		88071	AUTRE MATERIEL TRANSPORT
792	AIRCRAFT ETC		135182	W 499	121714	W 425	92068	W 391	84478	APP NAVIGATION AERIENNE
7928	AIRCRAFT NES,ASSOC EQUIP		22061				1		1	APP NAVIG AERIENNE NDA
79281	GLIDERS,KITES,ROTOCHUTES	N 4	22050							ROTOCHUTES
7929	AIRCRAFT PARTS NES	W 464	113120	W 499	121714	W 425	92066	W 391	84477	PIECES DU 792
8	MISC MANUFACTURED GOODS		220971		214475		218164		220319	ART MANUFACTURES DIVERS
812	*PLUMBG,HEATNG,LGHTNG EQ	W 8798	12081	W 9621	14841	W 6850	11905	W 6375	11835	APPAR SANITAIRES CHAUFFAGE

4. General Imports C.I.F. by Commodities according to the S.I.T.C. (Rev. 2) in thousand U.S. Dollars
Importations Générales C.A.F. par Produits d'après la C.T.C.I. (Rév. 2) en milliers de Dollars E.U.

SITC CTCI	COMMODITY	1992		1993		1994		1995		PRODUIT
		WEIGHT POIDS	VALUE VALEUR	WEIGHT POIDS	VALUE VALEUR	WEIGHT POIDS	VALUE VALEUR	WEIGHT POIDS	VALUE VALEUR	
821	*FURNITURE,PARTS THEREOF	W 1214	5344	W 1578	5809	W 1732	11388	W 2040	8551	MEUBLES ET PIECES
84	CLOTHING AND ACCESSORIES		53242		53110		52602		56286	VETEMENTS
842	MENS OUTERWEAR NOT KNIT	W 2536	13844	W 2503	12859	W 1675	11139	W 3152	19975	VET DESSUS POUR HOMMES
8422	— SUITS	W 2513	13651	W 2493	12818	W 447	3195	W 1746	11529	COMPLETS HOMMES MAT TEXT
84223	—— OF MAN–MADE FIBRES	W 2513	13651	W 2493	12818	W 130	970	W 226	1638	COMPLETS HOMMES FIB SYNT
843	WOMENS OUTERWEAR NONKNIT	W 5391	34115	W 5404	33927	W 2527	16488	W 2671	17428	VET DESSUS FEMMES MAT TEX
8431	— COATS AND JACKETS	W 5391	34115	W 5404	33927	W 334	2121	W 397	3219	MANT,VEST FEM MAT TEXTIL
84319	—— OF OTHER FIBRES	W 5382	34055	W 5399	33900					MANT,VEST FEM AUT FIBRES
845	OUTERWEAR KNIT NONELASTC					W 1690	13495	W 1125	10089	VET DESSOUS,ACCES BONNET
8459	— OTHER,CLTHG ACCESRYS					W 1466	11892	W 984	8885	AUT VET DESSUS DE BONNE
87	PRECISION INSTRUMNTS NES		52008		48611		52203		46932	INSTRUM,APPAR SCIENT NDA
872	MEDICAL INSTRUMENTS NES	W 1905	33218	W 784	27677	W 846	28101	W 855	27916	INSTR,APP MEDIC–CHIR NDA
87202	OTH MEDICAL INSTRUMENTS	W 1855	31078	W 741	26427	W 787	25664	W 764	25195	INSTRUM,APP MEDECINE
874	MEASURNG,CONTROLNG INSTR	W 343	11253	W 618	18869	W 460	18605	W 485	16121	INSTRUMENTS DE MESURE
88	PHOTO EQU,OPTICL GDS ETC		18912		15612		15397		16860	APP,FOURN PHOTO,OP,MONTR
89	MISC MANUFCTRD GOODS NES		69544		67619		65159		71712	ART MANUFACTURES DIVERS
892	PRINTED MATTER	W 2433	12363	W 2809	13048	W 1862	11595	W 1712	10256	IMPRIMES
893	ARTICLES OF PLASTIC NES	W 4053	15247	W 3371	16910		18604		27068	OUVRAGES EN MAT DIVIS 58
8939	MISC PLASTIC ARTICLES	W 3417	12178	W 2653	13657	W 4622	14124	W 6700	22086	ART DIVERS EN MAT DIV 58
89399	OTHR PLASTC ARTICLES NES	W 3352	11833	W 2590	13333	W 3165	12599	W 5647	20817	AUT OUV MAT DIV 58
897	GOLD,SILVER WARE,JEWELRY		11208		9240		7480		9100	BIJOUTERIE,ORFEVRERIE
9	GOODS NOT CLASSD BY KIND		26462		44176		31277		51927	ART TRANSACT NON CLASSES
931	*SPECIAL TRANSACTIONS	W 3258	20244	W 6021	37974	W 4062	17057	W 1387	19786	TRANS.SPECIALES
971	*GOLD,NON MONETARY NES	K 535	5955	K 502	5743	K 1174	13740	K 2550	31957	OR NON MONETAIRE
97101	NONMON GLD UNWRT,SEMIMFD	K 535	5955	K 502	5743	K 1174	13740	K 2550	31957	OR,ALLIAGES D'OR BRUTS

5. General Exports F.O.B. by Commodities according to the S.I.T.C. (Rev. 2) in thousand U.S. Dollars
Exportations Générales F.O.B. par Produits d'après la C.T.C.I. (Rév. 2) en milliers de Dollars E.U.

SITC CTCI	COMMODITY	1992 WEIGHT POIDS	1992 VALUE VALEUR	1993 WEIGHT POIDS	1993 VALUE VALEUR	1994 WEIGHT POIDS	1994 VALUE VALEUR	1995 WEIGHT POIDS	1995 VALUE VALEUR	PRODUIT
	ALL COMMODITIES		1219361		1245795		1424330		1768853	TOUS PRODUITS
0	FOOD AND LIVE ANIMALS		167324		218788		148342		169480	ALIMENTS,ANIMAUX VIVANTS
001	*LIVE ANIMALS FOR FOOD		22434		26591	W 907	18850	W 340	22055	ANIMAUX VIVANTS
0012	SHEEP AND GOATS,LIVE	N 552092	17429	N 790178	21963	W 410	16220	W 298	21405	ESPECES OVINE ET CAPRINE
00121	SHEEP,LIVE	N 549112	17344	N 789571	21945	W 409	16215	W 298	21399	ESPECE OVINE
0014	LIVE POULTRY	W 954	4972	W 1115	4579	W 498	2596	W 41	568	VOLAILLES VIVANTES
00141	LIVE PLTRY 185 GR OR LES	W 954	4969	W 1115	4579	W 153	1104	W 40	554	VOL VIVANTES MOINS 185 GR.
01	MEAT AND PREPARATIONS		13702		10731		6966		8572	VIANDES ET PREPARATIONS
011	MEAT FRESH,CHILLD,FROZEN	W 17775	13702		10660	W 2358	3707	W 3565	6189	VIANDES FRAICHES,REF,CONGE
0111	BOVINE MEAT FRESH,FROZEN	W 16915	12977	W 2439	2122	W 1317	1680	W 465	603	VIANDES BOVIN FRAI,REF
01111	BOVINE MEAT WITH BONE IN	W 16915	12977	W 2439	2122	W 584	752	W 221	261	VIANDES BOVIN NON DESOSS
0114	POULTRY FRESH CHLLD,FRZN	W 139	147	W 5606	8199	W 1020	1984	W 2845	5164	VOLAILLES MORTES
02	DAIRY PRODCTS,BIRDS'EGGS		25247		56914		6175		8914	PRODUITS LAITIERS,OEUFS
023	BUTTER	W 13053	11049	W 63992	48740	W 185	343	W 114	221	BEURRE
025	EGGS,BIRDS,FRESH,PRSRVD	W 66040	10616	W 36530	5667	W 42098	3438	W 14530	3093	OEUFS
0251	— IN SHELL	W 66040	10616	W 36530	5667	W 42098	3438	W 14530	3088	OEUFS EN COQUILLE
04	CEREALS AND PREPARATIONS		3350		2583		3283		7625	CEREALES ET PRODUITS
05	VEGETABLES AND FRUIT		77476		100935		96213		99649	LEGUMES ET FRUITS
054	VEG ETC FRSH,SMPLY PRSVD	W 268064	57608	W 214710	54729	W 188412	63205	W 276084	76872	LEGUMES FRAIS,CONG,SECS
0541	POTATOES FRSH EXCL SWEET	W 2636	658	W 2819	729	W 4625	1633	W 11972	5586	POMMES DE TERRE
0544	TOMATOES FRESH	W 488	51	W 265	171	W 100924	26726	W 135745	24696	TOMATES FRAICHES
0545	OTHER FRESH VEGETABLES	W 262277	55530	W 210950	53419	W 76815	29860	W 119521	38346	AUTRES LEGUMES FRAIS,REF
05459	FRESH VEGETABLES NES	W 261634	55409	W 210899	53396	W 76214	29612	W 119400	38312	LEGUMES FRAIS,REFRI NDA
0546	VEGETABLES SIMPLY PRESVD	W 55	68	W 40	27	W 5405	4554	W 7949	7535	LEGUMES CONG,CONSER
05461	VEGETABLES FROZEN	W 55	68	W 40	27	W 5373	4510	W 7949	7535	LEGUMES CONGELES
056	VEGTBLES ETC PRSVD,PREPD	W 3660	2686	W 21723	14575	W 1108	717	W 858	663	CONSERVES DE LEGUMES
0565	VEGTBLES PRSVD,PREPD NES	W 3465	2534	W 21719	14571	W 1101	712	W 855	659	LEGUMES PREPARES CONSERVE
05659	OTH VEG PRESVD,PREPD NES	W 3417	2454	W 21702	14553	W 1094	700	W 855	659	LEGUM PREPAP,CONSERV NDA
057	FRUIT,NUTS,FRESH,DRIED	W 77119	16867	W 86196	31236	W 90646	31608	W 62817	21804	FRUITS FRAIS OU SECS
0571	ORANGES, MANDARINS ETC	W 38827	8524	W 57123	22271	W 51625	19660	W 23597	8998	ORANGES,MAND,CLEMENTINES
05711	ORANGES,FRESH OR DRIED	W 25090	6846	W 38085	17834	W 33569	14039	W 6425	3720	ORANGES FRAICHES,SECHEES
05712	MANDARINS ETC FRESH, DRY	W 13736	1677	W 19038	4437	W 18056	5621	W 17171	5278	MANDARINES,CLEMENTINES
0572	LEMONS,GRAPEFRUIT ETC	W 10458	1878	W 13492	4169	W 18368	5034	W 13683	4348	AUTRES AGRUMES FRAIS,SECS
0579	FRUIT FRESH OR DRIED NES	W 26441	4856	W 14187	3479	W 18869	5120	W 23406	6415	FRUITS FRAIS,SECS NDA
05798	OTHER FRESH FRUIT	W 25903	4611	W 13818	3217	W 17760	4447	W 22667	5902	AUTRES FRUITS FRAIS
07	COFFEE,TEA,COCOA,SPICES		2656		1740		4094		9495	CAFE,THE,CACAO,EPICES
071	COFFEE AND SUBSTITUTES	W 706	849	W 287	420	W 423	1612	W 1892	6188	CAFE ET SUCCEDANES
0711	COFFEE GREEN,ROASTED,SUB	W 698	807	W 270	353	W 423	1612	W 1892	6188	CAFE TORREFIE OU DECAFEINE
07111	COFFEE GREEN,HUSKS,SKINS	W 698	807	W 270	353	W 423	1612	W 1838	6002	CAFE NON TORREFIE
081	*FEEDING STUFF FOR ANIML	W 37829	13022	W 33831	12015	W 16244	5517	W 12576	4831	NOURRITURE POUR ANIMAUX
0819	FOOD WASTE AND FEED NES	W 34303	12113	W 32152	11473	W 10526	4137	W 5898	2918	DECHETS,ALIMENTS NDA
08199	FODDER NES,INCL SWEETNED	W 34303	12113	W 32152	11473	W 10526	4137	W 5898	2918	PREPARATIONS FOURRAGERES
09	MISC EDIBLE PRODUCTS		5718		5755		4162		4937	PREP ALIMENTAIRES DIVERSES
098	EDIBLE PRODCTS,PREPS NES	W 3318	5718	W 3140	5755	W 2524	4151	W 2631	4838	PREP ALIMENTAIRES NDA
1	BEVERAGES AND TOBACCO		8867		5692		6130		8104	BOISSONS ET TABACS
11	BEVERAGES		3753		4536		4636		7575	BOISSONS
112	ALCOHOLIC BEVERAGES	W 2277	3565	W 2823	4023	W 1976	2354	W 3470	4097	BOISSONS ALCOOLIQUES
1124	DISTILLED ALCOHOLIC BEVS	W 1856	3256	W 2800	4011	W 1761	2266	W 3025	3814	ALCOOLS,EAUX-DE-VIE
12	TOBACCO AND MANUFACTURES		5114		1156		1494		529	TABACS BRUTS FABRIQUES
122	TOBACCO,MANUFACTURED	W 1319	5109	W 104	1152	W 106	1488	W 20	307	TABACS FABRIQUES
2	CRUDE MATERLS,EXCL FUELS		321021		277718		306346		375249	MAT BRUTES NON COMESTIBLES
21	HIDES,SKINS,FURS UNDRSSD		4109		2474		5760		19916	CUIRS,PEAUX BRUTS
211	HIDES,SKINS,EXC FURS,RAW	W 3185	4109	W 2347	2474	W 2284	5760	W 6670	19916	CUIRS ET PEAUX
2116	SHEEP SKIN WITH WOOL	W 2874	3595	W 2126	2353	W 1749	4599	W 1419	4376	PEAUX LAINEES D'OVINS
2117	SHEEP SKIN WITHOUT WOOL					W 124	793	W 2388	13712	PEAUX EPILEES D'OVINS
26	TEXTILE FIBRES AND WASTE		1736		2383		2109		6635	FIBRES TEXTILES
27	CRUDE FERTLZR,MINRLS NES		308374		267410		277540		325630	ENGRAIS MINERAUX BRUTS
271	FERTILIZERS,CRUDE	W 5499076	306838		264982		276180		323879	ENGRAIS BRUTS
2713	NAT CALCM PHOSPHATES ETC	W 4263880	180065		141030		143682		150347	PHOSPHATES DE CALCIUM
27131	— UNGROUND	W 4263880	180065		141030		143681		150347	PHOSPHATES NON MOULUS
2714	NTRL POTASSIC SALTS,CRDE	W 1235196	126773		123942		132493		173327	SELS DE POTASSIUM
28	METALLIFEROUS ORES,SCRAP		3620		3039		10592		17757	MINERAIS METAL,DECHETS
288	NONFERR METAL SCRAP NES	W 2887	3475	W 2033	2577	W 9024	9957	W 11117	15018	DECHETS NON FERREUX
2882	OTHER BASE MTL SCRAP NES	W 2887	3475	W 2033	2577	W 8924	9930	W 11117	15018	AUTRES DECHETS
28821	COPPER WASTE AND SCRAP	W 2866	3467	W 2033	2577	W 2207	3387	W 2906	5516	DECHETS DE CUIVRE
28823	ALUMINIUM WSTE AND SCRAP	W 21	8			W 4680	5914	W 4818	7959	DECHETS D'ALUMINIUM
29	CRUDE ANIMAL,VEG MAT NES		2085		1568		9023		4465	MATIERES BRUTES ANIM,VEGET
292	CRUDE VEG MATERIALS NES	W 1089	1334		1291	W 1876	8405	W 1256	2700	MAT BRUTES VEGETALES NDA
2925	SEEDS,ETC FOR PLANTING	W 73	757	W 46	403	W 678	7042	W 156	1744	SEMENCES NDA
4	ANIMAL,VEGETABLE OIL,FAT		3964		2623		89838		216798	HUILES,GRAISSES ANIM,VEG
42	FIXED VEGETABLE OIL,FAT		3761		2500		1325		9459	HUILES VEGETALES FIXES
424	FIXED VEG OIL NONSOFT	W 869	980	W 358	295	W 752	592	W 10100	8626	AUTRES HUILES VEG FIXES
4242	PALM OIL	W 99	77	W 307	233	W 173	146	W 8115	6081	HUILE DE PALME
431	*PROCESD ANML VEG OIL,ET	W 300	203	W 374	123	W 123115	88508	W 203414	207339	HUILES,GRAISSES PREPAREES
4312	HYDROGENATED OIL,FAT					W 122260	88133	W 195654	200329	HUILES HYDROGENEES
4313	FATTY ACIDS ETC,RESIDUES	W 101	19	W 204	36	W 854	374	W 7732	6973	ACIDES GRAS INDUST,RESIDUS
43131	FATTY ACIDS,ACID OILS	W 101	19	W 204	36	W 834	370	W 7732	6973	ACIDES GRAS INDUSTRIELS
5	CHEMCLS,RELATED PROD NES		328054		310103		392937		467681	PRODUITS CHIMIQUES
51	ORGANIC CHEMICALS		1860		1955		2108		6063	PROD CHIMIQ ORGANIQUES
52	INORGANIC CHEMICALS		30129		16191		22239		38259	PROD CHIM INORGANIQUES
522	INORG ELEMNTS,OXIDES,ETC	W 23982	9103	W 3586	2586	W 16838	8619	W 16294	9629	ELEMENTS INORGANIQUES
5222	INORGANIC ACIDS ETC	W 19261	6982	W 2571	1993	W 14889	7699	W 15535	9058	ACIDES INORGANIQUES
52222	SULPHURIC ACID;OLEUM		1			W 6609	4136	W 13998	8714	ACIDE SULFURIQUE,OLEUM
52224	PHOSPHORIC ACIDS ETC	W 18165	5949	W 23	14	W 5820	1686	W 1536	344	ACIDES PHOSPHORIQUES
523	OTHR INORG CHEMICALS ETC	W 107478	20628	W 108001	13429	W 96386	13382	W 137144	28259	AUT PRODUITS CHIMIQUES INORG
5231	METAL CMPD OF INORG ACID	W 14613	13229	W 10416	6948	W 9935	6403	W 22427	14842	SELS METALLIQUES
52311	FLUORIDES ETC	W 13292	12875	W 10329	6908	W 9697	6313	W 21700	14592	FLUORURES
5232	OTH MTL CMPD OF INRG ACD	W 92707	7319	W 96683	6111	W 86390	6922	W 114526	13221	SELS METALLIQUES
52324	CARBONATE NES,PERCBONATE	W 91961	6952	W 96484	6026	W 85406	6654	W 114227	12876	CARBONATES,PERCARBONATES
53	DYES,TANNING,COLOUR PROD		3990		8453		6785		12029	PROD TEINTURE,COLORANTS
533	PIGMENTS,PAINTS,ETC	W 3055	3545	W 4634	8264	W 4062	6246	W 5676	11316	PIGMENTS,PEINTURES,VERNIS
5334	VARNISHES,DISTEMPERS ETC	W 2264	2716	W 3540	6222	W 2823	4601	W 5130	10404	PEINTURES A L'EAU
53341	WATER-THINNED PAINTS		1	W 23	20	W 1518	2793	W 5041	10124	PEINTURES DILUEES
53344	DISTEMPERS,DYES NES ETC	W 2260	2694	W 3516	6201	W 1236	1703	W 39	142	PEINTURES A L'EAU
541	*MEDICINAL,PHARM PRODUCT	K 7720992	88350	K 5960449	119193	K 7134121	138903	K 6759753	147403	PROD MEDICINAUX PHARMACEUT
5417	MEDICAMENTS	K 7649766	87019	K 5913885	116640	K 7033713	136855	K 6611713	139970	MEDICAMENTS
54171	— CONTAINNG ANTIBIOTICS	K 7038453	80270	K 5161842	105366	K 4025	128	K 7125	412	MED CONTN ANTIBIOTIQUES
54172	— CONTAINING HORMONES	K 611313	6749	K 752043	11274	K 1481680	14898	K 924697	12360	MED CONTENANT HORMONES
54179	— CONTNG OTH SUBSTANCES					K 5548008	121829	K 5679891	127199	MED CONT AUT SUBSTANCES
55	PERFUME,CLEANING ETC PRD		55274		58350		43400		53299	PROD POUR PARFUM,TOILETTE
553	PERFUMERY,COSMETICS,ETC	W 1863	3254	W 3579	6533	W 1973	4849	W 1750	5030	PRODUITS DE PARFUMERIE

5. General Exports F.O.B. by Commodities according to the S.I.T.C. (Rev. 2) in thousand U.S. Dollars
Exportations Générales F.O.B. par Produits d'après la C.T.C.I. (Rév. 2) en milliers de Dollars E.U.

SITC CTCI	COMMODITY	1992		1993		1994		1995		PRODUIT
		WEIGHT POIDS	VALUE VALEUR	WEIGHT POIDS	VALUE VALEUR	WEIGHT POIDS	VALUE VALEUR	WEIGHT POIDS	VALUE VALEUR	
554	SOAP,CLEANSING ETC PREPS	W 54194	51667	W 57893	51591	W 54179	38266	W 60762	47560	SAVONS,PRODUITS DETERSIFS
5541	SOAPS	W 16502	19067	W 22791	24595	W 9513	9818	W 10344	9986	SAVONS,PROD TENSIO–ACTIFS
5542	WASHING PREPARATIONS ETC	W 37292	32357	W 33761	25288	W 44104	27938	W 50079	37198	PROD ORG TENSIO–ACT NDA
562	*FERTILIZERS,MANUFACTURE	W 597918	106660		81899		127857		161511	ENGRAIS MANUFACTURES
5621	CHEM NITROGENOUS FERTLZR	W 594386	105116		77967		124077		156602	ENGRAIS AZOTES
56219	CHEM NITROG FERTILZR NES	W 594186	105079		77967		124077		156602	ENGRAIS AZOTES NDA
58	PLASTIC MATERIALS ETC		14328		9588		7937		18540	MAT PLAST ARTIFICIELLES
582	PROD OF CONDENSATION ETC	W 5153	4746	W 3373	1996	W 6620	3948	W 13128	13150	PROD CONDENS,POLYCOND
5823	ALKYDS,OTHER POLYESTERS					W 6602	3912	W 12667	12599	ALKYDES ET AUT POLYESTERS
58231	— IN PRIMARY FORMS					W 6602	3912	W 12667	12599	SOUS FORMES PRIMAIRES
5828	ION EXCH,CONDEN ETC TYPE	W 5153	4746	W 3208	1846					ECHANGEURS D'IONS
583	POLYMERIZATION ETC PRODS	W 8328	9290	W 7375	7469	W 3780	3715	W 4339	4999	PROD POLYMERISATION
5831	POLYETHYLENE	W 6724	8052	W 5965	6727	W 497	497	W 199	236	POLYETHYLENE
58311	— IN PRIMARY FORMS	W 4985	5027	W 4013	3208	W 361	242	W 71	119	POLYETHYLENE PRIMAIRES
59	CHEMICAL MATERIALS NES		27463		14452		43678		30578	MAT PROD CHIMIQUES NDA
591	PESTICIDES,DISINFECTANTS	W 3760	17633	W 2298	7901	W 7774	38294	W 5220	20356	DESINF,INSECT,FONG,HERB
5912	FUNGICIDES,FOR RETAIL	W 3760	17633	W 2298	7901	W 3	17	W 11	141	FONGICIDES VENTE AU DET
5913	HERBICIDES,FOR RETAIL					W 6998	37634	W 2667	15067	HERBICIDES VENTE AU DET
592	STARCH,INULIN,GLUTEN,ETC	W 1888	3924	W 654	2710	W 997	2501	W 893	2608	AMIDONS,INUL,GLUT FROM
598	MISCEL CHEM PRODUCTS NES	W 4476	5906		3840	W 1725	2883	W 3694	7613	PROD DIV INDUST CHIM NDA
5989	CHEM PRODUCTS,PREPS NES	W 4440	5895	W 1721	3822	W 1703	2681	W 3193	6562	PROD PREP CHIMIQUES NDA
59899	OTH CHEM PRODS,PREPS,NES	W 3248	5356	W 1338	3518	W 639	1938	W 1319	5084	AUT PRODUITS CHIMIQUES NDA
6	BASIC MANUFACTURES		132256		148289		154029		182544	ART MANUFACTURES
61	LEATHER,DRESSED FUR,ETC		1954		1720		1557		8175	CUIRS,PELLETERIES
62	RUBBER MANUFACTURES NES		2280		1377		8228		11348	CAOUTCHOUC MANUFACTURE
625	RUBBER TYRES, TUBES ETC	W 722	1815		1048	W 1697	6390	W 2240	10446	PNEUS CAOUTCHOUC VULCANISE
6251	TYRES NEW FOR MOTOR CARS					W 1226	5403	W 2137	9984	PNEUS POUR VOITURES
64	PAPER,PAPERBOARD AND MFR		14245		22780		20690		22064	PAPIERS,CARTONS & OUVRAGES
641	PAPER AND PAPERBOARD	W 5660	8493	W 10230	10433	W 10153	11840	W 7653	10835	PAPIERS ET CARTONS
6412	PRINTG,WRITING PAPER NES	W 2260	4347	W 7466	6481	W 629	2164	W 540	2231	PAPIERS POUR L'IMPRESSION
64121	— UNCOATED	W 2246	4334	W 7284	6313	W 492	2023	W 494	2170	PAPIERS IMPRES NON COUCHES
6415	PAPER,PAPERBRD,BULK,NES	W 244	394	W 125	618	W 5558	4968	W 2165	2901	PAPIERS,CARTONS ROULEAUX
64159	OTHER PAPER ETC,BULK,NES	W 37	165	W 30	119	W 5550	4927	W 598	792	AUT PAPIER ROULEAUX FEUILLES
642	PAPER,ETC,PRECUT,ARTS OF	W 3539	5752	W 8482	12347	W 8095	8850	W 8085	11229	PAP,CARTONS DECOUPES
6421	PAPER ETC CONTAINERS	W 1840	2704	W 4109	6493	W 2161	2073	W 2897	3864	BOITES,SACS EMBALLAGES
65	TEXTILE YARN,FABRICS,ETC		30238		35283		37983		44008	FILS,TISSUS,ARTICLES TEXTILE
651	TEXTILE YARN	W 2616	8430	W 3934	9921	W 4660	14947	W 2429	10495	FILS TEXTILES
6513	COTTON YARN	W 762	3095	W 655	2044	W 1660	5997	W 965	4128	FILS DE COTON
6514	SYN FIB YRN,BULK,MONOFIL	W 845	1902	W 1589	3330	W 1583	5038	W 800	3812	FILS CONT 85% FIB TEXT SYNTH
652	COTTON FABRICS,WOVEN	W 604	4624	W 409	3157	W 73	305	W 90	763	TISSUS DE COTON
6522	WOVEN COTTON BLEACHD,ETC	W 604	4624	W 409	3157	W 73	305	W 80	712	TISSUS COTON BLANCHIS ETC
65224	BLCHED COTTON FABRIC NES	W 604	4624	W 409	3157	W 7	22	W 58	611	AUT TIS PLUS 85% COT BLANCHI
653	WOVN MAN–MADE FIB FABRIC	W 1357	8672	W 1411	9620	W 1580	11246	W 1479	14767	TISSUS FIBRES SYNTH,ARTIF
6531	CONT SYNT WEAVES NONPILE	W 1357	8670	W 1387	9538	W 858	4379	W 595	4489	TISSUS FIBRES SYNTH CONTINUE
65314	CONT SYN TYRE CORD FABRC	W 1297	7801	W 1357	9438	W 283	1392			TIS ARMATURE PNEUMATIQUES
6534	DISC SYN BLEND FABRC NES	W 1	2	W 24	81	W 695	6737	W 670	8910	TISSUS FIBRES SYNTH DISCONT
65349	OTH DISC SYN BLEND FABRC					W 647	6556	W 623	8216	TISSUS FIB SYNT MEL MAT AUT
657	SPECIAL TXTL FABRC,PRODS	W 879	3112	W 700	2102	W 1202	3213	W 1646	7900	TISSUS SPECIAUX
659	FLOOR COVERINGS,ETC	W 1327	4020	W 1418	6497	W 1749	5819	W 1846	5929	COUVRE–PARQUETS,TAPIS ETC
6594	WOOL CARPETS ETC NES	W 970	3477	W 1265	5986	W 20	69	W 27	130	TAPIS DE LAINE
65941	— TUFTED	W 970	3477	W 1265	5986					TAPIS DE LAINE TOUFFETES
6596	OTH TXTL CARPETS ETC NES				12	W 1394	4536	W 1721	5204	TAPIS AUT MAT TEXT NDA
65962	— OTHR THAN KNOTTED ETC					W 1394	4536	W 1721	5167	TAPIS AUT QUE NOUES TOUF
66	NONMETAL MINERAL MFS NES		40751		33521		49106		61281	ART MIN NON METALLIQUES
661	LIME,CEMENT,BLDG PRODS	W 1093295	34765	W 909542	27284	W 1063911	43870	W 934369	56184	CHAUX,CIMENTS MAT CONSTR
6612	CEMENT	W 1045352	32662	W 823299	25015	W 923210	39121	W 753908	42182	CIMENTS HYDRAULIQUES
6613	BUILDING STONE ETC WORKD	W 18586	844	W 43812	807	W 74170	2338	W 120008	10715	PIERRES A BATIR
66132	BUILDING STONE WORKED	W 18586	844	W 43812	807	W 74167	2334	W 120008	10713	OUVR EN PIERRES DE TAILLE
67	IRON AND STEEL		10627		12756		6263		9370	FER ET ACIER
674	IRN,STL UNIV,PLATE,SHEET	W 3094	2109	W 7612	4489	W 1607	1537	W 2174	2202	LARGES PLATS,TOLES
678	IRON,STL TUBES,PIPES,ETC	W 9427	6699	W 8856	6485	W 3714	3341	W 7366	4796	TUBES,TUYAUX EN FONTE,FER
6782	IRON,STL SEAMLESS TUBES	W 5204	3810	W 2286	2173	W 2155	1654	W 3	8	TUBES,TUYAUX SANS SOUDURE
6783	IRON,STL TUBES,PIPES NES	W 3964	2509	W 6562	4266	W 1528	1518	W 7340	4596	AUT TUBES,TUYAUX FER,ACIER
68	NON–FERROUS METALS		5167		4503		2118		6331	METAUX NON FERREUX
684	ALUMINIUM	W 2716	4733	W 2752	3694	W 584	1803	W 746	5662	ALUMINIUM
6842	ALUMINIUM,ALLOYS WORKED	W 346	2588	W 265	1140	W 584	1803	W 746	5662	ALUMINIUM,ALLIAGES OUVRE
69	METAL MANUFACTURES NES		25579		33332		25560		19474	ART MANUFACT EN METAL NDA
691	STRUCTURES AND PARTS NES	W 3101	9342	W 5689	15379	W 8242	17789	W 3723	4154	CONSTRUCT FER,ACIER,ALU
6911	STRUCTURES,PARTS IRN,STL	W 2689	7802	W 5489	14818	W 8138	17411	W 3548	3454	CONSTRUCT FER,ACIER,FONTE
692	METAL TANKS,BOXES,ETC	W 1445	1211	W 2432	5342	W 1565	841	W 1533	1196	RECIPIENTS METALLIQUES
697	BASE MTL HOUSEHOLD EQUIP		10010		9667	W 869	4716	W 770	7659	ART MENAGE MET COMMUNS
6973	DMSTC HEATG,COOKG APPARA		9200		8518	W 516	4238	W 448	6374	APPS CHAUF NON ELECTRIQ
69732	IRN,STL DOM HEATG APPARA	N 32911	3962	N 40694	6986	W 75	442	W 128	997	POELES,RECHAUDS NON ELECTRS
69735	DMSTC WATERHEATRS NONELE	W 771	4297	W 10	13					CHAUFFE–EAU NON ELECTR.
7	MACHINES,TRANSPORT EQUIP		126268		155838		224674		230949	MACHINES MATERIEL TRANSPORT
71	POWER GENERATING EQUIPMT		2829		5122		2496		3186	MACHINES GENERATRICES
72	MACHS FOR SPCL INDUSTRYS		11473		15737		25253		17214	MAC SPECIALES POUR INDUST
723	CIVIL ENGNEERG EQUIP ETC		5220		6748	W 1146	12751	W 175	5453	APPAREILS DE GENIE CIVIL
7234	CONST,MINING MACHNRY NES		4906		6337	W 51	10050	W 131	4871	MACH POUR LA CONST, MINES
72341	SELF–PROPELLD DOZERS,ETC	N 165	4420	N 84	2861		3563		3286	BULLDOZERS
72343	SLFPRP CONST ETC MCH NES						4663		182	AUT MACH EXTR,TERRASSEM
728	OTH MACHY FOR SPCL INDUS	W 1112	2723	W 2193	6631	W 1490	8202	W 1394	7647	AUT MACH IND PARTICULIERES
7281	MACH–TOOLS FR SPCL INDUS	W 544	1043	W 1094	4647	W 570	2980	W 505	1345	MACH–OUTILS SPEC IND PART
72811	MACH–TOOLS TO WRK MINRLS	W 345	921	W 1055	4592	W 428	2069	W 463	1259	MACH POUR TRAVAIL PIERRE
74	GENRL INDUSTRL MACHY NES		14235		17204		32443		36172	MACH APP INDUSTRIE
741	HEATING,COOLING EQUIPMNT		2104		5364	W 1622	15451	W 1152	11655	MACH CHAUFFAGE,PIECES
7414	NONDOM REFRIG EQUIPT,PTS		361		899	W 400	6248	W 504	6069	MAT PRODUCTION DU FROID
74149	PTS NES OF REFRIG EQUIPT	W 18	225	W 47	898	W 387	5522	W 482	5953	PIECES POUR MACH FROID
7415	AIR–CONDITIONING MACHNRY	W 145	1279	W 360	2668	W 624	4795	W 350	2906	GROUPES CONDITION AIR
743	PUMPS NES,CENTRFUGES ETC	W 228	1606	W 238	1316	W 592	3843	W 815	5455	POMPES COMPRES,VENT ETC
749	NONELEC MACH PTS,ACC NES	W 541	4971	W 534	5617	W 620	4547	W 774	8442	PIECES MACH NON ELEC NDA
75	OFFICE MACHNES,ADP EQUIP		1560		2960		3728		6476	MACH BUREAU TRAIT AUTOM
76	TELECOMM,SOUND EQUIPMENT		3405		3548		3921		5400	EQUIPMENT DE TELECOM
77	ELECTRIC MACHNRY NES ETC		9467		13564		13355		21209	MACH APP ELECT NDA
772	SWITCHGEAR ETC,PARTS NES	W 159	2351	W 318	5011	W 161	4185	W 129	2375	APP COUPURE,SECT ETC
7722	PRINTED CIRCUITS,PTS NES	W 110	1879	W 263	3983				12	CIRCUITS ET PIECES
773	ELECTR DISTRIBUTNG EQUIP	W 1096	2645	W 1751	4049	W 1057	2817	W 2743	10477	EQUIPMT DISTRIBUTION ELECT
7731	INSULATED WIRE,CABLE ETC	W 1081	2542	W 1663	3839	W 1055	2793	W 2739	10449	FILS,CABLES ISOLES ELECT
78	ROAD VEHICLES		42241		48414		69230		74433	VEHICULES ROUTIERS
781	PASS MOTOR VEH EXC BUSES	N 2832	20895	N 1101	8883	W 1	13707	W 1	13466	AUTO TRANSPORT PERSONNES
782	LORRIES,SPCL MTR VEH NES	N 321	6171	N 627	13957		11946	W 1	14139	VEHICULES SPECIAUX,MARCH

5. General Exports F.O.B. by Commodities according to the S.I.T.C. (Rev. 2) in thousand U.S. Dollars
Exportations Générales F.O.B. par Produits d'après la C.T.C.I. (Rév. 2) en milliers de Dollars E.U.

SITC CTCI	COMMODITY	1992		1993		1994		1995		PRODUIT
		WEIGHT POIDS	VALUE VALEUR	WEIGHT POIDS	VALUE VALEUR	WEIGHT POIDS	VALUE VALEUR	WEIGHT POIDS	VALUE VALEUR	
7821	LORRIES,TRUCKS	N 295	5239	N 580	12865		8103	W 1	13029	VEHICULES TRANSP MARCHAND
783	ROAD MOTOR VEHICLES NES	N 175	3313	N 343	14055		29648	W 1	29888	VEHICULES ROUTIERS NDA
7831	BUSES	N 175	3313	N 343	14055		29648	W 1	29888	VOITURES TRANSPORT COMMUN
784	MOTOR VEH PRTS,ACCES NES		10742		9680	W 2369	13128	W 1858	14149	PIECES 722,781,782,783
7849	OTHER MOTOR VEHCL PARTS	W 1559	10684	W 1432	9622	W 2369	13097	W 1858	14144	PIECES 722,781,782,783
79	OTHR TRANSPORT EQUIPMENT		40335		47851		72165		63910	AUTRE MATERIEL TRANSPORT
792	AIRCRAFT ETC		40208	W 29	47751	W 68	71955	W 38	62927	APP NAVIGATION AERIENNE
7924	AIRCRFT NES OVER 15000KG						5009			AERODYNES PLUS 15000 KG
7928	AIRCRAFT NES,ASSOC EQUIP		8162		2312		93			APP NAVIG AERIENNE NDA
79281	GLIDERS,KITES,ROTOCHUTES	N 6	8161							ROTOCHUTES
7929	AIRCRAFT PARTS NES	W 31	32046	W 29	45439	W 68	66853	W 38	61139	PIECES DU 792
8	MISC MANUFACTURED GOODS		77865		95885		82741		96554	ART MANUFACTURES DIVERS
821	*FURNITURE,PARTS THEREOF	W 2074	5230	W 1769	3340	W 1652	4182	W 1700	4688	MEUBLES ET PIECES
8219	FURNITURE AND PARTS NES	W 2035	5101	W 1758	3292	W 1215	3145	W 1334	3903	AUTRES MEUBLES ET PIECES
82199	OTHR FURN,FURN PARTS NES	W 2035	5101	W 1758	3292	W 17	44	W 17	106	MEUBLES NDA AUTRES MATIERES
84	CLOTHING AND ACCESSORIES		17649		21312		20331		28725	VETEMENTS
842	MENS OUTERWEAR NOT KNIT	W 572	6476	W 759	9234	W 502	6118	W 355	4986	VET DESSUS POUR HOMMES
8422	— SUITS	W 558	6311	W 736	8745	W 67	488	W 34	391	COMPLETS HOMMES MAT TEXT
84223	—— OF MAN–MADE FIBRES	W 553	6123	W 726	8519	W 63	458	W 29	353	COMPLETS HOMMES FIB SYNT
8423	— TROUSERS,BREECHES ETC					W 366	4690	W 277	4007	PANTALONS HOMMES MAT TEX
843	WOMENS OUTERWEAR NONKNIT	W 1044	10189	W 1040	10363	W 820	8269	W 1584	16339	VET DESSUS FEMMES MAT TEX
8431	— COATS AND JACKETS	W 1044	10189	W 1040	10363	W 24	185	W 42	601	MANT,VEST FEM MAT TEXTIL
84319	—— OF OTHER FIBRES	W 982	10028	W 1033	10274					MANT,VEST FEM AUT FIBRES
8433	— DRESSES					W 184	1862	W 521	5858	ROBES EN MAT–TEXTILES
8435	— BLOUSES					W 171	1364	W 584	5546	BLOUSES FEM MAT TEXTILES
8439	— OTHER OUTER GARMENTS					W 401	4642	W 385	3959	AUT VET DES FEM MAT TEXT
851	*FOOTWEAR	W 2508	5024	W 2297	4703	W 1606	3977	W 2041	5899	CHAUSSURES
87	PRECISION INSTRUMNTS NES		5486		10398		12245		6224	INSTRUM,APPAR SCIENT NDA
872	MEDICAL INSTRUMENTS NES	W 343	3776	W 247	4496	W 415	8198	W 151	3607	INSTR,APP MEDIC–CHIR NDA
87202	OTH MEDICAL INSTRUMENTS	W 343	3762	W 247	4490	W 414	8162	W 148	3439	INSTRUM,APP MEDECINE
874	MEASURNG,CONTROLNG INSTR	W 21	1650	W 88	5825	W 87	3395	W 27	2020	INSTRUMENTS DE MESURE
88	PHOTO EQU,OPTICL GDS ETC		5043		4590		3420		2830	APP,FOURN PHOTO,OP,MONTR
89	MISC MANUFCTRD GOODS NES		38777		50469		37323		46337	ART MANUFACTURES DIVERS
892	PRINTED MATTER	W 4490	11044	W 7432	18997	W 3390	7405	W 6978	16343	IMPRIMES
8921	PRINTED BOOKS,GLOBES,ETC	W 4338	10542	W 7368	18662	W 3253	6737	W 6784	15797	LIVRES,BROCHURES,CARTES
89211	PRINTED BOOKS,PAMPHLETS	W 4338	10540	W 7368	18661	W 3253	6733	W 6784	15797	LIVRES,BROCHURES
893	ARTICLES OF PLASTIC NES	W 7670	15400	W 9387	22550		20733		20586	OUVRAGES EN MAT DIVIS 58
8931	PLSTC PACKG CONTNRS,LIDS	W 105	863	W 1	2	W 5272	11027	W 4443	8840	ART TRANSP EMBALLAGE ETC
8932	PLSTC SANITRY,TOILET ART	W 675	1305	W 903	4708	W 1	4	W 30	121	OBJETS HYGIEN MAT DU 58
8939	MISC PLASTIC ARTICLES	W 6820	13056	W 8389	17640	W 4129	9594	W 4458	11461	ART DIVERS EN MAT DIV 58
89399	OTHR PLASTC ARTICLES NES	W 6770	12723	W 8269	17009	W 4109	9475	W 4429	11422	AUT OUV MAT DIV 58
897	GOLD,SILVER WARE,JEWELRY		7663		5588		4874		5602	BIJOUTERIE,ORFEVRERIE
8973	PREC JEWLRY,GLD–SILVWARE		7571		5547		4806		5396	BIJOUX OR,ARGENT ORFEVRE
89731	PRECIOUS METAL JEWELLERY		7571		5544		4803		5383	ART BIJOUTERIE,JOAILLER
9	GOODS NOT CLASSD BY KIND		52600		30605		17774		20926	ART TRANSACT NON CLASSES
931	*SPECIAL TRANSACTIONS		21	W 81	275	W 1223	4458	W 1454	20914	TRANS.SPECIALES
971	*GOLD,NON MONETARY NES	K 5282	52579	K 4106	30315	K 1579	13274	K 1	12	OR NON MONETAIRE
97101	NONMON GLD UNWRT,SEMIMFD	K 5282	52579	K 4106	30315	K 1579	13274	K 1	12	OR,ALLIAGES D'OR BRUTS

FOOT NOTES – NOTES

TABLE 1 –
1 Prior to 1981, special trade.
TABLEAU 1 –
1 Avant 1981, commerce spécial.

1. HISTORICAL SERIES, 1992–1996 GENERAL TRADE, IMPORTS C.I.F., EXPORTS F.O.B.
SERIES HISTORIQUES, 1992–1996 COMMERCE GENERAL, IMPORTATIONS C.A.F., EXPORTATIONS F.O.B

YEAR ANNEE	VALUE IN MILLION U.S. DOLLARS VALEUR EN MILLION U.S. DOLLARS MERCHANDISE – MARCHANDISE		GOLD – OR		CONVERSION FACTORS FACTEURS DE CONVERSION CENTS E.U. PAR		INDEX NUMBERS – INDICES QUANTUM		UNIT VALUE VALEUR UNITAIRE	
	IMPORTS	EXPORTS	IMPORTS	EXPORTS	IMPORTS	EXPORTS	IMPORTS	EXPORTS	IMPORTS	EXPORTS
1992	468.80	1398.40								
1993	494.00	1501.00								
1994	4499.00	3231.00								
1995	3882.00	5064.00								
1996	4261.30	6230.40								

2. IMPORTS BY BROAD ECONOMIC CATEGORY AND EXPORTS BY INDUSTRIAL ORIGIN. (PERCENTAGE OF TOTAL VALUE)
IMPORTATIONS PAR CATEGORIES ECONOMIQUES ET EXPORTATIONS PAR BRANCHE D'ACTIVITE. (EN POURCENTAGE DE LA VALEUR TOTALE)

IMPORTS – IMPORTATIONS

	1990	1991	1992	1993	1994	1995	1996
TOTAL IMPORTS–IMPORTATIONS TOTALES							
1 FOOD BEV–ALIMENTATION BOISSONS							
11 PRIMARY–PRODUITS DE BASE							
111 FOR INDUSTRY–POUR L'INDUSTRIE							
112 FOR HOUSEHOLDS–POUR LES MENAGES							
12 PROCESSED–PRODUITS ELABORES							
121 FOR INDUSTRY–POUR L'INDUSTRIE							
122 FOR HOUSEHOLDS–POUR LES MENAGES							
2 IND SUPPLIES–APPROV INDUSTRIELS							
21 PRIMARY–PRODUITS DE BASE							
22 PROCESSED–PRODUITS ELABORES							
3 FUELS–COMBUSTIBLES							
31 PRIMARY–PRODUITS DE BASE							
32 PROCESSED–PRODUITS ELABORES							
321 MOTOR SPIRIT–ESSENCE							
322 OTHER–AUTRES							
4 MACHINERY–EQUIPEMENT							
41 CAPITAL EQUIPMENT–MACHINES							
42 PARTS–PIECES ACCESSOIRES							
5 TRANSPORT–TRANSPORT							
51 PASSENGER CARS–AUTOMOBILES							
52 OTHER–AUTRES							
521 INDUSTRIAL–INDUSTRIELS							
522 NON INDUSTRIAL–NON INDUSTRIEL							
53 PARTS–PIECES ACCESSOIRES							
6 CONSUM GOODS–BIENS CONSOMMATION							
61 DURABLE–DURABLES							
62 SEMI DURABLE–SEMI DURABLES							
63 NON DURABLE–NON DURABLES							
7 GOODS NES–BIENS NDA							

EXPORTS – EXPORTATIONS

	1990	1991	1992	1993	1994	1995	1996
TOTAL EXPORTS–EXPORTATIONS TOTALES							
1 AGRICULTURE							
2 MINING QUARRY–INDUS EXTRACTIVES							
3 MANUFACTURING–IND MANUFACTUR							
31 FOOD BEV TOBACCO–ALIM BOISS TAB							
32 TEXTILES–INDUSTRIES TEXTILES							
33 WOOD & PRODUCTS–BOIS & PRODUITS							
34 PAPER & PRODUCTS–PAPIER & PRODT							
35 CHEMICALS–INDUSTRIES CHIMIQUES							
36 NON METAL MIN–MIN NON METAL							
37 BASIC METAL–IND METAL BASE							
38 METAL MANUF–MANUF METAL							
39 OTH MANUF IND–AUTRES MANUF							

3. TRADE BY PRINCIPAL COUNTRIES OF PURCHASE AND SALE (VALUE IN THOUSAND U.S. DOLLARS)
ECHANGES SELON LES PRINCIPAUX PAYS D'ACHAT ET DE VENTE (VALEUR EN MILLIERS DE DOLLARS EU)

COUNTRIES–PAYS	GENERAL IMPORTS C.I.F. IMPORTATIONS GENERALES C.A.F				
	1991	1992	1993	1994	1995
World		468800	358300	4499000	3882000
Africa				1400	500
Americas		36300	45700	133600	80400
Northern America		6900	41500	124300	80400
LAIA		100	700		
CACM					
Caribbean		29300	3500	9300	
Rest of America					
As.ex F.USSR		235700	97900	320100	284600
Eur.x F.USSR		196800	210700	774800	635700
EU		112000	122400	580300	494800
EFTA		13700	17600	67800	57600
East Europe		44200	70300	121800	81400
Other Europe					
Former USSR				2206400	2645000
Oceania			2500	7500	2900
Russian Federation				1292100	1854400
Germany/Allemagne		18400	55000	293600	201500
Uzbekistan/Ouzbékistan				276600	268200
Turkmenistan/Turkménistn				277600	241300
China/Chine		204600	56200	69800	34200
Turkey/Turquie		3500	7700	87200	123900
USA/Etats–Unis d'Amer		5900	24200	109300	72500
Ukraine				119800	86700
United Kingdom		18600	14000	66400	82800
Switz.Liecht		13700	17600	65200	57300
Belarus/Bélarus				64100	79800
Austria/Autriche		29800	21500	39400	51600
Kyrgyzstan/Kirghizistan				104000	30800
Korea, Republic of		200	3800	67000	43200
Italy/Italie		2300	13200	60700	30100
Hungary/Hongrie		27100	19700	31200	21400
Mongolia/Mongolie		300	600	22400	60700
Finland/Finlande		25000	4600	15900	31300
France,Monac		6600	5900	30600	26400
Japan/Japon		4100	3000	53200	8400
Netherlands/Pays–Bas		500	500	31100	30900
Poland/Pologne		7900	1800	23400	20800
Czech Republic				29500	22400
India/Inde		9200	13400	10600	14000
Cuba		29300	3500	9300	
Czechoslovakia		2600	38900		
Canada		1000	17300	15000	7900
Sweden/Suède		9900	1900	11700	16500
Azerbaijan				11700	24900
Lithuania/Lituanie				16500	18000
Yugoslavia/Yougoslavie		26900		4900	1900
Tajikistan/Tadjikistan				17900	12100
Bulgaria/Bulgarie		1700	3600	16500	7400
Romania/Roumanie		4900	1500	17000	2300
Belgium–Luxembourg		100	5300	12800	7000
Latvia/Lettonie				10400	11500
Slovakia			4800	4200	7100
Ireland/Irlande				7000	7800
Israel/Israël		10000	4300		
Republic of Moldova				8100	5600
Australia/Australie			2500	7500	2900
Spain/Espagne			200	6100	6300
Estonia/Estonie				3400	6800
Pakistan			2500	7000	
Denmark/Danemark				5000	2600
Georgia/Géorgie				2900	2200
Armenia/Arménie				1300	2700
Afghanistan		2400	300	300	100
Iran (Islamic Rp. of)		100	2400		
Egypt/Egypte				1400	400

COUNTRIES–PAYS	GENERAL EXPORTS F.O.B. EXPORTATIONS GENERALES F.O.B.				
	1991	1992	1993	1994	1995
Monde		1489300	1270600	3231000	5064000
Afrique			500	6000	200
Amériques		115200	145700	88000	47300
Amérique du Nord		93800	143100	88000	47100
ALAI		300	200		
MCAC					
Caraïbes		18900			200
Autre Amérique		2200	2400		
Asie l'URSS exclus		447300	349500	310900	559400
Europe l'URSS exclus		913200	750100	831500	1362600
UE		620500	497300	486100	1074500
AELE		126800	183200	132400	187900
Europe de l'Est		152000	68100	212300	100200
Autre de l'Europe					
Ancienne URSS			1900	1905900	2801100
Océanie		500	21800	200	100
Russian Federation				1438900	2102600
Netherlands/Pays–Bas		51800	38500	247800	492800
China/Chine		226700	148800	148900	294200
Switz.Liecht		124200	183200	130000	186700
Germany/Allemagne		119300	119500	73200	170400
United Kingdom		91500	87600	64900	111700
USA/Etats–Unis d'Amer		93600	135500	75100	44700
Sweden/Suède		175100	90000	10000	2800
Uzbekistan/Ouzbékistan				117200	159600
Italy/Italie		27700	58700	42300	142600
Ukraine				128000	121400
Korea Dem People's Rp		16600	22000	60100	91600
Turkey/Turquie		16200	53800	49100	70800
Poland/Pologne		48000	14900	55700	38000
Lithuania/Lituanie				13400	120800
Kyrgyzstan/Kirghizistan				59900	73300
Finland/Finlande		42700	9200	16600	50500
Austria/Autriche		50200	32300	12500	15600
Czech Republic			9900	70600	26700
Belarus/Bélarus				43900	57200
Hungary/Hongrie		19400	16800	49000	8400
Japan/Japon		48400	34200	3600	900
Turkmenistan/Turkménistn				25300	51100
Belgium–Luxembourg		37500	16400	6400	15100
Ireland/Irlande		200	400	1900	71600
Iraq				27100	45000
Oman		70600			
Azerbaijan				46300	22400
India/Inde		700	1900	11800	48500
Czechoslovakia		62900			
Korea, Republic of		12600	41200	1500	2400
France,Monac		18500	30500	7200	
Tajikistan/Tadjikistan				9500	40800
Bulgaria/Bulgarie		16800	15400	12300	5700
Latvia/Lettonie			1900	14500	33200
Slovakia			9500	13700	20900
Cyprus/Chypre		32600	4100		
Thailand/Thaïlande		3700	23800		
Canada		200	7600	12900	2400
Australia/Australie		500	20700	200	100
Estonia/Estonie				3600	15700
Cuba		18900			200
Romania/Roumanie		4900	1600	11000	500
Yugoslavia/Yougoslavie		13900		700	
Philippines		7200	5400		
Denmark/Danemark		3000	8200	100	
Afghanistan		3000	2300	1800	3200
Egypt/Egypte			200	6000	200
Norway,SVD,JM		2600		2400	1200
Hong Kong		5700	400		

(VALUE AS PERCENTAGE OF WORLD TOTAL)(VALEURS EN POURCENTAGE DU TOTAL MONDIAL)

	1986	1987	1988	1989	1990	1991	1992	1993	1994	1995
Africa									0.0	0.0
Americas							7.7	12.8	3.0	2.1
Northern America							1.5	11.6	2.8	2.1
LAIA							0.0	0.2		
CACM										
Caribbean							6.2	1.0	0.2	
Rest of America										
As.ex F.USSR							50.3	27.3	7.1	7.3
Eur.x F.USSR							42.0	58.8	17.2	16.4
EU							23.9	34.2	12.9	12.7
EFTA							2.9	4.9	1.5	1.5
East Europe							9.4	19.6	2.7	2.1
Other Europe										
Former USSR									49.0	68.1
Oceania								0.7	0.2	0.1
Russian Federation									28.7	47.8
Germany/Allemagne							3.9	15.4	6.5	5.2
Uzbekistan/Ouzbékistan									6.1	6.9
Turkmenistan/Turkménistn									6.2	6.2
China/Chine							43.6	15.7	1.6	0.9
Turkey/Turquie							0.7	2.1	1.9	3.2
USA/Etats–Unis d'Amer							1.3	6.8	2.4	1.9
Ukraine									2.7	2.2
United Kingdom							4.0	3.9	1.5	2.1
Switz.Liecht							2.9	4.9	1.4	1.5

	1986	1987	1988	1989	1990	1991	1992	1993	1994	1995
Afrique								0.0	0.2	0.0
Amériques							7.7	11.5	2.7	0.9
Amérique du Nord							6.3	11.3	2.7	0.9
ALAI							0.0	0.0		
MCAC										
Caraïbes							1.3			0.0
Autre Amérique							0.1	0.2		
Asie l'URSS exclus							30.0	27.5	9.6	11.0
Europe l'URSS exclus							61.3	59.0	25.7	26.9
UE							41.7	39.1	15.0	21.2
AELE							8.5	14.4	4.1	3.7
Europe de l'Est							10.2	5.4	6.6	2.0
Autre de l'Europe										
Ancienne URSS								0.1	59.0	55.3
Océanie							0.0	1.7	0.0	0.0
Russian Federation									44.5	41.5
Netherlands/Pays–Bas							3.5	3.0	7.7	9.7
China/Chine							15.2	11.7	4.6	5.8
Switz.Liecht							8.3	14.4	4.0	3.7
Germany/Allemagne							8.0	9.4	2.3	3.4
United Kingdom							6.1	6.9	2.0	2.2
USA/Etats–Unis d'Amer							6.3	10.7	2.3	0.9
Sweden/Suède							11.8	7.1	0.3	0.1
Uzbekistan/Ouzbékistan									3.6	3.2
Italy/Italie							1.9	4.6	1.3	2.8

4. General Imports C.I.F. by Commodities according to the S.I.T.C. (Rev. 2) in thousand U.S. Dollars
Importations Générales C.A.F. par Produits d'après la C.T.C.I. (Rév. 2) en milliers de Dollars E.U.

SITC CTCI	COMMODITY	1992		1993		1994		1995		PRODUIT
		WEIGHT POIDS	VALUE VALEUR	WEIGHT POIDS	VALUE VALEUR	WEIGHT POIDS	VALUE VALEUR	WEIGHT POIDS	VALUE VALEUR	
	ALL COMMODITIES		468800		358300		4499000		3882000	TOUS PRODUITS

5. General Exports F.O.B. by Commodities according to the S.I.T.C. (Rev. 2) in thousand U.S. Dollars
Exportations Générales F.O.B. par Produits d'après la C.T.C.I. (Rév. 2) en milliers de Dollars E.U.

SITC CTCI	COMMODITY	1992 WEIGHT POIDS	1992 VALUE VALEUR	1993 WEIGHT POIDS	1993 VALUE VALEUR	1994 WEIGHT POIDS	1994 VALUE VALEUR	1995 WEIGHT POIDS	1995 VALUE VALEUR	PRODUIT
	ALL COMMODITIES		1489300		1270600		3231000		5064000	TOUS PRODUITS

1. HISTORICAL SERIES, 1961–1996 GENERAL TRADE, IMPORTS C.I.F., EXPORTS F.O.B.
SERIES HISTORIQUES, 1961–1996 COMMERCE GENERAL, IMPORTATIONS C.A.F., EXPORTATIONS F.O.B

YEAR ANNEE	VALUE IN MILLION KENYA SHILLINGS VALEUR EN MILLION KENYA SHILLINGS MERCHANDISE –MARCHANDISE IMPORTS	EXPORTS	GOLD –OR IMPORTS	EXPORTS	CONVERSION FACTORS U.S. CENTS PER KENYA SHILLING FACTEURS DE CONVERSION CENTS E.U. PAR KENYA SHILLING IMPORTS	EXPORTS	INDEX NUMBERS # 1 –INDICES QUANTUM IMPORTS	EXPORTS	UNIT VALUE VALEUR UNITAIRE IMPORTS	EXPORTS
1961	1518.60	1153.80			14.0000	14.0000	116	66	6	13
1962	1536.70	1249.30			14.0000	14.0000	114	73	6	13
1963	1657.00	1415.40			14.0000	14.0000	113	81	6	13
1964	1759.00	1558.60			14.0000	14.0000	117	86	6	13
1965	2014.80	1629.40			14.0000	14.0000	133	87	6	13
1966	2470.00	1824.20			14.0000	14.0000	167	108	6	13
1967	2401.00	1715.30			14.0000	14.0000	159	105	6	12
1968	2542.10	1785.30			14.0000	14.0000	169	113	7	12
1969	2582.30	1962.00			14.0000	14.0000	171	123	7	12
1970	3160.20	2178.00			14.0000	14.0000	112	76	5	12
1971	4015.30	2232.20			14.0000	14.0000	132	58	6	12
1972	3956.90	2654.30			14.0000	14.0000	117	86	6	13
1973	4571.00	3614.30			14.3340	14.2860	113	101	8	15
1974	7678.70	4718.00			14.0000	14.0000	129	96	11	20
1975	7256.90	4761.70			13.5000	13.5160	96	87	14	23
1976	8139.90	6901.20			11.9480	11.9500	92	92	17	32
1977	10625.70	9892.90			12.0840	12.0840	112	96	18	45
1978	13223.10	7915.00			12.9300	12.9160	131	88	19	38
1979	12386.00	8269.00			13.3800	13.3820	107	87	22	41
1980	19180.60	10314.10			13.4930	13.4660	139	100	11	26
1981	18507.20	10647.00			11.1790	11.1600	109	95	14	29
1982	18117.80	11371.80			8.9030	8.5900	84	82	42	59
1983	18112.40	13101.40			7.4959	7.5048	66	79	54	71
1984	22297.10	15533.40			6.9555	6.9708	78	78	55	85
1985	24023.00	16047.00			6.0930	6.0943	72	81	65	84
1986	26163.01	19460.00			6.1658	6.1643	85	93	62	90
1987	28904.00	15790.00			6.0730	6.0838	89	90	63	75
1988	35072.00	19012.00			5.6300	5.6350	100	95	69	86
1989	44235.01	19904.00			4.8552	4.8749	105	94	83	92
1990	48661.01	23677.01			4.3658	4.3551	100	100	100	100
1991	49147.01	30376.00			3.6610	3.6458	93	103	111	128
1992	58635.01	44494.00			3.1184	3.0609	90	103	129	144
1993	101128.00	78297.01			1.7543	1.7631	97	121	208	259
1994	115079.00	85642.00			1.8162	1.8277	121	137	187	266
1995	155168.00	97338.00			1.9372	1.9417	141	143	216	289
1996	162985.00	118223.00			1.7502	1.7488	140	164	235	307

2. IMPORTS BY BROAD ECONOMIC CATEGORY AND EXPORTS BY INDUSTRIAL ORIGIN. (PERCENTAGE OF TOTAL VALUE)
IMPORTATIONS PAR CATEGORIES ECONOMIQUES ET EXPORTATIONS PAR BRANCHE D'ACTIVITE.(EN POURCENTAGE DE LA VALEUR TOTALE)

IMPORTS – IMPORTATIONS

	1990	1991	1992	1993	1994	1995	1996
TOTAL IMPORTS–IMPORTATIONS TOTALES	100.	100.	100.	100.			
1 FOOD BEV–ALIMENTATION BOISSONS	8.8	9.4	12.7	12.1			
11 PRIMARY–PRODUITS DE BASE	4.1	2.5	1.9	5.0			
111 FOR INDUSTRY–POUR L'INDUSTRIE	3.9	2.4	1.7	4.4			
112 FOR HOUSEHOLDS–POUR LES MENAGES	0.2	0.0	0.2	0.7			
12 PROCESSED–PRODUITS ELABORES	4.6	6.9	10.8	7.1			
121 FOR INDUSTRY–POUR L'INDUSTRIE	3.4	5.0	8.6	5.7			
122 FOR HOUSEHOLDS–POUR LES MENAGES	1.3	1.9	2.2	1.4			
2 IND SUPPLIES–APPROV INDUSTRIELS	27.2	32.5	36.8	35.9			
21 PRIMARY–PRODUITS DE BASE	2.3	1.7	6.0	2.7			
22 PROCESSED–PRODUITS ELABORES	25.0	30.8	30.8	33.2			
3 FUELS–COMBUSTIBLES	19.4	17.9	19.2	14.5			
31 PRIMARY–PRODUITS DE BASE	9.3	0.6	0.9	0.7			
32 PROCESSED–PRODUITS ELABORES	10.1	17.3	18.3	13.8			
321 MOTOR SPIRIT–ESSENCE	3.0	5.8	5.7	4.2			
322 OTHER–AUTRES	7.0	11.6	12.6	9.6			
4 MACHINERY–EQUIPEMENT	20.5	24.7	19.1	16.5			
41 CAPITAL EQUIPMENT–MACHINES	18.2	22.1	16.7	14.1			
42 PARTS–PIECES ACCESSOIRES	2.3	2.6	2.4	2.4			
5 TRANSPORT–TRANSPORT	19.5	8.6	5.3	10.8			
51 PASSENGER CARS–AUTOMOBILES	3.6	2.3	1.9	3.3			
52 OTHER–AUTRES	12.0	2.1	1.1	4.1			
521 INDUSTRIAL–INDUSTRIELS	11.8	1.9	0.9	3.9			
522 NON INDUSTRIAL–NON INDUSTRIEL	0.2	0.2	0.2	0.2			
53 PARTS–PIECES ACCESSOIRES	3.8	4.2	2.2	3.4			
6 CONSUM GOODS–BIENS CONSOMMATION	3.9	6.2	6.1	8.7			
61 DURABLE–DURABLES	0.9	1.2	0.9	1.2			
62 SEMI DURABLE–SEMI DURABLES	1.0	1.4	1.7	1.7			
63 NON DURABLE–NON DURABLES	2.0	3.6	3.5	5.8			
7 GOODS NES–BIENS NDA	0.7	0.7	0.8	1.5			

EXPORTS – EXPORTATIONS

	1990	1991	1992	1993	1994	1995	1996
TOTAL EXPORTS–EXPORTATIONS TOTALES	100.	100.	100.	100.			
1 AGRICULTURE	44.9	50.9	42.0	49.8			
2 MINING QUARRY–INDUS EXTRACTIVES	2.7	3.1	2.1	2.6			
3 MANUFACTURING–IND MANUFACTUR	52.4	46.0	56.0	47.6			
31 FOOD BEV TOBACCO–ALIM BOISS TAB	8.5	7.4	7.0	8.8			
32 TEXTILES–INDUSTRIES TEXTILES	6.1	4.0	3.4	4.3			
33 WOOD & PRODUCTS–BOIS & PRODUITS	0.3	0.2	0.3	0.6			
34 PAPER & PRODUCTS–PAPIER & PRODT	1.3	1.7	0.7	1.5			
35 CHEMICALS–INDUSTRIES CHIMIQUES	18.8	21.4	15.3	14.9			
36 NON METAL MIN–MIN NON METAL	1.5	1.4	1.4	2.8			
37 BASIC METAL–IND METAL BASE	1.8	1.9	2.4	4.8			
38 METAL MANUF–MANUF METAL	13.4	2.4	3.0	3.2			
39 OTH MANUF IND–AUTRES MANUF	0.7	5.6	22.5	6.7			

3. TRADE BY PRINCIPAL COUNTRIES OF CONSIGNMENT (VALUE IN THOUSAND U.S. DOLLARS)
ECHANGES SELON LES PRINCIPAUX PAYS DE CONSIGNATION (VALEUR EN MILLIERS DE DOLLARS EU)

COUNTRIES–PAYS	GENERAL IMPORTS C.I.F. IMPORTATIONS GENERALES C.A.F				
	1992	1993	1994	1995	1996
World	1793040	1695948	2090027	3014541	2950024
Africa	94914	106602	287300	249796	105888
Americas	199282	180036	166025	194423	218026
Northern America	164513	159160	148256	137118	185534
LAIA	34620	20638	17696	57201	32247
CACM	103	171			
Caribbean	46	68	73	103	244
Rest of America					
As.ex F.USSR	418876	415247	810621	1147720	1186576
Eur.x F.USSR	641999	749837	796364	1278212	1196025
EU	594485	711366	739397	1214286	1111632
EFTA	38050	28940	41481	37651	62364
East Europe	7720	8020	13990	23801	20624
Other Europe					22
Former USSR	1046	4388	8325	16701	14592
Oceania	5296	5107	7045	9545	29685
United Kingdom	195514	243077	275202	353135	389829
Japan/Japon	126422	142139	180448	286098	219007
Germany/Allemagne	111097	126264	129885	193779	179389
United Arab Emirates	5812	5944	233794	249055	242680
USA/Etats–Unis d'Amer	147027	140031	138612	123726	154155
So. Africa Customs Un	47644	58821	226076	210836	48143
France,Monac	68630	74883	84353	144485	144610
India/Inde	50415	54433	78847	154569	168312
Italy/Italie	48968	88686	63685	142426	96189
Belgium–Luxembourg	45645	49102	50571	151465	93766
Saudi Arabia	17615	28270	49568	100403	148297
Netherlands/Pays–Bas	43442	48689	59547	83945	83767
Indonesia/Indonésie	3359	13886	46198	70600	116470
Malaysia/Malaisie	66540	38305	28778	54903	19586
China/Chine	26160	29080	27752	59946	50880
Switz.Liecht	26156	21582	36050	32474	48490
Singapore/Singapour	30415	20592	31935	32156	38961
Korea, Republic of	9234	12446	17636	30452	40584
Israel/Israël	16248	14152	17271	25535	24696
Denmark/Danemark	21035	22997	16085	13572	18731
Sweden/Suède	14149	13961	13317	21819	29043
Argentina/Argentine	9207	17639	2882	37511	24617
Canada	17485	19129	9644	13392	31379
Finland/Finlande	20122	17194	15517	16495	16051
Pakistan	19185	8335	38446	7237	9631
Ireland/Irlande	1957	3592	3980	63549	6596
Spain/Espagne	8740	12737	17160	16064	22190
Hong Kong	10966	17793	16593	18821	11970
Thailand/Thaïlande	14246	9700	13850	9251	20081
Brazil/Brésil	25219	1676	14691	19023	6124
Un. Rep. of Tanzania	9965	8750	19810	10909	16248
Zimbabwe	12623	14820	23394	4030	4816
Australia/Australie	4712	4789	6283	8873	28830
Austria/Autriche	12571	7459	7284	10207	15125
Russian Federation	1046	4388	8325	16701	14592
Norway,SVD,JM	11893	7358	5431	5177	13874
Bahrain/Bahreïn	39	4934	547	6058	24131
Kuwait/ Koweït	64	131	300	22789	9370
Iran (Islamic Rp. of)	5	69	17481	10365	2128
Yemen/Yémen	1	1	1808	216	24164
Zambia/Zambie	8051	6849	2585	3727	4625
Romania/Roumanie	2596	2653	4582	5124	6095
Uganda/Ouganda	5076	8219	3375	3394	520
Libyan Arab Jamahiriya					17529
Sri Lanka	491	3021	1498	5273	5849
Egypt/Egypte	345	378	1546	7355	6318
Greece/Grèce	519	922	591	627	13113
Bulgaria/Bulgarie	0	1772	3896	5662	2970
Portugal	2097	1803	2218	2717	3231
Czech Republic		1129	1005	3512	6109

COUNTRIES–PAYS	GENERAL EXPORTS F.O.B. EXPORTATIONS GENERALES F.O.B.				
	1992	1993	1994	1995	1996
Monde	1361703	1391890	1524651	1915587	1994730
Afrique	285407	456416	672052	834130	893212
Amériques	47260	60009	65219	63355	56606
Amérique du Nord	46886	59023	64214	61758	620
ALAI	248	702	1004	465	55907
MCAC	117	283			
Caraïbes	10	1	1	1132	79
Autre Amérique					
Asie l'URSS exclus	424467	282462	201827	228781	232438
Europe l'URSS exclus	504340	516412	541774	666121	725027
UE	455050	503349	529989	640011	688137
AELE	48722	11954	9399	22468	20581
Europe de l'Est	274	737	2136	2217	4390
Autre de l'Europe					1
Ancienne URSS	23	1259	186	889	404
Océanie	4813	5760	7202	5469	8613
United Kingdom	195802	211397	181245	197696	215837
Uganda/Ouganda	74772	118068	186431	277236	306419
Un. Rep. of Tanzania	48843	95457	155614	216030	239060
Germany/Allemagne	71567	94449	121583	152946	154425
Pakistan	84190	97625	108225	110631	91608
United Arab Emirates	256772	89083	4902	9690	9223
Netherlands/Pays–Bas	44364	51503	66533	86068	111742
Egypt/Egypte	40956	55202	46186	57992	75209
Rwanda	13393	24047	87819	33975	35433
USA/Etats–Unis d'Amer	39849	48478	53644	49758	492
Somalia/Somalie	30097	41390	44568	31735	40312
Ethiopia/Ethiopie	11364	29931	37097	53263	40103
Belgium–Luxembourg	25239	30330	33329	43433	39015
France,Monac	28337	25724	29898	38800	39393
Italy/Italie	33978	23373	28678	31930	35894
So. Africa Customs Un	6819	7536	17168	51757	41956
Dem. Rep. of the Congo	7885	10168	22947	40589	33445
Sudan/Soudan	12627	29046	24983	21449	23485
Switz.Liecht	47529	11371	8104	19735	17698
Sweden/Suède	13487	21885	18196	29427	20782
Spain/Espagne	12511	16756	15951	16643	23917
Finland/Finlande	11079	12113	12590	15767	17048
Japan/Japon	14499	11883	12173	13120	16588
Mexico/Mexique	169	194	216	14	55571
India/Inde	6889	10562	9401	13519	12720
Israel/Israël	11437	11082	8158	8600	11801
Singapore/Singapour	11434	10400	10359	6172	9817
Ireland/Irlande	8568	7313	8025	9229	9143
Saudi Arabia	7290	9581	6011	10950	7595
Canada	7037	10545	10570	12000	128
Burundi	6575	7802	11359	7695	6252
Mauritius/Maurice	6028	9782	233	8478	10054
Thailand/Thaïlande	5646	7346	6244	6903	8074
Yemen/Yémen	3531	6804	4315	6372	7710
Iran (Islamic Rp. of)	501	7	144	5081	22106
Australia/Australie	4063	4527	5929	4726	7210
Portugal	3878	2782	3584	5222	7798
Denmark/Danemark	2545	2533	4787	7067	5776
Greece/Grèce	2883	2884	4876	4494	6410
Malaysia/Malaisie	2061	3347	2552	10268	3177
Hong Kong	3131	2656	5436	2885	6363
Zimbabwe	2622	3989	4529	2669	5152
Sri Lanka	1350	3878	3159	5285	4815
Comoros/Comores	4261	5344	2818	2162	3045
Zambia/Zambie	3528	3011	3082	3340	3486
Djibouti	3486	3454	5712	1420	1635
Reunion/Réunion	3335	2001	2247	7686	
Philippines	1479	3061	3767	2775	3928
Korea, Republic of	2805	4188	2604	3058	1442
Nigeria/Nigéria	3667	2262	1630	3132	3245

(VALUE AS PERCENTAGE OF WORLD TOTAL)(VALEURS EN POURCENTAGE DU TOTAL MONDIAL)

	1987	1988	1989	1990	1991	1992	1993	1994	1995	1996
Africa	3.0	3.0	1.7	6.6	3.2	5.3	6.3	13.7	8.3	3.6
Americas	8.5	5.9	7.7	9.8	6.9	11.1	10.6	7.9	6.4	7.4
Northern America	7.8	5.5	7.2	8.6	6.0	9.2	9.4	7.1	4.5	6.3
LAIA	0.7	0.4	0.5	0.7	1.0	1.9	1.2	0.8	1.9	1.1
CACM		0.0		0.5	0.0	0.0	0.0			
Caribbean	0.0	0.0	0.0	0.0	0.0	0.0	0.0	0.0	0.0	0.0
Rest of America										
As.ex F.USSR	38.7	36.2	28.4	30.3	23.7	23.4	24.5	38.8	38.1	40.2
Eur.x F.USSR	49.2	54.2	51.1	44.1	48.1	35.8	44.2	38.1	42.4	40.5
EU	46.4	51.3	49.9	42.2	45.2	33.2	41.9	35.4	40.3	37.7
EFTA	2.1	1.9	0.9	1.2	2.1	2.1	1.7	2.0	1.2	2.1
East Europe	0.4	0.7	0.1	0.6	0.7	0.4	0.5	0.7	0.8	0.7
Other Europe	0.2	0.3	0.1	0.1	0.1					0.0
Former USSR	0.1	0.1		0.0	0.0	0.1	0.3	0.4	0.6	0.5
Oceania	0.5	0.6	0.4	0.3	0.2	0.3	0.3	0.3	0.3	1.0
United Kingdom	17.0	18.9	18.8	14.4	17.3	10.9	14.3	13.2	11.7	13.2
Japan/Japon	10.9	12.3	12.7	11.4	9.0	7.1	8.4	8.6	9.5	7.4
Germany/Allemagne	8.3	9.5	9.7	7.1	8.7	6.2	7.4	6.2	6.4	6.1
United Arab Emirates	16.0	11.4	5.7	7.2	0.2	0.3	0.4	11.2	8.3	8.2
USA/Etats–Unis d'Amer	7.1	5.0	6.8	8.1	5.1	8.2	8.3	6.6	4.1	5.2
So. Africa Customs Un	0.2	0.3	0.1	0.4	0.6	2.7	3.5	10.8	7.0	1.6
France,Monac	6.9	6.2	9.0	5.5	5.1	3.8	4.4	4.0	4.8	4.9
India/Inde	1.3	1.6	1.9	1.6	1.9	2.8	3.2	3.8	5.1	5.7
Italy/Italie	3.4	3.6	4.5	4.5	3.3	2.7	5.2	3.0	4.7	3.3
Belgium–Luxembourg	2.4	2.2	1.3	2.4	3.4	2.5	2.9	2.4	5.0	3.2

	1987	1988	1989	1990	1991	1992	1993	1994	1995	1996
Afrique	27.8	25.6	12.0	43.0	23.6	21.0	32.8	44.1	43.5	44.8
Amériques	6.2	5.8	7.4	3.0	4.3	3.5	4.3	4.3	3.3	2.8
Amérique du Nord	6.2	5.8	7.3	2.9	4.1	3.4	4.2	4.2	3.2	0.0
ALAI	0.0	0.1	0.0	0.0	0.0	0.0	0.1	0.1	0.0	2.8
MCAC		0.0	0.0	0.0	0.2	0.0	0.0			
Caraïbes	0.0	0.0	0.0		0.0	0.0	0.0	0.0	0.1	0.0
Autre Amérique			0.0							
Asie l'URSS exclus	13.3	10.0	9.4	12.8	13.3	31.2	20.3	13.2	11.9	11.7
Europe l'URSS exclus	46.4	52.6	54.2	34.9	47.1	37.0	37.1	35.5	34.8	36.3
UE	44.8	51.0	52.8	33.6	41.1	33.4	36.2	34.8	33.4	34.5
AELE	0.7	1.1	0.9	0.7	5.9	3.6	0.9	0.6	1.2	1.0
Europe de l'Est	0.7	0.3	0.2	0.4	0.1	0.0	0.1	0.1	0.1	0.2
Autre de l'Europe	0.2	0.2	0.3	0.2	0.1					0.0
Ancienne URSS	0.2	0.2		0.9	0.0	0.0	0.1	0.0	0.0	0.0
Océanie	0.6	0.6	0.6	0.3	0.5	0.4	0.4	0.5	0.3	0.4
United Kingdom	16.9	19.6	21.5	13.3	16.3	14.4	15.2	11.9	10.3	10.8
Uganda/Ouganda	8.5	8.8	3.3	18.5	6.6	5.5	8.5	12.2	14.5	15.4
Un. Rep. of Tanzania	2.9	2.6	1.4	2.2	3.4	3.6	6.9	10.2	11.3	12.0
Germany/Allemagne	9.6	12.0	12.8	7.7	7.6	5.3	6.8	8.0	8.0	7.7
Pakistan	5.7	2.8	3.8	5.8	6.4	6.2	7.0	7.1	5.8	4.6
United Arab Emirates	0.3	0.2	0.1	0.3	0.3	18.9	6.4	0.3	0.5	0.5
Netherlands/Pays–Bas	7.2	5.1	5.8	3.9	3.9	3.3	3.7	4.4	4.5	5.6
Egypt/Egypte	0.9	1.1	1.1	1.5	2.9	3.0	4.0	3.0	3.0	3.8
Rwanda	3.0	2.5	0.8	7.3	1.8	1.0	1.7	5.8	1.8	1.8
USA/Etats–Unis d'Amer	5.4	4.9	6.3	2.4	3.4	2.9	3.5	3.5	2.6	0.0

4. General Imports C.I.F. by Commodities according to the S.I.T.C. (Rev. 2) in thousand U.S. Dollars
Importations Générales C.A.F. par Produits d'après la C.T.C.I. (Rév. 2) en milliers de Dollars E.U.

SITC CTCI	COMMODITY	1992 WEIGHT POIDS	1992 VALUE VALEUR	1993 WEIGHT POIDS	1993 VALUE VALEUR	1994 WEIGHT POIDS	1994 VALUE VALEUR	1995 WEIGHT POIDS	1995 VALUE VALEUR	PRODUIT
	ALL COMMODITIES		1793040		1695948		2090027		3014541	TOUS PRODUITS
0	FOOD AND LIVE ANIMALS		204270		152575					ALIMENTS,ANIMAUX VIVANTS
02	DAIRY PRODCTS,BIRDS'EGGS		9958		4360					PRODUITS LAITIERS,OEUFS
022	MILK AND CREAM	W 8113	6962	W 1984	3931					LAIT ET CREME
0224	MILK,CREAM PRESERVED ETC	W 8093	6667	W 1983	3926					LAIT,CREME CONS,CONC
04	CEREALS AND PREPARATIONS		123203		102131		3540		2701	CEREALES ET PRODUITS
041	WHEAT ETC UNMILLED	W 132568	23957	W 366650	62050		2286		2266	FROMENT,EPEAUTRE
0412	OTHER WHEAT ETC UNMILLED	W 132568	23957	W 351006	59519					AUTRE FROMENT NON MOULU
042	RICE	W 59597	18035	W 36182	8282		1254		435	RIZ
0422	RICE SEMI–MILLED,MILLED	W 59596	18034	W 36174	8277					RIZ POLI,GLACE INCL BRISURES
04221	RICE MILLED UNBROKEN	W 59441	17948	W 17555	4092					RIZ POLI,GLACE EXCL BRISURES
044	MAIZE UNMILLED	W 415113	70104	W 80051	13355					MAIS NON MOULU
045	CEREALS NES UNMILLED	W 1664	1049	W 43875	8016					AUTRES CEREALES NON MOULUES
0459	OTHER CEREALS UNMILLED	W 1664	1049	W 43870	8012					SARRASIN,MILLET,SORGHO
046	WHEAT ETC MEAL OR FLOUR	W 21443	7174	W 19515	7554					SEMOULE FARINE,FROMENT
04601	FLOUR OF WHEAT OR MESLIN	W 21436	7165	W 19515	7554					FARINE DE FROMENT
05	VEGETABLES AND FRUIT		7414		12216					LEGUMES ET FRUITS
054	VEG ETC FRSH,SMPLY PRSVD	W 4549	6532		11084					LEGUMES FRAIS,CONG,SECS
0542	LEGUMINOUS VEGETBLES DRY	W 3411	2506	W 28522	7481					LEGUMES A COSSE SECS
06	SUGAR AND PREPS,HONEY		51105		25061					SUCRES ET PRODUITS
061	SUGAR AND HONEY	W 151499	51076		24995					SUCRES ET MIEL
0611	RAW BEET AND CANE SUGAR	W 149560	50088		24095					SUCRES BRUTS
1	BEVERAGES AND TOBACCO		1175		6962					BOISSONS ET TABACS
2	CRUDE MATERLS,EXCL FUELS		49597		50806					MAT BRUTES NON COMESTIBLES
23	RUBBER, CRUDE		6446		8926					CAOUTCHOUC BRUT
26	TEXTILE FIBRES AND WASTE		14794		22967					FIBRES TEXTILES
263	COTTON	W 3805	5967	W 5156	4781					COTON
2631	RAW COTTON,EXCL LINTERS	W 3769	5851	W 4703	4250					COTON EN MASSE
266	SYNTHETIC FIBRES TO SPIN	W 3390	6114	W 9570	14742					FIBRES SYNTHETIQUES
2665	DISCN SYNTH FIBRE UNCMBD	W 2651	3524	W 6759	7740					DISCONTINUES EN MASSE
2666	CONTIN FILAMNT TOW SYNTH	W 609	2347	W 2558	6555					CABLES POUR DISCONTINUS
27	CRUDE FERTLZR,MINRLS NES		11205		3750					ENGRAIS MINERAUX BRUTS
278	OTHER CRUDE MINERALS	W 66270	9054	W 12825	2891					AUTRES MINERAUX BRUTS
2789	MINERALS CRUDE NES	W 42715	6421	W 9308	1519					MINERAUX BRUTS NDA
29	CRUDE ANIMAL,VEG MAT NES		7442		10709					MATIERES BRUTES ANIM,VEGET
292	CRUDE VEG MATERIALS NES	W 784	7266		10611					MAT BRUTES VEGETALES NDA
2926	LIVE PLANTS,BULBS,ETC	W 164	3326	W 224	5729					BULBES,TUBERCULES
29269	LIVE PLANTS NES	W 120	2882	W 193	5477					AUTRES PLANTES VIVANTES
3	MINERAL FUELS ETC		451362		253889				19503	COMBUSTIBLES MINERAUX LUB
32	COAL,COKE AND BRIQUETTES		9233		7221					HOUILLES,COKES,BRIQUETTES
322	COAL,LIGNITE AND PEAT	W 157324	8883	W 130094	7051					HOUILLES,LIGNITES,TOURBE
3222	OTH COAL,NOT AGGLOMERATD	W 157288	8865	W 130094	7051					AUTRES HOUILLES
33	PETROLEUM AND PRODUCTS		435416		241823		16717			PETROLE ET DERIVES
333	CRUDE PETROLEUM						13084		11229	HUILES BRUTES DE PETROLE
334	PETROLEUM PRODUCTS,REFIN	W 1532214	328468		234346		3634		8067	PRODUITS RAFFINES
3341	GASOLINE,OTH LIGHT OILS	W 355775	102058		71323		580		1461	ESSENCES POUR MOTEURS
33411	MOTOR,AVIATION SPIRIT	W 355775	102057		71316		580		1461	ESSENCES MOTEURS D'AVIONS
3342	KEROSENE,OTH MEDIUM OILS	W 250452	65177		37619					PETR LAMPANTS,AUT HUIL
33421	KEROSENE INCL JET FUEL	W 249682	64934		37619					PETROLES LAMPANTS
3343	GAS OILS	W 585403	126026		90319					GAS OILS
3344	FUEL OILS,NES	W 319548	31509		26813					FUEL OILS
3345	LUBS,PETROLEUM OILS NES	W 21037	3698		8272					HUILES LUBRIFIANTES
33451	LUBS(HIGH PETR CONT) ETC	W 20906	3345		7453					HUILES LUBRIF,H LOURDES
335	RESIDUAL PETRLM PROD NES		106948		7476					PRODUITS RESIDUELS NDA
3351	PETRLM JELLY,MINERAL WAX	W 5228	4180		5333					VASELINE,CIRES MINERALES
3354	PETROLM BITUMEN,COKE ETC		102202	W 12900	1456					BITUME,COKE DE PETROLE
33541	PETROLEUM BITUMEN, ETC		97625	W 12857	1426					BITUME DE PETROLE
341	*GAS,NATURAL AND MANUFCT	W 25766	6713		4846					GAZ NATUREL,GAZ MANUFACT
3413	PETROLM GASES,LIQUEFIED	W 25765	6708		4844					GAZ DE PETROLE LIQUEFIE
34131	LIQUEFIED PROPANE,BUTANE	W 23693	6384		4818					PROPANE,BUTANE LIQUEFIES
4	ANIMAL,VEGETABLE OIL,FAT		98687		70737					HUILES,GRAISSES ANIM,VEG
42	FIXED VEGETABLE OIL,FAT		93109		66914					HUILES VEGETALES FIXES
423	FIXED VEG OILS,SOFT	W 3421	2610	W 11903	7477					HUILES VEGET DOUCES FIXES
424	FIXED VEG OIL NONSOFT	W 192464	90498		59437					AUTRES HUILES VEG FIXES
4242	PALM OIL	W 188219	85701		53696					HUILE DE PALME
5	CHEMCLS,RELATED PROD NES		272464		346571					PRODUITS CHIMIQUES
51	ORGANIC CHEMICALS		23152		32762					PROD CHIMIQ ORGANIQUES
511	HYDROCARBONS NES,DERIVS	W 4493	4635		5883					HYDROCARBURES NDA
513	CARBOXYLIC ACIDS ETC	W 3740	5062	W 7029	8121					ACIDES CARBOXYLIQUES
516	OTHER ORGANIC CHEMICALS	W 1850	5080		9089					AUTRES PROD ORGANIQUES
5169	ORGANIC CHEMICALS,NES	W 438	3283	W 409	6124					PROD CHIM ORGANIQUES NDA
52	INORGANIC CHEMICALS		24922		26103					PROD CHIM INORGANIQUES
522	INORG ELEMNTS,OXIDES,ETC	W 23938	13372		12527					ELEMENTS INORGANIQUES
5225	INORGANIC BASES ETC NES	W 17139	8073		5262					AUTRES BASES OXYDES METAL
52252	SODIUM HYDROXIDE, SOLID	W 10874	6049	W 7950	3412					HYDROXYDE DE SODIUM
523	OTHR INORG CHEMICALS ETC	W 18084	11208		13254					AUT PRODUITS CHIMIQUES INORG
5231	METAL CMPD OF INORG ACID	W 9141	4154	W 9300	6034					SELS METALLIQUES
5232	OTH MTL CMPD OF INRG ACD	W 6596	5514		5584					SELS METALLIQUES
53	DYES,TANNING,COLOUR PROD		13627		13176					PROD TEINTURE,COLORANTS
531	SYNT DYE,NAT INDGO,LAKES	W 858	8029	W 991	6668					MAT COLOR ORGAN,LAQUES
541	*MEDICINAL,PHARM PRODUCT	K 4042754	63847		98230		3153		4599	PROD MEDICINAUX PHARMACEUT
5413	ANTIBIOTICS IN BULK	K 197051	5542	K 200655	4756					ANTIBIOTIQUES NDA
5415	HORMONES,NAT,SYN IN BULK	K 2767	255		6346					HORMONES
54153	ADRENAL CORTICAL HORMONE	K 2753	255		6265					HORMONES CORTICO–SURRENAL
5416	GLYCOSIDES,GLANDS,SERA	K 144946	8569	K 180899	5006					HETEROSIDES
54164	ANTISERA,MICROB VACCINES	K 94531	6526	K 59062	2618					SERUMS,VACCINS
5417	MEDICAMENTS	K 2852249	41255		73441					MEDICAMENTS
54171	— CONTAINNG ANTIBIOTICS	K 1081628	15800		12922					MED CONTN ANTIBIOTIQUES
54172	— CONTAINING HORMONES	K 411307	8251		47645					MED CONTENANT HORMONES
54179	— CONTNG OTH SUBSTANCES	K 1264825	15228	K 1421771	11451					MED CONT AUT SUBSTANCES
5419	PHARMACEUTICAL GOODS NES	K 768257	6663	K 516404	6720					PREP,ART PHARMACEUTIQUES
55	PERFUME,CLEANING ETC PRD		5456		7862					PROD POUR PARFUM,TOILETTE
562	*FERTILIZERS,MANUFACTURE	W 241512	46950	W 295280	58484		3098		2335	ENGRAIS MANUFACTURES
5621	CHEM NITROGENOUS FERTLZR	W 49381	9940	W 49787	10319					ENGRAIS AZOTES
5629	FERTILIZERS NES	W 182414	34643	W 198347	40002					ENGRAIS NDA
56291	NIT–PHOS–POT FERTLZR NES	W 77095	14314	W 108263	17673					ENGRAIS CONT N P K
56292	NITROG–PHOS FERTILZR NES	W 105173	20197	W 90012	22295					ENGRAIS NDA CONT N P
58	PLASTIC MATERIALS ETC		51140		61973		3873		8965	MAT PLAST ARTIFICIELLES
582	PROD OF CONDENSATION ETC	W 7450	10553		15086					PROD CONDENS,POLYCOND
5823	ALKYDS,OTHER POLYESTERS	W 5251	6563		8381					ALKYDES ET AUT POLYESTERS
58231	— IN PRIMARY FORMS	W 5152	6146		7909					SOUS FORMES PRIMAIRES

4. General Imports C.I.F. by Commodities according to the S.I.T.C. (Rev. 2) in thousand U.S. Dollars
Importations Générales C.A.F. par Produits d'après la C.T.C.I. (Rév. 2) en milliers de Dollars E.U.

SITC CTCI	COMMODITY	1992 WEIGHT POIDS	1992 VALUE VALEUR	1993 WEIGHT POIDS	1993 VALUE VALEUR	1994 WEIGHT POIDS	1994 VALUE VALEUR	1995 WEIGHT POIDS	1995 VALUE VALEUR	PRODUIT
583	POLYMERIZATION ETC PRODS	W 43427	39104		44710					PROD POLYMERISATION
5831	POLYETHYLENE	W 26784	20929		21358					POLYETHYLENE
58311	— IN PRIMARY FORMS	W 26614	20215		20721					POLYETHYLENE PRIMAIRES
5832	POLYPROPYLENE	W 3949	4177	W 9403	6073					POLYPROPYLENE
5834	POLYVINYL CHLORIDE	W 8273	7795		8073					CHLORURE DE POLYVINYLE
58341	— IN PRIMARY FORMS	W 7640	5912		7103					SOUS FORMES PRIMAIRES
5839	OTH POLYMRZTION ETC PROD	W 3100	4263	W 4935	6258					AUT PROD POLYMER COPOLYM
59	CHEMICAL MATERIALS NES		43079		47670					MAT PROD CHIMIQUES NDA
591	PESTICIDES,DISINFECTANTS		30049	W 4845	26959					DESINF,INSECT,FONG,HERB
5911	INSECTICIDES,FOR RETAIL		11874	W 1109	11661					INSECTICIDES VENTE DET
5912	FUNGICIDES,FOR RETAIL	W 2266	11339	W 1808	8998					FONGICIDES VENTE AU DET
5913	HERBICIDES,FOR RETAIL	W 1293	5416	W 1296	4506					HERBICIDES VENTE AU DET
598	MISCEL CHEM PRODUCTS NES		11868		19675					PROD DIV INDUST CHIM NDA
5982	ANTI–KNOCK PREPARTNS ETC	W 596	1450		7845					PREPARAT ANTIDETONANTES
5989	CHEM PRODUCTS,PREPS NES		8797		10186					PROD PREP CHIMIQUES NDA
59899	OTH CHEM PRODS,PREPS,NES		5100		5260					AUT PRODUITS CHIMIQUES NDA
6	BASIC MANUFACTURES		213367		269639					ART MANUFACTURES
62	RUBBER MANUFACTURES NES		10140		13420					CAOUTCHOUC MANUFACTURE
628	RUBBER ARTICLES NES		4858		5894					OUVRAGES CAOUTCHOUC NDA
64	PAPER,PAPERBOARD AND MFR		25617		27598		1458		4543	PAPIERS,CARTONS & OUVRAGES
641	PAPER AND PAPERBOARD		22835		21183					PAPIERS ET CARTONS
6412	PRINTG,WRITING PAPER NES	W 4797	4874		5617					PAPIERS POUR L'IMPRESSION
64122	— COATED,IMPREGNATD ETC	W 4733	4756		5216					PAPIERS IMPRESSION COUCHES
6415	PAPER,PAPERBRD,BULK,NES		6478	W 7247	3979					PAPIERS,CARTONS ROULEAUX
6418	COATED ETC PAPER NES BLK	W 3548	3970		7278					PAP,CARTONS COUCHES,ENDUITS
64189	COATED PAPER ETC NES	W 3222	3443		5887					PAPIERS,CARTONS COUCHES
642	PAPER,ETC,PRECUT,ARTS OF		2782		6414					PAP,CARTONS DECOUPES
65	TEXTILE YARN,FABRICS,ETC		28171		37047					FILS,TISSUS,ARTICLES TEXTILE
652	COTTON FABRICS,WOVEN		4507		15625					TISSUS DE COTON
6522	WOVEN COTTON BLEACHD,ETC		3605		13843					TISSUS COTON BLANCHIS ETC
65224	BLCHED COTTON FABRIC NES	A 1269	1355	A 8972	5461					AUT TIS PLUS 85% COT BLANCHI
65225	BLCHD COTN BLEND FAB NES		2134		8195					AUT TIS MOINS 85% COT BLANCH
657	SPECIAL TXTL FABRC,PRODS		7215		8500					TISSUS SPECIAUX
6573	COATED ETC TEXTILES NES		4735		5413					TISSUS,ART MATIERE TEXT NDA
658	TEXTILE ARTICLES NES		11164		3712					ART FACONNES MAT TEXTILES
6582	MADE–UP CANVAS GOODS		7209		1332					BACHES,TENTES ETC
66	NONMETAL MINERAL MFS NES		17290		17876					ART MIN NON METALLIQUES
67	IRON AND STEEL		81154		108573		5641		9940	FER ET ACIER
672	IRON,STEEL PRIMARY FORMS	W 121363	42211	W 179899	62877					LINGOTS FER,ACIER
6725	IRN,STL BLOOMS,SLABS,ETC	W 54747	13267	W 50392	11371					BLOOMS,BILLETTES FER ACIER
67251	IRN,SMPLE STL BLOOMS,ETC	W 54746	13261	W 50389	11326					BLOOMS ETC NON ACIER FIN
6727	IRN,STL COIL FR REROLLNG	W 63956	28267	W 127803	51119					EBAUCHES POUR TOLES FER
67271	IRON,SIMPLE STEEL COILS	W 63852	28151	W 127135	50892					EBAUCHES NON EN ACIER
673	IRON,STEEL SHAPES ETC	W 19614	7720		9587					BARRES,PROFIL FER,ACIER
6731	IRON,STEEL WIRE ROD	W 14402	4698	W 19088	5301					FIL MACHINE FER,ACIER
67311	IRON,SIMPLE STL WIRE ROD	W 14382	4668	W 18974	5215					FIL MACH AUT ACIER FIN
674	IRN,STL UNIV,PLATE,SHEET		20548		27413					LARGES PLATS,TOLES
6747	TINNED PLATES,SHEETS	W 20353	18187	W 23634	21772					TOLES ETAMEES EN ACIER
678	IRON,STL TUBES,PIPES,ETC	W 6634	9425		6694					TUBES,TUYAUX EN FONTE,FER
68	NON–FERROUS METALS		19017		32932					METAUX NON FERREUX
684	ALUMINIUM	W 1198	4950		11836					ALUMINIUM
6842	ALUMINIUM,ALLOYS WORKED	W 798	4138		8398					ALUMINIUM,ALLIAGES OUVRE
68423	ALUMINIUM FOIL	W 493	2514	W 1146	5730					FEUILLES,BANDES MINCES AL
686	ZINC	W 6633	9133	W 8956	16364					ZINC
6861	ZINC,ALLOYS UNWROUGHT	W 6445	8760	W 8822	16144					ZINC ET ALLIAGES BRUTS
69	METAL MANUFACTURES NES		28875		30301					ART MANUFACT EN METAL NDA
691	STRUCTURES AND PARTS NES	W 2386	5490	W 1435	4423					CONSTRUCT FER,ACIER,ALU
695	TOOLS		6027		6693					OUTILS A MAIN
699	BASE METAL MFRS NES		9060		9400					ART MANUFACTURES MET NDA
7	MACHINES,TRANSPORT EQUIP		428210		454836				54486	MACHINES MATERIEL TRANSPORT
71	POWER GENERATING EQUIPMT		29185		25927					MACHINES GENERATRICES
713	INTRNL COMBUS PSTN ENGIN		8175		10801					MOTEURS EXPL COMB INT, PIECE
7139	PISTON ENGINE PARTS NES		5217		5303					PIECES POUR 713.2,3,8
716	ROTATING ELECTRIC PLANT		17513		9071					APP ELECTR ROTATIFS,PIECES
7161	DC MOTORS AND GENERATORS		6563		1537					MOTEURS COURANT CONTINU
7162	AC MTRS,GENRTRS,GEN SETS		10653		6667					MOTEURS ELECTRIQUES
71623	GEN SETS WITH PISTN ENGN		6103	N 731	3996					GROUPES MOTEUR EXPLOSION
72	MACHS FOR SPCL INDUSTRYS		101638		69421		893			MAC SPECIALES POUR INDUST
721	AGRIC MACHY,EXC TRACTORS		13966		4999		893		1717	MACHINES AGRICOLES
722	TRACTORS NON–ROAD		9088	N 468	11974					TRACTEURS
7224	WHEELED TRACTORS NES		8831	N 446	11411					TRACTEURS A ROUES
723	CIVIL ENGNEERG EQUIP ETC		16603		7509					APPAREILS DE GENIE CIVIL
7234	CONST,MINING MACHNRY NES		14755		6149					MACH POUR LA CONST, MINES
72341	SELF–PROPELLD DOZERS,ETC	N 79	10376		2176					BULLDOZERS
724	TEXTILE,LEATHER MACHNRY		14885		9816					MACH POUR INDUSTRIE TEXTILE
7244	SPINNING,EXTRDNG,ETC MCH		5500		2286					MACH POUR LE FILAGE
727	FOOD MACHRY NON–DOMESTIC		21561		7723					MACH INDUSTRIES ALIMENT
7272	OTH FOOD PROC MCHY,PARTS		19149		6971					AUT MACH IND ALIMENTAIRE
72721	ANML,VEGTBL OIL,FAT MACH		12475	N 23	2305					MACH IND HUILES,GRAISSES
72722	INDUS FOOD PROC MACH NES		6674		4666					MACHINES BOULANGERIE
728	OTH MACHY FOR SPCL INDUS		17619		21400					AUT MACH IND PARTICULIERES
7284	MACHY FOR SPCL INDUS NES		11279		18118					MACH SPEC IND PARTICUL.
72841	GLASS–WORKING MACHY NES		108		8260					MACH TRAVAIL VERRE ETC
72842	RUBBER,PLASTICS WRKG MCH	N 3133	6967	N 7713	4902					MACH IND CAOUT MAT PLAST
73	METALWORKING MACHINERY		7658		8117					MACH TRAVAIL DES METAUX
736	METALWORKING MACH–TOOLS		4698		5223					MACH–OUTILS TRAVAIL METAUX
74	GENRL INDUSTRL MACHY NES		79228		70711					MACH APP INDUSTRIE
741	HEATING,COOLING EQUIPMNT		10232		8035					MACH CHAUFFAGE,PIECES
742	PUMPS FOR LIQUIDS ETC		9147		9073					POMPES MOTO–POMPES
743	PUMPS NES,CENTRFUGES ETC		7172		7106					POMPES COMPRES,VENT ETC
744	MECHANICAL HANDLING EQU		16020		9642					EQUIP MANUTENTION PIECES
7442	LIFTING,LOADING MACH NES	N 6720	5450		3751					APP LEVAGE,MANUTENTION
7449	PTS NES OF MACHY OF 7442	W 526	8279		3590					PIECES DU 744.2
745	NONELEC MACHY,TOOLS NES		8845		9057					AUT MACH NON ELEC,PIECES
7452	OTH NONELEC MCHS,PTS NES		8436		8743					AUT MACH NON ELEC,PIECES
749	NONELEC MACH PTS,ACC NES		27813		27798					PIECES MACH NON ELEC NDA
7491	BALL,ROLLER,ETC BEARINGS	W 299	4405		5348					ROULEMENTS BILLES ETC
7492	COCKS,VALVES ETC NES		8512		6110					ART ROB,SIM POUR TUYAUX
7493	SHAFT,CRANK,PULLEY ETC		7509		8443					ARBRES TRANS,VILEBREQUINS
7499	OTH NONELEC MCHY PTS NES		7387		7896					PIECES NON ELECT NDA
74991	FOUNDRY MOULDS ETC NES	N 4199	1746		5327					MOULES POUR METAUX

4. General Imports C.I.F. by Commodities according to the S.I.T.C. (Rev. 2) in thousand U.S. Dollars
Importations Générales C.A.F. par Produits d'après la C.T.C.I. (Rév. 2) en milliers de Dollars E.U.

SITC CTCI	COMMODITY	1992 WEIGHT POIDS	1992 VALUE VALEUR	1993 WEIGHT POIDS	1993 VALUE VALEUR	1994 WEIGHT POIDS	1994 VALUE VALEUR	1995 WEIGHT POIDS	1995 VALUE VALEUR	PRODUIT
75	OFFICE MACHNES,ADP EQUIP		15075		16818					MACH BUREAU TRAIT AUTOM
752	AUTOMTIC DATA PROC EQUIP		9825		10904					MACH TRAIT INFORMATION
76	TELECOMM,SOUND EQUIPMENT		68452		58575					EQUIPMENT DE TELECOM
764	TELECOM EQPT,PTS,ACC NES		64458		52580					EQUIP TELECOM,PIECES
7641	LINE TELEPHONE,ETC EQUIP	N 106868	25289		38210					APP TELEPHON PAR FIL
7643	TV,RADIO TRANSMITTRS ETC	N 6937	33512	N 3093	6450					APP EMET TELE RADIO
77	ELECTRIC MACHNRY NES ETC		48225		43814					MACH APP ELECT NDA
771	ELECTRIC POWER MACHY NES		7150		6502					MACH PROD,TRANS ELECTR
7711	TRANSFORMERS,ELECTRICAL		5668		5092					TRANSFO ELECTRIQUES
772	SWITCHGEAR ETC,PARTS NES		9223		10321					APP COUPURE,SECT ETC
7721	SWITCHGEAR ETC		8147		9856					APP COUPURE,SECTIONMNT
773	ELECTR DISTRIBUTNG EQUIP	W 1032	5465		3400					EQUIPMT DISTRIBUTION ELECT
774	ELECTRO–MEDCL,XRAY EQUIP		5913		2030					APPAREILS MEDICAUX
778	ELECTRICAL MACHINERY NES		13464		15185					AUTRES MACH ELECT NDA
78	ROAD VEHICLES		67527		127760		12822			VEHICULES ROUTIERS
781	PASS MOTOR VEH EXC BUSES		34446		55255		9465		7651	AUTO TRANSPORT PERSONNES
782	LORRIES,SPCL MTR VEH NES	N 431	9959		35145				11850	VEHICULES SPECIAUX,MARCH
7821	LORRIES,TRUCKS	N 389	6916		29910					VEHICULES TRANSP MARCHAND
7822	SPECIAL MOTOR VEHCLS NES	N 42	3043	N 37	5235					VEHICULES USAGES SPECIAUX
783	ROAD MOTOR VEHICLES NES		1444		13882					VEHICULES ROUTIERS NDA
7831	BUSES		1070		13629					VOITURES TRANSPORT COMMUN
784	MOTOR VEH PRTS,ACCES NES		15737		15278					PIECES 722,781,782,783
7849	OTHER MOTOR VEHCL PARTS		15652		14165		3356		6047	PIECES 722,781,782,783
79	OTHR TRANSPORT EQUIPMENT		11222		33694					AUTRE MATERIEL TRANSPORT
792	AIRCRAFT ETC		8956		27019					APP NAVIGATION AERIENNE
7923	AIRCRFT NES2000–15000KG	N 11	699	N 21	8804					AERODYNES 2000 A 15000 KG
7929	AIRCRAFT PARTS NES		4490		14711					PIECES DU 792
8	MISC MANUFACTURED GOODS		73552		86581					ART MANUFACTURES DIVERS
87	PRECISION INSTRUMNTS NES		17664		18813					INSTRUM,APPAR SCIENT NDA
872	MEDICAL INSTRUMENTS NES	MN 109678	7080		7656					INSTR,APP MEDIC–CHIR NDA
87202	OTH MEDICAL INSTRUMENTS	MN 109094	5886		7378					INSTRUM,APP MEDECINE
874	MEASURNG,CONTROLNG INSTR		8921		9665					INSTRUMENTS DE MESURE
88	PHOTO EQU,OPTICL GDS ETC		6175		5129					APP,FOURN PHOTO,OP,MONTR
89	MISC MANUFCTRD GOODS NES		38563		51816					ART MANUFACTURES DIVERS
892	PRINTED MATTER		25406		34896					IMPRIMES
8921	PRINTED BOOKS,GLOBES,ETC		7969		9198					LIVRES,BROCHURES,CARTES
89211	PRINTED BOOKS,PAMPHLETS		7544		8745					LIVRES,BROCHURES
8928	PRINTED MATTER NES		16394		24095					IMPRIMES NDA
89283	UNISSUED BANKNOTES ETC	W 312	13456		20019					TIMBRES–POSTE FISCAUX
893	ARTICLES OF PLASTIC NES		7653		8192					OUVRAGES EN MAT DIVIS 58
8939	MISC PLASTIC ARTICLES		5442		5198					ART DIVERS EN MAT DIV 58
9	GOODS NOT CLASSD BY KIND		356		3351				10565	ART TRANSACT NON CLASSES

5. General Exports F.O.B. by Commodities according to the S.I.T.C. (Rev. 2) in thousand U.S. Dollars
Exportations Générales F.O.B. par Produits d'après la C.T.C.I. (Rév. 2) en milliers de Dollars E.U.

SITC CTCI	COMMODITY	1992 WEIGHT POIDS	1992 VALUE VALEUR	1993 WEIGHT POIDS	1993 VALUE VALEUR	1994 WEIGHT POIDS	1994 VALUE VALEUR	1995 WEIGHT POIDS	1995 VALUE VALEUR	PRODUIT
	ALL COMMODITIES		1361703		1391890		1524651		1915587	TOUS PRODUITS
0	FOOD AND LIVE ANIMALS		556168		679918					ALIMENTS,ANIMAUX VIVANTS
03	FISH AND PREPARATIONS		25777		30497					POISSONS ET PREPARATIONS
034	FISH,FRESH,CHILLED,FROZN	W 13501	23985	W 17007	29431					POISSON FRAIS, REFRIG,CONG
0344	FISH FILLETS,FROZEN	W 12784	22751	W 16663	28810					FILETS CONGELES
04	CEREALS AND PREPARATIONS		5966		5916					CEREALES ET PRODUITS
048	CEREAL ETC PREPARATIONS	W 6235	4089		4746					PREPTNS A BASE CEREALES
05	VEGETABLES AND FRUIT		96758		95293					LEGUMES ET FRUITS
054	VEG ETC FRSH,SMPLY PRSVD		27885		25512					LEGUMES FRAIS,CONG,SECS
0545	OTHER FRESH VEGETABLES		26063		23950					AUTRES LEGUMES FRAIS,REF
05459	FRESH VEGETABLES NES		25941		23716					LEGUMES FRAIS,REFRI NDA
056	VEGTBLES ETC PRSVD,PREPD	W 4256	6757	W 8034	12372					CONSERVES DE LEGUMES
0565	VEGTBLES PRSVD,PREPD NES	W 4207	6652	W 7986	12306					LEGUMES PREPARES CONSERVE
05659	OTH VEG PRESVD,PREPD NES	W 4207	6652	W 7975	12296					LEGUM PREPAP,CONSERV NDA
057	FRUIT,NUTS,FRESH,DRIED		15138		14042					FRUITS FRAIS OU SECS
0577	NUTS EDIBLE,FRESH,DRIED	W 1700	6820	W 1284	5884					FRUITS A COQUES
05779	NUTS EDIBLE,FRSH,DRY,NES	W 776	5258	W 763	5634					FRUITS A COQUES NDA
0579	FRUIT FRESH OR DRIED NES		8093		7832					FRUITS FRAIS,SECS NDA
05797	OTH TROP FRUIT,FRESH,DRY		6565	W 9767	5934					AVOCATS,MANGUES,GOYAVES
058	FRUIT PRESERVED,PREPARED	W 79459	46979		43366					CONSERVES DE FRUITS
0585	FRUIT OR VEGETABLE JUICE	W 10855	8932	W 10378	6846					JUS DE FRUITS
05854	PINEAPPLE JUICE	W 9949	7609	W 9865	6154					JUS D'ANANAS
0589	FRUIT PREPRD,PRESRVD,NES	W 68584	38005	W 68048	36342					FRUITS PREPARES CONSERV
05899	FRUIT,NUTS NES,PRESERVED	W 67549	34865	W 67401	34208					FRUITS PREP CONSERV NDA
07	COFFEE,TEA,COCOA,SPICES		416583		532699		27360			CAFE,THE,CACAO,EPICES
071	COFFEE AND SUBSTITUTES	W 78148	126329	W 88414	194830	W 79679	11933		14022	CAFE ET SUCCEDANES
0711	COFFEE GREEN,ROASTED,SUB	W 78147	126325	W 88411	194814	W 79679	11933	W 88519	14022	CAFE TORREFIE OU DECAFEINE
07111	COFFEE GREEN,HUSKS,SKINS	W 78145	126315	W 88337	194531	W 79679	11933	W 88519	14022	CAFE NON TORREFIE
074	TEA AND MATE	W 165598	289721		336871	W 174926	15427		17465	THE ET MATE
0741	TEA	W 165598	289721		336871	W 174926	15427	W 217937	17465	THE
1	BEVERAGES AND TOBACCO		23044		38337					BOISSONS ET TABACS
11	BEVERAGES		11783		26038					BOISSONS
112	ALCOHOLIC BEVERAGES	W 20983	11293		25536					BOISSONS ALCOOLIQUES
1123	BEER,ALE,STOUT,PORTER	W 20773	9808		24258					BIERES
12	TOBACCO AND MANUFACTURES		11260		12299					TABACS BRUTS FABRIQUES
121	TOBACCO UNMNFCTRD,REFUSE	W 2026	4225	W 1424	2431					TABACS BRUTS,DECHETS
122	TOBACCO,MANUFACTURED		7035		9868					TABACS FABRIQUES
1222	CIGARETTES	W 947	7024		9853					CIGARETTES
2	CRUDE MATERLS,EXCL FUELS		103474		116861					MAT BRUTES NON COMESTIBLES
26	TEXTILE FIBRES AND WASTE		12156		13437		605			FIBRES TEXTILES
265	VEG FIBRE,EXCL COTN,JUTE	W 32026	10676		12794					FIBRES VEGETALES
2654	SISAL,AGAVE FIBRES,WASTE	W 32026	10676		12793	W 27000	605		571	SISAL,AUTRES AGAVES
27	CRUDE FERTLZR,MINRLS NES		24916		31903		1102			ENGRAIS MINERAUX BRUTS
278	OTHER CRUDE MINERALS		24716		31628					AUTRES MINERAUX BRUTS
2783	COMMON SALT,ETC	W 48533	3393		4231					SEL
2785	QUARTZ,MICA,FELSPAR,ETC	W 66640	4321	W 71095	4519	W 71040	214		251	QUARTZ,MICA,FELDSPATH
27854	FELSPAR,FLOURSPAR,ETC	W 66639	4320	W 71095	4519	W 71040	214	W 64434	251	FELDSPATH,LEUCITE ETC.
2789	MINERALS CRUDE NES		16961	W 222787	22854					MINERAUX BRUTS NDA
27899	MINERAL SUBSTANCES NES		16691	W 220829	22410	W 215024	888		1001	MATIERES MINERALES NDA
29	CRUDE ANIMAL,VEG MAT NES		60051		65510					MATIERES BRUTES ANIM,VEGET
292	CRUDE VEG MATERIALS NES		58540		64000					MAT BRUTES VEGETALES NDA
2927	CUT FLOWERS AND FOLIAGE		27869		38466					FLEURS,FEUILLAGES COUPES
29271	CUT FLOWERS		27146	W 22400	36236					FLEURS ET BOUTONS
2929	OTH CRUDE VEG MATERIALS	W 2904	23775	W 1853	18924					MATIERES VEGETALES NDA
29291	VEGETABLE SAPS,EXTRACTS	W 492	22777	W 382	17935					SUCS,EXTRAITS VEGETAUX
3	MINERAL FUELS ETC		152388		129197				4757	COMBUSTIBLES MINERAUX LUB
33	PETROLEUM AND PRODUCTS		152006		128836		4981			PETROLE ET DERIVES
334	PETROLEUM PRODUCTS,REFIN	W 654360	150233		123295		4981		4756	PRODUITS RAFFINES
3341	GASOLINE,OTH LIGHT OILS	W 66197	20879		20179				1399	ESSENCES POUR MOTEURS
33411	MOTOR,AVIATION SPIRIT	W 66195	20877		20166		755		1399	ESSENCES MOTEURS D'AVIONS
3342	KEROSENE,OTH MEDIUM OILS	W 251175	81274		61394					PETR LAMPANTS,AUT HUIL
33421	KEROSENE INCL JET FUEL	W 251159	81269		61301					PETROLES LAMPANTS
3343	GAS OILS	W 86242	21137		18758					GAS OILS
3344	FUEL OILS,NES	W 245061	21680		17151					FUEL OILS
3345	LUBS,PETROLEUM OILS NES	W 5686	5264		5813					HUILES LUBRIFIANTES
33451	LUBS(HIGH PETR CONT) ETC	W 5626	5199		5705					HUILES LUBRIF,H LOURDES
335	RESIDUAL PETRLM PROD NES	W 4395	1772		5541					PRODUITS RESIDUELS NDA
4	ANIMAL,VEGETABLE OIL,FAT		4095		6346					HUILES,GRAISSES ANIM,VEG
431	*PROCESD ANML VEG OIL,ET	W 2340	2374		4978					HUILES,GRAISSES PREPAREES
4312	HYDROGENATED OIL,FAT	W 2140	2147		4761					HUILES HYDROGENEES
5	CHEMCLS,RELATED PROD NES		43687		58016					PRODUITS CHIMIQUES
51	ORGANIC CHEMICALS		4673		3285					PROD CHIMIQ ORGANIQUES
512	ALCOHOLS,PHENOLS ETC		4312		2974					PHENOLS,PHENOLS–ALCOOLS
5121	ACYCLIC ALCOHOLS,DERIVS		4303		2969					ALCOOLS ACYCLIQUES
53	DYES,TANNING,COLOUR PROD		7519		8771		269			PROD TEINTURE,COLORANTS
532	DYES NES,TANNING PROD	W 7751	6081	W 8159	6895					EXTRAITS TEINTURE,TANNAGE
5322	DYE,TANN EXTRCTS,TANNINS	W 7751	6081	W 8158	6888					EXT TAN ORIG VEG,TANNINS
53221	VEG TANN EXTRCTS,TANNINS	W 7751	6080	W 8154	6853		269		209	EXTR TANNANTS ORIG VEGET
541	*MEDICINAL,PHARM PRODUCT	K 1419692	9749		11473					PROD MEDICINAUX PHARMACEUT
5417	MEDICAMENTS	K 1241470	8856		10208					MEDICAMENTS
54171	— CONTAINNG ANTIBIOTICS	K 430456	4450	K 476633	3522					MED CONTN ANTIBIOTIQUES
55	PERFUME,CLEANING ETC PRD		13702		22762					PROD POUR PARFUM,TOILETTE
554	SOAP,CLEANSING ETC PREPS		9174		16123					SAVONS,PRODUITS DETERSIFS
5541	SOAPS		5799		12001					SAVONS,PROD TENSIO–ACTIFS
59	CHEMICAL MATERIALS NES		3324		5721		1432			MAT PROD CHIMIQUES NDA
591	PESTICIDES,DISINFECTANTS	W 568	2151		4232					DESINF,INSECT,FONG,HERB
6	BASIC MANUFACTURES		115588		190220					ART MANUFACTURES
61	LEATHER,DRESSED FUR,ETC		24485		27565					CUIRS,PELLETERIES
611	LEATHER	W 17055	24402		27508					CUIRS,PEAUX PREPARES
6113	CALF LEATHER	W 7822	8532	W 7085	6386					CUIRS,PEAUX DE VEAUX
6114	LEATHR BOVINE NES,EQUINE	W 4586	6971	W 3464	9049					CUIRS DE BOVINS
6116	LEATHER OF OTH HIDE,SKIN	W 3004	5804		9767					PEAUX PREP D'AUTRES ANIMAUX
61161	LEATHER FROM GOAT,KID	W 3004	5803		9756					PEAUX DE CAPRINS PREPAREES
63	WOOD,CORK MANUFACTRS NES		3432		7310		196			OUVRAGES LIEGE ET BOIS
635	WOOD MANUFACTURES NES		2923		4245					ART MANUF EN BOIS NDA
64	PAPER,PAPERBOARD AND MFR		5837		10559					PAPIERS,CARTONS & OUVRAGES
642	PAPER,ETC,PRECUT,ARTS OF		3914		6389					PAP,CARTONS DECOUPES
6421	PAPER ETC CONTAINERS		2809		4798					BOITES,SACS EMBALLAGES
65	TEXTILE YARN,FABRICS,ETC		13477		19294					FILS,TISSUS,ARTICLES TEXTILE
651	TEXTILE YARN	W 1893	5467		4972					FILS TEXTILES
658	TEXTILE ARTICLES NES		4354		7284					ART FACONNES MAT TEXTILES

5. General Exports F.O.B. by Commodities according to the S.I.T.C. (Rev. 2) in thousand U.S. Dollars
Exportations Générales F.O.B. par Produits d'après la C.T.C.I. (Rév. 2) en milliers de Dollars E.U.

SITC CTCI	COMMODITY	1992		1993		1994		1995		PRODUIT
		WEIGHT POIDS	VALUE VALEUR	WEIGHT POIDS	VALUE VALEUR	WEIGHT POIDS	VALUE VALEUR	WEIGHT POIDS	VALUE VALEUR	
6583	BLANKETS ETC NON ELECTRC	N 968849	3052		4724					COUVERTURES
66	NONMETAL MINERAL MFS NES		20845		41399		1492			ART MIN NON METALLIQUES
661	LIME,CEMENT,BLDG PRODS		15895		32484					CHAUX,CIMENTS MAT CONSTR
6612	CEMENT	W 413696	15616	W 623469	31872	W 522125	1492		1570	CIMENTS HYDRAULIQUES
67	IRON AND STEEL		30020		61085					FER ET ACIER
673	IRON,STEEL SHAPES ETC	W 14565	5391		10163					BARRES,PROFIL FER,ACIER
6732	IRON,STEEL BARS ETC	W 9603	3626		5687					BARRES FER,ACIER
67326	IRN,OTH STL BARS HOTROLD	W 8361	3085	W 12409	5182					BARRES PLEINES FER,ACIER
674	IRN,STL UNIV,PLATE,SHEET	W 26728	20752	W 50840	44120					LARGES PLATS,TOLES
6749	OTH IRN,STL PLATES,SHEET	W 21336	17292	W 45264	40870					AUTRES TOLES FER,ACIER
67491	— OF IRON OR SIMPLE STL	W 21336	17292	W 45250	40863					AUT TOLES AUTRES ACIER FIN
68	NON–FERROUS METALS		3141		5703		132			METAUX NON FERREUX
684	ALUMINIUM	W 661	1688		5050					ALUMINIUM
6842	ALUMINIUM,ALLOYS WORKED	W 659	1683		5031					ALUMINIUM,ALLIAGES OUVRE
69	METAL MANUFACTURES NES		10971		14685					ART MANUFACT EN METAL NDA
697	BASE MTL HOUSEHOLD EQUIP		2601		4325					ART MENAGE MET COMMUNS
7	MACHINES,TRANSPORT EQUIP		20314		19964				1735	MACHINES MATERIEL TRANSPORT
72	MACHS FOR SPCL INDUSTRYS		2246		5291					MAC SPECIALES POUR INDUST
74	GENRL INDUSTRL MACHY NES		9761		1234					MACH APP INDUSTRIE
745	NONELEC MACHY,TOOLS NES		8404		259					AUT MACH NON ELEC,PIECES
7452	OTH NONELEC MCHS,PTS NES		8399		254					AUT MACH NON ELEC,PIECES
74522	PACKAGNG,BOTTLNG,ETC MCH	N 387	8047	N 12082	51					MACH NETT BOUTEILLES,ETC
78	ROAD VEHICLES		4182		7961		859			VEHICULES ROUTIERS
8	MISC MANUFACTURED GOODS		324264		137657					ART MANUFACTURES DIVERS
821	*FURNITURE,PARTS THEREOF		1772		5376					MEUBLES ET PIECES
8212	MED FURN,STUFFD FURNSHGS	N 101611	1013		4246					MOB MEDICO–CHIRUR,PIECES
82122	MATTRESSES ETC	N 100981	970		4204					SOMMIERS,ARTICLES DE LITERIE
84	CLOTHING AND ACCESSORIES		6068		8790					VETEMENTS
851	*FOOTWEAR		2279		7975					CHAUSSURES
85101	FOOTWEAR RUBBER,PLASTIC	P 1529756	1352		4192					CHAUS SEMELLES CAOUTCH
89	MISC MANUFCTRD GOODS NES		311151		113195					ART MANUFACTURES DIVERS
892	PRINTED MATTER		4280		10384					IMPRIMES
8928	PRINTED MATTER NES		3181		9804					IMPRIMES NDA
89283	UNISSUED BANKNOTES ETC	W 2	2257	W 4	9255					TIMBRES–POSTE FISCAUX
893	ARTICLES OF PLASTIC NES		4063		10796					OUVRAGES EN MAT DIVIS 58
8931	PLSTC PACKG CONTNRS,LIDS	W 720	1395		4459					ART TRANSP EMBALLAGE ETC
8939	MISC PLASTIC ARTICLES		2424		5865					ART DIVERS EN MAT DIV 58
89399	OTHR PLASTC ARTICLES NES		2185		5563					AUT OUV MAT DIV 58
897	GOLD,SILVER WARE,JEWELRY		296013		85054					BIJOUTERIE,ORFEVRERIE
8973	PREC JEWLRY,GLD–SILVWARE		295399		83723					BIJOUX OR,ARGENT ORFEVRE
89733	JEWELLERY NES		295376		83464					OUV PERLES,PIERRES
9	GOODS NOT CLASSD BY KIND		18682		15373				13364	ART TRANSACT NON CLASSES
971	*GOLD,NON MONETARY NES	K 1831	18397	K 1502	15113					OR NON MONETAIRE
97101	NONMON GLD UNWRT,SEMIMFD	K 1831	18397	K 1502	15113					OR,ALLIAGES D'OR BRUTS

FOOT NOTES – NOTES

TABLE 1 –

1 The export indices relate to national exports only.

TABLEAU 1 –

1 Les indices des exportations se rapportent seulement aux exportations nationales.

1. HISTORICAL SERIES, 1960–1995 GENERAL TRADE, IMPORTS F.O.B., EXPORTS F.O.B.
SERIES HISTORIQUES, 1960–1995 COMMERCE GENERAL, IMPORTATIONS F.O.B., EXPORTATIONS F.O.B

YEAR ANNEE	VALUE IN MILLION ASTL. DOLLARS VALEUR EN MILLION ASTL. DOLLARS MERCHANDISE –MARCHANDISE		GOLD –OR		CONVERSION FACTORS U.S. CENTS PER ASTL. DOLLAR FACTEURS DE CONVERSION CENTS E.U. PAR ASTL. DOLLAR		INDEX NUMBERS –INDICES QUANTUM		UNIT VALUE VALEUR UNITAIRE	
	IMPORTS	EXPORTS	IMPORTS	EXPORTS	IMPORTS	EXPORTS	IMPORTS	EXPORTS	IMPORTS	EXPORTS
1960	2.59	1.88			112.0000	112.0000				
1961	3.48	1.96			112.0000	112.0000				
1962	3.84	1.79			112.0000	112.0000				
1963	3.57	2.68			112.0000	112.0000				
1964	3.25	2.64			112.0000	112.0000				
1965	3.65	3.73			112.0000	112.0000				
1966	2.70	4.80			112.0000	112.0000				
1967	3.94	6.20			112.0000	112.0000				
1968	4.13	6.80			112.0000	112.0000				
1969	3.15	7.31			112.0000	112.0000				
1970	3.92	6.97			112.0000	112.0000				
1971	4.73	8.69			113.4000	113.4000				
1972	5.42	6.60			119.1000	119.1000				
1973	6.82	11.69			142.2680	142.2690				
1974	7.55	24.05			142.9070	140.9340				
1975	9.28	27.73			131.0470	131.4290				
1976	10.06	18.15			122.4040	122.5440				
1977	11.69	18.21			110.9040	110.9040				
1978	14.11	21.40			114.4730	114.4680				
1979	15.55	21.21			111.7760	111.7760				
1980	16.62	2.54			114.9420	114.9420				
1981	19.91	3.58			114.9300	114.9300				
1982	22.77	2.35			110.1740	110.1740				
1983	19.61	4.00			94.4800	94.4800				
1984	20.88	8.80			87.9600	87.9600				
1985	21.58	6.06			70.0800	70.0800				
1986	21.45	2.50			67.0900	67.0900				
1987	25.14	2.87			70.0900	70.0900				
1988	28.18	6.67			78.4200	78.4200				
1989	28.60	6.44			79.2500	79.2500				
1990	34.45	3.68			79.3110	79.3110				
1991	33.23	3.70			77.9100	77.9100				
1992	50.53	6.51			73.5298	73.5298				
1993	40.87	5.07			67.9312	67.9312				
1994	36.11	7.11			73.3267	73.3267				
1995	47.55	10.03			71.6932	71.6932				

2. IMPORTS BY BROAD ECONOMIC CATEGORY AND EXPORTS BY INDUSTRIAL ORIGIN. (PERCENTAGE OF TOTAL VALUE)
IMPORTATIONS PAR CATEGORIES ECONOMIQUES ET EXPORTATIONS PAR BRANCHE D'ACTIVITE.(EN POURCENTAGE DE LA VALEUR TOTALE)

IMPORTS – IMPORTATIONS

	1990	1991	1992	1993	1994	1995	1996
TOTAL IMPORTS–IMPORTATIONS TOTALES	100.	100.	100.				
1 FOOD BEV–ALIMENTATION BOISSONS	28.6	33.4	23.1				
11 PRIMARY–PRODUITS DE BASE	2.7	3.7	2.3				
111 FOR INDUSTRY–POUR L'INDUSTRIE	0.4	0.5	0.3				
112 FOR HOUSEHOLDS–POUR LES MENAGES	2.3	3.1	2.1				
12 PROCESSED–PRODUITS ELABORES	25.9	29.7	20.8				
121 FOR INDUSTRY–POUR L'INDUSTRIE	5.5	6.5	4.4				
122 FOR HOUSEHOLDS–POUR LES MENAGES	20.4	23.1	16.3				
2 IND SUPPLIES–APPROV INDUSTRIELS	18.9	14.5	9.6				
21 PRIMARY–PRODUITS DE BASE	0.8	0.6	0.3				
22 PROCESSED–PRODUITS ELABORES	18.1	13.9	9.3				
3 FUELS–COMBUSTIBLES	10.6	10.9	7.8				
31 PRIMARY–PRODUITS DE BASE	0.1	0.1	0.1				
32 PROCESSED–PRODUITS ELABORES	10.6	10.8	7.7				
321 MOTOR SPIRIT–ESSENCE	2.6	2.7	1.9				
322 OTHER–AUTRES	8.0	8.1	5.9				
4 MACHINERY–EQUIPEMENT	21.1	12.6	26.5				
41 CAPITAL EQUIPMENT–MACHINES	20.2	12.0	25.5				
42 PARTS–PIECES ACCESSOIRES	0.9	0.6	1.0				
5 TRANSPORT–TRANSPORT	7.1	11.1	21.3				
51 PASSENGER CARS–AUTOMOBILES							
52 OTHER–AUTRES	4.7	6.5	19.5				
521 INDUSTRIAL–INDUSTRIELS	3.8	5.8	18.7				
522 NON INDUSTRIAL–NON INDUSTRIEL	0.9	0.7	0.8				
53 PARTS–PIECES ACCESSOIRES	2.4	4.6	1.8				
6 CONSUM GOODS–BIENS CONSOMMATION	12.9	16.9	11.3				
61 DURABLE–DURABLES	1.9	2.1	1.2				
62 SEMI DURABLE–SEMI DURABLES	5.8	6.5	3.7				
63 NON DURABLE–NON DURABLES	5.2	8.3	6.4				
7 GOODS NES–BIENS NDA	0.7	0.6	0.4				

EXPORTS – EXPORTATIONS

	1990	1991	1992	1993	1994	1995	1996
TOTAL EXPORTS–EXPORTATIONS TOTALES	100.	100.	100.				
1 AGRICULTURE	74.5	79.4	82.5				
2 MINING QUARRY–INDUS EXTRACTIVES							
3 MANUFACTURING–IND MANUFACTUR	25.5	20.5	17.4				
31 FOOD BEV TOBACCO–ALIM BOISS TAB							
32 TEXTILES–INDUSTRIES TEXTILES							
33 WOOD & PRODUCTS–BOIS & PRODUITS							
34 PAPER & PRODUCTS–PAPIER & PRODT							
35 CHEMICALS–INDUSTRIES CHIMIQUES			0.0				
36 NON METAL MIN–MIN NON METAL							
37 BASIC METAL–IND METAL BASE	1.2		1.5				
38 METAL MANUF–MANUF METAL		9.7					
39 OTH MANUF IND–AUTRES MANUF	24.2	10.8	15.9				

3. TRADE BY PRINCIPAL COUNTRIES OF ORIGIN AND DESTINATION (VALUE IN THOUSAND U.S. DOLLARS)
ECHANGES SELON LES PRINCIPAUX PAYS D'ORIGINE ET DE DESTINATION (VALEUR EN MILLIERS DE DOLLARS EU)

COUNTRIES–PAYS	GENERAL IMPORTS F.O.B. IMPORTATIONS GENERALES F.O.B.				
	1989	1990	1991	1992	1993
World	22663	26916	25888	36710	27765
Africa	0		0		0
Americas	1467	1802	938	1083	780
Northern America	1460	1781	920	1059	771
LAIA	6	21	19	24	10
CACM					
Caribbean	1				
Rest of America					
As.ex F.USSR	5935	8761	7811	10841	7294
Eur.x F.USSR	506	501	502	3933	2050
EU	475	470	383	3865	2025
EFTA	27	29	119	60	25
East Europe	3	2	0	7	0
Other Europe					
Former USSR					
Oceania	14755	15852	16636	20854	17642
Australia/Australie	10397	8981	10442	14093	11864
Japan/Japon	3456	6360	4753	8319	4078
Fiji/Fidji	2870	5203	4447	4156	3165
New Zealand	1107	1505	1680	1986	1777
China/Chine	1088	1195	1358	1210	1622
USA/Etats–Unis d'Amer	1458	1781	920	1051	754
France,Monac	16	12	5	3467	1566
Hong Kong	626	349	377	365	239
Papua New Guinea	6	93	9	570	772
Singapore/Singapour	167	167	419	242	345
United Kingdom	326	286	287	192	149
Korea, Republic of	235	184	136	136	385
Germany/Allemagne	32	39	84	181	269
Thailand/Thaïlande	59	100	98	54	108
American Samoa	357	0		1	
India/Inde	41	36	107	94	75
Malaysia/Malaisie	1	16	47	122	80
Netherlands/Pays–Bas	34	113	1	21	29
Nauru	15	49	12	25	12
Bangladesh	10		24	19	10
Sweden/Suède	51	3	1	1	0
Denmark/Danemark	3	11	4	2	11
Pacific Isld (Tr Terr.)	3	15	6		
Tonga	0		6		1
Samoa	0				

COUNTRIES–PAYS	GENERAL EXPORTS F.O.B. EXPORTATIONS GENERALES F.O.B.				
	1989	1990	1991	1992	1993
Monde	5099	2876	2880	4734	3040
Afrique					
Amériques	265	444	643	582	598
Amérique du Nord	265	444	643	582	598
ALAI					
MCAC					
Caraïbes					
Autre Amérique					
Asie l'URSS exclus	7	42	1144	3285	615
Europe l'URSS exclus	2332	1231	567	282	1386
UE	2332	1231	567	282	1386
AELE		0			0
Europe de l'Est					
Autre de l'Europe					
Ancienne URSS					
Océanie	2495	1159	526	586	431
Bangladesh			1107	3162	7
Netherlands/Pays–Bas	2190	608			1192
Fiji/Fidji	1944	539	108	194	145
USA/Etats–Unis d'Amer	265	443	643	582	598
Denmark/Danemark	67	565	526	215	125
Australia/Australie	160	310	158	227	124
Hong Kong	0		35	32	523
Pacific Isld (Tr Terr.)	334	215	16		
New Zealand	29	33	48	75	33
United Kingdom	34	54	39	42	48
Samoa	0	6	159		
Singapore/Singapour		2		79	43
Nauru	0	12	14	51	18
France,Monac	40				7
Japan/Japon	2	7	1	0	34
Germany/Allemagne		4	2	13	14
India/Inde	0	10		4	
Tonga	8	4		0	
Korea, Republic of				0	2
Thailand/Thaïlande				1	
Papua New Guinea			0		

(VALUE AS PERCENTAGE OF WORLD TOTAL)(VALEURS EN POURCENTAGE DU TOTAL MONDIAL)

	1984	1985	1986	1987	1988	1989	1990	1991	1992	1993
Africa	0.0	0.1		0.0		0.0		0.0		0.0
Americas	2.7	2.6	3.7	4.8	4.9	6.5	6.7	3.6	2.9	2.8
Northern America	2.7	2.6	3.4	4.4	4.8	6.4	6.6	3.6	2.9	2.8
LAIA		0.0	0.3	0.5	0.1	0.0	0.1	0.1	0.1	0.0
CACM										
Caribbean						0.0				
Rest of America										
As.ex F.USSR	21.6	29.4	26.2	23.4	22.1	26.2	32.6	30.2	29.5	26.3
Eur.x F.USSR	9.5	6.9	4.0	4.6	3.4	2.2	1.9	1.9	10.7	7.4
EU	9.4	6.2	3.5	4.5	3.3	2.1	1.7	1.5	10.5	7.3
EFTA	0.1	0.7	0.4	0.1	0.0	0.1	0.1	0.5	0.2	0.1
East Europe	0.1	0.0	0.0		0.0	0.0	0.0	0.0	0.0	0.0
Other Europe										
Former USSR			0.0							
Oceania	66.2	61.0	66.1	67.2	69.6	65.1	58.9	64.3	56.8	63.5
Australia/Australie	40.7	38.8	40.5	43.7	43.8	45.9	33.4	40.3	38.4	42.7
Japan/Japon	16.6	21.2	19.4	11.9	10.9	15.3	23.6	18.4	22.7	14.7
Fiji/Fidji	8.1	6.1	11.9	7.3	15.3	12.7	19.3	17.2	11.3	11.4
New Zealand	10.3	6.4	5.0	7.2	4.9	4.9	5.6	6.5	5.4	6.4
China/Chine	2.0	3.6	2.8	4.5	5.2	4.8	4.4	5.2	3.3	5.8
USA/Etats–Unis d'Amer	2.6	2.6	3.3	4.3	4.8	6.4	6.6	3.6	2.9	2.7
France,Monac	4.8	0.1	0.0	0.2	0.0	0.1	0.0	0.0	9.4	5.6
Hong Kong	1.7	2.0	2.0	2.9	2.9	2.8	1.3	1.5	1.0	0.9
Papua New Guinea	3.3	1.1	1.6	0.2	0.0	0.0	0.3	0.0	1.6	2.8
Singapore/Singapour	0.3	1.5	0.3	0.3	0.4	0.7	0.6	1.6	0.7	1.2

	1984	1985	1986	1987	1988	1989	1990	1991	1992	1993
Afrique				0.1	0.9					
Amériques	2.6	8.4	19.5	11.6	3.8	5.2	15.4	22.3	12.3	19.7
Amérique du Nord	2.6	8.4	19.5	11.6	3.8	5.2	15.4	22.3	12.3	19.7
ALAI										
MCAC										
Caraïbes										
Autre Amérique										
Asie l'URSS exclus	0.0	22.0	1.3	2.1	1.6	0.1	1.5	39.7	69.4	20.2
Europe l'URSS exclus	52.5	45.4	17.9	38.2	62.6	45.7	42.8	19.7	5.9	45.6
UE	52.5	45.4	17.9	38.2	62.6	45.7	42.8	19.7	5.9	45.6
AELE							0.0			0.0
Europe de l'Est										
Autre de l'Europe										
Ancienne URSS										
Océanie	44.8	24.2	61.3	47.9	29.8	48.9	40.3	18.3	12.4	14.2
Bangladesh								38.4	66.8	0.2
Netherlands/Pays–Bas		20.0	6.4	36.1	60.8	43.0	21.1			39.2
Fiji/Fidji	0.0	3.5	46.2	16.1	22.5	38.1	18.7	3.7	4.1	4.8
USA/Etats–Unis d'Amer	2.6	8.4	19.5	11.6	3.8	5.2	15.4	22.3	12.3	19.7
Denmark/Danemark	52.5					1.3	19.7	18.3	4.5	4.1
Australia/Australie	0.6	0.7	3.1	20.8	2.4	3.1	10.8	5.5	4.8	4.1
Hong Kong	0.0		0.0			0.0		1.2	0.7	17.2
Pacific Isld (Tr Terr.)	19.0	12.3	1.4	0.2	0.3	6.5	7.5	0.5		
New Zealand	0.0	0.0	3.0	3.3	1.3	0.6	1.1	1.7	1.6	1.1
United Kingdom			0.7	1.9	1.1	0.7	1.9	1.4	0.9	1.6

4. General Imports F.O.B. by Commodities according to the S.I.T.C. (Rev. 2) in thousand U.S. Dollars
Importations Générales F.O.B. par Produits d'après la C.T.C.I. (Rév. 2) en milliers de Dollars E.U.

SITC CTCI	COMMODITY	1990 WEIGHT POIDS	1990 VALUE VALEUR	1991 WEIGHT POIDS	1991 VALUE VALEUR	1992 WEIGHT POIDS	1992 VALUE VALEUR	1993 WEIGHT POIDS	1993 VALUE VALEUR	PRODUIT
	ALL COMMODITIES		26916		25888		36710		27765	TOUS PRODUITS
0	FOOD AND LIVE ANIMALS		7148		7755		7740		8100	ALIMENTS,ANIMAUX VIVANTS
01	MEAT AND PREPARATIONS		1032		1472		1542		1542	VIANDES ET PREPARATIONS
011	MEAT FRESH,CHILLD,FROZEN	W 106	225	W 192	376	W 186	345	W 300	462	VIANDES FRAICHES,REF,CONGE
0114	POULTRY FRESH CHLLD,FRZN	W 77	115	W 155	251	W 160	248	W 257	330	VOLAILLES MORTES
014	MEAT PREPD,PRSVD,NES ETC	W 284	792	W 376	1082	W 413	1173	W 393	1053	CONSERVES DE VIANDES
0149	OTH PREPARD,PRESRVD MEAT	W 270	750	W 357	1019	W 405	1145	W 369	983	AUTRES PREP DE VIANDES
02	DAIRY PRODCTS,BIRDS'EGGS		536		570		520		530	PRODUITS LAITIERS,OEUFS
022	MILK AND CREAM	W 182	478	W 148	467	W 170	421		439	LAIT ET CREME
0224	MILK,CREAM PRESERVED ETC	W 173	470	W 138	459	W 164	416		424	LAIT,CREME CONS,CONC
02242	MILK DRY,1.5% FAT OR LES	W 67	272	W 79	360	W 73	308	W 86	345	LAIT POUDRE INF 1.5%
02249	MILK(EX DRY) PRSVD,SWEET	W 105	198	W 57	96	W 91	107	W 62	78	LAIT CONS,CONC SUCRE
023	BUTTER	W 11	29	W 36	86	W 33	74	W 21	51	BEURRE
03	FISH AND PREPARATIONS		256		234		289		310	POISSONS ET PREPARATIONS
037	FISH ETC PREPD,PRSVD NES	W 251	254	W 273	233	W 371	288	W 334	310	POIS,CRUST,MOL PREPARES
0371	FISH PREPARD,PRESRVD NES	W 240	235	W 268	226	W 371	288	W 318	299	CONSERVES DE POISSONS
04	CEREALS AND PREPARATIONS		3348		3238		3335		3132	CEREALES ET PRODUITS
042	RICE	W 4621	1978	W 4659	1893	W 5191	1935	W 5220	1896	RIZ
046	WHEAT ETC MEAL OR FLOUR	W 2552	744	W 2761	733	W 2751	816	W 2098	602	SEMOULE FARINE,FROMENT
047	OTHER CEREAL MEALS,FLOUR							W 1122	343	AUTRES SEMOULES,FARINES
048	CEREAL ETC PREPARATIONS	W 319	626	W 296	612	W 304	582	W 189	289	PREPTNS A BASE CEREALES
0481	PREPD BREAKFAST FOOD ETC	W 38	105	W 50	127	W 40	120	W 49	90	CEREALES TRAVAILLEES
0484	BAKERY PRODUCTS	W 212	303	W 173	262	W 161	224	W 139	197	PRODUITS DE BOULANGERIE
04841	BREAD,BISCUIT,COM WAFERS	W 178	221	W 129	167	W 140	172	W 101	112	PAINS,BISCUITS DE MER
04842	PASTRY, CAKES ETC	W 35	81	W 45	95	W 22	52	W 38	85	PATISSERIE ETC.
0488	OTH CEREAL PREPS,MALT EX	W 65	212	W 71	221	W 101	234			EXTRAITS DE MALT
05	VEGETABLES AND FRUIT		394		406		380		388	LEGUMES ET FRUITS
054	VEG ETC FRSH,SMPLY PRSVD		115	W 179	129	W 223	135	W 227	148	LEGUMES FRAIS,CONG,SECS
0545	OTHER FRESH VEGETABLES		91	W 132	107	W 160	107	W 169	123	AUTRES LEGUMES FRAIS,REF
056	VEGTBLES ETC PRSVD,PREPD	W 69	81	W 74	75	W 63	72	W 87	103	CONSERVES DE LEGUMES
058	FRUIT PRESERVED,PREPARED		139	W 116	136	W 98	113	W 49	64	CONSERVES DE FRUITS
0585	FRUIT OR VEGETABLE JUICE			W 89	79	W 82	78	W 26	26	JUS DE FRUITS
06	SUGAR AND PREPS,HONEY		789		1008		893		849	SUCRES ET PRODUITS
061	SUGAR AND HONEY	W 2288	634	W 2908	843	W 2770	731	W 2850	741	SUCRES ET MIEL
0611	RAW BEET AND CANE SUGAR	W 2277	625	W 2878	826	W 2744	721	W 2789	715	SUCRES BRUTS
062	SUGAR CANDY NON–CHOCLATE	W 40	155	W 40	165	W 42	162	W 34	108	SUCRERIES
07	COFFEE,TEA,COCOA,SPICES		343		383		320		410	CAFE,THE,CACAO,EPICES
071	COFFEE AND SUBSTITUTES	W 8	105	W 11	133	W 8	103	W 10	129	CAFE ET SUCCEDANES
074	TEA AND MATE	W 40	188	W 42	198	W 32	152	W 49	230	THE ET MATE
09	MISC EDIBLE PRODUCTS		377		386		367		878	PREP ALIMENTAIRES DIVERSES
091	MARGARINE AND SHORTENING	W 67	111	W 131	122	W 295	127	W 112	125	MARGARINE ET GRAISSES
0914	MARGARINE,EDIBLE FAT NES							W 112	125	MARGARINES,SIMILI SAINDOUX
098	EDIBLE PRODCTS,PREPS NES		265	W 166	264	W 159	240		753	PREP ALIMENTAIRES NDA
09804	SAUCES,MIXED SEASONINGS	W 79	109	W 88	90	W 69	72	W 252	330	SAUCES,ASSAISONNEMENTS
09809	MISC FOOD PREPRTIONS NES		65	W 16	57	W 18	51	W 172	321	PREP ALIMENTAIRES NDA
1	BEVERAGES AND TOBACCO		1196		1780		1841		1794	BOISSONS ET TABACS
11	BEVERAGES		585		878		795		803	BOISSONS
111	NON–ALCOHL BEVERAGES NES	W 213	153	W 270	195	W 159	129	W 223	158	BOISSONS NON ALCOOLIQUES
11102	FLAVORED WATERS NON–ALCO	W 212	153	W 266	192	W 158	128	W 218	153	LIMONADES,EAUX GAZEUSES
112	ALCOHOLIC BEVERAGES	W 511	432	W 798	683	W 808	666	W 861	645	BOISSONS ALCOOLIQUES
1123	BEER,ALE,STOUT,PORTER	W 492	331	W 779	568	W 796	592	W 849	582	BIERES
1124	DISTILLED ALCOHOLIC BEVS	W 11	80	W 11	85	W 7	63	W 7	51	ALCOOLS,EAUX–DE–VIE
12	TOBACCO AND MANUFACTURES		610		903		1046		992	TABACS BRUTS FABRIQUES
122	TOBACCO,MANUFACTURED	W 43	610	W 51	903	W 57	1046	W 70	992	TABACS FABRIQUES
1222	CIGARETTES	W 8	169	W 13	274	W 15	305	W 28	292	CIGARETTES
1223	OTH MANUFACTURED TOBACCO	W 34	440	W 39	629	W 43	741	W 40	668	TABACS FUMER,CHIQUER,PRISER
2	CRUDE MATERLS,EXCL FUELS		745		392		454		605	MAT BRUTES NON COMESTIBLES
24	CORK AND WOOD		565		264		361		410	LIEGE ET BOIS
247	OTH WOOD ROUGH,SQUARED		41	W 39	21	W 33	17	W 419	167	BOIS BRUTS EQUARRIS
248	WOOD SHAPED,SLEEPERS	W 764	522	W 416	243	W 822	343	W 2322	243	BOIS SIMPLEMENT TRAVAILLES
26	TEXTILE FIBRES AND WASTE		118		94		57		64	FIBRES TEXTILES
269	WASTE OF TEXTILE FABRICS		103	W 1117	86	W 659	51	W 369	30	FRIPERIE DRILLES,CHIFFONS
27	CRUDE FERTLZR,MINRLS NES		58		30		34		130	ENGRAIS MINERAUX BRUTS
278	OTHER CRUDE MINERALS	W 372	58	W 150	30	W 226	34	W 349	130	AUTRES MINERAUX BRUTS
2789	MINERALS CRUDE NES	W 112	13	W 18	9	W 8	4	W 121	97	MINERAUX BRUTS NDA
3	MINERAL FUELS ETC		2887		2829		2870		2059	COMBUSTIBLES MINERAUX LUB
33	PETROLEUM AND PRODUCTS		2866		2796		2848		2043	PETROLE ET DERIVES
334	PETROLEUM PRODUCTS,REFIN	W 9939	2843	W 9440	2795	W 10584	2842	W 9504	2042	PRODUITS RAFFINES
3341	GASOLINE,OTH LIGHT OILS	W 3114	1233	W 3628	1236	W 4207	1250	W 2377	593	ESSENCES POUR MOTEURS
33411	MOTOR,AVIATION SPIRIT	W 2167	697	W 2294	689	W 2402	681	W 1650	413	ESSENCES MOTEURS D'AVIONS
33412	SPIRIT TYPE JET FUEL	W 947	536	W 1334	547	W 1805	569	W 727	180	CARBUREACTEURS
3342	KEROSENE,OTH MEDIUM OILS	W 902	246	W 691	194	W 686	198	W 1041	291	PETR LAMPANTS,AUT HUIL
33421	KEROSENE INCL JET FUEL	W 902	246	W 691	194	W 686	198	W 1041	291	PETROLES LAMPANTS
3343	GAS OILS	W 5864	1300	W 5023	1255	W 5579	1302	W 5961	1070	GAS OILS
3345	LUBS,PETROLEUM OILS NES	W 59	65	W 98	110	W 112	92	W 126	88	HUILES LUBRIFIANTES
33451	LUBS(HIGH PETR CONT) ETC	W 59	65	W 98	110	W 112	92	W 126	88	HUILES LUBRIF,H LOURDES
4	ANIMAL,VEGETABLE OIL,FAT		117		65		69		81	HUILES,GRAISSES ANIM,VEG
5	CHEMCLS,RELATED PROD NES		1208		1250		1110		1669	PRODUITS CHIMIQUES
53	DYES,TANNING,COLOUR PROD		155		133		136		199	PROD TEINTURE,COLORANTS
533	PIGMENTS,PAINTS,ETC		150		132		134		195	PIGMENTS,PEINTURES,VERNIS
5334	VARNISHES,DISTEMPERS ETC	V 86	127	W 26	107	W 22	101	V 51	166	PEINTURES A L'EAU
541	*MEDICINAL,PHARM PRODUCT		349		390		337		615	PROD MEDICINAUX PHARMACEUT
5419	PHARMACEUTICAL GOODS NES		304		360		263		540	PREP,ART PHARMACEUTIQUES
54199	OTH PHARMACEUTICAL GOODS		304		360		263		540	AUT PREP PHARMACEUTIQUES
55	PERFUME,CLEANING ETC PRD		459		520		462		595	PROD POUR PARFUM,TOILETTE
553	PERFUMERY,COSMETICS,ETC		157		152		141		233	PRODUITS DE PARFUMERIE
554	SOAP,CLEANSING ETC PREPS		298		364		318		359	SAVONS,PRODUITS DETERSIFS
5541	SOAPS	W 253	295	W 316	359	W 291	316	W 365	354	SAVONS,PROD TENSIO–ACTIFS
59	CHEMICAL MATERIALS NES		110		97		99		166	MAT PROD CHIMIQUES NDA
6	BASIC MANUFACTURES		3195		3205		2943		3407	ART MANUFACTURES
62	RUBBER MANUFACTURES NES		179		284		160		214	CAOUTCHOUC MANUFACTURE
625	RUBBER TYRES, TUBES ETC	N 10288	148	N 19307	192	N 12875	142	N 14334	184	PNEUS CAOUTCHOUC VULCANISE
6251	TYRES NEW FOR MOTOR CARS	N 3025	131	N 6242	155	N 4840	110	N 7371	161	PNEUS POUR VOITURES
63	WOOD,CORK MANUFACTRS NES		233		161		310		372	OUVRAGES LIEGE ET BOIS
634	VENEERS,PLYWOOD,ETC		157	W 263	146		280	A 1	284	PLACAGES,CONTRE–PLAQUES
635	WOOD MANUFACTURES NES		76		15		30		87	ART MANUF EN BOIS NDA
64	PAPER,PAPERBOARD AND MFR		334		456		425		381	PAPIERS,CARTONS & OUVRAGES
641	PAPER AND PAPERBOARD		94		143		76		105	PAPIERS ET CARTONS
6419	CONVERTED PAPER ETC NES		46		136		68		92	PAP,CART TRANSFORMES NDA
64192	COMPOSITE PAPER ETC,BULK								92	PAP,CART SIMPL ASSEMBLE
642	PAPER,ETC,PRECUT,ARTS OF		239		313		349		276	PAP,CARTONS DECOUPES

4. General Imports F.O.B. by Commodities according to the S.I.T.C. (Rev. 2) in thousand U.S. Dollars
Importations Générales F.O.B. par Produits d'après la C.T.C.I. (Rév. 2) en milliers de Dollars E.U.

SITC CTCI	COMMODITY	1990 WEIGHT POIDS	1990 VALUE VALEUR	1991 WEIGHT POIDS	1991 VALUE VALEUR	1992 WEIGHT POIDS	1992 VALUE VALEUR	1993 WEIGHT POIDS	1993 VALUE VALEUR	PRODUIT
6422	CORRESPONDENCE STATIONRY				293		301		245	ARTICLES CORRESPONDANCE
6428	PAPER ETC ARTICLES NES		222							OUVRAGES EN PATE A PAPIER
65	TEXTILE YARN,FABRICS,ETC		646		840		670		664	FILS,TISSUS,ARTICLES TEXTILE
651	TEXTILE YARN		83		97		41		72	FILS TEXTILES
652	COTTON FABRICS,WOVEN	A 254	237	A 243	245	A 268	244	A 272	232	TISSUS DE COTON
653	WOVN MAN–MADE FIB FABRIC		74		26		15	A 168	131	TISSUS FIBRES SYNTH,ARTIF
654	OTH WOVEN TEXTILE FABRIC	A 20	26	A 67	97	A 73	91	A 25	22	TISSUS AUT COTON SYNT,ARTIF
656	LACE,RIBBONS,TULLE,ETC		86		48		27		17	TULLES,BRODERIE
657	SPECIAL TXTL FABRC,PRODS		81		139		113		77	TISSUS SPECIAUX
6575	CORDAGE AND MANUFACTURES	W 17	58	W 10	125	W 27	102	W 11	61	FICELLES,CORDES,CORDAGES
65751	CORDAGE,CABLE,ROPE,TWINE	W 15	38	W 6	91	W 14	60	W 7	28	CORDAGES TRESSES OU NON
658	TEXTILE ARTICLES NES		54		169		137		99	ART FACONNES MAT TEXTILES
6584	LINENS ETC		41		102		52		69	LINGE DE MAISON
66	NONMETAL MINERAL MFS NES		404		436		231		468	ART MIN NON METALLIQUES
661	LIME,CEMENT,BLDG PRODS	W 3232	305	W 2830	363	W 1369	166	W 2813	308	CHAUX,CIMENTS MAT CONSTR
6612	CEMENT	W 3232	305	W 2830	363	W 1369	166	W 2813	308	CIMENTS HYDRAULIQUES
67	IRON AND STEEL		275		156		247		268	FER ET ACIER
673	IRON,STEEL SHAPES ETC	W 195	135	W 12	21	W 28	29	W 128	109	BARRES,PROFIL FER,ACIER
677	IRN,STL WIRE(EXCL W ROD)	W 34	19	W 51	59	W 98	129	W 43	96	FILS EN FER,ACIER
68	NON–FERROUS METALS		8		60		132		80	METAUX NON FERREUX
684	ALUMINIUM	W 4	8	W 17	47	W 56	128	W 34	77	ALUMINIUM
69	METAL MANUFACTURES NES		1103		812		769		961	ART MANUFACT EN METAL NDA
691	STRUCTURES AND PARTS NES	W 103	201	W 104	236	W 102	156	W 205	279	CONSTRUCT FER,ACIER,ALU
693	WIRE PRODUCTS NON ELECTR	W 69	135	W 37	56		120	W 108039	191	OUVRAGES FILS METALLIQUES
6931	WIRE CABLES, ROPES ETC	W 16	23	W 4	8	W 4	4	W 42838	85	CORDAGES EN FILS DE FER
6935	METAL FENCING,GAUZE,ETC	W 45	68	W 30	45	W 63	115	W 64329	103	TOILES EN FER,ACIER,CUIVRE
695	TOOLS		206		144		114		114	OUTILS A MAIN
6953	OTHER HAND TOOLS		191							AUTRES OUTILS A MAIN
69539	HAND TOOLS ETC NES		191							OUTILLAGE A MAIN NDA
697	BASE MTL HOUSEHOLD EQUIP		91		159		124		99	ART MENAGE MET COMMUNS
699	BASE METAL MFRS NES		330		91		114		124	ART MANUFACTURES MET NDA
6991	LOCKSMITHS WARES,ETC		174		48		59		84	ARTICLES DE SERRURERIE
69911	LOCKS,KEYS AND PARTS								84	SERRURES,VERROUS,CADENAS
6999	OTHR BASE METAL MFRS ETC		148		32		42		38	OUVRAGES EN TUNGST,MOLYB
7	MACHINES,TRANSPORT EQUIP		5131		6421		17352		6854	MACHINES MATERIEL TRANSPORT
71	POWER GENERATING EQUIPMT		474		526		1214		466	MACHINES GENERATRICES
713	INTRNL COMBUS PSTN ENGIN		227		373		223		266	MOTEURS EXPL COMB INT, PIECE
7133	MARINE PISTON ENGINES	N 212	199	N 319	282	N 180	160	N 631	211	MOTEURS EXPL POUR BATEAUX
71331	—— OUTBOARD	N 209	192	N 319	282	N 180	160			MOTEURS BATEAUX HORSBORD
7139	PISTON ENGINE PARTS NES		22		88		52		42	PIECES POUR 713.2,3,8
716	ROTATING ELECTRIC PLANT		197		138		930		185	APP ELECTR ROTATIFS,PIECES
7162	AC MTRS,GENRTRS,GEN SETS	N 92	142							MOTEURS ELECTRIQUES
72	MACHS FOR SPCL INDUSTRYS		325		496		266		368	MAC SPECIALES POUR INDUST
721	AGRIC MACHY,EXC TRACTORS		70		112		28		17	MACHINES AGRICOLES
723	CIVIL ENGNEERG EQUIP ETC	N 1	132	N 16	158	N 4	144	N 6	228	APPAREILS DE GENIE CIVIL
728	OTH MACHY FOR SPCL INDUS		75		146		34		37	AUT MACH IND PARTICULIERES
73	METALWORKING MACHINERY		86		18		23		30	MACH TRAVAIL DES METAUX
736	METALWORKING MACH–TOOLS	N 300	86	N 61	18		23		30	MACH–OUTILS TRAVAIL METAUX
74	GENRL INDUSTRL MACHY NES		910		1392		703		520	MACH APP INDUSTRIE
741	HEATING,COOLING EQUIPMNT		445		897		256		116	MACH CHAUFFAGE,PIECES
7413	INDUS FURNACES ETC,PARTS		281		49		27		8	FOURS IND,LABOR,PIECES
7414	NONDOM REFRIG EQUIPT,PTS		104		780		139		26	MAT PRODUCTION DU FROID
74141	REFRIG EQUIP NONDOMESTIC				780		139			REFIG INDUSTRIELS
74149	PTS NES OF REFRIG EQUIPT		104							PIECES POUR MACH FROID
742	PUMPS FOR LIQUIDS ETC		61		144		151		77	POMPES MOTO–POMPES
7428	OTHER PUMPS FOR LIQUIDS	N 88	50	N 211	90	N 1045	149	N 218	70	AUTRES POMPES POUR LIQ
743	PUMPS NES,CENTRFUGES ETC		54		38		147		39	POMPES COMPRES,VENT ETC
7431	PUMPS FOR GASES ETC	N 2921	45		38		147	N 1285	36	POMPES AIR A VIDE,COMPRES
744	MECHANICAL HANDLING EQU		253		232		33		190	EQUIP MANUTENTION PIECES
7441	FORK LIFT TRCKS,ETC,PTS		17		113		8	N 5	94	CHARIOTS POUR USINES ETC
74411	FORK LIFT TRUCKS ETC	N 2	16		113		8			CHARIOTS POUR LES GARES
7449	PTS NES OF MACHY OF 7442		232		87		22		95	PIECES DU 744.2
75	OFFICE MACHNES,ADP EQUIP		267		223		272		284	MACH BUREAU TRAIT AUTOM
752	AUTOMTIC DATA PROC EQUIP	N 79	100	N 50	117	N 93	147	N 183	182	MACH TRAIT INFORMATION
759	OFFICE,ADP MCH PTS,ACCES		87		31		25		51	PIECES DU 751 ET 752
76	TELECOMM,SOUND EQUIPMENT		316		212		6336		1197	EQUIPMENT DE TELECOM
764	TELECOM EQPT,PTS,ACC NES	N 379	180	N 103	116	N 2801	6251	N 1761	1086	EQUIP TELECOM,PIECES
77	ELECTRIC MACHNRY NES ETC		1293		1449		1068		1818	MACH APP ELECT NDA
771	ELECTRIC POWER MACHY NES		239	N 263	25	N 273	5	N 563	46	MACH PROD,TRANS ELECTR
772	SWITCHGEAR ETC,PARTS NES		100		768		375		576	APP COUPURE,SECT ETC
773	ELECTR DISTRIBUTNG EQUIP		502		120		67		81	EQUIPMT DISTRIBUTION ELECT
7731	INSULATED WIRE,CABLE ETC		502		120		67		81	FILS,CABLES ISOLES ELECT
775	HOUSEHOLD TYPE EQUIP NES		121		169		90		193	MACH,APP USAGE DOMESTQUE
7752	DOM REFRIGERATRS,FREEZRS	N 151	43	N 299	135	N 169	57	N 662	69	REFRIG,CONGEL MENAGER
776	TRANSISTORS,VALVES,ETC		47		43		225		8	LAMPES,TUBES,VALVES
778	ELECTRICAL MACHINERY NES		283		324		306		914	AUTRES MACH ELECT NDA
7781	BATTERIES,ACCUMULATORS	N 877312	144	N 888386	167	N 1038961	190	N 944559	283	PILES ET ACCUMULATEURS
77811	PRIMARY BATTERIES,CELLS	N 876537	105	N 887408	128	N 1038243	135	N 943916	239	PILES ELECTRIQUES,PIECES
7788	OTH ELEC MACHY,EQUIP NES		128		130		82		584	AUT MACH APP ELEC NDA
77886	OTH ELEC MACHINERY NES								584	AUT MACH APP ELECTRIQUES
78	ROAD VEHICLES		1130		2040		1443		2107	VEHICULES ROUTIERS
781	PASS MOTOR VEH EXC BUSES							N 1402	1024	AUTO TRANSPORT PERSONNES
782	LORRIES,SPCL MTR VEH NES	N 96	583	N 82	1194	N 116	815	N 27	402	VEHICULES SPECIAUX,MARCH
7821	LORRIES,TRUCKS	N 96	583	N 82	1194	N 116	815	N 27	402	VEHICULES TRANSP MARCHAND
783	ROAD MOTOR VEHICLES NES	N 16	99	N 32	284	N 17	126	N 35	284	VEHICULES ROUTIERS NDA
7831	BUSES	N 14	86	N 32	284	N 17	126	N 23	203	VOITURES TRANSPORT COMMUN
784	MOTOR VEH PRTS,ACCES NES		154		357		161		154	PIECES 722,781,782,783
785	CYCLES,ETC MOTRZD OR NOT		268		200		332		213	MOTOCYCLES SCOOTERS
7852	CYCLES, ETC NON–MOTOR	N 3945	204	N 1869	117	N 3751	200	N 1995	139	VELOCIPEDES SANS MOTEUR
79	OTHR TRANSPORT EQUIPMENT		328		65		6028		64	AUTRE MATERIEL TRANSPORT
791	RAILWAY VEHICLES		169		1					VEHIC MAT CHEMINS DE FER
793	SHIPS AND BOATS ETC	N 22	144		17		6026		46	NAVIRES BATEAUX,ETC
7932	SHIPS AND BOATS NES	N 21	137	N 6	17		5903	N 17	43	NAVIRES ET BATEAUX
7938	TUGS,SPECIAL VESSELS ETC	N 1	6		1		122		3	REMORQUEURS,BATEAUX SPEC
8	MISC MANUFACTURED GOODS		5137		2038		2184		3042	ART MANUFACTURES DIVERS
812	*PLUMBG,HEATNG,LGHTNG EQ		92		78		101		91	APPAR SANITAIRES CHAUFFAGE
8124	LIGHTING EQUIPMENT NES		86		72		91		78	APPAREILS ECLAIRAGE ETC
821	*FURNITURE,PARTS THEREOF		164		139		119		985	MEUBLES ET PIECES
84	CLOTHING AND ACCESSORIES		362		494		345		227	VETEMENTS
842	MENS OUTERWEAR NOT KNIT		91		177		94			VET DESSUS POUR HOMMES
844	UNDER GARMENTS NOT KNIT		106		86		69		31	VETEMENT DESSOUS MAT TEX

Kiribati

4. General Imports F.O.B. by Commodities according to the S.I.T.C. (Rev. 2) in thousand U.S. Dollars
Importations Générales F.O.B. par Produits d'après la C.T.C.I. (Rév. 2) en milliers de Dollars E.U.

SITC CTCI	COMMODITY	1990		1991		1992		1993		PRODUIT
		WEIGHT POIDS	VALUE VALEUR	WEIGHT POIDS	VALUE VALEUR	WEIGHT POIDS	VALUE VALEUR	WEIGHT POIDS	VALUE VALEUR	
87	PRECISION INSTRUMNTS NES		3168		48		413		139	INSTRUM,APPAR SCIENT NDA
872	MEDICAL INSTRUMENTS NES		3059		3		23		10	INSTR,APP MEDIC–CHIR NDA
874	MEASURNG,CONTROLNG INSTR		70		40		388		128	INSTRUMENTS DE MESURE
8742	MEASUR,DRAW ETC INST,PTS								128	INST DESSIN,TRACAGE,PCS
88	PHOTO EQU,OPTICL GDS ETC		127		58		82		75	APP,FOURN PHOTO,OP,MONTR
884	OPTICAL GOODS NES		87		12		17		7	ELEMENTS OPTIQ,ART LUNET
8841	OPTICAL ELEMENTS		84		12		17			LENTILLES,PRISMES,MIROIR
89	MISC MANUFCTRD GOODS NES		1142		1118		1062		1441	ART MANUFACTURES DIVERS
892	PRINTED MATTER		121		147		252		588	IMPRIMES
893	ARTICLES OF PLASTIC NES		529		456		367		348	OUVRAGES EN MAT DIVIS 58
8931	PLSTC PACKG CONTNRS,LIDS		367		274		208			ART TRANSP EMBALLAGE ETC
8939	MISC PLASTIC ARTICLES		162		182		159		348	ART DIVERS EN MAT DIV 58
89399	OTHR PLASTC ARTICLES NES		162		182		159		348	AUT OUV MAT DIV 58
894	TOYS,SPORTING GOODS,ETC		245		222		200		142	VOITURES ENFANTS,JOUETS
8947	OTH SPORT GDS,FAIR AMUSM		199		190		171		123	AUT ART DE SPORT
89471	FISHNG,HUNTNG EQUIP NES		162		146		140		91	HAMECONS ET EPUISETTES
895	OFFICE SUPPLIES NES		80		74		66		104	ART PAPET NDA
899	OTHER MANUFACTURED GOODS		140		191		147		228	AUT ART MANUF DIVERS NDA
8998	SMALLWARES,TOILETRYS ETC		27		63		31		101	ART MERCERIE,TOILETTE
89983	BUTTONS,STUDS,ETC								101	BOUTONS,BOUTONS–PRESSION
9	GOODS NOT CLASSD BY KIND		154		153		145		154	ART TRANSACT NON CLASSES
931	*SPECIAL TRANSACTIONS		154		153		145		150	TRANS.SPECIALES

5. General Exports F.O.B. by Commodities according to the S.I.T.C. (Rev. 2) in thousand U.S. Dollars
Exportations Générales F.O.B. par Produits d'après la C.T.C.I. (Rév. 2) en milliers de Dollars E.U.

SITC CTCI	COMMODITY	1990		1991		1992		1993		PRODUIT
		WEIGHT POIDS	VALUE VALEUR	WEIGHT POIDS	VALUE VALEUR	WEIGHT POIDS	VALUE VALEUR	WEIGHT POIDS	VALUE VALEUR	
	ALL COMMODITIES		2876		2880		4734		3040	TOUS PRODUITS
0	FOOD AND LIVE ANIMALS		779		497		537		1281	ALIMENTS,ANIMAUX VIVANTS
03	FISH AND PREPARATIONS		779		497		537		1281	POISSONS ET PREPARATIONS
034	FISH,FRESH,CHILLED,FROZN	W 861	753		478		451	W 354	711	POISSON FRAIS, REFRIG,CONG
0341	FISH FRSH,CHLLD,EX FILLT							W 354	711	POISSON FRAIS,REFRIGERE
035	FISH SALTED,DRIED,SMOKED	W 1	25	W 1	19	W 6	86	W 2	83	POISSON SECHE,SALE,FUME
03503	FISH(EX COD)DRIED,SALTED							W 2	83	POISSONS SECHES,SALES
036	SHELL FISH FRESH,FROZEN							W 97	487	CRUSTACES,MOLLUSQUES
2	CRUDE MATERLS,EXCL FUELS		1364		2073		3370		1346	MAT BRUTES NON COMESTIBLES
22	OIL SEEDS,OLEAGINOUS FRT		799		1266		3162		1192	GRAINES,FRUITS OLEAGINEUX
223	SEEDS FOR OTH FIXED OILS	W 4682	799	W 7817	1266	W 9907	3162	W 6352	1192	GRAINES AUTRES HUILES FIXES
2231	COPRA	W 4682	799	W 7817	1266	W 9907	3162	W 6352	1192	COPRAH
28	METALLIFEROUS ORES,SCRAP				280				8	MINERAIS METAL,DECHETS
282	IRON AND STEEL SCRAP			W 456	280			W 19	8	FERRAILLES
29	CRUDE ANIMAL,VEG MAT NES		565		526		208		147	MATIERES BRUTES ANIM,VEGET
292	CRUDE VEG MATERIALS NES	W 798	565	W 693	526	W 388	208	W 373	147	MAT BRUTES VEGETALES NDA
2924	VEG USED IN PHARMACY ETC	W 798	565	W 693	526					PLANTES MEDICINALES
2929	OTH CRUDE VEG MATERIALS					W 388	208	W 373	147	MATIERES VEGETALES NDA
29298	OTH CRD VEG MATERIAL NES							W 373	147	PRODUITS ORIGINE VEGET NDA
6	BASIC MANUFACTURES		36				72			ART MANUFACTURES
68	NON-FERROUS METALS		36				72			METAUX NON FERREUX
684	ALUMINIUM					W 79	72			ALUMINIUM
689	NON-FER BASE METALS NES	W 41	36							AUT METAUX NON FERREUX
6899	BASE METALS NES,CERMETS	W 41	36							METAUX COMMUNS NDA
8	MISC MANUFACTURED GOODS		22		7		9		16	ART MANUFACTURES DIVERS
88	PHOTO EQU,OPTICL GDS ETC		20		7		2		16	APP,FOURN PHOTO,OP,MONTR
883	DEVELOPED CINEMA FILM	N 75	20	N 15	7				16	FILMS CINE IMPRES NEG,POS
9	GOODS NOT CLASSD BY KIND		675		304		747		396	ART TRANSACT NON CLASSES
931	*SPECIAL TRANSACTIONS		675		304		747		396	TRANS.SPECIALES

1. HISTORICAL SERIES, 1961–1996 SPECIAL TRADE, IMPORTS C.I.F., EXPORTS F.O.B.
SERIES HISTORIQUES, 1961–1996 COMMERCE SPECIAL, IMPORTATIONS C.A.F., EXPORTATIONS F.O.B

YEAR ANNEE	VALUE IN MILLION U.S. DOLLARS / VALEUR EN MILLION U.S. DOLLARS: MERCHANDISE – MARCHANDISE IMPORTS	MERCHANDISE – MARCHANDISE EXPORTS	GOLD – OR IMPORTS	GOLD – OR EXPORTS	CONVERSION FACTORS FACTEURS DE CONVERSION CENTS E.U. PAR IMPORTS	CONVERSION FACTORS EXPORTS	INDEX NUMBERS – INDICES: QUANTUM IMPORTS	QUANTUM EXPORTS	UNIT VALUE / VALEUR UNITAIRE IMPORTS	UNIT VALUE / VALEUR UNITAIRE EXPORTS
1961	316.10	40.90								
1962	421.80	54.80								
1963	560.30	86.80					35	33	92	74
1964	404.40	119.10					25	45	93	76
1965	463.40	175.10					28	63	95	79
1966	716.40	250.30					44	82	94	87
1967	996.20	320.20					60	101	96	90
1968	1462.50	455.40					91	139	94	93
1969	1822.80	622.50					20	6	41	48
1970	1983.30	835.20					21	8	43	50
1971	2393.60	1067.60					25	10	42	49
1972	2522.00	1624.10					26	16	43	50
1973	4240.30	3225.00					33	25	58	63
1974	6851.80	4460.40					34	27	90	80
1975	7274.40	5081.00					18	16	59	44
1976	8773.60	7715.10					22	22	58	49
1977	10810.50	10046.50					26	26	59	54
1978	14971.90	12710.60					35	30	63	60
1979	20338.60	15055.50					39	30	77	71
1980	22291.60	17504.90					33	33	97	75
1981	26131.40	21253.80					37	39	102	77
1982	24250.80	21853.30					37	41	95	75
1983	26192.00	24445.10					42	48	90	72
1984	30631.40	29244.90					49	55	91	74
1985	31135.70	30283.10					51	60	88	72
1986	31598.64	34747.24					56	67	91	76
1987	41157.03	47358.22					67	83	88	80
1988	51968.66	60993.43					77	93	98	91
1989	61476.98	62384.04					88	94	100	100
1990	69739.79	64879.61					100	100	100	100
1991	81525.01	71870.00					117	110	104	104
1992	81775.01	76632.00					119	119	109	109
1993	83800.00	82236.00					127	127	107	111
1994	102348.00	96013.01					154	146	108	115
1995	135119.00	125058.00					187	181	113	116
1996	150676.50	130345.70					209	216	117	106

2. IMPORTS BY BROAD ECONOMIC CATEGORY AND EXPORTS BY INDUSTRIAL ORIGIN. (PERCENTAGE OF TOTAL VALUE)
IMPORTATIONS PAR CATEGORIES ECONOMIQUES ET EXPORTATIONS PAR BRANCHE D'ACTIVITE.(EN POURCENTAGE DE LA VALEUR TOTALE)

IMPORTS – IMPORTATIONS

	1990	1991	1992	1993	1994	1995	1996
TOTAL IMPORTS–IMPORTATIONS TOTALES	100.	100.	100.	100.	100.	100.	100.
1 FOOD BEV–ALIMENTATION BOISSONS	3.7	4.3	4.3	4.1	4.3	3.7	4.1
11 PRIMARY–PRODUITS DE BASE	2.4	3.0	2.8	2.6	2.8	2.3	2.6
111 FOR INDUSTRY–POUR L'INDUSTRIE	1.3	1.3	1.4	1.4	1.4	1.0	1.3
112 FOR HOUSEHOLDS–POUR LES MENAGES	1.1	1.7	1.4	1.2	1.4	1.2	1.3
12 PROCESSED–PRODUITS ELABORES	1.3	1.3	1.5	1.5	1.5	1.5	1.5
121 FOR INDUSTRY–POUR L'INDUSTRIE	0.8	0.7	0.7	0.7	0.7	0.6	0.6
122 FOR HOUSEHOLDS–POUR LES MENAGES	0.5	0.6	0.8	0.8	0.8	0.8	0.9
2 IND SUPPLIES–APPROV INDUSTRIELS	39.9	38.9	35.7	36.4	35.5	36.2	32.7
21 PRIMARY–PRODUITS DE BASE	11.2	9.7	8.9	9.1	7.7	7.5	6.7
22 PROCESSED–PRODUITS ELABORES	28.7	29.2	26.8	27.4	27.8	28.7	26.0
3 FUELS–COMBUSTIBLES	15.8	15.7	18.0	18.0	15.2	14.3	16.7
31 PRIMARY–PRODUITS DE BASE	12.2	13.1	15.1	14.7	12.0	11.4	13.6
32 PROCESSED–PRODUITS ELABORES	3.6	2.6	2.8	3.3	3.2	3.0	3.2
321 MOTOR SPIRIT–ESSENCE	0.7		1.4	1.6			
322 OTHER–AUTRES	2.9	2.6	1.4	1.8	3.2	3.0	3.2
4 MACHINERY–EQUIPEMENT	30.9	31.1	31.2	30.3	32.5	34.0	34.6
41 CAPITAL EQUIPMENT–MACHINES	21.2	21.4	20.8	20.5	22.6	23.5	23.6
42 PARTS–PIECES ACCESSOIRES	9.7	9.7	10.4	9.7	9.9	10.5	11.0
5 TRANSPORT–TRANSPORT	5.4	5.8	6.4	6.0	7.1	6.3	6.0
51 PASSENGER CARS–AUTOMOBILES	0.1	0.0	0.1	0.1	0.1	0.2	0.3
52 OTHER–AUTRES	2.5	2.7	3.2	2.5	3.1	2.6	2.9
521 INDUSTRIAL–INDUSTRIELS	2.5	2.7	3.2	2.5	3.1	2.6	2.9
522 NON INDUSTRIAL–NON INDUSTRIEL	0.0	0.0	0.0	0.0	0.0	0.0	0.0
53 PARTS–PIECES ACCESSOIRES	2.8	3.0	3.1	3.4	3.9	3.5	2.8
6 CONSUM GOODS–BIENS CONSOMMATION	3.8	3.7	3.9	4.5	4.9	5.1	5.6
61 DURABLE–DURABLES	1.3	1.1	1.0	1.2	1.2	1.2	1.3
62 SEMI DURABLE–SEMI DURABLES	1.6	1.7	1.9	2.2	2.5	2.7	3.1
63 NON DURABLE–NON DURABLES	0.9	0.9	1.0	1.1	1.1	1.1	1.3
7 GOODS NES–BIENS NDA	0.5	0.6	0.5	0.7	0.5	0.3	0.3

EXPORTS – EXPORTATIONS

	1990	1991	1992	1993	1994	1995	1996
TOTAL EXPORTS–EXPORTATIONS TOTALES	100.	100.	100.	100.	100.	100.	100.
1 AGRICULTURE	2.6	2.5	2.1	1.7	1.6	1.4	1.3
2 MINING QUARRY–INDUS EXTRACTIVES	0.2	0.2	0.2	0.2	0.2	0.1	0.1
3 MANUFACTURING–IND MANUFACTUR	97.2	97.3	97.7	98.1	98.2	98.5	98.6
31 FOOD BEV TOBACCO–ALIM BOISS TAB	1.3	1.2	1.2	1.2	1.2	1.2	1.4
32 TEXTILES–INDUSTRIES TEXTILES	30.0	27.7	25.6	23.0	20.8	16.8	16.1
33 WOOD & PRODUCTS–BOIS & PRODUITS	0.2	0.2	0.1	0.1	0.1	0.1	0.1
34 PAPER & PRODUCTS–PAPIER & PRODT	0.8	0.7	0.8	0.8	1.0	1.1	1.1
35 CHEMICALS–INDUSTRIES CHIMIQUES	8.6	9.8	11.6	11.8	11.8	12.4	13.6
36 NON METAL MIN–MIN NON METAL	1.0	0.9	0.8	0.8	0.7	0.6	0.6
37 BASIC METAL–IND METAL BASE	6.4	6.1	6.7	6.7	5.8	5.4	5.1
38 METAL MANUF–MANUF METAL	45.2	47.3	48.0	51.1	54.5	58.9	58.8
39 OTH MANUF IND–AUTRES MANUF	3.7	3.4	3.0	2.5	2.1	1.9	1.8

3. TRADE BY PRINCIPAL COUNTRIES OF PRODUCTION AND LAST DESTINATION (VALUE IN THOUSAND U.S. DOLLARS)
ECHANGES SELON LES PRINCIPAUX PAYS DE PRODUCTION ET DE DERNIERE DESTINATION (VALEUR EN MILLIERS DE DOLLARS EU)

COUNTRIES–PAYS	SPECIAL IMPORTS C.I.F. IMPORTATIONS SPECIALES C.A.F					COUNTRIES–PAYS	SPECIAL EXPORTS F.O.B. EXPORTATIONS SPECIALES F.O.B.				
	1992	1993	1994	1995	1996		1992	1993	1994	1995	1996
World	81758356	83793990	102342559	135112928	150334321	Monde	76631487	82232153	96007709	125056492	129714569
Africa	1080200	954017	1428042	2271708	2865818	Afrique	2577321	2004107	3146096	3060248	3356065
Americas	22376384	22004683	26860341	36969784	40419143	Amériques	24660606	24429601	28367606	33291040	31797179
Northern America	19888408	19644528	23604193	33022801	36043882	Amérique du Nord	19762931	19736073	22094824	26182775	23130964
LAIA	2034866	2006415	2547508	3435334	3703528	ALAI	2564563	3162466	3785719	4280155	4568912
CACM	22367	26806	36778	50203	43346	MCAC	218121	251323	287707	324949	356892
Caribbean	57027	43960	62634	45727	74223	Caraïbes	261888	186147	221074	244899	537065
Rest of America	373716	282975	609228	415719	554163	Autre Amérique	1853102	1093591	1978282	2258261	3203346
As.ex F.USSR	42019507	43111275	51220242	66345749	72164160	Asie l'URSS exclus	36572488	42457217	49119458	66037260	70635140
Eur.x F.USSR	11493127	11995290	15852814	20264991	24111754	Europe l'URSS exclus	10757997	10928721	12339133	18648597	18362368
EU	10473827	11124077	14537927	18192773	21206597	UE	9832505	9941853	11248629	16304312	15376952
EFTA	831557	722526	1007870	1681496	2505033	AELE	535731	328075	423702	965860	953101
East Europe	170129	117343	251877	300602	329626	Europe de l'Est	309907	557773	586665	1132426	1786043
Other Europe	172	200	516	33206	19680	Autre de l'Europe	25330	49601	21541	114244	59365
Former USSR	586145	1120263	1521510	2286761	2300225	Ancienne URSS	493687	774930	1263786	1787033	2780869
Oceania	3807415	4357469	4787705	6050472	7405575	Océanie	1346560	1404396	1507969	1897002	2443062
Japan/Japon	19457570	20015237	25388468	32604105	31447758	USA/Etats–Unis d'Amer	18153105	18218621	20703449	24343751	21925609
USA/Etats–Unis d'Amer	18319023	17951660	21598616	30418743	33319820	Japan/Japon	11599451	11564397	13522851	17048846	15766820
China/Chine	3724743	3928572	5462720	7400943	8538223	Hong Kong	5909029	6430766	8014737	10681996	11130967
Germany/Allemagne	3742532	3954694	5159377	6583839	7239188	China/Chine	2653639	5150992	6202986	9143588	11377060
Saudi Arabia	3797384	3734746	3815521	5432072	6666853	Singapore/Singapour	3221772	3109470	4151772	6689351	6438779
Australia/Australie	3077431	3344308	3780867	4897114	6271664	Germany/Allemagne	2876978	3592794	4313491	5965217	4705163
Indonesia/Indonésie	2291970	2588386	2842867	3325220	4013022	Indonesia/Indonésie	1934667	2094819	2539694	2957855	3198051
Malaysia/Malaisie	1758214	1946508	1875974	2515191	3006505	Malaysia/Malaisie	1135884	1429970	1651687	2950889	4333016
Canada	1568454	1692515	2004292	2603484	2723338	United Kingdom	1829720	1661128	1782589	2874016	3221748
Italy/Italie	1348478	1397604	1954351	2425407	3070225	Panama	1841799	1081655	1968486	2246316	3195244
United Kingdom	1354926	1400812	1662049	2387194	2994298	Thailand/Thaïlande	1532339	1760580	1835148	2427505	2664053
Singapore/Singapour	1788324	1539933	1659793	2168003	2527240	Canada	1608321	1374032	1389709	1790428	1203340
France,Monac	1381173	1486080	1819869	1948584	2208245	Australia/Australie	1094517	1184732	1231895	1569276	1807675
United Arab Emirates	1282853	1233146	1080834	1558099	2259201	Netherlands/Pays–Bas	1014287	950021	1121421	1542263	1675642
Russian Federation	569333	974789	1229650	1892870	1810265	Philippines	745871	934891	1212373	1493058	1905549
Iran (Islamic Rp. of)	1062012	1092921	1280238	1258446	1634355	Liberia/Libéria	1340593	782139	1779363	998363	875304
Switz.Liecht	671780	608188	869847	1474382	2251657	United Arab Emirates	803427	1053328	1171247	1321126	1377933
Oman	1329362	1117103	787899	927901	1221576	India/Inde	438256	1803690	1160012	1125814	1176965
Brazil/Brésil	796881	779334	1019063	1388224	1324568	France,Monac	982477	895043	1003037	1469670	1249107
So. Africa Customs Un	651651	549784	764208	1240874	1723862	Russian Federation	482693	601171	961911	1415881	1967534
Netherlands/Pays–Bas	628553	770241	815661	1112765	1207922	Mexico/Mexique	905362	997081	1289229	941147	1191004
Kuwait/ Koweït	340583	713476	864337	1067987	1444491	Viet Nam	436182	728268	1027359	1351014	1599141
Hong Kong	793929	934750	659958	837375	1142592	Saudi Arabia	940768	943976	878023	1106926	1096865
Thailand/Thaïlande	637822	538546	619828	935526	1218769	Brazil/Brésil	164465	448526	844175	1518649	1497155
Chile/Chili	365511	537988	705426	1020939	1102532	Italy/Italie	869215	606342	756152	1031155	921820
India/Inde	477505	523417	584556	798297	975718	Spain/Espagne	574208	526326	631691	847464	899918
New Zealand	488142	570715	662879	817197	816227	Turkey/Turquie	399122	610218	276027	574725	745948
Sweden/Suède	476037	418377	614365	755641	795698	Iran (Islamic Rp. of)	560068	430711	260669	352076	883903
Belgium–Luxembourg	474078	416154	532359	742328	728562	Belgium–Luxembourg	480137	443119	418747	573806	561575
Spain/Espagne	266023	345167	691402	562291	698839	Chile/Chili	326018	372868	408544	636517	640242
Panama	370083	278905	599868	406204	547651	So. Africa Customs Un	294890	285562	364403	606082	724877
Philippines	264929	317509	411831	610791	581332	Bangladesh	332621	366818	452379	567650	517645
Finland/Finlande	203357	303047	393858	538308	653833	Argentina/Argentine	463288	531349	472220	303761	443082
Denmark/Danemark	223149	224972	368018	425747	551756	Pakistan	371603	462223	363278	358356	358088
Brunei Darussalam	313585	273437	311604	375963	474839	Poland/Pologne	119555	240537	275888	411266	781960
Austria/Autriche	211271	231323	290942	430005	579423	Egypt/Egypte	187573	251428	354385	468943	473586
Ecuador/Equateur	393651	310078	327588	311940	346128	Switz.Liecht	242332	207174	225093	368638	643121
Yemen/Yémen	23763	103133	565693	462295	380681	Greece/Grèce	171806	221249	170955	404896	520555
Qatar	355020	308980	277982	231241	343713	Sweden/Suède	283594	230997	350772	307003	311600
Mexico/Mexique	172223	157572	228586	306745	408241	Norway,SVD,JM	286463	114083	190153	589977	298263
Pakistan	210227	179399	239016	279043	282763	Sri Lanka	209657	254625	307103	331008	345437
Nigeria/Nigéria	79204	53802	117161	353820	541968	Denmark/Danemark	239274	291654	172461	288890	317602
Papua New Guinea	171391	316681	273482	223435	150242	Israel/Israël	103131	118323	278083	415758	328535
Israel/Israël	91827	133954	144491	293874	390955	Venezuela	427800	391409	98461	116683	123644
Ireland/Irlande	107001	125534	190038	201220	381112	Portugal	99704	77853	173136	454371	328433
Bahrain/Bahreïn	137692	127448	171404	230375	233045	Libyan Arab Jamahiriya	162258	173586	150406	206618	437875
Turkey/Turquie	310593	140652	134065	115005	157165	Austria/Autriche	229755	215114	194695	228263	186505
Norway,SVD,JM	157375	109257	135094	199860	245191	Uzbekistan/Ouzbékistan	3361	70096	237281	244246	493833
Viet Nam	57333	90629	113775	193598	232048	Romania/Roumanie	38191	79929	82388	352344	475343
Argentina/Argentine	115707	66568	68267	132365	224340	Syrian Arab Republic	92182	142957	175284	244201	291630

(VALUE AS PERCENTAGE OF WORLD TOTAL)(VALEURS EN POURCENTAGE DU TOTAL MONDIAL)

	1987	1988	1989	1990	1991	1992	1993	1994	1995	1996		1987	1988	1989	1990	1991	1992	1993	1994	1995	1996
Africa	0.9	0.9	0.8	0.9	0.2	1.3	1.1	1.4	1.7	1.9	Afrique	1.8	2.0	2.0	1.9	3.9	3.4	2.4	3.3	2.4	2.6
Americas	26.5	29.7	31.1	28.8	28.3	27.4	26.3	26.2	27.4	26.9	Amériques	44.4	40.8	38.9	35.7	32.1	32.2	29.7	29.5	26.6	24.5
Northern America	23.7	26.9	28.6	26.4	25.5	24.3	23.4	23.1	24.4	24.0	Amérique du Nord	42.0	38.3	36.3	32.6	28.2	25.8	24.0	23.0	20.9	17.8
LAIA	2.3	2.6	2.3	2.2	2.6	2.5	2.4	2.5	2.5	2.5	ALAI	1.0	1.1	1.5	1.7	2.4	3.3	3.8	3.9	3.4	3.5
CACM	0.0	0.0	0.0	0.0	0.1	0.0	0.0	0.0	0.0	0.0	MCAC	0.2	0.1	0.2	0.2	0.4	0.3	0.3	0.3	0.3	0.3
Caribbean	0.0	0.0	0.1	0.0	0.1	0.1	0.1	0.1	0.0	0.0	Caraïbes	0.2	0.3	0.2	0.3	0.2	0.3	0.2	0.2	0.2	0.4
Rest of America	0.6	0.2	0.1	0.1	0.0	0.5	0.3	0.6	0.3	0.4	Autre Amérique	1.1	0.9	0.7	0.9	0.9	2.4	1.3	2.1	1.8	2.5
As.ex F.USSR	49.7	46.2	45.0	46.0	50.5	51.4	51.4	50.0	49.1	48.0	Asie l'URSS exclus	33.8	38.0	40.5	40.6	44.2	47.7	51.6	51.2	52.8	54.5
Eur.x F.USSR	13.3	13.5	12.4	14.0	14.5	14.1	14.3	15.5	15.0	16.0	Europe l'URSS exclus	16.4	15.6	13.9	16.2	16.3	14.0	13.3	12.9	14.9	14.2
EU	12.3	12.6	11.4	13.0	13.1	12.8	13.3	14.2	13.5	14.1	UE	15.6	14.7	13.2	15.4	14.7	12.8	12.1	11.7	13.0	11.9
EFTA	1.0	0.9	0.9	1.0	1.0	1.0	0.9	1.0	1.2	1.7	AELE	0.8	0.9	0.8	0.7	0.7	0.7	0.4	0.4	0.8	0.7
East Europe					0.4	0.2	0.1	0.2	0.2	0.2	Europe de l'Est					0.7	0.4	0.7	0.6	0.9	1.4
Other Europe	0.0	0.0	0.0	0.0	0.0	0.0	0.0	0.0	0.0	0.0	Autre de l'Europe	0.0	0.0	0.0	0.0	0.4	0.0	0.1	0.0	0.1	0.0
Former USSR					0.7	0.7	1.3	1.5	1.7	1.5	Ancienne URSS					0.9	0.6	0.9	1.3	1.4	2.1
Oceania	4.0	4.2	4.5	4.6	4.6	4.7	5.2	4.7	4.5	4.9	Océanie	1.7	1.8	2.1	1.9	1.7	1.8	1.7	1.6	1.5	1.9
Japan/Japon	33.3	30.7	28.4	26.6	25.9	23.8	23.9	24.8	24.1	20.9	USA/Etats–Unis d'Amer	38.9	35.4	33.2	29.9	25.9	23.7	22.2	21.6	19.5	16.9
USA/Etats–Unis d'Amer	21.4	24.6	25.9	24.3	23.2	22.4	21.4	21.1	22.5	22.2	Japan/Japon	17.8	19.8	21.6	19.4	17.2	15.1	14.1	14.1	13.6	12.2
China/Chine			2.2	2.1	4.2	4.6	4.7	5.3	5.5	5.7	Hong Kong	4.7	5.9	5.4	5.8	6.6	7.7	7.8	8.3	8.5	8.6
Germany/Allemagne	4.4	4.0	4.3	4.7	4.5	4.6	4.7	5.0	4.9	4.8	China/Chine			2.1	2.1	1.4	3.5	6.3	6.5	7.3	8.8
Saudi Arabia	2.6	1.6	1.7	2.5	4.0	4.6	4.5	3.7	4.0	4.4	Singapore/Singapour	2.0	2.2	2.5	2.8	3.8	4.2	3.8	4.3	5.3	5.0
Australia/Australie	3.1	3.5	3.6	3.7	3.7	3.8	4.0	3.7	3.6	4.2	Germany/Allemagne	4.2	3.9	3.4	4.4	4.4	3.8	4.4	4.5	4.8	3.6
Indonesia/Indonésie	2.0	1.7	1.8	2.3	2.5	2.8	3.1	2.8	2.5	2.7	Indonesia/Indonésie	0.5	0.7	1.1	1.7	1.9	2.5	2.5	2.6	2.4	2.5
Malaysia/Malaisie	2.6	2.6	2.4	2.3	2.3	2.2	2.3	1.8	1.9	2.0	Malaysia/Malaisie	0.6	0.7	0.9	1.1	1.4	1.5	1.7	1.7	2.4	3.3
Canada	2.3	2.3	2.7	2.1	2.3	1.9	2.0	2.0	1.9	1.8	United Kingdom	3.2	3.2	3.0	2.7	2.5	2.4	2.0	1.9	2.3	2.5
Italy/Italie	1.3	1.2	1.4	1.7	1.8	1.6	1.7	1.9	1.8	2.0	Panama	1.1	0.9	0.7	0.8	0.9	2.4	1.3	2.1	1.8	2.5

4. Special Imports C.I.F. by Commodities according to the S.I.T.C. (Rev. 2) in thousand U.S. Dollars
Importations Spéciales C.A.F. par Produits d'après la C.T.C.I. (Rév. 2) en milliers de Dollars E.U.

SITC CTCI	COMMODITY	1993		1994		1995		1996		PRODUIT
		WEIGHT POIDS	VALUE VALEUR	WEIGHT POIDS	VALUE VALEUR	WEIGHT POIDS	VALUE VALEUR	WEIGHT POIDS	VALUE VALEUR	
	ALL COMMODITIES		83793990		102342559		135112928		150334321	TOUS PRODUITS
0	FOOD AND LIVE ANIMALS		3989674		4749210		5912307		7249332	ALIMENTS,ANIMAUX VIVANTS
01	MEAT AND PREPARATIONS		408259		594661		766142		769359	VIANDES ET PREPARATIONS
011	MEAT FRESH,CHILLD,FROZEN		385534	W 214167	572571	W 269556	737523	W 266042	736199	VIANDES FRAICHES,REF,CONGE
0111	BOVINE MEAT FRESH,FROZEN		329698	W 142496	429499	W 168367	537603	W 163191	496472	VIANDES BOVIN FRAI,REF
03	FISH AND PREPARATIONS		507956		680999		784267		1008755	POISSONS ET PREPARATIONS
034	FISH,FRESH,CHILLED,FROZN	W 242702	360338	W 232159	431803	W 261265	505279	W 332771	614665	POISSON FRAIS, REFRIG,CONG
0342	FISH FROZEN,EXCL FILLETS	W 231496	260299	W 205420	259686	W 225141	299039	W 287892	365355	POISSONS CONGELES
04	CEREALS AND PREPARATIONS		1458366		1576011		1982937		2688779	CEREALES ET PRODUITS
041	WHEAT ETC UNMILLED	W 4938837	673929	W 6056524	783446		467083	W 3222977	723825	FROMENT,EPEAUTRE
0412	OTHER WHEAT ETC UNMILLED	W 4938837	673929	W 6056524	783446	W 2341779	467079	W 3222975	723821	AUTRE FROMENT NON MOULU
044	MAIZE UNMILLED		702320	W 5748702	696179	MW 9035	1265436	W 8704563	1571859	MAIS NON MOULU
05	VEGETABLES AND FRUIT		396099		493619		533807		675033	LEGUMES ET FRUITS
06	SUGAR AND PREPS,HONEY		386914		452436		555554		581848	SUCRES ET PRODUITS
061	SUGAR AND HONEY		362922	W 1864447	425304	W 1969612	521242	W 2138783	546214	SUCRES ET MIEL
0611	RAW BEET AND CANE SUGAR		315171	W 1274410	366995	W 1305791	440416	W 1399928	443074	SUCRES BRUTS
081	*FEEDING STUFF FOR ANIML		396350	W 2231402	391310	W 3179180	551896	W 3613241	765675	NOURRITURE POUR ANIMAUX
0813	OILCAKE AND OTH RESIDUES		271622	W 1372652	230880	W 2206276	348101	W 2544302	503732	TOURTEAUX
1	BEVERAGES AND TOBACCO		262741		348612		534544		664756	BOISSONS ET TABACS
2	CRUDE MATERLS,EXCL FUELS		8772127		9269864		11550035		10820395	MAT BRUTES NON COMESTIBLES
21	HIDES,SKINS,FURS UNDRSSD		973319		1092072		1189300		1175496	CUIRS,PEAUX BRUTS
211	HIDES,SKINS,EXC FURS,RAW	W 389043	881049	W 370822	921954	W 353757	991020	W 353301	890686	CUIRS ET PEAUX
2111	BOVINE,EQUINE HIDES,RAW	W 371741	799438	W 356058	837761	W 341908	914373	W 340553	802499	PEAUX DE BOVINS
22	OIL SEEDS,OLEAGINOUS FRT		346110		447010		482924		577745	GRAINES,FRUITS OLEAGINEUX
222	SEEDS FOR'SOFT'FIXED OIL	W 1170179	331940	W 1341213	429019	W 1551363	462155	W 1588616	560917	GRAINES HUILES FIXES
2222	SOYA BEANS	W 1087995	290337	W 1228408	351497	W 1467706	401835	W 1469619	473274	FEVES DE SOJA
23	RUBBER, CRUDE		447247		551738		728537		702602	CAOUTCHOUC BRUT
232	NATURAL RUBBER,GUMS	W 292692	251732	W 321199	332304	W 307664	476680	W 321440	460422	LATEX CAOUTCHOUC NATUREL
24	CORK AND WOOD		1776996		1570247		1694662		1696739	LIEGE ET BOIS
247	OTH WOOD ROUGH,SQUARED	W 6856299	1182563	W 6934653	1011575	W 7369760	1047332	W 7239492	963172	BOIS BRUTS EQUARRIS
2471	SAW–,VENEER–LOGS CONIFER	W 4871935	710196	W 5141971	616422	W 5796477	727908	W 5987727	705371	CONIFERES POUR SCIAGE,PLACAG
24711	— IN THE ROUGH	W 4871935	710196	W 5141971	616422	W 5796477	727908	W 5987727	705371	ECORCES OU DEGROSSIS
2472	SAW–,VENEER–LOGS NON–CON	W 1984364	472367	W 1792682	395153	W 1573283	319424	W 1251765	257801	NON CONIFERES SCIAGE,PLAC
24721	— IN THE ROUGH	W 1984364	472367	W 1792682	395153	W 1573283	319424	W 1251765	257801	BRUTS ECORCES DEGROSSIS
248	WOOD SHAPED,SLEEPERS		515020	W 765457	462631	W 773714	522767	W 791904	607595	BOIS SIMPLEMENT TRAVAILLES
2483	LUMBER SHAPED NON–CONIFR		447776	W 649122	408339	W 620990	420800	W 562454	435936	NON CONIFERES SCIES,RABOTES
24831	LUMBER SAWN ETC NON–CON		386712	W 564487	320903	W 523193	310360	W 449314	299888	SCIES LONGITUDINALEMENT
251	*PULP AND WASTE PAPER		839494	W 3251698	1044037	W 3231572	1857989	W 3683038	1473315	PATES A PAPIER,DECHETS
2517	SODA,SULPHATE WOOD PULP	W 1497959	585314	W 1723127	766074	W 1749647	1334738	W 2045202	1096148	PATES CHIMIQUES AU SULFATE
25172	— BLEACHED.NONDISSOLVNG	W 1251446	493730	W 1451678	657346	W 1479126	1146069	W 1773674	959505	PATES BLANCHIES
26	TEXTILE FIBRES AND WASTE		1043511		1143477		1387714		1221778	FIBRES TEXTILES
263	COTTON	W 371013	539456	W 373157	593059	W 372042	774685	W 351625	717276	COTON
2631	RAW COTTON,EXCL LINTERS	W 366251	534621	W 370666	589857	W 369046	771510	W 347094	713512	COTON EN MASSE
27	CRUDE FERTLZR,MINRLS NES		487628		523193		604533		599403	ENGRAIS MINERAUX BRUTS
28	METALLIFEROUS ORES,SCRAP		2572305		2585765		3237631		2981314	MINERAIS METAL,DECHETS
281	IRON ORE,CONCENTRATES		887528	MW 34250	796904	MW 35075	850681	MW 34824	918280	MINERAIS DE FER
2815	IRON ORE,CONC,NOT AGGLOM		865204	MW 33883	786049	MW 34372	820739	MW 33280	853737	MINERAIS NON AGGLOMERES
282	IRON AND STEEL SCRAP		775724	W 4969623	846833	W 5003108	996117	W 5209919	940058	FERRAILLES
28209	— OF OTHR IRON OR STEEL		709260	W 4761020	758596	W 4717685	831801	W 5061170	830413	FERRAILLES DE FER
287	BASE METAL ORES,CONC NES		630514	W 1816659	661895	W 1952971	908046		773330	MINERAIS METAUX COMMUNS
2871	CPR ORE ETC,CEMENT COPPR	W 573932	342685	W 428869	301915	W 468714	464575	W 439732	315475	MINERAIS DE CUIVRE,MATTES
28711	COPPER ORES,EXCL MATTE	W 571187	340990	W 426421	300536	W 468714	464575	W 439732	315473	MINERAIS DE CUIVRE
288	NONFERR METAL SCRAP NES		278033	W 170144	279967	W 215514	481660	W 193007	349552	DECHETS NON FERREUX
2882	OTHER BASE MTL SCRAP NES		270256	W 161629	273621	W 209034	476237	W 185826	343755	AUTRES DECHETS
29	CRUDE ANIMAL,VEG MAT NES		285518		312324		366744		392001	MATIERES BRUTES ANIM,VEGET
3	MINERAL FUELS ETC		15155224		15532241		19150109		24423063	COMBUSTIBLES MINERAUX LUB
32	COAL,COKE AND BRIQUETTES		1732840		1776578		2081319		2337056	HOUILLES,COKES,BRIQUETTES
322	COAL,LIGNITE AND PEAT		1712140		1753169	MW 43848	2057297	MW 46289	2310307	HOUILLES,LIGNITES,TOURBE
3222	OTH COAL,NOT AGGLOMERATD		1670648	MW 38507	1718066	MW 43113	2018532	MW 45398	2259985	AUTRES HOUILLES
33	PETROLEUM AND PRODUCTS		12039856		12194107		14896931		19188899	PETROLE ET DERIVES
333	CRUDE PETROLEUM	MW 74153	9150936	MW 77693	8878269	MW 84282	10809127	MW 94103	14431515	HUILES BRUTES DE PETROLE
334	PETROLEUM PRODUCTS,REFIN		2752735	MW 19768	3140706	MW 21829	3864511	MW 21462	4459969	PRODUITS RAFFINES
3341	GASOLINE,OTH LIGHT OILS		1324339							ESSENCES POUR MOTEURS
33419	OTH LIGHT PETROLEUM OILS		1318922							AUTRES HUILES LEGERES
3342	KEROSENE,OTH MEDIUM OILS		437161							PETR LAMPANTS,AUT HUIL
33421	KEROSENE INCL JET FUEL	W 2033936	427426							PETROLES LAMPANTS
3343	GAS OILS	W 1501006	285709							GAS OILS
3344	FUEL OILS,NES	W 5203321	570720							FUEL OILS
341	*GAS,NATURAL AND MANUFCT		1382528		1561557		2171859	MW 13835	2897108	GAZ NATUREL,GAZ MANUFACT
3413	PETROLM GASES,LIQUEFIED		1382486	MW 10042	1561516	MW 11161	2171816	MW 13835	2897082	GAZ DE PETROLE LIQUEFIE
34131	LIQUEFIED PROPANE,BUTANE		601017	W 4045425	600038	W 4405815	896388	W 4577041	1018572	PROPANE,BUTANE LIQUEFIES
34139	OTH HYDROCARBON GAS LQFD		781469	W 5996546	961477	W 6755683	1275428	MW 9258	1878510	HYDROCARBURES GAZEUX NDA
4	ANIMAL,VEGETABLE OIL,FAT		258000		322582		392026		368618	HUILES,GRAISSES ANIM,VEG
5	CHEMCLS,RELATED PROD NES		8029903		9510722		12840126		12917111	PRODUITS CHIMIQUES
51	ORGANIC CHEMICALS		2916988		3489402		5365860		4882263	PROD CHIMIQ ORGANIQUES
511	HYDROCARBONS NES,DERIVS		655104	W 1625476	747715	W 2386940	1634866	W 2532177	1310022	HYDROCARBURES NDA
5112	CYCLIC HYDROCARBONS		360772	W 995156	447255	W 1478128	1095912	W 1576650	816508	HYDROCARBURES CYCLIQUES
51124	XYLENES,CHEMICALLY PURE	W 551241	206469	W 525064	235444	W 904803	765597	W 905631	532872	XYLENES PURS
512	ALCOHOLS,PHENOLS ETC	W 1157008	437256	W 1321678	643511	W 1541136	1003296	W 1822201	971259	PHENOLS,PHENOLS–ALCOOLS
5121	ACYCLIC ALCOHOLS,DERIVS	W 1107803	348926	W 1259353	533972	W 1469700	864152	W 1741478	813374	ALCOOLS ACYCLIQUES
513	CARBOXYLIC ACIDS ETC		427427	W 511066	512657	W 429175	620286	W 435891	559064	ACIDES CARBOXYLIQUES
514	NITROGEN–FNCTN COMPOUNDS		598793	W 325686	647297	W 372487	932028	W 366612	832543	COMPOSES FONCT AZOTEES
5148	OTH NITROGN–FNCTN CMPNDS		356670	W 252030	386745	W 285989	623171	W 267680	492185	AUTRES COMPOSES AZOTES
515	ORG–INORG COMPOUNDS ETC		555326	W 252639	631721	W 265961	762419	W 273232	813579	COMPOSES ORGANO–MINERAUX
5156	HETEROCYCLIC CMPDS ETC		420181	W 228382	478762	W 241631	592561	W 246519	613917	COMPOSES HETEROCYCLIQUES
516	OTHER ORGANIC CHEMICALS	W 165974	243081	W 249734	306502	W 381605	412966	W 358614	395796	AUTRES PROD ORGANIQUES
52	INORGANIC CHEMICALS		870183		1034375		1253398		1404238	PROD CHIM INORGANIQUES
522	INORG ELEMNTS,OXIDES,ETC		436913	W 1262074	501434	W 1323180	646287	W 1485506	704186	ELEMENTS INORGANIQUES
523	OTHR INORG CHEMICALS ETC		279681	W 827154	321663	W 852556	379124	W 847890	387850	AUT PRODUITS CHIMIQUES INORG
53	DYES,TANNING,COLOUR PROD		690638		806910		906845		914823	PROD TEINTURE,COLORANTS
531	SYNT DYE,NAT INDGO,LAKES	W 22225	329388	W 26055	348815	W 27209	352540	W 29352	353601	MAT COLOR ORGAN,LAQUES
5311	SYNTHIC ORGNIC DYESTUFFS	W 21315	311765	W 25087	329747	W 26173	332307	W 28374	333920	MAT COLOR ORGAN SYNTHET
533	PIGMENTS,PAINTS,ETC		307803	W 131016	404598	W 137950	496375	W 137494	502965	PIGMENTS,PEINTURES,VERNIS
541	*MEDICINAL,PHARM PRODUCT		470112		546411		659885	MK 104005	764470	PROD MEDICINAUX PHARMACEUT
55	PERFUME,CLEANING ETC PRD		329909		427613		528203		679212	PROD POUR PARFUM,TOILETTE
58	PLASTIC MATERIALS ETC		1414828		1629260		1973650		1983921	MAT PLAST ARTIFICIELLES
582	PROD OF CONDENSATION ETC		595469	W 211334	720292	W 246140	931816	W 243634	927252	PROD CONDENS,POLYCOND
583	POLYMERIZATION ETC PRODS		714030	W 339162	801887	W 326343	923253	W 358556	941925	PROD POLYMERISATION
5839	OTH POLYMRZTION ETC PROD		395744	W 127019	443617	W 121633	513261	W 121514	519049	AUT PROD POLYMER COPOLYM
59	CHEMICAL MATERIALS NES		1213165		1468627		1995304		2150684	MAT PROD CHIMIQUES NDA
598	MISCEL CHEM PRODUCTS NES		1005806	W 396942	1220654	W 465815	1715063	W 490457	1869854	PROD DIV INDUST CHIM NDA

4. Special Imports C.I.F. by Commodities according to the S.I.T.C. (Rev. 2) in thousand U.S. Dollars
Importations Spéciales C.A.F. par Produits d'après la C.T.C.I. (Rév. 2) en milliers de Dollars E.U.

SITC CTCI	COMMODITY	1993		1994		1995		1996		PRODUIT
		WEIGHT POIDS	VALUE VALEUR	WEIGHT POIDS	VALUE VALEUR	WEIGHT POIDS	VALUE VALEUR	WEIGHT POIDS	VALUE VALEUR	
5989	CHEM PRODUCTS,PREPS NES		816232	W 250398	1012393	W 304673	1471692	W 312414	1598989	PROD PREP CHIMIQUES NDA
59899	OTH CHEM PRODS,PREPS,NES		609560	W 193840	772898	W 226108	1069244	W 222335	1181681	AUT PRODUITS CHIMIQUES NDA
6	BASIC MANUFACTURES		12327947		16276265		21707911		21428580	ART MANUFACTURES
61	LEATHER,DRESSED FUR,ETC		792267		998764		1090486		1156748	CUIRS,PELLETERIES
611	LEATHER		468657	W 75009	576863	W 79019	540127	W 71712	498035	CUIRS,PEAUX PREPARES
613	FUR SKINS TANNED,DRESSED	W 3929	212956	W 5137	279754	W 5217	368176	W 5882	473825	PELLETERIES
63	WOOD,CORK MANUFACTRS NES		782993		804498		915141		911454	OUVRAGES LIEGE ET BOIS
634	VENEERS,PLYWOOD,ETC		682721	W 965813	666908	W 1571190	738675	W 1037622	678488	PLACAGES,CONTRE–PLAQUES
6342	PLYWOOD OF WOOD SHEETS		551926	W 651148	535927	W 848583	593861	W 695755	531451	BOIS CONTRE–PLAQUES
64	PAPER,PAPERBOARD AND MFR		588364		675571		929204		881898	PAPIERS,CARTONS & OUVRAGES
641	PAPER AND PAPERBOARD	W 632138	509180	W 709177	591109	W 771910	825823	W 729576	756086	PAPIERS ET CARTONS
65	TEXTILE YARN,FABRICS,ETC		2706080		3481691		4142819		4001082	FILS,TISSUS,ARTICLES TEXTILE
651	TEXTILE YARN		1068768	W 458889	1456032	W 454686	1765042	W 459072	1701108	FILS TEXTILES
6514	SYN FIB YRN,BULK,MONOFIL	W 108814	275468	W 168272	411653	W 166358	513657	W 155786	433517	FILS CONT 85% FIB TEXT SYNTH
652	COTTON FABRICS,WOVEN		260689	W 68969	318980	W 70045	363849	W 68731	372365	TISSUS DE COTON
653	WOVN MAN–MADE FIB FABRIC		594104	W 164341	843856	W 164222	967959	W 138227	848075	TISSUS FIBRES SYNTH,ARTIF
654	OTH WOVEN TEXTILE FABRIC	W 23014	400208	W 22354	407786	W 24735	472163	W 23501	483229	TISSUS AUT COTON SYNT,ARTIF
66	NONMETAL MINERAL MFS NES		816607		1093672		1563241		1673851	ART MIN NON METALLIQUES
664	GLASS		269544	W 310352	401333	W 532233	641714	W 331183	558634	VERRE
67	IRON AND STEEL		3161374		4565966		6630554		6679445	FER ET ACIER
671	PIG IRON ETC		592464	W 2754151	692359	W 3328883	967870	W 3969470	1123863	FONTE,SPIEGEL,POUDRES
6716	FERRO–ALLOYS		295734	W 427130	310620	W 496311	466947	W 571445	553504	FERRO–ALLIAGES
672	IRON,STEEL PRIMARY FORMS		1134215	W 4673753	1614089	W 5636960	2385919	W 6369234	2220463	LINGOTS FER,ACIER
6725	IRN,STL BLOOMS,SLABS,ETC		612089	W 3027144	786406	W 3187115	989882	W 4186345	1153000	BLOOMS,BILLETTES FER ACIER
67251	IRN,SMPLE STL BLOOMS,ETC		541742	W 2928952	703298	W 3099519	852115	W 4113201	1078991	BLOOMS ETC NON ACIER FIN
6727	IRN,STL COIL FR REROLLNG		512367	W 1598764	814794	W 2385175	1363286	W 2175661	1041627	EBAUCHES POUR TOLES FER
67271	IRON,SIMPLE STEEL COILS		223627	W 1333567	455760	W 2090468	826198	W 1924571	653495	EBAUCHES NON EN ACIER
67274	STNLESS STEEL ETC COILS		282560	W 262781	356824	W 285613	532208	W 244193	383346	EBAUCHES ACIER INOXYDBLE
673	IRON,STEEL SHAPES ETC		468113	W 1616056	702010	W 2022077	945022	W 1695821	826624	BARRES,PROFIL FER,ACIER
6733	IRON,STEEL PROFILES ETC		141732	W 802991	316672	W 989051	423715	W 887164	373657	PROFILES,PALPLAN FER,ACIER
674	IRN,STL UNIV,PLATE,SHEET		608433	W 1695088	1025456	W 2470861	1573658	W 2552854	1629439	LARGES PLATS,TOLES
6744	IRN,STL HVY PLATE,ROLLED		226746	W 1000750	453412	W 1611181	785490	W 1580957	786753	TOLES LAMINEES PLUS 4.75 MM
67441	— OF IRON OR SIMPLE STL		195521	W 981358	419263	W 1591207	733813	W 1565939	742197	TOLES NON ACIER FIN CARB
678	IRON,STL TUBES,PIPES,ETC		277242	W 215417	391999	W 373500	599036	W 436581	671684	TUBES,TUYAUX EN FONTE,FER
68	NON–FERROUS METALS		2226389		3066303		4617368		4141268	METAUX NON FERREUX
682	COPPER EXC CEMENT COPPER		751214	W 405139	1052613	W 484684	1697865	W 535535	1554338	CUIVRE
6821	COPPER NES,ALLOYS,UNWRT		526810	W 351857	767034	W 406877	1235593	W 433788	1098179	CUIVRE BRUT
68212	COPPER REFINED,UNWROUGHT		365588	W 264376	576222	W 326716	978347	W 346163	865775	CUIVRE AFFINE BRUT
6822	COPPER,ALLOYS WORKED		224404	W 53282	285580	W 77807	462272	W 101747	456160	CUIVRE,ALLIAGES OUVRES
684	ALUMINIUM		1102484	W 822510	1459419	W 915328	2140761	W 838221	1728316	ALUMINIUM
6841	ALUMINIUM,ALLOYS,UNWRGHT	W 579343	718540	W 689328	1013585	W 783423	1569849	W 724458	1209442	ALUMINIUM,ALLIAGES BRUTS
6842	ALUMINIUM,ALLOYS WORKED		383944	W 133181	445834	W 131905	570913	W 113763	518874	ALUMINIUM,ALLIAGES OUVRE
68422	ALUMNM PLATE,SHEET,STRIP	W 99662	252390	W 113178	279641	W 107114	349095	W 88649	302658	TOLES, PLANCHES EN ALU
69	METAL MANUFACTURES NES		1029986		1318660		1489813		1642708	ART MANUFACT EN METAL NDA
695	TOOLS		279669	W 20661	323398	W 22711	370305	W 26571	445339	OUTILS A MAIN
699	BASE METAL MFRS NES		393390	W 63672	516037	W 74711	584163	W 78996	591027	ART MANUFACTURES MET NDA
7	MACHINES,TRANSPORT EQUIP		28397890		37381845		49403844		54654541	MACHINES MATERIEL TRANSPORT
71	POWER GENERATING EQUIPMT		2492801		2767822		3891333		3665985	MACHINES GENERATRICES
713	INTRNL COMBUS PSTN ENGIN		748360	W 70134	1047639	W 85232	1218314	W 89336	1173901	MOTEURS EXPL COMB INT, PIECE
7139	PISTON ENGINE PARTS NES		386324	W 31379	534209	W 30675	597551	W 43422	597295	PIECES POUR 713.2,3,8
714	ENGINES AND MOTORS NES		751770	W 2651	772296	W 12165	1154899	W 12765	742726	MOTEURS NON ELECTRIQUES
7144	REACTION ENGINES	W 414	405631	W 411	389470	W 327	315307	W 173	140266	PROPULSEURS A REACTION
7149	ENGINE & MOTOR PARTS NES		308479	W 1283	318679	W 7957	555216	W 9432	404134	PIECES 714 ET 718.88
716	ROTATING ELECTRIC PLANT		590442	W 29949	646150	W 38691	812789	W 50709	924628	APP ELECTR ROTATIFS,PIECES
7162	AC MTRS,GENRTRS,GEN SETS	W 15377	265792	W 19632	376461	W 29248	553283	W 36923	684477	MOTEURS ELECTRIQUES
72	MACHS FOR SPCL INDUSTRYS		4379064		5924208		8078656		8003485	MAC SPECIALES POUR INDUST
724	TEXTILE,LEATHER MACHNRY		1006179	W 61313	1315724	W 52304	1180160	W 35081	825515	MACH POUR INDUSTRIE TEXTILE
7244	SPINNING,EXTRDNG,ETC MCH	W 17489	446776	W 17750	420984	W 21218	489562	W 12992	311667	MACH POUR LE FILAGE
7245	WEAVING,FELT MFG,ETC MCH	W 15662	318795	W 30632	572592	W 19627	403591	W 11269	256280	METIERS A TISSER,PIECES
72451	WEAVING MACHINES (LOOMS)	W 9801	152157	W 21552	320996	W 13817	230705	W 6380	92985	METIERS A TISSER
725	PAPER ETC MILL MACHINERY		246881	W 6299	170590	W 23833	443930	W 20251	430463	MACHINES FABR PATE PAPIER
726	PRINTG,BKBINDG MACHY,PTS		327773	W 19413	544777	W 17699	536420	W 20897	499932	MACHINES POUR IMPRIMERIE
7264	PRINTING PRESSES		222822	W 14881	368609	W 13999	353398	W 17705	368932	MACHINES A IMPRIMER
72641	ROTARY PRINTING PRESSES		222822	W 14881	368609	W 13999	353398	W 17705	368932	MACH IMPRIMER ROTATIVES
728	OTH MACHY FOR SPCL INDUS		2190947	W 67448	3301793	W 89979	5215357	W 109988	5409410	AUT MACH IND PARTICULIERES
7284	MACHY FOR SPCL INDUS NES		1980248	W 51028	3014966	W 73061	4857078	W 94321	5063237	MACH SPEC IND PARTICUL.
72848	OTH MCHY WITH INDIV FNCT		1397037	W 30925	2221303	W 43283	3543969	W 58423	3668140	AUTRES MACHINES NDA
72849	PTS OF MACHS OF 7284 ETC	W 4759	248196	W 6609	406692	W 7220	663149	W 9299	729530	PIECES DU 728.4 ETC
73	METALWORKING MACHINERY		1154400		1740908		2270602		3109263	MACH TRAVAIL DES METAUX
736	METALWORKING MACH–TOOLS		788965	W 54958	1102669	W 72579	1580645	104024	2056697	MACH–OUTILS TRAVAIL METAUX
7361	METAL CUTTING MACH–TOOLS		321381	W 23337	476293	W 28550	789102	W 32741	968299	MACH–OUT ENLEVEMENT METAL
7362	METAL FORMING MACH–TOOLS		202711	W 17490	224810	W 30480	421803	W 48646	490178	MACH–OUTILS DEFORM METAL
737	METALWORKING MACHNRY NES		365435	W 36464	638239	W 45210	689957	W 71794	1052565	MACH TRAV METAUX PIECES
7372	ROLLING MILLS AND ROLLS		145637	W 22350	294994	W 31466	235767	W 55970	542564	LAMINOIRS CYLINDRES PIEC
74	GENRL INDUSTRL MACHY NES		4266166		5775486		7751336		8797220	MACH APP INDUSTRIE
741	HEATING,COOLING EQUIPMNT		794815	W 76260	1337334	W 92434	1783742	W 111636	2159938	MACH CHAUFFAGE,PIECES
7413	INDUS FURNACES ETC,PARTS		226902	W 15230	393258	W 15614	558573	W 31706	813275	FOURS IND,LABOR,PIECES
74131	INDUS FURNACES ETC ELCTR	W 5143	126300	W 7333	299744	W 7466	421418	W 9707	391390	FOURS ELECTRIQUES
7416	HEATING,COOLING EQU NES		275467	W 38674	545198	W 47389	705973	W 51458	856216	APP CHANGEMENT TEMP
742	PUMPS FOR LIQUIDS ETC		481504	W 25774	617371	W 32510	781248	W 34473	800635	POMPES MOTO–POMPES
743	PUMPS NES,CENTRFUGES ETC		710048	W 54771	956480	W 79297	1315705	W 89974	1521412	POMPES COMPRES,VENT ETC
7431	PUMPS FOR GASES ETC	W 19618	273042	W 31284	352991	W 48531	581268	W 57211	696704	POMPES AIR A VIDE,COMPRES
744	MECHANICAL HANDLING EQU		647786	W 79700	903053	W 113792	1241815	W 155353	1578813	EQUIP MANUTENTION PIECES
7442	LIFTING,LOADING MACH NES		335273	W 34989	516909	W 42971	686709	W 68223	960002	APP LEVAGE,MANUTENTION
74428	OTH HANDLING ETC MCH NES		237669	W 20001	329369	W 25012	485489	W 38937	672011	AUT APP LEVAGE ETC
745	NONELEC MACHY,TOOLS NES		376934	W 12353	411539	W 17815	611603	W 18800	620795	AUT MACH NON ELEC,PIECES
7452	OTH NONELEC MCHS,PTS NES	W 11335	331639	W 10885	354425	W 16396	549948	W 17269	557239	AUT MACH NON ELEC,PIECES
749	NONELEC MACH PTS,ACC NES		1255079	W 80075	1549708	W 103216	2017223	W 120690	2115627	PIECES MACH NON ELEC NDA
7491	BALL,ROLLER,ETC BEARINGS		312720	W 24295	400343	W 29964	516985	W 32293	495748	ROULEMENTS BILLES ETC
7492	COCKS,VALVES ETC NES	W 17757	465682	W 23642	603141	W 27371	805491	W 32488	828783	ART ROB,SIM POUR TUYAUX
7493	SHAFT,CRANK,PULLEY ETC		292024	W 25190	339984	W 35423	427844	W 42259	460729	ARBRES TRANS,VILEBREQUINS
75	OFFICE MACHNES,ADP EQUIP		2000559		2615034		3569888		3998149	MACH BUREAU TRAIT AUTOM
752	AUTOMTIC DATA PROC EQUIP		1185081	W 15104	1602692	W 19327	2164757	W 23698	2525852	MACH TRAIT INFORMATION
7523	DIGITL CENTRL PROCESSORS	W 1836	406077	W 2395	516955	W 3364	728204	W 3421	734101	UNITES CENTRALES
7524	DIGITL CENTRL STOR UNITS	W 1502	329517	W 1950	449629	W 2702	572477	W 2799	712236	UNITES MEMOIRE CENTRALES
7525	ADP PERIPHERAL UNITS	W 5658	275727	W 9412	395127	W 11906	576803	W 15205	612156	UNITES PERIPHERIQUES
759	OFFICE,ADP MCH PTS,ACCES	W 7028	633680	W 7423	813742	W 8595	1142481	W 10916	1300647	PIECES DU 751 ET 752
7599	ACCTG,ETC,ADP MCH PTS,AC	W 4112	538222	W 4311	679191	W 5523	971751	W 7612	1130681	PIECES DU 751 ET 752
76	TELECOMM,SOUND EQUIPMENT		1872226		2520373		3058763		3505259	EQUIPMENT DE TELECOM
764	TELECOM EQPT,PTS,ACC NES		1645041	W 23618	2221017	W 27796	2658459	W 31550	3070189	EQUIP TELECOM,PIECES
7641	LINE TELEPHONE,ETC EQUIP		117837	W 1812	230868	W 2395	375582	W 3604	485315	APP TELEPHON PAR FIL

4. Special Imports C.I.F. by Commodities according to the S.I.T.C. (Rev. 2) in thousand U.S. Dollars
Importations Spéciales C.A.F. par Produits d'après la C.T.C.I. (Rév. 2) en milliers de Dollars E.U.

SITC CTCI	COMMODITY	1993 WEIGHT POIDS	1993 VALUE VALEUR	1994 WEIGHT POIDS	1994 VALUE VALEUR	1995 WEIGHT POIDS	1995 VALUE VALEUR	1996 WEIGHT POIDS	1996 VALUE VALEUR	PRODUIT
7643	TV,RADIO TRANSMITTRS ETC	W 1421	302517	W 2726	636000	W 2415	575257	W 2229	640726	APP EMET TELE RADIO
7649	PTS NES OF EQUIPMT OF 76	W 11627	1008739	W 11947	1070566	W 13867	1339308	W 17285	1603264	PIECES DE LA DIV 76
76493	TELECOMM EQUIPMT PTS NES	W 4311	460731	W 4867	465211	W 5094	574434	W 5992	801112	PIECES 761,762,764.3,8
76499	PARTS ETC OF SOUND EQUIP	W 3460	396759	W 3442	391206	W 4029	454815	W 4833	458102	PIECES NDA POUR 763
77	ELECTRIC MACHNRY NES ETC		8557827		10722882		14550060		16571025	MACH APP ELECT NDA
771	ELECTRIC POWER MACHY NES	W 13252	360254	W 16315	417386	W 19693	483188	W 22349	576039	MACH PROD,TRANS ELECTR
7712	OTH ELEC POWER MACHY NES	W 7276	259226	W 9164	316573	W 11761	357675	W 14501	458557	AUT APP PROD TRANSF ELEC
772	SWITCHGEAR ETC,PARTS NES		1076686	W 19359	1319816	W 23885	1697481	W 26482	1725140	APP COUPURE,SECT ETC
7721	SWITCHGEAR ETC		866515	W 16339	1048972	W 20152	1370261	W 22408	1394880	APP COUPURE,SECTIONMNT
774	ELECTRO–MEDCL,XRAY EQUIP		197956	W 2514	319674	W 2643	355099	W 3264	385708	APPAREILS MEDICAUX
776	TRANSISTORS,VALVES,ETC		5649676	W 52822	6982537	W 66485	9838184	W 92133	11460009	LAMPES,TUBES,VALVES
7762	OTH ELECTRONIC TUBES ETC		347468	W 16064	340451	W 25633	584078	W 24722	584769	AUT LAMPES ELECTRONIQUES
7763	DIODES,TRANSISTORS,ETC		457300	W 3033	632684	W 3437	785316	W 3620	832642	DIODES,TRANSISTORS
7764	ELECTRONIC MICROCIRCUITS		3344235	W 4075	4230994	W 5029	6773149	W 5819	8206876	MICROSTRUCTURES ELECTRON
7768	ELCTRNC COMP PTS,CRYSTLS		1274191	W 12275	1606217	W 12986	1492642	W 12574	1427768	CRIST PIEZO–ELEC,PCS 776
77689	ELECTRNIC COMPON PTS NES		1146277	W 11760	1397235	W 12490	1210627	W 11976	1160677	PIECES DU GROUPE 776
778	ELECTRICAL MACHINERY NES		938682	W 67827	1267236	W 79825	1580635	W 91575	1681018	AUTRES MACH ELECT NDA
7788	OTH ELEC MACHY,EQUIP NES		630487	W 48360	863757	W 56642	1088248	W 62085	1118003	AUT MACH APP ELEC NDA
77884	ELECTRICAL CONDENSERS		219483	W 3043	308295	W 3186	362482	W 4469	332745	CONDENSATEURS ELECTRIQUES
78	ROAD VEHICLES		984249		1467390		1910376		2067762	VEHICULES ROUTIERS
784	MOTOR VEH PRTS,ACCES NES		774346	W 74745	1118234	W 80215	1303651	W 84070	1245271	PIECES 722,781,782,783
7849	OTHER MOTOR VEHCL PARTS		769917	W 73780	1111037	W 80118	1301194	W 83946	1240271	PIECES 722,781,782,783
79	OTHR TRANSPORT EQUIPMENT		2690598		3847743		4322831		4936394	AUTRE MATERIEL TRANSPORT
792	AIRCRAFT ETC		1846426		2207478		2479377	W 4560	2765780	APP NAVIGATION AERIENNE
7924	AIRCRFT NES OVER 15000KG	W 1611	1292764	W 1802	1377663	W 2048	1603049	W 2499	1928662	AERODYNES PLUS 15000 KG
7929	AIRCRAFT PARTS NES	W 1448	376773	W 2210	676221	W 1819	741457	W 1837	698135	PIECES DU 792
793	SHIPS AND BOATS ETC		718796		1467464	W 1430133	1556221	W 1346445	1934307	NAVIRES BATEAUX,ETC
7932	SHIPS AND BOATS NES		475446	W 1263006	1433644	W 1373137	1447969	W 1190060	1740001	NAVIRES ET BATEAUX
79322	TANKERS OF ALL KINDS	W 117318	57823	W 433048	604324	W 611253	426088	W 388084	579166	BATEAUX–CITERNES
79323	OTHER CARGO VESSELS	W 444907	415488	W 818356	772449	W 736506	960607	W 783822	1124870	AUT BATEAUX TRANS MARCH
8	MISC MANUFACTURED GOODS		5870270		7805419		10551089		11844077	ART MANUFACTURES DIVERS
84	CLOTHING AND ACCESSORIES		361235		699735		1081299		1516793	VETEMENTS
87	PRECISION INSTRUMNTS NES		2456641		3248828		4292628		4565071	INSTRUM,APPAR SCIENT NDA
871	OPTICAL INSTRUMENTS		225742	W 1731	328157	W 2164	416655	W 2356	389764	APPAR,INSTRUM D'OPTIQUE
874	MEASURNG,CONTROLNG INSTR		2010075	W 18584	2618715	W 22021	3558933	W 26324	3846285	INSTRUMENTS DE MESURE
8742	MEASUR,DRAW ETC INST,PTS	W 5844	642127	W 6858	703140	W 8140	933868	W 10511	1101870	INST DESSIN,TRACAGE,PCS
87421	MEASURNG,DRAWNG ETC INST	W 5528	594041	W 6512	628432	W 7603	830324	W 9759	967489	INSTRUM DESSIN,TRACAGE
8743	GAS,LIQUID CONTROL INSTR	W 3687	428746	W 4777	515026	W 5011	629198	W 5439	562527	APP,INSTR MESURE FLUIDES
8748	ELEC MEAS,CONTRL EQU NES		615081	W 3563	928090	W 5022	1436147	W 5406	1559066	APP ELEC ELECTRO MESURE
87483	OTH ELCTRNC MEAS ETC EQU		587612	W 3279	901870	W 4729	1406028	W 5168	1530495	AUT APP ELECTRO DE MESURE
88	PHOTO EQU,OPTICL GDS ETC		1135365		1470201		2016915		2071989	APP,FOURN PHOTO,OP,MONTR
881	PHOTO APPARAT,EQUIPT NES		383573	W 3841	606472	W 4718	958638	W 5391	952551	APP,EQUIP PHOTO NDA
8813	OTH PHOTO,CINE EQUIP NES		233903	W 2425	438902	W 2932	755459	W 3244	753541	APP,MAT PHOTO,CINEMA
88139	PHOTO,CINE LAB EQUIP NES	W 1379	223987	W 2055	423068	W 2515	736421	W 2781	733997	APP TYPES UTIL LABOR
882	PHOTO,CINEMA SUPPLIES		400202	W 33129	468633	W 39144	593310	W 41354	663889	PRODUITS PHOTO,CINEMA
8822	PHOTO FILM EXC DEV CINMA		299863	W 18451	337162	W 21283	396856	W 21893	441001	PLAQUES,PELLICULES,FILMS
89	MISC MANUFCTRD GOODS NES		1644387		1986292		2524236		2800382	ART MANUFACTURES DIVERS
893	ARTICLES OF PLASTIC NES		298495		371500		491711		533296	OUVRAGES EN MAT DIVIS 58
894	TOYS,SPORTING GOODS,ETC		406050	W 45182	446666	W 48936	604756	W 55771	715004	VOITURES ENFANTS,JOUETS
898	MUSICAL INSTRUMENTS,PTS		423904	W 18382	565318	W 23854	701162	W 18257	734999	INSTRUMENTS DE MUSIQUE
8983	SOUND RECRDNG TAPE,DISCS		351167	W 8761	479729	W 8680	598639	W 7527	643560	SUPPORTS SON POUR 763
89832	RECORDED DISCS,TAPES ETC		245025	W 1265	340967	W 1209	431089	W 1255	499022	DISQUES,PHONO,BANDES
9	GOODS NOT CLASSD BY KIND		730214		1145798		3070937		5963849	ART TRANSACT NON CLASSES
951	*WAR FIREARMS,AMMUNITION	W 2694	243256	W 2502	322612	W 2211	198700	W 2225	222091	VEHIC BLINDES ARMES
971	*GOLD,NON MONETARY NES		396355	K 58545	713751	K 217180	2737428	K 446807	5610100	OR NON MONETAIRE
97101	NONMON GLD UNWRT,SEMIMFD		396173	K 58324	713442	K 217118	2737294	K 446755	5609985	OR,ALLIAGES D'OR BRUTS

5. Special Exports F.O.B. by Commodities according to the S.I.T.C. (Rev. 2) in thousand U.S. Dollars
Exportations Spéciales F.O.B. par Produits d'après la C.T.C.I. (Rév. 2) en milliers de Dollars E.U.

SITC CTCI	COMMODITY	1993 WEIGHT POIDS	1993 VALUE VALEUR	1994 WEIGHT POIDS	1994 VALUE VALEUR	1995 WEIGHT POIDS	1995 VALUE VALEUR	1996 WEIGHT POIDS	1996 VALUE VALEUR	PRODUIT
	ALL COMMODITIES		82232153		96007709		125056492		129714569	TOUS PRODUITS
0	FOOD AND LIVE ANIMALS		2042148		2280257		2645396		2717246	ALIMENTS,ANIMAUX VIVANTS
03	FISH AND PREPARATIONS		1325283		1400420		1550508		1493747	POISSONS ET PREPARATIONS
034	FISH,FRESH,CHILLED,FROZN	W 216426	636054	W 200373	697363	W 220400	744973	W 227180	694019	POISSON FRAIS, REFRIG,CONG
0342	FISH FROZEN,EXCL FILLETS	W 178388	385338	W 161461	376146	W 178055	395642	W 194932	431606	POISSONS CONGELES
036	SHELL FISH FRESH,FROZEN	W 43359	327842	W 43159	327256	W 93017	398899	W 90116	372468	CRUSTACES,MOLLUSQUES
037	FISH ETC PREPD,PRSVD NES	W 57897	344140	W 64374	362326	W 66539	395382	W 77769	416879	POIS,CRUST,MOL PREPARES
2	CRUDE MATERLS,EXCL FUELS		1156738		1426221		1785267		1604409	MAT BRUTES NON COMESTIBLES
26	TEXTILE FIBRES AND WASTE		565283		773584		1056660		923517	FIBRES TEXTILES
266	SYNTHETIC FIBRES TO SPIN	W 453287	521064	W 541248	718334	W 559659	974474	W 690303	835241	FIBRES SYNTHETIQUES
2665	DISCN SYNTH FIBRE UNCMBD	W 412972	461895	W 486676	632708	W 510393	875271	W 637695	749194	DISCONTINUES EN MASSE
26652	— POLYESTER	W 357579	386890	W 405194	509225	W 434585	724331	W 564444	639427	FIBRES EN POLYESTERS
29	CRUDE ANIMAL,VEG MAT NES		299249		315516		341734		289254	MATIERES BRUTES ANIM,VEGET
292	CRUDE VEG MATERIALS NES		281653	W 33918	296356	W 30957	316189	W 26681	252477	MAT BRUTES VEGETALES NDA
3	MINERAL FUELS ETC		1858790		1756353		2486759		3893219	COMBUSTIBLES MINERAUX LUB
33	PETROLEUM AND PRODUCTS		1838269		1723636		2432399		3820044	PETROLE ET DERIVES
334	PETROLEUM PRODUCTS,REFIN		1738926	MW 12627	1618628	MW 15878	2305943	MW 20507	3705024	PRODUITS RAFFINES
3343	GAS OILS	W 4501946	806658							GAS OILS
3344	FUEL OILS,NES	MW 9084	625803							FUEL OILS
5	CHEMCLS,RELATED PROD NES		4850190		6248567		8827092		9009523	PRODUITS CHIMIQUES
51	ORGANIC CHEMICALS		1461944		1892269		2668364		2664625	PROD CHIMIQ ORGANIQUES
511	HYDROCARBONS NES,DERIVS	W 2007944	641237	W 2518217	965668	W 2684507	1213933	W 3214124	1216782	HYDROCARBURES NDA
5112	CYCLIC HYDROCARBONS	W 1317984	435112	W 1625813	661368	W 1804028	861477	W 2269381	857502	HYDROCARBURES CYCLIQUES
513	CARBOXYLIC ACIDS ETC	W 468923	271979	W 396403	301238	W 617761	693677	W 796562	578790	ACIDES CARBOXYLIQUES
5138	POLYACIDS AND DERIVATIVS	W 331579	187184	W 242058	192565	W 472049	543679	W 642341	440872	ACIDES POLYCARBOXYLIQUES
514	NITROGEN–FNCTN COMPOUNDS	W 137702	305168	W 174739	370199	W 182315	437481	W 224469	503330	COMPOSES FONCT AZOTEES
53	DYES,TANNING,COLOUR PROD		271711		342826		417770		465849	PROD TEINTURE,COLORANTS
58	PLASTIC MATERIALS ETC		2257246		2915764		4399841		4267248	MAT PLAST ARTIFICIELLES
582	PROD OF CONDENSATION ETC	W 400514	578234	W 502970	764752	W 578614	1244935	W 763939	1161237	PROD CONDENS,POLYCOND
5823	ALKYDS,OTHER POLYESTERS	W 325768	451307	W 401004	584920	W 454086	984978	W 631688	892507	ALKYDES ET AUT POLYESTERS
58231	— IN PRIMARY FORMS	W 264623	276225	W 336971	396435	W 379776	697641	W 540540	540867	SOUS FORMES PRIMAIRES
583	POLYMERIZATION ETC PRODS		1676003	W 2533251	2147133	W 2944547	3146740	W 3298347	3095898	PROD POLYMERISATION
5831	POLYETHYLENE	W 949785	538016	W 935633	649135	W 1110070	977168	W 1153620	936475	POLYETHYLENE
58311	— IN PRIMARY FORMS	W 936894	516464	W 918167	617545	W 1085689	928683	W 1127488	883831	POLYETHYLENE PRIMAIRES
5832	POLYPROPYLENE	W 780354	437474	W 841722	617348	W 857593	855683	W 943660	787350	POLYPROPYLENE
58321	— IN PRIMARY FORMS	W 746642	375894	W 805497	550283	W 810844	751023	W 898671	697915	POLYPROPYLENE PRIMAIRES
5833	POLYSTYRENE,ITS COPOLYMR	W 471212	389063	W 472765	474084	W 605559	742413	W 721445	698276	POLYPROPYLENE COPOLYMERES
58331	— IN PRIMARY FORMS	W 468783	385727	W 470407	470612	W 603261	737856	W 720014	695300	SOUS FORMES PRIMAIRES
59	CHEMICAL MATERIALS NES		222577		298766		400563		567927	MAT PROD CHIMIQUES NDA
598	MISCEL CHEM PRODUCTS NES	W 155645	174493	W 198139	231425	W 220727	311838	W 222473	458862	PROD DIV INDUST CHIM NDA
5989	CHEM PRODUCTS,PREPS NES	W 152215	168861	W 193982	223518	W 213952	300859	W 215668	448711	PROD PREP CHIMIQUES NDA
59899	OTH CHEM PRODS,PREPS,NES	W 143754	151979	W 182201	196325	W 192347	265801	W 194289	404545	AUT PRODUITS CHIMIQUES NDA
6	BASIC MANUFACTURES		20901359		23216516		27899606		27373172	ART MANUFACTURES
61	LEATHER,DRESSED FUR,ETC		1167556		1553426		1808104		1986585	CUIRS,PELLETERIES
611	LEATHER	W 86936	970692	W 107753	1302482	W 116694	1525510	W 118588	1599358	CUIRS,PEAUX PREPARES
6114	LEATHR BOVINE NES,EQUINE	W 60006	670547	W 74054	878533	W 83352	1047725	W 88786	1123329	CUIRS DE BOVINS
62	RUBBER MANUFACTURES NES		1279635		1391173		1518011		1763624	CAOUTCHOUC MANUFACTURE
625	RUBBER TYRES, TUBES ETC	W 448426	1132027	W 507928	1232922	W 502871	1329785	W 553783	1548662	PNEUS CAOUTCHOUC VULCANISE
6251	TYRES NEW FOR MOTOR CARS	W 174785	480282	W 220300	583247	W 227744	656481	W 244157	738765	PNEUS POUR VOITURES
6252	TYRES,NEW,BUS OR LORRY	W 182850	437284	W 186762	432353	W 166117	421868	W 194453	529144	PNEUS POUR AUTOBUS,CAMIONS
64	PAPER,PAPERBOARD AND MFR		572840		832179		1178008		1239188	PAPIERS,CARTONS & OUVRAGES
641	PAPER AND PAPERBOARD		416874	W 952538	633750	W 1013294	884839	W 1416259	937873	PAPIERS ET CARTONS
6412	PRINTG,WRITING PAPER NES	W 593059	336628	W 727310	498550	W 700884	626263	W 958741	675407	PAPIERS POUR L'IMPRESSION
64122	— COATED,IMPREGNATD ETC	W 592640	333270	W 726856	495026	W 700113	622357	W 958106	671767	PAPIERS IMPRESSION COUCHES
65	TEXTILE YARN,FABRICS,ETC		8963241		10702212		12319997		12717328	FILS,TISSUS,ARTICLES TEXTILE
651	TEXTILE YARN		947994	W 262317	1059350	W 311592	1335810	W 454080	1473734	FILS TEXTILES
6514	SYN FIB YRN,BULK,MONOFIL	W 143819	512927	W 164643	552189	W 220202	828600	W 365569	999905	FILS CONT 85% FIB TEXT SYNTH
65142	— NONTXT ETC CONT PAMID	W 125405	416071	W 137598	419462	W 190774	659085	W 328298	832066	FILS NON TEX FI CON POLYAMID
652	COTTON FABRICS,WOVEN	W 47533	392133	W 53342	469581	W 52392	520421	W 53856	557434	TISSUS DE COTON
6522	WOVEN COTTON BLEACHD,ETC	W 35692	338148	W 45134	426465	W 47089	488616	W 49629	531565	TISSUS COTON BLANCHIS ETC
653	WOVN MAN–MADE FIB FABRIC	W 472404	4724746	W 591791	5781680	W 655051	6561446	W 693707	6273964	TISSUS FIBRES SYNTH,ARTIF
6531	CONT SYNT WEAVES NONPILE	W 342657	3531659	W 437663	4341095	W 505274	5038348	W 559849	4925217	TISSUS FIBRES SYNTH CONTINUE
65315	CONT SYN TXTL FABRIC NES	W 338599	3479706	W 433382	4282881	W 500533	4968821	W 554937	4862676	TIS PLUS 85% TEXT SYNT CONT
6534	DISC SYN BLEND FABRC NES	W 45282	350401	W 46385	355382	W 40048	317738	W 37734	298251	TISSUS FIBRES SYNTH DISCONT
65341	DISC SYN FIB–COTTN FABRC	W 37472	274509	W 39594	284104	W 33755	247474	W 31656	228876	TISSUS FIB SYNT DIS MEL COTO
6535	CONT REGN WEAVES NONPILE	W 25230	262279	W 25481	270564	W 27254	315066	W 28245	328883	TISSUS FIB TEXT ART CONTINU
6536	DISC REGN TXTL FABRC NES	W 31808	247646	W 47106	388696	W 43528	366749	W 29690	235975	TISSUS 85% TEXT ART DISC
654	OTH WOVEN TEXTILE FABRIC	W 16460	497178	W 14639	476545	W 14049	436329	W 11283	439028	TISSUS AUT COTON SYNT,ARTIF
6541	SILK FABRICS WOVEN	W 3155	306210	W 3144	297581	W 2966	266235	W 3401	297126	TISSUS DE SOIE
655	KNITTED,ETC FABRICS	W 111084	839958	W 141801	1121534	W 152420	1227311	W 172119	1447449	ETOF BONNETERIE PIECES ETC
6552	OTHER KNIT ETC FAB NONEL	W 111084	839958	W 141801	1121534	W 152420	1227311	W 172119	1447449	ETOF BON NON ELAS NON SYNT
656	LACE,RIBBONS,TULLE,ETC	W 23608	269031	W 23442	298010	W 26359	369085	W 30601	449871	TULLES,BRODERIE
657	SPECIAL TXTL FABRC,PRODS	W 194319	923808	W 230850	1114178	W 269530	1438709	W 292335	1695063	TISSUS SPECIAUX
6573	COATED ETC TEXTILES NES	W 130858	654325	W 158730	787352	W 185949	1000386	W 202038	1172886	TISSUS,ART MATIERE TEXT NDA
65732	PLASTIC COATED TEXTILES	W 93532	491113	W 117902	609008	W 144678	800970	W 160161	972957	TISSUS IMPREGNES
658	TEXTILE ARTICLES NES	W 61489	344388	W 55319	353629	W 58154	397119	W 52298	339098	ART FACONNES MAT TEXTILES
66	NONMETAL MINERAL MFS NES		648148		661129		690097		660399	ART MIN NON METALLIQUES
661	LIME,CEMENT,BLDG PRODS		358204	W 4455209	339128	W 3598534	290634	W 2407191	213101	CHAUX,CIMENTS MAT CONSTR
67	IRON AND STEEL		5022471		4787608		5557963		5372849	FER ET ACIER
672	IRON,STEEL PRIMARY FORMS		1246374	W 3110158	1119027	W 3152589	1289359	W 3606147	1267409	LINGOTS FER,ACIER
6727	IRN,STL COIL FR REROLLNG		1168176	W 2924588	1067534	W 2711069	1157656	W 3171887	1161650	EBAUCHES POUR TOLES FER
67271	IRON,SIMPLE STEEL COILS	W 3309636	1112092	W 2885564	1013482	W 2666736	1079163	W 3109424	1066512	EBAUCHES NON EN ACIER
673	IRON,STEEL SHAPES ETC		673962	W 1494614	668951	W 962086	574119	W 1321889	609125	BARRES,PROFIL FER,ACIER
6732	IRON,STEEL BARS ETC		271452	W 871524	300766	W 291890	170197	W 453612	203687	BARRES FER,ACIER
6733	IRON,STEEL PROFILES ETC		269995	W 446132	250710	W 509020	281208	W 706982	299595	PROFILES,PALPLAN FER,ACIER
674	IRN,STL UNIV,PLATE,SHEET		2269046	W 3897800	2142451	W 3951012	2633402	W 4021732	2487385	LARGES PLATS,TOLES
6744	IRN,STL HVY PLATE,ROLLED		326108	W 593923	252800	W 615139	310811	W 510944	224764	TOLES LAMINEES PLUS 4.75 MM
67441	— OF IRON OR SIMPLE STL		321585	W 591311	248178	W 609716	297214	W 499297	201243	TOLES NON ACIER FIN CARB
6746	IRN,STL THIN PLATE,ROLLD		1080277	W 1890817	1042994	W 1902334	1285144	W 1991183	1252439	TOLES LAM MOINS 3MM
67461	— OF IRON OR SIMPLE STL		819480	W 1738600	760603	W 1752675	923636	W 1773298	858213	TOL NON AC FIN MOINS 3 MM
67463	— OF STAINLESS ETC STL		257634	W 152209	282388	W 135808	353257	W 189412	378898	TOL ACIER INOX MOINS 3 MM
6749	OTH IRN,STL PLATES,SHEET		652817	W 1025520	625399	W 1047445	794493	W 1078236	735287	AUTRES TOLES FER,ACIER
67491	— OF IRON OR SIMPLE STL		641981	W 1019258	612252	W 1040524	774135	W 1069153	718099	AUT TOLES AUTRES ACIER FIN
678	IRON,STL TUBES,PIPES,ETC		554640	W 884850	525009	W 895539	610483	W 856883	572480	TUBES,TUYAUX EN FONTE,FER
6783	IRON,STL TUBES,PIPES NES		463640	W 823860	414770	W 826320	466351	W 806335	441486	AUT TUBES,TUYAUX FER,ACIER
68	NON–FERROUS METALS		475944		750929		1099703		1010046	METAUX NON FERREUX
682	COPPER EXC CEMENT COPPER		243607	W 106057	318309	W 115663	430311	W 148724	448002	CUIVRE
6822	COPPER,ALLOYS WORKED	W 79707	231130	W 98790	301604	W 111047	416627	W 140080	427373	CUIVRE,ALLIAGES OUVRES
684	ALUMINIUM		153490	W 121215	283314	W 185381	522837	W 141616	395297	ALUMINIUM
69	METAL MANUFACTURES NES		2692604		2422913		3581294		2490928	ART MANUFACT EN METAL NDA
691	STRUCTURES AND PARTS NES		1026154	W 227729	534669	W 607109	1352823	W 196022	405137	CONSTRUCT FER,ACIER,ALU

5. Special Exports F.O.B. by Commodities according to the S.I.T.C. (Rev. 2) in thousand U.S. Dollars
Exportations Spéciales F.O.B. par Produits d'après la C.T.C.I. (Rév. 2) en milliers de Dollars E.U.

SITC CTCI	COMMODITY	1993 WEIGHT POIDS	1993 VALUE VALEUR	1994 WEIGHT POIDS	1994 VALUE VALEUR	1995 WEIGHT POIDS	1995 VALUE VALEUR	1996 WEIGHT POIDS	1996 VALUE VALEUR	PRODUIT
6911	STRUCTURES,PARTS IRN,STL		989052	W 220286	493899	W 595521	1286284	W 185583	328838	CONSTRUCT FER,ACIER,FONTE
697	BASE MTL HOUSEHOLD EQUIP	W 66953	464226	W 73402	488363	W 68674	487938	W 62751	436200	ART MENAGE MET COMMUNS
6974	BASE MTL DMSTC ARTIC NES	W 47751	352445	W 55356	388687	W 49931	387438	W 46950	345609	ARTICLES NDA FONTE,FER,ETC
69741	— OF IRON OR STEEL	W 33769	248968	W 35987	258586	W 33417	267373	W 29147	228911	ART NDA EN FONTE,FER
699	BASE METAL MFRS NES		316510	W 119406	377553	W 147101	507300	W 136082	474948	ART MANUFACTURES MET NDA
7	MACHINES,TRANSPORT EQUIP		36934770		47037272		65624625		67550577	MACHINES MATERIEL TRANSPORT
71	POWER GENERATING EQUIPMT		845265		1002289		1212193		692738	MACHINES GENERATRICES
714	ENGINES AND MOTORS NES	W 832	520841	W 1254	541896	W 1565	608075	W 684	141564	MOTEURS NON ELECTRIQUES
7144	REACTION ENGINES	W 337	326138	W 297	290036	W 231	246542	W 100	72479	PROPULSEURS A REACTION
72	MACHS FOR SPCL INDUSTRYS		1210075		1729440		2588398		3047546	MAC SPECIALES POUR INDUST
723	CIVIL ENGNEERG EQUIP ETC	W 79004	240739	W 134062	429960	W 194079	672887	W 206559	723592	APPAREILS DE GENIE CIVIL
7234	CONST,MINING MACHNRY NES	W 64795	210574	W 117707	392547	W 168387	604767	W 180182	665277	MACH POUR LA CONST, MINES
72342	SLFPRP SHOVELS,EXCAVATRS	W 62651	199054	W 114617	377798	W 163211	579495	W 175819	632386	PELLES MECANIQUES
724	TEXTILE,LEATHER MACHNRY		462884	W 92119	612844	W 97375	745059	W 115100	816809	MACH POUR INDUSTRIE TEXTILE
728	OTH MACHY FOR SPCL INDUS		391904	W 59107	550654	W 72350	1001663	W 87783	1315498	AUT MACH IND PARTICULIERES
7284	MACHY FOR SPCL INDUS NES		334554	W 38118	461645	W 52895	881503	W 65611	1167786	MACH SPEC IND PARTICUL.
72848	OTH MCHY WITH INDIV FNCT	W 10622	132619	W 15768	211105	W 22791	430095	W 27453	558681	AUTRES MACHINES NDA
73	METALWORKING MACHINERY		171820		329182		472446		614597	MACH TRAVAIL DES METAUX
736	METALWORKING MACH–TOOLS	W 16018	123818	W 20049	199079	W 35223	356066	W 47837	509976	MACH–OUTILS TRAVAIL METAUX
74	GENRL INDUSTRL MACHY NES		1715248		2199501		2953213		3150634	MACH APP INDUSTRIE
741	HEATING,COOLING EQUIPMNT	W 68489	472725	W 78207	564686	W 104006	783635	W 97326	759162	MACH CHAUFFAGE,PIECES
7415	AIR–CONDITIONING MACHNRY	W 26430	206136	W 32291	244013	W 46845	396771	W 53057	450705	GROUPES CONDITION AIR
743	PUMPS NES,CENTRFUGES ETC		254237	W 44327	277759	W 68696	455451	W 75919	528465	POMPES COMPRES,VENT ETC
7431	PUMPS FOR GASES ETC	W 29489	171736	W 33177	192904	W 54374	333597	W 57371	390890	POMPES AIR A VIDE,COMPRES
744	MECHANICAL HANDLING EQU	W 93296	470529	W 134431	678905	W 159850	835981	W 186590	890787	EQUIP MANUTENTION PIECES
7442	LIFTING,LOADING MACH NES	W 38881	220622	W 70109	371330	W 66738	424044	W 71135	426896	APP LEVAGE,MANUTENTION
74428	OTH HANDLING ETC MCH NES	W 27797	156078	W 57291	306198	W 43706	300491	W 48664	305019	AUT APP LEVAGE ETC
749	NONELEC MACH PTS,ACC NES		404216	W 46613	459811	W 56753	653818	W 62676	773924	PIECES MACH NON ELEC NDA
7499	OTH NONELEC MCHY PTS NES		167952	W 13253	200882	W 16825	296288	W 22281	447089	PIECES NON ELECT NDA
74991	FOUNDRY MOULDS ETC NES	W 9949	158440	W 11801	190514	W 14853	279510	W 19633	408060	MOULES POUR METAUX
75	OFFICE MACHNES,ADP EQUIP		3474332		3607205		4966919		5673306	MACH BUREAU TRAIT AUTOM
752	AUTOMTIC DATA PROC EQUIP	W 134097	2584738	W 145438	2799829	W 190097	3956041	W 206123	4706854	MACH TRAIT INFORMATION
7522	DIGITAL COMPUTERS	W 7247	344863	W 4013	256932	W 3136	169351	W 526	74223	MACH DIGITALES COMPLETES
7524	DIGITL CENTRL STOR UNITS	W 881	116500	W 1459	222065	W 2628	374965	W 5657	684507	UNITES MEMOIRE CENTRALES
7525	ADP PERIPHERAL UNITS	W 123868	1990845	W 138487	2229585	W 181995	3239602	W 197783	3745499	UNITES PERIPHERIQUES
759	OFFICE,ADP MCH PTS,ACCES		739870	W 5803	624424	W 7265	805517	W 9272	733460	PIECES DU 751 ET 752
7599	ACCTG,ETC,ADP MCH PTS,AC		722813	W 4164	595609	W 4961	768127	W 8072	716827	PIECES DU 751 ET 752
76	TELECOMM,SOUND EQUIPMENT		7092909		8234335		8877460		8887242	EQUIPMENT DE TELECOM
761	TELEVISION RECEIVERS	W 140758	1462755	W 160385	1698219	W 173061	1900728	W 201018	2206484	RECEPTEURS DE TELEVISION
7611	COLOUR TV RECEIVERS	W 134982	1406259	W 156845	1648713	W 169778	1843917	W 198679	2157089	RECEPTEURS COULEUR
762	RADIO BROADCAST RECEIVRS	W 55752	1125993	W 52689	1092393	W 41420	908367	W 18577	530092	RECEPTEURS RADIODIFFUSION
7621	MTR VEHC RADIO RECEIVERS	W 14399	468928	W 14237	464844	W 12163	424056	W 8640	333022	RECEPTEURS RADIO AUTO
7628	OTHER RADIO RECEIVERS	W 36761	567265	W 32032	500846	W 25383	409701	W 8423	156619	AUTRES RECEPT RADIO
763	SOUND RECORDRS,PHONOGRPH	W 56125	1581845	W 62696	1756715	W 58595	1824208	W 47293	1747057	PHONO,APP ENREGISTREMENT
7638	OTHR SOUND APPARATUS ETC	W 51425	1524335	W 59255	1715782	W 56547	1797792	W 45515	1723948	AUT APP D'ENREGIS,REPROD
76381	TV IMAGE,SND RECRDRS ETC	W 43174	1309940	W 49056	1479609	W 45354	1498580	W 36691	1434789	APP ENREG,REPRO IMAG,SON
764	TELECOM EQPT,PTS,ACC NES	W 127621	2922316	W 144787	3687009	W 149975	4243658	W 168243	4403609	EQUIP TELECOM,PIECES
7641	LINE TELEPHONE,ETC EQUIP	W 12973	591673	W 14256	669670	W 16788	792397	W 17094	766435	APP TELEPHON PAR FIL
7642	MICROPH,LOUDSPKR,AMPLIFR	W 43130	348757	W 45316	399847	W 46811	447546	W 42585	458072	MICRO,HAUT–PARLEUR,AMPLI
7643	TV,RADIO TRANSMITTRS ETC	W 2033	277675	W 2135	453527	W 2533	584483	W 2052	529265	APP EMET TELE RADIO
7648	TELECOMM EQUIPMENT NES	W 9259	411438	W 9274	485254	W 9241	551340	W 9759	398126	APP TELECOM NDA
7649	PTS NES OF EQUIPMT OF 76	W 60227	1292772	W 73807	1678710	W 74602	1867891	W 96754	2251711	PIECES DE LA DIV 76
76493	TELECOMM EQUIPMT PTS NES	W 44159	765429	W 56081	1026493	W 51836	1040407	W 67249	1354868	PIECES 761,762,764.3,8
76499	PARTS ETC OF SOUND EQUIP	W 8937	410382	W 9423	500731	W 12292	612984	W 18201	644039	PIECES NDA POUR 763
77	ELECTRIC MACHNRY NES ETC		12340745		18114361		28499099		25498660	MACH APP ELECT NDA
771	ELECTRIC POWER MACHY NES		406157	W 62737	442625	W 78470	564987	W 86304	711852	MACH PROD,TRANS ELECTR
7712	OTH ELEC POWER MACHY NES		201346	W 21941	211734	W 31261	309902	W 37437	426765	AUT APP PROD TRANSF ELEC
772	SWITCHGEAR ETC,PARTS NES		469565	W 23556	662015	W 25663	756993	W 32127	908979	APP COUPURE,SECT ETC
7721	SWITCHGEAR ETC		250256	W 15915	331781	W 16553	373955	W 21437	453478	APP COUPURE,SECTIONMNT
773	ELECTR DISTRIBUTNG EQUIP	W 115921	394823	W 100136	360076	W 129107	489955	W 158150	620213	EQUIPMT DISTRIBUTION ELECT
7731	INSULATED WIRE,CABLE ETC	W 112020	385980	W 98086	352369	W 125656	478811	W 155835	601443	FILS,CABLES ISOLES ELECT
775	HOUSEHOLD TYPE EQUIP NES		1217733	W 273308	1487616	W 302994	1691209	W 336126	1921688	MACH,APP USAGE DOMESTQUE
7752	DOM REFRIGERATRS,FREEZRS	W 74584	338707	W 79765	367914	W 84210	393112	W 102479	480444	REFRIG,CONGEL MENAGER
77521	DOMESTIC REFRIGERATORS	W 74073	336108	W 78943	363236	W 83168	386269	W 101598	475563	REFRIGERATEURS
7758	ELECTRO–THERMIC APPL NES		743293	W 158754	925153	W 168703	1007711	W 171467	1059563	APP ELECTROTHERMIQ NDA
77586	ELECTROTHERM DOM APP NES	W 117379	680702	W 146491	816874	W 145059	837452	W 143565	864246	APP ELECTRO THERMIQUES
776	TRANSISTORS,VALVES,ETC		8078346	W 199742	11847982	W 245138	19372850	W 291802	17305165	LAMPES,TUBES,VALVES
7761	TV PICTURE TUBES	W 151167	889038	W 159850	913475	W 181016	1087533	W 192271	1098126	TUBES CATHODIQUES
7762	OTH ELECTRONIC TUBES ETC		124346	W 20748	238910	W 36747	506349	W 60895	876581	AUT LAMPES ELECTRONIQUES
7763	DIODES,TRANSISTORS,ETC		438838	W 2542	511029	W 2989	669570	W 3407	673888	DIODES,TRANSISTORS
7764	ELECTRONIC MICROCIRCUITS		6425700	W 8714	9917853	W 10433	16734530	W 11262	14161173	MICROSTRUCTURES ELECTRON
7768	ELCTRNC COMP PTS,CRYSTLS		200424	W 7888	266716	W 13954	374868	W 23967	495397	CRIST PIEZO–ELEC,PCS 776
77689	ELECTRNIC COMPON PTS NES		133248	W 7575	181884	W 13547	255732	W 23585	396299	PIECES DU GROUPE 776
778	ELECTRICAL MACHINERY NES		1733913	W 148151	3258467	W 181803	5556186	W 206354	3954230	AUTRES MACH ELECT NDA
7788	OTH ELEC MACHY,EQUIP NES		1336465	W 30187	2788577	W 34668	5015383	W 36961	3399480	AUT MACH APP ELEC NDA
77889	ELEC PARTS OF MACHY NES	W 315	1001901	W 503	2347506	W 691	4419737	W 678	2605239	PIECES ELEC DE MACH NDA
78	ROAD VEHICLES		5725056		6631676		10121863		12350572	VEHICULES ROUTIERS
781	PASS MOTOR VEH EXC BUSES	W 588214	3883985	W 670197	4470416	W 1015619	7241992	W 1277117	9087606	AUTO TRANSPORT PERSONNES
782	LORRIES,SPCL MTR VEH NES	W 91250	334423	W 144222	507755	W 239859	796500	W 257232	872434	VEHICULES SPECIAUX,MARCH
7821	LORRIES,TRUCKS	W 87800	323380	W 133524	462925	W 217418	698664	W 241994	814161	VEHICULES TRANSP MARCHAND
783	ROAD MOTOR VEHICLES NES	W 57019	256072	W 77359	279057	W 91622	363650	W 102286	465156	VEHICULES ROUTIERS NDA
7831	BUSES	W 56801	255270	W 77131	278916	W 91500	363562	W 102174	465051	VOITURES TRANSPORT COMMUN
784	MOTOR VEH PRTS,ACCES NES	W 70202	385061	W 82003	500839	W 113604	667397	W 166235	1036878	PIECES 722,781,782,783
7849	OTHER MOTOR VEHCL PARTS	W 69452	382276	W 81166	497038	W 109507	652937	W 161545	1008790	PIECES 722,781,782,783
786	TRAILERS,NONMOTR VEH,NES	W 193603	725692	W 297621	711741	W 295856	874099	W 194407	700458	REMORQUES,CADRES,CONTAIN
7861	TRAILERS,TRANSP CONTAINR	W 176872	688968	W 275774	665326	W 272841	823412	W 175739	659715	REMORQUES TOUS VEHICULES
78613	CONTAINERS INC ROAD–RAIL	W 176439	687882	W 275027	663657	W 272050	821580	W 174932	657724	CADRES ET CONTAINERS
79	OTHR TRANSPORT EQUIPMENT		4359320		5189282		5933034		7635283	AUTRE MATERIEL TRANSPORT
792	AIRCRAFT ETC		286364		224811		281958	W 1268	236727	APP NAVIGATION AERIENNE
793	SHIPS AND BOATS ETC		4060623	MW 13943	4944844		5532786	MW 16125	7127303	NAVIRES BATEAUX,ETC
7932	SHIPS AND BOATS NES		3583771	MW 13925	4888664	MW 16431	5427090	MW 16050	7009420	NAVIRES ET BATEAUX
79322	TANKERS OF ALL KINDS		1467803	W 2500999	2086404	W 2696805	1896771	W 2613019	2290887	BATEAUX–CITERNES
79323	OTHER CARGO VESSELS		2084352	MW 11421	2790704	MW 13727	3512664	MW 13428	4697572	AUT BATEAUX TRANS MARCH
7938	TUGS,SPECIAL VESSELS ETC		473865	W 12831	53412		103033	W 55967	86561	REMORQUEURS,BATEAUX SPEC
79382	SPECL PURPOSE VESSLS ETC	W 64731	471897	W 11971	49127	W 35966	82764	W 50105	47958	BAT–PHARES,–POMPES,DRAGUES
8	MISC MANUFACTURED GOODS		14068266		13293566		13135814		11978271	ART MANUFACTURES DIVERS
831	*TRAVEL GOODS,HANDBAGS	W 51438	796333	W 45773	706179	W 42408	681368	W 30882	540800	ARTICLES DE VOYAGE ETC
83102	TRAVEL GDS,TOILET–CASES	W 23107	306391	W 21139	277832	W 19762	260162	W 12954	191967	ARTICLES DE VOYAGE
83109	OTHER TRAVEL BAGS,CASES	W 20469	303149	W 18439	280685	W 18917	309111	W 15858	278089	AUT CONTENANTS SIMILAIRES
84	CLOTHING AND ACCESSORIES		6229124		5692645		4981672		4237303	VETEMENTS
842	MENS OUTERWEAR NOT KNIT	W 30222	748451	W 32763	667220	W 23417	543368	W 20087	463820	VET DESSUS POUR HOMMES

5. Special Exports F.O.B. by Commodities according to the S.I.T.C. (Rev. 2) in thousand U.S. Dollars
Exportations Spéciales F.O.B. par Produits d'après la C.T.C.I. (Rév. 2) en milliers de Dollars E.U.

SITC CTCI	COMMODITY	1993 WEIGHT POIDS	1993 VALUE VALEUR	1994 WEIGHT POIDS	1994 VALUE VALEUR	1995 WEIGHT POIDS	1995 VALUE VALEUR	1996 WEIGHT POIDS	1996 VALUE VALEUR	PRODUIT
8429	— OTHER OUTER GARMENTS	W 16481	367616	W 16274	347646	W 14006	294574	W 12260	259483	AUT VET DES HOM MAT TEX
843	WOMENS OUTERWEAR NONKNIT		1059724	W 42410	1034974	W 33893	887800	W 29976	733447	VET DESSUS FEMMES MAT TEX
8431	— COATS AND JACKETS	W 8508	249387	W 7216	235387	W 5346	199720	W 4131	160845	MANT,VEST FEM MAT TEXTIL
8435	— BLOUSES	W 15904	267013	W 14136	250129	W 8062	198970	W 7010	148668	BLOUSES FEM MAT TEXTILES
8439	— OTHER OUTER GARMENTS		301317	W 12184	280792	W 12707	279086	W 10622	226654	AUT VET DES FEM MAT TEXT
844	UNDER GARMENTS NOT KNIT	W 29969	565352	W 28604	517475	W 24566	465313	W 20473	366920	VETEMENT DESSOUS MAT TEX
8441	— MENS SHIRTS	W 27653	510006	W 27622	484411	W 23892	439937	W 19776	350146	CHEMISES HOMMES MAT TEXT
84412	—— OF SYNTHETIC FIBRES	W 18867	313010	W 19898	308841	W 16807	273305	W 14223	226190	CHEMISES HOMMES FIB SYNT
845	OUTERWEAR KNIT NONELASTC		1412311	W 81983	1468393	W 63438	1275469	W 52326	1062618	VET DESSOUS,ACCES BONNET
8451	— JERSEYS,PULLOVERS ETC		744388	W 39700	660818	W 26981	498867	W 22576	412914	CHANDAILS,PULL–OVERS ETC
8459	— OTHER,CLTHG ACCESRYS	W 33847	602152	W 38751	728456	W 32627	682301	W 26433	574112	AUT VET DESSUS DE BONNE
846	UNDER GARMENTS KNITTED		650280	W 35544	652833	W 39797	741088	W 37384	667947	SOUS VETS DE BONNETERIE
8463	— OF SYNTH FBR NONELAST	W 20514	346226	W 18131	327637	W 15286	310337	W 13706	284385	SOUS–VET BONNET FIB SYNT
84632	—— MENS SHIRTS	W 18872	317435	W 16792	303002	W 14162	284804	W 12419	254127	CHEMISES DE BON FIB SYNMT
847	TEXTILE CLTHNG ACCES NES		561131	W 26723	547469	W 26887	539811	W 28314	548072	ACCES VET MAT TEXT NDA
8471	— NOT KNITTED		257911	W 6197	232304	W 5137	197757	W 6565	219779	ACCES VET MAT TEX NON BON
8472	CLTHNG ACCESRYS ETC KNIT		303220	W 20526	315165	W 21750	342053	W 21749	328293	ACCES VET BONNE NDA
84722	KNIT SOCKS,ETC NONELASTC		277540	W 17178	287929	W 18185	314267	W 17868	301282	CHAUSSETTES BON. NON ELAS
848	HEADGEAR,NONTXTL CLOTHNG		1231876	W 20813	804280	W 14689	528824	W 11853	394479	VET ACCES MAT AUT QUE TEX
8481	LEATHER CLOTHES,ACCESSOR	W 19554	1003094	W 11015	602791	W 5871	335734	W 4011	220946	VET ACCES MAT CUIR ARTIF
851	*FOOTWEAR	W 110290	2128047	W 85870	1556674	W 65335	1245728	W 48399	890461	CHAUSSURES
85101	FOOTWEAR RUBBER,PLASTIC	W 20263	388455	W 17209	264967	W 16153	297746	W 11899	227888	CHAUS SEMELLES CAOUTCH
85102	FOOTWEAR LEATHER	W 89038	1719227	W 67717	1278136	W 48761	943262	W 36122	659283	CHAUS SEMELLES EN CUIR
87	PRECISION INSTRUMNTS NES		521315		612704		806069		778865	INSTRUM,APPAR SCIENT NDA
871	OPTICAL INSTRUMENTS	W 2049	142776	W 2125	176525	W 2500	246087	W 3692	392615	APPAR,INSTRUM D'OPTIQUE
874	MEASURNG,CONTROLNG INSTR		322634	W 6916	362739	W 7738	474439	W 8104	302464	INSTRUMENTS DE MESURE
88	PHOTO EQU,OPTICL GDS ETC		657884		748661		891418		887660	APP,FOURN PHOTO,OP,MONTR
89	MISC MANUFCTRD GOODS NES		3499383		3675370		4217758		4324364	ART MANUFACTURES DIVERS
893	ARTICLES OF PLASTIC NES		521366		623129		756138		763615	OUVRAGES EN MAT DIVIS 58
8939	MISC PLASTIC ARTICLES		435640	W 243922	517028	W 258267	622393	W 258017	601245	ART DIVERS EN MAT DIV 58
89399	OTHR PLASTC ARTICLES NES		347610	W 153602	401837	W 161161	480184	W 160373	462285	AUT OUV MAT DIV 58
894	TOYS,SPORTING GOODS,ETC		715364	W 46041	660805	W 51083	774666	W 50729	845999	VOITURES ENFANTS,JOUETS
8942	TOYS,INDOOR GAMES ETC		332470	W 25190	238194	W 25881	271949	W 25502	296006	JOUETS,JEUX ETC
8947	OTH SPORT GDS,FAIR AMUSM	W 17702	366209	W 19994	408777	W 24648	496781	W 24792	543612	AUT ART DE SPORT
89471	FISHNG,HUNTNG EQUIP NES	W 10154	286974	W 11396	312387	W 13961	384093	W 12869	423284	HAMECONS ET EPUISETTES
897	GOLD,SILVER WARE,JEWELRY		337044		338435		328259		328036	BIJOUTERIE,ORFEVRERIE
8972	IMITATION JEWELLERY		290257		293588		272604		273273	BIJOUTERIE DE FANTAISIE
898	MUSICAL INSTRUMENTS,PTS	W 169859	1133240	W 182224	1198588	W 184717	1385329	W 184945	1451051	INSTRUMENTS DE MUSIQUE
8983	SOUND RECRDNG TAPE,DISCS	W 146671	843903	W 159621	897550	W 160304	1021519	W 165046	1114919	SUPPORTS SON POUR 763
89831	PREPD SND RECORDNG MEDIA	W 146324	824138	W 159131	872312	W 159699	987636	W 164373	1073744	SUPPORTS PREPARES
899	OTHER MANUFACTURED GOODS		555933		580428		642744		597012	AUT ART MANUF DIVERS NDA
9	GOODS NOT CLASSD BY KIND		342093		639735		2483891		5372261	ART TRANSACT NON CLASSES
971	*GOLD,NON MONETARY NES		290462		567704	K 197821	2431086	K 429320	5310861	OR NON MONETAIRE
97101	NONMON GLD UNWRT,SEMIMFD		290159	K 48357	567329	K 197671	2430808	K 427268	5310284	OR,ALLIAGES D'OR BRUTS

1. HISTORICAL SERIES, 1961–1996 SPECIAL TRADE, IMPORTS C.I.F., EXPORTS F.O.B.
SERIES HISTORIQUES, 1961–1996 COMMERCE SPECIAL, IMPORTATIONS C.A.F., EXPORTATIONS F.O.B

YEAR ANNEE	VALUE IN MILLION KUWAITI DINARS / VALEUR EN MILLION KUWAITI DINARS: MERCHANDISE – MARCHANDISE IMPORTS	EXPORTS	GOLD – OR IMPORTS	EXPORTS	CONVERSION FACTORS U.S. CENTS PER KUWAITI DINAR / FACTEURS DE CONVERSION CENTS E.U. PAR KUWAITI DINAR IMPORTS	EXPORTS	INDEX NUMBERS – INDICES: QUANTUM IMPORTS	EXPORTS	UNIT VALUE / VALEUR UNITAIRE IMPORTS	EXPORTS
1961	89.10	336.80			280.0000	280.0000				
1962	101.90	375.30			280.0000	280.0000				
1963	115.70	395.30			280.0000	280.0000				
1964	115.10	434.80			280.0000	280.0000				
1965	134.70	444.10			280.0000	280.0000				
1966	165.30	479.40			280.0000	280.0000				
1967	211.90	484.40			280.0000	280.0000				
1968	218.30	513.20			280.0000	280.0000				
1969	230.80	550.00			280.0000	280.0000				
1970	223.30	679.10			280.0000	280.0000				
1971	232.30	918.80			280.0000	280.0000				
1972	262.20	1005.40			304.0000	304.0000				
1973	310.60	1129.70			338.7460	338.7080				
1974	455.10	3214.70			341.4810	340.9120				
1975	693.20	2663.00			344.5620	344.8930				
1976	972.00	2875.80			342.2760	342.5400				
1977	1387.00	2796.60			349.3440	349.2760				
1978	1263.90	2868.20			363.7790	364.0810				
1979	1437.00	5172.90			362.1230	361.2400				
1980	1765.00	5369.00			370.0710	369.7990				
1981	1945.40	4553.50			358.2264	359.7197				
1982	2384.60	3156.40			347.3700	347.1835				
1983	2149.10	3373.60			343.1681	343.0791				
1984	2041.70	3631.00			338.0041	337.9205				
1985	1784.70	3151.90			342.6100	332.4677				
1986	1661.20	2105.00			342.3271	343.0552				
1987	1530.70	2304.40			359.0400	358.6852				
1988	1714.20	2166.00			358.5079	358.2112				
1989	1849.40	3378.00			340.4900	340.4900				
1990	1145.70	2031.40			342.4096	342.4343				
1991	1353.30	309.40			351.7800	351.7800				
1992	2129.20	1931.10			340.5632	340.0697				
1993	2123.80	3091.20			331.5726	331.4038				
1994	1988.20	3341.60			335.9886	336.0161				
1995	2323.10	3814.50			335.4347	335.1575				
1996	2258.00	4432.30			333.9900	333.9900				

2. IMPORTS BY BROAD ECONOMIC CATEGORY AND EXPORTS BY INDUSTRIAL ORIGIN. (PERCENTAGE OF TOTAL VALUE)
IMPORTATIONS PAR CATEGORIES ECONOMIQUES ET EXPORTATIONS PAR BRANCHE D'ACTIVITE.(EN POURCENTAGE DE LA VALEUR TOTALE)

IMPORTS – IMPORTATIONS

	1990	1991	1992	1993	1994	1995	1996
TOTAL IMPORTS–IMPORTATIONS TOTALES	100.	100.	100.	100.	100.	100.	
1 FOOD BEV–ALIMENTATION BOISSONS	15.3	9.5	12.3	13.6	15.2	13.8	
11 PRIMARY–PRODUITS DE BASE	9.7	5.3	7.5	8.5	9.3	8.4	
111 FOR INDUSTRY–POUR L'INDUSTRIE	3.7	2.3	3.1	3.4	3.9	3.3	
112 FOR HOUSEHOLDS–POUR LES MENAGES	6.0	3.0	4.4	5.1	5.3	5.1	
12 PROCESSED–PRODUITS ELABORES	5.6	4.2	4.7	5.0	5.9	5.5	
121 FOR INDUSTRY–POUR L'INDUSTRIE	1.0	0.3	0.5	0.5	0.7	0.6	
122 FOR HOUSEHOLDS–POUR LES MENAGES	4.6	3.9	4.3	4.6	5.2	4.8	
2 IND SUPPLIES–APPROV INDUSTRIELS	26.8	11.0	18.7	22.0	24.6	24.5	
21 PRIMARY–PRODUITS DE BASE	1.3	0.4	0.7	1.0	1.2	1.1	
22 PROCESSED–PRODUITS ELABORES	25.5	10.7	18.1	21.0	23.4	23.4	
3 FUELS–COMBUSTIBLES	0.6	0.7	0.4	0.3	0.5	0.4	
31 PRIMARY–PRODUITS DE BASE	0.1	0.0	0.1	0.1	0.0	0.1	
32 PROCESSED–PRODUITS ELABORES	0.5	0.7	0.4	0.3	0.4	0.3	
321 MOTOR SPIRIT–ESSENCE							
322 OTHER–AUTRES	0.5	0.7	0.4	0.3	0.4	0.3	
4 MACHINERY–EQUIPEMENT	14.6	23.6	19.5	18.8	17.6	15.3	
41 CAPITAL EQUIPMENT–MACHINES	13.8	22.1	18.0	17.2	16.1	13.9	
42 PARTS–PIECES ACCESSOIRES	0.8	1.5	1.4	1.6	1.5	1.4	
5 TRANSPORT–TRANSPORT	17.2	34.3	23.6	23.2	19.1	24.9	
51 PASSENGER CARS–AUTOMOBILES	8.5	23.6	12.7	8.0	8.4	8.4	
52 OTHER–AUTRES	4.2	6.8	6.3	10.6	6.5	11.9	
521 INDUSTRIAL–INDUSTRIELS	4.1	6.7	6.2	10.5	6.4	11.8	
522 NON INDUSTRIAL–NON INDUSTRIEL	0.1	0.0	0.1	0.1	0.1	0.1	
53 PARTS–PIECES ACCESSOIRES	4.5	3.9	4.5	4.6	4.2	4.6	
6 CONSUM GOODS–BIENS CONSOMMATION	25.3	20.4	25.4	22.1	23.0	21.1	
61 DURABLE–DURABLES	8.2	10.4	12.1	8.3	8.2	7.2	
62 SEMI DURABLE–SEMI DURABLES	12.0	7.0	9.6	9.2	9.7	9.1	
63 NON DURABLE–NON DURABLES	5.0	2.9	3.7	4.6	5.1	4.8	
7 GOODS NES–BIENS NDA	0.2	0.5	0.1	0.1	0.2	0.1	

EXPORTS – EXPORTATIONS

	1990	1991	1992	1993	1994	1995	1996
TOTAL EXPORTS–EXPORTATIONS TOTALES	100.	100.	100.	100.	100.	100.	
1 AGRICULTURE	0.3	0.3	0.1	0.1	0.1	0.1	
2 MINING QUARRY–INDUS EXTRACTIVES	92.4	80.4	94.5	94.9	93.6	94.4	
3 MANUFACTURING–IND MANUFACTUR	7.3	19.3	5.4	5.0	6.3	5.5	
31 FOOD BEV TOBACCO–ALIM BOISS TAB	0.5	0.2	0.3	0.2	0.2	0.2	
32 TEXTILES–INDUSTRIES TEXTILES	0.7	0.5	0.2	0.2	0.2	0.2	
33 WOOD & PRODUCTS–BOIS & PRODUITS	0.1	0.0	0.0	0.0	0.0	0.0	
34 PAPER & PRODUCTS–PAPIER & PRODT	0.2	0.1	0.2	0.2	0.3	0.3	
35 CHEMICALS–INDUSTRIES CHIMIQUES	2.3	1.0	1.0	1.2	1.7	2.4	
36 NON METAL MIN–MIN NON METAL	0.2	0.2	0.3	0.3	0.3	0.3	
37 BASIC METAL–IND METAL BASE	0.2	0.0	0.0	0.0	0.0	0.0	
38 METAL MANUF–MANUF METAL	3.1	17.1	3.2	2.7	3.6	2.1	
39 OTH MANUF IND–AUTRES MANUF	0.1	0.1	0.0	0.1	0.1	0.0	

3. TRADE BY PRINCIPAL COUNTRIES OF PRODUCTION AND LAST CONSIGNMENT (VALUE IN THOUSAND U.S. DOLLARS)
ECHANGES SELON LES PRINCIPAUX PAYS DE PRODUCTION ET DE DERNIERE CONSIGNATION (VALEUR EN MILLIERS DE DOLLARS EU)

COUNTRIES–PAYS	SPECIAL IMPORTS C.I.F. IMPORTATIONS SPECIALES C.A.F				
	1991	1992	1993	1994	1995
World	3490873	7251400	7042072	6680391	7789758
Africa	29588	82273	88350	104455	110909
Americas	1091849	1641556	1218107	1110387	1487556
Northern America	1068278	1530151	1106674	1030920	1362563
LAIA	23125	105135	107522	74369	119051
CACM	223	6115	3874	4966	5544
Caribbean	201	154	19	127	389
Rest of America	22	1	19	5	10
As.ex F.USSR	1207245	2789530	2689065	2753268	2941632
Eur.x F.USSR	1110352	2608008	2927913	2581970	3122055
EU	1052296	2428362	2745880	2421916	2964080
EFTA	34972	134412	125342	101255	101232
East Europe	19624	37259	48626	52818	50673
Other Europe	3460	1670	6760	3277	3873
Former USSR	1877	12282	9650	7348	22060
Oceania	40819	116274	108725	122574	104211
USA/Etats–Unis d'Amer	1025025	1476295	1048726	971227	1255233
Japan/Japon	567011	917799	892353	783052	728661
Germany/Allemagne	318592	668346	556263	549478	564659
France,Monac	88588	369933	775897	424086	867953
United Kingdom	243707	444980	472144	463546	466871
Italy/Italie	152755	418688	420012	399686	459559
Saudi Arabia	189743	318674	347084	383705	475262
India/Inde	45538	167875	162557	193909	224998
United Arab Emirates	53855	215241	121001	134829	171800
China/Chine	35717	124193	134376	153877	179329
Korea, Republic of	71091	134782	132938	134405	152347
Netherlands/Pays–Bas	55718	108614	125305	158156	115118
Turkey/Turquie	12295	88739	114120	162283	140719
Switz.Liecht	33947	128025	120755	96682	94823
Australia/Australie	37066	103448	88949	104110	89514
Sweden/Suède	57101	72885	82256	83838	77286
Spain/Espagne	22304	79938	67917	77992	113807
Thailand/Thaïlande	22788	71663	76206	88686	101911
Belgium–Luxembourg	31760	97930	76794	75913	75393
Malaysia/Malaisie	23089	66597	53951	78474	101697
Syrian Arab Republic	7324	95097	84671	64852	71646
Canada	43253	53856	57948	59693	107329
Singapore/Singapour	26900	64072	72383	75640	68684
Egypt/Egypte	26005	72626	72991	65202	65763
Indonesia/Indonésie	19807	53205	68864	78366	75538
Bahrain/Bahreïn	6963	92523	60501	55953	66410
Iran (Islamic Rp. of)	14997	37634	50656	87673	82610
Lebanon/Liban	23377	78179	64127	53913	48669
Brazil/Brésil	14219	51731	70538	45114	77955
Denmark/Danemark	30829	60899	50676	57135	59361
Austria/Autriche	23661	34360	33693	41907	68551
Pakistan	9687	50509	41138	31837	33281
Ireland/Irlande	8079	22749	28893	38176	39086
Finland/Finlande	8526	25206	23805	20374	26388
Greece/Grèce	5204	16451	25709	18015	16556
Argentina/Argentine	6466	36700	20808	2610	15263
Qatar	1220	11605	22194	19741	25538
Hungary/Hongrie	13722	11557	15777	21336	16220
Hong Kong	12478	17659	12810	15672	17789
New Zealand	3753	12825	19725	18465	14697
Philippines	4651	11957	15074	15547	18937
So. Africa Customs Un	1332	3812	7837	20351	27714
Mexico/Mexique	1599	10035	6754	19013	18483
Oman	4793	8111	12386	13720	14121
Portugal	5474	7381	6515	13614	13491
Romania/Roumanie	1400	5137	13874	12620	12819
Russian Federation		12282	9650	6919	16938
Cyprus/Chypre	4090	10484	9660	9127	8212
Poland/Pologne	1434	8367	8292	8176	9132
Sri Lanka	3003	5126	6926	7748	10081

COUNTRIES–PAYS	SPECIAL EXPORTS F.O.B. EXPORTATIONS SPECIALES F.O.B.				
	1991	1992	1993	1994	1995
Monde	1088933	6585282	10519039	11964516	12944424
Afrique	5675	11786	22232	33527	45852
Amériques	1214	9998	15055	15372	35738
Amérique du Nord	1182	9920	13731	15105	32480
ALAI	25	78	1310	263	3257
MCAC	3		13	0	
Caraïbes			0	4	
Autre Amérique	3	0	1		
Asie l'URSS exclus	145257	316670	471514	556211	618285
Europe l'URSS exclus	60075	21977	23451	161105	26944
UE	7725	20360	21518	159939	25517
AELE	135	1183	758	743	663
Europe de l'Est	52177	398	966	364	657
Autre de l'Europe	38	3	71	18	41
Ancienne URSS	1627	530	461	792	891
Océanie	86	261	327	508	715
Saudi Arabia	25417	93091	111139	111339	113009
United Arab Emirates	31833	91659	96239	105736	75811
India/Inde	308	17325	67860	103378	119334
Hong Kong	476	8009	43437	63517	30802
France,Monac	3671	1200	1480	120297	1387
China/Chine	1	48	5644	25143	86962
USA/Etats–Unis d'Amer	1064	9486	13021	14493	30561
Bahrain/Bahreïn	1999	11736	18695	15032	17151
Philippines	4721	6964	9823	15449	26325
Egypt/Egypte	2866	8923	15158	16774	19383
Iran (Islamic Rp. of)	10846	16698	10673	8678	13715
Pakistan	79	13950	10388	21781	12624
Singapore/Singapour	3460	10127	12981	13974	17289
Jordan/Jordanie	48281			3373	4067
Syrian Arab Republic	1342	8637	14257	9316	16059
Qatar	1174	8261	11222	12929	14896
Lebanon/Liban	2587	7704	10920	10594	13895
Romania/Roumanie	41610	104	108	92	236
Oman	980	6250	12611	9121	10919
Japan/Japon	257	3539	12258	9278	12048
Italy/Italie	291	3172	2285	15745	7388
United Kingdom	2201	6484	5512	8510	5820
Germany/Allemagne	496	4391	6908	5783	6715
Morocco/Maroc	42	208	1122	10560	10455
Sri Lanka	266	1572	8116	2296	9863
Turkey/Turquie	165	1350	5040	5621	4129
Viet Nam			2343	2158	8838
Tunisia/Tunisie	49	271	1394	3330	7063
Iraq	10713				
Libyan Arab Jamahiriya	44	981	1247	31	7521
Netherlands/Pays–Bas	213	1519	1610	3569	1927
Bangladesh	67	768	951	2725	2095
Bulgaria/Bulgarie	5907	125	64	58	94
Korea, Republic of	26	4909	153	373	510
Sweden/Suède	206	2178	1009	1367	626
Hungary/Hongrie	4603	68	97	58	74
Malaysia/Malaisie	15	186	170	2107	1763
Canada	118	434	710	612	1919
Spain/Espagne	499	916	597	1421	296
Belgium–Luxembourg	32	70	944	1629	658
Brazil/Brésil	10	57	8	109	3129
Switz.Liecht	22	1142	715	734	660
Sudan/Soudan	2616			45	119
Russian Federation		530	461	789	647
Un. Rep. of Tanzania	1	34	2026	175	12
Thailand/Thaïlande	0	982	245	241	427
Nigeria/Nigéria		598	36	1173	26
Cyprus/Chypre	33	256	448	928	75
Australia/Australie	86	223	284	466	653
Greece/Grèce	19	41	530	989	82

(VALUE AS PERCENTAGE OF WORLD TOTAL)(VALEURS EN POURCENTAGE DU TOTAL MONDIAL)

	1986	1987	1988	1989	1990	1991	1992	1993	1994	1995
Africa	0.6	0.8	0.8	0.9	0.9	0.8	1.1	1.3	1.6	1.4
Americas	13.8	11.9	14.8	15.3	15.6	31.3	22.6	17.3	16.6	19.1
Northern America	12.7	10.7	13.0	13.8	13.9	30.6	21.1	15.7	15.4	17.5
LAIA	0.9	0.9	1.6	1.4	1.6	0.7	1.4	1.5	1.1	1.5
CACM	0.1	0.2	0.1	0.1	0.1	0.0	0.1	0.1	0.1	0.1
Caribbean	0.0	0.0	0.0	0.0	0.0	0.0	0.0	0.0	0.0	0.0
Rest of America		0.0	0.0	0.0	0.0	0.0	0.0	0.0	0.0	0.0
As.ex F.USSR	45.9	49.0	47.2	46.4	43.5	34.6	38.5	38.2	41.2	37.8
Eur.x F.USSR	35.7	36.1	35.1	35.6	37.8	31.8	36.0	41.6	38.6	40.1
EU	33.3	32.1	29.5	31.7	33.6	30.1	33.5	39.0	36.3	38.1
EFTA	1.2	2.6	3.7	2.1	2.7	1.0	1.9	1.8	1.5	1.3
East Europe	0.9	1.1	1.4	1.5	1.2	0.6	0.5	0.7	0.8	0.7
Other Europe	0.3	0.4	0.4	0.3	0.3	0.1	0.0	0.1	0.0	0.0
Former USSR	0.1	0.1	0.2	0.2	0.2	0.1	0.2	0.1	0.1	0.3
Oceania	2.7	2.1	2.0	1.6	2.0	1.2	1.6	1.5	1.8	1.3
USA/Etats–Unis d'Amer	12.3	10.4	12.3	13.2	13.0	29.4	20.4	14.9	14.5	16.1
Japan/Japon	23.6	19.2	13.5	12.9	12.2	16.2	12.7	12.7	11.7	9.4
Germany/Allemagne	9.5	7.8	7.6	8.0	9.0	9.1	9.2	7.9	8.2	7.2
France,Monac	4.1	4.0	3.1	3.4	3.3	2.5	5.1	11.0	6.3	11.1
United Kingdom	6.4	6.8	6.1	6.6	6.0	7.0	6.1	6.7	6.9	6.0
Italy/Italie	5.5	5.0	4.7	5.4	5.5	4.4	5.8	6.0	6.0	5.9
Saudi Arabia	1.8	3.0	3.7	4.5	5.1	5.4	4.4	4.9	5.7	6.1
India/Inde	2.1	2.2	1.8	2.8	2.2	1.3	2.3	2.3	2.9	2.9
United Arab Emirates	1.1	1.9	2.5	1.6	1.6	1.5	3.0	1.7	2.0	2.2
China/Chine	1.6	2.2	3.0	3.5	3.2	1.0	1.7	1.9	2.3	2.3

	1986	1987	1988	1989	1990	1991	1992	1993	1994	1995
Afrique	7.0	7.4	3.6	6.9	0.6	0.5	0.2	0.2	0.3	0.4
Amériques	8.3	3.7	1.1	2.5	0.1	0.1	0.2	0.1	0.1	0.3
Amérique du Nord	8.3	3.7	1.0	2.4	0.1	0.1	0.2	0.1	0.1	0.3
ALAI	0.0	0.0	0.1	0.1	0.0	0.0	0.0	0.0	0.0	0.0
MCAC	0.0				0.0	0.0		0.0	0.0	
Caraïbes	0.0	0.0	0.0	0.0	0.0			0.0	0.0	
Autre Amérique		0.0	0.0			0.0	0.0	0.0		
Asie l'URSS exclus	69.6	80.0	89.4	84.2	6.5	13.3	4.8	4.5	4.6	4.8
Europe l'URSS exclus	13.8	8.8	4.9	6.5	0.8	5.5	0.3	0.2	1.3	0.2
UE	11.7	5.7	3.8	5.5	0.6	0.7	0.3	0.2	1.3	0.2
AELE	0.8	2.3	0.6	0.6	0.2	0.0	0.0	0.0	0.0	0.0
Europe de l'Est	1.2	0.4	0.3	0.2	0.0	4.8	0.0	0.0	0.0	0.0
Autre de l'Europe	0.1	0.4	0.2	0.1	0.0	0.0	0.0	0.0	0.0	0.0
Ancienne URSS	0.0	0.0	0.0	0.0	0.0	0.1	0.0	0.0	0.0	0.0
Océanie	0.1	0.1	0.1	0.0	0.0	0.0	0.0	0.0	0.0	0.0
Saudi Arabia	3.4	26.0	18.4	15.6	1.2	2.3	1.4	1.1	0.9	0.9
United Arab Emirates	6.5	7.0	6.6	6.4	0.6	2.9	1.4	0.9	0.9	0.6
India/Inde	6.7	5.7	3.3	3.4	0.2	0.0	0.3	0.6	0.9	0.9
Hong Kong	0.6	0.5	0.4	1.1	0.0	0.0	0.1	0.4	0.5	0.2
France,Monac	3.1	0.6	0.5	0.3	0.0	0.3	0.0	0.0	1.0	0.0
China/Chine	4.7	4.7	5.7	4.1	0.3	0.0	0.0	0.1	0.2	0.7
USA/Etats–Unis d'Amer	8.2	3.7	1.0	2.3	0.1	0.1	0.1	0.1	0.1	0.2
Bahrain/Bahreïn	1.2	1.3	1.9	2.2	0.2	0.2	0.2	0.2	0.1	0.1
Philippines	1.8	1.8	2.2	1.2	0.2	0.4	0.1	0.1	0.1	0.2
Egypt/Egypte	2.3	2.9	2.4	2.2	0.2	0.3	0.1	0.1	0.1	0.1

4. Special Imports C.I.F. by Commodities according to the S.I.T.C. (Rev. 2) in thousand U.S. Dollars
Importations Spéciales C.A.F. par Produits d'après la C.T.C.I. (Rév. 2) en milliers de Dollars E.U.

SITC CTCI	COMMODITY	1992		1993		1994		1995		PRODUIT
		WEIGHT POIDS	VALUE VALEUR	WEIGHT POIDS	VALUE VALEUR	WEIGHT POIDS	VALUE VALEUR	WEIGHT POIDS	VALUE VALEUR	
	ALL COMMODITIES		7251400		7042072		6680391		7789758	TOUS PRODUITS
0	FOOD AND LIVE ANIMALS		860407		933513		990959		1061157	ALIMENTS,ANIMAUX VIVANTS
001	*LIVE ANIMALS FOR FOOD		119635		132053		137117		98218	ANIMAUX VIVANTS
0012	SHEEP AND GOATS,LIVE	W 90353	112355	W 99129	126628	W 113445	128130	W 84518	92355	ESPECES OVINE ET CAPRINE
00121	SHEEP,LIVE	W 90238	111578	W 99038	126146	W 112503	126676	W 84422	92173	ESPECE OVINE
01	MEAT AND PREPARATIONS		103019		115956		105851		126577	VIANDES ET PREPARATIONS
011	MEAT FRESH,CHILLD,FROZEN	W 51806	90642	W 68232	105032	W 59811	93697	W 70341	114369	VIANDES FRAICHES,REF,CONGE
0111	BOVINE MEAT FRESH,FROZEN	W 8569	21420	W 13177	27033	W 11138	22782	W 11802	23556	VIANDES BOVIN FRAI,REF
01111	BOVINE MEAT WITH BONE IN	W 8569	21420	W 13177	27033	W 11138	22782	W 11802	23556	VIANDES BOVIN NON DESOSS
0114	POULTRY FRESH CHLLD,FRZN	W 38173	55523	W 50158	65573	W 43958	59882	W 54692	81778	VOLAILLES MORTES
02	DAIRY PRODCTS,BIRDS'EGGS		112857		147012		147752		152203	PRODUITS LAITIERS,OEUFS
022	MILK AND CREAM	W 29346	49472	W 50584	79654	W 48129	81125	W 46978	82857	LAIT ET CREME
0223	MILK AND CREAM FRESH	W 12420	13365	W 25142	24386	W 21362	25248	W 21666	28000	LAIT,CREME FRAIS
0224	MILK,CREAM PRESERVED ETC	W 16926	36108	W 25442	55268	W 26767	55878	W 25312	54856	LAIT,CREME CONS,CONC
02242	MILK DRY,1.5% FAT OR LES	W 6786	19626	W 14120	38970	W 15773	39593	W 13847	37374	LAIT POUDRE INF 1.5%
024	CHEESE AND CURD	W 10475	34468	W 11611	36611	W 13173	41101	W 12461	42148	FROMAGE ET CAILLEBOTTE
025	EGGS,BIRDS,FRESH,PRSRVD	W 16870	21085	W 17585	22788	W 11419	15422	W 11788	17003	OEUFS
0251	— IN SHELL	W 16846	20991	W 17585	22788	W 11413	15409	W 11718	16808	OEUFS EN COQUILLE
04	CEREALS AND PREPARATIONS		122118		132724		146408		184259	CEREALES ET PRODUITS
041	WHEAT ETC UNMILLED	W 103125	12343	W 211213	28179	W 123437	17011	W 182728	34539	FROMENT,EPEAUTRE
0411	DURUM WHEAT UNMILLED	W 103125	12343	W 211213	28179	W 123437	17011	W 182728	34539	FROMENT DUR NON MOULU
042	RICE	W 84992	57330	W 83366	55332	W 102835	66496	W 88612	60620	RIZ
0421	RICE IN HUSK OR HUSKED	W 84992	57330	W 83354	55321	W 102817	66478	W 88562	60581	RIZ SANS AUTRE PREPARATION
04211	RICE IN THE HUSK	W 84992	57330	W 83354	55321	W 102817	66478	W 88562	60581	RIZ PADDY
043	BARLEY UNMILLED	W 86513	12847	W 57942	6997	W 169035	16593	W 157985	25576	ORGE NON MONDEE
048	CEREAL ETC PREPARATIONS	W 10232	31265	W 11409	32743	W 11909	36548	W 13577	47812	PREPTNS A BASE CEREALES
05	VEGETABLES AND FRUIT		220338		219634		241741		255737	LEGUMES ET FRUITS
054	VEG ETC FRSH,SMPLY PRSVD	W 198459	106228	W 204959	97604	W 202621	105587	W 204923	114878	LEGUMES FRAIS,CONG,SECS
0545	OTHER FRESH VEGETABLES	W 88963	43722	W 87872	34705	W 83842	40258	W 83601	42141	AUTRES LEGUMES FRAIS,REF
05459	FRESH VEGETABLES NES	W 57033	35053	W 52773	23652	W 45381	28184	W 40655	29365	LEGUMES FRAIS,REFRI NDA
0546	VEGETABLES SIMPLY PRESVD	W 22803	24104	W 22790	23748	W 29041	29331	W 32004	35665	LEGUMES CONG,CONSER
057	FRUIT,NUTS,FRESH,DRIED	W 127644	82969	W 160406	97904	W 185607	109508	W 194174	109600	FRUITS FRAIS OU SECS
0579	FRUIT FRESH OR DRIED NES	W 50984	38581	W 68351	44440	W 77746	45381	W 75593	44607	FRUITS FRAIS,SECS NDA
05798	OTHER FRESH FRUIT	W 34899	19447	W 50932	22973	W 56919	23935	W 53157	22770	AUTRES FRUITS FRAIS
058	FRUIT PRESERVED,PREPARED	W 20039	23225	W 16180	16888	W 19345	18662	W 18708	19567	CONSERVES DE FRUITS
06	SUGAR AND PREPS,HONEY		42788		32121		45088		48379	SUCRES ET PRODUITS
061	SUGAR AND HONEY	W 52718	24080	W 48576	20134	W 68411	31175	W 57279	32640	SUCRES ET MIEL
0611	RAW BEET AND CANE SUGAR	W 50998	19133	W 46679	15622	W 66376	26116	W 54535	25652	SUCRES BRUTS
07	COFFEE,TEA,COCOA,SPICES		66726		69775		73473		89525	CAFE,THE,CACAO,EPICES
073	CHOCOLATE AND PRODUCTS	W 7391	36533	W 7052	37799	W 6211	33406	W 7470	40620	CHOCOLAT
074	TEA AND MATE	W 2731	14146	W 3551	16521	W 4433	22743	W 5050	26282	THE ET MATE
0741	TEA	W 2731	14146	W 3548	16518	W 4433	22743	W 5050	26282	THE
081	*FEEDING STUFF FOR ANIML	W 38229	12095	W 54001	17246	W 72285	24166	W 84354	27750	NOURRITURE POUR ANIMAUX
09	MISC EDIBLE PRODUCTS		45116		51253		54093		58059	PREP ALIMENTAIRES DIVERSES
098	EDIBLE PRODCTS,PREPS NES	W 13694	42877	W 16120	48587	W 15268	51213	W 16522	54672	PREP ALIMENTAIRES NDA
09809	MISC FOOD PREPRTIONS NES	W 8422	31579	W 9992	35533	W 8801	37340	W 9136	38660	PREP ALIMENTAIRES NDA
1	BEVERAGES AND TOBACCO		72662		96573		106875		93697	BOISSONS ET TABACS
11	BEVERAGES		25532		26258		31339		28575	BOISSONS
111	NON–ALCOHL BEVERAGES NES	W 62098	25532	W 62099	26258	W 71719	31339	W 73192	28575	BOISSONS NON ALCOOLIQUES
12	TOBACCO AND MANUFACTURES		47130		70315		75536		65123	TABACS BRUTS FABRIQUES
122	TOBACCO,MANUFACTURED	W 2470	47130	W 3566	70315	W 4060	75536	W 3671	65051	TABACS FABRIQUES
1222	CIGARETTES	W 2376	43789	W 3531	69453	W 4052	75183	W 3667	64802	CIGARETTES
2	CRUDE MATERLS,EXCL FUELS		59551		90043		103731		120960	MAT BRUTES NON COMESTIBLES
24	CORK AND WOOD		22580		34577		40142		53157	LIEGE ET BOIS
248	WOOD SHAPED,SLEEPERS	W 34587	14865	W 60210	26163	W 69401	35686	W 82218	44951	BOIS SIMPLEMENT TRAVAILLES
2481	RAILWAY SLEEPERS,TIES	W 34587	14865	W 60210	26163	W 69401	35686	W 82218	44951	TRAVERSES VOIES FERREES
27	CRUDE FERTLZR,MINRLS NES		12065		26446		32961		30582	ENGRAIS MINERAUX BRUTS
273	STONE,SAND AND GRAVEL	W 380947	8187	W 728492	21523	W 949601	26794	W 672102	24920	PIERRES,SABLES,GRAVIERS
3	MINERAL FUELS ETC		34143		31545		43597		41166	COMBUSTIBLES MINERAUX LUB
33	PETROLEUM AND PRODUCTS		32429		30259		42229		40131	PETROLE ET DERIVES
334	PETROLEUM PRODUCTS,REFIN	W 21197	25573	W 15422	17074	W 21956	25646	W 21668	23319	PRODUITS RAFFINES
3345	LUBS,PETROLEUM OILS NES	W 21197	25573	W 15422	17074	W 21956	25646	W 21668	23319	HUILES LUBRIFIANTES
33451	LUBS(HIGH PETR CONT) ETC	W 21197	25573	W 15422	17074	W 21956	25646	W 21668	23319	HUILES LUBRIF,H LOURDES
4	ANIMAL,VEGETABLE OIL,FAT		31279		26251		29432		47622	HUILES,GRAISSES ANIM,VEG
42	FIXED VEGETABLE OIL,FAT		31149		26080		29136		46937	HUILES VEGETALES FIXES
424	FIXED VEG OIL NONSOFT	W 20336	21224	W 19718	18850	W 20101	19513	W 34348	34487	AUTRES HUILES VEG FIXES
4249	FIXED VEGETABLE OILS NES	W 14567	17362	W 11410	13736	W 12054	14011	W 23964	24723	HUILES VEGET FIXES NDA
5	CHEMCLS,RELATED PROD NES		358696		429628		492232		550404	PRODUITS CHIMIQUES
52	INORGANIC CHEMICALS		56763		63383		67921		62268	PROD CHIM INORGANIQUES
523	OTHR INORG CHEMICALS ETC	W 29595	50493	W 51161	56420	W 39218	60040	W 56436	51935	AUT PRODUITS CHIMIQUES INORG
5239	INORG CHEM PRODUCTS NES	W 20120	47735	W 20920	47415	W 17979	54274	W 33099	46399	PROD CHIM INORGANIQ NDA
52399	OTH INORG CMPNDS NES ETC	W 19168	47260	W 20674	47284	W 17370	54012	W 32119	45956	AUT COMP INORGANIQUES NDA
53	DYES,TANNING,COLOUR PROD		28773		29509		30920		31654	PROD TEINTURE,COLORANTS
533	PIGMENTS,PAINTS,ETC	W 12349	25961	W 12311	27051	W 11171	26972	W 11466	28348	PIGMENTS,PEINTURES,VERNIS
541	*MEDICINAL,PHARM PRODUCT	K 4782541	74228	K 5432404	107043	K 5552036	105622	K 6303820	124726	PROD MEDICINAUX PHARMACEUT
5417	MEDICAMENTS	K 3536080	61641	K 3357181	85781	K 3294190	82049	K 4543348	102190	MEDICAMENTS
54171	— CONTAINNG ANTIBIOTICS	K 3536080	61641	K 3357181	85781	K 3294190	82049	K 4543348	102190	MED CONTN ANTIBIOTIQUES
5419	PHARMACEUTICAL GOODS NES	K 1246461	12587	K 2071917	21227	K 2248864	23450	K 1758091	22423	PREP,ART PHARMACEUTIQUES
54191	BANDAGES PREPARED ETC	K 1246461	12587	K 2071917	21227	K 2248864	23450	K 1758091	22423	OUATES,GAZES,BANDES
55	PERFUME,CLEANING ETC PRD		117247		122407		135262		158399	PROD POUR PARFUM,TOILETTE
553	PERFUMERY,COSMETICS,ETC	W 7774	79227	W 7438	78804	W 8652	86089	W 9730	104602	PRODUITS DE PARFUMERIE
554	SOAP,CLEANSING ETC PREPS	W 20377	35105	W 26363	39745	W 30039	44940	W 31899	48568	SAVONS,PRODUITS DETERSIFS
5542	WASHING PREPARATIONS ETC	W 15110	21674	W 21545	27528	W 24417	30809	W 26173	34078	PROD ORG TENSIO–ACT NDA
58	PLASTIC MATERIALS ETC		41912		57040		73939		87509	MAT PLAST ARTIFICIELLES
583	POLYMERIZATION ETC PRODS	W 28532	27224	W 40206	35258	W 57158	55405	W 46609	56590	PROD POLYMERISATION
5832	POLYPROPYLENE	W 11178	12396	W 14514	14358	W 21822	23070	W 15096	22883	POLYPROPYLENE
58321	— IN PRIMARY FORMS	W 11178	12396	W 14514	14358	W 21822	23070	W 15096	22883	POLYPROPYLENE PRIMAIRES
59	CHEMICAL MATERIALS NES		34883		47520		75940		82505	MAT PROD CHIMIQUES NDA
598	MISCEL CHEM PRODUCTS NES	W 12923	23622	W 19694	36175	W 25597	61553	W 27179	65029	PROD DIV INDUST CHIM NDA
5982	ANTI–KNOCK PREPARTNS ETC	W 238	1169	W 2749	12510	W 6372	35580	W 4985	29206	PREPARAT ANTIDETONANTES
5989	CHEM PRODUCTS,PREPS NES	W 12475	22242	W 16849	23547	W 19033	25763	W 22084	35734	PROD PREP CHIMIQUES NDA
59899	OTH CHEM PRODS,PREPS,NES	W 7474	16369	W 10916	17459	W 11606	18516	W 13110	25313	AUT PRODUITS CHIMIQUES NDA
6	BASIC MANUFACTURES		1242437		1317564		1288742		1523580	ART MANUFACTURES
62	RUBBER MANUFACTURES NES		63224		84538		65341		76634	CAOUTCHOUC MANUFACTURE
625	RUBBER TYRES, TUBES ETC	W 17630	58464	W 24127	75114	W 18763	58103	W 20835	68780	PNEUS CAOUTCHOUC VULCANISE
6251	TYRES NEW FOR MOTOR CARS	W 16427	54799	W 22329	69782	W 17273	53907	W 19894	65937	PNEUS POUR VOITURES
63	WOOD,CORK MANUFACTRS NES		43475		56102		61296		51263	OUVRAGES LIEGE ET BOIS
634	VENEERS,PLYWOOD,ETC	W 48111	33601	W 57467	46750	W 65487	49726	W 45666	37027	PLACAGES,CONTRE–PLAQUES
6342	PLYWOOD OF WOOD SHEETS	W 46117	32338	W 55267	45496	W 62217	47598	W 40664	33661	BOIS CONTRE–PLAQUES
64	PAPER,PAPERBOARD AND MFR		97962		121068		142918		171588	PAPIERS,CARTONS & OUVRAGES
641	PAPER AND PAPERBOARD	W 47239	49275	W 76157	68540	W 92051	88707	W 88274	108485	PAPIERS ET CARTONS

4. Special Imports C.I.F. by Commodities according to the S.I.T.C. (Rev. 2) in thousand U.S. Dollars
Importations Spéciales C.A.F. par Produits d'après la C.T.C.I. (Rév. 2) en milliers de Dollars E.U.

SITC CTCI	COMMODITY	1992 WEIGHT POIDS	1992 VALUE VALEUR	1993 WEIGHT POIDS	1993 VALUE VALEUR	1994 WEIGHT POIDS	1994 VALUE VALEUR	1995 WEIGHT POIDS	1995 VALUE VALEUR	PRODUIT
6412	PRINTG,WRITING PAPER NES	W 28664	24227	W 45005	34648	W 42746	35318	W 40033	45716	PAPIERS POUR L'IMPRESSION
64121	— UNCOATED	W 28664	24227	W 45005	34648	W 42746	35318	W 40033	45716	PAPIERS IMPRES NON COUCHES
642	PAPER,ETC,PRECUT,ARTS OF	W 16044	48687	W 17335	52528	W 18091	54212	W 20726	63103	PAP,CARTONS DECOUPES
6428	PAPER ETC ARTICLES NES	W 7512	25962	W 8257	31500	W 9271	35301	W 10989	41548	OUVRAGES EN PATE A PAPIER
64285	PAPER ETC DIAPERS ETC	W 4444	18846	W 5334	24172	W 6949	28917	W 8082	33828	SERVIETTES HYGIENIQUES
65	TEXTILE YARN,FABRICS,ETC		301584		254388		244141		263040	FILS,TISSUS,ARTICLES TEXTILE
653	WOVN MAN–MADE FIB FABRIC	W 9656	124267	W 10918	117799	W 11069	109924	W 11905	128426	TISSUS FIBRES SYNTH,ARTIF
6531	CONT SYNT WEAVES NONPILE	W 9335	117568	W 10528	111517	W 10761	104696	W 11612	122222	TISSUS FIBRES SYNTH CONTINUE
65315	CONT SYN TXTL FABRIC NES	W 9335	117568	W 10528	111517	W 10761	104696	W 11612	122222	TIS PLUS 85% TEXT SYNT CONT
658	TEXTILE ARTICLES NES	W 8307	46401	W 7239	36568	W 5694	27910	W 6517	30477	ART FACONNES MAT TEXTILES
6583	BLANKETS ETC NON ELECTRC	W 3228	22603	W 3349	23275	W 2457	14903	W 2758	15857	COUVERTURES
65831	WOOL BLANKETS ETC NES	W 3228	22603	W 3349	23275	W 2457	14903	W 2758	15857	COUVERTURES DE LAINE
659	FLOOR COVERINGS,ETC	W 21140	88955	W 17154	62297	W 18858	65298	W 17825	64566	COUVRE–PARQUETS,TAPIS ETC
6594	WOOL CARPETS ETC NES	W 20702	78499	W 16738	55672	W 18488	58365	W 17433	59203	TAPIS DE LAINE
65941	— TUFTED	W 8211	38983	W 7378	31986	W 5865	26988	W 5120	24571	TAPIS DE LAINE TOUFFETES
65942	— WOVEN	W 12491	39516	W 9359	23686	W 12623	31377	W 12313	34632	TAPIS DE LAINE TISSES
66	NONMETAL MINERAL MFS NES		133317		213068		250845		345609	ART MIN NON METALLIQUES
661	LIME,CEMENT,BLDG PRODS	W 358277	58781	W 1755869	132171	W 1891664	152969	W 2722196	221643	CHAUX,CIMENTS MAT CONSTR
6612	CEMENT	W 271778	15274	W 1642243	88342	W 1714180	89252	W 2502978	138637	CIMENTS HYDRAULIQUES
6613	BUILDING STONE ETC WORKD	W 85229	43044	W 112115	43340	W 175415	63172	W 216126	82246	PIERRES A BATIR
66132	BUILDING STONE WORKED	W 85229	43044	W 112115	43340	W 175415	63172	W 216126	82246	OUVR EN PIERRES DE TAILLE
662	CLAY,REFRACTORY BLDG PRD	W 38577	24167	W 52256	29554	W 67722	36559	W 94226	49431	MAT CONST REFRACTAIRES
6624	BRICKS ETC NONREFRACTORY	W 37902	23357	W 51768	29257	W 66914	35251	W 93044	48736	BRIQUES ETC CERAM NON REFR
66245	GLAZED CERAMIC SETTS ETC	W 31952	21729	W 41502	25558	W 58036	31845	W 77048	42406	AUT CARREAUX CERAMIQUE
664	GLASS	W 14267	17275	W 16896	21609	W 24003	24404	W 25720	30889	VERRE
67	IRON AND STEEL		349264		316586		246514		299377	FER ET ACIER
673	IRON,STEEL SHAPES ETC	W 150423	56052	W 258697	97279	W 387184	130987	W 345804	119516	BARRES,PROFIL FER,ACIER
6731	IRON,STEEL WIRE ROD	W 107160	33550	W 204154	70588	W 326584	103573	W 288352	93216	FIL MACHINE FER,ACIER
67311	IRON,SIMPLE STL WIRE ROD	W 107160	33550	W 204154	70588	W 326584	103573	W 288352	93216	FIL MACH AUT ACIER FIN
6733	IRON,STEEL PROFILES ETC	W 34146	18580	W 47034	23493	W 45969	21225	W 44702	20831	PROFILES,PALPLAN FER,ACIER
67331	SMALL U,I,H SECTIONS ETC	W 34146	18580	W 47034	23493	W 45969	21225	W 44702	20831	PROFILES MOINS 80MM
674	IRN,STL UNIV,PLATE,SHEET	W 43738	36462	W 58487	43453	W 51579	40182	W 76531	66307	LARGES PLATS,TOLES
6749	OTH IRN,STL PLATES,SHEET	W 41543	31405	W 56903	39379	W 49776	36192	W 74974	61501	AUTRES TOLES FER,ACIER
67491	— OF IRON OR SIMPLE STL	W 41543	31405	W 56903	39379	W 49776	36192	W 74974	61501	AUT TOLES AUTRES ACIER FIN
678	IRON,STL TUBES,PIPES,ETC	W 266580	237186	W 160273	152964	W 52851	56703	W 96366	92339	TUBES,TUYAUX EN FONTE,FER
6783	IRON,STL TUBES,PIPES NES	W 244348	216334	W 135093	129901	W 44671	41794	W 85441	68134	AUT TUBES,TUYAUX FER,ACIER
6785	IRON,STEEL TUBE FITTINGS	W 20832	20277	W 24851	22915	W 7788	14693	W 10925	24205	ACCESSOIRES DE TUYAUTERIE
68	NON–FERROUS METALS		53504		72653		79503		99351	METAUX NON FERREUX
682	COPPER EXC CEMENT COPPER	W 4553	16517	W 9928	28379	W 10673	31019	W 9223	35381	CUIVRE
6821	COPPER NES,ALLOYS,UNWRT	W 4553	16517	W 9928	28379	W 10673	31019	W 9223	35381	CUIVRE BRUT
68211	COPPER UNREF,EXC CEMENT	W 4553	16517	W 9928	28379	W 10673	31019	W 9223	35381	CUIVRE POUR AFFINAGE
684	ALUMINIUM	W 12453	36365	W 21147	43911	W 21602	48172	W 23632	63075	ALUMINIUM
6842	ALUMINIUM,ALLOYS WORKED	W 12453	36365	W 21147	43911	W 21602	48172	W 23632	63075	ALUMINIUM,ALLIAGES OUVRE
68421	ALUMINIUM BARS,WIRE,ETC	W 6489	14205	W 13402	23335	W 13790	25259	W 17091	40422	BARRES,PROFILES FILS ALU
69	METAL MANUFACTURES NES		198241		197494		196272		214888	ART MANUFACT EN METAL NDA
691	STRUCTURES AND PARTS NES	W 15008	24586	W 11508	23405	W 12402	27818	W 29885	49876	CONSTRUCT FER,ACIER,ALU
6911	STRUCTURES,PARTS IRN,STL	W 13898	19763	W 10077	16494	W 10300	18495	W 26544	34853	CONSTRUCT FER,ACIER,FONTE
697	BASE MTL HOUSEHOLD EQUIP	W 13481	77577	W 14546	75819	W 11111	66299	W 9612	61386	ART MENAGE MET COMMUNS
6974	BASE MTL DMSTC ARTIC NES	W 4184	24732	W 4237	24294	W 3487	18949	W 2425	14103	ARTICLES NDA FONTE,FER,ETC
69741	— OF IRON OR STEEL	W 3280	21309	W 3556	21473	W 2674	16080	W 1809	11532	ART NDA EN FONTE,FER
6975	BASE MTL INDR SANIT WARE	W 5534	29066	W 7481	34939	W 4925	31717	W 3899	27654	ART HYG NDA FER,AC,CU,ALU
69751	IRON,STL INDR SANIT WARE	W 5534	29066	W 7481	34939	W 4925	31717	W 3899	27654	ART HYGIENE NDA FER,ACIER
699	BASE METAL MFRS NES	W 9714	42835	W 14213	51277	W 13931	54135	W 12003	50641	ART MANUFACTURES MET NDA
6991	LOCKSMITHS WARES,ETC	W 4938	24054	W 5219	26209	W 4987	27018	W 5765	29577	ARTICLES DE SERRURERIE
69913	BASE MTL DOOR,ETC FITTNG	W 2665	14987	W 3240	17690	W 3711	20641	W 4667	23539	GARNITURES POUR MEUBLES
6996	BASE MTL MISC ARTICLES	W 4234	17289	W 5195	18077	W 5877	20125	W 5427	18273	ART DIVERS METAUX COMMUNS
69961	BASE MTL FLEXIBLE TUBING	W 4234	17289	W 5195	18077	W 5877	20125	W 5427	18273	TUYAUX FLEXIBLES
7	MACHINES,TRANSPORT EQUIP		3177904		2992418		2547963		3212507	MACHINES MATERIEL TRANSPORT
71	POWER GENERATING EQUIPMT		76940		131308		127173		179227	MACHINES GENERATRICES
716	ROTATING ELECTRIC PLANT	W 1926	22168	W 1986	30648	W 1636	24858	W 2277	29645	APP ELECTR ROTATIFS,PIECES
718	OTH POWER GENERATG MACHY	W 783	26076	W 2864	70685	W 3392	86624	W 4467	129956	AUTRES MOTEURS PARTIES
7188	WIND,WATER,ETC ENGINES	W 783	26076	W 2864	70685	W 3392	86624	W 4467	129956	MOT MACHINES MOTRICES NDA
71889	PARTS NES OF 71881,71882	W 783	26076	W 2857	70642	W 3388	86554	W 4467	129949	PARTIES DES POS 718.81,82
72	MACHS FOR SPCL INDUSTRYS		471663		333327		239619		188292	MAC SPECIALES POUR INDUST
722	TRACTORS NON–ROAD	W 4669	25036	W 3225	15543	W 3092	11970	W 997	3910	TRACTEURS
7224	WHEELED TRACTORS NES	W 4669	25036	W 3225	15543	W 3092	11970	W 997	3910	TRACTEURS A ROUES
723	CIVIL ENGNEERG EQUIP ETC	W 46195	273111	W 14680	134598	W 10170	85779	W 7042	70014	APPAREILS DE GENIE CIVIL
7234	CONST,MINING MACHNRY NES	W 44533	254672	W 13303	119786	W 8782	70788	W 5715	55997	MACH POUR LA CONST, MINES
72343	SLFPRP CONST ETC MCH NES	W 38605	226695	W 7048	91149	W 4215	49700	W 3199	42775	AUT MACH EXTR,TERRASSEM
726	PRINTG,BKBINDG MACHY,PTS	W 1392	26831	W 760	16989	W 689	14522	W 541	11217	MACHINES POUR IMPRIMERIE
728	OTH MACHY FOR SPCL INDUS	W 6047	100826	W 9295	138817	W 7672	92301	W 5789	76696	AUT MACH IND PARTICULIERES
7284	MACHY FOR SPCL INDUS NES	W 4295	83436	W 6381	115994	W 5027	74511	W 2870	52518	MACH SPEC IND PARTICUL.
72848	OTH MCHY WITH INDIV FNCT	W 4159	80213	W 6317	114541	W 4967	72911	W 2775	49788	AUTRES MACHINES NDA
74	GENRL INDUSTRL MACHY NES		307551		346202		297680		328434	MACH APP INDUSTRIE
741	HEATING,COOLING EQUIPMNT	W 18843	175132	W 20206	186896	W 18148	160629	W 20476	171057	MACH CHAUFFAGE,PIECES
7415	AIR–CONDITIONING MACHNRY	W 14640	111229	W 16599	127771	W 14594	119758	W 17560	134791	GROUPES CONDITION AIR
7416	HEATING,COOLING EQU NES	W 2418	46560	W 1838	44132	W 1238	22427	W 794	17640	APP CHANGEMENT TEMP
742	PUMPS FOR LIQUIDS ETC	W 1335	28026	W 1803	41958	W 1505	34871	W 1879	35688	POMPES MOTO–POMPES
7429	PTS NES OF PUMPS OF 742	W 404	13860	W 477	22680	W 567	22663	W 569	19347	PIECES POUR GROUPE 742
743	PUMPS NES,CENTRFUGES ETC	W 2120	23434	W 2294	34212	W 2363	31752	W 1944	38668	POMPES COMPRES,VENT ETC
7436	GAS,LIQUID FILTERS ETC	W 519	7331	W 886	12603	W 883	11338	W 871	24092	APP POUR FILT DES LIQUIDES
744	MECHANICAL HANDLING EQU	W 7721	51146	W 6867	37906	W 6343	35530	W 9088	46523	EQUIP MANUTENTION PIECES
7442	LIFTING,LOADING MACH NES	W 5845	36450	W 5680	27415	W 4919	23708	W 7573	30454	APP LEVAGE,MANUTENTION
74422	SHIP DERRICKS,CRANES ETC	W 5426	33862	W 4824	20656	W 3306	12974	W 4882	13843	GRUES,PONTS ROULANTS
749	NONELEC MACH PTS,ACC NES	W 1154	9829	W 3536	33294	W 2290	18538	W 2696	21592	PIECES MACH NON ELEC NDA
7492	COCKS,VALVES ETC NES	W 1137	9607	W 3519	33110	W 2186	17327	W 2583	19803	ART ROB,SIM POUR TUYAUX
75	OFFICE MACHNES,ADP EQUIP		153528		113377		115271		116041	MACH BUREAU TRAIT AUTOM
751	OFFICE MACHINES	W 760	24813	W 575	18118	W 407	16077	W 339	14651	MACH,APPAREILS DE BUREAU
752	AUTOMTIC DATA PROC EQUIP	W 689	62535	W 577	43673	W 516	36760	W 442	26945	MACH TRAIT INFORMATION
7522	DIGITAL COMPUTERS	W 682	62170	W 574	43446	W 512	36538	W 441	26841	MACH DIGITALES COMPLETES
759	OFFICE,ADP MCH PTS,ACCES	W 983	66181	W 782	51586	W 773	62434	W 779	74444	PIECES DU 751 ET 752
7591	OFFICE MACHINE PARTS NES	W 983	66181	W 782	51586	W 773	62434	W 779	74444	PIECES DU 7511,7518
75911	TYPEWRTR PARTS,ACCES NES	W 983	66181	W 782	51586	W 773	62434	W 779	74444	PIECES DU 7511
76	TELECOMM,SOUND EQUIPMENT		228467		214500		196385		222606	EQUIPMENT DE TELECOM
761	TELEVISION RECEIVERS	W 2466	39053	W 2105	30154	W 2239	32487	W 2789	41173	RECEPTEURS DE TELEVISION
7611	COLOUR TV RECEIVERS	W 2461	38922	W 2105	30140	W 2228	32410	W 2779	41057	RECEPTEURS COULEUR
762	RADIO BROADCAST RECEIVRS	W 1333	23528	W 1210	21104	W 1302	22891	W 1543	26758	RECEPTEURS RADIODIFFUSION
7622	PORTABLE RADIO RECEIVERS	W 1296	22070	W 1171	20072	W 1213	20622	W 1489	24902	RECEPT PORTATIFS RADIO
763	SOUND RECORDRS,PHONOGRPH	W 527	22808	W 409	17805	W 536	20760	W 507	20044	PHONO,APP ENREGISTREMENT
7638	OTHR SOUND APPARATUS ETC	W 527	22808	W 409	17805	W 536	20760	W 507	20044	AUT APP D'ENREGIS,REPROD
76381	TV IMAGE,SND RECRDRS ETC	W 490	22053	W 374	17046	W 470	19599	W 431	18672	APP ENREG,REPRO IMAG,SON

4. Special Imports C.I.F. by Commodities according to the S.I.T.C. (Rev. 2) in thousand U.S. Dollars
Importations Spéciales C.A.F. par Produits d'après la C.T.C.I. (Rév. 2) en milliers de Dollars E.U.

SITC CTCI	COMMODITY	1992		1993		1994		1995		PRODUIT
		WEIGHT POIDS	VALUE VALEUR	WEIGHT POIDS	VALUE VALEUR	WEIGHT POIDS	VALUE VALEUR	WEIGHT POIDS	VALUE VALEUR	
764	TELECOM EQPT,PTS,ACC NES	W 3182	143077	W 3579	145437	W 3615	120246	W 4209	134631	EQUIP TELECOM,PIECES
7641	LINE TELEPHONE,ETC EQUIP	W 409	26981	W 273	21668	W 335	30585	W 329	35497	APP TELEPHON PAR FIL
7648	TELECOMM EQUIPMENT NES	W 516	42813	W 510	44460	W 289	22562	W 105	17396	APP TELECOM NDA
76481	RADIOTELEPHONE ETC RCVRS	W 516	42813	W 510	44460	W 289	22562	W 105	17396	RECEP RADIOTELEPHONIE
7649	PTS NES OF EQUIPMT OF 76	W 1866	59815	W 2420	66273	W 2719	58503	W 3486	74992	PIECES DE LA DIV 76
76491	PTS NES OF APPAR OF 7641	W 1866	59815	W 2420	66273	W 2719	58503	W 3486	74992	PIECES POUR 764.1
77	ELECTRIC MACHNRY NES ETC		313070		311636		341731		291257	MACH APP ELECT NDA
771	ELECTRIC POWER MACHY NES	W 2249	20970	W 2561	22948	W 5408	30177	W 2008	12773	MACH PROD,TRANS ELECTR
7711	TRANSFORMERS,ELECTRICAL	W 2249	20970	W 2561	22948	W 5408	30177	W 2008	12773	TRANSFO ELECTRIQUES
77111	LIQUID DIELEC TRANSFRMRS	W 2249	20970	W 2561	22948	W 5408	30177	W 2008	12773	TRANSFO DIELEC LIQUIDE
772	SWITCHGEAR ETC,PARTS NES	W 6132	53092	W 5341	55322	W 5482	71028	W 5377	60372	APP COUPURE,SECT ETC
7722	PRINTED CIRCUITS,PTS NES	W 6132	53092	W 5341	55322	W 5482	71028	W 5377	60372	CIRCUITS ET PIECES
773	ELECTR DISTRIBUTNG EQUIP	W 11058	43063	W 11778	51643	W 14067	72296	W 12271	55788	EQUIPMT DISTRIBUTION ELECT
7731	INSULATED WIRE,CABLE ETC	W 10577	39368	W 11622	49997	W 13970	71434	W 9598	41349	FILS,CABLES ISOLES ELECT
774	ELECTRO–MEDCL,XRAY EQUIP	W 370	25731	W 258	23814	W 265	27045	W 186	19124	APPAREILS MEDICAUX
7741	ELECTRO–MEDICAL EQUIPMNT	W 343	23228	W 228	21792	W 205	21801	W 132	16251	APP ELECTRICITE MEDICALE
775	HOUSEHOLD TYPE EQUIP NES	W 16929	107899	W 12469	89359	W 11930	80725	W 12237	81176	MACH,APP USAGE DOMESTQUE
7752	DOM REFRIGERATRS,FREEZRS	W 5863	32589	W 3563	19609	W 3452	19124	W 3355	18387	REFRIG,CONGEL MENAGER
77521	DOMESTIC REFRIGERATORS	W 4530	25271	W 2848	15652	W 2687	15123	W 2521	13963	REFRIGERATEURS
7757	DOMESTIC ELECTRC EQU NES	W 2771	28347	W 2756	30838	W 2434	26879	W 2588	26501	APP ELECTR DOMEST NDA
7758	ELECTRO–THERMIC APPL NES	W 5711	30751	W 4625	28872	W 4226	23243	W 4159	23120	APP ELECTROTHERMIQ NDA
778	ELECTRICAL MACHINERY NES	W 7049	61159	W 8013	65733	W 8634	58735	W 8527	60079	AUTRES MACH ELECT NDA
7788	OTH ELEC MACHY,EQUIP NES	W 923	25712	W 803	26724	W 533	20533	W 439	18841	AUT MACH APP ELEC NDA
77889	ELEC PARTS OF MACHY NES	W 793	22204	W 621	20166	W 375	12142	W 256	10453	PIECES ELEC DE MACH NDA
78	ROAD VEHICLES		1408739		933398		916171		1007646	VEHICULES ROUTIERS
781	PASS MOTOR VEH EXC BUSES	W 81033	915022	W 53479	560783	W 53612	557835	W 59540	650411	AUTO TRANSPORT PERSONNES
782	LORRIES,SPCL MTR VEH NES	W 38701	270066	W 21425	150623	W 22285	152423	W 20756	138614	VEHICULES SPECIAUX,MARCH
7821	LORRIES,TRUCKS	W 36202	239902	W 20074	140605	W 21198	144471	W 19858	132982	VEHICULES TRANSP MARCHAND
7822	SPECIAL MOTOR VEHCLS NES	W 2499	30163	W 1351	10018	W 1086	7952	W 898	5632	VEHICULES USAGES SPECIAUX
783	ROAD MOTOR VEHICLES NES	W 7010	38242	W 7563	48715	W 5085	42584	W 4782	33949	VEHICULES ROUTIERS NDA
7831	BUSES	W 5166	29302	W 6567	45017	W 3946	37852	W 3961	31760	VOITURES TRANSPORT COMMUN
784	MOTOR VEH PRTS,ACCES NES	W 17502	174216	W 16325	162302	W 15747	154120	W 16717	175695	PIECES 722,781,782,783
7849	OTHER MOTOR VEHCL PARTS	W 17280	173700	W 16024	161010	W 15582	153736	W 16587	175302	PIECES 722,781,782,783
79	OTHR TRANSPORT EQUIPMENT		203284		595175		301735		861097	AUTRE MATERIEL TRANSPORT
792	AIRCRAFT ETC	W 241	165856	W 168	552743	W 148	212595	W 165	809197	APP NAVIGATION AERIENNE
7922	AIRCRFT NES 2000KG OR LS		108841	W 1	508973		169702	W 1	723718	AERODYNES MOINS 2000 KG
7929	AIRCRAFT PARTS NES	W 241	57016	W 167	43770	W 147	42893	W 164	85479	PIECES DU 792
793	SHIPS AND BOATS ETC		37428		42432		89140		51900	NAVIRES BATEAUX,ETC
7932	SHIPS AND BOATS NES		26010		18467		14246		17085	NAVIRES ET BATEAUX
79321	YACHTS,SPORTS VESSLS ETC		24265		13787		12577		8217	BATEAUX DE PLAISANCE
7938	TUGS,SPECIAL VESSELS ETC	W 577	11418		23916		63669		34800	REMORQUEURS,BATEAUX SPEC
79381	TUGS						41760			BATEAUX REMORQUEURS
79383	FLOATING STRUCTURES NES	W 577	11418	W 2418	17661	W 473	10847	W 1976	33173	ENGINS FLOTTANTS DIVERS
8	MISC MANUFACTURED GOODS		1346241		1067730		1042825		1107120	ART MANUFACTURES DIVERS
812	*PLUMBG,HEATNG,LGHTNG EQ	W 6511	41906	W 7133	36096	W 9984	47687	W 9676	51080	APPAR SANITAIRES CHAUFFAGE
8124	LIGHTING EQUIPMENT NES	W 2278	29455	W 2621	24698	W 3040	29446	W 2497	29638	APPAREILS ECLAIRAGE ETC
81242	LAMPS,FITTINGS BASE METL	W 2105	27390	W 2194	19249	W 2549	25330	W 2172	26371	APPAREILS D'ECLAIRAGE
821	*FURNITURE,PARTS THEREOF	W 49345	210004	W 37497	144949	W 30189	120821	W 29870	132733	MEUBLES ET PIECES
8219	FURNITURE AND PARTS NES	W 45944	192900	W 34550	126389	W 27719	104118	W 27048	112636	AUTRES MEUBLES ET PIECES
82191	METAL FURNITURE NES	W 10137	39002	W 10307	30046	W 7388	23328	W 6799	22383	MEUBLES NDA EN METAL
82192	WOOD FURNITURE NES	W 33749	147387	W 23010	92521	W 18514	74218	W 18161	81741	MEUBLES NDA EN BOIS
831	*TRAVEL GOODS,HANDBAGS	W 2953	23039	W 4066	26029	W 4154	26943	W 4432	33999	ARTICLES DE VOYAGE ETC
84	CLOTHING AND ACCESSORIES		308199		287783		291381		318964	VETEMENTS
842	MENS OUTERWEAR NOT KNIT	W 4838	68007	W 5234	71298	W 4753	60025	W 4859	59690	VET DESSUS POUR HOMMES
8421	— OVERCOATS,OTHER COATS	W 4838	68007	W 5234	71298	W 4753	60025	W 4859	59690	MANTEAUX HOMMES MAT TEXT
84211	—— OF WOOL,FINE HAIR	W 4838	68007	W 5234	71298	W 4753	60025	W 4859	59690	MANTEAUX HOMMES DE LAINE
843	WOMENS OUTERWEAR NONKNIT	W 7653	164661	W 6728	131929	W 6525	140474	W 6726	152978	VET DESSUS FEMMES MAT TEX
8431	— COATS AND JACKETS	W 5382	121825	W 4240	95485	W 3887	94417	W 4385	111806	MANT,VEST FEM MAT TEXTIL
8439	— OTHER OUTER GARMENTS	W 2271	42836	W 2488	36444	W 2638	46058	W 2341	41173	AUT VET DES FEM MAT TEXT
844	UNDER GARMENTS NOT KNIT	W 3243	46893	W 4081	54632	W 4409	62375	W 4708	70537	VETEMENT DESSOUS MAT TEX
8443	— WOMENS	W 1773	31451	W 1891	32520	W 2076	35625	W 2216	39854	VET DESSOUS FEM MAT TEXT
851	*FOOTWEAR	W 4392	72485	W 4372	64661	W 4685	62217	W 4792	69541	CHAUSSURES
85102	FOOTWEAR LEATHER	W 3764	64603	W 3512	55922	W 3882	53988	W 3619	58289	CHAUS SEMELLES EN CUIR
87	PRECISION INSTRUMNTS NES		93145		75723		71213		63080	INSTRUM,APPAR SCIENT NDA
874	MEASURNG,CONTROLNG INSTR	W 1361	76081	W 969	59737	W 918	56503	W 785	47624	INSTRUMENTS DE MESURE
8748	ELEC MEAS,CONTRL EQU NES	W 1012	62908	W 734	42913	W 606	48036	W 442	31934	APP ELEC ELECTRO MESURE
87483	OTH ELCTRNC MEAS ETC EQU	W 1012	62908	W 734	42913	W 606	48036	W 442	31934	AUT APP ELECTRO DE MESURE
88	PHOTO EQU,OPTICL GDS ETC		87754		78391		83074		78649	APP,FOURN PHOTO,OP,MONTR
885	WATCHES AND CLOCKS		48894		42077		43667		37510	HORLOGERIE
8851	WATCHES,MOVEMENTS,CASES		40819		33410		37717		32383	MONTRES,MOUVEMENTS,BOITES
88511	WATCHES		40819		33410		37717		32383	MONTRES POCHE,BRACELET
89	MISC MANUFCTRD GOODS NES		509710		354098		339488		359073	ART MANUFACTURES DIVERS
892	PRINTED MATTER	W 5528	34446	W 4683	31185	W 5426	28090	W 4887	29381	IMPRIMES
893	ARTICLES OF PLASTIC NES	W 13944	40143	W 15608	42566	W 17960	51394	W 18592	64350	OUVRAGES EN MAT DIVIS 58
8939	MISC PLASTIC ARTICLES	W 6678	20633	W 7865	23659	W 9698	29079	W 10165	36836	ART DIVERS EN MAT DIV 58
894	TOYS,SPORTING GOODS,ETC	W 8796	60932	W 8867	56309	W 8901	54393	W 8406	60070	VOITURES ENFANTS,JOUETS
8942	TOYS,INDOOR GAMES ETC	W 6322	41788	W 6647	37628	W 6099	34729	W 5301	35199	JOUETS,JEUX ETC
89421	LARGE SIZE WHEELED TOYS	W 5722	32288	W 5898	26880	W 5482	26109	W 4716	27422	VOITURES AMUSEM ENFANTS
895	OFFICE SUPPLIES NES	W 2863	26453	W 2257	19513	W 2096	19900	W 2241	22450	ART PAPET NDA
897	GOLD,SILVER WARE,JEWELRY		305549		155149		140419		140607	BIJOUTERIE,ORFEVRERIE
8973	PREC JEWLRY,GLD–SILVWARE		296516		149352		135134		133364	BIJOUX OR,ARGENT ORFEVRE
89731	PRECIOUS METAL JEWELLERY		296067		148950		134758		133121	ART BIJOUTERIE,JOAILLER
898	MUSICAL INSTRUMENTS,PTS	W 2294	22559	W 2391	28098	W 2450	22776	W 1592	17691	INSTRUMENTS DE MUSIQUE
8983	SOUND RECRDNG TAPE,DISCS	W 2083	17126	W 2179	24019	W 2289	19530	W 1459	14817	SUPPORTS SON POUR 763
899	OTHER MANUFACTURED GOODS		18079		20668		19790		24191	AUT ART MANUF DIVERS NDA
9	GOODS NOT CLASSD BY KIND		68079		56808		34034		31544	ART TRANSACT NON CLASSES
971	*GOLD,NON MONETARY NES	K 5274	60563	K 4588	52785	K 9991	30295	K 2254	28108	OR NON MONETAIRE
97101	NONMON GLD UNWRT,SEMIMFD	K 5274	60563	K 4588	52785	K 2491	30225	K 2254	28108	OR,ALLIAGES D'OR BRUTS

5. Special Exports F.O.B. by Commodities according to the S.I.T.C. (Rev. 2) in thousand U.S. Dollars
Exportations Spéciales F.O.B. par Produits d'après la C.T.C.I. (Rév. 2) en milliers de Dollars E.U.

SITC CTCI	COMMODITY	1992		1993		1994		1995		PRODUIT
		WEIGHT POIDS	VALUE VALEUR	WEIGHT POIDS	VALUE VALEUR	WEIGHT POIDS	VALUE VALEUR	WEIGHT POIDS	VALUE VALEUR	
	ALL COMMODITIES		6585282		10519039		11964516		12944424	TOUS PRODUITS
0	FOOD AND LIVE ANIMALS		21193		25458		25392		27371	ALIMENTS,ANIMAUX VIVANTS
2	CRUDE MATERLS,EXCL FUELS		19394		36062		44518		42448	MAT BRUTES NON COMESTIBLES
28	METALLIFEROUS ORES,SCRAP		16546		32359		40610		36470	MINERAIS METAL,DECHETS
3	MINERAL FUELS ETC		6224911		10000141		11230905		12255137	COMBUSTIBLES MINERAUX LUB
33	PETROLEUM AND PRODUCTS		6224911		10000082		11230897		12255112	PETROLE ET DERIVES
333	CRUDE PETROLEUM		6224000		9986000		11197000		12216000	HUILES BRUTES DE PETROLE
5	CHEMCLS,RELATED PROD NES		56122		100747		150873		260177	PRODUITS CHIMIQUES
52	INORGANIC CHEMICALS		6698		11641		38050		58624	PROD CHIM INORGANIQUES
522	INORG ELEMNTS,OXIDES,ETC	W 363877	6154	W 241020	10658	W 539029	37307	W 635405	58353	ELEMENTS INORGANIQUES
5221	CHEMICAL ELEMENTS	W 352682	2949	W 227639	7803	W 470298	24128	W 555288	40988	ELEMENTS CHIMIQUES
52215	SULPHUR,PURIFIED	W 350000	2287	W 225095	6978	W 467924	23389	W 553000	40414	SOUFRE SUBLIME,PRECIPITE
562	*FERTILIZERS,MANUFACTURE	W 233795	34416	W 673580	69944	W 716573	94503	W 945183	180288	ENGRAIS MANUFACTURES
5621	CHEM NITROGENOUS FERTLZR	W 233795	34415	W 673540	69927	W 716573	94503	W 945183	180288	ENGRAIS AZOTES
56216	UREA	W 233795	34415	W 673540	69927	W 716573	94503	W 945183	180288	UREE
6	BASIC MANUFACTURES		59259		91596		113721		133540	ART MANUFACTURES
66	NONMETAL MINERAL MFS NES		18347		28301		32482		41428	ART MIN NON METALLIQUES
7	MACHINES,TRANSPORT EQUIP		172219		216593		343726		182281	MACHINES MATERIEL TRANSPORT
74	GENRL INDUSTRL MACHY NES		22023		13496		11977		13307	MACH APP INDUSTRIE
77	ELECTRIC MACHNRY NES ETC		21156		40199		36532		31199	MACH APP ELECT NDA
78	ROAD VEHICLES		78720		115466		117627		109846	VEHICULES ROUTIERS
781	PASS MOTOR VEH EXC BUSES	W 4922	33390	W 5093	44530	W 4398	42363	W 3643	32048	AUTO TRANSPORT PERSONNES
782	LORRIES,SPCL MTR VEH NES	W 4328	22110	W 7643	34547	W 6079	36377	W 6328	26942	VEHICULES SPECIAUX,MARCH
7821	LORRIES,TRUCKS	W 4062	21259	W 7492	34064	W 5988	35617	W 6155	25900	VEHICULES TRANSP MARCHAND
79	OTHR TRANSPORT EQUIPMENT		10732		978		123745		1062	AUTRE MATERIEL TRANSPORT
792	AIRCRAFT ETC		4035				122047			APP NAVIGATION AERIENNE
7922	AIRCRFT NES 2000KG OR LS						122047			AERODYNES MOINS 2000 KG
8	MISC MANUFACTURED GOODS		28495		42206		49598		37465	ART MANUFACTURES DIVERS

1. HISTORICAL SERIES, 1992–1996 GENERAL TRADE, IMPORTS C.I.F., EXPORTS F.O.B.
SERIES HISTORIQUES, 1992–1996 COMMERCE GENERAL, IMPORTATIONS C.A.F., EXPORTATIONS F.O.B

YEAR ANNEE	VALUE IN MILLION U.S. DOLLARS VALEUR EN MILLION U.S. DOLLARS MERCHANDISE –MARCHANDISE		GOLD –OR		CONVERSION FACTORS FACTEURS DE CONVERSION CENTS E.U. PAR		INDEX NUMBERS –INDICES QUANTUM		UNIT VALUE VALEUR UNITAIRE	
	IMPORTS	EXPORTS	IMPORTS	EXPORTS	IMPORTS	EXPORTS	IMPORTS	EXPORTS	IMPORTS	EXPORTS
1992	70.47	76.45								
1993	112.00	112.10								
1994	369.00	340.00								
1995	439.00	380.00								
1996	837.93	507.07								

2. IMPORTS BY BROAD ECONOMIC CATEGORY AND EXPORTS BY INDUSTRIAL ORIGIN. (PERCENTAGE OF TOTAL VALUE)
IMPORTATIONS PAR CATEGORIES ECONOMIQUES ET EXPORTATIONS PAR BRANCHE D'ACTIVITE.(EN POURCENTAGE DE LA VALEUR TOTALE)

IMPORTS – IMPORTATIONS

	1990	1991	1992	1993	1994	1995	1996
TOTAL IMPORTS–IMPORTATIONS TOTALES						100.	100.
1 FOOD BEV–ALIMENTATION BOISSONS						11.6	20.3
11 PRIMARY–PRODUITS DE BASE						2.4	4.0
111 FOR INDUSTRY–POUR L'INDUSTRIE						1.9	2.9
112 FOR HOUSEHOLDS–POUR LES MENAGES						0.5	1.1
12 PROCESSED–PRODUITS ELABORES						9.2	16.3
121 FOR INDUSTRY–POUR L'INDUSTRIE						5.5	12.3
122 FOR HOUSEHOLDS–POUR LES MENAGES						3.7	4.1
2 IND SUPPLIES–APPROV INDUSTRIELS						14.1	18.7
21 PRIMARY–PRODUITS DE BASE						2.6	1.8
22 PROCESSED–PRODUITS ELABORES						11.5	16.9
3 FUELS–COMBUSTIBLES						24.0	28.4
31 PRIMARY–PRODUITS DE BASE						9.8	13.2
32 PROCESSED–PRODUITS ELABORES						14.2	15.2
321 MOTOR SPIRIT–ESSENCE						13.1	11.9
322 OTHER–AUTRES						1.1	3.3
4 MACHINERY–EQUIPEMENT						8.5	20.6
41 CAPITAL EQUIPMENT–MACHINES						6.6	13.4
42 PARTS–PIECES ACCESSOIRES						1.9	7.2
5 TRANSPORT–TRANSPORT						4.1	6.2
51 PASSENGER CARS–AUTOMOBILES						0.1	0.0
52 OTHER–AUTRES						2.0	2.3
521 INDUSTRIAL–INDUSTRIELS						2.0	2.3
522 NON INDUSTRIAL–NON INDUSTRIEL						0.0	0.0
53 PARTS–PIECES ACCESSOIRES						2.0	3.9
6 CONSUM GOODS–BIENS CONSOMMATION						4.2	5.6
61 DURABLE–DURABLES						0.8	1.2
62 SEMI DURABLE–SEMI DURABLES						1.4	1.2
63 NON DURABLE–NON DURABLES						2.0	3.2
7 GOODS NES–BIENS NDA						0.0	0.1

EXPORTS – EXPORTATIONS

	1990	1991	1992	1993	1994	1995	1996
TOTAL EXPORTS–EXPORTATIONS TOTALES						100.	100.
1 AGRICULTURE						12.9	17.9
2 MINING QUARRY–INDUS EXTRACTIVES						0.8	1.1
3 MANUFACTURING–IND MANUFACTUR						53.0	81.0
31 FOOD BEV TOBACCO–ALIM BOISS TAB						8.2	20.5
32 TEXTILES–INDUSTRIES TEXTILES						8.3	7.8
33 WOOD & PRODUCTS–BOIS & PRODUITS						0.0	0.1
34 PAPER & PRODUCTS–PAPIER & PRODT						0.1	0.3
35 CHEMICALS–INDUSTRIES CHIMIQUES						9.5	14.4
36 NON METAL MIN–MIN NON METAL						1.8	4.1
37 BASIC METAL–IND METAL BASE						7.2	4.8
38 METAL MANUF–MANUF METAL						10.7	14.0
39 OTH MANUF IND–AUTRES MANUF						7.2	15.0

3. TRADE BY PRINCIPAL COUNTRIES OF CONSIGNMENT AND LAST DESTINATION(VALUE IN THOUSAND U.S. DOLLARS)
ECHANGES SELON LES PRINCIPAUX PAYS DE CONSIGNATION ET DE DESTINATION FINALE (VALEUR EN MILLIERS DE DOLLARS EU)

COUNTRIES–PAYS	GENERAL IMPORTS C.I.F. IMPORTATIONS GENERALES C.A.F				
	1992	1993	1994	1995	1996
World	70472	112000	369000	522364	837933
Africa					70
Americas	134			47715	132699
Northern America	134			24967	78239
LAIA					32349
CACM					
Caribbean				22748	22063
Rest of America					47
As.ex F.USSR	110	9000	16000	65929	88451
Eur.x F.USSR	121			43606	115889
EU	76			34098	93161
EFTA	1			2858	16234
East Europe	44			6503	6378
Other Europe					
Former USSR			2000	357118	497729
Oceania					50
Russian Federation				114347	174471
Kazakhstan				112534	139670
Uzbekistan/Ouzbékistan				88926	131564
Turkey/Turquie	18	9000	15000	38334	47595
USA/Etats–Unis d'Amer	120			19082	35726
Germany/Allemagne	32			18705	31819
Canada	14			5885	42513
Cuba				22748	22063
Brazil/Brésil					32349
Turkmenistan/Turkménistn				18582	13606
France,Monac	2			1825	19090
Japan/Japon	1			7176	12512
Ukraine				4940	12291
China/Chine	84			6261	7818
Switz.Liecht	1			1176	12495
Belgium–Luxembourg				3830	8680
Austria/Autriche				1325	9818
Belarus/Bélarus				5034	6104
Tajikistan/Tadjikistan				4825	6303
Latvia/Lettonie				1513	6427
Korea, Republic of	4			2509	5139
Italy/Italie	9			1697	5793
Pakistan				2959	4095
Iran (Islamic Rp. of)			1000	2313	3448
Azerbaijan			2000	3263	1382
Denmark/Danemark				1865	4169
Norway,SVD,JM				1682	3736
United Kingdom	17			1671	3597
Netherlands/Pays–Bas	12			1506	3416
Lithuania/Lituanie				1742	2923
Finland/Finlande				1315	3132
Bulgaria/Bulgarie	6			3013	876
Poland/Pologne	1			1920	1589
India/Inde	0			550	2882
Afghanistan	0			3026	8
Hungary/Hongrie	19			1008	1761
Sweden/Suède	0			86	2380
United Arab Emirates				661	1748
Georgia/Géorgie				330	1555
Czech Republic				276	1262
Estonia/Estonie				247	1274
Israel/Israël				627	715
Greece/Grèce				189	1124
Korea Dem People's Rp	2			783	499
Cyprus/Chypre				473	366
Slovakia				224	545
Armenia/Arménie				601	1
Singapore/Singapour	0			122	400
Malaysia/Malaisie				128	348
Romania/Roumanie	0			62	344

COUNTRIES–PAYS	GENERAL EXPORTS F.O.B. EXPORTATIONS GENERALES F.O.B.				
	1992	1993	1994	1995	1996
Monde	76454	112100	340000	412042	507071
Afrique					
Amériques	8			5418	17859
Amérique du Nord	8			5418	17859
ALAI	0				
MCAC					
Caraïbes					
Autre Amérique					
Asie l'URSS exclus	191	6000	7000	84272	60961
Europe l'URSS exclus	192			47249	32296
UE	161			38858	19857
AELE	21			1766	892
Europe de l'Est	5			6545	11547
Autre de l'Europe					
Ancienne URSS			2000	275102	395954
Océanie	1			1	1
Russian Federation				106570	134664
Uzbekistan/Ouzbékistan				70828	116813
Kazakhstan				67235	112992
China/Chine	145			68464	36429
United Kingdom	60			27370	5326
USA/Etats–Unis d'Amer				4010	17642
Ukraine				8343	9391
Tajikistan/Tadjikistan				8265	8295
Turkey/Turquie	9	3000	4000	3220	5259
Afghanistan	0	3000	2000	2998	6499
Belarus/Bélarus				5034	5602
Iran (Islamic Rp. of)				4143	6302
Czech Republic				1177	8195
Azerbaijan			2000	2134	3213
Italy/Italie	3			2925	2513
France,Monac	35			3633	1759
Turkmenistan/Turkménistn				2217	3165
Germany/Allemagne	31			2067	2886
Belgium–Luxembourg	2			217	3655
Bulgaria/Bulgarie	2			2853	701
Netherlands/Pays–Bas	17			860	2059
Austria/Autriche	5			1719	1163
Cyprus/Chypre	0			1418	1266
Switz.Liecht	21			1766	892
Latvia/Lettonie				2255	349
Mongolia/Mongolie	1			891	1361
United Arab Emirates			1000	80	980
Poland/Pologne	1			1343	536
Republic of Moldova				978	764
Canada	8			1409	217
Japan/Japon	14			569	1046
India/Inde	3			521	1026
Romania/Roumanie	0			155	981
Hungary/Hongrie	0			177	954
Slovakia				840	179
Pakistan				605	408
Lithuania/Lituanie				428	491
Korea, Republic of	0			809	71
Korea Dem People's Rp	18			514	279
Georgia/Géorgie				689	97
Finland/Finlande	1			49	168
Estonia/Estonie				87	118
Spain/Espagne					144
Ireland/Irlande					132
Sweden/Suède	8				49
Armenia/Arménie				38	
Israel/Israël				16	9
Greece/Grèce				14	0
Denmark/Danemark				2	0
Thailand/Thaïlande	0				

(VALUE AS PERCENTAGE OF WORLD TOTAL)(VALEURS EN POURCENTAGE DU TOTAL MONDIAL)

	1987	1988	1989	1990	1991	1992	1993	1994	1995	1996
Africa										0.0
Americas						0.2			9.1	15.8
Northern America						0.2			4.8	9.3
LAIA										3.9
CACM										
Caribbean									4.4	2.6
Rest of America										0.0
As.ex F.USSR						0.2	8.0	4.3	12.6	10.6
Eur.x F.USSR						0.2			8.3	13.8
EU						0.1			6.5	11.1
EFTA						0.0			0.5	1.9
East Europe						0.1			1.2	0.8
Other Europe										
Former USSR								0.5	68.4	59.4
Oceania										0.0
Russian Federation									21.9	20.8
Kazakhstan									21.5	16.7
Uzbekistan/Ouzbékistan									17.0	15.7
Turkey/Turquie						0.0	8.0	4.1	7.3	5.7
USA/Etats–Unis d'Amer						0.2			3.7	4.3
Germany/Allemagne						0.0			3.6	3.8
Canada						0.0			1.1	5.1
Cuba									4.4	2.6
Brazil/Brésil										3.9
Turkmenistan/Turkménistn									3.6	1.6

	1987	1988	1989	1990	1991	1992	1993	1994	1995	1996
Afrique										
Amériques						0.0			1.3	3.5
Amérique du Nord						0.0			1.3	3.5
ALAI						0.0				
MCAC										
Caraïbes										
Autre Amérique										
Asie l'URSS exclus						0.2	5.4	2.1	20.5	12.0
Europe l'URSS exclus						0.3			11.5	6.4
UE						0.2			9.4	3.9
AELE						0.0			0.4	0.2
Europe de l'Est						0.0			1.6	2.3
Autre de l'Europe										
Ancienne URSS								0.6	66.8	78.1
Océanie						0.0			0.0	0.0
Russian Federation									25.9	26.6
Uzbekistan/Ouzbékistan									17.2	23.0
Kazakhstan									16.3	22.3
China/Chine						0.2			16.6	7.2
United Kingdom						0.1			6.6	1.1
USA/Etats–Unis d'Amer									1.0	3.5
Ukraine									2.0	1.9
Tajikistan/Tadjikistan									2.0	1.6
Turkey/Turquie						0.0	2.7	1.2	0.8	1.0
Afghanistan						0.0	2.7	0.6	0.7	1.3

4. General Imports C.I.F. by Commodities according to the S.I.T.C. (Rev. 2) in thousand U.S. Dollars
Importations Générales C.A.F. par Produits d'après la C.T.C.I. (Rév. 2) en milliers de Dollars E.U.

SITC CTCI	COMMODITY	1993 WEIGHT POIDS	1993 VALUE VALEUR	1994 WEIGHT POIDS	1994 VALUE VALEUR	1995 WEIGHT POIDS	1995 VALUE VALEUR	1996 WEIGHT POIDS	1996 VALUE VALEUR	PRODUIT
	ALL COMMODITIES						522364		837933	TOUS PRODUITS
0	FOOD AND LIVE ANIMALS						77720		149752	ALIMENTS,ANIMAUX VIVANTS
02	DAIRY PRODCTS,BIRDS'EGGS						1035		4212	PRODUITS LAITIERS,OEUFS
022	MILK AND CREAM					W 1126	654	W 1714	3749	LAIT ET CREME
0223	MILK AND CREAM FRESH					W 1126	654	W 1714	3749	LAIT,CREME FRAIS
04	CEREALS AND PREPARATIONS						28569		39550	CEREALES ET PRODUITS
041	WHEAT ETC UNMILLED					W 84116	12448	W 109377	22304	FROMENT,EPEAUTRE
0411	DURUM WHEAT UNMILLED					W 84116	12448	W 109377	22304	FROMENT DUR NON MOULU
042	RICE					W 3505	1856	W 3560	1544	RIZ
0421	RICE IN HUSK OR HUSKED					W 3505	1856	W 3560	1544	RIZ SANS AUTRE PREPARATION
04211	RICE IN THE HUSK					W 3505	1856	W 3560	1544	RIZ PADDY
046	WHEAT ETC MEAL OR FLOUR					W 56324	10541	W 30115	11592	SEMOULE FARINE,FROMENT
04601	FLOUR OF WHEAT OR MESLIN					W 56324	10541	W 30115	11592	FARINE DE FROMENT
048	CEREAL ETC PREPARATIONS						2088		2355	PREPTNS A BASE CEREALES
05	VEGETABLES AND FRUIT						1326		3316	LEGUMES ET FRUITS
06	SUGAR AND PREPS,HONEY						36387		92681	SUCRES ET PRODUITS
061	SUGAR AND HONEY					W 144140	34661	W 241765	91530	SUCRES ET MIEL
0611	RAW BEET AND CANE SUGAR					W 72316	25790	W 197558	83662	SUCRES BRUTS
0612	REFINED SUGAR ETC					W 8304	3226	W 4760	2706	SUCRES RAFFINES
0615	MOLASSES					W 63518	5644	W 39447	5162	MELASSES
062	SUGAR CANDY NON–CHOCLATE						1725		1151	SUCRERIES
07	COFFEE,TEA,COCOA,SPICES						4626		3621	CAFE,THE,CACAO,EPICES
073	CHOCOLATE AND PRODUCTS					W 1699	3716	W 1263	1898	CHOCOLAT
09	MISC EDIBLE PRODUCTS						4808		3594	PREP ALIMENTAIRES DIVERSES
098	EDIBLE PRODCTS,PREPS NES						4150		2953	PREP ALIMENTAIRES NDA
09809	MISC FOOD PREPRTIONS NES						2323		1422	PREP ALIMENTAIRES NDA
1	BEVERAGES AND TOBACCO						12553		20311	BOISSONS ET TABACS
11	BEVERAGES						11594		17730	BOISSONS
111	NON–ALCOHL BEVERAGES NES					W 28533	2261	W 5273	537	BOISSONS NON ALCOOLIQUES
11102	FLAVORED WATERS NON–ALCO					W 28533	2261	W 5273	537	LIMONADES,EAUX GAZEUSES
112	ALCOHOLIC BEVERAGES					W 53232	9333	W 148857	17193	BOISSONS ALCOOLIQUES
1121	WINE OF FRESH GRAPES ETC					W 13690	2520	W 48783	5965	VINS DE RAISINS FRAIS
11212	WINE OF FRESH GRAPES					W 13690	2520	W 48783	5965	VINS DE MOUTS DE RAISINS
1123	BEER,ALE,STOUT,PORTER					W 26559	2844	W 36565	3200	BIERES
1124	DISTILLED ALCOHOLIC BEVS					W 10809	3658	W 32363	5959	ALCOOLS,EAUX–DE–VIE
11249	OTH ALCOHOLC BEVS,CMPNDS					W 10809	3658	W 32363	5959	BOISSONS ALCOOLIQUES NDA
12	TOBACCO AND MANUFACTURES						959		2581	TABACS BRUTS FABRIQUES
122	TOBACCO,MANUFACTURED					W 204	889	W 1385	2575	TABACS FABRIQUES
1222	CIGARETTES					W 204	889	W 1385	2575	CIGARETTES
2	CRUDE MATERLS,EXCL FUELS						23964		21208	MAT BRUTES NON COMESTIBLES
24	CORK AND WOOD						3862		5259	LIEGE ET BOIS
248	WOOD SHAPED,SLEEPERS					W 16161	2605	W 27297	4321	BOIS SIMPLEMENT TRAVAILLES
2482	LUMBER SHAPED CONIFER					W 14955	2287	W 26135	4117	CONIFERES SCIES,RABOTES
24822	LUMBER PLANED ETC CONIFR					W 14955	2287	W 26135	4117	CONIFER RABOTES,RAINES
26	TEXTILE FIBRES AND WASTE						9805		6813	FIBRES TEXTILES
263	COTTON					W 5689	4865	W 1575	409	COTON
2631	RAW COTTON,EXCL LINTERS					W 2746	3943	W 94	149	COTON EN MASSE
268	WOOL(EXC TOPS),ANML HAIR					W 1269	1661	W 1049	1532	LAINES ET POILS
27	CRUDE FERTLZR,MINRLS NES						4414		5611	ENGRAIS MINERAUX BRUTS
278	OTHER CRUDE MINERALS						3482		4948	AUTRES MINERAUX BRUTS
2784	ASBESTOS CRDE,SMPLY WRKD					W 11446	2017	W 12542	2417	AMIANTE (ASBESTE)
28	METALLIFEROUS ORES,SCRAP						5515		2855	MINERAIS METAL,DECHETS
287	BASE METAL ORES,CONC NES					W 2178	2253	W 1197	1400	MINERAIS METAUX COMMUNS
2879	OTH NONFER ORE,CONCNTRTE					W 2178	2253	W 1197	1400	MINERAIS D'AUTRES METAUX
28799	OTH BASE MTL ORE,CON NES					W 2178	2253	W 1197	1400	AUTRES MINERAIS
288	NONFERR METAL SCRAP NES					W 6113	3087	W 2121	1383	DECHETS NON FERREUX
2882	OTHER BASE MTL SCRAP NES					W 6113	3087	W 2121	1383	AUTRES DECHETS
28821	COPPER WASTE AND SCRAP					W 5080	2779	W 1781	1307	DECHETS DE CUIVRE
3	MINERAL FUELS ETC						188412		240056	COMBUSTIBLES MINERAUX LUB
32	COAL,COKE AND BRIQUETTES						17041		25788	HOUILLES,COKES,BRIQUETTES
322	COAL,LIGNITE AND PEAT					W 4099709	17001	W 7144500	25143	HOUILLES,LIGNITES,TOURBE
3222	OTH COAL,NOT AGGLOMERATD					W 4092267	16875	W 7092911	23881	AUTRES HOUILLES
33	PETROLEUM AND PRODUCTS						103246		103176	PETROLE ET DERIVES
334	PETROLEUM PRODUCTS,REFIN					W 1440853	102473	W 3276155	99624	PRODUITS RAFFINES
341	*GAS,NATURAL AND MANUFCT						59546		84374	GAZ NATUREL,GAZ MANUFACT
3413	PETROLM GASES,LIQUEFIED						55511		71796	GAZ DE PETROLE LIQUEFIE
34139	OTH HYDROCARBON GAS LQFD						55511		71796	HYDROCARBURES GAZEUX NDA
3414	PETROLEUM GASES, GASEOUS						4036		12578	GAZ DE PETROLE GAZEUX
351	*ELECTRIC CURRENT					H 254400	8579	H 815100	26718	ENERGIE ELECTRIQUE
4	ANIMAL,VEGETABLE OIL,FAT						5328		4543	HUILES,GRAISSES ANIM,VEG
42	FIXED VEGETABLE OIL,FAT						5143		4450	HUILES VEGETALES FIXES
423	FIXED VEG OILS,SOFT					W 7758	3152	W 5239	3711	HUILES VEGET DOUCES FIXES
4236	SUNFLOWER SEED OIL					W 7007	2578	W 4643	3303	HUILE DE TOURNESOL
424	FIXED VEG OIL NONSOFT					W 1662	1991	W 741	739	AUTRES HUILES VEG FIXES
4249	FIXED VEGETABLE OILS NES					W 1625	1882	W 711	698	HUILES VEGET FIXES NDA
5	CHEMCLS,RELATED PROD NES						31919		64451	PRODUITS CHIMIQUES
51	ORGANIC CHEMICALS						3581		13826	PROD CHIMIQ ORGANIQUES
512	ALCOHOLS,PHENOLS ETC						2068		12280	PHENOLS,PHENOLS–ALCOOLS
5121	ACYCLIC ALCOHOLS,DERIVS						2068		12194	ALCOOLS ACYCLIQUES
51216	ETHYL ALC,DENATRD SPIRIT					V 12549	2034	V 109540	12192	ALCOOL ETHYLIQUE NON DENAT
52	INORGANIC CHEMICALS						6204		9702	PROD CHIM INORGANIQUES
522	INORG ELEMNTS,OXIDES,ETC					W 15680	3256	W 13970	3702	ELEMENTS INORGANIQUES
5225	INORGANIC BASES ETC NES					W 11580	2424	W 11727	2927	AUTRES BASES OXYDES METAL
523	OTHR INORG CHEMICALS ETC						2948		5999	AUT PRODUITS CHIMIQUES INORG
5239	INORG CHEM PRODUCTS NES						1988		4221	PROD CHIM INORGANIQ NDA
52399	OTH INORG CMPNDS NES ETC						1957		3632	AUT COMP INORGANIQUES NDA
53	DYES,TANNING,COLOUR PROD						2442		1909	PROD TEINTURE,COLORANTS
531	SYNT DYE,NAT INDGO,LAKES					W 1011	2372	W 699	1894	MAT COLOR ORGAN,LAQUES
541	*MEDICINAL,PHARM PRODUCT						8863		17762	PROD MEDICINAUX PHARMACEUT
5417	MEDICAMENTS						7680		15872	MEDICAMENTS
54171	— CONTAINNG ANTIBIOTICS						7680		15872	MED CONTN ANTIBIOTIQUES
55	PERFUME,CLEANING ETC PRD						3696		2454	PROD POUR PARFUM,TOILETTE
554	SOAP,CLEANSING ETC PREPS					W 3765	2525	W 1583	1500	SAVONS,PRODUITS DETERSIFS
562	*FERTILIZERS,MANUFACTURE					W 22517	3742	W 89763	10709	ENGRAIS MANUFACTURES
5621	CHEM NITROGENOUS FERTLZR					W 16415	3205	W 62899	8758	ENGRAIS AZOTES
56216	UREA					W 16415	3205	W 62899	8758	UREE
58	PLASTIC MATERIALS ETC						1518		3810	MAT PLAST ARTIFICIELLES
583	POLYMERIZATION ETC PRODS					W 1287	1518	W 2713	3810	PROD POLYMERISATION
59	CHEMICAL MATERIALS NES						914		3479	MAT PROD CHIMIQUES NDA
6	BASIC MANUFACTURES						67023		93950	ART MANUFACTURES
62	RUBBER MANUFACTURES NES						4695		10774	CAOUTCHOUC MANUFACTURE

4. General Imports C.I.F. by Commodities according to the S.I.T.C. (Rev. 2) in thousand U.S. Dollars
Importations Générales C.A.F. par Produits d'après la C.T.C.I. (Rév. 2) en milliers de Dollars E.U.

SITC CTCI	COMMODITY	1993 WEIGHT POIDS	1993 VALUE VALEUR	1994 WEIGHT POIDS	1994 VALUE VALEUR	1995 WEIGHT POIDS	1995 VALUE VALEUR	1996 WEIGHT POIDS	1996 VALUE VALEUR	PRODUIT
625	RUBBER TYRES, TUBES ETC					N 78670	3983	N 60932	7100	PNEUS CAOUTCHOUC VULCANISE
6252	TYRES,NEW,BUS OR LORRY					N 26137	2136	N 18767	4262	PNEUS POUR AUTOBUS,CAMIONS
628	RUBBER ARTICLES NES						691		3552	OUVRAGES CAOUTCHOUC NDA
6289	OTH RUBBER ARTICLES NES						487		3292	AUT OUVR CAOUTCHOUC NDA
62898	UNHARD RUBBER PRODS NES						487		3292	OUV CAOUT VULC NON DURCI
63	WOOD,CORK MANUFACTRS NES						6784		6062	OUVRAGES LIEGE ET BOIS
635	WOOD MANUFACTURES NES						5570		4188	ART MANUF EN BOIS NDA
6353	BUILDERS WOODWRK,PREFABS						5410		3482	OUVRAGES DE MENUISERIE
64	PAPER,PAPERBOARD AND MFR						5735		11036	PAPIERS,CARTONS & OUVRAGES
641	PAPER AND PAPERBOARD						3496		7572	PAPIERS ET CARTONS
642	PAPER,ETC,PRECUT,ARTS OF						2239		3465	PAP,CARTONS DECOUPES
6423	EXERCISE BOOKS ETC						1856		1918	REGISTRES,CAHIERS,CARNETS
65	TEXTILE YARN,FABRICS,ETC						10003		8887	FILS,TISSUS,ARTICLES TEXTILE
651	TEXTILE YARN					W 1566	3315		2145	FILS TEXTILES
6513	COTTON YARN					W 875	1797	W 398	662	FILS DE COTON
652	COTTON FABRICS,WOVEN						1892		797	TISSUS DE COTON
657	SPECIAL TXTL FABRC,PRODS						1223		2720	TISSUS SPECIAUX
66	NONMETAL MINERAL MFS NES						6190		12107	ART MIN NON METALLIQUES
661	LIME,CEMENT,BLDG PRODS						1603		2319	CHAUX,CIMENTS MAT CONSTR
663	MINERAL MANUFCTURES NES						2717		3079	ART MIN MANUF NDA
6633	MINRL MFS NES NONCERAMIC						2255		1817	OUVR MAT MINERALE NDA
66332	CEMENT,ARTFCL STONE PROD						1715		719	OUVRAGES EN CIMENT
665	GLASSWARE						1062		5062	OUVRAGES EN VERRE
6658	GLASS ARTICLES NES						919		4861	ARTICLES FAB EN VERRE NDA
66581	LABORATORY ETC GLASS					MN 37255	798	MN 241451	4632	VERRERIE LABOR,HYG,PHAR ETC
67	IRON AND STEEL						16692		12512	FER ET ACIER
672	IRON,STEEL PRIMARY FORMS					W 21745	7087	W 9296	4117	LINGOTS FER,ACIER
6727	IRN,STL COIL FR REROLLNG					W 21111	6502	W 8636	3794	EBAUCHES POUR TOLES FER
67271	IRON,SIMPLE STEEL COILS					W 21111	6502	W 8636	3794	EBAUCHES NON EN ACIER
673	IRON,STEEL SHAPES ETC					W 8053	2716	W 6325	2295	BARRES,PROFIL FER,ACIER
6731	IRON,STEEL WIRE ROD					W 8053	2716	W 6325	2295	FIL MACHINE FER,ACIER
67311	IRON,SIMPLE STL WIRE ROD					W 8053	2716	W 6325	2295	FIL MACH AUT ACIER FIN
674	IRN,STL UNIV,PLATE,SHEET					W 6706	2369	W 2231	1371	LARGES PLATS,TOLES
678	IRON,STL TUBES,PIPES,ETC					W 5458	3595	W 5834	3616	TUBES,TUYAUX EN FONTE,FER
6782	IRON,STL SEAMLESS TUBES					W 1986	1517	W 4422	2882	TUBES,TUYAUX SANS SOUDURE
6783	IRON,STL TUBES,PIPES NES					W 3329	1969	W 1171	540	AUT TUBES,TUYAUX FER,ACIER
68	NON–FERROUS METALS						3375		1717	METAUX NON FERREUX
682	COPPER EXC CEMENT COPPER					W 2395	2757	W 316	1081	CUIVRE
6821	COPPER NES,ALLOYS,UNWRT					W 1915	1824	W 143	573	CUIVRE BRUT
69	METAL MANUFACTURES NES						12871		30025	ART MANUFACT EN METAL NDA
691	STRUCTURES AND PARTS NES					W 810	264	W 3762	6156	CONSTRUCT FER,ACIER,ALU
6911	STRUCTURES,PARTS IRN,STL					W 810	264	W 3762	6156	CONSTRUCT FER,ACIER,FONTE
693	WIRE PRODUCTS NON ELECTR					W 2198	3902	W 1410	3152	OUVRAGES FILS METALLIQUES
6931	WIRE CABLES, ROPES ETC					W 2198	3902	W 1410	3152	CORDAGES EN FILS DE FER
69312	COPPER CABLES, ROPES ETC					W 1476	2859	W 673	1810	CORDAGES DE CUIVRE
699	BASE METAL MFRS NES						6237		14259	ART MANUFACTURES MET NDA
6997	IRON,STEEL ARTICLES NES						2782		7333	OUV FONTE,FER,ACIER NDA
69979	IRN,STL MANUFACTURES NES						2782		7333	AUT OUVRAGES EN FER NDA
6998	MFRS NES OF CPR,NIKL,ETC						1846		3290	OUVRAGES EN CU,NI,AL,PB,ZN
7	MACHINES,TRANSPORT EQUIP						96109		218951	MACHINES MATERIEL TRANSPORT
72	MACHS FOR SPCL INDUSTRYS						32247		59573	MAC SPECIALES POUR INDUST
721	AGRIC MACHY,EXC TRACTORS						452		5260	MACHINES AGRICOLES
7212	HARVESTING ETC MACHINES					N 38	89	N 301	3937	ENGINS POUR LA RECOLTE
72123	OTH HARVSTER,MOWRS,BALER					N 10	74	N 93	3834	AUT MACH POUR LA RECOLTE
723	CIVIL ENGNEERG EQUIP ETC						20154		34181	APPAREILS DE GENIE CIVIL
7234	CONST,MINING MACHNRY NES						20154		34181	MACH POUR LA CONST, MINES
72345	PILE DRIVERS,ETC					N 1893	15911	N 5608	28008	CHASSE–NEIGE
72348	PUBLIC WORKS MACHNRY NES						3068		5347	MACHINES TRAVAUX PUBLICS
724	TEXTILE,LEATHER MACHNRY						5848		6660	MACH POUR INDUSTRIE TEXTILE
7244	SPINNING,EXTRDNG,ETC MCH						5822		4437	MACH POUR LE FILAGE
72442	FIBRE PROCESSNG MACH NES						5822		4437	MACH PREP MAT TEXTILES
727	FOOD MACHRY NON–DOMESTIC						4054		3518	MACH INDUSTRIES ALIMENT
7272	OTH FOOD PROC MCHY,PARTS						4054		3518	AUT MACH IND ALIMENTAIRE
72722	INDUS FOOD PROC MACH NES						4054		3518	MACHINES BOULANGERIE
728	OTH MACHY FOR SPCL INDUS						650		6707	AUT MACH IND PARTICULIERES
7281	MACH–TOOLS FR SPCL INDUS							N 1223	3938	MACH–OUTILS SPEC IND PART
72811	MACH–TOOLS TO WRK MINRLS							N 832	3763	MACH POUR TRAVAIL PIERRE
73	METALWORKING MACHINERY						3516		2353	MACH TRAVAIL DES METAUX
737	METALWORKING MACHNRY NES						2750		2087	MACH TRAV METAUX PIECES
7373	WELDING,BRAZING,ETC MCHS						2743		2087	MACH SOUDAGE ETC PIECES
73732	ELECTRIC WELDERS,ETC						2717		2063	MACH ELECT POUR SOUDER
74	GENRL INDUSTRL MACHY NES						14220		32732	MACH APP INDUSTRIE
749	NONELEC MACH PTS,ACC NES						9904		28638	PIECES MACH NON ELEC NDA
7499	OTH NONELEC MCHY PTS NES						9589		28418	PIECES NON ELECT NDA
74999	MACH PARTS NONELEC NES						9589		28418	PIECES MACHINES NDA
75	OFFICE MACHNES,ADP EQUIP						2007		7621	MACH BUREAU TRAIT AUTOM
752	AUTOMTIC DATA PROC EQUIP						1733		7183	MACH TRAIT INFORMATION
7528	OFF–LINE DATA PROC EQUIP						1285		5498	MACH AUXIL TRAIT INFORM
76	TELECOMM,SOUND EQUIPMENT						2819		11136	EQUIPMENT DE TELECOM
764	TELECOM EQPT,PTS,ACC NES						2184		10044	EQUIP TELECOM,PIECES
7641	LINE TELEPHONE,ETC EQUIP						391		3436	APP TELEPHON PAR FIL
7643	TV,RADIO TRANSMITTRS ETC						1793		6607	APP EMET TELE RADIO
77	ELECTRIC MACHNRY NES ETC						11460		60775	MACH APP ELECT NDA
771	ELECTRIC POWER MACHY NES					N 260	593	N 2520	7213	MACH PROD,TRANS ELECTR
7711	TRANSFORMERS,ELECTRICAL					N 260	593	N 2520	7213	TRANSFO ELECTRIQUES
77111	LIQUID DIELEC TRANSFRMRS					N 260	593	N 2520	7213	TRANSFO DIELEC LIQUIDE
773	ELECTR DISTRIBUTNG EQUIP						3746		9920	EQUIPMT DISTRIBUTION ELECT
7731	INSULATED WIRE,CABLE ETC						2831	W 342	8983	FILS,CABLES ISOLES ELECT
774	ELECTRO–MEDCL,XRAY EQUIP						2670		12176	APPAREILS MEDICAUX
7741	ELECTRO–MEDICAL EQUIPMNT						2670		12176	APP ELECTRICITE MEDICALE
776	TRANSISTORS,VALVES,ETC						366		8650	LAMPES,TUBES,VALVES
7768	ELCTRNC COMP PTS,CRYSTLS						126		8544	CRIST PIEZO–ELEC,PCS 776
77689	ELECTRNIC COMPON PTS NES						126		8544	PIECES DU GROUPE 776
778	ELECTRICAL MACHINERY NES						2485		18896	AUTRES MACH ELECT NDA
7788	OTH ELEC MACHY,EQUIP NES						1903		15763	AUT MACH APP ELEC NDA
77886	OTH ELEC MACHINERY NES						967		3138	AUT MACH APP ELECTRIQUES
77889	ELEC PARTS OF MACHY NES						675		12236	PIECES ELEC DE MACH NDA
78	ROAD VEHICLES						27530		41720	VEHICULES ROUTIERS
782	LORRIES,SPCL MTR VEH NES					N 1192	12406	N 1421	16040	VEHICULES SPECIAUX,MARCH
7821	LORRIES,TRUCKS					N 1153	10984	N 1313	13732	VEHICULES TRANSP MARCHAND
783	ROAD MOTOR VEHICLES NES					N 110	2303	N 55	1537	VEHICULES ROUTIERS NDA

4. General Imports C.I.F. by Commodities according to the S.I.T.C. (Rev. 2) in thousand U.S. Dollars
Importations Générales C.A.F. par Produits d'après la C.T.C.I. (Rév. 2) en milliers de Dollars E.U.

SITC CTCI	COMMODITY	1993		1994		1995		1996		PRODUIT
		WEIGHT POIDS	VALUE VALEUR	WEIGHT POIDS	VALUE VALEUR	WEIGHT POIDS	VALUE VALEUR	WEIGHT POIDS	VALUE VALEUR	
7831	BUSES					N 110	2303	N 55	1537	VOITURES TRANSPORT COMMUN
784	MOTOR VEH PRTS,ACCES NES						11118		22284	PIECES 722,781,782,783
7849	OTHER MOTOR VEHCL PARTS						10272		22195	PIECES 722,781,782,783
79	OTHR TRANSPORT EQUIPMENT						1652		1824	AUTRE MATERIEL TRANSPORT
8	MISC MANUFACTURED GOODS						19172		24079	ART MANUFACTURES DIVERS
821	*FURNITURE,PARTS THEREOF						3098		3664	MEUBLES ET PIECES
8211	CHAIRS,SEATS AND PARTS						3060		3514	SIEGES ET PIECES
82111	CHAIRS AND OTHER SEATS						3060		3514	SIEGES
84	CLOTHING AND ACCESSORIES						4251		2127	VETEMENTS
842	MENS OUTERWEAR NOT KNIT						1955		1313	VET DESSUS POUR HOMMES
8421	— OVERCOATS,OTHER COATS						1955		1313	MANTEAUX HOMMES MAT TEXT
84219	—— OF OTHER FIBRES						1955		1313	MANTEAUX HOMMES AUT FIBR
851	*FOOTWEAR						2628		1889	CHAUSSURES
87	PRECISION INSTRUMNTS NES						1133		6643	INSTRUM,APPAR SCIENT NDA
874	MEASURNG,CONTROLNG INSTR						832		6275	INSTRUMENTS DE MESURE
8749	INSTR PTS NES,ACCESSORYS						611		5986	PIECES 873,874.3,54,874.8
89	MISC MANUFCTRD GOODS NES						6210		7862	ART MANUFACTURES DIVERS
893	ARTICLES OF PLASTIC NES						1695		3806	OUVRAGES EN MAT DIVIS 58
8939	MISC PLASTIC ARTICLES						1296		3303	ART DIVERS EN MAT DIV 58
89399	OTHR PLASTC ARTICLES NES						1296		3303	AUT OUV MAT DIV 58

5. General Exports F.O.B. by Commodities according to the S.I.T.C. (Rev. 2) in thousand U.S. Dollars
Exportations Générales F.O.B. par Produits d'après la C.T.C.I. (Rév. 2) en milliers de Dollars E.U.

SITC CTCI	COMMODITY	1993		1994		1995		1996		PRODUIT
		WEIGHT POIDS	VALUE VALEUR	WEIGHT POIDS	VALUE VALEUR	WEIGHT POIDS	VALUE VALEUR	WEIGHT POIDS	VALUE VALEUR	
	ALL COMMODITIES						412042		507071	TOUS PRODUITS
0	FOOD AND LIVE ANIMALS						60218		112590	ALIMENTS,ANIMAUX VIVANTS
01	MEAT AND PREPARATIONS						5215		6378	VIANDES ET PREPARATIONS
011	MEAT FRESH,CHILLD,FROZEN					W 3333	2827	W 1996	2153	VIANDES FRAICHES,REF,CONGE
0111	BOVINE MEAT FRESH,FROZEN					W 3333	2827	W 1996	2153	VIANDES BOVIN FRAI,REF
01111	BOVINE MEAT WITH BONE IN					W 3333	2827	W 1996	2153	VIANDES BOVIN NON DESOSS
014	MEAT PREPD,PRSVD,NES ETC						2388		4224	CONSERVES DE VIANDES
0149	OTH PREPARD,PRESRVD MEAT						2366		4162	AUTRES PREP DE VIANDES
02	DAIRY PRODCTS,BIRDS'EGGS						2912		1433	PRODUITS LAITIERS,OEUFS
022	MILK AND CREAM					W 1166	1371	W 801	622	LAIT ET CREME
0223	MILK AND CREAM FRESH					W 1166	1371	W 801	622	LAIT,CREME FRAIS
023	BUTTER					W 889	1344	W 165	457	BEURRE
04	CEREALS AND PREPARATIONS						2466		13592	CEREALES ET PRODUITS
041	WHEAT ETC UNMILLED					W 52	6	W 6152	3521	FROMENT,EPEAUTRE
0411	DURUM WHEAT UNMILLED					W 52	6	W 6152	3521	FROMENT DUR NON MOULU
044	MAIZE UNMILLED					W 132	20	W 5469	3583	MAIS NON MOULU
046	WHEAT ETC MEAL OR FLOUR					W 3357	734	W 11053	4367	SEMOULE FARINE,FROMENT
04601	FLOUR OF WHEAT OR MESLIN					W 3357	734	W 11053	4367	FARINE DE FROMENT
048	CEREAL ETC PREPARATIONS						1171		1698	PREPTNS A BASE CEREALES
05	VEGETABLES AND FRUIT						24833		27279	LEGUMES ET FRUITS
054	VEG ETC FRSH,SMPLY PRSVD						12865		12804	LEGUMES FRAIS,CONG,SECS
0544	TOMATOES FRESH					W 10970	2059	W 11985	1875	TOMATES FRAICHES
0545	OTHER FRESH VEGETABLES					W 72981	9578	W 77368	9755	AUTRES LEGUMES FRAIS,REF
05451	ALLIACEOUS VEGTBLS,FRESH					W 60517	7550	W 64300	7282	OIGNONS,ECHALOTES,AULX
05459	FRESH VEGETABLES NES					W 12465	2029	W 13068	2473	LEGUMES FRAIS,REFRI NDA
056	VEGTBLES ETC PRSVD,PREPD						1307		1013	CONSERVES DE LEGUMES
0565	VEGTBLES PRSVD,PREPD NES						1245		916	LEGUMES PREPARES CONSERVE
05651	VEGTBLS,FRUIT IN VINEGAR						1245		916	LEGUM CONSERV AU VINAIGRE
057	FRUIT,NUTS,FRESH,DRIED					W 49003	10239	W 68353	12929	FRUITS FRAIS OU SECS
0574	APPLES FRESH					W 36588	7126	W 47300	8095	POMMES FRAICHES
0579	FRUIT FRESH OR DRIED NES					W 9478	2362	W 12773	3085	FRUITS FRAIS,SECS NDA
05799	OTHER DRIED FRUIT					W 3898	1618	W 6756	2291	AUTRES FRUITS SECHES
06	SUGAR AND PREPS,HONEY						21586		56900	SUCRES ET PRODUITS
061	SUGAR AND HONEY					W 32203	18777	W 106247	56599	SUCRES ET MIEL
0612	REFINED SUGAR ETC					W 26346	15366	W 96763	52059	SUCRES RAFFINES
0615	MOLASSES					W 5598	3049	W 9208	4118	MELASSES
062	SUGAR CANDY NON–CHOCLATE					W 3129	2810		301	SUCRERIES
09	MISC EDIBLE PRODUCTS						1030		4209	PREP ALIMENTAIRES DIVERSES
098	EDIBLE PRODCTS,PREPS NES						930		4093	PREP ALIMENTAIRES NDA
09807	VINEGAR AND SUBSTITUTES					V 1136	453	V 15103	3361	VINAIGRES COMESTIBLES
1	BEVERAGES AND TOBACCO						32050		27809	BOISSONS ET TABACS
11	BEVERAGES						9426		8347	BOISSONS
112	ALCOHOLIC BEVERAGES					W 44821	9194	W 45242	8138	BOISSONS ALCOOLIQUES
1121	WINE OF FRESH GRAPES ETC					W 11323	2971	W 9254	1908	VINS DE RAISINS FRAIS
11212	WINE OF FRESH GRAPES					W 11323	2971	W 9254	1908	VINS DE MOUTS DE RAISINS
1124	DISTILLED ALCOHOLIC BEVS					W 28297	5582	W 28851	5446	ALCOOLS,EAUX–DE–VIE
11249	OTH ALCOHOLC BEVS,CMPNDS					W 28297	5582	W 28851	5446	BOISSONS ALCOOLIQUES NDA
12	TOBACCO AND MANUFACTURES						22624		19462	TABACS BRUTS FABRIQUES
121	TOBACCO UNMNFCTRD,REFUSE					W 36527	21647	W 19113	16276	TABACS BRUTS,DECHETS
1211	TOBACCO,NOT STRIPPED					W 22840	12917	W 10675	9439	TABACS NON ECOTES
1212	TOBACCO STRIPPED OR PART					W 13678	8728	W 8363	6826	TABACS PART ECOTES
122	TOBACCO,MANUFACTURED						977		3186	TABACS FABRIQUES
1222	CIGARETTES						977		3186	CIGARETTES
2	CRUDE MATERLS,EXCL FUELS						70060		73400	MAT BRUTES NON COMESTIBLES
21	HIDES,SKINS,FURS UNDRSSD						3965		15104	CUIRS,PEAUX BRUTS
211	HIDES,SKINS,EXC FURS,RAW						3962		15103	CUIRS ET PEAUX
2112	CALF AND KIP SKINS,RAW					N 4064674	2131	MN 17060	10818	PEAUX DE VEAUX
2116	SHEEP SKIN WITH WOOL					MN 13214	1820	MN 19222	4236	PEAUX LAINEES D'OVINS
22	OIL SEEDS,OLEAGINOUS FRT						977		3176	GRAINES,FRUITS OLEAGINEUX
223	SEEDS FOR OTH FIXED OILS					W 704	977	W 8434	3176	GRAINES AUTRES HUILES FIXES
2234	LINSEED					W 704	977	W 8434	3176	GRAINES DE LIN
26	TEXTILE FIBRES AND WASTE						47144		41402	FIBRES TEXTILES
261	SILK					W 2015	1824	W 1847	1795	SOIE
2614	SILK WORM COCOONS,WASTE					W 2001	1663	W 1798	1279	COCONS ET DECHETS
26142	SILK WASTE					W 1858	1370	W 1704	1126	DECHETS DE SOIE
263	COTTON					W 27383	25530	W 26139	34345	COTON
2631	RAW COTTON,EXCL LINTERS					W 17799	21619	W 22180	32000	COTON EN MASSE
2634	COTTON,CARDED OR COMBED					W 1487	2043	W 626	856	COTON CARDE OU PEIGNE
268	WOOL(EXC TOPS),ANML HAIR					W 14895	19725	W 4340	5044	LAINES ET POILS
2681	WOOL GREASY,FLEECE–WSHED					W 9161	8117	W 2439	1866	LAINE EN SUINT
2682	WOOL DEGREASED,UNCOMBED					W 5194	11056	W 1721	2960	LAINE DEGRAISSEE
28	METALLIFEROUS ORES,SCRAP						16497		11975	MINERAIS METAL,DECHETS
288	NONFERR METAL SCRAP NES					W 29955	15758	W 13392	10223	DECHETS NON FERREUX
2882	OTHER BASE MTL SCRAP NES					W 29955	15758	W 13392	10223	AUTRES DECHETS
28821	COPPER WASTE AND SCRAP					W 17485	11775	W 9262	8668	DECHETS DE CUIVRE
28823	ALUMINIUM WSTE AND SCRAP					W 12460	3983	W 3832	1508	DECHETS D'ALUMINIUM
3	MINERAL FUELS ETC						45584		77658	COMBUSTIBLES MINERAUX LUB
32	COAL,COKE AND BRIQUETTES						3139		2028	HOUILLES,COKES,BRIQUETTES
322	COAL,LIGNITE AND PEAT					W 170638	3139	W 100377	2028	HOUILLES,LIGNITES,TOURBE
3222	OTH COAL,NOT AGGLOMERATD					W 170638	3139	W 92277	1843	AUTRES HOUILLES
33	PETROLEUM AND PRODUCTS						1374		2068	PETROLE ET DERIVES
333	CRUDE PETROLEUM					W 24600	894	W 21103	1649	HUILES BRUTES DE PETROLE
351	*ELECTRIC CURRENT					H 1622000	40968	H 2880800	73551	ENERGIE ELECTRIQUE
5	CHEMCLS,RELATED PROD NES						48686		65358	PRODUITS CHIMIQUES
51	ORGANIC CHEMICALS						23759		30258	PROD CHIMIQ ORGANIQUES
512	ALCOHOLS,PHENOLS ETC					V 183393	23748		30245	PHENOLS,PHENOLS–ALCOOLS
5121	ACYCLIC ALCOHOLS,DERIVS					V 183393	23748		30245	ALCOOLS ACYCLIQUES
51216	ETHYL ALC,DENATRD SPIRIT					V 183393	23748	V 237199	30235	ALCOOL ETHYLIQUE NON DENAT
52	INORGANIC CHEMICALS						20357		32209	PROD CHIM INORGANIQUES
522	INORG ELEMNTS,OXIDES,ETC					W 418	1428	W 830	5140	ELEMENTS INORGANIQUES
5221	CHEMICAL ELEMENTS					W 342	1413	W 780	5090	ELEMENTS CHIMIQUES
52216	MERCURY					W 261	988	W 628	2512	MERCURE
52217	ALKALI,RARE EARTH METALS					W 65	259	W 137	1747	METAUX ALCALINS
523	OTHR INORG CHEMICALS ETC						9876		5864	AUT PRODUITS CHIMIQUES INORG
5231	METAL CMPD OF INORG ACID					W 749	1415	W 152	804	SELS METALLIQUES
52319	OTH SULPHATES,PERSLPHTES					W 749	1415	W 152	804	AUTRE SULFATES,ALUNS
5239	INORG CHEM PRODUCTS NES						8462		5041	PROD CHIM INORGANIQ NDA
52399	OTH INORG CMPNDS NES ETC						8457		4987	AUT COMP INORGANIQUES NDA
524	RADIOACTIVE ETC MATERIAL						9053		21205	MATIERES RADIOACTIVES
5241	RADIOACTIVE ELEMENTS ETC						9053		21205	RADIOELEMENTS,ISOTOPES
541	*MEDICINAL,PHARM PRODUCT						2563		1544	PROD MEDICINAUX PHARMACEUT

5. General Exports F.O.B. by Commodities according to the S.I.T.C. (Rev. 2) in thousand U.S. Dollars
Exportations Générales F.O.B. par Produits d'après la C.T.C.I. (Rév. 2) en milliers de Dollars E.U.

SITC CTCI	COMMODITY	1993 WEIGHT POIDS	1993 VALUE VALEUR	1994 WEIGHT POIDS	1994 VALUE VALEUR	1995 WEIGHT POIDS	1995 VALUE VALEUR	1996 WEIGHT POIDS	1996 VALUE VALEUR	PRODUIT
5417	MEDICAMENTS						1350		852	MEDICAMENTS
54171	— CONTAINNG ANTIBIOTICS						1350		852	MED CONTN ANTIBIOTIQUES
6	BASIC MANUFACTURES						92271		78764	ART MANUFACTURES
62	RUBBER MANUFACTURES NES						1253		1056	CAOUTCHOUC MANUFACTURE
65	TEXTILE YARN,FABRICS,ETC						25679		22133	FILS,TISSUS,ARTICLES TEXTILE
651	TEXTILE YARN					W 3020	6533		2805	FILS TEXTILES
6512	WOOL,HAIR YARN,INCL TOPS					W 802	4043	W 330	1966	FILS DE LAINE,DE POILS
65122	CARDED WOOL YARN IN BULK					W 802	4043	W 330	1966	FILS CONT 85% LAINE CARDEE
6513	COTTON YARN					W 2181	2451	W 399	801	FILS DE COTON
652	COTTON FABRICS,WOVEN						6438		4766	TISSUS DE COTON
6521	GREY WOVEN COTTON FABRIC						6339		4748	TISSUS COT ECRUS NON MERCER
65214	GREY WOVEN COTTON NES						6269		4642	AUT TISSUS 85% COTON ECRUS
654	OTH WOVEN TEXTILE FABRIC						4082		3505	TISSUS AUT COTON SYNT,ARTIF
6542	WOVEN WOOL,HAIR NONPILE						2799		2217	TIS PLUS 85% LAINE,POILS
65421	WOVN CARD WOOL,FINE HAIR						2799		2217	TISSUS 85% LAINE,PLS CARD
657	SPECIAL TXTL FABRC,PRODS						3756		4474	TISSUS SPECIAUX
6577	TEXTILES FOR MACHINERY						2906		3334	OUATES,MECHES ART TEXT
65773	TEXTLS FOR MACHINES NES						2314		3102	TISSUS USAGE TECH MAT TEX
658	TEXTILE ARTICLES NES						1229		3068	ART FACONNES MAT TEXTILES
6589	OTH TEXTILE ARTICLES NES						975		2386	AUT ART EN TEXTILES NDA
65898	KNITTED ETC ARTICLES NES						867		2223	ART BONNET NON ELASTIQUE
659	FLOOR COVERINGS,ETC						3392		3287	COUVRE–PARQUETS,TAPIS ETC
6592	CARPETS ETC KNOTTED					A 1154	2856	A 1143	2778	TAPIS POINTS NOUES,ENROULES
65921	— OF WOOL OR FINE HAIR					A 1154	2856	A 1143	2778	TAP NOUES,ENROULES LAINE
66	NONMETAL MINERAL MFS NES						11220		20992	ART MIN NON METALLIQUES
661	LIME,CEMENT,BLDG PRODS						4123		9631	CHAUX,CIMENTS MAT CONSTR
6612	CEMENT					W 82042	2067	W 1142603	6032	CIMENTS HYDRAULIQUES
6618	MNRL BLDG PRD UNFIRD NES						1732		3086	MAT CONST AMIANTE–CIMENT
66183	ASBESTOS–,FIBRE–CMNT PRD						1729		3077	OUVRAGES AMIANTE–CIMENT
663	MINERAL MANUFCTURES NES						1833		2653	ART MIN MANUF NDA
6633	MINRL MFS NES NONCERAMIC						1434		1372	OUVR MAT MINERALE NDA
664	GLASS						4747		7832	VERRE
6645	CAST,ROLLED GLASS UNWRKD					A 14189	4174	A 20157	7364	VERRE COULE NON TRAVAILLE
67	IRON AND STEEL						9588		5728	FER ET ACIER
672	IRON,STEEL PRIMARY FORMS					W 22966	5701	W 2960	1024	LINGOTS FER,ACIER
6727	IRN,STL COIL FR REROLLNG					W 22601	5594	W 2890	956	EBAUCHES POUR TOLES FER
67271	IRON,SIMPLE STEEL COILS					W 22601	5594	W 2890	956	EBAUCHES NON EN ACIER
677	IRN,STL WIRE(EXCL W ROD)						1931		55	FILS EN FER,ACIER
67705	OTHER ALLOY STEEL WIRE						1931		55	FILS ACIER AUT ACIERS ALLIES
678	IRON,STL TUBES,PIPES,ETC					W 851	720	W 5995	3522	TUBES,TUYAUX EN FONTE,FER
6782	IRON,STL SEAMLESS TUBES					W 259	137	W 3701	2093	TUBES,TUYAUX SANS SOUDURE
68	NON–FERROUS METALS						31078		18501	METAUX NON FERREUX
682	COPPER EXC CEMENT COPPER					W 6191	4782	W 138	197	CUIVRE
6821	COPPER NES,ALLOYS,UNWRT					W 5392	3982			CUIVRE BRUT
68212	COPPER REFINED,UNWROUGHT					W 5392	3982			CUIVRE AFFINE BRUT
689	NON–FER BASE METALS NES					W 6363	25052	W 4733	18006	AUT METAUX NON FERREUX
6899	BASE METALS NES,CERMETS					W 6354	25029	W 4733	18006	METAUX COMMUNS NDA
68999	BASE MTL NES UNWRT,WASTE					W 6354	25029	W 4733	18006	AUT METAUX COM BRUTS NDA
69	METAL MANUFACTURES NES						11899		7377	ART MANUFACT EN METAL NDA
693	WIRE PRODUCTS NON ELECTR					W 2708	2900	W 97	77	OUVRAGES FILS METALLIQUES
6931	WIRE CABLES, ROPES ETC					W 2708	2900	W 97	77	CORDAGES EN FILS DE FER
69312	COPPER CABLES, ROPES ETC					W 2556	2795	W 61	48	CORDAGES DE CUIVRE
695	TOOLS						2029		2572	OUTILS A MAIN
6954	BLADES,TIPS,ETC FR TOOLS						1633		2479	OUTILS POUR MACHINE–OUTIL
69541	PARTS TO INSERT IN TOOLS						1633		2479	OUTILS DE FORAGE
699	BASE METAL MFRS NES						6556		4125	ART MANUFACTURES MET NDA
6997	IRON,STEEL ARTICLES NES						1416		2480	OUV FONTE,FER,ACIER NDA
69979	IRN,STL MANUFACTURES NES						1416		2480	AUT OUVRAGES EN FER NDA
6999	OTHR BASE METAL MFRS ETC					W 190	3823		39	OUVRAGES EN TUNGST,MOLYB
69995	BERYLLIUM WRGHT,MFRS NES					W 190	3823		17	BERYLLIUM OUVRE NDA
7	MACHINES,TRANSPORT EQUIP						38420		49661	MACHINES MATERIEL TRANSPORT
71	POWER GENERATING EQUIPMT						2151		2875	MACHINES GENERATRICES
716	ROTATING ELECTRIC PLANT					N 114699	2013	N 92538	2761	APP ELECTR ROTATIFS,PIECES
7162	AC MTRS,GENRTRS,GEN SETS					N 114699	2013	N 92538	2761	MOTEURS ELECTRIQUES
71621	AC MTRS,INC UNIVRSL MTRS					N 114101	1892	N 91513	2642	MOT ELEC NON COUR CONTINU
72	MACHS FOR SPCL INDUSTRYS						3440		5249	MAC SPECIALES POUR INDUST
723	CIVIL ENGNEERG EQUIP ETC						2192		2192	APPAREILS DE GENIE CIVIL
7234	CONST,MINING MACHNRY NES						2192		2192	MACH POUR LA CONST, MINES
72348	PUBLIC WORKS MACHNRY NES						2170		1297	MACHINES TRAVAUX PUBLICS
73	METALWORKING MACHINERY						1437		2665	MACH TRAVAIL DES METAUX
736	METALWORKING MACH–TOOLS						1018		2284	MACH–OUTILS TRAVAIL METAUX
74	GENRL INDUSTRL MACHY NES						7340		7186	MACH APP INDUSTRIE
742	PUMPS FOR LIQUIDS ETC					N 8772	1417	N 8710	1474	POMPES MOTO–POMPES
7422	CENTRIFUGAL PUMPS NES					N 8772	1417	N 8710	1474	POMPES CENTRIF NON 742.81
743	PUMPS NES,CENTRFUGES ETC					N 9148	1540	N 7303	1176	POMPES COMPRES,VENT ETC
7439	PTS NES OF APP OF 7435,6					N 8801	1486	N 7040	1089	PIECES 743.5 ET 743.6
744	MECHANICAL HANDLING EQU						1336		2013	EQUIP MANUTENTION PIECES
749	NONELEC MACH PTS,ACC NES						2882		2394	PIECES MACH NON ELEC NDA
7499	OTH NONELEC MCHY PTS NES						2636		1986	PIECES NON ELECT NDA
74999	MACH PARTS NONELEC NES						2636		1986	PIECES MACHINES NDA
76	TELECOMM,SOUND EQUIPMENT						623		3494	EQUIPMENT DE TELECOM
764	TELECOM EQPT,PTS,ACC NES						109		3321	EQUIP TELECOM,PIECES
7643	TV,RADIO TRANSMITTRS ETC						103		3307	APP EMET TELE RADIO
77	ELECTRIC MACHNRY NES ETC						15912		20975	MACH APP ELECT NDA
773	ELECTR DISTRIBUTNG EQUIP						1884		1908	EQUIPMT DISTRIBUTION ELECT
7731	INSULATED WIRE,CABLE ETC					W 449	1718		1653	FILS,CABLES ISOLES ELECT
778	ELECTRICAL MACHINERY NES						11290		16190	AUTRES MACH ELECT NDA
7782	ELECTRIC LAMPS,BULBS					MN 1238645	10068	MN 1419510	14108	LAMPES, TUBES ELECTRIQUES
77821	ELEC FILAMENT LAMPS NES					MN 1238645	10068	MN 1419510	14108	LAMPES NON INFRAROUGES
7788	OTH ELEC MACHY,EQUIP NES						924		1758	AUT MACH APP ELEC NDA
78	ROAD VEHICLES						6927		6697	VEHICULES ROUTIERS
782	LORRIES,SPCL MTR VEH NES					N 216	1505	N 148	1832	VEHICULES SPECIAUX,MARCH
7821	LORRIES,TRUCKS					N 212	1446	N 130	1486	VEHICULES TRANSP MARCHAND
784	MOTOR VEH PRTS,ACCES NES						4429		3983	PIECES 722,781,782,783
7849	OTHER MOTOR VEHCL PARTS						4359		3964	PIECES 722,781,782,783
8	MISC MANUFACTURED GOODS						20869		19484	ART MANUFACTURES DIVERS
84	CLOTHING AND ACCESSORIES						7794		8348	VETEMENTS
842	MENS OUTERWEAR NOT KNIT						4508		4357	VET DESSUS POUR HOMMES
8421	— OVERCOATS,OTHER COATS						4508		4357	MANTEAUX HOMMES MAT TEXT
84219	—— OF OTHER FIBRES						4508		4357	MANTEAUX HOMMES AUT FIBR
851	*FOOTWEAR						1538		1408	CHAUSSURES

5. General Exports F.O.B. by Commodities according to the S.I.T.C. (Rev. 2) in thousand U.S. Dollars
Exportations Générales F.O.B. par Produits d'après la C.T.C.I. (Rév. 2) en milliers de Dollars E.U.

SITC CTCI	COMMODITY	1993		1994		1995		1996		PRODUIT
		WEIGHT POIDS	VALUE VALEUR	WEIGHT POIDS	VALUE VALEUR	WEIGHT POIDS	VALUE VALEUR	WEIGHT POIDS	VALUE VALEUR	
89	MISC MANUFCTRD GOODS NES						9844		7458	ART MANUFACTURES DIVERS
894	TOYS,SPORTING GOODS,ETC						8278		5175	VOITURES ENFANTS,JOUETS
8946	NON-MILITARY ARMS,AMMO						7806		4544	ARMES NON MILITAIRES
89463	HUNTNG,SPORTNG AMMUNTION						7806		4544	MUNITIONS
9	GOODS NOT CLASSD BY KIND						3143		1955	ART TRANSACT NON CLASSES
931	*SPECIAL TRANSACTIONS						3099		1669	TRANS.SPECIALES

1. HISTORICAL SERIES, 1993–1996 SPECIAL TRADE, IMPORTS C.I.F., EXPORTS F.O.B.
SERIES HISTORIQUES, 1993–1996 COMMERCE SPECIAL, IMPORTATIONS C.A.F., EXPORTATIONS F.O.B

YEAR ANNEE	VALUE IN MILLION U.S. DOLLARS VALEUR EN MILLION U.S. DOLLARS MERCHANDISE –MARCHANDISE IMPORTS	EXPORTS	GOLD –OR IMPORTS	EXPORTS	CONVERSION FACTORS FACTEURS DE CONVERSION CENTS E.U. PAR IMPORTS	EXPORTS	INDEX NUMBERS –INDICES QUANTUM IMPORTS	EXPORTS	UNIT VALUE VALEUR UNITAIRE IMPORTS	EXPORTS
1993	960.97	1003.62								
1994	1244.41	990.73								
1995	1748.62	1304.23								
1996	2219.40	1442.99								

2. IMPORTS BY BROAD ECONOMIC CATEGORY AND EXPORTS BY INDUSTRIAL ORIGIN. (PERCENTAGE OF TOTAL VALUE)
IMPORTATIONS PAR CATEGORIES ECONOMIQUES ET EXPORTATIONS PAR BRANCHE D'ACTIVITE.(EN POURCENTAGE DE LA VALEUR TOTALE)

IMPORTS – IMPORTATIONS

	1990	1991	1992	1993	1994	1995	1996
TOTAL IMPORTS–IMPORTATIONS TOTALES					100.	100.	100.
1 FOOD BEV–ALIMENTATION BOISSONS					9.8	9.7	11.8
11 PRIMARY–PRODUITS DE BASE					4.2	3.8	5.3
111 FOR INDUSTRY–POUR L'INDUSTRIE					1.5	1.1	2.4
112 FOR HOUSEHOLDS–POUR LES MENAGES					2.8	2.7	2.9
12 PROCESSED–PRODUITS ELABORES					5.6	5.9	6.5
121 FOR INDUSTRY–POUR L'INDUSTRIE					2.2	1.8	1.9
122 FOR HOUSEHOLDS–POUR LES MENAGES					3.4	4.1	4.6
2 IND SUPPLIES–APPROV INDUSTRIELS					21.3	27.9	28.1
21 PRIMARY–PRODUITS DE BASE					1.3	2.0	2.3
22 PROCESSED–PRODUITS ELABORES					20.0	25.9	25.8
3 FUELS–COMBUSTIBLES					28.8	21.1	21.6
31 PRIMARY–PRODUITS DE BASE					7.8	5.7	4.1
32 PROCESSED–PRODUITS ELABORES					21.0	15.5	17.4
321 MOTOR SPIRIT–ESSENCE							
322 OTHER–AUTRES					21.0	15.5	17.4
4 MACHINERY–EQUIPEMENT					16.5	16.7	16.8
41 CAPITAL EQUIPMENT–MACHINES					14.8	14.9	14.3
42 PARTS–PIECES ACCESSOIRES					1.7	1.8	2.5
5 TRANSPORT–TRANSPORT					7.5	8.9	6.7
51 PASSENGER CARS–AUTOMOBILES					2.1	2.8	1.7
52 OTHER–AUTRES					2.2	2.7	2.3
521 INDUSTRIAL–INDUSTRIELS					2.1	2.7	2.3
522 NON INDUSTRIAL–NON INDUSTRIEL					0.0	0.0	0.0
53 PARTS–PIECES ACCESSOIRES					3.2	3.4	2.6
6 CONSUM GOODS–BIENS CONSOMMATION					13.4	15.4	14.8
61 DURABLE–DURABLES					2.4	2.7	2.4
62 SEMI DURABLE–SEMI DURABLES					5.4	7.1	6.7
63 NON DURABLE–NON DURABLES					5.5	5.6	5.7
7 GOODS NES–BIENS NDA					2.7	0.2	0.2

EXPORTS – EXPORTATIONS

	1990	1991	1992	1993	1994	1995	1996
TOTAL EXPORTS–EXPORTATIONS TOTALES					100.	100.	100.
1 AGRICULTURE					9.0	13.2	6.3
2 MINING QUARRY–INDUS EXTRACTIVES					0.9	0.7	0.7
3 MANUFACTURING–IND MANUFACTUR					90.2	86.1	93.0
31 FOOD BEV TOBACCO–ALIM BOISS TAB					10.5	12.8	13.9
32 TEXTILES–INDUSTRIES TEXTILES					15.2	15.7	18.5
33 WOOD & PRODUCTS–BOIS & PRODUITS					13.9	15.4	19.8
34 PAPER & PRODUCTS–PAPIER & PRODT					1.1	1.5	2.5
35 CHEMICALS–INDUSTRIES CHIMIQUES					10.4	9.5	10.0
36 NON METAL MIN–MIN NON METAL					1.0	1.0	1.2
37 BASIC METAL–IND METAL BASE					7.6	5.1	4.0
38 METAL MANUF–MANUF METAL					26.5	22.5	20.7
39 OTH MANUF IND–AUTRES MANUF					4.0	2.5	2.2

3. TRADE BY PRINCIPAL COUNTRIES OF ORIGIN AND DESTINATION (VALUE IN THOUSAND U.S. DOLLARS)
ECHANGES SELON LES PRINCIPAUX PAYS D'ORIGINE ET DE DESTINATION (VALEUR EN MILLIERS DE DOLLARS EU)

COUNTRIES–PAYS	SPECIAL IMPORTS C.I.F. IMPORTATIONS SPECIALES C.A.F					COUNTRIES–PAYS	SPECIAL EXPORTS F.O.B. EXPORTATIONS SPECIALES F.O.B.				
	1992	1993	1994	1995	1996		1992	1993	1994	1995	1996
World	863041	961340	1241491	1818021	2319512	Monde	916310	1003044	989695	1305012	1443307
Africa	3540	501	3772	1877	3129	Afrique	4635	8699	5841	7180	21929
Americas	33482	16930	46239	49387	88074	Amériques	9313	12851	17582	18440	11616
Northern America	29593	12256	25790	38223	54948	Amérique du Nord	3863	7000	12803	18021	10286
LAIA	500	1289	5577	9954	12067	ALAI	124	2514	2220	165	161
CACM	29		497	911	6140	MCAC	5	3	416	13	42
Caribbean	3307	3385	14245	136	14858	Caraïbes	4862	2689	1890	36	964
Rest of America	54		130	164	61	Autre Amérique	458	646	254	206	164
As.ex F.USSR	7248	18361	37644	36419	35981	Asie l'URSS exclus	6601	47816	24343	16020	32900
Eur.x F.USSR	292620	290149	564845	1008496	1318884	Europe l'URSS exclus	408821	388848	438942	650570	699405
EU	253805	263086	505342	906785	1142335	UE	362718	334579	389153	574795	645225
EFTA	8493	7604	13322	30877	60550	AELE	4595	7190	20565	28578	16568
East Europe	24096	17759	44153	67856	109575	Europe de l'Est	38707	45631	27140	46456	34319
Other Europe			34	107	1646	Autre de l'Europe		10	251	11	271
Former USSR	404874	497564	494623	705887	870562	Ancienne URSS	448542	539699	502824	612570	677026
Oceania		14	2448	15956	2882	Océanie	476	396	163	231	431
Russian Federation	239570	273614	292085	394689	468952	Russian Federation	236254	297085	278340	330582	329624
Germany/Allemagne	128940	95764	168757	280054	320987	Germany/Allemagne	72259	66138	104377	177553	198888
Finland/Finlande	22288	40496	106080	189572	213671	United Kingdom	31862	46986	96127	118247	160247
Sweden/Suède	32639	50840	79797	145794	182615	Sweden/Suède	68402	64999	68440	121451	94630
Lithuania/Lituanie	27048	92079	73851	100875	146314	Ukraine	74801	59521	58375	71540	89058
Estonia/Estonie	55066	37971	43728	91895	132144	Lithuania/Lituanie	32897	42862	54735	72316	107356
Belarus/Bélarus	31533	39827	37919	57410	39708	Belarus/Bélarus	42783	51063	42697	56667	64077
Ukraine	30848	28716	37566	41771	59289	Netherlands/Pays–Bas	68034	81761	18655	25679	27710
Denmark/Danemark	6924	17712	28593	52578	91327	Finland/Finlande	33780	20193	23893	42061	34277
Netherlands/Pays–Bas	30094	9870	19382	55362	81451	Estonia/Estonie	12004	19389	25753	40624	52798
United Kingdom	5361	17932	29660	49464	63864	Poland/Pologne	20527	29634	16015	32588	19897
USA/Etats–Unis d'Amer	22363	11502	24635	35230	49076	Denmark/Danemark	6925	8903	15515	26308	52810
Italy/Italie	5344	7340	22324	42080	61531	Belgium–Luxembourg	51755	15868	4598	11925	15041
Poland/Pologne	10759	9405	19916	34544	59471	Kazakhstan	16075	22684	19111	15362	8257
France, Monac	7428	7844	18886	28313	35911	France, Monac	11133	10379	14078	16756	18664
Belgium–Luxembourg	4997	6629	13296	25058	41599	Italy/Italie	6889	13399	9434	14915	15831
Austria/Autriche	8579	5292	9066	21524	22000	Uzbekistan/Ouzbékistan	8790	8716	9969	13775	16092
Switz.Liecht	7968	6303	6461	16820	27736	USA/Etats–Unis d'Amer	3375	6440	11996	16981	9330
Norway,SVD,JM	525	1280	6772	13866	31699	Norway,SVD,JM	2611	2944	6397	22504	9573
Czech Republic			9846	14432	20630	Azerbaijan	13340	15299	5628	2057	1838
Japan/Japon	6673	4170	15404	10447	5593	Austria/Autriche	5713	2343	20536	3567	5991
Kazakhstan	9282	9631	2715	8028	10447	Ireland/Irlande	96	1026	9956	13987	4599
Hungary/Hongrie	4375	2626	7877	8331	14399	Switz.Liecht	1984	4043	13565	4112	5449
Spain/Espagne	1076	2343	5670	7896	14365	Hungary/Hongrie	8958	6274	4640	2509	2975
Cuba	3299	296	14136	34	10692	Japan/Japon	6498	6567	3766	3825	4405
Australia/Australie		14	1666	15567	2731	Thailand/Thaïlande		18364	6352	14	232
Republic of Moldova	3221	4257	3185	6483	2744	Republic of Moldova	6150	5210	3692	4697	3848
Bulgaria/Bulgarie	2262	1528	4063	3928	6386	Spain/Espagne	3886	1467	913	1564	15561
Israel/Israël	575	1149	3886	6315	6214	Turkmenistan/Turkménistn	2795	11662	1990	1221	300
Ireland/Irlande	23	567	2868	5831	8844	Czech Republic			3696	6779	6929
Canada	7230	755	1155	2940	5805	China/Chine		10496	4825	73	1153
Slovakia			2243	6447	8261	Egypt/Egypte	540	13	269	2206	13057
Azerbaijan	3749	8115	1129	572	1126	Mauritania/Mauritanie		4531	4981	3937	1785
Turkey/Turquie		6991	2281	1837	2427	Lebanon/Liban		3732	4011	2086	3209
India/Inde		2850	3354	3319	3638	Bulgaria/Bulgarie	2583	4599	1346	1928	1029
Brazil/Brésil	136	477	493	5064	6917	Czechoslovakia	6049	4295			
Uzbekistan/Ouzbékistan	1085	1146	711	2341	7727	Yugoslavia/Yougoslavie	2594	1035	1475	14	2059
Czechoslovakia	6499	3964				Slovakia			1073	2421	3352
Slovenia/Slovénia	1051	1337	1391	2410	3763	Turkey/Turquie		3462	618	1376	1220
Ecuador/Equateur	5	18	2335	3009	1823	Algeria/Algérie			0		6340
China/Chine		429	1415	1766	3396	Georgia/Géorgie	2655	1200	498	232	1458
Korea, Republic of			931	2554	3348	Portugal	1845	383	2460	475	429
Korea Dem People's Rp		759	2472	1813	1676	Singapore/Singapour		1	266	645	4664
Greece/Grèce	111	143	480	2789	3106	Kyrgyzstan/Kirghizistan		1422	476	1911	1272
Turkmenistan/Turkménistn	2749	934	497	894	1380	Nigeria/Nigéria	1028	3250	47	3	2
Guatemala			30	66	5724	Iceland/Islande		203	603	1962	1546
Yugoslavia/Yougoslavie	5175	173	175	98	112	Cuba	3771	49	95	10	138
Hong Kong		749	1633	2134	1088	Tajikistan/Tadjikistan		1572	524	1392	551
British Virgin Islds					3617	Yemen/Yémen		475	527	864	2029
United Arab Emirates		27	599	1153	1594	Canada	488	560	806	1040	956

(VALUE AS PERCENTAGE OF WORLD TOTAL)(VALEURS EN POURCENTAGE DU TOTAL MONDIAL)

	1987	1988	1989	1990	1991	1992	1993	1994	1995	1996
Africa						0.4	0.1	0.3	0.1	0.1
Americas						3.9	1.8	3.7	2.7	3.8
Northern America						3.4	1.3	2.1	2.1	2.4
LAIA						0.1	0.1	0.4	0.5	0.5
CACM						0.0		0.0	0.1	0.3
Caribbean						0.4	0.4	1.1	0.0	0.6
Rest of America						0.0		0.0	0.0	0.0
As.ex F.USSR						0.8	1.9	3.0	2.0	1.6
Eur.x F.USSR						33.9	30.2	45.5	55.5	56.9
EU						29.4	27.4	40.7	49.9	49.2
EFTA						1.0	0.8	1.1	1.7	2.6
East Europe						2.8	1.8	3.6	3.7	4.7
Other Europe								0.0	0.0	0.1
Former USSR						46.9	51.8	39.8	38.8	37.5
Oceania							0.0	0.2	0.9	0.1
Russian Federation						27.8	28.5	23.5	21.7	20.2
Germany/Allemagne						14.9	10.0	13.6	15.4	13.8
Finland/Finlande						2.6	4.2	8.5	10.4	9.2
Sweden/Suède						3.8	5.3	6.4	8.0	7.9
Lithuania/Lituanie						3.1	9.6	5.9	5.5	6.3
Estonia/Estonie						6.4	3.9	3.5	5.1	5.7
Belarus/Bélarus						3.7	4.1	3.1	3.2	1.7
Ukraine						3.6	3.0	3.0	2.3	2.6
Denmark/Danemark						0.8	1.8	2.3	2.9	3.9
Netherlands/Pays–Bas						3.5	1.0	1.6	3.0	3.5

	1987	1988	1989	1990	1991	1992	1993	1994	1995	1996
Afrique						0.5	0.9	0.6	0.6	1.5
Amériques						1.0	1.3	1.8	1.4	0.8
Amérique du Nord						0.4	0.7	1.3	1.4	0.7
ALAI						0.0	0.3	0.2	0.0	0.0
MCAC						0.0	0.0	0.0	0.0	0.0
Caraïbes						0.5	0.3	0.2	0.0	0.1
Autre Amérique						0.1	0.1	0.0	0.0	0.0
Asie l'URSS exclus						0.7	4.8	2.5	1.2	2.3
Europe l'URSS exclus						44.6	38.8	44.4	49.9	48.5
UE						39.6	33.4	39.3	44.0	44.7
AELE						0.5	0.7	2.1	2.2	1.1
Europe de l'Est						4.2	4.5	2.7	3.6	2.4
Autre de l'Europe							0.0	0.0	0.0	0.0
Ancienne URSS						49.0	53.8	50.8	46.9	46.9
Océanie						0.1	0.0	0.0	0.0	0.0
Russian Federation						25.8	29.6	28.1	25.3	22.8
Germany/Allemagne						7.9	6.6	10.5	13.6	13.8
United Kingdom						3.5	4.7	9.7	9.1	11.1
Sweden/Suède						7.5	6.5	6.9	9.3	6.6
Ukraine						8.2	5.9	5.9	5.5	6.2
Lithuania/Lituanie						3.6	4.3	5.5	5.5	7.4
Belarus/Bélarus						4.7	5.1	4.3	4.3	4.4
Netherlands/Pays–Bas						7.4	8.2	1.9	2.0	1.9
Finland/Finlande						3.7	2.0	2.4	3.2	2.4
Estonia/Estonie						1.3	1.9	2.6	3.1	3.7

4. Special Imports C.I.F. by Commodities according to the S.I.T.C. (Rev. 2) in thousand U.S. Dollars
Importations Spéciales C.A.F. par Produits d'après la C.T.C.I. (Rév. 2) en milliers de Dollars E.U.

SITC CTCI	COMMODITY	1993		1994		1995		1996		PRODUIT
		WEIGHT POIDS	VALUE VALEUR	WEIGHT POIDS	VALUE VALEUR	WEIGHT POIDS	VALUE VALEUR	WEIGHT POIDS	VALUE VALEUR	
	ALL COMMODITIES		961340		1241491		1818021		2319512	TOUS PRODUITS
0	FOOD AND LIVE ANIMALS		16258		101434		138159		226814	ALIMENTS,ANIMAUX VIVANTS
001	*LIVE ANIMALS FOR FOOD			W 11783	9229	W 1920	3189	W 384	1463	ANIMAUX VIVANTS
0013	SWINE,LIVE			W 4426	4485	W 531	580	W 111	126	ESPECE PORCINE
01	MEAT AND PREPARATIONS				6993		4768		11954	VIANDES ET PREPARATIONS
011	MEAT FRESH,CHILLD,FROZEN			W 5294	5011	W 4338	4353	W 11092	11006	VIANDES FRAICHES,REF,CONGE
03	FISH AND PREPARATIONS				11054		17499		26785	POISSONS ET PREPARATIONS
034	FISH,FRESH,CHILLED,FROZN			W 29621	9987	W 31772	16136	W 43808	24912	POISSON FRAIS, REFRIG,CONG
0342	FISH FROZEN,EXCL FILLETS			W 27867	9010	W 29707	14895	W 40128	22128	POISSONS CONGELES
04	CEREALS AND PREPARATIONS				13051		17672		54989	CEREALES ET PRODUITS
041	WHEAT ETC UNMILLED			W 34070	2281	W 35984	4813	W 123472	25040	FROMENT,EPEAUTRE
0412	OTHER WHEAT ETC UNMILLED			W 32054	2171	W 28731	3858	W 116382	23818	AUTRE FROMENT NON MOULU
045	CEREALS NES UNMILLED			W 3011	487	W 2221	339	W 50157	7844	AUTRES CEREALES NON MOULUES
0451	RYE UNMILLED					W 12	3	W 46193	7206	SEIGLE NON MOULU
048	CEREAL ETC PREPARATIONS			W 15987	5532	W 18395	9213	W 16993	11017	PREPTNS A BASE CEREALES
05	VEGETABLES AND FRUIT		5733		22297		33515		40375	LEGUMES ET FRUITS
054	VEG ETC FRSH,SMPLY PRSVD			W 14440	3887	W 16548	6531	W 18939	7405	LEGUMES FRAIS,CONG,SECS
057	FRUIT,NUTS,FRESH,DRIED	W 37877	5733	W 33969	13529	W 53680	19135	W 55873	21332	FRUITS FRAIS OU SECS
0573	BANANA,PLANTAIN,FRSH,DRY			W 14013	3915	W 17118	5983	W 16989	5529	BANANES FRAICHES,SECHEES
058	FRUIT PRESERVED,PREPARED			W 11895	3375	W 8085	6041	W 9913	9424	CONSERVES DE FRUITS
06	SUGAR AND PREPS,HONEY		5340		16877		22360		32252	SUCRES ET PRODUITS
061	SUGAR AND HONEY	W 38000	5340	W 52384	14872	W 184828	20491	W 82208	29218	SUCRES ET MIEL
0611	RAW BEET AND CANE SUGAR	W 34000	3495	W 47900	14115	W 179785	18590	W 65647	22556	SUCRES BRUTS
07	COFFEE,TEA,COCOA,SPICES		5185		8073		14996		27139	CAFE,THE,CACAO,EPICES
071	COFFEE AND SUBSTITUTES			W 1289	2605	W 1613	7137	W 2937	12708	CAFE ET SUCCEDANES
0711	COFFEE GREEN,ROASTED,SUB			W 1128	2216	W 1506	6339	W 2408	8776	CAFE TORREFIE OU DECAFEINE
081	*FEEDING STUFF FOR ANIML			W 11844	2573	W 22209	6561	W 34892	8410	NOURRITURE POUR ANIMAUX
09	MISC EDIBLE PRODUCTS				9390		13965		20832	PREP ALIMENTAIRES DIVERSES
098	EDIBLE PRODCTS,PREPS NES			W 15736	7886	W 13076	10946	W 15776	16882	PREP ALIMENTAIRES NDA
09809	MISC FOOD PREPRTIONS NES			W 9485	5354	W 10636	8947	W 13173	12500	PREP ALIMENTAIRES NDA
1	BEVERAGES AND TOBACCO		5441		21844		37345		50152	BOISSONS ET TABACS
11	BEVERAGES		5441		16555		32635		38696	BOISSONS
111	NON–ALCOHL BEVERAGES NES			W 22079	6355	W 30943	9758	W 29548	11832	BOISSONS NON ALCOOLIQUES
11102	FLAVORED WATERS NON–ALCO			W 16128	4940	W 23075	7507	W 24691	10213	LIMONADES,EAUX GAZEUSES
112	ALCOHOLIC BEVERAGES			W 18192	10200	W 24741	22876	W 27110	26864	BOISSONS ALCOOLIQUES
1121	WINE OF FRESH GRAPES ETC			W 12521	4607	W 19473	13459	W 21161	15688	VINS DE RAISINS FRAIS
11212	WINE OF FRESH GRAPES			W 5092	2497	W 16470	10726	W 19329	12893	VINS DE MOUTS DE RAISINS
1124	DISTILLED ALCOHOLIC BEVS			W 1655	3713	W 2056	6909	W 2657	8786	ALCOOLS,EAUX–DE–VIE
12	TOBACCO AND MANUFACTURES				5289		4710		11456	TABACS BRUTS FABRIQUES
122	TOBACCO,MANUFACTURED			W 1149	3248	W 281	3050	W 733	7851	TABACS FABRIQUES
1222	CIGARETTES			W 156	2152	W 185	2545	W 624	7297	CIGARETTES
2	CRUDE MATERLS,EXCL FUELS				20120		43044		59740	MAT BRUTES NON COMESTIBLES
22	OIL SEEDS,OLEAGINOUS FRT				3842		4091		4642	GRAINES,FRUITS OLEAGINEUX
24	CORK AND WOOD				1682		7000		4157	LIEGE ET BOIS
26	TEXTILE FIBRES AND WASTE				7289		15230		24073	FIBRES TEXTILES
263	COTTON			W 1269	1170	W 3760	4686	W 6986	9230	COTON
2631	RAW COTTON,EXCL LINTERS			W 1195	1121	W 3750	4628	W 6370	7568	COTON EN MASSE
268	WOOL(EXC TOPS),ANML HAIR			W 1274	3786	W 2374	7152	W 1836	7419	LAINES ET POILS
2682	WOOL DEGREASED,UNCOMBED			W 1113	2966	W 2127	5656	W 1671	6504	LAINE DEGRAISSEE
27	CRUDE FERTLZR,MINRLS NES				4019		6758		9965	ENGRAIS MINERAUX BRUTS
278	OTHER CRUDE MINERALS			W 103178	3077	W 106672	4736	W 145594	7094	AUTRES MINERAUX BRUTS
29	CRUDE ANIMAL,VEG MAT NES				1541		6459		8635	MATIERES BRUTES ANIM,VEGET
3	MINERAL FUELS ETC		438725		358400		385891		501704	COMBUSTIBLES MINERAUX LUB
32	COAL,COKE AND BRIQUETTES				11389		6477		9791	HOUILLES,COKES,BRIQUETTES
322	COAL,LIGNITE AND PEAT			W 465858	10810	W 160065	5847	W 207396	9159	HOUILLES,LIGNITES,TOURBE
3222	OTH COAL,NOT AGGLOMERATD			W 380487	8834	W 115698	4122	W 164152	7156	AUTRES HOUILLES
33	PETROLEUM AND PRODUCTS		299631		225858		231586		325831	PETROLE ET DERIVES
334	PETROLEUM PRODUCTS,REFIN	W 3291000	299631	W 2395709	223031	W 1764752	225846	W 2203001	320171	PRODUITS RAFFINES
3341	GASOLINE,OTH LIGHT OILS	W 534000	83407							ESSENCES POUR MOTEURS
3343	GAS OILS	W 1220000	122529							GAS OILS
3344	FUEL OILS,NES	W 1320000	75268							FUEL OILS
341	*GAS,NATURAL AND MANUFCT	MV 943358	77921		85871		96798		87003	GAZ NATUREL,GAZ MANUFACT
3413	PETROLM GASES,LIQUEFIED			W 44694	5609	W 38308	5334	W 31043	5008	GAZ DE PETROLE LIQUEFIE
3414	PETROLEUM GASES, GASEOUS				80261		91464		81996	GAZ DE PETROLE GAZEUX
351	*ELECTRIC CURRENT	H 2672000	35499		35283		51031		79078	ENERGIE ELECTRIQUE
4	ANIMAL,VEGETABLE OIL,FAT		3408		3638		10600		18565	HUILES,GRAISSES ANIM,VEG
42	FIXED VEGETABLE OIL,FAT				2625		9282		15888	HUILES VEGETALES FIXES
423	FIXED VEG OILS,SOFT			W 4867	2300	W 11729	8087	W 20954	13062	HUILES VEGET DOUCES FIXES
4239	OTH FIXED VEG OILS,SOFT			W 413	141	W 5254	3051	W 13644	7072	AUTRES HUILES FIXES
42391	RAPE,COLZA,MUSTARD OILS			W 413	141	W 5254	3051	W 13644	7072	H NAVETTE COLZA MOUTARDE
5	CHEMCLS,RELATED PROD NES		67951		135982		221720		275587	PRODUITS CHIMIQUES
51	ORGANIC CHEMICALS		22047		29732		46983		39810	PROD CHIMIQ ORGANIQUES
515	ORG–INORG COMPOUNDS ETC				22039	W 24954	35083	W 17342	24775	COMPOSES ORGANO–MINERAUX
5156	HETEROCYCLIC CMPDS ETC			W 23588	21917	W 24899	34761	W 17273	24414	COMPOSES HETEROCYCLIQUES
51561	LACTAMS			W 23562	21846	W 24790	34534	W 17213	24109	LACTAMES .
52	INORGANIC CHEMICALS				6140		7753		10891	PROD CHIM INORGANIQUES
523	OTHR INORG CHEMICALS ETC			W 22032	3800	W 18961	3458	W 21827	5881	AUT PRODUITS CHIMIQUES INORG
53	DYES,TANNING,COLOUR PROD				12807		19946		23194	PROD TEINTURE,COLORANTS
533	PIGMENTS,PAINTS,ETC			W 7176	10006	W 9167	18059	W 11417	20005	PIGMENTS,PEINTURES,VERNIS
5334	VARNISHES,DISTEMPERS ETC			W 4314	6875	W 5281	12242	W 4958	11937	PEINTURES A L'EAU
53342	OTH PAINTS,VARNISHES ETC			W 2812	4937	W 3491	8795	W 2723	8178	AUTRES PEINTURES,VERNIS
541	*MEDICINAL,PHARM PRODUCT	K 2392000	17167	MK 9464	52123	K 7950581	66396	K 7537077	79599	PROD MEDICINAUX PHARMACEUT
5417	MEDICAMENTS			K 4640558	43865	K 4436181	54656	K 5145625	66907	MEDICAMENTS
54171	— CONTAINNG ANTIBIOTICS			K 1028382	14092	K 415814	9317	K 408966	7061	MED CONTN ANTIBIOTIQUES
54172	— CONTAINING HORMONES			K 402858	4861	K 594445	8783	K 323519	5042	MED CONTENANT HORMONES
54179	— CONTNG OTH SUBSTANCES			K 3123641	23942	K 3396264	36108	K 4348302	53773	MED CONT AUT SUBSTANCES
5419	PHARMACEUTICAL GOODS NES			K 1229720	5760	K 1316260	7417	K 673192	7183	PREP,ART PHARMACEUTIQUES
54191	BANDAGES PREPARED ETC			K 1168628	4203	K 1219044	4358	K 578500	2925	OUATES,GAZES,BANDES
55	PERFUME,CLEANING ETC PRD		6882		14170		31839		43373	PROD POUR PARFUM,TOILETTE
553	PERFUMERY,COSMETICS,ETC			W 1530	6971	W 3261	19756	W 4292	27774	PRODUITS DE PARFUMERIE
554	SOAP,CLEANSING ETC PREPS			W 6359	6655	W 7444	11006	W 10900	14497	SAVONS,PRODUITS DETERSIFS
5542	WASHING PREPARATIONS ETC			W 5690	5390	W 6353	8234	W 9131	10658	PROD ORG TENSIO–ACT NDA
562	*FERTILIZERS,MANUFACTURE			W 45855	2959	W 86609	9176	W 205862	26296	ENGRAIS MANUFACTURES
5621	CHEM NITROGENOUS FERTLZR			W 33085	2190	W 51781	5113	W 127810	14537	ENGRAIS AZOTES
56211	AMMONIUM NITRATE			W 25077	1523	W 42169	3802	W 110878	12298	NITRATE D'AMMONIUM
5629	FERTILIZERS NES			W 6020	463	W 13805	2452	W 42036	8222	ENGRAIS NDA
56291	NIT–PHOS–POT FERTLZR NES			W 2694	241	W 11959	2209	W 36338	7101	ENGRAIS CONT N P K
58	PLASTIC MATERIALS ETC		11742		11397		21160		26974	MAT PLAST ARTIFICIELLES
582	PROD OF CONDENSATION ETC			W 12476	4824	W 10464	8026	W 14587	9984	PROD CONDENS,POLYCOND
583	POLYMERIZATION ETC PRODS			W 6506	5945	W 8643	12714	W 10648	16355	PROD POLYMERISATION
59	CHEMICAL MATERIALS NES				6633		18357		25318	MAT PROD CHIMIQUES NDA

4. Special Imports C.I.F. by Commodities according to the S.I.T.C. (Rev. 2) in thousand U.S. Dollars
Importations Spéciales C.A.F. par Produits d'après la C.T.C.I. (Rév. 2) en milliers de Dollars E.U.

SITC CTCI	COMMODITY	1993 WEIGHT POIDS	1993 VALUE VALEUR	1994 WEIGHT POIDS	1994 VALUE VALEUR	1995 WEIGHT POIDS	1995 VALUE VALEUR	1996 WEIGHT POIDS	1996 VALUE VALEUR	PRODUIT
592	STARCH,INULIN,GLUTEN,ETC			W 5439	2926	W 6531	7597	W 8024	10390	AMIDONS,INUL,GLUT FROM
5922	ALBUMINOID SUBSTAN,GLUES			W 2010	2070	W 3471	6571	W 4598	8823	MAT ALBUMIN,COLLES
598	MISCEL CHEM PRODUCTS NES				2704	W 8029	7754	W 6986	9331	PROD DIV INDUST CHIM NDA
5989	CHEM PRODUCTS,PREPS NES				2313	W 6227	6915	W 5523	7893	PROD PREP CHIMIQUES NDA
6	BASIC MANUFACTURES		124997		164386		321889		418115	ART MANUFACTURES
61	LEATHER,DRESSED FUR,ETC		3543		4198		5879		7272	CUIRS,PELLETERIES
62	RUBBER MANUFACTURES NES		17075		9709		17428		23278	CAOUTCHOUC MANUFACTURE
621	MATERIALS OF RUBBER	W 6234	5333	W 798	1364	W 745	2647	W 878	2914	PRODUITS EN CAOUTCHOUC
625	RUBBER TYRES, TUBES ETC			W 4010	6670	W 5365	11758	W 5603	16887	PNEUS CAOUTCHOUC VULCANISE
6251	TYRES NEW FOR MOTOR CARS			W 1521	3662	W 2275	5466	W 1417	6382	PNEUS POUR VOITURES
6252	TYRES,NEW,BUS OR LORRY			W 1419	1853	W 1539	4009	W 2254	7101	PNEUS POUR AUTOBUS,CAMIONS
63	WOOD,CORK MANUFACTRS NES		2773		5134		16214		12974	OUVRAGES LIEGE ET BOIS
635	WOOD MANUFACTURES NES			W 2186	3405	W 3557	11724	W 9252	8133	ART MANUF EN BOIS NDA
6353	BUILDERS WOODWRK,PREFABS			W 1731	3142	W 2961	11058	W 8034	7262	OUVRAGES DE MENUISERIE
64	PAPER,PAPERBOARD AND MFR		13141		29322		71256		93712	PAPIERS,CARTONS & OUVRAGES
641	PAPER AND PAPERBOARD	W 39000	11299	W 43089	19074	W 44088	44785	W 55243	61510	PAPIERS ET CARTONS
6411	NEWSPRINT			W 11641	2757	W 14317	8633	W 10909	7404	PAPIER JOURNAL
6412	PRINTG,WRITING PAPER NES			W 4740	4099	W 8222	8743	W 12147	11657	PAPIERS POUR L'IMPRESSION
64122	— COATED,IMPREGNATD ETC			W 2666	2196	W 7007	7011	W 9378	8671	PAPIERS IMPRESSION COUCHES
6415	PAPER,PAPERBRD,BULK,NES			W 11665	3943	W 6360	5750	W 9224	7189	PAPIERS,CARTONS ROULEAUX
6418	COATED ETC PAPER NES BLK			W 8087	3883	W 8583	14435	W 13013	25489	PAP,CARTONS COUCHES,ENDUITS
64181	PLASTIC COATED PAPER ETC			W 985	1678	W 2896	7486	W 4967	16084	PAP,CARTONS ENDUITS,RESINES
64189	COATED PAPER ETC NES			W 1296	1638	W 3446	6429	W 5360	8538	PAPIERS,CARTONS COUCHES
642	PAPER,ETC,PRECUT,ARTS OF			W 11201	10248	W 15445	26471	W 18753	32202	PAP,CARTONS DECOUPES
6421	PAPER ETC CONTAINERS			W 8611	5374	W 10209	12154	W 11409	13495	BOITES,SACS EMBALLAGES
6428	PAPER ETC ARTICLES NES			W 1670	2859	W 3680	10287	W 4658	12748	OUVRAGES EN PATE A PAPIER
64285	PAPER ETC DIAPERS ETC			W 490	1412	W 1336	6323	W 1632	7018	SERVIETTES HYGIENIQUES
65	TEXTILE YARN,FABRICS,ETC		34622		36823		62272		92792	FILS,TISSUS,ARTICLES TEXTILE
651	TEXTILE YARN			W 3035	10106	W 2822	15084	W 3339	21075	FILS TEXTILES
6514	SYN FIB YRN,BULK,MONOFIL			W 1770	6589	W 1979	11040	W 2157	15688	FILS CONT 85% FIB TEXT SYNTH
65142	— NONTXT ETC CONT PAMID			W 961	2031	W 1012	5052	W 1213	6980	FILS NON TEX FI CON POLYAMID
652	COTTON FABRICS,WOVEN			W 537	3603	W 655	5857	W 844	8010	TISSUS DE COTON
653	WOVN MAN–MADE FIB FABRIC			W 767	8269	W 1206	17699	W 1859	30879	TISSUS FIBRES SYNTH,ARTIF
6531	CONT SYNT WEAVES NONPILE			W 221	3025	W 457	6311	W 707	10136	TISSUS FIBRES SYNTH CONTINUE
65315	CONT SYN TXTL FABRIC NES			W 196	2883	W 451	6195	W 662	9326	TIS PLUS 85% TEXT SYNT CONT
6534	DISC SYN BLEND FABRC NES			W 246	2284	W 259	3482	W 595	10315	TISSUS FIBRES SYNTH DISCONT
655	KNITTED,ETC FABRICS			W 311	2646	W 524	5434	W 839	10766	ETOF BONNETERIE PIECES ETC
6552	OTHER KNIT ETC FAB NONEL			W 311	2646	W 524	5434	W 839	10766	ETOF BON NON ELAS NON SYNT
657	SPECIAL TXTL FABRC,PRODS			W 1725	5240	W 1802	9798	W 1939	10518	TISSUS SPECIAUX
6577	TEXTILES FOR MACHINERY			W 839	2949	W 833	5903	W 689	4769	OUATES,MECHES ART TEXT
65771	TEXTILE WADDING NES ETC			W 814	2856	W 798	5659	W 605	4276	OUATES,ARTICLES EN OUATE
66	NONMETAL MINERAL MFS NES		11186		18432		33514		45540	ART MIN NON METALLIQUES
661	LIME,CEMENT,BLDG PRODS			W 66224	2269	W 74894	5265	W 108640	7121	CHAUX,CIMENTS MAT CONSTR
662	CLAY,REFRACTORY BLDG PRD			W 25770	3672	W 51033	6343	W 43316	8599	MAT CONST REFRACTAIRES
663	MINERAL MANUFCTURES NES			W 30441	4498	W 41492	7608	W 56188	11719	ART MIN MANUF NDA
664	GLASS			W 11470	4578	W 13386	5685	W 11279	7236	VERRE
665	GLASSWARE			W 10836	3230	W 17141	8228	W 18656	10379	OUVRAGES EN VERRE
6651	BOTTLES ETC OF GLASS			W 9393	1741	W 16565	7003	W 18051	8673	RECIPIENTS EN VERRE
66511	GLASS BOTTLES ETC NONVAC			W 9393	1740	W 16565	7003	W 18051	8673	BONBONNES,BOUTEILLES,ETC
67	IRON AND STEEL		21627		30417		54344		71261	FER ET ACIER
671	PIG IRON ETC	W 246000	18173	W 36827	5860	W 12179	3922	W 5918	3785	FONTE,SPIEGEL,POUDRES
673	IRON,STEEL SHAPES ETC			W 13212	2180	W 19970	5778	W 28513	9469	BARRES,PROFIL FER,ACIER
674	IRN,STL UNIV,PLATE,SHEET			W 55469	10524	W 59140	25125	W 56677	32255	LARGES PLATS,TOLES
6746	IRN,STL THIN PLATE,ROLLD			W 21884	4599	W 16231	7108	W 10651	4570	TOLES LAM MOINS 3MM
67461	— OF IRON OR SIMPLE STL			W 21757	4541	W 15937	6756	W 10227	4057	TOL NON AC FIN MOINS 3 MM
6747	TINNED PLATES,SHEETS			W 9320	2764	W 16282	8720	W 19183	12868	TOLES ETAMEES EN ACIER
6749	OTH IRN,STL PLATES,SHEET			W 6160	1271	W 9421	3907	W 11867	10106	AUTRES TOLES FER,ACIER
67491	— OF IRON OR SIMPLE STL			W 3990	928	W 7400	2862	W 11491	9505	AUT TOLES AUTRES ACIER FIN
678	IRON,STL TUBES,PIPES,ETC			W 13348	5339	W 13024	10643	W 15852	15180	TUBES,TUYAUX EN FONTE,FER
6783	IRON,STL TUBES,PIPES NES			W 6239	1524	W 6095	3423	W 10208	8874	AUT TUBES,TUYAUX FER,ACIER
68	NON–FERROUS METALS		7307		6113		11270		11492	METAUX NON FERREUX
684	ALUMINIUM			W 1718	4776	W 2003	7791	W 2076	7856	ALUMINIUM
6842	ALUMINIUM,ALLOYS WORKED			W 1265	4420	W 1352	6859	W 1765	7454	ALUMINIUM,ALLIAGES OUVRE
69	METAL MANUFACTURES NES		13723		24239		49713		59793	ART MANUFACT EN METAL NDA
691	STRUCTURES AND PARTS NES			W 2520	6429	W 3338	13504	W 5712	11050	CONSTRUCT FER,ACIER,ALU
6911	STRUCTURES,PARTS IRN,STL			W 2061	4123	W 3088	11531	W 5506	9562	CONSTRUCT FER,ACIER,FONTE
692	METAL TANKS,BOXES,ETC			W 4295	3113	W 5164	7326	W 4264	7804	RECIPIENTS METALLIQUES
697	BASE MTL HOUSEHOLD EQUIP			W 1229	2781	W 1282	4943	W 1839	10173	ART MENAGE MET COMMUNS
699	BASE METAL MFRS NES			W 7430	6098	W 6114	13289	W 7533	18490	ART MANUFACTURES MET NDA
6991	LOCKSMITHS WARES,ETC			W 763	2081	W 881	5468	W 1145	7549	ARTICLES DE SERRURERIE
7	MACHINES,TRANSPORT EQUIP		260513		283027		460866		522309	MACHINES MATERIEL TRANSPORT
71	POWER GENERATING EQUIPMT				10949		22030		14036	MACHINES GENERATRICES
713	INTRNL COMBUS PSTN ENGIN			W 2176	5676	W 1478	7812	W 659	5455	MOTEURS EXPL COMB INT, PIECE
716	ROTATING ELECTRIC PLANT			W 1104	2822	W 1342	7283	W 805	3016	APP ELECTR ROTATIFS,PIECES
72	MACHS FOR SPCL INDUSTRYS		9127		50575		67342		72150	MAC SPECIALES POUR INDUST
721	AGRIC MACHY,EXC TRACTORS			W 2054	5457	W 2018	6264	W 2076	7558	MACHINES AGRICOLES
722	TRACTORS NON–ROAD	N 3171	9127	W 2147	4299	W 2494	5220	W 1154	6824	TRACTEURS
7224	WHEELED TRACTORS NES			W 2130	4277	W 2492	5206	W 1128	6730	TRACTEURS A ROUES
724	TEXTILE,LEATHER MACHNRY			W 592	7606	W 599	9824	W 663	6633	MACH POUR INDUSTRIE TEXTILE
7244	SPINNING,EXTRDNG,ETC MCH			W 219	4512	W 216	5060	W 257	1061	MACH POUR LE FILAGE
72443	SPINNING,REELING,ETC MCH			W 76	4087	W 180	4427	W 17	188	MACH POUR LA FILATURE
726	PRINTG,BKBINDG MACHY,PTS			W 282	2505	W 358	7298	W 355	4901	MACHINES POUR IMPRIMERIE
727	FOOD MACHRY NON–DOMESTIC			W 1315	9734	W 972	12680	W 1242	16550	MACH INDUSTRIES ALIMENT
7272	OTH FOOD PROC MCHY,PARTS			W 1179	9539	W 810	11755	W 1188	16088	AUT MACH IND ALIMENTAIRE
72722	INDUS FOOD PROC MACH NES			W 1080	8410	W 803	11703	W 1140	15836	MACHINES BOULANGERIE
728	OTH MACHY FOR SPCL INDUS			W 4682	17105	W 2347	21360	W 3161	22682	AUT MACH IND PARTICULIERES
7281	MACH–TOOLS FR SPCL INDUS			W 3823	10617	W 1506	11043	W 2347	15624	MACH–OUTILS SPEC IND PART
72812	MACH–TOOLS TO WORK WOOD			W 3385	8544	W 1330	7365	W 2114	13400	MACH–OUT POUR TRAVAIL BOIS
7284	MACHY FOR SPCL INDUS NES			W 551	4705	W 429	8675	W 484	6337	MACH SPEC IND PARTICUL.
73	METALWORKING MACHINERY				4240		5042		5926	MACH TRAVAIL DES METAUX
74	GENRL INDUSTRL MACHY NES		66880		34120		61860		83560	MACH APP INDUSTRIE
741	HEATING,COOLING EQUIPMNT			W 2139	7849	W 2308	17496	W 1860	19627	MACH CHAUFFAGE,PIECES
7414	NONDOM REFRIG EQUIPT,PTS			W 958	3172	W 934	5794	W 732	6115	MAT PRODUCTION DU FROID
7416	HEATING,COOLING EQU NES			W 663	2729	W 948	7904	W 659	8126	APP CHANGEMENT TEMP
742	PUMPS FOR LIQUIDS ETC			W 648	2763	W 558	5571	W 694	8514	POMPES MOTO–POMPES
743	PUMPS NES,CENTRFUGES ETC			W 649	3453	W 576	6108	W 887	8782	POMPES COMPRES,VENT ETC
744	MECHANICAL HANDLING EQU			W 3169	9126	W 3374	10117	W 3926	14003	EQUIP MANUTENTION PIECES
7441	FORK LIFT TRCKS,ETC,PTS			W 923	3785	W 719	2713	W 878	3608	CHARIOTS POUR USINES ETC
74411	FORK LIFT TRUCKS ETC			W 902	3734	W 695	2602	W 725	3027	CHARIOTS POUR LES GARES
7442	LIFTING,LOADING MACH NES			W 1762	3334	W 2479	5974	W 2744	7458	APP LEVAGE,MANUTENTION
745	NONELEC MACHY,TOOLS NES			W 661	6723	W 628	14645	W 889	18002	AUT MACH NON ELEC,PIECES

4. Special Imports C.I.F. by Commodities according to the S.I.T.C. (Rev. 2) in thousand U.S. Dollars
Importations Spéciales C.A.F. par Produits d'après la C.T.C.I. (Rév. 2) en milliers de Dollars E.U.

SITC CTCI	COMMODITY	1993 WEIGHT POIDS	1993 VALUE VALEUR	1994 WEIGHT POIDS	1994 VALUE VALEUR	1995 WEIGHT POIDS	1995 VALUE VALEUR	1996 WEIGHT POIDS	1996 VALUE VALEUR	PRODUIT
7451	POWER TOOLS NONELEC, PTS			W 122	2842	W 199	7045	W 132	3892	OUT MACH PNEUM A MOTEUR
7452	OTH NONELEC MCHS,PTS NES			W 538	3881	W 429	7600	W 757	14110	AUT MACH NON ELEC,PIECES
74522	PACKAGNG,BOTTLNG,ETC MCH			W 182	2674	W 179	5058	W 378	10026	MACH NETT BOUTEILLES,ETC
749	NONELEC MACH PTS,ACC NES			W 947	4206	W 804	7922	W 1429	14633	PIECES MACH NON ELEC NDA
7492	COCKS,VALVES ETC NES			W 472	1833	W 349	3748	W 900	8439	ART ROB,SIM POUR TUYAUX
75	OFFICE MACHNES,ADP EQUIP				28909		39552		60982	MACH BUREAU TRAIT AUTOM
751	OFFICE MACHINES			W 243	8382	W 263	7636	W 195	6576	MACH,APPAREILS DE BUREAU
7518	OFFICE MACHINES NES			W 98	4465	W 152	4733	W 128	4103	MACH,APP DE BUREAU NDA
752	AUTOMTIC DATA PROC EQUIP			W 195	9172	W 215	16077	W 283	21472	MACH TRAIT INFORMATION
759	OFFICE,ADP MCH PTS,ACCES			W 348	11355	W 326	15839	W 512	32933	PIECES DU 751 ET 752
7599	ACCTG,ETC,ADP MCH PTS,AC			W 309	10126	W 263	13511	W 443	29948	PIECES DU 751 ET 752
76	TELECOMM,SOUND EQUIPMENT				34097		45190		63916	EQUIPMENT DE TELECOM
761	TELEVISION RECEIVERS			W 215	2678	W 445	5054	W 521	7063	RECEPTEURS DE TELEVISION
764	TELECOM EQPT,PTS,ACC NES			W 1398	27913	W 1038	35241	W 1067	52831	EQUIP TELECOM,PIECES
7641	LINE TELEPHONE,ETC EQUIP			W 181	8603	W 223	7788	W 96	10824	APP TELEPHON PAR FIL
7643	TV,RADIO TRANSMITTRS ETC			W 43	4518	W 49	10168	W 84	14017	APP EMET TELE RADIO
7648	TELECOMM EQUIPMENT NES			W 41	5082	W 26	2837	W 36	4903	APP TELECOM NDA
76481	RADIOTELEPHONE ETC RCVRS			W 28	3983	W 4	1937	W 5	2757	RECEP RADIOTELEPHONIE
7649	PTS NES OF EQUIPMT OF 76			W 1092	9356	W 701	13783	W 810	22425	PIECES DE LA DIV 76
76491	PTS NES OF APPAR OF 7641			W 976	6837	W 458	5025	W 600	15417	PIECES POUR 764.1
76493	TELECOMM EQUIPMT PTS NES			W 102	2262	W 218	8103	W 175	6010	PIECES 761,762,764.3,8
77	ELECTRIC MACHNRY NES ETC		94922		41177		79181		92434	MACH APP ELECT NDA
771	ELECTRIC POWER MACHY NES			W 687	2481	W 683	7223	W 496	11551	MACH PROD,TRANS ELECTR
7712	OTH ELEC POWER MACHY NES			W 393	1214	W 343	4997	W 221	7449	AUT APP PROD TRANSF ELEC
772	SWITCHGEAR ETC,PARTS NES			W 727	6762	W 979	15901	W 901	19877	APP COUPURE,SECT ETC
7721	SWITCHGEAR ETC			W 722	6660	W 876	14704	W 875	18350	APP COUPURE,SECTIONMNT
773	ELECTR DISTRIBUTNG EQUIP			W 4390	7971	W 4704	17955	W 3589	14126	EQUIPMT DISTRIBUTION ELECT
7731	INSULATED WIRE,CABLE ETC			W 3992	7217	W 4287	16312	W 3395	13083	FILS,CABLES ISOLES ELECT
774	ELECTRO–MEDCL,XRAY EQUIP			W 121	4596	W 159	5882	W 143	8055	APPAREILS MEDICAUX
775	HOUSEHOLD TYPE EQUIP NES			W 1851	6682	W 2775	14200	W 2754	15452	MACH,APP USAGE DOMESTQUE
7758	ELECTRO–THERMIC APPL NES			W 617	2884	W 1125	6751	W 1302	7749	APP ELECTROTHERMIQ NDA
778	ELECTRICAL MACHINERY NES			W 3116	11876	W 3164	16054	W 3720	22039	AUTRES MACH ELECT NDA
78	ROAD VEHICLES		85195		70008		118927		112785	VEHICULES ROUTIERS
781	PASS MOTOR VEH EXC BUSES	N 5940	47134	W 4427	26230	W 13741	51522	W 8959	38904	AUTO TRANSPORT PERSONNES
782	LORRIES,SPCL MTR VEH NES			W 7807	18940	W 6518	27005	W 7082	36330	VEHICULES SPECIAUX,MARCH
7821	LORRIES,TRUCKS	N 677	5351	W 6756	14219	W 5209	20168	W 6310	33421	VEHICULES TRANSP MARCHAND
7822	SPECIAL MOTOR VEHCLS NES			W 1051	4721	W 1309	6836	W 772	2909	VEHICULES USAGES SPECIAUX
783	ROAD MOTOR VEHICLES NES			W 1312	3459	W 1078	5584	W 828	3473	VEHICULES ROUTIERS NDA
784	MOTOR VEH PRTS,ACCES NES			W 5130	17944	W 4174	27664	W 2622	24114	PIECES 722,781,782,783
7849	OTHER MOTOR VEHCL PARTS			W 5015	17746	W 4053	27508	W 2591	24029	PIECES 722,781,782,783
786	TRAILERS,NONMOTR VEH,NES			W 4181	2764	W 3352	6247	W 3790	8702	REMORQUES,CADRES,CONTAIN
79	OTHR TRANSPORT EQUIPMENT		4388		8952		21740		16520	AUTRE MATERIEL TRANSPORT
791	RAILWAY VEHICLES		2887	W 17081	8517	W 26573	18739	W 46816	11453	VEHIC MAT CHEMINS DE FER
7915	FRT,MAINT CARS NOT POWRD			W 1333	952	W 4521	7661	W 4035	401	WAGONS DE SERVICE
79151	RY SERV CARS NOT POWERED			W 131	899	W 2660	7610	W 28	182	WAGONS–ATELIERS,–GRUES
7919	RY TRACK FIXT,ETC,PARTS			W 9818	7417	W 11077	10006	W 7238	8928	MATER FIXE VOIES FERREES
79199	PARTS NES OF 7911–7915			W 9306	6273	W 9190	9060	W 6545	8087	PIECES 791.1 ET 5
8	MISC MANUFACTURED GOODS		41854		118986		196512		243667	ART MANUFACTURES DIVERS
812	*PLUMBG,HEATNG,LGHTNG EQ			W 3426	8491	W 2429	11415	W 3140	15527	APPAR SANITAIRES CHAUFFAGE
8124	LIGHTING EQUIPMENT NES			W 517	2995	W 635	6119	W 712	7955	APPAREILS ECLAIRAGE ETC
821	*FURNITURE,PARTS THEREOF	W 5222	9787	W 4763	14088	W 5306	19944	W 5236	21046	MEUBLES ET PIECES
8219	FURNITURE AND PARTS NES			W 3781	9574	W 4394	14075	W 4138	14100	AUTRES MEUBLES ET PIECES
82192	WOOD FURNITURE NES			W 2824	7079	W 3228	9134	W 2734	7925	MEUBLES NDA EN BOIS
84	CLOTHING AND ACCESSORIES		9553		30907		66954		72638	VETEMENTS
842	MENS OUTERWEAR NOT KNIT	W 654	9553	W 168	3746	W 132	3797	W 215	5754	VET DESSUS POUR HOMMES
843	WOMENS OUTERWEAR NONKNIT			W 327	4334	W 167	5191	W 253	7224	VET DESSUS FEMMES MAT TEX
844	UNDER GARMENTS NOT KNIT			W 673	13015	W 1858	44163	W 1397	34092	VETEMENT DESSOUS MAT TEX
8441	— MENS SHIRTS			W 662	12950	W 1844	43991	W 1387	33892	CHEMISES HOMMES MAT TEXT
84412	—— OF SYNTHETIC FIBRES			W 639	12798	W 1824	43695	W 1364	33255	CHEMISES HOMMES FIB SYNT
846	UNDER GARMENTS KNITTED			W 242	3950	W 288	7056	W 320	9430	SOUS VETS DE BONNETERIE
847	TEXTILE CLTHNG ACCES NES			W 226	2534	W 162	2721	W 391	8726	ACCES VET MAT TEXT NDA
8471	— NOT KNITTED			W 78	1587	W 84	1900	W 288	7409	ACCES VET MAT TEX NON BON
851	*FOOTWEAR			W 954	8326	W 794	10103	W 833	12579	CHAUSSURES
85102	FOOTWEAR LEATHER			W 846	7835	W 617	8889	W 705	11368	CHAUS SEMELLES EN CUIR
87	PRECISION INSTRUMNTS NES		9793		19005		23759		33021	INSTRUM,APPAR SCIENT NDA
871	OPTICAL INSTRUMENTS	W 876	9676	W 4	1025	W 7	617	W 9	793	APPAR,INSTRUM D'OPTIQUE
872	MEDICAL INSTRUMENTS NES			W 382	9041	W 456	10458	W 522	12059	INSTR,APP MEDIC–CHIR NDA
87202	OTH MEDICAL INSTRUMENTS			W 305	6879	W 349	8410	W 407	9681	INSTRUM,APP MEDECINE
873	METERS AND COUNTERS NES			W 292	4763	W 227	4377	W 296	7167	COMPTEURS,INST DE MESURE
8731	GAS SUPPLY METERS ETC			W 292	4750	W 225	4183	W 295	6977	COMPTEURS GAZ,LIQ ELECT
874	MEASURNG,CONTROLNG INSTR			W 184	4176	W 188	8307	W 290	13001	INSTRUMENTS DE MESURE
88	PHOTO EQU,OPTICL GDS ETC				4032		6879		11484	APP,FOURN PHOTO,OP,MONTR
89	MISC MANUFCTRD GOODS NES		2409		33451		56367		76103	ART MANUFACTURES DIVERS
892	PRINTED MATTER			W 2890	7889	W 2223	9307	W 2039	11241	IMPRIMES
8928	PRINTED MATTER NES			W 1187	4351	W 532	4047	W 563	5604	IMPRIMES NDA
893	ARTICLES OF PLASTIC NES				14408		29245		37369	OUVRAGES EN MAT DIVIS 58
8931	PLSTC PACKG CONTNRS,LIDS			W 1381	2882	W 2073	6434	W 3198	10037	ART TRANSP EMBALLAGE ETC
8939	MISC PLASTIC ARTICLES			W 3545	10966	W 5121	21896	W 5978	25858	ART DIVERS EN MAT DIV 58
89399	OTHR PLASTC ARTICLES NES			W 2500	8078	W 3620	15905	W 3969	18753	AUT OUV MAT DIV 58
894	TOYS,SPORTING GOODS,ETC			W 1107	4765	W 1305	8413	W 1305	9364	VOITURES ENFANTS,JOUETS
899	OTHER MANUFACTURED GOODS		2409		3021		4158		7174	AUT ART MANUF DIVERS NDA
9	GOODS NOT CLASSD BY KIND		926		33673		1994		2859	ART TRANSACT NON CLASSES
931	*SPECIAL TRANSACTIONS			W 58657	32401	W 75	210	W 198	1064	TRANS.SPECIALES

5. Special Exports F.O.B. by Commodities according to the S.I.T.C. (Rev. 2) in thousand U.S. Dollars
Exportations Spéciales F.O.B. par Produits d'après la C.T.C.I. (Rév. 2) en milliers de Dollars E.U.

SITC CTCI	COMMODITY	1993		1994		1995		1996		PRODUIT
		WEIGHT POIDS	VALUE VALEUR	WEIGHT POIDS	VALUE VALEUR	WEIGHT POIDS	VALUE VALEUR	WEIGHT POIDS	VALUE VALEUR	
	ALL COMMODITIES		1003044		989695		1305012		1443307	TOUS PRODUITS
0	FOOD AND LIVE ANIMALS		96558		104026		162507		204644	ALIMENTS,ANIMAUX VIVANTS
01	MEAT AND PREPARATIONS		21973		4479		4633		6860	VIANDES ET PREPARATIONS
014	MEAT PREPD,PRSVD,NES ETC			W 1458	2118	W 1870	3337	W 3609	6041	CONSERVES DE VIANDES
0142	SAUSAGES INCLDING TINNED			W 1158	1719	W 1286	1784	W 3453	5535	SAUCISSES,SAUCISSONS
02	DAIRY PRODCTS,BIRDS'EGGS		30901		12426		16321		26632	PRODUITS LAIT!ERS,OEUFS
022	MILK AND CREAM			W 19906	5684	W 17788	8121	W 30497	11096	LAIT ET CREME
0224	MILK,CREAM PRESERVED ETC			W 10982	5115	W 5939	6557	W 6772	7899	LAIT,CREME CONS,CONC
02249	MILK(EX DRY) PRSVD,SWEET			W 10698	4737	W 5361	5610	W 5526	6058	LAIT CONS,CONC SUCRE
023	BUTTER			W 2320	3103	W 1084	2262	W 3182	6891	BEURRE
024	CHEESE AND CURD			W 2124	3429	W 2399	5875	W 3322	8462	FROMAGE ET CAILLEBOTTE
03	FISH AND PREPARATIONS		26998		53046		87269		110999	POISSONS ET PREPARATIONS
034	FISH,FRESH,CHILLED,FROZN			W 17513	10358	W 26233	15284	W 22399	12967	POISSON FRAIS, REFRIG,CONG
0342	FISH FROZEN,EXCL FILLETS			W 15322	7713	W 22131	12161	W 15996	8600	POISSONS CONGELES
035	FISH SALTED,DRIED,SMOKED			W 2603	2275	W 3367	3261	W 5895	5101	POISSON SECHE,SALE,FUME
037	FISH ETC PREPD,PRSVD NES			W 24978	40380	W 34510	68695	W 52653	92913	POIS,CRUST,MOL PREPARES
0371	FISH PREPARD,PRESRVD NES			W 24968	40364	W 34508	68690	W 52652	92905	CONSERVES DE POISSONS
04	CEREALS AND PREPARATIONS				5724		5144		4709	CEREALES ET PRODUITS
045	CEREALS NES UNMILLED			W 67405	3096	W 23057	968			AUTRES CEREALES NON MOULUES
0451	RYE UNMILLED			W 67385	3091	W 23043	959			SEIGLE NON MOULU
048	CEREAL ETC PREPARATIONS			W 1494	2579	W 1900	3934	W 2440	4679	PREPTNS A BASE CEREALES
05	VEGETABLES AND FRUIT		16686		5467		14087		13760	LEGUMES ET FRUITS
058	FRUIT PRESERVED,PREPARED			W 4132	2363	W 18125	11105	W 17097	9932	CONSERVES DE FRUITS
0585	FRUIT OR VEGETABLE JUICE			W 2850	1516	W 17926	10748	W 16450	9096	JUS DE FRUITS
05857	JUICE OF OTHER FRUIT,VEG			W 1752	1042	W 7727	5298	W 3199	1911	JUS AUTRES FRUITS,LEGUMES
05858	MIXTURES OF DIFF JUICES			W 14	9	W 704	383	W 8333	4411	MELANGES JUS FRUITS,LEGUMES
06	SUGAR AND PREPS,HONEY				7319		20012		21072	SUCRES ET PRODUITS
061	SUGAR AND HONEY			W 4636	779	W 28857	9967	W 27992	6798	SUCRES ET MIEL
0612	REFINED SUGAR ETC			W 940	501	W 22184	9435	W 15815	5717	SUCRES RAFFINES
062	SUGAR CANDY NON–CHOCLATE			W 5202	6540	W 8200	10045	W 11241	14274	SUCRERIES
07	COFFEE,TEA,COCOA,SPICES				10433		9359		12936	CAFE,THE,CACAO,EPICES
073	CHOCOLATE AND PRODUCTS			W 2126	6881	W 1592	5529	W 3237	8229	CHOCOLAT
09	MISC EDIBLE PRODUCTS				1539		1917		4490	PREP ALIMENTAIRES DIVERSES
098	EDIBLE PRODCTS,PREPS NES			W 1081	1253	W 1509	1579	W 6463	4336	PREP ALIMENTAIRES NDA
1	BEVERAGES AND TOBACCO		15553		18059		23930		16348	BOISSONS ET TABACS
11	BEVERAGES		15553		11153		15564		12653	BOISSONS
111	NON–ALCOHL BEVERAGES NES			W 12097	3381	W 18004	4568	W 5408	1431	BOISSONS NON ALCOOLIQUES
11102	FLAVORED WATERS NON–ALCO			W 10948	3055	W 12000	3152	W 2634	746	LIMONADES,EAUX GAZEUSES
112	ALCOHOLIC BEVERAGES			W 8246	7773	W 12364	10995	W 13335	11222	BOISSONS ALCOOLIQUES
1121	WINE OF FRESH GRAPES ETC			W 4747	4576	W 7552	7626	W 8216	7672	VINS DE RAISINS FRAIS
11212	WINE OF FRESH GRAPES			W 4747	4576	W 7552	7626	W 8216	7672	VINS DE MOUTS DE RAISINS
12	TOBACCO AND MANUFACTURES				6905		8367		3695	TABACS BRUTS FABRIQUES
122	TOBACCO,MANUFACTURED			W 2210	6849	W 2146	8351	W 887	3693	TABACS FABRIQUES
1222	CIGARETTES			W 2210	6849	W 2146	8351	W 875	3619	CIGARETTES
2	CRUDE MATERLS,EXCL FUELS				175471		307871		289739	MAT BRUTES NON COMESTIBLES
21	HIDES,SKINS,FURS UNDRSSD				2626		4553		3947	CUIRS,PEAUX BRUTS
24	CORK AND WOOD				161668		285062		269196	LIEGE ET BOIS
245	FUEL WOOD NES, CHARCOAL			W 108099	2186	W 322384	10307	W 397564	13780	BOIS DE CHAUFFAGE
24501	FUEL WOOD IN LOGS,ETC			W 107964	2155	W 322246	10255	W 394852	12841	RONDINS,BUCHES ETC.
247	OTH WOOD ROUGH,SQUARED			W 1793956	60066	W 3048171	132246	W 1288520	49071	BOIS BRUTS EQUARRIS
2471	SAW–,VENEER–LOGS CONIFER			W 1088089	37822	W 1615041	72831	W 674957	28378	CONIFERES POUR SCIAGE,PLACAG
24711	— IN THE ROUGH			W 1088089	37822	W 1615041	72831	W 674957	28378	ECORCES OU DEGROSSIS
2472	SAW–,VENEER–LOGS NON–CON			W 705868	22245	W 1433130	59416	W 613563	20693	NON CONIFERES SCIAGE,PLAC
24721	— IN THE ROUGH			W 705868	22245	W 1433130	59416	W 613563	20693	BRUTS ECORCES DEGROSSIS
248	WOOD SHAPED,SLEEPERS			W 629855	97723	W 780751	141133	W 1172875	204045	BOIS SIMPLEMENT TRAVAILLES
2481	RAILWAY SLEEPERS,TIES			W 18969	2599	W 20375	3237	W 56285	11016	TRAVERSES VOIES FERREES
2482	LUMBER SHAPED CONIFER			W 397637	65256	W 695174	127018	W 1043543	179924	CONIFERES SCIES,RABOTES
24821	LUMBER SAWN ETC CONIFER			W 396320	64812	W 693063	126113	W 1039781	178909	CONIFERES SCIES LONGITUD
2483	LUMBER SHAPED NON–CONIFR			W 213249	29868	W 65203	10878	W 73047	13105	NON CONIFERES SCIES,RABOTES
24831	LUMBER SAWN ETC NON–CON			W 212958	29744	W 63772	10264	W 71427	12286	SCIES LONGITUDINALEMENT
26	TEXTILE FIBRES AND WASTE				4382		5553		3295	FIBRES TEXTILES
28	METALLIFEROUS ORES,SCRAP				2729		6963		7807	MINERAIS METAL,DECHETS
288	NONFERR METAL SCRAP NES			W 5094	1459	W 14408	4605	W 9330	2992	DECHETS NON FERREUX
2882	OTHER BASE MTL SCRAP NES			W 4985	1445	W 14314	4589	W 8891	2963	AUTRES DECHETS
3	MINERAL FUELS ETC		143061		17593		22908		29337	COMBUSTIBLES MINERAUX LUB
32	COAL,COKE AND BRIQUETTES				6405		4457		4221	HOUILLES,COKES,BRIQUETTES
322	COAL,LIGNITE AND PEAT			W 223923	6405	W 134922	4457	W 132885	4221	HOUILLES,LIGNITES,TOURBE
3224	PEAT,NOT AGGLOMERATED			W 130129	4052	W 126581	4189	W 128267	3974	TOURBE
33	PETROLEUM AND PRODUCTS		139882		4358		12416		21349	PETROLE ET DERIVES
334	PETROLEUM PRODUCTS,REFIN	W 848000	128415	W 21195	3659	W 51444	9230	W 109701	17294	PRODUITS RAFFINES
3341	GASOLINE,OTH LIGHT OILS	W 44000	8231							ESSENCES POUR MOTEURS
3342	KEROSENE,OTH MEDIUM OILS	W 120000	21256							PETR LAMPANTS,AUT HUIL
3343	GAS OILS	W 506000	84540							GAS OILS
3344	FUEL OILS,NES	W 171000	12584							FUEL OILS
351	*ELECTRIC CURRENT		1538		6625		6017		3756	ENERGIE ELECTRIQUE
5	CHEMCLS,RELATED PROD NES		68846		77499		89398		96074	PRODUITS CHIMIQUES
51	ORGANIC CHEMICALS				6360		7716		7086	PROD CHIMIQ ORGANIQUES
53	DYES,TANNING,COLOUR PROD				6428		10788		13704	PROD TEINTURE,COLORANTS
533	PIGMENTS,PAINTS,ETC			W 5987	6362	W 5717	10712	W 7501	13621	PIGMENTS,PEINTURES,VERNIS
5334	VARNISHES,DISTEMPERS ETC			W 5484	5951	W 5531	10310	W 6685	12619	PEINTURES A L'EAU
53342	OTH PAINTS,VARNISHES ETC			W 4804	5094	W 4745	8871	W 5795	10848	AUTRES PEINTURES,VERNIS
541	*MEDICINAL,PHARM PRODUCT	K 2851000	15587		28229	K 3189533	38598	K 3768407	41028	PROD MEDICINAUX PHARMACEUT
5417	MEDICAMENTS			K 1856549	25092	K 2115051	33214	K 2723550	36553	MEDICAMENTS
54171	— CONTAINNG ANTIBIOTICS			K 489600	6261	K 406712	6197	K 188115	2048	MED CONTN ANTIBIOTIQUES
54179	— CONTNG OTH SUBSTANCES			K 1333880	18269	K 1427984	23537	K 2395451	32787	MED CONT AUT SUBSTANCES
5419	PHARMACEUTICAL GOODS NES			K 702453	2445	K 762450	3986	K 518444	3500	PREP,ART PHARMACEUTIQUES
55	PERFUME,CLEANING ETC PRD				21755		11597		10263	PROD POUR PARFUM,TOILETTE
553	PERFUMERY,COSMETICS,ETC			W 2937	19676	W 2129	9855	W 1119	6510	PRODUITS DE PARFUMERIE
562	*FERTILIZERS,MANUFACTURE			W 14130	1184	W 24913	2509	W 62040	7640	ENGRAIS MANUFACTURES
58	PLASTIC MATERIALS ETC				4792		6670		3375	MAT PLAST ARTIFICIELLES
582	PROD OF CONDENSATION ETC			W 3733	3989	W 3205	5132	W 648	1178	PROD CONDENS,POLYCOND
5824	POLYAMIDES			W 3518	3798	W 3126	4983	W 619	1035	POLYAMIDES
58241	— IN PRIMARY FORMS			W 3518	3798	W 3126	4983	W 619	1035	POLYAMIDES PRIMAIRES
59	CHEMICAL MATERIALS NES				7220		10806		12201	MAT PROD CHIMIQUES NDA
592	STARCH,INULIN,GLUTEN,ETC			W 3575	6082	W 2297	7866	W 3390	8354	AMIDONS,INUL,GLUT FROM
5922	ALBUMINOID SUBSTAN,GLUES			W 2864	5910	W 2050	7690	W 2757	7998	MAT ALBUMIN,COLLES
59221	CASEIN AND DERIVATVS,ETC			W 1953	5241	W 1672	6960	W 2427	7396	CASEINES,CASEINATES
6	BASIC MANUFACTURES		306746		251631		323128		371910	ART MANUFACTURES
61	LEATHER,DRESSED FUR,ETC		15259		14431		16362		16834	CUIRS,PELLETERIES
611	LEATHER			W 2962	5542	W 2182	6606	W 1342	4096	CUIRS,PEAUX PREPARES
613	FUR SKINS TANNED,DRESSED			W 73	7899	W 90	8553	W 79	10956	PELLETERIES

5. Special Exports F.O.B. by Commodities according to the S.I.T.C. (Rev. 2) in thousand U.S. Dollars
Exportations Spéciales F.O.B. par Produits d'après la C.T.C.I. (Rév. 2) en milliers de Dollars E.U.

SITC CTCI	COMMODITY	1993 WEIGHT POIDS	1993 VALUE VALEUR	1994 WEIGHT POIDS	1994 VALUE VALEUR	1995 WEIGHT POIDS	1995 VALUE VALEUR	1996 WEIGHT POIDS	1996 VALUE VALEUR	PRODUIT
62	RUBBER MANUFACTURES NES		6175		1041		1624		3641	CAOUTCHOUC MANUFACTURE
63	WOOD,CORK MANUFACTRS NES		88176		38972		58967		81139	OUVRAGES LIEGE ET BOIS
634	VENEERS,PLYWOOD,ETC			W 112376	34535	W 110350	50341	W 144482	70022	PLACAGES,CONTRE-PLAQUES
6341	VENEER SHEETS ETC	V 1374000	57175	W 3918	3629	W 4199	7679	W 3297	8056	BOIS SIMPLEMENT SCIES
6342	PLYWOOD OF WOOD SHEETS	V 44000	16082	W 35589	21871	W 39851	30872	W 61431	47192	BOIS CONTRE-PLAQUES
6343	IMPROVED,RECONSTIT WOOD		9799	W 71384	8883	W 65976	11757	W 78559	14635	BOIS AMELIORES,RECONST
63432	RECONSTITUTED WOOD			W 71383	8882	W 65549	11699	W 77518	13746	BOIS RECONSTITUES
635	WOOD MANUFACTURES NES			W 12177	4436	W 24724	8550	W 33254	11102	ART MANUF EN BOIS NDA
6353	BUILDERS WOODWRK,PREFABS			W 4720	1850	W 11561	3945	W 12243	4079	OUVRAGES DE MENUISERIE
64	PAPER,PAPERBOARD AND MFR		8350		8569		15358		26177	PAPIERS,CARTONS & OUVRAGES
641	PAPER AND PAPERBOARD			W 18986	6441	W 25711	11186	W 26249	16170	PAPIERS ET CARTONS
6416	FIBRE BUILDING BOARD			W 13477	2159	W 17963	3990	W 18593	4927	PLAQUES CONSTRUCT EN PATE
64161	HARDBOARD			W 11571	1854	W 17645	3919	W 17773	4600	PLAQUES CONSTR COMPRIMES
6418	COATED ETC PAPER NES BLK			W 270	393	W 944	2211	W 1936	6537	PAP,CARTONS COUCHES,ENDUITS
64181	PLASTIC COATED PAPER ETC			W 79	58	W 228	739	W 1138	4594	PAP,CARTONS ENDUITS,RESINES
642	PAPER,ETC,PRECUT,ARTS OF			W 1768	2129	W 2641	4172	W 5783	10007	PAP,CARTONS DECOUPES
6421	PAPER ETC CONTAINERS			W 547	1010	W 1148	2206	W 2061	4980	BOITES,SACS EMBALLAGES
6428	PAPER ETC ARTICLES NES			W 993	704	W 1125	1384	W 3248	4423	OUVRAGES EN PATE A PAPIER
65	TEXTILE YARN,FABRICS,ETC		63579		80866		121216		131104	FILS,TISSUS,ARTICLES TEXTILE
651	TEXTILE YARN			W 15441	34845	W 18508	52947	W 17535	55689	FILS TEXTILES
6512	WOOL,HAIR YARN,INCL TOPS			W 686	2878	W 1298	6430	W 786	5433	FILS DE LAINE,DE POILS
6513	COTTON YARN			W 1577	3772	W 1435	4601	W 2221	7489	FILS DE COTON
6514	SYN FIB YRN,BULK,MONOFIL			W 11311	23248	W 11653	30913	W 10224	31562	FILS CONT 85% FIB TEXT SYNTH
65141	— TEXTRD,CONT POLYAMIDE			W 7129	14882	W 8759	22426	W 7292	21354	FILS TEXT FIB CONT POLYAMID
65142	— NONTXT ETC CONT PAMID			W 4030	8092	W 2735	8085	W 2731	9711	FILS NON TEX FI CON POLYAMID
6515	YARN OF 6514 FOR RETAIL	W 150000	16434			W 38	100	W 28	112	FILS CONT 85% FI SYNTHETIQ
6519	TEXTILE FIBRE YARN NES			W 1256	3009	W 3411	8724	W 3216	7104	FILS TEXT NDA FILE FIB VER
65195	YARN ETC OF GLASS FIBRE			W 1088	2574	W 3137	8134	W 3079	6870	FILS DE FIBRES DE VERRE
652	COTTON FABRICS,WOVEN			W 707	2113	W 458	2768	W 1101	4724	TISSUS DE COTON
654	OTH WOVEN TEXTILE FABRIC			W 1742	6245	W 2567	9530	W 2435	10568	TISSUS AUT COTON SYNT,ARTIF
6546	GLASS FIBRE FABRIC ETC			W 1015	3601	W 2180	8002	W 2178	9585	TISSUS DE FIBRES DE VERRE
655	KNITTED,ETC FABRICS			W 1125	8585	W 1348	12720	W 1722	18457	ETOF BONNETERIE PIECES ETC
6552	OTHER KNIT ETC FAB NONEL			W 1125	8585	W 1348	12720	W 1722	18457	ETOF BON NON ELAS NON SYNT
656	LACE,RIBBONS,TULLE,ETC			W 392	3048	W 380	4406	W 375	5117	TULLES,BRODERIE
657	SPECIAL TXTL FABRC,PRODS			W 5392	13566	W 5347	17670	W 4555	16939	TISSUS SPECIAUX
6573	COATED ETC TEXTILES NES			W 4848	12714	W 4524	15097	W 4074	15337	TISSUS,ART MATIERE TEXT NDA
65733	RUBBERIZED TEXT NOT KNIT			W 4821	12636	W 4496	14842	W 4037	15002	TISSUS CAOUTCHOUTES
6575	CORDAGE AND MANUFACTURES	W 14418	20090	W 279	363	W 439	779	W 312	746	FICELLES,CORDES,CORDAGES
658	TEXTILE ARTICLES NES			W 2213	10300	W 2839	18916	W 2776	17695	ART FACONNES MAT TEXTILES
6584	LINENS ETC			W 1818	8407	W 2373	15212	W 2246	12862	LINGE DE MAISON
65845	OTHER LINEN OF COTTON			W 1296	5918	W 1987	12062	W 2174	12017	LINGE DE TOILETTE COTON
66	NONMETAL MINERAL MFS NES		22390		9734		13048		18261	ART MIN NON METALLIQUES
661	LIME,CEMENT,BLDG PRODS			W 108944	3233	W 96856	3568	W 163962	6399	CHAUX,CIMENTS MAT CONSTR
6612	CEMENT			W 88933	2663	W 88708	3046	W 151558	5653	CIMENTS HYDRAULIQUES
665	GLASSWARE			W 2428	1232	W 13117	2930	W 25743	4426	OUVRAGES EN VERRE
667	PEARL,PREC-,SEMI-P STONE		8347						1005	PERLES, PIERRES GEMMES
67	IRON AND STEEL		84420		73553		63790		54528	FER ET ACIER
671	PIG IRON ETC	W 334000	59447	W 60	8	W 706	21	W 229	202	FONTE,SPIEGEL,POUDRES
673	IRON,STEEL SHAPES ETC			W 293358	61146	W 252599	52743	W 232148	44627	BARRES,PROFIL FER,ACIER
6731	IRON,STEEL WIRE ROD			W 243238	51027	W 230105	48030	W 198765	37343	FIL MACHINE FER,ACIER
67311	IRON,SIMPLE STL WIRE ROD			W 196151	41165	W 229994	47976	W 198627	37295	FIL MACH AUT ACIER FIN
67312	HIGH CARBON STL WIRE ROD			W 47088	9863			W 5	2	FIL MACH ACIER FIN CARBONE
6732	IRON,STEEL BARS ETC			W 48438	9882	W 16300	3277	W 31981	6841	BARRES FER,ACIER
67326	IRN,OTH STL BARS HOTROLD			W 47673	9756	W 11727	2284	W 30802	6514	BARRES PLEINES FER,ACIER
674	IRN,STL UNIV,PLATE,SHEET			W 22816	4641	W 9533	2869	W 6697	2791	LARGES PLATS,TOLES
677	IRN,STL WIRE(EXCL W ROD)			W 21503	4928	W 20501	4857	W 14431	3799	FILS EN FER,ACIER
67701	IRON, SIMPLE STEEL WIRE			W 21461	4920	W 20427	4817	W 14359	3766	FILS NON ACIER FIN CARBONE
69	METAL MANUFACTURES NES		18398		22624		29701		37086	ART MANUFACT EN METAL NDA
6911	STRUCTURES,PARTS IRN,STL	W 33000	18398	W 479	138	W 396	306	W 1826	829	CONSTRUCT FER,ACIER,FONTE
692	METAL TANKS,BOXES,ETC			W 2188	1980	W 3619	2845	W 4177	6356	RECIPIENTS METALLIQUES
6924	MTL TRANSPORT BOXES ETC			W 1897	1736	W 3190	2659	W 3805	6063	FUTS,TAMBOURS,BIDONS
69241	STL TRANSPORT BOXES ETC			W 1635	1475	W 2864	2161	W 3447	5596	FUTS,TAMBOURS,BIDONS FER
699	BASE METAL MFRS NES			W 10222	16659	W 8801	21289	W 5731	19553	ART MANUFACTURES MET NDA
6992	IRON,STL CHAIN AND PARTS			W 4173	12071	W 5337	17382	W 3902	14422	CHAINES EN FONTE,FER
7	MACHINES,TRANSPORT EQUIP		221088		189253		195896		187530	MACHINES MATERIEL TRANSPORT
71	POWER GENERATING EQUIPMT				11806		6827		6001	MACHINES GENERATRICES
713	INTRNL COMBUS PSTN ENGIN			W 2369	3720	W 419	1495	W 329	1174	MOTEURS EXPL COMB INT, PIECE
716	ROTATING ELECTRIC PLANT			W 5826	7533	W 1038	4904	W 672	3992	APP ELECTR ROTATIFS,PIECES
7161	DC MOTORS AND GENERATORS			W 4386	4162	W 495	2375	W 197	795	MOTEURS COURANT CONTINU
72	MACHS FOR SPCL INDUSTRYS				11913		12900		12716	MAC SPECIALES POUR INDUST
721	AGRIC MACHY,EXC TRACTORS			W 6249	5435	W 3158	4664	W 2010	4196	MACHINES AGRICOLES
728	OTH MACHY FOR SPCL INDUS			W 2458	2450	W 1170	4449	W 1420	5706	AUT MACH IND PARTICULIERES
73	METALWORKING MACHINERY				1407		2761		6311	MACH TRAVAIL DES METAUX
736	METALWORKING MACH-TOOLS			W 855	875	W 547	1364	W 1135	5214	MACH-OUTILS TRAVAIL METAUX
74	GENRL INDUSTRL MACHY NES		23713		7699		11167		10085	MACH APP INDUSTRIE
75	OFFICE MACHNES,ADP EQUIP				4721		4338		8460	MACH BUREAU TRAIT AUTOM
759	OFFICE,ADP MCH PTS,ACCES			W 37	1237	W 24	1240	W 82	5134	PIECES DU 751 ET 752
7599	ACCTG,ETC,ADP MCH PTS,AC			W 25	1132	W 14	974	W 81	5073	PIECES DU 751 ET 752
76	TELECOMM,SOUND EQUIPMENT				20025		17403		15485	EQUIPMENT DE TELECOM
764	TELECOM EQPT,PTS,ACC NES			W 3611	18637	W 3061	16446	W 1977	13058	EQUIP TELECOM,PIECES
7641	LINE TELEPHONE,ETC EQUIP			W 1997	14706	W 1620	12267	W 974	8891	APP TELEPHON PAR FIL
77	ELECTRIC MACHNRY NES ETC		71432		34525		58099		69360	MACH APP ELECT NDA
771	ELECTRIC POWER MACHY NES			W 554	1350	W 435	7072	W 266	10107	MACH PROD,TRANS ELECTR
7712	OTH ELEC POWER MACHY NES			W 538	1316	W 434	7063	W 265	10101	AUT APP PROD TRANSF ELEC
77129	PTS NES OF MACHY OF 771			W 14	252	W 385	5935	W 254	9809	PIECES MACH DU 771
772	SWITCHGEAR ETC,PARTS NES			W 820	2865	W 713	4006	W 463	3200	APP COUPURE,SECT ETC
7721	SWITCHGEAR ETC			W 816	2860	W 713	3986	W 462	3109	APP COUPURE,SECTIONMNT
778	ELECTRICAL MACHINERY NES			W 5259	26473	W 7272	43307	W 7251	51579	AUTRES MACH ELECT NDA
7784	ELECTRO-MECH HAND TOOLS			W 3650	20872	W 4478	30718	W 4356	35547	OUTILS ELECTROMEC,PIECES
7788	OTH ELEC MACHY,EQUIP NES			W 664	3412	W 1755	9957	W 1659	12209	AUT MACH APP ELEC NDA
77889	ELEC PARTS OF MACHY NES			W 577	2834	W 1740	9428	W 1584	10681	PIECES ELEC DE MACH NDA
78	ROAD VEHICLES		105012		57632		48958		30545	VEHICULES ROUTIERS
781	PASS MOTOR VEH EXC BUSES	N 1416	13907	W 503	2606	W 772	3883	W 572	3068	AUTO TRANSPORT PERSONNES
782	LORRIES,SPCL MTR VEH NES			W 4233	13281	W 1724	6013	W 753	3274	VEHICULES SPECIAUX,MARCH
7822	SPECIAL MOTOR VEHCLS NES			W 3424	12408	W 1429	5352	W 437	2843	VEHICULES USAGES SPECIAUX
783	ROAD MOTOR VEHICLES NES			W 8620	31517	W 6568	25115	W 1926	7827	VEHICULES ROUTIERS NDA
7831	BUSES	N 9035	53394	W 8538	31299	W 6518	25059	W 1820	7422	VOITURES TRANSPORT COMMUN
784	MOTOR VEH PRTS,ACCES NES			W 1772	6388	W 1922	8237	W 1137	8785	PIECES 722,781,782,783
7849	OTHER MOTOR VEHCL PARTS			W 1663	6129	W 1817	7950	W 1065	8518	PIECES 722,781,782,783
786	TRAILERS,NONMOTR VEH,NES			W 1263	1179	W 3555	3217	W 6386	5659	REMORQUES,CADRES,CONTAIN
79	OTHR TRANSPORT EQUIPMENT		20931		39524		33444		28567	AUTRE MATERIEL TRANSPORT

5. Special Exports F.O.B. by Commodities according to the S.I.T.C. (Rev. 2) in thousand U.S. Dollars
Exportations Spéciales F.O.B. par Produits d'après la C.T.C.I. (Rév. 2) en milliers de Dollars E.U.

SITC CTCI	COMMODITY	1993 WEIGHT POIDS	1993 VALUE VALEUR	1994 WEIGHT POIDS	1994 VALUE VALEUR	1995 WEIGHT POIDS	1995 VALUE VALEUR	1996 WEIGHT POIDS	1996 VALUE VALEUR	PRODUIT
791	RAILWAY VEHICLES		19563	W 71789	35607	W 12126	31522	W 11521	24287	VEHIC MAT CHEMINS DE FER
7912	OTH RAIL LOCOMOTIVES ETC			W 45577	7418		304	W 2631	922	AUTRES LOCOMOTIVES
7913	MECHAN–PROPELLED RY CARS			W 17536	23244	W 7452	25300	W 3992	18143	AUTOMOTRICES,DRAISINES
7914	RY COACHES NES NOT POWRD	N 530	17617	W 522	753	W 1401	2793	W 362	1812	VOITURES A VOYAGEURS
7919	RY TRACK FIXT,ETC,PARTS			W 3907	3321	W 2076	3076	W 1912	3312	MATER FIXE VOIES FERREES
79199	PARTS NES OF 7911–7915			W 3791	3112	W 2044	3038	W 1228	3126	PIECES 791.1 ET 5
8	MISC MANUFACTURED GOODS		126673		128134		155223		225847	ART MANUFACTURES DIVERS
812	*PLUMBG,HEATNG,LGHTNG EQ			W 2066	4343	W 1474	4308	W 788	3238	APPAR SANITAIRES CHAUFFAGE
8124	LIGHTING EQUIPMENT NES			W 1949	4116	W 1289	4065	W 736	3045	APPAREILS ECLAIRAGE ETC
81242	LAMPS,FITTINGS BASE METL			W 1813	3812	W 1001	3469	W 483	2406	APPAREILS D'ECLAIRAGE
821	*FURNITURE,PARTS THEREOF	W 43000	30247	W 29810	35501	W 27740	46824	W 27361	44903	MEUBLES ET PIECES
8211	CHAIRS,SEATS AND PARTS			W 5152	7954	W 2048	5007	W 1391	5029	SIEGES ET PIECES
82111	CHAIRS AND OTHER SEATS			W 4928	7686	W 2038	4925	W 1332	4740	SIEGES
8219	FURNITURE AND PARTS NES			W 24211	26609	W 24787	39898	W 25819	39322	AUTRES MEUBLES ET PIECES
82192	WOOD FURNITURE NES			W 16208	19109	W 13449	23354	W 9523	18269	MEUBLES NDA EN BOIS
82199	OTHR FURN,FURN PARTS NES			W 7949	7415	W 11070	16169	W 16218	20869	MEUBLES NDA AUTRES MATIERES
84	CLOTHING AND ACCESSORIES		63579		52899		73043		126952	VETEMENTS
842	MENS OUTERWEAR NOT KNIT	W 2573	22267	W 1059	7417	W 1502	10847	W 1443	20904	VET DESSUS POUR HOMMES
8423	— TROUSERS,BREECHES ETC			W 226	1870	W 462	3694	W 567	8876	PANTALONS HOMMES MAT TEX
8429	— OTHER OUTER GARMENTS			W 430	1867	W 610	3374	W 471	6179	AUT VET DES HOM MAT TEX
843	WOMENS OUTERWEAR NONKNIT			W 1092	6307	W 1167	10841	W 1975	35596	VET DESSUS FEMMES MAT TEX
8431	— COATS AND JACKETS			W 103	597	W 247	2201	W 395	6147	MANT,VEST FEM MAT TEXTIL
8433	— DRESSES			W 52	331	W 113	1492	W 312	7641	ROBES EN MAT–TEXTILES
8434	— SKIRTS			W 133	637	W 84	777	W 246	4922	JUPES EN MAT TEXTILES
8435	— BLOUSES			W 109	717	W 100	1217	W 221	4909	BLOUSES FEM MAT TEXTILES
8439	— OTHER OUTER GARMENTS			W 515	3330	W 524	4197	W 712	10475	AUT VET DES FEM MAT TEXT
845	OUTERWEAR KNIT NONELASTC	W 3543	21863	W 1921	15331	W 1265	15610	W 1420	26877	VET DESSOUS,ACCES BONNET
8451	— JERSEYS,PULLOVERS ETC			W 377	4556	W 317	6136	W 658	12587	CHANDAILS,PULL–OVERS ETC
8452	— WOMENS DRESSES ETC			W 441	4945	W 261	4258	W 336	8317	ROBES,JUPES BONNETERIE
8459	— OTHER,CLTHG ACCESRYS			W 1103	5830	W 686	5216	W 426	5973	AUT VET DESSUS DE BONNE
846	UNDER GARMENTS KNITTED			W 1323	18874	W 1479	29866	W 1760	37538	SOUS VETS DE BONNETERIE
8462	— OF COTTON NON ELASTIC			W 214	1403	W 310	3087	W 486	6057	SOUS–VET BONNET COTON
84629	—— OTHER			W 212	1388	W 310	3087	W 486	6057	AUT SOUS–VET BONNET COTON
8463	— OF SYNTH FBR NONELAST			W 744	5231	W 830	8386	W 950	9895	SOUS–VET BONNET FIB SYNT
84631	—— PANTY HOSE (TIGHTS)			W 721	5123	W 816	8155	W 930	9506	COLLANTS BON FIBR SYNT
8465	CORSETS,GARTERS,ETC			W 364	12241	W 339	18393	W 323	21586	CORSETS,GAINES ART SIM
84651	BRASSIERES			W 205	7647	W 175	9895	W 206	11228	SOUTIENS–GORGE,BUSTIERS
84652	CORSETS,BRACES ETC			W 159	4594	W 164	8498	W 117	10358	CORSETS,GAINES,JARRETEL
847	TEXTILE CLTHNG ACCES NES			W 498	3050	W 324	3620	W 324	3407	ACCES VET MAT TEXT NDA
851	*FOOTWEAR		22727	W 3700	16180	W 1966	7728	W 2449	7591	CHAUSSURES
85101	FOOTWEAR RUBBER,PLASTIC			W 2193	3464	W 1460	2295	W 1848	2556	CHAUS SEMELLES CAOUTCH
85102	FOOTWEAR LEATHER			W 1281	10637	W 274	3187	W 165	1789	CHAUS SEMELLES EN CUIR
88	PHOTO EQU,OPTICL GDS ETC		6022		2549		701		1256	APP,FOURN PHOTO,OP,MONTR
89	MISC MANUFCTRD GOODS NES		4099		13246		17987		38144	ART MANUFACTURES DIVERS
892	PRINTED MATTER			W 1231	1561	W 784	2643		8445	IMPRIMES
8928	PRINTED MATTER NES			W 412	809	W 373	1773		7006	IMPRIMES NDA
893	ARTICLES OF PLASTIC NES				3044		5411		5655	OUVRAGES EN MAT DIVIS 58
894	TOYS,SPORTING GOODS,ETC			W 745	2922	W 683	3322	W 775	5340	VOITURES ENFANTS,JOUETS
898	MUSICAL INSTRUMENTS,PTS			W 93	1102	W 64	1361		11882	INSTRUMENTS DE MUSIQUE
8983	SOUND RECRDNG TAPE,DISCS			W 29	964	W 21	1233		11828	SUPPORTS SON POUR 763
89832	RECORDED DISCS,TAPES ETC			W 9	850	W 12	1183		11765	DISQUES,PHONO,BANDES
899	OTHER MANUFACTURED GOODS		4099		3257		4362		5840	AUT ART MANUF DIVERS NDA
8993	COMBUSTIBLE PRODUCTS ETC			W 1933	1781	W 2969	3003	W 4105	4445	BOUGIES,ALLUMETTES ETC
9	GOODS NOT CLASSD BY KIND		246		27106		23040		21104	ART TRANSACT NON CLASSES
931	*SPECIAL TRANSACTIONS			W 62616	26743	W 60807	21834	W 54221	20417	TRANS.SPECIALES

1. HISTORICAL SERIES, 1960–1996 GENERAL TRADE, IMPORTS C.I.F., EXPORTS F.O.B.
SERIES HISTORIQUES, 1960–1996 COMMERCE GENERAL, IMPORTATIONS C.A.F., EXPORTATIONS F.O.B

YEAR ANNEE	VALUE IN MILLION U.S. DOLLARS / VALEUR EN MILLION U.S. DOLLARS — MERCHANDISE –MARCHANDISE		GOLD –OR		CONVERSION FACTORS U.S. CENTS PER LEBANESE POUND FACTEURS DE CONVERSION CENTS E.U. PAR LEBANESE POUND		INDEX NUMBERS –INDICES — QUANTUM		UNIT VALUE VALEUR UNITAIRE	
	IMPORTS	EXPORTS	IMPORTS	EXPORTS	IMPORTS	EXPORTS	IMPORTS	EXPORTS	IMPORTS	EXPORTS
1960	306.75	40.13								
1961	331.71	40.38								
1962	355.93	55.17								
1963	384.73	57.28								
1964	428.24	62.32								
1965	481.72	85.37								
1966	518.20	102.66								
1967	471.03	119.27								
1968	521.14	146.05								
1969	531.98	170.48								
1970	567.44	197.80								
1971	677.06	255.93								
1972	849.28	350.47								
1973	1292.03	618.30								
1975	2330.90	1121.00								
1976	838.30	496.00								
1977	1692.29	394.32								
1978	2049.85	755.00								
1979	2938.72	773.00								
1980	3650.00	868.18								
1981	3499.00	836.36								
1982	3391.00	727.27								
1983	3661.00	690.91								
1984	2948.00	581.82								
1985	2203.00	481.82								
1986	2203.00	500.00								
1987	1879.00	590.91								
1988	2457.09	709.15								
1989	2234.56	485.36								
1990	2524.34	494.04								
1991	3744.37	539.07								
1992	4202.38	560.12								
1993	2215.09	451.67								
1994	2856.22	572.71								
1995	5334.71	732.71								
1996	7568.57	1014.41								

2. IMPORTS BY BROAD ECONOMIC CATEGORY AND EXPORTS BY INDUSTRIAL ORIGIN. (PERCENTAGE OF TOTAL VALUE)
IMPORTATIONS PAR CATEGORIES ECONOMIQUES ET EXPORTATIONS PAR BRANCHE D'ACTIVITE.(EN POURCENTAGE DE LA VALEUR TOTALE)

IMPORTS – IMPORTATIONS

	1990	1991	1992	1993	1994	1995	1996
TOTAL IMPORTS–IMPORTATIONS TOTALES							
1 FOOD BEV–ALIMENTATION BOISSONS							
11 PRIMARY–PRODUITS DE BASE							
111 FOR INDUSTRY–POUR L'INDUSTRIE							
112 FOR HOUSEHOLDS–POUR LES MENAGES							
12 PROCESSED–PRODUITS ELABORES							
121 FOR INDUSTRY–POUR L'INDUSTRIE							
122 FOR HOUSEHOLDS–POUR LES MENAGES							
2 IND SUPPLIES–APPROV INDUSTRIELS							
21 PRIMARY–PRODUITS DE BASE							
22 PROCESSED–PRODUITS ELABORES							
3 FUELS–COMBUSTIBLES							
31 PRIMARY–PRODUITS DE BASE							
32 PROCESSED–PRODUITS ELABORES							
321 MOTOR SPIRIT–ESSENCE							
322 OTHER–AUTRES							
4 MACHINERY–EQUIPEMENT							
41 CAPITAL EQUIPMENT–MACHINES							
42 PARTS–PIECES ACCESSOIRES							
5 TRANSPORT–TRANSPORT							
51 PASSENGER CARS–AUTOMOBILES							
52 OTHER–AUTRES							
521 INDUSTRIAL–INDUSTRIELS							
522 NON INDUSTRIAL–NON INDUSTRIEL							
53 PARTS–PIECES ACCESSOIRES							
6 CONSUM GOODS–BIENS CONSOMMATION							
61 DURABLE–DURABLES							
62 SEMI DURABLE–SEMI DURABLES							
63 NON DURABLE–NON DURABLES							
7 GOODS NES–BIENS NDA							

EXPORTS – EXPORTATIONS

	1990	1991	1992	1993	1994	1995	1996
TOTAL EXPORTS–EXPORTATIONS TOTALES							
1 AGRICULTURE							
2 MINING QUARRY–INDUS EXTRACTIVES							
3 MANUFACTURING–IND MANUFACTUR							
31 FOOD BEV TOBACCO–ALIM BOISS TAB							
32 TEXTILES–INDUSTRIES TEXTILES							
33 WOOD & PRODUCTS–BOIS & PRODUITS							
34 PAPER & PRODUCTS–PAPIER & PRODT							
35 CHEMICALS–INDUSTRIES CHIMIQUES							
36 NON METAL MIN–MIN NON METAL							
37 BASIC METAL–IND METAL BASE							
38 METAL MANUF–MANUF METAL							
39 OTH MANUF IND–AUTRES MANUF							

3. TRADE BY PRINCIPAL COUNTRIES OF PRODUCTION AND LAST CONSIGNMENT (VALUE IN THOUSAND U.S. DOLLARS)
ECHANGES SELON LES PRINCIPAUX PAYS DE PRODUCTION ET DE DERNIERE CONSIGNATION (VALEUR EN MILLIERS DE DOLLARS EU)

GENERAL IMPORTS C.I.F. IMPORTATIONS GENERALES C.A.F

COUNTRIES–PAYS	1992	1993	1994	1995	1996
World		2215000	2861010	7295289	7570762
Africa		20000	55492	141767	133012
Americas			342111	911046	957867
Northern America			282654	814567	881097
LAIA			52402	96479	76770
CACM			1562		
Caribbean			4984		
Rest of America			508		
As.ex F.USSR		500000	633324	1369709	1418297
Eur.x F.USSR			1619534	3714916	3684887
EU			1389726	3322306	3317061
EFTA			104585	333437	258463
East Europe			118800	59173	109363
Other Europe			4267		
Former USSR			108769	249137	279081
Oceania			5099		
Italy/Italie			384915	945299	916107
USA/Etats–Unis d'Amer			266898	771346	825796
Germany/Allemagne			288507	610967	645003
France,Monac			256720	555568	589594
Syrian Arab Republic		284000	124708	234835	308037
United Kingdom			119806	284660	305185
Japan/Japon			121457	287404	293019
Switz.Liecht			99779	333437	258463
China/Chine			88877	239550	220431
Greece/Grèce			69788	224353	190832
Ukraine			66203	184479	190663
Turkey/Turquie		110000	63093	88122	173299
Spain/Espagne			62610	144867	142245
Korea, Republic of			54942	144790	134393
Saudi Arabia		47000	39989	126061	112663
Belgium–Luxembourg			52637	137982	111725
Netherlands/Pays–Bas			50019	120978	114499
Sweden/Suède			31305	101123	93881
Brazil/Brésil			40148	96479	76770
Jordan/Jordanie		28000	13472	119061	35636
Russian Federation			39449	64658	88418
Egypt/Egypte			21484	63405	54672
Denmark/Danemark			23426	58270	50154
Bulgaria/Bulgarie			22312	59173	47732
Canada			15756	43221	55301
Finland/Finlande			16121	48341	47483
Austria/Autriche			17016	42420	52027
Romania/Roumanie			45228		61631
Indonesia/Indonésie		16000	10184	30857	40785
Libyan Arab Jamahiriya			12075	36965	39299
Singapore/Singapour			10967	32736	32243
Ireland/Irlande			10375	29477	30300
Cyprus/Chypre			10890	29211	28143
United Arab Emirates			5929	23800	27651
Portugal			6480	18002	28025
Sudan/Soudan		11000	5657	18247	15866
Morocco/Maroc		4000	3239	8496	13121
Malaysia/Malaisie		11000	13627		
Czech Republic			23571		
Thailand/Thaïlande			22287		
Tunisia/Tunisie		5000	1619	5832	7521
Kuwait/ Koweït			3636	9038	7191
Hungary/Hongrie			14091		
Cote d'Ivoire			2276	8822	2532
Iran (Islamic Rp. of)			12055		
Philippines			2869	4246	4806
India/Inde			8627		
Pakistan		3000	5530		
Hong Kong			7902		
Poland/Pologne			7436		

GENERAL EXPORTS F.O.B. EXPORTATIONS GENERALES F.O.B.

COUNTRIES–PAYS	1992	1993	1994	1995	1996
Monde		452000	572712	826209	1019411
Afrique		70000	41996	44705	50792
Amériques			27529	37887	38864
Amérique du Nord			24258	35203	35016
ALAI			2970	2684	3848
MCAC			1		
Caraïbes			137		
Autre Amérique			163		
Asie l'URSS exclus		301000	354710	516255	634267
Europe l'URSS exclus			118583	157486	193044
UE			86532	130236	165355
AELE			13441	9312	14805
Europe de l'Est			17777	17938	12884
Autre de l'Europe			260		
Ancienne URSS			15511	15397	11377
Océanie			2651	3821	4060
United Arab Emirates		76000	102944	236948	238877
Saudi Arabia		99000	87283	91438	139055
Syrian Arab Republic		59000	63068	69182	70248
Kuwait/ Koweït			32276	32474	77881
Jordan/Jordanie		32000	22877	29564	50012
France,Monac			26452	49519	46991
USA/Etats–Unis d'Amer			20717	30960	30663
Egypt/Egypte		18000	11887	15929	16858
Italy/Italie			11117	12233	38603
Libyan Arab Jamahiriya		24000	7168	11199	13567
Germany/Allemagne			9643	18276	22941
United Kingdom			11049	13874	15958
Turkey/Turquie		5000	5096	15382	12687
Switz.Liecht			13092	9312	14805
Netherlands/Pays–Bas			9377	12373	14356
Bahrain/Bahreïn		11000	5981	5994	11293
Qatar		12000	6328	7298	6921
Romania/Roumanie			10558	12624	9210
Russian Federation			12135	11656	7861
Cyprus/Chypre			12315	10811	8343
Belgium–Luxembourg			5900	7149	11330
Greece/Grèce			5699	4488	7666
Bulgaria/Bulgarie			6288	5314	3674
Algeria/Algérie		14000	1262		
Oman		2000	2722	3020	6649
Japan/Japon			3663	5932	4295
Spain/Espagne			3560	7967	2345
Canada			3541	4243	4353
Australia/Australie			2649	3821	4060
Ukraine			2518	3741	3516
Morocco/Maroc		5000	1878	1858	674
Guinea/Guinée			2672	3353	2501
Sudan/Soudan		2000	1744	1919	2842
Brazil/Brésil			1820	2684	3848
Yemen/Yémen		3000	1458	972	2879
Cote d'Ivoire			1187	3004	3993
Sweden/Suède			1842	2379	3074
Ghana			954	2435	3589
Iran (Islamic Rp. of)		2000	2095	1195	1577
Indonesia/Indonésie			1787	3722	798
Tunisia/Tunisie		3000	755	406	1789
Denmark/Danemark			1403	1978	2091
Korea, Republic of			893	1375	2529
Liberia/Libéria			1836	1507	1006
Sierra Leone			1399	1029	1847
Niger				2066	2126
Nigeria/Nigéria		2000	1948		
Singapore/Singapour			1454	946	221
Dem. Rep. of the Congo			2003		
Senegal/Sénégal		1000	432		

(VALUE AS PERCENTAGE OF WORLD TOTAL)(VALEURS EN POURCENTAGE DU TOTAL MONDIAL)

	1987	1988	1989	1990	1991	1992	1993	1994	1995	1996
Africa							0.9	1.9	1.9	1.8
Americas								12.0	12.5	12.7
Northern America								9.9	11.2	11.6
LAIA								1.8	1.3	1.0
CACM								0.1		
Caribbean								0.2		
Rest of America								0.0		
As.ex F.USSR							22.6	22.1	18.8	18.7
Eur.x F.USSR								56.6	50.9	48.7
EU								48.6	45.5	43.8
EFTA								3.7	4.6	3.4
East Europe								4.2	0.8	1.4
Other Europe								0.1		
Former USSR								3.8	3.4	3.7
Oceania								0.2		
Italy/Italie								13.5	13.0	12.1
USA/Etats–Unis d'Amer								9.3	10.6	10.9
Germany/Allemagne								10.1	8.4	8.5
France,Monac								9.0	7.6	7.8
Syrian Arab Republic							12.8	4.4	3.2	4.1
United Kingdom								4.2	3.9	4.0
Japan/Japon								4.2	3.9	3.9
Switz.Liecht								3.5	4.6	3.4
China/Chine								3.1	3.3	2.9
Greece/Grèce								2.4	3.1	2.5

	1987	1988	1989	1990	1991	1992	1993	1994	1995	1996
Afrique							15.5	7.3	5.4	5.0
Amériques								4.8	4.6	3.8
Amérique du Nord								4.2	4.3	3.4
ALAI								0.5	0.3	0.4
MCAC								0.0		
Caraïbes								0.0		
Autre Amérique								0.0		
Asie l'URSS exclus							66.6	61.9	62.5	62.2
Europe l'URSS exclus								20.7	19.1	18.9
UE								15.1	15.8	16.2
AELE								2.3	1.1	1.5
Europe de l'Est								3.1	2.2	1.3
Autre de l'Europe								0.0		
Ancienne URSS								2.7	1.9	1.1
Océanie								0.5	0.5	0.4
United Arab Emirates							16.8	18.0	28.7	23.4
Saudi Arabia							21.9	15.2	11.1	13.6
Syrian Arab Republic							13.1	11.0	8.4	6.9
Kuwait/ Koweït								5.6	3.9	7.6
Jordan/Jordanie							7.1	4.0	3.6	4.9
France,Monac								4.6	6.0	4.6
USA/Etats–Unis d'Amer								3.6	3.7	3.0
Egypt/Egypte							4.0	2.1	1.9	1.7
Italy/Italie								1.9	1.5	3.8
Libyan Arab Jamahiriya							5.3	1.3	1.4	1.3

4. General Imports C.I.F. by Commodities according to the S.I.T.C. (Rev. 2) in thousand U.S. Dollars
Importations Générales C.A.F. par Produits d'après la C.T.C.I. (Rév. 2) en milliers de Dollars E.U.

SITC CTCI	COMMODITY	1993		1994		1995		1996		PRODUIT
		WEIGHT POIDS	VALUE VALEUR	WEIGHT POIDS	VALUE VALEUR	WEIGHT POIDS	VALUE VALEUR	WEIGHT POIDS	VALUE VALEUR	
	ALL COMMODITIES						7295289		7570762	TOUS PRODUITS
001	*LIVE ANIMALS FOR FOOD						290737		385085	ANIMAUX VIVANTS
1	BEVERAGES AND TOBACCO						573271		573561	BOISSONS ET TABACS
3	MINERAL FUELS ETC						642253		727031	COMBUSTIBLES MINERAUX LUB
4	ANIMAL,VEGETABLE OIL,FAT						67046		65497	HUILES,GRAISSES ANIM,VEG
5	CHEMCLS,RELATED PROD NES						486719		520184	PRODUITS CHIMIQUES
61	LEATHER,DRESSED FUR,ETC						26205		26770	CUIRS,PELLETERIES
63	WOOD,CORK MANUFACTRS NES						115043		122906	OUVRAGES LIEGE ET BOIS
66	NONMETAL MINERAL MFS NES						203045		185546	ART MIN NON METALLIQUES
77	ELECTRIC MACHNRY NES ETC						1140301		1337507	MACH APP ELECT NDA
78	ROAD VEHICLES						828686		892578	VEHICULES ROUTIERS
897	GOLD,SILVER WARE,JEWELRY						367891		324186	BIJOUTERIE,ORFEVRERIE
931	*SPECIAL TRANSACTIONS						131845		159612	TRANS.SPECIALES

5. General Exports F.O.B. by Commodities according to the S.I.T.C. (Rev. 2) in thousand U.S. Dollars
Exportations Générales F.O.B. par Produits d'après la C.T.C.I. (Rév. 2) en milliers de Dollars E.U.

SITC CTCI	COMMODITY	1993		1994		1995		1996		PRODUIT
		WEIGHT POIDS	VALUE VALEUR	WEIGHT POIDS	VALUE VALEUR	WEIGHT POIDS	VALUE VALEUR	WEIGHT POIDS	VALUE VALEUR	
	ALL COMMODITIES						826209		1019411	TOUS PRODUITS
001	*LIVE ANIMALS FOR FOOD						5837		5559	ANIMAUX VIVANTS
1	BEVERAGES AND TOBACCO						58722		61325	BOISSONS ET TABACS
3	MINERAL FUELS ETC						7577		6781	COMBUSTIBLES MINERAUX LUB
4	ANIMAL,VEGETABLE OIL,FAT						9209		17505	HUILES,GRAISSES ANIM,VEG
5	CHEMCLS,RELATED PROD NES						47696		34778	PRODUITS CHIMIQUES
61	LEATHER,DRESSED FUR,ETC						9174		7953	CUIRS,PELLETERIES
66	NONMETAL MINERAL MFS NES						32084		23138	ART MIN NON METALLIQUES
77	ELECTRIC MACHNRY NES ETC						65254		77959	MACH APP ELECT NDA
78	ROAD VEHICLES						28968		52116	VEHICULES ROUTIERS
897	GOLD,SILVER WARE,JEWELRY						69414		81781	BIJOUTERIE,ORFEVRERIE
931	*SPECIAL TRANSACTIONS						15402		14047	TRANS.SPECIALES

1. HISTORICAL SERIES, 1958–1994 GENERAL TRADE, IMPORTS C.I.F., EXPORTS F.O.B.
SERIES HISTORIQUES, 1958–1994 COMMERCE GENERAL, IMPORTATIONS C.A.F., EXPORTATIONS F.O.B

YEAR ANNEE	VALUE IN MILLION LIBYAN DINARS VALEUR EN MILLION LIBYAN DINARS MERCHANDISE –MARCHANDISE		GOLD –OR		CONVERSION FACTORS U.S. CENTS PER LIBYAN DINAR FACTEURS DE CONVERSION CENTS E.U. PAR LIBYAN DINAR		INDEX NUMBERS –INDICES QUANTUM		UNIT VALUE VALEUR UNITAIRE	
	IMPORTS	EXPORTS	IMPORTS	EXPORTS	IMPORTS	EXPORTS	IMPORTS	EXPORTS	IMPORTS	EXPORTS
1958	34.50	5.10			280.0000	280.0000				
1959	40.60	4.30			280.0000	280.0000				
1960	60.40	4.00			280.0000	280.0000				
1961	53.30	7.90			280.0000	280.0000				
1962	73.40	50.50			280.0000	280.0000				
1963	85.30	119.90			280.0000	280.0000				
1964	104.40	221.40			280.0000	280.0000				
1965	114.40	284.30			280.0000	280.0000				
1966	144.70	360.90			280.0000	280.0000				
1967	170.20	420.00			280.0000	280.0000				
1968	230.20	669.90			280.0000	280.0000				
1969	241.30	773.90			280.0000	280.0000				
1970	198.00	844.90			280.0000	280.0000				
1971	250.40	962.50			282.5560	282.0500				
1972	343.20	968.10			304.0000	304.0000				
1973	539.90	1197.10			335.7970	335.5820				
1974	817.80	2446.20			337.7800	337.7800				
1975	1048.70	2025.10			337.7810	337.7810				
1976	950.80	2830.70			337.7810	337.7810				
1977	1117.10	3381.80			337.7800	337.7800				
1978	1362.60	2933.00			337.7800	337.7800				
1979	1572.40	4761.90			337.7800	337.7800				
1980	2006.20	6489.20			337.7800	337.7800				
1981	2481.40	4611.20			337.7800	337.7800				
1982	2124.30	3908.80			337.7800	337.7800				
1983	1784.80	3616.60			337.7800	337.7800				
1984	1841.70	3300.40			337.7800	337.7800				
1985	1214.40	3645.60			337.7800	337.7800				
1986	1316.00	2432.00			318.6000	318.6000				
1987	1278.00	2372.00			369.5100	369.5100				
1988	1677.00	1907.00			350.5100	350.5100				
1989	1475.00	2407.00			342.2900	342.2900				
1990	1511.00	3745.00			370.5500	370.5500				
1991	1505.00	3154.00			355.8743	355.5068				
1993	1575.90	3248.55			324.2721	324.2368				
1994	1618.28	3456.85			310.5776	310.4849				

2. IMPORTS BY BROAD ECONOMIC CATEGORY AND EXPORTS BY INDUSTRIAL ORIGIN. (PERCENTAGE OF TOTAL VALUE)
IMPORTATIONS PAR CATEGORIES ECONOMIQUES ET EXPORTATIONS PAR BRANCHE D'ACTIVITE.(EN POURCENTAGE DE LA VALEUR TOTALE)

IMPORTS – IMPORTATIONS

	1990	1991	1992	1993	1994	1995	1996
TOTAL IMPORTS–IMPORTATIONS TOTALES	100.	100.					
1 FOOD BEV–ALIMENTATION BOISSONS	18.5	19.7					
11 PRIMARY–PRODUITS DE BASE	7.5	7.6					
111 FOR INDUSTRY–POUR L'INDUSTRIE	5.7	6.0					
112 FOR HOUSEHOLDS–POUR LES MENAGES	1.8	1.6					
12 PROCESSED–PRODUITS ELABORES	11.0	12.1					
121 FOR INDUSTRY–POUR L'INDUSTRIE	4.7	4.6					
122 FOR HOUSEHOLDS–POUR LES MENAGES	6.3	7.5					
2 IND SUPPLIES–APPROV INDUSTRIELS	35.0	33.9					
21 PRIMARY–PRODUITS DE BASE	3.4	2.3					
22 PROCESSED–PRODUITS ELABORES	31.7	31.6					
3 FUELS–COMBUSTIBLES	0.3	0.2					
31 PRIMARY–PRODUITS DE BASE	0.0	0.0					
32 PROCESSED–PRODUITS ELABORES	0.2	0.2					
321 MOTOR SPIRIT–ESSENCE							
322 OTHER–AUTRES	0.2	0.2					
4 MACHINERY–EQUIPEMENT	24.6	23.8					
41 CAPITAL EQUIPMENT–MACHINES	19.5	18.3					
42 PARTS–PIECES ACCESSOIRES	5.1	5.5					
5 TRANSPORT–TRANSPORT	12.3	11.5					
51 PASSENGER CARS–AUTOMOBILES	2.8	2.9					
52 OTHER–AUTRES	2.8	2.8					
521 INDUSTRIAL–INDUSTRIELS	2.8	2.7					
522 NON INDUSTRIAL–NON INDUSTRIEL	0.0	0.1					
53 PARTS–PIECES ACCESSOIRES	6.7	5.9					
6 CONSUM GOODS–BIENS CONSOMMATION	9.2	10.7					
61 DURABLE–DURABLES	3.0	2.5					
62 SEMI DURABLE–SEMI DURABLES	4.1	5.5					
63 NON DURABLE–NON DURABLES	2.2	2.7					
7 GOODS NES–BIENS NDA	0.0	0.0					

EXPORTS – EXPORTATIONS

	1990	1991	1992	1993	1994	1995	1996
TOTAL EXPORTS–EXPORTATIONS TOTALES	100.	100.					
1 AGRICULTURE	0.4	0.6					
2 MINING QUARRY–INDUS EXTRACTIVES	83.6	85.9					
3 MANUFACTURING–IND MANUFACTUR	16.0	13.5					
31 FOOD BEV TOBACCO–ALIM BOISS TAB	0.2	0.1					
32 TEXTILES–INDUSTRIES TEXTILES	0.0	0.0					
33 WOOD & PRODUCTS–BOIS & PRODUITS							
34 PAPER & PRODUCTS–PAPIER & PRODT	0.0	0.0					
35 CHEMICALS–INDUSTRIES CHIMIQUES	15.0	12.9					
36 NON METAL MIN–MIN NON METAL	0.2	0.0					
37 BASIC METAL–IND METAL BASE	0.6	0.4					
38 METAL MANUF–MANUF METAL	0.0	0.0					
39 OTH MANUF IND–AUTRES MANUF	0.0	0.0					

3. TRADE BY PRINCIPAL COUNTRIES OF ORIGIN AND DESTINATION (VALUE IN THOUSAND U.S. DOLLARS)
ECHANGES SELON LES PRINCIPAUX PAYS D'ORIGINE ET DE DESTINATION (VALEUR EN MILLIERS DE DOLLARS EU)

COUNTRIES–PAYS	GENERAL IMPORTS C.I.F. IMPORTATIONS GENERALES C.A.F				
	1990	1991	1992	1993	1994
World	5598631	5357527		5110219	5026000
Africa	297435	401687		451000	437000
Americas	281215	272049			
Northern America	126201	132751			
LAIA	98477	110470			
CACM	22	281			
Caribbean	56506	28547			
Rest of America	10				
As.ex F.USSR	931302	1016213		365000	327000
Eur.x F.USSR	4076888	3642605			
EU	3657771	3355314			
EFTA	223048	132458			
East Europe	60431	39889			
Other Europe	135637	114944			
Former USSR	2629	6477			
Oceania	9161	18497			
Italy/Italie	1036349	1160525			
Germany/Allemagne	819436	700983			
Turkey/Turquie	290231	340255		270000	226000
United Kingdom	472038	441923			
France,Monac	412513	333183			
Morocco/Maroc	120941	191038		155000	167000
Tunisia/Tunisie	122544	114628		207000	174000
Netherlands/Pays–Bas	313237	207038			
Japan/Japon	244350	178575			
Switz.Liecht	214483	126330			
Korea, Republic of	115413	170355			
Belgium–Luxembourg	156065	110505			
Austria/Autriche	108452	155205			
Egypt/Egypte	38866	73270		65000	70000
Brazil/Brésil	95403	74983			
Sweden/Suède	92329	69131			
Greece/Grèce	81209	65160			
USA/Etats–Unis d'Amer	69962	69643			
Malta/Malte	60913	69070			
Fm Yugoslav	74724	45874			
Canada	56239	63108			
China/Chine	49491	62206			
Spain/Espagne	53751	47943			
Lebanon/Liban	19962	23580		26000	28000
Cuba	56463	28547			
Thailand/Thaïlande	41127	40399			
Syrian Arab Republic	11944	24087		21000	23000
Ireland/Irlande	53538	25211			
Malaysia/Malaisie	608	3390		26000	31000
Denmark/Danemark	35815	23389			
Poland/Pologne	36913	20159			
Jordan/Jordanie	1497	12133		11000	12000
Hong Kong	13582	22502			
Sri Lanka	21156	13094			
Benin/Bénin	12			16000	17000
Cyprus/Chypre	12927	16244			
India/Inde	7762	21345			
Finland/Finlande	13917	13534			
Algeria/Algérie	6715	8403		3000	3000
Singapore/Singapour	10791	8432			
Hungary/Hongrie	10414	7013			
Sudan/Soudan	1515	4655		5000	6000
Mexico/Mexique	252	15937			
Argentina/Argentine	2689	13396			
United Arab Emirates	5117	10655			
Australia/Australie	5418	9003			
Pakistan	3880	1368		6000	2000
New Zealand	3744	9493			
Indonesia/Indonésie	2689	2993		3000	3000
Norway,SVD,JM	6944	4534			

COUNTRIES–PAYS	GENERAL EXPORTS F.O.B. EXPORTATIONS GENERALES F.O.B.				
	1990	1991	1992	1993	1994
Monde	13876843	11211715		10533000	10733000
Afrique	457831	392367		297000	367000
Amériques	9987	30128			
Amérique du Nord	250	4			
ALAI	9736	30123			
MCAC					
Caraïbes					
Autre Amérique					
Asie l'URSS exclus	588185	351623		182000	309000
Europe l'URSS exclus	12617338	10437598			
UE	11711358	9668346			
AELE	11687	215599			
Europe de l'Est	485164	180000			
Autre de l'Europe	409129	373652			
Ancienne URSS	203502				
Océanie					
Italy/Italie	6642085	4565220			
Germany/Allemagne	900789	1869891			
Spain/Espagne	1276599	1077736			
France,Monac	1187634	865289			
Greece/Grèce	611748	581951			
Turkey/Turquie	506589	246231		120000	258000
Fm Yugoslav	369874	347195			
Sudan/Soudan	150732	152970		184000	188000
Belgium–Luxembourg	305618	308312			
Netherlands/Pays–Bas	387915	194593			
United Kingdom	247657	144887			
Romania/Roumanie	241994	87103			
Bulgaria/Bulgarie	242489	84397			
Tunisia/Tunisie	72138	96095		47000	111000
Morocco/Maroc	115392	122441		16000	17000
Switz.Liecht	4453	215011			
Former USSR/Anc. URSS	203502				
Egypt/Egypte	78645	19167		47000	48000
Portugal	108970	51153			
Jordan/Jordanie	791	14659		27000	28000
Malta/Malte	39255	26457			
Sweden/Suède	42285	8350			
China/Chine	7103	38488			
Un. Rep. of Tanzania	31071				
Syrian Arab Republic	9827	3310		7000	7000
Indonesia/Indonésie		659		13000	13000
Brazil/Brésil	3337	20715			
United Arab Emirates	13310	3257		2000	2000
Lebanon/Liban	11241	7269			
Thailand/Thaïlande	7488	9383			
Korea, Republic of	6239	9269			
India/Inde	6369	8264			
Malaysia/Malaisie				13000	1000
Iran (Islamic Rp. of)	13823				
Algeria/Algérie	5815	883		2000	2000
Poland/Pologne		8329			
Norway,SVD,JM	7234	588			
Singapore/Singapour		6370			
Colombia/Colombie	2699	2051			
Argentina/Argentine		4147			
Venezuela		3210			
Mauritania/Mauritanie	357	473		1000	1000
Senegal/Sénégal	2418	128			
Pakistan	2499				
Cyprus/Chypre	1442	963			
Ecuador/Equateur	2102				
Chile/Chili	1598				
Neutral Zone/Zone Neutre	946				
Finland/Finlande		878			
Czechoslovakia	677	170			

(VALUE AS PERCENTAGE OF WORLD TOTAL)(VALEURS EN POURCENTAGE DU TOTAL MONDIAL)

	1985	1986	1987	1988	1989	1990	1991	1992	1993	1994
Africa	2.1	1.3	2.3	2.9	2.8	5.3	7.5		8.8	8.7
Americas	7.3	5.3	2.6	2.7	3.9	5.0	5.1			
Northern America	6.6	4.4	1.7	1.9	2.6	2.3	2.5			
LAIA	0.2	0.6	0.6	0.7	1.2	1.8	2.1			
CACM	0.1	0.0			0.0	0.0	0.0			
Caribbean	0.4	0.3	0.3	0.0	0.1	1.0	0.5			
Rest of America				0.0		0.0				
As.ex F.USSR	16.4	18.5	18.6	25.4	17.4	16.6	19.0		7.1	6.5
Eur.x F.USSR	72.8	73.9	75.8	68.8	75.6	72.8	68.0			
EU	64.9	66.2	64.7	59.1	67.6	65.3	62.6			
EFTA	2.2	3.1	4.0	3.2	2.5	4.0	2.5			
East Europe	2.9	2.1	3.3	4.0	3.0	1.1	0.7			
Other Europe	2.9	2.5	3.7	2.5	2.4	2.4	2.1			
Former USSR	0.6	0.1	0.1	0.0	0.0	0.0	0.1			
Oceania	0.8	0.8	0.7	0.2	0.3	0.2	0.3			
Italy/Italie	21.2	22.8	23.4	21.4	24.2	18.5	21.7			
Germany/Allemagne	15.6	12.2	12.0	11.5	14.8	14.6	13.1			
Turkey/Turquie	2.3	3.7	3.4	3.6	4.8	5.2	6.4		5.3	4.5
United Kingdom	7.2	10.1	10.0	8.5	8.3	8.4	8.2			
France,Monac	4.5	4.9	5.4	4.7	6.8	7.4	6.2			
Morocco/Maroc	1.6	0.9	1.8	1.6	1.6	2.2	3.6		3.0	3.3
Tunisia/Tunisie	0.4	0.1	0.1	0.9	0.9	2.2	2.1		4.1	3.5
Netherlands/Pays–Bas	4.6	4.4	2.8	3.3	3.3	5.6	3.9			
Japan/Japon	6.5	4.8	5.9	11.7	4.6	4.4	3.3			
Switz.Liecht	2.0	2.8	3.9	3.1	2.5	3.8	2.4			

	1985	1986	1987	1988	1989	1990	1991	1992	1993	1994
Afrique	0.8	1.1	0.6	1.5	1.6	3.3	3.5		2.8	3.4
Amériques	1.8	0.2	0.1	0.4	0.1	0.1	0.3			
Amérique du Nord	0.8			0.1	0.1	0.0	0.0			
ALAI		0.0	0.1	0.3	0.0	0.1	0.3			
MCAC										
Caraïbes	0.1	0.2								
Autre Amérique	1.0									
Asie l'URSS exclus	9.9	7.2	7.6	2.5	3.9	4.2	3.1		1.7	2.9
Europe l'URSS exclus	85.3	90.1	90.4	94.0	92.8	90.9	93.1			
UE	76.1	77.2	80.6	88.0	88.4	84.4	86.2			
AELE	1.4	1.6	0.3	0.9		0.1	1.9			
Europe de l'Est	3.6	9.2	7.5	2.7	2.4	3.5	1.6			
Autre de l'Europe	4.2	2.2	1.9	2.4	2.1	2.9	3.3			
Ancienne URSS	2.3	1.4	1.2	1.7	1.6	1.5				
Océanie										
Italy/Italie	30.7	32.8	40.5	41.9	48.6	47.9	40.7			
Germany/Allemagne	8.4	2.6	2.0	7.1	5.4	6.5	16.7			
Spain/Espagne	8.9	12.7	7.0	6.7	8.7	9.2	9.6			
France,Monac	10.8	8.6	9.2	13.1	9.8	8.6	7.7			
Greece/Grèce	5.7	5.3	5.2	7.6	5.8	4.4	5.2			
Turkey/Turquie	5.7	4.5	4.1	1.2	3.2	3.7	2.2		1.1	2.4
Fm Yugoslav	4.1	1.8	1.8	2.3	1.8	2.7	3.1			
Sudan/Soudan	0.3	0.4		1.0	0.8	1.1	1.4		1.7	1.8
Belgium–Luxembourg	0.0	3.2	5.4	2.6	2.3	2.2	2.7			
Netherlands/Pays–Bas	8.9	6.9	7.1	5.0	5.5	2.8	1.7			

4. General Imports C.I.F. by Commodities according to the S.I.T.C. (Rev. 2) in thousand U.S. Dollars
Importations Générales C.A.F. par Produits d'après la C.T.C.I. (Rév. 2) en milliers de Dollars E.U.

SITC CTCI	COMMODITY	1988		1989		1990		1991		PRODUIT
		WEIGHT POIDS	VALUE VALEUR	WEIGHT POIDS	VALUE VALEUR	WEIGHT POIDS	VALUE VALEUR	WEIGHT POIDS	VALUE VALEUR	
	ALL COMMODITIES		5907478		5048725		5598631		5357527	TOUS PRODUITS
0	FOOD AND LIVE ANIMALS		782658		911593		1155174		1073477	ALIMENTS,ANIMAUX VIVANTS
001	*LIVE ANIMALS FOR FOOD		159915		100844		44862		81780	ANIMAUX VIVANTS
0011	BOVINE SPECIES,LIVE	N 124121	79775	N 92761	59880	N 73384	41003	N 111776	74800	ESPECE BOVINE
00119	— OTHR THAN FR BREEDING	N 123198	78705	N 91921	59018	N 71400	38617	N 110838	73506	BOVINS NON REPRODUCTEURS
0012	SHEEP AND GOATS,LIVE	N 1351747	75859	N 615859	40293			N 63055	5969	ESPECES OVINE ET CAPRINE
00121	SHEEP,LIVE	N 1351539	75828	N 615859	40293			N 63055	5969	ESPECE OVINE
01	MEAT AND PREPARATIONS		20846		19872		13289		7759	VIANDES ET PREPARATIONS
011	MEAT FRESH,CHILLD,FROZEN	W 8952	20679	W 10480	19017	W 5091	13253	W 3308	7748	VIANDES FRAICHES,REF,CONGE
02	DAIRY PRODCTS,BIRDS'EGGS		79590		99064		113481		80795	PRODUITS LAITIERS,OEUFS
022	MILK AND CREAM	W 34188	40275	W 45225	57975	W 44170	65752	W 42213	47628	LAIT ET CREME
0224	MILK,CREAM PRESERVED ETC	W 33427	38761	W 45218	57963	W 43651	64209	W 42125	47469	LAIT,CREME CONS,CONC
02242	MILK DRY,1.5% FAT OR LES	W 8699	14456	W 13439	26155	W 15467	30536	W 12199	22675	LAIT POUDRE INF 1.5%
02243	MILK DRY,OVER 1.5% FAT	W 24728	24305	W 31780	31807	W 28183	33673	W 29926	24795	LAIT POUDRE SUP 1.5%
023	BUTTER	W 4209	7262	W 6618	11906	W 9401	18706	W 7514	11335	BEURRE
024	CHEESE AND CURD	W 17027	31997	W 14244	28917	W 12324	28194	W 8307	21343	FROMAGE ET CAILLEBOTTE
03	FISH AND PREPARATIONS		11428		20246		15627		38873	POISSONS ET PREPARATIONS
037	FISH ETC PREPD,PRSVD NES	W 1013	6217	W 2292	13068	W 1961	12908	W 5499	33022	POIS,CRUST,MOL PREPARES
0371	FISH PREPARD,PRESRVD NES	W 827	5169	W 2287	13033	W 1958	12890	W 5491	32978	CONSERVES DE POISSONS
04	CEREALS AND PREPARATIONS		246108		365553		479579		439088	CEREALES ET PRODUITS
041	WHEAT ETC UNMILLED	W 228097	34152	W 339453	67574	W 380000	54590	W 614000	79880	FROMENT,EPEAUTRE
042	RICE	W 43447	15152	W 275505	79795	W 105248	42641	W 150956	56160	RIZ
0421	RICE IN HUSK OR HUSKED	W 43447	15152	W 275505	79795	W 105248	42641	W 150956	56160	RIZ SANS AUTRE PREPARATION
043	BARLEY UNMILLED	W 521197	86952	W 295568	53719	W 832238	149703	W 478792	80358	ORGE NON MONDEE
044	MAIZE UNMILLED	W 270176	36373	W 250284	53918	W 234421	54495	W 222506	47355	MAIS NON MOULU
046	WHEAT ETC MEAL OR FLOUR	W 345153	65337	W 391210	105403	W 591013	164964	W 643386	151687	SEMOULE FARINE,FROMENT
04601	FLOUR OF WHEAT OR MESLIN	W 339885	63850	W 391102	105349	W 591013	164964	W 643170	151588	FARINE DE FROMENT
048	CEREAL ETC PREPARATIONS	W 3312	5781	W 1520	3896	W 3577	9753	W 8452	18515	PREPTNS A BASE CEREALES
05	VEGETABLES AND FRUIT		66819		84423		102088		104865	LEGUMES ET FRUITS
054	VEG ETC FRSH,SMPLY PRSVD	W 9201	9040	W 10441	9495	W 7067	6704	W 17858	16814	LEGUMES FRAIS,CONG,SECS
0542	LEGUMINOUS VEGETBLES DRY	W 8713	8138	W 10055	8819	W 4428	4720	W 17151	16226	LEGUMES A COSSE SECS
056	VEGTBLES ETC PRSVD,PREPD	W 43553	42638	W 45189	48932	W 61043	73760	W 62216	59368	CONSERVES DE LEGUMES
0565	VEGTBLES PRSVD,PREPD NES	W 43499	42563	W 45012	48644	W 60987	73665	W 62169	59297	LEGUMES PREPARES CONSERVE
05651	VEGTBLS,FRUIT IN VINEGAR	W 43499	42563	W 45012	48644	W 60987	73665	W 62169	59297	LEGUM CONSERV AU VINAIGRE
057	FRUIT,NUTS,FRESH,DRIED	W 13093	10919	W 27774	19798	W 20444	17617	W 21277	22035	FRUITS FRAIS OU SECS
06	SUGAR AND PREPS,HONEY		40580		85428		100982		107688	SUCRES ET PRODUITS
061	SUGAR AND HONEY	W 148373	40006	W 221325	84899	W 220808	99972	W 322545	107010	SUCRES ET MIEL
0612	REFINED SUGAR ETC	W 147918	39554	W 220012	82602	W 220043	99124	W 322007	106198	SUCRES RAFFINES
07	COFFEE,TEA,COCOA,SPICES		52292		46870		71237		46155	CAFE,THE,CACAO,EPICES
074	TEA AND MATE	W 17893	38394	W 15929	35696	W 71156	51421	W 14323	30086	THE ET MATE
081	*FEEDING STUFF FOR ANIML	W 364960	93237	W 276385	74227	W 650032	188817	W 511891	141747	NOURRITURE POUR ANIMAUX
0811	HAY, FODDER, GREEN, DRY	W 80099	20225	W 91540	22594	W 278229	79056	W 74734	17684	FOIN ET FOURRAGE
08112	FODDER ROOTS,HAY,ETC	W 16010	3654	W 35480	8144	W 107250	28428	W 28341	7436	RACINES FOURRAGERES
08119	FODDER OF VEG ORIGIN NES	W 57262	15501	W 52756	13681	W 156900	47250	W 46394	10248	AUTRES FOURRAGES
0819	FOOD WASTE AND FEED NES	W 224328	56187	W 153338	37183	W 326910	95784	W 405519	114646	DECHETS,ALIMENTS NDA
09	MISC EDIBLE PRODUCTS		11841		15066		25214		24727	PREP ALIMENTAIRES DIVERSES
098	EDIBLE PRODCTS,PREPS NES	W 3937	11803	W 3614	14421	W 6239	24998	W 6429	24603	PREP ALIMENTAIRES NDA
09809	MISC FOOD PREPRTIONS NES	W 1368	7006	W 2098	11331	W 2784	15976	W 3293	16214	PREP ALIMENTAIRES NDA
1	BEVERAGES AND TOBACCO		25316		18439		7797		23347	BOISSONS ET TABACS
12	TOBACCO AND MANUFACTURES		25262		18290		6411		22896	TABACS BRUTS FABRIQUES
121	TOBACCO UNMNFCTRD,REFUSE	W 5157	17074	W 4522	16335	W 1259	4956	W 4471	17731	TABACS BRUTS,DECHETS
1211	TOBACCO,NOT STRIPPED	W 5157	17074	W 4522	16335	W 1259	4956	W 4296	17639	TABACS NON ECOTES
12111	— VIRGI TYPE,FLUE–CURED	W 5157	17074	W 4522	16335	W 1259	4956	W 4296	17639	VIRGINIE SECHES AIR CHAUD
2	CRUDE MATERLS,EXCL FUELS		67731		91770		118242		128259	MAT BRUTES NON COMESTIBLES
22	OIL SEEDS,OLEAGINOUS FRT		22341		16290		12903		7785	GRAINES,FRUITS OLEAGINEUX
222	SEEDS FOR'SOFT'FIXED OIL	W 56156	22336	W 39519	15569	W 25975	12039	W 13773	7393	GRAINES HUILES FIXES
2222	SOYA BEANS	W 55584	21900	W 38484	14683	W 25222	10579	W 12655	5357	FEVES DE SOJA
24	CORK AND WOOD		20926		40775		62180		81227	LIEGE ET BOIS
248	WOOD SHAPED,SLEEPERS	W 85	20072	W 340	36548	W 210	58322	W 323	78135	BOIS SIMPLEMENT TRAVAILLES
2482	LUMBER SHAPED CONIFER	W 85	20072	W 151	36468	W 210	58322	W 323	78135	CONIFERES SCIES,RABOTES
27	CRUDE FERTLZR,MINRLS NES		6322		12211		16850		13957	ENGRAIS MINERAUX BRUTS
29	CRUDE ANIMAL,VEG MAT NES		13024		11159		19261		18435	MATIERES BRUTES ANIM,VEGET
292	CRUDE VEG MATERIALS NES	W 1862	13024	W 1381	11159	W 1284	19261	W 1237	18274	MAT BRUTES VEGETALES NDA
3	MINERAL FUELS ETC		18733		16651		16049		19716	COMBUSTIBLES MINERAUX LUB
33	PETROLEUM AND PRODUCTS		18687		16439		12489		19461	PETROLE ET DERIVES
4	ANIMAL,VEGETABLE OIL,FAT		114445		89797		106554		164413	HUILES,GRAISSES ANIM,VEG
42	FIXED VEGETABLE OIL,FAT		110604		87437		104678		162503	HUILES VEGETALES FIXES
423	FIXED VEG OILS,SOFT	W 74324	109828	W 77701	86552	W 114878	102956	W 161277	160981	HUILES VEGET DOUCES FIXES
4235	OLIVE OIL	W 52383	88391	W 33002	48477	W 13	19	W 15	19	HUILE D'OLIVE
4236	SUNFLOWER SEED OIL	W 11482	11173	W 25239	20975	W 27071	19221	W 87570	76731	HUILE DE TOURNESOL
4239	OTH FIXED VEG OILS,SOFT	W 10412	10227	W 18015	16011	W 87070	82707	W 73480	83993	AUTRES HUILES FIXES
5	CHEMCLS,RELATED PROD NES		463870		390374		379681		407955	PRODUITS CHIMIQUES
52	INORGANIC CHEMICALS		19135		26010		29589		20417	PROD CHIM INORGANIQUES
522	INORG ELEMNTS,OXIDES,ETC	W 8149	12628	W 15194	18348	W 14614	17391	W 9443	12218	ELEMENTS INORGANIQUES
53	DYES,TANNING,COLOUR PROD		52500		52460		44536		71066	PROD TEINTURE,COLORANTS
533	PIGMENTS,PAINTS,ETC	W 19603	47331	W 20530	47657	W 15362	42555	W 29179	68817	PIGMENTS,PEINTURES,VERNIS
5334	VARNISHES,DISTEMPERS ETC	W 17201	42167	W 17059	39939	W 12811	36581	W 28009	65969	PEINTURES A L'EAU
53342	OTH PAINTS,VARNISHES ETC	W 15259	37668	W 12056	28301	W 8111	23888	W 26552	62546	AUTRES PEINTURES,VERNIS
541	*MEDICINAL,PHARM PRODUCT		121525		84614		47631		83842	PROD MEDICINAUX PHARMACEUT
5417	MEDICAMENTS		113159		75359		30687		76504	MEDICAMENTS
55	PERFUME,CLEANING ETC PRD		51283		41769		77673		23460	PROD POUR PARFUM,TOILETTE
553	PERFUMERY,COSMETICS,ETC	W 2241	16630	W 1331	20129	W 1365	13501	W 509	5835	PRODUITS DE PARFUMERIE
554	SOAP,CLEANSING ETC PREPS	W 19954	32875	W 12974	19994	W 38159	62087	W 9119	15766	SAVONS,PRODUITS DETERSIFS
5541	SOAPS	W 12400	21358	W 5513	8519	W 17267	28732	W 4217	8515	SAVONS,PROD TENSIO–ACTIFS
5542	WASHING PREPARATIONS ETC	W 7001	10380	W 7007	10565	W 20517	32798	W 4775	7003	PROD ORG TENSIO–ACT NDA
562	*FERTILIZERS,MANUFACTURE	W 111970	27573	W 104985	24905	W 42995	12981	W 134149	28788	ENGRAIS MANUFACTURES
58	PLASTIC MATERIALS ETC		59282		59490		50460		77412	MAT PLAST ARTIFICIELLES
582	PROD OF CONDENSATION ETC	W 27504	57393	W 27745	57726	W 22963	47837	W 44840	72529	PROD CONDENS,POLYCOND
5821	PHENOPLASTS	W 27504	57393	W 27745	57726	W 22963	47837	W 44840	72529	PHENOPLASTES
58211	— IN PRIMARY FORMS	W 27504	57393	W 27745	57726	W 22963	47837	W 44840	72529	PHENOPLASTES PRIMAIRES
59	CHEMICAL MATERIALS NES		110953		83990		98549		82996	MAT PROD CHIMIQUES NDA
591	PESTICIDES,DISINFECTANTS	W 21015	54306	W 5884	13385	W 8167	20481	W 6358	13637	DESINF,INSECT,FONG,HERB
5914	DISINFECTANTS,ETC,FR RET	W 10420	31960	W 1732	4784	W 327	1049	W 54	165	DESINFECTANTS VENTE DET
59141	DISINFECTANTS FOR RETAIL	W 10420	31960	W 1732	4784	W 327	1049	W 54	165	DESINFECTANTS VENTE DET
598	MISCEL CHEM PRODUCTS NES	W 30209	51142	W 35362	61870	W 37535	68709	W 38119	59797	PROD DIV INDUST CHIM NDA
5989	CHEM PRODUCTS,PREPS NES	W 27568	46124	W 30211	51541	W 32936	59170	W 31321	46982	PROD PREP CHIMIQUES NDA
59899	OTH CHEM PRODS,PREPS,NES	W 23864	38377	W 28100	46972	W 31456	56012	W 28477	40861	AUT PRODUITS CHIMIQUES NDA
6	BASIC MANUFACTURES		1058681		1238154		1331192		1213829	ART MANUFACTURES
61	LEATHER,DRESSED FUR,ETC		17000		23220		24129		42638	CUIRS,PELLETERIES
612	LEATHER ETC MANUFACTURES	W 2200	14413	W 3183	19531	W 2707	17949	W 5638	35260	OUVRAGES EN CUIRS NDA
6123	PREPRD PARTS OF FOOTWEAR	W 2034	13351	W 3032	18623	W 2671	17727	W 5597	34996	PARTIES DE CHAUSSURES

4. General Imports C.I.F. by Commodities according to the S.I.T.C. (Rev. 2) in thousand U.S. Dollars
Importations Générales C.A.F. par Produits d'après la C.T.C.I. (Rév. 2) en milliers de Dollars E.U.

SITC CTCI	COMMODITY	1988 WEIGHT POIDS	1988 VALUE VALEUR	1989 WEIGHT POIDS	1989 VALUE VALEUR	1990 WEIGHT POIDS	1990 VALUE VALEUR	1991 WEIGHT POIDS	1991 VALUE VALEUR	PRODUIT
62	RUBBER MANUFACTURES NES		60619		59382		72796		58762	CAOUTCHOUC MANUFACTURE
625	RUBBER TYRES, TUBES ETC		45856		41783		60694		40251	PNEUS CAOUTCHOUC VULCANISE
6251	TYRES NEW FOR MOTOR CARS	N 537650	20243	N 358040	13074	N 639574	21603	N 363680	15263	PNEUS POUR VOITURES
6252	TYRES,NEW,BUS OR LORRY	N 81033	21824	N 103051	27078	N 138556	37444	N 91341	22939	PNEUS POUR AUTOBUS,CAMIONS
63	WOOD,CORK MANUFACTRS NES		37740		41375		34769		33872	OUVRAGES LIEGE ET BOIS
634	VENEERS,PLYWOOD,ETC		23332		17447		13997		18283	PLACAGES,CONTRE–PLAQUES
635	WOOD MANUFACTURES NES	W 4179	14198	W 6278	23235	W 4337	20605	W 5205	15128	ART MANUF EN BOIS NDA
6353	BUILDERS WOODWRK,PREFABS	W 2049	10238	W 3795	18757	W 3550	18884	W 2203	10939	OUVRAGES DE MENUISERIE
64	PAPER,PAPERBOARD AND MFR		53883		75266		88116		93167	PAPIERS,CARTONS & OUVRAGES
641	PAPER AND PAPERBOARD	W 13287	15812	W 26680	20494	W 14743	17835	W 23957	23655	PAPIERS ET CARTONS
642	PAPER,ETC,PRECUT,ARTS OF	W 21636	38071	W 31582	54772	W 39980	70281	W 46060	69512	PAP,CARTONS DECOUPES
6421	PAPER ETC CONTAINERS	W 15665	20946	W 21139	28175	W 31522	44232	W 37786	48506	BOITES,SACS EMBALLAGES
6428	PAPER ETC ARTICLES NES	W 2976	7661	W 7673	18080	W 5310	14698	W 4935	10874	OUVRAGES EN PATE A PAPIER
65	TEXTILE YARN,FABRICS,ETC		235181		138317		129880		187442	FILS,TISSUS,ARTICLES TEXTILE
651	TEXTILE YARN	W 5244	40797	W 5896	26937	W 3425	33161	W 5023	40903	FILS TEXTILES
653	WOVN MAN–MADE FIB FABRIC	W 33815	78480	W 19180	36847	W 16188	40181	W 23146	51848	TISSUS FIBRES SYNTH,ARTIF
6531	CONT SYNT WEAVES NONPILE	W 7111	18332	W 6580	11198	W 4391	12119	W 8713	22789	TISSUS FIBRES SYNTH CONTINUE
65314	CONT SYN TYRE CORD FABRC	W 7111	18332	W 6580	11198	W 4391	12119	W 8713	22789	TIS ARMATURE PNEUMATIQUES
6535	CONT REGN WEAVES NONPILE	W 20491	41768	W 9504	18803	W 8428	19570	W 10612	20786	TISSUS FIB TEXT ART CONTINU
655	KNITTED,ETC FABRICS	W 4324	18695	W 4749	16300	W 1206	5940	W 2679	12280	ETOF BONNETERIE PIECES ETC
657	SPECIAL TXTL FABRC,PRODS	W 12654	31267	W 7919	16316	W 3748	12392	W 7313	20498	TISSUS SPECIAUX
658	TEXTILE ARTICLES NES	W 9120	43069	W 6944	21086	W 4467	18915	W 10585	38741	ART FACONNES MAT TEXTILES
6583	BLANKETS ETC NON ELECTRC	W 3790	26791	W 1011	6600	W 1598	9737	W 5186	26867	COUVERTURES
65833	SYN FIB BLANKETS ETC NES	W 1408	7970	W 703	3388	W 1363	7754	W 4071	20432	COUVERTURES FIBRES SYNTHET
66	NONMETAL MINERAL MFS NES		64394		75483		124814		81771	ART MIN NON METALLIQUES
661	LIME,CEMENT,BLDG PRODS	W 142746	27130	W 151045	32208	W 521405	71990	W 204577	24303	CHAUX,CIMENTS MAT CONSTR
6612	CEMENT	W 108311	9170	W 122144	17397	W 468453	40979	W 187982	17184	CIMENTS HYDRAULIQUES
6613	BUILDING STONE ETC WORKD	W 12321	5988	W 18227	8800	W 44252	25654	W 13440	5817	PIERRES A BATIR
66132	BUILDING STONE WORKED	W 10430	5051	W 14653	7052	W 35513	21458	W 6134	2828	OUVR EN PIERRES DE TAILLE
662	CLAY,REFRACTORY BLDG PRD	W 115448	21041	W 103022	21615	W 73490	24496	W 105769	41245	MAT CONST REFRACTAIRES
6623	REFRACTORY BUILDING PROD	W 6411	3103	W 15634	7415	W 21059	11883	W 43340	19835	BRIQUES REFRACTAIRES
66231	SILICE EARTH BRICKS ETC	W 6411	3103	W 15634	7415	W 21059	11883	W 43340	19835	BRIQUES ETC FARINE SILICE
6624	BRICKS ETC NONREFRACTORY	W 109037	17938	W 87388	14200	W 52430	12612	W 62429	21410	BRIQUES ETC CERAM NON REFR
66245	GLAZED CERAMIC SETTS ETC	W 69866	12121	W 63685	10813	W 33279	8442	W 43261	19153	AUT CARREAUX CERAMIQUE
67	IRON AND STEEL		320449		476349		516185		401446	FER ET ACIER
671	PIG IRON ETC	W 347	541	W 18482	28368	W 22710	22890	W 35130	54823	FONTE,SPIEGEL,POUDRES
6712	PIG IRN,SPIEGELEISEN ETC	W 347	541	W 18482	28368	W 22710	22890	W 35130	54823	FONTES BRUTES
672	IRON,STEEL PRIMARY FORMS	W 18202	11807	W 62592	29094	W 158457	78798	W 20577	14013	LINGOTS FER,ACIER
6725	IRN,STL BLOOMS,SLABS,ETC	W 5042	2233	W 40792	14870	W 134448	62158	W 1818	915	BLOOMS,BILLETTES FER ACIER
673	IRON,STEEL SHAPES ETC	W 167531	72938	W 212614	94465	W 179598	93119	W 163161	79643	BARRES,PROFIL FER,ACIER
6731	IRON,STEEL WIRE ROD	W 120511	49523	W 139851	58920	W 143607	64230	W 122784	59595	FIL MACHINE FER,ACIER
6733	IRON,STEEL PROFILES ETC	W 31719	15842	W 43201	20560	W 18392	16230	W 25156	12254	PROFILES,PALPLAN FER,ACIER
674	IRN,STL UNIV,PLATE,SHEET	W 98583	54177	W 98673	70309	W 103380	63556	W 92539	48744	LARGES PLATS,TOLES
6741	IRON OR STEEL UNIVERSALS	W 98583	54177	W 98673	70309	W 103380	63556	W 92539	48744	LARGES PLATS FER,ACIER
677	IRN,STL WIRE(EXCL W ROD)	W 155586	67193	W 241262	100219	W 173587	128416	W 128404	55435	FILS EN FER,ACIER
678	IRON,STL TUBES,PIPES,ETC	W 80644	104249	W 115772	143080	W 71576	117416	W 101172	144301	TUBES,TUYAUX EN FONTE,FER
6781	CAST IRON TUBES,PIPES	W 35550	52814	W 54425	74324	W 36659	64905	W 43062	69406	TUBES,TUYAUX EN FONTE
6783	IRON,STL TUBES,PIPES NES	W 33612	32318	W 47660	47535	W 22478	27827	W 35444	37577	AUT TUBES,TUYAUX FER,ACIER
6785	IRON,STEEL TUBE FITTINGS	W 11482	19117	W 13687	21222	W 12439	24684	W 22666	37317	ACCESSOIRES DE TUYAUTERIE
68	NON–FERROUS METALS		27328		31157		45965		38687	METAUX NON FERREUX
684	ALUMINIUM	W 3597	11058	W 6431	18468	W 4608	16746	W 5000	17188	ALUMINIUM
6842	ALUMINIUM,ALLOYS WORKED	W 3376	10509	W 6262	18064	W 4558	16607	W 4985	17152	ALUMINIUM,ALLIAGES OUVRE
69	METAL MANUFACTURES NES		242087		317605		294539		276045	ART MANUFACT EN METAL NDA
691	STRUCTURES AND PARTS NES	W 23231	70365	W 32293	93023	W 38259	129920	W 35767	109128	CONSTRUCT FER,ACIER,ALU
6911	STRUCTURES,PARTS IRN,STL	W 18940	48100	W 28407	74356	W 33190	102851	W 30267	82813	CONSTRUCT FER,ACIER,FONTE
6912	STRUCTURES,PARTS ALUMNM	W 4290	22266	W 3885	18667	W 5069	27070	W 5500	26315	CONSTRUCT ALUMINIUM
692	METAL TANKS,BOXES,ETC	W 21928	39189	W 24614	54488	W 24838	53275	W 26243	51634	RECIPIENTS METALLIQUES
6921	METAL STORAGE TANKS ETC	W 1438	5926	W 4180	16621	W 2642	12969	W 1544	7511	CUVES EN FONTE,FER,ALU
6924	MTL TRANSPORT BOXES ETC	W 20490	33263	W 20434	37867	W 22196	40306	W 24699	44123	FUTS,TAMBOURS,BIDONS
69241	STL TRANSPORT BOXES ETC	W 15444	25072	W 15510	29341	W 13667	23101	W 15087	26992	FUTS,TAMBOURS,BIDONS FER
695	TOOLS	W 5948	39573	W 6237	65360	W 2462	17257	W 3653	22281	OUTILS A MAIN
6953	OTHER HAND TOOLS	W 4638	30101	W 3566	21005	W 1722	12083	W 2990	18679	AUTRES OUTILS A MAIN
69539	HAND TOOLS ETC NES	W 3791	25274	W 2735	16197	W 1166	8491	W 2427	15212	OUTILLAGE A MAIN NDA
6954	BLADES,TIPS,ETC FR TOOLS	W 885	7903	W 2095	42346	W 482	4173	W 549	3187	OUTILS POUR MACHINE–OUTIL
69541	PARTS TO INSERT IN TOOLS	W 364	5160	W 1807	40686	W 166	1376	W 263	1479	OUTILS DE FORAGE
697	BASE MTL HOUSEHOLD EQUIP	W 5294	33856	W 6135	39004	W 4414	27747	W 4942	29571	ART MENAGE MET COMMUNS
6973	DMSTC HEATG,COOKG APPARA	W 2831	20514	W 3292	24055	W 2298	15182	W 2419	15782	APPS CHAUF NON ELECTRIQ
69731	IRN,STL DOM COOKG APPARA	W 2473	17334	W 3121	22529	W 2101	13582	W 2357	15377	APPS CUISSON FER,ACIER
699	BASE METAL MFRS NES	W 11142	33591	W 13449	35676	W 11184	37373	W 12832	38956	ART MANUFACTURES MET NDA
6991	LOCKSMITHS WARES,ETC	W 3658	16190	W 2967	12930	W 2925	15873	W 4518	20512	ARTICLES DE SERRURERIE
7	MACHINES,TRANSPORT EQUIP		2286783		1715808		1936551		1813362	MACHINES MATERIEL TRANSPORT
71	POWER GENERATING EQUIPMT		140373		106661		101741		95606	MACHINES GENERATRICES
713	INTRNL COMBUS PSTN ENGIN		79723		62135		43488		43596	MOTEURS EXPL COMB INT, PIECE
7132	MOTOR VEHCL PISTN ENGINS	N 19247	33078	N 6186	13303	N 1980	4293	N 881	1755	MOTEURS EXPL POUR VEHICULES
7139	PISTON ENGINE PARTS NES	W 3046	42072	W 3248	43160	W 2560	36214	W 3099	39142	PIECES POUR 713.2,3,8
714	ENGINES AND MOTORS NES	W 1036	15194	W 632	10255	W 1045	18577	W 1248	18331	MOTEURS NON ELECTRIQUES
7149	ENGINE & MOTOR PARTS NES	W 538	9085	W 535	9060	W 1025	18319	W 568	9813	PIECES 714 ET 718.88
716	ROTATING ELECTRIC PLANT	W 2565	42587	W 1933	30897	W 2189	34591	W 1929	31551	APP ELECTR ROTATIFS,PIECES
7162	AC MTRS,GENRTRS,GEN SETS	W 1487	23113	W 1382	21629	W 1198	18799	W 1598	26231	MOTEURS ELECTRIQUES
71622	AC GENERATORS	W 1229	19524	W 1127	18044	W 944	15019	W 1374	23154	GENER COURANT ALTERNATIF
72	MACHS FOR SPCL INDUSTRYS		328769		241090		334058		268828	MAC SPECIALES POUR INDUST
721	AGRIC MACHY,EXC TRACTORS	W 10873	79220	W 5653	45347	W 4439	37780	W 4657	39928	MACHINES AGRICOLES
7211	CULTIVATING MACHINERY	W 6556	43629	W 3198	20750	W 1719	11622	W 399	2710	MACH PREPARATION DU SOL
7219	AGRICULTURE MACHINES NES	W 1772	18398	W 1145	12244	W 1737	18394	W 1895	19939	ENGINS AGRICOLES NDA
72197	OTH AGRIC ETC MACHINERY	W 1543	15311	W 865	8533	W 1657	17267	W 1577	15601	AUT APP POUR AGRICULTURE
722	TRACTORS NON–ROAD	W 2	35020	W 1	11877	W 2	34969	W 1	16026	TRACTEURS
7223	TRACK–LAYING TRACTORS	W 2	35020	W 1	11877	W 2	34969	W 1	16026	TRACTEURS A CHENILLES
723	CIVIL ENGNEERG EQUIP ETC	W 11698	105240	W 9611	88172	W 16139	146945	W 11691	98106	APPAREILS DE GENIE CIVIL
7234	CONST,MINING MACHNRY NES	W 8439	63728	W 6414	55983	W 13687	118942	W 7295	52991	MACH POUR LA CONST, MINES
72341	SELF–PROPELLD DOZERS,ETC	W 4951	30313	W 1792	11595	W 5234	35920	W 4210	22939	BULLDOZERS
72343	SLFPRP CONST ETC MCH NES	W 2129	20603	W 3752	36361	W 7644	75082	W 2582	25244	AUT MACH EXTR,TERRASSEM
7239	CONSTR ETC MACHY PTS NES	W 3258	31721	W 3197	30730	W 2452	25058	W 4396	43981	PIECES 723.41–723.46
724	TEXTILE,LEATHER MACHNRY		19873		14323		8856		10505	MACH POUR INDUSTRIE TEXTILE
727	FOOD MACHRY NON–DOMESTIC	W 937	12156	W 1500	19185	W 2233	29478	W 1790	22217	MACH INDUSTRIES ALIMENT
7272	OTH FOOD PROC MCHY,PARTS	W 912	11827	W 1265	16212	W 1182	15725	W 1405	16670	AUT MACH IND ALIMENTAIRE
72722	INDUS FOOD PROC MACH NES	W 892	11607	W 1042	13809	W 1152	15361	W 1384	16443	MACHINES BOULANGERIE
728	OTH MACHY FOR SPCL INDUS	W 6660	72232	W 5332	59006	W 6341	70464	W 6804	74488	AUT MACH IND PARTICULIERES
7283	OTHR MINERAL WORKG MACHY	W 1165	10908	W 1640	16188	W 1247	12601	W 2349	22481	MACH TRIER,CRIBLER,BROYER
72833	MNRL MIXING,KNEADING MCH	W 478	4432	W 1096	9984	W 766	6771	W 2042	19274	MACH MELANGER MAT MINER
7284	MACHY FOR SPCL INDUS NES	W 4719	51671	W 3163	36615	W 4425	50304	W 3364	39946	MACH SPEC IND PARTICUL.
72842	RUBBER,PLASTICS WRKG MCH	W 2097	19555	W 1278	11604	W 1368	13253	W 731	6762	MACH IND CAOUT MAT PLAST

4. General Imports C.I.F. by Commodities according to the S.I.T.C. (Rev. 2) in thousand U.S. Dollars
Importations Générales C.A.F. par Produits d'après la C.T.C.I. (Rév. 2) en milliers de Dollars E.U.

SITC CTCI	COMMODITY	1988		1989		1990		1991		PRODUIT
		WEIGHT POIDS	VALUE VALEUR	WEIGHT POIDS	VALUE VALEUR	WEIGHT POIDS	VALUE VALEUR	WEIGHT POIDS	VALUE VALEUR	
72848	OTH MCHY WITH INDIV FNCT	W 1822	22725	W 1407	17690	W 1439	18454	W 2401	29906	AUTRES MACHINES NDA
73	METALWORKING MACHINERY		25105		17572		20388		25069	MACH TRAVAIL DES METAUX
736	METALWORKING MACH–TOOLS	W 1716	17217	W 1177	12220	W 1131	11513	W 1729	17424	MACH–OUTILS TRAVAIL METAUX
7361	METAL CUTTING MACH–TOOLS	W 1716	17217	W 1177	12220	W 1131	11513	W 1729	17424	MACH–OUT ENLEVEMENT METAL
74	GENRL INDUSTRL MACHY NES		470811		477393		489184		503577	MACH APP INDUSTRIE
741	HEATING,COOLING EQUIPMNT		66376		94716		93236		81299	MACH CHAUFFAGE,PIECES
7414	NONDOM REFRIG EQUIPT,PTS		14631		26409		22191		22782	MAT PRODUCTION DU FROID
7415	AIR–CONDITIONING MACHNRY		24693		41572		39157		32379	GROUPES CONDITION AIR
7416	HEATING,COOLING EQU NES	W 1590	15160	W 2484	22596	W 2892	29051	W 2396	24432	APP CHANGEMENT TEMP
742	PUMPS FOR LIQUIDS ETC		62077		52061		65106		95239	POMPES MOTO–POMPES
7428	OTHER PUMPS FOR LIQUIDS		56049		50789		63257		93768	AUTRES POMPES POUR LIQ
743	PUMPS NES,CENTRFUGES ETC		34820		45392		48096		45659	POMPES COMPRES,VENT ETC
7431	PUMPS FOR GASES ETC	N 12742	10987	N 12930	11884	N 17572	15647	N 20857	18468	POMPES AIR A VIDE,COMPRES
744	MECHANICAL HANDLING EQU		34771		41594		36679		34281	EQUIP MANUTENTION PIECES
7442	LIFTING,LOADING MACH NES		17611		21208		22615		21887	APP LEVAGE,MANUTENTION
745	NONELEC MACHY,TOOLS NES		33399		31367		31455		20221	AUT MACH NON ELEC,PIECES
7452	OTH NONELEC MCHS,PTS NES		29037		29637		27954		18837	AUT MACH NON ELEC,PIECES
74527	SPRAYING MACHINERY	W 2727	25036	W 1747	16004	W 829	8099	W 805	7652	APP PROJETER ETC LIQUID
749	NONELEC MACH PTS,ACC NES	W 25805	239368	W 22590	212261	W 23281	214612	W 25279	226878	PIECES MACH NON ELEC NDA
7492	COCKS,VALVES ETC NES	W 4587	35949	W 4227	41547	W 5564	44984	W 5531	43024	ART ROB,SIM POUR TUYAUX
7499	OTH NONELEC MCHY PTS NES	W 20741	198225	W 17763	164227	W 17210	164023	W 19309	179153	PIECES NON ELECT NDA
74991	FOUNDRY MOULDS ETC NES	W 1090	8196	W 1165	8892	W 2316	18421	W 1270	9747	MOULES POUR METAUX
74999	MACH PARTS NONELEC NES	W 18849	182767	W 16281	152429	W 14500	141887	W 17471	164324	PIECES MACHINES NDA
75	OFFICE MACHNES,ADP EQUIP		30983		34701		39045		44141	MACH BUREAU TRAIT AUTOM
752	AUTOMTIC DATA PROC EQUIP	N 206	6600	N 316	9862	N 398	12162	N 569	19874	MACH TRAIT INFORMATION
7521	ANALOG,HYBRID COMPUTERS	N 206	6600	N 316	9862	N 398	12162	N 569	19874	MACH POUR TRAIT INFORMAT
759	OFFICE,ADP MCH PTS,ACCES	W 380	19665	W 312	12589	W 359	17939	W 307	15602	PIECES DU 751 ET 752
7599	ACCTG,ETC,ADP MCH PTS,AC	W 380	19665	W 312	12589	W 359	17939	W 307	15602	PIECES DU 751 ET 752
76	TELECOMM,SOUND EQUIPMENT		81412		99866		104728		111782	EQUIPMENT DE TELECOM
764	TELECOM EQPT,PTS,ACC NES		57265	W 2271	74606		88277		94820	EQUIP TELECOM,PIECES
7641	LINE TELEPHONE,ETC EQUIP	W 105	6430	W 171	9783	W 235	14647	W 271	16751	APP TELEPHON PAR FIL
7649	PTS NES OF EQUIPMT OF 76	W 1278	41866	W 1728	51331	W 2077	66178	W 2280	69478	PIECES DE LA DIV 76
77	ELECTRIC MACHNRY NES ETC		299749		243916		292881		262937	MACH APP ELECT NDA
771	ELECTRIC POWER MACHY NES	W 4232	39372	W 2071	18323	W 2302	21404	W 3414	30639	MACH PROD,TRANS ELECTR
7711	TRANSFORMERS,ELECTRICAL	W 4232	39372	W 2071	18323	W 2302	21404	W 3414	30639	TRANSFO ELECTRIQUES
772	SWITCHGEAR ETC,PARTS NES	W 6137	57566	W 7883	71448	W 10570	101889	W 6812	60717	APP COUPURE,SECT ETC
7721	SWITCHGEAR ETC	W 5989	56208	W 7818	70847	W 10202	98534	W 6585	58623	APP COUPURE,SECTIONMNT
773	ELECTR DISTRIBUTNG EQUIP	W 16927	48955	W 15598	46001	W 15624	68031	W 20414	58239	EQUIPMT DISTRIBUTION ELECT
7731	INSULATED WIRE,CABLE ETC	W 15773	44814	W 13373	38100	W 13752	61382	W 18858	52965	FILS,CABLES ISOLES ELECT
775	HOUSEHOLD TYPE EQUIP NES		61093		23199		37563		42646	MACH,APP USAGE DOMESTQUE
7752	DOM REFRIGERATRS,FREEZRS	N 70141	21724	N 30173	9016	N 10507	4886	N 13532	4958	REFRIG,CONGEL MENAGER
7758	ELECTRO–THERMIC APPL NES	W 2790	21380	W 1229	9100	W 2929	20387	W 2412	15863	APP ELECTROTHERMIQ NDA
778	ELECTRICAL MACHINERY NES		83321		76678		61655		64769	AUTRES MACH ELECT NDA
7781	BATTERIES,ACCUMULATORS		21479		10329		7548		12537	PILES ET ACCUMULATEURS
77812	ELECTRIC ACCUMULATORS	N 475174	19029	N 315762	8610	N 137642	5637	N 239241	9136	ACCUMULATEURS ELECTRIQ
7788	OTH ELEC MACHY,EQUIP NES	W 3088	41081	W 3827	45120	W 3564	43737	W 2730	34931	AUT MACH APP ELEC NDA
77889	ELEC PARTS OF MACHY NES	W 2344	32992	W 2517	29811	W 1907	25808	W 1978	25674	PIECES ELEC DE MACH NDA
78	ROAD VEHICLES		874628		470636		534895		465913	VEHICULES ROUTIERS
781	PASS MOTOR VEH EXC BUSES	N 54889	315298	N 19889	109003	N 17740	154293	N 27338	154784	AUTO TRANSPORT PERSONNES
782	LORRIES,SPCL MTR VEH NES	N 14405	235184	N 4650	116597	N 5207	107246	N 2193	68674	VEHICULES SPECIAUX,MARCH
7821	LORRIES,TRUCKS	N 13675	203376	N 3863	85436	N 2241	62933	N 1595	37825	VEHICULES TRANSP MARCHAND
7822	SPECIAL MOTOR VEHCLS NES	N 730	31808	N 787	31161	N 2966	44313	N 598	30849	VEHICULES USAGES SPECIAUX
783	ROAD MOTOR VEHICLES NES	N 787	19211		13767	N 529	22840	N 377	17729	VEHICULES ROUTIERS NDA
7831	BUSES	N 787	19211		13767	N 529	22840	N 377	17729	VOITURES TRANSPORT COMMUN
784	MOTOR VEH PRTS,ACCES NES	W 30335	279662	W 20274	191551	W 23028	227127	W 20502	185317	PIECES 722,781,782,783
7849	OTHER MOTOR VEHCL PARTS	W 28707	267468	W 19403	185187	W 21934	217564	W 19425	176768	PIECES 722,781,782,783
786	TRAILERS,NONMOTR VEH,NES		19777		32420		20851		31874	REMORQUES,CADRES,CONTAIN
7861	TRAILERS,TRANSP CONTAINR	N 743	18316	N 881	29756	N 765	19859	N 1197	30713	REMORQUES TOUS VEHICULES
78611	HOUSING,CAMPING TRAILERS	N 743	18316	N 881	29756	N 765	19859	N 1197	30713	REMORQUES POUR CAMPING
79	OTHR TRANSPORT EQUIPMENT		34952		23974		19631		35511	AUTRE MATERIEL TRANSPORT
792	AIRCRAFT ETC	W 187	29668		19424	W 86	13639		20511	APP NAVIGATION AERIENNE
7929	AIRCRAFT PARTS NES	W 187	29668	W 129	19175	W 86	13639	W 76	11193	PIECES DU 792
8	MISC MANUFACTURED GOODS		1021985		547878		527953		494916	ART MANUFACTURES DIVERS
812	*PLUMBG,HEATNG,LGHTNG EQ	W 6359	27196	W 7753	34049	W 5169	25732	W 4214	20155	APPAR SANITAIRES CHAUFFAGE
8124	LIGHTING EQUIPMENT NES	W 3359	21052	W 4039	24233	W 3662	22505	W 2928	17578	APPAREILS ECLAIRAGE ETC
81242	LAMPS,FITTINGS BASE METL	W 3237	20013	W 3841	22774	W 3397	20115	W 2850	16996	APPAREILS D'ECLAIRAGE
821	*FURNITURE,PARTS THEREOF	W 18952	76956	W 17825	71055	W 17503	72447	W 11134	41747	MEUBLES ET PIECES
8219	FURNITURE AND PARTS NES	W 17886	69163	W 16269	61108	W 16416	65429	W 10549	38132	AUTRES MEUBLES ET PIECES
82191	METAL FURNITURE NES	W 4603	20003	W 5809	23005	W 5843	23896	W 1380	5435	MEUBLES NDA EN METAL
82192	WOOD FURNITURE NES	W 12607	46932	W 9971	36531	W 10427	41030	W 9164	32679	MEUBLES NDA EN BOIS
84	CLOTHING AND ACCESSORIES		515944		134638		88190		165767	VETEMENTS
842	MENS OUTERWEAR NOT KNIT	W 9300	203263	W 3357	70239	W 1766	40856	W 3956	79007	VET DESSUS POUR HOMMES
8421	— OVERCOATS,OTHER COATS	W 9300	203263	W 3357	70239	W 1766	40856	W 3956	79007	MANTEAUX HOMMES MAT TEXT
84211	—— OF WOOL,FINE HAIR	W 9300	203263	W 3357	70239	W 1766	40856	W 3956	79007	MANTEAUX HOMMES DE LAINE
843	WOMENS OUTERWEAR NONKNIT	W 6059	179068	W 804	24077	W 991	30581	W 1843	54986	VET DESSUS FEMMES MAT TEX
8431	— COATS AND JACKETS	W 6059	179068	W 804	24077	W 991	30581	W 1843	54986	MANT,VEST FEM MAT TEXTIL
84311	—— OF WOOL,FINE HAIR	W 6059	179068	W 804	24077	W 991	30581	W 1843	54986	MANT,VEST FEMMES LAINE
844	UNDER GARMENTS NOT KNIT	W 1779	40030	W 508	10804	W 126	3199	W 221	5674	VETEMENT DESSOUS MAT TEX
845	OUTERWEAR KNIT NONELASTC	W 2431	63428	W 571	14244	W 287	7568	W 644	16786	VET DESSOUS,ACCES BONNET
8451	— JERSEYS,PULLOVERS ETC	W 1237	30820	W 291	6964	W 101	2607	W 276	6798	CHANDAILS,PULL–OVERS ETC
8452	— WOMENS DRESSES ETC	W 971	27175	W 167	4625	W 52	1556	W 213	6139	ROBES,JUPES BONNETERIE
851	*FOOTWEAR		52949		42445	P 3437847	52413		32738	CHAUSSURES
85102	FOOTWEAR LEATHER	P 2890396	42457	P 2731305	39871	P 2782472	44279	P 1925917	29126	CHAUS SEMELLES EN CUIR
87	PRECISION INSTRUMNTS NES		101067		102966		118278		100754	INSTRUM,APPAR SCIENT NDA
872	MEDICAL INSTRUMENTS NES	W 886	33359	W 535	19891	W 788	31152	W 581	22446	INSTR,APP MEDIC–CHIR NDA
87202	OTH MEDICAL INSTRUMENTS	W 801	28557	W 473	16511	W 737	28113	W 476	16375	INSTRUM,APP MEDECINE
874	MEASURNG,CONTROLNG INSTR	W 2082	64421	W 2796	75166	W 2771	81397	W 2031	62675	INSTRUMENTS DE MESURE
8745	MEAS,CONTRL,SCI INST NES	W 1185	23560	W 1696	35220	W 1773	45072	W 941	21252	APP SCIENT MESURE NDA
87452	INSTRMNTS ETC FR DEMONST	W 1143	21995	W 1606	32361	W 1444	33392	W 762	15006	INSTR POUR DEMONSTRATION
88	PHOTO EQU,OPTICL GDS ETC		29933		25474		27797		15702	APP,FOURN PHOTO,OP,MONTR
882	PHOTO,CINEMA SUPPLIES	W 2727	19605	W 961	9070	W 660	7271	W 700	7085	PRODUITS PHOTO,CINEMA
89	MISC MANUFCTRD GOODS NES		208650		129193		136174		112181	ART MANUFACTURES DIVERS
892	PRINTED MATTER		35965		24587		27774		33562	IMPRIMES
8921	PRINTED BOOKS,GLOBES,ETC		32516		19142		19989		29146	LIVRES,BROCHURES,CARTES
89211	PRINTED BOOKS,PAMPHLETS	N 3791982	32498	N 2423106	19037	N 1890328	18512	N 3312285	28958	LIVRES,BROCHURES
893	ARTICLES OF PLASTIC NES	W 24590	92042	W 19293	71747	W 19321	76489	W 14125	54962	OUVRAGES EN MAT DIVIS 58
8939	MISC PLASTIC ARTICLES	W 24590	92042	W 19293	71747	W 19321	76489	W 14125	54962	ART DIVERS EN MAT DIV 58
897	GOLD,SILVER WARE,JEWELRY		45128		4		37		17	BIJOUTERIE,ORFEVRERIE
8973	PREC JEWLRY,GLD–SILVWARE		45128							BIJOUX OR,ARGENT ORFEVRE
89732	GOLD,SILVER,ETC WARE		45128							ORFEVRERIE MET PRECIEUX
9	GOODS NOT CLASSD BY KIND		67277		28261		19437		18252	ART TRANSACT NON CLASSES

4. General Imports C.I.F. by Commodities according to the S.I.T.C. (Rev. 2) in thousand U.S. Dollars
Importations Générales C.A.F. par Produits d'après la C.T.C.I. (Rév. 2) en milliers de Dollars E.U.

SITC CTCI	COMMODITY	1988			1989			1990			1991			PRODUIT
		WEIGHT POIDS		VALUE VALEUR	WEIGHT POIDS		VALUE VALEUR	WEIGHT POIDS		VALUE VALEUR	WEIGHT POIDS		VALUE VALEUR	
971	*GOLD,NON MONETARY NES	K	4725	67277	K	7423	28138	K	1500	19340	K	1540	18252	OR NON MONETAIRE
97101	NONMON GLD UNWRT,SEMIMFD	K	4725	67277	K	2200	27900	K	1500	19340	K	1540	18252	OR,ALLIAGES D'OR BRUTS

5. General Exports F.O.B. by Commodities according to the S.I.T.C. (Rev. 2) in thousand U.S. Dollars
Exportations Générales F.O.B. par Produits d'après la C.T.C.I. (Rév. 2) en milliers de Dollars E.U.

SITC CTCI	COMMODITY	1988		1989		1990		1991		PRODUIT
		WEIGHT POIDS	VALUE VALEUR	WEIGHT POIDS	VALUE VALEUR	WEIGHT POIDS	VALUE VALEUR	WEIGHT POIDS	VALUE VALEUR	
	ALL COMMODITIES		6683242		8240262		13876843		11211715	TOUS PRODUITS
0	FOOD AND LIVE ANIMALS						49334		52735	ALIMENTS,ANIMAUX VIVANTS
2	CRUDE MATERLS,EXCL FUELS		1070		1528		75868		21560	MAT BRUTES NON COMESTIBLES
28	METALLIFEROUS ORES,SCRAP						44820			MINERAIS METAL,DECHETS
287	BASE METAL ORES,CONC NES					W 40070	44755			MINERAIS METAUX COMMUNS
2879	OTH NONFER ORE,CONCNTRTE					W 40070	44755			MINERAIS D'AUTRES METAUX
3	MINERAL FUELS ETC		6273938		7850725		13097960		10697737	COMBUSTIBLES MINERAUX LUB
33	PETROLEUM AND PRODUCTS		6201682		7748049		12978368		10548676	PETROLE ET DERIVES
333	CRUDE PETROLEUM	MW 44851	5364496	MW 50518	6782556	MW 61122	11431668	MW 65894	9483481	HUILES BRUTES DE PETROLE
334	PETROLEUM PRODUCTS,REFIN	W 7226438	837187	W 6991742	965492	W 8086212	1546700	W 7250479	1065195	PRODUITS RAFFINES
3341	GASOLINE,OTH LIGHT OILS	W 770977	142335	W 713834	150412					ESSENCES POUR MOTEURS
33412	SPIRIT TYPE JET FUEL	W 770977	142335	W 713834	150412					CARBUREACTEURS
3342	KEROSENE,OTH MEDIUM OILS			W 57371	9866	W 859980	219218	W 803953	128593	PETR LAMPANTS,AUT HUIL
33421	KEROSENE INCL JET FUEL			W 57371	9866	W 859980	219218	W 803953	128593	PETROLES LAMPANTS
3343	GAS OILS	W 1230418	167455	W 1489453	198373					GAS OILS
3344	FUEL OILS,NES	W 5225043	527398	W 4731085	606841	W 7226233	1327481	W 6446526	936602	FUEL OILS
341	*GAS,NATURAL AND MANUFCT		72256	W 63730	102676	W 107463	119592	W 489983	149061	GAZ NATUREL,GAZ MANUFACT
3413	PETROLM GASES,LIQUEFIED			W 63730	102676	W 55074	118990	W 70781	145077	GAZ DE PETROLE LIQUEFIE
34131	LIQUEFIED PROPANE,BUTANE			W 63730	102676	W 55074	118990	W 70781	145077	PROPANE,BUTANE LIQUEFIES
3414	PETROLEUM GASES, GASEOUS		72256			W 52389	602	W 419202	3985	GAZ DE PETROLE GAZEUX
5	CHEMCLS,RELATED PROD NES		408116		387985		524710		375844	PRODUITS CHIMIQUES
51	ORGANIC CHEMICALS		331481		311334		439776		272157	PROD CHIMIQ ORGANIQUES
511	HYDROCARBONS NES,DERIVS	W 768000	234469	W 845904	233481	W 918187	363335	W 851831	197810	HYDROCARBURES NDA
5111	ACYCLIC HYDROCARBONS	W 397888	176634	W 442019	185895	W 484673	256204	W 403993	118892	HYDROCARBURES ACYCLIQUES
5112	CYCLIC HYDROCARBONS	W 370112	57835	W 403885	47586	W 433515	107131	W 447838	78918	HYDROCARBURES CYCLIQUES
512	ALCOHOLS,PHENOLS ETC	W 620540	97013	W 504737	77853	W 735631	76441	W 665074	74347	PHENOLS,PHENOLS–ALCOOLS
5121	ACYCLIC ALCOHOLS,DERIVS	W 620540	97013	W 504737	77853	W 735631	76441	W 665074	74347	ALCOOLS ACYCLIQUES
52	INORGANIC CHEMICALS		45634		36856		37413		17279	PROD CHIM INORGANIQUES
523	OTHR INORG CHEMICALS ETC	W 33235	34709	W 29936	24344	W 35255	22447			AUT PRODUITS CHIMIQUES INORG
5231	METAL CMPD OF INORG ACID	W 33235	34709	W 29936	24344	W 35255	22447			SELS METALLIQUES
562	*FERTILIZERS,MANUFACTURE	W 325611	31001	W 387125	39795	W 190710	25383	W 462794	59067	ENGRAIS MANUFACTURES
5621	CHEM NITROGENOUS FERTLZR	W 325611	31001	W 387125	39795	W 190710	25383	W 462794	59067	ENGRAIS AZOTES
56216	UREA	W 325611	31001	W 387125	39795	W 190710	25383	W 462794	59067	UREE
6	BASIC MANUFACTURES				20		112147		53680	ART MANUFACTURES
67	IRON AND STEEL						80487		48929	FER ET ACIER
674	IRN,STL UNIV,PLATE,SHEET					W 51953	50095			LARGES PLATS,TOLES
6741	IRON OR STEEL UNIVERSALS					W 51953	50095			LARGES PLATS FER,ACIER

1. HISTORICAL SERIES, 1992–1996 GENERAL TRADE, IMPORTS C.I.F., EXPORTS F.O.B.
SERIES HISTORIQUES, 1992–1996 COMMERCE GENERAL, IMPORTATIONS C.A.F., EXPORTATIONS F.O.B

YEAR ANNEE	VALUE IN MILLION U.S. DOLLARS VALEUR EN MILLION U.S. DOLLARS MERCHANDISE – MARCHANDISE		GOLD – OR		CONVERSION FACTORS FACTEURS DE CONVERSION CENTS E.U. PAR		INDEX NUMBERS – INDICES QUANTUM		UNIT VALUE VALEUR UNITAIRE	
	IMPORTS	EXPORTS	IMPORTS	EXPORTS	IMPORTS	EXPORTS	IMPORTS	EXPORTS	IMPORTS	EXPORTS
1992	601.90	852.30								
1993	2283.50	2029.12								
1994	2353.25	2028.58								
1995	3648.50	2705.00								
1996	4558.75	3355.00								

2. IMPORTS BY BROAD ECONOMIC CATEGORY AND EXPORTS BY INDUSTRIAL ORIGIN. (PERCENTAGE OF TOTAL VALUE)
IMPORTATIONS PAR CATEGORIES ECONOMIQUES ET EXPORTATIONS PAR BRANCHE D'ACTIVITE.(EN POURCENTAGE DE LA VALEUR TOTALE)

IMPORTS – IMPORTATIONS

	1990	1991	1992	1993	1994	1995	1996
TOTAL IMPORTS–IMPORTATIONS TOTALES			100.		100.		
1 FOOD BEV–ALIMENTATION BOISSONS			6.2		8.5		
11 PRIMARY–PRODUITS DE BASE			4.4		3.6		
111 FOR INDUSTRY–POUR L'INDUSTRIE			4.1		0.8		
112 FOR HOUSEHOLDS–POUR LES MENAGES			0.3		2.8		
12 PROCESSED–PRODUITS ELABORES			1.8		4.9		
121 FOR INDUSTRY–POUR L'INDUSTRIE			0.4		1.5		
122 FOR HOUSEHOLDS–POUR LES MENAGES			1.4		3.5		
2 IND SUPPLIES–APPROV INDUSTRIELS			28.9		25.7		
21 PRIMARY–PRODUITS DE BASE			5.9		3.5		
22 PROCESSED–PRODUITS ELABORES			23.0		22.2		
3 FUELS–COMBUSTIBLES			44.5		31.4		
31 PRIMARY–PRODUITS DE BASE			38.9		6.7		
32 PROCESSED–PRODUITS ELABORES			5.6		24.7		
321 MOTOR SPIRIT–ESSENCE							
322 OTHER–AUTRES			5.6		24.7		
4 MACHINERY–EQUIPEMENT			8.2		15.8		
41 CAPITAL EQUIPMENT–MACHINES			7.3		13.9		
42 PARTS–PIECES ACCESSOIRES			0.9		1.9		
5 TRANSPORT–TRANSPORT			1.7		6.7		
51 PASSENGER CARS–AUTOMOBILES			0.3		1.7		
52 OTHER–AUTRES			0.7		2.6		
521 INDUSTRIAL–INDUSTRIELS			0.6		2.6		
522 NON INDUSTRIAL–NON INDUSTRIEL			0.1		0.0		
53 PARTS–PIECES ACCESSOIRES			0.7		2.4		
6 CONSUM GOODS–BIENS CONSOMMATION			9.4		10.7		
61 DURABLE–DURABLES			2.4		2.2		
62 SEMI DURABLE–SEMI DURABLES			4.3		3.8		
63 NON DURABLE–NON DURABLES			2.7		4.8		
7 GOODS NES–BIENS NDA			1.1		1.1		

EXPORTS – EXPORTATIONS

	1990	1991	1992	1993	1994	1995	1996
TOTAL EXPORTS–EXPORTATIONS TOTALES			100.		100.		
1 AGRICULTURE			4.2		7.0		
2 MINING QUARRY–INDUS EXTRACTIVES			1.2		2.3		
3 MANUFACTURING–IND MANUFACTUR			94.6		90.7		
31 FOOD BEV TOBACCO–ALIM BOISS TAB			19.8		18.6		
32 TEXTILES–INDUSTRIES TEXTILES			19.4		13.0		
33 WOOD & PRODUCTS–BOIS & PRODUITS			0.4		2.7		
34 PAPER & PRODUCTS–PAPIER & PRODT			1.5		1.7		
35 CHEMICALS–INDUSTRIES CHIMIQUES			12.7		26.8		
36 NON METAL MIN–MIN NON METAL			2.0		1.7		
37 BASIC METAL–IND METAL BASE			0.7		3.6		
38 METAL MANUF–MANUF METAL			27.8		21.2		
39 OTH MANUF IND–AUTRES MANUF			10.3		1.5		

3. TRADE BY PRINCIPAL COUNTRIES OF PRODUCTION AND CONSIGNMENT (VALUE IN THOUSAND U.S. DOLLARS)
ECHANGES SELON LES PRINCIPAUX PAYS DE PRODUCTION ET DE CONSIGNATION (VALEUR EN MILLIERS DE DOLLARS EU)

COUNTRIES–PAYS	GENERAL IMPORTS C.I.F. IMPORTATIONS GENERALES C.A.F				
	1992	1993	1994	1995	1996
World	805776	2274495	2589000	3648554	4404544
Africa	417	859	3896	6314	1026
Americas	22682	34658	58982	123335	142874
Northern America	22677	31733	53837	84799	118690
LAIA		1973	4240	31472	5067
CACM		673	396	424	324
Caribbean	1	279	360	5455	17003
Rest of America	4		150	1184	1789
As.ex F.USSR	3579	28854	26647	58871	124782
Eur.x F.USSR	88548	620912	1072006	1740127	2436828
EU	72173	499576	828448	1354331	1877764
EFTA	4018	33009	48642	87835	141804
East Europe	12274	85727	187934	288690	403031
Other Europe		116	30	148	2182
Former USSR	675272	1586636	1388296	1651097	1687837
Oceania	186	1416	1829	2709	5631
Russian Federation	464928	1220236	995215	1076251	1144949
Germany/Allemagne	37727	219436	353891	521820	691069
Ukraine	61915	141439	128716	134221	140927
Poland/Pologne	8471	49793	102526	154452	223625
Belarus/Bélarus	46954	75629	97856	133117	104646
Denmark/Danemark	1976	55550	66620	127277	167426
Finland/Finlande	7049	29110	74817	120753	163947
Latvia/Lettonie	18256	33288	69839	114773	142987
United Kingdom	4681	21240	35934	112761	176654
Netherlands/Pays–Bas	2038	51975	69485	93971	123598
Italy/Italie	1915	41714	70618	86302	139602
Sweden/Suède	9206	24885	60933	103039	138105
USA/Etats–Unis d'Amer	22141	26788	50759	69790	92790
Estonia/Estonie	4634	18060	40666	65524	97374
Switz.Liecht	3992	29992	30944	55753	101587
France,Monac	1288	15855	45307	59581	94297
Czech Republic		15553	37256	61134	80934
Kazakhstan	26087	46659	16628	65569	23536
Belgium–Luxembourg	3221	14973	19522	54679	77697
Hungary/Hongrie	1406	10957	21443	40497	61301
Austria/Autriche	2224	19406	15454	36676	45055
Uzbekistan/Ouzbékistan	19365	10121	18812	27249	14151
Norway,SVD,JM	25	2902	17192	31025	37736
Korea, Republic of	6	1300	2374	7345	50006
Slovakia		3900	14516	20142	22040
Republic of Moldova	18256	9703	5621	10366	8345
Canada	536	4944	3077	15009	25900
Spain/Espagne	597	2762	6750	13998	23729
Turkey/Turquie	22	16458	3951	9747	11973
Tajikistan/Tadjikistan	314	16714	7387	10129	7062
Bulgaria/Bulgarie	145	4991	9658	11376	13298
Ireland/Irlande	251	882	2081	6617	28938
Japan/Japon		5455	5460	8907	11271
Slovenia/Slovénia	80	2321	6340	8758	11116
Ecuador/Equateur		766	2540	20783	2442
Portugal			5705	14498	4999
Azerbaijan	2955	6987	4512	4593	1960
Cyprus/Chypre	2622	93	2489	6799	7654
British Virgin Islds			250	5345	13154
Hong Kong		302	301	4546	12772
Israel/Israël	331	1741	2275	6578	6643
United Arab Emirates		789	2091	4350	9475
Turkmenistan/Turkménistn	3875	2252	2113	5557	1184
India/Inde	20	696	2661	4308	5072
Australia/Australie	186	1021	1306	2607	5511
Kyrgyzstan/Kirghizistan	4141	2414	862	753	219
Greece/Grèce		1787	1332	2360	2646
Georgia/Géorgie	2274	2414	33	2924	479
Morocco/Maroc			2136	5802	60
Brazil/Brésil		70	542	6352	

COUNTRIES–PAYS	GENERAL EXPORTS F.O.B. EXPORTATIONS GENERALES F.O.B.				
	1992	1993	1994	1995	1996
Monde	805014	2024700	2029000	2705670	3279706
Afrique	399	6581	22212	3555	1875
Amériques	4932	13929	23794	32282	40211
Amérique du Nord	4545	9301	17809	22090	30878
ALAI	37	1209	4735	7519	4951
MCAC		23	68	44	54
Caraïbes	350	3209	955	2390	3390
Autre Amérique		186	227	238	938
Asie l'URSS exclus	8251	44973	33103	56801	76353
Europe l'URSS exclus	228937	603224	772125	1216720	1293747
UE	169810	398545	605943	983503	1095990
AELE	7928	14255	19271	85986	52113
Europe de l'Est	50616	189959	144695	145263	142011
Autre de l'Europe			60	363	942
Ancienne URSS	562478	1354598	1163255	1395445	1862843
Océanie	17	953	621	223	470
Russian Federation	228205	670799	569005	551928	780293
Germany/Allemagne	37113	137662	229220	389165	427616
Belarus/Bélarus	97368	149103	131681	291027	331907
Ukraine	125275	227305	123981	202810	251167
Latvia/Lettonie	38371	147824	170618	191163	304316
Poland/Pologne	33427	141382	101481	104792	103877
Netherlands/Pays–Bas	18853	56669	106069	132371	104494
United Kingdom	27978	31672	46742	84426	111459
Estonia/Estonie	12252	50879	51215	60395	81796
Sweden/Suède	22971	35532	62687	68799	55523
Denmark/Danemark	18973	30323	35092	72016	83702
Italy/Italie	7717	43670	38273	52411	85433
Kazakhstan	12589	38903	42205	34212	29683
France,Monac	11107	16812	24093	45806	50542
Switz.Liecht	6597	9278	6922	66355	37024
Uzbekistan/Ouzbékistan	16094	16231	17288	26549	43886
Finland/Finlande	10918	17626	19379	29076	31663
Belgium–Luxembourg	10480	13720	15735	28419	33092
Spain/Espagne	322	8441	17799	22363	32454
Ireland/Irlande	486	1000	1765	30515	41336
Hungary/Hongrie	7412	18510	17356	13590	13565
USA/Etats–Unis d'Amer	2721	5186	12876	20229	24678
Turkey/Turquie	2361	5046	3561	25661	25211
Republic of Moldova	10114	13115	12594	13539	10125
Norway,SVD,JM	1331	3907	12118	16555	14563
Azerbaijan	8408	17324	9298	5223	5918
Czech Republic		8371	12165	10004	13598
Austria/Autriche	1994	4046	5616	13589	17493
Bulgaria/Bulgarie	3313	12022	7621	11060	7630
Turkmenistan/Turkménistn	4809	13162	11537	4285	7608
Korea, Republic of		1628	1630	14766	19187
Viet Nam	418	26323	6529	1249	1029
Portugal		558	1773	12869	19614
Georgia/Géorgie	1930	1279	14405	7763	5841
Nigeria/Nigéria	13	2442	20700	98	
Japan/Japon	854	721	2924	2078	15183
Canada	1824	4116	4933	1861	6200
Romania/Roumanie	2947	6092	3783	3655	1917
Tajikistan/Tadjikistan	1513	4488	4321	2645	2387
Kyrgyzstan/Kirghizistan	2249	2628	2946	2419	4820
Armenia/Arménie	3301	1558	2162	1487	3096
China/Chine	1	7930	2613	345	192
Slovakia		3535	2289	2119	1423
Hong Kong	1	70	3610	4663	876
Greece/Grèce	898	814	1700	1679	1568
Philippines		535	1199	205	4399
Cyprus/Chypre	3236	419	1370	732	331
India/Inde		23	1624	2941	1143
Pakistan	366	302	1795	737	2409
Peru/Pérou		512	2197	859	1470

(VALUE AS PERCENTAGE OF WORLD TOTAL)(VALEURS EN POURCENTAGE DU TOTAL MONDIAL)

	1987	1988	1989	1990	1991	1992	1993	1994	1995	1996
Africa						0.1	0.0	0.2	0.2	0.0
Americas						2.8	1.5	2.3	3.4	3.2
Northern America						2.8	1.4	2.1	2.3	2.7
LAIA							0.1	0.2	0.9	0.1
CACM							0.0	0.0	0.0	0.0
Caribbean						0.0	0.0	0.0	0.1	0.4
Rest of America						0.0		0.0	0.0	0.0
As.ex F.USSR						0.4	1.3	1.0	1.6	2.8
Eur.x F.USSR						11.0	27.3	41.4	47.7	55.3
EU						9.0	22.0	32.0	37.1	42.6
EFTA						0.5	1.5	1.9	2.4	3.2
East Europe						1.5	3.8	7.3	7.9	9.2
Other Europe							0.0	0.0	0.0	0.0
Former USSR						83.8	69.8	53.6	45.3	38.3
Oceania						0.0	0.1	0.1	0.1	0.1
Russian Federation						57.7	53.6	38.4	29.5	26.0
Germany/Allemagne						4.7	9.6	13.7	14.3	15.7
Ukraine						7.7	6.2	5.0	3.7	3.2
Poland/Pologne						1.1	2.2	4.0	4.2	5.1
Belarus/Bélarus						5.8	3.3	3.8	3.6	2.4
Denmark/Danemark						0.2	2.4	2.6	3.5	3.8
Finland/Finlande						0.9	1.3	2.9	3.3	3.7
Latvia/Lettonie						2.3	1.5	2.7	3.1	3.2
United Kingdom						0.6	0.9	1.4	3.1	4.0
Netherlands/Pays–Bas						0.3	2.3	2.7	2.6	2.8

	1987	1988	1989	1990	1991	1992	1993	1994	1995	1996
Afrique						0.0	0.3	1.1	0.1	0.1
Amériques						0.6	0.7	1.2	1.2	1.2
Amérique du Nord						0.6	0.5	0.9	0.8	0.9
ALAI						0.0	0.1	0.2	0.3	0.2
MCAC							0.0	0.0	0.0	0.0
Caraïbes						0.0	0.2	0.0	0.1	0.1
Autre Amérique							0.0	0.0	0.0	0.0
Asie l'URSS exclus						1.0	2.2	1.6	2.1	2.3
Europe l'URSS exclus						28.4	29.8	38.1	45.0	39.4
UE						21.1	19.7	29.9	36.3	33.4
AELE						1.0	0.7	0.9	3.2	1.6
Europe de l'Est						6.3	9.4	7.1	5.4	4.3
Autre de l'Europe								0.0	0.0	0.0
Ancienne URSS						69.9	66.9	57.3	51.6	56.8
Océanie						0.0	0.0	0.0	0.0	0.0
Russian Federation						28.3	33.1	28.0	20.4	23.8
Germany/Allemagne						4.6	6.8	11.3	14.4	13.0
Belarus/Bélarus						12.1	7.4	6.5	10.8	10.1
Ukraine						15.6	11.2	6.1	7.5	7.7
Latvia/Lettonie						4.8	7.3	8.4	7.1	9.3
Poland/Pologne						4.2	7.0	5.0	3.9	3.2
Netherlands/Pays–Bas						2.3	2.8	5.2	4.9	3.2
United Kingdom						3.5	1.6	2.3	3.1	3.4
Estonia/Estonie						1.5	2.5	2.5	2.2	2.5
Sweden/Suède						2.9	1.8	3.1	2.5	1.7

4. General Imports C.I.F. by Commodities according to the S.I.T.C. (Rev. 2) in thousand U.S. Dollars
Importations Générales C.A.F. par Produits d'après la C.T.C.I. (Rév. 2) en milliers de Dollars E.U.

SITC CTCI	COMMODITY	1992 WEIGHT POIDS	1992 VALUE VALEUR	1993 WEIGHT POIDS	1993 VALUE VALEUR	1994 WEIGHT POIDS	1994 VALUE VALEUR	1995 WEIGHT POIDS	1995 VALUE VALEUR	PRODUIT
	ALL COMMODITIES		805776		2274495		2589000		3648554	TOUS PRODUITS
0	FOOD AND LIVE ANIMALS		80472				168793		388904	ALIMENTS,ANIMAUX VIVANTS
01	MEAT AND PREPARATIONS		91				15567		10355	VIANDES ET PREPARATIONS
011	MEAT FRESH,CHILLD,FROZEN				2600	W 12509	12890	W 9677	9656	VIANDES FRAICHES,REF,CONGE
0113	PIG MEAT FRESH,CHLD,FRZN					W 6752	8395	W 1352	2018	VIANDE DE PORC
02	DAIRY PRODCTS,BIRDS'EGGS		697				5713		61389	PRODUITS LAITIERS,OEUFS
022	MILK AND CREAM					W 5509	3819	W 45045	53058	LAIT ET CREME
0224	MILK,CREAM PRESERVED ETC					W 4195	2358	W 42805	50677	LAIT,CREME CONS,CONC
02242	MILK DRY,1.5% FAT OR LES					W 3700	1856	W 41207	48621	LAIT POUDRE INF 1.5%
03	FISH AND PREPARATIONS		1024		14160		22235		38716	POISSONS ET PREPARATIONS
034	FISH,FRESH,CHILLED,FROZN					W 26452	15578	W 52110	33018	POISSON FRAIS, REFRIG,CONG
0342	FISH FROZEN,EXCL FILLETS					W 20179	10980	W 44243	26020	POISSONS CONGELES
04	CEREALS AND PREPARATIONS		36880				13275		39103	CEREALES ET PRODUITS
048	CEREAL ETC PREPARATIONS				4364	W 21014	8808	W 26918	16172	PREPTNS A BASE CEREALES
05	VEGETABLES AND FRUIT		3511				51807		89136	LEGUMES ET FRUITS
054	VEG ETC FRSH,SMPLY PRSVD				1695	W 29148	9343	W 47576	14244	LEGUMES FRAIS,CONG,SECS
057	FRUIT,NUTS,FRESH,DRIED					W 56412	29890	W 133319	58670	FRUITS FRAIS OU SECS
0573	BANANA,PLANTAIN,FRSH,DRY					W 22200	11674	W 91619	36660	BANANES FRAICHES,SECHEES
058	FRUIT PRESERVED,PREPARED					W 16543	9348	W 17483	11111	CONSERVES DE FRUITS
06	SUGAR AND PREPS,HONEY		2993		11978		6320		28356	SUCRES ET PRODUITS
061	SUGAR AND HONEY					W 12154	1829	W 44536	14313	SUCRES ET MIEL
0611	RAW BEET AND CANE SUGAR					W 234	77	W 30602	10993	SUCRES BRUTS
062	SUGAR CANDY NON–CHOCLATE					W 1621	4491	W 4090	14043	SUCRERIES
07	COFFEE,TEA,COCOA,SPICES		2082		8891		23078		57993	CAFE,THE,CACAO,EPICES
071	COFFEE AND SUBSTITUTES					W 2261	8775	W 4750	26361	CAFE ET SUCCEDANES
0711	COFFEE GREEN,ROASTED,SUB					W 1869	6942	W 3753	18750	CAFE TORREFIE OU DECAFEINE
07112	COFFEE ROASTED					W 1301	5152	W 2741	14495	CAFE TORREFIE
073	CHOCOLATE AND PRODUCTS					W 1823	5653	W 4501	19793	CHOCOLAT
081	*FEEDING STUFF FOR ANIML		29885		1207	W 42812	8138	W 122741	24447	NOURRITURE POUR ANIMAUX
0813	OILCAKE AND OTH RESIDUES					W 21000	2627	W 76949	14500	TOURTEAUX
08131	— OF SOYA BEANS					W 2800	762	W 47062	11545	TOURTEAUX DE SOJA
09	MISC EDIBLE PRODUCTS		3308		6894		21249		38719	PREP ALIMENTAIRES DIVERSES
091	MARGARINE AND SHORTENING					W 18922	6727	W 20674	22143	MARGARINE ET GRAISSES
0914	MARGARINE,EDIBLE FAT NES					W 4922	4187	W 19975	21667	MARGARINES,SIMILI SAINDOUX
09141	MARGARINE					W 4100	3505	W 12624	13759	MARGARINE
098	EDIBLE PRODCTS,PREPS NES						14522		16576	PREP ALIMENTAIRES NDA
1	BEVERAGES AND TOBACCO		3966				43741		62258	BOISSONS ET TABACS
11	BEVERAGES		2484		21263		22590		31602	BOISSONS
111	NON–ALCOHL BEVERAGES NES					W 82871	8351	W 35590	11988	BOISSONS NON ALCOOLIQUES
112	ALCOHOLIC BEVERAGES					W 11574	14239	W 33431	19614	BOISSONS ALCOOLIQUES
12	TOBACCO AND MANUFACTURES		1482		24304		21151		30657	TABACS BRUTS FABRIQUES
121	TOBACCO UNMNFCTRD,REFUSE					W 3598	6026	W 6523	13023	TABACS BRUTS,DECHETS
1211	TOBACCO,NOT STRIPPED					W 2700	4477	W 6523	13023	TABACS NON ECOTES
122	TOBACCO,MANUFACTURED					W 1706	15125	W 2124	17633	TABACS FABRIQUES
1222	CIGARETTES					W 1702	15065	W 1806	16062	CIGARETTES
2	CRUDE MATERLS,EXCL FUELS		61688				123715		255110	MAT BRUTES NON COMESTIBLES
21	HIDES,SKINS,FURS UNDRSSD		1901				5936		20280	CUIRS,PEAUX BRUTS
211	HIDES,SKINS,EXC FURS,RAW					W 7409	5019	W 14880	13848	CUIRS ET PEAUX
22	OIL SEEDS,OLEAGINOUS FRT						29532		8062	GRAINES,FRUITS OLEAGINEUX
223	SEEDS FOR OTH FIXED OILS					W 112929	24365	W 8802	2154	GRAINES AUTRES HUILES FIXES
2239	OIL SEED FLOUR AND MEAL					W 110800	23113	W 8060	1188	FARINES GRAINES OLEAG
23	RUBBER, CRUDE		891				1215		14094	CAOUTCHOUC BRUT
233	RUBBER,SYNTHTIC,RECLAIMD					W 1293	1213	W 8282	13970	LATEX CAOUTCH SYNTH REGEN
2331	SYNTHETIC RUBBER ETC					W 1122	1060	W 8217	13852	LATEX CAOUTCH SYNTHETIQUE
24	CORK AND WOOD		17007				2275		3447	LIEGE ET BOIS
26	TEXTILE FIBRES AND WASTE		27283				50765		82885	FIBRES TEXTILES
263	COTTON				29156	W 19306	23328	W 22978	39533	COTON
2631	RAW COTTON,EXCL LINTERS					W 17900	22155	W 22605	39023	COTON EN MASSE
266	SYNTHETIC FIBRES TO SPIN					W 6145	8882	W 10322	18467	FIBRES SYNTHETIQUES
2665	DISCN SYNTH FIBRE UNCMBD					W 5879	8442	W 8621	14460	DISCONTINUES EN MASSE
268	WOOL(EXC TOPS),ANML HAIR					W 3089	9334	W 3019	9858	LAINES ET POILS
27	CRUDE FERTLZR,MINRLS NES		6305				26092		39385	ENGRAIS MINERAUX BRUTS
271	FERTILIZERS,CRUDE					W 295995	12850	W 413463	23313	ENGRAIS BRUTS
2713	NAT CALCM PHOSPHATES ETC					W 295300	12782	W 412196	23207	PHOSPHATES DE CALCIUM
27132	— GROUND					W 295300	12782	W 403540	23133	PHOSPHATES MOULUS
278	OTHER CRUDE MINERALS					W 178707	8482	W 172262	7103	AUTRES MINERAUX BRUTS
28	METALLIFEROUS ORES,SCRAP		724				406		67410	MINERAIS METAL,DECHETS
288	NONFERR METAL SCRAP NES					W 210	1	W 39387	59804	DECHETS NON FERREUX
2882	OTHER BASE MTL SCRAP NES							W 39148	59796	AUTRES DECHETS
28821	COPPER WASTE AND SCRAP							W 28056	49075	DECHETS DE CUIVRE
29	CRUDE ANIMAL,VEG MAT NES		2808				6361		8763	MATIERES BRUTES ANIM,VEGET
3	MINERAL FUELS ETC		358490		977679		817924		709391	COMBUSTIBLES MINERAUX LUB
32	COAL,COKE AND BRIQUETTES		30584				19092		12273	HOUILLES,COKES,BRIQUETTES
322	COAL,LIGNITE AND PEAT					W 454200	18320	W 265778	11071	HOUILLES,LIGNITES,TOURBE
3222	OTH COAL,NOT AGGLOMERATD					W 319400	13314	W 216684	9420	AUTRES HOUILLES
33	PETROLEUM AND PRODUCTS		145808				624118		506265	PETROLE ET DERIVES
333	CRUDE PETROLEUM					W 90670	8768	W 3014528	295896	HUILES BRUTES DE PETROLE
334	PETROLEUM PRODUCTS,REFIN					W 6867475	613274	W 1847820	205333	PRODUITS RAFFINES
341	*GAS,NATURAL AND MANUFCT		177220			W 1142881	150513	W 1868064	190853	GAZ NATUREL,GAZ MANUFACT
3414	PETROLEUM GASES, GASEOUS					W 1088200	144152	W 1833506	186423	GAZ DE PETROLE GAZEUX
351	*ELECTRIC CURRENT		4876			H 1482100	24201			ENERGIE ELECTRIQUE
4	ANIMAL,VEGETABLE OIL,FAT		765		10400		9688		18384	HUILES,GRAISSES ANIM,VEG
42	FIXED VEGETABLE OIL,FAT		765				6148		15753	HUILES VEGETALES FIXES
423	FIXED VEG OILS,SOFT					W 7603	5611	W 15374	14458	HUILES VEGET DOUCES FIXES
5	CHEMCLS,RELATED PROD NES		70880		147800		261998		442086	PRODUITS CHIMIQUES
51	ORGANIC CHEMICALS		8697		11212		9423		42509	PROD CHIMIQ ORGANIQUES
512	ALCOHOLS,PHENOLS ETC						1102		24783	PHENOLS,PHENOLS–ALCOOLS
5121	ACYCLIC ALCOHOLS,DERIVS						986		23955	ALCOOLS ACYCLIQUES
51215	ETHYLENE GLYCOL					W 47	41	W 38588	22335	ETHYLENE–GLYCOL
52	INORGANIC CHEMICALS		10741				31457		21729	PROD CHIM INORGANIQUES
522	INORG ELEMNTS,OXIDES,ETC					W 66664	9578	W 54814	11209	ELEMENTS INORGANIQUES
524	RADIOACTIVE ETC MATERIAL						16102		420	MATIERES RADIOACTIVES
5241	RADIOACTIVE ELEMENTS ETC						15958		18	RADIOELEMENTS,ISOTOPES
53	DYES,TANNING,COLOUR PROD		4912		10609		26683		43424	PROD TEINTURE,COLORANTS
533	PIGMENTS,PAINTS,ETC					W 15201	20767	W 20573	36883	PIGMENTS,PEINTURES,VERNIS
5334	VARNISHES,DISTEMPERS ETC					W 11107	15761	W 13076	25651	PEINTURES A L'EAU
53342	OTH PAINTS,VARNISHES ETC					W 7784	11337	W 10021	20644	AUTRES PEINTURES,VERNIS
541	*MEDICINAL,PHARM PRODUCT		5091		49537	K 5674514	88271	MK 9045	109029	PROD MEDICINAUX PHARMACEUT
5417	MEDICAMENTS					K 4151800	73652	K 5103477	90875	MEDICAMENTS
54171	— CONTAINNG ANTIBIOTICS					K 1629000	29015	K 1041325	24767	MED CONTN ANTIBIOTIQUES
54172	— CONTAINING HORMONES					K 672700	12665	K 454069	10090	MED CONTENANT HORMONES

4. General Imports C.I.F. by Commodities according to the S.I.T.C. (Rev. 2) in thousand U.S. Dollars
Importations Générales C.A.F. par Produits d'après la C.T.C.I. (Rév. 2) en milliers de Dollars E.U.

SITC CTCI	COMMODITY	1992 WEIGHT POIDS	1992 VALUE VALEUR	1993 WEIGHT POIDS	1993 VALUE VALEUR	1994 WEIGHT POIDS	1994 VALUE VALEUR	1995 WEIGHT POIDS	1995 VALUE VALEUR	PRODUIT
54179	— CONTNG OTH SUBSTANCES					K 1767100	30856	K 3436456	53957	MED CONT AUT SUBSTANCES
55	PERFUME,CLEANING ETC PRD		2307		9703		26846		45239	PROD POUR PARFUM,TOILETTE
553	PERFUMERY,COSMETICS,ETC					W 3799	15860	W 6837	30315	PRODUITS DE PARFUMERIE
554	SOAP,CLEANSING ETC PREPS					W 8663	10241	W 11293	13556	SAVONS,PRODUITS DETERSIFS
5542	WASHING PREPARATIONS ETC					W 7955	8835	W 10008	11041	PROD ORG TENSIO-ACT NDA
562	*FERTILIZERS,MANUFACTURE		691		16621	W 190091	13591	W 260848	16703	ENGRAIS MANUFACTURES
5621	CHEM NITROGENOUS FERTLZR					W 120091	9120	W 95820	7066	ENGRAIS AZOTES
58	PLASTIC MATERIALS ETC		7778				41417		109400	MAT PLAST ARTIFICIELLES
582	PROD OF CONDENSATION ETC					W 8492	7169	W 7995	12919	PROD CONDENS,POLYCOND
583	POLYMERIZATION ETC PRODS					W 28098	23695	W 89250	78602	PROD POLYMERISATION
5831	POLYETHYLENE					W 13484	6739	W 63154	43914	POLYETHYLENE
58311	— IN PRIMARY FORMS					W 11875	5275	W 60408	41811	POLYETHYLENE PRIMAIRES
5833	POLYSTYRENE,ITS COPOLYMR					W 6348	6056	W 14655	14628	POLYPROPYLENE COPOLYMERES
58331	— IN PRIMARY FORMS					W 6173	5677	W 14290	13707	SOUS FORMES PRIMAIRES
584	CELLULOSE DERIVATIVS ETC					W 4757	10543	W 7976	17841	CEL REGEN NIT ACETATE
5843	CELLULOSE ACETATES					W 4646	10253	W 7864	17489	ACETATES DE CELLULOSE
58432	— PLASTICIZED					W 4449	9928	W 7396	16408	ACETAT CELLULOSE PLASTIF
59	CHEMICAL MATERIALS NES		30663				24107		53917	MAT PROD CHIMIQUES NDA
592	STARCH,INULIN,GLUTEN,ETC				9100	W 8224	7119	W 18293	31145	AMIDONS,INUL,GLUT FROM
5922	ALBUMINOID SUBSTAN,GLUES					W 7214	6976	W 16316	30181	MAT ALBUMIN,COLLES
59221	CASEIN AND DERIVATVS,ETC				1	W 2114	2789	W 8372	24210	CASEINES,CASEINATES
598	MISCEL CHEM PRODUCTS NES					W 8394	14039	W 9546	15524	PROD DIV INDUST CHIM NDA
5989	CHEM PRODUCTS,PREPS NES					W 6610	13003	W 7452	12195	PROD PREP CHIMIQUES NDA
6	BASIC MANUFACTURES		86456				390167		645694	ART MANUFACTURES
61	LEATHER,DRESSED FUR,ETC		672				5770		14164	CUIRS,PELLETERIES
62	RUBBER MANUFACTURES NES		2404				15054		29335	CAOUTCHOUC MANUFACTURE
625	RUBBER TYRES, TUBES ETC						10006	N 1305796	20687	PNEUS CAOUTCHOUC VULCANISE
63	WOOD,CORK MANUFACTRS NES		160				17912		24056	OUVRAGES LIEGE ET BOIS
634	VENEERS,PLYWOOD,ETC						9177		15980	PLACAGES,CONTRE-PLAQUES
635	WOOD MANUFACTURES NES					W 7903	8689	W 6278	7849	ART MANUF EN BOIS NDA
6353	BUILDERS WOODWRK,PREFABS					W 4211	7841	W 3742	6911	OUVRAGES DE MENUISERIE
64	PAPER,PAPERBOARD AND MFR		4194				45804		83660	PAPIERS,CARTONS & OUVRAGES
641	PAPER AND PAPERBOARD					W 55901	31926	W 56591	50388	PAPIERS ET CARTONS
642	PAPER,ETC,PRECUT,ARTS OF					W 9127	13878	W 15000	33272	PAP,CARTONS DECOUPES
6421	PAPER ETC CONTAINERS					W 5877	5082	W 10156	16042	BOITES,SACS EMBALLAGES
6428	PAPER ETC ARTICLES NES					W 2107	5541	W 3006	11605	OUVRAGES EN PATE A PAPIER
65	TEXTILE YARN,FABRICS,ETC		25763				105527		190758	FILS,TISSUS,ARTICLES TEXTILE
651	TEXTILE YARN					W 8973	28204	W 10038	50275	FILS TEXTILES
6513	COTTON YARN					W 3116	8617	W 2875	9333	FILS DE COTON
6514	SYN FIB YRN,BULK,MONOFIL					W 3650	11429	W 3562	15463	FILS CONT 85% FIB TEXT SYNTH
6517	REGEN FIBRE YARN,MONOFIL					W 638	2085	W 1173	12943	FILS TEXT ART NON VENTE DT
65171	CONT VISCOSE RAYON YARN					W 398	1244	W 1035	12515	FILS RAY,VIS NON VENTE DET
652	COTTON FABRICS,WOVEN					W 2795	12492	W 4379	22835	TISSUS DE COTON
6522	WOVEN COTTON BLEACHD,ETC					W 1568	9916	W 1580	14673	TISSUS COTON BLANCHIS ETC
653	WOVN MAN-MADE FIB FABRIC					W 2323	27432	W 4250	50839	TISSUS FIBRES SYNTH,ARTIF
6534	DISC SYN BLEND FABRC NES					W 746	8128	W 1198	14299	TISSUS FIBRES SYNTH DISCONT
654	OTH WOVEN TEXTILE FABRIC					W 804	10314	W 1174	17542	TISSUS AUT COTON SYNT,ARTIF
655	KNITTED,ETC FABRICS				2414	W 1727	7311	W 14301	12341	ETOF BONNETERIE PIECES ETC
6552	OTHER KNIT ETC FAB NONEL					W 1727	7311	W 14301	12341	ETOF BON NON ELAS NON SYNT
656	LACE,RIBBONS,TULLE,ETC				10214	W 185	2058	W 148	4263	TULLES,BRODERIE
657	SPECIAL TXTL FABRC,PRODS				1648		9061	W 2914	14451	TISSUS SPECIAUX
66	NONMETAL MINERAL MFS NES		7924		15553		33738		51413	ART MIN NON METALLIQUES
662	CLAY,REFRACTORY BLDG PRD						8256		13798	MAT CONST REFRACTAIRES
6624	BRICKS ETC NONREFRACTORY						6354		12796	BRIQUES ETC CERAM NON REFR
66245	GLAZED CERAMIC SETTS ETC						5406	A 1918	10961	AUT CARREAUX CERAMIQUE
67	IRON AND STEEL		20688		81433		96336		146241	FER ET ACIER
672	IRON,STEEL PRIMARY FORMS					W 33720	5808	W 234490	44843	LINGOTS FER,ACIER
6727	IRN,STL COIL FR REROLLNG					W 18557	3041	W 218860	40982	EBAUCHES POUR TOLES FER
67271	IRON,SIMPLE STEEL COILS					W 16660	2567	W 210544	38577	EBAUCHES NON EN ACIER
673	IRON,STEEL SHAPES ETC					W 124422	43319	W 58668	16976	BARRES,PROFIL FER,ACIER
6732	IRON,STEEL BARS ETC					W 88644	36319	W 24013	6891	BARRES FER,ACIER
67326	IRN,OTH STL BARS HOTROLD					W 79052	33932	W 10406	2617	BARRES PLEINES FER,ACIER
674	IRN,STL UNIV,PLATE,SHEET					W 54611	16299	W 139101	53707	LARGES PLATS,TOLES
6744	IRN,STL HVY PLATE,ROLLED					W 13720	4285	W 37027	11155	TOLES LAMINEES PLUS 4.75 MM
6747	TINNED PLATES,SHEETS					W 5874	2035	W 22457	13983	TOLES ETAMEES EN ACIER
678	IRON,STL TUBES,PIPES,ETC					W 25517	14735	W 26725	21500	TUBES,TUYAUX EN FONTE,FER
68	NON-FERROUS METALS		10943				24328		36937	METAUX NON FERREUX
682	COPPER EXC CEMENT COPPER					W 4173	10014	W 3876	10634	CUIVRE
684	ALUMINIUM					W 3707	11273	W 8704	22068	ALUMINIUM
6842	ALUMINIUM,ALLOYS WORKED					W 2759	10556	W 3603	15492	ALUMINIUM,ALLIAGES OUVRE
69	METAL MANUFACTURES NES		13707				45698		69130	ART MANUFACT EN METAL NDA
691	STRUCTURES AND PARTS NES					W 7279	9640	W 9274	16426	CONSTRUCT FER,ACIER,ALU
6911	STRUCTURES,PARTS IRN,STL					W 6663	5595	W 8601	11176	CONSTRUCT FER,ACIER,FONTE
697	BASE MTL HOUSEHOLD EQUIP						6383		10982	ART MENAGE MET COMMUNS
699	BASE METAL MFRS NES					W 7727	12847	W 6704	20566	ART MANUFACTURES MET NDA
7	MACHINES,TRANSPORT EQUIP		119382		427173		567008		791661	MACHINES MATERIEL TRANSPORT
71	POWER GENERATING EQUIPMT		122				19571		23658	MACHINES GENERATRICES
713	INTRNL COMBUS PSTN ENGIN						8535		14824	MOTEURS EXPL COMB INT, PIECE
72	MACHS FOR SPCL INDUSTRYS		38608				122516		115996	MAC SPECIALES POUR INDUST
721	AGRIC MACHY,EXC TRACTORS						10346		11956	MACHINES AGRICOLES
722	TRACTORS NON-ROAD					N 2809	9563	N 1759	10355	TRACTEURS
7224	WHEELED TRACTORS NES					N 2806	9315	N 1743	10200	TRACTEURS A ROUES
724	TEXTILE,LEATHER MACHNRY						25436		22315	MACH POUR INDUSTRIE TEXTILE
7247	TEXTILE MACHINERY NES						8277		5737	MACH LAVAGE,TEINTURE TEX
726	PRINTG,BKBINDG MACHY,PTS						8350		5689	MACHINES POUR IMPRIMERIE
727	FOOD MACHRY NON-DOMESTIC						13305		22898	MACH INDUSTRIES ALIMENT
7272	OTH FOOD PROC MCHY,PARTS						12857		21784	AUT MACH IND ALIMENTAIRE
72722	INDUS FOOD PROC MACH NES						10605	N 99162	14579	MACHINES BOULANGERIE
728	OTH MACHY FOR SPCL INDUS						43510		37468	AUT MACH IND PARTICULIERES
7281	MACH-TOOLS FR SPCL INDUS						20803		13920	MACH-OUTILS SPEC IND PART
72812	MACH-TOOLS TO WORK WOOD						19123	N 2430	11378	MACH-OUT POUR TRAVAIL BOIS
7284	MACHY FOR SPCL INDUS NES						19442		22782	MACH SPEC IND PARTICUL.
72848	OTH MCHY WITH INDIV FNCT						4986		11217	AUTRES MACHINES NDA
74	GENRL INDUSTRL MACHY NES		13957				92606		100744	MACH APP INDUSTRIE
741	HEATING,COOLING EQUIPMNT						50412		27207	MACH CHAUFFAGE,PIECES
7414	NONDOM REFRIG EQUIPT,PTS						8385		13542	MAT PRODUCTION DU FROID
74141	REFRIG EQUIP NONDOMESTIC						7410	N 23556	11272	REFIG INDUSTRIELS
7416	HEATING,COOLING EQU NES						33676	N 73724	8564	APP CHANGEMENT TEMP
742	PUMPS FOR LIQUIDS ETC						7521		11150	POMPES MOTO-POMPES
743	PUMPS NES,CENTRFUGES ETC						9086		17968	POMPES COMPRES,VENT ETC
744	MECHANICAL HANDLING EQU						8032		14413	EQUIP MANUTENTION PIECES

4. General Imports C.I.F. by Commodities according to the S.I.T.C. (Rev. 2) in thousand U.S. Dollars
Importations Générales C.A.F. par Produits d'après la C.T.C.I. (Rév. 2) en milliers de Dollars E.U.

SITC CTCI	COMMODITY	1992 WEIGHT POIDS	1992 VALUE VALEUR	1993 WEIGHT POIDS	1993 VALUE VALEUR	1994 WEIGHT POIDS	1994 VALUE VALEUR	1995 WEIGHT POIDS	1995 VALUE VALEUR	PRODUIT
745	NONELEC MACHY,TOOLS NES						10489		17062	AUT MACH NON ELEC,PIECES
7452	OTH NONELEC MCHS,PTS NES						7614		11662	AUT MACH NON ELEC,PIECES
749	NONELEC MACH PTS,ACC NES						7066		12945	PIECES MACH NON ELEC NDA
75	OFFICE MACHNES,ADP EQUIP		6462				58813		56690	MACH BUREAU TRAIT AUTOM
751	OFFICE MACHINES						16115	N 166696	13609	MACH,APPAREILS DE BUREAU
7512	CALCULATNG,ACCTG,ETC MCH						8094	N 112847	6150	MACHINE A CALCULER ETC
752	AUTOMTIC DATA PROC EQUIP						18513	N 116294	22998	MACH TRAIT INFORMATION
759	OFFICE,ADP MCH PTS,ACCES					W 535	24186	W 478	20084	PIECES DU 751 ET 752
7599	ACCTG,ETC,ADP MCH PTS,AC					W 429	20478	W 398	17183	PIECES DU 751 ET 752
76	TELECOMM,SOUND EQUIPMENT		7122				44191		80440	EQUIPMENT DE TELECOM
761	TELEVISION RECEIVERS						1942	N 66601	14062	RECEPTEURS DE TELEVISION
7611	COLOUR TV RECEIVERS					N 7600	1866	N 65732	13891	RECEPTEURS COULEUR
764	TELECOM EQPT,PTS,ACC NES						35578		58129	EQUIP TELECOM,PIECES
7641	LINE TELEPHONE,ETC EQUIP						8811	N 131674	16842	APP TELEPHON PAR FIL
7643	TV,RADIO TRANSMITTRS ETC						10235	N 36275	20062	APP EMET TELE RADIO
7648	TELECOMM EQUIPMENT NES					N 10505	9824	N 5020	1518	APP TELECOM NDA
76483	RADAR APPARATUS ETC					N 9105	8849	N 2695	488	APP DE RADIOGUIDAGE ETC
7649	PTS NES OF EQUIPMT OF 76					W 205	5338	W 486	18616	PIECES DE LA DIV 76
77	ELECTRIC MACHNRY NES ETC		19308				77070		122998	MACH APP ELECT NDA
772	SWITCHGEAR ETC,PARTS NES					W 977	9776	W 1359	11578	APP COUPURE,SECT ETC
7721	SWITCHGEAR ETC					W 941	9267	W 1341	11335	APP COUPURE,SECTIONMNT
773	ELECTR DISTRIBUTNG EQUIP					W 6321	15376	W 7123	38644	EQUIPMT DISTRIBUTION ELECT
7731	INSULATED WIRE,CABLE ETC					W 5931	14753	W 6700	37763	FILS,CABLES ISOLES ELECT
775	HOUSEHOLD TYPE EQUIP NES						12909		20731	MACH,APP USAGE DOMESTQUE
7758	ELECTRO–THERMIC APPL NES						8200		10476	APP ELECTROTHERMIQ NDA
776	TRANSISTORS,VALVES,ETC						13259		13548	LAMPES,TUBES,VALVES
778	ELECTRICAL MACHINERY NES						18129		25586	AUTRES MACH ELECT NDA
78	ROAD VEHICLES		10887				124994		240704	VEHICULES ROUTIERS
781	PASS MOTOR VEH EXC BUSES					N 30408	43089	N 117860	141079	AUTO TRANSPORT PERSONNES
782	LORRIES,SPCL MTR VEH NES						30085		34239	VEHICULES SPECIAUX,MARCH
7821	LORRIES,TRUCKS						25554		25130	VEHICULES TRANSP MARCHAND
783	ROAD MOTOR VEHICLES NES					N 2000	11317	N 1005	10621	VEHICULES ROUTIERS NDA
784	MOTOR VEH PRTS,ACCES NES						20410		32779	PIECES 722,781,782,783
7849	OTHER MOTOR VEHCL PARTS					W 8346	19405	W 10285	32078	PIECES 722,781,782,783
786	TRAILERS,NONMOTR VEH,NES						12477		12580	REMORQUES,CADRES,CONTAIN
7861	TRAILERS,TRANSP CONTAINR						8883	N 47221	9567	REMORQUES TOUS VEHICULES
78612	OTHER TRAILERS					N 17809	8023	N 13506	8854	REMORQUES TRANSP MARCH
79	OTHR TRANSPORT EQUIPMENT		22452				20673		44895	AUTRE MATERIEL TRANSPORT
791	RAILWAY VEHICLES						13949		14796	VEHIC MAT CHEMINS DE FER
792	AIRCRAFT ETC						5761		22706	APP NAVIGATION AERIENNE
7924	AIRCRFT NES OVER 15000KG							N 5	19233	AERODYNES PLUS 15000 KG
8	MISC MANUFACTURED GOODS		14650				176889		268343	ART MANUFACTURES DIVERS
812	*PLUMBG,HEATNG,LGHTNG EQ		615				11878		16596	APPAR SANITAIRES CHAUFFAGE
821	*FURNITURE,PARTS THEREOF		209				17423		24711	MEUBLES ET PIECES
8219	FURNITURE AND PARTS NES						11880		17043	AUTRES MEUBLES ET PIECES
82192	WOOD FURNITURE NES						8322	N 142451	12381	MEUBLES NDA EN BOIS
84	CLOTHING AND ACCESSORIES		5330				39743		50203	VETEMENTS
844	UNDER GARMENTS NOT KNIT						13951		11924	VETEMENT DESSOUS MAT TEX
8441	— MENS SHIRTS						13327		11720	CHEMISES HOMMES MAT TEXT
84412	—— OF SYNTHETIC FIBRES						12449	W 521	11003	CHEMISES HOMMES FIB SYNT
851	*FOOTWEAR		4156			P 1343500	10883	P 1539403	11950	CHAUSSURES
87	PRECISION INSTRUMNTS NES		62				28985		49530	INSTRUM,APPAR SCIENT NDA
872	MEDICAL INSTRUMENTS NES						4937		17389	INSTR,APP MEDIC–CHIR NDA
873	METERS AND COUNTERS NES					N 489500	9622	N 317223	8331	COMPTEURS,INST DE MESURE
8731	GAS SUPPLY METERS ETC					N 487900	9578	N 310483	7565	COMPTEURS GAZ,LIQ ELECT
874	MEASURNG,CONTROLNG INSTR						13757		22507	INSTRUMENTS DE MESURE
88	PHOTO EQU,OPTICL GDS ETC		599				12637		20433	APP,FOURN PHOTO,OP,MONTR
89	MISC MANUFCTRD GOODS NES		3406				54088		92959	ART MANUFACTURES DIVERS
892	PRINTED MATTER					W 2581	9937	W 3331	19088	IMPRIMES
8928	PRINTED MATTER NES					W 1590	6381	W 2250	11532	IMPRIMES NDA
893	ARTICLES OF PLASTIC NES						20956		39230	OUVRAGES EN MAT DIVIS 58
8931	PLSTC PACKG CONTNRS,LIDS					W 3260	6735	W 7418	16662	ART TRANSP EMBALLAGE ETC
8939	MISC PLASTIC ARTICLES					W 3206	13776	W 4629	21782	ART DIVERS EN MAT DIV 58
89399	OTHR PLASTC ARTICLES NES					W 2893	12859	W 4054	20058	AUT OUV MAT DIV 58
899	OTHER MANUFACTURED GOODS				35238		4882		10936	AUT ART MANUF DIVERS NDA
9	GOODS NOT CLASSD BY KIND						29077		66722	ART TRANSACT NON CLASSES
931	*SPECIAL TRANSACTIONS				12117		28755		66462	TRANS.SPECIALES

5. General Exports F.O.B. by Commodities according to the S.I.T.C. (Rev. 2) in thousand U.S. Dollars
Exportations Générales F.O.B. par Produits d'après la C.T.C.I. (Rév. 2) en milliers de Dollars E.U.

SITC CTCI	COMMODITY	1992 WEIGHT POIDS	1992 VALUE VALEUR	1993 WEIGHT POIDS	1993 VALUE VALEUR	1994 WEIGHT POIDS	1994 VALUE VALEUR	1995 WEIGHT POIDS	1995 VALUE VALEUR	PRODUIT
	ALL COMMODITIES		805014		2024700		2029000		2705670	TOUS PRODUITS
0	FOOD AND LIVE ANIMALS		164034				326866		452459	ALIMENTS,ANIMAUX VIVANTS
001	*LIVE ANIMALS FOR FOOD		10			N 982508	26661	N 569309	6196	ANIMAUX VIVANTS
0011	BOVINE SPECIES,LIVE					N 129400	21570	N 10213	1916	ESPECE BOVINE
00119	— OTHR THAN FR BREEDING					N 128900	21466	N 9181	1702	BOVINS NON REPRODUCTEURS
01	MEAT AND PREPARATIONS		45375				37366		33973	VIANDES ET PREPARATIONS
011	MEAT FRESH,CHILLD,FROZEN				40554	W 23067	30372	W 14148	22045	VIANDES FRAICHES,REF,CONGE
0111	BOVINE MEAT FRESH,FROZEN					W 16743	22784	W 8268	13445	VIANDES BOVIN FRAI,REF
01111	BOVINE MEAT WITH BONE IN					W 13602	16339	W 5657	7691	VIANDES BOVIN NON DESOSS
01112	BOVINE MEAT BONELESS					W 3142	6445	W 2612	5754	VIANDES BOVIN DESOSSEES
014	MEAT PREPD,PRSVD,NES ETC					W 4008	6895	W 5792	11896	CONSERVES DE VIANDES
0149	OTH PREPARD,PRESRVD MEAT					W 3282	5392	W 5222	10476	AUTRES PREP DE VIANDES
02	DAIRY PRODCTS,BIRDS'EGGS		84177				109511		167733	PRODUITS LAITIERS,OEUFS
022	MILK AND CREAM					W 86540	68328	W 83357	104769	LAIT ET CREME
0224	MILK,CREAM PRESERVED ETC					W 81205	64303	W 77389	100779	LAIT,CREME CONS,CONC
02242	MILK DRY,1.5% FAT OR LES					W 67000	52388	W 59892	84272	LAIT POUDRE INF 1.5%
02243	MILK DRY,OVER 1.5% FAT					W 10444	8882	W 7221	5424	LAIT POUDRE SUP 1.5%
02249	MILK(EX DRY) PRSVD,SWEET					W 3160	2509	W 9982	10790	LAIT CONS,CONC SUCRE
023	BUTTER					W 17800	21741	W 20005	35952	BEURRE
024	CHEESE AND CURD					W 11672	18899	W 11661	24604	FROMAGE ET CAILLEBOTTE
03	FISH AND PREPARATIONS		8446		5116		17957		39148	POISSONS ET PREPARATIONS
034	FISH,FRESH,CHILLED,FROZN					W 11816	8853	W 31788	23165	POISSON FRAIS, REFRIG,CONG
0342	FISH FROZEN,EXCL FILLETS					W 7599	5911	W 28300	19427	POISSONS CONGELES
037	FISH ETC PREPD,PRSVD NES					W 4855	6687	W 5677	8884	POIS,CRUST,MOL PREPARES
0371	FISH PREPARD,PRESRVD NES					W 4805	6334	W 5644	8696	CONSERVES DE POISSONS
04	CEREALS AND PREPARATIONS		452				14101		14755	CEREALES ET PRODUITS
05	VEGETABLES AND FRUIT		3297				46300		82067	LEGUMES ET FRUITS
054	VEG ETC FRSH,SMPLY PRSVD				18975	W 34809	14651	W 55836	22113	LEGUMES FRAIS,CONG,SECS
0545	OTHER FRESH VEGETABLES					W 19408	8806	W 25349	13394	AUTRES LEGUMES FRAIS,REF
05459	FRESH VEGETABLES NES					W 15956	7803	W 24527	13074	LEGUMES FRAIS,REFRI NDA
057	FRUIT,NUTS,FRESH,DRIED					W 38619	21317	W 91555	38978	FRUITS FRAIS OU SECS
0573	BANANA,PLANTAIN,FRSH,DRY					W 21600	10691	W 60490	26769	BANANES FRAICHES,SECHEES
058	FRUIT PRESERVED,PREPARED					W 15914	8737	W 24362	18394	CONSERVES DE FRUITS
0585	FRUIT OR VEGETABLE JUICE					W 13971	6675	W 23156	16932	JUS DE FRUITS
05857	JUICE OF OTHER FRUIT,VEG					W 6148	3088	W 8159	8926	JUS AUTRES FRUITS,LEGUMES
06	SUGAR AND PREPS,HONEY		2712		17068		15925		22768	SUCRES ET PRODUITS
062	SUGAR CANDY NON–CHOCLATE					W 8244	11236	W 9544	19472	SUCRERIES
07	COFFEE,TEA,COCOA,SPICES		279		1511		24830		48679	CAFE,THE,CACAO,EPICES
071	COFFEE AND SUBSTITUTES					W 547	2594	W 1709	11509	CAFE ET SUCCEDANES
073	CHOCOLATE AND PRODUCTS					W 9810	21036	W 12957	35164	CHOCOLAT
081	*FEEDING STUFF FOR ANIML		9288		1116	W 130806	22224	W 45562	10117	NOURRITURE POUR ANIMAUX
0812	BRAN,POLLARD,SHARPS,ETC					W 54645	14019	W 1133	105	SONS
08121	BRAN, ETC OF MAIZE, RICE					W 52790	13951	W 150	30	SONS DE MAIS OU DE RIZ
09	MISC EDIBLE PRODUCTS		9998		2279		11990		27022	PREP ALIMENTAIRES DIVERSES
091	MARGARINE AND SHORTENING					W 2330	1915	W 14654	16518	MARGARINE ET GRAISSES
0914	MARGARINE,EDIBLE FAT NES					W 2181	1763	W 14378	16308	MARGARINES,SIMILI SAINDOUX
09141	MARGARINE					W 1800	1485	W 8652	10461	MARGARINE
098	EDIBLE PRODCTS,PREPS NES						10075		10504	PREP ALIMENTAIRES NDA
1	BEVERAGES AND TOBACCO		1425				122786		16496	BOISSONS ET TABACS
11	BEVERAGES		1344		11046		81555		13945	BOISSONS
111	NON–ALCOHL BEVERAGES NES					W 54610	10317	W 26819	8692	BOISSONS NON ALCOOLIQUES
11102	FLAVORED WATERS NON–ALCO					W 41191	9979	W 24372	8013	LIMONADES,EAUX GAZEUSES
112	ALCOHOLIC BEVERAGES					W 69176	71238	W 3662	5252	BOISSONS ALCOOLIQUES
1121	WINE OF FRESH GRAPES ETC					W 15095	14683	W 296	520	VINS DE RAISINS FRAIS
11212	WINE OF FRESH GRAPES					W 14500	14209	W 296	520	VINS DE MOUTS DE RAISINS
1123	BEER,ALE,STOUT,PORTER					W 16800	9278	W 22	29	BIERES
1124	DISTILLED ALCOHOLIC BEVS					W 36638	46900	W 3343	4704	ALCOOLS,EAUX–DE–VIE
11249	OTH ALCOHOLC BEVS,CMPNDS					W 35281	45492	W 3319	4671	BOISSONS ALCOOLIQUES NDA
12	TOBACCO AND MANUFACTURES		81		9883		41230		2552	TABACS BRUTS FABRIQUES
122	TOBACCO,MANUFACTURED					W 5902	40242	W 194	963	TABACS FABRIQUES
1222	CIGARETTES					W 5901	40230	W 146	955	CIGARETTES
2	CRUDE MATERLS,EXCL FUELS		41472				132972		341088	MAT BRUTES NON COMESTIBLES
21	HIDES,SKINS,FURS UNDRSSD						6146		11886	CUIRS,PEAUX BRUTS
22	OIL SEEDS,OLEAGINOUS FRT		14123				5207		7736	GRAINES,FRUITS OLEAGINEUX
23	RUBBER, CRUDE		31				341		11740	CAOUTCHOUC BRUT
233	RUBBER,SYNTHTIC,RECLAIMD					W 275	331	W 7668	11726	LATEX CAOUTCH SYNTH REGEN
2331	SYNTHETIC RUBBER ETC					W 275	328	W 7650	11717	LATEX CAOUTCH SYNTHETIQUE
24	CORK AND WOOD		1219				53589		137756	LIEGE ET BOIS
247	OTH WOOD ROUGH,SQUARED						21199	W 1231863	53491	BOIS BRUTS EQUARRIS
2471	SAW–,VENEER–LOGS CONIFER						12366	W 934930	39709	CONIFERES POUR SCIAGE,PLACAG
24711	— IN THE ROUGH						12366	W 934930	39709	ECORCES OU DEGROSSIS
2472	SAW–,VENEER–LOGS NON–CON						8833	W 296933	13782	NON CONIFERES SCIAGE,PLAC
24721	— IN THE ROUGH						8833	W 296933	13782	BRUTS ECORCES DEGROSSIS
248	WOOD SHAPED,SLEEPERS						32292	W 467944	84188	BOIS SIMPLEMENT TRAVAILLES
2482	LUMBER SHAPED CONIFER					W 72301	27435	W 436915	77560	CONIFERES SCIES,RABOTES
24821	LUMBER SAWN ETC CONIFER					W 68064	26614	W 425657	74834	CONIFERES SCIES LONGITUD
251	*PULP AND WASTE PAPER					W 5644	555	W 76839	9222	PATES A PAPIER,DECHETS
26	TEXTILE FIBRES AND WASTE		2894				30185		38092	FIBRES TEXTILES
261	SILK				6232			W 9	35	SOIE
263	COTTON				21719	W 18241	22073	W 16518	25597	COTON
2631	RAW COTTON,EXCL LINTERS					W 17500	21595	W 15107	24675	COTON EN MASSE
27	CRUDE FERTLZR,MINRLS NES		3570				4692		3701	ENGRAIS MINERAUX BRUTS
28	METALLIFEROUS ORES,SCRAP		2357				29475		118210	MINERAIS METAL,DECHETS
282	IRON AND STEEL SCRAP					W 503605	25796	W 584090	51092	FERRAILLES
28202	— OF ALLOY STEEL					W 185560	9829	W 88079	12401	FERRAILLES D'ACIERS ALLIES
28209	— OF OTHR IRON OR STEEL					W 280246	13633	W 443611	34670	FERRAILLES DE FER
288	NONFERR METAL SCRAP NES					W 1492	501	W 42600	65951	DECHETS NON FERREUX
2882	OTHER BASE MTL SCRAP NES					W 1413	499	W 42503	65900	AUTRES DECHETS
28821	COPPER WASTE AND SCRAP							W 29152	53436	DECHETS DE CUIVRE
28823	ALUMINIUM WSTE AND SCRAP					W 1009	418	W 11031	10004	DECHETS D'ALUMINIUM
29	CRUDE ANIMAL,VEG MAT NES		17145				2780		2746	MATIERES BRUTES ANIM,VEGET
3	MINERAL FUELS ETC		79983		523929		322083		308231	COMBUSTIBLES MINERAUX LUB
32	COAL,COKE AND BRIQUETTES						34121		8810	HOUILLES,COKES,BRIQUETTES
322	COAL,LIGNITE AND PEAT					W 146785	34121	W 170076	8810	HOUILLES,LIGNITES,TOURBE
3224	PEAT,NOT AGGLOMERATED					W 137400	33678	W 168163	8742	TOURBE
33	PETROLEUM AND PRODUCTS		25213				272720		236802	PETROLE ET DERIVES
334	PETROLEUM PRODUCTS,REFIN					W 6004072	270335	W 1491938	234105	PRODUITS RAFFINES
341	*GAS,NATURAL AND MANUFCT		1007			W 31300	7218	W 100793	12505	GAZ NATUREL,GAZ MANUFACT
3413	PETROLM GASES,LIQUEFIED					W 31235	7209	W 100792	12505	GAZ DE PETROLE LIQUEFIE
34131	LIQUEFIED PROPANE,BUTANE					W 31235	7209	W 98034	12139	PROPANE,BUTANE LIQUEFIES
351	*ELECTRIC CURRENT		53763			H 506300	8023	H 2886900	50113	ENERGIE ELECTRIQUE

5. General Exports F.O.B. by Commodities according to the S.I.T.C. (Rev. 2) in thousand U.S. Dollars
Exportations Générales F.O.B. par Produits d'après la C.T.C.I. (Rév. 2) en milliers de Dollars E.U.

SITC CTCI	COMMODITY	1992 WEIGHT POIDS	1992 VALUE VALEUR	1993 WEIGHT POIDS	1993 VALUE VALEUR	1994 WEIGHT POIDS	1994 VALUE VALEUR	1995 WEIGHT POIDS	1995 VALUE VALEUR	PRODUIT
4	ANIMAL,VEGETABLE OIL,FAT		519		1884		7369		12198	HUILES,GRAISSES ANIM,VEG
42	FIXED VEGETABLE OIL,FAT		140				6206		11338	HUILES VEGETALES FIXES
423	FIXED VEG OILS,SOFT					W 6891	6107	W 9906	11076	HUILES VEGET DOUCES FIXES
5	CHEMCLS,RELATED PROD NES		74731		120594		257161		384240	PRODUITS CHIMIQUES
51	ORGANIC CHEMICALS		1019		9860		43271		53319	PROD CHIMIQ ORGANIQUES
512	ALCOHOLS,PHENOLS ETC						33887		42333	PHENOLS,PHENOLS–ALCOOLS
5121	ACYCLIC ALCOHOLS,DERIVS						33883		41679	ALCOOLS ACYCLIQUES
51211	METHYL ALCOHOL(METHANOL)					W 25200	8722	W 29631	12459	ALCOOLS METHYLIQUES
51215	ETHYLENE GLYCOL					W 4000	1561	W 38713	23559	ETHYLENE–GLYCOL
51216	ETHYL ALC,DENATRD SPIRIT					V 22725	23517	V 5523	3980	ALCOOL ETHYLIQUE NON DENAT
52	INORGANIC CHEMICALS		272				13122		33149	PROD CHIM INORGANIQUES
522	INORG ELEMNTS,OXIDES,ETC					W 51383	7974	W 146092	29609	ELEMENTS INORGANIQUES
5225	INORGANIC BASES ETC NES					W 49783	7169	W 144127	21107	AUTRES BASES OXYDES METAL
52251	AMMONIA,ANHYDROUS ETC					W 47800	6938	W 140267	20339	AMMONIAC LIQUEFIE
541	*MEDICINAL,PHARM PRODUCT		2587		7697	K 5481235	38560	K 5910567	51963	PROD MEDICINAUX PHARMACEUT
5417	MEDICAMENTS					K 3431000	31182	K 3602504	46973	MEDICAMENTS
54171	— CONTAINNG ANTIBIOTICS					K 954700	9742	K 562797	9648	MED CONTN ANTIBIOTIQUES
54179	— CONTNG OTH SUBSTANCES					K 2135700	15871	K 2644835	30562	MED CONT AUT SUBSTANCES
55	PERFUME,CLEANING ETC PRD		3132		23300		8329		14710	PROD POUR PARFUM,TOILETTE
553	PERFUMERY,COSMETICS,ETC					W 1594	4578	W 1339	9028	PRODUITS DE PARFUMERIE
562	*FERTILIZERS,MANUFACTURE		49284		44740	W 752422	90825	W 906503	120885	ENGRAIS MANUFACTURES
5621	CHEM NITROGENOUS FERTLZR					W 499572	43948	W 539945	67729	ENGRAIS AZOTES
56211	AMMONIUM NITRATE					W 299500	22654	W 222036	23744	NITRATE D'AMMONIUM
56216	UREA					W 147100	16554	W 224858	34963	UREE
5629	FERTILIZERS NES					W 165749	40097	W 251603	44312	ENGRAIS NDA
56291	NIT–PHOS–POT FERTLZR NES					W 42200	20223	W 20645	2193	ENGRAIS CONT N P K
56292	NITROG–PHOS FERTLZR NES					W 121776	19785	W 223805	41487	ENGRAIS NDA CONT N P
58	PLASTIC MATERIALS ETC		7099				18980		53582	MAT PLAST ARTIFICIELLES
583	POLYMERIZATION ETC PRODS					W 28658	17071	W 55363	51006	PROD POLYMERISATION
5831	POLYETHYLENE					W 18452	9714	W 43614	36362	POLYETHYLENE
58311	— IN PRIMARY FORMS					W 15625	7901	W 39515	31741	POLYETHYLENE PRIMAIRES
5833	POLYSTYRENE,ITS COPOLYMR					W 4641	3744	W 8460	9175	POLYPROPYLENE COPOLYMERES
58331	— IN PRIMARY FORMS					W 4637	3730	W 8443	9101	SOUS FORMES PRIMAIRES
59	CHEMICAL MATERIALS NES		10779				39806		50217	MAT PROD CHIMIQUES NDA
592	STARCH,INULIN,GLUTEN,ETC				22045	W 18469	34077	W 15964	44628	AMIDONS,INUL,GLUT FROM
5922	ALBUMINOID SUBSTAN,GLUES					W 18434	34055	W 15482	44321	MAT ALBUMIN,COLLES
59221	CASEIN AND DERIVATVS,ETC					W 13868	28418	W 10915	38014	CASEINES,CASEINATES
6	BASIC MANUFACTURES		139161				315815		429261	ART MANUFACTURES
61	LEATHER,DRESSED FUR,ETC		2078				17563		25753	CUIRS,PELLETERIES
611	LEATHER					W 8175	14477	W 7146	15525	CUIRS,PEAUX PREPARES
6113	CALF LEATHER					W 6038	9890	W 5021	10024	CUIRS,PEAUX DE VEAUX
613	FUR SKINS TANNED,DRESSED					W 73	2423	W 177	8975	PELLETERIES
63	WOOD,CORK MANUFACTRS NES		4506				21860		32693	OUVRAGES LIEGE ET BOIS
634	VENEERS,PLYWOOD,ETC						11238		13706	PLACAGES,CONTRE–PLAQUES
6342	PLYWOOD OF WOOD SHEETS						7854	V 18334	6464	BOIS CONTRE–PLAQUES
635	WOOD MANUFACTURES NES					W 32115	10616	W 53587	18959	ART MANUF EN BOIS NDA
6353	BUILDERS WOODWRK,PREFABS					W 8383	6360	W 28824	9652	OUVRAGES DE MENUISERIE
64	PAPER,PAPERBOARD AND MFR		10834				31111		38567	PAPIERS,CARTONS & OUVRAGES
641	PAPER AND PAPERBOARD					W 89491	24256	W 64780	25617	PAPIERS ET CARTONS
6416	FIBRE BUILDING BOARD					W 55928	9665	W 44819	10266	PLAQUES CONSTRUCT EN PATE
64161	HARDBOARD					W 51855	8405	W 41567	8834	PLAQUES CONSTR COMPRIMES
642	PAPER,ETC,PRECUT,ARTS OF					W 11353	6855	W 12060	12950	PAP,CARTONS DECOUPES
65	TEXTILE YARN,FABRICS,ETC		83924				114725		163377	FILS,TISSUS,ARTICLES TEXTILE
651	TEXTILE YARN					W 8767	26427	W 12125	45473	FILS TEXTILES
6516	DISCON SYN FIB BLEND YRN					W 467	1327	W 2182	8272	FILS FIBR TEX SYNT DIS MOINS
6517	REGEN FIBRE YARN,MONOFIL					W 5481	16961	W 7549	28635	FILS TEXT ART NON VENTE DT
65171	CONT VISCOSE RAYON YARN					W 3628	12246	W 7092	27352	FILS RAY,VIS NON VENTE DET
652	COTTON FABRICS,WOVEN					W 5775	17709	W 5548	23942	TISSUS DE COTON
6521	GREY WOVEN COTTON FABRIC					W 2727	6148	W 3934	13194	TISSUS COT ECRUS NON MERCER
65214	GREY WOVEN COTTON NES					W 2686	6011	W 3831	12692	AUT TISSUS 85% COTON ECRUS
6522	WOVEN COTTON BLEACHD,ETC					W 3048	11562	W 1614	10748	TISSUS COTON BLANCHIS ETC
65224	BLCHED COTTON FABRIC NES					W 2672	9956	W 1298	7876	AUT TIS PLUS 85% COT BLANCHI
653	WOVN MAN–MADE FIB FABRIC					W 2174	11627	W 3498	29725	TISSUS FIBRES SYNTH,ARTIF
6534	DISC SYN BLEND FABRC NES					W 279	842	W 1595	17106	TISSUS FIBRES SYNTH DISCONT
65342	DISC SYN FIB–WOOL FABRIC						2	W 844	12895	TISSUS FIB SYNT MEL LAINE
6535	CONT REGN WEAVES NONPILE					W 1558	8901	W 1445	9337	TISSUS FIB TEXT ART CONTINU
65356	CONT REG BLEND FABRC NES					W 828	4902	W 1340	8395	TIS MOINS 85% TEXT ART CONT
654	OTH WOVEN TEXTILE FABRIC					W 4034	29076	W 2489	22110	TISSUS AUT COTON SYNT,ARTIF
6542	WOVEN WOOL,HAIR NONPILE					W 912	7613	W 850	10538	TIS PLUS 85% LAINE,POILS
65421	WOVN CARD WOOL,FINE HAIR					W 866	7234	W 840	10362	TISSUS 85% LAINE,PLS CARD
6543	WOVEN WOOL ETC FABRC NES					W 1183	10453	W 548	4760	TISSUS LAINE,POILS FINS NDA
65432	WOOL–DISC SYN FIBR FABRC					W 1180	10432	W 537	4620	TISSUS LAINE MEL SYNT DISC
6544	WOVEN FLAX,RAMIE FABRICS					W 1845	10550	W 1023	6635	TISSUS DE LIN,RAMIE
657	SPECIAL TXTL FABRC,PRODS				6465		3560	W 3966	10649	TISSUS SPECIAUX
658	TEXTILE ARTICLES NES					W 3505	14506	W 3235	21000	ART FACONNES MAT TEXTILES
6584	LINENS ETC					W 2113	11393	W 1985	15168	LINGE DE MAISON
659	FLOOR COVERINGS,ETC				9999		7566		5254	COUVRE–PARQUETS,TAPIS ETC
66	NONMETAL MINERAL MFS NES		18460		19324		33213		44633	ART MIN NON METALLIQUES
661	LIME,CEMENT,BLDG PRODS					W 452365	12910	W 313467	11874	CHAUX,CIMENTS MAT CONSTR
6612	CEMENT					W 435772	12070	W 290838	9929	CIMENTS HYDRAULIQUES
663	MINERAL MANUFCTURES NES					W 305846	8791	W 170867	6940	ART MIN MANUF NDA
6633	MINRL MFS NES NONCERAMIC					W 302229	7481	W 168406	5708	OUVR MAT MINERALE NDA
66332	CEMENT,ARTFCL STONE PROD					W 302040	7443	W 168046	5573	OUVRAGES EN CIMENT
665	GLASSWARE					W 18062	4056	W 37890	10908	OUVRAGES EN VERRE
6651	BOTTLES ETC OF GLASS					W 17100	2905	W 36812	8461	RECIPIENTS EN VERRE
66511	GLASS BOTTLES ETC NONVAC					W 17100	2905	W 36812	8461	BONBONNES,BOUTEILLES,ETC
67	IRON AND STEEL		3205		49414		56154		80131	FER ET ACIER
672	IRON,STEEL PRIMARY FORMS					W 34549	5241	W 203333	35960	LINGOTS FER,ACIER
6727	IRN,STL COIL FR REROLLNG					W 31172	4801	W 199228	34974	EBAUCHES POUR TOLES FER
67271	IRON,SIMPLE STEEL COILS					W 22890	3401	W 194158	33928	EBAUCHES NON EN ACIER
673	IRON,STEEL SHAPES ETC					W 79689	12938	W 13015	3431	BARRES,PROFIL FER,ACIER
674	IRN,STL UNIV,PLATE,SHEET					W 109571	16951	W 91678	28083	LARGES PLATS,TOLES
6747	TINNED PLATES,SHEETS					W 9192	2455	W 15732	9415	TOLES ETAMEES EN ACIER
677	IRN,STL WIRE(EXCL W ROD)					W 45674	8598	W 8445	2669	FILS EN FER,ACIER
67701	IRON, SIMPLE STEEL WIRE					W 45013	8537	W 8287	2582	FILS NON ACIER FIN CARBONE
68	NON–FERROUS METALS		2064				15589		12757	METAUX NON FERREUX
682	COPPER EXC CEMENT COPPER					W 6996	10995	W 1298	2222	CUIVRE
6821	COPPER NES,ALLOYS,UNWRT					W 5938	9526	W 954	1259	CUIVRE BRUT
68212	COPPER REFINED,UNWROUGHT					W 5906	9473	W 953	1257	CUIVRE AFFINE BRUT
69	METAL MANUFACTURES NES		12996				22355		24926	ART MANUFACT EN METAL NDA
699	BASE METAL MFRS NES					W 5261	5528	W 6133	8333	ART MANUFACTURES MET NDA

5. General Exports F.O.B. by Commodities according to the S.I.T.C. (Rev. 2) in thousand U.S. Dollars
Exportations Générales F.O.B. par Produits d'après la C.T.C.I. (Rév. 2) en milliers de Dollars E.U.

SITC CTCI	COMMODITY	1992 WEIGHT POIDS	1992 VALUE VALEUR	1993 WEIGHT POIDS	1993 VALUE VALEUR	1994 WEIGHT POIDS	1994 VALUE VALEUR	1995 WEIGHT POIDS	1995 VALUE VALEUR	PRODUIT
7	MACHINES,TRANSPORT EQUIP		197006		479863		315349		425021	MACHINES MATERIEL TRANSPORT
71	POWER GENERATING EQUIPMT		450				19536		16288	MACHINES GENERATRICES
713	INTRNL COMBUS PSTN ENGIN						6748		6967	MOTEURS EXPL COMB INT, PIECE
716	ROTATING ELECTRIC PLANT						9559		7943	APP ELECTR ROTATIFS,PIECES
7162	AC MTRS,GENRTRS,GEN SETS					N 1306516	9337	N 418389	7222	MOTEURS ELECTRIQUES
71621	AC MTRS,INC UNIVRSL MTRS					N 1305704	9109	N 417088	6984	MOT ELEC NON COUR CONTINU
72	MACHS FOR SPCL INDUSTRYS		17806				14262		19108	MAC SPECIALES POUR INDUST
73	METALWORKING MACHINERY		18094				12320		10883	MACH TRAVAIL DES METAUX
737	METALWORKING MACHNRY NES						7886		7317	MACH TRAV METAUX PIECES
7373	WELDING,BRAZING,ETC MCHS						7868	N 14007	7174	MACH SOUDAGE ETC PIECES
73732	ELECTRIC WELDERS,ETC						7863	N 13504	7153	MACH ELECT POUR SOUDER
74	GENRL INDUSTRL MACHY NES		24898				47721		47719	MACH APP INDUSTRIE
742	PUMPS FOR LIQUIDS ETC						18529		15119	POMPES MOTO–POMPES
7428	OTHER PUMPS FOR LIQUIDS						11299	N 72748	6476	AUTRES POMPES POUR LIQ
74288	PUMPS FR LIQUIDS NES ETC						11277	N 72718	6430	POMPES POUR LIQUIDES NDA
7429	PTS NES OF PUMPS OF 742					W 552	6969	W 344	8137	PIECES POUR GROUPE 742
743	PUMPS NES,CENTRFUGES ETC						18111		15776	POMPES COMPRES,VENT ETC
7431	PUMPS FOR GASES ETC						15495	N 236373	11730	POMPES AIR A VIDE,COMPRES
75	OFFICE MACHNES,ADP EQUIP		1724				9410		7972	MACH BUREAU TRAIT AUTOM
76	TELECOMM,SOUND EQUIPMENT		15273				46048		34952	EQUIPMENT DE TELECOM
761	TELEVISION RECEIVERS						26959	N 90046	17266	RECEPTEURS DE TELEVISION
7611	COLOUR TV RECEIVERS					N 139200	25595	N 74163	16360	RECEPTEURS COULEUR
764	TELECOM EQPT,PTS,ACC NES						13408		12390	EQUIP TELECOM,PIECES
7649	PTS NES OF EQUIPMT OF 76					W 900	10132	W 575	6505	PIECES DE LA DIV 76
76493	TELECOMM EQUIPMT PTS NES					W 867	9667	W 556	6117	PIECES 761,762,764.3,8
77	ELECTRIC MACHNRY NES ETC		75446				95170		152870	MACH APP ELECT NDA
773	ELECTR DISTRIBUTNG EQUIP					W 3223	6786	W 3704	21943	EQUIPMT DISTRIBUTION ELECT
7731	INSULATED WIRE,CABLE ETC					W 3143	6767	W 3646	21885	FILS,CABLES ISOLES ELECT
775	HOUSEHOLD TYPE EQUIP NES						36344		45444	MACH,APP USAGE DOMESTQUE
7752	DOM REFRIGERATRS,FREEZRS						31883	N 250663	39261	REFRIG,CONGEL MENAGER
77521	DOMESTIC REFRIGERATORS						21997	N 171621	26658	REFRIGERATEURS
77522	DOMESTIC DEEP–FREEZERS					N 67100	9886	N 79042	12603	MEUBLES CONGELATEURS
776	TRANSISTORS,VALVES,ETC						41897		72552	LAMPES,TUBES,VALVES
7761	TV PICTURE TUBES						37862	N 1560012	70686	TUBES CATHODIQUES
78	ROAD VEHICLES		28553				55761		99417	VEHICULES ROUTIERS
781	PASS MOTOR VEH EXC BUSES					N 8418	33444	N 15067	71371	AUTO TRANSPORT PERSONNES
784	MOTOR VEH PRTS,ACCES NES						4865		10851	PIECES 722,781,782,783
7849	OTHER MOTOR VEHCL PARTS					W 2667	4748	W 3840	10643	PIECES 722,781,782,783
785	CYCLES,ETC MOTRZD OR NOT						9218		11809	MOTOCYCLES SCOOTERS
7852	CYCLES, ETC NON–MOTOR					N 116000	7985	N 97146	10012	VELOCIPEDES SANS MOTEUR
79	OTHR TRANSPORT EQUIPMENT		14762				15122		35813	AUTRE MATERIEL TRANSPORT
792	AIRCRAFT ETC						5654		8295	APP NAVIGATION AERIENNE
793	SHIPS AND BOATS ETC						5102	N 120	21682	NAVIRES BATEAUX,ETC
7932	SHIPS AND BOATS NES						629	N 94	13167	NAVIRES ET BATEAUX
79323	OTHER CARGO VESSELS						80	N 10	8745	AUT BATEAUX TRANS MARCH
8	MISC MANUFACTURED GOODS		78945				219897		335763	ART MANUFACTURES DIVERS
821	*FURNITURE,PARTS THEREOF		9248				36148		46196	MEUBLES ET PIECES
8211	CHAIRS,SEATS AND PARTS						7353		7944	SIEGES ET PIECES
82111	CHAIRS AND OTHER SEATS						7243	N 222633	7835	SIEGES
8219	FURNITURE AND PARTS NES						27450		35817	AUTRES MEUBLES ET PIECES
82192	WOOD FURNITURE NES						24722	N 700359	31326	MEUBLES NDA EN BOIS
84	CLOTHING AND ACCESSORIES		55804				109544		204892	VETEMENTS
842	MENS OUTERWEAR NOT KNIT						32619		47482	VET DESSUS POUR HOMMES
8423	— TROUSERS,BREECHES ETC					N 2090200	7846	N 1940389	17212	PANTALONS HOMMES MAT TEX
8424	— JACKETS,BLAZERS ETC					N 1061400	15722	N 5490280	21862	VESTES HOMMES MAT TEXTIL
843	WOMENS OUTERWEAR NONKNIT						22240	N 8692031	68220	VET DESSUS FEMMES MAT TEX
8431	— COATS AND JACKETS					N 561200	3972	N 865647	15312	MANT,VEST FEM MAT TEXTIL
8435	— BLOUSES					N 2034400	4394	N 2585619	16182	BLOUSES FEM MAT TEXTILES
8439	— OTHER OUTER GARMENTS						9438	N 3127730	22104	AUT VET DES FEM MAT TEXT
844	UNDER GARMENTS NOT KNIT						6018	N 3229794	8897	VETEMENT DESSOUS MAT TEX
845	OUTERWEAR KNIT NONELASTC						28835	MN 10126	36885	VET DESSOUS,ACCES BONNET
8451	— JERSEYS,PULLOVERS ETC					N 3909500	9374	N 3280256	13742	CHANDAILS,PULL–OVERS ETC
8459	— OTHER,CLTHG ACCESRYS						16066	N 5647600	19707	AUT VET DESSUS DE BONNE
846	UNDER GARMENTS KNITTED						9647		23999	SOUS VETS DE BONNETERIE
8462	— OF COTTON NON ELASTIC					N 4812200	3843	N 8086471	16397	SOUS–VET BONNET COTON
84629	—— OTHER					N 4585000	3594	N 7848666	15989	AUT SOUS–VET BONNET COTON
847	TEXTILE CLTHNG ACCES NES						5967		11339	ACCES VET MAT TEXT NDA
8472	CLTHNG ACCESRYS ETC KNIT					W 1451	5689	W 1218	10815	ACCES VET BONNE NDA
84722	KNIT SOCKS,ETC NONELASTC					W 1397	5439	W 1193	10668	CHAUSSETTES BON. NON ELAS
851	*FOOTWEAR		7252			P 2776608	19404	P 2142196	19362	CHAUSSURES
85102	FOOTWEAR LEATHER					P 2300600	16024	P 1777905	16821	CHAUS SEMELLES EN CUIR
87	PRECISION INSTRUMNTS NES						19676		20252	INSTRUM,APPAR SCIENT NDA
873	METERS AND COUNTERS NES					N 1068902	8693	N 716132	8901	COMPTEURS,INST DE MESURE
8731	GAS SUPPLY METERS ETC					N 1068900	8693	N 714489	8889	COMPTEURS GAZ,LIQ ELECT
88	PHOTO EQU,OPTICL GDS ETC		14				3516		8631	APP,FOURN PHOTO,OP,MONTR
89	MISC MANUFCTRD GOODS NES		4142				28116		32693	ART MANUFACTURES DIVERS
893	ARTICLES OF PLASTIC NES						9024		12112	OUVRAGES EN MAT DIVIS 58
899	OTHER MANUFACTURED GOODS				101061		1373		2303	AUT ART MANUF DIVERS NDA
9	GOODS NOT CLASSD BY KIND						8704		913	ART TRANSACT NON CLASSES
931	*SPECIAL TRANSACTIONS				2976		8576		870	TRANS.SPECIALES

1. HISTORICAL SERIES, 1961–1996 GENERAL TRADE, IMPORTS C.I.F., EXPORTS F.O.B.
SERIES HISTORIQUES, 1961–1996 COMMERCE GENERAL, IMPORTATIONS C.A.F., EXPORTATIONS F.O.B

YEAR ANNEE	VALUE IN MILLION PATACAS / VALEUR EN MILLION PATACAS: MERCHANDISE – MARCHANDISE		GOLD – OR		CONVERSION FACTORS U.S. CENTS PER PATACA FACTEURS DE CONVERSION CENTS E.U. PAR PATACA		INDEX NUMBERS – INDICES: QUANTUM		UNIT VALUE VALEUR UNITAIRE	
	IMPORTS	EXPORTS	IMPORTS	EXPORTS	IMPORTS	EXPORTS	IMPORTS	EXPORTS	IMPORTS	EXPORTS
1961	165.80	75.30			19.1290	19.1290				
1962	196.80	86.70			19.1290	19.1290				
1963	218.50	108.90			19.1290	19.1290				
1964	252.40	114.80			19.1290	19.1290				
1965	269.90	122.90			19.1290	19.1290				
1966	293.80	138.20			19.1290	19.1290				
1967	245.50	143.20			19.1290	19.1290				
1968	303.20	170.60			19.1290	19.1290				
1969	360.10	225.80			16.3185	16.5289				
1970	393.20	255.80			16.3908	16.5892				
1971	447.20	291.10			16.7001	16.9147				
1972	592.50	409.70			17.6667	17.8724				
1973	750.30	497.10			19.1567	19.5207				
1974	648.70	551.20			19.5564	20.0153				
1975	791.30	683.90			18.7112	18.7043				
1976	977.10	1146.20			18.6654	18.9789				
1977	1102.40	1221.50			19.6927	20.0260				
1978	1252.40	1302.90			19.7420	20.0944				
1979	1817.90	2291.60			19.2611	19.2264				
1980	2779.90	2742.00			19.5321	19.5710				
1981	4141.20	4015.30			17.4487	17.0836				
1982	4475.40	4521.10			15.8143	15.8753				
1983	5423.30	5673.00			13.5434	13.5220				
1984	6399.20	7324.70			12.4695	12.4669				
1985	6200.00	7207.00			12.5653	12.5722				
1986	7326.67	8653.25			12.1449	12.0869				
1987	9028.09	11245.69			12.4187	12.4189				
1988	10380.58	12007.06			12.4224	12.4224				
1989	11873.42	13208.65			12.4471	12.4456				
1990	12343.09	13638.19			12.4241	12.4239				
1991	14832.42	13326.06			12.4224	12.4224				
1992	15684.72	14080.16			12.4224	12.4224				
1993	16137.99	14236.22			12.3898	12.3869				
1994	16925.12	14853.89			12.3457	12.3457				
1995	16267.10	15913.45			12.4525	12.4603				
1996	15930.66	15898.51			12.5111	12.5121				

2. IMPORTS BY BROAD ECONOMIC CATEGORY AND EXPORTS BY INDUSTRIAL ORIGIN. (PERCENTAGE OF TOTAL VALUE)
IMPORTATIONS PAR CATEGORIES ECONOMIQUES ET EXPORTATIONS PAR BRANCHE D'ACTIVITE. (EN POURCENTAGE DE LA VALEUR TOTALE)

IMPORTS – IMPORTATIONS

	1990	1991	1992	1993	1994	1995	1996
TOTAL IMPORTS–IMPORTATIONS TOTALES	100.	100.	100.	100.	100.	100.	100.
1 FOOD BEV–ALIMENTATION BOISSONS	8.8	8.4	8.9	9.3	10.3	10.1	10.0
11 PRIMARY–PRODUITS DE BASE	3.8	3.3	3.3	3.2	3.2	3.4	3.5
111 FOR INDUSTRY–POUR L'INDUSTRIE	1.1	1.1	1.1	1.2	1.3	1.3	1.3
112 FOR HOUSEHOLDS–POUR LES MENAGES	2.6	2.2	2.1	2.0	1.9	2.1	2.2
12 PROCESSED–PRODUITS ELABORES	5.0	5.1	5.7	6.1	7.1	6.7	6.4
121 FOR INDUSTRY–POUR L'INDUSTRIE	0.4	0.4	0.4	0.4	0.5	0.5	0.5
122 FOR HOUSEHOLDS–POUR LES MENAGES	4.6	4.6	5.2	5.7	6.7	6.1	5.9
2 IND SUPPLIES–APPROV INDUSTRIELS	59.8	52.4	50.7	52.3	50.5	50.1	52.8
21 PRIMARY–PRODUITS DE BASE	4.0	3.9	3.7	6.9	3.1	2.5	3.0
22 PROCESSED–PRODUITS ELABORES	55.8	48.5	47.0	45.4	47.4	47.7	49.9
3 FUELS–COMBUSTIBLES	4.7	4.5	4.3	4.6	4.7	5.1	6.4
31 PRIMARY–PRODUITS DE BASE	0.4	0.4	0.4	0.5	0.5	0.7	0.8
32 PROCESSED–PRODUITS ELABORES	4.3	4.1	3.8	4.1	4.2	4.5	5.6
321 MOTOR SPIRIT–ESSENCE	0.5	0.4	0.5	0.6	0.6	0.6	0.8
322 OTHER–AUTRES	3.8	3.6	3.3	3.5	3.6	3.8	4.8
4 MACHINERY–EQUIPEMENT	10.7	12.5	11.7	10.7	12.2	12.2	9.1
41 CAPITAL EQUIPMENT–MACHINES	9.5	11.5	10.9	9.9	11.1	11.0	8.2
42 PARTS–PIECES ACCESSOIRES	1.1	1.0	0.8	0.8	1.1	1.2	0.9
5 TRANSPORT–TRANSPORT	2.9	2.4	3.5	3.7	4.2	4.0	4.7
51 PASSENGER CARS–AUTOMOBILES	1.1	1.1	2.1	2.3	2.3	1.5	1.8
52 OTHER–AUTRES	1.2	0.8	1.0	1.1	1.0	1.8	1.3
521 INDUSTRIAL–INDUSTRIELS	1.0	0.4	0.6	0.6	0.6	1.5	0.7
522 NON INDUSTRIAL–NON INDUSTRIEL	0.2	0.4	0.4	0.4	0.4	0.3	0.5
53 PARTS–PIECES ACCESSOIRES	0.5	0.5	0.5	0.4	0.9	0.7	1.5
6 CONSUM GOODS–BIENS CONSOMMATION	12.9	19.4	20.5	19.0	17.8	18.0	16.7
61 DURABLE–DURABLES	3.0	6.8	7.4	6.8	5.0	4.1	3.2
62 SEMI DURABLE–SEMI DURABLES	5.3	9.1	9.5	7.7	7.8	7.9	7.9
63 NON DURABLE–NON DURABLES	4.7	3.4	3.5	4.5	5.1	6.0	5.5
7 GOODS NES–BIENS NDA	0.2	0.4	0.4	0.4	0.3	0.4	0.4

EXPORTS – EXPORTATIONS

	1990	1991	1992	1993	1994	1995	1996
TOTAL EXPORTS–EXPORTATIONS TOTALES	100.	100.	100.	100.	100.	100.	100.
1 AGRICULTURE	0.6	0.8	0.9	1.7	1.7	1.6	1.8
2 MINING QUARRY–INDUS EXTRACTIVES	0.0	0.0	0.0	0.0	0.0	0.0	0.0
3 MANUFACTURING–IND MANUFACTUR	99.4	99.2	99.1	98.3	98.3	98.4	98.2
31 FOOD BEV TOBACCO–ALIM BOISS TAB	0.6	0.8	1.5	3.6	3.4	1.5	1.4
32 TEXTILES–INDUSTRIES TEXTILES	77.6	79.7	79.7	76.3	76.9	80.8	84.3
33 WOOD & PRODUCTS–BOIS & PRODUITS	0.2	0.2	0.1	0.1	0.2	0.1	0.1
34 PAPER & PRODUCTS–PAPIER & PRODT	0.2	0.2	0.2	0.2	0.2	0.2	1.5
35 CHEMICALS–INDUSTRIES CHIMIQUES	2.4	2.8	2.6	2.8	2.6	2.3	2.3
36 NON METAL MIN–MIN NON METAL	1.2	0.9	1.0	1.2	0.9	0.9	1.1
37 BASIC METAL–IND METAL BASE	0.1	0.1	0.1	0.3	0.2	0.1	0.1
38 METAL MANUF–MANUF METAL	3.6	6.9	7.5	8.3	8.4	7.4	5.2
39 OTH MANUF IND–AUTRES MANUF	13.6	7.6	6.4	5.5	5.7	5.1	2.2

3. TRADE BY PRINCIPAL COUNTRIES OF PRODUCTION AND LAST CONSIGNMENT (VALUE IN THOUSAND U.S. DOLLARS)
ECHANGES SELON LES PRINCIPAUX PAYS DE PRODUCTION ET DE DERNIERE CONSIGNATION (VALEUR EN MILLIERS DE DOLLARS EU)

COUNTRIES–PAYS	GENERAL IMPORTS C.I.F. IMPORTATIONS GENERALES C.A.F					COUNTRIES–PAYS	GENERAL EXPORTS F.O.B. EXPORTATIONS GENERALES F.O.B.				
	1992	1993	1994	1995	1996		1992	1993	1994	1995	1996
World	1948192	1890728	2089235	2018591	1991983	Monde	1786092	1716788	1872184	2017324	2100018
Africa	3413	4205	17502	7697	4808	Afrique	2321	581	1045	1895	1335
Americas	108440	124245	154209	176161	131627	Amériques	650892	605501	721936	871370	836741
Northern America	104727	118237	146452	173118	125511	Amérique du Nord	646186	588789	707177	860941	830435
LAIA	3697	5897	7672	2913	5884	ALAI	2833	15276	13854	8673	4798
CACM		80	7		18	MCAC	534	504	97	132	128
Caribbean	16	31	78	130	214	Caraïbes	95	4		76	197
Rest of America	0					Autre Amérique	1245	928	809	1548	1183
As.ex F.USSR	1610490	1493536	1556936	1507577	1549087	Asie l'URSS exclus	463010	500444	524762	488720	560748
Eur.x F.USSR	192409	239020	334315	305702	283969	Europe l'URSS exclus	652269	597603	612823	645078	684917
EU	184475	229681	323082	297165	272749	UE	634201	581048	598002	633422	672812
EFTA	7105	7447	9625	8255	9929	AELE	17130	15442	13499	10685	11415
East Europe	730	1885	1586	280	1211	Europe de l'Est	694	459	560	739	683
Other Europe					1	Autre de l'Europe	244	652	760	215	4
Former USSR	4553	3909	6775	5317	285	Ancienne URSS	831	505	450	116	97
Oceania	28887	25813	19499	16137	22207	Océanie	16769	12153	11167	10144	8485
Hong Kong	641012	565371	634178	583300	578844	USA/Etats–Unis d'Amer	619399	563707	681817	831177	802180
China/Chine	397950	402362	393386	439239	477002	China/Chine	183580	231170	241325	211797	264088
Japan/Japon	350784	299075	267231	212399	178998	Hong Kong	230359	222110	222608	204384	212739
USA/Etats–Unis d'Amer	100355	109579	142756	149681	117482	Germany/Allemagne	211883	194250	188982	196893	213393
United Kingdom	48849	66762	88219	84057	77039	France,Monac	156146	142181	131706	137252	136092
Korea, Republic of	42497	42880	51218	47517	52523	United Kingdom	117896	106495	130655	141681	151741
France,Monac	29432	38336	62062	41219	35424	Netherlands/Pays–Bas	40106	45096	45844	46463	56162
Germany/Allemagne	31969	35254	48049	42790	31854	Canada	26574	24807	25289	29695	28111
Denmark/Danemark	19113	24785	39386	34491	22856	Japan/Japon	28959	24866	25129	26109	27802
Portugal	21720	15688	25114	23466	30525	Italy/Italie	35429	20694	19140	18291	15845
Italy/Italie	8950	14605	20315	26558	25269	Denmark/Danemark	14263	18556	20630	24021	29400
Australia/Australie	24480	21674	15710	13567	18183	Sweden/Suède	11665	7067	7692	18575	22976
Singapore/Singapour	10088	9072	11311	17640	16973	Spain/Espagne	9124	7832	16449	10779	12466
Indonesia/Indonésie	9964	12421	14910	12552	12610	Belgium–Luxembourg	11043	12458	13304	10817	8103
Finland/Finlande	4695	11116	11875	15381	18654	Austria/Autriche	9843	8402	10446	8319	12021
Thailand/Thaïlande	10300	11198	9751	10133	15510	Australia/Australie	15490	10026	9331	7644	6012
Malaysia/Malaisie	7783	7290	11093	14061	14098	Portugal	7303	9971	6544	12439	5901
Canada	4371	8658	3696	23438	7942	Switz.Liecht	10586	10043	7006	5760	6543
Saudi Arabia	7819	10179	8853	9420	11387	Mexico/Mexique	1869	12468	9959	4253	1097
Sweden/Suède	9674	8466	7976	7485	11882	Singapore/Singapour	1849	2012	2951	7686	12147
So. Africa Customs Un	3113	4173	17485	6994	2522	Norway,SVD,JM	5626	4884	6265	4720	4744
Netherlands/Pays–Bas	6478	6818	5761	6425	8540	Finland/Finlande	6356	4168	2739	2464	2872
Spain/Espagne	1811	2430	11532	10314	3797	Ireland/Irlande	2447	3508	3267	4424	4754
Switz.Liecht	4336	5972	4537	5102	6174	Korea, Republic of	643	1124	3753	4262	5178
Russian Federation	4553	3837	6775	5301	274	Chile/Chili	561	2220	2878	3457	2928
New Zealand	4406	4139	3783	2570	4012	Viet Nam	168	99	1429	4890	3869
Brazil/Brésil	2893	5203	6133	1823	2744	Panama	1182	928	809	1548	1183
India/Inde	1265	1065	3853	4999	6024	New Zealand	1218	790	680	1235	1230
Norway,SVD,JM	2768	1113	5088	3153	3754	Thailand/Thaïlande	567	659	920	999	1964
Pakistan	333	1484	2691	4439	2521	Malaysia/Malaisie	649	510	585	1043	2078
Belgium–Luxembourg	780	1762	1688	2784	4263	Saudi Arabia	1720	370	1302	1040	276
Philippines	2181	2991	2230	1624	2033	So. Africa Customs Un	407	236	998	1320	1113
Turkey/Turquie	229	2943	2137	3085	2224	Lao People's Dem. Rp.	723	442	1150	963	635
Austria/Autriche	264	816	474	1381	897	Greece/Grèce	696	369	605	1004	1087
Ireland/Irlande	516	171	453	707	1584	Philippines	179	41	348	203	2966
Greece/Grèce	225	2670	177	108	167	American Samoa	1	1337	1153	198	54
Czech Republic		1341	1024	13	145	Northern Mariana Islands				1063	1154
Israel/Israël	213	433	331	156	1036	Iceland/Islande	917	515	227	205	128
Poland/Pologne	225	458	467	132	878	Turkey/Turquie	261	496	37	370	788
Bangladesh	950	529	651		2	Russian Federation	831	505	446	100	62
Argentina/Argentine	410	152	588	264	574	Malta/Malte	244	652	760	215	
Mauritius/Maurice	10	21		683	1168	United Arab Emirates	306	252	555	170	501
Uruguay	58	165	501	223	858	Brunei Darussalam				195	1559
Mexico/Mexique	17	70	109	429	1178	Mauritius/Maurice	901	242	25	418	161
Myanmar	0	104	585	173	547	Brazil/Brésil	34	267	536	466	138
Chile/Chili	244	286	249	125	438	Poland/Pologne	543	37	133	303	357
Sri Lanka	220	208	142	163	511	Argentina/Argentine	214	117	377	339	325
Korea Dem People's Rp	887	59	30	41	14	Hungary/Hongrie	111	323	314	229	177
Cyprus/Chypre	203	187	239	241	156	Qatar	285	381	184	187	90
Viet Nam	194	44	94	149	455	Bangladesh	335	134	236	120	287

(VALUE AS PERCENTAGE OF WORLD TOTAL)(VALEURS EN POURCENTAGE DU TOTAL MONDIAL)

	1987	1988	1989	1990	1991	1992	1993	1994	1995	1996		1987	1988	1989	1990	1991	1992	1993	1994	1995	1996
Africa	0.2	0.6	0.5	0.3	0.3	0.2	0.2	0.8	0.4	0.2	Afrique	0.5	0.3	0.3	0.4	0.1	0.1	0.0	0.1	0.1	0.1
Americas	5.2	5.8	6.4	5.5	5.0	5.6	6.6	7.4	8.7	6.6	Amériques	34.8	35.4	39.2	37.8	33.0	36.4	35.3	38.6	43.2	39.8
Northern America	5.1	5.6	6.1	5.3	4.8	5.4	6.3	7.0	8.6	6.3	Amérique du Nord	34.7	35.2	39.0	37.5	32.7	36.2	34.3	37.8	42.7	39.5
LAIA	0.1	0.2	0.2	0.2	0.1	0.2	0.3	0.4	0.1	0.3	ALAI	0.1	0.1	0.1	0.1	0.1	0.2	0.9	0.7	0.4	0.2
CACM	0.0				0.0		0.0	0.0		0.0	MCAC	0.0	0.0	0.0	0.0	0.0	0.0	0.0	0.0	0.0	0.0
Caribbean	0.0	0.0	0.0	0.0	0.0	0.0	0.0	0.0	0.0	0.0	Caraïbes	0.0	0.0	0.0	0.0	0.0	0.0	0.0		0.0	0.0
Rest of America			0.0			0.0					Autre Amérique	0.0	0.1	0.1	0.1	0.1	0.1	0.1	0.0	0.1	0.1
As.ex F.USSR	82.2	82.1	82.5	83.1	84.0	82.7	79.0	74.5	74.7	77.8	Asie l'URSS exclus	22.5	22.8	23.4	21.7	24.8	25.9	29.2	28.0	24.2	26.7
Eur.x F.USSR	8.6	8.2	7.6	9.5	9.0	9.9	12.6	16.0	15.1	14.3	Europe l'URSS exclus	40.3	39.5	35.1	38.5	40.8	36.5	34.8	32.7	32.0	32.6
EU	7.8	7.9	7.4	9.3	8.7	9.5	12.1	15.5	14.7	13.7	UE	38.9	37.9	33.7	36.8	39.6	35.5	33.8	31.9	31.4	32.0
EFTA	0.7	0.2	0.2	0.2	0.2	0.4	0.4	0.5	0.4	0.5	AELE	1.0	1.3	1.1	1.2	1.0	1.0	0.9	0.7	0.5	0.5
East Europe	0.1	0.0	0.0	0.0	0.1	0.0	0.1	0.1	0.0	0.1	Europe de l'Est	0.4	0.3	0.3	0.4	0.2	0.0	0.0	0.0	0.0	0.0
Other Europe	0.0	0.1	0.0	0.0	0.0					0.0	Autre de l'Europe	0.0	0.0	0.0	0.1	0.0	0.0	0.0	0.0	0.0	0.0
Former USSR	0.4	0.5	0.4	0.4	0.2	0.2	0.2	0.3	0.3	0.0	Ancienne URSS	0.1	0.1	0.1	0.0	0.0	0.0	0.0	0.0	0.0	0.0
Oceania	2.4	1.7	2.6	1.2	1.6	1.5	1.4	0.9	0.8	1.1	Océanie	1.8	2.0	1.9	1.6	1.3	0.9	0.7	0.6	0.5	0.4
Hong Kong	42.8	42.9	42.3	42.2	34.9	32.9	29.9	30.4	28.9	29.1	USA/Etats–Unis d'Amer	33.2	33.8	37.5	36.0	31.2	34.7	32.8	36.4	41.2	38.2
China/Chine	21.0	19.9	19.6	17.8	21.6	20.4	21.3	18.8	21.8	23.9	China/Chine	4.1	4.5	3.4	4.5	8.6	10.3	13.5	12.9	10.5	12.6
Japan/Japon	9.8	10.5	10.2	11.5	17.4	18.0	15.8	12.8	10.5	9.0	Hong Kong	15.5	14.0	14.7	13.1	13.2	12.9	12.9	11.9	10.1	10.1
USA/Etats–Unis d'Amer	4.8	4.5	5.5	5.1	4.6	5.2	5.8	6.8	7.4	5.9	Germany/Allemagne	12.4	12.0	10.4	11.7	13.6	11.9	11.3	10.1	9.8	10.2
United Kingdom	2.0	2.6	2.4	2.9	2.5	2.5	3.5	4.2	4.2	3.9	France,Monac	9.6	8.8	7.5	8.0	8.8	8.7	8.3	7.0	6.8	6.5
Korea, Republic of	1.9	1.7	1.6	2.0	2.0	2.2	2.3	2.5	2.4	2.6	United Kingdom	7.0	7.6	7.3	7.7	7.3	6.6	6.2	7.0	7.0	7.2
France,Monac	0.8	0.9	0.8	1.0	0.9	1.5	2.0	3.0	2.0	1.8	Netherlands/Pays–Bas	2.3	2.3	2.0	2.1	2.5	2.2	2.6	2.4	2.3	2.7
Germany/Allemagne	0.8	0.9	0.9	1.1	1.4	1.6	1.9	2.3	2.1	1.6	Canada	1.4	1.4	1.5	1.5	1.5	1.5	1.4	1.4	1.5	1.3
Denmark/Danemark	1.5	1.0	0.6	1.7	1.5	1.0	1.3	1.9	1.7	1.1	Japan/Japon	2.2	3.5	4.5	3.1	1.8	1.6	1.4	1.3	1.3	1.3
Portugal	1.0	0.6	0.5	0.7	0.9	1.1	0.8	1.2	1.2	1.5	Italy/Italie	2.2	2.1	1.6	1.9	2.5	2.0	1.2	1.0	0.9	0.8

4. General Imports C.I.F. by Commodities according to the S.I.T.C. (Rev. 2) in thousand U.S. Dollars
Importations Générales C.A.F. par Produits d'après la C.T.C.I. (Rév. 2) en milliers de Dollars E.U.

SITC CTCI	COMMODITY	1993 WEIGHT POIDS	1993 VALUE VALEUR	1994 WEIGHT POIDS	1994 VALUE VALEUR	1995 WEIGHT POIDS	1995 VALUE VALEUR	1996 WEIGHT POIDS	1996 VALUE VALEUR	PRODUIT
	ALL COMMODITIES		1890728		2089235		2018591		1991983	TOUS PRODUITS
0	FOOD AND LIVE ANIMALS		127891		139471		143745		148540	ALIMENTS,ANIMAUX VIVANTS
001	*LIVE ANIMALS FOR FOOD	W 22221	26072	W 23800	28242	W 23587	28331	N 4549875	29134	ANIMAUX VIVANTS
0013	SWINE,LIVE	W 13300	12293	W 14760	15013	W 15030	14959	N 163138	14816	ESPECE PORCINE
0014	LIVE POULTRY	W 6785	7279	W 6734	8199	W 6615	8254	N 4375873	8686	VOLAILLES VIVANTES
00149	LIVE POULTRY OVER 185 GR	W 6756	7175	W 6715	8117	W 6592	8157	N 3971008	8623	VOL VIVANTES PLUS 185 GR.
01	MEAT AND PREPARATIONS		11085		10570		11130		10697	VIANDES ET PREPARATIONS
011	MEAT FRESH,CHILLD,FROZEN	W 12611	6435	W 12642	5723	W 12906	5873		5415	VIANDES FRAICHES,REF,CONGE
02	DAIRY PRODCTS,BIRDS'EGGS		12978		14121		14670		16429	PRODUITS LAITIERS,OEUFS
022	MILK AND CREAM	W 6401	9168	W 6990	10141	W 7337	11279		12337	LAIT ET CREME
0224	MILK,CREAM PRESERVED ETC	W 3476	6403	W 4126	7247	W 4384	8267		9013	LAIT,CREME CONS,CONC
03	FISH AND PREPARATIONS		14255		16275		19051		18270	POISSONS ET PREPARATIONS
034	FISH,FRESH,CHILLED,FROZN	W 5511	5045	W 5869	5783	W 6740	7774		7406	POISSON FRAIS, REFRIG,CONG
0341	FISH FRSH,CHLLD,EX FILLT	W 4572	3953	W 4910	4521	W 5714	6302		6379	POISSON FRAIS,REFRIGERE
036	SHELL FISH FRESH,FROZEN	W 3891	4325	W 3351	5824	W 3056	6325		5612	CRUSTACES,MOLLUSQUES
04	CEREALS AND PREPARATIONS		14940		17980		18409		19321	CEREALES ET PRODUITS
048	CEREAL ETC PREPARATIONS	W 7124	8693	W 7680	10698	W 7624	11251		12193	PREPTNS A BASE CEREALES
05	VEGETABLES AND FRUIT		23632		26080		25635		26211	LEGUMES ET FRUITS
054	VEG ETC FRSH,SMPLY PRSVD	W 29621	4758	W 29758	5323	W 30232	5205		6063	LEGUMES FRAIS,CONG,SECS
057	FRUIT,NUTS,FRESH,DRIED	W 23101	11249	W 24120	11744	W 24059	11488		11047	FRUITS FRAIS OU SECS
06	SUGAR AND PREPS,HONEY		5812		6304		6667		6503	SUCRES ET PRODUITS
07	COFFEE,TEA,COCOA,SPICES		6560		6470		6060		7718	CAFE,THE,CACAO,EPICES
09	MISC EDIBLE PRODUCTS		11565		12313		12212		12203	PREP ALIMENTAIRES DIVERSES
098	EDIBLE PRODCTS,PREPS NES	W 7903	10306	W 8954	11045	W 7516	11492		11546	PREP ALIMENTAIRES NDA
1	BEVERAGES AND TOBACCO		96247		137257		130137		104146	BOISSONS ET TABACS
11	BEVERAGES		49907		74128		59063		49971	BOISSONS
111	NON–ALCOHL BEVERAGES NES	W 63594	12904	W 67385	16022	MW 53021479	17533	MW 54418	19252	BOISSONS NON ALCOOLIQUES
11101	WATERS,ICE AND SNOW	W 52764	6366	W 55791	7661	MW 53021467	8056	MW 54407	8981	EAU,EAUX MINERALES
11102	FLAVORED WATERS NON–ALCO	W 10830	6539	W 11594	8361	W 12140	9477	W 11574	10271	LIMONADES,EAUX GAZEUSES
112	ALCOHOLIC BEVERAGES	W 21585	37003	W 23550	58106	W 21929	41530	W 15838	30718	BOISSONS ALCOOLIQUES
1121	WINE OF FRESH GRAPES ETC	W 762	2088	W 837	2348	W 974	2896	W 1504	7136	VINS DE RAISINS FRAIS
11212	WINE OF FRESH GRAPES	W 759	2082	W 834	2342	W 972	2887	W 1495	7058	VINS DE MOUTS DE RAISINS
1123	BEER,ALE,STOUT,PORTER	W 19207	8387	W 20575	9882	W 19103	11831	W 12357	10634	BIERES
1124	DISTILLED ALCOHOLIC BEVS	W 1557	26423	W 2048	45724	W 1087	25843	W 481	10849	ALCOOLS,EAUX–DE–VIE
11242	DISTILLD WINE,GRAPE MARC	W 670	24158	W 1213	42913	W 733	24270	W 269	8702	EAUX–DE–VIE NATURELLES
12	TOBACCO AND MANUFACTURES		46340		63130		71075		54176	TABACS BRUTS FABRIQUES
122	TOBACCO,MANUFACTURED	W 3254	46268	W 5151	63015		71028		53923	TABACS FABRIQUES
1222	CIGARETTES	W 2682	44578	W 4407	58900		66151	W 1597	46744	CIGARETTES
1223	OTH MANUFACTURED TOBACCO	W 570	1553	W 739	3858	W 813	4362		6227	TABACS FUMER,CHIQUER,PRISER
2	CRUDE MATERLS,EXCL FUELS		137950		74258		58046		65834	MAT BRUTES NON COMESTIBLES
21	HIDES,SKINS,FURS UNDRSSD		25797		26862		28294		36431	CUIRS,PEAUX BRUTS
212	FURSKINS,RAW	W 191	25784	W 127	26837	W 157	28294	N 865278	36420	PELLETERIES BRUTES
21201	MINK SKINS,RAW	W 149	22652	W 93	21550	W 86	16600	N 625220	23807	PEAUX DE VISON BRUTES
21209	OTHER FURSKINS,RAW	W 42	3131	W 33	5286	W 71	11694	N 240058	12613	AUTRES PELLETERIES BRUTES
24	CORK AND WOOD		7231		7413		6761		4444	LIEGE ET BOIS
26	TEXTILE FIBRES AND WASTE		22039		19674		15224		20361	FIBRES TEXTILES
268	WOOL(EXC TOPS),ANML HAIR	W 3254	17734	W 3855	14873	W 3490	13022		16597	LAINES ET POILS
2682	WOOL DEGREASED,UNCOMBED	W 2794	14369	W 3360	12396	W 2870	10124		13224	LAINE DEGRAISSEE
27	CRUDE FERTLZR,MINRLS NES		79763		17713		4307		1847	ENGRAIS MINERAUX BRUTS
273	STONE,SAND AND GRAVEL	MW 50029	78893	MW 12699	16946	MW 1021	3415		1209	PIERRES,SABLES,GRAVIERS
2733	SAND,EXCL METAL–BEARING	MW 44720	55531	MW 11621	11440	MW 738	1172	V 37307	103	SABLES NATURELS
2734	GRAVEL,CRUSHED STONE,ETC	W 5280445	22260	W 1042787	3927	W 247349	1196	V 64082	222	PIERRES CONCASSEES
3	MINERAL FUELS ETC		87553		98809		104434		129481	COMBUSTIBLES MINERAUX LUB
33	PETROLEUM AND PRODUCTS		69370		77897		79012		101853	PETROLE ET DERIVES
334	PETROLEUM PRODUCTS,REFIN	W 376345	68276	W 410525	76689	MW 330361	77682		99212	PRODUITS RAFFINES
3341	GASOLINE,OTH LIGHT OILS	W 23267	10601	W 25568	11846	MW 22237	12885	W 34511	15650	ESSENCES POUR MOTEURS
33411	MOTOR,AVIATION SPIRIT	W 23151	10580	W 25426	11819	MW 22078	12849	W 34381	15622	ESSENCES MOTEURS D'AVIONS
3342	KEROSENE,OTH MEDIUM OILS	W 10235	2861	W 10851	3029	MW 13005	6819	W 62996	17144	PETR LAMPANTS,AUT HUIL
33421	KEROSENE INCL JET FUEL	W 10235	2861	W 10851	3029	W 5570865	3976	W 53979	14319	PETROLES LAMPANTS
3343	GAS OILS	W 86258	25765	W 95714	28955	MW 65646	24175	W 81813	27146	GAS OILS
3344	FUEL OILS,NES	W 251943	24426	W 273944	28377	MW 225958	29297	W 239572	34574	FUEL OILS
341	*GAS,NATURAL AND MANUFCT	W 16976	9482	W 18588	10542	W 20879	12548		14405	GAZ NATUREL,GAZ MANUFACT
3413	PETROLM GASES,LIQUEFIED	W 16976	9482	W 18588	10542	W 20879	12548		14405	GAZ DE PETROLE LIQUEFIE
34131	LIQUEFIED PROPANE,BUTANE	W 16976	9482	W 18588	10542	W 20879	12548		14405	PROPANE,BUTANE LIQUEFIES
351	*ELECTRIC CURRENT		8683		10353		12249	H 170761	12278	ENERGIE ELECTRIQUE
4	ANIMAL,VEGETABLE OIL,FAT		4633		5779		6543		7021	HUILES,GRAISSES ANIM,VEG
42	FIXED VEGETABLE OIL,FAT		4607		5754		6512		6994	HUILES VEGETALES FIXES
5	CHEMCLS,RELATED PROD NES		82949		89908		87190		87581	PRODUITS CHIMIQUES
53	DYES,TANNING,COLOUR PROD		9840		9542		9115		7448	PROD TEINTURE,COLORANTS
541	*MEDICINAL,PHARM PRODUCT		12721	K 1469686	15511	K 1661336	18311		21109	PROD MEDICINAUX PHARMACEUT
5417	MEDICAMENTS	K 1244626	11243	K 1395728	13182	K 1551948	15600		17397	MEDICAMENTS
54179	— CONTNG OTH SUBSTANCES	K 989603	8219	K 1174444	9777	K 1376544	10240		12396	MED CONT AUT SUBSTANCES
55	PERFUME,CLEANING ETC PRD		20339		23276		27041		33841	PROD POUR PARFUM,TOILETTE
553	PERFUMERY,COSMETICS,ETC	W 8554	11091	W 9798	13369	W 11158	15637		20843	PRODUITS DE PARFUMERIE
554	SOAP,CLEANSING ETC PREPS	W 13970	8553	W 13959	8946	W 12416	10532		12134	SAVONS,PRODUITS DETERSIFS
5541	SOAPS	W 7865	4240	W 6713	3765	W 5382	5120		6463	SAVONS,PROD TENSIO–ACTIFS
58	PLASTIC MATERIALS ETC		24925		24876		18417		12766	MAT PLAST ARTIFICIELLES
583	POLYMERIZATION ETC PRODS	W 19186	20641	W 18505	19037	W 13696	16900		11494	PROD POLYMERISATION
5833	POLYSTYRENE,ITS COPOLYMR	W 6627	7743	W 6721	7276	W 5571	7604		3735	POLYPROPYLENE COPOLYMERES
58331	— IN PRIMARY FORMS	W 6437	7446	W 6504	6866	W 5391	7273		3521	SOUS FORMES PRIMAIRES
5834	POLYVINYL CHLORIDE	W 5109	5677	W 5146	6321	W 3291	4610		3508	CHLORURE DE POLYVINYLE
59	CHEMICAL MATERIALS NES		6612		7994		8365		8188	MAT PROD CHIMIQUES NDA
6	BASIC MANUFACTURES		777775		888947		879791		917906	ART MANUFACTURES
61	LEATHER,DRESSED FUR,ETC		35007		39790		42913		23963	CUIRS,PELLETERIES
611	LEATHER	W 969	8321	W 914	8236		6613		4762	CUIRS,PEAUX PREPARES
612	LEATHER ETC MANUFACTURES	W 672	2582	W 1849	4427	W 2932	9426		6808	OUVRAGES EN CUIRS NDA
6123	PREPRD PARTS OF FOOTWEAR	W 664	2406	W 1844	4314	W 2929	9343		6630	PARTIES DE CHAUSSURES
613	FUR SKINS TANNED,DRESSED	W 141	24104	W 88	27127	W 103	26874	N 416669	12393	PELLETERIES
63	WOOD,CORK MANUFACTRS NES		8112		11399		7969		6854	OUVRAGES LIEGE ET BOIS
634	VENEERS,PLYWOOD,ETC	W 19720	5938	W 22196	7534	W 15522	4498		4550	PLACAGES,CONTRE–PLAQUES
6342	PLYWOOD OF WOOD SHEETS	W 19662	5911	W 22101	7476	W 15435	4406	V 28699	4519	BOIS CONTRE–PLAQUES
64	PAPER,PAPERBOARD AND MFR		25164		27917		25997		24644	PAPIERS,CARTONS & OUVRAGES
641	PAPER AND PAPERBOARD	W 20502	6988	W 19330	8673		8964		8417	PAPIERS ET CARTONS
642	PAPER,ETC,PRECUT,ARTS OF	W 14994	18176	W 14863	19244	W 12540	17032		16227	PAP,CARTONS DECOUPES
6421	PAPER ETC CONTAINERS	W 7770	8100	W 7098	6587	W 6014	5459		4080	BOITES,SACS EMBALLAGES
6428	PAPER ETC ARTICLES NES	W 4433	8146	W 4633	10299	W 3879	8887		9051	OUVRAGES EN PATE A PAPIER
65	TEXTILE YARN,FABRICS,ETC		583530		666822		695828		769044	FILS,TISSUS,ARTICLES TEXTILE
651	TEXTILE YARN	W 24420	113899	W 26238	133178	W 24360	124325		131807	FILS TEXTILES
6512	WOOL,HAIR YARN,INCL TOPS	W 6164	52859	W 6868	64778	W 5926	60427		57196	FILS DE LAINE,DE POILS
65122	CARDED WOOL YARN IN BULK	W 3845	28955	W 4595	41342	W 4170	41948		40038	FILS CONT 85% LAINE CARDEE
65123	COMBED WOOL YARN IN BULK	W 614	6705	W 685	8037	W 547	5367		5055	FILS CONT 85% LAINE PEIGNEE

4. General Imports C.I.F. by Commodities according to the S.I.T.C. (Rev. 2) in thousand U.S. Dollars
Importations Générales C.A.F. par Produits d'après la C.T.C.I. (Rév. 2) en milliers de Dollars E.U.

SITC CTCI	COMMODITY	1993			1994			1995			1996			PRODUIT
			WEIGHT POIDS	VALUE VALEUR		WEIGHT POIDS	VALUE VALEUR		WEIGHT POIDS	VALUE VALEUR		WEIGHT POIDS	VALUE VALEUR	
65127	CARDED WOOL BLEND YARN	W	936	9360	W	774	7591	W	712	7395			7637	LAINE CARD MOINS 85% LAINE
65128	COMBED WOOL BLEND YARN	W	643	7021	W	523	4811	W	314	3271			2948	LAINE PEIG MOINS 85% LAINE
6513	COTTON YARN	W	9718	29271	W	10033	31587	W	9190	32181			39437	FILS DE COTON
6514	SYN FIB YRN,BULK,MONOFIL	W	4021	12311	W	4644	14418	W	5106	15076			16698	FILS CONT 85% FIB TEXT SYNTH
65142	— NONTXT ETC CONT PAMID	W	2279	6375	W	2789	8969	W	2629	9163			10269	FILS NON TEX FI CON POLYAMID
6516	DISCON SYN FIB BLEND YRN	W	2701	8320	W	3162	10253	W	3244	8603			8719	FILS FIBR TEX SYNT DIS MOINS
652	COTTON FABRICS,WOVEN	W	23998	143792	W	23343	156992	W	24701	179888	A	110597	214146	TISSUS DE COTON
6522	WOVEN COTTON BLEACHD,ETC	W	23716	142801	W	23184	156293	W	24608	179318	A	110375	213917	TISSUS COTON BLANCHIS ETC
65223	PILE ETC COTTON FABRICS	W	803	4164	W	1146	6755	W	1591	12102	A	9398	19459	VELOURS TISSUS BOUCLES
65224	BLCHED COTTON FABRIC NES	W	22250	133412	W	20897	143575	W	21853	159456	A	95926	186131	AUT TIS PLUS 85% COT BLANCHI
65225	BLCHD COTN BLEND FAB NES	W	499	5026	W	568	5496	W	737	7478	A	4936	8205	AUT TIS MOINS 85% COT BLANCH
653	WOVN MAN-MADE FIB FABRIC	W	28529	85743	W	42848	98835	W	47575	102281	A	207347	100638	TISSUS FIBRES SYNTH,ARTIF
6531	CONT SYNT WEAVES NONPILE	W	24495	53916	W	37788	66126	W	41353	62697	A	181077	64596	TISSUS FIBRES SYNTH CONTINUE
65314	CONT SYN TYRE CORD FABRC	W	2267	13686	W	4141	14331	W	4301	12265	A	20364	11556	TIS ARMATURE PNEUMATIQUES
65315	CONT SYN TXTL FABRIC NES	W	22228	40230	W	33647	51795	W	37052	50432	A	160713	53039	TIS PLUS 85% TEXT SYNT CONT
6532	DISC SYN TXTL FABRIC NES	W	759	5871	W	686	6275	W	750	9652	A	5235	12816	TIS DISC MOINS 85% FIBR TEXT
6534	DISC SYN BLEND FABRC NES	W	2678	18695	W	3646	17912	W	4662	19822	A	16662	14771	TISSUS FIBRES SYNTH DISCONT
65341	DISC SYN FIB-COTTN FABRC	W	2467	18249	W	3505	17394	W	4456	18845	A	15781	14396	TISSUS FIB SYNT DIS MEL COTO
654	OTH WOVEN TEXTILE FABRIC	W	260	3647	W	760	10576	W	554	7419			6007	TISSUS AUT COTON SYNT,ARTIF
6544	WOVEN FLAX,RAMIE FABRICS	W	136	2007	W	497	7270	W	387	5113	A	1706	4986	TISSUS DE LIN,RAMIE
655	KNITTED,ETC FABRICS	W	34793	207125	W	40361	236191	W	43969	249027			282877	ETOF BONNETERIE PIECES ETC
6552	OTHER KNIT ETC FAB NONEL	W	34793	207125	W	40361	236191	W	43969	249027			282877	ETOF BON NON ELAS NON SYNT
656	LACE,RIBBONS,TULLE,ETC	W	2278	10893	W	2057	12588	W	1985	14913			17747	TULLES,BRODERIE
65601	NARROW FABRICS NES	W	1707	4329	W	1479	4200	W	1496	5252			6753	RUBANS SANS TRAME EN FILS
657	SPECIAL TXTL FABRC,PRODS	W	3257	8909	W	3482	12784	W	3774	12001			10729	TISSUS SPECIAUX
6573	COATED ETC TEXTILES NES	W	1330	4183	W	1922	7335	W	2281	6235			5316	TISSUS,ART MATIERE TEXT NDA
65732	PLASTIC COATED TEXTILES	W	1292	4012	W	1808	6792	W	2187	5630	A	5947	4799	TISSUS IMPREGNES
658	TEXTILE ARTICLES NES	W	1087	7556	W	617	3663	W	629	4587			3717	ART FACONNES MAT TEXTILES
6584	LINENS ETC	W	784	6363	W	396	2766	W	458	3463	N	4291449	3030	LINGE DE MAISON
66	NONMETAL MINERAL MFS NES			53634			58607			43062			39346	ART MIN NON METALLIQUES
661	LIME,CEMENT,BLDG PRODS	W	638649	24075	W	720718	26728	W	504104	21465			24404	CHAUX,CIMENTS MAT CONSTR
6612	CEMENT	W	628804	20743	W	712842	23721	W	492461	16618			21404	CIMENTS HYDRAULIQUES
662	CLAY,REFRACTORY BLDG PRD			6077	W	41755	8079	W	37608	10327			6699	MAT CONST REFRACTAIRES
6624	BRICKS ETC NONREFRACTORY	W	32924	5908	W	41504	7922	W	37565	10277			6658	BRIQUES ETC CERAM NON REFR
66245	GLAZED CERAMIC SETTS ETC	W	15364	4493	W	17836	5682	W	23273	7873	A	1582	4255	AUT CARREAUX CERAMIQUE
663	MINERAL MANUFCTURES NES	W	213966	15656	W	206849	17175	W	67494	4646			2575	ART MIN MANUF NDA
6633	MINRL MFS NES NONCERAMIC	W	213520	15172	W	206267	16497	W	67261	4212			2291	OUVR MAT MINERALE NDA
66332	CEMENT,ARTFCL STONE PROD	W	213216	15076	W	206003	16337	W	63939	4061			2190	OUVRAGES EN CIMENT
67	IRON AND STEEL			39162			45024			22580			18479	FER ET ACIER
673	IRON,STEEL SHAPES ETC	W	163438	29067	W	157595	31658	W	76138	13852			11842	BARRES,PROFIL FER,ACIER
6732	IRON,STEEL BARS ETC	W	132563	21019	W	132448	25187	W	65387	11159			9726	BARRES FER,ACIER
67326	IRN,OTH STL BARS HOTROLD	W	104070	17715	W	119324	21485	W	64843	10937			9461	BARRES PLEINES FER,ACIER
6733	IRON,STEEL PROFILES ETC	W	22254	5304	W	25147	6470	W	10750	2693			2115	PROFILES,PALPLAN FER,ACIER
678	IRON,STL TUBES,PIPES,ETC	W	13841	6010	W	15667	9849	W	10474	5607			3577	TUBES,TUYAUX EN FONTE,FER
68	NON-FERROUS METALS			6054			5046			7429			9322	METAUX NON FERREUX
69	METAL MANUFACTURES NES			22993			30350			30220			21941	ART MANUFACT EN METAL NDA
691	STRUCTURES AND PARTS NES	W	4066	4626	W	6547	8728	W	3786	8788			3853	CONSTRUCT FER,ACIER,ALU
6911	STRUCTURES,PARTS IRN,STL	W	3410	2979	W	5677	7418	W	2462	4891			2819	CONSTRUCT FER,ACIER,FONTE
699	BASE METAL MFRS NES	W	4455	8243	W	4712	9675			9420			8252	ART MANUFACTURES MET NDA
7	MACHINES,TRANSPORT EQUIP			378643			423700			381404			312777	MACHINES MATERIEL TRANSPORT
71	POWER GENERATING EQUIPMT			7985			26494			39298			8368	MACHINES GENERATRICES
716	ROTATING ELECTRIC PLANT	W	801	4877	W	1982	19721	W	3452	34560			5395	APP ELECTR ROTATIFS,PIECES
7162	AC MTRS,GENRTRS,GEN SETS	W	671	2106	W	1275	12730	W	3139	28347	N	1483801	2656	MOTEURS ELECTRIQUES
71622	AC GENERATORS	W	47	212	W	599	6915	W	602	6966	N	108	20	GENER COURANT ALTERNATIF
71623	GEN SETS WITH PISTN ENGN	W	142	821	W	306	4515	W	2173	20409	N	104	875	GROUPES MOTEUR EXPLOSION
7169	PTS NES OF ROT ELEC PLNT	W	130	2770	W	707	6989	W	313	6142			2722	PIECES MAC APP ROTATIFS
72	MACHS FOR SPCL INDUSTRYS			29400			22335			16620			12281	MAC SPECIALES POUR INDUST
723	CIVIL ENGNEERG EQUIP ETC	W	2669	7967	W	2194	6138	W	491	2235			797	APPAREILS DE GENIE CIVIL
7234	CONST,MINING MACHNRY NES	W	2553	7501	W	2029	5679	W	433	2036	N	54	655	MACH POUR LA CONST, MINES
724	TEXTILE,LEATHER MACHNRY	W	1124	13440			7538	W	526	5718			4887	MACH POUR INDUSTRIE TEXTILE
7247	TEXTILE MACHINERY NES	W	386	7001	W	173	2145	W	73	792			1021	MACH LAVAGE,TEINTURE TEX
728	OTH MACHY FOR SPCL INDUS	W	758	6205	W	968	7262			5324			4450	AUT MACH IND PARTICULIERES
74	GENRL INDUSTRL MACHY NES			65597			83363			65968			52486	MACH APP INDUSTRIE
741	HEATING,COOLING EQUIPMNT	W	5045	34481	W	4596	30490	W	4037	26153			23962	MACH CHAUFFAGE,PIECES
7415	AIR-CONDITIONING MACHNRY	W	4467	30022	W	3740	23880	W	3439	22296	N	40841	20830	GROUPES CONDITION AIR
743	PUMPS NES,CENTRFUGES ETC	W	835	3603	W	1173	10653	W	634	3055			2771	POMPES COMPRES,VENT ETC
744	MECHANICAL HANDLING EQU	W	4587	15806	W	6984	24189	W	5226	23932			15970	EQUIP MANUTENTION PIECES
7442	LIFTING,LOADING MACH NES	W	3314	11066	W	3851	14513	W	2752	13034	N	1531	9302	APP LEVAGE,MANUTENTION
74424	LIFTS AND SKIP HOISTS	W	1772	5286	W	1693	6275	W	1679	6857	N	99	4237	ASCENSEURS,MONTE-CHARGE
7449	PTS NES OF MACHY OF 7442	W	1029	3924	W	2947	9266	W	2160	8667			5680	PIECES DU 744.2
749	NONELEC MACH PTS,ACC NES	W	1521	8561	W	1554	12368	W	1433	8697			6205	PIECES MACH NON ELEC NDA
7499	OTH NONELEC MCHY PTS NES	W	721	5877	W	818	7978	W	426	3886			2232	PIECES NON ELECT NDA
74991	FOUNDRY MOULDS ETC NES	W	627	5243	W	722	7123	W	353	3666	N	46475	2049	MOULES POUR METAUX
75	OFFICE MACHNES,ADP EQUIP			24627			21852			26572			19421	MACH BUREAU TRAIT AUTOM
751	OFFICE MACHINES	W	599	11518	W	270	6227	W	269	5658	N	144897	3575	MACH,APPAREILS DE BUREAU
7518	OFFICE MACHINES NES	W	581	11236	W	260	6078	W	262	5508	N	76899	3297	MACH,APP DE BUREAU NDA
75182	PHOTO,THERMOCOPY APPARAT	W	537	9533	W	206	5513	W	207	4272	N	3436	2336	APPAREILS DE PHOTOCOPIE
752	AUTOMTIC DATA PROC EQUIP	W	193	10390	W	237	11319	W	239	13907	N	23780	10365	MACH TRAIT INFORMATION
7523	DIGITL CENTRL PROCESSORS	W	68	5346	W	74	7399	W	80	6339	N	6	72	UNITES CENTRALES
7525	ADP PERIPHERAL UNITS	W	107	3559	W	122	2855	W	150	6144	N	19458	3576	UNITES PERIPHERIQUES
759	OFFICE,ADP MCH PTS,ACCES	W	66	2718	W	106	4306	W	177	7007			5481	PIECES DU 751 ET 752
7599	ACCTG,ETC,ADP MCH PTS,AC	W	29	2029	W	80	3752	W	151	6464			4703	PIECES DU 751 ET 752
76	TELECOMM,SOUND EQUIPMENT			129475			96919			76544			60538	EQUIPMENT DE TELECOM
761	TELEVISION RECEIVERS	W	1911	21135	W	1240	15087	W	1244	19640	N	42991	14579	RECEPTEURS DE TELEVISION
7611	COLOUR TV RECEIVERS	W	1908	21080	W	1238	15078	W	1242	19603	N	42800	14536	RECEPTEURS COULEUR
762	RADIO BROADCAST RECEIVRS	W	4705	35990	W	4624	29742	W	1990	11527	N	40606	2689	RECEPTEURS RADIODIFFUSION
7628	OTHER RADIO RECEIVERS	W	4584	34261	W	4576	28836	W	1965	11096	N	28596	1847	AUTRES RECEPT RADIO
763	SOUND RECORDRS,PHONOGRPH	W	1909	28780	W	512	8620	W	352	6825	N	45848	8241	PHONO,APP ENREGISTREMENT
7638	OTHR SOUND APPARATUS ETC	W	1896	28599	W	511	8607	W	350	6794	N	45832	8241	AUT APP D'ENREGIS,REPROD
76381	TV IMAGE,SND RECRDRS ETC	W	1455	24319	W	367	6560	W	298	5906	N	38632	7418	APP ENREG,REPRO IMAG,SON
764	TELECOM EQPT,PTS,ACC NES			43570	W	1014	43470	W	756	38553			35029	EQUIP TELECOM,PIECES
7641	LINE TELEPHONE,ETC EQUIP	W	210	11683	W	93	6759	W	58	3826			5663	APP TELEPHON PAR FIL
7643	TV,RADIO TRANSMITTRS ETC	W	35	11036	W	21	11920	W	37	16969	N	26229	14903	APP EMET TELE RADIO
7648	TELECOMM EQUIPMENT NES	W	29	11397	W	121	12281	W	27	9013	N	22350	4967	APP TELECOM NDA
76481	RADIOTELEPHONE ETC RCVRS	W	13	9781	W	5	4729	W	7	6862	N	21176	2983	RECEP RADIOTELEPHONIE
76483	RADAR APPARATUS ETC	W	1	44	W	104	6281	W	1	316	N	347	122	APP DE RADIOGUIDAGE ETC
7649	PTS NES OF EQUIPMT OF 76			5629	W	134	7829	W	199	6326			6141	PIECES DE LA DIV 76
77	ELECTRIC MACHNRY NES ETC			55148			99756			83013			75661	MACH APP ELECT NDA
771	ELECTRIC POWER MACHY NES	W	437	3309	W	794	10393	W	834	16803			20746	MACH PROD,TRANS ELECTR
7712	OTH ELEC POWER MACHY NES	W	140	1617	W	433	6828	W	487	15180			14839	AUT APP PROD TRANSF ELEC
77122	INDUCTORS	W	27	131	W	60	1485	W	132	6072	MN	27177	3914	BOBINES REACTANCE,SELFS

4. General Imports C.I.F. by Commodities according to the S.I.T.C. (Rev. 2) in thousand U.S. Dollars
Importations Générales C.A.F. par Produits d'après la C.T.C.I. (Rév. 2) en milliers de Dollars E.U.

SITC CTCI	COMMODITY	1993 WEIGHT POIDS	1993 VALUE VALEUR	1994 WEIGHT POIDS	1994 VALUE VALEUR	1995 WEIGHT POIDS	1995 VALUE VALEUR	1996 WEIGHT POIDS	1996 VALUE VALEUR	PRODUIT
77129	PTS NES OF MACHY OF 771	W 74	658	W 345	4745	W 302	6096		9933	PIECES MACH DU 771
772	SWITCHGEAR ETC,PARTS NES	W 726	8195	W 919	20233	W 694	14157		8476	APP COUPURE,SECT ETC
7721	SWITCHGEAR ETC	W 707	7876	W 894	18853	W 675	12685		6901	APP COUPURE,SECTIONMNT
773	ELECTR DISTRIBUTNG EQUIP	W 3753	11211	W 4063	13826	W 2532	7453		6530	EQUIPMT DISTRIBUTION ELECT
7731	INSULATED WIRE,CABLE ETC	W 3752	11169	W 4059	13762	W 2526	7420	L 28575	6492	FILS,CABLES ISOLES ELECT
775	HOUSEHOLD TYPE EQUIP NES	W 2901	16906	W 4419	25022		17077		16586	MACH,APP USAGE DOMESTQUE
7752	DOM REFRIGERATRS,FREEZRS	W 925	4761	W 2011	10633	W 1202	6326	N 34541	6405	REFRIG,CONGEL MENAGER
77521	DOMESTIC REFRIGERATORS	W 915	4717	W 2002	10586	W 1196	6273	N 34471	6369	REFRIGERATEURS
7758	ELECTRO–THERMIC APPL NES	W 989	7124	W 956	7005		5103		5167	APP ELECTROTHERMIQ NDA
776	TRANSISTORS,VALVES,ETC		3772	W 34	6515	W 55	9214		6398	LAMPES,TUBES,VALVES
7764	ELECTRONIC MICROCIRCUITS	W 22	2099	W 19	4161	W 40	6310	MN 9331	4389	MICROSTRUCTURES ELECTRON
778	ELECTRICAL MACHINERY NES		10911		23206	W 1571	16918		15299	AUTRES MACH ELECT NDA
7781	BATTERIES,ACCUMULATORS	W 1167	3942	W 1276	9955	W 945	6823		6698	PILES ET ACCUMULATEURS
77812	ELECTRIC ACCUMULATORS	W 327	1658	W 373	7752	W 329	4330	N 6638958	5382	ACCUMULATEURS ELECTRIQ
7788	OTH ELEC MACHY,EQUIP NES		4001		10077	W 186	7172		6066	AUT MACH APP ELEC NDA
78	ROAD VEHICLES		64400		70383		50975		62790	VEHICULES ROUTIERS
781	PASS MOTOR VEH EXC BUSES	W 5286	43009	W 5581	47266	W 3600	31190	N 5347	36699	AUTO TRANSPORT PERSONNES
782	LORRIES,SPCL MTR VEH NES	W 1445	8930	W 1106	8654	W 655	7173	N 213	4267	VEHICULES SPECIAUX,MARCH
7821	LORRIES,TRUCKS	W 1390	8436	W 948	6008	W 447	3670	N 204	3466	VEHICULES TRANSP MARCHAND
783	ROAD MOTOR VEHICLES NES	W 333	2252	W 400	3428	W 400	4566	N 135	7897	VEHICULES ROUTIERS NDA
7831	BUSES	W 307	2095	W 259	2341	W 380	4414	N 126	7317	VOITURES TRANSPORT COMMUN
785	CYCLES,ETC MOTRZD OR NOT	W 644	8346	W 1010	9544	W 461	5697		10806	MOTOCYCLES SCOOTERS
7851	MOTORCYCLES ETC	W 538	8029	W 549	8702	W 366	5382	N 10286	10481	MOTO VELO MOTEUR AUXIL
79	OTHR TRANSPORT EQUIPMENT		583		629		21501		19952	AUTRE MATERIEL TRANSPORT
792	AIRCRAFT ETC	W 3	149	W 1	336	W 18	20696		19513	APP NAVIGATION AERIENNE
7923	AIRCRFT NES2000–15000KG					W 14	17842			AERODYNES 2000 A 15000 KG
7929	AIRCRAFT PARTS NES	W 1	130	W 1	336	W 4	2854		17656	PIECES DU 792
8	MISC MANUFACTURED GOODS		193422		214470		219272		215794	ART MANUFACTURES DIVERS
821	*FURNITURE,PARTS THEREOF	W 8682	16759	W 7589	13317	W 7718	14725		12731	MEUBLES ET PIECES
8219	FURNITURE AND PARTS NES	W 5909	9615	W 5098	7863	W 5480	9742		7864	AUTRES MEUBLES ET PIECES
82192	WOOD FURNITURE NES	W 4841	6662	W 4253	6296	W 4475	7609	N 135867	6381	MEUBLES NDA EN BOIS
84	CLOTHING AND ACCESSORIES		85615		86996		88574		101556	VETEMENTS
845	OUTERWEAR KNIT NONELASTC	W 5259	70960	W 5521	68578	W 5182	68656	MN 15340	74006	VET DESSOUS,ACCES BONNET
8451	— JERSEYS,PULLOVERS ETC	W 5056	67739	W 5308	65002	W 5015	65382	MN 13828	68224	CHANDAILS,PULL–OVERS ETC
847	TEXTILE CLTHNG ACCES NES	W 569	4522	W 549	4869	W 561	5579		8750	ACCES VET MAT TEXT NDA
8471	— NOT KNITTED	W 471	4183	W 459	4606	W 495	5221		8336	ACCES VET MAT TEX NON BON
84719	MADE–UP CLTHG ACCESS NES	W 444	3814	W 422	4091	W 448	4507		7440	AUT ACCES VET MAT TEXTIL
851	*FOOTWEAR	W 883	5880	W 1087	7125	W 1406	8705	P 2929933	9341	CHAUSSURES
85102	FOOTWEAR LEATHER	W 576	4904	W 628	5851	W 938	7261	P 2065539	8271	CHAUS SEMELLES EN CUIR
87	PRECISION INSTRUMNTS NES		7080		7005		7749		7960	INSTRUM,APPAR SCIENT NDA
89	MISC MANUFCTRD GOODS NES		66965		86647		87244		70891	ART MANUFACTURES DIVERS
892	PRINTED MATTER	W 1495	6747	W 1608	7263	W 1593	9654		10224	IMPRIMES
8928	PRINTED MATTER NES	W 1195	5213	W 1274	5904	W 1227	8266		8642	IMPRIMES NDA
893	ARTICLES OF PLASTIC NES		22113		31154		26836		17381	OUVRAGES EN MAT DIVIS 58
8931	PLSTC PACKG CONTNRS,LIDS	W 7490	9273	W 8102	9940	W 4338	9535		6073	ART TRANSP EMBALLAGE ETC
8939	MISC PLASTIC ARTICLES	W 6817	12562	W 8012	20912	W 6684	17047		11098	ART DIVERS EN MAT DIV 58
89399	OTHR PLASTC ARTICLES NES	W 6406	12128	W 7756	20557	W 6383	16515		10583	AUT OUV MAT DIV 58
894	TOYS,SPORTING GOODS,ETC	W 2652	10393	W 3394	12039	W 1391	11272		11276	VOITURES ENFANTS,JOUETS
8942	TOYS,INDOOR GAMES ETC	W 2573	9686	W 3332	11513	W 1295	10752		9784	JOUETS,JEUX ETC
89424	INDOOR GAME EQUIPMENT	W 231	3824	W 284	5920	W 275	4917		6114	ART,JEUX DE SOCIETE
897	GOLD,SILVER WARE,JEWELRY		3423		7342		6726		4397	BIJOUTERIE,ORFEVRERIE
898	MUSICAL INSTRUMENTS,PTS	W 1864	5452	W 1754	9123	W 1222	7374		3418	INSTRUMENTS DE MUSIQUE
8983	SOUND RECRDNG TAPE,DISCS	W 1275	3116	W 1123	6755	W 739	5409		1707	SUPPORTS SON POUR 763
899	OTHER MANUFACTURED GOODS		17475		18114		21099		22056	AUT ART MANUF DIVERS NDA
8998	SMALLWARES,TOILETRYS ETC	W 1619	14887	W 1677	15035	W 1789	16339		18101	ART MERCERIE,TOILETTE
89983	BUTTONS,STUDS,ETC	W 787	6239	W 845	7287	W 815	7944		7966	BOUTONS,BOUTONS–PRESSION
89984	SLIDE FASTENERS,PARTS	W 774	8520	W 774	7605	W 910	8199		9976	FERMETURES A GLISSIERE
9	GOODS NOT CLASSD BY KIND		3665		16636		8029		2903	ART TRANSACT NON CLASSES
971	*GOLD,NON MONETARY NES				13760		5048		181	OR NON MONETAIRE
97101	NONMON GLD UNWRT,SEMIMFD				13760		5047		181	OR,ALLIAGES D'OR BRUTS

5. General Exports F.O.B. by Commodities according to the S.I.T.C. (Rev. 2) in thousand U.S. Dollars
Exportations Générales F.O.B. par Produits d'après la C.T.C.I. (Rév. 2) en milliers de Dollars E.U.

SITC CTCI	COMMODITY	1993				1994				1995				1996				PRODUIT
		WEIGHT POIDS		VALUE VALEUR		WEIGHT POIDS		VALUE VALEUR		WEIGHT POIDS		VALUE VALEUR		WEIGHT POIDS		VALUE VALEUR	
	ALL COMMODITIES			1716788			1872184			2017324			2100018	TOUS PRODUITS
0	FOOD AND LIVE ANIMALS			17688			15165			9036			7238	ALIMENTS,ANIMAUX VIVANTS
03	FISH AND PREPARATIONS			5681			4285			2520			2603	POISSONS ET PREPARATIONS
036	SHELL FISH FRESH,FROZEN	W	2810	5172	W	1571	3890	W	821	2320			2321	CRUSTACES,MOLLUSQUES
1	BEVERAGES AND TOBACCO			50165			52458			24208			25329	BOISSONS ET TABACS
11	BEVERAGES			28628			33369			10804			9048	BOISSONS
112	ALCOHOLIC BEVERAGES	W	2436	25437	W	2420	29820	W	3313	7453	W	2136	7476	BOISSONS ALCOOLIQUES
1124	DISTILLED ALCOHOLIC BEVS	W	878	24128	W	989	28601	W	294	4548	W	260	4864	ALCOOLS,EAUX-DE-VIE
11242	DISTILLD WINE,GRAPE MARC	W	576	22953	W	723	27110	W	117	4074	W	119	4459	EAUX-DE-VIE NATURELLES
12	TOBACCO AND MANUFACTURES			21536			19089			13404			16281	TABACS BRUTS FABRIQUES
122	TOBACCO,MANUFACTURED	W	2296	21536	W	2318	19089			13404			16281	TABACS FABRIQUES
1222	CIGARETTES	W	2220	21222	W	2261	18826			13158	W	1433	15995	CIGARETTES
2	CRUDE MATERLS,EXCL FUELS			34309			43046			48269			48210	MAT BRUTES NON COMESTIBLES
21	HIDES,SKINS,FURS UNDRSSD			20313			25725			27735			33043	CUIRS,PEAUX BRUTS
212	FURSKINS,RAW	W	148	20305	W	122	25716	W	148	27727	N	799350	33035	PELLETERIES BRUTES
21201	MINK SKINS,RAW	W	120	18678	W	98	21938	W	80	16480	N	594168	20876	PEAUX DE VISON BRUTES
21209	OTHER FURSKINS,RAW	W	28	1627	W	24	3778	W	68	11247	N	205182	12158	AUTRES PELLETERIES BRUTES
26	TEXTILE FIBRES AND WASTE			11113			14720			17741			12910	FIBRES TEXTILES
268	WOOL(EXC TOPS),ANML HAIR	W	2090	10774	W	2651	14542	W	3005	17488			12738	LAINES ET POILS
2682	WOOL DEGREASED,UNCOMBED	W	1945	9576	W	2526	14071	W	2828	16414			11191	LAINE DEGRAISSEE
3	MINERAL FUELS ETC			474			320			238			8085	COMBUSTIBLES MINERAUX LUB
33	PETROLEUM AND PRODUCTS			218			203			216			8055	PETROLE ET DERIVES
334	PETROLEUM PRODUCTS,REFIN	W	197	212	W	217	143	W	177	195			8053	PRODUITS RAFFINES
3342	KEROSENE,OTH MEDIUM OILS										W	31080	7757	PETR LAMPANTS,AUT HUIL
33421	KEROSENE INCL JET FUEL										W	30882	7695	PETROLES LAMPANTS
5	CHEMCLS,RELATED PROD NES			24439			22477			20968			18647	PRODUITS CHIMIQUES
541	*MEDICINAL,PHARM PRODUCT	K	317979	4774	K	304134	6049	K	196627	8911			7621	PROD MEDICINAUX PHARMACEUT
5413	ANTIBIOTICS IN BULK	K	17228	2429	K	23287	3573	K	42851	7031			5382	ANTIBIOTIQUES NDA
54133	TETRACYCLINES AND DERIVS	K	17228	2429	K	23287	3573	K	42251	7006			5382	TETRACYCLINES ET DERIVES
55	PERFUME,CLEANING ETC PRD			5880			5123			3975			3267	PROD POUR PARFUM,TOILETTE
6	BASIC MANUFACTURES			238604			232722			243632			214968	ART MANUFACTURES
61	LEATHER,DRESSED FUR,ETC			46515			39615			40818			23818	CUIRS,PELLETERIES
611	LEATHER	W	489	9780	W	532	6920	W	360	3439			1895	CUIRS,PEAUX PREPARES
6116	LEATHER OF OTH HIDE,SKIN	W	238	8824	W	276	5802	W	110	2191			358	PEAUX PREP D'AUTRES ANIMAUX
61161	LEATHER FROM GOAT,KID	W	237	8803	W	272	5740	W	106	2119	A	21	233	PEAUX DE CAPRINS PREPAREES
613	FUR SKINS TANNED,DRESSED	W	159	31729	W	94	27935	W	106	31882	N	537867	16425	PELLETERIES
65	TEXTILE YARN,FABRICS,ETC			152926			158574			168354			154574	FILS,TISSUS,ARTICLES TEXTILE
651	TEXTILE YARN	W	9849	70921	W	9369	70492	W	9055	63285			71548	FILS TEXTILES
6511	SILK YARN, SILKWORM GUT	W	648	8002	W	145	2089	W	125	1791			1330	FILS DE SOIE
65111	SILK YARN NON WASTE,BULK	W	637	7900	W	142	2086	W	125	1791			1330	FILS SOIE POUR VENT DETAIL
6512	WOOL,HAIR YARN,INCL TOPS	W	4986	45274	W	4704	50411	W	4290	44316			47434	FILS DE LAINE,DE POILS
65122	CARDED WOOL YARN IN BULK	W	3465	27848	W	3387	35098	W	3037	30666			34500	FILS CONT 85% LAINE CARDEE
65127	CARDED WOOL BLEND YARN	W	907	10282	W	699	7702	W	809	8646			7103	LAINE CARD MOINS 85% LAINE
6513	COTTON YARN	W	1496	7229	W	1434	7122	W	1153	6399			13852	FILS DE COTON
652	COTTON FABRICS,WOVEN	W	8011	31927	W	8250	33767	W	7738	35225	A	19938	33421	TISSUS DE COTON
6522	WOVEN COTTON BLEACHD,ETC	W	7898	31562	W	8136	33292	W	7724	35080	A	19865	33363	TISSUS COTON BLANCHIS ETC
65224	BLCHED COTTON FABRIC NES	W	7822	31112	W	8022	32698	W	7510	33841	A	18740	31618	AUT TIS PLUS 85% COT BLANCHI
653	WOVN MAN-MADE FIB FABRIC	W	3617	11780	W	4541	14339	W	5944	13949	A	39532	12651	TISSUS FIBRES SYNTH,ARTIF
6531	CONT SYNT WEAVES NONPILE	W	3224	9358	W	4040	11071	W	5498	11667	A	36561	10747	TISSUS FIBRES SYNTH CONTINUE
65315	CONT SYN TXTL FABRIC NES	W	2945	7229	W	3540	9530	W	5150	11148	A	34880	10126	TIS PLUS 85% TEXT SYNT CONT
654	OTH WOVEN TEXTILE FABRIC	W	161	6948	W	267	6387	W	554	5877	A	1144	4988	TISSUS AUT COTON SYNT,ARTIF
6541	SILK FABRICS WOVEN	W	130	6746	W	101	5790	W	99	5263	A	935	4502	TISSUS DE SOIE
655	KNITTED,ETC FABRICS	W	4374	19134	W	4796	22794	W	6589	35457			25638	ETOF BONNETERIE PIECES ETC
6552	OTHER KNIT ETC FAB NONEL	W	4374	19134	W	4796	22794	W	6589	35457			25638	ETOF BON NON ELAS NON SYNT
658	TEXTILE ARTICLES NES	W	920	7907	W	552	4686	W	694	7171			1948	ART FACONNES MAT TEXTILES
6584	LINENS ETC	W	678	6376	W	359	3529	W	319	3459	N	452918	1368	LINGE DE MAISON
66	NONMETAL MINERAL MFS NES			20134			16536			18637			23530	ART MIN NON METALLIQUES
661	LIME,CEMENT,BLDG PRODS	W	331895	17329	W	270449	14891	W	307449	17046			22154	CHAUX,CIMENTS MAT CONSTR
6612	CEMENT	W	331181	17093	W	269348	14603	W	306400	16743			21950	CIMENTS HYDRAULIQUES
69	METAL MANUFACTURES NES			8618			9632			9756			8291	ART MANUFACT EN METAL NDA
692	METAL TANKS,BOXES,ETC	W	17645	4856	W	18610	5730	W	17816	6056			4646	RECIPIENTS METALLIQUES
6924	MTL TRANSPORT BOXES ETC	W	17588	4592	W	18579	5688	W	17739	5996			4578	FUTS,TAMBOURS,BIDONS
7	MACHINES,TRANSPORT EQUIP			75712			78307			88347			76852	MACHINES MATERIEL TRANSPORT
72	MACHS FOR SPCL INDUSTRYS			9599			8721			14730			6164	MAC SPECIALES POUR INDUST
723	CIVIL ENGNEERG EQUIP ETC	W	1477	2604	W	1553	2959	W	1877	6293			697	APPAREILS DE GENIE CIVIL
74	GENRL INDUSTRL MACHY NES			17419			17161			12025			3730	MACH APP INDUSTRIE
741	HEATING,COOLING EQUIPMNT	W	1184	9217	W	648	4421	W	580	3130			603	MACH CHAUFFAGE,PIECES
7415	AIR-CONDITIONING MACHNRY	W	1131	8765	W	575	3996	W	442	2687	N	951	287	GROUPES CONDITION AIR
744	MECHANICAL HANDLING EQU	W	1567	3792	W	4198	8697	W	1758	4883			983	EQUIP MANUTENTION PIECES
7441	FORK LIFT TRCKS,ETC,PTS	W	1243	2629	W	1760	6607	W	848	2679	N	5	308	CHARIOTS POUR USINES ETC
74411	FORK LIFT TRUCKS ETC	W	1243	2629	W	1760	6607	W	848	2679	N	5	308	CHARIOTS POUR LES GARES
75	OFFICE MACHNES,ADP EQUIP			4940			9028			19921			18605	MACH BUREAU TRAIT AUTOM
759	OFFICE,ADP MCH PTS,ACCES	W	30	2789	W	65	6959	W	140	18040			17752	PIECES DU 751 ET 752
7599	ACCTG,ETC,ADP MCH PTS,AC	W	13	2701	W	43	6886	W	93	17951			17700	PIECES DU 751 ET 752
76	TELECOMM,SOUND EQUIPMENT			30067			19001			9234			4486	EQUIPMENT DE TELECOM
762	RADIO BROADCAST RECEIVRS	W	672	9735	W	916	6785	W	421	1886	N	3395	253	RECEPTEURS RADIODIFFUSION
7628	OTHER RADIO RECEIVERS	W	561	6595	W	897	6562	W	420	1876	N	2555	241	AUTRES RECEPT RADIO
764	TELECOM EQPT,PTS,ACC NES	W	807	14123	W	829	9475	W	529	4258			2268	EQUIP TELECOM,PIECES
7641	LINE TELEPHONE,ETC EQUIP	W	95	5882	W	19	1235	W	8	656			278	APP TELEPHON PAR FIL
77	ELECTRIC MACHNRY NES ETC			5890			15080			23676			27750	MACH APP ELECT NDA
771	ELECTRIC POWER MACHY NES	W	310	1437	W	378	3331	W	775	10491			12532	MACH PROD,TRANS ELECTR
7712	OTH ELEC POWER MACHY NES	W	66	725	W	158	2539	W	290	9053			8706	AUT APP PROD TRANSF ELEC
77122	INDUCTORS	W	46	535	W	58	803	W	166	7219	N	3698466	6987	BOBINES REACTANCE,SELFS
778	ELECTRICAL MACHINERY NES			2383	W	1121	9131			8750			7931	AUTRES MACH ELECT NDA
7781	BATTERIES,ACCUMULATORS	W	601	1765	W	948	8161	W	574	7152			7002	PILES ET ACCUMULATEURS
77812	ELECTRIC ACCUMULATORS	W	16	148	W	179	6370	W	141	5978	N	1576497	6444	ACCUMULATEURS ELECTRIQ
78	ROAD VEHICLES			5119			6796			6833			2521	VEHICULES ROUTIERS
79	OTHR TRANSPORT EQUIPMENT			228			394			86			8679	AUTRE MATERIEL TRANSPORT
792	AIRCRAFT ETC	W	1	56			199						8385	APP NAVIGATION AERIENNE
7929	AIRCRAFT PARTS NES			46			199						8385	PIECES DU 792
8	MISC MANUFACTURED GOODS			1274426			1427202			1581727			1700229	ART MANUFACTURES DIVERS
812	*PLUMBG,HEATNG,LGHTNG EQ	W	2443	14035	W	2054	12900			21176			20181	APPAR SANITAIRES CHAUFFAGE
8124	LIGHTING EQUIPMENT NES	W	2360	13969	W	1941	12745			21082			20090	APPAREILS ECLAIRAGE ETC
81243	PORTABLE BATTERY LAMPS	W	1724	10306	W	1643	10104			18247			14161	LAMPES ELECT PORTATIVES
84	CLOTHING AND ACCESSORIES			1090138			1203804			1372317			1546902	VETEMENTS
842	MENS OUTERWEAR NOT KNIT	W	12896	172824	W	13437	182850	W	13104	187688	MN	25456	207154	VET DESSUS POUR HOMMES
8421	— OVERCOATS,OTHER COATS	W	1514	22756	W	1689	25717	W	1289	21290	N	1005239	12301	MANTEAUX HOMMES MAT TEXT
84219	—— OF OTHER FIBRES	W	1507	22598	W	1679	25483	W	1273	20666	N	1005239	12301	MANTEAUX HOMMES AUT FIBR
8423	— TROUSERS,BREECHES ETC	W	8464	101192	W	8298	101180	W	8270	107895	MN	17070	119260	PANTALONS HOMMES MAT TEX
8429	— OTHER OUTER GARMENTS	W	2798	47515	W	3268	52884	W	3369	55903	N	7283636	74654	AUT VET DES HOM MAT TEX
843	WOMENS OUTERWEAR NONKNIT	W	10342	178527	W	11698	199794	W	12581	237639	MN	37977	282796	VET DESSUS FEMMES MAT TEX

5. General Exports F.O.B. by Commodities according to the S.I.T.C. (Rev. 2) in thousand U.S. Dollars
Exportations Générales F.O.B. par Produits d'après la C.T.C.I. (Rév. 2) en milliers de Dollars E.U.

SITC CTCI	COMMODITY	1993 WEIGHT POIDS	1993 VALUE VALEUR	1994 WEIGHT POIDS	1994 VALUE VALEUR	1995 WEIGHT POIDS	1995 VALUE VALEUR	1996 WEIGHT POIDS	1996 VALUE VALEUR	PRODUIT
8431	— COATS AND JACKETS	W 820	14939	W 1097	18146	W 608	10698	N 982139	10441	MANT,VEST FEM MAT TEXTIL
8433	— DRESSES	W 175	4922	W 367	9928	W 1227	31874	N 2463502	26773	ROBES EN MAT–TEXTILES
8434	— SKIRTS	W 337	7285	W 513	10857	W 682	15352	N 2026197	14979	JUPES EN MAT TEXTILES
8435	— BLOUSES	W 1371	37839	W 1437	38509	W 1780	44348	N 6686637	47517	BLOUSES FEM MAT TEXTILES
8439	— OTHER OUTER GARMENTS	W 7634	113449	W 8273	122104	W 8273	135139	MN 25801	182844	AUT VET DES FEM MAT TEXT
844	UNDER GARMENTS NOT KNIT	W 6551	121892	W 6505	129689	W 6413	137350		137793	VETEMENT DESSOUS MAT TEX
8441	— MENS SHIRTS	W 4029	77573	W 3912	82306	W 4061	88696		85263	CHEMISES HOMMES MAT TEXT
84411	—— OF COTTON	W 3240	63911	W 3102	66725	W 3284	72018	MN 9142	74256	CHEMISES HOMMES DE COTON
84412	—— OF SYNTHETIC FIBRES	W 789	13662	W 810	15581	W 777	16678		11007	CHEMISES HOMMES FIB SYNT
8442	— MENS,OTHR THAN SHIRTS	W 1057	14230	W 1247	17522	W 1125	20584	N 5106318	21805	SOUS–VET HOMMES MAT TEXT
8443	— WOMENS	W 1465	30088	W 1346	29862	W 1226	28071	N 4668550	30725	VET DESSOUS FEM MAT TEXT
845	OUTERWEAR KNIT NONELASTC	W 19844	443016	W 22548	507642	W 24954	591811	MN 99124	687992	VET DESSOUS,ACCES BONNET
8451	— JERSEYS,PULLOVERS ETC	W 10408	248373	W 10801	263338	W 10494	274172	MN 40585	336027	CHANDAILS,PULL–OVERS ETC
8452	— WOMENS DRESSES ETC	W 789	19268	W 1020	24889	W 1430	37006	N 4255189	35466	ROBES,JUPES BONNETERIE
8459	— OTHER,CLTHG ACCESRYS	W 8647	175376	W 10727	219415	W 13029	280633	MN 54283	316499	AUT VET DESSUS DE BONNE
846	UNDER GARMENTS KNITTED	W 8003	162002	W 8304	169399	W 9070	198424		205707	SOUS VETS DE BONNETERIE
8462	— OF COTTON NON ELASTIC	W 4673	87786	W 4720	89304	W 5234	104911	MN 36653	112726	SOUS–VET BONNET COTON
84629	—— OTHER	W 4673	87786	W 4720	89304	W 5234	104911	MN 36653	112726	AUT SOUS–VET BONNET COTON
8463	— OF SYNTH FBR NONELAST	W 2816	56774	W 2905	58010	W 2939	61437		61057	SOUS–VET BONNET FIB SYNT
84632	—— MENS SHIRTS	W 2816	56760	W 2897	58006	W 2939	61437	N 8293097	61052	CHEMISES DE BON FIB SYNMT
8465	CORSETS,GARTERS,ETC	W 514	17443	W 678	22084	W 897	32077	MN 18591	31924	CORSETS,GAINES ART SIM
84651	BRASSIERES	W 491	16653	W 652	21213	W 880	31264	MN 18427	31253	SOUTIENS–GORGE,BUSTIERS
847	TEXTILE CLTHNG ACCES NES	W 879	6991	W 905	7282	W 985	7830		14311	ACCES VET MAT TEXT NDA
8471	— NOT KNITTED	W 317	3126	W 442	4118	W 390	3394		12189	ACCES VET MAT TEX NON BON
84719	MADE–UP CLTHG ACCESS NES	W 184	1031	W 186	1270	W 201	1634		11595	AUT ACCES VET MAT TEXTIL
848	HEADGEAR,NONTXTL CLOTHNG	W 635	4885	W 1091	7148	W 765	11574		11149	VET ACCES MAT AUT QUE TEX
8484	HEADGEAR	W 113	1945	W 116	2515	W 506	9101		9237	COIFFURES ET PARTIES NDA
84843	HEADGEAR TEXTILE NONFELT	W 76	1265	W 99	2251	W 503	9084	N 7782365	9219	CHAPEAUX EN BONNETERIE
851	*FOOTWEAR	W 2256	21087	W 4313	33254	W 4684	40060	P 6209018	37586	CHAUSSURES
85101	FOOTWEAR RUBBER,PLASTIC	W 1352	9913	W 1658	10816	W 1163	8232	P 1247077	4790	CHAUS SEMELLES CAOUTCH
85102	FOOTWEAR LEATHER	W 892	11079	W 2647	22352	W 3517	31794	P 4957393	32768	CHAUS SEMELLES EN CUIR
87	PRECISION INSTRUMNTS NES		6679		1639		2812		2495	INSTRUM,APPAR SCIENT NDA
871	OPTICAL INSTRUMENTS	W 398	6061		3	W 2	35	N 4548	36	APPAR,INSTRUM D'OPTIQUE
88	PHOTO EQU,OPTICL GDS ETC		4808		6950		6927		6822	APP,FOURN PHOTO,OP,MONTR
882	PHOTO,CINEMA SUPPLIES	W 836	4052	W 886	4573	W 1699	6238		6468	PRODUITS PHOTO,CINEMA
89	MISC MANUFCTRD GOODS NES		134952		163811		134606		84375	ART MANUFACTURES DIVERS
892	PRINTED MATTER	W 210	459	W 150	452	W 165	449		28782	IMPRIMES
8928	PRINTED MATTER NES	W 103	334	W 99	325	W 126	363		28714	IMPRIMES NDA
89283	UNISSUED BANKNOTES ETC								28379	TIMBRES–POSTE FISCAUX
894	TOYS,SPORTING GOODS,ETC		83392	W 16202	95951	W 11456	72731		34041	VOITURES ENFANTS,JOUETS
8942	TOYS,INDOOR GAMES ETC		82582	W 16093	95009	W 11338	72145		33350	JOUETS,JEUX ETC
89422	DOLLS	W 2726	21007	W 3135	25935	W 1246	9592	N 1925574	587	POUPEES
89423	TOYS NES	W 10024	49744	W 11725	63977	W 9971	62200		32398	JOUETS,MODELES REDUITS
89425	XMAS DECORATIONS ETC	W 2779	11780	W 1164	4651	W 6	60		63	ART DIVERTIS,FETES
896	WORKS OF ART ETC		2449		1421		17827		406	OBJETS D'ART
89601	HAND PAINTINGS ETC NES		1685		107		6485		366	TABLEAUX,PEINTURES
89606	ANTIQUES NES		371		1229		8875		9	OBJETS D'ANTIQUITE
898	MUSICAL INSTRUMENTS,PTS	W 6758	35634	W 7399	49613	W 3360	25346		2011	INSTRUMENTS DE MUSIQUE
8983	SOUND RECRDNG TAPE,DISCS	W 6159	33637	W 6893	47829	W 2900	23289		502	SUPPORTS SON POUR 763
89831	PREPD SND RECORDNG MEDIA	W 6156	33608	W 6889	47723	W 2877	23114		360	SUPPORTS PREPARES
899	OTHER MANUFACTURED GOODS		5390		6416		8412		11094	AUT ART MANUF DIVERS NDA
8993	COMBUSTIBLE PRODUCTS ETC	W 1895	2412	W 2777	3904	W 3213	5934		8971	BOUGIES,ALLUMETTES ETC

1. HISTORICAL SERIES, 1960–1995 SPECIAL TRADE, IMPORTS C.I.F., EXPORTS F.O.B.
SERIES HISTORIQUES, 1960–1995 COMMERCE SPECIAL, IMPORTATIONS C.A.F., EXPORTATIONS F.O.B

YEAR ANNEE	VALUE IN MILLION MALAGASY FRANCS / VALEUR EN MILLION MALAGASY FRANCS — MERCHANDISE –MARCHANDISE		GOLD –OR		CONVERSION FACTORS U.S. CENTS PER MALAGASY FRANC / FACTEURS DE CONVERSION CENTS E.U. PAR MALAGASY FRANC		INDEX NUMBERS –INDICES — QUANTUM		UNIT VALUE / VALEUR UNITAIRE	
	IMPORTS	EXPORTS	IMPORTS	EXPORTS	IMPORTS	EXPORTS	IMPORTS	EXPORTS	IMPORTS	EXPORTS
1960	27512.00	18485.00	27.80		0.4051	0.4051				
1961	25498.00	19137.00	33.00		0.4051	0.4051				
1962	30000.00	23286.00	28.00		0.4051	0.4051				
1963	31459.00	20262.00	21.10		0.4051	0.4051				
1964	33429.00	22654.00	22.60		0.4051	0.4051				
1965	34089.00	22632.00	22.40		0.4051	0.4051				
1966	35004.00	24132.00	21.80		0.4051	0.4051				
1967	35847.00	25711.00	26.00		0.4051	0.4051				
1968	41937.00	28608.00	45.70		0.4051	0.4051				
1969	47198.00	29154.00	24.50		0.3881	0.3831				
1970	47320.00	40222.00	26.20		0.3601	0.3601				
1971	59228.00	40807.00	33.50		0.3601	0.3601				
1972	51754.00	41864.00	52.60		0.3967	0.3966				
1973	45089.00	44751.00	66.20		0.4495	0.4532				
1974	67257.00	58504.00			0.4180	0.4177				
1975	78047.00	63044.00			0.4702	0.4668				
1976	68434.00	66035.00			0.4168	0.4165				
1977	85217.00	82927.00			0.4075	0.4080				
1978	99632.00	87214.00			0.4450	0.4432				
1979	135319.00	83826.00			0.4736	0.4706				
1980	126775.00	84781.00			0.4730	0.4736				
1981	147977.00	85741.60			0.3646	0.3690				
1982	148601.00	108347.00			0.2860	0.2860				
1983	166750.00	127249.40			0.2319	0.2325				
1984	213531.00	192332.00			0.1715	0.1730				
1985	265916.00	181630.40			0.1511	0.1509				
1986	238458.00	212736.00			0.1479	0.1479				
1987	323046.90	353975.00			0.0935	0.0941				
1988	538361.00	385095.90			0.0711	0.0711				
1989	595640.00	514845.90			0.0624	0.0624				
1990	969540.10	476681.90			0.0672	0.0670				
1991	785690.10	559073.00			0.0555	0.0546				
1992	833773.00	516822.00			0.0537	0.0538				
1993	895687.90	498995.90			0.0523	0.0523				
1994	1408620.00	1246720.00			0.0318	0.0301				
1995	2274340.00	1554010.00			0.0233	0.0235				

2. IMPORTS BY BROAD ECONOMIC CATEGORY AND EXPORTS BY INDUSTRIAL ORIGIN. (PERCENTAGE OF TOTAL VALUE)
IMPORTATIONS PAR CATEGORIES ECONOMIQUES ET EXPORTATIONS PAR BRANCHE D'ACTIVITE.(EN POURCENTAGE DE LA VALEUR TOTALE)

IMPORTS – IMPORTATIONS

	1990	1991	1992	1993	1994	1995	1996
TOTAL IMPORTS–IMPORTATIONS TOTALES	100.	100.	100.	100.	100.	100.	
1 FOOD BEV–ALIMENTATION BOISSONS	10.0	9.7	11.6	11.8	14.1	14.6	
11 PRIMARY–PRODUITS DE BASE	0.8	2.4	3.5	3.7	2.8	4.0	
111 FOR INDUSTRY–POUR L'INDUSTRIE	0.8	1.4	0.9	2.0	1.7	2.4	
112 FOR HOUSEHOLDS–POUR LES MENAGES	0.0	1.0	2.6	1.7	1.1	1.6	
12 PROCESSED–PRODUITS ELABORES	9.2	7.3	8.1	8.1	11.4	10.6	
121 FOR INDUSTRY–POUR L'INDUSTRIE	2.0	3.1	2.5	5.5	2.4	5.2	
122 FOR HOUSEHOLDS–POUR LES MENAGES	7.1	4.2	5.6	2.6	8.9	5.4	
2 IND SUPPLIES–APPROV INDUSTRIELS	28.2	26.3	27.2	28.5	26.8	31.9	
21 PRIMARY–PRODUITS DE BASE	0.8	0.9	1.7	1.6	0.9	1.5	
22 PROCESSED–PRODUITS ELABORES	27.4	25.4	25.5	26.9	26.0	30.4	
3 FUELS–COMBUSTIBLES	16.3	11.8	19.1	18.1	14.4	13.7	
31 PRIMARY–PRODUITS DE BASE	6.0	6.8	13.2	13.2	7.5	11.3	
32 PROCESSED–PRODUITS ELABORES	10.2	5.1	6.0	4.9	6.9	2.4	
321 MOTOR SPIRIT–ESSENCE	10.2	5.1	6.0	4.8	6.9	2.4	
322 OTHER–AUTRES	0.0	0.0	0.0	0.0		0.0	
4 MACHINERY–EQUIPEMENT	17.3	23.4	16.0	16.8	17.2	14.2	
41 CAPITAL EQUIPMENT–MACHINES	14.5	20.3	13.8	14.5	14.7	12.0	
42 PARTS–PIECES ACCESSOIRES	2.8	3.1	2.3	2.3	2.5	2.2	
5 TRANSPORT–TRANSPORT	16.7	19.8	13.6	14.4	14.5	13.1	
51 PASSENGER CARS–AUTOMOBILES	2.8	3.3	2.8	2.4	2.0	2.4	
52 OTHER–AUTRES	7.9	11.1	5.9	7.5	7.7	5.9	
521 INDUSTRIAL–INDUSTRIELS	7.7	10.7	5.7	7.0	7.3	5.5	
522 NON INDUSTRIAL–NON INDUSTRIEL	0.1	0.4	0.2	0.4	0.4	0.4	
53 PARTS–PIECES ACCESSOIRES	6.0	5.3	5.0	4.5	4.8	4.8	
6 CONSUM GOODS–BIENS CONSOMMATION	9.9	7.7	8.7	8.8	9.3	8.7	
61 DURABLE–DURABLES	2.2	1.6	2.2	1.9	1.7	1.4	
62 SEMI DURABLE–SEMI DURABLES	2.9	2.3	2.0	2.5	3.3	2.9	
63 NON DURABLE–NON DURABLES	4.8	3.9	4.5	4.3	4.4	4.4	
7 GOODS NES–BIENS NDA	1.7	1.3	3.7	1.6	3.6	3.8	

EXPORTS – EXPORTATIONS

	1990	1991	1992	1993	1994	1995	1996
TOTAL EXPORTS–EXPORTATIONS TOTALES	100.	100.	100.	100.	100.	100.	
1 AGRICULTURE	65.7	65.0	64.6	64.1	75.0	66.3	
2 MINING QUARRY–INDUS EXTRACTIVES	9.0	7.9	7.6	7.2	4.6	7.8	
3 MANUFACTURING–IND MANUFACTUR	25.3	27.1	27.8	28.7	20.4	25.9	
31 FOOD BEV TOBACCO–ALIM BOISS TAB	10.2	5.8	6.1	5.6	6.6	6.4	
32 TEXTILES–INDUSTRIES TEXTILES	7.8	11.2	9.9	9.8	6.2	6.9	
33 WOOD & PRODUCTS–BOIS & PRODUITS	0.5	0.6	1.2	1.0	0.6	1.4	
34 PAPER & PRODUCTS–PAPIER & PRODT	0.1	0.1	0.1	0.1	2.9	1.2	
35 CHEMICALS–INDUSTRIES CHIMIQUES	2.1	3.4	4.9	5.0	1.9	6.2	
36 NON METAL MIN–MIN NON METAL	0.0	0.0	0.0	0.0	0.0	0.0	
37 BASIC METAL–IND METAL BASE	0.1	0.1	0.0	0.4	0.0	0.0	
38 METAL MANUF–MANUF METAL	2.4	2.6	2.2	4.2	0.5	1.3	
39 OTH MANUF IND–AUTRES MANUF	2.0	3.1	3.4	2.5	1.6	2.5	

3. TRADE BY PRINCIPAL COUNTRIES OF ORIGIN AND DESTINATION (VALUE IN THOUSAND U.S. DOLLARS)
ECHANGES SELON LES PRINCIPAUX PAYS D'ORIGINE ET DE DESTINATION (VALEUR EN MILLIERS DE DOLLARS EU)

COUNTRIES–PAYS	SPECIAL IMPORTS C.I.F. IMPORTATIONS SPECIALES C.A.F				
	1991	1992	1993	1994	1995
World	406328	391350	468604	431715	549528
Africa	29088	37648	52686	55271	42142
Americas	32136	23328	37666	21356	29010
Northern America	26018	19752	31171	19908	21637
LAIA	6049	2572	4697	1307	7304
CACM	21	44	3	1	6
Caribbean	18	327	1794	133	53
Rest of America	29	633	1	7	10
As.ex F.USSR	97988	117033	156276	140035	172105
Eur.x F.USSR	244813	210038	218287	213471	288570
EU	235090	200090	208668	202138	277849
EFTA	5601	5275	4491	6025	7677
East Europe	4057	3934	4538	5283	2701
Other Europe	64	613	574	17	11
Former USSR	989	1362	2830	819	969
Oceania	1315	1940	849	764	1772
France,Monac	136549	117890	127053	131596	162956
Germany/Allemagne	36535	24119	32138	24923	55512
Iran (Islamic Rp. of)	26472	13280	55578	21969	55314
Japan/Japon	28654	23029	41074	42596	32765
So. Africa Customs Un	17656	21821	24491	44933	34553
USA/Etats–Unis d'Amer	25423	19132	29399	19256	20791
United Kingdom	11613	20429	9541	12689	12988
Saudi Arabia	1812	41905	8574	7080	7174
China/Chine	7560	9113	13542	14100	18127
Italy/Italie	14053	11661	10424	8646	12677
Belgium–Luxembourg	8102	6878	9964	7761	13042
Singapore/Singapour	4550	5059	11850	6688	8967
Netherlands/Pays–Bas	9634	8334	5677	5148	7018
Spain/Espagne	10179	5191	5505	5431	4026
India/Inde	7185	2724	6317	5775	7089
Switz.Liecht	5390	5007	4303	5303	7270
Malaysia/Malaisie	3298	2103	5010	6601	8547
Mauritius/Maurice	875	3081	14783	2263	2598
Korea, Republic of	4223	2673	2183	4252	5416
Pakistan	71	192	501	8367	7845
Brazil/Brésil	4295	1441	3408	729	6150
Romania/Roumanie	2692	2286	3849	4709	1408
Sweden/Suède	4784	1313	1521	1418	3769
Thailand/Thaïlande	1532	1601	3327	1774	4485
Denmark/Danemark	1816	2180	3892	1763	2715
Nigeria/Nigéria		2672	7985	1129	28
Hong Kong	1398	1168	2344	1482	4098
Myanmar		18		7071	2344
Viet Nam	2	3142	874	4463	23
Zimbabwe	3227	1880	1496	533	7
Russian Federation		1362	2830	819	969
Australia/Australie	1250	1937	455	531	1741
Ireland/Irlande	485	1056	1142	1396	1148
Kenya	1812	625	772	974	631
Bahrain/Bahreïn	4184	171		417	0
Morocco/Maroc	404	1633	1428	861	388
United Arab Emirates	1769	2445	49	48	360
Canada	595	621	1772	652	846
Mozambique	61	3564	44	11	782
Cote d'Ivoire	3640	68	2	173	367
Austria/Autriche	1114	412	1023	533	947
Un. Rep. of Tanzania	184	743	4	2073	567
Sri Lanka	160	105	19	13	3213
Reunion/Réunion	516	255	320	880	535
Israel/Israël	212	1685	65	50	370
Turkey/Turquie	244	576	432	485	571
Korea Dem People's Rp	796	495	543	206	62
Venezuela	1413	656			
Finland/Finlande	85	245	534	611	542
Peru/Pérou	249	283	388	470	542

COUNTRIES–PAYS	SPECIAL EXPORTS F.O.B. EXPORTATIONS SPECIALES F.O.B.				
	1991	1992	1993	1994	1995
Monde	295380	268889	261729	326614	359874
Afrique	29414	30172	32758	37023	55058
Amériques	43555	42950	20871	29943	24563
Amérique du Nord	43220	42453	20154	29460	23930
ALAI	101	115	63	131	339
MCAC		12	12		6
Caraïbes	67	82	459	342	283
Autre Amérique	168	289	183	10	4
Asie l'URSS exclus	48679	40772	34589	41376	41450
Europe l'URSS exclus	157011	141966	167602	217793	226355
UE	150812	134238	162839	211553	215715
AELE	4862	3340	1860	1115	5781
Europe de l'Est	1332	4362	2864	5122	2657
Autre de l'Europe	5	20	39	3	2060
Ancienne URSS	16441	12824	5769	322	659
Océanie	279	205	140	157	327
France,Monac	78364	71582	87199	111805	102167
Germany/Allemagne	30472	26681	32907	37142	29917
USA/Etats–Unis d'Amer	42593	41758	19272	25980	23677
Japan/Japon	25950	23120	17893	26394	22299
Reunion/Réunion	15271	13319	16162	20788	21396
Italy/Italie	8621	8418	8762	15089	18890
United Kingdom	9329	6903	9610	16148	13610
Belgium–Luxembourg	8935	8861	8550	9681	17626
Singapore/Singapour	16802	5221	10241	7116	8392
Mauritius/Maurice	8824	8493	9726	6349	13960
Netherlands/Pays–Bas	2994	5859	4858	9108	7478
Spain/Espagne	1820	2743	4057	8228	12501
Russian Federation		12824	5769	322	659
Portugal	7421	891	2909	2296	4218
Former USSR/Anc. URSS	16441				
Sweden/Suède	2502	1177	1934	1681	8413
Switz.Liecht	3685	3311	1813	1075	5769
Poland/Pologne	988	3753	2256	4791	2157
Hong Kong	1327	2080	2156	2624	2979
Comoros/Comores	1774	1458	1481	1471	4508
India/Inde	1400	2632	746	1662	2882
United Arab Emirates	120	5492	2173	444	984
So. Africa Customs Un	783	2300	1633	1572	2745
Tunisia/Tunisie	475	663	1732	4114	1369
Algeria/Algérie	404	258		1236	5008
Canada	626	695	882	3480	254
Kenya	364	1242	507	124	1622
Greece/Grèce	227	907	1911	224	566
China/Chine	1168	2	30	442	1679
Gibraltar					2054
Seychelles	325	36	579	640	440
Saudi Arabia	1091	491	121	106	103
Thailand/Thaïlande	142	189	96	370	640
Norway,SVD,JM	1177	28	47	40	12
Zimbabwe	6	5	21	3	1241
Senegal/Sénégal	27	1144	15	35	42
Morocco/Maroc	150	305	277	126	403
Mozambique	277	4	1	166	740
Pakistan	113	62	355	330	263
Hungary/Hongrie	311	584	18	75	14
Australia/Australie	262	138	101	156	294
Bulgaria/Bulgarie	12	0	178	120	420
Czech Republic			411	135	61
Panama	120	289	183	10	4
Un. Rep. of Tanzania	88	387	81	31	4
Br. Indian Ocean Terr	2		7		573
Korea, Republic of	13	95	20	256	183
Egypt/Egypte	94	264	109	6	77
Turkey/Turquie	63	213	190	32	39
Austria/Autriche	99	131	102	53	121

(VALUE AS PERCENTAGE OF WORLD TOTAL)(VALEURS EN POURCENTAGE DU TOTAL MONDIAL)

	1986	1987	1988	1989	1990	1991	1992	1993	1994	1995
Africa	1.6		1.4	1.9	7.5	7.2	9.6	11.2	12.8	7.7
Americas	11.3		5.2	6.3	5.8	7.9	6.0	8.0	4.9	5.3
Northern America	11.0		5.0	5.3	4.4	6.4	5.0	6.7	4.6	3.9
LAIA	0.3		0.2	0.9	1.4	1.5	0.7	1.0	0.3	1.3
CACM	0.0				0.0	0.0	0.0	0.0	0.0	0.0
Caribbean	0.0		0.0		0.0	0.0	0.1	0.4	0.0	0.0
Rest of America	0.0				0.0	0.0	0.2	0.0	0.0	0.0
As.ex F.USSR	16.7		17.3	19.2	31.7	24.1	29.9	33.3	32.4	31.3
Eur.x F.USSR	51.6		66.5	64.3	54.3	60.3	53.7	46.6	49.4	52.5
EU	49.0		64.4	61.7	50.9	57.9	51.1	44.5	46.8	50.6
EFTA	2.3		1.7	2.2	1.7	1.4	1.3	1.0	1.4	1.4
East Europe	0.3		0.4	0.3	1.6	1.0	1.0	1.0	1.2	0.5
Other Europe	0.1		0.0	0.0	0.1	0.0	0.2	0.1	0.0	0.0
Former USSR	10.0		4.5	0.4	0.4	0.2	0.3	0.6	0.2	0.2
Oceania	0.1		0.1	0.1	0.4	0.3	0.5	0.2	0.2	0.3
France,Monac	31.3		41.1	40.3	30.6	33.6	30.1	27.1	30.5	29.7
Germany/Allemagne	6.7		8.8	7.7	6.5	9.0	6.2	6.9	5.8	10.1
Iran (Islamic Rp. of)			0.8	3.2	5.7	6.5	3.4	11.9	5.1	10.1
Japan/Japon	6.5		5.8	5.7	6.3	7.1	5.9	8.8	9.9	6.0
So. Africa Customs Un	0.2				1.5	4.3	5.6	5.2	10.4	6.3
USA/Etats–Unis d'Amer	10.7		4.1	4.4	4.1	6.3	4.9	6.3	4.5	3.8
United Kingdom	3.2		3.3	3.1	4.7	2.9	5.2	2.0	2.9	2.4
Saudi Arabia	0.1		2.0	0.0	0.5	0.4	10.7	1.8	1.6	1.3
China/Chine	1.6		0.9	2.0	2.3	1.9	2.3	2.9	3.3	3.3
Italy/Italie	2.8		4.7	3.9	3.0	3.5	3.0	2.2	2.0	2.3

	1986	1987	1988	1989	1990	1991	1992	1993	1994	1995
Afrique	3.7		6.4	7.3	12.0	10.0	11.2	12.5	11.3	15.3
Amériques	15.4		14.2	13.9	18.1	14.7	16.0	8.0	9.2	6.8
Amérique du Nord	15.4		13.9	13.7	17.9	14.6	15.8	7.7	9.0	6.6
ALAI	0.0		0.1	0.0	0.0	0.0	0.0	0.0	0.0	0.1
MCAC				0.0	0.0		0.0	0.0		0.0
Caraïbes			0.2	0.2	0.0	0.0	0.0	0.2	0.1	0.1
Autre Amérique	0.0		0.0	0.0	0.1	0.1	0.1	0.1	0.0	0.0
Asie l'URSS exclus	17.8		15.3	17.7	14.6	16.5	15.2	13.2	12.7	11.5
Europe l'URSS exclus	60.0		58.6	53.8	54.3	53.2	52.8	64.0	66.7	62.9
UE	58.3		57.3	52.4	52.2	51.1	49.9	62.2	64.8	59.9
AELE	0.4		0.7	0.5	1.1	1.6	1.2	0.7	0.3	1.6
Europe de l'Est	1.3		0.4	0.5	0.9	0.5	1.6	1.1	1.6	0.7
Autre de l'Europe	0.0		0.3	0.3	0.2	0.0	0.0	0.0	0.0	0.6
Ancienne URSS	2.3		1.4	1.3	0.8	5.6	4.8	2.2	0.1	0.2
Océanie	0.0		0.0	0.0	0.1	0.1	0.1	0.1	0.0	0.1
France,Monac	33.3		34.3	30.5	28.9	26.5	26.6	33.3	34.2	28.4
Germany/Allemagne	6.7		7.8	8.1	8.5	10.3	9.9	12.6	11.4	8.3
USA/Etats–Unis d'Amer	14.8		13.8	13.6	17.8	14.4	15.5	7.4	8.0	6.6
Japan/Japon	10.9		12.6	12.0	6.9	8.8	8.6	6.8	8.1	6.2
Reunion/Réunion	2.6		4.9	3.8	5.2	5.2	5.0	6.2	6.4	5.9
Italy/Italie	4.3		4.5	4.1	2.7	2.9	3.1	3.3	4.6	5.2
United Kingdom	1.9		3.2	2.6	1.6	3.2	2.6	3.7	4.9	3.8
Belgium–Luxembourg	0.9		2.6	2.7	4.9	3.0	3.3	3.3	3.0	4.9
Singapore/Singapour	1.0		0.8	0.8	6.1	5.7	1.9	3.9	2.2	2.3
Mauritius/Maurice	0.5		0.7	1.1	2.4	3.0	3.2	3.7	1.9	3.9

4. Special Imports C.I.F. by Commodities according to the S.I.T.C. (Rev. 2) in thousand U.S. Dollars
Importations Spéciales C.A.F. par Produits d'après la C.T.C.I. (Rév. 2) en milliers de Dollars E.U.

SITC CTCI	COMMODITY	1992 WEIGHT POIDS	1992 VALUE VALEUR	1993 WEIGHT POIDS	1993 VALUE VALEUR	1994 WEIGHT POIDS	1994 VALUE VALEUR	1995 WEIGHT POIDS	1995 VALUE VALEUR	PRODUIT
	ALL COMMODITIES		391350		468604		431715		549528	TOUS PRODUITS
0	FOOD AND LIVE ANIMALS		44661		50257		53260		68086	ALIMENTS,ANIMAUX VIVANTS
02	DAIRY PRODCTS,BIRDS'EGGS		5947		3713		3420		5180	PRODUITS LAITIERS,OEUFS
022	MILK AND CREAM	W 3861	4884	W 1610	3180	W 1488	2517	W 1675	4147	LAIT ET CREME
0224	MILK,CREAM PRESERVED ETC	W 3449	4517	W 1432	3007	W 1304	2363	W 1440	3919	LAIT,CREME CONS,CONC
02243	MILK DRY,OVER 1.5% FAT	W 1847	2878	W 1028	2488	W 716	1229	W 902	2650	LAIT POUDRE SUP 1.5%
03	FISH AND PREPARATIONS		8659		7323		5042		8713	POISSONS ET PREPARATIONS
034	FISH,FRESH,CHILLED,FROZN	W 15038	8491	W 13540	7217	W 7746	4346	W 10533	8545	POISSON FRAIS, REFRIG,CONG
0342	FISH FROZEN,EXCL FILLETS	W 14876	8406	W 13540	7216	W 7744	4342	W 10533	8544	POISSONS CONGELES
04	CEREALS AND PREPARATIONS		24919		34500		37302		41284	CEREALES ET PRODUITS
041	WHEAT ETC UNMILLED	W 32561	3174	W 60818	9002	W 53444	6772	W 70133	12650	FROMENT,EPEAUTRE
0411	DURUM WHEAT UNMILLED	W 2000	204	W 10500	1569					FROMENT DUR NON MOULU
0412	OTHER WHEAT ETC UNMILLED	W 30561	2970	W 50318	7433	W 53444	6772	W 70133	12650	AUTRE FROMENT NON MOULU
042	RICE	W 52413	12371	W 15468	4770	W 79847	26736	W 125061	17187	RIZ
0422	RICE SEMI–MILLED,MILLED	W 51364	12135	W 15407	4743	W 79844	26734	W 124349	16965	RIZ POLI,GLACE INCL BRISURES
04221	RICE MILLED UNBROKEN	W 45224	10910	W 14807	4571	W 78575	26373	W 122038	16385	RIZ POLI,GLACE EXCL BRISURES
04222	RICE BROKEN	W 6140	1225	W 601	172	W 1269	361	W 2312	580	BRISURES DE RIZ
044	MAIZE UNMILLED	W 24324	3809	W 15364	3465	W 2106	348	W 34	31	MAIS NON MOULU
046	WHEAT ETC MEAL OR FLOUR	W 18414	3666	W 13565	13623	W 3621	829	W 14112	6495	SEMOULE FARINE,FROMENT
04601	FLOUR OF WHEAT OR MESLIN	W 18391	3654	W 13457	13579	W 3512	790	W 14111	6494	FARINE DE FROMENT
047	OTHER CEREAL MEALS,FLOUR	W 2368	898	W 3339	1768	W 1684	769	W 558	274	AUTRES SEMOULES,FARINES
04701	CEREAL FLOUR(NON–WHEAT)	W 2368	898	W 3320	1761	W 819	423	W 550	265	FARINES DE CEREALES
048	CEREAL ETC PREPARATIONS	W 1203	922	W 2622	1866	W 2598	1846	W 6586	4645	PREPTNS A BASE CEREALES
0482	MALT INCLUDING FLOUR	W 200	92	W 1650	1043	W 1600	841	W 3300	2623	MALT MEME TORREFIE
05	VEGETABLES AND FRUIT		1806		911		630		802	LEGUMES ET FRUITS
054	VEG ETC FRSH,SMPLY PRSVD	W 3252	1521	W 1694	671	W 263	371	W 364	422	LEGUMES FRAIS,CONG,SECS
0542	LEGUMINOUS VEGETBLES DRY	W 3094	1425	W 1632	572	W 194	169	W 134	65	LEGUMES A COSSE SECS
06	SUGAR AND PREPS,HONEY		1271		1250		4283		8368	SUCRES ET PRODUITS
061	SUGAR AND HONEY	W 4727	1197	W 2116	1144	W 15348	4159	W 21219	8211	SUCRES ET MIEL
0611	RAW BEET AND CANE SUGAR	W 1992	262	W 135	73	W 1522	484	W 20617	7858	SUCRES BRUTS
0612	REFINED SUGAR ETC	W 2531	795	W 1093	445	W 13585	3553	W 59	31	SUCRES RAFFINES
09	MISC EDIBLE PRODUCTS		1322		1998		1876		2953	PREP ALIMENTAIRES DIVERSES
098	EDIBLE PRODCTS,PREPS NES	W 543	1272	W 562	1946	W 525	1862	W 715	2769	PREP ALIMENTAIRES NDA
1	BEVERAGES AND TOBACCO		869		1385		1351		2036	BOISSONS ET TABACS
2	CRUDE MATERLS,EXCL FUELS		6485		8015		5852		11532	MAT BRUTES NON COMESTIBLES
251	*PULP AND WASTE PAPER	W 4501	1902	W 5603	2173	W 5412	1335	W 6905	1656	PATES A PAPIER,DECHETS
26	TEXTILE FIBRES AND WASTE		3328		4669		2492		6452	FIBRES TEXTILES
266	SYNTHETIC FIBRES TO SPIN	W 970	1532	W 1215	2047	W 827	1374	W 681	1705	FIBRES SYNTHETIQUES
2665	DISCN SYNTH FIBRE UNCMBD	W 738	1248	W 764	1389	W 668	1169	W 679	1700	DISCONTINUES EN MASSE
267	OTHER MAN–MADE FIBRES	W 447	1337	W 592	1468	W 460	870	W 776	2232	AUTR FIBR TEXT ARTIF SYNTH
2671	REGENERATD FIBRE TO SPIN	W 349	1221	W 414	1245	W 302	704	W 408	1760	FIBRES TEXT ARTIFIC
26711	DISCN REGEN FIBRE UNCMBD	W 349	1221	W 414	1245	W 302	704	W 408	1760	FIBRES TEX ARTIF DISCONT
269	WASTE OF TEXTILE FABRICS	W 657	438	W 363	250	W 481	233	W 1944	2070	FRIPERIE DRILLES,CHIFFONS
26901	BULK TEXT WSTE,OLD CLTHG	W 625	382	W 343	237	W 480	232	W 1944	2070	ART ET ACCESS D'HABILLEMENT
29	CRUDE ANIMAL,VEG MAT NES		234		513		1581		1708	MATIERES BRUTES ANIM,VEGET
292	CRUDE VEG MATERIALS NES	W 22	217	W 65	510	W 556	1567	W 572	1676	MAT BRUTES VEGETALES NDA
3	MINERAL FUELS ETC		77402		88756		64363		77160	COMBUSTIBLES MINERAUX LUB
33	PETROLEUM AND PRODUCTS		76848		88244		63944		76495	PETROLE ET DERIVES
333	CRUDE PETROLEUM	W 332791	50939	W 468281	61549	W 235208	31985	W 435754	61655	HUILES BRUTES DE PETROLE
334	PETROLEUM PRODUCTS,REFIN	W 114598	23413	W 107787	22691	W 183188	29937	W 57870	13050	PRODUITS RAFFINES
335	RESIDUAL PETRLM PROD NES	W 6407	2496	W 11904	4004	W 3802	2022	W 5511	1791	PRODUITS RESIDUELS NDA
3351	PETRLM JELLY,MINERAL WAX	W 2331	1645	W 1947	1413	W 2249	1701	W 889	614	VASELINE,CIRES MINERALES
33512	MINERAL WAXES	W 2283	1563	W 1903	1357	W 2232	1676	W 805	489	PARAFFINES,CIRES DE PETROLE
3354	PETROLM BITUMEN,COKE ETC	W 4074	841	W 9953	2584	W 1553	320	W 4622	1163	BITUME,COKE DE PETROLE
33541	PETROLEUM BITUMEN, ETC	W 4009	703	W 9918	2507	W 1225	182	W 4575	1082	BITUME DE PETROLE
4	ANIMAL,VEGETABLE OIL,FAT		6878		13846		11486		19206	HUILES,GRAISSES ANIM,VEG
411	*ANIMAL OILS AND FATS	W 3036	910	W 2402	1064	W 119	100	W 3809	2120	HUILES,GRAISSES ANIMALES
4113	ANIML OIL,FAT,GREASE NES	W 3035	905	W 2402	1063	W 118	96	W 3809	2119	HUILES,GRAISSES ANIMALES NDA
41132	FATS OF BOVINE,SHEEP,ETC	W 3028	883	W 2402	1062	W 100	91	W 3698	2098	SUIFS BRUTS FONDUS
42	FIXED VEGETABLE OIL,FAT		4037		7051		6827		10509	HUILES VEGETALES FIXES
423	FIXED VEG OILS,SOFT	W 7020	3153	W 7273	4635	W 2719	2001	W 5998	4958	HUILES VEGET DOUCES FIXES
4232	SOYA BEAN OIL	W 6533	2792	W 6719	4214	W 2387	1697	W 2949	3005	HUILE DE SOJA
424	FIXED VEG OIL NONSOFT	W 4989	884	W 3366	2416	W 7776	4826	W 8413	5551	AUTRES HUILES VEG FIXES
4242	PALM OIL	W 4830	774	W 2471	1798	W 7284	4569	W 7344	4815	HUILE DE PALME
431	*PROCESD ANML VEG OIL,ET	W 5326	1931	W 11116	5730	W 10333	4559	W 9812	6576	HUILES,GRAISSES PREPAREES
4313	FATTY ACIDS ETC,RESIDUES	W 4875	1714	W 9825	4410	W 9906	4080	W 9258	5736	ACIDES GRAS INDUST,RESIDUS
43131	FATTY ACIDS,ACID OILS	W 4875	1714	W 9825	4410	W 9906	4080	W 9258	5736	ACIDES GRAS INDUSTRIELS
5	CHEMCLS,RELATED PROD NES		50597		61108		56285		69768	PRODUITS CHIMIQUES
51	ORGANIC CHEMICALS		2434		4341		3755		4244	PROD CHIMIQ ORGANIQUES
511	HYDROCARBONS NES,DERIVS	W 267	426	W 501	1590	W 463	1640	W 495	1000	HYDROCARBURES NDA
5113	HALOG DERIV OF HYDROCARB	W 164	231	W 415	1449	W 446	1619	W 421	897	DERIVES HALOGENES HYDROCAR
51139	OTH HALOG HYDRCARB DERIV	W 151	220	W 391	1428	W 442	1615	W 393	871	AUTRE DERIVES HALOGENES
52	INORGANIC CHEMICALS		6216		5155		4895		6360	PROD CHIM INORGANIQUES
522	INORG ELEMNTS,OXIDES,ETC	W 5202	3733	W 2951	2559	W 4971	2883		3881	ELEMENTS INORGANIQUES
5224	ZINC,IRON,LEAD ETC OXIDE	W 716	1250	W 667	1177	W 585	835	W 738	1499	OXYDES METALLIQUES
5225	INORGANIC BASES ETC NES	W 3895	2020	W 1991	1031	W 4186	1683	W 3182	1807	AUTRES BASES OXYDES METAL
52252	SODIUM HYDROXIDE, SOLID	W 2881	1635	W 1409	755	W 3213	1386	W 2623	1497	HYDROXYDE DE SODIUM
523	OTHR INORG CHEMICALS ETC	W 3171	2404	W 2788	2569	W 3488	2002	W 2410	2477	AUT PRODUITS CHIMIQUES INORG
5231	METAL CMPD OF INORG ACID	W 2001	1638	W 1570	1725	W 2124	1240	W 1071	1535	SELS METALLIQUES
53	DYES,TANNING,COLOUR PROD		4311		5316		5711		4419	PROD TEINTURE,COLORANTS
531	SYNT DYE,NAT INDGO,LAKES	W 197	2928	W 209	3331	W 275	4137	W 137	2395	MAT COLOR ORGAN,LAQUES
5311	SYNTHIC ORGNIC DYESTUFFS	W 135	2525	W 138	2873	W 202	3646	W 122	2162	MAT COLOR ORGAN SYNTHET
533	PIGMENTS,PAINTS,ETC	W 969	1367	W 1289	1927	W 707	1456	W 857	1972	PIGMENTS,PEINTURES,VERNIS
541	*MEDICINAL,PHARM PRODUCT	K 1133038	12870	K 1076133	12666	K 884885	13466	K 1021357	16145	PROD MEDICINAUX PHARMACEUT
5417	MEDICAMENTS	K 876778	10775	K 931439	10459	K 776543	11636	K 878740	13337	MEDICAMENTS
54171	— CONTAINNG ANTIBIOTICS	K 103065	1809	K 105813	1939	K 125119	2787	K 165072	2745	MED CONTN ANTIBIOTIQUES
54179	— CONTNG OTH SUBSTANCES	K 723076	7686	K 793762	7748	K 615005	7601	K 673487	9507	MED CONT AUT SUBSTANCES
55	PERFUME,CLEANING ETC PRD		2486		3459		2796		4337	PROD POUR PARFUM,TOILETTE
554	SOAP,CLEANSING ETC PREPS	W 836	859	W 1182	1385	W 1536	1392	W 1369	1555	SAVONS,PRODUITS DETERSIFS
562	*FERTILIZERS,MANUFACTURE	W 11740	2851	W 16984	4754	W 17506	5913	W 18914	7060	ENGRAIS MANUFACTURES
5621	CHEM NITROGENOUS FERTLZR	W 5439	1132	W 7734	2182	W 7235	1817	W 6650	2225	ENGRAIS AZOTES
56216	UREA	W 4775	962	W 7279	2014	W 6929	1737	W 6445	2145	UREE
5623	CHEM POTASSIC FERTILIZER	W 2905	646	W 3790	983	W 1275	382	W 7908	3319	ENGRAIS POTASSIQUES
56239	CHEM POTASS FERTILZR NES		1			W 1	2	W 3854	2167	ENGRAIS POTASSIQUES NDA
5629	FERTILIZERS NES	W 3316	1056	W 5178	1508	W 8597	3575	W 4037	1412	ENGRAIS NDA
56291	NIT–PHOS–POT FERTLZR NES	W 3291	1026	W 4857	1357	W 8139	3303	W 3446	1131	ENGRAIS CONT N P K
58	PLASTIC MATERIALS ETC		10456		13080		9813		16220	MAT PLAST ARTIFICIELLES
582	PROD OF CONDENSATION ETC	W 681	1907	W 919	2783	W 783	1535	W 850	1844	PROD CONDENS,POLYCOND
583	POLYMERIZATION ETC PRODS	W 5925	8330	W 7324	9883	W 6475	7828	W 8703	14000	PROD POLYMERISATION
5831	POLYETHYLENE	W 1494	1942	W 2056	2328	W 2040	1829	W 2866	4036	POLYETHYLENE
58311	— IN PRIMARY FORMS	W 1491	1920	W 2047	2305	W 2023	1790	W 2857	4004	POLYETHYLENE PRIMAIRES

4. Special Imports C.I.F. by Commodities according to the S.I.T.C. (Rev. 2) in thousand U.S. Dollars
Importations Spéciales C.A.F. par Produits d'après la C.T.C.I. (Rév. 2) en milliers de Dollars E.U.

SITC CTCI	COMMODITY	1992 WEIGHT POIDS	1992 VALUE VALEUR	1993 WEIGHT POIDS	1993 VALUE VALEUR	1994 WEIGHT POIDS	1994 VALUE VALEUR	1995 WEIGHT POIDS	1995 VALUE VALEUR	PRODUIT
5832	POLYPROPYLENE	W 1740	1687	W 2421	2414	W 1932	1739	W 2148	2494	POLYPROPYLENE
58321	— IN PRIMARY FORMS	W 1697	1508	W 2398	2287	W 1926	1694	W 2147	2480	POLYPROPYLENE PRIMAIRES
5834	POLYVINYL CHLORIDE	W 1098	1584	W 1039	1640	W 900	1213	W 1500	2271	CHLORURE DE POLYVINYLE
58341	— IN PRIMARY FORMS	W 1002	1346	W 949	1409	W 770	959	W 1258	1786	SOUS FORMES PRIMAIRES
5839	OTH POLYMRZTION ETC PROD	W 678	1392	W 609	1410	W 492	1145	W 813	2514	AUT PROD POLYMER COPOLYM
59	CHEMICAL MATERIALS NES		8617		11640		9812		10589	MAT PROD CHIMIQUES NDA
591	PESTICIDES,DISINFECTANTS	W 1155	5242	W 1141	5025	W 1230	4833	W 1020	4654	DESINF,INSECT,FONG,HERB
5911	INSECTICIDES,FOR RETAIL	W 976	4090	W 943	3609	W 1032	3856	W 812	3417	INSECTICIDES VENTE DET
598	MISCEL CHEM PRODUCTS NES	W 1178	2651	W 2046	5653	W 1080	4128	W 1374	4573	PROD DIV INDUST CHIM NDA
5982	ANTI-KNOCK PREPARTNS ETC	W 85	177	W 1104	2822	W 311	1089	W 709	2230	PREPARAT ANTIDETONANTES
5989	CHEM PRODUCTS,PREPS NES	W 1065	2412	W 914	2754	W 752	2955	W 644	2250	PROD PREP CHIMIQUES NDA
59899	OTH CHEM PRODS,PREPS,NES	W 757	1288	W 492	1448	W 359	1426	W 356	1250	AUT PRODUITS CHIMIQUES NDA
6	BASIC MANUFACTURES		58140		72541		67412		111133	ART MANUFACTURES
62	RUBBER MANUFACTURES NES		10138		10401		8531		12456	CAOUTCHOUC MANUFACTURE
621	MATERIALS OF RUBBER	W 271	1386	W 373	1214	W 239	741	W 499	1618	PRODUITS EN CAOUTCHOUC
625	RUBBER TYRES, TUBES ETC	W 3420	7011	W 3191	7224	W 2535	6160	W 3614	8655	PNEUS CAOUTCHOUC VULCANISE
6251	TYRES NEW FOR MOTOR CARS	W 627	1749	W 366	1076	W 416	1377	W 562	1733	PNEUS POUR VOITURES
6252	TYRES,NEW,BUS OR LORRY	W 1395	3605	W 1605	4327	W 1189	3036	W 1741	4339	PNEUS POUR AUTOBUS,CAMIONS
6259	OTH TYRES,TYRE CASES,ETC	W 1322	1377	W 1146	1572	W 849	1383	W 1169	2118	AUTRES PNEUS RECHAPES FLAPS
62599	TYRES NES,TYRE CASES,ETC	W 1169	893	W 1003	1198	W 710	1035	W 1082	1833	PNEUS,FLAPS
628	RUBBER ARTICLES NES	W 110	1741	W 153	1962	W 102	1630	W 142	2183	OUVRAGES CAOUTCHOUC NDA
64	PAPER,PAPERBOARD AND MFR		5994		7277		6387		11842	PAPIERS,CARTONS & OUVRAGES
641	PAPER AND PAPERBOARD	W 4245	3671	W 5108	4487	W 4292	4034	W 5313	7694	PAPIERS ET CARTONS
6412	PRINTG,WRITING PAPER NES	W 677	791	W 1211	1402	W 1319	1445	W 1741	2760	PAPIERS POUR L'IMPRESSION
642	PAPER,ETC,PRECUT,ARTS OF	W 1003	2323	W 1223	2790	W 986	2353	W 1523	4148	PAP,CARTONS DECOUPES
65	TEXTILE YARN,FABRICS,ETC		4747		9475		7194		8514	FILS,TISSUS,ARTICLES TEXTILE
651	TEXTILE YARN	W 340	1101	W 835	2961	W 409	1173	W 450	1492	FILS TEXTILES
6514	SYN FIB YRN,BULK,MONOFIL	W 298	937	W 590	2208	W 335	969	W 323	1023	FILS CONT 85% FIB TEXT SYNTH
653	WOVN MAN-MADE FIB FABRIC	W 1091	1081	W 1934	2077	W 1977	2633	W 2667	2586	TISSUS FIBRES SYNTH,ARTIF
6534	DISC SYN BLEND FABRC NES	W 497	632	W 573	843	W 1023	1910	W 994	1126	TISSUS FIBRES SYNTH DISCONT
65341	DISC SYN FIB-COTTN FABRC	W 377	183	W 344	243	W 815	1500	W 535	388	TISSUS FIB SYNT DIS MEL COTO
66	NONMETAL MINERAL MFS NES		8824		12311		11705		15118	ART MIN NON METALLIQUES
661	LIME,CEMENT,BLDG PRODS	W 99724	5187	W 77564	7059	W 96451	7243	W 86305	7410	CHAUX,CIMENTS MAT CONSTR
6612	CEMENT	W 99354	4909	W 77336	6689	W 96122	6885	W 85967	7076	CIMENTS HYDRAULIQUES
665	GLASSWARE	W 1307	917	W 2444	2107	W 2077	1567	W 4536	3784	OUVRAGES EN VERRE
6651	BOTTLES ETC OF GLASS	W 373	302	W 1143	976	W 966	712	W 3491	2664	RECIPIENTS EN VERRE
66511	GLASS BOTTLES ETC NONVAC	W 373	302	W 1143	975	W 961	707	W 3491	2664	BONBONNES,BOUTEILLES,ETC
67	IRON AND STEEL		13128		15636		17489		44072	FER ET ACIER
673	IRON,STEEL SHAPES ETC	W 9984	4104	W 6421	2857	W 12158	5035	W 43337	27906	BARRES,PROFIL FER,ACIER
6732	IRON,STEEL BARS ETC	W 5035	1883	W 4088	1634	W 6848	2695	W 38772	25365	BARRES FER,ACIER
67322	HIGH CARBON STL BARS ETC	W 975	407	W 481	194	W 666	251	W 31828	22091	BARRES ACIER FIN CARBONE
67326	IRN,OTH STL BARS HOTROLD	W 3568	1218	W 3446	1344	W 5805	2302	W 6741	3101	BARRES PLEINES FER,ACIER
6733	IRON,STEEL PROFILES ETC	W 2813	1316	W 1484	764	W 2779	1206	W 2927	1616	PROFILES,PALPLAN FER,ACIER
674	IRN,STL UNIV,PLATE,SHEET	W 7760	5171	W 8650	8042	W 12527	9457	W 13177	12658	LARGES PLATS,TOLES
6749	OTH IRN,STL PLATES,SHEET	W 4177	3014	W 5639	5827	W 8426	7180	W 9385	9778	AUTRES TOLES FER,ACIER
67491	— OF IRON OR SIMPLE STL	W 4158	2974	W 5637	5804	W 8412	7142	W 9367	9717	AUT TOLES AUTRES ACIER FIN
678	IRON,STL TUBES,PIPES,ETC	W 1381	1644	W 2396	3640	W 1489	1876	W 998	1684	TUBES,TUYAUX EN FONTE,FER
6782	IRON,STL SEAMLESS TUBES	W 771	626	W 1135	1835	W 924	748	W 669	605	TUBES,TUYAUX SANS SOUDURE
68	NON-FERROUS METALS		1822		2238		1743		2107	METAUX NON FERREUX
684	ALUMINIUM	W 289	1335	W 553	1811	W 465	1477	W 324	1601	ALUMINIUM
6842	ALUMINIUM,ALLOYS WORKED	W 289	1335	W 530	1754	W 465	1477	W 324	1601	ALUMINIUM,ALLIAGES OUVRE
69	METAL MANUFACTURES NES		13087		13493		13992		16493	ART MANUFACT EN METAL NDA
691	STRUCTURES AND PARTS NES	W 715	2173	W 446	1129	W 1489	3364	W 1440	2955	CONSTRUCT FER,ACIER,ALU
6911	STRUCTURES,PARTS IRN,STL	W 661	2036	W 426	1096	W 1440	3210	W 1424	2864	CONSTRUCT FER,ACIER,FONTE
694	STL,COPPR NAILS,NUTS,ETC	W 591	1256	W 523	1180	W 441	1265	W 441	1726	CLOUS,VIS,ECROUS
695	TOOLS	W 256	1953	W 341	2402	W 507	2651	W 293	2016	OUTILS A MAIN
6954	BLADES,TIPS,ETC FR TOOLS	W 57	826	W 74	1057	W 78	1577	W 36	700	OUTILS POUR MACHINE-OUTIL
69541	PARTS TO INSERT IN TOOLS	W 54	684	W 70	858	W 71	1436	W 30	506	OUTILS DE FORAGE
697	BASE MTL HOUSEHOLD EQUIP	W 240	679	W 326	1021	W 448	952	W 644	1820	ART MENAGE MET COMMUNS
699	BASE METAL MFRS NES	W 2045	5487	W 2283	5886	W 1952	4088	W 1925	5777	ART MANUFACTURES MET NDA
6991	LOCKSMITHS WARES,ETC	W 560	1418	W 505	1261	W 398	877	W 371	1148	ARTICLES DE SERRURERIE
6997	IRON,STEEL ARTICLES NES	W 759	1757	W 830	1969	W 456	933	W 420	1265	OUV FONTE,FER,ACIER NDA
69979	IRN,STL MANUFACTURES NES	W 758	1754	W 830	1969	W 456	932	W 419	1256	AUT OUVRAGES EN FER NDA
7	MACHINES,TRANSPORT EQUIP		112179		137020		129848		140858	MACHINES MATERIEL TRANSPORT
71	POWER GENERATING EQUIPMT		10439		7791		7497		8794	MACHINES GENERATRICES
713	INTRNL COMBUS PSTN ENGIN	W 452	5020	W 558	4140	W 428	3725	W 639	5510	MOTEURS EXPL COMB INT, PIECE
7139	PISTON ENGINE PARTS NES	W 140	3981	W 157	2891	W 106	2512	W 204	4080	PIECES POUR 713.2,3,8
714	ENGINES AND MOTORS NES	W 3	736	W 6	934	W 32	1746	W 3	680	MOTEURS NON ELECTRIQUES
716	ROTATING ELECTRIC PLANT	W 301	4363	W 382	2448	W 269	1782	W 164	2248	APP ELECTR ROTATIFS,PIECES
7162	AC MTRS,GENRTRS,GEN SETS	W 227	3397	W 311	2038	W 156	1208	W 130	1634	MOTEURS ELECTRIQUES
71623	GEN SETS WITH PSTN ENGN	W 193	2987	W 269	1707	W 104	673	W 98	1260	GROUPES MOTEUR EXPLOSION
72	MACHS FOR SPCL INDUSTRYS		13108		24473		16091		18028	MAC SPECIALES POUR INDUST
721	AGRIC MACHY,EXC TRACTORS	W 119	752	W 117	644	W 116	1027	W 154	1905	MACHINES AGRICOLES
722	TRACTORS NON-ROAD	W 375	1750	W 306	1478	W 174	730	W 346	1704	TRACTEURS
7224	WHEELED TRACTORS NES	W 375	1750	W 306	1478	W 166	716	W 326	1680	TRACTEURS A ROUES
723	CIVIL ENGNEERG EQUIP ETC	W 1188	3079	W 2056	11406	W 505	1063	W 931	2541	APPAREILS DE GENIE CIVIL
7234	CONST,MINING MACHNRY NES	W 878	2234	W 1692	8700	W 404	678	W 782	2026	MACH POUR LA CONST, MINES
72341	SELF-PROPELLD DOZERS,ETC	W 215	216	W 652	3200	W 36	94	W 260	601	BULLDOZERS
72342	SLFPRP SHOVELS,EXCAVATRS	W 268	721	W 683	2206	W 356	487	W 422	1266	PELLES MECANIQUES
72344	BORING,SINKING MACHINERY	W 334	1121	W 317	3092				8	MACHINES DE FORAGE
7239	CONSTR ETC MACHY PTS NES	W 165	591	W 120	1575	W 91	335	W 37	293	PIECES 723.41-723.46
724	TEXTILE,LEATHER MACHNRY	W 263	2820	W 369	3490	W 424	2746	W 484	3769	MACH POUR INDUSTRIE TEXTILE
726	PRINTG,BKBINDG MACHY,PTS	W 61	335	W 50	667	W 100	1565	W 80	1262	MACHINES POUR IMPRIMERIE
727	FOOD MACHRY NON-DOMESTIC	W 119	1202	W 340	1461	W 322	2248	W 216	1955	MACH INDUSTRIES ALIMENT
728	OTH MACHY FOR SPCL INDUS	W 945	2976	W 764	4730	W 916	6201	W 728	4356	AUT MACH IND PARTICULIERES
7283	OTHR MINERAL WORKG MACHY	W 616	925	W 391	1512	W 526	974	W 298	862	MACH TRIER,CRIBLER,BROYER
7284	MACHY FOR SPCL INDUS NES	W 118	1255	W 225	2266	W 251	4680	W 202	2482	MACH SPEC IND PARTICUL.
72848	OTH MCHY WITH INDIV FNCT	W 45	497	W 81	1026	W 158	3560	W 42	564	AUTRES MACHINES NDA
73	METALWORKING MACHINERY		1171		1414		1004		1135	MACH TRAVAIL DES METAUX
74	GENRL INDUSTRL MACHY NES		15806		19216		16124		23854	MACH APP INDUSTRIE
741	HEATING,COOLING EQUIPMNT	W 228	2230	W 258	2380	W 273	2313	W 269	2309	MACH CHAUFFAGE,PIECES
742	PUMPS FOR LIQUIDS ETC	W 125	2305	W 221	3118	W 101	1887	W 134	2391	POMPES MOTO-POMPES
7428	OTHER PUMPS FOR LIQUIDS	W 77	1292	W 124	1641	W 73	1151	W 86	1345	AUTRES POMPES POUR LIQ
74288	PUMPS FR LIQUIDS NES ETC	W 75	1213	W 117	1487	W 73	1149	W 85	1334	POMPES POUR LIQUIDES NDA
743	PUMPS NES,CENTRFUGES ETC	W 235	2456	W 222	2868	W 207	2621	W 257	3854	POMPES COMPRES,VENT ETC
7436	GAS,LIQUID FILTERS ETC	W 108	1039	W 84	867	W 113	1308	W 98	1358	APP POUR FILT DES LIQUIDES
744	MECHANICAL HANDLING EQU	W 421	2173	W 802	3219	W 1085	2227	W 899	5574	EQUIP MANUTENTION PIECES
7441	FORK LIFT TRCKS,ETC,PTS	W 184	335	W 325	901	W 237	613	W 478	2902	CHARIOTS POUR USINES ETC
74411	FORK LIFT TRUCKS ETC	W 181	329	W 325	893	W 236	594	W 476	2845	CHARIOTS POUR LES GARES
7442	LIFTING,LOADING MACH NES	W 167	708	W 409	1582	W 790	1188	W 291	1620	APP LEVAGE,MANUTENTION
745	NONELEC MACHY,TOOLS NES	W 114	1274	W 167	1494	W 194	1415	W 203	2564	AUT MACH NON ELEC,PIECES

4. Special Imports C.I.F. by Commodities according to the S.I.T.C. (Rev. 2) in thousand U.S. Dollars
Importations Spéciales C.A.F. par Produits d'après la C.T.C.I. (Rév. 2) en milliers de Dollars E.U.

SITC CTCI	COMMODITY	1992 WEIGHT POIDS	1992 VALUE VALEUR	1993 WEIGHT POIDS	1993 VALUE VALEUR	1994 WEIGHT POIDS	1994 VALUE VALEUR	1995 WEIGHT POIDS	1995 VALUE VALEUR	PRODUIT
7452	OTH NONELEC MCHS,PTS NES	W 108	1164	W 156	1327	W 170	1271	W 195	2353	AUT MACH NON ELEC,PIECES
749	NONELEC MACH PTS,ACC NES	W 383	5368	W 472	6136	W 447	5661	W 469	7162	PIECES MACH NON ELEC NDA
7491	BALL,ROLLER,ETC BEARINGS	W 49	928	W 62	1170	W 75	1308	W 70	1413	ROULEMENTS BILLES ETC
7492	COCKS,VALVES ETC NES	W 180	1460	W 237	1857	W 146	1102	W 186	1543	ART ROB,SIM POUR TUYAUX
7493	SHAFT,CRANK,PULLEY ETC	W 79	1979	W 122	2379	W 108	2334	W 129	3094	ARBRES TRANS,VILEBREQUINS
75	OFFICE MACHINES,ADP EQUIP		5677		7607		6806		7192	MACH BUREAU TRAIT AUTOM
751	OFFICE MACHINES	W 78	959	W 120	1925	W 147	1177	W 112	2247	MACH,APPAREILS DE BUREAU
7518	OFFICE MACHINES NES	W 39	606	W 68	1410	W 112	886	W 68	1830	MACH,APP DE BUREAU NDA
752	AUTOMTIC DATA PROC EQUIP	W 59	4166	W 84	4912	W 80	4746	W 86	3995	MACH TRAIT INFORMATION
7522	DIGITAL COMPUTERS	W 26	2269	W 37	3162	W 32	2429	W 34	1741	MACH DIGITALES COMPLETES
7525	ADP PERIPHERAL UNITS	W 23	1318	W 19	1085	W 22	1386	W 28	1270	UNITES PERIPHERIQUES
76	TELECOMM,SOUND EQUIPMENT		8080		5881		17808		10318	EQUIPMENT DE TELECOM
762	RADIO BROADCAST RECEIVRS	W 377	1661	W 540	1303	W 594	972	W 432	883	RECEPTEURS RADIODIFFUSION
764	TELECOM EQPT,PTS,ACC NES	W 101	5469	W 112	3299	W 813	15969	W 205	8435	EQUIP TELECOM,PIECES
7641	LINE TELEPHONE,ETC EQUIP	W 41	3716	W 22	1215	W 110	4235	W 32	2584	APP TELEPHON PAR FIL
7643	TV,RADIO TRANSMITTRS ETC	W 13	848	W 8	635	W 19	2551	W 14	1476	APP EMET TELE RADIO
7649	PTS NES OF EQUIPMT OF 76	W 27	619	W 46	712	W 605	8536	W 115	3747	PIECES DE LA DIV 76
76491	PTS NES OF APPAR OF 7641	W 2	192	W 1	137	W 14	1479	W 14	2386	PIECES POUR 764.1
76493	TELECOMM EQUIPMT PTS NES	W 17	402	W 40	541	W 585	7034	W 71	1233	PIECES 761,762,764.3,8
77	ELECTRIC MACHNRY NES ETC		18948		17610		15744		16344	MACH APP ELECT NDA
771	ELECTRIC POWER MACHY NES	W 224	2627	W 205	2051	W 127	1802	W 101	1431	MACH PROD,TRANS ELECTR
7711	TRANSFORMERS,ELECTRICAL	W 192	1794	W 180	1221	W 95	818	W 65	437	TRANSFO ELECTRIQUES
77111	LIQUID DIELEC TRANSFRMRS	W 157	1281	W 114	702	W 72	599	W 31	206	TRANSFO DIELEC LIQUIDE
772	SWITCHGEAR ETC,PARTS NES	W 204	4682	W 242	4851	W 233	3631	W 199	3980	APP COUPURE,SECT ETC
7721	SWITCHGEAR ETC	W 203	4622	W 241	4786	W 232	3513	W 196	3857	APP COUPURE,SECTIONMNT
773	ELECTR DISTRIBUTNG EQUIP	W 667	3237	W 484	1957	W 559	1891	W 451	2100	EQUIPMT DISTRIBUTION ELECT
7731	INSULATED WIRE,CABLE ETC	W 651	3031	W 438	1616	W 547	1834	W 441	2017	FILS,CABLES ISOLES ELECT
774	ELECTRO-MEDCL,XRAY EQUIP	W 14	577	W 27	1651	W 14	628	W 14	219	APPAREILS MEDICAUX
775	HOUSEHOLD TYPE EQUIP NES	W 534	3769	W 641	2486	W 624	2439	W 593	2075	MACH,APP USAGE DOMESTQUE
7752	DOM REFRIGERATRS,FREEZRS	W 299	2971	W 331	1143	W 341	1213	W 278	782	REFRIG,CONGEL MENAGER
77521	DOMESTIC REFRIGERATORS	W 229	2727	W 284	929	W 255	883	W 236	649	REFRIGERATEURS
778	ELECTRICAL MACHINERY NES	W 1425	3411	W 1200	3923	W 1763	4453	W 2344	5693	AUTRES MACH ELECT NDA
7781	BATTERIES,ACCUMULATORS	W 1017	1011	W 758	1203	W 1364	1215	W 1744	1960	PILES ET ACCUMULATEURS
78	ROAD VEHICLES		33634		51536		44905		50692	VEHICULES ROUTIERS
781	PASS MOTOR VEH EXC BUSES	W 2580	10947	W 2383	11206	W 1965	8617	W 2359	13106	AUTO TRANSPORT PERSONNES
782	LORRIES,SPCL MTR VEH NES	W 4163	14859	W 6092	26131	W 5981	18399	W 6135	21439	VEHICULES SPECIAUX,MARCH
7821	LORRIES,TRUCKS	W 3929	13574	W 5704	23766	W 5758	16966	W 5903	18864	VEHICULES TRANSP MARCHAND
7822	SPECIAL MOTOR VEHCLS NES	W 234	1285	W 387	2365	W 223	1433	W 233	2575	VEHICULES USAGES SPECIAUX
783	ROAD MOTOR VEHICLES NES	W 610	2160	W 1195	4820	W 1639	8524	W 1039	6070	VEHICULES ROUTIERS NDA
7831	BUSES	W 345	1871	W 630	3867	W 923	6235	W 491	4824	VOITURES TRANSPORT COMMUN
7832	TRACTORS FOR TR-TRAILERS	W 265	289	W 565	954	W 716	2288	W 547	1246	TRACTEURS ROUTIERS
784	MOTOR VEH PRTS,ACCES NES	W 804	3884	W 1337	5772	W 1104	5307	W 1215	6488	PIECES 722,781,782,783
7849	OTHER MOTOR VEHCL PARTS	W 757	3863	W 1225	5719	W 957	5238	W 1013	6355	PIECES 722,781,782,783
785	CYCLES,ETC MOTRZD OR NOT	W 264	1081	W 527	2414	W 586	2059	W 704	2835	MOTOCYCLES SCOOTERS
7851	MOTORCYCLES ETC	W 64	549	W 146	1544	W 115	1123	W 162	1705	MOTO VELO MOTEUR AUXIL
786	TRAILERS,NONMOTR VEH,NES	W 839	703	W 903	1194	W 1072	1999	W 907	754	REMORQUES,CADRES,CONTAIN
7861	TRAILERS,TRANSP CONTAINR	W 579	392	W 665	754	W 820	1655	W 563	407	REMORQUES TOUS VEHICULES
78612	OTHER TRAILERS	W 198	199	W 343	473	W 407	1487	W 266	241	REMORQUES TRANSP MARCH
79	OTHR TRANSPORT EQUIPMENT		5316		1491		3869		4502	AUTRE MATERIEL TRANSPORT
792	AIRCRAFT ETC	W 15	2360	W 7	904	W 19	2293	W 47	1941	APP NAVIGATION AERIENNE
7923	AIRCRFT NES2000-15000KG	W 6	1517	W 2	122					AERODYNES 2000 A 15000 KG
7929	AIRCRAFT PARTS NES	W 3	647	W 3	662	W 5	1313	W 8	1541	PIECES DU 792
793	SHIPS AND BOATS ETC	W 1156	2735	W 245	456	W 97	757	W 1131	2495	NAVIRES BATEAUX,ETC
7932	SHIPS AND BOATS NES	W 1113	2706	W 241	427	W 74	279	W 1063	1760	NAVIRES ET BATEAUX
79324	FISHING VESSELS ETC	W 1074	2471	W 129	276	W 23	120	W 699	1475	BATEAUX DE PECHE
8	MISC MANUFACTURED GOODS		28982		29284		35033		37653	ART MANUFACTURES DIVERS
812	*PLUMBG,HEATNG,LGHTNG EQ	W 595	984	W 714	1463	W 456	1005	W 454	1625	APPAR SANITAIRES CHAUFFAGE
821	*FURNITURE,PARTS THEREOF	W 325	1238	W 542	2354	W 524	1515	W 434	1708	MEUBLES ET PIECES
8219	FURNITURE AND PARTS NES	W 244	828	W 374	1474	W 351	927	W 294	953	AUTRES MEUBLES ET PIECES
84	CLOTHING AND ACCESSORIES		654		1186		1469		1466	VETEMENTS
851	*FOOTWEAR	W 373	474	W 705	1036	W 1089	1340	W 1440	2276	CHAUSSURES
87	PRECISION INSTRUMNTS NES		5077		6281		4838		6342	INSTRUM,APPAR SCIENT NDA
872	MEDICAL INSTRUMENTS NES	W 124	1789	W 139	2439	W 177	1595	W 132	1426	INSTR,APP MEDIC-CHIR NDA
87202	OTH MEDICAL INSTRUMENTS	W 120	1691	W 133	2251	W 173	1564	W 126	1288	INSTRUM,APP MEDECINE
874	MEASURNG,CONTROLNG INSTR	W 108	2765	W 100	3200	W 138	2619	W 89	3948	INSTRUMENTS DE MESURE
88	PHOTO EQU,OPTICL GDS ETC		1677		2530		2709		2508	APP,FOURN PHOTO,OP,MONTR
882	PHOTO,CINEMA SUPPLIES	W 125	968	W 147	1429	W 176	1585	W 137	1201	PRODUITS PHOTO,CINEMA
8822	PHOTO FILM EXC DEV CINMA	W 103	754	W 115	1113	W 136	1298	W 105	862	PLAQUES,PELLICULES,FILMS
89	MISC MANUFCTRD GOODS NES		18662		14011		21754		21150	ART MANUFACTURES DIVERS
892	PRINTED MATTER	W 618	12306	W 866	6359	W 771	12503	W 814	12251	IMPRIMES
8921	PRINTED BOOKS,GLOBES,ETC	W 320	1609	W 647	3902	W 441	2182	W 506	2505	LIVRES,BROCHURES,CARTES
89211	PRINTED BOOKS,PAMPHLETS	W 309	1576	W 632	3737	W 432	2156	W 488	2443	LIVRES,BROCHURES
8928	PRINTED MATTER NES	W 226	9910	W 141	1721	W 251	9538	W 191	8505	IMPRIMES NDA
89283	UNISSUED BANKNOTES ETC	W 152	9374	W 37	1132	W 133	8881	W 99	8116	TIMBRES-POSTE FISCAUX
893	ARTICLES OF PLASTIC NES		2533		3004		4634		3816	OUVRAGES EN MAT DIVIS 58
8939	MISC PLASTIC ARTICLES	W 532	1929	W 1133	2280	W 1081	4007	W 911	2785	ART DIVERS EN MAT DIV 58
89399	OTHR PLASTC ARTICLES NES	W 484	1822	W 590	1960	W 1026	3844	W 756	2553	AUT OUV MAT DIV 58
898	MUSICAL INSTRUMENTS,PTS	W 138	834	W 157	1172	W 332	1534	W 121	1106	INSTRUMENTS DE MUSIQUE
8983	SOUND RECRDNG TAPE,DISCS	W 124	748	W 145	1044	W 322	1485	W 109	1036	SUPPORTS SON POUR 763
899	OTHER MANUFACTURED GOODS		1479		1198		936		1535	AUT ART MANUF DIVERS NDA
9	GOODS NOT CLASSD BY KIND		5156		6393		6826		12096	ART TRANSACT NON CLASSES
931	*SPECIAL TRANSACTIONS		4928		6386		6808		12076	TRANS.SPECIALES

5. Special Exports F.O.B. by Commodities according to the S.I.T.C. (Rev. 2) in thousand U.S. Dollars
Exportations Spéciales F.O.B. par Produits d'après la C.T.C.I. (Rév. 2) en milliers de Dollars E.U.

SITC CTCI	COMMODITY	1992 WEIGHT POIDS	1992 VALUE VALEUR	1993 WEIGHT POIDS	1993 VALUE VALEUR	1994 WEIGHT POIDS	1994 VALUE VALEUR	1995 WEIGHT POIDS	1995 VALUE VALEUR	PRODUIT
	ALL COMMODITIES		268889		261729		326614		359874	TOUS PRODUITS
0	FOOD AND LIVE ANIMALS		181381		172903		254283		241135	ALIMENTS,ANIMAUX VIVANTS
001	*LIVE ANIMALS FOR FOOD	W 1350	884						1	ANIMAUX VIVANTS
0011	BOVINE SPECIES,LIVE	W 1324	863							ESPECE BOVINE
00119	— OTHR THAN FR BREEDING	W 1324	863							BOVINS NON REPRODUCTEURS
01	MEAT AND PREPARATIONS		3301		4118		4437		9000	VIANDES ET PREPARATIONS
011	MEAT FRESH,CHILLD,FROZEN	W 1320	3258	W 1717	4084	W 2357	4388	W 3841	8949	VIANDES FRAICHES,REF,CONGE
0111	BOVINE MEAT FRESH,FROZEN	W 1278	2908	W 1695	3855	W 2311	4189	W 3774	8809	VIANDES BOVIN FRAI,REF
01112	BOVINE MEAT BONELESS	W 1254	2879	W 1678	3777	W 2296	4172	W 3740	8764	VIANDES BOVIN DESOSSEES
03	FISH AND PREPARATIONS		47626		48223		60846		56686	POISSONS ET PREPARATIONS
034	FISH,FRESH,CHILLED,FROZN	W 253	409	W 192	454	W 541	1009	W 428	973	POISSON FRAIS, REFRIG,CONG
035	FISH SALTED,DRIED,SMOKED	W 308	748	W 243	979	W 254	576	W 179	667	POISSON SECHE,SALE,FUME
03503	FISH(EX COD)DRIED,SALTED	W 276	662	W 230	952	W 201	416	W 157	493	POISSONS SECHES,SALES
036	SHELL FISH FRESH,FROZEN	W 7725	46456	W 8614	46789	W 9282	59159	W 7927	55046	CRUSTACES,MOLLUSQUES
04	CEREALS AND PREPARATIONS		762		3936		2717		1293	CEREALES ET PRODUITS
044	MAIZE UNMILLED	W 1465	140	W 32172	3087	W 18827	1964	W 6620	934	MAIS NON MOULU
05	VEGETABLES AND FRUIT		20828		20624		22260		29889	LEGUMES ET FRUITS
054	VEG ETC FRSH,SMPLY PRSVD	W 10975	4851	W 14215	4319	W 19800	4852	W 23160	9059	LEGUMES FRAIS,CONG,SECS
0542	LEGUMINOUS VEGETBLES DRY	W 9448	3882	W 6247	2653	W 7835	3148	W 12723	5827	LEGUMES A COSSE SECS
0545	OTHER FRESH VEGETABLES	W 1482	937	W 2345	1208	W 2502	1204	W 2713	2312	AUTRES LEGUMES FRAIS,REF
05459	FRESH VEGETABLES NES	W 212	546	W 488	538	W 415	642	W 843	1397	LEGUMES FRAIS,REFRI NDA
056	VEGTBLES ETC PRSVD,PREPD	W 1169	1202	W 1029	1461	W 1383	1638	W 1480	1879	CONSERVES DE LEGUMES
0565	VEGTBLES PRSVD,PREPD NES	W 560	1008	W 720	1309	W 800	1480	W 882	1717	LEGUMES PREPARES CONSERVE
05651	VEGTBLS,FRUIT IN VINEGAR	W 525	806	W 669	1088	W 763	1350	W 830	1477	LEGUM CONSERV AU VINAIGRE
057	FRUIT,NUTS,FRESH,DRIED	W 7106	8293	W 5737	7293	W 6729	8444	W 8166	9104	FRUITS FRAIS OU SECS
0577	NUTS EDIBLE,FRESH,DRIED	W 3652	2845	W 1286	812	W 3528	1527	W 3278	2030	FRUITS A COQUES
05773	CASHEW NUTS,FRESH,DRIED	W 3613	2830	W 1196	786	W 3366	1495	W 3142	1977	NOIX DE CAJOU
0579	FRUIT FRESH OR DRIED NES	W 3418	5424	W 4404	6460	W 3192	6907	W 4876	7053	FRUITS FRAIS,SECS NDA
05798	OTHER FRESH FRUIT	W 3385	5403	W 4391	6449	W 3182	6898	W 4855	7025	AUTRES FRUITS FRAIS
058	FRUIT PRESERVED,PREPARED	W 3563	6482	W 4673	7551	W 2847	7325	W 6434	9848	CONSERVES DE FRUITS
0586	FRUIT TEMPORARILY PRESVD	W 3484	6271	W 4560	7327	W 2819	7279	W 6397	9810	FRUITS CONSERV TEMPORAIRE
05863	FRUIT TEMP PRSVD,UNFROZN	W 3484	6270	W 4553	7323	W 2808	7273	W 6391	9809	FRUITS CONSERVES PROVIS
06	SUGAR AND PREPS,HONEY		9588		6860		13304		9179	SUCRES ET PRODUITS
061	SUGAR AND HONEY	W 24240	9545	W 19269	6777	W 23560	13223	W 15075	9098	SUCRES ET MIEL
0611	RAW BEET AND CANE SUGAR	W 17237	9177	W 11266	6514	W 23558	13222	W 14802	8938	SUCRES BRUTS
07	COFFEE,TEA,COCOA,SPICES		98114		88767		150328		134691	CAFE,THE,CACAO,EPICES
071	COFFEE AND SUBSTITUTES	W 49500	31783	W 50918	40511	W 36526	79027	W 35244	82786	CAFE ET SUCCEDANES
0711	COFFEE GREEN,ROASTED,SUB	W 49500	31783	W 50918	40511	W 36526	79027	W 35242	82779	CAFE TORREFIE OU DECAFEINE
07111	COFFEE GREEN,HUSKS,SKINS	W 49448	31658	W 50917	40510	W 36509	78967	W 35240	82766	CAFE NON TORREFIE
072	COCOA	W 2730	2508	W 4081	3595	W 2838	3383	W 2464	2898	CACAO
0721	COCOA BEANS,RAW,ROASTED	W 2730	2508	W 4080	3595	W 2838	3382	W 2464	2898	CACAO EN FEVES
075	SPICES	W 14502	63619	W 15251	44365	W 18377	67748	W 19825	48851	EPICES
0751	PEPPER AND PIMENTO	W 1958	2271	W 2021	2433	W 2086	3008	W 1291	2611	POIVRE,PIMENTS
0752	SPICES,EX PEPPER,PIMENTO	W 12544	61347	W 13230	41932	W 16291	64739	W 18534	46240	AUTRES EPICES
07521	VANILLA	W 700	51401	W 485	34512	W 934	56253	W 602	34029	VANILLE
07522	CINNAMON,ETC	W 1240	922	W 1364	1048	W 1221	967	W 784	893	CANNELLE
07523	CLOVES	W 10585	8990	W 11358	6353	W 14117	7495	W 17128	11270	GIROFLES
2	CRUDE MATERLS,EXCL FUELS		26845		26323		24067		45512	MAT BRUTES NON COMESTIBLES
21	HIDES,SKINS,FURS UNDRSSD		644		1000		1063		1844	CUIRS,PEAUX BRUTS
211	HIDES,SKINS,EXC FURS,RAW	W 633	644	W 1252	1000	W 1059	1063	W 1482	1844	CUIRS ET PEAUX
2111	BOVINE,EQUINE HIDES,RAW	W 422	361	W 912	684	W 795	668	W 989	1107	PEAUX DE BOVINS
24	CORK AND WOOD		1683		1803		1120		3168	LIEGE ET BOIS
248	WOOD SHAPED,SLEEPERS	W 8726	1604	W 4804	1475	W 4429	1016	W 8228	2569	BOIS SIMPLEMENT TRAVAILLES
2483	LUMBER SHAPED NON–CONIFR	W 2278	983	W 2606	1112	W 2443	718	W 6644	2314	NON CONIFERES SCIES,RABOTES
24831	LUMBER SAWN ETC NON–CON	W 2188	954	W 1645	677	W 2179	623	W 5797	1806	SCIES LONGITUDINALEMENT
26	TEXTILE FIBRES AND WASTE		1832		2638		3057		6367	FIBRES TEXTILES
263	COTTON					W 537	726	W 1200	2290	COTON
2631	RAW COTTON,EXCL LINTERS					W 537	726	W 1200	2290	COTON EN MASSE
265	VEG FIBRE,EXCL COTN,JUTE	W 7078	1829	W 9397	2631	W 7836	2330	W 10482	4078	FIBRES VEGETALES
2654	SISAL,AGAVE FIBRES,WASTE	W 7078	1829	W 9397	2631	W 7815	2301	W 10482	4078	SISAL,AUTRES AGAVES
27	CRUDE FERTLZR,MINRLS NES		9268		8474		7891		11579	ENGRAIS MINERAUX BRUTS
278	OTHER CRUDE MINERALS	W 19673	8908	W 20618	8035	W 27071	7559	W 28460	11358	AUTRES MINERAUX BRUTS
2782	REFRACTORY MINERALS NES	W 10672	7426	W 11214	6726	W 12716	6231	W 16523	9762	ARGILE MINERAUX REFRACTAIRES
27822	NATURAL GRAPHITE	W 10671	7425	W 11182	6715	W 12715	6231	W 16522	9761	GRAPHITE NATUREL
2783	COMMON SALT,ETC	W 7768	659	W 7985	662	W 13666	993	W 10814	937	SEL
2785	QUARTZ,MICA,FELSPAR,ETC	W 1231	823	W 1323	623	W 662	302	W 1089	648	QUARTZ,MICA,FELDSPATH
28	METALLIFEROUS ORES,SCRAP		8236		7775		3833		12721	MINERAIS METAL,DECHETS
287	BASE METAL ORES,CONC NES	W 108451	7733	W 137800	7736	W 74191	3788	W 128544	12479	MINERAIS METAUX COMMUNS
2879	OTH NONFER ORE,CONCNTRTE	W 108451	7733	W 137800	7736	W 74191	3788	W 128543	12477	MINERAIS D'AUTRES METAUX
28791	CHROMIUM ORE,CONCENTRATE	W 108450	7733	W 137800	7736	W 74191	3788	W 128543	12477	MINERAIS DE CHROME
29	CRUDE ANIMAL,VEG MAT NES		4464		4558		6784		9644	MATIERES BRUTES ANIM,VEGET
292	CRUDE VEG MATERIALS NES	W 2522	4340	W 2917	4420	W 3318	6582	W 4611	9226	MAT BRUTES VEGETALES NDA
2923	VEG PLAITING MATERIALS	W 1615	1815	W 1756	2041	W 2520	3225	W 3215	5139	MAT VEGET POUR VANNERIE
2924	VEG USED IN PHARMACY ETC	W 405	789	W 658	863	W 196	382	W 371	730	PLANTES MEDICINALES
2929	OTH CRUDE VEG MATERIALS	W 495	1591	W 465	1357	W 569	2769	W 975	3111	MATIERES VEGETALES NDA
29291	VEGETABLE SAPS,EXTRACTS	W 18	1229	W 20	1028	W 56	2351	W 95	2444	SUCS,EXTRAITS VEGETAUX
3	MINERAL FUELS ETC		9369		8547		2030		14517	COMBUSTIBLES MINERAUX LUB
33	PETROLEUM AND PRODUCTS		9362		8547		2030		14516	PETROLE ET DERIVES
334	PETROLEUM PRODUCTS,REFIN	W 101898	9362	W 99506	8547	W 22217	2002	W 128911	14474	PRODUITS RAFFINES
5	CHEMCLS,RELATED PROD NES		3688		4374		4175		7498	PRODUITS CHIMIQUES
55	PERFUME,CLEANING ETC PRD		3427		3982		3912		7277	PROD POUR PARFUM,TOILETTE
551	ESSENTL OILS,PERFUME,ETC	W 1013	3426	W 1451	3980	W 1142	3881	W 1657	7271	HUILES ESSENTIELLES
5513	ESSENTL OIL,RESINOID,ETC	W 1012	3399	W 1451	3980	W 1142	3881	W 1657	7271	HUILES ESSENTIELLES,RESIN
6	BASIC MANUFACTURES		21398		20007		16572		26509	ART MANUFACTURES
61	LEATHER,DRESSED FUR,ETC		719		1195		2055		1275	CUIRS,PELLETERIES
611	LEATHER	W 162	718	W 330	1193	W 830	2051	W 441	1268	CUIRS,PEAUX PREPARES
6114	LEATHR BOVINE NES,EQUINE	W 161	714	W 330	1192	W 349	1266	W 225	972	CUIRS DE BOVINS
63	WOOD,CORK MANUFACTRS NES		1544		1269		992		2347	OUVRAGES LIEGE ET BOIS
634	VENEERS,PLYWOOD,ETC	W 1895	544	W 1580	286	W 1480	237	W 5073	1265	PLACAGES,CONTRE–PLAQUES
6343	IMPROVED,RECONSTIT WOOD	W 1541	404	W 1494	245	W 1449	211	W 5041	1221	BOIS AMELIORES,RECONST
63431	IMPROVED WOOD	W 1541	404	W 1494	245	W 1449	211	W 5026	1205	BOIS AMELIORES
635	WOOD MANUFACTURES NES	W 1246	1000	W 1364	983	W 594	755	W 1172	1081	ART MANUF EN BOIS NDA
65	TEXTILE YARN,FABRICS,ETC		14857		12783		10071		18084	FILS,TISSUS,ARTICLES TEXTILE
651	TEXTILE YARN	W 460	1691	W 481	1597	W 357	1351	W 810	3373	FILS TEXTILES
6513	COTTON YARN	W 460	1691	W 481	1597	W 357	1351	W 801	3311	FILS DE COTON
652	COTTON FABRICS,WOVEN	W 2634	9474	W 2049	7244	W 1927	6866	W 2038	11679	TISSUS DE COTON
6521	GREY WOVEN COTTON FABRIC	W 2527	7933	W 1913	5754	W 1808	5560	W 1489	5122	TISSUS COT ECRUS NON MERCER
65214	GREY WOVEN COTTON NES	W 2527	7932	W 1913	5754	W 1808	5560	W 1489	5118	AUT TISSUS 85% COTON ECRUS
6522	WOVEN COTTON BLEACHD,ETC	W 107	1541	W 135	1490	W 119	1306	W 549	6558	TISSUS COTON BLANCHIS ETC
65224	BLCHED COTTON FABRIC NES	W 105	1523	W 135	1481	W 117	1300	W 536	6525	AUT TIS PLUS 85% COT BLANCHI
653	WOVN MAN–MADE FIB FABRIC	W 39	621	W 96	1751	W 1	6	W 13	143	TISSUS FIBRES SYNTH,ARTIF

5. Special Exports F.O.B. by Commodities according to the S.I.T.C. (Rev. 2) in thousand U.S. Dollars
Exportations Spéciales F.O.B. par Produits d'après la C.T.C.I. (Rév. 2) en milliers de Dollars E.U.

SITC CTCI	COMMODITY	1992		1993		1994		1995		PRODUIT
		WEIGHT POIDS	VALUE VALEUR	WEIGHT POIDS	VALUE VALEUR	WEIGHT POIDS	VALUE VALEUR	WEIGHT POIDS	VALUE VALEUR	
6534	DISC SYN BLEND FABRC NES	W 1	8	W 95	1739		4	W 12	141	TISSUS FIBRES SYNTH DISCONT
65349	OTH DISC SYN BLEND FABRC	W 1	8	W 95	1739			W 9	89	TISSUS FIB SYNT MEL MAT AUT
657	SPECIAL TXTL FABRC,PRODS	W 1779	1013	W 1384	629	W 927	422	W 1807	1144	TISSUS SPECIAUX
6575	CORDAGE AND MANUFACTURES	W 1779	1011	W 1383	628	W 927	422	W 1806	1143	FICELLES,CORDES,CORDAGES
65751	CORDAGE,CABLE,ROPE,TWINE	W 1774	1001	W 1383	628	W 927	422	W 1806	1141	CORDAGES TRESSES OU NON
658	TEXTILE ARTICLES NES	W 406	1669	W 397	1382	W 208	923	W 234	1484	ART FACONNES MAT TEXTILES
6584	LINENS ETC	W 99	613	W 111	552	W 135	727	W 153	1223	LINGE DE MAISON
65843	TABLE LINEN OF COTTON	W 90	490	W 98	470	W 126	647	W 135	1093	LINGE DE TABLE DE COTON
66	NONMETAL MINERAL MFS NES		3463		2611		3266		4190	ART MIN NON METALLIQUES
667	PEARL,PREC–,SEMI–P STONE		3384		2550		3196		4109	PERLES, PIERRES GEMMES
6673	PREC–,SEMI–PR STONES NES		3372		2548		3193		4102	AUTRES PIERRES NON SERTIES
67	IRON AND STEEL		87		1101		4		43	FER ET ACIER
678	IRON,STL TUBES,PIPES,ETC	W 25	78	W 450	1101					TUBES,TUYAUX EN FONTE,FER
6782	IRON,STL SEAMLESS TUBES			W 447	1062					TUBES,TUYAUX SANS SOUDURE
69	METAL MANUFACTURES NES		525		880		49		239	ART MANUFACT EN METAL NDA
7	MACHINES,TRANSPORT EQUIP		4199		9227		1117		3229	MACHINES MATERIEL TRANSPORT
72	MACHS FOR SPCL INDUSTRYS		2024		2464		32		272	MAC SPECIALES POUR INDUST
723	CIVIL ENGNEERG EQUIP ETC	W 688	1954	W 216	2112			W 41	146	APPAREILS DE GENIE CIVIL
7234	CONST,MINING MACHNRY NES	W 568	1351	W 179	1282			W 39	130	MACH POUR LA CONST, MINES
72344	BORING,SINKING MACHINERY	W 545	1320	W 179	1282					MACHINES DE FORAGE
7239	CONSTR ETC MACHY PTS NES	W 120	603	W 37	830			W 1	3	PIECES 723.41–723.46
74	GENRL INDUSTRL MACHY NES		299		1136		58		233	MACH APP INDUSTRIE
79	OTHR TRANSPORT EQUIPMENT		66		4262		629		880	AUTRE MATERIEL TRANSPORT
792	AIRCRAFT ETC		38	W 11	4206	W 3	601		104	APP NAVIGATION AERIENNE
7921	HELICOPTERS			W 10	4197				4	HELICOPTERES
8	MISC MANUFACTURED GOODS		14194		15048		19942		13402	ART MANUFACTURES DIVERS
84	CLOTHING AND ACCESSORIES		10292		10992		7649		5116	VETEMENTS
842	MENS OUTERWEAR NOT KNIT	W 132	2481	W 111	1941	W 70	1189	W 80	1296	VET DESSUS POUR HOMMES
8423	— TROUSERS,BREECHES ETC	W 65	1107	W 76	1329	W 57	1047	W 72	1145	PANTALONS HOMMES MAT TEX
8429	— OTHER OUTER GARMENTS	W 67	1373	W 35	612	W 12	141	W 8	151	AUT VET DES HOM MAT TEX
843	WOMENS OUTERWEAR NONKNIT	W 208	3146	W 232	4366	W 256	4198	W 102	2113	VET DESSUS FEMMES MAT TEX
8435	— BLOUSES	W 72	1258	W 57	1186	W 76	1073	W 27	510	BLOUSES FEM MAT TEXTILES
8439	— OTHER OUTER GARMENTS	W 96	1323	W 127	2205	W 134	2366	W 44	837	AUT VET DES FEM MAT TEXT
844	UNDER GARMENTS NOT KNIT	W 38	740	W 104	2010	W 83	1137	W 31	632	VETEMENT DESSOUS MAT TEX
8441	— MENS SHIRTS	W 17	288	W 52	1045	W 8	108	W 8	174	CHEMISES HOMMES MAT TEXT
84411	—— OF COTTON	W 16	279	W 45	862	W 7	88	W 6	142	CHEMISES HOMMES DE COTON
8443	— WOMENS	W 21	440	W 40	756	W 72	982	W 21	411	VET DESSOUS FEM MAT TEXT
846	UNDER GARMENTS KNITTED	W 141	3145	W 108	2042	W 37	389	W 19	312	SOUS VETS DE BONNETERIE
8462	— OF COTTON NON ELASTIC	W 140	3112	W 107	2028	W 36	378	W 18	305	SOUS–VET BONNET COTON
84629	—— OTHER	W 140	3112	W 107	2028	W 36	378	W 18	305	AUT SOUS–VET BONNET COTON
89	MISC MANUFCTRD GOODS NES		2806		2501		11301		7147	ART MANUFACTURES DIVERS
892	PRINTED MATTER	W 4	43	W 12	58		9309	W 115	4142	IMPRIMES
8928	PRINTED MATTER NES		12	W 3	23		9288	W 111	4059	IMPRIMES NDA
89283	UNISSUED BANKNOTES ETC						9285		1143	TIMBRES–POSTE FISCAUX
89284	CALENDARS ON PAPER							W 111	2915	CALENDRIERS,BLOCS
899	OTHER MANUFACTURED GOODS	W 264	1451	W 313	1121	W 286	809	W 365	1863	AUT ART MANUF DIVERS NDA
8994	UMBRELLAS,CANES ETC	W 71	810	W 84	438	W 32	80	W 36	175	PARAPLUIES,CANNES ETC
9	GOODS NOT CLASSD BY KIND		6996		4768		3845		7151	ART TRANSACT NON CLASSES
931	*SPECIAL TRANSACTIONS		6478		4237		3239		6031	TRANS.SPECIALES
941	*ZOO ANIMALS,PETS ETC	W 6	517	W 6	531	W 8	606	W 6	1120	ANIMAUX DE ZOO ETC

1. HISTORICAL SERIES, 1960–1995 GENERAL TRADE, IMPORTS C.I.F., EXPORTS F.O.B.
SERIES HISTORIQUES, 1960–1995 COMMERCE GENERAL, IMPORTATIONS C.A.F., EXPORTATIONS F.O.B

YEAR ANNEE	VALUE IN MILLION MALAWI KWACHA / VALEUR EN MILLION MALAWI KWACHA — MERCHANDISE–MARCHANDISE		GOLD–OR		CONVERSION FACTORS U.S. CENTS PER MALAWI KWACHA / FACTEURS DE CONVERSION CENTS E.U. PAR MALAWI KWACHA		INDEX NUMBERS–INDICES — QUANTUM		UNIT VALUE / VALEUR UNITAIRE	
	IMPORTS	EXPORTS	IMPORTS	EXPORTS	IMPORTS	EXPORTS	IMPORTS	EXPORTS	IMPORTS	EXPORTS
1960		18.00			140.0000	140.0000				
1961		18.60			140.0000	140.0000				
1962		20.40			140.0000	140.0000				
1963		21.60			140.0000	140.0000				
1964	28.60	25.00			140.0000	140.0000				9
1965	40.80	28.80			140.0000	140.0000				9
1966	54.30	34.80			140.0000	140.0000				9
1967	50.90	40.90			138.4000	138.0300				9
1968	58.20	40.00			120.0000	120.0000				9
1969	61.50	44.00			120.0000	120.0000				10
1970	71.40	49.70			120.0000	120.0000				11
1971	89.80	59.30			121.5500	120.3500				12
1972	102.90	64.50			124.2850	122.8440				11
1973	114.70	79.90			122.7160	122.7600				12
1974	157.70	101.30			119.1280	119.0470				16
1975	218.70	122.10			114.6350	113.9270				19
1976	188.50	151.60			109.2000	109.1800				21
1977	209.80	180.30			110.8790	110.8370				27
1978	284.80	155.70			118.8050	119.0260				12
1979	324.80	189.80			122.4960	122.5730				12
1980	357.20	231.00			123.2430	123.4380				23
1981	313.00	243.70			111.8494	110.6412				27
1982	322.10	256.60			96.6153	95.7387				30
1983	363.80	270.60			85.5543	84.4785				29
1984	381.70	440.70			70.5320	70.1519				44
1985	492.60	429.70			58.3389	58.9372				40
1986	477.97	462.10			54.0515	53.0795				45
1987	653.94	615.06			45.1839	44.9795				59
1988	1080.15	751.69			38.8453	38.3223				71
1989	1398.80	743.22			36.2398	35.9122				83
1990	1572.47	1123.52			36.5942	37.1076				100
1991	1975.81	1326.36			35.5787	35.3779				116
1992	2653.83	1488.90			27.7121	26.6120				122
1993	2404.86	1410.91			22.6722	22.6326				124
1994	4264.01	2805.75			11.6071	11.5844				292
1995	7255.00	6193.40			6.5435	6.5447				467

2. IMPORTS BY BROAD ECONOMIC CATEGORY AND EXPORTS BY INDUSTRIAL ORIGIN. (PERCENTAGE OF TOTAL VALUE)
IMPORTATIONS PAR CATEGORIES ECONOMIQUES ET EXPORTATIONS PAR BRANCHE D'ACTIVITE.(EN POURCENTAGE DE LA VALEUR TOTALE)

IMPORTS – IMPORTATIONS

	1990	1991	1992	1993	1994	1995	1996
TOTAL IMPORTS–IMPORTATIONS TOTALES	100.	100.					
1 FOOD BEV–ALIMENTATION BOISSONS	7.3	6.6					
11 PRIMARY–PRODUITS DE BASE	1.3	1.7					
111 FOR INDUSTRY–POUR L'INDUSTRIE	1.2	1.5					
112 FOR HOUSEHOLDS–POUR LES MENAGES	0.1	0.2					
12 PROCESSED–PRODUITS ELABORES	6.0	4.9					
121 FOR INDUSTRY–POUR L'INDUSTRIE	4.3	2.8					
122 FOR HOUSEHOLDS–POUR LES MENAGES	1.7	2.1					
2 IND SUPPLIES–APPROV INDUSTRIELS	37.2	40.7					
21 PRIMARY–PRODUITS DE BASE	2.4	2.2					
22 PROCESSED–PRODUITS ELABORES	34.8	38.5					
3 FUELS–COMBUSTIBLES	10.3	10.4					
31 PRIMARY–PRODUITS DE BASE	0.3	0.2					
32 PROCESSED–PRODUITS ELABORES	10.0	10.2					
321 MOTOR SPIRIT–ESSENCE	10.0	10.2					
322 OTHER–AUTRES	0.0	0.0					
4 MACHINERY–EQUIPEMENT	16.8	16.4					
41 CAPITAL EQUIPMENT–MACHINES	14.3	14.2					
42 PARTS–PIECES ACCESSOIRES	2.4	2.1					
5 TRANSPORT–TRANSPORT	20.2	16.6					
51 PASSENGER CARS–AUTOMOBILES	3.2	2.4					
52 OTHER–AUTRES	9.9	7.6					
521 INDUSTRIAL–INDUSTRIELS	9.6	7.1					
522 NON INDUSTRIAL–NON INDUSTRIEL	0.4	0.5					
53 PARTS–PIECES ACCESSOIRES	7.1	6.5					
6 CONSUM GOODS–BIENS CONSOMMATION	7.0	7.8					
61 DURABLE–DURABLES	1.3	1.7					
62 SEMI DURABLE–SEMI DURABLES	2.9	3.2					
63 NON DURABLE–NON DURABLES	2.8	2.9					
7 GOODS NES–BIENS NDA	1.2	1.6					

EXPORTS – EXPORTATIONS

	1990	1991	1992	1993	1994	1995	1996
TOTAL EXPORTS–EXPORTATIONS TOTALES	100.	100.					
1 AGRICULTURE	84.7	87.5					
2 MINING QUARRY–INDUS EXTRACTIVES	0.0	0.0					
3 MANUFACTURING–IND MANUFACTUR	15.3	12.4					
31 FOOD BEV TOBACCO–ALIM BOISS TAB	7.8	6.0					
32 TEXTILES–INDUSTRIES TEXTILES	2.5	2.8					
33 WOOD & PRODUCTS–BOIS & PRODUITS	1.0	0.4					
34 PAPER & PRODUCTS–PAPIER & PRODT	0.0	0.0					
35 CHEMICALS–INDUSTRIES CHIMIQUES	0.5	0.5					
36 NON METAL MIN–MIN NON METAL	0.0	0.0					
37 BASIC METAL–IND METAL BASE	0.0	0.1					
38 METAL MANUF–MANUF METAL	3.1	2.3					
39 OTH MANUF IND–AUTRES MANUF	0.3	0.3					

3. TRADE BY PRINCIPAL COUNTRIES OF PRODUCTION AND LAST CONSIGNMENT (VALUE IN THOUSAND U.S. DOLLARS)
ECHANGES SELON LES PRINCIPAUX PAYS DE PRODUCTION ET DE DERNIERE CONSIGNATION (VALEUR EN MILLIERS DE DOLLARS EU)

COUNTRIES–PAYS	GENERAL IMPORTS C.I.F. IMPORTATIONS GENERALES C.A.F					COUNTRIES–PAYS	GENERAL EXPORTS F.O.B. EXPORTATIONS GENERALES F.O.B.				
	1991	1992	1993	1994	1995		1991	1992	1993	1994	1995
World	647402			539280	500409	Monde	482987			337088	433345
Africa	270151			252709	226604	Afrique	63027			74653	81999
Americas	36131			23055	21368	Amériques	76574			34978	63721
Northern America	31008			18679	17006	Amérique du Nord	71928			33502	57774
LAIA	5115			4259	4130	ALAI	4646			1121	5907
CACM				5	1	MCAC				16	0
Caribbean	8			78	130	Caraïbes				195	38
Rest of America				34	101	Autre Amérique				144	1
As.ex F.USSR	89498			101460	84237	Asie l'URSS exclus	70298			34649	32713
Eur.x F.USSR	242931			160872	166300	Europe l'URSS exclus	261669			182256	243336
EU	230247			156090	159763	UE	229486			154739	206879
EFTA	12267			3697	4367	AELE	32170			16476	18819
East Europe	417			1072	2169	Europe de l'Est	4			8547	13745
Other Europe	1			12	1	Autre de l'Europe	10			10	12
Former USSR				161	64	Ancienne URSS				5	1453
Oceania	6603			996	1820	Océanie	7727			8193	8816
So. Africa Customs Un	229394			174075	159790	Germany/Allemagne	71458			51691	58899
United Kingdom	132742			82161	78949	USA/Etats–Unis d'Amer	71094			32598	56983
Zimbabwe	30547			54959	39904	So. Africa Customs Un	43420			45532	44805
Japan/Japon	47662			35126	24925	United Kingdom	54158			41225	29966
Germany/Allemagne	27619			21734	46626	Netherlands/Pays–Bas	43262			25962	39378
USA/Etats–Unis d'Amer	21592			18442	13128	Japan/Japon	56706			27467	21778
India/Inde	6642			21685	15937	France, Monac	15499			10397	43302
France, Monac	16909			12687	8355	Switz.Liecht	30971			15874	17457
China/Chine	235			17624	15827	Spain/Espagne	15014			4286	12619
Zambia/Zambie	5396			13359	6097	Belgium–Luxembourg	14244			8238	6472
Italy/Italie	9189			9221	5010	Mozambique	1560			7575	9891
Austria/Autriche	2100			11035	8031	Zimbabwe	3425			7959	7051
Mozambique	1656			4436	15052	Australia/Australie	6421			4199	5649
Netherlands/Pays–Bas	9322			4485	3846	Zambia/Zambie	3233			4090	5137
Switz.Liecht	10577			3010	3846	Hungary/Hongrie	4			4813	6375
Hong Kong	8551			5058	3507	Un. Rep. of Tanzania	2145			2242	6482
Korea, Republic of	3140			6932	5606	Denmark/Danemark	4913			2217	3503
Malaysia/Malaisie	3479			4040	6820	Austria/Autriche	3375			3418	3617
Denmark/Danemark	10331			2007	1275	Pakistan	4013			2130	2070
Canada	9416			238	3878	New Zealand	1195			3408	2466
Belgium–Luxembourg	4493			4182	1692	Czech Republic				1869	4720
Finland/Finlande	3753			3074	2778	Egypt/Egypte	3779			322	2447
Brazil/Brésil	4106			2081	2730	Portugal	2386			1185	2641
Sweden/Suède	3249			2470	2369	Sweden/Suède	3223			2114	853
Portugal	6372			906	239	Croatia/Croatie				2370	3795
Kenya	2000			2358	2443	China/Chine	0			4148	1467
Australia/Australie	4688			755	807	Brazil/Brésil	324			1083	3541
Pakistan	263			2035	3812	India/Inde	2			22	4674
Thailand/Thaïlande	488			4060	449	Poland/Pologne				1784	2392
Spain/Espagne	3677			783	434	Mexico/Mexique	3902				
Singapore/Singapour	2208			785	1502	Finland/Finlande	658			1555	1423
Indonesia/Indonésie	38			2291	2146	Italy/Italie	652			911	2053
Argentina/Argentine	874			2125	1114	Uganda/Ouganda	65			2264	1202
Un. Rep. of Tanzania	491			1369	2099	Greece/Grèce	379			1164	1815
New Zealand	1915			163	984	Burundi	2110			600	507
Mauritius/Maurice	59			1847	1002	Norway, SVD, JM	1199			580	1363
Norway, SVD, JM	1690			635	256	Kenya	259			1598	798
Saudi Arabia				33	2323	Singapore/Singapour	1295			560	698
Romania/Roumanie	22			242	2065	Canada	834			905	791
Israel/Israël	1072			649	358	Argentina/Argentine	222				2266
Ireland/Irlande	378			1290	132	Dem. Rep. of the Congo	942			767	497
Bangladesh	965			144	77	Gambia/Gambie				739	997
United Arab Emirates				719	451	Turkey/Turquie	1				1509
Nigeria/Nigéria	510			14	34	Russian Federation					1421
Poland/Pologne				432	22	Philippines	1363				
Hungary/Hongrie	175			219	7	Mauritius/Maurice	452			73	585
Cyprus/Chypre	201			168	26	Ireland/Irlande	264			377	340
Iceland/Islande				52	265	Guinea/Guinée	157			510	300
Chile/Chili				49	257	Papua New Guinea	111			245	321
Turkey/Turquie	133			41	116	Solomon Isls				305	289

(VALUE AS PERCENTAGE OF WORLD TOTAL)(VALEURS EN POURCENTAGE DU TOTAL MONDIAL)

	1986	1987	1988	1989	1990	1991	1992	1993	1994	1995		1986	1987	1988	1989	1990	1991	1992	1993	1994	1995
Africa	36.3	44.8	40.1	47.3	38.5	41.7			46.9	45.3	Afrique	22.0	17.8	18.6	16.3	15.7	13.0			22.1	18.9
Americas	4.3	4.7	6.3	5.7	3.4	5.6			4.3	4.3	Amériques	8.8	11.0	11.6	12.9	13.1	15.9			10.4	14.7
Northern America	4.0	4.6	5.8	4.7	2.6	4.8			3.5	3.4	Amérique du Nord	8.8	10.9	11.6	12.7	11.9	14.9			9.9	13.3
LAIA	0.3	0.2	0.5	0.9	0.8	0.8			0.8	0.8	ALAI	0.1	0.1	0.0	0.2	1.2	1.0			0.3	1.4
CACM		0.0							0.0	0.0	MCAC		0.0							0.0	0.0
Caribbean		0.0		0.2	0.0	0.0			0.0	0.0	Caraïbes	0.0		0.0	0.0					0.1	0.0
Rest of America			0.0						0.0	0.0	Autre Amérique									0.0	0.0
As.ex F.USSR	14.6	9.4	13.8	11.4	14.2	13.8			18.8	16.8	Asie l'URSS exclus	7.2	12.2	14.7	15.2	15.9	14.6			10.3	7.5
Eur.x F.USSR	43.3	40.1	39.2	34.5	42.8	37.5			29.8	33.2	Europe l'URSS exclus	56.1	56.1	52.6	52.3	52.9	54.2			54.1	56.2
EU	41.1	38.3	36.9	33.3	41.2	35.6			28.9	31.9	UE	54.1	55.2	50.8	50.7	50.1	47.5			45.9	47.7
EFTA	2.2	1.4	1.7	1.0	1.4	1.9			0.7	0.9	AELE	2.0	0.8	1.7	1.6	2.3	6.7			4.9	4.3
East Europe	0.0	0.4	0.6	0.2	0.1	0.1			0.2	0.4	Europe de l'Est			0.0	0.0		0.0			2.5	3.2
Other Europe	0.0	0.0	0.0	0.0	0.0	0.0			0.0	0.0	Autre de l'Europe	0.0	0.0	0.0	0.0	0.5	0.0			0.0	0.0
Former USSR				0.0					0.0	0.0	Ancienne URSS									0.0	0.3
Oceania	1.6	1.0	0.7	1.1	0.5	1.0			0.2	0.4	Océanie	2.9	2.9	2.5	3.3	1.9	1.6			2.4	2.0
So. Africa Customs Un	29.6	36.2	32.2	37.6	31.7	35.4			32.3	31.9	Germany/Allemagne	9.5	9.3	12.4	10.3	16.0	14.8			15.3	13.6
United Kingdom	24.5	20.1	22.0	17.0	22.9	20.5			15.2	15.8	USA/Etats–Unis d'Amer	8.5	10.8	11.0	12.6	11.7	14.7			9.7	13.1
Zimbabwe	4.6	5.6	5.0	5.8	4.6	4.7			10.2	8.0	So. Africa Customs Un	8.1	11.2	11.3	10.5	8.0	9.0			13.5	10.3
Japan/Japon	9.2	5.6	9.2	6.3	7.5	7.4			6.5	5.0	United Kingdom	25.6	23.6	18.1	20.9	15.5	11.2			12.2	6.9
Germany/Allemagne	6.4	5.1	5.6	6.3	6.2	4.3			4.0	9.3	Netherlands/Pays–Bas	6.1	10.0	8.3	7.7	6.8	9.0			7.7	9.1
USA/Etats–Unis d'Amer	3.6	3.1	5.1	3.4	2.1	3.3			3.4	2.6	Japan/Japon	6.0	9.3	11.7	12.6	13.2	11.7			8.1	5.0
India/Inde	0.7	0.3	0.4	1.0	0.8	1.0			4.0	3.2	France, Monac	3.5	3.3	3.6	3.7	3.4	3.2			3.1	10.0
France, Monac	2.4	2.4	2.8	1.2	2.9	2.6			2.4	1.7	Switz.Liecht	1.7	0.5	1.4	1.3	1.8	6.4			4.7	4.0
China/Chine	0.0	0.0	0.0	0.0		0.0			3.3	3.2	Spain/Espagne	0.5	0.8	1.3	2.2	2.1	3.1			1.3	2.9
Zambia/Zambie	1.5	2.4	1.9	3.2	1.6	0.8			2.5	1.2	Belgium–Luxembourg	5.3	4.2	3.4	2.1	3.1	2.9			2.4	1.5

4. General Imports C.I.F. by Commodities according to the S.I.T.C. (Rev. 2) in thousand U.S. Dollars
Importations Générales C.A.F. par Produits d'après la C.T.C.I. (Rév. 2) en milliers de Dollars E.U.

SITC CTCI	COMMODITY	1992 WEIGHT POIDS	1992 VALUE VALEUR	1993 WEIGHT POIDS	1993 VALUE VALEUR	1994 WEIGHT POIDS	1994 VALUE VALEUR	1995 WEIGHT POIDS	1995 VALUE VALEUR	PRODUIT
	ALL COMMODITIES		735000		545231		539280		500409	TOUS PRODUITS
0	FOOD AND LIVE ANIMALS						75820		52860	ALIMENTS,ANIMAUX VIVANTS
02	DAIRY PRODCTS,BIRDS'EGGS						6132		3726	PRODUITS LAITIERS,OEUFS
022	MILK AND CREAM					W 2974	5444	W 1208	2718	LAIT ET CREME
0224	MILK,CREAM PRESERVED ETC					W 2877	5182	W 1075	2479	LAIT,CREME CONS,CONC
02243	MILK DRY,OVER 1.5% FAT					W 1446	2851	W 705	1782	LAIT POUDRE SUP 1.5%
02249	MILK(EX DRY) PRSVD,SWEET					W 1000	1845	W 205	297	LAIT CONS,CONC SUCRE
04	CEREALS AND PREPARATIONS						57509		42063	CEREALES ET PRODUITS
041	WHEAT ETC UNMILLED							W 14875	2690	FROMENT,EPEAUTRE
0412	OTHER WHEAT ETC UNMILLED							W 14875	2690	AUTRE FROMENT NON MOULU
044	MAIZE UNMILLED					W 259890	37734	W 154336	25783	MAIS NON MOULU
045	CEREALS NES UNMILLED					W 55280	8711	W 15875	4353	AUTRES CEREALES NON MOULUES
0459	OTHER CEREALS UNMILLED					W 55280	8711	W 15875	4353	SARRASIN,MILLET,SORGHO
04599	OTH CEREALS UNMILLED NES					W 55280	8711	W 15825	3209	AUTRES CEREALES NDA
046	WHEAT ETC MEAL OR FLOUR					W 25026	8734	W 19129	7758	SEMOULE FARINE,FROMENT
04601	FLOUR OF WHEAT OR MESLIN					W 25026	8734	W 19119	7753	FARINE DE FROMENT
048	CEREAL ETC PREPARATIONS					W 3508	2180	W 1838	1188	PREPTNS A BASE CEREALES
05	VEGETABLES AND FRUIT						1836		1540	LEGUMES ET FRUITS
06	SUGAR AND PREPS,HONEY						4048		299	SUCRES ET PRODUITS
061	SUGAR AND HONEY					W 12680	3870	W 457	221	SUCRES ET MIEL
0611	RAW BEET AND CANE SUGAR					W 11897	3417			SUCRES BRUTS
081	*FEEDING STUFF FOR ANIML					W 3131	1551	W 3211	1747	NOURRITURE POUR ANIMAUX
09	MISC EDIBLE PRODUCTS						2960		1805	PREP ALIMENTAIRES DIVERSES
098	EDIBLE PRODCTS,PREPS NES					W 1047	2905	W 466	1722	PREP ALIMENTAIRES NDA
09806	YEASTS,BAKING POWDERS					W 764	1863	W 202	498	LEVURES
1	BEVERAGES AND TOBACCO						2365		1486	BOISSONS ET TABACS
2	CRUDE MATERLS,EXCL FUELS						8092		6236	MAT BRUTES NON COMESTIBLES
26	TEXTILE FIBRES AND WASTE						2370		2611	FIBRES TEXTILES
27	CRUDE FERTLZR,MINRLS NES						3583		3180	ENGRAIS MINERAUX BRUTS
278	OTHER CRUDE MINERALS					W 26914	2979	W 26159	2788	AUTRES MINERAUX BRUTS
2783	COMMON SALT,ETC					W 24744	1974	W 25392	2384	SEL
3	MINERAL FUELS ETC						41146		55785	COMBUSTIBLES MINERAUX LUB
32	COAL,COKE AND BRIQUETTES						1276		1908	HOUILLES,COKES,BRIQUETTES
322	COAL,LIGNITE AND PEAT	W 10200	674	W 2100	113	W 26870	1269	W 135238	1895	HOUILLES,LIGNITES,TOURBE
3222	OTH COAL,NOT AGGLOMERATD					W 26869	1178	W 135238	1895	AUTRES HOUILLES
33	PETROLEUM AND PRODUCTS						39666		53336	PETROLE ET DERIVES
334	PETROLEUM PRODUCTS,REFIN					W 215916	37417	W 645200	51037	PRODUITS RAFFINES
3341	GASOLINE,OTH LIGHT OILS	W 55870	19335	W 55500	17480					ESSENCES POUR MOTEURS
33411	MOTOR,AVIATION SPIRIT	W 55870	19335	W 55500	17480					ESSENCES MOTEURS D'AVIONS
3343	GAS OILS	W 93873	24998	W 94221	21471					GAS OILS
335	RESIDUAL PETRLM PROD NES					W 3817	2209	W 3630	2299	PRODUITS RESIDUELS NDA
3351	PETRLM JELLY,MINERAL WAX					W 2146	1651	W 1658	1654	VASELINE,CIRES MINERALES
4	ANIMAL,VEGETABLE OIL,FAT						10909		15264	HUILES,GRAISSES ANIM,VEG
42	FIXED VEGETABLE OIL,FAT						9642		14620	HUILES VEGETALES FIXES
423	FIXED VEG OILS,SOFT					W 8638	5829	W 8270	6551	HUILES VEGET DOUCES FIXES
4232	SOYA BEAN OIL					W 6122	3638	W 6600	5215	HUILE DE SOJA
4236	SUNFLOWER SEED OIL					W 2511	2178	W 1461	1202	HUILE DE TOURNESOL
424	FIXED VEG OIL NONSOFT					W 9913	3813	W 10998	8069	AUTRES HUILES VEG FIXES
4242	PALM OIL					W 26	27	W 3130	2242	HUILE DE PALME
4244	PALM KERNEL OIL					W 486	295	W 4646	3507	HUILE DE PALMISTE
4249	FIXED VEGETABLE OILS NES					W 9396	3481	W 2865	1989	HUILES VEGET FIXES NDA
5	CHEMCLS,RELATED PROD NES						81504		112542	PRODUITS CHIMIQUES
51	ORGANIC CHEMICALS						4403		2569	PROD CHIMIQ ORGANIQUES
52	INORGANIC CHEMICALS						4543		3659	PROD CHIM INORGANIQUES
522	INORG ELEMNTS,OXIDES,ETC					W 2993	2213	W 4698	2366	ELEMENTS INORGANIQUES
5225	INORGANIC BASES ETC NES					W 1390	799	W 3777	1594	AUTRES BASES OXYDES METAL
523	OTHR INORG CHEMICALS ETC					W 4710	2330	W 2112	1290	AUT PRODUITS CHIMIQUES INORG
53	DYES,TANNING,COLOUR PROD						3510		1988	PROD TEINTURE,COLORANTS
533	PIGMENTS,PAINTS,ETC					W 977	1818	W 1520	1293	PIGMENTS,PEINTURES,VERNIS
541	*MEDICINAL,PHARM PRODUCT					K 1719613	11251	K 1581757	39628	PROD MEDICINAUX PHARMACEUT
5417	MEDICAMENTS					K 1180209	7906	K 1039724	36665	MEDICAMENTS
54171	— CONTAINNG ANTIBIOTICS					K 174921	2373	K 126711	3020	MED CONTN ANTIBIOTIQUES
54172	— CONTAINING HORMONES					K 366497	1245	K 145667	29911	MED CONTENANT HORMONES
54179	— CONTNG OTH SUBSTANCES					K 565220	3845	K 616849	2589	MED CONT AUT SUBSTANCES
5419	PHARMACEUTICAL GOODS NES					K 268459	2099	K 448762	1594	PREP,ART PHARMACEUTIQUES
54199	OTH PHARMACEUTICAL GOODS					K 61706	1626	K 171606	1183	AUT PREP PHARMACEUTIQUES
55	PERFUME,CLEANING ETC PRD						6656		6529	PROD POUR PARFUM,TOILETTE
551	ESSENTL OILS,PERFUME,ETC					W 505	3380	W 480	3648	HUILES ESSENTIELLES
5514	MIXED PERFUME SUBSTANCES					W 476	3282	W 452	3042	MELANGES SUBSTAN ODORIFER
554	SOAP,CLEANSING ETC PREPS					W 2642	2227	W 3074	2472	SAVONS,PRODUITS DETERSIFS
562	*FERTILIZERS,MANUFACTURE	W 194400	58518	W 201000	61442	W 92289	26647	W 132355	37607	ENGRAIS MANUFACTURES
5621	CHEM NITROGENOUS FERTLZR					W 59185	17696	W 82270	21514	ENGRAIS AZOTES
56212	AMMONIUM SULPHONITRATE					W 9813	4552	W 2757	337	SULFONITRATE D'AMMONIUM
56213	AMMONIUM SULPHATE					W 8355	3158	W 7562	1804	SULFATE D'AMMONIUM
56216	UREA					W 33459	7165	W 34674	10465	UREE
56219	CHEM NITROG FERTILZR NES					W 4958	2196	W 37201	8888	ENGRAIS AZOTES NDA
5623	CHEM POTASSIC FERTILIZER					W 2301	606	W 7152	2272	ENGRAIS POTASSIQUES
5629	FERTILIZERS NES					W 29178	7793	W 42541	13573	ENGRAIS NDA
56291	NIT–PHOS–POT FERTLZR NES					W 4443	1093	W 7753	2215	ENGRAIS CONT N P K
56292	NITROG–PHOS FERTILZR NES					W 24734	6031	W 34784	10053	ENGRAIS NDA CONT N P
58	PLASTIC MATERIALS ETC						13489		12134	MAT PLAST ARTIFICIELLES
583	POLYMERIZATION ETC PRODS					W 11797	11633	W 7786	11098	PROD POLYMERISATION
5834	POLYVINYL CHLORIDE					W 2553	2837	W 1439	1933	CHLORURE DE POLYVINYLE
58341	— IN PRIMARY FORMS					W 2445	2641	W 1349	1806	SOUS FORMES PRIMAIRES
5839	OTH POLYMRZTION ETC PROD					W 5397	5749	W 3933	5685	AUT PROD POLYMER COPOLYM
59	CHEMICAL MATERIALS NES						10695		8299	MAT PROD CHIMIQUES NDA
591	PESTICIDES,DISINFECTANTS					W 1712	6792	W 1420	5697	DESINF,INSECT,FONG,HERB
5911	INSECTICIDES,FOR RETAIL					W 1087	4465	W 723	3121	INSECTICIDES VENTE DET
598	MISCEL CHEM PRODUCTS NES					W 1215	2606	W 811	1714	PROD DIV INDUST CHIM NDA
5989	CHEM PRODUCTS,PREPS NES					W 910	2391	W 796	1660	PROD PREP CHIMIQUES NDA
59899	OTH CHEM PRODS,PREPS,NES					W 563	1929	W 497	1242	AUT PRODUITS CHIMIQUES NDA
6	BASIC MANUFACTURES						112352		90796	ART MANUFACTURES
62	RUBBER MANUFACTURES NES						14956		8279	CAOUTCHOUC MANUFACTURE
625	RUBBER TYRES, TUBES ETC					W 812	11599	W 635	5342	PNEUS CAOUTCHOUC VULCANISE
6251	TYRES NEW FOR MOTOR CARS					W 110	4140	W 43	1529	PNEUS POUR VOITURES
6252	TYRES,NEW,BUS OR LORRY					W 58	5268	W 20	1388	PNEUS POUR AUTOBUS,CAMIONS
628	RUBBER ARTICLES NES					W 304	1773	W 1316	1856	OUVRAGES CAOUTCHOUC NDA
64	PAPER,PAPERBOARD AND MFR						18532		15806	PAPIERS,CARTONS & OUVRAGES
641	PAPER AND PAPERBOARD					W 14320	13265	W 12579	12810	PAPIERS ET CARTONS
6413	KRAFT PAPER,PAPERBOARD					W 3964	3020	W 4670	4427	PAPIER ET CARTON KRAFT
64131	KRAFT LINER IN BULK					W 2395	1730	W 3806	3211	PAP KRAFT POUR COUVERTURES

4. General Imports C.I.F. by Commodities according to the S.I.T.C. (Rev. 2) in thousand U.S. Dollars
Importations Générales C.A.F. par Produits d'après la C.T.C.I. (Rév. 2) en milliers de Dollars E.U.

SITC CTCI	COMMODITY	1992 WEIGHT POIDS	1992 VALUE VALEUR	1993 WEIGHT POIDS	1993 VALUE VALEUR	1994 WEIGHT POIDS	1994 VALUE VALEUR	1995 WEIGHT POIDS	1995 VALUE VALEUR	PRODUIT
6415	PAPER,PAPERBRD,BULK,NES					W 5890	4327	W 3600	2620	PAPIERS,CARTONS ROULEAUX
64159	OTHER PAPER ETC,BULK,NES					W 4957	3909	W 2296	1883	AUT PAPIER ROULEAUX FEUILLES
6418	COATED ETC PAPER NES BLK					W 2873	3626	W 2772	3440	PAP,CARTONS COUCHES,ENDUITS
64181	PLASTIC COATED PAPER ETC					W 2396	3003	W 2282	2878	PAP,CARTONS ENDUITS,RESINES
642	PAPER,ETC,PRECUT,ARTS OF					W 6146	5267	W 2038	2996	PAP,CARTONS DECOUPES
6423	EXERCISE BOOKS ETC					W 513	1802	W 365	689	REGISTRES,CAHIERS,CARNETS
65	TEXTILE YARN,FABRICS,ETC						24713		25580	FILS,TISSUS,ARTICLES TEXTILE
651	TEXTILE YARN					W 1596	3522	W 505	2103	FILS TEXTILES
652	COTTON FABRICS,WOVEN					W 7450	8481	W 10207	9376	TISSUS DE COTON
6522	WOVEN COTTON BLEACHD,ETC					W 6818	8123	W 8744	8712	TISSUS COTON BLANCHIS ETC
65224	BLCHED COTTON FABRIC NES					W 2386	3030	W 4392	2899	AUT TIS PLUS 85% COT BLANCHI
65225	BLCHD COTN BLEND FAB NES					W 4408	5058	W 4238	5553	AUT TIS MOINS 85% COT BLANCH
653	WOVN MAN-MADE FIB FABRIC					W 17772	7210	W 16572	9655	TISSUS FIBRES SYNTH,ARTIF
6531	CONT SYNT WEAVES NONPILE					W 9099	1709	W 1181	1138	TISSUS FIBRES SYNTH CONTINUE
6534	DISC SYN BLEND FABRC NES					W 8054	4814	W 13797	6884	TISSUS FIBRES SYNTH DISCONT
65341	DISC SYN FIB-COTTN FABRC					W 7901	4704	W 12833	5959	TISSUS FIB SYNT DIS MEL COTO
658	TEXTILE ARTICLES NES					W 1200	1450	W 3386	1812	ART FACONNES MAT TEXTILES
66	NONMETAL MINERAL MFS NES						7284		7631	ART MIN NON METALLIQUES
661	LIME,CEMENT,BLDG PRODS					W 12787	1760	W 22069	3822	CHAUX,CIMENTS MAT CONSTR
6612	CEMENT					W 12358	1100	W 18450	1570	CIMENTS HYDRAULIQUES
6618	MNRL BLDG PRD UNFIRD NES					W 384	221	W 3557	1548	MAT CONST AMIANTE-CIMENT
67	IRON AND STEEL						19422		15056	FER ET ACIER
673	IRON,STEEL SHAPES ETC					W 7908	4558	W 30625	4152	BARRES,PROFIL FER,ACIER
6732	IRON,STEEL BARS ETC					W 5504	2175	W 29671	1821	BARRES FER,ACIER
674	IRN,STL UNIV,PLATE,SHEET					W 10404	11016	W 4838	6065	LARGES PLATS,TOLES
6749	OTH IRN,STL PLATES,SHEET					W 9616	9029	W 4293	4955	AUTRES TOLES FER,ACIER
67491	— OF IRON OR SIMPLE STL					W 9601	9010	W 4246	4863	AUT TOLES AUTRES ACIER FIN
678	IRON,STL TUBES,PIPES,ETC					W 1837	2157	W 5491	3958	TUBES,TUYAUX EN FONTE,FER
6783	IRON,STL TUBES,PIPES NES					W 1820	1068	W 5415	1962	AUT TUBES,TUYAUX FER,ACIER
68	NON-FERROUS METALS						1899		1125	METAUX NON FERREUX
684	ALUMINIUM					W 706	1676	W 347	1004	ALUMINIUM
6842	ALUMINIUM,ALLOYS WORKED					W 706	1676	W 347	1004	ALUMINIUM,ALLIAGES OUVRE
69	METAL MANUFACTURES NES						24285		16737	ART MANUFACT EN METAL NDA
691	STRUCTURES AND PARTS NES					W 895	9401	W 2650	6902	CONSTRUCT FER,ACIER,ALU
6911	STRUCTURES,PARTS IRN,STL					W 827	9108	W 2614	6715	CONSTRUCT FER,ACIER,FONTE
692	METAL TANKS,BOXES,ETC					W 255	1918	W 55	555	RECIPIENTS METALLIQUES
695	TOOLS					W 701	2294	W 168	1803	OUTILS A MAIN
699	BASE METAL MFRS NES					W 2699	6089	W 1300	4653	ART MANUFACTURES MET NDA
6991	LOCKSMITHS WARES,ETC					W 524	1950	W 283	1149	ARTICLES DE SERRURERIE
6996	BASE MTL MISC ARTICLES					W 995	2368	W 603	1710	ART DIVERS METAUX COMMUNS
7	MACHINES,TRANSPORT EQUIP						175263		137974	MACHINES MATERIEL TRANSPORT
71	POWER GENERATING EQUIPMT						7599		7685	MACHINES GENERATRICES
713	INTRNL COMBUS PSTN ENGIN					W 151	4253	W 67	1724	MOTEURS EXPL COMB INT, PIECE
716	ROTATING ELECTRIC PLANT					W 150	2808	W 209	3343	APP ELECTR ROTATIFS,PIECES
7162	AC MTRS,GENRTRS,GEN SETS					W 117	2033	W 81	1018	MOTEURS ELECTRIQUES
72	MACHS FOR SPCL INDUSTRYS						35909		21362	MAC SPECIALES POUR INDUST
723	CIVIL ENGNEERG EQUIP ETC					W 22	7428	W 27	5289	APPAREILS DE GENIE CIVIL
7234	CONST,MINING MACHNRY NES					W 21	5985	W 27	4940	MACH POUR LA CONST, MINES
72341	SELF-PROPELLD DOZERS,ETC						1526		2320	BULLDOZERS
72342	SLFPRP SHOVELS,EXCAVATRS					W 8	2938	W 20	1804	PELLES MECANIQUES
724	TEXTILE,LEATHER MACHNRY					W 237	2974	W 644	6705	MACH POUR INDUSTRIE TEXTILE
7244	SPINNING,EXTRDNG,ETC MCH					W 167	1729	W 568	5636	MACH POUR LE FILAGE
72443	SPINNING,REELING,ETC MCH					W 100	641	W 500	4781	MACH POUR LA FILATURE
726	PRINTG,BKBINDG MACHY,PTS					W 680	8503	W 78	773	MACHINES POUR IMPRIMERIE
7264	PRINTING PRESSES					W 612	7357	W 53	373	MACHINES A IMPRIMER
72641	ROTARY PRINTING PRESSES					W 612	7357	W 53	373	MACH IMPRIMER ROTATIVES
727	FOOD MACHRY NON-DOMESTIC					W 776	4451	W 376	2843	MACH INDUSTRIES ALIMENT
7272	OTH FOOD PROC MCHY,PARTS					W 290	3326	W 234	2077	AUT MACH IND ALIMENTAIRE
72722	INDUS FOOD PROC MACH NES					W 290	3321	W 231	2054	MACHINES BOULANGERIE
728	OTH MACHY FOR SPCL INDUS					W 1377	9984	W 322	2939	AUT MACH IND PARTICULIERES
7283	OTHR MINERAL WORKG MACHY					W 302	1649	W 114	460	MACH TRIER,CRIBLER,BROYER
7284	MACHY FOR SPCL INDUS NES					W 948	7727	W 145	2126	MACH SPEC IND PARTICUL.
72842	RUBBER,PLASTICS WRKG MCH					W 152	1794	W 11	147	MACH IND CAOUT MAT PLAST
72848	OTH MCHY WITH INDIV FNCT					W 332	2073	W 50	423	AUTRES MACHINES NDA
73	METALWORKING MACHINERY						1736		784	MACH TRAVAIL DES METAUX
74	GENRL INDUSTRL MACHY NES						18789		14015	MACH APP INDUSTRIE
741	HEATING,COOLING EQUIPMNT					W 166	2075	W 86	1302	MACH CHAUFFAGE,PIECES
742	PUMPS FOR LIQUIDS ETC					W 455	2658	W 290	2084	POMPES MOTO-POMPES
7428	OTHER PUMPS FOR LIQUIDS					W 348	1766	W 240	1556	AUTRES POMPES POUR LIQ
74288	PUMPS FR LIQUIDS NES ETC					W 346	1717	W 237	1513	POMPES POUR LIQUIDES NDA
743	PUMPS NES,CENTRFUGES ETC					W 337	2151	W 319	2006	POMPES COMPRES,VENT ETC
744	MECHANICAL HANDLING EQU					W 585	3822	W 474	3696	EQUIP MANUTENTION PIECES
7449	PTS NES OF MACHY OF 7442					W 221	2419	W 237	2041	PIECES DU 744.2
745	NONELEC MACHY,TOOLS NES					W 221	2279	W 232	1156	AUT MACH NON ELEC,PIECES
7452	OTH NONELEC MCHS,PTS NES					W 207	2124	W 217	1069	AUT MACH NON ELEC,PIECES
749	NONELEC MACH PTS,ACC NES					W 552	5803	W 344	3771	PIECES MACH NON ELEC NDA
7492	COCKS,VALVES ETC NES					W 143	1644	W 74	864	ART ROB,SIM POUR TUYAUX
7493	SHAFT,CRANK,PULLEY ETC					W 198	2222	W 143	1499	ARBRES TRANS,VILEBREQUINS
75	OFFICE MACHNES,ADP EQUIP						8231		7391	MACH BUREAU TRAIT AUTOM
751	OFFICE MACHINES					W 12	1939	W 35	3005	MACH,APPAREILS DE BUREAU
7518	OFFICE MACHINES NES					W 7	720	W 23	2280	MACH,APP DE BUREAU NDA
75188	OTHR OFFICE MACHINES NES					W 3	96	W 17	1754	AUTRES MACH DE BUREAU
752	AUTOMTIC DATA PROC EQUIP					W 10	3974	W 46	3213	MACH TRAIT INFORMATION
759	OFFICE,ADP MCH PTS,ACCES					W 33	2318	W 21	1173	PIECES DU 751 ET 752
7599	ACCTG,ETC,ADP MCH PTS,AC					W 22	2051	W 16	954	PIECES DU 751 ET 752
76	TELECOMM,SOUND EQUIPMENT						15551		4453	EQUIPMENT DE TELECOM
764	TELECOM EQPT,PTS,ACC NES					W 159	13006	W 84	3230	EQUIP TELECOM,PIECES
7641	LINE TELEPHONE,ETC EQUIP					W 43	2494	W 20	1014	APP TELEPHON PAR FIL
7649	PTS NES OF EQUIPMT OF 76					W 104	9768	W 36	801	PIECES DE LA DIV 76
76491	PTS NES OF APPAR OF 7641					W 67	9271	W 7	144	PIECES POUR 764.1
77	ELECTRIC MACHNRY NES ETC						17261		15890	MACH APP ELECT NDA
771	ELECTRIC POWER MACHY NES					W 106	1869	W 224	2674	MACH PROD,TRANS ELECTR
7711	TRANSFORMERS,ELECTRICAL					W 91	1501	W 157	1949	TRANSFO ELECTRIQUES
77118	OTHER ELEC TRANSFORMERS					W 91	1492	W 153	1674	AUTRES TRANSFO ELECTRIQ
772	SWITCHGEAR ETC,PARTS NES					W 273	3435	W 351	4232	APP COUPURE,SECT ETC
7721	SWITCHGEAR ETC					W 272	3412	W 351	4221	APP COUPURE,SECTIONMNT
773	ELECTR DISTRIBUTNG EQUIP					W 1273	2676	W 965	3346	EQUIPMT DISTRIBUTION ELECT
7731	INSULATED WIRE,CABLE ETC					W 1109	1901	W 746	2908	FILS,CABLES ISOLES ELECT
775	HOUSEHOLD TYPE EQUIP NES					W 766	2515	W 1781	1424	MACH,APP USAGE DOMESTQUE
778	ELECTRICAL MACHINERY NES					W 11104	5356	W 7258	3820	AUTRES MACH ELECT NDA
7781	BATTERIES,ACCUMULATORS					W 10555	2031	W 7046	1469	PILES ET ACCUMULATEURS

Malawi

4. General Imports C.I.F. by Commodities according to the S.I.T.C. (Rev. 2) in thousand U.S. Dollars
Importations Générales C.A.F. par Produits d'après la C.T.C.I. (Rév. 2) en milliers de Dollars E.U.

SITC CTCI	COMMODITY	1992 WEIGHT POIDS	1992 VALUE VALEUR	1993 WEIGHT POIDS	1993 VALUE VALEUR	1994 WEIGHT POIDS	1994 VALUE VALEUR	1995 WEIGHT POIDS	1995 VALUE VALEUR	PRODUIT
78	ROAD VEHICLES						66295		64891	VEHICULES ROUTIERS
781	PASS MOTOR VEH EXC BUSES					W 1152	15256	W 1057	14624	AUTO TRANSPORT PERSONNES
782	LORRIES,SPCL MTR VEH NES					W 2658	26036	W 1361	30034	VEHICULES SPECIAUX,MARCH
7821	LORRIES,TRUCKS					W 2658	22878	W 1361	29093	VEHICULES TRANSP MARCHAND
7822	SPECIAL MOTOR VEHCLS NES						3158		941	VEHICULES USAGES SPECIAUX
783	ROAD MOTOR VEHICLES NES						5582		9544	VEHICULES ROUTIERS NDA
7831	BUSES						3994		5248	VOITURES TRANSPORT COMMUN
7832	TRACTORS FOR TR–TRAILERS						1588		4296	TRACTEURS ROUTIERS
784	MOTOR VEH PRTS,ACCES NES					W 432	8493	W 264	4186	PIECES 722,781,782,783
7841	MOTOR VEHICLE CHASSIS						2561		728	CHASSIS 722,781,782,783
7849	OTHER MOTOR VEHCL PARTS					W 422	5160	W 257	3373	PIECES 722,781,782,783
785	CYCLES,ETC MOTRZD OR NOT					W 1912	10109	W 1295	5205	MOTOCYCLES SCOOTERS
7852	CYCLES, ETC NON–MOTOR					W 249	6297	W 311	2428	VELOCIPEDES SANS MOTEUR
7853	INVAL CARR, PTS OF 785					W 1662	2656	W 983	1837	FAUTEUILS INVALIDES,PIECES
78539	PARTS,ACCES NES OF 785					W 1662	2640	W 982	1832	PIECES DU 785
79	OTHR TRANSPORT EQUIPMENT						3893		1503	AUTRE MATERIEL TRANSPORT
791	RAILWAY VEHICLES					W 158	2413	W 63	832	VEHIC MAT CHEMINS DE FER
7919	RY TRACK FIXT,ETC,PARTS					W 158	2412	W 63	832	MATER FIXE VOIES FERREES
79199	PARTS NES OF 7911–7915					W 158	2412	W 63	832	PIECES 791.1 ET 5
8	MISC MANUFACTURED GOODS						31568		27186	ART MANUFACTURES DIVERS
812	*PLUMBG,HEATNG,LGHTNG EQ					W 916	1736	W 616	1578	APPAR SANITAIRES CHAUFFAGE
821	*FURNITURE,PARTS THEREOF					W 836	1921	W 351	2058	MEUBLES ET PIECES
84	CLOTHING AND ACCESSORIES						5361		2076	VETEMENTS
851	*FOOTWEAR					W 1044	2820	W 1218	1831	CHAUSSURES
87	PRECISION INSTRUMNTS NES						4910		3760	INSTRUM,APPAR SCIENT NDA
872	MEDICAL INSTRUMENTS NES					W 105	1440	W 166	1711	INSTR,APP MEDIC–CHIR NDA
87202	OTH MEDICAL INSTRUMENTS					W 87	1370	W 164	1648	INSTRUM,APP MEDECINE
874	MEASURNG,CONTROLNG INSTR					W 145	2373	W 121	1791	INSTRUMENTS DE MESURE
89	MISC MANUFCTRD GOODS NES						13171		14623	ART MANUFACTURES DIVERS
892	PRINTED MATTER					W 799	6551	W 1071	9711	IMPRIMES
8921	PRINTED BOOKS,GLOBES,ETC					W 436	2981	W 826	4759	LIVRES,BROCHURES,CARTES
89211	PRINTED BOOKS,PAMPHLETS					W 435	2943	W 800	4399	LIVRES,BROCHURES
8928	PRINTED MATTER NES					W 202	2812	W 137	4362	IMPRIMES NDA
89283	UNISSUED BANKNOTES ETC					W 68	1854	W 51	3585	TIMBRES–POSTE FISCAUX
893	ARTICLES OF PLASTIC NES						3461		2155	OUVRAGES EN MAT DIVIS 58

5. General Exports F.O.B. by Commodities according to the S.I.T.C. (Rev. 2) in thousand U.S. Dollars
Exportations Générales F.O.B. par Produits d'après la C.T.C.I. (Rév. 2) en milliers de Dollars E.U.

SITC CTCI	COMMODITY	1992 WEIGHT POIDS	1992 VALUE VALEUR	1993 WEIGHT POIDS	1993 VALUE VALEUR	1994 WEIGHT POIDS	1994 VALUE VALEUR	1995 WEIGHT POIDS	1995 VALUE VALEUR	PRODUIT
	ALL COMMODITIES		396000		319097		337088		433345	TOUS PRODUITS
0	FOOD AND LIVE ANIMALS						79875		79568	ALIMENTS,ANIMAUX VIVANTS
04	CEREALS AND PREPARATIONS						4171		3994	CEREALES ET PRODUITS
042	RICE	W 900	516	W 100	23	W 5908	2728	W 4712	1409	RIZ
0422	RICE SEMI–MILLED,MILLED					W 5883	2716	W 4712	1409	RIZ POLI,GLACE INCL BRISURES
04221	RICE MILLED UNBROKEN					W 5882	2716	W 4712	1409	RIZ POLI,GLACE EXCL BRISURES
044	MAIZE UNMILLED					W 1259	854	W 3126	1918	MAIS NON MOULU
05	VEGETABLES AND FRUIT						4833		10825	LEGUMES ET FRUITS
054	VEG ETC FRSH,SMPLY PRSVD					W 10336	3443	W 29426	8239	LEGUMES FRAIS,CONG,SECS
0542	LEGUMINOUS VEGETBLES DRY	W 5700	1806	W 3500	1358	W 9979	3383	W 29093	8185	LEGUMES A COSSE SECS
057	FRUIT,NUTS,FRESH,DRIED					W 361	1270	W 635	2495	FRUITS FRAIS OU SECS
0577	NUTS EDIBLE,FRESH,DRIED					W 301	1267	W 635	2495	FRUITS A COQUES
05779	NUTS EDIBLE,FRSH,DRY,NES					W 220	1234	W 337	2439	FRUITS A COQUES NDA
06	SUGAR AND PREPS,HONEY		25231				24772		19647	SUCRES ET PRODUITS
061	SUGAR AND HONEY		25231	W 26800	15571	W 33520	24748	W 66025	19646	SUCRES ET MIEL
0611	RAW BEET AND CANE SUGAR					W 25373	17521	W 56479	16130	SUCRES BRUTS
0612	REFINED SUGAR ETC					W 8110	7227	W 8414	3460	SUCRES RAFFINES
07	COFFEE,TEA,COCOA,SPICES						45275		44121	CAFE,THE,CACAO,EPICES
071	COFFEE AND SUBSTITUTES	W 8300	8026	W 5700	7921	W 4586	14774	W 5246	15480	CAFE ET SUCCEDANES
0711	COFFEE GREEN,ROASTED,SUB	W 8300	8026	W 5700	7921	W 4586	14774	W 5246	15480	CAFE TORREFIE OU DECAFEINE
07111	COFFEE GREEN,HUSKS,SKINS	W 8300	8026	W 5700	7921	W 4586	14774	W 5228	15421	CAFE NON TORREFIE
074	TEA AND MATE		27543	W 35300	35465	W 35138	29907	W 32387	26562	THE ET MATE
0741	TEA		27543	W 35300	35465	W 35138	29907	W 32387	26562	THE
075	SPICES					W 361	593	W 1187	2079	EPICES
0751	PEPPER AND PIMENTO					W 343	579	W 1086	1589	POIVRE,PIMENTS
1	BEVERAGES AND TOBACCO						198699		299962	BOISSONS ET TABACS
11	BEVERAGES						541		4307	BOISSONS
112	ALCOHOLIC BEVERAGES					W 290	527	W 829	4221	BOISSONS ALCOOLIQUES
1124	DISTILLED ALCOHOLIC BEVS					W 44	360	W 697	4125	ALCOOLS,EAUX–DE–VIE
11249	OTH ALCOHOLC BEVS,CMPNDS					W 29	127	W 685	4047	BOISSONS ALCOOLIQUES NDA
12	TOBACCO AND MANUFACTURES				212294		198158		295655	TABACS BRUTS FABRIQUES
121	TOBACCO UNMNFCTRD,REFUSE		265766	W 95700	212294	W 98313	196689	W 97955	293783	TABACS BRUTS,DECHETS
1211	TOBACCO,NOT STRIPPED					W 32808	67866	W 24756	70702	TABACS NON ECOTES
1212	TOBACCO STRIPPED OR PART					W 65505	128823	W 73198	223081	TABACS PART ECOTES
122	TOBACCO,MANUFACTURED					W 396	1469	W 158	1872	TABACS FABRIQUES
1222	CIGARETTES					W 353	1285	W 3	23	CIGARETTES
1223	OTH MANUFACTURED TOBACCO					W 6	25	W 136	1671	TABACS FUMER,CHIQUER,PRISER
2	CRUDE MATERLS,EXCL FUELS						10452		11299	MAT BRUTES NON COMESTIBLES
22	OIL SEEDS,OLEAGINOUS FRT						667		1733	GRAINES,FRUITS OLEAGINEUX
222	SEEDS FOR'SOFT'FIXED OIL					W 2555	635	W 7378	1675	GRAINES HUILES FIXES
23	RUBBER, CRUDE						2524		1582	CAOUTCHOUC BRUT
232	NATURAL RUBBER,GUMS					W 2312	2524	W 979	1582	LATEX CAOUTCHOUC NATUREL
23203	BALATA,GUTTA–PERCHA, ETC					W 2312	2524	W 939	1511	BALATA,GUTTA–PERCHA
26	TEXTILE FIBRES AND WASTE		4290				3969		4500	FIBRES TEXTILES
263	COTTON		4290	W 1900	2037	W 2219	3131	W 3044	3716	COTON
2631	RAW COTTON,EXCL LINTERS		4290	W 1900	2037					COTON EN MASSE
2634	COTTON,CARDED OR COMBED					W 2208	3130	W 3044	3716	COTON CARDE OU PEIGNE
29	CRUDE ANIMAL,VEG MAT NES						1621		1670	MATIERES BRUTES ANIM,VEGET
292	CRUDE VEG MATERIALS NES					W 581	1620	W 995	1668	MAT BRUTES VEGETALES NDA
2927	CUT FLOWERS AND FOLIAGE					W 352	1463	W 742	1565	FLEURS,FEUILLAGES COUPES
29271	CUT FLOWERS					W 352	1463	W 742	1565	FLEURS ET BOUTONS
5	CHEMCLS,RELATED PROD NES						2132		1680	PRODUITS CHIMIQUES
6	BASIC MANUFACTURES						19987		16964	ART MANUFACTURES
62	RUBBER MANUFACTURES NES						471		1391	CAOUTCHOUC MANUFACTURE
625	RUBBER TYRES, TUBES ETC					W 101	459	W 154	1353	PNEUS CAOUTCHOUC VULCANISE
63	WOOD,CORK MANUFACTRS NES						2522		2089	OUVRAGES LIEGE ET BOIS
634	VENEERS,PLYWOOD,ETC					W 3494	2047	W 15565	1826	PLACAGES,CONTRE–PLAQUES
6342	PLYWOOD OF WOOD SHEETS					W 3017	1882	W 15489	1779	BOIS CONTRE–PLAQUES
65	TEXTILE YARN,FABRICS,ETC						15073		11068	FILS,TISSUS,ARTICLES TEXTILE
652	COTTON FABRICS,WOVEN					W 19297	11959	W 14541	7004	TISSUS DE COTON
6521	GREY WOVEN COTTON FABRIC					W 17741	10708	W 10841	6481	TISSUS COT ECRUS NON MERCER
65214	GREY WOVEN COTTON NES					W 17741	10708	W 10841	6481	AUT TISSUS 85% COTON ECRUS
6522	WOVEN COTTON BLEACHD,ETC					W 1556	1251	W 3701	523	TISSUS COTON BLANCHIS ETC
653	WOVN MAN–MADE FIB FABRIC					W 3462	2219	W 4011	1811	TISSUS FIBRES SYNTH,ARTIF
6534	DISC SYN BLEND FABRC NES					W 3440	2156	W 3789	1286	TISSUS FIBRES SYNTH DISCONT
65341	DISC SYN FIB–COTTN FABRC					W 3440	2156	W 3789	1286	TISSUS FIB SYNT DIS MEL COTO
658	TEXTILE ARTICLES NES					W 358	653	W 963	2004	ART FACONNES MAT TEXTILES
6584	LINENS ETC					W 50	215	W 194	1518	LINGE DE MAISON
69	METAL MANUFACTURES NES						893		1709	ART MANUFACT EN METAL NDA
7	MACHINES,TRANSPORT EQUIP						13262		8589	MACHINES MATERIEL TRANSPORT
72	MACHS FOR SPCL INDUSTRYS						3258		1889	MAC SPECIALES POUR INDUST
724	TEXTILE,LEATHER MACHNRY					W 205	1482	W 12	36	MACH POUR INDUSTRIE TEXTILE
7245	WEAVING,FELT MFG,ETC MCH					W 201	1448	W 1	22	METIERS A TISSER,PIECES
72453	GIMPING,WARPING ETC MCHS					W 201	1448	W 1	22	METIERS A TULLE ETC
76	TELECOMM,SOUND EQUIPMENT						1960		749	EQUIPMENT DE TELECOM
763	SOUND RECORDRS,PHONOGRPH					W 6	1049	W 3	422	PHONO,APP ENREGISTREMENT
7638	OTHR SOUND APPARATUS ETC					W 6	1049	W 3	422	AUT APP D'ENREGIS,REPROD
76381	TV IMAGE,SND RECRDRS ETC					W 6	1039	W 3	420	APP ENREG,REPRO IMAG,SON
78	ROAD VEHICLES						5547		3799	VEHICULES ROUTIERS
781	PASS MOTOR VEH EXC BUSES						1206		1203	AUTO TRANSPORT PERSONNES
782	LORRIES,SPCL MTR VEH NES						1231		1208	VEHICULES SPECIAUX,MARCH
7821	LORRIES,TRUCKS						1050		868	VEHICULES TRANSP MARCHAND
786	TRAILERS,NONMOTR VEH,NES						1460	W 11	177	REMORQUES,CADRES,CONTAIN
7861	TRAILERS,TRANSP CONTAINR						1397	W 10	141	REMORQUES TOUS VEHICULES
78611	HOUSING,CAMPING TRAILERS						1393	W 1	7	REMORQUES POUR CAMPING
8	MISC MANUFACTURED GOODS						12596		14928	ART MANUFACTURES DIVERS
84	CLOTHING AND ACCESSORIES						11188		13372	VETEMENTS
842	MENS OUTERWEAR NOT KNIT					W 382	1824	W 486	2257	VET DESSUS POUR HOMMES
8423	— TROUSERS,BREECHES ETC					W 313	1694	W 476	2238	PANTALONS HOMMES MAT TEX
844	UNDER GARMENTS NOT KNIT					W 1636	2050	W 1463	2790	VETEMENT DESSOUS MAT TEX
8441	— MENS SHIRTS					W 1401	1876	W 1065	2547	CHEMISES HOMMES MAT TEXT
84411	—— OF COTTON					W 535	1290	W 849	2128	CHEMISES HOMMES DE COTON
845	OUTERWEAR KNIT NONELASTC					W 1181	1672	W 1127	2437	VET DESSOUS,ACCES BONNET
8459	— OTHER,CLTHG ACCESRYS					W 1102	1594	W 1004	2211	AUT VET DESSUS DE BONNE
846	UNDER GARMENTS KNITTED					W 2777	5012	W 2922	4729	SOUS VETS DE BONNETERIE
8462	— OF COTTON NON ELASTIC					W 1864	1335	W 1853	1596	SOUS–VET BONNET COTON
84629	—— OTHER					W 1864	1335	W 1853	1596	AUT SOUS–VET BONNET COTON
8463	— OF SYNTH FBR NONELAST					W 912	3677	W 1057	3092	SOUS–VET BONNET FIB SYNT
84632	—— MENS SHIRTS					W 912	3677	W 1057	3092	CHEMISES DE BON FIB SYNMT

1. HISTORICAL SERIES, 1964–1996 GENERAL TRADE, IMPORTS C.I.F., EXPORTS F.O.B.
SERIES HISTORIQUES, 1964–1996 COMMERCE GENERAL, IMPORTATIONS C.A.F., EXPORTATIONS F.O.B

YEAR ANNEE	VALUE IN MILLION RINGGIT VALEUR EN MILLION RINGGIT MERCHANDISE –MARCHANDISE		GOLD –OR		CONVERSION FACTORS U.S. CENTS PER RINGGIT FACTEURS DE CONVERSION CENTS E.U. PAR RINGGIT		INDEX NUMBERS –INDICES QUANTUM		UNIT VALUE VALEUR UNITAIRE	
	IMPORTS	EXPORTS	IMPORTS	EXPORTS	IMPORTS	EXPORTS	IMPORTS	EXPORTS	IMPORTS	EXPORTS
1964	3227.20	3387.50			32.6667	32.6667				
1965	3356.20	3782.60	5.01	0.20	32.6667	32.6667				
1966	3378.70	3845.80	7.21		32.6667	32.6667				
1967	3319.00	3722.80	3.31		32.6667	32.6667				
1968	3524.10	4122.50	4.35		32.6667	32.6667				
1969	3581.90	5051.60	18.78		32.6667	32.6667				
1970	4288.40	5163.10	12.77		32.6667	32.6667		36		43
1971	4416.20	5016.80	18.81		32.6667	32.6667		38		39
1972	4543.20	4854.20	7.91		35.4667	35.4667		38		36
1973	5933.90	7372.10	4.34		41.3055	41.3771		44		47
1974	9891.20	10194.70			41.5950	41.5582		42		72
1975	8530.40	9230.90			41.6313	41.5423		42		62
1976	9713.30	13442.90			39.3754	39.3769		54		73
1977	11164.70	14959.20			40.6500	40.6500		56		79
1978	13645.90	17073.90			43.3084	43.3634		61		82
1979	17161.10	24218.90			45.7101	45.7436		67		107
1980	23451.00	28171.60			45.9652	45.9499		65		126
1981	26603.80	27109.40			43.4004	43.4004		63		122
1982	29023.80	28108.20			42.8030	42.7872		67		114
1983	30795.20	32771.20			43.0760	43.0474		74		109
1984	32925.90	38646.90			42.5711	42.5688		72		114
1985	30437.80	38016.70			41.4037	41.4662		76		103
1986	27921.01	35319.01			38.7020	38.7552		82		77
1987	31934.00	45225.01			39.7100	39.7079		86		90
1988	43293.01	55260.00			38.1279	38.1505		70		102
1989	60858.00	67824.00			36.9400	36.9313		75		104
1990	79119.01	79646.00			36.9808	36.9800		100		100
1991	100831.00	94497.01			36.3466	36.3506		97		103
1992	101441.00	103657.00			39.2875	39.3331		96		112
1993	117422.00	121238.00			38.8828	38.8749		86		147
1994	155871.00	153688.00			38.2245	38.2300		84		191
1995	194517.00	184827.00			39.9007	39.8834		84		210
1996	197305.00	196862.00			39.7446	39.7509				215

2. IMPORTS BY BROAD ECONOMIC CATEGORY AND EXPORTS BY INDUSTRIAL ORIGIN. (PERCENTAGE OF TOTAL VALUE)
IMPORTATIONS PAR CATEGORIES ECONOMIQUES ET EXPORTATIONS PAR BRANCHE D'ACTIVITE.(EN POURCENTAGE DE LA VALEUR TOTALE)

IMPORTS – IMPORTATIONS

	1990	1991	1992	1993	1994	1995	1996
TOTAL IMPORTS–IMPORTATIONS TOTALES	100.	100.	100.	100.	100.	100.	100.
1 FOOD BEV–ALIMENTATION BOISSONS	6.0	5.5	5.4	5.0	4.5	3.9	4.3
11 PRIMARY–PRODUITS DE BASE	2.6	2.4	2.4	2.3	2.0	1.8	2.0
111 FOR INDUSTRY–POUR L'INDUSTRIE	1.1	1.1	0.9	0.9	0.8	0.7	0.7
112 FOR HOUSEHOLDS–POUR LES MENAGES	1.5	1.3	1.5	1.4	1.2	1.1	1.2
12 PROCESSED–PRODUITS ELABORES	3.4	3.1	3.0	2.7	2.4	2.1	2.3
121 FOR INDUSTRY–POUR L'INDUSTRIE	1.1	1.1	0.9	0.9	0.8	0.6	0.6
122 FOR HOUSEHOLDS–POUR LES MENAGES	2.3	2.0	2.0	1.8	1.6	1.5	1.7
2 IND SUPPLIES–APPROV INDUSTRIELS	30.3	28.7	28.8	28.2	26.0	25.8	24.8
21 PRIMARY–PRODUITS DE BASE	3.7	3.1	2.9	3.0	2.5	2.5	2.7
22 PROCESSED–PRODUITS ELABORES	26.6	25.7	26.0	25.2	23.4	23.2	22.1
3 FUELS–COMBUSTIBLES	5.2	4.3	4.2	3.7	2.6	2.3	2.7
31 PRIMARY–PRODUITS DE BASE	1.0	0.8	0.8	0.8	0.6	0.5	0.6
32 PROCESSED–PRODUITS ELABORES	4.2	3.5	3.4	2.8	2.0	1.8	2.1
321 MOTOR SPIRIT–ESSENCE	1.4	1.2	1.1	0.9	0.8	0.8	0.8
322 OTHER–AUTRES	2.8	2.3	2.3	1.9	1.2	1.1	1.3
4 MACHINERY–EQUIPEMENT	42.0	45.8	45.4	47.3	50.3	51.6	52.9
41 CAPITAL EQUIPMENT–MACHINES	24.4	28.4	26.7	26.5	26.9	26.1	25.1
42 PARTS–PIECES ACCESSOIRES	17.6	17.4	18.7	20.8	23.4	25.5	27.8
5 TRANSPORT–TRANSPORT	10.1	9.2	9.3	8.4	9.6	9.0	8.1
51 PASSENGER CARS–AUTOMOBILES	2.8	2.6	1.7	1.7	1.9	2.2	2.2
52 OTHER–AUTRES	4.6	4.2	5.0	4.6	6.0	5.1	3.8
521 INDUSTRIAL–INDUSTRIELS	4.5	4.0	4.9	4.5	5.8	4.9	3.7
522 NON INDUSTRIAL–NON INDUSTRIEL	0.1	0.1	0.1	0.2	0.1	0.1	0.1
53 PARTS–PIECES ACCESSOIRES	2.6	2.4	2.6	2.0	1.7	1.7	2.1
6 CONSUM GOODS–BIENS CONSOMMATION	6.1	5.9	6.2	5.9	5.7	4.8	4.7
61 DURABLE–DURABLES	2.1	2.0	1.9	1.8	1.8	1.5	1.3
62 SEMI DURABLE–SEMI DURABLES	2.3	2.2	2.5	2.5	2.5	2.1	2.1
63 NON DURABLE–NON DURABLES	1.7	1.6	1.8	1.5	1.4	1.3	1.3
7 GOODS NES–BIENS NDA	0.4	0.6	0.7	1.6	1.4	2.6	2.5

EXPORTS – EXPORTATIONS

	1990	1991	1992	1993	1994	1995	1996
TOTAL EXPORTS–EXPORTATIONS TOTALES	100.	100.	100.	100.	100.	100.	100.
1 AGRICULTURE	11.3	9.2	7.9	5.8	4.9	4.5	4.0
2 MINING QUARRY–INDUS EXTRACTIVES	17.5	14.9	12.2	9.6	6.6	6.0	6.8
3 MANUFACTURING–IND MANUFACTUR	71.3	75.8	79.9	84.6	88.5	89.6	89.1
31 FOOD BEV TOBACCO–ALIM BOISS TAB	9.4	8.8	8.8	7.9	8.6	8.5	7.7
32 TEXTILES–INDUSTRIES TEXTILES	6.1	6.2	6.4	5.9	5.3	4.9	5.1
33 WOOD & PRODUCTS–BOIS & PRODUITS	6.2	5.5	6.1	7.5	6.3	5.1	5.0
34 PAPER & PRODUCTS–PAPIER & PRODT	0.6	0.6	0.6	0.6	0.6	0.6	0.6
35 CHEMICALS–INDUSTRIES CHIMIQUES	4.6	4.5	4.8	4.7	5.1	5.7	5.8
36 NON METAL MIN–MIN NON METAL	0.8	0.7	0.7	0.7	0.8	0.8	0.8
37 BASIC METAL–IND METAL BASE	2.3	1.7	2.0	1.9	1.7	1.7	1.8
38 METAL MANUF–MANUF METAL	38.6	44.7	47.6	52.6	57.7	59.4	59.8
39 OTH MANUF IND–AUTRES MANUF	2.7	3.1	2.9	2.7	2.4	2.8	2.7

3. TRADE BY PRINCIPAL COUNTRIES OF ORIGIN AND DESTINATION (VALUE IN THOUSAND U.S. DOLLARS)
ECHANGES SELON LES PRINCIPAUX PAYS D'ORIGINE ET DE DESTINATION (VALEUR EN MILLIERS DE DOLLARS EU)

COUNTRIES–PAYS	GENERAL IMPORTS C.I.F. # 1 IMPORTATIONS GENERALES C.A.F				
	1992	1993	1994	1995	1996
World	39788414	45389995	59086023	77045624	77923386
Africa	147246	170294	295489	408767	564541
Americas	7127799	8484953	10788154	13876934	13596176
Northern America	6590051	7959537	10190585	12956681	12616602
LAIA	484480	522438	567895	889750	956345
CACM	3175	675	4868	9785	657
Caribbean	1585	1582	11145	7631	6150
Rest of America	48508	722	13661	13087	16423
As.ex F.USSR	24830548	28507701	35776349	46466560	47907360
Eur.x F.USSR	6111804	6528023	9966120	13565698	12747551
EU	5420799	5819045	8807612	11952409	11292253
EFTA	604713	636236	1060936	1475280	1294540
East Europe	76680	66166	92413	130497	147486
Other Europe	567	67	881	2040	1550
Former USSR	77361	104798	129862	235871	400387
Oceania	1365429	1592934	2129145	2489531	2647172
Japan/Japon	10358544	12541833	15911781	21183187	19238068
USA/Etats–Unis d'Amer	6301359	7726139	9955189	12546292	12144124
Singapore/Singapour	6272965	6949020	8402646	9607825	10471639
Germany/Allemagne	1677840	1750565	2500214	3434925	3350577
Korea, Republic of	1219063	1399313	1902966	3178270	4068519
United Kingdom	1360447	1427990	1910383	2186443	2043320
Australia/Australie	1058280	1292355	1765526	2109565	2223065
Thailand/Thaïlande	988321	1133838	1474161	2047551	2592352
China/Chine	974980	1096927	1367419	1715063	1875596
France,Monac	519420	651345	1555341	2361193	1574656
Hong Kong	904301	921868	1187218	1673343	1819547
Indonesia/Indonésie	636952	716972	940844	1219907	1424727
Switz.Liecht	568256	584733	978808	1392004	1162238
Italy/Italie	525613	585673	807888	982611	1089337
India/Inde	354393	397823	412492	549782	735305
Netherlands/Pays–Bas	337660	358127	404011	524024	690672
Sweden/Suède	260439	294721	475848	653596	620107
Philippines	240113	219140	321470	460269	799404
Belgium–Luxembourg	294218	258334	366449	460287	466022
Canada	288689	233392	235348	410361	472458
Ireland/Irlande	47775	51260	281038	547664	709321
New Zealand	262879	242487	275774	319553	365194
Brazil/Brésil	271906	285550	281621	308490	298058
Saudi Arabia	206717	259773	217421	227030	328455
Finland/Finlande	102630	136102	171431	257757	196550
Argentina/Argentine	84329	105168	80026	259196	275284
Spain/Espagne	49905	76141	94639	262444	228989
Russian Federation	77361	60448	73760	175125	265483
Viet Nam	126787	92844	111676	125912	150367
Chile/Chili	60817	80595	118522	164159	180452
So. Africa Customs Un	1308	7646	120896	204678	257124
Denmark/Danemark	121161	106732	96087	109894	145748
Austria/Autriche	91379	86859	102295	114365	116019
Turkey/Turquie	29671	55255	144052	123729	127137
Norway,SVD,JM	36435	51441	81975	83063	131232
Zambia/Zambie	86324	88180	85508	52410	33063
Peru/Pérou	34169	27955	67134	89535	87828
Pakistan	67177	59710	63257	66551	48862
Iran (Islamic Rp. of)	26241	59066	41957	46395	49687
Ukraine		36463	36381	35006	95036
Poland/Pologne	26685	19458	28524	46461	81552
United Arab Emirates	53600	30559	21896	36060	46468
Mexico/Mexique	10932	13137	14356	43929	99213
Portugal	27971	29955	35952	45686	40955
Myanmar	18521	22937	27749	41363	39987
Kuwait/ Koweït	3140	500	30617	68338	37158
Papua New Guinea	9828	21536	46841	26287	29975
Fiji/Fidji	26048	24397	31728	29764	21828
Jordan/Jordanie	16544	22763	25805	27520	35484
Romania/Roumanie	13936	11996	25174	44450	23246

COUNTRIES–PAYS	GENERAL EXPORTS F.O.B. # 1 EXPORTATIONS GENERALES F.O.B.				
	1992	1993	1994	1995	1996
Monde	40768515	47127195	58842665	73778170	78186076
Afrique	356750	453962	572669	803764	810793
Amériques	8413056	10690463	13898320	17021270	15844078
Amérique du Nord	7937622	10038206	12982202	15878922	14795100
ALAI	350230	484159	750438	927116	844795
MCAC	10076	23735	18733	15741	21976
Caraïbes	35571	37421	37201	36970	45678
Autre Amérique	79556	106942	109746	162522	136529
Asie l'URSS exclus	24574453	27810517	34416240	43687008	48801385
Europe l'URSS exclus	6398505	7226130	8648870	10765027	11057963
UE	6236113	7018014	8407875	10478867	10731876
AELE	117036	174846	145295	138407	164185
Europe de l'Est	35203	28218	85820	132485	142981
Autre de l'Europe	1707	1734	5290	5068	6379
Ancienne URSS	35823	46337	67957	114292	139843
Océanie	936761	899638	1238437	1379206	1522856
Singapore/Singapour	9384755	10208303	12173272	14990024	16016376
USA/Etats–Unis d'Amer	7585087	9582302	12438522	15278558	14247375
Japan/Japon	5475604	6119366	7091844	9352213	10483595
Hong Kong	1543824	1944427	2714651	3947812	4606590
United Kingdom	1642594	1990741	2233020	2984673	2695483
Thailand/Thaïlande	1488694	1694994	2218164	2894739	3207722
Germany/Allemagne	1634592	1723030	1944822	2363723	2377595
Korea, Republic of	1395958	1628585	1648136	2058789	2384667
China/Chine	771296	1203065	1935504	1956043	1881966
Netherlands/Pays–Bas	992593	1147721	1355143	1796845	2324515
Australia/Australie	681265	628588	921385	1126593	1215892
Indonesia/Indonésie	506837	543387	714223	973637	1218544
Belgium–Luxembourg	482314	567289	756045	793274	855623
France,Monac	565576	666003	800567	738873	642936
India/Inde	430648	209708	527552	831216	1205880
Philippines	478043	479709	608030	674916	938255
Pakistan	369473	425976	661965	714014	644799
United Arab Emirates	276601	352936	506238	685298	735193
Canada	352201	455703	543260	600109	547334
Italy/Italie	369622	341031	430905	565675	610617
Saudi Arabia	266604	279799	271229	337820	318638
Mexico/Mexique	135916	244640	388779	324929	199407
Spain/Espagne	170105	157224	258667	368109	328949
Brunei Darussalam	149922	187950	263272	296245	325183
Brazil/Brésil	73461	123969	207369	373213	403973
New Zealand	219380	200547	265253	194598	240415
Egypt/Egypte	151259	183255	201685	271339	240857
Ireland/Irlande	51081	84241	213839	326538	338949
Viet Nam	49793	137602	159294	268318	323101
Turkey/Turquie	116257	135570	195736	224854	213601
Myanmar	89703	103766	220298	230238	220839
Sri Lanka	110268	159810	148631	185959	157756
So. Africa Customs Un	197	10427	176371	272046	287615
Sweden/Suède	98296	95189	126261	172714	156097
Panama	72290	101036	107501	153748	135860
Denmark/Danemark	80625	75868	110924	134013	130242
Switz.Liecht	88994	75486	81489	103205	119310
Jordan/Jordanie	54028	82186	91413	133990	72014
Yemen/Yémen	84380	99566	49148	81860	69787
Bangladesh	64981	69334	65635	55201	126286
Iran (islamic Rp. of)	43250	58817	61146	115335	93320
Russian Federation	35823	37987	53011	99721	113137
Chile/Chili	84577	36742	39702	71042	67801
Austria/Autriche	52837	57094	60174	61949	60562
Norway,SVD,JM	27609	98938	63254	34098	43450
Kuwait/ Koweït	34657	38131	48965	68329	69852
Finland/Finlande	23946	32866	33753	61961	101067
Argentina/Argentine	24755	34603	57903	59611	73104
Portugal	39060	39963	42671	55837	51299
Oman	27710	33478	93045	38045	35597

(VALUE AS PERCENTAGE OF WORLD TOTAL)(VALEURS EN POURCENTAGE DU TOTAL MONDIAL)

	1987	1988	1989	1990	1991	1992	1993	1994	1995	1996
Africa	0.4	0.5	0.6	0.5	0.5	0.4	0.4	0.5	0.5	0.7
Americas	21.1	20.7	19.9	19.5	17.6	17.9	18.7	18.3	18.0	17.4
Northern America	19.8	18.9	17.8	17.8	16.2	16.6	17.5	17.2	16.8	16.2
LAIA	1.3	1.7	1.6	1.7	1.3	1.2	1.2	1.0	1.2	1.2
CACM				0.0	0.0	0.0	0.0	0.0	0.0	0.0
Caribbean	0.0	0.1	0.1	0.0	0.0	0.0	0.0	0.0	0.0	0.0
Rest of America	0.0	0.0	0.4	0.1	0.1	0.1	0.0	0.0	0.0	0.0
As.ex F.USSR	57.3	57.5	57.8	57.5	60.6	62.4	62.8	60.5	60.3	61.5
Eur.x F.USSR	15.7	15.7	16.6	17.6	17.0	15.4	14.4	16.9	17.6	16.4
EU	14.5	14.4	15.2	15.9	15.3	13.6	12.8	14.9	15.5	14.5
EFTA	0.9	0.9	1.1	1.4	1.5	1.5	1.4	1.8	1.9	1.7
East Europe	0.2	0.2	0.2	0.2	0.2	0.2	0.1	0.2	0.2	0.2
Other Europe	0.1	0.1	0.1	0.0	0.0	0.0	0.0	0.0	0.0	0.0
Former USSR	0.2	0.3	0.3	0.3	0.2	0.2	0.2	0.2	0.3	0.5
Oceania	5.2	5.2	4.7	4.5	3.8	3.4	3.5	3.6	3.2	3.4
Japan/Japon	21.7	23.5	24.2	24.1	26.1	26.0	27.6	26.9	27.5	24.7
USA/Etats–Unis d'Amer	18.7	17.7	16.9	16.8	15.4	15.8	17.0	16.8	16.3	15.6
Singapore/Singapour	14.7	13.2	13.6	15.0	15.6	15.8	15.3	14.2	12.5	13.4
Germany/Allemagne	4.2	3.9	3.8	4.3	4.4	4.2	3.9	4.2	4.5	4.3
Korea, Republic of	2.6	2.6	2.5	2.6	2.7	3.1	3.1	3.2	4.1	5.2
United Kingdom	4.3	4.9	5.4	5.5	4.6	3.4	3.1	3.2	2.8	2.6
Australia/Australie	4.2	4.1	3.8	3.7	3.1	2.7	2.8	3.0	2.7	2.9
Thailand/Thaïlande	3.5	3.1	3.0	2.4	2.4	2.5	2.5	2.5	2.7	3.3
China/Chine	3.0	2.9	2.7	1.9	2.2	2.5	2.4	2.3	2.2	2.4
France,Monac	1.6	1.5	1.2	1.5	1.4	1.3	1.4	2.6	3.1	2.0

	1987	1988	1989	1990	1991	1992	1993	1994	1995	1996
Afrique	0.6	0.7	0.9	0.8	0.8	0.9	1.0	1.0	1.1	1.0
Amériques	18.1	19.0	20.2	18.4	18.8	20.6	22.7	23.6	23.1	20.3
Amérique du Nord	17.4	18.1	19.4	17.7	17.7	19.5	21.3	22.1	21.5	18.9
ALAI	0.7	0.8	0.6	0.5	0.8	0.9	1.0	1.3	1.3	1.1
MCAC				0.0	0.0	0.0	0.1	0.0	0.0	0.0
Caraïbes	0.0	0.0	0.0	0.1	0.1	0.1	0.1	0.1	0.1	0.1
Autre Amérique	0.1	0.1	0.1	0.1	0.1	0.2	0.2	0.2	0.2	0.2
Asie l'URSS exclus	62.5	61.5	58.9	62.5	62.3	60.3	59.0	58.5	59.2	62.4
Europe l'URSS exclus	15.4	15.6	16.5	15.9	15.7	15.7	15.3	14.7	14.6	14.1
UE	14.7	14.9	15.8	15.3	15.2	15.3	14.9	14.3	14.2	13.7
AELE	0.3	0.2	0.2	0.3	0.3	0.3	0.4	0.2	0.2	0.2
Europe de l'Est	0.3	0.2	0.2	0.2	0.1	0.1	0.1	0.1	0.2	0.2
Autre de l'Europe	0.2	0.2	0.3	0.1	0.1	0.0	0.0	0.0	0.0	0.0
Ancienne URSS	0.8	0.6	1.0	0.5	0.2	0.1	0.1	0.1	0.2	0.2
Océanie	2.5	2.7	2.5	1.9	2.0	2.3	1.9	2.1	1.9	1.9
Singapore/Singapour	18.2	19.3	19.7	22.8	23.3	23.0	21.7	20.7	20.3	20.5
USA/Etats–Unis d'Amer	16.6	17.4	18.7	16.9	16.9	18.6	20.3	21.1	20.7	18.2
Japan/Japon	19.5	16.9	16.1	15.8	15.7	13.4	13.0	12.1	12.7	13.4
Hong Kong	2.8	3.5	3.1	3.2	3.4	3.8	4.1	4.6	5.4	5.9
United Kingdom	3.2	3.5	3.7	3.9	4.4	4.0	4.2	3.8	4.0	3.4
Thailand/Thaïlande	2.9	2.0	2.5	3.5	3.2	3.7	3.6	3.8	3.9	4.1
Germany/Allemagne	3.4	3.4	3.6	3.9	3.6	4.0	3.7	3.3	3.2	3.0
Korea, Republic of	5.3	5.0	5.0	4.6	4.4	3.4	3.5	2.8	2.8	3.0
China/Chine	1.6	2.0	1.9	2.1	1.9	1.9	2.6	3.3	2.7	2.4
Netherlands/Pays–Bas	3.5	3.0	3.6	2.6	2.4	2.4	2.4	2.3	2.4	3.0

4. General Imports C.I.F. by Commodities according to the S.I.T.C. (Rev. 2) in thousand U.S. Dollars
Importations Générales C.A.F. par Produits d'après la C.T.C.I. (Rév. 2) en milliers de Dollars E.U.

SITC CTCI	COMMODITY	1993 WEIGHT POIDS	1993 VALUE VALEUR	1994 WEIGHT POIDS	1994 VALUE VALEUR	1995 WEIGHT POIDS	1995 VALUE VALEUR	1996 WEIGHT POIDS	1996 VALUE VALEUR	PRODUIT
	ALL COMMODITIES		45389995		59086023		77045624		77923386	TOUS PRODUITS
0	FOOD AND LIVE ANIMALS		2258372		2544837		3128951		3607613	ALIMENTS,ANIMAUX VIVANTS
02	DAIRY PRODCTS,BIRDS'EGGS		274714		270485		369905		381191	PRODUITS LAITIERS,OEUFS
022	MILK AND CREAM	W 132799	247659	W 142554	240180	W 164242	333140		345328	LAIT ET CREME
0224	MILK,CREAM PRESERVED ETC	W 127382	241826	W 134749	232905	W 156434	321308		315806	LAIT,CREME CONS,CONC
03	FISH AND PREPARATIONS		254168		290171		307233		331536	POISSONS ET PREPARATIONS
034	FISH,FRESH,CHILLED,FROZN		159489	W 176197	180430		185289		220048	POISSON FRAIS, REFRIG,CONG
04	CEREALS AND PREPARATIONS		673792		725949		924494		1141785	CEREALES ET PRODUITS
041	WHEAT ETC UNMILLED	W 1094185	184666	W 1176223	214774	W 1117646	239431		269490	FROMENT,EPEAUTRE
0412	OTHER WHEAT ETC UNMILLED	W 1094181	184664	W 1176133	214758	W 1111930	238053		257590	AUTRE FROMENT NON MOULU
044	MAIZE UNMILLED	W 1799607	222811	W 1730884	226932	W 2084387	331906		372390	MAIS NON MOULU
048	CEREAL ETC PREPARATIONS	W 334723	142515	W 341104	157875	W 405453	197749		266056	PREPTNS A BASE CEREALES
05	VEGETABLES AND FRUIT		334099		377306		451386		506701	LEGUMES ET FRUITS
054	VEG ETC FRSH,SMPLY PRSVD		167926	W 494127	178905		233206		270913	LEGUMES FRAIS,CONG,SECS
06	SUGAR AND PREPS,HONEY		235663		279017		339184		345089	SUCRES ET PRODUITS
061	SUGAR AND HONEY	W 892068	225530	W 970966	266112	W 1057603	323072		326343	SUCRES ET MIEL
0611	RAW BEET AND CANE SUGAR	W 877550	215511	W 959502	253802	W 1033099	307960		310486	SUCRES BRUTS
081	*FEEDING STUFF FOR ANIML	W 657041	175741	W 747535	206827	W 821386	232422		338474	NOURRITURE POUR ANIMAUX
1	BEVERAGES AND TOBACCO		150477		163642		221137		197632	BOISSONS ET TABACS
2	CRUDE MATERLS,EXCL FUELS		1267114		1435249		1850815		1970491	MAT BRUTES NON COMESTIBLES
22	OIL SEEDS,OLEAGINOUS FRT		154325		166490		165929		172249	GRAINES,FRUITS OLEAGINEUX
222	SEEDS FOR'SOFT'FIXED OIL	W 533807	149627	W 530745	160077	W 540502	159448		163191	GRAINES HUILES FIXES
23	RUBBER, CRUDE		171994		227695		325416		371624	CAOUTCHOUC BRUT
232	NATURAL RUBBER,GUMS	W 167375	98035	W 235313	159025		229354		276178	LATEX CAOUTCHOUC NATUREL
26	TEXTILE FIBRES AND WASTE		189775		257943		347305		412815	FIBRES TEXTILES
27	CRUDE FERTLZR,MINRLS NES		148262		160856		201986		221860	ENGRAIS MINERAUX BRUTS
28	METALLIFEROUS ORES,SCRAP		440437		407828		536970		498953	MINERAIS METAL,DECHETS
282	IRON AND STEEL SCRAP	W 1417058	219242	W 869436	143737	W 1064477	174863		168330	FERRAILLES
28202	— OF ALLOY STEEL	W 959659	152492	W 615887	103698	W 480108	79764		109940	FERRAILLES D'ACIERS ALLIES
287	BASE METAL ORES,CONC NES		127608	W 142073	178240		206798		201911	MINERAIS METAUX COMMUNS
3	MINERAL FUELS ETC		1673706		1558246		1778414		2111333	COMBUSTIBLES MINERAUX LUB
33	PETROLEUM AND PRODUCTS		1473836		1379558		1570331		1816487	PETROLE ET DERIVES
333	CRUDE PETROLEUM	W 1672456	173218	W 1539983	176480	W 1276588	150704		184937	HUILES BRUTES DE PETROLE
334	PETROLEUM PRODUCTS,REFIN	W 7071127	1252247	W 6806536	1150328	W 7439278	1372005		1577872	PRODUITS RAFFINES
3341	GASOLINE,OTH LIGHT OILS	W 1761874	415223	W 2166979	449781	W 2724713	574373		626590	ESSENCES POUR MOTEURS
33411	MOTOR,AVIATION SPIRIT	W 1710907	403353	W 1832647	389083	W 1533586	348059		538638	ESSENCES MOTEURS D'AVIONS
3343	GAS OILS	W 1933155	379379	W 1677333	296083	W 1604230	287226		348690	GAS OILS
3344	FUEL OILS,NES	W 2736024	240119	W 2581895	235680	W 2782869	310244		382376	FUEL OILS
4	ANIMAL,VEGETABLE OIL,FAT		157005		213639		151496		104470	HUILES,GRAISSES ANIM,VEG
42	FIXED VEGETABLE OIL,FAT		149021		203509		132823		88888	HUILES VEGETALES FIXES
5	CHEMCLS,RELATED PROD NES		3327908		3910163		5322846		5145718	PRODUITS CHIMIQUES
51	ORGANIC CHEMICALS		562806		660477		1230741		1064800	PROD CHIMIQ ORGANIQUES
511	HYDROCARBONS NES,DERIVS		177919		195464		416437		268241	HYDROCARBURES NDA
5112	CYCLIC HYDROCARBONS		54203		115420		274695		182027	HYDROCARBURES CYCLIQUES
51125	STYRENE	V 70059	33013	V 124322	90121	V 262793	249745		82342	STYRENE
513	CARBOXYLIC ACIDS ETC	W 116365	104762	W 140897	136736	W 222522	281456		261707	ACIDES CARBOXYLIQUES
52	INORGANIC CHEMICALS		331874		413876		545364		589934	PROD CHIM INORGANIQUES
522	INORG ELEMNTS,OXIDES,ETC		178894		240676		306958		320690	ELEMENTS INORGANIQUES
523	OTHR INORG CHEMICALS ETC	W 549497	146544	W 588020	166266		227275		262155	AUT PRODUITS CHIMIQUES INORG
53	DYES,TANNING,COLOUR PROD		245437		308829		355655		368185	PROD TEINTURE,COLORANTS
533	PIGMENTS,PAINTS,ETC		162058		206486		239217		259254	PIGMENTS,PEINTURES,VERNIS
541	*MEDICINAL,PHARM PRODUCT		231955		271480		318478		332887	PROD MEDICINAUX PHARMACEUT
5417	MEDICAMENTS		179696		212119		246713		249108	MEDICAMENTS
54179	— CONTNG OTH SUBSTANCES		143223		175406		204098		200563	MED CONT AUT SUBSTANCES
55	PERFUME,CLEANING ETC PRD		244998		295801		345337		368695	PROD POUR PARFUM,TOILETTE
562	*FERTILIZERS,MANUFACTURE	W 1900893	246063	W 2114472	270057	W 2286279	339251		335282	ENGRAIS MANUFACTURES
58	PLASTIC MATERIALS ETC		1087070		1230666		1628605		1477046	MAT PLAST ARTIFICIELLES
582	PROD OF CONDENSATION ETC	W 191696	341396	W 266096	461692	W 414262	622131		532025	PROD CONDENS,POLYCOND
5823	ALKYDS,OTHER POLYESTERS	W 60536	108633	W 116069	183804	W 105242	243891		179391	ALKYDES ET AUT POLYESTERS
583	POLYMERIZATION ETC PRODS		727845	W 666457	746356		980143		919525	PROD POLYMERISATION
5831	POLYETHYLENE	W 277478	227934	W 202797	181372	W 213836	244987		233843	POLYETHYLENE
58311	— IN PRIMARY FORMS	W 272123	202312	W 196335	157613	W 205520	218725		204426	POLYETHYLENE PRIMAIRES
5833	POLYSTYRENE,ITS COPOLYMR	W 141115	171585	W 156030	210431	W 189577	314188		263944	POLYPROPYLENE COPOLYMERES
58331	— IN PRIMARY FORMS	W 140038	169074	W 154643	207834	W 187852	309864		253476	SOUS FORMES PRIMAIRES
5839	OTH POLYMRZTION ETC PROD		162943	W 55702	149431		166317		173792	AUT PROD POLYMER COPOLYM
59	CHEMICAL MATERIALS NES		369240		448236		550269		597051	MAT PROD CHIMIQUES NDA
598	MISCEL CHEM PRODUCTS NES		260445		321651		380437		418350	PROD DIV INDUST CHIM NDA
5989	CHEM PRODUCTS,PREPS NES		202497		258349		300560		329059	PROD PREP CHIMIQUES NDA
59899	OTH CHEM PRODS,PREPS,NES		126022		178264		198182		204752	AUT PRODUITS CHIMIQUES NDA
6	BASIC MANUFACTURES		6925417		8319365		10844376		10580305	ART MANUFACTURES
62	RUBBER MANUFACTURES NES		144752		170902		182973		192078	CAOUTCHOUC MANUFACTURE
64	PAPER,PAPERBOARD AND MFR		736842		900261		1343086		1087950	PAPIERS,CARTONS & OUVRAGES
641	PAPER AND PAPERBOARD		625032		752271		1164288		909836	PAPIERS ET CARTONS
6411	NEWSPRINT	W 218655	101703	W 253532	119633	W 322162	285295		176245	PAPIER JOURNAL
6413	KRAFT PAPER,PAPERBOARD	W 257366	136809	W 299977	146426	W 299044	224757		177378	PAPIER ET CARTON KRAFT
6415	PAPER,PAPERBRD,BULK,NES	W 226796	162465	W 491918	212737	W 290940	302537		247150	PAPIERS,CARTONS ROULEAUX
64159	OTHER PAPER ETC,BULK,NES	W 195847	149661	W 406470	190569	W 244984	273128		220834	AUT PAPIER ROULEAUX FEUILLES
65	TEXTILE YARN,FABRICS,ETC		1194277		1393108		1539269		1367700	FILS,TISSUS,ARTICLES TEXTILE
651	TEXTILE YARN		246575		325381		405049		296899	FILS TEXTILES
652	COTTON FABRICS,WOVEN		256347	A 38255	258366		252463		229289	TISSUS DE COTON
6522	WOVEN COTTON BLEACHD,ETC		163615	A 36493	161210		169079		138593	TISSUS COTON BLANCHIS ETC
65224	BLCHED COTTON FABRIC NES		139654	A 20032	140593		149530		120257	AUT TIS PLUS 85% COT BLANCHI
653	WOVN MAN–MADE FIB FABRIC		278055	A 177644	304089		317048		294818	TISSUS FIBRES SYNTH,ARTIF
6531	CONT SYNT WEAVES NONPILE		150159	A 1092	156684		160975		154106	TISSUS FIBRES SYNTH CONTINUE
655	KNITTED,ETC FABRICS	A 164641	204015	A 177155	231677	A 200612	225646		222946	ETOF BONNETERIE PIECES ETC
6552	OTHER KNIT ETC FAB NONEL	A 164641	204015	A 177155	231677	A 200612	225646		222946	ETOF BON NON ELAS NON SYNT
66	NONMETAL MINERAL MFS NES		682922		863474		1203625		1137883	ART MIN NON METALLIQUES
661	LIME,CEMENT,BLDG PRODS	W 1996079	111609	W 1630823	101363	W 2942430	183937		339799	CHAUX,CIMENTS MAT CONSTR
6612	CEMENT	W 1957706	89480	W 1583667	75325	W 2882861	153205		300767	CIMENTS HYDRAULIQUES
663	MINERAL MANUFCTURES NES		152774		181320		295238		206624	ART MIN MANUF NDA
664	GLASS		182234		287742		375882		288304	VERRE
6649	GLASS NES		135680		207590		252303		170019	VERRE NDA
66492	LAMP ETC ENVELOPES GLASS	MN 72297	116434	MN 127383	183526	MN 627929	207776		141025	AMPOULES EN VERRE
67	IRON AND STEEL		2111486		2449489		3320511		3533328	FER ET ACIER
672	IRON,STEEL PRIMARY FORMS	W 1669987	546820	W 1656653	544743	W 1896015	754811		792884	LINGOTS FER,ACIER
6725	IRN,STL BLOOMS,SLABS,ETC	W 687412	187157	W 715738	194836	W 580958	167750		244967	BLOOMS,BILLETTES FER ACIER
67251	IRN,SMPLE STL BLOOMS,ETC	W 686590	185483	W 712484	188489	W 580114	164202		240906	BLOOMS ETC NON ACIER FIN
6727	IRN,STL COIL FR REROLLNG	W 981060	358740	W 939566	348383	W 1313870	586496		546964	EBAUCHES POUR TOLES FER
67271	IRON,SIMPLE STEEL COILS	W 958077	327290	W 915244	320210	W 1282134	541541		487762	EBAUCHES NON EN ACIER
673	IRON,STEEL SHAPES ETC	W 527374	249245	W 646916	308341	W 1003365	510903		528638	BARRES,PROFIL FER,ACIER
6733	IRON,STEEL PROFILES ETC	W 322871	127450	W 418469	164717	W 599067	267835		275958	PROFILES,PALPLAN FER,ACIER

4. General Imports C.I.F. by Commodities according to the S.I.T.C. (Rev. 2) in thousand U.S. Dollars
Importations Générales C.A.F. par Produits d'après la C.T.C.I. (Rév. 2) en milliers de Dollars E.U.

SITC CTCI	COMMODITY	1993 WEIGHT POIDS	1993 VALUE VALEUR	1994 WEIGHT POIDS	1994 VALUE VALEUR	1995 WEIGHT POIDS	1995 VALUE VALEUR	1996 WEIGHT POIDS	1996 VALUE VALEUR	PRODUIT
674	IRN,STL UNIV,PLATE,SHEET	W 1412924	799642	W 1589966	933448	W 2348897	1507609		1436983	LARGES PLATS,TOLES
6744	IRN,STL HVY PLATE,ROLLED	W 324630	128292	W 388169	152302	W 592490	254151		275259	TOLES LAMINEES PLUS 4.75 MM
67441	— OF IRON OR SIMPLE STL	W 318952	120953	W 380687	140503	W 583162	236438		258276	TOLES NON ACIER FIN CARB
6746	IRN,STL THIN PLATE,ROLLD	W 541668	309132	W 535871	322133	W 734988	498215		410227	TOLES LAM MOINS 3MM
67461	— OF IRON OR SIMPLE STL	W 524110	274889	W 511326	272480	W 690395	410003		324413	TOL NON AC FIN MOINS 3 MM
6749	OTH IRN,STL PLATES,SHEET	W 395527	268495	W 440738	320128	W 679671	547299		528104	AUTRES TOLES FER,ACIER
67491	— OF IRON OR SIMPLE STL	W 388951	257953	W 433897	308790	W 672724	531393		502460	AUT TOLES AUTRES ACIER FIN
678	IRON,STL TUBES,PIPES,ETC	W 226928	341211	W 438406	457723	W 266487	283700		499261	TUBES,TUYAUX EN FONTE,FER
6783	IRON,STL TUBES,PIPES NES	W 91796	119776	W 280959	263040	W 114563	118530		233595	AUT TUBES,TUYAUX FER,ACIER
68	NON–FERROUS METALS		963744		1240138		1725804		1706875	METAUX NON FERREUX
682	COPPER EXC CEMENT COPPER	W 186743	507063	W 290616	661742	W 320839	874678		856206	CUIVRE
6821	COPPER NES,ALLOYS,UNWRT	W 94489	191097	W 110242	254892	W 116290	331300		332198	CUIVRE BRUT
68212	COPPER REFINED,UNWROUGHT	W 94290	190280	W 109556	253177	W 115360	328443		331429	CUIVRE AFFINE BRUT
6822	COPPER,ALLOYS WORKED	W 92254	315966	W 180374	406851	W 204549	543378		524007	CUIVRE,ALLIAGES OUVRES
684	ALUMINIUM	W 125630	262004	W 186026	384603	W 306401	605002		576645	ALUMINIUM
6841	ALUMINIUM,ALLOYS,UNWRGHT	W 88592	118283	W 105479	164289	W 202282	310317		267339	ALUMINIUM,ALLIAGES BRUTS
6842	ALUMINIUM,ALLOYS WORKED	W 37038	143721	W 80547	220314	W 104119	294686		309306	ALUMINIUM,ALLIAGES OUVRE
69	METAL MANUFACTURES NES		1002140		1180881		1314738		1380132	ART MANUFACT EN METAL NDA
694	STL,COPPR NAILS,NUTS,ETC	W 53419	128098	W 65144	182939	W 76087	166393		160770	CLOUS,VIS,ECROUS
695	TOOLS		184853		205341		246938		235956	OUTILS A MAIN
699	BASE METAL MFRS NES		462665		533789		634543		650140	ART MANUFACTURES MET NDA
6997	IRON,STEEL ARTICLES NES		160334		188956		245935		246931	OUV FONTE,FER,ACIER NDA
69979	IRN,STL MANUFACTURES NES		159124		187271		243425		244246	AUT OUVRAGES EN FER NDA
7	MACHINES,TRANSPORT EQUIP		25386463		35338580		46077930		46622981	MACHINES MATERIEL TRANSPORT
71	POWER GENERATING EQUIPMT		1204378		1779827		2052822		2026070	MACHINES GENERATRICES
712	STEAM ENGINES,TURBINES		10043		31246		325365		232699	MACHINES A VAPEUR D'EAU PIEC
7126	STEAM POWR UNITS,ENGINES	N 114	2286	N 623	20754	N 14402	252445		57602	MACHINES A VAPEUR D EAU
713	INTRNL COMBUS PSTN ENGIN		384173		422137		507826		640962	MOTEURS EXPL COMB INT, PIECE
7131	AIRCRAFT PSTN ENGINS,PTS		139656		130713		128143		249304	MOTEURS EXPL P.AVIATION, PIE
714	ENGINES AND MOTORS NES	N 131000	349301	N 1245127	530163	N 363259	401593		305536	MOTEURS NON ELECTRIQUES
7148	GAS TURBINES NES	N 750	242121	N 1464	336430	N 2049	275137		96199	TURBINES A GAZ
71488	OTHER GAS TURBINES NES	N 720	242070	N 1406	336068	N 1951	274844		95845	AUTRES TURBINES A GAZ
7149	ENGINE & MOTOR PARTS NES	N 130177	107130	N 1243516	193500	N 361098	125674		209158	PIECES 714 ET 718.88
71499	PARTS NES,OF 71488,71888	N 130132	107075	N 1190834	189935	N 359544	124787		206412	PIECES 714.88 ET 718.88
716	ROTATING ELECTRIC PLANT		426212		747149		763530		750290	APP ELECTR ROTATIFS,PIECES
7161	DC MOTORS AND GENERATORS	MN 16024	85471	MN 51047	185239	MN 60410	227464		164467	MOTEURS COURANT CONTINU
7162	AC MTRS,GENRTRS,GEN SETS	MN 145953	274655	MN 599373	448411	MN 223789	344968		436973	MOTEURS ELECTRIQUES
71621	AC MTRS,INC UNIVRSL MTRS	MN 145930	216539	MN 598926	302869	MN 223148	298506		351650	MOT ELEC NON COUR CONTINU
72	MACHS FOR SPCL INDUSTRYS		2415960		3102893		4461300		4408031	MAC SPECIALES POUR INDUST
723	CIVIL ENGNEERG EQUIP ETC		265420		345517		859881		953464	APPAREILS DE GENIE CIVIL
7234	CONST,MINING MACHNRY NES	N 6200	155888	N 10020	247813	N 19549	727623		811234	MACH POUR LA CONST, MINES
72342	SLFPRP SHOVELS,EXCAVATRS	N 3580	115287	N 5132	173995	N 9953	417541		505246	PELLES MECANIQUES
724	TEXTILE,LEATHER MACHNRY		265227		276991		476396		359256	MACH POUR INDUSTRIE TEXTILE
726	PRINTG,BKBINDG MACHY,PTS		154614		177166		182828		253617	MACHINES POUR IMPRIMERIE
728	OTH MACHY FOR SPCL INDUS		1549191		2113965		2688587		2555038	AUT MACH IND PARTICULIERES
7281	MACH–TOOLS FR SPCL INDUS		323145		524329		492783		431222	MACH–OUTILS SPEC IND PART
72812	MACH–TOOLS TO WORK WOOD	N 26147	278231	N 186541	418529	N 68649	375958		346416	MACH–OUT POUR TRAVAIL BOIS
7283	OTHR MINERAL WORKG MACHY	N 141759	110230	N 1138983	159497	N 1537585	206839		311524	MACH TRIER,CRIBLER,BROYER
7284	MACHY FOR SPCL INDUS NES		1115817		1430138		1988966		1812292	MACH SPEC IND PARTICUL.
72842	RUBBER,PLASTICS WRKG MCH	N 14687	259149	N 160702	323279	N 77657	417391		386766	MACH IND CAOUT MAT PLAST
72848	OTH MCHY WITH INDIV FNCT	N 62091	515832	N 542977	722053	N 408516	958303		903132	AUTRES MACHINES NDA
72849	PTS OF MACHS OF 7284 ETC		197227		251294		362578		354290	PIECES DU 728.4 ETC
73	METALWORKING MACHINERY		708164		952847		1689318		1139033	MACH TRAVAIL DES METAUX
736	METALWORKING MACH–TOOLS		537740		715276		784944		866041	MACH–OUTILS TRAVAIL METAUX
7361	METAL CUTTING MACH–TOOLS	N 41519	205874	N 81817	212330	N 89581	253816		279192	MACH–OUT ENLEVEMENT METAL
7362	METAL FORMING MACH–TOOLS	N 19827	168737	N 204291	259029	N 126135	250269		292066	MACH–OUTILS DEFORM METAL
737	METALWORKING MACHNRY NES		170423		237571		904374		272992	MACH TRAV METAUX PIECES
7371	FOUNDRY EQUIPMNT,PTS NES		19167		39548		342897		61978	CONVERTISSEURS ACIERIE,PIEC
73711	FOUNDRY EQUIPMENT NES	N 1379	9174	N 7596	30210	N 19587	321511		57076	CONVERTISSEURS ACIERIE
7372	ROLLING MILLS AND ROLLS		59311		71561		311983		53043	LAMINOIRS CYLINDRES PIEC
73721	ROLLING MILLS	N 340	49552	N 2556	61225	N 4306	287204		28382	LAMINOIRS ET TRAINS
7373	WELDING,BRAZING,ETC MCHS		91945	MN 117971	126462		249494		157972	MACH SOUDAGE ETC PIECES
73732	ELECTRIC WELDERS,ETC		88296	MN 117894	121147		244707		153199	MACH ELECT POUR SOUDER
74	GENRL INDUSTRL MACHY NES		2797548		3172216		3474656		3749580	MACH APP INDUSTRIE
741	HEATING,COOLING EQUIPMNT		687122		740846		778089		597560	MACH CHAUFFAGE,PIECES
7413	INDUS FURNACES ETC,PARTS		155637		127683		238635		183588	FOURS IND,LABOR,PIECES
7416	HEATING,COOLING EQU NES		398383	N 2205039	479684		344940		232591	APP CHANGEMENT TEMP
742	PUMPS FOR LIQUIDS ETC		148523		131674		163644		198307	POMPES MOTO–POMPES
743	PUMPS NES,CENTRFUGES ETC		523998		512835		501462		594626	POMPES COMPRES,VENT ETC
7431	PUMPS FOR GASES ETC		319851	N 1783830	226241		219528		263940	POMPES AIR A VIDE,COMPRES
744	MECHANICAL HANDLING EQU		507106		622254		842990		1049414	EQUIP MANUTENTION PIECES
7442	LIFTING,LOADING MACH NES	N 319523	327210	N 1325541	361176	N 1385933	562814		677383	APP LEVAGE,MANUTENTION
74428	OTH HANDLING ETC MCH NES	N 288760	155788	N 1133154	165504	N 1333433	282036		303770	AUT APP LEVAGE ETC
745	NONELEC MACHY,TOOLS NES		192142		231326		290258		338058	AUT MACH NON ELEC,PIECES
7452	OTH NONELEC MCHS,PTS NES		153923		186894		232837		279105	AUT MACH NON ELEC,PIECES
749	NONELEC MACH PTS,ACC NES		738656		933281		898212		971614	PIECES MACH NON ELEC NDA
7492	COCKS,VALVES ETC NES		245125	MN 64864	300008		177261		241492	ART ROB,SIM POUR TUYAUX
7499	OTH NONELEC MCHY PTS NES		310638		377804		434495		430428	PIECES NON ELECT NDA
74991	FOUNDRY MOULDS ETC NES	N 495984	245945	N 621675	299412	N 1135020	360177		352186	MOULES POUR METAUX
75	OFFICE MACHNES,ADP EQUIP		1376506		1893530		2790435		3905018	MACH BUREAU TRAIT AUTOM
752	AUTOMTIC DATA PROC EQUIP	N 203920	312132	N 1483629	405857	N 1363074	566827		944938	MACH TRAIT INFORMATION
7528	OFF–LINE DATA PROC EQUIP	N 43726	81469	N 168043	83780	N 529784	111150		301001	MACH AUXIL TRAIT INFORM
759	OFFICE,ADP MCH PTS,ACCES		1001917		1405986		2123657		2874377	PIECES DU 751 ET 752
7599	ACCTG,ETC,ADP MCH PTS,AC		978821		1376891		2075679		2827146	PIECES DU 751 ET 752
76	TELECOMM,SOUND EQUIPMENT		2485377		3173875		3857064		3201378	EQUIPMENT DE TELECOM
764	TELECOM EQPT,PTS,ACC NES		2284821		2908108		3576911		3007427	EQUIP TELECOM,PIECES
7641	LINE TELEPHONE,ETC EQUIP	MN 19576	91876	MN 27332	119080	MN 22430	263842		180146	APP TELEPHON PAR FIL
7643	TV,RADIO TRANSMITTRS ETC	N 441461	330985	N 837434	313473	N 1064046	499424		391411	APP EMET TELE RADIO
7649	PTS NES OF EQUIPMT OF 76		1734087		2288044		2622363		2217011	PIECES DE LA DIV 76
76491	PTS NES OF APPAR OF 7641		161456		208281		303230		292072	PIECES POUR 764.1
76493	TELECOMM EQUIPMT PTS NES		731973		964520		1229884		1025668	PIECES 761,762,764.3,8
76499	PARTS ETC OF SOUND EQUIP		799656		1055254		1011179		841784	PIECES NDA POUR 763
77	ELECTRIC MACHNRY NES ETC		11021300		16058953		21472485		22740522	MACH APP ELECT NDA
771	ELECTRIC POWER MACHY NES		475023		679527		685584		819205	MACH PROD,TRANS ELECTR
7711	TRANSFORMERS,ELECTRICAL		158714		246479		220999		343631	TRANSFO ELECTRIQUES
77118	OTHER ELEC TRANSFORMERS		140336		218958		207743		316346	AUTRES TRANSFO ELECTRIQ
7712	OTH ELEC POWER MACHY NES		316308		433048		464585		475574	AUT APP PROD TRANSF ELEC
77129	PTS NES OF MACHY OF 771		131221		199426		196575		213226	PIECES MACH DU 771
772	SWITCHGEAR ETC,PARTS NES		1768939		2530048		2675306		2653611	APP COUPURE,SECT ETC
7721	SWITCHGEAR ETC		893066	MN 11649	1168266		1306985		1325795	APP COUPURE,SECTIONMNT
7722	PRINTED CIRCUITS,PTS NES		597733		841795		1012427		995370	CIRCUITS ET PIECES

4. General Imports C.I.F. by Commodities according to the S.I.T.C. (Rev. 2) in thousand U.S. Dollars
Importations Générales C.A.F. par Produits d'après la C.T.C.I. (Rév. 2) en milliers de Dollars E.U.

SITC CTCI	COMMODITY	1993		1994		1995		1996		PRODUIT
		WEIGHT POIDS	VALUE VALEUR	WEIGHT POIDS	VALUE VALEUR	WEIGHT POIDS	VALUE VALEUR	WEIGHT POIDS	VALUE VALEUR	
7723	FIXED,VARIABLE RESISTORS		278140		519987		355893		332446	POTENTIOMETRES PIECES
773	ELECTR DISTRIBUTNG EQUIP		430222		481979		534571		508971	EQUIPMT DISTRIBUTION ELECT
7731	INSULATED WIRE,CABLE ETC	W 61883	349814	W 49269	387259	W 50203	441887		400083	FILS,CABLES ISOLES ELECT
776	TRANSISTORS,VALVES,ETC		7122482	MN 50666974	10616354		15516690		16698434	LAMPES,TUBES,VALVES
7761	TV PICTURE TUBES	N 6706872	466595	N 7249417	430597	MN 10272	827976		896226	TUBES CATHODIQUES
7762	OTH ELECTRONIC TUBES ETC		127252	N 6551598	246487	N 6897587	319796		482975	AUT LAMPES ELECTRONIQUES
7763	DIODES,TRANSISTORS,ETC	MN 11485908	648139	MN 12225466	1002758	MN 16649698	1183217		1457726	DIODES,TRANSISTORS
7764	ELECTRONIC MICROCIRCUITS	MN 3864993	2117755	MN 8157722	3691244	MN 9949087	5611477		6648729	MICROSTRUCTURES ELECTRON
7768	ELCTRNC COMP PTS,CRYSTLS		3762740	MN 30269985	5245269		7574225		7212778	CRIST PIEZO–ELEC,PCS 776
77689	ELECTRNIC COMPON PTS NES		3731493	MN 30049067	5175180		7481981		7117636	PIECES DU GROUPE 776
778	ELECTRICAL MACHINERY NES		1065330		1551923		1828397		1841992	AUTRES MACH ELECT NDA
7788	OTH ELEC MACHY,EQUIP NES		858170		1255131		1459773		1444069	AUT MACH APP ELEC NDA
77884	ELECTRICAL CONDENSERS		551641	MN 23216409	817607		997104		941024	CONDENSATEURS ELECTRIQUES
78	ROAD VEHICLES		1340618		1767772		2735671		3056623	VEHICULES ROUTIERS
781	PASS MOTOR VEH EXC BUSES	N 173308	770496	N 222879	1077289	N 310200	1674088		1698031	AUTO TRANSPORT PERSONNES
782	LORRIES,SPCL MTR VEH NES	N 19683	178626	N 24710	253066	N 41561	480140		670796	VEHICULES SPECIAUX,MARCH
7821	LORRIES,TRUCKS	N 18368	165894	N 23267	237742	N 39633	445693		637367	VEHICULES TRANSP MARCHAND
784	MOTOR VEH PRTS,ACCES NES	MN 101436	172382	MN 107670	230336	MN 128902	300950		380343	PIECES 722,781,782,783
7849	OTHER MOTOR VEHCL PARTS	MN 101433	157778	MN 107666	212234	MN 128897	259401		346426	PIECES 722,781,782,783
785	CYCLES,ETC MOTRZD OR NOT		164269	N 804293	147476		173199		153908	MOTOCYCLES SCOOTERS
79	OTHR TRANSPORT EQUIPMENT		2036613		3436668		3544180		2396725	AUTRE MATERIEL TRANSPORT
792	AIRCRAFT ETC		1698413		2061389		2523592		1396857	APP NAVIGATION AERIENNE
7924	AIRCRFT NES OVER 15000KG		1549885	N 36	1859635		2342515		1080481	AERODYNES PLUS 15000 KG
793	SHIPS AND BOATS ETC	N 15561	325381	N 32194	1328036	N 117840	906537		923754	NAVIRES BATEAUX,ETC
7932	SHIPS AND BOATS NES	N 1091	171551	N 4710	1033654	N 2717	613643		744876	NAVIRES ET BATEAUX
79322	TANKERS OF ALL KINDS	N 8	105213	N 17	410451		5147		120480	BATEAUX–CITERNES
79323	OTHER CARGO VESSELS	N 140	57963	N 1670	611477	N 710	595470		608592	AUT BATEAUX TRANS MARCH
7938	TUGS,SPECIAL VESSELS ETC	N 1764	150138	N 3546	291866	N 18307	278895		177559	REMORQUEURS,BATEAUX SPEC
79382	SPECL PURPOSE VESSLS ETC	N 83	144572	N 83	279011	N 85	270131		167426	BAT–PHARES,–POMPES,DRAGUES
8	MISC MANUFACTURED GOODS		2604026		3280473		3862408		3856207	ART MANUFACTURES DIVERS
87	PRECISION INSTRUMNTS NES		715450		938868		1216704		1182854	INSTRUM,APPAR SCIENT NDA
874	MEASURNG,CONTROLNG INSTR		609602		791535		1041625		988789	INSTRUMENTS DE MESURE
8742	MEASUR,DRAW ETC INST,PTS		229657	MN 24758	331400		457058		461963	INST DESSIN,TRACAGE,PCS
87421	MEASURNG,DRAWNG ETC INST		185361	N 149326	265733		350088		359715	INSTRUM DESSIN,TRACAGE
8748	ELEC MEAS,CONTRL EQU NES		120787		172393		235738		224658	APP ELEC ELECTRO MESURE
88	PHOTO EQU,OPTICL GDS ETC		587246		725766		824485		782932	APP,FOURN PHOTO,OP,MONTR
881	PHOTO APPARAT,EQUIPT NES		221530		288096		312819		280041	APP,EQUIP PHOTO NDA
8811	CAMERAS STILL,FLASH APP	MN 684615	203132	MN 640267	265329	MN 714606	287740		230080	APPAREILS PHOTO,PIECES
88119	PTS NES OF APPAR OF 8811	MN 683161	162259	MN 637282	209691	MN 706187	192017		148638	PIECES POUR 881.1
885	WATCHES AND CLOCKS		227678		276724		321101		306745	HORLOGERIE
89	MISC MANUFCTRD GOODS NES		1017824		1266208		1414583		1437603	ART MANUFACTURES DIVERS
893	ARTICLES OF PLASTIC NES		443737		573116		607487		575254	OUVRAGES EN MAT DIVIS 58
8939	MISC PLASTIC ARTICLES		338089	W 46924	436559		448871		430375	ART DIVERS EN MAT DIV 58
89399	OTHR PLASTC ARTICLES NES		328453	W 26259	424152		436846		419201	AUT OUV MAT DIV 58
898	MUSICAL INSTRUMENTS,PTS		195657		247098		285560		250537	INSTRUMENTS DE MUSIQUE
8983	SOUND RECRDNG TAPE,DISCS	MN 69668	174414	MN 115352	224712	MN 179149	264168		234445	SUPPORTS SON POUR 763
9	GOODS NOT CLASSD BY KIND		1639506		2321829		3807249		3726638	ART TRANSACT NON CLASSES
931	*SPECIAL TRANSACTIONS		650229		785041		1890740		1869150	TRANS.SPECIALES
971	*GOLD,NON MONETARY NES	K 81733	973492	K 121919	1515422	K 159855	1884679		1841107	OR NON MONETAIRE
97101	NONMON GLD UNWRT,SEMIMFD	K 81579	972111	K 121795	1514096	K 159806	1884090		1838482	OR,ALLIAGES D'OR BRUTS

5. General Exports F.O.B. by Commodities according to the S.I.T.C. (Rev. 2) in thousand U.S. Dollars
Exportations Générales F.O.B. par Produits d'après la C.T.C.I. (Rév. 2) en milliers de Dollars E.U.

SITC CTCI	COMMODITY	1993		1994		1995		1996		PRODUIT
		WEIGHT POIDS	VALUE VALEUR	WEIGHT POIDS	VALUE VALEUR	WEIGHT POIDS	VALUE VALEUR	WEIGHT POIDS	VALUE VALEUR	
	ALL COMMODITIES		47127195		58842665		73778170		78186076	TOUS PRODUITS
0	FOOD AND LIVE ANIMALS		1544283		1711157		1799351		1877314	ALIMENTS,ANIMAUX VIVANTS
001	*LIVE ANIMALS FOR FOOD	MN 51747	195003	MN 49083	207394	MN 48833	218921		243294	ANIMAUX VIVANTS
03	FISH AND PREPARATIONS		304073		323855		328876		320326	POISSONS ET PREPARATIONS
04	CEREALS AND PREPARATIONS		133645		183171		228052		233329	CEREALES ET PRODUITS
05	VEGETABLES AND FRUIT		215315		205157		198964		208130	LEGUMES ET FRUITS
07	COFFEE,TEA,COCOA,SPICES		298832		334567		310933		312002	CAFE,THE,CACAO,EPICES
072	COCOA	W 202767	242667	W 157989	251003	W 127707	225993		209799	CACAO
2	CRUDE MATERLS,EXCL FUELS		4241126		4367566		4737607		4230638	MAT BRUTES NON COMESTIBLES
23	RUBBER, CRUDE		834311		1125716		1618975		1404457	CAOUTCHOUC BRUT
232	NATURAL RUBBER,GUMS	W 937348	829981	W 1017725	1120518	W 1013456	1612910		1397906	LATEX CAOUTCHOUC NATUREL
23201	NATURAL RUBBER LATEX	W 120986	146617	W 120231	157837	W 109188	206257		210834	LATEX NATUREL
23202	OTHER NATURAL RUBBER	W 816356	683353	W 854854	920805	W 860451	1343719		1130856	CAOUTCHOUC NATUREL
24	CORK AND WOOD		3160091		2920887		2753292		2472052	LIEGE ET BOIS
247	OTH WOOD ROUGH,SQUARED	W 7069479	1137867	W 6417893	977048	W 5894434	907300		911411	BOIS BRUTS EQUARRIS
2472	SAW–,VENEER–LOGS NON–CON	W 7033337	1130830	W 6344009	961540	W 5828534	893415		897880	NON CONIFERES SCIAGE,PLAC
24721	— IN THE ROUGH	W 7033337	1130830	W 6344009	961540	W 5828534	893415		897880	BRUTS ECORCES DEGROSSIS
248	WOOD SHAPED,SLEEPERS		2011826		1934554		1833220		1543682	BOIS SIMPLEMENT TRAVAILLES
2483	LUMBER SHAPED NON–CONIFR		1954837		1882811		1784894		1512724	NON CONIFERES SCIES,RABOTES
24831	LUMBER SAWN ETC NON–CON	W 3807943	1741007	W 3309464	1642605	W 3085931	1552119		1291237	SCIES LONGITUDINALEMENT
24832	LUMBER PLANED ETC NONCON		213830		240206		232775		221487	RABOTES,RAINES,LANGUETES
3	MINERAL FUELS ETC		4848899		4336052		5159006		6201662	COMBUSTIBLES MINERAUX LUB
33	PETROLEUM AND PRODUCTS		3673366		3220830		3669809		4135991	PETROLE ET DERIVES
333	CRUDE PETROLEUM	MW 21589	3166122	MW 19371	2540772	MW 19247	2684578		3073676	HUILES BRUTES DE PETROLE
334	PETROLEUM PRODUCTS,REFIN	W 3433522	503070	W 4963823	670321	W 6557438	958300		1029345	PRODUITS RAFFINES
3341	GASOLINE,OTH LIGHT OILS	W 636253	105496	W 1534342	239771	W 2129448	355694		327157	ESSENCES POUR MOTEURS
33419	OTH LIGHT PETROLEUM OILS	W 636159	105474	W 1534325	239760	W 2128911	355589		326071	AUTRES HUILES LEGERES
3344	FUEL OILS,NES	W 1580998	169818	W 1938867	185158	W 2367317	239610		319362	FUEL OILS
341	*GAS,NATURAL AND MANUFCT	MW 9147	1174318	MW 9377	1113431	MW 11526	1486923		2065138	GAZ NATUREL,GAZ MANUFACT
3413	PETROLM GASES,LIQUEFIED	W 8096357	1070093	W 8114171	977875	MW 10257	1326166		1903649	GAZ DE PETROLE LIQUEFIE
34139	OTH HYDROCARBON GAS LQFD	W 7840708	1032068	W 8092963	974891	MW 9727	1223945		1772298	HYDROCARBURES GAZEUX NDA
4	ANIMAL,VEGETABLE OIL,FAT		2815382		4008358		5038836		4661088	HUILES,GRAISSES ANIM,VEG
42	FIXED VEGETABLE OIL,FAT		2269230		3178239		3947388		3702398	HUILES VEGETALES FIXES
424	FIXED VEG OIL NONSOFT		2227292		3106184		3833641		3603151	AUTRES HUILES VEG FIXES
4242	PALM OIL	W 5105852	2001137	W 5665842	2844429	W 5495599	3588661		3299496	HUILE DE PALME
4244	PALM KERNEL OIL	W 484104	192457	W 375803	211482	W 299330	194806		265142	HUILE DE PALMISTE
431	*PROCESD ANML VEG OIL,ET		546067		829929		1091281		950766	HUILES,GRAISSES PREPAREES
4312	HYDROGENATED OIL,FAT		338361	W 130	468722		598168		535544	HUILES HYDROGENEES
4313	FATTY ACIDS ETC,RESIDUES	W 582745	207507	W 676605	360470	W 766810	492395		413060	ACIDES GRAS INDUST,RESIDUS
43131	FATTY ACIDS,ACID OILS	W 563365	203129	W 650908	356483	W 748058	488404		407028	ACIDES GRAS INDUSTRIELS
5	CHEMCLS,RELATED PROD NES		1002987		1536141		2210538		2464088	PRODUITS CHIMIQUES
51	ORGANIC CHEMICALS		276321		438510		493609		534608	PROD CHIMIQ ORGANIQUES
512	ALCOHOLS,PHENOLS ETC		171181		286045		303388		272013	PHENOLS,PHENOLS–ALCOOLS
5121	ACYCLIC ALCOHOLS,DERIVS		168071		282678		291105		265290	ALCOOLS ACYCLIQUES
55	PERFUME,CLEANING ETC PRD		152045		177208		193431		207516	PROD POUR PARFUM,TOILETTE
58	PLASTIC MATERIALS ETC		208269		306422		545260		592763	MAT PLAST ARTIFICIELLES
583	POLYMERIZATION ETC PRODS		178587	W 220361	258980		449369		478923	PROD POLYMERISATION
59	CHEMICAL MATERIALS NES		118918		309092		602756		717030	MAT PROD CHIMIQUES NDA
598	MISCEL CHEM PRODUCTS NES		80248		254788		527277		622806	PROD DIV INDUST CHIM NDA
5989	CHEM PRODUCTS,PREPS NES		71485		241693		505487		602248	PROD PREP CHIMIQUES NDA
59899	OTH CHEM PRODS,PREPS,NES		53196		215599		475330		570305	AUT PRODUITS CHIMIQUES NDA
6	BASIC MANUFACTURES		4543168		5370033		6574694		7343847	ART MANUFACTURES
62	RUBBER MANUFACTURES NES		311342		346662		399257		407157	CAOUTCHOUC MANUFACTURE
621	MATERIALS OF RUBBER		163075		192823		217926		207417	PRODUITS EN CAOUTCHOUC
63	WOOD,CORK MANUFACTRS NES		1537369		1766219		1904312		2331582	OUVRAGES LIEGE ET BOIS
634	VENEERS,PLYWOOD,ETC		1364293		1563071		1687298		2086946	PLACAGES,CONTRE–PLAQUES
6341	VENEER SHEETS ETC	V 772953	298357	V 621999	257290	V 589983	230752		251408	BOIS SIMPLEMENT SCIES
6342	PLYWOOD OF WOOD SHEETS	V 2475213	1055479	V 3114019	1295616	V 3562097	1438616		1805485	BOIS CONTRE–PLAQUES
635	WOOD MANUFACTURES NES		173005		203045		216942		244596	ART MANUF EN BOIS NDA
64	PAPER,PAPERBOARD AND MFR		226008		288462		364028		353522	PAPIERS,CARTONS & OUVRAGES
65	TEXTILE YARN,FABRICS,ETC		698159		868870		1174678		1358064	FILS,TISSUS,ARTICLES TEXTILE
651	TEXTILE YARN		224906		302949		538528		688625	FILS TEXTILES
6514	SYN FIB YRN,BULK,MONOFIL	W 53695	90027	W 76499	136760	W 121392	268082		373361	FILS CONT 85% FIB TEXT SYNTH
65144	— TEXTRD,CONT POLYESTER	W 52155	84534	W 74329	130018	W 116689	255650		285556	FILS TEX FI CONT POLYESTERS
653	WOVN MAN–MADE FIB FABRIC		179568	A 149704	238232		265260		306896	TISSUS FIBRES SYNTH,ARTIF
66	NONMETAL MINERAL MFS NES		406313		547336		660292		646317	ART MIN NON METALLIQUES
663	MINERAL MANUFCTURES NES		115941		171893		230885		209562	ART MIN MANUF NDA
67	IRON AND STEEL		465454		419595		498041		598396	FER ET ACIER
678	IRON,STL TUBES,PIPES,ETC	W 356384	146043	W 189549	113935	W 156103	127998		211722	TUBES,TUYAUX EN FONTE,FER
68	NON–FERROUS METALS		448211		565858		783136		772185	METAUX NON FERREUX
682	COPPER EXC CEMENT COPPER	W 49366	176530	W 67567	224738	W 99402	359334		369714	CUIVRE
6822	COPPER,ALLOYS WORKED	W 49252	176170	W 67434	224527	W 97437	354008		369326	CUIVRE,ALLIAGES OUVRES
687	TIN	W 39386	198527	W 41160	204440	W 39224	231791		232793	ETAIN
6871	TIN,ALLOYS UNWROUGHT	W 36906	194651	W 38935	199864	W 37567	225248		221864	ETAIN ET ALLIAGES BRUTS
69	METAL MANUFACTURES NES		438611		550757		738980		796878	ART MANUFACT EN METAL NDA
699	BASE METAL MFRS NES		194774		252103		313954		371434	ART MANUFACTURES MET NDA
7	MACHINES,TRANSPORT EQUIP		22854440		31420523		40673132		43251531	MACHINES MATERIEL TRANSPORT
71	POWER GENERATING EQUIPMT		466617		549047		654980		789767	MACHINES GENERATRICES
713	INTRNL COMBUS PSTN ENGIN		160237		176745		137133		283791	MOTEURS EXPL COMB INT, PIECE
7131	AIRCRAFT PSTN ENGINS,PTS		146827		165558		118963		257942	MOTEURS EXPL P.AVIATION, PIE
716	ROTATING ELECTRIC PLANT		268793		332295		489429		458393	APP ELECTR ROTATIFS,PIECES
7162	AC MTRS,GENRTRS,GEN SETS	MN 160491	221796	MN 175056	293725	MN 245668	441482		418292	MOTEURS ELECTRIQUES
71621	AC MTRS,INC UNIVRSL MTRS	MN 160490	219497	MN 175053	289550	MN 245497	434296		410391	MOT ELEC NON COUR CONTINU
72	MACHS FOR SPCL INDUSTRYS		262444		285214		421027		564333	MAC SPECIALES POUR INDUST
728	OTH MACHY FOR SPCL INDUS		114357		129146		211511		301001	AUT MACH IND PARTICULIERES
7284	MACHY FOR SPCL INDUS NES		90248		101662		173504		235720	MACH SPEC IND PARTICUL.
74	GENRL INDUSTRL MACHY NES		953293		1264442		1648544		1507440	MACH APP INDUSTRIE
741	HEATING,COOLING EQUIPMNT		655788		821799		1061651		915665	MACH CHAUFFAGE,PIECES
7415	AIR–CONDITIONING MACHNRY		622567	N 2894554	785501		998784		818663	GROUPES CONDITION AIR
743	PUMPS NES,CENTRFUGES ETC		117033		189578		242505		219574	POMPES COMPRES,VENT ETC
75	OFFICE MACHNES,ADP EQUIP		3316413		5031961		7180506		9036303	MACH BUREAU TRAIT AUTOM
751	OFFICE MACHINES	MN 29197	208911	MN 22196	207477	MN 21022	227583		205915	MACH,APPAREILS DE BUREAU
7512	CALCULATNG,ACCTG,ETC MCH	MN 29158	194692	MN 22050	188289	MN 20487	189022		160524	MACHINE A CALCULER ETC
75121	CALCULATING MACHINES	MN 28945	177405	MN 21803	161538	MN 20148	153409		127075	MACHINES A CALCULER
752	AUTOMTIC DATA PROC EQUIP	N 1437007	448399	N 1012949	1181512	N 3813768	2185115		4112738	MACH TRAIT INFORMATION
7524	DIGITL CENTRL STOR UNITS	N 169	656	N 55489	60540	N 3641605	431525		1671772	UNITES MEMOIRE CENTRALES
7525	ADP PERIPHERAL UNITS	N 120892	112802	N 490530	935870	N 1723736	1473971		1502331	UNITES PERIPHERIQUES
7528	OFF–LINE DATA PROC EQUIP	N 1315015	331257	N 412467	97786	N 664169	175029		609171	MACH AUXIL TRAIT INFORM
759	OFFICE,ADP MCH PTS,ACCES		2659104		3642971		4767808		4717651	PIECES DU 751 ET 752
7599	ACCTG,ETC,ADP MCH PTS,AC		2615524		3540800		4690707		4653567	PIECES DU 751 ET 752
76	TELECOMM,SOUND EQUIPMENT		7112928		10046703		12300609		11888381	EQUIPMENT DE TELECOM

5. General Exports F.O.B. by Commodities according to the S.I.T.C. (Rev. 2) in thousand U.S. Dollars
Exportations Générales F.O.B. par Produits d'après la C.T.C.I. (Rév. 2) en milliers de Dollars E.U.

SITC CTCI	COMMODITY	1993 WEIGHT POIDS	1993 VALUE VALEUR	1994 WEIGHT POIDS	1994 VALUE VALEUR	1995 WEIGHT POIDS	1995 VALUE VALEUR	1996 WEIGHT POIDS	1996 VALUE VALEUR	PRODUIT
761	TELEVISION RECEIVERS	N 7742739	1236145	MN 19402	1731687	MN 24650	2239138		2084265	RECEPTEURS DE TELEVISION
7611	COLOUR TV RECEIVERS	N 7332613	1216793	MN 18050	1716688	MN 24132	2227879		2074772	RECEPTEURS COULEUR
762	RADIO BROADCAST RECEIVRS	MN 42787	2090076	MN 70052	2840355	MN 86882	3485092		3066784	RECEPTEURS RADIODIFFUSION
7621	MTR VEHC RADIO RECEIVERS	N 4467556	358851	N 6709822	443803	MN 13244	508816		452495	RECEPTEURS RADIO AUTO
7622	PORTABLE RADIO RECEIVERS	MN 24606	933072	MN 37469	1246416	MN 39203	1589167		1165187	RECEPT PORTATIFS RADIO
7628	OTHER RADIO RECEIVERS	MN 13713	798152	MN 25873	1150135	MN 34435	1387108		1449102	AUTRES RECEPT RADIO
763	SOUND RECORDRS,PHONOGRPH	MN 23889	1574579	MN 48555	2298889	MN 38109	2792018		2775171	PHONO,APP ENREGISTREMENT
7631	ELECTRIC GRAMOPHONES ETC	N 3312695	162253	N 6571098	290503	N 7957406	474618		371946	ELECTROPHON,TOURNE–DISQ
76318	OTH ELEC GRAMOPHONES ETC	N 3291318	160704	N 6474958	281352	N 7790267	463469		362041	AUT ELECTRO,TOURNE–DISQ
7638	OTHR SOUND APPARATUS ETC	MN 20576	1412326	MN 41984	2008386	MN 30151	2317399		2403225	AUT APP D'ENREGIS,REPROD
76381	TV IMAGE,SND RECRDRS ETC	N 6285492	1027446	MN 14936	1407775	MN 15761	1646247		1714460	APP ENREG,REPRO IMAG,SON
76388	DICTATING MACHINES ETC	MN 14290	384880	MN 27048	600611	MN 14391	671152		688764	MACHINES A DICTER
764	TELECOM EQPT,PTS,ACC NES		2212128		3175772		3784363		3962162	EQUIP TELECOM,PIECES
7641	LINE TELEPHONE,ETC EQUIP	MN 24355	505385	MN 39229	748755	MN 43231	875799		948522	APP TELEPHON PAR FIL
7642	MICROPH,LOUDSPKR,AMPLIFR	MN 58346	177922	MN 137130	270231	MN 125780	303818		322249	MICRO,HAUT–PARLEUR,AMPLI
7643	TV,RADIO TRANSMITTRS ETC	N 2367726	196031	N 6762902	180230	N 2974116	142555		123416	APP EMET TELE RADIO
7649	PTS NES OF EQUIPMT OF 76		1237210		1868701		2329096		2350334	PIECES DE LA DIV 76
76491	PTS NES OF APPAR OF 7641		90244		167775		180855		260723	PIECES POUR 764.1
76493	TELECOMM EQUIPMT PTS NES		645432		870940		1107058		1150736	PIECES 761,762,764.3,8
76499	PARTS ETC OF SOUND EQUIP		472399		784986		1000451		895193	PIECES NDA POUR 763
77	ELECTRIC MACHNRY NES ETC		9270627		11948236		16287060		17561106	MACH APP ELECT NDA
771	ELECTRIC POWER MACHY NES		455155		508882		538827		530228	MACH PROD,TRANS ELECTR
7711	TRANSFORMERS,ELECTRICAL		190957		208258		217916		210655	TRANSFO ELECTRIQUES
77118	OTHER ELEC TRANSFORMERS		190662		207209		216669		209053	AUTRES TRANSFO ELECTRIQ
7712	OTH ELEC POWER MACHY NES		264198		300623		320911		319573	AUT APP PROD TRANSF ELEC
77122	INDUCTORS	MN 511010	154557	MN 518691	155510	MN 690039	156238		77805	BOBINES REACTANCE,SELFS
772	SWITCHGEAR ETC,PARTS NES		771302		887567		1201008		1585132	APP COUPURE,SECT ETC
7721	SWITCHGEAR ETC		362077	N 282248	445786		477961		558080	APP COUPURE,SECTIONMNT
7722	PRINTED CIRCUITS,PTS NES		305593		292703		559756		870818	CIRCUITS ET PIECES
773	ELECTR DISTRIBUTNG EQUIP		211427		271677		351891		424468	EQUIPMT DISTRIBUTION ELECT
7731	INSULATED WIRE,CABLE ETC	W 38304	202773	W 83567	255430	W 73013	328825		350820	FILS,CABLES ISOLES ELECT
775	HOUSEHOLD TYPE EQUIP NES		174734		198810		236717		267451	MACH,APP USAGE DOMESTQUE
776	TRANSISTORS,VALVES,ETC		7289254	MN 39561757	9512071		13240029		14009625	LAMPES,TUBES,VALVES
7761	TV PICTURE TUBES	N 5280088	320423	MN 413656	465334	MN 13928	677182		818457	TUBES CATHODIQUES
7762	OTH ELECTRONIC TUBES ETC	N 682924	53289	N 5430910	235791	MN 15937	398225		613917	AUT LAMPES ELECTRONIQUES
7763	DIODES,TRANSISTORS,ETC	MN 19567227	1056124	MN 22034936	1311388	MN 26105842	1630564		1647437	DIODES,TRANSISTORS
7764	ELECTRONIC MICROCIRCUITS	MN 9231615	5262097	MN 10567871	6893064	MN 12443281	9845590		10064020	MICROSTRUCTURES ELECTRON
7768	ELCTRNC COMP PTS,CRYSTLS		597321	MN 6539863	606494		688468		865794	CRIST PIEZO–ELEC,PCS 776
77689	ELECTRNIC COMPON PTS NES		525527	MN 6126266	506037		553450		747932	PIECES DU GROUPE 776
778	ELECTRICAL MACHINERY NES		366432		566840		712979		736796	AUTRES MACH ELECT NDA
7788	OTH ELEC MACHY,EQUIP NES		288196		451064		566335		558996	AUT MACH APP ELEC NDA
77884	ELECTRICAL CONDENSERS		124821	MN 10925491	184103		243923		296422	CONDENSATEURS ELECTRIQUES
78	ROAD VEHICLES		381639		387509		466253		519140	VEHICULES ROUTIERS
781	PASS MOTOR VEH EXC BUSES	N 20438	157884	N 15299	123711	N 21002	168643		190135	AUTO TRANSPORT PERSONNES
79	OTHR TRANSPORT EQUIPMENT		1044202		1842192		1626510		1286873	AUTRE MATERIEL TRANSPORT
792	AIRCRAFT ETC		873082		1558683		1287225		932432	APP NAVIGATION AERIENNE
7924	AIRCRFT NES OVER 15000KG	N 35	709604	N 33	1445460	N 41	1164015		731919	AERODYNES PLUS 15000 KG
7929	AIRCRAFT PARTS NES		157953		103974		99660		194694	PIECES DU 792
793	SHIPS AND BOATS ETC	N 5744	170226	N 18444	282846	N 39385	338548		350829	NAVIRES BATEAUX,ETC
7938	TUGS,SPECIAL VESSELS ETC	N 3370	141755	N 7408	231632	N 22601	302627		340114	REMORQUEURS,BATEAUX SPEC
79382	SPECL PURPOSE VESSLS ETC	N 403	137924	N 262	224832	N 442	299276		336903	BAT–PHARES,–POMPES,DRAGUES
8	MISC MANUFACTURED GOODS		4884937		5589831		6455327		7068630	ART MANUFACTURES DIVERS
821	*FURNITURE,PARTS THEREOF		566264		768572		915980		1119490	MEUBLES ET PIECES
8211	CHAIRS,SEATS AND PARTS	MN 17725	118053	MN 22283	165546	MN 19911	196066		256727	SIEGES ET PIECES
82111	CHAIRS AND OTHER SEATS	N 4576181	109500	N 6643656	155053	N 7359515	184526		239744	SIEGES
8219	FURNITURE AND PARTS NES		432133		585842		703203		840817	AUTRES MEUBLES ET PIECES
82192	WOOD FURNITURE NES		297351		431971		528112		647437	MEUBLES NDA EN BOIS
84	CLOTHING AND ACCESSORIES		1959048		2076066		2269944		2378769	VETEMENTS
842	MENS OUTERWEAR NOT KNIT		183927	MN 23782	197487		199112		196699	VET DESSUS POUR HOMMES
843	WOMENS OUTERWEAR NONKNIT		216719	MN 28477	221255		204443		185639	VET DESSUS FEMMES MAT TEX
844	UNDER GARMENTS NOT KNIT		195891	MN 49563	214282		212645		185517	VETEMENT DESSOUS MAT TEX
8441	— MENS SHIRTS		178011	MN 41171	192693		190549		162292	CHEMISES HOMMES MAT TEXT
84411	—— OF COTTON	MN 21415	158267	MN 21556	152678	MN 18933	151225		146417	CHEMISES HOMMES DE COTON
845	OUTERWEAR KNIT NONELASTC		407832	MN 66190	397974		393584		390590	VET DESSOUS,ACCES BONNET
8459	— OTHER,CLTHG ACCESRYS		274090	MN 34906	255812		270112		257663	AUT VET DESSUS DE BONNE
846	UNDER GARMENTS KNITTED		224502		243026		249235		281864	SOUS VETS DE BONNETERIE
8462	— OF COTTON NON ELASTIC		172364	MN 76059	115567	MN 58932	128940		127503	SOUS–VET BONNET COTON
848	HEADGEAR,NONTXTL CLOTHNG		688104		755003		953579		1070610	VET ACCES MAT AUT QUE TEX
8482	PLASTC,RUBBR CLTHG,ACCES		654484		724436		924562		1042180	VET ACCES MAT PLAS ARTIF
84822	RUBBER CLOTHING,ACCESRYS	MN 13471601	654098	MN 16055069	724051	MN 18317515	924068		1041203	VET ACCES CAOUT VULCAN
87	PRECISION INSTRUMNTS NES		314280		371177		426444		507752	INSTRUM,APPAR SCIENT NDA
874	MEASURNG,CONTROLNG INSTR		141122		169354		205238		276443	INSTRUMENTS DE MESURE
88	PHOTO EQU,OPTICL GDS ETC		456781		591147		723659		732222	APP,FOURN PHOTO,OP,MONTR
881	PHOTO APPARAT,EQUIPT NES		268083		314707		426590		410848	APP,EQUIP PHOTO NDA
8811	CAMERAS STILL,FLASH APP	MN 68007	265761	MN 66045	311971	MN 112755	423942		398225	APPAREILS PHOTO,PIECES
88111	STILL CAMERAS	N 4957172	222853	N 4783701	272783	N 7251103	357478		332238	APPAREILS PHOTOGRAPHIQ
885	WATCHES AND CLOCKS		139679		225264		242340		244521	HORLOGERIE
89	MISC MANUFCTRD GOODS NES		1397114		1581361		1904988		2101628	ART MANUFACTURES DIVERS
893	ARTICLES OF PLASTIC NES		274645		335643		461903		469663	OUVRAGES EN MAT DIVIS 58
8931	PLSTC PACKG CONTNRS,LIDS	W 82400	130375	W 108637	163647	W 197047	227654		237801	ART TRANSP EMBALLAGE ETC
8939	MISC PLASTIC ARTICLES		137727	W 25452	165299		229052		226074	ART DIVERS EN MAT DIV 58
894	TOYS,SPORTING GOODS,ETC		359745		364618		436080		554853	VOITURES ENFANTS,JOUETS
8942	TOYS,INDOOR GAMES ETC		307656		302439		337125		444136	JOUETS,JEUX ETC
897	GOLD,SILVER WARE,JEWELRY		465281		461221		475808		438062	BIJOUTERIE,ORFEVRERIE
8973	PREC JEWLRY,GLD–SILVWARE		463787		458634		470220		421532	BIJOUX OR,ARGENT ORFEVRE
89731	PRECIOUS METAL JEWELLERY		460440		456008		466466		419464	ART BIJOUTERIE,JOAILLER
898	MUSICAL INSTRUMENTS,PTS		117441		208345		305957		392506	INSTRUMENTS DE MUSIQUE
8983	SOUND RECRDNG TAPE,DISCS	MN 176015	107789	MN 539192	203044	MN 278451	287412		369373	SUPPORTS SON POUR 763
89831	PREPD SND RECORDNG MEDIA	MN 160125	97371	MN 419423	162359	MN 236769	203867		320994	SUPPORTS PREPARES
9	GOODS NOT CLASSD BY KIND		321158		422540		971060		857916	ART TRANSACT NON CLASSES
931	*SPECIAL TRANSACTIONS		294975		391367		923907		819150	TRANS.SPECIALES

FOOT NOTES – NOTES

TABLE 3 –
1 Data for Singapore include value of commodities imported or exported via Singapore for which the country of production or of consumption is not known.

TABLEAU 3 –

1 Les données pour Singapour comprennent aussi les valeurs des produits importés ou exportés via Singapour pour lesquels le pays d'origine ou de consommation n'est pas connu.

1. HISTORICAL SERIES, 1988–1996 GENERAL TRADE, IMPORTS C.I.F., EXPORTS F.O.B.
SERIES HISTORIQUES, 1988–1996 COMMERCE GENERAL, IMPORTATIONS C.A.F., EXPORTATIONS F.O.B

YEAR ANNEE	VALUE IN MILLION U.S. DOLLARS VALEUR EN MILLION U.S. DOLLARS MERCHANDISE –MARCHANDISE IMPORTS	EXPORTS	GOLD –OR IMPORTS	EXPORTS	CONVERSION FACTORS U.S. CENTS PER RUFIYAA FACTEURS DE CONVERSION CENTS E.U. PAR RUFIYAA IMPORTS	EXPORTS	INDEX NUMBERS –INDICES QUANTUM IMPORTS	EXPORTS	UNIT VALUE VALEUR UNITAIRE IMPORTS	EXPORTS
1988	90.10	40.20								
1989	112.60	44.70								
1990	137.80	52.10								
1991	161.20	53.70								
1992	189.30	40.00								
1993	185.10	34.60								
1994	221.60	45.90								
1995	267.90	49.50								
1996	301.80	59.30								

2. IMPORTS BY BROAD ECONOMIC CATEGORY AND EXPORTS BY INDUSTRIAL ORIGIN. (PERCENTAGE OF TOTAL VALUE)
IMPORTATIONS PAR CATEGORIES ECONOMIQUES ET EXPORTATIONS PAR BRANCHE D'ACTIVITE.(EN POURCENTAGE DE LA VALEUR TOTALE)

IMPORTS – IMPORTATIONS

	1990	1991	1992	1993	1994	1995	1996
TOTAL IMPORTS–IMPORTATIONS TOTALES							
1 FOOD BEV–ALIMENTATION BOISSONS							
11 PRIMARY–PRODUITS DE BASE							
111 FOR INDUSTRY–POUR L'INDUSTRIE							
112 FOR HOUSEHOLDS–POUR LES MENAGES							
12 PROCESSED–PRODUITS ELABORES							
121 FOR INDUSTRY–POUR L'INDUSTRIE							
122 FOR HOUSEHOLDS–POUR LES MENAGES							
2 IND SUPPLIES–APPROV INDUSTRIELS							
21 PRIMARY–PRODUITS DE BASE							
22 PROCESSED–PRODUITS ELABORES							
3 FUELS–COMBUSTIBLES							
31 PRIMARY–PRODUITS DE BASE							
32 PROCESSED–PRODUITS ELABORES							
321 MOTOR SPIRIT–ESSENCE							
322 OTHER–AUTRES							
4 MACHINERY–EQUIPEMENT							
41 CAPITAL EQUIPMENT–MACHINES							
42 PARTS–PIECES ACCESSOIRES							
5 TRANSPORT–TRANSPORT							
51 PASSENGER CARS–AUTOMOBILES							
52 OTHER–AUTRES							
521 INDUSTRIAL–INDUSTRIELS							
522 NON INDUSTRIAL–NON INDUSTRIEL							
53 PARTS–PIECES ACCESSOIRES							
6 CONSUM GOODS–BIENS CONSOMMATION							
61 DURABLE–DURABLES							
62 SEMI DURABLE–SEMI DURABLES							
63 NON DURABLE–NON DURABLES							
7 GOODS NES–BIENS NDA							

EXPORTS – EXPORTATIONS

	1990	1991	1992	1993	1994	1995	1996
TOTAL EXPORTS–EXPORTATIONS TOTALES							
1 AGRICULTURE							
2 MINING QUARRY–INDUS EXTRACTIVES							
3 MANUFACTURING–IND MANUFACTUR							
31 FOOD BEV TOBACCO–ALIM BOISS TAB							
32 TEXTILES–INDUSTRIES TEXTILES							
33 WOOD & PRODUCTS–BOIS & PRODUITS							
34 PAPER & PRODUCTS–PAPIER & PRODT							
35 CHEMICALS–INDUSTRIES CHIMIQUES							
36 NON METAL MIN–MIN NON METAL							
37 BASIC METAL–IND METAL BASE							
38 METAL MANUF–MANUF METAL							
39 OTH MANUF IND–AUTRES MANUF							

3. TRADE BY PRINCIPAL COUNTRIES OF CONSIGNMENT AND LAST DESTINATION(VALUE IN THOUSAND U.S. DOLLARS)
ECHANGES SELON LES PRINCIPAUX PAYS DE CONSIGNATION ET DE DESTINATION FINALE (VALEUR EN MILLIERS DE DOLLARS EU)

COUNTRIES–PAYS	GENERAL IMPORTS C.I.F. IMPORTATIONS GENERALES C.A.F				
	1990	1991	1992	1993	1994
World		161303	189373	191358	222000
Africa		45	63	5	
Americas		1428	1882	1936	
Northern America		1249	1870	1929	
LAIA		26	1	4	
CACM					
Caribbean			2	0	
Rest of America		153	9	3	
As.ex F.USSR		141641	170113	171144	24000
Eur.x F.USSR		16526	15379	16596	
EU		15495	14561	15094	
EFTA		957	524	760	
East Europe		74	294	742	
Other Europe					
Former USSR		1	3	1	
Oceania		1185	1629	1349	
Singapore/Singapour		91981	110132	99073	
India/Inde		12478	13883	16403	
Sri Lanka		12295	12344	12803	
United Arab Emirates		3194	3857	12512	13000
United Kingdom		9295	7300	5669	
Japan/Japon		6523	7247	7434	
Malaysia/Malaisie		2434	4713	4329	6000
Thailand/Thaïlande		4531	6235	6320	
Hong Kong		3574	5194	5627	
Germany/Allemagne		2812	3467	3820	
Indonesia/Indonésie		276	1878	2440	3000
Myanmar		2663	2151	2615	
USA/Etats–Unis d'Amer		1220	1867	1886	
Netherlands/Pays–Bas		894	1237	2539	
Australia/Australie		1034	1569	1122	
Pakistan		589	1244	761	1000
Italy/Italie		906	814	570	
China/Chine		553	600	479	
Switz.Liecht		542	455	626	
Belgium–Luxembourg		543	320	606	
Denmark/Danemark		458	317	664	
Oman		0	82	31	1000
Bulgaria/Bulgarie		74	267	741	
Sweden/Suède		172	388	514	
France,Monac		210	345	486	
Korea, Republic of		458	88	222	
Norway,SVD,JM		415	69	134	
Finland/Finlande			251	188	
New Zealand		151	60	228	
Bangladesh		0	359	4	
Austria/Autriche		138	34	12	
Panama		153	9	3	
Canada		29	3	43	
Ireland/Irlande		24	28	1	
Turkey/Turquie		6		0	

COUNTRIES–PAYS	GENERAL EXPORTS F.O.B. EXPORTATIONS GENERALES F.O.B.				
	1990	1991	1992	1993	1994
Monde		53090	39727	34444	
Afrique				774	
Amériques		13179	5516	4010	
Amérique du Nord		13179	5516	4010	
ALAI					
MCAC					
Caraïbes					
Autre Amérique					
Asie l'URSS exclus		21741	16773	18783	
Europe l'URSS exclus		18152	17420	10823	
UE		18152	17388	10772	
AELE		0	32	50	
Europe de l'Est					
Autre de l'Europe					
Ancienne URSS					
Océanie		18		54	
United Kingdom		13198	11653	8423	
Sri Lanka		10140	10281	10439	
USA/Etats–Unis d'Amer		12253	5465	3902	
Thailand/Thaïlande		5795	2568	4788	
Germany/Allemagne		3477	4931	2024	
Singapore/Singapour		2726	2132	1222	
Japan/Japon		2075	1340	1426	
Hong Kong		973	405	354	
Netherlands/Pays–Bas		1115	348	152	
Canada		926	51	107	
Tunisia/Tunisie				774	
Turkey/Turquie				440	
Ireland/Irlande		107	186	46	
Italy/Italie		22	207	11	
France,Monac		81	29	72	
India/Inde		27	47	75	
Denmark/Danemark		134	1		
Switz.Liecht		0	32	50	
Australia/Australie		7		54	
Belgium–Luxembourg		14	22	17	
United Arab Emirates				39	
Austria/Autriche		3		26	
New Zealand		7			
Korea, Republic of		1			
Pakistan		1			
Finland/Finlande		0			
Sweden/Suède		0			

(VALUE AS PERCENTAGE OF WORLD TOTAL)(VALEURS EN POURCENTAGE DU TOTAL MONDIAL)

	1985	1986	1987	1988	1989	1990	1991	1992	1993	1994
Africa							0.0	0.0	0.0	
Americas							0.9	1.0	1.0	
Northern America							0.8	1.0	1.0	
LAIA							0.0	0.0	0.0	
CACM										
Caribbean								0.0	0.0	
Rest of America							0.1	0.0	0.0	
As.ex F.USSR							87.8	89.8	89.4	10.8
Eur.x F.USSR							10.2	8.1	8.7	
EU							9.6	7.7	7.9	
EFTA							0.6	0.3	0.4	
East Europe							0.0	0.2	0.4	
Other Europe										
Former USSR							0.0	0.0	0.0	
Oceania							0.7	0.9	0.7	
Singapore/Singapour							57.0	58.2	51.8	
India/Inde							7.7	7.3	8.6	
Sri Lanka							7.6	6.5	6.7	
United Arab Emirates							2.0	2.0	6.5	5.9
United Kingdom							5.8	3.9	3.0	
Japan/Japon							4.0	3.8	3.9	
Malaysia/Malaisie							1.5	2.5	2.3	2.7
Thailand/Thaïlande							2.8	3.3	3.3	
Hong Kong							2.2	2.7	2.9	
Germany/Allemagne							1.7	1.8	2.0	

	1985	1986	1987	1988	1989	1990	1991	1992	1993	1994
Afrique									2.2	
Amériques					21.2		24.8	13.9	11.6	
Amérique du Nord					21.2		24.8	13.9	11.6	
ALAI										
MCAC										
Caraïbes										
Autre Amérique										
Asie l'URSS exclus					52.3		41.0	42.2	54.5	
Europe l'URSS exclus					26.3		34.2	43.8	31.4	
UE					25.5		34.2	43.8	31.3	
AELE					0.9		0.0	0.1	0.1	
Europe de l'Est										
Autre de l'Europe										
Ancienne URSS										
Océanie					0.0		0.0		0.2	
United Kingdom					18.5		24.9	29.3	24.5	
Sri Lanka					13.0		19.1	25.9	30.3	
USA/Etats–Unis d'Amer					19.7		23.1	13.8	11.3	
Thailand/Thaïlande					30.1		10.9	6.5	13.9	
Germany/Allemagne					6.7		6.5	12.4	5.9	
Singapore/Singapour					3.6		5.1	5.4	3.5	
Japan/Japon					2.3		3.9	3.4	4.1	
Hong Kong					2.0		1.8	1.0	1.0	
Netherlands/Pays–Bas					0.2		2.1	0.9	0.4	
Canada					1.5		1.7	0.1	0.3	

4. General Imports C.I.F. by Commodities according to the S.I.T.C. (Rev. 2) in thousand U.S. Dollars
Importations Générales C.A.F. par Produits d'après la C.T.C.I. (Rév. 2) en milliers de Dollars E.U.

SITC CTCI	COMMODITY	1988 WEIGHT POIDS	1988 VALUE VALEUR	1989 WEIGHT POIDS	1989 VALUE VALEUR	1990 WEIGHT POIDS	1990 VALUE VALEUR	1991 WEIGHT POIDS	1991 VALUE VALEUR	PRODUIT
	ALL COMMODITIES								161303	TOUS PRODUITS
0	FOOD AND LIVE ANIMALS								31192	ALIMENTS,ANIMAUX VIVANTS
01	MEAT AND PREPARATIONS								3792	VIANDES ET PREPARATIONS
011	MEAT FRESH,CHILLD,FROZEN								3648	VIANDES FRAICHES,REF,CONGE
02	DAIRY PRODCTS,BIRDS'EGGS								5240	PRODUITS LAITIERS,OEUFS
04	CEREALS AND PREPARATIONS								7596	CEREALES ET PRODUITS
0481	PREPD BREAKFAST FOOD ETC								2747	CEREALES TRAVAILLEES
0482	MALT INCLUDING FLOUR								2100	MALT MEME TORREFIE
0488	OTH CEREAL PREPS,MALT EX								2749	EXTRAITS DE MALT
05	VEGETABLES AND FRUIT								8478	LEGUMES ET FRUITS
0548	EDIBLE VEG NES FRESH,DRY								4178	RACINES,TUBERCULES
057	FRUIT,NUTS,FRESH,DRIED								2496	FRUITS FRAIS OU SECS
06	SUGAR AND PREPS,HONEY								3384	SUCRES ET PRODUITS
07	COFFEE,TEA,COCOA,SPICES								1332	CAFE,THE,CACAO,EPICES
09	MISC EDIBLE PRODUCTS								954	PREP ALIMENTAIRES DIVERSES
098	EDIBLE PRODCTS,PREPS NES								954	PREP ALIMENTAIRES NDA
11	BEVERAGES								3850	BOISSONS
12	TOBACCO AND MANUFACTURES								4377	TABACS BRUTS FABRIQUES
2	CRUDE MATERLS,EXCL FUELS								19575	MAT BRUTES NON COMESTIBLES
24	CORK AND WOOD								4956	LIEGE ET BOIS
245	FUEL WOOD NES, CHARCOAL								4897	BOIS DE CHAUFFAGE
26	TEXTILE FIBRES AND WASTE								9504	FIBRES TEXTILES
263	COTTON								7835	COTON
266	SYNTHETIC FIBRES TO SPIN								1565	FIBRES SYNTHETIQUES
27	CRUDE FERTLZR,MINRLS NES								4932	ENGRAIS MINERAUX BRUTS
3	MINERAL FUELS ETC								23512	COMBUSTIBLES MINERAUX LUB
33	PETROLEUM AND PRODUCTS								23512	PETROLE ET DERIVES
334	PETROLEUM PRODUCTS,REFIN								23512	PRODUITS RAFFINES
4	ANIMAL,VEGETABLE OIL,FAT								1863	HUILES,GRAISSES ANIM,VEG
5	CHEMCLS,RELATED PROD NES								8690	PRODUITS CHIMIQUES
53	DYES,TANNING,COLOUR PROD								1682	PROD TEINTURE,COLORANTS
532	DYES NES,TANNING PROD								1682	EXTRAITS TEINTURE,TANNAGE
541	*MEDICINAL,PHARM PRODUCT								2398	PROD MEDICINAUX PHARMACEUT
55	PERFUME,CLEANING ETC PRD								3450	PROD POUR PARFUM,TOILETTE
551	ESSENTL OILS,PERFUME,ETC								1900	HUILES ESSENTIELLES
554	SOAP,CLEANSING ETC PREPS								1551	SAVONS,PRODUITS DETERSIFS
59	CHEMICAL MATERIALS NES								671	MAT PROD CHIMIQUES NDA
6	BASIC MANUFACTURES								19909	ART MANUFACTURES
61	LEATHER,DRESSED FUR,ETC								561	CUIRS,PELLETERIES
611	LEATHER								561	CUIRS,PEAUX PREPARES
64	PAPER,PAPERBOARD AND MFR								1871	PAPIERS,CARTONS & OUVRAGES
65	TEXTILE YARN,FABRICS,ETC								2721	FILS,TISSUS,ARTICLES TEXTILE
658	TEXTILE ARTICLES NES								647	ART FACONNES MAT TEXTILES
66	NONMETAL MINERAL MFS NES								2646	ART MIN NON METALLIQUES
6639	CERAMIC ARTICLES NES								1767	ARTICLES EN CERAMIQUE NDA
664	GLASS								496	VERRE
67	IRON AND STEEL								7419	FER ET ACIER
68	NON-FERROUS METALS								2849	METAUX NON FERREUX
684	ALUMINIUM								2640	ALUMINIUM
69	METAL MANUFACTURES NES								1420	ART MANUFACT EN METAL NDA
695	TOOLS								714	OUTILS A MAIN
699	BASE METAL MFRS NES								706	ART MANUFACTURES MET NDA
7	MACHINES,TRANSPORT EQUIP								35086	MACHINES MATERIEL TRANSPORT
71	POWER GENERATING EQUIPMT								13460	MACHINES GENERATRICES
77	ELECTRIC MACHNRY NES ETC								10603	MACH APP ELECT NDA
78	ROAD VEHICLES								8764	VEHICULES ROUTIERS
79	OTHR TRANSPORT EQUIPMENT								2259	AUTRE MATERIEL TRANSPORT
7928	AIRCRAFT NES,ASSOC EQUIP								1341	APP NAVIG AERIENNE NDA
7932	SHIPS AND BOATS NES								918	NAVIRES ET BATEAUX
8	MISC MANUFACTURED GOODS								12343	ART MANUFACTURES DIVERS
821	*FURNITURE,PARTS THEREOF								2303	MEUBLES ET PIECES
84	CLOTHING AND ACCESSORIES								2952	VETEMENTS
851	*FOOTWEAR								1070	CHAUSSURES
88	PHOTO EQU,OPTICL GDS ETC								1484	APP,FOURN PHOTO,OP,MONTR
89	MISC MANUFCTRD GOODS NES								4532	ART MANUFACTURES DIVERS
892	PRINTED MATTER								573	IMPRIMES
893	ARTICLES OF PLASTIC NES								2086	OUVRAGES EN MAT DIVIS 58
8942	TOYS,INDOOR GAMES ETC								624	JOUETS,JEUX ETC

Maldives

5. General Exports F.O.B. by Commodities according to the S.I.T.C. (Rev. 2) in thousand U.S. Dollars
Exportations Générales F.O.B. par Produits d'après la C.T.C.I. (Rév. 2) en milliers de Dollars E.U.

SITC CTCI	COMMODITY	1988 WEIGHT POIDS	1988 VALUE VALEUR	1989 WEIGHT POIDS	1989 VALUE VALEUR	1990 WEIGHT POIDS	1990 VALUE VALEUR	1991 WEIGHT POIDS	1991 VALUE VALEUR	PRODUIT
	ALL COMMODITIES								53090	TOUS PRODUITS
0	FOOD AND LIVE ANIMALS								34812	ALIMENTS,ANIMAUX VIVANTS
03	FISH AND PREPARATIONS								34812	POISSONS ET PREPARATIONS
0341	FISH FRSH,CHLLD,EX FILLT								338	POISSON FRAIS,REFRIGERE
0342	FISH FROZEN,EXCL FILLETS								7775	POISSONS CONGELES
03501	FISH MEAL FIT FOR FOOD								1044	FARINE DE POISSON
03503	FISH(EX COD)DRIED,SALTED								10119	POISSONS SECHES,SALES
0371	FISH PREPARD,PRESRVD NES								15414	CONSERVES DE POISSONS
2	CRUDE MATERLS,EXCL FUELS								2021	MAT BRUTES NON COMESTIBLES
29	CRUDE ANIMAL,VEG MAT NES								2011	MATIERES BRUTES ANIM,VEGET
29298	OTH CRD VEG MATERIAL NES								2002	PRODUITS ORIGINE VEGET NDA
4	ANIMAL,VEGETABLE OIL,FAT								177	HUILES,GRAISSES ANIM,VEG
41111	FISH LIVER OIL								177	HUILES DE FOIES
8	MISC MANUFACTURED GOODS								16080	ART MANUFACTURES DIVERS
84	CLOTHING AND ACCESSORIES								16059	VETEMENTS

1. HISTORICAL SERIES, 1961–1996 GENERAL TRADE, IMPORTS C.I.F., EXPORTS F.O.B.
SERIES HISTORIQUES, 1961–1996 COMMERCE GENERAL, IMPORTATIONS C.A.F., EXPORTATIONS F.O.B

YEAR ANNEE	VALUE IN MILLION MALTESE LIRI / VALEUR EN MILLION MALTESE LIRI — MERCHANDISE –MARCHANDISE IMPORTS	EXPORTS	GOLD –OR IMPORTS	EXPORTS	CONVERSION FACTORS U.S. CENTS PER MALTESE LIRA FACTEURS DE CONVERSION CENTS E.U. PAR MALTESE LIRA IMPORTS	EXPORTS	INDEX NUMBERS –INDICES QUANTUM IMPORTS	EXPORTS	UNIT VALUE VALEUR UNITAIRE IMPORTS	EXPORTS
1961	29.30	4.70			280.0000	280.0000			22	
1962	28.50	4.30			280.0000	280.0000			22	
1963	30.20	5.30			280.0000	280.0000			22	
1964	34.50	6.90			280.0000	280.0000			23	
1965	35.00	8.70			280.0000	280.0000			24	30
1966	38.70	10.80			280.0000	280.0000			24	29
1967	40.30	9.90			276.0000	275.0000			25	28
1968	51.20	14.10			240.0000	240.0000			26	30
1969	61.30	16.00			240.0000	240.0000			27	31
1970	66.90	16.10			240.0000	240.0000			28	35
1971	65.10	18.80			240.0000	240.0000			29	34
1972	66.90	25.70			260.5410	261.2830			32	38
1973	87.90	36.00			272.5280	272.8710			39	41
1974	137.40	51.60			259.8310	259.7420			54	54
1975	144.50	63.90			261.2910	261.2280			57	57
1976	179.90	97.40			235.0410	234.5430			62	63
1977	217.70	121.80			236.8720	236.9740			68	66
1978	221.50	132.00			259.7050	259.6030			72	71
1979	272.00	152.20			279.2560	278.9150			81	77
1980	323.70	166.70			289.7520	289.5700			88	80
1981	332.30	173.70			257.2947	257.6450			96	86
1982	325.10	169.00			242.6453	243.0725			96	89
1983	316.60	156.70			231.3645	231.3670			98	83
1984	330.50	181.40			216.8977	217.4057			96	85
1985	354.10	187.10			214.1725	213.4865			95	85
1986	348.10	194.70			254.9532	255.2462			91	87
1987	392.90	208.60			290.0488	290.0625			92	91
1988	447.40	235.90			302.3064	302.4701			93	101
1989	515.80	294.40			286.8896	286.7454			96	106
1990	620.50	357.90			316.0878	315.8176			100	100
1991	684.00	405.50			309.0511	308.7928			114	105
1992	747.80	490.90			314.0854	314.3505			114	105
1993	830.92	518.32			261.6693	261.4783			109	109
1994	918.80	592.50			265.6647	265.3693			114	126
1995	1037.70	674.90			283.5303	283.4626			112	124
1996	1010.10	628.60			277.3888	277.3775			116	127

2. IMPORTS BY BROAD ECONOMIC CATEGORY AND EXPORTS BY INDUSTRIAL ORIGIN. (PERCENTAGE OF TOTAL VALUE)
IMPORTATIONS PAR CATEGORIES ECONOMIQUES ET EXPORTATIONS PAR BRANCHE D'ACTIVITE.(EN POURCENTAGE DE LA VALEUR TOTALE)

IMPORTS – IMPORTATIONS

	1990	1991	1992	1993	1994	1995	1996
TOTAL IMPORTS–IMPORTATIONS TOTALES	100.	100.	100.	100.			
1 FOOD BEV–ALIMENTATION BOISSONS	8.8	9.2	9.0	8.5			
11 PRIMARY–PRODUITS DE BASE	3.1	3.3	3.3	3.0			
111 FOR INDUSTRY–POUR L'INDUSTRIE	0.7	0.5	0.7	0.6			
112 FOR HOUSEHOLDS–POUR LES MENAGES	2.4	2.8	2.6	2.4			
12 PROCESSED–PRODUITS ELABORES	5.7	5.9	5.7	5.5			
121 FOR INDUSTRY–POUR L'INDUSTRIE	0.5	0.4	0.4	0.5			
122 FOR HOUSEHOLDS–POUR LES MENAGES	5.2	5.5	5.2	5.1			
2 IND SUPPLIES–APPROV INDUSTRIELS	27.3	25.2	24.0	22.6			
21 PRIMARY–PRODUITS DE BASE	1.7	1.4	1.2	1.2			
22 PROCESSED–PRODUITS ELABORES	25.6	23.8	22.8	21.5			
3 FUELS–COMBUSTIBLES	5.2	5.0	4.6	4.6			
31 PRIMARY–PRODUITS DE BASE	0.8	0.7	0.6	0.5			
32 PROCESSED–PRODUITS ELABORES	4.4	4.3	4.0	4.1			
321 MOTOR SPIRIT–ESSENCE	4.4	4.3	4.0	0.6			
322 OTHER–AUTRES	0.0	0.0	0.0	3.5			
4 MACHINERY–EQUIPEMENT	37.5	39.7	40.5	40.0			
41 CAPITAL EQUIPMENT–MACHINES	15.2	14.7	12.0	12.0			
42 PARTS–PIECES ACCESSOIRES	22.3	25.0	28.5	28.0			
5 TRANSPORT–TRANSPORT	8.8	8.0	8.7	10.6			
51 PASSENGER CARS–AUTOMOBILES	3.0	3.1	3.4	2.7			
52 OTHER–AUTRES	3.2	1.3	3.1	5.3			
521 INDUSTRIAL–INDUSTRIELS	3.1	1.3	3.0	5.2			
522 NON INDUSTRIAL–NON INDUSTRIEL	0.0	0.1	0.1	0.0			
53 PARTS–PIECES ACCESSOIRES	2.7	3.6	2.2	2.6			
6 CONSUM GOODS–BIENS CONSOMMATION	11.8	12.2	12.7	13.0			
61 DURABLE–DURABLES	2.3	2.7	3.4	3.6			
62 SEMI DURABLE–SEMI DURABLES	6.3	6.1	5.9	6.0			
63 NON DURABLE–NON DURABLES	3.2	3.4	3.3	3.4			
7 GOODS NES–BIENS NDA	0.6	0.7	0.5	0.5			

EXPORTS – EXPORTATIONS

	1990	1991	1992	1993	1994	1995	1996
TOTAL EXPORTS–EXPORTATIONS TOTALES	100.	100.	100.	100.			
1 AGRICULTURE	0.9	0.7	0.5	1.0			
2 MINING QUARRY–INDUS EXTRACTIVES	0.4	0.2	0.1	0.0			
3 MANUFACTURING–IND MANUFACTUR	98.7	99.1	99.4	99.0			
31 FOOD BEV TOBACCO–ALIM BOISS TAB	2.5	2.6	2.4	2.3			
32 TEXTILES–INDUSTRIES TEXTILES	20.4	17.2	15.5	15.1			
33 WOOD & PRODUCTS–BOIS & PRODUITS	0.1	0.1	0.1	0.1			
34 PAPER & PRODUCTS–PAPIER & PRODT	4.0	4.3	3.8	4.9			
35 CHEMICALS–INDUSTRIES CHIMIQUES	7.0	7.3	7.3	7.9			
36 NON METAL MIN–MIN NON METAL	0.3	0.2	0.1	0.2			
37 BASIC METAL–IND METAL BASE	1.0	0.7	0.4	0.3			
38 METAL MANUF–MANUF METAL	60.2	62.5	65.4	62.6			
39 OTH MANUF IND–AUTRES MANUF	3.3	4.2	4.4	5.7			

3. TRADE BY PRINCIPAL COUNTRIES OF ORIGIN AND LAST DESTINATION (VALUE IN THOUSAND U.S. DOLLARS)
ECHANGES SELON LES PRINCIPAUX PAYS D'ORIGINE ET DE DERNIERE DESTINATION (VALEUR EN MILLIERS DE DOLLARS EU)

COUNTRIES–PAYS	GENERAL IMPORTS C.I.F. IMPORTATIONS GENERALES C.A.F					COUNTRIES–PAYS	GENERAL EXPORTS F.O.B. EXPORTATIONS GENERALES F.O.B.				
	1992	1993	1994	1995	1996		1992	1993	1994	1995	1996
World	2338533	2173432	2440560	2980993	2802781	Monde	1537319	1355384	1556159	1888424	1748027
Africa	62667	56174	64322	106446	133570	Afrique	87459	82819	90837	57719	53729
Americas	93525	210308	144382	204404	215446	Amériques	93056	109396	134414	196970	273352
Northern America	76139	192516	127757	179713	197827	Amérique du Nord	90093	108007	133593	191002	262095
LAIA	16696	16471	15533	22941	14177	ALAI	2812	687	448	5177	2194
CACM	428	1224	856	1134	2355	MCAC	16	413	14	247	53
Caribbean	67	83	175	252	927	Caraïbes	135	288	359	539	8996
Rest of America	196	14	61	363	161	Autre Amérique			1	6	14
As.ex F.USSR	279664	257552	247200	397127	404936	Asie l'URSS exclus	97035	105373	103963	205584	302513
Eur.x F.USSR	1871603	1630843	1951053	2227938	1993858	Europe l'URSS exclus	1180653	986517	1171032	1375382	1031018
EU	1820757	1576150	1871330	2174071	1920396	UE	1162565	976225	1156316	1343299	997632
EFTA	24773	36748	57352	32560	50676	AELE	13346	5433	5410	28701	15718
East Europe	17146	14759	18367	17922	17317	Europe de l'Est	3046	4356	9146	3317	15183
Other Europe	20	1	9		3	Autre de l'Europe	0	15			111
Former USSR	25578	12831	10220	14664	20291	Ancienne URSS	31924	25285	4503	5444	3315
Oceania	5496	5724	7442	8144	12312	Océanie	966	600	5440	1727	1515
Italy/Italie	882546	590957	645910	807901	548233	Italy/Italie	626917	437059	582955	574192	223410
United Kingdom	300913	291373	373790	476313	399032	Germany/Allemagne	218769	211836	220584	279705	250812
Germany/Allemagne	251178	310515	429123	359038	262949	France,Monac	139586	141071	153291	230514	260125
France,Monac	147442	182487	205144	262806	443458	USA/Etats–Unis d'Amer	89055	101736	116561	181261	234015
USA/Etats–Unis d'Amer	74012	189701	124734	176018	193665	United Kingdom	100634	109374	115107	139070	146808
Singapore/Singapour	46120	69956	87413	167783	161677	Singapore/Singapour	62771	67169	75439	139421	209639
Japan/Japon	96530	58431	55790	75125	89112	Libyan Arab Jamahiriya	64619	65732	52764	40473	44028
Libyan Arab Jamahiriya	50255	46656	50809	88206	119396	Belgium–Luxembourg	26786	26118	34212	66973	62589
Netherlands/Pays–Bas	75437	57354	57542	67448	74777	Netherlands/Pays–Bas	27447	33932	29914	28803	31947
Spain/Espagne	36332	31675	42619	59729	52840	Japan/Japon	1670	7499	11578	16152	49881
Switz.Liecht	21750	25750	51915	29469	39989	Canada	1037	6271	17032	9742	28035
Belgium–Luxembourg	30668	29684	28678	36247	41041	Nigeria/Nigéria	9364	2249	30058	6079	472
Korea, Republic of	27094	27886	19669	40977	36771	Russian Federation	24727	11974	3827	1979	1784
China/Chine	22974	21571	17032	30257	34338	Switz.Liecht	11620	3848	4085	10709	12575
Ireland/Irlande	23086	21538	18235	24061	23890	Saudi Arabia	8794	5807	4379	6853	9942
Turkey/Turquie	18053	14698	16866	22672	25266	United Arab Emirates	7310	6374	4535	5721	9149
Denmark/Danemark	16493	17405	17913	21983	19592	Spain/Espagne	7874	4142	6735	4945	2447
Greece/Grèce	16001	16496	20576	20534	19010	China/Chine	2	691	558	23847	816
Russian Federation	25286	12615	7556	11853	14388	Norway,SVD,JM	1723	1585	1324	17913	3118
Hong Kong	10962	13953	12914	14289	13816	Poland/Pologne	1399	364	5673	774	10808
Austria/Autriche	12212	10324	11592	14428	12562	Denmark/Danemark	4961	3228	3486	2991	2860
India/Inde	7820	10281	9124	13090	11294	Ukraine	7197	8654	72	261	649
Sweden/Suède	8485	7636	9249	10606	11006	Ireland/Irlande	2637	2521	1887	1999	4242
Portugal	12931	5984	7684	9973	7901	Sweden/Suède	2760	2426	2310	2889	2391
Brazil/Brésil	8709	8397	8003	11939	6517	Greece/Grèce	2196	1777	1672	3635	2827
Thailand/Thaïlande	7512	4831	7338	8490	9075	Turkey/Turquie	6025	3227	520	252	1995
Norway,SVD,JM	3023	10959	5251	2694	10443	Austria/Autriche	1464	1392	2110	2744	3346
Czech Republic		8542	8338	7169	7416	Angola	2882	4422		3039	
Malaysia/Malaisie	2905	2817	5786	10773	8195	Portugal	195	1074	1812	4732	2411
Australia/Australie	2796	2449	4563	4523	7960	Bahamas	135	271	12		8874
Finland/Finlande	7034	2721	3274	3003	4106	Egypt/Egypte	1719	1984	1380	1729	1881
Argentina/Argentine	3410	4853	3738	5022	2278	Afghanistan				4287	3767
New Zealand	2700	3247	2879	3562	4303	Kuwait/ Koweït	1310	2050	1278	1236	2117
Hungary/Hongrie	4685	2849	1916	4030	3057	Colombia/Colombie	164	180	196	4063	1645
Canada	2127	2815	3023	3692	4051	Hong Kong	1080	3279	687	422	730
Israel/Israël	554	2135	3436	4123	4150	Ethiopia/Ethiopie	4038	289		1446	133
Tunisia/Tunisie	1318	1708	2416	3664	3856	Turkmenistan/Turkménistn		2461		2849	513
So. Africa Customs Un	1656	2160	3362	3618	2064	Zambia/Zambie	742	5047			
Slovenia/Slovénia	1478	2401	2503	2986	3468	Oman	1384	1442	553	584	1332
Poland/Pologne	2953	2741	2187	2104	2353	Australia/Australie	959	584	574	1588	1337
Egypt/Egypte	2427	1090	649	5201	2433	New Zealand	7	16	4865	6	67
Philippines	5853	1825	2109	814	1021	Slovakia		2684	372	561	899
Pakistan	2116	2340	1875	2328	2350	Djibouti	1098	1222	600	[illegible]	735
Ukraine	45	77	2193	2640	4952	Morocco/Maroc	569	685	581	[illegible]	594
Yugoslavia/Yougoslavie	6394	495	1044	68	1795	Albania/Albanie	605	215	2365	105	652
Cyprus/Chypre	2368	1469	3282	1038	1346	Hungary/Hongrie	641	789	553	1168	771
Indonesia/Indonésie	1885	1289	1271	2030	2383	Yemen/Yémen	988	725	409	607	1171
Czechoslovakia	8690					Korea, Republic of	141	275	197	496	2558
Cote d'Ivoire	2431	1395	1964	1276	1337	Cyprus/Chypre	493	497	355	916	1359
Bulgaria/Bulgarie	511	240	4246	947	1556	Slovenia/Slovénia	785	257	11	65	2355

(VALUE AS PERCENTAGE OF WORLD TOTAL)(VALEURS EN POURCENTAGE DU TOTAL MONDIAL)

	1987	1988	1989	1990	1991	1992	1993	1994	1995	1996		1987	1988	1989	1990	1991	1992	1993	1994	1995	1996
Africa	4.3	3.3	0.5	3.6	2.7	2.7	2.6	2.6	3.6	4.8	Afrique	9.6	7.1	5.4	6.4	7.4	5.7	6.1	5.8	3.1	3.1
Americas	12.7	11.4	5.7	4.7	5.6	4.0	9.7	5.9	6.9	7.7	Amériques	8.1	11.5	5.7	4.0	4.4	6.1	8.1	8.6	10.4	15.6
Northern America	11.1	9.8	4.2	3.5	4.2	3.3	8.9	5.2	6.0	7.1	Amérique du Nord	7.9	11.5	5.6	3.9	4.3	5.9	8.0	8.6	10.1	15.0
LAIA	1.5	1.5	1.4	1.1	1.3	0.7	0.8	0.6	0.8	0.5	ALAI	0.1	0.0	0.0	0.0	0.1	0.2	0.1	0.0	0.3	0.1
CACM	0.1	0.1	0.1	0.1	0.0	0.0	0.1	0.0	0.0	0.1	MCAC				0.0	0.0	0.0	0.0	0.0	0.0	0.0
Caribbean	0.0	0.0	0.0	0.0	0.0	0.0	0.0	0.0	0.0	0.0	Caraïbes	0.0	0.0	0.0	0.0	0.0	0.0	0.0	0.0	0.0	0.5
Rest of America	0.0	0.0	0.0	0.0	0.0	0.0	0.0	0.0	0.0	0.0	Autre Amérique								0.0	0.0	0.0
As.ex F.USSR	6.9	8.5	9.6	9.7	10.9	12.0	11.8	10.1	13.3	14.4	Asie l'URSS exclus	5.2	6.4	6.0	5.3	5.0	6.3	7.8	6.7	10.9	17.3
Eur.x F.USSR	74.4	75.2	78.3	80.0	78.9	80.0	75.0	79.9	74.7	71.1	Europe l'URSS exclus	71.1	71.1	75.8	78.0	78.8	76.8	72.8	75.3	72.8	59.0
EU	69.8	71.4	75.6	77.5	76.6	77.9	72.5	76.7	72.9	68.5	UE	69.2	69.3	74.3	76.9	78.2	75.6	72.0	74.3	71.1	57.1
EFTA	1.2	1.1	0.9	1.0	1.0	1.1	1.7	2.3	1.1	1.8	AELE	0.6	0.5	0.6	0.5	0.4	0.9	0.4	0.3	1.5	0.9
East Europe	2.7	2.3	1.4	1.0	1.0	0.7	0.7	0.8	0.6	0.6	Europe de l'Est	1.3	1.2	0.8	0.6	0.2	0.2	0.3	0.6	0.2	0.9
Other Europe	0.7	0.4	0.5	0.5	0.3	0.0	0.0	0.0		0.0	Autre de l'Europe	0.0	0.1	0.0	0.0	0.0	0.0	0.0			0.0
Former USSR	1.3	1.2	0.8	1.6	1.6	1.1	0.6	0.4	0.5	0.7	Ancienne URSS	2.3	0.8	1.0	3.0	1.0	2.1	1.9	0.3	0.3	0.2
Oceania	0.4	0.4	0.3	0.3	0.3	0.2	0.3	0.3	0.3	0.4	Océanie	0.1	0.1	0.1	0.1	0.1	0.1	0.0	0.3	0.1	0.1
Italy/Italie	19.3	22.6	30.3	32.6	36.3	37.7	27.2	26.5	27.1	19.6	Italy/Italie	14.4	17.5	29.5	34.6	38.6	40.8	32.2	37.5	30.4	12.8
United Kingdom	17.1	16.9	15.3	14.9	14.7	12.9	13.4	15.3	16.0	14.2	Germany/Allemagne	30.9	27.1	22.5	20.5	17.8	14.2	15.6	14.2	14.8	14.3
Germany/Allemagne	16.6	15.0	13.0	11.7	11.1	10.7	14.3	17.6	12.0	9.4	France,Monac	2.3	4.2	5.3	7.1	9.1	9.1	10.4	9.9	12.2	14.9
France,Monac	3.5	5.0	5.6	7.2	4.6	6.3	8.4	8.4	8.8	15.8	USA/Etats–Unis d'Amer	7.7	11.2	5.4	3.8	4.2	5.8	7.5	7.5	9.6	13.4
USA/Etats–Unis d'Amer	10.9	9.7	3.9	3.3	4.1	3.2	8.7	5.1	5.9	6.9	United Kingdom	13.6	13.2	10.7	8.9	7.3	6.5	8.1	7.4	7.4	8.4
Singapore/Singapour	0.9	0.7	1.0	1.5	1.4	2.0	3.2	3.6	5.6	5.8	Singapore/Singapour	2.8	3.3	4.0	3.3	2.5	4.1	5.0	4.8	7.4	12.0
Japan/Japon	2.0	2.8	3.1	3.7	3.9	4.1	2.7	2.3	2.5	3.2	Libyan Arab Jamahiriya	8.9	6.2	4.9	5.1	5.5	4.2	4.8	3.4	2.1	2.5
Libyan Arab Jamahiriya	3.3	2.5	0.0	3.1	2.1	2.1	2.1	2.1	3.0	4.3	Belgium–Luxembourg	1.6	3.1	2.4	2.4	2.2	1.7	1.9	2.2	3.5	3.6
Netherlands/Pays–Bas	3.3	2.9	2.9	2.8	2.9	3.2	2.6	2.4	2.3	2.7	Netherlands/Pays–Bas	3.5	2.1	2.1	1.8	1.8	1.8	2.5	1.9	1.5	1.8
Spain/Espagne	1.9	2.1	2.3	1.6	1.5	1.6	1.5	1.7	2.0	1.9	Japan/Japon	0.2	0.1	0.1	0.1	0.1	0.1	0.6	0.7	0.9	2.9

4. General Imports C.I.F. by Commodities according to the S.I.T.C. (Rev. 2) in thousand U.S. Dollars
Importations Générales C.A.F. par Produits d'après la C.T.C.I. (Rév. 2) en milliers de Dollars E.U.

SITC CTCI	COMMODITY	1992		1993		1994		1995		PRODUIT
		WEIGHT POIDS	VALUE VALEUR	WEIGHT POIDS	VALUE VALEUR	WEIGHT POIDS	VALUE VALEUR	WEIGHT POIDS	VALUE VALEUR	
	ALL COMMODITIES		2338533		2173432		2440560		2980993	TOUS PRODUITS
0	FOOD AND LIVE ANIMALS		207492		184216					ALIMENTS,ANIMAUX VIVANTS
01	MEAT AND PREPARATIONS		36314		28976		14817		24217	VIANDES ET PREPARATIONS
011	MEAT FRESH,CHILLD,FROZEN	W 10211	26725	W 8980	20482					VIANDES FRAICHES,REF,CONGE
0111	BOVINE MEAT FRESH,FROZEN	W 8143	21495	W 7113	15858					VIANDES BOVIN FRAI,REF
01112	BOVINE MEAT BONELESS	W 5424	15694	W 6231	14184					VIANDES BOVIN DESOSSEES
014	MEAT PREPD,PRSVD,NES ETC		9564		8465					CONSERVES DE VIANDES
0149	OTH PREPARD,PRESRVD MEAT		7658		6754					AUTRES PREP DE VIANDES
02	DAIRY PRODCTS,BIRDS'EGGS		27846		25873		21960		29105	PRODUITS LAITIERS,OEUFS
022	MILK AND CREAM	W 5992	8907		7740					LAIT ET CREME
0224	MILK,CREAM PRESERVED ETC	W 5654	8418		7109					LAIT,CREME CONS,CONC
024	CHEESE AND CURD	W 5572	15869	W 5094	14851					FROMAGE ET CAILLEBOTTE
03	FISH AND PREPARATIONS		19038		14313		6189		7439	POISSONS ET PREPARATIONS
034	FISH,FRESH,CHILLED,FROZN		9009		7265					POISSON FRAIS, REFRIG,CONG
037	FISH ETC PREPD,PRSVD NES	W 2697	8640		5766					POIS,CRUST,MOL PREPARES
04	CEREALS AND PREPARATIONS		39491		34757		21785		31773	CEREALES ET PRODUITS
041	WHEAT ETC UNMILLED	W 59980	8546	W 45112	6168					FROMENT,EPEAUTRE
0412	OTHER WHEAT ETC UNMILLED	W 59980	8546	W 45112	6167					AUTRE FROMENT NON MOULU
044	MAIZE UNMILLED	W 60519	7883	W 53950	6617					MAIS NON MOULU
048	CEREAL ETC PREPARATIONS	W 6736	14899		13896					PREPTNS A BASE CEREALES
05	VEGETABLES AND FRUIT		31445		29459					LEGUMES ET FRUITS
057	FRUIT,NUTS,FRESH,DRIED	W 25490	17920	W 29064	15513		15935		21524	FRUITS FRAIS OU SECS
06	SUGAR AND PREPS,HONEY		10084		9096		12721		15137	SUCRES ET PRODUITS
07	COFFEE,TEA,COCOA,SPICES		17412		16983		9627		19232	CAFE,THE,CACAO,EPICES
073	CHOCOLATE AND PRODUCTS	W 1943	9776	W 1998	8657					CHOCOLAT
081	*FEEDING STUFF FOR ANIML	W 23311	11720		12432		12708		14356	NOURRITURE POUR ANIMAUX
09	MISC EDIBLE PRODUCTS		12733		11632					PREP ALIMENTAIRES DIVERSES
098	EDIBLE PRODCTS,PREPS NES		11620		10594		14567		22687	PREP ALIMENTAIRES NDA
1	BEVERAGES AND TOBACCO		23963		22921					BOISSONS ET TABACS
11	BEVERAGES		14120		12676		17739		20880	BOISSONS
112	ALCOHOLIC BEVERAGES	W 3031	12550		10402					BOISSONS ALCOOLIQUES
1124	DISTILLED ALCOHOLIC BEVS	W 1220	8491	W 1046	7071					ALCOOLS,EAUX–DE–VIE
12	TOBACCO AND MANUFACTURES		9843		10244		21203		19583	TABACS BRUTS FABRIQUES
122	TOBACCO,MANUFACTURED	W 506	8067	W 782	9869					TABACS FABRIQUES
1223	OTH MANUFACTURED TOBACCO	W 424	5599	W 691	7302					TABACS FUMER,CHIQUER,PRISER
2	CRUDE MATERLS,EXCL FUELS		31937		29636					MAT BRUTES NON COMESTIBLES
24	CORK AND WOOD		11731		8656					LIEGE ET BOIS
248	WOOD SHAPED,SLEEPERS	W 12618	9174		7488					BOIS SIMPLEMENT TRAVAILLES
263	COTTON	W 83	183		208		33380		42452	COTON
27	CRUDE FERTLZR,MINRLS NES		7749		9208		19561		17217	ENGRAIS MINERAUX BRUTS
3	MINERAL FUELS ETC		110277		102488		108318		118228	COMBUSTIBLES MINERAUX LUB
32	COAL,COKE AND BRIQUETTES		9307		8545					HOUILLES,COKES,BRIQUETTES
322	COAL,LIGNITE AND PEAT	W 211241	9174		8471					HOUILLES,LIGNITES,TOURBE
3222	OTH COAL,NOT AGGLOMERATD	W 210441	8912		8280					AUTRES HOUILLES
33	PETROLEUM AND PRODUCTS		97267		90688					PETROLE ET DERIVES
334	PETROLEUM PRODUCTS,REFIN	W 719998	93532		88606					PRODUITS RAFFINES
3341	GASOLINE,OTH LIGHT OILS				13870					ESSENCES POUR MOTEURS
3342	KEROSENE,OTH MEDIUM OILS				18102					PETR LAMPANTS,AUT HUIL
3343	GAS OILS				24128					GAS OILS
3344	FUEL OILS,NES				27894					FUEL OILS
4	ANIMAL,VEGETABLE OIL,FAT		6722		6081		7695		9519	HUILES,GRAISSES ANIM,VEG
5	CHEMCLS,RELATED PROD NES		153241		142941					PRODUITS CHIMIQUES
51	ORGANIC CHEMICALS		11565		11114		17280		20162	PROD CHIMIQ ORGANIQUES
52	INORGANIC CHEMICALS		8378		7514		8187		7253	PROD CHIM INORGANIQUES
53	DYES,TANNING,COLOUR PROD		16990		18805		20565		19067	PROD TEINTURE,COLORANTS
533	PIGMENTS,PAINTS,ETC		16201		18009					PIGMENTS,PEINTURES,VERNIS
5334	VARNISHES,DISTEMPERS ETC	W 1937	8579		8654					PEINTURES A L'EAU
53342	OTH PAINTS,VARNISHES ETC	W 1531	7167	W 1338	7365					AUTRES PEINTURES,VERNIS
541	*MEDICINAL,PHARM PRODUCT		27440		28657		28582		31864	PROD MEDICINAUX PHARMACEUT
5417	MEDICAMENTS		23388		23377					MEDICAMENTS
54179	— CONTNG OTH SUBSTANCES	K 649572	20715	K 473530	19035					MED CONT AUT SUBSTANCES
55	PERFUME,CLEANING ETC PRD		24866		21489		25405		41124	PROD POUR PARFUM,TOILETTE
553	PERFUMERY,COSMETICS,ETC		12035	W 88	11436					PRODUITS DE PARFUMERIE
554	SOAP,CLEANSING ETC PREPS	W 5264	9282		7193					SAVONS,PRODUITS DETERSIFS
58	PLASTIC MATERIALS ETC		49122		41702					MAT PLAST ARTIFICIELLES
582	PROD OF CONDENSATION ETC		18300		15085					PROD CONDENS,POLYCOND
5824	POLYAMIDES	W 5090	9223	W 3085	4811					POLYAMIDES
58241	— IN PRIMARY FORMS	W 5090	9223	W 3085	4811					POLYAMIDES PRIMAIRES
583	POLYMERIZATION ETC PRODS		27317		25041					PROD POLYMERISATION
5833	POLYSTYRENE,ITS COPOLYMR	W 3685	6203		6893					POLYPROPYLENE COPOLYMERES
58331	— IN PRIMARY FORMS	W 3644	6031	W 3034	6595					SOUS FORMES PRIMAIRES
5839	OTH POLYMRZTION ETC PROD		9388	W 1500	8239					AUT PROD POLYMER COPOLYM
59	CHEMICAL MATERIALS NES		13352		12839					MAT PROD CHIMIQUES NDA
598	MISCEL CHEM PRODUCTS NES		6783		6838		10830		13672	PROD DIV INDUST CHIM NDA
6	BASIC MANUFACTURES		408107		348796					ART MANUFACTURES
61	LEATHER,DRESSED FUR,ETC		24421		22318					CUIRS,PELLETERIES
611	LEATHER		17482		16583		17229		17306	CUIRS,PEAUX PREPARES
6114	LEATHR BOVINE NES,EQUINE	W 1750	15725		14846					CUIRS DE BOVINS
62	RUBBER MANUFACTURES NES		9595		7719		10450		15074	CAOUTCHOUC MANUFACTURE
63	WOOD,CORK MANUFACTRS NES		12473		9305					OUVRAGES LIEGE ET BOIS
634	VENEERS,PLYWOOD,ETC		8954		6584					PLACAGES,CONTRE–PLAQUES
64	PAPER,PAPERBOARD AND MFR		55003		49721		49575		65555	PAPIERS,CARTONS & OUVRAGES
641	PAPER AND PAPERBOARD		41313		36200					PAPIERS ET CARTONS
6415	PAPER,PAPERBRD,BULK,NES		25111		21730					PAPIERS,CARTONS ROULEAUX
64159	OTHER PAPER ETC,BULK,NES		24295	W 7062	21081					AUT PAPIER ROULEAUX FEUILLES
642	PAPER,ETC,PRECUT,ARTS OF		13690		13521					PAP,CARTONS DECOUPES
6421	PAPER ETC CONTAINERS		6316		7120					BOITES,SACS EMBALLAGES
65	TEXTILE YARN,FABRICS,ETC		135104		115864					FILS,TISSUS,ARTICLES TEXTILE
651	TEXTILE YARN		7868		5460					FILS TEXTILES
652	COTTON FABRICS,WOVEN		31891		33200					TISSUS DE COTON
6522	WOVEN COTTON BLEACHD,ETC		27598		30181					TISSUS COTON BLANCHIS ETC
65224	BLCHED COTTON FABRIC NES		23240	A 10798	26725					AUT TIS PLUS 85% COT BLANCHI
653	WOVN MAN–MADE FIB FABRIC		41233		29352					TISSUS FIBRES SYNTH,ARTIF
6534	DISC SYN BLEND FABRC NES	A 6174	22051	A 8307	15804					TISSUS FIBRES SYNTH DISCONT
65341	DISC SYN FIB–COTTN FABRC	A 3255	12085	A 4730	9719					TISSUS FIB SYNT DIS MEL COTO
6535	CONT REGN WEAVES NONPILE	A 3540	7952	A 3525	6366					TISSUS FIB TEXT ART CONTINU
654	OTH WOVEN TEXTILE FABRIC		20590		13566					TISSUS AUT COTON SYNT,ARTIF
6542	WOVEN WOOL,HAIR NONPILE	A 3230	15183	A 2960	9219					TIS PLUS 85% LAINE,POILS
65421	WOVN CARD WOOL,FINE HAIR	A 2558	10992	A 1206	4195					TISSUS 85% LAINE,PLS CARD
655	KNITTED,ETC FABRICS		8206	A 316	7428					ETOF BONNETERIE PIECES ETC
6552	OTHER KNIT ETC FAB NONEL		8206	A 316	7428					ETOF BON NON ELAS NON SYNT

4. General Imports C.I.F. by Commodities according to the S.I.T.C. (Rev. 2) in thousand U.S. Dollars
Importations Générales C.A.F. par Produits d'après la C.T.C.I. (Rév. 2) en milliers de Dollars E.U.

SITC CTCI	COMMODITY	1992 WEIGHT POIDS	1992 VALUE VALEUR	1993 WEIGHT POIDS	1993 VALUE VALEUR	1994 WEIGHT POIDS	1994 VALUE VALEUR	1995 WEIGHT POIDS	1995 VALUE VALEUR	PRODUIT
656	LACE,RIBBONS,TULLE,ETC		8005		7468		8676		9984	TULLES,BRODERIE
657	SPECIAL TXTL FABRC,PRODS		9210		11594		9921		9066	TISSUS SPECIAUX
66	NONMETAL MINERAL MFS NES		56703		45503					ART MIN NON METALLIQUES
661	LIME,CEMENT,BLDG PRODS		14048		12948					CHAUX,CIMENTS MAT CONSTR
6612	CEMENT	W 223845	11622		11341					CIMENTS HYDRAULIQUES
662	CLAY,REFRACTORY BLDG PRD		16080		13499					MAT CONST REFRACTAIRES
6624	BRICKS ETC NONREFRACTORY	W 23719	15876		13377					BRIQUES ETC CERAM NON REFR
66245	GLAZED CERAMIC SETTS ETC	W 21957	14572	W 24705	12072					AUT CARREAUX CERAMIQUE
665	GLASSWARE		7755		5033					OUVRAGES EN VERRE
666	POTTERY		4831		3814		20472		25047	POTERIE
67	IRON AND STEEL		37416		29324		20834		23288	FER ET ACIER
672	IRON,STEEL PRIMARY FORMS		7702		5603					LINGOTS FER,ACIER
673	IRON,STEEL SHAPES ETC		9755		6632					BARRES,PROFIL FER,ACIER
674	IRN,STL UNIV,PLATE,SHEET		7254		6548					LARGES PLATS,TOLES
678	IRON,STL TUBES,PIPES,ETC		9129		5843					TUBES,TUYAUX EN FONTE,FER
68	NON–FERROUS METALS		21669		19660					METAUX NON FERREUX
684	ALUMINIUM	W 4571	15102		13864					ALUMINIUM
6842	ALUMINIUM,ALLOYS WORKED	W 2782	11686		10246					ALUMINIUM,ALLIAGES OUVRE
68421	ALUMINIUM BARS,WIRE,ETC	W 2563	9509		8253					BARRES,PROFILES FILS ALU
69	METAL MANUFACTURES NES		55723		49381					ART MANUFACT EN METAL NDA
692	METAL TANKS,BOXES,ETC	W 2889	8263		6858					RECIPIENTS METALLIQUES
6924	MTL TRANSPORT BOXES ETC	W 2862	7900		6470					FUTS,TAMBOURS,BIDONS
695	TOOLS		7966		7705		12684		12198	OUTILS A MAIN
699	BASE METAL MFRS NES		18881		16373					ART MANUFACTURES MET NDA
6991	LOCKSMITHS WARES,ETC		8958		6570					ARTICLES DE SERRURERIE
6996	BASE MTL MISC ARTICLES		2772		2564		11013		14846	ART DIVERS METAUX COMMUNS
7	MACHINES,TRANSPORT EQUIP		1130530		1088145					MACHINES MATERIEL TRANSPORT
71	POWER GENERATING EQUIPMT		20622		31396		225479		265874	MACHINES GENERATRICES
713	INTRNL COMBUS PSTN ENGIN	N 24497	7808		14357					MOTEURS EXPL COMB INT, PIECE
7133	MARINE PISTON ENGINES	N 962	1550	N 3694	8764					MOTEURS EXPL POUR BATEAUX
71332	—— OTHER THAN OUTBOARD	N 203	756	N 2930	7846					MOT BATEAUX AUT HORSBORD
714	ENGINES AND MOTORS NES		6301		7546					MOTEURS NON ELECTRIQUES
72	MACHS FOR SPCL INDUSTRYS		50156		46780					MAC SPECIALES POUR INDUST
724	TEXTILE,LEATHER MACHNRY		8626		7897					MACH POUR INDUSTRIE TEXTILE
726	PRINTG,BKBINDG MACHY,PTS		5186		7876					MACHINES POUR IMPRIMERIE
728	OTH MACHY FOR SPCL INDUS		20919		21347					AUT MACH IND PARTICULIERES
7281	MACH–TOOLS FR SPCL INDUS		4911		7951					MACH–OUTILS SPEC IND PART
7284	MACHY FOR SPCL INDUS NES		13444		10022					MACH SPEC IND PARTICUL.
73	METALWORKING MACHINERY		16461		15037					MACH TRAVAIL DES METAUX
736	METALWORKING MACH–TOOLS		9978		7585					MACH–OUTILS TRAVAIL METAUX
737	METALWORKING MACHNRY NES		6483		7451					MACH TRAV METAUX PIECES
7373	WELDING,BRAZING,ETC MCHS		6326		7312					MACH SOUDAGE ETC PIECES
73732	ELECTRIC WELDERS,ETC		6230		7219					MACH ELECT POUR SOUDER
74	GENRL INDUSTRL MACHY NES		84349		80771					MACH APP INDUSTRIE
741	HEATING,COOLING EQUIPMNT		19305		17189					MACH CHAUFFAGE,PIECES
7415	AIR–CONDITIONING MACHNRY		8526	N 3050	7683					GROUPES CONDITION AIR
742	PUMPS FOR LIQUIDS ETC		8319		11257					POMPES MOTO–POMPES
7429	PTS NES OF PUMPS OF 742	W 361	4677	W 731	7516					PIECES POUR GROUPE 742
743	PUMPS NES,CENTRFUGES ETC		9498		9882					POMPES COMPRES,VENT ETC
744	MECHANICAL HANDLING EQU		16180		9928					EQUIP MANUTENTION PIECES
7442	LIFTING,LOADING MACH NES	N 16710	8167		6288					APP LEVAGE,MANUTENTION
745	NONELEC MACHY,TOOLS NES		10850		14269					AUT MACH NON ELEC,PIECES
7452	OTH NONELEC MCHS,PTS NES		10238		11446					AUT MACH NON ELEC,PIECES
749	NONELEC MACH PTS,ACC NES		20196		18245					PIECES MACH NON ELEC NDA
7499	OTH NONELEC MCHY PTS NES		12684		10070					PIECES NON ELECT NDA
74991	FOUNDRY MOULDS ETC NES	N 104306	11730	N 65295	9261					MOULES POUR METAUX
75	OFFICE MACHNES,ADP EQUIP		28999		40544					MACH BUREAU TRAIT AUTOM
752	AUTOMTIC DATA PROC EQUIP	N 23611	17550		19690					MACH TRAIT INFORMATION
7522	DIGITAL COMPUTERS	N 5742	7456	N 5347	7395					MACH DIGITALES COMPLETES
759	OFFICE,ADP MCH PTS,ACCES		8175		17556					PIECES DU 751 ET 752
7599	ACCTG,ETC,ADP MCH PTS,AC		7530		16667					PIECES DU 751 ET 752
76	TELECOMM,SOUND EQUIPMENT		38580		41389					EQUIPMENT DE TELECOM
764	TELECOM EQPT,PTS,ACC NES		31182		37047					EQUIP TELECOM,PIECES
7649	PTS NES OF EQUIPMT OF 76		19959		26717					PIECES DE LA DIV 76
76493	TELECOMM EQUIPMT PTS NES		17190		24257					PIECES 761,762,764.3,8
77	ELECTRIC MACHNRY NES ETC		709435		629277					MACH APP ELECT NDA
771	ELECTRIC POWER MACHY NES		8856		4996					MACH PROD,TRANS ELECTR
772	SWITCHGEAR ETC,PARTS NES		39398		29339					APP COUPURE,SECT ETC
7721	SWITCHGEAR ETC		38612	N 6231	27777					APP COUPURE,SECTIONMNT
773	ELECTR DISTRIBUTNG EQUIP		10457		11846					EQUIPMT DISTRIBUTION ELECT
7731	INSULATED WIRE,CABLE ETC		9714		11203					FILS,CABLES ISOLES ELECT
775	HOUSEHOLD TYPE EQUIP NES		20135		16958					MACH,APP USAGE DOMESTQUE
776	TRANSISTORS,VALVES,ETC		616686		553434					LAMPES,TUBES,VALVES
7761	TV PICTURE TUBES	N 181468	10135	N 287585	13289					TUBES CATHODIQUES
7764	ELECTRONIC MICROCIRCUITS		56152	MN 33032	64066					MICROSTRUCTURES ELECTRON
7768	ELCTRNC COMP PTS,CRYSTLS		548636		472733					CRIST PIEZO–ELEC,PCS 776
77689	ELECTRNIC COMPON PTS NES		548634	W 401	472721					PIECES DU GROUPE 776
778	ELECTRICAL MACHINERY NES		13074		11321					AUTRES MACH ELECT NDA
78	ROAD VEHICLES		116089		82199		109293		171168	VEHICULES ROUTIERS
781	PASS MOTOR VEH EXC BUSES	N 11196	78660	N 8931	58552					AUTO TRANSPORT PERSONNES
782	LORRIES,SPCL MTR VEH NES	N 2806	20991	N 1440	8629					VEHICULES SPECIAUX,MARCH
7821	LORRIES,TRUCKS	N 2699	17650	N 1357	7029					VEHICULES TRANSP MARCHAND
784	MOTOR VEH PRTS,ACCES NES	N 628108	11595		10466					PIECES 722,781,782,783
7849	OTHER MOTOR VEHCL PARTS	N 627908	11478		10320					PIECES 722,781,782,783
79	OTHR TRANSPORT EQUIPMENT		65839		120753					AUTRE MATERIEL TRANSPORT
792	AIRCRAFT ETC		57320		112573		93009		48651	APP NAVIGATION AERIENNE
7924	AIRCRFT NES OVER 15000KG	N 1	38622		93415					AERODYNES PLUS 15000 KG
7929	AIRCRAFT PARTS NES	W 31	18690		19029					PIECES DU 792
793	SHIPS AND BOATS ETC		8419		8164		6444		9719	NAVIRES BATEAUX,ETC
7932	SHIPS AND BOATS NES		7486		7514					NAVIRES ET BATEAUX
79321	YACHTS,SPORTS VESSLS ETC	N 195	2316		6852					BATEAUX DE PLAISANCE
8	MISC MANUFACTURED GOODS		237358		230301					ART MANUFACTURES DIVERS
812	*PLUMBG,HEATNG,LGHTNG EQ		9603		8231					APPAR SANITAIRES CHAUFFAGE
821	*FURNITURE,PARTS THEREOF		4799		7436					MEUBLES ET PIECES
84	CLOTHING AND ACCESSORIES		38712		35055					VETEMENTS
843	WOMENS OUTERWEAR NONKNIT	N 763129	7615	N 615802	6691					VET DESSUS FEMMES MAT TEX
844	UNDER GARMENTS NOT KNIT		7173		5687					VETEMENT DESSOUS MAT TEX
845	OUTERWEAR KNIT NONELASTC		11012		10273					VET DESSOUS,ACCES BONNET
851	*FOOTWEAR	P 1160343	6402		6879		10846		17827	CHAUSSURES
87	PRECISION INSTRUMNTS NES		30978		26919					INSTRUM,APPAR SCIENT NDA
872	MEDICAL INSTRUMENTS NES	W 74	7796		4253					INSTR,APP MEDIC–CHIR NDA

4. General Imports C.I.F. by Commodities according to the S.I.T.C. (Rev. 2) in thousand U.S. Dollars
Importations Générales C.A.F. par Produits d'après la C.T.C.I. (Rév. 2) en milliers de Dollars E.U.

SITC CTCI	COMMODITY	1992 WEIGHT POIDS	1992 VALUE VALEUR	1993 WEIGHT POIDS	1993 VALUE VALEUR	1994 WEIGHT POIDS	1994 VALUE VALEUR	1995 WEIGHT POIDS	1995 VALUE VALEUR	PRODUIT
87202	OTH MEDICAL INSTRUMENTS	W 72	7105	W 51	3547					INSTRUM,APP MEDECINE
874	MEASURNG,CONTROLNG INSTR		18993		21002					INSTRUMENTS DE MESURE
8749	INSTR PTS NES,ACCESSORYS		5491		7153					PIECES 873,874.3,54,874.8
88	PHOTO EQU,OPTICL GDS ETC		24157		22639					APP,FOURN PHOTO,OP,MONTR
884	OPTICAL GOODS NES		11931		12047					ELEMENTS OPTIQ,ART LUNET
8842	SPECTACLES AND FRAMES	MN 21647	11206		11375					LUNETTES ET MONTURES
88421	SPECTACLE FRAMES	MN 21481	10085	MN 16096	10147					MONTURES DE LUNETTES
89	MISC MANUFCTRD GOODS NES		120958		121655					ART MANUFACTURES DIVERS
892	PRINTED MATTER		21478		21440		18122		21544	IMPRIMES
8928	PRINTED MATTER NES		8307		8429					IMPRIMES NDA
893	ARTICLES OF PLASTIC NES		34079		31742					OUVRAGES EN MAT DIVIS 58
8931	PLSTC PACKG CONTNRS,LIDS		6806		6543					ART TRANSP EMBALLAGE ETC
8939	MISC PLASTIC ARTICLES		25670		23815					ART DIVERS EN MAT DIV 58
89399	OTHR PLASTC ARTICLES NES		24626		22983					AUT OUV MAT DIV 58
894	TOYS,SPORTING GOODS,ETC		11875		11050					VOITURES ENFANTS,JOUETS
8942	TOYS,INDOOR GAMES ETC		9218		8672		9077		13623	JOUETS,JEUX ETC
897	GOLD,SILVER WARE,JEWELRY		29649		35852		57106		58125	BIJOUTERIE,ORFEVRERIE
8973	PREC JEWLRY,GLD–SILVWARE		29034		35432					BIJOUX OR,ARGENT ORFEVRE
89731	PRECIOUS METAL JEWELLERY		7882		9207					ART BIJOUTERIE,JOAILLER
89732	GOLD,SILVER,ETC WARE		21098		26182					ORFEVRERIE MET PRECIEUX
898	MUSICAL INSTRUMENTS,PTS		7305		8194		932		1750	INSTRUMENTS DE MUSIQUE
8983	SOUND RECRDNG TAPE,DISCS		6050		7119					SUPPORTS SON POUR 763
899	OTHER MANUFACTURED GOODS		9525		8463		7799		26626	AUT ART MANUF DIVERS NDA
9	GOODS NOT CLASSD BY KIND		28907		17906					ART TRANSACT NON CLASSES
971	*GOLD,NON MONETARY NES		21972		11615					OR NON MONETAIRE
97101	NONMON GLD UNWRT,SEMIMFD	K 2132	21962		11614					OR,ALLIAGES D'OR BRUTS

5. General Exports F.O.B. by Commodities according to the S.I.T.C. (Rev. 2) in thousand U.S. Dollars
Exportations Générales F.O.B. par Produits d'après la C.T.C.I. (Rév. 2) en milliers de Dollars E.U.

SITC CTCI	COMMODITY	1992		1993		1994		1995		PRODUIT
		WEIGHT POIDS	VALUE VALEUR	WEIGHT POIDS	VALUE VALEUR	WEIGHT POIDS	VALUE VALEUR	WEIGHT POIDS	VALUE VALEUR	
	ALL COMMODITIES		1537319		1355384		1556159		1888424	TOUS PRODUITS
0	FOOD AND LIVE ANIMALS		29559		28418					ALIMENTS,ANIMAUX VIVANTS
03	FISH AND PREPARATIONS		2072		6249		6609		3999	POISSONS ET PREPARATIONS
034	FISH,FRESH,CHILLED,FROZN	W 260	1781		5966					POISSON FRAIS, REFRIG,CONG
0341	FISH FRSH,CHLLD,EX FILLT	W 247	1706		5943					POISSON FRAIS,REFRIGERE
05	VEGETABLES AND FRUIT		8079		3559					LEGUMES ET FRUITS
09	MISC EDIBLE PRODUCTS		11851		13421					PREP ALIMENTAIRES DIVERSES
098	EDIBLE PRODCTS,PREPS NES		11792		13413		10172		13124	PREP ALIMENTAIRES NDA
09809	MISC FOOD PREPRTIONS NES	W 5516	9963		11541					PREP ALIMENTAIRES NDA
1	BEVERAGES AND TOBACCO		14616		12721					BOISSONS ET TABACS
11	BEVERAGES		6806		6390		6495		6473	BOISSONS
112	ALCOHOLIC BEVERAGES	W 1511	6519	W 1780	6137					BOISSONS ALCOOLIQUES
1124	DISTILLED ALCOHOLIC BEVS	W 418	5343	W 443	4931					ALCOOLS,EAUX–DE–VIE
12	TOBACCO AND MANUFACTURES		7810		6332		5835		7642	TABACS BRUTS FABRIQUES
122	TOBACCO,MANUFACTURED	W 130	5610	W 135	5224					TABACS FABRIQUES
1222	CIGARETTES	W 119	4912	W 122	4552					CIGARETTES
2	CRUDE MATERLS,EXCL FUELS		5441		6931					MAT BRUTES NON COMESTIBLES
3	MINERAL FUELS ETC		30929		29980		29599		29793	COMBUSTIBLES MINERAUX LUB
33	PETROLEUM AND PRODUCTS		30929		29980					PETROLE ET DERIVES
334	PETROLEUM PRODUCTS,REFIN	W 181410	30893		29980					PRODUITS RAFFINES
3342	KEROSENE,OTH MEDIUM OILS				11440					PETR LAMPANTS,AUT HUIL
3343	GAS OILS				9714					GAS OILS
3344	FUEL OILS,NES				7327					FUEL OILS
5	CHEMCLS,RELATED PROD NES		38717		34420					PRODUITS CHIMIQUES
541	*MEDICINAL,PHARM PRODUCT	K 550046	12345		14765		19074		21436	PROD MEDICINAUX PHARMACEUT
5417	MEDICAMENTS	K 537430	12086		14311					MEDICAMENTS
54179	— CONTNG OTH SUBSTANCES	K 536764	12055		14283					MED CONT AUT SUBSTANCES
55	PERFUME,CLEANING ETC PRD		18247		15711		13746		13024	PROD POUR PARFUM,TOILETTE
553	PERFUMERY,COSMETICS,ETC		13256	W 123	10502					PRODUITS DE PARFUMERIE
554	SOAP,CLEANSING ETC PREPS	W 2122	3674	W 1642	4247					SAVONS,PRODUITS DETERSIFS
598	MISCEL CHEM PRODUCTS NES		252		148		13727		482	PROD DIV INDUST CHIM NDA
6	BASIC MANUFACTURES		112683		96980					ART MANUFACTURES
61	LEATHER,DRESSED FUR,ETC		27981		26921					CUIRS,PELLETERIES
612	LEATHER ETC MANUFACTURES	W 329	26394		24901					OUVRAGES EN CUIRS NDA
6123	PREPRD PARTS OF FOOTWEAR	W 281	25280		23830					PARTIES DE CHAUSSURES
62	RUBBER MANUFACTURES NES		28597		26183		31295		40254	CAOUTCHOUC MANUFACTURE
628	RUBBER ARTICLES NES		28425		26028					OUVRAGES CAOUTCHOUC NDA
6289	OTH RUBBER ARTICLES NES		28424		26028					AUT OUVR CAOUTCHOUC NDA
62898	UNHARD RUBBER PRODS NES		28424		26028					OUV CAOUT VULC NON DURCI
64	PAPER,PAPERBOARD AND MFR		5721		6649		4698		1884	PAPIERS,CARTONS & OUVRAGES
642	PAPER,ETC,PRECUT,ARTS OF		5610		6443					PAP,CARTONS DECOUPES
6428	PAPER ETC ARTICLES NES		4998		6154					OUVRAGES EN PATE A PAPIER
65	TEXTILE YARN,FABRICS,ETC		24236		15631					FILS,TISSUS,ARTICLES TEXTILE
651	TEXTILE YARN		13642		7522					FILS TEXTILES
6514	SYN FIB YRN,BULK,MONOFIL		13628	W 2075	7465					FILS CONT 85% FIB TEXT SYNTH
65142	— NONTXT ETC CONT PAMID	W 2696	13227	W 2066	7289					FILS NON TEX FI CON POLYAMID
68	NON–FERROUS METALS		5127		3090					METAUX NON FERREUX
684	ALUMINIUM	W 2165	5010		2809					ALUMINIUM
6842	ALUMINIUM,ALLOYS WORKED	W 2165	5010		2672					ALUMINIUM,ALLIAGES OUVRE
68421	ALUMINIUM BARS,WIRE,ETC	W 2160	4983	W 1351	2630					BARRES,PROFILES FILS ALU
69	METAL MANUFACTURES NES		15515		14139					ART MANUFACT EN METAL NDA
697	BASE MTL HOUSEHOLD EQUIP		7556		6978					ART MENAGE MET COMMUNS
6975	BASE MTL INDR SANIT WARE	W 1272	7084		6643					ART HYG NDA FER,AC,CU,ALU
69751	IRON,STL INDR SANIT WARE	W 1272	7084		6643					ART HYGIENE NDA FER,ACIER
7	MACHINES,TRANSPORT EQUIP		909432		774574					MACHINES MATERIEL TRANSPORT
71	POWER GENERATING EQUIPMT		21073		15987		68921		74509	MACHINES GENERATRICES
714	ENGINES AND MOTORS NES		16997		14362					MOTEURS NON ELECTRIQUES
7144	REACTION ENGINES	N 76	10140		6815					PROPULSEURS A REACTION
7149	ENGINE & MOTOR PARTS NES		6857		6203					PIECES 714 ET 718.88
71491	PARTS NES OF 7144,71481		6832		6203					PIECES DES PROPULSEURS
72	MACHS FOR SPCL INDUSTRYS		7836		4445					MAC SPECIALES POUR INDUST
726	PRINTG,BKBINDG MACHY,PTS		5416		1177					MACHINES POUR IMPRIMERIE
74	GENRL INDUSTRL MACHY NES		19375		21450					MACH APP INDUSTRIE
742	PUMPS FOR LIQUIDS ETC		11131		13794					POMPES MOTO–POMPES
7422	CENTRIFUGAL PUMPS NES	N 4	2		6414					POMPES CENTRIF NON 742.81
7428	OTHER PUMPS FOR LIQUIDS	N 6952	8032	N 1097	3540					AUTRES POMPES POUR LIQ
74288	PUMPS FR LIQUIDS NES ETC	N 6952	8032	N 1097	3540					POMPES POUR LIQUIDES NDA
749	NONELEC MACH PTS,ACC NES		4554		4507					PIECES MACH NON ELEC NDA
7499	OTH NONELEC MCHY PTS NES		4548		4384					PIECES NON ELECT NDA
75	OFFICE MACHNES,ADP EQUIP		6547		26995					MACH BUREAU TRAIT AUTOM
752	AUTOMTIC DATA PROC EQUIP	N 2296	2843		16213					MACH TRAIT INFORMATION
7523	DIGITL CENTRL PROCESSORS	N 12	55	N 541	6912					UNITES CENTRALES
7525	ADP PERIPHERAL UNITS	N 2031	563	N 77568	8842					UNITES PERIPHERIQUES
759	OFFICE,ADP MCH PTS,ACCES		2717		9214					PIECES DU 751 ET 752
7599	ACCTG,ETC,ADP MCH PTS,AC	W 8	2694		9103					PIECES DU 751 ET 752
76	TELECOMM,SOUND EQUIPMENT		33729		41499					EQUIPMENT DE TELECOM
761	TELEVISION RECEIVERS	N 185473	31037	N 279556	39728					RECEPTEURS DE TELEVISION
7611	COLOUR TV RECEIVERS	N 185473	31037	N 279556	39728					RECEPTEURS COULEUR
77	ELECTRIC MACHNRY NES ETC		797100		643620					MACH APP ELECT NDA
772	SWITCHGEAR ETC,PARTS NES		43824		40066					APP COUPURE,SECT ETC
7721	SWITCHGEAR ETC		43388		37994					APP COUPURE,SECTIONMNT
776	TRANSISTORS,VALVES,ETC		743457		595756					LAMPES,TUBES,VALVES
7763	DIODES,TRANSISTORS,ETC		742566		595518					DIODES,TRANSISTORS
78	ROAD VEHICLES		4083		4061		3136		6679	VEHICULES ROUTIERS
79	OTHR TRANSPORT EQUIPMENT		18780		14333					AUTRE MATERIEL TRANSPORT
792	AIRCRAFT ETC		18514		14211		27515		26937	APP NAVIGATION AERIENNE
7929	AIRCRAFT PARTS NES	W 24	18120		14090					PIECES DU 792
793	SHIPS AND BOATS ETC	N 76	267		122		520		39798	NAVIRES BATEAUX,ETC
8	MISC MANUFACTURED GOODS		389897		367743					ART MANUFACTURES DIVERS
821	*FURNITURE,PARTS THEREOF		5418		5018					MEUBLES ET PIECES
831	*TRAVEL GOODS,HANDBAGS		4991		5613					ARTICLES DE VOYAGE ETC
83102	TRAVEL GDS,TOILET–CASES	N 584663	4134		4144					ARTICLES DE VOYAGE
84	CLOTHING AND ACCESSORIES		176088		153197					VETEMENTS
842	MENS OUTERWEAR NOT KNIT	N 5585900	99210	N 5749305	94566					VET DESSUS POUR HOMMES
8422	— SUITS	N 211996	14877	N 181891	12335					COMPLETS HOMMES MAT TEXT
84223	—— OF MAN–MADE FIBRES	N 211996	14877	N 178147	12110					COMPLETS HOMMES FIB SYNT
8423	— TROUSERS,BREECHES ETC	N 4298146	58771	N 5036393	61183					PANTALONS HOMMES MAT TEX
8424	— JACKETS,BLAZERS ETC	N 341838	16078	N 375992	16857					VESTES HOMMES MAT TEXTIL
8429	— OTHER OUTER GARMENTS	N 661787	8339	N 114505	3306					AUT VET DES HOM MAT TEX
843	WOMENS OUTERWEAR NONKNIT	N 3299308	56456	N 2154130	38977					VET DESSUS FEMMES MAT TEX
8431	— COATS AND JACKETS	N 358319	18107	N 201509	12309					MANT,VEST FEM MAT TEXTIL

5. General Exports F.O.B. by Commodities according to the S.I.T.C. (Rev. 2) in thousand U.S. Dollars
Exportations Générales F.O.B. par Produits d'après la C.T.C.I. (Rév. 2) en milliers de Dollars E.U.

SITC CTCI	COMMODITY	1992		1993		1994		1995		PRODUIT
		WEIGHT POIDS	VALUE VALEUR	WEIGHT POIDS	VALUE VALEUR	WEIGHT POIDS	VALUE VALEUR	WEIGHT POIDS	VALUE VALEUR	
8433	— DRESSES	N 675840	7466	N 584205	5852					ROBES EN MAT–TEXTILES
8434	— SKIRTS	N 320446	6112	N 105897	2105					JUPES EN MAT TEXTILES
8435	— BLOUSES	N 395179	5424	N 331519	3664					BLOUSES FEM MAT TEXTILES
8439	— OTHER OUTER GARMENTS	N 1540081	19179	N 912664	14454					AUT VET DES FEM MAT TEXT
846	UNDER GARMENTS KNITTED	N 4812626	9585		11239					SOUS VETS DE BONNETERIE
8462	— OF COTTON NON ELASTIC	N 3191308	4879		5710					SOUS–VET BONNET COTON
84629	—— OTHER	N 3191308	4879		5710					AUT SOUS–VET BONNET COTON
8465	CORSETS,GARTERS,ETC	N 1402891	4508		5325					CORSETS,GAINES ART SIM
84651	BRASSIERES	N 1223264	3928	N 1248298	4828					SOUTIENS–GORGE,BUSTIERS
848	HEADGEAR,NONTXTL CLOTHNG		4990		3084					VET ACCES MAT AUT QUE TEX
8481	LEATHER CLOTHES,ACCESSOR		152		65		6816		9535	VET ACCES MAT CUIR ARTIF
851	*FOOTWEAR	P 205282	3839		3941		26211		33157	CHAUSSURES
87	PRECISION INSTRUMNTS NES		21611		22173					INSTRUM,APPAR SCIENT NDA
872	MEDICAL INSTRUMENTS NES	W 843	18118		16378					INSTR,APP MEDIC–CHIR NDA
87202	OTH MEDICAL INSTRUMENTS	W 843	18109		16212					INSTRUM,APP MEDECINE
874	MEASURNG,CONTROLNG INSTR		2978		5460					INSTRUMENTS DE MESURE
88	PHOTO EQU,OPTICL GDS ETC		48877		30049					APP,FOURN PHOTO,OP,MONTR
884	OPTICAL GOODS NES		42846		25099					ELEMENTS OPTIQ,ART LUNET
8842	SPECTACLES AND FRAMES	N 5916126	42831		25097					LUNETTES ET MONTURES
88421	SPECTACLE FRAMES	N 5415171	37297	N 1393211	20658					MONTURES DE LUNETTES
88422	SPECTACLES ETC	N 500955	5534		4439					LUNETTES
885	WATCHES AND CLOCKS		5843		4711		6241		3854	HORLOGERIE
8852	CLOCKS,CLOCK,WATCH PARTS		5793		4711					HORLOGES,MOUV,PARTIES
88524	TIME SWITCHES		5598		4581					APP DECLENC MECANISME
89	MISC MANUFCTRD GOODS NES		128985		147658					ART MANUFACTURES DIVERS
892	PRINTED MATTER		51837		60106		53551		50009	IMPRIMES
8928	PRINTED MATTER NES		49706		57322					IMPRIMES NDA
89283	UNISSUED BANKNOTES ETC	W 2080	49377		57159					TIMBRES–POSTE FISCAUX
893	ARTICLES OF PLASTIC NES		12399		13417					OUVRAGES EN MAT DIVIS 58
8931	PLSTC PACKG CONTNRS,LIDS		11376		12670					ART TRANSP EMBALLAGE ETC
894	TOYS,SPORTING GOODS,ETC		25147		30291					VOITURES ENFANTS,JOUETS
8942	TOYS,INDOOR GAMES ETC		25008		30243		32221		44624	JOUETS,JEUX ETC
89422	DOLLS		466		7555					POUPEES
89423	TOYS NES		24538		22667					JOUETS,MODELES REDUITS
897	GOLD,SILVER WARE,JEWELRY		35358		40697		34824		39958	BIJOUTERIE,ORFEVRERIE
8973	PREC JEWLRY,GLD–SILVWARE		35358		40696					BIJOUX OR,ARGENT ORFEVRE
89731	PRECIOUS METAL JEWELLERY		35325		40634					ART BIJOUTERIE,JOAILLER
9	GOODS NOT CLASSD BY KIND		6028		3617					ART TRANSACT NON CLASSES

Martinique

1. HISTORICAL SERIES, 1960–1995 SPECIAL TRADE, IMPORTS C.I.F., EXPORTS F.O.B.
SERIES HISTORIQUES, 1960–1995 COMMERCE SPECIAL, IMPORTATIONS C.A.F., EXPORTATIONS F.O.B

YEAR ANNEE	VALUE IN MILLION FRANCS VALEUR EN MILLION FRANCS				CONVERSION FACTORS U.S. CENTS PER FRANC FACTEURS DE CONVERSION CENTS E.U. PAR FRANC		INDEX NUMBERS –INDICES			
	MERCHANDISE –MARCHANDISE		GOLD –OR				QUANTUM		UNIT VALUE VALEUR UNITAIRE	
	IMPORTS	EXPORTS	IMPORTS	EXPORTS	IMPORTS	EXPORTS	IMPORTS	EXPORTS	IMPORTS	EXPORTS
1960	232.90	159.50			20.2600	20.2600				
1961	250.90	165.80			20.2600	20.2600				
1962	280.90	166.00			20.2600	20.2600				
1963	364.30	175.90			20.2600	20.2600				
1964	389.30	144.60			20.2600	20.2600				
1965	449.00	185.60			20.2600	20.2600				
1966	457.50	220.70			20.2600	20.2600				
1967	520.40	211.60			20.2600	20.2600				
1968	537.40	197.00			20.2600	20.2600				
1969	651.30	182.10			19.3700	19.5500				
1970	810.20	166.80			18.0000	18.0000				
1971	860.10	188.90			18.0700	18.0400				
1972	871.80	228.20			19.8401	19.8552				
1973	1083.20	244.30			22.5486	22.6188				
1974	1405.10	347.10			20.8484	20.8642				
1975	1453.50	407.70			23.4052	23.5237				
1976	1965.10	594.00			21.0526	20.9558				
1977	2098.60	630.30			20.3748	20.3755				
1978	2240.90	566.90			22.2405	21.9754				
1979	2869.90	567.00			23.5484	23.3940				
1980	3564.40	492.00			23.6632	23.7135				
1981	4188.00	894.70			18.5287	18.9077				
1982	4835.10	763.60			15.2139	15.1455				
1983	5577.70	866.60			13.1696	13.2143				
1984	5983.10	1350.80			11.4608	11.3692				
1985	6050.10	1456.20			11.2823	11.1508				
1986	6065.36	1496.35			14.4980	14.4582				
1987	6707.81	1169.74			16.6870	16.6208				
1988	7692.14	1171.28			16.7689	16.7764				
1989	8387.42	1277.24			15.7001	15.6506				
1990	9680.59	1512.15			18.3735	18.4115				
1991	9520.17	1207.64			17.8000	17.8717				
1992	9266.81	1312.12			18.8828	18.8225				
1993	8812.08	1078.15			17.6603	17.7520				
1994	9092.86	1214.76			18.0619	17.9814				
1995	9769.32	1111.60			20.0886	20.1268				

2. IMPORTS BY BROAD ECONOMIC CATEGORY AND EXPORTS BY INDUSTRIAL ORIGIN. (PERCENTAGE OF TOTAL VALUE)
IMPORTATIONS PAR CATEGORIES ECONOMIQUES ET EXPORTATIONS PAR BRANCHE D'ACTIVITE.(EN POURCENTAGE DE LA VALEUR TOTALE)

IMPORTS – IMPORTATIONS

	1990	1991	1992	1993	1994	1995	1996
TOTAL IMPORTS–IMPORTATIONS TOTALES	100.	100.	100.	100.	100.	100.	
1 FOOD BEV–ALIMENTATION BOISSONS	16.9	18.1	18.4	19.9	20.0	18.3	
11 PRIMARY–PRODUITS DE BASE	6.4	6.8	7.0	7.7	7.7	7.1	
111 FOR INDUSTRY–POUR L'INDUSTRIE	0.3	0.4	0.3	0.3	0.3	0.3	
112 FOR HOUSEHOLDS–POUR LES MENAGES	6.1	6.4	6.7	7.4	7.4	6.8	
12 PROCESSED–PRODUITS ELABORES	10.5	11.3	11.3	12.2	12.3	11.3	
121 FOR INDUSTRY–POUR L'INDUSTRIE	0.9	1.0	0.9	1.1	1.1	0.7	
122 FOR HOUSEHOLDS–POUR LES MENAGES	9.6	10.4	10.4	11.2	11.2	10.5	
2 IND SUPPLIES–APPROV INDUSTRIELS	19.7	20.4	18.9	18.4	19.2	18.2	
21 PRIMARY–PRODUITS DE BASE	0.7	0.7	0.8	0.8	0.8	0.8	
22 PROCESSED–PRODUITS ELABORES	19.0	19.7	18.1	17.6	18.4	17.4	
3 FUELS–COMBUSTIBLES	9.8	7.7	9.0	7.4	7.8	7.4	
31 PRIMARY–PRODUITS DE BASE	8.9	6.7	7.9	6.4	6.3	5.3	
32 PROCESSED–PRODUITS ELABORES	0.9	0.9	1.1	1.0	1.5	2.1	
321 MOTOR SPIRIT–ESSENCE		0.9	1.1	0.9		0.6	
322 OTHER–AUTRES	0.9	0.0	0.0	0.0	1.5	1.5	
4 MACHINERY–EQUIPEMENT	12.2	13.3	12.0	12.3	12.5	13.5	
41 CAPITAL EQUIPMENT–MACHINES	11.2	12.2	10.8	11.1	11.3	12.2	
42 PARTS–PIECES ACCESSOIRES	1.1	1.1	1.2	1.3	1.3	1.2	
5 TRANSPORT–TRANSPORT	19.0	16.0	16.2	16.6	14.1	18.4	
51 PASSENGER CARS–AUTOMOBILES	4.4	4.8	5.8	6.6	6.2	7.5	
52 OTHER–AUTRES	10.9	7.2	6.2	5.7	3.8	5.2	
521 INDUSTRIAL–INDUSTRIELS	10.6	6.9	5.9	5.4	3.6	4.9	
522 NON INDUSTRIAL–NON INDUSTRIEL	0.2	0.3	0.3	0.2	0.3	0.2	
53 PARTS–PIECES ACCESSOIRES	3.7	4.0	4.2	4.3	4.1	5.6	
6 CONSUM GOODS–BIENS CONSOMMATION	20.3	22.1	22.6	23.4	23.7	22.3	
61 DURABLE–DURABLES	4.7	5.4	5.5	5.4	5.5	5.1	
62 SEMI DURABLE–SEMI DURABLES	9.0	9.9	10.0	10.1	10.3	9.7	
63 NON DURABLE–NON DURABLES	6.5	6.7	7.1	7.9	7.9	7.5	
7 GOODS NES–BIENS NDA	2.1	2.4	2.9	1.9	2.7	2.0	

EXPORTS – EXPORTATIONS

	1990	1991	1992	1993	1994	1995	1996
TOTAL EXPORTS–EXPORTATIONS TOTALES	100.	100.	100.	100.	100.	100.	
1 AGRICULTURE	44.4	42.4	45.9	36.7	29.8	42.9	
2 MINING QUARRY–INDUS EXTRACTIVES	0.6	0.7	0.9	1.3	1.4	1.4	
3 MANUFACTURING–IND MANUFACTUR	55.0	56.8	53.2	62.0	68.8	55.7	
31 FOOD BEV TOBACCO–ALIM BOISS TAB	16.6	22.1	18.4	22.5	23.5	19.3	
32 TEXTILES–INDUSTRIES TEXTILES	0.3	0.4	0.5	0.3	0.4	0.5	
33 WOOD & PRODUCTS–BOIS & PRODUITS	0.2	0.4	0.1	0.1	0.1	0.1	
34 PAPER & PRODUCTS–PAPIER & PRODT	4.1	1.4	2.6	1.4	1.1	0.6	
35 CHEMICALS–INDUSTRIES CHIMIQUES	19.0	23.2	18.9	22.3	30.6	19.5	
36 NON METAL MIN–MIN NON METAL	0.4	0.3	0.3	0.2	0.1	0.1	
37 BASIC METAL–IND METAL BASE	0.3	0.4	0.5	0.3	0.3	0.3	
38 METAL MANUF–MANUF METAL	13.8	8.6	11.8	14.7	12.6	15.0	
39 OTH MANUF IND–AUTRES MANUF	0.3	0.3	0.1	0.2	0.2	0.2	

3. TRADE BY PRINCIPAL COUNTRIES OF PRODUCTION AND LAST CONSIGNMENT (VALUE IN THOUSAND U.S. DOLLARS)
ECHANGES SELON LES PRINCIPAUX PAYS DE PRODUCTION ET DE DERNIERE CONSIGNATION (VALEUR EN MILLIERS DE DOLLARS EU)

COUNTRIES–PAYS	SPECIAL IMPORTS C.I.F. IMPORTATIONS SPECIALES C.A.F				
	1991	1992	1993	1994	1995
World	1700305	1762690	1631250	1642265	1969815
Africa	31040	62804	19688	31174	58571
Americas	150837	158228	155605	156130	185494
Northern America	55199	57851	53225	50034	61843
LAIA	39912	42244	40622	36998	39550
CACM	2799	1877	2640	2967	2557
Caribbean	45663	47689	50226	54223	70600
Rest of America	7264	8567	8894	11907	10945
As.ex F.USSR	126181	157883	123710	131451	142140
Eur.x F.USSR	1361769	1348041	1295362	1268478	1529463
EU	1339787	1329709	1278059	1252086	1511980
EFTA	18574	15236	14361	11351	12921
East Europe	1859	1883	2157	4438	4341
Other Europe	1549	20	24	15	9
Former USSR	365	1220	683	956	178
Oceania	5715	6317	6489	5289	5109
France,Monac	1057059	1067067	1004051	1009123	1236359
Germany/Allemagne	60820	70287	59777	52991	64293
Italy/Italie	59385	54215	56927	57424	73372
United Kingdom	69665	36185	71723	51828	38021
USA/Etats–Unis d'Amer	48805	52389	47773	45192	56451
Japan/Japon	46596	42788	41060	34717	43701
Belgium–Luxembourg	24701	32209	33789	26444	27725
United Arab Emirates	32420	66638	24494	12063	65
Netherlands/Pays–Bas	19566	23898	26394	23725	26945
Cameroon/Cameroun	31	42733	14065	25325	28296
Spain/Espagne	30885	30174	11704	14444	21833
Brazil/Brésil	15672	14604	17685	19931	21684
Trinidad and Tobago	14269	9407	11243	17665	30167
Venezuela	19808	21095	17875	11490	11905
Guadeloupe	18539	17029	17858	18511	9195
Netherlands Antilles	6348	13774	12665	7953	16094
Korea, Republic of	5080	7268	10158	12235	18844
Saudi Arabia	13608	147	115	23166	12503
China/Chine	7291	8915	10023	10719	11488
Norway,SVD,JM	10008	9277	8269	7029	7844
Kuwait/ Koweït			12983	10415	13441
Denmark/Danemark	4139	3846	4428	5263	9991
Canada	6358	5458	5449	4841	5392
French Guiana	3715	4689	4809	7176	7025
Switz.Liecht	7743	5210	4998	3452	4634
New Zealand	4904	5510	5951	4804	4714
Nigeria/Nigéria	25746	10		2	6
Gabon					23259
Sweden/Suède	5661	3676	2137	2559	4752
Thailand/Thaïlande	3281	4100	3848	3296	4138
Angola	16	14964	144	50	28
Portugal	3215	2952	1900	3072	3512
Singapore/Singapour	2518	2760	1604	6260	1075
Suriname/Suriname	1885	2343	2677	3325	3409
Indonesia/Indonésie	1129	2253	2357	3946	3800
Iran (Islamic Rp. of)	78	179	17	19	12324
Colombia/Colombie	1363	3000	2530	2891	2780
India/Inde	1846	2314	1909	2577	2079
Hong Kong	2293	2166	2317	1860	1867
Malaysia/Malaisie	1196	1852	2454	2691	2282
Honduras	2009	1408	2201	2371	1665
Jamaica/Jamaïque	1342	1828	1121	2591	2583
Dominican Republic	1497	1454	2026	1673	2437
Ireland/Irlande	1544	1416	1885	1931	2187
Austria/Autriche	1538	1390	1926	1907	1966
Israel/Israël	292	1302	700	1731	3608
Czech Republic			1212	2844	3048
Turkey/Turquie	1890	1986	1144	1072	918
Morocco/Maroc	1667	1325	1464	1171	1185
St Vincent & Grenadines	626	1109	1536	1624	1701

COUNTRIES–PAYS	SPECIAL EXPORTS F.O.B. EXPORTATIONS SPECIALES F.O.B.				
	1991	1992	1993	1994	1995
Monde	216098	254541	201978	218605	241916
Afrique	51	45	11	96	1381
Amériques	86665	88375	68109	106547	50719
Amérique du Nord	868	2548	1334	2516	6716
ALAI	438	311	175	59	126
MCAC				38	
Caraïbes	71921	75814	61403	97718	36385
Autre Amérique	13438	9703	5197	6217	7492
Asie l'URSS exclus	181	107	724	7	816
Europe l'URSS exclus	129153	164592	132998	111894	188844
UE	129107	164416	132879	111804	188798
AELE	46	176	119	91	41
Europe de l'Est					
Autre de l'Europe					6
Ancienne URSS					
Océanie	28	1423	136	60	95
France,Monac	123325	160716	130411	96591	148476
Guadeloupe	68030	72762	58812	93299	30203
French Guiana	13348	9698	5197	6000	7479
Belgium–Luxembourg	233	734	202	10468	20727
United Kingdom	1616	619	347	2726	16900
USA/Etats–Unis d'Amer	826	1740	1291	2402	6406
Saint Lucia/St. Lucie	1855	1763	1439	2351	2421
Germany/Allemagne	3238	1337	712	787	487
Italy/Italie	167	790	577	753	1315
St Vincent & Grenadines	1006	89	30	85	885
Dominica/Dominique	471	283	616	279	276
French Polynesia	22	1412	79	21	17
British Virgin Islds	192	61	5		1228
Netherlands Antilles	132	131	295	331	588
Netherlands/Pays–Bas	22	182	571	423	231
Canada	42	808	44	109	311
Malaysia/Malaisie			647		564
Trinidad and Tobago	65	434	21	410	263
Cameroon/Cameroun					1157
Spain/Espagne	507	2	54	35	479
Venezuela	343	248	140	47	90
Dominican Republic	5	3		434	27
Grenada/Grenade	4	18	88	220	99
Switz.Liecht	40	152	105	39	14
Antigua and Barbuda		78			261
Barbados/Barbade	116	138	36	20	24
Panama	91			217	
Haiti/Haïti	32	46	57	103	40
Japan/Japon	20	80	26	7	29
Sweden/Suède		35		9	118
New Caledonia	6	11	20	38	78
United Arab Emirates					147
Turkey/Turquie	143				
Aruba				135	
Reunion/Réunion	29	10	10		83
Brazil/Brésil	49	9	28	5	36
Norway,SVD,JM	6	24	14	52	26
Mauritius/Maurice				9	103
Singapore/Singapour	18	24	51		
Denmark/Danemark				9	56
Cuba			5	37	5
Central African Rep.				46	
Cote d'Ivoire		32			8
Philippines					40
Costa Rica				38	
Australia/Australie			37		
Hong Kong					37
Guinea/Guinée		2			27
Tunisia/Tunisie				27	
Ecuador/Equateur	26				

(VALUE AS PERCENTAGE OF WORLD TOTAL)(VALEURS EN POURCENTAGE DU TOTAL MONDIAL)

	1986	1987	1988	1989	1990	1991	1992	1993	1994	1995
Africa	0.4	0.5	1.6	0.6	0.4	1.8	3.6	1.2	1.9	3.0
Americas	8.9	7.3	7.9	8.1	7.8	8.9	9.0	9.5	9.5	9.4
Northern America	2.5	2.3	2.5	2.7	2.9	3.2	3.3	3.3	3.0	3.1
LAIA	2.6	1.4	1.6	1.9	1.9	2.3	2.4	2.5	2.3	2.0
CACM	0.3	0.2	0.2	0.2	0.2	0.2	0.1	0.2	0.2	0.1
Caribbean	2.8	2.8	3.1	2.9	2.4	2.7	2.7	3.1	3.3	3.6
Rest of America	0.7	0.6	0.4	0.3	0.3	0.4	0.5	0.5	0.7	0.6
As.ex F.USSR	5.0	6.1	7.1	7.3	8.9	7.4	9.0	7.6	8.0	7.2
Eur.x F.USSR	85.1	85.2	82.5	83.0	81.2	80.1	76.5	79.4	77.2	77.6
EU	83.6	84.1	81.4	81.7	80.2	78.8	75.4	78.3	76.2	76.8
EFTA	1.1	0.9	0.9	1.0	0.8	1.1	0.9	0.9	0.7	0.7
East Europe	0.4	0.2	0.2	0.2	0.1	0.1	0.1	0.1	0.3	0.2
Other Europe	0.0	0.1	0.1	0.1	0.1	0.1	0.0	0.0	0.0	0.0
Former USSR	0.0	0.0	0.0	0.0	0.0	0.0	0.1	0.0	0.1	0.0
Oceania	0.3	0.3	0.3	0.4	0.3	0.3	0.4	0.4	0.3	0.3
France,Monac	63.7	65.2	64.4	62.7	63.5	62.2	60.5	61.6	61.4	62.8
Germany/Allemagne	2.7	3.0	4.1	3.9	3.7	3.6	4.0	3.7	3.2	3.3
Italy/Italie	4.1	3.7	3.8	4.0	3.2	3.5	3.1	3.5	3.5	3.7
United Kingdom	7.4	6.2	3.3	5.5	5.0	4.1	2.1	4.4	3.2	1.9
USA/Etats–Unis d'Amer	2.4	2.2	2.4	2.6	2.4	2.9	3.0	2.9	2.8	2.9
Japan/Japon	2.6	2.5	2.9	2.9	2.1	2.7	2.4	2.5	2.1	2.2
Belgium–Luxembourg	1.6	1.4	1.2	1.3	1.0	1.5	1.8	2.1	1.6	1.4
United Arab Emirates	1.1	2.1	2.4	0.9	5.1	1.9	3.8	1.5	0.7	0.0
Netherlands/Pays–Bas	1.8	1.8	1.6	1.5	1.1	1.2	1.4	1.6	1.4	1.4
Cameroon/Cameroun	0.0	0.0	0.0	0.0	0.0	0.0	2.4	0.9	1.5	1.4

	1986	1987	1988	1989	1990	1991	1992	1993	1994	1995
Afrique	0.0	0.0	0.0	0.1	0.0	0.0	0.0	0.0	0.0	0.6
Amériques	30.8	29.5	31.9	33.7	32.1	40.1	34.7	33.7	48.7	21.0
Amérique du Nord	0.3	0.3	0.9	1.5	0.7	0.4	1.0	0.7	1.2	2.8
ALAI	0.1	0.2	0.0	0.1	0.2	0.2	0.1	0.1	0.0	0.1
MCAC					0.0				0.0	
Caraïbes	27.9	26.0	26.8	29.0	26.8	33.3	29.8	30.4	44.7	15.0
Autre Amérique	2.5	3.1	4.1	3.1	4.4	6.2	3.8	2.6	2.8	3.1
Asie l'URSS exclus	0.0		0.0	0.0	0.0	0.1	0.0	0.4	0.0	0.3
Europe l'URSS exclus	69.2	70.4	68.1	66.2	67.8	59.8	64.7	65.8	51.2	78.1
UE	69.2	70.4	68.1	66.2	67.7	59.7	64.6	65.8	51.1	78.0
AELE	0.0		0.0	0.0	0.1	0.0	0.1	0.1	0.0	0.0
Europe de l'Est										
Autre de l'Europe										0.0
Ancienne URSS										
Océanie	0.0	0.0	0.0	0.0	0.0	0.0	0.6	0.1	0.0	0.0
France,Monac	65.1	64.6	64.7	62.7	61.7	57.1	63.1	64.6	44.2	61.4
Guadeloupe	25.8	24.1	24.4	26.5	25.0	31.5	28.6	29.1	42.7	12.5
French Guiana	2.5	3.0	4.1	3.1	4.3	6.2	3.8	2.6	2.7	3.1
Belgium–Luxembourg	0.0	0.0	0.1	0.0	0.1	0.1	0.3	0.1	4.8	8.6
United Kingdom	0.0	0.0	0.0	0.7	2.4	0.7	0.2	0.2	1.2	7.0
USA/Etats–Unis d'Amer	0.3	0.3	0.8	1.1	0.5	0.4	0.7	0.6	1.1	2.6
Saint Lucia/St. Lucie	1.1	1.0	1.1	1.1	0.6	0.9	0.7	0.7	1.1	1.0
Germany/Allemagne	4.0	5.6	2.6	2.7	1.4	1.5	0.5	0.4	0.4	0.2
Italy/Italie	0.0	0.0	0.4	0.0	1.6	0.1	0.3	0.3	0.3	0.5
St Vincent & Grenadines	0.1	0.1	0.3	0.1	0.1	0.5	0.0	0.0	0.0	0.4

4. Special Imports C.I.F. by Commodities according to the S.I.T.C. (Rev. 2) in thousand U.S. Dollars
Importations Spéciales C.A.F. par Produits d'après la C.T.C.I. (Rév. 2) en milliers de Dollars E.U.

SITC CTCI	COMMODITY	1992 WEIGHT POIDS	1992 VALUE VALEUR	1993 WEIGHT POIDS	1993 VALUE VALEUR	1994 WEIGHT POIDS	1994 VALUE VALEUR	1995 WEIGHT POIDS	1995 VALUE VALEUR	PRODUIT
	ALL COMMODITIES		1762690		1631250		1642265		1969815	TOUS PRODUITS
0	FOOD AND LIVE ANIMALS		287920		290603		293551		319593	ALIMENTS,ANIMAUX VIVANTS
01	MEAT AND PREPARATIONS		76935		78374		77386		82830	VIANDES ET PREPARATIONS
011	MEAT FRESH,CHILLD,FROZEN	W 17664	53863	W 19241	55597	W 19870	54603	W 20135	58657	VIANDES FRAICHES,REF,CONGE
0111	BOVINE MEAT FRESH,FROZEN	W 3276	20809	W 3351	21044	W 3497	20922	W 3426	22355	VIANDES BOVIN FRAI,REF
01111	BOVINE MEAT WITH BONE IN	W 792	5260	W 781	5384	W 584	3704	W 563	3830	VIANDES BOVIN NON DESOSS
01112	BOVINE MEAT BONELESS	W 2484	15549	W 2570	15660	W 2913	17218	W 2862	18525	VIANDES BOVIN DESOSSEES
0112	MUTTON ETC FRSH,CHLD,FRN	W 2069	5435	W 2069	5855	W 2044	5306	W 2001	5484	VIANDE DE MOUTON
0113	PIG MEAT FRESH,CHLD,FRZN	W 1263	4905	W 1642	5284	W 1835	5282	W 1872	6340	VIANDE DE PORC
0114	POULTRY FRESH CHLLD,FRZN	W 9283	19371	W 10230	19872	W 10352	19572	W 11074	20695	VOLAILLES MORTES
014	MEAT PREPD,PRSVD,NES ETC	W 5324	20915	W 5094	20351	W 5227	20256	W 5147	21530	CONSERVES DE VIANDES
0142	SAUSAGES INCLDING TINNED	W 2028	6631	W 1993	7438	W 2004	7286	W 2180	7771	SAUCISSES,SAUCISSONS
0149	OTH PREPARD,PRESRVD MEAT	W 3297	14284	W 3100	12912	W 3224	12970	W 2968	13758	AUTRES PREP DE VIANDES
02	DAIRY PRODCTS,BIRDS'EGGS		47611		48432		47489		53579	PRODUITS LAITIERS,OEUFS
022	MILK AND CREAM	W 20706	25726	W 22547	25264	W 23660	24308	W 25120	28667	LAIT ET CREME
0223	MILK AND CREAM FRESH	W 16154	11877	W 18212	13329	W 19171	12616	W 20483	14753	LAIT,CREME FRAIS
0224	MILK,CREAM PRESERVED ETC	W 4552	13849	W 4336	11935	W 4489	11692	W 4636	13915	LAIT,CREME CONS,CONC
02243	MILK DRY,OVER 1.5% FAT	W 1311	6100	W 1119	4663	W 1367	5298	W 1338	5488	LAIT POUDRE SUP 1.5%
024	CHEESE AND CURD	W 2381	15075	W 2846	16302	W 2889	16546	W 2920	18526	FROMAGE ET CAILLEBOTTE
03	FISH AND PREPARATIONS		33982		32711		34154		38630	POISSONS ET PREPARATIONS
034	FISH,FRESH,CHILLED,FROZN	W 3263	10960	W 3050	10144	W 3309	11224	W 3201	12055	POISSON FRAIS, REFRIG,CONG
0341	FISH FRSH,CHLLD,EX FILLT	W 1563	5683	W 1439	5247	W 1448	5103	W 1463	5867	POISSON FRAIS,REFRIGERE
0342	FISH FROZEN,EXCL FILLETS	W 1543	4658	W 1554	4641	W 1745	5603	W 1564	5364	POISSONS CONGELES
035	FISH SALTED,DRIED,SMOKED	W 2048	11962	W 2066	11003	W 2013	9495	W 2112	11503	POISSON SECHE,SALE,FUME
03503	FISH(EX COD)DRIED,SALTED	W 1654	9886	W 1701	9027	W 1712	8102	W 1764	9501	POISSONS SECHES,SALES
036	SHELL FISH FRESH,FROZEN	W 1324	7530	W 1407	7758	W 1389	9537	W 1356	10714	CRUSTACES,MOLLUSQUES
04	CEREALS AND PREPARATIONS		47160		45213		46774		45559	CEREALES ET PRODUITS
042	RICE	W 8472	6105	W 9403	6503	W 8108	6012	W 9059	7077	RIZ
0422	RICE SEMI–MILLED,MILLED	W 5012	4299	W 5910	4997	W 6607	4898	W 9015	6991	RIZ POLI,GLACE INCL BRISURES
04221	RICE MILLED UNBROKEN	W 4577	4005	W 5287	4698	W 5956	4633	W 8213	6644	RIZ POLI,GLACE EXCL BRISURES
044	MAIZE UNMILLED	W 25016	5623	W 16941	5390	W 20458	5604	W 16906	5057	MAIS NON MOULU
046	WHEAT ETC MEAL OR FLOUR	W 19308	10334	W 21864	10990	W 25554	12295	W 17491	8751	SEMOULE FARINE,FROMENT
04601	FLOUR OF WHEAT OR MESLIN	W 17757	9377	W 20628	10276	W 24164	11551	W 16310	8116	FARINE DE FROMENT
048	CEREAL ETC PREPARATIONS	W 11057	24257	W 9491	21848	W 8533	22251	W 9653	24229	PREPTNS A BASE CEREALES
0484	BAKERY PRODUCTS	W 3296	13068	W 3230	11971	W 4038	13633	W 5147	15315	PRODUITS DE BOULANGERIE
04841	BREAD,BISCUIT,COM WAFERS	W 1950	7622	W 2011	7369	W 2590	8771	W 3380	10026	PAINS,BISCUITS DE MER
04842	PASTRY, CAKES ETC	W 1346	5446	W 1219	4602	W 1448	4861	W 1767	5289	PATISSERIE ETC.
0488	OTH CEREAL PREPS,MALT EX	W 5080	6479	W 3515	4900	W 1113	3457	W 1091	3542	EXTRAITS DE MALT
05	VEGETABLES AND FRUIT		39601		41265		42910		49081	LEGUMES ET FRUITS
054	VEG ETC FRSH,SMPLY PRSVD	W 17830	14021	W 19333	15776	W 19451	16367	W 19426	19309	LEGUMES FRAIS,CONG,SECS
0545	OTHER FRESH VEGETABLES	W 7452	6343	W 7713	7025	W 8052	7119	W 8383	8439	AUTRES LEGUMES FRAIS,REF
056	VEGTBLES ETC PRSVD,PREPD	W 4279	7887	W 4476	7684	W 4703	7608	W 5062	8613	CONSERVES DE LEGUMES
0565	VEGTBLES PRSVD,PREPD NES	W 4084	7252	W 4287	7264	W 4510	7177	W 4880	8138	LEGUMES PREPARES CONSERVE
05659	OTH VEG PRESVD,PREPD NES	W 3977	6866	W 4154	6910	W 4300	6741	W 4686	7771	LEGUM PREPAP,CONSERV NDA
057	FRUIT,NUTS,FRESH,DRIED	W 6478	8394	W 7108	8338	W 6932	8454	W 8008	9610	FRUITS FRAIS OU SECS
058	FRUIT PRESERVED,PREPARED	W 4554	9299	W 5406	9466	W 6707	10481	W 7193	11548	CONSERVES DE FRUITS
0585	FRUIT OR VEGETABLE JUICE	W 3192	4812	W 3473	4284	W 4528	5003	W 4862	5638	JUS DE FRUITS
06	SUGAR AND PREPS,HONEY		10403		12730		12428		13413	SUCRES ET PRODUITS
061	SUGAR AND HONEY	W 6652	6985	W 8585	9196	W 8418	8848	W 8154	9552	SUCRES ET MIEL
0612	REFINED SUGAR ETC	W 5601	5777	W 7404	7658	W 7765	7953	W 7736	8834	SUCRES RAFFINES
07	COFFEE,TEA,COCOA,SPICES		9487		9045		9837		11117	CAFE,THE,CACAO,EPICES
073	CHOCOLATE AND PRODUCTS	W 1041	5967	W 1214	5924	W 1485	6075	W 1358	6301	CHOCOLAT
081	*FEEDING STUFF FOR ANIML	W 12484	6554	W 12122	6559	W 13219	6328	W 11079	6445	NOURRITURE POUR ANIMAUX
09	MISC EDIBLE PRODUCTS		15007		15224		15706		17703	PREP ALIMENTAIRES DIVERSES
098	EDIBLE PRODCTS,PREPS NES	W 3255	12979	W 3613	13154	W 4076	13711	W 4200	15521	PREP ALIMENTAIRES NDA
09809	MISC FOOD PREPRTIONS NES	W 1356	8101	W 1574	8537	W 1781	9045	W 2156	10658	PREP ALIMENTAIRES NDA
1	BEVERAGES AND TOBACCO		47232		46873		46721		51990	BOISSONS ET TABACS
11	BEVERAGES		40914		39798		38940		44868	BOISSONS
111	NON–ALCOHL BEVERAGES NES	W 10865	10465	W 11422	10274	W 13953	11110	W 19549	15169	BOISSONS NON ALCOOLIQUES
11102	FLAVORED WATERS NON–ALCO	W 7013	8360	W 7163	7985	W 9441	8930	W 12867	12136	LIMONADES,EAUX GAZEUSES
112	ALCOHOLIC BEVERAGES	W 13960	30448	W 14364	29524	W 13397	27830	W 13734	29699	BOISSONS ALCOOLIQUES
1121	WINE OF FRESH GRAPES ETC	W 6639	17848	W 6183	17830	W 6451	17055	W 5852	16733	VINS DE RAISINS FRAIS
11212	WINE OF FRESH GRAPES	W 5605	15562	W 5502	15801	W 5877	15321	W 5369	15127	VINS DE MOUTS DE RAISINS
1123	BEER,ALE,STOUT,PORTER	W 6226	8151	W 7169	7908	W 5920	7227	W 6770	9256	BIERES
12	TOBACCO AND MANUFACTURES		6319		7075		7781		7122	TABACS BRUTS FABRIQUES
122	TOBACCO,MANUFACTURED	W 273	6319	W 299	7075	W 324	7781	W 258	7122	TABACS FABRIQUES
1222	CIGARETTES	W 269	6104	W 293	6791	W 319	7511	W 251	6761	CIGARETTES
2	CRUDE MATERLS,EXCL FUELS		24231		22507		23665		26739	MAT BRUTES NON COMESTIBLES
24	CORK AND WOOD		15520		14254		14866		16304	LIEGE ET BOIS
248	WOOD SHAPED,SLEEPERS	W 27618	14705	W 25237	13662	W 25442	14056	W 24701	14279	BOIS SIMPLEMENT TRAVAILLES
2482	LUMBER SHAPED CONIFER	W 13168	6628	W 15210	7609	W 13045	6565	W 14139	7101	CONIFERES SCIES,RABOTES
2483	LUMBER SHAPED NON–CONIFR	W 14450	8077	W 10027	6052	W 12398	7491	W 10562	7178	NON CONIFERES SCIES,RABOTES
24831	LUMBER SAWN ETC NON–CON	W 11322	5560	W 8030	4307	W 9931	5405	W 8311	4921	SCIES LONGITUDINALEMENT
3	MINERAL FUELS ETC		162661		123472		128302		147977	COMBUSTIBLES MINERAUX LUB
33	PETROLEUM AND PRODUCTS		160471		122394		127702		146191	PETROLE ET DERIVES
333	CRUDE PETROLEUM	W 868875	136791	W 684297	104052	W 772200	103807	W 712768	102461	HUILES BRUTES DE PETROLE
334	PETROLEUM PRODUCTS,REFIN	W 60473	20015	W 63844	15794	W 98220	21464	W 191962	41076	PRODUITS RAFFINES
3341	GASOLINE,OTH LIGHT OILS	W 60404	19750	W 63728	15420			W 44339	10920	ESSENCES POUR MOTEURS
33411	MOTOR,AVIATION SPIRIT							W 44085	10687	ESSENCES MOTEURS D'AVIONS
33419	OTH LIGHT PETROLEUM OILS	W 60404	19750	W 63728	15420			W 254	233	AUTRES HUILES LEGERES
3344	FUEL OILS,NES							W 103733	14244	FUEL OILS
3345	LUBS,PETROLEUM OILS NES	W 68	265	W 116	374			W 6653	8491	HUILES LUBRIFIANTES
33451	LUBS(HIGH PETR CONT) ETC							W 6523	7932	HUILES LUBRIF,H LOURDES
4	ANIMAL,VEGETABLE OIL,FAT		7331		6991		7945		8332	HUILES,GRAISSES ANIM,VEG
42	FIXED VEGETABLE OIL,FAT		7029		6544		7470		7904	HUILES VEGETALES FIXES
423	FIXED VEG OILS,SOFT	W 5375	6257	W 5091	5920	W 5468	6820	W 5314	7200	HUILES VEGET DOUCES FIXES
4236	SUNFLOWER SEED OIL	W 4372	4956	W 4299	4792	W 4556	5490	W 4665	6053	HUILE DE TOURNESOL
5	CHEMCLS,RELATED PROD NES		161714		155820		164467		189505	PRODUITS CHIMIQUES
53	DYES,TANNING,COLOUR PROD		11845		9167		9109		9378	PROD TEINTURE,COLORANTS
533	PIGMENTS,PAINTS,ETC	W 5447	11633	W 4496	9020	W 4099	8739	W 3804	8907	PIGMENTS,PEINTURES,VERNIS
5334	VARNISHES,DISTEMPERS ETC	W 2186	8167	W 1506	5805	W 1503	5432	W 1422	5722	PEINTURES A L'EAU
53342	OTH PAINTS,VARNISHES ETC	W 1410	5618	W 1000	4028	W 805	3330	W 720	3420	AUTRES PEINTURES,VERNIS
541	*MEDICINAL,PHARM PRODUCT	K 2407697	63998	K 2319237	63590	K 2548031	70627	K 2480520	83931	PROD MEDICINAUX PHARMACEUT
5416	GLYCOSIDES,GLANDS,SERA	K 9339	2514	K 14040	2745	K 13805	4482	K 23684	6573	HETEROSIDES
54164	ANTISERA,MICROB VACCINES	K 7249	2327	K 11796	2585	K 11325	4357	K 22194	6491	SERUMS,VACCINS
5417	MEDICAMENTS	K 2232236	58681	K 2145361	58157	K 2381670	63613	K 2314597	74842	MEDICAMENTS
54179	— CONTNG OTH SUBSTANCES	K 2189193	57776	K 2061834	56354	K 2252470	61483	K 2206239	72809	MED CONT AUT SUBSTANCES
55	PERFUME,CLEANING ETC PRD		36803		37285		33540		35590	PROD POUR PARFUM,TOILETTE
553	PERFUMERY,COSMETICS,ETC	W 1952	21009	W 2039	21259	W 2012	19804	W 5341	21168	PRODUITS DE PARFUMERIE
554	SOAP,CLEANSING ETC PREPS	W 6752	13578	W 7670	13954	W 8035	12123	W 7815	12526	SAVONS,PRODUITS DETERSIFS
5542	WASHING PREPARATIONS ETC	W 4729	9027	W 5825	9944	W 5915	8142	W 5962	8839	PROD ORG TENSIO–ACT NDA

4. Special Imports C.I.F. by Commodities according to the S.I.T.C. (Rev. 2) in thousand U.S. Dollars
Importations Spéciales C.A.F. par Produits d'après la C.T.C.I. (Rév. 2) en milliers de Dollars E.U.

SITC CTCI	COMMODITY	1992 WEIGHT POIDS	1992 VALUE VALEUR	1993 WEIGHT POIDS	1993 VALUE VALEUR	1994 WEIGHT POIDS	1994 VALUE VALEUR	1995 WEIGHT POIDS	1995 VALUE VALEUR	PRODUIT
562	*FERTILIZERS,MANUFACTURE	W 45377	8677	W 25913	5036	W 47462	9355	W 38378	9092	ENGRAIS MANUFACTURES
58	PLASTIC MATERIALS ETC		10372		8851		10078		13037	MAT PLAST ARTIFICIELLES
583	POLYMERIZATION ETC PRODS	W 4271	8351	W 3830	7019	W 4422	8052	W 4876	11036	PROD POLYMERISATION
59	CHEMICAL MATERIALS NES		23429		25818		26052		31717	MAT PROD CHIMIQUES NDA
591	PESTICIDES,DISINFECTANTS	W 2016	11899	W 2777	14055	W 2343	13130	W 2593	16203	DESINF,INSECT,FONG,HERB
5911	INSECTICIDES,FOR RETAIL	W 1311	7314	W 1371	7559	W 1463	7870	W 1699	9910	INSECTICIDES VENTE DET
598	MISCEL CHEM PRODUCTS NES	W 2529	9414	W 3464	9970	W 4014	11101	W 3927	13675	PROD DIV INDUST CHIM NDA
5989	CHEM PRODUCTS,PREPS NES	W 2290	8207	W 3185	8501	W 3694	9089	W 3772	12570	PROD PREP CHIMIQUES NDA
59899	OTH CHEM PRODS,PREPS,NES	W 1537	6219	W 2063	6213	W 2694	7330	W 2755	10410	AUT PRODUITS CHIMIQUES NDA
6	BASIC MANUFACTURES		246372		220652		236564		260149	ART MANUFACTURES
62	RUBBER MANUFACTURES NES		16721		16212		16111		20645	CAOUTCHOUC MANUFACTURE
625	RUBBER TYRES, TUBES ETC	W 3045	14480	W 3329	14493	W 3353	14189	W 3404	17982	PNEUS CAOUTCHOUC VULCANISE
6251	TYRES NEW FOR MOTOR CARS	W 1218	6967	W 1447	7794	W 1506	8128	W 1623	10097	PNEUS POUR VOITURES
63	WOOD,CORK MANUFACTRS NES		17252		17433		20147		18642	OUVRAGES LIEGE ET BOIS
635	WOOD MANUFACTURES NES	W 5609	13836	W 5942	13253	W 8777	15298	W 6286	14145	ART MANUF EN BOIS NDA
6353	BUILDERS WOODWRK,PREFABS	W 4925	11205	W 5093	10729	W 7711	12693	W 5436	11606	OUVRAGES DE MENUISERIE
64	PAPER,PAPERBOARD AND MFR		40972		40211		38608		45072	PAPIERS,CARTONS & OUVRAGES
641	PAPER AND PAPERBOARD	W 14902	15356	W 16072	14627	W 10848	13043	W 9781	16163	PAPIERS ET CARTONS
642	PAPER,ETC,PRECUT,ARTS OF	W 6906	25616	W 7215	25584	W 8884	25566	W 7468	28910	PAP,CARTONS DECOUPES
6421	PAPER ETC CONTAINERS	W 2912	7034	W 3022	6797	W 4225	7542	W 3249	8724	BOITES,SACS EMBALLAGES
6423	EXERCISE BOOKS ETC	W 1243	5954	W 1201	5548	W 1338	5465	W 1167	6842	REGISTRES,CAHIERS,CARNETS
6428	PAPER ETC ARTICLES NES	W 2096	10376	W 2309	11228	W 2432	10250	W 2403	11289	OUVRAGES EN PATE A PAPIER
64285	PAPER ETC DIAPERS ETC	W 1267	7187	W 1386	7977	W 1463	7387	W 1480	7603	SERVIETTES HYGIENIQUES
65	TEXTILE YARN,FABRICS,ETC		25027		19909		19847		19056	FILS,TISSUS,ARTICLES TEXTILE
658	TEXTILE ARTICLES NES	W 857	9196	W 775	8039	W 976	8910	W 837	8311	ART FACONNES MAT TEXTILES
6584	LINENS ETC	W 477	6328	W 358	5218	W 506	5905	W 391	4856	LINGE DE MAISON
66	NONMETAL MINERAL MFS NES		48432		40991		42736		46564	ART MIN NON METALLIQUES
661	LIME,CEMENT,BLDG PRODS	W 232526	16686	W 182518	13566	W 188924	14106	W 158917	13673	CHAUX,CIMENTS MAT CONSTR
6612	CEMENT	W 230904	14459	W 180549	11462	W 186820	11918	W 155747	10867	CIMENTS HYDRAULIQUES
662	CLAY,REFRACTORY BLDG PRD	W 20076	12865	W 17056	10334	W 20227	11892	W 23128	13698	MAT CONST REFRACTAIRES
6624	BRICKS ETC NONREFRACTORY	W 19741	12627	W 16179	10066	W 19295	11488	W 22134	13225	BRIQUES ETC CERAM NON REFR
66245	GLAZED CERAMIC SETTS ETC	W 15854	10290	W 12860	8232	W 15496	9574	W 18853	11552	AUT CARREAUX CERAMIQUE
665	GLASSWARE	W 8141	8853	W 8573	8798	W 8177	8297	W 8927	9588	OUVRAGES EN VERRE
6651	BOTTLES ETC OF GLASS	W 7271	5334	W 7705	5590	W 7245	4902	W 8154	6085	RECIPIENTS EN VERRE
66511	GLASS BOTTLES ETC NONVAC	W 7271	5334	W 7705	5590	W 7245	4902	W 8154	6085	BONBONNES,BOUTEILLES,ETC
67	IRON AND STEEL		27521		23173		28596		31620	FER ET ACIER
673	IRON,STEEL SHAPES ETC	W 25402	9889	W 22814	10159	W 25821	10351	W 20648	9318	BARRES,PROFIL FER,ACIER
6731	IRON,STEEL WIRE ROD	W 17030	5645	W 14908	5285	W 17963	6101	W 15490	5727	FIL MACHINE FER,ACIER
67312	HIGH CARBON STL WIRE ROD	W 16883	5565	W 14890	5274	W 12839	4378	W 1	1	FIL MACH ACIER FIN CARBONE
674	IRN,STL UNIV,PLATE,SHEET	W 8279	7795	W 6350	6526	W 8288	8308	W 8244	9487	LARGES PLATS,TOLES
6749	OTH IRN,STL PLATES,SHEET	W 7268	6978	W 5309	5707	W 7604	7524	W 7699	8858	AUTRES TOLES FER,ACIER
67491	— OF IRON OR SIMPLE STL	W 7208	6911	W 5271	5650	W 7592	7460	W 7689	8825	AUT TOLES AUTRES ACIER FIN
678	IRON,STL TUBES,PIPES,ETC	W 4755	7870	W 2948	4932	W 4978	8171	W 5204	11020	TUBES,TUYAUX EN FONTE,FER
68	NON–FERROUS METALS		5905		5542		6562		6073	METAUX NON FERREUX
684	ALUMINIUM	W 724	4778	W 685	4193	W 886	5192	W 725	4444	ALUMINIUM
6842	ALUMINIUM,ALLOYS WORKED	W 724	4778	W 685	4192	W 886	5192	W 725	4444	ALUMINIUM,ALLIAGES OUVRE
69	METAL MANUFACTURES NES		64264		56900		63641		72140	ART MANUFACT EN METAL NDA
691	STRUCTURES AND PARTS NES	W 6734	20927	W 5489	17656	W 6765	22268	W 6694	23950	CONSTRUCT FER,ACIER,ALU
6911	STRUCTURES,PARTS IRN,STL	W 5719	15441	W 4512	12081	W 5938	16470	W 5574	16941	CONSTRUCT FER,ACIER,FONTE
6912	STRUCTURES,PARTS ALUMNM	W 1015	5486	W 978	5575	W 827	5798	W 1119	7010	CONSTRUCT ALUMINIUM
692	METAL TANKS,BOXES,ETC	W 1764	5906	W 1844	5656	W 2076	7975	W 1891	6894	RECIPIENTS METALLIQUES
6924	MTL TRANSPORT BOXES ETC	W 1539	4832	W 1602	4621	W 1651	5196	W 1461	4408	FUTS,TAMBOURS,BIDONS
695	TOOLS	W 501	4969	W 548	4769	W 639	4959	W 597	7095	OUTILS A MAIN
697	BASE MTL HOUSEHOLD EQUIP	W 1326	9592	W 1450	8891		8177	W 1255	8337	ART MENAGE MET COMMUNS
699	BASE METAL MFRS NES	W 2065	13419	W 1941	11780	W 2072	12709	W 2498	16138	ART MANUFACTURES MET NDA
6991	LOCKSMITHS WARES,ETC	W 646	5154	W 613	4933	W 703	5371	W 858	6964	ARTICLES DE SERRURERIE
7	MACHINES,TRANSPORT EQUIP		514096		490867		451173		637553	MACHINES MATERIEL TRANSPORT
71	POWER GENERATING EQUIPMT		26440		30201		22430		62833	MACHINES GENERATRICES
713	INTRNL COMBUS PSTN ENGIN	W 871	19273	W 916	16923	W 745	15522	W 2706	46076	MOTEURS EXPL COMB INT, PIECE
7138	PISTON ENGINES NES	W 498	8078	W 506	8063	W 402	6852	W 429	8900	MOTEURS A PISTONS NDA
7139	PISTON ENGINE PARTS NES	W 244	8721	W 182	6571	W 133	6138	W 1897	33915	PIECES POUR 713.2,3,8
714	ENGINES AND MOTORS NES	W 26	1993	W 111	8680	W 11	747	W 24	2939	MOTEURS NON ELECTRIQUES
716	ROTATING ELECTRIC PLANT	W 243	3750	W 266	3694	W 344	4406	W 904	13129	APP ELECTR ROTATIFS,PIECES
7169	PTS NES OF ROT ELEC PLNT	W 17	357	W 7	222	W 5	305	W 609	8470	PIECES MAC APP ROTATIFS
72	MACHS FOR SPCL INDUSTRYS		29846		20178		24194		35154	MAC SPECIALES POUR INDUST
723	CIVIL ENGNEERG EQUIP ETC	W 1062	7793	W 281	2413	W 1138	7670	W 1132	8869	APPAREILS DE GENIE CIVIL
7234	CONST,MINING MACHNRY NES	W 860	5973	W 212	1742	W 942	6485	W 1010	7921	MACH POUR LA CONST, MINES
72342	SLFPRP SHOVELS,EXCAVATRS	W 714	5111	W 160	1405	W 713	4365	W 939	7240	PELLES MECANIQUES
728	OTH MACHY FOR SPCL INDUS	W 987	10675	W 368	5633	W 690	5743	W 714	11576	AUT MACH IND PARTICULIERES
7284	MACHY FOR SPCL INDUS NES	W 357	5194	W 124	3582	W 180	2552	W 417	8830	MACH SPEC IND PARTICUL.
74	GENRL INDUSTRL MACHY NES		63042		54994		68760		83245	MACH APP INDUSTRIE
741	HEATING,COOLING EQUIPMNT	W 1187	14868	W 1532	16683	W 2024	20577	W 1911	23530	MACH CHAUFFAGE,PIECES
7414	NONDOM REFRIG EQUIPT,PTS	W 402	4838	W 626	5751	W 741	6733	W 903	10297	MAT PRODUCTION DU FROID
74141	REFRIG EQUIP NONDOMESTIC	W 346	4182	W 560	4974	W 601	5727	W 662	8392	REFIG INDUSTRIELS
7415	AIR–CONDITIONING MACHNRY	W 437	5436	W 498	6238	W 546	6217	W 594	7575	GROUPES CONDITION AIR
7416	HEATING,COOLING EQU NES	W 266	3648	W 357	3841	W 538	5843	W 361	4806	APP CHANGEMENT TEMP
742	PUMPS FOR LIQUIDS ETC	W 160	3750	W 135	3137	W 223	4879	W 291	6231	POMPES MOTO–POMPES
743	PUMPS NES,CENTRFUGES ETC	W 432	7379	W 459	8545	W 664	10857	W 547	10129	POMPES COMPRES,VENT ETC
744	MECHANICAL HANDLING EQU	W 2657	22389	W 1428	10348	W 1373	13595	W 1696	19001	EQUIP MANUTENTION PIECES
7442	LIFTING,LOADING MACH NES	W 2008	15774	W 956	4688	W 776	5902	W 968	9101	APP LEVAGE,MANUTENTION
74422	SHIP DERRICKS,CRANES ETC	W 1338	9337	W 430	595	W 197	852	W 157	957	GRUES,PONTS ROULANTS
7449	PTS NES OF MACHY OF 7442	W 192	3600	W 190	3820	W 311	5586	W 365	7248	PIECES DU 744.2
745	NONELEC MACHY,TOOLS NES	W 347	6879	W 431	8718	W 497	8691	W 826	12914	AUT MACH NON ELEC,PIECES
7452	OTH NONELEC MCHS,PTS NES	W 300	5613	W 373	7213	W 438	7274	W 735	11034	AUT MACH NON ELEC,PIECES
749	NONELEC MACH PTS,ACC NES	W 545	7778	W 574	7562	W 688	10161	W 1214	11440	PIECES MACH NON ELEC NDA
7492	COCKS,VALVES ETC NES	W 437	5631	W 358	4994	W 558	7754	W 1047	7674	ART ROB,SIM POUR TUYAUX
75	OFFICE MACHNES,ADP EQUIP		35130		33243		30910		35753	MACH BUREAU TRAIT AUTOM
751	OFFICE MACHINES		4903	W 103	4148	W 118	5277	W 138	5924	MACH,APPAREILS DE BUREAU
752	AUTOMTIC DATA PROC EQUIP	W 190	18304	W 214	16673	W 215	16273	W 226	20068	MACH TRAIT INFORMATION
7523	DIGITL CENTRL PROCESSORS	W 39	4112	W 66	6597	W 52	4896	W 53	6388	UNITES CENTRALES
7525	ADP PERIPHERAL UNITS	W 56	5214	W 67	4388	W 83	5521	W 67	4666	UNITES PERIPHERIQUES
759	OFFICE,ADP MCH PTS,ACCES	W 126	11923	W 156	12422	W 124	9360	W 122	9761	PIECES DU 751 ET 752
7591	OFFICE MACHINE PARTS NES	W 23	1327	W 122	8529	W 83	4971	W 54	3052	PIECES DU 7511,7518
75911	TYPEWRTR PARTS,ACCES NES	W 1	61	W 82	7043	W 49	3213	W 3	293	PIECES DU 7511
7599	ACCTG,ETC,ADP MCH PTS,AC	W 103	10596	W 35	3893	W 40	4389	W 68	6709	PIECES DU 751 ET 752
76	TELECOMM,SOUND EQUIPMENT		39658		45119		35320		41064	EQUIPMENT DE TELECOM
761	TELEVISION RECEIVERS	W 421	7056	W 544	8170	W 455	6824	W 421	6978	RECEPTEURS DE TELEVISION
7611	COLOUR TV RECEIVERS	W 413	6867	W 543	8141	W 452	6752	W 420	6963	RECEPTEURS COULEUR
762	RADIO BROADCAST RECEIVRS	W 253	6237	W 216	4722	W 331	5947	W 348	6358	RECEPTEURS RADIODIFFUSION
763	SOUND RECORDRS,PHONOGRPH	W 149	6285	W 96	4966	W 83	3701	W 125	5597	PHONO,APP ENREGISTREMENT
7638	OTHR SOUND APPARATUS ETC	W 144	6174	W 93	4901	W 80	3625	W 121	5556	AUT APP D'ENREGIS,REPROD

4. Special Imports C.I.F. by Commodities according to the S.I.T.C. (Rev. 2) in thousand U.S. Dollars
Importations Spéciales C.A.F. par Produits d'après la C.T.C.I. (Rév. 2) en milliers de Dollars E.U.

SITC CTCI	COMMODITY	1992 WEIGHT POIDS	1992 VALUE VALEUR	1993 WEIGHT POIDS	1993 VALUE VALEUR	1994 WEIGHT POIDS	1994 VALUE VALEUR	1995 WEIGHT POIDS	1995 VALUE VALEUR	PRODUIT
764	TELECOM EQPT,PTS,ACC NES	W 458	20081	W 522	27261	W 447	18849	W 407	22131	EQUIP TELECOM,PIECES
7641	LINE TELEPHONE,ETC EQUIP	W 129	7422	W 197	11394	W 177	9356	W 138	10976	APP TELEPHON PAR FIL
7649	PTS NES OF EQUIPMT OF 76	W 176	6489	W 142	8130	W 107	3513	W 111	4627	PIECES DE LA DIV 76
76491	PTS NES OF APPAR OF 7641	W 89	3726	W 40	5618	W 36	1982	W 47	2949	PIECES POUR 764.1
77	ELECTRIC MACHNRY NES ETC		68430		70372		64951		86048	MACH APP ELECT NDA
772	SWITCHGEAR ETC,PARTS NES	W 713	15352	W 740	16869	W 603	15922	W 879	25375	APP COUPURE,SECT ETC
7721	SWITCHGEAR ETC	W 713	15306	W 729	16767	W 602	15891	W 878	25326	APP COUPURE,SECTIONMNT
773	ELECTR DISTRIBUTNG EQUIP	W 2317	12012	W 2473	11046	W 2190	8563	W 3127	13500	EQUIPMT DISTRIBUTION ELECT
7731	INSULATED WIRE,CABLE ETC	W 2257	11614	W 2445	10830	W 2163	8317	W 3072	13064	FILS,CABLES ISOLES ELECT
775	HOUSEHOLD TYPE EQUIP NES	W 3310	19990	W 2915	17519	W 3570	20146	W 3782	22728	MACH,APP USAGE DOMESTQUE
7752	DOM REFRIGERATRS,FREEZRS	W 1404	7847	W 1315	6784	W 1692	8576	W 1446	8014	REFRIG,CONGEL MENAGER
77521	DOMESTIC REFRIGERATORS	W 1052	5759	W 974	4877	W 1268	6382	W 1043	5624	REFRIGERATEURS
7758	ELECTRO–THERMIC APPL NES	W 521	4663	W 553	4974	W 574	4920	W 661	5833	APP ELECTROTHERMIQ NDA
778	ELECTRICAL MACHINERY NES	W 1579	14564	W 1542	18956		13766	W 1680	17094	AUTRES MACH ELECT NDA
7781	BATTERIES,ACCUMULATORS	W 1204	5410	W 1151	5129	W 1295	5374	W 1226	5893	PILES ET ACCUMULATEURS
7782	ELECTRIC LAMPS,BULBS	W 111	1631	W 131	5649	W 91	1253	W 111	1679	LAMPES, TUBES ELECTRIQUES
78	ROAD VEHICLES		183394		180063		170216		240666	VEHICULES ROUTIERS
781	PASS MOTOR VEH EXC BUSES	W 9148	102992	W 9488	107953	W 9568	102145	W 12446	148523	AUTO TRANSPORT PERSONNES
782	LORRIES,SPCL MTR VEH NES	W 3113	31080	W 3515	25941	W 2524	24459	W 3378	38375	VEHICULES SPECIAUX,MARCH
7821	LORRIES,TRUCKS	W 2939	29282	W 3307	23830	W 2376	23124	W 3197	35946	VEHICULES TRANSP MARCHAND
783	ROAD MOTOR VEHICLES NES	W 531	7256	W 364	5215	W 299	4210	W 322	5103	VEHICULES ROUTIERS NDA
7831	BUSES	W 432	6640	W 331	4907	W 253	3733	W 220	3895	VOITURES TRANSPORT COMMUN
784	MOTOR VEH PRTS,ACCES NES	W 2061	31833	W 2039	32168	W 1996	30627	W 2176	36162	PIECES 722,781,782,783
7849	OTHER MOTOR VEHCL PARTS	W 1995	31219	W 2011	31833	W 1963	30299	W 2164	35990	PIECES 722,781,782,783
785	CYCLES,ETC MOTRZD OR NOT	W 412	5994	W 338	5200	W 390	5290	W 398	6299	MOTOCYCLES SCOOTERS
786	TRAILERS,NONMOTR VEH,NES	W 1373	4239	W 1059	3586	W 826	3486	W 1316	6205	REMORQUES,CADRES,CONTAIN
79	OTHR TRANSPORT EQUIPMENT		65428		55007		32565		51097	AUTRE MATERIEL TRANSPORT
793	SHIPS AND BOATS ETC	W 1861	61870	W 1945	52912	W 1436	32392	W 2911	50323	NAVIRES BATEAUX,ETC
7931	WARSHIPS	W 49	1516		2	W 138	5067	W 26	149	NAVIRES DE GUERRE
7932	SHIPS AND BOATS NES	W 1577	59063	W 1727	51835	W 1044	26398	W 1372	47418	NAVIRES ET BATEAUX
79321	YACHTS,SPORTS VESSLS ETC	W 1271	43212	W 1525	40139	W 835	19486	W 1284	43315	BATEAUX DE PLAISANCE
79323	OTHER CARGO VESSELS	W 267	15236	W 51	6117	W 201	6891	W 88	4103	AUT BATEAUX TRANS MARCH
79324	FISHING VESSELS ETC	W 11	137	W 151	5578		21			BATEAUX DE PECHE
8	MISC MANUFACTURED GOODS		260666		242645		251114		288462	ART MANUFACTURES DIVERS
812	*PLUMBG,HEATNG,LGHTNG EQ	W 1664	9849	W 1118	6445	W 1242	7078	W 1452	8659	APPAR SANITAIRES CHAUFFAGE
821	*FURNITURE,PARTS THEREOF	W 10653	43651	W 10125	38870	W 10710	40398	W 11700	46176	MEUBLES ET PIECES
8211	CHAIRS,SEATS AND PARTS	W 2030	11214	W 1895	10353	W 1865	9286	W 2192	11279	SIEGES ET PIECES
82111	CHAIRS AND OTHER SEATS	W 2023	11124	W 1881	10289	W 1842	9194	W 2168	11231	SIEGES
8219	FURNITURE AND PARTS NES	W 8048	29317	W 7802	26068	W 8313	27537	W 8959	31140	AUTRES MEUBLES ET PIECES
82191	METAL FURNITURE NES	W 896	5191	W 1023	5000	W 1094	5237	W 896	5189	MEUBLES NDA EN METAL
82192	WOOD FURNITURE NES	W 6599	21533	W 6068	18108	W 6422	18881	W 7255	22253	MEUBLES NDA EN BOIS
84	CLOTHING AND ACCESSORIES		57662		54845		56630		62552	VETEMENTS
842	MENS OUTERWEAR NOT KNIT	W 364	10874	W 336	9947	W 392	9728	W 395	9899	VET DESSUS POUR HOMMES
8423	— TROUSERS,BREECHES ETC	W 296	8226	W 264	7458	W 306	7357	W 310	7479	PANTALONS HOMMES MAT TEX
843	WOMENS OUTERWEAR NONKNIT	W 498	20022	W 519	19552	W 550	19152	W 679	23110	VET DESSUS FEMMES MAT TEX
8439	— OTHER OUTER GARMENTS	W 318	12564	W 347	13164	W 328	11947	W 433	14882	AUT VET DES FEM MAT TEXT
844	UNDER GARMENTS NOT KNIT	W 189	6423	W 194	5989	W 215	5354	W 202	5290	VETEMENT DESSOUS MAT TEX
8441	— MENS SHIRTS	W 148	5613	W 155	5350	W 183	4815	W 161	4646	CHEMISES HOMMES MAT TEXT
845	OUTERWEAR KNIT NONELASTC	W 165	6555	W 159	6006		7087	W 245	6815	VET DESSOUS,ACCES BONNET
8459	— OTHER,CLTHG ACCESRYS	W 148	6061	W 147	5434		6051	W 211	5969	AUT VET DESSUS DE BONNE
846	UNDER GARMENTS KNITTED	W 384	10374	W 397	9918	W 496	11773	W 591	13936	SOUS VETS DE BONNETERIE
8462	— OF COTTON NON ELASTIC	W 334	7962	W 331	7306	W 408	8513	W 467	9722	SOUS–VET BONNET COTON
84629	—— OTHER	W 334	7962	W 331	7306	W 408	8513	W 467	9722	AUT SOUS–VET BONNET COTON
851	*FOOTWEAR	W 1099	23870	W 1095	22617	W 1200	23940	W 1148	26199	CHAUSSURES
85102	FOOTWEAR LEATHER	W 713	19013	W 760	18677	W 857	19949	W 774	20735	CHAUS SEMELLES EN CUIR
87	PRECISION INSTRUMNTS NES		15614		13225		14432		17857	INSTRUM,APPAR SCIENT NDA
872	MEDICAL INSTRUMENTS NES	W 184	6601	W 177	6173	W 184	6543	W 182	6975	INSTR,APP MEDIC–CHIR NDA
87202	OTH MEDICAL INSTRUMENTS	W 172	5876	W 166	5693	W 161	5801	W 162	6104	INSTRUM,APP MEDECINE
874	MEASURNG,CONTROLNG INSTR	W 145	7689	W 112	5629	W 145	6550	W 132	8400	INSTRUMENTS DE MESURE
88	PHOTO EQU,OPTICL GDS ETC		9291		8368		7649		7827	APP,FOURN PHOTO,OP,MONTR
89	MISC MANUFCTRD GOODS NES		96359		94384		96745		114607	ART MANUFACTURES DIVERS
892	PRINTED MATTER	W 1832	21655	W 2140	21709	W 2350	22214	W 3623	27356	IMPRIMES
8921	PRINTED BOOKS,GLOBES,ETC	W 590	12079	W 728	12225	W 833	12798	W 1930	15269	LIVRES,BROCHURES,CARTES
89211	PRINTED BOOKS,PAMPHLETS	W 569	11893	W 718	12060	W 813	12695	W 1907	15097	LIVRES,BROCHURES
8928	PRINTED MATTER NES	W 1137	8181	W 1230	7719	W 1231	7429	W 1291	8471	IMPRIMES NDA
893	ARTICLES OF PLASTIC NES		35924		33969		34661		42848	OUVRAGES EN MAT DIVIS 58
8931	PLSTC PACKG CONTNRS,LIDS	W 1855	7906	W 2273	8520	W 2768	9406	W 2982	11973	ART TRANSP EMBALLAGE ETC
8939	MISC PLASTIC ARTICLES	W 6957	27232	W 6445	24586	W 6556	24330	W 6750	29849	ART DIVERS EN MAT DIV 58
89399	OTHR PLASTC ARTICLES NES	W 6330	24527	W 6136	23103	W 6248	22710	W 6425	28112	AUT OUV MAT DIV 58
894	TOYS,SPORTING GOODS,ETC	W 903	12307	W 1100	10559	W 1087	10798	W 1236	13286	VOITURES ENFANTS,JOUETS
8942	TOYS,INDOOR GAMES ETC	W 645	8760	W 767	7376	W 739	7325	W 828	9287	JOUETS,JEUX ETC
897	GOLD,SILVER WARE,JEWELRY		4902		5826		7622		5713	BIJOUTERIE,ORFEVRERIE
8973	PREC JEWLRY,GLD–SILVWARE		3118		5025		6831		4926	BIJOUX OR,ARGENT ORFEVRE
89731	PRECIOUS METAL JEWELLERY		3045		4970		6784		4782	ART BIJOUTERIE,JOAILLER
898	MUSICAL INSTRUMENTS,PTS	W 293	9533	W 383	10007	W 241	8882	W 278	10551	INSTRUMENTS DE MUSIQUE
8983	SOUND RECRDNG TAPE,DISCS	W 207	8579	W 311	9019	W 187	8038	W 209	9521	SUPPORTS SON POUR 763
89832	RECORDED DISCS,TAPES ETC	W 118	6931	W 148	6908	W 120	6697	W 130	8177	DISQUES,PHONO,BANDES
899	OTHER MANUFACTURED GOODS		8122		7981		8327		9223	AUT ART MANUF DIVERS NDA
9	GOODS NOT CLASSD BY KIND		50468		30820		38763		39515	ART TRANSACT NON CLASSES
911	*MAIL NOT CLASSED BY KIN		49666		30098					COLIS POSTAUX
931	*SPECIAL TRANSACTIONS						38158		38344	TRANS.SPECIALES

5. Special Exports F.O.B. by Commodities according to the S.I.T.C. (Rev. 2) in thousand U.S. Dollars
Exportations Spéciales F.O.B. par Produits d'après la C.T.C.I. (Rév. 2) en milliers de Dollars E.U.

SITC CTCI	COMMODITY	1992		1993		1994		1995		PRODUIT
		WEIGHT POIDS	VALUE VALEUR	WEIGHT POIDS	VALUE VALEUR	WEIGHT POIDS	VALUE VALEUR	WEIGHT POIDS	VALUE VALEUR	
	ALL COMMODITIES		254541		201978		218605		241916	TOUS PRODUITS
0	FOOD AND LIVE ANIMALS		129918		85522		80120		116775	ALIMENTS,ANIMAUX VIVANTS
02	DAIRY PRODCTS,BIRDS'EGGS		1240		1116		1528		973	PRODUITS LAITIERS,OEUFS
024	CHEESE AND CURD	W 269	817	W 277	852	W 365	1181	W 172	566	FROMAGE ET CAILLEBOTTE
04	CEREALS AND PREPARATIONS		4350		4463		4232		4318	CEREALES ET PRODUITS
042	RICE	W 2026	2537	W 2164	2719	W 2139	2655	W 1681	3961	RIZ
0422	RICE SEMI–MILLED,MILLED	W 1985	2504	W 2122	2672	W 2139	2655	W 1681	3961	RIZ POLI,GLACE INCL BRISURES
04221	RICE MILLED UNBROKEN	W 1985	2504	W 2122	2672	W 2065	2626	W 1618	3879	RIZ POLI,GLACE EXCL BRISURES
048	CEREAL ETC PREPARATIONS	W 748	1813	W 719	1742	W 693	1578	W 116	356	PREPTNS A BASE CEREALES
0484	BAKERY PRODUCTS	W 349	1035	W 367	1060	W 425	1048	W 96	304	PRODUITS DE BOULANGERIE
04841	BREAD,BISCUIT,COM WAFERS	W 338	1012	W 363	1043	W 414	1014	W 96	302	PAINS,BISCUITS DE MER
05	VEGETABLES AND FRUIT		122928		78604		70834		109429	LEGUMES ET FRUITS
054	VEG ETC FRSH,SMPLY PRSVD	W 603	739	W 662	996	W 604	815	W 496	838	LEGUMES FRAIS,CONG,SECS
0545	OTHER FRESH VEGETABLES	W 287	309	W 396	607	W 426	585	W 345	592	AUTRES LEGUMES FRAIS,REF
05459	FRESH VEGETABLES NES	W 287	309	W 396	607	W 426	585	W 345	592	LEGUMES FRAIS,REFRI NDA
057	FRUIT,NUTS,FRESH,DRIED	W 195238	114815	W 177516	71832	W 150217	63471	W 161261	102439	FRUITS FRAIS OU SECS
0573	BANANA,PLANTAIN,FRSH,DRY	W 193335	108323	W 176039	66713	W 148564	58154	W 158663	97711	BANANES FRAICHES,SECHEES
0579	FRUIT FRESH OR DRIED NES	W 1891	6474	W 1457	5007	W 1642	5267	W 2592	4716	FRUITS FRAIS,SECS NDA
05798	OTHER FRESH FRUIT	W 1798	6381	W 1433	4985	W 1606	5230	W 1608	4011	AUTRES FRUITS FRAIS
058	FRUIT PRESERVED,PREPARED	W 6995	7027	W 6605	5698	W 8442	6266	W 7510	5855	CONSERVES DE FRUITS
0585	FRUIT OR VEGETABLE JUICE	W 1851	1885	W 2581	2292	W 2244	1915	W 1802	1732	JUS DE FRUITS
05854	PINEAPPLE JUICE	W 1353	1088	W 2136	1639	W 1849	1279	W 1355	990	JUS D'ANANAS
0589	FRUIT PREPRD,PRESRVD,NES	W 4728	4218	W 3893	3037	W 6048	4044	W 5579	3717	FRUITS PREPARES CONSERV
05899	FRUIT,NUTS NES,PRESERVED	W 4704	3962	W 3865	2823	W 6034	3913	W 5574	3659	FRUITS PREP CONSERV NDA
06	SUGAR AND PREPS,HONEY		50		77		2108		988	SUCRES ET PRODUITS
061	SUGAR AND HONEY	W 27	50	W 27	53	W 2513	2108	W 1017	985	SUCRES ET MIEL
0611	RAW BEET AND CANE SUGAR	W 6	9	W 8	12	W 1934	1604	W 993	923	SUCRES BRUTS
1	BEVERAGES AND TOBACCO		32797		33037		35554		33172	BOISSONS ET TABACS
11	BEVERAGES		32797		33018		35500		33162	BOISSONS
111	NON–ALCOHL BEVERAGES NES	W 17541	11866	W 18361	12513	W 18931	14051	W 13177	8947	BOISSONS NON ALCOOLIQUES
11101	WATERS,ICE AND SNOW	W 5521	1738	W 5814	1703	W 4749	1398	W 5327	1723	EAU,EAUX MINERALES
11102	FLAVORED WATERS NON–ALCO	W 12020	10128	W 12546	10810	W 14182	12653	W 7850	7223	LIMONADES,EAUX GAZEUSES
112	ALCOHOLIC BEVERAGES	W 7988	20931	W 7794	20506	W 8237	21449	W 8680	24216	BOISSONS ALCOOLIQUES
1124	DISTILLED ALCOHOLIC BEVS	W 7840	20721	W 7668	20342	W 8097	21240	W 8617	24109	ALCOOLS,EAUX–DE–VIE
11249	OTH ALCOHOLC BEVS,CMPNDS	W 7833	20675	W 7668	20336	W 8080	21105	W 8614	24089	BOISSONS ALCOOLIQUES NDA
2	CRUDE MATERLS,EXCL FUELS		1960		1710		2523		3005	MAT BRUTES NON COMESTIBLES
27	CRUDE FERTLZR,MINRLS NES		528		567		1262		1555	ENGRAIS MINERAUX BRUTS
273	STONE,SAND AND GRAVEL	W 32911	515	W 18552	496	W 113779	1245	W 165324	1553	PIERRES,SABLES,GRAVIERS
2733	SAND,EXCL METAL–BEARING	W 27250	346	W 13358	342	W 70434	624	W 143785	1305	SABLES NATURELS
28	METALLIFEROUS ORES,SCRAP		388		394		548		789	MINERAIS METAL,DECHETS
288	NONFERR METAL SCRAP NES	W 436	388	W 408	394	W 1109	548	W 1061	787	DECHETS NON FERREUX
2882	OTHER BASE MTL SCRAP NES	W 310	387	W 408	394	W 538	546	W 582	783	AUTRES DECHETS
29	CRUDE ANIMAL,VEG MAT NES		874		657		490		516	MATIERES BRUTES ANIM,VEGET
292	CRUDE VEG MATERIALS NES	W 120	874	W 97	656	W 67	488	W 75	515	MAT BRUTES VEGETALES NDA
2927	CUT FLOWERS AND FOLIAGE	W 116	857	W 91	637	W 64	474	W 75	515	FLEURS,FEUILLAGES COUPES
29271	CUT FLOWERS	W 116	857	W 89	634	W 64	474	W 75	514	FLEURS ET BOUTONS
3	MINERAL FUELS ETC		43939		40241		62896		43177	COMBUSTIBLES MINERAUX LUB
33	PETROLEUM AND PRODUCTS		42067		38167		60996		41461	PETROLE ET DERIVES
334	PETROLEUM PRODUCTS,REFIN	W 279514	42057	W 247809	38157	W 379952	60991	W 267060	41458	PRODUITS RAFFINES
3341	GASOLINE,OTH LIGHT OILS	W 279513	42049	W 247808	38093			W 11110	3829	ESSENCES POUR MOTEURS
33411	MOTOR,AVIATION SPIRIT							W 11110	3826	ESSENCES MOTEURS D'AVIONS
33419	OTH LIGHT PETROLEUM OILS	W 279513	42049	W 247808	38093				2	AUTRES HUILES LEGERES
3342	KEROSENE,OTH MEDIUM OILS							W 11921	3616	PETR LAMPANTS,AUT HUIL
33421	KEROSENE INCL JET FUEL							W 11921	3616	PETROLES LAMPANTS
3343	GAS OILS							W 45294	11870	GAS OILS
3344	FUEL OILS,NES							W 198115	22111	FUEL OILS
341	*GAS,NATURAL AND MANUFCT	W 6633	1872	W 7141	2073	W 6590	1900	W 5149	1716	GAZ NATUREL,GAZ MANUFACT
3413	PETROLM GASES,LIQUEFIED	W 6633	1872	W 7141	2073	W 6590	1900	W 5149	1716	GAZ DE PETROLE LIQUEFIE
34131	LIQUEFIED PROPANE,BUTANE	W 6633	1872	W 7141	2073	W 6590	1900	W 5149	1716	PROPANE,BUTANE LIQUEFIES
5	CHEMCLS,RELATED PROD NES		5170		5892		5153		5167	PRODUITS CHIMIQUES
52	INORGANIC CHEMICALS		869		637		543		239	PROD CHIM INORGANIQUES
523	OTHR INORG CHEMICALS ETC	W 1611	862	W 1259	624	W 1089	529	W 491	221	AUT PRODUITS CHIMIQUES INORG
5231	METAL CMPD OF INORG ACID	W 1608	857	W 1257	624	W 975	496	W 380	177	SELS METALLIQUES
52313	HYPOCHLORITES ETC 51 51	W 1608	856	W 1257	624	W 975	496	W 380	177	CHLORITES,HYPOCHLORITES
53	DYES,TANNING,COLOUR PROD		1271		1278		1633		527	PROD TEINTURE,COLORANTS
533	PIGMENTS,PAINTS,ETC	W 671	1269	W 658	1278	W 870	1629	W 374	527	PIGMENTS,PEINTURES,VERNIS
5334	VARNISHES,DISTEMPERS ETC	W 587	1193	W 545	1175	W 692	1474	W 360	513	PEINTURES A L'EAU
53341	WATER–THINNED PAINTS	W 198	435	W 478	1003	W 188	362	W 91	133	PEINTURES DILUEES
53342	OTH PAINTS,VARNISHES ETC	W 388	759	W 67	171	W 502	1104	W 269	380	AUTRES PEINTURES,VERNIS
55	PERFUME,CLEANING ETC PRD		607		662		700		644	PROD POUR PARFUM,TOILETTE
562	*FERTILIZERS,MANUFACTURE	W 5171	1513	W 8296	2620	W 6599	1609	W 10933	3285	ENGRAIS MANUFACTURES
5629	FERTILIZERS NES	W 2529	933	W 8111	2562	W 6221	1519	W 10609	3203	ENGRAIS NDA
56291	NIT–PHOS–POT FERTLZR NES	W 2524	922	W 7961	2536	W 5737	1399	W 10328	3151	ENGRAIS CONT N P K
6	BASIC MANUFACTURES		13109		6141		5182		5173	ART MANUFACTURES
64	PAPER,PAPERBOARD AND MFR		5753		2365		1774		1143	PAPIERS,CARTONS & OUVRAGES
642	PAPER,ETC,PRECUT,ARTS OF	W 1316	5360	W 864	2149	W 683	1688	W 407	933	PAP,CARTONS DECOUPES
6421	PAPER ETC CONTAINERS	W 673	3358	W 120	245	W 26	108	W 2	8	BOITES,SACS EMBALLAGES
6424	PAPER ETC CT TO SIZE NES	W 380	921	W 475	1046	W 385	776	W 209	449	PAP,CARTONS DECOUPES
64243	TOILET PAPER CUT TO SIZE	W 378	893	W 474	1043	W 385	776	W 209	448	PAPIER HYGIENIQUE
6428	PAPER ETC ARTICLES NES	W 259	990	W 252	661	W 263	683	W 186	432	OUVRAGES EN PATE A PAPIER
67	IRON AND STEEL		973		532		617		675	FER ET ACIER
69	METAL MANUFACTURES NES		5012		2475		2209		2607	ART MANUFACT EN METAL NDA
691	STRUCTURES AND PARTS NES	W 1567	2004	W 176	556	W 215	427	W 253	546	CONSTRUCT FER,ACIER,ALU
6911	STRUCTURES,PARTS IRN,STL	W 1537	1601	W 158	370	W 213	391	W 232	441	CONSTRUCT FER,ACIER,FONTE
692	METAL TANKS,BOXES,ETC	W 390	1978	W 340	1308	W 295	1361	W 308	1372	RECIPIENTS METALLIQUES
6924	MTL TRANSPORT BOXES ETC	W 352	1882	W 340	1308	W 295	1361	W 307	1366	FUTS,TAMBOURS,BIDONS
69243	IRN,STL COMP GAS CYLINDR	W 282	1834	W 257	1258	W 284	1303	W 234	1050	RECIP FER,ACIER GAZ COMP
7	MACHINES,TRANSPORT EQUIP		22119		25255		22538		31423	MACHINES MATERIEL TRANSPORT
71	POWER GENERATING EQUIPMT		2492		3484		2390		4897	MACHINES GENERATRICES
713	INTRNL COMBUS PSTN ENGIN	W 29	459	W 38	1542	W 22	707	W 38	1759	MOTEURS EXPL COMB INT, PIECE
7131	AIRCRAFT PSTN ENGINS,PTS	W 1	220	W 10	754		66		41	MOTEURS EXPL P.AVIATION, PIE
71311	AIRCRAFT PISTON ENGINES	W 1	76	W 10	739					MOTEURS EXPL P.AVIATION
7139	PISTON ENGINE PARTS NES	W 24	160	W 32	713	W 16	598	W 31	1586	PIECES POUR 713.2,3,8
714	ENGINES AND MOTORS NES	W 4	1532	W 2	1282	W 2	1624	W 2	2668	MOTEURS NON ELECTRIQUES
7148	GAS TURBINES NES	W 4	1518	W 1	1272	W 2	1595	W 2	2662	TURBINES A GAZ
71481	TURBO–PROPELLERS	W 4	1518	W 1	1272	W 2	1595	W 2	2662	TURBO–PROPULSEURS
716	ROTATING ELECTRIC PLANT	W 11	131	W 38	657	W 4	56	W 86	464	APP ELECTR ROTATIFS,PIECES
72	MACHS FOR SPCL INDUSTRYS		1547		627		1401		312	MAC SPECIALES POUR INDUST
74	GENRL INDUSTRL MACHY NES		1898		1648		1435		1200	MACH APP INDUSTRIE
75	OFFICE MACHNES,ADP EQUIP		1486		857		1008		1837	MACH BUREAU TRAIT AUTOM
752	AUTOMTIC DATA PROC EQUIP	W 17	1169	W 4	249	W 2	285	W 6	1292	MACH TRAIT INFORMATION

5. Special Exports F.O.B. by Commodities according to the S.I.T.C. (Rev. 2) in thousand U.S. Dollars
Exportations Spéciales F.O.B. par Produits d'après la C.T.C.I. (Rév. 2) en milliers de Dollars E.U.

SITC CTCI	COMMODITY	1992		1993		1994		1995		PRODUIT
		WEIGHT POIDS	VALUE VALEUR	WEIGHT POIDS	VALUE VALEUR	WEIGHT POIDS	VALUE VALEUR	WEIGHT POIDS	VALUE VALEUR	
7528	OFF–LINE DATA PROC EQUIP	W 5	457	W 2	150		22	W 4	1038	MACH AUXIL TRAIT INFORM
759	OFFICE,ADP MCH PTS,ACCES	W 4	275	W 6	568		681	W 5	460	PIECES DU 751 ET 752
76	TELECOMM,SOUND EQUIPMENT		1445		1418		2190		2070	EQUIPMENT DE TELECOM
764	TELECOM EQPT,PTS,ACC NES	W 16	1000	W 9	1119		1895	W 27	1900	EQUIP TELECOM,PIECES
7641	LINE TELEPHONE,ETC EQUIP	W 4	237	W 6	665		751	W 19	514	APP TELEPHON PAR FIL
7649	PTS NES OF EQUIPMT OF 76	W 5	362	W 2	229	W 8	798	W 7	1188	PIECES DE LA DIV 76
76491	PTS NES OF APPAR OF 7641	W 5	349	W 1	180	W 7	703	W 6	1062	PIECES POUR 764.1
77	ELECTRIC MACHNRY NES ETC		1904		1258		613		575	MACH APP ELECT NDA
78	ROAD VEHICLES		2796		4263		1575		975	VEHICULES ROUTIERS
781	PASS MOTOR VEH EXC BUSES	W 82	727	W 106	951	W 104	773	W 53	430	AUTO TRANSPORT PERSONNES
782	LORRIES,SPCL MTR VEH NES	W 97	517	W 831	1992	W 44	124	W 20	39	VEHICULES SPECIAUX,MARCH
7821	LORRIES,TRUCKS	W 15	98	W 820	1880	W 19	67	W 17	31	VEHICULES TRANSP MARCHAND
786	TRAILERS,NONMOTR VEH,NES	W 62	661	W 90	937	W 67	395	W 66	373	REMORQUES,CADRES,CONTAIN
7861	TRAILERS,TRANSP CONTAINR	W 55	494	W 90	937	W 53	342	W 55	252	REMORQUES TOUS VEHICULES
78613	CONTAINERS INC ROAD–RAIL	W 33	422	W 90	937	W 53	342	W 37	223	CADRES ET CONTAINERS
79	OTHR TRANSPORT EQUIPMENT		8314		11558		11910		19367	AUTRE MATERIEL TRANSPORT
792	AIRCRAFT ETC	W 2	899	W 6	2329	W 1	546	W 1	513	APP NAVIGATION AERIENNE
7921	HELICOPTERS			W 5	1830					HELICOPTERES
7929	AIRCRAFT PARTS NES	W 2	899	W 1	494	W 1	546	W 1	513	PIECES DU 792
793	SHIPS AND BOATS ETC	W 573	7415	W 760	9229	W 657	11364	W 876	18804	NAVIRES BATEAUX,ETC
7932	SHIPS AND BOATS NES	W 572	7377	W 758	9210	W 629	11304	W 856	18575	NAVIRES ET BATEAUX
79321	YACHTS,SPORTS VESSLS ETC	W 520	5851	W 693	9121	W 595	10285	W 851	18418	BATEAUX DE PLAISANCE
79323	OTHER CARGO VESSELS	W 48	1482			W 17	725			AUT BATEAUX TRANS MARCH
8	MISC MANUFACTURED GOODS		5298		3756		4460		3955	ART MANUFACTURES DIVERS
821	*FURNITURE,PARTS THEREOF	W 120	789	W 83	550	W 53	350	W 42	313	MEUBLES ET PIECES
84	CLOTHING AND ACCESSORIES		795		459		608		716	VETEMENTS
87	PRECISION INSTRUMNTS NES		1408		657		1069		821	INSTRUM,APPAR SCIENT NDA
874	MEASURNG,CONTROLNG INSTR	W 1	951	W 2	404		793	W 5	494	INSTRUMENTS DE MESURE
89	MISC MANUFCTRD GOODS NES		1828		1723		2066		1415	ART MANUFACTURES DIVERS
893	ARTICLES OF PLASTIC NES	W 285	678		795	W 257	551	W 125	370	OUVRAGES EN MAT DIVIS 58
8939	MISC PLASTIC ARTICLES	W 114	427	W 121	721	W 111	289	W 49	192	ART DIVERS EN MAT DIV 58
89399	OTHR PLASTC ARTICLES NES	W 114	421	W 120	720	W 93	264	W 49	191	AUT OUV MAT DIV 58

1. HISTORICAL SERIES, 1961–1996 GENERAL TRADE, IMPORTS C.I.F., EXPORTS F.O.B.
SERIES HISTORIQUES, 1961–1996 COMMERCE GENERAL, IMPORTATIONS C.A.F., EXPORTATIONS F.O.B

YEAR ANNEE	VALUE IN MILLION MAUR. RUPEES / VALEUR EN MILLION MAUR. RUPEES — MERCHANDISE – MARCHANDISE		GOLD – OR		CONVERSION FACTORS U.S. CENTS PER MAUR. RUPEE FACTEURS DE CONVERSION CENTS E.U. PAR MAUR. RUPEE		INDEX NUMBERS – INDICES — QUANTUM		UNIT VALUE VALEUR UNITAIRE	
	IMPORTS	EXPORTS	IMPORTS	EXPORTS	IMPORTS	EXPORTS	IMPORTS	EXPORTS	IMPORTS	EXPORTS
1961	324.00	294.20	0.14		21.0000	21.0000			15	7
1962	322.70	305.90	0.03		21.0000	21.0000			15	7
1963	333.10	427.80	0.37		21.0000	21.0000			15	9
1964	388.90	366.90	0.39		21.0000	21.0000			16	9
1965	367.30	313.40	0.42		21.0000	21.0000			16	7
1966	333.20	337.60	0.48		21.0000	21.0000			17	7
1967	371.10	306.80	0.77		21.0000	21.0000			17	7
1968	421.10	354.00	0.87		18.0000	18.0000			20	7
1969	376.00	365.20	0.44		18.0000	18.0000			19	7
1970	419.90	383.40	0.25		18.0000	18.0000			8	6
1971	461.60	360.80	1.03		18.0000	18.0000			9	7
1972	635.80	573.80	1.82		18.8495	18.6417			10	8
1973	915.80	748.40			18.3641	18.2525			13	10
1974	1759.80	1787.50	7.10		17.5784	17.4854			21	24
1975	1995.30	1838.90			16.6315	16.2095			24	32
1976	2397.90	1769.80			14.9559	14.9756			26	26
1977	2950.80	2041.50		379.00	15.1551	15.1766			29	25
1978	3076.40	1987.10			16.2961	16.3937			31	25
1979	3634.40	2432.70			15.5665	15.4642			37	28
1980	4721.40	3341.30			13.1176	12.8877			54	39
1981	4976.80	2999.20			11.1325	10.8052			57	42
1982	5048.20	3988.70			9.1971	9.1971			71	47
1983	5175.00	4311.40			8.4120	8.3780			43	31
1984	6494.00	5180.30			7.2750	7.2016			49	34
1985	8119.00	6644.00			6.5143	6.5491			86	63
1986	9199.00	9062.00			7.4383	7.4582			69	67
1987	13037.00	11336.00			7.7676	7.7636			72	75
1988	17242.00	13455.00			7.4743	7.4113			79	80
1989	20217.01	15049.00			6.5570	6.5570			96	89
1990	24019.01	17677.01			6.7347	6.7517			100	100
1991	24383.01	18700.00			6.3942	6.3882			105	106
1992	25280.00	20244.00			6.4255	6.4255			107	114
1993	30319.01	22992.00			5.6584	5.6495			119	124
1994	34548.00	24097.01			5.5871	5.5895			127	130
1995	34071.01	26742.00			5.7511	5.7492			135	138
1996	40891.98	31540.99			5.5718	5.5765				149

2. IMPORTS BY BROAD ECONOMIC CATEGORY AND EXPORTS BY INDUSTRIAL ORIGIN. (PERCENTAGE OF TOTAL VALUE)
IMPORTATIONS PAR CATEGORIES ECONOMIQUES ET EXPORTATIONS PAR BRANCHE D'ACTIVITE.(EN POURCENTAGE DE LA VALEUR TOTALE)

IMPORTS – IMPORTATIONS

	1990	1991	1992	1993	1994	1995	1996
TOTAL IMPORTS–IMPORTATIONS TOTALES	100.	100.	100.	100.	100.	100.	
1 FOOD BEV–ALIMENTATION BOISSONS	11.6	11.5	12.2	12.8	13.3	15.5	
11 PRIMARY–PRODUITS DE BASE	4.5	4.3	4.8	4.8	5.3	5.8	
111 FOR INDUSTRY–POUR L'INDUSTRIE	1.1	0.7	1.1	1.5	1.7	1.7	
112 FOR HOUSEHOLDS–POUR LES MENAGES	3.4	3.6	3.6	3.3	3.6	4.1	
12 PROCESSED–PRODUITS ELABORES	7.1	7.2	7.5	8.0	8.0	9.7	
121 FOR INDUSTRY–POUR L'INDUSTRIE	1.0	1.3	1.3	1.2	1.2	1.6	
122 FOR HOUSEHOLDS–POUR LES MENAGES	6.0	5.9	6.2	6.8	6.8	8.1	
2 IND SUPPLIES–APPROV INDUSTRIELS	44.3	42.3	42.9	46.9	44.8	47.8	
21 PRIMARY–PRODUITS DE BASE	3.6	3.6	3.3	3.8	3.4	4.1	
22 PROCESSED–PRODUITS ELABORES	40.8	38.8	39.6	43.1	41.3	43.7	
3 FUELS–COMBUSTIBLES	7.7	10.2	8.5	6.7	5.9	6.7	
31 PRIMARY–PRODUITS DE BASE	0.6	0.7	0.8	0.8	0.7	0.9	
32 PROCESSED–PRODUITS ELABORES	7.1	9.5	7.7	5.9	5.2	5.8	
321 MOTOR SPIRIT–ESSENCE	1.0	1.8					
322 OTHER–AUTRES	6.1	7.7	7.7	5.9	5.2	5.9	
4 MACHINERY–EQUIPEMENT	12.5	14.3	12.7	13.5	12.5	12.0	
41 CAPITAL EQUIPMENT–MACHINES	11.4	13.0	11.3	12.3	11.4	10.7	
42 PARTS–PIECES ACCESSOIRES	1.1	1.3	1.4	1.2	1.1	1.3	
5 TRANSPORT–TRANSPORT	13.7	9.6	10.6	7.0	11.8	6.3	
51 PASSENGER CARS–AUTOMOBILES	2.9	2.3	2.8	1.8	1.9	1.9	
52 OTHER–AUTRES	7.5	3.9	3.9	3.3	8.3	2.2	
521 INDUSTRIAL–INDUSTRIELS	6.9	3.2	3.3	2.8	8.0	2.0	
522 NON INDUSTRIAL–NON INDUSTRIEL	0.6	0.7	0.6	0.5	0.3	0.2	
53 PARTS–PIECES ACCESSOIRES	3.3	3.5	4.0	1.9	1.6	2.2	
6 CONSUM GOODS–BIENS CONSOMMATION	9.9	11.7	12.7	12.9	11.6	11.5	
61 DURABLE–DURABLES	3.6	5.0	4.8	4.4	3.8	3.7	
62 SEMI DURABLE–SEMI DURABLES	3.8	4.0	4.8	5.3	4.7	4.6	
63 NON DURABLE–NON DURABLES	2.4	2.7	3.1	3.2	3.1	3.2	
7 GOODS NES–BIENS NDA	0.3	0.3	0.3	0.3	0.0	0.2	

EXPORTS – EXPORTATIONS

	1990	1991	1992	1993	1994	1995	1996
TOTAL EXPORTS–EXPORTATIONS TOTALES	100.	100.	100.	100.	100.	100.	
1 AGRICULTURE	1.4	1.6	1.4	1.4	1.4	1.4	
2 MINING QUARRY–INDUS EXTRACTIVES	2.1	2.1	1.6	1.9	1.9	1.8	
3 MANUFACTURING–IND MANUFACTUR	96.5	96.3	97.0	96.7	96.7	96.3	
31 FOOD BEV TOBACCO–ALIM BOISS TAB	31.0	30.2	30.1	28.4	28.0	28.1	
32 TEXTILES–INDUSTRIES TEXTILES	54.2	54.5	54.5	59.5	58.7	58.1	
33 WOOD & PRODUCTS–BOIS & PRODUITS	0.3	0.2	0.2	0.1	0.2	0.1	
34 PAPER & PRODUCTS–PAPIER & PRODT	0.2	0.1	0.3	0.1	0.2	0.2	
35 CHEMICALS–INDUSTRIES CHIMIQUES	2.4	2.9	3.0	1.1	0.9	1.0	
36 NON METAL MIN–MIN NON METAL	0.1	0.0	0.2	0.3	0.3	0.4	
37 BASIC METAL–IND METAL BASE	0.1	0.0	0.1	0.0	0.0	0.0	
38 METAL MANUF–MANUF METAL	4.5	4.8	4.4	3.6	5.0	5.1	
39 OTH MANUF IND–AUTRES MANUF	3.8	3.6	4.4	3.6	3.5	3.8	

3. TRADE BY PRINCIPAL COUNTRIES OF ORIGIN AND DESTINATION (VALUE IN THOUSAND U.S. DOLLARS)
ECHANGES SELON LES PRINCIPAUX PAYS D'ORIGINE ET DE DESTINATION (VALEUR EN MILLIERS DE DOLLARS EU)

COUNTRIES–PAYS	GENERAL IMPORTS C.I.F. IMPORTATIONS GENERALES C.A.F				
	1992	1993	1994	1995	1996
World	1782948	1919128	1923856	2000474	2276924
Africa	295049	336913	291692	302797	349280
Americas	82706	69728	72030	95737	106961
Northern America	54934	48008	45417	54755	59872
LAIA	27514	21484	22300	38997	45496
CACM	27	104	32	7	64
Caribbean	154	51	4137	1860	780
Rest of America	76	81	144	118	748
As.ex F.USSR	701434	739791	731257	776287	880327
Eur.x F.USSR	605300	688562	751939	729809	807903
EU	571299	652041	709198	672272	751787
EFTA	29374	35109	39735	50002	52999
East Europe	1606	1346	2975	7456	3080
Other Europe	14	56	27	44	9
Former USSR	4604	4411	330	2710	2984
Oceania	75383	79639	76506	88605	125733
France,Monac	231443	242429	356558	278928	255351
So. Africa Customs Un	232229	275388	234382	225690	277456
India/Inde	83970	112164	128169	166791	201637
United Kingdom	123408	135669	128752	131466	146156
Japan/Japon	168791	113412	97764	94438	100274
Germany/Allemagne	83831	92291	88767	89392	106025
Hong Kong	70169	88157	99060	94377	82229
China/Chine	55066	80806	69254	57793	97019
Australia/Australie	52824	56814	57217	63824	100930
Italy/Italie	53667	64854	55165	63789	77551
Singapore/Singapour	55695	56527	55403	52344	48362
Malaysia/Malaisie	48136	52803	45166	64489	53688
USA/Etats–Unis d'Amer	52893	45775	43050	51262	56980
Switz.Liecht	28756	34540	38924	46618	48999
Belgium–Luxembourg	24038	47623	30269	32147	38446
Pakistan	19610	29272	27779	20995	35916
Korea, Republic of	25895	28356	26540	25116	27489
Kuwait/ Koweït	0		16320	44638	69535
New Zealand	22476	22826	19289	24749	24800
Kenya	24954	22468	20499	21353	14292
Denmark/Danemark	4779	24170	5386	12714	54422
Indonesia/Indonésie	14991	25545	16503	16825	24902
Thailand/Thaïlande	22100	23260	17181	15800	15010
Spain/Espagne	9202	11454	14143	21668	33666
Madagascar	15590	16028	11677	20346	25884
Argentina/Argentine	17078	14762	17797	16462	15176
Saudi Arabia	4656	3763	25563	21681	11919
Netherlands/Pays–Bas	12445	13847	12569	12851	12324
Brazil/Brésil	9857	5173	3262	20559	11525
Bahrain/Bahreïn	24938	807	3575	4350	12301
Turkey/Turquie	3551	4929	10168	6705	10081
Ireland/Irlande	4426	5465	5971	8859	9444
Burkina Faso	2033	5464	7235	4369	12605
Zimbabwe	4123	6442	8264	9036	3417
Israel/Israël	8690	5209	6060	4388	6719
Philippines	4378	9871	3007	4374	2986
Jordan/Jordanie	2583	11242	4570	2121	2019
United Arab Emirates	9116	6740	1413	3547	1682
Sweden/Suède	4762	5828	2729	3918	4261
Chile/Chili	496	1481	889	935	16701
Greece/Grèce	10396	883	626	4324	2622
Macau/Macao	2987	1566	3316	5049	5049
Portugal	4157	2909	2687	3361	3857
Austria/Autriche	2824	2584	2859	3995	3722
Finland/Finlande	1921	2035	2718	4860	3941
Canada	2042	2233	2366	3470	2892
Russian Federation	3780	4411	330	1881	2547
Cameroon/Cameroun	98	2626	1328	7633	458
Myanmar	5676	1050	561	675	4011
Korea Dem People's Rp	2953	2560	2243	1772	2174

COUNTRIES–PAYS	GENERAL EXPORTS F.O.B. EXPORTATIONS GENERALES F.O.B.				
	1992	1993	1994	1995	1996
Monde	1335513	1467090	1348012	1538287	1699369
Afrique	73693	94367	83801	94463	79631
Amériques	175628	271189	272753	261485	242164
Amérique du Nord	171289	270265	255888	242252	238996
ALAI	353	494	16047	809	1849
MCAC	483	135	20		1
Caraïbes	986	257	694	18359	661
Autre Amérique	2517	39	104	64	657
Asie l'URSS exclus	35510	27828	31333	40045	33037
Europe l'URSS exclus	1025477	1069915	956842	1136826	1338609
UE	1008374	1049101	937986	1114613	1315587
AELE	16199	19491	17453	21474	22415
Europe de l'Est	221	222	331	415	407
Autre de l'Europe	661	1098	1071	323	174
Ancienne URSS	1581	277	1218	1065	290
Océanie	4020	3415	1883	3382	5430
United Kingdom	449846	476768	430903	527355	600294
France,Monac	272136	299997	270910	325541	362553
USA/Etats–Unis d'Amer	160749	262475	244250	227961	227524
Germany/Allemagne	114643	104025	79708	89721	93604
Italy/Italie	60255	58544	56112	63146	70468
Netherlands/Pays–Bas	23631	30545	28478	33270	42341
Madagascar	15160	29552	31734	39829	38960
Belgium–Luxembourg	23014	31616	28626	29379	39900
Spain/Espagne	30932	36356	24901	21122	36165
Reunion/Réunion	29125	30742	27185	28197	
Portugal	20813	4436	12247	14066	56274
Switz.Liecht	15515	19131	16867	20778	21138
Canada	10540	7790	11638	14291	11472
Hong Kong	5280	7940	12497	13514	10144
So. Africa Customs Un	12292	7625	5249	6814	11976
Japan/Japon	3124	5784	5476	9794	10358
Zimbabwe	3621	5382	4645	6614	8650
Singapore/Singapour	6253	6060	3431	3411	2033
Sweden/Suède	4467	1044	1850	3871	6710
Bahamas	346	14		17250	6
Brazil/Brésil	157	209	15714	53	704
Australia/Australie	3554	3086	1494	3019	4849
India/Inde	1013	978	3546	7111	2999
Seychelles	2666	3206	2932	2624	1933
Kenya	1643	3844	2065	1767	3544
Denmark/Danemark	2781	2640	1052	2056	2574
Comoros/Comores	2051	2057	2482	2363	1159
Austria/Autriche	2225	1660	1282	2137	2170
Un. Rep. of Tanzania	631	2061	147	938	4575
Ireland/Irlande	2405	923	1342	1843	1249
Mozambique	1110	4815	1045	194	31
Pakistan	2657	2203	1603	446	242
Rwanda	2074	1326	1122	914	1212
Malawi	134	591	1222	527	3780
Thailand/Thaïlande	398	107	676	976	2277
Burundi	222	638	2239	388	537
Uganda/Ouganda	121	804	675	1588	814
Israel/Israël	1978	780	496	101	207
Norway,SVD,JM	683	356	584	694	1218
Greece/Grèce	906	298	418	842	852
Malta/Malte	640	1098	1071	323	173
Panama	2447	35	103	58	657
Russian Federation	1581	277	1218	126	80
Malaysia/Malaisie	410	908	797	827	245
Zambia/Zambie	1078	1184	614	253	51
French So. & Antc Ter	15	37	102	594	1477
China/Chine	610	459	584	389	99
New Zealand	337	272	220	257	521
Sri Lanka	98	91	57	201	1061
Korea, Republic of	565	39	77	547	258

(VALUE AS PERCENTAGE OF WORLD TOTAL)(VALEURS EN POURCENTAGE DU TOTAL MONDIAL)

	1987	1988	1989	1990	1991	1992	1993	1994	1995	1996
Africa	2.3	9.6	10.2	12.1	15.8	16.5	17.6	15.2	15.1	15.3
Americas	1.0	12.8	2.9	5.6	4.4	4.6	3.6	3.7	4.8	4.7
Northern America	0.8	12.1	1.7	4.5	2.8	3.1	2.5	2.4	2.7	2.6
LAIA	0.2	0.7	1.1	1.0	1.5	1.5	1.1	1.2	1.9	2.0
CACM				0.0	0.0	0.0	0.0	0.0	0.0	0.0
Caribbean				0.0	0.0	0.0	0.0	0.2	0.1	0.0
Rest of America				0.1	0.0	0.0	0.0	0.0	0.0	0.0
As.ex F.USSR	31.6	40.1	45.8	39.5	41.0	39.3	38.5	38.0	38.8	38.7
Eur.x F.USSR	13.5	33.2	36.6	38.6	33.4	33.9	35.9	39.1	36.5	35.5
EU	13.0	31.2	34.6	36.7	31.9	32.0	34.0	36.9	33.6	33.0
EFTA	0.5	1.9	1.9	1.8	1.3	1.6	1.8	2.1	2.5	2.3
East Europe		0.1	0.1	0.1	0.1	0.1	0.1	0.2	0.4	0.1
Other Europe		0.0		0.0	0.0	0.0	0.0	0.0	0.0	0.0
Former USSR		0.0		0.0	0.3	0.3	0.2	0.0	0.1	0.1
Oceania	2.6	3.8	4.0	3.7	4.4	4.2	4.1	4.0	4.4	5.5
France,Monac	7.2	12.4	13.6	14.5	12.6	13.0	12.6	18.5	13.9	11.2
So. Africa Customs Un	2.0	8.6	9.0	8.8	11.6	13.0	14.3	12.2	11.3	12.2
India/Inde	1.9	3.7	3.8	4.1	4.3	4.7	5.8	6.7	8.3	8.9
United Kingdom	2.1	7.3	6.4	7.1	6.5	6.9	7.1	6.7	6.6	6.4
Japan/Japon	5.5	7.4	9.1	7.4	8.7	9.5	5.9	5.1	4.7	4.4
Germany/Allemagne	2.4	5.2	7.2	6.9	5.2	4.7	4.8	4.6	4.5	4.7
Hong Kong	4.3	5.5	4.8	3.7	4.0	3.9	4.6	5.1	4.7	3.6
China/Chine	3.6	3.9	4.9	3.3	3.6	3.1	4.2	3.6	2.9	4.3
Australia/Australie	1.4	2.6	2.5	2.4	3.1	3.0	3.0	3.0	3.2	4.4
Italy/Italie	0.6	3.0	3.1	2.8	3.3	3.0	3.4	2.9	3.2	3.4

	1987	1988	1989	1990	1991	1992	1993	1994	1995	1996
Afrique	0.4	3.4	3.7	4.2	4.9	5.5	6.4	6.2	6.1	4.7
Amériques	14.5	15.1	15.7	13.5	12.4	13.2	18.5	20.2	17.0	14.3
Amérique du Nord	14.5	15.1	14.8	13.2	12.1	12.8	18.4	19.0	15.7	14.1
ALAI				0.0	0.0	0.0	0.0	1.2	0.1	0.1
MCAC				0.0	0.0	0.0	0.0	0.0		0.0
Caraïbes			0.9	0.0	0.1	0.1	0.0	0.1	1.2	0.0
Autre Amérique				0.2	0.2	0.2	0.0	0.0	0.0	0.0
Asie l'URSS exclus	0.3	2.5	1.9	2.4	3.0	2.7	1.9	2.3	2.6	1.9
Europe l'URSS exclus	66.8	78.1	76.1	78.1	79.0	76.8	72.9	71.0	73.9	78.8
UE	66.8	77.4	75.3	77.0	77.6	75.5	71.5	69.6	72.5	77.4
AELE		0.7	0.8	1.1	1.3	1.2	1.3	1.3	1.4	1.3
Europe de l'Est				0.0	0.0	0.0	0.0	0.0	0.0	0.0
Autre de l'Europe				0.0	0.0	0.0	0.1	0.1	0.0	0.0
Ancienne URSS	0.3	0.0	1.3	0.1	0.1	0.1	0.0	0.1	0.1	0.0
Océanie	0.4	0.2	0.2	0.2	0.3	0.3	0.2	0.1	0.2	0.3
United Kingdom	33.1	35.7	35.8	35.3	35.4	33.7	32.5	32.0	34.3	35.3
France,Monac	21.4	22.5	19.8	22.1	19.6	20.4	20.4	20.1	21.2	21.3
USA/Etats–Unis d'Amer	12.6	13.3	13.8	12.7	11.6	12.0	17.9	18.1	14.8	13.4
Germany/Allemagne	6.3	9.5	9.2	8.5	10.8	8.6	7.1	5.9	5.8	5.5
Italy/Italie	1.9	3.8	3.8	4.4	4.8	4.5	4.0	4.2	4.1	4.1
Netherlands/Pays–Bas	1.2	1.2	2.3	1.7	1.9	1.8	2.1	2.1	2.2	2.5
Madagascar		0.2	0.3	0.8	0.6	1.1	2.0	2.4	2.6	2.3
Belgium–Luxembourg	1.3	2.3	2.0	2.3	1.8	1.7	2.2	2.1	1.9	2.3
Spain/Espagne				0.5	1.6	2.3	2.5	1.8	1.4	2.1
Reunion/Réunion	0.3	2.1	1.9	1.8	1.9	2.2	2.1	2.0	1.8	

4. General Imports C.I.F. by Commodities according to the S.I.T.C. (Rev. 2) in thousand U.S. Dollars
Importations Générales C.A.F. par Produits d'après la C.T.C.I. (Rév. 2) en milliers de Dollars E.U.

SITC CTCI	COMMODITY	1993 WEIGHT POIDS	1993 VALUE VALEUR	1994 WEIGHT POIDS	1994 VALUE VALEUR	1995 WEIGHT POIDS	1995 VALUE VALEUR	1996 WEIGHT POIDS	1996 VALUE VALEUR	PRODUIT
	ALL COMMODITIES		1919128		1923856		2000474		2276924	TOUS PRODUITS
0	FOOD AND LIVE ANIMALS		236821		236930		293013		329828	ALIMENTS,ANIMAUX VIVANTS
001	*LIVE ANIMALS FOR FOOD	N 182269	9738	N 332303	10415	N 198468	10527	N 160529	7661	ANIMAUX VIVANTS
0011	BOVINE SPECIES,LIVE	N 10641	8501	N 11171	8540	N 10063	9304	N 8971	6600	ESPECE BOVINE
00119	— OTHR THAN FR BREEDING	N 8896	7296	N 9873	7826	N 8801	8343	N 6018	4451	BOVINS NON REPRODUCTEURS
01	MEAT AND PREPARATIONS		26586		31214		31057		32193	VIANDES ET PREPARATIONS
011	MEAT FRESH,CHILLD,FROZEN	W 14584	21124	W 17818	25235	W 16442	25999	W 14713	26384	VIANDES FRAICHES,REF,CONGE
0111	BOVINE MEAT FRESH,FROZEN	W 7340	11149	W 10584	14750	W 9780	15316	W 7719	13366	VIANDES BOVIN FRAI,REF
01112	BOVINE MEAT BONELESS	W 7238	10938	W 10413	14259	W 9607	14717	W 7130	12517	VIANDES BOVIN DESOSSEES
0112	MUTTON ETC FRSH,CHLD,FRN	W 4489	7026	W 5098	7975	W 4643	8025	W 5099	10141	VIANDE DE MOUTON
014	MEAT PREPD,PRSVD,NES ETC	W 1952	5448	W 2341	5962	W 1632	5025	W 1761	5754	CONSERVES DE VIANDES
02	DAIRY PRODCTS,BIRDS'EGGS		41954		42448		72747		52432	PRODUITS LAITIERS,OEUFS
022	MILK AND CREAM	W 14048	32355	W 15965	32538	W 16240	62411	W 15241	40085	LAIT ET CREME
0224	MILK,CREAM PRESERVED ETC	W 12119	30769	W 13792	31052	W 13653	60688	W 12634	38051	LAIT,CREME CONS,CONC
02243	MILK DRY,OVER 1.5% FAT	W 10876	28017	W 12264	27841	W 12518	57863	W 11769	36019	LAIT POUDRE SUP 1.5%
024	CHEESE AND CURD	W 1731	7126	W 1742	7205	W 1818	7717	W 1964	9355	FROMAGE ET CAILLEBOTTE
03	FISH AND PREPARATIONS		23707		27295		36512		42148	POISSONS ET PREPARATIONS
034	FISH,FRESH,CHILLED,FROZN	W 12819	13590	W 16216	17695	W 25000	25500	W 26798	30813	POISSON FRAIS, REFRIG,CONG
0342	FISH FROZEN,EXCL FILLETS	W 12715	13073	W 15986	16944	W 24826	24749	W 26619	30026	POISSONS CONGELES
037	FISH ETC PREPD,PRSVD NES	W 3049	6217	W 3358	6007	W 3007	6034	W 3168	6362	POIS,CRUST,MOL PREPARES
0371	FISH PREPARD,PRESRVD NES	W 3041	6188	W 3340	5938	W 2992	5972	W 3163	6336	CONSERVES DE POISSONS
04	CEREALS AND PREPARATIONS		71069		63668		65815		103314	CEREALES ET PRODUITS
041	WHEAT ETC UNMILLED	W 124050	18183	W 134686	20057	W 112365	21824	W 123739	33350	FROMENT,EPEAUTRE
0411	DURUM WHEAT UNMILLED	W 52650	8111	W 110274	17008	W 55156	9259	W 5970	1495	FROMENT DUR NON MOULU
0412	OTHER WHEAT ETC UNMILLED	W 71400	10072	W 24412	3048	W 57209	12565	W 117769	31856	AUTRE FROMENT NON MOULU
042	RICE	W 90417	29372	W 79567	22199	W 56921	18965	W 88557	37202	RIZ
0422	RICE SEMI-MILLED,MILLED	W 90147	29237	W 79495	22168	W 56891	18947	W 88551	37191	RIZ POLI,GLACE INCL BRISURES
04221	RICE MILLED UNBROKEN	W 89968	29139	W 79429	22131	W 56868	18928	W 88534	37178	RIZ POLI,GLACE EXCL BRISURES
044	MAIZE UNMILLED	W 42584	7324	W 36574	5855	W 60293	10107	W 50277	12162	MAIS NON MOULU
048	CEREAL ETC PREPARATIONS	W 7753	12864	W 9442	14295	W 9011	14237	W 9236	15316	PREPTNS A BASE CEREALES
05	VEGETABLES AND FRUIT		29723		29169		30555		38628	LEGUMES ET FRUITS
054	VEG ETC FRSH,SMPLY PRSVD	W 25277	12210	W 23936	10765	W 26448	12146	W 30171	16403	LEGUMES FRAIS,CONG,SECS
0542	LEGUMINOUS VEGETBLES DRY	W 10433	6080	W 10523	5280	W 10515	5430	W 10862	6731	LEGUMES A COSSE SECS
057	FRUIT,NUTS,FRESH,DRIED		10151		10693	W 12268	10567	W 14405	14631	FRUITS FRAIS OU SECS
06	SUGAR AND PREPS,HONEY		3625		3464		12384		17908	SUCRES ET PRODUITS
061	SUGAR AND HONEY	W 723	1713	W 1017	1651	W 21355	10538	W 31751	16362	SUCRES ET MIEL
0611	RAW BEET AND CANE SUGAR	W 30	9			W 17535	7844			SUCRES BRUTS
0612	REFINED SUGAR ETC	W 2	1	W 10	2	W 2458	1182	W 30986	14646	SUCRES RAFFINES
07	COFFEE,TEA,COCOA,SPICES		6620		6164		6681		8059	CAFE,THE,CACAO,EPICES
081	*FEEDING STUFF FOR ANIML	W 21614	8423	W 18051	7765	W 27270	10283	W 23672	10574	NOURRITURE POUR ANIMAUX
09	MISC EDIBLE PRODUCTS		15375		15327		16453		16911	PREP ALIMENTAIRES DIVERSES
098	EDIBLE PRODCTS,PREPS NES		11975		12631		13371		12993	PREP ALIMENTAIRES NDA
09809	MISC FOOD PREPRTIONS NES	W 2489	8837	W 2919	9653	W 2671	10277	W 2294	9184	PREP ALIMENTAIRES NDA
1	BEVERAGES AND TOBACCO		9594		11185		12723		11808	BOISSONS ET TABACS
11	BEVERAGES		8304		9883		11282		10626	BOISSONS
112	ALCOHOLIC BEVERAGES	W 1754	6728		8313	W 2836	9445	W 2661	9306	BOISSONS ALCOOLIQUES
2	CRUDE MATERLS,EXCL FUELS		57772		54677		66823		85947	MAT BRUTES NON COMESTIBLES
24	CORK AND WOOD		20711		17396		17853		18447	LIEGE ET BOIS
248	WOOD SHAPED,SLEEPERS	W 23055	16789	W 20545	14308	W 25223	16320	W 19820	15120	BOIS SIMPLEMENT TRAVAILLES
2483	LUMBER SHAPED NON-CONIFR	W 21503	15997	W 18498	13123	W 23189	15014	W 18911	14270	NON CONIFERES SCIES,RABOTES
24831	LUMBER SAWN ETC NON-CON	W 21446	15870	W 18483	13083	W 23134	14955	W 18778	14095	SCIES LONGITUDINALEMENT
26	TEXTILE FIBRES AND WASTE		26904		27966		37494		46093	FIBRES TEXTILES
263	COTTON	W 6565	9646	W 7048	10189	W 10311	20193	W 12120	27578	COTON
2631	RAW COTTON,EXCL LINTERS	W 6481	9384	W 6862	9533	W 10243	19940	W 11995	26936	COTON EN MASSE
268	WOOL(EXC TOPS),ANML HAIR	W 3106	15477	W 3263	15732	W 2801	15064	W 3117	15919	LAINES ET POILS
2682	WOOL DEGREASED,UNCOMBED	W 2325	10164	W 2252	9192	W 1857	9666	W 2060	9703	LAINE DEGRAISSEE
27	CRUDE FERTLZR,MINRLS NES		3876		3423		5996		15086	ENGRAIS MINERAUX BRUTS
277	NATURAL ABRASIVES NES		1124		1183		3362		11948	ABRASIFS NATURELS NDA
2771	INDUSTRIAL DIAMONDS		210		123		2281		10581	DIAMANTS INDUSTRIELS
3	MINERAL FUELS ETC		133940		119833		138881		179982	COMBUSTIBLES MINERAUX LUB
33	PETROLEUM AND PRODUCTS		118592		106837		121909		162856	PETROLE ET DERIVES
334	PETROLEUM PRODUCTS,REFIN	W 612325	112578	W 655393	100041	W 696652	116919	W 710163	158263	PRODUITS RAFFINES
3341	GASOLINE,OTH LIGHT OILS							W 88695	21477	ESSENCES POUR MOTEURS
33411	MOTOR,AVIATION SPIRIT							W 88041	21229	ESSENCES MOTEURS D'AVIONS
3342	KEROSENE,OTH MEDIUM OILS							W 196021	50492	PETR LAMPANTS,AUT HUIL
33421	KEROSENE INCL JET FUEL							W 195988	50365	PETROLES LAMPANTS
3343	GAS OILS							W 416357	75915	GAS OILS
3345	LUBS,PETROLEUM OILS NES							W 9090	10380	HUILES LUBRIFIANTES
33451	LUBS(HIGH PETR CONT) ETC							W 8715	9399	HUILES LUBRIF,H LOURDES
335	RESIDUAL PETRLM PROD NES	W 22912	6014		6794	W 18185	4989	W 15761	4590	PRODUITS RESIDUELS NDA
341	*GAS,NATURAL AND MANUFCT	W 29545	11436	W 32678	10959	W 36223	13149	W 36585	14700	GAZ NATUREL,GAZ MANUFACT
3413	PETROLM GASES,LIQUEFIED	W 29544	11435	W 32677	10953	W 36223	13146	W 36585	14697	GAZ DE PETROLE LIQUEFIE
34131	LIQUEFIED PROPANE,BUTANE	W 29386	11373	W 32676	10947	W 36223	13142	W 36585	14697	PROPANE,BUTANE LIQUEFIES
4	ANIMAL,VEGETABLE OIL,FAT		18374		23158		25358		25861	HUILES,GRAISSES ANIM,VEG
42	FIXED VEGETABLE OIL,FAT		12825		19010		20785		18991	HUILES VEGETALES FIXES
423	FIXED VEG OILS,SOFT	W 19275	11099	W 28096	17500	W 26112	18403	W 26468	18056	HUILES VEGET DOUCES FIXES
4232	SOYA BEAN OIL	W 18191	10051	W 23669	14341	W 20604	14116	W 22954	15224	HUILE DE SOJA
5	CHEMCLS,RELATED PROD NES		134653		131304		149381		170623	PRODUITS CHIMIQUES
51	ORGANIC CHEMICALS		9261		7984		8857		9647	PROD CHIMIQ ORGANIQUES
52	INORGANIC CHEMICALS		11449		11033		14935		16395	PROD CHIM INORGANIQUES
522	INORG ELEMNTS,OXIDES,ETC	W 24398	6048	W 16925	5233	W 24415	7752	W 23482	7557	ELEMENTS INORGANIQUES
5225	INORGANIC BASES ETC NES	W 22907	4682	W 15251	3889	W 22885	6418	W 21703	6249	AUTRES BASES OXYDES METAL
523	OTHR INORG CHEMICALS ETC	W 10521	5355	W 13353	5718	W 16554	7163	W 19580	8808	AUT PRODUITS CHIMIQUES INORG
53	DYES,TANNING,COLOUR PROD		18653		17785		18711		23149	PROD TEINTURE,COLORANTS
531	SYNT DYE,NAT INDGO,LAKES	W 723	11229	W 779	10415	W 991	11596	W 1693	15217	MAT COLOR ORGAN,LAQUES
5311	SYNTHIC ORGNIC DYESTUFFS	W 658	10715	W 695	9916	W 904	11121	W 1576	14219	MAT COLOR ORGAN SYNTHET
533	PIGMENTS,PAINTS,ETC	W 3162	6721	W 3729	6672	W 2032	6037	W 3064	7520	PIGMENTS,PEINTURES,VERNIS
541	*MEDICINAL,PHARM PRODUCT	K 1731230	29917	K 1584028	27234	K 1825980	33049	K 1980037	37377	PROD MEDICINAUX PHARMACEUT
5417	MEDICAMENTS	K 1231218	25049	K 1298901	24157	K 1379463	28781	K 1767005	34028	MEDICAMENTS
54179	— CONTNG OTH SUBSTANCES	K 1192170	23978	K 1271779	23340	K 1355764	27648	K 1719393	32607	MED CONT AUT SUBSTANCES
55	PERFUME,CLEANING ETC PRD		13153		14096		15323		18162	PROD POUR PARFUM,TOILETTE
553	PERFUMERY,COSMETICS,ETC	W 733	7353	W 1031	7755	W 856	8556	W 1198	10387	PRODUITS DE PARFUMERIE
562	*FERTILIZERS,MANUFACTURE	W 63253	9840	W 54947	7755	W 46774	8377	W 55768	10543	ENGRAIS MANUFACTURES
58	PLASTIC MATERIALS ETC		21472		23665		25916		26527	MAT PLAST ARTIFICIELLES
583	POLYMERIZATION ETC PRODS	W 12055	16870	W 14322	19203	W 12446	21382	W 13746	21463	PROD POLYMERISATION
5839	OTH POLYMRZTION ETC PROD	W 5573	8488	W 6355	9360	W 5709	10357	W 5932	9651	AUT PROD POLYMER COPOLYM
59	CHEMICAL MATERIALS NES		20508		21368		23794		28345	MAT PROD CHIMIQUES NDA
591	PESTICIDES,DISINFECTANTS	W 1523	8768	W 1595	8763	W 1731	9496	W 1592	10490	DESINF,INSECT,FONG,HERB
598	MISCEL CHEM PRODUCTS NES	W 3466	9567	W 4258	10566	W 4556	11841	W 6525	15400	PROD DIV INDUST CHIM NDA
5989	CHEM PRODUCTS,PREPS NES	W 3342	8940	W 4128	10238	W 4441	11424	W 6197	14702	PROD PREP CHIMIQUES NDA
59891	PREPD GLAZINGS,DRESSINGS	W 1858	4739	W 2372	6201	W 2550	5942	W 3064	7722	PAREMENTS,APPRETS

4. General Imports C.I.F. by Commodities according to the S.I.T.C. (Rev. 2) in thousand U.S. Dollars
Importations Générales C.A.F. par Produits d'après la C.T.C.I. (Rév. 2) en milliers de Dollars E.U.

SITC CTCI	COMMODITY	1993 WEIGHT POIDS	1993 VALUE VALEUR	1994 WEIGHT POIDS	1994 VALUE VALEUR	1995 WEIGHT POIDS	1995 VALUE VALEUR	1996 WEIGHT POIDS	1996 VALUE VALEUR	PRODUIT
6	BASIC MANUFACTURES		704953		665235		730688		770665	ART MANUFACTURES
61	LEATHER,DRESSED FUR,ETC		11708		8596		11413		10291	CUIRS,PELLETERIES
611	LEATHER	W 255	8538	W 386	6081	W 318	8601	W 250	7486	CUIRS,PEAUX PREPARES
62	RUBBER MANUFACTURES NES		15176		14642		15348		16255	CAOUTCHOUC MANUFACTURE
625	RUBBER TYRES, TUBES ETC		9227	N 625242	8632	N 561864	9191	N 560274	9825	PNEUS CAOUTCHOUC VULCANISE
63	WOOD,CORK MANUFACTRS NES		13007		10897		11242		10878	OUVRAGES LIEGE ET BOIS
634	VENEERS,PLYWOOD,ETC	W 7413	10031		7896		7859		8597	PLACAGES,CONTRE–PLAQUES
6342	PLYWOOD OF WOOD SHEETS	W 6235	9403		7074	V 10897	6435	V 8710	6924	BOIS CONTRE–PLAQUES
64	PAPER,PAPERBOARD AND MFR		29785		30806		43641		39474	PAPIERS,CARTONS & OUVRAGES
641	PAPER AND PAPERBOARD	W 26264	20454	W 28223	21210	W 29835	31372	W 31077	28205	PAPIERS ET CARTONS
6413	KRAFT PAPER,PAPERBOARD	W 8811	5792	W 9139	5066	W 7828	6002	W 8692	5375	PAPIER ET CARTON KRAFT
6415	PAPER,PAPERBRD,BULK,NES	W 9807	7081	W 8896	6628	W 9519	10128	W 11083	10303	PAPIERS,CARTONS ROULEAUX
64159	OTHER PAPER ETC,BULK,NES	W 5412	5091	W 6285	5458	W 6451	8184	W 7435	8519	AUT PAPIER ROULEAUX FEUILLES
642	PAPER,ETC,PRECUT,ARTS OF	W 3487	9332	W 3626	9595	W 3810	12269	W 3544	11269	PAP,CARTONS DECOUPES
65	TEXTILE YARN,FABRICS,ETC		421802		402858		444672		460948	FILS,TISSUS,ARTICLES TEXTILE
651	TEXTILE YARN		145052	W 29609	129640	W 31297	155318	W 40026	194592	FILS TEXTILES
6512	WOOL,HAIR YARN,INCL TOPS	W 3081	37282	W 1460	15813	W 1231	13850	W 1666	17174	FILS DE LAINE,DE POILS
65122	CARDED WOOL YARN IN BULK	W 2132	26550	W 591	6623	W 298	3768	W 449	5205	FILS CONT 85% LAINE CARDEE
6513	COTTON YARN	W 22037	89551	W 25799	99440	W 27882	125775	W 36237	158401	FILS DE COTON
6514	SYN FIB YRN,BULK,MONOFIL		9221	W 1211	7954	W 1090	8374	W 1080	9611	FILS CONT 85% FIB TEXT SYNTH
6516	DISCON SYN FIB BLEND YRN	W 822	6933	W 848	4988	W 837	5583	W 724	5839	FILS FIBR TEX SYNT DIS MOINS
652	COTTON FABRICS,WOVEN	A 71860	111928		118030	W 24894	123674	W 11192	112009	TISSUS DE COTON
6521	GREY WOVEN COTTON FABRIC	A 7390	7426		4893	W 955	6740	W 940	7368	TISSUS COT ECRUS NON MERCER
65214	GREY WOVEN COTTON NES	A 6471	6384		4161	W 873	5970	W 832	6610	AUT TISSUS 85% COTON ECRUS
6522	WOVEN COTTON BLEACHD,ETC	A 64470	104502		113137	W 23938	116933	W 10252	104641	TISSUS COTON BLANCHIS ETC
65224	BLCHED COTTON FABRIC NES	A 27333	48963		54444	W 5389	50159	W 5675	58077	AUT TIS PLUS 85% COT BLANCHI
65225	BLCHD COTN BLEND FAB NES	A 34637	51349		55538	W 18228	63813	W 3882	40425	AUT TIS MOINS 85% COT BLANCH
653	WOVN MAN–MADE FIB FABRIC		59405		50640	W 5222	49325	W 5587	51912	TISSUS FIBRES SYNTH,ARTIF
6531	CONT SYNT WEAVES NONPILE	A 17704	19557		16567	W 1628	15745	W 1485	15516	TISSUS FIBRES SYNTH CONTINUE
65314	CONT SYN TYRE CORD FABRC	A 5266	5848		4877	W 497	4496	W 382	4198	TIS ARMATURE PNEUMATIQUES
65315	CONT SYN TXTL FABRIC NES	A 12439	13709		11690	W 1131	11249	W 1102	11318	TIS PLUS 85% TEXT SYNT CONT
6532	DISC SYN TXTL FABRIC NES	A 5390	6306		4661	W 452	4378	W 602	5541	TIS DISC MOINS 85% FIBR TEXT
6534	DISC SYN BLEND FABRC NES	A 14942	18830		19610	W 1887	17889	W 2101	19276	TISSUS FIBRES SYNTH DISCONT
65341	DISC SYN FIB–COTTN FABRC	A 10612	10800		12419	W 1289	10575	W 1271	10937	TISSUS FIB SYNT DIS MEL COTO
65349	OTH DISC SYN BLEND FABRC	A 3825	6044		5339	W 444	4583	W 693	6009	TISSUS FIB SYNT MEL MAT AUT
6538	DISC REG BLEND FABRC NES		7014		3798	W 427	3545	W 369	2800	TIS MOINS 85% TEXT ART DISC
654	OTH WOVEN TEXTILE FABRIC		25590		24265	W 794	27652	W 428	19591	TISSUS AUT COTON SYNT,ARTIF
6541	SILK FABRICS WOVEN	A 633	14858		13658	W 338	15825	W 31	9550	TISSUS DE SOIE
6542	WOVEN WOOL,HAIR NONPILE	A 941	7193		5067	W 152	6724	W 129	5720	TIS PLUS 85% LAINE,POILS
65421	WOVN CARD WOOL,FINE HAIR	A 892	6748		4627	W 140	6293	W 121	5405	TISSUS 85% LAINE,PLS CARD
655	KNITTED,ETC FABRICS	A 31690	48754		48928	W 7857	55888	W 4817	48055	ETOF BONNETERIE PIECES ETC
6552	OTHER KNIT ETC FAB NONEL	A 31690	48754		48928	W 7857	55888	W 4817	48055	ETOF BON NON ELAS NON SYNT
656	LACE,RIBBONS,TULLE,ETC		14227		13078	W 918	14969	W 908	16588	TULLES,BRODERIE
65601	NARROW FABRICS NES		6358		5776	W 501	8027	W 513	7194	RUBANS SANS TRAME EN FILS
657	SPECIAL TXTL FABRC,PRODS		13537		14866	W 1498	14270	W 1661	14852	TISSUS SPECIAUX
6573	COATED ETC TEXTILES NES	A 6382	8757		8852	W 871	7814	W 983	7814	TISSUS,ART MATIERE TEXT NDA
65732	PLASTIC COATED TEXTILES	A 6323	8604		8596	W 831	7502	W 902	7281	TISSUS IMPREGNES
66	NONMETAL MINERAL MFS NES		104544		96876		101738		106495	ART MIN NON METALLIQUES
661	LIME,CEMENT,BLDG PRODS	W 551988	43205	W 564279	40648	W 583985	41914	W 606806	45883	CHAUX,CIMENTS MAT CONSTR
6612	CEMENT	W 548276	39888	W 560504	36563	W 580660	39503	W 600815	42107	CIMENTS HYDRAULIQUES
662	CLAY,REFRACTORY BLDG PRD	W 22600	12733	W 24960	12387	W 24438	12396		16367	MAT CONST REFRACTAIRES
6624	BRICKS ETC NONREFRACTORY	W 22171	12576	W 24584	12245	W 24117	12162		16078	BRIQUES ETC CERAM NON REFR
66245	GLAZED CERAMIC SETTS ETC	W 19484	11228	W 22168	11087	W 21046	10779	W 25582	13477	AUT CARREAUX CERAMIQUE
664	GLASS		4473		4314		6190		5022	VERRE
665	GLASSWARE		8865		7611		7549		7992	OUVRAGES EN VERRE
667	PEARL,PREC–,SEMI–P STONE		30474		27886		29605		26391	PERLES, PIERRES GEMMES
6672	DIAMONDS NONINDUST,UNSET		26726		24624		23890		21047	DIAMANTS BRUTS
66722	— SRTD,ROUGH,SIMPLY WKD		21736		20859		20258		13662	DIAMANTS TRIES BRUTS
67	IRON AND STEEL		50257		52082		51667		70965	FER ET ACIER
672	IRON,STEEL PRIMARY FORMS	W 43505	13973	W 39421	13145	W 41151	14722	W 41008	15988	LINGOTS FER,ACIER
6725	IRN,STL BLOOMS,SLABS,ETC	W 43103	13731	W 37201	11812	W 39393	13470	W 39486	14726	BLOOMS,BILLETTES FER ACIER
67251	IRN,SMPLE STL BLOOMS,ETC	W 43102	13724	W 37199	11806	W 39390	13453	W 39479	14711	BLOOMS ETC NON ACIER FIN
673	IRON,STEEL SHAPES ETC	W 21457	9095	W 32749	13028		9404	W 28374	15479	BARRES,PROFIL FER,ACIER
6733	IRON,STEEL PROFILES ETC	W 9891	4519	W 15059	6438	W 11478	5476	W 14595	8759	PROFILES,PALPLAN FER,ACIER
674	IRN,STL UNIV,PLATE,SHEET	W 15742	13374	W 18277	14026	W 12603	13004	W 14678	16798	LARGES PLATS,TOLES
6749	OTH IRN,STL PLATES,SHEET	W 9636	10087	W 11331	10962	W 9779	11457	W 11407	14982	AUTRES TOLES FER,ACIER
67491	— OF IRON OR SIMPLE STL	W 9172	9548	W 10378	10276	W 9546	11255	W 10717	14583	AUT TOLES AUTRES ACIER FIN
678	IRON,STL TUBES,PIPES,ETC	W 11782	10941	W 11410	9119	W 13135	12514	W 16296	20143	TUBES,TUYAUX EN FONTE,FER
6783	IRON,STL TUBES,PIPES NES	W 6092	4728	W 4255	3049	W 5291	4513	W 6288	7884	AUT TUBES,TUYAUX FER,ACIER
68	NON–FERROUS METALS		10413		8922		10729		11100	METAUX NON FERREUX
684	ALUMINIUM	W 1331	5940	W 1447	5243	W 1396	6774	W 1061	4772	ALUMINIUM
6842	ALUMINIUM,ALLOYS WORKED	W 1331	5938	W 1447	5242	W 1396	6773	W 1061	4772	ALUMINIUM,ALLIAGES OUVRE
69	METAL MANUFACTURES NES		48261		39558		40237		44259	ART MANUFACT EN METAL NDA
691	STRUCTURES AND PARTS NES	W 4727	7733	W 1836	5134	W 1518	2903	W 1744	5058	CONSTRUCT FER,ACIER,ALU
6911	STRUCTURES,PARTS IRN,STL	W 4331	6076	W 1629	4015	W 1459	2642	W 1648	4788	CONSTRUCT FER,ACIER,FONTE
697	BASE MTL HOUSEHOLD EQUIP		9070		7115		7016		7106	ART MENAGE MET COMMUNS
699	BASE METAL MFRS NES		14365		12519	W 2805	14041	W 2568	15085	ART MANUFACTURES MET NDA
7	MACHINES,TRANSPORT EQUIP		430299		494666		381841		496847	MACHINES MATERIEL TRANSPORT
71	POWER GENERATING EQUIPMT		11350		22729		18305		42791	MACHINES GENERATRICES
713	INTRNL COMBUS PSTN ENGIN		5282		5525		6717		8411	MOTEURS EXPL COMB INT, PIECE
716	ROTATING ELECTRIC PLANT		3420		14384		9176		30757	APP ELECTR ROTATIFS,PIECES
7161	DC MOTORS AND GENERATORS	N 1600	797	N 5693	9806	N 2678	2104	N 27700	19450	MOTEURS COURANT CONTINU
72	MACHS FOR SPCL INDUSTRYS		100689		80916		71786		81823	MAC SPECIALES POUR INDUST
722	TRACTORS NON–ROAD	N 100	6821	N 91	3513	N 92	3348	N 67	2230	TRACTEURS
7224	WHEELED TRACTORS NES	N 93	6444	N 87	2393	N 84	2953	N 65	1849	TRACTEURS A ROUES
723	CIVIL ENGNEERG EQUIP ETC		9566		7088		3746		9589	APPAREILS DE GENIE CIVIL
7234	CONST,MINING MACHNRY NES	N 206	8186	N 1055	6129	N 159	3209	N 1029	9031	MACH POUR LA CONST, MINES
72342	SLFPRP SHOVELS,EXCAVATRS	N 121	6219	N 100	5116	N 52	2077	N 64	4584	PELLES MECANIQUES
724	TEXTILE,LEATHER MACHNRY		52229		41197		39229		42010	MACH POUR INDUSTRIE TEXTILE
7243	SEWING MACHS,NEEDLES ETC		11091		10228		10390		11187	MACHINES A COUDRE,PIECES
72431	SEWING MACHINES	N 17033	8678	N 14951	7298	N 11351	7518	N 11232	8227	MACHINES A COUDRE
7244	SPINNING,EXTRDNG,ETC MCH		9586		4395		2736		2994	MACH POUR LE FILAGE
7245	WEAVING,FELT MFG,ETC MCH	N 650	15333	N 1017	12561	N 727	9384	N 791	9985	METIERS A TISSER,PIECES
72453	GIMPING,WARPING ETC MCHS	N 412	6949	N 781	5133	N 424	3444	N 593	4996	METIERS A TULLE ETC
7247	TEXTILE MACHINERY NES		11694		10105		10893		12076	MACH LAVAGE,TEINTURE TEX
72474	OTH TEXTILE MACHNERY NES	N 2413	9908	N 723	7615	N 677	7728	N 1167	8254	MACH LAVAGE ETC MAT TEXT
726	PRINTG,BKBINDG MACHY,PTS		6414		5646		3658		6953	MACHINES POUR IMPRIMERIE
728	OTH MACHY FOR SPCL INDUS		15119		15414		12395		15679	AUT MACH IND PARTICULIERES
7284	MACHY FOR SPCL INDUS NES		7536		9932		6114		8326	MACH SPEC IND PARTICUL.
73	METALWORKING MACHINERY		5833		4657		3860		5521	MACH TRAVAIL DES METAUX
74	GENRL INDUSTRL MACHY NES		57410		55490		53723		67579	MACH APP INDUSTRIE

4. General Imports C.I.F. by Commodities according to the S.I.T.C. (Rev. 2) in thousand U.S. Dollars
Importations Générales C.A.F. par Produits d'après la C.T.C.I. (Rév. 2) en milliers de Dollars E.U.

SITC CTCI	COMMODITY	1993 WEIGHT POIDS	1993 VALUE VALEUR	1994 WEIGHT POIDS	1994 VALUE VALEUR	1995 WEIGHT POIDS	1995 VALUE VALEUR	1996 WEIGHT POIDS	1996 VALUE VALEUR	PRODUIT
741	HEATING,COOLING EQUIPMNT		12154		13920		12419		14215	MACH CHAUFFAGE,PIECES
743	PUMPS NES,CENTRFUGES ETC		8907		9775		7033		10451	POMPES COMPRES,VENT ETC
744	MECHANICAL HANDLING EQU		13541		9695		10484		15793	EQUIP MANUTENTION PIECES
7442	LIFTING,LOADING MACH NES	N 4998	9891	N 11012	6332	N 9550	6110	N 3764	6095	APP LEVAGE,MANUTENTION
745	NONELEC MACHY,TOOLS NES		8831		7864		7708		11123	AUT MACH NON ELEC,PIECES
7452	OTH NONELEC MCHS,PTS NES		8264		7223		7197		10447	AUT MACH NON ELEC,PIECES
749	NONELEC MACH PTS,ACC NES		10697		10782		12230		11908	PIECES MACH NON ELEC NDA
7492	COCKS,VALVES ETC NES		5799		4771	W 423	5662	W 617	5856	ART ROB,SIM POUR TUYAUX
75	OFFICE MACHINES,ADP EQUIP		25640		26249		26069		34621	MACH BUREAU TRAIT AUTOM
752	AUTOMTIC DATA PROC EQUIP	N 21908	16252	N 28742	16135	N 37742	16386	N 19745	21800	MACH TRAIT INFORMATION
7528	OFF-LINE DATA PROC EQUIP	N 14119	6238	N 16877	7023	N 20132	7378	N 10663	9395	MACH AUXIL TRAIT INFORM
759	OFFICE,ADP MCH PTS,ACCES	W 102	6522		5856	W 79	6347	W 107	8670	PIECES DU 751 ET 752
7599	ACCTG,ETC,ADP MCH PTS,AC	W 94	5960		5302	W 68	5631	W 98	7962	PIECES DU 751 ET 752
76	TELECOMM,SOUND EQUIPMENT		40969		37095		42128		56473	EQUIPMENT DE TELECOM
761	TELEVISION RECEIVERS		7847		6427	N 22426	5090	N 21349	5692	RECEPTEURS DE TELEVISION
7611	COLOUR TV RECEIVERS	N 34311	7844	N 29690	6415	N 22136	5070	N 20352	5649	RECEPTEURS COULEUR
763	SOUND RECORDRS,PHONOGRPH	N 30880	5962	N 47019	7181	N 38408	5134	N 37396	5610	PHONO,APP ENREGISTREMENT
7638	OTHR SOUND APPARATUS ETC	N 28980	5821	N 44243	7027	N 35731	4836	N 36549	5521	AUT APP D'ENREGIS,REPROD
764	TELECOM EQPT,PTS,ACC NES		23660		21054		29747		42706	EQUIP TELECOM,PIECES
7641	LINE TELEPHONE,ETC EQUIP	N 106145	14590	N 264377	14697	N 173042	14613	N 151483	28645	APP TELEPHON PAR FIL
7643	TV,RADIO TRANSMITTRS ETC	N 2779	1586	N 1545	1547	N 2852	8811	N 2092	8624	APP EMET TELE RADIO
77	ELECTRIC MACHNRY NES ETC		68568		57890		58821		78964	MACH APP ELECT NDA
772	SWITCHGEAR ETC,PARTS NES	W 605	13455	W 663	13480	W 463	11582	W 666	15284	APP COUPURE,SECT ETC
7721	SWITCHGEAR ETC	W 600	11746	W 652	11593	W 446	9132	W 650	13149	APP COUPURE,SECTIONMNT
773	ELECTR DISTRIBUTNG EQUIP	W 1564	9237	W 2599	9766	W 1890	7769	W 3220	13431	EQUIPMT DISTRIBUTION ELECT
7731	INSULATED WIRE,CABLE ETC	W 1488	8932	W 2417	8766	W 1876	7543	W 3114	12869	FILS,CABLES ISOLES ELECT
775	HOUSEHOLD TYPE EQUIP NES		28435		18214		18038		22226	MACH,APP USAGE DOMESTQUE
7751	HOUSEHOLD LDRY EQUIP NES	N 14698	9267	N 13725	3930	N 12499	3633	N 16978	5524	MACH A LAVER ET SECHOIRS
77511	DOMESTIC WASHING MACHNES	N 14654	9252	N 13664	3916	N 12313	3590	N 16755	5472	MACH LAVER LINGE MOINS 6 KG
7752	DOM REFRIGERATRS,FREEZRS	N 23377	8546	N 20866	6514	N 22576	7372	N 21542	7440	REFRIG,CONGEL MENAGER
77521	DOMESTIC REFRIGERATORS	N 20433	7481	N 19071	5837	N 20190	6586	N 18913	6287	REFRIGERATEURS
7758	ELECTRO–THERMIC APPL NES		6221		5353		4616		7137	APP ELECTROTHERMIQ NDA
778	ELECTRICAL MACHINERY NES		10473		10029		13492		19495	AUTRES MACH ELECT NDA
7783	AUTOMOTIVE ELECTR EQUIP		2167		2073		2326		9108	EQUIP ELECT MOTEURS EXPL
77831	IGNITION,STARTING EQUIP		1284		1069		1333		8162	APP ELEC ALLUM,DEMARRAGE
78	ROAD VEHICLES		88299		86326		85534		95347	VEHICULES ROUTIERS
781	PASS MOTOR VEH EXC BUSES	N 4036	34366	N 4198	35863	N 3844	37201	N 4019	44211	AUTO TRANSPORT PERSONNES
782	LORRIES,SPCL MTR VEH NES	N 1948	23104	N 2090	25948	N 1826	24271	N 2087	25809	VEHICULES SPECIAUX,MARCH
7821	LORRIES,TRUCKS	N 1943	22414	N 2076	24629	N 1809	22627	N 2068	24609	VEHICULES TRANSP MARCHAND
783	ROAD MOTOR VEHICLES NES	N 252	6403	N 255	5305	N 163	3926	N 241	5951	VEHICULES ROUTIERS NDA
7831	BUSES	N 249	6231	N 234	5051	N 150	3325	N 232	5605	VOITURES TRANSPORT COMMUN
784	MOTOR VEH PRTS,ACCES NES		11156		9847		13008		12499	PIECES 722,781,782,783
7849	OTHER MOTOR VEHCL PARTS	W 1344	8859	W 1276	7671	W 1213	7974		10690	PIECES 722,781,782,783
785	CYCLES,ETC MOTRZD OR NOT		10848		7977		5542		5902	MOTOCYCLES SCOOTERS
7851	MOTORCYCLES ETC	N 9083	7354	N 8048	4447	N 4350	2875	N 3626	2979	MOTO VELO MOTEUR AUXIL
79	OTHR TRANSPORT EQUIPMENT		31543		123313		21615		33729	AUTRE MATERIEL TRANSPORT
792	AIRCRAFT ETC		5595		114541		13699		14747	APP NAVIGATION AERIENNE
7924	AIRCRFT NES OVER 15000KG			N 1	111742					AERODYNES PLUS 15000 KG
7929	AIRCRAFT PARTS NES	W 4	5577		2795		10686		10587	PIECES DU 792
793	SHIPS AND BOATS ETC	N 3613	25793		8771	N 1229	7910		18974	NAVIRES BATEAUX,ETC
7931	WARSHIPS	N 2	3492		5			N 3	15317	NAVIRES DE GUERRE
7932	SHIPS AND BOATS NES	N 131	21094	N 8	742	N 131	7634		3416	NAVIRES ET BATEAUX
79324	FISHING VESSELS ETC	N 40	20088			N 7	7299	N 1	307	BATEAUX DE PECHE
7938	TUGS,SPECIAL VESSELS ETC	N 3479	1206		8024	N 1098	276	N 4589	242	REMORQUEURS,BATEAUX SPEC
79381	TUGS	N 1	173		7272					BATEAUX REMORQUEURS
8	MISC MANUFACTURED GOODS		181172		174370		186175		183254	ART MANUFACTURES DIVERS
812	*PLUMBG,HEATNG,LGHTNG EQ		8822		7454		6974		8816	APPAR SANITAIRES CHAUFFAGE
821	*FURNITURE,PARTS THEREOF		6435		8602		6376		5349	MEUBLES ET PIECES
8219	FURNITURE AND PARTS NES		4393		6683		4658		3614	AUTRES MEUBLES ET PIECES
84	CLOTHING AND ACCESSORIES		26826		22356		20232		19662	VETEMENTS
843	WOMENS OUTERWEAR NONKNIT	N 1890167	10430		10381		11348		10658	VET DESSUS FEMMES MAT TEX
8439	— OTHER OUTER GARMENTS	N 1520375	9299		9256	W 410	9711	W 418	9201	AUT VET DES FEM MAT TEXT
845	OUTERWEAR KNIT NONELASTC	N 1147705	6895	N 1065208	4703	N 805439	2294	N 622719	1570	VET DESSOUS,ACCES BONNET
8451	— JERSEYS,PULLOVERS ETC	N 858459	5854	N 886972	3895	N 554065	1411	N 402882	932	CHANDAILS,PULL–OVERS ETC
87	PRECISION INSTRUMNTS NES		11982		11115		14513		15857	INSTRUM,APPAR SCIENT NDA
874	MEASURNG,CONTROLNG INSTR		5272		5010		7195		8353	INSTRUMENTS DE MESURE
88	PHOTO EQU,OPTICL GDS ETC		38371		33116		36834		28291	APP,FOURN PHOTO,OP,MONTR
884	OPTICAL GOODS NES		8879		3089		3787		2674	ELEMENTS OPTIQ,ART LUNET
8842	SPECTACLES AND FRAMES		8436		2676		3363		2296	LUNETTES ET MONTURES
88421	SPECTACLE FRAMES	W 17	8225		2489	W 26	3103		2111	MONTURES DE LUNETTES
885	WATCHES AND CLOCKS		23231		23296		26981		19282	HORLOGERIE
8851	WATCHES,MOVEMENTS,CASES		5697		7618		11241		4206	MONTRES,MOUVEMENTS,BOITES
88511	WATCHES		5610		4456		8715		4172	MONTRES POCHE,BRACELET
8852	CLOCKS,CLOCK,WATCH PARTS		17534		15679		15740		15075	HORLOGES,MOUV,PARTIES
88529	CLOCK,WATCH PARTS NES		16720		15123		15172		14644	FOURNIT D HORLOG NDA
89	MISC MANUFCTRD GOODS NES		82350		84836		94225		98729	ART MANUFACTURES DIVERS
892	PRINTED MATTER	W 1718	17228	W 1851	17280	W 1890	19858	W 1946	20037	IMPRIMES
8921	PRINTED BOOKS,GLOBES,ETC	W 988	8687	W 1048	9199	W 1078	9817	W 1080	9778	LIVRES,BROCHURES,CARTES
89211	PRINTED BOOKS,PAMPHLETS	W 982	8597	W 1032	9049	W 1061	9531	W 1067	9642	LIVRES,BROCHURES
893	ARTICLES OF PLASTIC NES		27272		27793		32680		30537	OUVRAGES EN MAT DIVIS 58
8931	PLSTC PACKG CONTNRS,LIDS		6581		8019	W 1723	8633	W 1475	7953	ART TRANSP EMBALLAGE ETC
8939	MISC PLASTIC ARTICLES	W 6450	18927	W 6622	18941	W 7301	23026	W 6916	21337	ART DIVERS EN MAT DIV 58
89399	OTHR PLASTC ARTICLES NES	W 3224	15667	W 3973	16548	W 4746	20623	W 4773	19276	AUT OUV MAT DIV 58
894	TOYS,SPORTING GOODS,ETC		7652		6411		5595		6911	VOITURES ENFANTS,JOUETS
897	GOLD,SILVER WARE,JEWELRY		9734		10310		13567		17417	BIJOUTERIE,ORFEVRERIE
8973	PREC JEWLRY,GLD–SILVWARE		8323		8987		11603		15357	BIJOUX OR,ARGENT ORFEVRE
89731	PRECIOUS METAL JEWELLERY		8200		8147		10626		15029	ART BIJOUTERIE,JOAILLER
899	OTHER MANUFACTURED GOODS		12223		14604		14266		15875	AUT ART MANUF DIVERS NDA
8998	SMALLWARES,TOILETRYS ETC		9178		11246		11338		12818	ART MERCERIE,TOILETTE
89983	BUTTONS,STUDS,ETC	W 263	5125	W 362	6512	W 305	7031	W 312	7005	BOUTONS,BOUTONS–PRESSION
9	GOODS NOT CLASSD BY KIND		11550		12498		15592		22110	ART TRANSACT NON CLASSES
971	*GOLD,NON MONETARY NES		10119		12253	K 2060	14642	K 4256	21667	OR NON MONETAIRE
97101	NONMON GLD UNWRT,SEMIMFD		10114		12243	K 1656	14558	K 4151	21650	OR,ALLIAGES D'OR BRUTS

5. General Exports F.O.B. by Commodities according to the S.I.T.C. (Rev. 2) in thousand U.S. Dollars
Exportations Générales F.O.B. par Produits d'après la C.T.C.I. (Rév. 2) en milliers de Dollars E.U.

SITC CTCI	COMMODITY	1993 WEIGHT POIDS	1993 VALUE VALEUR	1994 WEIGHT POIDS	1994 VALUE VALEUR	1995 WEIGHT POIDS	1995 VALUE VALEUR	1996 WEIGHT POIDS	1996 VALUE VALEUR	PRODUIT
	ALL COMMODITIES		1467090		1348012		1538287		1699369	TOUS PRODUITS
0	FOOD AND LIVE ANIMALS		425950		384428		437634		523434	ALIMENTS,ANIMAUX VIVANTS
01	MEAT AND PREPARATIONS		6879		12301		14407		9589	VIANDES ET PREPARATIONS
014	MEAT PREPD,PRSVD,NES ETC	W 2391	6799	W 4820	12300	W 5122	14399	W 3335	9559	CONSERVES DE VIANDES
0149	OTH PREPARD,PRESRVD MEAT	W 2391	6799	W 4820	12300	W 5122	14399	W 3335	9559	AUTRES PREP DE VIANDES
03	FISH AND PREPARATIONS		25813		30392		37801		41895	POISSONS ET PREPARATIONS
037	FISH ETC PREPD,PRSVD NES	W 7830	24151	W 9319	28496	W 13241	36085	W 13264	39812	POIS,CRUST,MOL PREPARES
0371	FISH PREPARD,PRESRVD NES	W 7797	24056	W 9302	28454	W 13241	36085	W 13247	39757	CONSERVES DE POISSONS
04	CEREALS AND PREPARATIONS		4014		3910		3525		9473	CEREALES ET PRODUITS
046	WHEAT ETC MEAL OR FLOUR	W 14645	3512	W 16232	3698	W 16264	3349	W 28901	9310	SEMOULE FARINE,FROMENT
04601	FLOUR OF WHEAT OR MESLIN	W 14644	3511	W 16231	3697	W 8640	2477	W 26111	8986	FARINE DE FROMENT
06	SUGAR AND PREPS,HONEY		377119		328107		371880		454749	SUCRES ET PRODUITS
061	SUGAR AND HONEY	W 665325	376895	W 641962	327910	W 640659	371526	W 870498	454522	SUCRES ET MIEL
0611	RAW BEET AND CANE SUGAR	W 539984	370962	W 518782	321496	W 523889	363674	W 772524	447517	SUCRES BRUTS
0615	MOLASSES	W 125335	5927	W 123179	6413	W 116766	7850	W 97972	7002	MELASSES
07	COFFEE,TEA,COCOA,SPICES		7431		5472		4351		2428	CAFE,THE,CACAO,EPICES
074	TEA AND MATE	W 4367	6557	W 4029	4628	W 2898	2961	W 1397	1584	THE ET MATE
0741	TEA	W 4367	6557	W 4029	4628	W 2898	2961	W 1397	1584	THE
2	CRUDE MATERLS,EXCL FUELS		10245		9834		13155		12742	MAT BRUTES NON COMESTIBLES
29	CRUDE ANIMAL,VEG MAT NES		7426		6590		7977		7777	MATIERES BRUTES ANIM,VEGET
292	CRUDE VEG MATERIALS NES	W 612	7226		6369		7813		7548	MAT BRUTES VEGETALES NDA
2927	CUT FLOWERS AND FOLIAGE	W 587	7162	W 575	6319	W 601	7776	W 589	7531	FLEURS,FEUILLAGES COUPES
29271	CUT FLOWERS	W 583	7125	W 569	6260	W 596	7716	W 579	7415	FLEURS ET BOUTONS
5	CHEMCLS,RELATED PROD NES		14218		10062		11823		8487	PRODUITS CHIMIQUES
562	*FERTILIZERS,MANUFACTURE	W 31007	7821	W 21752	5176	W 22736	5915	W 25805	6921	ENGRAIS MANUFACTURES
5629	FERTILIZERS NES	W 27493	7163	W 19352	4778	W 19993	5273	W 25739	6905	ENGRAIS NDA
56291	NIT–PHOS–POT FERTLZR NES	W 27413	7143	W 15752	4020	W 19993	5273	W 25739	6905	ENGRAIS CONT N P K
6	BASIC MANUFACTURES		87305		90095		117432		127651	ART MANUFACTURES
65	TEXTILE YARN,FABRICS,ETC		48636		54060		76847		87833	FILS,TISSUS,ARTICLES TEXTILE
651	TEXTILE YARN	W 1342	12016	W 1458	12217	W 1509	12454	W 1280	11272	FILS TEXTILES
6512	WOOL,HAIR YARN,INCL TOPS	W 887	9434	W 837	8819	W 854	8834	W 658	8308	FILS DE LAINE,DE POILS
65123	COMBED WOOL YARN IN BULK	W 644	6858	W 620	6724	W 644	6581	W 561	7232	FILS CONT 85% LAINE PEIGNEE
652	COTTON FABRICS,WOVEN	A 13713	23284		26623	W 8789	42129	W 10485	49689	TISSUS DE COTON
6522	WOVEN COTTON BLEACHD,ETC	A 13683	23236		25076	W 8610	40275	W 10442	49114	TISSUS COTON BLANCHIS ETC
65224	BLCHED COTTON FABRIC NES	A 11358	19714		18402	W 8079	35275	W 10114	43848	AUT TIS PLUS 85% COT BLANCHI
65225	BLCHD COTN BLEND FAB NES	A 2301	3471		6648	W 527	4952	W 328	5266	AUT TIS MOINS 85% COT BLANCH
655	KNITTED,ETC FABRICS	A 2658	3818		4611	W 888	7746	W 1547	14193	ETOF BONNETERIE PIECES ETC
6552	OTHER KNIT ETC FAB NONEL	A 2658	3818		4611	W 888	7746	W 1547	14193	ETOF BON NON ELAS NON SYNT
658	TEXTILE ARTICLES NES		5098		6923	W 1111	10615	W 1099	11853	ART FACONNES MAT TEXTILES
6584	LINENS ETC	N 1639358	4795		6612	W 1064	10343	W 1073	11683	LINGE DE MAISON
65845	OTHER LINEN OF COTTON	N 800705	970		3601	W 887	8904	W 893	10201	LINGE DE TOILETTE COTON
66	NONMETAL MINERAL MFS NES		31574		29575		33150		34156	ART MIN NON METALLIQUES
664	GLASS		3278		3250	W 10	5468		5601	VERRE
6649	GLASS NES		3275	W 4	3228	W 7	5462	W 8	5599	VERRE NDA
66493	CLOCK,WATCH GLASSES ETC	W 4	3257	W 3	3223	W 4	5430	W 8	5599	VERRES D'HORLOGERIE
667	PEARL,PREC–,SEMI–P STONE		27803		25912		27239		28400	PERLES, PIERRES GEMMES
6672	DIAMONDS NONINDUST,UNSET		26640		24843		25703		26537	DIAMANTS BRUTS
66729	— CUT ETC NOT SET		26056		24553		24555		26272	DIAMANTS TAILLES
7	MACHINES,TRANSPORT EQUIP		15330		30065		35237		6218	MACHINES MATERIEL TRANSPORT
72	MACHS FOR SPCL INDUSTRYS		7532		4968		7625		804	MAC SPECIALES POUR INDUST
724	TEXTILE,LEATHER MACHNRY		3032		2995		5787		53	MACH POUR INDUSTRIE TEXTILE
74	GENRL INDUSTRL MACHY NES		1749		2711		4837		4356	MACH APP INDUSTRIE
79	OTHR TRANSPORT EQUIPMENT		581		15825		18074		18	AUTRE MATERIEL TRANSPORT
793	SHIPS AND BOATS ETC	N 36	569		15825		17270	N 2	18	NAVIRES BATEAUX,ETC
7932	SHIPS AND BOATS NES	N 36	569		15825		17270	N 1	4	NAVIRES ET BATEAUX
79323	OTHER CARGO VESSELS				15680					AUT BATEAUX TRANS MARCH
79324	FISHING VESSELS ETC						17248			BATEAUX DE PECHE
8	MISC MANUFACTURED GOODS		910295		817574		914795		1012121	ART MANUFACTURES DIVERS
831	*TRAVEL GOODS,HANDBAGS	N 1697170	3293		3496	N 3010389	4620	N 2272121	3996	ARTICLES DE VOYAGE ETC
84	CLOTHING AND ACCESSORIES		818029		731080		808272		918661	VETEMENTS
842	MENS OUTERWEAR NOT KNIT	MN 12652	105061	MN 12026	94743	MN 12058	104790	MN 16088	150364	VET DESSUS POUR HOMMES
8422	— SUITS	N 35768	2033	N 86212	6010	N 32494	2338	N 45767	3350	COMPLETS HOMMES MAT TEXT
84221	—— OF WOOL,FINE HAIR	N 20800	1733	N 78194	5796	N 22994	2151	N 16801	1499	COMPLETS HOMMES LAINE
8423	— TROUSERS,BREECHES ETC	MN 12075	92230	MN 11417	79685	MN 11360	88622	MN 15501	135830	PANTALONS HOMMES MAT TEX
8424	— JACKETS,BLAZERS ETC	N 412704	9917	N 378231	7516	N 412030	11852	N 407998	9649	VESTES HOMMES MAT TEXTIL
843	WOMENS OUTERWEAR NONKNIT	MN 10880	66457	N 8911886	54019	MN 9140	68639	MN 9277	73828	VET DESSUS FEMMES MAT TEX
8433	— DRESSES	N 498509	3905	N 520176	3493	N 766901	5195	N 760675	6280	ROBES EN MAT–TEXTILES
8434	— SKIRTS	N 367357	2831	N 304408	2088	N 857709	5901	N 1691412	12262	JUPES EN MAT TEXTILES
8435	— BLOUSES	N 2721947	19098	N 2157303	12700	N 1719798	15723	N 1517749	13944	BLOUSES FEM MAT TEXTILES
8439	— OTHER OUTER GARMENTS	N 7012166	37913	N 5844556	34415	N 5671720	40069	N 5168377	40016	AUT VET DES FEM MAT TEXT
844	UNDER GARMENTS NOT KNIT		162547	MN 15874	154416		143395	MN 13166	147181	VETEMENT DESSOUS MAT TEX
8441	— MENS SHIRTS		160124	MN 14984	150273	MN 12855	137583	MN 12317	141983	CHEMISES HOMMES MAT TEXT
84411	—— OF COTTON	MN 13221	141417	MN 12839	133709	MN 10842	123053	MN 10995	131537	CHEMISES HOMMES DE COTON
84412	—— OF SYNTHETIC FIBRES		18707	N 2144772	16565	N 2012802	14530	N 1321469	10446	CHEMISES HOMMES FIB SYNT
845	OUTERWEAR KNIT NONELASTC	MN 26877	240703		207801	MN 25806	216999	MN 24013	224357	VET DESSOUS,ACCES BONNET
8451	— JERSEYS,PULLOVERS ETC	MN 15891	187389		154660	MN 15531	161597	MN 15364	178614	CHANDAILS,PULL–OVERS ETC
8452	— WOMENS DRESSES ETC	N 1948415	14345	N 1869246	12088	N 2071149	14143	N 1051335	6492	ROBES,JUPES BONNETERIE
8459	— OTHER,CLTHG ACCESRYS	MN 9038	38968	MN 9250	41053	N 8204187	41259	N 7597959	39251	AUT VET DESSUS DE BONNE
846	UNDER GARMENTS KNITTED	MN 77903	222168		214115		270582		318421	SOUS VETS DE BONNETERIE
8462	— OF COTTON NON ELASTIC	MN 71643	203458	MN 69001	190781	MN 75599	242599	MN 75242	293409	SOUS–VET BONNET COTON
84629	—— OTHER	MN 71643	203458	MN 69001	190781	MN 75599	242599	MN 75242	293409	AUT SOUS–VET BONNET COTON
8463	— OF SYNTH FBR NONELAST	N 2641116	11689		16101		17984		14472	SOUS–VET BONNET FIB SYNT
84632	—— MENS SHIRTS	N 2620326	11636	N 3837420	16032	N 3231816	17888	N 2495440	14465	CHEMISES DE BON FIB SYNMT
8465	CORSETS,GARTERS,ETC	N 3618606	7020		7233	W 227	9999	W 236	10541	CORSETS,GAINES ART SIM
84651	BRASSIERES	N 3129486	5727		5813	W 192	8303	W 197	8543	SOUTIENS–GORGE,BUSTIERS
847	TEXTILE CLTHNG ACCES NES		19123		4069		2053		2993	ACCES VET MAT TEXT NDA
8471	— NOT KNITTED	N 986266	17740		3298		1199		1760	ACCES VET MAT TEX NON BON
84712	SHAWLS,VEILS ETC,NOT KNT	N 656108	16264	N 482288	2516		1029	N 496871	1615	ECHARPES ETC MAT TEXT
87	PRECISION INSTRUMNTS NES		4089		5485		7423		7120	INSTRUM,APPAR SCIENT NDA
874	MEASURNG,CONTROLNG INSTR		3475		4897		6500		6297	INSTRUMENTS DE MESURE
8748	ELEC MEAS,CONTRL EQU NES	N 437845	2701	N 500683	4740	N 709960	5469	N 1024824	6232	APP ELEC ELECTRO MESURE
87483	OTH ELCTRNC MEAS ETC EQU	N 334110	2364	N 495190	4534	N 709809	5461	N 1007456	6073	AUT APP ELECTRO DE MESURE
88	PHOTO EQU,OPTICL GDS ETC		38050		36273		41777		31475	APP,FOURN PHOTO,OP,MONTR
884	OPTICAL GOODS NES		11539		10856		13877		11889	ELEMENTS OPTIQ,ART LUNET
8842	SPECTACLES AND FRAMES		10486		9113	N 6042070	12364	N 5444805	10724	LUNETTES ET MONTURES
88422	SPECTACLES ETC	P 4133863	8779		7188	N 5238881	9263	N 4800799	8416	LUNETTES
885	WATCHES AND CLOCKS		25967		25079		27605		19586	HORLOGERIE
8851	WATCHES,MOVEMENTS,CASES		12925		13417		14941		13596	MONTRES,MOUVEMENTS,BOITES
88513	WATCH MOVEMENTS ASSEMBLD		12769		10581		10982		11504	MOUVEMENTS TERMINES
8852	CLOCKS,CLOCK,WATCH PARTS		13042		11662		12664		5989	HORLOGES,MOUV,PARTIES
88529	CLOCK,WATCH PARTS NES		12031		11616		12557		5989	FOURNIT D HORLOG NDA

5. General Exports F.O.B. by Commodities according to the S.I.T.C. (Rev. 2) in thousand U.S. Dollars
Exportations Générales F.O.B. par Produits d'après la C.T.C.I. (Rév. 2) en milliers de Dollars E.U.

SITC CTCI	COMMODITY	1993		1994		1995		1996		PRODUIT
		WEIGHT POIDS	VALUE VALEUR	WEIGHT POIDS	VALUE VALEUR	WEIGHT POIDS	VALUE VALEUR	WEIGHT POIDS	VALUE VALEUR	
89	MISC MANUFCTRD GOODS NES		44199		39356		50424		48481	ART MANUFACTURES DIVERS
894	TOYS,SPORTING GOODS,ETC		10648		9211		12110		10986	VOITURES ENFANTS,JOUETS
8942	TOYS,INDOOR GAMES ETC		9437		8620		11190		10683	JOUETS,JEUX ETC
89423	TOYS NES	N 2107765	7874	N 1743297	7163	N 2234128	9141	N 2025195	9046	JOUETS,MODELES REDUITS
897	GOLD,SILVER WARE,JEWELRY		26246		22534		29602		27309	BIJOUTERIE,ORFEVRERIE
8973	PREC JEWLRY,GLD–SILVWARE		25264		21324		26491		24193	BIJOUX OR,ARGENT ORFEVRE
89731	PRECIOUS METAL JEWELLERY		6952		7355		8124		9253	ART BIJOUTERIE,JOAILLER
89733	JEWELLERY NES		14305		10981		15348		11284	OUV PERLES,PIERRES
899	OTHER MANUFACTURED GOODS		3416		4230		4554		4456	AUT ART MANUF DIVERS NDA
9	GOODS NOT CLASSD BY KIND		2988		4673		5785		7475	ART TRANSACT NON CLASSES
941	*ZOO ANIMALS,PETS ETC	N 3847	2988	N 5508	4466	N 5627	5190	N 7037	7314	ANIMAUX DE ZOO ETC

1. HISTORICAL SERIES, 1960–1995 GENERAL TRADE, IMPORTS F.O.B., EXPORTS F.O.B.
SERIES HISTORIQUES, 1960–1995 COMMERCE GENERAL, IMPORTATIONS F.O.B., EXPORTATIONS F.O.B

YEAR ANNEE	VALUE IN MILLION U.S. DOLLARS / VALEUR EN MILLION U.S. DOLLARS — MERCHANDISE –MARCHANDISE IMPORTS	EXPORTS	GOLD –OR IMPORTS	GOLD –OR EXPORTS	CONVERSION FACTORS U.S. CENTS PER MEXICAN PESO / FACTEURS DE CONVERSION CENTS E.U. PAR MEXICAN PESO IMPORTS	EXPORTS	INDEX NUMBERS –INDICES QUANTUM IMPORTS	QUANTUM EXPORTS	UNIT VALUE / VALEUR UNITAIRE IMPORTS	UNIT VALUE / VALEUR UNITAIRE EXPORTS
1960	1186.48	739.79	0.02	0.02						
1961	1138.64	799.77		0.02						
1962	1142.96	882.33								
1963	1239.68	920.31	0.03							
1964	1492.56	999.37	0.04							
1965	1559.68	1088.78								
1966	1605.12	1162.76								
1967	1745.92	1103.81							22	26
1968	1960.11	1180.71	0.01						23	27
1969	2077.92	1384.95	0.01						24	27
1970	2319.51	1310.89	0.02						24	28
1971	2250.41	1395.46	0.02						27	30
1972	2718.48	1693.90	0.03						28	30
1973	3813.44	2256.79	0.0						28	32
1974	6056.71	2961.66	0.01	0.01					31	37
1975	6570.15	2992.27							37	46
1976	6032.15	3431.00							41	45
1977	5589.31	4285.18							54	74
1978	7918.00	6063.00							84	124
1979	11980.00	8816.00							93	140
1980	19431.00	15307.48							101	164
1981	25053.62	19419.62							73	130
1982	15056.73	21229.66								
1983	9005.76	22312.05								
1984	11788.19	24196.03								
1985	13762.49	21663.81								
1986	11918.16	16031.00								
1987	12760.76	20656.19								
1988	18954.40	20657.60								
1989	23633.44	22818.59								
1990	29968.80	27130.70								
1991	38138.73	27286.24							100	100
1992	48135.91	27729.64							100	92
1993	49622.91	30188.01							101	92
1994	60980.02	34531.99							102	89
1995	45976.89	47056.02								100
										103

2. IMPORTS BY BROAD ECONOMIC CATEGORY AND EXPORTS BY INDUSTRIAL ORIGIN. (PERCENTAGE OF TOTAL VALUE)
IMPORTATIONS PAR CATEGORIES ECONOMIQUES ET EXPORTATIONS PAR BRANCHE D'ACTIVITE.(EN POURCENTAGE DE LA VALEUR TOTALE)

IMPORTS – IMPORTATIONS

	1990	1991	1992	1993	1994	1995	1996
TOTAL IMPORTS–IMPORTATIONS TOTALES	100.	100.	100.	100.	100.	100.	
1 FOOD BEV–ALIMENTATION BOISSONS	12.2	9.5	7.9	7.3	7.2	5.2	
11 PRIMARY–PRODUITS DE BASE	5.5	5.7	4.6	4.0	4.0	2.9	
111 FOR INDUSTRY–POUR L'INDUSTRIE	2.9	3.2	2.8	2.3	2.2	1.9	
112 FOR HOUSEHOLDS–POUR LES MENAGES	2.7	2.5	1.9	1.7	1.8	1.0	
12 PROCESSED–PRODUITS ELABORES	6.7	3.8	3.3	3.3	3.2	2.3	
121 FOR INDUSTRY–POUR L'INDUSTRIE	1.2	0.8	0.5	0.4	0.5	0.4	
122 FOR HOUSEHOLDS–POUR LES MENAGES	5.5	2.9	2.8	2.9	2.7	1.9	
2 IND SUPPLIES–APPROV INDUSTRIELS	29.8	28.1	29.5	29.8	29.5	32.0	
21 PRIMARY–PRODUITS DE BASE	5.2	3.5	2.4	2.1	2.3	2.7	
22 PROCESSED–PRODUITS ELABORES	24.6	24.6	27.1	27.7	27.2	29.3	
3 FUELS–COMBUSTIBLES	3.6	3.4	2.7	2.3	1.8	2.0	
31 PRIMARY–PRODUITS DE BASE	0.7	0.5	0.6	0.5	0.4	0.5	
32 PROCESSED–PRODUITS ELABORES	3.0	2.9	2.1	1.8	1.4	1.4	
321 MOTOR SPIRIT–ESSENCE	1.3	1.8	1.2	1.0	0.6	0.7	
322 OTHER–AUTRES	1.6	1.1	0.9	0.8	0.8	0.8	
4 MACHINERY–EQUIPEMENT	27.8	25.8	29.9	30.2	29.6	31.7	
41 CAPITAL EQUIPMENT–MACHINES	22.1	21.4	22.6	22.3	22.4	21.5	
42 PARTS–PIECES ACCESSOIRES	5.7	4.5	7.3	7.8	7.3	10.1	
5 TRANSPORT–TRANSPORT	16.2	6.6	16.1	15.6	6.7	8.3	
51 PASSENGER CARS–AUTOMOBILES	0.8	0.8	0.6	0.6	1.6	0.6	
52 OTHER–AUTRES	2.6	2.0	2.0	1.3	1.4	0.5	
521 INDUSTRIAL–INDUSTRIELS	2.5	1.8	1.8	1.2	1.3	0.5	
522 NON INDUSTRIAL–NON INDUSTRIEL	0.1	0.2	0.2	0.1	0.1	0.0	
53 PARTS–PIECES ACCESSOIRES	12.7	3.8	13.5	13.7	3.7	7.2	
6 CONSUM GOODS–BIENS CONSOMMATION	10.2	10.8	13.6	14.3	14.8	14.0	
61 DURABLE–DURABLES	3.6	3.9	3.6	3.8	4.0	3.2	
62 SEMI DURABLE–SEMI DURABLES	4.8	4.8	7.7	8.1	8.3	8.4	
63 NON DURABLE–NON DURABLES	1.8	2.0	2.2	2.5	2.4	2.4	
7 GOODS NES–BIENS NDA	0.1	15.8	0.3	0.3	10.4	6.9	

EXPORTS – EXPORTATIONS

	1990	1991	1992	1993	1994	1995	1996
TOTAL EXPORTS–EXPORTATIONS TOTALES	100.	100.	100.	100.	100.	100.	
1 AGRICULTURE	9.4	10.0	5.2	5.5	5.1	5.8	
2 MINING QUARRY–INDUS EXTRACTIVES	37.2	29.6	17.1	13.2	11.7	10.2	
3 MANUFACTURING–IND MANUFACTUR	53.4	60.4	77.6	81.2	83.2	84.0	
31 FOOD BEV TOBACCO–ALIM BOISS TAB	2.9	3.3	2.2	2.1	2.3	2.3	
32 TEXTILES–INDUSTRIES TEXTILES	2.2	2.5	4.9	4.8	5.1	5.9	
33 WOOD & PRODUCTS–BOIS & PRODUITS	0.5	0.5	0.6	0.7	0.6	0.5	
34 PAPER & PRODUCTS–PAPIER & PRODT	0.8	0.9	1.4	1.3	0.9	1.1	
35 CHEMICALS–INDUSTRIES CHIMIQUES	10.3	10.7	8.3	8.0	7.5	7.8	
36 NON METAL MIN–MIN NON METAL	1.8	2.2	1.7	1.8	1.7	1.5	
37 BASIC METAL–IND METAL BASE	6.2	5.5	3.3	3.5	3.2	4.9	
38 METAL MANUF–MANUF METAL	28.0	33.4	53.3	57.1	60.0	58.2	
39 OTH MANUF IND–AUTRES MANUF	0.8	1.3	1.8	1.9	1.9	1.9	

3. TRADE BY PRINCIPAL COUNTRIES OF ORIGIN AND DESTINATION (VALUE IN THOUSAND U.S. DOLLARS)
ECHANGES SELON LES PRINCIPAUX PAYS D'ORIGINE ET DE DESTINATION (VALEUR EN MILLIERS DE DOLLARS EU)

COUNTRIES–PAYS	GENERAL IMPORTS F.O.B. IMPORTATIONS GENERALES F.O.B.					COUNTRIES–PAYS	GENERAL EXPORTS F.O.B. EXPORTATIONS GENERALES F.O.B.				
	1991	1992	1993	1994	1995		1991	1992	1993	1994	1995
World	38121500	61924225	65271994	79334975	72452988	Monde	27118759	46194885	51886415	60882213	79540655
Africa	62812	54134	60035	149275	128566	Afrique	148785	41832	14592	15690	46861
Americas	28453799	48847293	51716025	59344287	56972685	Amériques	21538464	41010317	47551972	56275911	73272593
Northern America	26827933	46544401	49360259	56450740	55347796	Amérique du Nord	19571492	38423594	44637298	53231252	68372020
LAIA	1188763	1680123	1800402	2585773	1414140	ALAI	981180	1372931	1597826	1597395	2853024
CACM	102149	102858	102162	144408	86458	MCAC	332121	477905	474101	532111	691136
Caribbean	65821	105097	78168	130713	112437	Caraïbes	530204	593703	656132	762542	1102373
Rest of America	269133	414814	375034	32653	11854	Autre Amérique	123467	142184	186615	152611	254040
As.ex F.USSR	2806290	4680955	4995280	9498844	7707146	Asie l'URSS exclus	1778937	1434709	1309846	1550354	2063523
Eur.x F.USSR	6564698	7998997	8091208	9746782	7265512	Europe l'URSS exclus	3487022	3581653	2839507	2944352	3996887
EU	5869605	7251856	7333429	9054289	6748932	UE	3319509	3433215	2680011	2769916	3351690
EFTA	621468	695131	702728	530548	414893	AELE	145720	137074	151684	169727	634502
East Europe	68681	48936	54847	159147	96784	Europe de l'Est	16647	10640	6851	3797	9972
Other Europe	4944	9	71	112	1059	Autre de l'Europe	5146	262	703	760	697
Former USSR	4186	19595	35532	147604	75045	Ancienne URSS	16969	6774	11734	5730	18195
Oceania	99078	197452	213847	316729	177573	Océanie	75580	57150	55824	68756	75085
USA/Etats–Unis d'Amer	26147733	45721054	48321169	54812851	53973135	USA/Etats–Unis d'Amer	18408160	37284306	42935367	51699002	66338809
Japan/Japon	1554756	2819026	3056523	4778296	3950985	Canada	1124578	1014991	1561953	1501253	1985761
Germany/Allemagne	2223652	2318482	2652377	3099712	2686270	Spain/Espagne	1142482	1233659	876191	909410	788923
France, Monac	831848	1260159	1011960	1526889	980486	Japan/Japon	1238851	845528	704969	1007007	979287
Canada	677527	810842	988164	1620139	1373916	France, Monac	598465	593727	444032	508628	483582
Spain/Espagne	537436	821942	1172281	1337744	693746	Germany/Allemagne	524936	488980	425606	394649	515408
Brazil/Brésil	650885	1029213	1077283	1224584	565141	Brazil/Brésil	186619	408648	292206	375979	800174
Italy/Italie	590230	954748	734777	1020796	770988	Belgium–Luxembourg	320965	284717	279738	340285	488801
Korea, Republic of	348098	463983	475764	937989	770560	United Kingdom	218149	241992	219812	266860	487581
United Kingdom	588041	589926	543772	706023	531223	Colombia/Colombie	154990	218506	238662	305793	453413
Switz.Liecht	591643	672072	678917	490446	389359	Argentina/Argentine	184507	188486	282321	247521	312923
Hong Kong	354383	586366	494425	286655	159278	Chile/Chili	126248	154263	198535	204285	489727
China/Chine		402271	454452	499361	520135	Switz.Liecht	119904	123987	140913	157532	617787
Sweden/Suède	328754	310649	245784	276939	200614	Venezuela	124963	200020	227365	173203	379554
Netherlands/Pays--Bas	235737	275191	362357	240011	217772	Cuba	105505	116700	188062	261979	394069
Belgium–Luxembourg	251065	286753	225421	346620	217923	Guatemala	143638	153087	203499	218095	302992
Singapore/Singapour	81700	190676	219398	289863	289110	Hong Kong	86887	97796	94445	173514	504340
Panama	250345	393740	355284	25058	8861	Dominican Republic	148878	178977	203144	161203	166999
Argentina/Argentine	202838	133330	160776	332544	190679	Netherlands/Pays--Bas	182749	162672	123972	117306	177094
Venezuela	122688	153784	205080	297381	213985	Panama	98749	115020	158426	123736	228982
Malaysia/Malaisie	20240	32459	28673	448282	435881	Cayman Is/Is Caïmans	109904	118197	116016	117424	252967
Ireland/Irlande	122229	182757	144030	137684	181057	Italy/Italie	171991	145976	75712	86127	197417
Chile/Chili	32525	89596	109613	230003	154216	El Salvador	115581	120427	113197	128463	146539
Peru/Pérou	69214	114729	79814	210868	98691	Peru/Pérou	77316	62616	93759	110181	178815
New Zealand	58081	137492	138454	146171	75837	Singapore/Singapour	36749	103626	130886	67259	173465
Indonesia/Indonésie	21636	28218	55548	251805	167353	Costa Rica		107313	99078	94755	141837
Korea Dem People's Rp		13611	18314	270301	203217	Israel/Israël	164041	159493	103324	3419	10522
Thailand/Thaïlande	17199	26787	49263	235844	166391	Portugal	88076	134430	70347	58003	81372
Denmark/Danemark	53791	104921	103128	130845	70832	Ecuador/Equateur	59413	62306	56104	109737	116026
Austria/Autriche	57124	89892	84592	120572	87431	Uruguay	27466	58692	179397	46757	76654
Australia/Australie	40256	42514	52702	166896	99229	Bermuda/Bermudes	38747	124295	139976	30997	47450
Colombia/Colombie	43806	54943	74090	120936	97413	Jamaica/Jamaïque	66021	105355	44570	53493	49972
India/Inde	29561	34567	49289	137023	120530	Honduras	54921	78850	37707	70005	68679
Guatemala	65968	68028	53403	83310	50998	Australia/Australie	51011	49083	47987	54020	63276
Russian Federation		19595	35112	140673	63605	Korea, Republic of	62775	43753	26947	37854	88337
Uruguay	44490	66110	70279	56060	17444	Indonesia/Indonésie	7934	43903	116844	35300	15994
Finland/Finlande	35684	35065	33886	66076	63427	Bahamas	13576	21208	44721	71430	59635
Israel/Israël	21639	34812	42442	84974	46589	Netherlands Antilles	68995	38453	26436	9734	63596
Morocco/Maroc	27043	32039	45861	55622	52668	Ireland/Irlande	7889	14937	81483	23455	70527
Ecuador/Equateur	9740	24765	9475	89454	68717	Austria/Autriche	24478	71751	41851	10043	12745
Trinidad and Tobago	12822	26625	20510	45363	67133	China/Chine		47180	23629	42171	37009
Philippines	5748	5406	8929	83312	68500	Belize/Bélize	22988	26137	26710	27370	22150
Poland/Pologne	31804	20866	24486	43936	41497	Sweden/Suède	21191	25722	16535	23895	30428
Netherlands Antilles	18252	43572	24054	51283	16861	India/Inde	35792	2513	9571	41649	25128
Norway,SVD,JM	29658	22891	23742	39957	24629	Saudi Arabia	22692	24641	8180	18328	36571
Czech Republic			22633	82231	21694	Nicaragua	17981	18228	20620	20793	31089
Sri Lanka	20677	17778	20890	22790	21729	Aruba			19352	45370	31373
So. Africa Customs Un	446	1610	1423	49688	43337	British Virgin Islds		7880	10352	29870	45211
Bermuda/Bermudes	2673	12505	50926	17750	745	Denmark/Danemark	17112	22673	17696	21610	7581
Turkey/Turquie	9884	8853	5130	42535	12931	Cote d'Ivoire	81531	715	518	1168	630

(VALUE AS PERCENTAGE OF WORLD TOTAL)(VALEURS EN POURCENTAGE DU TOTAL MONDIAL)

	1986	1987	1988	1989	1990	1991	1992	1993	1994	1995		1986	1987	1988	1989	1990	1991	1992	1993	1994	1995
Africa	0.3	0.5	0.4	0.3	0.2	0.2	0.1	0.1	0.2	0.2	Afrique	0.2	0.3	0.7	0.4	0.3	0.5	0.1	0.0	0.0	0.1
Americas	75.2	70.7	72.5	74.2	73.0	74.6	78.9	79.2	74.8	78.6	Amériques	79.2	74.3	75.3	78.9	78.1	79.4	88.8	91.6	92.4	92.1
Northern America	72.3	67.6	68.5	69.8	68.5	70.4	75.2	75.6	71.2	76.4	Amérique du Nord	73.0	66.1	67.3	71.3	71.0	72.2	83.2	86.0	87.4	86.0
LAIA	2.6	2.3	3.1	2.9	3.4	3.1	2.7	2.8	3.3	2.0	ALAI	3.3	3.9	4.1	3.2	3.3	3.6	3.0	3.1	2.6	3.6
CACM	0.1	0.2	0.2	0.3	0.3	0.3	0.2	0.2	0.2	0.1	MCAC	1.1	1.5	1.6	1.9	1.6	1.2	1.0	0.9	0.9	0.9
Caribbean	0.0	0.1	0.2	0.3	0.3	0.2	0.2	0.1	0.2	0.2	Caraïbes	1.2	2.0	2.0	2.0	1.9	2.0	1.3	1.3	1.3	1.4
Rest of America	0.1	0.4	0.4	0.8	0.5	0.7	0.7	0.6	0.0	0.0	Autre Amérique	0.6	0.8	0.4	0.5	0.3	0.5	0.3	0.4	0.3	0.3
As.ex F.USSR	7.0	8.1	8.7	6.4	7.3	7.4	7.6	7.7	12.0	10.6	Asie l'URSS exclus	8.2	9.8	9.4	8.0	7.7	6.6	3.1	2.5	2.5	2.6
Eur.x F.USSR	16.0	19.1	17.4	15.0	18.6	17.2	12.9	12.4	12.3	10.0	Europe l'URSS exclus	12.2	15.3	13.9	12.1	13.6	12.9	7.8	5.5	4.8	5.0
EU	14.3	17.4	15.8	13.1	16.8	15.4	11.7	11.2	11.4	9.3	UE	11.6	14.8	13.3	11.7	12.8	12.2	7.4	5.2	4.5	4.2
EFTA	1.2	1.5	1.3	1.4	1.5	1.6	1.1	1.1	0.7	0.6	AELE	0.3	0.4	0.4	0.3	0.8	0.5	0.3	0.3	0.3	0.8
East Europe	0.2	0.2	0.3	0.4	0.3	0.2	0.1	0.1	0.2	0.1	Europe de l'Est	0.2	0.1	0.2	0.1	0.0	0.1	0.0	0.0	0.0	0.0
Other Europe	0.2	0.0	0.0	0.0	0.0	0.0	0.0	0.0	0.0	0.0	Autre de l'Europe	0.0	0.0	0.0	0.0	0.0	0.0	0.0	0.0	0.0	0.0
Former USSR	0.0	0.1	0.0	0.0	0.0	0.0	0.0	0.1	0.2	0.1	Ancienne URSS	0.0	0.1	0.5	0.2	0.1	0.1	0.0	0.0	0.0	0.0
Oceania	0.4	0.3	0.6	0.5	0.8	0.3	0.3	0.3	0.4	0.2	Océanie	0.1	0.2	0.2	0.2	0.2	0.3	0.1	0.1	0.1	0.1
USA/Etats–Unis d'Amer	70.7	64.7	66.7	68.3	67.1	68.6	73.8	74.0	69.1	74.5	USA/Etats–Unis d'Amer	72.0	64.6	65.9	70.1	70.2	67.9	80.7	82.7	84.9	83.4
Japan/Japon	5.5	6.6	6.0	3.6	4.3	4.1	4.6	4.7	6.0	5.5	Canada	1.0	1.5	1.3	1.2	0.8	4.1	2.2	3.0	2.5	2.5
Germany/Allemagne	5.1	6.7	6.3	4.0	5.6	5.8	3.7	4.1	3.9	3.7	Spain/Espagne	4.4	6.0	4.8	4.9	5.5	4.2	2.7	1.7	1.5	1.0
France, Monac	1.7	2.8	2.3	2.1	2.4	2.2	2.0	1.6	1.9	1.4	Japan/Japon	5.5	6.6	6.0	5.7	5.5	4.6	1.8	1.4	1.7	1.2
Canada	1.6	2.9	1.8	1.6	1.3	1.8	1.3	1.5	2.0	1.9	France, Monac	2.2	2.8	2.7	2.1	2.1	2.2	1.3	0.9	0.8	0.6
Spain/Espagne	1.3	1.4	1.1	1.4	1.7	1.4	1.3	1.8	1.7	1.0	Germany/Allemagne	2.0	1.6	2.1	1.6	1.2	1.9	1.1	0.8	0.6	0.6
Brazil/Brésil	1.1	1.4	1.6	1.3	1.2	1.7	1.7	1.7	1.5	0.8	Brazil/Brésil	0.9	0.8	0.6	0.8	0.6	0.7	0.9	0.6	0.6	1.0
Italy/Italie	1.3	1.4	1.4	1.5	1.5	1.5	1.5	1.1	1.3	1.1	Belgium–Luxembourg	0.6	1.2	1.1	0.6	0.8	1.2	0.6	0.5	0.6	0.6
Korea, Republic of	0.1	0.2	0.6	0.7	0.6	0.9	0.7	0.7	1.2	1.1	United Kingdom	1.1	1.5	0.9	0.8	0.7	0.8	0.5	0.4	0.4	0.6
United Kingdom	1.4	1.8	1.9	1.2	2.0	1.5	1.0	0.8	0.9	0.7	Colombia/Colombie	0.6	0.7	0.9	0.5	0.4	0.6	0.5	0.5	0.5	0.6

4. General Imports F.O.B. by Commodities according to the S.I.T.C. (Rev. 2) in thousand U.S. Dollars
Importations Générales F.O.B. par Produits d'après la C.T.C.I. (Rév. 2) en milliers de Dollars E.U.

SITC CTCI	COMMODITY	1992 WEIGHT POIDS	1992 VALUE VALEUR	1993 WEIGHT POIDS	1993 VALUE VALEUR	1994 WEIGHT POIDS	1994 VALUE VALEUR	1995 WEIGHT POIDS	1995 VALUE VALEUR	PRODUIT
	ALL COMMODITIES		61924225		65271994		79334975		72452988	TOUS PRODUITS
0	FOOD AND LIVE ANIMALS		4157751		3863667		4883924		3095390	ALIMENTS,ANIMAUX VIVANTS
001	*LIVE ANIMALS FOR FOOD	N 2707253	261546	N 3013966	141888	N 3431098	196146	N 2091721	42805	ANIMAUX VIVANTS
0011	BOVINE SPECIES,LIVE	N 248669	198868	N 132592	95353	N 168912	138752	N 22105	21969	ESPECE BOVINE
01	MEAT AND PREPARATIONS		879642		783232		992477		503972	VIANDES ET PREPARATIONS
011	MEAT FRESH,CHILLD,FROZEN	W 569714	768716	W 531404	634769	W 616158	825221	W 415784	428449	VIANDES FRAICHES,REF,CONGE
0111	BOVINE MEAT FRESH,FROZEN	W 157475	386756	W 96874	229901	W 119328	336862	W 41115	107090	VIANDES BOVIN FRAI,REF
01112	BOVINE MEAT BONELESS	W 90464	273129	W 71232	178462	W 97760	286098	W 35364	94741	VIANDES BOVIN DESOSSEES
02	DAIRY PRODCTS,BIRDS'EGGS		606932		649390		545022		423733	PRODUITS LAITIERS,OEUFS
022	MILK AND CREAM	W 349251	461228	W 374914	490145	W 339105	371792	W 230224	320641	LAIT ET CREME
0224	MILK,CREAM PRESERVED ETC	W 235224	391162	W 255071	423187	W 195125	289397	W 160718	285031	LAIT,CREME CONS,CONC
02242	MILK DRY,1.5% FAT OR LES	W 155253	271346	W 190358	335017	W 118319	194735	W 106400	211472	LAIT POUDRE INF 1.5%
04	CEREALS AND PREPARATIONS		1242939		1051488		1418912		1126973	CEREALES ET PRODUITS
041	WHEAT ETC UNMILLED	W 1076520	163539	W 1741488	232807	W 1413743	189255	W 1222652	217121	FROMENT,EPEAUTRE
0412	OTHER WHEAT ETC UNMILLED	W 1068368	162257	W 1741398	232793	W 1372688	184437	W 1199329	212837	AUTRE FROMENT NON MOULU
044	MAIZE UNMILLED	W 1318272	185563	W 210643	69727	W 2746639	369528	W 2686920	376143	MAIS NON MOULU
045	CEREALS NES UNMILLED	W 4799256	555939	W 3855710	399908	W 3554859	416958	W 2162632	272729	AUTRES CEREALES NON MOULUES
0459	OTHER CEREALS UNMILLED	W 4754422	548578	W 3779753	388475	W 3511674	411314	W 2132029	267530	SARRASIN,MILLET,SORGHO
04592	SORGHUM UNMILLED	W 4726686	542138	W 3745190	380314	W 3473258	394815	W 2092492	254400	SORGHO NON MOULU
048	CEREAL ETC PREPARATIONS	W 524997	195863	W 548655	240743	W 560694	308736	W 252907	149985	PREPTNS A BASE CEREALES
05	VEGETABLES AND FRUIT		355324		410448		660735		310445	LEGUMES ET FRUITS
057	FRUIT,NUTS,FRESH,DRIED	W 209393	144502	W 258229	207466	W 381815	331255	W 193809	150643	FRUITS FRAIS OU SECS
081	*FEEDING STUFF FOR ANIML	W 1215912	292777	W 959116	257712	W 1189557	327708		219104	NOURRITURE POUR ANIMAUX
09	MISC EDIBLE PRODUCTS		211901		255709		309086		215357	PREP ALIMENTAIRES DIVERSES
098	EDIBLE PRODCTS,PREPS NES	W 106987	186891	W 120202	227851		274038		176629	PREP ALIMENTAIRES NDA
1	BEVERAGES AND TOBACCO		315258		306919		342537		139338	BOISSONS ET TABACS
11	BEVERAGES		257069		266144		324489		131124	BOISSONS
112	ALCOHOLIC BEVERAGES	W 107612	187002	W 104812	180969	W 110301	183265	W 49438	98540	BOISSONS ALCOOLIQUES
2	CRUDE MATERLS,EXCL FUELS		2596620		2621906		3030411		3034155	MAT BRUTES NON COMESTIBLES
22	OIL SEEDS,OLEAGINOUS FRT		694544		716409		870286		769611	GRAINES,FRUITS OLEAGINEUX
222	SEEDS FOR'SOFT'FIXED OIL	W 2911712	687525	W 2877480	706329	W 3245671	862211	W 2923357	765836	GRAINES HUILES FIXES
2222	SOYA BEANS	W 2101114	512136	W 2171379	523061	W 2496565	640472	W 2232453	542368	FEVES DE SOJA
24	CORK AND WOOD		316385		307641		302559		172842	LIEGE ET BOIS
248	WOOD SHAPED,SLEEPERS	W 589588	289832	W 477602	289362		277266		162624	BOIS SIMPLEMENT TRAVAILLES
2482	LUMBER SHAPED CONIFER	W 473279	219640	W 356195	194413		166937		79935	CONIFERES SCIES,RABOTES
24821	LUMBER SAWN ETC CONIFER	W 467263	209268	W 351470	185011	W 459331	154160	W 201147	69078	CONIFERES SCIES LONGITUD
251	*PULP AND WASTE PAPER	W 1474146	367212	W 1593522	372371	W 1704123	483773	W 1629024	677042	PATES A PAPIER,DECHETS
2511	WASTE PAPER,PPRBOARD ETC	W 1032746	140430	W 974150	116693	W 1091364	177799	W 1109907	266957	DECHETS DE PAPIER
2517	SODA,SULPHATE WOOD PULP	W 339005	172559	W 515687	205625	W 490321	242532	W 425169	340221	PATES CHIMIQUES AU SULFATE
25172	— BLEACHED,NONDISSOLVNG	W 330693	169065	W 512589	203951	W 487144	240849	W 422469	330246	PATES BLANCHIES
26	TEXTILE FIBRES AND WASTE		278966		353182		383043		342567	FIBRES TEXTILES
263	COTTON	W 145484	148595	W 213038	226861	W 184080	231165	W 142506	231366	COTON
2631	RAW COTTON,EXCL LINTERS	W 112070	139049	W 177708	216741	W 148488	222697	W 114784	219766	COTON EN MASSE
27	CRUDE FERTLZR,MINRLS NES		199137		170143		216521		259419	ENGRAIS MINERAUX BRUTS
28	METALLIFEROUS ORES,SCRAP		232602		218407		236644		315171	MINERAIS METAL,DECHETS
29	CRUDE ANIMAL,VEG MAT NES		206235		224434		245564		226103	MATIERES BRUTES ANIM,VEGET
3	MINERAL FUELS ETC		1752110		1595497		1507219		1540003	COMBUSTIBLES MINERAUX LUB
33	PETROLEUM AND PRODUCTS		1281892		1183872		1120546		1053493	PETROLE ET DERIVES
334	PETROLEUM PRODUCTS,REFIN	W 7555472	1202147	W 6744961	1091734	W 7618328	1015732	W 6929627	931474	PRODUITS RAFFINES
3341	GASOLINE,OTH LIGHT OILS	W 3574335	747135	W 3225856	640532	W 2517132	450262	W 2500805	471256	ESSENCES POUR MOTEURS
33411	MOTOR,AVIATION SPIRIT	W 13031	4730	W 13109	4644	W 2517132	450262	W 2500805	471256	ESSENCES MOTEURS D'AVIONS
33419	OTH LIGHT PETROLEUM OILS	W 3561304	742405	W 3212747	635888					AUTRES HUILES LEGERES
3344	FUEL OILS,NES	W 3670547	300238	W 2855307	228744	W 3669538	311245	W 3163524	244337	FUEL OILS
3345	LUBS,PETROLEUM OILS NES	W 309677	154339	W 662560	221914	W 1430848	253921	W 1262853	215024	HUILES LUBRIFIANTES
341	*GAS,NATURAL AND MANUFCT	W 2808053	380510	W 1705716	304006	MV 66076	271357	MV 127114	328665	GAZ NATUREL,GAZ MANUFACT
3413	PETROLM GASES,LIQUEFIED	W 919347	198184	W 965464	213274	V 2466587	198605	V 2702433	222792	GAZ DE PETROLE LIQUEFIE
4	ANIMAL,VEGETABLE OIL,FAT		382611		417896		496260		550347	HUILES,GRAISSES ANIM,VEG
42	FIXED VEGETABLE OIL,FAT		266279		275930		337474		344129	HUILES VEGETALES FIXES
423	FIXED VEG OILS,SOFT	W 432482	185574	W 447095	199725	W 388253	228555	W 392033	243777	HUILES VEGET DOUCES FIXES
5	CHEMCLS,RELATED PROD NES		4986606		5591419		6762317		6702853	PRODUITS CHIMIQUES
51	ORGANIC CHEMICALS		1496811		1503096		1794260		2022560	PROD CHIMIQ ORGANIQUES
511	HYDROCARBONS NES,DERIVS	W 705442	275230	W 730454	302073		406644		586684	HYDROCARBURES NDA
5112	CYCLIC HYDROCARBONS	W 251716	103991	W 265755	111776		170920		318045	HYDROCARBURES CYCLIQUES
51124	XYLENES,CHEMICALLY PURE	W 209537	83236	W 240822	97277	V 353793	134471	V 402021	275683	XYLENES PURS
512	ALCOHOLS,PHENOLS ETC	W 186281	121647	W 204835	106707		187475		228448	PHENOLS,PHENOLS-ALCOOLS
513	CARBOXYLIC ACIDS ETC	W 86572	181801	W 111626	191701	W 112625	220147	W 89475	233919	ACIDES CARBOXYLIQUES
514	NITROGEN-FNCTN COMPOUNDS	W 65354	386248	W 66156	385403	W 72520	410176	W 73946	386178	COMPOSES FONCT AZOTEES
5148	OTH NITROGN-FNCTN CMPNDS	W 21855	208847	W 22210	198733	W 22514	210438	W 23198	196132	AUTRES COMPOSES AZOTES
515	ORG-INORG COMPOUNDS ETC	W 34299	295919	W 30051	288971	W 41656	299104	W 29851	279771	COMPOSES ORGANO-MINERAUX
516	OTHER ORGANIC CHEMICALS	W 337996	235966	W 369739	228241	W 444858	270714	W 1399335	307560	AUTRES PROD ORGANIQUES
52	INORGANIC CHEMICALS		414845		396507		425388		443125	PROD CHIM INORGANIQUES
522	INORG ELEMNTS,OXIDES,ETC	W 777236	188968	W 595047	176226		181120		167280	ELEMENTS INORGANIQUES
523	OTHR INORG CHEMICALS ETC	W 611785	195493	W 549907	183827	W 672624	236131	W 674544	266430	AUT PRODUITS CHIMIQUES INORG
53	DYES,TANNING,COLOUR PROD		349206		364614		449438		403258	PROD TEINTURE,COLORANTS
533	PIGMENTS,PAINTS,ETC	W 151428	212401	W 77574	225139	W 112476	296277	W 88689	258676	PIGMENTS,PEINTURES,VERNIS
541	*MEDICINAL,PHARM PRODUCT	MK 13283	421850	MK 15793	533903		675914	MK 13574	584929	PROD MEDICINAUX PHARMACEUT
55	PERFUME,CLEANING ETC PRD		340860		409719		489542		371853	PROD POUR PARFUM,TOILETTE
553	PERFUMERY,COSMETICS,ETC	W 40455	197201	W 49010	227072	W 71301	277787		183335	PRODUITS DE PARFUMERIE
58	PLASTIC MATERIALS ETC		1267491		1478226		1809032		1948074	MAT PLAST ARTIFICIELLES
582	PROD OF CONDENSATION ETC	W 90187	265132	W 103479	312896	W 135671	415658	W 154913	501584	PROD CONDENS,POLYCOND
5823	ALKYDS,OTHER POLYESTERS	W 41215	114070	W 52738	138079	W 69141	191798	W 78621	248888	ALKYDES ET AUT POLYESTERS
583	POLYMERIZATION ETC PRODS	W 629052	905480	W 721575	1057617		1279950		1343949	PROD POLYMERISATION
5831	POLYETHYLENE	W 246950	217006	W 330698	277909	W 398988	373202	W 288123	321514	POLYETHYLENE
58311	— IN PRIMARY FORMS	W 230532	181253	W 311075	229472	W 364609	293093	W 255413	244397	POLYETHYLENE PRIMAIRES
5839	OTH POLYMRZTION ETC PROD	W 111712	291339	W 104532	333433	W 132373	392338	W 226688	448543	AUT PROD POLYMER COPOLYM
59	CHEMICAL MATERIALS NES		603110		729213		888728		825608	MAT PROD CHIMIQUES NDA
598	MISCEL CHEM PRODUCTS NES	W 246428	387801	W 322914	472975		556261		512488	PROD DIV INDUST CHIM NDA
5989	CHEM PRODUCTS,PREPS NES	W 204509	332298	W 277031	416317	W 318660	487377	W 331481	442948	PROD PREP CHIMIQUES NDA
59899	OTH CHEM PRODS,PREPS,NES	W 168381	238764	W 244219	311459	W 277158	338195	W 290757	306124	AUT PRODUITS CHIMIQUES NDA
6	BASIC MANUFACTURES		10130267		10785867		12950509		12024485	ART MANUFACTURES
61	LEATHER,DRESSED FUR,ETC		205305		220821		279860		325163	CUIRS,PELLETERIES
62	RUBBER MANUFACTURES NES		551981		585042		746906		785861	CAOUTCHOUC MANUFACTURE
625	RUBBER TYRES, TUBES ETC		271665		264668	MN 29739	327919		245877	PNEUS CAOUTCHOUC VULCANISE
628	RUBBER ARTICLES NES	W 19758	180257	W 20943	210487	W 27892	271944	W 30442	358296	OUVRAGES CAOUTCHOUC NDA
6289	OTH RUBBER ARTICLES NES	W 16390	145123	W 16230	170861	W 22429	229904	W 25887	319006	AUT OUVR CAOUTCHOUC NDA
62898	UNHARD RUBBER PRODS NES	W 15624	143291	W 15904	168558	W 21990	225795	W 25138	311791	OUV CAOUT VULC NON DURCI
63	WOOD,CORK MANUFACTRS NES		275347		295669		390076		185364	OUVRAGES LIEGE ET BOIS
64	PAPER,PAPERBOARD AND MFR		1402079		1514852		1980688		1809993	PAPIERS,CARTONS & OUVRAGES
641	PAPER AND PAPERBOARD	W 742360	601097	W 848336	687077	W 1126912	877209	W 744541	751067	PAPIERS ET CARTONS
642	PAPER,ETC,PRECUT,ARTS OF	W 546014	800982	W 506797	827775	W 654892	1103479	W 619804	1058926	PAP,CARTONS DECOUPES
6421	PAPER ETC CONTAINERS	W 387600	430297	W 340803	467087	W 450308	596105	W 457896	668291	BOITES,SACS EMBALLAGES

4. General Imports F.O.B. by Commodities according to the S.I.T.C. (Rev. 2) in thousand U.S. Dollars
Importations Générales F.O.B. par Produits d'après la C.T.C.I. (Rév. 2) en milliers de Dollars E.U.

SITC CTCI	COMMODITY	1992		1993		1994		1995		PRODUIT
		WEIGHT POIDS	VALUE VALEUR	WEIGHT POIDS	VALUE VALEUR	WEIGHT POIDS	VALUE VALEUR	WEIGHT POIDS	VALUE VALEUR	
6428	PAPER ETC ARTICLES NES	W 121784	276764	W 109820	242199	W 142087	366305	W 115925	285801	OUVRAGES EN PATE A PAPIER
65	TEXTILE YARN,FABRICS,ETC		1532225		1898899		2146913		1768839	FILS,TISSUS,ARTICLES TEXTILE
652	COTTON FABRICS,WOVEN	W 32776	187052	W 35606	224664		227667	A 115928	178529	TISSUS DE COTON
6522	WOVEN COTTON BLEACHD,ETC	W 30370	177676	W 33235	213778		211501	A 108088	168136	TISSUS COTON BLANCHIS ETC
653	WOVN MAN-MADE FIB FABRIC	W 69987	627537	W 83718	737038	A 528815	829407	A 337599	590557	TISSUS FIBRES SYNTH,ARTIF
6531	CONT SYNT WEAVES NONPILE	W 21130	183340	W 26121	212020	A 271495	270388	A 187476	216951	TISSUS FIBRES SYNTH CONTINUE
65315	CONT SYN TXTL FABRIC NES	W 17478	154408	W 19814	172897	A 223935	247706	A 177210	201315	TIS PLUS 85% TEXT SYNT CONT
6535	CONT REGN WEAVES NONPILE	W 20997	235895	W 23306	234902	A 76335	236915	A 41926	157539	TISSUS FIB TEXT ART CONTINU
657	SPECIAL TXTL FABRC,PRODS		196124		316023		415944		427885	TISSUS SPECIAUX
66	NONMETAL MINERAL MFS NES		574755		687247		815198		659556	ART MIN NON METALLIQUES
664	GLASS	W 169298	182124	W 173173	236254	W 172321	264125	W 165623	270747	VERRE
67	IRON AND STEEL		2119131		1876828		2163857		1938369	FER ET ACIER
672	IRON,STEEL PRIMARY FORMS	W 990887	375282	W 663349	297023	W 1124934	468005	W 429462	313860	LINGOTS FER,ACIER
6727	IRN,STL COIL FR REROLLNG	W 634566	312464	W 475781	258260	W 890752	400561	W 292029	268853	EBAUCHES POUR TOLES FER
67271	IRON,SIMPLE STEEL COILS	W 510397	172095	W 346205	120198	W 735786	244078	W 169960	74748	EBAUCHES NON EN ACIER
673	IRON,STEEL SHAPES ETC	W 1000892	379907	W 614856	293347	W 621923	324634	W 338448	227753	BARRES,PROFIL FER,ACIER
6732	IRON,STEEL BARS ETC	W 591358	220508	W 317542	161545	W 300751	170784	W 188998	137993	BARRES FER,ACIER
674	IRN,STL UNIV,PLATE,SHEET	W 1195583	720377	W 968443	638836	W 1149537	747807	W 1015722	717791	LARGES PLATS,TOLES
6746	IRN,STL THIN PLATE,ROLLD	W 448484	202461	W 365739	190858	W 399676	230621	W 249677	172836	TOLES LAM MOINS 3MM
6749	OTH IRN,STL PLATES,SHEET	W 288883	202213	W 271905	188531	W 299863	214953	W 278382	214444	AUTRES TOLES FER,ACIER
67491	— OF IRON OR SIMPLE STL	W 285849	196615	W 268842	181179	W 295126	206269	W 272564	196177	AUT TOLES AUTRES ACIER FIN
678	IRON,STL TUBES,PIPES,ETC	W 180755	379976	W 161459	383880	W 182470	305567	W 145228	270368	TUBES,TUYAUX EN FONTE,FER
6782	IRON,STL SEAMLESS TUBES	W 82524	207931	W 74718	216156	W 69103	94934	W 64698	104419	TUBES,TUYAUX SANS SOUDURE
68	NON-FERROUS METALS		809457		842304		1028489		1026518	METAUX NON FERREUX
682	COPPER EXC CEMENT COPPER	W 87992	282770	W 88626	284158	W 105174	341432	W 72398	296631	CUIVRE
6822	COPPER,ALLOYS WORKED	W 48162	182527	W 42133	191155	W 65123	243173	W 53218	238080	CUIVRE,ALLIAGES OUVRES
684	ALUMINIUM	W 211130	461406	W 250237	498015	W 272761	611458	W 230671	653918	ALUMINIUM
6842	ALUMINIUM,ALLOYS WORKED	W 114358	326213	W 119109	328943	W 155382	420111	W 153212	498409	ALUMINIUM,ALLIAGES OUVRE
68422	ALUMNM PLATE,SHEET,STRIP	W 75563	201756	W 77023	183175	W 95680	216774	W 97844	298958	TOLES, PLANCHES EN ALU
69	METAL MANUFACTURES NES		2659987		2864205		3398522		3524822	ART MANUFACT EN METAL NDA
694	STL,COPPR NAILS,NUTS,ETC	W 83800	289651	W 67239	324462	W 172025	396517	W 113402	463876	CLOUS,VIS,ECROUS
69402	IRN,STL NUTS,BOLTS,ETC	W 76602	267161	W 58556	299318	W 163568	367135	W 105793	431086	BOULONS,VIS,ECROUS FER,AC
695	TOOLS	W 30195	328635	W 24682	332161		364912		280497	OUTILS A MAIN
6954	BLADES,TIPS,ETC FR TOOLS	W 10955	209097	W 9687	213728		237019		202441	OUTILS POUR MACHINE-OUTIL
699	BASE METAL MFRS NES	W 237248	1596661	W 404945	1776572		2124998		2453367	ART MANUFACTURES MET NDA
6991	LOCKSMITHS WARES,ETC	W 32221	248848	W 42961	291976		293711		349057	ARTICLES DE SERRURERIE
6997	IRON,STEEL ARTICLES NES	W 125586	787807	W 281300	891800	W 329488	1074160	W 334002	1160228	OUV FONTE,FER,ACIER NDA
69979	IRN,STL MANUFACTURES NES	W 124165	778876	W 279831	880603	W 329405	1073975	W 333972	1160102	AUT OUVRAGES EN FER NDA
6998	MFRS NES OF CPR,NIKL,ETC	W 32049	291295	W 36065	311263	W 43464	362594	W 145849	494608	OUVRAGES EN CU,NI,AL,PB,ZN
69983	ALUMINIUM MANUFACTS NES	W 13667	188625	W 22320	188395	W 28274	196335	W 104966	256646	OUVRAGES EN ALUMINIUM
7	MACHINES,TRANSPORT EQUIP		30022994		31708391		30899625		31246930	MACHINES MATERIEL TRANSPORT
71	POWER GENERATING EQUIPMT		1356967		1542317		1534908		1915483	MACHINES GENERATRICES
713	INTRNL COMBUS PSTN ENGIN	W 89518	570717	W 76570	590696		647202		1098479	MOTEURS EXPL COMB INT, PIECE
7132	MOTOR VEHCL PISTN ENGINS	W 25123	117035	W 21790	178321	N 5102489	198656	W 35509	381326	MOTEURS EXPL POUR VEHICULES
7139	PISTON ENGINE PARTS NES	W 54906	342874	W 47162	321616	W 56363	376753	W 63681	665687	PIECES POUR 713.2,3,8
716	ROTATING ELECTRIC PLANT	W 93099	418155	W 104712	560670		641430		571693	APP ELECTR ROTATIFS,PIECES
7162	AC MTRS,GENRTRS,GEN SETS	W 21076	169492	W 21443	231671	MN 30079	252526	MN 50928	167118	MOTEURS ELECTRIQUES
71621	AC MTRS,INC UNIVRSL MTRS	W 15276	124568	W 17561	198574	MN 30004	203294	MN 50907	148413	MOT ELEC NON COUR CONTINU
7169	PTS NES OF ROT ELEC PLNT	W 64500	161424	W 72064	188194	W 92762	297909	W 110902	302395	PIECES MAC APP ROTATIFS
72	MACHS FOR SPCL INDUSTRYS		2685832		2329436		3235782		2445859	MAC SPECIALES POUR INDUST
723	CIVIL ENGNEERG EQUIP ETC	W 135130	491651	W 90466	382512		525920		160626	APPAREILS DE GENIE CIVIL
7234	CONST,MINING MACHNRY NES	W 115914	399778	W 75617	298311		438295		116280	MACH POUR LA CONST, MINES
72342	SLFPRP SHOVELS,EXCAVATRS	W 60582	198839	W 39513	137421	N 153493	211171	N 130288	54354	PELLES MECANIQUES
724	TEXTILE,LEATHER MACHNRY		508793		384997		527378		476946	MACH POUR INDUSTRIE TEXTILE
726	PRINTG,BKBINDG MACHY,PTS	W 14486	251109	W 10992	211475		238807		128664	MACHINES POUR IMPRIMERIE
728	OTH MACHY FOR SPCL INDUS	W 77458	1038075	W 64318	976685		1448823		1295012	AUT MACH IND PARTICULIERES
7284	MACHY FOR SPCL INDUS NES	W 44281	827162	W 37841	759060		1239932		1146484	MACH SPEC IND PARTICUL.
72842	RUBBER,PLASTICS WRKG MCH	W 17936	247820	W 16156	243669		325575		314493	MACH IND CAOUT MAT PLAST
72848	OTH MCHY WITH INDIV FNCT	W 18804	411753	W 15738	341338	N 3250538	716347	N 1933429	498773	AUTRES MACHINES NDA
73	METALWORKING MACHINERY		1011428		822352		918886		754395	MACH TRAVAIL DES METAUX
736	METALWORKING MACH-TOOLS	W 66743	831029	W 41803	602909		527325		529905	MACH-OUTILS TRAVAIL METAUX
7361	METAL CUTTING MACH-TOOLS	W 21928	222377	W 13115	145125	N 547894	140973	N 490604	137280	MACH-OUT ENLEVEMENT METAL
7362	METAL FORMING MACH-TOOLS	W 29898	202196	W 19416	196168	N 968452	172158	N 730188	170420	MACH-OUTILS DEFORM METAL
7367	OTH METALWRKG MACH-TOOLS	W 9619	313271	W 6354	172139	N 14428	123069	N 9064	115616	AUT MACH-OUT POUR METAUX
737	METALWORKING MACHNRY NES	W 19254	180399	W 16697	219443		391561		224490	MACH TRAV METAUX PIECES
74	GENRL INDUSTRL MACHY NES		3694326		3765671		4301012		3882589	MACH APP INDUSTRIE
741	HEATING,COOLING EQUIPMNT	W 66703	568562	W 61192	601741		671865		619256	MACH CHAUFFAGE,PIECES
7416	HEATING,COOLING EQU NES	W 14856	158025	W 17512	214346	N 1725507	217967	N 1182997	276453	APP CHANGEMENT TEMP
742	PUMPS FOR LIQUIDS ETC	W 18561	266432	W 15812	296717		261713		241313	POMPES MOTO-POMPES
743	PUMPS NES,CENTRFUGES ETC	W 70459	661199	W 84532	712742		916568		864352	POMPES COMPRES,VENT ETC
7431	PUMPS FOR GASES ETC	W 26877	204527	W 30943	196367	N 5624137	248879	MN 33809	247698	POMPES AIR A VIDE,COMPRES
7436	GAS,LIQUID FILTERS ETC	W 23773	238540	W 20666	285138	W 29831	379909	W 29953	352717	APP POUR FILT DES LIQUIDES
7439	PTS NES OF APP OF 7435,6	W 15403	157912	W 27812	161046	W 37068	240715	W 36193	211751	PIECES 743.5 ET 743.6
744	MECHANICAL HANDLING EQU		514534		433491		478324		360836	EQUIP MANUTENTION PIECES
7442	LIFTING,LOADING MACH NES		320229		293794	N 1463979	315222	N 545454	221451	APP LEVAGE,MANUTENTION
74428	OTH HANDLING ETC MCH NES		252281		199354	N 1160789	239836	N 454727	174246	AUT APP LEVAGE ETC
745	NONELEC MACHY,TOOLS NES	W 37987	538289	W 44045	574275		709169		516282	AUT MACH NON ELEC,PIECES
7452	OTH NONELEC MCHS,PTS NES	W 31294	458364	W 36356	482426		607156		438563	AUT MACH NON ELEC,PIECES
74522	PACKAGNG,BOTTLNG,ETC MCH	W 9653	240582	W 8957	245718	N 706800	314388	N 130541	209043	MACH NETT BOUTEILLES,ETC
749	NONELEC MACH PTS,ACC NES	W 88604	1145310	W 83593	1146705	W 146450	1263373	W 112827	1280550	PIECES MACH NON ELEC NDA
7492	COCKS,VALVES ETC NES	W 21574	326289	W 21435	356022	W 28942	370388	W 22320	340212	ART ROB,SIM POUR TUYAUX
7493	SHAFT,CRANK,PULLEY ETC	W 35310	326116	W 35463	318199	W 76606	329277	W 56899	369254	ARBRES TRANS,VILEBREQUINS
7499	OTH NONELEC MCHY PTS NES	W 17003	314605	W 13240	308650	W 19817	370234	W 19486	389781	PIECES NON ELECT NDA
74991	FOUNDRY MOULDS ETC NES	W 11400	231710	W 8745	225543	W 12360	279682	W 13045	292895	MOULES POUR METAUX
75	OFFICE MACHNES,ADP EQUIP		1876368		2253487		2280453		1891185	MACH BUREAU TRAIT AUTOM
751	OFFICE MACHINES	W 13828	249079	W 13480	261012	N 7115911	320804	N 4455494	200716	MACH,APPAREILS DE BUREAU
752	AUTOMTIC DATA PROC EQUIP	W 18237	931572	W 20071	1084777	MN 12809	1302965	N 6292701	979446	MACH TRAIT INFORMATION
7522	DIGITAL COMPUTERS	W 1533	145683	W 2113	220611	N 144238	136370	N 135619	97527	MACH DIGITALES COMPLETES
7523	DIGITL CENTRL PROCESSORS	W 2989	218712	W 2592	238015	N 280031	318848	N 113067	204618	UNITES CENTRALES
7525	ADP PERIPHERAL UNITS	W 11772	352832	W 13750	413839	MN 10730	544453	N 4356003	452470	UNITES PERIPHERIQUES
759	OFFICE,ADP MCH PTS,ACCES	W 15039	695717	W 20515	907698	W 16905	656684	W 32127	711023	PIECES DU 751 ET 752
7599	ACCTG,ETC,ADP MCH PTS,AC	W 9470	597987	W 10206	786757	W 9093	520947	W 23924	581133	PIECES DU 751 ET 752
76	TELECOMM,SOUND EQUIPMENT		2893751		3091907		3938696		3161859	EQUIPMENT DE TELECOM
761	TELEVISION RECEIVERS	W 41661	371213	W 31339	308069	N 7289885	319248	N 1453810	165656	RECEPTEURS DE TELEVISION
7611	COLOUR TV RECEIVERS	W 38907	355808	W 29705	298597	N 6926730	309026	N 1336233	161400	RECEPTEURS COULEUR
762	RADIO BROADCAST RECEIVRS		313850		252961	MN 10764	354474	N 7354323	320426	RECEPTEURS RADIODIFFUSION
7628	OTHER RADIO RECEIVERS		264766		211867	N 7489933	298550	N 4748168	216348	AUTRES RECEPT RADIO
763	SOUND RECORDRS,PHONOGRPH	W 11195	322304	W 17701	563147	MN 13975	821492	MN 12582	745566	PHONO,APP ENREGISTREMENT
7638	OTHR SOUND APPARATUS ETC	W 9085	265867	W 14648	484654	MN 12088	676857	MN 11002	598248	AUT APP D'ENREGIS,REPROD
76381	TV IMAGE,SND RECRDRS ETC	W 5791	173302	W 8217	278669	N 6018951	424932	N 4131670	316387	APP ENREG,REPRO IMAG,SON
76388	DICTATING MACHINES ETC	W 3294	92565	W 6430	205985	N 6068987	251925	N 6870040	281861	MACHINES A DICTER

4. General Imports F.O.B. by Commodities according to the S.I.T.C. (Rev. 2) in thousand U.S. Dollars
Importations Générales F.O.B. par Produits d'après la C.T.C.I. (Rév. 2) en milliers de Dollars E.U.

SITC CTCI	COMMODITY	1992 WEIGHT POIDS	1992 VALUE VALEUR	1993 WEIGHT POIDS	1993 VALUE VALEUR	1994 WEIGHT POIDS	1994 VALUE VALEUR	1995 WEIGHT POIDS	1995 VALUE VALEUR	PRODUIT
764	TELECOM EQPT,PTS,ACC NES	W 79677	1886384	W 79132	1967730		2443482		1930211	EQUIP TELECOM,PIECES
7641	LINE TELEPHONE,ETC EQUIP	W 7266	362377	W 8037	389911	N 7816383	500517	MN 9234	357481	APP TELEPHON PAR FIL
7643	TV,RADIO TRANSMITTRS ETC	W 2246	315575	W 2849	345848		507782		242326	APP EMET TELE RADIO
7649	PTS NES OF EQUIPMT OF 76	W 58524	1000035	W 54996	961460		1127470		1091940	PIECES DE LA DIV 76
76491	PTS NES OF APPAR OF 7641	W 2746	285577	W 2349	225025	MN 46183	214717	MN 107120	143493	PIECES POUR 764.1
76493	TELECOMM EQUIPMT PTS NES	W 48700	486523	W 46502	549502	W 56281	751980	W 58703	737433	PIECES 761,762,764.3,8
76499	PARTS ETC OF SOUND EQUIP	W 4209	209611	W 3155	157597		130343	W 2669	167636	PIECES NDA POUR 763
77	ELECTRIC MACHNRY NES ETC		7722813		8985043		10763968		13134603	MACH APP ELECT NDA
771	ELECTRIC POWER MACHY NES	W 44314	400982	W 47385	486834		612667		742266	MACH PROD,TRANS ELECTR
7711	TRANSFORMERS,ELECTRICAL	W 18925	234506	W 20763	266928	MN 478530	254696	MN 684505	291164	TRANSFO ELECTRIQUES
7712	OTH ELEC POWER MACHY NES	W 25389	166476	W 26622	219906		357971		451102	AUT APP PROD TRANSF ELEC
772	SWITCHGEAR ETC,PARTS NES	W 121311	1791101	W 109842	1976846		2469110		2804772	APP COUPURE,SECT ETC
7721	SWITCHGEAR ETC	W 100222	1375069	W 88209	1475291	W 72586	1707525	W 76712	1856183	APP COUPURE,SECTIONMNT
7722	PRINTED CIRCUITS,PTS NES	W 8507	249788	W 9626	317264	MN 314854	464883	MN 381497	655872	CIRCUITS ET PIECES
7723	FIXED,VARIABLE RESISTORS	W 12582	166244	W 12006	184291	W 11802	296702		292717	POTENTIOMETRES PIECES
773	ELECTR DISTRIBUTNG EQUIP	W 210779	1497944	W 234561	1707963	W 277666	1961124	W 319252	2315113	EQUIPMT DISTRIBUTION ELECT
7731	INSULATED WIRE,CABLE ETC	W 192760	1244271	W 217602	1420861	W 256530	1596982	W 299152	1883514	FILS,CABLES ISOLES ELECT
7732	ELECTRC INSULATING EQUIP	W 18019	253673	W 16959	287102	W 21136	364142	W 20100	431599	EQUIP ISOL ELECTRIQUE
775	HOUSEHOLD TYPE EQUIP NES		396526		401227		440084		240783	MACH,APP USAGE DOMESTQUE
776	TRANSISTORS,VALVES,ETC		1898092		2249892		3117225		4510363	LAMPES,TUBES,VALVES
7761	TV PICTURE TUBES	W 82269	434213	W 128015	631825	MN 34409	864240	MN 53560	1245700	TUBES CATHODIQUES
7763	DIODES,TRANSISTORS,ETC	W 5095	273688	W 5782	318711	W 10198	467208	W 12508	614920	DIODES,TRANSISTORS
7764	ELECTRONIC MICROCIRCUITS		951182		1111507		1535592		2299291	MICROSTRUCTURES ELECTRON
7768	ELCTRNC COMP PTS,CRYSTLS	W 17481	226694	W 10000	177396	W 14693	240269	W 14487	332842	CRIST PIEZO–ELEC,PCS 776
77689	ELECTRNIC COMPON PTS NES	W 17321	210301	W 9732	152658	W 14401	196567	W 13837	267876	PIECES DU GROUPE 776
778	ELECTRICAL MACHINERY NES		1623268		2004172		1968954		2422268	AUTRES MACH ELECT NDA
7781	BATTERIES,ACCUMULATORS	W 27033	233039	W 28521	277309		255349		331074	PILES ET ACCUMULATEURS
7782	ELECTRIC LAMPS,BULBS		136579		240492		187373		201419	LAMPES, TUBES ELECTRIQUES
7783	AUTOMOTIVE ELECTR EQUIP	W 22684	181944	W 25026	205176		268676		357367	EQUIP ELECT MOTEURS EXPL
77831	IGNITION,STARTING EQUIP	W 16683	118082	W 13925	123565		141752		225635	APP ELEC ALLUM,DEMARRAGE
7788	OTH ELEC MACHY,EQUIP NES		1035359		1243099		1204393		1503979	AUT MACH APP ELEC NDA
77884	ELECTRICAL CONDENSERS	W 11820	295200	W 10917	396251	MN 8865516	500217	MN 10443350	704109	CONDENSATEURS ELECTRIQUES
77889	ELEC PARTS OF MACHY NES	W 6918	433171	W 5676	471013	W 3825	285466	W 6983	422705	PIECES ELEC DE MACH NDA
78	ROAD VEHICLES		8105635		8457259		3179827		3831619	VEHICULES ROUTIERS
781	PASS MOTOR VEH EXC BUSES	N 187461	377043	N 129170	393865	N 140313	1239842	N 66554	438581	AUTO TRANSPORT PERSONNES
782	LORRIES,SPCL MTR VEH NES	N 269452	232104	N 44109	162748	N 56426	174983	N 32296	122571	VEHICULES SPECIAUX,MARCH
783	ROAD MOTOR VEHICLES NES	N 5654	240503	N 4449	176897	N 4604	157048	N 1242	15860	VEHICULES ROUTIERS NDA
7831	BUSES	N 4083	208914	N 3270	155792	N 3656	143913	N 736	11019	VOITURES TRANSPORT COMMUN
784	MOTOR VEH PRTS,ACCES NES		6991639		7480483	MN 347424	1342970	MN 1207116	3103870	PIECES 722,781,782,783
7841	MOTOR VEHICLE CHASSIS		6178252		6578121	N 104	1395	N 793	5535	CHASSIS 722,781,782,783
7849	OTHER MOTOR VEHCL PARTS		805278		893620	MN 347374	1289186	MN 1207109	3081428	PIECES 722,781,782,783
79	OTHR TRANSPORT EQUIPMENT		675874		460919		746093		229338	AUTRE MATERIEL TRANSPORT
792	AIRCRAFT ETC		564113		366602		536617		85351	APP NAVIGATION AERIENNE
7924	AIRCRFT NES OVER 15000KG	N 9	319145	N 10	172795	N 15	143518		1067	AERODYNES PLUS 15000 KG
8	MISC MANUFACTURED GOODS		7401458		8075022		10122755		9100205	ART MANUFACTURES DIVERS
821	*FURNITURE,PARTS THEREOF	W 112905	398769	W 120763	445553		611519		428823	MEUBLES ET PIECES
8211	CHAIRS,SEATS AND PARTS	W 35537	138012	W 40382	172457		231631		237973	SIEGES ET PIECES
8219	FURNITURE AND PARTS NES	W 73516	228173	W 75721	233311		326721		166221	AUTRES MEUBLES ET PIECES
84	CLOTHING AND ACCESSORIES		1122465		1303071		1823588		1912464	VETEMENTS
842	MENS OUTERWEAR NOT KNIT	W 27812	276255	W 29585	292808	MN 98547	423726	MN 150505	455481	VET DESSUS POUR HOMMES
8423	— TROUSERS,BREECHES ETC	W 20578	179752	W 23047	200210	MN 77520	327902	MN 119038	390665	PANTALONS HOMMES MAT TEX
843	WOMENS OUTERWEAR NONKNIT	W 27364	311606	W 30226	387441	MN 139544	491732		435305	VET DESSUS FEMMES MAT TEX
8439	— OTHER OUTER GARMENTS	W 20975	194108	W 22023	237676	MN 111370	323408	MN 143738	303092	AUT VET DES FEM MAT TEXT
845	OUTERWEAR KNIT NONELASTC	W 10629	139924	W 13383	173544	MN 71018	274955	MN 95980	309758	VET DESSOUS,ACCES BONNET
846	UNDER GARMENTS KNITTED	W 10167	125373	W 16394	167345	MN 262878	282832	MN 373433	325152	SOUS VETS DE BONNETERIE
851	*FOOTWEAR	MP 47015	234270	MP 33963	214024	MP 25780	215554	MP 9460	84832	CHAUSSURES
87	PRECISION INSTRUMNTS NES		1174484		1203289		1457863		1387521	INSTRUM,APPAR SCIENT NDA
874	MEASURNG,CONTROLNG INSTR	W 20614	931237	W 20155	918160		1044715		1007897	INSTRUMENTS DE MESURE
8742	MEASUR,DRAW ETC INST,PTS	W 5162	227879	W 4348	223427		232834		245340	INST DESSIN,TRACAGE,PCS
87421	MEASURNG,DRAWNG ETC INST	W 4816	211210	W 4184	210090	MN 10758	216777	N 6748722	226472	INSTRUM DESSIN,TRACAGE
8743	GAS,LIQUID CONTROL INSTR	W 8790	248674	W 7686	239708	MN 96662	278312	MN 87080	326018	APP,INSTR MESURE FLUIDES
8748	ELEC MEAS,CONTRL EQU NES	W 3510	268630	W 2257	264638	N 3739777	293165	N 5406423	248829	APP ELEC ELECTRO MESURE
87483	OTH ELCTRNC MEAS ETC EQU	W 3304	249286	W 2029	246234	N 3112914	273992	N 4521252	224202	AUT APP ELECTRO DE MESURE
88	PHOTO EQU,OPTICL GDS ETC		543763		602405		703927		503554	APP,FOURN PHOTO,OP,MONTR
882	PHOTO,CINEMA SUPPLIES	W 20473	229046	W 21519	245274	W 27192	279765	W 19798	257019	PRODUITS PHOTO,CINEMA
89	MISC MANUFCTRD GOODS NES		3763193		4122081		5100826		4642910	ART MANUFACTURES DIVERS
892	PRINTED MATTER		499602		587319		728732		581661	IMPRIMES
8921	PRINTED BOOKS,GLOBES,ETC	W 34565	204009	W 49113	254582		330325		204871	LIVRES,BROCHURES,CARTES
89211	PRINTED BOOKS,PAMPHLETS	W 32842	198564	W 48191	250740	MN 224817	324868	MN 203625	202859	LIVRES,BROCHURES
8928	PRINTED MATTER NES		180775		212522		256502		265501	IMPRIMES NDA
893	ARTICLES OF PLASTIC NES		1967610		2150317		2567698		2817476	OUVRAGES EN MAT DIVIS 58
8931	PLSTC PACKG CONTNRS,LIDS	W 115443	325436	W 105608	358674	W 199629	479727	W 195062	566218	ART TRANSP EMBALLAGE ETC
8939	MISC PLASTIC ARTICLES	W 375529	1631323	W 353827	1778897	W 389914	2070485	W 447365	2239245	ART DIVERS EN MAT DIV 58
89399	OTHR PLASTC ARTICLES NES	W 367329	1612740	W 342924	1756356	W 378678	2044551	W 441811	2224060	AUT OUV MAT DIV 58
894	TOYS,SPORTING GOODS,ETC		441651		421077		641587		357741	VOITURES ENFANTS,JOUETS
8942	TOYS,INDOOR GAMES ETC		336822		291310		477863		240641	JOUETS,JEUX ETC
898	MUSICAL INSTRUMENTS,PTS		420028		503603		604331		463929	INSTRUMENTS DE MUSIQUE
8983	SOUND RECRDNG TAPE,DISCS	W 47975	378700	W 25940	462553	W 30354	547588	W 26763	416692	SUPPORTS SON POUR 763
89831	PREPD SND RECORDNG MEDIA	W 44413	219640	W 21980	257205	W 24944	290250	W 23703	263249	SUPPORTS PREPARES
89832	RECORDED DISCS,TAPES ETC	W 3562	159060	W 3960	205348	W 5410	257338	W 3060	153443	DISQUES,PHONO,BANDES
899	OTHER MANUFACTURED GOODS		194030		197080		235058		180938	AUT ART MANUF DIVERS NDA
9	GOODS NOT CLASSD BY KIND		178550		305410		8339418		5019282	ART TRANSACT NON CLASSES
931	*SPECIAL TRANSACTIONS	W 2918	135736	W 12970	207446	W 1422786	8105591	W 799954	4955891	TRANS.SPECIALES

5. General Exports F.O.B. by Commodities according to the S.I.T.C. (Rev. 2) in thousand U.S. Dollars
Exportations Générales F.O.B. par Produits d'après la C.T.C.I. (Rév. 2) en milliers de Dollars E.U.

SITC CTCI	COMMODITY	1992 WEIGHT POIDS	1992 VALUE VALEUR	1993 WEIGHT POIDS	1993 VALUE VALEUR	1994 WEIGHT POIDS	1994 VALUE VALEUR	1995 WEIGHT POIDS	1995 VALUE VALEUR	PRODUIT
	ALL COMMODITIES		46194885		51886415		60882213		79540655	TOUS PRODUITS
0	FOOD AND LIVE ANIMALS		2802932		3355767		3751193		5445369	ALIMENTS,ANIMAUX VIVANTS
001	*LIVE ANIMALS FOR FOOD	N 1036708	331572	N 1391748	450591	N 1094808	362307	N 1679984	540293	ANIMAUX VIVANTS
0011	BOVINE SPECIES,LIVE	N 1029494	328923	N 1383237	448254	N 1093483	361657	N 1658153	536183	ESPECE BOVINE
00119	— OTHR THAN FR BREEDING	N 1028600	328391	N 1383147	448118	N 1092916	361385	N 1656663	535648	BOVINS NON REPRODUCTEURS
03	FISH AND PREPARATIONS		333413		407431		457049		689207	POISSONS ET PREPARATIONS
036	SHELL FISH FRESH,FROZEN	W 21430	239727	W 25718	325711	W 35065	376406	W 57904	537218	CRUSTACES,MOLLUSQUES
05	VEGETABLES AND FRUIT		1529339		1856366		2051108		2680423	LEGUMES ET FRUITS
054	VEG ETC FRSH,SMPLY PRSVD	W 1412212	929975	W 1741758	1250985	W 1881357	1336616	W 2471445	1795310	LEGUMES FRAIS,CONG,SECS
0544	TOMATOES FRESH	W 219261	166985	W 487562	394972	W 458555	394568	W 717287	585614	TOMATES FRAICHES
0545	OTHER FRESH VEGETABLES	W 914172	563319	W 987654	666349	W 1009147	703820	W 1299782	949388	AUTRES LEGUMES FRAIS,REF
05459	FRESH VEGETABLES NES	W 731419	440238	W 762789	520205	W 799603	549827	W 1062773	759138	LEGUMES FRAIS,REFRI NDA
0546	VEGETABLES SIMPLY PRESVD	W 201587	151666	W 209237	153873	W 235410	166269	W 264552	164803	LEGUMES CONG,CONSER
05461	VEGETABLES FROZEN	W 190208	147511	W 198949	150078	W 224927	162308	W 256346	162161	LEGUMES CONGELES
057	FRUIT,NUTS,FRESH,DRIED	W 888434	426012	W 911379	415115	W 861457	477038	W 1030875	572791	FRUITS FRAIS OU SECS
0579	FRUIT FRESH OR DRIED NES	W 436251	215475	W 427480	225097	W 444788	267453	W 555116	318333	FRUITS FRAIS,SECS NDA
06	SUGAR AND PREPS,HONEY		85600		91167		120975		258524	SUCRES ET PRODUITS
07	COFFEE,TEA,COCOA,SPICES		341296		346021		471632		874984	CAFE,THE,CACAO,EPICES
071	COFFEE AND SUBSTITUTES	W 208309	295272	W 200099	299710	W 183168	436675	W 196058	818824	CAFE ET SUCCEDANES
0711	COFFEE GREEN,ROASTED,SUB	W 204589	282532	W 195838	284965	W 178076	414718	W 188027	771075	CAFE TORREFIE OU DECAFEINE
07111	COFFEE GREEN,HUSKS,SKINS	W 195681	265617	W 183736	263626	W 170351	396173	W 187174	766700	CAFE NON TORREFIE
1	BEVERAGES AND TOBACCO		335855		377372		483785		590035	BOISSONS ET TABACS
11	BEVERAGES		304761		297398		427425		528652	BOISSONS
112	ALCOHOLIC BEVERAGES	W 470471	284984	W 462510	275444	W 580566	400750	W 792207	493038	BOISSONS ALCOOLIQUES
1123	BEER,ALE,STOUT,PORTER	W 416030	189783	W 424943	196459	W 503714	232505	W 687692	309621	BIERES
2	CRUDE MATERLS,EXCL FUELS		1219401		1121863		1379790		2017808	MAT BRUTES NON COMESTIBLES
24	CORK AND WOOD		189534		214027		182293		168004	LIEGE ET BOIS
248	WOOD SHAPED,SLEEPERS	W 109808	165297	W 116055	189601	W 119924	162792	W 184994	157467	BOIS SIMPLEMENT TRAVAILLES
2482	LUMBER SHAPED CONIFER	W 93536	132152	W 113923	185726	W 117416	158064	W 171801	145679	CONIFERES SCIES,RABOTES
26	TEXTILE FIBRES AND WASTE		212506		230619		348798		616278	FIBRES TEXTILES
266	SYNTHETIC FIBRES TO SPIN	W 68457	110495	W 72594	112387	W 145922	214439	W 182372	320518	FIBRES SYNTHETIQUES
27	CRUDE FERTLZR,MINRLS NES		251489		192205		226869		287548	ENGRAIS MINERAUX BRUTS
28	METALLIFEROUS ORES,SCRAP		299812		257613		361652		640470	MINERAIS METAL,DECHETS
288	NONFERR METAL SCRAP NES	W 107979	124428	W 86413	113065	W 124935	168275	W 239483	339991	DECHETS NON FERREUX
2882	OTHER BASE MTL SCRAP NES	W 104062	116521	W 80931	92343	W 117360	157074	W 213281	323893	AUTRES DECHETS
3	MINERAL FUELS ETC		8122253		7284228		7261691		8157272	COMBUSTIBLES MINERAUX LUB
33	PETROLEUM AND PRODUCTS		7939537		7099777		7050151		7929825	PETROLE ET DERIVES
333	CRUDE PETROLEUM	MW 68418	7419545	MW 67154	6485314	MW 65248	6624099	MW 64572	7419614	HUILES BRUTES DE PETROLE
334	PETROLEUM PRODUCTS,REFIN	W 6055462	513134	W 6092197	605540	W 3854056	416752	W 5300533	502403	PRODUITS RAFFINES
3343	GAS OILS	W 3954860	305196	W 2698753	311868	W 1869664	127871	W 2310650	110482	GAS OILS
5	CHEMCLS,RELATED PROD NES		2334275		2342542		2724849		3928854	PRODUITS CHIMIQUES
51	ORGANIC CHEMICALS		754535		816953		838001		1219224	PROD CHIMIQ ORGANIQUES
511	HYDROCARBONS NES,DERIVS	W 969319	186149	W 1277505	241078	W 605664	153932	W 238735	114225	HYDROCARBURES NDA
5111	ACYCLIC HYDROCARBONS	W 922850	161672	W 1177995	196452	W 515291	107038	W 183160	71679	HYDROCARBURES ACYCLIQUES
51119	OTH ACYCLIC HYDROCARBONS	W 758039	122196	W 1073679	174097	W 367301	63185	W 40090	7503	AUT HYDROCARBURES ACYCL
513	CARBOXYLIC ACIDS ETC	W 572625	351501	W 561902	352037	W 599017	423655	W 723589	740691	ACIDES CARBOXYLIQUES
5138	POLYACIDS AND DERIVATIVS	W 440848	233908	W 418733	233201	W 444331	270570	W 538232	528378	ACIDES POLYCARBOXYLIQUES
51384	TEREPHTHALIC ACID ESTERS	W 224508	113747	W 214831	115604	W 266798	152069	W 302337	277619	ESTERS DE L'ACIDE TEREPHTALI
52	INORGANIC CHEMICALS		353512		320991		369210		425540	PROD CHIM INORGANIQUES
522	INORG ELEMNTS,OXIDES,ETC	W 1282365	227973	W 708137	185850	W 896334	211409	W 1162942	228284	ELEMENTS INORGANIQUES
53	DYES,TANNING,COLOUR PROD		143219		145048		181111		241638	PROD TEINTURE,COLORANTS
541	*MEDICINAL,PHARM PRODUCT	MK 27701	219344	MK 13996	235693	MK 22906	298035		399402	PROD MEDICINAUX PHARMACEUT
55	PERFUME,CLEANING ETC PRD		126757		151950		185899		289185	PROD POUR PARFUM,TOILETTE
562	*FERTILIZERS,MANUFACTURE	W 615487	78660	W 477371	51949	W 842612	111690	W 1456539	263382	ENGRAIS MANUFACTURES
58	PLASTIC MATERIALS ETC		494206		449235		558333		842136	MAT PLAST ARTIFICIELLES
583	POLYMERIZATION ETC PRODS	W 461589	374833	W 353654	322764	W 370149	380812	W 762470	598504	PROD POLYMERISATION
59	CHEMICAL MATERIALS NES		160822		164599		175632		239304	MAT PROD CHIMIQUES NDA
6	BASIC MANUFACTURES		5041222		5572521		6001735		9034679	ART MANUFACTURES
61	LEATHER,DRESSED FUR,ETC		117640		118761		160747		242529	CUIRS,PELLETERIES
63	WOOD,CORK MANUFACTRS NES		132460		171297		190118		201784	OUVRAGES LIEGE ET BOIS
635	WOOD MANUFACTURES NES	W 99601	121249	W 240569	156929	W 272817	167521	W 320086	159640	ART MANUF EN BOIS NDA
64	PAPER,PAPERBOARD AND MFR		510634		486550		379499		641388	PAPIERS,CARTONS & OUVRAGES
641	PAPER AND PAPERBOARD	W 187649	91930	W 122641	64353	W 154426	88602	W 396900	295284	PAPIERS ET CARTONS
642	PAPER,ETC,PRECUT,ARTS OF	W 244396	418704	W 141212	422197	W 132279	290897	W 157530	346104	PAP,CARTONS DECOUPES
6428	PAPER ETC ARTICLES NES	W 143918	303761	W 68138	286716	W 35607	143607	W 46236	148922	OUVRAGES EN PATE A PAPIER
64284	PAPER TISSUES,TOWELS ETC	W 126037	266838	W 44267	241335	W 19403	109243	W 21379	102426	MOUCHOIRS SERVIETTES EN PAP
65	TEXTILE YARN,FABRICS,ETC		859465		870517		944048		1285381	FILS,TISSUS,ARTICLES TEXTILE
651	TEXTILE YARN	W 59204	172483	W 61564	182753	W 61755	190872	W 108158	346869	FILS TEXTILES
658	TEXTILE ARTICLES NES	W 73501	392290	W 48711	353988	W 48995	334119	W 59036	302912	ART FACONNES MAT TEXTILES
6589	OTH TEXTILE ARTICLES NES	W 63131	343667	W 38421	305393	W 18372	201525	W 15080	135321	AUT ART EN TEXTILES NDA
65898	KNITTED ETC ARTICLES NES	W 53493	248546	W 28316	166086	W 7358	87074	W 7238	66078	ART BONNET NON ELASTIQUE
66	NONMETAL MINERAL MFS NES		728790		763269		879884		1062841	ART MIN NON METALLIQUES
664	GLASS	W 123742	216601	W 158801	244109	W 183029	303594	W 232255	339351	VERRE
6647	SAFETY GLASS CUT OR NOT	W 51716	143564	W 63841	162689	W 77038	208436	W 75279	200097	GLACES DE SECURITE
665	GLASSWARE	W 275936	207830	W 257279	186856	W 262420	188380	W 293616	212222	OUVRAGES EN VERRE
67	IRON AND STEEL		749115		898572		1061474		2517795	FER ET ACIER
672	IRON,STEEL PRIMARY FORMS	W 814937	168696	W 1198884	275949	W 1291047	335999	W 3067103	968457	LINGOTS FER,ACIER
6725	IRN,STL BLOOMS,SLABS,ETC	W 791486	161508	W 1156356	261648	W 1261810	325161	W 2003532	594050	BLOOMS,BILLETTES FER ACIER
67251	IRN,SMPLE STL BLOOMS,ETC	W 790883	160983	W 1154546	259892	W 1260599	324144	W 1997710	590776	BLOOMS ETC NON ACIER FIN
6727	IRN,STL COIL FR REROLLNG	W 23308	7084	W 42436	14204	W 27199	10327	W 1062746	373982	EBAUCHES POUR TOLES FER
67271	IRON,SIMPLE STEEL COILS	W 23182	7007	W 41511	13114	W 26167	9536	W 1047715	368983	EBAUCHES NON EN ACIER
673	IRON,STEEL SHAPES ETC	W 97015	32161	W 156249	78347	W 153754	81201	W 1415054	449009	BARRES,PROFIL FER,ACIER
674	IRN,STL UNIV,PLATE,SHEET	W 320741	258907	W 289010	244325	W 268915	247836	W 824756	575055	LARGES PLATS,TOLES
6746	IRN,STL THIN PLATE,ROLLD	W 109186	130109	W 177666	169770	W 109515	137127	W 258350	244828	TOLES LAM MOINS 3MM
678	IRON,STL TUBES,PIPES,ETC	W 280072	204398	W 361206	235040	W 503094	326597	W 634518	427862	TUBES,TUYAUX EN FONTE,FER
6782	IRON,STL SEAMLESS TUBES	W 176016	120689	W 259696	159180	W 320907	210465	W 421772	293669	TUBES,TUYAUX SANS SOUDURE
68	NON–FERROUS METALS		756599		865654		835231		1359143	METAUX NON FERREUX
681	SILVER,PLATINUM,ETC		208249		187957		214824		301298	ARGENT ET PLATINE
6811	SILVER UNWKD,PARTLY WRKD		207405		186314		214324		300842	ARGENT BRUT MI–OUVRE
68113	SILVER UNWROUGHT		201179		179197		212648		299656	ARGENT ET ALLIAGES BRUTS
682	COPPER EXC CEMENT COPPER	W 156429	406812	W 200379	474830	W 173413	446371	W 250568	776327	CUIVRE
6821	COPPER NES,ALLOYS,UNWRT	W 118867	279426	W 163647	342356	W 142874	335634	W 194647	572004	CUIVRE BRUT
68211	COPPER UNREF,EXC CEMENT	W 103723	245673	W 147809	311770	W 120329	287691	W 124429	369834	CUIVRE POUR AFFINAGE
69	METAL MANUFACTURES NES		1118292		1297177		1404749		1487031	ART MANUFACT EN METAL NDA
697	BASE MTL HOUSEHOLD EQUIP	W 71032	228046	W 80306	238739	W 104147	307426	W 106861	332216	ART MENAGE MET COMMUNS
6973	DMSTC HEATG,COOKG APPARA	W 60668	175769	W 64657	188001	W 83157	236484	W 83320	251711	APPS CHAUF NON ELECTRIQ
69731	IRN,STL DOM COOKG APPARA	W 57946	169809	W 61319	180701	W 80149	227451	W 79635	242443	APPS CUISSON FER,ACIER
699	BASE METAL MFRS NES	W 446575	649274	W 244424	837168	W 257300	822993	W 381665	783936	ART MANUFACTURES MET NDA
6991	LOCKSMITHS WARES,ETC	W 34144	232985	W 63044	324709	W 59248	311874	W 44802	192028	ARTICLES DE SERRURERIE
69911	LOCKS,KEYS AND PARTS	W 27602	193947	W 53652	280246	W 25053	174513	W 29177	138835	SERRURES,VERROUS,CADENAS
6997	IRON,STEEL ARTICLES NES	W 323741	217527	W 90161	264546	W 77300	232551	W 195619	255869	OUV FONTE,FER,ACIER NDA

5. General Exports F.O.B. by Commodities according to the S.I.T.C. (Rev. 2) in thousand U.S. Dollars
Exportations Générales F.O.B. par Produits d'après la C.T.C.I. (Rév. 2) en milliers de Dollars E.U.

SITC CTCI	COMMODITY	1992			1993			1994			1995			PRODUIT
		WEIGHT POIDS		VALUE VALEUR	WEIGHT POIDS		VALUE VALEUR	WEIGHT POIDS		VALUE VALEUR	WEIGHT POIDS		VALUE VALEUR	
69979	IRN,STL MANUFACTURES NES	W	323562	216942	W	90075	264394	W	76214	231586	W	195316	255446	AUT OUVRAGES EN FER NDA
7	MACHINES,TRANSPORT EQUIP			21543670			25970931			32317722			41563897	MACHINES MATERIEL TRANSPORT
71	POWER GENERATING EQUIPMT			2188515			2527040			3300757			3876369	MACHINES GENERATRICES
713	INTRNL COMBUS PSTN ENGIN			1504616			1653492			2217798			2822352	MOTEURS EXPL COMB INT, PIECE
7132	MOTOR VEHCL PISTN ENGINS	N	1563559	1202722	N	1300125	1302180	N	1607061	1778113	N	1850155	2123218	MOTEURS EXPL POUR VEHICULES
7139	PISTON ENGINE PARTS NES	W	60949	266503	W	58733	309150	W	67132	400518	W	68552	463733	PIECES POUR 713.2,3,8
714	ENGINES AND MOTORS NES	W	830	145912	W	681	189187	W	1248	302636	W	1629	227038	MOTEURS NON ELECTRIQUES
716	ROTATING ELECTRIC PLANT	W	62213	478142	W	139942	633802	W	121861	742795	W	220447	781761	APP ELECTR ROTATIFS,PIECES
7162	AC MTRS,GENRTRS,GEN SETS	W	40291	310464	W	100537	419293	W	88744	488267	W	152407	494417	MOTEURS ELECTRIQUES
71621	AC MTRS,INC UNIVRSL MTRS	W	39236	306886	W	100160	413262	W	87450	464530	W	151871	486019	MOT ELEC NON COUR CONTINU
72	MACHS FOR SPCL INDUSTRYS			259524			272220			328758			659880	MAC SPECIALES POUR INDUST
74	GENRL INDUSTRL MACHY NES			1283906			1406044			1942282			2175338	MACH APP INDUSTRIE
741	HEATING,COOLING EQUIPMNT	W	75332	334540	W	72801	317604	W	93507	449015	W	108273	597637	MACH CHAUFFAGE,PIECES
7415	AIR–CONDITIONING MACHNRY	W	42539	175225	W	26104	158122	W	37464	251398	W	38165	319688	GROUPES CONDITION AIR
743	PUMPS NES,CENTRFUGES ETC	W	27724	241038	W	37386	270332	W	48058	490542	W	63777	515057	POMPES COMPRES,VENT ETC
7436	GAS,LIQUID FILTERS ETC	W	14388	160484	W	23088	166246	W	31678	330581	W	40307	314941	APP POUR FILT DES LIQUIDES
749	NONELEC MACH PTS,ACC NES	W	42267	425798	W	53103	548864	W	73484	700233	W	74966	715226	PIECES MACH NON ELEC NDA
7492	COCKS,VALVES ETC NES	W	21875	215946	W	25910	285569	W	32255	387554	W	40034	387103	ART ROB,SIM POUR TUYAUX
75	OFFICE MACHNES,ADP EQUIP			1172362			1518224			2282830			2924060	MACH BUREAU TRAIT AUTOM
751	OFFICE MACHINES	W	10694	201914	W	16502	300201	W	17476	387716	W	19663	385088	MACH,APPAREILS DE BUREAU
7511	TYPEWRITERS,CHEQUE–WRTRS	W	4089	51613	W	6783	104082	W	8907	191906	W	7769	116206	MACHINES A ECRIRE
7518	OFFICE MACHINES NES	W	6522	144036	W	9536	188772	W	8358	187259	W	11501	253264	MACH,APP DE BUREAU NDA
75182	PHOTO,THERMOCOPY APPARAT	W	6487	142834	W	9385	187354	W	7912	182463	W	10605	241329	APPAREILS DE PHOTOCOPIE
752	AUTOMTIC DATA PROC EQUIP	W	5658	440612	W	24222	826060	W	24663	1243314	W	51757	1734096	MACH TRAIT INFORMATION
7522	DIGITAL COMPUTERS	W	2129	238096	W	4626	356377	W	1915	310294	W	1874	396640	MACH DIGITALES COMPLETES
7523	DIGITL CENTRL PROCESSORS	W	143	19505	W	17	2461	W	3995	402312	W	6717	463941	UNITES CENTRALES
7525	ADP PERIPHERAL UNITS	W	2384	111049	W	8699	230857	W	16057	410872	W	39050	782552	UNITES PERIPHERIQUES
7528	OFF–LINE DATA PROC EQUIP	W	810	49856	W	10350	215549	W	2093	56827	W	3849	58751	MACH AUXIL TRAIT INFORM
759	OFFICE,ADP MCH PTS,ACCES	W	4146	529836	W	4929	391963	W	6898	651800	W	13226	804876	PIECES DU 751 ET 752
7599	ACCTG,ETC,ADP MCH PTS,AC	W	2202	498718	W	3006	361843	W	2662	599716	W	9230	757011	PIECES DU 751 ET 752
76	TELECOMM,SOUND EQUIPMENT			3833187			4606797			6275803			7560037	EQUIPMENT DE TELECOM
761	TELEVISION RECEIVERS	W	106728	1335994	W	243858	1774014	W	365009	2678290	W	537398	2977544	RECEPTEURS DE TELEVISION
7611	COLOUR TV RECEIVERS	W	106671	1335126	W	243807	1773535	W	364996	2678039	W	537360	2977178	RECEPTEURS COULEUR
762	RADIO BROADCAST RECEIVRS	W	16021	917261	W	27857	865995	W	26571	909112	W	27847	1048888	RECEPTEURS RADIODIFFUSION
7621	MTR VEHC RADIO RECEIVERS	W	5391	288678	W	4288	302261	W	6218	270602	W	7101	413157	RECEPTEURS RADIO AUTO
7622	PORTABLE RADIO RECEIVERS	W	2976	170670	W	611	12002	W	672	9665	W	1721	18695	RECEPT PORTATIFS RADIO
7628	OTHER RADIO RECEIVERS	W	7654	457913	W	22958	551732	W	19681	628845	W	19024	617036	AUTRES RECEPT RADIO
763	SOUND RECORDRS,PHONOGRPH	W	3491	138181	W	13320	247257	W	24096	354205	W	25791	529616	PHONO,APP ENREGISTREMENT
7638	OTHR SOUND APPARATUS ETC	W	3400	134726	W	13230	245068	W	23419	338615	W	23386	466634	AUT APP D'ENREGIS,REPROD
76388	DICTATING MACHINES ETC	W	3379	132331	W	9865	200043	W	15462	247743	W	12646	235783	MACHINES A DICTER
764	TELECOM EQPT,PTS,ACC NES	W	65099	1441751	W	76676	1719531	W	113237	2334196	W	143886	3003989	EQUIP TELECOM,PIECES
7641	LINE TELEPHONE,ETC EQUIP	W	5659	164328	W	9458	248201	W	15733	451320	W	18520	504096	APP TELEPHON PAR FIL
7642	MICROPH,LOUDSPKR,AMPLIFR	W	11596	143770	W	12845	169923	W	34322	194066	W	42742	238382	MICRO,HAUT–PARLEUR,AMPLI
7643	TV,RADIO TRANSMITTRS ETC	W	273	35670	W	869	43372	W	3438	270159	W	9841	516021	APP EMET TELE RADIO
7648	TELECOMM EQUIPMENT NES	W	765	72980	W	3513	124689	W	5614	117818	W	11916	274087	APP TELECOM NDA
7649	PTS NES OF EQUIPMT OF 76	W	46806	1025003	W	49991	1133346	W	54130	1300833	W	60867	1471403	PIECES DE LA DIV 76
76493	TELECOMM EQUIPMT PTS NES	W	35694	948054	W	45438	1004367	W	49844	1168879	W	56065	1276809	PIECES 761,762,764.3,8
77	ELECTRIC MACHNRY NES ETC			6889840			8305298			9564429			11685890	MACH APP ELECT NDA
771	ELECTRIC POWER MACHY NES	W	102190	667585	W	109830	765533	W	124572	819437	W	154054	955427	MACH PROD,TRANS ELECTR
7711	TRANSFORMERS,ELECTRICAL	W	39397	214891	W	32074	245182	W	36215	222613	W	44841	206964	TRANSFO ELECTRIQUES
77118	OTHER ELEC TRANSFORMERS	W	10688	145034	W	25838	182606	W	33172	178555	W	41588	168991	AUTRES TRANSFO ELECTRIQ
7712	OTH ELEC POWER MACHY NES	W	62793	452694	W	77757	520351	W	88357	596824	W	109213	748463	AUT APP PROD TRANSF ELEC
77121	STATIC CONVERTERS ETC	W	2675	176762	W	7277	205918	W	12353	311320	W	17393	349858	CONVERTISSEURS STATIQUES
77122	INDUCTORS	W	57357	258728	W	69480	299821	W	74525	248905	W	89468	357383	BOBINES REACTANCE,SELFS
772	SWITCHGEAR ETC,PARTS NES	W	303681	1301425	W	86433	1465697	W	101038	1810417	W	115927	2095781	APP COUPURE,SECT ETC
7721	SWITCHGEAR ETC	W	233455	1065153	W	80455	1133167	W	94674	1323178	W	109809	1374253	APP COUPURE,SECTIONMNT
7722	PRINTED CIRCUITS,PTS NES	W	1520	157054	W	1709	264480	W	2260	408123	W	2849	630931	CIRCUITS ET PIECES
773	ELECTR DISTRIBUTNG EQUIP	W	348696	2077421	W	275483	2778354	W	309509	2946531	W	404602	3427106	EQUIPMT DISTRIBUTION ELECT
7731	INSULATED WIRE,CABLE ETC	W	341563	2060876	W	273324	2762134	W	307265	2929838	W	401570	3410358	FILS,CABLES ISOLES ELECT
775	HOUSEHOLD TYPE EQUIP NES	W	82702	446261	W	122972	565118	W	141928	601287	W	241884	771529	MACH,APP USAGE DOMESTQUE
7757	DOMESTIC ELECTRC EQU NES	W	23513	158268	W	29311	175889	W	34293	199076	W	44309	234207	APP ELECTR DOMEST NDA
7758	ELECTRO–THERMIC APPL NES	W	18932	159483	W	45964	243744	W	48955	244552	W	64575	331269	APP ELECTROTHERMIQ NDA
776	TRANSISTORS,VALVES,ETC	W	37668	744022	W	16026	671103	W	26493	918274	W	26576	1132185	LAMPES,TUBES,VALVES
7763	DIODES,TRANSISTORS,ETC	W	12960	297475	W	3706	249697	W	8647	312741	W	6881	346470	DIODES,TRANSISTORS
7764	ELECTRONIC MICROCIRCUITS	W	1137	318920	W	2665	306880	W	4433	453518	W	2943	603469	MICROSTRUCTURES ELECTRON
778	ELECTRICAL MACHINERY NES	W	168940	1613118	W	140320	2008824	W	183225	2414817	W	229919	3265514	AUTRES MACH ELECT NDA
7781	BATTERIES,ACCUMULATORS	W	34004	234475	W	43912	278467	W	52588	324990	W	70085	386789	PILES ET ACCUMULATEURS
77811	PRIMARY BATTERIES,CELLS	W	5239	58117	W	7123	88463	W	12495	230379	W	20371	174915	PILES ELECTRIQUES,PIECES
77812	ELECTRIC ACCUMULATORS	W	18900	162422	W	29794	178208	W	32253	83033	W	47538	206846	ACCUMULATEURS ELECTRIQ
7782	ELECTRIC LAMPS,BULBS	W	44505	161931	W	12246	215083	W	14391	168151	W	17052	178500	LAMPES, TUBES ELECTRIQUES
7783	AUTOMOTIVE ELECTR EQUIP	W	11772	117093	W	26479	210879	W	35955	283505	W	40312	287041	EQUIP ELECT MOTEURS EXPL
77832	ELECT VEHICLE LGHTNG EQU	W	7003	68900	W	19901	146273	W	27521	212654	W	27204	196060	APP ELEC ECLAIR,SIGNAL AUTO
7788	OTH ELEC MACHY,EQUIP NES	W	76019	1070563	W	52772	1214772	W	74829	1586682	W	95833	2355617	AUT MACH APP ELEC NDA
77883	ELEC SIGNALLING EQU NES	W	4466	249013	W	14531	284679	W	20424	385560	W	22946	427271	APP ELECT SIGNAL ACOUS
77884	ELECTRICAL CONDENSERS	W	40750	269349	W	8880	273165	W	21377	416988	W	29871	946286	CONDENSATEURS ELECTRIQUES
77886	OTH ELEC MACHINERY NES	W	3690	172142	W	11562	218481	W	11066	231154	W	20177	312638	AUT MACH APP ELECTRIQUES
77889	ELEC PARTS OF MACHY NES	W	2487	336679	W	6487	392888	W	7209	503728	W	9041	616607	PIECES ELEC DE MACH NDA
78	ROAD VEHICLES			5717688			7083428			8409447			12156752	VEHICULES ROUTIERS
781	PASS MOTOR VEH EXC BUSES	N	347805	3368308	N	425272	4242481	N	489987	5062667	N	645012	7521751	AUTO TRANSPORT PERSONNES
782	LORRIES,SPCL MTR VEH NES	N	42406	586839			669549	N	52163	825346	N	120509	1850104	VEHICULES SPECIAUX,MARCH
7821	LORRIES,TRUCKS	N	42406	586839	N	44211	669279	N	52163	825346	N	120509	1850104	VEHICULES TRANSP MARCHAND
784	MOTOR VEH PRTS,ACCES NES			1602837			2013789			2310599			2498895	PIECES 722,781,782,783
7841	MOTOR VEHICLE CHASSIS	N	6513	80981	N	9664	134314	N	14814	212771	N	15298	217284	CHASSIS 722,781,782,783
7849	OTHER MOTOR VEHCL PARTS	W	314417	1499809	W	328502	1848229	W	430623	2058980	W	494744	2236003	PIECES 722,781,782,783
79	OTHR TRANSPORT EQUIPMENT			146976			188535			169319			418665	AUTRE MATERIEL TRANSPORT
792	AIRCRAFT ETC			118564			136177			143023			339002	APP NAVIGATION AERIENNE
8	MISC MANUFACTURED GOODS			4640334			5657654			6785469			8469796	ART MANUFACTURES DIVERS
812	*PLUMBG,HEATNG,LGHTNG EQ	W	74648	178643	W	94185	372089	W	157709	344209	W	151976	326749	APPAR SANITAIRES CHAUFFAGE
8124	LIGHTING EQUIPMENT NES	W	28570	122773	W	37251	304494	W	83270	251178	W	56498	220839	APPAREILS ECLAIRAGE ETC
821	*FURNITURE,PARTS THEREOF	W	181683	481460	W	241992	659019	W	283047	851296	W	295878	894750	MEUBLES ET PIECES
8211	CHAIRS,SEATS AND PARTS	W	69190	215987	W	63450	190360	W	128353	511947	W	117828	518441	SIEGES ET PIECES
82111	CHAIRS AND OTHER SEATS	W	65421	191160	W	26702	75169	W	56442	134565	W	39398	104494	SIEGES
82119	PTS NES OF CHAIRS ETC	W	3769	24827	W	36749	115191	W	71911	377382	W	78429	413947	PIECES DU 821.11
8212	MED FURN,STUFFD FURNSHGS	W	4308	18745	W	35615	191274	W	4412	33407	W	5302	39434	MOB MEDICO–CHIRUR,PIECES
82122	MATTRESSES ETC	W	4297	8704	W	35497	182054	W	4101	23604	W	3953	26712	SOMMIERS,ARTICLES DE LITERIE
8219	FURNITURE AND PARTS NES	W	108185	246728	W	142927	277385	W	150282	305942	W	172749	336875	AUTRES MEUBLES ET PIECES
82192	WOOD FURNITURE NES	W	44328	148179	W	80325	152760	W	87802	170813	W	103054	197534	MEUBLES NDA EN BOIS
84	CLOTHING AND ACCESSORIES			967235			1186433			1702642			2731526	VETEMENTS
842	MENS OUTERWEAR NOT KNIT	W	28265	253914	W	34738	290748	W	42226	386856	W	68833	603373	VET DESSUS POUR HOMMES
8423	— TROUSERS,BREECHES ETC	W	24704	213755	W	31037	252431	W	36690	313795	W	61904	507499	PANTALONS HOMMES MAT TEX
843	WOMENS OUTERWEAR NONKNIT	W	33441	297520	W	32145	330204	W	51640	505139	W	73087	725867	VET DESSUS FEMMES MAT TEX

5. General Exports F.O.B. by Commodities according to the S.I.T.C. (Rev. 2) in thousand U.S. Dollars
Exportations Générales F.O.B. par Produits d'après la C.T.C.I. (Rév. 2) en milliers de Dollars E.U.

SITC CTCI	COMMODITY	1992		1993		1994		1995		PRODUIT
		WEIGHT POIDS	VALUE VALEUR	WEIGHT POIDS	VALUE VALEUR	WEIGHT POIDS	VALUE VALEUR	WEIGHT POIDS	VALUE VALEUR	
8439	— OTHER OUTER GARMENTS	W 23666	218180	W 24639	241675	W 42339	371562	W 61656	550248	AUT VET DES FEM MAT TEXT
845	OUTERWEAR KNIT NONELASTC	W 4231	62877	W 11545	119702	W 24250	216655	W 53609	456266	VET DESSOUS,ACCES BONNET
846	UNDER GARMENTS KNITTED	W 30870	134989	W 14618	175339	W 22703	284629	W 50897	564284	SOUS VETS DE BONNETERIE
8462	— OF COTTON NON ELASTIC	W 3284	36299	W 7856	74213	W 16269	153404	W 38062	329475	SOUS–VET BONNET COTON
84629	—— OTHER	W 3284	36299	W 7856	74213	W 16269	153404	W 38062	329475	AUT SOUS–VET BONNET COTON
848	HEADGEAR,NONTXTL CLOTHNG	W 39006	145417	W 25989	187959	W 26202	202673	W 34718	211256	VET ACCES MAT AUT QUE TEX
851	*FOOTWEAR	W 15790	208447	W 13457	197757	W 10813	150087	W 19132	190891	CHAUSSURES
85102	FOOTWEAR LEATHER	W 14864	199694	W 12602	188932	W 9663	140389	W 16467	179335	CHAUS SEMELLES EN CUIR
87	PRECISION INSTRUMNTS NES		668544		764206		871723		960964	INSTRUM,APPAR SCIENT NDA
872	MEDICAL INSTRUMENTS NES	W 20722	313275	W 38656	333785	W 39173	353050	W 48288	422492	INSTR,APP MEDIC–CHIR NDA
87202	OTH MEDICAL INSTRUMENTS	W 16527	268325	W 32303	307064	W 31843	316149	W 36665	368716	INSTRUM,APP MEDECINE
874	MEASURNG,CONTROLNG INSTR	W 10995	312149	W 22804	364869	W 26462	457521	W 25770	476957	INSTRUMENTS DE MESURE
8743	GAS,LIQUID CONTROL INSTR	W 7533	169040	W 17273	214012	W 18411	264713	W 14641	229043	APP,INSTR MESURE FLUIDES
88	PHOTO EQU,OPTICL GDS ETC		255924		279308		312167		362987	APP,FOURN PHOTO,OP,MONTR
882	PHOTO,CINEMA SUPPLIES	W 25511	135099	W 5470	131982	W 7330	191817	W 9002	235544	PRODUITS PHOTO,CINEMA
89	MISC MANUFCTRD GOODS NES		1808193		2094386		2461673		2906520	ART MANUFACTURES DIVERS
893	ARTICLES OF PLASTIC NES		604487		772060		782332		833399	OUVRAGES EN MAT DIVIS 58
8931	PLSTC PACKG CONTNRS,LIDS	W 82658	125388	W 46833	224184	W 67117	240087	W 95159	290556	ART TRANSP EMBALLAGE ETC
8939	MISC PLASTIC ARTICLES	W 202712	468851	W 124509	536989	W 257359	528833	W 171364	525770	ART DIVERS EN MAT DIV 58
89399	OTHR PLASTC ARTICLES NES	W 196166	451235	W 117164	519908	W 246926	501302	W 158556	498697	AUT OUV MAT DIV 58
894	TOYS,SPORTING GOODS,ETC	W 181091	372174	W 83526	423059	W 99951	559981	W 130000	796629	VOITURES ENFANTS,JOUETS
8942	TOYS,INDOOR GAMES ETC	W 169784	259915	W 73905	301086	W 89330	415278	W 115724	616456	JOUETS,JEUX ETC
89423	TOYS NES	W 154893	216534	W 60338	246163	W 68969	284998	W 80072	335963	JOUETS,MODELES REDUITS
898	MUSICAL INSTRUMENTS,PTS	W 85693	423653	W 46354	448207	W 66525	570635	W 66542	607146	INSTRUMENTS DE MUSIQUE
8983	SOUND RECRDNG TAPE,DISCS	W 82299	387731	W 41934	403998	W 52836	497548	W 57547	516870	SUPPORTS SON POUR 763
89831	PREPD SND RECORDNG MEDIA	W 81238	338111	W 40067	353049	W 50085	447110	W 52334	424174	SUPPORTS PREPARES
9	GOODS NOT CLASSD BY KIND		123535		167103		134657		272541	ART TRANSACT NON CLASSES

1. HISTORICAL SERIES, 1992–1994 GENERAL TRADE, IMPORTS C.I.F., EXPORTS F.O.B.
SERIES HISTORIQUES, 1992–1994 COMMERCE GENERAL, IMPORTATIONS C.A.F., EXPORTATIONS F.O.B

YEAR ANNEE	VALUE IN MILLION U.S. DOLLARS VALEUR EN MILLION U.S. DOLLARS MERCHANDISE –MARCHANDISE IMPORTS	EXPORTS	GOLD –OR IMPORTS	EXPORTS	CONVERSION FACTORS FACTEURS DE CONVERSION CENTS E.U. PAR IMPORTS	EXPORTS	INDEX NUMBERS –INDICES QUANTUM IMPORTS	EXPORTS	UNIT VALUE VALEUR UNITAIRE IMPORTS	EXPORTS
1992	98.80	23.32								
1993	109.49	29.17								
1994	129.06	78.17								

2. IMPORTS BY BROAD ECONOMIC CATEGORY AND EXPORTS BY INDUSTRIAL ORIGIN. (PERCENTAGE OF TOTAL VALUE)
IMPORTATIONS PAR CATEGORIES ECONOMIQUES ET EXPORTATIONS PAR BRANCHE D'ACTIVITE.(EN POURCENTAGE DE LA VALEUR TOTALE)

IMPORTS – IMPORTATIONS

	1990	1991	1992	1993	1994	1995	1996
TOTAL IMPORTS–IMPORTATIONS TOTALES							
1 FOOD BEV–ALIMENTATION BOISSONS							
11 PRIMARY–PRODUITS DE BASE							
111 FOR INDUSTRY–POUR L'INDUSTRIE							
112 FOR HOUSEHOLDS–POUR LES MENAGES							
12 PROCESSED–PRODUITS ELABORES							
121 FOR INDUSTRY–POUR L'INDUSTRIE							
122 FOR HOUSEHOLDS–POUR LES MENAGES							
2 IND SUPPLIES–APPROV INDUSTRIELS							
21 PRIMARY–PRODUITS DE BASE							
22 PROCESSED–PRODUITS ELABORES							
3 FUELS–COMBUSTIBLES							
31 PRIMARY–PRODUITS DE BASE							
32 PROCESSED–PRODUITS ELABORES							
321 MOTOR SPIRIT–ESSENCE							
322 OTHER–AUTRES							
4 MACHINERY EQUIPEMENT							
41 CAPITAL EQUIPMENT–MACHINES							
42 PARTS–PIECES ACCESSOIRES							
5 TRANSPORT–TRANSPORT							
51 PASSENGER CARS–AUTOMOBILES							
52 OTHER–AUTRES							
521 INDUSTRIAL–INDUSTRIELS							
522 NON INDUSTRIAL–NON INDUSTRIEL							
53 PARTS–PIECES ACCESSOIRES							
6 CONSUM GOODS–BIENS CONSOMMATION							
61 DURABLE–DURABLES							
62 SEMI DURABLE–SEMI DURABLES							
63 NON DURABLE–NON DURABLES							
7 GOODS NES–BIENS NDA							

EXPORTS – EXPORTATIONS

	1990	1991	1992	1993	1994	1995	1996
TOTAL EXPORTS–EXPORTATIONS TOTALES							
1 AGRICULTURE							
2 MINING QUARRY–INDUS EXTRACTIVES							
3 MANUFACTURING–IND MANUFACTUR							
31 FOOD BEV TOBACCO–ALIM BOISS TAB							
32 TEXTILES–INDUSTRIES TEXTILES							
33 WOOD & PRODUCTS–BOIS & PRODUITS							
34 PAPER & PRODUCTS–PAPIER & PRODT							
35 CHEMICALS–INDUSTRIES CHIMIQUES							
36 NON METAL MIN–MIN NON METAL							
37 BASIC METAL–IND METAL BASE							
38 METAL MANUF–MANUF METAL							
39 OTH MANUF IND–AUTRES MANUF							

3. TRADE BY PRINCIPAL COUNTRIES OF FIRST AND LAST CONSIGNMENT (VALUE IN THOUSAND U.S. DOLLARS)
ECHANGES SELON LES PRINCIPAUX PAYS DE PREMIERE ET DE DERNIERE CONSIGNATION (VALEUR EN MILLIERS DE DOLLARS EU)

COUNTRIES–PAYS	GENERAL IMPORTS C.I.F. IMPORTATIONS GENERALES C.A.F 1990	1991	1992	1993	1994
World			98796		129060
Africa					
Americas			39807		42417
Northern America			39807		42417
LAIA					
CACM					
Caribbean					
Rest of America					
As.ex F.USSR			20238		41330
Eur.x F.USSR					
EU					
EFTA					
East Europe					
Other Europe					
Former USSR					
Oceania			32042		34532
USA/Etats–Unis d'Amer			39807		42417
Japan/Japon			20238		41330
Guam			28850		29959
Australia/Australie			3193		4574

COUNTRIES–PAYS	GENERAL EXPORTS F.O.B. EXPORTATIONS GENERALES F.O.B. 1990	1991	1992	1993	1994
Monde			23319	29169	78172
Afrique					
Amériques			2173	2685	2761
Amérique du Nord			2173	2685	2761
ALAI					
MCAC					
Caraïbes					
Autre Amérique					
Asie l'URSS exclus			18663	22369	56824
Europe l'URSS exclus					
UE					
AELE					
Europe de l'Est					
Autre de l'Europe					
Ancienne URSS					
Océanie			2246	4023	4232
Japan/Japon			18663	22369	56824
Guam			1931	3688	3951
USA/Etats–Unis d'Amer			2173	2685	2761
Pacific Isld (Tr Terr.)			261	269	254

(VALUE AS PERCENTAGE OF WORLD TOTAL)(VALEURS EN POURCENTAGE DU TOTAL MONDIAL)

	1985	1986	1987	1988	1989	1990	1991	1992	1993	1994
Africa										
Americas								40.3		32.9
Northern America								40.3		32.9
LAIA										
CACM										
Caribbean										
Rest of America										
As.ex F.USSR								20.5		32.0
Eur.x F.USSR										
EU										
EFTA										
East Europe										
Other Europe										
Former USSR										
Oceania								32.4		26.8
USA/Etats–Unis d'Amer								40.3		32.9
Japan/Japon								20.5		32.0
Guam								29.2		23.2
Australia/Australie								3.2		3.5

	1985	1986	1987	1988	1989	1990	1991	1992	1993	1994
Afrique										
Amériques								9.3	9.2	3.5
Amérique du Nord								9.3	9.2	3.5
ALAI										
MCAC										
Caraïbes										
Autre Amérique										
Asie l'URSS exclus								80.0	76.7	72.7
Europe l'URSS exclus										
UE										
AELE										
Europe de l'Est										
Autre de l'Europe										
Ancienne URSS										
Océanie								9.6	13.8	5.4
Japan/Japon								80.0	76.7	72.7
Guam								8.3	12.6	5.1
USA/Etats–Unis d'Amer								9.3	9.2	3.5
Pacific Isld (Tr Terr.)								1.1	0.9	0.3

4. General Imports C.I.F. by Commodities according to the S.I.T.C. (Rev. 2) in thousand U.S. Dollars
Importations Générales C.A.F. par Produits d'après la C.T.C.I. (Rév. 2) en milliers de Dollars E.U.

SITC CTCI	COMMODITY	1991		1992		1993		1994		PRODUIT
		WEIGHT POIDS	VALUE VALEUR	WEIGHT POIDS	VALUE VALEUR	WEIGHT POIDS	VALUE VALEUR	WEIGHT POIDS	VALUE VALEUR	
	ALL COMMODITIES				98796		109486		129060	TOUS PRODUITS
0	FOOD AND LIVE ANIMALS				19752		31170		25351	ALIMENTS,ANIMAUX VIVANTS
011	MEAT FRESH,CHILLD,FROZEN						2104			VIANDES FRAICHES,REF,CONGE
012	MEAT DRIED,SALTED,SMOKED						1526			VIANDE,ABATS SALES,SECHES
014	MEAT PREPD,PRSVD,NES ETC						2280			CONSERVES DE VIANDES
037	FISH ETC PREPD,PRSVD NES						5468			POIS,CRUST,MOL PREPARES
042	RICE						4006			RIZ
045	CEREALS NES UNMILLED						926			AUTRES CEREALES NON MOULUES
04601	FLOUR OF WHEAT OR MESLIN				575		584			FARINE DE FROMENT
0611	RAW BEET AND CANE SUGAR				870		691			SUCRES BRUTS
062	SUGAR CANDY NON-CHOCLATE						496			SUCRERIES
07112	COFFEE ROASTED				339		440			CAFE TORREFIE
09809	MISC FOOD PREPRTIONS NES				570		547			PREP ALIMENTAIRES NDA
1	BEVERAGES AND TOBACCO				8048		7035		6045	BOISSONS ET TABACS
11102	FLAVORED WATERS NON-ALCO				1996		1897			LIMONADES,EAUX GAZEUSES
1123	BEER,ALE,STOUT,PORTER				2968		2326			BIERES
1222	CIGARETTES				2499		2229			CIGARETTES
2	CRUDE MATERLS,EXCL FUELS				1620		2199		428	MAT BRUTES NON COMESTIBLES
248	WOOD SHAPED,SLEEPERS						2100			BOIS SIMPLEMENT TRAVAILLES
3	MINERAL FUELS ETC				16896		11221		18446	COMBUSTIBLES MINERAUX LUB
5	CHEMCLS,RELATED PROD NES				4416		4245		5696	PRODUITS CHIMIQUES
553	PERFUMERY,COSMETICS,ETC						754			PRODUITS DE PARFUMERIE
5541	SOAPS				738		645			SAVONS,PROD TENSIO-ACTIFS
6	BASIC MANUFACTURES				12313		16404		40770	ART MANUFACTURES
6342	PLYWOOD OF WOOD SHEETS				805		950			BOIS CONTRE-PLAQUES
6612	CEMENT				1355		1530			CIMENTS HYDRAULIQUES
7	MACHINES,TRANSPORT EQUIP				16793		22086		17402	MACHINES MATERIEL TRANSPORT
71331	—— OUTBOARD				702		913			MOTEURS BATEAUX HORSBORD
781	PASS MOTOR VEH EXC BUSES						6381			AUTO TRANSPORT PERSONNES
8	MISC MANUFACTURED GOODS				7619		12955		13379	ART MANUFACTURES DIVERS
821	*FURNITURE,PARTS THEREOF						420			MEUBLES ET PIECES
851	*FOOTWEAR						794			CHAUSSURES
8932	PLSTC SANITRY,TOILET ART				538		431			OBJETS HYGIEN MAT DU 58
89471	FISHNG,HUNTNG EQUIP NES				315		320			HAMECONS ET EPUISETTES
9	GOODS NOT CLASSD BY KIND				11327		2166		1491	ART TRANSACT NON CLASSES

5. General Exports F.O.B. by Commodities according to the S.I.T.C. (Rev. 2) in thousand U.S. Dollars
Exportations Générales F.O.B. par Produits d'après la C.T.C.I. (Rév. 2) en milliers de Dollars E.U.

SITC CTCI	COMMODITY	1991		1992		1993		1994		PRODUIT
		WEIGHT POIDS	VALUE VALEUR	WEIGHT POIDS	VALUE VALEUR	WEIGHT POIDS	VALUE VALEUR	WEIGHT POIDS	VALUE VALEUR	
	ALL COMMODITIES				23319		29169		78172	TOUS PRODUITS
0	FOOD AND LIVE ANIMALS				21071		27005		75732	ALIMENTS,ANIMAUX VIVANTS
03	FISH AND PREPARATIONS				20110		25320		74113	POISSONS ET PREPARATIONS
034	FISH,FRESH,CHILLED,FROZN				19485		25217		73573	POISSON FRAIS, REFRIG,CONG
037	FISH ETC PREPD,PRSVD NES				524		3		430	POIS,CRUST,MOL PREPARES
05	VEGETABLES AND FRUIT				401		1118		808	LEGUMES ET FRUITS
057	FRUIT,NUTS,FRESH,DRIED				390		1033		717	FRUITS FRAIS OU SECS
0573	BANANA,PLANTAIN,FRSH,DRY				278		754		456	BANANES FRAICHES,SECHEES
0577	NUTS EDIBLE,FRESH,DRIED				94		267		252	FRUITS A COQUES
05779	NUTS EDIBLE,FRSH,DRY,NES				94		267		252	FRUITS A COQUES NDA
081	*FEEDING STUFF FOR ANIML				222				390	NOURRITURE POUR ANIMAUX
8	MISC MANUFACTURED GOODS				2211		2140		2401	ART MANUFACTURES DIVERS
84	CLOTHING AND ACCESSORIES				2045		2055		2161	VETEMENTS
89	MISC MANUFCTRD GOODS NES				131					ART MANUFACTURES DIVERS
899	OTHER MANUFACTURED GOODS				131					AUT ART MANUF DIVERS NDA
8998	SMALLWARES,TOILETRYS ETC				131					ART MERCERIE,TOILETTE
89983	BUTTONS,STUDS,ETC				131					BOUTONS,BOUTONS–PRESSION

1. HISTORICAL SERIES, 1957–1996 SPECIAL TRADE, IMPORTS C.I.F., EXPORTS F.O.B.
SERIES HISTORIQUES, 1957–1996 COMMERCE SPECIAL, IMPORTATIONS C.A.F., EXPORTATIONS F.O.B

YEAR ANNEE	VALUE IN MILLION U.S. DOLLARS VALEUR EN MILLION U.S. DOLLARS MERCHANDISE – MARCHANDISE IMPORTS	EXPORTS	GOLD – OR IMPORTS	EXPORTS	CONVERSION FACTORS FACTEURS DE CONVERSION CENTS E.U. PAR IMPORTS	EXPORTS	INDEX NUMBERS – INDICES QUANTUM IMPORTS	EXPORTS	UNIT VALUE VALEUR UNITAIRE IMPORTS	EXPORTS
1957	75.00	57.00								
1958	77.00	55.00								
1959	83.00	62.00								
1960	97.00	72.00								
1962	97.00	72.00								
1963	125.00	70.00								
1965	98.00	81.00								
1966	109.00	82.00								
1967	116.00	86.00								
1968	116.00	77.00								
1969	110.00	77.00								
1970	121.00	84.00								
1971	128.00	101.70								
1972	157.00	130.00								
1973	230.00	167.00								
1974	225.00	200.00								
1975	266.00	218.00								
1976	301.00	232.00								
1977	375.00	232.00								
1978	417.00	280.00								
1979	498.00	343.00								
1980	547.80	402.80								
1985	1095.50	689.10								
1986	1139.70	716.10								
1987	1104.60	717.90								
1988	1113.60	739.10								
1989	963.00	721.50								
1990	924.00	660.70								
1991	360.90	348.00								
1992	418.30	388.50								
1993	361.50	380.90								
1994	222.70	324.20								
1995	415.30	473.30								
1996	438.50	423.00								

2. IMPORTS BY BROAD ECONOMIC CATEGORY AND EXPORTS BY INDUSTRIAL ORIGIN. (PERCENTAGE OF TOTAL VALUE)
IMPORTATIONS PAR CATEGORIES ECONOMIQUES ET EXPORTATIONS PAR BRANCHE D'ACTIVITE.(EN POURCENTAGE DE LA VALEUR TOTALE)

IMPORTS – IMPORTATIONS

	1990	1991	1992	1993	1994	1995	1996
TOTAL IMPORTS–IMPORTATIONS TOTALES							100.
1 FOOD BEV–ALIMENTATION BOISSONS							13.5
11 PRIMARY–PRODUITS DE BASE							1.0
111 FOR INDUSTRY–POUR L'INDUSTRIE							0.1
112 FOR HOUSEHOLDS–POUR LES MENAGES							0.8
12 PROCESSED–PRODUITS ELABORES							12.6
121 FOR INDUSTRY–POUR L'INDUSTRIE							7.4
122 FOR HOUSEHOLDS–POUR LES MENAGES							5.2
2 IND SUPPLIES–APPROV INDUSTRIELS							19.3
21 PRIMARY–PRODUITS DE BASE							0.8
22 PROCESSED–PRODUITS ELABORES							18.5
3 FUELS–COMBUSTIBLES							19.3
31 PRIMARY–PRODUITS DE BASE							0.2
32 PROCESSED–PRODUITS ELABORES							19.2
321 MOTOR SPIRIT–ESSENCE							
322 OTHER–AUTRES							19.2
4 MACHINERY–EQUIPEMENT							23.3
41 CAPITAL EQUIPMENT–MACHINES							21.7
42 PARTS–PIECES ACCESSOIRES							1.6
5 TRANSPORT–TRANSPORT							17.3
51 PASSENGER CARS–AUTOMOBILES							3.6
52 OTHER–AUTRES							10.2
521 INDUSTRIAL–INDUSTRIELS							9.9
522 NON INDUSTRIAL–NON INDUSTRIEL							0.3
53 PARTS–PIECES ACCESSOIRES							3.5
6 CONSUM GOODS–BIENS CONSOMMATION							7.3
61 DURABLE–DURABLES							3.1
62 SEMI DURABLE–SEMI DURABLES							1.6
63 NON DURABLE–NON DURABLES							2.6
7 GOODS NES–BIENS NDA							0.0

EXPORTS – EXPORTATIONS

	1990	1991	1992	1993	1994	1995	1996
TOTAL EXPORTS–EXPORTATIONS TOTALES							100.
1 AGRICULTURE							5.4
2 MINING QUARRY–INDUS EXTRACTIVES							57.2
3 MANUFACTURING–IND MANUFACTUR							37.4
31 FOOD BEV TOBACCO–ALIM BOISS TAB							8.8
32 TEXTILES–INDUSTRIES TEXTILES							19.7
33 WOOD & PRODUCTS–BOIS & PRODUITS							2.4
34 PAPER & PRODUCTS–PAPIER & PRODT							0.0
35 CHEMICALS–INDUSTRIES CHIMIQUES							0.9
36 NON METAL MIN–MIN NON METAL							0.0
37 BASIC METAL–IND METAL BASE							1.0
38 METAL MANUF–MANUF METAL							4.5
39 OTH MANUF IND–AUTRES MANUF							0.0

3. TRADE BY PRINCIPAL COUNTRIES OF ORIGIN AND LAST DESTINATION (VALUE IN THOUSAND U.S. DOLLARS)
ECHANGES SELON LES PRINCIPAUX PAYS D'ORIGINE ET DE DERNIERE DESTINATION (VALEUR EN MILLIERS DE DOLLARS EU)

COUNTRIES–PAYS	SPECIAL IMPORTS C.I.F. IMPORTATIONS SPECIALES C.A.F				
	1992	1993	1994	1995	1996
World	418300				450928
Africa					21
Americas					10947
Northern America					10835
LAIA					81
CACM					
Caribbean					30
Rest of America					
As.ex F.USSR	121900				162795
Eur.x F.USSR	74300				81280
EU	54700				66429
EFTA	5100				6007
East Europe	12100				8725
Other Europe					
Former USSR	214300				169444
Oceania					428
Russian Federation					163988
China/Chine	57500				69484
Japan/Japon	40100				52831
Germany/Allemagne	22100				33363
Korea, Republic of	8100				17658
Italy/Italie	1200				23163
Singapore/Singapour	6300				13934
Austria/Autriche	19400				591
Hong Kong	9600				3591
USA/Etats–Unis d'Amer					10563
France, Monac	7300				1126
Hungary/Hongrie	4900				2266
Switz.Liecht	5100				1119
Czechoslovakia	5400				
Denmark/Danemark	3000				1987
Norway,SVD,JM					4888
Poland/Pologne	1200				3520
United Kingdom	1500				2359
Ukraine					2807
Viet Nam					2687
Bulgaria/Bulgarie	500				2104
Fm Yugoslav	2400				
Netherlands/Pays–Bas	200				1616
Malaysia/Malaisie					1391
Belgium–Luxembourg					1013
Finland/Finlande					841
Kyrgyzstan/Kirghizistan					761
Kazakhstan					576
Uzbekistan/Ouzbékistan					490
Australia/Australie					428
India/Inde					416
Czech Republic					411
Korea Dem People's Rp	300				103
Canada					273
Romania/Roumanie	100				165
Turkmenistan/Turkménistn					263
Slovakia					259
Thailand/Thaïlande					226
Latvia/Lettonie					189
Lithuania/Lituanie					187
Pakistan					175
Spain/Espagne					169
Georgia/Géorgie					163
Greece/Grèce					121
Yugoslavia/Yougoslavie					120
Afghanistan					4

COUNTRIES–PAYS	SPECIAL EXPORTS F.O.B. EXPORTATIONS SPECIALES F.O.B.				
	1992	1993	1994	1995	1996
Monde	388500				424267
Afrique					
Amériques	4400				1349
Amérique du Nord	4400				1303
ALAI					
MCAC					
Caraïbes					
Autre Amérique					46
Asie l'URSS exclus	94400				93910
Europe l'URSS exclus	60110				58420
UE	27000				57911
AELE	16400				149
Europe de l'Est	14910				14
Autre de l'Europe					
Ancienne URSS	219700				267743
Océanie					
Russian Federation					267546
China/Chine	69400				75992
United Kingdom	3900				53859
Japan/Japon	18700				2213
Switz.Liecht	16400				149
Germany/Allemagne	12100				482
Hong Kong	3800				6082
Korea, Republic of					9184
Italy/Italie	8200				43
Bulgaria/Bulgarie	7300				1
USA/Etats–Unis d'Amer	4400				943
Netherlands/Pays–Bas	1700				3264
Czechoslovakia	4200				
Hungary/Hongrie	3000				0
Fm Yugoslav	1800				
Korea Dem People's Rp	1200				
France, Monac	800				4
Singapore/Singapour	600				169
Afghanistan	700				
Poland/Pologne	400				12
Canada					360
Croatia/Croatie					346
Austria/Autriche	300				7
Belgium–Luxembourg					249
Kazakhstan					151
Uzbekistan/Ouzbékistan					31
Georgia/Géorgie					14
Romania/Roumanie	10				

(VALUE AS PERCENTAGE OF WORLD TOTAL)(VALEURS EN POURCENTAGE DU TOTAL MONDIAL)

	1987	1988	1989	1990	1991	1992	1993	1994	1995	1996
Africa										0.0
Americas										2.4
Northern America										2.4
LAIA										0.0
CACM										
Caribbean										0.0
Rest of America										
As.ex F.USSR						29.1				36.1
Eur.x F.USSR						17.8				18.0
EU						13.1				14.7
EFTA						1.2				1.3
East Europe						2.9				1.9
Other Europe										
Former USSR						51.2				37.6
Oceania										0.1
Russian Federation										36.4
China/Chine						13.7				15.4
Japan/Japon						9.6				11.7
Germany/Allemagne						5.3				7.4
Korea, Republic of						1.9				3.9
Italy/Italie						0.3				5.1
Singapore/Singapour						1.5				3.1
Austria/Autriche						4.6				0.1
Hong Kong						2.3				0.8
USA/Etats–Unis d'Amer										2.3

	1987	1988	1989	1990	1991	1992	1993	1994	1995	1996
Afrique										
Amériques						1.1				0.3
Amérique du Nord						1.1				0.3
ALAI										
MCAC										
Caraïbes										
Autre Amérique										0.0
Asie l'URSS exclus						24.3				22.1
Europe l'URSS exclus						15.5				13.8
UE						6.9				13.6
AELE						4.2				0.0
Europe de l'Est						3.8				0.0
Autre de l'Europe										
Ancienne URSS						56.6				63.1
Océanie										
Russian Federation										63.1
China/Chine						17.9				17.9
United Kingdom						1.0				12.7
Japan/Japon						4.8				0.5
Switz.Liecht						4.2				0.0
Germany/Allemagne						3.1				0.1
Hong Kong						1.0				1.4
Korea, Republic of										2.2
Italy/Italie						2.1				0.0
Bulgaria/Bulgarie						1.9				0.0

4. Special Imports C.I.F. by Commodities according to the S.I.T.C. (Rev. 2) in thousand U.S. Dollars
Importations Spéciales C.A.F. par Produits d'après la C.T.C.I. (Rév. 2) en milliers de Dollars E.U.

SITC CTCI	COMMODITY	1993		1994		1995		1996		PRODUIT
		WEIGHT POIDS	VALUE VALEUR	WEIGHT POIDS	VALUE VALEUR	WEIGHT POIDS	VALUE VALEUR	WEIGHT POIDS	VALUE VALEUR	
	ALL COMMODITIES								450928	TOUS PRODUITS
0	FOOD AND LIVE ANIMALS								53919	ALIMENTS,ANIMAUX VIVANTS
04	CEREALS AND PREPARATIONS								33604	CEREALES ET PRODUITS
042	RICE							W 7900	3259	RIZ
0422	RICE SEMI-MILLED,MILLED							W 7900	3259	RIZ POLI,GLACE INCL BRISURES
04221	RICE MILLED UNBROKEN							W 7900	3259	RIZ POLI,GLACE EXCL BRISURES
046	WHEAT ETC MEAL OR FLOUR							W 100277	27201	SEMOULE FARINE,FROMENT
04601	FLOUR OF WHEAT OR MESLIN							W 100232	27197	FARINE DE FROMENT
048	CEREAL ETC PREPARATIONS							W 2589	2876	PREPTNS A BASE CEREALES
0484	BAKERY PRODUCTS							W 1761	2299	PRODUITS DE BOULANGERIE
04842	PASTRY, CAKES ETC							W 1430	1659	PATISSERIE ETC.
05	VEGETABLES AND FRUIT								6806	LEGUMES ET FRUITS
054	VEG ETC FRSH,SMPLY PRSVD								1695	LEGUMES FRAIS,CONG,SECS
057	FRUIT,NUTS,FRESH,DRIED								1530	FRUITS FRAIS OU SECS
058	FRUIT PRESERVED,PREPARED							W 2523	2244	CONSERVES DE FRUITS
0582	FRUIT PRESERVED BY SUGAR							W 1899	1639	FRUITS CONFITS AU SUCRE
06	SUGAR AND PREPS,HONEY								7398	SUCRES ET PRODUITS
061	SUGAR AND HONEY							W 10943	4143	SUCRES ET MIEL
0611	RAW BEET AND CANE SUGAR							W 10920	4049	SUCRES BRUTS
062	SUGAR CANDY NON-CHOCLATE							W 3067	3254	SUCRERIES
07	COFFEE,TEA,COCOA,SPICES								1913	CAFE,THE,CACAO,EPICES
09	MISC EDIBLE PRODUCTS								3137	PREP ALIMENTAIRES DIVERSES
098	EDIBLE PRODCTS,PREPS NES								2100	PREP ALIMENTAIRES NDA
1	BEVERAGES AND TOBACCO								7329	BOISSONS ET TABACS
11	BEVERAGES								4342	BOISSONS
111	NON-ALCOHL BEVERAGES NES							W 2666	1433	BOISSONS NON ALCOOLIQUES
11102	FLAVORED WATERS NON-ALCO							W 2503	1357	LIMONADES,EAUX GAZEUSES
112	ALCOHOLIC BEVERAGES							W 2876	2909	BOISSONS ALCOOLIQUES
12	TOBACCO AND MANUFACTURES								2987	TABACS BRUTS FABRIQUES
122	TOBACCO,MANUFACTURED								2987	TABACS FABRIQUES
1222	CIGARETTES							MN 672630	2193	CIGARETTES
2	CRUDE MATERLS,EXCL FUELS								4225	MAT BRUTES NON COMESTIBLES
26	TEXTILE FIBRES AND WASTE								2202	FIBRES TEXTILES
269	WASTE OF TEXTILE FABRICS							W 377	1398	FRIPERIE DRILLES,CHIFFONS
26901	BULK TEXT WSTE,OLD CLTHG							W 376	1396	ART ET ACCESS D'HABILLEMENT
3	MINERAL FUELS ETC								87184	COMBUSTIBLES MINERAUX LUB
33	PETROLEUM AND PRODUCTS								70598	PETROLE ET DERIVES
334	PETROLEUM PRODUCTS,REFIN							W 380321	70205	PRODUITS RAFFINES
351	*ELECTRIC CURRENT							H 374769	15746	ENERGIE ELECTRIQUE
4	ANIMAL,VEGETABLE OIL,FAT								3087	HUILES,GRAISSES ANIM,VEG
42	FIXED VEGETABLE OIL,FAT								1859	HUILES VEGETALES FIXES
423	FIXED VEG OILS,SOFT								1640	HUILES VEGET DOUCES FIXES
4236	SUNFLOWER SEED OIL							W 1721	1619	HUILE DE TOURNESOL
5	CHEMCLS,RELATED PROD NES								22058	PRODUITS CHIMIQUES
51	ORGANIC CHEMICALS								2311	PROD CHIMIQ ORGANIQUES
52	INORGANIC CHEMICALS								3779	PROD CHIM INORGANIQUES
523	OTHR INORG CHEMICALS ETC								2677	AUT PRODUITS CHIMIQUES INORG
5231	METAL CMPD OF INORG ACID								1924	SELS METALLIQUES
52317	SULPHITES,THIOSULPHATES							W 3801	1476	SULFITES,HYPOSULFITES
541	*MEDICINAL,PHARM PRODUCT							MK 782047	6114	PROD MEDICINAUX PHARMACEUT
5417	MEDICAMENTS							MK 477601	2986	MEDICAMENTS
54179	— CONTNG OTH SUBSTANCES							MK 420240	2270	MED CONT AUT SUBSTANCES
55	PERFUME,CLEANING ETC PRD								4501	PROD POUR PARFUM,TOILETTE
554	SOAP,CLEANSING ETC PREPS							W 4113	3040	SAVONS,PRODUITS DETERSIFS
5541	SOAPS							W 3277	1872	SAVONS,PROD TENSIO-ACTIFS
562	*FERTILIZERS,MANUFACTURE								2099	ENGRAIS MANUFACTURES
5621	CHEM NITROGENOUS FERTLZR								1504	ENGRAIS AZOTES
56211	AMMONIUM NITRATE							W 5989	1494	NITRATE D'AMMONIUM
6	BASIC MANUFACTURES								74761	ART MANUFACTURES
62	RUBBER MANUFACTURES NES								9415	CAOUTCHOUC MANUFACTURE
625	RUBBER TYRES, TUBES ETC							N 82475	5334	PNEUS CAOUTCHOUC VULCANISE
6252	TYRES,NEW,BUS OR LORRY							N 15693	4099	PNEUS POUR AUTOBUS,CAMIONS
628	RUBBER ARTICLES NES								3484	OUVRAGES CAOUTCHOUC NDA
6282	VULCANIZD RUBBER BELTING							W 122	3316	COURROIES EN CAOUTCHOUC
64	PAPER,PAPERBOARD AND MFR								3922	PAPIERS,CARTONS & OUVRAGES
641	PAPER AND PAPERBOARD								2293	PAPIERS ET CARTONS
642	PAPER,ETC,PRECUT,ARTS OF								1629	PAP,CARTONS DECOUPES
65	TEXTILE YARN,FABRICS,ETC								13931	FILS,TISSUS,ARTICLES TEXTILE
651	TEXTILE YARN								1623	FILS TEXTILES
652	COTTON FABRICS,WOVEN							L 3706	3940	TISSUS DE COTON
6521	GREY WOVEN COTTON FABRIC							L 3018	3388	TISSUS COT ECRUS NON MERCER
65214	GREY WOVEN COTTON NES							L 3018	3388	AUT TISSUS 85% COTON ECRUS
653	WOVN MAN-MADE FIB FABRIC							L 3818	3579	TISSUS FIBRES SYNTH,ARTIF
6531	CONT SYNT WEAVES NONPILE							L 3763	3534	TISSUS FIBRES SYNTH CONTINUE
65315	CONT SYN TXTL FABRIC NES							L 3677	3414	TIS PLUS 85% TEXT SYNT CONT
657	SPECIAL TXTL FABRC,PRODS								1555	TISSUS SPECIAUX
658	TEXTILE ARTICLES NES							N 686847	1545	ART FACONNES MAT TEXTILES
66	NONMETAL MINERAL MFS NES								12390	ART MIN NON METALLIQUES
661	LIME,CEMENT,BLDG PRODS							W 10508	1809	CHAUX,CIMENTS MAT CONSTR
6618	MNRL BLDG PRD UNFIRD NES							W 7092	1356	MAT CONST AMIANTE-CIMENT
662	CLAY,REFRACTORY BLDG PRD								2562	MAT CONST REFRACTAIRES
6623	REFRACTORY BUILDING PROD							W 1825	2188	BRIQUES REFRACTAIRES
66233	REFRACTORY CEMENT,MORTAR							W 408	1645	CIMENTS REFRACTAIRES
663	MINERAL MANUFCTURES NES								6119	ART MIN MANUF NDA
6633	MINRL MFS NES NONCERAMIC							W 4187	5578	OUVR MAT MINERALE NDA
66332	CEMENT,ARTFCL STONE PROD							W 3896	5498	OUVRAGES EN CIMENT
67	IRON AND STEEL								27224	FER ET ACIER
671	PIG IRON ETC								4906	FONTE,SPIEGEL,POUDRES
6713	IRON,STL POWDER,SHOT,ETC								3320	POUDRES,GREN FER,ACIER
67131	IRON,STEEL SHOT,GRIT,ETC							W 9745	3320	GRENAILLE FER,ACIER
6716	FERRO-ALLOYS							W 1562	1540	FERRO-ALLIAGES
674	IRN,STL UNIV,PLATE,SHEET								4150	LARGES PLATS,TOLES
6749	OTH IRN,STL PLATES,SHEET							W 9628	2675	AUTRES TOLES FER,ACIER
678	IRON,STL TUBES,PIPES,ETC							W 5730	9700	TUBES,TUYAUX EN FONTE,FER
6782	IRON,STL SEAMLESS TUBES							W 4040	8506	TUBES,TUYAUX SANS SOUDURE
679	IRN,STL CASTINGS UNWORKD								5914	OUVRAGES EN FONTE,FER,ACIER
6793	IRON,STL FORGINGS ROUGH							N 3651	1392	OUVRAGES FORGES,ESTAMPES
6794	IRON,STL CASTINGS ROUGH								4521	OUVRAGES COULES,MOULES
67941	IRON CASTINGS ROUGH								4521	OUVRAGES A L'ETAT BRUT
68	NON-FERROUS METALS								1723	METAUX NON FERREUX
69	METAL MANUFACTURES NES								5070	ART MANUFACT EN METAL NDA

4. Special Imports C.I.F. by Commodities according to the S.I.T.C. (Rev. 2) in thousand U.S. Dollars
Importations Spéciales C.A.F. par Produits d'après la C.T.C.I. (Rév. 2) en milliers de Dollars E.U.

SITC CTCI	COMMODITY	1993 WEIGHT POIDS	1993 VALUE VALEUR	1994 WEIGHT POIDS	1994 VALUE VALEUR	1995 WEIGHT POIDS	1995 VALUE VALEUR	1996 WEIGHT POIDS	1996 VALUE VALEUR	PRODUIT
7	MACHINES,TRANSPORT EQUIP								179195	MACHINES MATERIEL TRANSPORT
71	POWER GENERATING EQUIPMT								5608	MACHINES GENERATRICES
716	ROTATING ELECTRIC PLANT							N 7557	3403	APP ELECTR ROTATIFS,PIECES
72	MACHS FOR SPCL INDUSTRYS								46153	MAC SPECIALES POUR INDUST
722	TRACTORS NON–ROAD							N 38	2569	TRACTEURS
7223	TRACK–LAYING TRACTORS							N 27	1846	TRACTEURS A CHENILLES
723	CIVIL ENGNEERG EQUIP ETC							N 4329	8295	APPAREILS DE GENIE CIVIL
7234	CONST,MINING MACHNRY NES							N 1301	7413	MACH POUR LA CONST, MINES
72341	SELF–PROPELLD DOZERS,ETC							N 99	2627	BULLDOZERS
72342	SLFPRP SHOVELS,EXCAVATRS							N 57	3372	PELLES MECANIQUES
724	TEXTILE,LEATHER MACHNRY							N 179445	14481	MACH POUR INDUSTRIE TEXTILE
7244	SPINNING,EXTRDNG,ETC MCH							N 4705	4522	MACH POUR LE FILAGE
72442	FIBRE PROCESSNG MACH NES							N 69	2370	MACH PREP MAT TEXTILES
72443	SPINNING,REELING,ETC MCH							N 12	2093	MACH POUR LA FILATURE
7245	WEAVING,FELT MFG,ETC MCH							N 212	4305	METIERS A TISSER,PIECES
72453	GIMPING,WARPING ETC MCHS							N 90	3487	METIERS A TULLE ETC
7248	SKIN,LEATHER WORKNG MACH							N 36442	3253	MACHINES TRAVAIL DES CUIRS
727	FOOD MACHRY NON–DOMESTIC							N 10747	5448	MACH INDUSTRIES ALIMENT
7272	OTH FOOD PROC MCHY,PARTS							N 3574	4902	AUT MACH IND ALIMENTAIRE
72722	INDUS FOOD PROC MACH NES							N 1549	3506	MACHINES BOULANGERIE
72729	PTS NES OF MCHY OF 72722							N 2025	1396	PIECES MACH DU 727.22
728	OTH MACHY FOR SPCL INDUS							N 25256	12785	AUT MACH IND PARTICULIERES
7283	OTHR MINERAL WORKG MACHY							N 8600	4082	MACH TRIER,CRIBLER,BROYER
72839	PTS NES OF MACHY OF 7283							N 5892	2168	PIECES MACH DU 728.3
7284	MACHY FOR SPCL INDUS NES							N 16462	8252	MACH SPEC IND PARTICUL.
72842	RUBBER,PLASTICS WRKG MCH							N 1456	3561	MACH IND CAOUT MAT PLAST
72848	OTH MCHY WITH INDIV FNCT							N 109	2878	AUTRES MACHINES NDA
72849	PTS OF MACHS OF 7284 ETC							N 14761	1739	PIECES DU 728.4 ETC
73	METALWORKING MACHINERY								1974	MACH TRAVAIL DES METAUX
74	GENRL INDUSTRL MACHY NES								19558	MACH APP INDUSTRIE
741	HEATING,COOLING EQUIPMNT							N 7895	2354	MACH CHAUFFAGE,PIECES
742	PUMPS FOR LIQUIDS ETC							N 5433	1457	POMPES MOTO–POMPES
743	PUMPS NES,CENTRFUGES ETC							N 4920	1418	POMPES COMPRES,VENT ETC
744	MECHANICAL HANDLING EQU							N 51139	11738	EQUIP MANUTENTION PIECES
7442	LIFTING,LOADING MACH NES							N 2544	8211	APP LEVAGE,MANUTENTION
74422	SHIP DERRICKS,CRANES ETC							N 24	5872	GRUES,PONTS ROULANTS
74428	OTH HANDLING ETC MCH NES							N 2394	1811	AUT APP LEVAGE ETC
7449	PTS NES OF MACHY OF 7442							N 48467	3223	PIECES DU 744.2
749	NONELEC MACH PTS,ACC NES							N 22997	1932	PIECES MACH NON ELEC NDA
75	OFFICE MACHNES,ADP EQUIP								3772	MACH BUREAU TRAIT AUTOM
752	AUTOMTIC DATA PROC EQUIP							N 49334	2073	MACH TRAIT INFORMATION
76	TELECOMM,SOUND EQUIPMENT								14156	EQUIPMENT DE TELECOM
761	TELEVISION RECEIVERS							N 34660	2810	RECEPTEURS DE TELEVISION
7611	COLOUR TV RECEIVERS							N 34377	2773	RECEPTEURS COULEUR
764	TELECOM EQPT,PTS,ACC NES							N 139173	10678	EQUIP TELECOM,PIECES
7641	LINE TELEPHONE,ETC EQUIP							N 99735	8774	APP TELEPHON PAR FIL
7649	PTS NES OF EQUIPMT OF 76							N 33883	1557	PIECES DE LA DIV 76
77	ELECTRIC MACHNRY NES ETC								13538	MACH APP ELECT NDA
771	ELECTRIC POWER MACHY NES							N 4018	1606	MACH PROD,TRANS ELECTR
772	SWITCHGEAR ETC,PARTS NES							N 2334497	1405	APP COUPURE,SECT ETC
7721	SWITCHGEAR ETC							N 2334454	1404	APP COUPURE,SECTIONMNT
773	ELECTR DISTRIBUTNG EQUIP								1833	EQUIPMT DISTRIBUTION ELECT
7731	INSULATED WIRE,CABLE ETC							L 488	1520	FILS,CABLES ISOLES ELECT
775	HOUSEHOLD TYPE EQUIP NES							N 48215	3341	MACH,APP USAGE DOMESTQUE
7758	ELECTRO–THERMIC APPL NES							N 34045	1721	APP ELECTROTHERMIQ NDA
778	ELECTRICAL MACHINERY NES								4931	AUTRES MACH ELECT NDA
7781	BATTERIES,ACCUMULATORS								1591	PILES ET ACCUMULATEURS
7788	OTH ELEC MACHY,EQUIP NES								2356	AUT MACH APP ELEC NDA
78	ROAD VEHICLES								49526	VEHICULES ROUTIERS
781	PASS MOTOR VEH EXC BUSES							N 2994	16285	AUTO TRANSPORT PERSONNES
782	LORRIES,SPCL MTR VEH NES							N 340	14608	VEHICULES SPECIAUX,MARCH
7821	LORRIES,TRUCKS							N 299	13914	VEHICULES TRANSP MARCHAND
783	ROAD MOTOR VEHICLES NES							N 245	9130	VEHICULES ROUTIERS NDA
7831	BUSES							N 194	7972	VOITURES TRANSPORT COMMUN
784	MOTOR VEH PRTS,ACCES NES							N 261153	6719	PIECES 722,781,782,783
7849	OTHER MOTOR VEHCL PARTS							N 260287	6671	PIECES 722,781,782,783
785	CYCLES,ETC MOTRZD OR NOT							N 24682	2253	MOTOCYCLES SCOOTERS
79	OTHR TRANSPORT EQUIPMENT								24911	AUTRE MATERIEL TRANSPORT
791	RAILWAY VEHICLES							N 44811	24776	VEHIC MAT CHEMINS DE FER
7913	MECHAN–PROPELLED RY CARS							N 24	11174	AUTOMOTRICES,DRAISINES
7914	RY COACHES NES NOT POWRD							N 340	6125	VOITURES A VOYAGEURS
7915	FRT,MAINT CARS NOT POWRD							N 227	2887	WAGONS DE SERVICE
79152	RAILWAY FREIGHT CARS NES							N 227	2887	WAGONS MARCHANDISES
7919	RY TRACK FIXT,ETC,PARTS							N 44108	4548	MATER FIXE VOIES FERREES
79191	RY TRACK FIXTURES ETC							N 10738	3500	APP DE SIGNALISATION
8	MISC MANUFACTURED GOODS								19166	ART MANUFACTURES DIVERS
821	*FURNITURE,PARTS THEREOF							N 109182	5337	MEUBLES ET PIECES
8219	FURNITURE AND PARTS NES							N 61765	4619	AUTRES MEUBLES ET PIECES
82192	WOOD FURNITURE NES							N 37810	4278	MEUBLES NDA EN BOIS
87	PRECISION INSTRUMNTS NES								4494	INSTRUM,APPAR SCIENT NDA
872	MEDICAL INSTRUMENTS NES							N 21361	1901	INSTR,APP MEDIC–CHIR NDA
87202	OTH MEDICAL INSTRUMENTS							N 7241	1739	INSTRUM,APP MEDECINE
874	MEASURNG,CONTROLNG INSTR							N 21824	2498	INSTRUMENTS DE MESURE
89	MISC MANUFCTRD GOODS NES								5785	ART MANUFACTURES DIVERS
893	ARTICLES OF PLASTIC NES								2813	OUVRAGES EN MAT DIVIS 58
8939	MISC PLASTIC ARTICLES								1500	ART DIVERS EN MAT DIV 58
899	OTHER MANUFACTURED GOODS								1649	AUT ART MANUF DIVERS NDA

5. Special Exports F.O.B. by Commodities according to the S.I.T.C. (Rev. 2) in thousand U.S. Dollars
Exportations Spéciales F.O.B. par Produits d'après la C.T.C.I. (Rév. 2) en milliers de Dollars E.U.

SITC CTCI	COMMODITY	1993		1994		1995		1996		PRODUIT
		WEIGHT POIDS	VALUE VALEUR	WEIGHT POIDS	VALUE VALEUR	WEIGHT POIDS	VALUE VALEUR	WEIGHT POIDS	VALUE VALEUR	
	ALL COMMODITIES								424267	TOUS PRODUITS
0	FOOD AND LIVE ANIMALS								8734	ALIMENTS,ANIMAUX VIVANTS
01	MEAT AND PREPARATIONS								6180	VIANDES ET PREPARATIONS
011	MEAT FRESH,CHILLD,FROZEN							W 5553	5953	VIANDES FRAICHES,REF,CONGE
0111	BOVINE MEAT FRESH,FROZEN							W 3356	4761	VIANDES BOVIN FRAI,REF
01111	BOVINE MEAT WITH BONE IN							W 3296	4656	VIANDES BOVIN NON DESOSS
081	*FEEDING STUFF FOR ANIML							W 6962084	2097	NOURRITURE POUR ANIMAUX
0811	HAY, FODDER, GREEN, DRY							W 23146	1660	FOIN ET FOURRAGE
08112	FODDER ROOTS,HAY,ETC							W 23146	1660	RACINES FOURRAGERES
2	CRUDE MATERLS,EXCL FUELS								371351	MAT BRUTES NON COMESTIBLES
21	HIDES,SKINS,FURS UNDRSSD								22259	CUIRS,PEAUX BRUTS
211	HIDES,SKINS,EXC FURS,RAW								22111	CUIRS ET PEAUX
2111	BOVINE,EQUINE HIDES,RAW							N 207924	3627	PEAUX DE BOVINS
2112	CALF AND KIP SKINS,RAW							N 123646	2310	PEAUX DE VEAUX
2114	GOAT AND KID SKINS,RAW							N 387986	2283	PEAUX DE CAPRINS
2116	SHEEP SKIN WITH WOOL							N 1950081	13667	PEAUX LAINEES D'OVINS
24	CORK AND WOOD								10190	LIEGE ET BOIS
248	WOOD SHAPED,SLEEPERS							W 62808	9950	BOIS SIMPLEMENT TRAVAILLES
2482	LUMBER SHAPED CONIFER							W 62773	9946	CONIFERES SCIES,RABOTES
24821	LUMBER SAWN ETC CONIFER							W 62773	9946	CONIFERES SCIES LONGITUD
26	TEXTILE FIBRES AND WASTE								78568	FIBRES TEXTILES
268	WOOL(EXC TOPS),ANML HAIR							W 13430	78564	LAINES ET POILS
2681	WOOL GREASY,FLEECE-WSHED							W 6794	5857	LAINE EN SUINT
2683	FINE ANIMAL HAIR,UNCOMBD							W 1559	11867	POILS FINS EN MASSE
2685	COARSE HAIR UNCOMBED							W 3094	4615	CRINS EN MASSE
26851	HORSEHAIR AND ITS WASTE							W 997	1780	CRINS ET DECHETS
26859	COARSE HAIR NES UNCOMBED							W 2097	2836	AUTRES POILS EN MASSE
2687	WOOL OR HAIR COMBED ETC							W 773	53955	LAINE CARDEE PEIGNEE
27	CRUDE FERTLZR,MINRLS NES								23162	ENGRAIS MINERAUX BRUTS
278	OTHER CRUDE MINERALS								23160	AUTRES MINERAUX BRUTS
2785	QUARTZ,MICA,FELSPAR,ETC								23158	QUARTZ,MICA,FELDSPATH
27854	FELSPAR,FLOURSPAR,ETC							W 159424	23158	FELDSPATH,LEUCITE ETC.
28	METALLIFEROUS ORES,SCRAP								230835	MINERAIS METAL,DECHETS
282	IRON AND STEEL SCRAP							W 71913	8157	FERRAILLES
28209	— OF OTHR IRON OR STEEL							W 71082	8024	FERRAILLES DE FER
287	BASE METAL ORES,CONC NES								219480	MINERAIS METAUX COMMUNS
2871	CPR ORE ETC,CEMENT COPPR							W 473578	205166	MINERAIS DE CUIVRE,MATTES
28711	COPPER ORES,EXCL MATTE							W 473578	205166	MINERAIS DE CUIVRE
2879	OTH NONFER ORE,CONCNTRTE							W 5109	14184	MINERAIS D'AUTRES METAUX
28793	MOLYBD, NIOBIUM ETC ORES							W 5095	14160	MINERAIS DE MOLYBDENE,TITANE
288	NONFERR METAL SCRAP NES							W 3709	3198	DECHETS NON FERREUX
2882	OTHER BASE MTL SCRAP NES							W 3709	3198	AUTRES DECHETS
28823	ALUMINIUM WSTE AND SCRAP							W 2331	2171	DECHETS D'ALUMINIUM
29	CRUDE ANIMAL,VEG MAT NES								6248	MATIERES BRUTES ANIM,VEGET
291	CRUDE ANIMAL MTRIALS NES								6244	MATIERES BRUTES ANIMALES
2911	BONES,IVORY,HORNS,ETC							W 3753	2965	OS,CORNES,SABOTS
29116	IVORY,TORTOISE-SHELL ETC							W 772	2674	IVOIRE ECAILLE
2919	OTH ANIMAL MATERIALS NES								3279	MAT ORIGINE ANIMALE NDA
29193	GUT,BLADDERS,ETC NONFISH								3264	BOYAUX,VESSIES
5	CHEMCLS,RELATED PROD NES								2736	PRODUITS CHIMIQUES
562	*FERTILIZERS,MANUFACTURE								1958	ENGRAIS MANUFACTURES
5629	FERTILIZERS NES								1604	ENGRAIS NDA
56291	NIT-PHOS-POT FERTLZR NES							W 7994	1604	ENGRAIS CONT N P K
6	BASIC MANUFACTURES								6358	ART MANUFACTURES
67	IRON AND STEEL								4202	FER ET ACIER
672	IRON,STEEL PRIMARY FORMS							W 15894	2823	LINGOTS FER,ACIER
6724	IRN,STL INGOTS,LUMPS,ETC							W 15872	2811	FER,ACIER LINGOTS,MASSES
67241	IRON,SIMPLE STEEL INGOTS							W 15872	2811	LINGOTS EN FER ET ACIER
7	MACHINES,TRANSPORT EQUIP								7374	MACHINES MATERIEL TRANSPORT
78	ROAD VEHICLES								6086	VEHICULES ROUTIERS
781	PASS MOTOR VEH EXC BUSES							N 1682	5743	AUTO TRANSPORT PERSONNES
8	MISC MANUFACTURED GOODS								26955	ART MANUFACTURES DIVERS
84	CLOTHING AND ACCESSORIES								26587	VETEMENTS
842	MENS OUTERWEAR NOT KNIT							N 1021329	8801	VET DESSUS POUR HOMMES
8421	— OVERCOATS,OTHER COATS							N 510277	4688	MANTEAUX HOMMES MAT TEXT
84219	—— OF OTHER FIBRES							N 510277	4688	MANTEAUX HOMMES AUT FIBR
8429	— OTHER OUTER GARMENTS							N 371561	3603	AUT VET DES HOM MAT TEX
843	WOMENS OUTERWEAR NONKNIT							N 688564	4228	VET DESSUS FEMMES MAT TEX
8431	— COATS AND JACKETS							N 194653	2187	MANT,VEST FEM MAT TEXTIL
8439	— OTHER OUTER GARMENTS							N 457478	1951	AUT VET DES FEM MAT TEXT
844	UNDER GARMENTS NOT KNIT							N 986555	3214	VETEMENT DESSOUS MAT TEX
8441	— MENS SHIRTS							N 986517	3184	CHEMISES HOMMES MAT TEXT
84411	—— OF COTTON							N 919309	2995	CHEMISES HOMMES DE COTON
845	OUTERWEAR KNIT NONELASTC							N 349382	9385	VET DESSOUS,ACCES BONNET
8451	— JERSEYS,PULLOVERS ETC							N 192273	8686	CHANDAILS,PULL-OVERS ETC

1. HISTORICAL SERIES, 1958–1993 SPECIAL TRADE, IMPORTS C.I.F., EXPORTS F.O.B.
SERIES HISTORIQUES, 1958–1993 COMMERCE SPECIAL, IMPORTATIONS C.A.F., EXPORTATIONS F.O.B

YEAR ANNEE	VALUE IN MILLION E.C. DOLLARS VALEUR EN MILLION E.C. DOLLARS MERCHANDISE –MARCHANDISE		GOLD –OR		CONVERSION FACTORS U.S. CENTS PER E.C. DOLLAR FACTEURS DE CONVERSION CENTS E.U. PAR E.C. DOLLAR		INDEX NUMBERS –INDICES QUANTUM		UNIT VALUE VALEUR UNITAIRE	
	IMPORTS	EXPORTS	IMPORTS	EXPORTS	IMPORTS	EXPORTS	IMPORTS	EXPORTS	IMPORTS	EXPORTS
1958	1.54	0.38			58.3300	58.3300				
1959	8.50				58.3300					
1960	1.98	0.27			58.3300	58.3300				
1961	2.14	0.31			58.3300	58.3300				
1962	2.54	0.55			58.3300	58.3300				
1963	2.76	0.33			58.3300	58.3300				
1964	4.02	0.32			58.3300	58.3300				
1965	4.89	0.27			58.3300	58.3300				
1967	6.92	0.23			57.6500	57.6500				
1968	7.73	0.24			50.0000	50.0000				
1970	8.81	0.45			50.0000	50.0000				
1971	8.86	0.30			50.7166	50.7166				
1972	12.08	0.37			52.1216	52.1216				
1973	12.15	0.69			51.0860	51.0860				
1974	15.97	1.05			48.7301	48.7301				
1975	16.54	1.02			46.2878	46.2878				
1976	20.80	1.12			38.0480	38.0480				
1977	18.93	1.64			37.0370	37.0370				
1978	26.93	3.71			37.0370	37.0370				
1979	32.32	2.09			37.0370	37.0370				
1980	44.55	3.20			37.0370	37.0370				
1981	51.00	5.97			37.0370	37.0370				
1982	54.87	6.98			37.0370	37.0370				
1983	53.80	12.33			37.0370	37.0370				
1984	47.26	8.51			37.0370	37.0370				
1985	49.59	7.82			37.0370	37.0370				
1987	68.20	9.50			37.0370	37.0370				
1988	71.70	6.20			37.0370	37.0370				
1989	100.00	3.40			37.0370	37.0370				
1990	130.00	4.00			37.0370	37.0370				
1991	95.00	2.78			37.0370	37.0370				
1992	91.52	4.52			37.0370	37.0370				
1993	75.59	1.55			37.0370	37.0370				

2. IMPORTS BY BROAD ECONOMIC CATEGORY AND EXPORTS BY INDUSTRIAL ORIGIN. (PERCENTAGE OF TOTAL VALUE)
IMPORTATIONS PAR CATEGORIES ECONOMIQUES ET EXPORTATIONS PAR BRANCHE D'ACTIVITE.(EN POURCENTAGE DE LA VALEUR TOTALE)

IMPORTS – IMPORTATIONS

	1990	1991	1992	1993	1994	1995	1996
TOTAL IMPORTS–IMPORTATIONS TOTALES							
1 FOOD BEV–ALIMENTATION BOISSONS							
11 PRIMARY–PRODUITS DE BASE							
111 FOR INDUSTRY–POUR L'INDUSTRIE							
112 FOR HOUSEHOLDS–POUR LES MENAGES							
12 PROCESSED–PRODUITS ELABORES							
121 FOR INDUSTRY–POUR L'INDUSTRIE							
122 FOR HOUSEHOLDS–POUR LES MENAGES							
2 IND SUPPLIES–APPROV INDUSTRIELS							
21 PRIMARY–PRODUITS DE BASE							
22 PROCESSED–PRODUITS ELABORES							
3 FUELS–COMBUSTIBLES							
31 PRIMARY–PRODUITS DE BASE							
32 PROCESSED–PRODUITS ELABORES							
321 MOTOR SPIRIT–ESSENCE							
322 OTHER–AUTRES							
4 MACHINERY–EQUIPEMENT							
41 CAPITAL EQUIPMENT–MACHINES							
42 PARTS–PIECES ACCESSOIRES							
5 TRANSPORT–TRANSPORT							
51 PASSENGER CARS–AUTOMOBILES							
52 OTHER–AUTRES							
521 INDUSTRIAL–INDUSTRIELS							
522 NON INDUSTRIAL–NON INDUSTRIEL							
53 PARTS–PIECES ACCESSOIRES							
6 CONSUM GOODS–BIENS CONSOMMATION							
61 DURABLE–DURABLES							
62 SEMI DURABLE–SEMI DURABLES							
63 NON DURABLE–NON DURABLES							
7 GOODS NES–BIENS NDA							

EXPORTS – EXPORTATIONS

	1990	1991	1992	1993	1994	1995	1996
TOTAL EXPORTS–EXPORTATIONS TOTALES				100.			
1 AGRICULTURE				0.3			
2 MINING QUARRY–INDUS EXTRACTIVES							
3 MANUFACTURING–IND MANUFACTUR				99.1			
31 FOOD BEV TOBACCO–ALIM BOISS TAB				8.7			
32 TEXTILES–INDUSTRIES TEXTILES				3.8			
33 WOOD & PRODUCTS–BOIS & PRODUITS				1.4			
34 PAPER & PRODUCTS–PAPIER & PRODT				0.5			
35 CHEMICALS–INDUSTRIES CHIMIQUES				9.6			
36 NON METAL MIN–MIN NON METAL				1.2			
37 BASIC METAL–IND METAL BASE							
38 METAL MANUF–MANUF METAL				73.9			
39 OTH MANUF IND–AUTRES MANUF							

3. TRADE BY PRINCIPAL COUNTRIES OF ORIGIN AND LAST DESTINATION (VALUE IN THOUSAND U.S. DOLLARS)
ECHANGES SELON LES PRINCIPAUX PAYS D'ORIGINE ET DE DERNIERE DESTINATION (VALEUR EN MILLIERS DE DOLLARS EU)

COUNTRIES–PAYS	SPECIAL IMPORTS C.I.F. IMPORTATIONS SPECIALES C.A.F				
	1989	1990	1991	1992	1993
World	31547	43956	38786		28000
Africa					1
Americas	5567	7632	9527		21880
Northern America					13846
LAIA					604
CACM					6
Caribbean	5552	7597	9491		7030
Rest of America	15	35	36		394
As.ex F.USSR					883
Eur.x F.USSR					4689
EU					4686
EFTA					1
East Europe					1
Other Europe					1
Former USSR					
Oceania					1
Trinidad and Tobago	2763	3826	6442		4486
USA/Etats–Unis d'Amer					13347
United Kingdom					4048
Barbados/Barbade	839	889	673		432
Saint Lucia/St. Lucie	517	749	731		349
St Vincent & Grenadines	407	551	401		451
Jamaica/Jamaïque	511	408	404		373
Saint–Kitts–Nevis	297	313	420		269
Antigua and Barbuda	193	710	216		144
Japan/Japon					796
Canada					499
Dominica/Dominique	24	146	166		89
United States Virg Is					348
Colombia/Colombie					295
Suriname/Suriname					240
Netherlands/Pays–Bas					193
Venezuela					189
Germany/Allemagne					171
Denmark/Danemark					125

COUNTRIES–PAYS	SPECIAL EXPORTS F.O.B. EXPORTATIONS SPECIALES F.O.B.				
	1989	1990	1991	1992	1993
Monde	1633	1909	1499		574
Afrique					
Amériques	453	180	237		572
Amérique du Nord	369	134	157		373
ALAI					
MCAC					
Caraïbes	84	47	80		200
Autre Amérique					
Asie l'URSS exclus					2
Europe l'URSS exclus	8	4			
UE	8	4			
AELE					
Europe de l'Est					
Autre de l'Europe					
Ancienne URSS					
Océanie					
USA/Etats–Unis d'Amer	368	108	146		373
Antigua and Barbuda	32	23	28		105
Saint–Kitts–Nevis	20	20	51		58
Canada	0	26	11		
Barbados/Barbade	10				13
St Vincent & Grenadines	14	1			2
Dominica/Dominique	5	2			7
Saint Lucia/St. Lucie	2	1	1		9
United Kingdom	8	4			

(VALUE AS PERCENTAGE OF WORLD TOTAL)(VALEURS EN POURCENTAGE DU TOTAL MONDIAL)

	1984	1985	1986	1987	1988	1989	1990	1991	1992	1993
Africa										0.0
Americas						17.6	17.4	24.6		78.1
Northern America										49.4
LAIA										2.2
CACM										0.0
Caribbean						17.6	17.3	24.5		25.1
Rest of America						0.0	0.1	0.1		1.4
As.ex F.USSR										3.2
Eur.x F.USSR										16.7
EU										16.7
EFTA										0.0
East Europe										0.0
Other Europe										0.0
Former USSR										
Oceania										0.0
Trinidad and Tobago						8.8	8.7	16.6		16.0
USA/Etats–Unis d'Amer										47.7
United Kingdom										14.5
Barbados/Barbade						2.7	2.0	1.7		1.5
Saint Lucia/St. Lucie						1.6	1.7	1.9		1.2
St Vincent & Grenadines						1.3	1.3	1.0		1.6
Jamaica/Jamaïque						1.6	0.9	1.0		1.3
Saint–Kitts–Nevis						0.9	0.7	1.1		1.0
Antigua and Barbuda						0.6	1.6	0.6		0.5
Japan/Japon										2.8

	1984	1985	1986	1987	1988	1989	1990	1991	1992	1993
Afrique										
Amériques						27.7	9.4	15.8		99.7
Amérique du Nord						22.6	7.0	10.5		64.9
ALAI										
MCAC										
Caraïbes						5.2	2.4	5.4		34.8
Autre Amérique										
Asie l'URSS exclus										0.3
Europe l'URSS exclus						0.5	0.2			
UE						0.5	0.2			
AELE										
Europe de l'Est										
Autre de l'Europe										
Ancienne URSS										
Océanie										
USA/Etats–Unis d'Amer						22.5	5.7	9.7		64.9
Antigua and Barbuda						2.0	1.2	1.9		18.3
Saint–Kitts–Nevis						1.2	1.0	3.4		10.1
Canada						0.0	1.3	0.7		
Barbados/Barbade						0.6				2.2
St Vincent & Grenadines						0.9	0.1			0.4
Dominica/Dominique						0.3	0.1			1.2
Saint Lucia/St. Lucie						0.1	0.0	0.1		1.6
United Kingdom						0.5	0.2			

4. Special Imports C.I.F. by Commodities according to the S.I.T.C. (Rev. 2) in thousand U.S. Dollars
Importations Spéciales C.A.F. par Produits d'après la C.T.C.I. (Rév. 2) en milliers de Dollars E.U.

SITC CTCI	COMMODITY	1990		1991		1992		1993		PRODUIT
		WEIGHT POIDS	VALUE VALEUR	WEIGHT POIDS	VALUE VALEUR	WEIGHT POIDS	VALUE VALEUR	WEIGHT POIDS	VALUE VALEUR	
	ALL COMMODITIES		43956		38786				28000	TOUS PRODUITS
0	FOOD AND LIVE ANIMALS		6839		6236				5224	ALIMENTS,ANIMAUX VIVANTS
1	BEVERAGES AND TOBACCO		3178		2959				2329	BOISSONS ET TABACS
2	CRUDE MATERLS,EXCL FUELS		1688		756				477	MAT BRUTES NON COMESTIBLES
3	MINERAL FUELS ETC		4632		5876				4804	COMBUSTIBLES MINERAUX LUB
4	ANIMAL,VEGETABLE OIL,FAT		124		115				103	HUILES,GRAISSES ANIM,VEG
5	CHEMCLS,RELATED PROD NES		2585		2421				1801	PRODUITS CHIMIQUES
6	BASIC MANUFACTURES		9099		7206				4513	ART MANUFACTURES
7	MACHINES,TRANSPORT EQUIP		11493		9315				4078	MACHINES MATERIEL TRANSPORT
8	MISC MANUFACTURED GOODS		3977		3621				2335	ART MANUFACTURES DIVERS
9	GOODS NOT CLASSD BY KIND		341		280				2337	ART TRANSACT NON CLASSES

Montserrat

5. Special Exports F.O.B. by Commodities according to the S.I.T.C. (Rev. 2) in thousand U.S. Dollars
Exportations Spéciales F.O.B. par Produits d'après la C.T.C.I. (Rév. 2) en milliers de Dollars E.U.

SITC CTCI	COMMODITY	1990		1991		1992		1993		PRODUIT
		WEIGHT POIDS	VALUE VALEUR	WEIGHT POIDS	VALUE VALEUR	WEIGHT POIDS	VALUE VALEUR	WEIGHT POIDS	VALUE VALEUR	
	ALL COMMODITIES		1909		1499				574	TOUS PRODUITS
0	FOOD AND LIVE ANIMALS		6		13				6	ALIMENTS,ANIMAUX VIVANTS
01	MEAT AND PREPARATIONS								4	VIANDES ET PREPARATIONS
011	MEAT FRESH,CHILLD,FROZEN							W 1	4	VIANDES FRAICHES,REF,CONGE
0114	POULTRY FRESH CHLLD,FRZN							W 1	4	VOLAILLES MORTES
1	BEVERAGES AND TOBACCO		11		41				46	BOISSONS ET TABACS
11	BEVERAGES								46	BOISSONS
112	ALCOHOLIC BEVERAGES							W 18	46	BOISSONS ALCOOLIQUES
1124	DISTILLED ALCOHOLIC BEVS							W 18	46	ALCOOLS,EAUX-DE-VIE
11249	OTH ALCOHOLC BEVS,CMPNDS							W 18	46	BOISSONS ALCOOLIQUES NDA
2	CRUDE MATERLS,EXCL FUELS		14		3					MAT BRUTES NON COMESTIBLES
3	MINERAL FUELS ETC		11							COMBUSTIBLES MINERAUX LUB
5	CHEMCLS,RELATED PROD NES		18		13				6	PRODUITS CHIMIQUES
55	PERFUME,CLEANING ETC PRD								6	PROD POUR PARFUM,TOILETTE
551	ESSENTL OILS,PERFUME,ETC							W 2	6	HUILES ESSENTIELLES
5513	ESSENTL OIL,RESINOID,ETC							W 2	6	HUILES ESSENTIELLES,RESIN
6	BASIC MANUFACTURES		149		53				18	ART MANUFACTURES
63	WOOD,CORK MANUFACTRS NES								8	OUVRAGES LIEGE ET BOIS
635	WOOD MANUFACTURES NES								8	ART MANUF EN BOIS NDA
6359	OTHER WOOD MANUFACTURES								8	OUVRAGES EN BOIS NDA
63591	TOOLS,HANDLES ETC WOOD								8	OUTILS MANCHES D'OUTILS
66	NONMETAL MINERAL MFS NES								7	ART MIN NON METALLIQUES
663	MINERAL MANUFCTURES NES							W 1	2	ART MIN MANUF NDA
666	POTTERY								4	POTERIE
6666	CERAMIC ORNAMENTS ETC								4	OBJETS PORCELAINE,CERAM
7	MACHINES,TRANSPORT EQUIP		653		463				397	MACHINES MATERIEL TRANSPORT
74	GENRL INDUSTRL MACHY NES								3	MACH APP INDUSTRIE
741	HEATING,COOLING EQUIPMNT								3	MACH CHAUFFAGE,PIECES
7415	AIR–CONDITIONING MACHNRY								3	GROUPES CONDITION AIR
77	ELECTRIC MACHNRY NES ETC								366	MACH APP ELECT NDA
778	ELECTRICAL MACHINERY NES							W 7	366	AUTRES MACH ELECT NDA
7782	ELECTRIC LAMPS,BULBS								2	LAMPES, TUBES ELECTRIQUES
77822	ELEC DISCHARGE LAMPS NES								2	LAMPES NON ULTRA–VIOLETS
7783	AUTOMOTIVE ELECTR EQUIP							W 7	364	EQUIP ELECT MOTEURS EXPL
78	ROAD VEHICLES								29	VEHICULES ROUTIERS
784	MOTOR VEH PRTS,ACCES NES							W 3	29	PIECES 722,781,782,783
7849	OTHER MOTOR VEHCL PARTS							W 3	29	PIECES 722,781,782,783
8	MISC MANUFACTURED GOODS		740		403				101	ART MANUFACTURES DIVERS
812	*PLUMBG,HEATNG,LGHTNG EQ							W 2	26	APPAR SANITAIRES CHAUFFAGE
8124	LIGHTING EQUIPMENT NES							W 2	26	APPAREILS ECLAIRAGE ETC
81242	LAMPS,FITTINGS BASE METL							W 2	26	APPAREILS D'ECLAIRAGE
84	CLOTHING AND ACCESSORIES								22	VETEMENTS
846	UNDER GARMENTS KNITTED								22	SOUS VETS DE BONNETERIE
8462	— OF COTTON NON ELASTIC								22	SOUS–VET BONNET COTON
84629	—— OTHER								22	AUT SOUS–VET BONNET COTON
89	MISC MANUFCTRD GOODS NES								52	ART MANUFACTURES DIVERS
892	PRINTED MATTER								2	IMPRIMES
8921	PRINTED BOOKS,GLOBES,ETC								2	LIVRES,BROCHURES,CARTES
89211	PRINTED BOOKS,PAMPHLETS								2	LIVRES,BROCHURES
893	ARTICLES OF PLASTIC NES							W 10	49	OUVRAGES EN MAT DIVIS 58
8931	PLSTC PACKG CONTNRS,LIDS							W 10	49	ART TRANSP EMBALLAGE ETC
9	GOODS NOT CLASSD BY KIND		307		510					ART TRANSACT NON CLASSES

1. HISTORICAL SERIES, 1961–1996 SPECIAL TRADE, IMPORTS C.I.F., EXPORTS F.O.B.
SERIES HISTORIQUES, 1961–1996 COMMERCE SPECIAL, IMPORTATIONS C.A.F., EXPORTATIONS F.O.B

YEAR ANNEE	VALUE IN MILLION MOR. DIRHAMS / VALEUR EN MILLION MOR. DIRHAMS — MERCHANDISE –MARCHANDISE IMPORTS	MERCHANDISE –MARCHANDISE EXPORTS	GOLD –OR IMPORTS	GOLD –OR EXPORTS	CONVERSION FACTORS U.S. CENTS PER MOR. DIRHAM / FACTEURS DE CONVERSION CENTS E.U. PAR MOR. DIRHAM IMPORTS	CONVERSION FACTORS EXPORTS	INDEX NUMBERS –INDICES QUANTUM IMPORTS	QUANTUM EXPORTS	UNIT VALUE / VALEUR UNITAIRE IMPORTS	UNIT VALUE EXPORTS
1961	2225.00	1731.30	19.80		19.7600	19.7600	69	47	27	22
1962	2139.30	1762.50	6.80		19.7600	19.7600	68	50	26	21
1963	2235.60	1942.80	7.00		19.7600	19.7600	69	50	27	23
1964	2308.40	2185.80	14.40		19.7600	19.7600	63	56	30	23
1965	2250.80	2176.30	10.40		19.7600	19.7600	57	52	33	25
1966	2406.30	2168.10	6.10		19.7600	19.7600	68	51	29	25
1967	2616.50	2146.40	3.30		19.7600	19.7600	78	57	28	23
1968	2778.40	2278.00	4.70		19.7600	19.7600	81	56	28	24
1969	2835.20	2455.00	1.80		19.7600	19.7600	83	61	28	24
1970	3463.10	2471.10	7.70		19.7600	19.7600	32	38	29	24
1971	3537.10	2532.80	4.70		19.8140	19.8298	31	39	30	25
1972	3577.40	2952.90	10.60		21.7647	21.7547	29	45	32	25
1973	4683.60	3745.90			24.4186	24.2819	34	55	24	19
1974	8258.00	7439.90			22.9421	22.9355	41	52	33	40
1975	10399.00	6536.00			24.6947	24.7377	51	40	35	43
1976	11553.00	5579.30			22.6556	22.6214	57	46	34	33
1977	14400.00	5859.00			22.1783	22.1843	91	51	27	31
1978	12362.00	6261.10			24.0263	24.1392	70	43		
1979	14327.70	7622.00			25.6726	25.6996	73	44		
1980	16792.60	9645.00			24.9190	24.9190	69	44		
1981	22455.00	12002.60			19.3984	19.3314	61	56	63	59
1982	25990.20	12439.70			16.6059	16.5491	68	55	66	61
1983	25591.20	14724.20			14.0632	14.0048	58	61	75	65
1984	34395.50	19109.50			11.3583	11.3655	65	64	91	81
1985	38674.90	21740.00			9.9534	9.9586	66	66	102	90
1986	34604.00	22103.01			10.9912	11.0080	66	66	91	91
1987	35271.01	23390.00			11.9914	12.0020	68	72	89	88
1988	39133.01	29751.01			12.1962	12.1867	89	82		
1989	46594.00	28271.01			11.7883	11.8023	87	92	91	96
1990	57021.01	35135.01			12.1455	12.1395	100	100	100	100
1991	59720.00	37283.01			11.5440	11.4938	112	108	96	100
1992	62804.00	33954.00			11.7120	11.7120	128	101	92	95
1993	66576.00	31839.01			10.7583	10.7657	120	105	101	95
1994	66119.01	36815.01			10.8712	10.8800	96	115	114	94
1995	72868.99	40240.00			11.7222	11.7268				128
1996	84688.00	60210.00			11.4690	11.4659				125

2. IMPORTS BY BROAD ECONOMIC CATEGORY AND EXPORTS BY INDUSTRIAL ORIGIN. (PERCENTAGE OF TOTAL VALUE)
IMPORTATIONS PAR CATEGORIES ECONOMIQUES ET EXPORTATIONS PAR BRANCHE D'ACTIVITE.(EN POURCENTAGE DE LA VALEUR TOTALE)

IMPORTS – IMPORTATIONS

	1990	1991	1992	1993	1994	1995	1996
TOTAL IMPORTS–IMPORTATIONS TOTALES	100.	100.	100.	100.	100.	100.	100.
1 FOOD BEV–ALIMENTATION BOISSONS	8.7	8.7	12.2	14.2	12.3	16.7	16.1
11 PRIMARY–PRODUITS DE BASE	4.7	4.7	7.5	9.1	6.5	10.8	9.9
111 FOR INDUSTRY–POUR L'INDUSTRIE	3.1	3.3	5.9	7.3	4.8	8.5	8.3
112 FOR HOUSEHOLDS–POUR LES MENAGES	1.6	1.4	1.6	1.9	1.8	2.4	1.6
12 PROCESSED–PRODUITS ELABORES	4.0	4.0	4.8	5.1	5.7	5.9	6.2
121 FOR INDUSTRY–POUR L'INDUSTRIE	2.5	2.5	2.7	3.3	3.9	4.0	4.3
122 FOR HOUSEHOLDS–POUR LES MENAGES	1.5	1.4	2.1	1.8	1.8	1.9	1.9
2 IND SUPPLIES–APPROV INDUSTRIELS	39.8	41.6	38.6	36.5	39.2	40.6	38.4
21 PRIMARY–PRODUITS DE BASE	7.8	7.6	6.9	6.0	5.7	7.5	6.5
22 PROCESSED–PRODUITS ELABORES	32.1	33.9	31.6	30.5	33.5	33.2	31.9
3 FUELS–COMBUSTIBLES	16.7	14.3	15.1	14.1	15.2	13.5	15.2
31 PRIMARY–PRODUITS DE BASE	16.2	13.4	14.3	12.7	12.7	12.1	13.5
32 PROCESSED–PRODUITS ELABORES	0.5	0.9	0.9	1.4	2.5	1.4	1.7
321 MOTOR SPIRIT–ESSENCE	0.0	0.0	0.0	0.6	1.6	0.7	0.3
322 OTHER–AUTRES	0.5	0.8	0.8	0.8	0.8	0.7	1.4
4 MACHINERY–EQUIPEMENT	19.2	20.1	20.4	21.8	18.3	16.5	16.9
41 CAPITAL EQUIPMENT–MACHINES	15.9	16.8	17.8	19.9	16.5	14.7	14.6
42 PARTS–PIECES ACCESSOIRES	3.3	3.3	2.6	1.9	1.8	1.8	2.3
5 TRANSPORT–TRANSPORT	10.4	9.8	8.1	7.0	8.7	6.6	6.8
51 PASSENGER CARS–AUTOMOBILES	1.6	1.9	1.3	1.2	1.2	1.1	2.2
52 OTHER–AUTRES	6.3	4.9	3.8	3.7	5.2	3.4	2.2
521 INDUSTRIAL–INDUSTRIELS	6.2	4.8	3.7	3.6	5.1	3.4	2.1
522 NON INDUSTRIAL–NON INDUSTRIEL	0.1	0.1	0.1	0.1	0.1	0.0	0.1
53 PARTS–PIECES ACCESSOIRES	2.5	3.0	3.0	2.2	2.3	2.1	2.4
6 CONSUM GOODS–BIENS CONSOMMATION	5.0	5.4	5.4	6.1	6.2	6.0	6.7
61 DURABLE–DURABLES	1.3	1.3	1.1	1.2	1.2	1.5	1.9
62 SEMI DURABLE–SEMI DURABLES	1.5	1.7	1.8	2.0	1.9	2.1	2.1
63 NON DURABLE–NON DURABLES	2.2	2.4	2.5	2.9	3.0	2.5	2.8
7 GOODS NES–BIENS NDA	0.1	0.1	0.1	0.2	0.1	0.1	0.0

EXPORTS – EXPORTATIONS

	1990	1991	1992	1993	1994	1995	1996
TOTAL EXPORTS–EXPORTATIONS TOTALES	100.	100.	100.	100.	100.	100.	100.
1 AGRICULTURE	17.8	21.1	19.8	20.1	20.9	23.1	24.2
2 MINING QUARRY–INDUS EXTRACTIVES	12.9	10.6	10.3	9.5	10.4	9.3	10.5
3 MANUFACTURING–IND MANUFACTUR	69.3	68.3	69.9	70.5	68.8	67.7	65.2
31 FOOD BEV TOBACCO–ALIM BOISS TAB	10.0	9.0	9.0	8.5	9.5	10.3	10.5
32 TEXTILES–INDUSTRIES TEXTILES	24.7	25.2	27.4	27.9	25.0	23.2	22.7
33 WOOD & PRODUCTS–BOIS & PRODUITS	0.7	0.5	0.7	0.9	0.9	0.8	0.8
34 PAPER & PRODUCTS–PAPIER & PRODT	1.4	1.0	1.3	0.9	1.7	1.8	1.0
35 CHEMICALS–INDUSTRIES CHIMIQUES	23.6	23.1	22.3	22.9	23.2	23.9	22.7
36 NON METAL MIN–MIN NON METAL	0.6	0.6	0.6	0.7	0.9	0.9	1.0
37 BASIC METAL–IND METAL BASE	2.0	1.6	1.4	1.6	1.7	1.8	2.0
38 METAL MANUF–MANUF METAL	6.0	6.9	6.9	6.8	5.4	4.6	4.1
39 OTH MANUF IND–AUTRES MANUF	0.2	0.2	0.3	0.3	0.4	0.4	0.4

3. TRADE BY PRINCIPAL COUNTRIES OF PRODUCTION AND LAST CONSIGNMENT (VALUE IN THOUSAND U.S. DOLLARS)
ECHANGES SELON LES PRINCIPAUX PAYS DE PRODUCTION ET DE DERNIERE CONSIGNATION (VALEUR EN MILLIERS DE DOLLARS EU)

COUNTRIES–PAYS	SPECIAL IMPORTS C.I.F. IMPORTATIONS SPECIALES C.A.F				
	1992	1993	1994	1995	1996
World	7355618	6658856	7193691	8540491	8253885
Africa	427989	331228	507091	500733	661377
Americas	842452	1021461	1020979	1080679	1242465
Northern America	591812	774911	683709	721851	793217
LAIA	223591	217082	251776	344710	423502
CACM	4674	8471	12188	10035	9694
Caribbean	21435	20285	73011	2909	7000
Rest of America	940	711	294	1175	9053
As.ex F.USSR	1468357	1188094	1167308	1342150	1248085
Eur.x F.USSR	4470695	4008687	4328046	5209602	4746831
EU	4176500	3793288	4063454	4789617	4467783
EFTA	118128	91790	106864	119936	106476
East Europe	149989	117873	150984	292323	150902
Other Europe	247	287	208	1689	457
Former USSR	102593	85591	129856	378073	292362
Oceania	37804	22908	39692	28269	62704
France, Monac	1750719	1528796	1626807	1865610	1720768
Spain/Espagne	627857	699291	631408	728483	723244
USA/Etats–Unis d'Amer	434938	672342	620434	559149	612056
Italy/Italie	457040	417852	485706	489307	590400
Germany/Allemagne	436526	395282	506697	534921	501771
Saudi Arabia	405062	373780	384959	449047	491204
United Kingdom	201499	180745	202075	311538	231864
Belgium–Luxembourg	199404	154319	166036	238327	186506
Brazil/Brésil	152203	143619	150600	241550	248848
Netherlands/Pays–Bas	179245	145599	156168	207127	163724
Russian Federation	102593	83305	110059	284798	234336
Iran (Islamic Rp. of)	171903	166867	195151	207693	57942
China/Chine	145964	125738	123639	166343	145708
Sweden/Suède	132929	119198	126135	175526	118969
Japan/Japon	154217	114065	122356	124274	152277
Canada	156873	102569	63275	162703	179407
Algeria/Algérie	91217	107924	119313	111295	102167
United Arab Emirates	259827	110938	86530	17271	3340
Switz.Liecht	102843	74982	89204	92835	92610
Poland/Pologne	84062	69092	85795	134458	66210
Libyan Arab Jamahiriya	101940	17271	82645	55622	139106
Argentina/Argentine	37747	50445	74447	44264	134104
Portugal	53015	51310	59191	68098	85201
Nigeria/Nigéria	4090	21252	10485	61893	216565
Turkey/Turquie	86841	23617	42169	82288	57194
Korea, Republic of	42381	37175	27210	44577	59712
Finland/Finlande	48434	30228	33667	51641	45905
Gabon	22221	24365	85382	53287	20465
Tunisia/Tunisie	50843	36494	29054	32933	42220
Romania/Roumanie	26127	24661	33853	51940	50218
Denmark/Danemark	33587	25546	22968	46216	38002
Cameroon/Cameroun	69649	39861	34389	8295	8474
Kuwait/ Koweït	35893	80402	16041	10321	7097
New Zealand	33200	19929	22234	26072	39239
Cote d'Ivoire	26665	23760	29797	32775	25875
Ukraine		2114	15322	71309	46598
India/Inde	18402	20346	15955	25437	52273
Austria/Autriche	30953	16742	20794	27897	27150
Indonesia/Indonésie	16289	20493	30881	28801	25749
So. Africa Customs Un	1180	11047	46630	29287	32496
Benin/Bénin	19150	21097	24609	24097	25888
Hong Kong	19424	19121	21397	22576	23584
Syrian Arab Republic	10081	7693	17397	42329	23150
Ireland/Irlande	14924	19214	13852	27800	20821
Singapore/Singapour	14779	16874	12955	19743	27116
Norway,SVD,JM	15068	16803	17271	27046	13705
Egypt/Egypte	9530	10898	13042	37249	14093
Dominican Republic	10382	1654	65150	2375	5047
Bulgaria/Bulgarie	5947	3942	4672	53204	12603
Czech Republic		15860	23098	25517	14274

COUNTRIES–PAYS	SPECIAL EXPORTS F.O.B. EXPORTATIONS SPECIALES F.O.B.				
	1992	1993	1994	1995	1996
Monde	3977245	3695950	4034592	4718882	4741881
Afrique	352691	372642	308101	379288	346220
Amériques	248084	232821	239144	286858	314394
Amérique du Nord	172787	148942	160573	189491	201352
ALAI	65075	81053	74953	94443	111270
MCAC	673	290	628	488	950
Caraïbes	3888	2168	2382	1948	785
Autre Amérique	5661	368	607	488	36
Asie l'URSS exclus	668816	620794	759360	933122	963085
Europe l'URSS exclus	2670662	2433097	2673530	3047248	3031209
UE	2582360	2344316	2580488	2928568	2915614
AELE	41953	38075	41981	56039	47470
Europe de l'Est	29395	35614	36501	48315	52252
Autre de l'Europe	1750	4273	1233	1989	1163
Ancienne URSS	821	3484	13392	22766	34947
Océanie	13449	18702	23296	23169	39010
France, Monac	1303505	1227517	1279212	1400163	1343947
Spain/Espagne	359069	326646	373826	443111	468886
Japan/Japon	196542	217300	268109	361759	329541
India/Inde	237033	143637	258199	309635	299033
Italy/Italie	221847	193236	231081	268715	298936
Germany/Allemagne	187973	163374	172616	193918	185073
United Kingdom	133194	133763	155420	211358	183457
USA/Etats–Unis d'Amer	149007	126003	141740	159682	164173
Belgium–Luxembourg	137730	110303	135297	146647	167022
Libyan Arab Jamahiriya	131230	136892	99010	161489	125231
Netherlands/Pays–Bas	124377	96561	118219	114098	127433
Algeria/Algérie	71711	77782	96623	55958	35428
Saudi Arabia	65402	48287	54682	60588	62038
Tunisia/Tunisie	49554	39297	41866	52996	59285
Turkey/Turquie	29826	41459	33727	47165	76993
Mexico/Mexique	30972	39036	34108	37659	56734
Portugal	34798	25823	38910	49564	43673
Iran (Islamic Rp. of)	25402	53987	49468	22546	35973
Brazil/Brésil	22230	28569	30482	42969	28277
Ireland/Irlande	26243	17373	28981	39488	31040
Canada	23780	22939	18833	29809	37178
Indonesia/Indonésie	32171	28836	31451	16648	20037
Switz.Liecht	18032	19371	26039	38518	27060
China/Chine	30714	24095	14540	38503	16630
Poland/Pologne	16710	15530	22932	31928	33212
Pakistan	4188	24326	3065	21257	52600
Norway,SVD,JM	23376	18703	15931	17516	20373
Greece/Grèce	13358	11092	13762	20368	23898
New Zealand	9573	10371	12502	14207	29626
Sweden/Suède	16887	14483	10352	16573	16533
Russian Federation	821	2793	11891	15965	30374
Cote d'Ivoire	5949	7233	7155	19271	19603
Finland/Finlande	9220	13457	8638	13408	11589
Croatia/Croatie		10736	13298	11979	14646
Korea, Republic of	9894	6788	10331	10551	11221
Nigeria/Nigéria	12077	8993	10133	7926	9450
Austria/Autriche	9183	8702	11098	7397	10554
Romania/Roumanie	10721	13800	6450	7152	7272
Liberia/Libéria	86	41796	153	145	196
Australia/Australie	3650	8077	10451	8545	8989
Syrian Arab Republic	150	7333	8248	8090	15655
Gabon	7832	9204	5534	6982	8468
Mauritania/Mauritanie	6971	6898	7434	7718	8933
Guinea/Guinée	7668	6268	6290	11263	6188
Jordan/Jordanie	5568	4596	4993	8524	11126
Senegal/Sénégal	5978	4144	3188	5311	15049
Mali	5927	5524	3791	6675	8016
Dem. Rep. of the Congo	3153	4086	5141	8707	6885
Venezuela	7833	4396	3280	5571	5130
Argentina/Argentine	2708	2388	723	4828	15481

(VALUE AS PERCENTAGE OF WORLD TOTAL)(VALEURS EN POURCENTAGE DU TOTAL MONDIAL)

	1987	1988	1989	1990	1991	1992	1993	1994	1995	1996
Africa	3.2	2.1	2.6	5.8	6.0	5.8	5.0	7.0	5.9	8.0
Americas	17.2	17.7	13.0	11.8	12.6	11.5	15.3	14.2	12.7	15.1
Northern America	13.6	12.1	9.6	8.6	9.1	8.0	11.6	9.5	8.5	9.6
LAIA	3.2	5.0	2.8	2.8	3.2	3.0	3.3	3.5	4.0	5.1
CACM	0.0	0.1	0.1	0.0	0.0	0.1	0.1	0.2	0.1	0.1
Caribbean	0.3	0.4	0.3	0.3	0.2	0.3	0.3	1.0	0.0	0.1
Rest of America	0.0	0.1	0.2	0.1	0.0	0.0	0.0	0.0	0.0	0.1
As.ex F.USSR	17.4	17.1	17.9	17.7	16.4	20.0	17.8	16.2	15.7	15.1
Eur.x F.USSR	59.1	60.4	62.8	61.8	62.6	60.8	60.2	60.2	61.0	57.5
EU	55.1	55.0	57.9	57.2	58.6	56.8	57.0	56.5	56.1	54.1
EFTA	1.4	1.8	1.9	1.7	1.6	1.6	1.4	1.5	1.4	1.3
East Europe	2.2	3.1	2.5	2.6	2.1	2.0	1.8	2.1	3.4	1.8
Other Europe	0.4	0.6	0.5	0.3	0.3	0.0	0.0	0.0	0.0	0.0
Former USSR	2.9	2.4	3.5	2.7	2.1	1.4	1.3	1.8	4.4	3.5
Oceania	0.2	0.2	0.1	0.1	0.1	0.5	0.3	0.6	0.3	0.8
France, Monac	21.8	22.2	24.4	22.9	24.2	23.8	23.0	22.6	21.8	20.8
Spain/Espagne	8.8	7.8	8.7	8.4	8.3	8.5	10.5	8.8	8.5	8.8
USA/Etats–Unis d'Amer	9.1	7.0	6.8	6.3	5.8	5.9	10.1	8.6	6.5	7.4
Italy/Italie	5.5	5.5	6.3	6.8	6.9	6.2	6.3	6.8	5.7	7.2
Germany/Allemagne	6.7	7.1	6.2	6.3	5.9	5.9	5.9	7.0	6.3	6.1
Saudi Arabia	0.2	0.8	0.7	2.7	4.9	5.5	5.6	5.4	5.3	6.0
United Kingdom	3.0	3.0	2.6	3.5	3.4	2.7	2.7	2.8	3.6	2.8
Belgium–Luxembourg	3.0	3.1	2.8	2.6	2.9	2.7	2.3	2.3	2.8	2.3
Brazil/Brésil	1.5	1.9	1.7	1.8	2.4	2.1	2.2	2.1	2.8	3.0
Netherlands/Pays–Bas	2.4	2.4	2.4	2.2	2.6	2.4	2.2	2.2	2.4	2.0

	1987	1988	1989	1990	1991	1992	1993	1994	1995	1996
Afrique	6.9	7.2	8.1	7.8	9.9	8.9	10.1	7.6	8.0	7.3
Amériques	5.6	5.2	4.6	3.9	4.5	6.2	6.3	5.9	6.1	6.6
Amérique du Nord	2.2	2.6	2.6	2.3	3.1	4.3	4.0	4.0	4.0	4.2
ALAI	3.3	2.3	1.7	1.4	1.3	1.6	2.2	1.9	2.0	2.3
MCAC	0.0	0.1	0.0	0.0	0.0	0.0	0.0	0.0	0.0	0.0
Caraïbes	0.0	0.1	0.1	0.1	0.1	0.1	0.1	0.1	0.0	0.0
Autre Amérique	0.1	0.1	0.2	0.1	0.0	0.1	0.0	0.0	0.0	0.0
Asie l'URSS exclus	16.3	21.6	14.2	18.0	20.0	16.8	16.8	18.8	19.8	20.3
Europe l'URSS exclus	68.2	64.3	71.5	69.4	65.2	67.1	65.8	66.3	64.6	63.9
UE	62.9	57.9	65.7	65.9	63.2	64.9	63.4	64.0	62.1	61.5
AELE	1.3	1.1	1.4	1.2	1.0	1.1	1.0	1.0	1.2	1.0
Europe de l'Est	3.4	4.7	3.6	1.9	0.7	0.7	1.0	0.9	1.0	1.1
Autre de l'Europe	0.6	0.7	0.8	0.4	0.3	0.0	0.1	0.0	0.0	0.0
Ancienne URSS	1.6	0.2	0.3	0.2	0.0	0.0	0.1	0.3	0.5	0.7
Océanie	0.8	1.0	0.8	0.3	0.2	0.3	0.5	0.6	0.5	0.8
France, Monac	29.5	26.0	29.3	31.5	31.8	32.8	33.2	31.7	29.7	28.3
Spain/Espagne	6.8	7.2	8.3	9.2	8.8	9.0	8.8	9.3	9.4	9.9
Japan/Japon	4.3	4.6	4.6	3.9	5.2	4.9	5.9	6.6	7.7	6.9
India/Inde	5.4	9.2	2.0	4.6	7.0	6.0	3.9	6.4	6.6	6.3
Italy/Italie	5.5	5.6	6.3	6.9	6.2	5.6	5.2	5.7	5.7	6.3
Germany/Allemagne	6.2	5.6	5.3	5.3	4.9	4.7	4.4	4.3	4.1	3.9
United Kingdom	2.7	2.9	3.9	3.3	2.7	3.3	3.6	3.9	4.5	3.9
USA/Etats–Unis d'Amer	1.6	2.1	2.2	1.9	2.5	3.7	3.4	3.5	3.4	3.5
Belgium–Luxembourg	4.0	3.7	5.7	3.9	3.4	3.5	3.0	3.4	3.1	3.5
Libyan Arab Jamahiriya	3.3	2.7	2.5	2.8	4.6	3.3	3.7	2.5	3.4	2.6

4. Special Imports C.I.F. by Commodities according to the S.I.T.C. (Rev. 2) in thousand U.S. Dollars
Importations Spéciales C.A.F. par Produits d'après la C.T.C.I. (Rév. 2) en milliers de Dollars E.U.

SITC CTCI	COMMODITY	1993		1994		1995		1996		PRODUIT
		WEIGHT POIDS	VALUE VALEUR	WEIGHT POIDS	VALUE VALEUR	WEIGHT POIDS	VALUE VALEUR	WEIGHT POIDS	VALUE VALEUR	
	ALL COMMODITIES		6658856		7193691		8540491		8253885	TOUS PRODUITS
0	FOOD AND LIVE ANIMALS		889644		699480		1303489		1196403	ALIMENTS,ANIMAUX VIVANTS
001	*LIVE ANIMALS FOR FOOD	W 5163	16110	W 23804	53559	W 11389	37984	W 21114	61493	ANIMAUX VIVANTS
0011	BOVINE SPECIES,LIVE	W 4515	9455	W 22986	45805	W 10518	29044	W 20397	52636	ESPECE BOVINE
00111	— PURE BRED FR BREEDING	W 4515	9455	W 13956	31825	W 10479	28946	W 20396	52635	BOVINS REPRODUCTEURS
02	DAIRY PRODCTS,BIRDS'EGGS		73280		83891		96274		84038	PRODUITS LAITIERS,OEUFS
022	MILK AND CREAM	W 13202	21718	W 15798	25438	W 22215	45568	W 11594	21837	LAIT ET CREME
0224	MILK,CREAM PRESERVED ETC	W 13098	21591	W 15701	25358	W 22046	45349	W 11394	21619	LAIT,CREME CONS,CONC
02242	MILK DRY,1.5% FAT OR LES	W 6916	11817	W 12267	20972	W 18476	40919	W 9330	19130	LAIT POUDRE INF 1.5%
023	BUTTER	W 25904	48002	W 29034	53367	W 21500	45827	W 28050	56451	BEURRE
04	CEREALS AND PREPARATIONS		473700		228313		628866		623464	CEREALES ET PRODUITS
041	WHEAT ETC UNMILLED	W 2694919	351517	W 1191452	162578	W 2549113	468545	W 2240101	474454	FROMENT,EPEAUTRE
0411	DURUM WHEAT UNMILLED	W 390392	55662	W 95454	24218	W 260932	64640	W 322624	77538	FROMENT DUR NON MOULU
0412	OTHER WHEAT ETC UNMILLED	W 2304527	295855	W 1095998	138360	W 2288181	403905	W 1917476	396916	AUTRE FROMENT NON MOULU
043	BARLEY UNMILLED	W 579305	65370	W 115090	9721	W 465029	62844	W 29684	5553	ORGE NON MONDEE
044	MAIZE UNMILLED	W 354250	45055	W 364025	46342	W 548610	82886	W 542963	102455	MAIS NON MOULU
05	VEGETABLES AND FRUIT		44831		44077		102681		57736	LEGUMES ET FRUITS
054	VEG ETC FRSH,SMPLY PRSVD	W 138282	37539	W 86498	36762	W 131544	86786	W 58527	37353	LEGUMES FRAIS,CONG,SECS
0541	POTATOES FRSH EXCL SWEET	W 41293	11338	W 51276	20678	W 54387	36490	W 20066	12702	POMMES DE TERRE
0542	LEGUMINOUS VEGETBLES DRY	W 41218	18513	W 19836	8355	W 72995	39296	W 32559	19384	LEGUMES A COSSE SECS
06	SUGAR AND PREPS,HONEY		95043		129216		158466		159219	SUCRES ET PRODUITS
061	SUGAR AND HONEY	W 416793	93783	W 455453	127818	W 479158	156681	W 514099	156922	SUCRES ET MIEL
0611	RAW BEET AND CANE SUGAR	W 416002	92887	W 454615	126938	W 477250	154403	W 512290	154458	SUCRES BRUTS
07	COFFEE,TEA,COCOA,SPICES		109703		125254		158219		119042	CAFE,THE,CACAO,EPICES
071	COFFEE AND SUBSTITUTES	W 20415	23657	W 21889	38515	W 20068	60613	W 22564	44370	CAFE ET SUCCEDANES
0711	COFFEE GREEN,ROASTED,SUB	W 20295	21716	W 21833	38083	W 20042	60215	W 22520	43896	CAFE TORREFIE OU DECAFEINE
07111	COFFEE GREEN,HUSKS,SKINS	W 20271	21554	W 21809	38022	W 20015	60008	W 22478	43527	CAFE NON TORREFIE
074	TEA AND MATE	W 27142	70958	W 34027	74246	W 37628	81424	W 28399	57439	THE ET MATE
0741	TEA	W 27142	70957	W 34027	74246	W 37628	81424	W 28399	57439	THE
081	*FEEDING STUFF FOR ANIML	W 336339	60064	W 33205	11719	W 411392	83648	W 174142	51070	NOURRITURE POUR ANIMAUX
0812	BRAN,POLLARD,SHARPS,ETC	W 219657	24863	W 20829	2090	W 291482	36190	W 98022	12298	SONS
08122	BRAN,ETC OF OTHR CEREALS	W 219157	24816	W 20829	2090	W 291482	36190	W 98022	12298	SONS D'AUTRES CEREALES
0819	FOOD WASTE AND FEED NES	W 8010	15697	W 2873	5057	W 12051	29195	W 5768	17264	DECHETS,ALIMENTS NDA
1	BEVERAGES AND TOBACCO		90519		107630		82460		92460	BOISSONS ET TABACS
11	BEVERAGES		12488		17277		22798		26287	BOISSONS
112	ALCOHOLIC BEVERAGES	W 3387	11279	W 13453	16176	W 19020	21575	W 26143	25259	BOISSONS ALCOOLIQUES
12	TOBACCO AND MANUFACTURES		78032		90353		59662		66173	TABACS BRUTS FABRIQUES
122	TOBACCO,MANUFACTURED	W 3885	63977	W 4111	73767	W 1990	45563	W 1950	41867	TABACS FABRIQUES
1222	CIGARETTES	W 3830	62562	W 3970	72090	W 1953	44270	W 1780	40486	CIGARETTES
2	CRUDE MATERLS,EXCL FUELS		510280		645518		843834		681368	MAT BRUTES NON COMESTIBLES
22	OIL SEEDS,OLEAGINOUS FRT		22803		71793		83938		70737	GRAINES,FRUITS OLEAGINEUX
222	SEEDS FOR'SOFT'FIXED OIL	W 76621	20887		70384	W 249063	82353	W 199058	68449	GRAINES HUILES FIXES
2222	SOYA BEANS	W 31672	7829	W 38093	9712	W 55977	14439	W 78813	25073	FEVES DE SOJA
2224	SUNFLOWER SEEDS	W 970	569	W 144843	48659	W 142985	49293	W 75479	26497	GRAINES DE TOURNESOL
23	RUBBER, CRUDE		16166		19407		28571		23854	CAOUTCHOUC BRUT
24	CORK AND WOOD		150272		188576		229902		176871	LIEGE ET BOIS
247	OTH WOOD ROUGH,SQUARED	W 230431	44910	W 341251	60825	W 419958	66440	W 277440	51104	BOIS BRUTS EQUARRIS
2472	SAW–,VENEER–LOGS NON–CON	W 205764	39446	W 306878	53164	W 391508	59394	W 216932	37704	NON CONIFERES SCIAGE,PLAC
24721	— IN THE ROUGH	W 205764	39446	W 306878	53164	W 391508	59394	W 216932	37704	BRUTS ECORCES DEGROSSIS
248	WOOD SHAPED,SLEEPERS	W 299050	105282	W 322801	127710	W 372143	163397	W 306133	125745	BOIS SIMPLEMENT TRAVAILLES
2482	LUMBER SHAPED CONIFER	W 252522	81418	W 268124	96586	W 321362	132166	W 257049	99450	CONIFERES SCIES,RABOTES
24821	LUMBER SAWN ETC CONIFER	W 252494	81395	W 268052	96555	W 321269	132119	W 256921	99396	CONIFERES SCIES LONGITUD
2483	LUMBER SHAPED NON–CONIFR	W 45882	23527	W 54152	30858	W 49899	30945	W 48952	26219	NON CONIFERES SCIES,RABOTES
24831	LUMBER SAWN ETC NON–CON	W 44721	22962	W 53870	30712	W 49395	30621	W 48577	26017	SCIES LONGITUDINALEMENT
251	*PULP AND WASTE PAPER	W 49224	16146	W 40049	15687	W 56024	35214	W 50478	19243	PATES A PAPIER,DECHETS
26	TEXTILE FIBRES AND WASTE		132137		171339		203450		170087	FIBRES TEXTILES
263	COTTON	W 41510	54774	W 46946	76840	W 45864	95925	W 40513	81678	COTON
2631	RAW COTTON,EXCL LINTERS	W 40211	53638	W 45330	75392	W 44167	93494	W 38968	78714	COTON EN MASSE
266	SYNTHETIC FIBRES TO SPIN	W 32626	54048	W 35762	64269	W 31531	74841	W 33249	60774	FIBRES SYNTHETIQUES
2665	DISCN SYNTH FIBRE UNCMBD	W 17297	24606	W 17799	28094	W 17287	37418	W 18232	29856	DISCONTINUES EN MASSE
27	CRUDE FERTLZR,MINRLS NES		136703		143407		211480		167158	ENGRAIS MINERAUX BRUTS
274	SULPHUR,UNRSTD IRN PYRTE	W 2588177	115419	W 2653784	123055	W 2806822	186272	W 2600810	141810	SOUFRE ET PYRITES
2741	SULPHUR,EX SULP IN 52215	W 2588171	115417	W 2653772	123042	W 2806820	186271	W 2600662	141770	SOUFRE
29	CRUDE ANIMAL,VEG MAT NES		27157		25355		31996		33677	MATIERES BRUTES ANIM,VEGET
292	CRUDE VEG MATERIALS NES	W 6367	26931	W 4748	25146	W 5628	31539	W 5651	33224	MAT BRUTES VEGETALES NDA
3	MINERAL FUELS ETC		957232		1116797		1178700		1289967	COMBUSTIBLES MINERAUX LUB
32	COAL,COKE AND BRIQUETTES		53177		63120		98185		109885	HOUILLES,COKES,BRIQUETTES
322	COAL,LIGNITE AND PEAT	W 986369	47675	W 1268110	56440	W 1894970	92397	W 2222414	104471	HOUILLES,LIGNITES,TOURBE
3222	OTH COAL,NOT AGGLOMERATD	W 973533	46129	W 1207486	50421	W 1852278	87238	W 2185560	99653	AUTRES HOUILLES
33	PETROLEUM AND PRODUCTS		776881		895880		915967		1004545	PETROLE ET DERIVES
333	CRUDE PETROLEUM	W 6122630	720029	W 6855120	752706	W 6751486	787875	W 5743317	848442	HUILES BRUTES DE PETROLE
334	PETROLEUM PRODUCTS,REFIN	W 179907	42512	W 677329	123544	W 500508	102143	W 517375	119725	PRODUITS RAFFINES
3341	GASOLINE,OTH LIGHT OILS	W 177817	38681	W 674410	117845	W 310206	60012	W 76620	21156	ESSENCES POUR MOTEURS
33419	OTH LIGHT PETROLEUM OILS	W 177817	38681	W 674410	117845	W 306128	58705	W 56761	16546	AUTRES HUILES LEGERES
3343	GAS OILS					W 185277	34171	W 432856	91423	GAS OILS
335	RESIDUAL PETRLM PROD NES	W 204464	14340	W 370804	19630	W 436875	25950	W 632180	36377	PRODUITS RESIDUELS NDA
3354	PETROLM BITUMEN,COKE ETC	W 190380	5974	W 358646	12267	W 422698	16475	W 617794	27011	BITUME,COKE DE PETROLE
33542	PETROLEUM COKE	W 190320	5883	W 358572	12198	W 417339	15887	W 617616	26856	COKE DE PETROLE
341	*GAS,NATURAL AND MANUFCT	W 420465	80523	W 636443	109286	W 686428	154749		163318	GAZ NATUREL,GAZ MANUFACT
3413	PETROLM GASES,LIQUEFIED	W 420465	80523	W 636388	109274	W 686427	154749		163309	GAZ DE PETROLE LIQUEFIE
34131	LIQUEFIED PROPANE,BUTANE	W 420465	80523	W 636388	109274	W 686427	154749	W 687899	163309	PROPANE,BUTANE LIQUEFIES
351	*ELECTRIC CURRENT		46651		48511		9799		12220	ENERGIE ELECTRIQUE
4	ANIMAL,VEGETABLE OIL,FAT		136862		162771		197298		198690	HUILES,GRAISSES ANIM,VEG
42	FIXED VEGETABLE OIL,FAT		114987		140219		166211		166891	HUILES VEGETALES FIXES
423	FIXED VEG OILS,SOFT		108995	W 219211	135341	W 242067	160772	W 283184	161663	HUILES VEGET DOUCES FIXES
4232	SOYA BEAN OIL	W 157439	73559	W 177790	105768	W 114849	77092	W 197682	108802	HUILE DE SOJA
4239	OTH FIXED VEG OILS,SOFT	W 68872	31527	W 37417	23692	W 124476	78007	W 75904	45283	AUTRES HUILES FIXES
42391	RAPE,COLZA,MUSTARD OILS	W 68870	31523	W 37413	23677	W 124476	78006	W 75904	45281	H NAVETTE COLZA MOUTARDE
5	CHEMCLS,RELATED PROD NES		720237		859836		998691		1023816	PRODUITS CHIMIQUES
51	ORGANIC CHEMICALS		96265		115802		134748		128667	PROD CHIMIQ ORGANIQUES
513	CARBOXYLIC ACIDS ETC	W 19738	21030	W 21836	27980	W 15368	27935	W 21844	28141	ACIDES CARBOXYLIQUES
514	NITROGEN–FNCTN COMPOUNDS	W 7344	25914	W 8365	29262	W 8258	34735	W 9017	35055	COMPOSES FONCT AZOTEES
515	ORG–INORG COMPOUNDS ETC	W 2102	24195	W 1652	25735	W 1621	30589	W 2161	29993	COMPOSES ORGANO–MINERAUX
52	INORGANIC CHEMICALS		120471		122017		150553		150705	PROD CHIM INORGANIQUES
522	INORG ELEMNTS,OXIDES,ETC	W 551120	81090	W 383158	82869	W 380144	102271	W 404375	94499	ELEMENTS INORGANIQUES
5225	INORGANIC BASES ETC NES	W 530558	66715	W 359927	67353	W 350165	81766	W 354160	75689	AUTRES BASES OXYDES METAL
52251	AMMONIA,ANHYDROUS ETC	W 520165	62776	W 342325	62264	W 334580	76158	W 333856	70218	AMMONIAC LIQUEFIE
523	OTHR INORG CHEMICALS ETC	W 81935	38904	W 84206	38588	W 93467	47568		55637	AUT PRODUITS CHIMIQUES INORG
5232	OTH MTL CMPD OF INRG ACD	W 55170	27916	W 53306	25769	W 62249	32364	W 71305	37748	SELS METALLIQUES
53	DYES,TANNING,COLOUR PROD		68949		74799		84299		78960	PROD TEINTURE,COLORANTS
531	SYNT DYE,NAT INDGO,LAKES	W 2859	24186	W 3062	23901	W 3499	27155	W 3473	25652	MAT COLOR ORGAN,LAQUES

4. Special Imports C.I.F. by Commodities according to the S.I.T.C. (Rev. 2) in thousand U.S. Dollars
Importations Spéciales C.A.F. par Produits d'après la C.T.C.I. (Rév. 2) en milliers de Dollars E.U.

SITC CTCI	COMMODITY	1993		1994		1995		1996		PRODUIT
		WEIGHT POIDS	VALUE VALEUR	WEIGHT POIDS	VALUE VALEUR	WEIGHT POIDS	VALUE VALEUR	WEIGHT POIDS	VALUE VALEUR	
5311	SYNTHIC ORGNIC DYESTUFFS	W 2307	20337	W 2381	19956	W 2532	22573	W 2575	21621	MAT COLOR ORGAN SYNTHET
533	PIGMENTS,PAINTS,ETC	W 27341	40654	W 30924	47105	W 33222	53359	W 28105	48865	PIGMENTS,PEINTURES,VERNIS
541	*MEDICINAL,PHARM PRODUCT		98402		114131		129833		130266	PROD MEDICINAUX PHARMACEUT
5413	ANTIBIOTICS IN BULK		19947		27034		25939		22376	ANTIBIOTIQUES NDA
5417	MEDICAMENTS	K 1879211	55036	K 1900518	59083	K 2034641	71891	K 2150063	74865	MEDICAMENTS
54179	— CONTNG OTH SUBSTANCES	K 1368351	33479	K 1401552	35432	K 1491745	42200	K 1613330	44715	MED CONT AUT SUBSTANCES
55	PERFUME,CLEANING ETC PRD		35054		40048		48071		49607	PROD POUR PARFUM,TOILETTE
562	*FERTILIZERS,MANUFACTURE	W 342296	48267	W 525414	67470	W 378327	62468		106692	ENGRAIS MANUFACTURES
5621	CHEM NITROGENOUS FERTLZR	W 288000	34876	W 418431	48704	W 290098	45457	W 488598	87968	ENGRAIS AZOTES
56211	AMMONIUM NITRATE	W 115890	15299	W 160100	20970	W 135929	21911	W 211685	37055	NITRATE D'AMMONIUM
56216	UREA	W 114010	15392	W 137727	19136	W 91226	17369	W 185679	40903	UREE
58	PLASTIC MATERIALS ETC		148481		198689		251212		232899	MAT PLAST ARTIFICIELLES
582	PROD OF CONDENSATION ETC	W 21934	30606	W 33163	45053	W 36071	63224	W 32780	53542	PROD CONDENS,POLYCOND
5823	ALKYDS,OTHER POLYESTERS	W 12992	16538	W 17233	22552	W 18503	35645	W 16782	26131	ALKYDES ET AUT POLYESTERS
58231	— IN PRIMARY FORMS	W 12832	15753	W 17067	21653	W 18308	34312	W 16616	25001	SOUS FORMES PRIMAIRES
583	POLYMERIZATION ETC PRODS	W 126839	111855	W 159259	147077	W 138405	180074	W 157707	173215	PROD POLYMERISATION
5831	POLYETHYLENE	W 77890	58010	W 96438	78651	W 84275	97093	W 94757	90617	POLYETHYLENE
58311	— IN PRIMARY FORMS	W 77488	57041	W 94772	74994	W 82238	91961	W 92567	85679	POLYETHYLENE PRIMAIRES
5832	POLYPROPYLENE	W 23082	14640	W 32376	23939	W 29867	33226	W 36710	35214	POLYPROPYLENE
58321	— IN PRIMARY FORMS	W 22354	12652	W 31349	21322	W 28704	29372	W 34993	29236	POLYPROPYLENE PRIMAIRES
59	CHEMICAL MATERIALS NES		102430		125050		136002		144401	MAT PROD CHIMIQUES NDA
591	PESTICIDES,DISINFECTANTS	W 7261	30017	W 9968	42892	W 9958	44753	W 11670	54453	DESINF,INSECT,FONG,HERB
598	MISCEL CHEM PRODUCTS NES	W 40290	64149	W 43017	70884	W 44546	80395	W 44172	77640	PROD DIV INDUST CHIM NDA
5989	CHEM PRODUCTS,PREPS NES	W 33228	48280	W 34377	51223	W 36775	62102	W 36578	60728	PROD PREP CHIMIQUES NDA
59899	OTH CHEM PRODS,PREPS,NES	W 25822	37866	W 27116	41573	W 30384	51788	W 28733	47571	AUT PRODUITS CHIMIQUES NDA
6	BASIC MANUFACTURES		1159060		1355729		1589217		1458483	ART MANUFACTURES
61	LEATHER,DRESSED FUR,ETC		27479		31296		30407		27779	CUIRS,PELLETERIES
62	RUBBER MANUFACTURES NES		47726		47122		54902		91321	CAOUTCHOUC MANUFACTURE
625	RUBBER TYRES, TUBES ETC	W 2837	11030	W 3452	12775	W 4680	19050	W 9508	35720	PNEUS CAOUTCHOUC VULCANISE
628	RUBBER ARTICLES NES	W 4030	27625	W 3163	25868	W 3089	25931	W 6720	43486	OUVRAGES CAOUTCHOUC NDA
6282	VULCANIZD RUBBER BELTING	W 3062	15395	W 2140	12155	W 1897	10949	W 5389	25784	COURROIES EN CAOUTCHOUC
64	PAPER,PAPERBOARD AND MFR		128397		132461		183191		162351	PAPIERS,CARTONS & OUVRAGES
641	PAPER AND PAPERBOARD	W 171485	107946	W 176749	117214	W 177841	156870	W 164336	138149	PAPIERS ET CARTONS
6413	KRAFT PAPER,PAPERBOARD	W 63272	34572	W 62950	34466	W 67992	54009	W 54871	42866	PAPIER ET CARTON KRAFT
64139	KRAFT PAPER PAPERBD,NES	W 58913	32180	W 54015	29763	W 59243	47236	W 46879	37403	PAPIER,CARTON KRAFT NDA
6415	PAPER,PAPERBRD,BULK,NES	W 40059	20665	W 40897	23895	W 39996	35101	W 34375	24351	PAPIERS,CARTONS ROULEAUX
6418	COATED ETC PAPER NES BLK	W 15530	26174	W 18722	29248	W 16802	29522	W 20620	33257	PAP,CARTONS COUCHES,ENDUITS
64189	COATED PAPER ETC NES	W 13488	22672	W 16974	25719	W 15272	26129	W 19452	29952	PAPIERS,CARTONS COUCHES
642	PAPER,ETC,PRECUT,ARTS OF	W 13261	20451	W 7527	15247	W 13073	26321	W 10529	24201	PAP,CARTONS DECOUPES
65	TEXTILE YARN,FABRICS,ETC		309529		346039		404494		404683	FILS,TISSUS,ARTICLES TEXTILE
651	TEXTILE YARN	W 26987	93994	W 30770	110188	W 25464	112389	W 30751	113074	FILS TEXTILES
6514	SYN FIB YRN,BULK,MONOFIL	W 12365	34029	W 13477	37381	W 11074	41848	W 16446	46238	FILS CONT 85% FIB TEXT SYNTH
65142	— NONTXT ETC CONT PAMID	W 9781	22614	W 10334	24888	W 8419	26906	W 14629	35553	FILS NON TEX FI CON POLYAMID
6516	DISCON SYN FIB BLEND YRN	W 6560	27417	W 7960	34144	W 6402	33319	W 6439	30198	FILS FIBR TEX SYNT DIS MOINS
65166	DISCON SYN FIB–COTTN YRN	W 5946	24801	W 7409	31412	W 6163	31992	W 6069	28115	FILS TEXT SYNT MELANGE COTON
652	COTTON FABRICS,WOVEN	W 15283	98520	W 17005	112374	W 15931	132130	W 18036	140512	TISSUS DE COTON
6522	WOVEN COTTON BLEACHD,ETC	W 14383	94286	W 16004	106995	W 14894	125941	W 17175	134391	TISSUS COTON BLANCHIS ETC
65224	BLCHED COTTON FABRIC NES	W 13088	78869	W 14685	89778	W 12952	101676	W 15488	114746	AUT TIS PLUS 85% COT BLANCHI
653	WOVN MAN–MADE FIB FABRIC	W 3714	46947	W 3588	42381	W 4010	51095	W 3142	41230	TISSUS FIBRES SYNTH,ARTIF
657	SPECIAL TXTL FABRC,PRODS	W 8687	46159	W 11126	51864	W 11002	63277	W 10292	59199	TISSUS SPECIAUX
6573	COATED ETC TEXTILES NES	W 3136	20442	W 3175	21330	W 3266	24426	W 3499	24360	TISSUS,ART MATIERE TEXT NDA
66	NONMETAL MINERAL MFS NES		78493		79832		101784		86499	ART MIN NON METALLIQUES
664	GLASS	W 34298	18769	W 37444	25382	W 39994	34081	W 39668	27808	VERRE
67	IRON AND STEEL		323865		475469		491724		366853	FER ET ACIER
672	IRON,STEEL PRIMARY FORMS	W 386908	104966	W 476179	124593	W 691994	205720	W 575578	147854	LINGOTS FER,ACIER
6725	IRN,STL BLOOMS,SLABS,ETC	W 315451	81817	W 411442	103259	W 536670	140685	W 523065	130706	BLOOMS,BILLETTES FER ACIER
67251	IRN,SMPLE STL BLOOMS,ETC	W 315293	81742	W 411285	103191	W 536452	140552	W 523064	130699	BLOOMS ETC NON ACIER FIN
6727	IRN,STL COIL FR REROLLNG	W 71457	23149	W 64737	21333	W 155324	65035	W 52514	17148	EBAUCHES POUR TOLES FER
67271	IRON,SIMPLE STEEL COILS	W 69866	22506	W 64708	21283	W 155279	64954	W 52502	17119	EBAUCHES NON EN ACIER
673	IRON,STEEL SHAPES ETC	W 257542	85819	W 198229	72586	W 196601	79368	W 161240	63192	BARRES,PROFIL FER,ACIER
6732	IRON,STEEL BARS ETC	W 144462	47746	W 75423	29093	W 73916	33073	W 58274	26853	BARRES FER,ACIER
67326	IRN,OTH STL BARS HOTROLD	W 130451	39569	W 65942	21899	W 63444	22638	W 47716	16405	BARRES PLEINES FER,ACIER
6733	IRON,STEEL PROFILES ETC	W 64834	22542	W 89153	31863	W 83204	31813	W 70586	25478	PROFILES,PALPLAN FER,ACIER
674	IRN,STL UNIV,PLATE,SHEET	W 158495	90745	W 152989	91508	W 237018	150510	W 173681	112995	LARGES PLATS,TOLES
6746	IRN,STL THIN PLATE,ROLLD	W 74173	34090	W 56893	28052	W 136305	70191	W 83006	43106	TOLES LAM MOINS 3MM
67461	— OF IRON OR SIMPLE STL	W 71617	29235	W 54334	23270	W 133655	64625	W 78869	36509	TOL NON AC FIN MOINS 3 MM
6747	TINNED PLATES,SHEETS	W 30168	26108	W 36964	30960	W 40958	39203	W 38838	36863	TOLES ETAMEES EN ACIER
678	IRON,STL TUBES,PIPES,ETC	W 20426	26065	W 256788	167943	W 26331	34539	W 14940	23777	TUBES,TUYAUX EN FONTE,FER
6783	IRON,STL TUBES,PIPES NES	W 8953	7893	W 244596	152088	W 12738	12141	W 3961	5113	AUT TUBES,TUYAUX FER,ACIER
68	NON–FERROUS METALS		95883		97496		120120		109813	METAUX NON FERREUX
682	COPPER EXC CEMENT COPPER	W 19511	49056	W 17529	46611	W 16230	57666		55097	CUIVRE
6822	COPPER,ALLOYS WORKED	W 18933	47942	W 16720	45225	W 15643	56145	W 17898	53807	CUIVRE,ALLIAGES OUVRES
68221	COPPER BARS,WIRE,ETC	W 14658	34129	W 13339	33348	W 12114	39481	W 14112	37877	BARRES,PROFILES ET FILS
684	ALUMINIUM	W 15797	35662	W 15397	38878	W 16114	48461	W 15770	43488	ALUMINIUM
6842	ALUMINIUM,ALLOYS WORKED	W 12952	31338	W 12937	34570	W 12880	40310	W 14171	40071	ALUMINIUM,ALLIAGES OUVRE
69	METAL MANUFACTURES NES		136385		131796		184795		188533	ART MANUFACT EN METAL NDA
692	METAL TANKS,BOXES,ETC	W 4656	17175	W 4982	12293	W 12786	31419	W 9638	35253	RECIPIENTS METALLIQUES
6924	MTL TRANSPORT BOXES ETC	W 3816	13421	W 4027	9910	W 8149	27437	W 8448	31083	FUTS,TAMBOURS,BIDONS
699	BASE METAL MFRS NES		51358		54797	W 27599	71080	W 15975	70981	ART MANUFACTURES MET NDA
7	MACHINES,TRANSPORT EQUIP		1907085		1944085		1974969		1942998	MACHINES MATERIEL TRANSPORT
71	POWER GENERATING EQUIPMT		438880		177203		100817		103900	MACHINES GENERATRICES
711	STEAM BOILERS & AUX PLNT	W 26523	262121	W 2587	19445	W 474	3384	W 1583	5742	GENERATEURS VAPEUR EAU ETC
7111	STEAM BOILERS ETC	W 26388	260960	W 2377	17775	W 242	1636	W 348	1251	GENERATEURS VAPEUR EAU
713	INTRNL COMBUS PSTN ENGIN	W 9651	46309	W 9392	46956	W 11102	61160	W 10324	61788	MOTEURS EXPL COMB INT, PIECE
7139	PISTON ENGINE PARTS NES	W 1725	24555	W 1771	25923	W 1923	32005	W 2578	37095	PIECES POUR 713.2,3,8
714	ENGINES AND MOTORS NES	W 2316	46436	W 2816	80664		1945	W 3	913	MOTEURS NON ELECTRIQUES
7148	GAS TURBINES NES	W 2298	45036	W 2807	78484	W 80	1301		1	TURBINES A GAZ
71488	OTHER GAS TURBINES NES	W 2298	45036	W 2807	78483	W 80	1301		1	AUTRES TURBINES A GAZ
716	ROTATING ELECTRIC PLANT	W 7069	71188	W 2337	27637	W 3351	27463	W 3487	26657	APP ELECTR ROTATIFS,PIECES
7162	AC MTRS,GENRTRS,GEN SETS	W 6600	63891	W 2074	22938	W 2993	23143	W 3156	22603	MOTEURS ELECTRIQUES
71622	AC GENERATORS	W 1990	30008	W 276	8132	W 723	4684	W 1445	9711	GENER COURANT ALTERNATIF
71623	GEN SETS WITH PISTN ENGN	W 3918	28448	W 1010	8747	W 1494	12070	W 684	4630	GROUPES MOTEUR EXPLOSION
72	MACHS FOR SPCL INDUSTRYS		327619		375493		505125		445613	MAC SPECIALES POUR INDUST
721	AGRIC MACHY,EXC TRACTORS	W 3629	18634	W 8421	36278	W 4853	28343	W 14399	51918	MACHINES AGRICOLES
7212	HARVESTING ETC MACHINES	W 917	7050	W 6017	27683	W 1519	8974	W 11153	38015	ENGINS POUR LA RECOLTE
722	TRACTORS NON–ROAD	W 3297	13935	W 9910	51173	W 5485	23101	W 9539	38589	TRACTEURS
7224	WHEELED TRACTORS NES	W 3229	13729	W 9810	51053	W 5462	23075	W 9498	38552	TRACTEURS A ROUES
723	CIVIL ENGNEERG EQUIP ETC	W 13065	43992	W 9559	27966	W 16744	91782	W 16169	57466	APPAREILS DE GENIE CIVIL
7234	CONST,MINING MACHNRY NES	W 12293	41409	W 8618	25008	W 15612	87664	W 14658	52671	MACH POUR LA CONST, MINES
72342	SLFPRP SHOVELS,EXCAVATRS	W 7674	30343	W 5369	13908	W 10238	68153	W 9191	34727	PELLES MECANIQUES
724	TEXTILE,LEATHER MACHNRY	W 9976	80088	W 7865	83706	W 8331	100385	W 9009	119942	MACH POUR INDUSTRIE TEXTILE

4. Special Imports C.I.F. by Commodities according to the S.I.T.C. (Rev. 2) in thousand U.S. Dollars
Importations Spéciales C.A.F. par Produits d'après la C.T.C.I. (Rév. 2) en milliers de Dollars E.U.

SITC CTCI	COMMODITY	1993 WEIGHT POIDS	1993 VALUE VALEUR	1994 WEIGHT POIDS	1994 VALUE VALEUR	1995 WEIGHT POIDS	1995 VALUE VALEUR	1996 WEIGHT POIDS	1996 VALUE VALEUR	PRODUIT
7243	SEWING MACHS,NEEDLES ETC	W 4437	27165	W 2017	21328	W 1877	29237	W 1610	31806	MACHINES A COUDRE,PIECES
72431	SEWING MACHINES	W 3860	23708	W 1796	18796	W 1712	25878	W 1319	25934	MACHINES A COUDRE
7245	WEAVING,FELT MFG,ETC MCH	W 1507	16384	W 1973	21116	W 1829	27529	W 3214	36207	METIERS A TISSER,PIECES
725	PAPER ETC MILL MACHINERY	W 1282	9174	W 1905	14675	W 3320	47539	W 576	8523	MACHINES FABR PATE PAPIER
7251	PAPER,PULP MAKING MACHRY	W 476	1217	W 1241	5915	W 2795	41387	W 122	2401	MACHINES FABR PATE CARTON
72511	CELLULOSE PULP MFG MACHY	W 24	232	W 24	1114	W 2460	39374	W 19	656	MACH FABR PATE CELLULOSE
727	FOOD MACHRY NON-DOMESTIC	W 2688	26402	W 2852	25441	W 4254	50350	W 3780	41733	MACH INDUSTRIES ALIMENT
7272	OTH FOOD PROC MCHY,PARTS	W 1989	17372	W 2245	21198	W 2801	33835	W 2577	28021	AUT MACH IND ALIMENTAIRE
72722	INDUS FOOD PROC MACH NES	W 1578	14180	W 1514	20158	W 2207	31069	W 1672	24319	MACHINES BOULANGERIE
728	OTH MACHY FOR SPCL INDUS	W 19948	123569	W 15229	116505	W 21686	142222	W 12226	113622	AUT MACH IND PARTICULIERES
7283	OTHR MINERAL WORKG MACHY	W 12179	40281	W 7270	25387	W 11142	43714	W 5393	24506	MACH TRIER,CRIBLER,BROYER
72834	MINRL MOULDING ETC MACHY	W 8178	27385	W 3863	14051	W 7988	29608	W 1741	7916	MACH AGGLO CIMENT ETC
7284	MACHY FOR SPCL INDUS NES	W 6394	76332	W 6634	84052	W 8699	88371	W 5547	81572	MACH SPEC IND PARTICUL.
72842	RUBBER,PLASTICS WRKG MCH	W 2125	21577	W 1862	17469	W 2171	23750	W 2428	27451	MACH IND CAOUT MAT PLAST
72843	TOBACCO WORKING MACH NES	W 827	21358	W 435	12618	W 54	7661	W 251	12480	MACH POUR IND DU TABAC
72848	OTH MCHY WITH INDIV FNCT	W 2092	21164	W 3415	43580	W 5658	46335	W 2247	32526	AUTRES MACHINES NDA
73	METALWORKING MACHINERY		28230		27184		34417		36826	MACH TRAVAIL DES METAUX
736	METALWORKING MACH-TOOLS	W 4048	24228	W 4558	22894	W 4189	23581	W 4047	28626	MACH-OUTILS TRAVAIL METAUX
74	GENRL INDUSTRL MACHY NES		309987		334185		380720		405041	MACH APP INDUSTRIE
741	HEATING,COOLING EQUIPMNT	W 4867	47428	W 6571	67251	W 8776	80867	W 8861	83682	MACH CHAUFFAGE,PIECES
7415	AIR-CONDITIONING MACHNRY	W 756	9260	W 1428	23556	W 1328	21762	W 1181	18699	GROUPES CONDITION AIR
742	PUMPS FOR LIQUIDS ETC	W 2657	31191	W 2706	27406	W 4443	37096	W 3559	43249	POMPES MOTO-POMPES
743	PUMPS NES,CENTRFUGES ETC	W 3993	38843	W 3916	43296	W 5490	53853	W 4927	49946	POMPES COMPRES,VENT ETC
7436	GAS,LIQUID FILTERS ETC	W 1025	17736	W 1009	22317	W 1668	24280	W 1162	17253	APP POUR FILT DES LIQUIDES
744	MECHANICAL HANDLING EQU	W 14084	78364	W 14004	86837	W 10552	71193	W 11518	65818	EQUIP MANUTENTION PIECES
7442	LIFTING,LOADING MACH NES	W 10058	57272	W 10720	70366	W 7704	56212	W 7151	44196	APP LEVAGE,MANUTENTION
74428	OTH HANDLING ETC MCH NES	W 7542	43179	W 7773	54881	W 3473	25326	W 2868	23628	AUT APP LEVAGE ETC
745	NONELEC MACHY,TOOLS NES	W 2493	45230	W 2413	36092	W 3282	42109	W 2745	57626	AUT MACH NON ELEC,PIECES
7452	OTH NONELEC MCHS,PTS NES	W 2438	43827	W 2352	34731	W 3228	40583	W 2661	55510	AUT MACH NON ELEC,PIECES
74522	PACKAGNG,BOTTLNG,ETC MCH	W 920	30780	W 883	22529	W 1311	22472	W 1097	37282	MACH NETT BOUTEILLES,ETC
749	NONELEC MACH PTS,ACC NES	W 4542	68931	W 5254	73303	W 17220	95602	W 6319	104720	PIECES MACH NON ELEC NDA
7492	COCKS,VALVES ETC NES	W 2229	24766	W 2528	25421	W 14324	42867	W 2522	32428	ART ROB,SIM POUR TUYAUX
7493	SHAFT,CRANK,PULLEY ETC	W 873	18289	W 1063	19338	W 1116	20428	W 1529	28558	ARBRES TRANS,VILEBREQUINS
7499	OTH NONELEC MCHY PTS NES	W 779	15798	W 947	17361	W 1078	20237	W 1247	25651	PIECES NON ELECT NDA
75	OFFICE MACHNES,ADP EQUIP		82784		87123		95611		118286	MACH BUREAU TRAIT AUTOM
752	AUTOMTIC DATA PROC EQUIP	W 837	56665	W 964	62283	W 976	68051	W 1310	81101	MACH TRAIT INFORMATION
7522	DIGITAL COMPUTERS	W 201	14055	W 161	10935	W 246	20566	W 369	26933	MACH DIGITALES COMPLETES
76	TELECOMM,SOUND EQUIPMENT		105833		160519		134713		158087	EQUIPMENT DE TELECOM
761	TELEVISION RECEIVERS	W 1488	16202	W 1524	17480	W 2695	31173	W 4314	49570	RECEPTEURS DE TELEVISION
7611	COLOUR TV RECEIVERS	W 1241	15136	W 1386	16893	W 2452	29667	W 3760	46204	RECEPTEURS COULEUR
764	TELECOM EQPT,PTS,ACC NES	W 1738	84464	W 2247	137200	W 2495	92216	W 2538	90702	EQUIP TELECOM,PIECES
7641	LINE TELEPHONE,ETC EQUIP	W 574	37853	W 1009	64145	W 713	45687	W 563	47548	APP TELEPHON PAR FIL
7643	TV,RADIO TRANSMITTRS ETC	W 573	23808	W 646	46293	W 315	25549	W 92	17560	APP EMET TELE RADIO
77	ELECTRIC MACHNRY NES ETC		209830		234971		257207		233881	MACH APP ELECT NDA
771	ELECTRIC POWER MACHY NES	W 1750	25771	W 2379	26242	W 3536	32815	W 4004	22271	MACH PROD,TRANS ELECTR
7711	TRANSFORMERS,ELECTRICAL	W 1051	21871	W 1349	20327	W 2283	22754	W 3079	15829	TRANSFO ELECTRIQUES
772	SWITCHGEAR ETC,PARTS NES	W 3250	62976	W 3005	62450	W 2766	57870	W 1954	52813	APP COUPURE,SECT ETC
7721	SWITCHGEAR ETC	W 3205	60990	W 2988	59732	W 2733	54408	W 1915	49816	APP COUPURE,SECTIONMNT
773	ELECTR DISTRIBUTNG EQUIP	W 6766	43212	W 8561	52976	W 11210	73180	W 6461	56382	EQUIPMT DISTRIBUTION ELECT
7731	INSULATED WIRE,CABLE ETC	W 5955	37314	W 5832	42196	W 8418	58020	W 5067	46060	FILS,CABLES ISOLES ELECT
775	HOUSEHOLD TYPE EQUIP NES	W 2197	13052	W 3838	19278	W 3572	23103	W 3649	24974	MACH,APP USAGE DOMESTQUE
778	ELECTRICAL MACHINERY NES	W 5516	48605	W 6058	46831	W 5571	48749	W 6709	59199	AUTRES MACH ELECT NDA
78	ROAD VEHICLES		222712		273561		310752		389704	VEHICULES ROUTIERS
781	PASS MOTOR VEH EXC BUSES	W 8907	76711	W 9348	83805	W 10210	89760	W 22083	183096	AUTO TRANSPORT PERSONNES
782	LORRIES,SPCL MTR VEH NES	W 13749	78541	W 16392	102297	W 14438	106172	W 17520	106897	VEHICULES SPECIAUX,MARCH
7821	LORRIES,TRUCKS	W 10940	68855	W 12986	91834	W 12304	88630	W 14047	95044	VEHICULES TRANSP MARCHAND
783	ROAD MOTOR VEHICLES NES	W 3851	19219	W 4193	31773	W 5986	55100	W 4643	37261	VEHICULES ROUTIERS NDA
7831	BUSES	W 3144	14134	W 2862	22327	W 3218	32040	W 2510	20709	VOITURES TRANSPORT COMMUN
784	MOTOR VEH PRTS,ACCES NES	W 8008	34960	W 8711	39866	W 8771	42038	W 8882	44212	PIECES 722,781,782,783
7849	OTHER MOTOR VEHCL PARTS	W 7658	34156	W 8286	38710	W 8290	40766	W 8407	42989	PIECES 722,781,782,783
79	OTHR TRANSPORT EQUIPMENT		181209		273845		155607		51660	AUTRE MATERIEL TRANSPORT
791	RAILWAY VEHICLES	W 693	7114	W 202	3520	W 2452	36273	W 285	3427	VEHIC MAT CHEMINS DE FER
7913	MECHAN-PROPELLED RY CARS					W 915	33610			AUTOMOTRICES,DRAISINES
792	AIRCRAFT ETC	W 312	104452	W 484	249610		109744	W 165	25604	APP NAVIGATION AERIENNE
7924	AIRCRFT NES OVER 15000KG	W 67	67698	W 220	208573	W 67	69871			AERODYNES PLUS 15000 KG
7929	AIRCRAFT PARTS NES	W 196	25647	W 254	40762	W 220	31805	W 165	25595	PIECES DU 792
793	SHIPS AND BOATS ETC	W 46793	69643		20715		9589		22629	NAVIRES BATEAUX,ETC
7932	SHIPS AND BOATS NES	W 46714	68791		572	W 4566	7213	W 5626	18297	NAVIRES ET BATEAUX
79323	OTHER CARGO VESSELS	W 39200	54436			W 4499	6368	W 4531	11792	AUT BATEAUX TRANS MARCH
8	MISC MANUFACTURED GOODS		286933		299511		370887		369033	ART MANUFACTURES DIVERS
821	*FURNITURE,PARTS THEREOF	W 2887	14380	W 3984	18177	W 6038	27526	W 6040	24032	MEUBLES ET PIECES
87	PRECISION INSTRUMNTS NES		65450		64864		84117		78636	INSTRUM,APPAR SCIENT NDA
874	MEASURNG,CONTROLNG INSTR	W 1064	46853	W 1148	45010	W 1482	59729	W 1132	52202	INSTRUMENTS DE MESURE
88	PHOTO EQU,OPTICL GDS ETC		32543		33430		36998		38213	APP,FOURN PHOTO,OP,MONTR
882	PHOTO,CINEMA SUPPLIES	W 1959	19275	W 2097	21964	W 1911	21119	W 2261	22623	PRODUITS PHOTO,CINEMA
89	MISC MANUFCTRD GOODS NES		140685		151931		193667		198137	ART MANUFACTURES DIVERS
892	PRINTED MATTER	W 8617	37989	W 8472	42628	W 7564	43767	W 9214	52195	IMPRIMES
8921	PRINTED BOOKS,GLOBES,ETC	W 6480	23973	W 5885	24956	W 5239	24352	W 5255	24659	LIVRES,BROCHURES,CARTES
89211	PRINTED BOOKS,PAMPHLETS	W 6136	23264	W 5233	23887	W 4282	22580	W 4612	23738	LIVRES,BROCHURES
893	ARTICLES OF PLASTIC NES		49115		54110		79547		67371	OUVRAGES EN MAT DIVIS 58
8939	MISC PLASTIC ARTICLES	W 7182	38182	W 7506	40903	W 9289	55676	W 8873	50642	ART DIVERS EN MAT DIV 58
89399	OTHR PLASTC ARTICLES NES	W 6754	37041	W 7003	39580	W 8458	53232	W 8469	49267	AUT OUV MAT DIV 58
899	OTHER MANUFACTURED GOODS		17279		20523		23017		27630	AUT ART MANUF DIVERS NDA

5. Special Exports F.O.B. by Commodities according to the S.I.T.C. (Rev. 2) in thousand U.S. Dollars
Exportations Spéciales F.O.B. par Produits d'après la C.T.C.I. (Rév. 2) en milliers de Dollars E.U.

SITC CTCI	COMMODITY	1993 WEIGHT POIDS	1993 VALUE VALEUR	1994 WEIGHT POIDS	1994 VALUE VALEUR	1995 WEIGHT POIDS	1995 VALUE VALEUR	1996 WEIGHT POIDS	1996 VALUE VALEUR	PRODUIT
	ALL COMMODITIES		3695950		4034592		4718882		4741881	TOUS PRODUITS
0	FOOD AND LIVE ANIMALS		977603		1127869		1444294		1497261	ALIMENTS,ANIMAUX VIVANTS
03	FISH AND PREPARATIONS		538333		620546		773860		737054	POISSONS ET PREPARATIONS
034	FISH,FRESH,CHILLED,FROZN	W 31542	78574	W 31319	79513	W 28339	88031	W 29517	91396	POISSON FRAIS, REFRIG,CONG
0341	FISH FRSH,CHLLD,EX FILLT	W 19438	61125	W 17116	58037	W 15024	70020	W 17875	74282	POISSON FRAIS,REFRIGERE
0342	FISH FROZEN,EXCL FILLETS	W 11266	16207	W 13566	19996	W 12692	16610	W 11259	16282	POISSONS CONGELES
036	SHELL FISH FRESH,FROZEN	W 105395	312938	W 107872	381907	W 108044	503350	W 91651	467979	CRUSTACES,MOLLUSQUES
037	FISH ETC PREPD,PRSVD NES	W 56397	146002	W 59517	157750	W 68064	181087	W 61625	176072	POIS,CRUST,MOL PREPARES
0371	FISH PREPARD,PRESRVD NES	W 56294	145630	W 59381	156954	W 68028	180802	W 61613	176009	CONSERVES DE POISSONS
05	VEGETABLES AND FRUIT		406402		451541		585566		671630	LEGUMES ET FRUITS
054	VEG ETC FRSH,SMPLY PRSVD	W 267564	127305	W 293040	135419	W 297730	182556	W 247434	167431	LEGUMES FRAIS,CONG,SECS
0541	POTATOES FRSH EXCL SWEET	W 60974	19918	W 86871	26728	W 96853	48675	W 52934	25635	POMMES DE TERRE
0544	TOMATOES FRESH	W 162355	52867	W 150876	44016	W 156221	71806	W 153046	82394	TOMATES FRAICHES
0545	OTHER FRESH VEGETABLES	W 17137	11661	W 18901	14743	W 14356	12918	W 16745	18389	AUTRES LEGUMES FRAIS,REF
05459	FRESH VEGETABLES NES	W 15615	10872	W 16301	14050	W 13517	12212	W 16409	17991	LEGUMES FRAIS,REFRI NDA
0546	VEGETABLES SIMPLY PRESVD	W 12547	29022	W 14436	32086	W 13013	35554	W 9891	26396	LEGUMES CONG,CONSER
05461	VEGETABLES FROZEN	W 8773	18839	W 8624	19343	W 7603	19740	W 4403	10524	LEGUMES CONGELES
05462	VEG PRSVD UNFRZN UNTINND	W 3773	10182	W 5812	12742	W 5410	15814	W 5489	15872	LEGUMES CONSER PROVISOIR
0548	EDIBLE VEG NES FRESH,DRY	W 12860	12601	W 14988	13536	W 11273	6828	W 9698	8968	RACINES,TUBERCULES
05488	VEG PRODTS NES FRESH,DRY	W 12860	12601	W 14986	13526	W 11273	6828	W 9697	8966	PROD VEGET ALIM HUMAINE
056	VEGTBLES ETC PRSVD,PREPD	W 61403	82853	W 71742	99934	W 86136	132359	W 77242	130241	CONSERVES DE LEGUMES
0561	VEG DRIED EXC LEGUMINOUS	W 9402	13644	W 7471	9331	W 3607	4203	W 1331	3207	LEGUM DESSECH,DESHYDRAT
0565	VEGTBLES PRSVD,PREPD NES	W 52001	69209	W 64271	90603	W 82528	128155	W 75911	127034	LEGUMES PREPARES CONSERVE
05651	VEGTBLS,FRUIT IN VINEGAR	W 6196	11623	W 5558	11600	W 6086	14743	W 5471	12496	LEGUM CONSERV AU VINAIGRE
05659	OTH VEG PRESVD,PREPD NES	W 45806	57586	W 58712	79003	W 76442	113413	W 70440	114538	LEGUM PREPAP,CONSERV NDA
057	FRUIT,NUTS,FRESH,DRIED	W 525656	170184	W 518691	171024		226530	W 654814	333085	FRUITS FRAIS OU SECS
0571	ORANGES, MANDARINS ETC	W 508161	153793	W 498321	150614	W 414282	201114	W 631054	308914	ORANGES,MAND,CLEMENTINES
05711	ORANGES,FRESH OR DRIED	W 314741	89551	W 314217	84084	W 253618	112805	W 428042	177359	ORANGES FRAICHES,SECHEES
05712	MANDARINS ETC FRESH, DRY	W 193419	64242	W 184104	66529	W 160664	88309	W 203012	131555	MANDARINES,CLEMENTINES
0579	FRUIT FRESH OR DRIED NES	W 13372	10529	W 17911	15954	W 24069	19804	W 21380	18519	FRUITS FRAIS,SECS NDA
058	FRUIT PRESERVED,PREPARED		26061	W 50797	45161		44121	W 34961	40873	CONSERVES DE FRUITS
0585	FRUIT OR VEGETABLE JUICE	W 11608	9652	W 27912	24539	W 10231	10478	W 13196	16899	JUS DE FRUITS
05851	ORANGE JUICE	W 10632	8755	W 27112	23983	W 10000	10256	W 12754	16497	JUS D'ORANGE
0589	FRUIT PREPRD,PRESRVD,NES		14540	W 15205	14512		24735	W 15978	20479	FRUITS PREPARES CONSERV
05899	FRUIT,NUTS NES,PRESERVED	W 16292	14539	W 15205	14509	W 17676	24726	W 15978	20479	FRUITS PREP CONSERV NDA
07	COFFEE,TEA,COCOA,SPICES		9846		18168		31795		34756	CAFE,THE,CACAO,EPICES
071	COFFEE AND SUBSTITUTES	W 104	642		7027	W 816	13925	W 1321	16534	CAFE ET SUCCEDANES
0712	COFFEE EXTRACTS,ESSENCES	W 72	545	W 576	6937	W 800	13905	W 1320	16530	EXTRAITS DE CAFE
075	SPICES	W 7844	9121	W 9340	10477		17204	W 15935	18138	EPICES
09	MISC EDIBLE PRODUCTS		15561		11938		19819		12055	PREP ALIMENTAIRES DIVERSES
098	EDIBLE PRODCTS,PREPS NES	W 2950	8369	W 1587	9236	W 2957	19712	W 1363	11997	PREP ALIMENTAIRES NDA
09809	MISC FOOD PREPRTIONS NES	W 571	5264	W 549	6985	W 1938	17245	W 1000	10716	PREP ALIMENTAIRES NDA
1	BEVERAGES AND TOBACCO		7641		13041		14184		9750	BOISSONS ET TABACS
2	CRUDE MATERLS,EXCL FUELS		466842		586340		633986		642434	MAT BRUTES NON COMESTIBLES
251	*PULP AND WASTE PAPER	W 62951	21248	W 112357	54898	W 74183	66704	W 68282	32688	PATES A PAPIER,DECHETS
2516	CHEM WOOD PULP DISSOLVNG	W 62951	21248	W 3134	977	W 1435	1115			PATES CHIMIQUES DE BOIS
2517	SODA,SULPHATE WOOD PULP			W 109199	53919	W 72748	65589	W 68282	32688	PATES CHIMIQUES AU SULFATE
25172	— BLEACHED,NONDISSOLVNG			W 109199	53919	W 72748	65589	W 68282	32688	PATES BLANCHIES
27	CRUDE FERTLZR,MINRLS NES		290843		322156		326637		389302	ENGRAIS MINERAUX BRUTS
271	FERTILIZERS,CRUDE	W 8399144	259954	MW 9527	281720	MW 9420	284542	MW 10140	347437	ENGRAIS BRUTS
2713	NAT CALCM PHOSPHATES ETC	W 8398409	259851	MW 9527	281720	MW 9420	284542	MW 10140	347437	PHOSPHATES DE CALCIUM
27131	— UNGROUND	W 8398409	259851	MW 9527	281720	MW 9420	284542	MW 10140	347437	PHOSPHATES NON MOULUS
273	STONE,SAND AND GRAVEL	W 1195848	11086	W 2038890	16588	W 1052399	8915	W 868584	8740	PIERRES,SABLES,GRAVIERS
278	OTHER CRUDE MINERALS	W 426800	19803	W 519490	23848	W 601395	33161	W 535376	33089	AUTRES MINERAUX BRUTS
2789	MINERALS CRUDE NES	W 311121	12387	W 334473	13867	W 381593	18507	W 326237	17765	MINERAUX BRUTS NDA
27892	NAT BARIUM SULPHATE,CARB	W 306647	12148	W 333863	13587	W 371308	16559	W 321520	15679	SULFATE DE BARYUM NATUREL
28	METALLIFEROUS ORES,SCRAP		85387		125860		146015		133094	MINERAIS METAL,DECHETS
282	IRON AND STEEL SCRAP	W 153150	12746	W 108104	10880	W 120747	13700	W 90590	10133	FERRAILLES
287	BASE METAL ORES,CONC NES	W 229160	58820	W 285615	99028	W 282981	111619	W 300648	109973	MINERAIS METAUX COMMUNS
2871	CPR ORE ETC,CEMENT COPPR	W 46045	22344	W 44057	30900	W 42194	33220	W 41993	22439	MINERAIS DE CUIVRE,MATTES
28711	COPPER ORES,EXCL MATTE	W 44342	21686	W 41831	26964	W 40080	31304	W 40650	21959	MINERAIS DE CUIVRE
2874	LEAD ORES,CONCENTRATES	W 32543	4391	W 55423	15648	W 36905	12972	W 45720	18328	MINERAIS DE PLOMB
2875	ZINC ORES,CONCENTRATES	W 111780	23211	W 151161	36769	W 171466	44246	W 178175	45015	MINERAIS DE ZINC
2879	OTH NONFER ORE,CONCNTRTE	W 366	565	W 4208	8891	W 4544	14038	W 4890	16193	MINERAIS D'AUTRES METAUX
28799	OTH BASE MTL ORE,CON NES	W 366	565	W 4208	8891	W 4544	14037	W 4890	16193	AUTRES MINERAIS
288	NONFERR METAL SCRAP NES	W 9611	11091	W 12809	14771	W 12196	19760	W 9927	12725	DECHETS NON FERREUX
2882	OTHER BASE MTL SCRAP NES	W 8939	10906	W 11804	14460	W 11612	19592	W 8804	12484	AUTRES DECHETS
28821	COPPER WASTE AND SCRAP	W 6920	9821	W 6632	10039	W 7158	14514	W 5526	9761	DECHETS DE CUIVRE
29	CRUDE ANIMAL,VEG MAT NES		55342		69275		86263		81707	MATIERES BRUTES ANIM,VEGET
292	CRUDE VEG MATERIALS NES	W 16484	51224	W 19623	64673		81258		74786	MAT BRUTES VEGETALES NDA
2924	VEG USED IN PHARMACY ETC	W 5510	10540	W 7199	12993	W 7753	15019	W 8028	16451	PLANTES MEDICINALES
2927	CUT FLOWERS AND FOLIAGE	W 2496	13817	W 3018	16381	W 3780	18717	W 3144	15735	FLEURS,FEUILLAGES COUPES
29271	CUT FLOWERS	W 2475	13756	W 2980	16236	W 3737	18538	W 3138	15725	FLEURS ET BOUTONS
2929	OTH CRUDE VEG MATERIALS	W 6566	23303	W 7400	32689	W 5235	44099	W 6522	39884	MATIERES VEGETALES NDA
29291	VEGETABLE SAPS,EXTRACTS	W 3954	21805	W 4494	30479	W 2995	42105	W 3747	36326	SUCS,EXTRAITS VEGETAUX
3	MINERAL FUELS ETC		98347		83968		103941		77146	COMBUSTIBLES MINERAUX LUB
33	PETROLEUM AND PRODUCTS		98339		83968		103941		77108	PETROLE ET DERIVES
334	PETROLEUM PRODUCTS,REFIN	W 535579	98282	W 514542	83964	W 555801	103939	W 364385	77099	PRODUITS RAFFINES
3341	GASOLINE,OTH LIGHT OILS	W 535574	98270	W 514542	83960	W 553335	103393	W 268971	50651	ESSENCES POUR MOTEURS
33411	MOTOR,AVIATION SPIRIT					W 63506	9975	W 119630	21480	ESSENCES MOTEURS D'AVIONS
33419	OTH LIGHT PETROLEUM OILS	W 535574	98270	W 514542	83960	W 489829	93418	W 149341	29171	AUTRES HUILES LEGERES
3345	LUBS,PETROLEUM OILS NES	W 4	12		4		50	W 73354	21434	HUILES LUBRIFIANTES
33451	LUBS(HIGH PETR CONT) ETC				3		7	W 73351	21427	HUILES LUBRIF,H LOURDES
4	ANIMAL,VEGETABLE OIL,FAT		1093		4229		23015		50607	HUILES,GRAISSES ANIM,VEG
42	FIXED VEGETABLE OIL,FAT		752		2785		17109		47671	HUILES VEGETALES FIXES
423	FIXED VEG OILS,SOFT	W 425	751	W 2520	2785	W 6449	17104	W 14661	47588	HUILES VEGET DOUCES FIXES
4235	OLIVE OIL	W 422	748	W 250	612	W 6449	17104	W 14660	47572	HUILE D'OLIVE
5	CHEMCLS,RELATED PROD NES		721439		813266		980154		954557	PRODUITS CHIMIQUES
52	INORGANIC CHEMICALS		351216		472226		551479		527672	PROD CHIM INORGANIQUES
522	INORG ELEMNTS,OXIDES,ETC	W 1434523	350659	W 1675561	471728	W 1723014	551189	W 1618463	527324	ELEMENTS INORGANIQUES
5222	INORGANIC ACIDS ETC	W 1434104	350405	W 1675503	471658	W 1722959	551082	W 1618433	527250	ACIDES INORGANIQUES
52224	PHOSPHORIC ACIDS ETC	W 1433916	350143	W 1675496	471651	W 1722958	551082	W 1618433	527249	ACIDES PHOSPHORIQUES
541	*MEDICINAL,PHARM PRODUCT		24336		29602		18608		10080	PROD MEDICINAUX PHARMACEUT
5417	MEDICAMENTS	K 2047407	22049	K 2686333	27173	K 653996	15005	K 337065	6619	MEDICAMENTS
54179	— CONTNG OTH SUBSTANCES	K 1804555	16717	K 2619966	23983	K 556675	10050	K 299211	4858	MED CONT AUT SUBSTANCES
55	PERFUME,CLEANING ETC PRD		21125		24535		32421		26161	PROD POUR PARFUM,TOILETTE
551	ESSENTL OILS,PERFUME,ETC	W 698	16096	W 1484	16080	W 1075	22060	W 810	17838	HUILES ESSENTIELLES
5513	ESSENTL OIL,RESINOID,ETC	W 487	14531	W 1403	15549	W 826	20056	W 606	15439	HUILES ESSENTIELLES,RESIN
562	*FERTILIZERS,MANUFACTURE	W 2408486	311274	W 1674075	272034	W 1784150	360673	W 1884573	380802	ENGRAIS MANUFACTURES
5622	CHEM PHOSPHATIC FERTILZR	W 2247642	290236	W 1623355	263255	W 1761162	355517	W 1749647	351001	ENGRAIS PHOSPHATES
56222	SUPERPHOSPHATES	W 473771	52454	W 445141	57370	W 491908	76279	W 660486	112244	SUPERPHOSPHATES

5. Special Exports F.O.B. by Commodities according to the S.I.T.C. (Rev. 2) in thousand U.S. Dollars
Exportations Spéciales F.O.B. par Produits d'après la C.T.C.I. (Rév. 2) en milliers de Dollars E.U.

SITC CTCI	COMMODITY	1993		1994		1995		1996		PRODUIT
		WEIGHT POIDS	VALUE VALEUR	WEIGHT POIDS	VALUE VALEUR	WEIGHT POIDS	VALUE VALEUR	WEIGHT POIDS	VALUE VALEUR	
56229	CHEM PHOSPH FERTILZR NES	W 1773871	237782	W 1178214	205885	W 1269254	279238	W 1089161	238756	ENGRAIS PHOSPHATES NDA
5629	FERTILIZERS NES	W 160820	21015	W 50577	8746	W 22988	5156	W 134926	29801	ENGRAIS NDA
56292	NITROG–PHOS FERTILZR NES	W 160737	20973	W 50577	8746	W 22988	5156	W 134925	29796	ENGRAIS NDA CONT N P
6	BASIC MANUFACTURES		328898		373243		431964		445318	ART MANUFACTURES
61	LEATHER,DRESSED FUR,ETC		21194		45043		44426		66311	CUIRS,PELLETERIES
611	LEATHER	W 1254	9452	W 4361	33657	W 1875	37219	W 2761	58563	CUIRS,PEAUX PREPARES
6115	LEATHER FROM SHEEP,LAMBS	W 479	3841	W 2591	23456	W 1370	31424	W 2498	51827	PEAUX D'OVINS PREPAREES
612	LEATHER ETC MANUFACTURES	W 1043	11741	W 1139	11369	W 862	7207	W 561	7733	OUVRAGES EN CUIRS NDA
62	RUBBER MANUFACTURES NES		10770		20948		22532		20300	CAOUTCHOUC MANUFACTURE
625	RUBBER TYRES, TUBES ETC	W 3231	10492	W 6374	20397	W 6592	22215	W 6019	20182	PNEUS CAOUTCHOUC VULCANISE
63	WOOD,CORK MANUFACTRS NES		32179		34188		36137		36166	OUVRAGES LIEGE ET BOIS
634	VENEERS,PLYWOOD,ETC	W 18581	19046	W 15682	20077	W 16856	21746	W 16329	21114	PLACAGES,CONTRE–PLAQUES
6342	PLYWOOD OF WOOD SHEETS	W 13349	15788	W 15186	18977	W 14195	20061	W 15175	20174	BOIS CONTRE–PLAQUES
64	PAPER,PAPERBOARD AND MFR		8354		8003		14950		13371	PAPIERS,CARTONS & OUVRAGES
65	TEXTILE YARN,FABRICS,ETC		165581		155415		177443		158476	FILS,TISSUS,ARTICLES TEXTILE
651	TEXTILE YARN	W 9937	44833	W 12115	55514	W 10908	57555	W 7457	39681	FILS TEXTILES
6513	COTTON YARN	W 5795	24920	W 6913	31016	W 6829	34004	W 5158	24978	FILS DE COTON
6516	DISCON SYN FIB BLEND YRN	W 2510	13415	W 3154	18156	W 2408	15786	W 1326	9068	FILS FIBR TEX SYNT DIS MOINS
652	COTTON FABRICS,WOVEN	W 2891	14157	W 1584	9386	W 1841	11178	W 573	5034	TISSUS DE COTON
653	WOVN MAN–MADE FIB FABRIC	W 3328	28980	W 3103	26329	W 3478	33981	W 2962	34117	TISSUS FIBRES SYNTH,ARTIF
658	TEXTILE ARTICLES NES	W 4246	21629	W 1994	12298	W 4097	24679	W 6684	33250	ART FACONNES MAT TEXTILES
659	FLOOR COVERINGS,ETC	W 7551	39194	W 6890	38656	W 4120	35532	W 3515	29993	COUVRE–PARQUETS,TAPIS ETC
6592	CARPETS ETC KNOTTED	W 3753	29811	W 3953	30677	W 3575	31908	W 3121	27239	TAPIS POINTS NOUES,ENROULES
65921	— OF WOOL OR FINE HAIR	W 3747	29790	W 3939	30546	W 3570	31852	W 3120	27228	TAP NOUES,ENROULES LAINE
66	NONMETAL MINERAL MFS NES		17483		27608		34517		37243	ART MIN NON METALLIQUES
661	LIME,CEMENT,BLDG PRODS	W 5291	1486		9339	W 451924	15023	W 244942	11894	CHAUX,CIMENTS MAT CONSTR
67	IRON AND STEEL		12987		5911		11585		16506	FER ET ACIER
68	NON–FERROUS METALS		46451		59232		72179		77871	METAUX NON FERREUX
681	SILVER,PLATINUM,ETC		19556		28353		37491		31602	ARGENT ET PLATINE
6811	SILVER UNWKD,PARTLY WRKD		19556		28353		37491		31602	ARGENT BRUT MI–OUVRE
68113	SILVER UNWROUGHT		19298		28353		37055		31436	ARGENT ET ALLIAGES BRUTS
685	LEAD		24008	W 58212	28033	W 63922	33753	W 54522	42483	PLOMB
6851	LEAD,ALLOYS UNWROUGHT		24007	W 58212	28033	W 63922	33753	W 54522	42483	PLOMB,ALLIAGES BRUTS
68511	UNREFINED LEAD	W 74939	24007	W 58212	28033	W 63922	33753	W 54454	42397	PLOMB POUR AFFINAGE
69	METAL MANUFACTURES NES		13898		16895		18195		19075	ART MANUFACT EN METAL NDA
7	MACHINES,TRANSPORT EQUIP		203947		167236		152711		138165	MACHINES MATERIEL TRANSPORT
74	GENRL INDUSTRL MACHY NES		11332		9239		26771		26221	MACH APP INDUSTRIE
741	HEATING,COOLING EQUIPMNT	W 92	589		477		19667	W 1455	21210	MACH CHAUFFAGE,PIECES
7413	INDUS FURNACES ETC,PARTS	W 29	140	W 2	25	W 5600	19011	W 1442	21051	FOURS IND,LABOR,PIECES
74132	INDUST FURNACES NONELECT	W 9	17	W 1	6	W 5600	19011	W 1442	21051	FOURS NON ELECTRIQUES
77	ELECTRIC MACHNRY NES ETC		103290		125142		90177		80642	MACH APP ELECT NDA
773	ELECTR DISTRIBUTNG EQUIP	W 3175	51180	W 3753	59836	W 4199	72517	W 5148	71705	EQUIPMT DISTRIBUTION ELECT
7731	INSULATED WIRE,CABLE ETC	W 3171	51091	W 3746	59656	W 4195	72473	W 5140	71547	FILS,CABLES ISOLES ELECT
775	HOUSEHOLD TYPE EQUIP NES		2068		16643		5207		193	MACH,APP USAGE DOMESTQUE
7752	DOM REFRIGERATRS,FREEZRS	W 330	1719	W 2819	15824	W 832	4971	W 2	9	REFRIG,CONGEL MENAGER
776	TRANSISTORS,VALVES,ETC	W 1202	36671		36062	W 21	597	W 1	95	LAMPES,TUBES,VALVES
7763	DIODES,TRANSISTORS,ETC	W 999	35034	W 1085	31672	W 21	575	W 1	70	DIODES,TRANSISTORS
78	ROAD VEHICLES		18492		20346		23161		20101	VEHICULES ROUTIERS
784	MOTOR VEH PRTS,ACCES NES	W 2041	17067	W 2322	18325	W 2345	19452	W 2333	16978	PIECES 722,781,782,783
7849	OTHER MOTOR VEHCL PARTS	W 2035	17009	W 2322	18325	W 2345	19452	W 2333	16978	PIECES 722,781,782,783
79	OTHR TRANSPORT EQUIPMENT		53379		753		3290		705	AUTRE MATERIEL TRANSPORT
793	SHIPS AND BOATS ETC	W 82320	53070	W 3659	752	W 2022	1741	W 842	705	NAVIRES BATEAUX,ETC
7932	SHIPS AND BOATS NES	W 82319	53052	W 3659	748	W 2022	1741	W 842	705	NAVIRES ET BATEAUX
79323	OTHER CARGO VESSELS	W 82314	52630	W 3651	637			W 842	705	AUT BATEAUX TRANS MARCH
8	MISC MANUFACTURED GOODS		889685		863957		933141		925025	ART MANUFACTURES DIVERS
812	*PLUMBG,HEATNG,LGHTNG EQ	W 2710	11837	W 2329	12059	W 3377	12235	W 6642	15979	APPAR SANITAIRES CHAUFFAGE
831	*TRAVEL GOODS,HANDBAGS	W 1569	18050	W 1253	16685	W 830	16158	W 528	12829	ARTICLES DE VOYAGE ETC
84	CLOTHING AND ACCESSORIES		760268		738913		796841		779008	VETEMENTS
842	MENS OUTERWEAR NOT KNIT	W 24108	259247	W 22348	254961	W 19899	281216	W 16770	256908	VET DESSUS POUR HOMMES
8421	— OVERCOATS,OTHER COATS	W 1606	18281	W 1477	17841	W 859	13434	W 291	7232	MANTEAUX HOMMES MAT TEXT
84219	—— OF OTHER FIBRES	W 1578	17655	W 1439	17328	W 847	13087	W 291	7201	MANTEAUX HOMMES AUT FIBR
8423	— TROUSERS,BREECHES ETC	W 17218	178572	W 16329	166865	W 15277	202619	W 14489	208399	PANTALONS HOMMES MAT TEX
8429	— OTHER OUTER GARMENTS	W 5039	57377	W 4144	56700	W 3593	59546	W 1864	34232	AUT VET DES HOM MAT TEX
843	WOMENS OUTERWEAR NONKNIT	W 7282	97068	W 5911	89085	W 4500	81719	W 4621	83040	VET DESSUS FEMMES MAT TEX
8439	— OTHER OUTER GARMENTS	W 5299	67931	W 4320	60863	W 3516	56613	W 3905	62900	AUT VET DES FEM MAT TEXT
844	UNDER GARMENTS NOT KNIT	W 3780	80569	W 3312	75721	W 2448	69331	W 1926	53300	VETEMENT DESSOUS MAT TEX
8441	— MENS SHIRTS	W 3436	75489	W 3001	69811	W 2283	64752	W 1779	50115	CHEMISES HOMMES MAT TEXT
84411	—— OF COTTON	W 2161	48110	W 1904	44326	W 1348	39857	W 1026	31243	CHEMISES HOMMES DE COTON
84412	—— OF SYNTHETIC FIBRES	W 1275	27379	W 1097	25485	W 935	24895	W 753	18872	CHEMISES HOMMES FIB SYNT
845	OUTERWEAR KNIT NONELASTC	W 15668	210769	W 16231	221198	W 14833	248987	W 14242	265653	VET DESSOUS,ACCES BONNET
8451	— JERSEYS,PULLOVERS ETC	W 7061	100142	W 7518	109310	W 7038	125031	W 7198	139321	CHANDAILS,PULL–OVERS ETC
8459	— OTHER,CLTHG ACCESRYS	W 8242	105300	W 8457	106918	W 7541	117371	W 6832	120663	AUT VET DESSUS DE BONNE
846	UNDER GARMENTS KNITTED	W 4593	90201	W 3892	77671	W 3990	92800	W 3679	95750	SOUS VETS DE BONNETERIE
8462	— OF COTTON NON ELASTIC	W 4250	75203	W 3605	65936	W 3475	72123	W 3274	72194	SOUS–VET BONNET COTON
84629	—— OTHER	W 4250	75203	W 3605	65936	W 3475	72123	W 3274	72194	AUT SOUS–VET BONNET COTON
8465	CORSETS,GARTERS,ETC	W 214	12557	W 148	8792	W 331	16303	W 245	19579	CORSETS,GAINES ART SIM
84652	CORSETS,BRACES ETC	W 151	10395	W 125	7847	W 327	16063	W 232	18896	CORSETS,GAINES,JARRETEL
848	HEADGEAR,NONTXTL CLOTHNG	W 603	20774	W 498	18485		14799	W 502	13834	VET ACCES MAT AUT QUE TEX
8481	LEATHER CLOTHES,ACCESSOR	W 530	19915	W 448	17682	W 345	14107	W 322	12852	VET ACCES MAT CUIR ARTIF
851	*FOOTWEAR	W 5407	71758	W 4718	61570	W 4626	71350	W 4375	71982	CHAUSSURES
85102	FOOTWEAR LEATHER	W 3487	57540	W 3109	50643	W 2887	57444	W 2880	58753	CHAUS SEMELLES EN CUIR
89	MISC MANUFCTRD GOODS NES		20837		28969		28908		37760	ART MANUFACTURES DIVERS

1. HISTORICAL SERIES, 1960–1995 SPECIAL TRADE, IMPORTS C.I.F., EXPORTS F.O.B.
SERIES HISTORIQUES, 1960–1995 COMMERCE SPECIAL, IMPORTATIONS C.A.F., EXPORTATIONS F.O.B

YEAR ANNEE	VALUE IN MILLION U.S. DOLLARS VALEUR EN MILLION U.S. DOLLARS MERCHANDISE –MARCHANDISE IMPORTS	EXPORTS	GOLD –OR IMPORTS	EXPORTS	CONVERSION FACTORS FACTEURS DE CONVERSION CENTS E.U. PAR IMPORTS	EXPORTS	INDEX NUMBERS –INDICES QUANTUM IMPORTS	EXPORTS	UNIT VALUE VALEUR UNITAIRE IMPORTS	EXPORTS
1960	128.43	73.04	119.60	134.50						
1961	137.27	95.09	112.60	399.70						
1962	135.91	90.98	113.20	229.00						
1963	141.71	100.73	112.50	398.50						
1964	156.19	105.84								
1965	173.24	108.02	135.30	325.30						
1966	207.91	112.12	271.80	299.30						
1967	199.20	121.78	301.10	301.10						
1968	234.29	155.10	299.90	298.30						
1969	260.20	141.90								
1970	323.53	156.40								
1971	340.91	163.34								
1972	330.02	176.64								
1973	467.08	226.55								
1974	468.08	301.39								
1975	427.61	200.97								
1976	288.38	0.15								
1977	330.79	150.00								
1978	523.09	162.53								
1979	567.87	254.08								
1980	800.00	281.00								
1981	801.00	281.00								
1982	836.00	229.00								
1983	636.00	132.00								
1984	540.00	96.00								
1985	424.00	77.00								
1986	543.00	79.00								
1987	642.00	97.00								
1988	736.00	103.00								
1989	808.00	105.00								
1990	878.00	126.00								
1991	899.00	162.00								
1992	855.00	139.00								
1993	955.00	132.00								
1994	1019.00	150.00								
1995	784.00	169.00								

2. IMPORTS BY BROAD ECONOMIC CATEGORY AND EXPORTS BY INDUSTRIAL ORIGIN. (PERCENTAGE OF TOTAL VALUE)
IMPORTATIONS PAR CATEGORIES ECONOMIQUES ET EXPORTATIONS PAR BRANCHE D'ACTIVITE.(EN POURCENTAGE DE LA VALEUR TOTALE)

IMPORTS – IMPORTATIONS

	1990	1991	1992	1993	1994	1995	1996
TOTAL IMPORTS–IMPORTATIONS TOTALES					100.		
1 FOOD BEV–ALIMENTATION BOISSONS					16.3		
11 PRIMARY–PRODUITS DE BASE					6.7		
111 FOR INDUSTRY–POUR L'INDUSTRIE					5.7		
112 FOR HOUSEHOLDS–POUR LES MENAGES					1.0		
12 PROCESSED–PRODUITS ELABORES					9.6		
121 FOR INDUSTRY–POUR L'INDUSTRIE					5.1		
122 FOR HOUSEHOLDS–POUR LES MENAGES					4.6		
2 IND SUPPLIES–APPROV INDUSTRIELS					21.5		
21 PRIMARY–PRODUITS DE BASE					2.2		
22 PROCESSED–PRODUITS ELABORES					19.4		
3 FUELS–COMBUSTIBLES					13.9		
31 PRIMARY–PRODUITS DE BASE					0.0		
32 PROCESSED–PRODUITS ELABORES					13.8		
321 MOTOR SPIRIT–ESSENCE					10.8		
322 OTHER–AUTRES					3.1		
4 MACHINERY–EQUIPEMENT					17.9		
41 CAPITAL EQUIPMENT–MACHINES					16.7		
42 PARTS–PIECES ACCESSOIRES					1.3		
5 TRANSPORT–TRANSPORT					17.5		
51 PASSENGER CARS–AUTOMOBILES							
52 OTHER–AUTRES					14.3		
521 INDUSTRIAL–INDUSTRIELS					13.4		
522 NON INDUSTRIAL–NON INDUSTRIEL					0.9		
53 PARTS–PIECES ACCESSOIRES					3.2		
6 CONSUM GOODS–BIENS CONSOMMATION					10.8		
61 DURABLE–DURABLES					1.9		
62 SEMI DURABLE–SEMI DURABLES					2.4		
63 NON DURABLE–NON DURABLES					6.5		
7 GOODS NES–BIENS NDA					2.0		

EXPORTS – EXPORTATIONS

	1990	1991	1992	1993	1994	1995	1996
TOTAL EXPORTS–EXPORTATIONS TOTALES					100.		
1 AGRICULTURE					64.8		
2 MINING QUARRY–INDUS EXTRACTIVES					1.3		
3 MANUFACTURING–IND MANUFACTUR					33.9		
31 FOOD BEV TOBACCO–ALIM BOISS TAB					8.6		
32 TEXTILES–INDUSTRIES TEXTILES					5.2		
33 WOOD & PRODUCTS–BOIS & PRODUITS					1.5		
34 PAPER & PRODUCTS–PAPIER & PRODT					0.7		
35 CHEMICALS–INDUSTRIES CHIMIQUES					12.1		
36 NON METAL MIN–MIN NON METAL					0.2		
37 BASIC METAL–IND METAL BASE					0.2		
38 METAL MANUF–MANUF METAL					4.7		
39 OTH MANUF IND–AUTRES MANUF					0.7		

3. TRADE BY PRINCIPAL COUNTRIES OF PRODUCTION AND CONSUMPTION (VALUE IN THOUSAND U.S. DOLLARS)
ECHANGES SELON LES PRINCIPAUX PAYS DE PRODUCTION ET DE COMSOMMATION (VALEUR EN MILLIERS DE DOLLARS EU)

COUNTRIES–PAYS	SPECIAL IMPORTS C.I.F. IMPORTATIONS SPECIALES C.A.F				
	1990	1991	1992	1993	1994
World				955000	544015
Africa				1000	186627
Americas					27323
Northern America					26403
LAIA					920
CACM					
Caribbean					
Rest of America					
As.ex F.USSR				120000	75471
Eur.x F.USSR					191299
EU					179351
EFTA					11780
East Europe					
Other Europe					168
Former USSR					
Oceania					3643
So. Africa Customs Un					163487
Saudi Arabia				63000	
Japan/Japon					45673
United Kingdom					36145
United Arab Emirates				32000	2161
Portugal					25180
Germany/Allemagne					22956
USA/Etats–Unis d'Amer					22382
France,Monac					21509
Zimbabwe					21193
Denmark/Danemark					21093
Italy/Italie					16893
Malaysia/Malaisie				15000	296
Netherlands/Pays–Bas					12734
Spain/Espagne					10070
Indonesia/Indonésie				7000	2068
Switz.Liecht					8620
Hong Kong					6040
India/Inde					5599
Pakistan					5295
Sweden/Suède					5248
Canada					4021
Australia/Australie					3486
Belgium–Luxembourg					3478
Norway,SVD,JM					3160
Bangladesh				3000	118
Thailand/Thaïlande					2432
Finland/Finlande					2114
Myanmar					1817
Korea, Republic of					1304
Austria/Autriche					1073
Egypt/Egypte				1000	
Malawi					824
China/Chine					766
Ireland/Irlande					693
Brazil/Brésil					661
Mauritius/Maurice					633
Singapore/Singapour					565
Kenya					261
Bolivia/Bolivie					259
Viet Nam					250
Sri Lanka					183
Gibraltar					168
Greece/Grèce					165
New Zealand					157
Korea Dem People's Rp					136
Mauritania/Mauritanie					126
Zambia/Zambie					103

COUNTRIES–PAYS	SPECIAL EXPORTS F.O.B. EXPORTATIONS SPECIALES F.O.B.				
	1990	1991	1992	1993	1994
Monde				132000	163977
Afrique				1000	40457
Amériques					13864
Amérique du Nord					13864
ALAI					
MCAC					
Caraïbes					
Autre Amérique					
Asie l'URSS exclus				9000	37923
Europe l'URSS exclus					56973
UE					56973
AELE					
Europe de l'Est					
Autre de l'Europe					
Ancienne URSS					
Océanie					
Spain/Espagne					31557
So. Africa Customs Un					28956
Japan/Japon					24069
Portugal					14599
USA/Etats–Unis d'Amer					13788
India/Inde					11644
Zimbabwe					7282
Iran (Islamic Rp. of)				4000	
Belgium–Luxembourg					3733
United Kingdom					3129
Malaysia/Malaisie				2000	550
Indonesia/Indonésie				2000	
Netherlands/Pays–Bas					1118
Un. Rep. of Tanzania					1080
United Arab Emirates				1000	72
Morocco/Maroc				1000	
Germany/Allemagne					948
Italy/Italie					869
Malawi					785
Rwanda					738
Angola					730
Singapore/Singapour					553
Kenya					375
Ireland/Irlande					366
France,Monac					341
Dem. Rep. of the Congo					288
Hong Kong					267
Sweden/Suède					194
Thailand/Thaïlande					189
Burundi					119
Denmark/Danemark					119
Zambia/Zambie					104
Canada					76
China/Chine					74

(VALUE AS PERCENTAGE OF WORLD TOTAL)(VALEURS EN POURCENTAGE DU TOTAL MONDIAL)

	1985	1986	1987	1988	1989	1990	1991	1992	1993	1994
Africa	7.2	11.9	11.1	12.7	17.5				0.1	34.3
Americas	17.2	4.8	7.1	8.7	11.7					5.0
Northern America	6.9	3.8	5.8	7.3	10.1					4.9
LAIA	10.3	1.0	1.2	1.4	1.6					0.2
CACM		0.0	0.0							
Caribbean				0.0	0.0					
Rest of America										
As.ex F.USSR	19.1	19.9	18.6	16.7	13.8				12.6	13.9
Eur.x F.USSR	36.6	46.1	51.0	47.9	44.1					35.2
EU	32.3	41.9	48.6	45.3	40.9					33.0
EFTA	1.4	2.3	1.7	1.2	1.2					2.2
East Europe	2.6	1.9	0.7	1.3	2.0					
Other Europe	0.3	0.0	0.0	0.0	0.0					0.0
Former USSR	12.3	7.3	4.6	5.7	5.3					
Oceania	0.1	0.3	0.2	0.2	0.2					0.7
So. Africa Customs Un	5.7	6.2	6.4	7.6	12.4					30.1
Saudi Arabia									6.6	
Japan/Japon	2.6	5.2	5.1	3.9	5.0					8.4
United Kingdom	3.1	4.4	5.4	5.8	5.2					6.6
United Arab Emirates	5.5	7.5	5.3	4.4					3.4	0.4
Portugal	4.3	5.9	4.8	5.3	5.8					4.6
Germany/Allemagne	2.6	5.6	5.6	5.2	4.8					4.2
USA/Etats–Unis d'Amer	5.4	2.6	4.2	4.4	8.2					4.1
France,Monac	7.4	6.7	6.6	5.6	5.6					4.0
Zimbabwe	0.4	4.9	4.1	5.0	4.1					3.9

	1985	1986	1987	1988	1989	1990	1991	1992	1993	1994
Afrique	2.1	4.7	3.4	3.3	3.6				0.8	24.7
Amériques	7.8	9.8	9.1	6.1	9.0					8.5
Amérique du Nord	7.7	9.7	9.1	6.1	8.8					8.5
ALAI	0.0	0.0	0.0	0.0	0.2					
MCAC					0.0					
Caraïbes	0.1	0.1	0.0	0.0						
Autre Amérique	0.0	0.0								
Asie l'URSS exclus	54.4	54.8	53.2	58.1	40.7				6.8	23.1
Europe l'URSS exclus	31.6	26.0	30.4	27.6	29.5					34.7
UE	26.4	22.7	26.9	25.4	24.8					34.7
AELE	0.0	0.2	0.2	0.2	0.1					
Europe de l'Est	5.2	3.0	3.3	2.1	4.6					
Autre de l'Europe				0.0						
Ancienne URSS	0.8	1.1	1.8	1.4	2.2					
Océanie	0.0	0.0	0.1	0.1	0.1					
Spain/Espagne	10.9	11.8	12.1	11.8	13.6					19.2
So. Africa Customs Un	1.4	1.7	1.2	1.7	2.5					17.7
Japan/Japon	12.0	17.1	11.3	9.8	8.3					14.7
Portugal	4.5	2.4	4.8	4.6	5.9					8.9
USA/Etats–Unis d'Amer	7.6	9.7	8.7	5.8	8.7					8.4
India/Inde		4.3	2.6							7.1
Zimbabwe	0.0	0.3	0.3	0.3	0.6					4.4
Iran (Islamic Rp. of)									3.0	
Belgium–Luxembourg		0.1	0.3	0.3	0.1					2.3
United Kingdom	4.3	1.7	3.8	3.0	1.8					1.9

4. Special Imports C.I.F. by Commodities according to the S.I.T.C. (Rev. 2) in thousand U.S. Dollars
Importations Spéciales C.A.F. par Produits d'après la C.T.C.I. (Rév. 2) en milliers de Dollars E.U.

SITC CTCI	COMMODITY	1991		1992		1993		1994		PRODUIT
		WEIGHT POIDS	VALUE VALEUR	WEIGHT POIDS	VALUE VALEUR	WEIGHT POIDS	VALUE VALEUR	WEIGHT POIDS	VALUE VALEUR	
	ALL COMMODITIES								544015	TOUS PRODUITS
0	FOOD AND LIVE ANIMALS								78665	ALIMENTS,ANIMAUX VIVANTS
02	DAIRY PRODCTS,BIRDS'EGGS								4329	PRODUITS LAITIERS,OEUFS
022	MILK AND CREAM								3279	LAIT ET CREME
0224	MILK,CREAM PRESERVED ETC								2427	LAIT,CREME CONS,CONC
03	FISH AND PREPARATIONS								2249	POISSONS ET PREPARATIONS
04	CEREALS AND PREPARATIONS								52652	CEREALES ET PRODUITS
041	WHEAT ETC UNMILLED								8621	FROMENT,EPEAUTRE
0411	DURUM WHEAT UNMILLED								8621	FROMENT DUR NON MOULU
042	RICE								19639	RIZ
0421	RICE IN HUSK OR HUSKED								19639	RIZ SANS AUTRE PREPARATION
04211	RICE IN THE HUSK								19639	RIZ PADDY
044	MAIZE UNMILLED								3203	MAIS NON MOULU
046	WHEAT ETC MEAL OR FLOUR								11926	SEMOULE FARINE,FROMENT
04601	FLOUR OF WHEAT OR MESLIN								11744	FARINE DE FROMENT
048	CEREAL ETC PREPARATIONS								8824	PREPTNS A BASE CEREALES
0481	PREPD BREAKFAST FOOD ETC								6779	CEREALES TRAVAILLEES
05	VEGETABLES AND FRUIT								2196	LEGUMES ET FRUITS
06	SUGAR AND PREPS,HONEY								9781	SUCRES ET PRODUITS
061	SUGAR AND HONEY								9532	SUCRES ET MIEL
0611	RAW BEET AND CANE SUGAR								8033	SUCRES BRUTS
081	*FEEDING STUFF FOR ANIML								2613	NOURRITURE POUR ANIMAUX
0819	FOOD WASTE AND FEED NES								1983	DECHETS,ALIMENTS NDA
08199	FODDER NES,INCL SWEETNED								1927	PREPARATIONS FOURRAGERES
09	MISC EDIBLE PRODUCTS								2505	PREP ALIMENTAIRES DIVERSES
098	EDIBLE PRODCTS,PREPS NES								2223	PREP ALIMENTAIRES NDA
1	BEVERAGES AND TOBACCO								8396	BOISSONS ET TABACS
11	BEVERAGES								7190	BOISSONS
111	NON–ALCOHL BEVERAGES NES								3180	BOISSONS NON ALCOOLIQUES
11102	FLAVORED WATERS NON–ALCO								2703	LIMONADES,EAUX GAZEUSES
112	ALCOHOLIC BEVERAGES								4010	BOISSONS ALCOOLIQUES
1121	WINE OF FRESH GRAPES ETC								2510	VINS DE RAISINS FRAIS
2	CRUDE MATERLS,EXCL FUELS								10330	MAT BRUTES NON COMESTIBLES
22	OIL SEEDS,OLEAGINOUS FRT								1769	GRAINES,FRUITS OLEAGINEUX
222	SEEDS FOR'SOFT'FIXED OIL								1660	GRAINES HUILES FIXES
2221	GROUNDNUTS,GREEN								1645	ARACHIDES NON GRILLEES
26	TEXTILE FIBRES AND WASTE								4133	FIBRES TEXTILES
269	WASTE OF TEXTILE FABRICS								3879	FRIPERIE DRILLES,CHIFFONS
26901	BULK TEXT WSTE,OLD CLTHG								3879	ART ET ACCESS D'HABILLEMENT
3	MINERAL FUELS ETC								76445	COMBUSTIBLES MINERAUX LUB
33	PETROLEUM AND PRODUCTS								59520	PETROLE ET DERIVES
334	PETROLEUM PRODUCTS,REFIN								58542	PRODUITS RAFFINES
351	*ELECTRIC CURRENT								16757	ENERGIE ELECTRIQUE
4	ANIMAL,VEGETABLE OIL,FAT								8737	HUILES,GRAISSES ANIM,VEG
42	FIXED VEGETABLE OIL,FAT								5317	HUILES VEGETALES FIXES
423	FIXED VEG OILS,SOFT								3522	HUILES VEGET DOUCES FIXES
4236	SUNFLOWER SEED OIL								2406	HUILE DE TOURNESOL
424	FIXED VEG OIL NONSOFT								1795	AUTRES HUILES VEG FIXES
431	*PROCESD ANML VEG OIL,ET								1969	HUILES,GRAISSES PREPAREES
4312	HYDROGENATED OIL,FAT								1898	HUILES HYDROGENEES
5	CHEMCLS,RELATED PROD NES								70771	PRODUITS CHIMIQUES
52	INORGANIC CHEMICALS								3071	PROD CHIM INORGANIQUES
53	DYES,TANNING,COLOUR PROD								2383	PROD TEINTURE,COLORANTS
533	PIGMENTS,PAINTS,ETC								2048	PIGMENTS,PEINTURES,VERNIS
541	*MEDICINAL,PHARM PRODUCT								33103	PROD MEDICINAUX PHARMACEUT
5417	MEDICAMENTS								29084	MEDICAMENTS
54171	— CONTAINNG ANTIBIOTICS								29084	MED CONTN ANTIBIOTIQUES
55	PERFUME,CLEANING ETC PRD								2689	PROD POUR PARFUM,TOILETTE
554	SOAP,CLEANSING ETC PREPS								1668	SAVONS,PRODUITS DETERSIFS
58	PLASTIC MATERIALS ETC								3349	MAT PLAST ARTIFICIELLES
583	POLYMERIZATION ETC PRODS								2729	PROD POLYMERISATION
59	CHEMICAL MATERIALS NES								24235	MAT PROD CHIMIQUES NDA
591	PESTICIDES,DISINFECTANTS								20811	DESINF,INSECT,FONG,HERB
598	MISCEL CHEM PRODUCTS NES								3130	PROD DIV INDUST CHIM NDA
5989	CHEM PRODUCTS,PREPS NES								1650	PROD PREP CHIMIQUES NDA
6	BASIC MANUFACTURES								65303	ART MANUFACTURES
62	RUBBER MANUFACTURES NES								3924	CAOUTCHOUC MANUFACTURE
625	RUBBER TYRES, TUBES ETC								2563	PNEUS CAOUTCHOUC VULCANISE
6251	TYRES NEW FOR MOTOR CARS								2045	PNEUS POUR VOITURES
63	WOOD,CORK MANUFACTRS NES								2241	OUVRAGES LIEGE ET BOIS
635	WOOD MANUFACTURES NES								1695	ART MANUF EN BOIS NDA
64	PAPER,PAPERBOARD AND MFR								7758	PAPIERS,CARTONS & OUVRAGES
641	PAPER AND PAPERBOARD								4636	PAPIERS ET CARTONS
6411	NEWSPRINT								1656	PAPIER JOURNAL
6412	PRINTG,WRITING PAPER NES								1845	PAPIERS POUR L'IMPRESSION
64121	— UNCOATED								1845	PAPIERS IMPRES NON COUCHES
642	PAPER,ETC,PRECUT,ARTS OF								3122	PAP,CARTONS DECOUPES
6421	PAPER ETC CONTAINERS								1750	BOITES,SACS EMBALLAGES
65	TEXTILE YARN,FABRICS,ETC								11910	FILS,TISSUS,ARTICLES TEXTILE
652	COTTON FABRICS,WOVEN								2309	TISSUS DE COTON
6521	GREY WOVEN COTTON FABRIC								2309	TISSUS COT ECRUS NON MERCER
65214	GREY WOVEN COTTON NES								2017	AUT TISSUS 85% COTON ECRUS
655	KNITTED,ETC FABRICS								3976	ETOF BONNETERIE PIECES ETC
6552	OTHER KNIT ETC FAB NONEL								3976	ETOF BON NON ELAS NON SYNT
658	TEXTILE ARTICLES NES								2196	ART FACONNES MAT TEXTILES
6581	BAGS,SACKS OF TEXTILES								1680	SACS EMBALLAGE TEXTILES
66	NONMETAL MINERAL MFS NES								11060	ART MIN NON METALLIQUES
661	LIME,CEMENT,BLDG PRODS								5910	CHAUX,CIMENTS MAT CONSTR
6612	CEMENT								4577	CIMENTS HYDRAULIQUES
665	GLASSWARE								2066	OUVRAGES EN VERRE
67	IRON AND STEEL								7813	FER ET ACIER
673	IRON,STEEL SHAPES ETC								2453	BARRES,PROFIL FER,ACIER
678	IRON,STL TUBES,PIPES,ETC								3091	TUBES,TUYAUX EN FONTE,FER
6785	IRON,STEEL TUBE FITTINGS								1917	ACCESSOIRES DE TUYAUTERIE
68	NON–FERROUS METALS								3273	METAUX NON FERREUX
69	METAL MANUFACTURES NES								17098	ART MANUFACT EN METAL NDA
691	STRUCTURES AND PARTS NES								6863	CONSTRUCT FER,ACIER,ALU
6911	STRUCTURES,PARTS IRN,STL								6640	CONSTRUCT FER,ACIER,FONTE
695	TOOLS								3094	OUTILS A MAIN
699	BASE METAL MFRS NES								2909	ART MANUFACTURES MET NDA
7	MACHINES,TRANSPORT EQUIP								192863	MACHINES MATERIEL TRANSPORT

4. Special Imports C.I.F. by Commodities according to the S.I.T.C. (Rev. 2) in thousand U.S. Dollars
Importations Spéciales C.A.F. par Produits d'après la C.T.C.I. (Rév. 2) en milliers de Dollars E.U.

SITC CTCI	COMMODITY	1991		1992		1993		1994		PRODUIT
		WEIGHT POIDS	VALUE VALEUR	WEIGHT POIDS	VALUE VALEUR	WEIGHT POIDS	VALUE VALEUR	WEIGHT POIDS	VALUE VALEUR	
71	POWER GENERATING EQUIPMT								5453	MACHINES GENERATRICES
713	INTRNL COMBUS PSTN ENGIN								2718	MOTEURS EXPL COMB INT, PIECE
7131	AIRCRAFT PSTN ENGINS,PTS								2351	MOTEURS EXPL P.AVIATION, PIE
71319	PTS NES OF ENGN OF 71311								2236	PIECES POUR 713.11
716	ROTATING ELECTRIC PLANT								2130	APP ELECTR ROTATIFS,PIECES
7162	AC MTRS,GENRTRS,GEN SETS								1817	MOTEURS ELECTRIQUES
72	MACHS FOR SPCL INDUSTRYS								21680	MAC SPECIALES POUR INDUST
721	AGRIC MACHY,EXC TRACTORS								5257	MACHINES AGRICOLES
7212	HARVESTING ETC MACHINES								4792	ENGINS POUR LA RECOLTE
722	TRACTORS NON-ROAD								5551	TRACTEURS
7224	WHEELED TRACTORS NES								5551	TRACTEURS A ROUES
723	CIVIL ENGNEERG EQUIP ETC								5504	APPAREILS DE GENIE CIVIL
7234	CONST,MINING MACHNRY NES								5504	MACH POUR LA CONST, MINES
72341	SELF-PROPELLD DOZERS,ETC								4039	BULLDOZERS
728	OTH MACHY FOR SPCL INDUS								2366	AUT MACH IND PARTICULIERES
73	METALWORKING MACHINERY								9688	MACH TRAVAIL DES METAUX
736	METALWORKING MACH-TOOLS								5714	MACH-OUTILS TRAVAIL METAUX
7362	METAL FORMING MACH-TOOLS								1722	MACH-OUTILS DEFORM METAL
7367	OTH METALWRKG MACH-TOOLS								3260	AUT MACH-OUT POUR METAUX
737	METALWORKING MACHNRY NES								3974	MACH TRAV METAUX PIECES
7371	FOUNDRY EQUIPMNT,PTS NES								2082	CONVERTISSEURS ACIERIE,PIEC
7373	WELDING,BRAZING,ETC MCHS								1860	MACH SOUDAGE ETC PIECES
73732	ELECTRIC WELDERS,ETC								1687	MACH ELECT POUR SOUDER
74	GENRL INDUSTRL MACHY NES								26921	MACH APP INDUSTRIE
741	HEATING,COOLING EQUIPMNT								7706	MACH CHAUFFAGE,PIECES
7413	INDUS FURNACES ETC,PARTS								2951	FOURS IND,LABOR,PIECES
742	PUMPS FOR LIQUIDS ETC								5330	POMPES MOTO-POMPES
7428	OTHER PUMPS FOR LIQUIDS								5330	AUTRES POMPES POUR LIQ
743	PUMPS NES,CENTRFUGES ETC								3194	POMPES COMPRES,VENT ETC
7431	PUMPS FOR GASES ETC								1717	POMPES AIR A VIDE,COMPRES
744	MECHANICAL HANDLING EQU								6291	EQUIP MANUTENTION PIECES
7441	FORK LIFT TRCKS,ETC,PTS								2497	CHARIOTS POUR USINES ETC
7442	LIFTING,LOADING MACH NES								1916	APP LEVAGE,MANUTENTION
7449	PTS NES OF MACHY OF 7442								1878	PIECES DU 744.2
749	NONELEC MACH PTS,ACC NES								3178	PIECES MACH NON ELEC NDA
75	OFFICE MACHNES,ADP EQUIP								5692	MACH BUREAU TRAIT AUTOM
752	AUTOMTIC DATA PROC EQUIP								2795	MACH TRAIT INFORMATION
7521	ANALOG,HYBRID COMPUTERS								2795	MACH POUR TRAIT INFORMAT
76	TELECOMM,SOUND EQUIPMENT								13270	EQUIPMENT DE TELECOM
763	SOUND RECORDRS,PHONOGRPH								2818	PHONO,APP ENREGISTREMENT
7631	ELECTRIC GRAMOPHONES ETC								2565	ELECTROPHON,TOURNE-DISQ
764	TELECOM EQPT,PTS,ACC NES								9830	EQUIP TELECOM,PIECES
7641	LINE TELEPHONE,ETC EQUIP								4976	APP TELEPHON PAR FIL
7643	TV,RADIO TRANSMITTRS ETC								3746	APP EMET TELE RADIO
77	ELECTRIC MACHNRY NES ETC								23776	MACH APP ELECT NDA
772	SWITCHGEAR ETC,PARTS NES								5477	APP COUPURE,SECT ETC
7721	SWITCHGEAR ETC								5407	APP COUPURE,SECTIONMNT
773	ELECTR DISTRIBUTNG EQUIP								2523	EQUIPMT DISTRIBUTION ELECT
7731	INSULATED WIRE,CABLE ETC								2377	FILS,CABLES ISOLES ELECT
774	ELECTRO-MEDCL,XRAY EQUIP								5052	APPAREILS MEDICAUX
7741	ELECTRO-MEDICAL EQUIPMNT								5006	APP ELECTRICITE MEDICALE
775	HOUSEHOLD TYPE EQUIP NES								3885	MACH,APP USAGE DOMESTQUE
778	ELECTRICAL MACHINERY NES								4896	AUTRES MACH ELECT NDA
7781	BATTERIES,ACCUMULATORS								2256	PILES ET ACCUMULATEURS
78	ROAD VEHICLES								80649	VEHICULES ROUTIERS
782	LORRIES,SPCL MTR VEH NES								57849	VEHICULES SPECIAUX,MARCH
7821	LORRIES,TRUCKS								56194	VEHICULES TRANSP MARCHAND
7822	SPECIAL MOTOR VEHCLS NES								1655	VEHICULES USAGES SPECIAUX
783	ROAD MOTOR VEHICLES NES								10215	VEHICULES ROUTIERS NDA
7831	BUSES								10215	VOITURES TRANSPORT COMMUN
784	MOTOR VEH PRTS,ACCES NES								6258	PIECES 722,781,782,783
7849	OTHER MOTOR VEHCL PARTS								4671	PIECES 722,781,782,783
785	CYCLES,ETC MOTRZD OR NOT								4770	MOTOCYCLES SCOOTERS
7851	MOTORCYCLES ETC								4024	MOTO VELO MOTEUR AUXIL
79	OTHR TRANSPORT EQUIPMENT								5734	AUTRE MATERIEL TRANSPORT
791	RAILWAY VEHICLES								3710	VEHIC MAT CHEMINS DE FER
8	MISC MANUFACTURED GOODS								21809	ART MANUFACTURES DIVERS
821	*FURNITURE,PARTS THEREOF								4388	MEUBLES ET PIECES
8219	FURNITURE AND PARTS NES								3435	AUTRES MEUBLES ET PIECES
82191	METAL FURNITURE NES								3435	MEUBLES NDA EN METAL
84	CLOTHING AND ACCESSORIES								2624	VETEMENTS
87	PRECISION INSTRUMNTS NES								3022	INSTRUM,APPAR SCIENT NDA
874	MEASURNG,CONTROLNG INSTR								2072	INSTRUMENTS DE MESURE
89	MISC MANUFCTRD GOODS NES								7814	ART MANUFACTURES DIVERS
892	PRINTED MATTER								1816	IMPRIMES
893	ARTICLES OF PLASTIC NES								4383	OUVRAGES EN MAT DIVIS 58
8939	MISC PLASTIC ARTICLES								3538	ART DIVERS EN MAT DIV 58
89399	OTHR PLASTC ARTICLES NES								3132	AUT OUV MAT DIV 58
9	GOODS NOT CLASSD BY KIND								10696	ART TRANSACT NON CLASSES
931	*SPECIAL TRANSACTIONS								10589	TRANS.SPECIALES

5. Special Exports F.O.B. by Commodities according to the S.I.T.C. (Rev. 2) in thousand U.S. Dollars
Exportations Spéciales F.O.B. par Produits d'après la C.T.C.I. (Rév. 2) en milliers de Dollars E.U.

SITC CTCI	COMMODITY	1991 WEIGHT POIDS	1991 VALUE VALEUR	1992 WEIGHT POIDS	1992 VALUE VALEUR	1993 WEIGHT POIDS	1993 VALUE VALEUR	1994 WEIGHT POIDS	1994 VALUE VALEUR	PRODUIT
	ALL COMMODITIES								163977	TOUS PRODUITS
0	FOOD AND LIVE ANIMALS								100724	ALIMENTS,ANIMAUX VIVANTS
02	DAIRY PRODCTS,BIRDS'EGGS								691	PRODUITS LAITIERS,OEUFS
022	MILK AND CREAM								691	LAIT ET CREME
0224	MILK,CREAM PRESERVED ETC								691	LAIT,CREME CONS,CONC
03	FISH AND PREPARATIONS								68578	POISSONS ET PREPARATIONS
034	FISH,FRESH,CHILLED,FROZN								502	POISSON FRAIS, REFRIG,CONG
036	SHELL FISH FRESH,FROZEN								68001	CRUSTACES,MOLLUSQUES
04	CEREALS AND PREPARATIONS								1020	CEREALES ET PRODUITS
044	MAIZE UNMILLED								667	MAIS NON MOULU
05	VEGETABLES AND FRUIT								17883	LEGUMES ET FRUITS
057	FRUIT,NUTS,FRESH,DRIED								17674	FRUITS FRAIS OU SECS
0571	ORANGES, MANDARINS ETC								1220	ORANGES,MAND,CLEMENTINES
0577	NUTS EDIBLE,FRESH,DRIED								16454	FRUITS A COQUES
06	SUGAR AND PREPS,HONEY								11136	SUCRES ET PRODUITS
061	SUGAR AND HONEY								11136	SUCRES ET MIEL
0611	RAW BEET AND CANE SUGAR								11136	SUCRES BRUTS
07	COFFEE,TEA,COCOA,SPICES								523	CAFE,THE,CACAO,EPICES
074	TEA AND MATE								523	THE ET MATE
0741	TEA								523	THE
081	*FEEDING STUFF FOR ANIML								855	NOURRITURE POUR ANIMAUX
0813	OILCAKE AND OTH RESIDUES								643	TOURTEAUX
1	BEVERAGES AND TOBACCO								1041	BOISSONS ET TABACS
12	TOBACCO AND MANUFACTURES								1041	TABACS BRUTS FABRIQUES
121	TOBACCO UNMNFCTRD,REFUSE								1041	TABACS BRUTS,DECHETS
2	CRUDE MATERLS,EXCL FUELS								24873	MAT BRUTES NON COMESTIBLES
22	OIL SEEDS,OLEAGINOUS FRT								5071	GRAINES,FRUITS OLEAGINEUX
223	SEEDS FOR OTH FIXED OILS								5071	GRAINES AUTRES HUILES FIXES
24	CORK AND WOOD								2777	LIEGE ET BOIS
247	OTH WOOD ROUGH,SQUARED								1504	BOIS BRUTS EQUARRIS
2471	SAW-,VENEER-LOGS CONIFER								1504	CONIFERES POUR SCIAGE,PLACAG
24711	— IN THE ROUGH								1504	ECORCES OU DEGROSSIS
248	WOOD SHAPED,SLEEPERS								1273	BOIS SIMPLEMENT TRAVAILLES
2482	LUMBER SHAPED CONIFER								1071	CONIFERES SCIES,RABOTES
24821	LUMBER SAWN ETC CONIFER								1071	CONIFERES SCIES LONGITUD
26	TEXTILE FIBRES AND WASTE								13965	FIBRES TEXTILES
263	COTTON								13826	COTON
2631	RAW COTTON,EXCL LINTERS								9282	COTON EN MASSE
2633	COTTON WASTE,UNCOMBED								828	DECHETS DE COTON
2634	COTTON,CARDED OR COMBED								3716	COTON CARDE OU PEIGNE
28	METALLIFEROUS ORES,SCRAP								2426	MINERAIS METAL,DECHETS
282	IRON AND STEEL SCRAP								876	FERRAILLES
28201	— OF PIG OR CAST IRON								876	FERRAILLES DE FONTE
287	BASE METAL ORES,CONC NES								1426	MINERAIS METAUX COMMUNS
2873	ALUMINIUM ORES,ALUMINA								1426	MINERAIS D'ALUMINIUM
28731	ALUMINIUM ORE,CONCNTRATE								1426	MINERAIS D'ALUMINIUM
3	MINERAL FUELS ETC								14767	COMBUSTIBLES MINERAUX LUB
33	PETROLEUM AND PRODUCTS								14580	PETROLE ET DERIVES
334	PETROLEUM PRODUCTS,REFIN								14580	PRODUITS RAFFINES
4	ANIMAL,VEGETABLE OIL,FAT								639	HUILES,GRAISSES ANIM,VEG
42	FIXED VEGETABLE OIL,FAT								506	HUILES VEGETALES FIXES
424	FIXED VEG OIL NONSOFT								506	AUTRES HUILES VEG FIXES
4241	LINSEED OIL								506	HUILE DE LIN
6	BASIC MANUFACTURES								10805	ART MANUFACTURES
62	RUBBER MANUFACTURES NES								2781	CAOUTCHOUC MANUFACTURE
625	RUBBER TYRES, TUBES ETC								2741	PNEUS CAOUTCHOUC VULCANISE
6251	TYRES NEW FOR MOTOR CARS								2588	PNEUS POUR VOITURES
63	WOOD,CORK MANUFACTRS NES								1155	OUVRAGES LIEGE ET BOIS
634	VENEERS,PLYWOOD,ETC								1023	PLACAGES,CONTRE-PLAQUES
6341	VENEER SHEETS ETC								962	BOIS SIMPLEMENT SCIES
64	PAPER,PAPERBOARD AND MFR								1058	PAPIERS,CARTONS & OUVRAGES
642	PAPER,ETC,PRECUT,ARTS OF								1042	PAP,CARTONS DECOUPES
6421	PAPER ETC CONTAINERS								1042	BOITES,SACS EMBALLAGES
65	TEXTILE YARN,FABRICS,ETC								4186	FILS,TISSUS,ARTICLES TEXTILE
651	TEXTILE YARN								1670	FILS TEXTILES
6513	COTTON YARN								1617	FILS DE COTON
657	SPECIAL TXTL FABRC,PRODS								2379	TISSUS SPECIAUX
6573	COATED ETC TEXTILES NES								1990	TISSUS,ART MATIERE TEXT NDA
65733	RUBBERIZED TEXT NOT KNIT								1816	TISSUS CAOUTCHOUTES
69	METAL MANUFACTURES NES								879	ART MANUFACT EN METAL NDA
7	MACHINES,TRANSPORT EQUIP								5338	MACHINES MATERIEL TRANSPORT
71	POWER GENERATING EQUIPMT								643	MACHINES GENERATRICES
72	MACHS FOR SPCL INDUSTRYS								1138	MAC SPECIALES POUR INDUST
723	CIVIL ENGNEERG EQUIP ETC								764	APPAREILS DE GENIE CIVIL
7234	CONST,MINING MACHNRY NES								764	MACH POUR LA CONST, MINES
72341	SELF-PROPELLD DOZERS,ETC								624	BULLDOZERS
74	GENRL INDUSTRL MACHY NES								1295	MACH APP INDUSTRIE
78	ROAD VEHICLES								1882	VEHICULES ROUTIERS
782	LORRIES,SPCL MTR VEH NES								1722	VEHICULES SPECIAUX,MARCH
7821	LORRIES,TRUCKS								1633	VEHICULES TRANSP MARCHAND
8	MISC MANUFACTURED GOODS								2028	ART MANUFACTURES DIVERS
84	CLOTHING AND ACCESSORIES								1363	VETEMENTS
843	WOMENS OUTERWEAR NONKNIT								618	VET DESSUS FEMMES MAT TEX
8432	— SUITS AND COSTUMES								560	COSTUMES-TAIL MAT TEXIL
9	GOODS NOT CLASSD BY KIND								3620	ART TRANSACT NON CLASSES
931	*SPECIAL TRANSACTIONS								1073	TRANS.SPECIALES
971	*GOLD,NON MONETARY NES								2547	OR NON MONETAIRE
97101	NONMON GLD UNWRT,SEMIMFD								2547	OR,ALLIAGES D'OR BRUTS

1. HISTORICAL SERIES, 1961–1996 GENERAL TRADE, IMPORTS C.I.F., EXPORTS F.O.B.
SERIES HISTORIQUES, 1961–1996 COMMERCE GENERAL, IMPORTATIONS C.A.F., EXPORTATIONS F.O.B

YEAR ANNEE	VALUE IN MILLION KYATS VALEUR EN MILLION KYATS MERCHANDISE –MARCHANDISE		GOLD –OR		CONVERSION FACTORS U.S. CENTS PER KYAT FACTEURS DE CONVERSION CENTS E.U. PAR KYAT		INDEX NUMBERS –INDICES QUANTUM		UNIT VALUE VALEUR UNITAIRE	
	IMPORTS	EXPORTS	IMPORTS	EXPORTS	IMPORTS	EXPORTS	IMPORTS	EXPORTS	IMPORTS	EXPORTS
1961	1027.50	1057.00			21.0000	21.0000				
1962	1042.00	1263.00			21.0000	21.0000				
1963	1115.30	1288.00			21.0000	21.0000				
1964	1292.70	1126.00			21.0000	21.0000				
1965	1177.90	1076.00			21.0000	21.0000				
1966	751.90	934.00			21.0000	21.0000				
1967	741.20	590.30			21.0000	21.0000				
1968	858.70	529.40			21.0000	21.0000				
1969	784.80	629.10			21.0000	21.0000				
1970	807.00	515.80			21.0000	21.0000				
1971	933.30	609.60			21.0000	21.0000				
1972	866.63	654.70			18.3404	18.3379				
1973	702.70	698.60			20.3605	20.4048				
1974	1047.20	958.40			20.6012	20.5788		54		108
1975	1612.60	1104.60			15.4769	15.5273		54		108
1976	1311.11	1304.39			14.7860	14.7724		85		96
1977	1946.50	1474.70			14.0539	14.0574		86		110
1978	2240.40	1608.40			14.6056	14.5567		69		116
1979	2116.00	2548.80			15.0679	15.0664		105		116
1980	2337.30	3122.70			15.1222	15.1234		107		140
1981	2702.50	3352.70			13.8019	13.7660		112		159
1982	3178.10	3040.00			12.8610	12.8609		119		130
1983	2150.80	3039.40			12.4487	12.4396		136		123
1984	2016.20	2512.00			11.8483	11.9676		129		124
1985	2401.50	2575.90			11.8251	11.8041		100		132
1986	2245.20	2116.50			13.5609	13.5967		119		105
1987	1785.60	1449.80			15.0338	15.0782		88		81
1988	1538.00	1051.40			15.8628	15.7500		59		93
1989	1280.50	1410.40			14.9257	14.9048		72		116
1990	1709.40	2037.00			15.7995	15.9544		100		100
1991	4058.80	2633.00			15.9192	15.9275		97		101
1992	3971.00	3241.10			16.4040	16.3974		108		88
1993	5007.00	3609.40			16.2624	16.2390		149		81
1994	5285.90	4776.70			16.6127	16.5859		145		87
1995	7564.20	4825.80			17.6448	17.6383		151		136
1996	8064.40	4099.80			16.8736	16.8488		95		71

2. IMPORTS BY BROAD ECONOMIC CATEGORY AND EXPORTS BY INDUSTRIAL ORIGIN. (PERCENTAGE OF TOTAL VALUE)
IMPORTATIONS PAR CATEGORIES ECONOMIQUES ET EXPORTATIONS PAR BRANCHE D'ACTIVITE.(EN POURCENTAGE DE LA VALEUR TOTALE)

IMPORTS – IMPORTATIONS

	1990	1991	1992	1993	1994	1995	1996
TOTAL IMPORTS–IMPORTATIONS TOTALES		100.					
1 FOOD BEV–ALIMENTATION BOISSONS		12.2					
11 PRIMARY–PRODUITS DE BASE		0.6					
111 FOR INDUSTRY–POUR L'INDUSTRIE		0.0					
112 FOR HOUSEHOLDS–POUR LES MENAGES		0.5					
12 PROCESSED–PRODUITS ELABORES		11.6					
121 FOR INDUSTRY–POUR L'INDUSTRIE		7.3					
122 FOR HOUSEHOLDS–POUR LES MENAGES		4.3					
2 IND SUPPLIES–APPROV INDUSTRIELS		31.9					
21 PRIMARY–PRODUITS DE BASE		0.4					
22 PROCESSED–PRODUITS ELABORES		31.5					
3 FUELS–COMBUSTIBLES		3.3					
31 PRIMARY–PRODUITS DE BASE		1.5					
32 PROCESSED–PRODUITS ELABORES		1.8					
321 MOTOR SPIRIT–ESSENCE		0.1					
322 OTHER–AUTRES		1.7					
4 MACHINERY–EQUIPEMENT		16.7					
41 CAPITAL EQUIPMENT–MACHINES		15.1					
42 PARTS–PIECES ACCESSOIRES		1.7					
5 TRANSPORT–TRANSPORT		19.0					
51 PASSENGER CARS–AUTOMOBILES		3.2					
52 OTHER–AUTRES		9.2					
521 INDUSTRIAL–INDUSTRIELS		6.9					
522 NON INDUSTRIAL–NON INDUSTRIEL		2.3					
53 PARTS–PIECES ACCESSOIRES		6.7					
6 CONSUM GOODS–BIENS CONSOMMATION		15.8					
61 DURABLE–DURABLES		4.0					
62 SEMI DURABLE–SEMI DURABLES		6.9					
63 NON DURABLE–NON DURABLES		4.9					
7 GOODS NES–BIENS NDA		1.0					

EXPORTS – EXPORTATIONS

	1990	1991	1992	1993	1994	1995	1996
TOTAL EXPORTS–EXPORTATIONS TOTALES		100.					
1 AGRICULTURE		71.1					
2 MINING QUARRY–INDUS EXTRACTIVES		3.2					
3 MANUFACTURING–IND MANUFACTUR		25.7					
31 FOOD BEV TOBACCO–ALIM BOISS TAB		13.9					
32 TEXTILES–INDUSTRIES TEXTILES		3.6					
33 WOOD & PRODUCTS–BOIS & PRODUITS		2.6					
34 PAPER & PRODUCTS–PAPIER & PRODT		0.0					
35 CHEMICALS–INDUSTRIES CHIMIQUES		1.0					
36 NON METAL MIN–MIN NON METAL		0.2					
37 BASIC METAL–IND METAL BASE		0.3					
38 METAL MANUF–MANUF METAL		2.6					
39 OTH MANUF IND–AUTRES MANUF		1.5					

3. TRADE BY PRINCIPAL COUNTRIES OF PURCHASE AND SALE (VALUE IN THOUSAND U.S. DOLLARS)
ECHANGES SELON LES PRINCIPAUX PAYS D'ACHAT ET DE VENTE (VALEUR EN MILLIERS DE DOLLARS EU)

COUNTRIES–PAYS	GENERAL IMPORTS C.I.F. IMPORTATIONS GENERALES C.A.F				
	1991	1992	1993	1994	1995
World	845815	880125	1288525	1384225	1470323
Africa	5238	500	3373	1150	1221
Americas	28129	38572	48657	19463	20674
Northern America	27415	38520	48563	18528	19681
LAIA	569	52	94	935	993
CACM	144				
Caribbean	0				
Rest of America					
As.ex F.USSR	685492	765970	1104972	1186077	1259850
Eur.x F.USSR	112952	52114	87140	79166	83559
EU	95661	41763	76573	61062	64860
EFTA	9406	4906	7686	7964	8459
East Europe	6927	5403	2809	1545	1110
Other Europe	958				
Former USSR	1	1952		640	2656
Oceania	14002	1366	9208	15915	18915
Japan/Japon	185152	251987	328525	326057	346338
China/Chine	141844	155175	205139	169347	179880
Singapore/Singapour	105187	94459	133394	201957	214519
Thailand/Thaïlande	126433	114113	140738	137915	146494
Malaysia/Malaisie	60746	54028	92257	129893	137972
Korea, Republic of	21575	28843	47564	65647	69730
India/Inde	23423	20300	45754	51275	54464
Indonesia/Indonésie	8820	19184	52295	53167	56474
Germany/Allemagne	46129	18824	40327	22165	23543
USA/Etats–Unis d'Amer	26251	36796	45990	16975	18031
Hong Kong	4010	6570	21944	42030	44644
Australia/Australie	13947	1015	9208	15915	16905
United Kingdom	15593	8225	8427	7218	7667
Bangladesh	1248	5548	29822	2259	2400
Switz.Liecht	9278	4895	7593	7888	8378
France, Monac	6683	4657	10421	7678	8156
Netherlands/Pays–Bas	8741	3883	5734	8102	8606
Yugoslavia/Yougoslavie		41	73	8595	9130
Italy/Italie	3320	822	6059	2520	2677
Denmark/Danemark	7616	955	690	2696	2864
Belgium–Luxembourg	3380	2556	712	2866	3044
Turkey/Turquie	4	10543	1610		
Sweden/Suède	898	769	2064	2525	2682
Israel/Israël	1773	2667	509	1826	1939
Canada	1164	1724	2573	1553	1650
Pakistan	77	230	4871	1508	1602
Morocco/Maroc			3373	1130	1200
Romania/Roumanie	2704	2185	247		
Ireland/Irlande	151	686	1138	1427	1516
Philippines	8	36	377	2160	2294
Iran (Islamic Rp. of)		2285	141	1033	1098
Bulgaria/Bulgarie	2497	461	597	430	457
Austria/Autriche	1316	153	346	1062	1128
Portugal	0			1802	1915
Poland/Pologne	773	2529	33	63	67
Russian Federation		1952		640	679
Madagascar	2755				
Greece/Grèce	48	157	439	924	981
New Zealand	55	351			2010
Senegal/Sénégal	2305				
Brazil/Brésil	29	52	94	935	993
Czech Republic			932	500	531
Finland/Finlande	1786	44	24	47	49
Slovakia			932	500	
Czechoslovakia	927	28			
Fm Yugoslav	682				
Cyprus/Chypre	507				
Egypt/Egypte	1	500			
Kuwait/ Koweït	449				
Hungary/Hongrie	27	200	68	51	55

COUNTRIES–PAYS	GENERAL EXPORTS F.O.B. EXPORTATIONS GENERALES F.O.B.				
	1991	1992	1993	1994	1995
Monde	464950	599392	686554	896496	953796
Afrique	14306	10216	4617	1674	1897
Amériques	5312	12464	26132	47147	50161
Amérique du Nord	2157	12464	26132	47147	50161
ALAI	3156				
MCAC					
Caraïbes					
Autre Amérique					
Asie l'URSS exclus	433931	501003	573204	684585	728238
Europe l'URSS exclus	11350	18854	25562	19235	17923
UE	10095	17460	23842	19039	17715
AELE	1255	1394	1720	196	208
Europe de l'Est					
Autre de l'Europe					
Ancienne URSS					6986
Océanie	2	2589	1827	1798	2222
Singapore/Singapour	108320	98662	133124	146535	155901
Thailand/Thaïlande	91140	98430	119651	90020	95774
India/Inde	51328	100954	103074	115342	122714
Indonesia/Indonésie	8466	2320	11497	139756	148689
Hong Kong	34454	53992	73555	44636	47489
China/Chine	69515	55522	34073	46023	48964
Japan/Japon	30144	24667	30461	43447	46224
USA/Etats–Unis d'Amer	1972	12201	24841	45284	48179
Pakistan	10701	28768	18472	13531	14396
Malaysia/Malaisie	6187	9822	16033	16916	17997
Sri Lanka	8599	13079	7306	11048	11754
Bangladesh	5246	7859	15271	6127	6518
Germany/Allemagne	5218	10586	8303	3445	3665
Korea, Republic of	3728	4522	5708	6588	7009
United Kingdom	298	1746	3306	4473	4759
Cote d'Ivoire	357	5659	4615	1650	1756
Netherlands/Pays–Bas	2453	3193	2746	1413	1503
Maldives	1534	2146	2101	1377	1465
Kuwait/ Koweït	1792		1958	2282	2428
Italy/Italie	353	408	3485	2627	1570
Australia/Australie	2	2589	1827	1798	1913
France, Monac	356	348	773	2707	2880
Mauritius/Maurice	2107	4434			
Canada	185	262	1291	1863	1982
Sudan/Soudan	5261				
Sweden/Suède		202	1332	1805	1920
Switz.Liecht	1255	1390	1720	158	168
Belgium–Luxembourg	1375	926	763	771	821
Spain/Espagne	38	34	1846	1476	254
Peru/Pérou	3156				
Sierra Leone	2653		2	23	25
Philippines	722	71	404	408	434
Denmark/Danemark	4	16	1288	302	321
Democratic Kampuchea	1651				
Dem. Rep. of the Congo	1443				
Gambia/Gambie	1008	123			
United Arab Emirates	312	151	391	109	14
Egypt/Egypte	756				116
Saudi Arabia	71		71	295	314
Benin/Bénin	721				
Israel/Israël			54	126	134
New Zealand					309
Norway, SVD, JM		3		38	41
Viet Nam		39		20	21
Finland/Finlande				20	21

(VALUE AS PERCENTAGE OF WORLD TOTAL)(VALEURS EN POURCENTAGE DU TOTAL MONDIAL)

	1986	1987	1988	1989	1990	1991	1992	1993	1994	1995
Africa			0.2	0.1	0.1	0.6	0.1	0.3	0.1	0.1
Americas			1.9	2.0	12.5	3.3	4.4	3.8	1.4	1.4
Northern America			1.8	1.9	12.5	3.2	4.4	3.8	1.3	1.3
LAIA			0.1	0.1	0.0	0.1	0.0	0.0	0.1	0.1
CACM						0.0				
Caribbean						0.0				
Rest of America										
As.ex F.USSR			68.4	73.6	70.5	81.0	87.0	85.8	85.7	85.7
Eur.x F.USSR			25.6	24.0	13.8	13.4	5.9	6.8	5.7	5.7
EU			22.7	21.9	11.2	11.3	4.7	5.9	4.4	4.4
EFTA			0.5	0.6	0.6	1.1	0.6	0.6	0.6	0.6
East Europe			0.0	0.8	0.3	0.8	0.6	0.2	0.1	0.1
Other Europe			0.5	0.3		0.1				
Former USSR			0.0	0.0	0.0	0.0	0.2		0.0	0.2
Oceania			0.8	0.3	2.6	1.7	0.2	0.7	1.1	1.3
Japan/Japon			34.8	24.7	16.3	21.9	28.6	25.5	23.6	23.6
China/Chine			18.7	19.0	21.8	16.8	17.6	15.9	12.2	12.2
Singapore/Singapour			8.5	9.6	9.6	12.4	10.7	10.4	14.6	14.6
Thailand/Thaïlande			1.1	12.7	10.0	14.9	13.0	10.9	10.0	10.0
Malaysia/Malaisie			1.0	1.9	6.9	7.2	6.1	7.2	9.4	9.4
Korea, Republic of			2.9	3.1	3.6	2.6	3.3	3.7	4.7	4.7
India/Inde			0.4	1.0	0.7	2.8	2.3	3.6	3.7	3.7
Indonesia/Indonésie			0.2	0.3	0.3	1.0	2.2	4.1	3.8	3.8
Germany/Allemagne			8.9	8.2	3.3	5.5	2.1	3.1	1.6	1.6
USA/Etats–Unis d'Amer			1.7	1.8	12.3	3.1	4.2	3.6	1.2	1.2

	1986	1987	1988	1989	1990	1991	1992	1993	1994	1995
Afrique			1.4	1.6		3.1	1.7	0.7	0.2	0.2
Amériques			1.9	1.3	0.2	1.1	2.1	3.8	5.3	5.3
Amérique du Nord			1.9	1.3	0.2	0.5	2.1	3.8	5.3	5.3
ALAI			0.0	0.0		0.7				
MCAC										
Caraïbes										
Autre Amérique				0.0						
Asie l'URSS exclus			82.6	84.9	93.9	93.3	83.6	83.5	76.4	76.4
Europe l'URSS exclus			7.8	7.4	3.1	2.4	3.1	3.7	2.1	1.9
UE			7.2	6.6	3.1	2.2	2.9	3.5	2.1	1.9
AELE			0.5	0.5	0.0	0.3	0.2	0.3	0.0	0.0
Europe de l'Est			0.1	0.1						
Autre de l'Europe			0.0	0.0						
Ancienne URSS			0.0							0.7
Océanie			0.1	0.1	0.0	0.0	0.4	0.3	0.2	0.2
Singapore/Singapour			9.7	9.7	28.6	23.3	16.5	19.4	16.3	16.3
Thailand/Thaïlande			11.7	12.9	13.1	19.6	16.4	17.4	10.0	10.0
India/Inde			12.1	12.1	17.7	11.0	16.8	15.0	12.9	12.9
Indonesia/Indonésie			0.1	0.1		1.8	0.4	1.7	15.6	15.6
Hong Kong			4.7	6.0	8.4	7.4	9.0	10.7	5.0	5.0
China/Chine			30.7	28.6	13.4	15.0	9.3	5.0	5.1	5.1
Japan/Japon			6.6	5.8	7.5	6.5	4.1	4.4	4.8	4.8
USA/Etats–Unis d'Amer			1.9	1.3	0.1	0.4	2.0	3.6	5.1	5.1
Pakistan			0.8	1.1	0.4	2.3	4.8	2.7	1.5	1.5
Malaysia/Malaisie			2.1	1.4	1.4	1.3	1.6	2.3	1.9	1.9

4. General Imports C.I.F. by Commodities according to the S.I.T.C. (Rev. 2) in thousand U.S. Dollars
Importations Générales C.A.F. par Produits d'après la C.T.C.I. (Rév. 2) en milliers de Dollars E.U.

SITC CTCI	COMMODITY	1991 WEIGHT POIDS	1991 VALUE VALEUR	1992 WEIGHT POIDS	1992 VALUE VALEUR	1993 WEIGHT POIDS	1993 VALUE VALEUR	1994 WEIGHT POIDS	1994 VALUE VALEUR	PRODUIT
	ALL COMMODITIES # 1		845815		880125		1288525		1384225	TOUS PRODUITS
0	FOOD AND LIVE ANIMALS		44393		23856		26706		76927	ALIMENTS,ANIMAUX VIVANTS
02	DAIRY PRODCTS,BIRDS'EGGS		9175							PRODUITS LAITIERS,OEUFS
022	MILK AND CREAM	W 10954	8767							LAIT ET CREME
0224	MILK,CREAM PRESERVED ETC	W 10932	8757							LAIT,CREME CONS,CONC
02241	WHEY	W 5908	3792							LACTOSERUM (PETIT LAIT)
02242	MILK DRY,1.5% FAT OR LES	W 5024	4964							LAIT POUDRE INF 1.5%
02249	MILK(EX DRY) PRSVD,SWEET			W 8128	5764		11569		17247	LAIT CONS,CONC SUCRE
04	CEREALS AND PREPARATIONS		6570							CEREALES ET PRODUITS
046	WHEAT ETC MEAL OR FLOUR	W 22482	5835							SEMOULE FARINE,FROMENT
04601	FLOUR OF WHEAT OR MESLIN	W 22482	5835	W 2000	640	W 24	725	W 61	17608	FARINE DE FROMENT
07	COFFEE,TEA,COCOA,SPICES		4620							CAFE,THE,CACAO,EPICES
075	SPICES	W 1534	4493	W 15749	12734		3602		1663	EPICES
0752	SPICES,EX PEPPER,PIMENTO	W 1425	4277							AUTRES EPICES
07523	CLOVES	W 946	3237							GIROFLES
09	MISC EDIBLE PRODUCTS		21805							PREP ALIMENTAIRES DIVERSES
098	EDIBLE PRODCTS,PREPS NES		21720							PREP ALIMENTAIRES NDA
09809	MISC FOOD PREPRTIONS NES		21560	W 1219	1923		320		2422	PREP ALIMENTAIRES NDA
1	BEVERAGES AND TOBACCO		4083		2651		5885		5721	BOISSONS ET TABACS
11	BEVERAGES		3598							BOISSONS
111	NON–ALCOHL BEVERAGES NES		3402							BOISSONS NON ALCOOLIQUES
2	CRUDE MATERLS,EXCL FUELS		5807		3058		4197		8300	MAT BRUTES NON COMESTIBLES
26	TEXTILE FIBRES AND WASTE		3573							FIBRES TEXTILES
3	MINERAL FUELS ETC		40938		14068		53359		47127	COMBUSTIBLES MINERAUX LUB
32	COAL,COKE AND BRIQUETTES		29		180		5318		688	HOUILLES,COKES,BRIQUETTES
33	PETROLEUM AND PRODUCTS		40906							PETROLE ET DERIVES
333	CRUDE PETROLEUM	W 39134	12943							HUILES BRUTES DE PETROLE
334	PETROLEUM PRODUCTS,REFIN	W 23312	15044							PRODUITS RAFFINES
3344	FUEL OILS,NES	W 10207	4741							FUEL OILS
3345	LUBS,PETROLEUM OILS NES	W 10289	8927							HUILES LUBRIFIANTES
33451	LUBS(HIGH PETR CONT) ETC	W 10289	8927							HUILES LUBRIF,H LOURDES
335	RESIDUAL PETRLM PROD NES	W 42985	12919							PRODUITS RESIDUELS NDA
3351	PETRLM JELLY,MINERAL WAX	W 29362	8759							VASELINE,CIRES MINERALES
33512	MINERAL WAXES	W 29351	8745							PARAFFINES,CIRES DE PETROLE
33525	MINERAL TAR OILS ETC NES			MW 13031	13646				37525	AUTRES PRODUITS NDA
3353	MIN TAR PITCH,PITCH COKE	W 13614	4159							BRAI,COKE DE BRAI
33531	PITCH FROM MINERAL TARS	W 13614	4159							BRAI DE GOUDRON
4	ANIMAL,VEGETABLE OIL,FAT		61257		65198		86059		133742	HUILES,GRAISSES ANIM,VEG
42	FIXED VEGETABLE OIL,FAT		55474							HUILES VEGETALES FIXES
424	FIXED VEG OIL NONSOFT	W 110122	55464							AUTRES HUILES VEG FIXES
4242	PALM OIL	W 108322	54512							HUILE DE PALME
431	*PROCESD ANML VEG OIL,ET	W 15069	5709							HUILES,GRAISSES PREPAREES
4313	FATTY ACIDS ETC,RESIDUES	W 15052	5701							ACIDES GRAS INDUST,RESIDUS
43131	FATTY ACIDS,ACID OILS	W 15052	5701							ACIDES GRAS INDUSTRIELS
5	CHEMCLS,RELATED PROD NES		83190		100829		171259		100781	PRODUITS CHIMIQUES
5146	OXYGEN–FNCT AMINO–CMPNDS			W 7366	14340		25083		25989	COMP AMINES FONCT OXYGEN
52	INORGANIC CHEMICALS		7607							PROD CHIM INORGANIQUES
522	INORG ELEMNTS,OXIDES,ETC	W 33685	3424							ELEMENTS INORGANIQUES
523	OTHR INORG CHEMICALS ETC	W 7009	4172							AUT PRODUITS CHIMIQUES INORG
53	DYES,TANNING,COLOUR PROD		11901		4995		7614		7544	PROD TEINTURE,COLORANTS
531	SYNT DYE,NAT INDGO,LAKES	W 1153	7035							MAT COLOR ORGAN,LAQUES
5311	SYNTHIC ORGNIC DYESTUFFS	W 1153	7029							MAT COLOR ORGAN SYNTHET
533	PIGMENTS,PAINTS,ETC		4753							PIGMENTS,PEINTURES,VERNIS
5335	GLAZES,DRIERS,PUTTY ETC	W 3193	3572							PREPTNS COLOR UTILISES CERAM
53351	PREPRD PIGMENT,GLAZE ETC	W 2811	3316							PIGMENTS OPACIFIANTS
541	*MEDICINAL,PHARM PRODUCT		24187		9703		13974		13220	PROD MEDICINAUX PHARMACEUT
5417	MEDICAMENTS		20688							MEDICAMENTS
55	PERFUME,CLEANING ETC PRD		10750							PROD POUR PARFUM,TOILETTE
554	SOAP,CLEANSING ETC PREPS		8524							SAVONS,PRODUITS DETERSIFS
5541	SOAPS		3417	W 2540	2175		3630		4831	SAVONS,PROD TENSIO–ACTIFS
5542	WASHING PREPARATIONS ETC	W 5943	5029							PROD ORG TENSIO–ACT NDA
562	*FERTILIZERS,MANUFACTURE	W 37878	10563	W 30000	10051	W 4	20952	W 4	4861	ENGRAIS MANUFACTURES
5621	CHEM NITROGENOUS FERTLZR	W 27519	8108							ENGRAIS AZOTES
58	PLASTIC MATERIALS ETC		9627							MAT PLAST ARTIFICIELLES
582	PROD OF CONDENSATION ETC		9488							PROD CONDENS,POLYCOND
59	CHEMICAL MATERIALS NES		6797							MAT PROD CHIMIQUES NDA
598	MISCEL CHEM PRODUCTS NES		5413							PROD DIV INDUST CHIM NDA
5989	CHEM PRODUCTS,PREPS NES		4996							PROD PREP CHIMIQUES NDA
59899	OTH CHEM PRODS,PREPS,NES		4149							AUT PRODUITS CHIMIQUES NDA
6	BASIC MANUFACTURES		217807		141309		220152		242019	ART MANUFACTURES
61	LEATHER,DRESSED FUR,ETC		3009							CUIRS,PELLETERIES
62	RUBBER MANUFACTURES NES		17266		11325		13856		12546	CAOUTCHOUC MANUFACTURE
625	RUBBER TYRES, TUBES ETC	N 1408918	16594							PNEUS CAOUTCHOUC VULCANISE
64	PAPER,PAPERBOARD AND MFR		19699		7085		13535		7755	PAPIERS,CARTONS & OUVRAGES
641	PAPER AND PAPERBOARD	W 20963	18801							PAPIERS ET CARTONS
6411	NEWSPRINT	W 6997	4720							PAPIER JOURNAL
6412	PRINTG,WRITING PAPER NES	W 7133	5475							PAPIERS POUR L'IMPRESSION
64121	— UNCOATED	W 5711	4452							PAPIERS IMPRES NON COUCHES
6415	PAPER,PAPERBRD,BULK,NES	W 3202	6602							PAPIERS,CARTONS ROULEAUX
64153	GREASEPROOF ETC PAPER	W 2722	6181							PAP,CARTONS PARCHEMINES
65	TEXTILE YARN,FABRICS,ETC		74228							FILS,TISSUS,ARTICLES TEXTILE
651	TEXTILE YARN	W 6001	46237							FILS TEXTILES
6512	WOOL,HAIR YARN,INCL TOPS	W 522	5929							FILS DE LAINE,DE POILS
65126	WOOL ETC YARN AT RETAIL	W 221	3078							FILS CONT 85% LAINE FIN
6513	COTTON YARN	W 5145	39202	W 34	100		400		224	FILS DE COTON
652	COTTON FABRICS,WOVEN	A 17236	16498	A 946	3343		13496		23475	TISSUS DE COTON
6522	WOVEN COTTON BLEACHD,ETC	A 17234	16496							TISSUS COTON BLANCHIS ETC
65224	BLCHED COTTON FABRIC NES	A 15536	14159							AUT TIS PLUS 85% COT BLANCHI
653	WOVN MAN–MADE FIB FABRIC	A 2	19	A 105	820		1831		4627	TISSUS FIBRES SYNTH,ARTIF
657	SPECIAL TXTL FABRC,PRODS		3546							TISSUS SPECIAUX
6575	CORDAGE AND MANUFACTURES	W 7744	3139							FICELLES,CORDES,CORDAGES
658	TEXTILE ARTICLES NES		6616							ART FACONNES MAT TEXTILES
66	NONMETAL MINERAL MFS NES		21647							ART MIN NON METALLIQUES
661	LIME,CEMENT,BLDG PRODS	W 39739	4711							CHAUX,CIMENTS MAT CONSTR
6612	CEMENT	W 38601	3449	W 1000	5479		11306		17786	CIMENTS HYDRAULIQUES
662	CLAY,REFRACTORY BLDG PRD		4056							MAT CONST REFRACTAIRES
6623	REFRACTORY BUILDING PROD	N 2404321	2676							BRIQUES REFRACTAIRES
66231	SILICE EARTH BRICKS ETC	N 2403121	2672							BRIQUES ETC FARINE SILICE
665	GLASSWARE		2864							OUVRAGES EN VERRE
666	POTTERY		8158							POTERIE
6664	PORCELN,CHINA HOUSE WARE		5698							VAISSELLE,ARTS MEN PORC

4. General Imports C.I.F. by Commodities according to the S.I.T.C. (Rev. 2) in thousand U.S. Dollars
Importations Générales C.A.F. par Produits d'après la C.T.C.I. (Rév. 2) en milliers de Dollars E.U.

SITC CTCI	COMMODITY	1991 WEIGHT POIDS	1991 VALUE VALEUR	1992 WEIGHT POIDS	1992 VALUE VALEUR	1993 WEIGHT POIDS	1993 VALUE VALEUR	1994 WEIGHT POIDS	1994 VALUE VALEUR	PRODUIT
67	IRON AND STEEL		61211							FER ET ACIER
673	IRON,STEEL SHAPES ETC	W 52028	16170							BARRES,PROFIL FER,ACIER
6732	IRON,STEEL BARS ETC	W 32866	12872							BARRES FER,ACIER
6733	IRON,STEEL PROFILES ETC	W 18805	3195							PROFILES,PALPLAN FER,ACIER
674	IRN,STL UNIV,PLATE,SHEET	W 131685	40927							LARGES PLATS,TOLES
6749	OTH IRN,STL PLATES,SHEET	W 130796	40413							AUTRES TOLES FER,ACIER
69	METAL MANUFACTURES NES		20032							ART MANUFACT EN METAL NDA
691	STRUCTURES AND PARTS NES	W 12894	3237							CONSTRUCT FER,ACIER,ALU
6911	STRUCTURES,PARTS IRN,STL	W 11854	2927							CONSTRUCT FER,ACIER,FONTE
694	STL,COPPR NAILS,NUTS,ETC	W 38635	4471							CLOUS,VIS,ECROUS
69401	IRON,STEEL NAILS ETC	W 36698	4039							CLOUS,POINTES FER,ACIER
697	BASE MTL HOUSEHOLD EQUIP		4415							ART MENAGE MET COMMUNS
6974	BASE MTL DMSTC ARTIC NES		2600							ARTICLES NDA FONTE,FER,ETC
69741	— OF IRON OR STEEL		2552							ART NDA EN FONTE,FER
699	BASE METAL MFRS NES		4994		86246		110201		74181	ART MANUFACTURES MET NDA
6997	IRON,STEEL ARTICLES NES		2961							OUV FONTE,FER,ACIER NDA
69979	IRN,STL MANUFACTURES NES		2912							AUT OUVRAGES EN FER NDA
7	MACHINES,TRANSPORT EQUIP		328344		243767		405126		440781	MACHINES MATERIEL TRANSPORT
71	POWER GENERATING EQUIPMT		26103							MACHINES GENERATRICES
713	INTRNL COMBUS PSTN ENGIN		19124							MOTEURS EXPL COMB INT, PIECE
716	ROTATING ELECTRIC PLANT		6278							APP ELECTR ROTATIFS,PIECES
72	MACHS FOR SPCL INDUSTRYS		25011							MAC SPECIALES POUR INDUST
723	CIVIL ENGNEERG EQUIP ETC		8531							APPAREILS DE GENIE CIVIL
7234	CONST,MINING MACHNRY NES		8528							MACH POUR LA CONST, MINES
724	TEXTILE,LEATHER MACHNRY		4495							MACH POUR INDUSTRIE TEXTILE
7243	SEWING MACHS,NEEDLES ETC		4088							MACHINES A COUDRE,PIECES
728	OTH MACHY FOR SPCL INDUS		8235							AUT MACH IND PARTICULIERES
7284	MACHY FOR SPCL INDUS NES		7020							MACH SPEC IND PARTICUL.
74	GENRL INDUSTRL MACHY NES		30706							MACH APP INDUSTRIE
741	HEATING,COOLING EQUIPMNT		2849							MACH CHAUFFAGE,PIECES
744	MECHANICAL HANDLING EQU		7903							EQUIP MANUTENTION PIECES
7442	LIFTING,LOADING MACH NES		6344							APP LEVAGE,MANUTENTION
745	NONELEC MACHY,TOOLS NES		3122							AUT MACH NON ELEC,PIECES
7451	POWER TOOLS NONELEC, PTS		3060							OUT MACH PNEUM A MOTEUR
749	NONELEC MACH PTS,ACC NES		12928							PIECES MACH NON ELEC NDA
7499	OTH NONELEC MCHY PTS NES		12238							PIECES NON ELECT NDA
74999	MACH PARTS NONELEC NES		12208							PIECES MACHINES NDA
76	TELECOMM,SOUND EQUIPMENT		29246							EQUIPMENT DE TELECOM
761	TELEVISION RECEIVERS		15671							RECEPTEURS DE TELEVISION
762	RADIO BROADCAST RECEIVRS		3162							RECEPTEURS RADIODIFFUSION
763	SOUND RECORDRS,PHONOGRPH	N 19893	4904							PHONO,APP ENREGISTREMENT
7631	ELECTRIC GRAMOPHONES ETC	N 19893	4904							ELECTROPHON,TOURNE–DISQ
764	TELECOM EQPT,PTS,ACC NES		5509							EQUIP TELECOM,PIECES
7643	TV,RADIO TRANSMITTRS ETC		3028							APP EMET TELE RADIO
77	ELECTRIC MACHNRY NES ETC		65094		47593		70930		93234	MACH APP ELECT NDA
773	ELECTR DISTRIBUTNG EQUIP		6542							EQUIPMT DISTRIBUTION ELECT
7731	INSULATED WIRE,CABLE ETC		6534							FILS,CABLES ISOLES ELECT
775	HOUSEHOLD TYPE EQUIP NES		3698							MACH,APP USAGE DOMESTQUE
778	ELECTRICAL MACHINERY NES		53871							AUTRES MACH ELECT NDA
7781	BATTERIES,ACCUMULATORS		5116							PILES ET ACCUMULATEURS
77811	PRIMARY BATTERIES,CELLS	N 532816	4762							PILES ELECTRIQUES,PIECES
7782	ELECTRIC LAMPS,BULBS	MN 12613	3336							LAMPES, TUBES ELECTRIQUES
7788	OTH ELEC MACHY,EQUIP NES		45319							AUT MACH APP ELEC NDA
77886	OTH ELEC MACHINERY NES		44736							AUT MACH APP ELECTRIQUES
78	ROAD VEHICLES		107732							VEHICULES ROUTIERS
781	PASS MOTOR VEH EXC BUSES	N 6196	26782							AUTO TRANSPORT PERSONNES
782	LORRIES,SPCL MTR VEH NES	N 4582	43478							VEHICULES SPECIAUX,MARCH
7821	LORRIES,TRUCKS	N 4579	42853							VEHICULES TRANSP MARCHAND
784	MOTOR VEH PRTS,ACCES NES		12943							PIECES 722,781,782,783
7849	OTHER MOTOR VEHCL PARTS		12942							PIECES 722,781,782,783
785	CYCLES,ETC MOTRZD OR NOT		24264							MOTOCYCLES SCOOTERS
7851	MOTORCYCLES ETC	N 6877	9986							MOTO VELO MOTEUR AUXIL
7852	CYCLES, ETC NON–MOTOR	N 123182	9459							VELOCIPEDES SANS MOTEUR
7853	INVAL CARR, PTS OF 785		4819							FAUTEUILS INVALIDES,PIECES
78539	PARTS,ACCES NES OF 785		4819							PIECES DU 785
79	OTHR TRANSPORT EQUIPMENT		42380							AUTRE MATERIEL TRANSPORT
791	RAILWAY VEHICLES		2780							VEHIC MAT CHEMINS DE FER
7919	RY TRACK FIXT,ETC,PARTS		2780							MATER FIXE VOIES FERREES
79199	PARTS NES OF 7911–7915		2654							PIECES 791.1 ET 5
792	AIRCRAFT ETC		17583							APP NAVIGATION AERIENNE
7921	HELICOPTERS		14262							HELICOPTERES
7928	AIRCRAFT NES,ASSOC EQUIP		3272							APP NAVIG AERIENNE NDA
79283	AIRCRAFT LAUNCHERS ETC		3272							CATAPULTES
793	SHIPS AND BOATS ETC		22017							NAVIRES BATEAUX,ETC
7938	TUGS,SPECIAL VESSELS ETC		22017							REMORQUEURS,BATEAUX SPEC
79382	SPECL PURPOSE VESSLS ETC		22016							BAT–PHARES,–POMPES,DRAGUES
8	MISC MANUFACTURED GOODS		54768		26880		51028		59164	ART MANUFACTURES DIVERS
84	CLOTHING AND ACCESSORIES		9098							VETEMENTS
847	TEXTILE CLTHNG ACCES NES		8166							ACCES VET MAT TEXT NDA
8471	— NOT KNITTED		2969							ACCES VET MAT TEX NON BON
8472	CLTHNG ACCESRYS ETC KNIT		5197							ACCES VET BONNE NDA
851	*FOOTWEAR		7293							CHAUSSURES
87	PRECISION INSTRUMNTS NES		4904							INSTRUM,APPAR SCIENT NDA
874	MEASURNG,CONTROLNG INSTR		3202							INSTRUMENTS DE MESURE
8745	MEAS,CONTRL,SCI INST NES		1190		3614		6895		8260	APP SCIENT MESURE NDA
88	PHOTO EQU,OPTICL GDS ETC		5127							APP,FOURN PHOTO,OP,MONTR
882	PHOTO,CINEMA SUPPLIES		2615							PRODUITS PHOTO,CINEMA
89	MISC MANUFCTRD GOODS NES		25493							ART MANUFACTURES DIVERS
893	ARTICLES OF PLASTIC NES		9732							OUVRAGES EN MAT DIVIS 58
895	OFFICE SUPPLIES NES		4311							ART PAPET NDA
8952	PENS,PENCILS,FOUNTN PENS		2965							PLUMES,CRAYONS,STYLOS
898	MUSICAL INSTRUMENTS,PTS		5201							INSTRUMENTS DE MUSIQUE
8983	SOUND RECRDNG TAPE,DISCS	N 2500365	5082							SUPPORTS SON POUR 763
89831	PREPD SND RECORDNG MEDIA	N 2500365	5082							SUPPORTS PREPARES
899	OTHER MANUFACTURED GOODS		4771							AUT ART MANUF DIVERS NDA
9	GOODS NOT CLASSD BY KIND		5229		258511		264753		269662	ART TRANSACT NON CLASSES
931	*SPECIAL TRANSACTIONS		5228							TRANS.SPECIALES

5. General Exports F.O.B. by Commodities according to the S.I.T.C. (Rev. 2) in thousand U.S. Dollars
Exportations Générales F.O.B. par Produits d'après la C.T.C.I. (Rév. 2) en milliers de Dollars E.U.

SITC CTCI	COMMODITY	1991 WEIGHT POIDS	1991 VALUE VALEUR	1992 WEIGHT POIDS	1992 VALUE VALEUR	1993 WEIGHT POIDS	1993 VALUE VALEUR	1994 WEIGHT POIDS	1994 VALUE VALEUR	PRODUIT
	ALL COMMODITIES # 1		464950		599392		686554		896496	TOUS PRODUITS
0	FOOD AND LIVE ANIMALS		188912		215727		237037		453964	ALIMENTS,ANIMAUX VIVANTS
03	FISH AND PREPARATIONS		29717							POISSONS ET PREPARATIONS
034	FISH,FRESH,CHILLED,FROZN	W 4710	5610							POISSON FRAIS, REFRIG,CONG
035	FISH SALTED,DRIED,SMOKED	W 1672	3073							POISSON SECHE,SALE,FUME
036	SHELL FISH FRESH,FROZEN	W 5294	20647							CRUSTACES,MOLLUSQUES
04	CEREALS AND PREPARATIONS		44797							CEREALES ET PRODUITS
042	RICE	W 180222	39801	W 196000	40830	W 261	43521	W 1025	193392	RIZ
0422	RICE SEMI–MILLED,MILLED	W 180222	39801							RIZ POLI,GLACE INCL BRISURES
044	MAIZE UNMILLED	W 47722	4486	W 43000	4919	W 40	4547	W 69	8127	MAIS NON MOULU
05	VEGETABLES AND FRUIT		91456							LEGUMES ET FRUITS
054	VEG ETC FRSH,SMPLY PRSVD		81283							LEGUMES FRAIS,CONG,SECS
0542	LEGUMINOUS VEGETBLES DRY	W 250863	78486	W 442000	109371	W 514	117570	W 418	132521	LEGUMES A COSSE SECS
0548	EDIBLE VEG NES FRESH,DRY		2254							RACINES,TUBERCULES
057	FRUIT,NUTS,FRESH,DRIED		10053							FRUITS FRAIS OU SECS
0571	ORANGES, MANDARINS ETC		2155							ORANGES,MAND,CLEMENTINES
0577	NUTS EDIBLE,FRESH,DRIED		3078							FRUITS A COQUES
05771	COCONUTS FRESH OR DRIED		1502							NOIX DE COCO
05779	NUTS EDIBLE,FRSH,DRY,NES	W 944	1576							FRUITS A COQUES NDA
0579	FRUIT FRESH OR DRIED NES		4487							FRUITS FRAIS,SECS NDA
05795	PINEAPPLES,FRESH,DRIED		1724							ANANAS FRAIS OU SECS
05799	OTHER DRIED FRUIT	W 3304	1568							AUTRES FRUITS SECHES
06	SUGAR AND PREPS,HONEY		1516							SUCRES ET PRODUITS
07	COFFEE,TEA,COCOA,SPICES		6108							CAFE,THE,CACAO,EPICES
075	SPICES	W 2455	5076							EPICES
0751	PEPPER AND PIMENTO	W 1544	3595							POIVRE,PIMENTS
0752	SPICES,EX PEPPER,PIMENTO	W 910	1481							AUTRES EPICES
081	*FEEDING STUFF FOR ANIML	W 65573	8948			W 35	4222	W 14	1990	NOURRITURE POUR ANIMAUX
0811	HAY, FODDER, GREEN, DRY	W 55575	2407							FOIN ET FOURRAGE
08119	FODDER OF VEG ORIGIN NES	W 55570	2407							AUTRES FOURRAGES
0813	OILCAKE AND OTH RESIDUES	W 6842	4900	W 26000	2788	W 35	4222	W 14	1990	TOURTEAUX
09	MISC EDIBLE PRODUCTS		5372							PREP ALIMENTAIRES DIVERSES
098	EDIBLE PRODCTS,PREPS NES		5367							PREP ALIMENTAIRES NDA
09809	MISC FOOD PREPRTIONS NES		5367							PREP ALIMENTAIRES NDA
1	BEVERAGES AND TOBACCO		6641		5		2		53	BOISSONS ET TABACS
12	TOBACCO AND MANUFACTURES		6312							TABACS BRUTS FABRIQUES
122	TOBACCO,MANUFACTURED		5710							TABACS FABRIQUES
1221	CIGARS,CHEROOTS,ETC		1571							CIGARES
1222	CIGARETTES		4024							CIGARETTES
2	CRUDE MATERLS,EXCL FUELS		217957		199965		252435		252786	MAT BRUTES NON COMESTIBLES
22	OIL SEEDS,OLEAGINOUS FRT		42413							GRAINES,FRUITS OLEAGINEUX
222	SEEDS FOR'SOFT'FIXED OIL	W 156737	42357							GRAINES HUILES FIXES
2224	SUNFLOWER SEEDS	W 154607	41308							GRAINES DE TOURNESOL
23	RUBBER, CRUDE		5412							CAOUTCHOUC BRUT
232	NATURAL RUBBER,GUMS	W 8355	5412	W 18000	11642	W 23	14777	W 24	20235	LATEX CAOUTCHOUC NATUREL
23202	OTHER NATURAL RUBBER					W 23	14777	W 24	20235	CAOUTCHOUC NATUREL
24	CORK AND WOOD		148526							LIEGE ET BOIS
247	OTH WOOD ROUGH,SQUARED	W 392009	137505	V 193000	103140		120331		158064	BOIS BRUTS EQUARRIS
2472	SAW–,VENEER–LOGS NON–CON	W 391999	136552							NON CONIFERES SCIAGE,PLAC
24721	— IN THE ROUGH	W 379171	124566							BRUTS ECORCES DEGROSSIS
24722	— RGHLY OR HALF SQUARED	W 12828	11985							BOIS SIMPLEMENT EQUARRIS
248	WOOD SHAPED,SLEEPERS	W 158	11017	V 324000	52472		81195		17913	BOIS SIMPLEMENT TRAVAILLES
2483	LUMBER SHAPED NON–CONIFR	W 158	11017							NON CONIFERES SCIES,RABOTES
26	TEXTILE FIBRES AND WASTE		1658							FIBRES TEXTILES
28	METALLIFEROUS ORES,SCRAP		6931							MINERAIS METAL,DECHETS
287	BASE METAL ORES,CONC NES	W 13266	6913				4709		10117	MINERAIS METAUX COMMUNS
2871	CPR ORE ETC,CEMENT COPPR	W 1927	3794							MINERAIS DE CUIVRE,MATTES
28711	COPPER ORES,EXCL MATTE	W 1927	3794							MINERAIS DE CUIVRE
2876	TIN ORES,CONCENTRATES	W 1329	1897							MINERAIS D'ETAIN
29	CRUDE ANIMAL,VEG MAT NES		11704							MATIERES BRUTES ANIM,VEGET
291	CRUDE ANIMAL MTRIALS NES		1645							MATIERES BRUTES ANIMALES
292	CRUDE VEG MATERIALS NES		10059							MAT BRUTES VEGETALES NDA
2923	VEG PLAITING MATERIALS		5454							MAT VEGET POUR VANNERIE
2924	VEG USED IN PHARMACY ETC		2202							PLANTES MEDICINALES
2929	OTH CRUDE VEG MATERIALS		1790							MATIERES VEGETALES NDA
3	MINERAL FUELS ETC		1113		1318		1398		8258	COMBUSTIBLES MINERAUX LUB
5	CHEMCLS,RELATED PROD NES		3487		141		326		330	PRODUITS CHIMIQUES
55	PERFUME,CLEANING ETC PRD		2398							PROD POUR PARFUM,TOILETTE
553	PERFUMERY,COSMETICS,ETC		1736							PRODUITS DE PARFUMERIE
6	BASIC MANUFACTURES		16784		45860		32325		41017	ART MANUFACTURES
65	TEXTILE YARN,FABRICS,ETC		3862							FILS,TISSUS,ARTICLES TEXTILE
658	TEXTILE ARTICLES NES		2087							ART FACONNES MAT TEXTILES
66	NONMETAL MINERAL MFS NES		8887							ART MIN NON METALLIQUES
667	PEARL,PREC–,SEMI–P STONE		8047		17381					PERLES, PIERRES GEMMES
6673	PREC–,SEMI–PR STONES NES		7095							AUTRES PIERRES NON SERTIES
69	METAL MANUFACTURES NES		1454							ART MANUFACT EN METAL NDA
7	MACHINES,TRANSPORT EQUIP		9382		234		3456		4002	MACHINES MATERIEL TRANSPORT
79	OTHR TRANSPORT EQUIPMENT		9115							AUTRE MATERIEL TRANSPORT
792	AIRCRAFT ETC		9101							APP NAVIGATION AERIENNE
7928	AIRCRAFT NES,ASSOC EQUIP		8166							APP NAVIG AERIENNE NDA
79283	AIRCRAFT LAUNCHERS ETC		8166							CATAPULTES
8	MISC MANUFACTURED GOODS		20616		19544		40037		60822	ART MANUFACTURES DIVERS
84	CLOTHING AND ACCESSORIES		10496							VETEMENTS
847	TEXTILE CLTHNG ACCES NES		10061							ACCES VET MAT TEXT NDA
8472	CLTHNG ACCESRYS ETC KNIT		9689							ACCES VET BONNE NDA
851	*FOOTWEAR	P 331190	1662							CHAUSSURES
89	MISC MANUFCTRD GOODS NES		7202							ART MANUFACTURES DIVERS
894	TOYS,SPORTING GOODS,ETC		1928							VOITURES ENFANTS,JOUETS
8942	TOYS,INDOOR GAMES ETC		1928							JOUETS,JEUX ETC
89423	TOYS NES		1926							JOUETS,MODELES REDUITS
896	WORKS OF ART ETC		3402							OBJETS D'ART
89601	HAND PAINTINGS ETC NES		1511							TABLEAUX,PEINTURES
89606	ANTIQUES NES		1412							OBJETS D'ANTIQUITE
9	GOODS NOT CLASSD BY KIND		45		116597		119537		75021	ART TRANSACT NON CLASSES

FOOT NOTES – NOTES

TABLE 4 –

Foot Notes (Continued) – Notes (Suite)

1 In 1991 the data presented according to SITC, Revision 2 have been estimated from data reported according to the national classification.

TABLE 5 –

1 In 1991 the data presented according to SITC, Revision 2 have been estimated from data reported according to the national classification.

TABLEAU 4 –

1 En 1991 les données qui se présentent conformémen t à CTCI, Révision 2 sont les estimations des données rapportées d'après la classification nati onale.

TABLEAU 5 –

1 En 1991 les données qui se présentent conformémen t à CTCI, Révision 2 sont les estimations des données rapportées d'après la classification nati onale.

1. HISTORICAL SERIES, 1976–1995 SPECIAL TRADE, IMPORTS C.I.F., EXPORTS F.O.B. #1
SERIES HISTORIQUES, 1976–1995 COMMERCE SPECIAL, IMPORTATIONS C.A.F., EXPORTATIONS F.O.B

YEAR ANNEE	VALUE IN MILLION NEP. RUPEES / VALEUR EN MILLION NEP. RUPEES: MERCHANDISE – MARCHANDISE		GOLD – OR		CONVERSION FACTORS U.S. CENTS PER NEP. RUPEE FACTEURS DE CONVERSION CENTS E.U. PAR NEP. RUPEE		INDEX NUMBERS – INDICES: QUANTUM		UNIT VALUE VALEUR UNITAIRE	
	IMPORTS	EXPORTS	IMPORTS	EXPORTS	IMPORTS	EXPORTS	IMPORTS	EXPORTS	IMPORTS	EXPORTS
1976	2040.50	1211.20			8.0000	8.0000				
1977	2109.80	1047.40			8.0000	8.0000				
1978	2676.70	1099.70			8.2844	8.2826				
1979	3053.20	1305.70			8.3333	8.3333				
1980	4107.30	964.20			8.3333	8.3333				
1981	4720.50	1512.50			8.2637	8.2682				
1982	5237.10	1160.50			7.5494	7.5577				
1983	6746.40	1360.90			6.8801	6.8599				
1984	6846.70	2109.30			6.0867	6.0439				
1985	8454.40	2932.00			5.4805	5.4893				
1986	9750.60	3005.10			4.7144	4.7122				
1987	12443.80	3289.60			4.5852	4.5823				
1988	15850.20	4433.10			4.2832	4.3193				
1989	15780.20	4303.20			3.6858	3.6959				
1990	20156.70	6159.50			3.4057	3.4004				
1991	28234.80	9831.30			2.7089	2.6706				
1992	33843.10	15976.70			2.3410	2.3408				
1993	42751.90	18935.20			2.0575	2.0549				
1994	57249.01	17961.01			2.0245	2.0247				
1995	71315.01	18076.00			1.9321	1.9313				

2. IMPORTS BY BROAD ECONOMIC CATEGORY AND EXPORTS BY INDUSTRIAL ORIGIN. (PERCENTAGE OF TOTAL VALUE)
IMPORTATIONS PAR CATEGORIES ECONOMIQUES ET EXPORTATIONS PAR BRANCHE D'ACTIVITE.(EN POURCENTAGE DE LA VALEUR TOTALE)

IMPORTS – IMPORTATIONS

	1990	1991	1992	1993	1994	1995	1996
TOTAL IMPORTS–IMPORTATIONS TOTALES	100.	100.	100.	100.		100.	
1 FOOD BEV–ALIMENTATION BOISSONS	12.9	8.6	10.3	8.0		15.0	
11 PRIMARY–PRODUITS DE BASE	6.0	4.2	6.0	2.8		5.1	
111 FOR INDUSTRY–POUR L'INDUSTRIE	2.5	1.8	3.5	1.2		1.3	
112 FOR HOUSEHOLDS–POUR LES MENAGES	3.6	2.4	2.5	1.6		3.8	
12 PROCESSED–PRODUITS ELABORES	6.8	4.3	4.3	5.2		9.9	
121 FOR INDUSTRY–POUR L'INDUSTRIE	3.5	3.5	3.4	4.1		6.9	
122 FOR HOUSEHOLDS–POUR LES MENAGES	3.3	0.9	0.9	1.1		3.0	
2 IND SUPPLIES–APPROV INDUSTRIELS	47.4	37.6	40.9	42.9		30.8	
21 PRIMARY–PRODUITS DE BASE	8.8	9.0	12.8	14.4		5.4	
22 PROCESSED–PRODUITS ELABORES	38.5	28.7	28.1	28.5		25.3	
3 FUELS–COMBUSTIBLES	8.6	8.8	12.4	11.5		19.5	
31 PRIMARY–PRODUITS DE BASE	0.0	1.1	12.2	0.8		0.0	
32 PROCESSED–PRODUITS ELABORES	8.6	7.6	0.2	10.7		19.5	
321 MOTOR SPIRIT–ESSENCE	0.4						
322 OTHER–AUTRES	8.1	7.6	0.2	10.7		19.5	
4 MACHINERY–EQUIPEMENT	13.8	16.7	9.7	7.7		12.8	
41 CAPITAL EQUIPMENT–MACHINES	11.8	15.7	9.6	7.6		11.8	
42 PARTS–PIECES ACCESSOIRES	2.0	1.0	0.1	0.1		1.0	
5 TRANSPORT–TRANSPORT	4.4	3.0	3.2	4.4		5.1	
51 PASSENGER CARS–AUTOMOBILES	1.0	1.0	1.1	1.7			
52 OTHER–AUTRES	0.9	0.6	0.7	1.6		1.5	
521 INDUSTRIAL–INDUSTRIELS	0.6	0.5	0.4	1.6		1.5	
522 NON INDUSTRIAL–NON INDUSTRIEL	0.3	0.2	0.3	0.1			
53 PARTS–PIECES ACCESSOIRES	2.5	1.4	1.4	1.1		3.6	
6 CONSUM GOODS–BIENS CONSOMMATION	12.5	9.3	8.4	9.6		8.7	
61 DURABLE–DURABLES	1.5	1.5	1.4	2.0		2.2	
62 SEMI DURABLE–SEMI DURABLES	4.0	2.6	2.4	2.8		4.0	
63 NON DURABLE–NON DURABLES	7.0	5.1	4.7	4.8		2.5	
7 GOODS NES–BIENS NDA	14.1	16.0	15.1	15.9		8.1	

EXPORTS – EXPORTATIONS

	1990	1991	1992	1993	1994	1995	1996
TOTAL EXPORTS–EXPORTATIONS TOTALES	100.	100.	100.	100.		100.	
1 AGRICULTURE	12.7	14.4	14.3	11.2		1.1	
2 MINING QUARRY–INDUS EXTRACTIVES	0.2	0.2	0.2	0.1			
3 MANUFACTURING–IND MANUFACTUR	87.0	85.4	85.6	88.7		98.9	
31 FOOD BEV TOBACCO–ALIM BOISS TAB	3.5	2.5	1.2	1.0		0.0	
32 TEXTILES–INDUSTRIES TEXTILES	79.3	77.1	79.8	82.3		96.6	
33 WOOD & PRODUCTS–BOIS & PRODUITS	0.1	0.1	0.1	0.0		0.1	
34 PAPER & PRODUCTS–PAPIER & PRODT	0.0	0.1	0.2	0.1		0.3	
35 CHEMICALS–INDUSTRIES CHIMIQUES	0.5	2.1	1.6	0.6		0.1	
36 NON METAL MIN–MIN NON METAL	0.0	0.0					
37 BASIC METAL–IND METAL BASE	0.0						
38 METAL MANUF–MANUF METAL	0.3	0.7	0.5	0.8		1.1	
39 OTH MANUF IND–AUTRES MANUF	3.2	2.8	2.2	3.7		0.8	

3. TRADE BY PRINCIPAL COUNTRIES OF FIRST AND LAST CONSIGNMENT (VALUE IN THOUSAND U.S. DOLLARS)
ECHANGES SELON LES PRINCIPAUX PAYS DE PREMIERE ET DE DERNIERE CONSIGNATION (VALEUR EN MILLIERS DE DOLLARS EU)

COUNTRIES–PAYS	SPECIAL IMPORTS C.I.F. IMPORTATIONS SPECIALES C.A.F				
	1991	1992	1993	1994	1995
World	592137	695151	695975	1044051	855909
Africa	6224	4971	7799		317
Americas	8093	18275	18531		26700
Northern America	5348	9693	9933		11544
LAIA	2739	8582	8598		15121
CACM					36
Caribbean	5				
Rest of America					
As.ex F.USSR	465328	541686	534557	344882	691969
Eur.x F.USSR	76133	77963	71263		99461
EU	53931	51963	50736		91136
EFTA	8797	4267	2742		4537
East Europe	13286	21730	17783		3759
Other Europe	120				
Former USSR	376	244	3357		4373
Oceania	35978	52005	60460		33089
India/Inde	198383	263257	264968	344882	
Singapore/Singapour	91484	137293	128631		218127
Japan/Japon	84750	67252	55760		64024
Hong Kong	9148	9648	15087		218316
New Zealand	32922	47423	55068		27946
China/Chine	29864	16217	20376		45987
Germany/Allemagne	13429	18467	17561		35000
Korea, Republic of	14036	16021	14392		16379
France,Monac	19657	10867	13583		11605
United Kingdom	4146	7729	10082		16524
Poland/Pologne	9854	13554	8687		2552
Thailand/Thaïlande	5605	7101	7201		12758
Bangladesh	7293	828	4346		17572
USA/Etats–Unis d'Amer	4408	8538	5000		8576
United Arab Emirates	974	696	1594		19699
Brazil/Brésil	2457	5047	7044		8183
Bahrain/Bahreïn	4	69	124		20713
Madagascar	6188	4928	7328		
Australia/Australie	3055	4581	5391		5081
Switz.Liecht	8588	4091	1773		2872
Saudi Arabia	477	4822	2086		9256
Indonesia/Indonésie	2473	3161	3074		6470
Denmark/Danemark	779	2012	1356		9445
Finland/Finlande	4481	5227	575		3149
Belgium–Luxembourg	2146	3034	2172		5722
Argentina/Argentine		3473	1331		6663
Romania/Roumanie	2267	5317	3458		0
Jordan/Jordanie		3098	4598		2867
Canada	940	1155	4934		2967
Malaysia/Malaisie					9909
Spain/Espagne	3454	662	2096		1800
Russian Federation		244	3357		4310
Kuwait/ Koweït	6382				627
Italy/Italie	1960	1434	459		3125
Netherlands/Pays–Bas	1896	883	1287		2688
Oman	1	1	0		5868
Bulgaria/Bulgarie	8	768	3845		
Brunei Darussalam	505	188	167		3612
Pakistan	351	868	850		2294
Ireland/Irlande	806	1135	1057		1311
Norway,SVD,JM	209	176	969		1665
Hungary/Hongrie	72	1124	799		396
Czechoslovakia	1085	967			
Philippines	26	66	1544		280
Czech Republic			994		810
Iran (Islamic Rp. of)	1404	107	195		
Viet Nam	611	944			20
Sweden/Suède	612	346	293		313
Sri Lanka	348	131	259		308
Austria/Autriche	271	117	189		443

COUNTRIES–PAYS	SPECIAL EXPORTS F.O.B. EXPORTATIONS SPECIALES F.O.B.				
	1991	1992	1993	1994	1995
Monde	192934	319192	354604	390633	286323
Afrique	10	89	32		72
Amériques	38783	76811	81157		106788
Amérique du Nord	38781	76724	81051		106205
ALAI	2	87	94		518
MCAC					
Caraïbes					60
Autre Amérique			12		5
Asie l'URSS exclus	48042	63411	60336	48773	5295
Europe l'URSS exclus	105810	178119	210310		173368
UE	91775	163041	194548		163569
AELE	13429	15031	15601		9498
Europe de l'Est	599	45	159		283
Autre de l'Europe	7		0		
Ancienne URSS	106	4	34		113
Océanie	182	757	2736		687
Germany/Allemagne	72886	139788	172457		131247
USA/Etats–Unis d'Amer	37407	74004	75830		103033
India/Inde	41462	33944	34761	48773	
Switz.Liecht	13278	14898	15494		9307
Sri Lanka	2708	19969	16423		944
Belgium–Luxembourg	4707	6433	5865		5537
United Kingdom	4514	4233	4310		6623
Italy/Italie	3905	3888	3833		7189
Canada	1374	2720	5221		3166
Austria/Autriche	901	2029	1850		4041
Netherlands/Pays–Bas	2013	2301	1671		2724
France,Monac	1578	1604	2696		2824
Singapore/Singapour	849	3554	2570		480
Japan/Japon	776	1205	1748		1512
Australia/Australie	138	695	2616		566
Spain/Espagne	244	437	788		2306
Pakistan	230	2413	624		101
Hong Kong	220	1073	846		1099
Sweden/Suède	605	962	509		452
Korea, Republic of	1543	149	101		349
Bangladesh	55	560	1227		133
Ireland/Irlande	198	791	229		137
United Arab Emirates	3	161	801		42
Denmark/Danemark	188	335	191		258
Thailand/Thaïlande	46	6	495		167
Norway,SVD,JM	151	118	107		191
Czechoslovakia	531	0			
New Zealand	44	62	120		122
Finland/Finlande	38	82	79		129
Portugal	0	150	57		74
Brazil/Brésil	1	65	3		194
Mexico/Mexique		7	22		216
Hungary/Hongrie	1	16	50		164
Czech Republic			99		108
Iran (Islamic Rp. of)	6	80	72		1
Russian Federation		4	34		111
Argentina/Argentine	0	5	44		97
Poland/Pologne	68	29	10		9
Former USSR/Anc. URSS	106				
Indonesia/Indonésie	30	0	1		42
Greece/Grèce	0	7	13		28
Saudi Arabia	0	4	33		6
Brunei Darussalam	6	0	7		13
Bhutan/Bhoutan	8	2	13		3
Turkey/Turquie		0	7		11
Madagascar	3	3	7		
Oman		1	12		
Fm Yugoslav	7				
Cyprus/Chypre					5
Philippines	0	1	1		2

(VALUE AS PERCENTAGE OF WORLD TOTAL)(VALEURS EN POURCENTAGE DU TOTAL MONDIAL)

Imports / Importations

	1986	1987	1988	1989	1990	1991	1992	1993	1994	1995
Africa	0.5	0.4	0.7	1.4	1.1	1.1	0.7	1.1		0.0
Americas	1.9	1.0	1.6	1.6	1.4	1.4	2.6	2.7		3.1
Northern America	1.8	1.0	1.5	1.5	1.3	0.9	1.4	1.4		1.3
LAIA	0.1	0.0	0.1	0.1	0.1	0.5	1.2	1.2		1.8
CACM				0.0	0.0					0.0
Caribbean	0.0				0.0	0.0				
Rest of America	0.0				0.0					
As.ex F.USSR	88.1	83.3	76.7	73.6	78.8	78.6	77.9	76.8	33.0	80.8
Eur.x F.USSR	8.7	13.6	12.9	19.3	14.2	12.9	11.2	10.2		11.6
EU	6.7	11.3	11.5	14.9	11.5	9.1	7.5	7.3		10.6
EFTA	0.9	0.3	0.5	0.4	0.7	1.5	0.6	0.4		0.5
East Europe	1.1	1.9	0.9	4.1	2.0	2.2	3.1	2.6		0.4
Other Europe	0.1	0.0	0.0	0.0	0.0	0.0				
Former USSR	0.1	0.0	2.9	0.9	0.0	0.1	0.0	0.5		0.5
Oceania	0.7	1.6	4.8	3.1	4.4	6.1	7.5	8.7		3.9
India/Inde	53.4	40.4	37.3	31.0	27.6	33.5	37.9	38.1	33.0	
Singapore/Singapour	3.2	7.4	8.2	10.7	16.2	15.4	19.8	18.5		25.5
Japan/Japon	15.7	13.6	13.1	12.7	8.1	14.3	9.7	8.0		7.5
Hong Kong	2.4	1.9	1.5	1.9	5.0	1.5	1.4	2.2		25.5
New Zealand	0.3	1.3	4.1	2.5	4.0	5.6	6.8	7.9		3.3
China/Chine	5.5	2.6	3.4	3.2	7.5	5.0	2.3	2.9		5.4
Germany/Allemagne	3.2	3.0	5.1	6.6	2.5	2.3	2.7	2.5		4.1
Korea, Republic of	5.0	5.5	4.3	4.4	4.6	2.4	2.3	2.1		1.9
France,Monac	0.6	0.3	1.1	2.1	3.3	3.3	1.6	2.0		1.4
United Kingdom	1.0	1.8	1.9	2.7	1.1	0.7	1.1	1.4		1.9

Exports / Exportations

	1986	1987	1988	1989	1990	1991	1992	1993	1994	1995
Afrique	0.0	0.0	0.0	0.0	0.0	0.0	0.0	0.0		0.0
Amériques	29.4	21.0	23.2	29.3	34.4	20.1	24.1	22.9		37.3
Amérique du Nord	29.0	20.9	23.1	29.3	34.3	20.1	24.0	22.9		37.1
ALAI	0.2	0.1	0.1	0.0	0.0	0.0	0.0	0.0		0.2
MCAC	0.1				0.0					
Caraïbes										0.0
Autre Amérique	0.1				0.1			0.0		0.0
Asie l'URSS exclus	49.0	50.2	40.3	29.1	21.4	24.9	19.9	17.0	12.5	1.8
Europe l'URSS exclus	19.1	27.2	35.5	41.5	42.5	54.8	55.8	59.3		60.5
UE	15.7	20.5	27.3	33.0	35.0	47.6	51.1	54.9		57.1
AELE	2.0	5.8	6.9	7.9	6.9	7.0	4.7	4.4		3.3
Europe de l'Est	1.4	1.0	1.3	0.7	0.7	0.3	0.0	0.0		0.1
Autre de l'Europe		0.0	0.0	0.0		0.0		0.0		
Ancienne URSS	2.3	1.5	1.0		1.1	0.1	0.0	0.0		0.0
Océanie	0.2	0.1	0.1	0.1	0.4	0.1	0.2	0.8		0.2
Germany/Allemagne	7.5	10.2	16.4	21.4	24.8	37.8	43.8	48.6		45.8
USA/Etats–Unis d'Amer	28.5	20.4	22.8	28.7	33.8	19.4	23.2	21.4		36.0
India/Inde	33.8	44.0	38.6	25.4	12.1	21.5	10.6	9.8	12.5	
Switz.Liecht	2.0	5.4	6.6	7.7	6.5	6.9	4.7	4.4		3.3
Sri Lanka	5.3	0.7	0.0		0.0	1.4	6.3	4.6		0.3
Belgium–Luxembourg	0.7	0.9	1.4	2.3	3.1	2.4	2.0	1.7		1.9
United Kingdom	3.7	5.7	6.1	5.9	4.4	2.3	1.3	1.2		2.3
Italy/Italie	3.2	2.5	1.7	1.7	1.9	2.0	1.2	1.1		2.5
Canada	0.5	0.4	0.3	0.5	0.6	0.7	0.9	1.5		1.1
Austria/Autriche	0.0	0.0	0.1	0.1	0.1	0.5	0.6	0.5		1.4

4. Special Imports C.I.F. by Commodities according to the S.I.T.C. (Rev. 2) in thousand U.S. Dollars
Importations Spéciales C.A.F. par Produits d'après la C.T.C.I. (Rév. 2) en milliers de Dollars E.U.

SITC CTCI	COMMODITY	1992		1993		1994		1995		PRODUIT
		WEIGHT POIDS	VALUE VALEUR	WEIGHT POIDS	VALUE VALEUR	WEIGHT POIDS	VALUE VALEUR	WEIGHT POIDS	VALUE VALEUR	
	ALL COMMODITIES		695151		695975		1044051		855909	TOUS PRODUITS
0	FOOD AND LIVE ANIMALS		46622		30706		82697		40954	ALIMENTS,ANIMAUX VIVANTS
001	*LIVE ANIMALS FOR FOOD		12518		535				13	ANIMAUX VIVANTS
0019	LIVE ANIMALS FR FOOD NES		12510		535					ANIMAUX VIVANTS NDA
02	DAIRY PRODCTS,BIRDS'EGGS		9098		5346				704	PRODUITS LAITIERS,OEUFS
022	MILK AND CREAM		8170		5346				555	LAIT ET CREME
0223	MILK AND CREAM FRESH		3909		894					LAIT,CREME FRAIS
04	CEREALS AND PREPARATIONS		11005		8172				4660	CEREALES ET PRODUITS
041	WHEAT ETC UNMILLED		4605		1124					FROMENT,EPEAUTRE
0411	DURUM WHEAT UNMILLED		4605		1124					FROMENT DUR NON MOULU
042	RICE		5645		6122				1295	RIZ
0421	RICE IN HUSK OR HUSKED		5644		5691					RIZ SANS AUTRE PREPARATION
048	CEREAL ETC PREPARATIONS				571				2657	PREPTNS A BASE CEREALES
05	VEGETABLES AND FRUIT		6253		4692				21459	LEGUMES ET FRUITS
054	VEG ETC FRSH,SMPLY PRSVD		3211		3230				3992	LEGUMES FRAIS,CONG,SECS
0545	OTHER FRESH VEGETABLES				82				3043	AUTRES LEGUMES FRAIS,REF
05451	ALLIACEOUS VEGTBLS,FRESH								3043	OIGNONS,ECHALOTES,AULX
057	FRUIT,NUTS,FRESH,DRIED		2780		1462				12598	FRUITS FRAIS OU SECS
0577	NUTS EDIBLE,FRESH,DRIED		330		245				11680	FRUITS A COQUES
05779	NUTS EDIBLE,FRSH,DRY,NES		268						11067	FRUITS A COQUES NDA
058	FRUIT PRESERVED,PREPARED								4815	CONSERVES DE FRUITS
0582	FRUIT PRESERVED BY SUGAR								4815	FRUITS CONFITS AU SUCRE
06	SUGAR AND PREPS,HONEY		692		5045				5586	SUCRES ET PRODUITS
061	SUGAR AND HONEY		631		5014				5489	SUCRES ET MIEL
0611	RAW BEET AND CANE SUGAR		630		4980					SUCRES BRUTS
0612	REFINED SUGAR ETC								5487	SUCRES RAFFINES
07	COFFEE,TEA,COCOA,SPICES		6648		5773				7436	CAFE,THE,CACAO,EPICES
075	SPICES		4846		4405				6922	EPICES
0752	SPICES,EX PEPPER,PIMENTO		4501		4091				6580	AUTRES EPICES
07525	SEEDS OF ANISE,CUMIN,ETC		2503							GRAINES ANIS,FENOUIL
1	BEVERAGES AND TOBACCO		7091		6292		7442		2110	BOISSONS ET TABACS
12	TOBACCO AND MANUFACTURES		6018		5242				712	TABACS BRUTS FABRIQUES
121	TOBACCO UNMNFCTRD,REFUSE		5808		5176					TABACS BRUTS,DECHETS
2	CRUDE MATERLS,EXCL FUELS		85216		81578		63211		41853	MAT BRUTES NON COMESTIBLES
22	OIL SEEDS,OLEAGINOUS FRT		1423		3529				7356	GRAINES,FRUITS OLEAGINEUX
223	SEEDS FOR OTH FIXED OILS		1423		3529				6019	GRAINES AUTRES HUILES FIXES
2234	LINSEED				2106					GRAINES DE LIN
2238	OIL SEEDS AND FRUITS NES		1423		1065				6019	GRAINES D'OLEAGINEUX NDA
23	RUBBER, CRUDE		877		2579				575	CAOUTCHOUC BRUT
233	RUBBER,SYNTHTIC,RECLAIMD		877		2579					LATEX CAOUTCH SYNTH REGEN
2331	SYNTHETIC RUBBER ETC		877		2579					LATEX CAOUTCH SYNTHETIQUE
26	TEXTILE FIBRES AND WASTE		50415		57950				29104	FIBRES TEXTILES
263	COTTON		3078		3256					COTON
2631	RAW COTTON,EXCL LINTERS		3078		3256					COTON EN MASSE
268	WOOL(EXC TOPS),ANML HAIR		47337		54694				27292	LAINES ET POILS
2681	WOOL GREASY,FLEECE–WSHED		47337		54694					LAINE EN SUINT
2682	WOOL DEGREASED,UNCOMBED								27232	LAINE DEGRAISSEE
28	METALLIFEROUS ORES,SCRAP		31469		16201				4634	MINERAIS METAL,DECHETS
287	BASE METAL ORES,CONC NES		22894		11507					MINERAIS METAUX COMMUNS
288	NONFERR METAL SCRAP NES		8546		4694				3903	DECHETS NON FERREUX
2882	OTHER BASE MTL SCRAP NES		8546		4694				3903	AUTRES DECHETS
28821	COPPER WASTE AND SCRAP		6421		2628				3746	DECHETS DE CUIVRE
3	MINERAL FUELS ETC		88261		82000		97925		117400	COMBUSTIBLES MINERAUX LUB
32	COAL,COKE AND BRIQUETTES		6735		5607				3	HOUILLES,COKES,BRIQUETTES
322	COAL,LIGNITE AND PEAT		6735		5607					HOUILLES,LIGNITES,TOURBE
33	PETROLEUM AND PRODUCTS		81512		76394				117388	PETROLE ET DERIVES
333	CRUDE PETROLEUM		78214							HUILES BRUTES DE PETROLE
334	PETROLEUM PRODUCTS,REFIN		1538		74725				116732	PRODUITS RAFFINES
3341	GASOLINE,OTH LIGHT OILS								112354	ESSENCES POUR MOTEURS
3345	LUBS,PETROLEUM OILS NES		1538		3138				4378	HUILES LUBRIFIANTES
4	ANIMAL,VEGETABLE OIL,FAT		22894		23204		29501		40699	HUILES,GRAISSES ANIM,VEG
42	FIXED VEGETABLE OIL,FAT		22335		22572				40699	HUILES VEGETALES FIXES
423	FIXED VEG OILS,SOFT		13587		12233				28303	HUILES VEGET DOUCES FIXES
4232	SOYA BEAN OIL		13375		12096				11004	HUILE DE SOJA
4239	OTH FIXED VEG OILS,SOFT								16915	AUTRES HUILES FIXES
42391	RAPE,COLZA,MUSTARD OILS								16915	H NAVETTE COLZA MOUTARDE
424	FIXED VEG OIL NONSOFT		8748		10339				12395	AUTRES HUILES VEG FIXES
4242	PALM OIL		7097		7450				9586	HUILE DE PALME
4243	COCONUT (COPRA) OIL		1048		2477				2658	HJUILE DE COPRAH
5	CHEMCLS,RELATED PROD NES		84638		83208		112186		69412	PRODUITS CHIMIQUES
51	ORGANIC CHEMICALS		93		5769				7922	PROD CHIMIQ ORGANIQUES
514	NITROGEN–FNCTN COMPOUNDS								7124	COMPOSES FONCT AZOTEES
53	DYES,TANNING,COLOUR PROD		2534		1724				1864	PROD TEINTURE,COLORANTS
541	*MEDICINAL,PHARM PRODUCT		27758		28962				8970	PROD MEDICINAUX PHARMACEUT
55	PERFUME,CLEANING ETC PRD		2056		1514				3211	PROD POUR PARFUM,TOILETTE
562	*FERTILIZERS,MANUFACTURE		36425		27667				28832	ENGRAIS MANUFACTURES
5629	FERTILIZERS NES				27463					ENGRAIS NDA
56299	OTHER FERTILIZERS NES				27463					AUTRES ENGRAIS NDA
58	PLASTIC MATERIALS ETC		13044		12234				16797	MAT PLAST ARTIFICIELLES
582	PROD OF CONDENSATION ETC		2797		2110					PROD CONDENS,POLYCOND
583	POLYMERIZATION ETC PRODS		9909		10124				16608	PROD POLYMERISATION
5831	POLYETHYLENE								13604	POLYETHYLENE
5834	POLYVINYL CHLORIDE								2618	CHLORURE DE POLYVINYLE
58341	— IN PRIMARY FORMS								2581	SOUS FORMES PRIMAIRES
59	CHEMICAL MATERIALS NES		2639		5239				1816	MAT PROD CHIMIQUES NDA
6	BASIC MANUFACTURES		138980		131010		387641		87235	ART MANUFACTURES
62	RUBBER MANUFACTURES NES		28004		25102				5736	CAOUTCHOUC MANUFACTURE
621	MATERIALS OF RUBBER		23695		21612				2729	PRODUITS EN CAOUTCHOUC
62104	UNHARD VULC RUBBER,BASIC								2729	PLAQUES,FEUILLES CAOUT
625	RUBBER TYRES, TUBES ETC		4309		3288				1638	PNEUS CAOUTCHOUC VULCANISE
63	WOOD,CORK MANUFACTRS NES		530		2635				334	OUVRAGES LIEGE ET BOIS
635	WOOD MANUFACTURES NES		47		2341					ART MANUF EN BOIS NDA
6351	BOXES,CASES,CRATES,ETC				2161					CAISSES EMBALLAGES BOIS
64	PAPER,PAPERBOARD AND MFR		5772		6131				1700	PAPIERS,CARTONS & OUVRAGES
641	PAPER AND PAPERBOARD		5461		5715				1665	PAPIERS ET CARTONS
65	TEXTILE YARN,FABRICS,ETC		29224		31618				26098	FILS,TISSUS,ARTICLES TEXTILE
651	TEXTILE YARN		952		3635				17917	FILS TEXTILES
6511	SILK YARN, SILKWORM GUT								6442	FILS DE SOIE
6519	TEXTILE FIBRE YARN NES								10602	FILS TEXT NDA FILE FIB VER
652	COTTON FABRICS,WOVEN		27263		24887				1189	TISSUS DE COTON
653	WOVN MAN–MADE FIB FABRIC								2788	TISSUS FIBRES SYNTH,ARTIF

4. Special Imports C.I.F. by Commodities according to the S.I.T.C. (Rev. 2) in thousand U.S. Dollars
Importations Spéciales C.A.F. par Produits d'après la C.T.C.I. (Rév. 2) en milliers de Dollars E.U.

SITC CTCI	COMMODITY	1992		1993		1994		1995		PRODUIT
		WEIGHT POIDS	VALUE VALEUR	WEIGHT POIDS	VALUE VALEUR	WEIGHT POIDS	VALUE VALEUR	WEIGHT POIDS	VALUE VALEUR	
66	NONMETAL MINERAL MFS NES		26386		18932				3103	ART MIN NON METALLIQUES
661	LIME,CEMENT,BLDG PRODS		15260		11530				174	CHAUX,CIMENTS MAT CONSTR
6612	CEMENT		13510		10241					CIMENTS HYDRAULIQUES
662	CLAY,REFRACTORY BLDG PRD		9508		5533				1721	MAT CONST REFRACTAIRES
6623	REFRACTORY BUILDING PROD		9508		5533				1721	BRIQUES REFRACTAIRES
67	IRON AND STEEL		40284		26409				15823	FER ET ACIER
672	IRON,STEEL PRIMARY FORMS		16237		10660				2039	LINGOTS FER,ACIER
673	IRON,STEEL SHAPES ETC		3665		3367				5816	BARRES,PROFIL FER,ACIER
6733	IRON,STEEL PROFILES ETC				68				5753	PROFILES,PALPLAN FER,ACIER
67334	OTH PRFILES COLDFRMD ETC								5753	PROFILES OBTENUS A FROID
674	IRN,STL UNIV,PLATE,SHEET		10109		7464				7802	LARGES PLATS,TOLES
6747	TINNED PLATES,SHEETS								7721	TOLES ETAMEES EN ACIER
677	IRN,STL WIRE(EXCL W ROD)		3211		1720				18	FILS EN FER,ACIER
678	IRON,STL TUBES,PIPES,ETC		7063		3197				114	TUBES,TUYAUX EN FONTE,FER
6783	IRON,STL TUBES,PIPES NES		3490		1057				114	AUT TUBES,TUYAUX FER,ACIER
68	NON–FERROUS METALS		7012		17219				24702	METAUX NON FERREUX
681	SILVER,PLATINUM,ETC		318		379				16195	ARGENT ET PLATINE
682	COPPER EXC CEMENT COPPER		3295		8209				2123	CUIVRE
6821	COPPER NES,ALLOYS,UNWRT		106		2288				557	CUIVRE BRUT
68212	COPPER REFINED,UNWROUGHT		106		2288					CUIVRE AFFINE BRUT
684	ALUMINIUM		1198		2802				1428	ALUMINIUM
686	ZINC		160		1836				4120	ZINC
6861	ZINC,ALLOYS UNWROUGHT		160		1215				3782	ZINC ET ALLIAGES BRUTS
69	METAL MANUFACTURES NES		1559		2917				9312	ART MANUFACT EN METAL NDA
693	WIRE PRODUCTS NON ELECTR		72		138				3364	OUVRAGES FILS METALLIQUES
6935	METAL FENCING,GAUZE,ETC		72		8				3364	TOILES EN FER,ACIER,CUIVRE
69351	IRN,STL FENCNG,GAUZE ETC								3364	TOILES EN FER,ACIER
7	MACHINES,TRANSPORT EQUIP		118888		115641		203209		114792	MACHINES MATERIEL TRANSPORT
71	POWER GENERATING EQUIPMT								3254	MACHINES GENERATRICES
716	ROTATING ELECTRIC PLANT								3254	APP ELECTR ROTATIFS,PIECES
7162	AC MTRS,GENRTRS,GEN SETS								3254	MOTEURS ELECTRIQUES
72	MACHS FOR SPCL INDUSTRYS		22146		19988				1534	MAC SPECIALES POUR INDUST
721	AGRIC MACHY,EXC TRACTORS				2409					MACHINES AGRICOLES
728	OTH MACHY FOR SPCL INDUS		21906		16702					AUT MACH IND PARTICULIERES
74	GENRL INDUSTRL MACHY NES		25986		2955				7803	MACH APP INDUSTRIE
741	HEATING,COOLING EQUIPMNT		20069							MACH CHAUFFAGE,PIECES
742	PUMPS FOR LIQUIDS ETC		4428		942				463	POMPES MOTO–POMPES
7421	RECIPROCATING PUMPS NES		4428		401					POMPES ALTERN NON 742.81
749	NONELEC MACH PTS,ACC NES		626		355				5917	PIECES MACH NON ELEC NDA
75	OFFICE MACHNES,ADP EQUIP		5768		11904				25620	MACH BUREAU TRAIT AUTOM
752	AUTOMTIC DATA PROC EQUIP		5374		9844				23187	MACH TRAIT INFORMATION
76	TELECOMM,SOUND EQUIPMENT		5942		11300				31217	EQUIPMENT DE TELECOM
761	TELEVISION RECEIVERS		1554		2342				4348	RECEPTEURS DE TELEVISION
7611	COLOUR TV RECEIVERS		1554		2342					RECEPTEURS COULEUR
764	TELECOM EQPT,PTS,ACC NES		4184		8660				26517	EQUIP TELECOM,PIECES
7648	TELECOMM EQUIPMENT NES		4177							APP TELECOM NDA
77	ELECTRIC MACHNRY NES ETC		13277		21485				18078	MACH APP ELECT NDA
771	ELECTRIC POWER MACHY NES		375		120				5133	MACH PROD,TRANS ELECTR
7711	TRANSFORMERS,ELECTRICAL		356		113				5133	TRANSFO ELECTRIQUES
774	ELECTRO–MEDCL,XRAY EQUIP								5051	APPAREILS MEDICAUX
775	HOUSEHOLD TYPE EQUIP NES		6070		9091				4042	MACH,APP USAGE DOMESTQUE
7752	DOM REFRIGERATRS,FREEZRS		1238		975				2751	REFRIG,CONGEL MENAGER
7758	ELECTRO–THERMIC APPL NES		4650		7872				282	APP ELECTROTHERMIQ NDA
77586	ELECTROTHERM DOM APP NES		4553		7798				135	APP ELECTRO THERMIQUES
778	ELECTRICAL MACHINERY NES		2443		4732				3685	AUTRES MACH ELECT NDA
7783	AUTOMOTIVE ELECTR EQUIP		395		3400					EQUIP ELECT MOTEURS EXPL
78	ROAD VEHICLES		40543		39171				18165	VEHICULES ROUTIERS
781	PASS MOTOR VEH EXC BUSES		7864		11659				15135	AUTO TRANSPORT PERSONNES
783	ROAD MOTOR VEHICLES NES		2961		2331					VEHICULES ROUTIERS NDA
7831	BUSES		2677		2218					VOITURES TRANSPORT COMMUN
79	OTHR TRANSPORT EQUIPMENT		4858		8547				9122	AUTRE MATERIEL TRANSPORT
792	AIRCRAFT ETC		4840		8483				9117	APP NAVIGATION AERIENNE
7922	AIRCRFT NES 2000KG OR LS				8483					AERODYNES MOINS 2000 KG
7929	AIRCRAFT PARTS NES		4840							PIECES DU 792
8	MISC MANUFACTURED GOODS		28997		31588		58397		38715	ART MANUFACTURES DIVERS
812	*PLUMBG,HEATNG,LGHTNG EQ		1760		2619				742	APPAR SANITAIRES CHAUFFAGE
84	CLOTHING AND ACCESSORIES		8460		8770				6416	VETEMENTS
842	MENS OUTERWEAR NOT KNIT		7718		7668				6198	VET DESSUS POUR HOMMES
851	*FOOTWEAR		1808						3985	CHAUSSURES
87	PRECISION INSTRUMNTS NES		6490		7731				567	INSTRUM,APPAR SCIENT NDA
871	OPTICAL INSTRUMENTS		1378		2620				17	APPAR,INSTRUM D'OPTIQUE
872	MEDICAL INSTRUMENTS NES		4299		4165					INSTR,APP MEDIC–CHIR NDA
87202	OTH MEDICAL INSTRUMENTS		4299		4127					INSTRUM,APP MEDECINE
88	PHOTO EQU,OPTICL GDS ETC		2278		3102				16143	APP,FOURN PHOTO,OP,MONTR
882	PHOTO,CINEMA SUPPLIES		1381		2242				13998	PRODUITS PHOTO,CINEMA
8822	PHOTO FILM EXC DEV CINMA		1358		2242					PLAQUES,PELLICULES,FILMS
89	MISC MANUFCTRD GOODS NES		7611		8218				10498	ART MANUFACTURES DIVERS
892	PRINTED MATTER		2787		2852				484	IMPRIMES
895	OFFICE SUPPLIES NES		1024		2247				3290	ART PAPET NDA
899	OTHER MANUFACTURED GOODS		1619		964				3060	AUT ART MANUF DIVERS NDA
9	GOODS NOT CLASSD BY KIND		73564		110750		1842		302739	ART TRANSACT NON CLASSES
931	*SPECIAL TRANSACTIONS		70048		107756				45976	TRANS.SPECIALES
951	*WAR FIREARMS,AMMUNITION		3516		2291				2381	VEHIC BLINDES ARMES
971	*GOLD,NON MONETARY NES								254221	OR NON MONETAIRE

5. Special Exports F.O.B. by Commodities according to the S.I.T.C. (Rev. 2) in thousand U.S. Dollars
Exportations Spéciales F.O.B. par Produits d'après la C.T.C.I. (Rév. 2) en milliers de Dollars E.U.

SITC CTCI	COMMODITY	1992 WEIGHT POIDS	1992 VALUE VALEUR	1993 WEIGHT POIDS	1993 VALUE VALEUR	1994 WEIGHT POIDS	1994 VALUE VALEUR	1995 WEIGHT POIDS	1995 VALUE VALEUR	PRODUIT
	ALL COMMODITIES		319192		354604		390633		286323	TOUS PRODUITS
0	FOOD AND LIVE ANIMALS		40427		31763		23555		1359	ALIMENTS,ANIMAUX VIVANTS
001	*LIVE ANIMALS FOR FOOD		3713		1340			N 112	10	ANIMAUX VIVANTS
0019	LIVE ANIMALS FR FOOD NES		3713		1340					ANIMAUX VIVANTS NDA
05	VEGETABLES AND FRUIT		27485		22578				1039	LEGUMES ET FRUITS
054	VEG ETC FRSH,SMPLY PRSVD		27375		22561			W 2117	1032	LEGUMES FRAIS,CONG,SECS
0542	LEGUMINOUS VEGETBLES DRY		27256		22556			W 2117	1032	LEGUMES A COSSE SECS
07	COFFEE,TEA,COCOA,SPICES		5388		4266				311	CAFE,THE,CACAO,EPICES
075	SPICES		5326		4147			W 4	5	EPICES
0752	SPICES,EX PEPPER,PIMENTO		5326		4147			W 4	5	AUTRES EPICES
07524	NUTMEG,MACE,CARDAMOMS		2662							NOIX MUSCADES
07526	GINGER (EXCPT SWEETENED)		1980							GINGEMBRE
081	*FEEDING STUFF FOR ANIML		2921		2855					NOURRITURE POUR ANIMAUX
0812	BRAN,POLLARD,SHARPS,ETC		1332		1040					SONS
0813	OILCAKE AND OTH RESIDUES		1589		1815					TOURTEAUX
2	CRUDE MATERLS,EXCL FUELS		9534		12075		8755		1913	MAT BRUTES NON COMESTIBLES
21	HIDES,SKINS,FURS UNDRSSD		1276		2271					CUIRS,PEAUX BRUTS
211	HIDES,SKINS,EXC FURS,RAW		1276		2271					CUIRS ET PEAUX
2119	SKIN NES,WASTE,USED LTHR		1276		2271					CUIRS ET PEAUX NDA
22	OIL SEEDS,OLEAGINOUS FRT		7137		8101				1741	GRAINES,FRUITS OLEAGINEUX
223	SEEDS FOR OTH FIXED OILS		7137		8101			W 3847	1741	GRAINES AUTRES HUILES FIXES
2238	OIL SEEDS AND FRUITS NES		4937	W 7672	5568			W 3847	1741	GRAINES D'OLEAGINEUX NDA
2239	OIL SEED FLOUR AND MEAL		2201		2533					FARINES GRAINES OLEAG
4	ANIMAL,VEGETABLE OIL,FAT						2802			HUILES,GRAISSES ANIM,VEG
5	CHEMCLS,RELATED PROD NES		5051		2193		4294		133	PRODUITS CHIMIQUES
53	DYES,TANNING,COLOUR PROD		2387		960					PROD TEINTURE,COLORANTS
532	DYES NES,TANNING PROD		2387		960					EXTRAITS TEINTURE,TANNAGE
5322	DYE,TANN EXTRCTS,TANNINS		2387		960					EXT TAN ORIG VEG,TANNINS
59	CHEMICAL MATERIALS NES		2594		1113					MAT PROD CHIMIQUES NDA
598	MISCEL CHEM PRODUCTS NES		2594		1113					PROD DIV INDUST CHIM NDA
5981	CHEMCLS FROM WOOD,RESIN		2594		1113					PROD CHIM BASE BOIS RESIN
6	BASIC MANUFACTURES		179431		210344		220947		168185	ART MANUFACTURES
61	LEATHER,DRESSED FUR,ETC		5442		5549				8539	CUIRS,PELLETERIES
611	LEATHER		5082	A 663	4925			A 963	8486	CUIRS,PEAUX PREPARES
6114	LEATHR BOVINE NES,EQUINE	A 50	398	A 86	606			A 167	1362	CUIRS DE BOVINS
6116	LEATHER OF OTH HIDE,SKIN		4672	A 577	4319			A 796	7124	PEAUX PREP D'AUTRES ANIMAUX
61161	LEATHER FROM GOAT,KID			A 284	1917			A 796	7124	PEAUX DE CAPRINS PREPAREES
61169	LEATHER NES			A 293	2402					PEAUX PREPAREES NDA
65	TEXTILE YARN,FABRICS,ETC		171423		201484				156110	FILS,TISSUS,ARTICLES TEXTILE
654	OTH WOVEN TEXTILE FABRIC		1690		1446				1	TISSUS AUT COTON SYNT,ARTIF
6545	WEAVES OF FIBRES OF 2640		1690		1400					TISSUS DE JUTE
657	SPECIAL TXTL FABRC,PRODS		2100		2018					TISSUS SPECIAUX
6575	CORDAGE AND MANUFACTURES		2100		2011					FICELLES,CORDES,CORDAGES
658	TEXTILE ARTICLES NES		691		531				1665	ART FACONNES MAT TEXTILES
6584	LINENS ETC				1				1307	LINGE DE MAISON
659	FLOOR COVERINGS,ETC	A 2371	166935	A 3126	196638				154376	COUVRE–PARQUETS,TAPIS ETC
6592	CARPETS ETC KNOTTED	A 2371	166935	A 3126	196638				154376	TAPIS POINTS NOUES,ENROULES
65921	— OF WOOL OR FINE HAIR	A 2371	166935	A 3126	196638				154376	TAP NOUES,ENROULES LAINE
69	METAL MANUFACTURES NES		1709		2681				2589	ART MANUFACT EN METAL NDA
697	BASE MTL HOUSEHOLD EQUIP		1706		2662				2567	ART MENAGE MET COMMUNS
6978	BASE MTL HOUSE EQUIP NES		1706		2662					ART MENAGE MET COMMUNS
69782	BASE MTL DECOR ARTICLES		1706		2662					AUT OBJETS ORNEM INTERIEUR
8	MISC MANUFACTURED GOODS		79881		86268		129887		114157	ART MANUFACTURES DIVERS
84	CLOTHING AND ACCESSORIES		77867		84927				111292	VETEMENTS
842	MENS OUTERWEAR NOT KNIT		12871		10531				9918	VET DESSUS POUR HOMMES
8423	— TROUSERS,BREECHES ETC		11968		8651					PANTALONS HOMMES MAT TEX
843	WOMENS OUTERWEAR NONKNIT		34514		48876				51694	VET DESSUS FEMMES MAT TEX
8433	— DRESSES		1225		3909				13790	ROBES EN MAT–TEXTILES
8434	— SKIRTS		587		797				4759	JUPES EN MAT TEXTILES
8435	— BLOUSES		19255		33034				21353	BLOUSES FEM MAT TEXTILES
8439	— OTHER OUTER GARMENTS		12377		9709				10667	AUT VET DES FEM MAT TEXT
844	UNDER GARMENTS NOT KNIT		25475		17102				32788	VETEMENT DESSOUS MAT TEX
8441	— MENS SHIRTS		21457		14965				32788	CHEMISES HOMMES MAT TEXT
8442	— MENS,OTHR THAN SHIRTS		1072		530					SOUS–VET HOMMES MAT TEXT
8443	— WOMENS		2946		1607					VET DESSOUS FEM MAT TEXT
845	OUTERWEAR KNIT NONELASTC		4390		7030				13646	VET DESSOUS,ACCES BONNET
8451	— JERSEYS,PULLOVERS ETC		4379		6562					CHANDAILS,PULL–OVERS ETC
846	UNDER GARMENTS KNITTED				761				931	SOUS VETS DE BONNETERIE
847	TEXTILE CLTHNG ACCES NES		582		595				1728	ACCES VET MAT TEXT NDA
89	MISC MANUFCTRD GOODS NES		2014		1341				2182	ART MANUFACTURES DIVERS
897	GOLD,SILVER WARE,JEWELRY		1908		1306				2032	BIJOUTERIE,ORFEVRERIE
8973	PREC JEWLRY,GLD–SILVWARE		1467		1306				2032	BIJOUX OR,ARGENT ORFEVRE
9	GOODS NOT CLASSD BY KIND		4855		11907		4		55	ART TRANSACT NON CLASSES
931	*SPECIAL TRANSACTIONS		4855		11907				55	TRANS.SPECIALES

FOOT NOTES – NOTES

TABLE 1 –
1 Prior to 1986, general trade.
TABLEAU 1 –
1 Avant 1986, commerce général.

1. HISTORICAL SERIES, 1961–1996 SPECIAL TRADE, IMPORTS C.I.F., EXPORTS F.O.B.
SERIES HISTORIQUES, 1961–1996 COMMERCE SPECIAL, IMPORTATIONS C.A.F., EXPORTATIONS F.O.B

YEAR ANNEE	VALUE IN MILLION NETH. GUILDERS VALEUR EN MILLION NETH. GUILDERS MERCHANDISE –MARCHANDISE IMPORTS	EXPORTS	GOLD #1 –OR IMPORTS	EXPORTS	CONVERSION FACTORS U.S. CENTS PER NETH. GUILDER FACTEURS DE CONVERSION CENTS E.U. PAR NETH. GUILDER IMPORTS	EXPORTS	INDEX NUMBERS –INDICES QUANTUM IMPORTS	EXPORTS	UNIT VALUE VALEUR UNITAIRE IMPORTS	EXPORTS
1961	18652.00	15712.00	27.30	15.00	27.4081	27.4106	20	15	40	42
1962	19358.00	16596.00	27.40	13.00	27.6243	27.6243	21	16	39	43
1963	21602.00	17962.00	21.60	6.00	27.6243	27.6243	23	17	40	44
1964	25548.00	21025.00	26.60	8.00	27.6243	27.6243	26	19	41	44
1965	27010.00	23144.00	35.90	15.00	27.6243	27.6243	28	21	41	45
1966	29024.00	24443.00	40.10	28.00	27.6243	27.6243	30	22	41	45
1967	30181.00	26380.00	124.80	95.00	27.6243	27.6243	31	24	41	44
1968	33638.00	30197.00	166.40	121.00	27.6243	27.6243	36	28	40	44
1969	39797.00	36074.00	155.80	131.00	27.6243	27.6243	41	33	41	45
1970	48603.00	42622.00	114.80	54.00	27.6243	27.6243	47	37	43	47
1971	52294.00	49775.00	117.40	27.00	28.5600	28.5840	50	42	45	48
1972	55422.00	53879.00	60.00	17.00	31.1517	31.1488	52	46	45	49
1973	66560.00	66873.00	141.20	89.00	36.0457	35.9656	43	33	29	34
1974	87821.00	87993.00	278.00	162.00	37.3230	37.3154	42	35	39	43
1975	88010.00	88655.00			39.5815	39.5903	55	53	70	69
1976	104250.00	106017.00			37.9621	37.9328	61	60	74	74
1977	111974.00	107195.00			40.7577	40.7690	63	59	76	76
1978	114372.00	108205.00			46.3722	46.3483	67	61	75	74
1979	134885.00	127689.00			49.9034	49.8842	71	66	83	81
1980	152279.00	146967.00			50.3142	50.3185	69	66	96	92
1981	163999.00	170772.00			40.1962	40.2479	65	66	111	106
1982	167346.00	176761.00			37.4489	37.5014	64	65	113	111
1983	175456.00	186745.00			35.1295	35.1697	67	69	114	110
1984	198921.50	210691.30			31.2365	31.2690	72	74	121	118
1985	216008.00	226017.00			30.2682	30.2713	77	77	122	122
1986	185053.00	197286.00			40.9016	40.8096	80	80	101	103
1987	184844.00	188017.00			49.4987	49.5146	85	83	94	94
1988	195801.00	203778.00			50.8281	50.8326	90	91	94	94
1989	221412.00	229409.00			47.1823	47.2017	95	95	101	100
1990	229708.00	239181.00			55.0632	55.0994	100	100	100	100
1991	237118.00	249051.00			53.6658	53.6725	104	105	100	98
1992	236597.00	246541.00			56.9194	56.9301	106	108	97	95
1993	231637.00	258343.00			53.8524	53.8534	110	116	92	92
1994	256442.00	282209.00			55.1067	55.1202	121	129	92	92
1995	283537.90	314693.10			62.3809	62.3706	136	140	92	94
1996	304559.10	332620.00			59.3127	59.3005	144	147	93	94

2. IMPORTS BY BROAD ECONOMIC CATEGORY AND EXPORTS BY INDUSTRIAL ORIGIN. (PERCENTAGE OF TOTAL VALUE)
IMPORTATIONS PAR CATEGORIES ECONOMIQUES ET EXPORTATIONS PAR BRANCHE D'ACTIVITE.(EN POURCENTAGE DE LA VALEUR TOTALE)

IMPORTS – IMPORTATIONS

	1990	1991	1992	1993	1994	1995	1996
TOTAL IMPORTS–IMPORTATIONS TOTALES	100.	100.	100.	100.	100.	100.	100.
1 FOOD BEV–ALIMENTATION BOISSONS	10.3	11.0	11.7	12.1	12.4	11.7	11.3
11 PRIMARY–PRODUITS DE BASE	5.6	5.8	6.0	6.2	6.8	6.0	6.2
111 FOR INDUSTRY–POUR L'INDUSTRIE	2.9	2.9	2.9	3.0	3.4	2.9	3.1
112 FOR HOUSEHOLDS–POUR LES MENAGES	2.7	3.0	3.0	3.2	3.4	3.2	3.1
12 PROCESSED–PRODUITS ELABORES	4.7	5.1	5.7	5.9	5.7	5.6	5.1
121 FOR INDUSTRY–POUR L'INDUSTRIE	0.9	0.9	0.9	1.1	1.2	1.1	1.1
122 FOR HOUSEHOLDS–POUR LES MENAGES	3.8	4.3	4.8	4.8	4.5	4.6	4.1
2 IND SUPPLIES–APPROV INDUSTRIELS	31.1	29.6	29.2	28.8	30.2	31.2	28.5
21 PRIMARY–PRODUITS DE BASE	3.5	3.4	3.3	3.4	3.3	3.3	2.9
22 PROCESSED–PRODUITS ELABORES	27.5	26.2	25.9	25.4	26.9	27.9	25.7
3 FUELS–COMBUSTIBLES	10.0	9.0	8.2	9.2	7.8	7.4	8.5
31 PRIMARY–PRODUITS DE BASE	7.7	7.2	6.8	6.8	5.9	5.8	6.8
32 PROCESSED–PRODUITS ELABORES	2.3	1.8	1.4	2.4	1.9	1.6	1.8
321 MOTOR SPIRIT–ESSENCE	0.7	0.6	0.6	0.7	0.6	0.5	0.5
322 OTHER–AUTRES	1.5	1.2	0.8	1.7	1.3	1.1	1.2
4 MACHINERY–EQUIPEMENT	20.4	20.7	20.9	20.4	21.0	22.3	23.9
41 CAPITAL EQUIPMENT–MACHINES	15.7	15.9	16.1	15.3	15.8	16.6	17.8
42 PARTS–PIECES ACCESSOIRES	4.7	4.8	4.8	5.1	5.2	5.7	6.1
5 TRANSPORT–TRANSPORT	10.7	11.3	11.2	10.9	10.7	11.1	10.9
51 PASSENGER CARS–AUTOMOBILES	3.5	4.0	3.7	4.2	4.0	4.2	4.3
52 OTHER–AUTRES	2.7	2.6	3.0	2.4	2.7	2.6	2.4
521 INDUSTRIAL–INDUSTRIELS	2.5	2.4	2.7	2.1	2.4	2.4	2.0
522 NON INDUSTRIAL–NON INDUSTRIEL	0.2	0.3	0.3	0.3	0.3	0.2	0.4
53 PARTS–PIECES ACCESSOIRES	4.4	4.6	4.5	4.2	4.0	4.3	4.2
6 CONSUM GOODS–BIENS CONSOMMATION	16.8	17.8	18.1	18.0	17.2	15.8	16.1
61 DURABLE–DURABLES	4.7	4.7	4.5	4.3	4.0	3.8	4.1
62 SEMI DURABLE–SEMI DURABLES	8.9	9.6	9.9	9.7	9.1	7.9	8.3
63 NON DURABLE–NON DURABLES	3.3	3.4	3.7	4.0	4.2	4.1	3.8
7 GOODS NES–BIENS NDA	0.7	0.6	0.7	0.6	0.6	0.5	0.8

EXPORTS – EXPORTATIONS

	1990	1991	1992	1993	1994	1995	1996
TOTAL EXPORTS–EXPORTATIONS TOTALES	100.	100.	100.	100.	100.	100.	100.
1 AGRICULTURE	8.3	8.6	8.6	8.1	8.5	7.6	7.3
2 MINING QUARRY–INDUS EXTRACTIVES	3.4	3.9	3.5	3.5	2.9	2.9	3.3
3 MANUFACTURING–IND MANUFACTUR	88.3	87.5	87.8	88.4	88.5	89.5	89.4
31 FOOD BEV TOBACCO–ALIM BOISS TAB	15.6	15.7	16.7	17.1	16.4	15.7	15.0
32 TEXTILES–INDUSTRIES TEXTILES	4.4	4.5	4.6	4.3	4.2	4.1	4.0
33 WOOD & PRODUCTS–BOIS & PRODUITS	0.5	0.6	0.6	0.6	0.6	0.5	0.5
34 PAPER & PRODUCTS–PAPIER & PRODT	3.1	3.1	3.2	2.6	2.9	3.1	2.7
35 CHEMICALS–INDUSTRIES CHIMIQUES	24.5	23.3	22.2	22.4	22.7	23.1	23.0
36 NON METAL MIN–MIN NON METAL	1.1	1.1	1.2	1.1	1.0	0.9	0.8
37 BASIC METAL–IND METAL BASE	4.2	3.9	3.6	3.4	3.8	4.1	3.6
38 METAL MANUF–MANUF METAL	30.2	30.7	31.1	32.3	31.8	33.2	35.1
39 OTH MANUF IND–AUTRES MANUF	4.7	4.6	4.7	4.7	5.1	4.7	4.6

3. TRADE BY PRINCIPAL COUNTRIES OF PROVENANCE AND DESTINATION (VALUE IN THOUSAND U.S. DOLLARS)
ECHANGES SELON LES PRINCIPAUX PAYS DE PROVENANCE ET DE DESTINATION (VALEUR EN MILLIERS DE DOLLARS EU)

COUNTRIES–PAYS	SPECIAL IMPORTS C.I.F. IMPORTATIONS SPECIALES C.A.F				
	1992	1993	1994	1995	1996
World	134469978	115667665	130511732	157929414	160896310
Africa	3167759	2772606	2916127	3471726	3869206
Americas	13819606	13539505	15433637	18869175	18894774
Northern America	10952013	10508263	11013636	14251953	14421159
LAIA	2534094	2643289	3870309	3974364	3805427
CACM	123972	153738	200451	215966	261164
Caribbean	113281	147531	259233	325375	308225
Rest of America	96246	86684	90008	101517	98798
As.ex F.USSR	17695678	19403910	20041481	23932514	27013663
Eur.x F.USSR	96004383	75479824	86972711	104860963	103097322
EU	90832294	70426849	80924120	97063204	94569505
EFTA	3593069	3486803	4213495	5296726	5990794
East Europe	1291463	1311261	1594413	2226194	2267530
Other Europe	30917	39117	21883	27158	25478
Former USSR	1185066	1456126	1481956	2063084	2390852
Oceania	539863	447532	505038	457989	427836
Germany/Allemagne	33437930	25124148	28787670	34168214	32896000
Belgium–Luxembourg	18924714	12614900	14690334	17247047	16563598
United Kingdom	11394996	10056695	11379521	14614276	14364985
USA/Etats–Unis d'Amer	10225564	9833424	10268009	13291982	13497427
France,Monac	10545550	8081932	9395375	10937076	10924979
Japan/Japon	4732483	4701452	4754293	5626460	6176546
Italy/Italie	4852014	4067984	4669221	5323292	5312238
Sweden/Suède	2747829	2412074	3017920	4054656	4078383
Spain/Espagne	2182411	2212253	2457299	3112079	3363535
Norway,SVD,JM	1711015	1838038	2357008	3086346	3853492
Switz.Liecht	1846804	1608840	1818152	2137057	2061937
Saudi Arabia	2261614	1565515	1616636	1936592	2063917
China/Chine	979823	1442585	1746768	2168899	2456279
Hong Kong	1188776	1518520	1581582	1958293	2118672
Ireland/Irlande	1445879	1425118	1536844	2041040	1654061
Denmark/Danemark	1765484	1357054	1482989	1663646	1624006
Brazil/Brésil	1099799	1225966	1848456	1709671	1713136
Finland/Finlande	1250436	1194591	1490622	1544664	1346217
Austria/Autriche	1252806	1080045	1137039	1245893	1252331
Russian Federation	1100422	928109	940132	1296733	1573764
Singapore/Singapour	587938	706804	1107142	1421242	1637271
Iran (Islamic Rp. of)	1404033	1184982	991206	751480	739928
Kuwait/ Koweït	311505	1291292	922846	1148283	1384364
Indonesia/Indonésie	714017	814844	1009737	1084373	1181861
Thailand/Thaïlande	855921	903677	818840	958559	1261911
Malaysia/Malaisie	543325	773799	851573	1084977	1307524
Algeria/Algérie	781219	821732	625064	893116	864647
Canada	724955	668729	741337	925733	873195
Portugal	799096	587456	673738	894263	953838
Poland/Pologne	622070	624222	727509	934661	975492
Korea, Republic of	618568	634764	644256	801527	922162
Argentina/Argentine	584655	495234	810919	732871	725398
Turkey/Turquie	502958	598678	601529	739538	788188
Israel/Israël	463369	492048	524150	636366	778119
India/Inde	380657	479651	542956	680686	747665
Nigeria/Nigéria	569381	542618	669304	406977	620807
Cote d'Ivoire	337345	256170	358794	442554	560801
Australia/Australie	449230	362886	397077	347732	327964
So. Africa Customs Un	237596	266822	288739	386764	474179
Hungary/Hongrie	210644	218682	254152	402758	463404
Chile/Chili	257575	230564	296290	309311	262616
Philippines	186865	226097	218753	280870	372321
Czech Republic		223746	288104	358633	364351
Latvia/Lettonie	24515	271271	216452	315942	376675
Venezuela	81993	133428	274721	336614	303328
Colombia/Colombie	182778	177479	201141	266027	299317
Greece/Grèce	233149	212599	205548	217058	235336
Mexico/Mexique	134031	154489	142977	340882	218291
Cameroon/Cameroun	202474	141067	134168	191313	207716
Pakistan	129021	149284	160909	195111	190814

COUNTRIES–PAYS	SPECIAL EXPORTS F.O.B. EXPORTATIONS SPECIALES F.O.B.				
	1992	1993	1994	1995	1996
Monde	139934344	131143330	145825274	177626307	177369366
Afrique	2545437	2617158	2352564	3082802	2762716
Amériques	7234085	7519469	7815585	8830289	8232622
Amérique du Nord	5584390	5357773	5927766	6297692	6021142
ALAI	1049600	1465628	1208146	1714942	1576880
MCAC	67379	76461	103197	135065	125089
Caraïbes	416302	507632	476017	555454	396867
Autre Amérique	116414	111975	100459	127135	112643
Asie l'URSS exclus	7914504	9292705	9568883	12155106	12139179
Europe l'URSS exclus	109537687	97276978	109384098	134431071	133655762
UE	103819425	91910607	103211038	126783851	126464118
AELE	3623478	2999411	3419337	4260145	3717784
Europe de l'Est	1648826	1829773	2150259	2732883	2807343
Autre de l'Europe	132685	120875	134016	116349	108555
Ancienne URSS	765221	1342178	1646344	2214642	2350719
Océanie	593504	531520	663887	598455	574457
Germany/Allemagne	37946678	34730933	38267234	46123330	45896316
Belgium–Luxembourg	18987382	15526078	18050733	21162581	21240837
France,Monac	13729718	12409874	13978903	17636582	17478645
United Kingdom	11921212	10918555	12533855	15182991	14846792
Italy/Italie	8372784	6689779	7103994	8754797	9235184
USA/Etats–Unis d'Amer	5113017	4882972	5360520	5680466	5469884
Spain/Espagne	3471057	2911386	3345301	4609306	4492847
Sweden/Suède	1984207	1885243	2133338	3233430	3481215
Switz.Liecht	2413245	2121634	2375884	2887237	2525010
Denmark/Danemark	1945127	1749089	2164340	2664322	2622612
Austria/Autriche	1496660	1446929	1637000	2376167	2383799
Greece/Grèce	1429802	1249065	1411491	1586295	1389246
Japan/Japon	1110494	1096742	1335652	1698035	1759552
Russian Federation	683969	1018934	1243009	1576686	1589311
Portugal	1051101	1059077	986419	1173908	1119520
Norway,SVD,JM	1016125	810735	977016	1284176	1116301
Poland/Pologne	829837	846475	975401	1240593	1281364
Finland/Finlande	712837	649303	829589	1261192	1301465
Ireland/Irlande	770859	685296	768842	1018948	975640
Turkey/Turquie	555297	818040	644342	990824	1128316
Hong Kong	503099	615659	788415	1021159	963814
Singapore/Singapour	427747	720050	692960	992577	875914
Saudi Arabia	676716	684550	591748	629313	595501
Korea, Republic of	387343	487049	592785	761995	910693
China/Chine	334591	609580	562699	722642	645223
Canada	466055	454588	541654	610958	540686
Brazil/Brésil	326515	453875	343786	799905	617150
Indonesia/Indonésie	382770	539518	369737	733534	398192
Australia/Australie	476918	418679	535692	445236	430784
Israel/Israël	343620	381124	439629	513857	514884
So. Africa Customs Un	310404	360321	388678	478638	449035
Thailand/Thaïlande	278544	266129	407737	498701	498666
United Arab Emirates	345029	375879	385002	435544	405138
Czech Republic		341353	412589	554095	637352
Hungary/Hongrie	279368	332166	411738	458381	444443
India/Inde	235609	257528	262437	367946	451006
Nigeria/Nigéria	368402	358345	261669	271828	297832
Egypt/Egypte	263546	292326	315442	334480	298988
Malaysia/Malaisie	213048	254089	255062	327937	346270
Mexico/Mexique	298259	436962	224141	187971	231766
Iran (Islamic Rp. of)	429917	278307	206910	245427	203865
Morocco/Maroc	157378	178744	187709	248876	217088
Philippines	124703	140329	173026	203158	266058
Croatia/Croatie	45971	204417	211167	222748	207829
Netherlands Antilles	150875	179351	174674	187083	159598
Libyan Arab Jamahiriya	171363	211079	135380	152752	151732
Argentina/Argentine	109562	113952	185349	190068	203808
Romania/Roumanie	122077	135799	146933	215582	166622
Tunisia/Tunisie	122206	142340	138163	183668	172045
Pakistan	121711	150737	131234	135454	193009

(VALUE AS PERCENTAGE OF WORLD TOTAL)(VALEURS EN POURCENTAGE DU TOTAL MONDIAL)

	1987	1988	1989	1990	1991	1992	1993	1994	1995	1996
Africa	3.2	2.7	2.6	2.7	2.7	2.4	2.4	2.2	2.2	2.4
Americas	10.2	11.0	11.5	10.9	10.7	10.3	11.7	11.8	11.9	11.7
Northern America	7.8	8.3	9.0	8.4	8.4	8.1	9.1	8.4	9.0	9.0
LAIA	2.0	2.3	2.2	2.2	2.0	1.9	2.3	3.0	2.5	2.4
CACM	0.1	0.1	0.1	0.1	0.1	0.1	0.1	0.2	0.1	0.2
Caribbean	0.1	0.1	0.1	0.1	0.1	0.1	0.1	0.2	0.2	0.2
Rest of America	0.1	0.2	0.2	0.2	0.1	0.1	0.1	0.1	0.1	0.1
As.ex F.USSR	12.2	12.0	12.5	12.4	13.1	13.2	16.8	15.4	15.2	16.8
Eur.x F.USSR	72.4	71.5	70.3	71.1	71.1	71.4	65.3	66.6	66.4	64.1
EU	68.1	67.6	66.4	67.0	67.6	67.5	60.9	62.0	61.5	58.8
EFTA	3.0	2.6	2.6	2.8	2.4	2.7	3.0	3.2	3.4	3.7
East Europe	1.0	0.9	1.0	1.0	0.9	1.0	1.1	1.2	1.4	1.4
Other Europe	0.3	0.3	0.3	0.3	0.2	0.0	0.0	0.0	0.0	0.0
Former USSR	1.5	1.1	1.3	1.2	0.9	0.9	1.3	1.1	1.3	1.5
Oceania	0.5	0.5	0.4	0.4	0.4	0.4	0.4	0.4	0.3	0.3
Germany/Allemagne	26.6	26.0	25.3	25.4	25.4	24.9	21.7	22.1	21.6	20.4
Belgium–Luxembourg	14.5	14.5	13.9	13.7	14.0	14.1	10.9	11.3	10.9	10.3
United Kingdom	7.7	7.6	7.8	8.1	8.6	8.5	8.7	8.7	9.3	8.9
USA/Etats–Unis d'Amer	7.2	7.5	8.2	7.7	7.7	7.6	8.5	7.9	8.4	8.4
France,Monac	7.3	7.6	7.5	7.7	7.5	7.8	7.0	7.2	6.9	6.8
Japan/Japon	3.3	3.2	3.0	3.1	3.6	3.5	4.1	3.6	3.6	3.8
Italy/Italie	3.8	3.7	3.6	3.7	3.7	3.6	3.5	3.6	3.4	3.3
Sweden/Suède	2.2	2.2	2.2	2.1	2.0	2.0	2.1	2.3	2.6	2.5
Spain/Espagne	1.4	1.4	1.3	1.5	1.5	1.6	1.9	1.9	2.0	2.1
Norway,SVD,JM	1.5	1.2	1.3	1.4	1.1	1.3	1.6	1.8	2.0	2.4

	1987	1988	1989	1990	1991	1992	1993	1994	1995	1996
Afrique	2.7	2.5	2.3	2.0	1.8	1.8	2.0	1.6	1.7	1.6
Amériques	6.2	5.4	5.8	4.9	4.8	5.2	5.7	5.4	5.0	4.6
Amérique du Nord	4.9	4.4	4.7	4.0	3.8	4.0	4.1	4.1	3.5	3.4
ALAI	0.8	0.6	0.6	0.5	0.6	0.8	1.1	0.8	1.0	0.9
MCAC	0.1	0.1	0.1	0.1	0.0	0.0	0.1	0.1	0.1	0.1
Caraïbes	0.4	0.3	0.3	0.3	0.3	0.3	0.4	0.3	0.3	0.2
Autre Amérique	0.1	0.1	0.1	0.1	0.1	0.1	0.1	0.1	0.1	0.1
Asie l'URSS exclus	6.3	5.7	5.0	5.0	5.2	5.7	7.1	6.6	6.8	6.8
Europe l'URSS exclus	83.0	77.9	77.9	79.1	79.2	78.3	74.2	75.0	75.7	75.4
UE	78.6	74.0	74.3	75.3	75.0	74.2	70.1	70.8	71.4	71.3
AELE	3.1	2.8	2.4	2.4	2.8	2.6	2.3	2.3	2.4	2.1
Europe de l'Est	1.0	0.8	0.9	0.9	1.0	1.2	1.4	1.5	1.5	1.6
Autre de l'Europe	0.4	0.3	0.4	0.4	0.4	0.1	0.1	0.1	0.1	0.1
Ancienne URSS	0.4	0.4	0.5	0.4	0.4	0.5	1.0	1.1	1.2	1.3
Océanie	0.5	0.5	0.5	0.4	0.4	0.4	0.4	0.5	0.3	0.3
Germany/Allemagne	27.4	24.9	24.5	26.1	27.8	27.1	26.5	26.2	26.0	25.9
Belgium–Luxembourg	14.5	14.1	13.9	13.9	13.6	13.6	11.8	12.4	11.9	12.0
France,Monac	10.9	10.2	10.2	10.4	9.9	9.8	9.5	9.6	9.9	9.9
United Kingdom	10.3	10.1	10.4	9.5	8.6	8.5	8.3	8.6	8.5	8.4
Italy/Italie	6.4	5.9	6.0	6.1	5.9	6.0	5.1	4.9	4.9	5.2
USA/Etats–Unis d'Amer	4.3	3.9	4.1	3.6	3.4	3.7	3.7	3.7	3.2	3.1
Spain/Espagne	1.8	1.8	2.2	2.4	2.4	2.5	2.2	2.3	2.6	2.5
Sweden/Suède	1.9	1.7	1.8	1.6	1.5	1.4	1.4	1.5	1.8	2.0
Switz.Liecht	1.8	1.9	1.6	1.7	1.6	1.7	1.6	1.6	1.6	1.4
Denmark/Danemark	1.6	1.5	1.5	1.5	1.5	1.4	1.3	1.5	1.5	1.5

4. Special Imports C.I.F. by Commodities according to the S.I.T.C. (Rev. 2) in thousand U.S. Dollars
Importations Spéciales C.A.F. par Produits d'après la C.T.C.I. (Rév. 2) en milliers de Dollars E.U.

SITC CTCI	COMMODITY	1993		1994		1995		1996		PRODUIT
		WEIGHT POIDS	VALUE VALEUR	WEIGHT POIDS	VALUE VALEUR	WEIGHT POIDS	VALUE VALEUR	WEIGHT POIDS	VALUE VALEUR	
	ALL COMMODITIES # 1		115667665		130511732		157929414		160896310	TOUS PRODUITS
0	FOOD AND LIVE ANIMALS		13173715		14832330		16837028		16618932	ALIMENTS,ANIMAUX VIVANTS
001	*LIVE ANIMALS FOR FOOD	W 253211	495608	W 271980	529109	W 267708	514466	W 264845	450196	ANIMAUX VIVANTS
0011	BOVINE SPECIES,LIVE	W 138910	365538	W 153970	399420	W 111910	327690	W 93680	240169	ESPECE BOVINE
01	MEAT AND PREPARATIONS		989493		1168241		1277416		1313596	VIANDES ET PREPARATIONS
011	MEAT FRESH,CHILLD,FROZEN	W 304846	785794	W 346920	891512	W 344197	976797	W 362799	1002832	VIANDES FRAICHES,REF,CONGE
0111	BOVINE MEAT FRESH,FROZEN	W 96664	379397	W 107393	421937	W 112430	480055	W 118549	435135	VIANDES BOVIN FRAI,REF
02	DAIRY PRODCTS,BIRDS'EGGS		2067856		2004192		2963810		2283126	PRODUITS LAITIERS,OEUFS
022	MILK AND CREAM	W 1368774	1253423	W 1549622	1348873	W 1760799	2136760	W 1764392	1610992	LAIT ET CREME
0224	MILK,CREAM PRESERVED ETC	W 903177	999482	W 923094	1008262	W 1089819	1718458	W 1028555	1203750	LAIT,CREME CONS,CONC
02242	MILK DRY,1.5% FAT OR LES	W 228893	532751	W 229584	532865	W 294223	823059	W 221808	532327	LAIT POUDRE INF 1.5%
02243	MILK DRY,OVER 1.5% FAT	W 73705	214591	W 69484	197757	W 136761	488891	W 94378	297934	LAIT POUDRE SUP 1.5%
023	BUTTER	W 119835	406501	W 66191	233011	W 78496	343032	W 60534	228778	BEURRE
024	CHEESE AND CURD	W 81681	347577	W 87394	362392	W 88893	408496	W 90399	360438	FROMAGE ET CAILLEBOTTE
03	FISH AND PREPARATIONS		727384		786815		948191		943372	POISSONS ET PREPARATIONS
034	FISH,FRESH,CHILLED,FROZN	W 269978	364662	W 299004	425482	W 294802	499198	W 246896	496905	POISSON FRAIS, REFRIG,CONG
04	CEREALS AND PREPARATIONS		1666633		1936593		2100767		2135764	CEREALES ET PRODUITS
041	WHEAT ETC UNMILLED	W 2086470	439198	W 2490034	451452	W 2720648	540351	W 2930358	577964	FROMENT,EPEAUTRE
0412	OTHER WHEAT ETC UNMILLED	W 2085970	439052	W 2481665	449794	W 2711274	538340	W 2904028	571294	AUTRE FROMENT NON MOULU
044	MAIZE UNMILLED	W 1401605	346572	W 1987326	410269	W 1721684	430858	W 1597742	376121	MAIS NON MOULU
048	CEREAL ETC PREPARATIONS	W 423574	479660	W 475890	540160	W 492708	601662	W 484522	579576	PREPTNS A BASE CEREALES
05	VEGETABLES AND FRUIT		3692220		4039169		4348429		4494500	LEGUMES ET FRUITS
054	VEG ETC FRSH,SMPLY PRSVD	W 6285397	1476381	W 5866245	1490425	W 4327969	1516990	W 5177909	1545797	LEGUMES FRAIS,CONG,SECS
0548	EDIBLE VEG NES FRESH,DRY	W 3533760	513063	W 2874444	385630	W 1168695	184049	W 2071182	308125	RACINES,TUBERCULES
05481	ROOTS,TUBERS FRESH,DRY	W 3527877	505530	W 2823385	375899	W 1133023	171809	W 2032141	297646	RACINES DE MANIOC ETC
057	FRUIT,NUTS,FRESH,DRIED	W 1654827	1239994	W 1862932	1511270	W 1826406	1610009	W 1806011	1642673	FRUITS FRAIS OU SECS
0579	FRUIT FRESH OR DRIED NES	W 332753	325209	W 417242	415361	W 406958	441433	W 462287	468188	FRUITS FRAIS,SECS NDA
058	FRUIT PRESERVED,PREPARED	W 772160	729375	W 833207	802066	W 908661	975788	W 913393	1032074	CONSERVES DE FRUITS
0585	FRUIT OR VEGETABLE JUICE	W 516191	474555	W 555772	501257	W 646333	667690	W 617836	706694	JUS DE FRUITS
06	SUGAR AND PREPS,HONEY		418325		426810		466195		451837	SUCRES ET PRODUITS
07	COFFEE,TEA,COCOA,SPICES		1216273		1559334		1961044		2053692	CAFE,THE,CACAO,EPICES
071	COFFEE AND SUBSTITUTES	W 184470	367499	W 168762	493481	W 166658	725137	W 183202	599426	CAFE ET SUCCEDANES
0711	COFFEE GREEN,ROASTED,SUB	W 180021	333534	W 162800	440679	W 160678	660447	W 175359	533210	CAFE TORREFIE OU DECAFEINE
07111	COFFEE GREEN,HUSKS,SKINS	W 161421	262304	W 137446	324154	W 137918	519279	W 152338	415823	CAFE NON TORREFIE
072	COCOA	W 375269	504288	W 439357	678160	W 462622	799708	W 626544	1015691	CACAO
0721	COCOA BEANS,RAW,ROASTED	W 296598	326793	W 363965	492410	W 399182	621306	W 556841	819726	CACAO EN FEVES
081	*FEEDING STUFF FOR ANIML	W 8906230	1433933	MW 11085	1830942	MW 10252	1657780	MW 10877	1960406	NOURRITURE POUR ANIMAUX
0813	OILCAKE AND OTH RESIDUES	W 2777135	441361	W 4550473	717184	W 4063243	588360	W 4150794	729795	TOURTEAUX
0819	FOOD WASTE AND FEED NES	W 3724233	652655	W 3804258	687068	W 3908209	716609	W 4202053	828170	DECHETS,ALIMENTS NDA
08193	BEET-PULP,BAGASSE,ETC	W 3208928	361782	W 3133350	329575	W 3270687	364216	W 2089915	236462	PULPES,AUTRES DECHETS
08199	FODDER NES,INCL SWEETNED	W 507916	289211	W 659685	355338	W 613398	349532	W 2101333	589443	PREPARATIONS FOURRAGERES
09	MISC EDIBLE PRODUCTS		465990		551124		598930		532442	PREP ALIMENTAIRES DIVERSES
098	EDIBLE PRODCTS,PREPS NES	W 216940	411663	W 246653	472677	W 237695	504325	W 248655	461374	PREP ALIMENTAIRES NDA
1	BEVERAGES AND TOBACCO		1685558		1849402		2085437		2083545	BOISSONS ET TABACS
11	BEVERAGES		895214		977167		1084072		1111623	BOISSONS
112	ALCOHOLIC BEVERAGES	W 359088	697777	W 417126	763692	W 428191	841071	W 425969	850372	BOISSONS ALCOOLIQUES
1121	WINE OF FRESH GRAPES ETC	W 213643	458063	W 237446	513269	W 219301	539700	W 229183	568762	VINS DE RAISINS FRAIS
11212	WINE OF FRESH GRAPES	W 204390	444740	W 233903	508395	W 213183	528622	W 222992	557427	VINS DE MOUTS DE RAISINS
12	TOBACCO AND MANUFACTURES		790344		872235		1001365		971922	TABACS BRUTS FABRIQUES
121	TOBACCO UNMNFCTRD,REFUSE	W 83862	427784	W 87683	433397	W 89087	478131	W 97651	465404	TABACS BRUTS,DECHETS
122	TOBACCO,MANUFACTURED	W 36237	362560	W 38593	438838	W 38132	523235	W 39106	506519	TABACS FABRIQUES
2	CRUDE MATERLS,EXCL FUELS		5554205		7002363		7930157		7655345	MAT BRUTES NON COMESTIBLES
22	OIL SEEDS,OLEAGINOUS FRT		1188776		1909315		1695659		1908271	GRAINES,FRUITS OLEAGINEUX
222	SEEDS FOR'SOFT'FIXED OIL	W 4369015	1135961	W 6354151	1853902	W 5969008	1639748	W 5852693	1839643	GRAINES HUILES FIXES
2222	SOYA BEANS	W 3246453	751951	W 5232517	1377150	W 4880370	1191860	W 4736947	1378810	FEVES DE SOJA
24	CORK AND WOOD		1012973		1171254		1109576		1037627	LIEGE ET BOIS
248	WOOD SHAPED,SLEEPERS	W 2076411	938271	W 2168819	1092266	W 1843118	1028368	W 1899509	963689	BOIS SIMPLEMENT TRAVAILLES
2482	LUMBER SHAPED CONIFER	W 1458103	487048	W 1591602	659551	W 1371317	614906	W 1442323	565384	CONIFERES SCIES,RABOTES
24821	LUMBER SAWN ETC CONIFER	W 1451452	483035	W 1582766	651107	W 1363259	603656	W 1435730	559042	CONIFERES SCIES LONGITUD
2483	LUMBER SHAPED NON-CONIFR	W 596817	447518	W 559786	429024	W 462745	411553	W 450938	397163	NON CONIFERES SCIES,RABOTES
24831	LUMBER SAWN ETC NON-CON	W 561133	403628	W 520475	378856	W 409834	328047	W 396801	321036	SCIES LONGITUDINALEMENT
251	*PULP AND WASTE PAPER	W 1661036	324888	W 2007156	547429	W 2345070	969910	W 2348380	717922	PATES A PAPIER,DECHETS
2517	SODA,SULPHATE WOOD PULP	W 569251	211879	W 734312	348903	W 714129	545280	W 862540	488460	PATES CHIMIQUES AU SULFATE
25172	— BLEACHED,NONDISSOLVNG	W 568178	211393	W 731947	347824	W 709286	541677	W 856077	484921	PATES BLANCHIES
27	CRUDE FERTLZR,MINRLS NES		650165		679228		814259		840301	ENGRAIS MINERAUX BRUTS
28	METALLIFEROUS ORES,SCRAP		1121443		1235891		1679010		1412872	MINERAIS METAL,DECHETS
282	IRON AND STEEL SCRAP	W 3517874	407642	W 2933386	424544	W 3042422	544916	W 2810018	431392	FERRAILLES
288	NONFERR METAL SCRAP NES	W 281174	236094	W 297389	298178	W 364210	504306	W 340773	394040	DECHETS NON FERREUX
2882	OTHER BASE MTL SCRAP NES	W 257324	225849	W 268821	281274	W 329756	478625	W 302231	371341	AUTRES DECHETS
29	CRUDE ANIMAL,VEG MAT NES		762587		893075		991982		1154990	MATIERES BRUTES ANIM,VEGET
292	CRUDE VEG MATERIALS NES	W 368898	679199	W 475617	784912	W 344962	854530	W 560214	991029	MAT BRUTES VEGETALES NDA
2927	CUT FLOWERS AND FOLIAGE	W 89211	327324	W 101734	375573	W 107621	442768	W 137387	533873	FLEURS,FEUILLAGES COUPES
3	MINERAL FUELS ETC		11134215		10691407		12161762		14326261	COMBUSTIBLES MINERAUX LUB
32	COAL,COKE AND BRIQUETTES		812129		886580		987306		919910	HOUILLES,COKES,BRIQUETTES
322	COAL,LIGNITE AND PEAT	MW 17075	781178	MW 18886	833249	MW 19127	905709	MW 19600	882690	HOUILLES,LIGNITES,TOURBE
3222	OTH COAL,NOT AGGLOMERATD	MW 15160	699119	MW 16792	728832	MW 17438	815013	MW 17528	776791	AUTRES HOUILLES
33	PETROLEUM AND PRODUCTS		9493893		9005866		10290117		12463737	PETROLE ET DERIVES
333	CRUDE PETROLEUM	MW 55389	6496436	MW 56594	6400463	MW 59800	7635877	MW 61489	9371889	HUILES BRUTES DE PETROLE
334	PETROLEUM PRODUCTS,REFIN	MW 16897	2536700	MW 15041	2179232	MW 13451	2157926	MW 13538	2553650	PRODUITS RAFFINES
3341	GASOLINE,OTH LIGHT OILS	W 4128866	777330	W 4266901	730703	W 4404792	806760	W 4256214	874368	ESSENCES POUR MOTEURS
33419	OTH LIGHT PETROLEUM OILS	W 3799196	716023	W 3865607	660137	W 3971972	724884	W 4120151	848477	AUTRES HUILES LEGERES
3343	GAS OILS	W 5656808	958182	W 4887910	747482	W 3700448	592374	W 5178276	1016543	GAS OILS
3344	FUEL OILS,NES	W 6373329	535641	W 5163773	443432	W 4748568	463520	W 3523912	370557	FUEL OILS
335	RESIDUAL PETRLM PROD NES	W 2602235	460756	W 2624670	426171	W 2773432	496315	W 3007343	538198	PRODUITS RESIDUELS NDA
341	*GAS,NATURAL AND MANUFCT		612127	W 4915370	576427	W 4705458	631576	W 4933480	724387	GAZ NATUREL,GAZ MANUFACT
3413	PETROLM GASES,LIQUEFIED	W 2199897	363526	W 1947692	285272	W 1587658	281019	W 1670909	350007	GAZ DE PETROLE LIQUEFIE
4	ANIMAL,VEGETABLE OIL,FAT		779161		1089178		1353911		1227425	HUILES,GRAISSES ANIM,VEG
42	FIXED VEGETABLE OIL,FAT		476721		698687		840023		822473	HUILES VEGETALES FIXES
424	FIXED VEG OIL NONSOFT	W 622046	279169	W 773456	396148	W 764769	526016	W 829031	545871	AUTRES HUILES VEG FIXES
5	CHEMCLS,RELATED PROD NES		13021215		15805060		20217976		18497720	PRODUITS CHIMIQUES
51	ORGANIC CHEMICALS		3695469		4475243		5687695		5074728	PROD CHIMIQ ORGANIQUES
511	HYDROCARBONS NES,DERIVS	W 1331293	504147	W 1920678	765003	W 2047218	1064383	W 2334745	983107	HYDROCARBURES NDA
5112	CYCLIC HYDROCARBONS	W 671643	231162	W 949473	378059	W 1050879	491329	W 971846	353092	HYDROCARBURES CYCLIQUES
512	ALCOHOLS,PHENOLS ETC	W 1074457	491903	W 1319675	694488	W 1632878	947790	W 1977640	948322	PHENOLS,PHENOLS-ALCOOLS
5121	ACYCLIC ALCOHOLS,DERIVS	W 908240	341386	W 1095540	518881	W 1335076	697667	W 1534034	624534	ALCOOLS ACYCLIQUES
513	CARBOXYLIC ACIDS ETC	W 675206	644499	W 833854	803562	W 899743	1179241	W 812318	924143	ACIDES CARBOXYLIQUES
5137	MONOACIDS AND DERIVATIVS	W 394289	377646	W 446572	449433	W 527772	708773	W 520718	595589	ACIDES MONOCARBOXYLIQUES
514	NITROGEN-FNCTN COMPOUNDS	W 387718	1040266	W 318397	1135827	W 370071	1127198	W 375591	1039983	COMPOSES FONCT AZOTEES
5148	OTH NITROGN-FNCTN CMPNDS	W 176068	459525	W 130987	509424	W 175648	562406	W 175994	445194	AUTRES COMPOSES AZOTES
515	ORG-INORG COMPOUNDS ETC	W 114138	504591	W 120417	552887	W 131900	699047	W 77103	555536	COMPOSES ORGANO-MINERAUX
5156	HETEROCYCLIC CMPDS ETC	W 70546	331837	W 74155	357114	W 87215	481839	W 41514	348619	COMPOSES HETEROCYCLIQUES

4. Special Imports C.I.F. by Commodities according to the S.I.T.C. (Rev. 2) in thousand U.S. Dollars
Importations Spéciales C.A.F. par Produits d'après la C.T.C.I. (Rév. 2) en milliers de Dollars E.U.

SITC CTCI	COMMODITY	1993			1994			1995			1996			PRODUIT
		WEIGHT POIDS		VALUE VALEUR	WEIGHT POIDS		VALUE VALEUR	WEIGHT POIDS		VALUE VALEUR	WEIGHT POIDS		VALUE VALEUR	
516	OTHER ORGANIC CHEMICALS	W	689558	510061	W	740526	523476	W	637147	670035	W	585917	623637	AUTRES PROD ORGANIQUES
52	INORGANIC CHEMICALS			901756			891833			1018918			1048013	PROD CHIM INORGANIQUES
522	INORG ELEMNTS,OXIDES,ETC	W	2113926	428108	W	2717587	466306	W	2957553	586871	W	3259496	583765	ELEMENTS INORGANIQUES
53	DYES,TANNING,COLOUR PROD			726392			903420			1083855			1011721	PROD TEINTURE,COLORANTS
533	PIGMENTS,PAINTS,ETC	W	206058	479139	W	231462	583487	W	252882	710754	W	248046	659020	PIGMENTS,PEINTURES,VERNIS
541	*MEDICINAL,PHARM PRODUCT	MK	89164	2137660	MK	55525	2804965	MK	77907	3894167	MK	77269	3430951	PROD MEDICINAUX PHARMACEUT
5413	ANTIBIOTICS IN BULK	K	2061069	83293	K	3492731	209359	MK	10751	513988	MK	10621	446490	ANTIBIOTIQUES NDA
54139	OTHER ANTIBIOTICS	K	1019752	52801	K	2615807	183378	MK	9623	474563	K	8677063	368779	AUTRES ANTIBIOTIQUES
5417	MEDICAMENTS	MK	74216	1628977	MK	24288	2013883	MK	24139	2528926	MK	22290	2081567	MEDICAMENTS
54179	— CONTNG OTH SUBSTANCES	MK	43628	1333265	MK	20794	1648440	MK	20138	2015446	MK	17592	1504162	MED CONT AUT SUBSTANCES
55	PERFUME,CLEANING ETC PRD			1106646			1239785			1481639			1378615	PROD POUR PARFUM,TOILETTE
553	PERFUMERY,COSMETICS,ETC	W	68040	471851	W	68884	513335	W	77910	693161	W	80896	654647	PRODUITS DE PARFUMERIE
554	SOAP,CLEANSING ETC PREPS	W	312022	457356	W	344247	529833	W	319309	555100	W	313048	488032	SAVONS,PRODUITS DETERSIFS
5542	WASHING PREPARATIONS ETC	W	278437	385889	W	300378	434239	W	284961	465643	W	281070	411870	PROD ORG TENSIO–ACT NDA
58	PLASTIC MATERIALS ETC			2686250			3430857			4494733			4060333	MAT PLAST ARTIFICIELLES
582	PROD OF CONDENSATION ETC	W	366235	759399	W	530864	1022702	W	590833	1390227	W	562447	1245333	PROD CONDENS,POLYCOND
5823	ALKYDS,OTHER POLYESTERS	W	165741	356998	W	232834	480831	W	265104	655678	W	246764	585456	ALKYDES ET AUT POLYESTERS
58231	— IN PRIMARY FORMS	W	148427	246673	W	214911	365591	W	243638	513385	W	229390	462924	SOUS FORMES PRIMAIRES
583	POLYMERIZATION ETC PRODS	W	1401701	1821084	W	1712338	2268538	W	1666674	2930413	W	1724876	2596648	PROD POLYMERISATION
5831	POLYETHYLENE	W	460530	373265	W	478205	403811	W	485658	573186	W	461829	449090	POLYETHYLENE
5839	OTH POLYMRZTION ETC PROD	W	220637	480206	W	330381	670882	W	333886	864541	W	322450	806030	AUT PROD POLYMER COPOLYM
59	CHEMICAL MATERIALS NES			1548040			1786070			2210472			2163852	MAT PROD CHIMIQUES NDA
598	MISCEL CHEM PRODUCTS NES	W	946698	947257	W	1030235	1167161	W	1073039	1482584	W	1124052	1462176	PROD DIV INDUST CHIM NDA
5989	CHEM PRODUCTS,PREPS NES	W	769670	745048	W	816510	894474	W	854768	1173064	W	882463	1136932	PROD PREP CHIMIQUES NDA
59899	OTH CHEM PRODS,PREPS,NES	W	699132	598515	W	738534	704433	W	769072	980580	W	792400	880915	AUT PRODUITS CHIMIQUES NDA
6	BASIC MANUFACTURES			17180093			19944028			25296127			23386912	ART MANUFACTURES
62	RUBBER MANUFACTURES NES			1157899			1329430			1612633			1627792	CAOUTCHOUC MANUFACTURE
625	RUBBER TYRES, TUBES ETC	W	199296	780167	W	230306	906250	W	253141	1113992	W	257944	1099566	PNEUS CAOUTCHOUC VULCANISE
6251	TYRES NEW FOR MOTOR CARS	W	89371	442092	W	100621	501583	W	101964	560895	W	107353	552434	PNEUS POUR VOITURES
63	WOOD,CORK MANUFACTRS NES			911802			1019833			1081183			1065037	OUVRAGES LIEGE ET BOIS
634	VENEERS,PLYWOOD,ETC	W	783410	518437	W	802592	556495	W	829447	594703	W	775978	538395	PLACAGES,CONTRE–PLAQUES
635	WOOD MANUFACTURES NES	W	326613	378416	W	394554	449092	W	359012	469719	W	374638	509945	ART MANUF EN BOIS NDA
64	PAPER,PAPERBOARD AND MFR			3197548			3595121			4543259			4269657	PAPIERS,CARTONS & OUVRAGES
641	PAPER AND PAPERBOARD	W	2695159	2122618	W	3066362	2417391	W	3094798	3161404	W	3168472	2990180	PAPIERS ET CARTONS
6412	PRINTG,WRITING PAPER NES	W	521381	481926	W	619348	585088	W	553679	706044	W	621606	693201	PAPIERS POUR L'IMPRESSION
64122	— COATED,IMPREGNATD ETC	W	470894	417225	W	566921	517003	W	465774	568443	W	528112	568723	PAPIERS IMPRESSION COUCHES
6415	PAPER,PAPERBRD,BULK,NES	W	833259	607556	W	903407	645864	W	787916	766752	W	831077	700345	PAPIERS,CARTONS ROULEAUX
64159	OTHER PAPER ETC,BULK,NES	W	769140	563230	W	839615	600113	W	724030	704237	W	766668	650677	AUT PAPIER ROULEAUX FEUILLES
6418	COATED ETC PAPER NES BLK	W	288019	381081	W	352572	463198	W	519110	737829	W	560896	733471	PAP,CARTONS COUCHES,ENDUITS
642	PAPER,ETC,PRECUT,ARTS OF	W	530162	1074930	W	591989	1177729	W	595832	1381855	W	593696	1279477	PAP,CARTONS DECOUPES
6421	PAPER ETC CONTAINERS	W	278422	424797	W	306787	455822	W	327628	580612	W	339887	529196	BOITES,SACS EMBALLAGES
6428	PAPER ETC ARTICLES NES	W	156444	398625	W	171861	437314	W	172779	501064	W	155447	451891	OUVRAGES EN PATE A PAPIER
65	TEXTILE YARN,FABRICS,ETC			2873136			3049927			3507958			3441543	FILS,TISSUS,ARTICLES TEXTILE
651	TEXTILE YARN	W	152432	692457	W	163631	774313	W	157405	844744	W	160397	910867	FILS TEXTILES
6514	SYN FIB YRN,BULK,MONOFIL	W	83441	443562	W	88415	506674	W	80538	553238	W	90850	652686	FILS CONT 85% FIB TEXT SYNTH
653	WOVN MAN–MADE FIB FABRIC	W	51389	505668	W	48273	509972	W	51906	624512	W	56445	554609	TISSUS FIBRES SYNTH,ARTIF
657	SPECIAL TXTL FABRC,PRODS			351610	W	68716	362023	W	73605	433055	W	82133	431160	TISSUS SPECIAUX
658	TEXTILE ARTICLES NES	W	67945	387106	W	72271	446153	W	74252	484897	W	80614	475419	ART FACONNES MAT TEXTILES
66	NONMETAL MINERAL MFS NES			1709410			1986598			2202872			2108836	ART MIN NON METALLIQUES
661	LIME,CEMENT,BLDG PRODS	W	3693514	347571	W	4483271	418992	W	4448264	474542	W	4143679	446381	CHAUX,CIMENTS MAT CONSTR
664	GLASS	W	404330	375427	W	458381	451540	W	489539	523470	W	451625	458210	VERRE
67	IRON AND STEEL			2882778			3557229			5166445			4349924	FER ET ACIER
673	IRON,STEEL SHAPES ETC	W	1578786	653408	W	1865421	778332	W	1963862	1029109	W	1943430	854041	BARRES,PROFIL FER,ACIER
674	IRN,STL UNIV,PLATE,SHEET	W	1566406	1098663	W	1938340	1477178	W	2170228	2231914	W	2132607	1754458	LARGES PLATS,TOLES
6746	IRN,STL THIN PLATE,ROLLD	W	422727	372643	W	593755	577415	W	674140	955536	W	612742	670341	TOLES LAM MOINS 3MM
67463	— OF STAINLESS ETC STL	W	112250	201182	W	192879	350968	W	256842	661754	W	226452	437010	TOL ACIER INOX MOINS 3 MM
6749	OTH IRN,STL PLATES,SHEET	W	411562	288389	W	464358	343939	W	543928	474160	W	542244	428161	AUTRES TOLES FER,ACIER
678	IRON,STL TUBES,PIPES,ETC	W	616235	616538	W	642237	683873	W	658173	917617	W	677466	889555	TUBES,TUYAUX EN FONTE,FER
68	NON–FERROUS METALS			1577603			2015101			3099398			2419093	METAUX NON FERREUX
682	COPPER EXC CEMENT COPPER	W	132786	359115	W	142986	418482	W	154491	575040	W	164763	496410	CUIVRE
684	ALUMINIUM	W	527184	894325	W	652214	1209297	W	821356	1912421	W	666104	1454657	ALUMINIUM
6841	ALUMINIUM,ALLOYS,UNWRGHT	W	376319	420534	W	458322	631965	W	622326	1164433	W	464298	775768	ALUMINIUM,ALLIAGES BRUTS
6842	ALUMINIUM,ALLOYS WORKED	W	150864	473791	W	193893	577332	W	199030	747988	W	201806	678889	ALUMINIUM,ALLIAGES OUVRE
69	METAL MANUFACTURES NES			2667117			3135948			3811814			3841397	ART MANUFACT EN METAL NDA
691	STRUCTURES AND PARTS NES	W	181471	342076	W	207724	384743	W	232440	497359	W	218789	436258	CONSTRUCT FER,ACIER,ALU
692	METAL TANKS,BOXES,ETC	W	175897	370852	W	184037	427325	W	173384	469691	W	228467	512245	RECIPIENTS METALLIQUES
6924	MTL TRANSPORT BOXES ETC	W	160539	335692	W	170620	397884	W	160618	431184	W	214249	477395	FUTS,TAMBOURS,BIDONS
695	TOOLS	W	49625	459309	W	53063	558606	W	50425	786544	W	62037	819383	OUTILS A MAIN
6954	BLADES,TIPS,ETC FR TOOLS	W	6817	227770	W	10030	318555	W	9548	481808	W	13174	450867	OUTILS POUR MACHINE–OUTIL
699	BASE METAL MFRS NES	W	217248	860157	W	242800	1016815	W	257472	1171862	W	315406	1214945	ART MANUFACTURES MET NDA
7	MACHINES,TRANSPORT EQUIP			36086714			40800317			51947250			55316125	MACHINES MATERIEL TRANSPORT
71	POWER GENERATING EQUIPMT			2065222			1971095			2429737			2463030	MACHINES GENERATRICES
713	INTRNL COMBUS PSTN ENGIN	W	47465	567626	W	50815	626613	W	67019	873602	W	78706	1004054	MOTEURS EXPL COMB INT, PIECE
7139	PISTON ENGINE PARTS NES	W	24328	286186	W	27969	358633	W	38642	496258	W	39458	464763	PIECES POUR 713.2,3,8
714	ENGINES AND MOTORS NES	W	4926	1109706	W	5692	919813	W	5428	1027321	W	5067	965307	MOTEURS NON ELECTRIQUES
7149	ENGINE & MOTOR PARTS NES	W	4462	816344	W	5149	632041	W	4538	737217	W	4648	764266	PIECES 714 ET 718.88
71491	PARTS NES OF 7144,71481	W	500	581771	W	536	382847	W	605	463654	W	577	490745	PIECES DES PROPULSEURS
72	MACHS FOR SPCL INDUSTRYS			2097913			2379002			2659097			2715649	MAC SPECIALES POUR INDUST
723	CIVIL ENGNEERG EQUIP ETC	W	63383	362001	W	68741	414423	W	80463	515422	W	86212	507940	APPAREILS DE GENIE CIVIL
728	OTH MACHY FOR SPCL INDUS	W	43653	640396	W	46907	759504	W	48781	886028	W	52639	911272	AUT MACH IND PARTICULIERES
7284	MACHY FOR SPCL INDUS NES	W	27461	486681	W	29569	617244	W	30926	722700	W	31779	724430	MACH SPEC IND PARTICUL.
73	METALWORKING MACHINERY			367057			445085			464881			587899	MACH TRAVAIL DES METAUX
74	GENRL INDUSTRL MACHY NES			3458190			4074856			4885389			5325465	MACH APP INDUSTRIE
741	HEATING,COOLING EQUIPMNT	W	41306	527289	W	47866	580164	W	50230	715924	W	57810	933509	MACH CHAUFFAGE,PIECES
743	PUMPS NES,CENTRFUGES ETC	W	42223	526173	W	45440	667137	W	49805	721016	W	62490	787427	POMPES COMPRES,VENT ETC
744	MECHANICAL HANDLING EQU	W	94770	623304	W	110872	845492	W	130034	953775	W	142907	982248	EQUIP MANUTENTION PIECES
7449	PTS NES OF MACHY OF 7442	W	35607	281145	W	44319	358040	W	55932	489820	W	47410	423013	PIECES DU 744.2
745	NONELEC MACHY,TOOLS NES	W	22125	430918	W	24631	496678	W	23024	522446	W	31691	592363	AUT MACH NON ELEC,PIECES
7452	OTH NONELEC MCHS,PTS NES	W	20933	395812	W	23102	446653	W	21453	467364	W	28996	524093	AUT MACH NON ELEC,PIECES
749	NONELEC MACH PTS,ACC NES	W	70457	1050301	W	70297	1116408	W	93475	1546062	W	105718	1596479	PIECES MACH NON ELEC NDA
7492	COCKS,VALVES ETC NES	W	28095	474514	W	26670	497176	W	30831	618927	W	38506	659434	ART ROB,SIM POUR TUYAUX
75	OFFICE MACHNES,ADP EQUIP			8688602			10364285			13694692			15741182	MACH BUREAU TRAIT AUTOM
751	OFFICE MACHINES	W	34923	962311	W	35467	1061856	W	44935	1448427	W	40270	1176060	MACH,APPAREILS DE BUREAU
7518	OFFICE MACHINES NES	W	32338	879967	W	32179	956284	W	41000	1330069	W	37250	1082797	MACH,APP DE BUREAU NDA
75182	PHOTO,THERMOCOPY APPARAT	W	24700	602603	W	23964	639845	W	31544	933609	W	29735	818726	APPAREILS DE PHOTOCOPIE
752	AUTOMTIC DATA PROC EQUIP	W	84510	4840620	W	97856	5961739	W	130416	8230577	W	150718	9888990	MACH TRAIT INFORMATION
7522	DIGITAL COMPUTERS	W	1308	242663	W	2420	481396	W	3474	852359	W	4066	992177	MACH DIGITALES COMPLETES
7523	DIGITL CENTRL PROCESSORS	W	14170	1303703	W	17086	1685188	W	22963	2590110	W	26002	2588778	UNITES CENTRALES
7524	DIGITL CENTRL STOR UNITS	W	5963	1001254	W	7354	1360376	W	11647	1952095	W	12950	2891438	UNITES MEMOIRE CENTRALES
7525	ADP PERIPHERAL UNITS	W	57786	1661023	W	65915	1904635	W	84718	2364499	W	97693	2729941	UNITES PERIPHERIQUES
7528	OFF–LINE DATA PROC EQUIP	W	5280	630594	W	5061	526890	W	7585	464482	W	9812	667001	MACH AUXIL TRAIT INFORM

4. Special Imports C.I.F. by Commodities according to the S.I.T.C. (Rev. 2) in thousand U.S. Dollars
Importations Spéciales C.A.F. par Produits d'après la C.T.C.I. (Rév. 2) en milliers de Dollars E.U.

SITC CTCI	COMMODITY	1993			1994			1995			1996			PRODUIT
			WEIGHT POIDS	VALUE VALEUR		WEIGHT POIDS	VALUE VALEUR		WEIGHT POIDS	VALUE VALEUR		WEIGHT POIDS	VALUE VALEUR	
759	OFFICE,ADP MCH PTS,ACCES	W	44017	2885671	W	54053	3340690	W	58663	4015688	W	70274	4676131	PIECES DU 751 ET 752
7591	OFFICE MACHINE PARTS NES	W	15310	494993	W	16530	577691	W	14038	584758	W	17629	631177	PIECES DU 7511,7518
75919	COPY MACH PRTS,ACCES NES	W	13485	381256	W	14279	439069	W	12025	440701	W	15214	487328	PIECES DU 751.82
7599	ACCTG,ETC,ADP MCH PTS,AC	W	28707	2390678	W	37523	2762998	W	44625	3430930	W	52645	4044955	PIECES DU 751 ET 752
76	TELECOMM,SOUND EQUIPMENT			3104341			3115434			4190324			4454834	EQUIPMENT DE TELECOM
761	TELEVISION RECEIVERS	W	35750	564143	W	32136	508487	W	39190	640019	W	48094	771238	RECEPTEURS DE TELEVISION
7611	COLOUR TV RECEIVERS	W	35224	555258	W	31476	498158	W	38695	629400	W	47395	756001	RECEPTEURS COULEUR
762	RADIO BROADCAST RECEIVRS	W	21331	502898	W	22605	506721	W	27298	652669	W	30480	659889	RECEPTEURS RADIODIFFUSION
763	SOUND RECORDRS,PHONOGRPH	W	12709	531410	W	11481	522086	W	11126	563210	W	13415	780054	PHONO,APP ENREGISTREMENT
7638	OTHR SOUND APPARATUS ETC	W	12202	525134	W	11151	517827	W	10732	558725	W	13116	776435	AUT APP D'ENREGIS,REPROD
76381	TV IMAGE,SND RECRDRS ETC	W	4945	270513	W	5402	301672	W	5441	337567	W	7900	596801	APP ENREG,REPRO IMAG,SON
764	TELECOM EQPT,PTS,ACC NES	W	29990	1505890	W	31817	1578141	W	38330	2334427	W	43303	2243653	EQUIP TELECOM,PIECES
7641	LINE TELEPHONE,ETC EQUIP	W	5599	402409	W	6202	421887	W	8015	606111	W	8620	726370	APP TELEPHON PAR FIL
7649	PTS NES OF EQUIPMT OF 76	W	4945	448671	W	6764	566128	W	9539	975621	W	10898	1038379	PIECES DE LA DIV 76
76491	PTS NES OF APPAR OF 7641	W	1169	154298	W	1556	254909	W	2592	591569	W	4181	685825	PIECES POUR 764.1
77	ELECTRIC MACHNRY NES ETC			6153899			7009505			9125336			9693664	MACH APP ELECT NDA
772	SWITCHGEAR ETC,PARTS NES	W	27968	879068	W	32943	1041186	W	42483	1472316	W	50321	1530533	APP COUPURE,SECT ETC
7721	SWITCHGEAR ETC	W	26705	772532	W	31532	931858	W	41002	1326961	W	48762	1407841	APP COUPURE,SECTIONMNT
773	ELECTR DISTRIBUTNG EQUIP	W	48484	368172	W	56023	419817	W	64811	541236	W	69128	565474	EQUIPMT DISTRIBUTION ELECT
7731	INSULATED WIRE,CABLE ETC	W	45739	335756	W	52763	381172	W	61118	500607	W	65794	532838	FILS,CABLES ISOLES ELECT
774	ELECTRO–MEDCL,XRAY EQUIP	W	3686	409496	W	3458	403103	W	4237	495325	W	5363	580101	APPAREILS MEDICAUX
775	HOUSEHOLD TYPE EQUIP NES	W	149280	1135116	W	157278	1212153	W	165400	1379385	W	182837	1437571	MACH,APP USAGE DOMESTQUE
7758	ELECTRO–THERMIC APPL NES	W	33746	343587	W	40270	405279	W	40218	440332	W	44533	460584	APP ELECTROTHERMIQ NDA
776	TRANSISTORS,VALVES,ETC	W	8117	1668369	W	10072	1980211	W	10168	2873556	W	9526	3075597	LAMPES,TUBES,VALVES
7764	ELECTRONIC MICROCIRCUITS	W	2804	1355220	W	2802	1630300	W	4423	2409947	W	5357	2729794	MICROSTRUCTURES ELECTRON
778	ELECTRICAL MACHINERY NES	W	125146	1441505	W	120465	1677706	W	139630	2026629	W	156700	2099852	AUTRES MACH ELECT NDA
7782	ELECTRIC LAMPS,BULBS	W	18036	354831	W	20510	379628	W	20890	387633	W	21093	408592	LAMPES, TUBES ELECTRIQUES
7788	OTH ELEC MACHY,EQUIP NES	W	36860	490842	W	25913	587970	W	34939	797982	W	34395	781617	AUT MACH APP ELEC NDA
78	ROAD VEHICLES			8216924			9285253			12045895			13009100	VEHICULES ROUTIERS
781	PASS MOTOR VEH EXC BUSES	W	516823	4900933	W	529785	5248413	W	585552	6693789	W	625439	6889490	AUTO TRANSPORT PERSONNES
782	LORRIES,SPCL MTR VEH NES	W	124396	783076	W	140462	966798	W	149028	1241640	W	196326	1585007	VEHICULES SPECIAUX,MARCH
7821	LORRIES,TRUCKS	W	112716	727371	W	128856	904143	W	134535	1145977	W	175695	1453149	VEHICULES TRANSP MARCHAND
784	MOTOR VEH PRTS,ACCES NES	W	179835	1408931	W	246218	1907691	W	310332	2592981	W	360923	2856952	PIECES 722,781,782,783
7849	OTHER MOTOR VEHCL PARTS	W	172907	1340360	W	232216	1743866	W	292210	2358479	W	341933	2580806	PIECES 722,781,782,783
785	CYCLES,ETC MOTRZD OR NOT	W	53937	621585	W	48720	591880	W	47117	636510	W	58001	849082	MOTOCYCLES SCOOTERS
786	TRAILERS,NONMOTR VEH,NES	W	88368	344706	W	104941	413820	W	104480	472109	W	125045	475100	REMORQUES,CADRES,CONTAIN
79	OTHR TRANSPORT EQUIPMENT			1934565			2155802			2451899			1325301	AUTRE MATERIEL TRANSPORT
791	RAILWAY VEHICLES	W	19133	431828	W	13601	304408	W	13104	375783	W	11805	240448	VEHIC MAT CHEMINS DE FER
792	AIRCRAFT ETC	W	2413	1320878	W	2738	1709062	W	3307	1955735	W	2007	860382	APP NAVIGATION AERIENNE
7924	AIRCRFT NES OVER 15000KG	W	623	561989	W	1133	1159502	W	937	1147905	W	347	364557	AERODYNES PLUS 15000 KG
7929	AIRCRAFT PARTS NES	W	1670	730703	W	1469	517240	W	2160	739998	W	1535	450420	PIECES DU 792
8	MISC MANUFACTURED GOODS			16283096			17462484			19042841			20343958	ART MANUFACTURES DIVERS
812	*PLUMBG,HEATNG,LGHTNG EQ	W	91514	562508	W	106335	632890	W	101792	718024	W	117715	742752	APPAR SANITAIRES CHAUFFAGE
821	*FURNITURE,PARTS THEREOF	W	348554	1454382	W	398547	1611151	W	374811	1740638	W	388854	1841043	MEUBLES ET PIECES
8211	CHAIRS,SEATS AND PARTS	W	85929	474820	W	90510	504712	W	84019	537285	W	93722	615545	SIEGES ET PIECES
82111	CHAIRS AND OTHER SEATS	W	72103	417288	W	77173	444053	W	69626	456702	W	76937	486684	SIEGES
8219	FURNITURE AND PARTS NES	W	246490	825095	W	289672	931077	W	270318	1005513	W	274527	1020210	AUTRES MEUBLES ET PIECES
82192	WOOD FURNITURE NES	W	160040	540046	W	192876	636939	W	184052	686524	W	188563	703622	MEUBLES NDA EN BOIS
84	CLOTHING AND ACCESSORIES			4867527			5029080			5014785			5439249	VETEMENTS
842	MENS OUTERWEAR NOT KNIT	W	40068	976558	W	43677	1035542	W	41111	1059413	W	42659	1112955	VET DESSUS POUR HOMMES
8423	— TROUSERS,BREECHES ETC	W	20939	429396	W	22494	466378	W	20677	459222	W	23091	527755	PANTALONS HOMMES MAT TEX
843	WOMENS OUTERWEAR NONKNIT	W	42255	1263015	W	46762	1386417	W	44497	1419357	W	50809	1461052	VET DESSUS FEMMES MAT TEX
8439	— OTHER OUTER GARMENTS	W	23461	554211	W	26094	614181	W	23628	599111	W	27799	687307	AUT VET DES FEM MAT TEXT
845	OUTERWEAR KNIT NONELASTC	W	46563	1105832	W	44445	1051478	W	36656	977977	W	44719	1094013	VET DESSOUS,ACCES BONNET
8451	— JERSEYS,PULLOVERS ETC	W	24431	605865	W	23618	583209	W	19976	550824	W	25569	631540	CHANDAILS,PULL–OVERS ETC
8459	— OTHER,CLTHG ACCESRYS	W	18987	418134	W	17658	384981	W	14361	354613	W	16828	396435	AUT VET DESSUS DE BONNE
846	UNDER GARMENTS KNITTED	W	36860	734207	W	35874	752389	W	32819	778419	W	40155	913614	SOUS VETS DE BONNETERIE
8462	— OF COTTON NON ELASTIC	W	29796	513348	W	28867	516285	W	25856	520450	W	31690	618626	SOUS–VET BONNET COTON
84629	—— OTHER	W	29796	513348	W	28867	516285	W	25856	520450	W	31690	618626	AUT SOUS–VET BONNET COTON
851	*FOOTWEAR	W	67334	958302	W	70206	999293	W	65348	1020264	W	72603	1142201	CHAUSSURES
85102	FOOTWEAR LEATHER	W	52962	839679	W	57346	882197	W	51358	872585	W	55650	963336	CHAUS SEMELLES EN CUIR
87	PRECISION INSTRUMNTS NES			1846473			2001381			2541210			2760966	INSTRUM,APPAR SCIENT NDA
872	MEDICAL INSTRUMENTS NES	W	10019	469671	W	11215	536902	W	11386	654014	W	12957	733698	INSTR,APP MEDIC–CHIR NDA
87202	OTH MEDICAL INSTRUMENTS	W	8294	434296	W	9416	491882	W	9275	597506	W	10686	676270	INSTRUM,APP MEDECINE
874	MEASURNG,CONTROLNG INSTR	W	12492	1225959	W	13392	1296758	W	15706	1675823	W	19093	1783545	INSTRUMENTS DE MESURE
8748	ELEC MEAS,CONTRL EQU NES	W	1507	260902	W	1426	261454	W	1722	366660	W	2571	489594	APP ELEC ELECTRO MESURE
88	PHOTO EQU,OPTICL GDS ETC			1112985			1264650			1408476			1568471	APP,FOURN PHOTO,OP,MONTR
882	PHOTO,CINEMA SUPPLIES	W	37874	561823	W	38597	626962	W	36443	705574	W	39638	745390	PRODUITS PHOTO,CINEMA
8822	PHOTO FILM EXC DEV CINMA	W	22695	423367	W	23005	458600	W	18806	489755	W	18683	492133	PLAQUES,PELLICULES,FILMS
89	MISC MANUFCTRD GOODS NES			5248503			5699692			6312854			6522646	ART MANUFACTURES DIVERS
892	PRINTED MATTER	W	135522	717009	W	144851	779396	W	127317	754898	W	123278	751774	IMPRIMES
893	ARTICLES OF PLASTIC NES			1652271			1880183			2101454			2135392	OUVRAGES EN MAT DIVIS 58
8931	PLSTC PACKG CONTNRS,LIDS	W	211442	565208	W	246210	661378	W	222209	731478	W	230580	745732	ART TRANSP EMBALLAGE ETC
8939	MISC PLASTIC ARTICLES	W	243728	1029059	W	234278	1145849	W	241353	1281430	W	264558	1305877	ART DIVERS EN MAT DIV 58
89399	OTHR PLASTC ARTICLES NES	W	217309	932880	W	207367	1046030	W	211926	1165985	W	235102	1197421	AUT OUV MAT DIV 58
894	TOYS,SPORTING GOODS,ETC	W	114277	908210	W	118356	920414	W	112754	1046152	W	118446	1174481	VOITURES ENFANTS,JOUETS
8942	TOYS,INDOOR GAMES ETC	W	95600	743196	W	98449	754775	W	91551	870117	W	93567	969510	JOUETS,JEUX ETC
89423	TOYS NES	W	50445	352223	W	48283	348617	W	41483	308054	W	42166	315225	JOUETS,MODELES REDUITS
898	MUSICAL INSTRUMENTS,PTS	W	50216	1106066	W	46657	1111686	W	53819	1249821	W	44153	1246981	INSTRUMENTS DE MUSIQUE
8983	SOUND RECRDNG TAPE,DISCS	W	45009	1022115	W	41467	1038812	W	49154	1179889	W	40387	1173426	SUPPORTS SON POUR 763
89831	PREPD SND RECORDNG MEDIA	W	28275	392799	W	26310	389114	W	33606	514854	W	24998	425284	SUPPORTS PREPARES
89832	RECORDED DISCS,TAPES ETC	W	16734	629316	W	15156	649697	W	15547	665035	W	15390	748142	DISQUES,PHONO,BANDES
899	OTHER MANUFACTURED GOODS			523822			609461			743740			813246	AUT ART MANUF DIVERS NDA
9	GOODS NOT CLASSD BY KIND			769694			1035162			1056923			1440087	ART TRANSACT NON CLASSES
931	*SPECIAL TRANSACTIONS	W	541229	437009	W	665970	548506	W	670856	671119	W	838954	1007806	TRANS.SPECIALES

5. Special Exports F.O.B. by Commodities according to the S.I.T.C. (Rev. 2) in thousand U.S. Dollars
Exportations Spéciales F.O.B. par Produits d'après la C.T.C.I. (Rév. 2) en milliers de Dollars E.U.

SITC CTCI	COMMODITY	1993 WEIGHT POIDS	1993 VALUE VALEUR	1994 WEIGHT POIDS	1994 VALUE VALEUR	1995 WEIGHT POIDS	1995 VALUE VALEUR	1996 WEIGHT POIDS	1996 VALUE VALEUR	PRODUIT
	ALL COMMODITIES # 1		131143330		145825274		177626307		177369366	TOUS PRODUITS
0	FOOD AND LIVE ANIMALS		23424556		25172361		28729786		27057576	ALIMENTS,ANIMAUX VIVANTS
001	*LIVE ANIMALS FOR FOOD	W 442592	714715	W 472719	797867	W 492846	943694	W 499395	1039480	ANIMAUX VIVANTS
0013	SWINE,LIVE	W 316704	436215	W 340200	494785	W 359269	638686	W 371744	739391	ESPECE PORCINE
01	MEAT AND PREPARATIONS		4918171		5103785		5421686		5303470	VIANDES ET PREPARATIONS
011	MEAT FRESH,CHILLD,FROZEN	W 1755627	4241879	W 1791329	4428309	W 1746935	4637055	W 1706363	4387647	VIANDES FRAICHES,REF,CONGE
0111	BOVINE MEAT FRESH,FROZEN	W 378521	1602095	W 364756	1569701	W 343271	1604058	W 330053	1324861	VIANDES BOVIN FRAI,REF
01111	BOVINE MEAT WITH BONE IN	W 257685	1119615	W 241675	1026432	W 209269	988147	W 180637	730244	VIANDES BOVIN NON DESOSS
01112	BOVINE MEAT BONELESS	W 120836	482480	W 123082	543269	W 134002	615911	W 149417	594617	VIANDES BOVIN DESOSSEES
0113	PIG MEAT FRESH,CHLD,FRZN	W 846968	1598370	W 844929	1688934	W 767944	1773059	W 703193	1786669	VIANDE DE PORC
0114	POULTRY FRESH CHLLD,FRZN	W 388019	806455	W 407259	880225	W 465833	993227	W 499726	1042822	VOLAILLES MORTES
014	MEAT PREPD,PRSVD,NES ETC	W 144927	414041	W 136154	412723	W 144613	466513	W 147054	473984	CONSERVES DE VIANDES
02	DAIRY PRODCTS,BIRDS'EGGS		4594789		4269835		5049070		4839529	PRODUITS LAITIERS,OEUFS
022	MILK AND CREAM	W 971489	1435989	W 857758	1277290	W 975889	1686711	W 902227	1460439	LAIT ET CREME
0224	MILK,CREAM PRESERVED ETC	W 783459	1248976	W 652972	1058767	W 750779	1425650	W 656953	1180895	LAIT,CREME CONS,CONC
02243	MILK DRY,OVER 1.5% FAT	W 237760	536698	W 192234	463767	W 234069	622508	W 198557	529076	LAIT POUDRE SUP 1.5%
02249	MILK(EX DRY) PRSVD,SWEET	W 317882	420031	W 276249	386586	W 275774	420989	W 275573	405161	LAIT CONS,CONC SUCRE
023	BUTTER	W 255210	734703	W 168284	524049	W 186670	652015	W 163243	565494	BEURRE
024	CHEESE AND CURD	W 469665	1928794	W 486133	2028500	W 502057	2272698	W 525291	2288425	FROMAGE ET CAILLEBOTTE
025	EGGS,BIRDS,FRESH,PRSRVD	W 425506	495302	W 383494	439997	W 380288	437647	W 376537	525171	OEUFS
0251	— IN SHELL	W 388836	427382	W 341810	362194	W 345714	366915	W 342835	451010	OEUFS EN COQUILLE
03	FISH AND PREPARATIONS		1258834		1308670		1473631		1395761	POISSONS ET PREPARATIONS
034	FISH,FRESH,CHILLED,FROZN	W 476356	694022	W 440984	695237	W 442657	807879	W 423492	769920	POISSON FRAIS, REFRIG,CONG
04	CEREALS AND PREPARATIONS		1515956		1570404		1739586		1670161	CEREALES ET PRODUITS
048	CEREAL ETC PREPARATIONS	W 623741	1155291	W 636585	1204835	W 684872	1398635	W 645535	1271240	PREPTNS A BASE CEREALES
0484	BAKERY PRODUCTS	W 227051	584136	W 230697	600440	W 230151	657689	W 211165	590171	PRODUITS DE BOULANGERIE
0488	OTH CEREAL PREPS,MALT EX	W 156408	431725	W 166751	464563	W 182143	559074	W 166803	508724	EXTRAITS DE MALT
05	VEGETABLES AND FRUIT		5550691		6651441		7719028		6800679	LEGUMES ET FRUITS
054	VEG ETC FRSH,SMPLY PRSVD	W 6440261	3211543	W 6329538	3840252	W 5808254	4551585	W 5162041	3883335	LEGUMES FRAIS,CONG,SECS
0541	POTATOES FRSH EXCL SWEET	W 1854805	338041	W 2107264	474027	W 1835817	681650	W 1353561	406003	POMMES DE TERRE
0544	TOMATOES FRESH	W 667720	668686	W 701825	792073	W 747956	824463	W 660669	833777	TOMATES FRAICHES
0545	OTHER FRESH VEGETABLES	W 1959417	1503856	W 2138431	1751778	W 2021854	1947292	W 1940134	1766665	AUTRES LEGUMES FRAIS,REF
05459	FRESH VEGETABLES NES	W 1310525	1304530	W 1459791	1514674	W 1454210	1673027	W 1434159	1583074	LEGUMES FRAIS,REFRI NDA
0546	VEGETABLES SIMPLY PRESVD	W 1304709	537689	W 916155	688334	W 960283	988859	W 969137	782162	LEGUMES CONG,CONSER
05461	VEGETABLES FROZEN	W 1290038	523792	W 897293	669656	W 943821	973110	W 950463	764506	LEGUMES CONGELES
056	VEGTBLES ETC PRSVD,PREPD	W 749192	801039	W 754029	823134	W 751813	990979	W 649789	758510	CONSERVES DE LEGUMES
0565	VEGTBLES PRSVD,PREPD NES	W 678315	710686	W 676816	727678	W 681168	872665	W 578118	642807	LEGUMES PREPARES CONSERVE
05659	OTH VEG PRESVD,PREPD NES	W 595516	600931	W 622701	642606	W 632842	788700	W 547649	603943	LEGUM PREPAP,CONSERV NDA
057	FRUIT,NUTS,FRESH,DRIED	W 1064172	849184	W 1292853	1166589	W 1298705	1256365	W 1298007	1275615	FRUITS FRAIS OU SECS
058	FRUIT PRESERVED,PREPARED	W 533811	688925	W 597700	821467	W 607255	920100	W 576850	883220	CONSERVES DE FRUITS
0585	FRUIT OR VEGETABLE JUICE	W 327989	429548	W 395857	543897	W 387064	592874	W 346197	556346	JUS DE FRUITS
06	SUGAR AND PREPS,HONEY		634547		597062		679025		577615	SUCRES ET PRODUITS
07	COFFEE,TEA,COCOA,SPICES		1487377		1716566		2002198		1909596	CAFE,THE,CACAO,EPICES
072	COCOA	W 321326	671692	W 352773	819778	W 365632	951723	W 402002	985471	CACAO
0723	COCOA BUTTER AND PASTE	W 152284	446072	W 166272	560487	W 172539	665516	W 189678	699445	BEURRE ET PATE DE CACAO
07232	COCOA BUTTER	W 133473	411319	W 143327	514752	W 146823	606625	W 153429	623559	BEURRE DE CACAO
073	CHOCOLATE AND PRODUCTS	W 215860	639607	W 217160	648236	W 215988	741726	W 213389	655107	CHOCOLAT
081	*FEEDING STUFF FOR ANIML	W 6118048	1718695	W 7325816	2042885	W 7756875	2319236	W 6903344	2233389	NOURRITURE POUR ANIMAUX
0813	OILCAKE AND OTH RESIDUES	W 2287641	485843	W 2818858	569671	W 3218500	641086	W 2728413	658962	TOURTEAUX
08131	— OF SOYA BEANS	W 1846701	422474	W 2232015	490304	W 2489025	550197	W 2089493	566904	TOURTEAUX DE SOJA
0819	FOOD WASTE AND FEED NES	W 2782657	1058329	W 3225096	1246931	W 3373262	1470403	W 3090337	1376747	DECHETS,ALIMENTS NDA
08199	FODDER NES,INCL SWEETNED	W 1478731	879479	W 1749818	1044321	W 1790191	1245012	W 1877396	1195310	PREPARATIONS FOURRAGERES
09	MISC EDIBLE PRODUCTS		1030781		1113845		1382632		1287896	PREP ALIMENTAIRES DIVERSES
098	EDIBLE PRODCTS,PREPS NES	W 409713	853375	W 425503	924297	W 451237	1101803	W 427933	1015832	PREP ALIMENTAIRES NDA
09809	MISC FOOD PREPRTIONS NES	W 190117	474218	W 182385	501462	W 189817	551275	W 194116	554723	PREP ALIMENTAIRES NDA
1	BEVERAGES AND TOBACCO		3383085		3788857		4619203		4909398	BOISSONS ET TABACS
11	BEVERAGES		1316203		1471531		1788560		1862938	BOISSONS
112	ALCOHOLIC BEVERAGES	W 948457	1007213	W 1059663	1127999	W 1213249	1397338	W 1353694	1489067	BOISSONS ALCOOLIQUES
1123	BEER,ALE,STOUT,PORTER	W 848811	750210	W 940530	833718	W 1083982	1075720	W 1203143	1160887	BIERES
12	TOBACCO AND MANUFACTURES		2066882		2317327		2830643		3046461	TABACS BRUTS FABRIQUES
122	TOBACCO,MANUFACTURED	W 107552	2012127	W 118827	2259047	W 124989	2769200	W 138264	2988577	TABACS FABRIQUES
1222	CIGARETTES	W 73599	1569257	W 86373	1775419	W 89198	2186012	W 104837	2457594	CIGARETTES
2	CRUDE MATERLS,EXCL FUELS		7178949		8188120		9133795		8397475	MAT BRUTES NON COMESTIBLES
22	OIL SEEDS,OLEAGINOUS FRT		219842		464230		264395		241800	GRAINES,FRUITS OLEAGINEUX
28	METALLIFEROUS ORES,SCRAP		1291491		1119014		1428002		1110731	MINERAIS METAL,DECHETS
282	IRON AND STEEL SCRAP	W 5579006	768031	W 3658302	608607	W 3617656	747272	W 3046591	562569	FERRAILLES
28209	— OF OTHR IRON OR STEEL	W 5286089	621379	W 3316269	438837	W 3238211	462260	W 2742176	393054	FERRAILLES DE FER
29	CRUDE ANIMAL,VEG MAT NES		4236475		4931004		5399753		5289763	MATIERES BRUTES ANIM,VEGET
292	CRUDE VEG MATERIALS NES	W 1156716	4077456	W 1282365	4740753	W 1162220	5179038	W 1268146	5056055	MAT BRUTES VEGETALES NDA
2926	LIVE PLANTS,BULBS,ETC	W 721300	1797299	W 734680	2107411	W 701645	2261054	W 737697	2183627	BULBES,TUBERCULES
29261	BULBS,TUBERS,CORMS,ETC	W 147688	567990	W 167165	680362	W 156918	751468	W 159383	694129	BULBES,OIGNONS
29269	LIVE PLANTS NES	W 573611	1229310	W 567514	1427049	W 544728	1509586	W 578314	1489498	AUTRES PLANTES VIVANTES
2927	CUT FLOWERS AND FOLIAGE	W 347062	1915369	W 391795	2195876	W 366262	2425806	W 389989	2382111	FLEURS,FEUILLAGES COUPES
29271	CUT FLOWERS	W 338057	1876284	W 381831	2139586	W 355814	2363880	W 375999	2306384	FLEURS ET BOUTONS
3	MINERAL FUELS ETC		11820782		11143380		12745036		14701329	COMBUSTIBLES MINERAUX LUB
33	PETROLEUM AND PRODUCTS		7868096		7502096		8269293		9552016	PETROLE ET DERIVES
334	PETROLEUM PRODUCTS,REFIN	MW 49719	7499445	MW 49275	7043805	MW 49742	7792346	MW 49367	9101594	PRODUITS RAFFINES
3341	GASOLINE,OTH LIGHT OILS	MW 10845	2054531	MW 12574	2118807	MW 13214	2346652	MW 13043	2743688	ESSENCES POUR MOTEURS
33411	MOTOR,AVIATION SPIRIT	W 2662219	526661	W 2644435	469385	W 1694768	316786	W 1280515	276080	ESSENCES MOTEURS D'AVIONS
33419	OTH LIGHT PETROLEUM OILS	W 8182572	1527870	MW 9930	1649422	MW 11519	2029866	MW 11762	2467608	AUTRES HUILES LEGERES
3342	KEROSENE,OTH MEDIUM OILS	W 3556515	698488	W 3765649	653337	W 4122974	732569	W 4392590	895700	PETR LAMPANTS,AUT HUIL
33421	KEROSENE INCL JET FUEL	W 3478706	671774	W 3689547	630986	W 4063645	713359	W 4299721	865847	PETROLES LAMPANTS
3343	GAS OILS	MW 16079	2729192	MW 16037	2386718	MW 17667	2760598	MW 18377	3504592	GAS OILS
3344	FUEL OILS,NES	MW 18606	1613490	MW 16085	1410616	MW 13973	1427074	MW 12665	1383666	FUEL OILS
3345	LUBS,PETROLEUM OILS NES	W 632044	403743	W 813686	474327	W 763946	525452	W 889136	573949	HUILES LUBRIFIANTES
341	*GAS,NATURAL AND MANUFCT		3691530	MW 31454	3351205		4079811		4835936	GAZ NATUREL,GAZ MANUFACT
3414	PETROLEUM GASES, GASEOUS	MW 32482	3495892	MW 30387	3173086	MW 30225	3839131	MW 36004	4561899	GAZ DE PETROLE GAZEUX
4	ANIMAL,VEGETABLE OIL,FAT		1062440		1294480		1575757		1492151	HUILES,GRAISSES ANIM,VEG
42	FIXED VEGETABLE OIL,FAT		664747		830602		1018099		971557	HUILES VEGETALES FIXES
423	FIXED VEG OILS,SOFT	W 940394	499601	W 1007799	635828	W 1010976	748209	W 957639	641229	HUILES VEGET DOUCES FIXES
5	CHEMCLS,RELATED PROD NES		18189697		21797014		28502294		26942289	PRODUITS CHIMIQUES
51	ORGANIC CHEMICALS		4319983		5114681		7513216		6942177	PROD CHIMIQ ORGANIQUES
511	HYDROCARBONS NES,DERIVS	W 4138814	1517743	W 3879557	1660091	W 4678308	2763053	W 5093639	2373863	HYDROCARBURES NDA
5111	ACYCLIC HYDROCARBONS	W 1676415	560633	W 1497473	519887	W 1646831	864299	W 1846164	788074	HYDROCARBURES ACYCLIQUES
5112	CYCLIC HYDROCARBONS	W 2353591	863120	W 2254141	1027470	W 2865559	1677626	W 3068795	1362476	HYDROCARBURES CYCLIQUES
51125	STYRENE	W 684241	329309	W 940921	558147	W 979248	850879	W 1267195	695932	STYRENE
512	ALCOHOLS,PHENOLS ETC	W 1271625	368310	W 1376195	585503	W 1445081	789274	W 1721211	745100	PHENOLS,PHENOLS–ALCOOLS
5121	ACYCLIC ALCOHOLS,DERIVS	W 1230181	282531	W 1320445	486444	W 1380257	640870	W 1652420	600584	ALCOOLS ACYCLIQUES
513	CARBOXYLIC ACIDS ETC	W 457853	568398	W 591677	732726	W 648376	1009286	W 648861	891615	ACIDES CARBOXYLIQUES
5137	MONOACIDS AND DERIVATIVS	W 337150	390546	W 412152	499366	W 476366	712786	W 518169	655670	ACIDES MONOCARBOXYLIQUES
514	NITROGEN–FNCTN COMPOUNDS	W 432387	858023	W 463439	1027643	W 485670	1175510	W 532947	1070698	COMPOSES FONCT AZOTEES

5. Special Exports F.O.B. by Commodities according to the S.I.T.C. (Rev. 2) in thousand U.S. Dollars
Exportations Spéciales F.O.B. par Produits d'après la C.T.C.I. (Rév. 2) en milliers de Dollars E.U.

SITC CTCI	COMMODITY	1993 WEIGHT POIDS	1993 VALUE VALEUR	1994 WEIGHT POIDS	1994 VALUE VALEUR	1995 WEIGHT POIDS	1995 VALUE VALEUR	1996 WEIGHT POIDS	1996 VALUE VALEUR	PRODUIT
5148	OTH NITROGN–FNCTN CMPNDS	W 271469	500591	W 303996	622485	W 294777	755682	W 347601	689022	AUTRES COMPOSES AZOTES
515	ORG–INORG COMPOUNDS ETC	W 58758	438574	W 56620	516110	W 221023	891167	W 264913	997095	COMPOSES ORGANO–MINERAUX
5156	HETEROCYCLIC CMPDS ETC	W 26900	287286	W 24438	348819	W 187302	699737	W 239084	823100	COMPOSES HETEROCYCLIQUES
516	OTHER ORGANIC CHEMICALS	W 1020103	568935	W 986807	592608	W 1395897	884928	W 1461146	863806	AUTRES PROD ORGANIQUES
52	INORGANIC CHEMICALS		875742		1043942		1112668		1178923	PROD CHIM INORGANIQUES
522	INORG ELEMNTS,OXIDES,ETC	W 1786856	382768	W 2544553	490783	W 2368747	619127	W 3080266	647150	ELEMENTS INORGANIQUES
53	DYES,TANNING,COLOUR PROD		1041767		1231802		1479339		1659153	PROD TEINTURE,COLORANTS
533	PIGMENTS,PAINTS,ETC	W 264463	866179	W 308477	973852	W 285627	1112194	W 309325	1241743	PIGMENTS,PEINTURES,VERNIS
5334	VARNISHES,DISTEMPERS ETC	W 152326	503585	W 170398	534144	W 139399	573017	W 152327	655712	PEINTURES A L'EAU
53342	OTH PAINTS,VARNISHES ETC	W 113703	421764	W 125588	439413	W 103917	478392	W 115946	554873	AUTRES PEINTURES,VERNIS
541	*MEDICINAL,PHARM PRODUCT	MK 33489	1875981	MK 155578	2780660	MK 89627	3973753	MK 80110	3437918	PROD MEDICINAUX PHARMACEUT
5417	MEDICAMENTS	MK 24766	1346440	MK 32791	1998820	MK 47693	2636117	MK 30306	2016671	MEDICAMENTS
54179	— CONTNG OTH SUBSTANCES	MK 21042	1095989	MK 27952	1614499	MK 43259	2138668	MK 26345	1490710	MED CONT AUT SUBSTANCES
55	PERFUME,CLEANING ETC PRD		1188647		1346476		1393938		1452960	PROD POUR PARFUM,TOILETTE
554	SOAP,CLEANSING ETC PREPS	W 447597	547476	W 543008	658132	W 487914	647600	W 534885	647331	SAVONS,PRODUITS DETERSIFS
562	*FERTILIZERS,MANUFACTURE	W 6251991	698471	W 7056992	848163	W 6604331	1080340	W 6079681	1013515	ENGRAIS MANUFACTURES
5621	CHEM NITROGENOUS FERTLZR	W 4762282	462953	W 5032713	514482	W 4666261	669175	W 4456480	661845	ENGRAIS AZOTES
58	PLASTIC MATERIALS ETC		5593661		6516673		8635695		8018465	MAT PLAST ARTIFICIELLES
582	PROD OF CONDENSATION ETC	W 1374721	2046347	W 1161834	2152127	W 1228695	2849750	W 1320584	2856105	PROD CONDENS,POLYCOND
5823	ALKYDS,OTHER POLYESTERS	W 715958	1011390	W 415390	1026819	W 478691	1400422	W 506839	1378968	ALKYDES ET AUT POLYESTERS
58231	— IN PRIMARY FORMS	W 223196	858401	W 388582	871524	W 447619	1198743	W 473470	1173654	SOUS FORMES PRIMAIRES
583	POLYMERIZATION ETC PRODS	W 3284961	3475207	W 3873870	4281884	W 3691169	5681975	W 3795256	5041130	PROD POLYMERISATION
5831	POLYETHYLENE	W 1288290	882814	W 1394198	979005	W 1262011	1303309	W 1244194	1119996	POLYETHYLENE
58311	— IN PRIMARY FORMS	W 1161786	797422	W 1189131	848398	W 1152479	1170395	W 1133300	992600	POLYETHYLENE PRIMAIRES
5832	POLYPROPYLENE	W 489515	373451	W 591051	499927	W 560212	745496	W 593554	631208	POLYPROPYLENE
58321	— IN PRIMARY FORMS	W 449165	290900	W 542794	397889	W 508560	584199	W 535026	483261	POLYPROPYLENE PRIMAIRES
5833	POLYSTYRENE,ITS COPOLYMR	W 453211	576206	W 520426	656723	W 476846	844304	W 503722	760632	POLYPROPYLENE COPOLYMERES
58331	— IN PRIMARY FORMS	W 437428	557426	W 481079	636013	W 459883	816540	W 488316	735467	SOUS FORMES PRIMAIRES
5834	POLYVINYL CHLORIDE	W 439246	391179	W 509298	512986	W 476991	698384	W 498352	509840	CHLORURE DE POLYVINYLE
5839	OTH POLYMRZTION ETC PROD	W 440861	902382	W 665063	1235815	W 720322	1603507	W 777862	1570691	AUT PROD POLYMER COPOLYM
59	CHEMICAL MATERIALS NES		2586030		2904633		3303042		3226906	MAT PROD CHIMIQUES NDA
591	PESTICIDES,DISINFECTANTS	W 70192	376176	W 103763	488481	W 89531	486597	W 79813	435435	DESINF,INSECT,FONG,HERB
592	STARCH,INULIN,GLUTEN,ETC	W 1010009	775104	W 1013319	807634	W 1038994	909502	W 1052421	939949	AMIDONS,INUL,GLUT FROM
5922	ALBUMINOID SUBSTAN,GLUES	W 505076	539711	W 539357	581442	W 580307	661522	W 604125	693319	MAT ALBUMIN,COLLES
598	MISCEL CHEM PRODUCTS NES	W 1065883	1434751	W 1099829	1608518	W 1057996	1906943	W 1322308	1851521	PROD DIV INDUST CHIM NDA
5989	CHEM PRODUCTS,PREPS NES	W 989203	1281497	W 1017390	1414748	W 961806	1681494	W 1220033	1655624	PROD PREP CHIMIQUES NDA
59899	OTH CHEM PRODS,PREPS,NES	W 842066	895626	W 861285	1027779	W 820496	1286818	W 1065186	1269457	AUT PRODUITS CHIMIQUES NDA
6	BASIC MANUFACTURES		15413423		17802939		22421247		20268106	ART MANUFACTURES
62	RUBBER MANUFACTURES NES		984400		1098504		1320894		1272388	CAOUTCHOUC MANUFACTURE
625	RUBBER TYRES, TUBES ETC	W 180184	699688	W 189574	712445	W 216074	851741	W 204080	822851	PNEUS CAOUTCHOUC VULCANISE
6251	TYRES NEW FOR MOTOR CARS	W 76847	406119	W 78624	415329	W 85043	501051	W 84137	487942	PNEUS POUR VOITURES
63	WOOD,CORK MANUFACTRS NES		556549		701121		731557		661380	OUVRAGES LIEGE ET BOIS
635	WOOD MANUFACTURES NES	W 316852	433371	W 414852	540782	W 383591	594364	W 378998	550691	ART MANUF EN BOIS NDA
64	PAPER,PAPERBOARD AND MFR		2506911		3156695		4065371		3724150	PAPIERS,CARTONS & OUVRAGES
641	PAPER AND PAPERBOARD	W 2194380	1646619	W 2677681	2139636	W 2687693	2844338	W 2686107	2517719	PAPIERS ET CARTONS
6412	PRINTG,WRITING PAPER NES	W 500612	442169	W 635005	564677	W 609202	753401	W 627196	640044	PAPIERS POUR L'IMPRESSION
64122	— COATED,IMPREGNATD ETC	W 470718	401986	W 586190	508788	W 543783	644794	W 518043	504888	PAPIERS IMPRESSION COUCHES
6415	PAPER,PAPERBRD,BULK,NES	W 702548	373002	W 886230	537730	W 866219	733644	W 821699	535040	PAPIERS,CARTONS ROULEAUX
64159	OTHER PAPER ETC,BULK,NES	W 692747	365286	W 869916	526079	W 852593	718844	W 809733	524125	AUT PAPIER ROULEAUX FEUILLES
6418	COATED ETC PAPER NES BLK	W 158643	272245	W 211847	414582	W 247248	505725	W 279388	548603	PAP,CARTONS COUCHES,ENDUITS
642	PAPER,ETC,PRECUT,ARTS OF	W 416297	860292	W 486000	1017059	W 502608	1221032	W 541850	1206431	PAP,CARTONS DECOUPES
6428	PAPER ETC ARTICLES NES	W 146124	354626	W 173931	466350	W 177150	554711	W 203683	558151	OUVRAGES EN PATE A PAPIER
65	TEXTILE YARN,FABRICS,ETC		2484260		2700417		3532054		3242956	FILS,TISSUS,ARTICLES TEXTILE
652	COTTON FABRICS,WOVEN	W 30117	397753	W 31469	392482	W 33604	469467	W 34765	442977	TISSUS DE COTON
653	WOVN MAN–MADE FIB FABRIC	W 38066	390332	W 34913	418182	W 42759	562313	W 46039	475067	TISSUS FIBRES SYNTH,ARTIF
657	SPECIAL TXTL FABRC,PRODS	W 68340	490951	W 76580	564374	W 81831	666753	W 80773	617758	TISSUS SPECIAUX
659	FLOOR COVERINGS,ETC	W 129275	435763	W 138782	481323	W 185018	680714	W 193485	680368	COUVRE–PARQUETS,TAPIS ETC
66	NONMETAL MINERAL MFS NES		1348323		1409728		1514456		1429676	ART MIN NON METALLIQUES
67	IRON AND STEEL		2731615		3459479		4313253		3742759	FER ET ACIER
672	IRON,STEEL PRIMARY FORMS	W 2531646	667642	W 2811612	861140	W 2514247	956311	W 2773652	827580	LINGOTS FER,ACIER
6727	IRN,STL COIL FR REROLLNG	W 1022899	329004	W 1270129	466339	W 1300262	558023	W 1261276	439818	EBAUCHES POUR TOLES FER
67271	IRON,SIMPLE STEEL COILS	W 1015922	321472	W 1264361	459943	W 1292287	544233	W 1258470	434463	EBAUCHES NON EN ACIER
674	IRN,STL UNIV,PLATE,SHEET	W 2031860	1129607	W 2480537	1528749	W 2515319	1973639	W 2578416	1771856	LARGES PLATS,TOLES
6746	IRN,STL THIN PLATE,ROLLD	W 755733	405870	W 1045951	644131	W 986428	798687	W 1040256	718613	TOLES LAM MOINS 3MM
678	IRON,STL TUBES,PIPES,ETC	W 443232	442277	W 523864	487246	W 479401	618915	W 446389	555085	TUBES,TUYAUX EN FONTE,FER
68	NON–FERROUS METALS		1643816		2003086		2937853		2479753	METAUX NON FERREUX
684	ALUMINIUM	W 570073	1114827	W 652796	1371255	W 809463	2141555	W 702617	1669150	ALUMINIUM
6841	ALUMINIUM,ALLOYS,UNWRGHT	W 400995	540818	W 443871	676764	W 576826	1189340	W 483772	836815	ALUMINIUM,ALLIAGES BRUTS
6842	ALUMINIUM,ALLOYS WORKED	W 169078	574009	W 208926	694491	W 232638	952215	W 218845	832336	ALUMINIUM,ALLIAGES OUVRE
69	METAL MANUFACTURES NES		2953160		3050933		3773439		3501669	ART MANUFACT EN METAL NDA
691	STRUCTURES AND PARTS NES	W 370599	981869	W 321996	714504	W 327050	1093371	W 325955	785372	CONSTRUCT FER,ACIER,ALU
6911	STRUCTURES,PARTS IRN,STL	W 355087	855015	W 302812	571593	W 301121	903478	W 303552	611045	CONSTRUCT FER,ACIER,FONTE
695	TOOLS	W 35422	417394	W 30756	453204	W 29432	595035	W 34978	671203	OUTILS A MAIN
699	BASE METAL MFRS NES	W 162742	828709	W 186431	945162	W 178200	1091570	W 359271	1067736	ART MANUFACTURES MET NDA
7	MACHINES,TRANSPORT EQUIP		32665964		36255036		47165587		50488661	MACHINES MATERIEL TRANSPORT
71	POWER GENERATING EQUIPMT		1414485		1526190		1787463		1822572	MACHINES GENERATRICES
713	INTRNL COMBUS PSTN ENGIN	W 28298	387218	W 33031	429588	W 35040	582050	W 41583	611255	MOTEURS EXPL COMB INT, PIECE
714	ENGINES AND MOTORS NES	W 9416	675435	W 8295	742306	W 9910	862607	W 9081	873839	MOTEURS NON ELECTRIQUES
7149	ENGINE & MOTOR PARTS NES	W 8510	527495	W 7690	552542	W 9238	705728	W 8682	726570	PIECES 714 ET 718.88
72	MACHS FOR SPCL INDUSTRYS		2768765		3156306		3601990		3645643	MAC SPECIALES POUR INDUST
721	AGRIC MACHY,EXC TRACTORS	W 54423	471032	W 60221	499206	W 61729	578772	W 61069	513258	MACHINES AGRICOLES
727	FOOD MACHRY NON–DOMESTIC	W 18628	448782	W 26977	559924	W 29638	627950	W 25478	595775	MACH INDUSTRIES ALIMENT
7272	OTH FOOD PROC MCHY,PARTS	W 15460	422424	W 21310	525575	W 22871	587052	W 17618	560200	AUT MACH IND ALIMENTAIRE
72722	INDUS FOOD PROC MACH NES	W 15335	420345	W 21058	522361	W 22787	585085	W 17108	557297	MACHINES BOULANGERIE
728	OTH MACHY FOR SPCL INDUS	W 48895	909808	W 51622	1063226	W 58362	1265101	W 54863	1344897	AUT MACH IND PARTICULIERES
7284	MACHY FOR SPCL INDUS NES	W 34667	778630	W 38318	940389	W 43353	1111493	W 38998	1199543	MACH SPEC IND PARTICUL.
72849	PTS OF MACHS OF 7284 ETC	W 9274	250019	W 13287	407019	W 17150	474588	W 16390	575189	PIECES DU 728.4 ETC
74	GENRL INDUSTRL MACHY NES		3461486		3898762		4586504		4747581	MACH APP INDUSTRIE
741	HEATING,COOLING EQUIPMNT	W 44060	635183	W 54444	694713	W 50178	813509	W 51143	911820	MACH CHAUFFAGE,PIECES
743	PUMPS NES,CENTRFUGES ETC	W 30655	515429	W 30853	538381	W 32843	607608	W 42639	766517	POMPES COMPRES,VENT ETC
744	MECHANICAL HANDLING EQU	W 123005	823847	W 141165	1016289	W 168963	1278848	W 157769	1220308	EQUIP MANUTENTION PIECES
745	NONELEC MACHY,TOOLS NES	W 19677	438310	W 24204	494982	W 19916	543730		534209	AUT MACH NON ELEC,PIECES
7452	OTH NONELEC MCHS,PTS NES	W 18594	401666	W 22893	451431	W 18789	492490		476952	AUT MACH NON ELEC,PIECES
749	NONELEC MACH PTS,ACC NES	W 44033	727759	W 49924	791870	W 54819	977692	W 59776	960013	PIECES MACH NON ELEC NDA
75	OFFICE MACHNES,ADP EQUIP		8175675		10144722		13355586		15372640	MACH BUREAU TRAIT AUTOM
751	OFFICE MACHINES	W 37336	1114192	W 54178	1555771	W 53347	1796180	W 66126	1561780	MACH,APPAREILS DE BUREAU
7518	OFFICE MACHINES NES	W 36044	1075304	W 52310	1498573	W 51333	1735175	W 63954	1495971	MACH,APP DE BUREAU NDA
75182	PHOTO,THERMOCOPY APPARAT	W 30199	873486	W 44444	1232884	W 44099	1419120	W 39928	1198312	APPAREILS DE PHOTOCOPIE
752	AUTOMTIC DATA PROC EQUIP	W 56675	4267436	W 74824	5586607	W 96841	7697159	W 120938	9764369	MACH TRAIT INFORMATION
7522	DIGITAL COMPUTERS	W 775	187613	W 1988	479029	W 2785	840646	W 3879	936188	MACH DIGITALES COMPLETES
7523	DIGITL CENTRL PROCESSORS	W 10923	1120081	W 16771	1642059	W 17949	2187533	W 20162	2427190	UNITES CENTRALES

5. Special Exports F.O.B. by Commodities according to the S.I.T.C. (Rev. 2) in thousand U.S. Dollars
Exportations Spéciales F.O.B. par Produits d'après la C.T.C.I. (Rév. 2) en milliers de Dollars E.U.

SITC CTCI	COMMODITY	1993 WEIGHT POIDS	1993 VALUE VALEUR	1994 WEIGHT POIDS	1994 VALUE VALEUR	1995 WEIGHT POIDS	1995 VALUE VALEUR	1996 WEIGHT POIDS	1996 VALUE VALEUR	PRODUIT
7524	DIGITL CENTRL STOR UNITS	W 4783	847820	W 5045	986803	W 8080	1872784	W 12331	2849325	UNITES MEMOIRE CENTRALES
7525	ADP PERIPHERAL UNITS	W 37237	1518986	W 46728	2005748	W 63338	2432651	W 77963	2966802	UNITES PERIPHERIQUES
7528	OFF–LINE DATA PROC EQUIP	W 2948	591430	W 4255	469130	W 4578	355171	W 6412	562867	MACH AUXIL TRAIT INFORM
759	OFFICE,ADP MCH PTS,ACCES	W 38559	2794046	W 45067	3002344	W 47627	3862247	W 49892	4046491	PIECES DU 751 ET 752
7591	OFFICE MACHINE PARTS NES	W 22216	831045	W 26111	1039599	W 23363	1087480	W 16823	689404	PIECES DU 7511,7518
75919	COPY MACH PRTS,ACCES NES	W 20678	720005	W 23949	853053	W 20944	867003	W 14914	534649	PIECES DU 751.82
7599	ACCTG,ETC,ADP MCH PTS,AC	W 16343	1963001	W 18955	1962746	W 24264	2774767	W 33069	3357086	PIECES DU 751 ET 752
76	TELECOMM,SOUND EQUIPMENT		2246359		2398432		3121723		3482739	EQUIPMENT DE TELECOM
762	RADIO BROADCAST RECEIVRS	W 15472	345075	W 16793	388114	W 20272	527420	W 23172	592667	RECEPTEURS RADIODIFFUSION
764	TELECOM EQPT,PTS,ACC NES	W 24263	1439799	W 24454	1547384	W 26336	2030873	W 27370	2095961	EQUIP TELECOM,PIECES
7649	PTS NES OF EQUIPMT OF 76	W 10011	846247	W 9859	938152	W 10749	1245431	W 9755	1265225	PIECES DE LA DIV 76
76491	PTS NES OF APPAR OF 7641	W 2674	426317	W 2840	469413	W 4193	840617	W 4016	794202	PIECES POUR 764.1
77	ELECTRIC MACHNRY NES ETC		7098895		7883408		10264363		11502412	MACH APP ELECT NDA
772	SWITCHGEAR ETC,PARTS NES	W 24836	855123	W 32801	975786	W 29274	1423286	W 29536	1391524	APP COUPURE,SECT ETC
7721	SWITCHGEAR ETC	W 23207	685024	W 31076	781042	W 27429	1204572	W 27124	1167058	APP COUPURE,SECTIONMNT
774	ELECTRO–MEDCL,XRAY EQUIP	W 5400	860083	W 4754	963487	W 5197	1134168	W 5818	1069504	APPAREILS MEDICAUX
7742	X–RAY APPARATUS ETC	W 4666	694111	W 3885	729408	W 3991	770326	W 4478	770623	APPAREILS A RAYONS X
775	HOUSEHOLD TYPE EQUIP NES	W 42390	716115	W 42826	736316	W 50073	887545	W 56638	768525	MACH,APP USAGE DOMESTQUE
776	TRANSISTORS,VALVES,ETC	W 17294	2439905	W 15492	2819924	W 17606	3946445	W 20045	5322882	LAMPES,TUBES,VALVES
7763	DIODES,TRANSISTORS,ETC	W 2468	376452	W 1605	399847	W 1877	576697	W 1869	515658	DIODES,TRANSISTORS
7764	ELECTRONIC MICROCIRCUITS	W 3088	1725159	W 2811	2054464	W 3246	2923729	W 4622	4352439	MICROSTRUCTURES ELECTRON
778	ELECTRICAL MACHINERY NES	W 101689	1633706	W 102618	1700167	W 111982	2101176		2084317	AUTRES MACH ELECT NDA
7782	ELECTRIC LAMPS,BULBS	W 50240	751511	W 49021	708480	W 53259	803133	W 52782	721425	LAMPES, TUBES ELECTRIQUES
77822	ELEC DISCHARGE LAMPS NES	W 25804	398788	W 23896	362453	W 26610	417534	W 26155	379250	LAMPES NON ULTRA–VIOLETS
7788	OTH ELEC MACHY,EQUIP NES	W 14017	554037	W 15991	624346	W 16476	809422		877301	AUT MACH APP ELEC NDA
78	ROAD VEHICLES		4022874		5007081		7382128		8328362	VEHICULES ROUTIERS
781	PASS MOTOR VEH EXC BUSES	W 193089	1322026	W 189123	1474521	W 247307	2624881	W 303534	3325699	AUTO TRANSPORT PERSONNES
782	LORRIES,SPCL MTR VEH NES	W 111925	511857	W 158160	777802	W 175126	1124143	W 192830	1163975	VEHICULES SPECIAUX,MARCH
7821	LORRIES,TRUCKS	W 101834	463173	W 147018	720256	W 163012	1054427	W 175394	1061949	VEHICULES TRANSP MARCHAND
783	ROAD MOTOR VEHICLES NES	W 70917	558451	W 104690	865097	W 143036	1381626	W 153087	1399113	VEHICULES ROUTIERS NDA
7832	TRACTORS FOR TR–TRAILERS	W 61288	442419	W 92180	723060	W 130860	1239517	W 140278	1257307	TRACTEURS ROUTIERS
784	MOTOR VEH PRTS,ACCES NES	W 152577	931757	W 200784	1236578	W 222976	1575381	W 238535	1586593	PIECES 722,781,782,783
7849	OTHER MOTOR VEHCL PARTS	W 147505	893023	W 192487	1166242	W 216903	1511204	W 232094	1529607	PIECES 722,781,782,783
785	CYCLES,ETC MOTRZD OR NOT	W 29408	432580	W 21838	350828	W 16263	340458	W 25432	539166	MOTOCYCLES SCOOTERS
79	OTHR TRANSPORT EQUIPMENT		3163603		1886627		2684262		1204844	AUTRE MATERIEL TRANSPORT
792	AIRCRAFT ETC	W 3374	2652025	W 2046	1191793	W 2757	2008326	W 1885	847055	APP NAVIGATION AERIENNE
7924	AIRCRFT NES OVER 15000KG	W 1700	1904101	W 530	533741	W 1187	1159932	W 693	384376	AERODYNES PLUS 15000 KG
7929	AIRCRAFT PARTS NES	W 1349	419081	W 1238	406896	W 1162	415126	W 1063	377664	PIECES DU 792
793	SHIPS AND BOATS ETC		454975	W 87702	642448	W 46289	612428	W 1043253	309243	NAVIRES BATEAUX,ETC
8	MISC MANUFACTURED GOODS		12735703		13793198		15545892		15886405	ART MANUFACTURES DIVERS
812	*PLUMBG,HEATNG,LGHTNG EQ	W 86476	436734	W 90879	494997	W 81698	518659	W 81498	492408	APPAR SANITAIRES CHAUFFAGE
821	*FURNITURE,PARTS THEREOF	W 186910	877153	W 283565	878434	W 172742	960025	W 166020	971434	MEUBLES ET PIECES
8219	FURNITURE AND PARTS NES	W 124646	507950	W 223746	524758	W 120071	566981	W 111062	563020	AUTRES MEUBLES ET PIECES
84	CLOTHING AND ACCESSORIES		2366208		2623417		2772073		3054067	VETEMENTS
842	MENS OUTERWEAR NOT KNIT	W 14312	419719	W 14132	474167	W 14156	541991	W 16206	572212	VET DESSUS POUR HOMMES
843	WOMENS OUTERWEAR NONKNIT	W 18250	674679	W 19506	766420	W 19210	792543	W 21382	793623	VET DESSUS FEMMES MAT TEX
845	OUTERWEAR KNIT NONELASTC	W 17340	513729	W 18851	562744	W 16183	530998	W 22541	645110	VET DESSOUS,ACCES BONNET
846	UNDER GARMENTS KNITTED	W 17267	379023	W 13603	390148	W 14223	459733	W 18664	533865	SOUS VETS DE BONNETERIE
851	*FOOTWEAR	W 34390	499264	W 33804	488932	W 32614	564089	W 34141	559258	CHAUSSURES
85102	FOOTWEAR LEATHER	W 23387	408613	W 23724	410303	W 23697	466369	W 24097	452317	CHAUS SEMELLES EN CUIR
87	PRECISION INSTRUMNTS NES		1798229		1975770		2356494		2649297	INSTRUM,APPAR SCIENT NDA
872	MEDICAL INSTRUMENTS NES	W 8581	557029	W 7832	580234	W 7547	704225	W 9571	833559	INSTR,APP MEDIC–CHIR NDA
87202	OTH MEDICAL INSTRUMENTS	W 7890	538230	W 7022	555112	W 6575	671998	W 8566	788865	INSTRUM,APP MEDECINE
874	MEASURNG,CONTROLNG INSTR	W 13102	1149057	W 12756	1264779	W 12356	1498610	W 17497	1654367	INSTRUMENTS DE MESURE
8748	ELEC MEAS,CONTRL EQU NES	W 1411	291560	W 1449	320290	W 1501	378590	W 3071	533276	APP ELEC ELECTRO MESURE
88	PHOTO EQU,OPTICL GDS ETC		1098958		1419858		1477551		1803084	APP,FOURN PHOTO,OP,MONTR
881	PHOTO APPARAT,EQUIPT NES	W 3255	309619	W 3885	459306	W 3674	504727	W 4303	800223	APP,EQUIP PHOTO NDA
8813	OTH PHOTO,CINE EQUIP NES	W 1379	187969	W 1871	335917	W 1924	398210	W 2394	688585	APP,MAT PHOTO,CINEMA
88139	PHOTO,CINE LAB EQUIP NES	W 854	172109	W 1236	314451	W 1333	375550	W 1720	666081	APP TYPES UTIL LABOR
882	PHOTO,CINEMA SUPPLIES	W 37157	661467	W 41377	821104	W 40359	801375	W 37930	830752	PRODUITS PHOTO,CINEMA
8822	PHOTO FILM EXC DEV CINMA	W 32121	597384	W 34501	732233	W 30479	686171	W 30084	719354	PLAQUES,PELLICULES,FILMS
88221	PHOTO FILM FLAT UNEXPOSD	W 29253	522499	W 29953	600975	W 26189	555310	W 25279	595482	PLAQUES PHOTO,FILMS SENS
89	MISC MANUFCTRD GOODS NES		5521700		5770415		6707214		6172015	ART MANUFACTURES DIVERS
892	PRINTED MATTER	W 164344	816445	W 167537	863007	W 181258	989482	W 173507	884484	IMPRIMES
893	ARTICLES OF PLASTIC NES		1581716		1727193		1985505		1898015	OUVRAGES EN MAT DIVIS 58
8931	PLSTC PACKG CONTNRS,LIDS	W 209704	482647	W 174381	539330	W 174048	638995	W 173614	588909	ART TRANSP EMBALLAGE ETC
8939	MISC PLASTIC ARTICLES	W 297666	1050975	W 220081	1138883	W 222455	1290459	W 221858	1247862	ART DIVERS EN MAT DIV 58
89399	OTHR PLASTC ARTICLES NES	W 289315	988783	W 212136	1076563	W 214284	1225220	W 214293	1195119	AUT OUV MAT DIV 58
894	TOYS,SPORTING GOODS,ETC	W 76875	589782	W 72593	686455	W 62759	941359	W 65554	807362	VOITURES ENFANTS,JOUETS
8942	TOYS,INDOOR GAMES ETC	W 66933	487519	W 59404	561201	W 50285	814447	W 50883	659782	JOUETS,JEUX ETC
898	MUSICAL INSTRUMENTS,PTS	W 75207	1703334	W 71273	1581405	W 78800	1772075	W 65751	1504824	INSTRUMENTS DE MUSIQUE
8983	SOUND RECRDNG TAPE,DISCS	W 72750	1640499	W 69356	1542058	W 77148	1732916	W 64235	1474513	SUPPORTS SON POUR 763
89831	PREPD SND RECORDNG MEDIA	W 37063	564680	W 33211	559909	W 35789	660368	W 22185	340812	SUPPORTS PREPARES
89832	RECORDED DISCS,TAPES ETC	W 35687	1075819	W 36145	982149	W 41358	1072547	W 42050	1133702	DISQUES,PHONO,BANDES
899	OTHER MANUFACTURED GOODS		575779		639564		719627		820505	AUT ART MANUF DIVERS NDA
9	GOODS NOT CLASSD BY KIND		5268731		6589888		7187710		7225975	ART TRANSACT NON CLASSES
931	*SPECIAL TRANSACTIONS	W 3589483	5013312	W 4598731	6224965	W 4363002	6813005	W 4353344	6742257	TRANS.SPECIALES

FOOT NOTES – NOTES

TABLE 1 –

1 The gold trade includes gold bullion, bars, dust, concentrates, scrap, sweepings, specie and partly–worked gold.

TABLE 4 –

1 Victuals and stores of foreign origin for Netherlands' ships and aircraft are included at the section 9 level only.

TABLE 5 –

1 Victuals and stores supplied to foreign ships and aircraft are included at the section 9 level only.

TABLEAU 1 –

1 Le commerce d'or comprend l'or en lingots, les barres, la poussière, les concentrés, les déchets, les balayures, les pièces de monnaie et l'or partiellement travaillé.

TABLEAU 4 –

1 Les victuailles et l'approvisionnement d'origine étrangère des Pays–Bas sont compris au niveau de la section 9 seulement.

TABLEAU 5 –

1 Les victuailles et l'approvisionnement d'origine étrangère des Pays–Bas sont compris seulement au niveau de la section 9'

1. HISTORICAL SERIES, 1959–1994 SPECIAL TRADE, IMPORTS C.I.F., EXPORTS F.O.B. # 1
SERIES HISTORIQUES, 1959–1994 COMMERCE SPECIAL, IMPORTATIONS C.A.F., EXPORTATIONS F.O.B

YEAR ANNEE	VALUE IN MILLION N.A. GUILDERS VALEUR EN MILLION N.A. GUILDERS MERCHANDISE –MARCHANDISE IMPORTS	EXPORTS	GOLD –OR IMPORTS	EXPORTS	CONVERSION FACTORS U.S. CENTS PER N.A. GUILDER FACTEURS DE CONVERSION CENTS E.U. PAR N.A. GUILDER IMPORTS	EXPORTS	INDEX NUMBERS –INDICES QUANTUM IMPORTS	EXPORTS	UNIT VALUE VALEUR UNITAIRE IMPORTS	EXPORTS
1959	1465.00	1342.00			53.0264	53.0264				
1960	1286.00	1241.00			53.0264	53.0264				
1961	1353.00	1337.00			53.0264	53.0264				
1962	1360.00	1297.00			53.0264	53.0264				
1963	1313.00	1242.00			53.0264	53.0264				
1964	1225.00	1188.00			53.0264	53.0264				
1965	1164.00	1136.00			53.0264	53.0264				
1966	1165.00	1116.00			53.0264	53.0264				
1967	1261.00	1146.00			53.0264	53.0264				
1968	1267.00	1130.00			53.0264	53.0264				
1969	1307.00	1178.00			53.0264	53.0264				
1970	1504.00	1275.00			53.0264	53.0264				
1971	1660.00	1366.00			53.0259	53.0259				
1972	1565.00	1364.00			55.5550	55.5550				
1973	2868.00	2465.00			55.5543	55.5545				
1974	6536.00	5815.00			55.5555	55.5555				
1975	5088.00	4315.00			55.5559	55.5559				
1976	6601.00	4544.00			55.5556	55.5556				
1977	5631.00	4764.00			55.5556	55.5556				
1978	5682.00	4754.00			55.5556	55.5556				
1979	7911.00	7138.00			55.5556	55.5556				
1980	10216.00	9292.00			55.5556	55.5556				
1981	10551.00	9750.00			55.5556	55.5556				
1982	9150.00	8803.00			55.5556	55.5556				
1983	8148.00	7937.00			55.5555	55.5556				
1984	7258.00	6719.00			55.5536	55.5538				
1985	4061.00	3023.00			55.5556	55.5556				
1986	2002.00	1664.00			55.5500	55.5500				
1987	2703.00	2354.00			55.5500	55.5500				
1988	2526.00	2041.00			55.5500	55.5500				
1989	2888.00	2608.00			55.7633	55.7633				
1990	3833.00	3204.00			55.8700	55.8700				
1991	3828.00	2862.00			55.8700	55.8700				
1992	3344.00	2790.00			55.8700	55.8700				
1993	3485.00	2297.00			55.8700	55.8700				
1994	2622.00	1835.00			55.8700	55.8700				

2. IMPORTS BY BROAD ECONOMIC CATEGORY AND EXPORTS BY INDUSTRIAL ORIGIN. (PERCENTAGE OF TOTAL VALUE)
IMPORTATIONS PAR CATEGORIES ECONOMIQUES ET EXPORTATIONS PAR BRANCHE D'ACTIVITE.(EN POURCENTAGE DE LA VALEUR TOTALE)

IMPORTS – IMPORTATIONS

	1990	1991	1992	1993	1994	1995	1996
TOTAL IMPORTS–IMPORTATIONS TOTALES	100.	100.	100.				
1 FOOD BEV–ALIMENTATION BOISSONS	5.5	5.4	8.3				
11 PRIMARY–PRODUITS DE BASE	2.2	2.2	3.4				
111 FOR INDUSTRY–POUR L'INDUSTRIE	0.2	0.2	1.0				
112 FOR HOUSEHOLDS–POUR LES MENAGES	2.0	2.0	2.4				
12 PROCESSED–PRODUITS ELABORES	3.3	3.1	5.0				
121 FOR INDUSTRY–POUR L'INDUSTRIE	0.1	0.1	0.2				
122 FOR HOUSEHOLDS–POUR LES MENAGES	3.2	3.0	4.7				
2 IND SUPPLIES–APPROV INDUSTRIELS	7.4	7.5	8.8				
21 PRIMARY–PRODUITS DE BASE	0.4	0.3	0.5				
22 PROCESSED–PRODUITS ELABORES	7.0	7.1	8.3				
3 FUELS–COMBUSTIBLES	70.4	70.7	58.8				
31 PRIMARY–PRODUITS DE BASE	64.4	64.3	52.8				
32 PROCESSED–PRODUITS ELABORES	6.0	6.4	6.0				
321 MOTOR SPIRIT–ESSENCE	0.4	0.1	0.0				
322 OTHER–AUTRES	5.6	6.2	6.0				
4 MACHINERY–EQUIPEMENT	5.4	5.0	6.6				
41 CAPITAL EQUIPMENT–MACHINES	5.0	4.5	5.9				
42 PARTS–PIECES ACCESSOIRES	0.5	0.5	0.7				
5 TRANSPORT–TRANSPORT	3.9	3.7	6.4				
51 PASSENGER CARS–AUTOMOBILES	1.3	1.6	2.1				
52 OTHER–AUTRES	1.5	0.8	2.3				
521 INDUSTRIAL–INDUSTRIELS	1.4	0.8	2.3				
522 NON INDUSTRIAL–NON INDUSTRIEL	0.0	0.0	0.0				
53 PARTS–PIECES ACCESSOIRES	1.1	1.3	2.0				
6 CONSUM GOODS–BIENS CONSOMMATION	7.4	7.8	11.1				
61 DURABLE–DURABLES	1.8	1.8	2.9				
62 SEMI DURABLE–SEMI DURABLES	3.5	4.0	5.2				
63 NON DURABLE–NON DURABLES	2.1	2.1	3.0				
7 GOODS NES–BIENS NDA	0.0	0.0	0.0				

EXPORTS – EXPORTATIONS

	1990	1991	1992	1993	1994	1995	1996
TOTAL EXPORTS–EXPORTATIONS TOTALES	100.	100.	100.				
1 AGRICULTURE	0.0	0.1	2.6				
2 MINING QUARRY–INDUS EXTRACTIVES	12.0	9.6	7.3				
3 MANUFACTURING–IND MANUFACTUR	88.0	90.4	90.2				
31 FOOD BEV TOBACCO–ALIM BOISS TAB	0.5	0.5	0.5				
32 TEXTILES–INDUSTRIES TEXTILES	0.1	0.1	0.1				
33 WOOD & PRODUCTS–BOIS & PRODUITS	0.0	0.0	0.0				
34 PAPER & PRODUCTS–PAPIER & PRODT	0.2	0.1	0.2				
35 CHEMICALS–INDUSTRIES CHIMIQUES	86.2	88.3	85.6				
36 NON METAL MIN–MIN NON METAL	0.0	0.0	0.0				
37 BASIC METAL–IND METAL BASE	0.1	0.0	0.1				
38 METAL MANUF–MANUF METAL	0.9	1.2	3.6				
39 OTH MANUF IND–AUTRES MANUF	0.0	0.1	0.1				

3. TRADE BY PRINCIPAL COUNTRIES OF FIRST AND LAST CONSIGNMENT (VALUE IN THOUSAND U.S. DOLLARS)
ECHANGES SELON LES PRINCIPAUX PAYS DE PREMIERE ET DE DERNIERE CONSIGNATION (VALEUR EN MILLIERS DE DOLLARS EU)

COUNTRIES–PAYS	SPECIAL IMPORTS C.I.F. # 1 IMPORTATIONS SPECIALES C.A.F				
	1990	1991	1992	1993	1994
World	2147004	2188945	1868324	1946930	1464909
Africa	40	86	104		
Americas	1807659	1908416	1539781	334637	284936
Northern America	291504	324040	349624	334637	284936
LAIA	1463888	1545920	1106334		
CACM	1422	1834	2207		
Caribbean	40220	24553	45843		
Rest of America	10625	12070	35773		
As.ex F.USSR	99393	48594	56732	42458	32405
Eur.x F.USSR	207413	198265	235340	185475	175990
EU	188320	183045	218286	185475	175990
EFTA	4432	6162	13847		
East Europe	2380	2355	2220		
Other Europe	12282	6702	742		
Former USSR	344	411	141		
Oceania	1087	1334	1096		
Venezuela	1270780	1522375	1075733		
USA/Etats–Unis d'Amer	273405	316359	317365	334637	284936
Netherlands/Pays–Bas	122730	130082	152000	169833	163699
Japan/Japon	46736	38076	40963	42458	32405
Ecuador/Equateur	118508	14	81		
United Kingdom	20516	16871	18262	15642	12291
Trinidad and Tobago	26721	15981	34335		
Mexico/Mexique	54434	5001	6394		
Canada	17723	7292	31999		
Germany/Allemagne	14004	13886	13853		
Italy/Italie	16591	9164	15217		
Panama	9867	11375	13308		
Iran (Islamic Rp. of)	26975				
Aruba	11302	6954	8537		
Colombia/Colombie	7104	7915	10618		
Brazil/Brésil	7061	6181	9354		
Switz.Liecht	2519	4522	12004		
Suriname/Suriname	661	652	13334		
Hong Kong	4730	4339	5263		
France,Monac	5255	4150	4791		
Argentina/Argentine	5468	3789	3478		
Saudi Arabia	12588		17		
Guyana	97	43	9079		
Belgium–Luxembourg	3083	2014	4044		
Sweden/Suède	1665	2470	3755		
Korea, Republic of	2644	2027	2254		
Spain/Espagne	1922	1634	2288		
Hungary/Hongrie	2038	2000	1753		
Norway,SVD,JM	1912	1614	1844		
Denmark/Danemark	1653	1508	2020		
Singapore/Singapour	947	650	2770		
Costa Rica	951	1250	1411		
Thailand/Thaïlande	1093	603	853		
Dominican Republic	486	559	1311		
Portugal	401	811	893		
New Zealand	563	642	577		
Australia/Australie	524	692	519		
Barbados/Barbade	494	541	642		
Jamaica/Jamaïque	1021	166	202		
Israel/Israël	324	325	554		
Austria/Autriche	221	182	693		
Peru/Pérou	443	393	246		
El Salvador	227	427	389		
Bermuda/Bermudes	376	388	260		
Indonesia/Indonésie	84	284	572		
India/Inde	223	156	447		
Former USSR/Anc. URSS	344	411			
Ireland/Irlande	253	140	241		
Bahamas	111	273	159		
Guatemala	94	37	330		

COUNTRIES–PAYS	SPECIAL EXPORTS F.O.B. # 1 EXPORTATIONS SPECIALES F.O.B.				
	1990	1991	1992	1993	1994
Monde	1800612	1599210	1558890	1398885	
Afrique	66176	51730	68361		
Amériques	1577250	1359944	1231257	14525	
Amérique du Nord	637018	482334	480009	14525	
ALAI	248477	282116	215726		
MCAC	118860	83069	99081		
Caraïbes	490627	414646	351280		
Autre Amérique	82268	97779	85160		
Asie l'URSS exclus	52687	85696	101560		
Europe l'URSS exclus	73518	74192	154270	70447	
UE	73354	73625	126946	70447	
AELE	164	567	502		
Europe de l'Est					
Autre de l'Europe					
Ancienne URSS					
Océanie	2543	1067	788		
USA/Etats–Unis d'Amer	600824	453469	389602	14525	
Dominican Republic	132562	78037	109457		
Colombia/Colombie	57190	80839	111699		
Venezuela	82485	77663	28516		
Guadeloupe	55939	53840	51445		
Costa Rica	60044	44524	56174		
Netherlands/Pays–Bas	16865	16878	50108	68324	
Bahamas	54751	50737	43232		
Japan/Japon	48421	47163	47965		
Jamaica/Jamaïque	32695	67739	39906		
Brazil/Brésil	57017	64156	18405		
Canada	22874	16144	83368		
Guyana	38471	35748	46761		
Aruba	43997	39470	25785		
Honduras	42720	30380	30697		
Chile/Chili	34350	25727	36997		
Cuba	57044	25924	12154		
Germany/Allemagne	24178	30170	36362		
Singapore/Singapour	3598	32742	52715		
Haiti/Haïti	54675	31870	512		
Dominica/Dominique	23122	29731	26250		
Barbados/Barbade	29822	29264	12319		
Suriname/Suriname	20284	18663	18260		
Senegal/Sénégal	14330	12666	23597		
Panama	8177	27910	6923		
Belize/Bélize	14560	14188	13055		
Trinidad and Tobago	5427	7108	28928		
Nigeria/Nigéria	12842	6392	17755		
United Kingdom	12529	13085	8585	2123	
Spain/Espagne	8455	8072	16908		
Bermuda/Bermudes	13320	12722	6977		
Yugoslavia/Yougoslavie			26822		
Peru/Pérou	4694	9968	10518		
Ecuador/Equateur	6666	10398	6608		
Guatemala	9297	4449	6772		
So. Africa Customs Un	10338	6771			
Liberia/Libéria	12847				
Italy/Italie	9991	1526	783		
Argentina/Argentine	463	9973	1615		
Belgium–Luxembourg	830	1151	9463		
Un. Rep. of Tanzania	115		10517		
Nicaragua	2009	3716	3516		
Cote d'Ivoire	4619	3476			
Togo		7663			
Uruguay	2663	3372	1147		
El Salvador	4791		1922		
Cape Verde/Cap–Vert		3120	3195		
Pakistan		5246			
Gambia/Gambie		2702	1895		
Australia/Australie	2543	1067	788		

(VALUE AS PERCENTAGE OF WORLD TOTAL)(VALEURS EN POURCENTAGE DU TOTAL MONDIAL)

	1985	1986	1987	1988	1989	1990	1991	1992	1993	1994
Africa				0.0	0.0	0.0	0.0	0.0		
Americas	64.5			84.5	85.6	84.2	87.2	82.4	17.2	19.5
Northern America	46.9			14.1	13.6	13.6	14.8	18.7	17.2	19.5
LAIA	15.6			68.6	69.2	68.2	70.6	59.2		
CACM	0.0			0.1	0.1	0.1	0.1	0.1		
Caribbean	1.7			1.0	2.0	1.9	1.1	2.5		
Rest of America	0.3			0.7	0.7	0.5	0.6	1.9		
As.ex F.USSR	7.8			3.3	2.8	4.6	2.2	3.0	2.2	2.2
Eur.x F.USSR	27.4			11.5	10.8	9.7	9.1	12.6	9.5	12.0
EU	26.3			10.5	10.1	8.8	8.4	11.7	9.5	12.0
EFTA	1.2			0.8	0.4	0.2	0.3	0.7		
East Europe				0.1	0.1	0.1	0.1	0.1		
Other Europe				0.0	0.1	0.6	0.3	0.0		
Former USSR	0.2			0.1	0.0	0.0	0.0	0.0		
Oceania	0.1			0.1	0.1	0.1	0.1	0.1		
Venezuela				57.5	67.8	59.2	69.5	57.6		
USA/Etats–Unis d'Amer	46.2			13.6	13.2	12.7	14.5	17.0	17.2	19.5
Netherlands/Pays–Bas	9.2			7.1	6.6	5.7	5.9	8.1	8.7	11.2
Japan/Japon	4.6			1.9	1.7	2.2	1.7	2.2	2.2	2.2
Ecuador/Equateur				9.7	0.0	5.5	0.0	0.0		
United Kingdom	2.7			1.0	0.9	1.0	0.8	1.0	0.8	0.8
Trinidad and Tobago	1.5			0.1	0.1	1.2	0.7	1.8		
Mexico/Mexique				0.2	0.3	2.5	0.2	0.3		
Canada	0.7			0.5	0.4	0.8	0.3	1.7		
Germany/Allemagne	2.5			0.8	0.6	0.7	0.6	0.7		

	1985	1986	1987	1988	1989	1990	1991	1992	1993	1994
Afrique	0.3			0.2	2.2	3.7	3.2	4.4		
Amériques	76.7			83.4	81.8	87.6	85.0	79.0	1.0	
Amérique du Nord	60.6			31.2	36.1	35.4	30.2	30.8	1.0	
ALAI	8.0			16.5	10.1	13.8	17.6	13.8		
MCAC	0.5			5.3	5.6	6.6	5.2	6.4		
Caraïbes	5.4			24.1	24.0	27.2	25.9	22.5		
Autre Amérique	2.2			6.2	6.1	4.6	6.1	5.5		
Asie l'URSS exclus	1.2			4.3	4.3	2.9	5.4	6.5		
Europe l'URSS exclus	21.0			5.1	9.7	4.1	4.6	9.9	5.0	
UE	20.3			5.1	9.6	4.1	4.6	8.1	5.0	
AELE	0.5			0.0	0.0	0.0	0.0	0.0		
Europe de l'Est	0.0									
Autre de l'Europe	0.2			0.0	0.0					
Ancienne URSS	0.6									
Océanie	0.2			0.3	0.2	0.1	0.1	0.1		
USA/Etats–Unis d'Amer	57.0			28.1	33.8	33.4	28.4	25.0	1.0	
Dominican Republic	3.2			5.1	6.3	7.4	4.9	7.0		
Colombia/Colombie	6.1			1.8	1.2	3.2	5.1	7.2		
Venezuela				6.0	4.2	4.6	4.9	1.8		
Guadeloupe	1.6			2.6	3.2	3.1	3.4	3.3		
Costa Rica				1.1	1.9	3.3	2.8	3.6		
Netherlands/Pays–Bas	1.4			1.0	2.0	0.9	1.1	3.2	4.9	
Bahamas				2.4	2.8	3.0	3.2	2.8		
Japan/Japon	0.3			3.9	3.6	2.7	2.9	3.1		
Jamaica/Jamaïque				2.0	2.0	1.8	4.2	2.6		

4. Special Imports C.I.F. by Commodities according to the S.I.T.C. (Rev. 2) in thousand U.S. Dollars
Importations Spéciales C.A.F. par Produits d'après la C.T.C.I. (Rév. 2) en milliers de Dollars E.U.

SITC CTCI	COMMODITY	1991 WEIGHT POIDS	1991 VALUE VALEUR	1992 WEIGHT POIDS	1992 VALUE VALEUR	1993 WEIGHT POIDS	1993 VALUE VALEUR	1994 WEIGHT POIDS	1994 VALUE VALEUR	PRODUIT
	ALL COMMODITIES # 1		2188945		1868322		1946930		1464909	TOUS PRODUITS
0	FOOD AND LIVE ANIMALS		111245		144982		197207		186047	ALIMENTS,ANIMAUX VIVANTS
01	MEAT AND PREPARATIONS		29203		30247					VIANDES ET PREPARATIONS
011	MEAT FRESH,CHILLD,FROZEN		20737	W 10926	21363					VIANDES FRAICHES,REF,CONGE
0111	BOVINE MEAT FRESH,FROZEN	W 2334	6807	W 2339	6950					VIANDES BOVIN FRAI,REF
0114	POULTRY FRESH CHLLD,FRZN		7549	W 5630	7054					VOLAILLES MORTES
02	DAIRY PRODCTS,BIRDS'EGGS		13181		15438					PRODUITS LAITIERS,OEUFS
022	MILK AND CREAM		6048	W 4567	7460					LAIT ET CREME
0224	MILK,CREAM PRESERVED ETC		5110	W 3394	6151					LAIT,CREME CONS,CONC
024	CHEESE AND CURD		6330	W 2370	7267					FROMAGE ET CAILLEBOTTE
03	FISH AND PREPARATIONS		7168		8222					POISSONS ET PREPARATIONS
04	CEREALS AND PREPARATIONS		11766		36490				76542	CEREALES ET PRODUITS
042	RICE		2383	W 54618	23963					RIZ
0421	RICE IN HUSK OR HUSKED		318	W 31146	12958					RIZ SANS AUTRE PREPARATION
0422	RICE SEMI-MILLED,MILLED	W 6145	2065	W 23472	11005					RIZ POLI,GLACE INCL BRISURES
048	CEREAL ETC PREPARATIONS		4993	W 3122	6534					PREPTNS A BASE CEREALES
05	VEGETABLES AND FRUIT		27975		29757				27376	LEGUMES ET FRUITS
054	VEG ETC FRSH,SMPLY PRSVD		11817		10237					LEGUMES FRAIS,CONG,SECS
057	FRUIT,NUTS,FRESH,DRIED		6360		7223					FRUITS FRAIS OU SECS
058	FRUIT PRESERVED,PREPARED		6684	W 7078	8413					CONSERVES DE FRUITS
0585	FRUIT OR VEGETABLE JUICE		4890	W 5788	6050					JUS DE FRUITS
09	MISC EDIBLE PRODUCTS		9268		11112					PREP ALIMENTAIRES DIVERSES
098	EDIBLE PRODCTS,PREPS NES		7997	W 4431	9672					PREP ALIMENTAIRES NDA
1	BEVERAGES AND TOBACCO		11895		15972		18436		15644	BOISSONS ET TABACS
11	BEVERAGES		10493		14827					BOISSONS
112	ALCOHOLIC BEVERAGES	W 3955	9491	W 5026	13427					BOISSONS ALCOOLIQUES
2	CRUDE MATERLS,EXCL FUELS		7109		9475		12291		11733	MAT BRUTES NON COMESTIBLES
24	CORK AND WOOD		4280		5817					LIEGE ET BOIS
3	MINERAL FUELS ETC		1547383		1097872		1117320		727426	COMBUSTIBLES MINERAUX LUB
33	PETROLEUM AND PRODUCTS		1542053		1087985				727426	PETROLE ET DERIVES
333	CRUDE PETROLEUM	MW 12056	1402558	MW 9205	976524					HUILES BRUTES DE PETROLE
334	PETROLEUM PRODUCTS,REFIN		139327	W 968126	111165					PRODUITS RAFFINES
3341	GASOLINE,OTH LIGHT OILS	W 69106	14194	W 123102	24316					ESSENCES POUR MOTEURS
33412	SPIRIT TYPE JET FUEL	W 57099	11230	W 123100	24305					CARBUREACTEURS
3343	GAS OILS		29991	W 195001	32384					GAS OILS
3344	FUEL OILS,NES	W 5570000	80914	W 636000	47119					FUEL OILS
3345	LUBS,PETROLEUM OILS NES		14229	W 14023	7347					HUILES LUBRIFIANTES
33451	LUBS(HIGH PETR CONT) ETC		14229	W 14023	7347					HUILES LUBRIF,H LOURDES
341	*GAS,NATURAL AND MANUFCT	W 21058	5330	W 38377	9884					GAZ NATUREL,GAZ MANUFACT
3413	PETROLM GASES,LIQUEFIED	W 21000	5298	W 38000	9746					GAZ DE PETROLE LIQUEFIE
5	CHEMCLS,RELATED PROD NES		78081		68449		84916		67603	PRODUITS CHIMIQUES
52	INORGANIC CHEMICALS		9315		1409					PROD CHIM INORGANIQUES
522	INORG ELEMNTS,OXIDES,ETC		8090		979					ELEMENTS INORGANIQUES
541	*MEDICINAL,PHARM PRODUCT		16534	K 934000	19245					PROD MEDICINAUX PHARMACEUT
55	PERFUME,CLEANING ETC PRD		14349		17858					PROD POUR PARFUM,TOILETTE
553	PERFUMERY,COSMETICS,ETC		12948	W 1381	15298					PRODUITS DE PARFUMERIE
59	CHEMICAL MATERIALS NES		29475		22269					MAT PROD CHIMIQUES NDA
598	MISCEL CHEM PRODUCTS NES		26621	W 13985	17924					PROD DIV INDUST CHIM NDA
5989	CHEM PRODUCTS,PREPS NES		24805	W 13710	17413					PROD PREP CHIMIQUES NDA
59899	OTH CHEM PRODS,PREPS,NES		24669	W 13637	17217					AUT PRODUITS CHIMIQUES NDA
6	BASIC MANUFACTURES		106985		124537		132961		117885	ART MANUFACTURES
62	RUBBER MANUFACTURES NES		4997		6821					CAOUTCHOUC MANUFACTURE
63	WOOD,CORK MANUFACTRS NES		8487		9866					OUVRAGES LIEGE ET BOIS
64	PAPER,PAPERBOARD AND MFR		14913		18745					PAPIERS,CARTONS & OUVRAGES
641	PAPER AND PAPERBOARD		4862		6508					PAPIERS ET CARTONS
642	PAPER,ETC,PRECUT,ARTS OF		10052	W 3783	12237					PAP,CARTONS DECOUPES
65	TEXTILE YARN,FABRICS,ETC		10074		13346					FILS,TISSUS,ARTICLES TEXTILE
658	TEXTILE ARTICLES NES		4526		6089					ART FACONNES MAT TEXTILES
66	NONMETAL MINERAL MFS NES		20447		23615					ART MIN NON METALLIQUES
661	LIME,CEMENT,BLDG PRODS		8573	W 80399	8783					CHAUX,CIMENTS MAT CONSTR
6612	CEMENT		6696	W 75141	6460					CIMENTS HYDRAULIQUES
662	CLAY,REFRACTORY BLDG PRD		4030		5645					MAT CONST REFRACTAIRES
67	IRON AND STEEL		21294		15313		13966		12850	FER ET ACIER
678	IRON,STL TUBES,PIPES,ETC		14240	W 3976	9244					TUBES,TUYAUX EN FONTE,FER
69	METAL MANUFACTURES NES		23596		32353					ART MANUFACT EN METAL NDA
691	STRUCTURES AND PARTS NES		4668	W 2837	7383					CONSTRUCT FER,ACIER,ALU
699	BASE METAL MFRS NES		5986		9307					ART MANUFACTURES MET NDA
7	MACHINES,TRANSPORT EQUIP		203027		258324		238548		211188	MACHINES MATERIEL TRANSPORT
71	POWER GENERATING EQUIPMT		29205		33959					MACHINES GENERATRICES
713	INTRNL COMBUS PSTN ENGIN		15005	W 288	21311					MOTEURS EXPL COMB INT, PIECE
7131	AIRCRAFT PSTN ENGINS,PTS		11875	W 26	18109					MOTEURS EXPL P.AVIATION, PIE
716	ROTATING ELECTRIC PLANT		5950	W 350	6920					APP ELECTR ROTATIFS,PIECES
72	MACHS FOR SPCL INDUSTRYS		7576		10041					MAC SPECIALES POUR INDUST
74	GENRL INDUSTRL MACHY NES		34503		41102					MACH APP INDUSTRIE
741	HEATING,COOLING EQUIPMNT		5294		7118					MACH CHAUFFAGE,PIECES
742	PUMPS FOR LIQUIDS ETC		14005	W 543	11018					POMPES MOTO-POMPES
743	PUMPS NES,CENTRFUGES ETC		3296	W 205	5927					POMPES COMPRES,VENT ETC
7431	PUMPS FOR GASES ETC		3296	W 205	5927					POMPES AIR A VIDE,COMPRES
744	MECHANICAL HANDLING EQU		2574	W 696	6409					EQUIP MANUTENTION PIECES
749	NONELEC MACH PTS,ACC NES		9334	W 837	10630					PIECES MACH NON ELEC NDA
7499	OTH NONELEC MCHY PTS NES		8363	W 813	9663					PIECES NON ELECT NDA
75	OFFICE MACHNES,ADP EQUIP		14238		16730					MACH BUREAU TRAIT AUTOM
752	AUTOMTIC DATA PROC EQUIP		12394		13336					MACH TRAIT INFORMATION
76	TELECOMM,SOUND EQUIPMENT		21378		28251					EQUIPMENT DE TELECOM
764	TELECOM EQPT,PTS,ACC NES		11563		17324					EQUIP TELECOM,PIECES
7641	LINE TELEPHONE,ETC EQUIP		6989	W 95	12412					APP TELEPHON PAR FIL
77	ELECTRIC MACHNRY NES ETC		32928		33788					MACH APP ELECT NDA
773	ELECTR DISTRIBUTNG EQUIP		11764	W 1735	10907					EQUIPMT DISTRIBUTION ELECT
7731	INSULATED WIRE,CABLE ETC		6655	W 1375	7497					FILS,CABLES ISOLES ELECT
775	HOUSEHOLD TYPE EQUIP NES		7729		7742					MACH,APP USAGE DOMESTQUE
778	ELECTRICAL MACHINERY NES		8607		10222					AUTRES MACH ELECT NDA
7788	OTH ELEC MACHY,EQUIP NES		5488	W 269	6533					AUT MACH APP ELEC NDA
78	ROAD VEHICLES		55776		62130		63687		58663	VEHICULES ROUTIERS
781	PASS MOTOR VEH EXC BUSES	N 5522	35115	N 4294	38655					AUTO TRANSPORT PERSONNES
782	LORRIES,SPCL MTR VEH NES	N 1011	9469	N 955	11079					VEHICULES SPECIAUX,MARCH
7821	LORRIES,TRUCKS	N 989	8471	N 937	9341					VEHICULES TRANSP MARCHAND
784	MOTOR VEH PRTS,ACCES NES		8352		8954					PIECES 722,781,782,783
7849	OTHER MOTOR VEHCL PARTS		8286	W 1513	8919					PIECES 722,781,782,783
79	OTHR TRANSPORT EQUIPMENT		6404		31239					AUTRE MATERIEL TRANSPORT
792	AIRCRAFT ETC		1339		26325					APP NAVIGATION AERIENNE
7921	HELICOPTERS		32	N 2	24686					HELICOPTERES

4. Special Imports C.I.F. by Commodities according to the S.I.T.C. (Rev. 2) in thousand U.S. Dollars
Importations Spéciales C.A.F. par Produits d'après la C.T.C.I. (Rév. 2) en milliers de Dollars E.U.

SITC CTCI	COMMODITY	1991		1992		1993		1994		PRODUIT
		WEIGHT POIDS	VALUE VALEUR	WEIGHT POIDS	VALUE VALEUR	WEIGHT POIDS	VALUE VALEUR	WEIGHT POIDS	VALUE VALEUR	
8	MISC MANUFACTURED GOODS		122616		146907					ART MANUFACTURES DIVERS
821	*FURNITURE,PARTS THEREOF		9696		13623		17318		13967	MEUBLES ET PIECES
8219	FURNITURE AND PARTS NES		9430	W 3098	12880					AUTRES MEUBLES ET PIECES
84	CLOTHING AND ACCESSORIES		46341		41508					VETEMENTS
842	MENS OUTERWEAR NOT KNIT		11043		15596					VET DESSUS POUR HOMMES
843	WOMENS OUTERWEAR NONKNIT		13394		15135					VET DESSUS FEMMES MAT TEX
847	TEXTILE CLTHNG ACCES NES		17073		3368					ACCES VET MAT TEXT NDA
8471	— NOT KNITTED		15834		1678					ACCES VET MAT TEX NON BON
84719	MADE–UP CLTHG ACCESS NES		15603		1150					AUT ACCES VET MAT TEXTIL
851	*FOOTWEAR		7707		8870					CHAUSSURES
87	PRECISION INSTRUMNTS NES		11942		9712					INSTRUM,APPAR SCIENT NDA
874	MEASURNG,CONTROLNG INSTR		9176	W 75	6299					INSTRUMENTS DE MESURE
88	PHOTO EQU,OPTICL GDS ETC		10053		11222					APP,FOURN PHOTO,OP,MONTR
89	MISC MANUFCTRD GOODS NES		31837		54873					ART MANUFACTURES DIVERS
892	PRINTED MATTER		7363		10346					IMPRIMES
893	ARTICLES OF PLASTIC NES		9353		12840					OUVRAGES EN MAT DIVIS 58
894	TOYS,SPORTING GOODS,ETC		5158		7098					VOITURES ENFANTS,JOUETS
897	GOLD,SILVER WARE,JEWELRY		3886		14216					BIJOUTERIE,ORFEVRERIE
8973	PREC JEWLRY,GLD–SILVWARE		3413		13687					BIJOUX OR,ARGENT ORFEVRE

5. Special Exports F.O.B. by Commodities according to the S.I.T.C. (Rev. 2) in thousand U.S. Dollars
Exportations Spéciales F.O.B. par Produits d'après la C.T.C.I. (Rév. 2) en milliers de Dollars E.U.

SITC CTCI	COMMODITY	1991		1992		1993		1994		PRODUIT
		WEIGHT POIDS	VALUE VALEUR	WEIGHT POIDS	VALUE VALEUR	WEIGHT POIDS	VALUE VALEUR	WEIGHT POIDS	VALUE VALEUR	
	ALL COMMODITIES #1		1599209		1558890		1398885		1025214	TOUS PRODUITS
0	FOOD AND LIVE ANIMALS		4213		43360		91062		100789	ALIMENTS,ANIMAUX VIVANTS
04	CEREALS AND PREPARATIONS		839		39946					CEREALES ET PRODUITS
042	RICE	W 216	154	W 61087	39366					RIZ
2	CRUDE MATERLS,EXCL FUELS		7520		10622		12402		12962	MAT BRUTES NON COMESTIBLES
27	CRUDE FERTLZR,MINRLS NES		6469		10103					ENGRAIS MINERAUX BRUTS
278	OTHER CRUDE MINERALS	W 252239	5313	W 370629	7522					AUTRES MINERAUX BRUTS
2783	COMMON SALT,ETC	W 252237	5312	W 370503	7520					SEL
3	MINERAL FUELS ETC		1534591		1421840		1245253		829111	COMBUSTIBLES MINERAUX LUB
33	PETROLEUM AND PRODUCTS		1507767		1410064				829111	PETROLE ET DERIVES
333	CRUDE PETROLEUM	W 1116000	118895	W 956000	90303					HUILES BRUTES DE PETROLE
334	PETROLEUM PRODUCTS,REFIN		1350373	MW 11205	1285566					PRODUITS RAFFINES
3341	GASOLINE,OTH LIGHT OILS		595631	W 2908000	551037					ESSENCES POUR MOTEURS
33411	MOTOR,AVIATION SPIRIT		451865	W 2191000	418908					ESSENCES MOTEURS D'AVIONS
33412	SPIRIT TYPE JET FUEL		143765	W 717000	132130					CARBUREACTEURS
3343	GAS OILS	MW 40506	321465	W 2534000	249030					GAS OILS
3344	FUEL OILS,NES	MW 299939	275853	W 5465000	394614					FUEL OILS
3345	LUBS,PETROLEUM OILS NES	MW 23666	157424	W 298031	90884					HUILES LUBRIFIANTES
33451	LUBS(HIGH PETR CONT) ETC	MW 23666	157424	W 298031	90884					HUILES LUBRIF,H LOURDES
335	RESIDUAL PETRLM PROD NES		38499	W 507000	34194					PRODUITS RESIDUELS NDA
3354	PETROLM BITUMEN,COKE ETC		38499	W 507000	34194					BITUME,COKE DE PETROLE
33541	PETROLEUM BITUMEN, ETC	W 7336000	38498	W 507000	34194					BITUME DE PETROLE
341	*GAS,NATURAL AND MANUFCT		26823	W 49000	11777					GAZ NATUREL,GAZ MANUFACT
3413	PETROLM GASES,LIQUEFIED		26823	W 49000	11777					GAZ DE PETROLE LIQUEFIE
5	CHEMCLS,RELATED PROD NES		22370		13715		9274		6313	PRODUITS CHIMIQUES
51	ORGANIC CHEMICALS		9164		4601					PROD CHIMIQ ORGANIQUES
59	CHEMICAL MATERIALS NES		5984		1808					MAT PROD CHIMIQUES NDA
598	MISCEL CHEM PRODUCTS NES		5984	W 3150	1808					PROD DIV INDUST CHIM NDA
5989	CHEM PRODUCTS,PREPS NES		5984	W 3150	1808					PROD PREP CHIMIQUES NDA
59899	OTH CHEM PRODS,PREPS,NES		5984	W 3150	1808					AUT PRODUITS CHIMIQUES NDA
6	BASIC MANUFACTURES		6767		8924		8659		48719	ART MANUFACTURES
7	MACHINES,TRANSPORT EQUIP		13441		49453		21341		18661	MACHINES MATERIEL TRANSPORT
79	OTHR TRANSPORT EQUIPMENT		2811		34460					AUTRE MATERIEL TRANSPORT
792	AIRCRAFT ETC		2323	W 72	31746					APP NAVIGATION AERIENNE
8	MISC MANUFACTURED GOODS		5379		7103					ART MANUFACTURES DIVERS

FOOT NOTES – NOTES

TABLE 1 –
1 Prior to 1986, includes Aruba.
TABLE 3 –
1 Curacao and Bonaire only.
TABLE 4 –
1 Curacao and Bonaire only. In 1991 and 1992 the data presented according to SITC, Revision 2 have been estimated from data reported according to the national classification.
TABLE 5 –
1 Curacao and Bonaire only. In 1991 and 1992 the data presented according to SITC, Revision 2 have been estimated from data reported according to the national classification.
TABLEAU 1 –
1 Avant 1986 y compris Aruba.
TABLEAU 3 –
1 Y compris seulement Curaçao et Bonaire.
TABLEAU 4 –
1 Y compris seulement Curaçao et Bonaire. En 1991 et 1992 les données qui se présentent confor mément à CTCI, Révision 2 sont les estimations des données rapportées d'après la classification nati onale.
TABLEAU 5 –
1 Y compris seulement Curaçao et Bonaire. En 1991 et 1992 les données qui se présentent confor mément à CTCI, Révision 2 sont les estimations des données rapportées d'après la classification nati onale.

1. HISTORICAL SERIES, 1961–1996 SPECIAL TRADE, IMPORTS C.I.F., EXPORTS F.O.B.
SERIES HISTORIQUES, 1961–1996 COMMERCE SPECIAL, IMPORTATIONS C.A.F., EXPORTATIONS F.O.B

YEAR ANNEE	VALUE IN MILLION C.F.P. FRANCS VALEUR EN MILLION C.F.P. FRANCS MERCHANDISE –MARCHANDISE		GOLD –OR		CONVERSION FACTORS U.S. CENTS PER C.F.P. FRANC FACTEURS DE CONVERSION CENTS E.U. PAR C.F.P. FRANC		INDEX NUMBERS –INDICES QUANTUM		UNIT VALUE VALEUR UNITAIRE	
	IMPORTS	EXPORTS	IMPORTS	EXPORTS	IMPORTS	EXPORTS	IMPORTS	EXPORTS	IMPORTS	EXPORTS
1961	4284.00	5026.00			1.1140	1.1140				
1962	3683.00	3088.00			1.1140	1.1140				
1963	3451.00	4147.00			1.1140	1.1140				
1964	4888.00	5596.00			1.1140	1.1140				
1965	6885.00	5848.00			1.1140	1.1140				
1966	6037.00	6970.00			1.1140	1.1140				
1967	7068.00	6748.00			1.1140	1.1140				
1968	8350.00	10164.00			1.1140	1.1140				
1969	12098.00	12733.00			1.0510	1.0540				
1970	23271.00	19362.00			0.9902	0.9902				
1971	23529.00	20178.00			0.9902	0.9902				
1972	19144.00	17415.00			1.0907	1.0908				
1973	17748.00	15677.00			1.2335	1.2460				
1974	24635.00	24857.00			1.1489	1.1409				
1975	27049.00	25494.00			1.2849	1.2916				
1976	24074.00	26612.00			1.1422	1.1489				
1977	26032.00	27799.00			1.1183	1.1157				
1978	23926.00	17500.00			1.2208	1.2353				
1979	27791.00	27905.00			1.2973	1.2916				
1980	35041.00	31340.00			1.3055	1.2933				
1981	40480.00	34295.80			1.0081	0.9989				
1982	43735.00	32055.00			0.8393	0.8283				
1983	42201.00	21271.70			0.7201	0.7225				
1984	49605.00	33098.00			0.6273	0.6241				
1985	55931.00	43864.00			0.6228	0.6171				
1986	62938.99	26248.99			0.7281	0.7262				
1987	68532.98	24478.99			0.9139	0.9207				
1988	65386.98	50804.99			0.9233	0.9142				
1989	88607.98	77900.00			0.8644	0.8668				
1990	86929.98	43930.99			1.0162	1.0224				
1991	88748.00	45915.98			0.9730	0.9665				
1992	88120.98	39447.98			1.0401	1.0381				
1993	87419.98	36611.98			0.9809	0.9812				
1994	87304.98	36208.99			1.0035	1.0103				
1995	81933.97	46188.99			1.1133	1.1140				
1996	93086.99	50224.99			1.0866	1.0871				

2. IMPORTS BY BROAD ECONOMIC CATEGORY AND EXPORTS BY INDUSTRIAL ORIGIN. (PERCENTAGE OF TOTAL VALUE)
IMPORTATIONS PAR CATEGORIES ECONOMIQUES ET EXPORTATIONS PAR BRANCHE D'ACTIVITE.(EN POURCENTAGE DE LA VALEUR TOTALE)

IMPORTS – IMPORTATIONS

	1990	1991	1992	1993	1994	1995	1996
TOTAL IMPORTS–IMPORTATIONS TOTALES							
1 FOOD BEV–ALIMENTATION BOISSONS							
11 PRIMARY–PRODUITS DE BASE							
111 FOR INDUSTRY–POUR L'INDUSTRIE							
112 FOR HOUSEHOLDS–POUR LES MENAGES							
12 PROCESSED–PRODUITS ELABORES							
121 FOR INDUSTRY–POUR L'INDUSTRIE							
122 FOR HOUSEHOLDS–POUR LES MENAGES							
2 IND SUPPLIES–APPROV INDUSTRIELS							
21 PRIMARY–PRODUITS DE BASE							
22 PROCESSED–PRODUITS ELABORES							
3 FUELS–COMBUSTIBLES							
31 PRIMARY–PRODUITS DE BASE							
32 PROCESSED–PRODUITS ELABORES							
321 MOTOR SPIRIT–ESSENCE							
322 OTHER–AUTRES							
4 MACHINERY–EQUIPEMENT							
41 CAPITAL EQUIPMENT–MACHINES							
42 PARTS–PIECES ACCESSOIRES							
5 TRANSPORT–TRANSPORT							
51 PASSENGER CARS–AUTOMOBILES							
52 OTHER–AUTRES							
521 INDUSTRIAL–INDUSTRIELS							
522 NON INDUSTRIAL–NON INDUSTRIEL							
53 PARTS–PIECES ACCESSOIRES							
6 CONSUM GOODS–BIENS CONSOMMATION							
61 DURABLE–DURABLES							
62 SEMI DURABLE–SEMI DURABLES							
63 NON DURABLE–NON DURABLES							
7 GOODS NES–BIENS NDA							

EXPORTS – EXPORTATIONS

	1990	1991	1992	1993	1994	1995	1996
TOTAL EXPORTS–EXPORTATIONS TOTALES							
1 AGRICULTURE							
2 MINING QUARRY–INDUS EXTRACTIVES							
3 MANUFACTURING–IND MANUFACTUR							
31 FOOD BEV TOBACCO–ALIM BOISS TAB							
32 TEXTILES–INDUSTRIES TEXTILES							
33 WOOD & PRODUCTS–BOIS & PRODUITS							
34 PAPER & PRODUCTS–PAPIER & PRODT							
35 CHEMICALS–INDUSTRIES CHIMIQUES							
36 NON METAL MIN–MIN NON METAL							
37 BASIC METAL–IND METAL BASE							
38 METAL MANUF–MANUF METAL							
39 OTH MANUF IND–AUTRES MANUF							

3. TRADE BY PRINCIPAL COUNTRIES OF PRODUCTION AND LAST CONSIGNMENT (VALUE IN THOUSAND U.S. DOLLARS)
ECHANGES SELON LES PRINCIPAUX PAYS DE PRODUCTION ET DE DERNIERE CONSIGNATION (VALEUR EN MILLIERS DE DOLLARS EU)

COUNTRIES–PAYS	SPECIAL IMPORTS C.I.F. IMPORTATIONS SPECIALES C.A.F				
	1992	1993	1994	1995	1996
World	927264	855323	842231	841317	1007946
Africa					
Americas	49057	46203	38434	35378	46441
Northern America	49057	46203	38434	35378	46441
LAIA					
CACM					
Caribbean					
Rest of America					
As.ex F.USSR	58635	45036	40276	36317	46236
Eur.x F.USSR	429458	380850	368014	375361	417495
EU	429458	380850	368014	375361	417495
EFTA					
East Europe					
Other Europe					
Former USSR					
Oceania	135013	148549	147551	156684	199354
France,Monac	429458	380850	368014	375361	417495
Australia/Australie	94453	105429	99827	107218	132795
New Zealand	40560	43121	47724	49465	66560
Japan/Japon	58635	45036	40276	36317	46236
USA/Etats–Unis d'Amer	49057	46203	38434	35378	46441

COUNTRIES–PAYS	SPECIAL EXPORTS F.O.B. EXPORTATIONS SPECIALES F.O.B.				
	1992	1993	1994	1995	1996
Monde	409470	376737	354812		
Afrique	156				
Amériques	14843	28226	17080		
Amérique du Nord	14657	28226	17080		
ALAI					
MCAC					
Caraïbes	187				
Autre Amérique					
Asie l'URSS exclus	135013	134333	127946		
Europe l'URSS exclus	214171	177046	164143		
UE	214171	177046	164143		
AELE					
Europe de l'Est					
Autre de l'Europe					
Ancienne URSS					
Océanie	44727	33146	36815		
France,Monac	131681	121304	98274		
Japan/Japon	96399	101100	96030		
Australia/Australie	33330	25659	29916		
Korea, Republic of	30870	24988	26879		
Germany/Allemagne	27299	11794	26908		
USA/Etats–Unis d'Amer	14657	28226	17080		
Spain/Espagne	19421	15848	14826		
United Kingdom	9861	12348	12513		
Belgium–Luxembourg	4536	8488	6350		
Italy/Italie	13120	4735	951		
India/Inde	4754	6991	4762		
Wallis and Futuna Is	6155	5503	4341		
Sweden/Suède	8252	2528	4321		
French Polynesia	2948	1050	1666		
Hong Kong	1266	1254	274		
Vanuatu	851	933	892		
Pacific Isld (Tr Terr.)	519				
Malaysia/Malaisie	509				
Fiji/Fidji	488				
Indonesia/Indonésie	488				
Viet Nam	405				
Samoa	259				
Guadeloupe	187				
Singapore/Singapour	187				
New Zealand	176				
China/Chine	135				
Reunion/Réunion	62				

(VALUE AS PERCENTAGE OF WORLD TOTAL)(VALEURS EN POURCENTAGE DU TOTAL MONDIAL)

	1987	1988	1989	1990	1991	1992	1993	1994	1995	1996
Africa	0.0	0.0								
Americas	10.3	6.6	10.4	6.0	7.0	5.3	5.4	4.6	4.2	4.6
Northern America	10.3	6.6	10.4	6.0	7.0	5.3	5.4	4.6	4.2	4.6
LAIA	0.0	0.0								
CACM										
Caribbean	0.0	0.0								
Rest of America										
As.ex F.USSR	10.6	9.5	5.3	4.9	5.8	6.3	5.3	4.8	4.3	4.6
Eur.x F.USSR	53.6	57.9	44.1	47.5	45.7	46.3	44.5	43.7	44.6	41.4
EU	53.4	57.7	44.1	47.5	45.7	46.3	44.5	43.7	44.6	41.4
EFTA	0.2	0.2								
East Europe										
Other Europe										
Former USSR										
Oceania	11.9	14.0	12.4	11.8	13.4	14.6	17.4	17.5	18.6	19.8
France,Monac	47.0	50.4	44.1	47.5	45.7	46.3	44.5	43.7	44.6	41.4
Australia/Australie	8.6	10.4	9.1	8.5	9.7	10.2	12.3	11.9	12.7	13.2
New Zealand	3.2	3.6	3.3	3.3	3.7	4.4	5.0	5.7	5.9	6.6
Japan/Japon	4.5	4.9	5.3	4.9	5.8	6.3	5.3	4.8	4.3	4.6
USA/Etats–Unis d'Amer	10.1	6.3	10.4	6.0	7.0	5.3	5.4	4.6	4.2	4.6

	1987	1988	1989	1990	1991	1992	1993	1994	1995	1996
Afrique	0.0	0.0			0.0	0.0				
Amériques	9.7	11.2			4.8	3.6	7.5	4.8		
Amérique du Nord	9.7	11.2			4.8	3.6	7.5	4.8		
ALAI	0.0	0.0								
MCAC										
Caraïbes	0.0	0.0			0.0	0.0				
Autre Amérique										
Asie l'URSS exclus	23.4	24.9			39.3	33.0	35.7	36.1		
Europe l'URSS exclus	51.4	47.8			48.8	52.3	47.0	46.3		
UE	51.3	47.8			48.7	52.3	47.0	46.3		
AELE	0.0	0.0								
Europe de l'Est					0.1					
Autre de l'Europe										
Ancienne URSS										
Océanie	1.1	1.0			6.8	10.9	8.8	10.4		
France,Monac	37.0	32.2			27.8	32.2	32.2	27.7		
Japan/Japon	21.6	24.5			29.5	23.5	26.8	27.1		
Australia/Australie	1.0	0.9			4.3	8.1	6.8	8.4		
Korea, Republic of	0.0	0.0			8.0	7.5	6.6	7.6		
Germany/Allemagne	7.2	7.3			6.9	6.7	3.1	7.6		
USA/Etats–Unis d'Amer	9.6	11.1			4.8	3.6	7.5	4.8		
Spain/Espagne	3.1	3.2			4.7	4.7	4.2	4.2		
United Kingdom	0.6	1.4			2.5	2.4	3.3	3.5		
Belgium–Luxembourg	0.1	0.1			1.3	1.1	2.3	1.8		
Italy/Italie	1.7	1.8			3.8	3.2	1.3	0.3		

4. Special Imports C.I.F. by Commodities according to the S.I.T.C. (Rev. 2) in thousand U.S. Dollars
Importations Spéciales C.A.F. par Produits d'après la C.T.C.I. (Rév. 2) en milliers de Dollars E.U.

SITC CTCI	COMMODITY	1993		1994		1995		1996		PRODUIT
		WEIGHT POIDS	VALUE VALEUR	WEIGHT POIDS	VALUE VALEUR	WEIGHT POIDS	VALUE VALEUR	WEIGHT POIDS	VALUE VALEUR	
	ALL COMMODITIES		855323		842231		841317		1007946	TOUS PRODUITS
0	FOOD AND LIVE ANIMALS		148647		159147		156132		180914	ALIMENTS,ANIMAUX VIVANTS
01	MEAT AND PREPARATIONS				13216					VIANDES ET PREPARATIONS
0111	BOVINE MEAT FRESH,FROZEN	W 524	2732	W 532	2518	W 461	2523	W 344	1823	VIANDES BOVIN FRAI,REF
0114	POULTRY FRESH CHLLD,FRZN	W 3025	5113	W 3632	6444	W 241	514	W 219	455	VOLAILLES MORTES
0149	OTH PREPARD,PRESRVD MEAT	W 906	3620	W 920	3946	W 849	3627	W 871	4225	AUTRES PREP DE VIANDES
02	DAIRY PRODCTS,BIRDS'EGGS				16323					PRODUITS LAITIERS,OEUFS
0224	MILK,CREAM PRESERVED ETC	W 1371	4603					W 633	5573	LAIT,CREME CONS,CONC
02243	MILK DRY,OVER 1.5% FAT			W 1669	5547	W 1427	4739			LAIT POUDRE SUP 1.5%
024	CHEESE AND CURD	W 1340	6743	W 1392	6975	W 1246	6891	W 352	7733	FROMAGE ET CAILLEBOTTE
03	FISH AND PREPARATIONS				4901					POISSONS ET PREPARATIONS
0371	FISH PREPARD,PRESRVD NES	W 808	2752	W 936	3174	W 857	2715	W 1006	3631	CONSERVES DE POISSONS
04	CEREALS AND PREPARATIONS				8075					CEREALES ET PRODUITS
041	WHEAT ETC UNMILLED	W 17527	3802			W 26954	5744	W 17527	5632	FROMENT,EPEAUTRE
042	RICE	W 8195	3848	W 8171	3579	W 9929	4106	W 8593	4408	RIZ
0421	RICE IN HUSK OR HUSKED	W 8195	3848					W 8593	4408	RIZ SANS AUTRE PREPARATION
0481	PREPD BREAKFAST FOOD ETC			W 21631	4303					CEREALES TRAVAILLEES
05	VEGETABLES AND FRUIT				10544					LEGUMES ET FRUITS
05459	FRESH VEGETABLES NES	W 1336	2359	W 1550	2634	W 1188	2138	W 2780	2998	LEGUMES FRAIS,REFRI NDA
056	VEGTBLES ETC PRSVD,PREPD			W 2597	4032	W 2804	3899			CONSERVES DE LEGUMES
0565	VEGTBLES PRSVD,PREPD NES	W 2557	3803					W 2755	4073	LEGUMES PREPARES CONSERVE
06	SUGAR AND PREPS,HONEY				3540					SUCRES ET PRODUITS
061	SUGAR AND HONEY	W 5905	2849	W 6737	3540	W 6738	3312	W 7032	3849	SUCRES ET MIEL
0611	RAW BEET AND CANE SUGAR	W 5905	2849					W 7032	3849	SUCRES BRUTS
1	BEVERAGES AND TOBACCO		17159		17982					BOISSONS ET TABACS
11	BEVERAGES				17982					BOISSONS
1121	WINE OF FRESH GRAPES ETC	W 40459	9786	W 43262	10226	W 42467	10687	W 44058	11891	VINS DE RAISINS FRAIS
1123	BEER,ALE,STOUT,PORTER	W 32127	3025	W 37559	3425	W 36590	3286	W 27798	2965	BIERES
3	MINERAL FUELS ETC		83791		86321		82462		98611	COMBUSTIBLES MINERAUX LUB
32	COAL,COKE AND BRIQUETTES				6608		4994		7582	HOUILLES,COKES,BRIQUETTES
322	COAL,LIGNITE AND PEAT	W 129230	6045	W 175132	6608	W 135096	4994	W 177176	7582	HOUILLES,LIGNITES,TOURBE
3221	ANTHRACITE,NOT AGGLOMRTD			W 175132	6608	W 135096	4994	W 177176	7582	ANTHRACITE
33	PETROLEUM AND PRODUCTS				30398					PETROLE ET DERIVES
33411	MOTOR,AVIATION SPIRIT	W 74212	12486	W 81729	12146	W 82798	12413	W 74995	12963	ESSENCES MOTEURS D'AVIONS
3343	GAS OILS	W 79117	15949	W 75022	13515	W 92945	15414	W 84447	18603	GAS OILS
3345	LUBS,PETROLEUM OILS NES	W 3057	3800	W 2525	3396	W 2694	3583	W 3709	4609	HUILES LUBRIFIANTES
341	*GAS,NATURAL AND MANUFCT			W 6401	2392	W 6930	2660	W 5983	2667	GAZ NATUREL,GAZ MANUFACT
3414	PETROLEUM GASES, GASEOUS	W 7086	2587							GAZ DE PETROLE GAZEUX
5	CHEMCLS,RELATED PROD NES		63514		62638		85695		76641	PRODUITS CHIMIQUES
53342	OTH PAINTS,VARNISHES ETC	W 591	2569							AUTRES PEINTURES,VERNIS
541	*MEDICINAL,PHARM PRODUCT			K 806000	21619	K 799000	24631			PROD MEDICINAUX PHARMACEUT
5417	MEDICAMENTS	K 761000	21560	K 806000	21619	K 799000	24631	K 831000	29257	MEDICAMENTS
55	PERFUME,CLEANING ETC PRD				3965					PROD POUR PARFUM,TOILETTE
554	SOAP,CLEANSING ETC PREPS	W 2019	4652							SAVONS,PRODUITS DETERSIFS
5542	WASHING PREPARATIONS ETC			W 2155	3965	W 2244	3522	W 2115	3543	PROD ORG TENSIO–ACT NDA
6	BASIC MANUFACTURES		177326		144522					ART MANUFACTURES
62	RUBBER MANUFACTURES NES		33960		7293				45954	CAOUTCHOUC MANUFACTURE
6251	TYRES NEW FOR MOTOR CARS	W 122168	7261							PNEUS POUR VOITURES
6252	TYRES,NEW,BUS OR LORRY			N 147448	7293	N 124752	7473	W 147954	10258	PNEUS POUR AUTOBUS,CAMIONS
63	WOOD,CORK MANUFACTRS NES		12506		14615		13322		13827	OUVRAGES LIEGE ET BOIS
64	PAPER,PAPERBOARD AND MFR		25061		28208		29327		31412	PAPIERS,CARTONS & OUVRAGES
65	TEXTILE YARN,FABRICS,ETC		36770		34855		34177		39100	FILS,TISSUS,ARTICLES TEXTILE
66	NONMETAL MINERAL MFS NES				4216					ART MIN NON METALLIQUES
661	LIME,CEMENT,BLDG PRODS	W 89511	4738	W 80710	4216	W 83691	4003	W 68206	3927	CHAUX,CIMENTS MAT CONSTR
6612	CEMENT	W 89511	4738	W 80710	4216	W 83691	4003	W 68206	3927	CIMENTS HYDRAULIQUES
69	METAL MANUFACTURES NES		62862		53329		57288		69472	ART MANUFACT EN METAL NDA
7	MACHINES,TRANSPORT EQUIP		299400		277747					MACHINES MATERIEL TRANSPORT
7611	COLOUR TV RECEIVERS	W 7440	2237	N 8315	2277	N 6918	1967	W 12233	3140	RECEPTEURS COULEUR
77	ELECTRIC MACHNRY NES ETC		144912		139177		141803		181531	MACH APP ELECT NDA
78	ROAD VEHICLES		147713		133920		132363		171938	VEHICULES ROUTIERS
781	PASS MOTOR VEH EXC BUSES	W 5551	57446	N 4391	53830	N 5360	53435	W 4897	65748	AUTO TRANSPORT PERSONNES
7821	LORRIES,TRUCKS	W 1477	26296	N 1521	24725	N 1488	30508	W 1584	34227	VEHICULES TRANSP MARCHAND
7932	SHIPS AND BOATS NES			N 186	2373	N 173	2573	W 196	2466	NAVIRES ET BATEAUX
79328	OTHER SHIPS AND BOATS	W 133	2732							NAVIRES ET BATEAUX NDA
9	GOODS NOT CLASSD BY KIND		62647		91010					ART TRANSACT NON CLASSES
931	*SPECIAL TRANSACTIONS		62647	W 31700	91010		68926			TRANS.SPECIALES

5. Special Exports F.O.B. by Commodities according to the S.I.T.C. (Rev. 2) in thousand U.S. Dollars
Exportations Spéciales F.O.B. par Produits d'après la C.T.C.I. (Rév. 2) en milliers de Dollars E.U.

SITC CTCI	COMMODITY	1993		1994		1995		1996		PRODUIT
		WEIGHT POIDS	VALUE VALEUR	WEIGHT POIDS	VALUE VALEUR	WEIGHT POIDS	VALUE VALEUR	WEIGHT POIDS	VALUE VALEUR	
	ALL COMMODITIES		376737		354812		465791		543887	TOUS PRODUITS
2	CRUDE MATERLS,EXCL FUELS		122918		110503					MAT BRUTES NON COMESTIBLES
28	METALLIFEROUS ORES,SCRAP		122918		110503					MINERAIS METAL,DECHETS
287	BASE METAL ORES,CONC NES		122918	W 3181400	110503		175312		207559	MINERAIS METAUX COMMUNS
2872	NICKEL ORES,CONCENTRATES			W 3181400	110503	W 4531500	175157		207559	MINERAIS DE NICKEL
28721	NICKEL ORES,EXCL MATTE		76491	W 3169000	66280	W 4517000	111169		131031	MINERAIS DE NICKEL
28722	NICKEL MATTE,SINTERS,ETC		46427	W 12400	44223	W 14500	63988		76529	MATTES,SINTERS
6	BASIC MANUFACTURES		212389		208621					ART MANUFACTURES
67	IRON AND STEEL		212389		208621					FER ET ACIER
671	PIG IRON ETC		212389	W 133000	208621	W 144700	257260			FONTE,SPIEGEL,POUDRES
6716	FERRO–ALLOYS		212389	W 133000	208621	W 144700	257260			FERRO–ALLIAGES
67169	OTHER FERRO–ALLOYS		212389	W 133000	208621	W 144700	257260		303125	AUTRES FERRO–ALLIAGES
9	GOODS NOT CLASSD BY KIND		41430		35688					ART TRANSACT NON CLASSES
931	*SPECIAL TRANSACTIONS		41430		35688		33219			TRANS.SPECIALES

1. HISTORICAL SERIES, 1961–1996 GENERAL TRADE, IMPORTS C.I.F., EXPORTS F.O.B.
SERIES HISTORIQUES, 1961–1996 COMMERCE GENERAL, IMPORTATIONS C.A.F., EXPORTATIONS F.O.B

YEAR ANNEE	VALUE IN MILLION N.Z. DOLLARS / VALEUR EN MILLION N.Z. DOLLARS: MERCHANDISE–MARCHANDISE IMPORTS	MERCHANDISE–MARCHANDISE EXPORTS	GOLD–OR IMPORTS	GOLD–OR EXPORTS	CONVERSION FACTORS U.S. CENTS PER N.Z. DOLLAR / FACTEURS DE CONVERSION CENTS E.U. PAR N.Z. DOLLAR: IMPORTS	EXPORTS	INDEX NUMBERS–INDICES: QUANTUM IMPORTS	QUANTUM EXPORTS	UNIT VALUE / VALEUR UNITAIRE IMPORTS	UNIT VALUE / VALEUR UNITAIRE EXPORTS
1961	649.70	567.40	0.14	0.58	139.8400	139.8400	58	64	68	71
1962	541.60	573.80	0.22	0.44	139.0000	139.0000	50	66	66	72
1963	650.60	664.10	0.19	0.30	139.0000	139.0000	61	70	66	79
1964	701.50	773.80	0.27	0.18	139.0000	139.0000	65	73	67	86
1965	756.70	723.90	0.27	0.16	139.0000	139.0000	45	35	11	13
1966	787.50	780.00	0.24	0.09	139.0000	139.0000	47	41	11	13
1967	695.60	725.40	0.27	0.07	137.0000	136.0000	41	42	11	12
1968	799.10	920.90	0.17	0.05	112.0000	112.0000	39	49	13	13
1969	895.60	1080.90	0.25	0.03	112.0000	112.0000	42	54	14	14
1970	1111.80	1093.70	0.36	0.06	112.0000	112.0000	49	52	14	14
1971	1186.10	1199.80			113.6170	113.4520	50	54	15	15
1972	1273.90	1499.40	0.56		119.5000	119.5000	51	56	16	18
1973	1591.50	1913.10	0.90	0.20	136.8690	135.7620	61	55	17	23
1974	2615.00	1733.80	1.03	0.20	139.7100	140.4810	79	51	21	22
1975	2613.50	1796.40			120.1640	119.7570	60	52	28	22
1976	3270.80	2815.50			99.2790	99.1790	61	62	35	29
1977	3464.00	3294.90			97.0810	97.0440	59	63	35	33
1978	3359.40	3603.50			104.1680	103.9370	54	64	39	36
1979	4466.10	4606.70			101.5700	101.8250	64	69	44	43
1980	5615.90	5568.80			97.3950	97.2950	62	73	57	50
1981	6635.60	6465.90			85.6608	86.0289	64	74	65	56
1982	7800.30	7408.40			74.6812	74.7677	67	76	73	62
1983	7991.70	7907.50			66.7289	66.8189	63	80	79	66
1984	10933.50	9582.30			54.9687	55.9120	76	84	90	74
1985	12473.00	11316.00			49.6737	49.4017	76	93	100	81
1986	11622.10	11225.10			52.1817	52.3969	75	91	97	79
1987	12242.50	12149.70			59.4362	59.2258	85	94	93	84
1988	11216.90	13488.20			65.4549	65.6077	77	97	92	89
1989	14710.10	14819.50			59.7138	59.8900	93	95	99	101
1990	15895.50	15760.00			59.7719	59.6056	100	100	100	100
1991	14526.80	16671.00			57.8770	57.8791	90	110	101	96
1992	17132.00	18208.00			53.8042	53.8184	100	113	108	104
1993	17781.01	19492.00			54.1936	54.0815	104	118	107	106
1994	19981.01	20519.01			59.6236	59.3825	122	130	104	102
1995	21251.41	20928.21			65.6801	65.6434	129	134	103	100
1996	21400.00	20966.30			68.8086	68.7886	133	140	101	97

2. IMPORTS BY BROAD ECONOMIC CATEGORY AND EXPORTS BY INDUSTRIAL ORIGIN. (PERCENTAGE OF TOTAL VALUE)
IMPORTATIONS PAR CATEGORIES ECONOMIQUES ET EXPORTATIONS PAR BRANCHE D'ACTIVITE.(EN POURCENTAGE DE LA VALEUR TOTALE)

IMPORTS – IMPORTATIONS

	1990	1991	1992	1993	1994	1995	1996
TOTAL IMPORTS–IMPORTATIONS TOTALES	100.	100.	100.	100.	100.	100.	100.
1 FOOD BEV–ALIMENTATION BOISSONS	6.1	7.1	6.6	7.1	6.8	6.7	6.9
11 PRIMARY–PRODUITS DE BASE	1.7	1.9	1.9	2.0	1.9	1.9	1.9
111 FOR INDUSTRY–POUR L'INDUSTRIE	0.6	0.7	0.7	0.7	0.7	0.7	0.7
112 FOR HOUSEHOLDS–POUR LES MENAGES	1.1	1.2	1.2	1.3	1.2	1.2	1.2
12 PROCESSED–PRODUITS ELABORES	4.4	5.2	4.7	5.0	4.9	4.9	5.0
121 FOR INDUSTRY–POUR L'INDUSTRIE	1.2	1.4	1.3	1.3	1.2	1.2	1.1
122 FOR HOUSEHOLDS–POUR LES MENAGES	3.3	3.7	3.5	3.8	3.8	3.7	3.9
2 IND SUPPLIES–APPROV INDUSTRIELS	27.6	29.9	28.8	29.1	27.8	27.9	26.6
21 PRIMARY–PRODUITS DE BASE	1.7	1.7	1.9	2.1	1.8	1.8	1.6
22 PROCESSED–PRODUITS ELABORES	25.8	28.1	26.9	27.0	25.9	26.1	25.0
3 FUELS–COMBUSTIBLES	7.3	7.3	6.4	6.2	5.3	5.2	6.1
31 PRIMARY–PRODUITS DE BASE	5.7	5.6	4.9	4.8	4.0	3.7	3.8
32 PROCESSED–PRODUITS ELABORES	1.6	1.7	1.5	1.4	1.3	1.5	2.3
321 MOTOR SPIRIT–ESSENCE			0.7	0.8	0.8	0.9	1.1
322 OTHER–AUTRES	1.6	1.7	0.8	0.6	0.6	0.6	1.2
4 MACHINERY–EQUIPEMENT	22.9	21.4	21.9	22.5	23.2	24.2	24.6
41 CAPITAL EQUIPMENT–MACHINES	19.9	18.1	18.4	18.8	19.5	20.5	21.1
42 PARTS–PIECES ACCESSOIRES	3.1	3.3	3.4	3.6	3.6	3.7	3.5
5 TRANSPORT–TRANSPORT	19.0	15.1	17.2	15.9	18.2	17.6	17.2
51 PASSENGER CARS–AUTOMOBILES	7.5	6.1	6.4	7.1	8.1	8.2	9.6
52 OTHER–AUTRES	7.5	5.2	6.9	4.7	6.4	5.9	4.4
521 INDUSTRIAL–INDUSTRIELS	7.2	4.9	6.6	4.5	6.2	5.7	4.1
522 NON INDUSTRIAL–NON INDUSTRIEL	0.3	0.3	0.3	0.3	0.2	0.3	0.3
53 PARTS–PIECES ACCESSOIRES	4.0	3.9	4.0	4.1	3.7	3.5	3.3
6 CONSUM GOODS–BIENS CONSOMMATION	16.7	18.7	18.7	19.0	18.5	18.0	18.3
61 DURABLE–DURABLES	4.7	4.8	4.8	4.6	4.6	4.3	4.3
62 SEMI DURABLE–SEMI DURABLES	6.7	7.9	7.9	8.2	8.2	8.3	8.6
63 NON DURABLE–NON DURABLES	5.3	6.0	6.0	6.1	5.7	5.3	5.5
7 GOODS NES–BIENS NDA	0.4	0.5	0.4	0.3	0.3	0.4	0.2

EXPORTS – EXPORTATIONS

	1990	1991	1992	1993	1994	1995	1996
TOTAL EXPORTS–EXPORTATIONS TOTALES	100.	100.	100.	100.	100.	100.	100.
1 AGRICULTURE	17.4	16.8	17.6	17.6	16.7	17.2	16.1
2 MINING QUARRY–INDUS EXTRACTIVES	1.9	2.4	2.3	2.3	2.0	1.8	2.4
3 MANUFACTURING–IND MANUFACTUR	80.7	80.8	80.1	80.1	81.3	80.9	81.5
31 FOOD BEV TOBACCO–ALIM BOISS TAB	36.9	37.4	38.0	37.8	35.9	34.6	38.0
32 TEXTILES–INDUSTRIES TEXTILES	8.3	7.8	8.0	7.6	8.3	8.1	7.8
33 WOOD & PRODUCTS–BOIS & PRODUITS	2.0	2.5	2.8	3.6	3.8	3.8	3.4
34 PAPER & PRODUCTS–PAPIER & PRODT	6.2	5.8	5.5	5.2	5.4	6.1	5.4
35 CHEMICALS–INDUSTRIES CHIMIQUES	8.2	8.0	7.3	7.7	9.3	8.9	8.6
36 NON METAL MIN–MIN NON METAL	0.3	0.4	0.4	0.4	0.4	0.3	0.3
37 BASIC METAL–IND METAL BASE	6.8	6.5	5.8	5.4	5.2	6.0	5.3
38 METAL MANUF–MANUF METAL	9.3	9.9	10.2	10.3	11.4	11.6	10.9
39 OTH MANUF IND–AUTRES MANUF	2.6	2.5	2.1	2.1	1.7	1.7	1.9

3. TRADE BY PRINCIPAL COUNTRIES OF PRODUCTION AND LAST CONSIGNMENT (VALUE IN THOUSAND U.S. DOLLARS)
ECHANGES SELON LES PRINCIPAUX PAYS DE PRODUCTION ET DE DERNIERE CONSIGNATION (VALEUR EN MILLIERS DE DOLLARS EU)

COUNTRIES–PAYS	GENERAL IMPORTS C.I.F. IMPORTATIONS GENERALES C.A.F				
	1992	1993	1994	1995	1996
World	9204993	9654754	11901410	13957663	14724204
Africa	37528	44469	69385	88019	97440
Americas	2064726	2004706	2571708	3002912	2904354
Northern America	1948354	1894719	2451921	2854110	2746360
LAIA	91088	92390	101779	140160	149560
CACM	759	939	1678	1521	1400
Caribbean	16937	3954	5283	6015	6991
Rest of America	7588	12703	11047	1107	43
As.ex F.USSR	3063753	3357722	3942889	4479597	4793097
Eur.x F.USSR	1975620	2058337	2563117	3195261	3183733
EU	1830206	1917410	2393428	3011149	2978654
EFTA	134744	127596	148112	166352	186744
East Europe	8879	11370	18237	15085	14690
Other Europe	24	327	889	72	242
Former USSR	2495	7845	4690	4151	3555
Oceania	2018011	2134501	2695735	3124148	3673111
Australia/Australie	1946231	2060663	2558421	3010793	3569933
USA/Etats–Unis d'Amer	1800165	1733572	2279874	2610413	2458171
Japan/Japon	1353217	1565768	1826407	1935978	2103266
United Kingdom	581646	562478	737600	818136	770575
Germany/Allemagne	383562	416585	542613	664462	689650
China/Chine	242921	292570	388289	493862	548198
Italy/Italie	215641	242971	260681	345865	361434
France,Monac	159704	161272	205593	318885	259251
Singapore/Singapour	200205	137168	210990	270549	270715
Saudi Arabia	255066	227168	181006	180732	239869
Canada	148092	155965	171777	242977	287240
Korea, Republic of	141269	154248	191849	238543	271993
Sweden/Suède	114697	156695	193705	239319	245670
Malaysia/Malaisie	107680	126242	144892	245637	285618
Netherlands/Pays–Bas	100527	113247	127271	166695	155166
Hong Kong	119213	121365	130134	149566	114690
Switz.Liecht	97950	110930	119869	133915	138889
Indonesia/Indonésie	61623	76982	84227	171302	142363
United Arab Emirates	113538	140882	136578	53559	34217
Thailand/Thaïlande	75595	77146	89586	105233	117488
Belgium–Luxembourg	68303	73745	84571	115490	113345
Finland/Finlande	37836	45553	51929	78858	107993
Denmark/Danemark	44685	45353	62317	87935	75440
India/Inde	39866	44891	62118	75513	85799
Spain/Espagne	30739	30533	47325	55733	69899
Brazil/Brésil	34994	40336	43586	58365	51555
Papua New Guinea	11343	15823	82800	51223	42909
Austria/Autriche	30814	24762	30203	59753	58223
Ireland/Irlande	46655	29400	34307	42398	48512
So. Africa Customs Un	12114	19961	35943	54564	47553
Norway,SVD,JM	36728	15988	26702	28302	46699
Fiji/Fidji	30502	24327	30238	33851	31419
Pakistan	22431	26892	31174	29081	29548
Israel/Israël	24614	23034	28743	28857	29178
Philippines	15682	19786	30661	35581	30516
Oman	9115	5357	17461	46855	29162
Ecuador/Equateur	24476	18414	13245	21847	29185
Nauru	22460	24528	18130	19696	18197
Morocco/Maroc	14490	14793	18676	23077	30892
Mexico/Mexique	8035	9772	12889	20212	28404
Iran (Islamic Rp. of)	13416	13655	30185	10281	2541
Portugal	12063	10927	11909	13797	17269
Argentina/Argentine	10829	11668	16620	14332	10037
Chile/Chili	6083	5477	8380	18906	22644
Turkey/Turquie	6589	5138	8763	11524	13122
Jordan/Jordanie	2534	8778	10570	4402	10036
Sri Lanka	6493	5788	6271	7140	9499
Panama	7294	12193	10552	547	18
Viet Nam	853	891	4693	9041	12960
Poland/Pologne	2394	3082	10067	6158	5173

COUNTRIES–PAYS	GENERAL EXPORTS F.O.B. EXPORTATIONS GENERALES F.O.B.				
	1992	1993	1994	1995	1996
Monde	9829990	10558180	12185496	13745435	14354279
Afrique	151368	185602	174124	175535	215127
Amériques	1702470	1871830	1943360	2045802	2081835
Amérique du Nord	1357957	1409710	1555033	1606048	1527339
ALAI	247019	385788	298883	318999	408130
MCAC	16976	14731	24094	34375	63606
Caraïbes	70374	51211	55859	63946	67386
Autre Amérique	10143	10390	9490	22434	15373
Asie l'URSS exclus	3824811	4031169	4748131	5732781	5950229
Europe l'URSS exclus	1673470	1681858	1997000	2263000	2391729
UE	1630984	1633493	1944827	2196837	2313433
AELE	35508	40735	40392	51383	58249
Europe de l'Est	3917	3689	6230	7432	7885
Autre de l'Europe	3010	3723	3318	2710	9622
Ancienne URSS	15998	98096	113159	115273	130655
Océanie	2327196	2542699	3068063	3245137	3387206
Australia/Australie	1938316	2106289	2606556	2806628	2933254
Japan/Japon	1468027	1540860	1867614	2229482	2208946
USA/Etats–Unis d'Amer	1212891	1226924	1343623	1376111	1316967
United Kingdom	629061	641309	734917	832285	922278
Korea, Republic of	403212	502907	585702	708746	677345
Hong Kong	220769	241697	320203	417051	456261
Germany/Allemagne	240167	249335	314155	329608	347057
China/Chine	192825	212263	337840	348159	367289
Malaysia/Malaisie	266977	210103	235000	287298	327553
Canada	142599	180232	208958	223056	208394
Singapore/Singapour	163034	145781	163822	192144	202761
Indonesia/Indonésie	141791	126244	146483	199309	232719
Italy/Italie	110036	120144	171145	197191	237038
Thailand/Thaïlande	111371	107566	129716	183936	186242
Belgium–Luxembourg	133251	124300	136978	152935	168098
France,Monac	117472	122605	134359	145925	151217
Philippines	92179	118575	115213	137749	170240
Saudi Arabia	125028	130446	120543	107285	129283
Fiji/Fidji	102441	118632	126583	120598	128457
Mexico/Mexique	110508	166587	114593	73085	106047
Russian Federation	15983	89176	74970	113920	129986
India/Inde	61708	88694	76596	79890	79587
Turkey/Turquie	39146	51433	72097	102210	92768
Iran (Islamic Rp. of)	107303	49990	29125	53685	116895
Netherlands/Pays–Bas	48970	59427	74536	69938	85797
Papua New Guinea	52863	62925	59515	50322	65384
Algeria/Algérie	56053	85666	63461	40708	41063
French Polynesia	41624	57944	65027	54906	56058
Spain/Espagne	46357	37422	52437	65030	46364
Peru/Pérou	29376	46653	47520	59198	61747
Venezuela	36020	45803	53328	46803	61839
Samoa	54521	50217	47807	46106	35622
Sri Lanka	29805	36795	43444	59852	63202
New Caledonia	34741	38938	41489	50811	58630
Brazil/Brésil	7331	64627	14350	42359	75866
Switz.Liecht	31861	37179	35881	44462	50966
Chile/Chili	18969	22758	36334	58647	56024
Greece/Grèce	41665	37669	40931	26287	27319
Nepal/Népal	35441	45056	23469	33660	30431
So. Africa Customs Un	19480	22153	31434	44050	50868
United Arab Emirates	24863	22434	23978	42617	52567
Egypt/Egypte	24843	26264	33647	29591	50423
Argentina/Argentine	38959	35293	19484	26263	31569
Sweden/Suède	27410	23486	27273	36007	29550
American Samoa	22586	23450	31036	28094	28058
Denmark/Danemark	17496	17498	24601	33418	31606
Cook Islands/Iles Cook	24866	26163	26780	22433	20158
Viet Nam	5726	9487	19768	39329	42797
Tonga	16568	20571	25526	25179	22405
Morocco/Maroc	17250	17312	15082	21624	35506

(VALUE AS PERCENTAGE OF WORLD TOTAL)(VALEURS EN POURCENTAGE DU TOTAL MONDIAL)

	1987	1988	1989	1990	1991	1992	1993	1994	1995	1996
Africa	0.4	0.3	0.4	0.3	0.4	0.4	0.5	0.6	0.6	0.7
Americas	18.9	20.0	20.1	21.0	19.8	22.4	20.8	21.6	21.5	19.7
Northern America	17.8	18.7	18.8	19.8	18.4	21.2	19.6	20.6	20.4	18.7
LAIA	1.0	1.2	1.3	1.1	1.1	1.0	1.0	0.9	1.0	1.0
CACM	0.0	0.0	0.0	0.0	0.0	0.0	0.0	0.0	0.0	0.0
Caribbean	0.1	0.0	0.0	0.0	0.2	0.2	0.0	0.0	0.0	0.0
Rest of America	0.0	0.0	0.0	0.0	0.1	0.1	0.1	0.1	0.0	0.0
As.ex F.USSR	33.1	32.8	34.4	32.0	33.1	33.3	34.8	33.1	32.1	32.6
Eur.x F.USSR	26.3	23.5	22.8	24.6	23.2	21.5	21.3	21.5	22.9	21.6
EU	24.9	22.2	21.4	22.6	20.8	19.9	19.9	20.1	21.6	20.2
EFTA	1.2	1.2	1.2	1.9	2.3	1.5	1.3	1.2	1.2	1.3
East Europe	0.2	0.2	0.2	0.1	0.1	0.1	0.1	0.2	0.1	0.1
Other Europe	0.0	0.0	0.0	0.0	0.0	0.0	0.0	0.0	0.0	0.0
Former USSR	0.1	0.2	0.2	0.1	0.0	0.0	0.1	0.0	0.0	0.0
Oceania	20.7	22.4	21.7	21.4	23.0	21.9	22.1	22.7	22.4	24.9
Australia/Australie	20.0	21.6	20.7	20.3	22.1	21.1	21.3	21.5	21.6	24.2
USA/Etats–Unis d'Amer	16.1	16.7	16.8	17.9	16.8	19.6	18.0	19.2	18.7	16.7
Japan/Japon	18.8	17.0	18.4	15.5	15.6	14.7	16.2	15.3	13.9	14.3
United Kingdom	9.8	8.6	8.8	7.3	6.4	6.3	5.8	6.2	5.9	5.2
Germany/Allemagne	5.7	4.9	4.2	4.6	4.2	4.2	4.3	4.6	4.8	4.7
China/Chine	1.0	1.2	1.1	1.2	1.9	2.6	3.0	3.3	3.5	3.7
Italy/Italie	2.1	1.8	1.8	2.2	2.4	2.3	2.5	2.2	2.5	2.5
France,Monac	1.7	1.6	1.5	1.8	2.2	1.7	1.7	1.7	2.3	1.8
Singapore/Singapour	1.4	1.2	1.3	1.4	1.4	2.2	1.4	1.8	1.9	1.8
Saudi Arabia	2.6	2.5	3.0	3.4	3.6	2.8	2.4	1.5	1.3	1.6

	1987	1988	1989	1990	1991	1992	1993	1994	1995	1996
Afrique	0.9	0.9	0.8	1.4	1.7	1.5	1.8	1.4	1.3	1.5
Amériques	19.7	18.5	17.7	18.0	17.5	17.3	17.7	15.9	14.9	14.5
Amérique du Nord	16.8	15.8	14.9	14.9	14.2	13.8	13.4	12.8	11.7	10.6
ALAI	2.1	2.1	2.0	2.3	2.3	2.5	3.7	2.5	2.3	2.8
MCAC	0.1	0.1	0.1	0.1	0.1	0.2	0.1	0.2	0.3	0.4
Caraïbes	0.5	0.5	0.6	0.7	0.9	0.7	0.5	0.5	0.5	0.5
Autre Amérique	0.1	0.1	0.1	0.1	0.1	0.1	0.1	0.1	0.2	0.1
Asie l'URSS exclus	33.6	36.8	36.4	34.5	37.3	38.9	38.2	39.0	41.7	41.5
Europe l'URSS exclus	23.5	19.7	19.5	19.2	17.5	17.0	15.9	16.4	16.5	16.7
UE	22.7	18.8	19.0	18.6	17.0	16.6	15.5	16.0	16.0	16.1
AELE	0.3	0.4	0.3	0.3	0.3	0.4	0.4	0.3	0.4	0.4
Europe de l'Est	0.4	0.4	0.2	0.3	0.1	0.0	0.0	0.1	0.1	0.1
Autre de l'Europe	0.1	0.1	0.1	0.0	0.0	0.0	0.0	0.0	0.0	0.1
Ancienne URSS	1.5	1.9	2.0	1.8	1.4	0.2	0.9	0.9	0.8	0.9
Océanie	19.0	20.4	22.3	22.9	22.8	23.7	24.1	25.2	23.6	23.6
Australia/Australie	15.7	17.4	18.9	19.0	18.8	19.7	19.9	21.4	20.4	20.4
Japan/Japon	16.1	17.7	17.4	16.1	16.0	14.9	14.6	15.3	16.2	15.4
USA/Etats–Unis d'Amer	15.2	13.6	13.2	13.1	12.8	12.3	11.6	11.0	10.0	9.2
United Kingdom	9.5	7.2	7.1	7.0	6.2	6.4	6.1	6.0	6.1	6.4
Korea, Republic of	2.2	2.3	3.3	4.2	4.3	4.1	4.8	4.8	5.2	4.7
Hong Kong	1.4	1.4	1.7	1.5	1.6	2.2	2.3	2.6	3.0	3.2
Germany/Allemagne	2.4	2.2	2.1	2.4	2.4	2.4	2.4	2.6	2.4	2.4
China/Chine	2.7	4.6	2.0	1.0	1.7	2.0	2.0	2.8	2.5	2.6
Malaysia/Malaisie	1.1	1.5	1.6	1.7	2.5	2.7	2.0	1.9	2.1	2.3
Canada	1.6	1.7	1.7	1.8	1.4	1.5	1.7	1.7	1.6	1.5

4. General Imports C.I.F. by Commodities according to the S.I.T.C. (Rev. 2) in thousand U.S. Dollars
Importations Générales C.A.F. par Produits d'après la C.T.C.I. (Rév. 2) en milliers de Dollars E.U.

SITC CTCI	COMMODITY	1993		1994		1995		1996		PRODUIT
		WEIGHT POIDS	VALUE VALEUR	WEIGHT POIDS	VALUE VALEUR	WEIGHT POIDS	VALUE VALEUR	WEIGHT POIDS	VALUE VALEUR	
	ALL COMMODITIES		9654754		11901410		13957663		14724204	TOUS PRODUITS
0	FOOD AND LIVE ANIMALS		584312		696270		810312		888775	ALIMENTS,ANIMAUX VIVANTS
03	FISH AND PREPARATIONS		35432		39651		52577		43979	POISSONS ET PREPARATIONS
04	CEREALS AND PREPARATIONS		103489		116421		135086		159808	CEREALES ET PRODUITS
041	WHEAT ETC UNMILLED	W 229034	41987	W 242884	44556	W 169540	35999	W 214368	55588	FROMENT,EPEAUTRE
0412	OTHER WHEAT ETC UNMILLED	W 227660	41600	W 242884	44556	W 169530	35996	W 214295	55553	AUTRE FROMENT NON MOULU
048	CEREAL ETC PREPARATIONS	W 24746	42846	W 25367	50050		60153		77775	PREPTNS A BASE CEREALES
05	VEGETABLES AND FRUIT		155490		164946		202916		209741	LEGUMES ET FRUITS
057	FRUIT,NUTS,FRESH,DRIED	W 106058	81243	W 118340	86626	W 118016	92739	W 119921	107091	FRUITS FRAIS OU SECS
0573	BANANA,PLANTAIN,FRSH,DRY	W 65168	30821	W 73395	28358	W 71733	29598	W 70525	32821	BANANES FRAICHES,SECHEES
058	FRUIT PRESERVED,PREPARED	W 12147	35887	W 13208	39679	W 37736	55527	W 33718	52288	CONSERVES DE FRUITS
06	SUGAR AND PREPS,HONEY		72809		89427		97320		111939	SUCRES ET PRODUITS
061	SUGAR AND HONEY	W 193707	56246	W 231032	69479		75721	W 288000	87805	SUCRES ET MIEL
0611	RAW BEET AND CANE SUGAR	W 158813	39425	W 174101	49363	W 175659	55007	W 170734	50407	SUCRES BRUTS
07	COFFEE,TEA,COCOA,SPICES		61845		78001		95754		95064	CAFE,THE,CACAO,EPICES
081	*FEEDING STUFF FOR ANIML		27540		42049		44123		52135	NOURRITURE POUR ANIMAUX
09	MISC EDIBLE PRODUCTS		76799		107469		116634		140805	PREP ALIMENTAIRES DIVERSES
098	EDIBLE PRODCTS,PREPS NES		74505		104814		112217		128932	PREP ALIMENTAIRES NDA
09809	MISC FOOD PREPRTIONS NES		50490	W 1	77559		84066		95410	PREP ALIMENTAIRES NDA
1	BEVERAGES AND TOBACCO		103109		128336		135747		145660	BOISSONS ET TABACS
11	BEVERAGES		86760		110439		117627		122752	BOISSONS
112	ALCOHOLIC BEVERAGES	W 37202	82122	W 54590	101241	W 27087	105669	W 28476	110957	BOISSONS ALCOOLIQUES
1121	WINE OF FRESH GRAPES ETC	W 24756	37006	W 34547	47595	W 20978	45013	W 22553	51865	VINS DE RAISINS FRAIS
11212	WINE OF FRESH GRAPES	W 24682	36734	W 34488	47390	W 20904	44732	W 22482	51581	VINS DE MOUTS DE RAISINS
1124	DISTILLED ALCOHOLIC BEVS	W 3659	35608	W 4594	43172	W 4170	48640	W 4352	47791	ALCOOLS,EAUX–DE–VIE
2	CRUDE MATERLS,EXCL FUELS		361193		388002		440195		453727	MAT BRUTES NON COMESTIBLES
27	CRUDE FERTLZR,MINRLS NES		90170		91434		104249		96009	ENGRAIS MINERAUX BRUTS
271	FERTILIZERS,CRUDE	W 835418	57298	W 794377	53777	W 792623	55557	W 720604	51669	ENGRAIS BRUTS
2713	NAT CALCM PHOSPHATES ETC	W 835228	57014	W 793855	52494	W 792245	54789	W 720381	51084	PHOSPHATES DE CALCIUM
27131	— UNGROUND	W 604425	42483	W 231013	14951	W 223612	14981	W 165676	10370	PHOSPHATES NON MOULUS
27132	— GROUND	W 230803	14532	W 562842	37543	W 568634	39809	W 554704	40714	PHOSPHATES MOULUS
28	METALLIFEROUS ORES,SCRAP		139011		141206		147136		179841	MINERAIS METAL,DECHETS
287	BASE METAL ORES,CONC NES	W 544024	118254	W 537550	126326	W 492650	128961	W 617844	164600	MINERAIS METAUX COMMUNS
2873	ALUMINIUM ORES,ALUMINA	W 543144	117857	W 536810	126029	W 491730	128526	W 616961	164094	MINERAIS D'ALUMINIUM
28732	ALUMINA(ALUMINIUM OXIDE)	W 538489	116998	W 534692	125517	W 489303	127906	W 616958	164091	ALUMINE (OXYDE ALUMINIUM)
29	CRUDE ANIMAL,VEG MAT NES		33109		38866		45237		41603	MATIERES BRUTES ANIM,VEGET
3	MINERAL FUELS ETC		624173		670853		752420		937620	COMBUSTIBLES MINERAUX LUB
33	PETROLEUM AND PRODUCTS		622159		668986		751344		935229	PETROLE ET DERIVES
333	CRUDE PETROLEUM	W 3432510	464571	W 3774686	473015	W 3670356	514779	W 3576302	558987	HUILES BRUTES DE PETROLE
334	PETROLEUM PRODUCTS,REFIN		131513		158814		203571		336744	PRODUITS RAFFINES
3341	GASOLINE,OTH LIGHT OILS	W 325513	76801	W 441884	91398	W 581504	123331	W 707543	161854	ESSENCES POUR MOTEURS
33411	MOTOR,AVIATION SPIRIT	W 324760	75762	W 441262	90367	W 580528	122176	W 701343	159728	ESSENCES MOTEURS D'AVIONS
3343	GAS OILS	W 18224	1923	W 39558	6939	W 43179	10135	W 269578	59420	GAS OILS
3345	LUBS,PETROLEUM OILS NES		30282		35028		40163		48239	HUILES LUBRIFIANTES
335	RESIDUAL PETRLM PROD NES	W 132823	26075	W 236343	37158	W 172607	32994	W 147340	39497	PRODUITS RESIDUELS NDA
4	ANIMAL,VEGETABLE OIL,FAT		43793		52984		64848		59710	HUILES,GRAISSES ANIM,VEG
42	FIXED VEGETABLE OIL,FAT		35439		42243		48986		45921	HUILES VEGETALES FIXES
5	CHEMCLS,RELATED PROD NES		1295042		1498584		1756879		1783528	PRODUITS CHIMIQUES
51	ORGANIC CHEMICALS		127851		167139		198312		177243	PROD CHIMIQ ORGANIQUES
513	CARBOXYLIC ACIDS ETC		31774		34036		48555		40447	ACIDES CARBOXYLIQUES
514	NITROGEN–FNCTN COMPOUNDS		32167		43429		49766		46867	COMPOSES FONCT AZOTEES
515	ORG–INORG COMPOUNDS ETC		25144		43090		39790		45903	COMPOSES ORGANO–MINERAUX
52	INORGANIC CHEMICALS		93965		98809		123848		141360	PROD CHIM INORGANIQUES
522	INORG ELEMNTS,OXIDES,ETC		33333		37468		47871		57806	ELEMENTS INORGANIQUES
523	OTHR INORG CHEMICALS ETC		59311		60177		74913		82476	AUT PRODUITS CHIMIQUES INORG
53	DYES,TANNING,COLOUR PROD		82249		99777		109176		112685	PROD TEINTURE,COLORANTS
533	PIGMENTS,PAINTS,ETC		47428		62600		74137		79423	PIGMENTS,PEINTURES,VERNIS
541	*MEDICINAL,PHARM PRODUCT		305406		334359		372250		406377	PROD MEDICINAUX PHARMACEUT
5417	MEDICAMENTS		248484		266288		298466		331465	MEDICAMENTS
54171	— CONTAINNG ANTIBIOTICS		37134		39969		40238		44550	MED CONTN ANTIBIOTIQUES
54172	— CONTAINING HORMONES		36366		38211		45034		36804	MED CONTENANT HORMONES
54179	— CONTNG OTH SUBSTANCES		159315		172095		195778		223788	MED CONT AUT SUBSTANCES
55	PERFUME,CLEANING ETC PRD		118103		142593		162373		185273	PROD POUR PARFUM,TOILETTE
553	PERFUMERY,COSMETICS,ETC		64185		81232		96731		107472	PRODUITS DE PARFUMERIE
554	SOAP,CLEANSING ETC PREPS		39458		42968		48090		59681	SAVONS,PRODUITS DETERSIFS
5542	WASHING PREPARATIONS ETC	W 2	29933	W 6	32525		36706		45596	PROD ORG TENSIO–ACT NDA
562	*FERTILIZERS,MANUFACTURE	W 614579	92406	W 660962	111859	W 786438	159123		140015	ENGRAIS MANUFACTURES
5623	CHEM POTASSIC FERTILIZER	W 239494	33521	W 211011	30539	W 259661	41624	W 237020	35645	ENGRAIS POTASSIQUES
56231	POTASSIUM CHLORIDE	W 234469	32049	W 203561	28540	W 246239	38244	W 236234	35344	CHLORURE DE POTASSIUM
5629	FERTILIZERS NES	W 212035	39040	W 245457	53553	W 296548	76515		64388	ENGRAIS NDA
56292	NITROG–PHOS FERTILZR NES	W 198741	32679	W 237825	48664	W 290581	71832	W 211632	55667	ENGRAIS NDA CONT N P
58	PLASTIC MATERIALS ETC		309064		370382		420365		405660	MAT PLAST ARTIFICIELLES
582	PROD OF CONDENSATION ETC		73108		82173		97909		93504	PROD CONDENS,POLYCOND
5823	ALKYDS,OTHER POLYESTERS	W 16831	41047	W 19517	45351		57844		52623	ALKYDES ET AUT POLYESTERS
58231	— IN PRIMARY FORMS	W 16579	30166	W 19299	33449	W 19046	42983	W 20735	39372	SOUS FORMES PRIMAIRES
583	POLYMERIZATION ETC PRODS		225737		278760		313476		303955	PROD POLYMERISATION
5831	POLYETHYLENE		74359		95429		106589		108981	POLYETHYLENE
58311	— IN PRIMARY FORMS	W 80886	63960	W 103850	84156	W 89882	94080	W 101863	95103	POLYETHYLENE PRIMAIRES
5834	POLYVINYL CHLORIDE	W 27521	34414	W 33550	46202		51342		42016	CHLORURE DE POLYVINYLE
5839	OTH POLYMRZTION ETC PROD	W 31	52116	W 40	55566		62198		63961	AUT PROD POLYMER COPOLYM
59	CHEMICAL MATERIALS NES		161814		167677		205407		208635	MAT PROD CHIMIQUES NDA
591	PESTICIDES,DISINFECTANTS		41751		43562		58413		75694	DESINF,INSECT,FONG,HERB
598	MISCEL CHEM PRODUCTS NES		99725		100201		118255		105304	PROD DIV INDUST CHIM NDA
5989	CHEM PRODUCTS,PREPS NES		71402		75754		86991		80553	PROD PREP CHIMIQUES NDA
59899	OTH CHEM PRODS,PREPS,NES		46081		53077		59521		61411	AUT PRODUITS CHIMIQUES NDA
6	BASIC MANUFACTURES		1575103		1873522		2251195		2266800	ART MANUFACTURES
62	RUBBER MANUFACTURES NES		116041		127847		156156		162048	CAOUTCHOUC MANUFACTURE
625	RUBBER TYRES, TUBES ETC	N 2146043	65425	N 2215556	70088	N 3177659	88553	N 3118784	92534	PNEUS CAOUTCHOUC VULCANISE
628	RUBBER ARTICLES NES		32081		35851		40053		42209	OUVRAGES CAOUTCHOUC NDA
63	WOOD,CORK MANUFACTRS NES		21734		28949		39728		45138	OUVRAGES LIEGE ET BOIS
64	PAPER,PAPERBOARD AND MFR		257667		302445		412493		393413	PAPIERS,CARTONS & OUVRAGES
641	PAPER AND PAPERBOARD		187720		217905		306278		268768	PAPIERS ET CARTONS
6412	PRINTG,WRITING PAPER NES	W 51324	70565	W 62596	85659		127078		93908	PAPIERS POUR L'IMPRESSION
64122	— COATED,IMPREGNATD ETC	W 51323	54282	W 62594	64334	W 70384	91211	W 52362	62071	PAPIERS IMPRESSION COUCHES
6415	PAPER,PAPERBRD,BULK,NES	W 51131	50636	W 59132	57328	W 69987	81751	W 63495	70980	PAPIERS,CARTONS ROULEAUX
64159	OTHER PAPER ETC,BULK,NES	W 50354	48736	W 58464	55456	W 69159	79439	W 60838	67197	AUT PAPIER ROULEAUX FEUILLES
6418	COATED ETC PAPER NES BLK	W 18757	47798	W 18497	50993	W 21353	60958	W 21370	61381	PAP,CARTONS COUCHES,ENDUITS
64189	COATED PAPER ETC NES	W 12994	35133	W 13711	39072	W 14963	45775	W 14497	44965	PAPIERS,CARTONS COUCHES
642	PAPER,ETC,PRECUT,ARTS OF		69947		84541		106215		124645	PAP,CARTONS DECOUPES
6428	PAPER ETC ARTICLES NES		24671		31527		42055		52765	OUVRAGES EN PATE A PAPIER
65	TEXTILE YARN,FABRICS,ETC		406232		465601		479944		474807	FILS,TISSUS,ARTICLES TEXTILE

4. General Imports C.I.F. by Commodities according to the S.I.T.C. (Rev. 2) in thousand U.S. Dollars
Importations Générales C.A.F. par Produits d'après la C.T.C.I. (Rév. 2) en milliers de Dollars E.U.

SITC CTCI	COMMODITY	1993 WEIGHT POIDS	1993 VALUE VALEUR	1994 WEIGHT POIDS	1994 VALUE VALEUR	1995 WEIGHT POIDS	1995 VALUE VALEUR	1996 WEIGHT POIDS	1996 VALUE VALEUR	PRODUIT
651	TEXTILE YARN		65285		76061		69655		64432	FILS TEXTILES
652	COTTON FABRICS,WOVEN	A 34590	52135	A 34911	56213	A 30990	57235	A 28330	55990	TISSUS DE COTON
6522	WOVEN COTTON BLEACHD,ETC	A 29905	49269	A 30500	53241	A 26917	53916	A 25387	53611	TISSUS COTON BLANCHIS ETC
65224	BLCHED COTTON FABRIC NES	A 27017	42590	A 26983	44559	A 23721	44350	A 21751	42642	AUT TIS PLUS 85% COT BLANCHI
653	WOVN MAN–MADE FIB FABRIC	A 59780	90892	A 63517	100514	A 76439	102263	A 69693	93637	TISSUS FIBRES SYNTH,ARTIF
6534	DISC SYN BLEND FABRC NES	A 23718	32172	A 22851	30273	A 27898	30877	A 20584	28841	TISSUS FIBRES SYNTH DISCONT
657	SPECIAL TXTL FABRC,PRODS		67400		75059		73570		74793	TISSUS SPECIAUX
658	TEXTILE ARTICLES NES		48731		60005		70018		77392	ART FACONNES MAT TEXTILES
6584	LINENS ETC	MN 18688	32349	MN 22455	39533	MN 20359	43127	MN 19513	47267	LINGE DE MAISON
66	NONMETAL MINERAL MFS NES		151327		186844		235621		239894	ART MIN NON METALLIQUES
662	CLAY,REFRACTORY BLDG PRD		20598		25151		46132		39601	MAT CONST REFRACTAIRES
664	GLASS		43492		56099		62558		67182	VERRE
67	IRON AND STEEL		218988		285571		332203		369963	FER ET ACIER
673	IRON,STEEL SHAPES ETC	W 59543	41649	W 70729	50383	W 78750	61670	W 109690	80379	BARRES,PROFIL FER,ACIER
674	IRN,STL UNIV,PLATE,SHEET	W 121302	111830	W 161821	146353	W 149765	160049	W 160512	162248	LARGES PLATS,TOLES
6746	IRN,STL THIN PLATE,ROLLD	W 19514	30867	W 20785	30363	W 23518	47189	W 21965	34998	TOLES LAM MOINS 3MM
6747	TINNED PLATES,SHEETS	W 35054	28017	W 42528	35737	W 35518	31519	W 40249	39266	TOLES ETAMEES EN ACIER
6749	OTH IRN,STL PLATES,SHEET	W 39542	32439	W 64776	56305	W 49929	48025	W 50802	49705	AUTRES TOLES FER,ACIER
67491	— OF IRON OR SIMPLE STL	W 37795	28542	W 62131	50408	W 48256	44181	W 49587	46154	AUT TOLES AUTRES ACIER FIN
678	IRON,STL TUBES,PIPES,ETC	W 30211	32465	W 39179	45448	W 39892	51341	W 46638	65125	TUBES,TUYAUX EN FONTE,FER
68	NON–FERROUS METALS		157198		184949		236720		204735	METAUX NON FERREUX
682	COPPER EXC CEMENT COPPER		53410		60787		72715		66603	CUIVRE
6822	COPPER,ALLOYS WORKED		40923		40484		40212		38227	CUIVRE,ALLIAGES OUVRES
684	ALUMINIUM	W 29911	73263	W 36392	91653	W 41046	127853	W 34910	103218	ALUMINIUM
6842	ALUMINIUM,ALLOYS WORKED	W 25311	65934	W 28272	76574	W 29356	101405	W 22462	80553	ALUMINIUM,ALLIAGES OUVRE
68422	ALUMNM PLATE,SHEET,STRIP	W 17183	38892	W 20568	48754	W 20286	63041	W 15208	48430	TOLES, PLANCHES EN ALU
69	METAL MANUFACTURES NES		226285		269218		334524		352332	ART MANUFACT EN METAL NDA
695	TOOLS		50327		58646		69679		68039	OUTILS A MAIN
697	BASE MTL HOUSEHOLD EQUIP		26765		33069		41472		46825	ART MENAGE MET COMMUNS
699	BASE METAL MFRS NES		87018		102261		122905		135622	ART MANUFACTURES MET NDA
7	MACHINES,TRANSPORT EQUIP		3716718		4963750		5876547		6153555	MACHINES MATERIEL TRANSPORT
71	POWER GENERATING EQUIPMT		201263		215873		241377		293612	MACHINES GENERATRICES
713	INTRNL COMBUS PSTN ENGIN		69334		86105		105812		103539	MOTEURS EXPL COMB INT, PIECE
714	ENGINES AND MOTORS NES		89973		77617		66004		58471	MOTEURS NON ELECTRIQUES
7149	ENGINE & MOTOR PARTS NES		76913		70078		53859		50911	PIECES 714 ET 718.88
71491	PARTS NES OF 7144,71481		74383		64303		48939		46058	PIECES DES PROPULSEURS
716	ROTATING ELECTRIC PLANT		30919		36736		38729		61951	APP ELECTR ROTATIFS,PIECES
72	MACHS FOR SPCL INDUSTRYS		460964		580301		611327		667544	MAC SPECIALES POUR INDUST
721	AGRIC MACHY,EXC TRACTORS		46117		58953		75051		79171	MACHINES AGRICOLES
7212	HARVESTING ETC MACHINES		30431		35365		40988		45842	ENGINS POUR LA RECOLTE
722	TRACTORS NON–ROAD	N 6554	65843	N 7541	80370	N 4140	73108	N 8256	81603	TRACTEURS
7224	WHEELED TRACTORS NES	N 6553	65754	N 7538	79560	N 4129	72022	N 8253	81428	TRACTEURS A ROUES
723	CIVIL ENGNEERG EQUIP ETC		83493		126120		123694		126689	APPAREILS DE GENIE CIVIL
7234	CONST,MINING MACHNRY NES		72883		105563		107244		112476	MACH POUR LA CONST, MINES
72342	SLFPRP SHOVELS,EXCAVATRS		57804	N 5	81069		78926		85004	PELLES MECANIQUES
725	PAPER ETC MILL MACHINERY		38512		23106		33278		78849	MACHINES FABR PATE PAPIER
726	PRINTG,BKBINDG MACHY,PTS		52069		105944		91456		70712	MACHINES POUR IMPRIMERIE
7264	PRINTING PRESSES	W 1206	26276	W 3090	69482	W 1840	49324	W 1401	38006	MACHINES A IMPRIMER
72641	ROTARY PRINTING PRESSES	W 1206	26276	W 3090	69482	W 1840	49324	W 1401	38006	MACH IMPRIMER ROTATIVES
728	OTH MACHY FOR SPCL INDUS		124344		132372		150056		179715	AUT MACH IND PARTICULIERES
7281	MACH–TOOLS FR SPCL INDUS		36463		35740		31276		49442	MACH–OUTILS SPEC IND PART
72812	MACH–TOOLS TO WORK WOOD	W 2388	31448	W 2710	29364	W 2200	24946	W 3076	39395	MACH–OUT POUR TRAVAIL BOIS
7284	MACHY FOR SPCL INDUS NES		82765		85520		107494		118411	MACH SPEC IND PARTICUL.
72848	OTH MCHY WITH INDIV FNCT		30101	N 22264	36170	N 136663	51318	N 43619	57764	AUTRES MACHINES NDA
73	METALWORKING MACHINERY		42248		63502		77150		65915	MACH TRAVAIL DES METAUX
736	METALWORKING MACH–TOOLS		27568		46223		47704		44495	MACH–OUTILS TRAVAIL METAUX
74	GENRL INDUSTRL MACHY NES		422325		534380		685100		766520	MACH APP INDUSTRIE
741	HEATING,COOLING EQUIPMNT		64410		79074		122172		139582	MACH CHAUFFAGE,PIECES
7416	HEATING,COOLING EQU NES		32163		36597		39449		56732	APP CHANGEMENT TEMP
742	PUMPS FOR LIQUIDS ETC		41193		52956		59195		61764	POMPES MOTO–POMPES
743	PUMPS NES,CENTRFUGES ETC		67489		85442		102679		113784	POMPES COMPRES,VENT ETC
744	MECHANICAL HANDLING EQU		68305		94205		146224		178269	EQUIP MANUTENTION PIECES
7441	FORK LIFT TRCKS,ETC,PTS		25445		35820		55191		63937	CHARIOTS POUR USINES ETC
74411	FORK LIFT TRUCKS ETC		25249		35763		55134		63916	CHARIOTS POUR LES GARES
7442	LIFTING,LOADING MACH NES		26296		36174		62226		68012	APP LEVAGE,MANUTENTION
74428	OTH HANDLING ETC MCH NES	W 161	20978	W 160	29092		45909		55560	AUT APP LEVAGE ETC
7449	PTS NES OF MACHY OF 7442		16564		22210		28807		46319	PIECES DU 744.2
745	NONELEC MACHY,TOOLS NES		70826		87667		108993		114561	AUT MACH NON ELEC,PIECES
7452	OTH NONELEC MCHS,PTS NES		54765		69609		87957		93077	AUT MACH NON ELEC,PIECES
749	NONELEC MACH PTS,ACC NES		110101		135036		145837		158561	PIECES MACH NON ELEC NDA
7492	COCKS,VALVES ETC NES		50686		64276		67836	MN 15009	77650	ART ROB,SIM POUR TUYAUX
75	OFFICE MACHNES,ADP EQUIP		479275		635127		776848		767410	MACH BUREAU TRAIT AUTOM
751	OFFICE MACHINES		56049		61779		69754		69068	MACH,APPAREILS DE BUREAU
7518	OFFICE MACHINES NES		40248		50277		58707		52336	MACH,APP DE BUREAU NDA
75182	PHOTO,THERMOCOPY APPARAT	N 11826	30673	N 11751	33238	N 14178	42039	N 12855	39519	APPAREILS DE PHOTOCOPIE
752	AUTOMTIC DATA PROC EQUIP		273537		388273		481369		478435	MACH TRAIT INFORMATION
7522	DIGITAL COMPUTERS		95605		138336		152969		180690	MACH DIGITALES COMPLETES
7523	DIGITL CENTRL PROCESSORS		25074		49419		87902		50312	UNITES CENTRALES
7524	DIGITL CENTRL STOR UNITS		17091		45869		64500		62137	UNITES MEMOIRE CENTRALES
7525	ADP PERIPHERAL UNITS		81479		96118		123719		120461	UNITES PERIPHERIQUES
7528	OFF–LINE DATA PROC EQUIP		51822		56861		50953		54677	MACH AUXIL TRAIT INFORM
759	OFFICE,ADP MCH PTS,ACCES		149689		185074		225725		219907	PIECES DU 751 ET 752
7599	ACCTG,ETC,ADP MCH PTS,AC		131642		163568		201150		191117	PIECES DU 751 ET 752
76	TELECOMM,SOUND EQUIPMENT		380316		488915		663401		645327	EQUIPMENT DE TELECOM
761	TELEVISION RECEIVERS	N 272354	73994	N 358172	96394	N 330645	96908	N 230488	77842	RECEPTEURS DE TELEVISION
7611	COLOUR TV RECEIVERS	N 267191	73076	N 356007	95837	N 328860	96596	N 229514	77619	RECEPTEURS COULEUR
762	RADIO BROADCAST RECEIVRS	N 648771	40229	N 909177	62492	N 1112447	78803	N 813114	64126	RECEPTEURS RADIODIFFUSION
7628	OTHER RADIO RECEIVERS	N 221514	23492	N 322391	40834	N 351398	55266	N 287574	42255	AUTRES RECEPT RADIO
763	SOUND RECORDRS,PHONOGRPH	N 330881	47315	N 429092	53571	N 386986	57116	N 421162	63857	PHONO,APP ENREGISTREMENT
7638	OTHR SOUND APPARATUS ETC	N 307997	45910	N 416901	52595	N 380620	56213	N 415185	63163	AUT APP D'ENREGIS,REPROD
76381	TV IMAGE,SND RECRDRS ETC	N 111463	29882	N 128721	33988	N 152677	38822	N 160318	42683	APP ENREG,REPRO IMAG,SON
764	TELECOM EQPT,PTS,ACC NES		218778		276458		430574		439502	EQUIP TELECOM,PIECES
7641	LINE TELEPHONE,ETC EQUIP	N 756000	72666	N 1280200	82653		117365	N 1101409	138802	APP TELEPHON PAR FIL
7643	TV,RADIO TRANSMITTRS ETC		54502		85656		133185		105306	APP EMET TELE RADIO
7648	TELECOMM EQUIPMENT NES		30223		28119		37477		22423	APP TELECOM NDA
7649	PTS NES OF EQUIPMT OF 76		48982		64043		122462		150545	PIECES DE LA DIV 76
76491	PTS NES OF APPAR OF 7641		30109		37891		90379		108211	PIECES POUR 764.1
77	ELECTRIC MACHNRY NES ETC		447054		545802		654268		704239	MACH APP ELECT NDA
771	ELECTRIC POWER MACHY NES		27377		28332		55470		64642	MACH PROD,TRANS ELECTR
772	SWITCHGEAR ETC,PARTS NES	MN 103552	91405	MN 169353	120009		137021		141725	APP COUPURE,SECT ETC
7721	SWITCHGEAR ETC	N 9077	84295	N 33184	108667		123723		126811	APP COUPURE,SECTIONMNT

4. General Imports C.I.F. by Commodities according to the S.I.T.C. (Rev. 2) in thousand U.S. Dollars
Importations Générales C.A.F. par Produits d'après la C.T.C.I. (Rév. 2) en milliers de Dollars E.U.

SITC CTCI	COMMODITY	1993		1994		1995		1996		PRODUIT
		WEIGHT POIDS	VALUE VALEUR	WEIGHT POIDS	VALUE VALEUR	WEIGHT POIDS	VALUE VALEUR	WEIGHT POIDS	VALUE VALEUR	
773	ELECTR DISTRIBUTNG EQUIP		37332		45009		48792		55118	EQUIPMT DISTRIBUTION ELECT
7731	INSULATED WIRE,CABLE ETC	W 14000	35016	W 6900	40436	W 5661	44009	W 6821	48062	FILS,CABLES ISOLES ELECT
775	HOUSEHOLD TYPE EQUIP NES		103228		124942		138146		148056	MACH,APP USAGE DOMESTQUE
7758	ELECTRO–THERMIC APPL NES		46590		58294		65851		67446	APP ELECTROTHERMIQ NDA
776	TRANSISTORS,VALVES,ETC	MN 69804	39071	MN 87683	53425		74668		74265	LAMPES,TUBES,VALVES
7764	ELECTRONIC MICROCIRCUITS	MN 12610	22865	MN 19022	33618	MN 21048	49440	MN 22485	51678	MICROSTRUCTURES ELECTRON
778	ELECTRICAL MACHINERY NES		124859		151235		177406		192269	AUTRES MACH ELECT NDA
7788	OTH ELEC MACHY,EQUIP NES		48325		59105		71097		86484	AUT MACH APP ELEC NDA
78	ROAD VEHICLES		1035752		1402719		1679633		1947109	VEHICULES ROUTIERS
781	PASS MOTOR VEH EXC BUSES	N 108606	683321	N 139874	961240	N 158263	1140714	N 197925	1418565	AUTO TRANSPORT PERSONNES
782	LORRIES,SPCL MTR VEH NES	N 28871	206164	N 32107	262222	N 31907	321629	N 60540	307689	VEHICULES SPECIAUX,MARCH
7821	LORRIES,TRUCKS	N 28838	204052	N 32034	257335	N 31764	310499	N 32385	298759	VEHICULES TRANSP MARCHAND
784	MOTOR VEH PRTS,ACCES NES		80977		98122		117749		120156	PIECES 722,781,782,783
7849	OTHER MOTOR VEHCL PARTS		76574		91513		108453		114523	PIECES 722,781,782,783
785	CYCLES,ETC MOTRZD OR NOT		38955		41041		48035		53663	MOTOCYCLES SCOOTERS
79	OTHR TRANSPORT EQUIPMENT		247521		497132		487444		295879	AUTRE MATERIEL TRANSPORT
792	AIRCRAFT ETC		215063		444635		413621		124579	APP NAVIGATION AERIENNE
7923	AIRCRFT NES2000–15000KG	N 36	52551	N 46	41915	N 36	104046	N 34	62287	AERODYNES 2000 A 15000 KG
7924	AIRCRFT NES OVER 15000KG	N 3	100554	N 8	326339	N 3	239866			AERODYNES PLUS 15000 KG
7929	AIRCRAFT PARTS NES		41187		58184		54230		46874	PIECES DU 792
793	SHIPS AND BOATS ETC		25820		51242		70000	N 16582	165564	NAVIRES BATEAUX,ETC
7932	SHIPS AND BOATS NES	N 1980	24106	N 2402	49492	N 7671	57320	N 15545	163657	NAVIRES ET BATEAUX
79322	TANKERS OF ALL KINDS							N 2	94754	BATEAUX–CITERNES
8	MISC MANUFACTURED GOODS		1340955		1618244		1850140		2021508	ART MANUFACTURES DIVERS
812	*PLUMBG,HEATNG,LGHTNG EQ		27189		36892		46663		50102	APPAR SANITAIRES CHAUFFAGE
821	*FURNITURE,PARTS THEREOF		45673		63400		79754		102052	MEUBLES ET PIECES
8219	FURNITURE AND PARTS NES		18565		27526		37011		50717	AUTRES MEUBLES ET PIECES
84	CLOTHING AND ACCESSORIES		197674		266048		306411		351551	VETEMENTS
843	WOMENS OUTERWEAR NONKNIT	N 7893804	45647	N 8974005	58975	MN 9490	72867	MN 10264	85703	VET DESSUS FEMMES MAT TEX
845	OUTERWEAR KNIT NONELASTC	N 1078107	55538	N 991775	78129	MN 13253	80498	MN 13080	92476	VET DESSOUS,ACCES BONNET
8459	— OTHER,CLTHG ACCESRYS	N 566767	30674	N 528825	47614	MN 9965	48759	MN 9513	55116	AUT VET DESSUS DE BONNE
846	UNDER GARMENTS KNITTED	MN 16068	30562	MN 21788	45261		53602		64179	SOUS VETS DE BONNETERIE
8462	— OF COTTON NON ELASTIC	MN 13783	22958	MN 19277	33727	MN 19027	39595	MN 19570	48316	SOUS–VET BONNET COTON
851	*FOOTWEAR	P 7519863	65498	MP 9497	79755	MP 10373	89709	MP 9606	100093	CHAUSSURES
85102	FOOTWEAR LEATHER	P 4900693	50477	P 6267519	63176	P 6919089	70927	P 6517879	79850	CHAUS SEMELLES EN CUIR
87	PRECISION INSTRUMNTS NES		186274		226871		246276		260494	INSTRUM,APPAR SCIENT NDA
872	MEDICAL INSTRUMENTS NES		44328		53230		60810		70390	INSTR,APP MEDIC–CHIR NDA
87202	OTH MEDICAL INSTRUMENTS		39500		47011		52839		61966	INSTRUM,APP MEDECINE
874	MEASURNG,CONTROLNG INSTR		121980		149645		159118		160436	INSTRUMENTS DE MESURE
8748	ELEC MEAS,CONTRL EQU NES		30037		42421		43370		46897	APP ELEC ELECTRO MESURE
87483	OTH ELCTRNC MEAS ETC EQU		26377		36582		38348		41729	AUT APP ELECTRO DE MESURE
88	PHOTO EQU,OPTICL GDS ETC		135230		156628		170125		192346	APP,FOURN PHOTO,OP,MONTR
881	PHOTO APPARAT,EQUIPT NES		32236		32474		32804		41669	APP,EQUIP PHOTO NDA
882	PHOTO,CINEMA SUPPLIES		65999		77498		82136		93742	PRODUITS PHOTO,CINEMA
8822	PHOTO FILM EXC DEV CINMA		47946		56277		58165		60796	PLAQUES,PELLICULES,FILMS
89	MISC MANUFCTRD GOODS NES		659712		757223		876740		929163	ART MANUFACTURES DIVERS
892	PRINTED MATTER		179506		208415		218980		230826	IMPRIMES
8921	PRINTED BOOKS,GLOBES,ETC		90040		101088		105655		111198	LIVRES,BROCHURES,CARTES
89211	PRINTED BOOKS,PAMPHLETS		88416		99229		103624		108933	LIVRES,BROCHURES
8922	NEWSPAPERS,PERIODICALS		52097		60336		62197		65743	JOURNAUX ET PERIODIQUES
8928	PRINTED MATTER NES		33590		42291		45476		47243	IMPRIMES NDA
893	ARTICLES OF PLASTIC NES		142583		173726		208405		219606	OUVRAGES EN MAT DIVIS 58
8939	MISC PLASTIC ARTICLES		111871		132709		159267		168594	ART DIVERS EN MAT DIV 58
89399	OTHR PLASTC ARTICLES NES	W 7	90962	W 1	110495		133948		145979	AUT OUV MAT DIV 58
894	TOYS,SPORTING GOODS,ETC		110351		120849		158101		173641	VOITURES ENFANTS,JOUETS
8942	TOYS,INDOOR GAMES ETC		70036		74124		101610		113537	JOUETS,JEUX ETC
89423	TOYS NES		32730		35978		45828		51662	JOUETS,MODELES REDUITS
89424	INDOOR GAME EQUIPMENT		28512		27000		40879		46686	ART,JEUX DE SOCIETE
8947	OTH SPORT GDS,FAIR AMUSM		31454		37911		45157		47753	AUT ART DE SPORT
897	GOLD,SILVER WARE,JEWELRY		37881		30276		24331		30138	BIJOUTERIE,ORFEVRERIE
8973	PREC JEWLRY,GLD–SILVWARE		32941		23276		17781		23972	BIJOUX OR,ARGENT ORFEVRE
89731	PRECIOUS METAL JEWELLERY		31279		21194		14907		21666	ART BIJOUTERIE,JOAILLER
898	MUSICAL INSTRUMENTS,PTS		118210		140978		170025		169852	INSTRUMENTS DE MUSIQUE
8983	SOUND RECRDNG TAPE,DISCS		108098		129602		158289		157229	SUPPORTS SON POUR 763
89832	RECORDED DISCS,TAPES ETC		87759		108690		137624		136031	DISQUES,PHONO,BANDES
899	OTHER MANUFACTURED GOODS		43117		48210		56738		64306	AUT ART MANUF DIVERS NDA

5. General Exports F.O.B. by Commodities according to the S.I.T.C. (Rev. 2) in thousand U.S. Dollars
Exportations Générales F.O.B. par Produits d'après la C.T.C.I. (Rév. 2) en milliers de Dollars E.U.

SITC CTCI	COMMODITY	1993 WEIGHT POIDS	1993 VALUE VALEUR	1994 WEIGHT POIDS	1994 VALUE VALEUR	1995 WEIGHT POIDS	1995 VALUE VALEUR	1996 WEIGHT POIDS	1996 VALUE VALEUR	PRODUIT
	ALL COMMODITIES		10558180		12185496		13745435		14354279	TOUS PRODUITS
0	FOOD AND LIVE ANIMALS		4692096		5082551		5645798		6263453	ALIMENTS,ANIMAUX VIVANTS
001	*LIVE ANIMALS FOR FOOD	N 1661907	98596	N 1537871	100284	N 977737	80862	N 872282	91014	ANIMAUX VIVANTS
0012	SHEEP AND GOATS,LIVE	N 1245144	47877	N 831139	42757	N 629581	24136	N 551905	22145	ESPECES OVINE ET CAPRINE
00121	SHEEP,LIVE	N 1244944	47349	N 825486	30891	N 627906	22865	N 551155	21873	ESPECE OVINE
0015	EQUINE SPECIES, LIVE	N 3165	46527	N 3132	51399	N 3149	53508	N 3046	63504	CHEVAUX,ANES,MULETS
01	MEAT AND PREPARATIONS		1653178		1691262		1785821		1873293	VIANDES ET PREPARATIONS
011	MEAT FRESH,CHILLD,FROZEN	W 696851	1632350	W 722038	1660779	W 776455	1749554	W 776821	1836491	VIANDES FRAICHES,REF,CONGE
0111	BOVINE MEAT FRESH,FROZEN	W 313829	772956	W 319124	782023	W 347058	767504	W 343178	681818	VIANDES BOVIN FRAI,REF
01111	BOVINE MEAT WITH BONE IN	W 22486	33955	W 26697	49914	W 28459	45530	W 24921	41739	VIANDES BOVIN NON DESOSS
01112	BOVINE MEAT BONELESS	W 291344	739000	W 292427	732109	W 318600	721974	W 318257	640079	VIANDES BOVIN DESOSSEES
0112	MUTTON ETC FRSH,CHLD,FRN	W 327894	729386	W 344077	743539	W 365013	809812	W 371148	984095	VIANDE DE MOUTON
0116	EDIBLE OFFAL FRESH,CH,FR	W 38719	53766	W 43501	59667	W 48704	69076	W 49260	63923	ABATS COMESTIBLES
0118	MEAT NES FRESH,CHLD,FRZN	W 14855	72514	W 13953	71553	W 14200	98668	W 11568	102370	AUTRES VIANDES,ABATS
01189	OTHER MEAT NES FRESH,ETC	W 14855	72514	W 13953	71553	W 14199	98666	W 11568	102370	VIANDE,ABATS COMESTIBLES
02	DAIRY PRODCTS,BIRDS'EGGS		1520674		1661199		1788800		2309422	PRODUITS LAITIERS,OEUFS
022	MILK AND CREAM	W 436209	794032	W 516609	844909	W 443412	882412	W 564696	1175135	LAIT ET CREME
0223	MILK AND CREAM FRESH	W 30453	39666	W 48849	55620	W 45700	61872	W 66230	83014	LAIT,CREME FRAIS
0224	MILK,CREAM PRESERVED ETC	W 405756	754366	W 467760	789289	W 397712	820540	W 498465	1092121	LAIT,CREME CONS,CONC
02242	MILK DRY,1.5% FAT OR LES	W 107268	194859	W 149236	246972	W 113315	239228	W 169433	365457	LAIT POUDRE INF 1.5%
02243	MILK DRY,OVER 1.5% FAT	W 293700	552317	W 308117	530096	W 276008	567828	W 318997	706128	LAIT POUDRE SUP 1.5%
023	BUTTER	W 248660	448922	W 251671	469472	W 233273	510606	W 274250	624378	BEURRE
024	CHEESE AND CURD	W 126499	276267	W 159353	345439	W 168793	394127	W 204718	507668	FROMAGE ET CAILLEBOTTE
03	FISH AND PREPARATIONS		640962		686786		802230		796693	POISSONS ET PREPARATIONS
034	FISH,FRESH,CHILLED,FROZN	W 210197	437644	W 174931	418999	W 175758	479722	W 197169	484446	POISSON FRAIS, REFRIG,CONG
0341	FISH FRSH,CHLLD,EX FILLT	W 8537	45910	W 10401	54059	W 9258	54227	W 8844	51421	POISSON FRAIS,REFRIGERE
0342	FISH FROZEN,EXCL FILLETS	W 136161	155506	W 109079	148342	W 107820	184713	W 126610	205919	POISSONS CONGELES
0344	FISH FILLETS,FROZEN	W 64451	230799	W 54617	211861	W 57878	236003	W 60882	222548	FILETS CONGELES
036	SHELL FISH FRESH,FROZEN	W 14114	149368		213500	W 104004	266172	W 84275	257461	CRUSTACES,MOLLUSQUES
037	FISH ETC PREPD,PRSVD NES	W 7267	48876	W 7103	49042	W 7356	48893	W 7130	48444	POIS,CRUST,MOL PREPARES
04	CEREALS AND PREPARATIONS		39105		57746		81131		85995	CEREALES ET PRODUITS
048	CEREAL ETC PREPARATIONS		33250		53953		74013		79736	PREPTNS A BASE CEREALES
05	VEGETABLES AND FRUIT		596974		693861		888298		849624	LEGUMES ET FRUITS
054	VEG ETC FRSH,SMPLY PRSVD		132511		188738		213853		203540	LEGUMES FRAIS,CONG,SECS
0545	OTHER FRESH VEGETABLES	W 170197	71703	W 241435	105711	W 214592	116844	W 253639	107658	AUTRES LEGUMES FRAIS,REF
05451	ALLIACEOUS VEGTBLS,FRESH	W 92761	28963	W 136731	49880	W 132168	62596	W 160957	47874	OIGNONS,ECHALOTES,AULX
05459	FRESH VEGETABLES NES	W 77436	42740	W 104704	55830	W 82423	54248	W 92682	59784	LEGUMES FRAIS,REFRI NDA
0546	VEGETABLES SIMPLY PRESVD	W 47347	36434	W 68859	53794	W 79043	65695	W 76518	66370	LEGUMES CONG,CONSER
05461	VEGETABLES FROZEN	W 47347	36434	W 68859	53794	W 78990	65654	W 76518	66368	LEGUMES CONGELES
057	FRUIT,NUTS,FRESH,DRIED	W 459096	411602	W 422231	442025	W 520162	602592	W 544646	565131	FRUITS FRAIS OU SECS
0574	APPLES FRESH	W 237414	194248	W 209766	194022	W 313057	314666	W 310786	252637	POMMES FRAICHES
0579	FRUIT FRESH OR DRIED NES	W 220877	215839	W 211666	245917	W 205843	284867	W 232959	310053	FRUITS FRAIS,SECS NDA
05798	OTHER FRESH FRUIT	W 210663	194448	W 200103	220419	W 193262	250352	W 221617	280268	AUTRES FRUITS FRAIS
058	FRUIT PRESERVED,PREPARED	W 18223	38620	W 22904	48899		53715	W 45555	65989	CONSERVES DE FRUITS
06	SUGAR AND PREPS,HONEY		28818		35886		41241		64362	SUCRES ET PRODUITS
061	SUGAR AND HONEY	W 29695	24313	W 26909	29925	W 46469	34757	W 58166	57929	SUCRES ET MIEL
081	*FEEDING STUFF FOR ANIML		25015		31579		35746		47774	NOURRITURE POUR ANIMAUX
09	MISC EDIBLE PRODUCTS		63343		92886		113735		103980	PREP ALIMENTAIRES DIVERSES
098	EDIBLE PRODCTS,PREPS NES		59923		89140		111560		101366	PREP ALIMENTAIRES NDA
09809	MISC FOOD PREPRTIONS NES		39601		59559		78232		70225	PREP ALIMENTAIRES NDA
1	BEVERAGES AND TOBACCO		48694		60521		68142		81842	BOISSONS ET TABACS
11	BEVERAGES		46766		57705		64380		78134	BOISSONS
112	ALCOHOLIC BEVERAGES	W 20894	44728	W 20811	52299	W 20022	57691	W 15139	74376	BOISSONS ALCOOLIQUES
1121	WINE OF FRESH GRAPES ETC	W 8580	24843	W 8202	26333	W 8627	32044	W 12042	45077	VINS DE RAISINS FRAIS
11212	WINE OF FRESH GRAPES	W 8579	24841	W 8202	26330	W 8601	31994	W 12041	45075	VINS DE MOUTS DE RAISINS
2	CRUDE MATERLS,EXCL FUELS		1902786		2283569		2537293		2419219	MAT BRUTES NON COMESTIBLES
21	HIDES,SKINS,FURS UNDRSSD		201508		267339		293801		308582	CUIRS,PEAUX BRUTS
211	HIDES,SKINS,EXC FURS,RAW		200066		264676		293460		307544	CUIRS ET PEAUX
2111	BOVINE,EQUINE HIDES,RAW	N 833536	32767	N 864816	39830	N 905733	48122	N 874011	40573	PEAUX DE BOVINS
2117	SHEEP SKIN WITHOUT WOOL		149682		202205		217644		238580	PEAUX EPILEES D'OVINS
24	CORK AND WOOD		745436		774059		790255		781379	LIEGE ET BOIS
247	OTH WOOD ROUGH,SQUARED	W 3006395	440970	W 3386338	427567	W 3680484	427685	W 3948048	461612	BOIS BRUTS EQUARRIS
2471	SAW–,VENEER–LOGS CONIFER	W 3005754	440735	W 3384469	427152	W 3675808	427094	W 3947890	461547	CONIFERES POUR SCIAGE,PLACAG
24711	— IN THE ROUGH	W 3005754	440735	W 3384469	427152	W 3675808	427094	W 3947890	461547	ECORCES OU DEGROSSIS
248	WOOD SHAPED,SLEEPERS		282644		323447		321461		289530	BOIS SIMPLEMENT TRAVAILLES
2482	LUMBER SHAPED CONIFER		280959		322024		319938		287987	CONIFERES SCIES,RABOTES
24821	LUMBER SAWN ETC CONIFER	W 566022	255577	W 601034	292613	W 629025	287400	W 575360	253536	CONIFERES SCIES LONGITUD
251	*PULP AND WASTE PAPER	W 697590	189841	W 721318	238002	W 713834	351932	W 774082	279031	PATES A PAPIER,DECHETS
2512	MECHANICAL WOOD PULP	W 309128	72636	W 329627	95137	W 341256	127199	W 351124	99402	PATES MECANIQUES DE BOIS
2517	SODA,SULPHATE WOOD PULP	W 342534	112976	W 321421	135116	W 299555	210319	W 328756	168028	PATES CHIMIQUES AU SULFATE
25171	— UNBLEACHED	W 142913	45172	W 150932	58353	W 117872	70125	W 146226	78155	PATES ECRUES
25172	— BLEACHED,NONDISSOLVNG	W 199621	67805	W 170489	76763	W 181683	140194	W 182530	89873	PATES BLANCHIES
26	TEXTILE FIBRES AND WASTE		507796		712841		785808		713927	FIBRES TEXTILES
268	WOOL(EXC TOPS),ANML HAIR	W 214720	506614	W 246129	711523	W 219828	784331	W 203836	712479	LAINES ET POILS
2681	WOOL GREASY,FLEECE–WSHED	W 52048	114387	W 57827	168543	W 64391	213714	W 49567	162027	LAINE EN SUINT
2682	WOOL DEGREASED,UNCOMBED	W 160610	384940	W 185637	532480	W 152816	559790	W 151261	537682	LAINE DEGRAISSEE
28	METALLIFEROUS ORES,SCRAP		32822		36982		40521		34613	MINERAIS METAL,DECHETS
29	CRUDE ANIMAL,VEG MAT NES		208842		235269		256610		279528	MATIERES BRUTES ANIM,VEGET
291	CRUDE ANIMAL MTRIALS NES		145311		158683		169855		194333	MATIERES BRUTES ANIMALES
2911	BONES,IVORY,HORNS,ETC		61257		67373		70132		90680	OS,CORNES,SABOTS
29111	BONE,HORN–CORE AND WASTE		32887		31143		38503		50476	OS
2919	OTH ANIMAL MATERIALS NES		84054		91311		99722		103654	MAT ORIGINE ANIMALE NDA
29193	GUT,BLADDERS,ETC NONFISH		70132		75425		85948		86854	BOYAUX,VESSIES
292	CRUDE VEG MATERIALS NES		63531		76586		86755		85195	MAT BRUTES VEGETALES NDA
2927	CUT FLOWERS AND FOLIAGE		30822		41015		44182		39907	FLEURS,FEUILLAGES COUPES
3	MINERAL FUELS ETC		267380		243921		217956		323074	COMBUSTIBLES MINERAUX LUB
32	COAL,COKE AND BRIQUETTES		42581		49895		63390		75780	HOUILLES,COKES,BRIQUETTES
322	COAL,LIGNITE AND PEAT	W 790980	42581	W 1047235	49895	W 1337589	63390	W 1430008	75780	HOUILLES,LIGNITES,TOURBE
3222	OTH COAL,NOT AGGLOMERATD	W 787644	42059	W 1043606	49267	W 1333751	62703	W 1426258	74959	AUTRES HOUILLES
33	PETROLEUM AND PRODUCTS		221027		190748		151809		239006	PETROLE ET DERIVES
333	CRUDE PETROLEUM	W 1072877	162163	W 1137085	150719	W 1011386	144407	W 1312227	224054	HUILES BRUTES DE PETROLE
334	PETROLEUM PRODUCTS,REFIN		57972		39673		4968		13755	PRODUITS RAFFINES
4	ANIMAL,VEGETABLE OIL,FAT		65697		79653		110428		104176	HUILES,GRAISSES ANIM,VEG
411	*ANIMAL OILS AND FATS		38037		47569		66753		60564	HUILES,GRAISSES ANIMALES
4113	ANIML OIL,FAT,GREASE NES	W 122175	37223	W 139515	46450		65145	W 142025	58383	HUILES,GRAISSES ANIMALES NDA
41132	FATS OF BOVINE,SHEEP,ETC	W 120855	36351	W 137228	45390	W 134768	63597	W 138993	56878	SUIFS BRUTS FONDUS
431	*PROCESD ANML VEG OIL,ET		27076		31493		42914		42752	HUILES,GRAISSES PREPAREES
5	CHEMCLS,RELATED PROD NES		606043		920603		1030875		1032298	PRODUITS CHIMIQUES
51	ORGANIC CHEMICALS		90721		248053		286537		226534	PROD CHIMIQ ORGANIQUES
512	ALCOHOLS,PHENOLS ETC		83517		241318		278685		214784	PHENOLS,PHENOLS–ALCOOLS
5121	ACYCLIC ALCOHOLS,DERIVS		83446		241215		278634		214652	ALCOOLS ACYCLIQUES

5. General Exports F.O.B. by Commodities according to the S.I.T.C. (Rev. 2) in thousand U.S. Dollars
Exportations Générales F.O.B. par Produits d'après la C.T.C.I. (Rév. 2) en milliers de Dollars E.U.

SITC CTCI	COMMODITY	1993 WEIGHT POIDS	1993 VALUE VALEUR	1994 WEIGHT POIDS	1994 VALUE VALEUR	1995 WEIGHT POIDS	1995 VALUE VALEUR	1996 WEIGHT POIDS	1996 VALUE VALEUR	PRODUIT
51211	METHYL ALCOHOL(METHANOL)	V 972012	80532	V 1186600	238025	V 1599246	275748	V 2315943	210953	ALCOOLS METHYLIQUES
541	*MEDICINAL,PHARM PRODUCT		42733		46549		76610		74858	PROD MEDICINAUX PHARMACEUT
55	PERFUME,CLEANING ETC PRD		74209		98792		100020		111358	PROD POUR PARFUM,TOILETTE
553	PERFUMERY,COSMETICS,ETC		51496		57113		49442		47797	PRODUITS DE PARFUMERIE
554	SOAP,CLEANSING ETC PREPS		22018		40479		49439		62092	SAVONS,PRODUITS DETERSIFS
58	PLASTIC MATERIALS ETC		37601		52135		68481		71212	MAT PLAST ARTIFICIELLES
583	POLYMERIZATION ETC PRODS		26405		36659		49714		55240	PROD POLYMERISATION
59	CHEMICAL MATERIALS NES		332012		441478		457305		496862	MAT PROD CHIMIQUES NDA
591	PESTICIDES,DISINFECTANTS		8350		32640		43628		43636	DESINF,INSECT,FONG,HERB
592	STARCH,INULIN,GLUTEN,ETC		310688		387991		396942		435166	AMIDONS,INUL,GLUT FROM
5922	ALBUMINOID SUBSTAN,GLUES		310162		387684		396577		434659	MAT ALBUMIN,COLLES
59221	CASEIN AND DERIVATVS,ETC	W 65691	273791	W 87559	341636	W 73093	339488	W 72482	379556	CASEINES,CASEINATES
59222	ALBUMINS AND DERIVATIVES	W 6876	28273	W 8829	35702	W 11737	47155	W 9820	44920	ALBUMINES,ALBUMINATES
6	BASIC MANUFACTURES		1453469		1684307		2033407		2039122	ART MANUFACTURES
61	LEATHER,DRESSED FUR,ETC		145513		166295		199806		233858	CUIRS,PELLETERIES
611	LEATHER		118942		138137		155192		181217	CUIRS,PEAUX PREPARES
6114	LEATHR BOVINE NES,EQUINE	A 34	75323	A 151	88314		110170		127047	CUIRS DE BOVINS
6115	LEATHER FROM SHEEP,LAMBS		34468		41260		40456		48494	PEAUX D'OVINS PREPAREES
613	FUR SKINS TANNED,DRESSED	N 578812	21404	N 369266	19135	N 1684709	32620	N 2016052	44883	PELLETERIES
62	RUBBER MANUFACTURES NES		39649		47942		52612		51997	CAOUTCHOUC MANUFACTURE
63	WOOD,CORK MANUFACTRS NES		76325		115401		149721		169187	OUVRAGES LIEGE ET BOIS
634	VENEERS,PLYWOOD,ETC		54272		90475		119443		132448	PLACAGES,CONTRE–PLAQUES
6342	PLYWOOD OF WOOD SHEETS	V 6016	26869		53306	V 130581	69095		77332	BOIS CONTRE–PLAQUES
6343	IMPROVED,RECONSTIT WOOD	V 87963	23658	V 109730	31682	V 121416	41987	V 116661	49517	BOIS AMELIORES,RECONST
63432	RECONSTITUTED WOOD	V 87928	23640	V 109678	31641	V 121414	41986	V 116661	49517	BOIS RECONSTITUES
64	PAPER,PAPERBOARD AND MFR		329543		374737		428382		443885	PAPIERS,CARTONS & OUVRAGES
641	PAPER AND PAPERBOARD		295483		332134		378840		401794	PAPIERS ET CARTONS
6411	NEWSPRINT	W 254631	114680	W 251604	128597	W 228400	146810	W 257328	186933	PAPIER JOURNAL
6413	KRAFT PAPER,PAPERBOARD	W 82711	32574	W 62700	28970	W 50840	33246	W 77588	35011	PAPIER ET CARTON KRAFT
6416	FIBRE BUILDING BOARD	V 361007	103802	V 366925	121021	V 366724	135329	V 353967	117317	PLAQUES CONSTRUCT EN PATE
64162	INSULATING BOARD, ETC	V 358289	102429	V 363175	119168	V 363558	133692	V 351289	115914	PLAQUES CONST NON COMPR
642	PAPER,ETC,PRECUT,ARTS OF		34060		42603		49543		42091	PAP,CARTONS DECOUPES
65	TEXTILE YARN,FABRICS,ETC		129308		146740		160750		164098	FILS,TISSUS,ARTICLES TEXTILE
651	TEXTILE YARN		37515		42773		44958		45719	FILS TEXTILES
6512	WOOL,HAIR YARN,INCL TOPS	W 5768	35935	W 5822	39392	W 5635	41355	W 5838	43712	FILS DE LAINE,DE POILS
659	FLOOR COVERINGS,ETC		37550		48581		52911		55976	COUVRE–PARQUETS,TAPIS ETC
6594	WOOL CARPETS ETC NES		34507		45325		48558	A 2590	51260	TAPIS DE LAINE
66	NONMETAL MINERAL MFS NES		40944		43927		48815		42338	ART MIN NON METALLIQUES
67	IRON AND STEEL		173455		171595		205878		190480	FER ET ACIER
672	IRON,STEEL PRIMARY FORMS	W 232792	70026	W 251487	75670	W 220832	80992	W 247904	73712	LINGOTS FER,ACIER
6727	IRN,STL COIL FR REROLLNG	W 226508	68852	W 251415	75506	W 220717	80806	W 239706	71054	EBAUCHES POUR TOLES FER
67271	IRON,SIMPLE STEEL COILS	W 226435	68805	W 251002	75373	W 220589	80693	W 239682	71001	EBAUCHES NON EN ACIER
674	IRN,STL UNIV,PLATE,SHEET	W 120299	62474	W 104970	53214	W 146695	80503	W 153773	86993	LARGES PLATS,TOLES
6749	OTH IRN,STL PLATES,SHEET	W 78537	46106	W 44470	29819	W 56548	39872	W 76635	55053	AUTRES TOLES FER,ACIER
67491	— OF IRON OR SIMPLE STL	W 78481	45987	W 44435	29749	W 56490	39730	W 76535	54817	AUT TOLES AUTRES ACIER FIN
68	NON–FERROUS METALS		386416		453379		603322		551225	METAUX NON FERREUX
682	COPPER EXC CEMENT COPPER		42396		53945	W 14294	59664		56984	CUIVRE
6822	COPPER,ALLOYS WORKED		41280		53211	W 14204	59446		56838	CUIVRE,ALLIAGES OUVRES
684	ALUMINIUM	W 262944	341344	W 254483	395277	W 265367	535984	W 279362	484025	ALUMINIUM
6841	ALUMINIUM,ALLOYS,UNWRGHT	W 243257	286975	W 232281	327429	W 246230	470509	W 258179	407007	ALUMINIUM,ALLIAGES BRUTS
6842	ALUMINIUM,ALLOYS WORKED	W 19687	54369	W 22202	67848	W 19138	65475	W 21183	77018	ALUMINIUM,ALLIAGES OUVRE
68421	ALUMINIUM BARS,WIRE,ETC	W 10736	26368	W 11759	33259	W 9594	30556	W 13308	44383	BARRES,PROFILES FILS ALU
69	METAL MANUFACTURES NES		132316		164291		184119		192054	ART MANUFACT EN METAL NDA
699	BASE METAL MFRS NES		43564		55073		61573		68633	ART MANUFACTURES MET NDA
7	MACHINES,TRANSPORT EQUIP		785492		1001539		1175613		1173818	MACHINES MATERIEL TRANSPORT
71	POWER GENERATING EQUIPMT		22788		38646		28076		45908	MACHINES GENERATRICES
72	MACHS FOR SPCL INDUSTRYS		104107		116908		140062		152069	MAC SPECIALES POUR INDUST
721	AGRIC MACHY,EXC TRACTORS		40304		45030		56797		55326	MACHINES AGRICOLES
728	OTH MACHY FOR SPCL INDUS		23010		34425		39462		48813	AUT MACH IND PARTICULIERES
74	GENRL INDUSTRL MACHY NES		137850		191112		204056		233977	MACH APP INDUSTRIE
741	HEATING,COOLING EQUIPMNT		42351		71462		76854		92919	MACH CHAUFFAGE,PIECES
75	OFFICE MACHNES,ADP EQUIP		48879		54186		71923		73570	MACH BUREAU TRAIT AUTOM
759	OFFICE,ADP MCH PTS,ACCES		24849		25847		41245		41217	PIECES DU 751 ET 752
76	TELECOMM,SOUND EQUIPMENT		64554		88880		111735		104333	EQUIPMENT DE TELECOM
764	TELECOM EQPT,PTS,ACC NES		60674		85268		107483		99473	EQUIP TELECOM,PIECES
7643	TV,RADIO TRANSMITTRS ETC		24183		41691		54247		53816	APP EMET TELE RADIO
77	ELECTRIC MACHNRY NES ETC		206540		291254		324312		357364	MACH APP ELECT NDA
772	SWITCHGEAR ETC,PARTS NES	N 906874	34106	N 3478574	53994		61921		77795	APP COUPURE,SECT ETC
7721	SWITCHGEAR ETC	N 20986	31164	N 49382	48783		53775		69662	APP COUPURE,SECTIONMNT
773	ELECTR DISTRIBUTNG EQUIP		33130		38848		41446		26133	EQUIPMT DISTRIBUTION ELECT
775	HOUSEHOLD TYPE EQUIP NES		90570		126783		127330		145042	MACH,APP USAGE DOMESTQUE
7751	HOUSEHOLD LDRY EQUIP NES	N 88500	24649	N 141989	42903	N 147881	47970	N 174567	58947	MACH A LAVER ET SECHOIRS
77511	DOMESTIC WASHING MACHNES	N 55353	19550	N 101657	36543	N 104030	40411	N 119993	49028	MACH LAVER LINGE MOINS 6 KG
7752	DOM REFRIGERATRS,FREEZRS	N 109133	31644	N 133504	41427	N 118059	36691	N 123207	38052	REFRIG,CONGEL MENAGER
778	ELECTRICAL MACHINERY NES		36263		44192		54563		59491	AUTRES MACH ELECT NDA
78	ROAD VEHICLES		63189		69137		63149		66069	VEHICULES ROUTIERS
784	MOTOR VEH PRTS,ACCES NES		42655		47005		41877		42049	PIECES 722,781,782,783
7849	OTHER MOTOR VEHCL PARTS		42382		46616		41570		41532	PIECES 722,781,782,783
79	OTHR TRANSPORT EQUIPMENT		124221		138984		207194		126462	AUTRE MATERIEL TRANSPORT
792	AIRCRAFT ETC		97147		50417		146445		82701	APP NAVIGATION AERIENNE
7924	AIRCRFT NES OVER 15000KG	N 5	65807	N 3	17816	N 7	104869	N 10	39030	AERODYNES PLUS 15000 KG
793	SHIPS AND BOATS ETC		26908		88254		60327		43639	NAVIRES BATEAUX,ETC
7932	SHIPS AND BOATS NES		24714		35971		49062		23789	NAVIRES ET BATEAUX
7938	TUGS,SPECIAL VESSELS ETC	N 793	1387	N 164	50983	N 1062	2631	N 2202	4539	REMORQUEURS,BATEAUX SPEC
79382	SPECL PURPOSE VESSLS ETC	N 5	654		46804	N 1	624	N 4	95	BAT–PHARES,–POMPES,DRAGUES
8	MISC MANUFACTURED GOODS		459712		538956		562957		538827	ART MANUFACTURES DIVERS
821	*FURNITURE,PARTS THEREOF		42389		52746		47407		45242	MEUBLES ET PIECES
8219	FURNITURE AND PARTS NES		30603		38828		31920		29513	AUTRES MEUBLES ET PIECES
84	CLOTHING AND ACCESSORIES		107594		124115		141059		124225	VETEMENTS
848	HEADGEAR,NONTXTL CLOTHNG		29448		42242		37152		27532	VET ACCES MAT AUT QUE TEX
87	PRECISION INSTRUMNTS NES		83285		109922		105593		83622	INSTRUM,APPAR SCIENT NDA
874	MEASURNG,CONTROLNG INSTR		39937		62175		63615		44013	INSTRUMENTS DE MESURE
89	MISC MANUFCTRD GOODS NES		193601		212525		225621		238742	ART MANUFACTURES DIVERS
893	ARTICLES OF PLASTIC NES		89748		101300		111438		112337	OUVRAGES EN MAT DIVIS 58
8931	PLSTC PACKG CONTNRS,LIDS	N 42000	29528	N 36520	37244		35553		37094	ART TRANSP EMBALLAGE ETC
8939	MISC PLASTIC ARTICLES		51934		52862		65789		65722	ART DIVERS EN MAT DIV 58
89399	OTHR PLASTC ARTICLES NES	W 1	50893		51728		64767		64394	AUT OUV MAT DIV 58
897	GOLD,SILVER WARE,JEWELRY		38975		32080		21603		25682	BIJOUTERIE,ORFEVRERIE
8973	PREC JEWLRY,GLD–SILVWARE		36908		29779		19386		23658	BIJOUX OR,ARGENT ORFEVRE
89731	PRECIOUS METAL JEWELLERY		35958		27422		18150		22462	ART BIJOUTERIE,JOAILLER
9	GOODS NOT CLASSD BY KIND		276812		289876		362967		378452	ART TRANSACT NON CLASSES

5. General Exports F.O.B. by Commodities according to the S.I.T.C. (Rev. 2) in thousand U.S. Dollars
Exportations Générales F.O.B. par Produits d'après la C.T.C.I. (Rév. 2) en milliers de Dollars E.U.

SITC CTCI	COMMODITY	1993		1994		1995		1996		PRODUIT
		WEIGHT POIDS	VALUE VALEUR	WEIGHT POIDS	VALUE VALEUR	WEIGHT POIDS	VALUE VALEUR	WEIGHT POIDS	VALUE VALEUR	
931	*SPECIAL TRANSACTIONS		146837		141659		167908		197459	TRANS.SPECIALES
971	*GOLD,NON MONETARY NES		127791		145103		192212		177243	OR NON MONETAIRE
97101	NONMON GLD UNWRT,SEMIMFD	K 26328	127583	K 39682	144962	K 40091	192209	K 40897	177186	OR,ALLIAGES D'OR BRUTS

1. HISTORICAL SERIES, 1961–1996 SPECIAL TRADE, IMPORTS C.I.F., EXPORTS F.O.B.
SERIES HISTORIQUES, 1961–1996 COMMERCE SPECIAL, IMPORTATIONS C.A.F., EXPORTATIONS F.O.B

YEAR ANNEE	VALUE IN MILLION U.S. DOLLARS / VALEUR EN MILLION U.S. DOLLARS — MERCHANDISE –MARCHANDISE: IMPORTS	EXPORTS	GOLD –OR: IMPORTS	EXPORTS	CONVERSION FACTORS FACTEURS DE CONVERSION CENTS E.U. PAR: IMPORTS	EXPORTS	INDEX NUMBERS –INDICES — QUANTUM: IMPORTS	EXPORTS	UNIT VALUE / VALEUR UNITAIRE: IMPORTS	EXPORTS
1961	74.40	68.40		7.73						
1962	98.20	90.20	0.70	7.71						
1963	110.80	106.80		7.09						
1964	137.00	125.20	1.21	6.88						
1965	160.30	149.00		5.41						
1966	181.90	142.20		5.18						
1967	203.90	151.70	1.54	5.21						
1968	184.70	162.30	1.35	5.02						
1969	176.99	158.75	1.40	4.10						
1970	198.75	178.62	0.89	3.80						
1971	210.44	187.24		3.80						
1972	218.49	249.44	0.53	3.10						
1973	326.98	277.88	0.63	3.20						
1974	561.68	380.92								
1975	516.86	375.17								
1976	532.14	541.90								
1977	761.93	636.80								
1978	593.93	645.97								
1979	360.20	566.55								
1980	887.21	450.44								
1981	999.44	499.83								
1982	775.55	405.45								
1983	806.91	431.29								
1984	826.24	384.80								
1985	964.30	301.50								
1986	856.80	247.20								
1987	826.80	272.80								
1988	805.20	232.70								
1989	614.90	310.70								
1990	637.50	330.60								
1991	751.40	272.40								
1992	855.10	223.10								
1993	744.00	267.00								
1994	874.70	351.70								
1995	961.70	526.30								
1996	1119.90	634.80								

2. IMPORTS BY BROAD ECONOMIC CATEGORY AND EXPORTS BY INDUSTRIAL ORIGIN. (PERCENTAGE OF TOTAL VALUE)
IMPORTATIONS PAR CATEGORIES ECONOMIQUES ET EXPORTATIONS PAR BRANCHE D'ACTIVITE.(EN POURCENTAGE DE LA VALEUR TOTALE)

IMPORTS – IMPORTATIONS

	1990	1991	1992	1993	1994	1995	1996
TOTAL IMPORTS–IMPORTATIONS TOTALES	100.	100.	100.	100.	100.	100.	100.
1 FOOD BEV–ALIMENTATION BOISSONS	15.3	20.8	20.8	19.3	17.1	16.6	16.1
11 PRIMARY–PRODUITS DE BASE	3.8	7.1	4.8	6.7	5.0	3.9	4.8
111 FOR INDUSTRY–POUR L'INDUSTRIE	1.5	3.4	1.7	3.9	3.2	2.2	3.2
112 FOR HOUSEHOLDS–POUR LES MENAGES	2.3	3.7	3.1	2.7	1.8	1.7	1.5
12 PROCESSED–PRODUITS ELABORES	11.5	13.7	16.0	12.7	12.1	12.7	11.4
121 FOR INDUSTRY–POUR L'INDUSTRIE	4.1	2.5	5.1	3.8	3.7	3.3	3.4
122 FOR HOUSEHOLDS–POUR LES MENAGES	7.4	11.1	10.9	8.9	8.5	9.4	8.0
2 IND SUPPLIES–APPROV INDUSTRIELS	25.1	27.4	22.1	24.3	27.9	27.0	30.3
21 PRIMARY–PRODUITS DE BASE	4.7	1.5	1.8	1.3	2.0	1.6	1.9
22 PROCESSED–PRODUITS ELABORES	20.4	25.9	20.3	23.1	25.9	25.4	28.4
3 FUELS–COMBUSTIBLES	19.0	4.5	14.9	13.9	12.7	17.9	9.0
31 PRIMARY–PRODUITS DE BASE	16.7	4.0	12.2	11.7	10.3	13.9	4.5
32 PROCESSED–PRODUITS ELABORES	2.3	0.5	2.7	2.2	2.5	4.0	4.5
321 MOTOR SPIRIT–ESSENCE	0.2	0.0	0.3	0.2	0.3	0.6	0.3
322 OTHER–AUTRES	2.1	0.5	2.4	2.0	2.1	3.4	4.2
4 MACHINERY–EQUIPEMENT	14.7	16.6	16.4	15.8	17.4	14.8	16.4
41 CAPITAL EQUIPMENT–MACHINES	13.2	15.2	15.2	14.4	16.1	13.2	14.6
42 PARTS–PIECES ACCESSOIRES	1.4	1.5	1.2	1.4	1.3	1.6	1.8
5 TRANSPORT–TRANSPORT	18.4	15.0	10.8	11.0	9.3	9.2	11.6
51 PASSENGER CARS–AUTOMOBILES	13.2	9.9	7.3	3.0	2.0	2.9	3.7
52 OTHER–AUTRES	1.8	1.3	0.8	5.4	4.5	3.2	4.5
521 INDUSTRIAL–INDUSTRIELS	1.1	0.5	0.2	4.9	4.1	3.0	4.3
522 NON INDUSTRIAL–NON INDUSTRIEL	0.8	0.8	0.6	0.4	0.4	0.2	0.2
53 PARTS–PIECES ACCESSOIRES	3.4	3.8	2.7	2.7	2.8	3.1	3.4
6 CONSUM GOODS–BIENS CONSOMMATION	7.5	15.7	14.7	15.4	15.3	14.3	16.4
61 DURABLE–DURABLES	1.5	2.6	1.8	1.8	1.7	2.0	2.2
62 SEMI DURABLE–SEMI DURABLES	2.6	4.7	4.4	4.9	5.0	4.5	4.6
63 NON DURABLE–NON DURABLES	3.4	8.4	8.5	8.7	8.6	7.7	9.5
7 GOODS NES–BIENS NDA	0.0	0.0	0.4	0.2	0.2	0.2	0.3

EXPORTS – EXPORTATIONS

	1990	1991	1992	1993	1994	1995	1996
TOTAL EXPORTS–EXPORTATIONS TOTALES	100.	100.	100.	100.	100.	100.	100.
1 AGRICULTURE	51.2	54.4	54.0	43.3	55.9	53.1	44.1
2 MINING QUARRY–INDUS EXTRACTIVES	0.1	0.3	0.3	0.1	0.0	0.1	0.0
3 MANUFACTURING–IND MANUFACTUR	48.7	45.3	45.7	56.6	44.1	46.8	55.8
31 FOOD BEV TOBACCO–ALIM BOISS TAB	38.8	33.2	35.8	37.8	27.6	22.5	17.9
32 TEXTILES–INDUSTRIES TEXTILES	1.1	1.3	1.2	1.7	1.7	1.5	1.3
33 WOOD & PRODUCTS–BOIS & PRODUITS	0.7	0.9	0.6	0.8	1.5	2.3	2.9
34 PAPER & PRODUCTS–PAPIER & PRODT	0.1	0.1	0.1	0.1	0.2	0.1	0.0
35 CHEMICALS–INDUSTRIES CHIMIQUES	3.9	4.3	4.0	3.0	2.5	2.0	1.7
36 NON METAL MIN–MIN NON METAL	0.2	0.3	0.6	1.5	0.9	0.9	0.7
37 BASIC METAL–IND METAL BASE	2.7	3.1	2.1	5.3	0.8	0.4	0.3
38 METAL MANUF–MANUF METAL	1.2	2.1	1.1	2.6	3.3	9.7	17.4
39 OTH MANUF IND–AUTRES MANUF	0.0	0.0	0.0	3.9	5.4	7.4	13.6

3. TRADE BY PRINCIPAL COUNTRIES OF PROVENANCE AND LAST DESTINATION (VALUE IN THOUSAND U.S. DOLLARS)
ECHANGES SELON LES PRINCIPAUX PAYS DE PROVENANCE ET DE DERNIERE DESTINATION (VALEUR EN MILLIERS DE DOLLARS EU)

COUNTRIES–PAYS	SPECIAL IMPORTS C.I.F. IMPORTATIONS SPECIALES C.A.F					COUNTRIES–PAYS	SPECIAL EXPORTS F.O.B. EXPORTATIONS SPECIALES F.O.B.				
	1992	1993	1994	1995	1996		1992	1993	1994	1995	1996
World	906761	755121	852466	1009211	1076154	Monde	236493	267493	351108	509212	660183
Africa	189	1414	919	1062	2374	Afrique	21	2	154	146	180
Americas	692516	576939	599874	794150	828609	Amériques	148907	218971	258727	329701	434905
Northern America	240788	207287	227845	318403	387925	Amérique du Nord	77509	145606	152954	219536	300897
LAIA	180302	141516	145705	183967	105353	ALAI	22952	11321	13300	17645	16547
CACM	227617	197383	190155	228271	259977	MCAC	41657	57102	83901	83007	101191
Caribbean	3546	3595	2655	6465	8843	Caraïbes	4500	1344	3993	7410	11720
Rest of America	40263	27158	33515	57044	66512	Autre Amérique	2289	3598	4579	2103	4550
As.ex F.USSR	98545	92239	104985	91122	120204	Asie l'URSS exclus	24852	1768	2105	13042	7800
Eur.x F.USSR	98552	75521	122077	111750	118175	Europe l'URSS exclus	62010	45570	88456	166022	216899
EU	86976	65095	100369	101570	111125	UE	60749	44290	85172	161915	211161
EFTA	8303	7516	7073	7215	5911	AELE	1127	689	3081	4051	1670
East Europe	3274	2739	3975	2875	762	Europe de l'Est	134	591	182	8	3880
Other Europe		130	10661	89	374	Autre de l'Europe			21	49	188
Former USSR	13593	5223	21155	6995	2763	Ancienne URSS	237	968	1610	279	247
Oceania	2311	3556	3167	4132	4029	Océanie	149	215	57	2	153
USA/Etats–Unis d'Amer	232021	200738	214705	304405	365271	USA/Etats–Unis d'Amer	61431	117198	150276	214431	296294
Venezuela	123889	93626	101676	130800	19538	Germany/Allemagne	25996	24264	44119	57997	61062
Costa Rica	89402	77827	68238	82234	90577	El Salvador	13650	15258	37114	41284	58098
Guatemala	68946	66831	69256	79657	90403	Spain/Espagne	4902	2424	13586	39514	73258
Japan/Japon	54725	60494	61009	50462	82840	Costa Rica	17173	22926	25504	17309	13339
Panama	40244	27154	33512	56965	66248	Belgium–Luxembourg	21362	4718	9713	17491	16813
El Salvador	50318	34752	34354	40497	46556	Honduras	5540	11542	12575	14009	19594
Mexico/Mexique	27836	28691	26982	31559	55016	Canada	16078	28408	2678	5105	4603
Germany/Allemagne	25214	19234	23425	22664	25052	Mexico/Mexique	13708	10208	11010	8949	11277
Honduras	18952	17973	18306	25882	32440	Netherlands/Pays–Bas	4615	5538	3247	16835	16275
Spain/Espagne	6103	7169	19009	23762	30327	Guatemala	5294	7375	8708	10404	10160
Canada	8767	6526	13140	13998	22653	United Kingdom	276	1363	4953	9879	24405
France,Monac	10857	7816	11704	10709	14292	Japan/Japon	21411	1329	1282	6968	871
Russian Federation	13593	5223	21155	6995	2763	France,Monac	1588	1388	4428	9959	9089
Colombia/Colombie	9651	5469	8831	6364	12757	Italy/Italie	1424	3635	3703	8010	4488
Belgium–Luxembourg	4079	6539	16617	5718	9522	Panama	2109	3529	4532	2103	4517
Italy/Italie	7808	7201	8328	8218	10727	Venezuela	7845		587	2406	2664
Korea, Republic of	8895	3046	4689	9706	8507	Dominican Republic	427	715	1824	3124	5767
Brazil/Brésil	7699	5974	4928	5381	8669	Cuba	3955	432	946	2883	2598
Netherlands/Pays–Bas	7151	4126	5376	6694	6271	Switz.Liecht	1079	531	1687	3174	1549
Denmark/Danemark	5642	1301	5548	11540	2783	Colombia/Colombie	1171	956	1035	1859	2209
Switz.Liecht	4833	3677	6380	5448	4490	Jordan/Jordanie					3920
Viet Nam	4387	4031	14549			Bulgaria/Bulgarie					3720
United Kingdom	3665	3868	2228	5000	5790	Finland/Finlande	51	83	420	1236	1869
Argentina/Argentine	4226	6756	1491	1622	3755	Russian Federation	237	968	1610	279	247
Finland/Finlande	8554	4591	591	2670	165	Denmark/Danemark	179	252	158	694	2033
New Zealand	2144	3467	3065	4003	3346	Korea, Republic of				2933	80
Sweden/Suède	3343	2274	3004	2685	3890	Hong Kong	4	79	724	1572	575
Ecuador/Equateur	158	236	448	7127	3322	Jamaica/Jamaïque	117	117	765	795	1040
Norway,SVD,JM	3456	3759	684	1748	1421	Haiti/Haïti			153	470	2082
Korea Dem People's Rp	1318	4843	1204	188	1989	Norway,SVD,JM	48	158	1394	877	121
Cuba	2173	2902	1411	1006	1855	Austria/Autriche	346	365	466	284	552
Austria/Autriche	2056	778	1996	1398	1944	Chile/Chili		107	10	1559	19
Peru/Pérou	6375	173	326	150	784	Peru/Pérou	17	11	533	973	68
Israel/Israël	1768	747	821	1478	2166	Sweden/Suède	4	135	335	11	994
Hong Kong	112	494	461	4314	1166	Ecuador/Equateur	15	28	35	1338	32
Netherlands Antilles	979	151	512	3290	1085	Israel/Israël	411	238		6	192
Bulgaria/Bulgarie	2231	1788	1588		11	Poland/Pologne		440	182		
Trinidad and Tobago		25	467	1905	2964	Australia/Australie	149	146	57	2	97
China/Chine	125	97	895	1569	2444	Argentina/Argentine	2	13		215	215
India/Inde	1197	1468	607	770	990	Brazil/Brésil	193		85	53	33
Chile/Chili	408	527	900	747	1355	Portugal	6	76	39	5	227
Poland/Pologne	48	38	389	2612	610	Belize/Bélize	180	69	47		33
Ireland/Irlande	2465	193	263	208	175	Bolivia/Bolivie			3	292	5
So. Africa Customs Un	11	6	12		2332	Cayman Is/Is Caïmans		14	14	87	179
Bahamas		2		0	2266	Dominica/Dominique		10	224		26
Macau/Macao		199			1772	Romania/Roumanie	78	144			
Greece/Grèce			1819			Sri Lanka	169			3	
Thailand/Thaïlande	356	149	129	672	446	Czech Republic				8	160
Dominican Republic	256	382	170	204	621	Thailand/Thaïlande	12			152	

(VALUE AS PERCENTAGE OF WORLD TOTAL)(VALEURS EN POURCENTAGE DU TOTAL MONDIAL)

	1987	1988	1989	1990	1991	1992	1993	1994	1995	1996		1987	1988	1989	1990	1991	1992	1993	1994	1995	1996
Africa		0.0	0.0	0.6	0.0	0.0	0.2	0.1	0.1	0.2	Afrique				0.0	0.0	0.0	0.0	0.0	0.0	0.0
Americas		29.2	35.3	53.5	67.5	76.4	76.4	70.4	78.7	77.0	Amériques		32.5	51.2	51.7	58.6	63.0	81.9	73.7	64.7	65.9
Northern America		6.5	6.3	14.9	28.9	26.6	27.5	26.7	31.5	36.0	Amérique du Nord		17.1	22.3	27.6	31.2	32.8	54.4	43.6	43.1	45.6
LAIA		9.4	13.9	21.3	8.7	19.9	18.7	17.1	18.2	9.8	ALAI		0.2	1.8	7.6	5.4	9.7	4.2	3.8	3.5	2.5
CACM		4.9	7.1	10.8	23.5	25.1	26.1	22.3	22.6	24.2	MCAC		8.5	19.0	13.8	19.3	17.6	21.3	23.9	16.3	15.3
Caribbean		3.8	1.4	1.2	0.8	0.4	0.5	0.3	0.6	0.8	Caraïbes		4.5	5.4	2.4	1.5	1.9	0.5	1.1	1.5	1.8
Rest of America		4.5	6.5	5.3	5.6	4.4	3.6	3.9	5.7	6.2	Autre Amérique		2.1	2.7	0.3	1.2	1.0	1.3	1.3	0.4	0.7
As.ex F.USSR		7.9	8.0	14.6	12.8	10.9	12.2	12.3	9.0	11.2	Asie l'URSS exclus		17.1	8.1	8.7	14.2	10.5	0.7	0.6	2.6	1.2
Eur.x F.USSR		33.1	31.1	21.1	16.2	10.9	10.0	14.3	11.1	11.0	Europe l'URSS exclus		49.1	36.8	34.8	27.1	26.2	17.0	25.2	32.6	32.9
EU		22.1	21.2	14.9	14.2	9.6	8.6	11.8	10.1	10.3	UE		42.5	33.5	33.3	26.2	25.7	16.6	24.3	31.8	32.0
EFTA		3.6	3.1	1.2	1.4	0.9	1.0	0.8	0.7	0.5	AELE			0.0	1.1	0.0	0.5	0.3	0.9	0.8	0.3
East Europe		7.4	6.7	5.0	0.6	0.4	0.4	0.5	0.3	0.1	Europe de l'Est		6.6	3.2	0.4	0.2	0.1	0.2	0.1	0.0	0.6
Other Europe		0.0	0.0	0.0	0.0		0.0	1.3	0.0	0.0	Autre de l'Europe					0.7			0.0	0.0	0.0
Former USSR		29.8	25.4	10.1	3.4	1.5	0.7	2.5	0.7	0.3	Ancienne URSS		1.3	4.0	3.5	0.0	0.1	0.4	0.5	0.1	0.0
Oceania		0.0	0.0	0.0	0.0	0.3	0.5	0.4	0.4	0.4	Océanie					0.1	0.1	0.1	0.0	0.0	0.0
USA/Etats–Unis d'Amer		2.6	3.7	12.2	25.6	25.6	26.6	25.2	30.2	33.9	USA/Etats–Unis d'Amer		0.0	0.1	6.6	20.0	26.0	43.8	42.8	42.1	44.9
Venezuela		0.1	0.2	9.8	1.8	13.7	12.4	11.9	13.0	1.8	Germany/Allemagne		20.5	15.6	12.9	11.4	11.0	9.1	12.6	11.4	9.2
Costa Rica		1.7	3.0	4.0	9.8	9.9	10.3	8.0	8.1	8.4	El Salvador		1.3	4.2	2.8	7.2	5.8	5.7	10.6	8.1	8.8
Guatemala		2.2	2.7	4.6	8.6	7.6	8.9	8.1	7.9	8.4	Spain/Espagne		4.9	3.1	3.6	1.0	2.1	0.9	3.9	7.8	11.1
Japan/Japon		3.4	5.1	7.1	6.6	6.0	8.0	7.2	5.0	7.7	Costa Rica		4.0	6.6	4.6	4.5	7.3	8.6	7.3	3.4	2.0
Panama		4.5	6.4	5.3	5.6	4.4	3.6	3.9	5.6	6.2	Belgium–Luxembourg		10.6	10.4	11.2	11.3	9.0	1.8	2.8	3.4	2.5
El Salvador		0.9	0.9	1.7	3.8	5.5	4.6	4.0	4.0	4.3	Honduras		0.8	3.9	2.6	3.3	2.3	4.3	3.6	2.8	3.0
Mexico/Mexique		1.8	2.1	2.6	2.1	3.1	3.8	3.2	3.1	5.1	Canada		17.1	22.2	21.0	11.2	6.8	10.6	0.8	1.0	0.7
Germany/Allemagne		3.5	2.6	2.5	3.6	2.8	2.5	2.7	2.2	2.3	Mexico/Mexique		0.1	1.7	6.1	4.9	5.8	3.8	3.1	1.8	1.7
Honduras		0.2	0.4	0.6	1.3	2.1	2.4	2.1	2.6	3.0	Netherlands/Pays–Bas		3.0	1.4	1.3	1.2	2.0	2.1	0.9	3.3	2.5

4. Special Imports C.I.F. by Commodities according to the S.I.T.C. (Rev. 2) in thousand U.S. Dollars
Importations Spéciales C.A.F. par Produits d'après la C.T.C.I. (Rév. 2) en milliers de Dollars E.U.

SITC CTCI	COMMODITY	1993			1994			1995			1996			PRODUIT
		WEIGHT POIDS		VALUE VALEUR	WEIGHT POIDS		VALUE VALEUR	WEIGHT POIDS		VALUE VALEUR	WEIGHT POIDS		VALUE VALEUR	
	ALL COMMODITIES			755121			852466			1009211			1076154	TOUS PRODUITS
0	FOOD AND LIVE ANIMALS			126287			122463			138798			152356	ALIMENTS,ANIMAUX VIVANTS
01	MEAT AND PREPARATIONS			2748			2197			1650			1718	VIANDES ET PREPARATIONS
02	DAIRY PRODCTS,BIRDS'EGGS			16898			15328			18849			11486	PRODUITS LAITIERS,OEUFS
022	MILK AND CREAM	W	5500	13552	W	5715	11281	W	6106	13835	W	2602	5830	LAIT ET CREME
0224	MILK,CREAM PRESERVED ETC	W	5111	13065	W	5576	11162	W	6053	13793	W	2557	5786	LAIT,CREME CONS,CONC
02242	MILK DRY,1.5% FAT OR LES	W	1024	2704	W	2251	4281	W	1351	3239	W	867	2179	LAIT POUDRE INF 1.5%
02243	MILK DRY,OVER 1.5% FAT	W	3604	9789	W	3016	6504	W	4413	10206	W	1162	3050	LAIT POUDRE SUP 1.5%
025	EGGS,BIRDS,FRESH,PRSRVD	W	1118	2953	W	1114	3109	W	1244	3547	W	1137	3426	OEUFS
0251	— IN SHELL	W	1115	2951	W	1106	3086	W	1242	3543	W	1130	3398	OEUFS EN COQUILLE
04	CEREALS AND PREPARATIONS			45282			58332			60960			84867	CEREALES ET PRODUITS
041	WHEAT ETC UNMILLED	W	78014	14038	W	91900	14865	W	89369	17663	W	103338	26336	FROMENT,EPEAUTRE
0411	DURUM WHEAT UNMILLED	W	18543	3308	W	36385	5900	W	89369	17663	W	49828	13300	FROMENT DUR NON MOULU
0412	OTHER WHEAT ETC UNMILLED	W	59471	10730	W	55515	8966				W	53510	13036	AUTRE FROMENT NON MOULU
042	RICE	W	48270	15483	W	46648	24150	W	53299	21815	W	70014	32447	RIZ
0421	RICE IN HUSK OR HUSKED	W	33672	11793	W	13047	8254	W	4659	1635	W	12129	3789	RIZ SANS AUTRE PREPARATION
04211	RICE IN THE HUSK	W	20479	7298	W	4571	1993	W	1156	395	W	12066	3778	RIZ PADDY
04212	RICE HUSKED	W	13192	4495	W	8476	6261	W	3503	1240	W	63	12	RIZ CARGO
0422	RICE SEMI–MILLED,MILLED	W	14598	3690	W	33601	15896	W	48639	20180	W	57885	28657	RIZ POLI,GLACE INCL BRISURES
04221	RICE MILLED UNBROKEN	W	11010	3153	W	32713	15612	W	44120	19077	W	54391	28017	RIZ POLI,GLACE EXCL BRISURES
044	MAIZE UNMILLED	W	5183	883	W	35411	4986	W	32381	3157	W	18865	3944	MAIS NON MOULU
047	OTHER CEREAL MEALS,FLOUR	W	1703	928	W	3320	1474	W	6836	2749	W	11538	5524	AUTRES SEMOULES,FARINES
04701	CEREAL FLOUR(NON–WHEAT)	W	1689	913	W	3294	1450	W	6787	2730	W	11478	5490	FARINES DE CEREALES
048	CEREAL ETC PREPARATIONS	W	12611	12374	W	12229	11784	W	14879	14634	W	13726	14048	PREPTNS A BASE CEREALES
0481	PREPD BREAKFAST FOOD ETC	W	2098	2809	W	2557	3357	W	3567	3866	W	2925	3133	CEREALES TRAVAILLEES
04812	CEREAL ROASTED, PUFFED	W	1346	2157	W	1867	2963	W	2165	3231	W	1420	2375	PRODTS BASE CEREALES
0484	BAKERY PRODUCTS	W	1931	2487	W	2058	1854	W	2867	2313	W	3288	3186	PRODUITS DE BOULANGERIE
0488	OTH CEREAL PREPS,MALT EX	W	1608	4268	W	1528	3827	W	1878	4983	W	1580	4225	EXTRAITS DE MALT
05	VEGETABLES AND FRUIT			20290			14868			15934			16817	LEGUMES ET FRUITS
054	VEG ETC FRSH,SMPLY PRSVD	W	36913	12972	W	23863	8776	W	28193	10378	W	25366	10103	LEGUMES FRAIS,CONG,SECS
0541	POTATOES FRSH EXCL SWEET	W	10960	2532	W	12896	3669	W	14673	4332	W	12478	3579	POMMES DE TERRE
0542	LEGUMINOUS VEGETBLES DRY	W	8560	4629	W	2867	1751	W	4158	1539	W	3593	2004	LEGUMES A COSSE SECS
0545	OTHER FRESH VEGETABLES	W	15580	4345	W	7483	2812	W	8828	3907	W	7570	3120	AUTRES LEGUMES FRAIS,REF
05459	FRESH VEGETABLES NES	W	11296	3217	W	4110	1429	W	3714	2137	W	3080	1773	LEGUMES FRAIS,REFRI NDA
057	FRUIT,NUTS,FRESH,DRIED			3946	W	9925	2494	W	8769	2372	W	11361	2821	FRUITS FRAIS OU SECS
058	FRUIT PRESERVED,PREPARED	W	3605	2845	W	2766	2419	W	2644	2596	W	3974	3216	CONSERVES DE FRUITS
06	SUGAR AND PREPS,HONEY			10155			3008			2765			3120	SUCRES ET PRODUITS
061	SUGAR AND HONEY	W	19914	7221	W	686	468	W	637	445	W	537	376	SUCRES ET MIEL
0611	RAW BEET AND CANE SUGAR	W	5489	2677	W	387	152	W	4	3	W	41	21	SUCRES BRUTS
0612	REFINED SUGAR ETC	W	14311	4412	W	58	37	W	141	57	W	6	11	SUCRES RAFFINES
062	SUGAR CANDY NON–CHOCLATE	W	3741	2934	W	4205	2540	W	4284	2321	W	2685	2744	SUCRERIES
07	COFFEE,TEA,COCOA,SPICES			2973			1474			1898			2074	CAFE,THE,CACAO,EPICES
081	*FEEDING STUFF FOR ANIML	W	16677	5281	W	17746	5387	W	12942	5023	W	15007	5533	NOURRITURE POUR ANIMAUX
0813	OILCAKE AND OTH RESIDUES	W	15858	4471	W	17003	4838	W	11730	3293	W	13444	4609	TOURTEAUX
08131	— OF SOYA BEANS	W	15837	4462	W	17003	4838	W	10956	3089	W	13424	4605	TOURTEAUX DE SOJA
09	MISC EDIBLE PRODUCTS			20147			19332			28785			23311	PREP ALIMENTAIRES DIVERSES
091	MARGARINE AND SHORTENING	W	1904	1755	W	1288	1289	W	16587	9209	W	1547	1479	MARGARINE ET GRAISSES
0913	PIG,POULTRY FAT RENDERED	W	350	240				W	15242	7884				SAINDOUX
098	EDIBLE PRODCTS,PREPS NES	W	7703	18392	W	7017	18043	W	8476	19577	W	8465	21832	PREP ALIMENTAIRES NDA
09804	SAUCES,MIXED SEASONINGS	W	3631	3603	W	3286	3157	W	4599	4813	W	3971	4602	SAUCES,ASSAISONNEMENTS
09805	SOUPS AND BROTHS	W	1630	3303	W	1229	2792	W	1324	2759	W	1449	3011	SOUPES,POTAGES,BOUILLONS
09809	MISC FOOD PREPRTIONS NES	W	1427	10129	W	1423	10772	W	1390	10552	W	1604	12306	PREP ALIMENTAIRES NDA
1	BEVERAGES AND TOBACCO			5659			5021			5665			8251	BOISSONS ET TABACS
11	BEVERAGES			3641			1812			3171			3171	BOISSONS
112	ALCOHOLIC BEVERAGES	W	2762	2797	W	955	1365	W	1281	1957	W	1287	1843	BOISSONS ALCOOLIQUES
12	TOBACCO AND MANUFACTURES			2018			3209			2494			5079	TABACS BRUTS FABRIQUES
121	TOBACCO UNMNFCTRD,REFUSE	W	461	1324	W	1111	3112	W	791	2304	W	1844	4884	TABACS BRUTS,DECHETS
1212	TOBACCO STRIPPED OR PART	W	64	255	W	843	2588	W	624	2043	W	1666	4532	TABACS PART ECOTES
2	CRUDE MATERLS,EXCL FUELS			8282			11993			13857			13690	MAT BRUTES NON COMESTIBLES
26	TEXTILE FIBRES AND WASTE			3950			5098			6222			7637	FIBRES TEXTILES
269	WASTE OF TEXTILE FABRICS	W	2083	3514	W	3491	4224	W	4326	4693	W	4753	5745	FRIPERIE DRILLES,CHIFFONS
26901	BULK TEXT WSTE,OLD CLTHG	W	809	1860	W	1822	2714	W	2229	2853	W	1859	2693	ART ET ACCESS D'HABILLEMENT
3	MINERAL FUELS ETC			105256			109205			181052			97377	COMBUSTIBLES MINERAUX LUB
33	PETROLEUM AND PRODUCTS			103896			106872			176763			92391	PETROLE ET DERIVES
333	CRUDE PETROLEUM			86957	W	604171	85375	W	762808	136033	W	277039	42996	HUILES BRUTES DE PETROLE
334	PETROLEUM PRODUCTS,REFIN	W	69430	16494	W	97353	20946	W	211909	40134	W	284790	48563	PRODUITS RAFFINES
3341	GASOLINE,OTH LIGHT OILS	W	5799	1375	W	8957	2799	W	32272	6339	W	9697	2939	ESSENCES POUR MOTEURS
33411	MOTOR,AVIATION SPIRIT	W	5799	1375	W	8957	2799	W	32272	6339	W	9695	2934	ESSENCES MOTEURS D'AVIONS
3343	GAS OILS	W	54017	10115	W	78719	11353	W	146936	22468	W	169378	27693	GAS OILS
3344	FUEL OILS,NES	W	4680	1045	W	405	283	W	21650	3554	W	95008	10679	FUEL OILS
3345	LUBS,PETROLEUM OILS NES	W	4930	3954	W	9272	6511	W	11046	7760	W	10707	7252	HUILES LUBRIFIANTES
33451	LUBS(HIGH PETR CONT) ETC	W	4769	3699	W	9171	6332	W	10853	7478	W	10555	7022	HUILES LUBRIF,H LOURDES
341	*GAS,NATURAL AND MANUFCT	W	3812	1357	W	7591	2285	W	13719	4285	W	14297	4952	GAZ NATUREL,GAZ MANUFACT
3413	PETROLM GASES,LIQUEFIED	W	3812	1356	W	7591	2283	W	13719	4283	W	14297	4952	GAZ DE PETROLE LIQUEFIE
34131	LIQUEFIED PROPANE,BUTANE	W	3808	1353	W	7591	2282	W	13718	4281	W	6866	2479	PROPANE,BUTANE LIQUEFIES
4	ANIMAL,VEGETABLE OIL,FAT			29772			37079			34329			39235	HUILES,GRAISSES ANIM,VEG
411	*ANIMAL OILS AND FATS	W	17111	7353	W	13398	6383	W	259	134	W	13550	7109	HUILES,GRAISSES ANIMALES
4113	ANIML OIL,FAT,GREASE NES	W	17109	7350	W	13397	6379	W	253	122	W	13536	7103	HUILES,GRAISSES ANIMALES NDA
41132	FATS OF BOVINE,SHEEP,ETC	W	16724	7142	W	12997	6198	W	91	36	W	13533	7098	SUIFS BRUTS FONDUS
42	FIXED VEGETABLE OIL,FAT			20674			28520			30371			24660	HUILES VEGETALES FIXES
423	FIXED VEG OILS,SOFT	W	33107	17699	W	28240	18630	W	31814	24891	W	18445	13510	HUILES VEGET DOUCES FIXES
4232	SOYA BEAN OIL	W	20474	10486	W	11182	6680	W	8840	6355	W	6165	4757	HUILE DE SOJA
4233	COTTON SEED OIL	W	5556	3304	W	10552	6486	W	15157	11451	W	9111	6535	HUILE DE COTON
4234	GROUNDNUT(PEANUT) OIL	W	5467	2698	W	1	1	W	5	10				HUILE D'ARACHIDE
4236	SUNFLOWER SEED OIL	W	942	579	W	5586	4620	W	7312	6706	W	499	508	HUILE DE TOURNESOL
424	FIXED VEG OIL NONSOFT	W	5938	2975	W	19440	9890	W	8009	5480	W	18752	11149	AUTRES HUILES VEG FIXES
4242	PALM OIL	W	3743	1791	W	14798	7451	W	4752	3376	W	15781	9520	HUILE DE PALME
431	*PROCESD ANML VEG OIL,ET	W	2762	1745	W	3207	2176	W	6224	3824	W	11120	7467	HUILES,GRAISSES PREPAREES
4313	FATTY ACIDS ETC,RESIDUES	W	67	10	W	576	153	W	4360	2168	W	8479	5195	ACIDES GRAS INDUST,RESIDUS
43131	FATTY ACIDS,ACID OILS	W	7	6	W	476	147	W	4320	2165	W	8479	5195	ACIDES GRAS INDUSTRIELS
5	CHEMCLS,RELATED PROD NES			113637			137008			172178			197231	PRODUITS CHIMIQUES
51	ORGANIC CHEMICALS			3492			4678			5822			5202	PROD CHIMIQ ORGANIQUES
52	INORGANIC CHEMICALS			5770			5766			7208			6615	PROD CHIM INORGANIQUES
522	INORG ELEMNTS,OXIDES,ETC	W	10049	3086	W	9367	3003	W	8661	3757	W	29828	2929	ELEMENTS INORGANIQUES
523	OTHR INORG CHEMICALS ETC			2679	W	7369	2732	W	8696	3452	W	8793	3683	AUT PRODUITS CHIMIQUES INORG
53	DYES,TANNING,COLOUR PROD			4160			4342			7075			10653	PROD TEINTURE,COLORANTS
533	PIGMENTS,PAINTS,ETC	W	2078	3458	W	2508	3655	W	3046	5585	W	3253	7996	PIGMENTS,PEINTURES,VERNIS
5334	VARNISHES,DISTEMPERS ETC	W	1748	2807	W	1962	2708	W	2028	2724	W	2175	3288	PEINTURES A L'EAU
541	*MEDICINAL,PHARM PRODUCT			44703	K	3669680	51056	K	4653702	53232	K	6548036	74937	PROD MEDICINAUX PHARMACEUT
5416	GLYCOSIDES,GLANDS,SERA	K	707850	2430	K	539174	2838	K	1661632	3064	K	2860904	3960	HETEROSIDES
54164	ANTISERA,MICROB VACCINES	K	652960	1851	K	278803	1950	K	1307131	2248	K	2139264	3462	SERUMS,VACCINS

4. Special Imports C.I.F. by Commodities according to the S.I.T.C. (Rev. 2) in thousand U.S. Dollars
Importations Spéciales C.A.F. par Produits d'après la C.T.C.I. (Rév. 2) en milliers de Dollars E.U.

SITC CTCI	COMMODITY	1993			1994			1995			1996			PRODUIT
			WEIGHT POIDS	VALUE VALEUR		WEIGHT POIDS	VALUE VALEUR		WEIGHT POIDS	VALUE VALEUR		WEIGHT POIDS	VALUE VALEUR	
5417	MEDICAMENTS	K	2532706	37015	K	2547642	43899	K	2348414	44346	K	3084179	64257	MEDICAMENTS
54171	— CONTAINNG ANTIBIOTICS	K	331916	6202	K	414497	5703	K	314816	6848	K	429920	6374	MED CONTN ANTIBIOTIQUES
54172	— CONTAINING HORMONES	K	121500	2728	K	149933	3383	K	162169	4141	K	111723	3386	MED CONTENANT HORMONES
54179	— CONTNG OTH SUBSTANCES	K	2078210	28037	K	1890524	33821	K	1859961	33148	K	2533178	54281	MED CONT AUT SUBSTANCES
5419	PHARMACEUTICAL GOODS NES	K	337270	3653	K	188007	2293	K	221199	3355	K	287311	4403	PREP,ART PHARMACEUTIQUES
54199	OTH PHARMACEUTICAL GOODS	K	109060	1787	K	72612	1553	K	79544	2600	K	99148	3302	AUT PREP PHARMACEUTIQUES
55	PERFUME,CLEANING ETC PRD			14838			16461			22036			25633	PROD POUR PARFUM,TOILETTE
553	PERFUMERY,COSMETICS,ETC	W	3129	6123	W	3331	6448	W	4324	8831	W	4796	10130	PRODUITS DE PARFUMERIE
554	SOAP,CLEANSING ETC PREPS	W	8934	8023	W	9285	8424	W	11127	11494	W	14767	13784	SAVONS,PRODUITS DETERSIFS
5541	SOAPS	W	6404	4888	W	6672	4899	W	7321	6458	W	10523	8029	SAVONS,PROD TENSIO–ACTIFS
5542	WASHING PREPARATIONS ETC	W	2110	2365	W	2154	2757	W	3342	4270	W	3694	4775	PROD ORG TENSIO–ACT NDA
562	*FERTILIZERS,MANUFACTURE	W	47310	7911	W	65989	18276	W	78953	18996	W	68407	17690	ENGRAIS MANUFACTURES
5621	CHEM NITROGENOUS FERTLZR	W	39979	6385	W	43956	13523	W	52834	12530	W	51469	13520	ENGRAIS AZOTES
56216	UREA	W	38638	6111	W	43118	13314	W	44801	11244	W	39581	10641	UREE
5629	FERTILIZERS NES	W	6819	1415	W	17355	3873	W	20456	5391	W	13518	3570	ENGRAIS NDA
56292	NITROG–PHOS FERTILZR NES				W	16521	3536	W	14596	3585	W	7885	2066	ENGRAIS NDA CONT N P
58	PLASTIC MATERIALS ETC			13340			14182			31175			31040	MAT PLAST ARTIFICIELLES
582	PROD OF CONDENSATION ETC	W	1491	1769	W	3220	3397	W	10601	14316	W	11502	11354	PROD CONDENS,POLYCOND
5822	AMINOPLASTS	W	267	337	W	2057	1787	W	8899	9204	W	10350	7875	AMINOPLASTES
58221	— IN PRIMARY FORMS	W	267	337	W	2057	1787	W	8899	9204	W	10350	7875	AMINOPLASTES PRIMAIRES
5823	ALKYDS,OTHER POLYESTERS	W	548	600	W	905	1075	W	1401	4479	W	968	2262	ALKYDES ET AUT POLYESTERS
58231	— IN PRIMARY FORMS	W	548	588	W	905	1075	W	1401	4479	W	962	2236	SOUS FORMES PRIMAIRES
583	POLYMERIZATION ETC PRODS	W	6848	7855	W	9014	9412	W	12661	15566	W	14319	16630	PROD POLYMERISATION
5831	POLYETHYLENE	W	3868	3652	W	6337	5658	W	7338	8212	W	7661	7859	POLYETHYLENE
58311	— IN PRIMARY FORMS	W	3618	3047	W	5639	4492	W	6661	6655	W	6512	5872	POLYETHYLENE PRIMAIRES
585	PLASTIC MATERIAL NES	W	3360	2357	W	10	5							RESINES ARTIFICIELLES
5852	OTH ART PLASTIC MTLS NES	W	3360	2357	W	10	5							AUT MAT PLAST ARTIFICIEL
58522	ALGINIC ACID,SALTS,ESTRS	W	3358	2354										ACIDE ALGINIQUE
59	CHEMICAL MATERIALS NES			18951			21675			25827			24446	MAT PROD CHIMIQUES NDA
591	PESTICIDES,DISINFECTANTS	W	3334	13085	W	3811	15479	W	4446	19852	W	4701	18274	DESINF,INSECT,FONG,HERB
5911	INSECTICIDES,FOR RETAIL	W	791	3953	W	939	4142	W	1358	6058	W	1592	5606	INSECTICIDES VENTE DET
5912	FUNGICIDES,FOR RETAIL	W	315	1988	W	424	3059	W	572	4632	W	791	4377	FONGICIDES VENTE AU DET
5913	HERBICIDES,FOR RETAIL	W	1542	5918	W	1440	6963	W	1541	7974	W	1344	7075	HERBICIDES VENTE AU DET
598	MISCEL CHEM PRODUCTS NES	W	3111	4952	W	2768	4380	W	3007	4484	W	2646	4412	PROD DIV INDUST CHIM NDA
5989	CHEM PRODUCTS,PREPS NES	W	2404	3010	W	2246	3007	W	2350	3342	W	2118	3598	PROD PREP CHIMIQUES NDA
59899	OTH CHEM PRODS,PREPS,NES	W	1834	2268	W	1891	2489	W	1939	2362	W	1680	2761	AUT PRODUITS CHIMIQUES NDA
6	BASIC MANUFACTURES			106754			136646			150309			179127	ART MANUFACTURES
62	RUBBER MANUFACTURES NES			12249			15812			19850			20792	CAOUTCHOUC MANUFACTURE
625	RUBBER TYRES, TUBES ETC	W	3992	9484	W	6038	13109	W	6865	16771	W	6716	17392	PNEUS CAOUTCHOUC VULCANISE
6251	TYRES NEW FOR MOTOR CARS	W	1026	2643	W	1031	2943	W	1094	3487	W	1093	3570	PNEUS POUR VOITURES
6252	TYRES,NEW,BUS OR LORRY	W	1493	4239	W	2255	5626	W	2238	7641	W	2323	8129	PNEUS POUR AUTOBUS,CAMIONS
6259	OTH TYRES,TYRE CASES,ETC	W	1318	2231	W	2549	4085	W	3344	5268	W	3038	5223	AUTRES PNEUS RECHAPES FLAPS
62599	TYRES NES,TYRE CASES,ETC	W	1112	1695	W	2317	3544	W	3102	4593	W	2731	4513	PNEUS,FLAPS
64	PAPER,PAPERBOARD AND MFR			20248			19265			25574			31820	PAPIERS,CARTONS & OUVRAGES
641	PAPER AND PAPERBOARD	W	12921	10189	W	13566	9525	W	9338	11110	W	14859	14994	PAPIERS ET CARTONS
6415	PAPER,PAPERBRD,BULK,NES	W	3115	2177	W	5806	3248	W	2919	3642	W	5569	4871	PAPIERS,CARTONS ROULEAUX
64159	OTHER PAPER ETC,BULK,NES	W	3094	2118	W	5759	3140	W	2824	3468	W	5529	4768	AUT PAPIER ROULEAUX FEUILLES
642	PAPER,ETC,PRECUT,ARTS OF	W	5851	10058	W	6269	9740	W	9002	14464	W	10494	16827	PAP,CARTONS DECOUPES
6421	PAPER ETC CONTAINERS	W	1854	2613	W	1688	2513	W	3779	5807	W	5250	7168	BOITES,SACS EMBALLAGES
6423	EXERCISE BOOKS ETC	W	1067	2340	W	1533	2139	W	1941	2792	W	2258	3154	REGISTRES,CAHIERS,CARNETS
6424	PAPER ETC CT TO SIZE NES	W	2149	3109	W	2140	2764	W	2156	2909	W	1945	3554	PAP,CARTONS DECOUPES
64243	TOILET PAPER CUT TO SIZE	W	1905	2330	W	1880	1904	W	1937	2201	W	1668	2533	PAPIER HYGIENIQUE
65	TEXTILE YARN,FABRICS,ETC			11359			12841			13207			12851	FILS,TISSUS,ARTICLES TEXTILE
653	WOVN MAN–MADE FIB FABRIC	W	1841	6529	W	3303	7313	W	2679	7545	W	3067	5822	TISSUS FIBRES SYNTH,ARTIF
6531	CONT SYNT WEAVES NONPILE	W	1693	6065	W	3215	6823	W	2299	5286	W	2605	3433	TISSUS FIBRES SYNTH CONTINUE
65315	CONT SYN TXTL FABRIC NES	W	1651	5703	W	3191	6716	W	2257	5096	W	2590	3370	TIS PLUS 85% TEXT SYNT CONT
66	NONMETAL MINERAL MFS NES			15268			15342			17210			23815	ART MIN NON METALLIQUES
661	LIME,CEMENT,BLDG PRODS			2048	W	5952	2689	W	15467	4834	W	6350	3893	CHAUX,CIMENTS MAT CONSTR
6612	CEMENT	W	1110	799	W	2724	1597	W	6275	3204	W	3996	2132	CIMENTS HYDRAULIQUES
665	GLASSWARE	W	14318	9037	W	12495	7699	W	8966	5965	W	21181	12459	OUVRAGES EN VERRE
6651	BOTTLES ETC OF GLASS	W	13002	7298	W	11149	6292	W	7955	4557	W	19877	10855	RECIPIENTS EN VERRE
66511	GLASS BOTTLES ETC NONVAC	W	13002	7298	W	11149	6292	W	7955	4557	W	19874	10835	BONBONNES,BOUTEILLES,ETC
67	IRON AND STEEL			22977			42445			38519			49210	FER ET ACIER
672	IRON,STEEL PRIMARY FORMS	W	3090	719	W	5422	1664	W	2479	1386	W	8168	3589	LINGOTS FER,ACIER
6727	IRN,STL COIL FR REROLLNG	W	1565	308	W	2174	922	W	2371	1351	W	7030	3246	EBAUCHES POUR TOLES FER
67271	IRON,SIMPLE STEEL COILS	W	450	171	W	780	311	W	1869	996	W	7011	3239	EBAUCHES NON EN ACIER
673	IRON,STEEL SHAPES ETC	W	17232	7626	W	24868	10239	W	29067	13007	W	28963	11894	BARRES,PROFIL FER,ACIER
6731	IRON,STEEL WIRE ROD	W	4975	1708	W	11928	4128	W	11122	3954	W	14908	5106	FIL MACHINE FER,ACIER
67315	OTHER ALLOY STL WIRE ROD	W	2955	1009	W	11181	3870	W	9354	3350	W	11923	4063	FIL MACH NON ACIERS ALL
6732	IRON,STEEL BARS ETC	W	9738	4436	W	10343	4639	W	12926	5721	W	11351	5092	BARRES FER,ACIER
67326	IRN,OTH STL BARS HOTROLD	W	6068	2620	W	8906	3894	W	11675	5076	W	10120	4033	BARRES PLEINES FER,ACIER
6733	IRON,STEEL PROFILES ETC	W	2519	1482	W	2597	1472	W	5019	3332	W	2704	1697	PROFILES,PALPLAN FER,ACIER
674	IRN,STL UNIV,PLATE,SHEET	W	12062	9120	W	22091	16714	W	19645	14482	W	22863	19937	LARGES PLATS,TOLES
6746	IRN,STL THIN PLATE,ROLLD	W	1138	419	W	3863	2577	W	5329	4083	W	6400	4734	TOLES LAM MOINS 3MM
67461	— OF IRON OR SIMPLE STL	W	98	51	W	2771	1961	W	3993	3163	W	5921	4285	TOL NON AC FIN MOINS 3 MM
6749	OTH IRN,STL PLATES,SHEET	W	9143	7763	W	11724	11185	W	9508	7962	W	11530	12304	AUTRES TOLES FER,ACIER
67491	— OF IRON OR SIMPLE STL	W	9122	7717	W	11638	11129	W	9084	7676	W	11442	12227	AUT TOLES AUTRES ACIER FIN
678	IRON,STL TUBES,PIPES,ETC	W	3892	4315	W	11293	12715	W	5882	7951	W	8906	12224	TUBES,TUYAUX EN FONTE,FER
6783	IRON,STL TUBES,PIPES NES	W	3158	2774	W	9327	8430	W	4933	5486	W	6818	8590	AUT TUBES,TUYAUX FER,ACIER
68	NON–FERROUS METALS			2272			3116			3636			4820	METAUX NON FERREUX
684	ALUMINIUM	W	562	1454	W	1020	1803	W	678	2289	W	1100	3961	ALUMINIUM
6842	ALUMINIUM,ALLOYS WORKED	W	378	1295	W	391	1353	W	643	2204	W	1100	3961	ALUMINIUM,ALLIAGES OUVRE
69	METAL MANUFACTURES NES			20076			25228			29196			32384	ART MANUFACT EN METAL NDA
691	STRUCTURES AND PARTS NES	W	826	2164	W	3520	6957	W	1186	5147	W	1069	2506	CONSTRUCT FER,ACIER,ALU
6911	STRUCTURES,PARTS IRN,STL	W	619	1791	W	3410	6726	W	1109	4902	W	1005	2287	CONSTRUCT FER,ACIER,FONTE
693	WIRE PRODUCTS NON ELECTR	W	903	1174	W	809	1305	W	1475	2709	W	1891	3957	OUVRAGES FILS METALLIQUES
695	TOOLS			3979	W	741	3648	W	781	3817	W	1031	4761	OUTILS A MAIN
697	BASE MTL HOUSEHOLD EQUIP	W	806	2409	W	802	2531	W	1087	3249	W	1376	4286	ART MENAGE MET COMMUNS
699	BASE METAL MFRS NES	W	2012	5232	W	2683	6197	W	2858	7627	W	3249	9857	ART MANUFACTURES MET NDA
6996	BASE MTL MISC ARTICLES	W	1408	2641	W	1822	3190	W	1664	3025	W	1879	3443	ART DIVERS METAUX COMMUNS
7	MACHINES,TRANSPORT EQUIP			196805			224666			232357			287175	MACHINES MATERIEL TRANSPORT
71	POWER GENERATING EQUIPMT			8790			19302			19465			15962	MACHINES GENERATRICES
711	STEAM BOILERS & AUX PLNT	W	102	714	W	71	816	W	300	5514	W	149	2000	GENERATEURS VAPEUR EAU ETC
7119	PTS NES OF APP OF 711	W	8	151	W	36	611	W	231	5034	W	50	1406	PART,PIECES POUR 711
71191	PTS NES OF BOILERS	W	7	139	W	34	553	W	226	4792	W	49	1393	PART,PIECES POUR 711.1
712	STEAM ENGINES,TURBINES	W	35	568	W	271	6410	W	2	48	W	1	31	MACHINES A VAPEUR D'EAU PIEC
7129	STM ENGINE ETC PARTS NES	W	2	163	W	269	6391				W	1	31	PARTIES,PIECES DU 712.6
713	INTRNL COMBUS PSTN ENGIN	W	458	3924	W	432	3087	W	528	5194	W	648	5831	MOTEURS EXPL COMB INT, PIECE
7139	PISTON ENGINE PARTS NES	W	95	1494	W	158	2068	W	259	3842	W	320	3894	PIECES POUR 713.2,3,8
716	ROTATING ELECTRIC PLANT	W	324	3249	W	644	6892	W	955	8217	W	500	5879	APP ELECTR ROTATIFS,PIECES
7162	AC MTRS,GENRTRS,GEN SETS	W	284	2606	W	519	5324	W	613	4304	W	390	4445	MOTEURS ELECTRIQUES

4. Special Imports C.I.F. by Commodities according to the S.I.T.C. (Rev. 2) in thousand U.S. Dollars
Importations Spéciales C.A.F. par Produits d'après la C.T.C.I. (Rév. 2) en milliers de Dollars E.U.

SITC CTCI	COMMODITY	1993 WEIGHT POIDS	1993 VALUE VALEUR	1994 WEIGHT POIDS	1994 VALUE VALEUR	1995 WEIGHT POIDS	1995 VALUE VALEUR	1996 WEIGHT POIDS	1996 VALUE VALEUR	PRODUIT
71622	AC GENERATORS	W 42	468	W 319	3928	W 233	1897	W 157	2188	GENER COURANT ALTERNATIF
72	MACHS FOR SPCL INDUSTRYS		13115		36575		21845		35415	MAC SPECIALES POUR INDUST
721	AGRIC MACHY,EXC TRACTORS	W 628	3295	W 806	5087	W 1067	5130	W 1027	7578	MACHINES AGRICOLES
7212	HARVESTING ETC MACHINES	W 350	2215	W 383	3511	W 351	2308	W 525	4939	ENGINS POUR LA RECOLTE
722	TRACTORS NON–ROAD	W 496	1475	W 1100	3057	W 874	2411	W 587	2912	TRACTEURS
723	CIVIL ENGNEERG EQUIP ETC		2640	W 3934	22694	W 761	4479	W 1398	8397	APPAREILS DE GENIE CIVIL
7234	CONST,MINING MACHNRY NES	W 316	2520	W 3805	21662	W 704	4049	W 1064	6809	MACH POUR LA CONST, MINES
72342	SLFPRP SHOVELS,EXCAVATRS	W 52	193	W 391	2878	W 294	1429	W 252	1912	PELLES MECANIQUES
72343	SLFPRP CONST ETC MCH NES	W 160	1703	W 2972	15401	W 128	960	W 195	1463	AUT MACH EXTR,TERRASSEM
727	FOOD MACHRY NON–DOMESTIC	W 152	1335	W 132	939	W 278	2064	W 596	6387	MACH INDUSTRIES ALIMENT
7272	OTH FOOD PROC MCHY,PARTS	W 133	1260	W 100	702	W 183	1454	W 517	5314	AUT MACH IND ALIMENTAIRE
72722	INDUS FOOD PROC MACH NES	W 92	1185	W 59	547	W 133	1209	W 398	3620	MACHINES BOULANGERIE
728	OTH MACHY FOR SPCL INDUS	W 190	2062	W 348	2796	W 438	5483	W 1147	6538	AUT MACH IND PARTICULIERES
7284	MACHY FOR SPCL INDUS NES	W 97	957	W 109	1550	W 224	4492	W 132	2139	MACH SPEC IND PARTICUL.
74	GENRL INDUSTRL MACHY NES		25902		25397		38717		42770	MACH APP INDUSTRIE
741	HEATING,COOLING EQUIPMNT	W 782	5846	W 762	5557	W 1024	7522	W 1481	9441	MACH CHAUFFAGE,PIECES
7414	NONDOM REFRIG EQUIPT,PTS	W 226	1386	W 179	1150	W 364	2169	W 839	4897	MAT PRODUCTION DU FROID
74141	REFRIG EQUIP NONDOMESTIC	W 210	1248	W 124	672	W 248	1602	W 774	4477	REFIG INDUSTRIELS
742	PUMPS FOR LIQUIDS ETC	W 278	3835	W 360	4156	W 449	6886	W 547	9169	POMPES MOTO–POMPES
7428	OTHER PUMPS FOR LIQUIDS	W 246	2976	W 245	3041	W 378	5554	W 443	7637	AUTRES POMPES POUR LIQ
74288	PUMPS FR LIQUIDS NES ETC	W 188	2090	W 209	2464	W 354	5076	W 402	6846	POMPES POUR LIQUIDES NDA
743	PUMPS NES,CENTRFUGES ETC	W 465	4348	W 500	3464	W 711	5301	W 658	5194	POMPES COMPRES,VENT ETC
744	MECHANICAL HANDLING EQU	W 255	1211	W 472	3356	W 421	1834	W 584	3078	EQUIP MANUTENTION PIECES
745	NONELEC MACHY,TOOLS NES	W 513	5514	W 244	2850	W 456	6847	W 310	5386	AUT MACH NON ELEC,PIECES
7452	OTH NONELEC MCHS,PTS NES	W 464	4738	W 210	2230	W 405	5518	W 270	4182	AUT MACH NON ELEC,PIECES
74522	PACKAGNG,BOTTLNG,ETC MCH	W 277	3067	W 39	615	W 102	2119	W 55	868	MACH NETT BOUTEILLES,ETC
749	NONELEC MACH PTS,ACC NES	W 610	5147	W 751	6013	W 1261	10326	W 989	10501	PIECES MACH NON ELEC NDA
7492	COCKS,VALVES ETC NES	W 339	2347	W 476	2388	W 660	4647	W 434	3714	ART ROB,SIM POUR TUYAUX
75	OFFICE MACHNES,ADP EQUIP		12377		14033		16486		21312	MACH BUREAU TRAIT AUTOM
751	OFFICE MACHINES	W 185	1980	W 164	1876	W 240	2834	W 294	3701	MACH,APPAREILS DE BUREAU
752	AUTOMTIC DATA PROC EQUIP	W 228	8533	W 292	8937	W 352	10507	W 405	13743	MACH TRAIT INFORMATION
7521	ANALOG,HYBRID COMPUTERS	W 80	3040	W 57	1117	W 51	888	W 41	1578	MACH POUR TRAIT INFORMAT
7522	DIGITAL COMPUTERS	W 99	4098	W 151	5575	W 159	6254	W 168	7309	MACH DIGITALES COMPLETES
7525	ADP PERIPHERAL UNITS	W 27	837	W 55	1248	W 101	2159	W 170	3654	UNITES PERIPHERIQUES
759	OFFICE,ADP MCH PTS,ACCES	W 114	1864	W 121	3220	W 101	3145	W 111	3868	PIECES DU 751 ET 752
7599	ACCTG,ETC,ADP MCH PTS,AC	W 37	920	W 74	2241	W 95	2982	W 108	3780	PIECES DU 751 ET 752
76	TELECOMM,SOUND EQUIPMENT		35208		28174		25194		26180	EQUIPMENT DE TELECOM
761	TELEVISION RECEIVERS	W 389	1411	W 343	1767	W 568	2785	W 611	3363	RECEPTEURS DE TELEVISION
762	RADIO BROADCAST RECEIVRS	W 303	1032	W 360	1440	W 594	2617	W 556	3819	RECEPTEURS RADIODIFFUSION
764	TELECOM EQPT,PTS,ACC NES	W 1219	32339	W 1032	24457	W 675	19038	W 628	18303	EQUIP TELECOM,PIECES
7641	LINE TELEPHONE,ETC EQUIP	W 584	21173	W 428	14672	W 388	14778	W 315	13533	APP TELEPHON PAR FIL
7643	TV,RADIO TRANSMITTRS ETC	W 284	6250	W 70	3348	W 40	1407	W 42	2007	APP EMET TELE RADIO
7649	PTS NES OF EQUIPMT OF 76	W 303	4223	W 468	5765	W 117	1966	W 121	1689	PIECES DE LA DIV 76
76491	PTS NES OF APPAR OF 7641	W 66	2342	W 358	3255	W 59	920	W 18	586	PIECES POUR 764.1
77	ELECTRIC MACHNRY NES ETC		32446		37321		40686		47428	MACH APP ELECT NDA
771	ELECTRIC POWER MACHY NES	W 355	1488	W 588	3926	W 858	5557	W 682	5121	MACH PROD,TRANS ELECTR
7711	TRANSFORMERS,ELECTRICAL	W 176	609	W 379	3179	W 678	4963	W 509	4206	TRANSFO ELECTRIQUES
77111	LIQUID DIELEC TRANSFRMRS	W 29	183	W 127	1601	W 278	3294	W 226	2950	TRANSFO DIELEC LIQUIDE
772	SWITCHGEAR ETC,PARTS NES		4163	W 733	5920	W 657	7359	W 899	11605	APP COUPURE,SECT ETC
7721	SWITCHGEAR ETC		4122	W 672	5662	W 652	7279	W 896	11521	APP COUPURE,SECTIONMNT
773	ELECTR DISTRIBUTNG EQUIP	W 1782	6903	W 1859	8094	W 1920	8526	W 2245	9040	EQUIPMT DISTRIBUTION ELECT
7731	INSULATED WIRE,CABLE ETC	W 1613	6305	W 1717	7625	W 1792	7963	W 1710	7837	FILS,CABLES ISOLES ELECT
774	ELECTRO–MEDCL,XRAY EQUIP	W 465	5976	W 241	3308	W 52	1586	W 102	1784	APPAREILS MEDICAUX
7741	ELECTRO–MEDICAL EQUIPMNT	W 345	3813	W 236	3181	W 46	1430	W 80	1294	APP ELECTRICITE MEDICALE
775	HOUSEHOLD TYPE EQUIP NES	W 1350	4582	W 1475	4879	W 1928	6662	W 2021	7096	MACH,APP USAGE DOMESTQUE
7752	DOM REFRIGERATRS,FREEZRS	W 659	2564	W 740	2831	W 941	3820	W 1108	4614	REFRIG,CONGEL MENAGER
77521	DOMESTIC REFRIGERATORS	W 585	2254	W 673	2502	W 819	3284	W 981	4046	REFRIGERATEURS
778	ELECTRICAL MACHINERY NES	W 2891	9084	W 3235	10672	W 3339	10699	W 3239	12037	AUTRES MACH ELECT NDA
7781	BATTERIES,ACCUMULATORS	W 1996	4452	W 2558	5963	W 2532	6130	W 2438	6101	PILES ET ACCUMULATEURS
77811	PRIMARY BATTERIES,CELLS	W 1607	3560	W 1936	4384	W 1798	4324	W 1381	3566	PILES ELECTRIQUES,PIECES
78	ROAD VEHICLES		66262		54821		66465		91460	VEHICULES ROUTIERS
781	PASS MOTOR VEH EXC BUSES	W 4138	22394	W 3076	16946	W 5258	29202	W 6526	39830	AUTO TRANSPORT PERSONNES
782	LORRIES,SPCL MTR VEH NES	W 5100	22083	W 4013	21208	W 5259	23500	W 6869	34956	VEHICULES SPECIAUX,MARCH
7821	LORRIES,TRUCKS	W 4764	18901	W 3383	13702	W 5011	22816	W 6181	31021	VEHICULES TRANSP MARCHAND
7822	SPECIAL MOTOR VEHCLS NES	W 337	3182	W 630	7506	W 247	684	W 687	3935	VEHICULES USAGES SPECIAUX
783	ROAD MOTOR VEHICLES NES	W 2436	10976	W 2143	7588	W 2591	4538	W 2949	5918	VEHICULES ROUTIERS NDA
7831	BUSES	W 2124	10165	W 1759	6683	W 1990	3223	W 2347	4823	VOITURES TRANSPORT COMMUN
784	MOTOR VEH PRTS,ACCES NES	W 364	3867	W 375	3698	W 538	4469	W 649	5694	PIECES 722,781,782,783
7849	OTHER MOTOR VEHCL PARTS	W 350	3763	W 369	3645	W 530	4401	W 621	5503	PIECES 722,781,782,783
785	CYCLES,ETC MOTRZD OR NOT	W 1356	4357	W 1196	4576	W 1108	3680	W 1180	3973	MOTOCYCLES SCOOTERS
786	TRAILERS,NONMOTR VEH,NES	W 638	2586	W 458	805	W 726	1076	W 511	1089	REMORQUES,CADRES,CONTAIN
7861	TRAILERS,TRANSP CONTAINR	W 446	2451	W 241	622	W 400	675	W 302	804	REMORQUES TOUS VEHICULES
78612	OTHER TRAILERS	W 408	2422	W 204	576	W 342	626	W 191	349	REMORQUES TRANSP MARCH
79	OTHR TRANSPORT EQUIPMENT		1694		8017		1340		4762	AUTRE MATERIEL TRANSPORT
793	SHIPS AND BOATS ETC	W 471	1561	W 2594	7874	W 739	1256	W 1820	4566	NAVIRES BATEAUX,ETC
7932	SHIPS AND BOATS NES	W 459	1472	W 2292	5088	W 725	1155	W 1810	4303	NAVIRES ET BATEAUX
79324	FISHING VESSELS ETC	W 248	560	W 2169	4730	W 642	451	W 1725	4025	BATEAUX DE PECHE
7938	TUGS,SPECIAL VESSELS ETC	W 12	85	W 302	2786	W 14	71	W 5	122	REMORQUEURS,BATEAUX SPEC
79382	SPECL PURPOSE VESSLS ETC			W 300	2749	W 10	46		13	BAT–PHARES,–POMPES,DRAGUES
8	MISC MANUFACTURED GOODS		62297		68105		80490		101201	ART MANUFACTURES DIVERS
821	*FURNITURE,PARTS THEREOF	W 1320	3614	W 1732	4028	W 2192	6100	W 2315	8695	MEUBLES ET PIECES
8212	MED FURN,STUFFD FURNSHGS	W 428	1460	W 654	1558	W 849	3142	W 940	5108	MOB MEDICO–CHIRUR,PIECES
82121	MEDICAL FURNITURE,PARTS	W 65	818	W 123	537	W 211	1945	W 217	3565	MOBILIER MED,TABLE OPER ETC
84	CLOTHING AND ACCESSORIES		11015		12060		11376		9224	VETEMENTS
846	UNDER GARMENTS KNITTED	W 599	2266	W 646	2216	W 697	2284	W 620	2079	SOUS VETS DE BONNETERIE
851	*FOOTWEAR	W 1828	3100	W 1898	4015	W 2196	4747	W 1976	4363	CHAUSSURES
87	PRECISION INSTRUMNTS NES		11003		8764		14455		18344	INSTRUM,APPAR SCIENT NDA
872	MEDICAL INSTRUMENTS NES	W 333	3575	W 317	3021	W 449	9255	W 598	7921	INSTR,APP MEDIC–CHIR NDA
87202	OTH MEDICAL INSTRUMENTS	W 328	3396	W 314	2859	W 400	9050	W 521	7725	INSTRUM,APP MEDECINE
873	METERS AND COUNTERS NES	W 125	1102	W 197	1312	W 131	1790	W 360	3873	COMPTEURS,INST DE MESURE
8731	GAS SUPPLY METERS ETC	W 125	1078	W 192	1252	W 130	1752	W 358	3830	COMPTEURS GAZ,LIQ ELECT
874	MEASURNG,CONTROLNG INSTR	W 303	6009	W 327	4201	W 226	3118	W 345	6200	INSTRUMENTS DE MESURE
88	PHOTO EQU,OPTICL GDS ETC		4121		4197		4992		4856	APP,FOURN PHOTO,OP,MONTR
882	PHOTO,CINEMA SUPPLIES	W 260	2640	W 258	2780	W 275	3008	W 284	2883	PRODUITS PHOTO,CINEMA
89	MISC MANUFCTRD GOODS NES		27850		32543		36056		52336	ART MANUFACTURES DIVERS
892	PRINTED MATTER	W 1372	8204	W 1713	9656	W 1441	9250	W 1658	11298	IMPRIMES
8921	PRINTED BOOKS,GLOBES,ETC	W 879	4787	W 1151	5844	W 822	4972	W 825	5688	LIVRES,BROCHURES,CARTES
89211	PRINTED BOOKS,PAMPHLETS	W 865	4762	W 1140	5800	W 687	4567	W 789	5507	LIVRES,BROCHURES
8928	PRINTED MATTER NES	W 377	2908	W 417	3086	W 450	3512	W 649	4895	IMPRIMES NDA
893	ARTICLES OF PLASTIC NES		11401		13243		14603		18895	OUVRAGES EN MAT DIVIS 58
8931	PLSTC PACKG CONTNRS,LIDS	W 2483	6218	W 2250	5983	W 2357	6422	W 4176	9125	ART TRANSP EMBALLAGE ETC

Nicaragua

4. Special Imports C.I.F. by Commodities according to the S.I.T.C. (Rev. 2) in thousand U.S. Dollars
Importations Spéciales C.A.F. par Produits d'après la C.T.C.I. (Rév. 2) en milliers de Dollars E.U.

SITC CTCI	COMMODITY	1993			1994			1995			1996			PRODUIT
		WEIGHT POIDS		VALUE VALEUR	WEIGHT POIDS		VALUE VALEUR	WEIGHT POIDS		VALUE VALEUR	WEIGHT POIDS		VALUE VALEUR	
8939	MISC PLASTIC ARTICLES	W	2750	5018	W	3404	7121	W	3418	8013	W	4337	9628	ART DIVERS EN MAT DIV 58
89399	OTHR PLASTC ARTICLES NES	W	2661	4777	W	3329	6963	W	3344	7741	W	4214	9179	AUT OUV MAT DIV 58
894	TOYS,SPORTING GOODS,ETC	W	1081	2938	W	1228	3584	W	1275	3863	W	1312	2932	VOITURES ENFANTS,JOUETS
8942	TOYS,INDOOR GAMES ETC	W	949	2219	W	1117	2669	W	1062	2653	W	1142	2233	JOUETS,JEUX ETC
895	OFFICE SUPPLIES NES	W	442	2087	W	513	2351	W	525	3591	W	2148	13724	ART PAPET NDA
8959	OTHER OFFICE SUPPLIES	W	129	892	W	145	862	W	161	1681	W	1615	11040	AUT ART DE PAPETERIE
89591	INK EXCL PRINTING INK	W	82	269	W	64	281	W	103	984	W	1550	10205	ENCRES A ECRIRE

5. Special Exports F.O.B. by Commodities according to the S.I.T.C. (Rev. 2) in thousand U.S. Dollars
Exportations Spéciales F.O.B. par Produits d'après la C.T.C.I. (Rév. 2) en milliers de Dollars E.U.

SITC CTCI	COMMODITY	1993		1994		1995		1996		PRODUIT
		WEIGHT POIDS	VALUE VALEUR	WEIGHT POIDS	VALUE VALEUR	WEIGHT POIDS	VALUE VALEUR	WEIGHT POIDS	VALUE VALEUR	
	ALL COMMODITIES		267493		351108		509212		660183	TOUS PRODUITS
0	FOOD AND LIVE ANIMALS		174622		260195		339878		343854	ALIMENTS,ANIMAUX VIVANTS
001	*LIVE ANIMALS FOR FOOD	W 16071	13512	W 13697	11440	W 4684	3256	W 3673	2863	ANIMAUX VIVANTS
0011	BOVINE SPECIES,LIVE	W 15975	13399	W 13648	11390	W 3456	2859	W 3289	2722	ESPECE BOVINE
00119	— OTHR THAN FR BREEDING	W 15820	13267	W 13642	11385	W 2232	1841	W 3248	2684	BOVINS NON REPRODUCTEURS
01	MEAT AND PREPARATIONS		62067		65095		55846		42076	VIANDES ET PREPARATIONS
011	MEAT FRESH,CHILLD,FROZEN	W 26113	61944	W 27392	64726	W 26200	55711	W 22696	41828	VIANDES FRAICHES,REF,CONGE
0111	BOVINE MEAT FRESH,FROZEN	W 25321	60820	W 26352	63355	W 25360	54747	W 21491	40705	VIANDES BOVIN FRAI,REF
01111	BOVINE MEAT WITH BONE IN	W 5860	12472	W 1445	2709	W 3948	7273	W 6229	10927	VIANDES BOVIN NON DESOSS
01112	BOVINE MEAT BONELESS	W 19461	48347	W 24907	60647	W 21412	47474	W 15263	29777	VIANDES BOVIN DESOSSEES
02	DAIRY PRODCTS,BIRDS'EGGS		160		1846		7634		10969	PRODUITS LAITIERS,OEUFS
022	MILK AND CREAM	W 36	56	W 66	106	W 787	1686	W 1290	2935	LAIT ET CREME
0224	MILK,CREAM PRESERVED ETC	W 32	54	W 4	14	W 670	1472	W 1119	2683	LAIT,CREME CONS,CONC
02243	MILK DRY,OVER 1.5% FAT	W 32	54			W 644	1430	W 1036	2533	LAIT POUDRE SUP 1.5%
024	CHEESE AND CURD	W 29	53	W 830	1263	W 2807	4613	W 4783	8027	FROMAGE ET CAILLEBOTTE
03	FISH AND PREPARATIONS		28506		53082		97936		78305	POISSONS ET PREPARATIONS
034	FISH,FRESH,CHILLED,FROZN	W 1867	5531	W 3103	8796	W 2414	9459	W 2553	10754	POISSON FRAIS, REFRIG,CONG
0341	FISH FRSH,CHLLD,EX FILLT	W 1575	4216	W 2144	5765	W 1404	4514	W 1538	5475	POISSON FRAIS,REFRIGERE
0342	FISH FROZEN,EXCL FILLETS	W 212	1083	W 671	1870	W 518	2102	W 619	3081	POISSONS CONGELES
0344	FISH FILLETS,FROZEN	W 34	103	W 194	773	W 465	2670	W 340	1873	FILETS CONGELES
035	FISH SALTED,DRIED,SMOKED	W 79	599	W 91	1180	W 717	1580	W 1341	3580	POISSON SECHE,SALE,FUME
03503	FISH(EX COD)DRIED,SALTED	W 39	332	W 86	1167	W 717	1580	W 1340	3578	POISSONS SECHES,SALES
036	SHELL FISH FRESH,FROZEN	W 2324	22377	W 4839	43106	W 7123	69743	W 6972	63962	CRUSTACES,MOLLUSQUES
037	FISH ETC PREPD,PRSVD NES					W 50175	17154	W 5	7	POIS,CRUST,MOL PREPARES
0371	FISH PREPARD,PRESRVD NES					W 50175	17154	W 5	7	CONSERVES DE POISSONS
04	CEREALS AND PREPARATIONS		1733		8309		3970		4300	CEREALES ET PRODUITS
044	MAIZE UNMILLED	W 380	84	W 8957	1420	W 4172	533	W 4544	795	MAIS NON MOULU
045	CEREALS NES UNMILLED	W 881	150	W 21180	3085	W 648	82	W 1992	272	AUTRES CEREALES NON MOULUES
0459	OTHER CEREALS UNMILLED	W 881	150	W 21180	3085	W 648	82	W 1992	272	SARRASIN,MILLET,SORGHO
04592	SORGHUM UNMILLED	W 881	150	W 21180	3085	W 648	82	W 1990	270	SORGHO NON MOULU
048	CEREAL ETC PREPARATIONS	W 927	1385	W 1441	3020	W 1717	2814	W 1278	2231	PREPTNS A BASE CEREALES
0484	BAKERY PRODUCTS	W 905	1342	W 1370	2989	W 1632	2659	W 1186	2082	PRODUITS DE BOULANGERIE
04842	PASTRY, CAKES ETC	W 860	1275	W 1357	2978	W 1632	2659	W 1185	2081	PATISSERIE ETC.
05	VEGETABLES AND FRUIT		11317		22989		29790		33190	LEGUMES ET FRUITS
054	VEG ETC FRSH,SMPLY PRSVD	W 6032	2034	W 25701	13222	W 28786	11243	W 17417	7413	LEGUMES FRAIS,CONG,SECS
0542	LEGUMINOUS VEGETBLES DRY	W 3914	1431	W 19011	10951	W 22256	8740	W 11793	5089	LEGUMES A COSSE SECS
057	FRUIT,NUTS,FRESH,DRIED	W 39381	9244	W 42546	9572	W 68399	18142	W 95300	25471	FRUITS FRAIS OU SECS
0573	BANANA,PLANTAIN,FRSH,DRY	W 22174	4607	W 28544	6192	W 54635	14230	W 80900	22231	BANANES FRAICHES,SECHEES
0577	NUTS EDIBLE,FRESH,DRIED	W 5720	1814	W 10	8			W 2	2	FRUITS A COQUES
05771	COCONUTS FRESH OR DRIED	W 5563	1736							NOIX DE COCO
0579	FRUIT FRESH OR DRIED NES	W 11255	2741	W 13562	3230	W 13099	3687	W 14109	3134	FRUITS FRAIS,SECS NDA
05798	OTHER FRESH FRUIT	W 10396	2397	W 12631	2718	W 10743	2343	W 11751	1934	AUTRES FRUITS FRAIS
06	SUGAR AND PREPS,HONEY		19104		17875		16182		37028	SUCRES ET PRODUITS
061	SUGAR AND HONEY	W 98944	19102	W 101693	17854	W 99563	16107	W 171743	36934	SUCRES ET MIEL
0611	RAW BEET AND CANE SUGAR	W 57090	17453	W 55018	15827	W 45126	12478	W 121979	33430	SUCRES BRUTS
0615	MOLASSES	W 41800	1593	W 46590	1967	W 54283	3529	W 49537	3248	MELASSES
07	COFFEE,TEA,COCOA,SPICES		36469		77354		121498		129771	CAFE,THE,CACAO,EPICES
071	COFFEE AND SUBSTITUTES	W 30330	36335	W 38262	77235	W 38043	121064	W 53909	127928	CAFE ET SUCCEDANES
0711	COFFEE GREEN,ROASTED,SUB	W 29681	34475	W 37911	76227	W 37850	119897	W 53568	126275	CAFE TORREFIE OU DECAFEINE
07111	COFFEE GREEN,HUSKS,SKINS	W 29681	34475	W 37911	76227	W 37781	119303	W 53233	123780	CAFE NON TORREFIE
07113	COFFEE SUBST CONT COFFEE					W 67	589	W 335	2496	SUCCEDANES DU CAFE
0712	COFFEE EXTRACTS,ESSENCES	W 649	1860	W 352	1008	W 194	1167	W 341	1653	EXTRAITS DE CAFE
081	*FEEDING STUFF FOR ANIML	W 19628	1672	W 21576	1989	W 23704	2984	W 23208	2965	NOURRITURE POUR ANIMAUX
0812	BRAN,POLLARD,SHARPS,ETC	W 16970	1260	W 18777	1605	W 16073	1400	W 17659	1695	SONS
08122	BRAN,ETC OF OTHR CEREALS	W 11304	845	W 18460	1582	W 16035	1393	W 17210	1648	SONS D'AUTRES CEREALES
09	MISC EDIBLE PRODUCTS		84		214		782		2387	PREP ALIMENTAIRES DIVERSES
098	EDIBLE PRODCTS,PREPS NES	W 131	84	W 218	214	W 517	782	W 1574	2382	PREP ALIMENTAIRES NDA
1	BEVERAGES AND TOBACCO		2740		3954		5576		17006	BOISSONS ET TABACS
11	BEVERAGES		1004		1473		1492		2485	BOISSONS
112	ALCOHOLIC BEVERAGES	W 1228	1004	W 1789	1473	W 1932	1455	W 2722	1879	BOISSONS ALCOOLIQUES
1124	DISTILLED ALCOHOLIC BEVS	W 1228	1002	W 1788	1471	W 1931	1455	W 2645	1867	ALCOOLS,EAUX–DE–VIE
11249	OTH ALCOHOLC BEVS,CMPNDS	W 1184	964	W 1788	1471	W 1931	1455	W 2645	1867	BOISSONS ALCOOLIQUES NDA
12	TOBACCO AND MANUFACTURES		1736		2481		4083		14521	TABACS BRUTS FABRIQUES
121	TOBACCO UNMNFCTRD,REFUSE	W 557	1341	W 557	2149	W 457	2448	W 512	3889	TABACS BRUTS,DECHETS
1211	TOBACCO,NOT STRIPPED	W 520	1207	W 273	1055	W 205	1185	W 170	1952	TABACS NON ECOTES
1212	TOBACCO STRIPPED OR PART	W 29	126	W 264	1075	W 246	1261	W 323	1898	TABACS PART ECOTES
122	TOBACCO,MANUFACTURED	W 37	395	W 45	332	W 175	1635	W 566	10631	TABACS FABRIQUES
1221	CIGARS,CHEROOTS,ETC	W 29	368	W 30	295	W 126	1582	W 480	10494	CIGARES
2	CRUDE MATERLS,EXCL FUELS		20148		32451		43453		65549	MAT BRUTES NON COMESTIBLES
21	HIDES,SKINS,FURS UNDRSSD		2362		2856		1152		1674	CUIRS,PEAUX BRUTS
211	HIDES,SKINS,EXC FURS,RAW	W 3261	2362	W 3624	2856	W 1235	1152	W 1680	1674	CUIRS ET PEAUX
2111	BOVINE,EQUINE HIDES,RAW	W 1928	1365	W 3195	2510	W 1074	983	W 1493	1559	PEAUX DE BOVINS
2112	CALF AND KIP SKINS,RAW	W 1222	934	W 393	320	W 122	144	W 160	82	PEAUX DE VEAUX
22	OIL SEEDS,OLEAGINOUS FRT		12804		17511		24588		29772	GRAINES,FRUITS OLEAGINEUX
222	SEEDS FOR'SOFT'FIXED OIL	W 18929	12539	W 21725	17153	W 35163	24187	W 32789	28168	GRAINES HUILES FIXES
2221	GROUNDNUTS,GREEN	W 7363	4157	W 13913	9781	W 20664	12065	W 20159	13384	ARACHIDES NON GRILLEES
2222	SOYA BEANS	W 2463	1616			W 451	162	W 327	73	FEVES DE SOJA
2225	SESAME SEEDS	W 9024	6753	W 7584	7335	W 14048	11957	W 12068	14685	GRAINES DE SESAME
24	CORK AND WOOD		1660		4950		11319		17914	LIEGE ET BOIS
248	WOOD SHAPED,SLEEPERS	W 3580	1596	W 14659	4950	W 33127	11269	W 55601	17882	BOIS SIMPLEMENT TRAVAILLES
2482	LUMBER SHAPED CONIFER	W 1083	489	W 8126	1123	W 18368	2539	W 35372	5286	CONIFERES SCIES,RABOTES
24821	LUMBER SAWN ETC CONIFER	W 1054	408	W 8126	1123	W 18349	2536	W 35330	5262	CONIFERES SCIES LONGITUD
2483	LUMBER SHAPED NON–CONIFR	W 2496	1108	W 6533	3827	W 14758	8730	W 20229	12596	NON CONIFERES SCIES,RABOTES
24831	LUMBER SAWN ETC NON–CON	W 2489	1095	W 6517	3808	W 14714	8713	W 20229	12596	SCIES LONGITUDINALEMENT
26	TEXTILE FIBRES AND WASTE		499		4239		2199		10247	FIBRES TEXTILES
263	COTTON	W 483	421	W 1677	4225	W 1540	2195	W 6313	10247	COTON
2631	RAW COTTON,EXCL LINTERS	W 264	377	W 1677	4225	W 1540	2195	W 5844	10088	COTON EN MASSE
28	METALLIFEROUS ORES,SCRAP		2328		2392		3765		5231	MINERAIS METAL,DECHETS
282	IRON AND STEEL SCRAP	W 29433	1218	W 24613	1018	W 17600	738	W 26168	1820	FERRAILLES
288	NONFERR METAL SCRAP NES	W 1507	886	W 1647	1374	W 2783	2864	W 2795	3412	DECHETS NON FERREUX
2882	OTHER BASE MTL SCRAP NES	W 1507	886	W 1647	1374	W 2783	2864	W 2795	3412	AUTRES DECHETS
28821	COPPER WASTE AND SCRAP	W 775	635	W 782	1072	W 1044	1884	W 1606	2996	DECHETS DE CUIVRE
3	MINERAL FUELS ETC		4552		3547		3140		4564	COMBUSTIBLES MINERAUX LUB
33	PETROLEUM AND PRODUCTS		2306		3545		3137		4561	PETROLE ET DERIVES
334	PETROLEUM PRODUCTS,REFIN	W 6503	1481	W 13281	2866	W 10894	2402	W 20802	4330	PRODUITS RAFFINES
3341	GASOLINE,OTH LIGHT OILS	W 4850	1173	W 10739	2414	W 10006	1993	W 7986	1164	ESSENCES POUR MOTEURS
33419	OTH LIGHT PETROLEUM OILS	W 4850	1173	W 10739	2414	W 10006	1993	W 129	85	AUTRES HUILES LEGERES
3345	LUBS,PETROLEUM OILS NES	W 24	49	W 8	7	W 160	114	W 12816	3166	HUILES LUBRIFIANTES
33451	LUBS(HIGH PETR CONT) ETC	W 24	49	W 8	7	W 160	113	W 12806	3149	HUILES LUBRIF,H LOURDES
335	RESIDUAL PETRLM PROD NES	W 7845	824	W 6385	679	W 4044	734	W 970	231	PRODUITS RESIDUELS NDA
351	*ELECTRIC CURRENT	H 47548	2228							ENERGIE ELECTRIQUE

5. Special Exports F.O.B. by Commodities according to the S.I.T.C. (Rev. 2) in thousand U.S. Dollars
Exportations Spéciales F.O.B. par Produits d'après la C.T.C.I. (Rév. 2) en milliers de Dollars E.U.

SITC CTCI	COMMODITY	1993 WEIGHT POIDS	1993 VALUE VALEUR	1994 WEIGHT POIDS	1994 VALUE VALEUR	1995 WEIGHT POIDS	1995 VALUE VALEUR	1996 WEIGHT POIDS	1996 VALUE VALEUR	PRODUIT
4	ANIMAL,VEGETABLE OIL,FAT		229		38		3332		721	HUILES,GRAISSES ANIM,VEG
42	FIXED VEGETABLE OIL,FAT		196		35		3260		636	HUILES VEGETALES FIXES
423	FIXED VEG OILS,SOFT	W 261	196	W 40	33	W 3833	3250	W 786	627	HUILES VEGET DOUCES FIXES
4234	GROUNDNUT(PEANUT) OIL					W 3833	3250	W 783	614	HUILE D'ARACHIDE
5	CHEMCLS,RELATED PROD NES		4342		4755		5912		6117	PRODUITS CHIMIQUES
541	*MEDICINAL,PHARM PRODUCT	K 109900	712	K 540163	1298	K 170580	1156	K 144351	1059	PROD MEDICINAUX PHARMACEUT
55	PERFUME,CLEANING ETC PRD		917		1388		1955		1715	PROD POUR PARFUM,TOILETTE
554	SOAP,CLEANSING ETC PREPS	W 929	917	W 1451	1333	W 2548	1890	W 2190	1697	SAVONS,PRODUITS DETERSIFS
5542	WASHING PREPARATIONS ETC	W 691	777	W 1382	1296	W 1246	1150	W 485	499	PROD ORG TENSIO–ACT NDA
59	CHEMICAL MATERIALS NES		1352		839		658		545	MAT PROD CHIMIQUES NDA
591	PESTICIDES,DISINFECTANTS	W 184	1201	W 70	573	W 124	413	W 75	379	DESINF,INSECT,FONG,HERB
6	BASIC MANUFACTURES		19098		12020		11688		12515	ART MANUFACTURES
61	LEATHER,DRESSED FUR,ETC		1037		1204		3977		4274	CUIRS,PELLETERIES
611	LEATHER	W 238	937	W 671	1151	W 2384	3975	W 2701	4261	CUIRS,PEAUX PREPARES
6114	LEATHR BOVINE NES,EQUINE	W 156	195	W 466	595	W 1602	2218	W 2272	3213	CUIRS DE BOVINS
65	TEXTILE YARN,FABRICS,ETC		1747		3593		2689		2920	FILS,TISSUS,ARTICLES TEXTILE
658	TEXTILE ARTICLES NES	W 942	910	W 615	1099	W 811	1396	W 1283	2020	ART FACONNES MAT TEXTILES
6581	BAGS,SACKS OF TEXTILES	W 891	819	W 595	1045	W 446	796	W 663	971	SACS EMBALLAGE TEXTILES
66	NONMETAL MINERAL MFS NES		2046		1501		1760		1078	ART MIN NON METALLIQUES
661	LIME,CEMENT,BLDG PRODS	W 5152	1257	W 6880	1008	W 6632	1266	W 644	51	CHAUX,CIMENTS MAT CONSTR
6618	MNRL BLDG PRD UNFIRD NES	W 4196	1196	W 4390	852	W 6627	1266	W 21	5	MAT CONST AMIANTE–CIMENT
66183	ASBESTOS–,FIBRE–CMNT PRD	W 3476	1051	W 474	114	W 384	97	W 20	5	OUVRAGES AMIANTE–CIMENT
67	IRON AND STEEL		951		2330		1410		1790	FER ET ACIER
68	NON–FERROUS METALS		11407		292		421		266	METAUX NON FERREUX
681	SILVER,PLATINUM,ETC		9993				134		1	ARGENT ET PLATINE
6811	SILVER UNWKD,PARTLY WRKD		9993				134		1	ARGENT BRUT MI–OUVRE
68112	ROLLED SILVER		8724							PLAQUE ARGENT BRUT MI–OUV
68113	SILVER UNWROUGHT		1269				134		1	ARGENT ET ALLIAGES BRUTS
684	ALUMINIUM	W 440	1112	W 46	68	W 78	172	W 110	155	ALUMINIUM
6842	ALUMINIUM,ALLOYS WORKED	W 387	1084	W 46	68	W 78	172	W 110	155	ALUMINIUM,ALLIAGES OUVRE
68421	ALUMINIUM BARS,WIRE,ETC	W 377	1000	W 1	3	W 1	2	W 22	33	BARRES,PROFILES FILS ALU
69	METAL MANUFACTURES NES		1451		1953		731		720	ART MANUFACT EN METAL NDA
7	MACHINES,TRANSPORT EQUIP		2198		6069		31050		63066	MACHINES MATERIEL TRANSPORT
72	MACHS FOR SPCL INDUSTRYS		709		1917		1444		743	MAC SPECIALES POUR INDUST
75	OFFICE MACHNES,ADP EQUIP		96		424		22695		40981	MACH BUREAU TRAIT AUTOM
759	OFFICE,ADP MCH PTS,ACCES			W 5	423	W 138	22650	W 147	40970	PIECES DU 751 ET 752
7591	OFFICE MACHINE PARTS NES			W 5	418	W 138	22647	W 147	40969	PIECES DU 7511,7518
75919	COPY MACH PRTS,ACCES NES			W 5	418	W 138	22647	W 147	40969	PIECES DU 751.82
77	ELECTRIC MACHNRY NES ETC		200		1322		1333		17557	MACH APP ELECT NDA
771	ELECTRIC POWER MACHY NES			W 4	19	W 1	2	W 6400	16530	MACH PROD,TRANS ELECTR
7712	OTH ELEC POWER MACHY NES			W 1	3	W 1	2	W 6400	16530	AUT APP PROD TRANSF ELEC
77121	STATIC CONVERTERS ETC							W 6400	16529	CONVERTISSEURS STATIQUES
775	HOUSEHOLD TYPE EQUIP NES	W 26	82	W 235	1163	W 267	1088	W 237	793	MACH,APP USAGE DOMESTQUE
7752	DOM REFRIGERATRS,FREEZRS	W 26	80	W 234	1161	W 265	1087	W 236	789	REFRIG,CONGEL MENAGER
77522	DOMESTIC DEEP–FREEZERS	W 15	54	W 234	1160	W 265	1087	W 236	789	MEUBLES CONGELATEURS
78	ROAD VEHICLES		254		983		2584		1391	VEHICULES ROUTIERS
784	MOTOR VEH PRTS,ACCES NES	W 39	47	W 437	304	W 1576	1859	W 274	862	PIECES 722,781,782,783
7849	OTHER MOTOR VEHCL PARTS	W 32	44	W 126	110	W 1545	1849	W 274	862	PIECES 722,781,782,783
8	MISC MANUFACTURED GOODS		10752		23478		54962		138482	ART MANUFACTURES DIVERS
812	*PLUMBG,HEATNG,LGHTNG EQ	W 1386	1550	W 1508	1766	W 2006	2520	W 2529	3286	APPAR SANITAIRES CHAUFFAGE
8122	CERAMIC PLUMBNG FIXTURES	W 1386	1550	W 1503	1747	W 2005	2515	W 2529	3283	EVIERS,LAVABOS,CUVETTES
89	MISC MANUFCTRD GOODS NES		7537		19908		50745		133168	ART MANUFACTURES DIVERS
895	OFFICE SUPPLIES NES		341	W 123	8978	W 234	27950	W 192	51950	ART PAPET NDA
8959	OTHER OFFICE SUPPLIES	W 2	335	W 44	8893	W 177	27890	W 174	51936	AUT ART DE PAPETERIE
89594	TYPEWRTR RIBBON,INK PADS	W 2	335	W 43	8892	W 177	27890	W 174	51936	RUBANS ENCREURS
897	GOLD,SILVER WARE,JEWELRY		6661		9850		9128		36793	BIJOUTERIE,ORFEVRERIE
8973	PREC JEWLRY,GLD–SILVWARE		6661		9850		9127		36793	BIJOUX OR,ARGENT ORFEVRE
89731	PRECIOUS METAL JEWELLERY		6661		9850		9127		36793	ART BIJOUTERIE,JOAILLER
898	MUSICAL INSTRUMENTS,PTS		6		19	W 140	12365	W 133	43124	INSTRUMENTS DE MUSIQUE
8983	SOUND RECRDNG TAPE,DISCS		6			W 116	12353	W 132	43123	SUPPORTS SON POUR 763
89831	PREPD SND RECORDNG MEDIA		6			W 116	12353	W 132	43123	SUPPORTS PREPARES
9	GOODS NOT CLASSD BY KIND		28811		4602		10221		8311	ART TRANSACT NON CLASSES
971	*GOLD,NON MONETARY NES		28259		3578		9228	K 4571	6938	OR NON MONETAIRE
97101	NONMON GLD UNWRT,SEMIMFD		28259		3578		9228	K 4571	6938	OR,ALLIAGES D'OR BRUTS

Niger

1. HISTORICAL SERIES, 1960–1995 SPECIAL TRADE, IMPORTS C.I.F., EXPORTS F.O.B.
SERIES HISTORIQUES, 1960–1995 COMMERCE SPECIAL, IMPORTATIONS C.A.F., EXPORTATIONS F.O.B

YEAR ANNEE	VALUE IN MILLION C.F.A. FRANCS VALEUR EN MILLION C.F.A. FRANCS MERCHANDISE – MARCHANDISE		GOLD – OR		CONVERSION FACTORS U.S. CENTS PER C.F.A. FRANC FACTEURS DE CONVERSION CENTS E.U. PAR C.F.A. FRANC		INDEX NUMBERS – INDICES QUANTUM		UNIT VALUE VALEUR UNITAIRE	
	IMPORTS	EXPORTS	IMPORTS	EXPORTS	IMPORTS	EXPORTS	IMPORTS	EXPORTS	IMPORTS	EXPORTS
1960	3207.00	3108.00			0.4051	0.4051				
1961	4653.00	3824.00			0.4051	0.4051				
1962	6779.00	4834.00			0.4051	0.4051				
1963	5974.00	5339.00			0.4051	0.4051				
1964	8114.00	5260.00			0.4051	0.4051				
1965	9297.00	6250.00			0.4051	0.4051				
1966	11115.00	8574.00			0.4051	0.4051				
1967	11352.00	8226.00			0.4051	0.4051				
1968	10237.00	7125.00			0.4051	0.4051				
1969	12570.00	6250.00			0.3890	0.3920				
1970	16213.00	8795.00			0.3601	0.3601				
1971	14975.00	10670.00			0.3601	0.3601				
1972	16576.00	13712.00			0.3970	0.3962				
1973	19098.00	13817.00			0.4504	0.4463				
1974	23144.00	12621.00			0.4181	0.4181				
1975	21889.00	19556.00			0.4607	0.4643				
1976	30383.00	31979.00			0.4168	0.4198				
1977	48221.00	39335.00			0.4070	0.4070				
1978	68896.00	63706.00			0.4440	0.4440				
1979	98058.00	95241.00			0.4708	0.4704				
1980	125426.00	119523.00			0.4733	0.4733				
1981	138512.00	123589.00			0.3680	0.3680				
1982	153214.00	109124.00			0.3040	0.3040				
1983	123288.00	113896.00			0.2624	0.2624				
1984	124610.00	119495.00			0.2289	0.2289				
1985	154757.00	93901.00			0.2230	0.2230				
1986	127559.00	109645.00			0.2888	0.2888				
1987	93387.01	93863.01			0.3327	0.3327				
1988	115193.00	85941.01			0.3357	0.3357				
1989	115822.00	77710.00			0.3135	0.3135				
1990	105851.00	76939.01			0.3673	0.3673				
1991	100235.00	86626.00			0.3545	0.3545				
1992	126684.00	69394.00			0.3790	0.3777				
1993	106123.00	63756.00			0.3537	0.3542				
1994	182097.00	96017.01			0.1800	0.1800				
1995	186501.00	129300.00			0.2002	0.2002				

2. IMPORTS BY BROAD ECONOMIC CATEGORY AND EXPORTS BY INDUSTRIAL ORIGIN. (PERCENTAGE OF TOTAL VALUE)
IMPORTATIONS PAR CATEGORIES ECONOMIQUES ET EXPORTATIONS PAR BRANCHE D'ACTIVITE.(EN POURCENTAGE DE LA VALEUR TOTALE)

IMPORTS – IMPORTATIONS

	1990	1991	1992	1993	1994	1995	1996
TOTAL IMPORTS–IMPORTATIONS TOTALES							
1 FOOD BEV–ALIMENTATION BOISSONS							
11 PRIMARY–PRODUITS DE BASE							
111 FOR INDUSTRY–POUR L'INDUSTRIE							
112 FOR HOUSEHOLDS–POUR LES MENAGES							
12 PROCESSED–PRODUITS ELABORES							
121 FOR INDUSTRY–POUR L'INDUSTRIE							
122 FOR HOUSEHOLDS–POUR LES MENAGES							
2 IND SUPPLIES–APPROV INDUSTRIELS							
21 PRIMARY–PRODUITS DE BASE							
22 PROCESSED–PRODUITS ELABORES							
3 FUELS–COMBUSTIBLES							
31 PRIMARY–PRODUITS DE BASE							
32 PROCESSED–PRODUITS ELABORES							
321 MOTOR SPIRIT–ESSENCE							
322 OTHER–AUTRES							
4 MACHINERY–EQUIPEMENT							
41 CAPITAL EQUIPMENT–MACHINES							
42 PARTS–PIECES ACCESSOIRES							
5 TRANSPORT–TRANSPORT							
51 PASSENGER CARS–AUTOMOBILES							
52 OTHER–AUTRES							
521 INDUSTRIAL–INDUSTRIELS							
522 NON INDUSTRIAL–NON INDUSTRIEL							
53 PARTS–PIECES ACCESSOIRES							
6 CONSUM GOODS–BIENS CONSOMMATION							
61 DURABLE–DURABLES							
62 SEMI DURABLE–SEMI DURABLES							
63 NON DURABLE–NON DURABLES							
7 GOODS NES–BIENS NDA							

EXPORTS – EXPORTATIONS

	1990	1991	1992	1993	1994	1995	1996
TOTAL EXPORTS–EXPORTATIONS TOTALES							
1 AGRICULTURE							
2 MINING QUARRY–INDUS EXTRACTIVES							
3 MANUFACTURING–IND MANUFACTUR							
31 FOOD BEV TOBACCO–ALIM BOISS TAB							
32 TEXTILES–INDUSTRIES TEXTILES							
33 WOOD & PRODUCTS–BOIS & PRODUITS							
34 PAPER & PRODUCTS–PAPIER & PRODT							
35 CHEMICALS–INDUSTRIES CHIMIQUES							
36 NON METAL MIN–MIN NON METAL							
37 BASIC METAL–IND METAL BASE							
38 METAL MANUF–MANUF METAL							
39 OTH MANUF IND–AUTRES MANUF							

3. TRADE BY PRINCIPAL COUNTRIES OF PRODUCTION AND LAST DESTINATION (VALUE IN THOUSAND U.S. DOLLARS)
ECHANGES SELON LES PRINCIPAUX PAYS DE PRODUCTION ET DE DERNIERE DESTINATION (VALEUR EN MILLIERS DE DOLLARS EU)

COUNTRIES–PAYS	SPECIAL IMPORTS C.I.F. IMPORTATIONS SPECIALES C.A.F				
	1987	1988	1989	1990	1991
World		386703	363102	388791	355333
Africa		83435	96630	107931	108488
Americas		24207	15280	28587	19863
Northern America		22888	14540	28051	19136
LAIA		1319	740	536	727
CACM					
Caribbean					
Rest of America					
As.ex F.USSR		63639	50129	51815	40431
Eur.x F.USSR		196213	171895	173105	142977
EU		193346	169187	170747	140807
EFTA		1840	1859	1466	1177
East Europe		1027	850	893	993
Other Europe					
Former USSR					
Oceania		101	19	110	74
France, Monac		123165	105095	104662	88107
Nigeria/Nigéria		46196	47511	51407	55298
Cote d'Ivoire		22482	30319	35595	29356
Japan/Japon		36152	23459	23133	23298
USA/Etats–Unis d'Amer		19504	12126	22468	18267
Germany/Allemagne		16560	17377	16385	15818
Netherlands/Pays–Bas		13720	14625	14009	13825
Italy/Italie		15083	9850	11405	5902
Pakistan		12203	8160	11276	7512
United Kingdom		9050	8941	12213	7069
China/Chine		9262	6747	5950	5406
Belgium–Luxembourg		7207	7116	6384	5661
Algeria/Algérie		2239	4555	5987	12691
Ghana		3125	3878	5003	2928
Angola		2612	3775	3232	3152
Canada		3384	2414	5583	869
Spain/Espagne		4005	3151	1972	1652
Hong Kong		1504	1699	4253	2354
Burkina Faso		2964	1649	2612	2141
Togo		1722	2220	2351	1124
Denmark/Danemark		2568	1530	1429	1166
Switz.Liecht		1840	1859	1466	1177
Malaysia/Malaisie		1561	1768	2068	776
Saudi Arabia		611	2640	1987	596
Thailand/Thaïlande		2007	2439	1131	216
Sweden/Suède		1185	981	1612	915
Czechoslovakia		943	762	804	922
Brazil/Brésil		1319	740	536	727
Morocco/Maroc		880	784	444	535
Senegal/Sénégal		601	1107	632	209
Ireland/Irlande		366	414	544	596
Mali		134	279	492	734
Cameroon/Cameroun		480	555	176	298
Korea, Republic of		252	122	555	117
Austria/Autriche		436	107	132	96
Bangladesh		87	122	239	145
Romania/Roumanie		84	88	88	71
Australia/Australie		101	19	110	74
Egypt/Egypte					21

COUNTRIES–PAYS	SPECIAL EXPORTS F.O.B. EXPORTATIONS SPECIALES F.O.B.				
	1987	1988	1989	1990	1991
Monde		288504	243621	282597	311910
Afrique		32959	30886	40025	73357
Amériques		40	119	173	376
Amérique du Nord		40	119	173	376
ALAI					
MCAC					
Caraïbes					
Autre Amérique					
Asie l'URSS exclus		77412	57693	57446	58648
Europe l'URSS exclus		176279	153675	182111	175779
UE		176279	153675	182111	175779
AELE					
Europe de l'Est					
Autre de l'Europe					
Ancienne URSS					
Océanie					
France, Monac		158998	135043	165961	161181
Japan/Japon		77365	57693	57446	58648
Nigeria/Nigéria		13431	21838	24840	59085
Spain/Espagne		14455	16895	14266	12989
Cote d'Ivoire		5878	3013	3218	2099
Benin/Bénin		4176	1245	2509	3506
Togo		621	1596	2722	1570
Burkina Faso		2185	683	1726	865
Italy/Italie		1460	1107	1517	326
Libyan Arab Jamahiriya		524	179	507	2769
Algeria/Algérie		849	564	859	1546
Mali		134	141	2024	702
Chad/Tchad		1907	342	408	255
Ghana		799	191	720	259
Senegal/Sénégal		960	426	95	464
United Kingdom		916	191	217	50
Germany/Allemagne		121	150	92	915
Congo		1081		7	181
Egypt/Egypte		40	649	136	
USA/Etats–Unis d'Amer		23	88	169	305
Belgium–Luxembourg		50	219	29	266
Guinea/Guinée		252	16	22	32
Cameroon/Cameroun		97	3	191	7
Netherlands/Pays–Bas		185	19	15	35
Denmark/Danemark		94	50	15	18
Canada		17	31	4	71
China/Chine		47			

(VALUE AS PERCENTAGE OF WORLD TOTAL)(VALEURS EN POURCENTAGE DU TOTAL MONDIAL)

	1982	1983	1984	1985	1986	1987	1988	1989	1990	1991
Africa	20.3	25.8	20.8	15.0			21.6	26.6	27.8	30.5
Americas	5.7	4.1	5.5	11.6			6.3	4.2	7.4	5.6
Northern America	4.8	2.9	4.0	10.4			5.9	4.0	7.2	5.4
LAIA	0.9	1.1	1.5	1.2			0.3	0.2	0.1	0.2
CACM										
Caribbean										
Rest of America										
As.ex F.USSR	7.4	7.7	10.4	10.5			16.5	13.8	13.3	11.4
Eur.x F.USSR	59.0	60.6	55.5	56.4			50.7	47.3	44.5	40.2
EU	57.4	58.2	54.1	55.3			50.0	46.6	43.9	39.6
EFTA	1.5	2.3	1.3	1.0			0.5	0.5	0.4	0.3
East Europe	0.2	0.1	0.1	0.1			0.3	0.2	0.2	0.3
Other Europe	0.0			0.0						
Former USSR	1.1	0.4	0.1	0.3						
Oceania	0.0			0.1			0.0	0.0	0.0	0.0
France, Monac	35.4	36.7	34.2	33.5			31.9	28.9	26.9	24.8
Nigeria/Nigéria	7.7	14.3	9.0	4.0			11.9	13.1	13.2	15.6
Cote d'Ivoire	7.9	6.9	7.8	8.3			5.8	8.3	9.2	8.3
Japan/Japon	4.0	5.1	4.2	3.9			9.3	6.5	5.9	6.6
USA/Etats–Unis d'Amer	4.5	2.6	3.3	9.1			5.0	3.3	5.8	5.1
Germany/Allemagne	9.1	9.9	5.3	5.6			4.3	4.8	4.2	4.5
Netherlands/Pays–Bas	2.7	2.0	2.7	2.3			3.5	4.0	3.6	3.9
Italy/Italie	2.0	2.0	4.3	6.6			3.9	2.7	2.9	1.7
Pakistan	0.7	0.2	1.9	2.0			3.2	2.2	2.9	2.1
United Kingdom	4.4	4.5	4.0	3.9			2.3	2.5	3.1	2.0

	1982	1983	1984	1985	1986	1987	1988	1989	1990	1991
Afrique	7.2	6.5	10.0	10.8			11.4	12.7	14.2	23.5
Amériques	0.1	0.9	0.2	2.2			0.0	0.0	0.1	0.1
Amérique du Nord	0.1	0.9	0.1	2.2			0.0	0.0	0.1	0.1
ALAI			0.0	0.0						
MCAC										
Caraïbes		0.0	0.0	0.0						
Autre Amérique		0.0								
Asie l'URSS exclus	7.5	11.4	10.8	3.9			26.8	23.7	20.3	18.8
Europe l'URSS exclus	83.9	79.7	76.6	82.7			61.1	63.1	64.4	56.4
UE	83.9	79.6	76.6	82.6			61.1	63.1	64.4	56.4
AELE	0.0			0.0						
Europe de l'Est										
Autre de l'Europe		0.0								
Ancienne URSS	0.4	0.1	0.2	0.2						
Océanie	0.0	0.0	0.0							
France, Monac	77.3	68.7	70.0	77.6			55.1	55.4	58.7	51.7
Japan/Japon	7.5	11.4	10.8	3.9			26.8	23.7	20.3	18.8
Nigeria/Nigéria	5.9	5.1	6.1	6.9			4.7	9.0	8.8	18.9
Spain/Espagne	2.3	2.8	2.1	3.1			5.0	6.9	5.0	4.2
Cote d'Ivoire	0.3	0.2	0.6	1.2			2.0	1.2	1.1	0.7
Benin/Bénin	0.4	0.2	0.5	0.2			1.4	0.5	0.9	1.1
Togo	0.3	0.2	0.2	0.1			0.2	0.7	1.0	0.5
Burkina Faso	0.1	0.2	1.0	0.3			0.8	0.3	0.6	0.3
Italy/Italie	1.5	1.8	0.9	1.5			0.5	0.5	0.5	0.1
Libyan Arab Jamahiriya				0.0			0.2	0.1	0.2	0.9

4. Special Imports C.I.F. by Commodities according to the S.I.T.C. (Rev. 2) in thousand U.S. Dollars
Importations Spéciales C.A.F. par Produits d'après la C.T.C.I. (Rév. 2) en milliers de Dollars E.U.

SITC CTCI	COMMODITY	1988			1989			1990			1991			PRODUIT
		WEIGHT POIDS		VALUE VALEUR	WEIGHT POIDS		VALUE VALEUR	WEIGHT POIDS		VALUE VALEUR	WEIGHT POIDS		VALUE VALEUR	
	ALL COMMODITIES			386703			363102			388791			355333	TOUS PRODUITS
0	FOOD AND LIVE ANIMALS			86231			71406			84002			72949	ALIMENTS,ANIMAUX VIVANTS
01	MEAT AND PREPARATIONS			906			2013			654			613	VIANDES ET PREPARATIONS
014	MEAT PREPD,PRSVD,NES ETC	W	329	906	W	794	2013	W	244	654	W	204	613	CONSERVES DE VIANDES
0149	OTH PREPARD,PRESRVD MEAT	W	329	906	W	794	2013	W	244	654	W	204	613	AUTRES PREP DE VIANDES
02	DAIRY PRODCTS,BIRDS'EGGS			11931			7173			8602			7693	PRODUITS LAITIERS,OEUFS
022	MILK AND CREAM	W	8087	11538	W	4960	6878	W	4294	8187	W	6805	7416	LAIT ET CREME
0224	MILK,CREAM PRESERVED ETC	W	8087	11538	W	4960	6878	W	4294	8187	W	6805	7416	LAIT,CREME CONS,CONC
04	CEREALS AND PREPARATIONS			33835			26400			34886			31657	CEREALES ET PRODUITS
041	WHEAT ETC UNMILLED	W	30260	9943	W	23358	7982	W	24157	9873	W	32571	9274	FROMENT,EPEAUTRE
042	RICE	W	28396	11202	W	29202	11816	W	28680	10222	W	17054	5091	RIZ
044	MAIZE UNMILLED	W	7052	2719	W	3159	304	W	11438	973	W	11653	851	MAIS NON MOULU
045	CEREALS NES UNMILLED	W	25070	6613	W	3949	677	W	26168	9201	W	41559	2634	AUTRES CEREALES NON MOULUES
0459	OTHER CEREALS UNMILLED	W	25070	6613	W	3949	677	W	26168	9201	W	41559	2634	SARRASIN,MILLET,SORGHO
046	WHEAT ETC MEAL OR FLOUR	W	3505	974	W	6305	2928	W	2724	984	W	9003	10036	SEMOULE FARINE,FROMENT
04601	FLOUR OF WHEAT OR MESLIN	W	3505	974	W	6305	2928	W	2724	984	W	9003	10036	FARINE DE FROMENT
048	CEREAL ETC PREPARATIONS	W	3412	2383	W	3910	2693	W	5139	3633	W	6111	3772	PREPTNS A BASE CEREALES
0483	MACARONI,SPAGHETTI ETC	W	2030	1695	W	2736	1997	W	3998	2850	W	5168	3148	PATES ALMENTAIRES
05	VEGETABLES AND FRUIT			12988			10556			16326			12415	LEGUMES ET FRUITS
056	VEGTBLES ETC PRSVD,PREPD	W	2030	2743	W	1187	1646	W	1273	1803	W	1311	1627	CONSERVES DE LEGUMES
0565	VEGTBLES PRSVD,PREPD NES	W	2030	2743	W	1187	1646	W	1273	1803	W	1311	1627	LEGUMES PREPARES CONSERVE
057	FRUIT,NUTS,FRESH,DRIED	W	11170	10246	W	12770	8910	W	14466	14523	W	11397	10787	FRUITS FRAIS OU SECS
0577	NUTS EDIBLE,FRESH,DRIED	W	7036	9470	W	5982	7765	W	7115	12896	W	5465	9589	FRUITS A COQUES
05779	NUTS EDIBLE,FRSH,DRY,NES	W	7036	9470	W	5982	7765	W	7115	12896	W	5465	9589	FRUITS A COQUES NDA
0579	FRUIT FRESH OR DRIED NES	W	4134	775	W	6788	1144	W	7351	1627	W	5932	1198	FRUITS FRAIS,SECS NDA
05796	DATES,FRESH OR DRIED	W	4134	775	W	6788	1144	W	7351	1627	W	5932	1198	DATTES FRAICHES OU SECHES
06	SUGAR AND PREPS,HONEY			13851			16321			18508			15733	SUCRES ET PRODUITS
061	SUGAR AND HONEY	W	32856	13851	W	32966	16321	W	31712	18508	W	34308	15733	SUCRES ET MIEL
07	COFFEE,TEA,COCOA,SPICES			9128			5549			3445			2847	CAFE,THE,CACAO,EPICES
071	COFFEE AND SUBSTITUTES	W	165	2535	W	122	1831	W	57	907	W	30	432	CAFE ET SUCCEDANES
074	TEA AND MATE	W	2598	6593	W	1871	3718	W	1178	2538	W	9621	2414	THE ET MATE
0741	TEA	W	2598	6593	W	1871	3718	W	1178	2538	W	9621	2414	THE
09	MISC EDIBLE PRODUCTS			2498			2934			1047			1726	PREP ALIMENTAIRES DIVERSES
098	EDIBLE PRODCTS,PREPS NES	W	961	2498	W	3950	2934	W	543	1047	W	484	1726	PREP ALIMENTAIRES NDA
09805	SOUPS AND BROTHS	W	627	2128	W	849	2599	W	167	654	W	212	1379	SOUPES,POTAGES,BOUILLONS
1	BEVERAGES AND TOBACCO			4532			5527			11820			4651	BOISSONS ET TABACS
12	TOBACCO AND MANUFACTURES			3478			4486			11048			3949	TABACS BRUTS FABRIQUES
122	TOBACCO,MANUFACTURED	W	250	3478	W	293	4486	W	541	11048	W	267	3949	TABACS FABRIQUES
1222	CIGARETTES	W	250	3478	W	293	4486	W	541	11048	W	267	3949	CIGARETTES
2	CRUDE MATERLS,EXCL FUELS			9893			6533			10145			7842	MAT BRUTES NON COMESTIBLES
27	CRUDE FERTLZR,MINRLS NES			8272			5681			9194			7593	ENGRAIS MINERAUX BRUTS
274	SULPHUR,UNRSTD IRN PYRTE	W	20614	4925	W	9102	2110	W	17463	4768	W	17709	4523	SOUFRE ET PYRITES
2741	SULPHUR,EX SULP IN 52215	W	20614	4925	W	9102	2110	W	17463	4768	W	17709	4523	SOUFRE
278	OTHER CRUDE MINERALS	W	18274	3347	W	22871	3571	W	22344	4426	W	17985	3070	AUTRES MINERAUX BRUTS
2783	COMMON SALT,ETC	W	17498	2702	W	22514	3295	W	21704	3934	W	17807	2932	SEL
3	MINERAL FUELS ETC			20129			20851			25230			33571	COMBUSTIBLES MINERAUX LUB
33	PETROLEUM AND PRODUCTS			20129			20851			25230			33571	PETROLE ET DERIVES
334	PETROLEUM PRODUCTS,REFIN	W	48092	19655	W	52410	20418	W	60075	24690	W	78496	33461	PRODUITS RAFFINES
3341	GASOLINE,OTH LIGHT OILS	W	10077	5539	W	11699	5718	W	12052	6009	W	24028	10603	ESSENCES POUR MOTEURS
33411	MOTOR,AVIATION SPIRIT	W	10077	5539	W	11699	5718	W	12052	6009	W	24028	10603	ESSENCES MOTEURS D'AVIONS
3342	KEROSENE,OTH MEDIUM OILS	W	1808	665	W	1769	558	W	2079	981	W	9178	2350	PETR LAMPANTS,AUT HUIL
3343	GAS OILS	W	28501	8983	W	27724	9117	W	2858	10248	W	27003	10068	GAS OILS
3345	LUBS,PETROLEUM OILS NES	W	7706	4468	W	11218	5025	W	43086	7453	W	18287	10440	HUILES LUBRIFIANTES
33451	LUBS(HIGH PETR CONT) ETC	W	7706	4468	W	11218	5025	W	43086	7453	W	18287	10440	HUILES LUBRIF,H LOURDES
4	ANIMAL,VEGETABLE OIL,FAT			2709			13521			15173			13542	HUILES,GRAISSES ANIM,VEG
42	FIXED VEGETABLE OIL,FAT			789			10847			11996			11645	HUILES VEGETALES FIXES
424	FIXED VEG OIL NONSOFT	W	1318	789	W	12586	10847	W	12117	11996	W	12933	11645	AUTRES HUILES VEG FIXES
4242	PALM OIL	W	1318	789	W	12586	10847	W	12117	11996	W	12933	11645	HUILE DE PALME
431	*PROCESD ANML VEG OIL,ET	W	3537	1920	W	4664	2674	W	5294	3177	W	3291	1897	HUILES,GRAISSES PREPAREES
4313	FATTY ACIDS ETC,RESIDUES	W	3537	1920	W	4664	2674	W	5294	3177	W	3291	1897	ACIDES GRAS INDUST,RESIDUS
43131	FATTY ACIDS,ACID OILS	W	3537	1920	W	4664	2674	W	5294	3177	W	3291	1897	ACIDES GRAS INDUSTRIELS
5	CHEMCLS,RELATED PROD NES			30834			29864			31584			34078	PRODUITS CHIMIQUES
52	INORGANIC CHEMICALS			6902			5994			6663			3814	PROD CHIM INORGANIQUES
522	INORG ELEMNTS,OXIDES,ETC	W	2849	1585	W	2988	1812	W	2892	1943	W	1928	1340	ELEMENTS INORGANIQUES
5225	INORGANIC BASES ETC NES	W	2849	1585	W	2988	1812	W	2892	1943	W	1928	1340	AUTRES BASES OXYDES METAL
52252	SODIUM HYDROXIDE, SOLID	W	2849	1585	W	2988	1812	W	2892	1943	W	1928	1340	HYDROXYDE DE SODIUM
523	OTHR INORG CHEMICALS ETC	W	10560	5317	W	6942	4182	W	7088	4720	W	4765	2474	AUT PRODUITS CHIMIQUES INORG
5231	METAL CMPD OF INORG ACID	W	5274	3404	W	2704	2530	W	1489	1319	W	406	124	SELS METALLIQUES
52314	CHLORATES, BROMATES ETC	W	4067	2924	W	2571	2470	W	1131	1150	W	1	7	CHLORATES,PERCHLORATES
5232	OTH MTL CMPD OF INRG ACD	W	5286	1913	W	4238	1652	W	5599	3401	W	4359	2350	SELS METALLIQUES
52328	BORATES AND PERBORATES	W	5286	1913	W	4238	1652	W	5599	3401	W	4359	2350	BORATES ET PERBORATES
53	DYES,TANNING,COLOUR PROD			1997			2157			999			1450	PROD TEINTURE,COLORANTS
531	SYNT DYE,NAT INDGO,LAKES	W	114	1997	W	104	2157	W	76	999	W	82	1450	MAT COLOR ORGAN,LAQUES
5311	SYNTHIC ORGNIC DYESTUFFS	W	114	1997	W	104	2157	W	76	999	W	82	1450	MAT COLOR ORGAN SYNTHET
541	*MEDICINAL,PHARM PRODUCT	K	463000	8634	K	531000	11302	K	599000	12088	K	549000	17161	PROD MEDICINAUX PHARMACEUT
5416	GLYCOSIDES,GLANDS,SERA	K	10000	1047	K	11000	2151	K	11000	764	K	11000	8533	HETEROSIDES
54164	ANTISERA,MICROB VACCINES	K	10000	1047	K	11000	2151	K	11000	764	K	11000	8533	SERUMS,VACCINS
5417	MEDICAMENTS	K	453000	7587	K	520000	9151	K	588000	11324	K	538000	8629	MEDICAMENTS
54171	— CONTAINNG ANTIBIOTICS	K	453000	7587	K	520000	9151	K	588000	11324	K	538000	8629	MED CONTN ANTIBIOTIQUES
562	*FERTILIZERS,MANUFACTURE	W	5655	3921	W	9325	2743	W	3594	1131	W	5289	2350	ENGRAIS MANUFACTURES
5629	FERTILIZERS NES	W	4227	3250	W	9019	2615	W	2470	485	W	4098	1705	ENGRAIS NDA
572	*EXPLOSIVES,PYROTECH PRO	W	345	1007	W	235	658	W	409	1308	W	314	957	EXPLOSIFS
5721	PREPARED EXPLOSIVES	W	345	1007	W	235	658	W	409	1308	W	314	957	POUDRES,EXPLOSIFS
57212	PREPARED EXPLOSIVES NES	W	345	1007	W	235	658	W	409	1308	W	314	957	EXPLOSIFS PREPARES
59	CHEMICAL MATERIALS NES			7808			6148			8797			7799	MAT PROD CHIMIQUES NDA
591	PESTICIDES,DISINFECTANTS	W	891	6090	W	1136	4941	W	1135	7353	W	1403	6299	DESINF,INSECT,FONG,HERB
598	MISCEL CHEM PRODUCTS NES	W	399	1719	W	1069	1207	W	272	1443	W	250	1500	PROD DIV INDUST CHIM NDA
5989	CHEM PRODUCTS,PREPS NES	W	399	1719	W	1069	1207	W	272	1443	W	250	1500	PROD PREP CHIMIQUES NDA
6	BASIC MANUFACTURES			59815			51621			51224			44624	ART MANUFACTURES
62	RUBBER MANUFACTURES NES			5962			3640			5172			3765	CAOUTCHOUC MANUFACTURE
625	RUBBER TYRES, TUBES ETC	W	869	4223	W	714	2941	W	741	4378	W	5814	3074	PNEUS CAOUTCHOUC VULCANISE
63	WOOD,CORK MANUFACTRS NES			2303			1699			2571			2265	OUVRAGES LIEGE ET BOIS
634	VENEERS,PLYWOOD,ETC	W	5958	2303	W	4821	1699	W	6096	2571	W	38381	2265	PLACAGES,CONTRE–PLAQUES
6342	PLYWOOD OF WOOD SHEETS	W	1594	1527	W	1355	1147	W	1827	1708	W	1805	1560	BOIS CONTRE–PLAQUES
65	TEXTILE YARN,FABRICS,ETC			18722			20073			22571			17760	FILS,TISSUS,ARTICLES TEXTILE
652	COTTON FABRICS,WOVEN	W	2167	13807	W	2388	16340	W	1798	16330	W	1676	14084	TISSUS DE COTON
653	WOVN MAN–MADE FIB FABRIC	W	471	1088	W	391	696	W	589	1466	W	439	908	TISSUS FIBRES SYNTH,ARTIF
6531	CONT SYNT WEAVES NONPILE	W	471	1088	W	391	696	W	589	1466	W	439	908	TISSUS FIBRES SYNTH CONTINUE
658	TEXTILE ARTICLES NES	W	3779	3827	W	3501	3038	W	3142	4775	W	7641	2769	ART FACONNES MAT TEXTILES
6581	BAGS,SACKS OF TEXTILES	W	2768	1333	W	2452	997	W	1856	1594	W	6985	1305	SACS EMBALLAGE TEXTILES
6589	OTH TEXTILE ARTICLES NES	W	582	1393	W	717	1251	W	677	1238	W	444	798	AUT ART EN TEXTILES NDA

4. Special Imports C.I.F. by Commodities according to the S.I.T.C. (Rev. 2) in thousand U.S. Dollars
Importations Spéciales C.A.F. par Produits d'après la C.T.C.I. (Rév. 2) en milliers de Dollars E.U.

SITC CTCI	COMMODITY	1988 WEIGHT POIDS	1988 VALUE VALEUR	1989 WEIGHT POIDS	1989 VALUE VALEUR	1990 WEIGHT POIDS	1990 VALUE VALEUR	1991 WEIGHT POIDS	1991 VALUE VALEUR	PRODUIT
66	NONMETAL MINERAL MFS NES		10158		10988		7765		6406	ART MIN NON METALLIQUES
661	LIME,CEMENT,BLDG PRODS	W 62204	8486	W 9114	9825	W 57344	6758	W 40206	5424	CHAUX,CIMENTS MAT CONSTR
6612	CEMENT	W 62204	8486	W 9114	9825	W 57344	6758	W 40206	5424	CIMENTS HYDRAULIQUES
662	CLAY,REFRACTORY BLDG PRD	W 1585	1309	W 987	774	W 699	657	W 822	663	MAT CONST REFRACTAIRES
6624	BRICKS ETC NONREFRACTORY	W 1585	1309	W 987	774	W 699	657	W 822	663	BRIQUES ETC CERAM NON REFR
67	IRON AND STEEL		13270		8013		6402		8848	FER ET ACIER
673	IRON,STEEL SHAPES ETC	W 3577	2209	W 4608	2800	W 1890	1469	W 6102	3152	BARRES,PROFIL FER,ACIER
6732	IRON,STEEL BARS ETC	W 1111	621	W 1656	934	W 455	496	W 3099	1595	BARRES FER,ACIER
6733	IRON,STEEL PROFILES ETC	W 2466	1588	W 2952	1865	W 1435	973	W 3003	1556	PROFILES,PALPLAN FER,ACIER
674	IRN,STL UNIV,PLATE,SHEET	W 2443	7822	W 2471	2649	W 2496	2795	W 1875	1904	LARGES PLATS,TOLES
6744	IRN,STL HVY PLATE,ROLLED	W 2443	7822	W 2471	2649	W 2496	2795	W 1875	1904	TOLES LAMINEES PLUS 4.75 MM
69	METAL MANUFACTURES NES		8369		6182		6049		5013	ART MANUFACT EN METAL NDA
693	WIRE PRODUCTS NON ELECTR	W 661	1601	W 485	834	W 454	797	W 131	280	OUVRAGES FILS METALLIQUES
694	STL,COPPR NAILS,NUTS,ETC	W 387	1715	W 147	724	W 179	834	W 129	645	CLOUS,VIS,ECROUS
695	TOOLS	W 195	2588	W 162	1793	W 77	1425	W 115	1723	OUTILS A MAIN
6953	OTHER HAND TOOLS	W 126	1480	W 118	859	W 60	676	W 73	709	AUTRES OUTILS A MAIN
697	BASE MTL HOUSEHOLD EQUIP	W 410	987	W 408	1580	W 608	2204	W 713	1904	ART MENAGE MET COMMUNS
6973	DMSTC HEATG,COOKG APPARA	W 9	87	W 230	962	W 406	1535	W 359	1234	APPS CHAUF NON ELECTRIQ
69733	PTS NES OF APPAR OF 6973	W 9	87	W 230	962	W 406	1535	W 359	1234	PART PIECES POUR 697.3
7	MACHINES,TRANSPORT EQUIP		74878		63700		57912		48407	MACHINES MATERIEL TRANSPORT
71	POWER GENERATING EQUIPMT		4310		5254		3262		2212	MACHINES GENERATRICES
714	ENGINES AND MOTORS NES	W 123	2773	W 220	4311	W 158	2935	W 286	1691	MOTEURS NON ELECTRIQUES
7149	ENGINE & MOTOR PARTS NES	W 123	2773	W 220	4311	W 158	2935	W 286	1691	PIECES 714 ET 718.88
716	ROTATING ELECTRIC PLANT	W 142	1450	W 98	940	W 23	268	W 42	440	APP ELECTR ROTATIFS,PIECES
72	MACHS FOR SPCL INDUSTRYS		6257		3728		4834		4091	MAC SPECIALES POUR INDUST
722	TRACTORS NON-ROAD	W 799	2387	W 799	981	W 256	643	W 394	872	TRACTEURS
7224	WHEELED TRACTORS NES	W 799	2387	W 799	981	W 256	643	W 394	872	TRACTEURS A ROUES
723	CIVIL ENGNEERG EQUIP ETC	W 377	3454	W 537	2405	W 564	3511	W 555	3070	APPAREILS DE GENIE CIVIL
7234	CONST,MINING MACHNRY NES	W 145	769	W 286	680	W 196	698	W 409	1379	MACH POUR LA CONST, MINES
72341	SELF-PROPELLD DOZERS,ETC	W 145	769	W 286	680	W 196	698	W 409	1379	BULLDOZERS
7239	CONSTR ETC MACHY PTS NES	W 173	2336	W 134	1273	W 326	2512	W 112	1563	PIECES 723.41–723.46
74	GENRL INDUSTRL MACHY NES		12606		10270		8095		7792	MACH APP INDUSTRIE
741	HEATING,COOLING EQUIPMNT	W 213	2508	W 307	1975	W 129	882		1000	MACH CHAUFFAGE,PIECES
7415	AIR-CONDITIONING MACHNRY	W 195	1974	W 289	1796	W 110	753	W 319	925	GROUPES CONDITION AIR
742	PUMPS FOR LIQUIDS ETC	W 219	3750	W 235	3593	W 103	2494	W 150	2981	POMPES MOTO-POMPES
7429	PTS NES OF PUMPS OF 742	W 30	789	W 48	1151	W 15	705	W 10	617	PIECES POUR GROUPE 742
743	PUMPS NES,CENTRFUGES ETC	W 186	2195	W 107	1470	W 94	1230	W 100	1195	POMPES COMPRES,VENT ETC
749	NONELEC MACH PTS,ACC NES	W 195	4153	W 132	3232	W 122	3489	W 117	2616	PIECES MACH NON ELEC NDA
7492	COCKS,VALVES ETC NES	W 85	1269	W 44	931	W 46	801	W 28	528	ART ROB,SIM POUR TUYAUX
7493	SHAFT,CRANK,PULLEY ETC	W 42	1266	W 38	1003	W 30	1128	W 21	681	ARBRES TRANS,VILEBREQUINS
75	OFFICE MACHNES,ADP EQUIP		1853		2085		2556		5275	MACH BUREAU TRAIT AUTOM
752	AUTOMTIC DATA PROC EQUIP	W 21	1853	W 28	2085	W 29	2556	W 63	5275	MACH TRAIT INFORMATION
76	TELECOMM,SOUND EQUIPMENT		2357		1712		1543		1110	EQUIPMENT DE TELECOM
764	TELECOM EQPT,PTS,ACC NES	W 24	2357	W 31	1712	W 17	1543	W 30	1110	EQUIP TELECOM,PIECES
7641	LINE TELEPHONE,ETC EQUIP	W 19	1699	W 17	1260	W 13	962	W 8	656	APP TELEPHON PAR FIL
77	ELECTRIC MACHNRY NES ETC		7782		10142		10887		9380	MACH APP ELECT NDA
772	SWITCHGEAR ETC,PARTS NES	W 42	856	W 72	1677	W 35	716	W 25	518	APP COUPURE,SECT ETC
7721	SWITCHGEAR ETC	W 42	856	W 72	1677	W 35	716	W 25	518	APP COUPURE,SECTIONMNT
773	ELECTR DISTRIBUTNG EQUIP	W 242	900	W 536	2263	W 228	1282	W 174	596	EQUIPMT DISTRIBUTION ELECT
7731	INSULATED WIRE,CABLE ETC	W 242	900	W 536	2263	W 228	1282	W 174	596	FILS,CABLES ISOLES ELECT
775	HOUSEHOLD TYPE EQUIP NES	W 158	1192	W 125	865	W 136	1267	W 172	727	MACH,APP USAGE DOMESTQUE
776	TRANSISTORS,VALVES,ETC	W 43	1722	W 50	1072	W 74	1120	W 37	1060	LAMPES,TUBES,VALVES
7763	DIODES,TRANSISTORS,ETC	W 7	1386	W 16	734	W 3	738	W 4	755	DIODES,TRANSISTORS
778	ELECTRICAL MACHINERY NES	W 856	2578	W 3091	3931	W 3779	6031	W 4374	6356	AUTRES MACH ELECT NDA
7781	BATTERIES,ACCUMULATORS	W 822	1937	W 3076	3571	W 3753	5462	W 4354	6037	PILES ET ACCUMULATEURS
77811	PRIMARY BATTERIES,CELLS	W 459	661	W 2760	2539	W 3545	4639	W 4117	5360	PILES ELECTRIQUES,PIECES
77812	ELECTRIC ACCUMULATORS	W 363	1276	W 316	1031	W 208	823	W 237	677	ACCUMULATEURS ELECTRIQ
78	ROAD VEHICLES		39713		30510		26736		18547	VEHICULES ROUTIERS
781	PASS MOTOR VEH EXC BUSES	W 5357	19877	W 5357	7624	W 3575	8837	W 3759	6069	AUTO TRANSPORT PERSONNES
782	LORRIES,SPCL MTR VEH NES	W 2539	12085	W 2539	17462	W 1663	13131	W 4793	8753	VEHICULES SPECIAUX,MARCH
784	MOTOR VEH PRTS,ACCES NES	W 557	5546	W 557	4787	W 238	4173	W 240	3074	PIECES 722,781,782,783
786	TRAILERS,NONMOTR VEH,NES	W 401	1279	W 505	310	W 188	206	W 301	291	REMORQUES,CADRES,CONTAIN
8	MISC MANUFACTURED GOODS		16177		20337		24183		11929	ART MANUFACTURES DIVERS
821	*FURNITURE,PARTS THEREOF	W 209	1893	W 415	1937	W 246	2924	W 257	1060	MEUBLES ET PIECES
8219	FURNITURE AND PARTS NES	W 178	816	W 320	1135	W 167	2160	W 223	805	AUTRES MEUBLES ET PIECES
84	CLOTHING AND ACCESSORIES		1259		1113		1429		833	VETEMENTS
851	*FOOTWEAR	W 1473	2501	W 1936	2956	W 1701	4176	W 885	2457	CHAUSSURES
87	PRECISION INSTRUMNTS NES		6110		8722		6865		5250	INSTRUM,APPAR SCIENT NDA
872	MEDICAL INSTRUMENTS NES	W 21	645	W 52	962	W 102	3276	W 62	1914	INSTR,APP MEDIC-CHIR NDA
874	MEASURNG,CONTROLNG INSTR	W 94	5465	W 156	7759	W 77	3589	W 67	3336	INSTRUMENTS DE MESURE
8741	SURVEYING INSTRUMENTS	W 16	2179	W 102	1379	W 11	830	W 7	691	INST GEODESIE,TOPO ETC
8748	ELEC MEAS,CONTRL EQU NES	W 67	2853	W 48	6176	W 61	2512	W 56	2503	APP ELEC ELECTRO MESURE
89	MISC MANUFCTRD GOODS NES		4414		5609		8789		2329	ART MANUFACTURES DIVERS
892	PRINTED MATTER	W 197	3219	W 169	2392	W 250	4856	W 141	2113	IMPRIMES
8921	PRINTED BOOKS,GLOBES,ETC	W 148	2273	W 111	1376	W 196	3754	W 95	1110	LIVRES,BROCHURES,CARTES
893	ARTICLES OF PLASTIC NES	W 425	1195	W 953	3217	W 829	3934	W 113	216	OUVRAGES EN MAT DIVIS 58
8939	MISC PLASTIC ARTICLES	W 425	1195	W 953	3217	W 829	3934	W 113	216	ART DIVERS EN MAT DIV 58
89399	OTHR PLASTC ARTICLES NES	W 425	1195	W 953	3217	W 829	3934	W 113	216	AUT OUV MAT DIV 58
9	GOODS NOT CLASSD BY KIND		81505		79742		76270		83740	ART TRANSACT NON CLASSES
931	*SPECIAL TRANSACTIONS	W 52923	81505	W 98992	79742	W 37978	76270	W 42129	83740	TRANS.SPECIALES

Niger

5. Special Exports F.O.B. by Commodities according to the S.I.T.C. (Rev. 2) in thousand U.S. Dollars
Exportations Spéciales F.O.B. par Produits d'après la C.T.C.I. (Rév. 2) en milliers de Dollars E.U.

SITC CTCI	COMMODITY	1988		1989		1990		1991		PRODUIT
		WEIGHT POIDS	VALUE VALEUR	WEIGHT POIDS	VALUE VALEUR	WEIGHT POIDS	VALUE VALEUR	WEIGHT POIDS	VALUE VALEUR	
	ALL COMMODITIES		288504		243621		282597		311910	TOUS PRODUITS
0	FOOD AND LIVE ANIMALS		20273		18355		20385		60538	ALIMENTS,ANIMAUX VIVANTS
001	*LIVE ANIMALS FOR FOOD	W 16798	11625	W 15008	10154	W 33065	7339	W 77645	52434	ANIMAUX VIVANTS
03	FISH AND PREPARATIONS		3		865		437			POISSONS ET PREPARATIONS
04	CEREALS AND PREPARATIONS		124		812		147		21	CEREALES ET PRODUITS
05	VEGETABLES AND FRUIT		8047		5737		12033		7671	LEGUMES ET FRUITS
054	VEG ETC FRSH,SMPLY PRSVD	W 28319	7963	W 47088	5615	W 93569	11871	W 57939	7604	LEGUMES FRAIS,CONG,SECS
1	BEVERAGES AND TOBACCO		896		5295		6575		6583	BOISSONS ET TABACS
12	TOBACCO AND MANUFACTURES		896		5295		6575		6583	TABACS BRUTS FABRIQUES
2	CRUDE MATERLS,EXCL FUELS		257321		209869		239799		235941	MAT BRUTES NON COMESTIBLES
26	TEXTILE FIBRES AND WASTE		4989		4088		4444		2162	FIBRES TEXTILES
263	COTTON	W 1086	4270	W 380	3944	W 1651	4408	W 921	2088	COTON
28	METALLIFEROUS ORES,SCRAP		251691		204844		234396		233300	MINERAIS METAL,DECHETS
288	NONFERR METAL SCRAP NES	W 6695	251691	W 6649	204844	W 7114	234396	W 2954	233300	DECHETS NON FERREUX
3	MINERAL FUELS ETC		27		16		7		2549	COMBUSTIBLES MINERAUX LUB
6	BASIC MANUFACTURES		3542		3323		5352		1755	ART MANUFACTURES
61	LEATHER,DRESSED FUR,ETC		2175		2706		4330		1478	CUIRS,PELLETERIES
611	LEATHER	W 566	2152	W 857	2633	W 924	4319	W 444	1468	CUIRS,PEAUX PREPARES
67	IRON AND STEEL		987		370		683		96	FER ET ACIER
7	MACHINES,TRANSPORT EQUIP		5636		5414		9326		3790	MACHINES MATERIEL TRANSPORT
78	ROAD VEHICLES		2568		1674		2542		808	VEHICULES ROUTIERS
79	OTHR TRANSPORT EQUIPMENT		3				2909		606	AUTRE MATERIEL TRANSPORT
8	MISC MANUFACTURED GOODS		604		1069		687		507	ART MANUFACTURES DIVERS
88	PHOTO EQU,OPTICL GDS ETC		426		909		400		269	APP,FOURN PHOTO,OP,MONTR

1. HISTORICAL SERIES, 1959–1994 GENERAL TRADE, IMPORTS C.I.F., EXPORTS F.O.B.
SERIES HISTORIQUES, 1959–1994 COMMERCE GENERAL, IMPORTATIONS C.A.F., EXPORTATIONS F.O.B

YEAR ANNEE	VALUE IN MILLION NAIRA VALEUR EN MILLION NAIRA MERCHANDISE – MARCHANDISE		GOLD – OR		CONVERSION FACTORS U.S. CENTS PER NAIRA FACTEURS DE CONVERSION CENTS E.U. PAR NAIRA		INDEX NUMBERS – INDICES QUANTUM		UNIT VALUE VALEUR UNITAIRE	
	IMPORTS	EXPORTS	IMPORTS	EXPORTS	IMPORTS	EXPORTS	IMPORTS	EXPORTS	IMPORTS	EXPORTS
1959	356.80	327.00			140.0000	140.0000				122
1960	431.80	339.40			140.0000	140.0000				123
1961	444.80	346.90			140.0000	140.0000				115
1962	406.40	337.10			140.0000	140.0000				110
1963	415.10	379.30			140.0000	140.0000				115
1964	507.80	429.30			140.0000	140.0000				118
1965	550.30	536.50			140.0000	140.0000				
1966	512.70	568.20			140.0000	140.0000				
1967	447.10	483.60			140.0000	140.0000				
1968	386.40	422.20			140.0000	140.0000				
1969	497.40	636.20			140.0000	140.0000				
1970	756.40	885.40			140.0000	140.0000				
1971	1075.10	1293.30			140.0000	140.0000				
1972	990.10	1434.20			152.0000	152.0000				
1973	1224.80	2277.40			152.2670	152.1880				
1974	1737.30	5794.90			159.5650	158.6630				
1975	3721.50	4925.50			162.3340	162.2930				
1976	5148.50	6751.10			159.5280	159.5460				
1977	7089.70	7630.70			154.9650	155.1420				
1978	8140.80	6324.80			156.5050	156.2490				
1979	6169.20	10400.00			166.1990	166.7130				
1980	8217.10	13712.70			182.8530	182.3080				
1981	12602.60	11034.20			162.2908	163.9151				
1982	10100.10	9223.40			148.5400	148.5871				
1983	6555.70	7751.80			138.2300	137.5468				
1984	4484.50	9138.80			130.8500	131.5218				
1985	5536.90	11720.80			112.0600	111.8740				
1986	5975.40	9047.60			67.4204	65.1952				
1987	15698.00	29577.92			24.9600	24.9600				
1988	17645.10	31192.80			22.0410	22.0410				
1989	25177.60	59928.80			13.5790	13.5790				
1990	45717.90	104108.00			12.4500	12.4500				100
1991	89488.00	121534.00			10.1380	10.1380				97
1992	143151.00	205613.00			6.1280	6.1280				97
1993	165629.40	218765.20			4.5360	4.5360				95
1994	143226.00	206059.00			4.5500	4.5500				107

2. IMPORTS BY BROAD ECONOMIC CATEGORY AND EXPORTS BY INDUSTRIAL ORIGIN. (PERCENTAGE OF TOTAL VALUE)
IMPORTATIONS PAR CATEGORIES ECONOMIQUES ET EXPORTATIONS PAR BRANCHE D'ACTIVITE. (EN POURCENTAGE DE LA VALEUR TOTALE)

IMPORTS – IMPORTATIONS

	1990	1991	1992	1993	1994	1995	1996
TOTAL IMPORTS–IMPORTATIONS TOTALES		100.					
1 FOOD BEV–ALIMENTATION BOISSONS		5.9					
11 PRIMARY–PRODUITS DE BASE		2.5					
111 FOR INDUSTRY–POUR L'INDUSTRIE		0.2					
112 FOR HOUSEHOLDS–POUR LES MENAGES		2.3					
12 PROCESSED–PRODUITS ELABORES		3.4					
121 FOR INDUSTRY–POUR L'INDUSTRIE		0.5					
122 FOR HOUSEHOLDS–POUR LES MENAGES		2.9					
2 IND SUPPLIES–APPROV INDUSTRIELS		32.1					
21 PRIMARY–PRODUITS DE BASE		1.6					
22 PROCESSED–PRODUITS ELABORES		30.5					
3 FUELS–COMBUSTIBLES		0.3					
31 PRIMARY–PRODUITS DE BASE		0.0					
32 PROCESSED–PRODUITS ELABORES		0.3					
321 MOTOR SPIRIT–ESSENCE		0.1					
322 OTHER–AUTRES		0.2					
4 MACHINERY–EQUIPEMENT		19.8					
41 CAPITAL EQUIPMENT–MACHINES		15.1					
42 PARTS–PIECES ACCESSOIRES		4.7					
5 TRANSPORT–TRANSPORT		12.8					
51 PASSENGER CARS–AUTOMOBILES		5.0					
52 OTHER–AUTRES		3.0					
521 INDUSTRIAL–INDUSTRIELS		2.9					
522 NON INDUSTRIAL–NON INDUSTRIEL		0.1					
53 PARTS–PIECES ACCESSOIRES		4.8					
6 CONSUM GOODS–BIENS CONSOMMATION		5.6					
61 DURABLE–DURABLES		2.9					
62 SEMI DURABLE–SEMI DURABLES		1.3					
63 NON DURABLE–NON DURABLES		1.4					
7 GOODS NES–BIENS NDA		23.6					

EXPORTS – EXPORTATIONS

	1990	1991	1992	1993	1994	1995	1996
TOTAL EXPORTS–EXPORTATIONS TOTALES		100.					
1 AGRICULTURE		1.6					
2 MINING QUARRY–INDUS EXTRACTIVES		96.5					
3 MANUFACTURING–IND MANUFACTUR		1.9					
31 FOOD BEV TOBACCO–ALIM BOISS TAB		0.2					
32 TEXTILES–INDUSTRIES TEXTILES		0.3					
33 WOOD & PRODUCTS–BOIS & PRODUITS		0.0					
34 PAPER & PRODUCTS–PAPIER & PRODT		0.0					
35 CHEMICALS–INDUSTRIES CHIMIQUES		0.6					
36 NON METAL MIN–MIN NON METAL		0.0					
37 BASIC METAL–IND METAL BASE		0.0					
38 METAL MANUF–MANUF METAL		0.1					
39 OTH MANUF IND–AUTRES MANUF		0.6					

3. TRADE BY PRINCIPAL COUNTRIES OF PRODUCTION AND LAST CONSIGNMENT (VALUE IN THOUSAND U.S. DOLLARS)
ECHANGES SELON LES PRINCIPAUX PAYS DE PRODUCTION ET DE DERNIERE CONSIGNATION (VALEUR EN MILLIERS DE DOLLARS EU)

COUNTRIES–PAYS	GENERAL IMPORTS C.I.F. IMPORTATIONS GENERALES C.A.F				
	1990	1991	1992	1993	1994
World	4317921	7114360		7513000	6517000
Africa	32475	57349		38000	45000
Americas	581433	792520			
Northern America	393260	589209			
LAIA	186140	201550			
CACM					
Caribbean	659	538			
Rest of America	1375	1224			
As.ex F.USSR	711341	1162565		217000	180000
Eur.x F.USSR	2816851	4960973			
EU	2570821	4677048			
EFTA	143371	190862			
East Europe	81607	56538			
Other Europe	61	36524			
Former USSR	13293	15409			
Oceania	5203	5427			
United Kingdom	739417	2324956			
Germany/Allemagne	644589	881035			
USA/Etats–Unis d'Amer	373963	563039			
France,Monac	394209	440375			
Japan/Japon	257434	401280			
Netherlands/Pays–Bas	207208	298537			
Italy/Italie	193827	297904			
Brazil/Brésil	175801	179085			
China/Chine	128230	189776			
Belgium–Luxembourg	143671	160020			
Switz.Liecht	115829	142016			
Hong Kong	96415	126287			
Saudi Arabia	3495	39330		78000	76000
India/Inde	67082	85003			
Indonesia/Indonésie	10253	19626		59000	58000
Korea, Republic of	53977	80463			
Malaysia/Malaisie	9153	18012		68000	29000
Spain/Espagne	59463	55258			
Greece/Grèce	45896	58510			
Singapore/Singapour	34444	50349			
Austria/Autriche	33384	49845			
Israel/Israël	36603	31421			
Sweden/Suède	29728	38056			
Ireland/Irlande	34175	32240			
Denmark/Danemark	24875	28730			
Poland/Pologne	22143	28329			
Canada	18282	26132			
Iceland/Islande	12110	30155			
Morocco/Maroc	9796	10570		10000	11000
Norway,SVD,JM	15432	18691			
Bulgaria/Bulgarie	17355	12771			
Czechoslovakia	20914	8974			
Former USSR/Anc. URSS	13293	15409			
Niger	8487	4733		5000	6000
Yugoslavia/Yougoslavie	20990				
Finland/Finlande	13319	6980			
Pakistan	582	721		9000	9000
Cameroon/Cameroun	584	2503		6000	8000
Argentina/Argentine	6384	10435			
Thailand/Thaïlande	6518	9509			
Romania/Roumanie	10456	3042			
Togo	1075	11933			
Portugal	7060	4603			
Senegal/Sénégal	1266	1254		4000	5000
Turkey/Turquie	2206	4312			5000
Benin/Bénin	474	2013		4000	5000
Hungary/Hongrie	7758	3423			
Mexico/Mexique	1828	8736			
Cote d'Ivoire	4627	5392			
Australia/Australie	5120	4722			

COUNTRIES–PAYS	GENERAL EXPORTS F.O.B. EXPORTATIONS GENERALES F.O.B.				
	1990	1991	1992	1993	1994
Monde	10241646	12827941		9923000	9376000
Afrique	667756	668879		234000	238000
Amériques	5746329	6410137			
Amérique du Nord	5674514	6165371			
ALAI	70515	197663			
MCAC					
Caraïbes	9	41			
Autre Amérique	1291	47062			
Asie l'URSS exclus	37527	68497		10000	15000
Europe l'URSS exclus	3750438	5640599			
UE	3741402	5613368			
AELE	1759	1849			
Europe de l'Est	512	1751			
Autre de l'Europe	303	23631			
Ancienne URSS	14251	9540			
Océanie	10	2			
USA/Etats–Unis d'Amer	5551527	6011690			
Spain/Espagne	939451	2070045			
Netherlands/Pays–Bas	933627	878331			
Germany/Allemagne	591369	918662			
Italy/Italie	298146	935714			
France,Monac	292856	497179			
Cote d'Ivoire	224270	298050			
United Kingdom	298914	148715			
Portugal	282531	134992			
Ghana	224694	189966			
Cameroon/Cameroun	73763	78234		87000	91000
Canada	117584	150988			
Senegal/Sénégal	42877	157		66000	68000
Brazil/Brésil	9423	125754			
Chile/Chili	27464	52979			
Dem. Rep. of the Congo	32135	37722			
Gabon	105	20515		22000	21000
Sweden/Suède	54751	1628			
Chad/Tchad	24818	8264		10000	10000
Guinea/Guinée	5075	12861		17000	17000
Uruguay	32537	16978			
Morocco/Maroc	1961	5299		20000	20000
Philippines	9	40403			
Sierra Leone	15916	5894		7000	7000
Austria/Autriche	35471	2			
Belgium–Luxembourg	9372	25338			
Singapore/Singapour	16628	16006			
Former USSR/Anc. URSS	14251	9540			
Fm Yugoslav		23238			
Malaysia/Malaisie	130	225		8000	7000
Niger	3678	2519		3000	3000
Bermuda/Bermudes	5403	2693			
Liberia/Libéria	7270	689			
Saudi Arabia	2767	302		1000	3000
India/Inde	3878	3093			
Yugoslavia/Yougoslavie	6462				
China/Chine	5565	552			
Togo	3775	2092			
Kenya	3687	1993			
Japan/Japon	2998	2302			
Turkey/Turquie	107	670			4000
Hong Kong	2278	1661			
Denmark/Danemark	2261	726			
Switz.Liecht	1459	1494			
Ireland/Irlande	1143	1752			
Indonesia/Indonésie	4	856		1000	1000
Benin/Bénin	966	1241			
Gambia/Gambie	591	424		1000	
Algeria/Algérie		6		1000	1000
Poland/Pologne	242	1663			

(VALUE AS PERCENTAGE OF WORLD TOTAL)(VALEURS EN POURCENTAGE DU TOTAL MONDIAL)

	1985	1986	1987	1988	1989	1990	1991	1992	1993	1994
Africa	1.0		1.3	1.2	1.1	0.8	0.8		0.5	0.7
Americas	18.3		12.9	14.7	14.5	13.5	11.1			
Northern America	13.6		7.5	9.9	10.8	9.1	8.3			
LAIA	3.8		5.3	4.8	3.6	4.3	2.8			
CACM			0.0	0.0	0.0					
Caribbean	0.9		0.0	0.0	0.1	0.0	0.0			
Rest of America	0.0			0.0	0.0	0.0	0.0			
As.ex F.USSR	12.1		15.9	16.2	16.8	16.5	16.3		2.9	2.8
Eur.x F.USSR	68.6		69.9	65.7	66.0	65.2	69.7			
EU	63.1		64.5	60.5	61.5	59.5	65.7			
EFTA	4.7		3.3	3.3	3.0	3.3	2.7			
East Europe	0.2		1.6	1.4	0.9	1.9	0.8			
Other Europe	0.6		0.6	0.5	0.3	0.0	0.5			
Former USSR	0.0			0.8	0.2	0.3	0.2			
Oceania	0.1		0.0	0.1	0.1	0.1	0.1			
United Kingdom	21.2		18.3	17.0	17.1	17.1	32.7			
Germany/Allemagne	10.9		12.2	13.6	14.6	14.9	12.4			
USA/Etats–Unis d'Amer	12.6		7.1	9.4	10.3	8.7	7.9			
France,Monac	10.7		9.7	9.4	8.7	9.1	6.2			
Japan/Japon	6.6		8.3	7.9	7.5	6.0	5.6			
Netherlands/Pays–Bas	4.2		5.3	4.6	4.5	4.8	4.2			
Italy/Italie	6.7		7.7	6.1	6.5	4.5	4.2			
Brazil/Brésil	3.6		5.3	4.6	3.4	4.1	2.5			
China/Chine				1.3	1.5	3.0	2.7			
Belgium–Luxembourg			2.8	3.0	3.2	3.3	2.2			

	1985	1986	1987	1988	1989	1990	1991	1992	1993	1994
Afrique	1.8		2.4	3.3	4.1	6.5	5.2		2.4	2.5
Amériques	31.1		57.6	51.7	53.2	56.1	50.0			
Amérique du Nord	23.0		42.5	47.5	50.3	55.4	48.1			
ALAI	7.9		3.8	3.4	2.8	0.7	1.5			
MCAC				0.0	0.0					
Caraïbes	0.2		11.3	0.8	0.2	0.0	0.0			
Autre Amérique	0.0			0.0	0.0	0.0	0.4			
Asie l'URSS exclus	0.5		0.2	0.6	0.8	0.4	0.5		0.1	0.2
Europe l'URSS exclus	66.4		39.8	44.0	41.7	36.6	44.0			
UE	63.6		38.9	43.3	41.0	36.5	43.8			
AELE	2.8		0.8	0.6	0.6	0.0	0.0			
Europe de l'Est	0.0			0.0	0.0	0.0	0.0			
Autre de l'Europe	0.0		0.0	0.0	0.0	0.0	0.2			
Ancienne URSS	0.1			0.1	0.0	0.1	0.1			
Océanie	0.0		0.0	0.1	0.0	0.0	0.0			
USA/Etats–Unis d'Amer	21.8		40.5	45.5	48.9	54.2	46.9			
Spain/Espagne	5.9		9.0	10.0	10.5	9.2	16.1			
Netherlands/Pays–Bas	4.6		4.1	8.5	6.4	9.1	6.8			
Germany/Allemagne	15.0		8.2	8.4	6.9	5.8	7.2			
Italy/Italie	11.3		3.4	2.6	4.1	2.9	7.3			
France,Monac	12.0		6.2	7.2	5.8	2.9	3.9			
Cote d'Ivoire	1.4		2.1	1.1	1.2	2.2	2.3			
United Kingdom	5.9		2.8	2.6	2.5	2.9	1.2			
Portugal	1.9		1.7	1.7	2.5	2.8	1.1			
Ghana				0.7	1.0	2.2	1.5			

4. General Imports C.I.F. by Commodities according to the S.I.T.C. (Rev. 2) in thousand U.S. Dollars
Importations Générales C.A.F. par Produits d'après la C.T.C.I. (Rév. 2) en milliers de Dollars E.U.

SITC CTCI	COMMODITY	1989 WEIGHT POIDS	1989 VALUE VALEUR	1990 WEIGHT POIDS	1990 VALUE VALEUR	1991 WEIGHT POIDS	1991 VALUE VALEUR	1992 WEIGHT POIDS	1992 VALUE VALEUR	PRODUIT
	ALL COMMODITIES		3419079		4317921		7114360		7148944	TOUS PRODUITS
0	FOOD AND LIVE ANIMALS		233649		330174		402607		583648	ALIMENTS,ANIMAUX VIVANTS
02	DAIRY PRODCTS,BIRDS'EGGS						73695			PRODUITS LAITIERS,OEUFS
022	MILK AND CREAM		40309		21038	W 79999	72737			LAIT ET CREME
0224	MILK,CREAM PRESERVED ETC					W 60066	57424			LAIT,CREME CONS,CONC
02242	MILK DRY,1.5% FAT OR LES					W 41639	32273			LAIT POUDRE INF 1.5%
03	FISH AND PREPARATIONS						141969			POISSONS ET PREPARATIONS
034	FISH,FRESH,CHILLED,FROZN		1903		676	W 290045	128125			POISSON FRAIS, REFRIG,CONG
0342	FISH FROZEN,EXCL FILLETS					W 221119	87605			POISSONS CONGELES
0344	FISH FILLETS,FROZEN					W 38499	25296			FILETS CONGELES
06	SUGAR AND PREPS,HONEY						124638			SUCRES ET PRODUITS
061	SUGAR AND HONEY		78566		120831	W 477818	120039			SUCRES ET MIEL
0612	REFINED SUGAR ETC					W 449780	108360			SUCRES RAFFINES
09	MISC EDIBLE PRODUCTS						27810			PREP ALIMENTAIRES DIVERSES
098	EDIBLE PRODCTS,PREPS NES					W 37734	27782			PREP ALIMENTAIRES NDA
1	BEVERAGES AND TOBACCO		15074		19702		10864		14307	BOISSONS ET TABACS
2	CRUDE MATERLS,EXCL FUELS		119716		134638		127841		179445	MAT BRUTES NON COMESTIBLES
26	TEXTILE FIBRES AND WASTE						21672			FIBRES TEXTILES
27	CRUDE FERTLZR,MINRLS NES						52612			ENGRAIS MINERAUX BRUTS
278	OTHER CRUDE MINERALS					W 317539	43343			AUTRES MINERAUX BRUTS
2783	COMMON SALT,ETC					W 253578	24310			SEL
29	CRUDE ANIMAL,VEG MAT NES						22965			MATIERES BRUTES ANIM,VEGET
3	MINERAL FUELS ETC		28674		27343		35420		37781	COMBUSTIBLES MINERAUX LUB
33	PETROLEUM AND PRODUCTS						33051			PETROLE ET DERIVES
334	PETROLEUM PRODUCTS,REFIN		14454		10723	W 13864	18814			PRODUITS RAFFINES
4	ANIMAL,VEGETABLE OIL,FAT		7739		20656		35272		47358	HUILES,GRAISSES ANIM,VEG
411	*ANIMAL OILS AND FATS					W 70408	28927			HUILES,GRAISSES ANIMALES
4113	ANIML OIL,FAT,GREASE NES					W 57993	23554			HUILES,GRAISSES ANIMALES NDA
5	CHEMCLS,RELATED PROD NES		780144		851255		980189		1294712	PRODUITS CHIMIQUES
51	ORGANIC CHEMICALS						125555			PROD CHIMIQ ORGANIQUES
511	HYDROCARBONS NES,DERIVS					W 36201	28520			HYDROCARBURES NDA
512	ALCOHOLS,PHENOLS ETC					W 32456	25465			PHENOLS,PHENOLS–ALCOOLS
514	NITROGEN–FNCTN COMPOUNDS					W 19416	26840			COMPOSES FONCT AZOTEES
52	INORGANIC CHEMICALS						115463			PROD CHIM INORGANIQUES
522	INORG ELEMNTS,OXIDES,ETC					W 161004	73708			ELEMENTS INORGANIQUES
5225	INORGANIC BASES ETC NES					W 131219	46218			AUTRES BASES OXYDES METAL
52252	SODIUM HYDROXIDE, SOLID					W 118583	36193			HYDROXYDE DE SODIUM
523	OTHR INORG CHEMICALS ETC					W 75943	41465			AUT PRODUITS CHIMIQUES INORG
5231	METAL CMPD OF INORG ACID					W 37660	23663			SELS METALLIQUES
53	DYES,TANNING,COLOUR PROD						143453			PROD TEINTURE,COLORANTS
531	SYNT DYE,NAT INDGO,LAKES					W 30859	49767			MAT COLOR ORGAN,LAQUES
5311	SYNTHIC ORGNIC DYESTUFFS					W 27749	42343			MAT COLOR ORGAN SYNTHET
533	PIGMENTS,PAINTS,ETC					W 46986	74666			PIGMENTS,PEINTURES,VERNIS
5331	COLOURING MATERIAL NES					W 21609	31703			AUT MATIERES COLORANTES
5334	VARNISHES,DISTEMPERS ETC					W 13655	23477			PEINTURES A L'EAU
541	*MEDICINAL,PHARM PRODUCT		72152		79191		71106			PROD MEDICINAUX PHARMACEUT
5419	PHARMACEUTICAL GOODS NES						57073			PREP,ART PHARMACEUTIQUES
54199	OTH PHARMACEUTICAL GOODS						51444			AUT PREP PHARMACEUTIQUES
55	PERFUME,CLEANING ETC PRD						67894			PROD POUR PARFUM,TOILETTE
551	ESSENTL OILS,PERFUME,ETC					W 30967	51955			HUILES ESSENTIELLES
5513	ESSENTL OIL,RESINOID,ETC					W 21224	31328			HUILES ESSENTIELLES,RESIN
562	*FERTILIZERS,MANUFACTURE					W 129385	31398			ENGRAIS MANUFACTURES
58	PLASTIC MATERIALS ETC						237107			MAT PLAST ARTIFICIELLES
582	PROD OF CONDENSATION ETC					W 19367	24204			PROD CONDENS,POLYCOND
583	POLYMERIZATION ETC PRODS						196034			PROD POLYMERISATION
5831	POLYETHYLENE						173688			POLYETHYLENE
58311	— IN PRIMARY FORMS						169557			POLYETHYLENE PRIMAIRES
59	CHEMICAL MATERIALS NES						170956			MAT PROD CHIMIQUES NDA
598	MISCEL CHEM PRODUCTS NES					W 106966	135700			PROD DIV INDUST CHIM NDA
5981	CHEMCLS FROM WOOD,RESIN					W 12568	22645			PROD CHIM BASE BOIS RESIN
5989	CHEM PRODUCTS,PREPS NES					W 92032	109218			PROD PREP CHIMIQUES NDA
59899	OTH CHEM PRODS,PREPS,NES					W 84088	94028			AUT PRODUITS CHIMIQUES NDA
6	BASIC MANUFACTURES		724711		966128		1252050		1644141	ART MANUFACTURES
62	RUBBER MANUFACTURES NES						93734			CAOUTCHOUC MANUFACTURE
625	RUBBER TYRES, TUBES ETC					W 40844	70422			PNEUS CAOUTCHOUC VULCANISE
6251	TYRES NEW FOR MOTOR CARS					W 20058	44956			PNEUS POUR VOITURES
64	PAPER,PAPERBOARD AND MFR						129512			PAPIERS,CARTONS & OUVRAGES
641	PAPER AND PAPERBOARD					W 101120	107263			PAPIERS ET CARTONS
6412	PRINTG,WRITING PAPER NES					W 44347	46539			PAPIERS POUR L'IMPRESSION
64121	— UNCOATED					W 40212	40402			PAPIERS IMPRES NON COUCHES
642	PAPER,ETC,PRECUT,ARTS OF		113764		200201	W 16124	22249			PAP,CARTONS DECOUPES
65	TEXTILE YARN,FABRICS,ETC						54982			FILS,TISSUS,ARTICLES TEXTILE
651	TEXTILE YARN		20640		11402	W 7043	15796			FILS TEXTILES
657	SPECIAL TXTL FABRC,PRODS					W 13619	23989			TISSUS SPECIAUX
66	NONMETAL MINERAL MFS NES						197773			ART MIN NON METALLIQUES
661	LIME,CEMENT,BLDG PRODS		28916		61381	W 1521454	112963			CHAUX,CIMENTS MAT CONSTR
6612	CEMENT					W 1516532	107255			CIMENTS HYDRAULIQUES
662	CLAY,REFRACTORY BLDG PRD					W 24411	31386			MAT CONST REFRACTAIRES
665	GLASSWARE					W 14245	22162			OUVRAGES EN VERRE
67	IRON AND STEEL						571393			FER ET ACIER
671	PIG IRON ETC					W 29130	47026			FONTE,SPIEGEL,POUDRES
6713	IRON,STL POWDER,SHOT,ETC					W 27814	44679			POUDRES,GREN FER,ACIER
67131	IRON,STEEL SHOT,GRIT,ETC					W 18914	33850			GRENAILLE FER,ACIER
672	IRON,STEEL PRIMARY FORMS					W 30045	79210			LINGOTS FER,ACIER
6727	IRN,STL COIL FR REROLLNG					W 24252	63413			EBAUCHES POUR TOLES FER
67271	IRON,SIMPLE STEEL COILS					W 18175	54247			EBAUCHES NON EN ACIER
673	IRON,STEEL SHAPES ETC		59184		105621	W 238086	149030			BARRES,PROFIL FER,ACIER
6733	IRON,STEEL PROFILES ETC					W 223763	130205			PROFILES,PALPLAN FER,ACIER
67334	OTH PRFILES COLDFRMD ETC					W 208087	112251			PROFILES OBTENUS A FROID
674	IRN,STL UNIV,PLATE,SHEET		44535		41438	W 41086	91808			LARGES PLATS,TOLES
6747	TINNED PLATES,SHEETS					W 27092	57298			TOLES ETAMEES EN ACIER
678	IRON,STL TUBES,PIPES,ETC					W 84679	184807			TUBES,TUYAUX EN FONTE,FER
6781	CAST IRON TUBES,PIPES					W 16951	36340			TUBES,TUYAUX EN FONTE
6782	IRON,STL SEAMLESS TUBES					W 9285	28195			TUBES,TUYAUX SANS SOUDURE
6783	IRON,STL TUBES,PIPES NES					W 9455	25847			AUT TUBES,TUYAUX FER,ACIER
6785	IRON,STEEL TUBE FITTINGS					W 47252	91679			ACCESSOIRES DE TUYAUTERIE
68	NON–FERROUS METALS						69648			METAUX NON FERREUX
684	ALUMINIUM					W 19273	42141			ALUMINIUM
6842	ALUMINIUM,ALLOYS WORKED					W 13517	32196			ALUMINIUM,ALLIAGES OUVRE
69	METAL MANUFACTURES NES						131632			ART MANUFACT EN METAL NDA
697	BASE MTL HOUSEHOLD EQUIP					W 5102	28618			ART MENAGE MET COMMUNS

4. General Imports C.I.F. by Commodities according to the S.I.T.C. (Rev. 2) in thousand U.S. Dollars
Importations Générales C.A.F. par Produits d'après la C.T.C.I. (Rév. 2) en milliers de Dollars E.U.

SITC CTCI	COMMODITY	1989 WEIGHT POIDS	1989 VALUE VALEUR	1990 WEIGHT POIDS	1990 VALUE VALEUR	1991 WEIGHT POIDS	1991 VALUE VALEUR	1992 WEIGHT POIDS	1992 VALUE VALEUR	PRODUIT
6973	DMSTC HEATG,COOKG APPARA					W 3111	24961			APPS CHAUF NON ELECTRIQ
69734	COPPER DOMSTC STOVES,ETC					W 2315	23410			APP NON ELEC CUISSON CUIVRE
699	BASE METAL MFRS NES					W 16044	32799			ART MANUFACTURES MET NDA
7	MACHINES,TRANSPORT EQUIP		1369614		1747923		2340805		2990123	MACHINES MATERIEL TRANSPORT
71	POWER GENERATING EQUIPMT						131714			MACHINES GENERATRICES
713	INTRNL COMBUS PSTN ENGIN					W 13035	30971			MOTEURS EXPL COMB INT, PIECE
716	ROTATING ELECTRIC PLANT					W 19613	85734			APP ELECTR ROTATIFS,PIECES
7162	AC MTRS,GENRTRS,GEN SETS					W 16204	69109			MOTEURS ELECTRIQUES
71623	GEN SETS WITH PISTN ENGN					W 11070	50176			GROUPES MOTEUR EXPLOSION
72	MACHS FOR SPCL INDUSTRYS						438731			MAC SPECIALES POUR INDUST
721	AGRIC MACHY,EXC TRACTORS		41759		29810	W 6325	30205			MACHINES AGRICOLES
723	CIVIL ENGNEERG EQUIP ETC					W 31703	160224			APPAREILS DE GENIE CIVIL
7234	CONST,MINING MACHNRY NES					W 6704	54966			MACH POUR LA CONST, MINES
7239	CONSTR ETC MACHY PTS NES					W 24870	104639			PIECES 723.41–723.46
724	TEXTILE,LEATHER MACHNRY					W 25698	93758			MACH POUR INDUSTRIE TEXTILE
7245	WEAVING,FELT MFG,ETC MCH					W 3014	21369			METIERS A TISSER,PIECES
7247	TEXTILE MACHINERY NES					W 14408	46227			MACH LAVAGE,TEINTURE TEX
72479	TEXTILE MACHINRY PTS NES					W 9857	26364			PIECES POUR 724.7 775.1
728	OTH MACHY FOR SPCL INDUS					W 15835	104497			AUT MACH IND PARTICULIERES
7283	OTHR MINERAL WORKG MACHY					W 3941	25399			MACH TRIER,CRIBLER,BROYER
7284	MACHY FOR SPCL INDUS NES					W 11536	76647			MACH SPEC IND PARTICUL.
72848	OTH MCHY WITH INDIV FNCT					W 8134	60813			AUTRES MACHINES NDA
73	METALWORKING MACHINERY						36873			MACH TRAVAIL DES METAUX
736	METALWORKING MACH–TOOLS					W 7426	26484			MACH–OUTILS TRAVAIL METAUX
74	GENRL INDUSTRL MACHY NES						435456			MACH APP INDUSTRIE
741	HEATING,COOLING EQUIPMNT					W 5514	33386			MACH CHAUFFAGE,PIECES
742	PUMPS FOR LIQUIDS ETC					W 8361	41645			POMPES MOTO–POMPES
7428	OTHER PUMPS FOR LIQUIDS					W 5978	29370			AUTRES POMPES POUR LIQ
74288	PUMPS FR LIQUIDS NES ETC					W 5747	28193			POMPES POUR LIQUIDES NDA
743	PUMPS NES,CENTRFUGES ETC					W 21129	51907			POMPES COMPRES,VENT ETC
7431	PUMPS FOR GASES ETC					W 10387	25639			POMPES AIR A VIDE,COMPRES
744	MECHANICAL HANDLING EQU					W 6971	39663			EQUIP MANUTENTION PIECES
7442	LIFTING,LOADING MACH NES					W 3559	25883			APP LEVAGE,MANUTENTION
749	NONELEC MACH PTS,ACC NES					W 59541	255608			PIECES MACH NON ELEC NDA
7492	COCKS,VALVES ETC NES					W 10959	49131			ART ROB,SIM POUR TUYAUX
7499	OTH NONELEC MCHY PTS NES					W 42995	186889			PIECES NON ELECT NDA
74991	FOUNDRY MOULDS ETC NES					W 5667	24348			MOULES POUR METAUX
74999	MACH PARTS NONELEC NES					W 35990	157805			PIECES MACHINES NDA
75	OFFICE MACHNES,ADP EQUIP						42759			MACH BUREAU TRAIT AUTOM
76	TELECOMM,SOUND EQUIPMENT						242681			EQUIPMENT DE TELECOM
762	RADIO BROADCAST RECEIVRS					W 28254	90035			RECEPTEURS RADIODIFFUSION
7628	OTHER RADIO RECEIVERS					W 27230	85506			AUTRES RECEPT RADIO
763	SOUND RECORDRS,PHONOGRPH					W 8587	28323			PHONO,APP ENREGISTREMENT
764	TELECOM EQPT,PTS,ACC NES					W 8421	113902			EQUIP TELECOM,PIECES
7641	LINE TELEPHONE,ETC EQUIP					W 2640	62958			APP TELEPHON PAR FIL
77	ELECTRIC MACHNRY NES ETC						207986			MACH APP ELECT NDA
771	ELECTRIC POWER MACHY NES					W 4047	32082			MACH PROD,TRANS ELECTR
772	SWITCHGEAR ETC,PARTS NES					W 7202	22118			APP COUPURE,SECT ETC
773	ELECTR DISTRIBUTNG EQUIP					W 7151	27381			EQUIPMT DISTRIBUTION ELECT
7731	INSULATED WIRE,CABLE ETC					W 5876	23097			FILS,CABLES ISOLES ELECT
775	HOUSEHOLD TYPE EQUIP NES					W 7987	29485			MACH,APP USAGE DOMESTQUE
776	TRANSISTORS,VALVES,ETC					W 11897	28218			LAMPES,TUBES,VALVES
7768	ELCTRNC COMP PTS,CRYSTLS					W 11734	27457			CRIST PIEZO–ELEC,PCS 776
77689	ELECTRNIC COMPON PTS NES					W 11729	27440			PIECES DU GROUPE 776
778	ELECTRICAL MACHINERY NES					W 16912	68534			AUTRES MACH ELECT NDA
7788	OTH ELEC MACHY,EQUIP NES					W 11604	48021			AUT MACH APP ELEC NDA
78	ROAD VEHICLES						693420			VEHICULES ROUTIERS
781	PASS MOTOR VEH EXC BUSES		127487		239836	W 109849	358749			AUTO TRANSPORT PERSONNES
782	LORRIES,SPCL MTR VEH NES		24380		40382	W 9132	60847			VEHICULES SPECIAUX,MARCH
7821	LORRIES,TRUCKS					W 7321	43160			VEHICULES TRANSP MARCHAND
783	ROAD MOTOR VEHICLES NES					W 5247	45952			VEHICULES ROUTIERS NDA
7831	BUSES					W 2630	28772			VOITURES TRANSPORT COMMUN
784	MOTOR VEH PRTS,ACCES NES		137468		242025	W 146270	193096			PIECES 722,781,782,783
7849	OTHER MOTOR VEHCL PARTS					W 143141	187965			PIECES 722,781,782,783
785	CYCLES,ETC MOTRZD OR NOT					W 13109	30790			MOTOCYCLES SCOOTERS
7851	MOTORCYCLES ETC		16489		26640	W 3197	5678			MOTO VELO MOTEUR AUXIL
7853	INVAL CARR, PTS OF 785					W 9787	24697			FAUTEUILS INVALIDES,PIECES
78539	PARTS,ACCES NES OF 785					W 9486	24003			PIECES DU 785
79	OTHR TRANSPORT EQUIPMENT						111185			AUTRE MATERIEL TRANSPORT
793	SHIPS AND BOATS ETC						87247			NAVIRES BATEAUX,ETC
7932	SHIPS AND BOATS NES						73512			NAVIRES ET BATEAUX
79322	TANKERS OF ALL KINDS					W 5900	56082			BATEAUX–CITERNES
8	MISC MANUFACTURED GOODS		138501		207790		251789		350306	ART MANUFACTURES DIVERS
87	PRECISION INSTRUMNTS NES						75333			INSTRUM,APPAR SCIENT NDA
872	MEDICAL INSTRUMENTS NES					W 7762	29861			INSTR,APP MEDIC–CHIR NDA
87202	OTH MEDICAL INSTRUMENTS					W 7256	28372			INSTRUM,APP MEDECINE
874	MEASURNG,CONTROLNG INSTR					W 9889	38406			INSTRUMENTS DE MESURE
89	MISC MANUFCTRD GOODS NES						127291			ART MANUFACTURES DIVERS
892	PRINTED MATTER					W 22122	52166			IMPRIMES
8921	PRINTED BOOKS,GLOBES,ETC					W 16196	44897			LIVRES,BROCHURES,CARTES
89211	PRINTED BOOKS,PAMPHLETS					W 15237	31217			LIVRES,BROCHURES
893	ARTICLES OF PLASTIC NES					W 16634	27763			OUVRAGES EN MAT DIVIS 58
8939	MISC PLASTIC ARTICLES					W 13142	22042			ART DIVERS EN MAT DIV 58
9	GOODS NOT CLASSD BY KIND		735		12314		1677523		7124	ART TRANSACT NON CLASSES
931	*SPECIAL TRANSACTIONS					W 1052	1677133			TRANS.SPECIALES

5. General Exports F.O.B. by Commodities according to the S.I.T.C. (Rev. 2) in thousand U.S. Dollars
Exportations Générales F.O.B. par Produits d'après la C.T.C.I. (Rév. 2) en milliers de Dollars E.U.

SITC CTCI	COMMODITY	1989		1990		1991		1992		PRODUIT
		WEIGHT POIDS	VALUE VALEUR	WEIGHT POIDS	VALUE VALEUR	WEIGHT POIDS	VALUE VALEUR	WEIGHT POIDS	VALUE VALEUR	
	ALL COMMODITIES		8145435		10241646		12827941		11786765	TOUS PRODUITS
0	FOOD AND LIVE ANIMALS		172982		175818		181358		153230	ALIMENTS,ANIMAUX VIVANTS
07	COFFEE,TEA,COCOA,SPICES		146155		141309		145877			CAFE,THE,CACAO,EPICES
072	COCOA		144340		141238	W 160395	143824			CACAO
0721	COCOA BEANS,RAW,ROASTED		133414		134614	W 155692	133900			CACAO EN FEVES
2	CRUDE MATERLS,EXCL FUELS		122544		76211		78286		82491	MAT BRUTES NON COMESTIBLES
23	RUBBER, CRUDE		75327		47972		55963			CAOUTCHOUC BRUT
232	NATURAL RUBBER,GUMS		26715		11457	W 64221	35122			LATEX CAOUTCHOUC NATUREL
233	RUBBER,SYNTHTIC,RECLAIMD		48612		36515	W 35387	20841			LATEX CAOUTCH SYNTH REGEN
3	MINERAL FUELS ETC		7723788		9854811		12395967		11421376	COMBUSTIBLES MINERAUX LUB
33	PETROLEUM AND PRODUCTS		7560140		9824415		12395664			PETROLE ET DERIVES
333	CRUDE PETROLEUM		7544883		9820751		12375923			HUILES BRUTES DE PETROLE
5	CHEMCLS,RELATED PROD NES		34710		34423		31953		35370	PRODUITS CHIMIQUES
6	BASIC MANUFACTURES		24012		38985		46919		23561	ART MANUFACTURES
9	GOODS NOT CLASSD BY KIND		38068		45430		81290		58930	ART TRANSACT NON CLASSES
931	*SPECIAL TRANSACTIONS						81290			TRANS.SPECIALES

1. HISTORICAL SERIES, 1956–1993 GENERAL TRADE, IMPORTS C.I.F., EXPORTS F.O.B.
SERIES HISTORIQUES, 1956–1993 COMMERCE GENERAL, IMPORTATIONS C.A.F., EXPORTATIONS F.O.B

YEAR ANNEE	VALUE IN MILLION N.Z. DOLLARS VALEUR EN MILLION N.Z. DOLLARS MERCHANDISE –MARCHANDISE		GOLD –OR		CONVERSION FACTORS U.S. CENTS PER N.Z. DOLLAR FACTEURS DE CONVERSION CENTS E.U. PAR N.Z. DOLLAR		INDEX NUMBERS –INDICES QUANTUM		UNIT VALUE VALEUR UNITAIRE	
	IMPORTS	EXPORTS	IMPORTS	EXPORTS	IMPORTS	EXPORTS	IMPORTS	EXPORTS	IMPORTS	EXPORTS
1956	0.33	0.13			140.0000	140.0000				
1957	0.31	0.12			140.0000	140.0000				
1958	0.30	0.11			140.0000	140.0000				
1959	0.34	0.05			140.0000	140.0000				
1960	0.46	0.04			140.0000	140.0000				
1961	0.48	0.07			140.0000	140.0000				
1962	0.37	0.06			139.0000	139.0000				
1963	0.33	0.10			139.0000	139.0000				
1964	0.46	0.16			139.0000	139.0000				
1965	0.50	0.13			139.0000	139.0000				
1966	0.52	0.11			139.0000	139.0000				
1967	0.60	0.13			137.0000	137.0000				
1968	0.69	0.06			112.0000	112.0000				
1969	0.77	0.07			112.0000	112.0000				
1970	0.75	0.18			112.0000	112.0000				
1971	0.81	0.18			113.6080	113.6080				
1972	0.92	0.14			119.5000	119.5000				
1973	0.72	0.14			136.1970	136.3000				
1974	1.15	0.17			140.1000	140.1000				
1975	2.09	0.20			121.4560	121.4560				
1976	1.75	0.15			99.6370	99.4150				
1977	2.11	0.26			97.0830	96.9150				
1978	2.32	0.24			103.7760	103.9250				
1979	2.09	0.37			102.3470	102.3470				
1980	3.38	0.31			97.3400	97.3400				
1981	3.84	0.59			87.0000	87.0000				
1982	3.43	0.64			75.1875	75.1875				
1983	3.16	0.63			66.8800	66.8800				
1984	4.21	0.25			57.8500	57.8500				
1985	3.75	0.18			49.8400	49.8400				
1986		0.17				52.7457				
1987		0.12				57.8485				
1988		0.09				66.3134				
1991	5.86	0.08			57.9200	57.9200				
1992	7.22	0.19			53.8100	53.8100				
1993	6.96	0.54			54.0700	54.0700				

2. IMPORTS BY BROAD ECONOMIC CATEGORY AND EXPORTS BY INDUSTRIAL ORIGIN. (PERCENTAGE OF TOTAL VALUE)
IMPORTATIONS PAR CATEGORIES ECONOMIQUES ET EXPORTATIONS PAR BRANCHE D'ACTIVITE.(EN POURCENTAGE DE LA VALEUR TOTALE)

IMPORTS – IMPORTATIONS

	1990	1991	1992	1993	1994	1995	1996
TOTAL IMPORTS–IMPORTATIONS TOTALES							
1 FOOD BEV–ALIMENTATION BOISSONS							
11 PRIMARY–PRODUITS DE BASE							
111 FOR INDUSTRY–POUR L'INDUSTRIE							
112 FOR HOUSEHOLDS–POUR LES MENAGES							
12 PROCESSED–PRODUITS ELABORES							
121 FOR INDUSTRY–POUR L'INDUSTRIE							
122 FOR HOUSEHOLDS–POUR LES MENAGES							
2 IND SUPPLIES–APPROV INDUSTRIELS							
21 PRIMARY–PRODUITS DE BASE							
22 PROCESSED–PRODUITS ELABORES							
3 FUELS–COMBUSTIBLES							
31 PRIMARY–PRODUITS DE BASE							
32 PROCESSED–PRODUITS ELABORES							
321 MOTOR SPIRIT–ESSENCE							
322 OTHER–AUTRES							
4 MACHINERY–EQUIPEMENT							
41 CAPITAL EQUIPMENT–MACHINES							
42 PARTS–PIECES ACCESSOIRES							
5 TRANSPORT–TRANSPORT							
51 PASSENGER CARS–AUTOMOBILES							
52 OTHER–AUTRES							
521 INDUSTRIAL–INDUSTRIELS							
522 NON INDUSTRIAL–NON INDUSTRIEL							
53 PARTS–PIECES ACCESSOIRES							
6 CONSUM GOODS–BIENS CONSOMMATION							
61 DURABLE–DURABLES							
62 SEMI DURABLE–SEMI DURABLES							
63 NON DURABLE–NON DURABLES							
7 GOODS NES–BIENS NDA							

EXPORTS – EXPORTATIONS

	1990	1991	1992	1993	1994	1995	1996
TOTAL EXPORTS–EXPORTATIONS TOTALES							
1 AGRICULTURE							
2 MINING QUARRY–INDUS EXTRACTIVES							
3 MANUFACTURING–IND MANUFACTUR							
31 FOOD BEV TOBACCO–ALIM BOISS TAB							
32 TEXTILES–INDUSTRIES TEXTILES							
33 WOOD & PRODUCTS–BOIS & PRODUITS							
34 PAPER & PRODUCTS–PAPIER & PRODT							
35 CHEMICALS–INDUSTRIES CHIMIQUES							
36 NON METAL MIN–MIN NON METAL							
37 BASIC METAL–IND METAL BASE							
38 METAL MANUF–MANUF METAL							
39 OTH MANUF IND–AUTRES MANUF							

3. TRADE BY PRINCIPAL COUNTRIES OF PROVENANCE AND DESTINATION (VALUE IN THOUSAND U.S. DOLLARS)
ECHANGES SELON LES PRINCIPAUX PAYS DE PROVENANCE ET DE DESTINATION (VALEUR EN MILLIERS DE DOLLARS EU)

COUNTRIES–PAYS	GENERAL IMPORTS C.I.F. IMPORTATIONS GENERALES C.A.F					COUNTRIES–PAYS	GENERAL EXPORTS F.O.B. EXPORTATIONS GENERALES F.O.B.				
	1989	1990	1991	1992	1993		1989	1990	1991	1992	1993
World				3887	3477	Monde					
Africa						Afrique					
Americas				6	100	Amériques					
Northern America				5	100	Amérique du Nord					
LAIA						ALAI					
CACM						MCAC					
Caribbean						Caraïbes					
Rest of America						Autre Amérique					
As.ex F.USSR				230	213	Asie l'URSS exclus					
Eur.x F.USSR				4	7	Europe l'URSS exclus					
EU				4	7	UE					
EFTA						AELE					
East Europe						Europe de l'Est					
Other Europe						Autre de l'Europe					
Former USSR						Ancienne URSS					
Oceania				3647	3157	Océanie					
New Zealand				3196	2994						
Australia/Australie				417	51						
Japan/Japon				222	192						
Fiji/Fidji				12	70						
Samoa				15	24						
United Kingdom				1	7						

(VALUE AS PERCENTAGE OF WORLD TOTAL)(VALEURS EN POURCENTAGE DU TOTAL MONDIAL)

	1984	1985	1986	1987	1988	1989	1990	1991	1992	1993		1984	1985	1986	1987	1988	1989	1990	1991	1992	1993
Africa										0.0	Afrique										
Americas	1.2	0.1							0.1	2.9	Amériques		1.3								
Northern America	1.2	0.1							0.1	2.9	Amérique du Nord		1.3								
LAIA									0.0	0.0	ALAI										
CACM											MCAC										
Caribbean											Caraïbes										
Rest of America											Autre Amérique										
As.ex F.USSR	5.1	14.6							5.9	6.1	Asie l'URSS exclus										
Eur.x F.USSR	3.1	0.0							0.1	0.2	Europe l'URSS exclus	4.4									
EU	3.1	0.0							0.1	0.2	UE	4.4									
EFTA										0.0	AELE										
East Europe											Europe de l'Est										
Other Europe											Autre de l'Europe										
Former USSR	0.7										Ancienne URSS	2.7									
Oceania	89.1	85.4							93.8	90.8	Océanie	92.7	98.7	100.0	100.0						
New Zealand	56.2	59.5							82.2	86.1											
Australia/Australie	0.7	1.6							10.7	1.5											
Japan/Japon	5.0	13.3							5.7	5.5											
Fiji/Fidji	29.0	20.1							0.3	2.0											
Samoa	2.4	2.4							0.4	0.7											
United Kingdom	3.0								0.0	0.2											

4. General Imports C.I.F. by Commodities according to the S.I.T.C. (Rev. 2) in thousand U.S. Dollars
Importations Générales C.A.F. par Produits d'après la C.T.C.I. (Rév. 2) en milliers de Dollars E.U.

SITC CTCI	COMMODITY	1990		1991		1992		1993		PRODUIT
		WEIGHT POIDS	VALUE VALEUR	WEIGHT POIDS	VALUE VALEUR	WEIGHT POIDS	VALUE VALEUR	WEIGHT POIDS	VALUE VALEUR	
	ALL COMMODITIES						3887		3477	TOUS PRODUITS
0	FOOD AND LIVE ANIMALS						1127		955	ALIMENTS,ANIMAUX VIVANTS
01	MEAT AND PREPARATIONS						190		223	VIANDES ET PREPARATIONS
011	MEAT FRESH,CHILLD,FROZEN						186		219	VIANDES FRAICHES,REF,CONGE
02	DAIRY PRODCTS,BIRDS'EGGS						82		71	PRODUITS LAITIERS,OEUFS
03	FISH AND PREPARATIONS						338		201	POISSONS ET PREPARATIONS
037	FISH ETC PREPD,PRSVD NES						330		195	POIS,CRUST,MOL PREPARES
04	CEREALS AND PREPARATIONS						173		144	CEREALES ET PRODUITS
048	CEREAL ETC PREPARATIONS						162		137	PREPTNS A BASE CEREALES
0484	BAKERY PRODUCTS						160		135	PRODUITS DE BOULANGERIE
05	VEGETABLES AND FRUIT						152		137	LEGUMES ET FRUITS
054	VEG ETC FRSH,SMPLY PRSVD						44		45	LEGUMES FRAIS,CONG,SECS
056	VEGTBLES ETC PRSVD,PREPD						80		68	CONSERVES DE LEGUMES
05651	VEGTBLS,FRUIT IN VINEGAR						79		65	LEGUM CONSERV AU VINAIGRE
057	FRUIT,NUTS,FRESH,DRIED						27		23	FRUITS FRAIS OU SECS
0572	LEMONS,GRAPEFRUIT ETC						26		22	AUTRES AGRUMES FRAIS,SECS
06	SUGAR AND PREPS,HONEY						43		36	SUCRES ET PRODUITS
061	SUGAR AND HONEY						42		33	SUCRES ET MIEL
07	COFFEE,TEA,COCOA,SPICES						30		24	CAFE,THE,CACAO,EPICES
081	*FEEDING STUFF FOR ANIML						26		32	NOURRITURE POUR ANIMAUX
09	MISC EDIBLE PRODUCTS						94		87	PREP ALIMENTAIRES DIVERSES
098	EDIBLE PRODCTS,PREPS NES						94		87	PREP ALIMENTAIRES NDA
09809	MISC FOOD PREPRTIONS NES						93		86	PREP ALIMENTAIRES NDA
1	BEVERAGES AND TOBACCO						369		194	BOISSONS ET TABACS
11	BEVERAGES						345		167	BOISSONS
112	ALCOHOLIC BEVERAGES						341		9	BOISSONS ALCOOLIQUES
1123	BEER,ALE,STOUT,PORTER						16	V 110	7	BIERES
12	TOBACCO AND MANUFACTURES						24		27	TABACS BRUTS FABRIQUES
122	TOBACCO,MANUFACTURED						24		27	TABACS FABRIQUES
1223	OTH MANUFACTURED TOBACCO						22		26	TABACS FUMER,CHIQUER,PRISER
2	CRUDE MATERLS,EXCL FUELS						98		50	MAT BRUTES NON COMESTIBLES
26	TEXTILE FIBRES AND WASTE						11		16	FIBRES TEXTILES
269	WASTE OF TEXTILE FABRICS						11		16	FRIPERIE DRILLES,CHIFFONS
26901	BULK TEXT WSTE,OLD CLTHG						11		16	ART ET ACCESS D'HABILLEMENT
27	CRUDE FERTLZR,MINRLS NES						72		20	ENGRAIS MINERAUX BRUTS
3	MINERAL FUELS ETC						419		115	COMBUSTIBLES MINERAUX LUB
33	PETROLEUM AND PRODUCTS						418		114	PETROLE ET DERIVES
334	PETROLEUM PRODUCTS,REFIN						117		83	PRODUITS RAFFINES
33411	MOTOR,AVIATION SPIRIT				W 266	32		25	ESSENCES MOTEURS D'AVIONS
33412	SPIRIT TYPE JET FUEL				W 269	21	W 81	17	CARBUREACTEURS
3344	FUEL OILS,NES				W 787	64	W 220	40	FUEL OILS
335	RESIDUAL PETRLM PROD NES					301		31	PRODUITS RESIDUELS NDA
4	ANIMAL,VEGETABLE OIL,FAT					20		19	HUILES,GRAISSES ANIM,VEG
431	*PROCESD ANML VEG OIL,ET					20		18	HUILES,GRAISSES PREPAREES
5	CHEMCLS,RELATED PROD NES					320		360	PRODUITS CHIMIQUES
53	DYES,TANNING,COLOUR PROD					44		31	PROD TEINTURE,COLORANTS
532	DYES NES,TANNING PROD					43		28	EXTRAITS TEINTURE,TANNAGE
541	*MEDICINAL,PHARM PRODUCT					14		66	PROD MEDICINAUX PHARMACEUT
55	PERFUME,CLEANING ETC PRD					108		92	PROD POUR PARFUM,TOILETTE
553	PERFUMERY,COSMETICS,ETC					36		30	PRODUITS DE PARFUMERIE
554	SOAP,CLEANSING ETC PREPS					72		62	SAVONS,PRODUITS DETERSIFS
58	PLASTIC MATERIALS ETC					51		85	MAT PLAST ARTIFICIELLES
59	CHEMICAL MATERIALS NES					89		77	MAT PROD CHIMIQUES NDA
592	STARCH,INULIN,GLUTEN,ETC					59		42	AMIDONS,INUL,GLUT FROM
5921	STARCH,INULIN,GLUTEN					55		39	AMID,INUL,GLUT FROMENT
6	BASIC MANUFACTURES					594		607	ART MANUFACTURES
62	RUBBER MANUFACTURES NES					30		38	CAOUTCHOUC MANUFACTURE
63	WOOD,CORK MANUFACTRS NES					169		172	OUVRAGES LIEGE ET BOIS
635	WOOD MANUFACTURES NES					24		2	ART MANUF EN BOIS NDA
6353	BUILDERS WOODWRK,PREFABS					24		1	OUVRAGES DE MENUISERIE
64	PAPER,PAPERBOARD AND MFR					104		88	PAPIERS,CARTONS & OUVRAGES
641	PAPER AND PAPERBOARD					100		85	PAPIERS ET CARTONS
65	TEXTILE YARN,FABRICS,ETC					60		43	FILS,TISSUS,ARTICLES TEXTILE
651	TEXTILE YARN					44		26	FILS TEXTILES
66	NONMETAL MINERAL MFS NES					37		45	ART MIN NON METALLIQUES
661	LIME,CEMENT,BLDG PRODS					12		21	CHAUX,CIMENTS MAT CONSTR
66181	ASPHALT ETC PRODUCTS					3		18	OUVRAGES EN ASPHALTE
665	GLASSWARE					13		14	OUVRAGES EN VERRE
67	IRON AND STEEL					16		11	FER ET ACIER
68	NON-FERROUS METALS					36		38	METAUX NON FERREUX
684	ALUMINIUM					33		36	ALUMINIUM
6841	ALUMINIUM,ALLOYS,UNWRGHT					32		35	ALUMINIUM,ALLIAGES BRUTS
69	METAL MANUFACTURES NES					136		169	ART MANUFACT EN METAL NDA
691	STRUCTURES AND PARTS NES					92		128	CONSTRUCT FER,ACIER,ALU
696	CUTLERY					20		24	COUTELLERIE
69606	BASE METAL TABLEWARE NES					20		24	CUILLERS,FOURCHETTES
699	BASE METAL MFRS NES					17		12	ART MANUFACTURES MET NDA
7	MACHINES,TRANSPORT EQUIP					645		935	MACHINES MATERIEL TRANSPORT
71	POWER GENERATING EQUIPMT					152		315	MACHINES GENERATRICES
716	ROTATING ELECTRIC PLANT							125	APP ELECTR ROTATIFS,PIECES
7163	ROTARY CONVERTERS							125	CONVERTISSEURS ROTATIFS
718	OTH POWER GENERATG MACHY					147		187	AUTRES MOTEURS PARTIES
7187	NUCLEAR REACTORS,PTS NES					147		187	REACTEURS NUCLEAIRES
72	MACHS FOR SPCL INDUSTRYS					23		8	MAC SPECIALES POUR INDUST
74	GENRL INDUSTRL MACHY NES					16		19	MACH APP INDUSTRIE
76	TELECOMM,SOUND EQUIPMENT					86		292	EQUIPMENT DE TELECOM
763	SOUND RECORDRS,PHONOGRPH					82		272	PHONO,APP ENREGISTREMENT
764	TELECOM EQPT,PTS,ACC NES					3		20	EQUIP TELECOM,PIECES
76481	RADIOTELEPHONE ETC RCVRS							18	RECEP RADIOTELEPHONIE
77	ELECTRIC MACHNRY NES ETC					14		12	MACH APP ELECT NDA
78	ROAD VEHICLES					339		269	VEHICULES ROUTIERS
781	PASS MOTOR VEH EXC BUSES				N 1683	9	N 13	13	AUTO TRANSPORT PERSONNES
782	LORRIES,SPCL MTR VEH NES				N 2307	11	N 59	31	VEHICULES SPECIAUX,MARCH
7821	LORRIES,TRUCKS				N 2307	11	N 59	31	VEHICULES TRANSP MARCHAND
783	ROAD MOTOR VEHICLES NES						N 2	14	VEHICULES ROUTIERS NDA
7831	BUSES						N 2	14	VOITURES TRANSPORT COMMUN
79	OTHR TRANSPORT EQUIPMENT					10		12	AUTRE MATERIEL TRANSPORT
793	SHIPS AND BOATS ETC					10		12	NAVIRES BATEAUX,ETC
8	MISC MANUFACTURED GOODS					295		241	ART MANUFACTURES DIVERS
821	*FURNITURE,PARTS THEREOF					42		13	MEUBLES ET PIECES
82122	MATTRESSES ETC					40		12	SOMMIERS,ARTICLES DE LITERIE

4. General Imports C.I.F. by Commodities according to the S.I.T.C. (Rev. 2) in thousand U.S. Dollars
Importations Générales C.A.F. par Produits d'après la C.T.C.I. (Rév. 2) en milliers de Dollars E.U.

SITC CTCI	COMMODITY	1990		1991		1992		1993		PRODUIT
		WEIGHT POIDS	VALUE VALEUR	WEIGHT POIDS	VALUE VALEUR	WEIGHT POIDS	VALUE VALEUR	WEIGHT POIDS	VALUE VALEUR	
84	CLOTHING AND ACCESSORIES						85		83	VETEMENTS
847	TEXTILE CLTHNG ACCES NES						71		76	ACCES VET MAT TEXT NDA
84719	MADE-UP CLTHG ACCESS NES						18		26	AUT ACCES VET MAT TEXTIL
84722	KNIT SOCKS,ETC NONELASTC						49		49	CHAUSSETTES BON. NON ELAS
851	*FOOTWEAR						21		30	CHAUSSURES
85105	GAITERS,LEGGINGS,ETC						20		28	GUETRES,JAMBIERES ETC
87	PRECISION INSTRUMNTS NES						10		25	INSTRUM,APPAR SCIENT NDA
88	PHOTO EQU,OPTICL GDS ETC						5		14	APP,FOURN PHOTO,OP,MONTR
89	MISC MANUFCTRD GOODS NES						132		76	ART MANUFACTURES DIVERS
892	PRINTED MATTER						104		57	IMPRIMES
89282	PLANS,ETC NOT PRINTED						103		46	PLANS ARCHITECTES,INGEN
894	TOYS,SPORTING GOODS,ETC						19		15	VOITURES ENFANTS,JOUETS
89423	TOYS NES						18		14	JOUETS,MODELES REDUITS

5. General Exports F.O.B. by Commodities according to the S.I.T.C. (Rev. 2) in thousand U.S. Dollars
Exportations Générales F.O.B. par Produits d'après la C.T.C.I. (Rév. 2) en milliers de Dollars E.U.

SITC CTCI	COMMODITY	1990 WEIGHT POIDS	1990 VALUE VALEUR	1991 WEIGHT POIDS	1991 VALUE VALEUR	1992 WEIGHT POIDS	1992 VALUE VALEUR	1993 WEIGHT POIDS	1993 VALUE VALEUR	PRODUIT
	ALL COMMODITIES						100		272	TOUS PRODUITS
0	FOOD AND LIVE ANIMALS						68		242	ALIMENTS,ANIMAUX VIVANTS
05	VEGETABLES AND FRUIT						68		242	LEGUMES ET FRUITS
054	VEG ETC FRSH,SMPLY PRSVD						47		237	LEGUMES FRAIS,CONG,SECS
0548	EDIBLE VEG NES FRESH,DRY						47		237	RACINES,TUBERCULES
05481	ROOTS,TUBERS FRESH,DRY						47		237	RACINES DE MANIOC ETC
056	VEGTBLES ETC PRSVD,PREPD						7			CONSERVES DE LEGUMES
0564	FLOUR ETC OF FRUIT,VEGET						7			FARINES,SEMOULES,FLOCONS
05645	TAPIOCA, SAGO, ETC						7			TAPIOCA
057	FRUIT,NUTS,FRESH,DRIED						14		5	FRUITS FRAIS OU SECS
0577	NUTS EDIBLE,FRESH,DRIED						14		5	FRUITS A COQUES
05771	COCONUTS FRESH OR DRIED						14		5	NOIX DE COCO
9	GOODS NOT CLASSD BY KIND						27			ART TRANSACT NON CLASSES

Norway, incl. Svalbard & Jan Mayen Islds

Norvège y compris iles Svalbard et Jan Mayen

1. HISTORICAL SERIES, 1961–1996 GENERAL TRADE, IMPORTS C.I.F., EXPORTS F.O.B.
SERIES HISTORIQUES, 1961–1996 COMMERCE GENERAL, IMPORTATIONS C.A.F., EXPORTATIONS F.O.B

YEAR ANNEE	VALUE IN MILLION NORWG. KRONER / VALEUR EN MILLION NORWG. KRONER — MERCHANDISE –MARCHANDISE — IMPORTS	EXPORTS	GOLD –OR — IMPORTS	EXPORTS	CONVERSION FACTORS U.S. CENTS PER NORWG. KRONE FACTEURS DE CONVERSION CENTS E.U. PAR NORWG. KRONE — IMPORTS	EXPORTS	INDEX NUMBERS –INDICES — QUANTUM — IMPORTS	EXPORTS	UNIT VALUE VALEUR UNITAIRE — IMPORTS	EXPORTS
1961	11543.00	6652.00	5.44	0.19	14.0000	14.0000	22	12	28	25
1962	11885.00	6942.00	5.72	0.14	14.0000	14.0000	24	13	28	25
1963	13013.00	7664.00	6.62	0.27	14.0000	14.0000	25	15	28	25
1964	14169.00	9219.00	9.30	0.52	14.0000	14.0000	28	17	29	25
1965	15787.00	10309.00	10.68	0.52	14.0000	14.0000	30	18	29	26
1966	17169.00	11168.00	9.39	0.41	14.0000	14.0000	34	19	29	27
1967	19627.00	12411.00	12.97	0.45	14.0000	14.0000	36	21	29	26
1968	19331.00	13841.00	13.57	0.65	14.0000	14.0000	39	23	28	26
1969	21011.00	15741.00	13.17	0.99	14.0000	14.0000	44	26	29	26
1970	26443.00	17549.00	15.46	0.84	14.0000	14.0000	50	27	31	28
1971	28715.00	18003.00	13.92	0.78	14.1800	14.1800	50	27	32	29
1972	28808.00	21625.00	16.09	1.48	15.0400	15.0400	51	31	32	29
1973	36040.00	27085.00	13.20	1.70	17.3130	17.3060	56	34	34	32
1974	46556.00	34720.00	18.97	2.80	18.0730	18.0710	62	34	43	42
1975	50545.00	37922.00			19.2020	19.0760	62	35	46	46
1976	60533.00	43330.00			18.3710	18.3510	69	41	49	47
1977	68579.00	47263.00			18.7860	18.7940	74	39	53	50
1978	60169.00	57084.00			19.1090	19.0540	66	48	56	51
1979	69339.00	68527.00			19.7690	19.7690	69	51	62	62
1980	83602.00	91672.00			20.2490	20.2300	77	54	69	80
1981	89687.80	104265.40			17.4518	17.4745	76	54	72	93
1982	99747.30	113236.30			15.5182	15.5385	77	53	78	100
1983	98407.80	131397.00			13.4519	13.4160	74	60	80	103
1984	113102.10	154034.50			12.2799	12.2648	84	64	83	113
1985	132563.40	170732.80			11.7377	11.7087	94	67	88	118
1986	150052.00	133847.00			13.5330	13.5194	108	69	88	88
1987	152041.00	144543.00			14.8913	14.8698	106	78	91	85
1988	151101.00	146166.00			15.3690	15.3419	95	81	93	85
1989	163380.00	187146.00			14.4940	14.4869	90	93	99	96
1990	169998.00	211579.00			16.0113	16.0907	100	100	100	100
1991	165181.00	220316.00			15.4834	15.4848	102	107	98	96
1992	160821.00	218474.00			16.1148	16.1084	106	115	97	88
1993	170069.00	225714.00			14.0487	14.0788	107	121	97	89
1994	192073.00	243809.00			14.2147	14.2264	122	136	97	85
1995	208627.00	265883.00			15.8049	15.7947	134	145	98	88
1996	229720.00	320130.00			15.5044	15.5079	148	162	98	95

2. IMPORTS BY BROAD ECONOMIC CATEGORY AND EXPORTS BY INDUSTRIAL ORIGIN. (PERCENTAGE OF TOTAL VALUE)
IMPORTATIONS PAR CATEGORIES ECONOMIQUES ET EXPORTATIONS PAR BRANCHE D'ACTIVITE.(EN POURCENTAGE DE LA VALEUR TOTALE)

IMPORTS – IMPORTATIONS

	1990	1991	1992	1993	1994	1995	1996
TOTAL IMPORTS–IMPORTATIONS TOTALES	100.	100.	100.	100.	100.	100.	100.
1 FOOD BEV–ALIMENTATION BOISSONS	5.1	5.5	5.9	5.9	6.1	6.0	6.2
11 PRIMARY–PRODUITS DE BASE	2.5	2.7	2.8	2.5	2.9	2.9	3.1
111 FOR INDUSTRY–POUR L'INDUSTRIE	0.9	0.7	0.7	0.5	1.0	0.8	0.9
112 FOR HOUSEHOLDS–POUR LES MENAGES	1.6	2.0	2.1	2.0	1.9	2.1	2.1
12 PROCESSED–PRODUITS ELABORES	2.6	2.9	3.1	3.4	3.2	3.1	3.1
121 FOR INDUSTRY–POUR L'INDUSTRIE	0.4	0.4	0.5	0.6	0.5	0.5	0.6
122 FOR HOUSEHOLDS–POUR LES MENAGES	2.2	2.4	2.6	2.8	2.7	2.6	2.6
2 IND SUPPLIES–APPROV INDUSTRIELS	30.3	31.0	30.5	30.0	32.1	32.6	30.1
21 PRIMARY–PRODUITS DE BASE	4.9	4.9	4.5	4.5	4.8	4.8	4.7
22 PROCESSED–PRODUITS ELABORES	25.4	26.1	26.0	25.5	27.3	27.8	25.4
3 FUELS–COMBUSTIBLES	4.0	3.9	3.1	3.0	2.7	2.5	4.1
31 PRIMARY–PRODUITS DE BASE	1.6	1.6	1.3	1.3	0.7	0.8	0.9
32 PROCESSED–PRODUITS ELABORES	2.4	2.3	1.8	1.7	2.0	1.7	3.2
321 MOTOR SPIRIT–ESSENCE	0.7	0.5	0.4	0.4	0.4	0.5	0.3
322 OTHER–AUTRES	1.7	1.8	1.5	1.3	1.7	1.3	2.9
4 MACHINERY–EQUIPEMENT	21.7	22.8	23.5	24.3	23.2	25.2	26.3
41 CAPITAL EQUIPMENT–MACHINES	17.6	18.5	18.9	19.4	18.5	20.3	21.8
42 PARTS–PIECES ACCESSOIRES	4.1	4.3	4.6	4.9	4.8	4.9	4.5
5 TRANSPORT–TRANSPORT	18.7	15.2	14.4	15.5	14.7	13.1	13.5
51 PASSENGER CARS–AUTOMOBILES	2.4	1.9	2.7	2.5	3.9	3.7	4.6
52 OTHER–AUTRES	13.1	9.9	8.3	9.6	7.1	5.7	5.1
521 INDUSTRIAL–INDUSTRIELS	12.9	9.7	8.0	9.3	6.8	5.4	4.9
522 NON INDUSTRIAL–NON INDUSTRIEL	0.2	0.2	0.2	0.2	0.3	0.2	0.3
53 PARTS–PIECES ACCESSOIRES	3.2	3.3	3.5	3.5	3.6	3.7	3.8
6 CONSUM GOODS–BIENS CONSOMMATION	18.2	19.4	20.6	20.2	19.5	19.0	18.5
61 DURABLE–DURABLES	4.3	4.5	4.6	4.5	4.4	4.3	4.3
62 SEMI DURABLE–SEMI DURABLES	10.1	10.8	11.6	11.4	10.8	10.3	9.9
63 NON DURABLE–NON DURABLES	3.8	4.2	4.3	4.4	4.3	4.4	4.2
7 GOODS NES–BIENS NDA	1.9	1.9	1.7	0.9	1.7	1.5	1.4

EXPORTS – EXPORTATIONS

	1990	1991	1992	1993	1994	1995	1996
TOTAL EXPORTS–EXPORTATIONS TOTALES	100.	100.	100.	100.	100.	100.	100.
1 AGRICULTURE	5.6	6.2	6.3	6.6	7.4	7.1	6.6
2 MINING QUARRY–INDUS EXTRACTIVES	43.7	45.6	46.1	47.6	46.0	44.1	51.1
3 MANUFACTURING–IND MANUFACTUR	50.7	47.3	46.8	45.1	46.7	48.7	42.3
31 FOOD BEV TOBACCO–ALIM BOISS TAB	1.8	1.8	2.1	1.9	1.8	1.6	1.5
32 TEXTILES–INDUSTRIES TEXTILES	0.8	0.8	0.8	0.8	0.9	0.8	0.7
33 WOOD & PRODUCTS–BOIS & PRODUITS	1.3	1.2	1.1	1.3	1.2	1.1	0.9
34 PAPER & PRODUCTS–PAPIER & PRODT	4.5	3.3	2.8	3.0	2.6	3.3	2.5
35 CHEMICALS–INDUSTRIES CHIMIQUES	12.0	10.8	11.0	11.0	7.6	7.1	7.2
36 NON METAL MIN–MIN NON METAL	0.7	0.6	0.6	0.5	0.4	0.4	0.4
37 BASIC METAL–IND METAL BASE	11.9	10.5	9.7	9.5	9.6	10.1	8.4
38 METAL MANUF–MANUF METAL	17.0	17.8	18.0	16.4	15.1	16.4	14.1
39 OTH MANUF IND–AUTRES MANUF	0.8	0.6	0.6	0.8	7.5	7.9	6.7

3. TRADE BY PRINCIPAL COUNTRIES OF PRODUCTION AND LAST CONSIGNMENT (VALUE IN THOUSAND U.S. DOLLARS)
ECHANGES SELON LES PRINCIPAUX PAYS DE PRODUCTION ET DE DERNIERE CONSIGNATION (VALEUR EN MILLIERS DE DOLLARS EU)

COUNTRIES–PAYS	GENERAL IMPORTS C.I.F. IMPORTATIONS GENERALES C.A.F				
	1992	1993	1994	1995	1996
World	26074786	24021241	27294925	32705876	34309175
Africa	367948	299553	260685	303207	423404
Americas	3261697	2921850	3300446	3734071	3760551
Northern America	2698995	2428325	2546198	2905113	2983239
LAIA	252067	221276	316492	380586	378006
CACM	22586	26525	23022	30626	36036
Caribbean	104464	115135	198389	233992	152741
Rest of America	183584	130590	216346	183754	210529
As.ex F.USSR	3217124	3512717	3363531	3514043	3925135
Eur.x F.USSR	18713072	16778594	19514359	24281667	25320770
EU	17979294	16132194	18810620	23365602	24295980
EFTA	428268	423519	409887	518947	564425
East Europe	207121	191097	246762	342645	388473
Other Europe	16732	7905	20604	22001	42310
Former USSR	420002	414048	756536	782724	731567
Oceania	94943	94479	99368	90163	147748
Sweden/Suède	4023899	3397653	4094401	5048322	5855292
Germany/Allemagne	3762026	3254681	3802853	4557999	4592302
United Kingdom	2419924	2197386	2830578	3203660	3191255
Denmark/Danemark	1954472	1784722	2015554	2473240	2654561
USA/Etats–Unis d'Amer	2225500	1938191	2009827	2189412	2220772
Japan/Japon	1640497	1923249	1629665	1254356	1332903
Netherlands/Pays–Bas	1028041	983864	1158394	1457843	1528392
France, Monac	1059162	1028299	1105735	1446073	1444098
Finland/Finlande	922022	786162	996708	1290570	1231797
Italy/Italie	875966	830580	947508	1155142	1312325
Belgium–Luxembourg	623443	584394	696081	947054	878565
Canada	468756	485293	533968	703268	741297
China/Chine	359581	425105	515807	621872	693928
Russian Federation	385340	344482	616609	592653	579248
Spain/Espagne	396671	484353	282946	614792	486363
Switz.Liecht	387638	370866	368008	457459	485264
Ireland/Irlande	239412	269321	320448	497220	464674
Austria/Autriche	311269	254888	270211	328858	325422
Portugal	298020	235068	249475	303062	291146
Korea, Republic of	234253	137930	219031	388914	203881
Singapore/Singapour	99472	225531	104064	134787	568986
Hong Kong	170396	156316	169506	207483	177174
Poland/Pologne	117736	112932	134668	172885	194510
So. Africa Customs Un	117100	124276	116855	160444	204833
Jamaica/Jamaïque	101130	105557	105399	147113	124660
Suriname/Suriname	88968	81052	111291	146544	129465
Brazil/Brésil	92662	82626	108823	130191	114653
Australia/Australie	87641	87847	90652	76382	135897
India/Inde	77653	76003	98816	108701	110744
Thailand/Thaïlande	65952	63084	76297	97460	103447
Panama	94399	49298	104799	37052	79889
Malaysia/Malaisie	53933	52389	71839	91066	95057
Turkey/Turquie	58743	45841	61431	93077	94523
Iceland/Islande	40631	52653	41879	61488	79162
Liberia/Libéria	90361	57982	22630	1381	83389
Czech Republic		37606	49530	81550	85489
Indonesia/Indonésie	36172	40980	43766	51158	64156
Greece/Grèce	64968	40823	39729	41766	39789
Colombia/Colombie	30542	29267	56074	49715	47099
Chile/Chili	27156	25500	28372	66922	60570
Israel/Israël	33442	34430	40993	43212	49239
Pakistan	39673	34484	37410	43038	39588
Argentina/Argentine	50144	21981	27727	36361	55858
Latvia/Lettonie	10492	21963	21361	79675	55310
Morocco/Maroc	47744	34208	27904	30042	34092
Hungary/Hongrie	28074	21090	31727	41843	49206
Bahamas	2057	8687	90639	49558	9019
Estonia/Estonie	8151	15793	32535	43216	43857
Peru/Pérou	7814	14042	33959	39228	26187
Mexico/Mexique	8362	9850	26836	32592	39664

COUNTRIES–PAYS	GENERAL EXPORTS F.O.B. EXPORTATIONS GENERALES F.O.B.				
	1992	1993	1994	1995	1996
Monde	35149008	31903873	34743549	41740342	48954986
Afrique	719287	499269	380878	282705	287214
Amériques	3553718	3490037	4063235	4911023	6382732
Amérique du Nord	2866484	2959231	3612611	4187583	5656482
ALAI	178178	223229	266772	418186	474876
MCAC	29415	9964	11004	11609	9753
Caraïbes	304962	72123	104924	225031	106248
Autre Amérique	174679	225489	67924	68613	135373
Asie l'URSS exclus	1957818	1838566	2020288	2816775	2911209
Europe l'URSS exclus	28685174	25872303	27977997	33283484	38767314
UE	27681333	24969751	27032099	32232498	37642278
AELE	449803	347641	409338	393334	467160
Europe de l'Est	373949	389173	417875	484352	464037
Autre de l'Europe	151155	142271	82006	93412	90738
Ancienne URSS	130603	122050	193341	311990	464728
Océanie	102408	81647	107809	133972	141789
United Kingdom	8510018	7842933	7231629	8362015	9713387
Germany/Allemagne	4623065	4149231	4322327	4981053	5456751
Sweden/Suède	3293467	2777779	3260227	4119138	4540644
Netherlands/Pays–Bas	2509719	2706109	3302849	3977353	5436302
France, Monac	2705633	2524396	2826964	3246606	4320586
USA/Etats–Unis d'Amer	1871116	1977677	2345116	2569108	3626798
Denmark/Danemark	1912278	1399919	1639361	2098968	2237246
Canada	914424	739994	1152901	1576631	1980451
Belgium–Luxembourg	1007951	731672	978684	1300659	1553865
Italy/Italie	915091	828705	998335	1145057	1318004
Finland/Finlande	898491	812155	1034473	1145402	1076111
Japan/Japon	578983	589461	650672	741490	904644
Spain/Espagne	428138	363289	481962	702609	938226
Ireland/Irlande	336595	319575	422360	386235	435370
Poland/Pologne	313889	316627	333196	359527	343421
Portugal	327140	285671	305520	372641	346794
Singapore/Singapour	160757	146581	192921	505989	196321
Liberia/Libéria	495360	272489	165941	81126	59674
Switz.Liecht	207600	184579	210430	226943	217321
Iceland/Islande	242203	163063	198908	166391	249839
China/Chine	142046	202486	170689	185062	202449
Brazil/Brésil	94492	107192	173614	252350	244649
Russian Federation	77228	96046	123665	190865	276964
Korea, Republic of	126041	96174	116730	179168	235008
Austria/Autriche	136367	116234	139483	181813	172233
Panama	173138	224651	66061	65788	131265
Israel/Israël	142021	111186	116815	132011	139087
Hong Kong	106851	97174	85041	168909	131889
Greece/Grèce	77379	112083	87926	212948	96759
Thailand/Thaïlande	65769	100443	86496	130620	159328
Australia/Australie	72256	71549	94408	100219	116340
Turkey/Turquie	113601	91707	52530	86607	109454
Bermuda/Bermudes	58954	226395	107868	33408	15448
Bahamas	169581	8081	69136	22909	55518
Saudi Arabia	60655	32602	61591	130871	39355
India/Inde	57463	27197	77414	99003	61833
Malaysia/Malaisie	95279	29353	80309	55046	51284
Malta/Malte	83857	103662	38266	48280	23605
Cyprus/Chypre	66547	75448	56687	68321	23952
Faeroe Islds/Is Féroé	59786	37410	43228	44648	61158
Czech Republic		38489	48232	66810	65224
United Arab Emirates	27431	33583	36823	49767	69206
Chile/Chili	26384	37250	17195	29806	100203
Nigeria/Nigéria	43677	43305	35085	17682	18498
Indonesia/Indonésie	23517	22784	26063	30846	52591
Latvia/Lettonie	34245	3171	15920	28139	72776
Argentina/Argentine	8131	26799	12310	62974	37954
So. Africa Customs Un	21747	24000	31833	32834	32707
Egypt/Egypte	14012	29509	26017	20777	45638
Philippines	7303	5771	10295	12516	98363

(VALUE AS PERCENTAGE OF WORLD TOTAL)(VALEURS EN POURCENTAGE DU TOTAL MONDIAL)

	1987	1988	1989	1990	1991	1992	1993	1994	1995	1996
Africa	1.1	3.9	5.1	4.5	2.7	1.4	1.2	1.0	0.9	1.2
Americas	10.3	12.8	17.2	15.2	13.1	12.5	12.2	12.1	11.4	11.0
Northern America	7.7	8.4	9.7	10.5	10.1	10.4	10.1	9.3	8.9	8.7
LAIA	1.2	1.3	1.5	1.0	1.1	1.0	0.9	1.2	1.2	1.1
CACM	0.1	0.1	0.1	0.1	0.1	0.1	0.1	0.1	0.1	0.1
Caribbean	0.3	0.8	1.7	1.1	0.7	0.4	0.5	0.7	0.7	0.4
Rest of America	1.1	2.2	4.1	2.5	1.2	0.7	0.5	0.8	0.6	0.6
As.ex F.USSR	10.1	10.0	10.6	9.2	11.8	12.3	14.6	12.3	10.7	11.4
Eur.x F.USSR	77.4	72.2	65.6	69.5	70.7	71.8	69.8	71.5	74.2	73.8
EU	74.0	68.3	62.2	66.2	67.9	69.0	67.2	68.9	71.4	70.8
EFTA	1.8	1.8	1.6	1.7	1.6	1.6	1.8	1.5	1.6	1.6
East Europe	1.3	1.5	1.3	1.1	0.7	0.8	0.8	0.9	1.0	1.1
Other Europe	0.3	0.5	0.5	0.5	0.6	0.1	0.0	0.1	0.1	0.1
Former USSR	0.6	0.7	1.1	1.4	1.4	1.6	1.7	2.8	2.4	2.1
Oceania	0.4	0.5	0.5	0.3	0.2	0.4	0.4	0.4	0.3	0.4
Sweden/Suède	18.9	17.6	15.2	15.8	15.4	15.4	14.1	15.0	15.4	17.1
Germany/Allemagne	15.5	13.6	12.6	14.0	14.1	14.4	13.5	13.9	13.9	13.4
United Kingdom	9.0	7.8	7.4	9.0	8.7	9.3	9.1	10.4	9.8	9.3
Denmark/Danemark	7.8	7.6	6.7	6.7	7.3	7.5	7.4	7.4	7.6	7.7
USA/Etats–Unis d'Amer	6.4	6.6	7.4	8.1	7.8	8.5	8.1	7.4	6.7	6.5
Japan/Japon	5.7	4.6	3.7	4.4	4.9	6.3	8.0	6.0	3.8	3.9
Netherlands/Pays–Bas	3.8	3.9	3.3	4.0	5.3	3.9	4.1	4.2	4.5	4.5
France, Monac	3.7	3.3	3.3	3.8	3.8	4.1	4.3	4.1	4.4	4.2
Finland/Finlande	4.3	3.5	3.0	3.1	3.1	3.5	3.3	3.7	3.9	3.6
Italy/Italie	4.0	3.3	2.9	3.2	3.4	3.4	3.5	3.5	3.5	3.8

	1987	1988	1989	1990	1991	1992	1993	1994	1995	1996
Afrique	1.3	1.6	1.4	1.1	2.3	2.0	1.6	1.1	0.7	0.6
Amériques	12.0	9.1	10.4	10.6	9.2	10.1	10.9	11.7	11.8	13.0
Amérique du Nord	6.7	7.6	9.2	9.0	7.6	8.2	9.3	10.4	10.0	11.6
ALAI	0.6	0.8	0.7	0.7	0.7	0.5	0.7	0.8	1.0	1.0
MCAC	0.0	0.0	0.1	0.0	0.0	0.1	0.0	0.0	0.0	0.0
Caraïbes	3.3	0.3	0.2	0.7	0.6	0.9	0.2	0.3	0.5	0.2
Autre Amérique	1.3	0.3	0.2	0.1	0.4	0.5	0.7	0.2	0.2	0.3
Asie l'URSS exclus	4.9	5.4	4.7	5.6	5.5	5.6	5.8	5.8	6.7	5.9
Europe l'URSS exclus	80.9	82.7	82.3	81.8	82.4	81.6	81.1	80.5	79.7	79.2
UE	78.1	79.7	80.1	79.5	80.0	78.8	78.3	77.8	77.2	76.9
AELE	1.5	1.8	1.2	1.1	0.9	1.3	1.1	1.2	0.9	1.0
Europe de l'Est	0.6	0.7	0.5	0.7	0.9	1.1	1.2	1.2	1.2	0.9
Autre de l'Europe	0.7	0.6	0.5	0.6	0.6	0.4	0.4	0.2	0.2	0.2
Ancienne URSS	0.4	0.6	0.6	0.5	0.3	0.4	0.4	0.6	0.7	0.9
Océanie	0.5	0.6	0.5	0.4	0.3	0.3	0.3	0.3	0.3	0.3
United Kingdom	26.6	26.0	26.7	26.0	26.5	24.2	24.6	20.8	20.0	19.8
Germany/Allemagne	14.9	12.4	11.2	11.2	11.1	13.2	13.0	12.4	11.9	11.1
Sweden/Suède	11.1	11.7	12.4	11.5	10.3	9.4	8.7	9.4	9.9	9.3
Netherlands/Pays–Bas	7.3	6.9	6.6	8.0	7.9	7.1	8.5	9.5	9.5	11.1
France, Monac	5.1	7.3	9.0	7.8	7.5	7.7	7.9	8.1	7.8	8.8
USA/Etats–Unis d'Amer	5.7	6.1	6.8	6.5	4.8	5.3	6.2	6.7	6.2	7.4
Denmark/Danemark	5.1	5.3	4.7	4.8	5.6	5.4	4.4	4.7	5.0	4.6
Canada	0.8	1.2	2.2	2.5	2.7	2.6	2.3	3.3	3.8	4.0
Belgium–Luxembourg	1.3	2.4	2.5	2.2	2.4	2.9	2.3	2.8	3.1	3.2
Italy/Italie	2.3	2.8	2.4	2.6	2.3	2.6	2.6	2.9	2.7	2.7

4. General Imports C.I.F. by Commodities according to the S.I.T.C. (Rev. 2) in thousand U.S. Dollars
Importations Générales C.A.F. par Produits d'après la C.T.C.I. (Rév. 2) en milliers de Dollars E.U.

SITC CTCI	COMMODITY	1993 WEIGHT POIDS	1993 VALUE VALEUR	1994 WEIGHT POIDS	1994 VALUE VALEUR	1995 WEIGHT POIDS	1995 VALUE VALEUR	1996 WEIGHT POIDS	1996 VALUE VALEUR	PRODUIT
	ALL COMMODITIES		24021241		27294925		32705876		34309175	TOUS PRODUITS
0	FOOD AND LIVE ANIMALS		1332194		1546501		1817155		1942095	ALIMENTS,ANIMAUX VIVANTS
03	FISH AND PREPARATIONS		243309		242238		342330		381778	POISSONS ET PREPARATIONS
034	FISH,FRESH,CHILLED,FROZN	W 164451	152038	W 171857	159005	W 198173	218142	W 243732	248676	POISSON FRAIS, REFRIG,CONG
0341	FISH FRSH,CHLLD,EX FILLT	W 123380	84178	W 134188	101340	W 163090	158510	W 192653	168614	POISSON FRAIS,REFRIGERE
04	CEREALS AND PREPARATIONS		155734		205474		208920		287738	CEREALES ET PRODUITS
048	CEREAL ETC PREPARATIONS	W 89042	110497	W 102463	118856	W 93632	141974	W 105230	156566	PREPTNS A BASE CEREALES
05	VEGETABLES AND FRUIT		366612		418988		469111		497981	LEGUMES ET FRUITS
054	VEG ETC FRSH,SMPLY PRSVD	W 71935	79303	W 110202	100528	W 120984	123527	W 132386	126566	LEGUMES FRAIS,CONG,SECS
057	FRUIT,NUTS,FRESH,DRIED	W 222836	190043	W 224277	205501	W 216253	230321	W 227563	250380	FRUITS FRAIS OU SECS
058	FRUIT PRESERVED,PREPARED	W 50064	69465	W 55381	83699	W 48757	83161	W 53577	90353	CONSERVES DE FRUITS
06	SUGAR AND PREPS,HONEY		113893		129533		149875		155681	SUCRES ET PRODUITS
07	COFFEE,TEA,COCOA,SPICES		170387		255442		270223		256549	CAFE,THE,CACAO,EPICES
071	COFFEE AND SUBSTITUTES	W 40175	72239	W 46752	142205	W 38528	150067	W 41594	126055	CAFE ET SUCCEDANES
0711	COFFEE GREEN,ROASTED,SUB	W 39267	61723	W 45729	128024	W 37639	135890	W 40447	109535	CAFE TORREFIE OU DECAFEINE
07111	COFFEE GREEN,HUSKS,SKINS	W 38437	58741	W 44786	123581	W 37201	133115	W 39790	106202	CAFE NON TORREFIE
081	*FEEDING STUFF FOR ANIML	W 273571	117727	W 278229	134356	W 242507	173750	W 271479	169114	NOURRITURE POUR ANIMAUX
09	MISC EDIBLE PRODUCTS		121520		109160		135534		117360	PREP ALIMENTAIRES DIVERSES
098	EDIBLE PRODCTS,PREPS NES	W 25941	118513	W 29720	106030	W 33428	132045	W 32393	114453	PREP ALIMENTAIRES NDA
09809	MISC FOOD PREPRTIONS NES	W 17169	96565	W 19452	80044	W 22708	98401	W 22209	83863	PREP ALIMENTAIRES NDA
1	BEVERAGES AND TOBACCO		177168		192128		219102		218854	BOISSONS ET TABACS
11	BEVERAGES		109359		127961		158039		158081	BOISSONS
112	ALCOHOLIC BEVERAGES	W 37181	98447	W 45678	112790	W 49571	146095	W 51153	149552	BOISSONS ALCOOLIQUES
2	CRUDE MATERLS,EXCL FUELS		1595958		2030213		2470972		2466561	MAT BRUTES NON COMESTIBLES
22	OIL SEEDS,OLEAGINOUS FRT		11171		66362		87236		107626	GRAINES,FRUITS OLEAGINEUX
222	SEEDS FOR'SOFT'FIXED OIL	W 16165	10084	W 230587	65190	W 315243	85921	W 334691	106206	GRAINES HUILES FIXES
24	CORK AND WOOD		237676		421109		583251		492714	LIEGE ET BOIS
247	OTH WOOD ROUGH,SQUARED	W 806613	59508	W 2033676	137048	W 3008581	248767	W 1917089	161654	BOIS BRUTS EQUARRIS
2471	SAW–,VENEER–LOGS CONIFER	W 571451	39120	W 1416484	98437	W 2216653	181036	W 1435983	120843	CONIFERES POUR SCIAGE,PLACAG
24711	— IN THE ROUGH	W 571451	39120	W 1416484	98437	W 2216653	181036	W 1435983	120843	ECORCES OU DEGROSSIS
248	WOOD SHAPED,SLEEPERS		158972	W 449520	256530	W 433777	296338	W 462400	290153	BOIS SIMPLEMENT TRAVAILLES
2482	LUMBER SHAPED CONIFER		125424	W 408048	214333	W 385380	240112	W 414704	234091	CONIFERES SCIES,RABOTES
24821	LUMBER SAWN ETC CONIFER	W 340834	114556	W 393234	198521	W 370248	221716	W 397890	216238	CONIFERES SCIES LONGITUD
27	CRUDE FERTLZR,MINRLS NES		168995		178755		202851		212726	ENGRAIS MINERAUX BRUTS
278	OTHER CRUDE MINERALS	W 1753457	104850	W 1896876	109636	W 1973585	126126	W 2011554	127536	AUTRES MINERAUX BRUTS
28	METALLIFEROUS ORES,SCRAP		1005680		1145933		1313313		1412558	MINERAIS METAL,DECHETS
287	BASE METAL ORES,CONC NES		882666	W 2821408	974710	W 2658560	1120789	W 2754033	1226511	MINERAIS METAUX COMMUNS
2872	NICKEL ORES,CONCENTRATES	W 141931	455671	W 146274	521835	W 109318	594744	W 141941	703328	MINERAIS DE NICKEL
28722	NICKEL MATTE,SINTERS,ETC	W 141929	455657	W 146274	521835	W 109318	594744	W 141941	703328	MATTES,SINTERS
2873	ALUMINIUM ORES,ALUMINA	W 1748507	306438	W 1760049	322587	W 1609533	395316	W 1716114	401318	MINERAIS D'ALUMINIUM
28732	ALUMINA(ALUMINIUM OXIDE)	W 1722893	305344	W 1720504	320911	W 1576786	393746	W 1693565	400205	ALUMINE (OXYDE ALUMINIUM)
288	NONFERR METAL SCRAP NES	W 274119	70178	W 265870	128503	W 276764	142841	W 290584	128546	DECHETS NON FERREUX
2882	OTHER BASE MTL SCRAP NES	W 44264	45620	W 77206	102958	W 67712	119854	W 71356	99952	AUTRES DECHETS
28823	ALUMINIUM WSTE AND SCRAP	W 35666	35112	W 68505	90426	W 60576	108052	W 63038	87669	DECHETS D'ALUMINIUM
29	CRUDE ANIMAL,VEG MAT NES		98214		106809		130977		127386	MATIERES BRUTES ANIM,VEGET
292	CRUDE VEG MATERIALS NES	W 18762	87346	W 23952	93874	W 29826	116964	W 29858	114165	MAT BRUTES VEGETALES NDA
3	MINERAL FUELS ETC		802934		845774		961474		1550403	COMBUSTIBLES MINERAUX LUB
32	COAL,COKE AND BRIQUETTES		105751		124780		142362		150613	HOUILLES,COKES,BRIQUETTES
33	PETROLEUM AND PRODUCTS		594445		608029		769287		869988	PETROLE ET DERIVES
333	CRUDE PETROLEUM	W 1332434	157605	W 981515	107922	W 1398124	166123	W 1332752	213128	HUILES BRUTES DE PETROLE
334	PETROLEUM PRODUCTS,REFIN	MW 93416	337693	W 2318361	384298	W 2358882	452056	W 2362430	486796	PRODUITS RAFFINES
3341	GASOLINE,OTH LIGHT OILS	W 417276	90591	W 606267	109642	W 810097	153328	W 517702	114305	ESSENCES POUR MOTEURS
33411	MOTOR,AVIATION SPIRIT	W 393534	83607	W 551468	96678	W 697005	130104	W 484912	104657	ESSENCES MOTEURS D'AVIONS
3343	GAS OILS	W 479180	74543	W 441689	68132	W 638567	104604	W 520303	106157	GAS OILS
3344	FUEL OILS,NES	W 919397	85247	W 1022492	103363	W 695546	81803	W 1074128	140721	FUEL OILS
3345	LUBS,PETROLEUM OILS NES	MW 91537	74686	W 107370	78105	W 121614	95561	W 122931	95233	HUILES LUBRIFIANTES
335	RESIDUAL PETRLM PROD NES	W 709688	99148	W 792490	115809	W 885750	151108	W 855641	170064	PRODUITS RESIDUELS NDA
3354	PETROLM BITUMEN,COKE ETC	W 594130	68731	W 652592	77240	W 742022	101685	W 713356	119901	BITUME,COKE DE PETROLE
341	*GAS,NATURAL AND MANUFCT	W 770448	94796	W 87457	9716	W 84745	10624	W 72169	11144	GAZ NATUREL,GAZ MANUFACT
3413	PETROLM GASES,LIQUEFIED	W 770434	94640	W 85689	9050	W 84289	10326	W 71694	10931	GAZ DE PETROLE LIQUEFIE
34131	LIQUEFIED PROPANE,BUTANE	W 740042	91147							PROPANE,BUTANE LIQUEFIES
351	*ELECTRIC CURRENT	H 594138	7943	H 4519728	103250	H 2200513	39202	MH 13212	518658	ENERGIE ELECTRIQUE
4	ANIMAL,VEGETABLE OIL,FAT		88929		86737		107840		119572	HUILES,GRAISSES ANIM,VEG
5	CHEMCLS,RELATED PROD NES		2190927		2415410		3026082		3001903	PRODUITS CHIMIQUES
51	ORGANIC CHEMICALS		297737		294439		372213		372606	PROD CHIMIQ ORGANIQUES
511	HYDROCARBONS NES,DERIVS		96007	W 280596	77770	W 350188	119780	W 316727	89842	HYDROCARBURES NDA
52	INORGANIC CHEMICALS		174434		188961		238501		240674	PROD CHIM INORGANIQUES
522	INORG ELEMNTS,OXIDES,ETC		95815	W 355619	102323	W 455392	155519	W 473754	150743	ELEMENTS INORGANIQUES
523	OTHR INORG CHEMICALS ETC		72904	W 243123	79854	W 195476	76665	W 209848	83974	AUT PRODUITS CHIMIQUES INORG
53	DYES,TANNING,COLOUR PROD		213761		246049		309696		297278	PROD TEINTURE,COLORANTS
531	SYNT DYE,NAT INDGO,LAKES	W 3329	66816	W 4256	85719	W 4430	115125	W 4395	96412	MAT COLOR ORGAN,LAQUES
5311	SYNTHIC ORGNIC DYESTUFFS	W 2790	64571	W 3371	81674	W 3728	112304	W 3443	93258	MAT COLOR ORGAN SYNTHET
533	PIGMENTS,PAINTS,ETC		144321	W 71869	157360	W 77551	191535	W 82091	197555	PIGMENTS,PEINTURES,VERNIS
541	*MEDICINAL,PHARM PRODUCT	MK 9185	446569	MK 9989	474472	MK 9899	607897		617585	PROD MEDICINAUX PHARMACEUT
5417	MEDICAMENTS	K 5433823	366470	K 5984999	381457	K 5801256	498323	K 6290821	504776	MEDICAMENTS
54179	— CONTNG OTH SUBSTANCES	K 4969940	315210	K 5541724	336763	K 5272627	425130	K 5976079	451418	MED CONT AUT SUBSTANCES
55	PERFUME,CLEANING ETC PRD		271780		353994		408986		437898	PROD POUR PARFUM,TOILETTE
553	PERFUMERY,COSMETICS,ETC	W 19277	149674	W 20529	175409	W 20375	201850	W 21340	194251	PRODUITS DE PARFUMERIE
554	SOAP,CLEANSING ETC PREPS	W 62722	98957	W 69380	114050	W 74019	134187	W 84365	148192	SAVONS,PRODUITS DETERSIFS
5542	WASHING PREPARATIONS ETC	W 50546	72084	W 57362	85229	W 61944	100549	W 71372	110510	PROD ORG TENSIO–ACT NDA
562	*FERTILIZERS,MANUFACTURE		97250	W 707473	98696	W 716454	106993	W 718424	107791	ENGRAIS MANUFACTURES
58	PLASTIC MATERIALS ETC		395054		458847		598412		555547	MAT PLAST ARTIFICIELLES
582	PROD OF CONDENSATION ETC		95310	W 50663	112102	W 53895	144244	W 54752	137228	PROD CONDENS,POLYCOND
583	POLYMERIZATION ETC PRODS		283481	W 210249	326820	W 221470	433929	W 225979	399671	PROD POLYMERISATION
5831	POLYETHYLENE	W 75159	76854	W 83079	91847	W 85117	126922	W 79862	105305	POLYETHYLENE
5839	OTH POLYMRZTION ETC PROD	W 28977	87940	W 31341	96667	W 34058	124273	W 38626	128128	AUT PROD POLYMER COPOLYM
59	CHEMICAL MATERIALS NES		274231		280317		357920		343232	MAT PROD CHIMIQUES NDA
598	MISCEL CHEM PRODUCTS NES		204290	W 149021	207441	W 164854	266970	W 157903	244188	PROD DIV INDUST CHIM NDA
5989	CHEM PRODUCTS,PREPS NES	W 97261	160538	W 71099	159307	W 84547	210412	W 85249	191688	PROD PREP CHIMIQUES NDA
59899	OTH CHEM PRODS,PREPS,NES	W 67096	117449	W 50885	117277	W 62496	158888	W 71453	154607	AUT PRODUITS CHIMIQUES NDA
6	BASIC MANUFACTURES		4140661		5145356		6163014		5886243	ART MANUFACTURES
62	RUBBER MANUFACTURES NES		236432		264359		304298		312908	CAOUTCHOUC MANUFACTURE
625	RUBBER TYRES, TUBES ETC		147302	W 41694	166437	W 39969	183308	W 40910	188817	PNEUS CAOUTCHOUC VULCANISE
6251	TYRES NEW FOR MOTOR CARS	N 2301162	87966	W 21982	100605	W 19704	105924	W 21324	116168	PNEUS POUR VOITURES
63	WOOD,CORK MANUFACTRS NES		191481		212881		276746		299552	OUVRAGES LIEGE ET BOIS
635	WOOD MANUFACTURES NES		119417	W 66222	130292	W 75639	178386	W 82345	196091	ART MANUF EN BOIS NDA
6353	BUILDERS WOODWRK,PREFABS		83546	W 39856	87753	W 46471	125283	W 51115	142502	OUVRAGES DE MENUISERIE
64	PAPER,PAPERBOARD AND MFR		647610		717016		957925		960693	PAPIERS,CARTONS & OUVRAGES
641	PAPER AND PAPERBOARD		353876	W 440302	396702	W 468046	553505	W 489072	544007	PAPIERS ET CARTONS
6412	PRINTG,WRITING PAPER NES	W 120272	110066	W 129970	121781	W 116138	153200	W 121500	144657	PAPIERS POUR L'IMPRESSION
64122	— COATED,IMPREGNATD ETC	W 95963	86393	W 104903	95596	W 93592	118629	W 97457	112708	PAPIERS IMPRESSION COUCHES

4. General Imports C.I.F. by Commodities according to the S.I.T.C. (Rev. 2) in thousand U.S. Dollars
Importations Générales C.A.F. par Produits d'après la C.T.C.I. (Rév. 2) en milliers de Dollars E.U.

SITC CTCI	COMMODITY	1993 WEIGHT POIDS	1993 VALUE VALEUR	1994 WEIGHT POIDS	1994 VALUE VALEUR	1995 WEIGHT POIDS	1995 VALUE VALEUR	1996 WEIGHT POIDS	1996 VALUE VALEUR	PRODUIT
6415	PAPER,PAPERBRD,BULK,NES	W 99233	70761	W 114144	83402	W 126236	125735	W 138472	128492	PAPIERS,CARTONS ROULEAUX
64159	OTHER PAPER ETC,BULK,NES	W 71865	56090	W 85847	69553	W 104734	110408	W 112607	112720	AUT PAPIER ROULEAUX FEUILLES
6418	COATED ETC PAPER NES BLK	W 65527	103704	W 64108	98305	W 60131	118373	W 62791	119236	PAP,CARTONS COUCHES,ENDUITS
642	PAPER,ETC,PRECUT,ARTS OF	W 133915	293733	W 142857	320313	W 148429	404420	W 154330	416686	PAP,CARTONS DECOUPES
6421	PAPER ETC CONTAINERS	W 30102	65492	W 39592	76480	W 45844	99194	W 48616	99465	BOITES,SACS EMBALLAGES
6428	PAPER ETC ARTICLES NES	W 58516	133602	W 59670	149245	W 58530	182206	W 59795	188791	OUVRAGES EN PATE A PAPIER
65	TEXTILE YARN,FABRICS,ETC		483013		535536		620406		641204	FILS,TISSUS,ARTICLES TEXTILE
657	SPECIAL TXTL FABRC,PRODS	W 11100	88589	W 12054	95652	W 13673	118345	W 15133	127167	TISSUS SPECIAUX
658	TEXTILE ARTICLES NES		103559	W 13862	112365	W 15476	140093	W 16625	149225	ART FACONNES MAT TEXTILES
66	NONMETAL MINERAL MFS NES		320379		354524		448373		485738	ART MIN NON METALLIQUES
663	MINERAL MANUFCTURES NES	W 146975	80688	W 173826	87187	W 192934	109550	W 197099	121417	ART MIN MANUF NDA
664	GLASS	W 74703	74261	W 83240	78554	W 90981	102396	W 99233	103158	VERRE
67	IRON AND STEEL		1131585		1212048		1465569		1383821	FER ET ACIER
672	IRON,STEEL PRIMARY FORMS	W 325157	98382	W 330580	101844	W 402206	148756	W 305484	110287	LINGOTS FER,ACIER
673	IRON,STEEL SHAPES ETC	W 242562	127076	W 252412	137591	W 277546	186048	W 278438	174613	BARRES,PROFIL FER,ACIER
674	IRN,STL UNIV,PLATE,SHEET	W 406576	239044	W 475477	301735	W 513992	421845	W 527623	401653	LARGES PLATS,TOLES
6744	IRN,STL HVY PLATE,ROLLED	W 162951	86997	W 214520	123205	W 229331	172207	W 215334	155520	TOLES LAMINEES PLUS 4.75 MM
67441	— OF IRON OR SIMPLE STL	W 155412	68944	W 203151	91854	W 215589	124579	W 202806	110145	TOLES NON ACIER FIN CARB
6749	OTH IRN,STL PLATES,SHEET	W 107163	72397	W 102738	77183	W 117056	109768	W 142951	127531	AUTRES TOLES FER,ACIER
67491	— OF IRON OR SIMPLE STL	W 103815	65630	W 97970	67693	W 111351	93940	W 137499	113549	AUT TOLES AUTRES ACIER FIN
678	IRON,STL TUBES,PIPES,ETC		598515	W 443609	603572	W 435743	620984	W 388843	595849	TUBES,TUYAUX EN FONTE,FER
6782	IRON,STL SEAMLESS TUBES	W 95994	149579	W 90634	168290	W 99409	179285	W 122216	207492	TUBES,TUYAUX SANS SOUDURE
6783	IRON,STL TUBES,PIPES NES	W 354267	344321	W 331963	336974	W 312944	318947	W 241351	248234	AUT TUBES,TUYAUX FER,ACIER
6785	IRON,STEEL TUBE FITTINGS		98453	W 12553	91998	W 13882	114651	W 15285	131591	ACCESSOIRES DE TUYAUTERIE
68	NON-FERROUS METALS		320507		570838		673234		613538	METAUX NON FERREUX
682	COPPER EXC CEMENT COPPER	W 20076	61408	W 26098	85044	W 29128	118695	W 28631	109502	CUIVRE
6822	COPPER,ALLOYS WORKED	W 17463	56443	W 23464	79184	W 25864	109207	W 25475	100891	CUIVRE,ALLIAGES OUVRES
684	ALUMINIUM	W 130239	203027	W 232755	407927	W 190313	450837	W 188960	393998	ALUMINIUM
6841	ALUMINIUM,ALLOYS,UNWRGHT	W 102715	113156	W 198663	292712	W 152303	287398	W 149540	234788	ALUMINIUM,ALLIAGES BRUTS
6842	ALUMINIUM,ALLOYS WORKED	W 27524	89871	W 34091	115216	W 38010	163440	W 39420	159210	ALUMINIUM,ALLIAGES OUVRE
69	METAL MANUFACTURES NES		774366		1233339		1369218		1141040	ART MANUFACT EN METAL NDA
691	STRUCTURES AND PARTS NES	W 58290	163209	W 75122	472360	W 88087	438927	W 82455	230825	CONSTRUCT FER,ACIER,ALU
6911	STRUCTURES,PARTS IRN,STL	W 54792	143048	W 70658	445973	W 82537	400202	W 77217	190519	CONSTRUCT FER,ACIER,FONTE
694	STL,COPPR NAILS,NUTS,ETC	W 17788	69024	W 19669	76064	W 22424	101160	W 22479	100777	CLOUS,VIS,ECROUS
695	TOOLS		115357	W 6839	129827	W 7888	161355	W 7736	169567	OUTILS A MAIN
699	BASE METAL MFRS NES	W 51491	254040	W 66302	343399	W 67777	434149	W 68223	388175	ART MANUFACTURES MET NDA
6991	LOCKSMITHS WARES,ETC	W 7453	60106	W 9025	71674	W 10426	90635	W 12100	108007	ARTICLES DE SERRURERIE
6996	BASE MTL MISC ARTICLES	W 9856	36829	W 16181	94437	W 15456	126475	W 9951	46965	ART DIVERS METAUX COMMUNS
6997	IRON,STEEL ARTICLES NES	W 16644	70150	W 21156	82641	W 23008	104218	W 24215	104915	OUV FONTE,FER,ACIER NDA
69979	IRN,STL MANUFACTURES NES	W 15203	67023	W 19859	80235	W 21120	101260	W 21350	98575	AUT OUVRAGES EN FER NDA
7	MACHINES,TRANSPORT EQUIP		9348362		10097237		12307070		13449726	MACHINES MATERIEL TRANSPORT
71	POWER GENERATING EQUIPMT		413609		490766		555124		617294	MACHINES GENERATRICES
713	INTRNL COMBUS PSTN ENGIN		161103	W 12101	183018	W 13138	220663	W 12853	219241	MOTEURS EXPL COMB INT, PIECE
714	ENGINES AND MOTORS NES		94976	W 1574	157586	W 1965	157943	W 2572	189257	MOTEURS NON ELECTRIQUES
7149	ENGINE & MOTOR PARTS NES	W 988	64933	W 1398	82565	W 1556	90567	W 2191	114375	PIECES 714 ET 718.88
716	ROTATING ELECTRIC PLANT		126413	W 9760	116898	W 10636	132681	W 11546	132596	APP ELECTR ROTATIFS,PIECES
7162	AC MTRS,GENRTRS,GEN SETS	N 960941	85846	W 8002	87653	W 8841	99005	W 9763	104920	MOTEURS ELECTRIQUES
72	MACHS FOR SPCL INDUSTRYS		893910		1038627		1449055		1624054	MAC SPECIALES POUR INDUST
721	AGRIC MACHY,EXC TRACTORS		89980	W 15239	107037	W 16576	132412	W 17491	152567	MACHINES AGRICOLES
722	TRACTORS NON-ROAD	N 2818	55398	W 13638	93425	W 17193	135971	W 17492	142083	TRACTEURS
7224	WHEELED TRACTORS NES	N 2676	54840	W 13569	92585	W 17072	134918	W 17399	140621	TRACTEURS A ROUES
723	CIVIL ENGNEERG EQUIP ETC		290869	W 31526	318529	W 43789	476542	W 51262	535943	APPAREILS DE GENIE CIVIL
7234	CONST,MINING MACHNRY NES	N 4346	97204	W 20424	127956	W 30545	212667	W 34399	229265	MACH POUR LA CONST, MINES
72342	SLFPRP SHOVELS,EXCAVATRS	N 1077	60275	W 17001	92235	W 25501	159935	W 26676	162673	PELLES MECANIQUES
7239	CONSTR ETC MACHY PTS NES	W 11537	191674	W 10914	189191	W 12812	260706	W 16491	303204	PIECES 723.41–723.46
725	PAPER ETC MILL MACHINERY		47546	W 2564	48004	W 6273	108419	W 4244	92628	MACHINES FABR PATE PAPIER
726	PRINTG,BKBINDG MACHY,PTS		65019	W 2391	90989	W 2412	96153	W 3754	123725	MACHINES POUR IMPRIMERIE
727	FOOD MACHRY NON-DOMESTIC		58123	W 2559	66091	W 2758	80243	W 3438	107805	MACH INDUSTRIES ALIMENT
728	OTH MACHY FOR SPCL INDUS		256834	W 19882	276954	W 26606	375869	W 27971	425082	AUT MACH IND PARTICULIERES
7284	MACHY FOR SPCL INDUS NES		197242	W 10702	194967	W 13574	243021	W 14909	286258	MACH SPEC IND PARTICUL.
72848	OTH MCHY WITH INDIV FNCT	N 83716	109486	W 5595	98011	W 7532	119545	W 8077	144435	AUTRES MACHINES NDA
72849	PTS OF MACHS OF 7284 ETC	W 2780	55693	W 3735	66341	W 4165	83749	W 5217	103570	PIECES DU 728.4 ETC
73	METALWORKING MACHINERY		88980		117770		166196		190370	MACH TRAVAIL DES METAUX
736	METALWORKING MACH-TOOLS		60639	W 5948	75291	W 7640	117507	W 8379	140784	MACH-OUTILS TRAVAIL METAUX
74	GENRL INDUSTRL MACHY NES		1286489		1399868		1830972		1930458	MACH APP INDUSTRIE
741	HEATING,COOLING EQUIPMNT		157587	W 13840	186033	W 21134	261710	W 25700	311082	MACH CHAUFFAGE,PIECES
7416	HEATING,COOLING EQU NES		56075	W 4174	75041	W 9597	112439	W 10184	127923	APP CHANGEMENT TEMP
742	PUMPS FOR LIQUIDS ETC		125688	W 5943	127081	W 7019	164322	W 7252	165551	POMPES MOTO-POMPES
743	PUMPS NES,CENTRFUGES ETC		220763	W 13839	217875	W 16926	289294	W 15861	292123	POMPES COMPRES,VENT ETC
7431	PUMPS FOR GASES ETC	N 245974	78432	W 3725	54824	W 4853	86517	W 4627	79690	POMPES AIR A VIDE,COMPRES
744	MECHANICAL HANDLING EQU		214333	W 37073	270846	W 46449	405060	W 50028	426349	EQUIP MANUTENTION PIECES
7442	LIFTING,LOADING MACH NES	N 123338	88306	W 14708	104010	W 20350	155832	W 21252	182544	APP LEVAGE,MANUTENTION
74428	OTH HANDLING ETC MCH NES	N 87889	49622	W 7734	56116	W 10316	86494	W 11760	110270	AUT APP LEVAGE ETC
7449	PTS NES OF MACHY OF 7442	W 10072	88981	W 13179	111188	W 15384	176693	W 14934	154419	PIECES DU 744.2
745	NONELEC MACHY,TOOLS NES		162215	W 8711	171224	W 11203	212402	W 10898	214882	AUT MACH NON ELEC,PIECES
7452	OTH NONELEC MCHS,PTS NES		140466	W 7626	144331	W 10153	185262	W 9848	186664	AUT MACH NON ELEC,PIECES
749	NONELEC MACH PTS,ACC NES	W 19089	405902	W 23976	426809	W 25337	498185	W 25775	520472	PIECES MACH NON ELEC NDA
7492	COCKS,VALVES ETC NES	W 8874	260423	W 11751	263569	W 11493	292035	W 10851	298740	ART ROB,SIM POUR TUYAUX
7493	SHAFT,CRANK,PULLEY ETC	W 5454	63100	W 6413	74620	W 6969	96027	W 7992	108023	ARBRES TRANS,VILEBREQUINS
75	OFFICE MACHNES,ADP EQUIP		1060546		1185308		1585544		1562826	MACH BUREAU TRAIT AUTOM
751	OFFICE MACHINES	N 1208272	88247	W 3029	105557		124542	W 3443	116112	MACH,APPAREILS DE BUREAU
7518	OFFICE MACHINES NES	N 552769	69516	W 2587	82449	W 2913	102118	W 2992	95488	MACH,APP DE BUREAU NDA
752	AUTOMTIC DATA PROC EQUIP	N 902101	597826	W 8834	648126	W 11786	908839	W 12936	950849	MACH TRAIT INFORMATION
7522	DIGITAL COMPUTERS	N 44801	68425	W 621	84695	W 806	99259	W 931	133375	MACH DIGITALES COMPLETES
7523	DIGITL CENTRL PROCESSORS	N 150439	194826	W 2550	220289	W 3798	368714	W 4158	364179	UNITES CENTRALES
7525	ADP PERIPHERAL UNITS	N 483858	203697	W 4462	229742	W 5841	305586	W 4774	220751	UNITES PERIPHERIQUES
7528	OFF-LINE DATA PROC EQUIP	N 127493	75284	W 793	64226	W 805	62265	W 2467	129851	MACH AUXIL TRAIT INFORM
759	OFFICE,ADP MCH PTS,ACCES	W 4386	374473	W 5226	431625	W 5586	552163	W 5718	495866	PIECES DU 751 ET 752
7599	ACCTG,ETC,ADP MCH PTS,AC	W 3334	331623	W 4212	386269	W 4505	500379	W 4578	449647	PIECES DU 751 ET 752
76	TELECOMM,SOUND EQUIPMENT		732152		895622		1168831		1140988	EQUIPMENT DE TELECOM
761	TELEVISION RECEIVERS	N 239729	86233	W 7011	107471	W 6878	117242	W 7456	116422	RECEPTEURS DE TELEVISION
7611	COLOUR TV RECEIVERS	N 236433	84151	W 6982	105856	W 6835	113774	W 7438	115498	RECEPTEURS COULEUR
764	TELECOM EQPT,PTS,ACC NES		529426	W 7937	651856	W 9202	893988	W 9352	859042	EQUIP TELECOM,PIECES
7641	LINE TELEPHONE,ETC EQUIP	N 912835	101165	W 1194	107502	W 1686	180807	W 1896	211473	APP TELEPHON PAR FIL
7643	TV,RADIO TRANSMITTRS ETC	N 194186	105231	W 708	175138	W 1189	293894	W 925	240010	APP EMET TELE RADIO
7649	PTS NES OF EQUIPMT OF 76	W 3109	233867	W 3169	259184	W 3187	315592	W 3221	309020	PIECES DE LA DIV 76
76491	PTS NES OF APPAR OF 7641	W 1124	137346	W 980	138789	W 1306	174832	W 1513	192765	PIECES POUR 764.1
76493	TELECOMM EQUIPMT PTS NES	W 1741	88881	W 1934	112062	W 1618	129947	W 1446	105368	PIECES 761,762,764.3,8
77	ELECTRIC MACHNRY NES ETC		1296587		1419321		1796940		1875355	MACH APP ELECT NDA
771	ELECTRIC POWER MACHY NES		96683	W 5203	92140	W 6449	125070	W 9695	147222	MACH PROD,TRANS ELECTR
772	SWITCHGEAR ETC,PARTS NES	W 8668	285350	W 9003	309891	W 10715	432536	W 11803	432926	APP COUPURE,SECT ETC

Norway, incl. Svalbard & Jan Mayen Islds

Norvège y compris iles Svalbard et Jan Mayen

4. General Imports C.I.F. by Commodities according to the S.I.T.C. (Rev. 2) in thousand U.S. Dollars
Importations Générales C.A.F. par Produits d'après la C.T.C.I. (Rév. 2) en milliers de Dollars E.U.

SITC CTCI	COMMODITY	1993		1994		1995		1996		PRODUIT
		WEIGHT POIDS	VALUE VALEUR	WEIGHT POIDS	VALUE VALEUR	WEIGHT POIDS	VALUE VALEUR	WEIGHT POIDS	VALUE VALEUR	
7721	SWITCHGEAR ETC	W 8433	254023	W 8704	272285	W 10304	375993	W 11402	383261	APP COUPURE,SECTIONMNT
773	ELECTR DISTRIBUTNG EQUIP	W 15403	107112	W 17201	111806	W 19287	142744	W 20330	153652	EQUIPMT DISTRIBUTION ELECT
7731	INSULATED WIRE,CABLE ETC	W 14203	94077	W 15778	99024	W 17949	126214	W 19169	137680	FILS,CABLES ISOLES ELECT
775	HOUSEHOLD TYPE EQUIP NES		238846	W 38913	274671	W 41060	315364	W 42697	327755	MACH,APP USAGE DOMESTQUE
7758	ELECTRO-THERMIC APPL NES		68873	W 9994	84852	W 10395	94306	W 11451	102365	APP ELECTROTHERMIQ NDA
776	TRANSISTORS,VALVES,ETC		134362	W 593	175601	W 600	213732	W 455	200409	LAMPES,TUBES,VALVES
7764	ELECTRONIC MICROCIRCUITS	MN 47032	102841	W 197	137174	W 232	160839	W 236	155861	MICROSTRUCTURES ELECTRON
778	ELECTRICAL MACHINERY NES		380802	W 170212	408639	W 187023	514792	W 184917	533870	AUTRES MACH ELECT NDA
7788	OTH ELEC MACHY,EQUIP NES		191797	W 146722	193829	W 162036	251654	W 158037	258728	AUT MACH APP ELEC NDA
77887	ELECTRICAL CARBONS	W 142784	80795	W 144589	85501	W 159397	103018	W 154871	108272	PIECES CHARBON,GRAPHITE
78	ROAD VEHICLES		1410803		2113556		2624127		2982457	VEHICULES ROUTIERS
781	PASS MOTOR VEH EXC BUSES	N 66422	592788	W 127681	1063310	W 126440	1221307	W 157657	1564607	AUTO TRANSPORT PERSONNES
782	LORRIES,SPCL MTR VEH NES	N 18015	333234	W 54730	462901	W 65421	642150	W 60097	616009	VEHICULES SPECIAUX,MARCH
7821	LORRIES,TRUCKS	N 17797	312165	W 52007	437526	W 61907	605026	W 55747	576058	VEHICULES TRANSP MARCHAND
783	ROAD MOTOR VEHICLES NES	N 2347	73784	W 5162	70530	W 8140	114414	W 5237	79139	VEHICULES ROUTIERS NDA
7831	BUSES	N 2298	70053	W 4376	62104	W 7459	106905	W 4849	76442	VOITURES TRANSPORT COMMUN
784	MOTOR VEH PRTS,ACCES NES		249589	W 35278	308932	W 40316	383999	W 40111	428060	PIECES 722,781,782,783
7849	OTHER MOTOR VEHCL PARTS	W 26757	233238	W 33616	298076	W 38430	370401	W 37085	393791	PIECES 722,781,782,783
785	CYCLES,ETC MOTRZD OR NOT		92599	W 7916	114630	W 7141	128340	W 9430	149075	MOTOCYCLES SCOOTERS
786	TRAILERS,NONMOTR VEH,NES		68809	W 23529	93253	W 28397	133916	W 32897	145566	REMORQUES,CADRES,CONTAIN
7861	TRAILERS,TRANSP CONTAINR		42976	W 17635	61082	W 21750	92830	W 25795	104314	REMORQUES TOUS VEHICULES
79	OTHR TRANSPORT EQUIPMENT		2165286		1436400		1130283		1525923	AUTRE MATERIEL TRANSPORT
791	RAILWAY VEHICLES		46840	W 10333	64181		61331	W 8776	159998	VEHIC MAT CHEMINS DE FER
792	AIRCRAFT ETC		338396	W 854	311669	W 1768	262838	W 1528	283632	APP NAVIGATION AERIENNE
7924	AIRCRFT NES OVER 15000KG	N 6	146890	W 149	90696	W 10	10529	W 53	30475	AERODYNES PLUS 15000 KG
7929	AIRCRAFT PARTS NES	W 596	103692	W 565	132350	W 1595	161142	W 1300	167428	PIECES DU 792
793	SHIPS AND BOATS ETC		1780050	W 906594	1060550	W 664203	806113		1082293	NAVIRES BATEAUX,ETC
7932	SHIPS AND BOATS NES		1503697	W 891233	1019568	W 654859	770589	W 590459	616582	NAVIRES ET BATEAUX
79322	TANKERS OF ALL KINDS	W 1053839	1134544	W 295846	358432	W 289990	357063	W 28653	30138	BATEAUX-CITERNES
79323	OTHER CARGO VESSELS	W 344374	320657	W 591281	627432	W 354104	335517	W 551969	513388	AUT BATEAUX TRANS MARCH
7938	TUGS,SPECIAL VESSELS ETC		238821	W 7946	25495	W 2907	10689		448922	REMORQUEURS,BATEAUX SPEC
79382	SPECL PURPOSE VESSLS ETC	N 14	230917	W 2059	11783	W 506	1626	W 80500	438464	BAT-PHARES,-POMPES,DRAGUES
8	MISC MANUFACTURED GOODS		4157923		4481353		5150483		5220575	ART MANUFACTURES DIVERS
812	*PLUMBG,HEATNG,LGHTNG EQ		126069	W 15742	145670	W 18572	184116	W 20137	197231	APPAR SANITAIRES CHAUFFAGE
8124	LIGHTING EQUIPMENT NES	W 9114	106644	W 9663	115370	W 12305	152352	W 12887	157983	APPAREILS ECLAIRAGE ETC
81242	LAMPS,FITTINGS BASE METL	W 7579	84571	W 8089	90931	W 9874	115083	W 10438	122175	APPAREILS D'ECLAIRAGE
821	*FURNITURE,PARTS THEREOF		446612	W 116175	506150	W 120552	610628	W 123041	650989	MEUBLES ET PIECES
8211	CHAIRS,SEATS AND PARTS	W 17694	110914	W 18398	118579	W 21088	149408	W 22384	160394	SIEGES ET PIECES
82111	CHAIRS AND OTHER SEATS	W 16362	102306	W 16677	107762	W 19181	136497	W 20493	147667	SIEGES
8219	FURNITURE AND PARTS NES	W 79866	283754	W 92152	330719	W 93951	395441	W 95564	424928	AUTRES MEUBLES ET PIECES
82192	WOOD FURNITURE NES	W 57046	203019	W 63797	229689	W 66836	283271	W 68141	305568	MEUBLES NDA EN BOIS
84	CLOTHING AND ACCESSORIES		1199763		1294566		1420803		1382353	VETEMENTS
842	MENS OUTERWEAR NOT KNIT	MN 10676	192764	W 8393	229659	W 9449	272088	W 8328	242132	VET DESSUS POUR HOMMES
8423	— TROUSERS,BREECHES ETC	N 6139916	68124	W 3827	87477	W 4013	102355	W 3876	100388	PANTALONS HOMMES MAT TEX
8429	— OTHER OUTER GARMENTS	N 2884300	66854	W 3295	86438	W 4129	105900	W 3203	82447	AUT VET DES HOM MAT TEX
843	WOMENS OUTERWEAR NONKNIT	MN 24842	340400	W 10660	367794	W 10174	396845	W 9305	364426	VET DESSUS FEMMES MAT TEX
8439	— OTHER OUTER GARMENTS	MN 15314	145847	W 6006	163534	W 5505	166755	W 4980	155238	AUT VET DES FEM MAT TEXT
845	OUTERWEAR KNIT NONELASTC		340929	W 13147	329186	W 11976	327057	W 12862	353853	VET DESSOUS,ACCES BONNET
8451	— JERSEYS,PULLOVERS ETC	MN 18548	195824	W 7968	188971	W 6693	176843	W 7527	200502	CHANDAILS,PULL-OVERS ETC
8459	— OTHER,CLTHG ACCESRYS		115754	W 4365	111547	W 4454	118478	W 4521	123448	AUT VET DESSUS DE BONNE
846	UNDER GARMENTS KNITTED	MN 65429	140055	W 7068	145514	W 7224	173967	W 7392	176585	SOUS VETS DE BONNETERIE
8462	— OF COTTON NON ELASTIC	MN 43129	95050	W 5953	102745	W 5962	122730	W 6131	125279	SOUS-VET BONNET COTON
84629	—— OTHER	MN 43129	95050	W 5638	97447	W 5709	117248	W 5844	118863	AUT SOUS-VET BONNET COTON
848	HEADGEAR,NONTXTL CLOTHNG		84902	W 5362	104882	W 5824	112539	W 5844	106309	VET ACCES MAT AUT QUE TEX
851	*FOOTWEAR	MP 16594	230521	W 13398	259260	W 13185	283319	W 13031	285076	CHAUSSURES
85102	FOOTWEAR LEATHER	MP 12120	191288	W 9288	215862	W 9296	235956	W 9275	236155	CHAUS SEMELLES EN CUIR
87	PRECISION INSTRUMNTS NES		504425		533659		580047		569730	INSTRUM,APPAR SCIENT NDA
872	MEDICAL INSTRUMENTS NES	W 1932	91488	W 2263	114235	W 2794	153120	W 2828	159626	INSTR,APP MEDIC-CHIR NDA
87202	OTH MEDICAL INSTRUMENTS	W 1586	76440	W 1851	93637	W 2230	118766	W 2311	135121	INSTRUM,APP MEDECINE
874	MEASURNG,CONTROLNG INSTR		340276	W 4342	335691	W 4041	355868	W 4297	343433	INSTRUMENTS DE MESURE
8749	INSTR PTS NES,ACCESSORYS		74251	W 581	68627	W 614	68423	W 692	69828	PIECES 873,874.3,54,874.8
88	PHOTO EQU,OPTICL GDS ETC		222996		229209		271206		282555	APP,FOURN PHOTO,OP,MONTR
882	PHOTO,CINEMA SUPPLIES	W 7033	92848	W 7232	93667	W 7711	108557	W 7220	99787	PRODUITS PHOTO,CINEMA
8822	PHOTO FILM EXC DEV CINMA	W 5091	73100	W 5134	72035	W 5454	82200	W 5435	76531	PLAQUES,PELLICULES,FILMS
89	MISC MANUFCTRD GOODS NES		1364171		1446259		1717792		1770384	ART MANUFACTURES DIVERS
892	PRINTED MATTER	W 48246	269507	W 51593	278023	W 54790	349342	W 56171	359481	IMPRIMES
8921	PRINTED BOOKS,GLOBES,ETC	W 12593	89823	W 13362	88933	W 14666	118438	W 13570	114650	LIVRES,BROCHURES,CARTES
89211	PRINTED BOOKS,PAMPHLETS	W 12013	84919	W 12722	83577	W 13891	111518	W 13012	108646	LIVRES,BROCHURES
8928	PRINTED MATTER NES	W 27585	137105	W 29301	144444	W 31599	178750	W 34364	181739	IMPRIMES NDA
89286	TRADE ADV MATRL,CATALOGS	W 21429	78096	W 22038	80475	W 23614	99079	W 27283	109038	IMPRIMES PUBLICITAIRES
893	ARTICLES OF PLASTIC NES		413137		454819		525377		562322	OUVRAGES EN MAT DIVIS 58
8931	PLSTC PACKG CONTNRS,LIDS	W 38298	134801	W 41149	137113	W 40785	166083	W 45560	172880	ART TRANSP EMBALLAGE ETC
8939	MISC PLASTIC ARTICLES	W 53878	262073	W 61869	299914	W 58259	338087	W 64156	365336	ART DIVERS EN MAT DIV 58
89399	OTHR PLASTC ARTICLES NES	W 36266	205793	W 41756	237075	W 39284	268445	W 44221	289382	AUT OUV MAT DIV 58
894	TOYS,SPORTING GOODS,ETC		206743	W 20910	219604	W 23803	267660	W 23221	274016	VOITURES ENFANTS,JOUETS
8942	TOYS,INDOOR GAMES ETC		126624	W 13751	129776	W 16131	164432	W 15880	174434	JOUETS,JEUX ETC
898	MUSICAL INSTRUMENTS,PTS		235481	W 6356	254207	W 6859	298863	W 6712	293377	INSTRUMENTS DE MUSIQUE
8983	SOUND RECRDNG TAPE,DISCS		214219	W 5599	234024	W 5991	274821	W 5905	270760	SUPPORTS SON POUR 763
89832	RECORDED DISCS,TAPES ETC		185878	W 3914	205463	W 4409	246210	W 4370	235903	DISQUES,PHONO,BANDES
899	OTHER MANUFACTURED GOODS		113970		121175		145319		151249	AUT ART MANUF DIVERS NDA
9	GOODS NOT CLASSD BY KIND		186185		454215		482683		453242	ART TRANSACT NON CLASSES
931	*SPECIAL TRANSACTIONS	W 1462	14132		256203		286525		270528	TRANS.SPECIALES
951	*WAR FIREARMS,AMMUNITION		152267	W 1274	178311	W 2409	169728	W 5225	159435	VEHIC BLINDES ARMES
95106	AMMUNITION NES	W 636	78239	W 604	123267	W 503	118704	W 1865	97174	PROJECTILES,MUNITIONS

Norway, incl. Svalbard & Jan Mayen Islds

Norvège y compris iles Svalbard et Jan Mayen

5. General Exports F.O.B. by Commodities according to the S.I.T.C. (Rev. 2) in thousand U.S. Dollars
Exportations Générales F.O.B. par Produits d'après la C.T.C.I. (Rév. 2) en milliers de Dollars E.U.

SITC CTCI	COMMODITY	1993		1994		1995		1996		PRODUIT
		WEIGHT POIDS	VALUE VALEUR	WEIGHT POIDS	VALUE VALEUR	WEIGHT POIDS	VALUE VALEUR	WEIGHT POIDS	VALUE VALEUR	
	ALL COMMODITIES		31903873		34743549		41740342		48954986	TOUS PRODUITS
0	FOOD AND LIVE ANIMALS		2507800		3002489		3405601		3730000	ALIMENTS,ANIMAUX VIVANTS
03	FISH AND PREPARATIONS		2210385		2678729		3045421		3321608	POISSONS ET PREPARATIONS
034	FISH,FRESH,CHILLED,FROZN	W 865305	1419655	W 1023885	1751602	W 1135785	2066747	W 1291846	2360208	POISSON FRAIS, REFRIG,CONG
0341	FISH FRSH,CHLLD,EX FILLT	W 310356	715583	W 309157	848989	W 344719	936333	W 370704	949141	POISSON FRAIS,REFRIGERE
0342	FISH FROZEN,EXCL FILLETS	W 415346	347028	W 521024	425848	W 582622	555490	W 692756	788439	POISSONS CONGELES
0344	FISH FILLETS,FROZEN	W 128386	316381	W 177366	418949	W 187290	500638	W 195185	514912	FILETS CONGELES
035	FISH SALTED,DRIED,SMOKED	W 129925	537049	W 167811	659569	W 167913	719818	W 169245	696269	POISSON SECHE,SALE,FUME
03502	COD(NOT IN FILLETS)DRIED	W 37714	210678	W 36877	226202	W 44309	293371	W 46497	286663	MORUE SECHEE,SALEE
03503	FISH(EX COD)DRIED,SALTED	W 88800	289647	W 127053	393206	W 119442	382117	W 118672	365124	POISSONS SECHES,SALES
037	FISH ETC PREPD,PRSVD NES	W 46407	198186	W 50734	211279	W 40769	204130	W 43762	214028	POIS,CRUST,MOL PREPARES
0371	FISH PREPARD,PRESRVD NES	W 30241	103159	W 34307	105789	W 29489	101100	W 30092	104857	CONSERVES DE POISSONS
0372	SHELL FISH PREPRD,PRESVD	W 16167	95027	W 16426	105490	W 11280	103030	W 13670	109170	CRUSTACES,COQUIL PREPARES
081	*FEEDING STUFF FOR ANIML	W 166158	80391	W 217325	98718	W 262516	117640	W 289365	159470	NOURRITURE POUR ANIMAUX
2	CRUDE MATERLS,EXCL FUELS		863889		799425		1022953		933769	MAT BRUTES NON COMESTIBLES
24	CORK AND WOOD		204263		201906		223046		204162	LIEGE ET BOIS
248	WOOD SHAPED,SLEEPERS		168701	W 385882	180178	W 365313	191849	W 385732	176027	BOIS SIMPLEMENT TRAVAILLES
2482	LUMBER SHAPED CONIFER		166678	W 383814	177398	W 364145	189865	W 381385	172855	CONIFERES SCIES,RABOTES
24821	LUMBER SAWN ETC CONIFER	W 609209	153671	W 366600	163858	W 352401	177710	W 363317	157400	CONIFERES SCIES LONGITUD
251	*PULP AND WASTE PAPER			W 493795	163624	W 555836	281625	W 505932	209134	PATES A PAPIER,DECHETS
2516	CHEM WOOD PULP DISSOLVNG	W 106045	63519	W 104443	67196	W 136488	126173	W 148854	124669	PATES CHIMIQUES DE BOIS
27	CRUDE FERTLZR,MINRLS NES		213428		198944		229078		232927	ENGRAIS MINERAUX BRUTS
273	STONE,SAND AND GRAVEL	W 8685717	124968	MW 9064	143305	MW 10050	166217	MW 9944	164722	PIERRES,SABLES,GRAVIERS
28	METALLIFEROUS ORES,SCRAP		156042		135643		151914		142898	MINERAIS METAL,DECHETS
3	MINERAL FUELS ETC		16368267		17236676		19736815		26758860	COMBUSTIBLES MINERAUX LUB
33	PETROLEUM AND PRODUCTS		13943492		14618704		16756045		22886837	PETROLE ET DERIVES
333	CRUDE PETROLEUM	MW 99582	12590487	MW 111261	13168552	MW 121730	15330928	MW 136824	20987835	HUILES BRUTES DE PETROLE
334	PETROLEUM PRODUCTS,REFIN	MW 17500	1317243	MW 9706	1428610	MW 9156	1390527	MW 10259	1858744	PRODUITS RAFFINES
3341	GASOLINE,OTH LIGHT OILS	W 2716377	498000	W 3781886	600965	W 3933145	639372	W 4785090	907790	ESSENCES POUR MOTEURS
33411	MOTOR,AVIATION SPIRIT	W 1681759	336975	W 1848450	317450	W 1360671	244965	W 1949153	397098	ESSENCES MOTEURS D'AVIONS
33419	OTH LIGHT PETROLEUM OILS	W 1034618	161025	W 1931212	283148	W 2561372	392562	W 2817768	507053	AUTRES HUILES LEGERES
3343	GAS OILS	W 3655789	559508	W 3742631	569870	W 2980056	464707	W 3097136	595316	GAS OILS
3344	FUEL OILS,NES	W 1767504	176459	W 1754615	175954	W 1902145	216044	W 1906757	242771	FUEL OILS
341	*GAS,NATURAL AND MANUFCT	MW 26140	2285192	MW 23973	2522733	MW 25199	2790965	MW 33664	3716038	GAZ NATUREL,GAZ MANUFACT
3413	PETROLM GASES,LIQUEFIED	W 1468910	223946	W 2325798	325021	W 2910821	506664	W 3156414	637908	GAZ DE PETROLE LIQUEFIE
34131	LIQUEFIED PROPANE,BUTANE	W 1376060	212672	W 2212117	304855	W 2770622	457760	W 2986189	594334	PROPANE,BUTANE LIQUEFIES
3414	PETROLEUM GASES, GASEOUS	MW 24671	2061247	MW 21647	2197706	MW 22288	2284302	MW 30507	3078131	GAZ DE PETROLE GAZEUX
351	*ELECTRIC CURRENT	H 8376769	124732	H 4740918	93371	H 8563380	188751	H 4236276	153199	ENERGIE ELECTRIQUE
5	CHEMCLS,RELATED PROD NES		2004269		990573		1268055		1369780	PRODUITS CHIMIQUES
51	ORGANIC CHEMICALS		357758		202836		247680		276261	PROD CHIMIQ ORGANIQUES
511	HYDROCARBONS NES,DERIVS		141133	W 1209	3846	W 792	1327		509	HYDROCARBURES NDA
5113	HALOG DERIV OF HYDROCARB		140570	W 1042	3331	W 129	224	W 37	136	DERIVES HALOGENES HYDROCAR
51131	VINYL CHLORIDE		140427							CHLORURE DE VINYLE
514	NITROGEN–FNCTN COMPOUNDS		171853	W 2171	173334	W 3891	219963	W 6057	244828	COMPOSES FONCT AZOTEES
5147	AMIDE–FNCT CMPD,EXC UREA	W 938	138238	W 1133	160916	W 1584	197452	W 1948	220454	COMPOSES CARBOXYAMIDE
52	INORGANIC CHEMICALS		297010		158574		201482		234994	PROD CHIM INORGANIQUES
522	INORG ELEMNTS,OXIDES,ETC		160044	W 515946	142760	W 839451	179126	W 983824	207617	ELEMENTS INORGANIQUES
5221	CHEMICAL ELEMENTS		97882	W 97072	117659	W 105855	146842	W 111124	163610	ELEMENTS CHIMIQUES
52212	NON–METALS NES		96524	W 91798	116931	W 97689	145279	W 97136	161895	SELENIUM,PHOSPHORE
523	OTHR INORG CHEMICALS ETC		135678	W 103590	14746	W 144670	21241	W 199358	26067	AUT PRODUITS CHIMIQUES INORG
541	*MEDICINAL,PHARM PRODUCT	MK 18797	193347	MK 14232	189994		210126		225438	PROD MEDICINAUX PHARMACEUT
562	*FERTILIZERS,MANUFACTURE		306620	W 8505	1311	W 51	43	W 2923	359	ENGRAIS MANUFACTURES
5629	FERTILIZERS NES		242699	W 4475	838	W 10	4	W 2802	345	ENGRAIS NDA
56291	NIT–PHOS–POT FERTLZR NES		224576							ENGRAIS CONT N P K
58	PLASTIC MATERIALS ETC		507364		156087		201313		185588	MAT PLAST ARTIFICIELLES
582	PROD OF CONDENSATION ETC		108795	W 10697	30412	W 11454	40143	W 11291	38849	PROD CONDENS,POLYCOND
583	POLYMERIZATION ETC PRODS		358072	W 84729	124646	W 76673	160139	W 74234	145321	PROD POLYMERISATION
5831	POLYETHYLENE	W 241979	159246	W 7225	11959	W 7343	12884	W 8489	14932	POLYETHYLENE
58311	— IN PRIMARY FORMS	W 235575	148851							POLYETHYLENE PRIMAIRES
59	CHEMICAL MATERIALS NES		178049		184027		270354		294370	MAT PROD CHIMIQUES NDA
598	MISCEL CHEM PRODUCTS NES		165253	W 1161556	171294	W 1626140	256869	W 1966029	280068	PROD DIV INDUST CHIM NDA
5989	CHEM PRODUCTS,PREPS NES	W 878458	106539	W 1039452	128003	W 1450716	187738	W 1815864	208898	PROD PREP CHIMIQUES NDA
59899	OTH CHEM PRODS,PREPS,NES	W 850310	92531	W 1007738	112300	W 1418625	163991	W 1781770	188597	AUT PRODUITS CHIMIQUES NDA
6	BASIC MANUFACTURES		4871915		4908392		6325185		6155362	ART MANUFACTURES
63	WOOD,CORK MANUFACTRS NES		230441		226205		256624		243151	OUVRAGES LIEGE ET BOIS
635	WOOD MANUFACTURES NES		200135	W 61853	185660	W 59798	206571	W 56132	189156	ART MANUF EN BOIS NDA
6353	BUILDERS WOODWRK,PREFABS		193904	W 60187	179743	W 57459	198573	W 54010	181847	OUVRAGES DE MENUISERIE
64	PAPER,PAPERBOARD AND MFR		910682		688128		1053108		938652	PAPIERS,CARTONS & OUVRAGES
641	PAPER AND PAPERBOARD		832159	W 990391	603412	W 1111117	948952	W 1008853	829855	PAPIERS ET CARTONS
6413	KRAFT PAPER,PAPERBOARD		84823	W 222324	128914	W 214567	182960	W 221367	147516	PAPIER ET CARTON KRAFT
64131	KRAFT LINER IN BULK	W 117154	49504	W 181947	92416	W 180332	141232	W 187961	113311	PAP KRAFT POUR COUVERTURES
6415	PAPER,PAPERBRD,BULK,NES			W 682855	407685	W 810374	675344	W 708389	599524	PAPIERS,CARTONS ROULEAUX
64159	OTHER PAPER ETC,BULK,NES	W 471787	266769	W 640779	350762	W 769557	606613	W 669107	533212	AUT PAPIER ROULEAUX FEUILLES
65	TEXTILE YARN,FABRICS,ETC		145456		169900		186332		197291	FILS,TISSUS,ARTICLES TEXTILE
66	NONMETAL MINERAL MFS NES		142942		124066		137860		153312	ART MIN NON METALLIQUES
67	IRON AND STEEL		868245		759710		942650		1044491	FER ET ACIER
671	PIG IRON ETC		367819	W 643306	413150	W 790347	558072	W 652076	582175	FONTE,SPIEGEL,POUDRES
6716	FERRO–ALLOYS		354395	W 612529	407378	W 621183	514308	W 651376	581645	FERRO–ALLIAGES
67162	FERRO–SILICON		237470	W 423410	283694	W 415723	347758	W 414036	371957	FERRO–SILICIUM
67169	OTHER FERRO–ALLOYS	W 208746	116925	W 189118	123685	W 205460	166550	W 237340	209688	AUTRES FERRO–ALLIAGES
673	IRON,STEEL SHAPES ETC	W 369192	121383	W 314973	116347	W 249565	115949	W 311937	129131	BARRES,PROFIL FER,ACIER
674	IRN,STL UNIV,PLATE,SHEET	W 155034	104487	W 168187	115618	W 182032	143889	W 170716	135842	LARGES PLATS,TOLES
68	NON–FERROUS METALS		2112397		2564189		3260132		3059510	METAUX NON FERREUX
682	COPPER EXC CEMENT COPPER	W 42014	89148	W 47442	114254	W 40520	131835	W 40187	104819	CUIVRE
683	NICKEL	W 59873	320352	W 67211	408374	W 52660	448415	W 61060	474492	NICKEL
6831	NICKEL,ALLOYS UNWROUGHT	W 59860	320305	W 67188	408233	W 52644	448216	W 61030	474404	NICKEL ET ALLIAGES BRUTS
684	ALUMINIUM	W 967304	1394579	W 1041851	1718620	W 978348	2298690	W 1072138	2125495	ALUMINIUM
6841	ALUMINIUM,ALLOYS,UNWRGHT	W 788322	1050715	W 866704	1333552	W 810570	1781901	W 875679	1600306	ALUMINIUM,ALLIAGES BRUTS
6842	ALUMINIUM,ALLOYS WORKED	W 178982	343863	W 175148	385069	W 167778	516790	W 196459	525189	ALUMINIUM,ALLIAGES OUVRE
68421	ALUMINIUM BARS,WIRE,ETC	W 55282	108163	W 65394	140129	W 62976	190152	W 87317	212776	BARRES,PROFILES FILS ALU
68422	ALUMNM PLATE,SHEET,STRIP	W 120509	225722	W 105536	230538	W 101632	306798	W 105089	281951	TOLES, PLANCHES EN ALU
686	ZINC		138150	W 125648	126694	W 121262	130387	W 122227	128964	ZINC
6861	ZINC,ALLOYS UNWROUGHT	W 126887	124012	W 124539	125767	W 120148	129484	W 121410	128228	ZINC ET ALLIAGES BRUTS
689	NON–FER BASE METALS NES		131867	W 4042	138176	W 3974	178043	W 3562	174393	AUT METAUX NON FERREUX
6899	BASE METALS NES,CERMETS	W 3099	73860	W 4005	137000	W 3969	178040	W 3477	174335	METAUX COMMUNS NDA
68999	BASE MTL NES UNWRT,WASTE	W 3099	73860	W 3853	136966	W 3969	178040	W 3477	174335	AUT METAUX COM BRUTS NDA
69	METAL MANUFACTURES NES		397341		298389		407965		439052	ART MANUFACT EN METAL NDA
691	STRUCTURES AND PARTS NES	W 25788	161662	W 17098	50739	W 22834	90983	W 23541	90860	CONSTRUCT FER,ACIER,ALU
6911	STRUCTURES,PARTS IRN,STL	W 23678	145900	W 15215	36686	W 19839	69413	W 20785	69601	CONSTRUCT FER,ACIER,FONTE
699	BASE METAL MFRS NES	W 24634	107953	W 20703	121428	W 22212	150633	W 26627	187270	ART MANUFACTURES MET NDA
7	MACHINES,TRANSPORT EQUIP		4138036		4196784		5553376		5417976	MACHINES MATERIEL TRANSPORT

Norway, incl. Svalbard & Jan Mayen Islds

Norvège y compris iles Svalbard et Jan Mayen

5. General Exports F.O.B. by Commodities according to the S.I.T.C. (Rev. 2) in thousand U.S. Dollars
Exportations Générales F.O.B. par Produits d'après la C.T.C.I. (Rév. 2) en milliers de Dollars E.U.

SITC CTCI	COMMODITY	1993		1994		1995		1996		PRODUIT
		WEIGHT POIDS	VALUE VALEUR	WEIGHT POIDS	VALUE VALEUR	WEIGHT POIDS	VALUE VALEUR	WEIGHT POIDS	VALUE VALEUR	
71	POWER GENERATING EQUIPMT		260024		260951		311744		338211	MACHINES GENERATRICES
713	INTRNL COMBUS PSTN ENGIN		111538	W 6901	130282	W 6975	148419	W 6624	146609	MOTEURS EXPL COMB INT, PIECE
714	ENGINES AND MOTORS NES		102226	W 569	73573	W 617	78053	W 733	97320	MOTEURS NON ELECTRIQUES
72	MACHS FOR SPCL INDUSTRYS		364312		390572		522440		650552	MAC SPECIALES POUR INDUST
721	AGRIC MACHY,EXC TRACTORS		91786	W 22278	113307	W 23226	135684	W 26242	148443	MACHINES AGRICOLES
723	CIVIL ENGNEERG EQUIP ETC		77197	W 13666	84279	W 14464	126945	W 14835	163742	APPAREILS DE GENIE CIVIL
728	OTH MACHY FOR SPCL INDUS		100812	W 9280	102406	W 11867	139421	W 12890	186475	AUT MACH IND PARTICULIERES
7284	MACHY FOR SPCL INDUS NES		82777	W 5260	81158	W 7618	115394	W 9145	158124	MACH SPEC IND PARTICUL.
74	GENRL INDUSTRL MACHY NES		504624		566556		812825		910658	MACH APP INDUSTRIE
741	HEATING,COOLING EQUIPMNT		71174	W 8357	94472	W 9220	122336	W 11479	158168	MACH CHAUFFAGE,PIECES
742	PUMPS FOR LIQUIDS ETC		96294	W 3145	91841	W 4048	133912	W 4496	145924	POMPES MOTO–POMPES
744	MECHANICAL HANDLING EQU		128723	W 19996	154442	W 27849	245779	W 26741	242708	EQUIP MANUTENTION PIECES
7442	LIFTING,LOADING MACH NES		67238	W 10504	88013	W 16382	155102	W 14168	136682	APP LEVAGE,MANUTENTION
749	NONELEC MACH PTS,ACC NES	W 4091	75653	W 4664	78267	W 7083	122909	W 8638	162030	PIECES MACH NON ELEC NDA
75	OFFICE MACHNES,ADP EQUIP		258801		326820		353260		409575	MACH BUREAU TRAIT AUTOM
752	AUTOMTIC DATA PROC EQUIP	N 308983	167748	W 1386	201364	W 1150	209120	W 1262	222449	MACH TRAIT INFORMATION
759	OFFICE,ADP MCH PTS,ACCES	W 782	73029	W 1340	98485	W 964	105710	W 1974	159597	PIECES DU 751 ET 752
7599	ACCTG,ETC,ADP MCH PTS,AC	W 649	66672	W 1197	95455	W 803	103207	W 1751	154336	PIECES DU 751 ET 752
76	TELECOMM,SOUND EQUIPMENT		316837		379135		574360		565164	EQUIPMENT DE TELECOM
764	TELECOM EQPT,PTS,ACC NES		300165	W 3166	359243	W 4564	555593	W 4492	547065	EQUIP TELECOM,PIECES
7641	LINE TELEPHONE,ETC EQUIP	N 173969	74790	W 487	89697	W 917	167132	W 486	143179	APP TELEPHON PAR FIL
7643	TV,RADIO TRANSMITTRS ETC	N 12799	67346	W 246	85697	W 326	129160	W 475	163674	APP EMET TELE RADIO
7649	PTS NES OF EQUIPMT OF 76	W 1463	119353	W 1489	129663	W 2472	220973	W 2450	200542	PIECES DE LA DIV 76
77	ELECTRIC MACHNRY NES ETC		418467		486742		641765		783301	MACH APP ELECT NDA
772	SWITCHGEAR ETC,PARTS NES	W 3744	81778	W 4657	101695	W 5764	141678	W 6379	165419	APP COUPURE,SECT ETC
7721	SWITCHGEAR ETC	W 3724	78678	W 4640	98338	W 5742	133840	W 6363	160637	APP COUPURE,SECTIONMNT
773	ELECTR DISTRIBUTNG EQUIP	W 10434	59252	W 10427	67744	W 11155	92937	W 27978	199404	EQUIPMT DISTRIBUTION ELECT
7731	INSULATED WIRE,CABLE ETC	W 9131	52894	W 10266	66122	W 10981	91488	W 27755	197344	FILS,CABLES ISOLES ELECT
778	ELECTRICAL MACHINERY NES		83524	W 5690	99206	W 9464	142674	W 26566	151065	AUTRES MACH ELECT NDA
78	ROAD VEHICLES		292890		389469		536443		553152	VEHICULES ROUTIERS
784	MOTOR VEH PRTS,ACCES NES		186694	W 31489	250740	W 36823	339331	W 37706	353257	PIECES 722,781,782,783
7849	OTHER MOTOR VEHCL PARTS	W 23579	185959	W 31267	248719	W 36529	337079	W 37552	351698	PIECES 722,781,782,783
79	OTHR TRANSPORT EQUIPMENT		1699150		1364926		1761307		1167355	AUTRE MATERIEL TRANSPORT
792	AIRCRAFT ETC		114899	W 215	39258		44031	W 140	45150	APP NAVIGATION AERIENNE
793	SHIPS AND BOATS ETC		1582256	W 1428798	1322928	W 1814488	1705517	W 982206	1101691	NAVIRES BATEAUX,ETC
7931	WARSHIPS	N 181	110536	W 6496	114404	W 1344	108198	W 2711	61799	NAVIRES DE GUERRE
7932	SHIPS AND BOATS NES		1314453	W 1246372	1050017	W 1810510	1528379	W 961130	947235	NAVIRES ET BATEAUX
79322	TANKERS OF ALL KINDS	W 1588323	448260	W 281632	283485	W 390546	264078	W 145681	181137	BATEAUX–CITERNES
79323	OTHER CARGO VESSELS	W 1234768	727626	W 948996	619158	W 1400516	1081567	W 789052	529915	AUT BATEAUX TRANS MARCH
79324	FISHING VESSELS ETC	W 15951	100780	W 13292	94102	W 17461	139233	W 24690	198626	BATEAUX DE PECHE
7938	TUGS,SPECIAL VESSELS ETC		152716	W 1681	138307	W 2634	68939	W 1447	89839	REMORQUEURS,BATEAUX SPEC
79382	SPECL PURPOSE VESSLS ETC	N 7	145526	W 57	112382	W 51	34644	W 1370	86285	BAT–PHARES,–POMPES,DRAGUES
8	MISC MANUFACTURED GOODS		943725		1051600		1252147		1357267	ART MANUFACTURES DIVERS
821	*FURNITURE,PARTS THEREOF		168784	W 25929	202637	W 30045	265790	W 35923	311649	MEUBLES ET PIECES
8211	CHAIRS,SEATS AND PARTS	W 7216	99991	W 7806	118522	W 8564	153604	W 10282	177767	SIEGES ET PIECES
82111	CHAIRS AND OTHER SEATS	W 6356	93821	W 7148	113866	W 7820	147028	W 9168	166353	SIEGES
87	PRECISION INSTRUMNTS NES		270718		322879		367396		421370	INSTRUM,APPAR SCIENT NDA
874	MEASURNG,CONTROLNG INSTR		230484	W 2109	278530	W 2134	312975		352517	INSTRUMENTS DE MESURE
89	MISC MANUFCTRD GOODS NES		338875		306118		366706		388826	ART MANUFACTURES DIVERS
893	ARTICLES OF PLASTIC NES		114664		131487		177696		172975	OUVRAGES EN MAT DIVIS 58
9	GOODS NOT CLASSD BY KIND		109604		2488540		3104236		3150848	ART TRANSACT NON CLASSES
931	*SPECIAL TRANSACTIONS	W 437	3662		2410950		3017824		3028480	TRANS.SPECIALES

Oman

1. HISTORICAL SERIES, 1965–1996 GENERAL TRADE, IMPORTS C.I.F., EXPORTS F.O.B.
SERIES HISTORIQUES, 1965–1996 COMMERCE GENERAL, IMPORTATIONS C.A.F., EXPORTATIONS F.O.B

YEAR ANNEE	VALUE IN MILLION RIALS OMANI / VALEUR EN MILLION RIALS OMANI — MERCHANDISE–MARCHANDISE IMPORTS	EXPORTS	GOLD–OR IMPORTS	EXPORTS	CONVERSION FACTORS U.S. CENTS PER RIAL OMANI / FACTEURS DE CONVERSION CENTS E.U. PAR RIAL OMANI — IMPORTS	EXPORTS	INDEX NUMBERS–INDICES — QUANTUM IMPORTS	EXPORTS	UNIT VALUE / VALEUR UNITAIRE IMPORTS	EXPORTS
1965	6.50	0.80			280.0000	280.0000				
1966	6.80	0.70			280.0000	280.0000				
1967	7.20	13.40			276.7000	276.7000				
1968	8.10	62.90			240.0000	240.0000				
1969	11.20	84.70			240.0000	240.0000				
1970	14.40	85.90			240.0000	240.0000				
1971	40.20	88.00			240.0000	240.0000				
1972	61.60	88.60			260.6000	260.6000				
1973	85.80	115.00			286.8610	286.8610				
1974	135.60	419.10			289.5190	289.5190				
1975	264.30	489.20			289.5190	289.5190				
1976	250.50	545.20			289.5190	289.5190				
1977	302.10	547.40			289.5190	289.5190				
1978	327.20	552.00			289.5190	289.5190				
1979	430.50	787.40			289.5190	289.5190				
1980	598.20	1294.50			289.5190	289.5190				
1981	790.30	1621.90			289.5194	289.5194				
1982	926.50	1526.90			289.5192	289.5192				
1983	860.90	1467.30			289.5192	289.5192				
1984	949.20	1527.50			289.5191	289.5193				
1985	1088.90	1778.10			289.5191	289.5190				
1986	916.70	1122.50			260.0776	262.7984				
1987	700.70	1484.90			260.0776	260.0776				
1988	846.50	1291.40			260.0778	260.0779				
1989	867.90	1564.00			260.0780	260.0780				
1990	1031.00	2118.00			260.0778	260.0780				
1991	1228.00	1872.00			260.0797	260.0780				
1992	1449.30	2086.00			260.0797	260.0796				
1993	1581.80	2037.00			260.0797	260.0796				
1994	1505.30	2132.00			260.0800	260.0800				
1995	1633.20	2196.00			260.0796	260.0796				
1996	1760.20				260.0797					

2. IMPORTS BY BROAD ECONOMIC CATEGORY AND EXPORTS BY INDUSTRIAL ORIGIN. (PERCENTAGE OF TOTAL VALUE)
IMPORTATIONS PAR CATEGORIES ECONOMIQUES ET EXPORTATIONS PAR BRANCHE D'ACTIVITE.(EN POURCENTAGE DE LA VALEUR TOTALE)

IMPORTS – IMPORTATIONS

	1990	1991	1992	1993	1994	1995	1996
TOTAL IMPORTS–IMPORTATIONS TOTALES	100.	100.	100.	100.	100.	100.	
1 FOOD BEV–ALIMENTATION BOISSONS	17.0	15.1	13.9	13.3	14.8	15.2	
11 PRIMARY–PRODUITS DE BASE	8.9	7.9	7.2	6.5	7.4	8.0	
111 FOR INDUSTRY–POUR L'INDUSTRIE	2.5	1.9	1.9	1.5	2.1	3.3	
112 FOR HOUSEHOLDS–POUR LES MENAGES	6.4	6.0	5.2	5.0	5.3	4.7	
12 PROCESSED–PRODUITS ELABORES	8.1	7.2	6.7	6.8	7.3	7.1	
121 FOR INDUSTRY–POUR L'INDUSTRIE	0.4	0.5	0.4	0.5	0.6	0.8	
122 FOR HOUSEHOLDS–POUR LES MENAGES	7.7	6.7	6.4	6.3	6.7	6.3	
2 IND SUPPLIES–APPROV INDUSTRIELS	21.2	21.4	18.8	19.1	19.9	22.2	
21 PRIMARY–PRODUITS DE BASE	1.1	0.9	0.8	1.6	2.2	2.3	
22 PROCESSED–PRODUITS ELABORES	20.1	20.5	17.9	17.5	17.6	19.9	
3 FUELS–COMBUSTIBLES	4.2	1.9	1.9	3.2	1.1	1.6	
31 PRIMARY–PRODUITS DE BASE	0.1	0.0	0.1	0.1	0.1	0.1	
32 PROCESSED–PRODUITS ELABORES	4.1	1.8	1.9	3.1	0.9	1.5	
321 MOTOR SPIRIT–ESSENCE		1.7	1.7	2.9	0.9		
322 OTHER–AUTRES	4.1	0.1	0.1	0.2	0.1	1.5	
4 MACHINERY–EQUIPEMENT	17.0	21.6	18.0	17.5	18.2	18.3	
41 CAPITAL EQUIPMENT–MACHINES	15.4	19.7	16.5	16.0	16.7	16.7	
42 PARTS–PIECES ACCESSOIRES	1.6	1.9	1.5	1.5	1.5	1.6	
5 TRANSPORT–TRANSPORT	18.7	20.4	25.9	25.9	25.4	21.5	
51 PASSENGER CARS–AUTOMOBILES	11.1	12.1	16.3	15.7	13.3	9.8	
52 OTHER–AUTRES	2.0	2.2	3.0	4.1	6.0	4.8	
521 INDUSTRIAL–INDUSTRIELS	2.0	2.1	2.9	4.1	5.9	4.8	
522 NON INDUSTRIAL–NON INDUSTRIEL	0.1	0.1	0.1	0.1	0.1	0.0	
53 PARTS–PIECES ACCESSOIRES	5.6	6.1	6.6	6.1	6.2	6.8	
6 CONSUM GOODS–BIENS CONSOMMATION	15.0	16.3	18.1	16.4	17.1	16.6	
61 DURABLE–DURABLES	6.4	6.0	6.1	5.0	5.1	5.0	
62 SEMI DURABLE–SEMI DURABLES	4.4	4.2	3.7	3.4	3.6	3.6	
63 NON DURABLE–NON DURABLES	4.2	6.1	8.4	8.0	8.5	8.0	
7 GOODS NES–BIENS NDA	6.9	3.3	3.4	4.6	3.5	4.7	

EXPORTS – EXPORTATIONS

	1990	1991	1992	1993	1994	1995	1996
TOTAL EXPORTS–EXPORTATIONS TOTALES	100.	100.	100.	100.	100.	100.	
1 AGRICULTURE	1.4	1.4	1.3	1.7	1.8	2.1	
2 MINING QUARRY–INDUS EXTRACTIVES	89.1	84.1	83.3	78.3	75.9	78.1	
3 MANUFACTURING–IND MANUFACTUR	9.5	14.5	15.4	20.0	22.3	19.7	
31 FOOD BEV TOBACCO–ALIM BOISS TAB	0.3	1.2	2.0	3.0	3.1	2.9	
32 TEXTILES–INDUSTRIES TEXTILES	0.6	0.8	1.0	1.2	1.4	1.7	
33 WOOD & PRODUCTS–BOIS & PRODUITS	0.0	0.0	0.0	0.0	0.0	0.0	
34 PAPER & PRODUCTS–PAPIER & PRODT	0.0	0.1	0.1	0.1	0.1	0.1	
35 CHEMICALS–INDUSTRIES CHIMIQUES	3.2	4.1	1.2	1.5	1.5	1.7	
36 NON METAL MIN–MIN NON METAL	0.1	0.1	0.1	0.2	0.2	0.2	
37 BASIC METAL–IND METAL BASE	0.8	0.9	0.9	1.2	1.5	1.5	
38 METAL MANUF–MANUF METAL	4.1	7.1	9.9	12.5	13.8	11.0	
39 OTH MANUF IND–AUTRES MANUF	0.3	0.3	0.3	0.4	0.7	0.6	

3. TRADE BY PRINCIPAL COUNTRIES OF ORIGIN AND LAST CONSIGNMENT (VALUE IN THOUSAND U.S. DOLLARS)
ECHANGES SELON LES PRINCIPAUX PAYS D'ORIGINE ET DE DERNIERE CONSIGNATION (VALEUR EN MILLIERS DE DOLLARS EU)

COUNTRIES–PAYS	GENERAL IMPORTS C.I.F. IMPORTATIONS GENERALES C.A.F				
	1991	1992	1993	1994	1995
World	3193972	3769161	4114043	3915035	4248557
Africa	11956	11014	15043	19172	15801
Americas	267488	290441	398916	297756	342193
Northern America	250666	272188	372028	273285	298205
LAIA	14002	14278	25336	23210	42080
CACM	2767	3961	1519	1220	1756
Caribbean	53	14	25	41	151
Rest of America			9	0	
As.ex F.USSR	1887307	2379024	2585954	2484063	2489764
Eur.x F.USSR	927376	979774	945583	993573	1242749
EU	891648	928338	909696	937365	1185065
EFTA	28593	44908	30006	37065	44471
East Europe	3573	3397	2848	16973	9437
Other Europe	3561	1493	1529	1315	2307
Former USSR	2962	973	1970	264	5671
Oceania	73592	86449	143074	99253	125542
United Arab Emirates	808415	1053154	1154039	1139827	1012825
Japan/Japon	654010	876914	859727	779025	671349
United Kingdom	320672	319811	343216	346237	444713
USA/Etats–Unis d'Amer	243865	256996	331824	263782	276123
Germany/Allemagne	166893	200605	181504	192144	215623
France,Monac	104709	116293	102067	106039	163825
India/Inde	86495	95559	105875	122122	141415
Netherlands/Pays–Bas	128147	118337	87677	101108	105903
Saudi Arabia	83770	75062	87739	97171	161709
Australia/Australie	59807	74906	132193	87331	114352
Italy/Italie	57859	58082	73279	74193	81989
Korea, Republic of	32721	50898	76335	50792	109021
Malaysia/Malaisie	33069	32730	37068	72370	53088
Switz.Liecht	26232	41212	26985	33710	40904
Singapore/Singapour	43316	25988	31114	30208	36176
Belgium–Luxembourg	25619	26506	26120	23606	52488
Pakistan	31522	23886	39143	26237	33244
Bahrain/Bahreïn	19325	27990	70635	13790	19126
Indonesia/Indonésie	10070	8866	15871	36149	66232
Sweden/Suède	23320	24399	25184	27392	36435
Denmark/Danemark	23924	23781	25725	24267	29078
Thailand/Thaïlande	23624	25041	21102	16014	24243
China/Chine	13388	16436	19333	20707	38111
Canada	6801	15192	40204	9503	22082
Hong Kong	16837	20337	15035	17524	18878
Spain/Espagne	11689	12626	11811	14063	18426
Turkey/Turquie	2510	13529	11136	14808	19027
New Zealand	13785	11493	10876	11922	11113
Qatar	13726	9364	8123	5873	14875
Austria/Autriche	7588	10336	12197	9498	12098
Argentina/Argentine	5713	3813	10883	7675	17256
Iran (Islamic Rp. of)	251	1449	2454	9463	30701
Finland/Finlande	10528	7607	6406	8368	8301
Chile/Chili	4900	3762	10737	9116	12064
Ireland/Irlande	5293	5944	8834	7576	12232
Kuwait/ Koweït	832	4486	8389	8419	9584
Brazil/Brésil	2953	6340	3536	5117	10619
So. Africa Customs Un		191	6483	11493	4313
Cyprus/Chypre	2539	3229	4239	8701	3531
Egypt/Egypte	6755	4572	3755	2782	3844
Philippines	1974	2056	2063	2302	11143
Bulgaria/Bulgarie	62	85	170	12549	4408
Sri Lanka	2993	3235	3145	3844	4051
Greece/Grèce	4653	2751	4244	1944	2688
Norway,SVD,JM	2361	3697	3022	3081	3490
Jordan/Jordanie	2060	1912	3484	2186	3322
Syrian Arab Republic	171	379	4590	1238	3209
Malta/Malte	1317	1493	1527	1315	2307
Lebanon/Liban	584	1814	1987	1223	1323
Bangladesh	1345	1429	1150	1465	1255

COUNTRIES–PAYS	GENERAL EXPORTS F.O.B. EXPORTATIONS GENERALES F.O.B.				
	1991	1992	1993	1994	1995
Monde	4873508	5451161	5299511	5418298	5917390
Afrique	46932	60193	99310	118470	129852
Amériques	24512	53763	211111	54975	164432
Amérique du Nord	24390	53734	210860	54576	164163
ALAI	31	28	13	386	270
MCAC	91		13		
Caraïbes			3	13	
Autre Amérique		0	222		
Asie l'URSS exclus	501614	5271007	4872984	5165171	5305664
Europe l'URSS exclus	49212	51314	58587	50837	53325
UE	48366	50961	57952	50049	52603
AELE	762	263	261	234	576
Europe de l'Est	10	32	184	62	66
Autre de l'Europe	74	57	4	214	64
Ancienne URSS	28		894	1413	14912
Océanie	11357	1820	18891	783	1534
Japan/Japon	4363	1840029	1418662	1887088	1688468
Korea, Republic of	17756	1283329	1069683	769435	936340
United Arab Emirates	317061	458799	505436	549058	604566
China/Chine	5	380211	432697	436365	573491
Thailand/Thaïlande	719	243210	274839	447270	506590
Yemen/Yémen	1919	190065	189431	250768	167403
Singapore/Singapour	14246	227137	276802	29200	161204
Hong Kong	22005	94150	143365	222089	129020
Iran (Islamic Rp. of)	54052	109924	131378	119661	124838
USA/Etats–Unis d'Amer	23128	53448	210476	53451	163875
Saudi Arabia	24655	38277	42035	54698	55240
Un. Rep. of Tanzania	21533	27828	44930	47911	58708
United Kingdom	33140	21393	29000	31574	29047
India/Inde	12929	15709	19914	24498	27275
Zambia/Zambie	11244	13071	20878	19618	29171
Kenya	10759	14413	20512	18360	28466
Kuwait/ Koweït	13253	9607	9632	13699	18042
France,Monac	3386	19208	16729	5724	5809
Bahrain/Bahreïn	9162	6879	7547	7948	9305
Qatar	5890	5899	7168	6925	8529
Australia/Australie	11357	1727	18825	666	1426
Syrian Arab Republic	202	2693	9124	6612	3757
So. Africa Customs Un			11	21653	130
Netherlands/Pays–Bas	3993	2946	2418	3384	4855
Germany/Allemagne	3119	1856	3529	2743	4683
Italy/Italie	2245	2009	2363	3334	3515
Sri Lanka	378	665	1574	8398	1968
Tunisia/Tunisie	567	1191	5000	4032	2172
Egypt/Egypte	565	845	2693	3048	4786
Pakistan	1725	1240	1620	2065	2297
Greece/Grèce	717	2594	2829	1139	1634
Libyan Arab Jamahiriya	653	1293	3284	926	2197
Malaysia/Malaisie	26	735	536	4176	2351
Russian Federation			894	860	5624
Jordan/Jordanie	369	933	1632	1634	2126
Lebanon/Liban	439	1577	1546	1310	1722
Kazakhstan				213	5580
Philippines	135	134	1070	3110	1088
Sudan/Soudan	638	932	726	819	1710
Belgium–Luxembourg	1075	446	567	740	993
Canada	1261	286	385	1125	287
Indonesia/Indonésie			1	1270	2008
Spain/Espagne	195	245	305	1047	1219
Dem. Rep. of the Congo		102	86	862	310
Azerbaijan				202	1154
Bangladesh	20	44	33	1144	78
Switz.Liecht	249	214	258	132	362
Cyprus/Chypre	150	133	407	210	284
Viet Nam			35		1050
Morocco/Maroc	49	194	158	234	318

(VALUE AS PERCENTAGE OF WORLD TOTAL)(VALEURS EN POURCENTAGE DU TOTAL MONDIAL)

	1986	1987	1988	1989	1990	1991	1992	1993	1994	1995
Africa	0.2	0.2	0.2	0.2	0.5	0.4	0.3	0.4	0.5	0.4
Americas	8.4	7.6	9.9	9.6	10.0	8.4	7.7	9.7	7.6	8.1
Northern America	7.8	6.9	9.0	8.9	9.6	7.8	7.2	9.0	7.0	7.0
LAIA	0.6	0.5	0.7	0.5	0.3	0.4	0.4	0.6	0.6	1.0
CACM	0.0	0.1	0.2	0.2	0.0	0.1	0.1	0.0	0.0	0.0
Caribbean	0.0	0.0	0.0	0.0	0.0	0.0	0.0	0.0	0.0	0.0
Rest of America		0.0		0.0				0.0	0.0	
As.ex F.USSR	43.8	48.8	51.4	53.2	53.8	59.1	63.1	62.9	63.4	58.6
Eur.x F.USSR	45.0	39.6	34.9	32.5	32.1	29.0	26.0	23.0	25.4	29.3
EU	43.7	38.0	32.9	29.7	29.3	27.9	24.6	22.1	23.9	27.9
EFTA	1.2	1.3	1.7	2.5	2.3	0.9	1.2	0.7	0.9	1.0
East Europe	0.0	0.1	0.1	0.1	0.2	0.1	0.1	0.1	0.4	0.2
Other Europe	0.1	0.2	0.2	0.2	0.4	0.1	0.0	0.0	0.0	0.1
Former USSR		0.0	0.0	0.2	0.1	0.1	0.0	0.0	0.0	0.1
Oceania	2.5	3.2	2.9	3.6	2.7	2.3	2.3	3.5	2.5	3.0
United Arab Emirates	18.7	21.0	21.0	24.2	23.2	25.3	27.9	28.1	29.1	23.8
Japan/Japon	14.4	15.2	16.8	15.7	17.0	20.5	23.3	20.9	19.9	15.8
United Kingdom	17.9	14.7	13.3	11.7	11.5	10.0	8.5	8.3	8.8	10.5
USA/Etats–Unis d'Amer	7.6	6.7	8.8	8.5	9.4	7.6	6.8	8.1	6.7	6.5
Germany/Allemagne	9.0	8.0	5.2	5.5	4.9	5.2	5.3	4.4	4.9	5.1
France,Monac	3.6	3.6	3.5	3.3	4.3	3.3	3.1	2.5	2.7	3.9
India/Inde	2.2	3.7	3.7	2.8	2.8	2.7	2.5	2.6	3.1	3.3
Netherlands/Pays–Bas	4.0	4.5	2.9	3.2	3.4	4.0	3.1	2.1	2.6	2.5
Saudi Arabia	0.6	1.1	1.3	2.0	2.2	2.6	2.0	2.1	2.5	3.8
Australia/Australie	2.0	2.6	2.3	2.9	2.3	1.9	2.0	3.2	2.2	2.7

	1986	1987	1988	1989	1990	1991	1992	1993	1994	1995
Afrique	3.5	0.3	0.2	0.1	0.4	1.0	1.1	1.9	2.2	2.2
Amériques	4.0	5.6	1.6	2.8	0.3	0.5	1.0	4.0	1.0	2.8
Amérique du Nord	4.0	5.6	1.6	2.8	0.3	0.5	1.0	4.0	1.0	2.8
ALAI	0.0	0.0	0.0	0.0	0.0	0.0	0.0	0.0	0.0	0.0
MCAC	0.0	0.0				0.0		0.0		
Caraïbes								0.0	0.0	
Autre Amérique	0.0						0.0	0.0		
Asie l'URSS exclus	71.8	82.3	85.7	86.4	6.4	10.3	96.7	92.0	95.3	89.7
Europe l'URSS exclus	16.9	6.6	3.0	2.0	1.0	1.0	0.9	1.1	0.9	0.9
UE	16.3	6.6	3.0	2.0	0.9	1.0	0.9	1.1	0.9	0.9
AELE	0.6	0.0	0.1	0.1	0.0	0.0	0.0	0.0	0.0	0.0
Europe de l'Est		0.0		0.0		0.0	0.0	0.0	0.0	0.0
Autre de l'Europe	0.0		0.0	0.0	0.0	0.0	0.0	0.0	0.0	0.0
Ancienne URSS					0.0	0.0		0.0	0.0	0.3
Océanie	3.9	0.4	0.4	0.4	0.1	0.2	0.0	0.4	0.0	0.0
Japan/Japon	4.2	38.1	44.2	34.6	0.2	0.1	33.8	26.8	34.8	28.5
Korea, Republic of	4.1	14.8	20.6	28.8	0.3	0.4	23.5	20.2	14.2	15.8
United Arab Emirates	40.0	3.8	5.7	5.4	3.9	6.5	8.4	9.5	10.1	10.2
China/Chine		0.0	0.0	0.0	0.0	0.0	7.0	8.2	8.1	9.7
Thailand/Thaïlande	0.0	3.3	1.7	1.2	0.0	0.0	4.5	5.2	8.3	8.6
Yemen/Yémen						0.0	3.5	3.6	4.6	2.8
Singapore/Singapour	2.3	6.6	2.4	5.2	0.2	0.3	4.2	5.2	0.5	2.7
Hong Kong	0.2	0.0	0.0	0.0	0.1	0.5	1.7	2.7	4.1	2.2
Iran (Islamic Rp. of)	0.8	0.1	0.1	0.3	0.3	1.1	2.0	2.5	2.2	2.1
USA/Etats–Unis d'Amer	2.9	5.5	1.6	2.8	0.3	0.5	1.0	4.0	1.0	2.8

Oman

4. General Imports C.I.F. by Commodities according to the S.I.T.C. (Rev. 2) in thousand U.S. Dollars
Importations Générales C.A.F. par Produits d'après la C.T.C.I. (Rév. 2) en milliers de Dollars E.U.

SITC CTCI	COMMODITY	1993		1994		1995		1996		PRODUIT
		WEIGHT POIDS	VALUE VALEUR	WEIGHT POIDS	VALUE VALEUR	WEIGHT POIDS	VALUE VALEUR	WEIGHT POIDS	VALUE VALEUR	
	ALL COMMODITIES		4114043		3915035		4248557		4577923	TOUS PRODUITS
0	FOOD AND LIVE ANIMALS		482082		499080		568135			ALIMENTS,ANIMAUX VIVANTS
001	*LIVE ANIMALS FOR FOOD	W 19550	20619	W 25388	26782	W 30537	45671			ANIMAUX VIVANTS
0012	SHEEP AND GOATS,LIVE	W 19437	19537	W 25271	26060	W 30453	45197			ESPECES OVINE ET CAPRINE
00121	SHEEP,LIVE	W 16897	16421	W 23380	22773	W 22673	24907			ESPECE OVINE
00122	GOATS,LIVE	W 2540	3116	W 1891	3287	W 7780	20290			ESPECE CAPRINE
01	MEAT AND PREPARATIONS		70533		75197		86791			VIANDES ET PREPARATIONS
011	MEAT FRESH,CHILLD,FROZEN	W 52888	68045	W 53824	71314	W 58935	82312			VIANDES FRAICHES,REF,CONGE
0111	BOVINE MEAT FRESH,FROZEN	W 8593	10975	W 8841	10620	W 11557	15842			VIANDES BOVIN FRAI,REF
01112	BOVINE MEAT BONELESS	W 7925	10263	W 8637	10255	W 11361	15537			VIANDES BOVIN DESOSSEES
0112	MUTTON ETC FRSH,CHLD,FRN	W 8874	14359	W 8043	14722	W 6982	14376			VIANDE DE MOUTON
0114	POULTRY FRESH CHLLD,FRZN	W 34933	41855	W 36590	44970	W 40122	51370			VOLAILLES MORTES
02	DAIRY PRODCTS,BIRDS'EGGS		83530		87807		97725			PRODUITS LAITIERS,OEUFS
022	MILK AND CREAM	W 31476	52083	W 35917	57458	W 35995	62225			LAIT ET CREME
0224	MILK,CREAM PRESERVED ETC	W 24982	42752	W 28297	46533	W 27853	51156			LAIT,CREME CONS,CONC
02243	MILK DRY,OVER 1.5% FAT	W 10565	24657	W 12854	27904	W 11385	28477			LAIT POUDRE SUP 1.5%
02249	MILK(EX DRY) PRSVD,SWEET	W 13740	16474	W 15285	18247	W 15789	20612			LAIT CONS,CONC SUCRE
023	BUTTER	W 6090	12714	W 5130	10649	W 5381	12322			BEURRE
024	CHEESE AND CURD	W 4253	10315	W 4156	10575	W 4679	13062			FROMAGE ET CAILLEBOTTE
04	CEREALS AND PREPARATIONS		102554		104673		137836			CEREALES ET PRODUITS
041	WHEAT ETC UNMILLED	W 156503	23562	W 184561	32564	W 195846	41819			FROMENT,EPEAUTRE
0411	DURUM WHEAT UNMILLED	W 155602	23311	W 183458	32257	W 194807	41533			FROMENT DUR NON MOULU
042	RICE	W 106833	50373	W 75962	37520	W 139876	42080			RIZ
0422	RICE SEMI–MILLED,MILLED	W 94815	45958	W 73443	36464	W 73979	37273			RIZ POLI,GLACE INCL BRISURES
04221	RICE MILLED UNBROKEN	W 94815	45958	W 73441	36461	W 73979	37273			RIZ POLI,GLACE EXCL BRISURES
043	BARLEY UNMILLED	W 47400	5782	W 158076	12899	W 71366	32538			ORGE NON MONDEE
048	CEREAL ETC PREPARATIONS	W 10010	14991	W 10086	13052	W 9021	16519			PREPTNS A BASE CEREALES
05	VEGETABLES AND FRUIT		126176		118153		102310			LEGUMES ET FRUITS
054	VEG ETC FRSH,SMPLY PRSVD	W 63349	34698	W 70377	34123	W 68867	28363			LEGUMES FRAIS,CONG,SECS
0545	OTHER FRESH VEGETABLES	W 27613	15101	W 32673	13366	W 33235	10578			AUTRES LEGUMES FRAIS,REF
056	VEGTBLES ETC PRSVD,PREPD	W 14770	13170	W 14122	13765	W 15815	14648			CONSERVES DE LEGUMES
057	FRUIT,NUTS,FRESH,DRIED	W 103530	67976	W 76478	62274	W 73025	52201			FRUITS FRAIS OU SECS
0571	ORANGES, MANDARINS ETC	W 35483	19687	W 27922	18868	W 40244	16574			ORANGES,MAND,CLEMENTINES
05711	ORANGES,FRESH OR DRIED	W 34130	18314	W 27828	18501	W 39957	15679			ORANGES FRAICHES,SECHEES
0579	FRUIT FRESH OR DRIED NES	W 40007	22000	W 29431	18205	W 17499	11181			FRUITS FRAIS,SECS NDA
05798	OTHER FRESH FRUIT	W 34046	15194	W 25146	11943	W 14579	7535			AUTRES FRUITS FRAIS
06	SUGAR AND PREPS,HONEY		15522		17343		17701			SUCRES ET PRODUITS
061	SUGAR AND HONEY	W 35250	13130	W 36185	15320	W 34059	16147			SUCRES ET MIEL
0612	REFINED SUGAR ETC	W 33669	11048	W 34595	13416	W 32916	14348			SUCRES RAFFINES
07	COFFEE,TEA,COCOA,SPICES		28024		33205		39154			CAFE,THE,CACAO,EPICES
073	CHOCOLATE AND PRODUCTS	W 4109	9517	W 4367	11909	W 4196	12695			CHOCOLAT
09	MISC EDIBLE PRODUCTS		25543		23615		27551			PREP ALIMENTAIRES DIVERSES
098	EDIBLE PRODCTS,PREPS NES	W 10032	25073	W 10422	23287	W 11073	27013			PREP ALIMENTAIRES NDA
09809	MISC FOOD PREPRTIONS NES	W 8434	22728	W 8464	19958	W 8439	22594			PREP ALIMENTAIRES NDA
1	BEVERAGES AND TOBACCO		243627		251955		228323			BOISSONS ET TABACS
11	BEVERAGES		47814		49780		35316			BOISSONS
111	NON–ALCOHL BEVERAGES NES	W 94617	38235	W 99986	41209	W 72742	26648			BOISSONS NON ALCOOLIQUES
11102	FLAVORED WATERS NON–ALCO	W 63083	32760	W 65152	35676	W 41095	21458			LIMONADES,EAUX GAZEUSES
12	TOBACCO AND MANUFACTURES		195813		202175		193006			TABACS BRUTS FABRIQUES
122	TOBACCO,MANUFACTURED	W 12589	195465	W 18175	201937	W 22502	192867			TABACS FABRIQUES
1222	CIGARETTES	W 12002	186790	W 18093	201647	W 22395	192518			CIGARETTES
2	CRUDE MATERLS,EXCL FUELS		84603		96640		115911			MAT BRUTES NON COMESTIBLES
24	CORK AND WOOD		25388		25843		27044			LIEGE ET BOIS
248	WOOD SHAPED,SLEEPERS	W 139601	23982	W 74046	17390	W 78245	20599			BOIS SIMPLEMENT TRAVAILLES
2483	LUMBER SHAPED NON–CONIFR	W 133701	22566	W 72655	16823	W 77880	20367			NON CONIFERES SCIES,RABOTES
24831	LUMBER SAWN ETC NON–CON	W 133701	22566	W 72655	16823	W 77879	20363			SCIES LONGITUDINALEMENT
27	CRUDE FERTLZR,MINRLS NES		13809		11133		14370			ENGRAIS MINERAUX BRUTS
28	METALLIFEROUS ORES,SCRAP		37341		51550		65664			MINERAIS METAL,DECHETS
287	BASE METAL ORES,CONC NES	W 66797	32193	W 103681	51507	W 104876	65434			MINERAIS METAUX COMMUNS
2871	CPR ORE ETC,CEMENT COPPR	W 57004	31089	W 103673	51479	W 94927	64702			MINERAIS DE CUIVRE,MATTES
28711	COPPER ORES,EXCL MATTE	W 57004	31089	W 103673	51479	W 94909	64700			MINERAIS DE CUIVRE
3	MINERAL FUELS ETC		131496		42111		64628			COMBUSTIBLES MINERAUX LUB
33	PETROLEUM AND PRODUCTS		125952		37076		60922			PETROLE ET DERIVES
334	PETROLEUM PRODUCTS,REFIN	W 462946	123902	W 44534	35206	W 180583	58954			PRODUITS RAFFINES
3341	GASOLINE,OTH LIGHT OILS	W 456585	115581	W 42864	32568					ESSENCES POUR MOTEURS
33419	OTH LIGHT PETROLEUM OILS	W 456585	115581	W 42864	32568					AUTRES HUILES LEGERES
4	ANIMAL,VEGETABLE OIL,FAT		21239		30162		39596			HUILES,GRAISSES ANIM,VEG
42	FIXED VEGETABLE OIL,FAT		21201		30088		38920			HUILES VEGETALES FIXES
424	FIXED VEG OIL NONSOFT	W 35953	17987	W 39647	23799	W 37635	29656			AUTRES HUILES VEG FIXES
4242	PALM OIL	W 23694	10853	W 25342	14534	W 30325	21504			HUILE DE PALME
5	CHEMCLS,RELATED PROD NES		231762		228541		279074		276205	PRODUITS CHIMIQUES
52	INORGANIC CHEMICALS		13787		14925		16212			PROD CHIM INORGANIQUES
53	DYES,TANNING,COLOUR PROD		13482		11364		13483			PROD TEINTURE,COLORANTS
541	*MEDICINAL,PHARM PRODUCT	K 4596397	61241	K 4559248	57515	K 4811848	69043			PROD MEDICINAUX PHARMACEUT
5413	ANTIBIOTICS IN BULK	K 5281	104	K 444655	7045	K 1073204	17309			ANTIBIOTIQUES NDA
54139	OTHER ANTIBIOTICS	K 5281	104	K 444655	7045	K 1073204	17309			AUTRES ANTIBIOTIQUES
5417	MEDICAMENTS	K 4407431	59239	K 3609827	48022	K 3558816	49231			MEDICAMENTS
54171	— CONTAINNG ANTIBIOTICS	K 734759	15115	K 336018	9834	K 297965	4253			MED CONTN ANTIBIOTIQUES
54179	— CONTNG OTH SUBSTANCES	K 3654430	43860	K 3270451	37943	K 3249487	44656			MED CONT AUT SUBSTANCES
55	PERFUME,CLEANING ETC PRD		55285		57625		72045			PROD POUR PARFUM,TOILETTE
553	PERFUMERY,COSMETICS,ETC	W 5738	36629	W 6423	39769	W 6704	48795			PRODUITS DE PARFUMERIE
554	SOAP,CLEANSING ETC PREPS	W 10672	16110	W 9493	13310	W 9666	14606			SAVONS,PRODUITS DETERSIFS
58	PLASTIC MATERIALS ETC		26745		25113		32334			MAT PLAST ARTIFICIELLES
583	POLYMERIZATION ETC PRODS	W 20159	22005	W 20892	20942	W 21900	28823			PROD POLYMERISATION
5831	POLYETHYLENE	W 10704	8174	W 13501	12206	W 13481	15836			POLYETHYLENE
58311	— IN PRIMARY FORMS	W 10704	8174	W 13501	12206	W 12880	14326			POLYETHYLENE PRIMAIRES
59	CHEMICAL MATERIALS NES		44119		48197		59114			MAT PROD CHIMIQUES NDA
598	MISCEL CHEM PRODUCTS NES	W 21713	34606	W 28737	39377	W 27887	47205			PROD DIV INDUST CHIM NDA
5989	CHEM PRODUCTS,PREPS NES	W 20679	32582	W 28007	38249	W 25354	43591			PROD PREP CHIMIQUES NDA
59899	OTH CHEM PRODS,PREPS,NES	W 17957	26535	W 26146	35976	W 23639	41347			AUT PRODUITS CHIMIQUES NDA
6	BASIC MANUFACTURES		616787		560356		655954			ART MANUFACTURES
62	RUBBER MANUFACTURES NES		47923		38218		52108			CAOUTCHOUC MANUFACTURE
625	RUBBER TYRES, TUBES ETC	W 15353	46390	W 12410	36764	W 15466	51155			PNEUS CAOUTCHOUC VULCANISE
6251	TYRES NEW FOR MOTOR CARS	W 8763	28134	W 7676	25204	W 7270	24203			PNEUS POUR VOITURES
6252	TYRES,NEW,BUS OR LORRY	W 6459	17806	W 4612	11188	W 7983	26268			PNEUS POUR AUTOBUS,CAMIONS
63	WOOD,CORK MANUFACTRS NES		23592		18841		22130			OUVRAGES LIEGE ET BOIS
634	VENEERS,PLYWOOD,ETC	W 33642	18063	W 17930	15216	W 24446	17849			PLACAGES,CONTRE–PLAQUES
6342	PLYWOOD OF WOOD SHEETS	W 28691	14140	W 17677	14417	W 23781	16650			BOIS CONTRE–PLAQUES
64	PAPER,PAPERBOARD AND MFR		45299		47360		63154			PAPIERS,CARTONS & OUVRAGES
641	PAPER AND PAPERBOARD	W 13710	12566	W 18349	15093	W 19968	23513			PAPIERS ET CARTONS
6415	PAPER,PAPERBRD,BULK,NES	W 10365	8880	W 11977	9726	W 14562	17230			PAPIERS,CARTONS ROULEAUX

4. General Imports C.I.F. by Commodities according to the S.I.T.C. (Rev. 2) in thousand U.S. Dollars
Importations Générales C.A.F. par Produits d'après la C.T.C.I. (Rév. 2) en milliers de Dollars E.U.

SITC CTCI	COMMODITY	1993		1994		1995		1996		PRODUIT
		WEIGHT POIDS	VALUE VALEUR	WEIGHT POIDS	VALUE VALEUR	WEIGHT POIDS	VALUE VALEUR	WEIGHT POIDS	VALUE VALEUR	
64159	OTHER PAPER ETC,BULK,NES	W 7503	7012	W 11534	9253	W 13010	15897			AUT PAPIER ROULEAUX FEUILLES
642	PAPER,ETC,PRECUT,ARTS OF	W 17968	32733	W 22816	32267	W 26001	39641			PAP,CARTONS DECOUPES
6421	PAPER ETC CONTAINERS	W 11290	13622	W 13415	14770	W 14314	16211			BOITES,SACS EMBALLAGES
6428	PAPER ETC ARTICLES NES	W 4680	14644	W 7907	13679	W 10545	20028			OUVRAGES EN PATE A PAPIER
65	TEXTILE YARN,FABRICS,ETC		131297		129435		162621			FILS,TISSUS,ARTICLES TEXTILE
652	COTTON FABRICS,WOVEN	W 4967	25828	W 6104	29377	W 4887	29716			TISSUS DE COTON
6521	GREY WOVEN COTTON FABRIC	W 4944	25506	W 6103	29334	W 4878	29572			TISSUS COT ECRUS NON MERCER
65214	GREY WOVEN COTTON NES	W 4684	24225	W 5356	28855	W 4787	29129			AUT TISSUS 85% COTON ECRUS
653	WOVN MAN–MADE FIB FABRIC	W 6728	63633	W 7345	59704	W 11598	91033			TISSUS FIBRES SYNTH,ARTIF
6531	CONT SYNT WEAVES NONPILE	W 671	6859	W 1286	10449	W 2006	17547			TISSUS FIBRES SYNTH CONTINUE
65314	CONT SYN TYRE CORD FABRC	W 671	6859	W 1286	10449	W 2006	17547			TIS ARMATURE PNEUMATIQUES
6534	DISC SYN BLEND FABRC NES	W 5353	48460	W 5530	44175	W 8966	68772			TISSUS FIBRES SYNTH DISCONT
65341	DISC SYN FIB–COTTN FABRC	W 5348	48355	W 5510	44054	W 8966	68767			TISSUS FIB SYNT DIS MEL COTO
659	FLOOR COVERINGS,ETC	W 5069	15686	W 4420	14975	W 4889	13827			COUVRE–PARQUETS,TAPIS ETC
6596	OTH TXTL CARPETS ETC NES	W 4793	14026	W 4220	13866	W 4489	12719			TAPIS AUT MAT TEXT NDA
65961	— TUFTED	W 4574	12722	W 4060	12392	W 4317	11686			TAPIS AUT MAT TEXT TOUFF
66	NONMETAL MINERAL MFS NES		89357		84418		88835			ART MIN NON METALLIQUES
661	LIME,CEMENT,BLDG PRODS	W 496660	40416	W 449251	34710	W 351397	25125			CHAUX,CIMENTS MAT CONSTR
6612	CEMENT	W 472371	33092	W 437975	31722	W 336228	22103			CIMENTS HYDRAULIQUES
662	CLAY,REFRACTORY BLDG PRD	W 25670	14717	W 25944	14408	W 22285	14163			MAT CONST REFRACTAIRES
665	GLASSWARE	W 30684	20242	W 39023	23305	W 39851	28302			OUVRAGES EN VERRE
6651	BOTTLES ETC OF GLASS	W 28966	13246	W 36935	14358	W 37862	19557			RECIPIENTS EN VERRE
66511	GLASS BOTTLES ETC NONVAC	W 28941	13187	W 36932	14284	W 37860	19523			BONBONNES,BOUTEILLES,ETC
67	IRON AND STEEL		153762		131771		134692			FER ET ACIER
673	IRON,STEEL SHAPES ETC	W 184233	61141	W 167433	52423	W 155218	55973			BARRES,PROFIL FER,ACIER
6732	IRON,STEEL BARS ETC	W 151488	47995	W 143450	43756	W 132925	44444			BARRES FER,ACIER
67322	HIGH CARBON STL BARS ETC					W 129389	43310			BARRES ACIER FIN CARBONE
67326	IRN,OTH STL BARS HOTROLD	W 123214	39049	W 119626	37331					BARRES PLEINES FER,ACIER
674	IRN,STL UNIV,PLATE,SHEET	W 21063	10848	W 10911	6990	W 20987	14117			LARGES PLATS,TOLES
6747	TINNED PLATES,SHEETS					W 20672	13833			TOLES ETAMEES EN ACIER
678	IRON,STL TUBES,PIPES,ETC	W 97893	77480	W 83021	68998	W 51639	62254			TUBES,TUYAUX EN FONTE,FER
6782	IRON,STL SEAMLESS TUBES	W 55758	37215	W 54122	42214	W 30010	32568			TUBES,TUYAUX SANS SOUDURE
6783	IRON,STL TUBES,PIPES NES	W 38761	31834	W 26475	19287	W 17326	18532			AUT TUBES,TUYAUX FER,ACIER
68	NON–FERROUS METALS		15314		15783		21200			METAUX NON FERREUX
69	METAL MANUFACTURES NES		108881		93280		109920			ART MANUFACT EN METAL NDA
691	STRUCTURES AND PARTS NES	W 16328	29144	W 15083	15072	W 17301	27810			CONSTRUCT FER,ACIER,ALU
6911	STRUCTURES,PARTS IRN,STL	W 10506	21204	W 10795	7834	W 8077	12384			CONSTRUCT FER,ACIER,FONTE
6912	STRUCTURES,PARTS ALUMNM	W 5821	7940	W 4288	7238	W 9224	15426			CONSTRUCT ALUMINIUM
692	METAL TANKS,BOXES,ETC	W 15708	27222	W 18839	25691	W 12827	22428			RECIPIENTS METALLIQUES
6924	MTL TRANSPORT BOXES ETC	W 15186	26195	W 17619	23136	W 11953	20314			FUTS,TAMBOURS,BIDONS
697	BASE MTL HOUSEHOLD EQUIP	W 3893	14212	W 3027	12589	W 2608	13933			ART MENAGE MET COMMUNS
699	BASE METAL MFRS NES	W 9930	20917	W 12616	23840	W 9414	23292			ART MANUFACTURES MET NDA
6991	LOCKSMITHS WARES,ETC	W 7209	16160	W 8694	18657	W 7215	17837			ARTICLES DE SERRURERIE
69913	BASE MTL DOOR,ETC FITTNG	W 6955	14144	W 8093	15889	W 6879	15341			GARNITURES POUR MEUBLES
7	MACHINES,TRANSPORT EQUIP		1778458		1670041		1672316		1901183	MACHINES MATERIEL TRANSPORT
71	POWER GENERATING EQUIPMT		95087		126752		126476			MACHINES GENERATRICES
713	INTRNL COMBUS PSTN ENGIN	W 2299	24180	W 1287	14203	W 1236	16472			MOTEURS EXPL COMB INT, PIECE
7139	PISTON ENGINE PARTS NES	W 1112	13494	W 755	10302	W 557	11126			PIECES POUR 713.2,3,8
714	ENGINES AND MOTORS NES	W 1171	9414	W 4947	60538	W 2311	56446			MOTEURS NON ELECTRIQUES
7148	GAS TURBINES NES	W 1120	8146	W 2770	29298	W 456	20117			TURBINES A GAZ
71488	OTHER GAS TURBINES NES	W 1120	8146	W 2770	29298	W 456	20117			AUTRES TURBINES A GAZ
7149	ENGINE & MOTOR PARTS NES	W 48	1255	W 2176	31240	W 1851	36315			PIECES 714 ET 718.88
71499	PARTS NES,OF 71488,71888	W 48	1255	W 2176	31240	W 1851	36315			PIECES 714.88 ET 718.88
716	ROTATING ELECTRIC PLANT	W 2601	60003	W 2432	48360	W 2691	51599			APP ELECTR ROTATIFS,PIECES
7162	AC MTRS,GENRTRS,GEN SETS	W 831	9024	W 885	8351	W 1433	15019			MOTEURS ELECTRIQUES
71623	GEN SETS WITH PISTN ENGN	W 480	6287	W 798	7689	W 1346	14419			GROUPES MOTEUR EXPLOSION
7169	PTS NES OF ROT ELEC PLNT	W 1459	49973	W 1489	39828	W 1136	34120			PIECES MAC APP ROTATIFS
72	MACHS FOR SPCL INDUSTRYS		244590		216716		210454			MAC SPECIALES POUR INDUST
723	CIVIL ENGNEERG EQUIP ETC	W 23688	197861	W 20449	173326	W 14453	151056			APPAREILS DE GENIE CIVIL
7234	CONST,MINING MACHNRY NES	W 3654	13140	W 2657	13459	W 3903	17500			MACH POUR LA CONST, MINES
7239	CONSTR ETC MACHY PTS NES	W 19941	184368	W 17707	159530	W 10429	132683			PIECES 723.41–723.46
727	FOOD MACHRY NON–DOMESTIC	W 262	4156	W 580	5283	W 940	15237			MACH INDUSTRIES ALIMENT
728	OTH MACHY FOR SPCL INDUS	W 3426	25103	W 2665	21789	W 3328	27902			AUT MACH IND PARTICULIERES
7284	MACHY FOR SPCL INDUS NES	W 1547	16923	W 1690	16375	W 2478	22642			MACH SPEC IND PARTICUL.
74	GENRL INDUSTRL MACHY NES		160170		146821		139076			MACH APP INDUSTRIE
741	HEATING,COOLING EQUIPMNT	W 11383	50377	W 11063	53188	W 10042	54665			MACH CHAUFFAGE,PIECES
7415	AIR–CONDITIONING MACHNRY	W 10216	42370	W 10199	46218	W 8513	43732			GROUPES CONDITION AIR
742	PUMPS FOR LIQUIDS ETC	W 2338	17850	W 2597	17865	W 2994	20296			POMPES MOTO–POMPES
743	PUMPS NES,CENTRFUGES ETC	W 1173	21716	W 2342	9179	W 1404	9757			POMPES COMPRES,VENT ETC
7431	PUMPS FOR GASES ETC	W 717	17392	W 473	3240	W 306	2368			POMPES AIR A VIDE,COMPRES
744	MECHANICAL HANDLING EQU	W 4943	45053	W 3905	33788	W 4765	29345			EQUIP MANUTENTION PIECES
7442	LIFTING,LOADING MACH NES	W 2298	17053	W 1272	8021	W 2274	7648			APP LEVAGE,MANUTENTION
7449	PTS NES OF MACHY OF 7442	W 2040	25268	W 1190	20424	W 1858	18959			PIECES DU 744.2
745	NONELEC MACHY,TOOLS NES	W 952	8373	W 1301	15329	W 1069	11087			AUT MACH NON ELEC,PIECES
7452	OTH NONELEC MCHS,PTS NES	W 942	8294	W 1282	15247	W 1044	10987			AUT MACH NON ELEC,PIECES
749	NONELEC MACH PTS,ACC NES	W 1322	16802	W 1391	17472	W 1129	13926			PIECES MACH NON ELEC NDA
7492	COCKS,VALVES ETC NES	W 1209	13659	W 1224	15200	W 1017	12427			ART ROB,SIM POUR TUYAUX
75	OFFICE MACHNES,ADP EQUIP		75846		46854		52614			MACH BUREAU TRAIT AUTOM
752	AUTOMTIC DATA PROC EQUIP	W 1314	30006	W 241	6273	W 197	6118			MACH TRAIT INFORMATION
7522	DIGITAL COMPUTERS	W 1125	25471	W 127	3140	W 92	2738			MACH DIGITALES COMPLETES
759	OFFICE,ADP MCH PTS,ACCES	W 573	38178	W 525	35006	W 713	38120			PIECES DU 751 ET 752
7599	ACCTG,ETC,ADP MCH PTS,AC	W 473	35813	W 461	32817	W 625	35563			PIECES DU 751 ET 752
76	TELECOMM,SOUND EQUIPMENT		99464		88731		126201			EQUIPMENT DE TELECOM
761	TELEVISION RECEIVERS	W 1567	17732	W 1251	14228	W 2399	25960			RECEPTEURS DE TELEVISION
7611	COLOUR TV RECEIVERS	W 1450	16088	W 1219	13961	W 2364	25777			RECEPTEURS COULEUR
763	SOUND RECORDRS,PHONOGRPH	W 1521	22154	W 869	16169	W 509	10692			PHONO,APP ENREGISTREMENT
7638	OTHR SOUND APPARATUS ETC	W 1504	21893	W 845	15757	W 504	10601			AUT APP D'ENREGIS,REPROD
76381	TV IMAGE,SND RECRDRS ETC	W 1473	21479	W 791	15048	W 461	9616			APP ENREG,REPRO IMAG,SON
764	TELECOM EQPT,PTS,ACC NES	W 1211	49421	W 1602	51877	W 2152	78990			EQUIP TELECOM,PIECES
7649	PTS NES OF EQUIPMT OF 76	W 896	33447	W 1305	38517	W 1596	56482			PIECES DE LA DIV 76
76491	PTS NES OF APPAR OF 7641	W 97	9857	W 322	14023	W 567	25555			PIECES POUR 764.1
76493	TELECOMM EQUIPMT PTS NES	W 763	23161	W 955	24009	W 1020	30691			PIECES 761,762,764.3,8
77	ELECTRIC MACHNRY NES ETC		129144		132770		201402			MACH APP ELECT NDA
771	ELECTRIC POWER MACHY NES	W 1603	4921	W 1936	6618	W 3570	29739			MACH PROD,TRANS ELECTR
7711	TRANSFORMERS,ELECTRICAL	W 1476	4092	W 1868	5963	W 3353	28315			TRANSFO ELECTRIQUES
77111	LIQUID DIELEC TRANSFRMRS	W 969	2859	W 1679	5561	W 3072	27021			TRANSFO DIELEC LIQUIDE
772	SWITCHGEAR ETC,PARTS NES	W 5069	38319	W 5103	38851	W 6782	58231			APP COUPURE,SECT ETC
7721	SWITCHGEAR ETC	W 5069	38319	W 5100	38813	W 6748	58074			APP COUPURE,SECTIONMNT
773	ELECTR DISTRIBUTNG EQUIP	W 12419	31873	W 17102	32826	W 18285	53769			EQUIPMT DISTRIBUTION ELECT
7731	INSULATED WIRE,CABLE ETC	W 11708	30630	W 16272	31545	W 16695	49595			FILS,CABLES ISOLES ELECT
775	HOUSEHOLD TYPE EQUIP NES	W 7381	37436	W 6606	34567	W 6347	36127			MACH,APP USAGE DOMESTQUE

4. General Imports C.I.F. by Commodities according to the S.I.T.C. (Rev. 2) in thousand U.S. Dollars
Importations Générales C.A.F. par Produits d'après la C.T.C.I. (Rév. 2) en milliers de Dollars E.U.

SITC CTCI	COMMODITY	1993		1994		1995		1996		PRODUIT
		WEIGHT POIDS	VALUE VALEUR	WEIGHT POIDS	VALUE VALEUR	WEIGHT POIDS	VALUE VALEUR	WEIGHT POIDS	VALUE VALEUR	
7752	DOM REFRIGERATRS,FREEZRS	W 3447	13592	W 2987	14095	W 2990	14190			REFRIG,CONGEL MENAGER
77521	DOMESTIC REFRIGERATORS	W 2801	10448	W 2536	11901	W 2409	11354			REFRIGERATEURS
7757	DOMESTIC ELECTRC EQU NES	W 2044	13197	W 1393	9207	W 1431	9274			APP ELECTR DOMEST NDA
778	ELECTRICAL MACHINERY NES	W 4141	13369	W 4588	13282	W 8125	18410			AUTRES MACH ELECT NDA
78	ROAD VEHICLES		898993		854856		787522			VEHICULES ROUTIERS
781	PASS MOTOR VEH EXC BUSES	W 69939	632760	W 50978	500877	W 37120	406062			AUTO TRANSPORT PERSONNES
782	LORRIES,SPCL MTR VEH NES	W 11254	67514	W 14988	107360	W 22036	127277			VEHICULES SPECIAUX,MARCH
7821	LORRIES,TRUCKS	W 10025	59582	W 14265	104268	W 15466	105609			VEHICULES TRANSP MARCHAND
7822	SPECIAL MOTOR VEHCLS NES	W 1229	7932	W 723	3091	W 6570	21668			VEHICULES USAGES SPECIAUX
783	ROAD MOTOR VEHICLES NES	W 4419	22110	W 7164	59673	W 5645	50086			VEHICULES ROUTIERS NDA
7831	BUSES	W 4410	22048	W 7113	59415	W 5645	50086			VOITURES TRANSPORT COMMUN
784	MOTOR VEH PRTS,ACCES NES	W 13759	159209	W 12813	158990	W 14144	182703			PIECES 722,781,782,783
7849	OTHER MOTOR VEHCL PARTS	W 12718	156234	W 12006	157249	W 13624	181657			PIECES 722,781,782,783
786	TRAILERS,NONMOTR VEH,NES	W 4800	13864	W 4062	25273	W 3598	19576			REMORQUES,CADRES,CONTAIN
7861	TRAILERS,TRANSP CONTAINR	W 3865	10509	W 3507	20209	W 3158	14305			REMORQUES TOUS VEHICULES
78612	OTHER TRAILERS	W 3685	10272	W 3499	20180	W 3031	13545			REMORQUES TRANSP MARCH
79	OTHR TRANSPORT EQUIPMENT		71672		48923		24394			AUTRE MATERIEL TRANSPORT
792	AIRCRAFT ETC	W 664	68004	W 513	45734	W 182	22508			APP NAVIGATION AERIENNE
7924	AIRCRFT NES OVER 15000KG	W 561	58576	W 350	29697					AERODYNES PLUS 15000 KG
7929	AIRCRAFT PARTS NES	W 103	9428	W 163	16037	W 181	22437			PIECES DU 792
8	MISC MANUFACTURED GOODS		259617		267526		309548			ART MANUFACTURES DIVERS
812	*PLUMBG,HEATNG,LGHTNG EQ	W 5267	21607	W 5779	27641	W 5060	27267			APPAR SANITAIRES CHAUFFAGE
8122	CERAMIC PLUMBNG FIXTURES	W 4025	11693	W 3685	13437	W 3375	11123			EVIERS,LAVABOS,CUVETTES
8124	LIGHTING EQUIPMENT NES	W 1139	9629	W 1903	14021	W 1656	16034			APPAREILS ECLAIRAGE ETC
821	*FURNITURE,PARTS THEREOF	W 12699	40199	W 10263	36311	W 11299	33132			MEUBLES ET PIECES
8219	FURNITURE AND PARTS NES	W 11729	34968	W 9358	31094	W 10455	29386			AUTRES MEUBLES ET PIECES
82192	WOOD FURNITURE NES	W 9879	29375	W 8308	27397	W 9055	25863			MEUBLES NDA EN BOIS
84	CLOTHING AND ACCESSORIES		30356		27843		30535			VETEMENTS
845	OUTERWEAR KNIT NONELASTC	W 1377	17852	W 1121	16070	W 1267	18670			VET DESSOUS,ACCES BONNET
8459	— OTHER,CLTHG ACCESRYS	W 1358	17665	W 1111	16015	W 1253	18356			AUT VET DESSUS DE BONNE
851	*FOOTWEAR	W 2340	16089	W 2091	14534	W 1882	16746			CHAUSSURES
85102	FOOTWEAR LEATHER	W 1146	11760	W 975	10194	W 943	12858			CHAUS SEMELLES EN CUIR
87	PRECISION INSTRUMNTS NES		22115		21384		37355			INSTRUM,APPAR SCIENT NDA
872	MEDICAL INSTRUMENTS NES	W 607	13159	W 397	11202	W 482	11242			INSTR,APP MEDIC–CHIR NDA
874	MEASURNG,CONTROLNG INSTR	W 250	7214	W 302	8100	W 376	24806			INSTRUMENTS DE MESURE
88	PHOTO EQU,OPTICL GDS ETC		46978		46965		62364			APP,FOURN PHOTO,OP,MONTR
882	PHOTO,CINEMA SUPPLIES	W 783	8360	W 612	9642	W 1132	14848			PRODUITS PHOTO,CINEMA
8822	PHOTO FILM EXC DEV CINMA	W 611	7350	W 540	9242	W 861	13775			PLAQUES,PELLICULES,FILMS
885	WATCHES AND CLOCKS		30890		31813		35057			HORLOGERIE
8851	WATCHES,MOVEMENTS,CASES		29155		31271		34741			MONTRES,MOUVEMENTS,BOITES
88511	WATCHES		28970		30204		33458			MONTRES POCHE,BRACELET
89	MISC MANUFCTRD GOODS NES		78377		88002		97943			ART MANUFACTURES DIVERS
893	ARTICLES OF PLASTIC NES	W 10385	23825	W 13343	26152	W 12924	33679			OUVRAGES EN MAT DIVIS 58
8939	MISC PLASTIC ARTICLES	W 7675	19776	W 6999	20302	W 7126	23820			ART DIVERS EN MAT DIV 58
89399	OTHR PLASTC ARTICLES NES	W 6858	17167	W 6432	18130	W 6109	20667			AUT OUV MAT DIV 58
896	WORKS OF ART ETC		15		6		14		227830	OBJETS D'ART
897	GOLD,SILVER WARE,JEWELRY		18547		28993		26724			BIJOUTERIE,ORFEVRERIE
8973	PREC JEWLRY,GLD–SILVWARE		16684		28119		24830			BIJOUX OR,ARGENT ORFEVRE
89731	PRECIOUS METAL JEWELLERY		16622		28095		24685			ART BIJOUTERIE,JOAILLER
9	GOODS NOT CLASSD BY KIND		264373		268625		315072			ART TRANSACT NON CLASSES
931	*SPECIAL TRANSACTIONS	W 10884	179524	W 10174	127441	W 7891	187843			TRANS.SPECIALES
971	*GOLD,NON MONETARY NES	K 7132	80375	K 11229	137884	K 10819	123154			OR NON MONETAIRE
97101	NONMON GLD UNWRT,SEMIMFD	K 7018	80371	K 11229	137884	K 7717	123119			OR,ALLIAGES D'OR BRUTS

5. General Exports F.O.B. by Commodities according to the S.I.T.C. (Rev. 2) in thousand U.S. Dollars
Exportations Générales F.O.B. par Produits d'après la C.T.C.I. (Rév. 2) en milliers de Dollars E.U.

SITC CTCI	COMMODITY	1993 WEIGHT POIDS	1993 VALUE VALEUR	1994 WEIGHT POIDS	1994 VALUE VALEUR	1995 WEIGHT POIDS	1995 VALUE VALEUR	1996 WEIGHT POIDS	1996 VALUE VALEUR	PRODUIT
	ALL COMMODITIES		5299511		5418298		5917390		7344391	TOUS PRODUITS
0	FOOD AND LIVE ANIMALS		98334		112069		149681			ALIMENTS,ANIMAUX VIVANTS
001	*LIVE ANIMALS FOR FOOD	W 930	3646	W 2795	9056	W 9099	24240			ANIMAUX VIVANTS
0012	SHEEP AND GOATS,LIVE	W 906	3551	W 2774	8991	W 9062	23996			ESPECES OVINE ET CAPRINE
00122	GOATS,LIVE	W 906	3551	W 2763	8957	W 9054	23962			ESPECE CAPRINE
03	FISH AND PREPARATIONS		51477		49464		61422			POISSONS ET PREPARATIONS
034	FISH,FRESH,CHILLED,FROZN	W 45022	45759	W 43476	43674	W 57675	55531			POISSON FRAIS, REFRIG,CONG
0342	FISH FROZEN,EXCL FILLETS	W 45022	45759	W 43473	43672	W 57670	55528			POISSONS CONGELES
04	CEREALS AND PREPARATIONS		12703		17720		23175			CEREALES ET PRODUITS
1	BEVERAGES AND TOBACCO		124576		119947		112918			BOISSONS ET TABACS
12	TOBACCO AND MANUFACTURES		121457		117190		107549			TABACS BRUTS FABRIQUES
122	TOBACCO,MANUFACTURED	W 16615	120427	W 16147	116311	W 18198	106849			TABACS FABRIQUES
1222	CIGARETTES	W 16586	120345	W 16147	116311	W 18168	106673			CIGARETTES
2	CRUDE MATERLS,EXCL FUELS		13404		17153		26639			MAT BRUTES NON COMESTIBLES
3	MINERAL FUELS ETC		4181741		4144268		4650589			COMBUSTIBLES MINERAUX LUB
33	PETROLEUM AND PRODUCTS		4181741		4144252		4650580			PETROLE ET DERIVES
333	CRUDE PETROLEUM	MW 36556	4147979	MW 34192	4107703	MW 35734	4606883	MW 40498	5764667	HUILES BRUTES DE PETROLE
334	PETROLEUM PRODUCTS,REFIN	W 30366	33758	W 33639	36548	W 36703	43657		122498	PRODUITS RAFFINES
3341	GASOLINE,OTH LIGHT OILS	W 30255	33461	W 33534	36311					ESSENCES POUR MOTEURS
33419	OTH LIGHT PETROLEUM OILS	W 30255	33461	W 33534	36311					AUTRES HUILES LEGERES
4	ANIMAL,VEGETABLE OIL,FAT		11840		17060		21984			HUILES,GRAISSES ANIM,VEG
42	FIXED VEGETABLE OIL,FAT		11840		17043		21958			HUILES VEGETALES FIXES
424	FIXED VEG OIL NONSOFT	W 15205	11828	W 20721	16846	W 23370	21924			AUTRES HUILES VEG FIXES
4249	FIXED VEGETABLE OILS NES	W 15200	11818	W 20639	16726	W 23303	21796			HUILES VEGET FIXES NDA
5	CHEMCLS,RELATED PROD NES		22090		17611		21081		19506	PRODUITS CHIMIQUES
55	PERFUME,CLEANING ETC PRD		17011		11568		13804			PROD POUR PARFUM,TOILETTE
6	BASIC MANUFACTURES		102762		127645		161596			ART MANUFACTURES
62	RUBBER MANUFACTURES NES		15153		14767		22359			CAOUTCHOUC MANUFACTURE
625	RUBBER TYRES, TUBES ETC	W 5208	15137	W 5473	14745	W 6703	22271			PNEUS CAOUTCHOUC VULCANISE
68	NON–FERROUS METALS		58138		77097		82597			METAUX NON FERREUX
682	COPPER EXC CEMENT COPPER	W 20363	42340	W 23073	54453	W 22158	72905			CUIVRE
6821	COPPER NES,ALLOYS,UNWRT	W 20326	42278	W 23064	54413	W 22098	72739			CUIVRE BRUT
68212	COPPER REFINED,UNWROUGHT	W 20300	39864	W 23017	49366	W 22011	61303			CUIVRE AFFINE BRUT
684	ALUMINIUM	W 5672	15733	W 8395	22628	W 3322	9672			ALUMINIUM
6842	ALUMINIUM,ALLOYS WORKED	W 5672	15733	W 8395	22628	W 3322	9672			ALUMINIUM,ALLIAGES OUVRE
68421	ALUMINIUM BARS,WIRE,ETC	W 5672	15733	W 8395	22628	W 3198	9208			BARRES,PROFILES FILS ALU
69	METAL MANUFACTURES NES		8344		12217		24070			ART MANUFACT EN METAL NDA
7	MACHINES,TRANSPORT EQUIP		619712		695964		569815		679588	MACHINES MATERIEL TRANSPORT
72	MACHS FOR SPCL INDUSTRYS		25247		27278		26187			MAC SPECIALES POUR INDUST
723	CIVIL ENGNEERG EQUIP ETC	W 4770	23342	W 5585	25534	W 4546	24765			APPAREILS DE GENIE CIVIL
7239	CONSTR ETC MACHY PTS NES	W 2809	19429	W 4660	23061	W 4100	23919			PIECES 723.41–723.46
76	TELECOMM,SOUND EQUIPMENT		9876		12308		23123			EQUIPMENT DE TELECOM
77	ELECTRIC MACHNRY NES ETC		14637		16863		23648			MACH APP ELECT NDA
78	ROAD VEHICLES		514562		578645		460939			VEHICULES ROUTIERS
781	PASS MOTOR VEH EXC BUSES	W 36710	401329	W 35659	417992	W 18492	246401			AUTO TRANSPORT PERSONNES
782	LORRIES,SPCL MTR VEH NES	W 3142	11800	W 4864	19107	W 6091	38133			VEHICULES SPECIAUX,MARCH
7821	LORRIES,TRUCKS	W 3095	11695	W 4864	19107	W 5962	37857			VEHICULES TRANSP MARCHAND
783	ROAD MOTOR VEHICLES NES	W 2840	17381	W 4587	43289	W 4635	53128			VEHICULES ROUTIERS NDA
7831	BUSES	W 2840	17381	W 4587	43289	W 4635	53128			VOITURES TRANSPORT COMMUN
784	MOTOR VEH PRTS,ACCES NES	W 6920	82716	W 8332	94508	W 9405	121240			PIECES 722,781,782,783
7849	OTHER MOTOR VEHCL PARTS	W 6920	82716	W 8332	94508	W 9405	121240			PIECES 722,781,782,783
79	OTHR TRANSPORT EQUIPMENT		45425		43944		16776			AUTRE MATERIEL TRANSPORT
792	AIRCRAFT ETC	W 47	45158	W 49	43482	W 49	16682			APP NAVIGATION AERIENNE
7929	AIRCRAFT PARTS NES	W 47	45158	W 49	43482	W 49	16682			PIECES DU 792
8	MISC MANUFACTURED GOODS		94611		115351		150393			ART MANUFACTURES DIVERS
84	CLOTHING AND ACCESSORIES		59283		73322		89079			VETEMENTS
843	WOMENS OUTERWEAR NONKNIT	W 818	7914	W 898	9595	W 1853	18561			VET DESSUS FEMMES MAT TEX
844	UNDER GARMENTS NOT KNIT	W 4047	34468	W 5114	46991	W 2929	31211			VETEMENT DESSOUS MAT TEX
8441	— MENS SHIRTS	W 4047	34468	W 5114	46991	W 2929	31211			CHEMISES HOMMES MAT TEXT
84412	—— OF SYNTHETIC FIBRES	W 4047	34468	W 5114	46991	W 2929	31211			CHEMISES HOMMES FIB SYNT
845	OUTERWEAR KNIT NONELASTC	W 1948	16264	W 1870	15726	W 3900	34993			VET DESSOUS,ACCES BONNET
8459	— OTHER,CLTHG ACCESRYS	W 1936	16139	W 1650	14436	W 3558	31577			AUT VET DESSUS DE BONNE
88	PHOTO EQU,OPTICL GDS ETC		16365		14966		24347			APP,FOURN PHOTO,OP,MONTR
896	WORKS OF ART ETC								51496	OBJETS D'ART
9	GOODS NOT CLASSD BY KIND		30441		51229		52693			ART TRANSACT NON CLASSES
931	*SPECIAL TRANSACTIONS	W 4931	17431	W 7604	34739	W 9008	30628			TRANS.SPECIALES

1. HISTORICAL SERIES, 1961–1996 GENERAL TRADE, IMPORTS C.I.F., EXPORTS F.O.B.
SERIES HISTORIQUES, 1961–1996 COMMERCE GENERAL, IMPORTATIONS C.A.F., EXPORTATIONS F.O.B

YEAR ANNEE	VALUE IN MILLION PAK. RUPEES VALEUR EN MILLION PAK. RUPEES MERCHANDISE –MARCHANDISE		GOLD –OR		CONVERSION FACTORS U.S. CENTS PER PAK. RUPEE FACTEURS DE CONVERSION CENTS E.U. PAR PAK. RUPEE		INDEX NUMBERS –INDICES QUANTUM		UNIT VALUE VALEUR UNITAIRE	
	IMPORTS	EXPORTS	IMPORTS	EXPORTS	IMPORTS	EXPORTS	IMPORTS	EXPORTS	IMPORTS	EXPORTS
1961	3056.30	1905.00			21.0000	21.0000	11	10	4	7
1962	3514.90	1891.70			21.0000	21.0000	10	13	4	6
1963	4231.70	1983.40			21.0000	21.0000	12	14	4	6
1964	4749.30	2351.90			21.0000	21.0000	14	15	4	6
1965	4967.00	2515.20			21.0000	21.0000	13	14	4	7
1966	4284.40	2860.80			21.0000	21.0000	13	14	4	7
1967	5243.40	3071.80			21.0000	21.0000	15	15	4	7
1968	4742.20	3429.50			21.0000	21.0000	13	17	4	7
1969	4929.50	3245.00			21.0000	21.0000	14	16	5	7
1970	5575.70	3444.10			21.0000	21.0000	15	16	5	7
1971	4409.20	3171.50			21.0000	21.0000	15	21	6	7
1972	5936.90	5818.40			11.2172	11.6734	20	30	11	14
1973	9698.30	9523.80			9.9872	9.9839	26	31	15	24
1974	17201.30	10857.40			10.1010	10.1010	31	28	25	31
1975	21361.30	10242.10			10.1010	10.1010	36	32	29	28
1976	21587.60	11550.80			10.1010	10.1010	41	35	25	30
1977	24297.80	11626.10			10.1010	10.1010	47	34	29	36
1978	32521.00	14603.90			10.1010	10.1010	57	38	30	41
1979	40158.30	20354.40			10.1010	10.1010	67	53	34	48
1980	52966.00	25620.90			10.1010	10.1010	67	51	42	51
1981	54936.50	28516.00			10.1010	10.1010	72	61	49	48
1982	63803.00	28246.20			8.4399	8.4781	66	49	56	56
1983	70048.20	40308.60			7.6251	7.6266	66	56	60	56
1984	82058.50	36636.40			7.1576	7.1343	74	44	70	61
1985	93811.00	43646.00			6.2792	6.2774	77	56	73	62
1986	89355.41	56245.31			6.0174	6.0068	75	75	65	65
1987	101440.50	72685.89			5.7467	5.7476	77	82	76	79
1988	119212.60	81442.10			5.5530	5.5588	100	90	78	84
1989	146444.30	98412.40			4.8615	4.8561	105	94	92	91
1990	160134.00	121345.00			4.6060	4.6056	100	100	100	100
1991	201409.00	155398.00			4.1900	4.2009	105	113	107	104
1992	235296.00	183599.00			3.9861	3.9854	122	124	110	106
1993	265142.00	187786.00			3.5833	3.5615	124	112	118	116
1994	271744.00	225200.00			3.2711	3.2706	120	139	138	136
1995	362685.90	252714.00			3.1600	3.1623	129	110	156	171
1996	437768.90	335312.90			2.7711	2.7798	127	130	172	189

2. IMPORTS BY BROAD ECONOMIC CATEGORY AND EXPORTS BY INDUSTRIAL ORIGIN. (PERCENTAGE OF TOTAL VALUE)
IMPORTATIONS PAR CATEGORIES ECONOMIQUES ET EXPORTATIONS PAR BRANCHE D'ACTIVITE.(EN POURCENTAGE DE LA VALEUR TOTALE)

IMPORTS – IMPORTATIONS

	1990	1991	1992	1993	1994	1995	1996
TOTAL IMPORTS–IMPORTATIONS TOTALES	100.	100.	100.	100.	100.	100.	100.
1 FOOD BEV–ALIMENTATION BOISSONS	16.3	11.5	14.5	13.6	15.6	17.3	14.5
11 PRIMARY–PRODUITS DE BASE	7.9	5.1	8.2	7.2	6.4	7.2	6.7
111 FOR INDUSTRY–POUR L'INDUSTRIE	4.5	1.9	4.9	3.7	3.3	4.0	4.1
112 FOR HOUSEHOLDS–POUR LES MENAGES	3.4	3.2	3.3	3.5	3.1	3.2	2.5
12 PROCESSED–PRODUITS ELABORES	8.4	6.4	6.3	6.4	9.1	10.1	7.9
121 FOR INDUSTRY–POUR L'INDUSTRIE	5.8	5.0	5.1	5.8	8.5	9.3	6.0
122 FOR HOUSEHOLDS–POUR LES MENAGES	2.6	1.4	1.2	0.6	0.6	0.8	1.9
2 IND SUPPLIES–APPROV INDUSTRIELS	33.2	32.5	31.9	30.5	33.4	33.5	33.0
21 PRIMARY–PRODUITS DE BASE	4.7	4.4	4.6	4.0	6.0	5.5	3.5
22 PROCESSED–PRODUITS ELABORES	28.5	28.1	27.3	26.5	27.4	28.0	29.5
3 FUELS–COMBUSTIBLES	20.8	17.9	16.3	17.1	18.3	16.4	20.7
31 PRIMARY–PRODUITS DE BASE	8.7	6.6	6.6	5.9	7.7	5.6	6.1
32 PROCESSED–PRODUITS ELABORES	12.1	11.3	9.7	11.1	10.6	10.8	14.5
321 MOTOR SPIRIT–ESSENCE	0.5	0.4	0.2	1.4	0.4	0.3	0.6
322 OTHER–AUTRES	11.6	10.8	9.6	9.8	10.2	10.5	14.0
4 MACHINERY–EQUIPEMENT	18.2	23.8	25.6	21.4	21.9	23.6	20.6
41 CAPITAL EQUIPMENT–MACHINES	16.4	21.9	23.5	19.6	19.2	21.9	18.7
42 PARTS–PIECES ACCESSOIRES	1.8	1.9	2.0	1.8	2.7	1.7	1.9
5 TRANSPORT–TRANSPORT	7.9	10.7	8.6	14.1	7.1	5.5	7.1
51 PASSENGER CARS–AUTOMOBILES	2.4	1.9	2.2	4.2	2.0	1.9	2.1
52 OTHER–AUTRES	2.8	5.5	3.7	6.6	2.6	1.6	2.1
521 INDUSTRIAL–INDUSTRIELS	2.4	5.2	3.2	6.2	2.3	1.2	1.6
522 NON INDUSTRIAL–NON INDUSTRIEL	0.4	0.4	0.4	0.4	0.4	0.4	0.5
53 PARTS–PIECES ACCESSOIRES	2.7	3.3	2.8	3.3	2.5	2.1	3.0
6 CONSUM GOODS–BIENS CONSOMMATION	3.4	3.4	2.9	3.2	3.2	3.4	3.6
61 DURABLE–DURABLES	0.8	0.6	0.7	0.6	0.5	0.6	0.4
62 SEMI DURABLE–SEMI DURABLES	0.8	0.9	0.6	0.8	0.8	0.9	1.2
63 NON DURABLE–NON DURABLES	1.9	1.8	1.6	1.8	2.0	1.9	2.0
7 GOODS NES–BIENS NDA	0.1	0.2	0.1	0.2	0.5	0.2	0.5

EXPORTS – EXPORTATIONS

	1990	1991	1992	1993	1994	1995	1996
TOTAL EXPORTS–EXPORTATIONS TOTALES	100.	100.	100.	100.	100.	100.	100.
1 AGRICULTURE	12.3	10.0	11.2	7.2	4.0	5.2	7.5
2 MINING QUARRY–INDUS EXTRACTIVES	1.3	1.1	1.1	1.0	0.6	0.7	0.8
3 MANUFACTURING–IND MANUFACTUR	86.4	88.9	87.6	91.8	95.3	94.1	91.8
31 FOOD BEV TOBACCO–ALIM BOISS TAB	6.0	7.7	7.2	5.7	6.8	9.4	6.7
32 TEXTILES–INDUSTRIES TEXTILES	73.4	73.7	74.0	79.0	81.3	77.6	77.9
33 WOOD & PRODUCTS–BOIS & PRODUITS	0.0	0.0	0.0	0.1	0.0	0.0	0.0
34 PAPER & PRODUCTS–PAPIER & PRODT	0.1	0.1	0.1	0.1	0.1	0.1	0.1
35 CHEMICALS–INDUSTRIES CHIMIQUES	1.0	1.1	0.9	0.7	1.0	1.1	1.1
36 NON METAL MIN–MIN NON METAL	0.3	0.3	0.2	0.2	0.2	0.2	0.2
37 BASIC METAL–IND METAL BASE	0.0	0.0	0.0	0.0	0.0	0.0	0.0
38 METAL MANUF–MANUF METAL	2.9	3.0	2.7	2.9	2.3	2.4	2.5
39 OTH MANUF IND–AUTRES MANUF	2.6	3.0	2.5	3.0	3.6	3.2	3.2

3. TRADE BY PRINCIPAL COUNTRIES OF PRODUCTION AND FIRST CONSIGNMENT(VALUE IN THOUSAND U.S. DOLLARS)
ECHANGES SELON LES PRINCIPAUX PAYS DE PRODUCTION ET DE PREMIERE CONSIGNATION (VALEUR EN MILLIERS DE DOLLARS EU)

COUNTRIES--PAYS	GENERAL IMPORTS C.I.F. IMPORTATIONS GENERALES C.A.F				
	1992	1993	1994	1995	1996
World	9362901	9739750	8881540	11703553	12140621
Africa	194695	211333	205966	316050	338843
Americas	1227464	1119859	1017230	1421120	1599382
Northern America	1081740	971781	937886	1225446	1391322
LAIA	144409	147166	77489	191014	204542
CACM	685	640	526	2417	1294
Caribbean	480	137	399	537	1465
Rest of America	150	136	929	1707	759
As.ex F.USSR	4678891	5417572	4749994	6350995	6597360
Eur.x F.USSR	2941670	2701259	2554378	3266184	3208983
EU	2548326	2372079	2289162	2754121	2528811
EFTA	265606	239846	202717	377927	582280
East Europe	110297	77561	57111	125620	92691
Other Europe	3591	3489	1132	2341	938
Former USSR	92088	33894	154735	170304	141929
Oceania	228093	255832	199236	178880	254124
Japan/Japon	1329576	1515348	831286	1254004	1241753
USA/Etats--Unis d'Amer	978941	906802	867650	1093206	1308714
Germany/Allemagne	725998	694822	699215	734555	601403
Malaysia/Malaisie	418193	492836	658137	988249	642759
Saudi Arabia	497218	518698	487713	583986	706086
Kuwait/ Koweït	178741	361884	565919	668300	905376
United Kingdom	549745	465602	474009	553935	565781
China/Chine	420784	436591	420810	515267	574273
United Arab Emirates	286218	335003	295537	562115	621015
Italy/Italie	382730	290729	276102	585069	351884
Korea, Republic of	344401	456233	286710	350279	324129
Switz.Liecht	247666	223602	193807	366310	549821
France,Monac	303877	356871	360805	257791	204938
Australia/Australie	210276	241064	181284	164777	238809
Iran (Islamic Rp. of)	184481	152697	129368	191070	271964
Singapore/Singapour	145043	167242	163292	225015	197124
Netherlands/Pays--Bas	183194	170027	136590	152984	249518
Bahrain/Bahreïn	117124	157750	138277	68865	135940
Indonesia/Indonésie	89972	124178	116252	119113	139254
Belgium--Luxembourg	112209	121367	114102	116786	107002
Kenya	85479	112326	96658	123949	109434
Russian Federation	91675	32676	147654	107507	122668
Qatar	138526	155088	99368	71379	31970
India/Inde	52129	68299	72157	82370	187800
Brazil/Brésil	104264	76287	46577	108600	119756
Sweden/Suède	100356	110750	72730	81171	84024
Thailand/Thaïlande	77441	61117	70970	110320	126440
Canada	101185	59827	69044	130010	81888
Turkey/Turquie	49754	59462	56138	86869	74974
Denmark/Danemark	59726	29447	35525	76271	98257
Spain/Espagne	40026	44406	44747	63999	79605
Argentina/Argentine	27622	64216	23471	65375	55339
Hong Kong	54581	48489	31293	49827	46384
Finland/Finlande	22202	16706	27513	47347	115348
Sri Lanka	33037	42314	42115	50694	44422
Oman	7437	24021	64043	53572	40626
Bangladesh	49580	39166	23948	35657	36271
Ireland/Irlande	22148	21598	22896	44504	37494
Austria/Autriche	38381	27309	20208	20689	23274
Hungary/Hongrie	27615	28493	24324	21874	21884
Morocco/Maroc	5435	30476	5831	24252	54601
Myanmar	32451	27227	11756	30795	16418
Egypt/Egypte	24911	5544	20455	36866	30197
Romania/Roumanie	10462	17161	13742	24304	44823
Jordan/Jordanie	12507	7408	34401	24008	24664
Poland/Pologne	12144	9030	9387	54294	11429
Un. Rep. of Tanzania	17727	20848	15667	18695	15523
Yemen/Yémen	580	14682	14398	38100	13716
Norway,SVD,JM	17885	16146	8907	11318	24354
New Zealand	17130	14437	17689	13503	15083

COUNTRIES--PAYS	GENERAL EXPORTS F.O.B. EXPORTATIONS GENERALES F.O.B.				
	1992	1993	1994	1995	1996
Monde	7304489	6877530	7356903	8157874	9322199
Afrique	293732	249941	334046	359430	428763
Amériques	1121449	1262632	1409433	1508073	1858013
Amérique du Nord	1077315	1179902	1323280	1375757	1700156
ALAI	31333	67008	64764	108334	126530
MCAC	2714	4091	10225	11760	17497
Caraïbes	2117	2207	2585	5818	3741
Autre Amérique	7969	9425	8579	6404	10088
Asie l'URSS exclus	3419850	2885121	2940215	3515732	3826888
Europe l'URSS exclus	2294367	2281650	2475726	2580344	2916614
UE	2191572	2193811	2388745	2486851	2809469
AELE	65648	66461	66908	57576	68716
Europe de l'Est	26329	14467	13464	30032	30822
Autre de l'Europe	2695	3712	3602	2722	3403
Ancienne URSS	48160	65220	56325	76236	120991
Océanie	126932	132965	141158	118058	170931
USA/Etats--Unis d'Amer	933054	1006163	1159190	1230761	1556639
Hong Kong	572072	375608	566560	617543	875137
Germany/Allemagne	509300	569358	541280	561573	664024
Japan/Japon	560375	502067	537219	552426	605951
United Kingdom	508239	508226	563723	529132	628965
United Arab Emirates	378154	414667	402360	373987	448374
France,Monac	295248	300106	271529	274591	270015
Saudi Arabia	315379	293594	206954	229583	246554
Netherlands/Pays--Bas	178458	197559	228570	271930	276205
Korea, Republic of	169123	175359	219664	277398	273158
Italy/Italie	223330	166507	213578	235936	256825
Belgium--Luxembourg	111957	136408	188684	206051	232757
Canada	143758	173008	163333	144401	143107
Bangladesh	135876	118959	118630	154727	107014
Spain/Espagne	120230	92177	125721	129923	129963
Australia/Australie	99241	104462	112728	92438	136888
Singapore/Singapour	130918	131064	94850	95054	90361
Indonesia/Indonésie	94277	51107	39808	108403	139125
China/Chine	54121	59969	54109	121161	118876
Sweden/Suède	94277	72297	76536	71569	81754
Turkey/Turquie	43098	103927	35663	136537	76093
Thailand/Thaïlande	113832	64368	39798	61971	96649
Sri Lanka	84413	58675	69984	56464	82640
Portugal	39976	49271	64657	74144	101537
Iran (Islamic Rp. of)	90564	18334	26401	124702	67297
India/Inde	135328	48999	46464	39790	42207
Malaysia/Malaisie	74726	50308	48737	47079	39009
Denmark/Danemark	38431	37859	39988	49907	52930
Switz.Liecht	35087	38836	34503	27792	34800
Philippines	26991	27706	24204	30840	50945
Brazil/Brésil	5037	21184	16539	58359	59180
Norway,SVD,JM	30429	27459	32123	29613	33455
Kuwait/ Koweït	37943	33373	22950	25108	32498
Oman	23532	28498	22849	32512	42951
Greece/Grèce	15096	17014	20573	31351	59424
Bahrain/Bahreïn	28463	20826	20211	31706	40941
Cyprus/Chypre	32573	36703	28164	25212	17989
Austria/Autriche	28301	26721	29094	26727	23500
Russian Federation	45930	35406	15732	14537	21193
Egypt/Egypte	3566	10057	21402	46390	50613
Kenya	26577	14623	30086	19918	36046
New Zealand	20919	24474	25072	23756	30053
Yemen/Yémen	28232	22004	20150	30224	17116
Uzbekistan/Ouzbékistan	795	14583	17934	36069	44800
So. Africa Customs Un	27688	17839	14284	9790	43549
Afghanistan	15997	15784	32914	20171	13078
Jordan/Jordanie	41466	10469	10124	15267	11950
Mauritius/Maurice	16006	18227	17391	16553	20052
Chile/Chili	6311	12907	14667	18116	33228
Finland/Finlande	17199	14027	15772	14977	20322

(VALUE AS PERCENTAGE OF WORLD TOTAL)(VALEURS EN POURCENTAGE DU TOTAL MONDIAL)

	1987	1988	1989	1990	1991	1992	1993	1994	1995	1996
Africa	1.7	1.1	1.8	2.6	2.2	2.1	2.2	2.3	2.7	2.8
Americas	11.7	15.8	17.6	15.1	14.0	13.1	11.5	11.5	12.1	13.2
Northern America	10.5	14.5	16.2	14.1	12.0	11.6	10.0	10.6	10.5	11.5
LAIA	1.1	1.2	1.3	0.9	1.9	1.5	1.5	0.9	1.6	1.7
CACM	0.0	0.0	0.1	0.0	0.0	0.0	0.0	0.0	0.0	0.0
Caribbean	0.0	0.0	0.0	0.0	0.1	0.0	0.0	0.0	0.0	0.0
Rest of America	0.1	0.0	0.0	0.0	0.0	0.0	0.0	0.0	0.0	0.0
As.ex F.USSR	52.1	48.7	50.2	50.7	49.2	50.0	55.6	53.5	54.3	54.3
Eur.x F.USSR	32.0	31.8	27.2	28.5	31.2	31.4	27.7	28.8	27.9	26.4
EU	27.2	27.4	22.8	24.1	27.0	27.2	24.4	25.8	23.5	20.8
EFTA	3.0	2.6	2.6	2.8	2.6	2.8	2.5	2.3	3.2	4.8
East Europe	1.4	1.4	1.4	1.3	1.2	1.2	0.8	0.6	1.1	0.8
Other Europe	0.4	0.4	0.4	0.3	0.4	0.0	0.0	0.0	0.0	0.0
Former USSR	0.7	0.4	0.5	0.9	1.0	1.0	0.3	1.7	1.5	1.2
Oceania	1.8	2.2	2.8	2.4	1.9	2.4	2.6	2.2	1.5	2.1
Japan/Japon	15.9	14.7	13.0	11.9	14.7	14.2	15.6	9.4	10.7	10.2
USA/Etats--Unis d'Amer	9.4	13.0	15.3	12.8	11.1	10.5	9.3	9.8	9.3	10.8
Germany/Allemagne	8.1	7.6	7.2	7.4	7.9	7.8	7.1	7.9	6.3	5.0
Malaysia/Malaisie	3.2	3.9	3.4	3.3	4.5	4.5	5.1	7.4	8.4	5.3
Saudi Arabia	5.0	4.4	4.6	6.3	5.1	5.3	5.3	5.5	5.0	5.8
Kuwait/ Koweït	8.3	7.3	10.2	6.0	0.4	1.9	3.7	6.4	5.7	7.5
United Kingdom	7.0	6.3	5.5	4.9	5.1	5.9	4.8	5.3	4.7	4.7
China/Chine	4.0	3.8	4.5	4.6	4.2	4.5	4.5	4.7	4.4	4.7
United Arab Emirates	2.9	1.5	1.6	2.1	3.7	3.1	3.4	3.3	4.8	5.1
Italy/Italie	2.7	3.1	2.1	3.1	3.2	4.1	3.0	3.1	5.0	2.9

	1987	1988	1989	1990	1991	1992	1993	1994	1995	1996
Afrique	5.6	4.2	4.4	4.2	4.3	4.0	3.6	4.5	4.4	4.6
Amériques	12.7	12.9	14.1	14.4	13.9	15.4	18.4	19.2	18.5	19.9
Amérique du Nord	12.4	12.8	13.8	14.1	13.2	14.7	17.2	18.0	16.9	18.2
ALAI	0.1	0.1	0.1	0.2	0.5	0.4	1.0	0.9	1.3	1.4
MCAC	0.0	0.0	0.1	0.0	0.0	0.0	0.1	0.1	0.1	0.2
Caraïbes	0.1	0.0	0.0	0.0	0.1	0.0	0.0	0.0	0.1	0.0
Autre Amérique	0.0	0.0	0.0	0.1	0.1	0.1	0.1	0.1	0.1	0.1
Asie l'URSS exclus	41.1	44.1	45.6	39.4	44.0	46.8	41.9	40.0	43.1	41.1
Europe l'URSS exclus	36.4	34.9	32.7	39.3	35.3	31.4	33.2	33.7	31.6	31.3
UE	33.3	32.1	30.4	36.0	32.3	30.0	31.9	32.5	30.5	30.1
AELE	1.6	1.4	1.3	1.2	1.0	0.9	1.0	0.9	0.7	0.7
Europe de l'Est	1.5	1.2	1.0	1.9	1.7	0.4	0.2	0.2	0.4	0.3
Autre de l'Europe	0.0	0.1	0.1	0.3	0.3	0.0	0.1	0.0	0.0	0.0
Ancienne URSS	2.7	2.0	1.4	1.3	0.9	0.7	0.9	0.8	0.9	1.3
Océanie	1.5	1.9	1.8	1.4	1.4	1.7	1.9	1.9	1.4	1.8
USA/Etats--Unis d'Amer	11.1	11.2	12.2	12.4	11.5	12.8	14.6	15.8	15.1	16.7
Hong Kong	2.4	4.5	5.2	5.0	5.9	7.8	5.5	7.7	7.6	9.4
Germany/Allemagne	7.1	6.9	6.7	8.5	8.3	7.0	8.3	7.4	6.9	7.1
Japan/Japon	11.4	11.5	10.5	8.2	8.0	7.7	7.3	7.3	6.8	6.5
United Kingdom	7.0	6.8	6.3	7.4	6.9	7.0	7.4	7.7	6.5	6.7
United Arab Emirates	3.7	4.2	3.7	3.3	3.7	5.2	6.0	5.5	4.6	4.8
France,Monac	3.2	3.1	3.2	4.0	3.9	4.0	4.4	3.7	3.4	2.9
Saudi Arabia	5.5	3.8	2.3	2.9	3.9	4.3	4.3	2.8	2.8	2.6
Netherlands/Pays--Bas	1.8	2.1	1.7	2.0	2.0	2.4	2.9	3.1	3.3	3.0
Korea, Republic of	2.7	3.0	3.2	3.0	4.1	2.3	2.5	3.0	3.4	2.9

4. General Imports C.I.F. by Commodities according to the S.I.T.C. (Rev. 2) in thousand U.S. Dollars
Importations Générales C.A.F. par Produits d'après la C.T.C.I. (Rév. 2) en milliers de Dollars E.U.

SITC CTCI	COMMODITY	1993 WEIGHT POIDS	1993 VALUE VALEUR	1994 WEIGHT POIDS	1994 VALUE VALEUR	1995 WEIGHT POIDS	1995 VALUE VALEUR	1996 WEIGHT POIDS	1996 VALUE VALEUR	PRODUIT
	ALL COMMODITIES		9739750		8881540		11703553		12140621	TOUS PRODUITS
0	FOOD AND LIVE ANIMALS		756041		626617		898825		1030033	ALIMENTS,ANIMAUX VIVANTS
04	CEREALS AND PREPARATIONS		362545		300356		463515		486846	CEREALES ET PRODUITS
041	WHEAT ETC UNMILLED	W 2198679	344732	W 2228361	282465	W 2285520	444368	W 2112697	465962	FROMENT,EPEAUTRE
0411	DURUM WHEAT UNMILLED	W 2176687	341587	W 2228361	282465	W 2285520	444368	W 2112661	465939	FROMENT DUR NON MOULU
05	VEGETABLES AND FRUIT		115799		100418		162453		136579	LEGUMES ET FRUITS
054	VEG ETC FRSH,SMPLY PRSVD	W 309427	82573	W 206973	58602	W 385314	116525	W 239631	84027	LEGUMES FRAIS,CONG,SECS
0542	LEGUMINOUS VEGETBLES DRY	W 276213	74295	W 169796	49985	W 298982	102599	W 162514	65690	LEGUMES A COSSE SECS
057	FRUIT,NUTS,FRESH,DRIED	W 71441	31875	W 97635	39481	W 89395	42014	W 133165	49676	FRUITS FRAIS OU SECS
0577	NUTS EDIBLE,FRESH,DRIED	W 33540	24978	W 36357	28145	W 39099	31679	W 38732	33064	FRUITS A COQUES
06	SUGAR AND PREPS,HONEY		20387		6834		7654		194221	SUCRES ET PRODUITS
061	SUGAR AND HONEY	W 49946	19421	W 13161	6213	W 9035	6381	W 493336	193234	SUCRES ET MIEL
0612	REFINED SUGAR ETC	W 45661	15739	W 7859	2660	W 3724	1755	W 403284	163358	SUCRES RAFFINES
07	COFFEE,TEA,COCOA,SPICES		230900		188216		216964		179661	CAFE,THE,CACAO,EPICES
074	TEA AND MATE	W 125252	217456	W 106549	174338	W 115719	181980	W 110773	163458	THE ET MATE
0741	TEA	W 125252	217456	W 106549	174338	W 115719	181980	W 110773	163458	THE
2	CRUDE MATERLS,EXCL FUELS		539885		719369		817502		628144	MAT BRUTES NON COMESTIBLES
21	HIDES,SKINS,FURS UNDRSSD		34327		41207		27215		28933	CUIRS,PEAUX BRUTS
211	HIDES,SKINS,EXC FURS,RAW	W 22626	34324	W 18414	41194	W 10456	27201	W 13464	28122	CUIRS ET PEAUX
22	OIL SEEDS,OLEAGINOUS FRT		22929		27157		35546		34780	GRAINES,FRUITS OLEAGINEUX
223	SEEDS FOR OTH FIXED OILS	W 82960	22196	W 119639	26666	W 111657	27361	W 100056	26692	GRAINES AUTRES HUILES FIXES
23	RUBBER, CRUDE		35768		41376		63917		63781	CAOUTCHOUC BRUT
232	NATURAL RUBBER,GUMS	W 24282	22517	W 28309	26272	W 29558	42339	W 29613	39334	LATEX CAOUTCHOUC NATUREL
251	*PULP AND WASTE PAPER	W 79650	27077	W 77501	23288	W 70344	37816	W 71006	25976	PATES A PAPIER,DECHETS
26	TEXTILE FIBRES AND WASTE		202065		405781		458890		263102	FIBRES TEXTILES
263	COTTON	W 15509	11832	W 138784	218410	W 134020	223005	W 42062	54439	COTON
2631	RAW COTTON,EXCL LINTERS	W 6687	11814	W 121507	218310	W 107708	222853	W 27359	54194	COTON EN MASSE
266	SYNTHETIC FIBRES TO SPIN	W 72577	87857	W 62644	96401	W 53474	113310	W 48391	81837	FIBRES SYNTHETIQUES
2665	DISCN SYNTH FIBRE UNCMBD	W 46107	64813	W 52811	78440	W 43968	92643	W 39962	64709	DISCONTINUES EN MASSE
26652	— POLYESTER	W 31354	38035	W 29860	41821	W 23548	49360	W 21105	31676	FIBRES EN POLYESTERS
26653	— ACRYLIC	W 14499	26218	W 22251	35450	W 19597	41456	W 18261	32009	FIBRES ACRYLIQUES
267	OTHER MAN–MADE FIBRES	W 23564	48103	W 21758	40364	W 22125	50609	W 26416	53834	AUTR FIBR TEXT ARTIF SYNTH
2671	REGENERATD FIBRE TO SPIN	W 23562	48100	W 21707	40297	W 22010	50482	W 26408	53820	FIBRES TEXT ARTIFIC
26711	DISCN REGEN FIBRE UNCMBD	W 22520	44184	W 20226	35225	W 20326	44012	W 24367	45967	FIBRES TEX ARTIF DISCONT
269	WASTE OF TEXTILE FABRICS	W 86178	23146	W 87699	20620	W 83099	31789	W 99050	37131	FRIPERIE DRILLES,CHIFFONS
26901	BULK TEXT WSTE,OLD CLTHG	W 84349	22381	W 86939	20305	W 82586	31551	W 98797	37044	ART ET ACCESS D'HABILLEMENT
27	CRUDE FERTLZR,MINRLS NES		32066		27967		33982		31059	ENGRAIS MINERAUX BRUTS
28	METALLIFEROUS ORES,SCRAP		138534		109931		109251		124566	MINERAIS METAL,DECHETS
281	IRON ORE,CONCENTRATES	W 1982537	55938	W 1888647	49306	W 1697986	54989	W 1591355	51630	MINERAIS DE FER
2816	IRON ORE AGGLOMERATES	W 1982434	55874	W 1888617	49284	W 1697978	54983	W 1591353	51630	MINERAIS AGGLOMERES
282	IRON AND STEEL SCRAP	W 354041	51139	W 184425	28582	W 120606	22115	W 257965	41398	FERRAILLES
28209	— OF OTHR IRON OR STEEL	W 246313	35388	W 132674	20616	W 87157	15351	W 127091	18148	FERRAILLES DE FER
288	NONFERR METAL SCRAP NES	W 81185	30334	W 89019	29991	W 64781	30034	W 59826	28777	DECHETS NON FERREUX
2882	OTHER BASE MTL SCRAP NES	W 81091	30303	W 88380	29674	W 64588	29954	W 59616	28702	AUTRES DECHETS
28823	ALUMINIUM WSTE AND SCRAP	W 78728	29400	W 82991	28131	W 58891	28284	W 53440	25671	DECHETS D'ALUMINIUM
29	CRUDE ANIMAL,VEG MAT NES		36403		32129		38935		39471	MATIERES BRUTES ANIM,VEGET
292	CRUDE VEG MATERIALS NES	W 45415	35860	W 43776	31719	W 51114	38207	W 54358	38741	MAT BRUTES VEGETALES NDA
3	MINERAL FUELS ETC		1668118		1631754		1901748		2446689	COMBUSTIBLES MINERAUX LUB
32	COAL,COKE AND BRIQUETTES		76134		56569		53999		63527	HOUILLES,COKES,BRIQUETTES
322	COAL,LIGNITE AND PEAT	W 1217819	76066	W 1050200	56537	W 884495	53964	W 982141	63036	HOUILLES,LIGNITES,TOURBE
3222	OTH COAL,NOT AGGLOMERATD	W 1217603	76010	W 1049284	56105	W 884069	53835	W 981989	62970	AUTRES HOUILLES
33	PETROLEUM AND PRODUCTS		1581721		1401674		1780152		2290091	PETROLE ET DERIVES
333	CRUDE PETROLEUM	W 4188895	490261	W 3907964	454054	W 4174043	529429	W 3858984	567739	HUILES BRUTES DE PETROLE
334	PETROLEUM PRODUCTS,REFIN	W 7256429	1084292	W 7393565	941965	MW 9185	1244163	MW 10340	1715653	PRODUITS RAFFINES
3341	GASOLINE,OTH LIGHT OILS	W 683602	132676	W 209986	39450	W 133876	28978	W 314405	65472	ESSENCES POUR MOTEURS
33411	MOTOR,AVIATION SPIRIT	W 428360	83802	W 200148	37895	W 129639	28164	W 314101	65324	ESSENCES MOTEURS D'AVIONS
33419	OTH LIGHT PETROLEUM OILS	W 255223	48867	W 9838	1555	W 4237	815			AUTRES HUILES LEGERES
3342	KEROSENE,OTH MEDIUM OILS	W 201962	40562	W 161185	28343	W 68748	13380	W 148431	31905	PETR LAMPANTS,AUT HUIL
33421	KEROSENE INCL JET FUEL	W 201896	40495	W 161185	28343	W 68738	13376	W 148360	31878	PETROLES LAMPANTS
3343	GAS OILS	W 3484849	650449	W 3530662	541221	W 4401427	716087	W 5044838	1022147	GAS OILS
3344	FUEL OILS,NES	W 2869257	243674	W 3453840	308300	W 4548146	458154	W 4759162	554299	FUEL OILS
3345	LUBS,PETROLEUM OILS NES	W 16759	16932	W 37892	24650	W 32503	27564	W 72821	41830	HUILES LUBRIFIANTES
341	*GAS,NATURAL AND MANUFCT		10263		173510		67597		93072	GAZ NATUREL,GAZ MANUFACT
3413	PETROLM GASES,LIQUEFIED	W 32773	10167	W 460370	173479	W 324031	67595	W 340941	93062	GAZ DE PETROLE LIQUEFIE
34139	OTH HYDROCARBON GAS LQFD	W 32293	10159	W 458930	173466	W 324031	67595	W 340941	93062	HYDROCARBURES GAZEUX NDA
4	ANIMAL,VEGETABLE OIL,FAT		601314		789495		1102964		724887	HUILES,GRAISSES ANIM,VEG
411	*ANIMAL OILS AND FATS	W 51638	22702	W 73855	32568	W 22940	14591	W 72608	41892	HUILES,GRAISSES ANIMALES
4113	ANIML OIL,FAT,GREASE NES	W 51448	22568	W 73749	32494	W 22853	14498	W 72521	41827	HUILES,GRAISSES ANIMALES NDA
41132	FATS OF BOVINE,SHEEP,ETC	W 50074	21118	W 70389	29781	W 20633	12450	W 72383	41652	SUIFS BRUTS FONDUS
42	FIXED VEGETABLE OIL,FAT		548750		723757		1062532		651051	HUILES VEGETALES FIXES
423	FIXED VEG OILS,SOFT	W 225851	104438	W 201309	125202	W 228074	181146	W 150281	93160	HUILES VEGET DOUCES FIXES
4232	SOYA BEAN OIL	W 221186	101593	W 198072	122628	W 196549	157203	W 140357	86222	HUILE DE SOJA
424	FIXED VEG OIL NONSOFT	W 921571	444312	W 1106337	598555	W 1057237	881386	W 905838	557891	AUTRES HUILES VEG FIXES
4242	PALM OIL	W 915586	439822	W 1099783	593956	W 1049173	874187	W 899455	552288	HUILE DE PALME
431	*PROCESD ANML VEG OIL,ET	W 83370	29862	W 106569	33170	W 62047	25841	W 85984	31944	HUILES,GRAISSES PREPAREES
4313	FATTY ACIDS ETC,RESIDUES	W 80199	26702	W 103770	30226	W 59759	22712	W 84096	29199	ACIDES GRAS INDUST,RESIDUS
43131	FATTY ACIDS,ACID OILS	W 78457	26470	W 96603	29184	W 52730	21803	W 62897	25609	ACIDES GRAS INDUSTRIELS
5	CHEMCLS,RELATED PROD NES		1544889		1443780		1965866		2141845	PRODUITS CHIMIQUES
51	ORGANIC CHEMICALS		378595		373557		498517		529883	PROD CHIMIQ ORGANIQUES
512	ALCOHOLS,PHENOLS ETC		37452		41523		50663	W 161687	91547	PHENOLS,PHENOLS–ALCOOLS
5121	ACYCLIC ALCOHOLS,DERIVS		33745		37869		46377	W 158310	87199	ALCOOLS ACYCLIQUES
51215	ETHYLENE GLYCOL	V 44143	18971	V 40680	17071	V 34378	23452	W 103751	58874	ETHYLENE–GLYCOL
513	CARBOXYLIC ACIDS ETC	W 176714	121529	W 176154	135532	W 216089	225429	W 206167	203421	ACIDES CARBOXYLIQUES
5138	POLYACIDS AND DERIVATIVS	W 150305	90218	W 148535	104213	W 187129	183909	W 175047	156380	ACIDES POLYCARBOXYLIQUES
51389	OTH POLYACIDS ETC,DERIVS	W 118647	74395	W 131291	91626	W 180237	173474	W 161118	144352	ACIDES POLYCARBOXYLIQUES
514	NITROGEN–FNCTN COMPOUNDS	W 14288	110154	W 11869	81357	W 14962	113329	W 20187	118507	COMPOSES FONCT AZOTEES
5146	OXYGEN–FNCT AMINO–CMPNDS	W 3222	31271	W 1962	19852	W 2251	18486	W 3545	21376	COMP AMINES FONCT OXYGEN
5148	OTH NITROGN–FNCTN CMPNDS	W 7423	62498	W 6265	46866	W 8291	70571	W 12510	78288	AUTRES COMPOSES AZOTES
51482	IMIDE–,IMIDE–FNCT CMPNDS	W 2223	44840	W 1491	35402	W 2416	47632	W 6636	53922	COMPOSES A FONCTION IMIDE
515	ORG–INORG COMPOUNDS ETC	W 13167	55273	W 14205	55464	W 9816	61907	W 8032	61054	COMPOSES ORGANO–MINERAUX
5156	HETEROCYCLIC CMPDS ETC	W 2709	28219	W 2046	31833	W 2924	37077	W 2766	33522	COMPOSES HETEROCYCLIQUES
51569	OTH HETEROCYC CMPDS,ETC	W 2482	27770	W 1922	31399	W 2606	36308	W 2322	31921	AUT COMP HETEROCYCLIQUES
516	OTHER ORGANIC CHEMICALS	W 56859	35021	W 70545	39604	W 15122	30205	W 14839	24959	AUTRES PROD ORGANIQUES
5161	ETHERS,EPOXIDES,ACETALS	W 50606	22628	W 64416	28453	W 8977	7823	W 6388	6744	ETHERS–OXYDES,ALCOOLS
51611	ETHERS,ETHER–ALCOHOL,ETC	W 50426	21445	W 64385	28240	W 8926	7558	W 5657	5777	ETHERS–OXYDES
52	INORGANIC CHEMICALS		58736		52188		63821		66780	PROD CHIM INORGANIQUES
523	OTHR INORG CHEMICALS ETC	W 80275	33492	W 78714	32409	W 94268	40527	W 93215	44027	AUT PRODUITS CHIMIQUES INORG
53	DYES,TANNING,COLOUR PROD		138234		132651		147822		139558	PROD TEINTURE,COLORANTS
531	SYNT DYE,NAT INDGO,LAKES	W 13959	84475	W 16735	80164	W 15845	85226	W 14056	80780	MAT COLOR ORGAN,LAQUES
5311	SYNTHIC ORGNIC DYESTUFFS	W 13195	81657	W 15747	76939	W 14972	81589	W 13242	77168	MAT COLOR ORGAN SYNTHET
533	PIGMENTS,PAINTS,ETC	W 20440	35382	W 21383	32461	W 20375	40175	W 21139	38651	PIGMENTS,PEINTURES,VERNIS

4. General Imports C.I.F. by Commodities according to the S.I.T.C. (Rev. 2) in thousand U.S. Dollars
Importations Générales C.A.F. par Produits d'après la C.T.C.I. (Rév. 2) en milliers de Dollars E.U.

SITC CTCI	COMMODITY	1993 WEIGHT POIDS	1993 VALUE VALEUR	1994 WEIGHT POIDS	1994 VALUE VALEUR	1995 WEIGHT POIDS	1995 VALUE VALEUR	1996 WEIGHT POIDS	1996 VALUE VALEUR	PRODUIT
541	*MEDICINAL,PHARM PRODUCT	MK 11455	235310	MK 10732	242694	MK 11707	297526	MK 11612	315583	PROD MEDICINAUX PHARMACEUT
5413	ANTIBIOTICS IN BULK	K 740698	53952	K 830283	54095	K 953784	66474	K 862462	65551	ANTIBIOTIQUES NDA
54139	OTHER ANTIBIOTICS	K 285667	42671	K 386805	44426	K 504193	57369	K 428784	54298	AUTRES ANTIBIOTIQUES
5417	MEDICAMENTS	K 8371385	129759	K 8045936	136186	K 8679710	167634	K 8919084	180391	MEDICAMENTS
54179	— CONTNG OTH SUBSTANCES	K 6247498	93971	K 5370160	102117	K 5464484	113814	K 5594671	124836	MED CONT AUT SUBSTANCES
55	PERFUME,CLEANING ETC PRD		24679		21448		43550		36607	PROD POUR PARFUM,TOILETTE
562	*FERTILIZERS,MANUFACTURE	W 1505833	258413	W 913792	170570	W 1159038	275989	W 1844473	433183	ENGRAIS MANUFACTURES
5621	CHEM NITROGENOUS FERTLZR	W 393585	58572	W 79052	11348	W 190542	53256	W 673168	154530	ENGRAIS AZOTES
56216	UREA	W 389189	57638	W 77531	10976	W 189226	52863	W 641460	147215	UREE
5629	FERTILIZERS NES	W 1110826	199723	W 787158	152726	W 847874	198816	W 1078984	260036	ENGRAIS NDA
56292	NITROG–PHOS FERTILZR NES	W 988038	172680	W 725928	139302	W 700320	161340	W 970988	233277	ENGRAIS NDA CONT N P
58	PLASTIC MATERIALS ETC		263880		274703		367253		353686	MAT PLAST ARTIFICIELLES
582	PROD OF CONDENSATION ETC	W 42559	57120	W 110937	64689	W 52078	92459	W 61113	84845	PROD CONDENS,POLYCOND
5823	ALKYDS,OTHER POLYESTERS	W 25549	29180	W 92671	39626	W 36596	66039	W 46635	56925	ALKYDES ET AUT POLYESTERS
58231	— IN PRIMARY FORMS	W 24338	26090	W 91550	37108	W 34846	60338	W 46051	55156	SOUS FORMES PRIMAIRES
583	POLYMERIZATION ETC PRODS	W 247693	196140	W 240426	201132	W 226055	264206	W 277285	257131	PROD POLYMERISATION
5831	POLYETHYLENE	W 73838	48168	W 86303	53622	W 76647	68328	W 95531	74179	POLYETHYLENE
58311	— IN PRIMARY FORMS	W 63869	45536	W 75372	51039	W 61144	63250	W 82074	69872	POLYETHYLENE PRIMAIRES
5832	POLYPROPYLENE	W 64541	42965	W 69315	49418	W 54590	67167	W 62486	57906	POLYPROPYLENE
58321	— IN PRIMARY FORMS	W 62909	38236	W 67713	44926	W 52669	60473	W 60388	52290	POLYPROPYLENE PRIMAIRES
5834	POLYVINYL CHLORIDE	W 70228	54114	W 44541	42298	W 50276	58122	W 70018	54289	CHLORURE DE POLYVINYLE
58341	— IN PRIMARY FORMS	W 63835	42635	W 39435	33378	W 41059	44562	W 53787	41245	SOUS FORMES PRIMAIRES
5839	OTH POLYMRZTION ETC PROD	W 13700	19144	W 14826	21414	W 22677	33471	W 26281	38088	AUT PROD POLYMER COPOLYM
59	CHEMICAL MATERIALS NES		185699		175200		269119		265492	MAT PROD CHIMIQUES NDA
591	PESTICIDES,DISINFECTANTS	W 13523	68792	W 14695	64101	W 29127	147950	W 29211	139481	DESINF,INSECT,FONG,HERB
5911	INSECTICIDES,FOR RETAIL	W 10342	55861	W 10276	48517	W 23019	121852	W 23525	114942	INSECTICIDES VENTE DET
598	MISCEL CHEM PRODUCTS NES	W 52657	112951	W 56126	105824	W 58152	115659	W 69711	120812	PROD DIV INDUST CHIM NDA
5982	ANTI–KNOCK PREPARTNS ETC	W 12590	28697	W 14561	32489	W 13447	27719	W 16797	34779	PREPARAT ANTIDETONANTES
5989	CHEM PRODUCTS,PREPS NES	W 34084	78576	W 34179	67055	W 36445	79316	W 45052	77723	PROD PREP CHIMIQUES NDA
59899	OTH CHEM PRODS,PREPS,NES	W 24753	61741	W 24811	51690	W 25333	60706	W 32877	58391	AUT PRODUITS CHIMIQUES NDA
6	BASIC MANUFACTURES		902186		881886		1166897		1231728	ART MANUFACTURES
62	RUBBER MANUFACTURES NES		60173		58033		74347		90059	CAOUTCHOUC MANUFACTURE
625	RUBBER TYRES, TUBES ETC	N 2505462	45874	N 2772194	48558	N 3412461	58923	N 2811407	69611	PNEUS CAOUTCHOUC VULCANISE
6259	OTH TYRES,TYRE CASES,ETC	N 2063909	39874	N 2210491	38246	N 2386721	34976	N 1999708	47478	AUTRES PNEUS RECHAPES FLAPS
62599	TYRES NES,TYRE CASES,ETC	N 1248547	38598	N 1216123	37221	N 1049381	33170	N 1254808	45050	PNEUS,FLAPS
64	PAPER,PAPERBOARD AND MFR		134270		122634		153816		140767	PAPIERS,CARTONS & OUVRAGES
641	PAPER AND PAPERBOARD	W 221511	126800	W 193610	115685	W 154052	143076	W 154840	129985	PAPIERS ET CARTONS
6411	NEWSPRINT	W 71450	35868	W 78343	36535	W 67000	56384	W 61470	45064	PAPIER JOURNAL
6418	COATED ETC PAPER NES BLK	W 73606	30580	W 37384	25551	W 32573	29088	W 40636	31419	PAP,CARTONS COUCHES,ENDUITS
65	TEXTILE YARN,FABRICS,ETC		100373		76731		121406		110495	FILS,TISSUS,ARTICLES TEXTILE
651	TEXTILE YARN	W 23287	73865	W 19120	53532	W 16013	55093	W 17224	62129	FILS TEXTILES
6514	SYN FIB YRN,BULK,MONOFIL	W 11760	35939	W 8417	23909	W 5856	19110	W 7746	22621	FILS CONT 85% FIB TEXT SYNTH
66	NONMETAL MINERAL MFS NES		59471		75310		66807		61401	ART MIN NON METALLIQUES
661	LIME,CEMENT,BLDG PRODS	W 204116	10126	W 564663	28000	W 232030	12778	W 22485	2404	CHAUX,CIMENTS MAT CONSTR
6612	CEMENT	W 161854	9742	W 495821	27292	W 207475	12185	W 16968	1912	CIMENTS HYDRAULIQUES
67	IRON AND STEEL		352536		332828		447548		490855	FER ET ACIER
672	IRON,STEEL PRIMARY FORMS	W 22739	8228	W 41233	14553	W 101422	39128	W 114066	41845	LINGOTS FER,ACIER
674	IRN,STL UNIV,PLATE,SHEET	W 411620	202077	W 378046	181716	W 501749	238944	W 573420	245563	LARGES PLATS,TOLES
6747	TINNED PLATES,SHEETS	W 135238	49198	W 89653	41960	W 158538	59563	W 119541	47341	TOLES ETAMEES EN ACIER
6749	OTH IRN,STL PLATES,SHEET	W 200727	110997	W 228505	100210	W 229592	116576	W 293637	120401	AUTRES TOLES FER,ACIER
67491	— OF IRON OR SIMPLE STL	W 183059	82422	W 215468	80964	W 210575	94488	W 280584	102009	AUT TOLES AUTRES ACIER FIN
678	IRON,STL TUBES,PIPES,ETC	W 109882	94231	W 98302	92615	W 105605	112774	W 191734	134042	TUBES,TUYAUX EN FONTE,FER
6782	IRON,STL SEAMLESS TUBES	W 23281	23772	W 23626	33184	W 25435	22560	W 51598	51677	TUBES,TUYAUX SANS SOUDURE
6783	IRON,STL TUBES,PIPES NES	W 62096	48496	W 51840	39531	W 62828	63215	W 122003	57289	AUT TUBES,TUYAUX FER,ACIER
68	NON–FERROUS METALS		112156		102766		161849		163904	METAUX NON FERREUX
682	COPPER EXC CEMENT COPPER	W 13416	38077	W 12578	33136	W 18465	63897	W 19934	58330	CUIVRE
6821	COPPER NES,ALLOYS,UNWRT	W 5280	13357	W 5456	12127	W 10657	35452	W 11697	27455	CUIVRE BRUT
68212	COPPER REFINED,UNWROUGHT	W 5240	13270	W 5452	12114	W 10646	35409	W 11689	27424	CUIVRE AFFINE BRUT
684	ALUMINIUM	W 18843	41462	W 22535	45510	W 29863	61704	W 26033	66806	ALUMINIUM
69	METAL MANUFACTURES NES		68604		97823		125548		157534	ART MANUFACT EN METAL NDA
691	STRUCTURES AND PARTS NES	W 10706	14704	W 31848	41523	W 42632	50766	W 46069	63374	CONSTRUCT FER,ACIER,ALU
6911	STRUCTURES,PARTS IRN,STL	W 10598	14178	W 31830	41416	W 42541	50205	W 45972	62711	CONSTRUCT FER,ACIER,FONTE
699	BASE METAL MFRS NES	W 13389	28355	W 15617	30777	W 14528	42227	W 18633	40387	ART MANUFACTURES MET NDA
7	MACHINES,TRANSPORT EQUIP		3454801		2524788		3381098		3226566	MACHINES MATERIEL TRANSPORT
71	POWER GENERATING EQUIPMT		155232		331219		797043		736653	MACHINES GENERATRICES
711	STEAM BOILERS & AUX PLNT		6985		45698		157209		110049	GENERATEURS VAPEUR EAU ETC
7112	AUXILIARY BOILER PLANT	N 14	765	N 581	23787	N 217	37443	N 303	10934	APPAREILS AUXIL DU 711.1
7119	PTS NES OF APP OF 711	W 734	5122	W 3293	13896	W 17043	107513	W 5423	96253	PART,PIECES POUR 711
71191	PTS NES OF BOILERS	W 719	4991	W 3193	13458	W 16269	105266	W 4038	82366	PART,PIECES POUR 711.1
712	STEAM ENGINES,TURBINES		15756		70977		313920		234453	MACHINES A VAPEUR D'EAU PIEC
7126	STEAM POWR UNITS,ENGINES	N 66	10828	N 99	34920	N 39	4822	N 581	81194	MACHINES A VAPEUR D EAU
7129	STM ENGINE ETC PARTS NES	W 279	4927	W 2152	36057	W 95934	309098	W 15807	153259	PARTIES,PIECES DU 712.6
713	INTRNL COMBUS PSTN ENGIN		22766		29967		43417		102905	MOTEURS EXPL COMB INT, PIECE
7138	PISTON ENGINES NES	N 13463	3091	N 130413	9611	N 350900	20219	N 493120	57825	MOTEURS A PISTONS NDA
714	ENGINES AND MOTORS NES		4648		35184		41719		21860	MOTEURS NON ELECTRIQUES
716	ROTATING ELECTRIC PLANT		103700		133412		201118		220234	APP ELECTR ROTATIFS,PIECES
7162	AC MTRS,GENRTRS,GEN SETS	N 112084	92728	N 103675	105912	N 74574	170626	N 150391	133742	MOTEURS ELECTRIQUES
71623	GEN SETS WITH PISTN ENGN	N 8841	88011	N 12928	101142	N 4990	155559	N 4714	123111	GROUPES MOTEUR EXPLOSION
7169	PTS NES OF ROT ELEC PLNT	W 399	5222	W 2049	18112	W 1486	22453	W 5159	81564	PIECES MAC APP ROTATIFS
718	OTH POWER GENERATG MACHY		1377		15980		39660		47151	AUTRES MOTEURS PARTIES
7188	WIND,WATER,ETC ENGINES		1371		15980		39660		47151	MOT MACHINES MOTRICES NDA
71889	PARTS NES OF 71881,71882	W 37	374	W 526	4547	W 1631	36761	W 3041	41142	PARTIES DES POS 718.81,82
72	MACHS FOR SPCL INDUSTRYS		1021663		664414		799099		631929	MAC SPECIALES POUR INDUST
722	TRACTORS NON–ROAD		43569		37191	N 241	141384		50233	TRACTEURS
7224	WHEELED TRACTORS NES		43170		37180	N 240	141351		50225	TRACTEURS A ROUES
723	CIVIL ENGINEERG EQUIP ETC		96914		83814		70918		100110	APPAREILS DE GENIE CIVIL
7234	CONST,MINING MACHNRY NES		79164	N 19675	72217	N 44044	64252	N 80700	96315	MACH POUR LA CONST, MINES
72341	SELF–PROPELLD DOZERS,ETC	N 1144	29546	N 311	15457	N 280	21971	N 273	10671	BULLDOZERS
724	TEXTILE,LEATHER MACHNRY		690169		304469		291269		165176	MACH POUR INDUSTRIE TEXTILE
7244	SPINNING,EXTRDNG,ETC MCH		380473		135433		176908		90815	MACH POUR LE FILAGE
72441	TEXTILE EXTRUDING MACHS	N 317	42442	N 290	17341	N 4164	114533	N 512	34775	MACH FILAGE TEXT SYNTH
72442	FIBRE PROCESSNG MACH NES	N 11399	136983	N 5931	48556	N 714	16807	N 701	14165	MACH PREP MAT TEXTILES
72443	SPINNING,REELING,ETC MCH	N 149014	162218	N 26067	53421	N 6870	28845	N 3088	15451	MACH POUR LA FILATURE
72449	PTS NES OF MACHS OF 7244	W 3814	38830	W 1767	16115	W 1788	16724	W 2739	26424	PIECES DES MACH DU 724.4
7245	WEAVING,FELT MFG,ETC MCH	N 30973	183346	N 17758	79950	N 15165	35974	N 12631	23842	METIERS A TISSER,PIECES
72451	WEAVING MACHINES (LOOMS)	N 15545	110686	N 9732	50492	N 7910	16088	N 8193	15065	METIERS A TISSER
72452	KNITTING MACHINES	N 3629	40756	N 3134	15056	N 1439	12244	N 1454	4322	METIERS A BONNETERIE
72453	GIMPING,WARPING ETC MCHS	N 11791	31743	N 4891	14402	N 5815	7641	N 2978	4453	METIERS A TULLE ETC
7247	TEXTILE MACHINERY NES		69986		51912		48263		32745	MACH LAVAGE,TEINTURE TEX
72474	OTH TEXTILE MACHNERY NES	N 62511	63379	N 15677	46275	N 22440	45393	N 13620	29101	MACH LAVAGE ETC MAT TEXT
728	OTH MACHY FOR SPCL INDUS		135054		174674		240868		257579	AUT MACH IND PARTICULIERES

4. General Imports C.I.F. by Commodities according to the S.I.T.C. (Rev. 2) in thousand U.S. Dollars
Importations Générales C.A.F. par Produits d'après la C.T.C.I. (Rév. 2) en milliers de Dollars E.U.

SITC CTCI	COMMODITY	1993 WEIGHT POIDS	1993 VALUE VALEUR	1994 WEIGHT POIDS	1994 VALUE VALEUR	1995 WEIGHT POIDS	1995 VALUE VALEUR	1996 WEIGHT POIDS	1996 VALUE VALEUR	PRODUIT
7283	OTHR MINERAL WORKG MACHY		29467		49203		37285		28166	MACH TRIER,CRIBLER,BROYER
72834	MINRL MOULDING ETC MACHY	N 3864	8880	N 5727	30250	N 4798	25552	N 450	2573	MACH AGGLO CIMENT ETC
7284	MACHY FOR SPCL INDUS NES		103153		123260		199423		224542	MACH SPEC IND PARTICUL.
72848	OTH MCHY WITH INDIV FNCT	N 124648	45374	N 71756	78799	N 72430	128336	N 39694	81915	AUTRES MACHINES NDA
72849	PTS OF MACHS OF 7284 ETC	W 2574	36039	W 2844	31241	W 4116	50126	W 21966	133239	PIECES DU 728.4 ETC
74	GENRL INDUSTRL MACHY NES		337243		413282		487443		529814	MACH APP INDUSTRIE
741	HEATING,COOLING EQUIPMNT		63843		120299		99024		144202	MACH CHAUFFAGE,PIECES
7416	HEATING,COOLING EQU NES		23523		65744		46015	N 16961	98893	APP CHANGEMENT TEMP
743	PUMPS NES,CENTRFUGES ETC		55786		55080		122313		97036	POMPES COMPRES,VENT ETC
7431	PUMPS FOR GASES ETC	N 328483	22339	N 362425	28796	N 625626	53159	N 401687	36745	POMPES AIR A VIDE,COMPRES
7436	GAS,LIQUID FILTERS ETC	N 1418501	23469	N 1359784	12939	N 1108653	37214	N 920309	33432	APP POUR FILT DES LIQUIDES
744	MECHANICAL HANDLING EQU		105929		138973		127984		118945	EQUIP MANUTENTION PIECES
7449	PTS NES OF MACHY OF 7442	W 11952	77139	W 18037	110888	W 9118	98258	W 12739	90391	PIECES DU 744.2
749	NONELEC MACH PTS,ACC NES		72980		58649		91294		108349	PIECES MACH NON ELEC NDA
7492	COCKS,VALVES ETC NES		27877		22496		30893	MN 11775	54812	ART ROB,SIM POUR TUYAUX
75	OFFICE MACHNES,ADP EQUIP		64262		62748		85688		54954	MACH BUREAU TRAIT AUTOM
752	AUTOMTIC DATA PROC EQUIP		47199	N 158027	46822	N 243525	60684	N 196487	34797	MACH TRAIT INFORMATION
76	TELECOMM,SOUND EQUIPMENT		265791		163803		202707		140327	EQUIPMENT DE TELECOM
764	TELECOM EQPT,PTS,ACC NES		252885		156700		174750		128420	EQUIP TELECOM,PIECES
7641	LINE TELEPHONE,ETC EQUIP	N 560572	38708	N 156453	6867	N 76125	10059	N 91585	11413	APP TELEPHON PAR FIL
7649	PTS NES OF EQUIPMT OF 76	W 6410	208287	W 7191	134483	W 5812	152534	W 5514	97449	PIECES DE LA DIV 76
76491	PTS NES OF APPAR OF 7641	W 2655	162277	W 2087	98746	W 1220	92686	W 1108	51823	PIECES POUR 764.1
76493	TELECOMM EQUIPMT PTS NES	W 2584	28383	W 3236	24615	W 3276	44330	W 2659	36610	PIECES 761,762,764.3,8
77	ELECTRIC MACHNRY NES ETC		234608		298389		364986		438903	MACH APP ELECT NDA
771	ELECTRIC POWER MACHY NES		29364		34569		95007		86122	MACH PROD,TRANS ELECTR
7711	TRANSFORMERS,ELECTRICAL	N 4177	21027	N 9075	23372	N 17322	71149	N 7339	72108	TRANSFO ELECTRIQUES
77118	OTHER ELEC TRANSFORMERS	N 3750	20389	N 6075	22558	N 17032	71131	N 4850	72056	AUTRES TRANSFO ELECTRIQ
772	SWITCHGEAR ETC,PARTS NES		39544		41308		82880	MN 102454	106195	APP COUPURE,SECT ETC
7721	SWITCHGEAR ETC		36378		37865		78071	MN 67507	103486	APP COUPURE,SECTIONMNT
773	ELECTR DISTRIBUTNG EQUIP	W 17252	64569	W 15019	40305	W 17921	57545	W 47413	117917	EQUIPMT DISTRIBUTION ELECT
7731	INSULATED WIRE,CABLE ETC	W 15692	61857	W 9809	30784	W 11274	43837	W 33331	92501	FILS,CABLES ISOLES ELECT
778	ELECTRICAL MACHINERY NES		51779		134997		63410		78750	AUTRES MACH ELECT NDA
7788	OTH ELEC MACHY,EQUIP NES		34301		121425		42826		57969	AUT MACH APP ELEC NDA
77889	ELEC PARTS OF MACHY NES	W 7644	22886	W 19077	113794	W 1053	15817	W 5149	40413	PIECES ELEC DE MACH NDA
78	ROAD VEHICLES		1021501		386761		453772		551269	VEHICULES ROUTIERS
781	PASS MOTOR VEH EXC BUSES	N 75738	412961	N 29786	173988	N 35123	217210	N 186468	244852	AUTO TRANSPORT PERSONNES
782	LORRIES,SPCL MTR VEH NES	N 25458	261778		114361	N 15523	109494	N 14111	162021	VEHICULES SPECIAUX,MARCH
7821	LORRIES,TRUCKS	N 24727	236514	N 9111	100313	N 15355	93313	N 13780	132866	VEHICULES TRANSP MARCHAND
783	ROAD MOTOR VEHICLES NES	N 18779	237502	N 1612	13743	N 924	15368	N 2043	25769	VEHICULES ROUTIERS NDA
7831	BUSES	N 18519	235549	N 1607	13670	N 856	11667	N 1660	21064	VOITURES TRANSPORT COMMUN
784	MOTOR VEH PRTS,ACCES NES		47990		35723		42572		46903	PIECES 722,781,782,783
7849	OTHER MOTOR VEHCL PARTS		43938		34319		41505		45872	PIECES 722,781,782,783
785	CYCLES,ETC MOTRZD OR NOT		58984		47490		66769		69786	MOTOCYCLES SCOOTERS
7851	MOTORCYCLES ETC	N 95156	42721	N 76863	31890	N 96071	45572	N 122414	54088	MOTO VELO MOTEUR AUXIL
79	OTHR TRANSPORT EQUIPMENT		325388		180607		158253		118589	AUTRE MATERIEL TRANSPORT
792	AIRCRFT ETC		242600		136749		45460		85291	APP NAVIGATION AERIENNE
7924	AIRCRFT NES OVER 15000KG	N 16	55179	N 217	64508		46		81	AERODYNES PLUS 15000 KG
7929	AIRCRAFT PARTS NES	W 1241	153788	W 1233	69537	W 698	43050	W 1080	84120	PIECES DU 792
793	SHIPS AND BOATS ETC		54850		26770		89929		6659	NAVIRES BATEAUX,ETC
7933	VESSELS FOR BREAKING UP	N 25	41914	N 5	12460	N 30	67248			BATEAUX A DEPECER
8	MISC MANUFACTURED GOODS		249995		217854		270412		317673	ART MANUFACTURES DIVERS
87	PRECISION INSTRUMNTS NES		118682		90372		97344		115901	INSTRUM,APPAR SCIENT NDA
872	MEDICAL INSTRUMENTS NES	MN 165898	37104	MN 178825	25083	MN 244972	27217	MN 278052	32640	INSTR,APP MEDIC-CHIR NDA
874	MEASURNG,CONTROLNG INSTR		78306		58880		65137		70769	INSTRUMENTS DE MESURE
8749	INSTR PTS NES,ACCESSORYS	W 943	31024	W 1276	23028	W 699	31709	W 887	27331	PIECES 873,874.3,54,874.8
88	PHOTO EQU,OPTICL GDS ETC		31811		32273		43667		40430	APP,FOURN PHOTO,OP,MONTR
882	PHOTO,CINEMA SUPPLIES		26419		27230		32906		29107	PRODUITS PHOTO,CINEMA
89	MISC MANUFCTRD GOODS NES		93893		86921		118433		148143	ART MANUFACTURES DIVERS
899	OTHER MANUFACTURED GOODS		38309		35127		56131		78666	AUT ART MANUF DIVERS NDA
8991	CARVED,MOULDED GOODS		29205		27212		47591		68336	MAT A TAILLER,A MOULER
89911	GOODS OF ANML CARVNG MTL		26430		24551		45000		66088	ECAILLE,NACRE,IVOIRE ETC
9	GOODS NOT CLASSD BY KIND		19592		41383		189314		384885	ART TRANSACT NON CLASSES
931	*SPECIAL TRANSACTIONS		15028		37311		19281		55067	TRANS.SPECIALES
971	*GOLD,NON MONETARY NES	K 271	3101	K 188	2234	K 12843	168279	K 28916	328772	OR NON MONETAIRE
97101	NONMON GLD UNWRT,SEMIMFD	K 271	3101	K 188	2234	K 12843	168279	K 28450	325816	OR,ALLIAGES D'OR BRUTS

5. General Exports F.O.B. by Commodities according to the S.I.T.C. (Rev. 2) in thousand U.S. Dollars
Exportations Générales F.O.B. par Produits d'après la C.T.C.I. (Rév. 2) en milliers de Dollars E.U.

SITC CTCI	COMMODITY	1993 WEIGHT POIDS	1993 VALUE VALEUR	1994 WEIGHT POIDS	1994 VALUE VALEUR	1995 WEIGHT POIDS	1995 VALUE VALEUR	1996 WEIGHT POIDS	1996 VALUE VALEUR	PRODUIT
	ALL COMMODITIES		6877530		7356903		8157874		9322199	TOUS PRODUITS
0	FOOD AND LIVE ANIMALS		633283		700407		930803		818074	ALIMENTS,ANIMAUX VIVANTS
03	FISH AND PREPARATIONS		201872		143155		150435		147095	POISSONS ET PREPARATIONS
034	FISH,FRESH,CHILLED,FROZN	W 34979	86684	W 20007	31653	W 21076	31519	W 26465	33973	POISSON FRAIS, REFRIG,CONG
0342	FISH FROZEN,EXCL FILLETS	W 27447	70581	W 12968	21346	W 12708	18962	W 15650	19424	POISSONS CONGELES
036	SHELL FISH FRESH,FROZEN	W 23216	94117	W 23891	97119	W 21943	97145	W 25160	95216	CRUSTACES,MOLLUSQUES
04	CEREALS AND PREPARATIONS		272898		319124		482305		506508	CEREALES ET PRODUITS
042	RICE	W 933782	270024	W 1398506	316477	W 1579244	478798	W 1677545	500657	RIZ
0422	RICE SEMI–MILLED,MILLED	W 933782	270024	W 1398506	316477	W 1579244	478798	W 1677545	500657	RIZ POLI,GLACE INCL BRISURES
04221	RICE MILLED UNBROKEN	W 933782	270024	W 1398506	316477	W 1579244	478798	W 1677545	500657	RIZ POLI,GLACE EXCL BRISURES
05	VEGETABLES AND FRUIT		61768		55772		53198		84660	LEGUMES ET FRUITS
057	FRUIT,NUTS,FRESH,DRIED	W 128041	46798	W 133377	42839	W 119255	37216	W 179033	60588	FRUITS FRAIS OU SECS
0579	FRUIT FRESH OR DRIED NES	W 84845	34675	W 100624	34733	W 78085	29563	W 126328	50056	FRUITS FRAIS,SECS NDA
06	SUGAR AND PREPS,HONEY		75897		143243		229948		57428	SUCRES ET PRODUITS
061	SUGAR AND HONEY	W 1209961	67019	W 1858368	135344	W 1953681	222024	W 751695	51887	SUCRES ET MIEL
0612	REFINED SUGAR ETC			W 148862	49097	W 317623	123365	W 100	46	SUCRES RAFFINES
0615	MOLASSES	W 1208646	65277	W 1707164	83783	W 1630505	95443	W 746787	47744	MELASSES
07	COFFEE,TEA,COCOA,SPICES		12236		30780		10353		13625	CAFE,THE,CACAO,EPICES
2	CRUDE MATERLS,EXCL FUELS		326795		187944		347955		598987	MAT BRUTES NON COMESTIBLES
26	TEXTILE FIBRES AND WASTE		252317		103778		246476		481459	FIBRES TEXTILES
263	COTTON	W 275221	237131	W 127133	84942	W 172582	224581	W 468171	458658	COTON
2631	RAW COTTON,EXCL LINTERS	W 179330	186604	W 17129	19309	W 84197	161038	W 260365	403681	COTON EN MASSE
2633	COTTON WASTE,UNCOMBED	W 92609	49970	W 109802	65564	W 83465	61420	W 95534	52799	DECHETS DE COTON
29	CRUDE ANIMAL,VEG MAT NES		49659		55292		66074		83264	MATIERES BRUTES ANIM,VEGET
291	CRUDE ANIMAL MTRIALS NES	W 29320	14441	W 24870	13826	W 34027	19545	W 38701	28602	MATIERES BRUTES ANIMALES
292	CRUDE VEG MATERIALS NES	W 68814	35218	W 62989	41466	W 62335	46530	W 59094	54662	MAT BRUTES VEGETALES NDA
2922	NAT GUMS,RESINS,LACS,ETC	W 41326	25483	W 41270	30329	W 42700	33429	W 36384	38435	GOMME LAQUE
3	MINERAL FUELS ETC		67558		57236		79767		70509	COMBUSTIBLES MINERAUX LUB
33	PETROLEUM AND PRODUCTS		67558		57236		78891		69375	PETROLE ET DERIVES
333	CRUDE PETROLEUM	W 379218	56195	W 235159	36428	W 308217	44290	W 347075	50757	HUILES BRUTES DE PETROLE
334	PETROLEUM PRODUCTS,REFIN	W 44000	6376		14233	W 179023	27412	W 112021	16851	PRODUITS RAFFINES
3344	FUEL OILS,NES	W 44000	6376	W 113300	14233	W 172709	25471	W 112010	16847	FUEL OILS
5	CHEMCLS,RELATED PROD NES		31833		45243		54787		72591	PRODUITS CHIMIQUES
541	*MEDICINAL,PHARM PRODUCT	K 3034359	19829	K 3597978	31963	K 3636271	32312	K 5590706	43592	PROD MEDICINAUX PHARMACEUT
5417	MEDICAMENTS	K 2138074	13926	K 2760781	24322	K 2750759	25635	K 3529443	28864	MEDICAMENTS
54179	— CONTNG OTH SUBSTANCES	K 2138074	13926	K 2760781	24322	K 2747574	25523	K 3529257	28856	MED CONT AUT SUBSTANCES
6	BASIC MANUFACTURES		3800712		4295865		4584004		5248245	ART MANUFACTURES
61	LEATHER,DRESSED FUR,ETC		240262		268546		279535		275308	CUIRS,PELLETERIES
611	LEATHER	A 14820	216484	A 17244	248064	A 16794	266315	A 16379	263112	CUIRS,PEAUX PREPARES
6113	CALF LEATHER	A 2567	43109	A 2823	46551	A 2384	47467	A 2496	50818	CUIRS,PEAUX DE VEAUX
6114	LEATHR BOVINE NES,EQUINE	A 3934	64086	A 5029	75144	A 4588	71377	A 4632	70896	CUIRS DE BOVINS
6115	LEATHER FROM SHEEP,LAMBS	A 1107	18596	A 1870	28945	A 1676	27477	A 1663	29450	PEAUX D'OVINS PREPAREES
6116	LEATHER OF OTH HIDE,SKIN	A 7062	90177	A 7519	97404	A 8141	119973	A 7589	111949	PEAUX PREP D'AUTRES ANIMAUX
61161	LEATHER FROM GOAT,KID	A 7058	90117	A 7485	96962	A 8078	118612	A 7468	110182	PEAUX DE CAPRINS PREPAREES
612	LEATHER ETC MANUFACTURES		23778	W 2160	20482	W 1280	13220		12155	OUVRAGES EN CUIRS NDA
65	TEXTILE YARN,FABRICS,ETC		3506944		3977689		4255967		4919099	FILS,TISSUS,ARTICLES TEXTILE
651	TEXTILE YARN	W 591608	1200305	W 562229	1421569	W 526644	1648199	W 594825	1672574	FILS TEXTILES
6513	COTTON YARN	W 568497	1148186	W 533329	1345267	W 507338	1587430	W 570045	1601595	FILS DE COTON
6514	SYN FIB YRN,BULK,MONOFIL	W 22869	51517	W 27973	73387	W 14626	46095	W 20544	59031	FILS CONT 85% FIB TEXT SYNTH
65144	— TEXTRD,CONT POLYESTER	W 22383	50009	W 27217	71246	W 13476	42466	W 19583	55250	FILS TEX FI CONT POLYESTERS
652	COTTON FABRICS,WOVEN	A 1068081	837990	A 1123817	962462	A 1062294	1072543	A 1448568	1403068	TISSUS DE COTON
6521	GREY WOVEN COTTON FABRIC	A 499813	370084	A 525235	461506	A 502205	515974	A 603827	583884	TISSUS COT ECRUS NON MERCER
65214	GREY WOVEN COTTON NES	A 478726	351764	A 493878	437415	A 444244	468596	A 476621	492472	AUT TISSUS 85% COTON ECRUS
65215	GREY WOVN COTN BLEND NES	A 17121	15099	A 27909	20728	A 54874	44226	A 121946	86382	AUT TIS MOINS 85% COT ECRUS
6522	WOVEN COTTON BLEACHD,ETC	A 568268	467906	A 598582	500956	A 560089	556569	A 844741	819184	TISSUS COTON BLANCHIS ETC
65221	COTTON GAUZE BLEACHD,ETC	A 24949	28093	A 14742	18016	A 27803	32313	A 23422	25943	TISSUS COTON POINT DE GAZE
65224	BLCHED COTTON FABRIC NES	A 493258	396087	A 482641	385839	A 407499	378669	A 478384	432395	AUT TIS PLUS 85% COT BLANCHI
65225	BLCHD COTN BLEND FAB NES	A 45438	39921	A 96615	93361	A 123186	143865	A 341957	359782	AUT TIS MOINS 85% COT BLANCH
653	WOVN MAN–MADE FIB FABRIC		536883		651697		503047		519113	TISSUS FIBRES SYNTH,ARTIF
6531	CONT SYNT WEAVES NONPILE	A 645907	534400	A 853452	650288	A 533268	502270	A 594849	517877	TISSUS FIBRES SYNTH CONTINUE
65314	CONT SYN TYRE CORD FABRC	A 237336	172238	A 299876	224470	A 132912	129513	A 148529	139396	TIS ARMATURE PNEUMATIQUES
65315	CONT SYN TXTL FABRIC NES	A 408571	362162	A 553576	425818	A 400357	372756	A 446320	378481	TIS PLUS 85% TEXT SYNT CONT
655	KNITTED,ETC FABRICS		91030		91914		94111	W 19353	93500	ETOF BONNETERIE PIECES ETC
6552	OTHER KNIT ETC FAB NONEL		91030		91914		94111	W 19353	93500	ETOF BON NON ELAS NON SYNT
657	SPECIAL TXTL FABRC,PRODS	W 18382	39163	W 10723	34708	W 9917	40576	W 10300	41587	TISSUS SPECIAUX
6577	TEXTILES FOR MACHINERY	W 8791	33533	W 8293	31047	W 7947	36787	W 8402	37612	OUATES,MECHES ART TEXT
65771	TEXTILE WADDING NES ETC	W 8608	31987	W 8146	30091	W 7759	36205	W 8260	37104	OUATES,ARTICLES EN OUATE
658	TEXTILE ARTICLES NES		631243		611384		726083		929274	ART FACONNES MAT TEXTILES
6581	BAGS,SACKS OF TEXTILES	W 17143	19744	W 5722	18498	W 4685	20874	W 6970	29601	SACS EMBALLAGE TEXTILES
6582	MADE–UP CANVAS GOODS	W 20297	39314	W 15100	33775	W 14653	38597	W 14601	36065	BACHES,TENTES ETC
6584	LINENS ETC		447729		448799		536437		703359	LINGE DE MAISON
65841	BED LINEN OF COTTON	W 35745	220386	W 37096	234149	W 41536	288581	W 51958	336988	LINGE DE LIT DE COTON
65842	BED LINEN OF OTHR FIBRES	W 9239	60999	W 8220	53015	W 9761	68770	W 17756	120564	LINGE DE LIT AUT FIBRES
65845	OTHER LINEN OF COTTON	W 33599	144359	W 30280	137193	W 30641	154526	W 42249	205395	LINGE DE TOILETTE COTON
65849	OTH FURN ART OF OTH FIBR	N 4456824	11587	N 6172308	16124	N 4473024	15602	N 8951760	28266	AUT ART AMEUBLEMENT AUT FIBR
6589	OTH TEXTILE ARTICLES NES		123007		109002		125100		154760	AUT ART EN TEXTILES NDA
65898	KNITTED ETC ARTICLES NES		107253		90452		105180	MN 532303718	119467	ART BONNET NON ELASTIQUE
65899	TXTL ARTCLES NONKNIT NES	MN 16961	15752	MN 17491	18550	MN 17143	19917	MN 28382	35284	ART TIS AUT QUE BONNETERIE
659	FLOOR COVERINGS,ETC	A 3064	160225	A 3430	191163	A 2602	151746	A 4450	238495	COUVRE–PARQUETS,TAPIS ETC
6592	CARPETS ETC KNOTTED	A 2785	157728	A 3011	187503	A 2317	148909	A 3789	230884	TAPIS POINTS NOUES,ENROULES
65921	— OF WOOL OR FINE HAIR	A 2785	157728	A 3011	187495	A 2317	148909	A 3789	230884	TAP NOUES,ENROULES LAINE
69	METAL MANUFACTURES NES		30684		28590		30012		29671	ART MANUFACT EN METAL NDA
7	MACHINES,TRANSPORT EQUIP		51230		34220		43808		55125	MACHINES MATERIEL TRANSPORT
72	MACHS FOR SPCL INDUSTRYS		26862		13537		14210		19554	MAC SPECIALES POUR INDUST
8	MISC MANUFACTURED GOODS		1938262		2011198		2090593		2441011	ART MANUFACTURES DIVERS
84	CLOTHING AND ACCESSORIES		1584558		1615072		1665023		1940961	VETEMENTS
842	MENS OUTERWEAR NOT KNIT	MN 84971	223844	MN 100924	242589	MN 82900	222587	MN 290891	279931	VET DESSUS POUR HOMMES
8422	— SUITS	N 6911940	17049	MN 12942	28673	MN 14902	27546	MN 15036	29917	COMPLETS HOMMES MAT TEXT
84223	—— OF MAN–MADE FIBRES	N 6890352	16983	MN 12932	28645	MN 14898	27536	MN 15036	29917	COMPLETS HOMMES FIB SYNT
8423	— TROUSERS,BREECHES ETC	MN 47029	118052	MN 48503	112056	MN 44614	123357	MN 50492	159197	PANTALONS HOMMES MAT TEX
8424	— JACKETS,BLAZERS ETC	MN 10207	36967	MN 10869	34002	N 5595624	23269	MN 156661	31602	VESTES HOMMES MAT TEXTIL
8429	— OTHER OUTER GARMENTS	MN 20753	51521	MN 28554	67682	MN 17786	48409	MN 68683	59129	AUT VET DES HOM MAT TEX
843	WOMENS OUTERWEAR NONKNIT	MN 76445	203372	MN 73255	184696	MN 61332	163645	MN 72752	220900	VET DESSUS FEMMES MAT TEX
8432	-- SUITS AND COSTUMES	N 4831404	14062	N 7889052	19433	MN 10856	27463	MN 24083	58321	COSTUMES–TAIL MAT TEXIL
8433	— DRESSES	MN 13733	37676	MN 16751	38889	MN 12432	36801	MN 9962	32138	ROBES EN MAT–TEXTILES
8435	— BLOUSES	MN 16017	43742	MN 13423	34873	N 7723668	21199	MN 9123	26958	BLOUSES FEM MAT TEXTILES
8439	— OTHER OUTER GARMENTS	MN 36674	93081	MN 30907	80395	MN 27253	68721	MN 25425	90326	AUT VET DES FEM MAT TEXT
844	UNDER GARMENTS NOT KNIT	MN 52743	153893	MN 61919	155795	MN 54767	167883	MN 62650	204540	VETEMENT DESSOUS MAT TEX
8441	— MENS SHIRTS	MN 34460	100464	MN 43131	109579	MN 40443	122173	MN 49142	165637	CHEMISES HOMMES MAT TEXT
84411	—— OF COTTON	MN 31527	93194	MN 39786	102386	MN 38201	116417	MN 46669	158511	CHEMISES HOMMES DE COTON
8442	— MENS,OTHR THAN SHIRTS	MN 17792	52283	MN 18182	45236	MN 14065	44984	MN 13362	38572	SOUS–VET HOMMES MAT TEXT

5. General Exports F.O.B. by Commodities according to the S.I.T.C. (Rev. 2) in thousand U.S. Dollars
Exportations Générales F.O.B. par Produits d'après la C.T.C.I. (Rév. 2) en milliers de Dollars E.U.

SITC CTCI	COMMODITY	1993 WEIGHT POIDS	1993 VALUE VALEUR	1994 WEIGHT POIDS	1994 VALUE VALEUR	1995 WEIGHT POIDS	1995 VALUE VALEUR	1996 WEIGHT POIDS	1996 VALUE VALEUR	PRODUIT
845	OUTERWEAR KNIT NONELASTC	MN 67528	192059	MN 65212	183279	MN 63858	195047	MN 783382	238336	VET DESSOUS,ACCES BONNET
8459	— OTHER,CLTHG ACCESRYS	MN 55918	165063	MN 53926	157788	MN 55471	171800	MN 396737	209073	AUT VET DESSUS DE BONNE
846	UNDER GARMENTS KNITTED	MN 107609	257034	MN 132654	319875	MN 125016	365693	MN 1186200	398033	SOUS VETS DE BONNETERIE
8462	— OF COTTON NON ELASTIC	MN 49247	103308	MN 54070	118450	MN 42200	110260	MN 399582	117965	SOUS–VET BONNET COTON
84629	——— OTHER	MN 49247	103308	MN 54070	118450	MN 42200	110260	MN 399582	117965	AUT SOUS–VET BONNET COTON
8463	— OF SYNTH FBR NONELAST	MN 57653	153010	MN 77733	200303	MN 81921	254104	MN 784875	278953	SOUS–VET BONNET FIB SYNT
84632	——— MENS SHIRTS	MN 57468	152759	MN 77362	199943	MN 81637	253872	MN 211395	278897	CHEMISES DE BON FIB SYNMT
847	TEXTILE CLTHNG ACCES NES	MN 225778	123093	MN 257976	138999	MN 254893	167342	MN 246196	160985	ACCES VET MAT TEXT NDA
8471	— NOT KNITTED	MN 98041	56853	MN 106023	51538	MN 79455	46679	MN 110926	48611	ACCES VET MAT TEX NON BON
84712	SHAWLS,VEILS ETC,NOT KNT	MN 25700	36955	MN 26467	28761	MN 20944	28019	MN 15033	20477	ECHARPES ETC MAT TEXT
8472	CLTHNG ACCESRYS ETC KNIT	MN 127737	66240	MN 151953	87460	MN 175438	120663	MN 135270	112373	ACCES VET BONNE NDA
84721	KNIT GLOVES,ETC NONELAST	MN 84711	21059	MN 95403	27800	MN 107009	38485	MN 103195	35136	GANTERIE BONNET NON ELAS
84722	KNIT SOCKS,ETC NONELASTC	MN 43026	45181	MN 56551	59660	MN 68429	82177	MN 32074	77238	CHAUSSETTES BON. NON ELAS
848	HEADGEAR,NONTXTL CLOTHNG	MN 53607	431263	MN 56733	389839	MN 64048	382828	MN 55904	438237	VET ACCES MAT AUT QUE TEX
8481	LEATHER CLOTHES,ACCESSOR	MN 53197	430612	MN 56286	389442	MN 63864	382505	MN 55261	437780	VET ACCES MAT CUIR ARTIF
851	*FOOTWEAR	P 8423471	30441	P 8440551	31628	MP 10078	47952	P 8085522	47960	CHAUSSURES
85102	FOOTWEAR LEATHER	P 8285281	29716	P 8332896	30935	MP 9923	47196	P 7729997	45291	CHAUS SEMELLES EN CUIR
87	PRECISION INSTRUMNTS NES		107174		94667		110705		138198	INSTRUM,APPAR SCIENT NDA
872	MEDICAL INSTRUMENTS NES	MN 81493	102038	MN 65698	93882	MN 76250	108189	MN 96893	135581	INSTR,APP MEDIC–CHIR NDA
87202	OTH MEDICAL INSTRUMENTS	MN 81493	102038	MN 65698	93882	MN 76250	108185	MN 96891	135532	INSTRUM,APP MEDECINE
89	MISC MANUFCTRD GOODS NES		206208		257490		257856		305702	ART MANUFACTURES DIVERS
894	TOYS,SPORTING GOODS,ETC		140028		194569	MN 57130	189086		223358	VOITURES ENFANTS,JOUETS
8947	OTH SPORT GDS,FAIR AMUSM	MN 52572	139549	MN 68722	193936	MN 55622	188142	MN 4665086	222494	AUT ART DE SPORT
89472	OTH OUTDOOR SPORT GOODS	MN 50049	139418	MN 66871	193635	MN 55217	188019	MN 61407	222250	ART POUR JEUX PLEIN AIR
899	OTHER MANUFACTURED GOODS		42351		43405		47457		58913	AUT ART MANUF DIVERS NDA
8991	CARVED,MOULDED GOODS		38011		41623		44841		53880	MAT A TAILLER,A MOULER
89911	GOODS OF ANML CARVNG MTL		38001		41614		44742		53871	ECAILLE,NACRE,IVOIRE ETC

1. HISTORICAL SERIES, 1961–1996 SPECIAL TRADE, IMPORTS C.I.F., EXPORTS F.O.B. #1
SERIES HISTORIQUES, 1961–1996 COMMERCE SPECIAL, IMPORTATIONS C.A.F., EXPORTATIONS F.O.B

YEAR ANNEE	VALUE IN MILLION BALBOAS VALEUR EN MILLION BALBOAS MERCHANDISE –MARCHANDISE IMPORTS	EXPORTS	GOLD –OR IMPORTS	EXPORTS	CONVERSION FACTORS U.S. CENTS PER BALBOA FACTEURS DE CONVERSION CENTS E.U. PAR BALBOA IMPORTS	EXPORTS	INDEX NUMBERS –INDICES QUANTUM IMPORTS	EXPORTS	UNIT VALUE VALEUR UNITAIRE IMPORTS	EXPORTS
1961	124.00	30.30	0.21		100.0000	100.0000				
1962	145.20	48.00	0.39		100.0000	100.0000				
1963	162.80	60.00	0.31		100.0000	100.0000				
1964	181.40	69.70	0.53		100.0000	100.0000				
1965	208.40	79.30	0.43		100.0000	100.0000				
1966	234.80	89.50	0.34		100.0000	100.0000				
1967	250.70	93.90	0.66		100.0000	100.0000				
1968	266.30	99.80	0.71		100.0000	100.0000				
1969	305.40	112.70	2.30		100.0000	100.0000				
1970	357.00	106.30	0.86		100.0000	100.0000		105		35
1971	395.80	114.90	0.95		100.0000	100.0000		112		35
1972	440.50	121.10	0.57		100.0000	100.0000		108		37
1973	508.00	135.30	0.66		100.0000	100.0000		122		60
1974	829.20	204.30			100.0000	100.0000		158		85
1975	952.50	304.90			100.0000	100.0000				99
1976	912.20	256.50			100.0000	100.0000		139		90
1977	938.10	270.80			100.0000	100.0000		147		81
1978	845.00	247.00			100.0000	100.0000		147		79
1979	1063.00	295.00			100.0000	100.0000		134		96
1980	1288.90	353.40			100.0000	100.0000		124		123
1981	1562.10	319.40			100.0000	100.0000		106		129
1982	1568.30	309.30			100.0000	100.0000		121		104
1983	1413.00	303.50			100.0000	100.0000		107		115
1984	1429.60	256.30			100.0000	100.0000		81		113
1985	1391.80	306.50			100.0000	100.0000		97		106
1986	1283.75	327.05			100.0000	100.0000		94		93
1987	1306.36	336.16			100.0000	100.0000		94		103
1988	815.07	292.45			100.0000	100.0000		79		93
1989	964.76	297.21			100.0000	100.0000		93		95
1990	1538.60	340.10			100.0000	100.0000		100		100
1991	1695.00	358.40			100.0000	100.0000		95		101
1992	2023.60	501.50			100.0000	100.0000		97		
1993	2187.80	553.20			100.0000	100.0000		116		
1994	2404.10	583.30			100.0000	100.0000				
1995	2510.70	625.20			100.0000	100.0000				
1996		619.55				100.0000				

2. IMPORTS BY BROAD ECONOMIC CATEGORY AND EXPORTS BY INDUSTRIAL ORIGIN. (PERCENTAGE OF TOTAL VALUE)
IMPORTATIONS PAR CATEGORIES ECONOMIQUES ET EXPORTATIONS PAR BRANCHE D'ACTIVITE.(EN POURCENTAGE DE LA VALEUR TOTALE)

IMPORTS – IMPORTATIONS

	1990	1991	1992	1993	1994	1995	1996
TOTAL IMPORTS–IMPORTATIONS TOTALES	100.	100.	100.	100.	100.	100.	
1 FOOD BEV–ALIMENTATION BOISSONS	10.7	9.3	8.7	8.2	8.4	8.3	
11 PRIMARY–PRODUITS DE BASE	2.9	2.4	2.1	2.0	2.1	2.3	
111 FOR INDUSTRY–POUR L'INDUSTRIE	1.3	1.1	1.0	0.9	1.1	1.1	
112 FOR HOUSEHOLDS–POUR LES MENAGES	1.6	1.3	1.1	1.0	1.0	1.2	
12 PROCESSED–PRODUITS ELABORES	7.8	6.9	6.6	6.3	6.3	6.0	
121 FOR INDUSTRY–POUR L'INDUSTRIE	2.2	1.8	1.3	1.4	1.5	1.5	
122 FOR HOUSEHOLDS–POUR LES MENAGES	5.6	5.1	5.3	4.8	4.8	4.5	
2 IND SUPPLIES–APPROV INDUSTRIELS	29.6	28.1	28.7	28.2	29.0	29.7	
21 PRIMARY–PRODUITS DE BASE	1.3	1.0	1.8	2.0	2.0	2.1	
22 PROCESSED–PRODUITS ELABORES	28.3	27.0	26.9	26.2	27.1	27.6	
3 FUELS–COMBUSTIBLES	16.4	14.9	15.0	12.6	12.8	13.5	
31 PRIMARY–PRODUITS DE BASE	14.1	10.0	12.3	9.6	6.1	6.8	
32 PROCESSED–PRODUITS ELABORES	2.3	4.9	2.7	3.0	6.7	6.7	
321 MOTOR SPIRIT–ESSENCE	0.9	1.5	0.9	1.2	1.5	0.6	
322 OTHER–AUTRES	1.4	3.4	1.8	1.8	5.2	6.2	
4 MACHINERY–EQUIPEMENT	9.1	12.2	13.2	16.0	15.6	15.7	
41 CAPITAL EQUIPMENT–MACHINES	7.9	10.8	11.6	14.1	13.5	13.7	
42 PARTS–PIECES ACCESSOIRES	1.2	1.3	1.6	1.8	2.0	2.0	
5 TRANSPORT–TRANSPORT	9.4	13.1	13.9	14.7	14.3	13.2	
51 PASSENGER CARS–AUTOMOBILES	3.5	5.2	5.3	5.8	5.5	6.8	
52 OTHER–AUTRES	2.5	3.9	4.4	4.9	4.9	2.6	
521 INDUSTRIAL–INDUSTRIELS	2.3	3.8	4.2	4.7	4.7	2.4	
522 NON INDUSTRIAL–NON INDUSTRIEL	0.1	0.2	0.2	0.2	0.2	0.1	
53 PARTS–PIECES ACCESSOIRES	3.5	3.9	4.2	4.0	3.9	3.9	
6 CONSUM GOODS–BIENS CONSOMMATION	24.7	22.4	20.3	20.3	19.8	19.5	
61 DURABLE–DURABLES	4.8	4.9	4.5	4.4	4.4	4.2	
62 SEMI DURABLE–SEMI DURABLES	12.5	10.7	9.7	9.7	9.0	8.9	
63 NON DURABLE–NON DURABLES	7.4	6.9	6.1	6.2	6.4	6.4	
7 GOODS NES–BIENS NDA	0.1	0.1	0.1	0.1	0.1	0.0	

EXPORTS – EXPORTATIONS

	1990	1991	1992	1993	1994	1995	1996
TOTAL EXPORTS–EXPORTATIONS TOTALES	100.	100.	100.	100.	100.	100.	100.
1 AGRICULTURE	53.9	67.3	68.4	65.0	65.0	63.9	60.6
2 MINING QUARRY–INDUS EXTRACTIVES	0.0	0.0	0.0	0.0	0.0	0.0	0.1
3 MANUFACTURING–IND MANUFACTUR	46.1	32.7	31.6	35.0	35.0	36.0	39.3
31 FOOD BEV TOBACCO–ALIM BOISS TAB	23.4	15.8	13.4	16.4	13.2	11.3	12.3
32 TEXTILES–INDUSTRIES TEXTILES	8.1	7.1	7.6	6.8	6.2	6.0	6.0
33 WOOD & PRODUCTS–BOIS & PRODUITS	0.2	0.1	0.2	0.3	0.4	0.4	0.4
34 PAPER & PRODUCTS–PAPIER & PRODT	1.9	1.4	1.3	1.2	2.0	2.9	2.3
35 CHEMICALS–INDUSTRIES CHIMIQUES	5.5	5.4	6.0	6.8	7.8	8.7	10.5
36 NON METAL MIN–MIN NON METAL	0.5	0.5	0.6	0.6	0.6	0.5	0.4
37 BASIC METAL–IND METAL BASE	0.8	0.6	0.5	0.4	0.6	0.2	0.5
38 METAL MANUF–MANUF METAL	4.5	1.4	1.5	1.4	1.8	2.6	4.2
39 OTH MANUF IND–AUTRES MANUF	1.2	0.5	0.5	1.1	2.6	3.4	2.6

3. TRADE BY PRINCIPAL COUNTRIES OF PRODUCTION AND LAST DESTINATION (VALUE IN THOUSAND U.S. DOLLARS)
ECHANGES SELON LES PRINCIPAUX PAYS DE PRODUCTION ET DE DERNIERE DESTINATION (VALEUR EN MILLIERS DE DOLLARS EU)

COUNTRIES–PAYS	SPECIAL IMPORTS C.I.F. IMPORTATIONS SPECIALES C.A.F				
	1992	1993	1994	1995	1996
World	2018424	2199785	2402083	2510712	
Africa	5609	4826	8542	5217	
Americas	1250023	1335998	1475156	1632158	
Northern America	762157	837095	969499	1042090	
LAIA	307085	303066	329916	422403	
CACM	95704	107808	125285	137992	
Caribbean	85067	87995	50428	29668	
Rest of America	10	34	29	6	
As.ex F.USSR	261948	271159	287836	252046	
Eur.x F.USSR	157598	197512	231326	222212	
EU	144205	170837	204695	202797	
EFTA	11194	15782	10796	12961	
East Europe	2071	10844	15648	4184	
Other Europe				1448	
Former USSR	18	4216	3095	2571	
Oceania	9228	9064	9280	12128	
USA/Etats–Unis d'Amer	746573	819045	943722	1009154	
Japan/Japon	165276	170936	172971	126841	
Ecuador/Equateur	126762	84288	104932	134042	
Costa Rica	54679	60984	68218	74993	
Mexico/Mexique	40597	60891	47313	85814	
Venezuela	41897	38163	53368	77991	
Korea, Republic of	40912	38809	56187	54743	
Colombia/Colombie	35342	52370	47563	48937	
Germany/Allemagne	34477	41520	43581	46858	
Aruba	64517	66384	15600	9305	
Brazil/Brésil	31098	32885	40716	37229	
Guatemala	25549	29316	32688	37445	
Netherlands/Pays–Bas	9451	8756	42115	33935	
Spain/Espagne	15379	22478	24625	31222	
Canada	15542	18030	25777	32525	
Italy/Italie	15953	18566	33261	22965	
Hong Kong	20233	22286	21594	21659	
France, Monac	16881	18123	14282	14062	
United Kingdom	17113	14927	14013	16018	
Chile/Chili	12080	14047	15246	17520	
Trinidad and Tobago	9117	17021	15893	9884	
El Salvador	11165	12255	13377	14830	
Argentina/Argentine	10671	14162	14099	12209	
New Zealand	8316	8841	8842	11751	
Belgium–Luxembourg	7961	7707	9050	12404	
Switz.Liecht	9030	7854	8809	9722	
Denmark/Danemark	8293	8443	7384	8908	
Sweden/Suède	9440	9744	7074	5776	
Peru/Pérou	8516	6160	6586	8495	
Honduras	3841	4954	9416	8991	
Netherlands Antilles	4867	1504	14420	6322	
So. Africa Customs Un	5116	4770	8538	5197	
Ireland/Irlande	6065	5942	5541	5183	
Norway,SVD,JM	2164	7928	1987	3168	
Bulgaria/Bulgarie	16	4609	6784	1876	
China/Chine	1415	1590	2517	6462	
Greece/Grèce	73	11439	295	157	
Russian Federation	18	4216	3095	2571	
Thailand/Thaïlande	1717	1780	2806	3377	
Dominican Republic	422	2485	3886	2543	
Poland/Pologne	386	3892	2526	2262	
Israel/Israël	1554	2152	1490	3568	
Austria/Autriche	1691	838	1905	2488	
Dominica/Dominique	5915			129	
Romania/Roumanie	0	1378	4448	0	
Malaysia/Malaisie	901	1053	1280	2144	
Finland/Finlande	968	1246	922	1948	
Nicaragua	470	298	1587	1733	
India/Inde	830	831	1397	951	
Turkey/Turquie	220	1074	596	1611	

COUNTRIES–PAYS	SPECIAL EXPORTS F.O.B. EXPORTATIONS SPECIALES F.O.B.				
	1992	1993	1994	1995	1996
Monde	480912	506828	539823	577209	569201
Afrique		3	184	71	27
Amériques	238327	297035	334802	384449	418010
Amérique du Nord	153568	190899	225331	264755	299025
ALAI	18739	28769	22355	21913	25686
MCAC	56357	64030	72424	83385	76437
Caraïbes	9390	12493	14184	14195	16382
Autre Amérique	273	844	508	199	478
Asie l'URSS exclus	2873	2696	4205	7242	7856
Europe l'URSS exclus	219705	193269	182825	177243	130300
UE	218896	193269	182261	176820	130152
AELE	808	0	157	183	70
Europe de l'Est			406	241	16
Autre de l'Europe					62
Ancienne URSS		15	2561	1449	652
Océanie	4596	7960	8229	540	1089
USA/Etats–Unis d'Amer	151305	187243	220682	257396	286342
Germany/Allemagne	134867	72447	69004	71743	25182
Sweden/Suède	21961	49099	48497	28010	57782
Costa Rica	30905	32371	36451	41781	37673
Belgium–Luxembourg	9971	27858	37896	27520	23676
Italy/Italie	39942	27794	9533	6161	5813
Guatemala	7594	9089	11572	14810	15037
Spain/Espagne	8831	7396	10651	12619	14411
El Salvador	9686	8104	10855	9907	9436
Honduras	5053	11380	8957	12357	9925
Mexico/Mexique	6291	18105	7562	487	2051
Portugal		3930	926	26267	
Colombia/Colombie	2751	3845	5708	9047	9176
Canada	2248	3536	4625	7228	11445
New Zealand	4567	7953	7421		
Ecuador/Equateur	1794	2040	3470	6995	5433
Nicaragua	3119	3086	4590	4529	4366
Netherlands Antilles	3652	3461	4434	3004	3977
Cuba	979	2035	1805	3448	4534
Venezuela	3866	2065	1921	891	2790
Hong Kong	1116	1930	2209	3224	2740
Japan/Japon	976	434	1864	3489	4444
Netherlands/Pays–Bas	1991	1967	3759	2067	308
Dominican Republic	1173	1167	1473	1992	3484
Aruba	1597	1431	1545	1978	1664
Peru/Pérou	1014	938	1057	2126	2320
United Kingdom	139	905	689	1980	2030
Haiti/Haïti	20	2177	1997	1117	122
Russian Federation		15	2561	1449	652
Jamaica/Jamaïque	253	866	971	1047	1509
France, Monac	1006	1758	888	313	615
Bolivia/Bolivie	444	322	933	684	1906
Chile/Chili	222	518	381	962	1392
Argentina/Argentine	1842	556	226	196	163
Australia/Australie	30	7	807	540	1063
Barbados/Barbade	516	424	1029	3	51
Bahamas	155	332	263	857	331
Trinidad and Tobago	140	156	475	492	663
Brazil/Brésil	218	136	863	292	350
Belize/Bélize	177	691	282	137	478
Bermuda/Bermudes	15	120	24	131	1226
Dominica/Dominique	815	211	9		4
Norway,SVD,JM	511		154	181	63
Finland/Finlande		75	370		279
Iran (Islamic Rp. of)	620				
Paraguay	120	190	160	86	5
Martinique	36	175	148	199	
Uruguay	176	54	74	148	95
Suriname/Suriname	82	151	175	48	
Bulgaria/Bulgarie			406		

(VALUE AS PERCENTAGE OF WORLD TOTAL)(VALEURS EN POURCENTAGE DU TOTAL MONDIAL)

	1987	1988	1989	1990	1991	1992	1993	1994	1995	1996
Africa	0.0	0.0	0.2	0.1	0.3	0.3	0.2	0.4	0.2	
Americas	61.3	66.2	65.0	62.2	60.6	61.9	60.7	61.4	65.0	
Northern America	35.4	38.6	39.1	35.7	37.3	37.8	38.1	40.4	41.5	
LAIA	20.2	21.0	17.4	20.2	15.8	15.2	13.8	13.7	16.8	
CACM	5.0	6.2	6.1	5.0	4.8	4.7	4.9	5.2	5.5	
Caribbean	0.7	0.3	2.5	1.3	2.7	4.2	4.0	2.1	1.2	
Rest of America	0.0	0.0	0.0	0.0	0.0	0.0	0.0	0.0	0.0	
As.ex F.USSR	14.7	8.9	9.6	9.5	12.2	13.0	12.3	12.0	10.0	
Eur.x F.USSR	11.0	12.3	10.8	8.7	8.6	7.8	9.0	9.6	8.9	
EU	10.2	11.3	9.7	7.7	7.7	7.1	7.8	8.5	8.1	
EFTA	0.7	0.8	0.8	0.7	0.6	0.6	0.7	0.4	0.5	
East Europe	0.2	0.2	0.2	0.2	0.2	0.1	0.5	0.7	0.2	
Other Europe	0.0	0.0	0.0	0.1	0.1				0.1	
Former USSR	0.0	0.0	0.0	0.0	0.0	0.0	0.2	0.1	0.1	
Oceania	0.4	0.6	0.7	0.4	0.4	0.5	0.4	0.4	0.5	
USA/Etats–Unis d'Amer	34.4	37.7	38.4	34.9	35.8	37.0	37.2	39.3	40.2	
Japan/Japon	7.4	4.6	4.3	5.0	6.8	8.2	7.8	7.2	5.1	
Ecuador/Equateur	2.0	4.1	6.2	11.1	6.2	6.3	3.8	4.4	5.3	
Costa Rica	3.0	3.3	3.4	2.9	2.7	2.7	2.8	2.8	3.0	
Mexico/Mexique	8.5	7.6	2.9	1.7	1.8	2.0	2.8	2.0	3.4	
Venezuela	4.0	4.2	3.2	2.4	2.7	2.1	1.7	2.2	3.1	
Korea, Republic of	2.0	1.4	1.3	1.7	2.3	2.0	1.8	2.3	2.2	
Colombia/Colombie	1.7	1.3	1.2	1.8	2.0	1.8	2.4	2.0	1.9	
Germany/Allemagne	2.7	2.2	2.8	2.0	2.3	1.7	1.9	1.8	1.9	
Aruba			0.0	0.0	1.0	3.2	3.0	0.6	0.4	

	1987	1988	1989	1990	1991	1992	1993	1994	1995	1996
Afrique	0.0	0.2	0.1	0.0			0.0	0.0	0.0	0.0
Amériques	80.9	69.1	69.0	66.5	49.8	49.6	58.6	62.0	66.6	73.4
Amérique du Nord	68.9	50.7	47.4	46.2	32.3	31.9	37.7	41.7	45.9	52.5
ALAI	2.1	4.3	4.1	5.4	5.5	3.9	5.7	4.1	3.8	4.5
MCAC	8.6	11.5	12.2	13.2	10.2	11.7	12.6	13.4	14.4	13.4
Caraïbes	1.3	2.4	4.5	1.7	1.7	2.0	2.5	2.6	2.5	2.9
Autre Amérique	0.1	0.1	0.8	0.1	0.1	0.1	0.2	0.1	0.0	0.1
Asie l'URSS exclus	1.8	1.5	1.1	1.0	1.7	0.6	0.5	0.8	1.3	1.4
Europe l'URSS exclus	16.5	27.8	28.0	30.1	44.5	45.7	38.1	33.9	30.7	22.9
UE	16.2	25.7	27.3	29.9	44.4	45.5	38.1	33.8	30.6	22.9
AELE	0.3	0.0	0.0	0.1	0.1	0.2	0.0	0.0	0.0	0.0
Europe de l'Est	0.0	2.1	0.7	0.2	0.0			0.1	0.0	0.0
Autre de l'Europe		0.0		0.1						0.0
Ancienne URSS				0.0			0.0	0.5	0.3	0.1
Océanie		0.0		0.0	0.4	1.0	1.6	1.5	0.1	0.2
USA/Etats–Unis d'Amer	67.5	49.0	46.1	45.1	31.6	31.5	36.9	40.9	44.6	50.3
Germany/Allemagne	5.9	11.5	13.3	15.4	25.6	28.0	14.3	12.8	12.4	4.4
Sweden/Suède	1.6	2.1	1.6	1.9	3.6	4.6	9.7	9.0	4.9	10.2
Costa Rica	5.8	7.0	8.2	9.0	5.9	6.4	6.4	6.8	7.2	6.6
Belgium–Luxembourg	4.1	4.3	6.0	5.4	4.7	2.1	5.5	7.0	4.8	4.2
Italy/Italie	2.5	4.7	3.7	4.5	8.6	8.3	5.5	1.8	1.1	1.0
Guatemala	0.8	1.3	1.6	1.1	1.4	1.6	1.8	2.1	2.6	2.6
Spain/Espagne	0.9	1.1	1.6	2.1	1.6	1.8	1.5	2.0	2.2	2.5
El Salvador	0.8	1.0	0.9	1.1	1.4	2.0	1.6	2.0	1.7	1.7
Honduras	0.6	0.7	0.9	1.1	0.8	1.1	2.2	1.7	2.1	1.7

4. Special Imports C.I.F. by Commodities according to the S.I.T.C. (Rev. 2) in thousand U.S. Dollars
Importations Spéciales C.A.F. par Produits d'après la C.T.C.I. (Rév. 2) en milliers de Dollars E.U.

SITC CTCI	COMMODITY	1992		1993		1994		1995		PRODUIT
		WEIGHT POIDS	VALUE VALEUR	WEIGHT POIDS	VALUE VALEUR	WEIGHT POIDS	VALUE VALEUR	WEIGHT POIDS	VALUE VALEUR	
	ALL COMMODITIES		2018424		2199785		2402083		2510712	TOUS PRODUITS
0	FOOD AND LIVE ANIMALS		190122		198999		215711		233191	ALIMENTS,ANIMAUX VIVANTS
01	MEAT AND PREPARATIONS		11733		10915		11717		8848	VIANDES ET PREPARATIONS
014	MEAT PREPD,PRSVD,NES ETC	W 3317	7594	W 3073	6772	W 3672	7206	W 2854	6088	CONSERVES DE VIANDES
0149	OTH PREPARD,PRESRVD MEAT	W 3070	6795	W 2826	5959	W 3429	6424	W 2679	5509	AUTRES PREP DE VIANDES
02	DAIRY PRODCTS,BIRDS'EGGS		18004		11358		12995		15637	PRODUITS LAITIERS,OEUFS
022	MILK AND CREAM	W 4040	7816	W 2142	4248	W 3010	5588	W 5163	11225	LAIT ET CREME
0224	MILK,CREAM PRESERVED ETC	W 4025	7805	W 2132	4240	W 3010	5587	W 2945	6453	LAIT,CREME CONS,CONC
024	CHEESE AND CURD	W 2473	6220	W 2314	5326	W 2594	5742	W 531	1861	FROMAGE ET CAILLEBOTTE
03	FISH AND PREPARATIONS		12774		11951		11154		11237	POISSONS ET PREPARATIONS
037	FISH ETC PREPD,PRSVD NES	W 5127	11439	W 4606	10076	W 4599	9109	W 4782	8890	POIS,CRUST,MOL PREPARES
0371	FISH PREPARD,PRESRVD NES	W 5099	11296	W 4575	9884	W 4569	8913	W 4753	8732	CONSERVES DE POISSONS
04	CEREALS AND PREPARATIONS		58450		64260		69971		79842	CEREALES ET PRODUITS
041	WHEAT ETC UNMILLED	W 89726	16876	W 82818	17037	W 116722	22419	W 94304	19841	FROMENT,EPEAUTRE
0411	DURUM WHEAT UNMILLED	W 89726	16876	W 82818	17037	W 116722	22419	W 94304	19841	FROMENT DUR NON MOULU
044	MAIZE UNMILLED	W 120247	17409	W 166754	23514	W 148519	22087	W 165307	26062	MAIS NON MOULU
048	CEREAL ETC PREPARATIONS	W 21442	21510	W 18996	21019	W 22376	22368	W 24252	27900	PREPTNS A BASE CEREALES
0481	PREPD BREAKFAST FOOD ETC	W 2067	8844	W 1941	8714	W 1970	8000	W 3309	10322	CEREALES TRAVAILLEES
04812	CEREAL ROASTED, PUFFED	W 2067	8844	W 1941	8714	W 1970	8000	W 2548	9593	PRODTS BASE CEREALES
0482	MALT INCLUDING FLOUR	W 17188	6517	W 14400	5277	W 15925	5162	W 16610	6406	MALT MEME TORREFIE
05	VEGETABLES AND FRUIT		36048		40385		42958		43934	LEGUMES ET FRUITS
054	VEG ETC FRSH,SMPLY PRSVD	W 8430	6287	W 8711	6415	W 6655	5439	W 12919	9987	LEGUMES FRAIS,CONG,SECS
056	VEGTBLES ETC PRSVD,PREPD	W 6898	5990	W 5212	7696	W 4754	7669	W 4072	6920	CONSERVES DE LEGUMES
057	FRUIT,NUTS,FRESH,DRIED	W 9193	11146	W 11276	12597	W 13801	14780	W 12227	13012	FRUITS FRAIS OU SECS
058	FRUIT PRESERVED,PREPARED	W 6194	12625	W 6728	13678	W 7339	15070	W 6623	14015	CONSERVES DE FRUITS
0585	FRUIT OR VEGETABLE JUICE	W 4102	9349	W 4737	10479	W 4861	11295	W 4323	9998	JUS DE FRUITS
06	SUGAR AND PREPS,HONEY		5133		5970		7093		10753	SUCRES ET PRODUITS
07	COFFEE,TEA,COCOA,SPICES		8583		8901		9924		10755	CAFE,THE,CACAO,EPICES
073	CHOCOLATE AND PRODUCTS	W 2219	6344	W 2205	6490	W 2063	6568	W 1722	5986	CHOCOLAT
081	*FEEDING STUFF FOR ANIML	W 55084	17781	W 66342	21428	W 76138	24438	W 91944	28622	NOURRITURE POUR ANIMAUX
0813	OILCAKE AND OTH RESIDUES	W 47391	11860	W 54838	14203	W 66189	16839	W 73072	17389	TOURTEAUX
08131	— OF SOYA BEANS							W 73070	17387	TOURTEAUX DE SOJA
0819	FOOD WASTE AND FEED NES	W 7437	5841	W 11330	7159	W 9742	7540	W 18622	11152	DECHETS,ALIMENTS NDA
08199	FODDER NES,INCL SWEETNED	W 7437	5841	W 11330	7159	W 9742	7540	W 12088	9050	PREPARATIONS FOURRAGERES
09	MISC EDIBLE PRODUCTS		19761		22003		23630		21488	PREP ALIMENTAIRES DIVERSES
098	EDIBLE PRODCTS,PREPS NES	W 5584	19567	W 6149	21826	W 6877	23545	W 7164	21459	PREP ALIMENTAIRES NDA
09809	MISC FOOD PREPRTIONS NES	W 3106	12502	W 3398	14191	W 3670	15438	W 3986	14385	PREP ALIMENTAIRES NDA
1	BEVERAGES AND TOBACCO		9509		10457		13796		12734	BOISSONS ET TABACS
11	BEVERAGES		7890		8320		10329		10563	BOISSONS
112	ALCOHOLIC BEVERAGES	W 1836	7385	W 2322	7721	W 2866	8878	W 3138	8948	BOISSONS ALCOOLIQUES
2	CRUDE MATERLS,EXCL FUELS		21304		22941		30998		27251	MAT BRUTES NON COMESTIBLES
251	*PULP AND WASTE PAPER	W 8031	3286	W 8419	3074	W 12014	4823	W 17218	7810	PATES A PAPIER,DECHETS
3	MINERAL FUELS ETC		303056		278920		310267		343256	COMBUSTIBLES MINERAUX LUB
33	PETROLEUM AND PRODUCTS		281411		259404		289691		317688	PETROLE ET DERIVES
333	CRUDE PETROLEUM	W 1830400	225795	W 1720857	191952	W 1188791	125475	W 1223452	144654	HUILES BRUTES DE PETROLE
334	PETROLEUM PRODUCTS,REFIN	W 255498	53386	W 352155	65288	W 1040743	161071	W 1056746	168164	PRODUITS RAFFINES
3341	GASOLINE,OTH LIGHT OILS	W 51330	17553	W 102685	25824	W 150313	37246	W 118654	27983	ESSENCES POUR MOTEURS
33411	MOTOR,AVIATION SPIRIT	W 13597	6760	W 14301	6907	W 8585	7416	W 56311	12999	ESSENCES MOTEURS D'AVIONS
33412	SPIRIT TYPE JET FUEL	W 61	42	W 148	103	W 93	57	W 60450	14164	CARBUREACTEURS
33419	OTH LIGHT PETROLEUM OILS	W 37672	10751	W 88237	18813	W 141635	29773	W 1893	820	AUTRES HUILES LEGERES
3342	KEROSENE,OTH MEDIUM OILS	W 166839	30170	W 237070	36069	W 521846	86965	W 65453	15929	PETR LAMPANTS,AUT HUIL
33421	KEROSENE INCL JET FUEL	W 23397	6064	W 15341	3729	W 78486	18197	W 65416	15897	PETROLES LAMPANTS
33429	OTH MEDIUM PETROLEUM OIL	W 143442	24106	W 221729	32340	W 443360	68769	W 36	32	AUTRES HUILES MOYENNES
3343	GAS OILS	W 35499	3039	W 10555	719	W 351366	31100	W 858065	113695	GAS OILS
341	*GAS,NATURAL AND MANUFCT	W 59461	19326	W 66103	17376	W 71488	18100	W 76990	22856	GAZ NATUREL,GAZ MANUFACT
3413	PETROLM GASES,LIQUEFIED	W 59459	19318	W 66102	17374	W 71488	18099	W 76989	22843	GAZ DE PETROLE LIQUEFIE
34131	LIQUEFIED PROPANE,BUTANE							W 76975	22816	PROPANE,BUTANE LIQUEFIES
4	ANIMAL,VEGETABLE OIL,FAT		8886		14429		20149		21959	HUILES,GRAISSES ANIM,VEG
42	FIXED VEGETABLE OIL,FAT		7738		13581		18681		19965	HUILES VEGETALES FIXES
423	FIXED VEG OILS,SOFT	W 13567	7738	W 24771	13581	W 28108	18681	W 23815	18248	HUILES VEGET DOUCES FIXES
4232	SOYA BEAN OIL							W 23327	17019	HUILE DE SOJA
5	CHEMCLS,RELATED PROD NES		258942		284132		310099		331611	PRODUITS CHIMIQUES
51	ORGANIC CHEMICALS		17338		18457		19257		20959	PROD CHIMIQ ORGANIQUES
52	INORGANIC CHEMICALS		17090		17317		17889		18244	PROD CHIM INORGANIQUES
522	INORG ELEMNTS,OXIDES,ETC	W 11138	6432	W 9068	5118	W 18149	6453	W 19333	6530	ELEMENTS INORGANIQUES
523	OTHR INORG CHEMICALS ETC	W 21450	10639	W 24688	12194	W 23762	11423	W 25618	11695	AUT PRODUITS CHIMIQUES INORG
5232	OTH MTL CMPD OF INRG ACD	W 14817	7601	W 17849	9017	W 16231	7918	W 15641	7447	SELS METALLIQUES
53	DYES,TANNING,COLOUR PROD		11329		13669		14302		17067	PROD TEINTURE,COLORANTS
533	PIGMENTS,PAINTS,ETC	W 4059	8630	W 5724	10524	W 7036	11074	W 9187	12996	PIGMENTS,PEINTURES,VERNIS
541	*MEDICINAL,PHARM PRODUCT	K 1904278	65828	K 3985664	77585	K 3935997	80276	K 4868530	95039	PROD MEDICINAUX PHARMACEUT
5417	MEDICAMENTS	K 1557095	56317	K 2088971	65207	K 2627681	70265	K 3523894	82127	MEDICAMENTS
54171	— CONTAINNG ANTIBIOTICS							K 900925	27803	MED CONTN ANTIBIOTIQUES
54172	— CONTAINING HORMONES							K 379784	15033	MED CONTENANT HORMONES
54179	— CONTNG OTH SUBSTANCES							K 2238837	39192	MED CONT AUT SUBSTANCES
55	PERFUME,CLEANING ETC PRD		33778		37992		40859		40239	PROD POUR PARFUM,TOILETTE
553	PERFUMERY,COSMETICS,ETC	W 3441	22474	W 3618	24070	W 5193	26827	W 4394	26542	PRODUITS DE PARFUMERIE
554	SOAP,CLEANSING ETC PREPS	W 3370	6113	W 4929	7763	W 6098	8689	W 5732	7610	SAVONS,PRODUITS DETERSIFS
562	*FERTILIZERS,MANUFACTURE	W 86047	17138	W 95092	15974	W 100896	19831	W 105199	23362	ENGRAIS MANUFACTURES
5621	CHEM NITROGENOUS FERTLZR	W 58947	11660	W 62918	9979	W 59695	11436	W 52021	11440	ENGRAIS AZOTES
58	PLASTIC MATERIALS ETC		45680		48438		55963		56116	MAT PLAST ARTIFICIELLES
582	PROD OF CONDENSATION ETC	W 3647	8008	W 4171	8517	W 4527	9586	W 6465	10053	PROD CONDENS,POLYCOND
583	POLYMERIZATION ETC PRODS	W 32125	33232	W 33769	34851	W 38287	41084	W 32527	43170	PROD POLYMERISATION
5831	POLYETHYLENE							W 17056	17631	POLYETHYLENE
58311	— IN PRIMARY FORMS							W 16902	17333	POLYETHYLENE PRIMAIRES
5839	OTH POLYMRZTION ETC PROD							W 3768	8328	AUT PROD POLYMER COPOLYM
59	CHEMICAL MATERIALS NES		49821		53724		60369		58638	MAT PROD CHIMIQUES NDA
591	PESTICIDES,DISINFECTANTS	W 7286	24716	W 9312	28664	W 9196	32037	W 8386	34579	DESINF,INSECT,FONG,HERB
5912	FUNGICIDES,FOR RETAIL							W 1456	12454	FONGICIDES VENTE AU DET
5913	HERBICIDES,FOR RETAIL							W 2981	12080	HERBICIDES VENTE AU DET
5914	DISINFECTANTS,ETC,FR RET	W 7286	24716	W 9312	28664	W 9196	32037	W 2468	3168	DESINFECTANTS VENTE DET
592	STARCH,INULIN,GLUTEN,ETC	W 16708	9540	W 16097	10315	W 16415	10896	W 5567	7091	AMIDONS,INUL,GLUT FROM
598	MISCEL CHEM PRODUCTS NES	W 5955	15565	W 6891	14746	W 8151	17436	W 7212	16968	PROD DIV INDUST CHIM NDA
5982	ANTI-KNOCK PREPARTNS ETC	W 2306	7630	W 2172	4967	W 2582	5808	W 2092	4913	PREPARAT ANTIDETONANTES
5989	CHEM PRODUCTS,PREPS NES	W 3500	7580	W 4502	9250	W 5332	11118	W 4820	11396	PROD PREP CHIMIQUES NDA
59898	COMPOUND CATALYSTS	W 2033	5822	W 2754	7286	W 3443	8674	W 47	212	CATALYSEURS COMPOSITES
59899	OTH CHEM PRODS,PREPS,NES							W 2956	8740	AUT PRODUITS CHIMIQUES NDA
6	BASIC MANUFACTURES		395167		419198		457819		484084	ART MANUFACTURES
61	LEATHER,DRESSED FUR,ETC		8258		9553		6514		8001	CUIRS,PELLETERIES
612	LEATHER ETC MANUFACTURES	W 905	7244	W 1028	8505	W 947	5889	W 1087	7033	OUVRAGES EN CUIRS NDA
6123	PREPRD PARTS OF FOOTWEAR	W 896	7117	W 1016	8366	W 938	5774	W 1073	6924	PARTIES DE CHAUSSURES
62	RUBBER MANUFACTURES NES		30627		31759		31405		37124	CAOUTCHOUC MANUFACTURE

4. Special Imports C.I.F. by Commodities according to the S.I.T.C. (Rev. 2) in thousand U.S. Dollars
Importations Spéciales C.A.F. par Produits d'après la C.T.C.I. (Rév. 2) en milliers de Dollars E.U.

SITC CTCI	COMMODITY	1992 WEIGHT POIDS	1992 VALUE VALEUR	1993 WEIGHT POIDS	1993 VALUE VALEUR	1994 WEIGHT POIDS	1994 VALUE VALEUR	1995 WEIGHT POIDS	1995 VALUE VALEUR	PRODUIT
625	RUBBER TYRES, TUBES ETC	W 8591	24084	W 8952	25045	W 8920	24343	W 14001	29733	PNEUS CAOUTCHOUC VULCANISE
6251	TYRES NEW FOR MOTOR CARS	W 8479	23801	W 8826	24763	W 8803	24077	W 7280	13200	PNEUS POUR VOITURES
6252	TYRES,NEW,BUS OR LORRY							W 3257	9476	PNEUS POUR AUTOBUS,CAMIONS
63	WOOD,CORK MANUFACTRS NES		5595		6479		10782		9783	OUVRAGES LIEGE ET BOIS
64	PAPER,PAPERBOARD AND MFR		94253		96557		110546		121230	PAPIERS,CARTONS & OUVRAGES
641	PAPER AND PAPERBOARD	W 112044	70325	W 106189	66192	W 135829	82659	W 112885	94137	PAPIERS ET CARTONS
6411	NEWSPRINT	W 101992	59408	W 96828	55364	W 124758	70656	W 12495	8151	PAPIER JOURNAL
6413	KRAFT PAPER,PAPERBOARD							W 57739	41197	PAPIER ET CARTON KRAFT
64132	SACK KRAFT PAPER IN BULK							W 30399	21796	PAPIER KRAFT POUR SACS
64139	KRAFT PAPER PAPERBD,NES							W 19835	15120	PAPIER,CARTON KRAFT NDA
6415	PAPER,PAPERBRD,BULK,NES	W 45	171	W 114	207	W 67	210	W 16729	19987	PAPIERS,CARTONS ROULEAUX
64159	OTHER PAPER ETC,BULK,NES							W 15122	18801	AUT PAPIER ROULEAUX FEUILLES
6418	COATED ETC PAPER NES BLK	W 1578	3578	W 1855	3910	W 1721	3860	W 20016	17534	PAP,CARTONS COUCHES,ENDUITS
64181	PLASTIC COATED PAPER ETC							W 14544	11703	PAP,CARTONS ENDUITS,RESINES
642	PAPER,ETC,PRECUT,ARTS OF	W 11026	23928	W 15489	30365	W 12517	27887	W 10873	27093	PAP,CARTONS DECOUPES
6421	PAPER ETC CONTAINERS	W 7245	11685	W 11255	17086	W 7882	12630	W 6445	12569	BOITES,SACS EMBALLAGES
6428	PAPER ETC ARTICLES NES	W 1754	6089	W 2006	7173	W 2251	8391	W 2714	8830	OUVRAGES EN PATE A PAPIER
65	TEXTILE YARN,FABRICS,ETC		78594		81586		73738		74657	FILS,TISSUS,ARTICLES TEXTILE
651	TEXTILE YARN	W 1714	8461	W 1365	6545	W 1562	6094	W 1099	6872	FILS TEXTILES
652	COTTON FABRICS,WOVEN	W 1463	10801	W 1531	11976	W 1772	10596	W 1197	9017	TISSUS DE COTON
6521	GREY WOVEN COTTON FABRIC	W 1355	10308	W 1452	11640	W 1711	10262	W 247	1577	TISSUS COT ECRUS NON MERCER
65214	GREY WOVEN COTTON NES	W 1349	10263	W 1440	11589	W 1702	10229	W 166	916	AUT TISSUS 85% COTON ECRUS
653	WOVN MAN–MADE FIB FABRIC	W 4526	29320	W 5004	32131	W 4760	26960	W 3969	25632	TISSUS FIBRES SYNTH,ARTIF
6531	CONT SYNT WEAVES NONPILE	W 3862	24403	W 4504	28279	W 4207	23330	W 2480	14508	TISSUS FIBRES SYNTH CONTINUE
65315	CONT SYN TXTL FABRIC NES							W 2317	13266	TIS PLUS 85% TEXT SYNT CONT
657	SPECIAL TXTL FABRC,PRODS	W 2301	10134	W 2380	8114	W 2109	8239	W 1923	7958	TISSUS SPECIAUX
658	TEXTILE ARTICLES NES	W 610	6633	W 1211	8650	W 876	6634	W 1278	9148	ART FACONNES MAT TEXTILES
6584	LINENS ETC	W 515	5577	W 998	7333	W 733	5500	W 1124	7831	LINGE DE MAISON
66	NONMETAL MINERAL MFS NES		21984		30218		38345		40028	ART MIN NON METALLIQUES
661	LIME,CEMENT,BLDG PRODS	W 8810	2420	W 65766	3876	W 166342	9676	W 31025	7897	CHAUX,CIMENTS MAT CONSTR
6612	CEMENT	W 5740	1040	W 62682	2533	W 161685	7613	W 24775	4767	CIMENTS HYDRAULIQUES
662	CLAY,REFRACTORY BLDG PRD	W 10731	5994	W 18653	9494	W 23698	11061	W 20575	10328	MAT CONST REFRACTAIRES
6624	BRICKS ETC NONREFRACTORY	W 9931	5375	W 18023	8785	W 22397	10210	W 19227	9281	BRIQUES ETC CERAM NON REFR
66245	GLAZED CERAMIC SETTS ETC	W 9909	5358	W 17997	8750	W 22363	10195	W 18721	9167	AUT CARREAUX CERAMIQUE
664	GLASS	W 4736	3568	W 5779	4996	W 6710	5661	W 7239	8706	VERRE
67	IRON AND STEEL		78817		78627		94272		90416	FER ET ACIER
672	IRON,STEEL PRIMARY FORMS	W 35632	9435	W 35357	9870	W 36713	10018	W 35128	10791	LINGOTS FER,ACIER
6725	IRN,STL BLOOMS,SLABS,ETC	W 35620	9400	W 35356	9862	W 36712	10013	W 34594	10198	BLOOMS,BILLETTES FER ACIER
67251	IRN,SMPLE STL BLOOMS,ETC	W 35620	9400	W 35356	9862	W 36712	10013	W 34584	10161	BLOOMS ETC NON ACIER FIN
673	IRON,STEEL SHAPES ETC	W 24419	10923	W 41980	17726	W 42333	17440	W 29192	12912	BARRES,PROFIL FER,ACIER
6732	IRON,STEEL BARS ETC	W 8715	3709	W 18583	7621	W 24752	9266	W 11870	4711	BARRES FER,ACIER
67326	IRN,OTH STL BARS HOTROLD	W 8715	3709	W 18583	7621	W 24752	9266	W 7358	2670	BARRES PLEINES FER,ACIER
6733	IRON,STEEL PROFILES ETC	W 11336	5333	W 18247	7946	W 13068	6234	W 13977	6787	PROFILES,PALPLAN FER,ACIER
674	IRN,STL UNIV,PLATE,SHEET	W 61757	41614	W 53366	34735	W 69803	44718	W 64084	49635	LARGES PLATS,TOLES
6745	IRN,STL MED PLATE,ROLLED	W 45607	29765	W 30683	18861	W 47526	29466	W 1920	1094	TOLES 3 A 4.75 MM
67451	— OF IRON OR SIMPLE STL	W 45607	29765	W 30683	18861	W 47526	29466	W 1672	895	TOLES AUT NON ACIER FIN
6747	TINNED PLATES,SHEETS	W 7627	7327	W 11052	10296	W 8652	8062	W 11963	11487	TOLES ETAMEES EN ACIER
6749	OTH IRN,STL PLATES,SHEET	W 1339	1169	W 2368	1574	W 3645	2422	W 43249	32924	AUTRES TOLES FER,ACIER
67491	— OF IRON OR SIMPLE STL	W 1339	1169	W 2368	1574	W 3645	2422	W 42638	32425	AUT TOLES AUTRES ACIER FIN
678	IRON,STL TUBES,PIPES,ETC	W 9324	7866	W 10999	8982	W 17469	12927	W 13243	11286	TUBES,TUYAUX EN FONTE,FER
6783	IRON,STL TUBES,PIPES NES	W 5618	3962	W 7065	4703	W 6118	4522	W 11032	8098	AUT TUBES,TUYAUX FER,ACIER
68	NON–FERROUS METALS		14573		15480		20082		28367	METAUX NON FERREUX
682	COPPER EXC CEMENT COPPER	W 1606	4882	W 1877	5175	W 2217	6484	W 2214	8306	CUIVRE
6822	COPPER,ALLOYS WORKED	W 1605	4875	W 1875	5163	W 2215	6473	W 2210	8264	CUIVRE,ALLIAGES OUVRES
684	ALUMINIUM	W 2869	9298	W 3370	9666	W 4949	13086	W 5988	19572	ALUMINIUM
6842	ALUMINIUM,ALLOYS WORKED	W 2863	9294	W 3370	9666	W 4949	13086	W 4361	15811	ALUMINIUM,ALLIAGES OUVRE
68422	ALUMNM PLATE,SHEET,STRIP	W 1925	5278	W 2070	5195	W 3094	7148	W 2555	8025	TOLES, PLANCHES EN ALU
69	METAL MANUFACTURES NES		62465		68939		72136		74478	ART MANUFACT EN METAL NDA
692	METAL TANKS,BOXES,ETC	W 1606	7356	W 2018	8131	W 1789	6570	W 4118	12472	RECIPIENTS METALLIQUES
6924	MTL TRANSPORT BOXES ETC	W 1292	6076	W 1699	5572	W 1322	5247	W 3729	10795	FUTS,TAMBOURS,BIDONS
69242	ALUMNM TRNSPRT BOXES ETC	W 834	4691	W 1114	4278	W 647	3558	W 2354	7736	FUTS,TAMBOURS,BIDONS ALU
695	TOOLS	W 1121	6934	W 1176	8006	W 1412	8825	W 1402	8962	OUTILS A MAIN
697	BASE MTL HOUSEHOLD EQUIP	W 3273	13952	W 3366	15368	W 4040	14698	W 2709	10260	ART MENAGE MET COMMUNS
6973	DMSTC HEATG,COOKG APPARA	W 2488	10029	W 2542	11102	W 3074	10069	W 1932	5998	APPS CHAUF NON ELECTRIQ
699	BASE METAL MFRS NES	W 4971	21117	W 5828	21563	W 7276	24228	W 6117	24405	ART MANUFACTURES MET NDA
6991	LOCKSMITHS WARES,ETC	W 1376	7959	W 1675	8777	W 1895	9937	W 1645	9074	ARTICLES DE SERRURERIE
6996	BASE MTL MISC ARTICLES	W 1824	6825	W 1933	6244	W 2125	6191	W 2355	8057	ART DIVERS METAUX COMMUNS
7	MACHINES,TRANSPORT EQUIP		564167		686701		741144		727711	MACHINES MATERIEL TRANSPORT
71	POWER GENERATING EQUIPMT		28040		42958		33510		25350	MACHINES GENERATRICES
713	INTRNL COMBUS PSTN ENGIN	W 880	7400	W 909	12047	W 970	11699	W 781	14403	MOTEURS EXPL COMB INT, PIECE
7139	PISTON ENGINE PARTS NES	W 241	3932	W 304	6118	W 453	7722	W 330	7068	PIECES POUR 713.2,3,8
716	ROTATING ELECTRIC PLANT	W 1926	14008	W 2774	23238	W 2407	14290	W 945	9515	APP ELECTR ROTATIFS,PIECES
7161	DC MOTORS AND GENERATORS	W 758	8014	W 1077	13131	W 516	4482	W 381	3530	MOTEURS COURANT CONTINU
7163	ROTARY CONVERTERS	W 946	3623	W 1450	7378	W 1591	7095	W 4	40	CONVERTISSEURS ROTATIFS
72	MACHS FOR SPCL INDUSTRYS		58858		83551		77023		78302	MAC SPECIALES POUR INDUST
722	TRACTORS NON–ROAD	W 4843	8485	W 4317	8586	W 5512	11635	W 2013	11417	TRACTEURS
7223	TRACK–LAYING TRACTORS	W 4843	8485	W 4317	8586	W 5512	11635	W 221	620	TRACTEURS A CHENILLES
7224	WHEELED TRACTORS NES							W 1791	10797	TRACTEURS A ROUES
723	CIVIL ENGNEERG EQUIP ETC	W 2530	11602	W 5522	24196	W 4044	17145	W 3471	19621	APPAREILS DE GENIE CIVIL
7234	CONST,MINING MACHNRY NES	W 2519	11521	W 5486	24067	W 4021	17051	W 3190	18182	MACH POUR LA CONST, MINES
72342	SLFPRP SHOVELS,EXCAVATRS							W 1785	9315	PELLES MECANIQUES
724	TEXTILE,LEATHER MACHNRY	W 1887	8677	W 2392	9890	W 2173	8967	W 690	6091	MACH POUR INDUSTRIE TEXTILE
7247	TEXTILE MACHINERY NES	W 1467	6099	W 2015	7271	W 1816	6370	W 302	1693	MACH LAVAGE,TEINTURE TEX
725	PAPER ETC MILL MACHINERY	W 153	2877	W 297	8930	W 102	2116	W 281	3846	MACHINES FABR PATE PAPIER
726	PRINTG,BKBINDG MACHY,PTS	W 412	6498	W 477	7814	W 719	12572	W 307	5942	MACHINES POUR IMPRIMERIE
7264	PRINTING PRESSES	W 259	3919	W 263	3530	W 414	7947	W 75	1172	MACHINES A IMPRIMER
727	FOOD MACHRY NON–DOMESTIC	W 673	5260	W 567	5008	W 803	5938	W 1204	9663	MACH INDUSTRIES ALIMENT
7272	OTH FOOD PROC MCHY,PARTS	W 453	3919	W 295	3675	W 667	5010	W 1034	8602	AUT MACH IND ALIMENTAIRE
72722	INDUS FOOD PROC MACH NES							W 1034	8593	MACHINES BOULANGERIE
728	OTH MACHY FOR SPCL INDUS	W 1186	10156	W 1307	12997	W 1760	12804	W 1294	14223	AUT MACH IND PARTICULIERES
7283	OTHR MINERAL WORKG MACHY	W 755	3544	W 938	6753	W 1219	6278	W 642	3933	MACH TRIER,CRIBLER,BROYER
73	METALWORKING MACHINERY		5072		9460		10059		8265	MACH TRAVAIL DES METAUX
736	METALWORKING MACH–TOOLS	W 348	4351	W 505	6331	W 758	8856	W 609	5443	MACH–OUTILS TRAVAIL METAUX
74	GENRL INDUSTRL MACHY NES		56596		76518		82242		102017	MACH APP INDUSTRIE
741	HEATING,COOLING EQUIPMNT	W 1606	12231	W 2266	16390	W 2561	20069	W 4166	28119	MACH CHAUFFAGE,PIECES
7415	AIR–CONDITIONING MACHNRY	W 980	7432	W 1316	9734	W 1652	12346	W 2418	14071	GROUPES CONDITION AIR
742	PUMPS FOR LIQUIDS ETC	W 432	5221	W 574	7136	W 586	7572	W 724	7819	POMPES MOTO–POMPES
743	PUMPS NES,CENTRFUGES ETC	W 860	8613	W 1215	12658	W 1310	12975	W 1383	12025	POMPES COMPRES,VENT ETC
744	MECHANICAL HANDLING EQU	W 2928	10749	W 4031	14508	W 3589	14005	W 3839	19998	EQUIP MANUTENTION PIECES
7442	LIFTING,LOADING MACH NES	W 1507	4053	W 1808	6410	W 1475	5699	W 2797	12645	APP LEVAGE,MANUTENTION
74424	LIFTS AND SKIP HOISTS							W 1862	7746	ASCENSEURS,MONTE–CHARGE

4. Special Imports C.I.F. by Commodities according to the S.I.T.C. (Rev. 2) in thousand U.S. Dollars
Importations Spéciales C.A.F. par Produits d'après la C.T.C.I. (Rév. 2) en milliers de Dollars E.U.

SITC CTCI	COMMODITY	1992 WEIGHT POIDS	1992 VALUE VALEUR	1993 WEIGHT POIDS	1993 VALUE VALEUR	1994 WEIGHT POIDS	1994 VALUE VALEUR	1995 WEIGHT POIDS	1995 VALUE VALEUR	PRODUIT
745	NONELEC MACHY,TOOLS NES	W 411	7013	W 553	8080	W 719	8943	W 994	17398	AUT MACH NON ELEC,PIECES
7452	OTH NONELEC MCHS,PTS NES	W 351	6085	W 491	6993	W 631	7484	W 922	16411	AUT MACH NON ELEC,PIECES
74522	PACKAGNG,BOTTLNG,ETC MCH	W 2	19	W 1	13	W 12	235	W 323	8038	MACH NETT BOUTEILLES,ETC
749	NONELEC MACH PTS,ACC NES	W 1567	12769	W 2245	17746	W 1937	18677	W 1625	16659	PIECES MACH NON ELEC NDA
7492	COCKS,VALVES ETC NES	W 727	5991	W 714	6852	W 818	8416	W 988	7181	ART ROB,SIM POUR TUYAUX
75	OFFICE MACHNES,ADP EQUIP		41546		41966		51772		61369	MACH BUREAU TRAIT AUTOM
751	OFFICE MACHINES	W 362	7715	W 401	9084	W 349	8146	W 392	8945	MACH,APPAREILS DE BUREAU
752	AUTOMTIC DATA PROC EQUIP	W 349	19680	W 353	17332	W 359	22840	W 411	26110	MACH TRAIT INFORMATION
7521	ANALOG,HYBRID COMPUTERS							W 205	11894	MACH POUR TRAIT INFORMAT
7522	DIGITAL COMPUTERS							W 106	7915	MACH DIGITALES COMPLETES
759	OFFICE,ADP MCH PTS,ACCES	W 356	14151	W 404	15551	W 460	20786	W 621	26313	PIECES DU 751 ET 752
7591	OFFICE MACHINE PARTS NES	W 356	14151	W 404	15551	W 460	20786	W 46	1688	PIECES DU 7511,7518
75911	TYPEWRTR PARTS,ACCES NES	W 343	13743	W 390	15178	W 450	20392	W 2	112	PIECES DU 7511
7599	ACCTG,ETC,ADP MCH PTS,AC							W 575	24625	PIECES DU 751 ET 752
76	TELECOMM,SOUND EQUIPMENT		65002		68545		81846		79556	EQUIPMENT DE TELECOM
761	TELEVISION RECEIVERS	W 14	399	W 5	255	W 7	345	W 1150	12325	RECEPTEURS DE TELEVISION
7611	COLOUR TV RECEIVERS	W 5	265	W 4	235	W 7	283	W 1080	11841	RECEPTEURS COULEUR
762	RADIO BROADCAST RECEIVRS	W 1927	23663	W 2098	25824	W 2223	28295	W 442	9600	RECEPTEURS RADIODIFFUSION
7621	MTR VEHC RADIO RECEIVERS	W 826	10620	W 828	11825	W 824	11365	W 238	5480	RECEPTEURS RADIO AUTO
7628	OTHER RADIO RECEIVERS	W 1087	11827	W 1237	12872	W 1378	14782	W 85	1881	AUTRES RECEPT RADIO
763	SOUND RECORDRS,PHONOGRPH	W 305	9882	W 278	9492	W 373	10471	W 660	12116	PHONO,APP ENREGISTREMENT
7638	OTHR SOUND APPARATUS ETC	W 220	7660	W 203	7275	W 267	7542	W 464	9702	AUT APP D'ENREGIS,REPROD
76388	DICTATING MACHINES ETC	W 157	7216	W 144	6708	W 152	5995	W 331	4798	MACHINES A DICTER
764	TELECOM EQPT,PTS,ACC NES	W 892	31058	W 944	32974	W 1067	42735	W 1064	45515	EQUIP TELECOM,PIECES
7641	LINE TELEPHONE,ETC EQUIP	W 344	17556	W 351	17412	W 405	19811	W 305	20588	APP TELEPHON PAR FIL
7643	TV,RADIO TRANSMITTRS ETC	W 50	5768	W 70	7803	W 114	12032	W 103	9726	APP EMET TELE RADIO
77	ELECTRIC MACHNRY NES ETC		65145		84871		105010		93840	MACH APP ELECT NDA
771	ELECTRIC POWER MACHY NES	W 71	3752	W 79	3470	W 136	3826	W 2018	9447	MACH PROD,TRANS ELECTR
772	SWITCHGEAR ETC,PARTS NES	W 1191	9800	W 1788	16914	W 1919	19764	W 1376	12972	APP COUPURE,SECT ETC
7721	SWITCHGEAR ETC	W 551	4895	W 1180	10062	W 1344	13305	W 1372	12684	APP COUPURE,SECTIONMNT
773	ELECTR DISTRIBUTNG EQUIP	W 1602	7112	W 1425	6996	W 2778	11334	W 2638	11821	EQUIPMT DISTRIBUTION ELECT
7731	INSULATED WIRE,CABLE ETC	W 1350	5642	W 1269	6433	W 2554	10266	W 2469	11005	FILS,CABLES ISOLES ELECT
774	ELECTRO–MEDCL,XRAY EQUIP	W 45	3375	W 69	5172	W 87	9180	W 87	5889	APPAREILS MEDICAUX
775	HOUSEHOLD TYPE EQUIP NES	W 4568	24001	W 5256	29271	W 5827	36211	W 6980	28693	MACH,APP USAGE DOMESTQUE
7752	DOM REFRIGERATRS,FREEZRS	W 2819	13103	W 3131	14011	W 3365	15511	W 3755	13579	REFRIG,CONGEL MENAGER
77521	DOMESTIC REFRIGERATORS							W 2606	10683	REFRIGERATEURS
7753	DOMSTC DISHWASHING MACHS	W 137	2364	W 202	5879	W 630	11437	W 7	50	MACH A LAVER VAISSELLE
778	ELECTRICAL MACHINERY NES	W 3850	16414	W 4580	22109	W 5028	23501	W 4967	23310	AUTRES MACH ELECT NDA
7781	BATTERIES,ACCUMULATORS	W 2767	7084	W 3020	7819	W 3318	9059	W 3515	9393	PILES ET ACCUMULATEURS
78	ROAD VEHICLES		239190		273425		292333		273391	VEHICULES ROUTIERS
781	PASS MOTOR VEH EXC BUSES	W 17182	107310	W 19609	127499	W 21037	130781	W 22723	170210	AUTO TRANSPORT PERSONNES
782	LORRIES,SPCL MTR VEH NES	W 640	2017	W 750	2955	W 1243	5393	W 6359	28722	VEHICULES SPECIAUX,MARCH
7821	LORRIES,TRUCKS	W 31	88	W 41	430	W 81	677	W 4167	15925	VEHICULES TRANSP MARCHAND
7822	SPECIAL MOTOR VEHCLS NES	W 609	1929	W 708	2525	W 1162	4716	W 2192	12797	VEHICULES USAGES SPECIAUX
783	ROAD MOTOR VEHICLES NES	W 14942	78502	W 18661	93081	W 18895	101328	W 6556	24395	VEHICULES ROUTIERS NDA
7831	BUSES	W 14804	78072	W 18135	90769	W 18721	100658	W 4412	18643	VOITURES TRANSPORT COMMUN
784	MOTOR VEH PRTS,ACCES NES	W 4363	43136	W 4475	40946	W 4785	45312	W 4591	41695	PIECES 722,781,782,783
7849	OTHER MOTOR VEHCL PARTS	W 4322	43086	W 4367	40813	W 4717	45237	W 4472	41217	PIECES 722,781,782,783
79	OTHR TRANSPORT EQUIPMENT		4717		5408		7349		5622	AUTRE MATERIEL TRANSPORT
8	MISC MANUFACTURED GOODS		255853		281979		298042		320027	ART MANUFACTURES DIVERS
812	*PLUMBG,HEATNG,LGHTNG EQ	W 879	3962	W 1493	5329	W 1699	6510	W 2969	8119	APPAR SANITAIRES CHAUFFAGE
821	*FURNITURE,PARTS THEREOF	W 759	4208	W 1117	6165	W 2569	9807	W 4437	15757	MEUBLES ET PIECES
8219	FURNITURE AND PARTS NES	W 428	2174	W 681	3117	W 1801	6023	W 3464	9797	AUTRES MEUBLES ET PIECES
831	*TRAVEL GOODS,HANDBAGS	W 591	5446	W 613	6623	W 616	6277	W 783	6924	ARTICLES DE VOYAGE ETC
84	CLOTHING AND ACCESSORIES		76013		78883		75383		74765	VETEMENTS
842	MENS OUTERWEAR NOT KNIT	W 1447	18051	W 1514	18380	W 1445	17538	W 1046	13379	VET DESSUS POUR HOMMES
8423	— TROUSERS,BREECHES ETC							W 732	9610	PANTALONS HOMMES MAT TEX
843	WOMENS OUTERWEAR NONKNIT	W 1467	22614	W 1403	21053	W 1363	22923	W 1545	26585	VET DESSUS FEMMES MAT TEX
8439	— OTHER OUTER GARMENTS							W 1117	17905	AUT VET DES FEM MAT TEXT
844	UNDER GARMENTS NOT KNIT	W 339	5821	W 437	6266	W 456	6968	W 513	7925	VETEMENT DESSOUS MAT TEX
845	OUTERWEAR KNIT NONELASTC	W 1453	12316	W 1783	14044	W 1373	9860	W 1212	15162	VET DESSOUS,ACCES BONNET
8451	— JERSEYS,PULLOVERS ETC	W 772	8384	W 1050	9813	W 731	6742	W 634	8733	CHANDAILS,PULL–OVERS ETC
846	UNDER GARMENTS KNITTED	W 1040	12017	W 1286	13270	W 1168	12553	W 401	5908	SOUS VETS DE BONNETERIE
851	*FOOTWEAR	W 2480	31275	W 2977	33716	W 3100	36660	W 2855	36246	CHAUSSURES
85101	FOOTWEAR RUBBER,PLASTIC	W 102	413	W 115	418	W 192	1567	W 1574	20049	CHAUS SEMELLES CAOUTCH
85102	FOOTWEAR LEATHER	W 2367	30758	W 2849	33167	W 2899	34941	W 1267	15970	CHAUS SEMELLES EN CUIR
87	PRECISION INSTRUMNTS NES		18260		24795		24617		30666	INSTRUM,APPAR SCIENT NDA
872	MEDICAL INSTRUMENTS NES	W 392	7258	W 540	12469	W 390	11244	W 564	12913	INSTR,APP MEDIC–CHIR NDA
87201	DENTAL INSTRUMENTS	W 368	5915	W 507	10135	W 359	9462	W 17	356	INSTRUM,APPAR DENTAIRE
87202	OTH MEDICAL INSTRUMENTS							W 507	11309	INSTRUM,APP MEDECINE
874	MEASURNG,CONTROLNG INSTR	W 404	10276	W 343	9169	W 492	11200	W 527	14029	INSTRUMENTS DE MESURE
88	PHOTO EQU,OPTICL GDS ETC		21812		24363		23796		24418	APP,FOURN PHOTO,OP,MONTR
882	PHOTO,CINEMA SUPPLIES	W 664	6895	W 894	8384	W 873	8207	W 873	8517	PRODUITS PHOTO,CINEMA
8822	PHOTO FILM EXC DEV CINMA	W 462	5624	W 647	6608	W 666	7166	W 696	7626	PLAQUES,PELLICULES,FILMS
885	WATCHES AND CLOCKS		7283		7327		7493		7255	HORLOGERIE
8851	WATCHES,MOVEMENTS,CASES		6602		6485		6824		6911	MONTRES,MOUVEMENTS,BOITES
89	MISC MANUFCTRD GOODS NES		94876		102105		114991		123133	ART MANUFACTURES DIVERS
892	PRINTED MATTER	W 2252	19121	W 2495	19377	W 2860	23253	W 3136	24190	IMPRIMES
8921	PRINTED BOOKS,GLOBES,ETC	W 1243	10492	W 1195	9745	W 1465	11966	W 1801	13459	LIVRES,BROCHURES,CARTES
89211	PRINTED BOOKS,PAMPHLETS	W 1213	10178	W 1167	9564	W 1394	11429	W 1749	12871	LIVRES,BROCHURES
893	ARTICLES OF PLASTIC NES	W 6731	26035	W 7805	30528	W 8496	33559		36239	OUVRAGES EN MAT DIVIS 58
8931	PLSTC PACKG CONTNRS,LIDS	W 5469	20498	W 6126	24040	W 6863	26981	W 3095	13336	ART TRANSP EMBALLAGE ETC
8939	MISC PLASTIC ARTICLES	W 1262	5537	W 1679	6488	W 1633	6577	W 5966	22246	ART DIVERS EN MAT DIV 58
89399	OTHR PLASTC ARTICLES NES	W 1262	5537	W 1679	6488	W 1633	6577	W 4976	20711	AUT OUV MAT DIV 58
894	TOYS,SPORTING GOODS,ETC	W 3038	19587	W 3632	20841	W 4054	23663	W 3909	24612	VOITURES ENFANTS,JOUETS
8942	TOYS,INDOOR GAMES ETC	W 2380	15527	W 3009	17138	W 3365	19719	W 3346	20621	JOUETS,JEUX ETC
89423	TOYS NES	W 1449	10048	W 1851	10432	W 2109	12446	W 1656	10579	JOUETS,MODELES REDUITS
895	OFFICE SUPPLIES NES	W 529	4934	W 597	5047	W 583	6966	W 646	8628	ART PAPET NDA
897	GOLD,SILVER WARE,JEWELRY		8503		10334		8818		8829	BIJOUTERIE,ORFEVRERIE
898	MUSICAL INSTRUMENTS,PTS	W 504	9798	W 485	8919	W 515	10862	W 508	11847	INSTRUMENTS DE MUSIQUE
8983	SOUND RECRDNG TAPE,DISCS	W 406	8120	W 398	7729	W 433	9610	W 416	10588	SUPPORTS SON POUR 763
89832	RECORDED DISCS,TAPES ETC							W 180	8231	DISQUES,PHONO,BANDES
899	OTHER MANUFACTURED GOODS		6535		6820		7488		8293	AUT ART MANUF DIVERS NDA
9	GOODS NOT CLASSD BY KIND		11419		2029		4058		8888	ART TRANSACT NON CLASSES
971	*GOLD,NON MONETARY NES	K 840	9773	K 115	409	K 264	2718	K 865	8572	OR NON MONETAIRE
97101	NONMON GLD UNWRT,SEMIMFD	K 822	9748	K 43	357	K 254	2715	K 836	8565	OR,ALLIAGES D'OR BRUTS

5. Special Exports F.O.B. by Commodities according to the S.I.T.C. (Rev. 2) in thousand U.S. Dollars
Exportations Spéciales F.O.B. par Produits d'après la C.T.C.I. (Rév. 2) en milliers de Dollars E.U.

SITC CTCI	COMMODITY	1993 WEIGHT POIDS	1993 VALUE VALEUR	1994 WEIGHT POIDS	1994 VALUE VALEUR	1995 WEIGHT POIDS	1995 VALUE VALEUR	1996 WEIGHT POIDS	1996 VALUE VALEUR	PRODUIT
	ALL COMMODITIES		506828		539823		577209		569201	TOUS PRODUITS
0	FOOD AND LIVE ANIMALS		389987		399472		413859		392461	ALIMENTS,ANIMAUX VIVANTS
001	*LIVE ANIMALS FOR FOOD	W 93	121	W 221	657	W 78	290	W 672	2800	ANIMAUX VIVANTS
0011	BOVINE SPECIES,LIVE	W 72	101	W 204	624	W 61	213	W 603	2649	ESPECE BOVINE
00111	— PURE BRED FR BREEDING	W 72	101	W 204	624	W 61	213	W 603	2649	BOVINS REPRODUCTEURS
01	MEAT AND PREPARATIONS		16660		5424		4112		6339	VIANDES ET PREPARATIONS
011	MEAT FRESH,CHILLD,FROZEN	W 4619	16634	W 1592	5424	W 1460	4108	W 2697	5786	VIANDES FRAICHES,REF,CONGE
0111	BOVINE MEAT FRESH,FROZEN	W 4547	16306	W 1565	5320	W 1284	3711	W 2340	5053	VIANDES BOVIN FRAI,REF
01112	BOVINE MEAT BONELESS					W 1275	3684	W 2340	5053	VIANDES BOVIN DESOSSEES
02	DAIRY PRODCTS,BIRDS'EGGS		8172		9135		9689		11943	PRODUITS LAITIERS,OEUFS
022	MILK AND CREAM	W 3604	5261	W 4060	5606	W 4571	6323	W 5853	8011	LAIT ET CREME
0224	MILK,CREAM PRESERVED ETC	W 3581	5221	W 4013	5530	W 4523	6266	W 5850	8005	LAIT,CREME CONS,CONC
02249	MILK(EX DRY) PRSVD,SWEET					W 4523	6266	W 5847	7997	LAIT CONS,CONC SUCRE
024	CHEESE AND CURD	W 708	2781	W 703	2714	W 610	2470	W 500	2033	FROMAGE ET CAILLEBOTTE
025	EGGS,BIRDS,FRESH,PRSRVD	W 124	130	W 554	815	W 558	897	W 1003	1900	OEUFS
0251	— IN SHELL	W 124	130	W 554	815	W 558	897	W 1003	1900	OEUFS EN COQUILLE
03	FISH AND PREPARATIONS		86986		102586		118399		112633	POISSONS ET PREPARATIONS
034	FISH,FRESH,CHILLED,FROZN	W 6366	18609	W 6188	18431	W 6512	19399	W 7223	22017	POISSON FRAIS, REFRIG,CONG
0341	FISH FRSH,CHLLD,EX FILLT	W 111	65	W 26	17	W 4767	12727	W 5135	14102	POISSON FRAIS,REFRIGERE
0343	FISH FILLETS,FRESH,CHLLD					W 1720	6595	W 2035	7738	FILETS FRAIS,REFRIGERES
0344	FISH FILLETS,FROZEN	W 6254	18544	W 6162	18414			W 5	19	FILETS CONGELES
035	FISH SALTED,DRIED,SMOKED	W 75	2430	W 84	2766	W 109	3723	W 194	4564	POISSON SECHE,SALE,FUME
03503	FISH(EX COD)DRIED,SALTED					W 86	3388	W 153	4040	POISSONS SECHES,SALES
036	SHELL FISH FRESH,FROZEN	W 9282	65885	W 10321	81389	W 13254	95277	W 13131	85966	CRUSTACES,MOLLUSQUES
05	VEGETABLES AND FRUIT		225344		231258		208036		199801	LEGUMES ET FRUITS
054	VEG ETC FRSH,SMPLY PRSVD	W 6147	2398	W 12196	5113	W 12043	3623	W 20578	5853	LEGUMES FRAIS,CONG,SECS
0545	OTHER FRESH VEGETABLES	W 3465	863	W 6227	1448	W 9179	1972	W 17564	4058	AUTRES LEGUMES FRAIS,REF
05459	FRESH VEGETABLES NES	W 3465	863	W 6227	1448	W 9113	1946	W 17564	4058	LEGUMES FRAIS,REFRI NDA
0548	EDIBLE VEG NES FRESH,DRY	W 2574	1478	W 3855	2579	W 1280	854	W 2885	1673	RACINES,TUBERCULES
05481	ROOTS,TUBERS FRESH,DRY	W 2574	1478	W 3855	2579	W 1280	854	W 2885	1673	RACINES DE MANIOC ETC
057	FRUIT,NUTS,FRESH,DRIED	W 729081	216651	W 782518	220090	W 718205	203762	W 656797	192717	FRUITS FRAIS OU SECS
0573	BANANA,PLANTAIN,FRSH,DRY	W 694167	201853	W 747016	206844	W 690028	190365	W 632264	184162	BANANES FRAICHES,SECHEES
0579	FRUIT FRESH OR DRIED NES	W 34885	14795	W 35502	13246	W 28161	13396	W 24533	8554	FRUITS FRAIS,SECS NDA
05798	OTHER FRESH FRUIT	W 34885	14795	W 35502	13245	W 27980	13326	W 23339	8133	AUTRES FRUITS FRAIS
058	FRUIT PRESERVED,PREPARED	W 10523	5728	W 19376	5566	W 431	649	W 726	1226	CONSERVES DE FRUITS
0582	FRUIT PRESERVED BY SUGAR	W 10022	4902	W 19214	5322					FRUITS CONFITS AU SUCRE
06	SUGAR AND PREPS,HONEY		22287		17757		19989		22892	SUCRES ET PRODUITS
061	SUGAR AND HONEY	W 65221	21959	W 54777	17073	W 45775	18978	W 46645	22598	SUCRES ET MIEL
0611	RAW BEET AND CANE SUGAR	W 63110	21899	W 54777	17073	W 44215	17972	W 46645	22598	SUCRES BRUTS
07	COFFEE,TEA,COCOA,SPICES		13291		15707		36047		20970	CAFE,THE,CACAO,EPICES
071	COFFEE AND SUBSTITUTES	W 8079	11888	W 5266	13989	W 10945	33408	W 8400	18803	CAFE ET SUCCEDANES
0711	COFFEE GREEN,ROASTED,SUB	W 8079	11888	W 5266	13989	W 10945	33408	W 8400	18803	CAFE TORREFIE OU DECAFEINE
07111	COFFEE GREEN,HUSKS,SKINS					W 10945	33402	W 8345	18705	CAFE NON TORREFIE
081	*FEEDING STUFF FOR ANIML	W 16290	4819	W 20365	5675	W 21226	5406	W 8013	2605	NOURRITURE POUR ANIMAUX
0814	MEAT OR FISH MEAL FODDER	W 15734	4480	W 19082	5085	W 20468	4988	W 7095	2192	FARINES DE VIANDES,POISSONS
08142	FISH MEAL FODDER					W 20468	4988	W 7095	2192	FARINES DE POISSONS
09	MISC EDIBLE PRODUCTS		11950		10804		11659		10935	PREP ALIMENTAIRES DIVERSES
098	EDIBLE PRODCTS,PREPS NES	W 5910	11950	W 5610	10784	W 6136	11598	W 5639	10935	PREP ALIMENTAIRES NDA
09804	SAUCES,MIXED SEASONINGS	W 3165	5446	W 5005	9690	W 5504	10348	W 4956	9888	SAUCES,ASSAISONNEMENTS
09809	MISC FOOD PREPRTIONS NES	W 2581	6160	W 356	677	W 484	977	W 412	650	PREP ALIMENTAIRES NDA
1	BEVERAGES AND TOBACCO		14518		14101		10278		10587	BOISSONS ET TABACS
11	BEVERAGES		6248		7490		5491		4734	BOISSONS
112	ALCOHOLIC BEVERAGES	W 5052	5639	W 5607	6977	W 2623	4539	W 2273	4450	BOISSONS ALCOOLIQUES
1124	DISTILLED ALCOHOLIC BEVS	W 4189	5065	W 3589	5627	W 2485	4444	W 2069	4307	ALCOOLS,EAUX-DE-VIE
11249	OTH ALCOHOLC BEVS,CMPNDS					W 2478	4401	W 2060	4285	BOISSONS ALCOOLIQUES NDA
12	TOBACCO AND MANUFACTURES		8270		6612		4788		5853	TABACS BRUTS FABRIQUES
121	TOBACCO UNMNFCTRD,REFUSE	W 1290	5610	W 559	1688	W 248	494	W 170	658	TABACS BRUTS,DECHETS
1211	TOBACCO,NOT STRIPPED	W 1290	5610	W 559	1688	W 248	494	W 163	634	TABACS NON ECOTES
122	TOBACCO,MANUFACTURED	W 400	2659	W 746	4924	W 710	4294	W 822	5195	TABACS FABRIQUES
1222	CIGARETTES	W 400	2659	W 745	4847	W 709	4198	W 822	5189	CIGARETTES
2	CRUDE MATERLS,EXCL FUELS		5691		4947		10840		9774	MAT BRUTES NON COMESTIBLES
22	OIL SEEDS,OLEAGINOUS FRT						2812		453	GRAINES,FRUITS OLEAGINEUX
223	SEEDS FOR OTH FIXED OILS					W 37874	2812	W 8300	453	GRAINES AUTRES HUILES FIXES
2232	PALM NUTS AND KERNELS					W 37874	2812	W 8300	453	NOIX,AMANDES DE PALMISTE
28	METALLIFEROUS ORES,SCRAP		1498		1894		5283		6681	MINERAIS METAL,DECHETS
288	NONFERR METAL SCRAP NES	W 1148	845	W 1118	815	W 5332	4313	W 6861	5832	DECHETS NON FERREUX
2882	OTHER BASE MTL SCRAP NES	W 1148	845	W 1118	815	W 5332	4313	W 6861	5832	AUTRES DECHETS
28823	ALUMINIUM WSTE AND SCRAP	W 313	215	W 80	56	W 4387	3212	W 5973	4976	DECHETS D'ALUMINIUM
29	CRUDE ANIMAL,VEG MAT NES		2845		2488		2249		1966	MATIERES BRUTES ANIM,VEGET
292	CRUDE VEG MATERIALS NES	W 786	1897	W 685	1599	W 572	1282	W 546	1305	MAT BRUTES VEGETALES NDA
3	MINERAL FUELS ETC		10129		12973		18181		28027	COMBUSTIBLES MINERAUX LUB
33	PETROLEUM AND PRODUCTS		10129		12973		18181		27743	PETROLE ET DERIVES
334	PETROLEUM PRODUCTS,REFIN	W 81601	10128	W 96712	12966	W 143313	18180	W 76094	27741	PRODUITS RAFFINES
3341	GASOLINE,OTH LIGHT OILS	W 3430	1173	W 5465	1515	W 2259	795	W 36329	7157	ESSENCES POUR MOTEURS
33411	MOTOR,AVIATION SPIRIT					W 2259	795	W 36329	7157	ESSENCES MOTEURS D'AVIONS
3342	KEROSENE,OTH MEDIUM OILS			W 11610	1912					PETR LAMPANTS,AUT HUIL
3343	GAS OILS	W 75884	6484	W 77325	7219	W 139014	15560	W 24406	3975	GAS OILS
3344	FUEL OILS,NES	W 2287	2471	W 2312	2320			W 13024	14256	FUEL OILS
3345	LUBS,PETROLEUM OILS NES					W 2041	1825	W 2335	2354	HUILES LUBRIFIANTES
33451	LUBS(HIGH PETR CONT) ETC					W 2041	1825	W 2335	2354	HUILES LUBRIF,H LOURDES
4	ANIMAL,VEGETABLE OIL,FAT		2077		2461		1879		1681	HUILES,GRAISSES ANIM,VEG
411	*ANIMAL OILS AND FATS	W 8645	2062	W 12623	2461	W 7357	1868	W 2323	679	HUILES,GRAISSES ANIMALES
4111	OILS OF FISH,WHALES ETC	W 8645	2062	W 12623	2461	W 7357	1868	W 2323	679	GRAISSES,HUILES DE POISSONS
41112	OTHER FISH OILS AND FATS					W 7357	1868	W 2323	679	AUTRES HUILES ET GRAISSES
5	CHEMCLS,RELATED PROD NES		22173		26615		28742		28466	PRODUITS CHIMIQUES
51	ORGANIC CHEMICALS		1951		3119		1388		3152	PROD CHIMIQ ORGANIQUES
512	ALCOHOLS,PHENOLS ETC	W 6043	1948	W 8751	3040	W 3360	1385	W 5540	2838	PHENOLS,PHENOLS-ALCOOLS
5121	ACYCLIC ALCOHOLS,DERIVS	W 6043	1948	W 8751	3040	W 3360	1385	W 5540	2838	ALCOOLS ACYCLIQUES
51216	ETHYL ALC,DENATRD SPIRIT	W 6043	1948	W 8751	3039	W 3360	1385	W 5540	2838	ALCOOL ETHYLIQUE NON DENAT
53	DYES,TANNING,COLOUR PROD		3814		3839		5627		6801	PROD TEINTURE,COLORANTS
531	SYNT DYE,NAT INDGO,LAKES	W 1110	3009	W 844	2275	W 796	2544	W 848	2810	MAT COLOR ORGAN,LAQUES
5311	SYNTHIC ORGNIC DYESTUFFS	W 1110	3009	W 844	2275	W 791	2502	W 845	2792	MAT COLOR ORGAN SYNTHET
533	PIGMENTS,PAINTS,ETC	W 269	804	W 480	1564	W 1138	3083	W 1608	3991	PIGMENTS,PEINTURES,VERNIS
5334	VARNISHES,DISTEMPERS ETC	W 206	477	W 294	882	W 1006	2622	W 1530	3632	PEINTURES A L'EAU
53342	OTH PAINTS,VARNISHES ETC					W 672	1845	W 1355	3280	AUTRES PEINTURES,VERNIS
541	*MEDICINAL,PHARM PRODUCT	K 559515	9962	K 712344	12113	K 984812	15811	K 866164	13041	PROD MEDICINAUX PHARMACEUT
5417	MEDICAMENTS	K 559515	9962	K 711997	12083	K 983807	15792	K 865691	13036	MEDICAMENTS
54179	— CONTNG OTH SUBSTANCES					K 978508	15148	K 863861	12973	MED CONT AUT SUBSTANCES
55	PERFUME,CLEANING ETC PRD		5184		5801		4466		3593	PROD POUR PARFUM,TOILETTE
553	PERFUMERY,COSMETICS,ETC	W 726	4571	W 948	5551	W 610	4070	W 618	3299	PRODUITS DE PARFUMERIE
6	BASIC MANUFACTURES		24699		33627		39184		44222	ART MANUFACTURES

5. Special Exports F.O.B. by Commodities according to the S.I.T.C. (Rev. 2) in thousand U.S. Dollars
Exportations Spéciales F.O.B. par Produits d'après la C.T.C.I. (Rév. 2) en milliers de Dollars E.U.

SITC CTCI	COMMODITY	1993		1994		1995		1996		PRODUIT
		WEIGHT POIDS	VALUE VALEUR	WEIGHT POIDS	VALUE VALEUR	WEIGHT POIDS	VALUE VALEUR	WEIGHT POIDS	VALUE VALEUR	
61	LEATHER,DRESSED FUR,ETC		7995		9071		8643		9032	CUIRS,PELLETERIES
611	LEATHER	W 4519	7995	W 4957	9071	W 4373	8643	W 4945	8992	CUIRS,PEAUX PREPARES
6114	LEATHR BOVINE NES,EQUINE	W 4519	7995	W 4956	9038	W 4373	8643	W 4945	8992	CUIRS DE BOVINS
63	WOOD,CORK MANUFACTRS NES		931		1629		1846		2238	OUVRAGES LIEGE ET BOIS
635	WOOD MANUFACTURES NES	W 525	752	W 775	1107	W 1175	1796	W 1396	2195	ART MANUF EN BOIS NDA
6359	OTHER WOOD MANUFACTURES	W 525	751	W 748	1041	W 1144	1741	W 1284	1990	OUVRAGES EN BOIS NDA
63591	TOOLS,HANDLES ETC WOOD	W 522	733	W 744	1027	W 1135	1727	W 1260	1947	OUTILS MANCHES D'OUTILS
64	PAPER,PAPERBOARD AND MFR		5368		10234		16034		12798	PAPIERS,CARTONS & OUVRAGES
641	PAPER AND PAPERBOARD	W 1224	688	W 4969	2100	W 8817	5384	W 7889	3522	PAPIERS ET CARTONS
6411	NEWSPRINT	W 1218	654	W 4953	2064	W 8377	4776	W 7498	2931	PAPIER JOURNAL
642	PAPER,ETC,PRECUT,ARTS OF	W 4647	4680	W 7277	8135	W 9447	10650	W 5279	9276	PAP,CARTONS DECOUPES
6421	PAPER ETC CONTAINERS	W 3522	2298	W 5096	3379	W 6907	5256	W 1939	2601	BOITES,SACS EMBALLAGES
6428	PAPER ETC ARTICLES NES	W 1086	2266	W 2085	4592	W 2420	5072	W 3267	6498	OUVRAGES EN PATE A PAPIER
64283	PAPER DISHES,CUPS,ETC					W 1066	2595	W 1196	2794	ASSIETTES ETC EN PAPIER
64284	PAPER TISSUES,TOWELS ETC		1	W 496	1896	W ^	15			MOUCHOIRS SERVIETTES EN PAP
64285	PAPER ETC DIAPERS ETC	W 1025	2225	W 1036	2348	W 410	1757	W 693	2885	SERVIETTES HYGIENIQUES
66	NONMETAL MINERAL MFS NES		2823		3129		2989		2029	ART MIN NON METALLIQUES
68	NON–FERROUS METALS		1547		2276		1194		2470	METAUX NON FERREUX
684	ALUMINIUM	W 2192	1517	W 3072	2265	W 135	476	W 297	1194	ALUMINIUM
6841	ALUMINIUM,ALLOYS,UNWRGHT	W 2168	1403	W 3051	2158					ALUMINIUM,ALLIAGES BRUTS
69	METAL MANUFACTURES NES		4596		6685		7928		14719	ART MANUFACT EN METAL NDA
692	METAL TANKS,BOXES,ETC	W 1184	3149	W 1118	5293	W 1476	6112	W 3577	12365	RECIPIENTS METALLIQUES
6924	MTL TRANSPORT BOXES ETC	W 1181	3136	W 1118	5293	W 1476	6112	W 3571	12356	FUTS,TAMBOURS,BIDONS
69242	ALUMNM TRNSPRT BOXES ETC	W 1172	3104	W 1118	5293	W 1476	6112	W 3531	12274	FUTS,TAMBOURS,BIDONS ALU
8	MISC MANUFACTURED GOODS		32888		40259		48629		41598	ART MANUFACTURES DIVERS
84	CLOTHING AND ACCESSORIES		24053		23239		25724		24125	VETEMENTS
842	MENS OUTERWEAR NOT KNIT	W 74	2455	W 63	2258	W 56	1904	W 55	1592	VET DESSUS POUR HOMMES
843	WOMENS OUTERWEAR NONKNIT	W 105	4510	W 114	4246	W 137	5127	W 132	4997	VET DESSUS FEMMES MAT TEX
8439	— OTHER OUTER GARMENTS					W 92	3170	W 82	2744	AUT VET DES FEM MAT TEXT
844	UNDER GARMENTS NOT KNIT	W 354	11581	W 311	11481	W 419	15110	W 375	13415	VETEMENT DESSOUS MAT TEX
8441	— MENS SHIRTS	W 288	10044	W 278	10399	W 328	12736	W 285	10831	CHEMISES HOMMES MAT TEXT
84412	—— OF SYNTHETIC FIBRES					W 328	12736	W 285	10831	CHEMISES HOMMES FIB SYNT
8442	— MENS,OTHR THAN SHIRTS		9		10	W 75	1851	W 70	1878	SOUS–VET HOMMES MAT TEXT
8443	— WOMENS	W 65	1528	W 33	1072	W 16	522	W 20	706	VET DESSOUS FEM MAT TEXT
847	TEXTILE CLTHNG ACCES NES	W 97	2484	W 83	2139			W 3	79	ACCES VET MAT TEXT NDA
8471	— NOT KNITTED	W 92	2310	W 77	1941				3	ACCES VET MAT TEX NON BON
84714	GLOVES,SOCKS ETC,NOT KNT	W 92	2310	W 77	1940					BAS,CHAUSSETTES MAT TEXT
848	HEADGEAR,NONTXTL CLOTHNG	W 854	2621	W 882	2711	W 1072	3567	W 1086	3951	VET ACCES MAT AUT QUE TEX
8482	PLASTC,RUBBR CLTHG,ACCES	W 853	2599	W 880	2645	W 1072	3556	W 1085	3922	VET ACCES MAT PLAS ARTIF
84822	RUBBER CLOTHING,ACCESRYS	W 853	2599	W 880	2645	W 1072	3556	W 1085	3922	VET ACCES CAOUT VULCAN
89	MISC MANUFCTRD GOODS NES		7689		16317		22369		16692	ART MANUFACTURES DIVERS
893	ARTICLES OF PLASTIC NES	W 889	1778	W 969	1728		2011	W 770	1611	OUVRAGES EN MAT DIVIS 58
8931	PLSTC PACKG CONTNRS,LIDS	W 883	1751	W 925	1644	W 428	1147	W 257	739	ART TRANSP EMBALLAGE ETC
897	GOLD,SILVER WARE,JEWELRY		1049		6723		7810		1785	BIJOUTERIE,ORFEVRERIE
8973	PREC JEWLRY,GLD–SILVWARE		1049		6723		7809		1785	BIJOUX OR,ARGENT ORFEVRE
89731	PRECIOUS METAL JEWELLERY		1048		6055		7809		1778	ART BIJOUTERIE,JOAILLER
899	OTHER MANUFACTURED GOODS	W 1899	4749	W 3058	7537	W 4722	10548	W 4690	11558	AUT ART MANUF DIVERS NDA
8997	BASKETWORK,BROOMS ETC	W 1768	4043	W 2823	6590	W 4439	9657	W 4581	11194	OUVRAGES VANNERIE NDA
89972	BRUSHES,BROOMS,MOPS ETC	W 1767	4007	W 2822	6589	W 4439	9647	W 4581	11194	BALAIS ET BALAYETTES
9	GOODS NOT CLASSD BY KIND		3259		3989		4427		10865	ART TRANSACT NON CLASSES
971	*GOLD,NON MONETARY NES	K 850	3158	K 585	3765	K 1234	4427	K 2442	10865	OR NON MONETAIRE
97101	NONMON GLD UNWRT,SEMIMFD	K 468	3085	K 577	3743	K 1075	4384	K 2427	10807	OR,ALLIAGES D'OR BRUTS

FOOT NOTES – NOTES

TABLE 1 –
1 Prior to 1964, imports f.o.b.
TABLEAU 1 –
1 Avant 1964, les importations sont f.a.b.

1. HISTORICAL SERIES, 1960–1995 GENERAL TRADE, IMPORTS F.O.B., EXPORTS F.O.B.
SERIES HISTORIQUES, 1960–1995 COMMERCE GENERAL, IMPORTATIONS F.O.B., EXPORTATIONS F.O.B

YEAR ANNEE	VALUE IN MILLION KINA VALEUR EN MILLION KINA MERCHANDISE # 1 –MARCHANDISE IMPORTS	EXPORTS	GOLD –OR IMPORTS	EXPORTS	CONVERSION FACTORS U.S. CENTS PER KINA FACTEURS DE CONVERSION CENTS E.U. PAR KINA IMPORTS	EXPORTS	INDEX NUMBERS –INDICES QUANTUM IMPORTS	EXPORTS	UNIT VALUE VALEUR UNITAIRE IMPORTS	EXPORTS
1960	42.10	36.40		1.27	112.0000	112.0000				
1961	53.50	31.90		1.36	112.0000	112.0000				
1962	51.90	30.40		1.44	112.0000	112.0000				
1963	57.10	35.00		1.34	112.0000	112.0000				
1964	70.70	39.60		1.32	112.0000	112.0000				
1965	86.90	48.10		1.08	112.0000	112.0000				
1966	110.40	48.90		0.95	112.0000	112.0000				
1967	127.40	52.30		0.91	112.0000	112.0000				
1968	145.30	69.40		0.82	112.0000	112.0000				
1969	150.50	74.40		0.81	112.0000	112.0000				
1970	239.50	91.70		0.80	112.0000	112.0000				
1971	275.40	106.30		0.70	113.8760	113.7580				
1972	247.40	182.00		0.81	119.0990	119.0990				
1973	214.40	362.70		0.95	142.1660	143.0970				
1974	298.90	477.80		1.62	143.2280	145.1130				
1975	362.80	335.90			131.0860	131.1220				
1976	351.50	435.50			122.2990	122.4960				
1977	448.30	539.80			126.5470	126.5680				
1978	478.30	504.00			141.2820	141.6820				
1979	561.60	629.10			140.4000	140.3790				
1980	684.20	694.20			149.4710	148.7350				
1981	738.10	581.80			148.5438	148.3945				71
1982	751.70	570.90			135.3008	135.1002				72
1983	821.70	682.20			119.5202	119.1071				82
1984	851.10	783.50			111.7249	111.5829				93
1985	866.90	917.00			99.8319	99.7706				91
1986	1037.38	1000.80			102.9352	102.9934				96
1987	1144.94	1123.20			110.2289	110.5110				105
1988	1378.85	1256.30			115.5184	115.5419				81
1989	1324.80	1111.60			116.7165	116.9369				68
1990	1138.61	1122.40			104.6084	104.8583				100
1991	1535.94	1390.50			105.0583	104.9507				99
1992	1431.17	1862.60			103.7504	103.4645				101
1993	1270.50	2527.30			102.2448	102.2374				113
1994	1534.10	2662.00			99.1461	98.8071				132
1995	1862.90	3395.90			77.9239	78.0400				

2. IMPORTS BY BROAD ECONOMIC CATEGORY AND EXPORTS BY INDUSTRIAL ORIGIN. (PERCENTAGE OF TOTAL VALUE)
IMPORTATIONS PAR CATEGORIES ECONOMIQUES ET EXPORTATIONS PAR BRANCHE D'ACTIVITE.(EN POURCENTAGE DE LA VALEUR TOTALE)

IMPORTS – IMPORTATIONS

	1990	1991	1992	1993	1994	1995	1996
TOTAL IMPORTS–IMPORTATIONS TOTALES	100.						
1 FOOD BEV–ALIMENTATION BOISSONS	16.9						
11 PRIMARY–PRODUITS DE BASE	4.7						
111 FOR INDUSTRY–POUR L'INDUSTRIE	1.2						
112 FOR HOUSEHOLDS–POUR LES MENAGES	3.5						
12 PROCESSED–PRODUITS ELABORES	12.2						
121 FOR INDUSTRY–POUR L'INDUSTRIE	0.5						
122 FOR HOUSEHOLDS–POUR LES MENAGES	11.7						
2 IND SUPPLIES–APPROV INDUSTRIELS	24.0						
21 PRIMARY–PRODUITS DE BASE	1.1						
22 PROCESSED–PRODUITS ELABORES	23.0						
3 FUELS–COMBUSTIBLES	6.8						
31 PRIMARY–PRODUITS DE BASE	0.1						
32 PROCESSED–PRODUITS ELABORES	6.7						
321 MOTOR SPIRIT–ESSENCE	1.2						
322 OTHER–AUTRES	5.5						
4 MACHINERY–EQUIPEMENT	23.7						
41 CAPITAL EQUIPMENT–MACHINES	20.8						
42 PARTS–PIECES ACCESSOIRES	2.9						
5 TRANSPORT–TRANSPORT	16.7						
51 PASSENGER CARS–AUTOMOBILES	2.8						
52 OTHER–AUTRES	7.6						
521 INDUSTRIAL–INDUSTRIELS	7.5						
522 NON INDUSTRIAL–NON INDUSTRIEL	0.1						
53 PARTS–PIECES ACCESSOIRES	6.3						
6 CONSUM GOODS–BIENS CONSOMMATION	10.3						
61 DURABLE–DURABLES	1.6						
62 SEMI DURABLE–SEMI DURABLES	5.2						
63 NON DURABLE–NON DURABLES	3.5						
7 GOODS NES–BIENS NDA	1.6						

EXPORTS – EXPORTATIONS

	1990	1991	1992	1993	1994	1995	1996
TOTAL EXPORTS–EXPORTATIONS TOTALES	100.	100.	100.	100.			
1 AGRICULTURE	24.9	21.8	27.2	28.1			
2 MINING QUARRY–INDUS EXTRACTIVES	56.6	53.8	50.3	62.3			
3 MANUFACTURING–IND MANUFACTUR	18.4	24.4	22.5	9.6			
31 FOOD BEV TOBACCO–ALIM BOISS TAB	5.4	6.2	9.1	4.9			
32 TEXTILES–INDUSTRIES TEXTILES	0.0	0.2	0.1	0.1			
33 WOOD & PRODUCTS–BOIS & PRODUITS	0.9	0.7	0.7	0.5			
34 PAPER & PRODUCTS–PAPIER & PRODT	0.0	0.0	0.0	0.0			
35 CHEMICALS–INDUSTRIES CHIMIQUES	0.5	0.4	0.2	0.1			
36 NON METAL MIN–MIN NON METAL	0.1	0.0	0.0	0.0			
37 BASIC METAL–IND METAL BASE	1.5	1.3	1.0	0.4			
38 METAL MANUF–MANUF METAL	8.6	15.0	10.8	3.4			
39 OTH MANUF IND–AUTRES MANUF	1.5	0.5	0.5	0.2			

3. TRADE BY PRINCIPAL COUNTRIES OF PRODUCTION AND LAST CONSIGNMENT (VALUE IN THOUSAND U.S. DOLLARS)
ECHANGES SELON LES PRINCIPAUX PAYS DE PRODUCTION ET DE DERNIERE CONSIGNATION (VALEUR EN MILLIERS DE DOLLARS EU)

COUNTRIES–PAYS	GENERAL IMPORTS F.O.B. IMPORTATIONS GENERALES F.O.B.				
	1989	1990	1991	1992	1993
World	1576451	1233083			
Africa	2475	3236			
Americas	245324	149204			
Northern America	239681	143267			
LAIA	5586	5914			
CACM	1				
Caribbean	30	12			
Rest of America	26	11			
As.ex F.USSR	477393	366121			
Eur.x F.USSR	170781	87594			
EU	164070	84234			
EFTA	4895	1922			
East Europe	812	353			
Other Europe	1004	1084			
Former USSR	117	13636			
Oceania	678270	609862			
Australia/Australie	625426	567901			
Japan/Japon	236663	160453			
USA/Etats–Unis d'Amer	205658	119553			
Singapore/Singapour	106213	105686			
New Zealand	49534	40805			
United Kingdom	45067	29022			
France,Monac	56056	13992			
Canada	34023	23714			
China/Chine	31259	25016			
Hong Kong	33815	19691			
Germany/Allemagne	22991	16326			
Korea, Republic of	16212	11318			
Netherlands/Pays–Bas	21235	4902			
Malaysia/Malaisie	11731	9231			
Indonesia/Indonésie	7499	11621			
Thailand/Thaïlande	8752	7962			
Former USSR/Anc. URSS	117	13636			
Italy/Italie	3851	8939			
Denmark/Danemark	4940	3737			
Chile/Chili	3985	4652			
Belgium–Luxembourg	4595	2183			
Saudi Arabia	6042	25			
Sweden/Suède	2637	2798			
Philippines	1835	3161			
Norway,SVD,JM	3433	940			
Sudan/Soudan	1365	2193			
India/Inde	1375	1189			
Switz.Liecht	1462	982			
Fiji/Fidji	1656	727			
Brazil/Brésil	1327	970			
Fm Yugoslav	1002	1081			
Malawi	963	1014			
Bangladesh	1002	772			
Vanuatu	1503	174			
Ireland/Irlande	923	517			
Spain/Espagne	907	451			
Finland/Finlande	430	898			
Israel/Israël	426	436			
Austria/Autriche	320	448			
Korea Dem People's Rp	178	352			
Hungary/Hongrie	423	15			
Mexico/Mexique	189	242			
Sri Lanka	217	148			
Czechoslovakia	197	156			
Solomon Isls	110	139			
Jordan/Jordanie	152	70			
Pakistan	83	134			
Poland/Pologne	37	152			
Portugal	115	16			
Mali	111	0			

COUNTRIES–PAYS	GENERAL EXPORTS F.O.B. EXPORTATIONS GENERALES F.O.B.				
	1989	1990	1991	1992	1993
Monde	1453785	1261730	1641763	1698897	2624576
Afrique	130	2138	1739	66	53
Amériques	28529	34301	37225	39975	110940
Amérique du Nord	28350	34259	36415	39937	110901
ALAI	164	32	810	3	39
MCAC					
Caraïbes	16	10		34	1
Autre Amérique					
Asie l'URSS exclus	740374	568758	645706	641975	1234549
Europe l'URSS exclus	509316	312120	300853	309704	318403
UE	461438	304783	262150	309119	318373
AELE	1747	7336	602	567	30
Europe de l'Est	46131		38101	18	
Autre de l'Europe					
Ancienne URSS			14983	4164	
Océanie	174420	343964	639781	700822	960201
Australia/Australie	165539	328528	608041	691849	933711
Japan/Japon	543957	351422	361678	360034	563233
Germany/Allemagne	341636	201225	147322	163940	167004
Korea, Republic of	126820	124939	147761	133823	262349
United Kingdom	66033	54240	65706	72917	81255
Philippines	31639	53677	69521	47231	70334
USA/Etats–Unis d'Amer	28063	30131	36109	36004	109718
Singapore/Singapour	9884	18499	34293	62410	82816
China/Chine	1064	2467	4159	4599	173196
Finland/Finlande	5590	35801	32956	40934	26843
Netherlands/Pays–Bas	21514	8145	8418	25634	26980
New Zealand	5748	11616	27447	5294	19465
Hong Kong	7130	2721	9485	10353	8251
Bulgaria/Bulgarie			37791	18	
Czechoslovakia	30753				
Indonesia/Indonésie	3423	4026	479	6602	12542
Belgium–Luxembourg	6556	2165	4858	3509	3156
Thailand/Thaïlande	527	843	1260	1893	15521
Malaysia/Malaisie	1916	1014	2411	2557	10561
Spain/Espagne	14278	56	765	95	26
Jordan/Jordanie	5001	205	1000	6898	2047
Former USSR/Anc. URSS			14983		
India/Inde	3325	4952	1842	3720	306
Poland/Pologne	11660		310		
Solomon Isls	2185	2658	2976	2689	1304
Denmark/Danemark	26		0		11263
France,Monac	5430	2619	1345	860	445
Switz.Liecht	1746	7299	602	567	30
Canada	287	4127	307	3933	1183
Myanmar			9481		
Fiji/Fidji	488	513	275	236	4807
Russian Federation				4164	
Korea Dem People's Rp	2488				
Italy/Italie	206	319	449	543	579
Hungary/Hongrie	1991				
So. Africa Customs Un	65	1848	18	0	
Former GDR	1727				
New Caledonia	87	115	479	540	123
Pakistan	435	189	238	229	161
Vanuatu	69	352	26	91	572
Ireland/Irlande	147	137	171	257	220
Un. Rep. of Tanzania		8	852	30	10
Iran (Islamic Rp. of)			887		
Chile/Chili			809	2	
Sweden/Suède	13	61	3	345	378
Sri Lanka	4	290	91	73	319
Angola			497		
French Polynesia	269		152	40	35
Egypt/Egypte	11	273	192	20	1
Portugal	9	13	156	87	224

(VALUE AS PERCENTAGE OF WORLD TOTAL)(VALEURS EN POURCENTAGE DU TOTAL MONDIAL)

	1984	1985	1986	1987	1988	1989	1990	1991	1992	1993
Africa	0.1	0.1	0.1	0.1	0.1	0.2	0.3			
Americas	12.0	12.3	12.9	14.0	11.9	15.6	12.1			
Northern America	11.7	12.0	12.3	13.3	11.5	15.2	11.6			
LAIA	0.2	0.3	0.6	0.4	0.5	0.4	0.5			
CACM	0.0	0.0	0.0	0.1		0.0				
Caribbean	0.0	0.0	0.0	0.0	0.0	0.0	0.0			
Rest of America	0.0	0.0	0.0	0.2	0.0	0.0	0.0			
As.ex F.USSR	35.1	33.8	31.3	32.4	31.9	30.3	29.7			
Eur.x F.USSR	7.6	8.1	10.8	9.1	8.5	10.8	7.1			
EU	7.2	7.7	10.4	8.7	8.3	10.4	6.8			
EFTA	0.2	0.3	0.3	0.3	0.2	0.3	0.2			
East Europe	0.1	0.0	0.0	0.0	0.0	0.1	0.0			
Other Europe	0.2	0.1	0.1	0.1	0.1	0.1	0.1			
Former USSR	0.0	0.0	0.0	0.0	0.0	0.0	1.1			
Oceania	44.9	45.2	44.4	44.2	47.4	43.0	49.5			
Australia/Australie	39.5	39.6	39.9	40.6	43.6	39.7	46.1			
Japan/Japon	15.8	17.0	17.7	17.6	17.8	15.0	13.0			
USA/Etats–Unis d'Amer	11.1	11.6	10.2	10.9	10.4	13.0	9.7			
Singapore/Singapour	11.9	10.0	6.2	6.5	5.9	6.7	8.6			
New Zealand	5.2	5.4	4.4	3.5	3.7	3.1	3.3			
United Kingdom	3.5	2.9	3.4	2.9	3.1	2.9	2.4			
France,Monac	0.8	0.9	0.8	0.7	0.7	3.6	1.1			
Canada	0.6	0.4	2.2	2.4	1.1	2.2	1.9			
China/Chine	2.0	1.7	1.9	1.9	2.2	2.0	2.0			
Hong Kong	2.3	2.3	1.8	2.0	2.0	2.1	1.6			

	1984	1985	1986	1987	1988	1989	1990	1991	1992	1993
Afrique	0.0	0.0	0.0		0.0	0.0	0.2	0.1	0.0	0.0
Amériques	3.7	7.9	3.2	2.0	3.2	2.0	2.7	2.3	2.4	4.2
Amérique du Nord	3.7	7.9	3.2	2.0	3.2	2.0	2.7	2.2	2.4	4.2
ALAI			0.0	0.0	0.0	0.0	0.0	0.0	0.0	0.0
MCAC										
Caraïbes			0.0			0.0	0.0		0.0	0.0
Autre Amérique										
Asie l'URSS exclus	41.0	32.0	37.0	51.3	56.8	50.9	45.1	39.3	37.8	47.0
Europe l'URSS exclus	44.8	47.6	44.4	38.1	33.0	35.0	24.7	18.3	18.2	12.1
UE	43.1	47.5	44.4	38.1	32.1	31.7	24.2	16.0	18.2	12.1
AELE	0.8	0.0	0.0	0.0	0.0	0.1	0.6	0.0	0.0	0.0
Europe de l'Est	1.0	0.1			1.0	3.2		2.3	0.0	
Autre de l'Europe										
Ancienne URSS	0.0		0.3					0.9	0.2	
Océanie	10.4	12.2	15.0	8.5	6.9	12.0	27.3	39.0	41.3	36.6
Australia/Australie	9.0	10.6	13.7	7.7	6.4	11.4	26.0	37.0	40.7	35.6
Japan/Japon	28.7	22.3	26.4	28.2	41.2	37.4	27.9	22.0	21.2	21.5
Germany/Allemagne	20.9	29.5	34.8	27.7	21.6	23.5	15.9	9.0	9.6	6.4
Korea, Republic of	5.7	6.1	6.3	16.4	6.6	8.7	9.9	9.0	7.9	10.0
United Kingdom	11.2	7.8	4.5	4.6	5.0	4.5	4.3	4.0	4.3	3.1
Philippines	0.1	0.3	0.0	2.5	5.8	2.2	4.3	4.2	2.8	2.7
USA/Etats–Unis d'Amer	3.4	3.9	3.2	2.0	3.0	1.9	2.4	2.2	2.1	4.2
Singapore/Singapour	1.2	0.6	1.7	0.5	0.5	0.7	1.5	2.1	3.7	3.2
China/Chine	3.1	1.9	1.9	2.1	0.1	0.1	0.2	0.3	0.3	6.6
Finland/Finlande	0.0	0.0	0.0	0.0	0.0	0.4	2.8	2.0	2.4	1.0

4. General Imports F.O.B. by Commodities according to the S.I.T.C. (Rev. 2) in thousand U.S. Dollars
Importations Générales F.O.B. par Produits d'après la C.T.C.I. (Rév. 2) en milliers de Dollars E.U.

SITC CTCI	COMMODITY	1987		1988		1989		1990		PRODUIT
		WEIGHT POIDS	VALUE VALEUR	WEIGHT POIDS	VALUE VALEUR	WEIGHT POIDS	VALUE VALEUR	WEIGHT POIDS	VALUE VALEUR	
	ALL COMMODITIES		1178145		1347072		1576451		1233088	TOUS PRODUITS
0	FOOD AND LIVE ANIMALS		189494		211667		225285		206032	ALIMENTS,ANIMAUX VIVANTS
01	MEAT AND PREPARATIONS		40532		44726		48880		43864	VIANDES ET PREPARATIONS
011	MEAT FRESH,CHILLD,FROZEN	W 44486	33769	W 39100	38536	W 38657	39299	W 43009	36447	VIANDES FRAICHES,REF,CONGE
0111	BOVINE MEAT FRESH,FROZEN	W 14148	17466	W 13263	17512	W 13388	19075	W 10156	15042	VIANDES BOVIN FRAI,REF
01112	BOVINE MEAT BONELESS	W 12312	15080	W 12454	16432	W 12737	17725	W 9784	14204	VIANDES BOVIN DESOSSEES
0112	MUTTON ETC FRSH,CHLD,FRN	W 19657	11126	W 22537	17386	W 22649	16461	W 30095	18056	VIANDE DE MOUTON
012	MEAT DRIED,SALTED,SMOKED	W 1611	2508	W 1938	3221	W 2818	4758	W 2387	4501	VIANDE,ABATS SALES,SECHES
014	MEAT PREPD,PRSVD,NES ETC	W 2542	4255	W 1782	2969	W 2652	4823	W 1921	2915	CONSERVES DE VIANDES
0149	OTH PREPARD,PRESRVD MEAT	W 2353	3875	W 1656	2695	W 2506	4427	W 1816	2646	AUTRES PREP DE VIANDES
02	DAIRY PRODCTS,BIRDS'EGGS		10573		12814		14285		14123	PRODUITS LAITIERS,OEUFS
022	MILK AND CREAM	W 7609	7988	W 8265	9804	W 7815	11217	W 9814	10858	LAIT ET CREME
0224	MILK,CREAM PRESERVED ETC	W 6111	7170	W 7475	9263	W 5346	9710	W 9199	10420	LAIT,CREME CONS,CONC
02243	MILK DRY,OVER 1.5% FAT	W 1713	3678	W 1881	4645	W 1869	5497	W 1614	5325	LAIT POUDRE SUP 1.5%
02249	MILK(EX DRY) PRSVD,SWEET	W 4310	3364	W 5371	4258	W 3228	3603	W 7473	4846	LAIT CONS,CONC SUCRE
03	FISH AND PREPARATIONS		36814		43690		40349		36198	POISSONS ET PREPARATIONS
037	FISH ETC PREPD,PRSVD NES	W 33820	35130	W 33677	42489	W 32765	39210	W 31721	34970	POIS,CRUST,MOL PREPARES
0371	FISH PREPARD,PRESRVD NES	W 33798	35028	W 33658	42410	W 32747	39120	W 31705	34891	CONSERVES DE POISSONS
04	CEREALS AND PREPARATIONS		56921		58119		70518		64955	CEREALES ET PRODUITS
041	WHEAT ETC UNMILLED	W 35617	4417	W 51991	7687	W 51777	10531	W 52851	11645	FROMENT,EPEAUTRE
0412	OTHER WHEAT ETC UNMILLED	W 19901	2478	W 43140	6293	W 40033	8784	W 36882	9180	AUTRE FROMENT NON MOULU
042	RICE	W 132058	38031	W 117279	37379	W 291112	42876	W 154182	41013	RIZ
0422	RICE SEMI–MILLED,MILLED	W 130942	37732	W 116403	37099	W 242486	42190	W 148896	40045	RIZ POLI,GLACE INCL BRISURES
04221	RICE MILLED UNBROKEN	W 130938	37732	W 116379	37092	W 242486	42190	W 148896	40045	RIZ POLI,GLACE EXCL BRISURES
045	CEREALS NES UNMILLED	W 17926	1967	W 4100	266	W 29194	4782	W 17652	1821	AUTRES CEREALES NON MOULUES
048	CEREAL ETC PREPARATIONS	W 12575	9884	W 9966	10419	W 11071	10404	W 17155	9659	PREPTNS A BASE CEREALES
0484	BAKERY PRODUCTS	W 2159	3742	W 2131	4593	W 2034	4373	W 1733	3176	PRODUITS DE BOULANGERIE
04842	PASTRY, CAKES ETC	W 1956	3526	W 1889	4333	W 1802	4080	W 1593	3056	PATISSERIE ETC.
05	VEGETABLES AND FRUIT		9671		12708		12554		11420	LEGUMES ET FRUITS
054	VEG ETC FRSH,SMPLY PRSVD	W 4267	2266	W 12094	4205	W 4528	2763	W 4952	2681	LEGUMES FRAIS,CONG,SECS
058	FRUIT PRESERVED,PREPARED	W 3702	3607	W 3414	3913	W 4276	4936	W 4471	4420	CONSERVES DE FRUITS
06	SUGAR AND PREPS,HONEY		4403		3132		2804		3197	SUCRES ET PRODUITS
07	COFFEE,TEA,COCOA,SPICES		4821		6265		4567		4478	CAFE,THE,CACAO,EPICES
081	*FEEDING STUFF FOR ANIML	W 43361	8085	W 33743	10299	W 34088	10687		8991	NOURRITURE POUR ANIMAUX
0819	FOOD WASTE AND FEED NES	W 37822	6894	W 30011	8876	W 27692	8079	W 19645	6519	DECHETS,ALIMENTS NDA
08199	FODDER NES,INCL SWEETNED	W 37603	6847	W 30011	8876	W 27692	8077	W 19628	6516	PREPARATIONS FOURRAGERES
09	MISC EDIBLE PRODUCTS		17602		19816		20564		18757	PREP ALIMENTAIRES DIVERSES
091	MARGARINE AND SHORTENING	W 6171	5944	W 6540	7418	W 6911	7878	W 5864	6719	MARGARINE ET GRAISSES
0914	MARGARINE,EDIBLE FAT NES	W 6104	5866	W 6386	7208	W 6868	7823	W 5827	6675	MARGARINES,SIMILI SAINDOUX
09149	OTH PREPARED EDIBLE FATS	W 4069	3568	W 4302	4521	W 5111	5333	W 4021	3800	SIMILI–SAINDOUX
098	EDIBLE PRODCTS,PREPS NES	W 6703	11658	W 6385	12398	W 6441	12686	W 12366	12038	PREP ALIMENTAIRES NDA
09809	MISC FOOD PREPRTIONS NES	W 4122	7277	W 4308	7750	W 4176	7492	W 10226	6911	PREP ALIMENTAIRES NDA
1	BEVERAGES AND TOBACCO		13433		18076		17509		15495	BOISSONS ET TABACS
11	BEVERAGES		7348		9292		10947		10298	BOISSONS
111	NON–ALCOHL BEVERAGES NES	W 5573	3108	W 7690	4648	W 6558	6314	W 10570	5969	BOISSONS NON ALCOOLIQUES
11102	FLAVORED WATERS NON–ALCO	W 5562	3086	W 7640	4611	W 6511	6271	W 10517	5929	LIMONADES,EAUX GAZEUSES
112	ALCOHOLIC BEVERAGES	W 1840	4240	W 1330	4645	W 1762	4634	W 751	4330	BOISSONS ALCOOLIQUES
12	TOBACCO AND MANUFACTURES		6085		8784		6561		5197	TABACS BRUTS FABRIQUES
121	TOBACCO UNMNFCTRD,REFUSE	W 1000	4367	W 1532	6596	W 963	4603	W 762	3309	TABACS BRUTS,DECHETS
1212	TOBACCO STRIPPED OR PART	W 1000	4367	W 1532	6596	W 963	4603	W 762	3309	TABACS PART ECOTES
12129	— OTHER TYPES	W 1000	4365	W 1532	6596	W 963	4603	W 762	3309	AUTRES SECHES AIR CHAUD
2	CRUDE MATERLS,EXCL FUELS		9670		9910		9353		9441	MAT BRUTES NON COMESTIBLES
26	TEXTILE FIBRES AND WASTE		4024		4095		4276		4150	FIBRES TEXTILES
269	WASTE OF TEXTILE FABRICS	W 2171	3731	W 1872	3683	W 2585	3795	W 1704	3654	FRIPERIE DRILLES,CHIFFONS
26901	BULK TEXT WSTE,OLD CLTHG	W 1980	3589	W 1595	3391	W 2323	3472	W 1543	3426	ART ET ACCESS D'HABILLEMENT
27	CRUDE FERTLZR,MINRLS NES		3894		3889		3359		3802	ENGRAIS MINERAUX BRUTS
3	MINERAL FUELS ETC		125744		113424		74484		83810	COMBUSTIBLES MINERAUX LUB
33	PETROLEUM AND PRODUCTS		125075		112952		73965		83066	PETROLE ET DERIVES
334	PETROLEUM PRODUCTS,REFIN	W 863333	124453	W 828829	112319	W 480865	73513	W 377292	82768	PRODUITS RAFFINES
3341	GASOLINE,OTH LIGHT OILS	W 136332	27948	W 121499	23760	W 60770	13320	W 56448	14816	ESSENCES POUR MOTEURS
33411	MOTOR,AVIATION SPIRIT	W 106824	22150	W 86809	17381	W 59911	12721	W 56029	14439	ESSENCES MOTEURS D'AVIONS
33419	OTH LIGHT PETROLEUM OILS	W 29508	5797	W 34690	6378	W 859	599	W 419	376	AUTRES HUILES LEGERES
3342	KEROSENE,OTH MEDIUM OILS	W 59255	10604	W 26942	4705	W 30264	5111	W 58905	11625	PETR LAMPANTS,AUT HUIL
33421	KEROSENE INCL JET FUEL	W 57910	10359	W 26890	4670	W 29028	5058	W 58507	11414	PETROLES LAMPANTS
3343	GAS OILS	W 278764	42785	W 338781	48084	W 231841	35443	W 240202	45848	GAS OILS
3344	FUEL OILS,NES	W 375458	34720	W 326741	24502	W 146639	9985	W 11341	1846	FUEL OILS
3345	LUBS,PETROLEUM OILS NES	W 13524	8397	W 14865	11267	W 11351	9654	W 10396	8634	HUILES LUBRIFIANTES
33451	LUBS(HIGH PETR CONT) ETC	W 13507	8361	W 14857	11235	W 11312	9584	W 10375	8574	HUILES LUBRIF,H LOURDES
4	ANIMAL,VEGETABLE OIL,FAT		3973		3871		3904		5018	HUILES,GRAISSES ANIM,VEG
5	CHEMCLS,RELATED PROD NES		94667		97606		92071		86130	PRODUITS CHIMIQUES
51	ORGANIC CHEMICALS		5370		5710		5299		3739	PROD CHIMIQ ORGANIQUES
52	INORGANIC CHEMICALS		30113		18994		12218		16823	PROD CHIM INORGANIQUES
522	INORG ELEMNTS,OXIDES,ETC	W 12055	7126	W 4841	4252	W 4323	5429	W 13028	5660	ELEMENTS INORGANIQUES
5225	INORGANIC BASES ETC NES	W 9000	4806	W 1467	1144	W 2146	2318	W 9048	1835	AUTRES BASES OXYDES METAL
523	OTHR INORG CHEMICALS ETC	W 55814	22758	W 16164	14739		6551		11147	AUT PRODUITS CHIMIQUES INORG
5232	OTH MTL CMPD OF INRG ACD	W 8761	8464	W 8296	8164	W 1962	3979	W 10656	9013	SELS METALLIQUES
52325	CYANIDES,COMPLEX CYANIDE	W 6319	7078	W 6171	6951	W 1025	2505	W 4074	6338	CYANURES SIMPLES,COMPLEXES
5239	INORG CHEM PRODUCTS NES	W 45093	13198	W 5281	5347		1252		560	PROD CHIM INORGANIQ NDA
52391	HYDROGEN PEROXIDE	W 42849	10602	W 2698	1896		40		23	PEROXYDE D'HYDROGENE
53	DYES,TANNING,COLOUR PROD		3285		4288		4672		3613	PROD TEINTURE,COLORANTS
541	*MEDICINAL,PHARM PRODUCT		10808		12477		13126		12578	PROD MEDICINAUX PHARMACEUT
5417	MEDICAMENTS	K 1160764	5880	K 948800	6707	K 938527	7201	K 8694262	7853	MEDICAMENTS
54179	— CONTNG OTH SUBSTANCES	K 384498	3939	K 391734	4368	K 291334	5060	K 412654	4142	MED CONT AUT SUBSTANCES
5419	PHARMACEUTICAL GOODS NES		3799		4881		5064		4127	PREP,ART PHARMACEUTIQUES
55	PERFUME,CLEANING ETC PRD		15540		16292		17230		12776	PROD POUR PARFUM,TOILETTE
553	PERFUMERY,COSMETICS,ETC		3614		3715		4547		2907	PRODUITS DE PARFUMERIE
554	SOAP,CLEANSING ETC PREPS		11332		12044		12317		9522	SAVONS,PRODUITS DETERSIFS
5541	SOAPS	W 3183	3627	W 2887	4066	W 2411	3688	W 1944	2727	SAVONS,PROD TENSIO–ACTIFS
5542	WASHING PREPARATIONS ETC	W 6418	7481	W 6187	7781	W 6159	8399	W 5742	6600	PROD ORG TENSIO–ACT NDA
562	*FERTILIZERS,MANUFACTURE	W 26807	5936	W 36446	7613	W 29368	7159	W 34840	6538	ENGRAIS MANUFACTURES
5621	CHEM NITROGENOUS FERTLZR	W 15192	2911	W 18292	3779	W 19147	4743	W 26342	4098	ENGRAIS AZOTES
58	PLASTIC MATERIALS ETC		9135		11063		11403		9818	MAT PLAST ARTIFICIELLES
583	POLYMERIZATION ETC PRODS	W 3531	6703	W 3579	7976	W 2760	7667	W 2864	5635	PROD POLYMERISATION
59	CHEMICAL MATERIALS NES		13127		19129		18702		17852	MAT PROD CHIMIQUES NDA
591	PESTICIDES,DISINFECTANTS	W 2181	6215	W 2464	8337	W 1860	7274	W 2263	5082	DESINF,INSECT,FONG,HERB
598	MISCEL CHEM PRODUCTS NES	W 2550	4914		8320	W 2960	9716	W 3303	11428	PROD DIV INDUST CHIM NDA
5989	CHEM PRODUCTS,PREPS NES	W 2373	4541	W 5104	7909	W 2560	8669	W 3020	10521	PROD PREP CHIMIQUES NDA
59899	OTH CHEM PRODS,PREPS,NES	W 1168	2729	W 4676	6739	W 2106	7457	W 2470	9254	AUT PRODUITS CHIMIQUES NDA
6	BASIC MANUFACTURES		208703		241190		297377		237345	ART MANUFACTURES
62	RUBBER MANUFACTURES NES		27621		33376		34525		27936	CAOUTCHOUC MANUFACTURE
621	MATERIALS OF RUBBER		3317		4685		3746		3548	PRODUITS EN CAOUTCHOUC

4. General Imports F.O.B. by Commodities according to the S.I.T.C. (Rev. 2) in thousand U.S. Dollars
Importations Générales F.O.B. par Produits d'après la C.T.C.I. (Rév. 2) en milliers de Dollars E.U.

SITC CTCI	COMMODITY	1987		1988		1989		1990		PRODUIT
		WEIGHT POIDS	VALUE VALEUR	WEIGHT POIDS	VALUE VALEUR	WEIGHT POIDS	VALUE VALEUR	WEIGHT POIDS	VALUE VALEUR	
625	RUBBER TYRES, TUBES ETC	N 476921	19231	N 441236	21649	N 471268	24812	N 385632	18408	PNEUS CAOUTCHOUC VULCANISE
6251	TYRES NEW FOR MOTOR CARS	N 100991	3578	N 88864	2996	N 101396	3553	N 65691	2220	PNEUS POUR VOITURES
6252	TYRES,NEW,BUS OR LORRY	N 144324	8426	N 106401	7126	N 159112	8226	N 124408	6163	PNEUS POUR AUTOBUS,CAMIONS
6259	OTH TYRES,TYRE CASES,ETC	N 221766	7023	N 230422	11381	N 200354	12759	N 186212	9838	AUTRES PNEUS RECHAPES FLAPS
62599	TYRES NES,TYRE CASES,ETC	N 33691	5039	N 59459	10048	N 48668	11120	N 32148	7587	PNEUS,FLAPS
628	RUBBER ARTICLES NES		5072		7042		5967		5980	OUVRAGES CAOUTCHOUC NDA
6289	OTH RUBBER ARTICLES NES		3191		4108		4132		4294	AUT OUVR CAOUTCHOUC NDA
62898	UNHARD RUBBER PRODS NES		3017		3993		4003		4048	OUV CAOUT VULC NON DURCI
64	PAPER,PAPERBOARD AND MFR		24951		25786		28804		25269	PAPIERS,CARTONS & OUVRAGES
641	PAPER AND PAPERBOARD		11541		11333		12403		12314	PAPIERS ET CARTONS
6412	PRINTG,WRITING PAPER NES	W 2236	3714	W 2832	3756	W 1740	3746	W 4022	3681	PAPIERS POUR L'IMPRESSION
642	PAPER,ETC,PRECUT,ARTS OF		13410		14453		16400		12955	PAP,CARTONS DECOUPES
6421	PAPER ETC CONTAINERS		4451		5045		5264		3795	BOITES,SACS EMBALLAGES
65	TEXTILE YARN,FABRICS,ETC		23333		28265		29980		24169	FILS,TISSUS,ARTICLES TEXTILE
652	COTTON FABRICS,WOVEN	A 15007	5116	A 6300	6339	A 6179	7149	A 6050	6579	TISSUS DE COTON
6522	WOVEN COTTON BLEACHD,ETC	A 12617	2995	A 4160	4048	A 4320	4908	A 4340	4281	TISSUS COTON BLANCHIS ETC
657	SPECIAL TXTL FABRC,PRODS		3233		4371		4885		3387	TISSUS SPECIAUX
658	TEXTILE ARTICLES NES		8530		10655		11476		8256	ART FACONNES MAT TEXTILES
6584	LINENS ETC		4070		4052		4751		3006	LINGE DE MAISON
66	NONMETAL MINERAL MFS NES		19004		17402		22799		23231	ART MIN NON METALLIQUES
661	LIME,CEMENT,BLDG PRODS		7141		8728		12247		12344	CHAUX,CIMENTS MAT CONSTR
6612	CEMENT		4999		5774	W 201267	6931	W 1026641	7547	CIMENTS HYDRAULIQUES
662	CLAY,REFRACTORY BLDG PRD		4266		1278		1180		1997	MAT CONST REFRACTAIRES
664	GLASS		2443		2743		3483		3951	VERRE
67	IRON AND STEEL		38135		49752		76603		52682	FER ET ACIER
672	IRON,STEEL PRIMARY FORMS	W 13334	3664	W 10427	4462		6284		6253	LINGOTS FER,ACIER
6727	IRN,STL COIL FR REROLLNG	W 8479	3460	W 5961	3452		5694		4613	EBAUCHES POUR TOLES FER
673	IRON,STEEL SHAPES ETC	W 105415	5274	W 29972	7823		6901	W 154094	9839	BARRES,PROFIL FER,ACIER
6732	IRON,STEEL BARS ETC	W 11825	3786	W 24856	6008		4165	W 12850	5574	BARRES FER,ACIER
674	IRN,STL UNIV,PLATE,SHEET	W 301926	9377	W 51455	10405	W 46926	11141		7602	LARGES PLATS,TOLES
6749	OTH IRN,STL PLATES,SHEET	W 28304	3849	W 12459	6039	W 12575	4408		3414	AUTRES TOLES FER,ACIER
67494	— OF OTHER ALLOY STEEL	W 14232	2240	W 8251	4389	W 5220	2042		746	AUT TOLES ACIERS ALLIES
678	IRON,STL TUBES,PIPES,ETC	W 10060	10479	W 14274	17230	W 30332	41333	W 14131	22100	TUBES,TUYAUX EN FONTE,FER
6782	IRON,STL SEAMLESS TUBES	W 4395	2983	W 5055	5133	W 5201	8315	W 2713	5131	TUBES,TUYAUX SANS SOUDURE
6783	IRON,STL TUBES,PIPES NES	W 3779	3346	W 7071	7436	W 23155	26934	W 8181	9576	AUT TUBES,TUYAUX FER,ACIER
6785	IRON,STEEL TUBE FITTINGS	W 840	3333	W 1275	3836	W 1137	5493	W 904	5251	ACCESSOIRES DE TUYAUTERIE
679	IRN,STL CASTINGS UNWORKD	W 16083	7809	W 10909	7883	W 10959	8136	W 6797	4368	OUVRAGES EN FONTE,FER,ACIER
6793	IRON,STL FORGINGS ROUGH	W 4662	2598	W 8988	6336	W 5198	4403	W 5649	3637	OUVRAGES FORGES,ESTAMPES
6794	IRON,STL CASTINGS ROUGH	W 11422	5211	W 1921	1547	W 5761	3733	W 1148	731	OUVRAGES COULES,MOULES
67942	STEEL CASTINGS ROUGH	W 8792	4111	W 1384	1235	W 5640	3087	W 1125	662	OUVR COULES,MOULES ACIER
68	NON–FERROUS METALS		3299		3883		4347		4299	METAUX NON FERREUX
69	METAL MANUFACTURES NES		70343		80357		97703		77340	ART MANUFACT EN METAL NDA
691	STRUCTURES AND PARTS NES		15533		21002		27945		20406	CONSTRUCT FER,ACIER,ALU
6911	STRUCTURES,PARTS IRN,STL		13714		19807		25988		19205	CONSTRUCT FER,ACIER,FONTE
692	METAL TANKS,BOXES,ETC	MN 52239	7821	MN 50877	7768	MN 56437	11014	MN 69440	10649	RECIPIENTS METALLIQUES
6924	MTL TRANSPORT BOXES ETC	MN 52238	5590	MN 50876	6577	MN 56435	9000	MN 69438	7575	FUTS,TAMBOURS,BIDONS
69241	STL TRANSPORT BOXES ETC	MN 49601	4730	MN 49860	5889	MN 56164	7922	MN 69368	6863	FUTS,TAMBOURS,BIDONS FER
693	WIRE PRODUCTS NON ELECTR		3426	W 2946	4188	W 2382	4660	W 3519	4854	OUVRAGES FILS METALLIQUES
694	STL,COPPR NAILS,NUTS,ETC	W 2137	6649	W 2066	7868	W 6346	7338	W 3445	6205	CLOUS,VIS,ECROUS
69402	IRN,STL NUTS,BOLTS,ETC	W 1642	5708	W 1532	6787	W 5801	6165	W 2472	5444	BOULONS,VIS,ECROUS FER,AC
695	TOOLS		12944		12845		17751		12616	OUTILS A MAIN
6953	OTHER HAND TOOLS	N 1389662	4800	N 1355804	5461	N 1362134	7392	MN 73069	5182	AUTRES OUTILS A MAIN
6954	BLADES,TIPS,ETC FR TOOLS		6673		5536		8321		6129	OUTILS POUR MACHINE–OUTIL
69541	PARTS TO INSERT IN TOOLS	N 453721	6245	N 362392	5089	N 211089	7428	N 195525	5574	OUTILS DE FORAGE
697	BASE MTL HOUSEHOLD EQUIP		5630		6687		7543		5983	ART MENAGE MET COMMUNS
699	BASE METAL MFRS NES		16517		17639		19214		15178	ART MANUFACTURES MET NDA
6991	LOCKSMITHS WARES,ETC		3916		4369		5683		4722	ARTICLES DE SERRURERIE
6997	IRON,STEEL ARTICLES NES		6097		6387		4296		3910	OUV FONTE,FER,ACIER NDA
69979	IRN,STL MANUFACTURES NES		5998		6343		4124		3839	AUT OUVRAGES EN FER NDA
7	MACHINES,TRANSPORT EQUIP		428901		533122		712213		472195	MACHINES MATERIEL TRANSPORT
71	POWER GENERATING EQUIPMT		34322		49508		58370		37964	MACHINES GENERATRICES
713	INTRNL COMBUS PSTN ENGIN		15797		18655		36518		20184	MOTEURS EXPL COMB INT, PIECE
7131	AIRCRAFT PSTN ENGINS,PTS		5262		4572		15795		10305	MOTEURS EXPL P.AVIATION, PIE
71311	AIRCRAFT PISTON ENGINES	N 65	4289	N 46	3466	N 64	11178	N 79	7894	MOTEURS EXPL P.AVIATION
7138	PISTON ENGINES NES	N 2033	1137	N 2049	1948	N 1701	5805	N 1414	1844	MOTEURS A PISTONS NDA
7139	PISTON ENGINE PARTS NES		5332		9021		9573		4179	PIECES POUR 713.2,3,8
714	ENGINES AND MOTORS NES		3832		9784		4815		2506	MOTEURS NON ELECTRIQUES
7148	GAS TURBINES NES	N 58	2684	N 163	8541	N 54	3508	N 48	1563	TURBINES A GAZ
71488	OTHER GAS TURBINES NES	N 44	2442	N 30	8528	N 17	3491	N 24	1304	AUTRES TURBINES A GAZ
716	ROTATING ELECTRIC PLANT		9764		14840		11806		13358	APP ELECTR ROTATIFS,PIECES
7162	AC MTRS,GENRTRS,GEN SETS	N 6685	7081	N 8383	10524	N 7998	8920	N 5609	10150	MOTEURS ELECTRIQUES
71622	AC GENERATORS	N 379	2837	N 851	5127	N 510	3495	N 457	1992	GENER COURANT ALTERNATIF
71623	GEN SETS WITH PISTN ENGN	N 1926	3025	N 2230	2705	N 2576	3323	N 1099	6630	GROUPES MOTEUR EXPLOSION
718	OTH POWER GENERATG MACHY		4153		2227		2356		668	AUTRES MOTEURS PARTIES
7188	WIND,WATER,ETC ENGINES		4150		2226		2348		667	MOT MACHINES MOTRICES NDA
72	MACHS FOR SPCL INDUSTRYS		96889		135182		166017		101576	MAC SPECIALES POUR INDUST
721	AGRIC MACHY,EXC TRACTORS		4351		5972		8666		3462	MACHINES AGRICOLES
7219	AGRICULTURE MACHINES NES		2845		4577		6401		2003	ENGINS AGRICOLES NDA
72197	OTH AGRIC ETC MACHINERY		2109		3378		5374		1089	AUT APP POUR AGRICULTURE
722	TRACTORS NON–ROAD	N 268	3777	N 214	5764	N 352	6515	N 146	3820	TRACTEURS
723	CIVIL ENGNEERG EQUIP ETC		68116		93621		120368		74146	APPAREILS DE GENIE CIVIL
7234	CONST,MINING MACHNRY NES		42885		52476		76472		37854	MACH POUR LA CONST, MINES
72341	SELF–PROPELLD DOZERS,ETC	N 156	11510	N 187	13933	N 277	20539	N 259	12467	BULLDOZERS
72342	SLFPRP SHOVELS,EXCAVATRS	N 83	10892	N 101	11787	N 93	22283	N 65	5551	PELLES MECANIQUES
72343	SLFPRP CONST ETC MCH NES	N 277	8254	N 700	15487	N 1689	16284	N 275	12114	AUT MACH EXTR,TERRASSEM
72344	BORING,SINKING MACHINERY	N 636	4126	N 226	1614	N 153	1426	N 131	1117	MACHINES DE FORAGE
72346	OTH CONST,MINING MCH NES	N 349	7720	N 571	9559	N 551	15773	N 1471	6044	AUT MACH EXTRACTION,EXCAV ET
7239	CONSTR ETC MACHY PTS NES		25086		41047		43736		36159	PIECES 723.41–723.46
728	OTH MACHY FOR SPCL INDUS		15303		23278		24108		14292	AUT MACH IND PARTICULIERES
7283	OTHR MINERAL WORKG MACHY		10595		18510		18020		9714	MACH TRIER,CRIBLER,BROYER
72839	PTS NES OF MACHY OF 7283		8840		11808		10679		3646	PIECES MACH DU 728.3
73	METALWORKING MACHINERY		14541		4081		6121		4621	MACH TRAVAIL DES METAUX
736	METALWORKING MACH–TOOLS		12832		2268		4014		3023	MACH–OUTILS TRAVAIL METAUX
7361	METAL CUTTING MACH–TOOLS		8605	N 5700	1184	N 3602	1500	N 7425	1674	MACH–OUT ENLEVEMENT METAL
73615	DRILLING ETC MCH,MTLWRKG		8048	N 1425	338	N 717	614	N 682	335	MACHINES A PERCER
74	GENRL INDUSTRL MACHY NES		56141		66648		86349		64630	MACH APP INDUSTRIE
741	HEATING,COOLING EQUIPMNT		7497		8875		10546		12228	MACH CHAUFFAGE,PIECES
7414	NONDOM REFRIG EQUIPT,PTS		4305		3303		3550		3192	MAT PRODUCTION DU FROID
74141	REFRIG EQUIP NONDOMESTIC	N 3330	3607	N 3296	2522	N 2512	2900	N 2583	2565	REFIG INDUSTRIELS
7416	HEATING,COOLING EQU NES		812		1300		1289		5119	APP CHANGEMENT TEMP
742	PUMPS FOR LIQUIDS ETC		7641		9508		12136		8744	POMPES MOTO–POMPES

4. General Imports F.O.B. by Commodities according to the S.I.T.C. (Rev. 2) in thousand U.S. Dollars
Importations Générales F.O.B. par Produits d'après la C.T.C.I. (Rév. 2) en milliers de Dollars E.U.

SITC CTCI	COMMODITY	1987 WEIGHT POIDS	1987 VALUE VALEUR	1988 WEIGHT POIDS	1988 VALUE VALEUR	1989 WEIGHT POIDS	1989 VALUE VALEUR	1990 WEIGHT POIDS	1990 VALUE VALEUR	PRODUIT
7428	OTHER PUMPS FOR LIQUIDS	N 35331	4530	N 40215	5670	N 41369	9310	N 46898	6573	AUTRES POMPES POUR LIQ
74288	PUMPS FR LIQUIDS NES ETC	N 34395	4150	N 38921	4438	N 40828	8333	N 44778	5962	POMPES POUR LIQUIDES NDA
743	PUMPS NES,CENTRFUGES ETC		6910		8557		10414		9327	POMPES COMPRES,VENT ETC
7436	GAS,LIQUID FILTERS ETC	N 294492	2384	N 293753	3313	N 292746	3697	N 283478	4082	APP POUR FILT DES LIQUIDES
744	MECHANICAL HANDLING EQU		10967		13319		22957		12727	EQUIP MANUTENTION PIECES
7441	FORK LIFT TRCKS,ETC,PTS		4330		4161		6056		4045	CHARIOTS POUR USINES ETC
74411	FORK LIFT TRUCKS ETC	N 194	3796	N 232	2956	N 244	4972	N 137	3468	CHARIOTS POUR LES GARES
7442	LIFTING,LOADING MACH NES	N 5724	4992	N 9510	6762	N 6788	12910	N 7055	6193	APP LEVAGE,MANUTENTION
74428	OTH HANDLING ETC MCH NES	N 1672	1603	N 6442	2889	N 4208	5975	N 5302	3592	AUT APP LEVAGE ETC
745	NONELEC MACHY,TOOLS NES		4624		5339		7464		4215	AUT MACH NON ELEC,PIECES
7452	OTH NONELEC MCHS,PTS NES		3460		4075		5201		2844	AUT MACH NON ELEC,PIECES
749	NONELEC MACH PTS,ACC NES		18501		21050		22833		17388	PIECES MACH NON ELEC NDA
7491	BALL,ROLLER,ETC BEARINGS	N 257654	4128	N 272420	4617	N 227128	4969	N 160557	3833	ROULEMENTS BILLES ETC
7492	COCKS,VALVES ETC NES	N 204057	4677	N 341703	6614	N 297690	8603	N 342757	7589	ART ROB,SIM POUR TUYAUX
7493	SHAFT,CRANK,PULLEY ETC		7165		7658		7159		4127	ARBRES TRANS,VILEBREQUINS
75	OFFICE MACHNES,ADP EQUIP		18353		23676		25724		22191	MACH BUREAU TRAIT AUTOM
751	OFFICE MACHINES	N 137386	3723	N 125829	4757	N 159716	5410	N 172877	4168	MACH,APPAREILS DE BUREAU
752	AUTOMTIC DATA PROC EQUIP	N 8712	9081	N 12351	12034	N 11922	11424		11779	MACH TRAIT INFORMATION
7528	OFF–LINE DATA PROC EQUIP	N 4578	5200	N 9044	7640	N 7906	6856	N 12429	7808	MACH AUXIL TRAIT INFORM
759	OFFICE,ADP MCH PTS,ACCES		5549		6885		8889		6244	PIECES DU 751 ET 752
7599	ACCTG,ETC,ADP MCH PTS,AC		4538		5559		7339		5208	PIECES DU 751 ET 752
76	TELECOMM,SOUND EQUIPMENT		28053		27041		20745		19985	EQUIPMENT DE TELECOM
764	TELECOM EQPT,PTS,ACC NES		19666		22808		14479		16245	EQUIP TELECOM,PIECES
7641	LINE TELEPHONE,ETC EQUIP		4333		4062		3372		2325	APP TELEPHON PAR FIL
7643	TV,RADIO TRANSMITTRS ETC	N 39194	6367	N 25712	9566	N 13115	3028	N 14682	4907	APP EMET TELE RADIO
7648	TELECOMM EQUIPMENT NES		5261		4467		4505		5458	APP TELECOM NDA
76483	RADAR APPARATUS ETC		5049		4328		4022		5183	APP DE RADIOGUIDAGE ETC
7649	PTS NES OF EQUIPMT OF 76		3047		4073		2910		3028	PIECES DE LA DIV 76
77	ELECTRIC MACHNRY NES ETC		43634		53947		60358		58325	MACH APP ELECT NDA
771	ELECTRIC POWER MACHY NES		3288		6563		7350		5538	MACH PROD,TRANS ELECTR
7711	TRANSFORMERS,ELECTRICAL	N 5631	2099	N 6140	4487	N 3945	3333	N 3903	3919	TRANSFO ELECTRIQUES
77118	OTHER ELEC TRANSFORMERS	N 5530	2083	N 5817	3588	N 3817	3114	N 3892	3874	AUTRES TRANSFO ELECTRIQ
772	SWITCHGEAR ETC,PARTS NES		9654		13469		16212		14398	APP COUPURE,SECT ETC
7721	SWITCHGEAR ETC		9309		12683		15677		14017	APP COUPURE,SECTIONMNT
773	ELECTR DISTRIBUTNG EQUIP		7126		10672		10588		15315	EQUIPMT DISTRIBUTION ELECT
7731	INSULATED WIRE,CABLE ETC		6204		9309		9281		14026	FILS,CABLES ISOLES ELECT
775	HOUSEHOLD TYPE EQUIP NES		6345		5525		7647		5452	MACH,APP USAGE DOMESTQUE
778	ELECTRICAL MACHINERY NES		15753		15044		17285		15570	AUTRES MACH ELECT NDA
7781	BATTERIES,ACCUMULATORS		7683		6615		8000		7020	PILES ET ACCUMULATEURS
77811	PRIMARY BATTERIES,CELLS		5385		4394		5186		5300	PILES ELECTRIQUES,PIECES
78	ROAD VEHICLES		92728		115931		150513		98492	VEHICULES ROUTIERS
781	PASS MOTOR VEH EXC BUSES	N 5571	45472	N 2894	26019	N 4091	37899	N 3029	34824	AUTO TRANSPORT PERSONNES
782	LORRIES,SPCL MTR VEH NES	N 2221	24653	N 5509	59230	N 4032	77031	N 4628	43275	VEHICULES SPECIAUX,MARCH
7821	LORRIES,TRUCKS	N 2196	23791	N 5462	58031	N 3971	67814	N 4581	35308	VEHICULES TRANSP MARCHAND
7822	SPECIAL MOTOR VEHCLS NES	N 25	862	N 47	1199	N 61	9217	N 47	7967	VEHICULES USAGES SPECIAUX
783	ROAD MOTOR VEHICLES NES	N 700	6888	N 1022	12392	N 1241	12859	N 708	6158	VEHICULES ROUTIERS NDA
7831	BUSES	N 697	6878	N 1011	11994	N 1231	12153	N 706	5981	VOITURES TRANSPORT COMMUN
784	MOTOR VEH PRTS,ACCES NES		12002		13489		16938		10028	PIECES 722,781,782,783
7849	OTHER MOTOR VEHCL PARTS		10395		13211		15740		9210	PIECES 722,781,782,783
79	OTHR TRANSPORT EQUIPMENT		44239		57109		138018		64411	AUTRE MATERIEL TRANSPORT
792	AIRCRAFT ETC		37789		46357		116163		51069	APP NAVIGATION AERIENNE
7921	HELICOPTERS	N 10	7426	N 21	14723	N 16	10089	N 15	18631	HELICOPTERES
7923	AIRCRFT NES2000–15000KG	N 10	21460	N 9	2352	N 2	1295	N 3	790	AERODYNES 2000 A 15000 KG
7924	AIRCRFT NES OVER 15000KG		149	N 11	7888	N 9	75121	N 2	6743	AERODYNES PLUS 15000 KG
7929	AIRCRAFT PARTS NES		8133		18989		26744		23899	PIECES DU 792
793	SHIPS AND BOATS ETC	N 1594	6285	N 1036	10553	N 1210	21829	N 1071	13226	NAVIRES BATEAUX,ETC
7932	SHIPS AND BOATS NES	N 1195	4317	N 737	10137	N 765	21101	N 733	12142	NAVIRES ET BATEAUX
79323	OTHER CARGO VESSELS	N 32	1896	N 109	6474	N 319	15970	N 260	9115	AUT BATEAUX TRANS MARCH
8	MISC MANUFACTURED GOODS		101418		116629		131300		105466	ART MANUFACTURES DIVERS
812	*PLUMBG,HEATNG,LGHTNG EQ		3245		4381		4731		3543	APPAR SANITAIRES CHAUFFAGE
821	*FURNITURE,PARTS THEREOF		5509		6902		6424		4669	MEUBLES ET PIECES
84	CLOTHING AND ACCESSORIES		22036		26509		26781		20393	VETEMENTS
842	MENS OUTERWEAR NOT KNIT	MN 28566	8298	N 5369317	10884	MN 85071	10743	N 3793582	8110	VET DESSUS POUR HOMMES
8423	— TROUSERS,BREECHES ETC	MN 27642	6242	N 4492415	8456	N 4363920	8522	N 3254922	6356	PANTALONS HOMMES MAT TEX
84232	—— OF COTTON	MN 27189	5265	N 3622827	6694	N 3721884	7190	N 2965113	5260	PANTALONS HOMMES COTON
843	WOMENS OUTERWEAR NONKNIT	N 2314552	3768	N 2095218	3880	N 2103922	3888	N 1551512	2873	VET DESSUS FEMMES MAT TEX
844	UNDER GARMENTS NOT KNIT	N 4911640	4483	N 6385073	5223	N 5972941	5814	N 4699231	4311	VETEMENT DESSOUS MAT TEX
851	*FOOTWEAR		6963		6844		9329		7205	CHAUSSURES
85102	FOOTWEAR LEATHER		4753		3942		5920		4348	CHAUS SEMELLES EN CUIR
87	PRECISION INSTRUMNTS NES		17906		21623		24192		20076	INSTRUM,APPAR SCIENT NDA
874	MEASURNG,CONTROLNG INSTR		15903		18077		21665		17900	INSTRUMENTS DE MESURE
8741	SURVEYING INSTRUMENTS		5005		7792		5691		3084	INST GEODESIE,TOPO ETC
87412	SURVEY INSTR ETC NONELEC		4467		5078		4972		2529	INSTR GEODESIE,TOPO ETC
8743	GAS,LIQUID CONTROL INSTR	N 33280	3042	N 35369	2316	N 46634	4939	N 28886	2764	APP,INSTR MESURE FLUIDES
8748	ELEC MEAS,CONTRL EQU NES	N 17827	4092	N 20443	4636	N 22152	6803	N 24712	8887	APP ELEC ELECTRO MESURE
87483	OTH ELCTRNC MEAS ETC EQU	N 5759	1963	N 10609	3084	N 11191	4687	N 13786	7123	AUT APP ELECTRO DE MESURE
88	PHOTO EQU,OPTICL GDS ETC		6060		7197		7298		6362	APP,FOURN PHOTO,OP,MONTR
89	MISC MANUFCTRD GOODS NES		36592		39956		48551		40444	ART MANUFACTURES DIVERS
892	PRINTED MATTER		12757		13027		17468		14891	IMPRIMES
8921	PRINTED BOOKS,GLOBES,ETC	N 3432792	4349	N 3319756	4966	N 2706620	5559	N 2192305	5204	LIVRES,BROCHURES,CARTES
89211	PRINTED BOOKS,PAMPHLETS	N 3411315	4293	N 3279835	4861	N 2693917	5444	N 2169259	5125	LIVRES,BROCHURES
8928	PRINTED MATTER NES		7776		7362		11439		9239	IMPRIMES NDA
89283	UNISSUED BANKNOTES ETC		5761		4924		8793		7019	TIMBRES–POSTE FISCAUX
893	ARTICLES OF PLASTIC NES		11595		13405		15498		12717	OUVRAGES EN MAT DIVIS 58
8939	MISC PLASTIC ARTICLES		9094		11681		13133		10178	ART DIVERS EN MAT DIV 58
89399	OTHR PLASTC ARTICLES NES		7761		10285		11444		8972	AUT OUV MAT DIV 58
894	TOYS,SPORTING GOODS,ETC		3684		3715		4349		4498	VOITURES ENFANTS,JOUETS
9	GOODS NOT CLASSD BY KIND		2143		1577		12956		12156	ART TRANSACT NON CLASSES
931	*SPECIAL TRANSACTIONS						11680		8584	TRANS.SPECIALES

5. General Exports F.O.B. by Commodities according to the S.I.T.C. (Rev. 2) in thousand U.S. Dollars
Exportations Générales F.O.B. par Produits d'après la C.T.C.I. (Rév. 2) en milliers de Dollars E.U.

SITC CTCI	COMMODITY	1990 WEIGHT POIDS	1990 VALUE VALEUR	1991 WEIGHT POIDS	1991 VALUE VALEUR	1992 WEIGHT POIDS	1992 VALUE VALEUR	1993 WEIGHT POIDS	1993 VALUE VALEUR	PRODUIT
	ALL COMMODITIES		1261730		1641763		1698897		2624576	TOUS PRODUITS
0	FOOD AND LIVE ANIMALS		168152		140887		133903		150985	ALIMENTS,ANIMAUX VIVANTS
03	FISH AND PREPARATIONS		10747		13979		12934		9167	POISSONS ET PREPARATIONS
036	SHELL FISH FRESH,FROZEN	W 1294	9831	W 1490	13085	W 1527	12229	W 1110	8990	CRUSTACES,MOLLUSQUES
06	SUGAR AND PREPS,HONEY		4829		3031		3105			SUCRES ET PRODUITS
061	SUGAR AND HONEY	W 9712	4829	W 7664	3031	W 6923	3105			SUCRES ET MIEL
0611	RAW BEET AND CANE SUGAR	W 9700	4814	W 7664	3031	W 6909	3087			SUCRES BRUTS
07	COFFEE,TEA,COCOA,SPICES		150282		121537		113367		137103	CAFE,THE,CACAO,EPICES
071	COFFEE AND SUBSTITUTES	W 63426	108531	W 44911	80082	W 55125	70558	W 63576	94523	CAFE ET SUCCEDANES
0711	COFFEE GREEN,ROASTED,SUB	W 63426	108530	W 44911	80082	W 55125	70558	W 63576	94523	CAFE TORREFIE OU DECAFEINE
07111	COFFEE GREEN,HUSKS,SKINS	W 63416	108467	W 44892	79971	W 55093	70337	W 63545	94326	CAFE NON TORREFIE
072	COCOA	W 36433	34178	W 37618	36746	W 39327	35695	W 38325	34889	CACAO
0721	COCOA BEANS,RAW,ROASTED	W 36433	34178	W 37615	36740	W 39327	35695	W 38325	34889	CACAO EN FEVES
074	TEA AND MATE	W 5408	7022	W 3747	4407	W 5638	6755	W 6441	7343	THE ET MATE
0741	TEA	W 5408	7022	W 3747	4407	W 5638	6755	W 6441	7343	THE
2	CRUDE MATERLS,EXCL FUELS		691905		711242		716526		965990	MAT BRUTES NON COMESTIBLES
22	OIL SEEDS,OLEAGINOUS FRT		10351		7438		14542		16646	GRAINES,FRUITS OLEAGINEUX
223	SEEDS FOR OTH FIXED OILS	W 71919	10351	W 59286	7438	W 59131	14542	W 75645	16646	GRAINES AUTRES HUILES FIXES
2231	COPRA	W 60699	9377	W 45341	5624	W 45640	12270	W 58461	14114	COPRAH
24	CORK AND WOOD		90040		101576		154583		432344	LIEGE ET BOIS
246	PULPWOOD,CHIPS,WOODWASTE	W 156957	7432	W 105543	5732	W 57024	6272	W 96170	7032	BOIS DE TRITURATION
24602	PULPWOOD CHIPS,PARTICLES	W 156957	7432	W 105543	5732	W 55580	5226	W 96132	7005	EN FORME DE PLAQUETTES
247	OTH WOOD ROUGH,SQUARED	W 970895	80845	W 1047927	93825	W 1463167	146591	W 2130544	423735	BOIS BRUTS EQUARRIS
2471	SAW–,VENEER–LOGS CONIFER	W 35043	4836	W 44384	7585	W 83330	15818	W 89051	27629	CONIFERES POUR SCIAGE,PLACAG
24711	— IN THE ROUGH	W 35043	4836	W 44196	7556	W 83330	15818	W 89051	27629	ECORCES OU DEGROSSIS
2472	SAW–,VENEER–LOGS NON–CON	W 429989	44330	W 419553	47717	W 536110	66690	W 852511	212870	NON CONIFERES SCIAGE,PLAC
24721	— IN THE ROUGH	W 429132	44185	W 419484	47707	W 535539	66648	W 852511	212870	BRUTS ECORCES DEGROSSIS
2479	PTPROPS,POLES,PILING,ETC	W 505863	31680	W 583990	38524	W 843726	64083	W 1188982	183236	POTEAUX DE MINES
28	METALLIFEROUS ORES,SCRAP		583578		595865		541809		510688	MINERAIS METAL,DECHETS
287	BASE METAL ORES,CONC NES	W 471939	582656	W 576039	595032	W 550099	541188	W 556231	510302	MINERAIS METAUX COMMUNS
2871	CPR ORE ETC,CEMENT COPPR	W 471939	582656	W 576039	595032	W 550099	541188	W 556231	510302	MINERAIS DE CUIVRE,MATTES
28711	COPPER ORES,EXCL MATTE	W 471934	582653	W 576039	595032	W 550099	541188	W 556188	510290	MINERAIS DE CUIVRE
29	CRUDE ANIMAL,VEG MAT NES		4331		3072		2230		1746	MATIERES BRUTES ANIM,VEGET
3	MINERAL FUELS ETC		1648		3680		1739		803429	COMBUSTIBLES MINERAUX LUB
33	PETROLEUM AND PRODUCTS		1648		3680		1739		803429	PETROLE ET DERIVES
333	CRUDE PETROLEUM		15		10			W 6187316	802020	HUILES BRUTES DE PETROLE
4	ANIMAL,VEGETABLE OIL,FAT		43718		61294		88628		96594	HUILES,GRAISSES ANIM,VEG
42	FIXED VEGETABLE OIL,FAT		43716		61115		87780		95871	HUILES VEGETALES FIXES
424	FIXED VEG OIL NONSOFT	W 160924	43716	W 199596	61115	W 227411	87780	W 268934	95871	AUTRES HUILES VEG FIXES
4242	PALM OIL	W 115623	28468	W 166295	47286	W 178410	58661	W 213217	72338	HUILE DE PALME
4243	COCONUT (COPRA) OIL	W 37865	12771	W 25771	11665	W 40913	25013	W 36502	16192	HJUILE DE COPRAH
6	BASIC MANUFACTURES		22381		20010		18511		13668	ART MANUFACTURES
68	NON–FERROUS METALS		14708		14052		10581		8499	METAUX NON FERREUX
681	SILVER,PLATINUM,ETC		14652		13945		10580		8481	ARGENT ET PLATINE
6811	SILVER UNWKD,PARTLY WRKD		14652		13945		10580		8481	ARGENT BRUT MI–OUVRE
68113	SILVER UNWROUGHT		14652		13938		10580		8481	ARGENT ET ALLIAGES BRUTS
69	METAL MANUFACTURES NES		4517		4091		6380		1587	ART MANUFACT EN METAL NDA
7	MACHINES,TRANSPORT EQUIP		72218		135562		102886		66330	MACHINES MATERIEL TRANSPORT
71	POWER GENERATING EQUIPMT		8284		1617		2408		2817	MACHINES GENERATRICES
713	INTRNL COMBUS PSTN ENGIN		7828		837		93		415	MOTEURS EXPL COMB INT, PIECE
7131	AIRCRAFT PSTN ENGINS,PTS		7033		517				113	MOTEURS EXPL P.AVIATION, PIE
71311	AIRCRAFT PISTON ENGINES	N 190	6413	N 6	435			N 10	102	MOTEURS EXPL P.AVIATION
72	MACHS FOR SPCL INDUSTRYS		20113		16840		42975		17137	MAC SPECIALES POUR INDUST
723	CIVIL ENGNEERG EQUIP ETC		18306		14558		36223		16245	APPAREILS DE GENIE CIVIL
7234	CONST,MINING MACHNRY NES	N 302	12209	N 261	10096	N 1193	32177	N 401	8858	MACH POUR LA CONST, MINES
72341	SELF–PROPELLD DOZERS,ETC	N 36	1840	N 35	2066	N 67	10834	N 37	2492	BULLDOZERS
72342	SLFPRP SHOVELS,EXCAVATRS	N 100	5650	N 17	1624	N 7	199	N 5	255	PELLES MECANIQUES
72343	SLFPRP CONST ETC MCH NES	N 22	1028	N 42	1461	N 1070	18693	N 88	2907	AUT MACH EXTR,TERRASSEM
7239	CONSTR ETC MACHY PTS NES		6096		4443		3983		7387	PIECES 723.41–723.46
74	GENRL INDUSTRL MACHY NES		6155		4079		7836		2914	MACH APP INDUSTRIE
78	ROAD VEHICLES		10807		11593		3818		3079	VEHICULES ROUTIERS
782	LORRIES,SPCL MTR VEH NES	N 151	9612	N 197	7978	N 51	2706	N 59	2084	VEHICULES SPECIAUX,MARCH
7822	SPECIAL MOTOR VEHCLS NES	N 142	6677	N 163	7277	N 12	450	N 28	1079	VEHICULES USAGES SPECIAUX
79	OTHR TRANSPORT EQUIPMENT		23434		99399		41815		38043	AUTRE MATERIEL TRANSPORT
792	AIRCRAFT ETC		21203		96387		38811		22215	APP NAVIGATION AERIENNE
7921	HELICOPTERS	N 4	2948	N 17	26245	N 13	12855	N 9	2775	HELICOPTERES
7922	AIRCRFT NES 2000KG OR LS	N 1	107		18689			N 3	1133	AERODYNES MOINS 2000 KG
7924	AIRCRFT NES OVER 15000KG	N 1	3859		36849	N 2	18306	N 5	4526	AERODYNES PLUS 15000 KG
7929	AIRCRAFT PARTS NES		14183		14603		6759		13463	PIECES DU 792
793	SHIPS AND BOATS ETC	N 100	2231	N 29	3012	N 63	2996	N 327	15828	NAVIRES BATEAUX,ETC
7932	SHIPS AND BOATS NES	N 86	2070	N 26	2982	N 26	1853	N 77	14333	NAVIRES ET BATEAUX
79323	OTHER CARGO VESSELS	N 3	348	N 6	2008	N 10	1421	N 50	14171	AUT BATEAUX TRANS MARCH
8	MISC MANUFACTURED GOODS		11049		27574		7822		4863	ART MANUFACTURES DIVERS
87	PRECISION INSTRUMNTS NES		9954		24988		5603		2937	INSTRUM,APPAR SCIENT NDA
874	MEASURNG,CONTROLNG INSTR		9933		24954		5261		2726	INSTRUMENTS DE MESURE
8741	SURVEYING INSTRUMENTS		6913		23655		2550		2194	INST GEODESIE,TOPO ETC
87412	SURVEY INSTR ETC NONELEC		5857		23655		1501		2194	INSTR GEODESIE,TOPO ETC
9	GOODS NOT CLASSD BY KIND		248849		540457		628166		521909	ART TRANSACT NON CLASSES
931	*SPECIAL TRANSACTIONS		15662		5386		5097		4273	TRANS.SPECIALES
971	*GOLD,NON MONETARY NES	K 18742	233135	K 45383	535054	K 58489	623067	K 44773	517602	OR NON MONETAIRE
97101	NONMON GLD UNWRT,SEMIMFD	K 18742	233135	K 45383	535054	K 58435	622608	K 44773	517602	OR,ALLIAGES D'OR BRUTS

FOOT NOTES – NOTES

TABLE 1 –
1 Merchandise imports for 1968 and exports for 1970 include a floating oil rig valued at kina 8 million. Prior to 1981, special trade.

TABLEAU 1 –
1 Les importations de marchandises pour 1968 et les exportations pour 1970, comprennent une plate–forme flottante pétrolière évaluée à 8 millions de kinas. Avant 1981, commerce spéciale.

Paraguay

1. HISTORICAL SERIES, 1960–1995 SPECIAL TRADE, IMPORTS C.I.F., EXPORTS F.O.B.
SERIES HISTORIQUES, 1960–1995 COMMERCE SPECIAL, IMPORTATIONS C.A.F., EXPORTATIONS F.O.B

YEAR ANNEE	VALUE IN MILLION U.S. DOLLARS VALEUR EN MILLION U.S. DOLLARS MERCHANDISE –MARCHANDISE IMPORTS	EXPORTS	GOLD –OR IMPORTS	EXPORTS	CONVERSION FACTORS FACTEURS DE CONVERSION CENTS E.U. PAR IMPORTS	EXPORTS	INDEX NUMBERS –INDICES QUANTUM IMPORTS	EXPORTS	UNIT VALUE VALEUR UNITAIRE IMPORTS	EXPORTS
1960	32.40	27.00								
1961	34.70	30.70								
1962	34.70	33.50								
1963	32.60	40.20								
1964	33.80	49.80								
1965	47.40	57.30								
1966	50.20	49.40								
1967	60.70	48.30								
1968	61.50	47.60								
1969	70.40	51.00								
1970	63.80	64.10								
1971	70.30	65.21								
1972	69.85	86.19								
1973	104.79	126.93								
1974	171.39	169.81								
1975	178.67	176.71								
1976	180.14	181.25								
1977	255.38	278.91								
1978	317.74	256.96								
1979	437.72	305.08								
1980	614.74	310.24								
1981	599.68	295.56								
1982	729.69	375.09								
1983	631.24	342.55								
1984	643.56	386.13								
1985	630.60	305.14								
1986	831.90	274.67								
1987	678.85	379.26								
1988	777.99	657.02								
1989	818.54	1119.28								
1990	1352.00	958.70								
1991	1460.30	737.10								
1992	1421.60	656.60								
1993	1688.80	725.20								
1994	2370.20	816.80								
1995	3143.80	919.30								

2. IMPORTS BY BROAD ECONOMIC CATEGORY AND EXPORTS BY INDUSTRIAL ORIGIN. (PERCENTAGE OF TOTAL VALUE)
IMPORTATIONS PAR CATEGORIES ECONOMIQUES ET EXPORTATIONS PAR BRANCHE D'ACTIVITE.(EN POURCENTAGE DE LA VALEUR TOTALE)

IMPORTS – IMPORTATIONS

	1990	1991	1992	1993	1994	1995	1996
TOTAL IMPORTS–IMPORTATIONS TOTALES	100.	100.	100.	100.	100.	100.	
1 FOOD BEV–ALIMENTATION BOISSONS	6.1	7.5	9.5	8.3	10.6	12.0	
11 PRIMARY–PRODUITS DE BASE	0.3	0.5	1.4	1.3	2.2	2.5	
111 FOR INDUSTRY–POUR L'INDUSTRIE	0.2	0.4	1.3	1.1	1.9	2.2	
112 FOR HOUSEHOLDS–POUR LES MENAGES	0.1	0.1	0.1	0.2	0.3	0.3	
12 PROCESSED–PRODUITS ELABORES	5.8	7.0	8.0	7.0	8.4	9.5	
121 FOR INDUSTRY–POUR L'INDUSTRIE	0.5	0.4	0.5	0.5	0.4	0.5	
122 FOR HOUSEHOLDS–POUR LES MENAGES	5.3	6.6	7.5	6.5	8.0	9.1	
2 IND SUPPLIES–APPROV INDUSTRIELS	16.7	17.7	18.0	18.6	18.5	16.3	
21 PRIMARY–PRODUITS DE BASE	0.5	1.0	0.9	0.8	0.9	0.7	
22 PROCESSED–PRODUITS ELABORES	16.2	16.6	17.1	17.8	17.6	15.6	
3 FUELS–COMBUSTIBLES	14.2	11.8	13.5	11.9	8.1	6.5	
31 PRIMARY–PRODUITS DE BASE	6.4	5.4	4.9	3.5	2.2	1.5	
32 PROCESSED–PRODUITS ELABORES	7.8	6.3	8.6	8.4	5.8	5.0	
321 MOTOR SPIRIT–ESSENCE	1.7	1.5	1.6	1.7	1.2	3.5	
322 OTHER–AUTRES	6.1	4.8	7.1	6.7	4.6	1.6	
4 MACHINERY–EQUIPEMENT	15.9	15.3	17.9	19.1	18.9	17.2	
41 CAPITAL EQUIPMENT–MACHINES	14.3	13.6	16.2	16.8	16.8	15.7	
42 PARTS–PIECES ACCESSOIRES	1.6	1.7	1.7	2.2	2.2	1.5	
5 TRANSPORT–TRANSPORT	10.4	13.9	15.7	15.4	14.0	13.8	
51 PASSENGER CARS–AUTOMOBILES	2.3	3.9	6.0	5.4	4.1	4.3	
52 OTHER–AUTRES	4.4	5.1	6.1	6.2	6.0	5.9	
521 INDUSTRIAL–INDUSTRIELS	4.2	4.8	5.5	5.3	5.2	5.1	
522 NON INDUSTRIAL–NON INDUSTRIEL	0.2	0.4	0.6	0.9	0.8	0.8	
53 PARTS–PIECES ACCESSOIRES	3.6	4.8	3.7	3.8	4.0	3.6	
6 CONSUM GOODS–BIENS CONSOMMATION	36.5	33.8	25.4	26.4	29.4	33.9	
61 DURABLE–DURABLES	23.6	18.3	11.1	11.6	12.5	14.4	
62 SEMI DURABLE–SEMI DURABLES	8.7	9.0	7.0	7.9	8.3	9.3	
63 NON DURABLE–NON DURABLES	4.2	6.5	7.2	6.9	8.5	10.1	
7 GOODS NES–BIENS NDA	0.3	0.0	0.0	0.2	0.5	0.3	

EXPORTS – EXPORTATIONS

	1990	1991	1992	1993	1994	1995	1996
TOTAL EXPORTS–EXPORTATIONS TOTALES	100.	100.	100.	100.	100.	100.	
1 AGRICULTURE	68.1	67.0	53.7	55.2	52.5	54.0	
2 MINING QUARRY–INDUS EXTRACTIVES	0.0	0.0	0.1	0.1	0.1	0.1	
3 MANUFACTURING–IND MANUFACTUR	31.9	33.0	46.2	44.6	47.4	45.9	
31 FOOD BEV TOBACCO–ALIM BOISS TAB	18.7	16.5	24.1	21.5	19.4	19.4	
32 TEXTILES–INDUSTRIES TEXTILES	5.6	5.7	8.4	9.4	11.2	10.6	
33 WOOD & PRODUCTS–BOIS & PRODUITS	3.9	6.0	8.0	8.7	9.6	9.6	
34 PAPER & PRODUCTS–PAPIER & PRODT	0.1	0.1	0.3	0.3	0.4	0.5	
35 CHEMICALS–INDUSTRIES CHIMIQUES	3.2	3.5	3.6	2.2	2.8	3.2	
36 NON METAL MIN–MIN NON METAL	0.0	0.0	0.1	0.1	0.2	0.2	
37 BASIC METAL–IND METAL BASE	0.2	0.8	1.3	1.7	2.5	1.0	
38 METAL MANUF–MANUF METAL	0.2	0.3	0.3	0.8	1.3	1.3	
39 OTH MANUF IND–AUTRES MANUF	0.0	0.0	0.0	0.0	0.0	0.0	

Paraguay

3. TRADE BY PRINCIPAL COUNTRIES OF FIRST AND LAST CONSIGNMENT (VALUE IN THOUSAND U.S. DOLLARS)
ECHANGES SELON LES PRINCIPAUX PAYS DE PREMIERE ET DE DERNIERE CONSIGNATION (VALEUR EN MILLIERS DE DOLLARS EU)

COUNTRIES–PAYS	SPECIAL IMPORTS C.I.F. IMPORTATIONS SPECIALES C.A.F				
	1991	1992	1993	1994	1995
World	1460309	1420431	1688033	2424603	3135881
Africa	62433	44283	64993	51058	28229
Americas	756753	817844	980165	1422366	1774373
Northern America	223172	201112	245407	309153	410938
LAIA	494743	596847	706698	1093946	1353123
CACM	207	420	146	236	423
Caribbean	13973	620	94	8	580
Rest of America	24657	18844	27818	19023	9309
As.ex F.USSR	416354	338013	426904	628211	961234
Eur.x F.USSR	220837	216850	212886	314844	363722
EU	207756	202778	199383	275701	346223
EFTA	10105	10088	10938	16054	15283
East Europe	2930	3937	2445	23060	2216
Other Europe	46	32			
Former USSR	3751	3129	2758	7225	37
Oceania	181	313	328	898	1269
Brazil/Brésil	251275	283109	369501	598725	681290
Argentina/Argentine	175150	231005	242379	349393	518585
USA/Etats–Unis d'Amer	219040	199032	237702	284529	392415
Japan/Japon	191914	174236	204155	226576	272502
Korea, Republic of	69712	55520	67048	119242	207194
Hong Kong	51120	21185	23297	90592	169734
Germany/Allemagne	59103	55695	57798	81969	83303
United Kingdom	60285	59649	55146	61641	96076
Chile/Chili	39764	39641	47657	84530	85220
Italy/Italie	34471	28185	21197	49497	66193
Algeria/Algérie	54762	37390	60563	29164	15841
France, Monac	23353	24440	23734	33729	37816
Uruguay	11107	12016	20716	31704	36878
Panama	24657	18844	27818	19023	9309
Mexico/Mexique	11910	12318	15339	14243	20131
Singapore/Singapour	2153	7914	6853	19416	36316
Spain/Espagne	9727	10774	9603	15914	21848
Netherlands/Pays–Bas	8250	10722	20822	10227	13797
Switz.Liecht	9831	9886	10828	15774	15035
Canada	4133	2078	7705	24624	18524
So. Africa Customs Un	7630	6887	4372	21840	12329
Venezuela	1595	14871	4692	9128	1497
Sweden/Suède	4248	4289	4837	4949	11166
India/Inde	1949	2833	5093	7482	10048
Belgium–Luxembourg	4272	4564	2981	8229	7200
Malaysia/Malaisie	634	1399	3605	4745	15615
Romania/Roumanie	217	441	139	20306	938
Aruba	13938				
Russian Federation		3129	2758	7225	37
Austria/Autriche	1990	1459	874	3503	2722
Colombia/Colombie	1095	1248	1029	2137	4673
Denmark/Danemark	1111	1164	1717	2817	3056
Bolivia/Bolivie	1940	1309	2378	1945	2096
Indonesia/Indonésie	508	419	758	2633	4450
Thailand/Thaïlande	297	1074	1416	1601	4168
Israel/Israël	1388	1384	1200	2246	1856
Peru/Pérou	530	823	2120	996	1324
Ecuador/Equateur	377	508	888	1146	1429
Czechoslovakia	1800	2540			
Former USSR/Anc. URSS	3751				
Czech Republic			1718	1816	5
Poland/Pologne	704	567	339	733	558
Ireland/Irlande	306	1582	323	233	370
Finland/Finlande	82	117	98	1869	320
Australia/Australie	181	78	309	886	873
Greece/Grèce	338	4	115	675	1157
Portugal	219	135	139	449	1200
Pakistan	341	415	13	432	755
Hungary/Hongrie	209	344	204	158	406
Norway,SVD,JM	274	203	110	280	249

COUNTRIES–PAYS	SPECIAL EXPORTS F.O.B. EXPORTATIONS SPECIALES F.O.B.				
	1991	1992	1993	1994	1995
Monde	737041	656555	725218	816833	919331
Afrique	2715	3572	2148	4731	5748
Amériques	401012	384541	434973	553527	656869
Amérique du Nord	56586	49514	68537	76742	55854
ALAI	326581	312364	342840	468585	596312
MCAC	864	3199	270	653	567
Caraïbes	14901	14314	17069	7486	3682
Autre Amérique	2079	5149	6257	61	454
Asie l'URSS exclus	61541	32062	12032	19909	73439
Europe l'URSS exclus	271560	236151	275215	237781	182439
UE	235962	225144	248409	226748	178087
AELE	35197	10832	26757	10953	4294
Europe de l'Est	84	161	49	79	35
Autre de l'Europe	317	15			
Ancienne URSS	194	203	837	685	365
Océanie	20	12	14	110	262
Brazil/Brésil	203042	171447	215123	323698	410825
Netherlands/Pays–Bas	109605	138879	189254	160042	89676
Argentina/Argentine	45031	64149	64943	90701	83278
USA/Etats–Unis d'Amer	35006	34994	53168	57115	43869
Chile/Chili	47633	47382	42248	32788	31051
Italy/Italie	39324	22487	17103	24227	29100
Germany/Allemagne	36222	20330	6698	13244	10460
Switz.Liecht	35175	8751	25982	10868	4268
Bermuda/Bermudes	21497	13730	12555	18652	11519
Uruguay	11319	10804	7211	10447	33946
France, Monac	11226	14063	11557	12200	19739
Venezuela	11582	8302	395	2188	21572
Spain/Espagne	13201	7453	5209	5575	9474
United Kingdom	3803	5337	13965	4688	6997
Portugal	13995	7757	1938	4318	3254
Bahamas	14524	8780	6253		591
Belgium–Luxembourg	7524	8285	2077	1250	9016
Israel/Israël	2305	5919	3282	5218	2651
Peru/Pérou	4018	4826	5180	495	3181
Cayman Is/Is Caïmans		4277	7120	2826	1550
Hong Kong	2040	1057	1436	2734	7452
Panama	2079	5140	6257	61	454
Korea, Republic of	8018	2634	278	280	2172
Bolivia/Bolivie	2196	1506	2881	3125	3638
Mexico/Mexique	1026	1601	3412	3887	925
So. Africa Customs Un	1478	2570	1203	1579	3739
Colombia/Colombie	565	1250	982	784	6930
Indonesia/Indonésie	2848	2216	127	72	3786
British Virgin Islds	306	1117	3362	2970	1158
Japan/Japon	3811	2449	755	1036	677
Thailand/Thaïlande	982	2136	156	4	1895
Canada	84	790	2813	975	465
China/Chine	3613		528		
Tunisia/Tunisie	226	580	471	1680	943
Singapore/Singapour	1876	1479	53	119	284
Ecuador/Equateur	170	1096	464	471	967
Guatemala	726	1476	25	474	374
Iceland/Islande		2081	772	84	26
Philippines	613			28	2049
Ireland/Irlande	790	307	312	781	63
Malaysia/Malaisie	747	131	139	8	1067
Russian Federation		203	837	685	150
Turkey/Turquie	106	1230	198	59	
Dominican Republic	10	3	81	1231	220
Saudi Arabia	29	51	572	601	253
Lebanon/Liban	409	31		284	604
El Salvador	6	1207		39	41
India/Inde	22	189	195	375	380
Egypt/Egypte	517	72	2	224	320
Morocco/Maroc				421	536

(VALUE AS PERCENTAGE OF WORLD TOTAL)(VALEURS EN POURCENTAGE DU TOTAL MONDIAL)

	1986	1987	1988	1989	1990	1991	1992	1993	1994	1995
Africa	7.6	10.8	11.0	10.0	6.0	4.3	3.1	3.9	2.1	0.9
Americas	60.9	56.0	54.9	55.3	47.7	51.8	57.6	58.1	58.7	56.6
Northern America	13.7	10.5	10.3	14.2	12.9	15.3	14.2	14.5	12.8	13.1
LAIA	46.3	44.5	44.2	39.7	32.9	33.9	42.0	41.9	45.1	43.1
CACM	0.0	0.0	0.0	0.0	0.0	0.0	0.0	0.0	0.0	0.0
Caribbean		0.0		0.0	0.0	1.0	0.0	0.0	0.0	0.0
Rest of America	0.9	1.0	0.4	1.3	1.8	1.7	1.3	1.6	0.8	0.3
As.ex F.USSR	11.6	11.0	13.0	20.5	30.4	28.5	23.8	25.3	25.9	30.7
Eur.x F.USSR	19.8	22.2	21.1	14.2	15.9	15.1	15.3	12.6	13.0	11.6
EU	18.6	21.0	19.6	13.1	15.0	14.2	14.3	11.8	11.4	11.0
EFTA	1.2	1.0	1.2	0.9	0.7	0.7	0.7	0.6	0.7	0.5
East Europe	0.1	0.2	0.3	0.2	0.1	0.2	0.3	0.1	1.0	0.1
Other Europe	0.0	0.0	0.0	0.0	0.0	0.0	0.0			
Former USSR	0.0			0.0	0.0	0.3	0.2	0.2	0.3	0.0
Oceania	0.0	0.0		0.0	0.0	0.0	0.0	0.0	0.0	0.0
Brazil/Brésil	30.1	31.2	29.0	25.5	16.5	17.2	19.9	21.9	24.7	21.7
Argentina/Argentine	14.3	8.9	12.0	10.7	12.8	12.0	16.3	14.4	14.4	16.5
USA/Etats–Unis d'Amer	13.6	10.4	10.0	14.1	12.7	15.0	14.0	14.1	11.7	12.5
Japan/Japon	6.0	6.0	7.6	12.2	15.5	13.1	12.3	12.1	9.3	8.7
Korea, Republic of	0.3	0.5	0.8	2.0	4.4	4.8	3.9	4.0	4.9	6.6
Hong Kong	1.4	1.2	1.1	2.4	4.0	3.5	1.5	1.4	3.7	5.4
Germany/Allemagne	6.3	5.6	5.9	4.3	4.8	4.0	3.9	3.4	3.4	2.7
United Kingdom	6.2	6.3	6.5	3.8	3.6	4.1	4.2	3.3	2.5	3.1
Chile/Chili	0.9	1.2	1.7	2.1	2.1	2.7	2.8	2.8	3.5	2.7
Italy/Italie	1.3	4.5	1.7	0.9	1.9	2.4	2.0	1.3	2.0	2.1

	1986	1987	1988	1989	1990	1991	1992	1993	1994	1995
Afrique	1.2	0.7	1.8	0.4	0.3	0.4	0.5	0.3	0.6	0.6
Amériques	71.0	53.0	50.2	56.7	58.0	54.4	58.6	60.0	67.8	71.5
Amérique du Nord	4.2	4.2	8.1	6.3	5.6	7.7	7.5	9.5	9.4	6.1
ALAI	65.2	44.6	38.5	41.8	44.4	44.3	47.6	47.3	57.4	64.9
MCAC	0.1	0.0	0.0	0.0	0.1	0.1	0.5	0.0	0.1	0.1
Caraïbes	0.1	0.1	0.0	2.9	4.2	2.0	2.2	2.4	0.9	0.4
Autre Amérique	1.5	4.1	3.6	5.6	3.7	0.3	0.8	0.9	0.0	0.0
Asie l'URSS exclus	1.2	3.4	8.0	3.3	4.6	8.3	4.9	1.7	2.4	8.0
Europe l'URSS exclus	26.6	42.8	40.0	39.6	37.0	36.8	36.0	37.9	29.1	19.8
UE	20.7	36.0	32.2	32.2	31.7	32.0	34.3	34.3	27.8	19.4
AELE	5.9	6.8	7.6	7.3	5.2	4.8	1.6	3.7	1.3	0.5
Europe de l'Est			0.0	0.1	0.0	0.0	0.0	0.0	0.0	0.0
Autre de l'Europe	0.0		0.1	0.0	0.1	0.0	0.0			
Ancienne URSS						0.0	0.0	0.1	0.1	0.0
Océanie					0.0	0.0	0.0	0.0	0.0	0.0
Brazil/Brésil	39.5	17.6	23.0	32.5	32.6	27.5	26.1	29.7	39.6	44.7
Netherlands/Pays–Bas	9.7	18.0	13.3	18.5	15.3	14.9	21.2	26.1	19.6	9.8
Argentina/Argentine	15.1	15.2	6.6	4.9	5.8	6.1	9.8	9.0	11.1	9.1
USA/Etats–Unis d'Amer	4.0	4.2	3.8	4.2	4.3	4.7	5.3	7.3	7.0	4.8
Chile/Chili	5.9	6.0	5.2	2.8	3.1	6.5	7.2	5.8	4.0	3.4
Italy/Italie	1.8	3.4	2.5	2.4	2.7	5.3	3.4	2.4	3.0	3.2
Germany/Allemagne	3.3	3.8	3.8	2.3	4.6	4.9	3.1	0.9	1.6	1.1
Switz.Liecht	5.9	6.8	7.6	7.3	5.2	4.8	1.3	3.6	1.3	0.5
Bermuda/Bermudes	0.1		4.3	2.2	1.3	2.9	2.1	1.7	2.3	1.3
Uruguay	2.8	3.2	0.9	1.0	1.2	1.5	1.6	1.0	1.3	3.7

Paraguay

4. Special Imports C.I.F. by Commodities according to the S.I.T.C. (Rev. 2) in thousand U.S. Dollars
Importations Spéciales C.A.F. par Produits d'après la C.T.C.I. (Rév. 2) en milliers de Dollars E.U.

SITC CTCI	COMMODITY	1992 WEIGHT POIDS	1992 VALUE VALEUR	1993 WEIGHT POIDS	1993 VALUE VALEUR	1994 WEIGHT POIDS	1994 VALUE VALEUR	1995 WEIGHT POIDS	1995 VALUE VALEUR	PRODUIT
	ALL COMMODITIES		1420431		1688033		2424603		3135881	TOUS PRODUITS
0	FOOD AND LIVE ANIMALS		55340		71673		150655		217467	ALIMENTS,ANIMAUX VIVANTS
001	*LIVE ANIMALS FOR FOOD	W 880	1716	W 2913	3039	W 60096	43084	W 82954	56950	ANIMAUX VIVANTS
0011	BOVINE SPECIES,LIVE	W 684	940	W 2814	2397	W 59658	41130	W 82417	54187	ESPECE BOVINE
00111	— PURE BRED FR BREEDING	W 634	868	W 119	163	W 719	1108	W 28849	19298	BOVINS REPRODUCTEURS
00119	— OTHR THAN FR BREEDING	W 50	73	W 2695	2234	W 58938	40022	W 53568	34889	BOVINS NON REPRODUCTEURS
02	DAIRY PRODCTS,BIRDS'EGGS		8156		6061		18949		22010	PRODUITS LAITIERS,OEUFS
022	MILK AND CREAM	W 4237	8059	W 2889	5781	W 7645	17445	W 7241	18923	LAIT ET CREME
0224	MILK,CREAM PRESERVED ETC	W 4237	8059	W 2850	5737	W 7510	17342	W 7129	18782	LAIT,CREME CONS,CONC
02243	MILK DRY,OVER 1.5% FAT	W 1591	3649	W 1954	4411	W 4521	11858	W 6534	17919	LAIT POUDRE SUP 1.5%
04	CEREALS AND PREPARATIONS		19947		27639		24492		53974	CEREALES ET PRODUITS
041	WHEAT ETC UNMILLED	W 42535	5869	W 81914	11185	W 7000	873	W 38059	5937	FROMENT,EPEAUTRE
0411	DURUM WHEAT UNMILLED	W 38725	5341	W 79814	10869	W 7000	873	W 133	33	FROMENT DUR NON MOULU
048	CEREAL ETC PREPARATIONS	W 23038	12614	W 26309	15551	W 33211	21270	W 37074	42768	PREPTNS A BASE CEREALES
0482	MALT INCLUDING FLOUR	W 16607	5436	W 19153	6849	W 21957	6640	W 18873	10910	MALT MEME TORREFIE
0484	BAKERY PRODUCTS	W 5453	5553	W 5375	5997	W 8325	10151	W 12554	22420	PRODUITS DE BOULANGERIE
04842	PASTRY, CAKES ETC	W 5260	5234	W 5255	5793	W 7938	9474	W 10445	20316	PATISSERIE ETC.
05	VEGETABLES AND FRUIT		5129		5853		10353		15920	LEGUMES ET FRUITS
06	SUGAR AND PREPS,HONEY		4661		5203		12419		19318	SUCRES ET PRODUITS
062	SUGAR CANDY NON-CHOCLATE	W 2417	3704	W 2641	4421	W 5082	8621	W 7663	14323	SUCRERIES
07	COFFEE,TEA,COCOA,SPICES		2723		4236		7076		11575	CAFE,THE,CACAO,EPICES
09	MISC EDIBLE PRODUCTS		11204		15952		24001		26225	PREP ALIMENTAIRES DIVERSES
098	EDIBLE PRODCTS,PREPS NES	W 3860	11090	W 5338	15884	W 8948	23719	W 9221	25757	PREP ALIMENTAIRES NDA
09809	MISC FOOD PREPRTIONS NES	W 1876	8665	W 2387	11846	W 4020	17283	W 4140	16948	PREP ALIMENTAIRES NDA
1	BEVERAGES AND TOBACCO		120050		116721		197641		355812	BOISSONS ET TABACS
11	BEVERAGES		69671		65394		107941		157956	BOISSONS
111	NON-ALCOHL BEVERAGES NES	W 697	446	W 5475	3021	W 12214	6523	W 18396	11175	BOISSONS NON ALCOOLIQUES
11102	FLAVORED WATERS NON-ALCO	W 678	434	W 5403	3006	W 12161	6503	W 18220	10891	LIMONADES,EAUX GAZEUSES
112	ALCOHOLIC BEVERAGES	W 32803	69225	W 37455	62372	W 85433	101418	W 97860	146781	BOISSONS ALCOOLIQUES
1121	WINE OF FRESH GRAPES ETC	W 8727	9115	W 6633	8258	W 11396	10721	W 10957	15801	VINS DE RAISINS FRAIS
11212	WINE OF FRESH GRAPES	W 8463	8895	W 6281	7539	W 10864	10249	W 10434	15336	VINS DE MOUTS DE RAISINS
1123	BEER,ALE,STOUT,PORTER	W 7201	3930	W 16220	9519	W 54010	30334	W 56481	33606	BIERES
1124	DISTILLED ALCOHOLIC BEVS	W 14555	54742	W 13949	44291	W 17317	59120	W 27333	94668	ALCOOLS,EAUX-DE-VIE
11241	WHISKY	W 11400	50862	W 12697	41463	W 15065	53822	W 24202	87202	WHISKY
12	TOBACCO AND MANUFACTURES		50379		51327		89700		197856	TABACS BRUTS FABRIQUES
122	TOBACCO,MANUFACTURED	W 3762	47604	W 3692	46731	W 9039	84238	W 22971	190532	TABACS FABRIQUES
1222	CIGARETTES	W 3747	47532	W 3668	46524	W 9024	84108	W 22811	190008	CIGARETTES
2	CRUDE MATERLS,EXCL FUELS		20059		13176		17520		15838	MAT BRUTES NON COMESTIBLES
22	OIL SEEDS,OLEAGINOUS FRT		10338		3992		976		3991	GRAINES,FRUITS OLEAGINEUX
222	SEEDS FOR'SOFT'FIXED OIL	W 10294	10336	W 2809	3973	W 303	941	W 4666	3927	GRAINES HUILES FIXES
2223	COTTON SEEDS	W 6068	9535	W 1970	3210			W 4103	3162	GRAINES DE COTON
27	CRUDE FERTLZR,MINRLS NES		3446		3134		10357		4421	ENGRAIS MINERAUX BRUTS
3	MINERAL FUELS ETC		193994		206525		201753		206429	COMBUSTIBLES MINERAUX LUB
33	PETROLEUM AND PRODUCTS		177790		191912		189659		192425	PETROLE ET DERIVES
333	CRUDE PETROLEUM	W 242910	52888	W 219913	44435	W 234222	43287	W 228423	31496	HUILES BRUTES DE PETROLE
334	PETROLEUM PRODUCTS,REFIN	W 485247	122615	W 567973	142400	W 664735	140072	W 716850	157759	PRODUITS RAFFINES
3341	GASOLINE,OTH LIGHT OILS	W 80833	22407	W 116376	29223	W 143140	29163	W 543327	108541	ESSENCES POUR MOTEURS
33411	MOTOR,AVIATION SPIRIT	W 79997	22059	W 115381	28884	W 142269	28847	W 530537	104792	ESSENCES MOTEURS D'AVIONS
3342	KEROSENE,OTH MEDIUM OILS	W 27168	6285	W 18387	4323	W 22902	4717			PETR LAMPANTS,AUT HUIL
33421	KEROSENE INCL JET FUEL	W 27168	6285	W 18387	4323	W 22902	4717			PETROLES LAMPANTS
3343	GAS OILS	W 363335	82755	W 415033	94674	W 478145	88972	W 15051	11023	GAS OILS
3345	LUBS,PETROLEUM OILS NES	W 13867	11142	W 17895	13936	W 20274	17041	W 158424	38177	HUILES LUBRIFIANTES
33451	LUBS(HIGH PETR CONT) ETC	W 13290	10071	W 16862	11578	W 19100	14599	W 157519	36751	HUILES LUBRIF,H LOURDES
335	RESIDUAL PETRLM PROD NES	W 11105	2287	W 28552	5078	W 44692	6300	W 21688	3170	PRODUITS RESIDUELS NDA
341	*GAS,NATURAL AND MANUFCT	W 57163	16204	W 55587	14613	W 70328	11120	W 70367	14003	GAZ NATUREL,GAZ MANUFACT
3413	PETROLM GASES,LIQUEFIED	W 57118	16197	W 55587	14613	W 70328	11120	W 70352	13925	GAZ DE PETROLE LIQUEFIE
34139	OTH HYDROCARBON GAS LQFD	W 56869	16134	W 55587	14613	W 70328	11119	W 69501	13732	HYDROCARBURES GAZEUX NDA
5	CHEMCLS,RELATED PROD NES		141995		179908		269942		278540	PRODUITS CHIMIQUES
51	ORGANIC CHEMICALS		14427		18082		15157		17615	PROD CHIMIQ ORGANIQUES
514	NITROGEN-FNCTN COMPOUNDS	W 963	4327	W 1048	4058		4809	W 1245	5436	COMPOSES FONCT AZOTEES
515	ORG-INORG COMPOUNDS ETC	W 310	4685	W 294	4752	W 307	4064	W 539	5494	COMPOSES ORGANO-MINERAUX
52	INORGANIC CHEMICALS		9097		7849		8453		8835	PROD CHIM INORGANIQUES
523	OTHR INORG CHEMICALS ETC	W 16931	5032	W 21739	3949	W 30806	5353	W 11809	4139	AUT PRODUITS CHIMIQUES INORG
53	DYES,TANNING,COLOUR PROD		7726		12715		23109		16414	PROD TEINTURE,COLORANTS
531	SYNT DYE,NAT INDGO,LAKES	W 314	1964	W 423	2845	W 1540	10981	W 538	3411	MAT COLOR ORGAN,LAQUES
5312	SYNTH LUMIN,INDIGO,LAKES	W 85	383	W 102	466	W 1211	8464	W 152	570	LUMINOPHORES ORGAN SYNTH
53121	SYN ORG LUMIN ETC,INDIGO	W 53	248	W 56	287	W 1152	8266	W 126	460	PROD ORGANIQ SYNTH LUMIN
533	PIGMENTS,PAINTS,ETC	W 3414	4837	W 4924	8444	W 6376	10516	W 6944	12057	PIGMENTS,PEINTURES,VERNIS
5334	VARNISHES,DISTEMPERS ETC	W 2135	2451	W 3353	5169	W 3918	5709	W 3760	6180	PEINTURES A L'EAU
541	*MEDICINAL,PHARM PRODUCT	K 2514350	29416	K 2496304	36121	K 7191099	62021	K 6128531	51059	PROD MEDICINAUX PHARMACEUT
5417	MEDICAMENTS	K 2029437	21381	K 2192642	27391	K 6759462	51073	K 5569281	37364	MEDICAMENTS
54179	— CONTNG OTH SUBSTANCES	K 1900688	15301	K 2051396	20597	K 5935772	41126	K 5185152	29087	MED CONT AUT SUBSTANCES
55	PERFUME,CLEANING ETC PRD		21118		27468		45034		55328	PROD POUR PARFUM,TOILETTE
553	PERFUMERY,COSMETICS,ETC	W 5340	16923	W 5425	19568	W 10747	32658	W 11269	38931	PRODUITS DE PARFUMERIE
554	SOAP,CLEANSING ETC PREPS	W 2706	2547	W 2970	3190	W 9515	9273	W 14571	14384	SAVONS,PRODUITS DETERSIFS
5542	WASHING PREPARATIONS ETC	W 1291	1682	W 2211	2149	W 7645	7473	W 11479	11519	PROD ORG TENSIO-ACT NDA
562	*FERTILIZERS,MANUFACTURE	W 58051	11639	W 74892	11943	W 107407	18076	W 81268	22644	ENGRAIS MANUFACTURES
5629	FERTILIZERS NES	W 49985	9915	W 66887	10621	W 87379	14916	W 64899	18216	ENGRAIS NDA
56291	NIT-PHOS-POT FERTLZR NES	W 37516	6707	W 37146	5365	W 56619	9263	W 41945	13066	ENGRAIS CONT N P K
58	PLASTIC MATERIALS ETC		20601		25377		38198		44337	MAT PLAST ARTIFICIELLES
582	PROD OF CONDENSATION ETC	W 2282	2354	W 4402	4420	W 8219	7887	W 7433	8844	PROD CONDENS,POLYCOND
583	POLYMERIZATION ETC PRODS	W 17602	17652	W 22188	20524	W 31688	29663	W 32994	34669	PROD POLYMERISATION
5831	POLYETHYLENE	W 8492	6563	W 11991	8269	W 16996	11883	W 13320	17662	POLYETHYLENE
58311	— IN PRIMARY FORMS	W 8262	6237	W 11725	7775	W 16717	11360	W 12996	16591	POLYETHYLENE PRIMAIRES
59	CHEMICAL MATERIALS NES		27682		39008		59144		61292	MAT PROD CHIMIQUES NDA
591	PESTICIDES,DISINFECTANTS	W 3420	20783	W 3733	26005	W 8111	46440	W 8549	46944	DESINF,INSECT,FONG,HERB
5911	INSECTICIDES,FOR RETAIL	W 1693	9027	W 1176	8946	W 2083	11933	W 1593	9455	INSECTICIDES VENTE DET
5913	HERBICIDES,FOR RETAIL	W 1397	9288	W 1937	12651	W 3300	27896	W 3987	30810	HERBICIDES VENTE AU DET
598	MISCEL CHEM PRODUCTS NES	W 2925	5460	W 4395	10677	W 5704	9400	W 5381	10069	PROD DIV INDUST CHIM NDA
5982	ANTI-KNOCK PREPARTNS ETC	W 686	1476	W 1459	5945	W 1001	2275	W 988	2841	PREPARAT ANTIDETONANTES
6	BASIC MANUFACTURES		169543		209981		314782		372142	ART MANUFACTURES
62	RUBBER MANUFACTURES NES		27747		36067		56620		63943	CAOUTCHOUC MANUFACTURE
625	RUBBER TYRES, TUBES ETC	W 8030	22961	W 10212	30617	W 16119	50158	W 18511	54453	PNEUS CAOUTCHOUC VULCANISE
6251	TYRES NEW FOR MOTOR CARS	W 2989	8652	W 2384	6629	W 3940	12430	W 4518	13211	PNEUS POUR VOITURES
6252	TYRES,NEW,BUS OR LORRY	W 3299	10420	W 5511	18764	W 7837	28949	W 9207	29952	PNEUS POUR AUTOBUS,CAMIONS
6259	OTH TYRES,TYRE CASES,ETC	W 1493	3185	W 2013	4411	W 3816	7477	W 4083	9470	AUTRES PNEUS RECHAPES FLAPS
64	PAPER,PAPERBOARD AND MFR		31046		36553		51398		71380	PAPIERS,CARTONS & OUVRAGES
641	PAPER AND PAPERBOARD	W 30665	23181	W 35248	24512	W 50385	33539	W 46790	44127	PAPIERS ET CARTONS
6411	NEWSPRINT	W 13265	8236	W 14440	9319	W 19959	12156	W 17500	14290	PAPIER JOURNAL
6415	PAPER,PAPERBRD,BULK,NES	W 9266	6699	W 9840	7001	W 12193	8925	W 11136	13402	PAPIERS,CARTONS ROULEAUX
64159	OTHER PAPER ETC,BULK,NES	W 9096	6298	W 9705	6788	W 11943	8593	W 9989	12582	AUT PAPIER ROULEAUX FEUILLES

4. Special Imports C.I.F. by Commodities according to the S.I.T.C. (Rev. 2) in thousand U.S. Dollars
Importations Spéciales C.A.F. par Produits d'après la C.T.C.I. (Rév. 2) en milliers de Dollars E.U.

SITC CTCI	COMMODITY	1992 WEIGHT POIDS	1992 VALUE VALEUR	1993 WEIGHT POIDS	1993 VALUE VALEUR	1994 WEIGHT POIDS	1994 VALUE VALEUR	1995 WEIGHT POIDS	1995 VALUE VALEUR	PRODUIT
642	PAPER,ETC,PRECUT,ARTS OF	W 3704	7866	W 5107	12041	W 8811	17859	W 10920	27253	PAP,CARTONS DECOUPES
6428	PAPER ETC ARTICLES NES	W 2583	6176	W 3598	9297	W 5575	13355	W 7223	20870	OUVRAGES EN PATE A PAPIER
64285	PAPER ETC DIAPERS ETC	W 2292	5716	W 3085	8525	W 4634	12008	W 5955	18704	SERVIETTES HYGIENIQUES
65	TEXTILE YARN,FABRICS,ETC		23351		37592		57516		64565	FILS,TISSUS,ARTICLES TEXTILE
652	COTTON FABRICS,WOVEN	W 1156	2931	W 1968	6102	W 3893	13495	W 3634	10295	TISSUS DE COTON
6522	WOVEN COTTON BLEACHD,ETC	W 1142	2854	W 1955	6059	W 3857	13409	W 3626	10266	TISSUS COTON BLANCHIS ETC
65224	BLCHED COTTON FABRIC NES	W 703	1869	W 1762	5572	W 3691	12746	W 2770	9701	AUT TIS PLUS 85% COT BLANCHI
653	WOVN MAN-MADE FIB FABRIC	W 3266	11035	W 4416	17018	W 6896	22597	W 7741	29966	TISSUS FIBRES SYNTH,ARTIF
6531	CONT SYNT WEAVES NONPILE	W 2049	6136	W 2773	10456	W 4282	12511	W 4310	15568	TISSUS FIBRES SYNTH CONTINUE
65315	CONT SYN TXTL FABRIC NES	W 1920	5737	W 2609	9700	W 4082	11720	W 4144	14680	TIS PLUS 85% TEXT SYNT CONT
66	NONMETAL MINERAL MFS NES		14867		19128		26914		34278	ART MIN NON METALLIQUES
665	GLASSWARE	W 4890	5099	W 7315	6377	W 8388	7533	W 7114	8787	OUVRAGES EN VERRE
67	IRON AND STEEL		22590		24226		39135		41378	FER ET ACIER
674	IRN,STL UNIV,PLATE,SHEET	W 26125	14400	W 27118	14426	W 35270	22229	W 40793	25808	LARGES PLATS,TOLES
6749	OTH IRN,STL PLATES,SHEET	W 12412	7957	W 7583	5211	W 17346	14196	W 18477	12347	AUTRES TOLES FER,ACIER
67491	-- OF IRON OR SIMPLE STL	W 7364	4270	W 5328	3372	W 15453	9778	W 18108	11885	AUT TOLES AUTRES ACIER FIN
68	NON-FERROUS METALS		7624		10178		11641		16470	METAUX NON FERREUX
684	ALUMINIUM	W 1316	4249	W 1932	6506	W 2225	7736	W 2432	10323	ALUMINIUM
6842	ALUMINIUM,ALLOYS WORKED	W 1193	4086	W 1864	6417	W 2185	7671	W 2382	10213	ALUMINIUM,ALLIAGES OUVRE
69	METAL MANUFACTURES NES		41418		45302		70246		76730	ART MANUFACT EN METAL NDA
691	STRUCTURES AND PARTS NES	W 3134	5162	W 974	2204	W 2664	4743	W 1560	2514	CONSTRUCT FER,ACIER,ALU
6911	STRUCTURES,PARTS IRN,STL	W 3102	5083	W 963	2077	W 2588	3855	W 1529	2160	CONSTRUCT FER,ACIER,FONTE
692	METAL TANKS,BOXES,ETC	W 1557	5002	W 2220	6078	W 4082	13908	W 3148	8138	RECIPIENTS METALLIQUES
693	WIRE PRODUCTS NON ELECTR	W 2061	4815	W 1596	3432	W 1764	3395	W 3572	9000	OUVRAGES FILS METALLIQUES
6931	WIRE CABLES, ROPES ETC	W 1925	4677	W 1311	3079	W 1277	2923	W 2948	8280	CORDAGES EN FILS DE FER
695	TOOLS	W 1743	7050	W 2194	7234	W 4813	11416	W 7385	12691	OUTILS A MAIN
6953	OTHER HAND TOOLS	W 1278	4783	W 1740	5076	W 3976	7566	W 6636	9557	AUTRES OUTILS A MAIN
696	CUTLERY	W 632	3550	W 1074	4524	W 2167	7490	W 4057	8324	COUTELLERIE
697	BASE MTL HOUSEHOLD EQUIP	W 2903	5481	W 3798	7756	W 8375	13052	W 18498	16936	ART MENAGE MET COMMUNS
6974	BASE MTL DMSTC ARTIC NES	W 819	1606	W 1712	2901	W 4975	5231	W 9301	9897	ARTICLES NDA FONTE,FER,ETC
699	BASE METAL MFRS NES	W 2974	7903	W 3533	10913	W 5288	12203	W 5995	14486	ART MANUFACTURES MET NDA
7	MACHINES,TRANSPORT EQUIP		583100		704314		999387		1323564	MACHINES MATERIEL TRANSPORT
71	POWER GENERATING EQUIPMT		22062		30495		41060		37425	MACHINES GENERATRICES
713	INTRNL COMBUS PSTN ENGIN	W 2145	8276	W 1705	9409	W 2239	11071	W 3134	13809	MOTEURS EXPL COMB INT, PIECE
7139	PISTON ENGINE PARTS NES	W 342	4574	W 495	6213	W 1081	8157	W 2349	8657	PIECES POUR 713.2,3,8
718	OTH POWER GENERATG MACHY	W 1584	8291	W 2174	16979	W 2481	26159	W 1038	13489	AUTRES MOTEURS PARTIES
7188	WIND,WATER,ETC ENGINES	W 1584	8291	W 2174	16979	W 2462	26151	W 1038	13489	MOT MACHINES MOTRICES NDA
71889	PARTS NES OF 71881,71882	W 1574	8189	W 2159	16858	W 2451	26022	W 1027	13402	PARTIES DES POS 718.81,82
72	MACHS FOR SPCL INDUSTRYS		62069		70556		103111		100447	MAC SPECIALES POUR INDUST
721	AGRIC MACHY,EXC TRACTORS	W 2114	5261	W 3466	9023	W 5609	15524	W 4601	15268	MACHINES AGRICOLES
7212	HARVESTING ETC MACHINES	W 864	2154	W 1591	4264	W 2750	10458	W 1926	9201	ENGINS POUR LA RECOLTE
72122	COMBINE HARVESTR-THRESHR	W 438	815	W 1063	2625	W 1975	7868	W 1290	6343	MOISSONNEUSES-BATTEUSES
722	TRACTORS NON-ROAD	W 2323	7842	W 2861	11417	W 3219	13832	W 2610	13357	TRACTEURS
7224	WHEELED TRACTORS NES	W 2183	7128	W 2761	11037	W 3042	12838	W 2503	12854	TRACTEURS A ROUES
723	CIVIL ENGNEERG EQUIP ETC	W 2306	11546	W 3970	16973	W 3419	17217	W 4525	25555	APPAREILS DE GENIE CIVIL
7234	CONST,MINING MACHNRY NES	W 1957	9983	W 3736	16260	W 2968	15490	W 4117	24147	MACH POUR LA CONST, MINES
72341	SELF-PROPELLD DOZERS,ETC	W 709	3800	W 2259	10701	W 842	3839	W 1702	12624	BULLDOZERS
72342	SLFPRP SHOVELS,EXCAVATRS	W 896	5110	W 1084	4579	W 1334	6062	W 1965	9576	PELLES MECANIQUES
724	TEXTILE,LEATHER MACHNRY	W 1723	12474	W 1288	9302	W 2495	19418	W 1712	13589	MACH POUR INDUSTRIE TEXTILE
7244	SPINNING,EXTRDNG,ETC MCH	W 720	4657	W 437	2874	W 1440	11526	W 636	4895	MACH POUR LE FILAGE
726	PRINTG,BKBINDG MACHY,PTS	W 320	3192	W 646	7171	W 1038	10798	W 1175	8592	MACHINES POUR IMPRIMERIE
727	FOOD MACHRY NON-DOMESTIC	W 1463	8647	W 879	4703	W 1073	6587	W 1059	5882	MACH INDUSTRIES ALIMENT
7272	OTH FOOD PROC MCHY,PARTS	W 1307	7510	W 622	3449	W 936	5093	W 944	4966	AUT MACH IND ALIMENTAIRE
72722	INDUS FOOD PROC MACH NES	W 1112	7212	W 483	2587	W 887	4819	W 889	4318	MACHINES BOULANGERIE
728	OTH MACHY FOR SPCL INDUS	W 2228	11680	W 1740	10593	W 2081	18718	W 2069	13500	AUT MACH IND PARTICULIERES
7284	MACHY FOR SPCL INDUS NES	W 678	5578	W 902	6768	W 993	12927	W 981	9306	MACH SPEC IND PARTICUL.
72842	RUBBER,PLASTICS WRKG MCH	W 277	2495	W 409	4437	W 710	8183	W 329	4507	MACH IND CAOUT MAT PLAST
73	METALWORKING MACHINERY		4805		2713		2225		3309	MACH TRAVAIL DES METAUX
74	GENRL INDUSTRL MACHY NES		58085		64246		109247		98937	MACH APP INDUSTRIE
741	HEATING,COOLING EQUIPMNT	W 3010	18895	W 3634	17506	W 4756	31636	W 4693	31280	MACH CHAUFFAGE,PIECES
7414	NONDOM REFRIG EQUIPT,PTS	W 640	5022	W 519	3051	W 784	4327	W 1025	7213	MAT PRODUCTION DU FROID
74141	REFRIG EQUIP NONDOMESTIC	W 566	4781	W 450	2678	W 675	3949	W 871	6285	REFIG INDUSTRIELS
7415	AIR-CONDITIONING MACHNRY	W 1056	5748	W 1493	8812	W 2137	15285	W 2682	18578	GROUPES CONDITION AIR
7416	HEATING,COOLING EQU NES	W 1192	7304	W 1454	4594	W 1151	9756	W 771	4304	APP CHANGEMENT TEMP
742	PUMPS FOR LIQUIDS ETC	W 426	3985	W 463	4661	W 981	8126	W 1388	7554	POMPES MOTO-POMPES
743	PUMPS NES,CENTRFUGES ETC	W 1196	8561	W 1577	8038	W 2515	14287	W 3254	14965	POMPES COMPRES,VENT ETC
7431	PUMPS FOR GASES ETC	W 751	4482	W 853	3282	W 1222	5305	W 1546	4552	POMPES AIR A VIDE,COMPRES
744	MECHANICAL HANDLING EQU	W 2062	7400	W 2078	9852	W 2335	9722	W 2123	9605	EQUIP MANUTENTION PIECES
7442	LIFTING,LOADING MACH NES	W 1306	4130	W 1624	7182	W 1623	5566	W 1512	6441	APP LEVAGE,MANUTENTION
745	NONELEC MACHY,TOOLS NES	W 1111	10548	W 1233	11319	W 3191	25068	W 1207	13794	AUT MACH NON ELEC,PIECES
7452	OTH NONELEC MCHS,PTS NES	W 1045	9170	W 1160	9848	W 3076	22405	W 1052	10724	AUT MACH NON ELEC,PIECES
74522	PACKAGNG,BOTTLNG,ETC MCH	W 632	6994	W 376	5435	W 720	13050	W 171	4842	MACH NETT BOUTEILLES,ETC
749	NONELEC MACH PTS,ACC NES	W 1071	8695	W 1348	12870	W 2280	20408	W 2531	21739	PIECES MACH NON ELEC NDA
75	OFFICE MACHNES,ADP EQUIP		45686		56719		77043		152082	MACH BUREAU TRAIT AUTOM
751	OFFICE MACHINES	W 766	5457	W 1882	7273	W 2387	11199	W 1845	15033	MACH,APPAREILS DE BUREAU
752	AUTOMTIC DATA PROC EQUIP	W 2387	32412	W 2880	36443	W 3097	48046	W 11234	119325	MACH TRAIT INFORMATION
7522	DIGITAL COMPUTERS	W 221	5770	W 177	4965	W 100	5643	W 268	4071	MACH DIGITALES COMPLETES
7524	DIGITL CENTRL STOR UNITS		4	W 2	85	W 1	65	W 485	14000	UNITES MEMOIRE CENTRALES
7525	ADP PERIPHERAL UNITS	W 11	244	W 1492	18284	W 2603	37118	W 9612	87932	UNITES PERIPHERIQUES
7528	OFF-LINE DATA PROC EQUIP	W 2137	25963	W 1139	12438	W 330	4297	W 370	7834	MACH AUXIL TRAIT INFORM
759	OFFICE,ADP MCH PTS,ACCES	W 2306	7817	W 2962	13003	W 4669	17798	W 3242	17723	PIECES DU 751 ET 752
7599	ACCTG,ETC,ADP MCH PTS,AC	W 2288	7342	W 2941	12488	W 4611	16898	W 3107	16200	PIECES DU 751 ET 752
76	TELECOMM,SOUND EQUIPMENT		127722		181102		269848		428756	EQUIPMENT DE TELECOM
761	TELEVISION RECEIVERS	W 9783	53171	W 14111	64104	W 18039	101660	W 17328	118429	RECEPTEURS DE TELEVISION
7611	COLOUR TV RECEIVERS	W 4595	34161	W 7903	47214	W 11096	81613	W 11064	96818	RECEPTEURS COULEUR
7612	MONOCHROME TV RECEIVERS	W 5188	19010	W 6208	16890	W 6943	20046	W 6265	21611	RECEPTEURS NOIR ET BLANC
762	RADIO BROADCAST RECEIVRS	W 9318	29619	W 11974	42978	W 17152	72964	W 27078	143870	RECEPTEURS RADIODIFFUSION
7621	MTR VEHC RADIO RECEIVERS	W 665	3894	W 1419	11087	W 2340	19349	W 2572	30510	RECEPTEURS RADIO AUTO
7622	PORTABLE RADIO RECEIVERS	W 3156	8817	W 4114	11325	W 5475	17030	W 8552	36834	RECEPT PORTATIFS RADIO
7628	OTHER RADIO RECEIVERS	W 5498	16907	W 6441	20565	W 9338	36586	W 15953	76526	AUTRES RECEPT RADIO
763	SOUND RECORDRS,PHONOGRPH	W 1517	24133	W 1821	30104	W 2079	39813	W 2921	78514	PHONO,APP ENREGISTREMENT
7638	OTHR SOUND APPARATUS ETC	W 1487	22782	W 1716	28711	W 1845	36393	W 2835	77658	AUT APP D'ENREGIS,REPROD
76381	TV IMAGE,SND RECRDRS ETC	W 1332	20978	W 1389	25719	W 1428	32674	W 2241	66528	APP ENREG,REPRO IMAG,SON
76388	DICTATING MACHINES ETC	W 155	1805	W 327	2992	W 417	3719	W 594	11130	MACHINES A DICTER
764	TELECOM EQPT,PTS,ACC NES	W 1718	20799	W 2901	43917	W 4844	55411	W 6620	87942	EQUIP TELECOM,PIECES
7641	LINE TELEPHONE,ETC EQUIP	W 1129	11524	W 1810	22431	W 2427	30979	W 2894	39165	APP TELEPHON PAR FIL
7642	MICROPH,LOUDSPKR,AMPLIFR	W 214	1642	W 480	2661	W 1529	6724	W 2394	9868	MICRO,HAUT-PARLEUR,AMPLI
7643	TV,RADIO TRANSMITTRS ETC	W 78	3725	W 116	3647	W 144	3648	W 343	12204	APP EMET TELE RADIO
7648	TELECOMM EQUIPMENT NES	W 113	1677	W 147	7926	W 286	9945	W 502	18588	APP TELECOM NDA
76482	TELEVISION CAMERAS	W 14	710	W 101	2701	W 128	8626	W 294	16844	APP PRISE DE VUES TELE
7649	PTS NES OF EQUIPMT OF 76	W 184	2230	W 348	7251	W 458	4116	W 487	8117	PIECES DE LA DIV 76

4. Special Imports C.I.F. by Commodities according to the S.I.T.C. (Rev. 2) in thousand U.S. Dollars
Importations Spéciales C.A.F. par Produits d'après la C.T.C.I. (Rév. 2) en milliers de Dollars E.U.

SITC CTCI	COMMODITY	1992 WEIGHT POIDS	1992 VALUE VALEUR	1993 WEIGHT POIDS	1993 VALUE VALEUR	1994 WEIGHT POIDS	1994 VALUE VALEUR	1995 WEIGHT POIDS	1995 VALUE VALEUR	PRODUIT
76491	PTS NES OF APPAR OF 7641	W 54	1026	W 131	5629	W 65	963	W 67	5218	PIECES POUR 764.1
77	ELECTRIC MACHNRY NES ETC		75058		83524		129134		150089	MACH APP ELECT NDA
771	ELECTRIC POWER MACHY NES	W 2255	11323	W 1592	7219	W 4719	10771	W 4043	12752	MACH PROD,TRANS ELECTR
7711	TRANSFORMERS,ELECTRICAL	W 1616	8763	W 1280	5332	W 2943	8059	W 2416	8822	TRANSFO ELECTRIQUES
77118	OTHER ELEC TRANSFORMERS	W 1592	8733	W 1188	5067	W 1429	2470	W 2133	7129	AUTRES TRANSFO ELECTRIQ
772	SWITCHGEAR ETC,PARTS NES	W 887	8829	W 832	12807	W 1792	13372	W 1542	15188	APP COUPURE,SECT ETC
7721	SWITCHGEAR ETC	W 885	8758	W 823	12654	W 1741	13158	W 1539	15068	APP COUPURE,SECTIONMNT
773	ELECTR DISTRIBUTNG EQUIP	W 1769	8314	W 1095	3547	W 2164	8094	W 2290	9695	EQUIPMT DISTRIBUTION ELECT
7731	INSULATED WIRE,CABLE ETC	W 1443	7506	W 857	3213	W 1505	6601	W 1967	8594	FILS,CABLES ISOLES ELECT
775	HOUSEHOLD TYPE EQUIP NES	W 10379	28344	W 13083	33722	W 20316	55588	W 27347	70637	MACH,APP USAGE DOMESTQUE
7751	HOUSEHOLD LDRY EQUIP NES	W 1104	4060	W 1479	5346	W 2140	9453	W 1858	7491	MACH A LAVER ET SECHOIRS
77511	DOMESTIC WASHING MACHNES	W 1076	4001	W 1413	5040	W 2069	9073	W 1794	7157	MACH LAVER LINGE MOINS 6 KG
7752	DOM REFRIGERATRS,FREEZRS	W 5144	9870	W 5685	11689	W 4550	12363	W 3117	9536	REFRIG,CONGEL MENAGER
77521	DOMESTIC REFRIGERATORS	W 3855	7144	W 3917	7646	W 2817	7881	W 2187	6549	REFRIGERATEURS
7757	DOMESTIC ELECTRC EQU NES	W 3033	9332	W 3800	9813	W 10403	22777	W 16079	33717	APP ELECTR DOMEST NDA
77572	DOM ELEC ROOM FANS ETC	W 2575	5988	W 3391	6909	W 9671	17986	W 15135	28102	HOTTES ASPIRANTES,VENTIL
7758	ELECTRO–THERMIC APPL NES	W 1003	4598	W 1903	6150	W 2893	9905	W 5546	17887	APP ELECTROTHERMIQ NDA
77586	ELECTROTHERM DOM APP NES	W 596	3046	W 1004	4023	W 1998	6952	W 3691	12968	APP ELECTRO THERMIQUES
776	TRANSISTORS,VALVES,ETC	W 249	3908	W 629	8080	W 941	9454	W 339	4450	LAMPES,TUBES,VALVES
7764	ELECTRONIC MICROCIRCUITS	W 238	3595	W 601	7700	W 914	9089	W 316	4074	MICROSTRUCTURES ELECTRON
778	ELECTRICAL MACHINERY NES	W 3866	12205	W 4926	16469	W 11762	27340	W 13973	34065	AUTRES MACH ELECT NDA
7781	BATTERIES,ACCUMULATORS	W 2244	4239	W 3037	5281	W 6914	9108	W 8729	13664	PILES ET ACCUMULATEURS
78	ROAD VEHICLES		183856		211202		258903		336227	VEHICULES ROUTIERS
781	PASS MOTOR VEH EXC BUSES	W 10861	84585	W 12134	91044	W 13671	98944	W 20109	135297	AUTO TRANSPORT PERSONNES
782	LORRIES,SPCL MTR VEH NES	W 9537	55006	W 10972	65768	W 13935	76335	W 18230	99340	VEHICULES SPECIAUX,MARCH
7821	LORRIES,TRUCKS	W 9395	54174	W 10559	63459	W 12981	70628	W 17182	92799	VEHICULES TRANSP MARCHAND
783	ROAD MOTOR VEHICLES NES	W 3613	18469	W 4194	20514	W 6673	39472	W 8526	41351	VEHICULES ROUTIERS NDA
7831	BUSES	W 2673	14961	W 2852	15489	W 3789	26967	W 3907	23251	VOITURES TRANSPORT COMMUN
7832	TRACTORS FOR TR–TRAILERS	W 940	3507	W 1342	5025	W 2884	12506	W 4620	18100	TRACTEURS ROUTIERS
784	MOTOR VEH PRTS,ACCES NES	W 1980	14975	W 2113	14052	W 3690	19861	W 5356	25513	PIECES 722,781,782,783
7849	OTHER MOTOR VEHCL PARTS	W 1762	14037	W 1905	12913	W 3324	17874	W 4826	21662	PIECES 722,781,782,783
785	CYCLES,ETC MOTRZD OR NOT	W 2789	9961	W 4482	18504	W 6533	22619	W 6773	30356	MOTOCYCLES SCOOTERS
7851	MOTORCYCLES ETC	W 833	4298	W 1151	7417	W 1276	7629	W 2014	16218	MOTO VELO MOTEUR AUXIL
7852	CYCLES, ETC NON–MOTOR	W 1536	4181	W 2787	7635	W 4374	11202	W 3405	8343	VELOCIPEDES SANS MOTEUR
79	OTHR TRANSPORT EQUIPMENT		3759		3758		8816		16292	AUTRE MATERIEL TRANSPORT
793	SHIPS AND BOATS ETC	W 892	2114	W 1477	2062		6361	W 5495	12975	NAVIRES BATEAUX,ETC
8	MISC MANUFACTURED GOODS		135743		183902		258960		354127	ART MANUFACTURES DIVERS
831	*TRAVEL GOODS,HANDBAGS	W 1021	1972	W 1190	2855	W 4071	5796	W 5794	9956	ARTICLES DE VOYAGE ETC
84	CLOTHING AND ACCESSORIES		7987		13537		26587		28414	VETEMENTS
846	UNDER GARMENTS KNITTED	W 897	3891	W 1373	5541	W 2564	9865	W 2090	9325	SOUS VETS DE BONNETERIE
851	*FOOTWEAR	W 2852	8987	W 3841	13106	W 8301	24870	W 10512	41708	CHAUSSURES
85102	FOOTWEAR LEATHER	W 2647	8397	W 3566	12303	W 6630	20066	W 8960	36618	CHAUS SEMELLES EN CUIR
87	PRECISION INSTRUMNTS NES		12332		17889		18765		18522	INSTRUM,APPAR SCIENT NDA
874	MEASURNG,CONTROLNG INSTR	W 433	5963	W 794	11093	W 1239	9283	W 2354	8563	INSTRUMENTS DE MESURE
88	PHOTO EQU,OPTICL GDS ETC		19670		24810		28464		38047	APP,FOURN PHOTO,OP,MONTR
882	PHOTO,CINEMA SUPPLIES	W 534	6362	W 792	9141	W 815	10716	W 1636	13263	PRODUITS PHOTO,CINEMA
8822	PHOTO FILM EXC DEV CINMA	W 359	5222	W 533	7148	W 520	8915	W 576	10805	PLAQUES,PELLICULES,FILMS
885	WATCHES AND CLOCKS		9256		9255		10245		15079	HORLOGERIE
8851	WATCHES,MOVEMENTS,CASES		8137		6147		4799		6368	MONTRES,MOUVEMENTS,BOITES
88511	WATCHES		7517		5573		3922		5838	MONTRES POCHE,BRACELET
89	MISC MANUFCTRD GOODS NES		80270		105587		144950		203930	ART MANUFACTURES DIVERS
892	PRINTED MATTER	W 509	3002	W 869	6083	W 1191	6406	W 1831	9621	IMPRIMES
893	ARTICLES OF PLASTIC NES		14262		18950		23813		30424	OUVRAGES EN MAT DIVIS 58
8931	PLSTC PACKG CONTNRS,LIDS	W 1386	4244	W 1694	6622	W 2204	6894	W 3544	9837	ART TRANSP EMBALLAGE ETC
8939	MISC PLASTIC ARTICLES	W 3870	9806	W 4119	12134	W 10312	15548	W 15200	20042	ART DIVERS EN MAT DIV 58
89399	OTHR PLASTC ARTICLES NES	W 3726	9586	W 4017	11903	W 9910	14961	W 14817	19253	AUT OUV MAT DIV 58
894	TOYS,SPORTING GOODS,ETC	W 16302	27635	W 20298	36689	W 34198	56972	W 46676	97191	VOITURES ENFANTS,JOUETS
8942	TOYS,INDOOR GAMES ETC	W 15526	24415	W 18691	30438	W 30903	44114	W 41193	79477	JOUETS,JEUX ETC
89423	TOYS NES	W 11877	16244	W 12756	15425	W 21031	23746	W 28472	47207	JOUETS,MODELES REDUITS
89424	INDOOR GAME EQUIPMENT	W 1385	4537	W 1758	9293	W 2776	11664	W 3224	16289	ART,JEUX DE SOCIETE
8947	OTH SPORT GDS,FAIR AMUSM	W 396	1935	W 1150	3544	W 1566	5340	W 4526	11059	AUT ART DE SPORT
895	OFFICE SUPPLIES NES	W 1560	5125	W 2018	6265	W 4578	7826	W 4584	10847	ART PAPET NDA
898	MUSICAL INSTRUMENTS,PTS	W 4109	20296	W 5175	23414	W 7148	32370	W 8479	32075	INSTRUMENTS DE MUSIQUE
8983	SOUND RECRDNG TAPE,DISCS	W 3280	17429	W 3709	18870	W 5408	26405	W 6390	26083	SUPPORTS SON POUR 763
89831	PREPD SND RECORDNG MEDIA	W 3096	15511	W 3546	17029	W 5140	22126	W 6195	20638	SUPPORTS PREPARES
899	OTHER MANUFACTURED GOODS		8754		13362		16411		22042	AUT ART MANUF DIVERS NDA
9	GOODS NOT CLASSD BY KIND		117		1082		11736		8038	ART TRANSACT NON CLASSES
951	*WAR FIREARMS,AMMUNITION	W 30	117	W 205	1075	W 1463	11736	W 1068	7725	VEHIC BLINDES ARMES

5. Special Exports F.O.B. by Commodities according to the S.I.T.C. (Rev. 2) in thousand U.S. Dollars
Exportations Spéciales F.O.B. par Produits d'après la C.T.C.I. (Rév. 2) en milliers de Dollars E.U.

SITC CTCI	COMMODITY	1992		1993		1994		1995		PRODUIT
		WEIGHT POIDS	VALUE VALEUR	WEIGHT POIDS	VALUE VALEUR	WEIGHT POIDS	VALUE VALEUR	WEIGHT POIDS	VALUE VALEUR	
	ALL COMMODITIES		656555		725218		816833		919331	TOUS PRODUITS
0	FOOD AND LIVE ANIMALS		120567		123752		136925		152170	ALIMENTS,ANIMAUX VIVANTS
001	*LIVE ANIMALS FOR FOOD	W 275	184	W 8838	6132	W 19841	14504	W 12400	12152	ANIMAUX VIVANTS
0011	BOVINE SPECIES,LIVE	W 258	138	W 8808	6097	W 19831	14474	W 12366	12050	ESPECE BOVINE
00119	— OTHR THAN FR BREEDING	W 249	122	W 8500	5895	W 19741	14381	W 11897	11608	BOVINS NON REPRODUCTEURS
01	MEAT AND PREPARATIONS		47496		47082		55419		54862	VIANDES ET PREPARATIONS
011	MEAT FRESH,CHILLD,FROZEN	W 30553	47061	W 29383	46211	W 32098	52744	W 29065	51053	VIANDES FRAICHES,REF,CONGE
0111	BOVINE MEAT FRESH,FROZEN	W 26703	43863	W 25967	43705	W 27004	46979	W 25531	48000	VIANDES BOVIN FRAI,REF
01111	BOVINE MEAT WITH BONE IN	W 10324	13792	W 7953	9744	W 8478	10831	W 9647	13916	VIANDES BOVIN NON DESOSS
01112	BOVINE MEAT BONELESS	W 16379	30071	W 18014	33961	W 18526	36148	W 15884	34084	VIANDES BOVIN DESOSSEES
0116	EDIBLE OFFAL FRESH,CH,FR	W 3850	3198	W 3416	2506	W 4895	5560	W 3386	2919	ABATS COMESTIBLES
014	MEAT PREPD,PRSVD,NES ETC	W 209	435	W 647	871	W 1526	2675	W 1576	3809	CONSERVES DE VIANDES
0149	OTH PREPARD,PRESRVD MEAT	W 182	426	W 647	871	W 1526	2675	W 1503	3575	AUTRES PREP DE VIANDES
04	CEREALS AND PREPARATIONS		831		739		24531		26824	CEREALES ET PRODUITS
041	WHEAT ETC UNMILLED					W 78440	15109	W 37000	4960	FROMENT,EPEAUTRE
0411	DURUM WHEAT UNMILLED					W 78440	15109	W 37000	4960	FROMENT DUR NON MOULU
044	MAIZE UNMILLED	W 6000	648	W 1676	178	W 74288	9029	W 187917	21629	MAIS NON MOULU
05	VEGETABLES AND FRUIT		6039		3951		5911		5754	LEGUMES ET FRUITS
058	FRUIT PRESERVED,PREPARED	W 1017	3064	W 698	2015	W 556	3298	W 1806	3892	CONSERVES DE FRUITS
0589	FRUIT PREPRD,PRESRVD,NES	W 797	2871	W 602	1946	W 527	3265	W 686	2531	FRUITS PREPARES CONSERV
05899	FRUIT,NUTS NES,PRESERVED	W 792	2857	W 602	1946	W 527	3265	W 686	2531	FRUITS PREP CONSERV NDA
06	SUGAR AND PREPS,HONEY		2515		2381		1144		6021	SUCRES ET PRODUITS
061	SUGAR AND HONEY	W 6720	2515	W 5940	2277	W 1408	540	W 11144	5965	SUCRES ET MIEL
0611	RAW BEET AND CANE SUGAR	W 6720	2515	W 5940	2277	W 1408	540	W 11144	5965	SUCRES BRUTS
07	COFFEE,TEA,COCOA,SPICES		3286		4535		5586		2915	CAFE,THE,CACAO,EPICES
071	COFFEE AND SUBSTITUTES	W 1622	3004	W 2150	4404	W 1625	5355	W 635	2651	CAFE ET SUCCEDANES
0712	COFFEE EXTRACTS,ESSENCES	W 529	1902	W 770	2600	W 798	3588	W 376	1858	EXTRAITS DE CAFE
081	*FEEDING STUFF FOR ANIML	W 424728	60048	W 413540	58628	W 184172	28975	W 308048	43330	NOURRITURE POUR ANIMAUX
0813	OILCAKE AND OTH RESIDUES	W 424310	59241	W 412560	57598	W 180889	27417	W 306235	40852	TOURTEAUX
08131	— OF SOYA BEANS	W 379873	56986	W 344094	51153	W 155100	25590	W 272662	37955	TOURTEAUX DE SOJA
08133	— OF COTTON SEEDS	W 44172	2203	W 43965	3255	W 21181	1541	W 32925	2859	TOURTEAUX DE COTON
08139	— OF OTHER OILSEEDS ETC	W 264	53	W 17000	2745					TOURTEAUX D'AUTRES OLEAGINEU
1	BEVERAGES AND TOBACCO		6925		7250		7761		9351	BOISSONS ET TABACS
12	TOBACCO AND MANUFACTURES		6893		7138		6945		6804	TABACS BRUTS FABRIQUES
121	TOBACCO UNMNFCTRD,REFUSE	W 6224	6893	W 6524	7011	W 6531	6943	W 5903	6804	TABACS BRUTS,DECHETS
1211	TOBACCO,NOT STRIPPED	W 1621	2275	W 1514	1894	W 1514	1229	W 5153	5782	TABACS NON ECOTES
1212	TOBACCO STRIPPED OR PART	W 4484	4591	W 4926	5104	W 4961	5699	W 727	1018	TABACS PART ECOTES
2	CRUDE MATERLS,EXCL FUELS		383579		430881		432118		514484	MAT BRUTES NON COMESTIBLES
21	HIDES,SKINS,FURS UNDRSSD		503		2550		1275		1355	CUIRS,PEAUX BRUTS
211	HIDES,SKINS,EXC FURS,RAW	W 2763	503	W 4739	2550	W 3348	1275	W 3130	1355	CUIRS ET PEAUX
22	OIL SEEDS,OLEAGINOUS FRT		139201		226657		224777		177710	GRAINES,FRUITS OLEAGINEUX
222	SEEDS FOR'SOFT'FIXED OIL	W 859690	138119	W 1364085	225620	W 1190075	223965	W 1076731	177502	GRAINES HUILES FIXES
2222	SOYA BEANS	W 857466	137222	W 1360434	223689	W 1186520	222259	W 1074110	175923	FEVES DE SOJA
24	CORK AND WOOD		40283		41712		48140		57633	LIEGE ET BOIS
248	WOOD SHAPED,SLEEPERS	W 236671	39956	W 224186	41383	W 216615	47844	W 271083	57049	BOIS SIMPLEMENT TRAVAILLES
2483	LUMBER SHAPED NON–CONIFR	W 235511	39916	W 223786	41363	W 215465	47798	W 268834	56745	NON CONIFERES SCIES,RABOTES
24831	LUMBER SAWN ETC NON–CON	W 206662	22319	W 194339	22737	W 180581	25152	W 231585	29296	SCIES LONGITUDINALEMENT
24832	LUMBER PLANED ETC NONCON	W 28849	17598	W 29446	18627	W 34884	22646	W 37249	27450	RABOTES,RAINES,LANGUETES
26	TEXTILE FIBRES AND WASTE		202056		157484		155275		273971	FIBRES TEXTILES
263	COTTON	W 182614	201339	W 136127	156766	W 108014	153910	W 143975	271010	COTON
2631	RAW COTTON,EXCL LINTERS	W 179156	200298	W 132179	155523	W 96264	151425	W 135858	268064	COTON EN MASSE
3	MINERAL FUELS ETC		3029		1588		2085		1861	COMBUSTIBLES MINERAUX LUB
33	PETROLEUM AND PRODUCTS		3029		1588		2085		1861	PETROLE ET DERIVES
334	PETROLEUM PRODUCTS,REFIN	W 33701	3029	W 13653	1588	W 23756	2085	W 19899	1861	PRODUITS RAFFINES
3343	GAS OILS	W 33701	3029	W 13652	1584	W 23752	2076			GAS OILS
4	ANIMAL,VEGETABLE OIL,FAT		42476		40717		63729		64309	HUILES,GRAISSES ANIM,VEG
42	FIXED VEGETABLE OIL,FAT		42105		40424		63166		63943	HUILES VEGETALES FIXES
423	FIXED VEG OILS,SOFT	W 83626	33519	W 75864	33881	W 123426	55499	W 206886	59424	HUILES VEGET DOUCES FIXES
4232	SOYA BEAN OIL	W 79794	32035	W 72350	31979	W 115314	51550	W 204099	57800	HUILE DE SOJA
4236	SUNFLOWER SEED OIL	W 397	288	W 3	2	W 6650	3010	W 922	540	HUILE DE TOURNESOL
424	FIXED VEG OIL NONSOFT	W 8293	8586	W 7826	6544	W 9099	7666	W 5183	4518	AUTRES HUILES VEG FIXES
4244	PALM KERNEL OIL	W 3303	2244	W 3224	2261	W 3908	2649	W 486	412	HUILE DE PALMISTE
4249	FIXED VEGETABLE OILS NES	W 4221	6147	W 4302	4064	W 4606	4614	W 4593	4002	HUILES VEGET FIXES NDA
5	CHEMCLS,RELATED PROD NES		20784		14142		20591		23552	PRODUITS CHIMIQUES
51	ORGANIC CHEMICALS		2690		1628		1764		2990	PROD CHIMIQ ORGANIQUES
512	ALCOHOLS,PHENOLS ETC	W 229	2683	W 129	1573	W 331	1759	W 184	2881	PHENOLS,PHENOLS–ALCOOLS
5122	CYCLIC ALCOHOLS,DERIVATS	W 201	2671	W 129	1573	W 131	1710	W 184	2881	ALCOOLS CYCLIQUES
53	DYES,TANNING,COLOUR PROD		3924		3439		5621		3504	PROD TEINTURE,COLORANTS
532	DYES NES,TANNING PROD	W 4794	3905	W 3896	3408	W 7266	5607	W 4336	3499	EXTRAITS TEINTURE,TANNAGE
5322	DYE,TANN EXTRCTS,TANNINS	W 4794	3905	W 3896	3408	W 7264	5604	W 4333	3490	EXT TAN ORIG VEG,TANNINS
53221	VEG TANN EXTRCTS,TANNINS	W 4794	3905	W 3896	3408	W 7264	5604	W 4333	3490	EXTR TANNANTS ORIG VEGET
541	*MEDICINAL,PHARM PRODUCT		1411		2025	K 956329	3703	K 2876135	5888	PROD MEDICINAUX PHARMACEUT
5417	MEDICAMENTS	K 224582	1245	K 763544	1940	K 769297	3603	K 2310379	3646	MEDICAMENTS
54179	— CONTNG OTH SUBSTANCES	K 189506	782	K 693870	1329	K 541499	2502	K 2240061	3527	MED CONT AUT SUBSTANCES
55	PERFUME,CLEANING ETC PRD		12391		6807		8794		8357	PROD POUR PARFUM,TOILETTE
551	ESSENTL OILS,PERFUME,ETC	W 1048	12051	W 726	6578	W 678	8468	W 595	7960	HUILES ESSENTIELLES
5513	ESSENTL OIL,RESINOID,ETC	W 1048	12049	W 726	6573	W 678	8468	W 595	7957	HUILES ESSENTIELLES,RESIN
6	BASIC MANUFACTURES		68374		95185		137834		134622	ART MANUFACTURES
61	LEATHER,DRESSED FUR,ETC		37437		51880		63683		55695	CUIRS,PELLETERIES
611	LEATHER	W 4760	36143	W 8440	50407	W 7742	60531	W 6938	54732	CUIRS,PEAUX PREPARES
6113	CALF LEATHER	W 38	223	W 416	868	W 838	2264	W 2966	9341	CUIRS,PEAUX DE VEAUX
6114	LEATHR BOVINE NES,EQUINE	W 3625	26705	W 6606	37861	W 5697	42390	W 3201	35427	CUIRS DE BOVINS
6116	LEATHER OF OTH HIDE,SKIN	W 42	360	W 55	815	W 160	4330	W 80	1759	PEAUX PREP D'AUTRES ANIMAUX
61169	LEATHER NES	W 42	360	W 55	815	W 160	4330	W 80	1759	PEAUX PREPAREES NDA
6118	LEATHER SPECIALLY FINSHD	W 855	8500	W 938	10391	W 972	11469	W 691	8205	CUIRS,PEAUX TANNES
61183	LEATHER PATENT,METALIZED	W 855	8500	W 938	10391	W 972	11469	W 691	8205	CUIRS,PEAUX VERNIS
612	LEATHER ETC MANUFACTURES	W 169	1294	W 275	1473	W 143	3151	W 202	962	OUVRAGES EN CUIRS NDA
6129	LEATHER MANUFACTURES NES	W 132	804	W 196	916	W 77	2473	W 27	839	AUT OUV CUIR NAT,ARTIF
62	RUBBER MANUFACTURES NES		11		9		38		3196	CAOUTCHOUC MANUFACTURE
625	RUBBER TYRES, TUBES ETC	W 9	7	W 1	1			W 450	3172	PNEUS CAOUTCHOUC VULCANISE
6259	OTH TYRES,TYRE CASES,ETC	W 9	7	W 1	1			W 450	3172	AUTRES PNEUS RECHAPES FLAPS
62599	TYRES NES,TYRE CASES,ETC	W 9	7	W 1	1			W 450	3172	PNEUS,FLAPS
63	WOOD,CORK MANUFACTRS NES		12664		21622		30411		31295	OUVRAGES LIEGE ET BOIS
634	VENEERS,PLYWOOD,ETC	W 42902	11245	W 57732	19822	W 71252	28030	W 66453	25869	PLACAGES,CONTRE–PLAQUES
6341	VENEER SHEETS ETC	W 27403	6935	W 35296	10981	W 29169	9188	W 27435	8696	BOIS SIMPLEMENT SCIES
6342	PLYWOOD OF WOOD SHEETS	W 15453	4297	W 22264	8751	W 42010	18822	W 34742	15261	BOIS CONTRE–PLAQUES
635	WOOD MANUFACTURES NES	W 3741	1419	W 3710	1799	W 3903	2381	W 9600	5426	ART MANUF EN BOIS NDA
6353	BUILDERS WOODWRK,PREFABS	W 950	346	W 1199	730	W 2175	1589	W 6727	4206	OUVRAGES DE MENUISERIE
65	TEXTILE YARN,FABRICS,ETC		8969		8490		18495		28107	FILS,TISSUS,ARTICLES TEXTILE
651	TEXTILE YARN	W 472	1559	W 1497	3490	W 5747	10353	W 4014	13442	FILS TEXTILES

5. Special Exports F.O.B. by Commodities according to the S.I.T.C. (Rev. 2) in thousand U.S. Dollars
Exportations Spéciales F.O.B. par Produits d'après la C.T.C.I. (Rév. 2) en milliers de Dollars E.U.

SITC CTCI	COMMODITY	1992		1993		1994		1995		PRODUIT
		WEIGHT POIDS	VALUE VALEUR	WEIGHT POIDS	VALUE VALEUR	WEIGHT POIDS	VALUE VALEUR	WEIGHT POIDS	VALUE VALEUR	
6513	COTTON YARN	W 472	1559	W 1497	3490	W 5747	10353	W 4014	13442	FILS DE COTON
652	COTTON FABRICS,WOVEN	W 2049	6517	W 1110	4653	W 1310	6624	W 2070	12837	TISSUS DE COTON
6521	GREY WOVEN COTTON FABRIC	W 1390	3654	W 690	2363	W 628	2763	W 484	2676	TISSUS COT ECRUS NON MERCER
65214	GREY WOVEN COTTON NES	W 1390	3654	W 690	2363	W 628	2763	W 484	2676	AUT TISSUS 85% COTON ECRUS
6522	WOVEN COTTON BLEACHD,ETC	W 660	2863	W 420	2291	W 682	3861	W 1586	10162	TISSUS COTON BLANCHIS ETC
65224	BLCHED COTTON FABRIC NES	W 660	2863	W 420	2291	W 663	3849	W 1405	9007	AUT TIS PLUS 85% COT BLANCHI
67	IRON AND STEEL		8251		11984		20727		9481	FER ET ACIER
672	IRON,STEEL PRIMARY FORMS	W 5146	1031	W 12327	2950	W 1211	268	W 26108	5688	LINGOTS FER,ACIER
6725	IRN,STL BLOOMS,SLABS,ETC	W 5146	1031	W 12327	2950	W 1211	268	W 26108	5688	BLOOMS,BILLETTES FER ACIER
67251	IRN,SMPLE STL BLOOMS,ETC	W 5146	1031	W 12327	2950	W 1211	268	W 26108	5688	BLOOMS ETC NON ACIER FIN
673	IRON,STEEL SHAPES ETC	W 22381	6983	W 30465	8880	W 96839	20390	W 10124	3318	BARRES,PROFIL FER,ACIER
6732	IRON,STEEL BARS ETC	W 16996	5348	W 24554	7170	W 94519	19660	W 5943	1980	BARRES FER,ACIER
67326	IRN,OTH STL BARS HOTROLD	W 14524	4567	W 21353	6198	W 93646	19517	W 1686	564	BARRES PLEINES FER,ACIER
7	MACHINES,TRANSPORT EQUIP		1224		4538		7679		7159	MACHINES MATERIEL TRANSPORT
72	MACHS FOR SPCL INDUSTRYS		111		326		352		3849	MAC SPECIALES POUR INDUST
78	ROAD VEHICLES		289		2253		6532		1168	VEHICULES ROUTIERS
783	ROAD MOTOR VEHICLES NES	W 25	216	W 198	1507	W 543	4650	W 10	101	VEHICULES ROUTIERS NDA
7831	BUSES	W 25	216	W 198	1507	W 543	4650	W 10	101	VOITURES TRANSPORT COMMUN
8	MISC MANUFACTURED GOODS		9505		7158		8110		11824	ART MANUFACTURES DIVERS
84	CLOTHING AND ACCESSORIES		6026		3296		3392		6326	VETEMENTS
843	WOMENS OUTERWEAR NONKNIT	W 262	3402	W 117	1677	W 104	1536	W 247	3540	VET DESSUS FEMMES MAT TEX
8439	— OTHER OUTER GARMENTS	W 242	2574	W 86	818	W 96	1324	W 236	3232	AUT VET DES FEM MAT TEXT

1. HISTORICAL SERIES, 1961–1996 SPECIAL TRADE, IMPORTS C.I.F., EXPORTS F.O.B.
SERIES HISTORIQUES, 1961–1996 COMMERCE SPECIAL, IMPORTATIONS C.A.F., EXPORTATIONS F.O.B

YEAR ANNEE	VALUE IN MILLION U.S. DOLLARS VALEUR EN MILLION U.S. DOLLARS MERCHANDISE # 1 –MARCHANDISE		GOLD # 1 –OR		CONVERSION FACTORS FACTEURS DE CONVERSION CENTS E.U. PAR		INDEX NUMBERS –INDICES QUANTUM		UNIT VALUE VALEUR UNITAIRE	
	IMPORTS	EXPORTS	IMPORTS	EXPORTS	IMPORTS	EXPORTS	IMPORTS	EXPORTS	IMPORTS	EXPORTS
1961	468.10	496.30								
1962	539.00	542.90								
1963	552.80	539.70								
1964	570.90	666.20								
1965	718.70	666.20								
1966	816.50	762.80								
1967	819.80	755.20								
1968	629.70	866.10								
1969	600.00	865.50								
1970	621.70	1044.40						185		42
1971	749.60	892.90						170		38
1972	796.30	944.40						178		41
1973	1024.20	1049.50						142		67
1974	1595.30	1517.40						144		82
1975	2379.60	1314.60						79		56
1976	1798.00	1296.10						89		64
1977	1598.30	1647.40						98		70
1978	1356.30	1805.30						114		68
1979	1475.50	3379.60						138		104
1980	2573.30	3265.50						120		137
1981	3803.00	3249.00						121		113
1982	3079.80	3227.00						133		98
1983	2147.20	3027.10						115		104
1984	1869.50	3130.50						115		93
1985	1806.00	2978.00						118		85
1986	2908.80	2530.60						106		69
1987	3562.30	2660.80						96		86
1988	3348.00	2701.00						85		95
1989	2749.20	3488.00						100		104
1990	3469.80	3230.90						100		100
1991	4194.70	3329.10						104		93
1992	4861.30	3484.40						111		94
1993	4859.20	3514.50						121		75
1994	6690.70	4554.60						132		86
1995	9224.00	5575.10						133		106
1996	9472.30	5897.10						142		107

2. IMPORTS BY BROAD ECONOMIC CATEGORY AND EXPORTS BY INDUSTRIAL ORIGIN. (PERCENTAGE OF TOTAL VALUE)
IMPORTATIONS PAR CATEGORIES ECONOMIQUES ET EXPORTATIONS PAR BRANCHE D'ACTIVITE.(EN POURCENTAGE DE LA VALEUR TOTALE)

IMPORTS – IMPORTATIONS

	1990	1991	1992	1993	1994	1995	1996
TOTAL IMPORTS–IMPORTATIONS TOTALES	100.	100.	100.	100.	100.	100.	100.
1 FOOD BEV–ALIMENTATION BOISSONS	19.0	16.3	17.4	16.3	14.5	10.6	13.7
11 PRIMARY–PRODUITS DE BASE	6.4	5.2	6.5	6.0	5.0	3.7	4.9
111 FOR INDUSTRY–POUR L'INDUSTRIE	5.0	3.3	4.6	4.8	3.6	2.8	3.9
112 FOR HOUSEHOLDS–POUR LES MENAGES	1.4	1.9	1.9	1.2	1.3	0.9	1.0
12 PROCESSED–PRODUITS ELABORES	12.6	11.1	10.9	10.3	9.5	6.9	8.8
121 FOR INDUSTRY–POUR L'INDUSTRIE	4.3	2.7	3.6	2.5	2.6	1.4	1.6
122 FOR HOUSEHOLDS–POUR LES MENAGES	8.3	8.4	7.3	7.9	6.9	5.5	7.2
2 IND SUPPLIES–APPROV INDUSTRIELS	30.3	30.1	29.1	31.0	30.2	31.2	28.7
21 PRIMARY–PRODUITS DE BASE	4.5	3.7	4.3	3.6	3.6	3.5	3.0
22 PROCESSED–PRODUITS ELABORES	25.9	26.3	24.8	27.4	26.6	27.6	25.7
3 FUELS–COMBUSTIBLES	12.3	10.8	9.9	7.9	6.4	8.6	10.0
31 PRIMARY–PRODUITS DE BASE	5.5	6.8	5.5	3.7	2.7	4.7	6.0
32 PROCESSED–PRODUITS ELABORES	6.8	4.0	4.4	4.2	3.7	4.0	4.0
321 MOTOR SPIRIT–ESSENCE	0.3	0.3	0.1	0.1	0.1	0.2	0.2
322 OTHER–AUTRES	6.5	3.7	4.3	4.1	3.6	3.8	3.8
4 MACHINERY–EQUIPEMENT	23.7	19.7	18.1	22.6	21.8	22.7	25.5
41 CAPITAL EQUIPMENT–MACHINES	20.5	16.9	15.5	19.5	18.9	19.9	22.8
42 PARTS–PIECES ACCESSOIRES	3.2	2.8	2.6	3.1	2.9	2.8	2.7
5 TRANSPORT–TRANSPORT	10.2	15.7	18.3	13.4	15.6	14.8	10.7
51 PASSENGER CARS–AUTOMOBILES	0.5	6.1	5.4	3.9	4.5	4.6	3.7
52 OTHER–AUTRES	4.8	4.6	8.5	5.1	6.8	6.4	3.9
521 INDUSTRIAL–INDUSTRIELS	4.8	4.4	8.2	4.8	6.4	5.8	3.4
522 NON INDUSTRIAL–NON INDUSTRIEL	0.0	0.2	0.3	0.2	0.4	0.6	0.4
53 PARTS–PIECES ACCESSOIRES	4.9	5.0	4.4	4.4	4.3	3.7	3.2
6 CONSUM GOODS–BIENS CONSOMMATION	4.2	7.3	7.0	8.7	11.5	12.1	11.4
61 DURABLE–DURABLES	1.0	2.1	2.3	2.7	4.5	4.2	3.7
62 SEMI DURABLE–SEMI DURABLES	1.0	2.4	2.3	2.9	3.8	4.5	4.5
63 NON DURABLE–NON DURABLES	2.2	2.8	2.4	3.1	3.3	3.4	3.2
7 GOODS NES–BIENS NDA	0.4	0.2	0.2	0.1	0.0	0.1	0.1

EXPORTS – EXPORTATIONS

	1990	1991	1992	1993	1994	1995	1996
TOTAL EXPORTS–EXPORTATIONS TOTALES	100.	100.	100.	100.	100.	100.	100.
1 AGRICULTURE	7.2	8.8	7.0	7.0	10.3	11.5	10.0
2 MINING QUARRY–INDUS EXTRACTIVES	20.2	15.8	17.5	15.0	16.6	20.3	20.4
3 MANUFACTURING–IND MANUFACTUR	72.6	75.5	75.5	78.0	73.1	68.2	69.6
31 FOOD BEV TOBACCO–ALIM BOISS TAB	15.9	20.1	19.3	24.4	25.5	21.2	23.3
32 TEXTILES–INDUSTRIES TEXTILES	11.1	11.8	10.1	9.8	9.3	8.2	8.5
33 WOOD & PRODUCTS–BOIS & PRODUITS	0.1	0.2	0.2	0.4	0.5	0.3	0.5
34 PAPER & PRODUCTS–PAPIER & PRODT	0.2	0.1	0.4	0.1	0.1	0.3	0.1
35 CHEMICALS–INDUSTRIES CHIMIQUES	13.7	9.7	9.8	9.6	7.7	5.9	6.4
36 NON METAL MIN–MIN NON METAL	0.4	0.5	0.5	0.6	0.5	0.5	0.5
37 BASIC METAL–IND METAL BASE	26.5	28.9	31.2	28.8	26.5	28.2	26.6
38 METAL MANUF–MANUF METAL	2.6	2.3	2.0	2.0	1.5	1.4	1.2
39 OTH MANUF IND–AUTRES MANUF	2.1	1.9	2.0	2.2	1.6	2.3	2.5

3. TRADE BY PRINCIPAL COUNTRIES OF PROVENANCE AND DESTINATION (VALUE IN THOUSAND U.S. DOLLARS)
ECHANGES SELON LES PRINCIPAUX PAYS DE PROVENANCE ET DE DESTINATION (VALEUR EN MILLIERS DE DOLLARS EU)

COUNTRIES–PAYS	SPECIAL IMPORTS C.I.F. IMPORTATIONS SPECIALES C.A.F				
	1992	1993	1994	1995	1996
World	3964266	4230756	5626292	7584060	7947194
Africa	10165	10510	18038	15199	15325
Americas	2617063	2758306	3507003	4692827	5078713
Northern America	1224280	1317416	1669349	2063979	2299393
LAIA	1326966	1375966	1735820	2530210	2693725
CACM	4422	23822	35982	42205	50347
Caribbean	21194	15482	24703	25584	19940
Rest of America	40202	25620	41149	30849	15308
As.ex F.USSR	556225	665713	990978	1273609	1193695
Eur.x F.USSR	671804	674654	1018897	1462361	1513081
EU	610758	608099	925511	1353861	1423298
EFTA	47253	47686	66017	71892	63220
East Europe	13191	18461	25487	35717	24511
Other Europe	78	205	54	44	18
Former USSR	8160	19407	19381	14372	37996
Oceania	44981	63556	68087	72313	106717
USA/Etats–Unis d'Amer	1145596	1251526	1583118	1911406	2089314
Japan/Japon	317818	330758	490431	532627	439747
Colombia/Colombie	312621	230722	254894	611708	677178
Brazil/Brésil	214011	256274	372825	426823	363451
Argentina/Argentine	256508	274982	299151	347211	278761
Venezuela	136249	118179	154334	384702	590976
Germany/Allemagne	190602	173745	262333	260418	305831
Chile/Chili	124484	155160	216475	284465	284571
Mexico/Mexique	89842	111401	162569	241728	272406
Spain/Espagne	38235	47487	75017	325432	338418
Korea, Republic of	65018	100160	171890	229709	241175
Italy/Italie	105188	83780	165542	180557	185357
China/Chine	21909	90591	109812	241987	190034
Canada	78353	65888	85771	152524	210078
Ecuador/Equateur	114643	127070	159881	70468	44454
France, Monac	53411	63237	91948	130765	142140
Bolivia/Bolivie	33128	46161	74940	123448	124341
Sweden/Suède	48564	49524	90689	130300	79647
United Kingdom	53496	52377	73673	98420	109679
Belgium–Luxembourg	43601	48297	58901	66362	60852
Switz.Liecht	44980	42765	60646	62113	52608
New Zealand	30883	46154	54079	55031	74929
Netherlands/Pays–Bas	42523	43909	51717	60240	60008
Panama	40093	25120	40584	30683	15008
Uruguay	14261	36136	24733	23845	39346
Thailand/Thaïlande	35981	21704	8601	24289	37920
Denmark/Danemark	9926	23133	22050	27980	44159
Guatemala	2723	19083	28697	34935	35052
Hong Kong	12901	12351	22786	37018	22669
Paraguay	31220	19881	16018	15814	18241
Australia/Australie	13766	17354	13908	17238	31762
India/Inde	5663	9915	12087	22783	40523
Finland/Finlande	4885	6689	8426	26095	42808
Russian Federation	8084	15270	16493	13696	33976
Viet Nam	18260	6609	28843	832	30358
Austria/Autriche	6467	9278	12382	25473	29117
Singapore/Singapour	10468	10525	14474	21269	18211
Ireland/Irlande	11474	5544	10914	19463	21277
Malaysia/Malaisie	2677	5343	12830	19862	18137
So. Africa Customs Un	9392	8804	10900	14005	14099
Netherlands Antilles	18336	11705	13226	8080	274
Indonesia/Indonésie	1534	3695	8399	14327	19944
Israel/Israël	5003	7405	7614	11068	12785
Norway,SVD,JM	2271	4921	5370	9780	10548
Turkey/Turquie	286	551	9278	17131	3560
Czech Republic		9379	12484	2540	5761
Costa Rica	1347	4438	4719	5366	11134
Hungary/Hongrie	1060	2546	5463	9539	7334
Bulgaria/Bulgarie	518	3809	777	15034	3140
Pakistan	319	344	953	1689	17410

COUNTRIES–PAYS	SPECIAL EXPORTS F.O.B. EXPORTATIONS SPECIALES F.O.B.				
	1992	1993	1994	1995	1996
Monde	3359376	3343382	4388901	5439700	5835016
Afrique	17632	18795	30038	38122	65714
Amériques	1479717	1420889	1674046	2031294	2312134
Amérique du Nord	817653	800364	851605	1078234	1318014
ALAI	635809	581868	782064	888690	919948
MCAC	14213	20121	25160	21872	28905
Caraïbes	5043	10384	5634	22584	19501
Autre Amérique	6998	8152	9583	19914	25766
Asie l'URSS exclus	801572	771598	1098270	1396737	1447264
Europe l'URSS exclus	1001210	1065646	1510804	1905461	1934492
UE	936774	998306	1404095	1660553	1558457
AELE	37551	53354	75912	207232	315568
Europe de l'Est	14106	6074	19805	21874	40080
Autre de l'Europe	20	480	89	475	113
Ancienne URSS	5253	10564	21267	11674	20467
Océanie	15675	17525	26320	12753	20115
USA/Etats–Unis d'Amer	705792	717376	726969	937562	1159577
Japan/Japon	291664	298833	384601	455487	388020
United Kingdom	218121	283784	405325	409506	424223
China/Chine	251799	140519	284836	349016	419386
Germany/Allemagne	147673	204019	279350	331925	300717
Italy/Italie	193809	162005	197501	246483	198719
Netherlands/Pays–Bas	119747	116101	233571	277554	208387
Brazil/Brésil	157899	124254	180858	199881	239260
Canada	111664	82680	123484	139869	157750
Belgium–Luxembourg	95150	85215	118098	155335	154224
Switz.Liecht	31318	43894	53669	179849	291241
Mexico/Mexique	96932	91174	165530	96272	95609
Venezuela	96629	75865	83991	163155	125664
Colombia/Colombie	88382	87122	99486	118247	120323
Chile/Chili	70127	72594	86192	152127	123189
Spain/Espagne	57208	57425	76566	121720	139928
Korea, Republic of	58813	59358	61465	111215	145136
Bolivia/Bolivie	43124	62765	78044	76936	101247
France, Monac	68820	66196	63593	71172	80070
Ecuador/Equateur	47543	43347	60584	46819	70320
Malaysia/Malaisie	22873	26576	57536	70284	73750
Hong Kong	42541	28599	33791	49538	54593
Iran (Islamic Rp. of)	41143	24473	9709	32674	52293
Philippines	13266	24042	31802	41721	31972
Argentina/Argentine	29946	19053	22655	30838	37748
Indonesia/Indonésie	258	12306	32624	25490	29983
Norway,SVD,JM	6228	9460	22237	27378	24322
Australia/Australie	13858	14989	23460	11476	18492
Thailand/Thaïlande	5566	1813	11818	22906	34944
So. Africa Customs Un	379	1136	7050	19699	41700
Panama	6948	8122	9472	19711	25646
Russian Federation	5253	9909	20991	9930	20121
Denmark/Danemark	11780	11282	13108	14731	14730
Algeria/Algérie	7750	10812	9847	13572	12821
Yugoslavia/Yougoslavie	12758	7428	6799	9493	13709
Israel/Israël	1201	10008	19565	15072	3801
Poland/Pologne	2002	1997	10765	12678	17092
Costa Rica	7866	7877	10319	9712	8589
Turkey/Turquie	3264	9282	5978	7304	15469
Bulgaria/Bulgarie	6820	3150	8578	7877	12435
Finland/Finlande	996	1607	6028	14761	12879
Guatemala	3480	5139	6587	7972	6328
Sweden/Suède	6686	6586	4069	6148	5999
Portugal	13062	1214	3568	4150	4949
India/Inde	1820	2738	2539	2364	14960
Netherlands Antilles	455	738	575	9661	11976
El Salvador	1262	3993	2916	2063	10525
Uruguay	3235	2362	3244	3172	5105
Singapore/Singapour	551	1107	1744	2204	10960
Honduras	1551	2935	5009	2069	3098

(VALUE AS PERCENTAGE OF WORLD TOTAL)(VALEURS EN POURCENTAGE DU TOTAL MONDIAL)

	1987	1988	1989	1990	1991	1992	1993	1994	1995	1996
Africa	0.9	1.0	0.9	0.6	0.4	0.3	0.2	0.3	0.2	0.2
Americas	51.0	48.0	65.1	66.2	66.3	66.0	65.2	62.3	61.9	63.9
Northern America	25.9	23.9	32.7	29.9	28.0	30.9	31.1	29.7	27.2	28.9
LAIA	24.2	23.4	30.9	35.5	36.8	33.5	32.5	30.9	33.4	33.9
CACM	0.1	0.1	0.0	0.0	0.0	0.1	0.6	0.6	0.6	0.6
Caribbean	0.3	0.1	0.8	0.2	0.3	0.5	0.4	0.4	0.3	0.3
Rest of America	0.4	0.5	0.7	0.5	1.1	1.0	0.6	0.7	0.4	0.2
As.ex F.USSR	12.1	6.1	8.2	7.3	10.9	14.0	15.7	17.6	16.8	15.0
Eur.x F.USSR	33.8	23.1	24.1	22.6	20.8	16.9	15.9	18.1	19.3	19.0
EU	30.4	20.8	20.9	19.8	19.0	15.4	14.4	16.4	17.9	17.9
EFTA	2.6	1.8	1.9	2.3	1.5	1.2	1.1	1.2	0.9	0.8
East Europe	0.7	0.5	1.1	0.5	0.3	0.3	0.4	0.5	0.5	0.3
Other Europe	0.0	0.0	0.2	0.1	0.0	0.0	0.0	0.0	0.0	0.0
Former USSR	0.1	0.1	0.2	0.3	0.3	0.2	0.5	0.3	0.2	0.5
Oceania	2.3	2.1	1.3	2.5	1.1	1.1	1.5	1.2	1.0	1.3
USA/Etats–Unis d'Amer	22.5	22.2	30.9	28.2	25.7	28.9	29.6	28.1	25.2	26.3
Japan/Japon	8.0	3.9	4.3	3.4	6.2	8.0	7.8	8.7	7.0	5.5
Colombia/Colombie	3.5	2.4	3.6	3.8	7.5	7.9	5.5	4.5	8.1	8.5
Brazil/Brésil	6.4	6.5	6.2	6.4	5.9	5.4	6.1	6.6	5.6	4.6
Argentina/Argentine	5.9	6.8	8.2	8.8	7.3	6.5	6.5	5.3	4.6	3.5
Venezuela	1.7	1.9	1.8	2.1	3.5	3.4	2.8	2.7	5.1	7.4
Germany/Allemagne	8.6	6.8	6.0	6.6	5.9	4.8	4.1	4.7	3.4	3.8
Chile/Chili	3.0	2.3	2.2	3.4	3.0	3.1	3.7	3.8	3.8	3.6
Mexico/Mexique	1.5	1.8	2.4	3.8	3.0	2.3	2.6	2.9	3.2	3.4
Spain/Espagne	2.1	1.8	1.2	1.2	1.0	1.0	1.1	1.3	4.3	4.3

	1987	1988	1989	1990	1991	1992	1993	1994	1995	1996
Afrique	1.0	0.9	0.8	0.7	0.6	0.5	0.6	0.7	0.7	1.1
Amériques	48.5	37.5	43.0	38.7	39.2	44.0	42.5	38.1	37.3	39.6
Amérique du Nord	30.8	24.8	27.5	23.8	20.7	24.3	23.9	19.4	19.8	22.6
ALAI	15.9	11.4	14.0	13.0	17.5	18.9	17.4	17.8	16.3	15.8
MCAC	0.8	0.5	0.6	0.7	0.6	0.4	0.6	0.6	0.4	0.5
Caraïbes	0.2	0.6	0.7	0.8	0.1	0.2	0.3	0.1	0.4	0.3
Autre Amérique	0.8	0.2	0.3	0.5	0.2	0.2	0.2	0.2	0.4	0.4
Asie l'URSS exclus	17.9	22.2	20.3	20.4	26.8	23.9	23.1	25.0	25.7	24.8
Europe l'URSS exclus	28.1	37.8	31.2	35.7	31.4	29.8	31.9	34.4	35.0	33.2
UE	24.0	34.6	27.6	32.6	29.4	27.9	29.9	32.0	30.5	26.7
AELE	0.6	0.4	0.6	0.2	0.3	1.1	1.6	1.7	3.8	5.4
Europe de l'Est	2.1	1.8	1.9	1.5	0.9	0.4	0.2	0.5	0.4	0.7
Autre de l'Europe	1.4	1.0	1.1	1.5	0.8	0.0	0.0	0.0	0.0	0.0
Ancienne URSS	3.0	1.0	4.4	1.9	0.8	0.2	0.3	0.5	0.2	0.4
Océanie	0.2	0.2	0.1	0.1	0.2	0.5	0.5	0.6	0.2	0.3
USA/Etats–Unis d'Amer	29.2	23.9	26.5	23.1	19.1	21.0	21.5	16.6	17.2	19.9
Japan/Japon	10.0	10.8	10.9	12.7	10.1	8.7	8.9	8.8	8.4	6.6
United Kingdom	5.6	9.8	4.6	4.5	3.7	6.5	8.5	9.2	7.5	7.3
China/Chine	1.8	4.4	2.6	1.7	7.2	7.5	4.2	6.5	6.4	7.2
Germany/Allemagne	4.2	5.5	7.5	7.6	6.1	4.4	6.1	6.4	6.1	5.2
Italy/Italie	2.8	4.7	4.2	8.3	7.8	5.8	4.8	4.5	4.5	3.4
Netherlands/Pays–Bas	1.8	3.6	3.2	3.3	4.0	3.6	3.5	5.3	5.1	3.6
Brazil/Brésil	4.5	2.5	3.7	3.2	3.5	4.7	3.7	4.1	3.7	4.1
Canada	1.6	0.9	1.0	0.7	1.6	3.3	2.5	2.8	2.6	2.7
Belgium–Luxembourg	5.6	4.9	4.2	4.6	3.0	2.8	2.5	2.7	2.9	2.6

4. Special Imports C.I.F. by Commodities according to the S.I.T.C. (Rev. 2) in thousand U.S. Dollars
Importations Spéciales C.A.F. par Produits d'après la C.T.C.I. (Rév. 2) en milliers de Dollars E.U.

SITC CTCI	COMMODITY	1993 WEIGHT POIDS	1993 VALUE VALEUR	1994 WEIGHT POIDS	1994 VALUE VALEUR	1995 WEIGHT POIDS	1995 VALUE VALEUR	1996 WEIGHT POIDS	1996 VALUE VALEUR	PRODUIT
	ALL COMMODITIES		4230756		5626292		7584060		7947194	TOUS PRODUITS
0	FOOD AND LIVE ANIMALS		762422		856289		909603		1195811	ALIMENTS,ANIMAUX VIVANTS
01	MEAT AND PREPARATIONS		20847		22946		24289		31874	VIANDES ET PREPARATIONS
011	MEAT FRESH,CHILLD,FROZEN	W 31682	19570	W 16025	21172	W 16827	22132	W 23540	29250	VIANDES FRAICHES,REF,CONGE
02	DAIRY PRODCTS,BIRDS'EGGS		85526		102703		112103		134635	PRODUITS LAITIERS,OEUFS
022	MILK AND CREAM	W 40348	76301	W 51279	88623	W 52055	97422	W 59314	117787	LAIT ET CREME
0224	MILK,CREAM PRESERVED ETC	W 39537	75230	W 50030	87237	W 50284	94586	W 57171	115840	LAIT,CREME CONS,CONC
02242	MILK DRY,1.5% FAT OR LES	W 9023	18239	W 10499	18387	W 8956	18036	W 9254	21283	LAIT POUDRE INF 1.5%
02243	MILK DRY,OVER 1.5% FAT	W 23551	50348	W 30243	59787	W 29727	65229	W 33015	80154	LAIT POUDRE SUP 1.5%
04	CEREALS AND PREPARATIONS		433961		434296		475691		681505	CEREALES ET PRODUITS
041	WHEAT ETC UNMILLED	W 1008094	166773	W 1079559	175364	W 1008872	188179	W 1125638	264239	FROMENT,EPEAUTRE
0411	DURUM WHEAT UNMILLED	W 968206	158524	W 1031467	166683	W 987367	184215	W 1065202	250249	FROMENT DUR NON MOULU
042	RICE	W 329940	98539	W 245811	76141	W 174613	59584	W 411900	159368	RIZ
0422	RICE SEMI–MILLED,MILLED	W 295097	88618	W 219675	69307	W 159001	55937	W 372507	147021	RIZ POLI,GLACE INCL BRISURES
04221	RICE MILLED UNBROKEN	W 294958	88568	W 216462	68242	W 159001	55937	W 371844	146690	RIZ POLI,GLACE EXCL BRISURES
044	MAIZE UNMILLED	W 610279	86272	W 855105	118269	W 1066392	154323	W 776962	146092	MAIS NON MOULU
046	WHEAT ETC MEAL OR FLOUR	W 75713	23804	W 41871	12361	W 12935	4195	W 51313	19796	SEMOULE FARINE,FROMENT
04601	FLOUR OF WHEAT OR MESLIN	W 63870	19996	W 32644	9464	W 12935	4195	W 50383	19511	FARINE DE FROMENT
048	CEREAL ETC PREPARATIONS	W 68050	37072	W 76903	37208	W 97320	55250	W 104193	64448	PREPTNS A BASE CEREALES
0482	MALT INCLUDING FLOUR	W 31561	14204	W 46419	14851	W 52771	20122	W 39637	17988	MALT MEME TORREFIE
05	VEGETABLES AND FRUIT		41064		59672		49568		58269	LEGUMES ET FRUITS
054	VEG ETC FRSH,SMPLY PRSVD	W 53894	21069	W 55125	27383	W 29441	15874	W 48942	25895	LEGUMES FRAIS,CONG,SECS
0542	LEGUMINOUS VEGETBLES DRY	W 42815	16482	W 44715	20904	W 27120	13008	W 45404	22935	LEGUMES A COSSE SECS
057	FRUIT,NUTS,FRESH,DRIED	W 17937	11027	W 35729	20634	W 36968	20909	W 34859	17896	FRUITS FRAIS OU SECS
06	SUGAR AND PREPS,HONEY		99830		128598		118580		143719	SUCRES ET PRODUITS
061	SUGAR AND HONEY	W 304431	93164	W 333742	107836	W 239716	91735	W 316136	117973	SUCRES ET MIEL
0612	REFINED SUGAR ETC	W 259976	80009	W 301608	97145	W 237222	90080	W 313118	116241	SUCRES RAFFINES
062	SUGAR CANDY NON–CHOCLATE	W 3146	6666	W 10162	20762	W 12935	26846	W 12373	25747	SUCRERIES
07	COFFEE,TEA,COCOA,SPICES		8704		20262		18381		17137	CAFE,THE,CACAO,EPICES
081	*FEEDING STUFF FOR ANIML	W 146499	45890	W 186134	49253	W 246689	61898	W 237060	75185	NOURRITURE POUR ANIMAUX
0813	OILCAKE AND OTH RESIDUES	W 138597	36785	W 174887	40398	W 233057	52624	W 228576	64117	TOURTEAUX
08131	— OF SOYA BEANS	W 137078	36506	W 174065	40275	W 228390	51830	W 220512	62557	TOURTEAUX DE SOJA
09	MISC EDIBLE PRODUCTS		21301		29312		38704		42147	PREP ALIMENTAIRES DIVERSES
098	EDIBLE PRODCTS,PREPS NES	W 4492	20924	W 5401	28472	W 7291	36030	W 8933	38914	PREP ALIMENTAIRES NDA
09809	MISC FOOD PREPRTIONS NES	W 2359	17185	W 3009	23697	W 4278	30135	W 5042	31953	PREP ALIMENTAIRES NDA
1	BEVERAGES AND TOBACCO		18885		31454		36383		36037	BOISSONS ET TABACS
11	BEVERAGES		15443		27151		31799		30007	BOISSONS
112	ALCOHOLIC BEVERAGES	W 6892	14145	W 10662	25073	W 12696	29182	W 11473	28254	BOISSONS ALCOOLIQUES
2	CRUDE MATERLS,EXCL FUELS		96322		129133		175699		139831	MAT BRUTES NON COMESTIBLES
23	RUBBER, CRUDE		13784		14861		23276		19868	CAOUTCHOUC BRUT
251	*PULP AND WASTE PAPER	W 19045	7494	W 28461	13912		23243	W 24830	13246	PATES A PAPIER,DECHETS
26	TEXTILE FIBRES AND WASTE		41203		51974		67099		42142	FIBRES TEXTILES
263	COTTON	W 24843	22772	W 19634	29955	W 21521	44008	W 12921	23220	COTON
2631	RAW COTTON,EXCL LINTERS	W 24145	22283	W 19110	29436	W 21503	43994	W 12902	23181	COTON EN MASSE
3	MINERAL FUELS ETC		343565		367433		666547		806887	COMBUSTIBLES MINERAUX LUB
32	COAL,COKE AND BRIQUETTES		31079		33488		34829		41254	HOUILLES,COKES,BRIQUETTES
322	COAL,LIGNITE AND PEAT	W 262096	13386	W 354703	17862	W 287030	15632	W 360483	18989	HOUILLES,LIGNITES,TOURBE
3222	OTH COAL,NOT AGGLOMERATD	W 262086	13381	W 354702	17861	W 287007	15606	W 360236	18838	AUTRES HOUILLES
323	BRIQUETS,COKE,SEMI–COKE	W 121082	17693	W 158748	15626	W 196087	19196	W 214934	22265	BRIQUETTES
3232	COKE,SEMI–COKE,RTRT CRBN	W 121082	17693	W 158747	15626	W 196081	19184	W 214897	22226	COKES ET SEMI–COKES
33	PETROLEUM AND PRODUCTS		295132		311044		598435		733352	PETROLE ET DERIVES
333	CRUDE PETROLEUM	W 833510	125364	W 965667	112255	W 2463147	304854	W 2909915	426726	HUILES BRUTES DE PETROLE
334	PETROLEUM PRODUCTS,REFIN		161454	W 1166056	191127	W 1507926	282848	W 1303913	296622	PRODUITS RAFFINES
3343	GAS OILS	W 681805	121839	W 1050573	148433	W 1311551	216974	W 1130700	233701	GAS OILS
3345	LUBS,PETROLEUM OILS NES	W 54186	26542	W 70717	32180	W 75482	39670	W 68672	36585	HUILES LUBRIFIANTES
33451	LUBS(HIGH PETR CONT) ETC	W 53655	25021	W 70014	30067	W 74376	36815	W 67718	33984	HUILES LUBRIF,H LOURDES
341	*GAS,NATURAL AND MANUFCT	W 66886	17354	W 92698	22901	W 114041	33283	W 112238	32281	GAZ NATUREL,GAZ MANUFACT
3413	PETROLM GASES,LIQUEFIED	W 66866	17333	W 92687	22878	W 114041	33276	W 112238	32275	GAZ DE PETROLE LIQUEFIE
34139	OTH HYDROCARBON GAS LQFD	W 66865	17330	W 92687	22877	W 114035	33261	W 112236	32265	HYDROCARBURES GAZEUX NDA
4	ANIMAL,VEGETABLE OIL,FAT		46884		97148		71215		73288	HUILES,GRAISSES ANIM,VEG
42	FIXED VEGETABLE OIL,FAT		41939		92763		66158		66627	HUILES VEGETALES FIXES
423	FIXED VEG OILS,SOFT	W 68000	41200	W 136572	89798	W 87721	64825	W 97223	65677	HUILES VEGET DOUCES FIXES
4232	SOYA BEAN OIL	W 61999	36684	W 122399	79623	W 82384	59941	W 86013	57140	HUILE DE SOJA
5	CHEMCLS,RELATED PROD NES		595420		747565		971669		963114	PRODUITS CHIMIQUES
51	ORGANIC CHEMICALS		100450		121707		151966		135327	PROD CHIMIQ ORGANIQUES
513	CARBOXYLIC ACIDS ETC	W 15796	19840	W 22125	25670	W 18592	33547	W 20665	28139	ACIDES CARBOXYLIQUES
514	NITROGEN–FNCTN COMPOUNDS	W 16058	30642	W 20691	35949	W 12422	40571	W 23189	41781	COMPOSES FONCT AZOTEES
5148	OTH NITROGN–FNCTN CMPNDS	W 13882	20402	W 18388	26246	W 9923	26968	W 19883	29905	AUTRES COMPOSES AZOTES
515	ORG–INORG COMPOUNDS ETC	W 2069	20543	W 2682	21487	W 3541	27811	W 2986	20970	COMPOSES ORGANO–MINERAUX
52	INORGANIC CHEMICALS		46556		47292		53118		58775	PROD CHIM INORGANIQUES
522	INORG ELEMNTS,OXIDES,ETC	W 20909	12804		15586	W 18920	17326	W 18387	15827	ELEMENTS INORGANIQUES
523	OTHR INORG CHEMICALS ETC	W 59437	33675	W 60563	31648	W 64488	35699	W 80002	42867	AUT PRODUITS CHIMIQUES INORG
5232	OTH MTL CMPD OF INRG ACD	W 46759	24922	W 47633	22505	W 48928	24275	W 57976	28510	SELS METALLIQUES
52322	PHOSPHITES,PHOSPHATES	W 20774	16513	W 18254	13383	W 19727	14708	W 23768	16894	PHOSPHITES,PHOSPHATES
53	DYES,TANNING,COLOUR PROD		40792		54230		61259		62459	PROD TEINTURE,COLORANTS
531	SYNT DYE,NAT INDGO,LAKES	W 2095	21343	W 2516	29017	W 3218	29855	W 2434	28279	MAT COLOR ORGAN,LAQUES
5311	SYNTHIC ORGNIC DYESTUFFS	W 1750	18228	W 2172	25412	W 2711	25709	W 2131	25164	MAT COLOR ORGAN SYNTHET
533	PIGMENTS,PAINTS,ETC	W 5400	15185	W 7977	21697	W 8485	27461	W 9579	30958	PIGMENTS,PEINTURES,VERNIS
541	*MEDICINAL,PHARM PRODUCT		83308	K 5407638	100320		160527	K 5589175	151713	PROD MEDICINAUX PHARMACEUT
5413	ANTIBIOTICS IN BULK	K 154014	12890	K 178722	12300	K 259431	19350	K 164929	10843	ANTIBIOTIQUES NDA
5417	MEDICAMENTS	K 2188188	50116	K 4428273	62849	K 3946475	105498	K 4200250	103248	MEDICAMENTS
54171	— CONTAINNG ANTIBIOTICS	K 446879	16786	K 2472862	16812	K 479553	25319	K 495214	23786	MED CONTN ANTIBIOTIQUES
54179	— CONTNG OTH SUBSTANCES	K 1488329	24569	K 1806877	35939	K 3048390	62016	K 3334779	60423	MED CONT AUT SUBSTANCES
55	PERFUME,CLEANING ETC PRD		39953		62680		74224		79144	PROD POUR PARFUM,TOILETTE
553	PERFUMERY,COSMETICS,ETC	W 4973	18188	W 8463	32582	W 8377	38381	W 8884	39660	PRODUITS DE PARFUMERIE
562	*FERTILIZERS,MANUFACTURE		54330	W 400994	63522	W 345145	79690	W 412604	95409	ENGRAIS MANUFACTURES
5621	CHEM NITROGENOUS FERTLZR	W 226874	36246	W 249191	38653	W 268068	61788	W 299742	69230	ENGRAIS AZOTES
56216	UREA	W 209115	30778	W 220509	32701	W 235773	54371	W 223180	52923	UREE
58	PLASTIC MATERIALS ETC		136548		186962		254079		246947	MAT PLAST ARTIFICIELLES
582	PROD OF CONDENSATION ETC	W 19741	30341	W 18403	31977	W 22128	48265	W 24581	47697	PROD CONDENS,POLYCOND
5823	ALKYDS,OTHER POLYESTERS	W 11487	15202	W 8304	12516	W 12723	26932	W 14796	24502	ALKYDES ET AUT POLYESTERS
58231	— IN PRIMARY FORMS	W 11297	14319	W 7968	11197	W 12175	24034	W 14541	23024	SOUS FORMES PRIMAIRES
583	POLYMERIZATION ETC PRODS	W 106152	95420	W 148706	146628	W 143071	196692	W 170701	191435	PROD POLYMERISATION
5831	POLYETHYLENE	W 45655	34567	W 64255	49611	W 55403	63588	W 68363	66952	POLYETHYLENE
58311	— IN PRIMARY FORMS	W 45560	34293	W 62704	47211	W 54628	61537	W 67474	63995	POLYETHYLENE PRIMAIRES
5832	POLYPROPYLENE	W 16738	14551	W 23594	22886	W 21719	34593	W 24740	32115	POLYPROPYLENE
58321	— IN PRIMARY FORMS	W 15229	11087	W 21070	17284	W 18011	23286	W 20437	20420	POLYPROPYLENE PRIMAIRES
5834	POLYVINYL CHLORIDE	W 31217	25368	W 40958	41927	W 46768	55850	W 55497	50165	CHLORURE DE POLYVINYLE
58341	— IN PRIMARY FORMS	W 30732	23924	W 40121	39614	W 45492	52372	W 54223	46265	SOUS FORMES PRIMAIRES
59	CHEMICAL MATERIALS NES		91604		108331		134405		130202	MAT PROD CHIMIQUES NDA
591	PESTICIDES,DISINFECTANTS	W 4356	26262	W 5316	34793	W 5597	33863	W 5998	36778	DESINF,INSECT,FONG,HERB

4. Special Imports C.I.F. by Commodities according to the S.I.T.C. (Rev. 2) in thousand U.S. Dollars
Importations Spéciales C.A.F. par Produits d'après la C.T.C.I. (Rév. 2) en milliers de Dollars E.U.

SITC CTCI	COMMODITY	1993		1994		1995		1996		PRODUIT
		WEIGHT POIDS	VALUE VALEUR	WEIGHT POIDS	VALUE VALEUR	WEIGHT POIDS	VALUE VALEUR	WEIGHT POIDS	VALUE VALEUR	
5911	INSECTICIDES,FOR RETAIL	W 1903	14305	W 2120	17879	W 2428	18132	W 2397	18597	INSECTICIDES VENTE DET
598	MISCEL CHEM PRODUCTS NES	W 29580	55202	W 31774	62649	W 36799	84012	W 38218	76446	PROD DIV INDUST CHIM NDA
5982	ANTI–KNOCK PREPARTNS ETC	W 5469	16404	W 7559	19469	W 10672	32957	W 8073	19959	PREPARAT ANTIDETONANTES
5989	CHEM PRODUCTS,PREPS NES	W 20419	35659	W 22388	39934	W 23768	46444	W 27901	51779	PROD PREP CHIMIQUES NDA
59899	OTH CHEM PRODS,PREPS,NES	W 17741	29275	W 18980	30965	W 20377	36727	W 23054	40039	AUT PRODUITS CHIMIQUES NDA
6	BASIC MANUFACTURES		597280		822599		1200952		1156899	ART MANUFACTURES
62	RUBBER MANUFACTURES NES		56087		77618		93113		94392	CAOUTCHOUC MANUFACTURE
625	RUBBER TYRES, TUBES ETC	W 10744	34717	W 22167	49356	W 18897	58364	W 19605	61557	PNEUS CAOUTCHOUC VULCANISE
6252	TYRES,NEW,BUS OR LORRY	W 3799	12532	W 11698	18614	W 6893	21797	W 6478	21802	PNEUS POUR AUTOBUS,CAMIONS
6259	OTH TYRES,TYRE CASES,ETC	W 4400	14184	W 6041	17604	W 6781	20999	W 8162	23810	AUTRES PNEUS RECHAPES FLAPS
628	RUBBER ARTICLES NES	W 1820	13132	W 1817	17009	W 2356	21507	W 2146	19759	OUVRAGES CAOUTCHOUC NDA
64	PAPER,PAPERBOARD AND MFR		119173		142282		230738		244447	PAPIERS,CARTONS & OUVRAGES
641	PAPER AND PAPERBOARD	W 152118	98380	W 166885	116033	W 175571	179717	W 190255	181063	PAPIERS ET CARTONS
6411	NEWSPRINT	W 50356	23614	W 54551	28303	W 55540	41344	W 54784	42764	PAPIER JOURNAL
6412	PRINTG,WRITING PAPER NES	W 13320	12032	W 18675	16844	W 27595	35090	W 27283	31354	PAPIERS POUR L'IMPRESSION
64122	— COATED,IMPREGNATD ETC	W 10670	9796	W 13929	12683	W 21654	26897	W 19102	22131	PAPIERS IMPRESSION COUCHES
6415	PAPER,PAPERBRD,BULK,NES	W 54577	39803	W 60285	45214	W 48240	58283	W 60208	62992	PAPIERS,CARTONS ROULEAUX
64159	OTHER PAPER ETC,BULK,NES	W 49283	36101	W 58704	42553	W 46852	55447	W 58938	61048	AUT PAPIER ROULEAUX FEUILLES
6418	COATED ETC PAPER NES BLK	W 14998	12572	W 13907	13548	W 18303	23321	W 18586	21002	PAP,CARTONS COUCHES,ENDUITS
642	PAPER,ETC,PRECUT,ARTS OF	W 12537	20793	W 14736	26249	W 24223	51021	W 27657	63385	PAP,CARTONS DECOUPES
6428	PAPER ETC ARTICLES NES	W 2079	6654	W 3163	10369	W 5676	20401	W 8303	28017	OUVRAGES EN PATE A PAPIER
65	TEXTILE YARN,FABRICS,ETC		95309		131761		153158		153948	FILS,TISSUS,ARTICLES TEXTILE
651	TEXTILE YARN	W 9424	36853		32782		42061	W 12315	45145	FILS TEXTILES
6514	SYN FIB YRN,BULK,MONOFIL	W 8124	31833	W 6733	25295	W 8840	32385	W 9274	34327	FILS CONT 85% FIB TEXT SYNTH
65142	— NONTXT ETC CONT PAMID	W 4139	14406	W 4022	13815	W 5705	20451	W 6495	23996	FILS NON TEX FI CON POLYAMID
653	WOVN MAN–MADE FIB FABRIC	W 6507	25592	W 7824	43056	W 7705	42221	W 6350	35238	TISSUS FIBRES SYNTH,ARTIF
657	SPECIAL TXTL FABRC,PRODS	W 4050	13691	W 4798	24400	W 6236	31580	W 5365	29335	TISSUS SPECIAUX
66	NONMETAL MINERAL MFS NES		57225		84761		147743		126370	ART MIN NON METALLIQUES
661	LIME,CEMENT,BLDG PRODS	W 18144	2725	W 62385	5737	W 779039	41474	W 380314	24490	CHAUX,CIMENTS MAT CONSTR
6612	CEMENT	W 17681	2286	W 61608	4765	W 777382	39935	W 377478	21835	CIMENTS HYDRAULIQUES
664	GLASS	W 39945	24180	W 48532	30808	W 60502	52929	W 56870	39820	VERRE
665	GLASSWARE	W 10696	10814	W 13233	17469	W 23116	17492	W 13137	17977	OUVRAGES EN VERRE
67	IRON AND STEEL		144037		202344		321470		280271	FER ET ACIER
671	PIG IRON ETC		9069	W 78942	17059	W 83884	18395	W 72038	16976	FONTE,SPIEGEL,POUDRES
672	IRON,STEEL PRIMARY FORMS	W 13622	5901	W 41733	13362	W 72573	23456	W 98198	30156	LINGOTS FER,ACIER
673	IRON,STEEL SHAPES ETC	W 55723	24131	W 125740	48198	W 223193	81339	W 98940	41312	BARRES,PROFIL FER,ACIER
6731	IRON,STEEL WIRE ROD	W 30284	10843	W 61281	21224	W 71682	25506	W 56885	19607	FIL MACHINE FER,ACIER
67311	IRON,SIMPLE STL WIRE ROD	W 19513	7071	W 52820	18086	W 44416	15951	W 44355	15498	FIL MACH AUT ACIER FIN
6732	IRON,STEEL BARS ETC	W 22302	11516	W 59041	23176	W 139212	49754	W 27628	14149	BARRES FER,ACIER
67326	IRN,OTH STL BARS HOTROLD	W 986	655	W 42353	13538	W 121013	37899	W 18573	6288	BARRES PLEINES FER,ACIER
674	IRN,STL UNIV,PLATE,SHEET	W 79722	61767	W 96232	70251	W 168561	123941	W 146407	107562	LARGES PLATS,TOLES
6746	IRN,STL THIN PLATE,ROLLD	W 29676	18215	W 32049	20666	W 55541	37168	W 47449	30461	TOLES LAM MOINS 3MM
67461	— OF IRON OR SIMPLE STL	W 26294	12662	W 26190	12587	W 50252	26658	W 43024	22128	TOL NON AC FIN MOINS 3 MM
6747	TINNED PLATES,SHEETS	W 26686	23811	W 28446	23341	W 31543	27961	W 32209	31344	TOLES ETAMEES EN ACIER
6749	OTH IRN,STL PLATES,SHEET	W 13462	12960	W 21517	16553	W 40408	34584	W 22481	21597	AUTRES TOLES FER,ACIER
67491	— OF IRON OR SIMPLE STL	W 12038	11813	W 20353	15256	W 38195	31636	W 21838	19518	AUT TOLES AUTRES ACIER FIN
678	IRON,STL TUBES,PIPES,ETC	W 24236	30025	W 35180	39307	W 47828	61689	W 51385	67018	TUBES,TUYAUX EN FONTE,FER
6782	IRON,STL SEAMLESS TUBES	W 19982	20470	W 21652	21061	W 33180	32093	W 33860	37492	TUBES,TUYAUX SANS SOUDURE
68	NON–FERROUS METALS		17399		22606		35215		31253	METAUX NON FERREUX
69	METAL MANUFACTURES NES		96189		143670		199423		199474	ART MANUFACT EN METAL NDA
695	TOOLS	W 3247	23558	W 5535	31883	W 8719	49932	W 5105	41278	OUTILS A MAIN
697	BASE MTL HOUSEHOLD EQUIP	W 3555	10199	W 7338	19102	W 7449	25497	W 6606	25677	ART MENAGE MET COMMUNS
699	BASE METAL MFRS NES	W 6239	26333	W 8853	37979	W 9309	50568	W 14572	53826	ART MANUFACTURES MET NDA
7	MACHINES,TRANSPORT EQUIP		1521138		2189092		2952613		2955822	MACHINES MATERIEL TRANSPORT
71	POWER GENERATING EQUIPMT		174757		152178		174442		232527	MACHINES GENERATRICES
713	INTRNL COMBUS PSTN ENGIN	W 7586	66189	W 10477	81764	W 13589	94285	W 10276	89213	MOTEURS EXPL COMB INT, PIECE
7132	MOTOR VEHCL PISTN ENGINS	W 4425	12960	W 5287	19046	W 5788	18237	W 5142	11134	MOTEURS EXPL POUR VEHICULES
7139	PISTON ENGINE PARTS NES	W 1844	37095	W 2247	40935	W 2239	47180	W 2178	41656	PIECES POUR 713.2,3,8
716	ROTATING ELECTRIC PLANT	W 6517	83346	W 5527	46755	W 6411	53096	W 10269	122404	APP ELECTR ROTATIFS,PIECES
7162	AC MTRS,GENRTRS,GEN SETS	W 6044	77052	W 4000	35609	W 5250	43831	W 9578	111765	MOTEURS ELECTRIQUES
71622	AC GENERATORS	W 1960	45306	W 471	6572	W 281	2293	W 4296	52156	GENER COURANT ALTERNATIF
71623	GEN SETS WITH PISTN ENGN	W 1835	19845	W 1596	16746	W 2232	26272	W 3271	43769	GROUPES MOTEUR EXPLOSION
718	OTH POWER GENERATG MACHY	W 300	16058	W 208	6539	W 189	5971	W 367	7428	AUTRES MOTEURS PARTIES
7188	WIND,WATER,ETC ENGINES	W 300	16049	W 207	6512	W 189	5968	W 354	7388	MOT MACHINES MOTRICES NDA
72	MACHS FOR SPCL INDUSTRYS		221354		312232		371014		444361	MAC SPECIALES POUR INDUST
721	AGRIC MACHY,EXC TRACTORS	W 3988	12794	W 732	6362	W 3673	13671	W 1560	15611	MACHINES AGRICOLES
722	TRACTORS NON–ROAD	W 11413	27175	W 3693	24121	W 5085	18183	W 2061	12426	TRACTEURS
7224	WHEELED TRACTORS NES	W 11122	25212	W 2742	18341	W 4388	13951	W 1908	11331	TRACTEURS A ROUES
723	CIVIL ENGNEERG EQUIP ETC		66125	W 17196	102255	W 19744	126857	W 21106	145824	APPAREILS DE GENIE CIVIL
7234	CONST,MINING MACHNRY NES		48002	W 16919	100739	W 16694	103041	W 20269	141938	MACH POUR LA CONST, MINES
72341	SELF–PROPELLD DOZERS,ETC	W 1599	10310	W 4288	26883	W 3502	22029	W 5057	32624	BULLDOZERS
72342	SLFPRP SHOVELS,EXCAVATRS	W 3867	24784	W 10421	59566	W 10510	63078	W 11968	79517	PELLES MECANIQUES
7239	CONSTR ETC MACHY PTS NES	W 1952	16999			W 2679	21864	W 226	775	PIECES 723.41–723.46
724	TEXTILE,LEATHER MACHNRY	W 4165	40795	W 6522	65283	W 6283	71844	W 4975	71105	MACH POUR INDUSTRIE TEXTILE
7245	WEAVING,FELT MFG,ETC MCH	W 705	9758	W 1677	18433	W 1629	21052	W 1311	19415	METIERS A TISSER,PIECES
726	PRINTG,BKBINDG MACHY,PTS	W 764	13061	W 1460	18786	W 1756	23132	W 2603	43686	MACHINES POUR IMPRIMERIE
7264	PRINTING PRESSES	W 475	7776	W 791	8748	W 1155	13359	W 1956	31018	MACHINES A IMPRIMER
72641	ROTARY PRINTING PRESSES	W 475	7776	W 791	8748	W 1155	13359	W 1956	31018	MACH IMPRIMER ROTATIVES
727	FOOD MACHRY NON–DOMESTIC	W 2054	14270	W 3143	26253	W 4108	21711	W 2088	24150	MACH INDUSTRIES ALIMENT
7272	OTH FOOD PROC MCHY,PARTS	W 1695	11505	W 2412	20669	W 1472	12938	W 1344	18414	AUT MACH IND ALIMENTAIRE
72722	INDUS FOOD PROC MACH NES	W 1694	11458	W 2252	17577	W 1224	11573	W 1214	17090	MACHINES BOULANGERIE
728	OTH MACHY FOR SPCL INDUS	W 4899	43948	W 7337	65812	W 9502	86147	W 11927	118128	AUT MACH IND PARTICULIERES
7283	OTHR MINERAL WORKG MACHY	W 1874	10170	W 3461	19668	W 4729	27332	W 6434	44015	MACH TRIER,CRIBLER,BROYER
72839	PTS NES OF MACHY OF 7283	W 888	5039	W 1073	6974	W 1116	7909	W 3612	26001	PIECES MACH DU 728.3
7284	MACHY FOR SPCL INDUS NES	W 2576	30298	W 3131	42958	W 3356	51862	W 4480	67703	MACH SPEC IND PARTICUL.
72842	RUBBER,PLASTICS WRKG MCH	W 1138	14205	W 1382	16837	W 1463	22711	W 1696	26679	MACH IND CAOUT MAT PLAST
72848	OTH MCHY WITH INDIV FNCT	W 1128	8435	W 1138	12607	W 1399	17460	W 2199	30801	AUTRES MACHINES NDA
73	METALWORKING MACHINERY		12476		24303		38007		38890	MACH TRAVAIL DES METAUX
736	METALWORKING MACH–TOOLS	W 1869	7992	W 2593	15273	W 5226	24320	W 6699	28316	MACH–OUTILS TRAVAIL METAUX
74	GENRL INDUSTRL MACHY NES		274018		334446		406869		470977	MACH APP INDUSTRIE
741	HEATING,COOLING EQUIPMNT		80229	W 6017	49885	W 7044	64414	W 12497	98706	MACH CHAUFFAGE,PIECES
7415	AIR–CONDITIONING MACHNRY		43371	W 664	6045	W 1060	10207	W 1107	11327	GROUPES CONDITION AIR
7416	HEATING,COOLING EQU NES	W 2879	21683	W 2359	25525	W 2268	22913	W 4250	42997	APP CHANGEMENT TEMP
742	PUMPS FOR LIQUIDS ETC	W 2744	32920	W 2872	39224	W 9086	60123	W 3932	59958	POMPES MOTO–POMPES
7428	OTHER PUMPS FOR LIQUIDS	W 1058	12045	W 1439	18511	W 4692	31959	W 1553	27156	AUTRES POMPES POUR LIQ
74288	PUMPS FR LIQUIDS NES ETC	W 832	8993	W 1122	13387	W 4241	23889	W 1050	18625	POMPES POUR LIQUIDES NDA
7429	PTS NES OF PUMPS OF 742	W 1047	14704	W 868	14261	W 799	16214	W 1172	18000	PIECES POUR GROUPE 742
743	PUMPS NES,CENTRFUGES ETC	W 4102	43572	W 6027	58314	W 7256	74677	W 5987	74606	POMPES COMPRES,VENT ETC
7431	PUMPS FOR GASES ETC	W 2157	14697	W 3531	19873	W 4526	29561	W 3158	23686	POMPES AIR A VIDE,COMPRES
744	MECHANICAL HANDLING EQU	W 3208	21689	W 7051	51319	W 6045	36972	W 10641	74712	EQUIP MANUTENTION PIECES
7442	LIFTING,LOADING MACH NES	W 2028	14596	W 2800	20073	W 3123	21620	W 4166	28257	APP LEVAGE,MANUTENTION

4. Special Imports C.I.F. by Commodities according to the S.I.T.C. (Rev. 2) in thousand U.S. Dollars
Importations Spéciales C.A.F. par Produits d'après la C.T.C.I. (Rév. 2) en milliers de Dollars E.U.

SITC CTCI	COMMODITY	1993 WEIGHT POIDS	1993 VALUE VALEUR	1994 WEIGHT POIDS	1994 VALUE VALEUR	1995 WEIGHT POIDS	1995 VALUE VALEUR	1996 WEIGHT POIDS	1996 VALUE VALEUR	PRODUIT
7449	PTS NES OF MACHY OF 7442	W 186	2206	W 2447	24478	W 538	4301	W 4051	35732	PIECES DU 744.2
745	NONELEC MACHY,TOOLS NES	W 1386	24504	W 2980	42031	W 3472	55655	W 2679	53146	AUT MACH NON ELEC,PIECES
7452	OTH NONELEC MCHS,PTS NES	W 1226	19704	W 2702	33784	W 3090	46153	W 2364	44735	AUT MACH NON ELEC,PIECES
74522	PACKAGNG,BOTTLNG,ETC MCH	W 504	9186	W 1112	17944	W 1113	19926	W 938	21952	MACH NETT BOUTEILLES,ETC
749	NONELEC MACH PTS,ACC NES	W 4980	71103	W 5695	93672	W 7692	115029	W 6514	109849	PIECES MACH NON ELEC NDA
7491	BALL,ROLLER,ETC BEARINGS	W 1007	15652	W 1167	19262	W 1171	21970	W 1030	19947	ROULEMENTS BILLES ETC
7492	COCKS,VALVES ETC NES	W 1739	19645	W 2160	28149	W 2944	36806	W 2915	37451	ART ROB,SIM POUR TUYAUX
7493	SHAFT,CRANK,PULLEY ETC	W 1355	22845	W 1542	29514	W 2620	34278	W 1757	34812	ARBRES TRANS,VILEBREQUINS
7499	OTH NONELEC MCHY PTS NES	W 879	12962	W 826	16747	W 957	21974	W 812	17639	PIECES NON ELECT NDA
75	OFFICE MACHNES,ADP EQUIP		93742		135319		207720		259661	MACH BUREAU TRAIT AUTOM
751	OFFICE MACHINES	W 803	15640	W 1070	22159	W 1517	32129	W 1485	33765	MACH,APPAREILS DE BUREAU
7518	OFFICE MACHINES NES	W 477	10457	W 613	14392	W 862	20904	W 1020	24760	MACH,APP DE BUREAU NDA
752	AUTOMTIC DATA PROC EQUIP	W 1721	58468	W 2671	91568	W 3202	144139	W 4012	182049	MACH TRAIT INFORMATION
7522	DIGITAL COMPUTERS	W 425	22526	W 691	35916	W 961	61432	W 1265	79951	MACH DIGITALES COMPLETES
7525	ADP PERIPHERAL UNITS	W 1093	24109	W 1730	38694	W 1893	54972	W 2305	66122	UNITES PERIPHERIQUES
759	OFFICE,ADP MCH PTS,ACCES	W 1064	19635	W 765	21592	W 4794	31452	W 1020	43847	PIECES DU 751 ET 752
7599	ACCTG,ETC,ADP MCH PTS,AC	W 895	16980	W 688	18310	W 4697	27227	W 906	38775	PIECES DU 751 ET 752
76	TELECOMM,SOUND EQUIPMENT		134491		269271		460963		490301	EQUIPMENT DE TELECOM
761	TELEVISION RECEIVERS	W 2408	22180	W 6173	72149	W 6933	76814	W 5987	69406	RECEPTEURS DE TELEVISION
7611	COLOUR TV RECEIVERS	W 1404	17421	W 5132	67130	W 5433	70889	W 5416	66586	RECEPTEURS COULEUR
762	RADIO BROADCAST RECEIVRS	W 2448	16590	W 4696	42549	W 4547	53932	W 3332	44155	RECEPTEURS RADIODIFFUSION
7628	OTHER RADIO RECEIVERS	W 1816	12348	W 4000	36897	W 4000	47562	W 2945	38732	AUTRES RECEPT RADIO
763	SOUND RECORDRS,PHONOGRPH	W 308	9234	W 808	20739	W 813	25241	W 593	20289	PHONO,APP ENREGISTREMENT
7638	OTHR SOUND APPARATUS ETC	W 295	9005	W 763	19993	W 780	24499	W 585	20134	AUT APP D'ENREGIS,REPROD
76381	TV IMAGE,SND RECRDRS ETC	W 208	7047	W 650	17406	W 672	21339	W 504	17637	APP ENREG,REPRO IMAG,SON
764	TELECOM EQPT,PTS,ACC NES	W 2535	86488	W 3866	133834	W 6993	304976	W 7022	356451	EQUIP TELECOM,PIECES
7641	LINE TELEPHONE,ETC EQUIP	W 544	41217	W 1367	60107	W 3506	179663	W 2823	132557	APP TELEPHON PAR FIL
7643	TV,RADIO TRANSMITTRS ETC	W 510	19805	W 255	33237	W 780	66150	W 689	85770	APP EMET TELE RADIO
7649	PTS NES OF EQUIPMT OF 76	W 1152	18371	W 1550	26291	W 1405	40601	W 2392	117108	PIECES DE LA DIV 76
76491	PTS NES OF APPAR OF 7641	W 86	4023	W 248	11818	W 943	28724	W 1727	97682	PIECES POUR 764.1
77	ELECTRIC MACHNRY NES ETC		156022		231734		351399		347182	MACH APP ELECT NDA
771	ELECTRIC POWER MACHY NES	W 1580	13187	W 2353	16825	W 4338	25293	W 4369	31872	MACH PROD,TRANS ELECTR
772	SWITCHGEAR ETC,PARTS NES	W 1710	30684	W 2680	45348	W 2783	58659	W 3436	64725	APP COUPURE,SECT ETC
7721	SWITCHGEAR ETC	W 1626	27091	W 2586	39570	W 2689	55300	W 3365	62276	APP COUPURE,SECTIONMNT
773	ELECTR DISTRIBUTNG EQUIP	W 3164	17441	W 6233	26801	W 15145	79932	W 11257	74108	EQUIPMT DISTRIBUTION ELECT
7731	INSULATED WIRE,CABLE ETC	W 2618	14550	W 4149	21585	W 12972	66125	W 8830	51647	FILS,CABLES ISOLES ELECT
775	HOUSEHOLD TYPE EQUIP NES	W 5533	30103	W 9490	53356	W 14516	75566	W 10477	66293	MACH,APP USAGE DOMESTQUE
778	ELECTRICAL MACHINERY NES	W 8140	48088	W 11350	71183	W 15942	80631	W 12531	84971	AUTRES MACH ELECT NDA
7788	OTH ELEC MACHY,EQUIP NES	W 1492	13603	W 2425	24094	W 2457	16979	W 2607	25885	AUT MACH APP ELEC NDA
78	ROAD VEHICLES		441534		699280		895495		652399	VEHICULES ROUTIERS
781	PASS MOTOR VEH EXC BUSES	W 28732	165647	W 46679	252421	W 91264	352068	W 51980	291247	AUTO TRANSPORT PERSONNES
782	LORRIES,SPCL MTR VEH NES	W 18262	91433	W 45085	194394	W 70505	234520	W 34489	190512	VEHICULES SPECIAUX,MARCH
7821	LORRIES,TRUCKS	W 17088	86086	W 42007	183380	W 68555	226212	W 32219	173037	VEHICULES TRANSP MARCHAND
783	ROAD MOTOR VEHICLES NES	W 36024	104349	W 48813	131002	W 59092	155913	W 17920	60358	VEHICULES ROUTIERS NDA
7831	BUSES	W 33153	97178	W 38783	111855	W 42816	122712	W 13554	47991	VOITURES TRANSPORT COMMUN
7832	TRACTORS FOR TR–TRAILERS	W 2871	7171	W 10030	19147	W 16276	33201	W 4366	12367	TRACTEURS ROUTIERS
784	MOTOR VEH PRTS,ACCES NES	W 8174	54138	W 10247	76450	W 13587	88042	W 9305	64535	PIECES 722,781,782,783
7849	OTHER MOTOR VEHCL PARTS	W 7359	47629	W 8747	65049	W 12479	80548	W 8685	61037	PIECES 722,781,782,783
785	CYCLES,ETC MOTRZD OR NOT	W 4637	23986	W 6775	36021	W 10609	56891	W 6641	39837	MOTOCYCLES SCOOTERS
7851	MOTORCYCLES ETC	W 782	6296	W 1706	17110	W 4538	35121	W 2259	25092	MOTO VELO MOTEUR AUXIL
7853	INVAL CARR, PTS OF 785	W 2290	13488	W 2616	10932	W 2661	10326	W 2111	6933	FAUTEUILS INVALIDES,PIECES
78539	PARTS,ACCES NES OF 785	W 2275	13412	W 2599	10844	W 2593	9879	W 2077	6717	PIECES DU 785
79	OTHR TRANSPORT EQUIPMENT		12743		30329		46705		19525	AUTRE MATERIEL TRANSPORT
791	RAILWAY VEHICLES	W 1186	8403	W 2106	19079	W 1123	24075	W 553	5408	VEHIC MAT CHEMINS DE FER
8	MISC MANUFACTURED GOODS		248041		384806		598361		618596	ART MANUFACTURES DIVERS
821	*FURNITURE,PARTS THEREOF	W 1905	7582	W 3364	14068	W 4603	23881	W 6500	36176	MEUBLES ET PIECES
84	CLOTHING AND ACCESSORIES		10940		25059		36356		42604	VETEMENTS
851	*FOOTWEAR	W 5527	13156	W 6610	24768	W 6061	31191	W 2825	27252	CHAUSSURES
85102	FOOTWEAR LEATHER	W 2634	9803	W 5528	18549	W 4330	18521	W 1454	16296	CHAUS SEMELLES EN CUIR
87	PRECISION INSTRUMNTS NES		59045		80233		133875		114636	INSTRUM,APPAR SCIENT NDA
872	MEDICAL INSTRUMENTS NES	W 1596	20768	W 649	17682	W 1303	31580	W 1134	29364	INSTR,APP MEDIC–CHIR NDA
87202	OTH MEDICAL INSTRUMENTS	W 1543	19418	W 590	16176	W 1150	26537	W 987	25416	INSTRUM,APP MEDECINE
874	MEASURNG,CONTROLNG INSTR	W 1194	33480	W 1648	45525	W 2398	77646	W 1654	66123	INSTRUMENTS DE MESURE
88	PHOTO EQU,OPTICL GDS ETC		32126		51263		66302		68247	APP,FOURN PHOTO,OP,MONTR
882	PHOTO,CINEMA SUPPLIES	W 1862	19872	W 3334	30544	W 3278	40446	W 3124	42142	PRODUITS PHOTO,CINEMA
8822	PHOTO FILM EXC DEV CINMA	W 1240	17037	W 2425	24735	W 2089	31049	W 2317	32041	PLAQUES,PELLICULES,FILMS
89	MISC MANUFCTRD GOODS NES		116425		176433		285146		305417	ART MANUFACTURES DIVERS
892	PRINTED MATTER	W 3497	23924	W 4359	30221	W 5156	42362	W 6928	50654	IMPRIMES
8921	PRINTED BOOKS,GLOBES,ETC	W 1586	11840	W 2264	16310	W 2881	22630	W 4572	30447	LIVRES,BROCHURES,CARTES
89211	PRINTED BOOKS,PAMPHLETS	W 1569	11741	W 2207	15987	W 2777	21977	W 4488	29806	LIVRES,BROCHURES
893	ARTICLES OF PLASTIC NES		29747		49253		89342		83220	OUVRAGES EN MAT DIVIS 58
8931	PLSTC PACKG CONTNRS,LIDS	W 4009	12541	W 5821	21044	W 9185	34211	W 7715	26321	ART TRANSP EMBALLAGE ETC
8939	MISC PLASTIC ARTICLES	W 3465	16860	W 6789	27576	W 13454	54117	W 15215	55781	ART DIVERS EN MAT DIV 58
89399	OTHR PLASTC ARTICLES NES	W 3061	15727	W 6019	25686	W 11781	50566	W 12447	50021	AUT OUV MAT DIV 58
894	TOYS,SPORTING GOODS,ETC	W 4758	18928	W 8311	33759	W 11113	67365	W 10375	80331	VOITURES ENFANTS,JOUETS
8942	TOYS,INDOOR GAMES ETC	W 4365	16358	W 7719	30256	W 9880	60158	W 8774	71277	JOUETS,JEUX ETC
89423	TOYS NES	W 2547	8523	W 4072	13511	W 5396	26492	W 4557	24212	JOUETS,MODELES REDUITS
89424	INDOOR GAME EQUIPMENT	W 410	2807	W 1254	7597	W 1695	19653	W 1980	35847	ART,JEUX DE SOCIETE
898	MUSICAL INSTRUMENTS,PTS	W 1399	18326	W 2461	25982	W 3284	35607	W 3150	39688	INSTRUMENTS DE MUSIQUE
8983	SOUND RECRDNG TAPE,DISCS	W 1283	16921	W 2273	23702	W 3028	32247	W 2930	36661	SUPPORTS SON POUR 763
899	OTHER MANUFACTURED GOODS		11253		17077		23314		23855	AUT ART MANUF DIVERS NDA

5. Special Exports F.O.B. by Commodities according to the S.I.T.C. (Rev. 2) in thousand U.S. Dollars
Exportations Spéciales F.O.B. par Produits d'après la C.T.C.I. (Rév. 2) en milliers de Dollars E.U.

SITC CTCI	COMMODITY	1993		1994		1995		1996		PRODUIT
		WEIGHT POIDS	VALUE VALEUR	WEIGHT POIDS	VALUE VALEUR	WEIGHT POIDS	VALUE VALEUR	WEIGHT POIDS	VALUE VALEUR	
	ALL COMMODITIES		3343382		4388901		5439700		5835016	TOUS PRODUITS
0	FOOD AND LIVE ANIMALS		919741		1349363		1481126		1573151	ALIMENTS,ANIMAUX VIVANTS
03	FISH AND PREPARATIONS		119589		168728		207995		209177	POISSONS ET PREPARATIONS
034	FISH,FRESH,CHILLED,FROZN	W 34121	43864	W 48074	51834	W 56533	69564	W 79331	87217	POISSON FRAIS, REFRIG,CONG
0342	FISH FROZEN,EXCL FILLETS	W 15139	18551	W 15367	12531	W 10375	10112	W 18261	17006	POISSONS CONGELES
0344	FISH FILLETS,FROZEN	W 13057	15926	W 30628	35784	W 45436	57025	W 59790	65954	FILETS CONGELES
036	SHELL FISH FRESH,FROZEN	W 17304	48031	W 24690	83622	W 26322	103273	W 17410	76285	CRUSTACES,MOLLUSQUES
037	FISH ETC PREPD,PRSVD NES	W 13865	24043	W 20424	31177	W 22890	31432	W 25057	38687	POIS,CRUST,MOL PREPARES
0371	FISH PREPARD,PRESRVD NES	W 13190	18709	W 19715	24894	W 22552	29246	W 24434	35362	CONSERVES DE POISSONS
04	CEREALS AND PREPARATIONS		5769		13655		9574		5759	CEREALES ET PRODUITS
05	VEGETABLES AND FRUIT		118079		139625		171367		207458	LEGUMES ET FRUITS
054	VEG ETC FRSH,SMPLY PRSVD		35284	W 41342	48647	W 50394	59093	W 67853	68724	LEGUMES FRAIS,CONG,SECS
0545	OTHER FRESH VEGETABLES	W 13790	15546	W 12485	19318	W 21101	26504	W 40617	35595	AUTRES LEGUMES FRAIS,REF
05459	FRESH VEGETABLES NES	W 11245	14953	W 11314	18628	W 14555	24167	W 14615	27896	LEGUMES FRAIS,REFRI NDA
0546	VEGETABLES SIMPLY PRESVD	W 7656	12697	W 14389	17832	W 11894	18950	W 14005	23293	LEGUMES CONG,CONSER
05461	VEGETABLES FROZEN	W 6881	11073	W 13477	16052	W 10503	16187	W 11087	18253	LEGUMES CONGELES
056	VEGTBLES ETC PRSVD,PREPD		66784	W 48248	70753	W 45956	88293	W 47204	103717	CONSERVES DE LEGUMES
0565	VEGTBLES PRSVD,PREPD NES	W 57449	60811	W 47786	63986	W 44581	81030	W 45450	94574	LEGUMES PREPARES CONSERVE
05659	OTH VEG PRESVD,PREPD NES	W 57353	60714	W 47656	63887	W 44347	80684	W 45341	94417	LEGUM PREPAP,CONSERV NDA
057	FRUIT,NUTS,FRESH,DRIED		9134	W 12241	12086	W 14994	13172	W 33676	22462	FRUITS FRAIS OU SECS
06	SUGAR AND PREPS,HONEY		15085		31694		30599		39183	SUCRES ET PRODUITS
061	SUGAR AND HONEY	W 50654	14476	W 69795	31005		30472	W 98881	38480	SUCRES ET MIEL
0611	RAW BEET AND CANE SUGAR	W 49507	13966	W 56014	24868	W 64633	30281	W 82515	37193	SUCRES BRUTS
07	COFFEE,TEA,COCOA,SPICES		73433		223155		310384		247453	CAFE,THE,CACAO,EPICES
071	COFFEE AND SUBSTITUTES	W 48531	60075	W 68861	206791	W 105262	286121	W 100337	223460	CAFE ET SUCCEDANES
0711	COFFEE GREEN,ROASTED,SUB	W 48486	59880	W 68861	206791	W 105204	285674	W 100296	223100	CAFE TORREFIE OU DECAFEINE
07111	COFFEE GREEN,HUSKS,SKINS	W 46613	57171	W 66022	199471	W 104733	283980	W 100098	222638	CAFE NON TORREFIE
072	COCOA	W 6196	11233	W 4639	14050	W 6631	21579	W 7485	20081	CACAO
0723	COCOA BUTTER AND PASTE	W 4209	9571	W 4266	13862	W 6432	21470	W 6825	19669	BEURRE ET PATE DE CACAO
07232	COCOA BUTTER	W 3567	8692	W 4194	13823	W 5428	20597	W 4957	18836	BEURRE DE CACAO
081	*FEEDING STUFF FOR ANIML		582754	W 2323311	766211	W 1859432	739033	W 1627559	856203	NOURRITURE POUR ANIMAUX
0811	HAY, FODDER, GREEN, DRY	W 9765	19850	W 11170	19314	W 8789	13900	W 7732	14966	FOIN ET FOURRAGE
08119	FODDER OF VEG ORIGIN NES	W 9765	19850	W 11170	19314	W 8749	13893	W 7716	14963	AUTRES FOURRAGES
0814	MEAT OR FISH MEAL FODDER	W 1597472	560838	W 2306016	743496	W 1845589	722100	W 1611805	836127	FARINES DE VIANDES,POISSONS
08142	FISH MEAL FODDER	W 1596080	560394	W 2305369	743247	W 1845242	721956	W 1611805	836127	FARINES DE POISSONS
2	CRUDE MATERLS,EXCL FUELS		557401		772963		1014017		973822	MAT BRUTES NON COMESTIBLES
26	TEXTILE FIBRES AND WASTE		53714		66474		92825		73330	FIBRES TEXTILES
263	COTTON	W 2030	4577	W 2248	5040	W 8127	24390	W 11576	30274	COTON
2631	RAW COTTON,EXCL LINTERS	W 2005	4559	W 2133	4815	W 8006	24195	W 11509	30172	COTON EN MASSE
266	SYNTHETIC FIBRES TO SPIN		32194		36778	W 21889	44347	W 14484	26913	FIBRES SYNTHETIQUES
2666	CONTIN FILAMNT TOW SYNTH		18390	W 10944	19415	W 11757	23749	W 8890	16066	CABLES POUR DISCONTINUS
26663	— OF ACRYLIC FIBRES	W 9424	18390	W 10944	19415	W 11757	23749	W 8890	16066	DE FIBRES ACRYLIQUES
268	WOOL(EXC TOPS),ANML HAIR	W 7092	16459	W 4411	24565	W 4283	24041	W 3443	16123	LAINES ET POILS
2687	WOOL OR HAIR COMBED ETC	W 5765	13852	W 2712	21119	W 2628	21165	W 1419	13171	LAINE CARDEE PEIGNEE
28	METALLIFEROUS ORES,SCRAP		469848		666345		872354		823245	MINERAIS METAL,DECHETS
281	IRON ORE,CONCENTRATES	W 3202312	81175	W 6547332	108812	W 6007510	100316	W 4030664	84095	MINERAIS DE FER
2815	IRON ORE,CONC,NOT AGGLOM	W 1505032	29353	W 3471635	43434	W 3023187	34979	W 1584219	20586	MINERAIS NON AGGLOMERES
2816	IRON ORE AGGLOMERATES	W 1697256	51799	W 3074773	65024	W 2983255	65063	W 2445812	63298	MINERAIS AGGLOMERES
287	BASE METAL ORES,CONC NES	W 1207436	379246	W 1369206	540296	W 1451488	736483	W 1565511	711041	MINERAIS METAUX COMMUNS
2871	CPR ORE ETC,CEMENT COPPR	W 154584	49237	W 150734	89783	W 217386	176009	W 242419	137375	MINERAIS DE CUIVRE,MATTES
28711	COPPER ORES,EXCL MATTE	W 152612	44980	W 150734	89783	W 217386	176009	W 242419	137375	MINERAIS DE CUIVRE
2874	LEAD ORES,CONCENTRATES	W 177820	92965	W 222366	141565	W 231524	177621	W 234993	183345	MINERAIS DE PLOMB
2875	ZINC ORES,CONCENTRATES	W 846756	176902	W 944942	208849	W 956836	236389	W 1041170	273327	MINERAIS DE ZINC
2876	TIN ORES,CONCENTRATES	W 21822	46168	W 44863	81582	W 37099	81472	W 38271	87790	MINERAIS D'ETAIN
2879	OTH NONFER ORE,CONCNTRTE	W 6099	13869	W 5622	17809	W 8596	64978	W 8658	29204	MINERAIS D'AUTRES METAUX
28793	MOLYBD, NIOBIUM ETC ORES	W 5461	12442	W 4844	16059	W 7326	60441	W 7683	26784	MINERAIS DE MOLYBDENE,TITANE
289	PREC MTAL ORES,WASTE NES	K 8140848	7767	K 7630759	13234	MK 12107	27506	MK 10675	22945	MINERAIS,DECHETS MET PREC
28901	PRECIOUS METAL ORES,CONC	K 8140848	7767	K 7630759	13234	MK 12107	27506	MK 10675	22945	MINERAIS METAUX PRECIEUX
29	CRUDE ANIMAL,VEG MAT NES		18599		16793		31366		49602	MATIERES BRUTES ANIM,VEGET
291	CRUDE ANIMAL MTRIALS NES		2474	W 500	3119	W 1065	13686	W 921	33055	MATIERES BRUTES ANIMALES
2919	OTH ANIMAL MATERIALS NES		2474	W 257	3058	W 414	13532	W 746	32994	MAT ORIGINE ANIMALE NDA
29199	ANIMAL PRODUCTS,NES	W 166	2351	W 168	2711	W 246	12917	W 602	32309	PROD ORIGINE ANIMALE NDA
292	CRUDE VEG MATERIALS NES	W 12146	16125	W 10778	13674	W 11219	17679	W 10780	16547	MAT BRUTES VEGETALES NDA
3	MINERAL FUELS ETC		199577		177088		268262		384829	COMBUSTIBLES MINERAUX LUB
33	PETROLEUM AND PRODUCTS		199576		177085		268254		384826	PETROLE ET DERIVES
333	CRUDE PETROLEUM					W 1522089	140406	W 2019579	236589	HUILES BRUTES DE PETROLE
334	PETROLEUM PRODUCTS,REFIN	W 1608689	199468		177010	W 1209976	127825	W 1228442	146916	PRODUITS RAFFINES
3341	GASOLINE,OTH LIGHT OILS	W 54482	12173	W 145295	22374	W 75562	12974	W 115956	22361	ESSENCES POUR MOTEURS
33411	MOTOR,AVIATION SPIRIT	W 54289	12119	W 145295	22374	W 75562	12973	W 115956	22361	ESSENCES MOTEURS D'AVIONS
3343	GAS OILS	W 137701	16291		149959	W 60984	15690	W 66274	16156	GAS OILS
3344	FUEL OILS,NES	W 1415688	169647			W 1069020	96543	W 1042601	106210	FUEL OILS
4	ANIMAL,VEGETABLE OIL,FAT		35735		72747		82924		78395	HUILES,GRAISSES ANIM,VEG
411	*ANIMAL OILS AND FATS	W 119875	35509	W 285597	67490	W 270145	77628	W 225145	75224	HUILES,GRAISSES ANIMALES
4111	OILS OF FISH,WHALES ETC	W 119875	35509	W 285597	67490	W 270145	77628	W 225145	75223	GRAISSES,HUILES DE POISSONS
41112	OTHER FISH OILS AND FATS	W 119875	35509	W 285562	67485	W 268467	76811	W 225145	75223	AUTRES HUILES ET GRAISSES
5	CHEMCLS,RELATED PROD NES		70335		96818		118874		153519	PRODUITS CHIMIQUES
52	INORGANIC CHEMICALS		20185		26060		32127		39149	PROD CHIM INORGANIQUES
522	INORG ELEMNTS,OXIDES,ETC	W 54833	14381	W 103204	19049	W 152387	23034	W 219519	24651	ELEMENTS INORGANIQUES
53	DYES,TANNING,COLOUR PROD		10552		17558		28835		41409	PROD TEINTURE,COLORANTS
531	SYNT DYE,NAT INDGO,LAKES	W 15	215		423	W 12	1527	W 70	19735	MAT COLOR ORGAN,LAQUES
5312	SYNTH LUMIN,INDIGO,LAKES	W 1	113	W 3	239	W 7	1378	W 66	19631	LUMINOPHORES ORGAN SYNTH
53122	COLOUR LAKES	W 1	106	W 2	235	W 6	1374	W 65	19625	LAQUES COLORANTES
532	DYES NES,TANNING PROD	W 1120	9952	W 1248	16657	W 1944	26645	W 2435	20992	EXTRAITS TEINTURE,TANNAGE
5322	DYE,TANN EXTRCTS,TANNINS	W 340	8785	W 423	15837	W 568	25597	W 1050	19909	EXT TAN ORIG VEG,TANNINS
53222	DYEING EXTRCTS VEG,ANMAL	W 137	8204	W 258	15439	W 346	25111	W 618	19164	MATI COLOR VEGET ANIMALE
541	*MEDICINAL,PHARM PRODUCT		6466	K 301243	12884	K 399674	16050		21768	PROD MEDICINAUX PHARMACEUT
55	PERFUME,CLEANING ETC PRD		16853		21064		20282		24817	PROD POUR PARFUM,TOILETTE
554	SOAP,CLEANSING ETC PREPS		10649	W 9682	13295	W 7744	10877	W 9773	11848	SAVONS,PRODUITS DETERSIFS
5542	WASHING PREPARATIONS ETC	W 7567	10142	W 8608	11821	W 6760	9263	W 7375	9255	PROD ORG TENSIO–ACT NDA
6	BASIC MANUFACTURES		1073996		1279829		1642696		1605513	ART MANUFACTURES
65	TEXTILE YARN,FABRICS,ETC		120656		149820		171527		159345	FILS,TISSUS,ARTICLES TEXTILE
651	TEXTILE YARN		65369	W 16279	88907	W 13942	102534	W 13664	84659	FILS TEXTILES
6512	WOOL,HAIR YARN,INCL TOPS	W 3080	20288	W 3032	29511	W 3266	35035	W 2186	22888	FILS DE LAINE,DE POILS
6513	COTTON YARN	W 9306	41054	W 12018	55211	W 10001	63752	W 10810	58073	FILS DE COTON
652	COTTON FABRICS,WOVEN		22581	W 15342	26872	W 3409	27972	W 5473	35323	TISSUS DE COTON
6522	WOVEN COTTON BLEACHD,ETC		16115	W 1556	16133	W 2708	24577	W 4386	30682	TISSUS COTON BLANCHIS ETC
65224	BLCHED COTTON FABRIC NES	W 1221	15489	W 1549	16084	W 2600	23399	W 4077	27794	AUT TIS PLUS 85% COT BLANCHI
654	OTH WOVEN TEXTILE FABRIC		15808	W 794	20522	W 804	22391	W 1027	21963	TISSUS AUT COTON SYNT,ARTIF
6542	WOVEN WOOL,HAIR NONPILE	W 2412	14904	W 760	19490	W 762	21013	W 567	15560	TIS PLUS 85% LAINE,POILS
65422	WOVN COMB WOOL,FINE HAIR	W 2238	12326	W 568	15740	W 621	17230	W 508	14062	TISSUS 85% LAINE,PLS PEIG
66	NONMETAL MINERAL MFS NES		19606		20190		22927		28037	ART MIN NON METALLIQUES

5. Special Exports F.O.B. by Commodities according to the S.I.T.C. (Rev. 2) in thousand U.S. Dollars
Exportations Spéciales F.O.B. par Produits d'après la C.T.C.I. (Rév. 2) en milliers de Dollars E.U.

SITC CTCI	COMMODITY	1993 WEIGHT POIDS	1993 VALUE VALEUR	1994 WEIGHT POIDS	1994 VALUE VALEUR	1995 WEIGHT POIDS	1995 VALUE VALEUR	1996 WEIGHT POIDS	1996 VALUE VALEUR	PRODUIT
68	NON–FERROUS METALS		889364		1062447		1389811		1376077	METAUX NON FERREUX
681	SILVER,PLATINUM,ETC		74081		100154		111128		125263	ARGENT ET PLATINE
6811	SILVER UNWKD,PARTLY WRKD		74081		100154		110951		125263	ARGENT BRUT MI–OUVRE
68113	SILVER UNWROUGHT		73516		99991		109633		124841	ARGENT ET ALLIAGES BRUTS
682	COPPER EXC CEMENT COPPER	W 294664	649861	W 360747	771675	W 375457	1077551	W 425968	959715	CUIVRE
6821	COPPER NES,ALLOYS,UNWRT	W 271854	599131	W 342717	729723	W 356465	1017493	W 407724	911302	CUIVRE BRUT
68211	COPPER UNREF,EXC CEMENT	W 59465	165846	W 105518	216887	W 91046	246390	W 82722	175378	CUIVRE POUR AFFINAGE
68212	COPPER REFINED,UNWROUGHT	W 212308	433248	W 237199	512836	W 265419	771103	W 325002	735924	CUIVRE AFFINE BRUT
6822	COPPER,ALLOYS WORKED	W 22810	50730	W 18030	41952	W 18993	60058	W 18244	48412	CUIVRE,ALLIAGES OUVRES
68221	COPPER BARS,WIRE,ETC	W 22138	48379	W 17469	40331	W 18485	58126	W 15059	39714	BARRES,PROFILES ET FILS
685	LEAD	W 74366	30139	W 76401	40487	W 80224	53277	W 87898	70051	PLOMB
6851	LEAD,ALLOYS UNWROUGHT	W 74262	29627	W 76173	40390	W 80222	53273	W 87898	70051	PLOMB,ALLIAGES BRUTS
68512	REF LEAD(EXC ALLOY)UNWRT	W 73668	29241	W 75529	40047	W 79762	52950	W 85932	68491	PLOMB AFFINE BRUT
686	ZINC	W 134920	130451	W 140547	141247	W 120023	140117	W 171366	193071	ZINC
6861	ZINC,ALLOYS UNWROUGHT	W 133316	127532	W 136337	133377	W 112350	127520	W 151304	162516	ZINC ET ALLIAGES BRUTS
6863	ZINC,ALLOYS WKD,INC DUST	W 1604	2919	W 4210	7870	W 7673	12598	W 20062	30555	ZINC ET ALLIAGES OUVRES
68632	ZINC SHEETS,STRIP,FOIL	W 1529	2743	W 4140	7796	W 5546	10142	W 19806	30476	PLANCHES,FEUILLES EN ZINC
687	TIN	W 35	81	W 40	216	W 78	452	W 4523	20943	ETAIN
6871	TIN,ALLOYS UNWROUGHT	W 5	32	W 34	201	W 65	414	W 4510	20905	ETAIN ET ALLIAGES BRUTS
69	METAL MANUFACTURES NES		22523		21201		24802		7394	ART MANUFACT EN METAL NDA
699	BASE METAL MFRS NES		19167	W 15957	18948	W 15707	22453	W 1920	4085	ART MANUFACTURES MET NDA
6998	MFRS NES OF CPR,NIKL,ETC	W 14090	17906	W 14746	17831	W 14657	20326	W 840	1462	OUVRAGES EN CU,NI,AL,PB,ZN
69985	ZINC MANUFACTURES NES	W 13862	17242	W 13392	16454	W 14267	19768	W 707	957	OUVRAGES EN ZINC
7	MACHINES,TRANSPORT EQUIP		34469		31448		31816		35166	MACHINES MATERIEL TRANSPORT
8	MISC MANUFACTURED GOODS		239368		265522		334013		416696	ART MANUFACTURES DIVERS
84	CLOTHING AND ACCESSORIES		158691		189512		202022		256770	VETEMENTS
845	OUTERWEAR KNIT NONELASTC		73769	W 4316	79120	W 3090	71572	W 3522	90738	VET DESSOUS,ACCES BONNET
8451	— JERSEYS,PULLOVERS ETC	W 978	34816	W 808	37216	W 1360	34575	W 1644	44716	CHANDAILS,PULL–OVERS ETC
8459	— OTHER,CLTHG ACCESRYS		37839	W 3479	41038	W 1654	34485	W 1754	42232	AUT VET DESSUS DE BONNE
846	UNDER GARMENTS KNITTED	W 4907	71303	W 3317	94945	W 5460	114429	W 6481	143134	SOUS VETS DE BONNETERIE
8462	— OF COTTON NON ELASTIC	W 4047	51472	W 2105	56632	W 4172	84292	W 3550	69253	SOUS–VET BONNET COTON
84629	—— OTHER	W 4047	51472	W 2105	56632	W 4172	84292	W 3550	69253	AUT SOUS–VET BONNET COTON
8463	— OF SYNTH FBR NONELAST	W 860	19825	W 1211	38288	W 1287	30097	W 2930	73868	SOUS–VET BONNET FIB SYNT
84632	—— MENS SHIRTS	W 860	19821	W 1211	38283	W 1286	30062	W 2930	73868	CHEMISES DE BON FIB SYNMT
89	MISC MANUFCTRD GOODS NES		75144		69702		126416		145069	ART MANUFACTURES DIVERS
897	GOLD,SILVER WARE,JEWELRY		67540		59456		111306		126575	BIJOUTERIE,ORFEVRERIE
8973	PREC JEWLRY,GLD–SILVWARE		63391		54783		106678		101808	BIJOUX OR,ARGENT ORFEVRE
89731	PRECIOUS METAL JEWELLERY		61325		52483		104541		99200	ART BIJOUTERIE,JOAILLER
8974	PREC MTL INDUS,LAB EQUIP		3		1		2		19222	AUT OUV METAUX PRECIEUX
9	GOODS NOT CLASSD BY KIND		211362		341682		464231		611461	ART TRANSACT NON CLASSES
971	*GOLD,NON MONETARY NES		209685	K 33919	340511	K 49051	462918	K 67105	609158	OR NON MONETAIRE
97101	NONMON GLD UNWRT,SEMIMFD	K 57900	209685	K 33919	340511	K 49029	462918	K 66383	601284	OR,ALLIAGES D'OR BRUTS

FOOT NOTES – NOTES

TABLE 1 –

1 Beginning 1969: merchandise imports include gold; merchandise exports include gold coins; gold exports exclude gold coins and include gold content of all mineral exports.

TABLEAU 1 –

1 A partir de 1969, les importations de marchandises comprennent l'or, les exportations de marchandises comprennent les pièces de monnaie qui sont donc exclues des exportations d'or et comprennent le contenu en or de toutes les exportations de minerais et métaux.

1. HISTORICAL SERIES, 1961–1996 GENERAL TRADE, IMPORTS C.I.F., EXPORTS F.O.B.
SERIES HISTORIQUES, 1961–1996 COMMERCE GENERAL, IMPORTATIONS C.A.F., EXPORTATIONS F.O.B

YEAR ANNEE	VALUE IN MILLION U.S. DOLLARS VALEUR EN MILLION U.S. DOLLARS MERCHANDISE –MARCHANDISE		GOLD –OR		CONVERSION FACTORS FACTEURS DE CONVERSION CENTS E.U. PAR		INDEX NUMBERS –INDICES QUANTUM		UNIT VALUE VALEUR UNITAIRE	
	IMPORTS	EXPORTS	IMPORTS	EXPORTS	IMPORTS	EXPORTS	IMPORTS	EXPORTS	IMPORTS	EXPORTS
1961	690.60	540.80		9.96			46	22		43
1962	655.20	580.30	5.83	20.79			43	24		44
1963	716.40	770.60		8.86			43	30		46
1964	890.30	779.40		8.62			53	31		46
1965	928.00	795.70		1.56			42	32		47
1966	1177.70	877.40		16.10			45	34		47
1967	1178.70	891.50		16.75			54	33		48
1968	1331.40	962.10		16.15			59	33		50
1969	1327.20	983.20		18.44			56	32		51
1970	1286.20	1142.20		22.87			39	28		52
1971	1404.80	1189.30		11.45			42	31		49
1972	1485.00	1168.40		8.96			42	32		47
1973	1789.50	1837.20		39.15			40	34		68
1974	3467.60	2725.00		48.06			47	31		113
1975	3776.20	2294.50		53.50			49	32		90
1976	3953.30	2573.70		65.35			52	41		79
1977	4269.80	3150.90		71.27			50	50		80
1978	5143.40	3424.90		75.74			60	48		89
1979	6612.90	4601.20		103.28			65	53		110
1980	8295.20	5787.80		238.38			66	64		114
1981	7945.70	5722.20		210.70			61	65		112
1982	8255.30	5020.60					69	68		93
1983	7979.50	5005.30					66	65		98
1984	6051.20	5321.60					47	63		108
1985	5445.00	4629.00					41	60		97
1986	5134.29	4841.78					53	74		83
1987	6811.48	5720.24					64	74		96
1988	8731.40	7034.80					78	84		115
1989	10732.07	7746.74					93	93		112
1990	13041.00	8067.90					100	100		100
1991	12785.70	8767.10					102	103		115
1992	15449.20	9751.50								118
1993	18754.40	11088.70								122
1994	22545.50	13304.00								128
1995	28336.70	17501.81								135
1996	34121.90	20416.80								144

2. IMPORTS BY BROAD ECONOMIC CATEGORY AND EXPORTS BY INDUSTRIAL ORIGIN. (PERCENTAGE OF TOTAL VALUE)
IMPORTATIONS PAR CATEGORIES ECONOMIQUES ET EXPORTATIONS PAR BRANCHE D'ACTIVITE.(EN POURCENTAGE DE LA VALEUR TOTALE)

IMPORTS – IMPORTATIONS

	1990	1991	1992	1993	1994	1995	1996
TOTAL IMPORTS–IMPORTATIONS TOTALES	100.	100.	100.	100.	100.	100.	100.
1 FOOD BEV–ALIMENTATION BOISSONS	7.8	6.3	6.3	5.7	6.2	6.6	6.9
11 PRIMARY–PRODUITS DE BASE	3.3	3.2	3.2	2.9	3.2	3.0	2.8
111 FOR INDUSTRY–POUR L'INDUSTRIE	2.4	2.1	2.2	2.0	2.2	2.0	1.8
112 FOR HOUSEHOLDS–POUR LES MENAGES	0.9	1.1	1.0	0.8	1.0	0.9	0.9
12 PROCESSED–PRODUITS ELABORES	4.5	3.1	3.1	2.8	3.1	3.7	4.1
121 FOR INDUSTRY–POUR L'INDUSTRIE	0.8	0.7	0.7	0.5	0.5	0.7	1.0
122 FOR HOUSEHOLDS–POUR LES MENAGES	3.7	2.4	2.4	2.4	2.5	2.9	3.1
2 IND SUPPLIES–APPROV INDUSTRIELS	33.1	39.9	32.0	30.5	28.9	28.7	28.2
21 PRIMARY–PRODUITS DE BASE	4.3	5.3	3.8	3.3	3.3	3.5	3.4
22 PROCESSED–PRODUITS ELABORES	28.8	34.6	28.2	27.2	25.6	25.2	24.8
3 FUELS–COMBUSTIBLES	14.8	15.0	13.8	11.3	9.4	9.1	9.2
31 PRIMARY–PRODUITS DE BASE	13.5	12.8	11.8	8.4	6.9	8.1	8.3
32 PROCESSED–PRODUITS ELABORES	1.4	2.2	1.9	3.0	2.5	1.0	0.8
321 MOTOR SPIRIT–ESSENCE	0.0	0.0	0.0	0.2	0.3	0.2	0.2
322 OTHER–AUTRES	1.3	2.2	1.9	2.8	2.2	0.8	0.6
4 MACHINERY–EQUIPEMENT	18.0	27.7	20.6	22.6	25.5	23.3	41.4
41 CAPITAL EQUIPMENT–MACHINES	13.3	14.0	14.9	17.1	19.5	17.2	20.0
42 PARTS–PIECES ACCESSOIRES	4.7	13.7	5.7	5.5	6.0	6.1	21.4
5 TRANSPORT–TRANSPORT	7.7	6.8	7.4	10.0	7.5	8.7	9.7
51 PASSENGER CARS–AUTOMOBILES	1.4	1.8	1.9	2.1	2.4	2.4	2.3
52 OTHER–AUTRES	3.0	2.9	3.2	4.4	1.8	2.9	4.6
521 INDUSTRIAL–INDUSTRIELS	2.7	2.7	2.9	4.0	1.4	2.6	4.1
522 NON INDUSTRIAL–NON INDUSTRIEL	0.3	0.2	0.3	0.4	0.4	0.4	0.4
53 PARTS–PIECES ACCESSOIRES	3.3	2.1	2.4	3.4	3.4	3.4	2.9
6 CONSUM GOODS–BIENS CONSOMMATION	2.8	4.0	3.5	3.8	4.3	4.3	4.6
61 DURABLE–DURABLES	0.5	0.7	0.7	0.7	0.9	1.1	1.2
62 SEMI DURABLE–SEMI DURABLES	1.0	1.9	1.3	1.5	1.5	1.7	1.9
63 NON DURABLE–NON DURABLES	1.3	1.4	1.4	1.6	1.8	1.5	1.4
7 GOODS NES–BIENS NDA	15.8	0.4	16.4	16.1	18.2	19.3	0.1

EXPORTS – EXPORTATIONS

	1990	1991	1992	1993	1994	1995	1996
TOTAL EXPORTS–EXPORTATIONS TOTALES	100.	100.	100.	100.	100.	100.	100.
1 AGRICULTURE	8.8	9.5	7.6	7.7	6.8	5.7	4.6
2 MINING QUARRY–INDUS EXTRACTIVES	4.9	5.0	4.4	2.9	2.5	2.1	1.7
3 MANUFACTURING–IND MANUFACTUR	86.3	85.6	87.9	89.4	90.7	92.2	93.7
31 FOOD BEV TOBACCO–ALIM BOISS TAB	11.3	10.4	10.6	8.8	8.2	8.2	6.3
32 TEXTILES–INDUSTRIES TEXTILES	10.8	24.8	11.6	10.5	10.2	9.1	15.1
33 WOOD & PRODUCTS–BOIS & PRODUITS	2.6	2.8	1.7	1.4	1.2	1.0	1.0
34 PAPER & PRODUCTS–PAPIER & PRODT	0.5	0.6	0.6	0.6	0.5	0.5	0.5
35 CHEMICALS–INDUSTRIES CHIMIQUES	5.5	6.4	4.6	3.9	3.6	3.4	3.8
36 NON METAL MIN–MIN NON METAL	0.7	0.9	0.8	0.8	0.7	0.6	0.5
37 BASIC METAL–IND METAL BASE	4.6	3.4	2.7	3.0	2.7	3.0	2.3
38 METAL MANUF–MANUF METAL	15.5	32.3	19.7	22.0	24.8	25.1	61.6
39 OTH MANUF IND–AUTRES MANUF	34.9	4.1	35.4	38.3	38.7	41.2	2.5

3. TRADE BY PRINCIPAL COUNTRIES OF PRODUCTION AND LAST DESTINATION (VALUE IN THOUSAND U.S. DOLLARS)
ECHANGES SELON LES PRINCIPAUX PAYS DE PRODUCTION ET DE DERNIERE DESTINATION (VALEUR EN MILLIERS DE DOLLARS EU)

COUNTRIES–PAYS	GENERAL IMPORTS C.I.F. IMPORTATIONS GENERALES C.A.F					COUNTRIES–PAYS	GENERAL EXPORTS F.O.B. EXPORTATIONS GENERALES F.O.B.				
	1992	1993	1994	1995	1996		1992	1993	1994	1995	1996
World	15465254	18772699	22737984	28487359	34701209	Monde	9824314	11374805	13482896	17447186	20542482
Africa	120981	173000	122813	174691	161054	Afrique	29346	40517	51411	43952	62964
Americas	3341614	4269326	4769234	6151485	7712079	Amériques	4134260	4703557	5525184	6638756	7406008
Northern America	3043128	3929406	4342473	5658706	7058379	Amérique du Nord	4003358	4579280	5390074	6447313	7243972
LAIA	297383	318009	418693	471472	645096	ALAI	53002	72372	77621	114711	116402
CACM	462	541	727	16155	2478	MCAC	493	845	746	596	1263
Caribbean	199	21089	6682	3577	3673	Caraïbes	29261	15666	17081	26828	12492
Rest of America	442	281	660	1576	2453	Autre Amérique	48146	35394	39661	49309	31878
As.ex F.USSR	9217762	11162568	13992284	17302943	20810567	Asie l'URSS exclus	3553851	4401220	5286767	7426950	9170783
Eur.x F.USSR	2053606	2288266	2712134	3263064	4261622	Europe l'URSS exclus	1944868	2061676	2407945	3128610	3669797
EU	1859935	2051490	2506513	3035077	3868573	UE	1906025	2016949	2358643	3073405	3602875
EFTA	91263	115954	131813	186772	296685	AELE	27967	33571	36079	36234	42928
East Europe	99985	120175	72836	38378	94246	Europe de l'Est	4793	8621	10512	13256	17927
Other Europe	625	26	0	1568	1035	Autre de l'Europe	5875	1947	2270	516	2772
Former USSR	100522	113753	271862	500456	562884	Ancienne URSS	7794	11722	20221	11813	16330
Oceania	630693	765785	869654	1092098	1192598	Océanie	153685	156113	187825	197093	216601
Japan/Japon	3277367	4282976	5561411	6304733	7578175	USA/Etats–Unis d'Amer	3843279	4384803	5194240	6245130	7037834
USA/Etats–Unis d'Amer	2823842	3763440	4187901	5386447	6770766	Japan/Japon	1745049	1827035	2034730	2747452	3671211
Singapore/Singapour	574970	1016086	1494320	1635989	1826451	Singapore/Singapour	252323	379450	708458	995708	1223545
Saudi Arabia	921350	796479	994345	1718713	1751185	United Kingdom	466758	540505	638623	923185	936413
Korea, Republic of	740040	943656	1172428	1429308	1785950	Hong Kong	463657	548175	651406	823983	868252
Hong Kong	745390	913769	1164761	1384956	1459018	Germany/Allemagne	521740	586004	665264	699122	847005
Germany/Allemagne	702265	647231	797642	977090	1283097	Netherlands/Pays–Bas	406262	361847	516119	805091	1114585
Australia/Australie	458169	534450	638997	828548	887440	Thailand/Thaïlande	98434	168719	363824	798887	780079
Malaysia/Malaisie	409751	378244	458096	623676	857618	Malaysia/Malaisie	127819	161066	222063	315406	687058
Indonesia/Indonésie	196478	368100	399409	620735	707904	Korea, Republic of	175819	221008	292067	443715	370660
United Kingdom	313835	393424	406285	573425	506314	France, Monac	178916	208942	185020	203202	227715
China/Chine	200174	201903	332930	660813	763429	China/Chine	113895	173874	164485	213966	327922
Thailand/Thaïlande	146016	189473	212187	427921	660414	Canada	159830	194128	195759	202107	205807
Netherlands/Pays–Bas	191963	249014	294902	343488	358343	Australia/Australie	112596	114448	139843	143291	160760
France, Monac	223179	215381	258018	323272	417095	United Arab Emirates	110543	149690	130190	105110	123955
Russian Federation	98718	106844	216227	406811	530557	Belgium–Luxembourg	76844	94110	97196	105374	107744
Brazil/Brésil	211319	235406	282166	290855	338589	Italy/Italie	99490	85475	90490	111173	93854
United Arab Emirates	276358	272202	230201	184007	318158	Indonesia/Indonésie	40273	48259	71123	129126	142453
Canada	219286	165966	154571	272220	287613	Viet Nam	29702	37373	62510	123626	129990
Italy/Italie	125745	143162	178871	244412	324986	Spain/Espagne	69662	50270	55135	79528	88799
Belgium–Luxembourg	99734	118132	245870	192069	236824	India/Inde	8595	225619	12989	20228	36563
Israel/Israël	101178	170218	203654	162468	183948	Saudi Arabia	57037	68129	58707	64906	54582
India/Inde	95375	123243	148192	176133	241987	Panama	47432	35291	39621	49127	31677
Iran (Islamic Rp. of)	173702	72509	71188	114878	298311	Mexico/Mexique	21325	35025	39875	38659	35985
Switz.Liecht	86905	112553	125208	177356	208401	Ireland/Irlande	9411	13084	20942	53934	67754
New Zealand	101439	133150	136695	147015	171320	Switz.Liecht	21579	27125	28094	27517	34196
Sweden/Suède	29219	68169	76723	104919	224187	Chile/Chili	17476	17463	16926	33939	39420
Kuwait/ Koweït	86835	202282	86777	35646	20419	Denmark/Danemark	20290	23519	23966	26866	28254
Ireland/Irlande	30446	34777	36841	78805	246219	So. Africa Customs Un	8509	19001	29202	24257	30304
Papua New Guinea	59478	82104	77662	88408	101992	Sweden/Suède	23622	17003	17859	20185	24515
Finland/Finlande	22172	85494	82809	64041	96914	New Zealand	12520	13809	18180	22287	20469
Spain/Espagne	65892	43723	61728	64538	86648	American Samoa	16289	13398	15929	17212	16836
So. Africa Customs Un	24517	76231	54894	65130	75617	Finland/Finlande	7447	9703	19690	14442	27202
Oman	2	266	25143	88758	178546	Austria/Autriche	11195	14360	15510	13726	19848
Chile/Chili	49326	38603	47706	44209	111017	Netherlands Antilles	23830	11873	13413	18354	5973
Viet Nam	15771	13748	16885	42933	196924	Egypt/Egypte	9741	11706	11802	10617	21704
Poland/Pologne	61313	71360	35682	14455	60683	Russian Federation	7751	10412	20203	11374	15382
Brunei Darussalam	94018	52044	36313	7854	415	Brazil/Brésil	4337	5285	9264	20855	13445
Qatar	77072	28764	23773	15526	44731	Kuwait/ Koweït	6883	10189	8609	9779	17702
Mexico/Mexique	7810	7034	22108	58864	93535	Israel/Israël	6172	7776	12357	9728	10881
Peru/Pérou	18208	29861	37980	51475	39867	Portugal	9122	6715	4791	8336	11246
Denmark/Danemark	34807	29717	34819	32592	43463	Palau	6077	6299	7575	8323	10526
Pakistan	30650	29969	24649	33086	52591	Norway,SVD,JM	6047	6355	7856	8655	8617
Ukraine	21	1202	43360	73695	20499	Argentina/Argentine	3844	6008	7216	7040	12973
Turkey/Turquie	29994	6480	18103	19140	59696	Greece/Grèce	5267	5411	8039	9239	7941
Austria/Autriche	16588	21060	25793	25292	33450	Pakistan	1230	1907	3991	7233	17826
Zimbabwe	33304	22980	28614	17984	16415	Bahrain/Bahreïn	5622	7323	7287	5599	3509
Norway,SVD,JM	3729	3389	6443	9416	87190	Sri Lanka	2592	3685	7371	9434	6217
Argentina/Argentine	9150	4744	12211	19669	56607	Hungary/Hongrie	2039	3376	4932	6983	8039
Romania/Roumanie	16698	18587	13676	7101	18225	Turkey/Turquie	6352	4993	2300	3335	5603

(VALUE AS PERCENTAGE OF WORLD TOTAL)(VALEURS EN POURCENTAGE DU TOTAL MONDIAL)

	1987	1988	1989	1990	1991	1992	1993	1994	1995	1996		1987	1988	1989	1990	1991	1992	1993	1994	1995	1996
Africa	1.3	1.1	1.0	0.7	0.5	0.8	0.9	0.5	0.6	0.5	Afrique	0.3	0.3	0.3	0.3	0.3	0.3	0.4	0.4	0.3	0.3
Americas	24.7	24.2	23.9	23.7	23.9	21.6	22.7	21.0	21.6	22.2	Amériques	38.5	37.9	40.7	40.3	38.4	42.1	41.4	41.0	38.1	36.1
Northern America	23.3	22.2	20.7	21.0	21.6	19.7	20.9	19.1	19.9	20.3	Amérique du Nord	37.6	37.2	39.4	39.4	37.3	40.7	40.3	40.0	37.0	35.3
LAIA	1.5	2.0	3.2	2.7	2.3	1.9	1.7	1.8	1.7	1.9	ALAI	0.1	0.1	0.4	0.2	0.4	0.5	0.6	0.6	0.7	0.6
CACM	0.0	0.0	0.0	0.0	0.0	0.0	0.0	0.0	0.1	0.0	MCAC	0.0	0.0	0.0	0.0	0.0	0.0	0.0	0.0	0.0	0.0
Caribbean	0.0	0.0	0.0	0.0	0.0	0.0	0.1	0.0	0.0	0.0	Caraïbes	0.1	0.1	0.2	0.3	0.2	0.3	0.1	0.1	0.2	0.1
Rest of America	0.0	0.0	0.0	0.0	0.0	0.0	0.0	0.0	0.0	0.0	Autre Amérique	0.6	0.5	0.7	0.5	0.5	0.5	0.3	0.3	0.3	0.2
As.ex F.USSR	56.0	54.6	57.1	58.2	58.6	59.6	59.5	61.5	60.7	60.0	Asie l'URSS exclus	38.9	40.7	38.9	38.9	40.0	36.2	38.7	39.2	42.6	44.6
Eur.x F.USSR	13.8	14.6	13.0	12.9	12.2	13.3	12.2	11.9	11.5	12.3	Europe l'URSS exclus	19.9	18.4	17.7	18.6	19.5	19.8	18.1	17.9	17.9	17.9
EU	12.2	13.2	11.9	11.7	10.8	12.0	10.9	11.0	10.7	11.1	UE	19.4	18.1	17.4	18.2	19.1	19.4	17.7	17.5	17.6	17.5
EFTA	1.1	0.9	0.6	0.7	0.7	0.6	0.6	0.6	0.7	0.9	AELE	0.3	0.3	0.2	0.3	0.3	0.3	0.3	0.3	0.2	0.2
East Europe	0.5	0.4	0.5	0.5	0.6	0.6	0.6	0.3	0.1	0.3	Europe de l'Est	0.1	0.0	0 0	0.0	0.1	0.0	0.1	0.1	0.1	0.1
Other Europe	0.0	0.1	0.0	0.0	0.1	0.0	0.0	0.0	0.0	0.0	Autre de l'Europe	0.0	0.0	0.0	0.0	0.0	0.1	0.0	0.0	0.0	0.0
Former USSR	0.2	0.4	0.2	0.2	0.3	0.6	0.6	1.2	1.8	1.6	Ancienne URSS	0.5	0.3	0.3	0.2	0.2	0.1	0.1	0.1	0.1	0.1
Oceania	3.9	5.1	4.8	4.3	4.5	4.1	4.1	3.8	3.8	3.4	Océanie	2.1	2.4	2.1	1.6	1.6	1.6	1.4	1.4	1.1	1.1
Japan/Japon	16.9	17.4	19.5	18.4	19.6	21.2	22.8	24.5	22.1	21.8	USA/Etats–Unis d'Amer	36.2	35.7	37.8	37.9	35.7	39.1	38.5	38.5	35.8	34.3
USA/Etats–Unis d'Amer	22.0	21.2	19.1	19.5	20.3	18.3	20.0	18.4	18.9	19.5	Japan/Japon	17.2	20.1	20.3	19.8	20.0	17.8	16.1	15.1	15.7	17.9
Singapore/Singapour	3.4	4.0	4.7	3.9	3.7	3.7	5.4	6.6	5.7	5.3	Singapore/Singapour	3.4	3.2	2.8	2.9	2.6	2.6	3.3	5.3	5.7	6.0
Saudi Arabia	3.2	1.4	2.4	4.4	5.4	6.0	4.2	4.4	6.0	5.0	United Kingdom	4.3	4.6	4.2	4.3	4.2	4.8	4.8	4.7	5.3	4.6
Korea, Republic of	2.9	4.0	4.0	3.8	5.0	4.8	5.0	5.2	5.0	5.1	Hong Kong	4.9	4.9	3.9	4.0	4.4	4.7	4.8	4.8	4.7	4.2
Hong Kong	4.6	4.4	4.5	4.4	4.8	4.8	4.9	5.1	4.9	4.2	Germany/Allemagne	5.1	4.2	4.3	4.8	5.7	5.3	5.2	4.9	4.0	4.1
Germany/Allemagne	4.2	3.9	3.9	4.3	3.8	4.5	3.4	3.5	3.4	3.7	Netherlands/Pays–Bas	5.4	4.5	4.2	4.4	3.8	4.1	3.2	3.8	4.6	5.4
Australia/Australie	3.0	3.6	3.5	3.1	3.3	3.0	2.8	2.8	2.9	2.6	Thailand/Thaïlande	2.2	1.7	2.0	1.9	2.5	1.0	1.5	2.7	4.6	3.8
Malaysia/Malaisie	4.0	3.0	2.5	2.2	2.5	2.6	2.0	2.0	2.2	2.5	Malaysia/Malaisie	2.1	1.7	1.3	1.5	1.4	1.3	1.4	1.6	1.8	3.3
Indonesia/Indonésie	1.3	1.0	1.6	1.5	1.4	1.3	2.0	1.8	2.2	2.0	Korea, Republic of	1.9	2.3	2.2	2.8	2.6	1.8	1.9	2.2	2.5	1.8

4. General Imports C.I.F. by Commodities according to the S.I.T.C. (Rev. 2) in thousand U.S. Dollars
Importations Générales C.A.F. par Produits d'après la C.T.C.I. (Rév. 2) en milliers de Dollars E.U.

SITC CTCI	COMMODITY	1993 WEIGHT POIDS	1993 VALUE VALEUR	1994 WEIGHT POIDS	1994 VALUE VALEUR	1995 WEIGHT POIDS	1995 VALUE VALEUR	1996 WEIGHT POIDS	1996 VALUE VALEUR	PRODUIT
	ALL COMMODITIES		18772699		22737984		28487359		34701209	TOUS PRODUITS
0	FOOD AND LIVE ANIMALS		1267594		1505859		2107296		2548809	ALIMENTS,ANIMAUX VIVANTS
001	*LIVE ANIMALS FOR FOOD	W 26571	43671	N 1119330	53526	N 2254861	88047	W 53129	84812	ANIMAUX VIVANTS
01	MEAT AND PREPARATIONS		32900		66097		79554		109447	VIANDES ET PREPARATIONS
02	DAIRY PRODCTS,BIRDS'EGGS		272613		332018		438834		404190	PRODUITS LAITIERS,OEUFS
022	MILK AND CREAM	W 148031	230339	W 182944	278886	W 201838	379004	W 191069	342197	LAIT ET CREME
0224	MILK,CREAM PRESERVED ETC	W 127385	202194	W 154707	243214	W 166333	330767	W 151480	293785	LAIT,CREME CONS,CONC
02242	MILK DRY,1.5% FAT OR LES	W 77031	130829	W 88424	146857	W 103592	229858	W 83237	177830	LAIT POUDRE INF 1.5%
02243	MILK DRY,OVER 1.5% FAT	W 29123	57181	W 35379	73994	W 34239	80218	W 36982	90122	LAIT POUDRE SUP 1.5%
04	CEREALS AND PREPARATIONS		425828		516726		688522		1051436	CEREALES ET PRODUITS
041	WHEAT ETC UNMILLED	W 1802564	297757	W 2146889	368859	W 2101745	409586	W 1887093	426956	FROMENT,EPEAUTRE
0412	OTHER WHEAT ETC UNMILLED	W 1802564	297757	W 2146889	368859	W 2101745	409586	W 1887093	426956	AUTRE FROMENT NON MOULU
042	RICE	W 203943	37144	W 1638	682	W 263251	82725	W 866949	308945	RIZ
0422	RICE SEMI–MILLED,MILLED	W 203943	37144	W 1638	682	W 263248	82707	W 866949	308945	RIZ POLI,GLACE INCL BRISURES
04221	RICE MILLED UNBROKEN	W 203943	37144	W 1638	682	W 263248	82707	W 866905	308922	RIZ POLI,GLACE EXCL BRISURES
048	CEREAL ETC PREPARATIONS	W 166529	82760	W 222654	132021	W 192809	145248	W 189449	166328	PREPTNS A BASE CEREALES
05	VEGETABLES AND FRUIT		74049		117994		122412		151291	LEGUMES ET FRUITS
06	SUGAR AND PREPS,HONEY		25585		43721		190747		287299	SUCRES ET PRODUITS
061	SUGAR AND HONEY	W 45738	23466	W 71529	35997	W 464846	176779	W 904423	279902	SUCRES ET MIEL
0611	RAW BEET AND CANE SUGAR					W 235754	87484	W 439371	135637	SUCRES BRUTS
081	*FEEDING STUFF FOR ANIML	W 973498	276255	W 812597	227380	W 1094516	313441	W 595511	230406	NOURRITURE POUR ANIMAUX
0813	OILCAKE AND OTH RESIDUES	W 828591	206565	W 657120	151199	W 901335	204350	W 446194	116939	TOURTEAUX
08131	— OF SOYA BEANS	W 825710	206180	W 655066	150832	W 898392	203941	W 431147	112829	TOURTEAUX DE SOJA
1	BEVERAGES AND TOBACCO		136142		237308		169416		123035	BOISSONS ET TABACS
12	TOBACCO AND MANUFACTURES		98598		183000		123048		82038	TABACS BRUTS FABRIQUES
121	TOBACCO UNMNFCTRD,REFUSE	W 14410	57215	W 26642	93512	W 25233	91153	W 15318	72012	TABACS BRUTS,DECHETS
1212	TOBACCO STRIPPED OR PART	W 14409	57190	W 26642	93512	W 25190	91029	W 15305	71822	TABACS PART ECOTES
122	TOBACCO,MANUFACTURED	W 4951	41382	W 9833	89488	W 4418	31895	W 1168	10026	TABACS FABRIQUES
1222	CIGARETTES	W 4949	41303	W 9789	88943	W 4413	31791	W 1154	9729	CIGARETTES
2	CRUDE MATERLS,EXCL FUELS		775012		977311		1236233		1474720	MAT BRUTES NON COMESTIBLES
24	CORK AND WOOD		127749		122965		164499		289125	LIEGE ET BOIS
247	OTH WOOD ROUGH,SQUARED	W 480975	82451	W 300896	56216	W 513120	82036	W 728411	126465	BOIS BRUTS EQUARRIS
2472	SAW–,VENEER–LOGS NON–CON	W 396039	57109	W 270751	47411	W 399784	62630	W 630957	105158	NON CONIFERES SCIAGE,PLAC
24721	— IN THE ROUGH	W 396039	57109	W 270751	47411	W 399784	62630	W 630957	105158	BRUTS ECORCES DEGROSSIS
248	WOOD SHAPED,SLEEPERS	W 201476	45256	W 207948	66690	W 259623	82259	W 461988	162388	BOIS SIMPLEMENT TRAVAILLES
2483	LUMBER SHAPED NON–CONIFR	W 198709	43958	W 201322	63223	W 227468	67260	W 394861	118336	NON CONIFERES SCIES,RABOTES
24831	LUMBER SAWN ETC NON–CON	W 198705	43956	W 201235	63150	W 227465	67244	W 394825	118262	SCIES LONGITUDINALEMENT
251	*PULP AND WASTE PAPER	W 323450	80920	W 322009	79308	W 360088	139009	W 351006	113991	PATES A PAPIER,DECHETS
26	TEXTILE FIBRES AND WASTE		156354		240932		248273		272440	FIBRES TEXTILES
263	COTTON	W 59194	72286	W 76673	113913	W 61605	116661	W 77824	143544	COTON
2631	RAW COTTON,EXCL LINTERS	W 55299	69858	W 74102	111532	W 59295	113349	W 75228	140732	COTON EN MASSE
266	SYNTHETIC FIBRES TO SPIN	W 34474	47716	W 45052	73192	W 37997	73910	W 52886	71280	FIBRES SYNTHETIQUES
2665	DISCN SYNTH FIBRE UNCMBD	W 32433	42686	W 43255	68729	W 36416	69595	W 50558	66202	DISCONTINUES EN MASSE
27	CRUDE FERTLZR,MINRLS NES		74292		101110		149173		144757	ENGRAIS MINERAUX BRUTS
28	METALLIFEROUS ORES,SCRAP		244096		318319		412882		505104	MINERAIS METAL,DECHETS
287	BASE METAL ORES,CONC NES	W 383977	233977	W 429687	312274	W 532280	402395	W 533170	382307	MINERAIS METAUX COMMUNS
2871	CPR ORE ETC,CEMENT COPPR	W 371318	229631	W 420065	307773	W 499033	394210	W 509068	373503	MINERAIS DE CUIVRE,MATTES
28711	COPPER ORES,EXCL MATTE	W 371318	229631	W 420065	307773	W 499033	394210	W 509068	373503	MINERAIS DE CUIVRE
3	MINERAL FUELS ETC		2166939		2165953		2629497		3200176	COMBUSTIBLES MINERAUX LUB
32	COAL,COKE AND BRIQUETTES		57687		44696		80443		126093	HOUILLES,COKES,BRIQUETTES
322	COAL,LIGNITE AND PEAT	W 925979	51626	W 1061580	38137	W 1629454	66566	W 3356925	112167	HOUILLES,LIGNITES,TOURBE
33	PETROLEUM AND PRODUCTS		1952126		1942172		2324862		2849450	PETROLE ET DERIVES
333	CRUDE PETROLEUM	MW 11251	1366326	MW 11764	1350606	MW 15975	2010352	MW 17065	2555129	HUILES BRUTES DE PETROLE
334	PETROLEUM PRODUCTS,REFIN	W 2897321	549164	W 3657277	567097	W 1374175	282056	W 1263858	267377	PRODUITS RAFFINES
3341	GASOLINE,OTH LIGHT OILS	W 142614	32541	W 332210	72866	W 230696	67018	W 242454	56575	ESSENCES POUR MOTEURS
3343	GAS OILS	W 2310519	426489	W 2002085	324844	W 585391	99939	W 535458	117540	GAS OILS
3344	FUEL OILS,NES	W 357469	30324	W 1176243	115835	W 463698	56322	W 427632	55346	FUEL OILS
341	*GAS,NATURAL AND MANUFCT	W 882953	157125	W 1100668	179086	W 1066188	224193	W 960734	224632	GAZ NATUREL,GAZ MANUFACT
3413	PETROLM GASES,LIQUEFIED	W 882953	157125	W 1100659	179065	W 1066186	224147	W 960711	224552	GAZ DE PETROLE LIQUEFIE
34131	LIQUEFIED PROPANE,BUTANE	W 744666	120779	W 962210	151790	W 957623	196255	W 835992	192834	PROPANE,BUTANE LIQUEFIES
5	CHEMCLS,RELATED PROD NES		1784222		2150920		2566315		2833811	PRODUITS CHIMIQUES
51	ORGANIC CHEMICALS		343409		384609		488068		463115	PROD CHIMIQ ORGANIQUES
511	HYDROCARBONS NES,DERIVS	W 97330	56524	W 95513	64174	W 103714	90211	W 122763	74469	HYDROCARBURES NDA
513	CARBOXYLIC ACIDS ETC	W 94021	86736	W 96309	94654	W 93319	124099	W 83405	107358	ACIDES CARBOXYLIQUES
514	NITROGEN–FNCTN COMPOUNDS	W 24128	66690	W 23390	80234	W 27948	103270	W 32950	112487	COMPOSES FONCT AZOTEES
52	INORGANIC CHEMICALS		171924		190637		244712		260960	PROD CHIM INORGANIQUES
522	INORG ELEMNTS,OXIDES,ETC	W 438716	82810	W 513690	86827	W 406979	111014	W 525429	118043	ELEMENTS INORGANIQUES
523	OTHR INORG CHEMICALS ETC	W 284638	88807	W 346321	103296	W 419523	133015	W 379091	142288	AUT PRODUITS CHIMIQUES INORG
53	DYES,TANNING,COLOUR PROD		140048		148416		175033		179802	PROD TEINTURE,COLORANTS
531	SYNT DYE,NAT INDGO,LAKES	W 8641	59990	W 8266	54719	W 8612	57925	W 8091	55734	MAT COLOR ORGAN,LAQUES
533	PIGMENTS,PAINTS,ETC	W 37986	77125	W 42849	90608	W 46840	113007	W 49820	120788	PIGMENTS,PEINTURES,VERNIS
541	*MEDICINAL,PHARM PRODUCT	MK 11661	206510	MK 12095	269405	MK 11415	303800	MK 15686	341777	PROD MEDICINAUX PHARMACEUT
5417	MEDICAMENTS	K 7044269	112543	K 8467024	165772	K 6633596	184409	K 8940545	223318	MEDICAMENTS
54179	— CONTNG OTH SUBSTANCES	K 6349455	88376	K 7718466	129379	K 5539328	138267	K 8043036	167368	MED CONT AUT SUBSTANCES
55	PERFUME,CLEANING ETC PRD		108723		126397		155103		160596	PROD POUR PARFUM,TOILETTE
551	ESSENTL OILS,PERFUME,ETC	W 7095	62016	W 7192	69692	W 6596	81444	W 7628	83792	HUILES ESSENTIELLES
562	*FERTILIZERS,MANUFACTURE	W 1212873	147462	W 1379070	199762	W 1267879	227896	W 1342922	243213	ENGRAIS MANUFACTURES
5621	CHEM NITROGENOUS FERTLZR	W 796526	101128	W 999814	137445	W 906291	158604	W 961674	170470	ENGRAIS AZOTES
56216	UREA	W 596775	78959	W 689279	102217	W 630865	125264	W 650415	124814	UREE
58	PLASTIC MATERIALS ETC		458742		590503		710581		847976	MAT PLAST ARTIFICIELLES
582	PROD OF CONDENSATION ETC	W 30959	69271	W 43142	92032	W 42410	113088	W 51603	143621	PROD CONDENS,POLYCOND
583	POLYMERIZATION ETC PRODS	W 468600	373697	W 567894	482211	W 463617	578627	W 637510	685466	PROD POLYMERISATION
5831	POLYETHYLENE	W 172701	121158	W 224150	165383	W 161145	167306	W 241144	221309	POLYETHYLENE
58311	— IN PRIMARY FORMS	W 159818	107999	W 218665	150507	W 154632	150091	W 231560	200303	POLYETHYLENE PRIMAIRES
5832	POLYPROPYLENE	W 187063	122616	W 184074	139291	W 159865	183103	W 202367	196180	POLYPROPYLENE
58321	— IN PRIMARY FORMS	W 182974	115224	W 177982	126634	W 151953	161565	W 189913	168392	POLYPROPYLENE PRIMAIRES
5834	POLYVINYL CHLORIDE	W 59903	47363	W 104291	79775	W 75204	85869	W 101885	89509	CHLORURE DE POLYVINYLE
5839	OTH POLYMRZTION ETC PROD	W 27392	50056	W 29480	57985	W 38559	92092	W 55956	121252	AUT PROD POLYMER COPOLYM
59	CHEMICAL MATERIALS NES		204149		237781		257234		332563	MAT PROD CHIMIQUES NDA
598	MISCEL CHEM PRODUCTS NES	W 78878	139214	W 79405	162902	W 95196	169395	W 125862	208780	PROD DIV INDUST CHIM NDA
5989	CHEM PRODUCTS,PREPS NES	W 53101	99977	W 56401	126722	W 66819	121417	W 94196	156975	PROD PREP CHIMIQUES NDA
59899	OTH CHEM PRODS,PREPS,NES	W 32585	67665	W 37938	87052	W 40804	85281	W 67283	113403	AUT PRODUITS CHIMIQUES NDA
6	BASIC MANUFACTURES		2846451		3177999		4002599		4919487	ART MANUFACTURES
61	LEATHER,DRESSED FUR,ETC		99355		94999		93691		125914	CUIRS,PELLETERIES
611	LEATHER	W 5953	71725	W 7114	68088	W 6358	69615	W 7607	94548	CUIRS,PEAUX PREPARES
6114	LEATHR BOVINE NES,EQUINE	W 4755	61703	W 4822	56363	W 4437	60034	W 5202	73392	CUIRS DE BOVINS
62	RUBBER MANUFACTURES NES		116891		130865		165013		222146	CAOUTCHOUC MANUFACTURE
625	RUBBER TYRES, TUBES ETC	W 32600	72401	N 5015734	81850	N 6530425	110977	W 65279	158459	PNEUS CAOUTCHOUC VULCANISE
64	PAPER,PAPERBOARD AND MFR		223154		306527		363210		403794	PAPIERS,CARTONS & OUVRAGES
641	PAPER AND PAPERBOARD	W 310447	178168	W 430161	244968	W 392861	299379	W 475544	310646	PAPIERS ET CARTONS
6413	KRAFT PAPER,PAPERBOARD	W 108644	50068	W 152527	70777	W 137591	84877	W 175456	90719	PAPIER ET CARTON KRAFT

4. General Imports C.I.F. by Commodities according to the S.I.T.C. (Rev. 2) in thousand U.S. Dollars
Importations Générales C.A.F. par Produits d'après la C.T.C.I. (Rév. 2) en milliers de Dollars E.U.

SITC CTCI	COMMODITY	1993 WEIGHT POIDS	1993 VALUE VALEUR	1994 WEIGHT POIDS	1994 VALUE VALEUR	1995 WEIGHT POIDS	1995 VALUE VALEUR	1996 WEIGHT POIDS	1996 VALUE VALEUR	PRODUIT
65	TEXTILE YARN,FABRICS,ETC		740350		821804		943485		1256272	FILS,TISSUS,ARTICLES TEXTILE
651	TEXTILE YARN	W 41693	110284	W 39072	122252	W 45008	160469	W 50813	176649	FILS TEXTILES
652	COTTON FABRICS,WOVEN	W 30297	151598		166005		205278	W 39729	252237	TISSUS DE COTON
6522	WOVEN COTTON BLEACHD,ETC	W 29421	148913		162256		200040	W 38453	246002	TISSUS COTON BLANCHIS ETC
65224	BLCHED COTTON FABRIC NES	W 27055	132368		146257		179512	W 34578	215131	AUT TIS PLUS 85% COT BLANCHI
653	WOVN MAN-MADE FIB FABRIC	W 22457	140625		157960		186208	W 40405	274182	TISSUS FIBRES SYNTH,ARTIF
6531	CONT SYNT WEAVES NONPILE	W 11059	74162		72678		90951	W 23615	137579	TISSUS FIBRES SYNTH CONTINUE
65315	CONT SYN TXTL FABRIC NES	W 10907	73078		72021		89529	W 23328	135797	TIS PLUS 85% TEXT SYNT CONT
655	KNITTED,ETC FABRICS		175943	W 29408	197120	W 30126	213168	W 38055	261527	ETOF BONNETERIE PIECES ETC
6552	OTHER KNIT ETC FAB NONEL		175943	W 29408	197120	W 30126	213168	W 38055	261527	ETOF BON NON ELAS NON SYNT
657	SPECIAL TXTL FABRC,PRODS	W 24064	98787		111704		105622	W 29929	138338	TISSUS SPECIAUX
6573	COATED ETC TEXTILES NES	W 19807	75514	W 21038	82016	W 17823	73730	W 22717	97235	TISSUS,ART MATIERE TEXT NDA
66	NONMETAL MINERAL MFS NES		121838		138853		247583		388022	ART MIN NON METALLIQUES
661	LIME,CEMENT,BLDG PRODS	W 753531	42914	W 705229	37357	W 1467974	87612	W 2598312	160703	CHAUX,CIMENTS MAT CONSTR
6612	CEMENT	W 745694	38306	W 696467	31935	W 1452740	78881	W 2572057	145559	CIMENTS HYDRAULIQUES
67	IRON AND STEEL		924966		973427		1475734		1620279	FER ET ACIER
672	IRON,STEEL PRIMARY FORMS	W 1706461	446980	W 1800409	439679	W 2443828	697806	W 2284057	631942	LINGOTS FER,ACIER
6725	IRN,STL BLOOMS,SLABS,ETC	W 1273004	301435	W 1627115	375599	W 2223571	614427	W 1950977	505910	BLOOMS,BILLETTES FER ACIER
67251	IRN,SMPLE STL BLOOMS,ETC	W 1273004	301435	W 1627083	375519	W 2223469	613987	W 1950974	505903	BLOOMS ETC NON ACIER FIN
6727	IRN,STL COIL FR REROLLNG	W 433454	145543	W 173290	64073	W 219684	83230	W 333028	125922	EBAUCHES POUR TOLES FER
67271	IRON,SIMPLE STEEL COILS	W 427898	134252	W 169078	57254	W 214861	73706	W 323469	117995	EBAUCHES NON EN ACIER
673	IRON,STEEL SHAPES ETC	W 154447	71807	W 249081	111575	W 387052	158997	W 750324	317699	BARRES,PROFIL FER,ACIER
6731	IRON,STEEL WIRE ROD	W 69313	25307	W 127254	45147	W 224400	72161	W 288360	120567	FIL MACHINE FER,ACIER
67311	IRON,SIMPLE STL WIRE ROD	W 62454	21362	W 114632	37608	W 217845	68456	W 270928	110407	FIL MACH AUT ACIER FIN
6732	IRON,STEEL BARS ETC	W 36499	25783	W 27282	26319	W 64150	37701	W 273374	108731	BARRES FER,ACIER
674	IRN,STL UNIV,PLATE,SHEET	W 477362	272297	W 469640	290366	W 835118	511224	W 844343	489073	LARGES PLATS,TOLES
6744	IRN,STL HVY PLATE,ROLLED	W 123502	49342	W 91708	38147	W 235270	94942	W 260999	102947	TOLES LAMINEES PLUS 4.75 MM
67441	— OF IRON OR SIMPLE STL	W 121911	46740	W 90080	35405	W 233230	90806	W 258249	95954	TOLES NON ACIER FIN CARB
6746	IRN,STL THIN PLATE,ROLLD	W 207015	124429	W 192145	131077	W 301968	213846	W 304257	191197	TOLES LAM MOINS 3MM
67461	— OF IRON OR SIMPLE STL	W 191831	97174	W 169050	90619	W 282066	169328	W 277705	143021	TOL NON AC FIN MOINS 3 MM
6749	OTH IRN,STL PLATES,SHEET	W 65936	46294	W 84023	61052	W 131983	102981	W 132517	104169	AUTRES TOLES FER,ACIER
67491	— OF IRON OR SIMPLE STL	W 61274	39715	W 82087	57877	W 127624	97692	W 128802	100401	AUT TOLES AUTRES ACIER FIN
678	IRON,STL TUBES,PIPES,ETC	W 49638	72434	W 59366	91960	W 51984	64019	W 82590	122317	TUBES,TUYAUX EN FONTE,FER
68	NON-FERROUS METALS		219669		269999		359185		365785	METAUX NON FERREUX
682	COPPER EXC CEMENT COPPER	W 30402	73108	W 38219	99399	W 32239	115538	W 48953	115983	CUIVRE
684	ALUMINIUM	W 49853	88091	W 86653	106732	W 55652	155680	W 66649	162834	ALUMINIUM
6842	ALUMINIUM,ALLOYS WORKED	W 26815	56998	W 18616	59633	W 22387	86849	W 28985	97062	ALUMINIUM,ALLIAGES OUVRE
69	METAL MANUFACTURES NES		388747		424203		325031		474051	ART MANUFACT EN METAL NDA
691	STRUCTURES AND PARTS NES	W 57212	215511	W 60745	205094	W 40632	75630	W 64237	125599	CONSTRUCT FER,ACIER,ALU
6911	STRUCTURES,PARTS IRN,STL	W 57072	215083	W 60452	203725	W 39860	71127	W 62589	119270	CONSTRUCT FER,ACIER,FONTE
699	BASE METAL MFRS NES	W 75460	81259		95578		98297	W 57985	149827	ART MANUFACTURES MET NDA
7	MACHINES,TRANSPORT EQUIP		6139242		7576030		9238044		17955644	MACHINES MATERIEL TRANSPORT
71	POWER GENERATING EQUIPMT		815496		886439		561884		595916	MACHINES GENERATRICES
711	STEAM BOILERS & AUX PLNT	W 4407	59293		21552		10669	W 6532	28559	GENERATEURS VAPEUR EAU ETC
712	STEAM ENGINES,TURBINES	W 5043	92231		367178		73752	W 4764	43423	MACHINES A VAPEUR D'EAU PIEC
7129	STM ENGINE ETC PARTS NES	W 4912	91393	W 20347	359011	W 7993	72084	W 4703	41024	PARTIES,PIECES DU 712.6
713	INTRNL COMBUS PSTN ENGIN	W 74179	195703		293269		293895	W 84222	306681	MOTEURS EXPL COMB INT, PIECE
7132	MOTOR VEHCL PISTN ENGINS	W 55852	59415	N 438603	99533	N 247051	174009	W 65315	174065	MOTEURS EXPL POUR VEHICULES
7138	PISTON ENGINES NES	W 6999	34239	N 208500	97325	N 169944	53273	W 12905	67145	MOTEURS A PISTONS NDA
7139	PISTON ENGINE PARTS NES	W 10411	94035	W 9239	88838	W 5559	59301	W 4902	56238	PIECES POUR 713.2,3,8
714	ENGINES AND MOTORS NES	W 5690	126897		40708		28811	W 2086	19885	MOTEURS NON ELECTRIQUES
7149	ENGINE & MOTOR PARTS NES	W 5047	111093	W 3261	39952	W 1001	28406	W 2085	19857	PIECES 714 ET 718.88
71499	PARTS NES,OF 71488,71888	W 5045	110640	W 3260	39882	W 1000	28351	W 2085	19857	PIECES 714.88 ET 718.88
716	ROTATING ELECTRIC PLANT	W 43275	339558		162602		151780	W 25111	192649	APP ELECTR ROTATIFS,PIECES
7162	AC MTRS,GENRTRS,GEN SETS	W 38411	304052	N 1710991	128770	N 1978786	116862	W 21133	158398	MOTEURS ELECTRIQUES
71623	GEN SETS WITH PISTN ENGN	W 29826	279171	N 6339	93537	N 3625	85370	W 10761	107889	GROUPES MOTEUR EXPLOSION
72	MACHS FOR SPCL INDUSTRYS		635387		893333		1365020		1833336	MAC SPECIALES POUR INDUST
723	CIVIL ENGNEERG EQUIP ETC	W 39972	55700		66157		129950	W 112999	265295	APPAREILS DE GENIE CIVIL
7234	CONST,MINING MACHNRY NES	W 36079	45043	N 7162	47690	N 28638	110438	W 101562	227656	MACH POUR LA CONST, MINES
72342	SLFPRP SHOVELS,EXCAVATRS	W 21171	23161	N 1942	28381	N 3064	63050	W 60964	107861	PELLES MECANIQUES
724	TEXTILE,LEATHER MACHNRY	W 13374	110533		162689		159193	W 13130	117131	MACH POUR INDUSTRIE TEXTILE
727	FOOD MACHRY NON-DOMESTIC	W 4023	35162		68468		90835	W 9952	106814	MACH INDUSTRIES ALIMENT
728	OTH MACHY FOR SPCL INDUS	W 30241	374297		472446		840143	W 67079	1183239	AUT MACH IND PARTICULIERES
7283	OTHR MINERAL WORKG MACHY	W 5036	24806		21346		65454	W 24448	164815	MACH TRIER,CRIBLER,BROYER
7284	MACHY FOR SPCL INDUS NES	W 22792	337333		440678		748507	W 38721	994313	MACH SPEC IND PARTICUL.
72848	OTH MCHY WITH INDIV FNCT	W 6228	108444	N 5	163551	N 40	272751	W 12213	400853	AUTRES MACHINES NDA
72849	PTS OF MACHS OF 7284 ETC	W 5464	168517	W 5194	169465	W 10003	312997	W 11015	421628	PIECES DU 728.4 ETC
73	METALWORKING MACHINERY		104331		91968		210573		281601	MACH TRAVAIL DES METAUX
736	METALWORKING MACH-TOOLS	W 15985	76935		68404		165367	W 28449	223439	MACH-OUTILS TRAVAIL METAUX
74	GENRL INDUSTRL MACHY NES		621086		754113		914660		1265749	MACH APP INDUSTRIE
741	HEATING,COOLING EQUIPMNT	W 18186	124131		164600		199478	W 29845	287809	MACH CHAUFFAGE,PIECES
7416	HEATING,COOLING EQU NES	W 7750	51366		64530		63634	W 9531	110241	APP CHANGEMENT TEMP
742	PUMPS FOR LIQUIDS ETC	W 6609	60479		66846		74546	W 11739	97343	POMPES MOTO-POMPES
743	PUMPS NES,CENTRFUGES ETC	W 17680	99366		127312		174902	W 35616	205606	POMPES COMPRES,VENT ETC
744	MECHANICAL HANDLING EQU	W 31316	129287		165694		187489	W 68505	302319	EQUIP MANUTENTION PIECES
7442	LIFTING,LOADING MACH NES	W 15551	76461	N 254667	86790	N 213193	92390	W 34080	159019	APP LEVAGE,MANUTENTION
745	NONELEC MACHY,TOOLS NES	W 7119	68221		86150		102871	W 10792	140559	AUT MACH NON ELEC,PIECES
7452	OTH NONELEC MCHS,PTS NES	W 6701	64318		81266		97397	W 9605	125578	AUT MACH NON ELEC,PIECES
749	NONELEC MACH PTS,ACC NES	W 16804	139601	W 17916	143512	W 20209	175375	W 26007	232112	PIECES MACH NON ELEC NDA
75	OFFICE MACHNES,ADP EQUIP		280643		341922		541461		1942788	MACH BUREAU TRAIT AUTOM
752	AUTOMTIC DATA PROC EQUIP	W 2993	96906	N 463050	115021	N 768285	172676	W 7614	244055	MACH TRAIT INFORMATION
7525	ADP PERIPHERAL UNITS	W 2424	62660	N 401769	72411	N 688011	95217	W 5612	140760	UNITES PERIPHERIQUES
759	OFFICE,ADP MCH PTS,ACCES	W 4126	149327	W 5268	186303	W 6392	310255	W 15767	1636646	PIECES DU 751 ET 752
7599	ACCTG,ETC,ADP MCH PTS,AC	W 3833	142625	W 4824	176685	W 5925	298117	W 15074	1617941	PIECES DU 751 ET 752
76	TELECOMM,SOUND EQUIPMENT		613130		895313		1321662		2007470	EQUIPMENT DE TELECOM
764	TELECOM EQPT,PTS,ACC NES	W 21338	572818		824637		1205911	W 53410	1917369	EQUIP TELECOM,PIECES
7641	LINE TELEPHONE,ETC EQUIP	W 1587	111781		246766		282736	W 7777	355336	APP TELEPHON PAR FIL
7643	TV,RADIO TRANSMITTRS ETC	W 740	78267		108459		294454	W 10210	323774	APP EMET TELE RADIO
7649	PTS NES OF EQUIPMT OF 76	W 17627	371122		449615		602481	W 32794	1208663	PIECES DE LA DIV 76
76491	PTS NES OF APPAR OF 7641	W 2913	99700	W 5226	135562	W 3466	186736	W 9968	471304	PIECES POUR 764.1
76493	TELECOMM EQUIPMT PTS NES	W 8968	213501		237714		329731	W 14709	574241	PIECES 761,762,764.3,8
76499	PARTS ETC OF SOUND EQUIP	W 2754	42620	W 2890	42005	W 2715	49492	W 3631	125610	PIECES NDA POUR 763
77	ELECTRIC MACHNRY NES ETC		1419139		1802622		2183157		7129099	MACH APP ELECT NDA
771	ELECTRIC POWER MACHY NES	W 12557	100538		100440		113592	W 31722	243640	MACH PROD,TRANS ELECTR
7711	TRANSFORMERS,ELECTRICAL	W 6719	54456	N 4781588	42891	N 7415206	48425	W 21047	109703	TRANSFO ELECTRIQUES
7712	OTH ELEC POWER MACHY NES	W 5837	46082	W 6378	57550	W 6443	65166	W 10675	133937	AUT APP PROD TRANSF ELEC
772	SWITCHGEAR ETC,PARTS NES	W 19720	277986		303474		322535	W 32412	601292	APP COUPURE,SECT ETC
7721	SWITCHGEAR ETC	W 18693	241983		251458		233864	W 22131	389944	APP COUPURE,SECTIONMNT
7722	PRINTED CIRCUITS,PTS NES	W 565	19283	W 1010	23440	W 1418	52946	W 9456	161355	CIRCUITS ET PIECES
773	ELECTR DISTRIBUTNG EQUIP	W 40369	179034	W 38808	243063	W 48644	298544	W 72235	457592	EQUIPMT DISTRIBUTION ELECT
7731	INSULATED WIRE,CABLE ETC	W 25389	100756	W 25464	141415	W 30683	174495	W 49744	335151	FILS,CABLES ISOLES ELECT

4. General Imports C.I.F. by Commodities according to the S.I.T.C. (Rev. 2) in thousand U.S. Dollars
Importations Générales C.A.F. par Produits d'après la C.T.C.I. (Rév. 2) en milliers de Dollars E.U.

SITC CTCI	COMMODITY	1993 WEIGHT POIDS	1993 VALUE VALEUR	1994 WEIGHT POIDS	1994 VALUE VALEUR	1995 WEIGHT POIDS	1995 VALUE VALEUR	1996 WEIGHT POIDS	1996 VALUE VALEUR	PRODUIT
7732	ELECTRC INSULATING EQUIP	W 14980	78278	W 13344	101648	W 17961	124049	W 22491	122441	EQUIP ISOL ELECTRIQUE
77327	OTH ELEC INSUL FITTG NES	W 4017	48586	W 5251	80787	W 5921	96385	W 6861	96206	PIECES ISOL EN AUT MATIERES
776	TRANSISTORS,VALVES,ETC	W 7677	670962		929123		1125539	W 24253	5345845	LAMPES,TUBES,VALVES
7763	DIODES,TRANSISTORS,ETC	W 675	38400	W 570	52350	W 898	92658	W 1151	182535	DIODES,TRANSISTORS
7764	ELECTRONIC MICROCIRCUITS	W 556	107392	W 786	131545	W 781	189179	W 2202	857542	MICROSTRUCTURES ELECTRON
7768	ELCTRNC COMP PTS,CRYSTLS	W 2268	497609		707714	W 3925	787090	W 9815	4238310	CRIST PIEZO–ELEC,PCS 776
77689	ELECTRNIC COMPON PTS NES	W 2209	484272	W 2572	686445	W 3846	735158	W 9725	4200191	PIECES DU GROUPE 776
778	ELECTRICAL MACHINERY NES	W 50273	159856		187161		262668	W 52951	404111	AUTRES MACH ELECT NDA
7788	OTH ELEC MACHY,EQUIP NES	W 9752	93587		112992		162215	W 16282	256803	AUT MACH APP ELEC NDA
77884	ELECTRICAL CONDENSERS	W 1386	42486	W 1722	69495	W 2036	101756	W 2387	159408	CONDENSATEURS ELECTRIQUES
78	ROAD VEHICLES		911354		1096981		1516970		1869914	VEHICULES ROUTIERS
781	PASS MOTOR VEH EXC BUSES	W 72688	402398	N 106959	540534	N 129586	694680	W 112022	785870	AUTO TRANSPORT PERSONNES
782	LORRIES,SPCL MTR VEH NES	W 62358	191567	N 29447	194245	N 60173	251303	W 100525	284271	VEHICULES SPECIAUX,MARCH
7821	LORRIES,TRUCKS	W 50365	163106	N 28787	176671	N 58996	217222	W 78650	228573	VEHICULES TRANSP MARCHAND
783	ROAD MOTOR VEHICLES NES	W 18202	31918	N 2532	37667	N 16904	139913	W 60405	294286	VEHICULES ROUTIERS NDA
7831	BUSES	W 10637	20882	N 1630	21508	N 14951	104927	W 43906	258825	VOITURES TRANSPORT COMMUN
784	MOTOR VEH PRTS,ACCES NES	W 92946	187323		202905		276934	W 163130	300103	PIECES 722,781,782,783
7849	OTHER MOTOR VEHCL PARTS	W 87833	182289	W 243623	187845	W 106183	246772	W 129361	275143	PIECES 722,781,782,783
785	CYCLES,ETC MOTRZD OR NOT	W 18229	89638		112559		138209	W 30658	182993	MOTOCYCLES SCOOTERS
7851	MOTORCYCLES ETC	W 8539	75681	N 106628	86010	N 113899	105966	W 14085	146123	MOTO VELO MOTEUR AUXIL
79	OTHR TRANSPORT EQUIPMENT		738676		813338		622657		1029771	AUTRE MATERIEL TRANSPORT
792	AIRCRAFT ETC	W 1227	622082		140695		468957	W 2855	918225	APP NAVIGATION AERIENNE
7924	AIRCRFT NES OVER 15000KG	W 724	489126	N 2	8120	N 8	271589	W 1950	747355	AERODYNES PLUS 15000 KG
7929	AIRCRAFT PARTS NES	W 470	130225	W 644	118749	W 853	185826	W 778	137944	PIECES DU 792
793	SHIPS AND BOATS ETC	W 48657	110607	N 4091	668016	N 40043	147771	W 63205	100714	NAVIRES BATEAUX,ETC
7938	TUGS,SPECIAL VESSELS ETC	W 6182	81182	N 3751	607002	N 3553	107129	W 3132	47892	REMORQUEURS,BATEAUX SPEC
79382	SPECL PURPOSE VESSLS ETC	W 6051	80490	N 13	606125	N 36	105100	W 2557	45144	BAT–PHARES,–POMPES,DRAGUES
8	MISC MANUFACTURED GOODS		618339		779107		1014498		1527503	ART MANUFACTURES DIVERS
87	PRECISION INSTRUMNTS NES		157554		172400		219526		294628	INSTRUM,APPAR SCIENT NDA
874	MEASURNG,CONTROLNG INSTR	W 3915	114415		119234		158477	W 5666	209678	INSTRUMENTS DE MESURE
88	PHOTO EQU,OPTICL GDS ETC		105876		145378		158244		363885	APP,FOURN PHOTO,OP,MONTR
881	PHOTO APPARAT,EQUIPT NES	W 923	32231		60011		67114	W 1982	185132	APP,EQUIP PHOTO NDA
8811	CAMERAS STILL,FLASH APP	W 270	19434		36581		37656	W 1233	151830	APPAREILS PHOTO,PIECES
88119	PTS NES OF APPAR OF 8811	W 152	16715	W 202	32710	W 238	31700	W 1004	144738	PIECES POUR 881.1
882	PHOTO,CINEMA SUPPLIES	W 6160	56886		66696		68538	W 8497	76088	PRODUITS PHOTO,CINEMA
89	MISC MANUFCTRD GOODS NES		269194		355589		478725		627022	ART MANUFACTURES DIVERS
892	PRINTED MATTER	W 9629	50053		68239		92252	W 14398	104499	IMPRIMES
893	ARTICLES OF PLASTIC NES		90606		118404		171740		264936	OUVRAGES EN MAT DIVIS 58
8939	MISC PLASTIC ARTICLES	W 20218	70014		91674		130108	W 44597	192394	ART DIVERS EN MAT DIV 58
89399	OTHR PLASTC ARTICLES NES	W 16794	66284	W 10890	83477	W 13854	119906	W 36735	181494	AUT OUV MAT DIV 58
9	GOODS NOT CLASSD BY KIND		3012971		4126809		5481830		54935	ART TRANSACT NON CLASSES
931	*SPECIAL TRANSACTIONS	W 4724649	3009870	W 1972407	4120984		5473765			TRANS.SPECIALES

5. General Exports F.O.B. by Commodities according to the S.I.T.C. (Rev. 2) in thousand U.S. Dollars
Exportations Générales F.O.B. par Produits d'après la C.T.C.I. (Rév. 2) en milliers de Dollars E.U.

SITC CTCI	COMMODITY	1993 WEIGHT POIDS	1993 VALUE VALEUR	1994 WEIGHT POIDS	1994 VALUE VALEUR	1995 WEIGHT POIDS	1995 VALUE VALEUR	1996 WEIGHT POIDS	1996 VALUE VALEUR	PRODUIT
	ALL COMMODITIES		11374805		13482896		17447186		20542482	TOUS PRODUITS
0	FOOD AND LIVE ANIMALS		1327550		1329811		1337147		1397589	ALIMENTS,ANIMAUX VIVANTS
03	FISH AND PREPARATIONS		476567		532480		501944		436902	POISSONS ET PREPARATIONS
034	FISH,FRESH,CHILLED,FROZN	W 38058	58351	W 39128	66736	W 41496	84565	W 34899	72815	POISSON FRAIS, REFRIG,CONG
0341	FISH FRSH,CHLLD,EX FILLT	W 23380	36556	W 19156	31339	W 24749	51278	W 20289	40276	POISSON FRAIS,REFRIGERE
036	SHELL FISH FRESH,FROZEN	W 55370	282196	W 38688	310306	W 34498	290957	W 39755	219457	CRUSTACES,MOLLUSQUES
037	FISH ETC PREPD,PRSVD NES	W 73685	133899	W 63224	153219	W 50306	124321	W 73497	142059	POIS,CRUST,MOL PREPARES
0371	FISH PREPARD,PRESRVD NES	W 71801	127440	W 61219	144412	W 48559	115224	W 71103	134244	CONSERVES DE POISSONS
05	VEGETABLES AND FRUIT		600333		571769		581516		632380	LEGUMES ET FRUITS
057	FRUIT,NUTS,FRESH,DRIED	W 1450180	370114		348103		368806	W 1522050	393877	FRUITS FRAIS OU SECS
0573	BANANA,PLANTAIN,FRSH,DRY	W 1153468	226072	W 1155182	215274	W 1213411	223742	W 1253175	236417	BANANES FRAICHES,SECHEES
0577	NUTS EDIBLE,FRESH,DRIED	W 105826	87564		72907		70529	W 78218	86874	FRUITS A COQUES
05771	COCONUTS FRESH OR DRIED	W 101771	85307		72096		69663	W 77914	86641	NOIX DE COCO
0579	FRUIT FRESH OR DRIED NES	W 190885	56477	W 197016	59914	W 213968	74521	W 190653	70577	FRUITS FRAIS,SECS NDA
058	FRUIT PRESERVED,PREPARED	W 405217	200120	W 367333	192591	W 349863	178904	W 441931	202954	CONSERVES DE FRUITS
0585	FRUIT OR VEGETABLE JUICE	W 96728	38413	W 91997	39084	W 101845	43240	W 120544	47254	JUS DE FRUITS
0589	FRUIT PREPRD,PRESRVD,NES	W 295202	147728	W 265466	142912	W 238590	125497	W 311729	144279	FRUITS PREPARES CONSERV
05899	FRUIT,NUTS NES,PRESERVED	W 294072	145840	W 264394	140430	W 237521	122795	W 309823	140524	FRUITS PREP CONSERV NDA
06	SUGAR AND PREPS,HONEY		137741		85101		88769		157843	SUCRES ET PRODUITS
061	SUGAR AND HONEY	W 824663	128096	W 438329	75704	W 246810	74631	W 352837	140102	SUCRES ET MIEL
0611	RAW BEET AND CANE SUGAR	W 324739	102240	W 183013	61410	W 153837	66490	W 319657	136683	SUCRES BRUTS
081	*FEEDING STUFF FOR ANIML	W 509947	55328	W 596210	63040	W 776928	80345	W 512609	71981	NOURRITURE POUR ANIMAUX
0813	OILCAKE AND OTH RESIDUES	W 490791	45441	W 575370	53160	W 757002	66945	W 474568	56281	TOURTEAUX
08137	— OF COCONUT(COPRA)	W 489369	45303	W 574223	53016	W 756343	66872	W 471423	55901	TOURTEAUX DE COPRAH
1	BEVERAGES AND TOBACCO		44382		44637		41842		58696	BOISSONS ET TABACS
12	TOBACCO AND MANUFACTURES		34808		32626		27939		45031	TABACS BRUTS FABRIQUES
2	CRUDE MATERLS,EXCL FUELS		387736		411008		531071		521973	MAT BRUTES NON COMESTIBLES
24	CORK AND WOOD		38921		20646		27064		36650	LIEGE ET BOIS
28	METALLIFEROUS ORES,SCRAP		200314		226684		283529		261510	MINERAIS METAL,DECHETS
281	IRON ORE,CONCENTRATES	W 17506	525	W 10385	454			W 4481872	70159	MINERAIS DE FER
2816	IRON ORE AGGLOMERATES							W 4481872	70159	MINERAIS AGGLOMERES
287	BASE METAL ORES,CONC NES	W 1031786	132076	W 846589	135606	W 1008978	170938	W 1501464	92909	MINERAIS METAUX COMMUNS
2871	CPR ORE ETC,CEMENT COPPR	W 370805	109541	W 309107	113511	W 282284	134228	W 178678	52198	MINERAIS DE CUIVRE,MATTES
28711	COPPER ORES,EXCL MATTE	W 370789	109406	W 309007	113486	W 282266	134222	W 178678	52198	MINERAIS DE CUIVRE
289	PREC MTAL ORES,WASTE NES	K 32880	53444	K 22104	67322	K 22485	64759	K 31613	58934	MINERAIS,DECHETS MET PREC
28901	PRECIOUS METAL ORES,CONC	K 23544	52686	K 22104	67322	K 22485	64759	K 30716	57074	MINERAIS METAUX PRECIEUX
29	CRUDE ANIMAL,VEG MAT NES		54212		64384		93709		104618	MATIERES BRUTES ANIM,VEGET
292	CRUDE VEG MATERIALS NES	W 35139	50698	W 37164	59532	W 43449	89070	W 42616	100558	MAT BRUTES VEGETALES NDA
2929	OTH CRUDE VEG MATERIALS	W 32146	46507	W 34560	56093	W 40455	84225	W 39207	94833	MATIERES VEGETALES NDA
3	MINERAL FUELS ETC		228809		215523		262803		382203	COMBUSTIBLES MINERAUX LUB
33	PETROLEUM AND PRODUCTS		136486		119706		154823		273921	PETROLE ET DERIVES
334	PETROLEUM PRODUCTS,REFIN	W 675932	103311	W 730993	100979	W 960754	143062	W 1517084	272674	PRODUITS RAFFINES
3341	GASOLINE,OTH LIGHT OILS	W 455038	75752	W 579800	77229	W 609510	90644	W 663715	124808	ESSENCES POUR MOTEURS
33419	OTH LIGHT PETROLEUM OILS	W 417357	68141	W 569253	75560	W 562348	82621	W 663715	124808	AUTRES HUILES LEGERES
3343	GAS OILS	W 24613	3838	W 7288	1059	W 107857	22165	W 488717	89658	GAS OILS
341	*GAS,NATURAL AND MANUFCT	W 528636	92323	W 553534	95817	W 491217	107981	W 475775	108281	GAZ NATUREL,GAZ MANUFACT
3413	PETROLM GASES,LIQUEFIED	W 528636	92323	W 553534	95817	W 491217	107981	W 475774	108281	GAZ DE PETROLE LIQUEFIE
34139	OTH HYDROCARBON GAS LQFD	W 500382	86871	W 542825	94056	W 487438	107201	W 474774	108074	HYDROCARBURES GAZEUX NDA
4	ANIMAL,VEGETABLE OIL,FAT		370239		490689		844419		588818	HUILES,GRAISSES ANIM,VEG
42	FIXED VEGETABLE OIL,FAT		358850		475802		826479		570728	HUILES VEGETALES FIXES
424	FIXED VEG OIL NONSOFT	W 860880	358832	W 849465	475802	W 1340768	826479	W 792732	570728	AUTRES HUILES VEG FIXES
4243	COCONUT (COPRA) OIL	W 859208	357608	W 848756	475165	W 1340410	826089	W 792652	570641	HJUILE DE COPRAH
5	CHEMCLS,RELATED PROD NES		257403		298213		329587		342553	PRODUITS CHIMIQUES
51	ORGANIC CHEMICALS		41341		43393		48664		45898	PROD CHIMIQ ORGANIQUES
512	ALCOHOLS,PHENOLS ETC	W 34797	35570	W 31475	38428	W 30639	43390	W 31333	40214	PHENOLS,PHENOLS–ALCOOLS
5121	ACYCLIC ALCOHOLS,DERIVS	W 34797	35569	W 31475	38428	W 30639	43390	W 31314	40167	ALCOOLS ACYCLIQUES
562	*FERTILIZERS,MANUFACTURE	W 555327	85455	W 584602	101250	W 670444	119916	W 583967	104637	ENGRAIS MANUFACTURES
5629	FERTILIZERS NES	W 520805	77947	W 552189	92259	W 641539	110774	W 531133	90751	ENGRAIS NDA
56292	NITROG–PHOS FERTILZR NES	W 239681	33580	W 230305	41853	W 169915	31210	W 98249	20170	ENGRAIS NDA CONT N P
56299	OTHER FERTILIZERS NES	W 150127	20975	W 287984	42220	W 471624	79565	W 432885	70581	AUTRES ENGRAIS NDA
6	BASIC MANUFACTURES		806744		879963		1123957		1298021	ART MANUFACTURES
63	WOOD,CORK MANUFACTRS NES		125504		145873		154328		178161	OUVRAGES LIEGE ET BOIS
635	WOOD MANUFACTURES NES	W 65759	100715		126972		131526	W 79066	159589	ART MANUF EN BOIS NDA
6353	BUILDERS WOODWRK,PREFABS	W 52234	54006		74213		68027	W 55929	93663	OUVRAGES DE MENUISERIE
6354	WOOD MFRS DOMESTIC ETC	W 12258	43689		47857		56532	W 12941	58125	ART MANUF USAGE DOMESTIQUE
64	PAPER,PAPERBOARD AND MFR		32612		33233		54689		55541	PAPIERS,CARTONS & OUVRAGES
65	TEXTILE YARN,FABRICS,ETC		123165		177660		213000		318622	FILS,TISSUS,ARTICLES TEXTILE
651	TEXTILE YARN	W 11568	26430	W 16639	42662	W 17767	49287	W 25674	60117	FILS TEXTILES
655	KNITTED,ETC FABRICS	W 6068	18717	W 12092	43706	W 12171	49790	W 16467	67067	ETOF BONNETERIE PIECES ETC
6552	OTHER KNIT ETC FAB NONEL	W 6068	18717	W 12092	43706	W 12171	49790	W 16467	67067	ETOF BON NON ELAS NON SYNT
658	TEXTILE ARTICLES NES	W 2877	28605		30814		43321	W 10931	81015	ART FACONNES MAT TEXTILES
66	NONMETAL MINERAL MFS NES		86883		96127		108029		103524	ART MIN NON METALLIQUES
666	POTTERY	W 17775	47564	MN 31734	51451	MN 36360	56390	W 21691	57599	POTERIE
67	IRON AND STEEL		54003		56959		60990		87459	FER ET ACIER
68	NON–FERROUS METALS		284735		297783		445909		369130	METAUX NON FERREUX
682	COPPER EXC CEMENT COPPER	W 141567	273268	W 145414	286267	W 148057	430661	W 145878	348740	CUIVRE
6821	COPPER NES,ALLOYS,UNWRT	W 136920	264617	W 137465	269895	W 139637	406318	W 143329	343059	CUIVRE BRUT
68212	COPPER REFINED,UNWROUGHT	W 136920	264617	W 137465	269895	W 139637	406318	W 143329	343059	CUIVRE AFFINE BRUT
69	METAL MANUFACTURES NES		81890		54692		61474		142487	ART MANUFACT EN METAL NDA
691	STRUCTURES AND PARTS NES	W 82716	48518	W 9377	6775	W 6646	7815	W 44152	46202	CONSTRUCT FER,ACIER,ALU
6911	STRUCTURES,PARTS IRN,STL	W 82609	47913	W 6924	5041	W 6589	7381	W 44026	45546	CONSTRUCT FER,ACIER,FONTE
7	MACHINES,TRANSPORT EQUIP		2119307		2906623		3869530		11624031	MACHINES MATERIEL TRANSPORT
72	MACHS FOR SPCL INDUSTRYS		11567		13107		17065		89557	MAC SPECIALES POUR INDUST
74	GENRL INDUSTRL MACHY NES		22304		29408		36992		119513	MACH APP INDUSTRIE
75	OFFICE MACHNES,ADP EQUIP		215033		232932		442613		2772211	MACH BUREAU TRAIT AUTOM
752	AUTOMTIC DATA PROC EQUIP	W 4609	187949	MN 12874	179232	MN 10073	268877	W 15173	1081722	MACH TRAIT INFORMATION
7525	ADP PERIPHERAL UNITS	W 4593	187378	MN 12863	177865	MN 9787	195377	W 14678	1014619	UNITES PERIPHERIQUES
7528	OFF–LINE DATA PROC EQUIP	W 2	173	N 9	33	N 286482	73438	W 317	63337	MACH AUXIL TRAIT INFORM
759	OFFICE,ADP MCH PTS,ACCES	W 253	27004	W 774	53698	W 3553	171981	W 15257	1677297	PIECES DU 751 ET 752
7599	ACCTG,ETC,ADP MCH PTS,AC	W 253	27004	W 774	53698	W 3552	171961	W 14935	1672132	PIECES DU 751 ET 752
76	TELECOMM,SOUND EQUIPMENT		506015		681199		805551		1156755	EQUIPMENT DE TELECOM
761	TELEVISION RECEIVERS	W 1314	17656	N 257341	35609	N 493512	70939	W 10901	121186	RECEPTEURS DE TELEVISION
7611	COLOUR TV RECEIVERS	W 856	12240	N 160920	24697	N 438622	63289	W 10738	115252	RECEPTEURS COULEUR
762	RADIO BROADCAST RECEIVRS	W 3561	69307	N 2448368	120949	N 2575805	119499	W 3717	86533	RECEPTEURS RADIODIFFUSION
7621	MTR VEHC RADIO RECEIVERS	W 546	29525	N 1027979	62848	N 1346291	76955	W 1294	55251	RECEPTEURS RADIO AUTO
7628	OTHER RADIO RECEIVERS	W 2976	39016	N 1413191	58024	N 1229514	42544	W 2339	30311	AUTRES RECEPT RADIO
764	TELECOM EQPT,PTS,ACC NES	W 13773	393501		499851		596139	W 31444	931228	EQUIP TELECOM,PIECES
7641	LINE TELEPHONE,ETC EQUIP	W 3055	65342		105291		150617	W 16636	430456	APP TELEPHON PAR FIL
7643	TV,RADIO TRANSMITTRS ETC	W 5234	173258	N 4752989	193407	N 4231453	190970	W 3575	141825	APP EMET TELE RADIO
7648	TELECOMM EQUIPMENT NES	W 794	57619	N 1228093	61023	N 845575	37239	W 815	38599	APP TELECOM NDA
76483	RADAR APPARATUS ETC	W 625	45733	N 1129744	50274	N 735361	25895	W 622	24604	APP DE RADIOGUIDAGE ETC

5. General Exports F.O.B. by Commodities according to the S.I.T.C. (Rev. 2) in thousand U.S. Dollars
Exportations Générales F.O.B. par Produits d'après la C.T.C.I. (Rév. 2) en milliers de Dollars E.U.

SITC CTCI	COMMODITY	1993 WEIGHT POIDS	1993 VALUE VALEUR	1994 WEIGHT POIDS	1994 VALUE VALEUR	1995 WEIGHT POIDS	1995 VALUE VALEUR	1996 WEIGHT POIDS	1996 VALUE VALEUR	PRODUIT
7649	PTS NES OF EQUIPMT OF 76	W 3101	85165		118170		196269	W 7724	296036	PIECES DE LA DIV 76
76491	PTS NES OF APPAR OF 7641	W 262	13790	W 258	13969	W 673	49592	W 1390	106343	PIECES POUR 764.1
76493	TELECOMM EQUIPMT PTS NES	W 2476	58488		89755		132213	W 5689	154458	PIECES 761,762,764.3,8
77	ELECTRIC MACHNRY NES ETC		1249297		1756637		2313098		7055806	MACH APP ELECT NDA
772	SWITCHGEAR ETC,PARTS NES	W 1354	56788		93960	W 2526	118693	W 5442	252661	APP COUPURE,SECT ETC
7721	SWITCHGEAR ETC	W 434	5176		5765	W 774	12363	W 3370	97671	APP COUPURE,SECTIONMNT
7722	PRINTED CIRCUITS,PTS NES	W 351	20586	W 358	20733	W 568	36139	W 1145	97916	CIRCUITS ET PIECES
7723	FIXED,VARIABLE RESISTORS	W 569	31026	W 1029	67462	W 1184	70191	W 926	57075	POTENTIOMETRES PIECES
773	ELECTR DISTRIBUTNG EQUIP	W 29131	310041	W 38051	450817	W 39213	477454	W 47014	521526	EQUIPMT DISTRIBUTION ELECT
7731	INSULATED WIRE,CABLE ETC	W 25598	303041	W 33407	442636	W 33624	467605	W 41703	513515	FILS,CABLES ISOLES ELECT
776	TRANSISTORS,VALVES,ETC	W 5859	805605		1100297		1586717	W 17350	6126974	LAMPES,TUBES,VALVES
7763	DIODES,TRANSISTORS,ETC	W 2705	197713	W 3369	263780	W 3646	383533	W 5067	682585	DIODES,TRANSISTORS
7764	ELECTRONIC MICROCIRCUITS	W 2854	575033	W 3193	798755	W 4191	1140313	W 11629	5302706	MICROSTRUCTURES ELECTRON
7768	ELCTRNC COMP PTS,CRYSTLS	W 288	32807	W 338	37290	W 322	62869	W 635	141405	CRIST PIEZO–ELEC,PCS 776
77689	ELECTRNIC COMPON PTS NES	W 196	20653	W 244	23530	W 257	49124	W 585	130999	PIECES DU GROUPE 776
778	ELECTRICAL MACHINERY NES	W 10858	30789		47333		65426	W 13113	67344	AUTRES MACH ELECT NDA
78	ROAD VEHICLES		109096		180185		238387		333554	VEHICULES ROUTIERS
784	MOTOR VEH PRTS,ACCES NES	W 9082	96232		165692		208566	W 25309	281669	PIECES 722,781,782,783
7849	OTHER MOTOR VEHCL PARTS	W 8829	95559	W 14488	164883	W 20495	208089	W 25170	281062	PIECES 722,781,782,783
8	MISC MANUFACTURED GOODS		1769289		1983543		2248808		4111050	ART MANUFACTURES DIVERS
821	*FURNITURE,PARTS THEREOF	W 57460	203271		240153		276201	W 74363	294147	MEUBLES ET PIECES
8211	CHAIRS,SEATS AND PARTS	W 10592	42169		47083		56148	W 12637	54870	SIEGES ET PIECES
82111	CHAIRS AND OTHER SEATS	W 10188	41251	N 1132216	45925	N 1236088	55117	W 12298	53877	SIEGES
8219	FURNITURE AND PARTS NES	W 46602	158989		191267		217345	W 61302	235214	AUTRES MEUBLES ET PIECES
82192	WOOD FURNITURE NES	W 8431	37658	N 746306	50861	N 1090926	76478	W 20157	86063	MEUBLES NDA EN BOIS
82199	OTHR FURN,FURN PARTS NES	W 35453	111157		120438		112128	W 33761	119276	MEUBLES NDA AUTRES MATIERES
831	*TRAVEL GOODS,HANDBAGS	W 9710	53736	MN 19264	76077	MN 27221	110213	W 32226	180546	ARTICLES DE VOYAGE ETC
83102	TRAVEL GDS,TOILET–CASES	W 6315	30440	N 8715312	53452	MN 9469	68325	W 21004	104732	ARTICLES DE VOYAGE
83109	OTHER TRAVEL BAGS,CASES	W 2515	17507	N 8193615	13600	MN 11470	23986	W 8971	62941	AUT CONTENANTS SIMILAIRES
84	CLOTHING AND ACCESSORIES		868334		924749		1091907		2411806	VETEMENTS
842	MENS OUTERWEAR NOT KNIT	W 7949	110395	MN 18929	129137	MN 22198	147801	W 24839	378603	VET DESSUS POUR HOMMES
8423	— TROUSERS,BREECHES ETC	W 4833	57687	MN 12311	66166	MN 14730	81793	W 14312	195915	PANTALONS HOMMES MAT TEX
8424	— JACKETS,BLAZERS ETC	W 2057	34932	N 3456380	43529	N 3650329	43320	W 6055	102680	VESTES HOMMES MAT TEXTIL
843	WOMENS OUTERWEAR NONKNIT		163392	MN 40950	193343	MN 61863	264167	W 45129	721598	VET DESSUS FEMMES MAT TEX
8431	— COATS AND JACKETS	W 1585	28542	N 2218090	26952	N 1437010	19533	W 3965	76381	MANT,VEST FEM MAT TEXTIL
8433	— DRESSES	W 1509	23892	N 7016434	41876	MN 10873	65174	W 9976	160619	ROBES EN MAT–TEXTILES
8439	— OTHER OUTER GARMENTS		85150	MN 26183	101971	MN 41275	142014	W 23747	357607	AUT VET DES FEM MAT TEXT
844	UNDER GARMENTS NOT KNIT	W 2396	41135	N 6420812	38534		56272	W 11135	179191	VETEMENT DESSOUS MAT TEX
8441	— MENS SHIRTS	W 1647	29932	N 4287033	25114		41219	W 7327	123357	CHEMISES HOMMES MAT TEXT
84411	—— OF COTTON	W 1499	27428	N 3080261	19939	N 3474613	24412	W 4667	86843	CHEMISES HOMMES DE COTON
845	OUTERWEAR KNIT NONELASTC	W 26573	304666	MN 90745	314557	MN 98691	343682	W 41054	514706	VET DESSOUS,ACCES BONNET
8451	— JERSEYS,PULLOVERS ETC	W 5011	69133	MN 15322	82070	MN 14350	82141	W 7804	106537	CHANDAILS,PULL–OVERS ETC
8459	— OTHER,CLTHG ACCESRYS	W 20024	218384	MN 71690	218210	MN 79203	241291	W 30240	367897	AUT VET DESSUS DE BONNE
846	UNDER GARMENTS KNITTED	W 18945	181798	MN 68829	173849	MN 71568	198956	W 29432	423505	SOUS VETS DE BONNETERIE
8462	— OF COTTON NON ELASTIC	W 12762	112339	MN 42365	87472	MN 31572	70621	W 16641	220554	SOUS–VET BONNET COTON
84621	—— MENS SHIRTS							W 11536	162499	CHEMISES DE COTON
84629	—— OTHER	W 12762	112339	MN 42365	87472	MN 31572	70621	W 5105	58055	AUT SOUS–VET BONNET COTON
8463	— OF SYNTH FBR NONELAST	W 6124	67825	MN 24560	83759	MN 38277	126641	W 9358	100399	SOUS–VET BONNET FIB SYNT
84632	—— MENS SHIRTS	W 6119	67776	MN 23028	82394	MN 35093	124445	W 9237	98819	CHEMISES DE BON FIB SYNMT
8465	CORSETS,GARTERS,ETC	W 59	1634	N 1904164	2618	N 1718849	1695	W 3433	102553	CORSETS,GAINES ART SIM
84651	BRASSIERES	W 55	1494	N 1696301	2079	N 631781	1114	W 2925	87931	SOUTIENS–GORGE,BUSTIERS
848	HEADGEAR,NONTXTL CLOTHNG	W 3093	51745		48941		46266	W 8113	134190	VET ACCES MAT AUT QUE TEX
8481	LEATHER CLOTHES,ACCESSOR	W 1656	40189		35725		32100	W 2426	70648	VET ACCES MAT CUIR ARTIF
851	*FOOTWEAR	W 15814	142144	MP 26516	175816	MP 21430	153894	W 15977	167807	CHAUSSURES
85102	FOOTWEAR LEATHER	W 9510	85173	MP 12020	72823	MP 9082	63082	W 13557	148472	CHAUS SEMELLES EN CUIR
85103	SHOES WOOD–,CORK–SOLED	W 3387	39371	MP 9241	91687	P 7396028	80404	W 74	436	CHAUS SEMELLES BOIS,LIEGE
87	PRECISION INSTRUMNTS NES		22958		21160		26848		78894	INSTRUM,APPAR SCIENT NDA
88	PHOTO EQU,OPTICL GDS ETC		11517		35297		34583		338082	APP,FOURN PHOTO,OP,MONTR
881	PHOTO APPARAT,EQUIPT NES	W 45	2827		24638		22693	W 774	175034	APP,EQUIP PHOTO NDA
8811	CAMERAS STILL,FLASH APP	W 35	2239		22634		21892	W 694	169120	APPAREILS PHOTO,PIECES
88111	STILL CAMERAS	W 28	1450	N 342219	22587	N 326016	21705	W 526	142202	APPAREILS PHOTOGRAPHIQ
885	WATCHES AND CLOCKS		754		715		1194		151371	HORLOGERIE
8851	WATCHES,MOVEMENTS,CASES		672		231		1018		119675	MONTRES,MOUVEMENTS,BOITES
88511	WATCHES		508		14		32		107893	MONTRES POCHE,BRACELET
89	MISC MANUFCTRD GOODS NES		452027		492325		537282		619041	ART MANUFACTURES DIVERS
893	ARTICLES OF PLASTIC NES		42206		50178		75920		109597	OUVRAGES EN MAT DIVIS 58
8939	MISC PLASTIC ARTICLES	W 10868	24134		29590		44805	W 29101	72439	ART DIVERS EN MAT DIV 58
89399	OTHR PLASTC ARTICLES NES	W 8362	21680	W 11656	27466	W 16228	42263	W 26075	69255	AUT OUV MAT DIV 58
894	TOYS,SPORTING GOODS,ETC	W 18735	137061		165734		206833	W 28914	246719	VOITURES ENFANTS,JOUETS
8942	TOYS,INDOOR GAMES ETC	W 16470	119342		141418		169373	W 24551	202180	JOUETS,JEUX ETC
89425	XMAS DECORATIONS ETC	W 10421	77480		96633		123533	W 17310	133677	ART DIVERTIS,FETES
897	GOLD,SILVER WARE,JEWELRY		54786		50510		29526		22926	BIJOUTERIE,ORFEVRERIE
8972	IMITATION JEWELLERY		51423		46659		25085		17759	BIJOUTERIE DE FANTAISIE
899	OTHER MANUFACTURED GOODS		207434		210719		201736		195076	AUT ART MANUF DIVERS NDA
8997	BASKETWORK,BROOMS ETC	W 35881	132154		134372		124948	W 27307	102125	OUVRAGES VANNERIE NDA
89971	BASKETWORK,WICKERWRK,ETC	W 35750	131929	MN 95329	134154	MN 89429	124675	W 27188	101627	OUVRAGES DE VANNERIE
9	GOODS NOT CLASSD BY KIND		4063346		4922884		6858023		217548	ART TRANSACT NON CLASSES
931	*SPECIAL TRANSACTIONS	W 4262093	3898218	W 5127154	4707441		6659455	W 1	2	TRANS.SPECIALES
971	*GOLD,NON MONETARY NES	K 49846	162711	K 61902	212091	K 50237	195672	K 60238	214913	OR NON MONETAIRE
97101	NONMON GLD UNWRT,SEMIMFD	K 49308	160623	K 61239	209458	K 50131	195459	K 60199	214628	OR,ALLIAGES D'OR BRUTS

1. HISTORICAL SERIES, 1961–1996 GENERAL TRADE, IMPORTS F.O.B., EXPORTS F.O.B.
SERIES HISTORIQUES, 1961–1996 COMMERCE GENERAL, IMPORTATIONS F.O.B., EXPORTATIONS F.O.B

YEAR ANNEE	VALUE IN MILLION U.S. DOLLARS VALEUR EN MILLION U.S. DOLLARS — MERCHANDISE –MARCHANDISE		GOLD –OR		CONVERSION FACTORS FACTEURS DE CONVERSION CENTS E.U. PAR		INDEX NUMBERS –INDICES — QUANTUM		UNIT VALUE VALEUR UNITAIRE	
	IMPORTS	EXPORTS	IMPORTS	EXPORTS	IMPORTS	EXPORTS	IMPORTS	EXPORTS	IMPORTS	EXPORTS
1961	1686.80	1503.50					27	15		
1962	1885.50	1646.30					30	17		
1963	1979.00	1770.00					31	18		
1964	2072.30	2096.50					32	21		
1965	2340.30	2227.80					37	22		
1966	2494.00	2272.00					40	23		
1967	2644.80	2526.50					43	26		
1968	2853.00	2857.80					47	30		
1969	3209.80	3141.50					47	33		
1970	3607.50	3547.80					57	36		
1971	4037.80	3872.30					65	38		
1972	5335.30	4932.00					80	43		
1973	7813.20	6373.60					98	48		
1974	10481.70	8315.10					112	54		
1975	12537.00	10282.50					117	59		
1976	13867.40	11016.60					129	62		
1977	14616.00	12265.10					129	66		
1978	16088.90	13667.10					131	70		
1979	17583.90	16249.00					130	75		
1980	19089.10	16996.90					127	72		
1981	12043.00	14508.00					106	58		
1982	10244.00	11172.00					91	63		
1983	10590.00	11572.00					96	70		
1984	10638.00	11750.00					104	76		
1985	10799.00	11488.00					113	77		
1986	11208.00	12074.00					118	81		
1987	10844.00	12205.00					124	85		
1988	12240.00	13956.00					136	92		
1989	10085.00	13155.00					138	94	14	16
1990	8413.00	13627.00					100	100	100	100
1991	15757.00	14903.00					156	103	136	118
1992	15701.00	13324.00								
1993	18834.00	14143.00					210	96	182	191
1994	21383.01	17042.00					238	114	231	246
1995	29050.00	22892.00								
1996	36965.89	24410.48								

2. IMPORTS BY BROAD ECONOMIC CATEGORY AND EXPORTS BY INDUSTRIAL ORIGIN. (PERCENTAGE OF TOTAL VALUE)
IMPORTATIONS PAR CATEGORIES ECONOMIQUES ET EXPORTATIONS PAR BRANCHE D'ACTIVITE.(EN POURCENTAGE DE LA VALEUR TOTALE)

IMPORTS – IMPORTATIONS

	1990	1991	1992	1993	1994	1995	1996
TOTAL IMPORTS–IMPORTATIONS TOTALES	100.	100.	100.	100.	100.	100.	100.
1 FOOD BEV–ALIMENTATION BOISSONS	5.1	8.9	9.4	8.9	8.5	7.7	8.1
11 PRIMARY–PRODUITS DE BASE	2.1	4.9	5.2	5.5	5.2	4.4	5.1
111 FOR INDUSTRY–POUR L'INDUSTRIE	0.8	1.4	2.0	2.4	2.0	2.1	2.9
112 FOR HOUSEHOLDS–POUR LES MENAGES	1.3	3.6	3.2	3.1	3.1	2.3	2.3
12 PROCESSED–PRODUITS ELABORES	2.9	4.0	4.3	3.4	3.3	3.3	3.0
121 FOR INDUSTRY–POUR L'INDUSTRIE	0.2	0.2	0.8	0.8	0.8	0.8	0.8
122 FOR HOUSEHOLDS–POUR LES MENAGES	2.7	3.8	3.5	2.6	2.5	2.4	2.1
2 IND SUPPLIES–APPROV INDUSTRIELS	23.5	16.9	27.5	33.9	37.7	39.5	36.2
21 PRIMARY–PRODUITS DE BASE	5.9	3.8	4.7	4.5	4.4	4.5	3.9
22 PROCESSED–PRODUITS ELABORES	17.6	13.1	22.9	29.3	33.3	35.0	32.2
3 FUELS–COMBUSTIBLES	21.9	18.8	16.7	12.3	10.4	9.2	9.2
31 PRIMARY–PRODUITS DE BASE	16.5	14.9	13.3	10.3	8.6	7.3	7.2
32 PROCESSED–PRODUITS ELABORES	5.4	3.9	3.4	2.0	1.9	1.8	2.0
321 MOTOR SPIRIT–ESSENCE			2.0	0.0	0.9		
322 OTHER–AUTRES	5.4	3.9	1.4	2.0	1.0	1.8	2.0
4 MACHINERY–EQUIPEMENT	25.0	21.1	23.8	22.6	22.7	22.9	23.8
41 CAPITAL EQUIPMENT–MACHINES	24.1	20.6	21.1	19.4	19.4	19.4	20.3
42 PARTS–PIECES ACCESSOIRES	0.9	0.5	2.7	3.3	3.3	3.5	3.5
5 TRANSPORT–TRANSPORT	5.9	8.5	6.1	7.2	6.9	7.4	9.4
51 PASSENGER CARS–AUTOMOBILES			2.0	2.3	1.8	1.6	2.5
52 OTHER–AUTRES	1.3	1.1	1.6	1.7	1.4	1.1	1.3
521 INDUSTRIAL–INDUSTRIELS	1.3	1.1	1.5	1.6	1.2	1.0	1.2
522 NON INDUSTRIAL–NON INDUSTRIEL			0.0	0.1	0.1	0.1	0.1
53 PARTS–PIECES ACCESSOIRES	4.7	7.4	2.5	3.1	3.8	4.7	5.5
6 CONSUM GOODS–BIENS CONSOMMATION	9.9	15.2	14.2	13.5	13.7	12.8	13.0
61 DURABLE–DURABLES	3.0	3.9	3.2	2.7	2.7	2.6	2.9
62 SEMI DURABLE–SEMI DURABLES	3.9	6.5	5.3	5.3	5.7	5.4	5.5
63 NON DURABLE–NON DURABLES	3.0	4.8	5.6	5.4	5.3	4.8	4.6
7 GOODS NES–BIENS NDA	0.0	0.0	0.1	0.1	0.1	0.5	0.1

EXPORTS – EXPORTATIONS

	1990	1991	1992	1993	1994	1995	1996
TOTAL EXPORTS–EXPORTATIONS TOTALES	100.	100.	100.	100.	100.	100.	100.
1 AGRICULTURE	5.9	8.4	7.1	4.2	3.6	3.5	2.8
2 MINING QUARRY–INDUS EXTRACTIVES	10.6	10.8	11.2	9.5	8.8	7.9	6.4
3 MANUFACTURING–IND MANUFACTUR	79.4	74.1	79.7	84.7	87.6	88.7	90.8
31 FOOD BEV TOBACCO–ALIM BOISS TAB	6.6	6.0	8.5	8.2	9.0	7.8	8.8
32 TEXTILES–INDUSTRIES TEXTILES	6.1	6.2	8.4	15.3	14.7	14.0	13.7
33 WOOD & PRODUCTS–BOIS & PRODUITS	1.3	3.1	3.4	3.4	3.8	3.6	3.3
34 PAPER & PRODUCTS–PAPIER & PRODT	0.8	0.9	1.5	1.4	1.7	2.8	2.7
35 CHEMICALS–INDUSTRIES CHIMIQUES	10.6	10.4	11.1	9.3	9.8	11.2	11.4
36 NON METAL MIN–MIN NON METAL	1.5	3.0	2.6	2.8	3.0	2.8	2.9
37 BASIC METAL–IND METAL BASE	13.6	13.5	15.0	13.9	13.8	12.3	10.3
38 METAL MANUF–MANUF METAL	32.3	25.2	28.3	29.6	30.4	32.9	36.2
39 OTH MANUF IND–AUTRES MANUF	10.5	12.6	3.0	2.4	1.4	1.4	1.5

3. TRADE BY PRINCIPAL COUNTRIES OF PURCHASE AND SALE (VALUE IN THOUSAND U.S. DOLLARS)
ECHANGES SELON LES PRINCIPAUX PAYS D'ACHAT ET DE VENTE (VALEUR EN MILLIERS DE DOLLARS EU)

COUNTRIES–PAYS	GENERAL IMPORTS F.O.B. IMPORTATIONS GENERALES F.O.B.				
	1992	1993	1994	1995	1996
World	15894136	18845337	21433480	29019476	37094949
Africa	187961	256462	305477	472053	474423
Americas	787211	1268713	1145277	1673155	2520876
Northern America	595446	1073073	816760	1252347	1829072
LAIA	168187	168787	311153	376843	627676
CACM	18295	22366	11778	36061	55342
Caribbean	3214	2126	3649	4641	5604
Rest of America	2069	2361	1937	3263	3182
As.ex F.USSR	1678738	1741522	1769669	2513904	3517190
Eur.x F.USSR	11336124	13740241	15466069	21519803	27012431
EU	9850301	12206120	13707542	18781594	23739197
EFTA	661972	685036	725129	901913	939196
East Europe	703939	719626	902308	1677231	2112276
Other Europe	900	1662	1494	2193	1808
Former USSR	1884555	1809132	2062542	2798516	3512449
Oceania	19354	29267	26229	42045	57580
Germany/Allemagne	3797962	5289365	5843929	7736568	9166315
Italy/Italie	1097893	1469154	1778451	2482609	3688226
Russian Federation	1351002	1271250	1439965	1959786	2525849
United Kingdom	1055570	1085036	1102932	1502689	2186877
France,Monac	705717	803743	937784	1421232	2027855
Netherlands/Pays–Bas	757035	876979	956927	1317979	1413016
USA/Etats–Unis d'Amer	538163	1000293	754206	1140398	1645926
Austria/Autriche	720917	613537	525515	737848	815366
Sweden/Suède	303648	421617	578846	909468	996874
Belgium–Luxembourg	400602	434059	513786	766941	950809
Czech Republic		350293	474511	891721	1150479
Denmark/Danemark	335389	455991	492576	635008	811800
Finland/Finlande	378834	383287	505773	540517	610838
Japan/Japon	334655	329632	335009	478652	604796
Switz.Liecht	306077	327982	354174	504242	557445
Spain/Espagne	190508	253533	326691	473417	757091
China/Chine	157946	224912	296107	465088	734797
Norway,SVD,JM	354864	355761	367888	393161	373899
Korea, Republic of	112253	165230	200087	262980	665355
Hungary/Hongrie	143554	165510	210352	352242	425988
Ukraine	161893	198975	194585	290760	418458
Slovakia		161450	185319	380803	432546
Iran (Islamic Rp. of)	400002	297015	180879	158055	28661
Belarus/Bélarus	161154	113935	157394	238397	257392
Brazil/Brésil	52372	58371	125424	154644	331145
Ireland/Irlande	46194	66594	82960	151414	189673
Singapore/Singapour	81808	86450	73910	129163	164573
Czechoslovakia	503456				
Canada	57005	72676	62554	111949	182804
Indonesia/Indonésie	35447	66342	88163	119710	166873
India/Inde	64253	75526	82382	108091	139913
Slovenia/Slovénia	4827	82056	86362	103565	151497
Hong Kong	87800	77560	63118	87209	92068
Turkey/Turquie	80461	64980	84597	76119	93160
Lithuania/Lituanie	57022	90430	71817	66704	109655
Uzbekistan/Ouzbékistan	47033	41038	78586	120488	108453
Thailand/Thaïlande	60716	34483	41802	86951	101584
Greece/Grèce	55111	47624	54287	79273	77212
Cote d'Ivoire	35327	38227	51277	89936	85060
Malaysia/Malaisie	11239	22346	38045	78198	137081
Ecuador/Equateur	28305	28771	68918	81167	78385
Kazakhstan	62696	44241	73673	61097	34738
So. Africa Customs Un	30954	39453	35033	78051	79284
Israel/Israël	24820	39298	32626	66066	84673
Argentina/Argentine	40478	35941	34795	22854	88009
Algeria/Algérie	2099	13359	26609	92376	80807
Croatia/Croatie	881	36737	38962	47580	52575
Colombia/Colombie	24718	21499	38496	32687	49890
Romania/Roumanie	30377	19963	14932	25307	70595
Morocco/Maroc	21879	22283	30459	38314	42121

COUNTRIES–PAYS	GENERAL EXPORTS F.O.B. EXPORTATIONS GENERALES F.O.B.				
	1992	1993	1994	1995	1996
Monde	13164571	14044104	17194369	22862130	24393116
Afrique	359146	380920	288051	303087	330375
Amériques	661104	666739	1024771	999856	914544
Amérique du Nord	343205	454980	729952	688914	678149
ALAI	234387	186380	210189	211085	183986
MCAC	7949	10817	3538	9689	9092
Caraïbes	51266	7247	77207	80553	15125
Autre Amérique	24297	7315	3885	9615	28192
Asie l'URSS exclus	966471	995232	1012426	1075373	1217904
Europe l'URSS exclus	9905687	10865500	12933382	17855202	18497408
UE	8642179	9761824	11752352	16038667	16250233
AELE	353672	266099	269813	359656	535604
Europe de l'Est	779449	757844	838625	1349683	1561584
Autre de l'Europe	7802	3598	3783	6352	6807
Ancienne URSS	1246844	1105064	1484015	2604062	3404341
Océanie	25291	30392	22087	24550	28544
Germany/Allemagne	4132662	5117312	6114637	8777546	8417332
Russian Federation	723298	644459	902910	1274249	1653799
Netherlands/Pays–Bas	790587	825694	996888	1288604	1169561
Italy/Italie	727563	740605	842247	1124267	1356873
United Kingdom	567004	609407	769683	916894	960795
France,Monac	478524	593811	672446	819164	1077416
Denmark/Danemark	330471	418897	534241	688157	742962
USA/Etats–Unis d'Amer	304211	407410	582886	622704	563653
Ukraine	188170	184896	257430	742620	977716
Czech Republic		342538	429441	698197	847219
Belgium–Luxembourg	355852	369463	414153	564079	607861
Sweden/Suède	328916	307145	426370	580977	582563
Austria/Autriche	421469	339833	366650	489001	484109
Finland/Finlande	259222	195928	293129	352810	315401
Hungary/Hongrie	171002	174222	172477	267362	310203
Switz.Liecht	188088	186805	159815	207951	225916
Slovakia		166720	169163	279383	280040
Spain/Espagne	117869	101535	171280	249821	249706
Belarus/Bélarus	158790	103195	114983	240634	272394
Norway,SVD,JM	159309	76891	107669	147064	299220
Lithuania/Lituanie	36377	45619	95964	189401	230289
Brazil/Brésil	105514	106396	128837	121677	100046
Thailand/Thaïlande	91342	70711	101534	94205	145173
Czechoslovakia	498038				
Greece/Grèce	47462	64597	61591	95348	182560
Cyprus/Chypre	42037	14525	165611	97974	66089
Morocco/Maroc	74754	56891	60032	101104	55076
China/Chine	49211	164860	61431	35419	33717
Ireland/Irlande	72930	63349	62998	54387	64863
Turkey/Turquie	87498	62171	31861	74422	58613
Egypt/Egypte	86737	43193	49656	60605	70151
Canada	38980	45094	58694	66210	84781
Korea, Republic of	24001	40578	39602	55297	121568
India/Inde	52411	42098	40492	80200	51381
Romania/Roumanie	66542	36357	27165	57609	73777
Singapore/Singapour	36523	48486	54460	57013	58350
Japan/Japon	67737	48717	36501	42873	52130
Iran (Islamic Rp. of)	110927	33726	23499	31758	24059
Hong Kong	33161	35093	58756	51013	43563
Liberia/Libéria	16363	117899	19576	1203	63847
Latvia/Lettonie	15066	23744	36548	61290	80774
Bulgaria/Bulgarie	43567	31600	39826	46137	47882
Yugoslavia/Yougoslavie	121480	10801	10754	8318	36618
Saudi Arabia	23011	27163	22319	38148	46298
United Arab Emirates	29564	7260	11517	32549	74470
Bahamas	40041	150	58512	49133	3045
Kazakhstan	23235	32143	23905	32745	36812
Mexico/Mexique	45165	34204	28013	24361	9919
Philippines	34948	27364	21529	18546	37474
Malaysia/Malaisie	15829	10018	15333	35674	61056

(VALUE AS PERCENTAGE OF WORLD TOTAL)(VALEURS EN POURCENTAGE DU TOTAL MONDIAL)

	1987	1988	1989	1990	1991	1992	1993	1994	1995	1996
Africa	0.6	0.5	0.5	0.5	0.4	1.2	1.4	1.4	1.6	1.3
Americas	4.3	4.8	3.8	2.7	3.2	5.0	6.7	5.3	5.8	6.8
Northern America	1.4	2.1	1.6	1.8	2.5	3.7	5.7	3.8	4.3	4.9
LAIA	2.5	2.5	2.0	0.8	0.6	1.1	0.9	1.5	1.3	1.7
CACM	0.0	0.0	0.0	0.0	0.0	0.1	0.1	0.1	0.1	0.1
Caribbean	0.3	0.2	0.2	0.0	0.0	0.0	0.0	0.0	0.0	0.0
Rest of America	0.1	0.0	0.0	0.0	0.0	0.0	0.0	0.0	0.0	0.0
As.ex F.USSR	7.3	7.8	9.0	9.2	11.3	10.6	9.2	8.3	8.7	9.5
Eur.x F.USSR	52.2	61.3	67.1	66.8	70.7	71.3	72.9	72.2	74.2	72.8
EU	28.2	35.6	42.6	51.4	59.0	62.0	64.8	64.0	64.7	64.0
EFTA	4.2	5.2	6.3	7.9	5.5	4.2	3.6	3.4	3.1	2.5
East Europe	16.0	17.2	14.1	5.4	4.9	4.4	3.8	4.2	5.8	5.7
Other Europe	3.7	3.3	4.1	2.1	1.3	0.0	0.0	0.0	0.0	0.0
Former USSR	24.7	23.3	18.1	19.8	14.1	11.9	9.6	9.6	9.6	9.5
Oceania	1.3	1.4	1.1	0.4	0.2	0.1	0.2	0.1	0.1	0.2
Germany/Allemagne	10.5	13.3	16.1	20.1	26.5	23.9	28.1	27.3	26.7	24.7
Italy/Italie	2.5	3.3	4.1	7.5	4.5	6.9	7.8	8.3	8.6	9.9
Russian Federation						8.5	6.7	6.7	6.8	6.8
United Kingdom	3.2	4.2	4.5	5.7	4.0	6.6	5.8	5.1	5.2	5.9
France,Monac	2.3	2.5	3.1	3.0	3.6	4.4	4.3	4.4	4.9	5.5
Netherlands/Pays–Bas	1.7	2.7	3.0	2.6	4.9	4.8	4.7	4.5	4.5	3.8
USA/Etats–Unis d'Amer	1.3	2.0	1.4	1.6	2.3	3.4	5.3	3.5	3.9	4.4
Austria/Autriche	3.6	4.4	6.0	5.7	6.3	4.5	3.3	2.5	2.5	2.2
Sweden/Suède	1.2	1.6	1.7	2.0	1.8	1.9	2.2	2.7	3.1	2.7
Belgium–Luxembourg	1.3	1.4	1.5	1.4	2.8	2.5	2.3	2.4	2.6	2.6

	1987	1988	1989	1990	1991	1992	1993	1994	1995	1996
Afrique	2.2	2.7	2.5	2.3	2.0	2.7	2.7	1.7	1.3	1.4
Amériques	4.8	4.6	4.7	4.7	4.2	5.0	4.7	6.0	4.4	3.7
Amérique du Nord	3.1	3.1	3.3	3.2	2.9	2.6	3.2	4.2	3.0	2.8
ALAI	1.3	1.3	0.9	1.4	1.2	1.8	1.3	1.2	0.9	0.8
MCAC	0.0	0.0	0.0	0.0	0.0	0.1	0.1	0.0	0.0	0.0
Caraïbes	0.3	0.2	0.2	0.1	0.0	0.4	0.1	0.4	0.4	0.1
Autre Amérique	0.0	0.0	0.3	0.0	0.1	0.2	0.1	0.0	0.0	0.1
Asie l'URSS exclus	7.6	7.6	8.8	7.5	5.1	7.3	7.1	5.9	4.7	5.0
Europe l'URSS exclus	51.6	57.8	60.7	68.9	76.8	75.2	77.4	75.2	78.1	75.8
UE	32.5	35.4	40.3	54.8	64.1	65.6	69.5	68.4	70.2	66.6
AELE	2.6	3.3	3.4	5.7	5.5	2.7	1.9	1.6	1.6	2.2
Europe de l'Est	13.7	16.2	14.0	6.8	5.8	5.9	5.4	4.9	5.9	6.4
Autre de l'Europe	2.7	2.8	3.1	1.6	1.4	0.1	0.0	0.0	0.0	0.0
Ancienne URSS	21.3	24.5	20.8	15.3	11.0	9.5	7.9	8.6	11.4	14.0
Océanie	0.2	0.2	0.2	0.2	0.1	0.2	0.2	0.1	0.1	0.1
Germany/Allemagne	10.7	13.1	14.8	25.1	29.3	31.4	36.4	35.6	38.4	34.5
Russian Federation						5.5	4.6	5.3	5.6	6.8
Netherlands/Pays–Bas	1.8	2.2	2.6	3.1	5.2	6.0	5.9	5.8	5.6	4.8
Italy/Italie	2.9	2.3	2.3	2.9	4.1	5.5	5.3	4.9	4.9	5.6
United Kingdom	4.3	5.0	6.5	7.1	7.1	4.3	4.3	4.5	4.0	3.9
France,Monac	2.3	2.3	2.4	3.2	3.8	3.6	4.2	3.9	3.6	4.4
Denmark/Danemark	1.2	1.3	1.4	1.8	2.3	2.5	3.0	3.1	3.0	3.0
USA/Etats–Unis d'Amer	2.6	2.6	2.8	2.8	2.5	2.3	2.9	3.4	2.7	2.3
Ukraine						1.4	1.3	1.5	3.2	4.0
Czech Republic							2.4	2.5	3.1	3.5

4. General Imports F.O.B. by Commodities according to the S.I.T.C. (Rev. 2) in thousand U.S. Dollars
Importations Générales F.O.B. par Produits d'après la C.T.C.I. (Rév. 2) en milliers de Dollars E.U.

SITC CTCI	COMMODITY	1993		1994		1995		1996		PRODUIT
		WEIGHT POIDS	VALUE VALEUR	WEIGHT POIDS	VALUE VALEUR	WEIGHT POIDS	VALUE VALEUR	WEIGHT POIDS	VALUE VALEUR	
	ALL COMMODITIES		18845337		21433480		29019476		37094949	TOUS PRODUITS
0	FOOD AND LIVE ANIMALS		1819044		1868372		2327015		3137000	ALIMENTS,ANIMAUX VIVANTS
01	MEAT AND PREPARATIONS		167431		206700		140852		189327	VIANDES ET PREPARATIONS
011	MEAT FRESH,CHILLD,FROZEN	W 157738	162732	W 190994	203054	W 96907	133282	W 118784	177766	VIANDES FRAICHES,REF,CONGE
0113	PIG MEAT FRESH,CHLD,FRZN	W 47365	69214	W 97803	114678	W 46178	76071	W 36523	79141	VIANDE DE PORC
0114	POULTRY FRESH CHLLD,FRZN	W 72595	60431	W 58314	59404	W 31095	35265	W 44017	51078	VOLAILLES MORTES
02	DAIRY PRODCTS,BIRDS'EGGS		89963		49575		40161		44535	PRODUITS LAITIERS,OEUFS
03	FISH AND PREPARATIONS		125981		169018		181053		241376	POISSONS ET PREPARATIONS
034	FISH,FRESH,CHILLED,FROZN	W 146304	92057	W 182450	136367	W 170010	140992	W 198491	203828	POISSON FRAIS, REFRIG,CONG
0342	FISH FROZEN,EXCL FILLETS	W 108225	56314	W 135477	81622	W 133813	92951	W 151763	135691	POISSONS CONGELES
04	CEREALS AND PREPARATIONS		423106		124953		323880		856638	CEREALES ET PRODUITS
041	WHEAT ETC UNMILLED	W 818054	104021	W 207540	35617	W 976617	125195	W 2187478	452954	FROMENT,EPEAUTRE
0412	OTHER WHEAT ETC UNMILLED	W 546277	67039	W 82469	7781	W 859474	103602	W 2142031	441306	AUTRE FROMENT NON MOULU
043	BARLEY UNMILLED	W 675480	76658	W 100953	7359	W 679963	56178	W 595766	100910	ORGE NON MONDEE
044	MAIZE UNMILLED	W 926688	118652	W 93027	13611	W 198930	29696	W 609352	118767	MAIS NON MOULU
05	VEGETABLES AND FRUIT		278463		308412		388298		485431	LEGUMES ET FRUITS
054	VEG ETC FRSH,SMPLY PRSVD	W 256725	65901	W 169016	64916	W 198494	76636	W 164770	73030	LEGUMES FRAIS,CONG,SECS
057	FRUIT,NUTS,FRESH,DRIED	W 533556	168615	W 587054	189786	W 699823	233176	W 796172	305118	FRUITS FRAIS OU SECS
0573	BANANA,PLANTAIN,FRSH,DRY	W 144598	52529	W 177889	73597	W 245426	99387	W 255862	125954	BANANES FRAICHES,SECHEES
06	SUGAR AND PREPS,HONEY		46033		47989		135541		99026	SUCRES ET PRODUITS
061	SUGAR AND HONEY	W 25636	8738	W 14792	6522	W 201284	90755	W 96310	49422	SUCRES ET MIEL
07	COFFEE,TEA,COCOA,SPICES		296103		447742		565679		531817	CAFE,THE,CACAO,EPICES
071	COFFEE AND SUBSTITUTES	W 91902	134881	W 101895	255948	W 99206	338758	W 106452	267145	CAFE ET SUCCEDANES
0711	COFFEE GREEN,ROASTED,SUB	W 89057	115918	W 97397	224305	W 94605	301848	W 100632	227320	CAFE TORREFIE OU DECAFEINE
07111	COFFEE GREEN,HUSKS,SKINS	W 68333	73754	W 85259	185969	W 90647	282472	W 97056	213011	CAFE NON TORREFIE
072	COCOA	W 43883	63720	W 51176	83406	W 53538	93743	W 62986	108502	CACAO
074	TEA AND MATE	W 32832	60504	W 32348	60091	W 32552	65776	W 33145	69711	THE ET MATE
0741	TEA	W 32824	60445	W 32348	60091	W 32552	65776	W 33145	69711	THE
081	*FEEDING STUFF FOR ANIML	W 716613	196079	W 937294	269663	W 1181306	316777	W 1451223	451746	NOURRITURE POUR ANIMAUX
0813	OILCAKE AND OTH RESIDUES	W 428540	102489	W 599544	133932	W 707631	159343	W 906955	255576	TOURTEAUX
08131	— OF SOYA BEANS	W 415298	100439	W 596407	133467	W 703545	158441	W 882139	251773	TOURTEAUX DE SOJA
0814	MEAT OR FISH MEAL FODDER	W 138985	40429	W 225198	73764	W 243531	81945	W 268841	100745	FARINES DE VIANDES,POISSONS
08141	MEAT MEAL FODDER	W 132287	38044	W 221405	72073	W 241739	80991	W 267213	99759	FARINES DE VIANDES
09	MISC EDIBLE PRODUCTS		165267		187172		201714		196840	PREP ALIMENTAIRES DIVERSES
098	EDIBLE PRODCTS,PREPS NES	W 71985	143974	W 96996	177230	W 95252	191821	W 93217	187271	PREP ALIMENTAIRES NDA
09809	MISC FOOD PREPRTIONS NES	W 45615	96350	W 71346	132237	W 64650	135204	W 57580	123825	PREP ALIMENTAIRES NDA
1	BEVERAGES AND TOBACCO		144516		184778		216014		249373	BOISSONS ET TABACS
12	TOBACCO AND MANUFACTURES		107482		141154		163197		165082	TABACS BRUTS FABRIQUES
121	TOBACCO UNMNFCTRD,REFUSE	W 28040	98310	W 41208	125670	W 44534	141971	W 42049	154567	TABACS BRUTS,DECHETS
1212	TOBACCO STRIPPED OR PART	W 15698	67962	W 28500	98072	W 31602	113655	W 29672	129493	TABACS PART ECOTES
2	CRUDE MATERLS,EXCL FUELS		836861		1085074		1524778		1695773	MAT BRUTES NON COMESTIBLES
22	OIL SEEDS,OLEAGINOUS FRT		34253		56846		39387		151850	GRAINES,FRUITS OLEAGINEUX
222	SEEDS FOR'SOFT'FIXED OIL	W 80022	29480	W 120497	49839	W 55287	35475	W 383264	144816	GRAINES HUILES FIXES
23	RUBBER, CRUDE		48312		81687		121496		127486	CAOUTCHOUC BRUT
251	*PULP AND WASTE PAPER	W 110900	37486	W 143335	58320	W 223356	138267	W 198703	103666	PATES A PAPIER,DECHETS
26	TEXTILE FIBRES AND WASTE		186751		269674		344398		321311	FIBRES TEXTILES
263	COTTON	W 69402	70640	W 88111	125390	W 90665	178495	W 85142	149853	COTON
2631	RAW COTTON,EXCL LINTERS	W 58565	65326	W 81688	121080	W 86472	174111	W 80573	144479	COTON EN MASSE
27	CRUDE FERTLZR,MINRLS NES		123026		147272		187838		212574	ENGRAIS MINERAUX BRUTS
278	OTHER CRUDE MINERALS		54882	W 426228	66039	W 463762	84289	W 492699	84877	AUTRES MINERAUX BRUTS
28	METALLIFEROUS ORES,SCRAP		261447		278453		390580		389512	MINERAIS METAL,DECHETS
281	IRON ORE,CONCENTRATES	W 8775959	191578	W 8447731	192547	MW 10875	278328	MW 9804	274509	MINERAIS DE FER
2815	IRON ORE,CONC,NOT AGGLOM	W 6926919	135289	W 6162680	124371	W 7544496	169758	W 6774335	167418	MINERAIS NON AGGLOMERES
2816	IRON ORE AGGLOMERATES	W 1849040	56289	W 2250918	67031	W 2984589	97128	W 2699187	95008	MINERAIS AGGLOMERES
287	BASE METAL ORES,CONC NES	W 509272	68592	W 604346	84172	W 585840	108811	W 570741	110501	MINERAIS METAUX COMMUNS
29	CRUDE ANIMAL,VEG MAT NES		104782		122400		171349		212029	MATIERES BRUTES ANIM,VEGET
292	CRUDE VEG MATERIALS NES		55325	W 28790	64170	W 47055	88514	W 38849	101188	MAT BRUTES VEGETALES NDA
3	MINERAL FUELS ETC		2353366		2271287		2676660		3421741	COMBUSTIBLES MINERAUX LUB
33	PETROLEUM AND PRODUCTS		2033233		1875072		2111604		2694698	PETROLE ET DERIVES
333	CRUDE PETROLEUM	MW 13674	1625161	MW 12720	1442321	MW 13037	1576351	MW 13351	1976367	HUILES BRUTES DE PETROLE
334	PETROLEUM PRODUCTS,REFIN	W 1763346	378132	W 2045991	396520	W 2432036	491601	W 2958144	674319	PRODUITS RAFFINES
3341	GASOLINE,OTH LIGHT OILS	W 1105534	213560	W 1065952	184645					ESSENCES POUR MOTEURS
33411	MOTOR,AVIATION SPIRIT	W 8678	3255	W 982119	172322					ESSENCES MOTEURS D'AVIONS
33412	SPIRIT TYPE JET FUEL	W 1075074	206084							CARBUREACTEURS
3343	GAS OILS	W 435339	75406	W 548502	83377					GAS OILS
3345	LUBS,PETROLEUM OILS NES	W 92912	66489	W 88170	70536					HUILES LUBRIFIANTES
341	*GAS,NATURAL AND MANUFCT		313469		351021	W 5473648	480635	W 5510161	608299	GAZ NATUREL,GAZ MANUFACT
3413	PETROLM GASES,LIQUEFIED	W 121949	18461	W 218491	36547	W 426639	75801	W 629202	112940	GAZ DE PETROLE LIQUEFIE
3414	PETROLEUM GASES, GASEOUS		295008		314474	W 5047009	404834	W 4880959	495359	GAZ DE PETROLE GAZEUX
4	ANIMAL,VEGETABLE OIL,FAT		113565		158002		187818		214594	HUILES,GRAISSES ANIM,VEG
42	FIXED VEGETABLE OIL,FAT		88614		119713		125003		140047	HUILES VEGETALES FIXES
423	FIXED VEG OILS,SOFT	W 142133	64851	W 151118	84985	W 125873	83417	W 157508	99623	HUILES VEGET DOUCES FIXES
5	CHEMCLS,RELATED PROD NES		2363578		3023692		4134196		4878108	PRODUITS CHIMIQUES
51	ORGANIC CHEMICALS		332403		510218		694621		634209	PROD CHIMIQ ORGANIQUES
511	HYDROCARBONS NES,DERIVS	W 287604	95356	W 483543	170249	W 488946	262106	W 435124	162022	HYDROCARBURES NDA
5111	ACYCLIC HYDROCARBONS	W 102662	30982	W 140573	45157	W 166390	87524	W 142093	61418	HYDROCARBURES ACYCLIQUES
5112	CYCLIC HYDROCARBONS	W 159434	49565	W 279139	98381	W 235496	118363	W 217130	71865	HYDROCARBURES CYCLIQUES
512	ALCOHOLS,PHENOLS ETC	W 137018	51883	W 179918	87047	W 139116	91838	W 173366	93194	PHENOLS,PHENOLS–ALCOOLS
514	NITROGEN–FNCTN COMPOUNDS	W 23061	62597	W 32056	84917	W 39319	121373	W 41333	139320	COMPOSES FONCT AZOTEES
52	INORGANIC CHEMICALS		93172		112141		142816		179154	PROD CHIM INORGANIQUES
53	DYES,TANNING,COLOUR PROD		213770		275287		362282		431900	PROD TEINTURE,COLORANTS
533	PIGMENTS,PAINTS,ETC	W 70443	170487	W 77564	221080	W 95934	297579	W 120738	357977	PIGMENTS,PEINTURES,VERNIS
5334	VARNISHES,DISTEMPERS ETC	W 25689	83396	W 31807	105390	W 39368	150912	W 45837	182278	PEINTURES A L'EAU
53342	OTH PAINTS,VARNISHES ETC	W 18097	60912	W 22923	77447	W 27991	111963	W 29224	126930	AUTRES PEINTURES,VERNIS
541	*MEDICINAL,PHARM PRODUCT	MK 24104	654079		737935	MK 25420	911736	MK 27709	1068160	PROD MEDICINAUX PHARMACEUT
5417	MEDICAMENTS	MK 15676	489786	MK 16677	561217	MK 16876	697790	MK 18332	846422	MEDICAMENTS
54171	— CONTAINNG ANTIBIOTICS	K 1955114	121360	K 1460000	84848	K 1591596	122866	K 2013417	151467	MED CONTN ANTIBIOTIQUES
54179	— CONTNG OTH SUBSTANCES	MK 12650	319196	MK 14567	414037	MK 14676	484136	MK 15700	586253	MED CONT AUT SUBSTANCES
55	PERFUME,CLEANING ETC PRD		295240		316620		407561		566674	PROD POUR PARFUM,TOILETTE
553	PERFUMERY,COSMETICS,ETC	W 35084	127655	W 37951	135715	W 41138	152387	W 56136	225577	PRODUITS DE PARFUMERIE
554	SOAP,CLEANSING ETC PREPS	W 121326	125648	W 171042	127006	W 163921	175212	W 230460	234784	SAVONS,PRODUITS DETERSIFS
5542	WASHING PREPARATIONS ETC	W 99805	95202	W 148619	94634	W 138375	134032	W 198394	184802	PROD ORG TENSIO–ACT NDA
562	*FERTILIZERS,MANUFACTURE	W 685778	51608	W 912084	65285	W 907709	76587	W 1089532	103102	ENGRAIS MANUFACTURES
58	PLASTIC MATERIALS ETC		412158		595248		1001183		1200388	MAT PLAST ARTIFICIELLES
582	PROD OF CONDENSATION ETC	W 43101	92304	W 65514	122689	W 86695	194725	W 115595	228787	PROD CONDENS,POLYCOND
583	POLYMERIZATION ETC PRODS	W 197472	305104	W 292113	448125	W 435662	769110	W 576861	927240	PROD POLYMERISATION
5831	POLYETHYLENE	W 49544	39526	W 88366	95097	W 137574	178915	W 178924	201135	POLYETHYLENE
58311	— IN PRIMARY FORMS	W 46387	35069	W 69469	59690	W 112845	129296	W 149496	141460	POLYETHYLENE PRIMAIRES
5832	POLYPROPYLENE	W 36355	54746	W 41857	58224	W 55260	103455	W 72848	118677	POLYPROPYLENE
5833	POLYSTYRENE,ITS COPOLYMR	W 35736	46243	W 53768	71930	W 59019	105604	W 96359	131321	POLYPROPYLENE COPOLYMERES
5834	POLYVINYL CHLORIDE	W 30801	42160	W 42293	60615	W 84759	128954	W 112016	166416	CHLORURE DE POLYVINYLE

4. General Imports F.O.B. by Commodities according to the S.I.T.C. (Rev. 2) in thousand U.S. Dollars
Importations Générales F.O.B. par Produits d'après la C.T.C.I. (Rév. 2) en milliers de Dollars E.U.

SITC CTCI	COMMODITY	1993 WEIGHT POIDS	1993 VALUE VALEUR	1994 WEIGHT POIDS	1994 VALUE VALEUR	1995 WEIGHT POIDS	1995 VALUE VALEUR	1996 WEIGHT POIDS	1996 VALUE VALEUR	PRODUIT
5839	OTH POLYMRZTION ETC PROD	W 30190	90823	W 42828	111900	W 64797	167595	W 70365	199404	AUT PROD POLYMER COPOLYM
59	CHEMICAL MATERIALS NES		309153		407721		531816		689512	MAT PROD CHIMIQUES NDA
591	PESTICIDES,DISINFECTANTS	W 12559	89778	W 14965	121298	W 18730	139328	W 23898	174110	DESINF,INSECT,FONG,HERB
592	STARCH,INULIN,GLUTEN,ETC	W 62042	58525	W 43776	78745	W 94975	120199	W 93710	147804	AMIDONS,INUL,GLUT FROM
5922	ALBUMINOID SUBSTAN,GLUES	W 28189	50419	W 38247	76220	W 48358	99236	W 51295	128822	MAT ALBUMIN,COLLES
598	MISCEL CHEM PRODUCTS NES	W 223082	160850	W 257879	207678	W 275114	272289	W 353187	367598	PROD DIV INDUST CHIM NDA
5989	CHEM PRODUCTS,PREPS NES	W 64967	118225	W 83355	150560	W 93534	198416	W 152743	277994	PROD PREP CHIMIQUES NDA
59899	OTH CHEM PRODS,PREPS,NES	W 49140	80954	W 67926	108063	W 78480	147617	W 109800	205922	AUT PRODUITS CHIMIQUES NDA
6	BASIC MANUFACTURES		3478516		4415557		6355312		7576608	ART MANUFACTURES
61	LEATHER,DRESSED FUR,ETC		101763		130769		188265		242941	CUIRS,PELLETERIES
611	LEATHER	W 6713	78135	W 9596	98522	W 10578	142155	W 14275	176915	CUIRS,PEAUX PREPARES
6114	LEATHR BOVINE NES,EQUINE	W 4265	52678	W 5731	67011	W 6648	106287	W 8947	136283	CUIRS DE BOVINS
62	RUBBER MANUFACTURES NES		137782		164428		222996		296259	CAOUTCHOUC MANUFACTURE
628	RUBBER ARTICLES NES	W 7666	53882	W 10297	67414	W 12052	90047	W 15207	115784	OUVRAGES CAOUTCHOUC NDA
63	WOOD,CORK MANUFACTRS NES		51324		72356		122315		163960	OUVRAGES LIEGE ET BOIS
64	PAPER,PAPERBOARD AND MFR		456874		599488		938450		1134778	PAPIERS,CARTONS & OUVRAGES
641	PAPER AND PAPERBOARD	W 282642	287936	W 362839	399827	W 479787	647140	W 673538	807842	PAPIERS ET CARTONS
6412	PRINTG,WRITING PAPER NES	W 57698	58229	W 99923	102441	W 137626	174946	W 169486	180553	PAPIERS POUR L'IMPRESSION
64122	— COATED,IMPREGNATD ETC	W 53179	53879	W 92392	94253	W 126684	159026	W 152652	161181	PAPIERS IMPRESSION COUCHES
6415	PAPER,PAPERBRD,BULK,NES	W 87165	63922	W 126179	79735	W 159300	148546	W 217613	175469	PAPIERS,CARTONS ROULEAUX
64159	OTHER PAPER ETC,BULK,NES	W 83278	62010	W 123511	76771	W 154686	141852	W 210993	167732	AUT PAPIER ROULEAUX FEUILLES
6418	COATED ETC PAPER NES BLK	W 57284	113858	W 69268	158775	W 88849	217640	W 118440	271350	PAP,CARTONS COUCHES,ENDUITS
64181	PLASTIC COATED PAPER ETC	W 13138	44485	W 17033	78389	W 21143	96779	W 29067	124567	PAP,CARTONS ENDUITS,RESINES
64189	COATED PAPER ETC NES	W 42744	68066	W 51709	79892	W 67375	120338	W 88696	145817	PAPIERS,CARTONS COUCHES
642	PAPER,ETC,PRECUT,ARTS OF	W 87854	168938	W 94718	199661	W 118884	291310	W 148473	326936	PAP,CARTONS DECOUPES
6421	PAPER ETC CONTAINERS	W 52565	80649	W 57251	103165	W 71981	146897	W 86040	166864	BOITES,SACS EMBALLAGES
6428	PAPER ETC ARTICLES NES	W 22201	57913	W 22037	56365	W 27022	76137	W 33000	82377	OUVRAGES EN PATE A PAPIER
65	TEXTILE YARN,FABRICS,ETC		1381249		1727905		2194000		2389125	FILS,TISSUS,ARTICLES TEXTILE
651	TEXTILE YARN		124833	W 33096	161918	W 37398	209923	W 62401	285956	FILS TEXTILES
6514	SYN FIB YRN,BULK,MONOFIL		55555	W 14289	77791	W 16891	102296	W 33107	141653	FILS CONT 85% FIB TEXT SYNTH
652	COTTON FABRICS,WOVEN	W 33345	258623	W 37390	322793	W 39737	402311	W 43430	419547	TISSUS DE COTON
6522	WOVEN COTTON BLEACHD,ETC	W 26032	223925	W 29936	293644	W 34409	383246	W 37818	397403	TISSUS COTON BLANCHIS ETC
65224	BLCHED COTTON FABRIC NES	W 19965	179258	W 25035	239621	W 29941	318456	W 33012	333206	AUT TIS PLUS 85% COT BLANCHI
653	WOVN MAN–MADE FIB FABRIC	W 37714	486841	W 52428	553065	W 64781	701350	W 97607	681292	TISSUS FIBRES SYNTH,ARTIF
6531	CONT SYNT WEAVES NONPILE	W 10292	107795	W 16701	124924	W 21028	145238	W 24742	147536	TISSUS FIBRES SYNTH CONTINUE
65315	CONT SYN TXTL FABRIC NES	W 9264	95699	W 15126	109283	W 19057	126791	W 22197	124845	TIS PLUS 85% TEXT SYNT CONT
6534	DISC SYN BLEND FABRC NES	W 9650	122505	W 13663	139995	W 15239	167731	W 42115	180498	TISSUS FIBRES SYNTH DISCONT
6535	CONT REGN WEAVES NONPILE	W 3838	74360	W 5232	92007	W 5375	136595	W 4796	109431	TISSUS FIB TEXT ART CONTINU
65355	CONT REGN TXTL FABRC NES	W 2671	49371	W 3853	63741	W 3747	94289	W 3431	75263	TISSUS 85% TEXT ART CONT
6538	DISC REG BLEND FABRC NES	W 4366	80787	W 3759	79728	W 4625	104097	W 4789	97628	TIS MOINS 85% TEXT ART DISC
654	OTH WOVEN TEXTILE FABRIC	W 7434	155391	W 9144	187854	W 9435	215983	W 11256	228968	TISSUS AUT COTON SYNT,ARTIF
6542	WOVEN WOOL,HAIR NONPILE	W 2769	71929	W 3194	85035	W 3345	93394	W 3287	97536	TIS PLUS 85% LAINE,POILS
6543	WOVEN WOOL ETC FABRC NES	W 2948	60230	W 3316	63704	W 3473	79058	W 4606	91621	TISSUS LAINE,POILS FINS NDA
655	KNITTED,ETC FABRICS	W 10758	103980	W 14592	135150	W 15415	157786	W 18597	187510	ETOF BONNETERIE PIECES ETC
6552	OTHER KNIT ETC FAB NONEL	W 10758	103980	W 14592	135150	W 15415	157786	W 18597	187510	ETOF BON NON ELAS NON SYNT
657	SPECIAL TXTL FABRC,PRODS	W 22779	158048	W 33745	231640	W 43857	317258	W 52075	362837	TISSUS SPECIAUX
6572	BONDED FIBRE TEXTLS NES	W 7359	44569	W 8134	64825	W 12309	91104	W 14720	90163	TISSUS NON TISSES
6573	COATED ETC TEXTILES NES	W 10109	76068	W 16267	116013	W 21305	157147	W 24419	184398	TISSUS,ART MATIERE TEXT NDA
658	TEXTILE ARTICLES NES	W 3859	28134	W 6855	57993	W 8271	88389	W 11603	103955	ART FACONNES MAT TEXTILES
66	NONMETAL MINERAL MFS NES		304011		394118		611881		798641	ART MIN NON METALLIQUES
662	CLAY,REFRACTORY BLDG PRD	W 248927	99126	W 335151	130313	W 457132	200771	W 634895	283919	MAT CONST REFRACTAIRES
6624	BRICKS ETC NONREFRACTORY	W 231846	80225	W 321216	112437	W 429506	164077	W 604127	236940	BRIQUES ETC CERAM NON REFR
66245	GLAZED CERAMIC SETTS ETC	W 129498	58871	W 172672	79363	W 215564	107315	W 305023	156267	AUT CARREAUX CERAMIQUE
663	MINERAL MANUFCTURES NES	W 61025	49997	W 90880	65706	W 184303	110903	W 319250	140600	ART MIN MANUF NDA
664	GLASS	W 76432	83820	W 114727	114081	W 148421	171377	W 168883	204867	VERRE
67	IRON AND STEEL		430408		566297		934768		1075018	FER ET ACIER
673	IRON,STEEL SHAPES ETC	W 69672	40167	W 142947	73379	W 200927	134280	W 199540	134191	BARRES,PROFIL FER,ACIER
674	IRN,STL UNIV,PLATE,SHEET	W 353922	195825	W 440460	258838	W 505115	391048	W 501868	398771	LARGES PLATS,TOLES
6744	IRN,STL HVY PLATE,ROLLED	W 114134	45207	W 121781	58656	W 155643	101805	W 105878	73432	TOLES LAMINEES PLUS 4.75 MM
6746	IRN,STL THIN PLATE,ROLLD	W 56920	38509	W 101536	62587	W 112054	103103	W 120372	110355	TOLES LAM MOINS 3MM
6749	OTH IRN,STL PLATES,SHEET	W 113772	72503	W 138267	97847	W 136660	122822	W 138853	133374	AUTRES TOLES FER,ACIER
67491	— OF IRON OR SIMPLE STL	W 109340	67793	W 135059	92656	W 132972	113928	W 134234	120779	AUT TOLES AUTRES ACIER FIN
678	IRON,STL TUBES,PIPES,ETC	W 71467	100940	W 76604	103346	W 157914	235988	W 244861	347877	TUBES,TUYAUX EN FONTE,FER
6783	IRON,STL TUBES,PIPES NES	W 31229	35613	W 35308	37888	W 97214	125853	W 173422	207930	AUT TUBES,TUYAUX FER,ACIER
68	NON–FERROUS METALS		196170		220542		367461		429534	METAUX NON FERREUX
684	ALUMINIUM	W 67480	137837	W 65795	165055	W 88133	268345	W 114210	319987	ALUMINIUM
6841	ALUMINIUM,ALLOYS,UNWRGHT	W 42317	49574	W 38258	58218	W 45141	87972	W 49529	81675	ALUMINIUM,ALLIAGES BRUTS
6842	ALUMINIUM,ALLOYS WORKED	W 25163	88263	W 27537	106837	W 42992	180373	W 64681	238312	ALUMINIUM,ALLIAGES OUVRE
69	METAL MANUFACTURES NES		418935		539654		775176		1046352	ART MANUFACT EN METAL NDA
691	STRUCTURES AND PARTS NES	W 37278	61714	W 39446	84507	W 48334	118339	W 62162	162114	CONSTRUCT FER,ACIER,ALU
695	TOOLS	W 5477	44456	W 6620	59983	W 9236	89709	W 13641	124222	OUTILS A MAIN
697	BASE MTL HOUSEHOLD EQUIP	W 13935	68463	W 13762	71612	W 16603	92968	W 23191	134162	ART MENAGE MET COMMUNS
699	BASE METAL MFRS NES	W 31062	136293	W 41509	189063	W 57276	287806	W 77702	388642	ART MANUFACTURES MET NDA
6991	LOCKSMITHS WARES,ETC	W 8003	60022	W 11386	81344	W 15508	123961	W 22546	168522	ARTICLES DE SERRURERIE
69913	BASE MTL DOOR,ETC FITTNG	W 6092	44746	W 9320	64372	W 12862	95913	W 18982	131464	GARNITURES POUR MEUBLES
7	MACHINES,TRANSPORT EQUIP		5496486		6207903		8667252		12237476	MACHINES MATERIEL TRANSPORT
71	POWER GENERATING EQUIPMT		283632		392967		562407		700143	MACHINES GENERATRICES
713	INTRNL COMBUS PSTN ENGIN	W 21253	166062	W 27004	243238	W 32409	336287	W 47499	447037	MOTEURS EXPL COMB INT, PIECE
7132	MOTOR VEHCL PISTN ENGINS	W 13663	104110	W 19091	171846	W 25266	236089	W 34942	306692	MOTEURS EXPL POUR VEHICULES
72	MACHS FOR SPCL INDUSTRYS		867421		1025581		1294666		1764021	MAC SPECIALES POUR INDUST
721	AGRIC MACHY,EXC TRACTORS	W 22663	48232	W 39333	77994	W 32612	135204	W 61243	237255	MACHINES AGRICOLES
7212	HARVESTING ETC MACHINES	W 14161	20303	W 24613	33282	W 16493	54706	W 37182	130402	ENGINS POUR LA RECOLTE
723	CIVIL ENGNEERG EQUIP ETC	W 15144	111566	W 14265	50006	W 21759	82630	W 41530	113161	APPAREILS DE GENIE CIVIL
7234	CONST,MINING MACHNRY NES	W 14262	104582	W 12762	45242	W 19136	68287	W 38768	99421	MACH POUR LA CONST, MINES
72344	BORING,SINKING MACHINERY	W 7778	71867	W 1181	8507	W 808	11799	W 1908	13613	MACHINES DE FORAGE
724	TEXTILE,LEATHER MACHNRY	W 10691	134261	W 14722	171803	W 14689	183735	W 19917	223553	MACH POUR INDUSTRIE TEXTILE
725	PAPER ETC MILL MACHINERY	W 3732	55361	W 3994	62999	W 6363	96173	W 7769	113702	MACHINES FABR PATE PAPIER
726	PRINTG,BKBINDG MACHY,PTS	W 6232	70381	W 7462	115748	W 8618	108550	W 12486	178176	MACHINES POUR IMPRIMERIE
727	FOOD MACHRY NON–DOMESTIC	W 11179	155627	W 11100	155913	W 17701	236783	W 14851	216212	MACH INDUSTRIES ALIMENT
7272	OTH FOOD PROC MCHY,PARTS	W 10216	154360	W 10371	152100	W 16957	232749	W 13732	210400	AUT MACH IND ALIMENTAIRE
72722	INDUS FOOD PROC MACH NES	W 10010	149378	W 10203	146676	W 16643	224951	W 13196	195165	MACHINES BOULANGERIE
728	OTH MACHY FOR SPCL INDUS	W 28268	283612	W 39460	381721	W 38876	438244	W 50975	633612	AUT MACH IND PARTICULIERES
7284	MACHY FOR SPCL INDUS NES	W 15214	212895	W 25234	299859	W 22332	327764	W 30816	492801	MACH SPEC IND PARTICUL.
72842	RUBBER,PLASTICS WRKG MCH	W 5476	41537	W 7957	56173	W 9607	93461	W 11091	107938	MACH IND CAOUT MAT PLAST
72844	WOOD TREATING MACHNS NES	W 1938	14207	W 6722	71287	W 2973	32093	W 3808	44502	MACH TRAITEMENT DU BOIS
72848	OTH MCHY WITH INDIV FNCT	W 4492	75851	W 7382	110389	W 5712	110098	W 10379	185068	AUTRES MACHINES NDA
73	METALWORKING MACHINERY		122390		186683		248396		310462	MACH TRAVAIL DES METAUX
736	METALWORKING MACH–TOOLS	W 8330	84378	W 12220	112025	W 13649	121023	W 24054	189503	MACH–OUTILS TRAVAIL METAUX
737	METALWORKING MACHNRY NES	W 3313	38012	W 7727	74658	W 23563	127373	W 17314	120959	MACH TRAV METAUX PIECES
74	GENRL INDUSTRL MACHY NES		1056841		1268613		1767554		2316309	MACH APP INDUSTRIE
741	HEATING,COOLING EQUIPMNT	W 21515	218618	W 28162	260223	W 32609	381973	W 60779	598652	MACH CHAUFFAGE,PIECES

4. General Imports F.O.B. by Commodities according to the S.I.T.C. (Rev. 2) in thousand U.S. Dollars
Importations Générales F.O.B. par Produits d'après la C.T.C.I. (Rév. 2) en milliers de Dollars E.U.

SITC CTCI	COMMODITY	1993		1994		1995		1996		PRODUIT
		WEIGHT POIDS	VALUE VALEUR	WEIGHT POIDS	VALUE VALEUR	WEIGHT POIDS	VALUE VALEUR	WEIGHT POIDS	VALUE VALEUR	
7413	INDUS FURNACES ETC,PARTS	W 6319	41738	W 11269	66996	W 8081	77383	W 18844	121014	FOURS IND,LABOR,PIECES
7416	HEATING,COOLING EQU NES	W 5955	72100	W 7204	88492	W 12216	156059	W 24008	267764	APP CHANGEMENT TEMP
742	PUMPS FOR LIQUIDS ETC	W 3787	70118	W 3922	77402	W 6234	113809	W 6535	129461	POMPES MOTO–POMPES
743	PUMPS NES,CENTRFUGES ETC	W 21431	217326	W 19710	264178	W 25801	365201	W 35266	466992	POMPES COMPRES,VENT ETC
7436	GAS,LIQUID FILTERS ETC	W 14185	132349	W 10833	155430	W 14401	225968	W 18742	274353	APP POUR FILT DES LIQUIDES
744	MECHANICAL HANDLING EQU	W 18964	127756	W 24770	160291	W 58161	201011	W 42640	233989	EQUIP MANUTENTION PIECES
7442	LIFTING,LOADING MACH NES	W 9165	75932	W 11931	96503	W 13705	125158	W 18450	133466	APP LEVAGE,MANUTENTION
74428	OTH HANDLING ETC MCH NES	W 7231	57588	W 8317	67964	W 10623	99081	W 13012	94366	AUT APP LEVAGE ETC
745	NONELEC MACHY,TOOLS NES	W 12371	190758	W 11899	208840	W 14113	286049	W 16230	364187	AUT MACH NON ELEC,PIECES
7452	OTH NONELEC MCHS,PTS NES	W 11751	170915	W 11017	179610	W 12935	244942	W 14707	311251	AUT MACH NON ELEC,PIECES
74522	PACKAGNG,BOTTLNG,ETC MCH	W 5088	108724	W 4621	103617	W 5115	144791	W 5515	172910	MACH NETT BOUTEILLES,ETC
749	NONELEC MACH PTS,ACC NES	W 18086	232265	W 22965	297679	W 30199	419511	W 39042	523028	PIECES MACH NON ELEC NDA
7492	COCKS,VALVES ETC NES	W 8946	143438	W 11027	169576	W 14156	231465	W 18451	289871	ART ROB,SIM POUR TUYAUX
75	OFFICE MACHNES,ADP EQUIP		577664		593792		841302		1120648	MACH BUREAU TRAIT AUTOM
751	OFFICE MACHINES	W 2654	60093	W 3119	65588	W 3186	82014	W 4408	114519	MACH,APPAREILS DE BUREAU
752	AUTOMTIC DATA PROC EQUIP		407570	W 7639	416233	W 10199	591052	W 15189	790475	MACH TRAIT INFORMATION
7522	DIGITAL COMPUTERS	W 1849	122259	W 1199	133201	W 1401	197020	W 1266	175792	MACH DIGITALES COMPLETES
7524	DIGITL CENTRL STOR UNITS		76962	W 486	76888	W 621	104420	W 1088	148449	UNITES MEMOIRE CENTRALES
7525	ADP PERIPHERAL UNITS	W 5245	157042	W 5585	158083	W 7799	225870	W 11766	310300	UNITES PERIPHERIQUES
759	OFFICE,ADP MCH PTS,ACCES	W 4619	110001	W 3017	111971	W 4462	168236	W 6771	215654	PIECES DU 751 ET 752
7599	ACCTG,ETC,ADP MCH PTS,AC	W 4247	98269	W 2662	98161	W 4040	149732	W 6277	192386	PIECES DU 751 ET 752
76	TELECOMM,SOUND EQUIPMENT		583856		546763		729797		1048271	EQUIPMENT DE TELECOM
762	RADIO BROADCAST RECEIVRS	W 9226	57867	W 8118	41993	W 8512	76367	W 9722	126336	RECEPTEURS RADIODIFFUSION
764	TELECOM EQPT,PTS,ACC NES	W 11884	451528	W 11804	425338	W 14200	568973	W 17347	804366	EQUIP TELECOM,PIECES
7641	LINE TELEPHONE,ETC EQUIP	W 4205	271679	W 2865	196527	W 2185	153962	W 2913	220204	APP TELEPHON PAR FIL
7643	TV,RADIO TRANSMITTRS ETC	W 419	57296	W 468	76852	W 514	94652	W 980	186942	APP EMET TELE RADIO
7649	PTS NES OF EQUIPMT OF 76	W 5969	97008	W 6827	123075	W 9010	268935	W 9968	339008	PIECES DE LA DIV 76
76491	PTS NES OF APPAR OF 7641	W 429	17264	W 702	40197	W 1090	103116	W 1257	159134	PIECES POUR 764.1
76493	TELECOMM EQUIPMT PTS NES	W 4944	66800	W 5784	74905	W 7320	124824	W 8050	146364	PIECES 761,762,764.3,8
77	ELECTRIC MACHNRY NES ETC		940163		1096818		1595616		2207571	MACH APP ELECT NDA
771	ELECTRIC POWER MACHY NES	W 5334	44888	W 7841	75235	W 9697	104695	W 12274	151544	MACH PROD,TRANS ELECTR
7712	OTH ELEC POWER MACHY NES	W 4975	38999	W 7320	65433	W 8918	92153	W 10537	122528	AUT APP PROD TRANSF ELEC
772	SWITCHGEAR ETC,PARTS NES	W 6340	179051	W 9222	239977	W 12006	361064	W 17957	500946	APP COUPURE,SECT ETC
7721	SWITCHGEAR ETC	W 6053	167855	W 8877	226199	W 11647	345108	W 17125	471263	APP COUPURE,SECTIONMNT
773	ELECTR DISTRIBUTNG EQUIP	W 11857	76194	W 13531	85914	W 17276	128251	W 24248	180290	EQUIPMT DISTRIBUTION ELECT
7731	INSULATED WIRE,CABLE ETC	W 10867	64458	W 12411	72275	W 16141	112470	W 22594	156760	FILS,CABLES ISOLES ELECT
774	ELECTRO–MEDCL,XRAY EQUIP	W 999	91938	W 699	64701	W 871	112703	W 1157	128829	APPAREILS MEDICAUX
775	HOUSEHOLD TYPE EQUIP NES	W 28749	134242	W 32924	170615	W 45942	254498	W 66105	385276	MACH,APP USAGE DOMESTQUE
7758	ELECTRO–THERMIC APPL NES	W 5157	46102	W 6367	63642	W 8661	91406	W 14679	137420	APP ELECTROTHERMIQ NDA
776	TRANSISTORS,VALVES,ETC	W 11310	167478	W 10756	174769	W 14043	243470	W 16901	366986	LAMPES,TUBES,VALVES
7761	TV PICTURE TUBES	W 9331	57870	W 9573	53117	W 12909	76818	W 15261	107061	TUBES CATHODIQUES
7764	ELECTRONIC MICROCIRCUITS	W 287	70506	W 278	82960	W 375	117303	W 720	193947	MICROSTRUCTURES ELECTRON
778	ELECTRICAL MACHINERY NES	W 33545	246372	W 33329	285607	W 40677	390935	W 48523	493700	AUTRES MACH ELECT NDA
7788	OTH ELEC MACHY,EQUIP NES	W 13995	100734	W 13502	114233	W 14784	161116	W 15634	200366	AUT MACH APP ELEC NDA
78	ROAD VEHICLES		1023251		1033189		1556272		2622288	VEHICULES ROUTIERS
781	PASS MOTOR VEH EXC BUSES	W 65758	441269	W 57246	376073	W 64308	466242	W 123474	919837	AUTO TRANSPORT PERSONNES
782	LORRIES,SPCL MTR VEH NES	W 49684	188434	W 35820	129424	W 23735	113147	W 33609	165987	VEHICULES SPECIAUX,MARCH
7821	LORRIES,TRUCKS	W 39249	140424	W 28699	101353	W 21864	96142	W 31293	141870	VEHICULES TRANSP MARCHAND
783	ROAD MOTOR VEHICLES NES	W 27639	68517	W 32393	66819	W 16492	64300	W 15580	46984	VEHICULES ROUTIERS NDA
784	MOTOR VEH PRTS,ACCES NES	W 42273	263293	W 82008	360790	W 109114	752521	W 198619	1262538	PIECES 722,781,782,783
7841	MOTOR VEHICLE CHASSIS	W 1292	12915	W 3395	35278	W 13634	143617	W 11462	107338	CHASSIS 722,781,782,783
7842	MOTOR VEHICLE BODIES	W 5129	39173	W 32984	79345	W 27658	187013	W 68217	440417	CARROS 722,781,782,783
7849	OTHER MOTOR VEHCL PARTS	W 35851	211205	W 45629	246167	W 67822	421891	W 118941	714783	PIECES 722,781,782,783
785	CYCLES,ETC MOTRZD OR NOT	W 4673	21920	W 9436	52296	W 13966	81287	W 19565	112519	MOTOCYCLES SCOOTERS
786	TRAILERS,NONMOTR VEH,NES	W 37877	39818	W 47497	47787	W 48533	78775	W 66603	114423	REMORQUES,CADRES,CONTAIN
79	OTHR TRANSPORT EQUIPMENT		41268		63497		71242		147763	AUTRE MATERIEL TRANSPORT
8	MISC MANUFACTURED GOODS		1938965		2208173		2794110		3558234	ART MANUFACTURES DIVERS
812	*PLUMBG,HEATNG,LGHTNG EQ	W 42215	89313	W 31016	114935	W 34999	157021	W 54702	215013	APPAR SANITAIRES CHAUFFAGE
8121	CENTRAL HEATING EQUIPMNT	W 33794	44125	W 18673	57284	W 21615	79938	W 37429	114147	CHAUDIERES,RADIATEURS
821	*FURNITURE,PARTS THEREOF	W 35830	117030	W 40321	121959	W 47135	166964	W 60337	212563	MEUBLES ET PIECES
8219	FURNITURE AND PARTS NES	W 23892	64905	W 26829	67438	W 30585	90385	W 38179	114801	AUTRES MEUBLES ET PIECES
84	CLOTHING AND ACCESSORIES		255712		268884		316454		452128	VETEMENTS
851	*FOOTWEAR	W 23186	82017	W 27798	99554	W 38318	122249	W 50636	171027	CHAUSSURES
85102	FOOTWEAR LEATHER	W 15856	56989	W 20509	74320	W 27856	87341	W 33084	114947	CHAUS SEMELLES EN CUIR
87	PRECISION INSTRUMNTS NES		356243		386742		503194		602821	INSTRUM,APPAR SCIENT NDA
872	MEDICAL INSTRUMENTS NES	W 2831	110946	W 3584	101790	W 3613	127225	W 4843	157384	INSTR,APP MEDIC–CHIR NDA
87202	OTH MEDICAL INSTRUMENTS	W 2234	88363	W 2909	84268	W 2771	104194	W 3612	125108	INSTRUM,APP MEDECINE
874	MEASURNG,CONTROLNG INSTR		223596	W 3879	256751	W 5330	333257	W 5888	391745	INSTRUMENTS DE MESURE
8748	ELEC MEAS,CONTRL EQU NES	W 1320	84495	W 645	95955	W 809	113669	W 890	131774	APP ELEC ELECTRO MESURE
87483	OTH ELCTRNC MEAS ETC EQU	W 1179	72304	W 442	82237	W 577	93538	W 618	110559	AUT APP ELECTRO DE MESURE
88	PHOTO EQU,OPTICL GDS ETC		113732		111776		134142		171256	APP,FOURN PHOTO,OP,MONTR
882	PHOTO,CINEMA SUPPLIES	W 4380	63916	W 5070	61731	W 5382	67820	W 5995	74578	PRODUITS PHOTO,CINEMA
89	MISC MANUFCTRD GOODS NES		910490		1084749		1367753		1699618	ART MANUFACTURES DIVERS
892	PRINTED MATTER	W 72426	239071	W 79002	232832	W 82042	277452	W 83253	339399	IMPRIMES
8921	PRINTED BOOKS,GLOBES,ETC	W 24283	102493	W 25984	90315	W 30806	109336	W 31077	121345	LIVRES,BROCHURES,CARTES
89211	PRINTED BOOKS,PAMPHLETS	W 23538	99530	W 24825	85200	W 29845	104675	W 30284	116520	LIVRES,BROCHURES
8922	NEWSPAPERS,PERIODICALS	W 36196	74614	W 42567	80572	W 38886	87296	W 35246	76517	JOURNAUX ET PERIODIQUES
8928	PRINTED MATTER NES	W 11210	54415	W 9682	52509	W 11578	70116	W 15998	128775	IMPRIMES NDA
893	ARTICLES OF PLASTIC NES	W 110302	353249	W 146317	480986	W 147185	621479	W 174483	756038	OUVRAGES EN MAT DIVIS 58
8931	PLSTC PACKG CONTNRS,LIDS	W 47017	115439	W 70868	170170	W 55271	179289	W 57843	190833	ART TRANSP EMBALLAGE ETC
8939	MISC PLASTIC ARTICLES	W 61871	228295	W 73664	297771	W 89061	419687	W 112804	534667	ART DIVERS EN MAT DIV 58
89399	OTHR PLASTC ARTICLES NES	W 47071	194073	W 55623	250127	W 67401	355920	W 86496	453375	AUT OUV MAT DIV 58
894	TOYS,SPORTING GOODS,ETC	W 17155	111069	W 21383	121773	W 24332	151984	W 32411	210296	VOITURES ENFANTS,JOUETS
8942	TOYS,INDOOR GAMES ETC	W 15085	88047	W 17310	96138	W 19741	112627	W 25295	144173	JOUETS,JEUX ETC
89423	TOYS NES	W 10536	70206	W 12323	76620	W 12250	82967	W 14917	99823	JOUETS,MODELES REDUITS
899	OTHER MANUFACTURED GOODS		105283		129079		161442		199951	AUT ART MANUF DIVERS NDA
8998	SMALLWARES,TOILETRYS ETC	W 2872	55616	W 3529	67347	W 3831	78334	W 4556	82776	ART MERCERIE,TOILETTE
9	GOODS NOT CLASSD BY KIND		12051		10642		136321		21135	ART TRANSACT NON CLASSES
931	*SPECIAL TRANSACTIONS						114995			TRANS.SPECIALES

5. General Exports F.O.B. by Commodities according to the S.I.T.C. (Rev. 2) in thousand U.S. Dollars
Exportations Générales F.O.B. par Produits d'après la C.T.C.I. (Rév. 2) en milliers de Dollars E.U.

SITC CTCI	COMMODITY	1993 WEIGHT POIDS	1993 VALUE VALEUR	1994 WEIGHT POIDS	1994 VALUE VALEUR	1995 WEIGHT POIDS	1995 VALUE VALEUR	1996 WEIGHT POIDS	1996 VALUE VALEUR	PRODUIT
	ALL COMMODITIES		14044104		17194369		22862130		24393116	TOUS PRODUITS
0	FOOD AND LIVE ANIMALS		1389302		1726035		2089470		2454919	ALIMENTS,ANIMAUX VIVANTS
001	*LIVE ANIMALS FOR FOOD	W 118339	166094	W 109900	175307	W 97771	174627	W 92802	171568	ANIMAUX VIVANTS
0011	BOVINE SPECIES,LIVE	W 33772	47542	W 49874	77275	W 50915	88772	W 37326	72876	ESPECE BOVINE
00119	— OTHR THAN FR BREEDING	W 33617	47265	W 48715	75135	W 50476	87770	W 37326	72876	BOVINS NON REPRODUCTEURS
0015	EQUINE SPECIES, LIVE	W 61561	92578	W 49764	81667	W 37513	68026	W 44258	79289	CHEVAUX,ANES,MULETS
01	MEAT AND PREPARATIONS		177995		215224		320121		437396	VIANDES ET PREPARATIONS
011	MEAT FRESH,CHILLD,FROZEN	W 31351	114360	W 30639	123663	W 59471	177139	W 81750	205712	VIANDES FRAICHES,REF,CONGE
0114	POULTRY FRESH CHLLD,FRZN	W 14680	51517	W 13832	54415	W 16043	66151	W 21105	81776	VOLAILLES MORTES
014	MEAT PREPD,PRSVD,NES ETC	W 22536	63564	W 39842	89192	W 71271	141705	W 132079	227534	CONSERVES DE VIANDES
0142	SAUSAGES INCLDING TINNED	W 3051	8308	W 18117	32817	W 44460	76082	W 86996	137379	SAUCISSES,SAUCISSONS
0149	OTH PREPARD,PRESRVD MEAT	W 19485	55256	W 21725	56375	W 26811	65623	W 45083	90155	AUTRES PREP DE VIANDES
02	DAIRY PRODCTS,BIRDS'EGGS		218044		207700		252655		221365	PRODUITS LAITIERS,OEUFS
022	MILK AND CREAM	W 129102	181777	W 119598	158746	W 104046	195845	W 86929	145480	LAIT ET CREME
0224	MILK,CREAM PRESERVED ETC	W 129015	181743	W 119112	158411	W 102144	193820	W 81859	140133	LAIT,CREME CONS,CONC
02242	MILK DRY,1.5% FAT OR LES	W 125610	176873	W 112024	150125	W 97654	184931	W 76777	132574	LAIT POUDRE INF 1.5%
03	FISH AND PREPARATIONS		68907		116640		148215		168211	POISSONS ET PREPARATIONS
037	FISH ETC PREPD,PRSVD NES	W 23540	39734	W 29585	61011	W 29822	66211	W 34108	71360	POIS,CRUST,MOL PREPARES
04	CEREALS AND PREPARATIONS		19918		45751		100353		126705	CEREALES ET PRODUITS
048	CEREAL ETC PREPARATIONS	W 13896	18686	W 28672	42390	W 47354	75119	W 70149	103939	PREPTNS A BASE CEREALES
0484	BAKERY PRODUCTS	W 5951	14146	W 12245	26977	W 25040	53713	W 40051	76081	PRODUITS DE BOULANGERIE
05	VEGETABLES AND FRUIT		532465		646108		708147		703642	LEGUMES ET FRUITS
054	VEG ETC FRSH,SMPLY PRSVD	W 663081	144707	W 554493	164790	W 410949	175667	W 395224	172555	LEGUMES FRAIS,CONG,SECS
0545	OTHER FRESH VEGETABLES	W 219181	55859	W 247362	67850	W 146865	59648	W 172117	74712	AUTRES LEGUMES FRAIS,REF
0546	VEGETABLES SIMPLY PRESVD	W 78756	38363	W 113023	58441	W 108633	78270	W 116719	74631	LEGUMES CONG,CONSER
056	VEGTBLES ETC PRSVD,PREPD	W 39580	34063	W 80996	63305	W 59978	67175	W 71796	92052	CONSERVES DE LEGUMES
057	FRUIT,NUTS,FRESH,DRIED	W 253895	91830	W 181464	101254	W 243962	136375	W 204890	95870	FRUITS FRAIS OU SECS
0579	FRUIT FRESH OR DRIED NES	W 69051	46616	W 51509	59586	W 81425	66260	W 80392	48098	FRUITS FRAIS,SECS NDA
05794	BERRIES FRESH	W 46245	39509	W 42747	54544	W 54776	50727	W 63914	36905	BAIES FRAICHES
058	FRUIT PRESERVED,PREPARED	W 310304	261865	W 312001	316759	W 280532	328930	W 350300	343165	CONSERVES DE FRUITS
0585	FRUIT OR VEGETABLE JUICE	W 119713	90913	W 128130	97520	W 107124	148292	W 120900	131211	JUS DE FRUITS
05857	JUICE OF OTHER FRUIT,VEG	W 116437	88685	W 120602	93186	W 99021	142998	W 112926	124464	JUS AUTRES FRUITS,LEGUMES
0586	FRUIT TEMPORARILY PRESVD	W 173240	154679	W 171019	204752	W 162852	165915	W 214792	191771	FRUITS CONSERV TEMPORAIRE
05861	FRUIT,FRZN WITHOUT SUGAR	W 164087	148899	W 165919	199400	W 158886	162980	W 208000	188235	FRUITS CONG SANS SUCRE
06	SUGAR AND PREPS,HONEY		108383		145525		112045		220222	SUCRES ET PRODUITS
061	SUGAR AND HONEY	W 597267	86148	W 602981	98171	W 366216	37504	W 636182	99789	SUCRES ET MIEL
062	SUGAR CANDY NON--CHOCLATE	W 12725	22235	W 25899	47354	W 36119	74541	W 56002	120433	SUCRERIES
07	COFFEE,TEA,COCOA,SPICES		38186		61568		129458		209095	CAFE,THE,CACAO,EPICES
073	CHOCOLATE AND PRODUCTS	W 5925	17803	W 12519	36188	W 29297	82932	W 48410	140030	CHOCOLAT
09	MISC EDIBLE PRODUCTS		32076		72670		98107		129174	PREP ALIMENTAIRES DIVERSES
098	EDIBLE PRODCTS,PREPS NES	W 18593	28202	W 37394	68299	W 43367	80233	W 61339	117181	PREP ALIMENTAIRES NDA
09809	MISC FOOD PREPRTIONS NES	W 15333	22563	W 25288	46652	W 28316	56944	W 40510	87463	PREP ALIMENTAIRES NDA
1	BEVERAGES AND TOBACCO		133803		239427		163240		130235	BOISSONS ET TABACS
11	BEVERAGES		87774		185931		136308		86680	BOISSONS
111	NON--ALCOHL BEVERAGES NES	W 192029	51838	W 514379	120196	W 203380	50763	W 104326	23610	BOISSONS NON ALCOOLIQUES
11102	FLAVORED WATERS NON--ALCO	W 189614	51096	W 501742	117291	W 180498	45630	W 78619	18831	LIMONADES,EAUX GAZEUSES
112	ALCOHOLIC BEVERAGES	W 39977	35936	W 87225	65735	W 115355	85545	W 73089	63070	BOISSONS ALCOOLIQUES
12	TOBACCO AND MANUFACTURES		46029		53496		26932		43555	TABACS BRUTS FABRIQUES
2	CRUDE MATERLS,EXCL FUELS		775494		803529		1019041		820210	MAT BRUTES NON COMESTIBLES
22	OIL SEEDS,OLEAGINOUS FRT		8368		2698		99214		15487	GRAINES,FRUITS OLEAGINEUX
222	SEEDS FOR'SOFT'FIXED OIL	W 34331	7423	W 5567	1583	W 369149	98300	W 48630	13686	GRAINES HUILES FIXES
2226	RAPE AND COLZA SEEDS	W 34283	7379	W 4978	1205	W 368858	97917	W 48533	13429	GRAINES DE NAVETTE,COLZA
23	RUBBER, CRUDE		25214		34484		70843		60680	CAOUTCHOUC BRUT
233	RUBBER,SYNTHTIC,RECLAIMD	W 39578	24980	W 49190	34484	W 57532	70171	W 58646	60253	LATEX CAOUTCH SYNTH REGEN
2331	SYNTHETIC RUBBER ETC	W 34332	24449	W 43738	33689	W 52107	69283	W 53881	59189	LATEX CAOUTCH SYNTHETIQUE
23315	POLYBUTADIENE--STYRN(SBR)	W 34158	24332	W 43704	33620	W 51918	68938	W 52963	57739	POLYBUTADIENE--STYRENE
24	CORK AND WOOD		280117		334642		326372		266377	LIEGE ET BOIS
247	OTH WOOD ROUGH,SQUARED	W 767018	70237	W 540408	65166	W 282307	44643	W 200391	30181	BOIS BRUTS EQUARRIS
2471	SAW--,VENEER--LOGS CONIFER	W 554585	51591	W 366889	46169	W 182813	33932	W 151577	22780	CONIFERES POUR SCIAGE,PLACAG
24711	— IN THE ROUGH	W 554585	51591	W 366889	46169	W 182813	33932	W 151577	22780	ECORCES OU DEGROSSIS
248	WOOD SHAPED,SLEEPERS	W 805147	194522	W 985897	252368	W 732701	264292	W 555571	217163	BOIS SIMPLEMENT TRAVAILLES
2482	LUMBER SHAPED CONIFER	W 622131	134714	W 735751	172182	W 507385	167830	W 351771	122176	CONIFERES SCIES,RABOTES
24821	LUMBER SAWN ETC CONIFER	W 601446	126762	W 713840	164310	W 486488	156176	W 325769	109489	CONIFERES SCIES LONGITUD
2483	LUMBER SHAPED NON--CONIFR	W 171713	57988	W 232507	77084	W 210876	94039	W 189858	92475	NON CONIFERES SCIES,RABOTES
24831	LUMBER SAWN ETC NON--CON	W 136781	40721	W 205591	60125	W 181163	70286	W 166691	70875	SCIES LONGITUDINALEMENT
26	TEXTILE FIBRES AND WASTE		37208		57790		65962		41287	FIBRES TEXTILES
27	CRUDE FERTLZR,MINRLS NES		152297		158373		195389		162319	ENGRAIS MINERAUX BRUTS
273	STONE,SAND AND GRAVEL		49735	W 7274052	54847	W 6872998	60518	W 6625735	61250	PIERRES,SABLES,GRAVIERS
274	SULPHUR,UNRSTD IRN PYRTE	W 2259662	77179	W 1813369	73431	W 1643505	96083	W 1302430	58405	SOUFRE ET PYRITES
2741	SULPHUR,EX SULP IN 52215	W 2259662	77179	W 1813369	73431	W 1643505	96083	W 1302430	58405	SOUFRE
28	METALLIFEROUS ORES,SCRAP		157044		90348		92809		97924	MINERAIS METAL,DECHETS
282	IRON AND STEEL SCRAP	W 988862	83766	W 432882	48533	W 422504	57422	W 414033	52707	FERRAILLES
28209	— OF OTHR IRON OR STEEL	W 849828	65815	W 405587	37408	W 402256	44625	W 399514	42009	FERRAILLES DE FER
29	CRUDE ANIMAL,VEG MAT NES		66143		75268		94843		105133	MATIERES BRUTES ANIM,VEGET
3	MINERAL FUELS ETC		1260528		1565577		1869891		1677411	COMBUSTIBLES MINERAUX LUB
32	COAL,COKE AND BRIQUETTES		1126475		1324167		1577000		1355538	HOUILLES,COKES,BRIQUETTES
322	COAL,LIGNITE AND PEAT	MW 23615	978865	MW 28381	1057217	MW 32281	1244901	MW 29015	1140200	HOUILLES,LIGNITES,TOURBE
3222	OTH COAL,NOT AGGLOMERATD	MW 22539	951073	MW 27474	1034949	MW 31794	1231508	MW 28885	1135291	AUTRES HOUILLES
323	BRIQUETS,COKE,SEMI--COKE	W 1987911	147610	W 3185368	266950	W 3429921	332099	W 2289065	215338	BRIQUETTES
3232	COKE,SEMI--COKE,RTRT CRBN	W 1873354	141817	W 3104690	261791	W 3331368	326302	W 2205006	210577	COKES ET SEMI--COKES
33	PETROLEUM AND PRODUCTS		132378		153491		188137		196013	PETROLE ET DERIVES
334	PETROLEUM PRODUCTS,REFIN	W 1159489	97217	W 1104459	108116	W 1121442	130949	W 1212475	150282	PRODUITS RAFFINES
3344	FUEL OILS,NES	W 964937	56010	W 893681	60875					FUEL OILS
351	*ELECTRIC CURRENT		53		84886		101742		122070	ENERGIE ELECTRIQUE
5	CHEMCLS,RELATED PROD NES		924918		1140056		1739427		1845208	PRODUITS CHIMIQUES
51	ORGANIC CHEMICALS		199849		268002		471398		393299	PROD CHIMIQ ORGANIQUES
512	ALCOHOLS,PHENOLS ETC	W 146874	61620	W 159661	87305	W 175747	173205	W 181380	111678	PHENOLS,PHENOLS--ALCOOLS
5121	ACYCLIC ALCOHOLS,DERIVS	W 134519	57011	W 125187	72571	W 139115	145593	W 140029	88322	ALCOOLS ACYCLIQUES
51214	OCTYL ALCOHOLS(OCTANOLS)	W 83207	38663	W 73101	44193	W 74453	97232	W 76849	52698	ALCOOLS OCTYLIQUES
515	ORG--INORG COMPOUNDS ETC	W 73175	75585	W 65966	77360	W 79743	134849	W 82948	128566	COMPOSES ORGANO--MINERAUX
5156	HETEROCYCLIC CMPDS ETC	W 72694	69966	W 64910	66018	W 78859	124093	W 82305	119418	COMPOSES HETEROCYCLIQUES
51561	LACTAMS	W 72571	68437	W 64816	64389	W 78828	123034	W 82204	113619	LACTAMES .
52	INORGANIC CHEMICALS		163715		213498		242446		226709	PROD CHIM INORGANIQUES
522	INORG ELEMNTS,OXIDES,ETC		63495	W 746170	101018	W 747883	112319	W 615080	101397	ELEMENTS INORGANIQUES
5225	INORGANIC BASES ETC NES	W 145421	21002	W 398819	56939	W 330399	58509	W 273120	48491	AUTRES BASES OXYDES METAL
523	OTHR INORG CHEMICALS ETC	W 570575	99162	W 721238	111306	W 699563	128938	W 635536	123935	AUT PRODUITS CHIMIQUES INORG
5232	OTH MTL CMPD OF INRG ACD	W 467913	72996	W 606830	85293	W 582855	93215	W 528266	88293	SELS METALLIQUES
52323	NEUTRAL SODIUM CARBONATE	W 260646	32492	W 490644	58753	W 482827	63637	W 384811	55432	CARBONATE NEUTRE SODIUM
541	*MEDICINAL,PHARM PRODUCT		206627	K 8956000	200111	MK 9395	223841	MK 12067	256023	PROD MEDICINAUX PHARMACEUT
5417	MEDICAMENTS	K 6423814	171074	K 5848000	153717	K 6219185	169426	K 7128606	190045	MEDICAMENTS
54179	— CONTNG OTH SUBSTANCES	K 4436241	122825	K 4202000	110329	K 4706068	138781	K 5792728	158108	MED CONT AUT SUBSTANCES

5. General Exports F.O.B. by Commodities according to the S.I.T.C. (Rev. 2) in thousand U.S. Dollars
Exportations Générales F.O.B. par Produits d'après la C.T.C.I. (Rév. 2) en milliers de Dollars E.U.

SITC CTCI	COMMODITY	1993		1994		1995		1996		PRODUIT
		WEIGHT POIDS	VALUE VALEUR	WEIGHT POIDS	VALUE VALEUR	WEIGHT POIDS	VALUE VALEUR	WEIGHT POIDS	VALUE VALEUR	
55	PERFUME,CLEANING ETC PRD		28883		63732		161724		303522	PROD POUR PARFUM,TOILETTE
553	PERFUMERY,COSMETICS,ETC	W 7669	17621	W 12819	30850	W 26464	75915	W 44668	159955	PRODUITS DE PARFUMERIE
554	SOAP,CLEANSING ETC PREPS	W 12364	9872	W 56595	31441	W 79684	82104	W 143531	138681	SAVONS,PRODUITS DETERSIFS
5542	WASHING PREPARATIONS ETC	W 10258	8219	W 53652	28002	W 75285	76194	W 130331	123490	PROD ORG TENSIO–ACT NDA
562	*FERTILIZERS,MANUFACTURE	W 1434417	108605	W 1795803	173607	W 2342344	297128	W 2317286	303752	ENGRAIS MANUFACTURES
5621	CHEM NITROGENOUS FERTLZR	W 1325271	94234	W 1431670	121027	W 1799200	209649	W 1675613	193733	ENGRAIS AZOTES
56219	CHEM NITROG FERTILZR NES	W 741184	57038	W 392412	34489	W 858462	101172	W 842479	99628	ENGRAIS AZOTES NDA
5629	FERTILIZERS NES	W 96961	13203	W 284965	43418	W 473113	79315	W 568101	99759	ENGRAIS NDA
58	PLASTIC MATERIALS ETC		108233		106741		191351		187484	MAT PLAST ARTIFICIELLES
583	POLYMERIZATION ETC PRODS	W 135258	82265	W 99518	72032	W 123861	129441	W 154646	132826	PROD POLYMERISATION
59	CHEMICAL MATERIALS NES		72786		61883		82120		103526	MAT PROD CHIMIQUES NDA
592	STARCH,INULIN,GLUTEN,ETC	W 16710	45179	W 13093	30885	W 17617	39965	W 34704	54824	AMIDONS,INUL,GLUT FROM
5922	ALBUMINOID SUBSTAN,GLUES	W 16710	45179	W 13093	30885	W 17590	39873	W 33973	54280	MAT ALBUMIN,COLLES
6	BASIC MANUFACTURES		3791947		4831955		6423895		6450806	ART MANUFACTURES
61	LEATHER,DRESSED FUR,ETC		132744		147420		201902		216796	CUIRS,PELLETERIES
611	LEATHER	W 11439	50206	W 9217	57222	W 8510	70987	W 5152	57970	CUIRS,PEAUX PREPARES
612	LEATHER ETC MANUFACTURES	W 4342	72439	W 5413	73047	W 6494	99116	W 9117	120099	OUVRAGES EN CUIRS NDA
6123	PREPRD PARTS OF FOOTWEAR	W 3868	67212	W 5083	66342	W 5704	77823	W 7809	89530	PARTIES DE CHAUSSURES
62	RUBBER MANUFACTURES NES		92205		140488		210107		237617	CAOUTCHOUC MANUFACTURE
625	RUBBER TYRES, TUBES ETC	W 30414	66130	W 46344	104679	W 59767	159268	W 58490	168767	PNEUS CAOUTCHOUC VULCANISE
6251	TYRES NEW FOR MOTOR CARS	W 12363	34032	W 19276	49571	W 26941	78602	W 28406	88630	PNEUS POUR VOITURES
63	WOOD,CORK MANUFACTRS NES		275805		405805		561646		596505	OUVRAGES LIEGE ET BOIS
634	VENEERS,PLYWOOD,ETC	W 133866	55420	W 217440	94323	W 227812	116953	W 189868	110826	PLACAGES,CONTRE–PLAQUES
635	WOOD MANUFACTURES NES	W 635200	220348	W 894295	311278	W 892188	444693	W 871100	485480	ART MANUF EN BOIS NDA
6351	BOXES,CASES,CRATES,ETC	W 482264	95394	W 648861	124485	W 606746	147196	W 525418	128046	CAISSES EMBALLAGES BOIS
6353	BUILDERS WOODWRK,PREFABS	W 64512	59589	W 105286	89884	W 114939	146515	W 121313	164271	OUVRAGES DE MENUISERIE
6359	OTHER WOOD MANUFACTURES	W 79157	48453	W 128945	74810	W 159255	123623	W 211267	158423	OUVRAGES EN BOIS NDA
63599	OTHER WOOD ARTICLES NES	W 77577	47202	W 127363	73071	W 157451	121263	W 209148	155906	AUTRES OUVRAGES EN BOIS NDA
64	PAPER,PAPERBOARD AND MFR		166648		240732		524921		541383	PAPIERS,CARTONS & OUVRAGES
641	PAPER AND PAPERBOARD	W 393567	123579	W 472367	174336	W 632700	417814	W 717309	397245	PAPIERS ET CARTONS
6412	PRINTG,WRITING PAPER NES	W 1818	1250	W 21439	16389	W 102439	96278	W 115774	83152	PAPIERS POUR L'IMPRESSION
64121	— UNCOATED	W 395	417	W 20094	15100	W 101095	94410	W 113968	79402	PAPIERS IMPRES NON COUCHES
6413	KRAFT PAPER,PAPERBOARD	W 123249	45545	W 144480	59895	W 127733	84068	W 148987	79095	PAPIER ET CARTON KRAFT
6415	PAPER,PAPERBRD,BULK,NES	W 115555	37556	W 129558	44786	W 148607	103176	W 182480	105539	PAPIERS,CARTONS ROULEAUX
64159	OTHER PAPER ETC,BULK,NES	W 43003	19036	W 35498	17709	W 62198	58581	W 103686	78520	AUT PAPIER ROULEAUX FEUILLES
6416	FIBRE BUILDING BOARD	W 128602	28976	W 157108	39126	W 195793	76689	W 185980	66756	PLAQUES CONSTRUCT EN PATE
642	PAPER,ETC,PRECUT,ARTS OF	W 67623	43069	W 82685	66396	W 79240	107107	W 87031	144138	PAP,CARTONS DECOUPES
65	TEXTILE YARN,FABRICS,ETC		309766		398627		515593		563238	FILS,TISSUS,ARTICLES TEXTILE
651	TEXTILE YARN	W 12189	41390	W 18223	61933	W 21727	96195	W 18240	87501	FILS TEXTILES
654	OTH WOVEN TEXTILE FABRIC	W 5119	48675	W 7183	62700	W 5943	55590	W 5005	40579	TISSUS AUT COTON SYNT,ARTIF
658	TEXTILE ARTICLES NES	W 19489	107123	W 24668	155689	W 27311	213164	W 29341	235566	ART FACONNES MAT TEXTILES
6584	LINENS ETC	W 7330	57235	W 9952	83727	W 11559	113491	W 12011	121001	LINGE DE MAISON
66	NONMETAL MINERAL MFS NES		388920		500358		617930		671031	ART MIN NON METALLIQUES
661	LIME,CEMENT,BLDG PRODS	W 3661230	151300	W 4773549	196351	W 4334188	215194	W 3798152	183953	CHAUX,CIMENTS MAT CONSTR
6612	CEMENT	W 3241313	130831	W 4401312	171572	W 4035343	186464	W 3480128	152506	CIMENTS HYDRAULIQUES
663	MINERAL MANUFCTURES NES	W 209575	28715	W 294354	42019	W 311076	58726	W 339687	100435	ART MIN MANUF NDA
664	GLASS		46303	W 125314	50385	W 134248	58161	W 141198	64826	VERRE
665	GLASSWARE	W 110236	99521	W 149384	131216	W 166593	173491	W 169629	189297	OUVRAGES EN VERRE
6652	HOUSEHLD,HOTEL ETC GLASS	W 22772	74776	W 32207	96901	W 39494	127161	W 45098	140493	OBJETS VERRE TABLE,CUISINE
666	POTTERY	W 28410	54028	W 33073	64526	W 35940	82037	W 38663	93477	POTERIE
67	IRON AND STEEL		1006447		1223433		1426300		1346115	FER ET ACIER
672	IRON,STEEL PRIMARY FORMS	W 1116170	238287	W 1537117	304662	W 721323	175085	W 1088728	246517	LINGOTS FER,ACIER
6725	IRN,STL BLOOMS,SLABS,ETC	W 1075989	226671	W 1446809	288313	W 682072	165355	W 1073443	241013	BLOOMS,BILLETTES FER ACIER
67251	IRN,SMPLE STL BLOOMS,ETC	W 1069385	219314	W 1428558	278062	W 679097	158487	W 1064555	231528	BLOOMS ETC NON ACIER FIN
673	IRON,STEEL SHAPES ETC	W 1504252	462253	W 1584028	436471	W 1668862	548311	W 1660938	493525	BARRES,PROFIL FER,ACIER
6732	IRON,STEEL BARS ETC	W 253116	78236	W 366572	101596	W 262898	113072	W 221583	90970	BARRES FER,ACIER
67326	IRN,OTH STL BARS HOTROLD	W 212779	55630	W 320260	76906	W 206553	66141	W 142601	41253	BARRES PLEINES FER,ACIER
6733	IRON,STEEL PROFILES ETC	W 1115158	347420	W 1044829	288340	W 1200797	372861	W 1187108	338667	PROFILES,PALPLAN FER,ACIER
67331	SMALL U,I,H SECTIONS ETC	W 86786	60069	W 51047	13701	W 22607	7956	W 11780	3869	PROFILES MOINS 80MM
67332	LARGE U,I,H SECTIONS ETC	W 899714	250629	W 789256	218204	W 939593	285825	W 1005883	280185	PROFILES PLUS 80MM
674	IRN,STL UNIV,PLATE,SHEET	W 299503	89757	W 561239	177706	W 639505	251794	W 487190	194253	LARGES PLATS,TOLES
6744	IRN,STL HVY PLATE,ROLLED	W 226981	59295	W 345303	96857	W 304499	114506	W 263865	103284	TOLES LAMINEES PLUS 4.75 MM
67441	— OF IRON OR SIMPLE STL	W 219002	57112	W 345002	96554	W 304144	114029	W 263598	102930	TOLES NON ACIER FIN CARB
676	RAILWY RAILS ETC IRN,STL	W 121281	30892	W 206201	62606	W 229414	75972	W 154654	59104	RAILS,ELEMENTS VOIES FERREE
67601	RAILWAY RAILS IRN,STL	W 114346	26055	W 191180	55299	W 218974	68328	W 145200	52055	RAILS,ELEMENTS FER,ACIER
678	IRON,STL TUBES,PIPES,ETC	W 82343	57980	W 128502	85296	W 156696	127637	W 121555	119170	TUBES,TUYAUX EN FONTE,FER
679	IRN,STL CASTINGS UNWORKD	W 83605	65899	W 109599	94665	W 137397	143213	W 132956	144896	OUVRAGES EN FONTE,FER,ACIER
6794	IRON,STL CASTINGS ROUGH	W 80159	61375	W 104269	87426	W 131186	124827	W 126441	124798	OUVRAGES COULES,MOULES
67941	IRON CASTINGS ROUGH	W 80159	61375	W 104269	87426	W 131186	124827	W 126441	124798	OUVRAGES A L'ETAT BRUT
68	NON–FERROUS METALS		943413		1130887		1370023		1162583	METAUX NON FERREUX
681	SILVER,PLATINUM,ETC		96045		166242		152706		151493	ARGENT ET PLATINE
6811	SILVER UNWKD,PARTLY WRKD		94665		165798		151849		150616	ARGENT BRUT MI–OUVRE
68113	SILVER UNWROUGHT		94276		165157		151215		150182	ARGENT ET ALLIAGES BRUTS
682	COPPER EXC CEMENT COPPER	W 332597	663341	W 350522	794143	W 336661	1005826	W 335120	811311	CUIVRE
6821	COPPER NES,ALLOYS,UNWRT	W 266212	520904	W 264516	590471	W 201683	596071	W 207969	474486	CUIVRE BRUT
68212	COPPER REFINED,UNWROUGHT	W 266212	520904	W 264058	589668	W 201344	595324	W 207903	474309	CUIVRE AFFINE BRUT
6822	COPPER,ALLOYS WORKED	W 66386	142437	W 86006	203672	W 134979	409755	W 127152	336825	CUIVRE,ALLIAGES OUVRES
68221	COPPER BARS,WIRE,ETC	W 50217	100951	W 62518	140469	W 111499	329072	W 104935	264529	BARRES,PROFILES ET FILS
68222	COPPER PLATE,SHEET,STRIP	W 14424	35591	W 21309	55030	W 20173	66216	W 18901	58849	TOLES DE PLUS 0.15 MM
684	ALUMINIUM	W 43608	61988	W 41828	72016	W 52747	112758	W 52375	99903	ALUMINIUM
686	ZINC		113928	W 89866	84909	W 78821	83743	W 75888	80594	ZINC
6861	ZINC,ALLOYS UNWROUGHT	W 71429	91901	W 81808	72596	W 69381	67451	W 65814	64347	ZINC ET ALLIAGES BRUTS
69	METAL MANUFACTURES NES		475999		644205		995473		1115538	ART MANUFACT EN METAL NDA
691	STRUCTURES AND PARTS NES	W 152966	164479	W 195853	226506	W 256241	355516	W 273907	386465	CONSTRUCT FER,ACIER,ALU
6911	STRUCTURES,PARTS IRN,STL	W 152259	160204	W 194516	216513	W 253369	333735	W 270183	360181	CONSTRUCT FER,ACIER,FONTE
692	METAL TANKS,BOXES,ETC	W 51943	58820	W 43980	53991	W 53580	84570	W 65969	124122	RECIPIENTS METALLIQUES
6924	MTL TRANSPORT BOXES ETC	W 13713	17207	W 14836	20026	W 21948	44273	W 30117	77999	FUTS,TAMBOURS,BIDONS
694	STL,COPPR NAILS,NUTS,ETC	W 56514	41759	W 65014	53228	W 69573	74447	W 54946	61685	CLOUS,VIS,ECROUS
699	BASE METAL MFRS NES	W 81335	112295	W 133513	199159	W 208229	335989	W 226085	388647	ART MANUFACTURES MET NDA
6997	IRON,STEEL ARTICLES NES	W 59021	64078	W 97158	111640	W 156987	191571	W 171126	223044	OUV FONTE,FER,ACIER NDA
69979	IRN,STL MANUFACTURES NES	W 59013	64046	W 96931	111258	W 156579	190981	W 170814	222442	AUT OUVRAGES EN FER NDA
6998	MFRS NES OF CPR,NIKL,ETC	W 4378	16494	W 10746	38878	W 16424	67983	W 19715	75276	OUVRAGES EN CU,NI,AL,PB,ZN
7	MACHINES,TRANSPORT EQUIP		2879900		3396937		4808593		5703153	MACHINES MATERIEL TRANSPORT
71	POWER GENERATING EQUIPMT		207716		211149		364619		421293	MACHINES GENERATRICES
713	INTRNL COMBUS PSTN ENGIN	W 16071	81459	W 17249	88075	W 18870	109355	W 24971	151996	MOTEURS EXPL COMB INT, PIECE
7139	PISTON ENGINE PARTS NES	W 11262	44640	W 13883	58022	W 14780	75420	W 17870	97521	PIECES POUR 713.2,3,8
716	ROTATING ELECTRIC PLANT	W 16128	53743	W 17133	59357	W 21983	87021	W 24759	104907	APP ELECTR ROTATIFS,PIECES
7162	AC MTRS,GENRTRS,GEN SETS	W 14456	44718	W 14284	40952	W 16424	57243	W 15611	57398	MOTEURS ELECTRIQUES
72	MACHS FOR SPCL INDUSTRYS		246183		327046		425178		460416	MAC SPECIALES POUR INDUST
722	TRACTORS NON–ROAD	W 10397	26296	W 18429	55940	W 17497	66225	W 14284	67951	TRACTEURS
7224	WHEELED TRACTORS NES	W 10352	26146	W 18429	55940	W 17417	66165	W 14284	67951	TRACTEURS A ROUES

5. General Exports F.O.B. by Commodities according to the S.I.T.C. (Rev. 2) in thousand U.S. Dollars
Exportations Générales F.O.B. par Produits d'après la C.T.C.I. (Rév. 2) en milliers de Dollars E.U.

SITC CTCI	COMMODITY	1993		1994		1995		1996		PRODUIT
		WEIGHT POIDS	VALUE VALEUR	WEIGHT POIDS	VALUE VALEUR	WEIGHT POIDS	VALUE VALEUR	WEIGHT POIDS	VALUE VALEUR	
723	CIVIL ENGNEERG EQUIP ETC	W 18234	64090	W 24220	88273	W 23439	97754	W 22059	102570	APPAREILS DE GENIE CIVIL
7234	CONST,MINING MACHNRY NES	W 15208	57939	W 20683	79224	W 19445	87633	W 18390	93407	MACH POUR LA CONST, MINES
728	OTH MACHY FOR SPCL INDUS	W 21023	70741	W 23258	77986	W 36087	118500	W 34969	133720	AUT MACH IND PARTICULIERES
7284	MACHY FOR SPCL INDUS NES	W 11266	38896	W 12764	45374	W 24773	77928	W 25458	97808	MACH SPEC IND PARTICUL.
73	METALWORKING MACHINERY		54805		57651		83055		97871	MACH TRAVAIL DES METAUX
736	METALWORKING MACH–TOOLS	W 11166	46633	W 11493	45508	W 15468	68123	W 16823	77171	MACH–OUTILS TRAVAIL METAUX
74	GENRL INDUSTRL MACHY NES		268684		340500		519528		622733	MACH APP INDUSTRIE
741	HEATING,COOLING EQUIPMNT	W 9193	25795	W 10263	39017	W 13859	60704	W 19699	86424	MACH CHAUFFAGE,PIECES
744	MECHANICAL HANDLING EQU	W 34192	87434	W 44909	96655	W 55478	145308	W 58307	159435	EQUIP MANUTENTION PIECES
7449	PTS NES OF MACHY OF 7442	W 20823	49526	W 29532	61204	W 37682	94381	W 37625	94840	PIECES DU 744.2
749	NONELEC MACH PTS,ACC NES	W 31471	104175	W 33678	130130	W 49323	207308	W 58893	243168	PIECES MACH NON ELEC NDA
7491	BALL,ROLLER,ETC BEARINGS	W 7520	41582	W 9789	57136	W 16004	93456	W 13779	91928	ROULEMENTS BILLES ETC
76	TELECOMM,SOUND EQUIPMENT		35140		81098		168442		286937	EQUIPMENT DE TELECOM
761	TELEVISION RECEIVERS	W 61	896	W 1736	22821	W 3877	47268	W 11098	133547	RECEPTEURS DE TELEVISION
7611	COLOUR TV RECEIVERS	W 60	848	W 1736	22821	W 3877	47268	W 10602	127133	RECEPTEURS COULEUR
764	TELECOM EQPT,PTS,ACC NES	W 3775	30789	W 4965	54234	W 6306	95514	W 9599	145225	EQUIP TELECOM,PIECES
7649	PTS NES OF EQUIPMT OF 76	W 1304	16261	W 2139	34890	W 3336	69898	W 6497	116109	PIECES DE LA DIV 76
76493	TELECOMM EQUIPMT PTS NES	W 915	10562	W 1644	27574	W 2239	45917	W 4607	75576	PIECES 761,762,764.3,8
77	ELECTRIC MACHNRY NES ETC		594721		702095		1023292		1223876	MACH APP ELECT NDA
771	ELECTRIC POWER MACHY NES	W 2842	14128	W 5669	32882	W 6614	50496	W 9396	91865	MACH PROD,TRANS ELECTR
772	SWITCHGEAR ETC,PARTS NES	W 8439	88438	W 9325	107909	W 8694	137785	W 9212	169192	APP COUPURE,SECT ETC
7721	SWITCHGEAR ETC	W 8382	84938	W 9253	102966	W 8626	133024	W 9048	159575	APP COUPURE,SECTIONMNT
773	ELECTR DISTRIBUTNG EQUIP	W 56031	144215	W 50958	156468	W 73710	278655	W 86581	338558	EQUIPMT DISTRIBUTION ELECT
7731	INSULATED WIRE,CABLE ETC	W 53557	137974	W 47915	149218	W 68880	268717	W 81835	326122	FILS,CABLES ISOLES ELECT
775	HOUSEHOLD TYPE EQUIP NES	W 19135	82484	W 19340	87704	W 18529	98930	W 20325	112893	MACH,APP USAGE DOMESTQUE
776	TRANSISTORS,VALVES,ETC	W 15912	86382	W 18944	112277	W 27510	205490	W 28640	201275	LAMPES,TUBES,VALVES
7761	TV PICTURE TUBES	W 15530	76631	W 18086	92366	W 26825	164968	W 27753	171349	TUBES CATHODIQUES
778	ELECTRICAL MACHINERY NES	W 57897	173838	W 56480	199984	W 64866	248654	W 74926	306703	AUTRES MACH ELECT NDA
7782	ELECTRIC LAMPS,BULBS	W 10691	86240	W 13514	103458	W 16580	132884	W 18978	147201	LAMPES, TUBES ELECTRIQUES
77822	ELEC DISCHARGE LAMPS NES	W 4256	50179	W 5873	56699	W 7339	70087	W 8574	85717	LAMPES NON ULTRA–VIOLETS
7788	OTH ELEC MACHY,EQUIP NES	W 40672	61832	W 37604	73916	W 41204	84431	W 38926	94779	AUT MACH APP ELEC NDA
77887	ELECTRICAL CARBONS	W 39203	51432	W 36060	55732	W 39034	65724	W 36969	69578	PIECES CHARBON,GRAPHITE
78	ROAD VEHICLES		730571		793904		1127744		1324282	VEHICULES ROUTIERS
781	PASS MOTOR VEH EXC BUSES	W 107745	553163	W 104822	523728	W 124212	658816	W 135182	783337	AUTO TRANSPORT PERSONNES
782	LORRIES,SPCL MTR VEH NES	W 8057	33428	W 10690	68404	W 19092	182107	W 17205	160881	VEHICULES SPECIAUX,MARCH
7821	LORRIES,TRUCKS	W 5098	21788	W 8698	62683	W 18465	179977	W 16408	158637	VEHICULES TRANSP MARCHAND
784	MOTOR VEH PRTS,ACCES NES	W 14378	47941	W 21155	62751	W 35513	123477	W 51471	206748	PIECES 722,781,782,783
7849	OTHER MOTOR VEHCL PARTS	W 13547	44799	W 20851	61556	W 34497	116570	W 49698	187005	PIECES 722,781,782,783
786	TRAILERS,NONMOTR VEH,NES	W 58720	77028	W 75630	101631	W 78810	116543	W 80651	119165	REMORQUES,CADRES,CONTAIN
7861	TRAILERS,TRANSP CONTAINR	W 44869	53772	W 59741	66696	W 59751	72803	W 58940	74384	REMORQUES TOUS VEHICULES
79	OTHR TRANSPORT EQUIPMENT		728144		854110		1065392		1202555	AUTRE MATERIEL TRANSPORT
791	RAILWAY VEHICLES	W 84029	51866	W 53664	38046	W 37284	51839	W 20304	30963	VEHIC MAT CHEMINS DE FER
792	AIRCRAFT ETC	W 479	30307	W 624	29480	W 765	37557	W 628	84863	APP NAVIGATION AERIENNE
793	SHIPS AND BOATS ETC		645971	W 2486822	786584	W 1670934	975996	W 962359	1086729	NAVIRES BATEAUX,ETC
7932	SHIPS AND BOATS NES	W 1691186	618817	W 2458414	770406	W 1646067	950377	W 924479	1012182	NAVIRES ET BATEAUX
79322	TANKERS OF ALL KINDS	W 37656	62048			W 778	323	W 391	384	BATEAUX–CITERNES
79323	OTHER CARGO VESSELS	W 1638528	528685	W 2448802	751209	W 1632468	930135	W 912643	978648	AUT BATEAUX TRANS MARCH
8	MISC MANUFACTURED GOODS		2607066		3415848		4624485		5239320	ART MANUFACTURES DIVERS
812	*PLUMBG,HEATNG,LGHTNG EQ	W 10419	34257	W 14148	52084	W 18496	78457	W 24409	104406	APPAR SANITAIRES CHAUFFAGE
8124	LIGHTING EQUIPMENT NES	W 8242	31147	W 10997	47417	W 14857	70336	W 16952	88290	APPAREILS ECLAIRAGE ETC
821	*FURNITURE,PARTS THEREOF	W 334578	580978	W 470367	894779	W 599374	1337815	W 722993	1617368	MEUBLES ET PIECES
8211	CHAIRS,SEATS AND PARTS	W 107297	230706	W 145667	379904	W 199821	583762	W 236522	700266	SIEGES ET PIECES
82111	CHAIRS AND OTHER SEATS	W 102468	209948	W 137575	348190	W 191247	547686	W 225140	651588	SIEGES
8212	MED FURN,STUFFD FURNSHGS	W 7348	29485	W 12369	40355	W 11931	63081	W 14655	74715	MOB MEDICO–CHIRUR,PIECES
8219	FURNITURE AND PARTS NES	W 219933	320787	W 312331	474520	W 387621	690972	W 471816	842387	AUTRES MEUBLES ET PIECES
82192	WOOD FURNITURE NES	W 198578	288383	W 280691	422152	W 343936	605679	W 415311	726666	MEUBLES NDA EN BOIS
82199	OTHR FURN,FURN PARTS NES	W 12630	18432	W 19816	32385	W 30401	56186	W 42873	81705	MEUBLES NDA AUTRES MATIERES
84	CLOTHING AND ACCESSORIES		1577762		1842699		2298648		2369287	VETEMENTS
842	MENS OUTERWEAR NOT KNIT	W 15536	396379	W 18078	466706	W 20016	550841	W 22560	616183	VET DESSUS POUR HOMMES
8421	— OVERCOATS,OTHER COATS	W 2012	56668	W 2254	70403	W 1615	60697	W 2058	69267	MANTEAUX HOMMES MAT TEXT
8422	— SUITS	W 1264	48709	W 1428	54108	W 1396	59790	W 1405	62665	COMPLETS HOMMES MAT TEXT
8423	— TROUSERS,BREECHES ETC	W 4877	99829	W 6246	123106	W 8090	170610	W 9585	203229	PANTALONS HOMMES MAT TEX
8424	— JACKETS,BLAZERS ETC	W 2983	104410	W 3127	106767	W 3584	128945	W 3731	141574	VESTES HOMMES MAT TEXTIL
8429	— OTHER OUTER GARMENTS	W 4400	86763	W 5023	112322	W 5331	130799	W 5781	139448	AUT VET DES HOM MAT TEX
843	WOMENS OUTERWEAR NONKNIT	W 22557	738872	W 26791	867671	W 30049	1115033	W 31482	1128187	VET DESSUS FEMMES MAT TEX
8431	— COATS AND JACKETS	W 5863	222964	W 6441	247957	W 6551	289278	W 6532	278265	MANT,VEST FEM MAT TEXTIL
8433	— DRESSES	W 860	34077	W 1139	38418	W 1900	71875	W 2088	77562	ROBES EN MAT–TEXTILES
8434	— SKIRTS	W 2308	69078	W 2824	82614	W 3689	124125	W 3593	119502	JUPES EN MAT TEXTILES
8435	— BLOUSES	W 4879	174185	W 5848	207231	W 6572	269926	W 6410	250151	BLOUSES FEM MAT TEXTILES
8439	— OTHER OUTER GARMENTS	W 7617	203193	W 9517	259342	W 10303	318037	W 11695	353782	AUT VET DES FEM MAT TEXT
844	UNDER GARMENTS NOT KNIT	W 3239	127156	W 3706	142551	W 4613	185988	W 4498	162840	VETEMENT DESSOUS MAT TEX
8441	— MENS SHIRTS	W 2924	119864	W 3382	137217	W 4214	179347	W 3932	154242	CHEMISES HOMMES MAT TEXT
84411	—— OF COTTON	W 1208	50804	W 1503	60756	W 2005	86957	W 2111	89960	CHEMISES HOMMES DE COTON
84412	—— OF SYNTHETIC FIBRES	W 1716	69060	W 1879	76461	W 2209	92390	W 1821	64282	CHEMISES HOMMES FIB SYNT
845	OUTERWEAR KNIT NONELASTC	W 11527	210070	W 12387	229139	W 13813	278620	W 15745	284864	VET DESSOUS,ACCES BONNET
8451	— JERSEYS,PULLOVERS ETC	W 4160	71634	W 4528	78648	W 5438	98811	W 6989	129066	CHANDAILS,PULL–OVERS ETC
8459	— OTHER,CLTHG ACCESRYS	W 6196	110406	W 6530	121069	W 6787	139607	W 6710	119519	AUT VET DESSUS DE BONNE
846	UNDER GARMENTS KNITTED	W 4332	66444	W 5467	91082	W 5664	114561	W 6376	123748	SOUS VETS DE BONNETERIE
8462	— OF COTTON NON ELASTIC	W 3324	46629	W 4316	64443	W 4422	82658	W 4906	87325	SOUS–VET BONNET COTON
84629	—— OTHER	W 3324	46629	W 4316	64443	W 4422	82658	W 4906	87325	AUT SOUS–VET BONNET COTON
851	*FOOTWEAR	W 10281	109387	W 11203	121873	W 13383	175140	W 15675	221635	CHAUSSURES
85102	FOOTWEAR LEATHER	W 4667	53315	W 5459	67186	W 7139	107600	W 7970	122186	CHAUS SEMELLES EN CUIR
85103	SHOES WOOD–,CORK–SOLED	W 3454	43198	W 3470	40172	W 2986	34148	W 1888	27126	CHAUS SEMELLES BOIS,LIEGE
87	PRECISION INSTRUMNTS NES		46796		94449		104949		117790	INSTRUM,APPAR SCIENT NDA
874	MEASURNG,CONTROLNG INSTR	W 1259	27698	W 1525	41037	W 1841	57923	W 2261	74077	INSTRUMENTS DE MESURE
89	MISC MANUFCTRD GOODS NES		233959		380630		593268		766656	ART MANUFACTURES DIVERS
892	PRINTED MATTER	W 4813	19373	W 8058	35487	W 12799	53836	W 18496	78111	IMPRIMES
893	ARTICLES OF PLASTIC NES		87481		149529		261465		333625	OUVRAGES EN MAT DIVIS 58
8931	PLSTC PACKG CONTNRS,LIDS	W 10768	16126	W 13101	25375	W 20042	58131	W 33379	74813	ART TRANSP EMBALLAGE ETC
8939	MISC PLASTIC ARTICLES	W 20844	66779	W 39568	116692	W 57742	191651	W 71864	244255	ART DIVERS EN MAT DIV 58
89399	OTHR PLASTC ARTICLES NES	W 19289	63834	W 35144	107993	W 48466	172183	W 63274	224486	AUT OUV MAT DIV 58
894	TOYS,SPORTING GOODS,ETC		51013	W 14150	67837	W 13651	86432	W 15659	101809	VOITURES ENFANTS,JOUETS
8942	TOYS,INDOOR GAMES ETC		32341	W 9928	49458	W 9618	64730	W 11007	77912	JOUETS,JEUX ETC
898	MUSICAL INSTRUMENTS,PTS		9559	W 1220	44363	W 1544	82214	W 1577	78369	INSTRUMENTS DE MUSIQUE
8983	SOUND RECRDNG TAPE,DISCS		5857	W 543	40313	W 644	75277	W 670	71209	SUPPORTS SON POUR 763
89832	RECORDED DISCS,TAPES ETC		4985	W 287	38373	W 338	72504	W 292	69048	DISQUES,PHONO,BANDES
899	OTHER MANUFACTURED GOODS		45373		54092		71658		76605	AUT ART MANUF DIVERS NDA
9	GOODS NOT CLASSD BY KIND		27847		57539		94731		34886	ART TRANSACT NON CLASSES

1. HISTORICAL SERIES, 1961–1996 SPECIAL TRADE, IMPORTS C.I.F., EXPORTS F.O.B.
SERIES HISTORIQUES, 1961–1996 COMMERCE SPECIAL, IMPORTATIONS C.A.F., EXPORTATIONS F.O.B

YEAR ANNEE	VALUE IN MILLION PORT. ESCUDOS VALEUR EN MILLION PORT. ESCUDOS MERCHANDISE –MARCHANDISE		GOLD # 1 –OR		CONVERSION FACTORS U.S. CENTS PER PORT. ESCUDO FACTEURS DE CONVERSION CENTS E.U. PAR PORT. ESCUDO		INDEX NUMBERS –INDICES QUANTUM		UNIT VALUE VALEUR UNITAIRE	
	IMPORTS	EXPORTS	IMPORTS	EXPORTS	IMPORTS	EXPORTS	IMPORTS	EXPORTS	IMPORTS	EXPORTS
1961	18857.00	9373.00	371.00	32.50	3.4780	3.4780				
1962	16829.00	10632.00	386.20	0.30	3.4780	3.4780				
1963	18865.00	12023.00	426.20	0.80	3.4780	3.4780				
1964	22376.00	14830.00	405.60	0.80	3.4780	3.4780				
1965	26551.00	16572.00	238.90	1.00	3.4780	3.4780				
1966	29406.00	17811.00	353.60	0.80	3.4780	3.4780				
1967	30451.00	20164.00	303.80	0.80	3.4780	3.4780				
1968	33856.00	21909.00	301.60	0.80	3.4780	3.4780				
1969	37261.00	24526.00	104.10	0.40	3.4780	3.4780				
1970	45493.00	27296.00	777.00	0.20	3.4780	3.4780				
1971	52416.00	30248.00	793.90	0.70	3.4780	3.4780				
1972	60684.00	35255.00	515.40	0.60	3.6700	3.6700				
1973	74776.00	45410.00	512.70	0.10	4.1100	4.1010				
1974	118095.00	58014.00	736.40	1.90	3.9680	3.9620				
1975	97692.00	49310.00			3.9350	3.9310				
1976	130859.00	55089.00			3.3000	3.3110				
1977	190685.00	77685.00			2.6020	2.6040				
1978	230128.00	106451.00			2.2720	2.2650				
1979	331927.00	176051.00			2.0400	2.0400				
1980	473018.40	231623.20			1.9970	1.9980				
1981	608965.40	256912.70			1.6342	1.6269				
1982	753980.90	331742.70			1.2731	1.2573				
1983	899340.30	508568.60			0.9163	0.9043				
1984	1160633.00	760580.00			0.6874	0.6847				
1985	1326529.00	971747.10			0.5874	0.5877				
1986	1442000.00	1082000.00			0.6691	0.6693				
1987	1964999.00	1311000.00			0.7107	0.7110				
1988	2580999.00	1582000.00			0.6951	0.6947	11	10	30	25
1989	3024000.00	2016000.00			0.6351	0.6350	12	12	32	27
1990	3603000.00	2336000.00			0.7038	0.7028	100	100	100	100
1991	3808000.00	2352000.00			0.6934	0.6938	106	101	100	100
1992	4086000.00	2474000.00			0.7415	0.7425	119	107	95	98
1993	3888999.00	2468999.00			0.6254	0.6231			97	102
1994	4453998.00	2958000.00			0.6048	0.6051			100	106
1995	4883001.00	3412999.00			0.6625	0.6628			101	107
1996	5260001.00	3671000.00			0.6482	0.6483			103	107

2. IMPORTS BY BROAD ECONOMIC CATEGORY AND EXPORTS BY INDUSTRIAL ORIGIN. (PERCENTAGE OF TOTAL VALUE)
IMPORTATIONS PAR CATEGORIES ECONOMIQUES ET EXPORTATIONS PAR BRANCHE D'ACTIVITE.(EN POURCENTAGE DE LA VALEUR TOTALE)

IMPORTS – IMPORTATIONS

	1990	1991	1992	1993	1994	1995	1996
TOTAL IMPORTS–IMPORTATIONS TOTALES	100.	100.	100.	100.	100.	100.	100.
1 FOOD BEV–ALIMENTATION BOISSONS	9.8	10.9	10.1	11.4	12.3	12.1	11.6
11 PRIMARY–PRODUITS DE BASE	7.4	7.9	7.2	7.9	8.4	7.9	7.4
111 FOR INDUSTRY–POUR L'INDUSTRIE	3.0	3.0	2.7	2.8	2.8	2.8	2.7
112 FOR HOUSEHOLDS–POUR LES MENAGES	4.4	4.9	4.5	5.1	5.6	5.1	4.7
12 PROCESSED–PRODUITS ELABORES	2.4	3.0	2.9	3.5	3.9	4.2	4.2
121 FOR INDUSTRY–POUR L'INDUSTRIE	0.7	0.9	0.7	0.6	0.6	0.7	0.8
122 FOR HOUSEHOLDS–POUR LES MENAGES	1.7	2.2	2.2	2.9	3.3	3.5	3.4
2 IND SUPPLIES–APPROV INDUSTRIELS	33.1	32.3	31.1	30.5	32.5	33.7	31.5
21 PRIMARY–PRODUITS DE BASE	5.0	4.5	4.2	4.3	4.5	4.1	3.7
22 PROCESSED–PRODUITS ELABORES	28.1	27.8	26.9	26.3	28.1	29.5	27.8
3 FUELS–COMBUSTIBLES	10.8	9.0	8.0	8.9	8.5	8.2	7.8
31 PRIMARY–PRODUITS DE BASE	8.7	6.7	6.1	6.8	7.0	6.3	6.1
32 PROCESSED–PRODUITS ELABORES	2.0	2.3	1.9	2.1	1.5	1.9	1.7
321 MOTOR SPIRIT–ESSENCE	1.1	0.9	0.7		0.7		
322 OTHER–AUTRES	0.9	1.3	1.2	2.1	0.8	1.9	1.7
4 MACHINERY–EQUIPEMENT	19.9	19.8	18.9	17.4	16.1	16.9	17.3
41 CAPITAL EQUIPMENT–MACHINES	17.2	17.0	16.4	14.9	13.5	13.4	14.1
42 PARTS–PIECES ACCESSOIRES	2.7	2.8	2.5	2.5	2.6	3.6	3.3
5 TRANSPORT–TRANSPORT	15.4	15.3	18.1	16.9	17.4	15.7	18.1
51 PASSENGER CARS–AUTOMOBILES	5.5	6.2	7.9	7.8	7.1	6.2	6.8
52 OTHER–AUTRES	3.9	3.1	4.0	3.0	4.5	3.4	2.9
521 INDUSTRIAL–INDUSTRIELS	3.7	2.8	3.6	2.5	4.2	3.1	2.7
522 NON INDUSTRIAL–NON INDUSTRIEL	0.2	0.4	0.5	0.5	0.3	0.3	0.3
53 PARTS–PIECES ACCESSOIRES	6.0	6.0	6.1	6.0	5.8	6.2	8.4
6 CONSUM GOODS–BIENS CONSOMMATION	10.9	12.7	13.7	14.8	13.1	13.2	13.5
61 DURABLE–DURABLES	4.0	4.4	4.4	4.4	3.7	3.5	3.6
62 SEMI DURABLE–SEMI DURABLES	4.9	6.0	6.6	7.1	6.3	6.3	6.4
63 NON DURABLE–NON DURABLES	2.0	2.3	2.7	3.3	3.2	3.4	3.6
7 GOODS NES–BIENS NDA	0.1	0.1	0.1	0.1	0.1	0.2	0.1

EXPORTS – EXPORTATIONS

	1990	1991	1992	1993	1994	1995	1996
TOTAL EXPORTS–EXPORTATIONS TOTALES	100.	100.	100.	100.	100.	100.	100.
1 AGRICULTURE	2.3	2.4	2.1	1.8	1.8	2.0	1.8
2 MINING QUARRY–INDUS EXTRACTIVES	2.8	2.5	2.1	2.1	2.0	1.9	1.5
3 MANUFACTURING–IND MANUFACTUR	94.9	95.0	95.8	96.1	96.2	96.2	96.7
31 FOOD BEV TOBACCO–ALIM BOISS TAB	5.6	6.1	6.1	6.0	6.0	6.0	6.1
32 TEXTILES–INDUSTRIES TEXTILES	37.5	38.6	38.4	38.0	35.6	31.3	30.6
33 WOOD & PRODUCTS–BOIS & PRODUITS	5.7	5.2	4.7	4.7	4.5	4.1	4.1
34 PAPER & PRODUCTS–PAPIER & PRODT	6.0	5.7	5.4	5.4	6.0	6.6	5.3
35 CHEMICALS–INDUSTRIES CHIMIQUES	10.2	8.7	8.6	9.3	10.6	9.6	8.8
36 NON METAL MIN–MIN NON METAL	4.2	4.5	4.5	4.6	4.8	4.4	4.0
37 BASIC METAL–IND METAL BASE	1.4	1.2	1.2	1.2	1.2	1.1	1.2
38 METAL MANUF–MANUF METAL	23.6	24.2	26.3	26.2	27.1	32.5	36.0
39 OTH MANUF IND–AUTRES MANUF	0.7	0.8	0.7	0.6	0.6	0.6	0.6

3. TRADE BY PRINCIPAL COUNTRIES OF PRODUCTION AND LAST CONSIGNMENT (VALUE IN THOUSAND U.S. DOLLARS)
ECHANGES SELON LES PRINCIPAUX PAYS DE PRODUCTION ET DE DERNIERE CONSIGNATION (VALEUR EN MILLIERS DE DOLLARS EU)

COUNTRIES–PAYS	SPECIAL IMPORTS C.I.F. IMPORTATIONS SPECIALES C.A.F				
	1992	1993	1994	1995	1996
World	30610494	24244270	27065084	33565156	34121907
Africa	1680153	1367231	1506870	1728669	1847280
Americas	2038555	1638611	1887884	2299688	2181871
Northern America	1100318	866676	1050995	1198960	1197795
LAIA	841706	650191	705465	955341	853902
CACM	33502	30705	30563	38658	38943
Caribbean	46071	81555	87723	69131	72993
Rest of America	16958	9485	13137	37599	18239
As.ex F.USSR	2163691	1971910	2468342	2948011	2839442
Eur.x F.USSR	24529114	18968087	20880269	26172496	26772568
EU	23441556	18066957	19891304	25020868	25819958
EFTA	992788	833875	896747	952019	809622
East Europe	59892	53661	74870	128701	110919
Other Europe	12206	2052	4712	55594	7883
Former USSR	121451	220402	263081	337975	397381
Oceania	65156	44265	48719	61972	72468
Spain/Espagne	5081301	4330816	5384705	7118322	7666344
Germany/Allemagne	4607495	3642884	3761024	4952148	5285425
France,Monac	3935819	3084043	3468257	3964800	3782179
Italy/Italie	3135262	2103650	2318440	2809071	2824999
United Kingdom	2188259	1795271	1775103	2216176	2295087
Netherlands/Pays-Bas	2098135	1193553	1168088	1513776	1511847
Belgium–Luxembourg	1160063	917621	919711	1114451	1128442
USA/Etats-Unis d'Amer	925968	768238	978778	1099615	1082140
Japan/Japon	936818	782679	770572	741995	759765
Switz.Liecht	515180	472155	447056	506648	483893
Nigeria/Nigéria	403422	344500	384493	464125	584087
Brazil/Brésil	363430	337120	412648	514436	471539
Norway,SVD,JM	435511	333855	429825	409595	275780
Sweden/Suède	389329	291202	306849	404489	401166
Saudi Arabia	158172	207644	304167	356888	356073
Denmark/Danemark	249093	185126	232239	282169	277762
Korea, Republic of	92195	79016	174706	446787	327955
Iran (Islamic Rp. of)	135044	70184	362320	342568	198343
Algeria/Algérie	215151	323950	252734	158091	127833
Austria/Autriche	244389	201436	211089	202150	213032
Russian Federation	97209	186576	192539	258888	306243
China/Chine	110192	185806	171998	198875	231678
Finland/Finlande	207134	157855	131052	198633	185284
Ireland/Irlande	118252	136127	183054	191306	189196
Egypt/Egypte	263852	92445	150426	116316	194834
So. Africa Customs Un	161253	106828	119170	153656	153152
Libyan Arab Jamahiriya	91763	161368	97291	180011	123749
Thailand/Thaïlande	134149	113316	105119	115762	114881
Canada	174113	98277	71851	99293	115207
Argentina/Argentine	127474	90955	74332	110096	90696
Mexico/Mexique	145030	81586	68376	108038	76656
India/Inde	69378	71420	80851	116966	138578
Pakistan	51653	55388	62262	88747	111277
Malaysia/Malaisie	45475	50987	71865	94923	94557
Turkey/Turquie	50405	48043	75302	76157	73400
Colombia/Colombie	39027	49461	47744	72945	84381
Singapore/Singapour	50472	51816	46139	48410	52315
Morocco/Maroc	25152	34171	48577	62105	63716
Cameroon/Cameroun	37616	37419	40299	58808	42157
Israel/Israël	34721	35092	40969	45231	49449
Gabon	54247	11757	56207	65865	16064
Greece/Grèce	27025	27372	31692	53377	59196
Indonesia/Indonésie	15269	28535	42394	57798	52788
Hong Kong	44493	34134	33772	42786	38064
Venezuela	40844	25240	15188	57416	45212
Australia/Australie	37411	30638	32887	37349	40645
Iceland/Islande	42098	27866	19866	35777	49949
Cote d'Ivoire	26075	23193	36101	40867	37114
Chile/Chili	57017	17462	25783	33094	28319
Chad/Tchad	25976	19909	19366	45964	47382

COUNTRIES–PAYS	SPECIAL EXPORTS F.O.B. EXPORTATIONS SPECIALES F.O.B.				
	1992	1993	1994	1995	1996
Monde	18564578	15417381	17980753	23370015	23185562
Afrique	1230404	771502	786410	888718	1019128
Amériques	897603	940516	1299907	1578848	1599306
Amérique du Nord	790517	801945	1052553	1183684	1202948
ALAI	82448	111287	219159	318191	360248
MCAC	3642	4320	5082	8495	7002
Caraïbes	13726	20565	19160	46904	14378
Autre Amérique	7270	2399	3953	21573	14729
Asie l'URSS exclus	523925	549105	614363	880353	917194
Europe l'URSS exclus	15614763	12905929	15002317	19690811	19255978
UE	14993664	12349636	14399746	18883055	18438058
AELE	558316	491459	521381	694583	645274
Europe de l'Est	28532	28128	48887	80386	152117
Autre de l'Europe	15213	28626	26401	28628	11355
Ancienne URSS	53781	75613	76059	92463	138290
Océanie	49910	50622	64454	82664	103347
Germany/Allemagne	3547915	3012179	3400926	5033226	4413566
Spain/Espagne	2781913	2248294	2639741	3559822	3425873
France,Monac	2634583	2331274	2645913	3294555	3376590
United Kingdom	2060519	1749519	2085602	2596780	2567669
Netherlands/Pays-Bas	1010644	801624	966798	1231964	1164465
USA/Etats-Unis d'Amer	646488	678938	929232	1056113	1087035
Belgium–Luxembourg	606002	541813	654860	717521	997277
Italy/Italie	712975	461362	603359	796840	885826
Sweden/Suède	629035	396248	436892	506971	488593
Angola	830021	346640	293566	347169	397332
Denmark/Danemark	402221	329818	413809	512844	423038
Switz.Liecht	336430	320112	333311	453602	402435
Austria/Autriche	205447	181391	196056	237151	287503
Norway,SVD,JM	211459	159420	179750	231098	233532
Finland/Finlande	226668	152832	186848	205871	185276
Japan/Japon	141742	121193	136023	177943	179266
Canada	143647	122416	122121	126624	115287
Brazil/Brésil	37839	60186	88139	191579	248786
Greece/Grèce	93662	80867	79769	94993	115851
Cape Verde/Cap-Vert	57984	58881	84075	119694	125428
Israel/Israël	61381	69517	85253	115159	112410
Ireland/Irlande	82083	62416	89174	94518	106531
Morocco/Maroc	53816	49757	70499	80121	95827
Russian Federation	40712	47614	58193	68913	116272
Australia/Australie	39348	40907	51830	67672	87644
Singapore/Singapour	21323	22410	26958	82644	124949
So. Africa Customs Un	37292	38480	46818	63261	80886
Turkey/Turquie	31137	47788	35910	60522	68624
Mozambique	34181	37352	43367	49119	49919
Hong Kong	23306	30144	41045	56497	58132
Liberia/Libéria	83637	79356	33	398	42561
Saudi Arabia	31054	34484	41158	37844	44813
Argentina/Argentine	7284	13635	64351	50805	30389
Algeria/Algérie	10691	48026	46848	32210	23299
Tunisia/Tunisie	5193	10482	54586	59687	24982
Malaysia/Malaisie	21523	27186	36617	34064	22585
Guinea–Bissau	26874	22767	30839	30422	27859
China/Chine	18741	30100	17771	33742	32365
Korea, Republic of	22367	15916	20424	35864	37920
Hungary/Hongrie	9248	10555	19945	29378	55393
Macau/Macao	21635	15406	22880	24129	35062
Chile/Chili	12124	9786	23200	33498	39152
Thailand/Thaïlande	14193	15458	21240	36045	26605
India/Inde	23097	21410	7457	26101	10720
United Arab Emirates	9332	17679	17882	14669	23880
Cyprus/Chypre	17500	14531	15168	16734	16004
Egypt/Egypte	11943	10281	13581	15855	22062
Nigeria/Nigéria	11584	15543	18549	14880	13127
Sao Tome and Principe	11814	12935	12712	17298	16781
Senegal/Sénégal	2629	2481	24010	11765	30590

(VALUE AS PERCENTAGE OF WORLD TOTAL)(VALEURS EN POURCENTAGE DU TOTAL MONDIAL)

	1987	1988	1989	1990	1991	1992	1993	1994	1995	1996
Africa	7.3	5.8	6.5	7.3	5.8	5.5	5.6	5.6	5.2	5.4
Americas	9.2	9.5	8.9	8.3	7.5	6.7	6.8	7.0	6.9	6.4
Northern America	6.0	5.3	5.3	4.7	4.0	3.6	3.6	3.9	3.6	3.5
LAIA	3.0	3.8	3.2	3.3	3.2	2.7	2.7	2.6	2.8	2.5
CACM	0.1	0.1	0.1	0.1	0.1	0.1	0.1	0.1	0.1	0.1
Caribbean	0.1	0.2	0.3	0.1	0.1	0.2	0.3	0.3	0.2	0.2
Rest of America	0.1	0.1	0.1	0.1	0.1	0.1	0.0	0.0	0.1	0.1
As.ex F.USSR	11.2	9.2	9.0	8.1	7.8	7.1	8.1	9.1	8.8	8.3
Eur.x F.USSR	71.3	74.8	74.8	75.8	78.3	80.1	78.2	77.1	78.0	78.5
EU	66.6	70.4	71.0	72.1	74.8	76.6	74.5	73.5	74.5	75.7
EFTA	4.2	4.1	3.4	3.4	3.2	3.2	3.4	3.3	2.8	2.4
East Europe	0.4	0.4	0.3	0.3	0.2	0.2	0.2	0.3	0.4	0.3
Other Europe	0.2	0.1	0.1	0.0	0.1	0.0	0.0	0.0	0.2	0.0
Former USSR	0.4	0.3	0.3	0.2	0.2	0.4	0.9	1.0	1.0	1.2
Oceania	0.4	0.4	0.4	0.3	0.2	0.2	0.2	0.2	0.2	0.2
Spain/Espagne	11.8	13.1	14.5	14.4	15.8	16.6	17.9	19.9	21.2	22.5
Germany/Allemagne	14.7	14.6	14.5	14.3	15.0	15.1	15.0	13.9	14.8	15.5
France,Monac	11.1	11.5	11.7	11.5	11.9	12.9	12.7	12.8	11.8	11.1
Italy/Italie	8.7	9.2	9.1	10.0	10.2	10.2	8.7	8.6	8.4	8.3
United Kingdom	8.1	8.3	7.5	7.6	7.5	7.1	7.4	6.6	6.6	6.7
Netherlands/Pays-Bas	4.1	4.8	5.5	5.7	6.1	6.9	4.9	4.3	4.5	4.4
Belgium–Luxembourg	3.2	4.1	3.9	4.1	4.0	3.8	3.8	3.4	3.3	3.3
USA/Etats-Unis d'Amer	4.9	4.3	4.4	3.9	3.4	3.0	3.2	3.6	3.3	3.2
Japan/Japon	4.0	3.6	3.1	2.7	2.9	3.1	3.2	2.8	2.2	2.2
Switz.Liecht	2.4	2.4	2.1	2.1	1.8	1.7	1.9	1.7	1.5	1.4

	1987	1988	1989	1990	1991	1992	1993	1994	1995	1996
Afrique	3.5	4.2	4.6	4.6	5.3	6.6	5.0	4.4	3.8	4.4
Amériques	8.0	7.4	7.6	6.3	5.1	4.8	6.1	7.2	6.8	6.9
Amérique du Nord	7.2	6.7	6.9	5.6	4.6	4.3	5.2	5.9	5.1	5.2
ALAI	0.6	0.5	0.5	0.4	0.5	0.4	0.7	1.2	1.4	1.6
MCAC	0.0	0.0	0.0	0.0	0.0	0.0	0.0	0.0	0.0	0.0
Caraïbes	0.1	0.1	0.1	0.1	0.1	0.1	0.1	0.1	0.2	0.1
Autre Amérique	0.1	0.0	0.1	0.1	0.0	0.0	0.0	0.0	0.1	0.1
Asie l'URSS exclus	3.6	3.2	3.1	3.0	2.9	2.8	3.6	3.4	3.8	4.0
Europe l'URSS exclus	83.2	82.9	82.2	84.2	85.1	84.1	83.7	83.4	84.3	83.1
UE	78.4	78.5	78.0	80.5	81.6	80.8	80.1	80.1	80.8	79.5
AELE	4.3	4.0	3.8	3.3	3.3	3.0	3.2	2.9	3.0	2.8
Europe de l'Est	0.4	0.3	0.2	0.2	0.1	0.2	0.2	0.3	0.3	0.7
Autre de l'Europe	0.1	0.1	0.1	0.1	0.1	0.1	0.2	0.1	0.1	0.0
Ancienne URSS	0.6	0.6	0.9	0.4	0.1	0.3	0.5	0.4	0.4	0.6
Océanie	0.3	0.4	0.5	0.3	0.3	0.3	0.3	0.4	0.4	0.4
Germany/Allemagne	15.4	14.7	15.6	16.6	19.1	19.1	19.5	18.9	21.5	19.0
Spain/Espagne	9.3	11.5	12.7	13.5	15.1	15.0	14.6	14.7	15.2	14.8
France,Monac	15.8	15.2	15.0	15.5	14.3	14.2	15.1	14.7	14.1	14.6
United Kingdom	14.0	14.3	12.2	12.1	10.8	11.1	11.3	11.6	11.1	11.1
Netherlands/Pays-Bas	6.5	5.9	5.8	5.7	5.7	5.4	5.2	5.4	5.3	5.0
USA/Etats-Unis d'Amer	6.5	5.9	5.9	4.8	3.8	3.5	4.4	5.2	4.5	4.7
Belgium–Luxembourg	3.0	3.2	3.1	3.1	3.2	3.3	3.5	3.6	3.1	4.3
Italy/Italie	3.9	4.2	4.2	4.1	4.0	3.8	3.0	3.4	3.4	3.8
Sweden/Suède	4.6	4.0	4.0	4.1	3.7	3.4	2.6	2.4	2.2	2.1
Angola	1.1	1.9	2.5	2.5	3.4	4.5	2.2	1.6	1.5	1.7

4. Special Imports C.I.F. by Commodities according to the S.I.T.C. (Rev. 2) in thousand U.S. Dollars
Importations Spéciales C.A.F. par Produits d'après la C.T.C.I. (Rév. 2) en milliers de Dollars E.U.

SITC CTCI	COMMODITY	1993 WEIGHT POIDS	1993 VALUE VALEUR	1994 WEIGHT POIDS	1994 VALUE VALEUR	1995 WEIGHT POIDS	1995 VALUE VALEUR	1996 WEIGHT POIDS	1996 VALUE VALEUR	PRODUIT
	ALL COMMODITIES		24244270		27065084		33565156		34121907	TOUS PRODUITS
0	FOOD AND LIVE ANIMALS		2746669		3147935		3676557		3698342	ALIMENTS,ANIMAUX VIVANTS
01	MEAT AND PREPARATIONS		336259		453549		490770		397212	VIANDES ET PREPARATIONS
011	MEAT FRESH,CHILLD,FROZEN	W 108202	315135	W 138348	423202	W 138549	449107	W 117147	350851	VIANDES FRAICHES,REF,CONGE
0111	BOVINE MEAT FRESH,FROZEN	W 52711	200344	W 72106	282306	W 63734	269773	W 32688	132974	VIANDES BOVIN FRAI,REF
01111	BOVINE MEAT WITH BONE IN	W 47261	175834	W 65006	245705	W 55304	221891	W 25513	95406	VIANDES BOVIN NON DESOSS
0113	PIG MEAT FRESH,CHLD,FRZN	W 34864	68749	W 43377	85977	W 51710	118282	W 57194	144445	VIANDE DE PORC
02	DAIRY PRODCTS,BIRDS'EGGS		64990		99673		138812		139969	PRODUITS LAITIERS,OEUFS
03	FISH AND PREPARATIONS		623753		705209		806548		776535	POISSONS ET PREPARATIONS
034	FISH,FRESH,CHILLED,FROZN		199050	W 159898	247267	W 161014	282832	W 155956	285737	POISSON FRAIS, REFRIG,CONG
0342	FISH FROZEN,EXCL FILLETS		148836	W 112743	180197	W 115917	205710	W 120535	207816	POISSONS CONGELES
035	FISH SALTED,DRIED,SMOKED		278071	W 75207	285508	W 79829	331333	W 84649	315282	POISSON SECHE,SALE,FUME
03502	COD(NOT IN FILLETS)DRIED	W 22111	104809	W 19458	92764	W 19957	110938	W 17710	90492	MORUE SECHEE,SALEE
03503	FISH(EX COD)DRIED,SALTED		172763	W 55696	192064	W 59814	219686	W 66876	223851	POISSONS SECHES,SALES
036	SHELL FISH FRESH,FROZEN		123783	W 35216	141392	W 38089	156410	W 35450	147461	CRUSTACES,MOLLUSQUES
04	CEREALS AND PREPARATIONS		635781		632560		722854		765774	CEREALES ET PRODUITS
041	WHEAT ETC UNMILLED	W 914928	210391	W 999696	200460	W 1092992	239541	W 1140383	238338	FROMENT,EPEAUTRE
0412	OTHER WHEAT ETC UNMILLED	W 790930	176970	W 917050	181573	W 946079	203187	W 1054678	220017	AUTRE FROMENT NON MOULU
042	RICE	W 151193	93445	W 136671	82871	W 126226	83670	W 116679	81790	RIZ
044	MAIZE UNMILLED		211594	W 1045914	197083	W 939454	181669	W 905776	198056	MAIS NON MOULU
048	CEREAL ETC PREPARATIONS	W 49812	89390	W 65714	113062	W 94083	161091	W 107396	169540	PREPTNS A BASE CEREALES
05	VEGETABLES AND FRUIT		433311		523393		591550		607641	LEGUMES ET FRUITS
054	VEG ETC FRSH,SMPLY PRSVD	W 793825	182109	W 773731	202841	W 598558	217291	W 579270	208500	LEGUMES FRAIS,CONG,SECS
057	FRUIT,NUTS,FRESH,DRIED	W 305792	201566	W 336184	253137	W 336109	277653	W 361621	290129	FRUITS FRAIS OU SECS
0573	BANANA,PLANTAIN,FRSH,DRY	W 122970	69262	W 142245	96343	W 154619	110092	W 161338	101101	BANANES FRAICHES,SECHEES
06	SUGAR AND PREPS,HONEY		109699		132308		199242		238486	SUCRES ET PRODUITS
061	SUGAR AND HONEY	W 418820	90350	W 433186	110889	W 465722	166620	W 440526	205041	SUCRES ET MIEL
0611	RAW BEET AND CANE SUGAR	W 248741	73222	W 292630	92632	W 310944	142567	W 310075	181878	SUCRES BRUTS
07	COFFEE,TEA,COCOA,SPICES		143464		180661		254478		232443	CAFE,THE,CACAO,EPICES
071	COFFEE AND SUBSTITUTES		64567	W 38921	102863	W 36955	152141	W 43090	132727	CAFE ET SUCCEDANES
0711	COFFEE GREEN,ROASTED,SUB		59827	W 38093	96150	W 35713	138851	W 42007	123259	CAFE TORREFIE OU DECAFEINE
07111	COFFEE GREEN,HUSKS,SKINS		52253	W 35537	82840	W 33052	120901	W 39503	107777	CAFE NON TORREFIE
081	*FEEDING STUFF FOR ANIML	W 1543463	284489		270548	W 1270101	257111	W 1340982	311867	NOURRITURE POUR ANIMAUX
0813	OILCAKE AND OTH RESIDUES	W 491096	96637	W 455633	83599	W 265561	40865	W 390755	84097	TOURTEAUX
08131	— OF SOYA BEANS	W 349236	79628	W 293943	63396	W 89569	18594	W 189238	52333	TOURTEAUX DE SOJA
0819	FOOD WASTE AND FEED NES	W 768491	149970		148740	W 825251	186057	W 720447	187816	DECHETS,ALIMENTS NDA
08193	BEET–PULP,BAGASSE,ETC	W 715411	95727	W 678674	93065	W 752110	106792	W 286800	48738	PULPES,AUTRES DECHETS
08199	FODDER NES,INCL SWEETNED	W 52518	53809		55138	W 73021	79011	W 433598	138978	PREPARATIONS FOURRAGERES
09	MISC EDIBLE PRODUCTS		84558		86426		115960		131423	PREP ALIMENTAIRES DIVERSES
098	EDIBLE PRODCTS,PREPS NES	W 26243	82269		83730	W 36323	107440	W 41396	119149	PREP ALIMENTAIRES NDA
1	BEVERAGES AND TOBACCO		215790		314169		330080		327226	BOISSONS ET TABACS
11	BEVERAGES		158410		243698		261804		241784	BOISSONS
112	ALCOHOLIC BEVERAGES		119243	W 193159	193076	W 144793	207417	W 99696	189686	BOISSONS ALCOOLIQUES
1124	DISTILLED ALCOHOLIC BEVS		91126	W 41478	114158	W 32083	121040	W 24356	122552	ALCOOLS,EAUX–DE–VIE
11241	WHISKY	W 12473	75612	W 13391	80943	W 12923	87832	W 13204	94381	WHISKY
2	CRUDE MATERLS,EXCL FUELS		982689		1224064		1609684		1465191	MAT BRUTES NON COMESTIBLES
22	OIL SEEDS,OLEAGINOUS FRT		218090		245616		319862		314933	GRAINES,FRUITS OLEAGINEUX
222	SEEDS FOR'SOFT'FIXED OIL	W 802512	217085	W 827721	244663	W 1158264	318678	W 976945	313487	GRAINES HUILES FIXES
2222	SOYA BEANS	W 579933	155270	W 584041	158488	W 895290	233043	W 709333	225937	FEVES DE SOJA
24	CORK AND WOOD		189118		263997		382245		312246	LIEGE ET BOIS
247	OTH WOOD ROUGH,SQUARED	W 346653	99072	W 837743	155537	W 1329984	235225	W 823803	163031	BOIS BRUTS EQUARRIS
2472	SAW–,VENEER–LOGS NON–CON	W 345783	98744	W 756481	149930	W 1186931	226149	W 784996	159667	NON CONIFERES SCIAGE,PLAC
24721	— IN THE ROUGH	W 345783	98744	W 756481	149930	W 1186931	226149	W 784996	159667	BRUTS ECORCES DEGROSSIS
26	TEXTILE FIBRES AND WASTE		284500		355247		441800		418490	FIBRES TEXTILES
263	COTTON	W 160057	212309	W 169225	263578	W 173355	343203	W 172428	336719	COTON
2631	RAW COTTON,EXCL LINTERS	W 157680	211269	W 167814	262075	W 171393	340338	W 169427	331631	COTON EN MASSE
29	CRUDE ANIMAL,VEG MAT NES		80018		82275		106829		107071	MATIERES BRUTES ANIM,VEGET
3	MINERAL FUELS ETC		2160168		2333050		2754136		2671406	COMBUSTIBLES MINERAUX LUB
32	COAL,COKE AND BRIQUETTES		188563		206132		260024		237256	HOUILLES,COKES,BRIQUETTES
322	COAL,LIGNITE AND PEAT	W 4711999	187098	W 5094903	203861	W 5735006	257581	W 5110885	235076	HOUILLES,LIGNITES,TOURBE
3222	OTH COAL,NOT AGGLOMERATD	W 4155932	166331	W 4416946	182317	W 5348886	240709	W 4776331	219807	AUTRES HOUILLES
33	PETROLEUM AND PRODUCTS		1842287		2001398		2316479		2215253	PETROLE ET DERIVES
333	CRUDE PETROLEUM	MW 10855	1330574	MW 13437	1581542	MW 13237	1695299	MW 11132	1653815	HUILES BRUTES DE PETROLE
334	PETROLEUM PRODUCTS,REFIN	W 3884064	477976	W 2750626	387510	W 3647141	558990	W 2567678	514324	PRODUITS RAFFINES
3341	GASOLINE,OTH LIGHT OILS			W 1152622	179719					ESSENCES POUR MOTEURS
33419	OTH LIGHT PETROLEUM OILS			W 1132812	176048					AUTRES HUILES LEGERES
3344	FUEL OILS,NES			W 1420552	137456					FUEL OILS
341	*GAS,NATURAL AND MANUFCT	W 630074	122930	W 611630	111395	W 919096	162702	W 721585	189726	GAZ NATUREL,GAZ MANUFACT
3413	PETROLM GASES,LIQUEFIED	W 630073	122905	W 611628	111378	W 640140	150379	W 663557	187170	GAZ DE PETROLE LIQUEFIE
34131	LIQUEFIED PROPANE,BUTANE	W 622162	121301	W 605342	109811	W 630353	148564	W 651700	184815	PROPANE,BUTANE LIQUEFIES
4	ANIMAL,VEGETABLE OIL,FAT		124566		146565		232561		208772	HUILES,GRAISSES ANIM,VEG
42	FIXED VEGETABLE OIL,FAT		112436		134124		215669		190276	HUILES VEGETALES FIXES
423	FIXED VEG OILS,SOFT		91854	W 54690	111178	W 82280	189749	W 62010	165001	HUILES VEGET DOUCES FIXES
4235	OLIVE OIL		79005	W 36892	98400	W 44666	161314	W 29985	143540	HUILE D'OLIVE
5	CHEMCLS,RELATED PROD NES		2265732		2640364		3373104		3349124	PRODUITS CHIMIQUES
51	ORGANIC CHEMICALS		429547		510039		651527		601476	PROD CHIMIQ ORGANIQUES
511	HYDROCARBONS NES,DERIVS		65568		85641	W 151344	111595		88597	HYDROCARBURES NDA
514	NITROGEN–FNCTN COMPOUNDS		151896		160558	W 49294	193650	W 77050	198478	COMPOSES FONCT AZOTEES
5148	OTH NITROGN–FNCTN CMPNDS		104390		102867	W 39624	138497	W 64478	132623	AUTRES COMPOSES AZOTES
515	ORG–INORG COMPOUNDS ETC		87013		106039	W 5136	121492	W 6328	115651	COMPOSES ORGANO–MINERAUX
52	INORGANIC CHEMICALS		129653		143548		172745		176691	PROD CHIM INORGANIQUES
523	OTHR INORG CHEMICALS ETC		73800		77651	W 205930	92705	W 217397	101797	AUT PRODUITS CHIMIQUES INORG
53	DYES,TANNING,COLOUR PROD		253629		283969		351034		358028	PROD TEINTURE,COLORANTS
531	SYNT DYE,NAT INDGO,LAKES		104657		107491	W 12159	116127	W 15359	109872	MAT COLOR ORGAN,LAQUES
5311	SYNTHIC ORGNIC DYESTUFFS		96266		98616	W 8448	106372	W 9332	96251	MAT COLOR ORGAN SYNTHET
533	PIGMENTS,PAINTS,ETC		135322		161165	W 86186	222120	W 90440	235373	PIGMENTS,PEINTURES,VERNIS
5334	VARNISHES,DISTEMPERS ETC	W 16801	54954	W 24619	65103	W 27513	95287	W 28431	106758	PEINTURES A L'EAU
541	*MEDICINAL,PHARM PRODUCT		418240		492798		630017	MK 18059	701306	PROD MEDICINAUX PHARMACEUT
5417	MEDICAMENTS		294829		337554	MK 18828	437471	MK 12964	503787	MEDICAMENTS
54179	— CONTNG OTH SUBSTANCES	K 6118992	209043	K 8329505	256478	MK 17776	344302	MK 11895	398271	MED CONT AUT SUBSTANCES
55	PERFUME,CLEANING ETC PRD		281702		306302		388148		392799	PROD POUR PARFUM,TOILETTE
553	PERFUMERY,COSMETICS,ETC		144206	W 26006	158339	W 29001	211567	W 33730	215352	PRODUITS DE PARFUMERIE
554	SOAP,CLEANSING ETC PREPS	W 82138	111727		116407	W 111674	142744	W 113595	139920	SAVONS,PRODUITS DETERSIFS
5542	WASHING PREPARATIONS ETC	W 72822	93251		94992	W 98422	115441	W 94811	111456	PROD ORG TENSIO–ACT NDA
58	PLASTIC MATERIALS ETC		445935		525643		726363		667284	MAT PLAST ARTIFICIELLES
582	PROD OF CONDENSATION ETC	W 56367	108040		116753	W 69449	162777	W 66886	159633	PROD CONDENS,POLYCOND
583	POLYMERIZATION ETC PRODS		322265		392371	W 334834	544453	W 361008	490018	PROD POLYMERISATION
5831	POLYETHYLENE	W 84606	69092	W 84772	74298	W 86403	110738	W 99774	105050	POLYETHYLENE
5832	POLYPROPYLENE	W 65372	56644	W 71051	66945	W 76286	103710	W 74096	84182	POLYPROPYLENE
5834	POLYVINYL CHLORIDE	W 64083	66223		75641	W 66717	102816	W 66626	82019	CHLORURE DE POLYVINYLE
5839	OTH POLYMRZTION ETC PROD		62601	W 41207	86854	W 45387	124079	W 49614	113645	AUT PROD POLYMER COPOLYM

4. Special Imports C.I.F. by Commodities according to the S.I.T.C. (Rev. 2) in thousand U.S. Dollars
Importations Spéciales C.A.F. par Produits d'après la C.T.C.I. (Rév. 2) en milliers de Dollars E.U.

SITC CTCI	COMMODITY	1993 WEIGHT POIDS	1993 VALUE VALEUR	1994 WEIGHT POIDS	1994 VALUE VALEUR	1995 WEIGHT POIDS	1995 VALUE VALEUR	1996 WEIGHT POIDS	1996 VALUE VALEUR	PRODUIT
59	CHEMICAL MATERIALS NES		257119		301854		373083		370022	MAT PROD CHIMIQUES NDA
598	MISCEL CHEM PRODUCTS NES		171920		192344	W 144961	233337	W 112226	218338	PROD DIV INDUST CHIM NDA
5989	CHEM PRODUCTS,PREPS NES		133727		148853	W 83659	181752	W 83510	181748	PROD PREP CHIMIQUES NDA
59899	OTH CHEM PRODS,PREPS,NES		90912	W 52568	99418	W 59687	124752	W 57807	122291	AUT PRODUITS CHIMIQUES NDA
6	BASIC MANUFACTURES		4405345		5209755		6800194		6485290	ART MANUFACTURES
61	LEATHER,DRESSED FUR,ETC		432435		548067		601903		573336	CUIRS,PELLETERIES
611	LEATHER	W 43244	333689		423145	W 50329	457951	W 51285	430840	CUIRS,PEAUX PREPARES
6114	LEATHR BOVINE NES,EQUINE	W 36247	240147		318714	W 42638	347069	W 44208	336031	CUIRS DE BOVINS
612	LEATHER ETC MANUFACTURES		95582		122802	W 9401	138427	W 10426	137161	OUVRAGES EN CUIRS NDA
6123	PREPRD PARTS OF FOOTWEAR		93076		119545	W 9162	134008	W 10092	131385	PARTIES DE CHAUSSURES
62	RUBBER MANUFACTURES NES		226629		247954		351106		402573	CAOUTCHOUC MANUFACTURE
625	RUBBER TYRES, TUBES ETC		135794	W 41804	153436	W 50260	206719	W 54897	227506	PNEUS CAOUTCHOUC VULCANISE
6251	TYRES NEW FOR MOTOR CARS	W 12932	62420	W 15165	72191	W 18617	98173	W 22319	115532	PNEUS POUR VOITURES
63	WOOD,CORK MANUFACTRS NES		101658		97870		115804		130927	OUVRAGES LIEGE ET BOIS
64	PAPER,PAPERBOARD AND MFR		461395		505808		710201		701703	PAPIERS,CARTONS & OUVRAGES
641	PAPER AND PAPERBOARD		314526		352025	W 438803	509890	W 465657	494126	PAPIERS ET CARTONS
6412	PRINTG,WRITING PAPER NES	W 64001	60480	W 81094	77171	W 81311	109458	W 94005	105151	PAPIERS POUR L'IMPRESSION
6418	COATED ETC PAPER NES BLK		114529	W 72844	132885	W 71857	165214	W 79444	170728	PAP,CARTONS COUCHES,ENDUITS
64189	COATED PAPER ETC NES		103801	W 66214	120017	W 52223	108194	W 43257	74747	PAPIERS,CARTONS COUCHES
642	PAPER,ETC,PRECUT,ARTS OF		146870		153783	W 75990	200311	W 86437	207577	PAP,CARTONS DECOUPES
6428	PAPER ETC ARTICLES NES		96642		99333	W 39304	118321	W 45244	122221	OUVRAGES EN PATE A PAPIER
65	TEXTILE YARN,FABRICS,ETC		1441794		1650551		2012255		1964246	FILS,TISSUS,ARTICLES TEXTILE
651	TEXTILE YARN		409307		500041	W 123901	628515	W 131914	616447	FILS TEXTILES
6513	COTTON YARN		123531	W 40733	146052	W 43561	186011	W 46581	186944	FILS DE COTON
6514	SYN FIB YRN,BULK,MONOFIL	W 26839	117960		136150	W 31115	162980	W 29570	149088	FILS CONT 85% FIB TEXT SYNTH
6516	DISCON SYN FIB BLEND YRN	W 19257	64268	W 24731	83788	W 27019	108786	W 33033	117793	FILS FIBR TEX SYNT DIS MOINS
652	COTTON FABRICS,WOVEN		201327	W 24639	242005	W 24938	279886	W 26504	291432	TISSUS DE COTON
6522	WOVEN COTTON BLEACHD,ETC		182669	W 18979	211176	W 17726	239114	W 19662	254219	TISSUS COTON BLANCHIS ETC
65224	BLCHED COTTON FABRIC NES	W 13911	139138	W 15589	157549	W 14143	177454	W 14858	189149	AUT TIS PLUS 85% COT BLANCHI
653	WOVN MAN–MADE FIB FABRIC		337373		348916	W 24257	414317	W 22806	378756	TISSUS FIBRES SYNTH,ARTIF
6531	CONT SYNT WEAVES NONPILE		106808	W 6861	105813	W 7857	132416	W 7007	118208	TISSUS FIBRES SYNTH CONTINUE
65315	CONT SYN TXTL FABRIC NES		93731	W 5777	91942	W 6535	112788	W 5943	100667	TIS PLUS 85% TEXT SYNT CONT
6534	DISC SYN BLEND FABRC NES		104894	W 8933	109955	W 9952	133557	W 9345	131573	TISSUS FIBRES SYNTH DISCONT
654	OTH WOVEN TEXTILE FABRIC		140554	W 6045	156786	W 5896	170821	W 5112	153693	TISSUS AUT COTON SYNT,ARTIF
6542	WOVEN WOOL,HAIR NONPILE	W 2308	73247	W 2474	79074	W 2394	90966	W 2362	90536	TIS PLUS 85% LAINE,POILS
655	KNITTED,ETC FABRICS	W 7255	86994	W 6724	102028	W 7084	124643	W 7631	131894	ETOF BONNETERIE PIECES ETC
6552	OTHER KNIT ETC FAB NONEL	W 7255	86994	W 6724	102028	W 7084	124643	W 7631	131894	ETOF BON NON ELAS NON SYNT
657	SPECIAL TXTL FABRC,PRODS		137707		175831	W 22793	235910	W 22074	226853	TISSUS SPECIAUX
6573	COATED ETC TEXTILES NES		78507	W 7794	106651	W 10275	149496	W 10503	143147	TISSUS,ART MATIERE TEXT NDA
65732	PLASTIC COATED TEXTILES		68860	W 6727	93547	W 7837	124541	W 8816	125096	TISSUS IMPREGNES
66	NONMETAL MINERAL MFS NES		375938		390375		454466		476620	ART MIN NON METALLIQUES
662	CLAY,REFRACTORY BLDG PRD	W 117564	63120	W 161991	75297	W 196906	109717	W 195645	101285	MAT CONST REFRACTAIRES
664	GLASS		62787		63825	W 87795	86878	W 107873	102822	VERRE
667	PEARL,PREC–,SEMI–P STONE		66329		86565		57597		63477	PERLES, PIERRES GEMMES
6672	DIAMONDS NONINDUST,UNSET		63018		84045		54240		60469	DIAMANTS BRUTS
67	IRON AND STEEL		591593		852201		1274125		1045754	FER ET ACIER
672	IRON,STEEL PRIMARY FORMS		109552	W 520614	158988	W 538588	256792	W 200167	82266	LINGOTS FER,ACIER
6727	IRN,STL COIL FR REROLLNG	W 373807	106956	W 493506	148791	W 527055	249022	W 196975	78055	EBAUCHES POUR TOLES FER
67271	IRON,SIMPLE STEEL COILS	W 372730	106060	W 492121	147776	W 525247	246718	W 196299	76859	EBAUCHES NON EN ACIER
673	IRON,STEEL SHAPES ETC		146860		194375	W 709392	322445	W 589773	244115	BARRES,PROFIL FER,ACIER
6732	IRON,STEEL BARS ETC	W 236456	92177	W 341499	131982	W 444847	203652	W 268285	115303	BARRES FER,ACIER
67326	IRN,OTH STL BARS HOTROLD	W 209476	66016	W 305179	100771	W 392310	150486	W 230125	77218	BARRES PLEINES FER,ACIER
674	IRN,STL UNIV,PLATE,SHEET	W 302689	203951	W 364680	252836	W 497282	427337	W 735132	484194	LARGES PLATS,TOLES
6745	IRN,STL MED PLATE,ROLLED	W 61045	36205	W 51189	34778	W 61889	50789	W 227914	102673	TOLES 3 A 4.75 MM
6746	IRN,STL THIN PLATE,ROLLD	W 59428	55358	W 86650	78753	W 145729	146668	W 151123	131091	TOLES LAM MOINS 3MM
6749	OTH IRN,STL PLATES,SHEET	W 92889	63811	W 130680	82153	W 166348	137591	W 183940	137360	AUTRES TOLES FER,ACIER
67491	— OF IRON OR SIMPLE STL	W 91106	59939	W 128252	77506	W 164035	130389	W 181461	131223	AUT TOLES AUTRES ACIER FIN
678	IRON,STL TUBES,PIPES,ETC		67995		174346	W 152297	167084	W 128864	141654	TUBES,TUYAUX EN FONTE,FER
6783	IRON,STL TUBES,PIPES NES	W 32386	23469	W 137555	127350	W 111915	100073	W 77100	61466	AUT TUBES,TUYAUX FER,ACIER
68	NON–FERROUS METALS		305786		400686		583029		496502	METAUX NON FERREUX
682	COPPER EXC CEMENT COPPER		116080		148737	W 65136	223644	W 62471	198295	CUIVRE
6822	COPPER,ALLOYS WORKED		94766		132654	W 63554	219046	W 58367	188634	CUIVRE,ALLIAGES OUVRES
68221	COPPER BARS,WIRE,ETC	W 22594	48756	W 34054	77181	W 46765	141412	W 42324	115535	BARRES,PROFILES ET FILS
684	ALUMINIUM		138469		192292	W 100364	280369	W 95966	216762	ALUMINIUM
6841	ALUMINIUM,ALLOYS,UNWRGHT		70177	W 68257	107618	W 73352	164298	W 67676	114444	ALUMINIUM,ALLIAGES BRUTS
6842	ALUMINIUM,ALLOYS WORKED	W 23414	68291		84674	W 27012	116071	W 28290	102319	ALUMINIUM,ALLIAGES OUVRE
69	METAL MANUFACTURES NES		468117		516242		697306		693629	ART MANUFACT EN METAL NDA
695	TOOLS		82049		76791	W 11485	99107	W 11756	104465	OUTILS A MAIN
699	BASE METAL MFRS NES		142486		160407	W 39237	226906	W 43395	232055	ART MANUFACTURES MET NDA
7	MACHINES,TRANSPORT EQUIP		8621671		9310784		11327417		12378884	MACHINES MATERIEL TRANSPORT
71	POWER GENERATING EQUIPMT		368394		441164		638313		815788	MACHINES GENERATRICES
713	INTRNL COMBUS PSTN ENGIN	W 35875	250209	W 42801	348759	W 50345	525827	W 45818	669802	MOTEURS EXPL COMB INT, PIECE
7132	MOTOR VEHCL PISTN ENGINS	W 8443	79967	W 13509	143299	W 16042	223425	W 24183	385820	MOTEURS EXPL POUR VEHICULES
7139	PISTON ENGINE PARTS NES	W 26108	148411	W 27698	174583	W 32660	266708	W 19821	249084	PIECES POUR 713.2,3,8
72	MACHS FOR SPCL INDUSTRYS		829035		815299		1034146		1087965	MAC SPECIALES POUR INDUST
722	TRACTORS NON–ROAD	W 8953	64336	W 9948	69657	W 12955	101500	W 16844	129100	TRACTEURS
7224	WHEELED TRACTORS NES	W 8923	64161	W 9904	69393	W 12773	100277	W 16543	127241	TRACTEURS A ROUES
723	CIVIL ENGNEERG EQUIP ETC	W 22334	106327	W 20759	119816	W 23456	135075	W 29977	176092	APPAREILS DE GENIE CIVIL
7234	CONST,MINING MACHNRY NES	W 19255	89024	W 18086	103422	W 18541	105045	W 24461	143063	MACH POUR LA CONST, MINES
72342	SLFPRP SHOVELS,EXCAVATRS	W 15091	63044	W 12728	60771	W 14422	72405	W 19743	103589	PELLES MECANIQUES
724	TEXTILE,LEATHER MACHNRY		198872		219455	W 11604	263696	W 10771	262962	MACH POUR INDUSTRIE TEXTILE
728	OTH MACHY FOR SPCL INDUS		283103		253621	W 22017	312279	W 20515	302622	AUT MACH IND PARTICULIERES
7284	MACHY FOR SPCL INDUS NES		182544		185796	W 11756	209231	W 10958	204441	MACH SPEC IND PARTICUL.
72848	OTH MCHY WITH INDIV FNCT		77184	W 3489	71253	W 5180	86984	W 3772	74885	AUTRES MACHINES NDA
73	METALWORKING MACHINERY		240123		134763		140526		148303	MACH TRAVAIL DES METAUX
736	METALWORKING MACH–TOOLS		206359		106451	W 8216	100354	W 9943	110851	MACH–OUTILS TRAVAIL METAUX
7369	PTS NES OF TOOLS OF 736		83298		22602	W 1788	22232	W 1375	16550	PIECES GROUPE 736
74	GENRL INDUSTRL MACHY NES		895807		835176		1092384		1185723	MACH APP INDUSTRIE
741	HEATING,COOLING EQUIPMNT		230291		211858	W 23372	277842	W 22197	303667	MACH CHAUFFAGE,PIECES
7415	AIR–CONDITIONING MACHNRY	W 6486	85601	W 5000	70116	W 6239	105622	W 8346	138032	GROUPES CONDITION AIR
743	PUMPS NES,CENTRFUGES ETC		139882		131552	W 18025	167481	W 20191	205497	POMPES COMPRES,VENT ETC
744	MECHANICAL HANDLING EQU		162869		139146	W 31427	179461	W 36231	195693	EQUIP MANUTENTION PIECES
745	NONELEC MACHY,TOOLS NES		147944		136191	W 10413	156463	W 11329	155169	AUT MACH NON ELEC,PIECES
7452	OTH NONELEC MCHS,PTS NES		127450		116599	W 9574	131437	W 10258	128846	AUT MACH NON ELEC,PIECES
749	NONELEC MACH PTS,ACC NES		153591		159605	W 15860	233255	W 14688	228856	PIECES MACH NON ELEC NDA
7492	COCKS,VALVES ETC NES		78525		78329	W 7728	95822	W 8633	108052	ART ROB,SIM POUR TUYAUX
75	OFFICE MACHNES,ADP EQUIP		594413		609885		802845		871131	MACH BUREAU TRAIT AUTOM
751	OFFICE MACHINES	W 2734	80864	W 2935	88829	W 2807	95875	W 3295	81542	MACH,APPAREILS DE BUREAU
752	AUTOMTIC DATA PROC EQUIP	W 8307	368713		365270	W 7063	493611	W 8694	535315	MACH TRAIT INFORMATION
7523	DIGITL CENTRL PROCESSORS	W 3420	143985	W 1365	112861	W 1251	126886	W 1732	158694	UNITES CENTRALES
7525	ADP PERIPHERAL UNITS	W 2986	109955	W 2924	111135	W 3920	158795	W 5066	165888	UNITES PERIPHERIQUES

4. Special Imports C.I.F. by Commodities according to the S.I.T.C. (Rev. 2) in thousand U.S. Dollars
Importations Spéciales C.A.F. par Produits d'après la C.T.C.I. (Rév. 2) en milliers de Dollars E.U.

SITC CTCI	COMMODITY	1993 WEIGHT POIDS	1993 VALUE VALEUR	1994 WEIGHT POIDS	1994 VALUE VALEUR	1995 WEIGHT POIDS	1995 VALUE VALEUR	1996 WEIGHT POIDS	1996 VALUE VALEUR	PRODUIT
759	OFFICE,ADP MCH PTS,ACCES		144836		155787	W 3359	213358	W 4361	254275	PIECES DU 751 ET 752
7599	ACCTG,ETC,ADP MCH PTS,AC	W 1679	121549	W 1754	130482	W 2524	177175	W 3509	223819	PIECES DU 751 ET 752
76	TELECOMM,SOUND EQUIPMENT		776160		758268		931886		896296	EQUIPMENT DE TELECOM
761	TELEVISION RECEIVERS	W 13073	180848	W 11404	156246	W 11405	170928	W 10762	153113	RECEPTEURS DE TELEVISION
7611	COLOUR TV RECEIVERS	W 12884	177769	W 11315	154478	W 11253	168636	W 10694	151263	RECEPTEURS COULEUR
762	RADIO BROADCAST RECEIVRS	W 3751	104923		89667	W 4050	96059	W 3557	83189	RECEPTEURS RADIODIFFUSION
763	SOUND RECORDRS,PHONOGRPH		88391	W 1803	74734	W 1838	82726	W 1792	94849	PHONO,APP ENREGISTREMENT
7638	OTHR SOUND APPARATUS ETC		86503	W 1736	73474	W 1801	81986	W 1764	94273	AUT APP D'ENREGIS,REPROD
764	TELECOM EQPT,PTS,ACC NES		401997		437622	W 10090	582173	W 10433	565145	EQUIP TELECOM,PIECES
7641	LINE TELEPHONE,ETC EQUIP	W 1053	78596	W 1104	72995	W 1188	85923	W 1344	95054	APP TELEPHON PAR FIL
7643	TV,RADIO TRANSMITTRS ETC		61665	W 273	60149	W 297	91111	W 423	123399	APP EMET TELE RADIO
7649	PTS NES OF EQUIPMT OF 76		179880		220125	W 5680	318978	W 5749	290773	PIECES DE LA DIV 76
76491	PTS NES OF APPAR OF 7641		79809		92440	W 667	121137	W 742	119552	PIECES POUR 764.1
76493	TELECOMM EQUIPMT PTS NES	W 2288	79819	W 2986	89127	W 2935	102409	W 2405	82270	PIECES 761,762,764.3,8
77	ELECTRIC MACHNRY NES ETC		1331924		1635305		2317663		2323689	MACH APP ELECT NDA
771	ELECTRIC POWER MACHY NES	W 7347	88544		97336	W 8665	104085	W 9795	111755	MACH PROD,TRANS ELECTR
7712	OTH ELEC POWER MACHY NES	W 5307	72994		81118	W 6703	84670	W 7725	91611	AUT APP PROD TRANSF ELEC
772	SWITCHGEAR ETC,PARTS NES		296130		378636	W 16468	497324	W 17798	521253	APP COUPURE,SECT ETC
7721	SWITCHGEAR ETC		255437		318119	W 15226	417215	W 16411	450460	APP COUPURE,SECTIONMNT
773	ELECTR DISTRIBUTNG EQUIP		208543		254423	W 42014	374461	W 44684	370080	EQUIPMT DISTRIBUTION ELECT
7731	INSULATED WIRE,CABLE ETC		141516		160951	W 34917	242436	W 36611	234594	FILS,CABLES ISOLES ELECT
7732	ELECTRC INSULATING EQUIP		67026	W 6646	93471	W 7097	132024	W 8073	135487	EQUIP ISOL ELECTRIQUE
77327	OTH ELEC INSUL FITTG NES		43211	W 4712	65426	W 5104	103717	W 5616	102644	PIECES ISOL EN AUT MATIERES
775	HOUSEHOLD TYPE EQUIP NES		277734		281062	W 54031	332149	W 56231	358656	MACH,APP USAGE DOMESTQUE
7758	ELECTRO–THERMIC APPL NES		89257		98441	W 13136	116873	W 14529	129431	APP ELECTROTHERMIQ NDA
776	TRANSISTORS,VALVES,ETC		143679		268846	W 1866	593997	W 1747	488143	LAMPES,TUBES,VALVES
7764	ELECTRONIC MICROCIRCUITS		109406		218837	W 1116	526138	W 1031	408606	MICROSTRUCTURES ELECTRON
778	ELECTRICAL MACHINERY NES		286461		318250	W 30543	376323	W 34512	425448	AUTRES MACH ELECT NDA
7783	AUTOMOTIVE ELECTR EQUIP		58747		68833	W 5997	98274	W 6784	131011	EQUIP ELECT MOTEURS EXPL
7788	OTH ELEC MACHY,EQUIP NES		125807		141716	W 5492	153917	W 5281	157743	AUT MACH APP ELEC NDA
78	ROAD VEHICLES		3463643		3551058		3868975		4899280	VEHICULES ROUTIERS
781	PASS MOTOR VEH EXC BUSES	W 204794	1881475	W 206048	1910846	W 197336	2064204	W 226953	2300887	AUTO TRANSPORT PERSONNES
782	LORRIES,SPCL MTR VEH NES		478977	W 81387	625602	W 62558	519863	W 85548	697807	VEHICULES SPECIAUX,MARCH
7821	LORRIES,TRUCKS		467108	W 79642	615893	W 60265	505029	W 83242	685441	VEHICULES TRANSP MARCHAND
784	MOTOR VEH PRTS,ACCES NES		886712		830016	W 119186	1026216	W 166018	1638139	PIECES 722,781,782,783
7849	OTHER MOTOR VEHCL PARTS		862395		810087	W 116142	997025	W 162580	1608298	PIECES 722,781,782,783
785	CYCLES,ETC MOTRZD OR NOT		152757	W 8600	120861	W 9284	135846	W 9017	127699	MOTOCYCLES SCOOTERS
7851	MOTORCYCLES ETC		122388	W 4413	86783	W 4276	93912	W 4156	86438	MOTO VELO MOTEUR AUXIL
79	OTHR TRANSPORT EQUIPMENT		122173		529866		500679		150709	AUTRE MATERIEL TRANSPORT
792	AIRCRAFT ETC	W 203	55223		368379	W 583	348492	W 564	93860	APP NAVIGATION AERIENNE
7924	AIRCRFT NES OVER 15000KG	W 24	25930	W 406	342936	W 422	303508	W 173	14971	AERODYNES PLUS 15000 KG
793	SHIPS AND BOATS ETC		27185	W 58588	87364	W 28974	72630	W 17823	41867	NAVIRES BATEAUX,ETC
7932	SHIPS AND BOATS NES	W 3729	22909	W 54571	83898	W 6162	57797	W 7646	32753	NAVIRES ET BATEAUX
8	MISC MANUFACTURED GOODS		2577049		2581378		3251080		3358143	ART MANUFACTURES DIVERS
812	*PLUMBG,HEATNG,LGHTNG EQ	W 12150	74110		72243	W 13948	94632	W 17117	108046	APPAR SANITAIRES CHAUFFAGE
821	*FURNITURE,PARTS THEREOF		175226		169682	W 41224	213626	W 45668	230809	MEUBLES ET PIECES
8219	FURNITURE AND PARTS NES	W 24185	96794	W 22708	89073	W 26003	112263	W 29964	119358	AUTRES MEUBLES ET PIECES
84	CLOTHING AND ACCESSORIES		691945		715679		852395		870020	VETEMENTS
842	MENS OUTERWEAR NOT KNIT		104595		114064	W 3756	130612	W 3521	131205	VET DESSUS POUR HOMMES
843	WOMENS OUTERWEAR NONKNIT		141854		144864	W 3573	185504	W 3817	189359	VET DESSUS FEMMES MAT TEX
845	OUTERWEAR KNIT NONELASTC		198328		197426	W 5302	211741	W 5067	212174	VET DESSOUS,ACCES BONNET
8451	— JERSEYS,PULLOVERS ETC	W 2721	111931		103285	W 2656	105782	W 2250	98787	CHANDAILS,PULL–OVERS ETC
8459	— OTHER,CLTHG ACCESRYS		74145		82325	W 2300	89879	W 2461	96547	AUT VET DESSUS DE BONNE
846	UNDER GARMENTS KNITTED		113171		121320	W 5613	157111	W 5351	163713	SOUS VETS DE BONNETERIE
8462	— OF COTTON NON ELASTIC		65860		74058	W 3990	97400	W 3917	102512	SOUS–VET BONNET COTON
851	*FOOTWEAR	W 7363	108699		117602	W 10947	158139	W 11183	158270	CHAUSSURES
85102	FOOTWEAR LEATHER	W 5672	93134		100098	W 8498	132038	W 8293	128773	CHAUS SEMELLES EN CUIR
87	PRECISION INSTRUMNTS NES		303002		332785		397464		420780	INSTRUM,APPAR SCIENT NDA
872	MEDICAL INSTRUMENTS NES		83125		95786	W 3555	117267	W 3684	130059	INSTR,APP MEDIC–CHIR NDA
87202	OTH MEDICAL INSTRUMENTS		75087	W 2222	84154	W 3239	105681	W 3313	117885	INSTRUM,APP MEDECINE
874	MEASURNG,CONTROLNG INSTR		190783		199684	W 3559	233903	W 3524	246998	INSTRUMENTS DE MESURE
88	PHOTO EQU,OPTICL GDS ETC		223960		219243		273977		274577	APP,FOURN PHOTO,OP,MONTR
882	PHOTO,CINEMA SUPPLIES		80722		77273	W 7240	93267	W 6947	89395	PRODUITS PHOTO,CINEMA
89	MISC MANUFCTRD GOODS NES		962720		919199		1214566		1245730	ART MANUFACTURES DIVERS
892	PRINTED MATTER		167673		164255	W 27074	232425	W 27400	220363	IMPRIMES
893	ARTICLES OF PLASTIC NES		247175		261712		371852		377424	OUVRAGES EN MAT DIVIS 58
8939	MISC PLASTIC ARTICLES		189935		199840	W 45708	293573	W 48706	298566	ART DIVERS EN MAT DIV 58
89399	OTHR PLASTC ARTICLES NES		173731		184118	W 40283	273963	W 42093	274544	AUT OUV MAT DIV 58
894	TOYS,SPORTING GOODS,ETC		190633		155814	W 20561	188262	W 23190	226452	VOITURES ENFANTS,JOUETS
8942	TOYS,INDOOR GAMES ETC		151695		119859	W 15081	140411	W 17164	176394	JOUETS,JEUX ETC
89423	TOYS NES		85134	W 7986	62786	W 8412	69437	W 9718	79415	JOUETS,MODELES REDUITS
897	GOLD,SILVER WARE,JEWELRY		74690		65531		87605		90765	BIJOUTERIE,ORFEVRERIE
898	MUSICAL INSTRUMENTS,PTS		120434		115165		153324	W 11550	138737	INSTRUMENTS DE MUSIQUE
8983	SOUND RECRDNG TAPE,DISCS		103694		102152	W 8285	137003	W 10827	122687	SUPPORTS SON POUR 763
899	OTHER MANUFACTURED GOODS		114704		114520		133628		138136	AUT ART MANUF DIVERS NDA
9	GOODS NOT CLASSD BY KIND		144592		157020		210342		179529	ART TRANSACT NON CLASSES
971	*GOLD,NON MONETARY NES		125268		129334	K 14091	171466	K 13380	142961	OR NON MONETAIRE
97101	NONMON GLD UNWRT,SEMIMFD		125105		129330	K 14088	171465	K 12375	142947	OR,ALLIAGES D'OR BRUTS

5. Special Exports F.O.B. by Commodities according to the S.I.T.C. (Rev. 2) in thousand U.S. Dollars
Exportations Spéciales F.O.B. par Produits d'après la C.T.C.I. (Rév. 2) en milliers de Dollars E.U.

SITC CTCI	COMMODITY	1993 WEIGHT POIDS	1993 VALUE VALEUR	1994 WEIGHT POIDS	1994 VALUE VALEUR	1995 WEIGHT POIDS	1995 VALUE VALEUR	1996 WEIGHT POIDS	1996 VALUE VALEUR	PRODUIT
	ALL COMMODITIES		15417381		17980753		23370015		23185562	TOUS PRODUITS
0	FOOD AND LIVE ANIMALS		560861		687738		940952		897736	ALIMENTS,ANIMAUX VIVANTS
01	MEAT AND PREPARATIONS		47031		37632		44433		39781	VIANDES ET PREPARATIONS
02	DAIRY PRODCTS,BIRDS'EGGS		58922		78879		124558		132097	PRODUITS LAITIERS,OEUFS
022	MILK AND CREAM	W 22250	29047	W 54316	46647	W 84757	70767	W 93366	79753	LAIT ET CREME
03	FISH AND PREPARATIONS		200635		234873		301242		268567	POISSONS ET PREPARATIONS
034	FISH,FRESH,CHILLED,FROZN	W 36351	79856	W 48718	90495	W 51795	106480	W 42123	88325	POISSON FRAIS, REFRIG,CONG
0342	FISH FROZEN,EXCL FILLETS	W 26980	47034	W 34178	51847	W 31093	55928	W 22798	48212	POISSONS CONGELES
037	FISH ETC PREPD,PRSVD NES	W 26295	90062	W 34591	112611	W 37348	136701	W 26696	107632	POIS,CRUST,MOL PREPARES
0371	FISH PREPARD,PRESRVD NES	W 26250	89839	W 34497	112240	W 37232	136164	W 26602	107175	CONSERVES DE POISSONS
04	CEREALS AND PREPARATIONS		35381		47044		81624		90850	CEREALES ET PRODUITS
048	CEREAL ETC PREPARATIONS	W 11974	20710	W 17267	35652	W 30716	61284	W 37135	70788	PREPTNS A BASE CEREALES
05	VEGETABLES AND FRUIT		161027		204173		272888		242736	LEGUMES ET FRUITS
054	VEG ETC FRSH,SMPLY PRSVD	W 152286	115180	W 173111	135699	W 200003	183879	W 165395	139351	LEGUMES FRAIS,CONG,SECS
0546	VEGETABLES SIMPLY PRESVD	W 118350	89939	W 122308	106172	W 146162	141379	W 120482	108301	LEGUMES CONG,CONSER
05461	VEGETABLES FROZEN	W 117509	89236	W 121968	105826	W 145278	140808	W 120352	108071	LEGUMES CONGELES
1	BEVERAGES AND TOBACCO		484983		514759		585412		632133	BOISSONS ET TABACS
11	BEVERAGES		477835		507589		575157		615473	BOISSONS
112	ALCOHOLIC BEVERAGES	W 263359	469551	W 256603	496315	W 247490	560847	W 268984	598910	BOISSONS ALCOOLIQUES
1121	WINE OF FRESH GRAPES ETC	W 216929	431145	W 190631	446948	W 169618	496008	W 196398	539343	VINS DE RAISINS FRAIS
11212	WINE OF FRESH GRAPES	W 215579	430280	W 190318	446245	W 169311	495226	W 196005	538223	VINS DE MOUTS DE RAISINS
2	CRUDE MATERLS,EXCL FUELS		900810		1092377		1466417		1045068	MAT BRUTES NON COMESTIBLES
24	CORK AND WOOD		149475		152801		203385		158619	LIEGE ET BOIS
248	WOOD SHAPED,SLEEPERS	W 473330	80227	W 456666	83938	W 444022	95193	W 393780	75342	BOIS SIMPLEMENT TRAVAILLES
2482	LUMBER SHAPED CONIFER	W 467355	76865	W 444523	78759	W 433151	90712	W 386534	72201	CONIFERES SCIES,RABOTES
24821	LUMBER SAWN ETC CONIFER	W 464721	76571	W 443008	78479	W 416886	87329	W 348145	66491	CONIFERES SCIES LONGITUD
251	*PULP AND WASTE PAPER	W 1049989	362063	W 1102760	509312	W 1015846	739180	W 1034748	462110	PATES A PAPIER,DECHETS
2517	SODA,SULPHATE WOOD PULP	W 921762	319204	W 967385	456697	W 904733	671261	W 929169	429895	PATES CHIMIQUES AU SULFATE
25171	— UNBLEACHED	W 85011	28553	W 116644	49201	W 100940	73120	W 89900	37960	PATES ECRUES
25172	— BLEACHED,NONDISSOLVNG	W 836751	290651	W 850740	407496	W 803793	598141	W 839270	391935	PATES BLANCHIES
26	TEXTILE FIBRES AND WASTE		56618		60763		66880		65759	FIBRES TEXTILES
27	CRUDE FERTLZR,MINRLS NES		49345		52607		62244		60123	ENGRAIS MINERAUX BRUTS
273	STONE,SAND AND GRAVEL	W 289340	46940	W 395623	49877	W 485262	59489	W 431901	55784	PIERRES,SABLES,GRAVIERS
28	METALLIFEROUS ORES,SCRAP		241671		264039		324252		232035	MINERAIS METAL,DECHETS
287	BASE METAL ORES,CONC NES	W 686477	204307	W 564665	218390	W 527288	275165	W 503450	197053	MINERAIS METAUX COMMUNS
2871	CPR ORE ETC,CEMENT COPPR	W 672073	172939	W 554815	195801	W 516154	244448	W 492279	167623	MINERAIS DE CUIVRE,MATTES
28711	COPPER ORES,EXCL MATTE	W 671241	171707	W 554815	195801	W 516154	244448	W 492279	167623	MINERAIS DE CUIVRE
3	MINERAL FUELS ETC		521605		735991		747235		560394	COMBUSTIBLES MINERAUX LUB
33	PETROLEUM AND PRODUCTS		521089		725720		708844		536320	PETROLE ET DERIVES
334	PETROLEUM PRODUCTS,REFIN	W 3709035	472579	W 5001879	670148	W 4117745	652071	W 2711559	487214	PRODUITS RAFFINES
3341	GASOLINE,OTH LIGHT OILS			W 782819	126977					ESSENCES POUR MOTEURS
33411	MOTOR,AVIATION SPIRIT			W 550609	92126					ESSENCES MOTEURS D'AVIONS
3342	KEROSENE,OTH MEDIUM OILS			W 810166	136550					PETR LAMPANTS,AUT HUIL
33421	KEROSENE INCL JET FUEL			W 810160	136546					PETROLES LAMPANTS
3343	GAS OILS			W 1461199	212972					GAS OILS
3344	FUEL OILS,NES			W 1845179	158131					FUEL OILS
335	RESIDUAL PETRLM PROD NES	W 279161	48510	W 339462	55572	W 325317	56773	W 266258	49106	PRODUITS RESIDUELS NDA
4	ANIMAL,VEGETABLE OIL,FAT		47929		70131		151101		165966	HUILES,GRAISSES ANIM,VEG
42	FIXED VEGETABLE OIL,FAT		38400		63268		141743		156705	HUILES VEGETALES FIXES
423	FIXED VEG OILS,SOFT	W 22967	38048	W 53528	61812	W 102967	130559	W 112890	154906	HUILES VEGET DOUCES FIXES
4235	OLIVE OIL	W 12532	29362	W 16931	37343	W 21782	69360	W 20297	90095	HUILE D'OLIVE
5	CHEMCLS,RELATED PROD NES		649229		842678		1083499		1028055	PRODUITS CHIMIQUES
51	ORGANIC CHEMICALS		164770		234015		315888		204139	PROD CHIMIQ ORGANIQUES
511	HYDROCARBONS NES,DERIVS	W 431254	124298	W 497105	168933	W 483806	252468	W 408703	155976	HYDROCARBURES NDA
5111	ACYCLIC HYDROCARBONS	W 238083	63621	W 238355	67901	W 204818	89973	W 174529	57227	HYDROCARBURES ACYCLIQUES
5112	CYCLIC HYDROCARBONS	W 177988	53710	W 246120	93504	W 261788	153589	W 218619	89940	HYDROCARBURES CYCLIQUES
51124	XYLENES,CHEMICALLY PURE	W 97609	35608	W 129525	64756	W 145469	126586	W 115876	66124	XYLENES PURS
541	*MEDICINAL,PHARM PRODUCT		85784		94715	K 6259685	143582	K 6079838	169280	PROD MEDICINAUX PHARMACEUT
5417	MEDICAMENTS		42937		55023	K 4268648	89272	K 4153669	121754	MEDICAMENTS
54179	— CONTNG OTH SUBSTANCES	K 2113100	37849	K 2007174	47677	K 3589649	69117	K 2227344	73658	MED CONT AUT SUBSTANCES
55	PERFUME,CLEANING ETC PRD		42712		50842		76135		91806	PROD POUR PARFUM,TOILETTE
58	PLASTIC MATERIALS ETC		172935		244010		253490		221674	MAT PLAST ARTIFICIELLES
583	POLYMERIZATION ETC PRODS		157319		227261	W 180639	218183	W 160002	182702	PROD POLYMERISATION
5831	POLYETHYLENE	W 131987	84239	W 178473	124990	W 108586	105973	W 76108	67515	POLYETHYLENE
58311	— IN PRIMARY FORMS	W 129825	81552	W 174216	121357	W 102429	99829	W 72203	61774	POLYETHYLENE PRIMAIRES
5834	POLYVINYL CHLORIDE	W 65945	47106	W 77064	66452	W 52633	67822	W 63688	66814	CHLORURE DE POLYVINYLE
58341	— IN PRIMARY FORMS	W 62914	40260	W 73648	58046	W 48075	54740	W 57417	45715	SOUS FORMES PRIMAIRES
59	CHEMICAL MATERIALS NES		109588		134221		178335		208096	MAT PROD CHIMIQUES NDA
598	MISCEL CHEM PRODUCTS NES		103727		118824	W 114669	159696	W 115802	194242	PROD DIV INDUST CHIM NDA
5989	CHEM PRODUCTS,PREPS NES		59254		81116	W 68704	113191	W 77089	150545	PROD PREP CHIMIQUES NDA
59899	OTH CHEM PRODS,PREPS,NES		57676		79589	W 68032	111358	W 76297	148528	AUT PRODUITS CHIMIQUES NDA
6	BASIC MANUFACTURES		3782480		4457276		5511628		5361201	ART MANUFACTURES
61	LEATHER,DRESSED FUR,ETC		171713		204413		218527		213295	CUIRS,PELLETERIES
612	LEATHER ETC MANUFACTURES	W 5908	131248	W 7171	148494	W 6585	158501	W 6988	151753	OUVRAGES EN CUIRS NDA
6123	PREPRD PARTS OF FOOTWEAR	W 5885	130420	W 7123	147440	W 6530	157131	W 6899	150154	PARTIES DE CHAUSSURES
62	RUBBER MANUFACTURES NES		56146		103514		147539		167044	CAOUTCHOUC MANUFACTURE
625	RUBBER TYRES, TUBES ETC		47622	W 27322	93349	W 35658	126411	W 38925	146284	PNEUS CAOUTCHOUC VULCANISE
6251	TYRES NEW FOR MOTOR CARS	W 10634	38692	W 24653	86229	W 32555	116337	W 35517	135474	PNEUS POUR VOITURES
63	WOOD,CORK MANUFACTRS NES		637324		718265		846480		860851	OUVRAGES LIEGE ET BOIS
633	CORK MANUFACTURES	W 90136	504973	W 94545	549567	W 92011	640974	W 95698	662246	OUVRAGES EN LIEGE
63301	NATURAL CORK ARTICLES	W 21393	300103	W 21774	320088	W 22487	386536	W 26834	407838	OUVRAGES EN LIEGE NATUREL
63302	AGGLOMERATD CORK,ARTS OF	W 68743	204870	W 72771	229478	W 69523	254438	W 68864	254409	LIEGE AGGLOM ET OUVRAGES
634	VENEERS,PLYWOOD,ETC	W 336425	72953	W 374068	100392	W 320466	109320	W 284002	94461	PLACAGES,CONTRE–PLAQUES
6343	IMPROVED,RECONSTIT WOOD	W 274113	50108	W 307967	75091	W 255543	79692	W 239828	70542	BOIS AMELIORES,RECONST
63432	RECONSTITUTED WOOD	W 274077	50073	W 307945	75068	W 255492	79627	W 239761	70409	BOIS RECONSTITUES
635	WOOD MANUFACTURES NES		59398	W 79503	68306	W 101138	96186	W 80809	104144	ART MANUF EN BOIS NDA
64	PAPER,PAPERBOARD AND MFR		439772		545939		763927		738389	PAPIERS,CARTONS & OUVRAGES
641	PAPER AND PAPERBOARD		400350		501986	W 763697	701985	W 916657	667465	PAPIERS ET CARTONS
6413	KRAFT PAPER,PAPERBOARD	W 245794	104171	W 220289	107300	W 223424	162878	W 209099	122602	PAPIER ET CARTON KRAFT
64131	KRAFT LINER IN BULK	W 209066	81966	W 180299	82312	W 180835	123069	W 165825	84594	PAP KRAFT POUR COUVERTURES
6415	PAPER,PAPERBRD,BULK,NES		189667	W 307627	252821	W 295574	354667	W 351528	316372	PAPIERS,CARTONS ROULEAUX
64159	OTHER PAPER ETC,BULK,NES		189596	W 307589	252724	W 295526	354481	W 351109	316146	AUT PAPIER ROULEAUX FEUILLES
6416	FIBRE BUILDING BOARD	W 190661	64162	W 203748	79825	W 186156	83869	W 256173	86283	PLAQUES CONSTRUCT EN PATE
64162	INSULATING BOARD, ETC	W 160406	53636	W 161305	63321	W 147518	67276	W 200202	67507	PLAQUES CONST NON COMPR
642	PAPER,ETC,PRECUT,ARTS OF		39423		43952	W 30998	61942	W 46095	70924	PAP,CARTONS DECOUPES
65	TEXTILE YARN,FABRICS,ETC		1206287		1348455		1632747		1615781	FILS,TISSUS,ARTICLES TEXTILE
651	TEXTILE YARN	W 25719	103557	W 27450	125290	W 25012	141371	W 28604	150980	FILS TEXTILES
6513	COTTON YARN	W 10962	46376	W 9716	49184	W 9172	55741	W 10473	55601	FILS DE COTON
652	COTTON FABRICS,WOVEN		136158		157502	W 13107	187444	W 12462	196622	TISSUS DE COTON
6522	WOVEN COTTON BLEACHD,ETC		123114		145599	W 11351	175862	W 11612	190811	TISSUS COTON BLANCHIS ETC
65224	BLCHED COTTON FABRIC NES		103527		123688	W 10137	155039	W 10572	171342	AUT TIS PLUS 85% COT BLANCHI

5. Special Exports F.O.B. by Commodities according to the S.I.T.C. (Rev. 2) in thousand U.S. Dollars
Exportations Spéciales F.O.B. par Produits d'après la C.T.C.I. (Rév. 2) en milliers de Dollars E.U.

SITC CTCI	COMMODITY	1993 WEIGHT POIDS	1993 VALUE VALEUR	1994 WEIGHT POIDS	1994 VALUE VALEUR	1995 WEIGHT POIDS	1995 VALUE VALEUR	1996 WEIGHT POIDS	1996 VALUE VALEUR	PRODUIT
653	WOVN MAN–MADE FIB FABRIC		172573		175038	W 13441	194384	W 13113	198990	TISSUS FIBRES SYNTH,ARTIF
6534	DISC SYN BLEND FABRC NES		102234	W 6806	103964	W 7002	117967	W 7194	122777	TISSUS FIBRES SYNTH DISCONT
65342	DISC SYN FIB–WOOL FABRIC	W 2528	56755	W 2576	53781	W 2678	63524	W 2742	65692	TISSUS FIB SYNT MEL LAINE
657	SPECIAL TXTL FABRC,PRODS		148609		154640	W 78774	206874	W 79090	195827	TISSUS SPECIAUX
6575	CORDAGE AND MANUFACTURES	W 64770	99050	W 66513	105495	W 66344	131113	W 67009	122587	FICELLES,CORDES,CORDAGES
65751	CORDAGE,CABLE,ROPE,TWINE	W 60887	81087	W 62140	86408	W 62770	110240	W 63630	102902	CORDAGES TRESSES OU NON
658	TEXTILE ARTICLES NES		565572		623996	W 70789	757757	W 70206	743728	ART FACONNES MAT TEXTILES
6584	LINENS ETC		488070		544408	W 58785	651441	W 58705	649185	LINGE DE MAISON
65841	BED LINEN OF COTTON	W 16516	158885	W 20221	190700	W 21825	233792	W 22709	252877	LINGE DE LIT DE COTON
65845	OTHER LINEN OF COTTON	W 26816	243912		255086	W 27793	304257	W 27456	292184	LINGE DE TOILETTE COTON
6589	OTH TEXTILE ARTICLES NES		50621		54016	W 6175	77475	W 5916	69085	AUT ART EN TEXTILES NDA
66	NONMETAL MINERAL MFS NES		737067		883960		1010368		908347	ART MIN NON METALLIQUES
661	LIME,CEMENT,BLDG PRODS	W 818678	157729	W 1230574	176635	W 887091	186660	W 807920	183648	CHAUX,CIMENTS MAT CONSTR
6613	BUILDING STONE ETC WORKD	W 742164	153586	W 738334	159626	W 719737	173665	W 634771	167192	PIERRES A BATIR
66132	BUILDING STONE WORKED	W 213918	109241	W 235570	117261	W 222586	126727	W 214751	126560	OUVR EN PIERRES DE TAILLE
662	CLAY,REFRACTORY BLDG PRD	W 229936	97481	W 263875	116883	W 275675	129836	W 264521	119141	MAT CONST REFRACTAIRES
6624	BRICKS ETC NONREFRACTORY	W 225190	96420	W 260452	116053	W 270602	127986	W 257758	116875	BRIQUES ETC CERAM NON REFR
66245	GLAZED CERAMIC SETTS ETC	W 175493	86995	W 183976	91449	W 194459	100726	W 193369	95484	AUT CARREAUX CERAMIQUE
665	GLASSWARE	W 257356	138915		168530	W 351921	215571	W 266440	170334	OUVRAGES EN VERRE
6651	BOTTLES ETC OF GLASS	W 242929	91490	W 303571	114806	W 333204	145091	W 249947	112339	RECIPIENTS EN VERRE
66511	GLASS BOTTLES ETC NONVAC	W 242922	91463	W 303571	114805	W 333203	145072	W 249947	112329	BONBONNES,BOUTEILLES,ETC
666	POTTERY	W 89620	230906	W 107278	288174	W 113770	342923	W 108459	317081	POTERIE
6665	COARSE CERAMIC HOUSEWARE	W 33866	75504	W 38776	91111	W 40296	103626	W 40354	102475	VAISSELLE,ART MEN CERAM
6666	CERAMIC ORNAMENTS ETC	W 50067	133728	W 57623	154573	W 62849	193875	W 55953	160974	OBJETS PORCELAINE,CERAM
667	PEARL,PREC–,SEMI–P STONE		72109		81838		65017		54487	PERLES, PIERRES GEMMES
6672	DIAMONDS NONINDUST,UNSET		72055		81825		64829		54289	DIAMANTS BRUTS
66729	— CUT ETC NOT SET		67337		76589		61119		53525	DIAMANTS TAILLES
67	IRON AND STEEL		160681		178160		223697		238143	FER ET ACIER
673	IRON,STEEL SHAPES ETC	W 228488	73128	W 187713	60203	W 178035	73563	W 80105	34335	BARRES,PROFIL FER,ACIER
674	IRN,STL UNIV,PLATE,SHEET	W 87066	46983	W 109143	66232	W 95294	72852	W 164793	96941	LARGES PLATS,TOLES
69	METAL MANUFACTURES NES		346609		444855		628011		582731	ART MANUFACT EN METAL NDA
692	METAL TANKS,BOXES,ETC	W 31272	54723		56388	W 33369	66604	W 34412	76085	RECIPIENTS METALLIQUES
6924	MTL TRANSPORT BOXES ETC	W 30394	49334		54243	W 32027	60745	W 32778	65965	FUTS,TAMBOURS,BIDONS
697	BASE MTL HOUSEHOLD EQUIP	W 14994	61553	W 19770	76512	W 24162	102679	W 25933	117253	ART MENAGE MET COMMUNS
699	BASE METAL MFRS NES		133944		184347		238198		214855	ART MANUFACTURES MET NDA
6991	LOCKSMITHS WARES,ETC		61923		80258	W 10675	106568	W 9613	86367	ARTICLES DE SERRURERIE
69913	BASE MTL DOOR,ETC FITTNG	W 5794	49078	W 7055	58750	W 7693	75472	W 6439	61271	GARNITURES POUR MEUBLES
7	MACHINES,TRANSPORT EQUIP		3265627		3888559		6252691		7080702	MACHINES MATERIEL TRANSPORT
71	POWER GENERATING EQUIPMT		232198		260119		399089		253821	MACHINES GENERATRICES
713	INTRNL COMBUS PSTN ENGIN	W 31865	197626		221519	W 47629	332086	W 34338	224118	MOTEURS EXPL COMB INT, PIECE
7132	MOTOR VEHCL PISTN ENGINS	W 19477	140341	W 20282	152965	W 31125	257662	W 17027	141331	MOTEURS EXPL POUR VEHICULES
7139	PISTON ENGINE PARTS NES	W 11932	54051		65371	W 16333	67958	W 17166	73825	PIECES POUR 713.2,3,8
72	MACHS FOR SPCL INDUSTRYS		119810		143753		184088		198548	MAC SPECIALES POUR INDUST
724	TEXTILE,LEATHER MACHNRY		49854		52218	W 1964	52570	W 2495	57398	MACH POUR INDUSTRIE TEXTILE
74	GENRL INDUSTRL MACHY NES		313778		371289		477920		546541	MACH APP INDUSTRIE
741	HEATING,COOLING EQUIPMNT	W 11335	89748		103434	W 16096	126252	W 19154	153048	MACH CHAUFFAGE,PIECES
7416	HEATING,COOLING EQU NES	W 6412	60674	W 6836	64589	W 8530	78460	W 9109	90150	APP CHANGEMENT TEMP
749	NONELEC MACH PTS,ACC NES		180615		209759	W 12420	276854	W 12862	313500	PIECES MACH NON ELEC NDA
7499	OTH NONELEC MCHY PTS NES		139629		160666	W 6617	204528	W 7339	241229	PIECES NON ELECT NDA
74991	FOUNDRY MOULDS ETC NES	W 5054	137190	W 5927	159094	W 6438	201607	W 7072	237817	MOULES POUR METAUX
76	TELECOMM,SOUND EQUIPMENT		433684		553724		726736		777844	EQUIPMENT DE TELECOM
762	RADIO BROADCAST RECEIVRS	W 4112	333265	W 5118	420607	W 6564	531675	W 7662	565220	RECEPTEURS RADIODIFFUSION
7621	MTR VEHC RADIO RECEIVERS	W 3285	311019	W 4310	392845	W 5377	499702	W 6220	538039	RECEPTEURS RADIO AUTO
764	TELECOM EQPT,PTS,ACC NES	W 3095	77445		99279	W 7367	141990	W 8731	160517	EQUIP TELECOM,PIECES
7649	PTS NES OF EQUIPMT OF 76	W 1013	36913	W 2871	59675	W 5608	92321	W 6165	109884	PIECES DE LA DIV 76
77	ELECTRIC MACHNRY NES ETC		1110123		1425044		2126539		2074319	MACH APP ELECT NDA
771	ELECTRIC POWER MACHY NES		108641		122016	W 14040	171201	W 20600	198693	MACH PROD,TRANS ELECTR
7711	TRANSFORMERS,ELECTRICAL		84965		94234	W 12956	135214	W 19104	174598	TRANSFO ELECTRIQUES
77111	LIQUID DIELEC TRANSFRMRS	W 6789	25463	W 6535	24732	W 9537	44700	W 15554	84549	TRANSFO DIELEC LIQUIDE
77118	OTHER ELEC TRANSFORMERS		59502		69502	W 3418	90514	W 3551	90050	AUTRES TRANSFO ELECTRIQ
772	SWITCHGEAR ETC,PARTS NES		111243		149226	W 7956	186197	W 8023	180216	APP COUPURE,SECT ETC
7721	SWITCHGEAR ETC		92252		127526	W 7599	163193	W 7746	161476	APP COUPURE,SECTIONMNT
773	ELECTR DISTRIBUTNG EQUIP		570196		717911	W 60210	958463	W 63311	1016686	EQUIPMT DISTRIBUTION ELECT
7731	INSULATED WIRE,CABLE ETC	W 41983	564789		711029	W 58523	948004	W 61271	1008171	FILS,CABLES ISOLES ELECT
775	HOUSEHOLD TYPE EQUIP NES		113886		145391	W 36046	179393	W 29216	158393	MACH,APP USAGE DOMESTQUE
7752	DOM REFRIGERATRS,FREEZRS	W 13003	53027	W 17655	68616	W 16538	70288	W 9285	42617	REFRIG,CONGEL MENAGER
7758	ELECTRO–THERMIC APPL NES		41747		54495	W 15901	89796	W 17650	95061	APP ELECTROTHERMIQ NDA
77586	ELECTROTHERM DOM APP NES	W 4399	32666	W 5279	37821	W 7757	62682	W 9305	71248	APP ELECTRO THERMIQUES
776	TRANSISTORS,VALVES,ETC		74931		145796	W 306	429434	W 248	296494	LAMPES,TUBES,VALVES
7764	ELECTRONIC MICROCIRCUITS		71911		142276	W 205	424140	W 162	291219	MICROSTRUCTURES ELECTRON
778	ELECTRICAL MACHINERY NES		128201		141180	W 28392	195916	W 27868	218556	AUTRES MACH ELECT NDA
7788	OTH ELEC MACHY,EQUIP NES		64046		88025	W 3412	123064	W 2956	102994	AUT MACH APP ELEC NDA
78	ROAD VEHICLES		824262		928389		2084020		2932261	VEHICULES ROUTIERS
781	PASS MOTOR VEH EXC BUSES	W 41047	335967	W 24640	228596	W 84450	1134107	W 221139	2004981	AUTO TRANSPORT PERSONNES
782	LORRIES,SPCL MTR VEH NES	W 27300	199568	W 51164	370976	W 62969	488576	W 51495	417672	VEHICULES SPECIAUX,MARCH
7821	LORRIES,TRUCKS	W 27103	198836	W 50970	370097	W 62828	487770	W 51359	416607	VEHICULES TRANSP MARCHAND
784	MOTOR VEH PRTS,ACCES NES		216175	W 53143	242091	W 61915	353486	W 63597	390454	PIECES 722,781,782,783
7849	OTHER MOTOR VEHCL PARTS		215621	W 53109	241230	W 61817	352298	W 63474	389354	PIECES 722,781,782,783
785	CYCLES,ETC MOTRZD OR NOT		43197		56422	W 11397	70970	W 12070	77459	MOTOCYCLES SCOOTERS
79	OTHR TRANSPORT EQUIPMENT		165365		134465		176540		207507	AUTRE MATERIEL TRANSPORT
792	AIRCRAFT ETC		33046		83795	W 471	85886	W 364	58935	APP NAVIGATION AERIENNE
7924	AIRCRFT NES OVER 15000KG	W 27	10691	W 66	63702	W 312	60061	W 191	30149	AERODYNES PLUS 15000 KG
793	SHIPS AND BOATS ETC	W 40954	129710	W 22146	43406	W 38665	82438	W 41707	119968	NAVIRES BATEAUX,ETC
7932	SHIPS AND BOATS NES	W 40720	127880	W 21602	43220	W 38599	82190	W 41699	119848	NAVIRES ET BATEAUX
79322	TANKERS OF ALL KINDS	W 23100	79228	W 556	110					BATEAUX–CITERNES
79323	OTHER CARGO VESSELS	W 16104	43046	W 19574	36367	W 36719	77897	W 34418	103603	AUT BATEAUX TRANS MARCH
8	MISC MANUFACTURED GOODS		5166473		5652380		6576457		6355621	ART MANUFACTURES DIVERS
812	*PLUMBG,HEATNG,LGHTNG EQ	W 29691	62303	W 36083	68877	W 43326	88061	W 50989	98575	APPAR SANITAIRES CHAUFFAGE
821	*FURNITURE,PARTS THEREOF	W 99793	190355	W 49011	218650	W 54946	285289	W 66784	308585	MEUBLES ET PIECES
8211	CHAIRS,SEATS AND PARTS	W 7128	80989	W 7636	105504	W 11388	142182	W 18110	162744	SIEGES ET PIECES
82119	PTS NES OF CHAIRS ETC	W 5273	66467	W 5753	94687	W 8564	125520	W 15540	145210	PIECES DU 821.11
8219	FURNITURE AND PARTS NES	W 35412	96858	W 37666	100376	W 39992	127314	W 45197	130882	AUTRES MEUBLES ET PIECES
82192	WOOD FURNITURE NES	W 26918	74807	W 31049	80911	W 33846	104401	W 38493	106655	MEUBLES NDA EN BOIS
84	CLOTHING AND ACCESSORIES		3133873		3286753		3805091		3590714	VETEMENTS
842	MENS OUTERWEAR NOT KNIT	W 20032	679897		741505	W 21967	859008	W 20806	807007	VET DESSUS POUR HOMMES
8422	— SUITS	W 1221	59612	W 1510	70736	W 1823	100879	W 1896	106976	COMPLETS HOMMES MAT TEXT
8423	— TROUSERS,BREECHES ETC	W 10047	278579	W 10806	307769	W 11781	369814	W 11018	347869	PANTALONS HOMMES MAT TEX
8424	— JACKETS,BLAZERS ETC	W 3668	171653	W 4199	193463	W 4021	212422	W 3889	195830	VESTES HOMMES MAT TEXTIL
8429	— OTHER OUTER GARMENTS	W 4553	148072		147111	W 3801	151910	W 3406	127938	AUT VET DES HOM MAT TEX
843	WOMENS OUTERWEAR NONKNIT		400698		419394	W 10709	486398	W 10577	463231	VET DESSUS FEMMES MAT TEX
8431	— COATS AND JACKETS	W 1753	73392		76733	W 1929	101048	W 1900	104263	MANT,VEST FEM MAT TEXTIL

Portugal

5. Special Exports F.O.B. by Commodities according to the S.I.T.C. (Rev. 2) in thousand U.S. Dollars
Exportations Spéciales F.O.B. par Produits d'après la C.T.C.I. (Rév. 2) en milliers de Dollars E.U.

SITC CTCI	COMMODITY	1993		1994		1995		1996		PRODUIT
		WEIGHT POIDS	VALUE VALEUR	WEIGHT POIDS	VALUE VALEUR	WEIGHT POIDS	VALUE VALEUR	WEIGHT POIDS	VALUE VALEUR	
8434	— SKIRTS	W 1396	51003	W 1269	49222	W 1114	54788	W 990	47497	JUPES EN MAT TEXTILES
8435	— BLOUSES		72885	W 1516	81752	W 1711	99180	W 1729	94095	BLOUSES FEM MAT TEXTILES
8439	— OTHER OUTER GARMENTS		184650		189395	W 5266	193665	W 5216	181184	AUT VET DES FEM MAT TEXT
844	UNDER GARMENTS NOT KNIT		256344		290910	W 9404	335798	W 8372	286602	VETEMENT DESSOUS MAT TEX
8441	— MENS SHIRTS		235061		266936	W 7822	308774	W 6420	256674	CHEMISES HOMMES MAT TEXT
84411	—— OF COTTON	W 6019	200531	W 7156	234153	W 6827	265491	W 5580	224506	CHEMISES HOMMES DE COTON
845	OUTERWEAR KNIT NONELASTC		1012892		1022997	W 42018	1180912	W 41557	1131568	VET DESSOUS,ACCES BONNET
8451	— JERSEYS,PULLOVERS ETC	W 22052	506125	W 20942	489543	W 22298	583359	W 22630	581729	CHANDAILS,PULL–OVERS ETC
8452	— WOMENS DRESSES ETC	W 1735	51542		61363	W 2221	77728	W 1844	62723	ROBES,JUPES BONNETERIE
8459	— OTHER,CLTHG ACCESRYS		455226		472091	W 17499	519825	W 17083	487116	AUT VET DESSUS DE BONNE
846	UNDER GARMENTS KNITTED	W 25526	638978		649469	W 24942	748217	W 24594	721142	SOUS VETS DE BONNETERIE
8462	— OF COTTON NON ELASTIC	W 22985	576274		575807	W 22734	665840	W 22217	635923	SOUS–VET BONNET COTON
84621	—— MENS SHIRTS	W 2690	74380	W 3034	83771	W 2886	87663	W 2804	86569	CHEMISES DE COTON
84629	—— OTHER	W 20295	501894		492036	W 19847	578176	W 19414	549353	AUT SOUS–VET BONNET COTON
847	TEXTILE CLTHNG ACCES NES		128569		144886	W 16179	170657	W 15254	155238	ACCES VET MAT TEXT NDA
8472	CLTHNG ACCESRYS ETC KNIT	W 13386	119931		136202	W 15798	160522	W 14899	146406	ACCES VET BONNE NDA
84722	KNIT SOCKS,ETC NONELASTC	W 12940	115045		127676	W 14710	146747	W 13999	134950	CHAUSSETTES BON. NON ELAS
851	*FOOTWEAR		1349711	W 73034	1555422	W 70239	1689690	W 75475	1709651	CHAUSSURES
85102	FOOTWEAR LEATHER	W 61344	1320119	W 70737	1529932	W 67309	1648836	W 70270	1637395	CHAUS SEMELLES EN CUIR
87	PRECISION INSTRUMNTS NES		79715		130040		204822		172853	INSTRUM,APPAR SCIENT NDA
874	MEASURNG,CONTROLNG INSTR		36209		76593	W 939	127796	W 1045	115734	INSTRUMENTS DE MESURE
8743	GAS,LIQUID CONTROL INSTR		14649		57602	W 346	82464	W 323	65744	APP,INSTR MESURE FLUIDES
89	MISC MANUFCTRD GOODS NES		291149		330609		427439		402754	ART MANUFACTURES DIVERS
893	ARTICLES OF PLASTIC NES		127614		156901		199028		175981	OUVRAGES EN MAT DIVIS 58
8939	MISC PLASTIC ARTICLES	W 30591	100457		118918	W 43749	159275	W 44175	135953	ART DIVERS EN MAT DIV 58
89399	OTHR PLASTC ARTICLES NES	W 29849	97635		116659	W 43031	156657	W 43546	134041	AUT OUV MAT DIV 58
894	TOYS,SPORTING GOODS,ETC	W 3757	47934		55832	W 5453	76839	W 5163	72327	VOITURES ENFANTS,JOUETS

FOOT NOTES – NOTES

TABLE 1 –

1 The gold trade is comprised of gold bullion and specie, including government gold transactions, and partly–worked gold, jewellers' sweepings, dust, concentrates, etc.

TABLEAU 1 –

1 Le commerce de l'or comprend l'or en lingots ou en pièces de monnaie, y compris les transactions en or du gouvernement, ainsi que l'or partiellement travaillé, les balayures des bijoutiers, les poussières, les concentrés etc.

1. HISTORICAL SERIES, 1969–1994 GENERAL TRADE, IMPORTS C.I.F., EXPORTS F.O.B.
SERIES HISTORIQUES, 1969–1994 COMMERCE GENERAL, IMPORTATIONS C.A.F., EXPORTATIONS F.O.B

YEAR ANNEE	VALUE IN MILLION QATAR RIYALS VALEUR EN MILLION QATAR RIYALS MERCHANDISE –MARCHANDISE		GOLD –OR		CONVERSION FACTORS U.S. CENTS PER QATAR RIYAL FACTEURS DE CONVERSION CENTS E.U. PAR QATAR RIYAL		INDEX NUMBERS –INDICES QUANTUM		UNIT VALUE VALEUR UNITAIRE	
	IMPORTS	EXPORTS	IMPORTS	EXPORTS	IMPORTS	EXPORTS	IMPORTS	EXPORTS	IMPORTS	EXPORTS
1969	252.20	1088.60			21.0000	21.0000				
1970	305.50	1124.30			21.0000	21.0000				
1971	561.90	1689.00			21.0000	21.0000				
1972	607.30	2092.60			22.8000	22.8000				
1973	778.50	2841.70			24.9850	24.9838				
1974	1068.90	7958.20			25.3330	25.3330				
1975	1609.80	7107.00			25.4592	25.4559				154
1976	3300.30	8754.10			25.2428	25.2389				160
1977	4850.10	7964.00			25.2603	25.2588				179
1978	4589.70	8993.00			25.8112	25.7997				178
1979	5377.70	14655.00			26.4920	26.5819				250
1980	5267.90	20787.00			27.4725	27.4725				436
1981	5524.90	21272.00			27.4725	27.4725				
1982	7087.50	16405.00			27.4492	27.4725				
1983	5298.00	12002.00			27.4730	27.4728				
1984	4229.60	16427.00			27.4730	27.4729				
1985	4146.50	12894.00			27.4730	27.4619				
1986	3999.70				27.4730					
1987	4127.90				27.4730					
1988	4613.10				27.4730					
1989	4826.70	9779.91			27.4725	27.4725				
1990	6169.40	12846.87			27.4725	27.4725				100
1991	6261.20	11307.96			27.4725	27.4725				95
1992	7336.00	13600.08			27.4725	27.4725				103
1993	6882.10	11578.23			27.4725	27.4725				102
1994	7015.60	11695.12			27.4725	27.4725				105

2. IMPORTS BY BROAD ECONOMIC CATEGORY AND EXPORTS BY INDUSTRIAL ORIGIN. (PERCENTAGE OF TOTAL VALUE)
IMPORTATIONS PAR CATEGORIES ECONOMIQUES ET EXPORTATIONS PAR BRANCHE D'ACTIVITE.(EN POURCENTAGE DE LA VALEUR TOTALE)

IMPORTS – IMPORTATIONS

	1990	1991	1992	1993	1994	1995	1996
TOTAL IMPORTS–IMPORTATIONS TOTALES	100.	100.	100.	100.	100.		
1 FOOD BEV–ALIMENTATION BOISSONS	15.6	15.1	12.6	12.8	13.4		
11 PRIMARY–PRODUITS DE BASE	10.1	9.3	7.6	7.2	7.5		
111 FOR INDUSTRY–POUR L'INDUSTRIE	4.9	4.1	2.7	2.3	2.4		
112 FOR HOUSEHOLDS–POUR LES MENAGES	5.2	5.2	4.9	4.9	5.1		
12 PROCESSED–PRODUITS ELABORES	5.4	5.7	5.0	5.6	5.9		
121 FOR INDUSTRY–POUR L'INDUSTRIE	0.4	0.3	0.3	0.4	0.4		
122 FOR HOUSEHOLDS–POUR LES MENAGES	5.1	5.4	4.7	5.2	5.5		
2 IND SUPPLIES–APPROV INDUSTRIELS	24.7	26.2	25.2	26.0	30.2		
21 PRIMARY–PRODUITS DE BASE	3.1	3.2	2.9	2.3	3.3		
22 PROCESSED–PRODUITS ELABORES	21.6	23.0	22.2	23.7	26.9		
3 FUELS–COMBUSTIBLES	0.6	0.7	0.7	0.6	0.6		
31 PRIMARY–PRODUITS DE BASE	0.0	0.0	0.0	0.0	0.0		
32 PROCESSED–PRODUITS ELABORES	0.6	0.7	0.7	0.6	0.6		
321 MOTOR SPIRIT–ESSENCE							
322 OTHER–AUTRES	0.6	0.7	0.7	0.6	0.6		
4 MACHINERY–EQUIPEMENT	29.0	25.5	23.6	20.8	21.3		
41 CAPITAL EQUIPMENT–MACHINES	28.4	22.6	21.6	19.4	19.8		
42 PARTS–PIECES ACCESSOIRES	0.6	2.8	2.1	1.4	1.5		
5 TRANSPORT–TRANSPORT	14.2	15.1	19.8	20.5	16.5		
51 PASSENGER CARS–AUTOMOBILES	8.0	8.3	10.5	11.8	8.8		
52 OTHER–AUTRES	2.6	2.7	4.5	3.8	3.4		
521 INDUSTRIAL–INDUSTRIELS	2.5	2.6	4.5	3.7	3.3		
522 NON INDUSTRIAL–NON INDUSTRIEL	0.1	0.1	0.1	0.1	0.1		
53 PARTS–PIECES ACCESSOIRES	3.6	4.1	4.8	5.0	4.3		
6 CONSUM GOODS–BIENS CONSOMMATION	15.8	17.4	17.9	19.0	17.8		
61 DURABLE–DURABLES	5.9	7.1	7.6	8.2	7.4		
62 SEMI DURABLE–SEMI DURABLES	6.3	6.6	6.7	6.7	6.5		
63 NON DURABLE–NON DURABLES	3.6	3.7	3.6	4.0	3.9		
7 GOODS NES–BIENS NDA	0.1	0.1	0.1	0.2	0.1		

EXPORTS – EXPORTATIONS

	1990	1991	1992	1993	1994	1995	1996
TOTAL EXPORTS–EXPORTATIONS TOTALES	100.	100.	100.	100.	100.		
1 AGRICULTURE	0.1	0.1	0.1	0.1	0.2		
2 MINING QUARRY–INDUS EXTRACTIVES	79.3	73.7	75.2	75.1	67.0		
3 MANUFACTURING–IND MANUFACTUR	20.6	26.2	24.7	24.9	32.8		
31 FOOD BEV TOBACCO–ALIM BOISS TAB	0.1	0.4	0.2	0.3	0.3		
32 TEXTILES–INDUSTRIES TEXTILES	0.2	0.5	0.9	1.2	2.0		
33 WOOD & PRODUCTS–BOIS & PRODUITS	0.0	0.0	0.0	0.0	0.0		
34 PAPER & PRODUCTS–PAPIER & PRODT	0.0	0.0	0.0	0.0	0.0		
35 CHEMICALS–INDUSTRIES CHIMIQUES	12.6	18.0	16.6	15.4	23.1		
36 NON METAL MIN–MIN NON METAL	0.0	0.1	0.0	0.0	0.0		
37 BASIC METAL–IND METAL BASE	4.9	4.4	4.7	6.3	5.8		
38 METAL MANUF–MANUF METAL	2.5	2.7	2.3	1.6	1.6		
39 OTH MANUF IND–AUTRES MANUF	0.2	0.0	0.0	0.1	0.0		

3. TRADE BY PRINCIPAL COUNTRIES OF ORIGIN AND DESTINATION (VALUE IN THOUSAND U.S. DOLLARS)
ECHANGES SELON LES PRINCIPAUX PAYS D'ORIGINE ET DE DESTINATION (VALEUR EN MILLIERS DE DOLLARS EU)

COUNTRIES–PAYS	GENERAL IMPORTS C.I.F. IMPORTATIONS GENERALES C.A.F					COUNTRIES–PAYS	GENERAL EXPORTS F.O.B. EXPORTATIONS GENERALES F.O.B.				
	1990	1991	1992	1993	1994		1990	1991	1992	1993	1994
World	1694876	1720095	2015396	1890697	1927365	Monde	3641214	3209807	3840694	3245416	3212942
Africa	11879	13639	24221	19225	16132	Afrique	22428	19370	7701	4086	32931
Americas	201638	249624	292453	254378	256029	Amériques	13048	18837	35395	46895	73322
Northern America	165220	206357	246149	224367	214785	Amérique du Nord	9195	18833	35359	46879	65063
LAIA	35550	42068	45257	29185	38930	ALAI	3853	4	36	9	4784
CACM	777	1191	970	753	2157	MCAC				8	
Caribbean	29	7	72	46	149	Caraïbes					
Rest of America	63		6	27	9	Autre Amérique					3475
As.ex F.USSR	658298	681419	838180	898069	890606	Asie l'URSS exclus	783927	856655	1222501	998812	1026395
Eur.x F.USSR	774959	710049	806537	665379	702306	Europe l'URSS exclus	25078	33460	30228	15481	15406
EU	735110	677667	763333	628561	652985	UE	22801	31406	28727	13446	14479
EFTA	25377	25608	25568	29317	42155	AELE	2237	2046	858	2015	914
East Europe	4356	2947	4426	4955	5699	Europe de l'Est			5	10	14
Other Europe	10117	3827	1128	1310	835	Autre de l'Europe	39	8		1	
Former USSR	1272	1435	4793	11693	20982	Ancienne URSS	67	32	3	18	215
Oceania	44200	63448	48407	41241	41082	Océanie	13864	46374	57926	63604	53997
Japan/Japon	248300	234112	314534	310326	257714	Japan/Japon	169481	187761	307666	180133	183359
United Kingdom	245926	203355	225206	194547	197929	United Arab Emirates	165660	142770	162331	162680	190004
USA/Etats–Unis d'Amer	160582	199634	230381	220169	204211	Korea, Republic of	32440	18957	149830	170257	143306
Germany/Allemagne	130845	146993	146196	150872	128125	Saudi Arabia	65756	77228	110327	101803	91602
Italy/Italie	158620	97052	132278	85533	83570	India/Inde	21917	35526	56677	82299	140987
United Arab Emirates	50300	73522	101739	136056	133697	China/Chine	51899	82755	59077	47504	52196
France,Monac	79753	89211	111195	64773	75914	Iran (Islamic Rp. of)	12933	50212	80487	83458	18471
Saudi Arabia	68859	70004	72451	100536	95416	Australia/Australie	13432	46116	57359	63339	53758
Netherlands/Pays–Bas	33881	35903	55838	45877	57669	Pakistan	16130	54126	75510	8849	21392
Australia/Australie	41345	59718	44540	38113	37986	USA/Etats–Unis d'Amer	8722	17808	34171	46557	64144
India/Inde	30170	30363	39232	53894	63163	Singapore/Singapour	27292	55176	35243	13784	23748
Korea, Republic of	24165	27795	36844	36147	38409	Kuwait/ Koweït	19110	27523	22119	24513	16552
Belgium–Luxembourg	18135	43877	30081	25215	25912	Philippines	19393	17185	27220	15128	24725
Brazil/Brésil	27228	28750	33955	22378	30183	Indonesia/Indonésie	19540	10351	25430	19602	13449
Switz.Liecht	21194	20780	23367	27075	39683	Bahrain/Bahreïn	13672	11184	10684	14387	16555
Singapore/Singapour	33825	25110	28511	19304	15374	Thailand/Thaïlande	23583	13376	13262	6461	8022
China/Chine	16708	21974	24684	27101	28291	Oman	11493	14279	10179	9006	6712
Bahrain/Bahreïn	16197	23232	27411	18081	30841	Hong Kong	22782	3988	10579	6159	5925
Spain/Espagne	15738	18151	13936	16499	23284	Malaysia/Malaisie	10616	4829	7665	11872	12383
Thailand/Thaïlande	13719	18902	19374	16931	16606	Sri Lanka	5025	2137	4636	7092	20140
Sweden/Suède	17066	14021	18152	9126	24202	Jordan/Jordanie	8034	5836	9902	7241	6585
Jordan/Jordanie	9322	19392	20263	18564	13085	France,Monac	3560	8401	11690	5625	3085
Malaysia/Malaisie	14962	10028	12678	17059	25261	United Kingdom	11454	2718	5090	4280	5153
Pakistan	17102	15148	13819	12925	17484	Viet Nam	2	4460	7939	4939	6317
Iran (Islamic Rp. of)	7372	14235	17289	15588	21885	Netherlands/Pays–Bas	682	12240	5841	449	3402
Indonesia/Indonésie	6379	10192	18087	18744	21811	Sudan/Soudan	5519	3072	2150	313	10645
Denmark/Danemark	17261	14161	12720	13450	14403	Former Democratic Yemen	20619				
Syrian Arab Republic	27317	11128	10982	9768	9060	Un. Rep. of Tanzania	38	49	1200		17437
Hong Kong	8014	12142	6201	8448	26269	Yemen/Yémen		13271	342	125	4360
Egypt/Egypte	6026	8155	17659	13114	8886	Bangladesh	8555	353	4765	1702	1488
Lebanon/Liban	8817	10903	12033	10392	9820	Egypt/Egypte	2129	2907	2679	2610	1139
Turkey/Turquie	8673	7518	8263	9926	9486	Italy/Italie	2225	4592	2540	215	268
Canada	4638	6723	15767	4198	10574	Brazil/Brésil	3850	3	20		4706
Austria/Autriche	6056	6213	8023	8498	8780	Algeria/Algérie	5548	23	5	0	2203
Russian Federation			4793	11693	20982	Germany/Allemagne	1382	1678	1186	728	2342
Kuwait/ Koweït	6881	1139	6748	9960	9316	Switz.Liecht	1871	1878	794	1872	740
Oman	3927	5206	6059	7424	8515	Lebanon/Liban	1209	1331	1340	1115	683
Ireland/Irlande	4083	3732	5408	6711	7171	Syrian Arab Republic	1207	501	1014	1332	709
Argentina/Argentine	4011	8782	7100	1877	2198	Spain/Espagne	1698	367	556	2025	41
Philippines	4627	3637	3854	4754	4742	Canada	473	1025	1188	321	918
Greece/Grèce	5935	3314	2346	4031	3827	Ethiopia/Ethiopie	110	3550	21	11	27
Chile/Chili	3832	3936	3557	3736	1903	Iraq	3699				
New Zealand	2852	3723	3868	3126	3096	Panama					3475
Norway,SVD,JM	4175	4820	2195	2242	2471	Morocco/Maroc	2747	132	43	415	19
Cyprus/Chypre	3904	3590	3129	3133	2131	Belgium–Luxembourg	321	1337	922	38	65
So. Africa Customs Un	1657	1722	3110	2847	4509	Turkey/Turquie	870	545	415	426	174
Yugoslavia/Yougoslavie			11709	901	507	Zambia/Zambie	2073				
Fm Yugoslav	9504	3344				Nigeria/Nigéria	1787	6	1		
Hungary/Hongrie	1462	1452	2237	1847	2045	New Zealand	431	258	567	252	240
Bangladesh	1263	1185	1822	1770	1757	Tunisia/Tunisie	500	410	194	302	194

(VALUE AS PERCENTAGE OF WORLD TOTAL)(VALEURS EN POURCENTAGE DU TOTAL MONDIAL)

	1985	1986	1987	1988	1989	1990	1991	1992	1993	1994
Africa	0.3	0.2	0.5	0.6	0.7	0.7	0.8	1.2	1.0	0.8
Americas	8.8	9.8	13.8	13.0	12.2	11.9	14.5	14.5	13.5	13.3
Northern America	6.9	6.9	10.3	9.7	9.1	9.7	12.0	12.2	11.9	11.1
LAIA	1.8	2.8	3.4	3.2	3.0	2.1	2.4	2.2	1.5	2.0
CACM	0.0	0.0	0.0	0.0	0.0	0.0	0.1	0.0	0.0	0.1
Caribbean	0.0			0.0	0.0	0.0	0.0	0.0	0.0	0.0
Rest of America			0.0	0.0	0.0	0.0		0.0	0.0	0.0
As.ex F.USSR	35.1	31.4	32.0	39.9	42.4	38.8	39.6	41.6	47.5	46.2
Eur.x F.USSR	50.1	52.4	49.5	40.7	41.5	45.7	41.3	40.0	35.2	36.4
EU	47.6	48.8	46.7	38.3	39.8	43.4	39.4	37.9	33.2	33.9
EFTA	1.7	2.7	2.1	1.3	1.0	1.5	1.5	1.3	1.6	2.2
East Europe	0.1	0.1	0.2	0.4	0.3	0.3	0.2	0.2	0.3	0.3
Other Europe	0.7	0.4	0.4	0.7	0.4	0.6	0.2	0.1	0.1	0.0
Former USSR	0.0		0.0	0.1	0.1	0.1	0.1	0.2	0.6	1.1
Oceania	2.7	2.9	2.4	3.3	3.0	2.6	3.7	2.4	2.2	2.1
Japan/Japon	18.2	16.7	16.4	17.6	18.8	14.7	13.6	15.6	16.4	13.4
United Kingdom	16.3	17.0	17.1	13.8	11.7	14.5	11.8	11.2	10.3	10.3
USA/Etats–Unis d'Amer	6.5	6.4	10.0	9.3	8.8	9.5	11.6	11.4	11.6	10.6
Germany/Allemagne	8.7	9.6	8.3	7.9	7.3	7.7	8.5	7.3	8.0	6.6
Italy/Italie	4.9	5.7	5.4	4.3	7.8	9.4	5.6	6.6	4.5	4.3
United Arab Emirates	2.7	1.5	1.5	3.1	4.4	3.0	4.3	5.0	7.2	6.9
France,Monac	7.6	6.9	6.6	4.0	4.7	4.7	5.2	5.5	3.4	3.9
Saudi Arabia	1.5	1.0	1.3	3.0	2.9	4.1	4.1	3.6	5.3	5.0
Netherlands/Pays–Bas	2.8	2.7	2.6	2.5	2.6	2.0	2.1	2.8	2.4	3.0
Australia/Australie	2.5	2.7	2.2	3.1	2.7	2.4	3.5	2.2	2.0	2.0

	1985	1986	1987	1988	1989	1990	1991	1992	1993	1994
Afrique					0.4	0.6	0.6	0.2	0.1	1.0
Amériques					1.0	0.4	0.6	0.9	1.4	2.3
Amérique du Nord					0.6	0.3	0.6	0.9	1.4	2.0
ALAI					0.4	0.1	0.0	0.0	0.0	0.1
MCAC									0.0	
Caraïbes										
Autre Amérique										0.1
Asie l'URSS exclus					26.4	21.5	26.7	31.8	30.8	31.9
Europe l'URSS exclus					0.5	0.7	1.0	0.8	0.5	0.5
UE					0.5	0.6	1.0	0.7	0.4	0.5
AELE					0.0	0.1	0.1	0.0	0.1	0.0
Europe de l'Est					0.0			0.0	0.0	0.0
Autre de l'Europe						0.0	0.0		0.0	
Ancienne URSS						0.0	0.0	0.0	0.0	0.0
Océanie					2.1	0.4	1.4	1.5	2.0	1.7
Japan/Japon					6.9	4.7	5.8	8.0	5.6	5.7
United Arab Emirates					4.7	4.5	4.4	4.2	5.0	5.9
Korea, Republic of					0.7	0.9	0.6	3.9	5.2	4.5
Saudi Arabia					3.0	1.8	2.4	2.9	3.1	2.9
India/Inde					1.4	0.6	1.1	1.5	2.5	4.4
China/Chine					2.3	1.4	2.6	1.5	1.5	1.6
Iran (Islamic Rp. of)					0.2	0.4	1.6	2.1	2.6	0.6
Australia/Australie					2.0	0.4	1.4	1.5	2.0	1.7
Pakistan					0.5	0.4	1.7	2.0	0.3	0.7
USA/Etats–Unis d'Amer					0.6	0.2	0.6	0.9	1.4	2.0

4. General Imports C.I.F. by Commodities according to the S.I.T.C. (Rev. 2) in thousand U.S. Dollars
Importations Générales C.A.F. par Produits d'après la C.T.C.I. (Rév. 2) en milliers de Dollars E.U.

SITC CTCI	COMMODITY	1991		1992		1993		1994		PRODUIT
		WEIGHT POIDS	VALUE VALEUR	WEIGHT POIDS	VALUE VALEUR	WEIGHT POIDS	VALUE VALEUR	WEIGHT POIDS	VALUE VALEUR	
	ALL COMMODITIES		1720095		2015396		1890697		1927365	TOUS PRODUITS
0	FOOD AND LIVE ANIMALS		260858		253849		241794		253552	ALIMENTS,ANIMAUX VIVANTS
001	*LIVE ANIMALS FOR FOOD	W 23256	61157	W 19986	40201		30915	W 20218	34240	ANIMAUX VIVANTS
0012	SHEEP AND GOATS,LIVE	W 22519	60121	W 19473	39439	W 16375	29631	W 19465	33045	ESPECES OVINE ET CAPRINE
01	MEAT AND PREPARATIONS		27836		32537		30888		33792	VIANDES ET PREPARATIONS
011	MEAT FRESH,CHILLD,FROZEN	W 15777	26465	W 19193	30569	W 18580	28440	W 21085	31170	VIANDES FRAICHES,REF,CONGE
0112	MUTTON ETC FRSH,CHLD,FRN	W 2938	5534	W 2595	4768	W 2536	5409	W 1820	4244	VIANDE DE MOUTON
0114	POULTRY FRESH CHLLD,FRZN	W 10667	15732	W 14020	20075	W 13702	17679	W 16714	21548	VOLAILLES MORTES
02	DAIRY PRODCTS,BIRDS'EGGS		33843		36266		36363		37774	PRODUITS LAITIERS,OEUFS
022	MILK AND CREAM	W 12682	23083	W 13779	25944	W 13274	25281	W 14666	26434	LAIT ET CREME
0223	MILK AND CREAM FRESH	W 4056	5389	W 3850	5089	W 3743	4887	W 5390	6868	LAIT,CREME FRAIS
0224	MILK,CREAM PRESERVED ETC	W 8626	17694	W 9929	20855	W 9531	20394	W 9276	19566	LAIT,CREME CONS,CONC
02243	MILK DRY,OVER 1.5% FAT	W 2283	6427	W 3257	10749	W 3776	10424	W 3889	10796	LAIT POUDRE SUP 1.5%
02249	MILK(EX DRY) PRSVD,SWEET	W 5200	7980	W 6339	8787	W 5386	7972	W 4984	7258	LAIT CONS,CONC SUCRE
024	CHEESE AND CURD	W 2165	5756	W 1818	5217	W 2267	6106	W 2522	6272	FROMAGE ET CAILLEBOTTE
04	CEREALS AND PREPARATIONS		33372		36759		37978		34534	CEREALES ET PRODUITS
041	WHEAT ETC UNMILLED	W 29340	5388	W 40747	7599	W 44623	8118	W 28848	5669	FROMENT,EPEAUTRE
0411	DURUM WHEAT UNMILLED	W 29340	5388	W 40747	7599	W 44623	8118	W 28848	5669	FROMENT DUR NON MOULU
042	RICE	W 24591	13646	W 26992	12854	W 29600	13182	W 29218	13071	RIZ
048	CEREAL ETC PREPARATIONS		7917	W 4018	7756	W 4523	8899	W 4340	8975	PREPTNS A BASE CEREALES
05	VEGETABLES AND FRUIT		57865		61152		58995		60273	LEGUMES ET FRUITS
054	VEG ETC FRSH,SMPLY PRSVD	W 61773	20888	W 58673	22914	W 60906	21968	W 60807	23898	LEGUMES FRAIS,CONG,SECS
0545	OTHER FRESH VEGETABLES	W 31117	12015	W 34913	13862	W 34990	13494	W 36094	14073	AUTRES LEGUMES FRAIS,REF
05459	FRESH VEGETABLES NES	W 17120	8257	W 21587	11154	W 21763	10710	W 23066	10942	LEGUMES FRAIS,REFRI NDA
056	VEGTBLES ETC PRSVD,PREPD	W 3411	4135	W 3793	4792	W 4115	5697	W 4530	5144	CONSERVES DE LEGUMES
057	FRUIT,NUTS,FRESH,DRIED	W 47048	26583	W 49114	28499	W 53680	26295	W 53226	26026	FRUITS FRAIS OU SECS
0571	ORANGES, MANDARINS ETC	W 12719	6170	W 12297	5681	W 14970	6566	W 13201	5378	ORANGES,MAND,CLEMENTINES
0579	FRUIT FRESH OR DRIED NES	W 16506	7873	W 18100	9441	W 18841	8233	W 20408	9699	FRUITS FRAIS,SECS NDA
058	FRUIT PRESERVED,PREPARED	W 5903	6258	W 4984	4946	W 4049	5035	W 3680	5206	CONSERVES DE FRUITS
06	SUGAR AND PREPS,HONEY		8056		8412		7804		10601	SUCRES ET PRODUITS
061	SUGAR AND HONEY	W 10882	5356	W 11230	4614	W 10014	4405	W 17038	7679	SUCRES ET MIEL
0612	REFINED SUGAR ETC	W 10359	4415	W 10968	3921	W 9727	3704	W 16708	7060	SUCRES RAFFINES
07	COFFEE,TEA,COCOA,SPICES		17422		16255		14962		18338	CAFE,THE,CACAO,EPICES
073	CHOCOLATE AND PRODUCTS	W 1296	7179	W 1021	5752	W 929	5731	W 1112	6700	CHOCOLAT
074	TEA AND MATE	W 964	5989	W 1135	6336	W 1022	5813	W 1170	6594	THE ET MATE
0741	TEA	W 964	5989	W 1135	6336	W 1022	5813	W 1170	6594	THE
081	*FEEDING STUFF FOR ANIML	W 51623	8744	W 45732	8986	W 40616	8078	W 55485	9460	NOURRITURE POUR ANIMAUX
09	MISC EDIBLE PRODUCTS		10451		10812		12835		10861	PREP ALIMENTAIRES DIVERSES
098	EDIBLE PRODCTS,PREPS NES	W 7047	10092	W 5480	10422	W 6288	12217	W 4274	10347	PREP ALIMENTAIRES NDA
09809	MISC FOOD PREPRTIONS NES	W 6023	7913	W 3937	7963	W 4355	9245	W 2162	7107	PREP ALIMENTAIRES NDA
1	BEVERAGES AND TOBACCO		21453		24157		24109		25593	BOISSONS ET TABACS
11	BEVERAGES		7362		9041		9438		12087	BOISSONS
111	NON–ALCOHL BEVERAGES NES	W 10954	5366	W 13642	6714	W 16501	7456	W 21490	9796	BOISSONS NON ALCOOLIQUES
11102	FLAVORED WATERS NON–ALCO	W 5965	4383	W 7511	5086	W 8450	5899	W 12509	7933	LIMONADES,EAUX GAZEUSES
12	TOBACCO AND MANUFACTURES		14092		15117		14672		13506	TABACS BRUTS FABRIQUES
122	TOBACCO,MANUFACTURED	W 972	14054	W 1079	15079	W 1138	14616	W 924	13482	TABACS FABRIQUES
1222	CIGARETTES	W 968	13986	W 1077	15016	W 1137	14552	W 773	12929	CIGARETTES
2	CRUDE MATERLS,EXCL FUELS		52213		63127		47997		66008	MAT BRUTES NON COMESTIBLES
24	CORK AND WOOD		7908		12166		11106		9764	LIEGE ET BOIS
248	WOOD SHAPED,SLEEPERS	W 15715	5915	W 22430	10547	W 26913	10595	W 19378	8383	BOIS SIMPLEMENT TRAVAILLES
27	CRUDE FERTLZR,MINRLS NES		7249		12545		21091		12668	ENGRAIS MINERAUX BRUTS
273	STONE,SAND AND GRAVEL	W 56652	3255	W 511637	8264		17743	W 821489	9524	PIERRES,SABLES,GRAVIERS
2731	BLDG,DIMENSION STONE	W 12006	1682	W 416647	6525	W 1512036	16348	W 786558	8128	PIERRES DE TAILLE
27313	GRANITE,SANDSTONE,ETC	W 6066	242	W 407384	4996	W 1507263	15615	W 782120	7226	GYPSE,BASALTE,GRES
28	METALLIFEROUS ORES,SCRAP		33425		32971		11094		38623	MINERAIS METAL,DECHETS
281	IRON ORE,CONCENTRATES	W 743475	32586	W 787205	32315	W 222630	9168	W 895266	38581	MINERAIS DE FER
3	MINERAL FUELS ETC		13085		14771		13190		13505	COMBUSTIBLES MINERAUX LUB
33	PETROLEUM AND PRODUCTS		12912		14669		13190		13505	PETROLE ET DERIVES
334	PETROLEUM PRODUCTS,REFIN	W 10451	11361	W 13343	12698	W 12186	11705	W 12373	11124	PRODUITS RAFFINES
3345	LUBS,PETROLEUM OILS NES	W 10451	11361	W 13035	12672	W 12186	11705	W 12373	11124	HUILES LUBRIFIANTES
33451	LUBS(HIGH PETR CONT) ETC	W 10013	10248	W 12494	11777	W 11728	10342	W 11817	10002	HUILES LUBRIF,H LOURDES
4	ANIMAL,VEGETABLE OIL,FAT		9016		10620		9487		10241	HUILES,GRAISSES ANIM,VEG
42	FIXED VEGETABLE OIL,FAT		8779		10531		9336		10241	HUILES VEGETALES FIXES
424	FIXED VEG OIL NONSOFT	W 8210	7821	W 9530	9343	W 8300	8139	W 9181	9202	AUTRES HUILES VEG FIXES
4249	FIXED VEGETABLE OILS NES	W 7271	7203	W 8761	8741	W 7544	7316	W 8576	8605	HUILES VEGET FIXES NDA
5	CHEMCLS,RELATED PROD NES		101404		119486		140556		126818	PRODUITS CHIMIQUES
52	INORGANIC CHEMICALS		10725		9890		7854		8665	PROD CHIM INORGANIQUES
523	OTHR INORG CHEMICALS ETC	W 10736	6434	W 7281	4030	W 5305	3619	W 7590	3892	AUT PRODUITS CHIMIQUES INORG
53	DYES,TANNING,COLOUR PROD		9387		9587		8996		10364	PROD TEINTURE,COLORANTS
533	PIGMENTS,PAINTS,ETC	W 4770	8122	W 5566	8422	W 5588	8427	W 5754	9924	PIGMENTS,PEINTURES,VERNIS
5334	VARNISHES,DISTEMPERS ETC	W 4317	7087	W 4214	6317	W 4882	7270	W 4976	8031	PEINTURES A L'EAU
53342	OTH PAINTS,VARNISHES ETC	W 3536	6037	W 2635	4418	W 3255	5469	W 3044	5538	AUTRES PEINTURES,VERNIS
541	*MEDICINAL,PHARM PRODUCT	K 1786658	23152	K 1225333	23858		32127	K 1604987	26649	PROD MEDICINAUX PHARMACEUT
5417	MEDICAMENTS	K 1409035	19350	K 992529	20992		27760	K 1138398	22953	MEDICAMENTS
54179	— CONTNG OTH SUBSTANCES	K 1409035	19350	K 992529	20992		27760	K 1138398	22953	MED CONT AUT SUBSTANCES
55	PERFUME,CLEANING ETC PRD		27976		33759		33480		37977	PROD POUR PARFUM,TOILETTE
551	ESSENTL OILS,PERFUME,ETC	W 304	3284	W 425	5540	W 617	7440	W 474	8986	HUILES ESSENTIELLES
553	PERFUMERY,COSMETICS,ETC	W 2215	16190	W 2460	18470	W 2333	17568	W 2739	19147	PRODUITS DE PARFUMERIE
554	SOAP,CLEANSING ETC PREPS	W 5281	8503	W 6017	9749	W 5519	8472	W 6720	9844	SAVONS,PRODUITS DETERSIFS
5542	WASHING PREPARATIONS ETC	W 3608	4905	W 3987	5749	W 4264	5697	W 4623	5912	PROD ORG TENSIO–ACT NDA
58	PLASTIC MATERIALS ETC		6799		7082		9679		10113	MAT PLAST ARTIFICIELLES
583	POLYMERIZATION ETC PRODS	W 4955	5699	W 5174	5537	W 7008	7941	W 7419	8231	PROD POLYMERISATION
59	CHEMICAL MATERIALS NES		17636		27971		43995		27153	MAT PROD CHIMIQUES NDA
598	MISCEL CHEM PRODUCTS NES	W 8972	13318	W 14662	23828	W 20129	39243	W 16236	22683	PROD DIV INDUST CHIM NDA
5983	ORGANIC CHEM PRODCTS NES	W 576	1421	W 1216	4234	W 8068	22801	W 1838	4626	PROD ORGAN NDA IND CHIMIQ
59832	ARTIFICIAL,ETC GRAPHITE	W 568	1377	W 1213	4213	W 8068	22801	W 1835	4611	GRAPHITE ARTIFICIEL COLLOIDA
5989	CHEM PRODUCTS,PREPS NES	W 7623	10431	W 12539	15644	W 11579	13666	W 13941	16660	PROD PREP CHIMIQUES NDA
59899	OTH CHEM PRODS,PREPS,NES	W 6759	8515	W 10538	11208	W 9469	9698	W 11232	11759	AUT PRODUITS CHIMIQUES NDA
6	BASIC MANUFACTURES		327928		376042		364145		424163	ART MANUFACTURES
62	RUBBER MANUFACTURES NES		18193		23508		24069		21863	CAOUTCHOUC MANUFACTURE
625	RUBBER TYRES, TUBES ETC	W 5324	16893	W 7209	21913	W 6988	22302	W 5956	19426	PNEUS CAOUTCHOUC VULCANISE
6251	TYRES NEW FOR MOTOR CARS	W 3949	12971	W 4669	13749	W 4295	14112	W 3609	12096	PNEUS POUR VOITURES
6252	TYRES,NEW,BUS OR LORRY	W 1212	3348	W 2440	7805	W 2503	7427	W 2028	5857	PNEUS POUR AUTOBUS,CAMIONS
63	WOOD,CORK MANUFACTRS NES		10652		24059		19054		26228	OUVRAGES LIEGE ET BOIS
634	VENEERS,PLYWOOD,ETC	W 11647	9572	W 18452	13318	W 21182	17159	W 25237	20627	PLACAGES,CONTRE–PLAQUES
6342	PLYWOOD OF WOOD SHEETS	W 9747	7645	W 13311	9649	W 13630	11098	W 14942	12878	BOIS CONTRE–PLAQUES
6349	WOOD SIMPLY SHAPED NES	W 1690	1767	W 4682	3428	W 7012	5670	W 9923	7557	BOIS SIMPL TRAVAILLES NDA
635	WOOD MANUFACTURES NES	W 820	1058	W 10587	10735	W 1078	1894	W 2800	5576	ART MANUF EN BOIS NDA
6353	BUILDERS WOODWRK,PREFABS	W 574	401	W 10201	9758	W 644	810	W 2176	4186	OUVRAGES DE MENUISERIE
64	PAPER,PAPERBOARD AND MFR		26231		24346		24291		22379	PAPIERS,CARTONS & OUVRAGES
641	PAPER AND PAPERBOARD	W 4964	4990	W 4941	5186	W 7323	6316	W 4582	4350	PAPIERS ET CARTONS

4. General Imports C.I.F. by Commodities according to the S.I.T.C. (Rev. 2) in thousand U.S. Dollars
Importations Générales C.A.F. par Produits d'après la C.T.C.I. (Rév. 2) en milliers de Dollars E.U.

SITC CTCI	COMMODITY	1991 WEIGHT POIDS	1991 VALUE VALEUR	1992 WEIGHT POIDS	1992 VALUE VALEUR	1993 WEIGHT POIDS	1993 VALUE VALEUR	1994 WEIGHT POIDS	1994 VALUE VALEUR	PRODUIT
642	PAPER,ETC,PRECUT,ARTS OF	W 11207	21241	W 9622	19160	W 23447	17974	W 9498	18029	PAP,CARTONS DECOUPES
6428	PAPER ETC ARTICLES NES	W 3792	11697	W 3513	10513	W 4112	11573	W 4415	11231	OUVRAGES EN PATE A PAPIER
64285	PAPER ETC DIAPERS ETC	W 1802	7244	W 1600	5493	W 1696	6602	W 2065	6591	SERVIETTES HYGIENIQUES
65	TEXTILE YARN,FABRICS,ETC		74915		81981		83091		98074	FILS,TISSUS,ARTICLES TEXTILE
652	COTTON FABRICS,WOVEN	W 748	4487	W 437	5083	W 1524	6741	W 3902	24596	TISSUS DE COTON
653	WOVN MAN-MADE FIB FABRIC	W 2670	29951	W 1784	25018	W 3349	31214	W 3013	30727	TISSUS FIBRES SYNTH,ARTIF
654	OTH WOVEN TEXTILE FABRIC	W 450	10257	W 657	12914	W 237	6885	W 222	7280	TISSUS AUT COTON SYNT,ARTIF
6541	SILK FABRICS WOVEN	W 194	6616	W 139	5531	W 67	4267	W 96	5633	TISSUS DE SOIE
658	TEXTILE ARTICLES NES	W 2453	11406	W 4070	18014	W 3663	17991	W 3235	14842	ART FACONNES MAT TEXTILES
6584	LINENS ETC	W 761	6745	W 1287	11427	W 1227	11132	W 471	5355	LINGE DE MAISON
659	FLOOR COVERINGS,ETC	W 4113	14644	W 7147	18327		18205	W 4319	16274	COUVRE-PARQUETS,TAPIS ETC
6592	CARPETS ETC KNOTTED	W 3979	13056	W 4695	15442	W 4476	15246	W 3990	13423	TAPIS POINTS NOUES,ENROULES
66	NONMETAL MINERAL MFS NES		41485		53290		74939		87732	ART MIN NON METALLIQUES
661	LIME,CEMENT,BLDG PRODS	W 114077	13590	W 304061	18938	W 545722	36606	W 537773	38524	CHAUX,CIMENTS MAT CONSTR
6612	CEMENT	W 94769	4437	W 291728	12146	W 526306	25441	W 516911	26859	CIMENTS HYDRAULIQUES
6613	BUILDING STONE ETC WORKD	W 5219	3016	W 7273	4679	W 10544	7059	W 12678	7847	PIERRES A BATIR
66132	BUILDING STONE WORKED	W 4965	2907	W 6621	4480	W 9466	6708	W 12161	7718	OUVR EN PIERRES DE TAILLE
6618	MNRL BLDG PRD UNFIRD NES	W 14027	6126	W 4921	2086	W 8716	4086	W 8126	3816	MAT CONST AMIANTE-CIMENT
66183	ASBESTOS-,FIBRE-CMNT PRD	W 13419	5530	W 3437	1177	W 3531	1186	W 2650	455	OUVRAGES AMIANTE-CIMENT
662	CLAY,REFRACTORY BLDG PRD	W 34736	14617	W 27784	15670	W 41501	20000	W 41396	18273	MAT CONST REFRACTAIRES
6623	REFRACTORY BUILDING PROD	W 15926	6948	W 8754	6714	W 16917	9006	W 10669	5543	BRIQUES REFRACTAIRES
66232	REFRACTRY BRICKS ETC NES	W 6092	4112	W 5367	3939	W 10800	6938	W 5200	3958	BRIQUES ETC REFRACTAIRES
6624	BRICKS ETC NONREFRACTORY	W 18811	7669	W 19030	8956	W 24584	10994	W 30727	12730	BRIQUES ETC CERAM NON REFR
66245	GLAZED CERAMIC SETTS ETC	W 8415	4478	W 7846	5550	W 11054	6933	W 13948	7613	AUT CARREAUX CERAMIQUE
663	MINERAL MANUFCTURES NES	W 3454	2193	W 5890	3161	W 7669	2995	W 22632	10336	ART MIN MANUF NDA
6633	MINRL MFS NES NONCERAMIC	W 2373	1004	W 3678	1056	W 5986	1303	W 19994	7497	OUVR MAT MINERALE NDA
66332	CEMENT,ARTFCL STONE PROD	W 1975	547	W 2226	569	W 4695	872	W 18435	7153	OUVRAGES EN CIMENT
664	GLASS	W 4818	4629	W 5652	6803	W 5311	6451	W 6672	10563	VERRE
6649	GLASS NES	W 1543	2883	W 2093	4009	W 1606	3358	W 1853	6795	VERRE NDA
665	GLASSWARE	W 5294	4686	W 5021	5576	W 7817	6206	W 7804	6875	OUVRAGES EN VERRE
67	IRON AND STEEL		81839		88347		63239		75221	FER ET ACIER
671	PIG IRON ETC	W 8522	6874	W 43612	11945	W 4329	2614	W 1144	1281	FONTE,SPIEGEL,POUDRES
6716	FERRO-ALLOYS	W 7901	6449	W 16071	8111	W 3969	2492	W 828	905	FERRO-ALLIAGES
672	IRON,STEEL PRIMARY FORMS	W 2278	2160	W 30647	8807	W 6671	3754	W 6281	4514	LINGOTS FER,ACIER
673	IRON,STEEL SHAPES ETC	W 15208	8485	W 21708	10479	W 24240	10395	W 23251	12326	BARRES,PROFIL FER,ACIER
6733	IRON,STEEL PROFILES ETC	W 9501	5383	W 11411	6398	W 11929	5859	W 14002	8757	PROFILES,PALPLAN FER,ACIER
678	IRON,STL TUBES,PIPES,ETC	W 36060	59649	W 40171	51891	W 38224	40245	W 48359	50662	TUBES,TUYAUX EN FONTE,FER
6783	IRON,STL TUBES,PIPES NES	W 33982	52213	W 37854	42758	W 36987	35059	W 46112	46237	AUT TUBES,TUYAUX FER,ACIER
6785	IRON,STEEL TUBE FITTINGS	W 2079	7436	W 2317	9133	W 1237	5186	W 2247	4425	ACCESSOIRES DE TUYAUTERIE
68	NON-FERROUS METALS		13650		18082		13994		21721	METAUX NON FERREUX
682	COPPER EXC CEMENT COPPER	W 1137	5294	W 1583	7537	W 1022	3878	W 1565	4765	CUIVRE
6822	COPPER,ALLOYS WORKED	W 1137	5294	W 1583	7537	W 1022	3878	W 1565	4765	CUIVRE,ALLIAGES OUVRES
68225	COPPER TUBES,PIPES,ETC	W 1137	5294	W 1583	7537	W 1022	3878	W 1565	4765	TUBES,TUYAUX EN CUIVRE
684	ALUMINIUM	W 2382	8183	W 3806	10336	W 3784	10067	W 4022	11816	ALUMINIUM
6842	ALUMINIUM,ALLOYS WORKED	W 2325	7898	W 3800	10321	W 3776	10051	W 4018	11781	ALUMINIUM,ALLIAGES OUVRE
68421	ALUMINIUM BARS,WIRE,ETC	W 1197	4179	W 2127	5584	W 2175	6748	W 2346	7479	BARRES,PROFILES FILS ALU
69	METAL MANUFACTURES NES		60445		61652		60662		70212	ART MANUFACT EN METAL NDA
691	STRUCTURES AND PARTS NES	W 10130	20428	W 8871	12687	W 6543	13533	W 10132	19450	CONSTRUCT FER,ACIER,ALU
6911	STRUCTURES,PARTS IRN,STL	W 9649	18592	W 8297	10252	W 6077	11009	W 9475	15330	CONSTRUCT FER,ACIER,FONTE
692	METAL TANKS,BOXES,ETC	W 2875	6016	W 3213	7763	W 2773	8842	W 2552	7401	RECIPIENTS METALLIQUES
697	BASE MTL HOUSEHOLD EQUIP	W 2045	10893	W 4034	13944	W 2442	11770	W 3365	12697	ART MENAGE MET COMMUNS
6974	BASE MTL DMSTC ARTIC NES	W 1083	5263	W 1355	4441	W 1247	4870	W 1360	4443	ARTICLES NDA FONTE,FER,ETC
699	BASE METAL MFRS NES	W 4776	10716	W 4878	13546	W 5115	11920	W 8733	16852	ART MANUFACTURES MET NDA
6991	LOCKSMITHS WARES,ETC	W 921	3667	W 1173	6051	W 1384	5570	W 2055	7133	ARTICLES DE SERRURERIE
7	MACHINES,TRANSPORT EQUIP		729691		888005		800742		764094	MACHINES MATERIEL TRANSPORT
71	POWER GENERATING EQUIPMT		100460		42480		70683		58980	MACHINES GENERATRICES
711	STEAM BOILERS & AUX PLNT	W 287	3369	W 635	4773		27690	W 676	5292	GENERATEURS VAPEUR EAU ETC
7111	STEAM BOILERS ETC	W 287	3369	W 631	4660	W 2970	25667	W 646	5005	GENERATEURS VAPEUR EAU
713	INTRNL COMBUS PSTN ENGIN	W 514	7600	W 802	13111	W 1171	14882	W 540	9585	MOTEURS EXPL COMB INT, PIECE
7139	PISTON ENGINE PARTS NES	W 257	5257	W 411	7230	W 889	11644	W 348	7484	PIECES POUR 713.2,3,8
714	ENGINES AND MOTORS NES	W 3017	81905	W 139	12444	W 101	15587	W 464	31627	MOTEURS NON ELECTRIQUES
7148	GAS TURBINES NES	W 2184	50599	W 87	4272	W 31	718	W 197	11172	TURBINES A GAZ
71488	OTHER GAS TURBINES NES	W 2184	50599	W 87	4272	W 31	718	W 197	11172	AUTRES TURBINES A GAZ
7149	ENGINE & MOTOR PARTS NES	W 834	31305	W 52	8172	W 70	14870	W 267	20456	PIECES 714 ET 718.88
71499	PARTS NES,OF 71488,71888	W 834	31305	W 52	8172	W 70	14870	W 267	20456	PIECES 714.88 ET 718.88
716	ROTATING ELECTRIC PLANT	W 1251	7586	W 1590	12152		12523	W 1044	12475	APP ELECTR ROTATIFS,PIECES
7162	AC MTRS,GENRTRS,GEN SETS	W 322	3333	W 461	6130	W 504	6539	W 716	7706	MOTEURS ELECTRIQUES
72	MACHS FOR SPCL INDUSTRYS		101693		165959		91373		107168	MAC SPECIALES POUR INDUST
723	CIVIL ENGINEERG EQUIP ETC	W 6404	85005	W 17124	139300	W 10587	65956	W 7336	62869	APPAREILS DE GENIE CIVIL
7234	CONST,MINING MACHNRY NES	W 2629	23444	W 7993	46216	W 4994	15872	W 3577	14416	MACH POUR LA CONST, MINES
72342	SLFPRP SHOVELS,EXCAVATRS	W 350	810	W 2763	9948	W 3763	11115	W 2506	7077	PELLES MECANIQUES
72343	SLFPRP CONST ETC MCH NES	W 1380	9915	W 3561	23121	W 197	464	W 23	71	AUT MACH EXTR,TERRASSEM
72346	OTH CONST,MINING MCH NES	W 599	9784	W 804	7262			W 321	2859	AUT MACH EXTRACTION,EXCAV ET
7239	CONSTR ETC MACHY PTS NES	W 3736	61499	W 9042	92403	W 5407	49721	W 3599	47795	PIECES 723.41-723.46
726	PRINTG,BKBINDG MACHY,PTS	W 169	1966	W 113	2181	W 480	6512	W 124	1812	MACHINES POUR IMPRIMERIE
727	FOOD MACHRY NON-DOMESTIC	W 75	899	W 93	2724		1843	W 859	20265	MACH INDUSTRIES ALIMENT
7272	OTH FOOD PROC MCHY,PARTS	W 45	681	W 72	2200	W 86	777	W 755	16248	AUT MACH IND ALIMENTAIRE
72722	INDUS FOOD PROC MACH NES	W 45	681	W 72	2200	W 86	777	W 739	15937	MACHINES BOULANGERIE
728	OTH MACHY FOR SPCL INDUS	W 757	10146	W 1652	15357	W 1167	12072	W 1748	18644	AUT MACH IND PARTICULIERES
7283	OTHR MINERAL WORKG MACHY	W 502	6753	W 1466	13590	W 756	8912	W 1367	16104	MACH TRIER,CRIBLER,BROYER
72839	PTS NES OF MACHY OF 7283	W 328	5469	W 628	8820	W 401	7129	W 759	12132	PIECES MACH DU 728.3
74	GENRL INDUSTRL MACHY NES		107915		121529		117102		140724	MACH APP INDUSTRIE
741	HEATING,COOLING EQUIPMNT	W 5572	46067	W 6124	51929	W 6384	58802	W 12891	85007	MACH CHAUFFAGE,PIECES
7413	INDUS FURNACES ETC,PARTS	W 724	5176	W 1298	4679	W 1278	11762	W 1391	8581	FOURS IND,LABOR,PIECES
74132	INDUST FURNACES NONELECT	W 724	5176	W 1298	4679	W 1278	11762	W 1391	8581	FOURS NON ELECTRIQUES
7415	AIR-CONDITIONING MACHNRY	W 3160	18951	W 3602	24810	W 4075	29889	W 4391	29677	GROUPES CONDITION AIR
7416	HEATING,COOLING EQU NES	W 974	15357	W 725	18713	W 520	13475	W 6361	42641	APP CHANGEMENT TEMP
742	PUMPS FOR LIQUIDS ETC	W 1025	9221	W 1009	16231		18671	W 1037	16980	POMPES MOTO-POMPES
7428	OTHER PUMPS FOR LIQUIDS	W 542	3852	W 581	4738	W 570	6445	W 681	6505	AUTRES POMPES POUR LIQ
74288	PUMPS FR LIQUIDS NES ETC	W 536	3608	W 558	4484	W 564	6259	W 640	6076	POMPES POUR LIQUIDES NDA
7429	PTS NES OF PUMPS OF 742	W 110	2424	W 177	7051	W 231	10414	W 224	8706	PIECES POUR GROUPE 742
743	PUMPS NES,CENTRFUGES ETC	W 572	8837	W 1329	13750	W 806	8287	W 951	7032	POMPES COMPRES,VENT ETC
7436	GAS,LIQUID FILTERS ETC	W 288	3689	W 572	6345	W 399	3554	W 346	2160	APP POUR FILT DES LIQUIDES
744	MECHANICAL HANDLING EQU	W 1037	5920	W 3251	16537	W 3713	16130	W 3376	15972	EQUIP MANUTENTION PIECES
7442	LIFTING,LOADING MACH NES	W 760	3240	W 2237	11642	W 1946	6175	W 2032	8696	APP LEVAGE,MANUTENTION
7449	PTS NES OF MACHY OF 7442	W 163	2292	W 318	2052	W 1023	6579	W 741	4338	PIECES DU 744.2
745	NONELEC MACHY,TOOLS NES	W 375	4471	W 542	6154	W 551	4699	W 759	5716	AUT MACH NON ELEC,PIECES
749	NONELEC MACH PTS,ACC NES	W 1461	33399	W 1098	16928		10513	W 877	10018	PIECES MACH NON ELEC NDA
7492	COCKS,VALVES ETC NES	W 1072	32132	W 839	15084	W 1134	8904	W 795	8665	ART ROB,SIM POUR TUYAUX
75	OFFICE MACHNES,ADP EQUIP		18142		25916		23039		26291	MACH BUREAU TRAIT AUTOM
752	AUTOMTIC DATA PROC EQUIP	W 121	6442	W 143	8626	W 143	9597	W 139	10303	MACH TRAIT INFORMATION

Qatar

4. General Imports C.I.F. by Commodities according to the S.I.T.C. (Rev. 2) in thousand U.S. Dollars
Importations Générales C.A.F. par Produits d'après la C.T.C.I. (Rév. 2) en milliers de Dollars E.U.

SITC CTCI	COMMODITY	1991 WEIGHT POIDS	1991 VALUE VALEUR	1992 WEIGHT POIDS	1992 VALUE VALEUR	1993 WEIGHT POIDS	1993 VALUE VALEUR	1994 WEIGHT POIDS	1994 VALUE VALEUR	PRODUIT
759	OFFICE,ADP MCH PTS,ACCES	W 168	8472	W 242	13114	W 212	9662	W 267	12045	PIECES DU 751 ET 752
76	TELECOMM,SOUND EQUIPMENT		68908		53376		54802		44603	EQUIPMENT DE TELECOM
761	TELEVISION RECEIVERS	W 692	8440	W 748	8685	W 522	7681	W 576	7997	RECEPTEURS DE TELEVISION
7611	COLOUR TV RECEIVERS	W 684	8406	W 744	8634	W 522	7676	W 574	7992	RECEPTEURS COULEUR
762	RADIO BROADCAST RECEIVRS	W 425	6562	W 305	5282	W 364	5760	W 414	5122	RECEPTEURS RADIODIFFUSION
7622	PORTABLE RADIO RECEIVERS	W 335	5371	W 275	4538	W 348	5490	W 393	4812	RECEPT PORTATIFS RADIO
763	SOUND RECORDRS,PHONOGRPH	W 234	6726	W 402	4991		5327	W 184	5609	PHONO,APP ENREGISTREMENT
7638	OTHR SOUND APPARATUS ETC	W 162	5374	W 120	3745	W 149	4246	W 143	4597	AUT APP D'ENREGIS,REPROD
76381	TV IMAGE,SND RECRDRS ETC	W 162	5338	W 120	3737	W 148	4169	W 143	4594	APP ENREG,REPRO IMAG,SON
764	TELECOM EQPT,PTS,ACC NES	W 580	47180	W 685	34419	W 808	36035	W 558	25874	EQUIP TELECOM,PIECES
7641	LINE TELEPHONE,ETC EQUIP	W 260	39432	W 378	22287	W 314	11171	W 228	14117	APP TELEPHON PAR FIL
7643	TV,RADIO TRANSMITTRS ETC	W 29	616	W 16	1987	W 100	7641	W 7	2196	APP EMET TELE RADIO
7649	PTS NES OF EQUIPMT OF 76	W 261	5362	W 256	8013	W 347	13973	W 289	7241	PIECES DE LA DIV 76
77	ELECTRIC MACHNRY NES ETC		96368		112355		92032		95494	MACH APP ELECT NDA
771	ELECTRIC POWER MACHY NES	W 971	7570	W 2065	6916	W 587	5343	W 964	4592	MACH PROD,TRANS ELECTR
7711	TRANSFORMERS,ELECTRICAL	W 969	7549	W 2052	6836	W 566	5265	W 932	4318	TRANSFO ELECTRIQUES
772	SWITCHGEAR ETC,PARTS NES	W 2934	23884	W 2732	29100	W 2669	22784	W 1931	15424	APP COUPURE,SECT ETC
7721	SWITCHGEAR ETC	W 2877	23388	W 2729	29057	W 2644	22613	W 1917	15337	APP COUPURE,SECTIONMNT
773	ELECTR DISTRIBUTNG EQUIP	W 11091	35089	W 9958	33605	W 26478	28366	W 17519	39497	EQUIPMT DISTRIBUTION ELECT
7731	INSULATED WIRE,CABLE ETC	W 10852	34584	W 9810	33042	W 26089	27237	W 17027	37950	FILS,CABLES ISOLES ELECT
775	HOUSEHOLD TYPE EQUIP NES	W 3013	19258	W 3941	25246		20399	W 3150	19414	MACH,APP USAGE DOMESTQUE
7752	DOM REFRIGERATRS,FREEZRS	W 682	4127	W 1035	6075	W 844	4506	W 933	4974	REFRIG,CONGEL MENAGER
7757	DOMESTIC ELECTRC EQU NES	W 642	6146	W 651	5866		6358	W 643	5700	APP ELECTR DOMEST NDA
7758	ELECTRO–THERMIC APPL NES	W 1135	6004	W 1677	9846	W 1195	6816	W 1197	6395	APP ELECTROTHERMIQ NDA
778	ELECTRICAL MACHINERY NES	W 1927	9892	W 2278	16812		14235	W 2553	15174	AUTRES MACH ELECT NDA
7788	OTH ELEC MACHY,EQUIP NES	W 268	2986	W 205	6304		2812	W 102	3713	AUT MACH APP ELEC NDA
78	ROAD VEHICLES		218752		345623		337978		271754	VEHICULES ROUTIERS
781	PASS MOTOR VEH EXC BUSES	W 13861	143274	W 17502	211922	W 18389	222237	W 12790	170306	AUTO TRANSPORT PERSONNES
782	LORRIES,SPCL MTR VEH NES	W 5557	31917	W 16729	69296	W 10633	55143	W 7707	45076	VEHICULES SPECIAUX,MARCH
7821	LORRIES,TRUCKS	W 5054	28478	W 11643	58274	W 9884	52166	W 6667	40605	VEHICULES TRANSP MARCHAND
7822	SPECIAL MOTOR VEHCLS NES	W 504	3438	W 5086	11022	W 749	2978	W 1040	4471	VEHICULES USAGES SPECIAUX
783	ROAD MOTOR VEHICLES NES	W 1529	3262	W 2101	9354	W 2167	9770	W 2671	10649	VEHICULES ROUTIERS NDA
7831	BUSES	W 688	2338	W 903	5788	W 1234	7396	W 1963	8955	VOITURES TRANSPORT COMMUN
784	MOTOR VEH PRTS,ACCES NES	W 4261	36161	W 4689	49627	W 4818	47132	W 3713	40644	PIECES 722,781,782,783
7849	OTHER MOTOR VEHCL PARTS	W 4180	35862	W 4273	48982	W 4233	45770	W 3367	39440	PIECES 722,781,782,783
79	OTHR TRANSPORT EQUIPMENT		15283		15213		9631		14820	AUTRE MATERIEL TRANSPORT
792	AIRCRAFT ETC	W 37	12175	W 34	8492	W 23	5860	W 62	11373	APP NAVIGATION AERIENNE
7921	HELICOPTERS	W 12	6334	W 3	1504			W 3	1930	HELICOPTERES
7929	AIRCRAFT PARTS NES	W 25	5842	W 31	6987	W 23	5860	W 59	9443	PIECES DU 792
793	SHIPS AND BOATS ETC	W 651	3108	W 827	6721	W 366	3770	W 1058	3448	NAVIRES BATEAUX,ETC
8	MISC MANUFACTURED GOODS		203137		263534		246276		241775	ART MANUFACTURES DIVERS
812	*PLUMBG,HEATNG,LGHTNG EQ	W 3034	12261	W 4082	17163	W 3678	16515	W 4286	18818	APPAR SANITAIRES CHAUFFAGE
8122	CERAMIC PLUMBNG FIXTURES	W 2408	7235	W 3136	9291	W 2876	9746	W 3361	10627	EVIERS,LAVABOS,CUVETTES
8124	LIGHTING EQUIPMENT NES	W 595	4824	W 854	7438	W 736	6494	W 845	7826	APPAREILS ECLAIRAGE ETC
81242	LAMPS,FITTINGS BASE METL	W 545	4420	W 799	7007	W 663	6047	W 709	6798	APPAREILS D'ECLAIRAGE
821	*FURNITURE,PARTS THEREOF	W 6889	24128	W 11577	37641	W 9484	30253	W 9768	31222	MEUBLES ET PIECES
8211	CHAIRS,SEATS AND PARTS	W 1663	4517	W 2865	8918	W 2641	7692	W 3026	8789	SIEGES ET PIECES
8219	FURNITURE AND PARTS NES	W 4860	18041	W 8079	26926	W 6136	20640	W 6049	20650	AUTRES MEUBLES ET PIECES
82192	WOOD FURNITURE NES	W 3659	13469	W 6822	22895	W 5156	17435	W 4842	16444	MEUBLES NDA EN BOIS
84	CLOTHING AND ACCESSORIES		34286		39059		39231		38373	VETEMENTS
842	MENS OUTERWEAR NOT KNIT	W 712	7124	W 733	8565	W 754	8930	W 668	9269	VET DESSUS POUR HOMMES
8422	— SUITS	W 459	4951	W 415	5560	W 542	6791	W 530	7524	COMPLETS HOMMES MAT TEXT
843	WOMENS OUTERWEAR NONKNIT	W 1129	14190	W 1093	14597	W 1315	15538	W 858	15809	VET DESSUS FEMMES MAT TEX
8432	— SUITS AND COSTUMES	W 402	5853	W 460	6462	W 756	7997	W 372	6945	COSTUMES–TAIL MAT TEXIL
8439	— OTHER OUTER GARMENTS	W 203	3070	W 389	5212	W 318	4740	W 303	5890	AUT VET DES FEM MAT TEXT
844	UNDER GARMENTS NOT KNIT	W 555	4546	W 852	8460	W 644	7532	W 629	7195	VETEMENT DESSOUS MAT TEX
851	*FOOTWEAR	W 1294	14085	W 1236	14877	W 1118	13288	W 1040	13041	CHAUSSURES
85101	FOOTWEAR RUBBER,PLASTIC	W 1294	14085	W 1236	14877	W 1118	13288	W 942	11880	CHAUS SEMELLES CAOUTCH
87	PRECISION INSTRUMNTS NES		21653		38467		20470		18810	INSTRUM,APPAR SCIENT NDA
872	MEDICAL INSTRUMENTS NES	W 448	9330	W 213	6214	W 252	9900	W 234	7478	INSTR,APP MEDIC–CHIR NDA
87202	OTH MEDICAL INSTRUMENTS	W 391	8458	W 120	4269	W 198	7564	W 203	6332	INSTRUM,APP MEDECINE
874	MEASURNG,CONTROLNG INSTR	W 211	11319	W 451	31885	W 210	9949	W 340	10553	INSTRUMENTS DE MESURE
8743	GAS,LIQUID CONTROL INSTR	W 115	6865	W 163	6378	W 89	4684	W 176	5798	APP,INSTR MESURE FLUIDES
8745	MEAS,CONTRL,SCI INST NES	W 4	103	W 132	18210	W 56	1445	W 59	1083	APP SCIENT MESURE NDA
87452	INSTRMNTS ETC FR DEMONST	W 4	89	W 127	18144	W 50	1207	W 58	1040	INSTR POUR DEMONSTRATION
88	PHOTO EQU,OPTICL GDS ETC		25627		28762		28347		27882	APP,FOURN PHOTO,OP,MONTR
885	WATCHES AND CLOCKS		16323		18564		19716		18473	HORLOGERIE
8851	WATCHES,MOVEMENTS,CASES		15457		17694		19017		17447	MONTRES,MOUVEMENTS,BOITES
88511	WATCHES		15457		17694		19017		17447	MONTRES POCHE,BRACELET
89	MISC MANUFCTRD GOODS NES		66556		82699		94001		88928	ART MANUFACTURES DIVERS
893	ARTICLES OF PLASTIC NES	W 7306	15850	W 9520	18584	W 7516	14922	W 7428	15366	OUVRAGES EN MAT DIVIS 58
8939	MISC PLASTIC ARTICLES	W 5419	11567	W 6563	13664	W 6193	12146	W 6480	13544	ART DIVERS EN MAT DIV 58
89399	OTHR PLASTC ARTICLES NES	W 5238	11249	W 6299	13063	W 5959	11664	W 6221	12997	AUT OUV MAT DIV 58
894	TOYS,SPORTING GOODS,ETC	W 1810	8197	W 2236	10833	W 1993	10003	W 2531	9833	VOITURES ENFANTS,JOUETS
8942	TOYS,INDOOR GAMES ETC	W 1129	5016	W 1053	4978	W 1091	5928	W 1332	6149	JOUETS,JEUX ETC
895	OFFICE SUPPLIES NES	W 1277	6759	W 2116	9352	W 1626	8646	W 1830	8938	ART PAPET NDA
8959	OTHER OFFICE SUPPLIES	W 1029	5056	W 1769	7141	W 1377	6676	W 1275	5976	AUT ART DE PAPETERIE
897	GOLD,SILVER WARE,JEWELRY		22219		30170		46847		34629	BIJOUTERIE,ORFEVRERIE
8973	PREC JEWLRY,GLD–SILVWARE		21116		28860		45140		33224	BIJOUX OR,ARGENT ORFEVRE
89732	GOLD,SILVER,ETC WARE		21033		28377		45010		33026	ORFEVRERIE MET PRECIEUX
899	OTHER MANUFACTURED GOODS		5916		5216		6349		11658	AUT ART MANUF DIVERS NDA
8998	SMALLWARES,TOILETRYS ETC	W 462	3103	W 177	1494	W 237	2672	W 1534	7564	ART MERCERIE,TOILETTE

5. General Exports F.O.B. by Commodities according to the S.I.T.C. (Rev. 2) in thousand U.S. Dollars
Exportations Générales F.O.B. par Produits d'après la C.T.C.I. (Rév. 2) en milliers de Dollars E.U.

SITC CTCI	COMMODITY	1991		1992		1993		1994		PRODUIT
		WEIGHT POIDS	VALUE VALEUR	WEIGHT POIDS	VALUE VALEUR	WEIGHT POIDS	VALUE VALEUR	WEIGHT POIDS	VALUE VALEUR	
	ALL COMMODITIES		3209807		3840694		3245416		3212942	TOUS PRODUITS
0	FOOD AND LIVE ANIMALS		12649		9214		10765		15946	ALIMENTS,ANIMAUX VIVANTS
3	MINERAL FUELS ETC		2647740		3200629		2641728		2372766	COMBUSTIBLES MINERAUX LUB
33	PETROLEUM AND PRODUCTS		2521783		2803724		2328012		2238736	PETROLE ET DERIVES
333	CRUDE PETROLEUM	MW 15751	2235079	MW 17000	2486932	MW 17341	2116521	MW 16666	2010671	HUILES BRUTES DE PETROLE
334	PETROLEUM PRODUCTS,REFIN	W 1882346	286671	W 2220910	316746	W 1683183	211433	W 1895074	227955	PRODUITS RAFFINES
3341	GASOLINE,OTH LIGHT OILS	W 210128	45106	W 236452	46183	W 114987	20943	W 216776	32540	ESSENCES POUR MOTEURS
33411	MOTOR,AVIATION SPIRIT	W 124451	27343	W 100815	20533	W 83844	15719	W 216776	32540	ESSENCES MOTEURS D'AVIONS
33419	OTH LIGHT PETROLEUM OILS	W 85677	17763	W 135637	25650	W 31143	5224			AUTRES HUILES LEGERES
3342	KEROSENE,OTH MEDIUM OILS	W 256775	59880	W 311726	63692	W 260668	51012	W 301625	50343	PETR LAMPANTS,AUT HUIL
33421	KEROSENE INCL JET FUEL	W 256775	59880	W 311726	63692	W 260668	51012	W 301625	50343	PETROLES LAMPANTS
3343	GAS OILS	W 482269	101830	W 631368	116636	W 423928	73168	W 472301	69512	GAS OILS
3344	FUEL OILS,NES	W 933109	79841	W 1041326	90051	W 883458	66254	W 904360	75528	FUEL OILS
341	*GAS,NATURAL AND MANUFCT	W 871473	125952	W 2468668	396906	W 2308711	313716	W 1087057	134030	GAZ NATUREL,GAZ MANUFACT
3413	PETROLM GASES,LIQUEFIED	W 871473	125952	W 2468668	396906	W 2308711	313716	W 1087057	134030	GAZ DE PETROLE LIQUEFIE
34131	LIQUEFIED PROPANE,BUTANE	W 871473	125952	W 1081471	154304	W 1102086	134933	W 1087057	134030	PROPANE,BUTANE LIQUEFIES
34139	OTH HYDROCARBON GAS LQFD			W 1387197	242602	W 1206625	178782			HYDROCARBURES GAZEUX NDA
5	CHEMCLS,RELATED PROD NES		290451		316110		285492		509988	PRODUITS CHIMIQUES
51	ORGANIC CHEMICALS		21284		33367		40347		56654	PROD CHIMIQ ORGANIQUES
511	HYDROCARBONS NES,DERIVS	W 70452	21275	W 144786	33254	W 168205	40306	W 175785	56587	HYDROCARBURES NDA
5111	ACYCLIC HYDROCARBONS	W 70451	21275	W 144726	33227	W 168205	40306	W 175785	56587	HYDROCARBURES ACYCLIQUES
51111	ETHYLENE	W 70451	21275	W 144678	33189	W 168205	40306	W 175785	56587	ETHYLENE
52	INORGANIC CHEMICALS		29222		23648		27714		47837	PROD CHIM INORGANIQUES
522	INORG ELEMNTS,OXIDES,ETC	W 242779	29007	W 260026	23552	W 281659	27670	W 297767	47778	ELEMENTS INORGANIQUES
5225	INORGANIC BASES ETC NES	W 242380	28859	W 241934	22930	W 281637	27638	W 297756	47775	AUTRES BASES OXYDES METAL
52251	AMMONIA,ANHYDROUS ETC	W 242380	28859	W 241934	22930	W 281637	27638	W 297756	47775	AMMONIAC LIQUEFIE
562	*FERTILIZERS,MANUFACTURE	W 676476	105609	W 769097	103949	W 872930	92424	W 885869	115429	ENGRAIS MANUFACTURES
5621	CHEM NITROGENOUS FERTLZR	W 676468	105575	W 769065	103918	W 872930	92424	W 885869	115429	ENGRAIS AZOTES
56216	UREA	W 676408	105565	W 769065	103918	W 872930	92424	W 885869	115429	UREE
58	PLASTIC MATERIALS ETC		128156		146780		119550		283980	MAT PLAST ARTIFICIELLES
582	PROD OF CONDENSATION ETC		12		18			W 1298984	181501	PROD CONDENS,POLYCOND
5829	OTH CONDNSATION,ETC PROD							W 1298984	181501	AUT PROD CONDENSATION
583	POLYMERIZATION ETC PRODS	W 159807	128140	W 180660	146762	W 173105	119550	W 156767	102477	PROD POLYMERISATION
5831	POLYETHYLENE	W 159758	128099	W 180497	146595	W 172928	119357	W 156599	102303	POLYETHYLENE
58311	— IN PRIMARY FORMS	W 159700	128095	W 180484	146593	W 172928	119357	W 156517	102271	POLYETHYLENE PRIMAIRES
6	BASIC MANUFACTURES		150801		187741		212316		194236	ART MANUFACTURES
67	IRON AND STEEL		141019		180199		204787		186160	FER ET ACIER
673	IRON,STEEL SHAPES ETC	W 408066	137999	W 519121	176339	W 551319	203165	W 529128	185069	BARRES,PROFIL FER,ACIER
6732	IRON,STEEL BARS ETC	W 407836	137864	W 519000	176261	W 551205	203092	W 528965	184925	BARRES FER,ACIER
67326	IRN,OTH STL BARS HOTROLD	W 407836	137864	W 519000	176261	W 551205	203092			BARRES PLEINES FER,ACIER
7	MACHINES,TRANSPORT EQUIP		75117		79534		41990		45779	MACHINES MATERIEL TRANSPORT
72	MACHS FOR SPCL INDUSTRYS		10306		11596		9117		12021	MAC SPECIALES POUR INDUST
723	CIVIL ENGNEERG EQUIP ETC	W 2155	9758	W 2705	11310		8674	W 2273	11578	APPAREILS DE GENIE CIVIL
7239	CONSTR ETC MACHY PTS NES	W 1457	8420	W 904	8421	W 1612	6634	W 1766	10365	PIECES 723.41–723.46
78	ROAD VEHICLES		48924		49309		21718		16891	VEHICULES ROUTIERS
781	PASS MOTOR VEH EXC BUSES	W 3461	26524	W 2739	24357	W 1492	13486	W 1190	8222	AUTO TRANSPORT PERSONNES
782	LORRIES,SPCL MTR VEH NES	W 4136	17485	W 3880	20990		5525	W 1087	5074	VEHICULES SPECIAUX,MARCH
7821	LORRIES,TRUCKS	W 3762	16722	W 3829	20794	W 1180	5438	W 980	4847	VEHICULES TRANSP MARCHAND
8	MISC MANUFACTURED GOODS		25296		38928		44678		64743	ART MANUFACTURES DIVERS
84	CLOTHING AND ACCESSORIES		14092		30983		36112		58229	VETEMENTS
842	MENS OUTERWEAR NOT KNIT	W 1694	10892	W 2399	18765	W 2943	25450	W 1976	28589	VET DESSUS POUR HOMMES
8422	— SUITS	W 1624	10363	W 2356	18366	W 2932	25330	W 1967	28483	COMPLETS HOMMES MAT TEXT
843	WOMENS OUTERWEAR NONKNIT	W 249	2420	W 1373	10379	W 968	9492	W 1809	28155	VET DESSUS FEMMES MAT TEX
8432	— SUITS AND COSTUMES	W 97	1004	W 1200	8722	W 929	9134	W 1786	27851	COSTUMES–TAIL MAT TEXIL

1. HISTORICAL SERIES, 1992–1996 GENERAL TRADE, IMPORTS C.I.F., EXPORTS F.O.B. #1
SERIES HISTORIQUES, 1992–1996 COMMERCE GENERAL, IMPORTATIONS C.A.F., EXPORTATIONS F.O.B

YEAR ANNEE	VALUE IN MILLION U.S. DOLLARS VALEUR EN MILLION U.S. DOLLARS MERCHANDISE –MARCHANDISE		GOLD –OR		CONVERSION FACTORS FACTEURS DE CONVERSION CENTS E.U. PAR		INDEX NUMBERS –INDICES QUANTUM		UNIT VALUE VALEUR UNITAIRE	
	IMPORTS	EXPORTS	IMPORTS	EXPORTS	IMPORTS	EXPORTS	IMPORTS	EXPORTS	IMPORTS	EXPORTS
1992	170.00	157.00								
1993	184.00	178.00								
1994	668.95	565.44								
1995	822.00	720.00								
1996	1079.20	801.56								

2. IMPORTS BY BROAD ECONOMIC CATEGORY AND EXPORTS BY INDUSTRIAL ORIGIN. (PERCENTAGE OF TOTAL VALUE)
IMPORTATIONS PAR CATEGORIES ECONOMIQUES ET EXPORTATIONS PAR BRANCHE D'ACTIVITE.(EN POURCENTAGE DE LA VALEUR TOTALE)

IMPORTS – IMPORTATIONS

	1990	1991	1992	1993	1994	1995	1996
TOTAL IMPORTS–IMPORTATIONS TOTALES					100.	100.	
1 FOOD BEV–ALIMENTATION BOISSONS					4.0	6.7	
11 PRIMARY–PRODUITS DE BASE					2.3	3.3	
111 FOR INDUSTRY–POUR L'INDUSTRIE					1.5	1.7	
112 FOR HOUSEHOLDS–POUR LES MENAGES					0.8	1.5	
12 PROCESSED–PRODUITS ELABORES					1.7	3.4	
121 FOR INDUSTRY–POUR L'INDUSTRIE					0.3	0.8	
122 FOR HOUSEHOLDS–POUR LES MENAGES					1.3	2.6	
2 IND SUPPLIES–APPROV INDUSTRIELS					20.5	26.1	
21 PRIMARY–PRODUITS DE BASE					3.6	3.5	
22 PROCESSED–PRODUITS ELABORES					16.9	22.7	
3 FUELS–COMBUSTIBLES					54.6	45.8	
31 PRIMARY–PRODUITS DE BASE					33.6	18.5	
32 PROCESSED–PRODUITS ELABORES					21.0	27.3	
321 MOTOR SPIRIT–ESSENCE					5.5	21.4	
322 OTHER–AUTRES					15.5	5.9	
4 MACHINERY–EQUIPEMENT					9.0	11.5	
41 CAPITAL EQUIPMENT–MACHINES					7.4	10.4	
42 PARTS–PIECES ACCESSOIRES					1.7	1.1	
5 TRANSPORT–TRANSPORT					3.9	3.9	
51 PASSENGER CARS–AUTOMOBILES					0.7	0.7	
52 OTHER–AUTRES					1.0	0.8	
521 INDUSTRIAL–INDUSTRIELS					0.9	0.8	
522 NON INDUSTRIAL–NON INDUSTRIEL					0.1	0.0	
53 PARTS–PIECES ACCESSOIRES					2.2	2.4	
6 CONSUM GOODS–BIENS CONSOMMATION					7.8	5.9	
61 DURABLE–DURABLES					1.3	0.9	
62 SEMI DURABLE–SEMI DURABLES					2.7	2.2	
63 NON DURABLE–NON DURABLES					3.7	2.8	
7 GOODS NES–BIENS NDA					0.1	0.0	

EXPORTS – EXPORTATIONS

	1990	1991	1992	1993	1994	1995	1996
TOTAL EXPORTS–EXPORTATIONS TOTALES					100.	100.	
1 AGRICULTURE					20.3	13.2	
2 MINING QUARRY–INDUS EXTRACTIVES					0.1	0.2	
3 MANUFACTURING–IND MANUFACTUR					79.6	86.6	
31 FOOD BEV TOBACCO–ALIM BOISS TAB					47.8	60.2	
32 TEXTILES–INDUSTRIES TEXTILES					6.2	5.6	
33 WOOD & PRODUCTS–BOIS & PRODUITS					0.4	0.2	
34 PAPER & PRODUCTS–PAPIER & PRODT					1.4	1.1	
35 CHEMICALS–INDUSTRIES CHIMIQUES					2.8	1.9	
36 NON METAL MIN–MIN NON METAL					1.0	2.1	
37 BASIC METAL–IND METAL BASE					1.6	1.3	
38 METAL MANUF–MANUF METAL					15.7	12.8	
39 OTH MANUF IND–AUTRES MANUF					2.8	1.3	

3. TRADE BY PRINCIPAL COUNTRIES OF ORIGIN AND DESTINATION (VALUE IN THOUSAND U.S. DOLLARS)
ECHANGES SELON LES PRINCIPAUX PAYS D'ORIGINE ET DE DESTINATION (VALEUR EN MILLIERS DE DOLLARS EU)

COUNTRIES–PAYS	GENERAL IMPORTS C.I.F. # 1 IMPORTATIONS GENERALES C.A.F				
	1991	1992	1993	1994	1995
World		163653	181207	659273	840713
Africa				584	194
Americas			18583	20029	11850
Northern America			15167	19775	11279
LAIA			1729	59	277
CACM					120
Caribbean			1662	195	0
Rest of America			25		174
As.ex F.USSR			5081	17782	16663
Eur.x F.USSR			157401	137223	230599
EU			72222	67452	115194
EFTA			1178	2450	8852
East Europe			83098	65379	104972
Other Europe				230	42
Former USSR		127824		483509	580966
Oceania				145	353
Russian Federation		73979		309341	277995
Ukraine		24779		122709	228487
Romania/Roumanie			68323	42553	55953
Germany/Allemagne			28980	35621	45579
Belarus/Bélarus		16437		20098	50688
Bulgaria/Bulgarie			5639	10120	31876
USA/Etats–Unis d'Amer			12955	19188	10676
Italy/Italie			8680	8670	19289
Hungary/Hongrie			6976	6952	8503
Azerbaijan		1945		11985	5524
Netherlands/Pays–Bas			8473	3177	6549
Belgium–Luxembourg			2910	4015	9425
France, Monac			7013	2006	6467
Lithuania/Lituanie		1503		4146	7341
Austria/Autriche			2871	2073	7779
Switz.Liecht			1175	2392	8580
Turkey/Turquie			503	3412	6816
United Kingdom			3039	2127	5477
Poland/Pologne			1536	4368	4166
Greece/Grèce			211	3768	4993
Israel/Israël			1373	1690	5757
Turkmenistan/Turkménistn		2984		5027	756
Kazakhstan		1315		3069	2484
Sweden/Suède			3338	2267	1222
Uzbekistan/Ouzbékistan		2632		1769	2073
Denmark/Danemark			390	1908	4147
China/Chine			659	5556	160
Spain/Espagne			4708	251	1315
Latvia/Lettonie		660		2258	3061
India/Inde			29	4255	1084
Czech Republic			484	1388	2597
Finland/Finlande			1600	398	1860
Canada			2212	586	603
Estonia/Estonie		163		1111	1657
Slovenia/Slovénia			244	1160	818
Kyrgyzstan/Kirghizistan		441		902	717
Slovakia			140		1877
Ireland/Irlande			9	1056	895
Cyprus/Chypre			68	1634	107
Georgia/Géorgie		636		942	103
Argentina/Argentine			1583		29
Japan/Japon			233	67	1272
Anguilla			1567		
Yugoslavia/Yougoslavie			659	219	353
Korea, Republic of				470	575
Viet Nam			485		160
Liberia/Libéria				584	
Hong Kong			476		59
Indonesia/Indonésie				168	293
Tfyr Macedonia				172	238

COUNTRIES–PAYS	GENERAL EXPORTS F.O.B. # 1 EXPORTATIONS GENERALES F.O.B.				
	1991	1992	1993	1994	1995
Monde		118817	174258	566001	745530
Afrique			9	149	584
Amériques			1042	3619	11902
Amérique du Nord			1042	3615	9557
ALAI				1	
MCAC					2285
Caraïbes				1	
Autre Amérique				1	61
Asie l'URSS exclus			5999	4968	19305
Europe l'URSS exclus			166066	142978	229965
UE			36764	39117	86209
AELE			1047	2456	4669
Europe de l'Est			128114	100728	138044
Autre de l'Europe					
Ancienne URSS		88986		414273	483636
Océanie			8	13	115
Russian Federation		46529		289703	360141
Romania/Roumanie			106299	83415	103667
Ukraine		23187		68561	58894
Germany/Allemagne			15328	19678	45440
Belarus/Bélarus		5163		23657	26474
Bulgaria/Bulgarie			16475	10387	21369
Italy/Italie			6176	7770	15600
Azerbaijan		2343		12990	5355
Kazakhstan		2292		7205	8600
Lithuania/Lituanie		1417		4088	9804
Turkey/Turquie			1677	1415	11483
Austria/Autriche			668	1075	9940
Hungary/Hongrie			3039	2588	5719
USA/Etats–Unis d'Amer			888	1795	7942
United Kingdom			1004	3450	6162
Greece/Grèce			930	5065	2712
Latvia/Lettonie		1076		2949	4589
Switz.Liecht			1047	2428	4102
Ireland/Irlande			5529	236	452
Poland/Pologne			707	2483	2973
Uzbekistan/Ouzbékistan		1782		1424	2839
Sweden/Suède			5947		57
Turkmenistan/Turkménistn		3155		1074	1465
Israel/Israël			247	896	3394
Netherlands/Pays–Bas			615	1362	2286
Estonia/Estonie		329		1128	2314
Canada			154	1821	1615
Cyprus/Chypre			1843	715	944
Czech Republic			1136	1561	696
Slovakia			244		2951
Armenia/Arménie		319		191	2631
El Salvador					2285
Spain/Espagne				60	1571
Viet Nam			282	21	1280
France, Monac			97	85	1393
Georgia/Géorgie		542		634	147
Kyrgyzstan/Kirghizistan		653		368	250
Lebanon/Liban			652	399	140
Albania/Albanie			214	294	670
Hong Kong			1130		
Syrian Arab Republic			54	866	63
Belgium–Luxembourg			455	70	317
China/Chine			58	298	401
Thailand/Thaïlande				115	623
Slovenia/Slovénia			79	352	270
Tajikistan/Tadjikistan		198		302	134
Tfyr Macedonia				237	248
Norway,SVD,JM				28	423
India/Inde			1	70	342
Yugoslavia/Yougoslavie			45		319

(VALUE AS PERCENTAGE OF WORLD TOTAL)(VALEURS EN POURCENTAGE DU TOTAL MONDIAL)

	1986	1987	1988	1989	1990	1991	1992	1993	1994	1995
Africa									0.1	0.0
Americas								10.3	3.0	1.4
Northern America								8.4	3.0	1.3
LAIA								1.0	0.0	0.0
CACM										0.0
Caribbean								0.9	0.0	0.0
Rest of America								0.0		0.0
As.ex F.USSR								2.8	2.7	2.0
Eur.x F.USSR								86.9	20.8	27.4
EU								39.9	10.2	13.7
EFTA								0.7	0.4	1.1
East Europe								45.9	9.9	12.5
Other Europe									0.0	0.0
Former USSR							78.1		73.3	69.1
Oceania									0.0	0.0
Russian Federation							45.2		46.9	33.1
Ukraine							15.1		18.6	27.2
Romania/Roumanie								37.7	6.5	6.7
Germany/Allemagne								16.0	5.4	5.4
Belarus/Bélarus							10.0		3.0	6.0
Bulgaria/Bulgarie								3.1	1.5	3.8
USA/Etats–Unis d'Amer								7.1	2.9	1.3
Italy/Italie								4.8	1.3	2.3
Hungary/Hongrie								3.8	1.1	1.0
Azerbaijan							1.2		1.8	0.7

	1986	1987	1988	1989	1990	1991	1992	1993	1994	1995
Afrique								0.0	0.0	0.1
Amériques								0.6	0.6	1.6
Amérique du Nord								0.6	0.6	1.3
ALAI									0.0	
MCAC										0.3
Caraïbes									0.0	
Autre Amérique									0.0	0.0
Asie l'URSS exclus								3.4	0.9	2.6
Europe l'URSS exclus								95.3	25.3	30.8
UE								21.1	6.9	11.6
AELE								0.6	0.4	0.6
Europe de l'Est								73.5	17.8	18.5
Autre de l'Europe										
Ancienne URSS							74.9		73.2	64.9
Océanie								0.0	0.0	0.0
Russian Federation							39.2		51.2	48.3
Romania/Roumanie								61.0	14.7	13.9
Ukraine							19.5		12.1	7.9
Germany/Allemagne								8.8	3.5	6.1
Belarus/Bélarus							4.3		4.2	3.6
Bulgaria/Bulgarie								9.5	1.8	2.9
Italy/Italie								3.5	1.4	2.1
Azerbaijan							2.0		2.3	0.7
Kazakhstan							1.9		1.3	1.2
Lithuania/Lituanie							1.2		0.7	1.3

4. General Imports C.I.F. by Commodities according to the S.I.T.C. (Rev. 2) in thousand U.S. Dollars
Importations Générales C.A.F. par Produits d'après la C.T.C.I. (Rév. 2) en milliers de Dollars E.U.

SITC CTCI	COMMODITY	1992		1993		1994		1995		PRODUIT
		WEIGHT POIDS	VALUE VALEUR	WEIGHT POIDS	VALUE VALEUR	WEIGHT POIDS	VALUE VALEUR	WEIGHT POIDS	VALUE VALEUR	
	ALL COMMODITIES						659273		840713	TOUS PRODUITS
0	FOOD AND LIVE ANIMALS						34560		49436	ALIMENTS,ANIMAUX VIVANTS
03	FISH AND PREPARATIONS						2348		5454	POISSONS ET PREPARATIONS
034	FISH,FRESH,CHILLED,FROZN					W 1495	835	W 4888	3365	POISSON FRAIS, REFRIG,CONG
0342	FISH FROZEN,EXCL FILLETS					W 1450	817	W 4543	3244	POISSONS CONGELES
04	CEREALS AND PREPARATIONS						19248		20447	CEREALES ET PRODUITS
041	WHEAT ETC UNMILLED					W 38574	6183	W 62753	5008	FROMENT,EPEAUTRE
0411	DURUM WHEAT UNMILLED					W 7198	1209	W 42194	3111	FROMENT DUR NON MOULU
0412	OTHER WHEAT ETC UNMILLED					W 31376	4974	W 20559	1897	AUTRE FROMENT NON MOULU
044	MAIZE UNMILLED					W 39266	9704	W 39224	6345	MAIS NON MOULU
045	CEREALS NES UNMILLED					W 16838	1041	W 64264	4701	AUTRES CEREALES NON MOULUES
0451	RYE UNMILLED					W 16470	1007	W 63559	4389	SEIGLE NON MOULU
05	VEGETABLES AND FRUIT						4412		7228	LEGUMES ET FRUITS
054	VEG ETC FRSH,SMPLY PRSVD					W 15911	2407	W 21937	4467	LEGUMES FRAIS,CONG,SECS
0541	POTATOES FRSH EXCL SWEET					W 13877	1779	W 18120	3264	POMMES DE TERRE
06	SUGAR AND PREPS,HONEY						2068		4844	SUCRES ET PRODUITS
061	SUGAR AND HONEY					W 15051	1836	W 19927	4590	SUCRES ET MIEL
0611	RAW BEET AND CANE SUGAR					W 3165	919	W 7306	2772	SUCRES BRUTS
07	COFFEE,TEA,COCOA,SPICES						2119		2061	CAFE,THE,CACAO,EPICES
081	*FEEDING STUFF FOR ANIML					W 7729	2297	W 19179	3421	NOURRITURE POUR ANIMAUX
1	BEVERAGES AND TOBACCO						6926		15657	BOISSONS ET TABACS
11	BEVERAGES						2961		13967	BOISSONS
111	NON-ALCOHL BEVERAGES NES					W 915	350	W 5020	2602	BOISSONS NON ALCOOLIQUES
112	ALCOHOLIC BEVERAGES					W 2801	2611	W 12924	11365	BOISSONS ALCOOLIQUES
1121	WINE OF FRESH GRAPES ETC					W 1737	1364	W 10501	7741	VINS DE RAISINS FRAIS
11212	WINE OF FRESH GRAPES					W 1725	1359	W 9991	7602	VINS DE MOUTS DE RAISINS
1124	DISTILLED ALCOHOLIC BEVS					W 309	952	W 1075	3187	ALCOOLS,EAUX-DE-VIE
11249	OTH ALCOHOLC BEVS,CMPNDS					W 279	715	W 1069	3138	BOISSONS ALCOOLIQUES NDA
12	TOBACCO AND MANUFACTURES						3964		1690	TABACS BRUTS FABRIQUES
121	TOBACCO UNMNFCTRD,REFUSE					W 1921	2302	W 1307	1241	TABACS BRUTS,DECHETS
2	CRUDE MATERLS,EXCL FUELS						19131		31562	MAT BRUTES NON COMESTIBLES
21	HIDES,SKINS,FURS UNDRSSD						2068		1689	CUIRS,PEAUX BRUTS
24	CORK AND WOOD						3863		6265	LIEGE ET BOIS
248	WOOD SHAPED,SLEEPERS						2745		4724	BOIS SIMPLEMENT TRAVAILLES
2482	LUMBER SHAPED CONIFER						2318		3560	CONIFERES SCIES,RABOTES
24821	LUMBER SAWN ETC CONIFER					W 24668	1836	W 33029	3194	CONIFERES SCIES LONGITUD
26	TEXTILE FIBRES AND WASTE						6513		6612	FIBRES TEXTILES
266	SYNTHETIC FIBRES TO SPIN					W 1390	3172	W 1217	2284	FIBRES SYNTHETIQUES
268	WOOL(EXC TOPS),ANML HAIR					W 1439	2258	W 778	1894	LAINES ET POILS
27	CRUDE FERTLZR,MINRLS NES						1751		3627	ENGRAIS MINERAUX BRUTS
28	METALLIFEROUS ORES,SCRAP						658		4368	MINERAIS METAL,DECHETS
288	NONFERR METAL SCRAP NES					W 837	643	W 4194	4118	DECHETS NON FERREUX
2882	OTHER BASE MTL SCRAP NES					W 837	643	W 4148	4118	AUTRES DECHETS
28821	COPPER WASTE AND SCRAP					W 767	609	W 2843	2922	DECHETS DE CUIVRE
29	CRUDE ANIMAL,VEG MAT NES						3214		5602	MATIERES BRUTES ANIM,VEGET
292	CRUDE VEG MATERIALS NES						3203		5478	MAT BRUTES VEGETALES NDA
2925	SEEDS,ETC FOR PLANTING					W 454	2695	W 846	4766	SEMENCES NDA
3	MINERAL FUELS ETC						364204		386895	COMBUSTIBLES MINERAUX LUB
32	COAL,COKE AND BRIQUETTES						55657		50278	HOUILLES,COKES,BRIQUETTES
322	COAL,LIGNITE AND PEAT					W 2443968	55360	W 1315092	48907	HOUILLES,LIGNITES,TOURBE
3221	ANTHRACITE,NOT AGGLOMRTD					W 2357931	53290	W 1106026	41471	ANTHRACITE
3222	OTH COAL,NOT AGGLOMERATD					W 85693	2062	W 208702	7432	AUTRES HOUILLES
33	PETROLEUM AND PRODUCTS						133271		183195	PETROLE ET DERIVES
334	PETROLEUM PRODUCTS,REFIN					W 998635	128058	W 1165896	180424	PRODUITS RAFFINES
3341	GASOLINE,OTH LIGHT OILS					W 208587	37382	W 1165357	179797	ESSENCES POUR MOTEURS
33411	MOTOR,AVIATION SPIRIT					W 183965	32382	W 1165357	179797	ESSENCES MOTEURS D'AVIONS
33419	OTH LIGHT PETROLEUM OILS					W 20087	4124			AUTRES HUILES LEGERES
3342	KEROSENE,OTH MEDIUM OILS					W 14225	2388			PETR LAMPANTS,AUT HUIL
3343	GAS OILS					W 263608	36940			GAS OILS
3344	FUEL OILS,NES					W 492633	42807			FUEL OILS
3345	LUBS,PETROLEUM OILS NES					W 19582	8542	W 539	627	HUILES LUBRIFIANTES
33451	LUBS(HIGH PETR CONT) ETC					W 18548	7664			HUILES LUBRIF,H LOURDES
335	RESIDUAL PETRLM PROD NES					W 27682	4496	W 19017	2617	PRODUITS RESIDUELS NDA
3352	MINERAL TARS AND PRODCTS					W 8141	2610	W 3237	720	GOUDRONS MINERAUX
341	*GAS,NATURAL AND MANUFCT						165307	W 30710	105845	GAZ NATUREL,GAZ MANUFACT
3413	PETROLM GASES,LIQUEFIED					W 45259	12506	W 30615	3614	GAZ DE PETROLE LIQUEFIE
34139	OTH HYDROCARBON GAS LQFD					W 44453	12407	W 13966	1357	HYDROCARBURES GAZEUX NDA
3414	PETROLEUM GASES, GASEOUS					W 393	152795	W 95	102231	GAZ DE PETROLE GAZEUX
351	*ELECTRIC CURRENT					H 615400	9969	H 1996709	47577	ENERGIE ELECTRIQUE
5	CHEMCLS,RELATED PROD NES						42932		76130	PRODUITS CHIMIQUES
51	ORGANIC CHEMICALS						5578		7904	PROD CHIMIQ ORGANIQUES
512	ALCOHOLS,PHENOLS ETC						4358		5332	PHENOLS,PHENOLS-ALCOOLS
5121	ACYCLIC ALCOHOLS,DERIVS						4342		5283	ALCOOLS ACYCLIQUES
51216	ETHYL ALC,DENATRD SPIRIT					V 7139	4254	V 8275	5149	ALCOOL ETHYLIQUE NON DENAT
52	INORGANIC CHEMICALS						3414		8764	PROD CHIM INORGANIQUES
523	OTHR INORG CHEMICALS ETC						2476		7006	AUT PRODUITS CHIMIQUES INORG
5232	OTH MTL CMPD OF INRG ACD					W 12291	1609	W 39268	5133	SELS METALLIQUES
52323	NEUTRAL SODIUM CARBONATE					W 9483	865	W 37471	4104	CARBONATE NEUTRE SODIUM
53	DYES,TANNING,COLOUR PROD						2089		4193	PROD TEINTURE,COLORANTS
533	PIGMENTS,PAINTS,ETC					W 1677	1764	W 2236	3609	PIGMENTS,PEINTURES,VERNIS
5334	VARNISHES,DISTEMPERS ETC					W 1330	1322	W 1938	2877	PEINTURES A L'EAU
53342	OTH PAINTS,VARNISHES ETC					W 1127	1221	W 1680	2602	AUTRES PEINTURES,VERNIS
541	*MEDICINAL,PHARM PRODUCT						17568	K 1636130	18185	PROD MEDICINAUX PHARMACEUT
5417	MEDICAMENTS					K 849400	15084	K 1234130	16264	MEDICAMENTS
54171	— CONTAINNG ANTIBIOTICS					K 243100	3546	K 185400	2928	MED CONTN ANTIBIOTIQUES
54179	— CONTNG OTH SUBSTANCES					K 565200	10665	K 1021430	12630	MED CONT AUT SUBSTANCES
55	PERFUME,CLEANING ETC PRD						5269		6891	PROD POUR PARFUM,TOILETTE
553	PERFUMERY,COSMETICS,ETC					W 699	2429		1628	PRODUITS DE PARFUMERIE
554	SOAP,CLEANSING ETC PREPS					W 3638	2405	W 4070	3928	SAVONS,PRODUITS DETERSIFS
5542	WASHING PREPARATIONS ETC					W 2470	1713	W 3106	2972	PROD ORG TENSIO-ACT NDA
58	PLASTIC MATERIALS ETC						4939		7692	MAT PLAST ARTIFICIELLES
583	POLYMERIZATION ETC PRODS					W 4493	3341	W 5335	6360	PROD POLYMERISATION
59	CHEMICAL MATERIALS NES						3403		21279	MAT PROD CHIMIQUES NDA
591	PESTICIDES,DISINFECTANTS					W 453	1930	W 2046	17753	DESINF,INSECT,FONG,HERB
5911	INSECTICIDES,FOR RETAIL					W 16	66	W 206	2532	INSECTICIDES VENTE DET
5912	FUNGICIDES,FOR RETAIL					W 68	61	W 286	4392	FONGICIDES VENTE AU DET
5913	HERBICIDES,FOR RETAIL					W 229	1730	W 1108	10086	HERBICIDES VENTE AU DET
6	BASIC MANUFACTURES						75396		121018	ART MANUFACTURES
62	RUBBER MANUFACTURES NES						2704		5663	CAOUTCHOUC MANUFACTURE
625	RUBBER TYRES, TUBES ETC						2250		4531	PNEUS CAOUTCHOUC VULCANISE
63	WOOD,CORK MANUFACTRS NES						3719		5263	OUVRAGES LIEGE ET BOIS

4. General Imports C.I.F. by Commodities according to the S.I.T.C. (Rev. 2) in thousand U.S. Dollars
Importations Générales C.A.F. par Produits d'après la C.T.C.I. (Rév. 2) en milliers de Dollars E.U.

SITC CTCI	COMMODITY	1992 WEIGHT POIDS	1992 VALUE VALEUR	1993 WEIGHT POIDS	1993 VALUE VALEUR	1994 WEIGHT POIDS	1994 VALUE VALEUR	1995 WEIGHT POIDS	1995 VALUE VALEUR	PRODUIT
64	PAPER,PAPERBOARD AND MFR						11083		27228	PAPIERS,CARTONS & OUVRAGES
641	PAPER AND PAPERBOARD						7500		18375	PAPIERS ET CARTONS
6411	NEWSPRINT					W 792	288	W 4203	2708	PAPIER JOURNAL
6415	PAPER,PAPERBRD,BULK,NES					W 12894	3752		8410	PAPIERS,CARTONS ROULEAUX
64159	OTHER PAPER ETC,BULK,NES					W 12148	3409		5742	AUT PAPIER ROULEAUX FEUILLES
642	PAPER,ETC,PRECUT,ARTS OF						3583	W 6930	8853	PAP,CARTONS DECOUPES
6421	PAPER ETC CONTAINERS					W 4832	2499	W 5531	5988	BOITES,SACS EMBALLAGES
65	TEXTILE YARN,FABRICS,ETC						23336		28120	FILS,TISSUS,ARTICLES TEXTILE
651	TEXTILE YARN					W 2244	4244		5330	FILS TEXTILES
652	COTTON FABRICS,WOVEN						3536		3179	TISSUS DE COTON
6522	WOVEN COTTON BLEACHD,ETC						3109		2126	TISSUS COTON BLANCHIS ETC
65224	BLCHED COTTON FABRIC NES						2494		1127	AUT TIS PLUS 85% COT BLANCHI
653	WOVN MAN-MADE FIB FABRIC						2844		5257	TISSUS FIBRES SYNTH,ARTIF
654	OTH WOVEN TEXTILE FABRIC						7156		6143	TISSUS AUT COTON SYNT,ARTIF
6543	WOVEN WOOL ETC FABRC NES					A 2003	4909	A 892	2206	TISSUS LAINE,POILS FINS NDA
65432	WOOL-DISC SYN FIBR FABRC					A 1941	4703	A 876	2158	TISSUS LAINE MEL SYNT DISC
655	KNITTED,ETC FABRICS					A 279	836	A 3444	2777	ETOF BONNETERIE PIECES ETC
6552	OTHER KNIT ETC FAB NONEL					A 279	836	A 3444	2777	ETOF BON NON ELAS NON SYNT
657	SPECIAL TXTL FABRC,PRODS						1512		3813	TISSUS SPECIAUX
658	TEXTILE ARTICLES NES						2430		999	ART FACONNES MAT TEXTILES
66	NONMETAL MINERAL MFS NES						13928		23622	ART MIN NON METALLIQUES
661	LIME,CEMENT,BLDG PRODS						3408		3591	CHAUX,CIMENTS MAT CONSTR
6618	MNRL BLDG PRD UNFIRD NES						2002		1737	MAT CONST AMIANTE-CIMENT
662	CLAY,REFRACTORY BLDG PRD						4077		1751	MAT CONST REFRACTAIRES
6623	REFRACTORY BUILDING PROD					W 4086	3326	W 4297	581	BRIQUES REFRACTAIRES
66233	REFRACTORY CEMENT,MORTAR					W 1726	3115	W 173	267	CIMENTS REFRACTAIRES
665	GLASSWARE						5125		14870	OUVRAGES EN VERRE
6651	BOTTLES ETC OF GLASS					MN 51106	4760		14593	RECIPIENTS EN VERRE
66511	GLASS BOTTLES ETC NONVAC					MN 51106	4760		14593	BONBONNES,BOUTEILLES,ETC
67	IRON AND STEEL						12093		16318	FER ET ACIER
673	IRON,STEEL SHAPES ETC					W 16066	2205	W 3269	1077	BARRES,PROFIL FER,ACIER
674	IRN,STL UNIV,PLATE,SHEET					W 21359	5366	W 16800	6755	LARGES PLATS,TOLES
6745	IRN,STL MED PLATE,ROLLED					W 2975	623	W 9608	3027	TOLES 3 A 4.75 MM
678	IRON,STL TUBES,PIPES,ETC					W 11145	2777	W 13000	6625	TUBES,TUYAUX EN FONTE,FER
6782	IRON,STL SEAMLESS TUBES					W 7245	1817	W 5538	3139	TUBES,TUYAUX SANS SOUDURE
6783	IRON,STL TUBES,PIPES NES					W 3368	794	W 6856	3074	AUT TUBES,TUYAUX FER,ACIER
68	NON-FERROUS METALS						2395		4829	METAUX NON FERREUX
684	ALUMINIUM					W 986	1763	W 1284	3644	ALUMINIUM
6842	ALUMINIUM,ALLOYS WORKED					W 895	1703	W 843	3410	ALUMINIUM,ALLIAGES OUVRE
69	METAL MANUFACTURES NES						5410		7891	ART MANUFACT EN METAL NDA
699	BASE METAL MFRS NES						2436		3498	ART MANUFACTURES MET NDA
7	MACHINES,TRANSPORT EQUIP						84366		127852	MACHINES MATERIEL TRANSPORT
71	POWER GENERATING EQUIPMT						3624		6575	MACHINES GENERATRICES
713	INTRNL COMBUS PSTN ENGIN						2030		4007	MOTEURS EXPL COMB INT, PIECE
72	MACHS FOR SPCL INDUSTRYS						16540		33866	MAC SPECIALES POUR INDUST
721	AGRIC MACHY,EXC TRACTORS						5823		9631	MACHINES AGRICOLES
7212	HARVESTING ETC MACHINES						918		2910	ENGINS POUR LA RECOLTE
7219	AGRICULTURE MACHINES NES						2850		4544	ENGINS AGRICOLES NDA
72191	WINE-MAKING ETC MACHNERY					N 36	2487	N 235	2905	APPAREILS DE VINIFICATION
727	FOOD MACHRY NON-DOMESTIC						6470		15552	MACH INDUSTRIES ALIMENT
7272	OTH FOOD PROC MCHY,PARTS						5753		14159	AUT MACH IND ALIMENTAIRE
72722	INDUS FOOD PROC MACH NES					N 2053	5198		10783	MACHINES BOULANGERIE
72729	PTS NES OF MCHY OF 72722					W 54	357		3094	PIECES MACH DU 727.22
728	OTH MACHY FOR SPCL INDUS						1512		4643	AUT MACH IND PARTICULIERES
7284	MACHY FOR SPCL INDUS NES						1118		4344	MACH SPEC IND PARTICUL.
72841	GLASS-WORKING MACHY NES							W 163	3454	MACH TRAVAIL VERRE ETC
74	GENRL INDUSTRL MACHY NES						12473		18827	MACH APP INDUSTRIE
741	HEATING,COOLING EQUIPMNT						2262		4049	MACH CHAUFFAGE,PIECES
743	PUMPS NES,CENTRFUGES ETC						2805		1643	POMPES COMPRES,VENT ETC
745	NONELEC MACHY,TOOLS NES						3744		8626	AUT MACH NON ELEC,PIECES
7452	OTH NONELEC MCHS,PTS NES						3718		8522	AUT MACH NON ELEC,PIECES
74522	PACKAGNG,BOTTLNG,ETC MCH					W 115	2877	W 211	6009	MACH NETT BOUTEILLES,ETC
75	OFFICE MACHNES,ADP EQUIP						5486		5410	MACH BUREAU TRAIT AUTOM
752	AUTOMTIC DATA PROC EQUIP						3285		2838	MACH TRAIT INFORMATION
76	TELECOMM,SOUND EQUIPMENT						8387		19343	EQUIPMENT DE TELECOM
764	TELECOM EQPT,PTS,ACC NES						6961		18451	EQUIP TELECOM,PIECES
7641	LINE TELEPHONE,ETC EQUIP						3089	N 480	5319	APP TELEPHON PAR FIL
7643	TV,RADIO TRANSMITTRS ETC					N 430	247	N 657	2697	APP EMET TELE RADIO
7649	PTS NES OF EQUIPMT OF 76					W 81	3354		9908	PIECES DE LA DIV 76
76491	PTS NES OF APPAR OF 7641					W 6	123	W 55	4426	PIECES POUR 764.1
76493	TELECOMM EQUIPMT PTS NES					W 57	3162		4998	PIECES 761,762,764.3,8
77	ELECTRIC MACHNRY NES ETC						18535		21512	MACH APP ELECT NDA
773	ELECTR DISTRIBUTNG EQUIP					W 841	2082	W 601	3464	EQUIPMT DISTRIBUTION ELECT
7731	INSULATED WIRE,CABLE ETC					W 765	2000	W 438	3118	FILS,CABLES ISOLES ELECT
776	TRANSISTORS,VALVES,ETC						3645		4927	LAMPES,TUBES,VALVES
7761	TV PICTURE TUBES					N 113676	2828	N 111484	3805	TUBES CATHODIQUES
778	ELECTRICAL MACHINERY NES						9219		6558	AUTRES MACH ELECT NDA
7781	BATTERIES,ACCUMULATORS						2385		2859	PILES ET ACCUMULATEURS
77812	ELECTRIC ACCUMULATORS					N 46524	2249		2359	ACCUMULATEURS ELECTRIQ
7788	OTH ELEC MACHY,EQUIP NES					W 1680	5913	W 135	1935	AUT MACH APP ELEC NDA
77887	ELECTRICAL CARBONS					W 1469	4398	W 11	137	PIECES CHARBON,GRAPHITE
78	ROAD VEHICLES						18338		19330	VEHICULES ROUTIERS
781	PASS MOTOR VEH EXC BUSES					N 947	4689	N 574	6115	AUTO TRANSPORT PERSONNES
782	LORRIES,SPCL MTR VEH NES					N 1129	4071	N 549	3285	VEHICULES SPECIAUX,MARCH
7821	LORRIES,TRUCKS					N 1043	3402	N 469	2553	VEHICULES TRANSP MARCHAND
784	MOTOR VEH PRTS,ACCES NES						7199		6533	PIECES 722,781,782,783
7849	OTHER MOTOR VEHCL PARTS					W 10721	7019		6187	PIECES 722,781,782,783
8	MISC MANUFACTURED GOODS						30488		29868	ART MANUFACTURES DIVERS
821	*FURNITURE,PARTS THEREOF						4364		2432	MEUBLES ET PIECES
8219	FURNITURE AND PARTS NES					W 2336	3874	W 1407	2016	AUTRES MEUBLES ET PIECES
82192	WOOD FURNITURE NES					W 2103	3576	W 1178	1744	MEUBLES NDA EN BOIS
84	CLOTHING AND ACCESSORIES						9702		7230	VETEMENTS
843	WOMENS OUTERWEAR NONKNIT						3610	N 14176	509	VET DESSUS FEMMES MAT TEX
8439	— OTHER OUTER GARMENTS						3099	N 717	142	AUT VET DES FEM MAT TEXT
844	UNDER GARMENTS NOT KNIT						1540		3407	VETEMENT DESSOUS MAT TEX
8441	— MENS SHIRTS						1504		3320	CHEMISES HOMMES MAT TEXT
84412	—— OF SYNTHETIC FIBRES						1320		3260	CHEMISES HOMMES FIB SYNT
845	OUTERWEAR KNIT NONELASTC						2316	N 32194	288	VET DESSOUS,ACCES BONNET
851	*FOOTWEAR					P 582996	2822	P 299902	1722	CHAUSSURES
87	PRECISION INSTRUMNTS NES						3429		3821	INSTRUM,APPAR SCIENT NDA
89	MISC MANUFCTRD GOODS NES						8754		11937	ART MANUFACTURES DIVERS

4. General Imports C.I.F. by Commodities according to the S.I.T.C. (Rev. 2) in thousand U.S. Dollars
Importations Générales C.A.F. par Produits d'après la C.T.C.I. (Rév. 2) en milliers de Dollars E.U.

SITC CTCI	COMMODITY	1992		1993		1994		1995		PRODUIT
		WEIGHT POIDS	VALUE VALEUR	WEIGHT POIDS	VALUE VALEUR	WEIGHT POIDS	VALUE VALEUR	WEIGHT POIDS	VALUE VALEUR	
892	PRINTED MATTER					W 1410	3781		2040	IMPRIMES
8921	PRINTED BOOKS,GLOBES,ETC					W 1181	2966	W 197	382	LIVRES,BROCHURES,CARTES
89211	PRINTED BOOKS,PAMPHLETS					W 1179	2964	W 196	374	LIVRES,BROCHURES
893	ARTICLES OF PLASTIC NES						2656		6758	OUVRAGES EN MAT DIVIS 58
8931	PLSTC PACKG CONTNRS,LIDS					W 712	1234	W 1704	4470	ART TRANSP EMBALLAGE ETC

5. General Exports F.O.B. by Commodities according to the S.I.T.C. (Rev. 2) in thousand U.S. Dollars
Exportations Générales F.O.B. par Produits d'après la C.T.C.I. (Rév. 2) en milliers de Dollars E.U.

SITC CTCI	COMMODITY	1992		1993		1994		1995		PRODUIT
		WEIGHT POIDS	VALUE VALEUR	WEIGHT POIDS	VALUE VALEUR	WEIGHT POIDS	VALUE VALEUR	WEIGHT POIDS	VALUE VALEUR	
	ALL COMMODITIES						566001		745530	TOUS PRODUITS
0	FOOD AND LIVE ANIMALS						230600		295993	ALIMENTS,ANIMAUX VIVANTS
001	*LIVE ANIMALS FOR FOOD					N 11928	709		7295	ANIMAUX VIVANTS
0011	BOVINE SPECIES,LIVE					N 1843	426	N 14622	3443	ESPECE BOVINE
00119	— OTHR THAN FR BREEDING					N 1698	351	N 14622	3443	BOVINS NON REPRODUCTEURS
0013	SWINE,LIVE					N 1243	193	N 29760	3273	ESPECE PORCINE
01	MEAT AND PREPARATIONS						34364		49029	VIANDES ET PREPARATIONS
011	MEAT FRESH,CHILLD,FROZEN					W 30066	32414	W 37128	44720	VIANDES FRAICHES,REF,CONGE
0111	BOVINE MEAT FRESH,FROZEN					W 23235	24070	W 29578	34967	VIANDES BOVIN FRAI,REF
01111	BOVINE MEAT WITH BONE IN					W 23161	24003	W 28867	34117	VIANDES BOVIN NON DESOSS
0113	PIG MEAT FRESH,CHLD,FRZN					W 5682	7738	W 4948	7461	VIANDE DE PORC
014	MEAT PREPD,PRSVD,NES ETC					W 1112	1945	W 1840	4304	CONSERVES DE VIANDES
0149	OTH PREPARD,PRESRVD MEAT					W 850	1451	W 1614	3638	AUTRES PREP DE VIANDES
02	DAIRY PRODCTS,BIRDS'EGGS						11495		15232	PRODUITS LAITIERS,OEUFS
022	MILK AND CREAM					W 6160	3859	W 8637	8722	LAIT ET CREME
0224	MILK,CREAM PRESERVED ETC					W 3886	3409	W 5950	8183	LAIT,CREME CONS,CONC
02242	MILK DRY,1.5% FAT OR LES					W 2836	2660	W 4772	6307	LAIT POUDRE INF 1.5%
023	BUTTER					W 3496	6597	W 1739	5186	BEURRE
04	CEREALS AND PREPARATIONS						31817		30732	CEREALES ET PRODUITS
041	WHEAT ETC UNMILLED					W 665	39	W 110529	12706	FROMENT,EPEAUTRE
0411	DURUM WHEAT UNMILLED					W 665	39	W 83949	9440	FROMENT DUR NON MOULU
0412	OTHER WHEAT ETC UNMILLED							W 26581	3266	AUTRE FROMENT NON MOULU
044	MAIZE UNMILLED					W 48628	30974	W 27573	12323	MAIS NON MOULU
046	WHEAT ETC MEAL OR FLOUR					W 78	16	W 13024	3724	SEMOULE FARINE,FROMENT
04601	FLOUR OF WHEAT OR MESLIN					W 78	16	W 12698	3686	FARINE DE FROMENT
05	VEGETABLES AND FRUIT						107444		118870	LEGUMES ET FRUITS
054	VEG ETC FRSH,SMPLY PRSVD					W 48799	15300	W 39250	16991	LEGUMES FRAIS,CONG,SECS
0544	TOMATOES FRESH					W 12849	2585	W 6989	1892	TOMATES FRAICHES
0545	OTHER FRESH VEGETABLES					W 17480	3595	W 14538	3580	AUTRES LEGUMES FRAIS,REF
05459	FRESH VEGETABLES NES					W 14452	2769	W 11975	2631	LEGUMES FRAIS,REFRI NDA
0546	VEGETABLES SIMPLY PRESVD					W 17759	8865	W 15232	11082	LEGUMES CONG,CONSER
05461	VEGETABLES FROZEN					W 17676	8833	W 15140	11048	LEGUMES CONGELES
056	VEGTBLES ETC PRSVD,PREPD					W 19499	8448	W 20825	12513	CONSERVES DE LEGUMES
0565	VEGTBLES PRSVD,PREPD NES					W 19464	8436	W 20825	12513	LEGUMES PREPARES CONSERVE
05651	VEGTBLS,FRUIT IN VINEGAR					W 12678	4426	W 12855	6414	LEGUM CONSERV AU VINAIGRE
05659	OTH VEG PRESVD,PREPD NES					W 6786	4010	W 7970	6099	LEGUM PREPAP,CONSERV NDA
057	FRUIT,NUTS,FRESH,DRIED					W 254933	55377	W 100859	31629	FRUITS FRAIS OU SECS
0574	APPLES FRESH					W 96393	23291	W 67189	18950	POMMES FRAICHES
0575	GRAPES FRESH OR DRIED					W 137014	23968	W 13703	3606	RAISINS FRAIS OU SECS
05751	GRAPES FRESH					W 136999	23962	W 13658	3600	RAISINS FRAIS
0577	NUTS EDIBLE,FRESH,DRIED					W 1694	3128	W 3459	4367	FRUITS A COQUES
05779	NUTS EDIBLE,FRSH,DRY,NES					W 1449	2749	W 3432	4354	FRUITS A COQUES NDA
0579	FRUIT FRESH OR DRIED NES					W 19805	4978	W 16487	4691	FRUITS FRAIS,SECS NDA
05793	STONE FRUIT FRESH NES					W 14632	3520	W 13439	3060	FRUITS A NOYAU NDA FRAIS
058	FRUIT PRESERVED,PREPARED					W 71271	28319	W 78815	57737	CONSERVES DE FRUITS
0583	FRUIT JAMS,JELLIES ETC					W 5628	2925	W 7476	4917	PATES DE FRUITS CONFITURES
0585	FRUIT OR VEGETABLE JUICE					W 53468	21380	W 61162	48179	JUS DE FRUITS
05855	TOMATO JUICE					W 3047	934	W 6508	2941	JUS DE TOMATE
05857	JUICE OF OTHER FRUIT,VEG					W 47495	19761	W 53350	44732	JUS AUTRES FRUITS,LEGUMES
0589	FRUIT PREPRD,PRESRVD,NES					W 9916	3483	W 8668	4349	FRUITS PREPARES CONSERV
05899	FRUIT,NUTS NES,PRESERVED					W 9737	3444	W 8668	4348	FRUITS PREP CONSERV NDA
06	SUGAR AND PREPS,HONEY						37755		65767	SUCRES ET PRODUITS
061	SUGAR AND HONEY					W 138592	33915	W 179458	63053	SUCRES ET MIEL
0611	RAW BEET AND CANE SUGAR					W 84456	25564	W 117478	51458	SUCRES BRUTS
0612	REFINED SUGAR ETC					W 16085	5412	W 17498	7449	SUCRES RAFFINES
0615	MOLASSES					W 36893	2465	W 44270	3820	MELASSES
062	SUGAR CANDY NON–CHOCLATE					W 3338	3840	W 2198	2713	SUCRERIES
07	COFFEE,TEA,COCOA,SPICES						1049		3118	CAFE,THE,CACAO,EPICES
09	MISC EDIBLE PRODUCTS						5340		4452	PREP ALIMENTAIRES DIVERSES
098	EDIBLE PRODCTS,PREPS NES						5336		4397	PREP ALIMENTAIRES NDA
09804	SAUCES,MIXED SEASONINGS					W 6430	4291	W 4723	3948	SAUCES,ASSAISONNEMENTS
1	BEVERAGES AND TOBACCO						132172		220846	BOISSONS ET TABACS
11	BEVERAGES						96610		174345	BOISSONS
112	ALCOHOLIC BEVERAGES					W 163091	96337	W 273253	173025	BOISSONS ALCOOLIQUES
1121	WINE OF FRESH GRAPES ETC					W 154662	62786	W 259751	113094	VINS DE RAISINS FRAIS
11211	GRAPE MUST					W 16538	3606	W 93462	20861	MOUTS DE RAISIN
11212	WINE OF FRESH GRAPES					W 137303	58675	W 165551	91280	VINS DE MOUTS DE RAISINS
1124	DISTILLED ALCOHOLIC BEVS					W 8210	33456	W 13459	59882	ALCOOLS,EAUX–DE–VIE
11242	DISTILLD WINE,GRAPE MARC					W 2210	16965	W 3000	29953	EAUX–DE–VIE NATURELLES
11249	OTH ALCOHOLC BEVS,CMPNDS					W 5999	16483	W 10436	29769	BOISSONS ALCOOLIQUES NDA
12	TOBACCO AND MANUFACTURES						35561		46501	TABACS BRUTS FABRIQUES
121	TOBACCO UNMNFCTRD,REFUSE					W 17429	14081	W 17804	15542	TABACS BRUTS,DECHETS
1211	TOBACCO,NOT STRIPPED					W 13491	11287	W 7794	5976	TABACS NON ECOTES
1212	TOBACCO STRIPPED OR PART					W 3810	2775	W 9949	9555	TABACS PART ECOTES
122	TOBACCO,MANUFACTURED						21481		30959	TABACS FABRIQUES
1222	CIGARETTES						9780	W 3002	24383	CIGARETTES
1223	OTH MANUFACTURED TOBACCO					W 13323	11642	W 7756	6491	TABACS FUMER,CHIQUER,PRISER
2	CRUDE MATERLS,EXCL FUELS						18632		40035	MAT BRUTES NON COMESTIBLES
21	HIDES,SKINS,FURS UNDRSSD						5254		8866	CUIRS,PEAUX BRUTS
211	HIDES,SKINS,EXC FURS,RAW						5253		8788	CUIRS ET PEAUX
2111	BOVINE,EQUINE HIDES,RAW					W 2294	2046	W 1984	2468	PEAUX DE BOVINS
2112	CALF AND KIP SKINS,RAW					W 2599	2358	W 3804	4370	PEAUX DE VEAUX
22	OIL SEEDS,OLEAGINOUS FRT						4279		6555	GRAINES,FRUITS OLEAGINEUX
222	SEEDS FOR'SOFT'FIXED OIL					W 21119	4259	W 25083	6520	GRAINES HUILES FIXES
2224	SUNFLOWER SEEDS					W 20622	4145	W 24988	6506	GRAINES DE TOURNESOL
26	TEXTILE FIBRES AND WASTE						801		2254	FIBRES TEXTILES
28	METALLIFEROUS ORES,SCRAP						5909		18602	MINERAIS METAL,DECHETS
288	NONFERR METAL SCRAP NES					W 8462	5675	W 19357	17314	DECHETS NON FERREUX
2882	OTHER BASE MTL SCRAP NES					W 8462	5675	W 19356	17281	AUTRES DECHETS
28821	COPPER WASTE AND SCRAP					W 6281	4657	W 11515	11556	DECHETS DE CUIVRE
28823	ALUMINIUM WSTE AND SCRAP					W 2081	919	W 7748	5570	DECHETS D'ALUMINIUM
29	CRUDE ANIMAL,VEG MAT NES						1708		1504	MATIERES BRUTES ANIM,VEGET
3	MINERAL FUELS ETC						14347		6545	COMBUSTIBLES MINERAUX LUB
351	*ELECTRIC CURRENT					H 264800	13487	H 126860	6470	ENERGIE ELECTRIQUE
4	ANIMAL,VEGETABLE OIL,FAT						11173		11109	HUILES,GRAISSES ANIM,VEG
411	*ANIMAL OILS AND FATS					W 1543	2695	W 772	443	HUILES,GRAISSES ANIMALES
4113	ANIML OIL,FAT,GREASE NES					W 1543	2695	W 772	443	HUILES,GRAISSES ANIMALES NDA
41139	ANIMAL OILS,FATS NES					W 1062	2243			GRAISSES,HUILES ANIM NDA
42	FIXED VEGETABLE OIL,FAT						8418		10559	HUILES VEGETALES FIXES
423	FIXED VEG OILS,SOFT					W 16031	8408	W 13612	10542	HUILES VEGET DOUCES FIXES
4236	SUNFLOWER SEED OIL					W 16029	8407	W 13606	10537	HUILE DE TOURNESOL

5. General Exports F.O.B. by Commodities according to the S.I.T.C. (Rev. 2) in thousand U.S. Dollars
Exportations Générales F.O.B. par Produits d'après la C.T.C.I. (Rév. 2) en milliers de Dollars E.U.

SITC CTCI	COMMODITY	1992 WEIGHT POIDS	1992 VALUE VALEUR	1993 WEIGHT POIDS	1993 VALUE VALEUR	1994 WEIGHT POIDS	1994 VALUE VALEUR	1995 WEIGHT POIDS	1995 VALUE VALEUR	PRODUIT
5	CHEMCLS,RELATED PROD NES						12032		10053	PRODUITS CHIMIQUES
51	ORGANIC CHEMICALS						3962		3511	PROD CHIMIQ ORGANIQUES
512	ALCOHOLS,PHENOLS ETC						2999	V 2018	1565	PHENOLS,PHENOLS–ALCOOLS
5121	ACYCLIC ALCOHOLS,DERIVS						2983	V 2018	1565	ALCOOLS ACYCLIQUES
51216	ETHYL ALC,DENATRD SPIRIT					V 4157	2974	V 2018	1565	ALCOOL ETHYLIQUE NON DENAT
55	PERFUME,CLEANING ETC PRD						4782		3535	PROD POUR PARFUM,TOILETTE
553	PERFUMERY,COSMETICS,ETC					W 1743	2823	W 883	2074	PRODUITS DE PARFUMERIE
6	BASIC MANUFACTURES						44828		53946	ART MANUFACTURES
61	LEATHER,DRESSED FUR,ETC						2407		4341	CUIRS,PELLETERIES
611	LEATHER						1995		4144	CUIRS,PEAUX PREPARES
6114	LEATHR BOVINE NES,EQUINE					A 220	1137	A 242	2470	CUIRS DE BOVINS
63	WOOD,CORK MANUFACTRS NES						2441		1639	OUVRAGES LIEGE ET BOIS
635	WOOD MANUFACTURES NES						2284		1392	ART MANUF EN BOIS NDA
6353	BUILDERS WOODWRK,PREFABS						2229	W 4482	1266	OUVRAGES DE MENUISERIE
64	PAPER,PAPERBOARD AND MFR						5495		6862	PAPIERS,CARTONS & OUVRAGES
641	PAPER AND PAPERBOARD						3453		3597	PAPIERS ET CARTONS
6415	PAPER,PAPERBRD,BULK,NES					W 5108	1928	W 3653	1904	PAPIERS,CARTONS ROULEAUX
64159	OTHER PAPER ETC,BULK,NES					W 4877	1855	W 3129	1625	AUT PAPIER ROULEAUX FEUILLES
642	PAPER,ETC,PRECUT,ARTS OF					W 3464	2042		3264	PAP,CARTONS DECOUPES
6421	PAPER ETC CONTAINERS					W 2808	1642	W 3205	2576	BOITES,SACS EMBALLAGES
65	TEXTILE YARN,FABRICS,ETC						15369		10759	FILS,TISSUS,ARTICLES TEXTILE
659	FLOOR COVERINGS,ETC						12083		9222	COUVRE–PARQUETS,TAPIS ETC
6594	WOOL CARPETS ETC NES					A 393	4444	A 304	4932	TAPIS DE LAINE
65942	— WOVEN					A 384	4388	A 302	4899	TAPIS DE LAINE TISSES
6596	OTH TXTL CARPETS ETC NES					A 803	7400	A 399	4084	TAPIS AUT MAT TEXT NDA
65962	— OTHR THAN KNOTTED ETC					A 802	7399	A 396	4052	TAPIS AUT QUE NOUES TOUF
66	NONMETAL MINERAL MFS NES						5640		15378	ART MIN NON METALLIQUES
661	LIME,CEMENT,BLDG PRODS						2329		1440	CHAUX,CIMENTS MAT CONSTR
6618	MNRL BLDG PRD UNFIRD NES						2121		996	MAT CONST AMIANTE–CIMENT
66183	ASBESTOS–,FIBRE–CMNT PRD						2103		985	OUVRAGES AMIANTE–CIMENT
665	GLASSWARE						1966		12193	OUVRAGES EN VERRE
6651	BOTTLES ETC OF GLASS					MN 22577	1879		12136	RECIPIENTS EN VERRE
66511	GLASS BOTTLES ETC NONVAC					MN 22577	1879		12136	BONBONNES,BOUTEILLES,ETC
67	IRON AND STEEL						7992		8046	FER ET ACIER
673	IRON,STEEL SHAPES ETC					W 16624	3469	W 13001	3163	BARRES,PROFIL FER,ACIER
674	IRN,STL UNIV,PLATE,SHEET						2702	W 7324	1902	LARGES PLATS,TOLES
69	METAL MANUFACTURES NES						4078		3875	ART MANUFACT EN METAL NDA
699	BASE METAL MFRS NES						2478		1984	ART MANUFACTURES MET NDA
7	MACHINES,TRANSPORT EQUIP						65143		58786	MACHINES MATERIEL TRANSPORT
72	MACHS FOR SPCL INDUSTRYS						10309		12740	MAC SPECIALES POUR INDUST
722	TRACTORS NON–ROAD					N 1311	6575	N 995	6496	TRACTEURS
7223	TRACK–LAYING TRACTORS					N 1236	6435	N 892	6283	TRACTEURS A CHENILLES
74	GENRL INDUSTRL MACHY NES						16052		16861	MACH APP INDUSTRIE
742	PUMPS FOR LIQUIDS ETC					N 92752	12980	N 95479	13598	POMPES MOTO–POMPES
7422	CENTRIFUGAL PUMPS NES					N 33327	7723	N 20222	10442	POMPES CENTRIF NON 742.81
7428	OTHER PUMPS FOR LIQUIDS					N 25372	4744	N 17964	2575	AUTRES POMPES POUR LIQ
74288	PUMPS FR LIQUIDS NES ETC					N 25044	4636	N 17250	2367	POMPES POUR LIQUIDES NDA
76	TELECOMM,SOUND EQUIPMENT						14777		6171	EQUIPMENT DE TELECOM
761	TELEVISION RECEIVERS					N 93572	13499	N 28505	4191	RECEPTEURS DE TELEVISION
7611	COLOUR TV RECEIVERS					N 60924	11037	N 13983	3020	RECEPTEURS COULEUR
7612	MONOCHROME TV RECEIVERS					N 32648	2462	N 14522	1171	RECEPTEURS NOIR ET BLANC
77	ELECTRIC MACHNRY NES ETC						17783		16027	MACH APP ELECT NDA
775	HOUSEHOLD TYPE EQUIP NES						12972		7814	MACH,APP USAGE DOMESTQUE
7751	HOUSEHOLD LDRY EQUIP NES					N 71124	6306	N 36234	3197	MACH A LAVER ET SECHOIRS
77511	DOMESTIC WASHING MACHNES					N 70680	6181	N 32374	2918	MACH LAVER LINGE MOINS 6 KG
7752	DOM REFRIGERATRS,FREEZRS					N 46704	5395	N 20545	2653	REFRIG,CONGEL MENAGER
77522	DOMESTIC DEEP–FREEZERS					N 45862	5344	N 20295	2567	MEUBLES CONGELATEURS
776	TRANSISTORS,VALVES,ETC						1176		2632	LAMPES,TUBES,VALVES
778	ELECTRICAL MACHINERY NES						1566		2407	AUTRES MACH ELECT NDA
78	ROAD VEHICLES						4136		3990	VEHICULES ROUTIERS
784	MOTOR VEH PRTS,ACCES NES						2264		1581	PIECES 722,781,782,783
7849	OTHER MOTOR VEHCL PARTS					W 1590	2259		1536	PIECES 722,781,782,783
8	MISC MANUFACTURED GOODS						37062		48201	ART MANUFACTURES DIVERS
812	*PLUMBG,HEATNG,LGHTNG EQ						2329		3394	APPAR SANITAIRES CHAUFFAGE
8124	LIGHTING EQUIPMENT NES						1832		2997	APPAREILS ECLAIRAGE ETC
81242	LAMPS,FITTINGS BASE METL					W 1487	1806	W 1309	2835	APPAREILS D'ECLAIRAGE
821	*FURNITURE,PARTS THEREOF						10304		9697	MEUBLES ET PIECES
8211	CHAIRS,SEATS AND PARTS						2021		1067	SIEGES ET PIECES
82111	CHAIRS AND OTHER SEATS					N 1011300	2018		1062	SIEGES
8219	FURNITURE AND PARTS NES					W 10196	8193	W 6469	8556	AUTRES MEUBLES ET PIECES
82192	WOOD FURNITURE NES					W 10011	7989	W 6360	8405	MEUBLES NDA EN BOIS
84	CLOTHING AND ACCESSORIES						14297		23315	VETEMENTS
842	MENS OUTERWEAR NOT KNIT					N 494091	5398	N 568920	7778	VET DESSUS POUR HOMMES
8421	— OVERCOATS,OTHER COATS					N 97079	932	N 120211	2687	MANTEAUX HOMMES MAT TEXT
84219	—— OF OTHER FIBRES					N 93585	885	N 99811	2442	MANTEAUX HOMMES AUT FIBR
8423	— TROUSERS,BREECHES ETC					N 254208	2063	N 264719	1784	PANTALONS HOMMES MAT TEX
843	WOMENS OUTERWEAR NONKNIT						3523		7947	VET DESSUS FEMMES MAT TEX
8431	— COATS AND JACKETS					N 305425	1921	N 362225	5003	MANT,VEST FEM MAT TEXTIL
845	OUTERWEAR KNIT NONELASTC						1507		2369	VET DESSOUS,ACCES BONNET
846	UNDER GARMENTS KNITTED					N 2616320	1837	N 1972124	2600	SOUS VETS DE BONNETERIE
8462	— OF COTTON NON ELASTIC					N 1726994	1578	N 1753283	2530	SOUS–VET BONNET COTON
851	*FOOTWEAR					P 1210420	2315	P 858700	2672	CHAUSSURES
89	MISC MANUFCTRD GOODS NES						5805		7052	ART MANUFACTURES DIVERS
892	PRINTED MATTER						2014		1482	IMPRIMES
893	ARTICLES OF PLASTIC NES						1339		2601	OUVRAGES EN MAT DIVIS 58
8931	PLSTC PACKG CONTNRS,LIDS					W 450	993	W 1167	2244	ART TRANSP EMBALLAGE ETC

FOOT NOTES – NOTES

TABLE 1 –
1 Excludes trade with the Commonwealth of Independent States in 1993.
TABLE 3 –
1 Excludes trade with the Commonwealth of Independent States in 1993.
TABLEAU 1 –
1 Y exclu le commerce avec la confédération des états indépendants en 1993.
TABLEAU 3 –
1 Y exclu le commerce avec la confédération des états indépendants en 1993.

1. HISTORICAL SERIES, 1960–1995 SPECIAL TRADE, IMPORTS C.I.F., EXPORTS F.O.B.
SERIES HISTORIQUES, 1960–1995 COMMERCE SPECIAL, IMPORTATIONS C.A.F., EXPORTATIONS F.O.B

YEAR ANNEE	VALUE IN MILLION REUNION FRANCS VALEUR EN MILLION REUNION FRANCS MERCHANDISE –MARCHANDISE IMPORTS	EXPORTS	GOLD –OR IMPORTS	EXPORTS	CONVERSION FACTORS U.S. CENTS PER REUNION FRANC FACTEURS DE CONVERSION CENTS E.U. PAR REUNION FRANC IMPORTS	EXPORTS	INDEX NUMBERS –INDICES QUANTUM IMPORTS	EXPORTS	UNIT VALUE VALEUR UNITAIRE IMPORTS	EXPORTS
1960	258.00	179.80			20.2550	20.2550				
1961	285.10	181.30			20.2550	20.2550				
1962	312.50	163.10			20.2550	20.2550				
1963	344.30	188.10			20.2550	20.2550				
1964	439.30	184.40			20.2550	20.2550				
1965	479.00	170.00			20.2550	20.2550				
1966	516.30	193.40			20.2550	20.2550				
1967	574.40	179.70			20.2550	20.2550				
1968	621.90	227.70			20.2550	20.2550				
1969	759.10	236.80			19.3000	18.8350				
1970	894.40	282.10			18.0050	18.0050				
1971	962.30	241.80			18.0050	18.0050				
1972	1000.50	282.10			19.8312	19.8234				
1973	1270.10	366.80			22.6450	22.5151				
1974	1593.40	326.80			20.7857	20.9856				
1975	1757.70	257.20			23.3186	22.9614				
1976	2138.90	450.30			20.8952	20.8787				
1977	2413.00	560.70			20.3678	20.3430				
1978	2696.40	519.50			22.3871	22.3973				
1979	3230.50	594.10			23.5569	23.5532				
1980	3748.90	552.90			23.6866	23.5595				
1981	4281.50	573.00			18.3585	18.6954				
1982	5303.70	689.00			15.1512	15.1948				
1983	6404.00	667.00			13.0764	13.0395				
1984	6894.20	695.40			11.4729	11.4658				
1985	7456.50	868.00			11.2734	11.1908				
1986	7860.80	930.36			14.4665	14.4751				
1987	8751.25	1009.36			16.7346	16.7213				
1988	10056.87	946.09			16.5229	16.7498				
1989	11061.84	1028.27			15.6553	15.6201				
1990	11738.04	1015.69			18.4060	18.6742				
1991	12004.00	823.30			17.7408	18.1636				
1992	12258.78	1122.87			18.9255	18.9930				
1993	11650.89	948.20			17.6586	17.7092				
1994	13062.36	953.14			18.1087	17.9200				
1995	13076.63	1026.90			20.0730	20.1231				

2. IMPORTS BY BROAD ECONOMIC CATEGORY AND EXPORTS BY INDUSTRIAL ORIGIN. (PERCENTAGE OF TOTAL VALUE)
IMPORTATIONS PAR CATEGORIES ECONOMIQUES ET EXPORTATIONS PAR BRANCHE D'ACTIVITE.(EN POURCENTAGE DE LA VALEUR TOTALE)

IMPORTS – IMPORTATIONS

	1990	1991	1992	1993	1994	1995	1996
TOTAL IMPORTS–IMPORTATIONS TOTALES	100.	100.	100.	100.	100.	100.	
1 FOOD BEV–ALIMENTATION BOISSONS	16.0	15.5	17.2	17.8	17.1	17.4	
11 PRIMARY–PRODUITS DE BASE	6.2	6.3	6.9	6.8	6.5	6.7	
111 FOR INDUSTRY–POUR L'INDUSTRIE	0.6	1.3	1.6	1.3	1.6	1.6	
112 FOR HOUSEHOLDS–POUR LES MENAGES	5.6	4.9	5.3	5.4	4.9	5.1	
12 PROCESSED–PRODUITS ELABORES	9.8	9.2	10.3	11.0	10.6	10.7	
121 FOR INDUSTRY–POUR L'INDUSTRIE	0.8	0.7	0.4	0.5	0.4	0.4	
122 FOR HOUSEHOLDS–POUR LES MENAGES	9.0	8.6	9.9	10.5	10.1	10.3	
2 IND SUPPLIES–APPROV INDUSTRIELS	21.8	19.7	21.2	21.1	20.9	22.0	
21 PRIMARY–PRODUITS DE BASE	1.3	1.0	1.4	1.9	1.1	1.4	
22 PROCESSED–PRODUITS ELABORES	20.6	18.7	19.9	19.2	19.8	20.7	
3 FUELS–COMBUSTIBLES	6.1	5.7	4.9	5.0	5.0	4.6	
31 PRIMARY–PRODUITS DE BASE	0.5	0.5	0.6	0.7	0.7	0.8	
32 PROCESSED–PRODUITS ELABORES	5.6	5.2	4.3	4.3	4.3	3.8	
321 MOTOR SPIRIT–ESSENCE	5.6	5.2	4.2	4.2		1.1	
322 OTHER–AUTRES	0.0	0.0	0.0	0.0	4.3	2.7	
4 MACHINERY–EQUIPEMENT	13.8	15.8	14.7	13.6	14.9	13.1	
41 CAPITAL EQUIPMENT–MACHINES	12.7	14.7	13.6	12.4	13.6	11.9	
42 PARTS–PIECES ACCESSOIRES	1.1	1.1	1.2	1.1	1.3	1.2	
5 TRANSPORT–TRANSPORT	16.3	18.3	15.2	15.1	15.9	16.3	
51 PASSENGER CARS–AUTOMOBILES	5.2	4.8	6.0	6.3	6.7	7.7	
52 OTHER–AUTRES	7.9	10.5	5.9	5.1	5.2	5.2	
521 INDUSTRIAL–INDUSTRIELS	7.4	10.0	5.4	4.6	4.7	4.7	
522 NON INDUSTRIAL–NON INDUSTRIEL	0.4	0.6	0.5	0.5	0.5	0.5	
53 PARTS–PIECES ACCESSOIRES	3.2	2.9	3.3	3.8	3.9	3.4	
6 CONSUM GOODS–BIENS CONSOMMATION	23.6	22.5	24.2	25.3	24.1	24.7	
61 DURABLE–DURABLES	5.7	5.8	5.4	5.3	5.2	5.3	
62 SEMI DURABLE–SEMI DURABLES	10.5	9.7	10.9	11.0	10.3	10.5	
63 NON DURABLE–NON DURABLES	7.4	7.0	7.9	8.9	8.6	8.9	
7 GOODS NES–BIENS NDA	2.4	2.5	2.5	2.2	2.2	2.0	

EXPORTS – EXPORTATIONS

	1990	1991	1992	1993	1994	1995	1996
TOTAL EXPORTS–EXPORTATIONS TOTALES	100.	100.	100.	100.	100.	100.	
1 AGRICULTURE	5.1	8.6	7.0	7.4	11.5	10.7	
2 MINING QUARRY–INDUS EXTRACTIVES	0.1	0.1	0.1	0.1	0.2	0.2	
3 MANUFACTURING–IND MANUFACTUR	94.9	91.3	92.8	92.5	88.4	89.1	
31 FOOD BEV TOBACCO–ALIM BOISS TAB	77.6	70.9	73.0	68.2	65.7	67.7	
32 TEXTILES–INDUSTRIES TEXTILES	0.7	0.9	0.8	2.1	2.3	1.1	
33 WOOD & PRODUCTS–BOIS & PRODUITS	0.5	0.5	0.0	0.2	0.1	0.2	
34 PAPER & PRODUCTS–PAPIER & PRODT	0.7	0.8	0.6	0.8	0.7	0.7	
35 CHEMICALS–INDUSTRIES CHIMIQUES	3.2	2.6	2.5	3.4	2.0	2.1	
36 NON METAL MIN–MIN NON METAL	0.2	0.2	0.1	0.2	0.3	0.3	
37 BASIC METAL–IND METAL BASE	0.8	1.5	1.1	1.5	1.4	0.9	
38 METAL MANUF–MANUF METAL	11.0	12.6	13.8	16.0	15.9	16.1	
39 OTH MANUF IND–AUTRES MANUF	0.2	1.1	0.8	0.1	0.1	0.2	

3. TRADE BY PRINCIPAL COUNTRIES OF PRODUCTION AND LAST CONSIGNMENT (VALUE IN THOUSAND U.S. DOLLARS)
ECHANGES SELON LES PRINCIPAUX PAYS DE PRODUCTION ET DE DERNIERE CONSIGNATION (VALEUR EN MILLIERS DE DOLLARS EU)

COUNTRIES–PAYS	SPECIAL IMPORTS C.I.F. IMPORTATIONS SPECIALES C.A.F				
	1991	1992	1993	1994	1995
World	2133470	2393853	2075942	2358365	2711086
Africa	142067	138712	129622	136481	163023
Americas	128260	21245	21670	62109	46655
Northern America	120983	7844	7431	45639	16733
LAIA	6971	13299	14197	16419	29762
CACM	293	3	4	21	54
Caribbean	5	95	38	30	107
Rest of America	8	4			
As.ex F.USSR	244738	276766	234794	273245	309145
Eur.x F.USSR	1610600	1948474	1679030	1876786	2179187
EU	1607369	1944492	1664191	1866774	2170570
EFTA	2462	3523	4375	7182	6270
East Europe	294	112	9808	2521	2007
Other Europe	474			7	6
Former USSR	5	20	95	39	426
Oceania	7230	8264	10082	8549	10943
France, Monac	1372134	1663540	1441534	1575588	1797968
Bahrain/Bahreïn	91700	103032	88116	82876	83792
Italy/Italie	60774	66421	60770	75131	95595
So. Africa Customs Un	60916	67591	57289	56991	70339
Germany/Allemagne	56363	62863	47642	64618	75970
Japan/Japon	47545	55154	40845	42530	57324
Belgium–Luxembourg	37073	49514	38222	51144	58986
USA/Etats–Unis d'Amer	120338	7042	6874	44977	15005
United Kingdom	21566	25174	21420	31605	39302
Netherlands/Pays–Bas	21899	31955	25840	24619	30013
Mauritius/Maurice	19708	27203	27181	26081	26585
Thailand/Thaïlande	20757	25582	21947	23976	32548
Spain/Espagne	21431	28302	1713	23571	42606
Malaysia/Malaisie	19072	21033	20224	22903	26393
Madagascar	16062	18176	22068	24012	27493
China/Chine	13194	15500	15848	22208	24295
Argentina/Argentine	6011	10859	10661	9462	21452
Korea, Republic of	4354	7553	10965	15744	17561
Kenya	11404	12929	7486	8993	11280
Saudi Arabia	1349	2951	3791	18223	18214
Singapore/Singapour	14409	8600	6233	5176	7499
Indonesia/Indonésie	4786	9276	7248	8966	8493
India/Inde	5428	5395	4604	10895	9014
Congo	5848	4938	5545	5008	4953
Finland/Finlande	621	491	13487	2545	8928
Australia/Australie	4381	5402	6294	4228	5011
Brazil/Brésil	876	2214	3350	6764	7667
New Zealand	2790	2849	3438	4290	5894
Ireland/Irlande	2132	3250	2470	3976	6770
Denmark/Danemark	3549	3280	3739	3091	3896
Sweden/Suède	2337	2659	2878	5060	3996
Cameroon/Cameroun	1193	1049	2722	4157	7354
Hong Kong	5354	2911	2283	2935	2708
Switz.Liecht	1976	2717	2284	5181	3965
Zimbabwe	5085	203	1190	2770	4532
Cote d'Ivoire	8314	1212	391	1233	2307
Morocco/Maroc	2149	2419	2768	2888	1946
Viet Nam	4835	3351	1092	1008	1580
Austria/Autriche	1699	2470	2352	3270	2071
Portugal	2203	2363	995	2179	3921
Poland/Pologne	170	5	9480	694	230
Seychelles	2213	1698	1636	1695	1640
Greece/Grèce	3588	2211	1128	377	548
Israel/Israël	1314	1922	1344	1068	1977
Pakistan	225	253	302	3442	2061
Gabon	6016			23	
Norway,SVD,JM	426	804	1437	1476	1800
Turkey/Turquie	599	2387	207	1416	1287
Canada	639	802	556	661	1728
Philippines	382	749	1195	750	882

COUNTRIES–PAYS	SPECIAL EXPORTS F.O.B. EXPORTATIONS SPECIALES F.O.B.				
	1991	1992	1993	1994	1995
Monde	149761	210234	175715	170980	208691
Afrique	18564	20667	20126	17238	22728
Amériques	1453	1344	1526	3282	2829
Amérique du Nord	226	134	228	399	1275
ALAI	32	60		48	12
MCAC			1		
Caraïbes	1155	1118	1251	2390	1486
Autre Amérique	40	32	46	445	56
Asie l'URSS exclus	9549	10516	7982	11285	13334
Europe l'URSS exclus	120101	177504	143760	137482	168873
UE	119842	177086	143402	137330	166800
AELE	259	345	333	146	499
Europe de l'Est		73	26	7	
Autre de l'Europe					1574
Ancienne URSS					
Océanie	51	146	2050	1161	503
France, Monac	114061	160613	122012	127119	148920
Japan/Japon	9098	10026	6677	10643	12731
Comoros/Comores	8719	9079	9975	7581	9852
Madagascar	5294	5891	5043	5652	6640
United Kingdom	2296	3056	10912	3180	4184
Mauritius/Maurice	3535	3745	4123	3408	4062
Portugal		9072	7825		6
Belgium–Luxembourg	49	107	170	665	10380
Germany/Allemagne	1741	1724	1309	2024	1329
Martinique	532	897	1193	1650	1144
Italy/Italie	589	1243	503	585	1022
Netherlands/Pays–Bas	158	103	200	2710	626
New Caledonia	14	119	1952	1029	444
So. Africa Customs Un	399	1267	700	144	440
Spain/Espagne	684	773	142	632	167
USA/Etats–Unis d'Amer	220	120	206	361	1262
Seychelles	311	334	162	70	1180
Guadeloupe	623	220	58	740	342
Singapore/Singapour	414	78	894	308	13
Switz.Liecht	259	345	333	143	499
Malta/Malte					1574
Denmark/Danemark	64	259	309	339	162
Djibouti	207	293	62	168	9
Malaysia/Malaisie	14	237	23	176	161
Belize/Bélize				412	
Ethiopia/Ethiopie			41		312
Sweden/Suède	148	5	2	66	
Australia/Australie	36	19	89	28	35
French Guiana	40	32	46	26	56
Greece/Grèce	46	126			
Gabon		0		5	140
Cote d'Ivoire	51	30			49
India/Inde		39		2	86
Senegal/Sénégal		1		110	7
Poland/Pologne		73	26	7	
French Polynesia		8	10	59	24
Philippines			100		
Indonesia/Indonésie					88
Canada	6	14	22	38	7
Turkey/Turquie	3	83	1		
Kenya				62	8
United Arab Emirates	8	5	5	24	6
Thailand/Thaïlande		44	1		
Morocco/Maroc			14	20	9
Hong Kong	9		10	0	24
New Zealand	0			42	
Mozambique	6	23			1
China/Chine				30	
Finland/Finlande	4			9	5
Austria/Autriche			16		

(VALUE AS PERCENTAGE OF WORLD TOTAL)(VALEURS EN POURCENTAGE DU TOTAL MONDIAL)

	1986	1987	1988	1989	1990	1991	1992	1993	1994	1995
Africa	8.1	7.0	6.6	7.0	6.3	6.7	5.8	6.2	5.8	6.0
Americas	0.7	0.8	0.7	0.6	0.9	6.0	0.9	1.0	2.6	1.7
Northern America	0.4	0.3	0.2	0.2	0.5	5.7	0.3	0.4	1.9	0.6
LAIA	0.2	0.4	0.5	0.3	0.4	0.3	0.6	0.7	0.7	1.1
CACM	0.0		0.0	0.0	0.0	0.0	0.0	0.0	0.0	0.0
Caribbean	0.0	0.0	0.0	0.0	0.0	0.0	0.0	0.0	0.0	0.0
Rest of America	0.1	0.0	0.0	0.0	0.0	0.0	0.0			
As.ex F.USSR	12.5	11.2	10.9	10.5	11.7	11.5	11.6	11.3	11.6	11.4
Eur.x F.USSR	78.4	80.8	81.4	81.6	80.7	75.5	81.4	80.9	79.6	80.4
EU	78.2	80.5	81.2	81.4	80.4	75.3	81.2	80.2	79.2	80.1
EFTA	0.2	0.2	0.2	0.2	0.2	0.1	0.1	0.2	0.3	0.2
East Europe	0.0	0.0	0.0	0.0	0.0	0.0	0.0	0.5	0.1	0.1
Other Europe	0.0	0.0	0.0	0.0	0.0	0.0			0.0	0.0
Former USSR	0.0	0.0	0.0	0.0	0.0	0.0	0.0	0.0	0.0	0.0
Oceania	0.2	0.2	0.2	0.3	0.3	0.3	0.3	0.5	0.4	0.4
France, Monac	67.2	67.9	67.6	67.8	68.5	64.3	69.5	69.4	66.8	66.3
Bahrain/Bahreïn	4.9	3.0	2.7	3.9	5.4	4.3	4.3	4.2	3.5	3.1
Italy/Italie	3.4	3.5	3.5	3.4	3.0	2.8	2.8	2.9	3.2	3.5
So. Africa Customs Un	3.5	3.0	2.7	2.9	2.9	2.9	2.8	2.8	2.4	2.6
Germany/Allemagne	2.0	2.9	3.5	3.5	3.1	2.6	2.6	2.3	2.7	2.8
Japan/Japon	2.7	2.6	2.6	2.3	2.2	2.2	2.3	2.0	1.8	2.1
Belgium–Luxembourg	1.6	1.9	1.9	1.8	1.7	1.7	2.1	1.8	2.2	2.2
USA/Etats–Unis d'Amer	0.4	0.3	0.2	0.2	0.5	5.6	0.3	0.3	1.9	0.6
United Kingdom	1.1	1.4	1.3	1.1	1.1	1.0	1.1	1.0	1.3	1.4
Netherlands/Pays–Bas	1.2	1.3	1.1	1.1	1.0	1.0	1.3	1.2	1.0	1.1

	1986	1987	1988	1989	1990	1991	1992	1993	1994	1995
Afrique	8.1	7.0	9.7	10.3	9.8	12.4	9.8	11.5	10.1	10.9
Amériques	0.2	0.3	0.3	0.4	0.8	1.0	0.6	0.9	1.9	1.4
Amérique du Nord	0.2	0.2	0.2	0.2	0.0	0.2	0.1	0.1	0.2	0.6
ALAI			0.0			0.0	0.0		0.0	0.0
MCAC					0.0			0.0		
Caraïbes	0.0	0.1	0.1	0.1	0.7	0.8	0.5	0.7	1.4	0.7
Autre Amérique		0.0		0.1	0.0	0.0	0.0	0.0	0.3	0.0
Asie l'URSS exclus	2.3	2.8	2.6	2.7	3.2	6.4	5.0	4.5	6.6	6.4
Europe l'URSS exclus	89.3	89.9	87.4	86.5	86.2	80.2	84.4	81.8	80.4	80.9
UE	88.3	89.3	86.6	85.9	85.7	80.0	84.2	81.6	80.3	79.9
AELE	1.0	0.6	0.8	0.7	0.5	0.2	0.2	0.2	0.1	0.2
Europe de l'Est		0.0			0.0		0.0	0.0	0.0	
Autre de l'Europe										0.8
Ancienne URSS										
Océanie	0.1	0.0	0.0	0.0	0.1	0.0	0.1	1.2	0.7	0.2
France, Monac	71.9	71.4	75.6	75.7	83.1	76.2	76.4	69.4	74.3	71.4
Japan/Japon	2.3	2.7	2.5	2.7	3.1	6.1	4.8	3.8	6.2	6.1
Comoros/Comores	3.8	3.6	5.2	4.8	4.2	5.8	4.3	5.7	4.4	4.7
Madagascar	3.2	2.3	2.8	3.2	3.2	3.5	2.8	2.9	3.3	3.2
United Kingdom	14.3	0.8	1.1	4.4	1.1	1.5	1.5	6.2	1.9	2.0
Mauritius/Maurice	0.9	0.8	0.8	1.2	1.6	2.4	1.8	2.3	2.0	1.9
Portugal		15.3	8.1	3.6	0.2		4.3	4.5		0.0
Belgium–Luxembourg	0.1	0.1	0.1	0.1	0.1	0.0	0.1	0.1	0.4	5.0
Germany/Allemagne	1.8	1.5	1.0	1.1	1.1	1.2	0.8	0.7	1.2	0.6
Martinique	0.0	0.1	0.1	0.0	0.3	0.4	0.4	0.7	1.0	0.5

4. Special Imports C.I.F. by Commodities according to the S.I.T.C. (Rev. 2) in thousand U.S. Dollars
Importations Spéciales C.A.F. par Produits d'après la C.T.C.I. (Rév. 2) en milliers de Dollars E.U.

SITC CTCI	COMMODITY	1992 WEIGHT POIDS	1992 VALUE VALEUR	1993 WEIGHT POIDS	1993 VALUE VALEUR	1994 WEIGHT POIDS	1994 VALUE VALEUR	1995 WEIGHT POIDS	1995 VALUE VALEUR	PRODUIT
	ALL COMMODITIES		2393853		2075942		2358365		2711086	TOUS PRODUITS
0	FOOD AND LIVE ANIMALS		396432		369119		381152		452102	ALIMENTS,ANIMAUX VIVANTS
01	MEAT AND PREPARATIONS		85562		77558		79515		100686	VIANDES ET PREPARATIONS
011	MEAT FRESH,CHILLD,FROZEN	W 17076	61082	W 18526	56666	W 18607	57079	W 21230	73021	VIANDES FRAICHES,REF,CONGE
0111	BOVINE MEAT FRESH,FROZEN	W 3234	21533	W 3099	19723	W 2983	19938	W 3468	25171	VIANDES BOVIN FRAI,REF
01112	BOVINE MEAT BONELESS	W 3030	19191	W 3002	18625	W 2844	18150	W 3369	23856	VIANDES BOVIN DESOSSEES
0113	PIG MEAT FRESH,CHLD,FRZN	W 5744	17777	W 6756	15588	W 6453	14136	W 7500	20046	VIANDE DE PORC
0114	POULTRY FRESH CHLLD,FRZN	W 5994	14461	W 6402	14298	W 6651	15159	W 7426	18073	VOLAILLES MORTES
014	MEAT PREPD,PRSVD,NES ETC	W 4974	23208	W 4828	19812	W 5256	21071	W 5891	25840	CONSERVES DE VIANDES
0142	SAUSAGES INCLDING TINNED	W 1379	7491	W 1059	5821	W 1520	6944	W 1852	9138	SAUCISSES,SAUCISSONS
0149	OTH PREPARD,PRESRVD MEAT	W 3595	15717	W 3769	13988	W 3735	14119	W 4039	16702	AUTRES PREP DE VIANDES
02	DAIRY PRODCTS,BIRDS'EGGS		57314		53267		53227		59554	PRODUITS LAITIERS,OEUFS
022	MILK AND CREAM	W 17497	25620	W 17310	23093	W 13350	21132	W 10739	19930	LAIT ET CREME
0223	MILK AND CREAM FRESH	W 13026	11518	W 13250	10286	W 8997	7542	W 6958	6969	LAIT,CREME FRAIS
0224	MILK,CREAM PRESERVED ETC	W 4471	14102	W 4060	12807	W 4353	13589	W 3781	12960	LAIT,CREME CONS,CONC
02242	MILK DRY,1.5% FAT OR LES	W 3365	7867	W 2551	7367	W 3158	9010	W 2841	9270	LAIT POUDRE INF 1.5%
023	BUTTER	W 1936	9028	W 1715	7470	W 1888	8715	W 1937	10198	BEURRE
024	CHEESE AND CURD	W 3042	21967	W 3309	22423	W 3309	22753	W 3785	29066	FROMAGE ET CAILLEBOTTE
03	FISH AND PREPARATIONS		39263		34135		37635		43572	POISSONS ET PREPARATIONS
034	FISH,FRESH,CHILLED,FROZN	W 2438	8363	W 2472	7561	W 2870	9067	W 2634	9423	POISSON FRAIS, REFRIG,CONG
035	FISH SALTED,DRIED,SMOKED	W 1597	8491	W 1369	5785	W 1468	6260	W 1443	7192	POISSON SECHE,SALE,FUME
036	SHELL FISH FRESH,FROZEN	W 1864	13121	W 1909	10842	W 1824	12217	W 2099	15954	CRUSTACES,MOLLUSQUES
037	FISH ETC PREPD,PRSVD NES	W 2334	9288	W 2804	9947	W 2920	10092	W 2838	11002	POIS,CRUST,MOL PREPARES
0371	FISH PREPARD,PRESRVD NES	W 2228	8703	W 2710	9474	W 2826	9553	W 2735	10354	CONSERVES DE POISSONS
04	CEREALS AND PREPARATIONS		100439		92648		89214		107951	CEREALES ET PRODUITS
041	WHEAT ETC UNMILLED	W 35444	9627	W 16025	4834	W 18942	5219	W 20687	5823	FROMENT,EPEAUTRE
0412	OTHER WHEAT ETC UNMILLED	W 35074	9434	W 16025	4833	W 18942	5219	W 20599	5783	AUTRE FROMENT NON MOULU
042	RICE	W 67561	24240	W 54956	18482	W 63147	22944	W 73710	26745	RIZ
0421	RICE IN HUSK OR HUSKED	W 60162	20587	W 46387	14607	W 56236	19609	W 67057	23593	RIZ SANS AUTRE PREPARATION
04212	RICE HUSKED	W 60160	20584	W 46386	14604	W 56215	19601	W 67057	23593	RIZ CARGO
044	MAIZE UNMILLED	W 94120	22860	W 121947	28076	W 71814	13121	W 110114	24779	MAIS NON MOULU
048	CEREAL ETC PREPARATIONS	W 10889	36340	W 11586	33971	W 13078	38720	W 14056	42897	PREPTNS A BASE CEREALES
0484	BAKERY PRODUCTS	W 4986	23480	W 5820	23566	W 6532	25774	W 6890	27349	PRODUITS DE BOULANGERIE
04841	BREAD,BISCUIT,COM WAFERS	W 2863	13839	W 4020	16656	W 4484	18474	W 5393	21942	PAINS,BISCUITS DE MER
04842	PASTRY, CAKES ETC	W 2122	9642	W 1800	6910	W 2048	7300	W 1498	5407	PATISSERIE ETC.
0488	OTH CEREAL PREPS,MALT EX	W 1373	6164	W 1124	4393	W 1572	6193	W 2197	8571	EXTRAITS DE MALT
05	VEGETABLES AND FRUIT		48782		47071		51803		56650	LEGUMES ET FRUITS
054	VEG ETC FRSH,SMPLY PRSVD	W 15813	13715	W 15659	12949	W 20787	15562	W 19760	16948	LEGUMES FRAIS,CONG,SECS
056	VEGTBLES ETC PRSVD,PREPD	W 5244	9420	W 6308	9608	W 5643	9650	W 6450	11418	CONSERVES DE LEGUMES
0565	VEGTBLES PRSVD,PREPD NES	W 4962	8337	W 6150	9175	W 5455	9081	W 6209	10794	LEGUMES PREPARES CONSERVE
05659	OTH VEG PRESVD,PREPD NES	W 4809	8014	W 6006	8873	W 5332	8775	W 6075	10504	LEGUM PREPAP,CONSERV NDA
057	FRUIT,NUTS,FRESH,DRIED	W 10132	12239	W 12854	12408	W 12085	12718	W 11551	13663	FRUITS FRAIS OU SECS
058	FRUIT PRESERVED,PREPARED	W 6296	13408	W 7147	12105	W 8384	13874	W 7137	14620	CONSERVES DE FRUITS
06	SUGAR AND PREPS,HONEY		6633		8117		8147		10308	SUCRES ET PRODUITS
07	COFFEE,TEA,COCOA,SPICES		18094		14713		18067		21949	CAFE,THE,CACAO,EPICES
071	COFFEE AND SUBSTITUTES	W 2128	3717	W 1816	3039	W 2026	5517	W 2006	8166	CAFE ET SUCCEDANES
073	CHOCOLATE AND PRODUCTS	W 2150	12318	W 2333	9978	W 2524	10809	W 2461	11739	CHOCOLAT
081	*FEEDING STUFF FOR ANIML	W 43104	18484	W 54353	20501	W 50597	19803	W 63593	23717	NOURRITURE POUR ANIMAUX
0813	OILCAKE AND OTH RESIDUES	W 30599	7179	W 33268	8100	W 27494	6364	W 41814	8769	TOURTEAUX
08131	— OF SOYA BEANS	W 27226	6623	W 31125	7766	W 24561	5927	W 35589	7853	TOURTEAUX DE SOJA
0819	FOOD WASTE AND FEED NES	W 7352	9574	W 7962	9573	W 8594	10038	W 9665	12016	DECHETS,ALIMENTS NDA
08199	FODDER NES,INCL SWEETNED	W 7352	9574	W 7962	9573	W 8405	9980	W 9551	11978	PREPARATIONS FOURRAGERES
09	MISC EDIBLE PRODUCTS		20422		19353		21654		25196	PREP ALIMENTAIRES DIVERSES
098	EDIBLE PRODCTS,PREPS NES	W 6015	18832	W 6038	17559	W 6746	19470	W 7250	22563	PREP ALIMENTAIRES NDA
09809	MISC FOOD PREPRTIONS NES	W 2845	12049	W 3094	12170	W 3325	13284	W 3641	15945	PREP ALIMENTAIRES NDA
1	BEVERAGES AND TOBACCO		63268		55793		61368		74582	BOISSONS ET TABACS
11	BEVERAGES		45917		40129		44567		55257	BOISSONS
111	NON–ALCOHL BEVERAGES NES	W 16024	14639	W 18167	15025	W 21984	17055	W 23504	20456	BOISSONS NON ALCOOLIQUES
11102	FLAVORED WATERS NON–ALCO	W 10243	10486	W 10719	10439	W 12823	11741	W 15098	14862	LIMONADES,EAUX GAZEUSES
112	ALCOHOLIC BEVERAGES	W 15902	31278	W 12031	25104	W 13778	27512	W 15504	34801	BOISSONS ALCOOLIQUES
1121	WINE OF FRESH GRAPES ETC	W 11953	20881	W 8671	16317	W 10517	18221	W 12027	24782	VINS DE RAISINS FRAIS
11212	WINE OF FRESH GRAPES	W 11666	20195	W 8532	15904	W 10360	17732	W 11850	24203	VINS DE MOUTS DE RAISINS
1124	DISTILLED ALCOHOLIC BEVS	W 1919	7322	W 1379	5985	W 1336	6628	W 1298	6960	ALCOOLS,EAUX–DE–VIE
12	TOBACCO AND MANUFACTURES		17350		15664		16801		19325	TABACS BRUTS FABRIQUES
122	TOBACCO,MANUFACTURED	W 867	17350	W 761	15664	W 851	16801	W 824	19325	TABACS FABRIQUES
1222	CIGARETTES	W 234	7475	W 209	6631	W 172	5180	W 175	6763	CIGARETTES
1223	OTH MANUFACTURED TOBACCO	W 630	9658	W 539	8749	W 676	11263	W 644	12169	TABACS FUMER,CHIQUER,PRISER
2	CRUDE MATERLS,EXCL FUELS		37234		33905		38793		48882	MAT BRUTES NON COMESTIBLES
24	CORK AND WOOD		26509		23281		26796		36251	LIEGE ET BOIS
248	WOOD SHAPED,SLEEPERS	W 48512	26266	W 39540	22891	W 39182	25873	W 47986	35650	BOIS SIMPLEMENT TRAVAILLES
2482	LUMBER SHAPED CONIFER	W 12089	6718	W 10749	6237	W 11875	7280	W 15834	10579	CONIFERES SCIES,RABOTES
24821	LUMBER SAWN ETC CONIFER	W 11723	5930	W 10008	4991	W 10669	5596	W 14416	8331	CONIFERES SCIES LONGITUD
2483	LUMBER SHAPED NON–CONIFR	W 36423	19548	W 28791	16653	W 27307	18593	W 32152	25071	NON CONIFERES SCIES,RABOTES
24831	LUMBER SAWN ETC NON–CON	W 35718	18415	W 28527	16088	W 27043	18016	W 31533	23796	SCIES LONGITUDINALEMENT
3	MINERAL FUELS ETC		121325		106954		116764		128237	COMBUSTIBLES MINERAUX LUB
33	PETROLEUM AND PRODUCTS		106090		91506		100368		106122	PETROLE ET DERIVES
334	PETROLEUM PRODUCTS,REFIN	W 423599	102232	W 381837	88616	W 430208	96403	W 464307	102693	PRODUITS RAFFINES
3341	GASOLINE,OTH LIGHT OILS	W 423335	101667	W 381666	88158			W 126158	29406	ESSENCES POUR MOTEURS
33411	MOTOR,AVIATION SPIRIT							W 125567	28973	ESSENCES MOTEURS D'AVIONS
33419	OTH LIGHT PETROLEUM OILS	W 423335	101667	W 381666	88158			W 591	433	AUTRES HUILES LEGERES
3342	KEROSENE,OTH MEDIUM OILS							W 104607	22776	PETR LAMPANTS,AUT HUIL
33421	KEROSENE INCL JET FUEL							W 104607	22776	PETROLES LAMPANTS
3343	GAS OILS							W 170271	34964	GAS OILS
341	*GAS,NATURAL AND MANUFCT	W 26672	12489	W 22815	10291	W 27328	11759	W 29316	15005	GAZ NATUREL,GAZ MANUFACT
3413	PETROLM GASES,LIQUEFIED	W 26672	12489	W 22815	10291	W 27328	11759	W 29316	15004	GAZ DE PETROLE LIQUEFIE
34131	LIQUEFIED PROPANE,BUTANE	W 26672	12489	W 22815	10291	W 27328	11759	W 29315	15003	PROPANE,BUTANE LIQUEFIES
4	ANIMAL,VEGETABLE OIL,FAT		10974		8109		10556		12037	HUILES,GRAISSES ANIM,VEG
42	FIXED VEGETABLE OIL,FAT		10382		7975		10348		11756	HUILES VEGETALES FIXES
423	FIXED VEG OILS,SOFT	W 10711	9550	W 9039	7397	W 10053	9549	W 10505	11141	HUILES VEGET DOUCES FIXES
4236	SUNFLOWER SEED OIL	W 9341	8191	W 8518	6796	W 9004	8280	W 10015	10333	HUILE DE TOURNESOL
5	CHEMCLS,RELATED PROD NES		224374		213536		240341		282994	PRODUITS CHIMIQUES
53	DYES,TANNING,COLOUR PROD		14896		14586		16637		19602	PROD TEINTURE,COLORANTS
533	PIGMENTS,PAINTS,ETC	W 12304	14047	W 15991	14042	W 16885	16037	W 18071	19105	PIGMENTS,PEINTURES,VERNIS
5335	GLAZES,DRIERS,PUTTY ETC	W 9955	6209	W 13357	7124	W 14251	8145	W 15239	9654	PREPTNS COLOR UTILISES CERAM
53354	PUTTY,OTHER FILLINGS ETC	W 9889	5668	W 13300	6734	W 14195	7722	W 15166	9118	MASTICS ENDUITS
541	*MEDICINAL,PHARM PRODUCT	K 3746466	99468	K 3601351	98976	K 3900837	116405	K 4165235	138630	PROD MEDICINAUX PHARMACEUT
5416	GLYCOSIDES,GLANDS,SERA	K 12870	2236	K 13800	3515	K 21362	9607	K 24318	10676	HETEROSIDES
54164	ANTISERA,MICROB VACCINES	K 10454	2128	K 11182	3415	K 18908	9487	K 20506	10524	SERUMS,VACCINS
5417	MEDICAMENTS	K 3523691	93312	K 3400496	92191	K 3669056	102870	K 3943359	124025	MEDICAMENTS
54172	— CONTAINING HORMONES	K 1099364	38723	K 898061	37368	K 952485	41471	K 976576	45234	MED CONTENANT HORMONES
54179	— CONTNG OTH SUBSTANCES	K 2415064	53716	K 2479586	54282	K 2701788	60917	K 2962132	78556	MED CONT AUT SUBSTANCES

4. Special Imports C.I.F. by Commodities according to the S.I.T.C. (Rev. 2) in thousand U.S. Dollars
Importations Spéciales C.A.F. par Produits d'après la C.T.C.I. (Rév. 2) en milliers de Dollars E.U.

SITC CTCI	COMMODITY	1992 WEIGHT POIDS	1992 VALUE VALEUR	1993 WEIGHT POIDS	1993 VALUE VALEUR	1994 WEIGHT POIDS	1994 VALUE VALEUR	1995 WEIGHT POIDS	1995 VALUE VALEUR	PRODUIT
55	PERFUME,CLEANING ETC PRD		52660		49904		49317		56967	PROD POUR PARFUM,TOILETTE
553	PERFUMERY,COSMETICS,ETC	W 2392	24289	W 3063	23087	W 2765	23279	W 2920	27061	PRODUITS DE PARFUMERIE
554	SOAP,CLEANSING ETC PREPS	W 13695	26487	W 15496	25214	W 15706	24074	W 16016	27834	SAVONS,PRODUITS DETERSIFS
5542	WASHING PREPARATIONS ETC	W 10078	19154	W 12366	19432	W 12672	18610	W 13056	21649	PROD ORG TENSIO–ACT NDA
562	*FERTILIZERS,MANUFACTURE	W 33008	9339	W 32836	8543	W 31730	8425	W 32625	10224	ENGRAIS MANUFACTURES
5629	FERTILIZERS NES	W 28007	8281	W 24308	6864	W 22240	6455	W 21560	7424	ENGRAIS NDA
56291	NIT–PHOS–POT FERTLZR NES	W 25472	7233	W 22796	6029	W 20648	5710	W 14129	4291	ENGRAIS CONT N P K
58	PLASTIC MATERIALS ETC		18307		14159		17216		20466	MAT PLAST ARTIFICIELLES
583	POLYMERIZATION ETC PRODS	W 9064	15849	W 7682	12521	W 9528	15249	W 8486	17786	PROD POLYMERISATION
59	CHEMICAL MATERIALS NES		22819		21429		25446		29258	MAT PROD CHIMIQUES NDA
591	PESTICIDES,DISINFECTANTS	W 1366	8599	W 1416	8786	W 1708	10956	W 1723	12252	DESINF,INSECT,FONG,HERB
598	MISCEL CHEM PRODUCTS NES	W 3160	11953	W 2748	10735	W 3223	12395	W 3600	14624	PROD DIV INDUST CHIM NDA
5989	CHEM PRODUCTS,PREPS NES	W 3132	11788	W 2707	10589	W 3201	12162	W 3558	14349	PROD PREP CHIMIQUES NDA
59899	OTH CHEM PRODS,PREPS,NES	W 2370	10033	W 2101	9343	W 2535	10326	W 2899	12228	AUT PRODUITS CHIMIQUES NDA
6	BASIC MANUFACTURES		370996		295420		347616		414632	ART MANUFACTURES
62	RUBBER MANUFACTURES NES		21978		18757		22335		23155	CAOUTCHOUC MANUFACTURE
625	RUBBER TYRES, TUBES ETC	W 3320	17565	W 2978	15488	W 3561	18416	W 3435	18751	PNEUS CAOUTCHOUC VULCANISE
6251	TYRES NEW FOR MOTOR CARS	W 1636	8440	W 1646	8842	W 2030	10829	W 1894	10591	PNEUS POUR VOITURES
63	WOOD,CORK MANUFACTRS NES		29804		24011		26664		27430	OUVRAGES LIEGE ET BOIS
634	VENEERS,PLYWOOD,ETC	W 12423	10011	W 10042	9350	W 10373	10758	W 11665	9528	PLACAGES,CONTRE–PLAQUES
6342	PLYWOOD OF WOOD SHEETS	W 10863	8587	W 8994	8469	W 9056	9653	W 10429	8190	BOIS CONTRE–PLAQUES
635	WOOD MANUFACTURES NES	W 6996	19687	W 5907	14561	W 6312	15819	W 6169	17815	ART MANUF EN BOIS NDA
6353	BUILDERS WOODWRK,PREFABS	W 6133	16596	W 4713	11207	W 5250	12904	W 5156	14341	OUVRAGES DE MENUISERIE
64	PAPER,PAPERBOARD AND MFR		63730		58961		60602		76733	PAPIERS,CARTONS & OUVRAGES
641	PAPER AND PAPERBOARD	W 15433	21377	W 14709	16497	W 17111	19763	W 20296	28996	PAPIERS ET CARTONS
642	PAPER,ETC,PRECUT,ARTS OF	W 10085	42353	W 10985	42464	W 10411	40839	W 11312	47738	PAP,CARTONS DECOUPES
6421	PAPER ETC CONTAINERS	W 2505	8494	W 3136	10098	W 2804	8519	W 2825	7638	BOITES,SACS EMBALLAGES
6423	EXERCISE BOOKS ETC	W 1932	9054	W 2263	9386	W 1996	8523	W 2755	12460	REGISTRES,CAHIERS,CARNETS
6428	PAPER ETC ARTICLES NES	W 4154	20422	W 4135	19314	W 4344	20374	W 4354	23209	OUVRAGES EN PATE A PAPIER
64285	PAPER ETC DIAPERS ETC	W 2973	15372	W 2961	14397	W 3000	15782	W 2932	16863	SERVIETTES HYGIENIQUES
65	TEXTILE YARN,FABRICS,ETC		26178		23297		25149		27978	FILS,TISSUS,ARTICLES TEXTILE
658	TEXTILE ARTICLES NES	W 1302	10912	W 1514	10331	W 1456	10830	W 1614	13434	ART FACONNES MAT TEXTILES
6584	LINENS ETC	W 665	6595	W 826	6379	W 891	7394	W 874	8401	LINGE DE MAISON
66	NONMETAL MINERAL MFS NES		75325		57134		67702		84104	ART MIN NON METALLIQUES
661	LIME,CEMENT,BLDG PRODS	W 368674	30799	W 256332	22062	W 312163	27633	W 400073	35526	CHAUX,CIMENTS MAT CONSTR
6612	CEMENT	W 362864	26416	W 250451	17800	W 304733	22106	W 392908	29672	CIMENTS HYDRAULIQUES
662	CLAY,REFRACTORY BLDG PRD	W 28367	18622	W 26064	13541	W 32228	16973	W 33235	20242	MAT CONST REFRACTAIRES
6624	BRICKS ETC NONREFRACTORY	W 27724	17989	W 25643	13199	W 31028	16329	W 32966	20049	BRIQUES ETC CERAM NON REFR
66245	GLAZED CERAMIC SETTS ETC	W 26101	16923	W 24861	12755	W 29891	15436	W 32055	19413	AUT CARREAUX CERAMIQUE
663	MINERAL MANUFCTURES NES	W 5131	5602	W 5941	5773	W 7130	6322	W 9029	8447	ART MIN MANUF NDA
665	GLASSWARE	W 11848	11202	W 9812	9126	W 10038	9239	W 11331	9988	OUVRAGES EN VERRE
67	IRON AND STEEL		55608		35793		49142		68060	FER ET ACIER
673	IRON,STEEL SHAPES ETC	W 34463	16247	W 14359	6976	W 29832	13685	W 31764	16855	BARRES,PROFIL FER,ACIER
6732	IRON,STEEL BARS ETC	W 22601	8980	W 6257	2522	W 13902	5356	W 14665	6816	BARRES FER,ACIER
67326	IRN,OTH STL BARS HOTROLD	W 21496	8418	W 5871	2312	W 13634	5197	W 14465	6626	BARRES PLEINES FER,ACIER
674	IRN,STL UNIV,PLATE,SHEET	W 26614	25085	W 21244	17663	W 25414	21848	W 31124	29196	LARGES PLATS,TOLES
6749	OTH IRN,STL PLATES,SHEET	W 22583	22945	W 19098	16280	W 24000	20769	W 28534	27312	AUTRES TOLES FER,ACIER
67491	— OF IRON OR SIMPLE STL	W 22528	22814	W 19097	16268	W 23968	20691	W 28528	27299	AUT TOLES AUTRES ACIER FIN
678	IRON,STL TUBES,PIPES,ETC	W 9456	10816	W 8011	8439	W 8333	11047	W 13782	17306	TUBES,TUYAUX EN FONTE,FER
6783	IRON,STL TUBES,PIPES NES	W 6701	6254	W 5080	4135	W 4835	4754	W 10943	12274	AUT TUBES,TUYAUX FER,ACIER
68	NON–FERROUS METALS		8162		7934		11622		19052	METAUX NON FERREUX
684	ALUMINIUM	W 671	4906	W 847	5558	W 1477	8853	W 2579	15580	ALUMINIUM
6842	ALUMINIUM,ALLOYS WORKED	W 640	4841	W 847	5558	W 1477	8853	W 2579	15580	ALUMINIUM,ALLIAGES OUVRE
69	METAL MANUFACTURES NES		89855		69196		83946		87537	ART MANUFACT EN METAL NDA
691	STRUCTURES AND PARTS NES	W 7120	19913	W 5449	14291	W 7328	18865	W 4331	14798	CONSTRUCT FER,ACIER,ALU
6911	STRUCTURES,PARTS IRN,STL	W 6364	12960	W 4843	9542	W 6692	14379	W 3664	9385	CONSTRUCT FER,ACIER,FONTE
692	METAL TANKS,BOXES,ETC	W 3640	11262	W 1943	5392	W 1851	5824	W 1732	4907	RECIPIENTS METALLIQUES
6924	MTL TRANSPORT BOXES ETC	W 2865	8858	W 1415	4117	W 1446	4221	W 1516	4085	FUTS,TAMBOURS,BIDONS
693	WIRE PRODUCTS NON ELECTR	W 8639	7221	W 6627	5304	W 7970	6165	W 6028	6164	OUVRAGES FILS METALLIQUES
695	TOOLS	W 738	7223	W 760	6135	W 769	6709	W 928	8204	OUTILS A MAIN
697	BASE MTL HOUSEHOLD EQUIP	W 1873	12037	W 1955	11391	W 2472	13493	W 2652	16154	ART MENAGE MET COMMUNS
6974	BASE MTL DMSTC ARTIC NES	W 651	5381	W 730	5051	W 1021	6551	W 1341	8751	ARTICLES NDA FONTE,FER,ETC
699	BASE METAL MFRS NES	W 4083	22191	W 3532	17943	W 4930	23017	W 4400	25275	ART MANUFACTURES MET NDA
6991	LOCKSMITHS WARES,ETC	W 838	6827	W 799	6119	W 998	7773	W 1041	9227	ARTICLES DE SERRURERIE
6997	IRON,STEEL ARTICLES NES	W 2079	8358	W 1691	6406	W 2959	9857	W 2267	9350	OUV FONTE,FER,ACIER NDA
69979	IRN,STL MANUFACTURES NES	W 2078	8351	W 1690	6403	W 2958	9851	W 2266	9339	AUT OUVRAGES EN FER NDA
7	MACHINES,TRANSPORT EQUIP		719519		602239		742294		807206	MACHINES MATERIEL TRANSPORT
71	POWER GENERATING EQUIPMT		23740		12850		47829		14806	MACHINES GENERATRICES
711	STEAM BOILERS & AUX PLNT	W 559	5390	W 410	2394	W 3548	26925	W 153	2073	GENERATEURS VAPEUR EAU ETC
7119	PTS NES OF APP OF 711	W 456	4389	W 392	2207	W 3416	25993	W 122	1675	PART,PIECES POUR 711
71191	PTS NES OF BOILERS	W 456	4389	W 392	2199	W 3416	25993	W 122	1674	PART,PIECES POUR 711.1
713	INTRNL COMBUS PSTN ENGIN	W 269	8917	W 259	5438	W 246	6326	W 235	6824	MOTEURS EXPL COMB INT, PIECE
7139	PISTON ENGINE PARTS NES	W 194	7471	W 165	3785	W 125	4588	W 132	5051	PIECES POUR 713.2,3,8
716	ROTATING ELECTRIC PLANT	W 1025	8206	W 268	3776	W 514	6808	W 422	5174	APP ELECTR ROTATIFS,PIECES
72	MACHS FOR SPCL INDUSTRYS		65566		37289		48458		51696	MAC SPECIALES POUR INDUST
723	CIVIL ENGNEERG EQUIP ETC	W 2927	18432	W 817	6437	W 1497	10515	W 2392	17934	APPAREILS DE GENIE CIVIL
7234	CONST,MINING MACHNRY NES	W 2269	14031	W 650	3998	W 1232	7582	W 2134	14665	MACH POUR LA CONST, MINES
72342	SLFPRP SHOVELS,EXCAVATRS	W 1562	9196	W 463	2746	W 925	5083	W 1839	11422	PELLES MECANIQUES
727	FOOD MACHRY NON–DOMESTIC	W 951	9749	W 520	6259	W 507	5817	W 431	5498	MACH INDUSTRIES ALIMENT
7272	OTH FOOD PROC MCHY,PARTS	W 934	9483	W 504	5967	W 472	5404	W 415	5074	AUT MACH IND ALIMENTAIRE
72722	INDUS FOOD PROC MACH NES	W 934	9483	W 504	5950	W 472	5404	W 415	5074	MACHINES BOULANGERIE
728	OTH MACHY FOR SPCL INDUS	W 2158	20269	W 1027	10949	W 1019	15498	W 1174	13648	AUT MACH IND PARTICULIERES
7283	OTHR MINERAL WORKG MACHY	W 1100	7751	W 521	4090	W 451	3521	W 538	4246	MACH TRIER,CRIBLER,BROYER
7284	MACHY FOR SPCL INDUS NES	W 424	9274	W 313	5069	W 433	10639	W 423	7082	MACH SPEC IND PARTICUL.
74	GENRL INDUSTRL MACHY NES		92296		85274		85514		99161	MACH APP INDUSTRIE
741	HEATING,COOLING EQUIPMNT	W 2601	28364	W 2012	21219	W 1680	19253	W 1694	20617	MACH CHAUFFAGE,PIECES
7414	NONDOM REFRIG EQUIPT,PTS	W 1142	13536	W 1184	10677	W 804	8245	W 813	8854	MAT PRODUCTION DU FROID
74141	REFRIG EQUIP NONDOMESTIC	W 801	9457	W 877	7869	W 663	6420	W 585	6435	REFIG INDUSTRIELS
7415	AIR–CONDITIONING MACHNRY	W 914	7440	W 361	4322	W 320	3969	W 445	5237	GROUPES CONDITION AIR
743	PUMPS NES,CENTRFUGES ETC	W 732	9965	W 668	8146	W 734	8651	W 826	10978	POMPES COMPRES,VENT ETC
744	MECHANICAL HANDLING EQU	W 3111	23207	W 3847	26165	W 2918	20167	W 3298	27885	EQUIP MANUTENTION PIECES
7442	LIFTING,LOADING MACH NES	W 1827	11808	W 3186	19550	W 2007	12701	W 2074	16573	APP LEVAGE,MANUTENTION
74422	SHIP DERRICKS,CRANES ETC	W 731	3017	W 2253	12712	W 395	1541	W 1220	9011	GRUES,PONTS ROULANTS
74428	OTH HANDLING ETC MCH NES	W 696	5278	W 518	3466	W 1295	7760	W 610	5351	AUT APP LEVAGE ETC
745	NONELEC MACHY,TOOLS NES	W 728	14392	W 782	13981	W 780	12919	W 908	17204	AUT MACH NON ELEC,PIECES
7452	OTH NONELEC MCHS,PTS NES	W 649	12378	W 732	12529	W 708	10946	W 811	14957	AUT MACH NON ELEC,PIECES
749	NONELEC MACH PTS,ACC NES	W 1475	12484	W 1160	12029	W 2533	17722	W 2015	17128	PIECES MACH NON ELEC NDA
7492	COCKS,VALVES ETC NES	W 556	7281	W 655	7584	W 975	9952	W 591	8246	ART ROB,SIM POUR TUYAUX
75	OFFICE MACHNES,ADP EQUIP		58302		43806		48249		59856	MACH BUREAU TRAIT AUTOM
751	OFFICE MACHINES	W 186	9130	W 152	6374	W 178	7547	W 181	9400	MACH,APPAREILS DE BUREAU
752	AUTOMTIC DATA PROC EQUIP	W 408	38818	W 396	28418	W 416	31007	W 504	39203	MACH TRAIT INFORMATION

4. Special Imports C.I.F. by Commodities according to the S.I.T.C. (Rev. 2) in thousand U.S. Dollars
Importations Spéciales C.A.F. par Produits d'après la C.T.C.I. (Rév. 2) en milliers de Dollars E.U.

SITC CTCI	COMMODITY	1992		1993		1994		1995		PRODUIT
		WEIGHT POIDS	VALUE VALEUR	WEIGHT POIDS	VALUE VALEUR	WEIGHT POIDS	VALUE VALEUR	WEIGHT POIDS	VALUE VALEUR	
7523	DIGITL CENTRL PROCESSORS	W 120	12568	W 81	6950	W 108	9395	W 131	12178	UNITES CENTRALES
7525	ADP PERIPHERAL UNITS	W 99	7103	W 75	4927	W 120	7370	W 167	9766	UNITES PERIPHERIQUES
7528	OFF-LINE DATA PROC EQUIP	W 91	11075	W 135	8049	W 79	5481	W 88	7405	MACH AUXIL TRAIT INFORM
759	OFFICE,ADP MCH PTS,ACCES	W 115	10353	W 117	9015	W 109	9694	W 123	11253	PIECES DU 751 ET 752
7599	ACCTG,ETC,ADP MCH PTS,AC	W 77	8633	W 82	7489	W 72	7925	W 82	9125	PIECES DU 751 ET 752
76	TELECOMM,SOUND EQUIPMENT		50845		48601		58819		65594	EQUIPMENT DE TELECOM
761	TELEVISION RECEIVERS	W 574	9528	W 586	8567	W 703	10180	W 635	10688	RECEPTEURS DE TELEVISION
7611	COLOUR TV RECEIVERS	W 573	9488	W 586	8545	W 696	10089	W 632	10631	RECEPTEURS COULEUR
762	RADIO BROADCAST RECEIVRS	W 362	8057	W 338	6872	W 445	7958	W 447	10011	RECEPTEURS RADIODIFFUSION
764	TELECOM EQPT,PTS,ACC NES	W 555	26206	W 817	28000	W 630	34440	W 729	37769	EQUIP TELECOM,PIECES
7641	LINE TELEPHONE,ETC EQUIP	W 152	8951	W 414	9303	W 266	18221	W 231	16534	APP TELEPHON PAR FIL
7643	TV,RADIO TRANSMITTRS ETC	W 98	8066	W 123	11088	W 89	9520	W 90	10815	APP EMET TELE RADIO
77	ELECTRIC MACHNRY NES ETC		90173		81190		103107		101312	MACH APP ELECT NDA
772	SWITCHGEAR ETC,PARTS NES	W 1055	21319	W 1046	19041	W 1288	25207	W 1291	24430	APP COUPURE,SECT ETC
7721	SWITCHGEAR ETC	W 1053	21256	W 1043	18958	W 1285	25116	W 1288	24354	APP COUPURE,SECTIONMNT
773	ELECTR DISTRIBUTNG EQUIP	W 3068	12584	W 3344	12545	W 4258	18994	W 3531	16465	EQUIPMT DISTRIBUTION ELECT
7731	INSULATED WIRE,CABLE ETC	W 3035	12415	W 3333	12425	W 4224	18640	W 3507	16150	FILS,CABLES ISOLES ELECT
775	HOUSEHOLD TYPE EQUIP NES	W 4272	26390	W 4253	23664	W 4927	26706	W 5211	30474	MACH,APP USAGE DOMESTQUE
7752	DOM REFRIGERATRS,FREEZRS	W 1656	9074	W 1686	8599	W 2051	10088	W 1758	9721	REFRIG,CONGEL MENAGER
77521	DOMESTIC REFRIGERATORS	W 1336	7062	W 1289	6489	W 1541	7542	W 1341	7244	REFRIGERATEURS
7758	ELECTRO-THERMIC APPL NES	W 899	7617	W 779	6142	W 997	7317	W 1114	9115	APP ELECTROTHERMIQ NDA
778	ELECTRICAL MACHINERY NES	W 1695	18394	W 1969	17677	W 2062	20203	W 2129	21413	AUTRES MACH ELECT NDA
78	ROAD VEHICLES		325380		248936		292439		379024	VEHICULES ROUTIERS
781	PASS MOTOR VEH EXC BUSES	W 13221	143041	W 12540	130480	W 14825	158241	W 17388	209125	AUTO TRANSPORT PERSONNES
782	LORRIES,SPCL MTR VEH NES	W 9688	100202	W 6128	57767	W 6856	66175	W 7635	85598	VEHICULES SPECIAUX,MARCH
7821	LORRIES,TRUCKS	W 8743	90312	W 5585	54102	W 6566	63586	W 7280	81505	VEHICULES TRANSP MARCHAND
7822	SPECIAL MOTOR VEHCLS NES	W 945	9890	W 543	3665	W 289	2589	W 355	4092	VEHICULES USAGES SPECIAUX
783	ROAD MOTOR VEHICLES NES	W 972	18339	W 427	6836	W 454	6584	W 721	11463	VEHICULES ROUTIERS NDA
7831	BUSES	W 751	16434	W 300	5924	W 340	5590	W 344	7524	VOITURES TRANSPORT COMMUN
784	MOTOR VEH PRTS,ACCES NES	W 2567	43836	W 2647	38392	W 2627	41984	W 2889	49504	PIECES 722,781,782,783
7849	OTHER MOTOR VEHCL PARTS	W 2465	42631	W 2607	37967	W 2587	41428	W 2841	49037	PIECES 722,781,782,783
785	CYCLES,ETC MOTRZD OR NOT	W 991	13333	W 881	12376	W 1119	15210	W 1164	16873	MOTOCYCLES SCOOTERS
7851	MOTORCYCLES ETC	W 425	7915	W 359	7519	W 411	8584	W 337	8614	MOTO VELO MOTEUR AUXIL
79	OTHR TRANSPORT EQUIPMENT		6305		40630		53176		30861	AUTRE MATERIEL TRANSPORT
792	AIRCRAFT ETC	W 11	975	W 50	13244	W 100	49711	W 41	9928	APP NAVIGATION AERIENNE
7924	AIRCRFT NES OVER 15000KG					W 60	30717			AERODYNES PLUS 15000 KG
7929	AIRCRAFT PARTS NES	W 4	713	W 35	12887	W 37	18654	W 17	8160	PIECES DU 792
793	SHIPS AND BOATS ETC	W 187	5023	W 6023	27368	W 232	3442	W 960	20924	NAVIRES BATEAUX,ETC
7932	SHIPS AND BOATS NES	W 147	4504	W 6004	27119	W 138	2428	W 949	20795	NAVIRES ET BATEAUX
79324	FISHING VESSELS ETC	W 88	3516	W 5897	24444	W 11	126	W 870	19180	BATEAUX DE PECHE
8	MISC MANUFACTURED GOODS		391978		347148		368871		438012	ART MANUFACTURES DIVERS
812	*PLUMBG,HEATNG,LGHTNG EQ	W 1787	11616	W 1535	9425	W 1706	10568	W 2630	16216	APPAR SANITAIRES CHAUFFAGE
8124	LIGHTING EQUIPMENT NES	W 646	7357	W 589	5800	W 633	6575	W 836	8997	APPAREILS ECLAIRAGE ETC
821	*FURNITURE,PARTS THEREOF	W 15216	64724	W 15677	52707	W 17516	59464	W 19802	72351	MEUBLES ET PIECES
8211	CHAIRS,SEATS AND PARTS	W 3279	18296	W 3392	15837	W 3690	17495	W 4639	20993	SIEGES ET PIECES
82111	CHAIRS AND OTHER SEATS	W 3206	17998	W 3362	15730	W 3643	17306	W 4588	20718	SIEGES
8219	FURNITURE AND PARTS NES	W 11266	41276	W 11578	31491	W 12986	36525	W 14031	43781	AUTRES MEUBLES ET PIECES
82191	METAL FURNITURE NES	W 1710	11532	W 1277	6070	W 1158	5994	W 1395	6552	MEUBLES NDA EN METAL
82192	WOOD FURNITURE NES	W 8750	26246	W 9674	23029	W 11014	27254	W 11816	33648	MEUBLES NDA EN BOIS
84	CLOTHING AND ACCESSORIES		101607		86925		92540		98250	VETEMENTS
842	MENS OUTERWEAR NOT KNIT	W 685	18039	W 670	15023	W 752	15429	W 711	15438	VET DESSUS POUR HOMMES
8423	— TROUSERS,BREECHES ETC	W 484	11901	W 407	8773	W 509	9820	W 525	10389	PANTALONS HOMMES MAT TEX
843	WOMENS OUTERWEAR NONKNIT	W 1004	41819	W 826	31798		35306	W 988	38558	VET DESSUS FEMMES MAT TEX
8439	— OTHER OUTER GARMENTS	W 816	33974	W 642	25679	W 793	28587	W 781	30504	AUT VET DES FEM MAT TEXT
844	UNDER GARMENTS NOT KNIT	W 253	8310	W 274	7348	W 257	6997	W 201	6314	VETEMENT DESSOUS MAT TEX
8441	— MENS SHIRTS	W 209	7148	W 224	6575	W 232	6451	W 166	5437	CHEMISES HOMMES MAT TEXT
845	OUTERWEAR KNIT NONELASTC	W 451	12696	W 505	13479	W 585	12935	W 579	14883	VET DESSOUS,ACCES BONNET
8459	— OTHER,CLTHG ACCESRYS	W 331	9599	W 387	10982	W 405	9651	W 412	11366	AUT VET DESSUS DE BONNE
846	UNDER GARMENTS KNITTED	W 563	15650	W 574	15289	W 756	17518	W 763	18359	SOUS VETS DE BONNETERIE
8462	— OF COTTON NON ELASTIC	W 479	11374	W 488	10708	W 659	13095	W 624	12644	SOUS-VET BONNET COTON
84629	—— OTHER	W 479	11374	W 488	10708	W 659	13095	W 624	12644	AUT SOUS-VET BONNET COTON
851	*FOOTWEAR	W 1679	32905	W 1661	26600	W 1914	29269	W 2015	35989	CHAUSSURES
85101	FOOTWEAR RUBBER,PLASTIC	W 604	6421	W 587	5424	W 722	6620	W 807	9094	CHAUS SEMELLES CAOUTCH
85102	FOOTWEAR LEATHER	W 1039	25820	W 1048	20674	W 1167	22027	W 1172	25821	CHAUS SEMELLES EN CUIR
87	PRECISION INSTRUMNTS NES		29748		28185		29047		34149	INSTRUM,APPAR SCIENT NDA
872	MEDICAL INSTRUMENTS NES	W 292	15479	W 358	15912	W 365	15629	W 430	20386	INSTR,APP MEDIC-CHIR NDA
87202	OTH MEDICAL INSTRUMENTS	W 262	14028	W 339	15145	W 347	14847	W 405	19517	INSTRUM,APP MEDECINE
874	MEASURNG,CONTROLNG INSTR	W 213	11602	W 222	9181	W 196	10237	W 261	10492	INSTRUMENTS DE MESURE
88	PHOTO EQU,OPTICL GDS ETC		13367		11968		12844		14738	APP,FOURN PHOTO,OP,MONTR
89	MISC MANUFCTRD GOODS NES		131024		125729		129371		159575	ART MANUFACTURES DIVERS
892	PRINTED MATTER	W 2119	28618	W 2853	31384	W 2908	34823	W 3219	42576	IMPRIMES
8921	PRINTED BOOKS,GLOBES,ETC	W 835	15317	W 1290	16249	W 1374	18706	W 1419	20861	LIVRES,BROCHURES,CARTES
89211	PRINTED BOOKS,PAMPHLETS	W 822	15020	W 1259	15780	W 1362	18436	W 1403	20558	LIVRES,BROCHURES
8922	NEWSPAPERS,PERIODICALS	W 389	5193	W 553	8017	W 663	9276	W 814	13656	JOURNAUX ET PERIODIQUES
8928	PRINTED MATTER NES	W 869	7703	W 987	6788	W 839	6509	W 957	7738	IMPRIMES NDA
893	ARTICLES OF PLASTIC NES		39680		33119		34569		40923	OUVRAGES EN MAT DIVIS 58
8931	PLSTC PACKG CONTNRS,LIDS	W 2300	9977	W 1959	7828	W 2546	8852	W 3155	13535	ART TRANSP EMBALLAGE ETC
8939	MISC PLASTIC ARTICLES	W 6388	28724	W 6644	24679	W 5909	24494	W 5315	26230	ART DIVERS EN MAT DIV 58
89399	OTHR PLASTC ARTICLES NES	W 4151	23552	W 4834	21381	W 4174	21076	W 3955	22813	AUT OUV MAT DIV 58
894	TOYS,SPORTING GOODS,ETC	W 1903	22282	W 2103	22742		23722	W 3186	30196	VOITURES ENFANTS,JOUETS
8942	TOYS,INDOOR GAMES ETC	W 1243	15995	W 1581	17059		16958	W 2101	20874	JOUETS,JEUX ETC
89423	TOYS NES	W 744	9159	W 907	9499	W 920	9424	W 1156	12971	JOUETS,MODELES REDUITS
8947	OTH SPORT GDS,FAIR AMUSM	W 606	5580	W 479	4813	W 671	5864	W 1016	8358	AUT ART DE SPORT
898	MUSICAL INSTRUMENTS,PTS	W 424	16187	W 400	17138	W 391	17002	W 532	21224	INSTRUMENTS DE MUSIQUE
8983	SOUND RECRDNG TAPE,DISCS	W 300	14404	W 329	15497	W 322	15540	W 424	19098	SUPPORTS SON POUR 763
89832	RECORDED DISCS,TAPES ETC	W 162	11969	W 190	13509	W 191	13729	W 237	16700	DISQUES,PHONO,BANDES
899	OTHER MANUFACTURED GOODS		12027		11356		9945		12015	AUT ART MANUF DIVERS NDA
9	GOODS NOT CLASSD BY KIND		57752		43719		50611		52401	ART TRANSACT NON CLASSES
911	*MAIL NOT CLASSED BY KIN		57081		42770					COLIS POSTAUX
931	*SPECIAL TRANSACTIONS						48536		49850	TRANS.SPECIALES

5. Special Exports F.O.B. by Commodities according to the S.I.T.C. (Rev. 2) in thousand U.S. Dollars
Exportations Spéciales F.O.B. par Produits d'après la C.T.C.I. (Rév. 2) en milliers de Dollars E.U.

SITC CTCI	COMMODITY	1992		1993		1994		1995		PRODUIT
		WEIGHT POIDS	VALUE VALEUR	WEIGHT POIDS	VALUE VALEUR	WEIGHT POIDS	VALUE VALEUR	WEIGHT POIDS	VALUE VALEUR	
	ALL COMMODITIES		210234		175715		170980		208691	TOUS PRODUITS
0	FOOD AND LIVE ANIMALS		160227		126748		124737		156142	ALIMENTS,ANIMAUX VIVANTS
03	FISH AND PREPARATIONS		10435		7995		13369		16507	POISSONS ET PREPARATIONS
034	FISH,FRESH,CHILLED,FROZN	W 493	1618	W 1020	2382	W 1568	6299	W 1468	7570	POISSON FRAIS, REFRIG,CONG
0341	FISH FRSH,CHLLD,EX FILLT	W 17	110	W 59	405	W 340	1956	W 178	1325	POISSON FRAIS,REFRIGERE
0342	FISH FROZEN,EXCL FILLETS	W 474	1501	W 961	1977	W 1054	3747	W 1154	5670	POISSONS CONGELES
0344	FISH FILLETS,FROZEN	W 2	6			W 174	596	W 136	576	FILETS CONGELES
036	SHELL FISH FRESH,FROZEN	W 367	8389	W 284	5437	W 391	7037	W 425	8807	CRUSTACES,MOLLUSQUES
05	VEGETABLES AND FRUIT		1862		1833		4331		2676	LEGUMES ET FRUITS
054	VEG ETC FRSH,SMPLY PRSVD	W 288	258	W 55	98	W 4134	2068	W 73	111	LEGUMES FRAIS,CONG,SECS
0545	OTHER FRESH VEGETABLES	W 129	145	W 21	49	W 4090	2025	W 19	56	AUTRES LEGUMES FRAIS,REF
05451	ALLIACEOUS VEGTBLS,FRESH	W 26	37			W 4082	2000			OIGNONS,ECHALOTES,AULX
057	FRUIT,NUTS,FRESH,DRIED	W 640	1421	W 759	1477	W 1018	1782	W 1223	2076	FRUITS FRAIS OU SECS
0579	FRUIT FRESH OR DRIED NES	W 572	1341	W 738	1444	W 1003	1757	W 1172	2006	FRUITS FRAIS,SECS NDA
05795	PINEAPPLES,FRESH,DRIED	W 491	873	W 608	1048	W 954	1554	W 1138	1876	ANANAS FRAIS OU SECS
06	SUGAR AND PREPS,HONEY		145495		113637		104194		131971	SUCRES ET PRODUITS
061	SUGAR AND HONEY	W 238094	145479	W 204598	113626	W 185915	104186	W 184038	131945	SUCRES ET MIEL
0611	RAW BEET AND CANE SUGAR	W 203959	143701	W 170323	112032	W 155125	102587	W 175256	131491	SUCRES BRUTS
0615	MOLASSES	W 34130	1772	W 34260	1569	W 30408	1288	W 8755	427	MELASSES
07	COFFEE,TEA,COCOA,SPICES		1792		2600		1624		3166	CAFE,THE,CACAO,EPICES
075	SPICES	W 65	1750	W 134	2569	W 107	1587	W 200	3095	EPICES
0752	SPICES,EX PEPPER,PIMENTO	W 42	1506	W 104	2226	W 69	1137	W 174	2684	AUTRES EPICES
07521	VANILLA	W 16	1257	W 28	1888	W 13	588	W 5	198	VANILLE
07528	THYME ETC, OTHER SPICES	W 21	220	W 70	287	W 54	528	W 162	2443	THYM,SAFRAN,LAURIER
1	BEVERAGES AND TOBACCO		7202		5533		6701		6751	BOISSONS ET TABACS
11	BEVERAGES		6674		5130		6399		6378	BOISSONS
112	ALCOHOLIC BEVERAGES	W 4845	6557	W 3648	5018	W 5030	6317	W 4881	6168	BOISSONS ALCOOLIQUES
1124	DISTILLED ALCOHOLIC BEVS	W 4794	6493	W 3608	4976	W 4978	6234	W 4809	6038	ALCOOLS,EAUX–DE–VIE
11249	OTH ALCOHOLC BEVS,CMPNDS	W 4793	6487	W 3608	4975	W 4976	6226	W 4808	6035	BOISSONS ALCOOLIQUES NDA
2	CRUDE MATERLS,EXCL FUELS		1651		1072		1145		2024	MAT BRUTES NON COMESTIBLES
28	METALLIFEROUS ORES,SCRAP		509		236		347		940	MINERAIS METAL,DECHETS
288	NONFERR METAL SCRAP NES	W 508	399	W 381	236	W 518	344	W 743	853	DECHETS NON FERREUX
2882	OTHER BASE MTL SCRAP NES	W 508	399	W 381	236	W 518	344	W 743	853	AUTRES DECHETS
28821	COPPER WASTE AND SCRAP	W 238	282	W 175	186	W 360	298	W 599	809	DECHETS DE CUIVRE
29	CRUDE ANIMAL,VEG MAT NES		798		530		479		532	MATIERES BRUTES ANIM,VEGET
292	CRUDE VEG MATERIALS NES	W 237	784	W 151	528	W 104	462	W 87	531	MAT BRUTES VEGETALES NDA
2926	LIVE PLANTS,BULBS,ETC	W 230	712	W 148	510	W 102	429	W 82	495	BULBES,TUBERCULES
29269	LIVE PLANTS NES	W 230	712	W 148	510	W 102	429	W 82	492	AUTRES PLANTES VIVANTES
5	CHEMCLS,RELATED PROD NES		4159		5286		2456		3407	PRODUITS CHIMIQUES
53	DYES,TANNING,COLOUR PROD		694		595		235		539	PROD TEINTURE,COLORANTS
533	PIGMENTS,PAINTS,ETC	W 446	693	W 187	591	W 86	227	W 161	535	PIGMENTS,PEINTURES,VERNIS
5334	VARNISHES,DISTEMPERS ETC	W 419	654	W 161	543	W 77	213	W 134	467	PEINTURES A L'EAU
541	*MEDICINAL,PHARM PRODUCT	K 142042	486	K 101730	473	K 120913	605	K 129782	506	PROD MEDICINAUX PHARMACEUT
55	PERFUME,CLEANING ETC PRD		2537		3590		957		1309	PROD POUR PARFUM,TOILETTE
551	ESSENTL OILS,PERFUME,ETC	W 16	2297	W 34	3400	W 7	655	W 9	1019	HUILES ESSENTIELLES
5513	ESSENTL OIL,RESINOID,ETC	W 16	2297	W 33	3359	W 7	653	W 8	1018	HUILES ESSENTIELLES,RESIN
59	CHEMICAL MATERIALS NES		210		220		349		680	MAT PROD CHIMIQUES NDA
6	BASIC MANUFACTURES		5178		6620		5996		6282	ART MANUFACTURES
66	NONMETAL MINERAL MFS NES		202		288		350		704	ART MIN NON METALLIQUES
67	IRON AND STEEL		2302		2572		2285		1719	FER ET ACIER
674	IRN,STL UNIV,PLATE,SHEET	W 1574	2202	W 1580	2009	W 1657	1943	W 1109	1373	LARGES PLATS,TOLES
6749	OTH IRN,STL PLATES,SHEET	W 1165	1653	W 1126	1441	W 1393	1689	W 965	1230	AUTRES TOLES FER,ACIER
67491	— OF IRON OR SIMPLE STL	W 1145	1616	W 1107	1431	W 1393	1689	W 957	1211	AUT TOLES AUTRES ACIER FIN
69	METAL MANUFACTURES NES		1808		2433		2091		2341	ART MANUFACT EN METAL NDA
692	METAL TANKS,BOXES,ETC	W 171	674	W 207	841	W 193	819	W 153	829	RECIPIENTS METALLIQUES
6924	MTL TRANSPORT BOXES ETC	W 168	645	W 202	827	W 193	819	W 153	826	FUTS,TAMBOURS,BIDONS
69243	IRN,STL COMP GAS CYLINDR	W 142	540	W 186	762	W 186	793	W 153	825	RECIP FER,ACIER GAZ COMP
699	BASE METAL MFRS NES	W 142	484	W 214	723	W 213	356	W 124	333	ART MANUFACTURES MET NDA
7	MACHINES,TRANSPORT EQUIP		24014		21585		21378		26558	MACHINES MATERIEL TRANSPORT
71	POWER GENERATING EQUIPMT		2344		2830		2335		1116	MACHINES GENERATRICES
711	STEAM BOILERS & AUX PLNT	W 145	646	W 361	412	W 1	5	W 1	13	GENERATEURS VAPEUR EAU ETC
713	INTRNL COMBUS PSTN ENGIN	W 66	1090	W 30	527	W 24	416	W 38	343	MOTEURS EXPL COMB INT, PIECE
7139	PISTON ENGINE PARTS NES	W 56	1062	W 27	511	W 17	355	W 14	273	PIECES POUR 713.2,3,8
716	ROTATING ELECTRIC PLANT	W 49	438	W 153	740	W 21	467	W 28	630	APP ELECTR ROTATIFS,PIECES
718	OTH POWER GENERATG MACHY	W 3	95	W 1	1151	W 6	1287	W 1	52	AUTRES MOTEURS PARTIES
7188	WIND,WATER,ETC ENGINES	W 3	95	W 1	1151	W 6	1287	W 1	52	MOT MACHINES MOTRICES NDA
71889	PARTS NES OF 71881,71882			W 1	1151	W 1	1164		4	PARTIES DES POS 718.81,82
72	MACHS FOR SPCL INDUSTRYS		2675		2316		1587		4131	MAC SPECIALES POUR INDUST
723	CIVIL ENGNEERG EQUIP ETC	W 169	581	W 156	500	W 211	492	W 301	1075	APPAREILS DE GENIE CIVIL
7234	CONST,MINING MACHNRY NES	W 147	524	W 125	385	W 174	376	W 290	1038	MACH POUR LA CONST, MINES
727	FOOD MACHRY NON–DOMESTIC	W 665	997	W 849	873	W 48	248	W 388	445	MACH INDUSTRIES ALIMENT
7272	OTH FOOD PROC MCHY,PARTS	W 665	997	W 849	873	W 47	244	W 386	441	AUT MACH IND ALIMENTAIRE
72722	INDUS FOOD PROC MACH NES	W 665	997	W 849	873	W 47	244	W 386	441	MACHINES BOULANGERIE
728	OTH MACHY FOR SPCL INDUS	W 115	616	W 211	646	W 109	579	W 162	1756	AUT MACH IND PARTICULIERES
7284	MACHY FOR SPCL INDUS NES	W 21	252	W 27	198	W 54	426	W 104	1622	MACH SPEC IND PARTICUL.
72842	RUBBER,PLASTICS WRKG MCH				1	W 4	116	W 62	1249	MACH IND CAOUT MAT PLAST
74	GENRL INDUSTRL MACHY NES		1630		2316		1926		2545	MACH APP INDUSTRIE
744	MECHANICAL HANDLING EQU	W 93	482	W 527	1324	W 123	684	W 117	528	EQUIP MANUTENTION PIECES
7441	FORK LIFT TRCKS,ETC,PTS	W 29	71	W 359	862	W 49	82	W 21	28	CHARIOTS POUR USINES ETC
74411	FORK LIFT TRUCKS ETC	W 29	71	W 359	857	W 48	78	W 21	26	CHARIOTS POUR LES GARES
7442	LIFTING,LOADING MACH NES	W 54	253	W 117	175	W 66	516	W 80	323	APP LEVAGE,MANUTENTION
745	NONELEC MACHY,TOOLS NES	W 47	444	W 7	227	W 45	263	W 64	751	AUT MACH NON ELEC,PIECES
7452	OTH NONELEC MCHS,PTS NES	W 47	436	W 6	221	W 31	231	W 62	687	AUT MACH NON ELEC,PIECES
75	OFFICE MACHNES,ADP EQUIP		1821		1906		2653		2858	MACH BUREAU TRAIT AUTOM
751	OFFICE MACHINES	W 5	582	W 4	646	W 5	1029	W 5	1399	MACH,APPAREILS DE BUREAU
7512	CALCULATNG,ACCTG,ETC MCH	W 3	498	W 2	581	W 3	923	W 3	1219	MACHINE A CALCULER ETC
75128	POSTAGE–FRANKING ETC MCH	W 2	430	W 2	557	W 3	909	W 3	1197	MACHINES A AFFRANCHIR
752	AUTOMTIC DATA PROC EQUIP	W 4	508	W 7	484	W 11	773	W 7	722	MACH TRAIT INFORMATION
759	OFFICE,ADP MCH PTS,ACCES	W 4	731	W 6	776	W 6	850	W 7	738	PIECES DU 751 ET 752
7599	ACCTG,ETC,ADP MCH PTS,AC	W 4	709	W 5	754	W 6	843	W 6	673	PIECES DU 751 ET 752
76	TELECOMM,SOUND EQUIPMENT		2101		1560		1570		1782	EQUIPMENT DE TELECOM
764	TELECOM EQPT,PTS,ACC NES	W 34	1832	W 28	1330	W 31	1191	W 22	1574	EQUIP TELECOM,PIECES
7641	LINE TELEPHONE,ETC EQUIP	W 10	466	W 24	1020	W 27	791	W 17	862	APP TELEPHON PAR FIL
77	ELECTRIC MACHNRY NES ETC		3819		1837		1601		1646	MACH APP ELECT NDA
772	SWITCHGEAR ETC,PARTS NES	W 62	1147	W 35	442	W 23	293	W 40	397	APP COUPURE,SECT ETC
7721	SWITCHGEAR ETC	W 62	1143	W 35	428	W 23	293	W 40	397	APP COUPURE,SECTIONMNT
775	HOUSEHOLD TYPE EQUIP NES	W 51	369	W 95	666	W 118	573	W 39	234	MACH,APP USAGE DOMESTQUE
778	ELECTRICAL MACHINERY NES	W 26	1338	W 19	166	W 10	331	W 57	514	AUTRES MACH ELECT NDA
7781	BATTERIES,ACCUMULATORS	W 21	1217	W 3	24	W 8	57	W 31	107	PILES ET ACCUMULATEURS
77811	PRIMARY BATTERIES,CELLS	W 16	1195	W 1	11	W 5	44	W 12	50	PILES ELECTRIQUES,PIECES
78	ROAD VEHICLES		5990		8262		8085		9159	VEHICULES ROUTIERS

5. Special Exports F.O.B. by Commodities according to the S.I.T.C. (Rev. 2) in thousand U.S. Dollars
Exportations Spéciales F.O.B. par Produits d'après la C.T.C.I. (Rév. 2) en milliers de Dollars E.U.

SITC CTCI	COMMODITY	1992		1993		1994		1995		PRODUIT
		WEIGHT POIDS	VALUE VALEUR	WEIGHT POIDS	VALUE VALEUR	WEIGHT POIDS	VALUE VALEUR	WEIGHT POIDS	VALUE VALEUR	
781	PASS MOTOR VEH EXC BUSES	W 1050	3479	W 1354	4829	W 1249	4936	W 1532	5956	AUTO TRANSPORT PERSONNES
782	LORRIES,SPCL MTR VEH NES	W 1224	1274	W 1326	1976	W 1397	1550	W 1491	2048	VEHICULES SPECIAUX,MARCH
7821	LORRIES,TRUCKS	W 1211	1198	W 1299	1905	W 1374	1536	W 1439	1975	VEHICULES TRANSP MARCHAND
784	MOTOR VEH PRTS,ACCES NES	W 165	831	W 395	595	W 529	827	W 475	629	PIECES 722,781,782,783
7849	OTHER MOTOR VEHCL PARTS	W 165	831	W 395	595	W 527	827	W 472	628	PIECES 722,781,782,783
79	OTHR TRANSPORT EQUIPMENT		3286		396		1288		2986	AUTRE MATERIEL TRANSPORT
792	AIRCRAFT ETC	W 21	3009	W 1	99	W 3	491	W 6	515	APP NAVIGATION AERIENNE
7924	AIRCRFT NES OVER 15000KG	W 15	2274							AERODYNES PLUS 15000 KG
793	SHIPS AND BOATS ETC	W 28	277	W 37	298	W 250	733	W 6919	2428	NAVIRES BATEAUX,ETC
7932	SHIPS AND BOATS NES	W 28	269	W 36	290	W 250	728	W 6919	2423	NAVIRES ET BATEAUX
79323	OTHER CARGO VESSELS		3					W 6627	1574	AUT BATEAUX TRANS MARCH
79324	FISHING VESSELS ETC	W 3	45	W 3	71	W 204	412	W 280	766	BATEAUX DE PECHE
8	MISC MANUFACTURED GOODS		7356		8536		8123		7034	ART MANUFACTURES DIVERS
821	*FURNITURE,PARTS THEREOF	W 89	585	W 132	1243	W 169	670	W 159	633	MEUBLES ET PIECES
8219	FURNITURE AND PARTS NES	W 51	259	W 76	923	W 87	312	W 86	377	AUTRES MEUBLES ET PIECES
82191	METAL FURNITURE NES	W 13	86	W 22	761	W 14	20	W 8	26	MEUBLES NDA EN METAL
84	CLOTHING AND ACCESSORIES		1287		3155		3381		1878	VETEMENTS
843	WOMENS OUTERWEAR NONKNIT	W 69	379	W 60	665	W 108	1598	W 38	835	VET DESSUS FEMMES MAT TEX
8439	— OTHER OUTER GARMENTS	W 68	368	W 60	639	W 103	1536	W 37	821	AUT VET DES FEM MAT TEXT
845	OUTERWEAR KNIT NONELASTC	W 30	671	W 89	1971	W 62	1297	W 38	873	VET DESSOUS,ACCES BONNET
8459	— OTHER,CLTHG ACCESRYS	W 30	661	W 89	1962	W 62	1292	W 38	853	AUT VET DESSUS DE BONNE
87	PRECISION INSTRUMNTS NES		1587		1531		1450		2935	INSTRUM,APPAR SCIENT NDA
872	MEDICAL INSTRUMENTS NES	W 19	634	W 4	694	W 15	733	W 7	1234	INSTR,APP MEDIC–CHIR NDA
87202	OTH MEDICAL INSTRUMENTS	W 19	593	W 4	674	W 14	702	W 7	1190	INSTRUM,APP MEDECINE
874	MEASURNG,CONTROLNG INSTR	W 43	930	W 33	711	W 8	625	W 13	1613	INSTRUMENTS DE MESURE
8741	SURVEYING INSTRUMENTS	W 40	261		176		145	W 1	955	INST GEODESIE,TOPO ETC
87411	NAVIG INSTR NONELEC ETC	W 40	90		1		1	W 1	848	INSTR NAVIGATION
89	MISC MANUFCTRD GOODS NES		3013		2257		2115		1335	ART MANUFACTURES DIVERS
892	PRINTED MATTER	W 98	692	W 92	816	W 34	461	W 89	382	IMPRIMES
893	ARTICLES OF PLASTIC NES	W 196	780		354		440		545	OUVRAGES EN MAT DIVIS 58
8939	MISC PLASTIC ARTICLES	W 180	686	W 56	234	W 46	165	W 105	332	ART DIVERS EN MAT DIV 58
89399	OTHR PLASTC ARTICLES NES	W 178	681	W 40	207	W 45	155	W 105	332	AUT OUV MAT DIV 58
897	GOLD,SILVER WARE,JEWELRY		663		4		8		106	BIJOUTERIE,ORFEVRERIE
899	OTHER MANUFACTURED GOODS		89		760		872		31	AUT ART MANUF DIVERS NDA
8999	OTHER MANUF GOODS NES	W 1	18	W 4	733	W 4	821			OUVRAGES DIVERS NDA
89998	PARACHUTES,PRTS,ACCES OF		10	W 4	733	W 4	821			PARACHUTES ET PARTIES

1. HISTORICAL SERIES, 1961–1996 GENERAL TRADE, IMPORTS C.I.F., EXPORTS F.O.B.
SERIES HISTORIQUES, 1961–1996 COMMERCE GENERAL, IMPORTATIONS C.A.F., EXPORTATIONS F.O.B

YEAR ANNEE	VALUE IN MILLION U.S. DOLLARS VALEUR EN MILLION U.S. DOLLARS MERCHANDISE –MARCHANDISE		GOLD –OR		CONVERSION FACTORS FACTEURS DE CONVERSION CENTS E.U. PAR		INDEX NUMBERS –INDICES QUANTUM		UNIT VALUE VALEUR UNITAIRE	
	IMPORTS	EXPORTS	IMPORTS	EXPORTS	IMPORTS	EXPORTS	IMPORTS	EXPORTS	IMPORTS	EXPORTS
1961	814.68	792.51								
1962	941.02	818.02								
1963	1022.02	915.02								
1964	1168.19	1000.02								
1965	1077.19	1101.52								
1966	1213.19	1186.19								
1967	1546.20	1395.36								
1968	1609.03	1468.53								
1969	1740.53	1633.20								
1970	1960.20	1850.87								
1971	2102.71	2101.04								
1972	2615.73	2599.10								
1973	3467.90	3698.52								
1974	5143.53	4874.40								
1975	5341.74	5341.42								
1976	6095.34	6137.72								
1977	7017.98	6978.66								
1978	8909.59	8076.60								
1979	10915.45	9724.17								
1980	13843.40	11209.00								
1981	13453.60	12610.00								
1982	10524.60	11559.00								
1983	10414.40	11512.00								
1984	11160.70	12646.00								
1985	11266.60	12167.00								
1986	11437.20	9763.10								
1987	8977.70	10491.80								
1988	8254.00	11392.40								
1989	9122.40	10487.30								
1990	9843.40	5775.40								
1991	5793.40	4265.70								
1992	6259.60	4363.40								
1993	6521.70	4892.20								
1994	7109.00	6151.30								
1995	10277.90	7910.00								
1996	11435.30	8084.50								

2. IMPORTS BY BROAD ECONOMIC CATEGORY AND EXPORTS BY INDUSTRIAL ORIGIN. (PERCENTAGE OF TOTAL VALUE)
IMPORTATIONS PAR CATEGORIES ECONOMIQUES ET EXPORTATIONS PAR BRANCHE D'ACTIVITE.(EN POURCENTAGE DE LA VALEUR TOTALE)

IMPORTS – IMPORTATIONS

	1990	1991	1992	1993	1994	1995	1996
TOTAL IMPORTS–IMPORTATIONS TOTALES	100.	100.	100.	100.	100.	100.	100.
1 FOOD BEV–ALIMENTATION BOISSONS	9.3	10.7	12.8	11.1	7.3	6.8	5.4
11 PRIMARY–PRODUITS DE BASE	5.6	5.9	6.2	6.8	2.7	2.1	1.6
111 FOR INDUSTRY–POUR L'INDUSTRIE	3.1	4.9	4.0	5.5	1.2	0.4	0.7
112 FOR HOUSEHOLDS–POUR LES MENAGES	2.5	1.0	2.2	1.2	1.6	1.6	0.9
12 PROCESSED–PRODUITS ELABORES	3.7	4.8	6.6	4.4	4.6	4.7	3.8
121 FOR INDUSTRY–POUR L'INDUSTRIE	1.4	1.5	1.9	0.9	1.2	1.3	1.7
122 FOR HOUSEHOLDS–POUR LES MENAGES	2.3	3.3	4.7	3.5	3.4	3.4	2.1
2 IND SUPPLIES–APPROV INDUSTRIELS	25.1	24.4	28.2	31.7	34.4	36.0	36.5
21 PRIMARY–PRODUITS DE BASE	8.5	8.7	6.0	5.8	4.8	4.4	4.2
22 PROCESSED–PRODUITS ELABORES	16.7	15.7	22.2	25.8	29.6	31.5	32.3
3 FUELS–COMBUSTIBLES	38.0	39.7	29.7	25.9	23.7	21.4	20.9
31 PRIMARY–PRODUITS DE BASE	33.7	31.4	24.3	22.0	21.1	17.6	17.1
32 PROCESSED–PRODUITS ELABORES	4.3	8.3	5.4	3.9	2.7	3.8	3.8
321 MOTOR SPIRIT–ESSENCE							
322 OTHER–AUTRES	4.3	8.3	5.4	3.9	2.7	3.8	3.8
4 MACHINERY–EQUIPEMENT	15.1	13.2	12.4	17.1	19.8	20.7	20.9
41 CAPITAL EQUIPMENT–MACHINES	13.1	11.7	10.7	14.7	17.3	17.9	18.1
42 PARTS–PIECES ACCESSOIRES	2.1	1.5	1.7	2.3	2.5	2.8	2.7
5 TRANSPORT–TRANSPORT	6.9	3.2	6.0	5.5	5.5	4.7	4.8
51 PASSENGER CARS–AUTOMOBILES	0.1		0.2	0.1	0.2	1.7	0.7
52 OTHER–AUTRES	0.6	1.4	3.9	3.6	3.6	1.3	1.2
521 INDUSTRIAL–INDUSTRIELS	0.6	1.4	3.8	3.6	3.6	1.3	1.2
522 NON INDUSTRIAL–NON INDUSTRIEL	0.0	0.0	0.1	0.0	0.0	0.0	0.0
53 PARTS–PIECES ACCESSOIRES	6.2	1.8	1.9	1.7	1.6	1.7	2.9
6 CONSUM GOODS–BIENS CONSOMMATION	5.2	8.1	8.3	8.3	8.2	9.3	9.9
61 DURABLE–DURABLES	1.1	2.8	2.7	1.6	1.5	1.8	2.2
62 SEMI DURABLE–SEMI DURABLES	1.2	2.8	3.3	3.8	4.2	4.4	4.3
63 NON DURABLE–NON DURABLES	2.9	2.5	2.3	3.0	2.5	3.2	3.4
7 GOODS NES–BIENS NDA	0.4	0.7	2.7	0.5	1.1	1.3	1.5

EXPORTS – EXPORTATIONS

	1990	1991	1992	1993	1994	1995	1996
TOTAL EXPORTS–EXPORTATIONS TOTALES	100.	100.	100.	100.	100.	100.	100.
1 AGRICULTURE	1.0	3.2	3.1	2.4	2.6	3.9	5.4
2 MINING QUARRY–INDUS EXTRACTIVES	0.5	0.5	0.5	0.4	0.5	0.5	0.5
3 MANUFACTURING–IND MANUFACTUR	98.6	96.3	96.4	97.1	96.9	95.7	94.1
31 FOOD BEV TOBACCO–ALIM BOISS TAB	0.5	3.0	3.7	4.6	4.2	3.0	3.4
32 TEXTILES–INDUSTRIES TEXTILES	12.0	11.4	11.8	19.3	23.8	25.2	27.8
33 WOOD & PRODUCTS–BOIS & PRODUITS	2.7	2.2	3.0	3.3	3.4	3.1	3.6
34 PAPER & PRODUCTS–PAPIER & PRODT	0.7	0.6	0.6	0.6	0.7	1.2	0.8
35 CHEMICALS–INDUSTRIES CHIMIQUES	25.3	21.1	23.4	19.1	21.0	20.1	18.6
36 NON METAL MIN–MIN NON METAL	2.4	3.3	3.6	3.4	2.8	2.8	2.8
37 BASIC METAL–IND METAL BASE	14.1	13.2	15.1	18.0	16.3	16.6	13.9
38 METAL MANUF–MANUF METAL	38.2	39.2	32.6	27.4	23.3	22.9	22.7
39 OTH MANUF IND–AUTRES MANUF	2.8	2.2	2.6	1.6	1.3	0.7	0.5

3. TRADE BY PRINCIPAL COUNTRIES OF PRODUCTION AND LAST CONSIGNMENT (VALUE IN THOUSAND U.S. DOLLARS)
ECHANGES SELON LES PRINCIPAUX PAYS DE PRODUCTION ET DE DERNIERE CONSIGNATION (VALEUR EN MILLIERS DE DOLLARS EU)

COUNTRIES–PAYS	GENERAL IMPORTS C.I.F. IMPORTATIONS GENERALES C.A.F				
	1992	1993	1994	1995	1996
World	6259625	6521705	7109048	10277898	11435274
Africa	290529	183386	169893	482474	308282
Americas	372890	565904	666195	670493	825758
Northern America	264208	436121	508502	449991	472196
LAIA	101215	117694	137359	174515	270396
CACM	1742	3299	1956	4978	3298
Caribbean	5190	8481	17422	36995	77939
Rest of America	535	309	956	4014	1929
As.ex F.USSR	1165483	1194186	948288	1349112	1504016
Eur.x F.USSR	3257098	3493691	3924977	5957183	6764397
EU	2583320	2955787	3391745	5125255	5889670
EFTA	133521	161487	161873	227926	209102
East Europe	376568	328058	336675	558624	600759
Other Europe	229	178	318	679	411
Former USSR	977543	1025673	1272139	1625516	1760274
Oceania	30704	28202	55511	73487	121445
Germany/Allemagne	826252	1031206	1258635	1766216	1949376
Russian Federation	687336	764069	980245	1228735	1432111
Italy/Italie	487219	614595	841503	1363744	1747338
France,Monac	474489	506713	359119	532029	555267
Iran (Islamic Rp. of)	466553	604102	443032	255792	314917
USA/Etats–Unis d'Amer	222300	372910	459755	407435	418922
United Kingdom	187662	170483	220838	299745	324203
Austria/Autriche	190558	165518	192172	308751	339910
Hungary/Hongrie	178338	167708	165987	314467	288035
Netherlands/Pays–Bas	151696	157044	175304	270086	259288
Egypt/Egypte	160491	86504	122924	400626	239711
Turkey/Turquie	176440	147227	150174	250405	218122
Korea, Republic of	23389	46836	48570	319815	418551
Switz.Liecht	126720	150906	149009	203326	189779
Ukraine	148107	133270	150070	193586	181656
Belgium–Luxembourg	72922	86998	83497	157976	190635
Greece/Grèce	74687	69495	89329	158120	185314
Republic of Moldova	120452	85185	92479	104495	79789
China/Chine	73577	93474	60081	89828	115013
Japan/Japon	75941	57685	57505	76178	104210
Bulgaria/Bulgarie	84149	67941	59006	76717	73243
Israel/Israël	40388	55405	58114	105268	100417
Brazil/Brésil	33466	51875	77618	85924	109626
Australia/Australie	30601	28114	53769	71084	120759
Spain/Espagne	24246	40882	46449	88118	101281
Sweden/Suède	56379	33519	39091	75711	75721
Denmark/Danemark	20771	48245	45497	53970	86688
Canada	34007	63211	48747	42556	53269
Poland/Pologne	35944	33093	29781	57015	85508
Czech Republic		35982	49983	61740	82069
Argentina/Argentine	55891	45737	31172	31646	50129
Yugoslavia/Yougoslavie	135050	229	20334	19927	30915
Slovakia		23240	31793	48583	59067
Saudi Arabia	98172	22418	181	9675	11877
Cuba	5163	7737	16996	36531	62918
India/Inde	2912	19254	18090	42173	36010
Hong Kong	13084	16005	16654	35938	30277
So. Africa Customs Un	23176	39779	14560	18775	15145
Singapore/Singapour	42688	21417	8884	21487	14441
Finland/Finlande	5439	13531	27459	23849	33551
Venezuela	3227	4110	10698	19319	59138
Cyprus/Chypre	21824	14667	9924	29268	18705
Libyan Arab Jamahiriya	71911	19132	402		530
Belarus/Bélarus	3595	10555	17367	26556	28757
Ireland/Irlande	9645	15226	10081	22731	25476
Czechoslovakia	77980				
Syrian Arab Republic	30792	8762	7465	23438	6236
Slovenia/Slovénia	4321	9859	12619	21838	25079
Thailand/Thaïlande	17064	20882	5597	9142	18528
Lebanon/Liban	23880	18841	10715	8839	7570

COUNTRIES–PAYS	GENERAL EXPORTS F.O.B. EXPORTATIONS GENERALES F.O.B.				
	1992	1993	1994	1995	1996
Monde	4363390	4892169	6151245	7910049	8084459
Afrique	158441	219401	395595	569353	536718
Amériques	174965	201374	352140	407369	408381
Amérique du Nord	101902	95274	237417	231923	216720
ALAI	44408	76598	88713	124137	150392
MCAC	3384	2170	4878	13384	5299
Caraïbes	6822	27012	16510	36658	34801
Autre Amérique	18450	319	4622	1267	1169
Asie l'URSS exclus	1182408	1475712	1446130	1606747	1462828
Europe l'URSS exclus	2153314	2480159	3484315	4833199	5214472
UE	1530727	2024392	2964180	4281882	4574038
AELE	104306	126600	56019	76832	65958
Europe de l'Est	278231	257869	364617	328419	365620
Autre de l'Europe	30118	20912	25920	44550	24241
Ancienne URSS	604648	446161	396268	451175	430416
Océanie	8913	6489	8490	6992	7000
Germany/Allemagne	479197	699421	985926	1434187	1485959
Italy/Italie	265928	409401	797953	1246613	1392877
France,Monac	171836	219293	315787	456490	459770
Turkey/Turquie	219171	277428	250731	346953	389667
China/Chine	198744	419049	275614	179326	92926
Russian Federation	414518	220394	207256	157858	164324
Netherlands/Pays–Bas	109863	212114	216060	238757	342992
United Kingdom	156971	183373	200166	235911	247310
Egypt/Egypte	77445	100955	157816	199082	232586
USA/Etats–Unis d'Amer	83491	69025	194067	201182	192555
Greece/Grèce	115549	84311	141149	205019	177328
Syrian Arab Republic	107495	132655	145856	164013	157873
Hungary/Hongrie	80811	117020	160884	174261	171399
Austria/Autriche	104699	75750	96414	154813	169218
Ukraine	104469	104690	94848	137405	64843
Belgium–Luxembourg	44426	76234	103154	134052	125301
Bulgaria/Bulgarie	116094	102279	102193	70936	70616
Yugoslavia/Yougoslavie	151663	7948	46968	68766	136801
Republic of Moldova	71730	94181	47868	81295	96984
Israel/Israël	30630	53861	95065	107028	89616
Switz.Liecht	99043	119905	45466	65364	41927
India/Inde	43539	24640	45770	73896	177063
Singapore/Singapour	39603	34271	107837	117699	43308
Spain/Espagne	43571	28208	55996	101596	94519
Lebanon/Liban	71390	46606	47083	66199	61455
Iran (Islamic Rp. of)	120925	81755	28692	22976	27281
Japan/Japon	59907	52820	52951	35472	38983
Jordan/Jordanie	45034	42826	35668	27110	37350
Cyprus/Chypre	44645	20359	48577	35687	36001
Nigeria/Nigéria	12882	32367	86540	27061	23930
Poland/Pologne	52743	20145	13978	39110	52872
Morocco/Maroc	19494	25545	38795	46152	47347
Algeria/Algérie	3462	4668	24180	95703	48419
Saudi Arabia	28345	31233	41881	35572	33737
Sweden/Suède	27455	21420	34143	38794	43932
Thailand/Thaïlande	16646	29936	21760	38258	41037
Pakistan	14279	17078	15579	59086	40759
United Arab Emirates	12050	28342	47978	26840	28351
Argentina/Argentine	13999	38345	39722	13259	35450
Canada	18411	26249	38608	30601	24136
Yemen/Yémen	43366	21069	41859	24915	5970
Korea, Republic of	3649	3062	34898	52582	42491
Brazil/Brésil	2880	3674	10994	63319	55769
Czech Republic		9548	75502	20962	17577
Tunisia/Tunisie	2800	1519	6994	46762	52018
Georgia/Géorgie	802	1396	9697	49829	46726
Sri Lanka	24996	44782	3494	15146	10633
Sudan/Soudan	14630	13025	20965	18291	24212
So. Africa Customs Un	2744	1329	6909	72346	6958
Colombia/Colombie	14500	22137	20791	14123	16263

(VALUE AS PERCENTAGE OF WORLD TOTAL)(VALEURS EN POURCENTAGE DU TOTAL MONDIAL)

	1987	1988	1989	1990	1991	1992	1993	1994	1995	1996
Africa			2.7	7.0	8.8	4.6	2.8	2.4	4.7	2.7
Americas			4.7	6.8	6.3	6.0	8.7	9.4	6.5	7.2
Northern America			2.6	4.7	3.6	4.2	6.7	7.2	4.4	4.1
LAIA			0.7	1.5	2.6	1.6	1.8	1.9	1.7	2.4
CACM				0.0	0.0	0.0	0.1	0.0	0.0	0.0
Caribbean			1.4	0.6	0.1	0.1	0.1	0.2	0.4	0.7
Rest of America				0.0	0.1	0.0	0.0	0.0	0.0	0.0
As.ex F.USSR			28.5	23.1	23.8	18.6	18.3	13.3	13.1	13.2
Eur.x F.USSR			30.8	38.2	41.7	52.0	53.6	55.2	58.0	59.2
EU			13.8	21.5	28.7	41.3	45.3	47.7	49.9	51.5
EFTA			0.5	2.1	2.2	2.1	2.5	2.3	2.2	1.8
East Europe			14.7	12.3	7.6	6.0	5.0	4.7	5.4	5.3
Other Europe			1.8	2.3	3.2	0.0	0.0	0.0	0.0	0.0
Former USSR			31.2	23.4	17.7	15.6	15.7	17.9	15.8	15.4
Oceania			1.2	1.2	1.1	0.5	0.4	0.8	0.7	1.1
Germany/Allemagne			9.5	11.4	10.2	13.2	15.8	17.7	17.2	17.0
Russian Federation						11.0	11.7	13.8	12.0	12.5
Italy/Italie			0.6	1.2	3.6	7.8	9.4	11.8	13.3	15.3
France,Monac			0.6	1.9	3.8	7.6	7.8	5.1	5.2	4.9
Iran (Islamic Rp. of)			12.0	5.9	7.9	7.5	9.3	6.2	2.5	2.8
USA/Etats–Unis d'Amer			2.0	4.6	3.2	3.6	5.7	6.5	4.0	3.7
United Kingdom			0.8	1.8	2.6	3.0	2.6	3.1	2.9	2.8
Austria/Autriche			0.6	1.6	3.2	3.0	2.5	2.7	3.0	3.0
Hungary/Hongrie			3.2	2.4	2.1	2.8	2.6	2.3	3.1	2.5
Netherlands/Pays–Bas			0.5	1.4	1.7	2.4	2.4	2.5	2.6	2.3

	1987	1988	1989	1990	1991	1992	1993	1994	1995	1996
Afrique			3.7	3.6	3.5	3.6	4.5	6.4	7.2	6.6
Amériques			8.9	8.1	4.2	4.0	4.1	5.7	5.2	5.1
Amérique du Nord			6.1	6.3	3.3	2.3	1.9	3.9	2.9	2.7
ALAI			1.2	0.6	0.7	1.0	1.6	1.4	1.6	1.9
MCAC			0.1	0.1	0.2	0.1	0.0	0.1	0.2	0.1
Caraïbes			1.3	1.1	0.0	0.2	0.6	0.3	0.5	0.4
Autre Amérique			0.2	0.0	0.0	0.4	0.0	0.1	0.0	0.0
Asie l'URSS exclus			17.6	14.9	18.1	27.1	30.2	23.5	20.3	18.1
Europe l'URSS exclus			46.2	46.5	49.5	49.3	50.7	56.6	61.1	64.5
UE			32.8	33.3	36.7	35.1	41.4	48.2	54.1	56.6
AELE			0.9	1.6	1.7	2.4	2.6	0.9	1.0	0.8
Europe de l'Est			10.7	9.2	7.1	6.4	5.3	5.9	4.2	4.5
Autre de l'Europe			1.7	2.3	4.0	0.7	0.4	0.4	0.6	0.3
Ancienne URSS			21.9	24.2	22.7	13.9	9.1	6.4	5.7	5.3
Océanie			0.2	0.1	0.1	0.2	0.1	0.1	0.1	0.1
Germany/Allemagne			11.9	11.0	10.9	11.0	14.3	16.0	18.1	18.4
Italy/Italie			9.5	8.8	6.1	6.1	8.4	13.0	15.8	17.2
France,Monac			2.4	3.4	4.1	3.9	4.5	5.1	5.8	5.7
Turkey/Turquie			3.0	2.8	3.6	5.0	5.7	4.1	4.4	4.8
China/Chine			3.3	2.6	3.3	4.6	8.6	4.5	2.3	1.1
Russian Federation						9.5	4.5	3.4	2.0	2.0
Netherlands/Pays–Bas			1.4	2.7	5.3	2.5	4.3	3.5	3.0	4.2
United Kingdom			2.4	2.2	3.6	3.6	3.7	3.3	3.0	3.1
Egypt/Egypte			1.8	1.4	1.6	1.8	2.1	2.6	2.5	2.9
USA/Etats–Unis d'Amer			5.4	5.8	2.9	1.9	1.4	3.2	2.5	2.4

4. General Imports C.I.F. by Commodities according to the S.I.T.C. (Rev. 2) in thousand U.S. Dollars
Importations Générales C.A.F. par Produits d'après la C.T.C.I. (Rév. 2) en milliers de Dollars E.U.

SITC CTCI	COMMODITY	1993		1994		1995		1996		PRODUIT
		WEIGHT POIDS	VALUE VALEUR	WEIGHT POIDS	VALUE VALEUR	WEIGHT POIDS	VALUE VALEUR	WEIGHT POIDS	VALUE VALEUR	
	ALL COMMODITIES		6521705		7109048		10277898		11435274	TOUS PRODUITS
0	FOOD AND LIVE ANIMALS		791208		532576		745717		657797	ALIMENTS,ANIMAUX VIVANTS
01	MEAT AND PREPARATIONS		38300		63898		94094		19919	VIANDES ET PREPARATIONS
011	MEAT FRESH,CHILLD,FROZEN	W 42411	33582	W 54349	57257		69209	W 14271	15205	VIANDES FRAICHES,REF,CONGE
0114	POULTRY FRESH CHLLD,FRZN	W 36689	28676	W 38579	41477	W 23325	35451	W 2944	1125	VOLAILLES MORTES
02	DAIRY PRODCTS,BIRDS'EGGS		25372		22663		22706		25898	PRODUITS LAITIERS,OEUFS
04	CEREALS AND PREPARATIONS		401629		86833		82785		57455	CEREALES ET PRODUITS
041	WHEAT ETC UNMILLED	W 1252136	205115	W 102	53	W 8725	1070	W 10	8	FROMENT,EPEAUTRE
0411	DURUM WHEAT UNMILLED	W 359935	50943	W 18	3	W 2944	399	W 10	8	FROMENT DUR NON MOULU
0412	OTHER WHEAT ETC UNMILLED	W 892201	154172	W 84	50	W 5781	671			AUTRE FROMENT NON MOULU
043	BARLEY UNMILLED	W 946040	103365	W 395741	35758	W 4061	475	W 47288	9067	ORGE NON MONDEE
044	MAIZE UNMILLED	W 326744	52486	W 2819	2768	W 3704	3509	W 342	1040	MAIS NON MOULU
046	WHEAT ETC MEAL OR FLOUR	W 26277	5902	W 52873	10831	W 144241	31177	W 19809	7548	SEMOULE FARINE,FROMENT
04601	FLOUR OF WHEAT OR MESLIN	W 26132	5860	W 52659	10769	W 143106	30906	W 18985	7284	FARINE DE FROMENT
048	CEREAL ETC PREPARATIONS	W 33143	17008	W 42658	25496	W 54131	39320	W 48981	31230	PREPTNS A BASE CEREALES
05	VEGETABLES AND FRUIT		56252		57055		107216		87633	LEGUMES ET FRUITS
057	FRUIT,NUTS,FRESH,DRIED		31664		31505		56109		46463	FRUITS FRAIS OU SECS
06	SUGAR AND PREPS,HONEY		73407		86479		127266		171352	SUCRES ET PRODUITS
061	SUGAR AND HONEY	W 232386	66456	W 288305	72742		111312		164836	SUCRES ET MIEL
0611	RAW BEET AND CANE SUGAR	W 102957	29845	W 141846	43099	W 156419	62282	W 336488	121358	SUCRES BRUTS
0612	REFINED SUGAR ETC	W 114568	33465	W 70180	23672	W 105619	42872	W 99127	37751	SUCRES RAFFINES
07	COFFEE,TEA,COCOA,SPICES		59335		62030		71266		62085	CAFE,THE,CACAO,EPICES
071	COFFEE AND SUBSTITUTES	W 15973	30701	W 14119	23600		27143	W 34515	33222	CAFE ET SUCCEDANES
073	CHOCOLATE AND PRODUCTS	W 12049	20156	W 20414	27281	W 22049	29824	W 11437	11846	CHOCOLAT
081	*FEEDING STUFF FOR ANIML	W 318815	86204		68502	W 302261	95937		99063	NOURRITURE POUR ANIMAUX
0813	OILCAKE AND OTH RESIDUES	W 259294	64353		47937	W 236950	55915		57724	TOURTEAUX
08131	— OF SOYA BEANS	W 201403	50418	W 205001	47838	W 236015	55718	W 191529	57699	TOURTEAUX DE SOJA
09	MISC EDIBLE PRODUCTS		42872		68490		107625		102567	PREP ALIMENTAIRES DIVERSES
098	EDIBLE PRODCTS,PREPS NES		35806	W 31420	57334		96163		99264	PREP ALIMENTAIRES NDA
09809	MISC FOOD PREPRTIONS NES	W 2889	20407	W 6662	41069	W 12097	66274	W 11893	69206	PREP ALIMENTAIRES NDA
1	BEVERAGES AND TOBACCO		109006		68751		96610		115826	BOISSONS ET TABACS
11	BEVERAGES		38179		22028		27585		8600	BOISSONS
112	ALCOHOLIC BEVERAGES	W 107641	29060	W 72457	18328	W 83920	22706	W 19480	7821	BOISSONS ALCOOLIQUES
12	TOBACCO AND MANUFACTURES		70826		46723		69025		107226	TABACS BRUTS FABRIQUES
122	TOBACCO,MANUFACTURED	W 14506	54277		36485	W 23202	63488	W 11535	84852	TABACS FABRIQUES
1222	CIGARETTES	W 14286	53685	W 13240	35754	W 22335	60462	W 8706	73240	CIGARETTES
2	CRUDE MATERLS,EXCL FUELS		400360		405917		532926		603104	MAT BRUTES NON COMESTIBLES
21	HIDES,SKINS,FURS UNDRSSD		22286		16771		12393		14834	CUIRS,PEAUX BRUTS
211	HIDES,SKINS,EXC FURS,RAW		22112	W 7292	16745	W 4196	12252	W 4785	14628	CUIRS ET PEAUX
22	OIL SEEDS,OLEAGINOUS FRT		23183		21171		9481		39242	GRAINES,FRUITS OLEAGINEUX
222	SEEDS FOR'SOFT'FIXED OIL	W 83134	23131	W 76598	21089	W 7447	9309	W 105799	38941	GRAINES HUILES FIXES
2222	SOYA BEANS	W 72760	20916	W 73602	19177	W 36	41	W 97879	31948	FEVES DE SOJA
23	RUBBER, CRUDE		40998		35840		62236		71089	CAOUTCHOUC BRUT
233	RUBBER,SYNTHTIC,RECLAIMD		25574	W 23551	22469		32835	W 25453	38081	LATEX CAOUTCH SYNTH REGEN
2331	SYNTHETIC RUBBER ETC	W 30318	25172	W 23067	21902	W 22613	32411	W 25077	37338	LATEX CAOUTCH SYNTHETIQUE
26	TEXTILE FIBRES AND WASTE		83348		78953		120599		120186	FIBRES TEXTILES
263	COTTON	W 43620	59325	W 30609	45861	W 43819	86489	W 40081	78849	COTON
2631	RAW COTTON,EXCL LINTERS	W 42143	57046	W 30293	45451	W 43734	86350	W 39352	77635	COTON EN MASSE
27	CRUDE FERTLZR,MINRLS NES		68828		62984		66157		75632	ENGRAIS MINERAUX BRUTS
271	FERTILIZERS,CRUDE		39286	W 830766	34618		31849		33669	ENGRAIS BRUTS
2713	NAT CALCM PHOSPHATES ETC	W 989684	39230	W 830765	34611	W 733321	31824	W 683211	32602	PHOSPHATES DE CALCIUM
27131	— UNGROUND	W 857887	33090	W 772130	31781	W 715854	30993	W 667895	31711	PHOSPHATES NON MOULUS
278	OTHER CRUDE MINERALS		20654	W 131269	22178		25874		33710	AUTRES MINERAUX BRUTS
28	METALLIFEROUS ORES,SCRAP		123262		167274		225162		245294	MINERAIS METAL,DECHETS
281	IRON ORE,CONCENTRATES	W 3573503	90876	W 5452091	128530	W 6278469	157043	W 5843451	158136	MINERAIS DE FER
2815	IRON ORE,CONC,NOT AGGLOM	W 1733659	47133	W 1493241	38722	W 2786480	70287	W 3252767	87870	MINERAIS NON AGGLOMERES
2816	IRON ORE AGGLOMERATES	W 1825604	43322	W 3958850	89808	W 3491989	86756	W 2590684	70266	MINERAIS AGGLOMERES
287	BASE METAL ORES,CONC NES	W 644386	32362	W 716549	38591		67712		86971	MINERAIS METAUX COMMUNS
2873	ALUMINIUM ORES,ALUMINA	W 533056	22076	W 562179	20673	W 674412	28603	W 643201	42845	MINERAIS D'ALUMINIUM
28731	ALUMINIUM ORE,CONCNTRATE	W 521045	20216	W 540716	18944	W 660493	24925	W 546446	20197	MINERAIS D'ALUMINIUM
3	MINERAL FUELS ETC		1683097		1681656		2197563		2394422	COMBUSTIBLES MINERAUX LUB
32	COAL,COKE AND BRIQUETTES		217226		241532		290625		315758	HOUILLES,COKES,BRIQUETTES
322	COAL,LIGNITE AND PEAT	W 3210356	188788	W 4090005	229857	W 4737827	279999	W 4730346	303288	HOUILLES,LIGNITES,TOURBE
3221	ANTHRACITE,NOT AGGLOMRTD	W 519618	31954	W 333902	21961	W 6011	445	W 9089	754	ANTHRACITE
3222	OTH COAL,NOT AGGLOMERATD	W 2643621	156036	W 3745593	207791	W 4726767	279196	W 4719027	302388	AUTRES HOUILLES
323	BRIQUETS,COKE,SEMI–COKE	W 463140	28438	W 147386	11675	W 73350	10626	W 89317	12470	BRIQUETTES
3232	COKE,SEMI–COKE,RTRT CRBN	W 454313	28186	W 146896	11665	W 73340	10612	W 83266	12285	COKES ET SEMI–COKES
33	PETROLEUM AND PRODUCTS		1001109		1053523		1424500		1447603	PETROLE ET DERIVES
333	CRUDE PETROLEUM	W 7580718	832563	W 8122294	895794	W 8657249	1053532	W 7155735	1036932	HUILES BRUTES DE PETROLE
334	PETROLEUM PRODUCTS,REFIN	W 1742128	165825	W 1631463	154518	W 2858488	364979	W 3220823	404834	PRODUITS RAFFINES
341	*GAS,NATURAL AND MANUFCT		408741		367235		478209		614354	GAZ NATUREL,GAZ MANUFACT
3414	PETROLEUM GASES, GASEOUS		406385		367223		478163		611900	GAZ DE PETROLE GAZEUX
351	*ELECTRIC CURRENT		56020		19366		4229		16707	ENERGIE ELECTRIQUE
5	CHEMCLS,RELATED PROD NES		575805		624818		1043149		1092635	PRODUITS CHIMIQUES
51	ORGANIC CHEMICALS		138425		128537		213818		179418	PROD CHIMIQ ORGANIQUES
511	HYDROCARBONS NES,DERIVS		24113	W 90054	34150		80897		40953	HYDROCARBURES NDA
5111	ACYCLIC HYDROCARBONS	W 36845	9278	W 37415	10737	W 104080	41583	W 64905	20150	HYDROCARBURES ACYCLIQUES
512	ALCOHOLS,PHENOLS ETC	W 72977	37772	W 37320	31473	W 46714	42322		40811	PHENOLS,PHENOLS–ALCOOLS
5121	ACYCLIC ALCOHOLS,DERIVS	W 56302	28910	W 19548	18669	W 23168	24160	W 42168	32820	ALCOOLS ACYCLIQUES
513	CARBOXYLIC ACIDS ETC	W 43234	30848	W 23261	21392	W 21977	31985	W 34828	32565	ACIDES CARBOXYLIQUES
514	NITROGEN–FNCTN COMPOUNDS	W 15167	24436	W 6480	18725	W 5671	23913	W 6665	24243	COMPOSES FONCT AZOTEES
52	INORGANIC CHEMICALS		45016		48745		60553		70422	PROD CHIM INORGANIQUES
522	INORG ELEMNTS,OXIDES,ETC	W 180446	24307	W 132312	24589		30765		30792	ELEMENTS INORGANIQUES
523	OTHR INORG CHEMICALS ETC		20316		23569		29257		38918	AUT PRODUITS CHIMIQUES INORG
53	DYES,TANNING,COLOUR PROD		61722		68850		109791		123194	PROD TEINTURE,COLORANTS
533	PIGMENTS,PAINTS,ETC	W 20031	43920	W 22135	49313	W 33399	83565	W 40009	95349	PIGMENTS,PEINTURES,VERNIS
5334	VARNISHES,DISTEMPERS ETC	W 14720	33664	W 15352	36194	W 20110	57959	W 22057	63254	PEINTURES A L'EAU
53342	OTH PAINTS,VARNISHES ETC	W 11862	27534	W 12830	29384	W 14992	44499	W 15130	50475	AUTRES PEINTURES,VERNIS
541	*MEDICINAL,PHARM PRODUCT		112165	MK 18806	105273		172713		195330	PROD MEDICINAUX PHARMACEUT
5417	MEDICAMENTS	K 3953000	84919	K 2239000	68230	K 3339326	115849	K 3773884	139055	MEDICAMENTS
54171	— CONTAINNG ANTIBIOTICS	K 380000	15671	K 696000	21629	K 975796	36113	K 835991	34560	MED CONTN ANTIBIOTIQUES
54179	— CONTNG OTH SUBSTANCES	K 2615000	47073	K 1184000	32965	K 2049396	61369	K 2425563	82033	MED CONT AUT SUBSTANCES
55	PERFUME,CLEANING ETC PRD		44353		74922		133166		143823	PROD POUR PARFUM,TOILETTE
553	PERFUMERY,COSMETICS,ETC	W 5911	21643	W 8531	27037	W 10928	54730	W 12934	63597	PRODUITS DE PARFUMERIE
554	SOAP,CLEANSING ETC PREPS	W 15469	16172	W 35040	39171	W 61647	66521	W 59786	65428	SAVONS,PRODUITS DETERSIFS
5542	WASHING PREPARATIONS ETC	W 10694	11531	W 26730	30985	W 51355	55481	W 47680	53491	PROD ORG TENSIO–ACT NDA
58	PLASTIC MATERIALS ETC		57569		70178		134669		141802	MAT PLAST ARTIFICIELLES
582	PROD OF CONDENSATION ETC	W 18144	21118	W 15735	22365	W 18331	47677	W 21970	44388	PROD CONDENS,POLYCOND
583	POLYMERIZATION ETC PRODS		34691	W 21899	44331		82218	W 35015	91546	PROD POLYMERISATION
59	CHEMICAL MATERIALS NES		108952		116567		206675		227777	MAT PROD CHIMIQUES NDA
591	PESTICIDES,DISINFECTANTS	W 5781	58106	W 5412	47820	W 9065	87686	W 12016	107202	DESINF,INSECT,FONG,HERB

4. General Imports C.I.F. by Commodities according to the S.I.T.C. (Rev. 2) in thousand U.S. Dollars
Importations Générales C.A.F. par Produits d'après la C.T.C.I. (Rév. 2) en milliers de Dollars E.U.

SITC CTCI	COMMODITY	1993		1994		1995		1996		PRODUIT
		WEIGHT POIDS	VALUE VALEUR	WEIGHT POIDS	VALUE VALEUR	WEIGHT POIDS	VALUE VALEUR	WEIGHT POIDS	VALUE VALEUR	
5912	FUNGICIDES,FOR RETAIL	W 2127	23618	W 1695	22109	W 2694	31113	W 2675	30305	FONGICIDES VENTE AU DET
5913	HERBICIDES,FOR RETAIL	W 2269	21960	W 1184	10941	W 2884	34028	W 5244	54303	HERBICIDES VENTE AU DET
598	MISCEL CHEM PRODUCTS NES		41868		55650		96822		94317	PROD DIV INDUST CHIM NDA
5989	CHEM PRODUCTS,PREPS NES		27921		38550		76050		73403	PROD PREP CHIMIQUES NDA
59899	OTH CHEM PRODS,PREPS,NES	W 5644	14112	W 9914	21306	W 18154	42346	W 18476	37970	AUT PRODUITS CHIMIQUES NDA
6	BASIC MANUFACTURES		1059587		1383266		2140018		2563935	ART MANUFACTURES
61	LEATHER,DRESSED FUR,ETC		104786		168677		265678		337692	CUIRS,PELLETERIES
611	LEATHER	W 5514	78423	W 7812	121985	W 9540	185868	W 11390	230213	CUIRS,PEAUX PREPARES
6113	CALF LEATHER	W 1601	23165	W 2519	28212	W 1521	27378	W 1951	33510	CUIRS,PEAUX DE VEAUX
6114	LEATHR BOVINE NES,EQUINE	W 2984	44762	W 4093	77702	W 7010	140659	W 8401	177213	CUIRS DE BOVINS
612	LEATHER ETC MANUFACTURES		25522	W 7245	45742		78356		103703	OUVRAGES EN CUIRS NDA
6123	PREPRD PARTS OF FOOTWEAR	W 4125	25270	W 7210	45445	W 11800	77752	W 15128	102989	PARTIES DE CHAUSSURES
62	RUBBER MANUFACTURES NES		58086		45054		52922		68967	CAOUTCHOUC MANUFACTURE
625	RUBBER TYRES, TUBES ETC	W 13464	27984	W 7423	13809	W 13880	25996	W 16728	31213	PNEUS CAOUTCHOUC VULCANISE
628	RUBBER ARTICLES NES	W 4746	21743	W 6532	24649	W 2796	18431	W 2753	24348	OUVRAGES CAOUTCHOUC NDA
63	WOOD,CORK MANUFACTRS NES		16120		21759		59422		50189	OUVRAGES LIEGE ET BOIS
634	VENEERS,PLYWOOD,ETC	W 11302	10329	W 23049	13743	W 28358	38531	W 41210	34352	PLACAGES,CONTRE–PLAQUES
64	PAPER,PAPERBOARD AND MFR		53975		89110		160862		190822	PAPIERS,CARTONS & OUVRAGES
641	PAPER AND PAPERBOARD	W 51786	36857	W 68079	56260	W 79727	99187	W 102614	114196	PAPIERS ET CARTONS
642	PAPER,ETC,PRECUT,ARTS OF	W 13625	17118	W 22805	32850	W 31244	61675		76626	PAP,CARTONS DECOUPES
6421	PAPER ETC CONTAINERS	W 9022	9462	W 15317	18726	W 18819	30448	W 25926	43965	BOITES,SACS EMBALLAGES
65	TEXTILE YARN,FABRICS,ETC		481225		624552		938843		1054883	FILS,TISSUS,ARTICLES TEXTILE
651	TEXTILE YARN		38260		46764		66192		73057	FILS TEXTILES
652	COTTON FABRICS,WOVEN	W 5779	69661	W 9758	102977		146838		170139	TISSUS DE COTON
6522	WOVEN COTTON BLEACHD,ETC	W 4649	60282	W 8020	92133		129059		146941	TISSUS COTON BLANCHIS ETC
65224	BLCHED COTTON FABRIC NES	W 2970	35510	W 5655	59597	W 6804	91365	W 7416	108893	AUT TIS PLUS 85% COT BLANCHI
65225	BLCHD COTN BLEND FAB NES	W 1061	17939	W 1663	24896	W 1581	26269	W 1613	23624	AUT TIS MOINS 85% COT BLANCH
653	WOVN MAN–MADE FIB FABRIC	W 13528	214991	W 16957	268249	W 21608	392288	W 25543	419605	TISSUS FIBRES SYNTH,ARTIF
6531	CONT SYNT WEAVES NONPILE	W 4347	64117	W 6134	96836	W 7450	133326	W 8446	126275	TISSUS FIBRES SYNTH CONTINUE
65314	CONT SYN TYRE CORD FABRC	W 382	7856	W 875	19689	W 1422	31387	W 1324	24990	TIS ARMATURE PNEUMATIQUES
65315	CONT SYN TXTL FABRIC NES	W 3965	56261	W 5259	77147	W 6029	101939	W 7122	101285	TIS PLUS 85% TEXT SYNT CONT
6534	DISC SYN BLEND FABRC NES	W 3480	54193	W 4622	67693	W 5908	100110	W 6800	115020	TISSUS FIBRES SYNTH DISCONT
6535	CONT REGN WEAVES NONPILE	W 1275	23347	W 1535	27822	W 2058	42466	W 2660	48837	TISSUS FIB TEXT ART CONTINU
6536	DISC REGN TXTL FABRC NES	W 1379	23351	W 1838	27247	W 2254	39734	W 2159	38443	TISSUS 85% TEXT ART DISC
6538	DISC REG BLEND FABRC NES	W 1893	31537	W 1739	34576	W 2146	52290	W 2581	56843	TIS MOINS 85% TEXT ART DISC
65383	DISC REG–CONT MAN–MD FAB	W 1170	19765	W 884	18648	W 1018	24766	W 1251	28118	TISSUS TEX ART CONT MEL SYNT
654	OTH WOVEN TEXTILE FABRIC	W 3810	79339	W 5068	100302		152178		162937	TISSUS AUT COTON SYNT,ARTIF
6542	WOVEN WOOL,HAIR NONPILE	W 1256	34343	W 2052	50470	W 2489	75128	W 2937	90187	TIS PLUS 85% LAINE,POILS
65422	WOVN COMB WOOL,FINE HAIR	W 777	23226	W 1457	37883	W 1706	56682	W 2189	71120	TISSUS 85% LAINE,PLS PEIG
6543	WOVEN WOOL ETC FABRC NES	W 1707	33382	W 1934	32476		51287	W 2611	51944	TISSUS LAINE,POILS FINS NDA
65432	WOOL–DISC SYN FIBR FABRC	W 1401	27629	W 1699	28302	W 2193	47172	W 2382	47349	TISSUS LAINE MEL SYNT DISC
655	KNITTED,ETC FABRICS	W 982	9673	W 1621	18445	W 2755	36200	W 4163	47316	ETOF BONNETERIE PIECES ETC
6552	OTHER KNIT ETC FAB NONEL	W 982	9673	W 1621	18445	W 2755	36200	W 4163	47316	ETOF BON NON ELAS NON SYNT
657	SPECIAL TXTL FABRC,PRODS		38990		55353		94862		122322	TISSUS SPECIAUX
6572	BONDED FIBRE TEXTLS NES	W 1038	16770	W 2265	27147	W 3509	41683	W 4474	47606	TISSUS NON TISSES
6573	COATED ETC TEXTILES NES	W 1426	12261	W 2153	17349	W 3295	34251	W 3689	42849	TISSUS,ART MATIERE TEXT NDA
66	NONMETAL MINERAL MFS NES		69541		83122		121347		156222	ART MIN NON METALLIQUES
662	CLAY,REFRACTORY BLDG PRD	W 39207	26701	W 41185	29198		43199	W 109065	52728	MAT CONST REFRACTAIRES
6623	REFRACTORY BUILDING PROD	W 22873	21555	W 24046	21808	W 29998	31681	W 32923	32473	BRIQUES REFRACTAIRES
663	MINERAL MANUFCTURES NES	W 14387	16866	W 8108	15370		30476		34809	ART MIN MANUF NDA
664	GLASS	W 9074	13228	W 9486	23584		22488	W 14496	35156	VERRE
67	IRON AND STEEL		163254		208349		292522		370603	FER ET ACIER
671	PIG IRON ETC		26288	W 59380	31722	W 71904	46140	W 56818	38338	FONTE,SPIEGEL,POUDRES
6716	FERRO–ALLOYS	W 37880	23235	W 54727	30269	W 61531	42912	W 47740	35943	FERRO–ALLIAGES
672	IRON,STEEL PRIMARY FORMS	W 153069	42466	W 287121	75117	W 361822	141049	W 416708	175535	LINGOTS FER,ACIER
6725	IRN,STL BLOOMS,SLABS,ETC	W 114661	28003	W 234659	52909	W 304445	88452	W 328255	116645	BLOOMS,BILLETTES FER ACIER
67251	IRN,SMPLE STL BLOOMS,ETC	W 112843	26272	W 220227	42851	W 234767	53685	W 248688	70817	BLOOMS ETC NON ACIER FIN
67255	OTH ALLOY STL BLOOMS ETC	W 1745	1356	W 13362	8259	W 68529	32258	W 78462	43403	BLOOMS ETC AUT AC ALLIES
6727	IRN,STL COIL FR REROLLNG	W 21101	11318	W 47913	21310	W 38626	45387	W 70736	50458	EBAUCHES POUR TOLES FER
674	IRN,STL UNIV,PLATE,SHEET	W 41596	39183	W 48112	38367	W 53519	44720	W 84142	64360	LARGES PLATS,TOLES
678	IRON,STL TUBES,PIPES,ETC	W 16807	22659	W 33550	38811	W 19552	32243	W 27641	51803	TUBES,TUYAUX EN FONTE,FER
6782	IRON,STL SEAMLESS TUBES	W 9944	15306	W 18026	26287	W 11678	18471	W 19780	33909	TUBES,TUYAUX SANS SOUDURE
68	NON–FERROUS METALS		39693		36493		75052		102305	METAUX NON FERREUX
684	ALUMINIUM	W 3343	10698	W 2491	12822		29330	W 6530	47250	ALUMINIUM
6842	ALUMINIUM,ALLOYS WORKED	W 1219	8478	W 2454	12788		29305	W 6432	47110	ALUMINIUM,ALLIAGES OUVRE
69	METAL MANUFACTURES NES		72906		106150		173370		232252	ART MANUFACT EN METAL NDA
692	METAL TANKS,BOXES,ETC	W 4099	8130	W 4686	9717	W 7267	22630		39104	RECIPIENTS METALLIQUES
699	BASE METAL MFRS NES		34171		50035		66890		87191	ART MANUFACTURES MET NDA
7	MACHINES,TRANSPORT EQUIP		1449705		1784636		2538368		2916665	MACHINES MATERIEL TRANSPORT
71	POWER GENERATING EQUIPMT		52081		55619		85116		129288	MACHINES GENERATRICES
713	INTRNL COMBUS PSTN ENGIN	W 2932	27212		24391		30766		70567	MOTEURS EXPL COMB INT, PIECE
7132	MOTOR VEHCL PISTN ENGINS	W 1243	6929	W 939	5825	W 1531	10294	W 6698	49165	MOTEURS EXPL POUR VEHICULES
72	MACHS FOR SPCL INDUSTRYS		325293		466771		602903		697568	MAC SPECIALES POUR INDUST
721	AGRIC MACHY,EXC TRACTORS		35198	W 12849	88075	W 15829	103386		79743	MACHINES AGRICOLES
7212	HARVESTING ETC MACHINES	W 2734	24885	W 11475	79228	W 12839	75350	W 4885	33098	ENGINS POUR LA RECOLTE
723	CIVIL ENGNEERG EQUIP ETC	W 2483	17749	W 3513	29933	W 5798	46770	W 6914	49284	APPAREILS DE GENIE CIVIL
7234	CONST,MINING MACHNRY NES	W 2305	14218	W 2909	16951	W 4216	31959	W 5796	40004	MACH POUR LA CONST, MINES
724	TEXTILE,LEATHER MACHNRY	W 4948	81654	W 6115	100548	W 7081	136565		154637	MACH POUR INDUSTRIE TEXTILE
7243	SEWING MACHS,NEEDLES ETC	W 980	22757	W 1451	31585	W 1587	43006	W 1534	44094	MACHINES A COUDRE,PIECES
72431	SEWING MACHINES	W 740	19373	W 1263	26705	W 1340	36556	W 1314	35272	MACHINES A COUDRE
7245	WEAVING,FELT MFG,ETC MCH	W 1573	22155	W 904	18275	W 1098	23710	W 1324	46988	METIERS A TISSER,PIECES
7247	TEXTILE MACHINERY NES	W 805	15917	W 872	18417	W 2394	37802	W 2674	35227	MACH LAVAGE,TEINTURE TEX
726	PRINTG,BKBINDG MACHY,PTS	W 1590	11519	W 1754	16260		32801		40186	MACHINES POUR IMPRIMERIE
727	FOOD MACHRY NON–DOMESTIC	W 4366	63344	W 5036	55455	W 6512	73278	W 8321	121771	MACH INDUSTRIES ALIMENT
7272	OTH FOOD PROC MCHY,PARTS	W 3260	52733	W 3802	41626	W 5080	64931	W 7127	112079	AUT MACH IND ALIMENTAIRE
72722	INDUS FOOD PROC MACH NES	W 3170	51644	W 3741	40864	W 4977	62628	W 6030	94928	MACHINES BOULANGERIE
728	OTH MACHY FOR SPCL INDUS		104767	W 11936	152796	W 16093	180483	W 20354	226513	AUT MACH IND PARTICULIERES
7281	MACH–TOOLS FR SPCL INDUS	W 3511	41175	W 4467	42462	W 6706	57971	W 7421	58504	MACH–OUTILS SPEC IND PART
72812	MACH–TOOLS TO WORK WOOD	W 2694	32551	W 3715	31503	W 4784	33314	W 6477	47413	MACH–OUT POUR TRAVAIL BOIS
7283	OTHR MINERAL WORKG MACHY	W 1185	18346	W 2790	24404	W 3387	25827	W 4794	28165	MACH TRIER,CRIBLER,BROYER
7284	MACHY FOR SPCL INDUS NES		45246	W 4679	85930	W 6000	96685	W 8139	139844	MACH SPEC IND PARTICUL.
72842	RUBBER,PLASTICS WRKG MCH	W 1316	24162	W 1882	38047	W 2069	33978	W 2617	37466	MACH IND CAOUT MAT PLAST
72848	OTH MCHY WITH INDIV FNCT	W 387	9359	W 1622	29062	W 1288	27016	W 1028	27499	AUTRES MACHINES NDA
72849	PTS OF MACHS OF 7284 ETC	W 355	9675	W 526	13554	W 1951	30883	W 2084	34822	PIECES DU 728.4 ETC
73	METALWORKING MACHINERY		61315		37624		81414		84125	MACH TRAVAIL DES METAUX
736	METALWORKING MACH–TOOLS	W 7446	39193	W 1743	22813		39961	W 3317	57639	MACH–OUTILS TRAVAIL METAUX
737	METALWORKING MACHNRY NES		22122	W 1318	14811		41453		26486	MACH TRAV METAUX PIECES
74	GENRL INDUSTRL MACHY NES		244811		282790		517736		619640	MACH APP INDUSTRIE
741	HEATING,COOLING EQUIPMNT	W 5549	63930	W 10525	95469	W 15324	171551	W 20546	245231	MACH CHAUFFAGE,PIECES
7413	INDUS FURNACES ETC,PARTS	W 1675	18227	W 4440	30813	W 3635	44582	W 6477	67286	FOURS IND,LABOR,PIECES
74132	INDUST FURNACES NONELECT	W 1314	11540	W 1749	14410	W 2378	29042	W 5471	53706	FOURS NON ELECTRIQUES

4. General Imports C.I.F. by Commodities according to the S.I.T.C. (Rev. 2) in thousand U.S. Dollars
Importations Générales C.A.F. par Produits d'après la C.T.C.I. (Rév. 2) en milliers de Dollars E.U.

SITC CTCI	COMMODITY	1993 WEIGHT POIDS	1993 VALUE VALEUR	1994 WEIGHT POIDS	1994 VALUE VALEUR	1995 WEIGHT POIDS	1995 VALUE VALEUR	1996 WEIGHT POIDS	1996 VALUE VALEUR	PRODUIT
7414	NONDOM REFRIG EQUIPT,PTS	W 1738	14007	W 3097	20302	W 7392	50512	W 5697	44379	MAT PRODUCTION DU FROID
74141	REFRIG EQUIP NONDOMESTIC	W 1414	11910	W 2484	16672	W 5026	37322	W 3894	34285	REFIG INDUSTRIELS
7415	AIR–CONDITIONING MACHNRY	W 737	9548	W 1129	15543	W 1652	33600	W 1680	26578	GROUPES CONDITION AIR
7416	HEATING,COOLING EQU NES	W 1083	13493	W 1314	14253	W 2015	28903	W 4594	76279	APP CHANGEMENT TEMP
742	PUMPS FOR LIQUIDS ETC	W 1520	23430	W 1567	22798	W 2528	34001	W 2083	45875	POMPES MOTO–POMPES
743	PUMPS NES,CENTRFUGES ETC	W 2598	34638	W 3231	37408	W 5340	62420	W 6660	91673	POMPES COMPRES,VENT ETC
7439	PTS NES OF APP OF 7435,6	W 264	10746	W 295	8533	W 763	16195	W 1172	37295	PIECES 743.5 ET 743.6
744	MECHANICAL HANDLING EQU	W 2751	19945	W 3774	24223	W 8548	72316	W 6539	40124	EQUIP MANUTENTION PIECES
7442	LIFTING,LOADING MACH NES	W 1139	8723	W 1139	8200	W 3856	33529	W 2222	16281	APP LEVAGE,MANUTENTION
745	NONELEC MACHY,TOOLS NES	W 3407	71154	W 3521	61343		110240		111841	AUT MACH NON ELEC,PIECES
7452	OTH NONELEC MCHS,PTS NES	W 3332	68108	W 3431	57658		96963		102122	AUT MACH NON ELEC,PIECES
74522	PACKAGNG,BOTTLNG,ETC MCH	W 1527	35301	W 1797	39143	W 2829	59407	W 2540	61240	MACH NETT BOUTEILLES,ETC
74523	PACKING ETC MCHY PTS NES	W 1376	24265	W 415	4723	W 893	12312	W 637	14328	PIECES POUR 745.22,775.3
749	NONELEC MACH PTS,ACC NES	W 1438	31715	W 2022	41549		67208		84896	PIECES MACH NON ELEC NDA
7492	COCKS,VALVES ETC NES	W 398	9050	W 610	15640	W 1758	29290	W 1986	41875	ART ROB,SIM POUR TUYAUX
75	OFFICE MACHNES,ADP EQUIP		107140		128768		188212		205823	MACH BUREAU TRAIT AUTOM
751	OFFICE MACHINES	W 673	20944		18508		25353		23726	MACH,APPAREILS DE BUREAU
752	AUTOMTIC DATA PROC EQUIP	W 673	48376	W 969	63484	W 1846	99341	W 2300	118224	MACH TRAIT INFORMATION
759	OFFICE,ADP MCH PTS,ACCES	W 919	37821	W 751	46776	W 1114	63518	W 1323	63873	PIECES DU 751 ET 752
7599	ACCTG,ETC,ADP MCH PTS,AC	W 815	33338	W 681	41905	W 1052	56861	W 1254	57216	PIECES DU 751 ET 752
76	TELECOMM,SOUND EQUIPMENT		178486		202462		249306		274018	EQUIPMENT DE TELECOM
764	TELECOM EQPT,PTS,ACC NES	W 5460	159287		186693		222874		240957	EQUIP TELECOM,PIECES
7643	TV,RADIO TRANSMITTRS ETC	W 79	11736	W 98	17951	W 193	31840	W 124	22847	APP EMET TELE RADIO
7649	PTS NES OF EQUIPMT OF 76	W 4754	118484		139432		151571	W 5911	169051	PIECES DE LA DIV 76
76491	PTS NES OF APPAR OF 7641	W 1014	58974	W 859	63588	W 636	49896	W 772	70458	PIECES POUR 764.1
76493	TELECOMM EQUIPMT PTS NES	W 3547	54598	W 3461	72174	W 5081	100207	W 5044	96356	PIECES 761,762,764.3,8
77	ELECTRIC MACHNRY NES ETC		203610		285581		428076		504165	MACH APP ELECT NDA
772	SWITCHGEAR ETC,PARTS NES	W 668	20345	W 1389	51760		49823		68084	APP COUPURE,SECT ETC
7721	SWITCHGEAR ETC	W 524	18545	W 1303	49641	W 1507	47622	W 1885	63878	APP COUPURE,SECTIONMNT
773	ELECTR DISTRIBUTNG EQUIP	W 10091	35786	W 13902	92319	W 12767	100880	W 14977	114755	EQUIPMT DISTRIBUTION ELECT
7731	INSULATED WIRE,CABLE ETC	W 9929	34107	W 13781	89198	W 12653	97680	W 14826	111352	FILS,CABLES ISOLES ELECT
774	ELECTRO–MEDCL,XRAY EQUIP	W 201	30712	W 66	20508	W 264	44136	W 197	20018	APPAREILS MEDICAUX
7742	X–RAY APPARATUS ETC	W 168	24510	W 34	9016	W 205	33043	W 143	9582	APPAREILS A RAYONS X
775	HOUSEHOLD TYPE EQUIP NES		29569		20968		45039		89399	MACH,APP USAGE DOMESTQUE
776	TRANSISTORS,VALVES,ETC	W 4813	38829	W 4905	41642		85730		90201	LAMPES,TUBES,VALVES
7761	TV PICTURE TUBES	W 4591	29636	W 4694	33381	W 7783	63927	W 7235	59978	TUBES CATHODIQUES
778	ELECTRICAL MACHINERY NES		43533		51784		91904		105453	AUTRES MACH ELECT NDA
7788	OTH ELEC MACHY,EQUIP NES		15779		23486		36245		41819	AUT MACH APP ELEC NDA
78	ROAD VEHICLES		131963		120707		310347		346526	VEHICULES ROUTIERS
781	PASS MOTOR VEH EXC BUSES	W 2969	8922	W 3029	16515	W 23013	175352	W 10908	79022	AUTO TRANSPORT PERSONNES
782	LORRIES,SPCL MTR VEH NES	W 19625	36731	W 13590	49010	W 14210	51606	W 14764	53453	VEHICULES SPECIAUX,MARCH
7821	LORRIES,TRUCKS	W 18315	29354	W 10881	23156	W 10984	34147	W 12276	42703	VEHICULES TRANSP MARCHAND
7822	SPECIAL MOTOR VEHCLS NES	W 1310	7377	W 2709	25854	W 3226	17459	W 2488	10750	VEHICULES USAGES SPECIAUX
783	ROAD MOTOR VEHICLES NES	W 11771	48803	W 7743	29804	W 10567	41703	W 8912	48979	VEHICULES ROUTIERS NDA
7832	TRACTORS FOR TR–TRAILERS	W 4566	42498	W 3219	11543	W 5172	15160	W 5539	32174	TRACTEURS ROUTIERS
784	MOTOR VEH PRTS,ACCES NES	W 3164	14655	W 4141	15435	W 5148	25995	W 20959	145095	PIECES 722,781,782,783
7849	OTHER MOTOR VEHCL PARTS	W 2243	11136	W 3749	14425	W 4342	23707	W 20039	142872	PIECES 722,781,782,783
786	TRAILERS,NONMOTR VEH,NES	W 9953	21690	W 5791	8911	W 7475	13521	W 7068	17251	REMORQUES,CADRES,CONTAIN
79	OTHR TRANSPORT EQUIPMENT		145006		204314		75258		55512	AUTRE MATERIEL TRANSPORT
791	RAILWAY VEHICLES		64053	W 8043	21067		44947		14152	VEHIC MAT CHEMINS DE FER
7914	RY COACHES NES NOT POWRD	W 3889	58697	W 1313	9946		4		4	VOITURES A VOYAGEURS
792	AIRCRAFT ETC		79866		181879		28260		38168	APP NAVIGATION AERIENNE
7923	AIRCRFT NES2000–15000KG			W 74	26021	W 25	183		6619	AERODYNES 2000 A 15000 KG
7924	AIRCRFT NES OVER 15000KG	W 150	68000	W 199	126320	W 195	1400	W 92	1477	AERODYNES PLUS 15000 KG
7929	AIRCRAFT PARTS NES	W 48	11694	W 115	27569		21565	W 57	25294	PIECES DU 792
8	MISC MANUFACTURED GOODS		389750		521753		842893		907441	ART MANUFACTURES DIVERS
812	*PLUMBG,HEATNG,LGHTNG EQ	W 6108	10099	W 6578	14976	W 10683	34886	W 11028	44699	APPAR SANITAIRES CHAUFFAGE
821	*FURNITURE,PARTS THEREOF	W 4679	13580	W 7563	23587	W 15100	45159	W 19416	60204	MEUBLES ET PIECES
8219	FURNITURE AND PARTS NES	W 3830	8590	W 6477	17610	W 12988	35314	W 16715	43505	AUTRES MEUBLES ET PIECES
84	CLOTHING AND ACCESSORIES		112029		122557		170130		189071	VETEMENTS
844	UNDER GARMENTS NOT KNIT	W 1519	18103	W 3949	27062	W 6863	46209	W 5266	83243	VETEMENT DESSOUS MAT TEX
8441	— MENS SHIRTS	W 1298	16808	W 3676	26516	W 6117	45284	W 4894	81914	CHEMISES HOMMES MAT TEXT
84412	—— OF SYNTHETIC FIBRES	W 1130	15775	W 2713	24409	W 4838	43649	W 4795	80314	CHEMISES HOMMES FIB SYNT
846	UNDER GARMENTS KNITTED	W 2119	23490	W 3106	27042	W 3179	34596		31503	SOUS VETS DE BONNETERIE
847	TEXTILE CLTHNG ACCES NES		23845	W 1555	28937		47469		30387	ACCES VET MAT TEXT NDA
8471	— NOT KNITTED	W 985	21989	W 1309	26555		45087		28477	ACCES VET MAT TEX NON BON
84719	MADE–UP CLTHG ACCESS NES	W 898	21037	W 1148	25780	W 1644	44148	W 1458	27916	AUT ACCES VET MAT TEXTIL
851	*FOOTWEAR	W 6101	20859	W 12362	18489	W 22033	21621	W 20232	17836	CHAUSSURES
87	PRECISION INSTRUMNTS NES		61814		111956		196935		171092	INSTRUM,APPAR SCIENT NDA
872	MEDICAL INSTRUMENTS NES	W 523	10213	W 974	15937		55774		44353	INSTR,APP MEDIC–CHIR NDA
87202	OTH MEDICAL INSTRUMENTS	W 510	8654	W 938	14678	W 1855	52964	W 2046	38937	INSTRUM,APP MEDECINE
874	MEASURNG,CONTROLNG INSTR		45566	W 998	83874		127580		111470	INSTRUMENTS DE MESURE
8742	MEASUR,DRAW ETC INST,PTS	W 99	4888	W 333	31375		50149		11955	INST DESSIN,TRACAGE,PCS
87421	MEASURNG,DRAWNG ETC INST	W 97	4357	W 267	30554	W 476	47632	W 330	10274	INSTRUM DESSIN,TRACAGE
8748	ELEC MEAS,CONTRL EQU NES		18012	W 120	24002		31718		39005	APP ELEC ELECTRO MESURE
87483	OTH ELCTRNC MEAS ETC EQU	W 134	15647	W 106	21693		28991		32684	AUT APP ELECTRO DE MESURE
88	PHOTO EQU,OPTICL GDS ETC		16947		19811		34859		40765	APP,FOURN PHOTO,OP,MONTR
89	MISC MANUFCTRD GOODS NES		153312		208066		335306		379543	ART MANUFACTURES DIVERS
892	PRINTED MATTER		26180		37578		59640		68658	IMPRIMES
8928	PRINTED MATTER NES		15107		20524		29112		35944	IMPRIMES NDA
893	ARTICLES OF PLASTIC NES	W 13601	43197	W 65598	70075	W 40620	130545	W 41961	157606	OUVRAGES EN MAT DIVIS 58
8931	PLSTC PACKG CONTNRS,LIDS	W 8401	16388	W 54951	29096	W 23858	48529	W 19068	42618	ART TRANSP EMBALLAGE ETC
8939	MISC PLASTIC ARTICLES	W 5112	26461	W 10266	40326	W 16451	80476	W 22483	112940	ART DIVERS EN MAT DIV 58
89399	OTHR PLASTC ARTICLES NES	W 4325	24419	W 8425	36235	W 13548	71429	W 19816	103918	AUT OUV MAT DIV 58
894	TOYS,SPORTING GOODS,ETC	W 5446	28413	W 8018	39271		55141		50333	VOITURES ENFANTS,JOUETS
8942	TOYS,INDOOR GAMES ETC	W 5039	24702	W 7496	33964	W 9898	42520	W 8893	39029	JOUETS,JEUX ETC
899	OTHER MANUFACTURED GOODS		33954		44274		62806		74945	AUT ART MANUF DIVERS NDA
8998	SMALLWARES,TOILETRYS ETC		28302		35045		48008		58349	ART MERCERIE,TOILETTE
89983	BUTTONS,STUDS,ETC	W 351	18652	W 581	22956	W 825	30499	W 899	33214	BOUTONS,BOUTONS–PRESSION
9	GOODS NOT CLASSD BY KIND		49142		86057		122969		164554	ART TRANSACT NON CLASSES
931	*SPECIAL TRANSACTIONS		28627		67389		103414		140656	TRANS.SPECIALES
971	*GOLD,NON MONETARY NES		20418		18404					OR NON MONETAIRE
97101	NONMON GLD UNWRT,SEMIMFD		20409		18403					OR,ALLIAGES D'OR BRUTS

5. General Exports F.O.B. by Commodities according to the S.I.T.C. (Rev. 2) in thousand U.S. Dollars
Exportations Générales F.O.B. par Produits d'après la C.T.C.I. (Rév. 2) en milliers de Dollars E.U.

SITC CTCI	COMMODITY	1993 WEIGHT POIDS	1993 VALUE VALEUR	1994 WEIGHT POIDS	1994 VALUE VALEUR	1995 WEIGHT POIDS	1995 VALUE VALEUR	1996 WEIGHT POIDS	1996 VALUE VALEUR	PRODUIT
	ALL COMMODITIES		4892169		6151245		7910049		8084459	TOUS PRODUITS
0	FOOD AND LIVE ANIMALS		233719		309990		398748		557413	ALIMENTS,ANIMAUX VIVANTS
001	*LIVE ANIMALS FOR FOOD	W 60828	55266	W 83137	85081	W 81754	85572	W 73018	71761	ANIMAUX VIVANTS
0011	BOVINE SPECIES,LIVE	W 16297	16057	W 24439	26376	W 24426	28613	W 13667	16068	ESPECE BOVINE
0012	SHEEP AND GOATS,LIVE	W 39929	35484	W 48318	50533	W 44049	44786	W 41027	39895	ESPECES OVINE ET CAPRINE
01	MEAT AND PREPARATIONS		107570		131955		75931		64700	VIANDES ET PREPARATIONS
011	MEAT FRESH,CHILLD,FROZEN	W 76081	93884	W 97869	118269	W 42061	65424	W 37492	59778	VIANDES FRAICHES,REF,CONGE
0113	PIG MEAT FRESH,CHLD,FRZN	W 61631	66857	W 86282	93901	W 37667	50195	W 34456	48596	VIANDE DE PORC
04	CEREALS AND PREPARATIONS		3958		7742		143622		305491	CEREALES ET PRODUITS
041	WHEAT ETC UNMILLED			W 100	32	W 649684	109312	W 1281017	232785	FROMENT,EPEAUTRE
0412	OTHER WHEAT ETC UNMILLED			W 100	32	W 649384	109217	W 1281017	232785	AUTRE FROMENT NON MOULU
043	BARLEY UNMILLED			W 175	42	W 8535	820	W 166669	24735	ORGE NON MONDEE
044	MAIZE UNMILLED	W 3086	3352	W 6985	7312	W 220546	29830	W 187578	27143	MAIS NON MOULU
05	VEGETABLES AND FRUIT		52288		62035		67268		73802	LEGUMES ET FRUITS
054	VEG ETC FRSH,SMPLY PRSVD		19757	W 53848	24752		24757	W 25460	24850	LEGUMES FRAIS,CONG,SECS
057	FRUIT,NUTS,FRESH,DRIED		18876	W 47060	18341		23492	W 133697	25708	FRUITS FRAIS OU SECS
1	BEVERAGES AND TOBACCO		17452		23543		31141		54911	BOISSONS ET TABACS
11	BEVERAGES		16537		23410		30359		54833	BOISSONS
112	ALCOHOLIC BEVERAGES	W 22929	16264	W 39014	20155		26245		36187	BOISSONS ALCOOLIQUES
1121	WINE OF FRESH GRAPES ETC	W 22072	15456	W 37809	19180		25321	W 49184	34639	VINS DE RAISINS FRAIS
11212	WINE OF FRESH GRAPES	W 20725	14771	W 36622	18695	W 33292	24590	W 45454	32908	VINS DE MOUTS DE RAISINS
2	CRUDE MATERLS,EXCL FUELS		196641		277760		295295		309283	MAT BRUTES NON COMESTIBLES
24	CORK AND WOOD		110713		156334		174849		217939	LIEGE ET BOIS
248	WOOD SHAPED,SLEEPERS	W 273347	108501	W 423937	154249	W 455285	171313	W 544004	214475	BOIS SIMPLEMENT TRAVAILLES
2482	LUMBER SHAPED CONIFER	W 149186	51930	W 221223	72310	W 265395	88701	W 290361	96365	CONIFERES SCIES,RABOTES
24821	LUMBER SAWN ETC CONIFER	W 149106	51892	W 220068	71760	W 260941	86392	W 285525	94348	CONIFERES SCIES LONGITUD
2483	LUMBER SHAPED NON–CONIFR	W 124159	56572	W 202714	81939	W 189890	82612	W 253643	118110	NON CONIFERES SCIES,RABOTES
24831	LUMBER SAWN ETC NON–CON	W 120735	55062	W 190362	77381	W 170799	74853	W 238461	108966	SCIES LONGITUDINALEMENT
26	TEXTILE FIBRES AND WASTE		34870		46197		61003		34231	FIBRES TEXTILES
266	SYNTHETIC FIBRES TO SPIN		18884	W 18505	26393	W 18604	37115	W 11438	16859	FIBRES SYNTHETIQUES
2665	DISCN SYNTH FIBRE UNCMBD	W 8341	12477	W 15183	21102	W 15625	30993	W 9968	13789	DISCONTINUES EN MASSE
27	CRUDE FERTLZR,MINRLS NES		14852		15471		14876		20869	ENGRAIS MINERAUX BRUTS
28	METALLIFEROUS ORES,SCRAP		14436		28556		11679		5774	MINERAIS METAL,DECHETS
3	MINERAL FUELS ETC		487736		613537		628232		596168	COMBUSTIBLES MINERAUX LUB
33	PETROLEUM AND PRODUCTS		481229		608158		605166		579130	PETROLE ET DERIVES
334	PETROLEUM PRODUCTS,REFIN	W 2676244	474093	W 4068913	598483	W 3847430	589389	W 2944234	563519	PRODUITS RAFFINES
4	ANIMAL,VEGETABLE OIL,FAT		62637		47814		81998		71234	HUILES,GRAISSES ANIM,VEG
42	FIXED VEGETABLE OIL,FAT		60554		45143		78477		65685	HUILES VEGETALES FIXES
423	FIXED VEG OILS,SOFT	W 127180	60518		45032	W 127742	78368	W 123767	65512	HUILES VEGET DOUCES FIXES
4236	SUNFLOWER SEED OIL	W 113041	54365	W 56790	33474	W 106589	66200	W 111645	59091	HUILE DE TOURNESOL
5	CHEMCLS,RELATED PROD NES		391316		589658		849376		794703	PRODUITS CHIMIQUES
51	ORGANIC CHEMICALS		73056		151319		204588		137462	PROD CHIMIQ ORGANIQUES
512	ALCOHOLS,PHENOLS ETC	W 66548	13992	W 241587	68653	W 159448	59259	W 135239	37415	PHENOLS,PHENOLS–ALCOOLS
5121	ACYCLIC ALCOHOLS,DERIVS	W 62720	12728	W 236535	66630	W 152073	55053	W 133570	35552	ALCOOLS ACYCLIQUES
513	CARBOXYLIC ACIDS ETC	W 21202	15194	W 33163	28489	W 25765	32532	W 17239	23033	ACIDES CARBOXYLIQUES
5138	POLYACIDS AND DERIVATIVS	W 17619	11485	W 29143	23054	W 18298	20962	W 12665	14519	ACIDES POLYCARBOXYLIQUES
514	NITROGEN–FNCTN COMPOUNDS	W 40200	23157		38237		75473		57864	COMPOSES FONCT AZOTEES
5148	OTH NITROGN–FNCTN CMPNDS	W 36315	20440	W 56488	34820		67919	W 65768	51932	AUTRES COMPOSES AZOTES
51483	ACRYLONITRILE	W 29356	15075	W 43915	24867	W 53049	54563	W 53221	35867	ACRYLONITRILE
52	INORGANIC CHEMICALS		60002		73544		114635		122762	PROD CHIM INORGANIQUES
522	INORG ELEMNTS,OXIDES,ETC		17115	W 193272	24690		41140		32548	ELEMENTS INORGANIQUES
5225	INORGANIC BASES ETC NES		15409	W 183495	22080	W 163705	36621	W 174553	28881	AUTRES BASES OXYDES METAL
523	OTHR INORG CHEMICALS ETC		42847		48837		73495		90001	AUT PRODUITS CHIMIQUES INORG
5232	OTH MTL CMPD OF INRG ACD	W 185369	24664	W 285681	33757	W 344532	46079	W 394278	54259	SELS METALLIQUES
52323	NEUTRAL SODIUM CARBONATE	W 166881	20216	W 263877	28663	W 309325	37158	W 362329	46609	CARBONATE NEUTRE SODIUM
541	*MEDICINAL,PHARM PRODUCT		22449		33075		43793		39409	PROD MEDICINAUX PHARMACEUT
562	*FERTILIZERS,MANUFACTURE	W 1760932	168253	W 2082531	208163		334775	W 2489514	353785	ENGRAIS MANUFACTURES
5621	CHEM NITROGENOUS FERTLZR	W 1362304	121617	W 1527492	143390	W 2133998	284996	W 2204099	306871	ENGRAIS AZOTES
56211	AMMONIUM NITRATE	W 134427	10658	W 245327	20417	W 233082	24500	W 288783	35904	NITRATE D'AMMONIUM
56216	UREA	W 819905	82171	W 974341	98127	W 1293827	204051	W 1340837	209909	UREE
56219	CHEM NITROG FERTILZR NES	W 325836	25378	W 252608	22259	W 499541	49206	W 496293	55731	ENGRAIS AZOTES NDA
5629	FERTILIZERS NES	W 268631	35500	W 407409	53937		47737	W 242632	42342	ENGRAIS NDA
56291	NIT–PHOS–POT FERTLZR NES	W 217089	30166	W 359841	46758	W 259019	41263	W 211924	36857	ENGRAIS CONT N P K
58	PLASTIC MATERIALS ETC		49401		102885		129549		109071	MAT PLAST ARTIFICIELLES
583	POLYMERIZATION ETC PRODS		48237	W 137645	99555		116633		95331	PROD POLYMERISATION
5834	POLYVINYL CHLORIDE	W 73991	38987	W 111502	83738	W 101146	92615		63641	CHLORURE DE POLYVINYLE
58341	— IN PRIMARY FORMS	W 73851	38896	W 111471	83718	W 101072	92553	W 108955	63404	SOUS FORMES PRIMAIRES
6	BASIC MANUFACTURES		1399469		1627112		2230971		2074008	ART MANUFACTURES
61	LEATHER,DRESSED FUR,ETC		57416		138205		185074		232189	CUIRS,PELLETERIES
612	LEATHER ETC MANUFACTURES		51495		125365		171842	W 9028	217530	OUVRAGES EN CUIRS NDA
6123	PREPRD PARTS OF FOOTWEAR	W 4565	50307	W 6686	124022	W 7696	170129	W 8956	215931	PARTIES DE CHAUSSURES
62	RUBBER MANUFACTURES NES		24208		31031		51503		59036	CAOUTCHOUC MANUFACTURE
625	RUBBER TYRES, TUBES ETC	W 12847	19758		23633	W 22887	40315	W 21905	41319	PNEUS CAOUTCHOUC VULCANISE
6259	OTH TYRES,TYRE CASES,ETC	W 7538	10599	W 11999	17656	W 18580	31686	W 16727	30215	AUTRES PNEUS RECHAPES FLAPS
62599	TYRES NES,TYRE CASES,ETC	W 7333	10375	W 11689	17341	W 17931	30504	W 16358	29443	PNEUS,FLAPS
63	WOOD,CORK MANUFACTRS NES		51157		54834		72185		76787	OUVRAGES LIEGE ET BOIS
634	VENEERS,PLYWOOD,ETC	W 74563	27548	W 76656	28413		31805		28095	PLACAGES,CONTRE–PLAQUES
6342	PLYWOOD OF WOOD SHEETS	W 34766	17359	W 36013	18531	W 41724	23856	W 35732	21116	BOIS CONTRE–PLAQUES
635	WOOD MANUFACTURES NES	W 49681	23608	W 47572	26421	W 63110	40379	W 82915	48647	ART MANUF EN BOIS NDA
6353	BUILDERS WOODWRK,PREFABS	W 12236	9524	W 15386	11449	W 33681	23683	W 50804	29997	OUVRAGES DE MENUISERIE
64	PAPER,PAPERBOARD AND MFR		26765		37855		91775		60296	PAPIERS,CARTONS & OUVRAGES
641	PAPER AND PAPERBOARD		25512	W 119253	36531		89124	W 122378	56198	PAPIERS ET CARTONS
6413	KRAFT PAPER,PAPERBOARD	W 6399	3191	W 20343	9772	W 53336	39825	W 42614	25468	PAPIER ET CARTON KRAFT
6415	PAPER,PAPERBRD,BULK,NES	W 14783	6995	W 33111	11887	W 63004	30032	W 35105	19052	PAPIERS,CARTONS ROULEAUX
65	TEXTILE YARN,FABRICS,ETC		130371		138483		180866		169904	FILS,TISSUS,ARTICLES TEXTILE
651	TEXTILE YARN		62152		62066		87974		81655	FILS TEXTILES
6514	SYN FIB YRN,BULK,MONOFIL	W 9864	22954	W 10334	-25980	W 11366	36960	W 11560	34396	FILS CONT 85% FIB TEXT SYNTH
6516	DISCON SYN FIB BLEND YRN	W 8111	24688	W 6504	19847	W 7621	26847	W 8802	29171	FILS FIBR TEX SYNT DIS MOINS
65168	OTH DISC SYN BLEND YARN	W 6838	21351	W 6173	19177	W 7014	24702	W 8270	26968	FILS TEXT SYNT MELANGE AUT F
653	WOVN MAN–MADE FIB FABRIC	W 2397	15482		12539		14714		9165	TISSUS FIBRES SYNTH,ARTIF
658	TEXTILE ARTICLES NES	W 3363	16036	W 4416	24874		32675		33721	ART FACONNES MAT TEXTILES
6584	LINENS ETC	W 2195	11600	W 3156	18486	W 3270	24007	W 3314	23916	LINGE DE MAISON
66	NONMETAL MINERAL MFS NES		153081		162872		214105		211327	ART MIN NON METALLIQUES
661	LIME,CEMENT,BLDG PRODS	W 2361754	64019	W 2400672	64023	W 2966859	81652	W 2663864	79224	CHAUX,CIMENTS MAT CONSTR
6612	CEMENT	W 2335218	61687	W 2378777	60721	W 2951903	78984	W 2638309	75618	CIMENTS HYDRAULIQUES
664	GLASS		22542	W 114916	22899		32379	W 114783	29655	VERRE
665	GLASSWARE	W 24482	36955	W 23331	46943		61947		61419	OUVRAGES EN VERRE
6652	HOUSEHLD,HOTEL ETC GLASS	W 9672	32741	W 11386	44539	W 12163	55002	W 13443	54222	OBJETS VERRE TABLE,CUISINE
666	POTTERY	W 11029	17099	W 14939	22425	W 20506	33789	W 23017	37279	POTERIE
67	IRON AND STEEL		742658		803940		1059392		886135	FER ET ACIER
671	PIG IRON ETC	W 14970	3972	W 45914	15643	W 113138	42024	W 156402	61744	FONTE,SPIEGEL,POUDRES

5. General Exports F.O.B. by Commodities according to the S.I.T.C. (Rev. 2) in thousand U.S. Dollars
Exportations Générales F.O.B. par Produits d'après la C.T.C.I. (Rév. 2) en milliers de Dollars E.U.

SITC CTCI	COMMODITY	1993 WEIGHT POIDS	1993 VALUE VALEUR	1994 WEIGHT POIDS	1994 VALUE VALEUR	1995 WEIGHT POIDS	1995 VALUE VALEUR	1996 WEIGHT POIDS	1996 VALUE VALEUR	PRODUIT
6716	FERRO–ALLOYS	W 8098	2968	W 25410	12586	W 60584	34037	W 86951	49261	FERRO–ALLIAGES
67169	OTHER FERRO–ALLOYS	W 3559	799	W 7639	2714	W 46022	24659	W 70216	37043	AUTRES FERRO–ALLIAGES
672	IRON,STEEL PRIMARY FORMS		75184	W 389953	104048	W 398156	123905	W 198173	58487	LINGOTS FER,ACIER
6725	IRN,STL BLOOMS,SLABS,ETC	W 69128	15083	W 788	377	W 422	552	W 1229	1166	BLOOMS,BILLETTES FER ACIER
67251	IRN,SMPLE STL BLOOMS,ETC	W 68757	14905	W 688	294	W 137	80	W 1072	971	BLOOMS ETC NON ACIER FIN
6727	IRN,STL COIL FR REROLLNG	W 227959	60098	W 388048	103381	W 397725	123350	W 196909	57311	EBAUCHES POUR TOLES FER
673	IRON,STEEL SHAPES ETC	W 1180394	323761		268567	W 967622	283192	W 630360	181233	BARRES,PROFIL FER,ACIER
6731	IRON,STEEL WIRE ROD	W 736798	177558		157300	W 472452	130925	W 333688	87952	FIL MACHINE FER,ACIER
67311	IRON,SIMPLE STL WIRE ROD	W 734814	177083	W 598371	157299	W 469030	129898	W 332501	87077	FIL MACH AUT ACIER FIN
6732	IRON,STEEL BARS ETC	W 69497	19928	W 199667	47943	W 183238	60146	W 79136	31116	BARRES FER,ACIER
67326	IRN,OTH STL BARS HOTROLD	W 44987	11344	W 164382	38610	W 147815	43244	W 55734	17554	BARRES PLEINES FER,ACIER
6733	IRON,STEEL PROFILES ETC	W 374099	126275	W 227738	63324	W 311932	92121	W 217536	62165	PROFILES,PALPLAN FER,ACIER
67331	SMALL U,I,H SECTIONS ETC	W 58895	15994	W 53956	14448	W 42409	12261	W 47285	13579	PROFILES MOINS 80MM
67332	LARGE U,I,H SECTIONS ETC	W 223474	60521	W 142036	39153	W 241924	71363	W 145946	41538	PROFILES PLUS 80MM
67333	OTH PRFILES HOTROLLD ETC	W 47007	36628	W 25906	7319	W 21532	6268	W 19635	5484	AUT PROFILES LAMINES,FILES
674	IRN,STL UNIV,PLATE,SHEET	W 935836	250877	W 1106631	307449	W 1158144	400751	W 1069750	375444	LARGES PLATS,TOLES
6744	IRN,STL HVY PLATE,ROLLED	W 730202	192768	W 972525	260021	W 1057425	328218	W 1021268	328214	TOLES LAMINEES PLUS 4.75 MM
67441	— OF IRON OR SIMPLE STL	W 730135	192752	W 972357	259907	W 1055695	327285	W 1021214	327993	TOLES NON ACIER FIN CARB
6745	IRN,STL MED PLATE,ROLLED	W 137124	33911	W 85258	20961	W 11791	5128	W 9352	4858	TOLES 3 A 4.75 MM
67451	— OF IRON OR SIMPLE STL	W 133612	32012	W 84925	20822	W 9464	3497	W 5300	1986	TOLES AUT NON ACIER FIN
6746	IRN,STL THIN PLATE,ROLLD	W 27519	11304	W 37652	22614	W 73486	60154	W 33589	39491	TOLES LAM MOINS 3MM
67463	— OF STAINLESS ETC STL	W 3602	2993	W 11769	13956	W 16697	36864	W 15923	30815	TOL ACIER INOX MOINS 3 MM
677	IRN,STL WIRE(EXCL W ROD)	W 82284	22401	W 82708	25070	W 206119	61263	W 102112	32739	FILS EN FER,ACIER
678	IRON,STL TUBES,PIPES,ETC	W 97917	59176	W 130701	72710	W 216930	127790	W 244343	152856	TUBES,TUYAUX EN FONTE,FER
6782	IRON,STL SEAMLESS TUBES	W 52120	29216	W 67346	32779	W 120535	65458	W 149597	89553	TUBES,TUYAUX SANS SOUDURE
6783	IRON,STL TUBES,PIPES NES	W 25749	12471	W 41064	18777	W 71444	33155	W 46171	21618	AUT TUBES,TUYAUX FER,ACIER
6785	IRON,STEEL TUBE FITTINGS	W 18367	16561	W 21924	20963	W 24793	29085	W 48443	41587	ACCESSOIRES DE TUYAUTERIE
68	NON–FERROUS METALS		122687		180054		247429		234192	METAUX NON FERREUX
682	COPPER EXC CEMENT COPPER	W 11963	18723	W 14182	21053		18647		30188	CUIVRE
684	ALUMINIUM	W 83793	101649	W 110469	154234	W 128502	221002	W 128375	191818	ALUMINIUM
6841	ALUMINIUM,ALLOYS,UNWRGHT	W 75075	88174	W 99568	133938	W 106243	169536	W 105345	149132	ALUMINIUM,ALLIAGES BRUTS
6842	ALUMINIUM,ALLOYS WORKED	W 8718	13475	W 10901	20296	W 22259	51466	W 23030	42686	ALUMINIUM,ALLIAGES OUVRE
68421	ALUMINIUM BARS,WIRE,ETC	W 1928	2761	W 3032	5396	W 12041	25280	W 17459	30367	BARRES,PROFILES FILS ALU
69	METAL MANUFACTURES NES		91127		79838		128642		144142	ART MANUFACT EN METAL NDA
691	STRUCTURES AND PARTS NES	W 25304	21878	W 13475	12425	W 13099	13482	W 97784	31895	CONSTRUCT FER,ACIER,ALU
6911	STRUCTURES,PARTS IRN,STL	W 25158	21568	W 13375	12202	W 13028	13302	W 97693	31455	CONSTRUCT FER,ACIER,FONTE
694	STL,COPPR NAILS,NUTS,ETC	W 12261	9530	W 33149	11579	W 27575	24749	W 24372	23102	CLOUS,VIS,ECROUS
697	BASE MTL HOUSEHOLD EQUIP		20802		16143		17459		20053	ART MENAGE MET COMMUNS
699	BASE METAL MFRS NES		8124		16436		26888		22320	ART MANUFACTURES MET NDA
7	MACHINES,TRANSPORT EQUIP		835851		879194		1036992		1100384	MACHINES MATERIEL TRANSPORT
71	POWER GENERATING EQUIPMT		74268		82412		101183		103119	MACHINES GENERATRICES
711	STEAM BOILERS & AUX PLNT	W 12548	28356	W 6555	27796		20736	W 3504	13907	GENERATEURS VAPEUR EAU ETC
7112	AUXILIARY BOILER PLANT	W 7214	15680	W 3679	16550	W 6	99	W 6	111	APPAREILS AUXIL DU 711.1
716	ROTATING ELECTRIC PLANT	W 12411	31359	W 13439	32481		57792		65071	APP ELECTR ROTATIFS,PIECES
7162	AC MTRS,GENRTRS,GEN SETS	W 8968	22760	W 12141	29199	W 18177	51028		58384	MOTEURS ELECTRIQUES
71621	AC MTRS,INC UNIVRSL MTRS	W 8853	22001	W 12036	28588	W 17995	50129	W 18526	56707	MOT ELEC NON COUR CONTINU
72	MACHS FOR SPCL INDUSTRYS		100917		89567		109885		103689	MAC SPECIALES POUR INDUST
722	TRACTORS NON–ROAD	W 20759	38462	W 11936	26020	W 14623	33001	W 12321	28577	TRACTEURS
7224	WHEELED TRACTORS NES	W 20263	37747	W 11639	25504	W 14153	32018	W 12048	27968	TRACTEURS A ROUES
723	CIVIL ENGNEERG EQUIP ETC	W 3350	24816	W 6063	28715	W 6933	33176	W 11098	30264	APPAREILS DE GENIE CIVIL
7239	CONSTR ETC MACHY PTS NES	W 2268	17477	W 2596	12478	W 2099	14357	W 1864	8308	PIECES 723.41–723.46
728	OTH MACHY FOR SPCL INDUS		25048		16648	W 12021	30226		28746	AUT MACH IND PARTICULIERES
7283	OTHR MINERAL WORKG MACHY	W 3691	10480	W 3352	11252	W 9916	24733	W 6898	19730	MACH TRIER,CRIBLER,BROYER
73	METALWORKING MACHINERY		54338		41033		53157		61717	MACH TRAVAIL DES METAUX
736	METALWORKING MACH–TOOLS	W 10612	28857	W 10650	25094	W 12418	38634	W 16988	46340	MACH–OUTILS TRAVAIL METAUX
7361	METAL CUTTING MACH–TOOLS	W 7441	20344	W 6446	15395	W 7391	22229	W 5879	19550	MACH–OUT ENLEVEMENT METAL
737	METALWORKING MACHNRY NES		25481		15939		14523	W 5677	15377	MACH TRAV METAUX PIECES
7372	ROLLING MILLS AND ROLLS	W 3796	23355	W 1573	11826	W 3981	11151	W 3710	10895	LAMINOIRS CYLINDRES PIEC
73729	ROLL–MILL PTS NES, ROLLS	W 3735	23280	W 1573	11826	W 3951	10971	W 3524	10304	CYLINDRES DE LAMINOIRS
74	GENRL INDUSTRL MACHY NES		169339		160642		214701		234904	MACH APP INDUSTRIE
741	HEATING,COOLING EQUIPMNT	W 4749	14554		14710	W 7023	36410		21538	MACH CHAUFFAGE,PIECES
742	PUMPS FOR LIQUIDS ETC	W 2366	17675	W 2301	8392		8923	W 2408	9674	POMPES MOTO–POMPES
744	MECHANICAL HANDLING EQU	W 9203	14293	W 6360	10190		15311	W 15047	25519	EQUIP MANUTENTION PIECES
749	NONELEC MACH PTS,ACC NES	W 32812	113543	W 32318	119816		142453	W 37267	165152	PIECES MACH NON ELEC NDA
7491	BALL,ROLLER,ETC BEARINGS	W 16430	66716	W 17038	77826	W 16743	99402	W 17462	107889	ROULEMENTS BILLES ETC
7492	COCKS,VALVES ETC NES	W 14699	39358	W 12497	29842	W 10814	24616	W 12708	31138	ART ROB,SIM POUR TUYAUX
77	ELECTRIC MACHNRY NES ETC		59538		131125		184790		178903	MACH APP ELECT NDA
772	SWITCHGEAR ETC,PARTS NES		12569	W 3666	25306		37815		24510	APP COUPURE,SECT ETC
7721	SWITCHGEAR ETC	W 1952	11626	W 3619	24675	W 4401	37405	W 3607	23978	APP COUPURE,SECTIONMNT
773	ELECTR DISTRIBUTNG EQUIP	W 3570	9652	W 6951	54845	W 9314	83255	W 8213	77351	EQUIPMT DISTRIBUTION ELECT
7731	INSULATED WIRE,CABLE ETC	W 3089	8740	W 6258	53407	W 8595	81425	W 7544	75992	FILS,CABLES ISOLES ELECT
778	ELECTRICAL MACHINERY NES		16319		20259		32013		35308	AUTRES MACH ELECT NDA
78	ROAD VEHICLES		220439		163666		172900		165870	VEHICULES ROUTIERS
781	PASS MOTOR VEH EXC BUSES	W 40762	146532	W 31101	104114	W 15026	74973	W 9310	59422	AUTO TRANSPORT PERSONNES
782	LORRIES,SPCL MTR VEH NES	W 9735	29540	W 6848	24163	W 5831	21885	W 4367	14508	VEHICULES SPECIAUX,MARCH
7821	LORRIES,TRUCKS	W 8654	28503	W 5594	18803	W 5109	17662	W 4020	13370	VEHICULES TRANSP MARCHAND
784	MOTOR VEH PRTS,ACCES NES	W 8652	29113	W 5378	19956	W 12913	52519	W 17147	72178	PIECES 722,781,782,783
7849	OTHER MOTOR VEHCL PARTS	W 8455	28455	W 4472	18067	W 7184	40703	W 11975	59081	PIECES 722,781,782,783
79	OTHR TRANSPORT EQUIPMENT		145558		193542		182317		236300	AUTRE MATERIEL TRANSPORT
791	RAILWAY VEHICLES	W 55230	82017	W 39325	39937	W 36108	25304	W 62423	64017	VEHIC MAT CHEMINS DE FER
7914	RY COACHES NES NOT POWRD	W 6847	42058					W 6	21	VOITURES A VOYAGEURS
7915	FRT,MAINT CARS NOT POWRD	W 28613	17853	W 26170	18714	W 19939	8984	W 31695	21423	WAGONS DE SERVICE
79152	RAILWAY FREIGHT CARS NES	W 28536	17603	W 26150	18344	W 19931	8874	W 31695	21423	WAGONS MARCHANDISES
7919	RY TRACK FIXT,ETC,PARTS	W 19683	22082	W 12894	19566	W 15992	15586	W 29143	30360	MATER FIXE VOIES FERREES
79199	PARTS NES OF 7911–7915	W 19502	21503	W 12651	19353	W 15449	15158	W 28846	30034	PIECES 791.1 ET 5
792	AIRCRAFT ETC	W 168	14440		26818		8339		9691	APP NAVIGATION AERIENNE
793	SHIPS AND BOATS ETC	W 48735	49101		126787	W 145226	148674	W 120579	162592	NAVIRES BATEAUX,ETC
7932	SHIPS AND BOATS NES	W 43031	44325	W 151924	113722	W 142757	146477	W 105541	147847	NAVIRES ET BATEAUX
79323	OTHER CARGO VESSELS	W 27022	43434	W 124022	104212	W 138232	142472	W 92433	131213	AUT BATEAUX TRANS MARCH
8	MISC MANUFACTURED GOODS		1198811		1687009		2258199		2469717	ART MANUFACTURES DIVERS
812	*PLUMBG,HEATNG,LGHTNG EQ	W 21427	18819	W 17292	35913		20157		16516	APPAR SANITAIRES CHAUFFAGE
8121	CENTRAL HEATING EQUIPMNT	W 2356	7734	W 4946	23427	W 2039	6762	W 445	1340	CHAUDIERES,RADIATEURS
821	*FURNITURE,PARTS THEREOF	W 241903	379175	W 334165	397480		514169		485521	MEUBLES ET PIECES
8211	CHAIRS,SEATS AND PARTS	W 17943	34970	W 18053	40120	W 18046	46258	W 18047	46547	SIEGES ET PIECES
82111	CHAIRS AND OTHER SEATS	W 17448	34349	W 17681	39427	W 17127	45297	W 15997	44362	SIEGES
8219	FURNITURE AND PARTS NES	W 222563	340836	W 315352	355335	W 233115	465295	W 233653	436939	AUTRES MEUBLES ET PIECES
82192	WOOD FURNITURE NES	W 208661	328846	W 299286	337347	W 213565	441004	W 214208	411221	MEUBLES NDA EN BOIS
84	CLOTHING AND ACCESSORIES		639760		995240		1360351		1559096	VETEMENTS
842	MENS OUTERWEAR NOT KNIT	W 10481	190293	W 14553	331466	W 15457	422825	W 17026	503575	VET DESSUS POUR HOMMES
8421	— OVERCOATS,OTHER COATS	W 1652	31322	W 1760	46321	W 1852	55474	W 1616	53030	MANTEAUX HOMMES MAT TEXT
84219	—— OF OTHER FIBRES	W 1288	23297	W 1466	36701	W 1678	50498	W 1404	46537	MANTEAUX HOMMES AUT FIBR

5. General Exports F.O.B. by Commodities according to the S.I.T.C. (Rev. 2) in thousand U.S. Dollars
Exportations Générales F.O.B. par Produits d'après la C.T.C.I. (Rév. 2) en milliers de Dollars E.U.

SITC CTCI	COMMODITY	1993		1994		1995		1996		PRODUIT
		WEIGHT POIDS	VALUE VALEUR	WEIGHT POIDS	VALUE VALEUR	WEIGHT POIDS	VALUE VALEUR	WEIGHT POIDS	VALUE VALEUR	
8422	— SUITS	W 1101	21972	W 1512	31459	W 1177	39501	W 1778	63274	COMPLETS HOMMES MAT TEXT
8423	— TROUSERS,BREECHES ETC	W 3840	58351	W 5629	115795	W 5974	153745	W 6750	188960	PANTALONS HOMMES MAT TEX
8424	— JACKETS,BLAZERS ETC	W 2064	49016	W 2667	81699	W 2869	100870	W 2939	97522	VESTES HOMMES MAT TEXTIL
8429	— OTHER OUTER GARMENTS	W 1824	29632	W 2985	56192	W 3585	73235	W 3943	100789	AUT VET DES HOM MAT TEX
843	WOMENS OUTERWEAR NONKNIT	W 12917	243160	W 17709	398589	W 22111	577104	W 24416	651464	VET DESSUS FEMMES MAT TEX
8431	— COATS AND JACKETS	W 5019	102472	W 6725	169788	W 6902	211890	W 7097	221089	MANT,VEST FEM MAT TEXTIL
8432	— SUITS AND COSTUMES	W 714	12177	W 726	17275	W 899	25135	W 1080	33304	COSTUMES–TAIL MAT TEXIL
8433	— DRESSES	W 834	14633	W 1161	24484	W 1877	51445	W 2118	53924	ROBES EN MAT–TEXTILES
8434	— SKIRTS	W 1182	21624	W 1633	27957	W 2287	50777	W 2527	54367	JUPES EN MAT TEXTILES
8435	— BLOUSES	W 1508	32988	W 2498	57342	W 2936	77291	W 2924	78002	BLOUSES FEM MAT TEXTILES
8439	— OTHER OUTER GARMENTS	W 3660	59267	W 4966	101743	W 7209	160566	W 8671	210778	AUT VET DES FEM MAT TEXT
844	UNDER GARMENTS NOT KNIT	W 4526	48515	W 4926	60320	W 5680	95064	W 5556	105825	VETEMENT DESSOUS MAT TEX
8441	— MENS SHIRTS	W 3880	43333	W 4378	56015	W 4865	84963	W 4730	93285	CHEMISES HOMMES MAT TEXT
84411	—— OF COTTON	W 1443	15045	W 2771	32699	W 3008	50244	W 2998	64350	CHEMISES HOMMES DE COTON
84412	—— OF SYNTHETIC FIBRES	W 2437	28288	W 1607	23316	W 1857	34719	W 1732	28935	CHEMISES HOMMES FIB SYNT
845	OUTERWEAR KNIT NONELASTC	W 7658	84815	W 8080	97109	W 8305	124460	W 10035	151383	VET DESSOUS,ACCES BONNET
8451	— JERSEYS,PULLOVERS ETC	W 4762	51351	W 5274	61210	W 5279	75282	W 6754	95524	CHANDAILS,PULL–OVERS ETC
8459	— OTHER,CLTHG ACCESRYS	W 2549	28825	W 2538	31575	W 2752	43524	W 2969	49891	AUT VET DESSUS DE BONNE
846	UNDER GARMENTS KNITTED	W 3280	48887	W 4467	82777		107805	W 6283	112392	SOUS VETS DE BONNETERIE
8462	— OF COTTON NON ELASTIC	W 1392	18240	W 2319	35010	W 3608	48868	W 4217	62886	SOUS–VET BONNET COTON
84629	—— OTHER	W 1392	18240	W 2319	35010	W 3608	48868	W 4217	62886	AUT SOUS–VET BONNET COTON
8463	— OF SYNTH FBR NONELAST	W 1644	23140	W 1794	33200	W 2078	39621	W 1529	27559	SOUS–VET BONNET FIB SYNT
84631	—— PANTY HOSE (TIGHTS)	W 997	16844	W 1121	25674	W 1292	29497	W 867	19390	COLLANTS BON FIBR SYNT
851	*FOOTWEAR	W 12107	104255	W 17983	182537	W 21492	252807	W 23791	284289	CHAUSSURES
85102	FOOTWEAR LEATHER	W 8332	71062	W 15030	154652	W 18551	225444	W 20470	257815	CHAUS SEMELLES EN CUIR
85103	SHOES WOOD–,CORK–SOLED	W 2953	27781	W 1174	12538	W 848	11503	W 551	6863	CHAUS SEMELLES BOIS,LIEGE
89	MISC MANUFCTRD GOODS NES		39427		53048		79673		90020	ART MANUFACTURES DIVERS
894	TOYS,SPORTING GOODS,ETC	W 3654	13397	W 5315	26642		44321		47268	VOITURES ENFANTS,JOUETS
8942	TOYS,INDOOR GAMES ETC	W 3234	12249	W 4633	24816	W 6616	34706	W 6786	37584	JOUETS,JEUX ETC
9	GOODS NOT CLASSD BY KIND		68536		95628		99097		56638	ART TRANSACT NON CLASSES
931	*SPECIAL TRANSACTIONS		62863		67443		30903		22446	TRANS.SPECIALES
951	*WAR FIREARMS,AMMUNITION	W 5	22	W 1174	7996		66613		32692	VEHIC BLINDES ARMES
95101	ARMORED FIGHTNG VEHICLES	W 5	22	W 1174	7996	W 4730	38454	W 4484	7718	CHARS DE COMBAT
971	*GOLD,NON MONETARY NES	K 11000	4915		18880					OR NON MONETAIRE
97101	NONMON GLD UNWRT,SEMIMFD	K 11000	4915		18858					OR,ALLIAGES D'OR BRUTS

1. HISTORICAL SERIES, 1992–1996 GENERAL TRADE, IMPORTS C.I.F., EXPORTS F.O.B.
SERIES HISTORIQUES, 1992–1996 COMMERCE GENERAL, IMPORTATIONS C.A.F., EXPORTATIONS F.O.B

YEAR ANNEE	VALUE IN MILLION U.S. DOLLARS VALEUR EN MILLION U.S. DOLLARS MERCHANDISE – MARCHANDISE IMPORTS	EXPORTS	GOLD – OR IMPORTS	EXPORTS	CONVERSION FACTORS FACTEURS DE CONVERSION CENTS E.U. PAR IMPORTS	EXPORTS	INDEX NUMBERS – INDICES QUANTUM IMPORTS	EXPORTS	UNIT VALUE VALEUR UNITAIRE IMPORTS	EXPORTS
1992	36984.00	42376.30								
1993	32806.00	44297.30								
1994	50518.00	67642.00								
1995	60916.00	81137.00								
1996	61147.00	88703.00								

2. IMPORTS BY BROAD ECONOMIC CATEGORY AND EXPORTS BY INDUSTRIAL ORIGIN. (PERCENTAGE OF TOTAL VALUE)
IMPORTATIONS PAR CATEGORIES ECONOMIQUES ET EXPORTATIONS PAR BRANCHE D'ACTIVITE.(EN POURCENTAGE DE LA VALEUR TOTALE)

IMPORTS – IMPORTATIONS

	1990	1991	1992	1993	1994	1995	1996
TOTAL IMPORTS–IMPORTATIONS TOTALES							
1 FOOD BEV–ALIMENTATION BOISSONS							
11 PRIMARY–PRODUITS DE BASE							
111 FOR INDUSTRY–POUR L'INDUSTRIE							
112 FOR HOUSEHOLDS–POUR LES MENAGES							
12 PROCESSED–PRODUITS ELABORES							
121 FOR INDUSTRY–POUR L'INDUSTRIE							
122 FOR HOUSEHOLDS–POUR LES MENAGES							
2 IND SUPPLIES–APPROV INDUSTRIELS							
21 PRIMARY–PRODUITS DE BASE							
22 PROCESSED–PRODUITS ELABORES							
3 FUELS–COMBUSTIBLES							
31 PRIMARY–PRODUITS DE BASE							
32 PROCESSED–PRODUITS ELABORES							
321 MOTOR SPIRIT–ESSENCE							
322 OTHER–AUTRES							
4 MACHINERY–EQUIPEMENT							
41 CAPITAL EQUIPMENT–MACHINES							
42 PARTS–PIECES ACCESSOIRES							
5 TRANSPORT–TRANSPORT							
51 PASSENGER CARS–AUTOMOBILES							
52 OTHER–AUTRES							
521 INDUSTRIAL–INDUSTRIELS							
522 NON INDUSTRIAL–NON INDUSTRIEL							
53 PARTS–PIECES ACCESSOIRES							
6 CONSUM GOODS–BIENS CONSOMMATION							
61 DURABLE–DURABLES							
62 SEMI DURABLE–SEMI DURABLES							
63 NON DURABLE–NON DURABLES							
7 GOODS NES–BIENS NDA							

EXPORTS – EXPORTATIONS

	1990	1991	1992	1993	1994	1995	1996
TOTAL EXPORTS–EXPORTATIONS TOTALES							
1 AGRICULTURE							
2 MINING QUARRY–INDUS EXTRACTIVES							
3 MANUFACTURING–IND MANUFACTUR							
31 FOOD BEV TOBACCO–ALIM BOISS TAB							
32 TEXTILES–INDUSTRIES TEXTILES							
33 WOOD & PRODUCTS–BOIS & PRODUITS							
34 PAPER & PRODUCTS–PAPIER & PRODT							
35 CHEMICALS–INDUSTRIES CHIMIQUES							
36 NON METAL MIN–MIN NON METAL							
37 BASIC METAL–IND METAL BASE							
38 METAL MANUF–MANUF METAL							
39 OTH MANUF IND–AUTRES MANUF							

3. TRADE BY PRINCIPAL COUNTRIES OF ORIGIN AND DESTINATION (VALUE IN THOUSAND U.S. DOLLARS)
ECHANGES SELON LES PRINCIPAUX PAYS D'ORIGINE ET DE DESTINATION (VALEUR EN MILLIERS DE DOLLARS EU)

COUNTRIES–PAYS	GENERAL IMPORTS C.I.F. IMPORTATIONS GENERALES C.A.F				
	1992	1993	1994	1995	1996
World		26806700	50518000	46708925	45916905
Africa		380300	61900	268253	329904
Americas		3286000	2754500	3957031	4351936
Northern America		2597300	684500	2872138	3243139
LAIA		232900		770075	543712
CACM		4900		47443	47097
Caribbean		437500	2070000	259570	468485
Rest of America		13400		7805	49503
As.ex F.USSR		7880300	3659300	4489718	5254692
Eur.x F.USSR		14704800	19126100	22945421	19989467
EU		11197600	15132300	17954705	15867207
EFTA		768800	664500	884532	780141
East Europe		2191000	2837300	3499231	2763122
Other Europe		52900		10069	8846
Former USSR		172000	10986600	14619797	15085044
Oceania		115400	180100	247214	250453
Germany/Allemagne		5142100	5675000	6483096	5192939
Ukraine			4404000	6616650	6293700
USA/Etats–Unis d'Amer		2303700	684500	2648319	2902367
Kazakhstan			1996000	2675089	3038641
Belarus/Bélarus			2094000	2067700	2907600
Italy/Italie		1105800	1596000	1850580	2339819
Finland/Finlande		723600	1628000	2040657	1674607
China/Chine		2334600	952000	865423	1002721
Netherlands/Pays–Bas		431100	1611000	1646023	1010225
France, Monac		899200	1005000	1083902	1276166
Japan/Japon		1366900	1114000	762556	977975
United Kingdom		652700	895800	1099615	1131327
Austria/Autriche		855200	979400	981546	667208
Cuba		436300	2070000	196190	405559
Hungary/Hongrie		622300	761200	842099	657216
Romania/Roumanie		101700	146300	1453253	1060334
Belgium–Luxembourg		472900	614400	899289	667536
India/Inde		632600	586900	614066	602326
Switz.Liecht		679600	539300	697423	502709
Uzbekistan/Ouzbékistan			851800	888734	653589
Turkey/Turquie		661200	400500	541539	578203
Korea, Republic of		305600	429100	502080	799560
Republic of Moldova			475800	635955	829170
Czech Republic		460700	429900	438189	534349
Sweden/Suède		313600	310500	546619	555413
Poland/Pologne		528800	945800		
Denmark/Danemark		189800	322700	483257	440548
Bulgaria/Bulgarie		309500	345300	471453	245224
Spain/Espagne		174700	244700	240969	358470
Ireland/Irlande		83300	249800	322786	319077
Lithuania/Lituanie		53400	274700	386929	254207
Slovakia		167900	208800	294166	265890
Latvia/Lettonie		77400	197400	376144	233712
Canada		293600		222404	340548
Slovenia/Slovénia		232200		340668	278883
Singapore/Singapour		290300		267741	228308
Yugoslavia/Yougoslavie		146700	492000	8359	122471
Afghanistan		679400	7600	13318	7981
Brazil/Brésil		113900		359448	204529
Estonia/Estonie		41200	197700	274759	147147
Israel/Israël		139100		242655	272523
Norway, SVD, JM		87600	110600	174226	249264
Greece/Grèce		134200		257169	204917
Australia/Australie		80900	180100	136039	98949
Hong Kong		319100		92322	47168
Turkmenistan/Turkménistn			60400	179425	188028
Azerbaijan			141200	107352	151413
Croatia/Croatie		104700		140978	118483
Kyrgyzstan/Kirghizistan			97800	101151	146968
Tajikistan/Tadjikistan			90000	166988	87999

COUNTRIES–PAYS	GENERAL EXPORTS F.O.B. EXPORTATIONS GENERALES F.O.B.				
	1992	1993	1994	1995	1996
Monde		44297400	67642000	78216922	84988431
Afrique		521600	305400	719552	770701
Amériques		2890100	3648000	6773823	8070325
Amérique du Nord		2245800	3561000	4477518	5147019
ALAI		202300		300736	226812
MCAC		17600		37446	30896
Caraïbes		347000	87000	1710690	2338064
Autre Amérique		77400		247433	327534
Asie l'URSS exclus		10567400	8099700	14477898	14972430
Europe l'URSS exclus		29431800	34806400	38851275	42247436
UE		19922300	23771300	26447140	27770988
AELE		2044100	4128900	3981169	4355544
Europe de l'Est		7137100	6595600	8034732	9298789
Autre de l'Europe		21700		29645	190868
Ancienne URSS		589400	15517400	16817517	18396798
Océanie		12400	500	30638	12226
Germany/Allemagne		5074400	6376000	6207599	6734546
Ukraine			6885000	7149031	7551493
USA/Etats–Unis d'Amer		1998100	3561000	4317760	4843104
United Kingdom		3353400	4259000	3207849	3511836
China/Chine		3067800	2889000	3371421	4722167
Switz.Liecht		1726300	3719000	3714831	3975325
Italy/Italie		2629200	2984000	3376329	2823341
Japan/Japon		2005100	2823000	3172793	2914521
Netherlands/Pays–Bas		979100	2471000	3191533	3324780
Belarus/Bélarus			2998000	2940000	3356949
Finland/Finlande		1364100	1891000	2386457	2637848
Ireland/Irlande		604900	926200	2634820	2905572
Kazakhstan			1938000	2554589	2547355
Hungary/Hongrie		2098200	1408000	1626994	1803899
France, Monac		1839600	1326000	1525523	1700623
Romania/Roumanie		475000	474700	2341613	2936386
Czech Republic		1378500	1279000	1676391	1747617
Slovakia		932400	1235000	1735697	1879358
Turkey/Turquie		1078400	1014000	1644422	1685973
Belgium–Luxembourg		1079000	1380000	1476716	1427351
Austria/Autriche		1404900	884200	889333	823095
Bulgaria/Bulgarie		941500	784900	652238	930329
Sweden/Suède		783000	855200	643048	1024574
Lithuania/Lituanie		299000	691900	1080855	1128972
British Virgin Islds		36700		1346158	1616560
Korea, Republic of		391200	567600	747205	1184787
Poland/Pologne		1311100	1414000		
Latvia/Lettonie		207600	627600	794860	1042077
Uzbekistan/Ouzbékistan			750300	824022	1087987
India/Inde		474000	379000	997797	793572
Iran (Islamic Rp. of)		1004500		249271	377087
Israel/Israël		168500		624363	564568
Republic of Moldova			530200	413233	389699
Estonia/Estonie		82800	337300	411489	490852
Singapore/Singapour		241600		489957	570419
Spain/Espagne		384800	200900	289775	408563
Norway, SVD, JM		284300	319300	254403	362887
Cyprus/Chypre		539600		270318	400697
Denmark/Danemark		189700	217800	454988	282017
Egypt/Egypte		169900	500	393571	387797
Cuba		102800	87000	211254	465218
Thailand/Thaïlande		233500		389213	220709
Hong Kong		236300		310620	216984
Malaysia/Malaisie		22800		572456	119324
Mongolia/Mongolie		156600	143800	197422	192013
Viet Nam		123900	120500	322248	121999
Panama		77300		244075	326016
Kuwait/Koweït		15700		300601	314695
Yugoslavia/Yougoslavie		27400	310600	1457	275341
Tajikistan/Tadjikistan			143300	190060	151575

(VALUE AS PERCENTAGE OF WORLD TOTAL)(VALEURS EN POURCENTAGE DU TOTAL MONDIAL)

	1987	1988	1989	1990	1991	1992	1993	1994	1995	1996
Africa							1.4	0.1	0.6	0.7
Americas							12.3	5.5	8.5	9.5
Northern America							9.7	1.4	6.1	7.1
LAIA							0.9		1.6	1.2
CACM							0.0		0.1	0.1
Caribbean							1.6	4.1	0.6	1.0
Rest of America							0.0		0.0	0.1
As.ex F.USSR							29.4	7.2	9.6	11.4
Eur.x F.USSR							54.9	37.9	49.1	43.5
EU							41.8	30.0	38.4	34.6
EFTA							2.9	1.3	1.9	1.7
East Europe							8.2	5.6	7.5	6.0
Other Europe							0.2		0.0	0.0
Former USSR							0.6	21.7	31.3	32.9
Oceania							0.4	0.4	0.5	0.5
Germany/Allemagne							19.2	11.2	13.9	11.3
Ukraine								8.7	14.2	13.7
USA/Etats–Unis d'Amer							8.6	1.4	5.7	6.3
Kazakhstan								4.0	5.7	6.6
Belarus/Bélarus								4.1	4.4	6.3
Italy/Italie							4.1	3.2	4.0	5.1
Finland/Finlande							2.7	3.2	4.4	3.6
China/Chine							8.7	1.9	1.9	2.2
Netherlands/Pays–Bas							1.6	3.2	3.5	2.2
France, Monac							3.4	2.0	2.3	2.8

	1987	1988	1989	1990	1991	1992	1993	1994	1995	1996
Afrique							1.2	0.5	0.9	0.9
Amériques							6.5	5.4	8.7	9.5
Amérique du Nord							5.1	5.3	5.7	6.1
ALAI							0.5		0.4	0.3
MCAC							0.0		0.0	0.0
Caraïbes							0.8	0.1	2.2	2.8
Autre Amérique							0.2		0.3	0.4
Asie l'URSS exclus							23.9	12.0	18.5	17.6
Europe l'URSS exclus							66.4	51.5	49.7	49.7
UE							45.0	35.1	33.8	32.7
AELE							4.6	6.1	5.1	5.1
Europe de l'Est							16.1	9.8	10.3	10.9
Autre de l'Europe							0.0		0.0	0.2
Ancienne URSS							1.3	22.9	21.5	21.6
Océanie							0.0	0.0	0.0	0.0
Germany/Allemagne							11.5	9.4	7.9	7.9
Ukraine								10.2	9.1	8.9
USA/Etats–Unis d'Amer							4.5	5.3	5.5	5.7
United Kingdom							7.6	6.3	4.1	4.1
China/Chine							6.9	4.3	4.3	5.6
Switz.Liecht							3.9	5.5	4.7	4.7
Italy/Italie							5.9	4.4	4.3	3.3
Japan/Japon							4.5	4.2	4.1	3.4
Netherlands/Pays–Bas							2.2	3.7	4.1	3.9
Belarus/Bélarus								4.4	3.8	3.9

4. General Imports C.I.F. by Commodities according to the S.I.T.C. (Rev. 2) in thousand U.S. Dollars
Importations Générales C.A.F. par Produits d'après la C.T.C.I. (Rév. 2) en milliers de Dollars E.U.

SITC CTCI	COMMODITY	1992		1993		1994		1995		PRODUIT
		WEIGHT POIDS	VALUE VALEUR	WEIGHT POIDS	VALUE VALEUR	WEIGHT POIDS	VALUE VALEUR	WEIGHT POIDS	VALUE VALEUR	
	ALL COMMODITIES		36984000		26806700		50518000		46708925	TOUS PRODUITS

5. General Exports F.O.B. by Commodities according to the S.I.T.C. (Rev. 2) in thousand U.S. Dollars
Exportations Générales F.O.B. par Produits d'après la C.T.C.I. (Rév. 2) en milliers de Dollars E.U.

SITC CTCI	COMMODITY	1992		1993		1994		1995		PRODUIT
		WEIGHT POIDS	VALUE VALEUR	WEIGHT POIDS	VALUE VALEUR	WEIGHT POIDS	VALUE VALEUR	WEIGHT POIDS	VALUE VALEUR	
	ALL COMMODITIES		42376000		44297400		67642000		78216922	TOUS PRODUITS

1. HISTORICAL SERIES, 1959–1994 GENERAL TRADE, IMPORTS C.I.F., EXPORTS F.O.B.
SERIES HISTORIQUES, 1959–1994 COMMERCE GENERAL, IMPORTATIONS C.A.F., EXPORTATIONS F.O.B

YEAR ANNEE	VALUE IN MILLION E.C. DOLLARS / VALEUR EN MILLION E.C. DOLLARS — MERCHANDISE –MARCHANDISE		GOLD –OR		CONVERSION FACTORS U.S. CENTS PER E.C. DOLLAR / FACTEURS DE CONVERSION CENTS E.U. PAR E.C. DOLLAR		INDEX NUMBERS –INDICES — QUANTUM		UNIT VALUE / VALEUR UNITAIRE	
	IMPORTS	EXPORTS	IMPORTS	EXPORTS	IMPORTS	EXPORTS	IMPORTS	EXPORTS	IMPORTS	EXPORTS
1959	12.10	9.61			58.3300	58.3300				
1960	12.10	10.00			58.3300	58.3300				
1961	13.43	9.82			58.3300	58.3300				
1963	12.28	8.29			58.3300	58.3300				
1964	13.45	9.77			58.3300	58.3300				
1965	14.63	8.81			58.3300	58.3300				
1966	15.82	8.61			58.3300	58.3300				
1967	16.24	9.05			57.6500	57.6500				
1968	17.07	6.95			50.0000	50.0000				
1969	19.30	8.62			50.0000	50.0000				
1970	23.43	8.29			50.0000	50.0000				
1971	30.50	8.06			50.7170	50.7170				
1972	30.56	12.12			52.1220	52.1220				
1973	35.59	16.58			51.0810	51.0810				
1974	39.37	24.13			48.7300	48.7300				
1975	51.36	46.84			46.2880	46.2880				
1976	57.77	46.40			38.3480	38.3480				
1977	59.18	40.54			37.0370	37.0370				
1978	65.41	45.21			37.0370	37.0370				
1979	86.71	45.47			37.0370	37.0370				
1980	121.07	65.13			37.0370	37.0370				
1981	128.83	65.51			37.0370	37.0370				
1982	118.15	50.86			37.0370	37.0370				
1983	132.00	64.00			37.0370	37.0370				
1984	132.00	64.00			37.0370	37.0370				
1985	144.72	58.86			37.0370	37.0370				
1986	169.82	67.90			37.0370	37.0370				
1987	214.63	75.58			37.0370	37.0370				
1988	251.52	74.10			37.0370	37.0370				
1989	276.71	77.25			37.0370	37.0370				
1990	298.97	74.66			37.0370	37.0370				
1991	302.40	56.70			37.0370	37.0370				
1992	258.19	70.62			37.0370	37.0370				
1993	318.89	72.87			37.0370	37.0370				
1994	251.10	105.30			37.0370	37.0370				

2. IMPORTS BY BROAD ECONOMIC CATEGORY AND EXPORTS BY INDUSTRIAL ORIGIN. (PERCENTAGE OF TOTAL VALUE)
IMPORTATIONS PAR CATEGORIES ECONOMIQUES ET EXPORTATIONS PAR BRANCHE D'ACTIVITE.(EN POURCENTAGE DE LA VALEUR TOTALE)

IMPORTS – IMPORTATIONS

	1990	1991	1992	1993	1994	1995	1996
TOTAL IMPORTS–IMPORTATIONS TOTALES							
1 FOOD BEV–ALIMENTATION BOISSONS							
11 PRIMARY–PRODUITS DE BASE							
111 FOR INDUSTRY–POUR L'INDUSTRIE							
112 FOR HOUSEHOLDS–POUR LES MENAGES							
12 PROCESSED–PRODUITS ELABORES							
121 FOR INDUSTRY–POUR L'INDUSTRIE							
122 FOR HOUSEHOLDS–POUR LES MENAGES							
2 IND SUPPLIES–APPROV INDUSTRIELS							
21 PRIMARY–PRODUITS DE BASE							
22 PROCESSED–PRODUITS ELABORES							
3 FUELS–COMBUSTIBLES							
31 PRIMARY–PRODUITS DE BASE							
32 PROCESSED–PRODUITS ELABORES							
321 MOTOR SPIRIT–ESSENCE							
322 OTHER–AUTRES							
4 MACHINERY–EQUIPEMENT							
41 CAPITAL EQUIPMENT–MACHINES							
42 PARTS–PIECES ACCESSOIRES							
5 TRANSPORT–TRANSPORT							
51 PASSENGER CARS–AUTOMOBILES							
52 OTHER–AUTRES							
521 INDUSTRIAL–INDUSTRIELS							
522 NON INDUSTRIAL–NON INDUSTRIEL							
53 PARTS–PIECES ACCESSOIRES							
6 CONSUM GOODS–BIENS CONSOMMATION							
61 DURABLE–DURABLES							
62 SEMI DURABLE–SEMI DURABLES							
63 NON DURABLE–NON DURABLES							
7 GOODS NES–BIENS NDA							

EXPORTS – EXPORTATIONS

	1990	1991	1992	1993	1994	1995	1996
TOTAL EXPORTS–EXPORTATIONS TOTALES							
1 AGRICULTURE							
2 MINING QUARRY–INDUS EXTRACTIVES							
3 MANUFACTURING–IND MANUFACTUR							
31 FOOD BEV TOBACCO–ALIM BOISS TAB							
32 TEXTILES–INDUSTRIES TEXTILES							
33 WOOD & PRODUCTS–BOIS & PRODUITS							
34 PAPER & PRODUCTS–PAPIER & PRODT							
35 CHEMICALS–INDUSTRIES CHIMIQUES							
36 NON METAL MIN–MIN NON METAL							
37 BASIC METAL–IND METAL BASE							
38 METAL MANUF–MANUF METAL							
39 OTH MANUF IND–AUTRES MANUF							

3. TRADE BY PRINCIPAL COUNTRIES OF ORIGIN AND LAST DESTINATION (VALUE IN THOUSAND U.S. DOLLARS)
ECHANGES SELON LES PRINCIPAUX PAYS D'ORIGINE ET DE DERNIERE DESTINATION (VALEUR EN MILLIERS DE DOLLARS EU)

COUNTRIES–PAYS	GENERAL IMPORTS C.I.F. IMPORTATIONS GENERALES C.A.F				
	1990	1991	1992	1993	1994
World	110729	110280	96000	118000	93000
Africa					
Americas	70103	71245	49300	50500	53000
Northern America	54034	50994	49300	50500	53000
LAIA					
CACM					
Caribbean	15976	20051			
Rest of America	92	200			
As.ex F.USSR					
Eur.x F.USSR	19928	16483	13400	13700	14400
EU	19928	16483	13400	13700	14400
EFTA					
East Europe					
Other Europe					
Former USSR					
Oceania					
USA/Etats–Unis d'Amer	48333	46820	49300	50500	53000
United Kingdom	13198	12466	13400	13700	14400
Trinidad and Tobago	7222	11023			
Canada	5701	4174			
Barbados/Barbade	3081	3429			
France,Monac	3177	1527			
Jamaica/Jamaïque	1799	1693			
St Vincent & Grenadines	1470	1169			
Antigua and Barbuda	883	1036			
Denmark/Danemark	1006	848			
Italy/Italie	1187	500			
Netherlands/Pays–Bas	774	677			
Dominica/Dominique	585	585			
Saint Lucia/St. Lucie	494	589			
Germany/Allemagne	366	334			
Grenada/Grenade	271	247			
British Virgin Islds	135	165			
Guyana	92	164			
Montserrat	36	101			

COUNTRIES–PAYS	GENERAL EXPORTS F.O.B. EXPORTATIONS GENERALES F.O.B.				
	1990	1991	1992	1993	1994
Monde	27650	27481	26000	27000	39000
Afrique					
Amériques	17898	15046	14200	16600	15100
Amérique du Nord	14136	11527	14200	16600	15100
ALAI					
MCAC					
Caraïbes	3708	3490			
Autre Amérique	54	30			
Asie l'URSS exclus					
Europe l'URSS exclus	5919	9739	8400	8700	8600
UE	5919	9739	8400	8700	8600
AELE					
Europe de l'Est					
Autre de l'Europe					
Ancienne URSS					
Océanie					
USA/Etats–Unis d'Amer	14086	11458	14200	16600	15100
United Kingdom	5773	9465	8400	8700	8600
Antigua and Barbuda	755	743			
Trinidad and Tobago	708	325			
Saint Lucia/St. Lucie	439	524			
Dominica/Dominique	468	494			
Montserrat	510	356			
Barbados/Barbade	217	473			
Grenada/Grenade	236	331			
France,Monac	104	197			
British Virgin Islds	170	100			
St Vincent & Grenadines	143	118			
Canada	50	69			
Italy/Italie	42	71			
Jamaica/Jamaïque	63	27			
Guyana	54				
Netherlands/Pays–Bas		4			
Germany/Allemagne		0			

(VALUE AS PERCENTAGE OF WORLD TOTAL)(VALEURS EN POURCENTAGE DU TOTAL MONDIAL)

	1985	1986	1987	1988	1989	1990	1991	1992	1993	1994
Africa	2.3	0.5	0.1	0.1						
Americas	75.7	72.2	74.2	72.1	61.9	63.3	64.6	51.4	42.8	57.0
Northern America	50.6	50.7	53.4	52.7	44.4	48.8	46.2	51.4	42.8	57.0
LAIA	0.9	0.6	1.0	1.6						
CACM	0.3	0.2	0.8	0.6						
Caribbean	23.4	20.3	18.7	16.9	17.4	14.4	18.2			
Rest of America	0.6	0.3	0.3	0.4	0.1	0.1	0.2			
As.ex F.USSR	4.1	5.1	5.9	5.8						
Eur.x F.USSR	17.3	22.2	19.8	21.9	18.5	18.0	14.9	14.0	11.6	15.5
EU	16.0	20.4	18.9	21.1	18.5	18.0	14.9	14.0	11.6	15.5
EFTA	1.3	1.6	0.7	0.7						
East Europe		0.1	0.1	0.1						
Other Europe		0.1	0.1	0.0						
Former USSR	0.1			0.0						
Oceania	0.0	0.1	0.0	0.1						
USA/Etats–Unis d'Amer	47.0	47.8	47.0	48.5	41.3	43.6	42.5	51.4	42.8	57.0
United Kingdom	12.1	15.1	14.7	18.0	14.0	11.9	11.3	14.0	11.6	15.5
Trinidad and Tobago	9.0	6.5	7.1	6.5	7.4	6.5	10.0			
Canada	3.6	2.8	6.4	4.2	3.2	5.1	3.8			
Barbados/Barbade	3.3	3.7	2.7	2.7	2.6	2.8	3.1			
France,Monac	0.4	0.3	0.4	0.4	1.0	2.9	1.4			
Jamaica/Jamaïque	1.2	2.0	2.0	1.3	1.8	1.6	1.5			
St Vincent & Grenadines	3.4	3.7	2.1	2.1	1.7	1.3	1.1			
Antigua and Barbuda	1.1	1.2	1.1	0.8	1.1	0.8	0.9			
Denmark/Danemark	1.0	1.1	0.8	0.9	0.8	0.9	0.8			

	1985	1986	1987	1988	1989	1990	1991	1992	1993	1994
Afrique	0.0	0.0	0.0	0.0						
Amériques	73.7	79.5	85.9	71.2	58.7	64.7	54.8	54.6	61.5	38.7
Amérique du Nord	39.8	63.5	72.3	58.0	49.6	51.1	41.9	54.6	61.5	38.7
ALAI	0.0		0.0	0.1						
MCAC			0.0	0.0						
Caraïbes	33.8	15.1	13.3	13.0	9.1	13.4	12.7			
Autre Amérique	0.0	0.9	0.4	0.1		0.2	0.1			
Asie l'URSS exclus	0.0	0.0	0.0	0.1						
Europe l'URSS exclus	25.2	20.2	13.1	22.4	24.6	21.4	35.4	32.3	32.2	22.1
UE	25.2	20.2	13.1	22.4	24.6	21.4	35.4	32.3	32.2	22.1
AELE	0.0		0.0	0.0						
Europe de l'Est										
Autre de l'Europe										
Ancienne URSS										
Océanie		0.0								
USA/Etats–Unis d'Amer	39.4	63.4	71.6	57.8	49.5	50.9	41.7	54.6	61.5	38.7
United Kingdom	25.2	20.2	12.9	21.8	23.3	20.9	34.4	32.3	32.2	22.1
Antigua and Barbuda	5.2	2.4	2.6	2.3	1.8	2.7	2.7			
Trinidad and Tobago	10.7	6.5	3.3	4.3	3.7	2.6	1.2			
Saint Lucia/St. Lucie	0.1	0.0	0.1	0.1	0.1	1.6	1.9			
Dominica/Dominique	0.6	0.7	0.4	0.5	0.3	1.7	1.8			
Montserrat	2.7	1.3	2.0	0.9	1.2	1.8	1.3			
Barbados/Barbade	9.1	0.5	0.2	0.5	0.9	0.8	1.7			
Grenada/Grenade	0.6	0.3	0.3	0.4	0.4	0.9	1.2			
France,Monac		0.0	0.0	0.1	1.1	0.4	0.7			

4. General Imports C.I.F. by Commodities according to the S.I.T.C. (Rev. 2) in thousand U.S. Dollars
Importations Générales C.A.F. par Produits d'après la C.T.C.I. (Rév. 2) en milliers de Dollars E.U.

SITC CTCI	COMMODITY	1988 WEIGHT POIDS	1988 VALUE VALEUR	1989 WEIGHT POIDS	1989 VALUE VALEUR	1990 WEIGHT POIDS	1990 VALUE VALEUR	1991 WEIGHT POIDS	1991 VALUE VALEUR	PRODUIT
	ALL COMMODITIES		93283		102487		110729		110280	TOUS PRODUITS
0	FOOD AND LIVE ANIMALS		14531		14997		16755		18463	ALIMENTS,ANIMAUX VIVANTS
01	MEAT AND PREPARATIONS		3522							VIANDES ET PREPARATIONS
011	MEAT FRESH,CHILLD,FROZEN	W 2027	2331							VIANDES FRAICHES,REF,CONGE
0111	BOVINE MEAT FRESH,FROZEN	W 89	360							VIANDES BOVIN FRAI,REF
0114	POULTRY FRESH CHLLD,FRZN	W 1749	1654							VOLAILLES MORTES
014	MEAT PREPD,PRSVD,NES ETC	W 470	965							CONSERVES DE VIANDES
0142	SAUSAGES INCLDING TINNED	W 199	320							SAUSISSES,SAUCISSONS
0149	OTH PREPARD,PRESRVD MEAT	W 270	644							AUTRES PREP DE VIANDES
02	DAIRY PRODCTS,BIRDS'EGGS		1746							PRODUITS LAITIERS,OEUFS
022	MILK AND CREAM	W 1341	1266							LAIT ET CREME
0224	MILK,CREAM PRESERVED ETC	W 1134	1075							LAIT,CREME CONS,CONC
02249	MILK(EX DRY) PRSVD,SWEET	W 1067	977							LAIT CONS,CONC SUCRE
024	CHEESE AND CURD	W 131	397							FROMAGE ET CAILLEBOTTE
03	FISH AND PREPARATIONS		937							POISSONS ET PREPARATIONS
035	FISH SALTED,DRIED,SMOKED	W 160	412							POISSON SECHE,SALE,FUME
03503	FISH(EX COD)DRIED,SALTED	W 147	374							POISSONS SECHES,SALES
037	FISH ETC PREPD,PRSVD NES	W 110	329							POIS,CRUST,MOL PREPARES
0371	FISH PREPARD,PRESRVD NES	W 107	305							CONSERVES DE POISSONS
04	CEREALS AND PREPARATIONS		2822							CEREALES ET PRODUITS
042	RICE		539							RIZ
046	WHEAT ETC MEAL OR FLOUR	W 2327	1050							SEMOULE FARINE,FROMENT
04601	FLOUR OF WHEAT OR MESLIN	W 2310	1034							FARINE DE FROMENT
048	CEREAL ETC PREPARATIONS	W 860	1131							PREPTNS A BASE CEREALES
0481	PREPD BREAKFAST FOOD ETC	W 170	300							CEREALES TRAVAILLEES
05	VEGETABLES AND FRUIT		2449							LEGUMES ET FRUITS
054	VEG ETC FRSH,SMPLY PRSVD	W 1466	1004							LEGUMES FRAIS,CONG,SECS
0545	OTHER FRESH VEGETABLES	W 565	423							AUTRES LEGUMES FRAIS,REF
057	FRUIT,NUTS,FRESH,DRIED	W 246	338							FRUITS FRAIS OU SECS
058	FRUIT PRESERVED,PREPARED		880							CONSERVES DE FRUITS
0585	FRUIT OR VEGETABLE JUICE		715							JUS DE FRUITS
06	SUGAR AND PREPS,HONEY		390							SUCRES ET PRODUITS
081	*FEEDING STUFF FOR ANIML		669							NOURRITURE POUR ANIMAUX
0819	FOOD WASTE AND FEED NES		659							DECHETS,ALIMENTS NDA
08199	FODDER NES,INCL SWEETNED		659							PREPARATIONS FOURRAGERES
09	MISC EDIBLE PRODUCTS		1741							PREP ALIMENTAIRES DIVERSES
098	EDIBLE PRODCTS,PREPS NES	W 808	1495							PREP ALIMENTAIRES NDA
09804	SAUCES,MIXED SEASONINGS	W 246	442							SAUCES,ASSAISONNEMENTS
09809	MISC FOOD PREPRTIONS NES	W 454	857							PREP ALIMENTAIRES NDA
1	BEVERAGES AND TOBACCO		2473		2720		2883		3144	BOISSONS ET TABACS
11	BEVERAGES		2106							BOISSONS
111	NON–ALCOHL BEVERAGES NES		794							BOISSONS NON ALCOOLIQUES
11102	FLAVORED WATERS NON–ALCO	W 813	790							LIMONADES,EAUX GAZEUSES
112	ALCOHOLIC BEVERAGES	W 154	1312							BOISSONS ALCOOLIQUES
1124	DISTILLED ALCOHOLIC BEVS		836							ALCOOLS,EAUX–DE–VIE
11249	OTH ALCOHOLC BEVS,CMPNDS		530							BOISSONS ALCOOLIQUES NDA
12	TOBACCO AND MANUFACTURES		367							TABACS BRUTS FABRIQUES
122	TOBACCO,MANUFACTURED		366							TABACS FABRIQUES
1222	CIGARETTES		348							CIGARETTES
2	CRUDE MATERLS,EXCL FUELS		1680		1950		3108		2079	MAT BRUTES NON COMESTIBLES
24	CORK AND WOOD		1330							LIEGE ET BOIS
248	WOOD SHAPED,SLEEPERS		1257							BOIS SIMPLEMENT TRAVAILLES
2482	LUMBER SHAPED CONIFER		600							CONIFERES SCIES,RABOTES
24822	LUMBER PLANED ETC CONIFR		328							CONIFER RABOTES,RAINES
2483	LUMBER SHAPED NON–CONIFR		657							NON CONIFERES SCIES,RABOTES
24832	LUMBER PLANED ETC NONCON		528							RABOTES,RAINES,LANGUETES
3	MINERAL FUELS ETC		5145		6259		5529		8648	COMBUSTIBLES MINERAUX LUB
33	PETROLEUM AND PRODUCTS		4570							PETROLE ET DERIVES
334	PETROLEUM PRODUCTS,REFIN		4513							PRODUITS RAFFINES
3341	GASOLINE,OTH LIGHT OILS		1556							ESSENCES POUR MOTEURS
33411	MOTOR,AVIATION SPIRIT		1550							ESSENCES MOTEURS D'AVIONS
3343	GAS OILS		2499							GAS OILS
3345	LUBS,PETROLEUM OILS NES		359							HUILES LUBRIFIANTES
33451	LUBS(HIGH PETR CONT) ETC		349							HUILES LUBRIF,H LOURDES
341	*GAS,NATURAL AND MANUFCT	W 1375	571							GAZ NATUREL,GAZ MANUFACT
3413	PETROLM GASES,LIQUEFIED	W 1375	571							GAZ DE PETROLE LIQUEFIE
34131	LIQUEFIED PROPANE,BUTANE	W 1364	570							PROPANE,BUTANE LIQUEFIES
4	ANIMAL,VEGETABLE OIL,FAT		926		1034		806		977	HUILES,GRAISSES ANIM,VEG
42	FIXED VEGETABLE OIL,FAT		305							HUILES VEGETALES FIXES
431	*PROCESD ANML VEG OIL,ET		604							HUILES,GRAISSES PREPAREES
4312	HYDROGENATED OIL,FAT	W 370	587							HUILES HYDROGENEES
5	CHEMCLS,RELATED PROD NES		6995		7710		8136		9110	PRODUITS CHIMIQUES
53	DYES,TANNING,COLOUR PROD		1082							PROD TEINTURE,COLORANTS
533	PIGMENTS,PAINTS,ETC	W 405	1078							PIGMENTS,PEINTURES,VERNIS
5334	VARNISHES,DISTEMPERS ETC	W 262	893							PEINTURES A L'EAU
53341	WATER–THINNED PAINTS	W 110	295							PEINTURES DILUEES
53342	OTH PAINTS,VARNISHES ETC	W 144	472							AUTRES PEINTURES,VERNIS
541	*MEDICINAL,PHARM PRODUCT		1089							PROD MEDICINAUX PHARMACEUT
5417	MEDICAMENTS	K 102695	944							MEDICAMENTS
54179	— CONTNG OTH SUBSTANCES	K 92275	795							MED CONT AUT SUBSTANCES
55	PERFUME,CLEANING ETC PRD		1881							PROD POUR PARFUM,TOILETTE
553	PERFUMERY,COSMETICS,ETC	W 144	936							PRODUITS DE PARFUMERIE
554	SOAP,CLEANSING ETC PREPS		944							SAVONS,PRODUITS DETERSIFS
5542	WASHING PREPARATIONS ETC		692							PROD ORG TENSIO–ACT NDA
562	*FERTILIZERS,MANUFACTURE		440							ENGRAIS MANUFACTURES
5621	CHEM NITROGENOUS FERTLZR		412							ENGRAIS AZOTES
56219	CHEM NITROG FERTILZR NES		341							ENGRAIS AZOTES NDA
58	PLASTIC MATERIALS ETC		804							MAT PLAST ARTIFICIELLES
583	POLYMERIZATION ETC PRODS		684							PROD POLYMERISATION
59	CHEMICAL MATERIALS NES		1342							MAT PROD CHIMIQUES NDA
591	PESTICIDES,DISINFECTANTS	W 410	863							DESINF,INSECT,FONG,HERB
5911	INSECTICIDES,FOR RETAIL	W 75	344							INSECTICIDES VENTE DET
5913	HERBICIDES,FOR RETAIL	W 174	335							HERBICIDES VENTE AU DET
598	MISCEL CHEM PRODUCTS NES	W 125	285							PROD DIV INDUST CHIM NDA
6	BASIC MANUFACTURES		18934		20422		24974		25443	ART MANUFACTURES
62	RUBBER MANUFACTURES NES		951							CAOUTCHOUC MANUFACTURE
625	RUBBER TYRES, TUBES ETC	W 155	710							PNEUS CAOUTCHOUC VULCANISE
6259	OTH TYRES,TYRE CASES,ETC	W 58	332							AUTRES PNEUS RECHAPES FLAPS
63	WOOD,CORK MANUFACTRS NES		1688							OUVRAGES LIEGE ET BOIS
634	VENEERS,PLYWOOD,ETC		879							PLACAGES,CONTRE–PLAQUES
6342	PLYWOOD OF WOOD SHEETS		808							BOIS CONTRE–PLAQUES

4. General Imports C.I.F. by Commodities according to the S.I.T.C. (Rev. 2) in thousand U.S. Dollars
Importations Générales C.A.F. par Produits d'après la C.T.C.I. (Rév. 2) en milliers de Dollars E.U.

SITC CTCI	COMMODITY	1988		1989		1990		1991		PRODUIT
		WEIGHT POIDS	VALUE VALEUR	WEIGHT POIDS	VALUE VALEUR	WEIGHT POIDS	VALUE VALEUR	WEIGHT POIDS	VALUE VALEUR	
635	WOOD MANUFACTURES NES		807							ART MANUF EN BOIS NDA
6353	BUILDERS WOODWRK,PREFABS		697							OUVRAGES DE MENUISERIE
64	PAPER,PAPERBOARD AND MFR		1810							PAPIERS,CARTONS & OUVRAGES
642	PAPER,ETC,PRECUT,ARTS OF		1641							PAP,CARTONS DECOUPES
6421	PAPER ETC CONTAINERS		508							BOITES,SACS EMBALLAGES
6424	PAPER ETC CT TO SIZE NES	W 109	459							PAP,CARTONS DECOUPES
6428	PAPER ETC ARTICLES NES	W 97	347							OUVRAGES EN PATE A PAPIER
65	TEXTILE YARN,FABRICS,ETC		2403							FILS,TISSUS,ARTICLES TEXTILE
652	COTTON FABRICS,WOVEN	W 39	324							TISSUS DE COTON
653	WOVN MAN–MADE FIB FABRIC	W 109	458							TISSUS FIBRES SYNTH,ARTIF
656	LACE,RIBBONS,TULLE,ETC	W 13	372							TULLES,BRODERIE
657	SPECIAL TXTL FABRC,PRODS		604							TISSUS SPECIAUX
6574	ELASTIC FAB ETC NOT KNIT	W 57	467							TISSUS ELASTIQUES
658	TEXTILE ARTICLES NES		318							ART FACONNES MAT TEXTILES
66	NONMETAL MINERAL MFS NES		2913							ART MIN NON METALLIQUES
661	LIME,CEMENT,BLDG PRODS		1197							CHAUX,CIMENTS MAT CONSTR
6612	CEMENT		994							CIMENTS HYDRAULIQUES
662	CLAY,REFRACTORY BLDG PRD		454							MAT CONST REFRACTAIRES
6624	BRICKS ETC NONREFRACTORY		432							BRIQUES ETC CERAM NON REFR
663	MINERAL MANUFCTURES NES	W 273	311							ART MIN MANUF NDA
665	GLASSWARE		603							OUVRAGES EN VERRE
6651	BOTTLES ETC OF GLASS		362							RECIPIENTS EN VERRE
66511	GLASS BOTTLES ETC NONVAC		362							BONBONNES,BOUTEILLES,ETC
67	IRON AND STEEL		2605							FER ET ACIER
673	IRON,STEEL SHAPES ETC		491							BARRES,PROFIL FER,ACIER
6732	IRON,STEEL BARS ETC		331							BARRES FER,ACIER
67326	IRN,OTH STL BARS HOTROLD		329							BARRES PLEINES FER,ACIER
674	IRN,STL UNIV,PLATE,SHEET		285							LARGES PLATS,TOLES
676	RAILWY RAILS ETC IRN,STL		346							RAILS,ELEMENTS VOIES FERREE
678	IRON,STL TUBES,PIPES,ETC		1460							TUBES,TUYAUX EN FONTE,FER
6781	CAST IRON TUBES,PIPES		566							TUBES,TUYAUX EN FONTE
6785	IRON,STEEL TUBE FITTINGS		630							ACCESSOIRES DE TUYAUTERIE
69	METAL MANUFACTURES NES		6379							ART MANUFACT EN METAL NDA
691	STRUCTURES AND PARTS NES		1482							CONSTRUCT FER,ACIER,ALU
6911	STRUCTURES,PARTS IRN,STL		687							CONSTRUCT FER,ACIER,FONTE
6912	STRUCTURES,PARTS ALUMNM	W 375	795							CONSTRUCT ALUMINIUM
692	METAL TANKS,BOXES,ETC		390							RECIPIENTS METALLIQUES
693	WIRE PRODUCTS NON ELECTR		702							OUVRAGES FILS METALLIQUES
6935	METAL FENCING,GAUZE,ETC	W 200	454							TOILES EN FER,ACIER,CUIVRE
69351	IRN,STL FENCNG,GAUZE ETC	W 200	454							TOILES EN FER,ACIER
694	STL,COPPR NAILS,NUTS,ETC		482							CLOUS,VIS,ECROUS
69402	IRN,STL NUTS,BOLTS,ETC		307							BOULONS,VIS,ECROUS FER,AC
695	TOOLS		334							OUTILS A MAIN
697	BASE MTL HOUSEHOLD EQUIP		631							ART MENAGE MET COMMUNS
6973	DMSTC HEATG,COOKG APPARA	W 53	285							APPS CHAUF NON ELECTRIQ
699	BASE METAL MFRS NES		2300							ART MANUFACTURES MET NDA
6997	IRON,STEEL ARTICLES NES		1526							OUV FONTE,FER,ACIER NDA
69979	IRN,STL MANUFACTURES NES		1480							AUT OUVRAGES EN FER NDA
7	MACHINES,TRANSPORT EQUIP		29860		33696		32569		25837	MACHINES MATERIEL TRANSPORT
71	POWER GENERATING EQUIPMT		2788							MACHINES GENERATRICES
713	INTRNL COMBUS PSTN ENGIN		884							MOTEURS EXPL COMB INT, PIECE
7139	PISTON ENGINE PARTS NES	W 65	619							PIECES POUR 713.2,3,8
716	ROTATING ELECTRIC PLANT	W 172	1779							APP ELECTR ROTATIFS,PIECES
7161	DC MOTORS AND GENERATORS	W 169	1747							MOTEURS COURANT CONTINU
72	MACHS FOR SPCL INDUSTRYS		5934							MAC SPECIALES POUR INDUST
721	AGRIC MACHY,EXC TRACTORS	W 146	886							MACHINES AGRICOLES
7212	HARVESTING ETC MACHINES	W 114	706							ENGINS POUR LA RECOLTE
72121	LAWN MOWERS	W 34	365							TONDEUSES A GAZON
72123	OTH HARVSTER,MOWRS,BALER	W 73	303							AUT MACH POUR LA RECOLTE
723	CIVIL ENGNEERG EQUIP ETC		2827							APPAREILS DE GENIE CIVIL
7234	CONST,MINING MACHNRY NES		2451							MACH POUR LA CONST, MINES
7239	CONSTR ETC MACHY PTS NES		376							PIECES 723.41–723.46
727	FOOD MACHRY NON–DOMESTIC	W 70	465							MACH INDUSTRIES ALIMENT
7272	OTH FOOD PROC MCHY,PARTS	W 70	465							AUT MACH IND ALIMENTAIRE
72722	INDUS FOOD PROC MACH NES	W 61	425							MACHINES BOULANGERIE
728	OTH MACHY FOR SPCL INDUS	W 44	1453							AUT MACH IND PARTICULIERES
7283	OTHR MINERAL WORKG MACHY	W 27	1108							MACH TRIER,CRIBLER,BROYER
7284	MACHY FOR SPCL INDUS NES	W 14	324							MACH SPEC IND PARTICUL.
72848	OTH MCHY WITH INDIV FNCT	W 13	288							AUTRES MACHINES NDA
74	GENRL INDUSTRL MACHY NES		3282							MACH APP INDUSTRIE
741	HEATING,COOLING EQUIPMNT	W 80	628							MACH CHAUFFAGE,PIECES
743	PUMPS NES,CENTRFUGES ETC		610							POMPES COMPRES,VENT ETC
7431	PUMPS FOR GASES ETC	W 23	382							POMPES AIR A VIDE,COMPRES
749	NONELEC MACH PTS,ACC NES		1410							PIECES MACH NON ELEC NDA
7493	SHAFT,CRANK,PULLEY ETC		957							ARBRES TRANS,VILEBREQUINS
75	OFFICE MACHNES,ADP EQUIP		869							MACH BUREAU TRAIT AUTOM
751	OFFICE MACHINES		321							MACH,APPAREILS DE BUREAU
752	AUTOMTIC DATA PROC EQUIP	W 8	461							MACH TRAIT INFORMATION
76	TELECOMM,SOUND EQUIPMENT		3344							EQUIPMENT DE TELECOM
764	TELECOM EQPT,PTS,ACC NES		2980							EQUIP TELECOM,PIECES
7641	LINE TELEPHONE,ETC EQUIP	W 18	861							APP TELEPHON PAR FIL
7643	TV,RADIO TRANSMITTRS ETC	W 4	354							APP EMET TELE RADIO
7648	TELECOMM EQUIPMENT NES		426							APP TELECOM NDA
76483	RADAR APPARATUS ETC	W 13	401							APP DE RADIOGUIDAGE ETC
7649	PTS NES OF EQUIPMT OF 76		1302							PIECES DE LA DIV 76
76493	TELECOMM EQUIPMT PTS NES	W 18	1093							PIECES 761,762,764.3,8
77	ELECTRIC MACHNRY NES ETC		6462							MACH APP ELECT NDA
771	ELECTRIC POWER MACHY NES		623							MACH PROD,TRANS ELECTR
7711	TRANSFORMERS,ELECTRICAL	W 43	362							TRANSFO ELECTRIQUES
772	SWITCHGEAR ETC,PARTS NES		980							APP COUPURE,SECT ETC
7721	SWITCHGEAR ETC	W 40	596							APP COUPURE,SECTIONMNT
7722	PRINTED CIRCUITS,PTS NES		329							CIRCUITS ET PIECES
773	ELECTR DISTRIBUTNG EQUIP	W 401	1864							EQUIPMT DISTRIBUTION ELECT
7731	INSULATED WIRE,CABLE ETC	W 395	1793							FILS,CABLES ISOLES ELECT
775	HOUSEHOLD TYPE EQUIP NES		876							MACH,APP USAGE DOMESTQUE
7752	DOM REFRIGERATRS,FREEZRS	W 109	543							REFRIG,CONGEL MENAGER
77521	DOMESTIC REFRIGERATORS	W 86	434							REFRIGERATEURS
778	ELECTRICAL MACHINERY NES		2087							AUTRES MACH ELECT NDA
7781	BATTERIES,ACCUMULATORS	W 71	290							PILES ET ACCUMULATEURS
7788	OTH ELEC MACHY,EQUIP NES		1406							AUT MACH APP ELEC NDA
77886	OTH ELEC MACHINERY NES	W 38	1217							AUT MACH APP ELECTRIQUES

4. General Imports C.I.F. by Commodities according to the S.I.T.C. (Rev. 2) in thousand U.S. Dollars
Importations Générales C.A.F. par Produits d'après la C.T.C.I. (Rév. 2) en milliers de Dollars E.U.

SITC CTCI	COMMODITY	1988 WEIGHT POIDS	1988 VALUE VALEUR	1989 WEIGHT POIDS	1989 VALUE VALEUR	1990 WEIGHT POIDS	1990 VALUE VALEUR	1991 WEIGHT POIDS	1991 VALUE VALEUR	PRODUIT
78	ROAD VEHICLES		6625							VEHICULES ROUTIERS
781	PASS MOTOR VEH EXC BUSES		2645							AUTO TRANSPORT PERSONNES
782	LORRIES,SPCL MTR VEH NES	W 525	1642							VEHICULES SPECIAUX,MARCH
7821	LORRIES,TRUCKS	W 516	1619							VEHICULES TRANSP MARCHAND
783	ROAD MOTOR VEHICLES NES	W 145	787							VEHICULES ROUTIERS NDA
7831	BUSES	W 138	774							VOITURES TRANSPORT COMMUN
784	MOTOR VEH PRTS,ACCES NES		793							PIECES 722,781,782,783
7849	OTHER MOTOR VEHCL PARTS		769							PIECES 722,781,782,783
786	TRAILERS,NONMOTR VEH,NES	W 246	604							REMORQUES,CADRES,CONTAIN
7861	TRAILERS,TRANSP CONTAINR	W 110	552							REMORQUES TOUS VEHICULES
78612	OTHER TRAILERS	W 95	512							REMORQUES TRANSP MARCH
79	OTHR TRANSPORT EQUIPMENT		398							AUTRE MATERIEL TRANSPORT
8	MISC MANUFACTURED GOODS		12192		12947		15514		16025	ART MANUFACTURES DIVERS
812	*PLUMBG,HEATNG,LGHTNG EQ	W 94	407							APPAR SANITAIRES CHAUFFAGE
821	*FURNITURE,PARTS THEREOF		1421							MEUBLES ET PIECES
8211	CHAIRS,SEATS AND PARTS	W 78	409							SIEGES ET PIECES
82111	CHAIRS AND OTHER SEATS	W 78	408							SIEGES
8219	FURNITURE AND PARTS NES		762							AUTRES MEUBLES ET PIECES
82192	WOOD FURNITURE NES	W 108	451							MEUBLES NDA EN BOIS
84	CLOTHING AND ACCESSORIES		4207							VETEMENTS
843	WOMENS OUTERWEAR NONKNIT		739							VET DESSUS FEMMES MAT TEX
8439	— OTHER OUTER GARMENTS		600							AUT VET DES FEM MAT TEXT
84394	—— OF MAN–MADE FIBRES	W 58	449							VET DES FEM NDA FIB SYNT
844	UNDER GARMENTS NOT KNIT		365							VETEMENT DESSOUS MAT TEX
846	UNDER GARMENTS KNITTED		2642							SOUS VETS DE BONNETERIE
8465	CORSETS,GARTERS,ETC		2571							CORSETS,GAINES ART SIM
84651	BRASSIERES		1417							SOUTIENS–GORGE,BUSTIERS
84652	CORSETS,BRACES ETC	W 36	1154							CORSETS,GAINES,JARRETEL
851	*FOOTWEAR	W 47	436							CHAUSSURES
87	PRECISION INSTRUMNTS NES		869							INSTRUM,APPAR SCIENT NDA
874	MEASURNG,CONTROLNG INSTR		701							INSTRUMENTS DE MESURE
8748	ELEC MEAS,CONTRL EQU NES		390							APP ELEC ELECTRO MESURE
87489	ELEC MEASUR ETC INST NES		362							AUT INSTRUM ELEC NDA
89	MISC MANUFCTRD GOODS NES		4505							ART MANUFACTURES DIVERS
892	PRINTED MATTER	W 95	1016							IMPRIMES
8921	PRINTED BOOKS,GLOBES,ETC	W 52	288							LIVRES,BROCHURES,CARTES
89211	PRINTED BOOKS,PAMPHLETS	W 51	282							LIVRES,BROCHURES
8928	PRINTED MATTER NES	W 23	620							IMPRIMES NDA
89283	UNISSUED BANKNOTES ETC	W 8	483							TIMBRES–POSTE FISCAUX
893	ARTICLES OF PLASTIC NES		2238							OUVRAGES EN MAT DIVIS 58
8931	PLSTC PACKG CONTNRS,LIDS	W 95	350							ART TRANSP EMBALLAGE ETC
8939	MISC PLASTIC ARTICLES		1813							ART DIVERS EN MAT DIV 58
89399	OTHR PLASTC ARTICLES NES		1754							AUT OUV MAT DIV 58
894	TOYS,SPORTING GOODS,ETC		473							VOITURES ENFANTS,JOUETS
8942	TOYS,INDOOR GAMES ETC	W 20	360							JOUETS,JEUX ETC
9	GOODS NOT CLASSD BY KIND		546		753		456		553	ART TRANSACT NON CLASSES
961	*COIN NONGOLD,NONCURRENT	W 41	532							MONNAIES NON EMISES

5. General Exports F.O.B. by Commodities according to the S.I.T.C. (Rev. 2) in thousand U.S. Dollars
Exportations Générales F.O.B. par Produits d'après la C.T.C.I. (Rév. 2) en milliers de Dollars E.U.

SITC CTCI	COMMODITY	1988 WEIGHT POIDS	1988 VALUE VALEUR	1989 WEIGHT POIDS	1989 VALUE VALEUR	1990 WEIGHT POIDS	1990 VALUE VALEUR	1991 WEIGHT POIDS	1991 VALUE VALEUR	PRODUIT
	ALL COMMODITIES		27445		28610		27650		27481	TOUS PRODUITS
0	FOOD AND LIVE ANIMALS		10227		11700		7247		11178	ALIMENTS,ANIMAUX VIVANTS
03	FISH AND PREPARATIONS		203							POISSONS ET PREPARATIONS
036	SHELL FISH FRESH,FROZEN	W 122	190							CRUSTACES,MOLLUSQUES
06	SUGAR AND PREPS,HONEY		8790							SUCRES ET PRODUITS
061	SUGAR AND HONEY		8790							SUCRES ET MIEL
0611	RAW BEET AND CANE SUGAR	W 23572	8651							SUCRES BRUTS
0615	MOLASSES		136							MELASSES
09	MISC EDIBLE PRODUCTS		1119							PREP ALIMENTAIRES DIVERSES
091	MARGARINE AND SHORTENING	W 669	1119							MARGARINE ET GRAISSES
0914	MARGARINE,EDIBLE FAT NES	W 669	1119							MARGARINES,SIMILI SAINDOUX
09141	MARGARINE	W 98	158							MARGARINE
09149	OTH PREPARED EDIBLE FATS	W 571	961							SIMILI–SAINDOUX
1	BEVERAGES AND TOBACCO		1133		1117		1765		1678	BOISSONS ET TABACS
11	BEVERAGES		1133							BOISSONS
111	NON–ALCOHL BEVERAGES NES	W 2165	864							BOISSONS NON ALCOOLIQUES
11102	FLAVORED WATERS NON–ALCO	W 2165	864							LIMONADES,EAUX GAZEUSES
112	ALCOHOLIC BEVERAGES		269							BOISSONS ALCOOLIQUES
1123	BEER,ALE,STOUT,PORTER		217							BIERES
2	CRUDE MATERLS,EXCL FUELS		166		70		55		40	MAT BRUTES NON COMESTIBLES
26	TEXTILE FIBRES AND WASTE		111							FIBRES TEXTILES
268	WOOL(EXC TOPS),ANML HAIR	W 21	88							LAINES ET POILS
2685	COARSE HAIR UNCOMBED	W 21	88							CRINS EN MASSE
26851	HORSEHAIR AND ITS WASTE	W 21	88							CRINS ET DECHETS
3	MINERAL FUELS ETC		258		6		7		3	COMBUSTIBLES MINERAUX LUB
33	PETROLEUM AND PRODUCTS		257							PETROLE ET DERIVES
334	PETROLEUM PRODUCTS,REFIN		256							PRODUITS RAFFINES
3342	KEROSENE,OTH MEDIUM OILS		253							PETR LAMPANTS,AUT HUIL
33421	KEROSENE INCL JET FUEL		253							PETROLES LAMPANTS
6	BASIC MANUFACTURES		484		597		1506		1380	ART MANUFACTURES
66	NONMETAL MINERAL MFS NES		209							ART MIN NON METALLIQUES
663	MINERAL MANUFCTURES NES	W 1530	148							ART MIN MANUF NDA
6633	MINRL MFS NES NONCERAMIC	W 1527	140							OUVR MAT MINERALE NDA
66332	CEMENT,ARTFCL STONE PROD	W 1527	140							OUVRAGES EN CIMENT
69	METAL MANUFACTURES NES		152							ART MANUFACT EN METAL NDA
7	MACHINES,TRANSPORT EQUIP		9381		10862		13481		8354	MACHINES MATERIEL TRANSPORT
71	POWER GENERATING EQUIPMT		2066							MACHINES GENERATRICES
716	ROTATING ELECTRIC PLANT		2043							APP ELECTR ROTATIFS,PIECES
7161	DC MOTORS AND GENERATORS		2031							MOTEURS COURANT CONTINU
72	MACHS FOR SPCL INDUSTRYS		149							MAC SPECIALES POUR INDUST
76	TELECOMM,SOUND EQUIPMENT		216							EQUIPMENT DE TELECOM
764	TELECOM EQPT,PTS,ACC NES	W 7	200							EQUIP TELECOM,PIECES
7643	TV,RADIO TRANSMITTRS ETC	W 3	88							APP EMET TELE RADIO
77	ELECTRIC MACHNRY NES ETC		6478							MACH APP ELECT NDA
771	ELECTRIC POWER MACHY NES	W 130	3542							MACH PROD,TRANS ELECTR
7711	TRANSFORMERS,ELECTRICAL	W 61	3350							TRANSFO ELECTRIQUES
7712	OTH ELEC POWER MACHY NES	W 69	192							AUT APP PROD TRANSF ELEC
77129	PTS NES OF MACHY OF 771	W 66	157							PIECES MACH DU 771
772	SWITCHGEAR ETC,PARTS NES	W 178	2622							APP COUPURE,SECT ETC
7721	SWITCHGEAR ETC	W 136	1895							APP COUPURE,SECTIONMNT
7722	PRINTED CIRCUITS,PTS NES	W 41	712							CIRCUITS ET PIECES
773	ELECTR DISTRIBUTNG EQUIP	W 8	149							EQUIPMT DISTRIBUTION ELECT
7731	INSULATED WIRE,CABLE ETC	W 8	149							FILS,CABLES ISOLES ELECT
778	ELECTRICAL MACHINERY NES		160							AUTRES MACH ELECT NDA
78	ROAD VEHICLES		286							VEHICULES ROUTIERS
781	PASS MOTOR VEH EXC BUSES	W 1044	142							AUTO TRANSPORT PERSONNES
8	MISC MANUFACTURED GOODS		5692		4126		3431		4582	ART MANUFACTURES DIVERS
84	CLOTHING AND ACCESSORIES		5402							VETEMENTS
843	WOMENS OUTERWEAR NONKNIT		295							VET DESSUS FEMMES MAT TEX
8439	— OTHER OUTER GARMENTS	W 87	286							AUT VET DES FEM MAT TEXT
84399	—— OF OTHER FIBRES	W 84	278							VET DES FEM NDA AUT FIBR
844	UNDER GARMENTS NOT KNIT	W 6	114							VETEMENT DESSOUS MAT TEX
8441	— MENS SHIRTS	W 1	93							CHEMISES HOMMES MAT TEXT
84419	—— OF OTHER FIBRES	W 1	90							CHEMISES HOMMES AUT FIBR
846	UNDER GARMENTS KNITTED	W 130	4943							SOUS VETS DE BONNETERIE
8464	— OF OTH FIBRE NONELAST	W 66	3309							SOUS–VET BON AUT FIBRES
84649	—— OF FIBRES NES	W 66	3309							SOUS–VET BON AUT FIBRES
8465	CORSETS,GARTERS,ETC	W 63	1634							CORSETS,GAINES ART SIM
84651	BRASSIERES	W 63	1633							SOUTIENS–GORGE,BUSTIERS
87	PRECISION INSTRUMNTS NES		173							INSTRUM,APPAR SCIENT NDA
874	MEASURNG,CONTROLNG INSTR	W 3	165							INSTRUMENTS DE MESURE
9	GOODS NOT CLASSD BY KIND		76		90		66		164	ART TRANSACT NON CLASSES

1. HISTORICAL SERIES, 1959–1995 GENERAL TRADE, IMPORTS C.I.F., EXPORTS F.O.B. # 1
SERIES HISTORIQUES, 1959–1995 COMMERCE GENERAL, IMPORTATIONS C.A.F., EXPORTATIONS F.O.B

YEAR ANNEE	VALUE IN MILLION E.C. DOLLARS VALEUR EN MILLION E.C. DOLLARS MERCHANDISE –MARCHANDISE IMPORTS	EXPORTS	GOLD –OR IMPORTS	EXPORTS	CONVERSION FACTORS U.S. CENTS PER E.C. DOLLAR FACTEURS DE CONVERSION CENTS E.U. PAR E.C. DOLLAR IMPORTS	EXPORTS	INDEX NUMBERS –INDICES QUANTUM IMPORTS	EXPORTS	UNIT VALUE VALEUR UNITAIRE IMPORTS	EXPORTS
1959	10.00	6.30			58.3300	58.3300				
1960	12.20	5.40			58.3300	58.3300				
1961	13.30	7.70			58.3300	58.3300				
1962	16.70	7.60			58.3300	58.3300				
1963	16.70	8.00			58.3300	58.3300				
1964	20.40	9.80			58.3300	58.3300				
1965	22.00	11.20			58.3300	58.3300				
1966	28.40	12.10			58.3300	58.3300				
1967	29.50	11.70			57.6500	57.6500				
1968	29.50	12.60			50.0000	50.0000				
1969	41.50	16.30			50.0000	50.0000				
1970	54.60	8.70			50.0000	50.0000				
1971	69.00	12.20			50.7166	50.7166				
1972	68.70	15.10			52.1216	52.1216				
1973	74.20	19.20			51.0808	51.0808				
1974	91.10	32.90			48.7301	48.7301				
1975	100.40	34.50			46.2878	46.2878				
1976	125.70	49.90			38.0480	38.0480				
1977	160.20	61.00			37.0370	37.0370				
1978	219.90	72.40			37.0370	37.0370				
1979	273.20	86.00			37.0370	37.0370				
1980	334.20	124.20			37.0370	37.0370				
1981	348.90	111.30			37.0370	37.0370				
1982	318.70	112.30			37.0370	37.0370				
1983	288.40	128.30			37.0370	37.0370				
1984	320.00	129.10			37.0370	37.0370				
1985	337.50	140.50			37.0370	37.0370				
1986	417.90	234.59			37.0370	37.0370				
1987	483.90	214.80			37.0370	37.0370				
1988	595.00	312.00			37.0370	37.0370				
1989	739.10	294.70			37.0370	37.0370				
1990	731.60	343.70			37.0370	37.0370				
1991	797.00	297.80			37.0370	37.0370				
1992	845.00	331.50			37.0370	37.0370				
1993	810.87	323.30			37.0370	37.0370				
1995	826.27	294.21			37.0370	37.0370				

2. IMPORTS BY BROAD ECONOMIC CATEGORY AND EXPORTS BY INDUSTRIAL ORIGIN. (PERCENTAGE OF TOTAL VALUE)
IMPORTATIONS PAR CATEGORIES ECONOMIQUES ET EXPORTATIONS PAR BRANCHE D'ACTIVITE.(EN POURCENTAGE DE LA VALEUR TOTALE)

IMPORTS – IMPORTATIONS

	1990	1991	1992	1993	1994	1995	1996
TOTAL IMPORTS–IMPORTATIONS TOTALES	100.	100.					
1 FOOD BEV–ALIMENTATION BOISSONS	22.3	22.8					
11 PRIMARY–PRODUITS DE BASE	6.7	6.9					
111 FOR INDUSTRY–POUR L'INDUSTRIE	0.1	0.2					
112 FOR HOUSEHOLDS–POUR LES MENAGES	6.6	6.7					
12 PROCESSED–PRODUITS ELABORES	15.6	16.0					
121 FOR INDUSTRY–POUR L'INDUSTRIE	2.8	2.8					
122 FOR HOUSEHOLDS–POUR LES MENAGES	12.7	13.2					
2 IND SUPPLIES–APPROV INDUSTRIELS	32.4	31.7					
21 PRIMARY–PRODUITS DE BASE	1.2	1.6					
22 PROCESSED–PRODUITS ELABORES	31.2	30.0					
3 FUELS–COMBUSTIBLES	7.2	6.5					
31 PRIMARY–PRODUITS DE BASE	0.8	0.7					
32 PROCESSED–PRODUITS ELABORES	6.4	5.9					
321 MOTOR SPIRIT–ESSENCE	2.7	2.3					
322 OTHER–AUTRES	3.7	3.6					
4 MACHINERY–EQUIPEMENT	11.5	11.9					
41 CAPITAL EQUIPMENT–MACHINES	10.6	10.7					
42 PARTS–PIECES ACCESSOIRES	0.9	1.2					
5 TRANSPORT–TRANSPORT	8.5	8.2					
51 PASSENGER CARS–AUTOMOBILES	2.8	3.8					
52 OTHER–AUTRES	3.4	2.1					
521 INDUSTRIAL–INDUSTRIELS	3.3	2.0					
522 NON INDUSTRIAL–NON INDUSTRIEL	0.1	0.1					
53 PARTS–PIECES ACCESSOIRES	2.3	2.4					
6 CONSUM GOODS–BIENS CONSOMMATION	18.0	18.8					
61 DURABLE–DURABLES	3.7	4.1					
62 SEMI DURABLE–SEMI DURABLES	9.9	10.3					
63 NON DURABLE–NON DURABLES	4.4	4.4					
7 GOODS NES–BIENS NDA	0.1	0.1					

EXPORTS – EXPORTATIONS

	1990	1991	1992	1993	1994	1995	1996
TOTAL EXPORTS–EXPORTATIONS TOTALES	100.	100.					
1 AGRICULTURE	59.3	56.1					
2 MINING QUARRY–INDUS EXTRACTIVES	0.0	0.0					
3 MANUFACTURING–IND MANUFACTUR	40.7	43.9					
31 FOOD BEV TOBACCO–ALIM BOISS TAB	8.6	8.9					
32 TEXTILES–INDUSTRIES TEXTILES	16.1	17.6					
33 WOOD & PRODUCTS–BOIS & PRODUITS	0.0	0.1					
34 PAPER & PRODUCTS–PAPIER & PRODT	5.7	4.8					
35 CHEMICALS–INDUSTRIES CHIMIQUES	1.3	1.9					
36 NON METAL MIN–MIN NON METAL	0.0	0.0					
37 BASIC METAL–IND METAL BASE	0.0	0.2					
38 METAL MANUF–MANUF METAL	8.6	9.8					
39 OTH MANUF IND–AUTRES MANUF	0.3	0.4					

3. TRADE BY PRINCIPAL COUNTRIES OF PRODUCTION AND LAST CONSIGNMENT (VALUE IN THOUSAND U.S. DOLLARS)
ECHANGES SELON LES PRINCIPAUX PAYS DE PRODUCTION ET DE DERNIERE CONSIGNATION (VALEUR EN MILLIERS DE DOLLARS EU)

COUNTRIES–PAYS	GENERAL IMPORTS C.I.F. IMPORTATIONS GENERALES C.A.F				
	1991	1992	1993	1994	1995
World	295237	313135	300320		306026
Africa	226		37		55
Americas	192137	186782	206324		217472
Northern America	120077	116081	131720		128346
LAIA	13015	12813	9136		8014
CACM	2715	2056	1866		2965
Caribbean	54287	53237	60962		74546
Rest of America	2043	2595	2641		3601
As.ex F.USSR	32025	23708	28938		28204
Eur.x F.USSR	69496	72565	58971		57467
EU	67408	70616	57349		56351
EFTA	1795	1810	1283		718
East Europe	219	139	336		396
Other Europe	74				0
Former USSR	69		76		81
Oceania	1262	2042	1548		2728
USA/Etats–Unis d'Amer	109727	105935	121618		116531
United Kingdom	39303	43038	37646		34053
Trinidad and Tobago	26507	28695	30308		37825
Japan/Japon	18085	19374	16780		14061
Canada	10348	10146	10100		11815
Barbados/Barbade	7806	8510	9267		10387
France,Monac	11707	9460	6591		6153
St Vincent & Grenadines	6592	6893	7006		7435
Netherlands/Pays–Bas	7153	6693	2633		4675
Jamaica/Jamaïque	3609	3793	4816		4076
Germany/Allemagne	3701	4016	3527		4527
Brazil/Brésil	3865	3770	2554		2793
China/Chine	1853	1798	3737		4279
Colombia/Colombie	3224	3015	2489		2238
Italy/Italie	2266	3227	2185		2240
Venezuela	3003	3057	1792		1686
Netherlands Antilles	1927		1978		4906
Honduras	2034	2056	1582		2267
Dominica/Dominique	1506	1478	2061		2804
Guyana	1073	1739	2026		2717
Grenada/Grenade	1785	1913	1674		1974
Hong Kong	1831	2134	1498		1027
Mexico/Mexique	2109	2212	1431		638
Korea, Republic of	1778		2517		1720
Martinique	1632		1587		2619
Belgium–Luxembourg	381	1026	2253		1449
New Zealand	697	1360			2110
Antigua and Barbuda	1171	1176	1175		591
Denmark/Danemark	1181	1207	759		818
Switz.Liecht	1196	1077	1041		507
Thailand/Thaïlande	1380		970		1431
Australia/Australie	555	682	1467		614
Panama	868	699	568		815
Ireland/Irlande	613	784	584		871
Dominican Republic	453		684		1469
Argentina/Argentine	738	662	687		398
Saint–Kitts–Nevis	828	719	315		349
India/Inde	463	401	528		486
Norway,SVD,JM	593	698	232		206
Sweden/Suède	302	388	424		610
Singapore/Singapour	556		653		418
Spain/Espagne	407	379	333		499
Indonesia/Indonésie	215		626		709
Malaysia/Malaisie	155		637		639
Korea Dem People's Rp	311		431		588
Guatemala			239		593
Finland/Finlande	154	144	327		203
Costa Rica	680		44		96
Turkey/Turquie	73		174		334
Portugal	121	99	22		177

COUNTRIES–PAYS	GENERAL EXPORTS F.O.B. EXPORTATIONS GENERALES F.O.B.				
	1991	1992	1993	1994	1995
Monde	109852	122787	119740		108969
Afrique	4				16
Amériques	46296	48562	55829		47934
Amérique du Nord	24243	26780	33006		29342
ALAI	1095	808	376		221
MCAC			67		
Caraïbes	20482	20626	21367		17727
Autre Amérique	476	348	1014		644
Asie l'URSS exclus	187	104	132		479
Europe l'URSS exclus	63360	72097	63754		59804
UE	63347	72085	63751		59742
AELE	14	12	3		62
Europe de l'Est					
Autre de l'Europe					
Ancienne URSS					
Océanie	2	10			20
United Kingdom	54940	63097	59404		57817
USA/Etats–Unis d'Amer	23845	26268	32640		28356
Dominica/Dominique	4443	5005	9176		5838
Italy/Italie	7078	7690	895		3
Barbados/Barbade	4250	4214	2324		2788
Trinidad and Tobago	2377	2354	2299		3235
Antigua and Barbuda	1467	1670	1386		1733
Germany/Allemagne	804	842	2913		1399
Grenada/Grenade	1654	1861	1055		1325
St Vincent & Grenadines	1297	1748	1181		772
Jamaica/Jamaïque	1023	2154	1452		279
Martinique	1773		1077		778
Saint–Kitts–Nevis	826	744	717		443
Montserrat	841	845	322		364
Canada	397	512	362		986
Venezuela	547	501	373		190
Guyana	194	143	738		442
Belize/Bélize	277	203	230		173
Brazil/Brésil	547	306	3		11
Netherlands/Pays–Bas	276	299	173		61
Japan/Japon	98	100	119		340
Belgium–Luxembourg	101	53	108		212
Guadeloupe	122		187		127
France,Monac	78	69	201		59
Austria/Autriche	9	4	44		187
Netherlands Antilles	111		82		25
Dominican Republic	147		0		1
Hong Kong	5	3	9		124
Bahamas	32	31	64		
Denmark/Danemark	60	32			3
Switz.Liecht	13	11	3		62
Guatemala			67		
Suriname/Suriname			42		8
Philippines	38				
Sri Lanka	36				1
Australia/Australie		5			14
Mexico/Mexique					12
Aruba	0		9		
Singapore/Singapour	8		0		
Chile/Chili					6
Panama	4	2			
China/Chine	2	1			2
Korea, Republic of	0		4		
New Zealand	0	4			
India/Inde			0		4
Norway,SVD,JM	1	1			
Argentina/Argentine					2
Sweden/Suède			1		0
Indonesia/Indonésie					1
Spain/Espagne	0				1

(VALUE AS PERCENTAGE OF WORLD TOTAL)(VALEURS EN POURCENTAGE DU TOTAL MONDIAL)

	1986	1987	1988	1989	1990	1991	1992	1993	1994	1995
Africa	0.1	0.1	0.0	0.0	0.0	0.1		0.0		0.0
Americas	61.8	60.7	61.4	61.2	65.1	65.1	59.6	68.7		71.1
Northern America	38.0	38.4	38.7	38.1	40.1	40.7	37.1	43.9		41.9
LAIA	2.4	3.2	3.1	3.2	3.8	4.4	4.1	3.0		2.6
CACM	1.5	1.6	1.7	1.7	1.3	0.9	0.7	0.6		1.0
Caribbean	19.2	17.0	17.0	17.5	19.0	18.4	17.0	20.3		24.4
Rest of America	0.6	0.5	0.9	0.7	1.0	0.7	0.8	0.9		1.2
As.ex F.USSR	11.7	12.5	14.0	12.5	9.1	10.8	7.6	9.6		9.2
Eur.x F.USSR	25.4	26.5	24.1	25.8	22.9	23.5	23.2	19.6		18.8
EU	24.7	25.8	23.4	25.2	22.2	22.8	22.6	19.1		18.4
EFTA	0.4	0.4	0.5	0.4	0.6	0.6	0.6	0.4		0.2
East Europe	0.2	0.2	0.2	0.2	0.1	0.1	0.0	0.1		0.1
Other Europe	0.0	0.1	0.0	0.0	0.0	0.0				0.0
Former USSR	0.0	0.0	0.0	0.0	0.1	0.0		0.0		0.0
Oceania	0.2	0.2	0.5	0.3	0.9	0.4	0.7	0.5		0.9
USA/Etats–Unis d'Amer	34.9	34.6	34.7	34.8	37.1	37.2	33.8	40.5		38.1
United Kingdom	15.7	15.5	15.4	14.6	14.2	13.3	13.7	12.5		11.1
Trinidad and Tobago	7.8	8.3	8.5	8.5	9.4	9.0	9.2	10.1		12.4
Japan/Japon	6.9	6.5	8.3	7.2	6.2	6.1	6.2	5.6		4.6
Canada	3.1	3.8	4.0	3.3	3.0	3.5	3.2	3.4		3.9
Barbados/Barbade	3.0	2.1	2.5	2.2	2.8	2.6	2.7	3.1		3.4
France,Monac	2.4	2.4	1.7	2.1	2.0	4.0	3.0	2.2		2.0
St Vincent & Grenadines	2.1	2.0	1.9	2.0	2.2	2.2	2.2	2.3		2.4
Netherlands/Pays–Bas	2.8	3.0	2.7	2.2	1.8	2.4	2.1	0.9		1.5
Jamaica/Jamaïque	1.3	1.3	1.1	1.2	1.2	1.2	1.2	1.6		1.3

	1986	1987	1988	1989	1990	1991	1992	1993	1994	1995
Afrique		0.0	0.0	0.0	0.0	0.0				0.0
Amériques	30.8	41.3	40.2	42.3	39.8	42.1	39.5	46.6		44.0
Amérique du Nord	12.6	19.3	20.3	19.7	22.0	22.1	21.8	27.6		26.9
ALAI	0.2	0.4	0.7	0.5	0.3	1.0	0.7	0.3		0.2
MCAC	0.0			0.2	0.0			0.1		
Caraïbes	17.0	21.3	18.9	21.6	17.3	18.6	16.8	17.8		16.3
Autre Amérique	0.9	0.3	0.3	0.4	0.1	0.4	0.3	0.8		0.6
Asie l'URSS exclus	0.0	0.2	0.0	0.1	0.1	0.2	0.1	0.1		0.4
Europe l'URSS exclus	69.1	58.5	59.7	57.6	60.1	57.7	58.7	53.2		54.9
UE	69.1	58.5	59.7	57.6	60.1	57.7	58.7	53.2		54.8
AELE	0.0	0.0	0.0	0.0	0.0	0.0	0.0	0.0		0.1
Europe de l'Est				0.0						
Autre de l'Europe										
Ancienne URSS										
Océanie	0.0	0.0	0.0	0.0	0.0	0.0	0.0			0.0
United Kingdom	67.4	53.2	52.6	50.1	53.1	50.0	51.4	49.6		53.1
USA/Etats–Unis d'Amer	12.4	18.9	20.0	19.2	21.5	21.7	21.4	27.3		26.0
Dominica/Dominique	5.3	7.8	5.8	3.5	4.1	4.0	4.1	7.7		5.4
Italy/Italie	1.3	4.4	6.8	6.8	6.2	6.4	6.3	0.7		0.0
Barbados/Barbade	3.6	4.5	4.2	5.3	3.0	3.9	3.4	1.9		2.6
Trinidad and Tobago	3.0	1.2	2.1	3.2	1.7	2.2	1.9	1.9		3.0
Antigua and Barbuda	1.1	1.2	1.1	1.5	1.4	1.3	1.4	1.2		1.6
Germany/Allemagne	0.3	0.3	0.2	0.4	0.6	0.7	0.7	2.4		1.3
Grenada/Grenade	1.3	1.7	1.9	1.8	1.5	1.5	1.5	0.9		1.2
St Vincent & Grenadines	1.1	1.1	1.2	2.0	1.6	1.2	1.4	1.0		0.7

4. General Imports C.I.F. by Commodities according to the S.I.T.C. (Rev. 2) in thousand U.S. Dollars
Importations Générales C.A.F. par Produits d'après la C.T.C.I. (Rév. 2) en milliers de Dollars E.U.

SITC CTCI	COMMODITY	1992		1993		1994		1995		PRODUIT
		WEIGHT POIDS	VALUE VALEUR	WEIGHT POIDS	VALUE VALEUR	WEIGHT POIDS	VALUE VALEUR	WEIGHT POIDS	VALUE VALEUR	
	ALL COMMODITIES		313135		300320				306026	TOUS PRODUITS
0	FOOD AND LIVE ANIMALS		61424		60980				69858	ALIMENTS,ANIMAUX VIVANTS
01	MEAT AND PREPARATIONS								19304	VIANDES ET PREPARATIONS
011	MEAT FRESH,CHILLD,FROZEN							W 10400	16363	VIANDES FRAICHES,REF,CONGE
0111	BOVINE MEAT FRESH,FROZEN							W 702	2863	VIANDES BOVIN FRAI,REF
01112	BOVINE MEAT BONELESS							W 685	2767	VIANDES BOVIN DESOSSEES
0112	MUTTON ETC FRSH,CHLD,FRN							W 583	1317	VIANDE DE MOUTON
0114	POULTRY FRESH CHLLD,FRZN							W 7696	10764	VOLAILLES MORTES
014	MEAT PREPD,PRSVD,NES ETC							W 772	2448	CONSERVES DE VIANDES
0142	SAUSAGES INCLDING TINNED							W 354	922	SAUCISSES,SAUCISSONS
0149	OTH PREPARD,PRESRVD MEAT							W 418	1526	AUTRES PREP DE VIANDES
02	DAIRY PRODCTS,BIRDS'EGGS								8449	PRODUITS LAITIERS,OEUFS
022	MILK AND CREAM							W 3164	5631	LAIT ET CREME
0224	MILK,CREAM PRESERVED ETC							W 2643	4859	LAIT,CREME CONS,CONC
02243	MILK DRY,OVER 1.5% FAT							W 451	1738	LAIT POUDRE SUP 1.5%
02249	MILK(EX DRY) PRSVD,SWEET							W 2056	2698	LAIT CONS,CONC SUCRE
024	CHEESE AND CURD							W 604	2058	FROMAGE ET CAILLEBOTTE
03	FISH AND PREPARATIONS								4342	POISSONS ET PREPARATIONS
035	FISH SALTED,DRIED,SMOKED							W 285	1340	POISSON SECHE,SALE,FUME
03503	FISH(EX COD)DRIED,SALTED							W 255	1215	POISSONS SECHES,SALES
036	SHELL FISH FRESH,FROZEN							W 93	999	CRUSTACES,MOLLUSQUES
037	FISH ETC PREPD,PRSVD NES							W 521	1630	POIS,CRUST,MOL PREPARES
0371	FISH PREPARD,PRESRVD NES							W 515	1594	CONSERVES DE POISSONS
04	CEREALS AND PREPARATIONS								14747	CEREALES ET PRODUITS
042	RICE							W 3089	2087	RIZ
0422	RICE SEMI–MILLED,MILLED							W 1481	1309	RIZ POLI,GLACE INCL BRISURES
04221	RICE MILLED UNBROKEN							W 1439	1273	RIZ POLI,GLACE EXCL BRISURES
046	WHEAT ETC MEAL OR FLOUR							W 10828	4860	SEMOULE FARINE,FROMENT
04601	FLOUR OF WHEAT OR MESLIN							W 10826	4856	FARINE DE FROMENT
048	CEREAL ETC PREPARATIONS							W 3824	7566	PREPTNS A BASE CEREALES
0481	PREPD BREAKFAST FOOD ETC							W 377	1399	CEREALES TRAVAILLEES
04812	CEREAL ROASTED, PUFFED							W 302	1168	PRODTS BASE CEREALES
0484	BAKERY PRODUCTS							W 1498	3780	PRODUITS DE BOULANGERIE
04841	BREAD,BISCUIT,COM WAFERS							W 684	1816	PAINS,BISCUITS DE MER
04842	PASTRY, CAKES ETC							W 814	1964	PATISSERIE ETC.
0488	OTH CEREAL PREPS,MALT EX							W 290	1101	EXTRAITS DE MALT
05	VEGETABLES AND FRUIT								9789	LEGUMES ET FRUITS
054	VEG ETC FRSH,SMPLY PRSVD							W 5176	4383	LEGUMES FRAIS,CONG,SECS
0541	POTATOES FRSH EXCL SWEET							W 1924	1011	POMMES DE TERRE
0545	OTHER FRESH VEGETABLES							W 1658	1746	AUTRES LEGUMES FRAIS,REF
057	FRUIT,NUTS,FRESH,DRIED							W 568	961	FRUITS FRAIS OU SECS
058	FRUIT PRESERVED,PREPARED							W 2709	3794	CONSERVES DE FRUITS
0585	FRUIT OR VEGETABLE JUICE							W 2426	3017	JUS DE FRUITS
05851	ORANGE JUICE							W 1407	1623	JUS D'ORANGE
06	SUGAR AND PREPS,HONEY								4357	SUCRES ET PRODUITS
061	SUGAR AND HONEY							W 11763	3685	SUCRES ET MIEL
0611	RAW BEET AND CANE SUGAR							W 3906	1429	SUCRES BRUTS
0612	REFINED SUGAR ETC							W 3360	1707	SUCRES RAFFINES
07	COFFEE,TEA,COCOA,SPICES								1914	CAFE,THE,CACAO,EPICES
081	*FEEDING STUFF FOR ANIML							W 4663	1580	NOURRITURE POUR ANIMAUX
0819	FOOD WASTE AND FEED NES							W 4408	1519	DECHETS,ALIMENTS NDA
08199	FODDER NES,INCL SWEETNED							W 4408	1519	PREPARATIONS FOURRAGERES
09	MISC EDIBLE PRODUCTS								5306	PREP ALIMENTAIRES DIVERSES
098	EDIBLE PRODCTS,PREPS NES							W 1597	4596	PREP ALIMENTAIRES NDA
09804	SAUCES,MIXED SEASONINGS							W 565	1018	SAUCES,ASSAISONNEMENTS
09809	MISC FOOD PREPRTIONS NES							W 766	2775	PREP ALIMENTAIRES NDA
1	BEVERAGES AND TOBACCO		10545		10931				10928	BOISSONS ET TABACS
11	BEVERAGES								9488	BOISSONS
111	NON–ALCOHL BEVERAGES NES							W 3019	2666	BOISSONS NON ALCOOLIQUES
11102	FLAVORED WATERS NON–ALCO							W 2193	2348	LIMONADES,EAUX GAZEUSES
112	ALCOHOLIC BEVERAGES							W 2490	6822	BOISSONS ALCOOLIQUES
1121	WINE OF FRESH GRAPES ETC							W 587	1661	VINS DE RAISINS FRAIS
11212	WINE OF FRESH GRAPES							W 528	1536	VINS DE MOUTS DE RAISINS
1123	BEER,ALE,STOUT,PORTER							W 766	1109	BIERES
1124	DISTILLED ALCOHOLIC BEVS							W 850	3690	ALCOOLS,EAUX–DE–VIE
11241	WHISKY							W 155	1071	WHISKY
11249	OTH ALCOHOLC BEVS,CMPNDS							W 597	2226	BOISSONS ALCOOLIQUES NDA
12	TOBACCO AND MANUFACTURES								1441	TABACS BRUTS FABRIQUES
122	TOBACCO,MANUFACTURED							W 64	1218	TABACS FABRIQUES
1222	CIGARETTES							W 45	1200	CIGARETTES
2	CRUDE MATERLS,EXCL FUELS		10011		8094				9879	MAT BRUTES NON COMESTIBLES
24	CORK AND WOOD								6483	LIEGE ET BOIS
248	WOOD SHAPED,SLEEPERS							W 12662	5850	BOIS SIMPLEMENT TRAVAILLES
2482	LUMBER SHAPED CONIFER							W 12148	5623	CONIFERES SCIES,RABOTES
24821	LUMBER SAWN ETC CONIFER							W 11093	4994	CONIFERES SCIES LONGITUD
27	CRUDE FERTLZR,MINRLS NES								2299	ENGRAIS MINERAUX BRUTS
273	STONE,SAND AND GRAVEL							W 91264	956	PIERRES,SABLES,GRAVIERS
278	OTHER CRUDE MINERALS							W 4630	1245	AUTRES MINERAUX BRUTS
2789	MINERALS CRUDE NES							W 3576	1012	MINERAUX BRUTS NDA
27896	NATURAL ASPHALT,BITUMEN							W 3536	965	BITUMES,ASPHALTES NATURELS
3	MINERAL FUELS ETC		21321		22917				23344	COMBUSTIBLES MINERAUX LUB
33	PETROLEUM AND PRODUCTS								20919	PETROLE ET DERIVES
334	PETROLEUM PRODUCTS,REFIN							W 80201	20792	PRODUITS RAFFINES
3341	GASOLINE,OTH LIGHT OILS							W 32754	7939	ESSENCES POUR MOTEURS
33411	MOTOR,AVIATION SPIRIT							W 31987	7783	ESSENCES MOTEURS D'AVIONS
3343	GAS OILS							W 43402	10495	GAS OILS
3345	LUBS,PETROLEUM OILS NES							W 1433	1783	HUILES LUBRIFIANTES
33451	LUBS(HIGH PETR CONT) ETC							W 1427	1753	HUILES LUBRIF,H LOURDES
341	*GAS,NATURAL AND MANUFCT							W 5184	2402	GAZ NATUREL,GAZ MANUFACT
3413	PETROLM GASES,LIQUEFIED							W 5184	2402	GAZ DE PETROLE LIQUEFIE
34139	OTH HYDROCARBON GAS LQFD							W 3398	1487	HYDROCARBURES GAZEUX NDA
4	ANIMAL,VEGETABLE OIL,FAT		1080		440				781	HUILES,GRAISSES ANIM,VEG
5	CHEMCLS,RELATED PROD NES		31301		27396				26797	PRODUITS CHIMIQUES
53	DYES,TANNING,COLOUR PROD								3393	PROD TEINTURE,COLORANTS
533	PIGMENTS,PAINTS,ETC							W 1422	3254	PIGMENTS,PEINTURES,VERNIS
5334	VARNISHES,DISTEMPERS ETC							W 776	2312	PEINTURES A L'EAU
53342	OTH PAINTS,VARNISHES ETC							W 591	1792	AUTRES PEINTURES,VERNIS
541	*MEDICINAL,PHARM PRODUCT							K 221820	3223	PROD MEDICINAUX PHARMACEUT
5417	MEDICAMENTS							K 195982	2800	MEDICAMENTS
54179	— CONTNG OTH SUBSTANCES							K 186774	2423	MED CONT AUT SUBSTANCES
55	PERFUME,CLEANING ETC PRD								7307	PROD POUR PARFUM,TOILETTE

4. General Imports C.I.F. by Commodities according to the S.I.T.C. (Rev. 2) in thousand U.S. Dollars
Importations Générales C.A.F. par Produits d'après la C.T.C.I. (Rév. 2) en milliers de Dollars E.U.

SITC CTCI	COMMODITY	1992 WEIGHT POIDS	1992 VALUE VALEUR	1993 WEIGHT POIDS	1993 VALUE VALEUR	1994 WEIGHT POIDS	1994 VALUE VALEUR	1995 WEIGHT POIDS	1995 VALUE VALEUR	PRODUIT
553	PERFUMERY,COSMETICS,ETC							W 596	3513	PRODUITS DE PARFUMERIE
554	SOAP,CLEANSING ETC PREPS							W 2158	3741	SAVONS,PRODUITS DETERSIFS
5541	SOAPS							W 744	1253	SAVONS,PROD TENSIO–ACTIFS
5542	WASHING PREPARATIONS ETC							W 1377	2338	PROD ORG TENSIO–ACT NDA
562	*FERTILIZERS,MANUFACTURE							W 7115	2472	ENGRAIS MANUFACTURES
5629	FERTILIZERS NES							W 6196	2057	ENGRAIS NDA
56299	OTHER FERTILIZERS NES							W 6195	2055	AUTRES ENGRAIS NDA
58	PLASTIC MATERIALS ETC								2551	MAT PLAST ARTIFICIELLES
583	POLYMERIZATION ETC PRODS							W 697	1759	PROD POLYMERISATION
5839	OTH POLYMRZTION ETC PROD							W 697	1757	AUT PROD POLYMER COPOLYM
59	CHEMICAL MATERIALS NES								6304	MAT PROD CHIMIQUES NDA
591	PESTICIDES,DISINFECTANTS							W 1037	4067	DESINF,INSECT,FONG,HERB
5911	INSECTICIDES,FOR RETAIL							W 495	1827	INSECTICIDES VENTE DET
5913	HERBICIDES,FOR RETAIL							W 352	1114	HERBICIDES VENTE AU DET
592	STARCH,INULIN,GLUTEN,ETC							W 1160	1121	AMIDONS,INUL,GLUT FROM
598	MISCEL CHEM PRODUCTS NES							W 351	1116	PROD DIV INDUST CHIM NDA
5989	CHEM PRODUCTS,PREPS NES							W 321	1007	PROD PREP CHIMIQUES NDA
6	BASIC MANUFACTURES		69718		57778				66112	ART MANUFACTURES
62	RUBBER MANUFACTURES NES								3943	CAOUTCHOUC MANUFACTURE
625	RUBBER TYRES, TUBES ETC							W 696	2288	PNEUS CAOUTCHOUC VULCANISE
6252	TYRES,NEW,BUS OR LORRY							W 310	1174	PNEUS POUR AUTOBUS,CAMIONS
63	WOOD,CORK MANUFACTRS NES								5467	OUVRAGES LIEGE ET BOIS
634	VENEERS,PLYWOOD,ETC							W 6088	3502	PLACAGES,CONTRE–PLAQUES
6342	PLYWOOD OF WOOD SHEETS							W 5983	3452	BOIS CONTRE–PLAQUES
635	WOOD MANUFACTURES NES							W 682	1931	ART MANUF EN BOIS NDA
6353	BUILDERS WOODWRK,PREFABS							W 455	1462	OUVRAGES DE MENUISERIE
64	PAPER,PAPERBOARD AND MFR								18936	PAPIERS,CARTONS & OUVRAGES
641	PAPER AND PAPERBOARD							W 19682	13992	PAPIERS ET CARTONS
6413	KRAFT PAPER,PAPERBOARD							W 18131	11156	PAPIER ET CARTON KRAFT
64139	KRAFT PAPER PAPERBD,NES							W 18131	11156	PAPIER,CARTON KRAFT NDA
6417	CORRUGATED PAPER ETC,BLK							W 928	1271	PAPIERS,CARTONS ONDULES
64172	CREPED HSHOLD PAPER ETC							W 727	1011	PAPIER NON KRAFT CREPE
642	PAPER,ETC,PRECUT,ARTS OF							W 1618	4943	PAP,CARTONS DECOUPES
6421	PAPER ETC CONTAINERS							W 856	1331	BOITES,SACS EMBALLAGES
6428	PAPER ETC ARTICLES NES							W 477	1978	OUVRAGES EN PATE A PAPIER
64285	PAPER ETC DIAPERS ETC							W 332	1450	SERVIETTES HYGIENIQUES
65	TEXTILE YARN,FABRICS,ETC								6977	FILS,TISSUS,ARTICLES TEXTILE
653	WOVN MAN–MADE FIB FABRIC							W 264	1260	TISSUS FIBRES SYNTH,ARTIF
657	SPECIAL TXTL FABRC,PRODS							W 274	1378	TISSUS SPECIAUX
6575	CORDAGE AND MANUFACTURES							W 176	1080	FICELLES,CORDES,CORDAGES
65751	CORDAGE,CABLE,ROPE,TWINE							W 167	1006	CORDAGES TRESSES OU NON
658	TEXTILE ARTICLES NES							W 149	1314	ART FACONNES MAT TEXTILES
6584	LINENS ETC							W 110	970	LINGE DE MAISON
66	NONMETAL MINERAL MFS NES								13220	ART MIN NON METALLIQUES
661	LIME,CEMENT,BLDG PRODS							W 61060	4565	CHAUX,CIMENTS MAT CONSTR
6612	CEMENT							W 59701	4194	CIMENTS HYDRAULIQUES
662	CLAY,REFRACTORY BLDG PRD							W 3017	1809	MAT CONST REFRACTAIRES
6624	BRICKS ETC NONREFRACTORY							W 3016	1803	BRIQUES ETC CERAM NON REFR
66245	GLAZED CERAMIC SETTS ETC							W 2443	1569	AUT CARREAUX CERAMIQUE
664	GLASS								1211	VERRE
665	GLASSWARE							W 6024	4118	OUVRAGES EN VERRE
6651	BOTTLES ETC OF GLASS							W 5838	3558	RECIPIENTS EN VERRE
66511	GLASS BOTTLES ETC NONVAC							W 5838	3558	BONBONNES,BOUTEILLES,ETC
67	IRON AND STEEL								4545	FER ET ACIER
673	IRON,STEEL SHAPES ETC							W 4256	2119	BARRES,PROFIL FER,ACIER
6732	IRON,STEEL BARS ETC							W 3846	1677	BARRES FER,ACIER
67322	HIGH CARBON STL BARS ETC							W 3645	1550	BARRES ACIER FIN CARBONE
674	IRN,STL UNIV,PLATE,SHEET							W 1365	1564	LARGES PLATS,TOLES
6749	OTH IRN,STL PLATES,SHEET							W 1304	1513	AUTRES TOLES FER,ACIER
67491	— OF IRON OR SIMPLE STL							W 1296	1504	AUT TOLES AUTRES ACIER FIN
69	METAL MANUFACTURES NES								12251	ART MANUFACT EN METAL NDA
691	STRUCTURES AND PARTS NES							W 598	2154	CONSTRUCT FER,ACIER,ALU
6912	STRUCTURES,PARTS ALUMNM							W 184	1271	CONSTRUCT ALUMINIUM
693	WIRE PRODUCTS NON ELECTR							W 925	1104	OUVRAGES FILS METALLIQUES
6935	METAL FENCING,GAUZE,ETC							W 873	948	TOILES EN FER,ACIER,CUIVRE
69351	IRN,STL FENCNG,GAUZE ETC							W 873	948	TOILES EN FER,ACIER
694	STL,COPPR NAILS,NUTS,ETC							W 318	988	CLOUS,VIS,ECROUS
695	TOOLS							W 117	1067	OUTILS A MAIN
697	BASE MTL HOUSEHOLD EQUIP							W 370	1935	ART MENAGE MET COMMUNS
6973	DMSTC HEATG,COOKG APPARA							W 199	1093	APPS CHAUF NON ELECTRIQ
69731	IRN,STL DOM COOKG APPARA							W 193	1038	APPS CUISSON FER,ACIER
699	BASE METAL MFRS NES								3670	ART MANUFACTURES MET NDA
6991	LOCKSMITHS WARES,ETC							W 144	1063	ARTICLES DE SERRURERIE
6997	IRON,STEEL ARTICLES NES							W 312	1142	OUV FONTE,FER,ACIER NDA
69979	IRN,STL MANUFACTURES NES							W 309	1132	AUT OUVRAGES EN FER NDA
7	MACHINES,TRANSPORT EQUIP		66745		68540				58067	MACHINES MATERIEL TRANSPORT
71	POWER GENERATING EQUIPMT								2876	MACHINES GENERATRICES
713	INTRNL COMBUS PSTN ENGIN							W 114	2039	MOTEURS EXPL COMB INT, PIECE
7139	PISTON ENGINE PARTS NES							W 61	1486	PIECES POUR 713.2,3,8
72	MACHS FOR SPCL INDUSTRYS								3665	MAC SPECIALES POUR INDUST
723	CIVIL ENGINEERG EQUIP ETC							W 319	1276	APPAREILS DE GENIE CIVIL
7234	CONST,MINING MACHNRY NES							W 317	1204	MACH POUR LA CONST, MINES
72342	SLFPRP SHOVELS,EXCAVATRS							W 257	1036	PELLES MECANIQUES
74	GENRL INDUSTRL MACHY NES								10738	MACH APP INDUSTRIE
741	HEATING,COOLING EQUIPMNT							W 255	2651	MACH CHAUFFAGE,PIECES
7414	NONDOM REFRIG EQUIPT,PTS							W 130	1177	MAT PRODUCTION DU FROID
742	PUMPS FOR LIQUIDS ETC							W 53	951	POMPES MOTO–POMPES
743	PUMPS NES,CENTRFUGES ETC							W 86	924	POMPES COMPRES,VENT ETC
744	MECHANICAL HANDLING EQU							W 211	1296	EQUIP MANUTENTION PIECES
745	NONELEC MACHY,TOOLS NES							W 72	1290	AUT MACH NON ELEC,PIECES
7452	OTH NONELEC MCHS,PTS NES							W 58	1073	AUT MACH NON ELEC,PIECES
749	NONELEC MACH PTS,ACC NES							W 911	3625	PIECES MACH NON ELEC NDA
7492	COCKS,VALVES ETC NES							W 855	1382	ART ROB,SIM POUR TUYAUX
7493	SHAFT,CRANK,PULLEY ETC							W 37	1651	ARBRES TRANS,VILEBREQUINS
75	OFFICE MACHNES,ADP EQUIP								4731	MACH BUREAU TRAIT AUTOM
752	AUTOMTIC DATA PROC EQUIP							W 63	3009	MACH TRAIT INFORMATION
7523	DIGITL CENTRL PROCESSORS							W 23	1244	UNITES CENTRALES
7525	ADP PERIPHERAL UNITS							W 29	1070	UNITES PERIPHERIQUES
759	OFFICE,ADP MCH PTS,ACCES							W 16	942	PIECES DU 751 ET 752
76	TELECOMM,SOUND EQUIPMENT								6561	EQUIPMENT DE TELECOM
761	TELEVISION RECEIVERS							W 107	1377	RECEPTEURS DE TELEVISION

4. General Imports C.I.F. by Commodities according to the S.I.T.C. (Rev. 2) in thousand U.S. Dollars
Importations Générales C.A.F. par Produits d'après la C.T.C.I. (Rév. 2) en milliers de Dollars E.U.

SITC CTCI	COMMODITY	1992 WEIGHT POIDS	1992 VALUE VALEUR	1993 WEIGHT POIDS	1993 VALUE VALEUR	1994 WEIGHT POIDS	1994 VALUE VALEUR	1995 WEIGHT POIDS	1995 VALUE VALEUR	PRODUIT
7611	COLOUR TV RECEIVERS							W 103	1359	RECEPTEURS COULEUR
764	TELECOM EQPT,PTS,ACC NES							W 94	3881	EQUIP TELECOM,PIECES
7641	LINE TELEPHONE,ETC EQUIP							W 29	1832	APP TELEPHON PAR FIL
7649	PTS NES OF EQUIPMT OF 76							W 18	964	PIECES DE LA DIV 76
77	ELECTRIC MACHNRY NES ETC								10792	MACH APP ELECT NDA
772	SWITCHGEAR ETC,PARTS NES							W 80	1705	APP COUPURE,SECT ETC
7721	SWITCHGEAR ETC							W 79	1695	APP COUPURE,SECTIONMNT
773	ELECTR DISTRIBUTNG EQUIP							W 438	2117	EQUIPMT DISTRIBUTION ELECT
7731	INSULATED WIRE,CABLE ETC							W 421	2025	FILS,CABLES ISOLES ELECT
775	HOUSEHOLD TYPE EQUIP NES							W 591	3551	MACH,APP USAGE DOMESTQUE
7752	DOM REFRIGERATRS,FREEZRS							W 332	1779	REFRIG,CONGEL MENAGER
77521	DOMESTIC REFRIGERATORS							W 266	1447	REFRIGERATEURS
778	ELECTRICAL MACHINERY NES							W 358	2470	AUTRES MACH ELECT NDA
7781	BATTERIES,ACCUMULATORS							W 250	966	PILES ET ACCUMULATEURS
78	ROAD VEHICLES								17067	VEHICULES ROUTIERS
781	PASS MOTOR VEH EXC BUSES							W 1085	7031	AUTO TRANSPORT PERSONNES
782	LORRIES,SPCL MTR VEH NES							W 1020	5395	VEHICULES SPECIAUX,MARCH
7821	LORRIES,TRUCKS							W 850	4399	VEHICULES TRANSP MARCHAND
7822	SPECIAL MOTOR VEHCLS NES							W 170	995	VEHICULES USAGES SPECIAUX
783	ROAD MOTOR VEHICLES NES							W 356	1971	VEHICULES ROUTIERS NDA
7831	BUSES							W 279	1875	VOITURES TRANSPORT COMMUN
784	MOTOR VEH PRTS,ACCES NES							W 185	2101	PIECES 722,781,782,783
7849	OTHER MOTOR VEHCL PARTS							W 171	2051	PIECES 722,781,782,783
79	OTHR TRANSPORT EQUIPMENT								1330	AUTRE MATERIEL TRANSPORT
8	MISC MANUFACTURED GOODS		40835		42769				40023	ART MANUFACTURES DIVERS
812	*PLUMBG,HEATNG,LGHTNG EQ							W 261	1444	APPAR SANITAIRES CHAUFFAGE
821	*FURNITURE,PARTS THEREOF							W 708	3570	MEUBLES ET PIECES
8219	FURNITURE AND PARTS NES							W 423	2153	AUTRES MEUBLES ET PIECES
82192	WOOD FURNITURE NES							W 179	974	MEUBLES NDA EN BOIS
84	CLOTHING AND ACCESSORIES								8481	VETEMENTS
842	MENS OUTERWEAR NOT KNIT							W 100	1145	VET DESSUS POUR HOMMES
8423	— TROUSERS,BREECHES ETC							W 88	944	PANTALONS HOMMES MAT TEX
843	WOMENS OUTERWEAR NONKNIT							W 125	2122	VET DESSUS FEMMES MAT TEX
8439	— OTHER OUTER GARMENTS							W 66	980	AUT VET DES FEM MAT TEXT
845	OUTERWEAR KNIT NONELASTC							W 58	933	VET DESSOUS,ACCES BONNET
846	UNDER GARMENTS KNITTED							W 122	2845	SOUS VETS DE BONNETERIE
8462	— OF COTTON NON ELASTIC							W 92	1297	SOUS–VET BONNET COTON
84629	—— OTHER							W 91	1278	AUT SOUS–VET BONNET COTON
8465	CORSETS,GARTERS,ETC							W 29	1523	CORSETS,GAINES ART SIM
84651	BRASSIERES							W 24	1446	SOUTIENS–GORGE,BUSTIERS
851	*FOOTWEAR							W 305	3334	CHAUSSURES
85101	FOOTWEAR RUBBER,PLASTIC							W 161	1361	CHAUS SEMELLES CAOUTCH
85102	FOOTWEAR LEATHER							W 135	1840	CHAUS SEMELLES EN CUIR
87	PRECISION INSTRUMNTS NES								2085	INSTRUM,APPAR SCIENT NDA
874	MEASURNG,CONTROLNG INSTR							W 32	1299	INSTRUMENTS DE MESURE
88	PHOTO EQU,OPTICL GDS ETC								1372	APP,FOURN PHOTO,OP,MONTR
89	MISC MANUFCTRD GOODS NES								19169	ART MANUFACTURES DIVERS
892	PRINTED MATTER							W 419	5074	IMPRIMES
8921	PRINTED BOOKS,GLOBES,ETC							W 185	2787	LIVRES,BROCHURES,CARTES
89211	PRINTED BOOKS,PAMPHLETS							W 178	2686	LIVRES,BROCHURES
8928	PRINTED MATTER NES							W 173	1564	IMPRIMES NDA
89281	LABELS PAPER,PAPERBOARD							W 82	975	ETIQUETTES TOUS GENRES
893	ARTICLES OF PLASTIC NES							W 3027	8984	OUVRAGES EN MAT DIVIS 58
8931	PLSTC PACKG CONTNRS,LIDS							W 834	3438	ART TRANSP EMBALLAGE ETC
8939	MISC PLASTIC ARTICLES							W 2172	5431	ART DIVERS EN MAT DIV 58
89399	OTHR PLASTC ARTICLES NES							W 1843	4917	AUT OUV MAT DIV 58
894	TOYS,SPORTING GOODS,ETC							W 159	1486	VOITURES ENFANTS,JOUETS
8942	TOYS,INDOOR GAMES ETC							W 117	995	JOUETS,JEUX ETC
898	MUSICAL INSTRUMENTS,PTS							W 694	1130	INSTRUMENTS DE MUSIQUE
8983	SOUND RECRDNG TAPE,DISCS							W 688	983	SUPPORTS SON POUR 763
899	OTHER MANUFACTURED GOODS								1529	AUT ART MANUF DIVERS NDA

5. General Exports F.O.B. by Commodities according to the S.I.T.C. (Rev. 2) in thousand U.S. Dollars
Exportations Générales F.O.B. par Produits d'après la C.T.C.I. (Rév. 2) en milliers de Dollars E.U.

SITC CTCI	COMMODITY	1992 WEIGHT POIDS	1992 VALUE VALEUR	1993 WEIGHT POIDS	1993 VALUE VALEUR	1994 WEIGHT POIDS	1994 VALUE VALEUR	1995 WEIGHT POIDS	1995 VALUE VALEUR	PRODUIT
	ALL COMMODITIES		122787		119740				108969	TOUS PRODUITS
0	FOOD AND LIVE ANIMALS		70317		60150				57883	ALIMENTS,ANIMAUX VIVANTS
05	VEGETABLES AND FRUIT								56885	LEGUMES ET FRUITS
057	FRUIT,NUTS,FRESH,DRIED							W 114294	56815	FRUITS FRAIS OU SECS
0573	BANANA,PLANTAIN,FRSH,DRY							W 112920	56041	BANANES FRAICHES,SECHEES
0579	FRUIT FRESH OR DRIED NES							W 1318	738	FRUITS FRAIS,SECS NDA
05798	OTHER FRESH FRUIT							W 833	396	AUTRES FRUITS FRAIS
07	COFFEE,TEA,COCOA,SPICES								536	CAFE,THE,CACAO,EPICES
075	SPICES							W 240	407	EPICES
0751	PEPPER AND PIMENTO							W 234	378	POIVRE,PIMENTS
09	MISC EDIBLE PRODUCTS								365	PREP ALIMENTAIRES DIVERSES
1	BEVERAGES AND TOBACCO		6747		5200				5625	BOISSONS ET TABACS
11	BEVERAGES								5625	BOISSONS
111	NON–ALCOHL BEVERAGES NES							W 536	520	BOISSONS NON ALCOOLIQUES
11102	FLAVORED WATERS NON–ALCO							W 276	387	LIMONADES,EAUX GAZEUSES
112	ALCOHOLIC BEVERAGES							W 4188	5104	BOISSONS ALCOOLIQUES
1123	BEER,ALE,STOUT,PORTER							W 3863	4705	BIERES
2	CRUDE MATERLS,EXCL FUELS		618		526				490	MAT BRUTES NON COMESTIBLES
4	ANIMAL,VEGETABLE OIL,FAT		3227		1615				248	HUILES,GRAISSES ANIM,VEG
5	CHEMCLS,RELATED PROD NES		437		1502				923	PRODUITS CHIMIQUES
59	CHEMICAL MATERIALS NES								651	MAT PROD CHIMIQUES NDA
592	STARCH,INULIN,GLUTEN,ETC							W 86	349	AMIDONS,INUL,GLUT FROM
5922	ALBUMINOID SUBSTAN,GLUES							W 86	349	MAT ALBUMIN,COLLES
59229	PREPARED GLUES NES,ETC							W 81	331	COLLES PREPAREES NDA
6	BASIC MANUFACTURES		6918		10736				9927	ART MANUFACTURES
64	PAPER,PAPERBOARD AND MFR								7759	PAPIERS,CARTONS & OUVRAGES
642	PAPER,ETC,PRECUT,ARTS OF							W 8442	7744	PAP,CARTONS DECOUPES
6421	PAPER ETC CONTAINERS							W 8257	7210	BOITES,SACS EMBALLAGES
6424	PAPER ETC CT TO SIZE NES							W 129	358	PAP,CARTONS DECOUPES
64243	TOILET PAPER CUT TO SIZE							W 129	358	PAPIER HYGIENIQUE
65	TEXTILE YARN,FABRICS,ETC								599	FILS,TISSUS,ARTICLES TEXTILE
69	METAL MANUFACTURES NES								990	ART MANUFACT EN METAL NDA
697	BASE MTL HOUSEHOLD EQUIP							W 36	418	ART MENAGE MET COMMUNS
6978	BASE MTL HOUSE EQUIP NES							W 31	397	ART MENAGE MET COMMUNS
69782	BASE MTL DECOR ARTICLES							W 31	397	AUT OBJETS ORNEM INTERIEUR
7	MACHINES,TRANSPORT EQUIP		4284		10270				12166	MACHINES MATERIEL TRANSPORT
71	POWER GENERATING EQUIPMT								413	MACHINES GENERATRICES
72	MACHS FOR SPCL INDUSTRYS								2245	MAC SPECIALES POUR INDUST
723	CIVIL ENGNEERG EQUIP ETC							W 119	1275	APPAREILS DE GENIE CIVIL
7234	CONST,MINING MACHNRY NES							W 119	1275	MACH POUR LA CONST, MINES
72341	SELF–PROPELLD DOZERS,ETC							W 34	744	BULLDOZERS
72345	PILE DRIVERS,ETC							W 51	418	CHASSE–NEIGE
728	OTH MACHY FOR SPCL INDUS							W 72	865	AUT MACH IND PARTICULIERES
7284	MACHY FOR SPCL INDUS NES							W 64	771	MACH SPEC IND PARTICUL.
72842	RUBBER,PLASTICS WRKG MCH							W 51	493	MACH IND CAOUT MAT PLAST
74	GENRL INDUSTRL MACHY NES								1996	MACH APP INDUSTRIE
742	PUMPS FOR LIQUIDS ETC							W 37	463	POMPES MOTO–POMPES
7428	OTHER PUMPS FOR LIQUIDS							W 37	453	AUTRES POMPES POUR LIQ
74288	PUMPS FR LIQUIDS NES ETC							W 27	333	POMPES POUR LIQUIDES NDA
744	MECHANICAL HANDLING EQU							W 44	850	EQUIP MANUTENTION PIECES
7442	LIFTING,LOADING MACH NES							W 17	617	APP LEVAGE,MANUTENTION
76	TELECOMM,SOUND EQUIPMENT								1862	EQUIPMENT DE TELECOM
764	TELECOM EQPT,PTS,ACC NES							W 33	1824	EQUIP TELECOM,PIECES
7643	TV,RADIO TRANSMITTRS ETC							W 30	1728	APP EMET TELE RADIO
77	ELECTRIC MACHNRY NES ETC								3998	MACH APP ELECT NDA
771	ELECTRIC POWER MACHY NES							W 13	379	MACH PROD,TRANS ELECTR
7711	TRANSFORMERS,ELECTRICAL							W 12	327	TRANSFO ELECTRIQUES
77118	OTHER ELEC TRANSFORMERS							W 12	327	AUTRES TRANSFO ELECTRIQ
772	SWITCHGEAR ETC,PARTS NES							W 41	2483	APP COUPURE,SECT ETC
7721	SWITCHGEAR ETC							W 24	391	APP COUPURE,SECTIONMNT
7723	FIXED,VARIABLE RESISTORS							W 15	1795	POTENTIOMETRES PIECES
776	TRANSISTORS,VALVES,ETC							W 1	1018	LAMPES,TUBES,VALVES
7763	DIODES,TRANSISTORS,ETC							W 1	1014	DIODES,TRANSISTORS
78	ROAD VEHICLES								560	VEHICULES ROUTIERS
79	OTHR TRANSPORT EQUIPMENT								868	AUTRE MATERIEL TRANSPORT
792	AIRCRAFT ETC							W 4	408	APP NAVIGATION AERIENNE
7929	AIRCRAFT PARTS NES							W 4	408	PIECES DU 792
793	SHIPS AND BOATS ETC							W 25	460	NAVIRES BATEAUX,ETC
7932	SHIPS AND BOATS NES							W 25	459	NAVIRES ET BATEAUX
8	MISC MANUFACTURED GOODS		21288		29721				21411	ART MANUFACTURES DIVERS
84	CLOTHING AND ACCESSORIES								17448	VETEMENTS
842	MENS OUTERWEAR NOT KNIT							W 124	781	VET DESSUS POUR HOMMES
8423	— TROUSERS,BREECHES ETC							W 123	762	PANTALONS HOMMES MAT TEX
843	WOMENS OUTERWEAR NONKNIT							W 78	360	VET DESSUS FEMMES MAT TEX
844	UNDER GARMENTS NOT KNIT							W 71	767	VETEMENT DESSOUS MAT TEX
8441	— MENS SHIRTS							W 70	748	CHEMISES HOMMES MAT TEXT
84411	—— OF COTTON							W 68	728	CHEMISES HOMMES DE COTON
845	OUTERWEAR KNIT NONELASTC							W 1325	11953	VET DESSOUS,ACCES BONNET
8451	— JERSEYS,PULLOVERS ETC							W 640	3984	CHANDAILS,PULL–OVERS ETC
8459	— OTHER,CLTHG ACCESRYS							W 685	7966	AUT VET DESSUS DE BONNE
846	UNDER GARMENTS KNITTED								3551	SOUS VETS DE BONNETERIE
8462	— OF COTTON NON ELASTIC								504	SOUS–VET BONNET COTON
84629	—— OTHER							W 56	504	AUT SOUS–VET BONNET COTON
8465	CORSETS,GARTERS,ETC							W 74	3047	CORSETS,GAINES ART SIM
84651	BRASSIERES							W 73	2979	SOUTIENS–GORGE,BUSTIERS
87	PRECISION INSTRUMNTS NES								342	INSTRUM,APPAR SCIENT NDA
89	MISC MANUFCTRD GOODS NES								3031	ART MANUFACTURES DIVERS
893	ARTICLES OF PLASTIC NES							W 91	1964	OUVRAGES EN MAT DIVIS 58
8939	MISC PLASTIC ARTICLES							W 90	1958	ART DIVERS EN MAT DIV 58
89399	OTHR PLASTC ARTICLES NES							W 90	1958	AUT OUV MAT DIV 58
899	OTHER MANUFACTURED GOODS								362	AUT ART MANUF DIVERS NDA
8998	SMALLWARES,TOILETRYS ETC							W 11	351	ART MERCERIE,TOILETTE
89985	COMBS,HAIR–SLIDES,ETC							W 11	351	PEIGNES,BARRETTES ETC
9	GOODS NOT CLASSD BY KIND		8950		9				288	ART TRANSACT NON CLASSES

FOOT NOTES – NOTES

TABLE 1 –

1 Prior to 1981, special trade.
TABLEAU 1 –
1 Avant 1981, commerce spécial.

1. HISTORICAL SERIES, 1959–1994 SPECIAL TRADE, IMPORTS C.I.F., EXPORTS F.O.B.
SERIES HISTORIQUES, 1959–1994 COMMERCE SPECIAL, IMPORTATIONS C.A.F., EXPORTATIONS F.O.B

YEAR ANNEE	VALUE IN MILLION FRANCS VALEUR EN MILLION FRANCS MERCHANDISE –MARCHANDISE		GOLD –OR		CONVERSION FACTORS U.S. CENTS PER FRANC FACTEURS DE CONVERSION CENTS E.U. PAR FRANC		INDEX NUMBERS –INDICES QUANTUM		UNIT VALUE VALEUR UNITAIRE	
	IMPORTS	EXPORTS	IMPORTS	EXPORTS	IMPORTS	EXPORTS	IMPORTS	EXPORTS	IMPORTS	EXPORTS
1959	20.10	8.90			20.2550	20.2550				
1960	21.80	8.90			20.2550	20.2550				
1961	22.60	12.20			20.2550	20.2550				
1962	21.20	8.30			20.2550	20.2550				
1963	25.40	6.20			20.2550	20.2550				
1964	25.10	7.10			20.2550	20.2550				
1965	27.30	6.60			20.2550	20.2550				
1966	32.30	7.60			20.2550	20.2550				
1967	38.40	6.70			20.2550	20.2550				
1968	39.10	5.10			20.2550	20.2550				
1969	49.70	5.90			19.3650	19.3650				
1970	65.20	15.00			18.0050	18.0050				
1971	62.30	14.30			18.0050	18.0050				
1972	73.70	21.30			19.8269	19.8315				
1973	77.90	23.60			22.5579	22.5660				
1974	125.60	25.20			20.8098	20.8216				
1975	102.30	26.70			23.3459	23.3824				
1976	129.40	39.00			20.9027	20.9217				
1977	126.00	16.90			20.3537	20.3616				
1978	134.40	17.10			22.1937	22.2006				
1979	148.60	19.00			23.5355	23.5297				
1980	177.20	24.20			23.6663	23.6566				
1981	220.40	38.60			18.4753	18.4478				
1982	276.30	41.20			15.2158	15.2158				
1983	281.00	44.40			13.1780	13.1600				
1984	359.50	64.20			12.2121	12.2121				
1985	280.00	44.00			12.0000	12.0000				
1986	348.30	113.30			14.4991	14.4686				
1987	343.48	134.45			16.6585	16.6382				
1988	366.72	74.89			16.7873	16.7873				
1989	533.13	127.49			15.6737	15.6737				
1990	470.99	139.94			18.3645	18.3645				
1991	458.72	170.78			17.7239	17.7239				
1992	404.19	134.08			18.8900	18.8900				
1993	344.05	4.42			20.2042	20.2042				
1994	413.65	68.67			17.0590	17.0590				

2. IMPORTS BY BROAD ECONOMIC CATEGORY AND EXPORTS BY INDUSTRIAL ORIGIN. (PERCENTAGE OF TOTAL VALUE)
IMPORTATIONS PAR CATEGORIES ECONOMIQUES ET EXPORTATIONS PAR BRANCHE D'ACTIVITE.(EN POURCENTAGE DE LA VALEUR TOTALE)

IMPORTS – IMPORTATIONS

	1990	1991	1992	1993	1994	1995	1996
TOTAL IMPORTS–IMPORTATIONS TOTALES							
1 FOOD BEV–ALIMENTATION BOISSONS							
11 PRIMARY–PRODUITS DE BASE							
111 FOR INDUSTRY–POUR L'INDUSTRIE							
112 FOR HOUSEHOLDS–POUR LES MENAGES							
12 PROCESSED–PRODUITS ELABORES							
121 FOR INDUSTRY–POUR L'INDUSTRIE							
122 FOR HOUSEHOLDS–POUR LES MENAGES							
2 IND SUPPLIES–APPROV INDUSTRIELS							
21 PRIMARY–PRODUITS DE BASE							
22 PROCESSED–PRODUITS ELABORES							
3 FUELS–COMBUSTIBLES							
31 PRIMARY–PRODUITS DE BASE							
32 PROCESSED–PRODUITS ELABORES							
321 MOTOR SPIRIT–ESSENCE							
322 OTHER–AUTRES							
4 MACHINERY–EQUIPEMENT							
41 CAPITAL EQUIPMENT–MACHINES							
42 PARTS–PIECES ACCESSOIRES							
5 TRANSPORT–TRANSPORT							
51 PASSENGER CARS–AUTOMOBILES							
52 OTHER–AUTRES							
521 INDUSTRIAL–INDUSTRIELS							
522 NON INDUSTRIAL–NON INDUSTRIEL							
53 PARTS–PIECES ACCESSOIRES							
6 CONSUM GOODS–BIENS CONSOMMATION							
61 DURABLE–DURABLES							
62 SEMI DURABLE–SEMI DURABLES							
63 NON DURABLE–NON DURABLES							
7 GOODS NES–BIENS NDA							

EXPORTS – EXPORTATIONS

	1990	1991	1992	1993	1994	1995	1996
TOTAL EXPORTS–EXPORTATIONS TOTALES							
1 AGRICULTURE							
2 MINING QUARRY–INDUS EXTRACTIVES							
3 MANUFACTURING–IND MANUFACTUR							
31 FOOD BEV TOBACCO–ALIM BOISS TAB							
32 TEXTILES–INDUSTRIES TEXTILES							
33 WOOD & PRODUCTS–BOIS & PRODUITS							
34 PAPER & PRODUCTS–PAPIER & PRODT							
35 CHEMICALS–INDUSTRIES CHIMIQUES							
36 NON METAL MIN–MIN NON METAL							
37 BASIC METAL–IND METAL BASE							
38 METAL MANUF–MANUF METAL							
39 OTH MANUF IND–AUTRES MANUF							

3. TRADE BY PRINCIPAL COUNTRIES OF PRODUCTION AND LAST CONSIGNMENT (VALUE IN THOUSAND U.S. DOLLARS)
ECHANGES SELON LES PRINCIPAUX PAYS DE PRODUCTION ET DE DERNIERE CONSIGNATION (VALEUR EN MILLIERS DE DOLLARS EU)

COUNTRIES–PAYS	SPECIAL IMPORTS C.I.F. IMPORTATIONS SPECIALES C.A.F				
	1990	1991	1992	1993	1994
World	86496	81304	76352	69513	70565
Africa					
Americas	46150	46031	41172	40643	32397
Northern America	46150	46031	41172	40643	32397
LAIA					
CACM					
Caribbean					
Rest of America					
As.ex F.USSR					
Eur.x F.USSR	31177	27594	27827	24362	33215
EU	31177	27594	27827	24362	33215
EFTA					
East Europe					
Other Europe					
Former USSR					
Oceania					
Canada	46150	46031	41172	38174	30175
France,Monac	31177	27594	27827	24362	33215
USA/Etats–Unis d'Amer				2469	2222

COUNTRIES–PAYS	SPECIAL EXPORTS F.O.B. # 1 EXPORTATIONS SPECIALES F.O.B.				
	1990	1991	1992	1993	1994
Monde	41610	43985	37719	5827	14111
Afrique					
Amériques	141	134	125	50	38
Amérique du Nord	141	134	125	50	38
ALAI					
MCAC					
Caraïbes					
Autre Amérique					
Asie l'URSS exclus					
Europe l'URSS exclus	16027	17288	12986	24	11333
UE	16027	17288	12986	24	11333
AELE					
Europe de l'Est					
Autre de l'Europe					
Ancienne URSS					
Océanie					
France,Monac	16027	17288	12986	24	11333
Canada	141	134	125	50	38

(VALUE AS PERCENTAGE OF WORLD TOTAL)(VALEURS EN POURCENTAGE DU TOTAL MONDIAL)

	1985	1986	1987	1988	1989	1990	1991	1992	1993	1994
Africa		0.1		0.2	0.1					
Americas		50.0		51.3	43.1	53.4	56.6	53.9	58.5	45.9
Northern America		49.9		51.3	43.1	53.4	56.6	53.9	58.5	45.9
LAIA		0.0		0.0	0.0					
CACM										
Caribbean		0.0		0.0	0.0					
Rest of America		0.0		0.0	0.0					
As.ex F.USSR		1.6		2.3	6.0					
Eur.x F.USSR		48.2		46.2	50.7	36.0	33.9	36.4	35.0	47.1
EU		48.0		46.0	50.4	36.0	33.9	36.4	35.0	47.1
EFTA		0.1		0.2	0.3					
East Europe		0.1		0.0	0.0					
Other Europe		0.0		0.0	0.0					
Former USSR		0.1			0.0					
Oceania		0.0		0.1	0.0					
Canada		48.4		49.5	42.3	53.4	56.6	53.9	54.9	42.8
France,Monac		35.0		38.0	47.6	36.0	33.9	36.4	35.0	47.1
USA/Etats–Unis d'Amer		1.5		1.7	0.9				3.6	3.1

	1985	1986	1987	1988	1989	1990	1991	1992	1993	1994
Afrique										
Amériques		46.3		26.7	35.1	0.3	0.3	0.3	0.9	0.3
Amérique du Nord		46.3		26.7	35.1	0.3	0.3	0.3	0.9	0.3
ALAI										
MCAC										
Caraïbes										
Autre Amérique										
Asie l'URSS exclus					24.0					
Europe l'URSS exclus		53.7		73.3	40.9	38.5	39.3	34.4	0.4	80.3
UE		53.7		73.3	40.9	38.5	39.3	34.4	0.4	80.3
AELE										
Europe de l'Est										
Autre de l'Europe										
Ancienne URSS										
Océanie										
France,Monac		35.7		57.2	25.2	38.5	39.3	34.4	0.4	80.3
Canada		3.9		2.4	12.0	0.3	0.3	0.3	0.9	0.3

4. Special Imports C.I.F. by Commodities according to the S.I.T.C. (Rev. 2) in thousand U.S. Dollars
Importations Spéciales C.A.F. par Produits d'après la C.T.C.I. (Rév. 2) en milliers de Dollars E.U.

SITC CTCI	COMMODITY	1991		1992		1993		1994		PRODUIT
		WEIGHT POIDS	VALUE VALEUR	WEIGHT POIDS	VALUE VALEUR	WEIGHT POIDS	VALUE VALEUR	WEIGHT POIDS	VALUE VALEUR	
	ALL COMMODITIES		81304		76352		69513		70565	TOUS PRODUITS
0	FOOD AND LIVE ANIMALS						15361		13128	ALIMENTS,ANIMAUX VIVANTS
3	MINERAL FUELS ETC						8812		6627	COMBUSTIBLES MINERAUX LUB
33	PETROLEUM AND PRODUCTS						8812		6627	PETROLE ET DERIVES
334	PETROLEUM PRODUCTS,REFIN		18106		15052	W 41104	8812	W 37646	6627	PRODUITS RAFFINES
9	GOODS NOT CLASSD BY KIND						45340		50810	ART TRANSACT NON CLASSES
931	*SPECIAL TRANSACTIONS					W 16647	45340	W 17327	50810	TRANS.SPECIALES

5. Special Exports F.O.B. by Commodities according to the S.I.T.C. (Rev. 2) in thousand U.S. Dollars
Exportations Spéciales F.O.B. par Produits d'après la C.T.C.I. (Rév. 2) en milliers de Dollars E.U.

SITC CTCI	COMMODITY	1991		1992		1993		1994		PRODUIT
		WEIGHT POIDS	VALUE VALEUR	WEIGHT POIDS	VALUE VALEUR	WEIGHT POIDS	VALUE VALEUR	WEIGHT POIDS	VALUE VALEUR	
	ALL COMMODITIES # 1		43985		37719		5827		14111	TOUS PRODUITS
0	FOOD AND LIVE ANIMALS						342		417	ALIMENTS,ANIMAUX VIVANTS
03	FISH AND PREPARATIONS						342		417	POISSONS ET PREPARATIONS
034	FISH,FRESH,CHILLED,FROZN		24860		19624			W 20	52	POISSON FRAIS, REFRIG,CONG
035	FISH SALTED,DRIED,SMOKED		5173		5478	W 34	342	W 43	365	POISSON SECHE,SALE,FUME
08142	FISH MEAL FODDER		236		225					FARINES DE POISSONS
9	GOODS NOT CLASSD BY KIND						5485		13694	ART TRANSACT NON CLASSES
931	*SPECIAL TRANSACTIONS		13716		12392	W 20834	5485	W 14654	13694	TRANS.SPECIALES

FOOT NOTES – NOTES

TABLE 3 –
1 Export data for 1993 reflect the moratorium on the shipment of fish products.
TABLE 5 –
1 Data for 1993 reflect the moratorium on the shipment of fish products.
TABLEAU 3 –
1 En 1993 les données des exportations réfléchissent l'application du moratoire sur les produits de la pêche.
TABLEAU 5 –
1 En 1993 les données réfléchissent l'application du moratoire sur les produits de la pêche.

1. HISTORICAL SERIES, 1961–1996 SPECIAL TRADE, IMPORTS C.I.F., EXPORTS F.O.B.
SERIES HISTORIQUES, 1961–1996 COMMERCE SPECIAL, IMPORTATIONS C.A.F., EXPORTATIONS F.O.B

YEAR ANNEE	VALUE IN MILLION E.C. DOLLARS VALEUR EN MILLION E.C. DOLLARS MERCHANDISE –MARCHANDISE		GOLD –OR		CONVERSION FACTORS U.S. CENTS PER E.C. DOLLAR FACTEURS DE CONVERSION CENTS E.U. PAR E.C. DOLLAR		INDEX NUMBERS INDICES QUANTUM		UNIT VALUE VALEUR UNITAIRE	
	IMPORTS	EXPORTS	IMPORTS	EXPORTS	IMPORTS	EXPORTS	IMPORTS	EXPORTS	IMPORTS	EXPORTS
1961	12.60	5.80			58.3300	58.3300				
1962	12.50	6.10			58.3300	58.3300				
1963	12.80	6.30			58.3300	58.3300				
1964	16.10	6.50			58.3300	58.3300				
1965	14.80	6.40			58.3300	58.3300				
1966	16.10	6.70			58.3300	58.3300				
1967	15.80	6.30			57.6500	57.6500				
1968	20.00	7.50			50.0000	50.0000				
1969	24.40	7.60			50.0000	50.0000				
1970	30.50	7.10			50.0000	50.0000				
1971	36.00	5.90			50.7166	50.7166				
1972	35.20	6.60			52.1216	52.1216				
1973	38.10	10.10			51.0808	51.0808				
1974	52.30	14.60			48.7301	48.7301				
1975	53.90	16.50			46.2878	46.2878				
1976	62.00	24.70			38.0480	38.0480				
1977	81.90	27.00			37.0370	37.0370				
1978	97.70	44.30			37.0370	37.0370				
1979	125.10	39.90			37.0370	37.0370				
1980	154.20	42.50			37.0370	37.0370				
1981	157.10	65.90			37.0370	37.0370				
1982	175.80	87.10			37.0370	37.0370				
1983	190.00	110.80			37.0370	37.0370				
1984	206.80	144.60			37.0370	37.0370				
1985	213.80	170.90			37.0370	37.0370				
1986	235.70	172.30			37.0370	37.0370				
1987	266.40	141.30			37.0370	37.0370				
1988	330.10	230.20			37.0370	37.0370				
1989	344.20	201.40			37.0370	37.0370				
1990	367.40	223.40			37.0370	37.0370				
1991	377.10	181.20			37.0370	37.0370				
1992	356.60	210.90			37.0370	37.0370				
1993	362.70	156.10			37.0370	37.0370				
1994	351.00	136.10			37.0370	37.0370				
1995	366.70	115.20			37.0370	37.0370				
1996	356.00	125.20			37.0370	37.0370				

2. IMPORTS BY BROAD ECONOMIC CATEGORY AND EXPORTS BY INDUSTRIAL ORIGIN. (PERCENTAGE OF TOTAL VALUE)
IMPORTATIONS PAR CATEGORIES ECONOMIQUES ET EXPORTATIONS PAR BRANCHE D'ACTIVITE.(EN POURCENTAGE DE LA VALEUR TOTALE)

IMPORTS – IMPORTATIONS	1990	1991	1992	1993	1994	1995	1996
TOTAL IMPORTS–IMPORTATIONS TOTALES							
1 FOOD BEV–ALIMENTATION BOISSONS							
11 PRIMARY–PRODUITS DE BASE							
111 FOR INDUSTRY–POUR L'INDUSTRIE							
112 FOR HOUSEHOLDS–POUR LES MENAGES							
12 PROCESSED–PRODUITS ELABORES							
121 FOR INDUSTRY–POUR L'INDUSTRIE							
122 FOR HOUSEHOLDS–POUR LES MENAGES							
2 IND SUPPLIES–APPROV INDUSTRIELS							
21 PRIMARY–PRODUITS DE BASE							
22 PROCESSED–PRODUITS ELABORES							
3 FUELS–COMBUSTIBLES							
31 PRIMARY–PRODUITS DE BASE							
32 PROCESSED–PRODUITS ELABORES							
321 MOTOR SPIRIT–ESSENCE							
322 OTHER–AUTRES							
4 MACHINERY–EQUIPEMENT							
41 CAPITAL EQUIPMENT–MACHINES							
42 PARTS–PIECES ACCESSOIRES							
5 TRANSPORT–TRANSPORT							
51 PASSENGER CARS–AUTOMOBILES							
52 OTHER–AUTRES							
521 INDUSTRIAL–INDUSTRIELS							
522 NON INDUSTRIAL–NON INDUSTRIEL							
53 PARTS–PIECES ACCESSOIRES							
6 CONSUM GOODS–BIENS CONSOMMATION							
61 DURABLE–DURABLES							
62 SEMI DURABLE–SEMI DURABLES							
63 NON DURABLE–NON DURABLES							
7 GOODS NES–BIENS NDA							

EXPORTS – EXPORTATIONS	1990	1991	1992	1993	1994	1995	1996
TOTAL EXPORTS–EXPORTATIONS TOTALES							
1 AGRICULTURE							
2 MINING QUARRY–INDUS EXTRACTIVES							
3 MANUFACTURING–IND MANUFACTUR							
31 FOOD BEV TOBACCO–ALIM BOISS TAB							
32 TEXTILES–INDUSTRIES TEXTILES							
33 WOOD & PRODUCTS–BOIS & PRODUITS							
34 PAPER & PRODUCTS–PAPIER & PRODT							
35 CHEMICALS–INDUSTRIES CHIMIQUES							
36 NON METAL MIN–MIN NON METAL							
37 BASIC METAL–IND METAL BASE							
38 METAL MANUF–MANUF METAL							
39 OTH MANUF IND–AUTRES MANUF							

3. TRADE BY PRINCIPAL COUNTRIES OF PRODUCTION AND LAST CONSIGNMENT (VALUE IN THOUSAND U.S. DOLLARS)
ECHANGES SELON LES PRINCIPAUX PAYS DE PRODUCTION ET DE DERNIERE CONSIGNATION (VALEUR EN MILLIERS DE DOLLARS EU)

COUNTRIES–PAYS	SPECIAL IMPORTS C.I.F. IMPORTATIONS SPECIALES C.A.F					COUNTRIES–PAYS	SPECIAL EXPORTS F.O.B. EXPORTATIONS SPECIALES F.O.B.				
	1990	1991	1992	1993	1994		1990	1991	1992	1993	1994
World	136077	139684	132084	134340	129892	Monde	82721	67118	78093	57820	50365
Africa	29	104	12	37	111	Afrique	0				
Americas	89340	94826	92344	92852	88458	Amériques	37516	29228	36241	32100	33501
Northern America	54855	53775	52585	54496	49465	Amérique du Nord	8828	3730	3739	4386	4764
LAIA	4124	3484	4086	4129	2786	ALAI	5	29	28	28	31
CACM	746	2028	1874	839	822	MCAC		3	9	17	0
Caribbean	28883	34816	32642	32105	33124	Caraïbes	27726	25367	32421	27481	27858
Rest of America	732	724	1158	1283	2261	Autre Amérique	957	100	44	187	847
As.ex F.USSR	7749	5819	6390	6424	6430	Asie l'URSS exclus	10	34	7	24	35
Eur.x F.USSR	36734	35974	31127	33091	33065	Europe l'URSS exclus	45150	37853	41841	25691	16636
EU	35800	35182	30380	32204	32148	UE	45149	37851	41835	25690	16636
EFTA	559	521	570	681	515	AELE		1	6	1	
East Europe	361	249	161	192	401	Europe de l'Est	1				
Other Europe	1	19	10			Autre de l'Europe					
Former USSR	11	16	9		2	Ancienne URSS					
Oceania	86	226	34	193	150	Océanie	0				
USA/Etats–Unis d'Amer	49576	48983	48536	49750	46527	United Kingdom	44643	36733	32506	23533	15832
Trinidad and Tobago	17040	22302	22035	20688	21847	Trinidad and Tobago	10295	8354	9627	5982	5236
United Kingdom	24036	17470	22571	15775	16368	Saint Lucia/St. Lucie	5602	6113	7960	6837	6487
Barbados/Barbade	5544	5476	4533	5194	5149	USA/Etats–Unis d'Amer	8710	3544	3518	4269	4687
Canada	5279	4792	4049	4747	2937	Antigua and Barbuda	2935	2182	3106	3747	3756
Italy/Italie	1277	990	672	9174	8019	Dominica/Dominique	2236	2597	2921	3056	2797
Japan/Japon	4517	3373	3663	3439	3627	Barbados/Barbade	2793	1889	2535	2098	3400
Netherlands/Pays–Bas	4060	8270	2254	1480	2124	Italy/Italie	378	847	8961	1935	370
Germany/Allemagne	2972	2757	2579	2589	1923	Saint–Kitts–Nevis	1867	1514	1710	1712	2596
Jamaica/Jamaïque	1774	2015	2027	2405	2223	Grenada/Grenade	679	937	1923	1804	1303
Brazil/Brésil	1211	1146	1631	2662	1307	Jamaica/Jamaïque	672	1085	1559	862	911
France, Monac	1109	2036	743	795	1480	Guyana	897	89	43	186	847
Saint Lucia/St. Lucie	2073	1030	1128	662	609	Montserrat	351	343	312	395	524
Guyana	423	629	1006	1148	1790	Martinique	73	36	118	408	594
China/Chine	939	828	993	1103	1133	Haiti/Haïti	134	136	167	243	148
Venezuela	889	730	1356	744	948	Netherlands/Pays–Bas	33	67	297	190	163
Dominica/Dominique	662	826	950	911	1096	Canada	118	186	220	117	77
Colombia/Colombie	1583	703	705	312	322	Guadeloupe	31	41	269		
Denmark/Danemark	709	475	858	674	671	Germany/Allemagne	91	148	21	17	37
Guatemala	237	1250	1436	217	187	Netherlands Antilles	23	82	149	22	10
Netherlands Antilles	532	1016	916	857		Aruba		1		199	14
Sweden/Suède	903	1513	206	128	122	Portugal					207
Korea, Republic of	915	479	522	245	546	France, Monac	4	56	49	8	14
Honduras	465	501	312	591	614	Venezuela	5	8	28	27	31
Grenada/Grenade	265	490	628	446	516	Japan/Japon	9	24	4	21	34
Hong Kong	412	426	519	348	279	Belize/Bélize	36	9		1	
Belgium–Luxembourg	175	666	273	414	437	Dominican Republic		30			
Spain/Espagne	166	226	86	930	490	Argentina/Argentine		20			
Ireland/Irlande	340	720	93	209	473	Belgium–Luxembourg				8	12
Martinique	287	1294	33	63	27	Guatemala		3		17	
Switz.Liecht	201	216	254	553	313	Honduras			9		
Argentina/Argentine	373	432	306	262	122	Norway, SVD, JM			6		
Antigua and Barbuda	208	185	235	343	454	Korea, Republic of				3	
Thailand/Thaïlande	307	203	179	507	52	Panama		1	1		
Norway, SVD, JM	283	262	313	121	176	Switz.Liecht		1		1	
Singapore/Singapour	219	201	180	180	216	Singapore/Singapour	0	1			
Panama	199	73	151	96	349	Brazil/Brésil				1	1
Mexico/Mexique	56	471	85	146	83	China/Chine					1
Indonesia/Indonésie	107	94	132	188	266	Former GDR	1				
Aruba	9	10	4	101	588	Ireland/Irlande		0	0		
Saint–Kitts–Nevis	134	68	34	193	202	Costa Rica					0
Dominican Republic	264	32	29	23	126						
New Zealand	53	186	7	99	128						
Czechoslovakia	42	42	102	80	50						
Poland/Pologne	84	11	18	55	127						
Romania/Roumanie	1	194	21	41	29						
Costa Rica	41	65	118	30	19						
Belize/Bélize	109			39	113						
Hungary/Hongrie	18	2	20	15	195						
El Salvador	3	213	9	1	2						

(VALUE AS PERCENTAGE OF WORLD TOTAL)(VALEURS EN POURCENTAGE DU TOTAL MONDIAL)

	1985	1986	1987	1988	1989	1990	1991	1992	1993	1994
Africa						0.0	0.1	0.0	0.0	0.1
Americas	58.5	60.2	59.6	15.9	63.7	65.7	67.9	69.9	69.1	68.1
Northern America	39.7	41.3	40.3		44.8	40.3	38.5	39.8	40.6	38.1
LAIA						3.0	2.5	3.1	3.1	2.1
CACM						0.5	1.5	1.4	0.6	0.6
Caribbean	18.2	18.1	18.5	15.5	18.6	21.2	24.9	24.7	23.9	25.5
Rest of America	0.6	0.8	0.8	0.4	0.4	0.5	0.5	0.9	1.0	1.7
As.ex F.USSR						5.7	4.2	4.8	4.8	5.0
Eur.x F.USSR	27.2	25.6	27.4		21.3	27.0	25.8	23.6	24.6	25.5
EU	27.2	25.6	27.4		21.3	26.3	25.2	23.0	24.0	24.8
EFTA						0.4	0.4	0.4	0.5	0.4
East Europe						0.3	0.2	0.1	0.1	0.3
Other Europe						0.0	0.0	0.0		
Former USSR						0.0	0.0	0.0		0.0
Oceania						0.1	0.2	0.0	0.1	0.1
USA/Etats–Unis d'Amer	36.3	34.1	35.6		41.8	36.4	35.1	36.7	37.0	35.8
Trinidad and Tobago	10.5	10.5	11.1	9.2	10.8	12.5	16.0	16.7	15.4	16.8
United Kingdom	13.8	16.5	17.8		14.5	17.7	12.5	17.1	11.7	12.6
Barbados/Barbade	3.4	3.5	3.8	3.2	3.9	4.1	3.9	3.4	3.9	4.0
Canada	3.4	7.2	4.7		3.0	3.9	3.4	3.1	3.5	2.3
Italy/Italie	0.6	0.7	1.3		0.9	0.9	0.7	0.5	6.8	6.2
Japan/Japon						3.3	2.4	2.8	2.6	2.8
Netherlands/Pays–Bas	3.3	2.5	1.8		1.9	3.0	5.9	1.7	1.1	1.6
Germany/Allemagne	4.9	2.4	1.8		2.0	2.2	2.0	2.0	1.9	1.5
Jamaica/Jamaïque	1.5	1.6	1.8	1.2	1.3	1.3	1.4	1.5	1.8	1.7

	1985	1986	1987	1988	1989	1990	1991	1992	1993	1994
Afrique						0.0				
Amériques	71.7	68.5	59.6	41.7	52.2	45.4	43.5	46.4	55.5	66.5
Amérique du Nord	10.1	9.9	15.6		14.8	10.7	5.6	4.8	7.6	9.5
ALAI						0.0	0.0	0.0	0.0	0.1
MCAC							0.0	0.0	0.0	0.0
Caraïbes	61.1	58.3	43.2	41.6	37.2	33.5	37.8	41.5	47.5	55.3
Autre Amérique	0.5	0.3	0.8	0.1	0.1	1.2	0.1	0.1	0.3	1.7
Asie l'URSS exclus						0.0	0.1	0.0	0.0	0.1
Europe l'URSS exclus	28.2	31.2	39.6		46.9	54.6	56.4	53.6	44.4	33.0
UE	28.2	31.2	39.6		46.9	54.6	56.4	53.6	44.4	33.0
AELE							0.0	0.0	0.0	
Europe de l'Est						0.0				
Autre de l'Europe										
Ancienne URSS										
Océanie						0.0				
United Kingdom	28.2	31.2	39.1		43.2	54.0	54.7	41.6	40.7	31.4
Trinidad and Tobago	44.9	43.0	21.9	25.9	14.0	12.4	12.4	12.3	10.3	10.4
Saint Lucia/St. Lucie	6.3	5.3	5.5	5.4	7.0	6.8	9.1	10.2	11.8	12.9
USA/Etats–Unis d'Amer	9.7	9.4	15.1		14.6	10.5	5.3	4.5	7.4	9.3
Antigua and Barbuda	2.7	2.7	3.5	2.5	3.9	3.5	3.3	4.0	6.5	7.5
Dominica/Dominique	2.9	2.2	2.8	1.8	2.7	2.7	3.9	3.7	5.3	5.6
Barbados/Barbade	1.2	1.4	2.2	2.0	3.7	3.4	2.8	3.2	3.6	6.8
Italy/Italie			0.4		3.2	0.5	1.3	11.5	3.3	0.7
Saint–Kitts–Nevis	1.8	1.7	2.6	1.3	2.2	2.3	2.3	2.2	3.0	5.2
Grenada/Grenade	0.5	1.0	1.6	0.6	1.1	0.8	1.4	2.5	3.1	2.6

4. Special Imports C.I.F. by Commodities according to the S.I.T.C. (Rev. 2) in thousand U.S. Dollars
Importations Spéciales C.A.F. par Produits d'après la C.T.C.I. (Rév. 2) en milliers de Dollars E.U.

SITC CTCI	COMMODITY	1991		1992		1993		1994		PRODUIT
		WEIGHT POIDS	VALUE VALEUR	WEIGHT POIDS	VALUE VALEUR	WEIGHT POIDS	VALUE VALEUR	WEIGHT POIDS	VALUE VALEUR	
	ALL COMMODITIES		139684		132084		134340		129892	TOUS PRODUITS
0	FOOD AND LIVE ANIMALS		29827		31016		31368		26994	ALIMENTS,ANIMAUX VIVANTS
01	MEAT AND PREPARATIONS		6620		6451		6733		6953	VIANDES ET PREPARATIONS
0114	POULTRY FRESH CHLLD,FRZN	W 4492	4034	W 4980	4179	W 5304	4423	W 4851	4659	VOLAILLES MORTES
0121	PIG MEAT DRIED,SLTD,SMKD	W 392	838	W 426	754	W 322	785	W 334	844	LARD,JAMBONS
02	DAIRY PRODCTS,BIRDS'EGGS		2533		2849		2766		2601	PRODUITS LAITIERS,OEUFS
0224	MILK,CREAM PRESERVED ETC					W 1019	1850	W 1240	1763	LAIT,CREME CONS,CONC
02249	MILK(EX DRY) PRSVD,SWEET	W 1380	1766	W 1254	2068					LAIT CONS,CONC SUCRE
024	CHEESE AND CURD					W 198	722	W 201	681	FROMAGE ET CAILLEBOTTE
03	FISH AND PREPARATIONS		837		896		782		847	POISSONS ET PREPARATIONS
04	CEREALS AND PREPARATIONS		10480		11393		12654		8016	CEREALES ET PRODUITS
041	WHEAT ETC UNMILLED					W 27382	5119	W 10105	2186	FROMENT,EPEAUTRE
042	RICE					W 13932	4528	W 6750	2948	RIZ
05	VEGETABLES AND FRUIT		2335		2101		1883		1746	LEGUMES ET FRUITS
06	SUGAR AND PREPS,HONEY		2776		2859		1863		2615	SUCRES ET PRODUITS
0611	RAW BEET AND CANE SUGAR	W 3415	1453	W 3912	1335	W 2020	623	W 4471	1418	SUCRES BRUTS
0612	REFINED SUGAR ETC	W 1809	949	W 2767	1182	W 1797	802	W 1898	825	SUCRES RAFFINES
07	COFFEE,TEA,COCOA,SPICES		585		769		656		635	CAFE,THE,CACAO,EPICES
09	MISC EDIBLE PRODUCTS		3399		3280		3624		3416	PREP ALIMENTAIRES DIVERSES
1	BEVERAGES AND TOBACCO		2624		2472		2196		2082	BOISSONS ET TABACS
11	BEVERAGES		2269		2103		1826		1753	BOISSONS
2	CRUDE MATERLS,EXCL FUELS		3951		4659		4530		4643	MAT BRUTES NON COMESTIBLES
24	CORK AND WOOD		3151		3340		3748		3796	LIEGE ET BOIS
2482	LUMBER SHAPED CONIFER		2900		2890		3463		3497	CONIFERES SCIES,RABOTES
27	CRUDE FERTLZR,MINRLS NES		264		924		329		515	ENGRAIS MINERAUX BRUTS
3	MINERAL FUELS ETC		12147		10196		7843		8135	COMBUSTIBLES MINERAUX LUB
33	PETROLEUM AND PRODUCTS		10962		8832		6460		6950	PETROLE ET DERIVES
3341	GASOLINE,OTH LIGHT OILS		3239		2699		2592	W 24688	2555	ESSENCES POUR MOTEURS
3343	GAS OILS		6643		5923		2536	W 20736	3213	GAS OILS
341	*GAS,NATURAL AND MANUFCT		1179		1361		1378		1183	GAZ NATUREL,GAZ MANUFACT
3414	PETROLEUM GASES, GASEOUS						1378		1182	GAZ DE PETROLE GAZEUX
5	CHEMCLS,RELATED PROD NES		16365		16628		15924		14386	PRODUITS CHIMIQUES
52	INORGANIC CHEMICALS		438		407		464		330	PROD CHIM INORGANIQUES
53	DYES,TANNING,COLOUR PROD		1760		1671		1840		2056	PROD TEINTURE,COLORANTS
533	PIGMENTS,PAINTS,ETC						1338		1534	PIGMENTS,PEINTURES,VERNIS
541	*MEDICINAL,PHARM PRODUCT		1763		1600		2046		1915	PROD MEDICINAUX PHARMACEUT
55	PERFUME,CLEANING ETC PRD		3096		3040		3143		3009	PROD POUR PARFUM,TOILETTE
562	*FERTILIZERS,MANUFACTURE		3067		3427	W 9405	2153		1630	ENGRAIS MANUFACTURES
572	*EXPLOSIVES,PYROTECH PRO		100		120		1283		891	EXPLOSIFS
58	PLASTIC MATERIALS ETC		2559		2924		987		1176	MAT PLAST ARTIFICIELLES
59	CHEMICAL MATERIALS NES		3540		3363		3941		3257	MAT PROD CHIMIQUES NDA
591	PESTICIDES,DISINFECTANTS					W 2808	2747	W 809	2507	DESINF,INSECT,FONG,HERB
6	BASIC MANUFACTURES		30738		28825		34363		32836	ART MANUFACTURES
62	RUBBER MANUFACTURES NES		1169		1333		1641		1374	CAOUTCHOUC MANUFACTURE
63	WOOD,CORK MANUFACTRS NES		1577		1554		1799		2361	OUVRAGES LIEGE ET BOIS
64	PAPER,PAPERBOARD AND MFR		9691		9558		7113		4729	PAPIERS,CARTONS & OUVRAGES
6412	PRINTG,WRITING PAPER NES					W 5869	4237			PAPIERS POUR L'IMPRESSION
642	PAPER,ETC,PRECUT,ARTS OF							W 1911	1611	PAP,CARTONS DECOUPES
65	TEXTILE YARN,FABRICS,ETC		2999		3186		2521		2961	FILS,TISSUS,ARTICLES TEXTILE
654	OTH WOVEN TEXTILE FABRIC						1068		903	TISSUS AUT COTON SYNT,ARTIF
66	NONMETAL MINERAL MFS NES		5367		5276		6687		8447	ART MIN NON METALLIQUES
6612	CEMENT	W 39061	2728	W 41465	3046	W 63650	3675	W 63261	3575	CIMENTS HYDRAULIQUES
67	IRON AND STEEL		3073		1678		5183		2844	FER ET ACIER
68	NON–FERROUS METALS		205		195		274		391	METAUX NON FERREUX
69	METAL MANUFACTURES NES		6637		6036		9138		9720	ART MANUFACT EN METAL NDA
691	STRUCTURES AND PARTS NES					W 691	4908	W 804	5190	CONSTRUCT FER,ACIER,ALU
6911	STRUCTURES,PARTS IRN,STL	W 841	2112	W 537	1946					CONSTRUCT FER,ACIER,FONTE
6973	DMSTC HEATG,COOKG APPARA					W 138	594	W 194	764	APPS CHAUF NON ELECTRIQ
69733	PTS NES OF APPAR OF 6973	W 170	774	W 230	771					PART PIECES POUR 697.3
7	MACHINES,TRANSPORT EQUIP		30325		23800		24354		26791	MACHINES MATERIEL TRANSPORT
71	POWER GENERATING EQUIPMT		4937		1555		2019		1403	MACHINES GENERATRICES
72	MACHS FOR SPCL INDUSTRYS		5095		1758		3002		3166	MAC SPECIALES POUR INDUST
73	METALWORKING MACHINERY		736		156		230		247	MACH TRAVAIL DES METAUX
74	GENRL INDUSTRL MACHY NES		3659		4054		4113		5141	MACH APP INDUSTRIE
75	OFFICE MACHNES,ADP EQUIP		2387		1030		1894		1639	MACH BUREAU TRAIT AUTOM
76	TELECOMM,SOUND EQUIPMENT		1597		2981		1452		3675	EQUIPMENT DE TELECOM
77	ELECTRIC MACHNRY NES ETC		3994		5034		5280		5711	MACH APP ELECT NDA
77521	DOMESTIC REFRIGERATORS	N 3064	577	N 1475	590	N 1673	624	N 1818	616	REFRIGERATEURS
78	ROAD VEHICLES		7391		7019		6135		5331	VEHICULES ROUTIERS
781	PASS MOTOR VEH EXC BUSES					N 371	2296	N 428	2109	AUTO TRANSPORT PERSONNES
79	OTHR TRANSPORT EQUIPMENT		507		214		227		476	AUTRE MATERIEL TRANSPORT
8	MISC MANUFACTURED GOODS		13553		14305		13530		13834	ART MANUFACTURES DIVERS
812	*PLUMBG,HEATNG,LGHTNG EQ		604		539		813		959	APPAR SANITAIRES CHAUFFAGE
821	*FURNITURE,PARTS THEREOF		1270		1674		1000		1674	MEUBLES ET PIECES
84	CLOTHING AND ACCESSORIES		4236		3778		3213		3593	VETEMENTS
851	*FOOTWEAR		1451		1292	P 290	1231	P 270	1080	CHAUSSURES
87	PRECISION INSTRUMNTS NES		842		671		802		688	INSTRUM,APPAR SCIENT NDA
88	PHOTO EQU,OPTICL GDS ETC		424		485		449		450	APP,FOURN PHOTO,OP,MONTR
89	MISC MANUFCTRD GOODS NES		4510		5661		5789		5212	ART MANUFACTURES DIVERS
893	ARTICLES OF PLASTIC NES					W 1272	2271	W 1094	2067	OUVRAGES EN MAT DIVIS 58

5. Special Exports F.O.B. by Commodities according to the S.I.T.C. (Rev. 2) in thousand U.S. Dollars
Exportations Spéciales F.O.B. par Produits d'après la C.T.C.I. (Rév. 2) en milliers de Dollars E.U.

SITC CTCI	COMMODITY	1991		1992		1993		1994		PRODUIT
		WEIGHT POIDS	VALUE VALEUR	WEIGHT POIDS	VALUE VALEUR	WEIGHT POIDS	VALUE VALEUR	WEIGHT POIDS	VALUE VALEUR	
	ALL COMMODITIES		67118		78093		57820		50365	TOUS PRODUITS
0	FOOD AND LIVE ANIMALS		55177		65450		47277		36506	ALIMENTS,ANIMAUX VIVANTS
03	FISH AND PREPARATIONS		90		140		364		290	POISSONS ET PREPARATIONS
04	CEREALS AND PREPARATIONS		10063		13996		14283		14736	CEREALES ET PRODUITS
042	RICE					W 9835	5441	W 13135	6040	RIZ
04601	FLOUR OF WHEAT OR MESLIN					W 19195	8404	W 18786	8473	FARINE DE FROMENT
05	VEGETABLES AND FRUIT		42331		48098		30194		19340	LEGUMES ET FRUITS
05481	ROOTS,TUBERS FRESH,DRY	W 6896	3804	W 8996	5015	W 6086	3373	W 2850	1731	RACINES DE MANIOC ETC
0573	BANANA,PLANTAIN,FRSH,DRY	W 62911	37238	W 80957	42023	W 65677	26156	W 35190	16963	BANANES FRAICHES,SECHEES
05771	COCONUTS FRESH OR DRIED	N 1625000	270	N 2148000	318		181		116	NOIX DE COCO
0582	FRUIT PRESERVED BY SUGAR	W 813	300	W 998	407					FRUITS CONFITS AU SUCRE
07	COFFEE,TEA,COCOA,SPICES		427		496		276		121	CAFE,THE,CACAO,EPICES
07526	GINGER (EXCPT SWEETENED)					W 620	253	W 192	89	GINGEMBRE
081	*FEEDING STUFF FOR ANIML		2243		2637		2076		1937	NOURRITURE POUR ANIMAUX
08199	FODDER NES,INCL SWEETNED					W 10508	1965	W 12273	1849	PREPARATIONS FOURRAGERES
1	BEVERAGES AND TOBACCO		648		1227		1288		1141	BOISSONS ET TABACS
11	BEVERAGES		603		1205		1250		1141	BOISSONS
1123	BEER,ALE,STOUT,PORTER	W 269	368	W 190	217	V 133	152	V 502	491	BIERES
2	CRUDE MATERLS,EXCL FUELS		61		82		224		224	MAT BRUTES NON COMESTIBLES
5	CHEMCLS,RELATED PROD NES		659		308		326		406	PRODUITS CHIMIQUES
58	PLASTIC MATERIALS ETC		513		122		129		214	MAT PLAST ARTIFICIELLES
59	CHEMICAL MATERIALS NES		88		126		156		180	MAT PROD CHIMIQUES NDA
6	BASIC MANUFACTURES		3579		3079		2140		2596	ART MANUFACTURES
64	PAPER,PAPERBOARD AND MFR		1666		661		722		754	PAPIERS,CARTONS & OUVRAGES
67	IRON AND STEEL		854		886		714		957	FER ET ACIER
6749	OTH IRN,STL PLATES,SHEET	W 618	797	W 634	784	W 313	414	W 778	603	AUTRES TOLES FER,ACIER
69	METAL MANUFACTURES NES		993		1279		617		833	ART MANUFACT EN METAL NDA
69731	IRN,STL DOM COOKG APPARA					W 40	259	W 147	587	APPS CUISSON FER,ACIER
69732	IRN,STL DOM HEATG APPARA	W 60	841	W 155	1188					POELES,RECHAUDS NON ELECTRS
7	MACHINES,TRANSPORT EQUIP		2930		3339		2910		6176	MACHINES MATERIEL TRANSPORT
71	POWER GENERATING EQUIPMT		256		355		389		122	MACHINES GENERATRICES
72	MACHS FOR SPCL INDUSTRYS		180		788		397		1574	MAC SPECIALES POUR INDUST
74	GENRL INDUSTRL MACHY NES		90		706		170		513	MACH APP INDUSTRIE
75	OFFICE MACHNES,ADP EQUIP		81		60		379		23	MACH BUREAU TRAIT AUTOM
76	TELECOMM,SOUND EQUIPMENT		533		230		325		1584	EQUIPMENT DE TELECOM
77	ELECTRIC MACHNRY NES ETC		1476		592		389		854	MACH APP ELECT NDA
78	ROAD VEHICLES		190		172		428		742	VEHICULES ROUTIERS
79	OTHR TRANSPORT EQUIPMENT		119		434		424		756	AUTRE MATERIEL TRANSPORT
8	MISC MANUFACTURED GOODS		3920		4535		3618		3210	ART MANUFACTURES DIVERS
84	CLOTHING AND ACCESSORIES		3147		2880		2131		2170	VETEMENTS
89	MISC MANUFCTRD GOODS NES		719		1495		1448		978	ART MANUFACTURES DIVERS

1. HISTORICAL SERIES, 1960–1995 GENERAL TRADE, IMPORTS C.I.F., EXPORTS F.O.B. # 1
SERIES HISTORIQUES, 1960–1995 COMMERCE GENERAL, IMPORTATIONS C.A.F., EXPORTATIONS F.O.B

YEAR ANNEE	VALUE IN MILLION S. ARABIAN RIYAL / VALEUR EN MILLION S. ARABIAN RIYAL — MERCHANDISE –MARCHANDISE IMPORTS	EXPORTS	GOLD –OR IMPORTS	EXPORTS	CONVERSION FACTORS U.S. CENTS PER S. ARABIAN RIYAL FACTEURS DE CONVERSION CENTS E.U. PAR S. ARABIAN RIYAL IMPORTS	EXPORTS	INDEX NUMBERS –INDICES — QUANTUM IMPORTS	EXPORTS	UNIT VALUE VALEUR UNITAIRE IMPORTS	EXPORTS
1960	917.60	3802.50			24.4450	24.4450				
1961	1053.00	4095.00			22.2222	22.2222				
1962	1155.10	4392.00			22.2222	22.2222				
1963	1266.00	4797.00			22.2222	22.2222				
1964	1270.70	5400.00	72.90	28.00	22.2222	22.2222				
1965	1574.90	6268.50	103.40	2.00	22.2222	22.2222				
1966	2327.70	7850.00	70.30		22.2222	22.2222				
1967	2280.90	8093.30	66.10		22.2222	22.2222				
1968	2534.80	9117.20	52.50		22.2222	22.2222				
1969	3361.50	9003.10	71.90		22.2222	22.2222				
1970	3114.40	10906.50	82.40		22.2222	22.2222				
1971	3625.10	17304.00	42.40		22.2222	22.2222				
1972	4664.50	22757.80	43.80	3.00	24.1270	24.1270				
1973	7310.00	33309.00	46.10	13.00	27.1993	27.2929				
1974	10148.90	126223.00	0.30		28.1690	28.1690				
1975	14822.50	104412.00	0.60	1.00	28.4298	28.4220				
1976	30691.00	135153.00	0.20		28.3286	28.3286				
1977	51638.90	153209.00	23.10		28.3716	28.3699				
1978	69179.70	138242.00			29.5224	29.4530				
1979	82223.00	213183.00			29.7510	29.7525				
1980	100350.00	362886.00			30.1059	30.0677				
1981	119298.00	405481.00			29.5425	29.6537				
1982	139335.10	271090.20			29.1769	29.1872				
1983	135417.00	158443.90			28.9521	28.9283				
1984	118737.00	129794.40			28.3785	28.3785				
1985	85563.60	99535.80			27.6083	27.6083				
1986	70779.01	74750.00			26.9974	27.0054				
1987	75312.00	86880.00			26.7023	26.7023				
1988	81582.00	91290.00			26.7023	26.7023				
1989	79220.00	106290.00			26.7023	26.7023				
1990	90140.00	166340.00			26.7023	26.7023				
1991	108900.00	179000.00			26.7023	26.7023				
1992	124600.00	188300.00			26.7023	26.7023				
1993	105600.00	158770.00			26.7023	26.7023				
1994	87400.00	159590.00			26.7023	26.7023				
1995	105200.00				26.7023					

2. IMPORTS BY BROAD ECONOMIC CATEGORY AND EXPORTS BY INDUSTRIAL ORIGIN. (PERCENTAGE OF TOTAL VALUE)
IMPORTATIONS PAR CATEGORIES ECONOMIQUES ET EXPORTATIONS PAR BRANCHE D'ACTIVITE.(EN POURCENTAGE DE LA VALEUR TOTALE)

IMPORTS – IMPORTATIONS

	1990	1991	1992	1993	1994	1995	1996
TOTAL IMPORTS–IMPORTATIONS TOTALES	100.	100.	100.	100.	100.		
1 FOOD BEV–ALIMENTATION BOISSONS	13.0	11.8	10.0	9.6	11.5		
11 PRIMARY–PRODUITS DE BASE	6.9	6.4	6.6	6.2	7.8		
111 FOR INDUSTRY–POUR L'INDUSTRIE	2.8	2.3	3.7	2.9	4.0		
112 FOR HOUSEHOLDS–POUR LES MENAGES	4.1	4.1	2.9	3.3	3.8		
12 PROCESSED–PRODUITS ELABORES	6.1	5.5	3.3	3.4	3.8		
121 FOR INDUSTRY–POUR L'INDUSTRIE	0.3	0.4	0.3	0.3	0.5		
122 FOR HOUSEHOLDS–POUR LES MENAGES	5.7	5.1	3.0	3.1	3.3		
2 IND SUPPLIES–APPROV INDUSTRIELS	25.4	25.2	23.9	27.5	27.5		
21 PRIMARY–PRODUITS DE BASE	1.3	1.0	1.0	2.1	1.6		
22 PROCESSED–PRODUITS ELABORES	24.2	24.1	22.9	25.4	25.9		
3 FUELS–COMBUSTIBLES	0.3	0.2	0.1	0.2	0.2		
31 PRIMARY–PRODUITS DE BASE	0.0	0.0	0.0	0.0	0.0		
32 PROCESSED–PRODUITS ELABORES	0.2	0.2	0.1	0.1	0.2		
321 MOTOR SPIRIT–ESSENCE	0.0	0.0	0.0	0.0			
322 OTHER–AUTRES	0.2	0.2	0.1	0.1	0.2		
4 MACHINERY–EQUIPEMENT	15.0	17.3	18.9	18.9	19.3		
41 CAPITAL EQUIPMENT–MACHINES	10.5	13.7	14.7	15.2	15.4		
42 PARTS–PIECES ACCESSOIRES	4.6	3.6	4.2	3.7	3.8		
5 TRANSPORT–TRANSPORT	24.2	24.7	27.7	23.7	22.1		
51 PASSENGER CARS–AUTOMOBILES	6.4	7.1	6.9	6.2	7.3		
52 OTHER–AUTRES	3.6	4.6	3.5	2.7	3.3		
521 INDUSTRIAL–INDUSTRIELS	3.5	4.5	3.4	2.6	3.2		
522 NON INDUSTRIAL–NON INDUSTRIEL	0.1	0.1	0.1	0.1	0.1		
53 PARTS–PIECES ACCESSOIRES	14.2	13.1	17.3	14.8	11.5		
6 CONSUM GOODS–BIENS CONSOMMATION	21.7	20.2	18.3	18.8	17.0		
61 DURABLE–DURABLES	6.6	6.3	5.9	6.1	5.4		
62 SEMI DURABLE–SEMI DURABLES	9.1	8.8	7.9	8.3	7.4		
63 NON DURABLE–NON DURABLES	6.1	5.1	4.5	4.4	4.1		
7 GOODS NES–BIENS NDA	0.4	0.5	1.1	1.2	2.5		

EXPORTS – EXPORTATIONS

	1990	1991	1992	1993	1994	1995	1996
TOTAL EXPORTS–EXPORTATIONS TOTALES	100.	100.	100.	100.			
1 AGRICULTURE	0.6	0.5	0.5	0.7			
2 MINING QUARRY–INDUS EXTRACTIVES	78.7	82.2	83.1	80.4			
3 MANUFACTURING–IND MANUFACTUR	20.7	17.3	16.3	19.0			
31 FOOD BEV TOBACCO–ALIM BOISS TAB	0.3	0.5	0.4	0.4			
32 TEXTILES–INDUSTRIES TEXTILES	0.2	0.2	0.1	0.1			
33 WOOD & PRODUCTS–BOIS & PRODUITS	0.0	0.1	0.0	0.0			
34 PAPER & PRODUCTS–PAPIER & PRODT	0.2	0.2	0.1	0.2			
35 CHEMICALS–INDUSTRIES CHIMIQUES	17.6	14.4	14.1	16.3			
36 NON METAL MIN–MIN NON METAL	0.2	0.2	0.2	0.2			
37 BASIC METAL–IND METAL BASE	0.5	0.3	0.2	0.2			
38 METAL MANUF–MANUF METAL	1.6	1.4	1.1	1.4			
39 OTH MANUF IND–AUTRES MANUF	0.2	0.0	0.1	0.1			

3. TRADE BY PRINCIPAL COUNTRIES OF ORIGIN AND LAST DESTINATION (VALUE IN THOUSAND U.S. DOLLARS)
ECHANGES SELON LES PRINCIPAUX PAYS D'ORIGINE ET DE DERNIERE DESTINATION (VALEUR EN MILLIERS DE DOLLARS EU)

COUNTRIES–PAYS	GENERAL IMPORTS C.I.F. IMPORTATIONS GENERALES C.A.F				
	1990	1991	1992	1993	1994
World	24069057	29073801	33254321	28201434	23342633
Africa	469379	516274	604149	656439	618914
Americas	4573851	6721631	8311986	6792596	5777713
Northern America	4187501	6146328	7778929	6119793	5374826
LAIA	346940	537380	493123	649282	387701
CACM	35955	33942	31774	21450	14751
Caribbean	3382	1044	5263	1909	435
Rest of America	72	2938	2898	161	
As.ex F.USSR	7934238	8942476	10138165	9061718	7331367
Eur.x F.USSR	10457883	12369995	13715629	11254408	9225624
EU	8647903	10687099	11966878	10038524	8097966
EFTA	1593107	1446555	1555909	1071112	996167
East Europe	177255	195947	144680	130933	116126
Other Europe	39618	40394	4451	2474	5762
Former USSR	47619	62286	60860	44297	28148
Oceania	372628	369929	328154	296120	265097
USA/Etats–Unis d'Amer	4017333	5875501	7494168	5801510	4981851
Japan/Japon	3684622	3982588	4696806	3558482	2742417
United Kingdom	2713352	3275458	3580808	3111496	1975936
Germany/Allemagne	1769436	2274923	2469153	1977436	1934955
Italy/Italie	1110989	1342704	1649119	1427289	1099179
Switz.Liecht	1578758	1410394	1520407	1043283	970480
France,Monac	948567	1165846	1601370	1161284	1016355
Korea, Republic of	786612	859762	888987	752788	661403
China/Chine	440757	626190	706291	629508	503524
Belgium–Luxembourg	417741	553946	621214	539471	454685
Netherlands/Pays–Bas	538531	560941	527007	486631	406033
Turkey/Turquie	294306	351456	358912	610214	460934
India/Inde	258323	290512	410584	514831	421314
Sweden/Suède	309465	382597	415449	391145	339864
Brazil/Brésil	250800	382836	349190	491853	274193
Spain/Espagne	259303	369756	386785	328282	353385
Indonesia/Indonésie	209327	308078	349774	348907	265197
Canada	170168	270818	284695	318244	392870
Thailand/Thaïlande	268940	315553	326545	276933	204147
United Arab Emirates	162016	215182	260977	281652	297651
Australia/Australie	286839	279518	203297	166175	202480
Egypt/Egypte	96684	147082	246628	284023	216625
Malaysia/Malaisie	125964	185283	220122	191762	193626
Singapore/Singapour	186347	226982	227160	161831	112006
Austria/Autriche	114263	197890	229591	176687	132343
Syrian Arab Republic	149071	249728	136699	119844	130574
Denmark/Danemark	181907	211499	139243	121079	122091
Pakistan	101082	158482	182776	187394	106926
Bahrain/Bahreïn	105449	104202	131056	158180	168228
Hong Kong	122366	133545	156437	147414	79359
Ireland/Irlande	109676	132238	138821	99565	82105
Lebanon/Liban	88186	122050	109625	108939	103682
New Zealand	85620	90219	124831	129934	62420
Morocco/Maroc	119602	144177	90171	53375	61853
Greece/Grèce	90000	102427	90377	96362	64700
Finland/Finlande	66273	96785	86570	94069	90418
Zambia/Zambie	84966	63093	72228	85593	116805
Jordan/Jordanie	85331	13509	97227	107532	78459
Qatar	51767	56205	98972	83451	69500
Kuwait/ Koweït	74442	5430	42714	71103	79480
Sudan/Soudan	43485	33536	65342	74900	55816
Somalia/Somalie	37781	27241	54622	66246	77483
Philippines	41118	39481	38764	52409	58102
Chile/Chili	37866	42305	29491	43371	36481
So. Africa Customs Un	36624	36657	22832	36344	53561
Oman	34889	26759	34567	38155	43818
Czechoslovakia	41055	81133	48981		
Sri Lanka	43566	42170	20595	30781	17306
Poland/Pologne	33754	39194	18297	30472	27765
Colombia/Colombie	9516	34293	36344	35612	24164

COUNTRIES–PAYS	GENERAL EXPORTS F.O.B. EXPORTATIONS GENERALES F.O.B.				
	1990	1991	1992	1993	1994
Monde	44416405	47790210	50287202	42395280	42614076
Afrique	464802	471711	554345	380716	1097553
Amériques	12562533	12688278	12586368	9079139	9575228
Amérique du Nord	11080322	11355125	11146043	7750426	8244156
ALAI	1482212	1333153	1440325	1328713	1328276
MCAC					
Caraïbes					2797
Autre Amérique					
Asie l'URSS exclus	20844086	20776864	22100048	19753528	20554116
Europe l'URSS exclus	8482706	10471871	11229855	9752374	9733243
UE	8163077	10138336	11079337	9748804	9626116
AELE					7256
Europe de l'Est	319629	333535	150518	3570	361
Autre de l'Europe					98826
Ancienne URSS					2043
Océanie	427347	609963	541212	504299	458398
USA/Etats–Unis d'Amer	11080322	11355125	11146043	7750426	7881854
Japan/Japon					6801141
Korea, Republic of					3471001
Australia/Australie	427347	609963	541212	504299	385238
France,Monac					2261964
Italy/Italie					2174063
Singapore/Singapour					2065486
Germany/Allemagne					2052021
Bahrain/Bahreïn					1339748
Brazil/Brésil					1311426
India/Inde					1251172
Turkey/Turquie					1214796
United Arab Emirates					953113
United Kingdom					840604
Philippines					711922
Spain/Espagne					571698
Austria/Autriche					571090
Greece/Grèce					557624
Indonesia/Indonésie					489406
Pakistan					465624
Morocco/Maroc					446935
Kuwait/ Koweït					392384
Canada					362302
Sweden/Suède					285069
Thailand/Thaïlande					231666
Iran (Islamic Rp. of)					207216
Portugal					202188
Hong Kong					136956
China/Chine					120352
Malaysia/Malaisie					104784
Netherlands/Pays–Bas					102203
Qatar					101796
Jordan/Jordanie					99456
Sudan/Soudan					95087
Bangladesh					87837
Nigeria/Nigéria					84451
Un. Rep. of Tanzania					84175
Oman					81744
Malta/Malte					74323
New Zealand					73161
Yemen/Yémen					62381
Mozambique					58447
Kenya					54580
Egypt/Egypte					52962
Syrian Arab Republic					51193
Ethiopia/Ethiopie					45874
Lebanon/Liban					44537
Sri Lanka					35342
So. Africa Customs Un					32742
Eritrea/Erythrée					30350

(VALUE AS PERCENTAGE OF WORLD TOTAL)(VALEURS EN POURCENTAGE DU TOTAL MONDIAL)

	1985	1986	1987	1988	1989	1990	1991	1992	1993	1994
Africa	1.3	1.4	1.4	1.7	1.3	2.0	1.8	1.8	2.3	2.7
Americas	19.1	19.6	17.6	18.8	20.8	19.0	23.1	25.0	24.1	24.8
Northern America	17.4	18.1	16.1	16.9	19.2	17.4	21.1	23.4	21.7	23.0
LAIA	1.4	1.2	1.2	1.7	1.5	1.4	1.8	1.5	2.3	1.7
CACM	0.3	0.3	0.3	0.2	0.1	0.1	0.1	0.1	0.1	0.1
Caribbean	0.0	0.0	0.0	0.0	0.0	0.0	0.0	0.0	0.0	0.0
Rest of America	0.0	0.0	0.0	0.0	0.0	0.0	0.0	0.0	0.0	
As.ex F.USSR	36.3	35.4	38.7	37.8	35.2	33.0	30.8	30.5	32.1	31.4
Eur.x F.USSR	40.8	41.1	40.2	39.6	41.0	43.4	42.5	41.2	39.9	39.5
EU	37.7	38.2	36.9	35.9	34.7	35.9	36.8	36.0	35.6	34.7
EFTA	2.4	2.1	2.6	2.4	5.1	6.6	5.0	4.7	3.8	4.3
East Europe	0.6	0.5	0.5	0.8	1.0	0.7	0.7	0.4	0.5	0.5
Other Europe	0.2	0.2	0.2	0.4	0.2	0.2	0.1	0.0	0.0	0.0
Former USSR	0.1	0.1	0.1	0.1	0.1	0.2	0.2	0.2	0.2	0.1
Oceania	2.0	1.9	1.6	1.4	1.2	1.5	1.3	1.0	1.1	1.1
USA/Etats–Unis d'Amer	17.0	17.5	15.3	16.2	18.2	16.7	20.2	22.5	20.6	21.3
Japan/Japon	19.0	15.7	17.3	16.0	14.2	15.3	13.7	14.1	12.6	11.7
United Kingdom	6.2	7.3	7.8	7.3	10.2	11.3	11.3	10.8	11.0	8.5
Germany/Allemagne	8.4	8.1	7.7	7.2	6.3	7.4	7.8	7.4	7.0	8.3
Italy/Italie	7.8	7.3	6.8	6.5	5.7	4.6	4.6	5.0	5.1	4.7
Switz.Liecht	2.3	2.0	2.5	2.3	5.0	6.6	4.9	4.6	3.7	4.2
France,Monac	5.1	5.6	5.3	5.2	4.3	3.9	4.0	4.8	4.1	4.4
Korea, Republic of	3.7	4.1	4.9	4.7	4.0	3.3	3.0	2.7	2.7	2.8
China/Chine	0.9	1.2	1.6	1.8	1.9	1.8	2.2	2.1	2.2	2.2
Belgium–Luxembourg	1.6	1.8	1.7	1.9	1.5	1.7	1.9	1.9	1.9	1.9

	1985	1986	1987	1988	1989	1990	1991	1992	1993	1994
Afrique						1.0	1.0	1.1	0.9	2.6
Amériques		19.7	23.3			28.3	26.5	25.0	21.4	22.5
Amérique du Nord		17.3	19.9			24.9	23.8	22.2	18.3	19.3
ALAI		2.4	3.4			3.3	2.8	2.9	3.1	3.1
MCAC										
Caraïbes										0.0
Autre Amérique										
Asie l'URSS exclus		23.6	25.7			46.9	43.5	43.9	46.6	48.2
Europe l'URSS exclus		33.0	20.4			19.1	21.9	22.3	23.0	22.8
UE		33.0	19.2			18.4	21.2	22.0	23.0	22.6
AELE										0.0
Europe de l'Est			1.2			0.7	0.7	0.3	0.0	0.0
Autre de l'Europe										0.2
Ancienne URSS		1.3								0.0
Océanie						1.0	1.3	1.1	1.2	1.1
USA/Etats–Unis d'Amer		17.3	19.9			24.9	23.8	22.2	18.3	18.5
Japan/Japon		14.4	15.1							16.0
Korea, Republic of		1.6	2.2							8.1
Australia/Australie						1.0	1.3	1.1	1.2	0.9
France,Monac		6.8	3.2							5.3
Italy/Italie		7.1	3.0							5.1
Singapore/Singapour		1.2	2.6							4.8
Germany/Allemagne		3.4	1.6							4.8
Bahrain/Bahreïn		4.7	4.9							3.1
Brazil/Brésil		2.4	3.4							3.1

4. General Imports C.I.F. by Commodities according to the S.I.T.C. (Rev. 2) in thousand U.S. Dollars
Importations Générales C.A.F. par Produits d'après la C.T.C.I. (Rév. 2) en milliers de Dollars E.U.

SITC CTCI	COMMODITY	1991 WEIGHT POIDS	1991 VALUE VALEUR	1992 WEIGHT POIDS	1992 VALUE VALEUR	1993 WEIGHT POIDS	1993 VALUE VALEUR	1994 WEIGHT POIDS	1994 VALUE VALEUR	PRODUIT
	ALL COMMODITIES		29073801		33254321		28201434		23342633	TOUS PRODUITS
0	FOOD AND LIVE ANIMALS		3188993		3171604		2732772		2694686	ALIMENTS,ANIMAUX VIVANTS
001	*LIVE ANIMALS FOR FOOD	W 216734	452291	W 181268	385102	W 250213	457519	W 211679	365864	ANIMAUX VIVANTS
0012	SHEEP AND GOATS,LIVE	W 203222	415118	W 167341	346835	W 234795	423145	W 196162	332433	ESPECES OVINE ET CAPRINE
00121	SHEEP,LIVE	W 191200	386411	W 148312	312994	W 209245	379661	W 171429	300018	ESPECE OVINE
01	MEAT AND PREPARATIONS		522405		376775		318372		297763	VIANDES ET PREPARATIONS
011	MEAT FRESH,CHILLD,FROZEN	W 330839	490633	W 262267	367291	W 221524	306647	W 202234	288809	VIANDES FRAICHES,REF,CONGE
0111	BOVINE MEAT FRESH,FROZEN	W 47474	88489	W 49676	72383	W 18575	33476	W 21530	39125	VIANDES BOVIN FRAI,REF
0112	MUTTON ETC FRSH,CHLD,FRN	W 32466	59475	W 34587	67494	W 32831	66075	W 38021	77906	VIANDE DE MOUTON
0114	POULTRY FRESH CHLLD,FRZN	W 245728	335783	W 174434	222268	W 168440	204813	W 140576	168805	VOLAILLES MORTES
02	DAIRY PRODCTS,BIRDS'EGGS		507712		206564		180508		174325	PRODUITS LAITIERS,OEUFS
022	MILK AND CREAM	W 146735	283467	W 62632	118159	W 50946	98488	W 51891	92000	LAIT ET CREME
0224	MILK,CREAM PRESERVED ETC	W 99145	221489	W 45776	96919	W 45750	92505	W 45993	84219	LAIT,CREME CONS,CONC
02243	MILK DRY,OVER 1.5% FAT	W 56218	142547	W 19563	52191	W 13373	39074	W 13385	36966	LAIT POUDRE SUP 1.5%
024	CHEESE AND CURD	W 61775	164868	W 21563	61578	W 18499	58465	W 21148	61084	FROMAGE ET CAILLEBOTTE
04	CEREALS AND PREPARATIONS		453822		1166668		792684		886925	CEREALES ET PRODUITS
042	RICE	W 253610	147067	W 490031	295788	W 576502	310178	W 433562	228593	RIZ
0422	RICE SEMI-MILLED,MILLED	W 253610	147067	W 489475	295560	W 576502	310178	W 433562	228593	RIZ POLI,GLACE INCL BRISURES
04221	RICE MILLED UNBROKEN	W 253610	147067	W 489475	295560	W 576502	310178	W 433562	228593	RIZ POLI,GLACE EXCL BRISURES
043	BARLEY UNMILLED	W 478810	67376	W 5845479	686687	W 1908381	233218	W 5140264	496650	ORGE NON MONDEE
044	MAIZE UNMILLED	W 99589	16705	W 351501	51231	W 1195406	168241	W 580513	83910	MAIS NON MOULU
048	CEREAL ETC PREPARATIONS	W 114731	167768	W 92091	92498	W 81255	67699	W 92064	71000	PREPTNS A BASE CEREALES
05	VEGETABLES AND FRUIT		610470		509104		557590		541740	LEGUMES ET FRUITS
054	VEG ETC FRSH,SMPLY PRSVD	W 564961	178483	W 636332	162257	W 632563	166175	W 566688	154178	LEGUMES FRAIS,CONG,SECS
057	FRUIT,NUTS,FRESH,DRIED	W 668529	260098	W 702145	249924	W 791629	314633	W 822662	314720	FRUITS FRAIS OU SECS
0571	ORANGES, MANDARINS ETC	W 232004	64906	W 247256	74570	W 285241	94907	W 297456	94729	ORANGES,MAND,CLEMENTINES
05711	ORANGES,FRESH OR DRIED	W 192352	54212	W 209175	63644	W 239638	80279	W 250430	80450	ORANGES FRAICHES,SECHEES
058	FRUIT PRESERVED,PREPARED	W 97180	116657	W 55774	64179	W 48625	53664	W 49112	50801	CONSERVES DE FRUITS
06	SUGAR AND PREPS,HONEY		78028		111099		76382		80966	SUCRES ET PRODUITS
07	COFFEE,TEA,COCOA,SPICES		268541		171071		134645		111753	CAFE,THE,CACAO,EPICES
081	*FEEDING STUFF FOR ANIML	W 80088	41210	W 240690	83642	W 212658	74326	W 352733	103744	NOURRITURE POUR ANIMAUX
0813	OILCAKE AND OTH RESIDUES	W 30421	7227	W 157066	41731	W 160513	41244	W 281717	71784	TOURTEAUX
08131	— OF SOYA BEANS	W 25913	6019	W 151474	40398	W 157650	40609	W 279717	71405	TOURTEAUX DE SOJA
09	MISC EDIBLE PRODUCTS		179145		110659		96235		86622	PREP ALIMENTAIRES DIVERSES
098	EDIBLE PRODCTS,PREPS NES	W 91369	173212	W 43495	108201	W 36127	94208	W 40580	84966	PREP ALIMENTAIRES NDA
09809	MISC FOOD PREPRTIONS NES	W 19159	90434	W 14529	79464	W 11904	68594	W 18310	58071	PREP ALIMENTAIRES NDA
1	BEVERAGES AND TOBACCO		388802		111512		63348		116860	BOISSONS ET TABACS
12	TOBACCO AND MANUFACTURES		345814		99530		56700		106603	TABACS BRUTS FABRIQUES
122	TOBACCO,MANUFACTURED	W 35829	344141	W 19513	98518	W 11129	55818	W 8485	106131	TABACS FABRIQUES
1222	CIGARETTES	W 19370	327611	W 5800	88036	W 2994	47639	W 4931	101966	CIGARETTES
2	CRUDE MATERLS,EXCL FUELS		512981		584859		756654		520818	MAT BRUTES NON COMESTIBLES
22	OIL SEEDS,OLEAGINOUS FRT		30465		33472		84729		11403	GRAINES,FRUITS OLEAGINEUX
24	CORK AND WOOD		159519		184564		191823		150707	LIEGE ET BOIS
248	WOOD SHAPED,SLEEPERS	W 310215	130749	W 355810	151997	W 345303	149499	W 315028	123709	BOIS SIMPLEMENT TRAVAILLES
2483	LUMBER SHAPED NON-CONIFR	W 156441	62323	W 177402	74668	W 149506	66193	W 195270	73935	NON CONIFERES SCIES,RABOTES
24831	LUMBER SAWN ETC NON-CON	W 148133	58927	W 175194	70929	W 146825	62806	W 191369	70142	SCIES LONGITUDINALEMENT
26	TEXTILE FIBRES AND WASTE		78287		124561		85984		78247	FIBRES TEXTILES
28	METALLIFEROUS ORES,SCRAP		155134		142014		294146		172546	MINERAIS METAL,DECHETS
281	IRON ORE,CONCENTRATES	W 1099844	67292	W 2170393	108775	W 2760457	255350	W 3277315	121144	MINERAIS DE FER
2815	IRON ORE,CONC,NOT AGGLOM	W 613123	33495	W 2036194	96940	W 2760377	255111	W 2902534	107665	MINERAIS NON AGGLOMERES
4	ANIMAL,VEGETABLE OIL,FAT		124234		142764		103409		119699	HUILES,GRAISSES ANIM,VEG
42	FIXED VEGETABLE OIL,FAT		114345		131803		96496		110797	HUILES VEGETALES FIXES
424	FIXED VEG OIL NONSOFT	W 150293	94200	W 184193	112907	W 142102	83836	W 130123	101943	AUTRES HUILES VEG FIXES
5	CHEMCLS,RELATED PROD NES		2424515		2479466		2275030		1920290	PRODUITS CHIMIQUES
51	ORGANIC CHEMICALS		190400		168289		182979		200747	PROD CHIMIQ ORGANIQUES
511	HYDROCARBONS NES,DERIVS	W 102465	89632	W 72668	68152	W 67494	66482	W 61820	58515	HYDROCARBURES NDA
52	INORGANIC CHEMICALS		242621		216474		178948		203943	PROD CHIM INORGANIQUES
522	INORG ELEMNTS,OXIDES,ETC	W 496478	140962	W 420936	111590	W 308797	81854	W 341666	93749	ELEMENTS INORGANIQUES
5222	INORGANIC ACIDS ETC	W 454604	98435	W 390750	69958	W 275464	50879	W 304849	56180	ACIDES INORGANIQUES
52224	PHOSPHORIC ACIDS ETC	W 447079	94411	W 379697	65078	W 265124	43712	W 294193	50057	ACIDES PHOSPHORIQUES
523	OTHR INORG CHEMICALS ETC	W 188750	97784	W 184407	99345	W 214228	91302	W 222251	93518	AUT PRODUITS CHIMIQUES INORG
53	DYES,TANNING,COLOUR PROD		88967		110034		98583		87314	PROD TEINTURE,COLORANTS
533	PIGMENTS,PAINTS,ETC	W 43127	77293	W 50182	95739	W 47389	84361	W 38092	72865	PIGMENTS,PEINTURES,VERNIS
541	*MEDICINAL,PHARM PRODUCT	MK 27112	622688	MK 27355	844702	MK 22248	733024		528714	PROD MEDICINAUX PHARMACEUT
5417	MEDICAMENTS	MK 22733	550230	MK 21522	768852	MK 16823	629280	MK 12180	453653	MEDICAMENTS
54171	— CONTAINNG ANTIBIOTICS	MK 13133	389229	MK 11932	466111	K 5361000	308444	K 3435000	216315	MED CONTN ANTIBIOTIQUES
54172	— CONTAINING HORMONES	K 3902188	63469	K 4435000	203804	K 5924000	172076	K 3362000	114934	MED CONTENANT HORMONES
54179	— CONTNG OTH SUBSTANCES	K 5659578	95576	K 4957000	92241	K 5533000	147456	K 5257000	121053	MED CONT AUT SUBSTANCES
55	PERFUME,CLEANING ETC PRD		326368		343926		305668		249013	PROD POUR PARFUM,TOILETTE
553	PERFUMERY,COSMETICS,ETC	W 41787	244579	W 37423	251618	W 35708	207470	W 23808	154991	PRODUITS DE PARFUMERIE
554	SOAP,CLEANSING ETC PREPS	W 41017	60624	W 46824	67524	W 55657	74145	W 62080	70770	SAVONS,PRODUITS DETERSIFS
562	*FERTILIZERS,MANUFACTURE	W 685079	108577	W 285646	79433	W 225799	53230	W 29192	13317	ENGRAIS MANUFACTURES
58	PLASTIC MATERIALS ETC		356962		317151		330708		329971	MAT PLAST ARTIFICIELLES
583	POLYMERIZATION ETC PRODS	W 198586	309515	W 179599	267519	W 211444	277837	W 221107	279153	PROD POLYMERISATION
5831	POLYETHYLENE	W 74489	102693	W 67561	79934	W 65935	71460	W 66544	74219	POLYETHYLENE
5839	OTH POLYMRZTION ETC PROD	W 49512	86898	W 50441	89657	W 63453	97090	W 56500	94883	AUT PROD POLYMER COPOLYM
59	CHEMICAL MATERIALS NES		426525		393254		383046		301800	MAT PROD CHIMIQUES NDA
591	PESTICIDES,DISINFECTANTS	W 22366	104350	W 19624	85958	W 15047	67219	W 11686	37797	DESINF,INSECT,FONG,HERB
598	MISCEL CHEM PRODUCTS NES	W 125019	275776	W 112980	262532	W 110968	276498	W 101172	230849	PROD DIV INDUST CHIM NDA
5989	CHEM PRODUCTS,PREPS NES	W 94687	187199	W 86173	190585	W 78094	190796	W 70039	158153	PROD PREP CHIMIQUES NDA
59899	OTH CHEM PRODS,PREPS,NES	W 54180	113071	W 57253	127791	W 53990	135677	W 48057	113621	AUT PRODUITS CHIMIQUES NDA
6	BASIC MANUFACTURES		5829404		6398230		6085128		4819643	ART MANUFACTURES
62	RUBBER MANUFACTURES NES		521433		454715		451639		352010	CAOUTCHOUC MANUFACTURE
625	RUBBER TYRES, TUBES ETC	W 156152	439319	W 136468	381320	W 136923	383839	W 105677	297227	PNEUS CAOUTCHOUC VULCANISE
6251	TYRES NEW FOR MOTOR CARS	W 60412	166817	W 44130	128013	W 48014	139615	W 35690	107600	PNEUS POUR VOITURES
6252	TYRES,NEW,BUS OR LORRY	W 77060	217963	W 72424	199231	W 67246	194077	W 54212	149010	PNEUS POUR AUTOBUS,CAMIONS
63	WOOD,CORK MANUFACTRS NES		335403		360381		314402		239438	OUVRAGES LIEGE ET BOIS
634	VENEERS,PLYWOOD,ETC	W 368131	208591	W 506700	224694	W 409775	246923	W 368224	196494	PLACAGES,CONTRE-PLAQUES
6341	VENEER SHEETS ETC	W 138105	69365	W 161688	71689	W 148086	75334	W 173897	85935	BOIS SIMPLEMENT SCIES
6342	PLYWOOD OF WOOD SHEETS	W 162295	99920	W 294185	124749	W 216772	143798	W 116495	74602	BOIS CONTRE-PLAQUES
635	WOOD MANUFACTURES NES	W 54863	125437	W 37399	134344	W 25668	67018	W 23627	42570	ART MANUF EN BOIS NDA
6353	BUILDERS WOODWRK,PREFABS	W 44554	111783	W 28788	116864	W 17928	53358	W 18966	32817	OUVRAGES DE MENUISERIE
64	PAPER,PAPERBOARD AND MFR		461120		463784		518677		517113	PAPIERS,CARTONS & OUVRAGES
641	PAPER AND PAPERBOARD	W 336635	353312	W 377662	338948	W 536783	396626	W 564010	402049	PAPIERS ET CARTONS
6413	KRAFT PAPER,PAPERBOARD	W 77689	54552	W 96722	59733	W 154522	75396	W 166089	89020	PAPIER ET CARTON KRAFT
6417	CORRUGATED PAPER ETC,BLK	W 78986	94378	W 68575	72766	W 93756	85497	W 99073	85903	PAPIERS,CARTONS ONDULES
642	PAPER,ETC,PRECUT,ARTS OF	W 64275	107807	W 74717	124836	W 75470	122051	W 79321	115064	PAP,CARTONS DECOUPES
65	TEXTILE YARN,FABRICS,ETC		1429863		1530604		1343878		1042442	FILS,TISSUS,ARTICLES TEXTILE
651	TEXTILE YARN	W 26983	88176	W 24844	92207	W 29388	97975	W 30701	98633	FILS TEXTILES
653	WOVN MAN-MADE FIB FABRIC	W 53268	582405	W 54978	621813	W 45744	507598	W 38603	416926	TISSUS FIBRES SYNTH,ARTIF
6531	CONT SYNT WEAVES NONPILE	W 23771	248665	W 16917	199901	W 17080	183182	W 11261	127295	TISSUS FIBRES SYNTH CONTINUE

4. General Imports C.I.F. by Commodities according to the S.I.T.C. (Rev. 2) in thousand U.S. Dollars
Importations Générales C.A.F. par Produits d'après la C.T.C.I. (Rév. 2) en milliers de Dollars E.U.

SITC CTCI	COMMODITY	1991 WEIGHT POIDS	1991 VALUE VALEUR	1992 WEIGHT POIDS	1992 VALUE VALEUR	1993 WEIGHT POIDS	1993 VALUE VALEUR	1994 WEIGHT POIDS	1994 VALUE VALEUR	PRODUIT
65315	CONT SYN TXTL FABRIC NES	W 23165	243131	W 16181	195114	W 16396	177796	W 10502	120335	TIS PLUS 85% TEXT SYNT CONT
6532	DISC SYN TXTL FABRIC NES	W 17540	186176	W 29619	305578	W 22890	255083	W 20560	221316	TIS DISC MOINS 85% FIBR TEXT
6534	DISC SYN BLEND FABRC NES	W 8496	112912	W 5327	82331	W 2360	30642	W 2756	29697	TISSUS FIBRES SYNTH DISCONT
655	KNITTED,ETC FABRICS	W 7189	75370	W 10976	113121	W 13225	99425	W 12252	95113	ETOF BONNETERIE PIECES ETC
6552	OTHER KNIT ETC FAB NONEL	W 7189	75370	W 10976	113121	W 13225	99425	W 12252	95113	ETOF BON NON ELAS NON SYNT
658	TEXTILE ARTICLES NES	W 68936	231908	W 57592	224527	W 58124	210286	W 32195	113672	ART FACONNES MAT TEXTILES
6583	BLANKETS ETC NON ELECTRC	W 17443	75954	W 17756	87067	W 20405	93245	W 14117	53651	COUVERTURES
659	FLOOR COVERINGS,ETC	W 89777	272434	W 77657	265689	W 64454	221166	W 41138	142810	COUVRE-PARQUETS,TAPIS ETC
6595	MAN-MADE TXTL CARPTS NES	W 71731	205695	W 57873	185796	W 50400	158932	W 29180	93766	TAPIS MAT TEXT SYNT ARTIF
65952	— WOVEN	W 49936	142898	W 43395	137221	W 40055	124282	W 24251	74394	TAPIS MAT TEXT SYNT TISSES
66	NONMETAL MINERAL MFS NES		487642		616725		626988		514426	ART MIN NON METALLIQUES
661	LIME,CEMENT,BLDG PRODS	W 460697	176472	W 576444	228599	W 2657282	262419	W 2357888	203858	CHAUX,CIMENTS MAT CONSTR
6612	CEMENT	W 189482	14234	W 254785	18430	W 2220078	106427	W 2002413	99944	CIMENTS HYDRAULIQUES
6613	BUILDING STONE ETC WORKD	W 257963	153540	W 307592	198330	W 420393	144487	W 335925	95394	PIERRES A BATIR
66132	BUILDING STONE WORKED	W 109982	66643	W 158869	117731	W 162459	84550	W 122317	55884	OUVR EN PIERRES DE TAILLE
662	CLAY,REFRACTORY BLDG PRD	W 154006	74957	W 185432	95551	W 250995	99791	W 254107	91290	MAT CONST REFRACTAIRES
664	GLASS	W 77726	95989	W 80579	101075	W 94861	103365	W 90466	86200	VERRE
67	IRON AND STEEL		1273816		1457497		1405026		918570	FER ET ACIER
672	IRON,STEEL PRIMARY FORMS	W 422325	247632	W 454433	233276	W 1495532	503718	W 605679	241524	LINGOTS FER,ACIER
6724	IRN,STL INGOTS,LUMPS,ETC	W 12301	4329	W 47818	15577	W 834504	208517	W 171424	49333	FER,ACIER LINGOTS,MASSES
67243	STNLESS STEEL ETC INGOTS	W 10209	2943	W 45149	13810	W 832022	206569	W 139095	39080	LINGOTS ACIER INOXYDABLE
6727	IRN,STL COIL FR REROLLNG	W 403578	237727	W 403010	213264	W 650406	286861	W 426819	187783	EBAUCHES POUR TOLES FER
67271	IRON,SIMPLE STEEL COILS	W 375138	218207	W 383271	199517	W 561313	245178	W 393200	171971	EBAUCHES NON EN ACIER
673	IRON,STEEL SHAPES ETC	W 354425	184730	W 524750	232225	W 705380	255201	W 498411	194530	BARRES,PROFIL FER,ACIER
6732	IRON,STEEL BARS ETC	W 115230	52438	W 281700	113851	W 397234	132908	W 205778	75161	BARRES FER,ACIER
6733	IRON,STEEL PROFILES ETC	W 231001	127378	W 214598	107160	W 289431	114457	W 249584	103417	PROFILES,PALPLAN FER,ACIER
674	IRN,STL UNIV,PLATE,SHEET	W 343050	216027	W 359974	243101	W 436538	241555	W 349632	208818	LARGES PLATS,TOLES
6749	OTH IRN,STL PLATES,SHEET	W 106675	63731	W 139251	85884	W 200846	115200	W 168647	100706	AUTRES TOLES FER,ACIER
67491	— OF IRON OR SIMPLE STL	W 89328	53960	W 123733	77261	W 177128	99900	W 142630	85696	AUT TOLES AUTRES ACIER FIN
678	IRON,STL TUBES,PIPES,ETC	W 485964	513458	W 518693	670156	W 303703	311762	W 175788	210740	TUBES,TUYAUX EN FONTE,FER
6782	IRON,STL SEAMLESS TUBES	W 264969	230552	W 161901	195151	W 109230	76545	W 68255	51359	TUBES,TUYAUX SANS SOUDURE
6783	IRON,STL TUBES,PIPES NES	W 158671	148221	W 275169	274329	W 110156	103601	W 79040	68963	AUT TUBES,TUYAUX FER,ACIER
6785	IRON,STEEL TUBE FITTINGS	W 38535	114289	W 64783	184573	W 68526	118665	W 22060	81359	ACCESSOIRES DE TUYAUTERIE
68	NON-FERROUS METALS		487685		518011		589715		603680	METAUX NON FERREUX
682	COPPER EXC CEMENT COPPER	W 71274	193707	W 92865	260786	W 98479	235664	W 124701	291293	CUIVRE
6821	COPPER NES,ALLOYS,UNWRT	W 51336	119388	W 57962	138942	W 58443	117495	W 88749	196951	CUIVRE BRUT
68212	COPPER REFINED,UNWROUGHT	W 51183	118876	W 57903	138668	W 58001	115966	W 88749	196951	CUIVRE AFFINE BRUT
6822	COPPER,ALLOYS WORKED	W 19938	74319	W 34903	121844	W 40036	118169	W 35952	94342	CUIVRE,ALLIAGES OUVRES
684	ALUMINIUM	W 99262	263651	W 101281	228814	W 249571	325969	W 190304	279577	ALUMINIUM
6842	ALUMINIUM,ALLOYS WORKED	W 83066	232226	W 96630	218649	W 243535	316422	W 139899	273604	ALUMINIUM,ALLIAGES OUVRE
68421	ALUMINIUM BARS,WIRE,ETC	W 30449	62611	W 51568	95693	W 65540	109797	W 77794	133889	BARRES,PROFILES FILS ALU
68422	ALUMNM PLATE,SHEET,STRIP	W 42508	133617	W 35336	94413	W 159146	175078	W 48750	104225	TOLES, PLANCHES EN ALU
69	METAL MANUFACTURES NES		818960		983283		821431		621983	ART MANUFACT EN METAL NDA
691	STRUCTURES AND PARTS NES	W 84185	129963	W 109377	182541	W 89817	137083	W 59236	85264	CONSTRUCT FER,ACIER,ALU
6911	STRUCTURES,PARTS IRN,STL	W 80120	108931	W 105733	162505	W 86786	122933	W 57420	75327	CONSTRUCT FER,ACIER,FONTE
697	BASE MTL HOUSEHOLD EQUIP	W 44625	205876	W 51623	216656	W 44810	175129	W 30242	128938	ART MENAGE MET COMMUNS
699	BASE METAL MFRS NES	W 71700	232751	W 90624	266539	W 83569	238368	W 64395	195750	ART MANUFACTURES MET NDA
6991	LOCKSMITHS WARES,ETC	W 21189	97170	W 24402	110004	W 24101	100958	W 20889	86921	ARTICLES DE SERRURERIE
7	MACHINES,TRANSPORT EQUIP		11740418		15017890		11795078		9347429	MACHINES MATERIEL TRANSPORT
71	POWER GENERATING EQUIPMT		579840		766625		738550		624266	MACHINES GENERATRICES
711	STEAM BOILERS & AUX PLNT	W 4577	38749	W 7289	105033	W 4386	45839	W 6552	98945	GENERATEURS VAPEUR EAU ETC
7112	AUXILIARY BOILER PLANT	W 398	2721	W 507	6735	W 758	4848	W 4951	82882	APPAREILS AUXIL DU 711.1
713	INTRNL COMBUS PSTN ENGIN	W 31060	248788	W 19956	414799	W 23347	301586	W 16485	159173	MOTEURS EXPL COMB INT, PIECE
7131	AIRCRAFT PSTN ENGINS,PTS	W 216	71467	W 566	215625	W 471	111152	W 261	45898	MOTEURS EXPL P.AVIATION, PIE
71311	AIRCRAFT PISTON ENGINES	W 150	70631	W 533	214405	W 326	109728	W 167	44243	MOTEURS EXPL P.AVIATION
714	ENGINES AND MOTORS NES	W 975	39097	W 962	43566	W 2130	129828	W 612	43663	MOTEURS NON ELECTRIQUES
716	ROTATING ELECTRIC PLANT	W 24408	209799	W 15747	167587	W 18445	191278	W 16124	144220	APP ELECTR ROTATIFS,PIECES
7162	AC MTRS,GENRTRS,GEN SETS	W 19870	162703	W 10832	105134	W 11918	115714	W 9370	69472	MOTEURS ELECTRIQUES
718	OTH POWER GENERATG MACHY	W 1811	38872	W 1844	30496	W 2088	63578	W 2826	171400	AUTRES MOTEURS PARTIES
7188	WIND,WATER,ETC ENGINES	W 1199	34910	W 1844	30496	W 1564	60604	W 2806	171129	MOT MACHINES MOTRICES NDA
71882	OTH HYDRAULIC ENGNS,MTRS	W 678	23527	W 679	6444	W 419	9790	W 1774	96766	MACH MOTRICES HYDRAULQUES
72	MACHS FOR SPCL INDUSTRYS		590684		670681		678811		574199	MAC SPECIALES POUR INDUST
721	AGRIC MACHY,EXC TRACTORS	W 11127	80562	W 13340	99776	W 12351	86690	W 6730	52263	MACHINES AGRICOLES
723	CIVIL ENGNEERG EQUIP ETC	W 48797	255991	W 46669	202347	W 53621	216172	W 28430	137205	APPAREILS DE GENIE CIVIL
7234	CONST,MINING MACHNRY NES	W 42270	202677	W 38489	134690	W 46708	146438	W 24398	102699	MACH POUR LA CONST, MINES
724	TEXTILE,LEATHER MACHNRY	W 7562	55478	W 8535	76711	W 5609	50062	W 6725	83532	MACH POUR INDUSTRIE TEXTILE
728	OTH MACHY FOR SPCL INDUS	W 9018	102556	W 14933	182109	W 20125	190600	W 18095	163393	AUT MACH IND PARTICULIERES
7284	MACHY FOR SPCL INDUS NES	W 4562	65673	W 6053	101119	W 8039	98670	W 5602	82945	MACH SPEC IND PARTICUL.
73	METALWORKING MACHINERY		85516		137013		145501		123050	MACH TRAVAIL DES METAUX
736	METALWORKING MACH-TOOLS	W 7722	59298	W 12896	91715	W 14666	111120	W 13527	102358	MACH-OUTILS TRAVAIL METAUX
74	GENRL INDUSTRL MACHY NES		1847638		2706702		1958570		1526471	MACH APP INDUSTRIE
741	HEATING,COOLING EQUIPMNT	W 52464	380395	W 81982	693558	W 57339	464579	W 44371	333281	MACH CHAUFFAGE,PIECES
7414	NONDOM REFRIG EQUIPT,PTS	W 16224	93802	W 12663	89042	W 10377	77754	W 11085	76565	MAT PRODUCTION DU FROID
7415	AIR-CONDITIONING MACHNRY	W 25125	170183	W 34668	226282	W 32343	219201	W 26379	190348	GROUPES CONDITION AIR
7416	HEATING,COOLING EQU NES	W 5208	55866	W 27578	297098	W 7384	83353	W 3173	36410	APP CHANGEMENT TEMP
742	PUMPS FOR LIQUIDS ETC	W 31293	251531	W 33014	338207	W 23329	209791	W 14297	149629	POMPES MOTO-POMPES
7428	OTHER PUMPS FOR LIQUIDS	W 20821	156247	W 18423	187951	W 14811	130149	W 9659	92533	AUTRES POMPES POUR LIQ
74288	PUMPS FR LIQUIDS NES ETC	W 20326	149741	W 17887	180762	W 14047	121553	W 9236	86921	POMPES POUR LIQUIDES NDA
7429	PTS NES OF PUMPS OF 742	W 9565	81081	W 13443	123798	W 7705	67160	W 3095	42278	PIECES POUR GROUPE 742
743	PUMPS NES,CENTRFUGES ETC	W 25296	194128	W 37936	293980	W 40434	301503	W 46529	259600	POMPES COMPRES,VENT ETC
7431	PUMPS FOR GASES ETC	W 15086	90372	W 23127	153144	W 26524	145510	W 34591	149203	POMPES AIR A VIDE,COMPRES
744	MECHANICAL HANDLING EQU	W 37162	203433	W 46288	259735	W 31340	187001	W 26959	153444	EQUIP MANUTENTION PIECES
7442	LIFTING,LOADING MACH NES	W 18638	92650	W 26265	145551	W 18195	101458	W 15360	79348	APP LEVAGE,MANUTENTION
745	NONELEC MACHY,TOOLS NES	W 29959	125831	W 24503	132809	W 20674	117496	W 7435	106895	AUT MACH NON ELEC,PIECES
7452	OTH NONELEC MCHS,PTS NES	W 28656	106745	W 22383	105373	W 18842	97013	W 5720	88525	AUT MACH NON ELEC,PIECES
749	NONELEC MACH PTS,ACC NES	W 55225	692319	W 69146	988413	W 49921	678200	W 33049	523621	PIECES MACH NON ELEC NDA
7492	COCKS,VALVES ETC NES	W 16969	199781	W 26159	360169	W 17824	204702	W 11678	151036	ART ROB,SIM POUR TUYAUX
7499	OTH NONELEC MCHY PTS NES	W 28915	414370	W 30995	517134	W 22641	380084	W 15631	309350	PIECES NON ELECT NDA
74999	MACH PARTS NONELEC NES	W 26544	375519	W 27539	433628	W 19482	328824	W 13165	272049	PIECES MACHINES NDA
75	OFFICE MACHNES,ADP EQUIP		399479		425441		400314		342525	MACH BUREAU TRAIT AUTOM
752	AUTOMTIC DATA PROC EQUIP	W 2059	151825	W 2142	145585	W 1732	115189	W 863	54099	MACH TRAIT INFORMATION
759	OFFICE,ADP MCH PTS,ACCES	W 2877	179541	W 4133	219373	W 5437	226741	W 4265	235455	PIECES DU 751 ET 752
7599	ACCTG,ETC,ADP MCH PTS,AC	W 2441	166492	W 3235	186678	W 3353	177187	W 3162	209264	PIECES DU 751 ET 752
76	TELECOMM,SOUND EQUIPMENT		925795		777333		703798		592779	EQUIPMENT DE TELECOM
761	TELEVISION RECEIVERS	W 10139	141043	W 10440	156460	W 9735	146099	W 9467	141544	RECEPTEURS DE TELEVISION
7611	COLOUR TV RECEIVERS	W 9737	133755	W 10214	152952	W 9421	141396	W 8730	129804	RECEPTEURS COULEUR
762	RADIO BROADCAST RECEIVRS	W 4866	90112	W 3895	70749	W 3108	50967	W 3084	51630	RECEPTEURS RADIODIFFUSION
763	SOUND RECORDRS,PHONOGRPH	W 6684	155491	W 6319	130566	W 7199	148114	W 4385	91309	PHONO,APP ENREGISTREMENT
7638	OTHR SOUND APPARATUS ETC	W 6256	148680	W 6092	127384	W 6964	143892	W 4156	89211	AUT APP D'ENREGIS,REPROD
76388	DICTATING MACHINES ETC	W 3658	62869	W 4346	64270	W 5227	85913	W 2602	45341	MACHINES A DICTER
764	TELECOM EQPT,PTS,ACC NES	W 9699	539149		419559	W 8331	358617	W 6441	308296	EQUIP TELECOM,PIECES

4. General Imports C.I.F. by Commodities according to the S.I.T.C. (Rev. 2) in thousand U.S. Dollars
Importations Générales C.A.F. par Produits d'après la C.T.C.I. (Rév. 2) en milliers de Dollars E.U.

SITC CTCI	COMMODITY	1991		1992		1993		1994		PRODUIT
		WEIGHT POIDS	VALUE VALEUR	WEIGHT POIDS	VALUE VALEUR	WEIGHT POIDS	VALUE VALEUR	WEIGHT POIDS	VALUE VALEUR	
7641	LINE TELEPHONE,ETC EQUIP	W 3088	78034	W 3233	107441	W 2888	111952	W 2301	71459	APP TELEPHON PAR FIL
7643	TV,RADIO TRANSMITTRS ETC	W 1346	78038	W 1295	72182	W 1157	63385	W 956	81978	APP EMET TELE RADIO
7648	TELECOMM EQUIPMENT NES	W 1034	265995		123951	W 378	55110	W 244	39753	APP TELECOM NDA
76483	RADAR APPARATUS ETC	W 775	251765		116583	W 204	49114	W 113	29452	APP DE RADIOGUIDAGE ETC
7649	PTS NES OF EQUIPMT OF 76	W 3081	97137	W 3380	102909	W 3227	116220	W 2492	107454	PIECES DE LA DIV 76
77	ELECTRIC MACHNRY NES ETC		1249366		1592459		1426783		1109120	MACH APP ELECT NDA
771	ELECTRIC POWER MACHY NES	W 10839	79709	W 14440	112438	W 15447	128521	W 15174	126169	MACH PROD,TRANS ELECTR
7711	TRANSFORMERS,ELECTRICAL	W 7010	49435	W 8851	75635	W 9675	90073	W 8633	88251	TRANSFO ELECTRIQUES
772	SWITCHGEAR ETC,PARTS NES	W 21621	280442	W 27753	452872	W 30347	384701	W 26015	338792	APP COUPURE,SECT ETC
7721	SWITCHGEAR ETC	W 20482	274741	W 27450	446103	W 30010	370263	W 25633	330590	APP COUPURE,SECTIONMNT
773	ELECTR DISTRIBUTNG EQUIP	W 31676	130492	W 41270	196285	W 48037	176660	W 36023	103287	EQUIPMT DISTRIBUTION ELECT
7731	INSULATED WIRE,CABLE ETC	W 27567	108389	W 36819	175940	W 43571	155011	W 31917	85731	FILS,CABLES ISOLES ELECT
774	ELECTRO–MEDCL,XRAY EQUIP	W 1512	96998	W 1361	98208	W 1183	84565	W 922	66496	APPAREILS MEDICAUX
775	HOUSEHOLD TYPE EQUIP NES	W 60478	348713	W 62845	372830	W 55157	321428	W 40605	228952	MACH,APP USAGE DOMESTQUE
7752	DOM REFRIGERATRS,FREEZRS	W 22689	124646	W 21641	115297	W 16732	90652	W 13363	71452	REFRIG,CONGEL MENAGER
77521	DOMESTIC REFRIGERATORS	W 19347	106755	W 19203	102166	W 14226	77868	W 10998	58938	REFRIGERATEURS
7757	DOMESTIC ELECTRC EQU NES	W 16395	99265	W 16749	109911	W 14809	94375	W 11098	63487	APP ELECTR DOMEST NDA
7758	ELECTRO–THERMIC APPL NES	W 10748	63485	W 15795	93232	W 15406	89021	W 10453	57719	APP ELECTROTHERMIQ NDA
778	ELECTRICAL MACHINERY NES	W 55701	300111	W 57933	340368	W 53111	307403		229813	AUTRES MACH ELECT NDA
7781	BATTERIES,ACCUMULATORS	W 35052	97724	W 33461	92551	W 28041	82291	W 19689	56049	PILES ET ACCUMULATEURS
7788	OTH ELEC MACHY,EQUIP NES	W 7415	97042	W 6337	102421	W 6541	94297		93263	AUT MACH APP ELEC NDA
78	ROAD VEHICLES		3687644		3970456		3013377		2830879	VEHICULES ROUTIERS
781	PASS MOTOR VEH EXC BUSES	W 225420	1954038	W 239711	2193792	W 183525	1707039	W 171480	1650641	AUTO TRANSPORT PERSONNES
782	LORRIES,SPCL MTR VEH NES	W 143090	924138	W 123330	808761	W 77147	531386	W 74583	520646	VEHICULES SPECIAUX,MARCH
7821	LORRIES,TRUCKS	W 137299	879159	W 117753	767904	W 72113	494912	W 70308	490297	VEHICULES TRANSP MARCHAND
783	ROAD MOTOR VEHICLES NES	W 33720	212552	W 42008	210704	W 17178	103002	W 25427	164832	VEHICULES ROUTIERS NDA
7831	BUSES	W 13842	106065	W 16548	107826	W 9442	64652	W 18206	124745	VOITURES TRANSPORT COMMUN
7832	TRACTORS FOR TR–TRAILERS	W 19877	106487	W 25460	102878	W 7736	38350	W 7221	40087	TRACTEURS ROUTIERS
784	MOTOR VEH PRTS,ACCES NES	W 66800	532064	W 87616	691813	W 78773	621018	W 60599	452655	PIECES 722,781,782,783
7849	OTHER MOTOR VEHCL PARTS	W 63510	518768	W 84059	673411	W 76078	605314	W 59223	447566	PIECES 722,781,782,783
79	OTHR TRANSPORT EQUIPMENT		2374455		3971179		2729374		1624139	AUTRE MATERIEL TRANSPORT
792	AIRCRAFT ETC	W 3961	2336733		3883471		2693303	W 3683	1602004	APP NAVIGATION AERIENNE
7929	AIRCRAFT PARTS NES	W 3896	2278169	W 9297	3872351	W 6364	2654094	W 3656	1592513	PIECES DU 792
8	MISC MANUFACTURED GOODS		3269480		3530526		3306065		2464783	ART MANUFACTURES DIVERS
812	*PLUMBG,HEATNG,LGHTNG EQ	W 27119	117445	W 32417	161056	W 33280	148827	W 34443	134086	APPAR SANITAIRES CHAUFFAGE
8124	LIGHTING EQUIPMENT NES	W 10500	78063	W 12361	111861	W 12922	95104	W 11179	87892	APPAREILS ECLAIRAGE ETC
81242	LAMPS,FITTINGS BASE METL	W 6819	49987	W 9068	86887	W 8767	68441	W 9034	74492	APPAREILS D'ECLAIRAGE
821	*FURNITURE,PARTS THEREOF	W 131327	352591	W 138875	425922	W 114585	345044	W 100709	266358	MEUBLES ET PIECES
8219	FURNITURE AND PARTS NES	W 111070	272410	W 121744	340691	W 97298	262511	W 84694	199964	AUTRES MEUBLES ET PIECES
82192	WOOD FURNITURE NES	W 88669	216886	W 100615	269909	W 81153	209859	W 71474	162725	MEUBLES NDA EN BOIS
831	*TRAVEL GOODS,HANDBAGS	W 22131	98694	W 23501	98301	W 23386	90348	W 22686	74536	ARTICLES DE VOYAGE ETC
84	CLOTHING AND ACCESSORIES		1023114		1040573		853532		645794	VETEMENTS
842	MENS OUTERWEAR NOT KNIT	W 26448	262791	W 32817	265406	W 26262	206695	W 22264	156320	VET DESSUS POUR HOMMES
8422	— SUITS	W 12301	119973	W 17524	130998	W 14786	100256	W 12733	71857	COMPLETS HOMMES MAT TEXT
84223	—— OF MAN–MADE FIBRES	W 8716	97188	W 17313	127956	W 14544	94084	W 12596	67958	COMPLETS HOMMES FIB SYNT
843	WOMENS OUTERWEAR NONKNIT	W 25971	253340	W 35332	317214	W 25497	263018	W 20916	246637	VET DESSUS FEMMES MAT TEX
8439	— OTHER OUTER GARMENTS	W 7604	81870	W 11222	119447	W 11784	126769	W 11401	132866	AUT VET DES FEM MAT TEXT
844	UNDER GARMENTS NOT KNIT	W 16582	133815	W 19989	159224	W 16787	123682	W 10326	79089	VETEMENT DESSOUS MAT TEX
845	OUTERWEAR KNIT NONELASTC	W 20801	196139	W 15060	146502	W 16255	113651	W 7340	57753	VET DESSOUS,ACCES BONNET
8459	— OTHER,CLTHG ACCESRYS	W 15742	145918	W 10522	102839	W 6857	58388	W 4757	36555	AUT VET DESSUS DE BONNE
851	*FOOTWEAR	W 36030	252206	W 30126	213840	W 33963	204793	W 24348	168711	CHAUSSURES
85102	FOOTWEAR LEATHER	W 25041	189373	W 17850	151884	W 16628	134899	W 11805	108827	CHAUS SEMELLES EN CUIR
87	PRECISION INSTRUMNTS NES		316300		360223		381389		273541	INSTRUM,APPAR SCIENT NDA
872	MEDICAL INSTRUMENTS NES	W 3953	110846	W 3427	108964	W 3086	104120	W 2573	85568	INSTR,APP MEDIC–CHIR NDA
87202	OTH MEDICAL INSTRUMENTS	W 2107	57333	W 2966	94098	W 2629	91082	W 2052	74408	INSTRUM,APP MEDECINE
874	MEASURNG,CONTROLNG INSTR	W 4684	181136	W 6230	226576	W 6078	240835		159172	INSTRUMENTS DE MESURE
88	PHOTO EQU,OPTICL GDS ETC		400003		418938		367621		298494	APP,FOURN PHOTO,OP,MONTR
885	WATCHES AND CLOCKS		234609		258382		227051		195608	HORLOGERIE
8851	WATCHES,MOVEMENTS,CASES		218038		234589		208429		181237	MONTRES,MOUVEMENTS,BOITES
88511	WATCHES		213220		229661		203300		177680	MONTRES POCHE,BRACELET
89	MISC MANUFCTRD GOODS NES		709128		811673		914511		603263	ART MANUFACTURES DIVERS
893	ARTICLES OF PLASTIC NES		224266		269843		257539		220742	OUVRAGES EN MAT DIVIS 58
8939	MISC PLASTIC ARTICLES	W 46985	165053	W 61675	203089	W 62866	196295	W 51407	165293	ART DIVERS EN MAT DIV 58
89399	OTHR PLASTC ARTICLES NES	W 41982	151474	W 53475	181139	W 56933	179761	W 45916	150364	AUT OUV MAT DIV 58
894	TOYS,SPORTING GOODS,ETC	W 25458	94808		104987	W 45819	172419	W 25410	84902	VOITURES ENFANTS,JOUETS
897	GOLD,SILVER WARE,JEWELRY		79291		100125		158367		50336	BIJOUTERIE,ORFEVRERIE
8973	PREC JEWLRY,GLD–SILVWARE		49986		62203		124170		23414	BIJOUX OR,ARGENT ORFEVRE
89731	PRECIOUS METAL JEWELLERY		39854		51624		119718		17679	ART BIJOUTERIE,JOAILLER
898	MUSICAL INSTRUMENTS,PTS	W 9659	108091	W 8270	71044		79517	W 6075	57130	INSTRUMENTS DE MUSIQUE
8983	SOUND RECRDNG TAPE,DISCS	W 8891	100744	W 7417	63621		72172	W 5384	50469	SUPPORTS SON POUR 763
899	OTHER MANUFACTURED GOODS		96958		112976		103935		86472	AUT ART MANUF DIVERS NDA
9	GOODS NOT CLASSD BY KIND		1513965		1768906		1031444		1285062	ART TRANSACT NON CLASSES
931	*SPECIAL TRANSACTIONS	W 127043	111159		163942		160256	W 307233	167903	TRANS.SPECIALES
951	*WAR FIREARMS,AMMUNITION	W 348	10291		130225	W 5692	157843		368715	VEHIC BLINDES ARMES
95101	ARMORED FIGHTNG VEHICLES			W 1242	15558	W 5398	98134	W 8041	348905	CHARS DE COMBAT
95102	MILITARY FIREARMS NES			W 4041	109645			W 914	16185	ARMES DE GUERRE
971	*GOLD,NON MONETARY NES	K 118509	1391370		1473043	K 62983	706080	K 59441	734290	OR NON MONETAIRE
97101	NONMON GLD UNWRT,SEMIMFD	K 118509	1391370	K 130201	1472883	K 62983	706080	K 59441	734290	OR,ALLIAGES D'OR BRUTS

5. General Exports F.O.B. by Commodities according to the S.I.T.C. (Rev. 2) in thousand U.S. Dollars
Exportations Générales F.O.B. par Produits d'après la C.T.C.I. (Rév. 2) en milliers de Dollars E.U.

SITC CTCI	COMMODITY	1991		1992		1993		1994		PRODUIT
		WEIGHT POIDS	VALUE VALEUR	WEIGHT POIDS	VALUE VALEUR	WEIGHT POIDS	VALUE VALEUR	WEIGHT POIDS	VALUE VALEUR	
	ALL COMMODITIES		47790210		50287202		42395280		42614076	TOUS PRODUITS
0	FOOD AND LIVE ANIMALS		383966		396461		426948		368492	ALIMENTS,ANIMAUX VIVANTS
04	CEREALS AND PREPARATIONS		107430		161598		204014		139920	CEREALES ET PRODUITS
041	WHEAT ETC UNMILLED	W 951427	84986	W 1181205	141017	W 1568949	180037			FROMENT,EPEAUTRE
0412	OTHER WHEAT ETC UNMILLED	W 745977	65413	W 1181205	141017	W 1568949	180037			AUTRE FROMENT NON MOULU
2	CRUDE MATERLS,EXCL FUELS		100032		130970		161119		156208	MAT BRUTES NON COMESTIBLES
3	MINERAL FUELS ETC		43696590		46519816		38612299		38132754	COMBUSTIBLES MINERAUX LUB
33	PETROLEUM AND PRODUCTS		41781274		44393852		36674863		36154647	PETROLE ET DERIVES
333	CRUDE PETROLEUM	MW 309830	37331889	MW 317156	39602635	MW 297454	32017784	MW 290831	31294993	HUILES BRUTES DE PETROLE
334	PETROLEUM PRODUCTS,REFIN	MW 32396	4312848		4664506		4585854			PRODUITS RAFFINES
3341	GASOLINE,OTH LIGHT OILS	MW 10703	2041938	MW 11619	1969440	MW 11861	1702022			ESSENCES POUR MOTEURS
33411	MOTOR,AVIATION SPIRIT	MW 10703	2041234	MW 11619	1969440	MW 11861	1702022			ESSENCES MOTEURS D'AVIONS
3342	KEROSENE,OTH MEDIUM OILS	W 3766899	683208	W 4469465	811630	W 4530291	777059			PETR LAMPANTS,AUT HUIL
33421	KEROSENE INCL JET FUEL	W 3766899	683208	W 4469465	811630	W 4530291	777059			PETROLES LAMPANTS
3343	GAS OILS	W 8997890	1121431	MW 12991	1461283	MW 22800	1982046			GAS OILS
3344	FUEL OILS,NES	W 8922565	459609		413245		113248			FUEL OILS
341	*GAS,NATURAL AND MANUFCT		1915136	MW 15148	2125964	MW 15574	1937436		1978106	GAZ NATUREL,GAZ MANUFACT
3413	PETROLM GASES,LIQUEFIED		1914738	MW 15148	2125964	MW 15574	1937436			GAZ DE PETROLE LIQUEFIE
34131	LIQUEFIED PROPANE,BUTANE		1806902	MW 14645	2014113	MW 14846	1802106			PROPANE,BUTANE LIQUEFIES
34139	OTH HYDROCARBON GAS LQFD		107836	W 503043	111851	W 727686	135329			HYDROCARBURES GAZEUX NDA
5	CHEMCLS,RELATED PROD NES		2382867		2239848		2195973		2986118	PRODUITS CHIMIQUES
51	ORGANIC CHEMICALS		935204		931736		968271		1439788	PROD CHIMIQ ORGANIQUES
511	HYDROCARBONS NES,DERIVS		208094		269191	W 1145157	318797			HYDROCARBURES NDA
512	ALCOHOLS,PHENOLS ETC	W 1950954	493215	W 3523247	585835		568890			PHENOLS,PHENOLS–ALCOOLS
5121	ACYCLIC ALCOHOLS,DERIVS	W 1919376	483786	W 3280589	512303		529934			ALCOOLS ACYCLIQUES
51211	METHYL ALCOHOL(METHANOL)	W 1150948	161803	W 2137915	182495	W 1647453	152051			ALCOOLS METHYLIQUES
51215	ETHYLENE GLYCOL	W 658392	286627	W 871519	268421	W 748386	271227			ETHYLENE–GLYCOL
52	INORGANIC CHEMICALS		298917		339122		275236		227237	PROD CHIM INORGANIQUES
522	INORG ELEMNTS,OXIDES,ETC		287892		335666		273308			ELEMENTS INORGANIQUES
5225	INORGANIC BASES ETC NES		189111		213231		132652			AUTRES BASES OXYDES METAL
52253	SODIUM HYDROXIDE, OTHER		124871	W 856208	212572	W 738297	132211			HYDROXYDE SODIUM AQUEUX
562	*FERTILIZERS,MANUFACTURE		145086	W 978999	141355	W 1165628	148754		266222	ENGRAIS MANUFACTURES
5621	CHEM NITROGENOUS FERTLZR		128353	W 958935	136874	W 1162780	147891			ENGRAIS AZOTES
572	*EXPLOSIVES,PYROTECH PRO	W 87	137	W 1447	1645		2711		859280	EXPLOSIFS
58	PLASTIC MATERIALS ETC		888569		708080		647249		20294	MAT PLAST ARTIFICIELLES
583	POLYMERIZATION ETC PRODS		879082		703570		640774			PROD POLYMERISATION
5831	POLYETHYLENE		751850		581127	W 1089403	533262			POLYETHYLENE
58311	— IN PRIMARY FORMS		749942	W 1045819	579267	W 1088703	532702			POLYETHYLENE PRIMAIRES
6	BASIC MANUFACTURES		610289		446258		445074		482778	ART MANUFACTURES
69	METAL MANUFACTURES NES		139541		135187		129819		139386	ART MANUFACT EN METAL NDA
7	MACHINES,TRANSPORT EQUIP		434159		368363		394604		364219	MACHINES MATERIEL TRANSPORT
78	ROAD VEHICLES		206187		132643		91005		75835	VEHICULES ROUTIERS

FOOT NOTES – NOTES

TABLE 1 –

1 Beginning 1968, years refer to calendar years. Prior to 1968, years refer to the Islamic lunar year, which is about 11 days shorter than the Gregorian year; the Gregorian calendar equivalent of the lunar years changes annually: 1960 = 7 July 1959 – 23 June 1960; 1961 = 24 June 1960 – 13 June 1961; 1962 = 14 June 1961 – 2 June 1962; 1963 = 3 June 1962 – 23 May 1963; 1964 = 24 May 1963 – 11 May 1964; 1965 = 12 May 1964 – 30 April 1965; 1966 = 1 May 1965 – 20 April 1966; 1967 = 21 April 1966 – 10 April 1967.

TABLEAU 1 –

1 A partir de 1968, les années sont calendaires. Avant 1968, les années se rapportent à l'année lunaire islamique qui est plus courte d'environ 11 jours que l'année grégorienne. Le calendrier grégorien équivalent aux années lunaires se change annuellement. 1960 = 7 juillet 1959 – 23 juin 1960; 1961 = 24 juin 1960 – 13 juin 196l; 1962 = 14 juin 1961 – 2 juin 1962; 1963 = 3 juin 1962 – 23 mai 1963; 1964 = 24 mai 1963 – 11 mai 1964; 1965 = 12 mai 1964 – 30 avril 1965; 1966 = 1 mai 1965 – 20 avril 1966; 1967 = 21 avril 1966 – 10 avril 1967.

1. HISTORICAL SERIES, 1961–1996 SPECIAL TRADE, IMPORTS C.I.F., EXPORTS F.O.B.
SERIES HISTORIQUES, 1961–1996 COMMERCE SPECIAL, IMPORTATIONS C.A.F., EXPORTATIONS F.O.B

YEAR ANNEE	VALUE IN MILLION C.F.A. FRANCS / VALEUR EN MILLION C.F.A. FRANCS — MERCHANDISE –MARCHANDISE		GOLD –OR		CONVERSION FACTORS U.S. CENTS PER C.F.A. FRANC / FACTEURS DE CONVERSION CENTS E.U. PAR C.F.A. FRANC		INDEX NUMBERS –INDICES — QUANTUM		UNIT VALUE / VALEUR UNITAIRE	
	IMPORTS	EXPORTS	IMPORTS	EXPORTS	IMPORTS	EXPORTS	IMPORTS	EXPORTS	IMPORTS	EXPORTS
1961	38332.00	30657.00	2.00		0.4051	0.4051				
1962	38204.00	30671.00	2.00		0.4051	0.4051				
1963	38508.00	27279.00	18.00		0.4051	0.4051				
1964	42371.00	30243.00	16.00		0.4051	0.4051				
1965	39568.00	31712.00	16.00		0.4051	0.4051				
1966	38283.00	36764.00	30.00		0.4051	0.4051				
1967	38898.00	33890.00	6.00		0.4051	0.4051				
1968	44527.00	37369.00	2.00		0.4051	0.4051				
1969	51294.00	31907.00	5.00		0.3905	0.3962				
1970	53557.00	42182.00	6.00		0.3601	0.3601				
1971	60561.00	34707.00	49.00	5.00	0.3601	0.3601				
1972	70289.00	54412.00	26.00		0.3966	0.3969				
1973	79767.00	43237.00			0.4506	0.4512				
1974	119382.00	93983.00			0.4167	0.4158				
1975	124616.00	99101.00			0.4678	0.4643				
1976	139164.00	117094.00			0.4160	0.4105				
1977	187547.00	152920.00			0.4074	0.4080				
1978	170314.00	84909.00			0.4440	0.4418				
1979	197979.00	113858.00			0.4704	0.4704				
1980	222256.00	100767.00			0.4733	0.4733				
1981	292341.00	135900.00			0.3679	0.3677				
1982	325935.10	180037.00			0.3043	0.3043				
1983	396079.10	206976.00			0.2624	0.2624				
1984	437100.00	233974.00			0.2310	0.2284				
1985	370970.90	252492.00			0.2189	0.2196				
1986	332930.00	216580.00			0.2888	0.2888				
1987	307600.10	182250.00			0.3327	0.3327				
1988	321570.00	176080.00			0.3357	0.3357				
1989	389540.10	221100.00			0.3135	0.3135				
1990	332120.00	207380.00			0.3673	0.3673				
1991	330939.90	197710.00			0.3555	0.3554				
1992	273720.00	178080.00			0.3785	0.3787				
1993	332300.00	180500.00			0.3541	0.3541				
1994	611200.00	395500.00			0.1800	0.1800				
1995	650000.10	430200.00			0.2002	0.2002				
1996	707300.10	445100.00			0.1956	0.1956				

2. IMPORTS BY BROAD ECONOMIC CATEGORY AND EXPORTS BY INDUSTRIAL ORIGIN. (PERCENTAGE OF TOTAL VALUE)
IMPORTATIONS PAR CATEGORIES ECONOMIQUES ET EXPORTATIONS PAR BRANCHE D'ACTIVITE.(EN POURCENTAGE DE LA VALEUR TOTALE)

IMPORTS – IMPORTATIONS

	1990	1991	1992	1993	1994	1995	1996
TOTAL IMPORTS–IMPORTATIONS TOTALES	100.	100.	100.	100.		100.	
1 FOOD BEV–ALIMENTATION BOISSONS	26.7	27.5	27.9	31.2		30.4	
11 PRIMARY–PRODUITS DE BASE	10.6	8.5	7.5	7.5		6.7	
111 FOR INDUSTRY–POUR L'INDUSTRIE	5.0	3.4	3.0	3.4		4.5	
112 FOR HOUSEHOLDS–POUR LES MENAGES	5.5	5.1	4.5	4.2		2.2	
12 PROCESSED–PRODUITS ELABORES	16.1	19.0	20.4	23.7		23.6	
121 FOR INDUSTRY–POUR L'INDUSTRIE	2.0	4.7	4.3	6.1		5.9	
122 FOR HOUSEHOLDS–POUR LES MENAGES	14.1	14.3	16.1	17.6		17.7	
2 IND SUPPLIES–APPROV INDUSTRIELS	27.3	29.1	29.1	27.2		32.0	
21 PRIMARY–PRODUITS DE BASE	4.1	2.8	3.4	3.9		3.5	
22 PROCESSED–PRODUITS ELABORES	23.3	26.3	25.7	23.3		28.5	
3 FUELS–COMBUSTIBLES	15.7	10.7	8.7	8.9		9.8	
31 PRIMARY–PRODUITS DE BASE	8.7	8.3	6.8	7.4		7.2	
32 PROCESSED–PRODUITS ELABORES	7.0	2.4	1.9	1.5		2.5	
321 MOTOR SPIRIT–ESSENCE	0.6	0.4	0.0	0.0		0.2	
322 OTHER–AUTRES	6.4	2.0	1.8	1.5		2.3	
4 MACHINERY–EQUIPEMENT	12.5	14.9	14.4	12.9		10.9	
41 CAPITAL EQUIPMENT–MACHINES	10.9	13.4	12.6	11.4		9.8	
42 PARTS–PIECES ACCESSOIRES	1.6	1.5	1.8	1.5		1.1	
5 TRANSPORT–TRANSPORT	9.0	8.2	9.3	9.2		7.7	
51 PASSENGER CARS–AUTOMOBILES	2.9	2.4	3.2	3.3		2.0	
52 OTHER–AUTRES	2.7	3.1	2.9	2.9		2.8	
521 INDUSTRIAL–INDUSTRIELS	2.6	3.0	2.7	2.8		2.7	
522 NON INDUSTRIAL–NON INDUSTRIEL	0.1	0.1	0.1	0.1		0.1	
53 PARTS–PIECES ACCESSOIRES	3.4	2.7	3.3	3.0		2.9	
6 CONSUM GOODS–BIENS CONSOMMATION	8.8	9.6	10.6	10.5		8.8	
61 DURABLE–DURABLES	1.7	1.2	1.6	1.5		1.3	
62 SEMI DURABLE–SEMI DURABLES	2.6	2.6	3.2	3.3		3.3	
63 NON DURABLE–NON DURABLES	4.5	5.8	5.9	5.8		4.2	
7 GOODS NES–BIENS NDA	0.0	0.0	0.0	0.0		0.5	

EXPORTS – EXPORTATIONS

	1990	1991	1992	1993	1994	1995	1996
TOTAL EXPORTS–EXPORTATIONS TOTALES	100.	100.	100.	100.		100.	
1 AGRICULTURE	20.4	17.6	17.6	20.1		10.7	
2 MINING QUARRY–INDUS EXTRACTIVES	9.0	8.6	12.2	10.8		9.9	
3 MANUFACTURING–IND MANUFACTUR	70.6	73.7	70.2	69.1		79.4	
31 FOOD BEV TOBACCO–ALIM BOISS TAB	35.1	35.9	28.4	21.2		13.4	
32 TEXTILES–INDUSTRIES TEXTILES	1.7	1.0	1.2	1.0		0.7	
33 WOOD & PRODUCTS–BOIS & PRODUITS	0.0	0.1	0.1	0.1		0.1	
34 PAPER & PRODUCTS–PAPIER & PRODT	0.9	1.0	2.0	2.6		2.7	
35 CHEMICALS–INDUSTRIES CHIMIQUES	28.3	31.4	31.9	32.7		56.5	
36 NON METAL MIN–MIN NON METAL	0.3	0.1	0.1	0.2		0.4	
37 BASIC METAL–IND METAL BASE	0.1	0.3	0.6	1.1		0.6	
38 METAL MANUF–MANUF METAL	3.8	3.8	5.7	9.7		4.9	
39 OTH MANUF IND–AUTRES MANUF	0.4	0.1	0.2	0.3		0.3	

3. TRADE BY PRINCIPAL COUNTRIES OF PRODUCTION AND LAST CONSIGNMENT (VALUE IN THOUSAND U.S. DOLLARS)
ECHANGES SELON LES PRINCIPAUX PAYS DE PRODUCTION ET DE DERNIERE CONSIGNATION (VALEUR EN MILLIERS DE DOLLARS EU)

COUNTRIES–PAYS	SPECIAL IMPORTS C.I.F. IMPORTATIONS SPECIALES C.A.F				
	1991	1992	1993	1994	1995
World	1096951	1172453	1139203	876754	1224422
Africa	178146	176894	170540	92190	144333
Americas	113585	118238	98862	72768	160486
Northern America	93269	94675	69717	51371	84247
LAIA	18606	20774	27152	18007	69876
CACM	196	13	10	7	47
Caribbean	928	2725	1410	3383	6316
Rest of America	585	51	574	0	
As.ex F.USSR	143075	178598	181831	126833	231164
Eur.x F.USSR	644090	680921	665720	569551	668252
EU	624626	661375	650389	556875	654351
EFTA	6788	9444	7393	7643	7615
East Europe	11232	9522	7468	4839	5878
Other Europe	1445	131	36	17	9
Former USSR	5932	5804	9817	9249	16385
Oceania	3460	9812	11797	5844	3678
France,Monac	376722	389735	403053	300922	386928
Nigeria/Nigéria	79540	71783	71037	39336	77857
USA/Etats–Unis d'Amer	79238	71192	59203	43757	69978
Italy/Italie	57494	70115	48063	55575	43404
Cote d'Ivoire	61581	70827	57810	34071	32246
Thailand/Thaïlande	57012	35018	46673	32783	60488
Germany/Allemagne	38689	42055	42380	28403	59902
Spain/Espagne	36495	42045	40095	46915	41792
Japan/Japon	32445	44248	40727	35360	45844
Belgium–Luxembourg	41022	37144	30350	32744	38033
Netherlands/Pays–Bas	29023	29348	38691	34360	33616
China/Chine	13714	24296	23353	21886	29269
Brazil/Brésil	15107	16457	20426	14811	44542
United Kingdom	17245	21982	17024	19784	22099
Gabon	23663	17084	19930	2056	13735
Canada	14032	23483	10514	7611	14266
India/Inde	2220	6367	3069	2599	43629
Pakistan	9467	21069	6984	524	12353
Korea, Republic of	7804	9493	9825	8142	11111
Russian Federation		5804	9817	9249	16385
Portugal	4452	2563	2143	23539	5797
Viet Nam	59	12129	16129	4939	1472
Hong Kong	3364	5642	9432	6040	10034
Switz.Liecht	5955	7571	5809	6021	5695
New Zealand	3354	9310	11094	4086	3172
Sweden/Suède	6336	7869	5923	3708	6177
Morocco/Maroc	5358	5832	10404	2547	4859
Finland/Finlande	6972	4850	5657	3482	5530
Cameroon/Cameroun	3284	3065	4038	2275	8518
Denmark/Danemark	3934	5121	5694	3355	2918
Ireland/Irlande	2153	4215	5120	1976	5409
Argentina/Argentine	1762	1016	1979	290	11137
Austria/Autriche	3455	3347	5745	1680	1487
Poland/Pologne	4529	6126	1664	1053	1719
Uruguay	9			1002	12464
Turkey/Turquie	1783	2457	2955	1723	2968
Indonesia/Indonésie	1140	2504	4519	1450	2088
Malaysia/Malaisie	2047	2642	1398	989	4070
Czechoslovakia	5929	3090			
Norway,SVD,JM	831	1856	1581	1563	1915
Czech Republic			2900	1639	3195
Netherlands Antilles	872	2701	775	2217	1104
Singapore/Singapour	1847	2376	1862	520	797
Saudi Arabia	3865	1096	1296	210	517
So. Africa Customs Un	47	282	31	3370	3004
Trinidad and Tobago	43		618	1097	4850
Tunisia/Tunisie	903	1020	1385	1355	1341
Former USSR/Anc. URSS	5932				
Myanmar	403	1706	3383		
Peru/Pérou	1196	1955	1116	559	160

COUNTRIES–PAYS	SPECIAL EXPORTS F.O.B. EXPORTATIONS SPECIALES F.O.B.				
	1991	1992	1993	1994	1995
Monde	652208	683031	605102	444402	530759
Afrique	93594	135535	141076	110457	141992
Amériques	15795	7677	23591	6085	5792
Amérique du Nord	11705	3269	18008	5142	3249
ALAI	1975	1265	3845	914	2486
MCAC	1775	1850	1656		
Caraïbes	338	1294	83	29	50
Autre Amérique	2				8
Asie l'URSS exclus	129122	175269	132394	102787	186268
Europe l'URSS exclus	333859	298889	244830	164017	127571
UE	333612	297004	244138	163235	126475
AELE	51	187	590	779	1093
Europe de l'Est		56	82	1	
Autre de l'Europe	197	1642	20	2	
Ancienne URSS	51	10	33	427	
Océanie	69	101	0	2	14
France,Monac	206056	185745	157265	80001	58895
India/Inde	76914	105183	76935	67003	136424
Italy/Italie	66014	39513	41403	22389	38145
Mali	24222	36727	31330	40661	44974
Netherlands/Pays–Bas	10199	25279	7074	22368	8054
Cote d'Ivoire	17803	19650	13365	7771	8138
Iran (Islamic Rp. of)	6697	21556	13522	7942	9852
Spain/Espagne	20299	14028	9412	11866	2067
Gambia/Gambie	9505	11893	12559	7007	8810
Guinea/Guinée	5430	15169	11808	7007	6688
Japan/Japon	11977	13693	10348	3526	1930
Germany/Allemagne	8261	9489	9561	9701	4176
Philippines	10638	12345	3296	3645	10034
Cameroon/Cameroun	10399	7843	7251	4461	8630
Benin/Bénin	5023	6343	10227	2863	13429
Mauritania/Mauritanie	32	4485	12401	7103	11603
USA/Etats–Unis d'Amer	6789	2940	12172	5075	3079
Belgium–Luxembourg	9113	9002	7063	2708	2003
Nigeria/Nigéria	1177	3999	3787	7478	11789
United Kingdom	4897	3574	4006	9776	4970
Congo	5072	4788	5873	3079	1903
Portugal	3594	3979	2101	2301	6214
Greece/Grèce	5009	3993	5415	1270	1946
Guinea–Bissau	2821	3183	3074	3467	4097
Togo	1343	2986	1625	3750	5309
Burkina Faso	2169	2874	3775	1439	4680
Gabon	2236	3524	4063	1908	862
Canada	4916	330	5835	67	170
Korea, Republic of	1038	5248	1981	957	
Hong Kong	903	2777	2763	1145	688
Tunisia/Tunisie	1579	2585	1006	2105	3
Thailand/Thaïlande	54	669	2343	3067	1057
Sierra Leone	367	1600	2141	1647	1416
China/Chine	816	2270	3017	36	105
Ethiopia/Ethiopie		0	6127		
Morocco/Maroc	181	445	4467	134	676
El Salvador	1775	1850	1656		
Angola	39	4719	134	108	160
Chad/Tchad	657	574	1462	738	1308
Cape Verde/Cap–Vert	88	54	66	655	2628
Central African Rep.	305	199	1223	711	961
Colombia/Colombie	861	1247	753	469	
Kenya		192	593	2385	9
Ireland/Irlande	143	2004	522	486	
United Arab Emirates	348	437		332	1951
Niger	151	541	300	1293	762
Saudi Arabia	2874	23	40	4	
Switz.Liecht	44	187	587	767	1093
Brazil/Brésil	2		23	441	2082
Ghana	19	335	393	828	750

(VALUE AS PERCENTAGE OF WORLD TOTAL)(VALEURS EN POURCENTAGE DU TOTAL MONDIAL)

	1986	1987	1988	1989	1990	1991	1992	1993	1994	1995
Africa	17.4	13.1	9.2	23.4	16.1	16.2	15.1	15.0	10.5	11.8
Americas	5.1	7.9	10.2	9.2	9.5	10.4	10.1	8.7	8.3	13.1
Northern America	4.5	6.4	8.2	7.2	6.4	8.5	8.1	6.1	5.9	6.9
LAIA	0.5	1.3	1.9	1.7	1.8	1.7	1.8	2.4	2.1	5.7
CACM	0.0	0.1	0.0	0.0	0.0	0.0	0.0	0.0	0.0	0.0
Caribbean	0.1	0.1	0.0	0.4	1.3	0.1	0.2	0.1	0.4	0.5
Rest of America		0.0	0.0	0.0	0.0	0.1	0.0	0.1	0.0	
As.ex F.USSR	9.6	10.1	13.0	14.0	14.0	13.0	15.2	16.0	14.5	18.9
Eur.x F.USSR	53.6	56.4	65.2	52.0	59.0	58.7	58.1	58.4	65.0	54.6
EU	52.2	54.5	63.4	50.1	57.3	56.9	56.4	57.1	63.5	53.4
EFTA	0.7	0.8	0.9	0.6	0.6	0.6	0.8	0.6	0.9	0.6
East Europe	0.6	1.0	0.7	1.1	1.1	1.0	0.8	0.7	0.6	0.5
Other Europe	0.1	0.1	0.1	0.2	0.0	0.1	0.0	0.0	0.0	0.0
Former USSR	0.1	0.2	0.1	0.2	0.4	0.5	0.5	0.9	1.1	1.3
Oceania	0.0	0.0	0.0	0.1	0.0	0.3	0.8	1.0	0.7	0.3
France,Monac	30.0	31.5	36.7	28.6	32.9	34.3	33.2	35.4	34.3	31.6
Nigeria/Nigéria	7.4	2.8	2.4	8.1	7.5	7.3	6.1	6.2	4.5	6.4
USA/Etats–Unis d'Amer	3.8	3.9	7.1	5.9	5.3	7.2	6.1	5.2	5.0	5.7
Italy/Italie	5.0	4.9	5.2	5.0	6.5	5.2	6.0	4.2	6.3	3.5
Cote d'Ivoire	3.8	4.4	3.1	4.4	4.5	5.6	6.0	5.1	3.9	2.6
Thailand/Thaïlande	1.1	0.9	1.9	2.5	2.9	5.2	3.0	4.1	3.7	4.9
Germany/Allemagne	4.8	4.6	4.3	2.8	3.6	3.5	3.6	3.7	3.2	4.9
Spain/Espagne	3.1	3.5	5.7	4.5	4.2	3.3	3.6	3.5	5.4	3.4
Japan/Japon	2.6	3.4	4.0	3.7	3.6	3.0	3.8	3.6	4.0	3.7
Belgium–Luxembourg	2.1	2.7	2.8	2.1	2.7	3.7	3.2	2.7	3.7	3.1

	1986	1987	1988	1989	1990	1991	1992	1993	1994	1995
Afrique	18.4	18.9	13.3	22.6	20.1	14.4	19.8	23.3	24.9	26.8
Amériques	0.4	5.3	1.3	0.6	0.3	2.4	1.1	3.9	1.4	1.1
Amérique du Nord	0.3	0.4	1.3	0.2	0.2	1.8	0.5	3.0	1.2	0.6
ALAI	0.1	0.1	0.0	0.2	0.0	0.3	0.2	0.6	0.2	0.5
MCAC			0.0			0.3	0.3	0.3		
Caraïbes	0.1	4.8	0.0	0.2	0.0	0.1	0.2	0.0	0.0	0.0
Autre Amérique	0.0	0.0	0.0		0.0	0.0				0.0
Asie l'URSS exclus	13.6	7.2	13.5	16.8	17.0	19.8	25.7	21.9	23.1	35.1
Europe l'URSS exclus	44.5	45.6	67.4	50.8	53.4	51.2	43.8	40.5	36.9	24.0
UE	43.4	45.2	66.1	50.6	53.4	51.2	43.5	40.3	36.7	23.8
AELE	0.5	0.3	0.2	0.0	0.0	0.0	0.0	0.1	0.2	0.2
Europe de l'Est	0.0	0.0	0.2	0.0	0.0		0.0	0.0	0.0	
Autre de l'Europe	0.6	0.1	0.5	0.2		0.0	0.2	0.0	0.0	
Ancienne URSS	0.0	0.0	0.0	0.0	0.0	0.0	0.0	0.0	0.1	
Océanie		0.0	0.1	0.0		0.0	0.0	0.0	0.0	0.0
France,Monac	28.8	32.9	42.9	33.4	34.9	31.6	27.2	26.0	18.0	11.1
India/Inde	8.7	2.8	5.6	9.3	10.6	11.8	15.4	12.7	15.1	25.7
Italy/Italie	2.7	3.5	5.7	6.2	7.0	10.1	5.8	6.8	5.0	7.2
Mali	2.7	2.9	2.4	6.5	7.1	3.7	5.4	5.2	9.1	8.5
Netherlands/Pays–Bas	4.2	1.3	2.9	3.0	5.3	1.6	3.7	1.2	5.0	1.5
Cote d'Ivoire	4.0	3.8	1.9	2.8	2.8	2.7	2.9	2.2	1.7	1.5
Iran (Islamic Rp. of)	0.0				1.8	1.0	3.2	2.2	1.8	1.9
Spain/Espagne	2.4	2.8	5.3	4.0	2.9	3.1	2.1	1.6	2.7	0.4
Gambia/Gambie	0.5	0.7	0.4	1.2	0.9	1.5	1.7	2.1	1.6	1.7
Guinea/Guinée	1.0	1.1	0.6	2.2	2.0	0.8	2.2	2.0	1.6	1.3

4. Special Imports C.I.F. by Commodities according to the S.I.T.C. (Rev. 2) in thousand U.S. Dollars
Importations Spéciales C.A.F. par Produits d'après la C.T.C.I. (Rév. 2) en milliers de Dollars E.U.

SITC CTCI	COMMODITY	1992		1993		1994		1995		PRODUIT
		WEIGHT POIDS	VALUE VALEUR	WEIGHT POIDS	VALUE VALEUR	WEIGHT POIDS	VALUE VALEUR	WEIGHT POIDS	VALUE VALEUR	
	ALL COMMODITIES		1172453		1139203		876754		1224422	TOUS PRODUITS
0	FOOD AND LIVE ANIMALS		282617		293706		174466		317146	ALIMENTS,ANIMAUX VIVANTS
01	MEAT AND PREPARATIONS		4648		3853		1727		1819	VIANDES ET PREPARATIONS
011	MEAT FRESH,CHILLD,FROZEN	W 2093	3520	W 2152	2792	W 909	1145	W 761	1549	VIANDES FRAICHES,REF,CONGE
02	DAIRY PRODCTS,BIRDS'EGGS		60605		70375		39649		34430	PRODUITS LAITIERS,OEUFS
022	MILK AND CREAM	W 28866	54509	W 30383	63329	W 21058	35345	W 15587	30495	LAIT ET CREME
0224	MILK,CREAM PRESERVED ETC	W 26831	53268	W 28097	61889	W 19097	34312	W 13849	29287	LAIT,CREME CONS,CONC
02242	MILK DRY,1.5% FAT OR LES	W 25983	52314	W 26822	60187	W 18775	33965	W 12635	28265	LAIT POUDRE INF 1.5%
023	BUTTER	W 2346	4370	W 2358	5044	W 1727	3032	W 1203	2634	BEURRE
03	FISH AND PREPARATIONS		21270		13431		7869		889	POISSONS ET PREPARATIONS
034	FISH,FRESH,CHILLED,FROZN	W 23541	16908	W 17445	12683	W 7299	6711	W 26	50	POISSON FRAIS, REFRIG,CONG
0341	FISH FRSH,CHLLD,EX FILLT	W 23541	16908	W 17445	12683	W 7299	6711	W 26	50	POISSON FRAIS,REFRIGERE
037	FISH ETC PREPD,PRSVD NES	W 1287	4074	W 228	716	W 511	1145	W 254	813	POIS,CRUST,MOL PREPARES
0371	FISH PREPARD,PRESRVD NES	W 1229	3964	W 209	669	W 438	1123	W 249	782	CONSERVES DE POISSONS
04	CEREALS AND PREPARATIONS		112710		126051		76631		195868	CEREALES ET PRODUITS
041	WHEAT ETC UNMILLED	W 159812	29936	W 177701	35188	W 185102	31574	W 223899	53910	FROMENT,EPEAUTRE
0411	DURUM WHEAT UNMILLED	W 19293	4116	W 3891	837			W 4386	904	FROMENT DUR NON MOULU
0412	OTHER WHEAT ETC UNMILLED	W 140520	25820	W 173810	34352	W 185097	31574	W 219513	53005	AUTRE FROMENT NON MOULU
042	RICE	W 382508	71931	W 384887	80656	W 335146	40985	W 441295	132454	RIZ
0422	RICE SEMI–MILLED,MILLED	W 382508	71931	W 384887	80656	W 335143	40984	W 441295	132454	RIZ POLI,GLACE INCL BRISURES
04222	RICE BROKEN	W 359119	69291	W 384849	80617	W 335082	40950	W 441033	132417	BRISURES DE RIZ
044	MAIZE UNMILLED	W 21911	3557	W 19812	3421	W 9355	1039	W 25549	4192	MAIS NON MOULU
048	CEREAL ETC PREPARATIONS	W 4793	4733	W 3517	4418	W 2222	1768	W 3310	3105	PREPTNS A BASE CEREALES
05	VEGETABLES AND FRUIT		23127		24352		11880		19458	LEGUMES ET FRUITS
054	VEG ETC FRSH,SMPLY PRSVD	W 28925	11207	W 34204	13658	W 19481	8243	W 22126	10952	LEGUMES FRAIS,CONG,SECS
0541	POTATOES FRSH EXCL SWEET	W 12502	4222	W 14537	5072	W 7438	2957	W 7248	3458	POMMES DE TERRE
0545	OTHER FRESH VEGETABLES	W 15507	5867	W 18436	7473	W 11550	4763	W 13389	6208	AUTRES LEGUMES FRAIS,REF
05451	ALLIACEOUS VEGTBLS,FRESH	W 15091	5555	W 18068	7147	W 11391	4670	W 12921	5988	OIGNONS,ECHALOTES,AULX
056	VEGTBLES ETC PRSVD,PREPD	W 1440	1462	W 1265	1311	W 989	846	W 4538	5032	CONSERVES DE LEGUMES
0565	VEGTBLES PRSVD,PREPD NES	W 1303	1311	W 1219	1202	W 937	763	W 4482	4919	LEGUMES PREPARES CONSERVE
05659	OTH VEG PRESVD,PREPD NES	W 1286	1279	W 1204	1169	W 924	735	W 4445	4878	LEGUM PREPAP,CONSERV NDA
057	FRUIT,NUTS,FRESH,DRIED	W 14403	8999	W 10331	7984	W 5028	2228	W 5365	2580	FRUITS FRAIS OU SECS
06	SUGAR AND PREPS,HONEY		9627		6070		10317		27407	SUCRES ET PRODUITS
061	SUGAR AND HONEY	W 16758	8639	W 9756	4753	W 20125	9614	W 58204	26141	SUCRES ET MIEL
0611	RAW BEET AND CANE SUGAR							W 30501	10891	SUCRES BRUTS
0612	REFINED SUGAR ETC	W 14798	7679	W 8089	3955	W 18668	9027	W 26557	14651	SUCRES RAFFINES
07	COFFEE,TEA,COCOA,SPICES		24972		22843		12124		17033	CAFE,THE,CACAO,EPICES
071	COFFEE AND SUBSTITUTES	W 2050	12615	W 856	12409	W 265	1606	W 486	4979	CAFE ET SUCCEDANES
0712	COFFEE EXTRACTS,ESSENCES	W 780	11809	W 780	12248	W 222	1505	W 449	4853	EXTRAITS DE CAFE
074	TEA AND MATE	W 2429	8517	W 1918	7064	W 3350	8806	W 3657	9613	THE ET MATE
0741	TEA	W 2429	8517	W 1918	7064	W 3350	8805	W 3657	9613	THE
09	MISC EDIBLE PRODUCTS		24139		25551		13695		19877	PREP ALIMENTAIRES DIVERSES
098	EDIBLE PRODCTS,PREPS NES	W 7838	21233	W 7668	22627	W 5958	12402	W 7060	18941	PREP ALIMENTAIRES NDA
09806	YEASTS,BAKING POWDERS	W 2084	3376	W 1991	3657	W 1797	2704	W 1998	3596	LEVURES
09809	MISC FOOD PREPRTIONS NES	W 3678	14940	W 3805	15733	W 2964	8609	W 3708	13340	PREP ALIMENTAIRES NDA
1	BEVERAGES AND TOBACCO		13060		14120		10418		13251	BOISSONS ET TABACS
12	TOBACCO AND MANUFACTURES		10219		11569		8260		9955	TABACS BRUTS FABRIQUES
121	TOBACCO UNMNFCTRD,REFUSE	W 1564	9538	W 1457	11068	W 1231	7962	W 999	9319	TABACS BRUTS,DECHETS
1212	TOBACCO STRIPPED OR PART	W 1562	9535	W 1447	11052	W 1207	7935	W 967	9267	TABACS PART ECOTES
2	CRUDE MATERLS,EXCL FUELS		42398		45859		33925		40750	MAT BRUTES NON COMESTIBLES
24	CORK AND WOOD		14633		15347		10572		15060	LIEGE ET BOIS
247	OTH WOOD ROUGH,SQUARED	W 20010	5108	W 17890	5483	W 15764	2880	W 21606	6483	BOIS BRUTS EQUARRIS
2472	SAW–,VENEER–LOGS NON–CON	W 17050	3313	W 13993	3054	W 15354	2689	W 21342	6279	NON CONIFERES SCIAGE,PLAC
24721	— IN THE ROUGH	W 17050	3313	W 13993	3054	W 15277	2677	W 21342	6279	BRUTS ECORCES DEGROSSIS
248	WOOD SHAPED,SLEEPERS	W 18041	9517	W 17113	9863	W 18181	7688	W 16577	8567	BOIS SIMPLEMENT TRAVAILLES
2483	LUMBER SHAPED NON–CONIFR	W 17954	9414	W 17037	9791	W 18144	7649	W 16551	8518	NON CONIFERES SCIES,RABOTES
24831	LUMBER SAWN ETC NON–CON	W 17951	9411	W 17036	9790	W 18143	7647	W 16551	8517	SCIES LONGITUDINALEMENT
26	TEXTILE FIBRES AND WASTE		11396		9514		6386		8977	FIBRES TEXTILES
266	SYNTHETIC FIBRES TO SPIN	W 635	4109	W 523	3755	W 460	2554	W 428	2112	FIBRES SYNTHETIQUES
2667	DISCON SYNTH FIBRE COMBD	W 635	4109	W 523	3754	W 456	2527	W 422	2106	FIBRES TEXT SYNTH DISCONT
269	WASTE OF TEXTILE FABRICS	W 5411	6543	W 4456	5686	W 4169	3805	W 6516	6818	FRIPERIE DRILLES,CHIFFONS
26901	BULK TEXT WSTE,OLD CLTHG	W 4564	6024	W 3898	5330	W 3942	3681	W 6051	6590	ART ET ACCESS D'HABILLEMENT
27	CRUDE FERTLZR,MINRLS NES		11528		15519		13563		13722	ENGRAIS MINERAUX BRUTS
274	SULPHUR,UNRSTD IRN PYRTE	W 109093	8214	W 202097	12551	W 390594	11760	W 121044	10827	SOUFRE ET PYRITES
2741	SULPHUR,EX SULP IN 52215	W 109093	8214	W 202097	12551	W 390594	11760	W 121044	10827	SOUFRE
3	MINERAL FUELS ETC		103415		103893		168788		122389	COMBUSTIBLES MINERAUX LUB
33	PETROLEUM AND PRODUCTS		103001		103448		157749		122051	PETROLE ET DERIVES
333	CRUDE PETROLEUM	W 541482	79441	W 545702	84129	W 302782	35845	W 650686	88646	HUILES BRUTES DE PETROLE
334	PETROLEUM PRODUCTS,REFIN	W 83574	21626	W 56874	16857	W 848601	119402	W 127631	30525	PRODUITS RAFFINES
3341	GASOLINE,OTH LIGHT OILS	W 933	398	W 1343	511	W 214636	38150	W 9510	2182	ESSENCES POUR MOTEURS
33411	MOTOR,AVIATION SPIRIT	W 304	175	W 484	244	W 61562	11809	W 9085	2105	ESSENCES MOTEURS D'AVIONS
33412	SPIRIT TYPE JET FUEL	W 140	32	W 155	34	W 153048	26335	W 405	73	CARBUREACTEURS
3343	GAS OILS	W 62138	11817	W 35953	7418	W 281444	41346	W 72390	12049	GAS OILS
3344	FUEL OILS,NES	W 6613	978	W 7125	950	W 331544	29949	W 21774	3269	FUEL OILS
3345	LUBS,PETROLEUM OILS NES	W 13890	8432	W 12449	7973	W 20790	9922	W 23742	12981	HUILES LUBRIFIANTES
33451	LUBS(HIGH PETR CONT) ETC	W 13223	7424	W 12305	7662	W 20704	9683	W 23657	12711	HUILES LUBRIF,H LOURDES
341	*GAS,NATURAL AND MANUFCT		109		86	W 49597	10842		75	GAZ NATUREL,GAZ MANUFACT
3413	PETROLM GASES,LIQUEFIED		86		86	W 49597	10842		71	GAZ DE PETROLE LIQUEFIE
34131	LIQUEFIED PROPANE,BUTANE		86		86	W 49597	10842		71	PROPANE,BUTANE LIQUEFIES
4	ANIMAL,VEGETABLE OIL,FAT		52132		63915		34461		67395	HUILES,GRAISSES ANIM,VEG
411	*ANIMAL OILS AND FATS	W 10849	5093	W 1562	867	W 4063	1873	W 15681	8589	HUILES,GRAISSES ANIMALES
4113	ANIML OIL,FAT,GREASE NES	W 10849	5093	W 1562	867	W 3959	1804	W 15681	8589	HUILES,GRAISSES ANIMALES NDA
41132	FATS OF BOVINE,SHEEP,ETC	W 10825	5033	W 1497	796	W 3922	1759	W 15372	8382	SUIFS BRUTS FONDUS
42	FIXED VEGETABLE OIL,FAT		44954		62191		32053		55989	HUILES VEGETALES FIXES
423	FIXED VEG OILS,SOFT	W 54384	27749	W 80007	45821	W 44404	24112	W 71363	50596	HUILES VEGET DOUCES FIXES
4232	SOYA BEAN OIL	W 42	30	W 37828	21273	W 4671	3005	W 28182	19405	HUILE DE SOJA
4239	OTH FIXED VEG OILS,SOFT	W 53693	26790	W 41969	24088	W 39613	20883	W 42781	30016	AUTRES HUILES FIXES
42391	RAPE,COLZA,MUSTARD OILS	W 53686	26779	W 41969	24088	W 39613	20883	W 42781	30016	H NAVETTE COLZA MOUTARDE
424	FIXED VEG OIL NONSOFT	W 28776	17205	W 29868	16370	W 20922	7940	W 8476	5393	AUTRES HUILES VEG FIXES
4242	PALM OIL	W 26547	15248	W 25288	13785	W 17998	5951	W 6212	3734	HUILE DE PALME
5	CHEMCLS,RELATED PROD NES		151023		134104		114688		170298	PRODUITS CHIMIQUES
51	ORGANIC CHEMICALS		9783		11692		9643		12858	PROD CHIMIQ ORGANIQUES
515	ORG–INORG COMPOUNDS ETC	W 583	2612	W 347	3437	W 330	1946	W 486	3693	COMPOSES ORGANO–MINERAUX
52	INORGANIC CHEMICALS		26723		11426		10728		28955	PROD CHIM INORGANIQUES
522	INORG ELEMNTS,OXIDES,ETC	W 191848	22837		7732		7465	W 209418	25478	ELEMENTS INORGANIQUES
5221	CHEMICAL ELEMENTS	W 147505	13955		825		834	W 167436	13793	ELEMENTS CHIMIQUES
52215	SULPHUR,PURIFIED	W 147096	12976		4			W 166987	12392	SOUFRE SUBLIME,PRECIPITE
5225	INORGANIC BASES ETC NES	W 42117	7444	W 36046	5878	W 38522	5803	W 39789	10373	AUTRES BASES OXYDES METAL
52251	AMMONIA,ANHYDROUS ETC	W 27761	3180	W 22480	3317	W 25564	3957	W 26412	6770	AMMONIAC LIQUEFIE
52252	SODIUM HYDROXIDE, SOLID	W 14308	4195	W 13541	2468	W 12909	1771	W 13323	3456	HYDROXYDE DE SODIUM
523	OTHR INORG CHEMICALS ETC	W 6889	3855	W 6274	3659	W 7533	3213	W 6281	3471	AUT PRODUITS CHIMIQUES INORG

4. Special Imports C.I.F. by Commodities according to the S.I.T.C. (Rev. 2) in thousand U.S. Dollars
Importations Spéciales C.A.F. par Produits d'après la C.T.C.I. (Rév. 2) en milliers de Dollars E.U.

SITC CTCI	COMMODITY	1992 WEIGHT POIDS	1992 VALUE VALEUR	1993 WEIGHT POIDS	1993 VALUE VALEUR	1994 WEIGHT POIDS	1994 VALUE VALEUR	1995 WEIGHT POIDS	1995 VALUE VALEUR	PRODUIT
53	DYES,TANNING,COLOUR PROD		8451		5101		4105		7724	PROD TEINTURE,COLORANTS
531	SYNT DYE,NAT INDGO,LAKES	W 477	6131	W 267	2094	W 294	1752	W 453	3851	MAT COLOR ORGAN,LAQUES
5311	SYNTHIC ORGNIC DYESTUFFS	W 415	5724	W 176	1754	W 208	1392	W 379	3470	MAT COLOR ORGAN SYNTHET
533	PIGMENTS,PAINTS,ETC	W 810	2295	W 949	2978	W 912	2338	W 1399	3747	PIGMENTS,PEINTURES,VERNIS
541	*MEDICINAL,PHARM PRODUCT	K 2304914	45817	K 2542043	44980	K 2296159	32725	K 2558881	36085	PROD MEDICINAUX PHARMACEUT
5417	MEDICAMENTS	K 2041174	42347	K 2235180	41204	K 2047397	28365	K 2229923	31874	MEDICAMENTS
55	PERFUME,CLEANING ETC PRD		10029		11029		6338		10275	PROD POUR PARFUM,TOILETTE
553	PERFUMERY,COSMETICS,ETC	W 1576	4575	W 1624	5004	W 1215	2599	W 1816	4311	PRODUITS DE PARFUMERIE
554	SOAP,CLEANSING ETC PREPS	W 1890	3205	W 4951	3828	W 1395	1912	W 1575	2815	SAVONS,PRODUITS DETERSIFS
562	*FERTILIZERS,MANUFACTURE	W 64271	6929	W 66496	9574	W 94593	9032	W 83921	13515	ENGRAIS MANUFACTURES
5621	CHEM NITROGENOUS FERTLZR	W 42055	4370	W 32298	5128	W 45190	4299	W 38895	7576	ENGRAIS AZOTES
56216	UREA	W 15495	2761	W 20187	3653	W 19577	2507	W 25884	6323	UREE
5623	CHEM POTASSIC FERTILIZER	W 21831	2419	W 34142	4391	W 33389	3261	W 44290	5524	ENGRAIS POTASSIQUES
56231	POTASSIUM CHLORIDE	W 21801	2408	W 33944	4294	W 33201	3174	W 44101	5432	CHLORURE DE POTASSIUM
58	PLASTIC MATERIALS ETC		25762		22436		23535		36196	MAT PLAST ARTIFICIELLES
582	PROD OF CONDENSATION ETC	W 1896	2475	W 1924	2742	W 2444	2885	W 2388	3903	PROD CONDENS,POLYCOND
583	POLYMERIZATION ETC PRODS	W 20338	21761	W 17939	18000	W 27304	19603	W 25755	30637	PROD POLYMERISATION
5831	POLYETHYLENE	W 6867	6494	W 7193	6639	W 9040	6083	W 9937	11682	POLYETHYLENE
58311	— IN PRIMARY FORMS	W 6758	6163	W 7062	6127	W 8930	5689	W 9776	10998	POLYETHYLENE PRIMAIRES
5832	POLYPROPYLENE	W 4432	4496	W 3522	3523	W 5062	4140	W 4949	6679	POLYPROPYLENE
58321	— IN PRIMARY FORMS	W 4201	3560	W 3338	2760	W 4856	3487	W 4768	6133	POLYPROPYLENE PRIMAIRES
5834	POLYVINYL CHLORIDE	W 7429	7845	W 5713	5255	W 12083	7700	W 9057	8937	CHLORURE DE POLYVINYLE
58341	— IN PRIMARY FORMS	W 4930	3870	W 3922	3091	W 9862	5837	W 7397	7222	SOUS FORMES PRIMAIRES
59	CHEMICAL MATERIALS NES		17309		17641		18397		23941	MAT PROD CHIMIQUES NDA
591	PESTICIDES,DISINFECTANTS	W 1450	6077	W 1631	7057	W 1381	7367	W 1164	8019	DESINF,INSECT,FONG,HERB
5914	DISINFECTANTS,ETC,FR RET	W 1137	5076	W 1373	6374	W 1085	6573	W 940	7328	DESINFECTANTS VENTE DET
59149	RAT POISONS ETC FR RTAIL	W 998	4745	W 1277	6000	W 1014	6407	W 843	7048	ANTIPARASITES VENTE DET
598	MISCEL CHEM PRODUCTS NES	W 4149	10107	W 3837	9213	W 7419	9520	W 10391	14233	PROD DIV INDUST CHIM NDA
5982	ANTI–KNOCK PREPARTNS ETC	W 1432	4224	W 1292	4095	W 1875	4360	W 2311	6988	PREPARAT ANTIDETONANTES
5989	CHEM PRODUCTS,PREPS NES	W 2580	5578	W 2299	4598	W 2370	3943	W 2701	4744	PROD PREP CHIMIQUES NDA
6	BASIC MANUFACTURES		190318		175537		132682		212593	ART MANUFACTURES
62	RUBBER MANUFACTURES NES		14032		11878		10576		17165	CAOUTCHOUC MANUFACTURE
625	RUBBER TYRES, TUBES ETC	W 3861	10000	W 3014	8149	W 3490	6916	W 4679	11654	PNEUS CAOUTCHOUC VULCANISE
6252	TYRES,NEW,BUS OR LORRY	W 1115	4589	W 857	3743	W 850	3122	W 1392	5987	PNEUS POUR AUTOBUS,CAMIONS
6259	OTH TYRES,TYRE CASES,ETC	W 2439	3865	W 1918	3227	W 2374	2773	W 2893	3833	AUTRES PNEUS RECHAPES FLAPS
628	RUBBER ARTICLES NES	W 300	2651	W 248	2463	W 338	2194	W 424	3726	OUVRAGES CAOUTCHOUC NDA
63	WOOD,CORK MANUFACTRS NES		7336		6580		3778		4768	OUVRAGES LIEGE ET BOIS
634	VENEERS,PLYWOOD,ETC	W 6569	6404	W 5105	5660	W 4542	3206	W 4460	3998	PLACAGES,CONTRE–PLAQUES
6342	PLYWOOD OF WOOD SHEETS	W 6317	6111	W 4943	5465	W 4288	2965	W 3972	3587	BOIS CONTRE–PLAQUES
64	PAPER,PAPERBOARD AND MFR		31697		29058		22434		36026	PAPIERS,CARTONS & OUVRAGES
641	PAPER AND PAPERBOARD	W 23119	21137	W 20051	17815	W 18821	14576	W 23129	25983	PAPIERS ET CARTONS
6412	PRINTG,WRITING PAPER NES	W 4534	4382	W 3997	3957	W 2818	2521	W 3493	4808	PAPIERS POUR L'IMPRESSION
64121	— UNCOATED	W 4071	3587	W 3595	3336	W 2509	2145	W 2870	3819	PAPIERS IMPRES NON COUCHES
6413	KRAFT PAPER,PAPERBOARD	W 9125	7155	W 8497	6446	W 7073	4271	W 9893	9277	PAPIER ET CARTON KRAFT
64131	KRAFT LINER IN BULK	W 9125	7155	W 8497	6446	W 7073	4271	W 9893	9277	PAP KRAFT POUR COUVERTURES
6415	PAPER,PAPERBRD,BULK,NES	W 4607	3451	W 4181	3071	W 4144	2566	W 4429	4386	PAPIERS,CARTONS ROULEAUX
6418	COATED ETC PAPER NES BLK	W 3841	5262	W 2550	3802	W 4210	4784	W 3762	5777	PAP,CARTONS COUCHES,ENDUITS
64189	COATED PAPER ETC NES	W 3724	5059	W 2438	3597	W 4114	4633	W 3680	5634	PAPIERS,CARTONS COUCHES
642	PAPER,ETC,PRECUT,ARTS OF	W 3573	10560	W 3812	11243	W 4137	7858	W 4166	10044	PAP,CARTONS DECOUPES
6424	PAPER ETC CT TO SIZE NES	W 2266	6174	W 2386	6614	W 2858	5030	W 2138	4570	PAP,CARTONS DECOUPES
64249	OTH PAPER CT TO SIZE NES	W 1918	4907	W 2113	5376	W 2586	4181	W 1779	3391	AUT PAP CARTON DECOUP NDA
65	TEXTILE YARN,FABRICS,ETC		34258		24320		16299		35600	FILS,TISSUS,ARTICLES TEXTILE
651	TEXTILE YARN	W 421	2753	W 382	2549	W 395	2121	W 760	3974	FILS TEXTILES
652	COTTON FABRICS,WOVEN	W 3248	15795	W 1091	6059	W 329	1197	W 2374	11083	TISSUS DE COTON
6521	GREY WOVEN COTTON FABRIC	W 2777	13289	W 983	5404	W 160	592	W 1887	9340	TISSUS COT ECRUS NON MERCER
65214	GREY WOVEN COTTON NES	W 2772	13275	W 983	5402	W 160	592	W 1886	9328	AUT TISSUS 85% COTON ECRUS
653	WOVN MAN–MADE FIB FABRIC	W 919	3649	W 847	3601	W 1261	4106	W 1496	5598	TISSUS FIBRES SYNTH,ARTIF
657	SPECIAL TXTL FABRC,PRODS	W 823	2778	W 875	3064	W 1066	3252	W 1651	5536	TISSUS SPECIAUX
658	TEXTILE ARTICLES NES	W 4584	7219	W 4358	6287	W 1620	4052	W 3713	6399	ART FACONNES MAT TEXTILES
6581	BAGS,SACKS OF TEXTILES	W 4155	5678	W 3910	4652	W 1269	2626	W 1164	2318	SACS EMBALLAGE TEXTILES
66	NONMETAL MINERAL MFS NES		17140		16758		14590		21574	ART MIN NON METALLIQUES
662	CLAY,REFRACTORY BLDG PRD	W 11294	5741	W 12461	6756	W 14290	5740	W 16072	7860	MAT CONST REFRACTAIRES
6624	BRICKS ETC NONREFRACTORY	W 10824	5152	W 12067	6156	W 13888	5272	W 14927	6577	BRIQUES ETC CERAM NON REFR
66245	GLAZED CERAMIC SETTS ETC	W 8511	3793	W 9694	4442	W 11076	3962	W 12536	5179	AUT CARREAUX CERAMIQUE
665	GLASSWARE	W 4547	5782	W 3455	5324	W 4166	4336	W 6230	7342	OUVRAGES EN VERRE
6651	BOTTLES ETC OF GLASS	W 2440	3081	W 2325	3406	W 3501	2818	W 4643	5287	RECIPIENTS EN VERRE
66511	GLASS BOTTLES ETC NONVAC	W 2440	3080	W 2325	3406	W 3501	2818	W 4643	5287	BONBONNES,BOUTEILLES,ETC
67	IRON AND STEEL		49180		51948		42727		58692	FER ET ACIER
673	IRON,STEEL SHAPES ETC	W 40497	16472	W 37885	15595	W 68747	20248	W 62056	24992	BARRES,PROFIL FER,ACIER
6731	IRON,STEEL WIRE ROD	W 10223	3744	W 22951	8441	W 60390	16974	W 51661	19601	FIL MACHINE FER,ACIER
67311	IRON,SIMPLE STL WIRE ROD	W 10223	3744	W 22951	8441	W 60390	16974	W 51661	19601	FIL MACH AUT ACIER FIN
6732	IRON,STEEL BARS ETC	W 26169	10214	W 11209	4959	W 6417	2268	W 6895	3258	BARRES FER,ACIER
67326	IRN,OTH STL BARS HOTROLD	W 26165	10194	W 11164	4884	W 6385	2219	W 6882	3177	BARRES PLEINES FER,ACIER
674	IRN,STL UNIV,PLATE,SHEET	W 18403	18675	W 25184	24020	W 31292	17449	W 26451	21307	LARGES PLATS,TOLES
6744	IRN,STL HVY PLATE,ROLLED	W 1524	1307	W 1288	1033	W 1026	706	W 7013	4416	TOLES LAMINEES PLUS 4.75 MM
6746	IRN,STL THIN PLATE,ROLLD	W 4338	2732	W 6798	3824	W 15948	5687	W 6882	3799	TOLES LAM MOINS 3MM
6747	TINNED PLATES,SHEETS	W 8561	10924	W 14255	16714	W 12909	10118	W 10088	10544	TOLES ETAMEES EN ACIER
678	IRON,STL TUBES,PIPES,ETC	W 6254	8182	W 4017	6431	W 2992	3760	W 4140	7458	TUBES,TUYAUX EN FONTE,FER
6782	IRON,STL SEAMLESS TUBES	W 1031	1214	W 557	754	W 511	462	W 1952	3813	TUBES,TUYAUX SANS SOUDURE
6783	IRON,STL TUBES,PIPES NES	W 4889	5533	W 1184	1701	W 1936	1737	W 995	1328	AUT TUBES,TUYAUX FER,ACIER
68	NON–FERROUS METALS		4544		3972		3505		6304	METAUX NON FERREUX
684	ALUMINIUM	W 591	3165	W 549	3006	W 582	2391	W 989	4468	ALUMINIUM
6842	ALUMINIUM,ALLOYS WORKED	W 591	3165	W 549	3006	W 582	2391	W 989	4468	ALUMINIUM,ALLIAGES OUVRE
69	METAL MANUFACTURES NES		31904		30856		18553		32174	ART MANUFACT EN METAL NDA
691	STRUCTURES AND PARTS NES	W 1656	3445	W 877	2556	W 547	1341	W 1494	6523	CONSTRUCT FER,ACIER,ALU
6911	STRUCTURES,PARTS IRN,STL	W 1408	2831	W 671	1825	W 433	874	W 1342	6206	CONSTRUCT FER,ACIER,FONTE
692	METAL TANKS,BOXES,ETC	W 691	2294	W 1260	3728	W 1219	2438	W 1800	5575	RECIPIENTS METALLIQUES
6924	MTL TRANSPORT BOXES ETC	W 637	2065	W 1180	3347	W 1203	2322	W 1543	4230	FUTS,TAMBOURS,BIDONS
695	TOOLS	W 808	6019	W 404	2968	W 490	1659	W 410	2037	OUTILS A MAIN
6954	BLADES,TIPS,ETC FR TOOLS	W 450	4175	W 53	1478	W 37	495	W 27	656	OUTILS POUR MACHINE–OUTIL
69541	PARTS TO INSERT IN TOOLS	W 436	4035	W 46	1337	W 25	390	W 19	527	OUTILS DE FORAGE
697	BASE MTL HOUSEHOLD EQUIP	W 1708	4584	W 941	6479	W 1152	2524	W 1340	3699	ART MENAGE MET COMMUNS
6974	BASE MTL DMSTC ARTIC NES	W 1479	2440	W 709	4247	W 923	1231	W 1102	1756	ARTICLES NDA FONTE,FER,ETC
69741	— OF IRON OR STEEL	W 1351	1986	W 598	3842	W 861	984	W 1032	1512	ART NDA EN FONTE,FER
699	BASE METAL MFRS NES	W 3685	12063	W 3036	10398	W 2846	7341	W 3624	10258	ART MANUFACTURES MET NDA
6998	MFRS NES OF CPR,NIKL,ETC	W 1232	3831	W 818	2588	W 728	1719	W 868	2325	OUVRAGES EN CU,NI,AL,PB,ZN
7	MACHINES,TRANSPORT EQUIP		271098		252385		161833		221317	MACHINES MATERIEL TRANSPORT
71	POWER GENERATING EQUIPMT		18038		19865		20283		17165	MACHINES GENERATRICES
711	STEAM BOILERS & AUX PLNT	W 48	771	W 191	3472	W 101	837	W 127	2690	GENERATEURS VAPEUR EAU ETC
713	INTRNL COMBUS PSTN ENGIN	W 3035	10120	W 2194	10263	W 2184	10776	W 3109	8697	MOTEURS EXPL COMB INT, PIECE
7138	PISTON ENGINES NES	W 2703	3997	W 1983	4385	W 2032	4164	W 2866	3867	MOTEURS A PISTONS NDA

4. Special Imports C.I.F. by Commodities according to the S.I.T.C. (Rev. 2) in thousand U.S. Dollars
Importations Spéciales C.A.F. par Produits d'après la C.T.C.I. (Rév. 2) en milliers de Dollars E.U.

SITC CTCI	COMMODITY	1992 WEIGHT POIDS	1992 VALUE VALEUR	1993 WEIGHT POIDS	1993 VALUE VALEUR	1994 WEIGHT POIDS	1994 VALUE VALEUR	1995 WEIGHT POIDS	1995 VALUE VALEUR	PRODUIT
7139	PISTON ENGINE PARTS NES	W 84	3264	W 80	3581	W 74	4220	W 83	2340	PIECES POUR 713.2,3,8
714	ENGINES AND MOTORS NES		39	W 7	150	W 56	4249	W 5	73	MOTEURS NON ELECTRIQUES
7148	GAS TURBINES NES			W 2	29	W 26	3377			TURBINES A GAZ
71488	OTHER GAS TURBINES NES			W 2	29	W 26	3377			AUTRES TURBINES A GAZ
716	ROTATING ELECTRIC PLANT	W 475	6073	W 466	5441	W 465	4133	W 405	4798	APP ELECTR ROTATIFS,PIECES
7161	DC MOTORS AND GENERATORS	W 348	3592	W 367	3827	W 346	3084	W 339	4073	MOTEURS COURANT CONTINU
72	MACHS FOR SPCL INDUSTRYS		49940		44041		24997		35907	MAC SPECIALES POUR INDUST
723	CIVIL ENGNEERG EQUIP ETC	W 7105	29689	W 7467	26545	W 3835	8820	W 3508	12627	APPAREILS DE GENIE CIVIL
7234	CONST,MINING MACHNRY NES	W 6640	25733	W 6789	21717	W 3542	6347	W 2843	8452	MACH POUR LA CONST, MINES
72341	SELF–PROPELLD DOZERS,ETC	W 1898	7483	W 1162	3722	W 555	701	W 863	2215	BULLDOZERS
72342	SLFPRP SHOVELS,EXCAVATRS	W 1630	6100	W 1528	3488	W 934	1556	W 321	1214	PELLES MECANIQUES
72344	BORING,SINKING MACHINERY	W 50	321	W 2085	7964	W 66	303	W 138	635	MACHINES DE FORAGE
72346	OTH CONST,MINING MCH NES	W 2126	8002	W 1597	4676	W 1444	1754	W 1078	1440	AUT MACH EXTRACTION,EXCAV ET
7239	CONSTR ETC MACHY PTS NES	W 291	3308	W 579	4583	W 202	2380	W 95	1341	PIECES 723.41–723.46
724	TEXTILE,LEATHER MACHNRY	W 191	1826	W 189	1925	W 819	3878	W 893	3679	MACH POUR INDUSTRIE TEXTILE
727	FOOD MACHRY NON–DOMESTIC	W 235	3148	W 275	2768	W 366	3872	W 631	3579	MACH INDUSTRIES ALIMENT
7272	OTH FOOD PROC MCHY,PARTS	W 159	2419	W 220	2115	W 308	3316	W 546	2993	AUT MACH IND ALIMENTAIRE
728	OTH MACHY FOR SPCL INDUS	W 874	7879	W 937	9190	W 744	5681	W 1157	11535	AUT MACH IND PARTICULIERES
7284	MACHY FOR SPCL INDUS NES	W 438	5637	W 521	7055	W 452	4576	W 534	8672	MACH SPEC IND PARTICUL.
73	METALWORKING MACHINERY		2606		4442		4029		2770	MACH TRAVAIL DES METAUX
736	METALWORKING MACH–TOOLS	W 210	1952	W 324	3667	W 212	3729	W 360	1850	MACH–OUTILS TRAVAIL METAUX
74	GENRL INDUSTRL MACHY NES		45480		44274		30292		41228	MACH APP INDUSTRIE
741	HEATING,COOLING EQUIPMNT	W 565	8152	W 583	6657	W 409	4272	W 522	6175	MACH CHAUFFAGE,PIECES
742	PUMPS FOR LIQUIDS ETC	W 287	5979	W 373	6942	W 356	6010	W 360	6301	POMPES MOTO–POMPES
743	PUMPS NES,CENTRFUGES ETC	W 469	5879	W 450	6187	W 468	4105	W 607	7105	POMPES COMPRES,VENT ETC
7436	GAS,LIQUID FILTERS ETC	W 150	1860	W 145	2132	W 125	1265	W 246	4094	APP POUR FILT DES LIQUIDES
744	MECHANICAL HANDLING EQU	W 1162	7759	W 1041	6186	W 976	4417	W 1394	6965	EQUIP MANUTENTION PIECES
7442	LIFTING,LOADING MACH NES	W 604	4622	W 624	3933	W 623	2907	W 970	4511	APP LEVAGE,MANUTENTION
745	NONELEC MACHY,TOOLS NES	W 238	5207	W 314	6191	W 193	2434	W 252	4737	AUT MACH NON ELEC,PIECES
7452	OTH NONELEC MCHS,PTS NES	W 219	5086	W 285	5277	W 179	2349	W 244	4465	AUT MACH NON ELEC,PIECES
749	NONELEC MACH PTS,ACC NES	W 762	12503	W 756	12111	W 683	9054	W 666	9944	PIECES MACH NON ELEC NDA
7492	COCKS,VALVES ETC NES	W 366	4059	W 354	3516	W 371	2943	W 354	3940	ART ROB,SIM POUR TUYAUX
7493	SHAFT,CRANK,PULLEY ETC	W 194	4170	W 206	4760	W 149	3473	W 110	3145	ARBRES TRANS,VILEBREQUINS
75	OFFICE MACHNES,ADP EQUIP		13177		8572		3429		4652	MACH BUREAU TRAIT AUTOM
752	AUTOMTIC DATA PROC EQUIP	W 99	9058	W 73	5359	W 39	1633	W 52	2500	MACH TRAIT INFORMATION
76	TELECOMM,SOUND EQUIPMENT		20856		16681		11380		16330	EQUIPMENT DE TELECOM
761	TELEVISION RECEIVERS	W 406	4149	W 278	3279	W 204	1827	W 319	2930	RECEPTEURS DE TELEVISION
764	TELECOM EQPT,PTS,ACC NES	W 463	16316	W 291	12810	W 352	9026	W 482	12982	EQUIP TELECOM,PIECES
7641	LINE TELEPHONE,ETC EQUIP	W 93	7452	W 30	2957	W 45	2317	W 42	2673	APP TELEPHON PAR FIL
7643	TV,RADIO TRANSMITTRS ETC	W 46	3612	W 14	2780	W 5	321	W 29	1178	APP EMET TELE RADIO
7649	PTS NES OF EQUIPMT OF 76	W 47	3516	W 40	4610	W 73	5016	W 80	6745	PIECES DE LA DIV 76
76491	PTS NES OF APPAR OF 7641	W 20	1811	W 25	3756	W 52	4164	W 73	6434	PIECES POUR 764.1
77	ELECTRIC MACHNRY NES ETC		35633		31095		19776		32469	MACH APP ELECT NDA
772	SWITCHGEAR ETC,PARTS NES	W 351	6897	W 289	5916	W 294	5005	W 360	6581	APP COUPURE,SECT ETC
7721	SWITCHGEAR ETC	W 322	6070	W 247	5275	W 281	4837	W 348	6435	APP COUPURE,SECTIONMNT
773	ELECTR DISTRIBUTNG EQUIP	W 1797	9649	W 2025	8882	W 1036	3104	W 1910	7940	EQUIPMT DISTRIBUTION ELECT
7731	INSULATED WIRE,CABLE ETC	W 1721	9190	W 1952	8525	W 1018	2983	W 1833	7434	FILS,CABLES ISOLES ELECT
775	HOUSEHOLD TYPE EQUIP NES	W 1075	5397	W 1063	5241	W 1112	4501	W 1249	6143	MACH,APP USAGE DOMESTQUE
7752	DOM REFRIGERATRS,FREEZRS	W 822	4447	W 884	4356	W 913	3794	W 1041	4735	REFRIG,CONGEL MENAGER
77521	DOMESTIC REFRIGERATORS	W 777	3584	W 821	3512	W 835	2270	W 793	2005	REFRIGERATEURS
778	ELECTRICAL MACHINERY NES	W 1908	8122	W 1645	7920	W 1354	4674	W 1601	7406	AUTRES MACH ELECT NDA
7781	BATTERIES,ACCUMULATORS	W 1368	3958	W 1094	3594	W 961	2168	W 1047	3300	PILES ET ACCUMULATEURS
78	ROAD VEHICLES		80890		79924		42617		66927	VEHICULES ROUTIERS
781	PASS MOTOR VEH EXC BUSES	W 6282	36978	W 6153	37208	W 2621	18030	W 3946	24131	AUTO TRANSPORT PERSONNES
782	LORRIES,SPCL MTR VEH NES	W 5789	18740	W 6936	22265	W 3227	11678	W 5769	20591	VEHICULES SPECIAUX,MARCH
7821	LORRIES,TRUCKS	W 5246	16322	W 6440	20548	W 2816	9902	W 5063	18450	VEHICULES TRANSP MARCHAND
783	ROAD MOTOR VEHICLES NES	W 1509	7753	W 1425	6728	W 723	2943	W 1774	7929	VEHICULES ROUTIERS NDA
7831	BUSES	W 398	3651	W 359	2565	W 214	1163	W 627	3282	VOITURES TRANSPORT COMMUN
7832	TRACTORS FOR TR–TRAILERS	W 1111	4102	W 1066	4163	W 509	1779	W 1147	4647	TRACTEURS ROUTIERS
784	MOTOR VEH PRTS,ACCES NES	W 1773	11717	W 1537	9011	W 1520	6834	W 2128	9342	PIECES 722,781,782,783
7849	OTHER MOTOR VEHCL PARTS	W 1632	10953	W 1516	8942	W 1508	6830	W 2098	9282	PIECES 722,781,782,783
79	OTHR TRANSPORT EQUIPMENT		4478		3491		5030		3869	AUTRE MATERIEL TRANSPORT
793	SHIPS AND BOATS ETC	W 1586	3006	W 57	206	W 217	2705	W 310	1035	NAVIRES BATEAUX,ETC
8	MISC MANUFACTURED GOODS		66278		55542		44196		54089	ART MANUFACTURES DIVERS
812	*PLUMBG,HEATNG,LGHTNG EQ	W 1268	3589	W 1131	4289	W 1100	2527	W 1374	4814	APPAR SANITAIRES CHAUFFAGE
821	*FURNITURE,PARTS THEREOF	W 1293	6014	W 1397	4407	W 1288	3602	W 1160	4045	MEUBLES ET PIECES
8219	FURNITURE AND PARTS NES	W 830	3650	W 792	2684	W 593	1711	W 575	1890	AUTRES MEUBLES ET PIECES
84	CLOTHING AND ACCESSORIES		5656		5630		5077		7497	VETEMENTS
851	*FOOTWEAR	W 786	3108	W 740	2746	W 580	1869	W 1134	3734	CHAUSSURES
87	PRECISION INSTRUMNTS NES		11469		6652		10567		5250	INSTRUM,APPAR SCIENT NDA
872	MEDICAL INSTRUMENTS NES	W 110	1857	W 113	1897	W 273	4350	W 144	1343	INSTR,APP MEDIC–CHIR NDA
87202	OTH MEDICAL INSTRUMENTS	W 102	1499	W 107	1602	W 270	4181	W 130	1235	INSTRUM,APP MEDECINE
874	MEASURNG,CONTROLNG INSTR	W 101	7564	W 102	3556	W 495	4120	W 127	2483	INSTRUMENTS DE MESURE
88	PHOTO EQU,OPTICL GDS ETC		4175		2629		2102		3173	APP,FOURN PHOTO,OP,MONTR
89	MISC MANUFCTRD GOODS NES		31115		28332		17918		24281	ART MANUFACTURES DIVERS
892	PRINTED MATTER	W 1276	11601	W 1344	10669	W 1020	5675	W 922	6899	IMPRIMES
8921	PRINTED BOOKS,GLOBES,ETC	W 671	6015	W 826	5804	W 607	3235	W 550	4513	LIVRES,BROCHURES,CARTES
89211	PRINTED BOOKS,PAMPHLETS	W 640	5957	W 818	5793	W 592	3203	W 537	4472	LIVRES,BROCHURES
8922	NEWSPAPERS,PERIODICALS	W 370	4216	W 315	3729	W 227	1709	W 115	1021	JOURNAUX ET PERIODIQUES
893	ARTICLES OF PLASTIC NES	W 2738	10932	W 2319	10406	W 2088	7916	W 2286	9835	OUVRAGES EN MAT DIVIS 58
8931	PLSTC PACKG CONTNRS,LIDS	W 1120	4544	W 1217	5295	W 1093	4068	W 1147	5251	ART TRANSP EMBALLAGE ETC
8939	MISC PLASTIC ARTICLES	W 1491	5910	W 983	4621	W 912	3497	W 937	3951	ART DIVERS EN MAT DIV 58
89399	OTHR PLASTC ARTICLES NES	W 1489	5880	W 978	4587	W 911	3492	W 935	3939	AUT OUV MAT DIV 58
9	GOODS NOT CLASSD BY KIND		114		142		1296		5194	ART TRANSACT NON CLASSES
951	*WAR FIREARMS,AMMUNITION		33		120	W 20	1287	W 79	5194	VEHIC BLINDES ARMES

5. Special Exports F.O.B. by Commodities according to the S.I.T.C. (Rev. 2) in thousand U.S. Dollars
Exportations Spéciales F.O.B. par Produits d'après la C.T.C.I. (Rév. 2) en milliers de Dollars E.U.

SITC CTCI	COMMODITY	1992		1993		1994		1995		PRODUIT
		WEIGHT POIDS	VALUE VALEUR	WEIGHT POIDS	VALUE VALEUR	WEIGHT POIDS	VALUE VALEUR	WEIGHT POIDS	VALUE VALEUR	
	ALL COMMODITIES		683031		605102		444402		530759	TOUS PRODUITS
0	FOOD AND LIVE ANIMALS		215905		176319		63544		21259	ALIMENTS,ANIMAUX VIVANTS
03	FISH AND PREPARATIONS		186875		143623		42854		9842	POISSONS ET PREPARATIONS
034	FISH,FRESH,CHILLED,FROZN	W 29663	50496	W 20318	57017	W 22467	21490	W 1607	8596	POISSON FRAIS, REFRIG,CONG
0341	FISH FRSH,CHLLD,EX FILLT	W 29663	50496	W 20318	57017	W 22467	21490	W 1607	8596	POISSON FRAIS,REFRIGERE
035	FISH SALTED,DRIED,SMOKED	W 2663	5256	W 2318	4313	W 2830	2348	W 1744	976	POISSON SECHE,SALE,FUME
03503	FISH(EX COD)DRIED,SALTED	W 2613	5209	W 2240	4213	W 2445	2265	W 1607	964	POISSONS SECHES,SALES
036	SHELL FISH FRESH,FROZEN	W 3475	22270	W 2315	15423	W 2569	10576	W 4	25	CRUSTACES,MOLLUSQUES
037	FISH ETC PREPD,PRSVD NES	W 40227	108853	W 24494	66870	W 3432	8439	W 212	245	POIS,CRUST,MOL PREPARES
0371	FISH PREPARD,PRESRVD NES	W 29148	82118	W 17567	48333	W 771	2155	W 175	168	CONSERVES DE POISSONS
0372	SHELL FISH PREPRD,PRESVD	W 11079	26735	W 6927	18538	W 2661	6284	W 38	76	CRUSTACES,COQUIL PREPARES
05	VEGETABLES AND FRUIT		4953		11184		2838		2305	LEGUMES ET FRUITS
054	VEG ETC FRSH,SMPLY PRSVD	W 737	1528	W 4467	8740	W 2712	1697	W 1738	821	LEGUMES FRAIS,CONG,SECS
0545	OTHER FRESH VEGETABLES	W 573	1337	W 3956	8057	W 2069	1467	W 187	127	AUTRES LEGUMES FRAIS,REF
05459	FRESH VEGETABLES NES	W 573	1337	W 3956	8057	W 2036	1453	W 186	126	LEGUMES FRAIS,REFRI NDA
057	FRUIT,NUTS,FRESH,DRIED	W 1746	1554	W 3073	2103	W 2149	1063	W 1895	1445	FRUITS FRAIS OU SECS
06	SUGAR AND PREPS,HONEY		344		2849		2295		848	SUCRES ET PRODUITS
061	SUGAR AND HONEY		134	W 42131	2590	W 35644	2129	W 7388	579	SUCRES ET MIEL
0615	MOLASSES			W 42104	2526	W 35636	2122	W 7200	488	MELASSES
081	*FEEDING STUFF FOR ANIML	W 127859	20388	W 77725	13574	W 90662	13584	W 43823	6342	NOURRITURE POUR ANIMAUX
0813	OILCAKE AND OTH RESIDUES	W 124174	18889	W 73598	11889	W 84851	12515	W 38163	5088	TOURTEAUX
08132	— OF GROUNDNUTS	W 116422	16961	W 69592	11375	W 83768	12372	W 37163	5028	TOURTEAUX D'ARACHIDES
09	MISC EDIBLE PRODUCTS		1772		1983		684		861	PREP ALIMENTAIRES DIVERSES
098	EDIBLE PRODCTS,PREPS NES	W 430	1772	W 437	1980	W 254	684	W 328	848	PREP ALIMENTAIRES NDA
1	BEVERAGES AND TOBACCO		2090		2647		790		1114	BOISSONS ET TABACS
2	CRUDE MATERLS,EXCL FUELS		126231		103392		62979		104571	MAT BRUTES NON COMESTIBLES
21	HIDES,SKINS,FURS UNDRSSD		1968		3775		3763		5032	CUIRS,PEAUX BRUTS
211	HIDES,SKINS,EXC FURS,RAW	W 1154	1968	W 2542	3775	W 1637	3763	W 1659	5032	CUIRS ET PEAUX
2111	BOVINE,EQUINE HIDES,RAW	W 928	1274	W 2181	2810	W 1168	1787	W 468	1116	PEAUX DE BOVINS
22	OIL SEEDS,OLEAGINOUS FRT		6542		1911		4540		3673	GRAINES,FRUITS OLEAGINEUX
222	SEEDS FOR'SOFT'FIXED OIL	W 13962	6542	W 3496	1910	W 13230	4540	W 6617	3673	GRAINES HUILES FIXES
2221	GROUNDNUTS,GREEN	W 11913	6294	W 2811	1805	W 6549	3846	W 6617	3673	ARACHIDES NON GRILLEES
26	TEXTILE FIBRES AND WASTE		28025		27375		19017		33536	FIBRES TEXTILES
263	COTTON	W 16481	27409	W 19790	27210	W 15242	19011	W 9079	33522	COTON
2631	RAW COTTON,EXCL LINTERS	W 16480	27407	W 19789	27201	W 15242	19011	W 9079	33522	COTON EN MASSE
27	CRUDE FERTLZR,MINRLS NES		82731		64891		29761		51636	ENGRAIS MINERAUX BRUTS
271	FERTILIZERS,CRUDE	W 1261120	66434	W 871711	51166	W 529991	16723	W 846468	43268	ENGRAIS BRUTS
2713	NAT CALCM PHOSPHATES ETC	W 1261120	66434	W 871711	51166	W 529990	16716	W 846468	43268	PHOSPHATES DE CALCIUM
27131	— UNGROUND	W 1260640	66354	W 871711	51166	W 529989	16716	W 846466	43267	PHOSPHATES NON MOULUS
278	OTHER CRUDE MINERALS	W 270436	15769	W 215696	13684	W 288842	12973	W 158856	8258	AUTRES MINERAUX BRUTS
2782	REFRACTORY MINERALS NES	W 112756	5370	W 88016	4486	W 121120	5500	W 58960	2815	ARGILE MINERAUX REFRACTAIRES
27821	CLAY ETC	W 112756	5370	W 88016	4486	W 121120	5500	W 58960	2814	ARGILES
2783	COMMON SALT,ETC	W 157315	10337	W 127660	9193	W 167427	7316	W 99558	5226	SEL
28	METALLIFEROUS ORES,SCRAP		1464		1373		1803		4095	MINERAIS METAL,DECHETS
282	IRON AND STEEL SCRAP	W 4845	609	W 6113	816	W 19912	1317	W 20867	2236	FERRAILLES
288	NONFERR METAL SCRAP NES	W 698	854	W 568	557	W 655	486	W 1340	1859	DECHETS NON FERREUX
2882	OTHER BASE MTL SCRAP NES	W 698	854	W 568	557	W 655	486	W 1340	1859	AUTRES DECHETS
28821	COPPER WASTE AND SCRAP	W 596	798	W 407	438	W 477	401	W 1276	1795	DECHETS DE CUIVRE
29	CRUDE ANIMAL,VEG MAT NES		5164		3698		3940		6495	MATIERES BRUTES ANIM,VEGET
292	CRUDE VEG MATERIALS NES	W 1820	5162	W 1301	3673	W 1739	3937	W 2102	6467	MAT BRUTES VEGETALES NDA
2922	NAT GUMS,RESINS,LACS,ETC	W 1740	5057	W 1233	3440	W 1656	3766	W 2038	6325	GOMME LAQUE
3	MINERAL FUELS ETC		80284		87445		73014		79969	COMBUSTIBLES MINERAUX LUB
33	PETROLEUM AND PRODUCTS		79923		86887		72602		79377	PETROLE ET DERIVES
334	PETROLEUM PRODUCTS,REFIN	W 405823	79695	W 436142	86401	W 438507	72427	W 396186	78861	PRODUITS RAFFINES
3341	GASOLINE,OTH LIGHT OILS	W 152920	38133	W 134532	33558	W 199799	31807	W 173968	35193	ESSENCES POUR MOTEURS
33411	MOTOR,AVIATION SPIRIT	W 19542	4562	W 20693	5081	W 25163	4462	W 19551	4339	ESSENCES MOTEURS D'AVIONS
33412	SPIRIT TYPE JET FUEL	W 133344	33563	W 113803	28469	W 174636	27345	W 154417	30854	CARBUREACTEURS
3343	GAS OILS	W 132067	24495	W 137302	28598	W 149555	23086	W 138793	22396	GAS OILS
3344	FUEL OILS,NES	W 113978	12156	W 153357	15885	W 68247	4801	W 64650	8147	FUEL OILS
3345	LUBS,PETROLEUM OILS NES	W 4371	4360	W 8135	7698	W 15176	11762	W 14709	12320	HUILES LUBRIFIANTES
33451	LUBS(HIGH PETR CONT) ETC	W 4362	4324	W 7040	7458	W 15168	11739	W 14704	12295	HUILES LUBRIF,H LOURDES
4	ANIMAL,VEGETABLE OIL,FAT		55699		34436		74125		55711	HUILES,GRAISSES ANIM,VEG
42	FIXED VEGETABLE OIL,FAT		55550		34325		73999		54389	HUILES VEGETALES FIXES
423	FIXED VEG OILS,SOFT	W 90938	55532	W 46775	34283	W 73704	73985	W 54653	54208	HUILES VEGET DOUCES FIXES
4234	GROUNDNUT(PEANUT) OIL	W 90640	55040	W 46424	33722	W 73471	73780	W 54518	53842	HUILE D'ARACHIDE
5	CHEMCLS,RELATED PROD NES		127506		103819		109373		209730	PRODUITS CHIMIQUES
51	ORGANIC CHEMICALS		1590		3573		3414		4215	PROD CHIMIQ ORGANIQUES
512	ALCOHOLS,PHENOLS ETC	W 1391	699	W 1550	1087	W 2875	1637	W 1540	1749	PHENOLS,PHENOLS–ALCOOLS
5121	ACYCLIC ALCOHOLS,DERIVS	W 1391	696	W 1540	1071	W 2870	1633	W 1535	1739	ALCOOLS ACYCLIQUES
52	INORGANIC CHEMICALS		82972		56715		71369		119659	PROD CHIM INORGANIQUES
522	INORG ELEMNTS,OXIDES,ETC	W 263641	82844	W 226735	56641	W 275333	71298	W 263168	119487	ELEMENTS INORGANIQUES
5221	CHEMICAL ELEMENTS	W 45	169	W 33	788	W 498	1388	W 45	293	ELEMENTS CHIMIQUES
52211	GASES,EXCL HALOGENS	W 40	160	W 26	774	W 496	1388	W 42	290	OXYGENE,AZOTE,HYDROGENE
5222	INORGANIC ACIDS ETC	W 263022	82322	W 225815	55415	W 273215	69375	W 262558	118947	ACIDES INORGANIQUES
52224	PHOSPHORIC ACIDS ETC	W 262630	82124	W 225638	55335	W 273177	69347	W 262488	118915	ACIDES PHOSPHORIQUES
55	PERFUME,CLEANING ETC PRD		3674		5556		4204		8499	PROD POUR PARFUM,TOILETTE
553	PERFUMERY,COSMETICS,ETC	W 626	3093	W 960	4738	W 1240	3719	W 1774	6968	PRODUITS DE PARFUMERIE
562	*FERTILIZERS,MANUFACTURE	W 185235	31794	W 157652	26813	W 143816	21224	W 170846	63569	ENGRAIS MANUFACTURES
5623	CHEM POTASSIC FERTILIZER			W 700	162			W 5755	15136	ENGRAIS POTASSIQUES
56239	CHEM POTASS FERTILZR NES							W 5755	15136	ENGRAIS POTASSIQUES NDA
5629	FERTILIZERS NES	W 140024	29024	W 141058	24791	W 112127	19646	W 134281	47087	ENGRAIS NDA
58	PLASTIC MATERIALS ETC		3520		3522		2489		5011	MAT PLAST ARTIFICIELLES
583	POLYMERIZATION ETC PRODS	W 3004	3519	W 3122	3106	W 3762	2376	W 3959	4718	PROD POLYMERISATION
5831	POLYETHYLENE	W 792	812	W 782	783	W 760	410	W 1513	1765	POLYETHYLENE
58311	— IN PRIMARY FORMS	W 762	765	W 737	702	W 732	359	W 1497	1719	POLYETHYLENE PRIMAIRES
59	CHEMICAL MATERIALS NES		2586		5120		4930		6870	MAT PROD CHIMIQUES NDA
591	PESTICIDES,DISINFECTANTS	W 364	1496	W 1666	3485	W 1092	3390	W 949	4650	DESINF,INSECT,FONG,HERB
5914	DISINFECTANTS,ETC,FR RET	W 323	1304	W 1535	3132	W 837	2881	W 907	4467	DESINFECTANTS VENTE DET
59149	RAT POISONS ETC FR RTAIL	W 320	1299	W 1535	3132	W 837	2881	W 907	4467	ANTIPARASITES VENTE DET
598	MISCEL CHEM PRODUCTS NES	W 418	867	W 547	1257	W 671	1200	W 755	1799	PROD DIV INDUST CHIM NDA
6	BASIC MANUFACTURES		41315		44225		23411		27875	ART MANUFACTURES
64	PAPER,PAPERBOARD AND MFR		13192		14645		7643		13726	PAPIERS,CARTONS & OUVRAGES
641	PAPER AND PAPERBOARD	W 3562	2946	W 3353	2903	W 4579	1928	W 3774	3172	PAPIERS ET CARTONS
642	PAPER,ETC,PRECUT,ARTS OF	W 5489	10246	W 4685	11742	W 3178	5715	W 4402	10554	PAP,CARTONS DECOUPES
6421	PAPER ETC CONTAINERS	W 3822	5971	W 3213	6192	W 2060	2847	W 3299	6805	BOITES,SACS EMBALLAGES
6423	EXERCISE BOOKS ETC	W 1567	3751	W 1169	3322	W 792	1339	W 747	1823	REGISTRES,CAHIERS,CARNETS
6424	PAPER ETC CT TO SIZE NES	W 76	381	W 279	2077	W 297	1400	W 307	1769	PAP,CARTONS DECOUPES
64249	OTH PAPER CT TO SIZE NES	W 69	329	W 263	1983	W 288	1359	W 261	1651	AUT PAP CARTON DECOUP NDA
65	TEXTILE YARN,FABRICS,ETC		7300		5174		3805		3164	FILS,TISSUS,ARTICLES TEXTILE
652	COTTON FABRICS,WOVEN	W 673	5112	W 419	2586	W 181	560	W 187	664	TISSUS DE COTON
6522	WOVEN COTTON BLEACHD,ETC	W 414	4322	W 166	1771	W 8	99	W 9	54	TISSUS COTON BLANCHIS ETC

5. Special Exports F.O.B. by Commodities according to the S.I.T.C. (Rev. 2) in thousand U.S. Dollars
Exportations Spéciales F.O.B. par Produits d'après la C.T.C.I. (Rév. 2) en milliers de Dollars E.U.

SITC CTCI	COMMODITY	1992 WEIGHT POIDS	1992 VALUE VALEUR	1993 WEIGHT POIDS	1993 VALUE VALEUR	1994 WEIGHT POIDS	1994 VALUE VALEUR	1995 WEIGHT POIDS	1995 VALUE VALEUR	PRODUIT
65224	BLCHED COTTON FABRIC NES	W 414	4322	W 156	1674	W 2	12	W 9	54	AUT TIS PLUS 85% COT BLANCHI
66	NONMETAL MINERAL MFS NES		788		1358		2090		2257	ART MIN NON METALLIQUES
661	LIME,CEMENT,BLDG PRODS	W 2282	343	W 282	69	W 7451	1497	W 7040	973	CHAUX,CIMENTS MAT CONSTR
67	IRON AND STEEL		3630		6457		2703		2654	FER ET ACIER
674	IRN,STL UNIV,PLATE,SHEET	W 2371	3078	W 4377	5773	W 4429	2243	W 1480	1184	LARGES PLATS,TOLES
6747	TINNED PLATES,SHEETS	W 2070	2846	W 3965	5475	W 3759	1962	W 654	705	TOLES ETAMEES EN ACIER
69	METAL MANUFACTURES NES		14539		15405		6190		5055	ART MANUFACT EN METAL NDA
692	METAL TANKS,BOXES,ETC	W 5458	12603	W 5129	12672	W 4136	4807	W 1936	4226	RECIPIENTS METALLIQUES
6924	MTL TRANSPORT BOXES ETC	W 5415	12521	W 5083	12534	W 4087	4711	W 1935	4223	FUTS,TAMBOURS,BIDONS
69241	STL TRANSPORT BOXES ETC	W 4775	11613	W 4575	11695	W 3588	4258	W 1473	3606	FUTS,TAMBOURS,BIDONS FER
7	MACHINES,TRANSPORT EQUIP		21805		39328		25514		13461	MACHINES MATERIEL TRANSPORT
71	POWER GENERATING EQUIPMT		1340		6374		7709		1771	MACHINES GENERATRICES
714	ENGINES AND MOTORS NES	W 5	74	W 16	4064	W 18	6880	W 11	441	MOTEURS NON ELECTRIQUES
7144	REACTION ENGINES			W 7	2585	W 6	6272		1	PROPULSEURS A REACTION
72	MACHS FOR SPCL INDUSTRYS		7126		13787		3612		3194	MAC SPECIALES POUR INDUST
723	CIVIL ENGNEERG EQUIP ETC	W 1730	5097	W 2033	11820	W 1510	2190	W 590	1518	APPAREILS DE GENIE CIVIL
7234	CONST,MINING MACHNRY NES	W 1694	4927	W 1994	11287	W 1496	2073	W 527	1325	MACH POUR LA CONST, MINES
72341	SELF-PROPELLD DOZERS,ETC	W 679	2655	W 553	2439	W 400	452	W 130	213	BULLDOZERS
72343	SLFPRP CONST ETC MCH NES	W 341	422	W 332	1895	W 506	801	W 68	81	AUT MACH EXTR,TERRASSEM
72344	BORING,SINKING MACHINERY	W 1	114	W 560	5120	W 43	127	W 13	94	MACHINES DE FORAGE
74	GENRL INDUSTRL MACHY NES		2339		1887		1762		1392	MACH APP INDUSTRIE
76	TELECOMM,SOUND EQUIPMENT		2053		861		661		596	EQUIPMENT DE TELECOM
78	ROAD VEHICLES		6219		5882		2696		4876	VEHICULES ROUTIERS
781	PASS MOTOR VEH EXC BUSES	W 239	2221	W 302	3104	W 268	1638	W 242	3540	AUTO TRANSPORT PERSONNES
782	LORRIES,SPCL MTR VEH NES	W 595	2325	W 684	1897	W 191	572	W 324	831	VEHICULES SPECIAUX,MARCH
79	OTHR TRANSPORT EQUIPMENT		736		8444		8258		314	AUTRE MATERIEL TRANSPORT
792	AIRCRAFT ETC		603	W 41	8365	W 89	8030	W 2	230	APP NAVIGATION AERIENNE
7929	AIRCRAFT PARTS NES		458	W 37	7470	W 89	8010	W 1	140	PIECES DU 792
8	MISC MANUFACTURED GOODS		12196		13486		11409		11788	ART MANUFACTURES DIVERS
851	*FOOTWEAR	W 867	2737	W 543	2065	W 648	1153	W 319	696	CHAUSSURES
85101	FOOTWEAR RUBBER,PLASTIC	W 866	2734	W 542	2062	W 646	1141	W 317	695	CHAUS SEMELLES CAOUTCH
87	PRECISION INSTRUMNTS NES		572		2274		2221		1217	INSTRUM,APPAR SCIENT NDA
874	MEASURNG,CONTROLNG INSTR	W 7	524	W 11	2226	W 23	2121	W 12	1205	INSTRUMENTS DE MESURE
88	PHOTO EQU,OPTICL GDS ETC		103		131		2055		5	APP,FOURN PHOTO,OP,MONTR
881	PHOTO APPARAT,EQUIPT NES	W 1	27	W 1	24	W 59	2033			APP,EQUIP PHOTO NDA
8813	OTH PHOTO,CINE EQUIP NES		8	W 1	10	W 59	2033			APP,MAT PHOTO,CINEMA
88139	PHOTO,CINE LAB EQUIP NES		8	W 1	9	W 59	2033			APP TYPES UTIL LABOR
89	MISC MANUFCTRD GOODS NES		8068		7895		5484		9538	ART MANUFACTURES DIVERS
893	ARTICLES OF PLASTIC NES	W 2474	6519	W 3382	4774	W 2059	3577	W 3147	7596	OUVRAGES EN MAT DIVIS 58
8931	PLSTC PACKG CONTNRS,LIDS	W 1205	4857	W 2623	3122	W 1004	1945	W 2040	5385	ART TRANSP EMBALLAGE ETC
8939	MISC PLASTIC ARTICLES	W 1239	1578	W 759	1651	W 1053	1627	W 861	1679	ART DIVERS EN MAT DIV 58
89399	OTHR PLASTC ARTICLES NES	W 1239	1578	W 759	1651	W 1053	1627	W 861	1679	AUT OUV MAT DIV 58
9	GOODS NOT CLASSD BY KIND				5		244		5281	ART TRANSACT NON CLASSES
951	*WAR FIREARMS,AMMUNITION					W 8	235	W 35	1610	VEHIC BLINDES ARMES
971	*GOLD,NON MONETARY NES							K 397	3631	OR NON MONETAIRE
97101	NONMON GLD UNWRT,SEMIMFD							K 397	3631	OR,ALLIAGES D'OR BRUTS

1. HISTORICAL SERIES, 1961–1996 GENERAL TRADE, IMPORTS C.I.F., EXPORTS F.O.B.
SERIES HISTORIQUES, 1961–1996 COMMERCE GENERAL, IMPORTATIONS C.A.F., EXPORTATIONS F.O.B

YEAR ANNEE	VALUE IN MILLION SEYCH. RUPEES / VALEUR EN MILLION SEYCH. RUPEES: MERCHANDISE # 1 –MARCHANDISE IMPORTS	EXPORTS	GOLD –OR IMPORTS	EXPORTS	CONVERSION FACTORS U.S. CENTS PER SEYCH. RUPEE / FACTEURS DE CONVERSION CENTS E.U. PAR SEYCH. RUPEE: IMPORTS	EXPORTS	INDEX NUMBERS –INDICES: QUANTUM IMPORTS	QUANTUM EXPORTS	UNIT VALUE / VALEUR UNITAIRE IMPORTS	UNIT VALUE / VALEUR UNITAIRE EXPORTS
1961	12.03	6.71			21.0000	21.0000				
1962	12.80	7.40			21.0000	21.0000				
1963	14.60	6.87			21.0000	21.0000				
1964	15.72	8.69			21.0000	21.0000				
1965	18.67	9.77			21.0000	21.0000				
1966	19.96	8.60			21.0000	21.0000				
1967	24.60	10.04			21.0000	21.0000				
1968	33.88	17.39			18.0000	18.0000				
1969	40.00	13.91			18.0000	18.0000				
1970	55.92	11.90			18.0000	18.0000				
1971	84.00	9.83			18.0801	18.0801				
1972	111.67	12.77			18.7567	18.7567				
1973	135.12	18.86			18.3824	18.3824				
1974	160.46	39.13			17.5448	17.5448				
1975	191.35	35.00			16.6616	16.6616				
1976	290.62	57.63			14.9652	14.9652				
1977	349.74	84.76			13.1142	13.0839				
1978	402.05	96.00			14.3544	14.3544				
1979	534.78	138.63			15.9782	15.9835				
1980	631.44	135.21			15.6446	15.6446				
1981	589.01	108.34			15.8638	15.7884				
1982	641.32	100.09			15.2835	15.1691				
1983	594.14	136.86			14.8031	14.8110				
1984	619.00	181.48			14.1596	14.1344				
1985	704.72	199.69			14.0930	13.9654				
1986	651.96	113.66			16.0901	15.9725	64	17	103	110
1987	633.90	124.07			17.9297	17.8579	63	44	102	112
1988	856.63	171.33			18.5649	18.5778	87	93	100	112
1989	930.15	193.52			17.7039	17.6545	97	102	96	94
1990	993.78	301.50			18.8052	18.9142	100	100	100	100
1991	910.42	258.27			18.9528	18.9750	95	136	97	88
1992	980.87	245.66			19.4576	19.4468	107	126	93	101
1993	1234.86	265.02			19.3068	19.2845	147	106	85	102
1994	1042.38	262.15			19.8173	19.8258				121
1995	1109.00	252.00			20.9893	20.9588				122
1996	1723.85	692.83			20.1133	20.1138				122

2. IMPORTS BY BROAD ECONOMIC CATEGORY AND EXPORTS BY INDUSTRIAL ORIGIN. (PERCENTAGE OF TOTAL VALUE)
IMPORTATIONS PAR CATEGORIES ECONOMIQUES ET EXPORTATIONS PAR BRANCHE D'ACTIVITE.(EN POURCENTAGE DE LA VALEUR TOTALE)

IMPORTS – IMPORTATIONS

	1990	1991	1992	1993	1994	1995	1996
TOTAL IMPORTS–IMPORTATIONS TOTALES	100.	100.	100.	100.	100.	100.	100.
1 FOOD BEV–ALIMENTATION BOISSONS	16.5	17.7	20.7	17.8	19.5	20.2	18.9
11 PRIMARY–PRODUITS DE BASE	6.1	7.2	6.7	7.0	7.8	7.3	8.5
111 FOR INDUSTRY–POUR L'INDUSTRIE	0.3	0.7	0.3	0.4	0.3	0.4	0.3
112 FOR HOUSEHOLDS–POUR LES MENAGES	5.9	6.5	6.4	6.5	7.5	6.8	8.2
12 PROCESSED–PRODUITS ELABORES	10.4	10.5	14.0	10.8	11.7	12.9	10.4
121 FOR INDUSTRY–POUR L'INDUSTRIE	1.7	1.9	3.3	1.6	2.1	2.3	1.8
122 FOR HOUSEHOLDS–POUR LES MENAGES	8.7	8.6	10.7	9.3	9.6	10.6	8.5
2 IND SUPPLIES–APPROV INDUSTRIELS	23.4	24.5	24.3	21.9	24.6	19.4	17.1
21 PRIMARY–PRODUITS DE BASE	2.2	1.7	0.9	1.1	1.7	0.8	0.9
22 PROCESSED–PRODUITS ELABORES	21.2	22.8	23.4	20.9	22.9	18.6	16.2
3 FUELS–COMBUSTIBLES	19.2	21.7	17.1	14.1	15.5	17.3	3.2
31 PRIMARY–PRODUITS DE BASE	0.3	0.2	0.2	0.2	0.2	0.2	0.2
32 PROCESSED–PRODUITS ELABORES	18.9	21.5	16.9	13.9	15.3	17.1	3.0
321 MOTOR SPIRIT–ESSENCE	1.2	1.2	0.8	0.7	15.3	17.1	0.6
322 OTHER–AUTRES	17.7	20.3	16.1	13.2	0.0	0.0	2.4
4 MACHINERY–EQUIPEMENT	18.2	17.5	14.2	21.5	18.0	17.7	15.6
41 CAPITAL EQUIPMENT–MACHINES	17.4	16.9	13.5	20.6	16.2	15.4	14.1
42 PARTS–PIECES ACCESSOIRES	0.8	0.6	0.7	0.9	1.7	2.3	1.5
5 TRANSPORT–TRANSPORT	8.2	5.4	6.3	9.5	6.2	10.2	33.7
51 PASSENGER CARS–AUTOMOBILES	1.9	0.8	0.5	2.5	1.0	1.8	1.6
52 OTHER–AUTRES	2.4	0.7	1.2	2.6	1.9	4.1	28.3
521 INDUSTRIAL–INDUSTRIELS	2.4	0.6	1.1	2.5	1.8	4.0	28.2
522 NON INDUSTRIAL–NON INDUSTRIEL	0.1	0.1	0.1	0.1	0.1	0.1	0.1
53 PARTS–PIECES ACCESSOIRES	3.9	3.9	4.6	4.5	3.3	4.3	3.7
6 CONSUM GOODS–BIENS CONSOMMATION	14.3	13.2	17.2	14.9	16.1	14.9	11.1
61 DURABLE–DURABLES	3.0	2.2	4.2	3.7	3.6	3.6	2.7
62 SEMI DURABLE–SEMI DURABLES	7.4	6.9	8.7	7.3	7.9	7.2	5.5
63 NON DURABLE–NON DURABLES	3.9	4.0	4.3	3.9	4.6	4.0	2.8
7 GOODS NES–BIENS NDA	0.2	0.1	0.2	0.2	0.2	0.3	0.5

EXPORTS – EXPORTATIONS

	1990	1991	1992	1993	1994	1995	1996
TOTAL EXPORTS–EXPORTATIONS TOTALES	100.	100.	100.	100.	100.	100.	100.
1 AGRICULTURE	5.5	8.4	9.6	7.3	10.4	9.8	4.8
2 MINING QUARRY–INDUS EXTRACTIVES			0.0	0.1	0.0	0.0	0.1
3 MANUFACTURING–IND MANUFACTUR	94.5	91.6	90.3	92.7	89.5	90.2	95.1
31 FOOD BEV TOBACCO–ALIM BOISS TAB	19.1	25.7	29.5	23.1	36.3	36.1	25.1
32 TEXTILES–INDUSTRIES TEXTILES		0.0	0.1	0.0	0.1	0.1	0.0
33 WOOD & PRODUCTS–BOIS & PRODUITS					0.0	0.0	0.0
34 PAPER & PRODUCTS–PAPIER & PRODT	0.0	0.0	0.1	0.0	0.0	0.0	0.0
35 CHEMICALS–INDUSTRIES CHIMIQUES	49.6	60.7	58.0	55.4	46.1	47.2	22.1
36 NON METAL MIN–MIN NON METAL		0.0		0.1	0.0	0.5	0.0
37 BASIC METAL–IND METAL BASE		0.0		0.0		0.0	
38 METAL MANUF–MANUF METAL	25.8	5.1	2.6	13.9	6.6	5.9	47.6
39 OTH MANUF IND–AUTRES MANUF	0.0	0.0	0.1	0.2	0.4	0.3	0.2

3. TRADE BY PRINCIPAL COUNTRIES OF ORIGIN AND LAST CONSIGNMENT (VALUE IN THOUSAND U.S. DOLLARS)
ECHANGES SELON LES PRINCIPAUX PAYS D'ORIGINE ET DE DERNIERE CONSIGNATION (VALEUR EN MILLIERS DE DOLLARS EU)

COUNTRIES–PAYS	GENERAL IMPORTS C.I.F. IMPORTATIONS GENERALES C.A.F				
	1992	1993	1994	1995	1996
World	191359	241580	206496	254662	346723
Africa	34224	41735	37842	41946	47847
Americas	5755	19487	8590	10168	100840
Northern America	4876	18704	8127	9637	100516
LAIA	798	703	436	403	295
CACM				0	1
Caribbean	14	32	23	51	5
Rest of America	67	48	4	77	24
As.ex F.USSR	89884	99094	82746	115843	81684
Eur.x F.USSR	57444	74878	73293	83248	110514
EU	56829	73722	72412	81955	109018
EFTA	597	1152	879	1242	1382
East Europe	11	3	2	50	114
Other Europe	4	0			
Former USSR	146	2		2	24
Oceania	3883	4309	4006	3406	5329
United Kingdom	24733	32203	36385	35415	42467
Singapore/Singapour	31005	31632	30206	37445	35209
So. Africa Customs Un	27541	31072	27576	31386	39366
USA/Etats–Unis d'Amer	4812	18689	7874	9428	100363
Yemen/Yémen		31665	29175	40623	9287
France,Monac	8699	14962	11889	18086	26879
Japan/Japon	9153	13940	6814	14510	8228
Italy/Italie	6763	6254	6493	8835	13943
Bahrain/Bahreïn	30864	45	22	120	53
Germany/Allemagne	4162	7780	2766	3756	7841
India/Inde	2336	5081	3090	4987	9063
Netherlands/Pays–Bas	4599	4271	4691	5691	5000
Thailand/Thaïlande	2401	5157	3729	5057	6704
Spain/Espagne	1884	2263	3403	5127	6672
Kenya	2357	3479	4573	4391	3531
Australia/Australie	3221	3580	3317	3061	4863
Mauritius/Maurice	2966	3566	3537	3596	4032
Malaysia/Malaisie	3422	2994	2422	2905	3501
Belgium–Luxembourg	3361	1295	2312	2397	2606
China/Chine	3319	2556	2102	2025	1458
Hong Kong	1811	1657	1484	1552	1548
Ireland/Irlande	464	1161	2719	1051	1601
Pakistan	2363	1308	863	2032	98
Sweden/Suède	890	2292	918	858	1184
United Arab Emirates	589	422	950	1458	2107
Switz.Liecht	560	1090	803	1206	1349
Reunion/Réunion	913	1781	1109	878	
Korea, Republic of	821	429	310	896	1083
Denmark/Danemark	1056	695	505	568	675
Madagascar	47	1405	864	773	123
New Zealand	662	729	689	345	466
Indonesia/Indonésie	699	413	357	572	494
Brazil/Brésil	438	679	432	392	285
Zimbabwe	322	365	13	766	689
Israel/Israël	13	4	35	146	653
Sri Lanka	122	163	140	127	271
Turkey/Turquie	7	278	1	53	410
Canada	60	15	253	180	153
Austria/Autriche	40	341	36	52	60
Jordan/Jordanie	0	249	270	0	
Portugal	12	79	197	91	14
Finland/Finlande	142	57	75	11	13
Argentina/Argentine	289	1	2	3	
Cyprus/Chypre	12	172	9	0	88
Malawi	53	38	40	79	50
Greece/Grèce	22	69	24	17	63
Russian Federation	146	2		2	24
Czech Republic		0	0	33	112
Philippines	62	38	10	17	5
Mozambique			116		0

COUNTRIES–PAYS	GENERAL EXPORTS F.O.B. EXPORTATIONS GENERALES F.O.B.				
	1992	1993	1994	1995	1996
Monde	48006	51641	51772	53128	139354
Afrique	3911	3581	3162	2645	2189
Amériques	1040	3580	2061	2149	52085
Amérique du Nord	1022	3575	2055	2127	52071
ALAI	15	0	0	0	0
MCAC					
Caraïbes	1	3	3	20	12
Autre Amérique	2	2	2	2	2
Asie l'URSS exclus	29022	29514	24412	26730	44239
Europe l'URSS exclus	13988	14919	22013	21545	40106
UE	13959	14813	21986	21329	39867
AELE	30	86	26	216	232
Europe de l'Est	0	0	0		6
Autre de l'Europe	0	0	0	0	
Ancienne URSS				0	1
Océanie	38	38	111	29	65
Yemen/Yémen		27980	23158	24286	29427
USA/Etats–Unis d'Amer	1017	3529	2050	1987	52039
United Kingdom	4259	10516	13317	12713	12834
Bahrain/Bahreïn	27254		2	0	0
France,Monac	8180	2486	1174	1130	10804
Germany/Allemagne	360	632	3442	4914	7856
Singapore/Singapour	672	841	526	786	12768
Italy/Italie	29	15	2320	149	6631
Reunion/Réunion	2040	1454	1888	1723	
Mauritius/Maurice	1454	1828	341	267	457
Japan/Japon	29	94	285	1379	1898
Belgium–Luxembourg	796	676	603	339	415
So. Africa Customs Un	403	279	459	424	1054
Netherlands/Pays–Bas	307	323	200	198	364
Spain/Espagne	8	146	152	786	257
Denmark/Danemark	6	1	650	600	9
Kenya	0	1	34	189	583
Hong Kong	185	212	101	65	135
Sweden/Suède	9	13	7	15	642
Thailand/Thaïlande	124	232	201	76	0
Switz.Liecht	26	86	26	216	232
Madagascar		3	438	17	95
Greece/Grèce		0	0	311	49
United Arab Emirates	203	1	138	12	6
Portugal	0	1	118	174	0
Australia/Australie	38	38	108	29	65
Canada	5	47	5	140	32
Pakistan	144	58			
Sri Lanka	146	0			
India/Inde	0		2	103	2
Malaysia/Malaisie		6	0	24	
Un. Rep. of Tanzania		0	1	21	0
Ireland/Irlande	3	4	2	0	5
Brazil/Brésil	15				
China/Chine	10				
Czech Republic					5
New Zealand			3	0	
Finland/Finlande	1		2		
Austria/Autriche	0	0			1
Zimbabwe	0	0	0	0	0
Russian Federation				0	1
Cyprus/Chypre	0	0	0		
Indonesia/Indonésie		0			
Korea, Republic of		0			
Israel/Israël		0			

(VALUE AS PERCENTAGE OF WORLD TOTAL)(VALEURS EN POURCENTAGE DU TOTAL MONDIAL)

	1987	1988	1989	1990	1991	1992	1993	1994	1995	1996
Africa	16.7	12.9	16.2	18.7	17.0	17.9	17.3	18.3	16.5	13.8
Americas	3.1	10.7	2.7	2.1	2.5	3.0	8.1	4.2	4.0	29.1
Northern America	3.0	10.6	2.2	1.9	2.5	2.5	7.7	3.9	3.8	29.0
LAIA	0.1	0.1	0.4	0.2	0.0	0.4	0.3	0.2	0.2	0.1
CACM									0.0	0.0
Caribbean	0.0	0.0	0.0	0.0	0.0	0.0	0.0	0.0	0.0	0.0
Rest of America	0.0	0.0	0.0	0.0	0.0	0.0	0.0	0.0	0.0	0.0
As.ex F.USSR	34.5	36.1	42.6	40.2	45.6	47.0	41.0	40.1	45.5	23.6
Eur.x F.USSR	44.6	38.3	37.2	37.3	33.5	30.0	31.0	35.5	32.7	31.9
EU	44.0	37.6	36.9	37.0	33.2	29.7	30.5	35.1	32.2	31.4
EFTA	0.5	0.6	0.3	0.3	0.3	0.3	0.5	0.4	0.5	0.4
East Europe	0.0	0.1	0.0	0.0	0.0	0.0	0.0	0.0	0.0	0.0
Other Europe	0.0	0.0	0.0	0.0	0.0	0.0	0.0			
Former USSR	0.0	0.9	0.1	0.1	0.1	0.1	0.0		0.0	0.0
Oceania	1.2	1.1	1.1	1.6	1.2	2.0	1.8	1.9	1.3	1.5
United Kingdom	19.9	14.9	14.3	14.4	11.5	12.9	13.3	17.6	13.9	12.2
Singapore/Singapour	7.5	10.3	10.0	10.2	11.6	16.2	13.1	14.6	14.7	10.2
So. Africa Customs Un	13.2	10.3	13.1	13.6	13.0	14.4	12.9	13.4	12.3	11.4
USA/Etats–Unis d'Amer	3.0	10.6	2.2	1.9	2.5	2.5	7.7	3.8	3.7	28.9
Yemen/Yémen							13.1	14.1	16.0	2.7
France,Monac	14.3	10.4	9.6	11.3	8.8	4.5	6.2	5.8	7.1	7.8
Japan/Japon	5.5	6.5	7.0	6.1	5.2	4.8	5.8	3.3	5.7	2.4
Italy/Italie	1.3	2.2	5.4	2.2	2.5	3.5	2.6	3.1	3.5	4.0
Bahrain/Bahreïn	0.0	0.0	0.0	8.1	16.2	16.1	0.0	0.0	0.0	0.0
Germany/Allemagne	2.5	3.7	2.0	2.8	3.2	2.2	3.2	1.3	1.5	2.3

	1987	1988	1989	1990	1991	1992	1993	1994	1995	1996
Afrique	3.5	5.1	7.9	6.2	6.0	8.1	6.9	6.1	5.0	1.6
Amériques	2.5	2.6	3.0	1.2	1.2	2.2	6.9	4.0	4.0	37.4
Amérique du Nord	2.4	2.3	2.5	1.1	1.2	2.1	6.9	4.0	4.0	37.4
ALAI	0.1	0.3	0.5	0.1	0.0	0.0	0.0	0.0	0.0	0.0
MCAC										
Caraïbes		0.0	0.0	0.0		0.0	0.0	0.0	0.0	0.0
Autre Amérique			0.0			0.0	0.0	0.0	0.0	0.0
Asie l'URSS exclus	5.1	39.9	30.3	25.4	2.7	60.5	57.2	47.2	50.3	31.7
Europe l'URSS exclus	25.9	45.3	32.0	17.2	28.9	29.1	28.9	42.5	40.6	28.8
UE	24.8	45.2	31.9	17.2	28.9	29.1	28.7	42.5	40.1	28.6
AELE	1.1	0.1	0.1			0.1	0.2	0.1	0.4	0.2
Europe de l'Est	0.0	0.0	0.0	0.0		0.0	0.0	0.0		0.0
Autre de l'Europe	0.0	0.0	0.0	0.0	0.0	0.0	0.0	0.0	0.0	
Ancienne URSS	0.0	1.9							0.0	0.0
Océanie	0.3	0.1	0.0	0.0	0.1	0.1	0.1	0.2	0.1	0.0
Yemen/Yémen							54.2	44.7	45.7	21.1
USA/Etats–Unis d'Amer	2.4	2.3	2.5	1.1	1.2	2.1	6.8	4.0	3.7	37.3
United Kingdom	5.9	12.2	3.7	4.0	18.9	8.9	20.4	25.7	23.9	9.2
Bahrain/Bahreïn		0.0				56.8		0.0	0.0	0.0
France,Monac	18.3	26.3	24.9	11.2	9.0	17.0	4.8	2.3	2.1	7.8
Germany/Allemagne	0.3	4.1	2.3	0.2	0.7	0.7	1.2	6.6	9.3	5.6
Singapore/Singapour	0.4	0.6	0.7	0.5	0.6	1.4	1.6	1.0	1.5	9.2
Italy/Italie	0.3	0.5	0.3	1.3	0.1	0.1	0.0	4.5	0.3	4.8
Reunion/Réunion	3.0	4.4	7.3	5.8	4.7	4.3	2.8	3.6	3.2	
Mauritius/Maurice	0.2	0.2	0.1	0.2	1.0	3.0	3.5	0.7	0.5	0.3

4. General Imports C.I.F. by Commodities according to the S.I.T.C. (Rev. 2) in thousand U.S. Dollars
Importations Générales C.A.F. par Produits d'après la C.T.C.I. (Rév. 2) en milliers de Dollars E.U.

SITC CTCI	COMMODITY	1993 WEIGHT POIDS	1993 VALUE VALEUR	1994 WEIGHT POIDS	1994 VALUE VALEUR	1995 WEIGHT POIDS	1995 VALUE VALEUR	1996 WEIGHT POIDS	1996 VALUE VALEUR	PRODUIT
	ALL COMMODITIES		241580		206496		254662		346723	TOUS PRODUITS
0	FOOD AND LIVE ANIMALS		37865		37763		42505		58157	ALIMENTS,ANIMAUX VIVANTS
01	MEAT AND PREPARATIONS		3433		2100		3209		3331	VIANDES ET PREPARATIONS
011	MEAT FRESH,CHILLD,FROZEN	W 928	2741	W 535	1654	W 851	2548	W 879	2728	VIANDES FRAICHES,REF,CONGE
0111	BOVINE MEAT FRESH,FROZEN	W 375	1027	W 380	1056	W 342	1212	W 367	1169	VIANDES BOVIN FRAI,REF
01112	BOVINE MEAT BONELESS	W 372	1000	W 378	1043	W 340	1195	W 366	1163	VIANDES BOVIN DESOSSEES
0113	PIG MEAT FRESH,CHLD,FRZN	W 320	892	W 49	146	W 95	338	W 191	655	VIANDE DE PORC
02	DAIRY PRODCTS,BIRDS'EGGS		4851		5940		6045		7337	PRODUITS LAITIERS,OEUFS
022	MILK AND CREAM	W 1482	3210	W 2069	4140	W 1410	3939	W 1624	4904	LAIT ET CREME
0224	MILK,CREAM PRESERVED ETC	W 1276	2850	W 1788	3790	W 1310	3680	W 1462	4613	LAIT,CREME CONS,CONC
02242	MILK DRY,1.5% FAT OR LES	W 39	91	W 860	2077	W 385	1447	W 766	3086	LAIT POUDRE INF 1.5%
02243	MILK DRY,OVER 1.5% FAT	W 489	1510	W 468	960	W 302	1020	W 181	402	LAIT POUDRE SUP 1.5%
02249	MILK(EX DRY) PRSVD,SWEET	W 748	1248	W 459	754	W 623	1212	W 515	1126	LAIT CONS,CONC SUCRE
024	CHEESE AND CURD	W 214	838	W 250	922	W 243	991	W 237	1067	FROMAGE ET CAILLEBOTTE
03	FISH AND PREPARATIONS		7060		7961		8856		18829	POISSONS ET PREPARATIONS
034	FISH,FRESH,CHILLED,FROZN	W 9702	6672	W 8210	7405	W 11955	8555	W 19391	17417	POISSON FRAIS, REFRIG,CONG
0342	FISH FROZEN,EXCL FILLETS	W 9700	6648	W 8192	7221	W 11953	8503	W 19390	17412	POISSONS CONGELES
036	SHELL FISH FRESH,FROZEN	W 39	374	W 59	506	W 19	296	W 146	1304	CRUSTACES,MOLLUSQUES
04	CEREALS AND PREPARATIONS		8150		7097		10288		12259	CEREALES ET PRODUITS
042	RICE	W 3263	1799	W 1191	994	W 5958	3541	W 5639	4826	RIZ
0422	RICE SEMI–MILLED,MILLED	W 1732	1254	W 1191	994	W 5957	3540	W 5638	4825	RIZ POLI,GLACE INCL BRISURES
04221	RICE MILLED UNBROKEN	W 1732	1254	W 581	514	W 3058	2191	W 5136	4573	RIZ POLI,GLACE EXCL BRISURES
04222	RICE BROKEN			W 610	480	W 2899	1348	W 502	253	BRISURES DE RIZ
044	MAIZE UNMILLED	W 6072	1618	W 6112	1577	W 2769	770	W 3730	1080	MAIS NON MOULU
046	WHEAT ETC MEAL OR FLOUR	W 2801	1328	W 2325	1255	W 2561	1510	W 3813	2023	SEMOULE FARINE,FROMENT
04601	FLOUR OF WHEAT OR MESLIN	W 2795	1321	W 2267	1098	W 2477	1359	W 2838	1753	FARINE DE FROMENT
048	CEREAL ETC PREPARATIONS	W 2094	3299	W 1922	2842	W 2057	3511	W 1921	3510	PREPTNS A BASE CEREALES
0484	BAKERY PRODUCTS	W 534	1857	W 415	1407	W 475	1716	W 463	1616	PRODUITS DE BOULANGERIE
04841	BREAD,BISCUIT,COM WAFERS	W 168	729		104	W 123	414	W 14	51	PAINS,BISCUITS DE MER
04842	PASTRY, CAKES ETC	W 366	1128	W 415	1303	W 353	1302	W 449	1565	PATISSERIE ETC.
05	VEGETABLES AND FRUIT		7164		8796		7935		9477	LEGUMES ET FRUITS
054	VEG ETC FRSH,SMPLY PRSVD	W 4087	3610	W 4254	4045	W 4000	4034	W 4479	4290	LEGUMES FRAIS,CONG,SECS
0541	POTATOES FRSH EXCL SWEET	W 1338	720	W 1581	926	W 1347	925	W 1779	1053	POMMES DE TERRE
0545	OTHER FRESH VEGETABLES	W 1763	1580	W 1997	2017	W 1606	1579	W 1799	1797	AUTRES LEGUMES FRAIS,REF
05451	ALLIACEOUS VEGTBLS,FRESH	W 1169	819	W 1064	847	W 846	671	W 1041	665	OIGNONS,ECHALOTES,AULX
05459	FRESH VEGETABLES NES	W 594	761	W 934	1170	W 759	908	W 758	1132	LEGUMES FRAIS,REFRI NDA
057	FRUIT,NUTS,FRESH,DRIED	W 908	1712	W 740	1342	W 821	1433	W 1078	1860	FRUITS FRAIS OU SECS
058	FRUIT PRESERVED,PREPARED	W 1345	1388	W 2025	2843	W 920	1999	W 1481	2847	CONSERVES DE FRUITS
0585	FRUIT OR VEGETABLE JUICE	W 1112	912	W 1758	2277	W 603	1259	W 1331	2447	JUS DE FRUITS
05857	JUICE OF OTHER FRUIT,VEG	W 743	392	W 1081	1266	W 328	735	W 509	1062	JUS AUTRES FRUITS,LEGUMES
06	SUGAR AND PREPS,HONEY		2113		1438		2226		2367	SUCRES ET PRODUITS
061	SUGAR AND HONEY	W 4493	1618	W 3077	1160	W 3141	1747	W 3360	1974	SUCRES ET MIEL
0612	REFINED SUGAR ETC	W 4215	1369	W 3050	1089	W 2922	1591	W 3348	1929	SUCRES RAFFINES
07	COFFEE,TEA,COCOA,SPICES		1726		1391		1394		1601	CAFE,THE,CACAO,EPICES
073	CHOCOLATE AND PRODUCTS	W 200	776	W 200	683	W 181	658	W 165	697	CHOCOLAT
081	*FEEDING STUFF FOR ANIML	W 2829	1350	W 2903	1549	W 855	803	W 1865	961	NOURRITURE POUR ANIMAUX
0819	FOOD WASTE AND FEED NES	W 355	580	W 647	977	W 493	685	W 217	176	DECHETS,ALIMENTS NDA
08199	FODDER NES,INCL SWEETNED	W 355	580	W 647	977	W 493	685	W 217	176	PREPARATIONS FOURRAGERES
09	MISC EDIBLE PRODUCTS		1839		1490		1717		1873	PREP ALIMENTAIRES DIVERSES
098	EDIBLE PRODCTS,PREPS NES	W 494	1241	W 381	1069	W 448	1140	W 461	1156	PREP ALIMENTAIRES NDA
1	BEVERAGES AND TOBACCO		8366		3822		6994		4282	BOISSONS ET TABACS
11	BEVERAGES		7451		3275		6110		3660	BOISSONS
112	ALCOHOLIC BEVERAGES	W 3810	6769	W 991	2994	W 1615	5814	W 885	3446	BOISSONS ALCOOLIQUES
1121	WINE OF FRESH GRAPES ETC	W 764	1892	W 407	1235	W 744	2246	W 431	1373	VINS DE RAISINS FRAIS
11211	GRAPE MUST	W 503	995		1	W 52	118	W 28	62	MOUTS DE RAISIN
11212	WINE OF FRESH GRAPES	W 112	516	W 347	1121	W 606	1885	W 346	1226	VINS DE MOUTS DE RAISINS
1123	BEER,ALE,STOUT,PORTER	W 2255	1968	W 394	476	W 339	497	W 209	313	BIERES
1124	DISTILLED ALCOHOLIC BEVS	W 783	2900	W 188	1278	W 529	3066	W 240	1744	ALCOOLS,EAUX–DE–VIE
11241	WHISKY	W 147	891	W 84	613	W 284	1750	W 129	978	WHISKY
11242	DISTILLD WINE,GRAPE MARC	W 449	1206	W 41	261	W 102	563	W 41	330	EAUX–DE–VIE NATURELLES
11249	OTH ALCOHOLC BEVS,CMPNDS	W 187	803	W 64	404	W 144	753	W 70	436	BOISSONS ALCOOLIQUES NDA
12	TOBACCO AND MANUFACTURES		916		546		883		622	TABACS BRUTS FABRIQUES
2	CRUDE MATERLS,EXCL FUELS		3326		3614		4166		5082	MAT BRUTES NON COMESTIBLES
24	CORK AND WOOD		2900		2584		3254		3569	LIEGE ET BOIS
248	WOOD SHAPED,SLEEPERS	W 5971	2749		1959	W 4701	3136	W 10687	3335	BOIS SIMPLEMENT TRAVAILLES
2482	LUMBER SHAPED CONIFER	W 5877	2706	W 3434	1691	W 4480	2878	W 10637	3236	CONIFERES SCIES,RABOTES
24821	LUMBER SAWN ETC CONIFER	W 5863	2699	W 3433	1598	W 4445	2769	W 10128	2970	CONIFERES SCIES LONGITUD
27	CRUDE FERTLZR,MINRLS NES		132		679		203		499	ENGRAIS MINERAUX BRUTS
3	MINERAL FUELS ETC		34361		32132		44330		11395	COMBUSTIBLES MINERAUX LUB
33	PETROLEUM AND PRODUCTS		33858		31785		43816		10711	PETROLE ET DERIVES
334	PETROLEUM PRODUCTS,REFIN	W 203891	33629	W 212666	31531	W 230498	43523	W 42844	10318	PRODUITS RAFFINES
3341	GASOLINE,OTH LIGHT OILS	W 11287	1829	W 212665	31515	W 230488	43461	W 10715	2166	ESSENCES POUR MOTEURS
33411	MOTOR,AVIATION SPIRIT	W 11138	1719					W 10715	2166	ESSENCES MOTEURS D'AVIONS
3342	KEROSENE,OTH MEDIUM OILS	W 55382	8815					W 16941	3902	PETR LAMPANTS,AUT HUIL
33421	KEROSENE INCL JET FUEL	W 55382	8814					W 16941	3902	PETROLES LAMPANTS
3343	GAS OILS	W 133179	20885					W 13745	3045	GAS OILS
3345	LUBS,PETROLEUM OILS NES	W 1756	1956	W 2	17	W 10	61	W 860	1131	HUILES LUBRIFIANTES
33451	LUBS(HIGH PETR CONT) ETC	W 1754	1939					W 856	1108	HUILES LUBRIF,H LOURDES
4	ANIMAL,VEGETABLE OIL,FAT		1879		2279		4317		5718	HUILES,GRAISSES ANIM,VEG
42	FIXED VEGETABLE OIL,FAT		1846		2270		4269		5610	HUILES VEGETALES FIXES
423	FIXED VEG OILS,SOFT	W 721	647	W 1135	1052	W 1846	2445	W 1806	3552	HUILES VEGET DOUCES FIXES
4232	SOYA BEAN OIL	W 511	396	W 877	721	W 1217	1164	W 1118	1048	HUILE DE SOJA
4235	OLIVE OIL	W 5	13	W 12	30	W 232	722	W 345	1966	HUILE D'OLIVE
424	FIXED VEG OIL NONSOFT	W 973	1199	W 919	1218	W 1137	1824	W 871	2059	AUTRES HUILES VEG FIXES
4242	PALM OIL		1	W 917	1214	W 1018	1620	W 869	2050	HUILE DE PALME
4249	FIXED VEGETABLE OILS NES	W 972	1196	W 2	3	W 115	194	W 1	3	HUILES VEGET FIXES NDA
5	CHEMCLS,RELATED PROD NES		14373		12787		15706		16178	PRODUITS CHIMIQUES
53	DYES,TANNING,COLOUR PROD		1358		1139		1730		1748	PROD TEINTURE,COLORANTS
533	PIGMENTS,PAINTS,ETC	W 408	1335	W 241	1109	W 484	1656	W 536	1733	PIGMENTS,PEINTURES,VERNIS
5334	VARNISHES,DISTEMPERS ETC	W 330	1038	W 179	795	W 368	1310	W 407	1408	PEINTURES A L'EAU
541	*MEDICINAL,PHARM PRODUCT	K 142765	3374	K 210303	2614	K 497879	3761	K 272334	2859	PROD MEDICINAUX PHARMACEUT
5413	ANTIBIOTICS IN BULK	K 6826	196	K 24223	782	K 19414	835	K 24490	574	ANTIBIOTIQUES NDA
54139	OTHER ANTIBIOTICS	K 6673	195	K 21010	747	K 16725	824	K 21201	539	AUTRES ANTIBIOTIQUES
5417	MEDICAMENTS	K 40896	1187	K 123832	1378	K 142468	1854	K 141791	1490	MEDICAMENTS
54179	— CONTNG OTH SUBSTANCES	K 35479	900	K 85470	818	K 108752	1271	K 113784	1104	MED CONT AUT SUBSTANCES
5419	PHARMACEUTICAL GOODS NES	K 77615	1890	K 48806	303	K 24271	291	K 26216	374	PREP,ART PHARMACEUTIQUES
54199	OTH PHARMACEUTICAL GOODS	K 63136	1687	K 4840	93	K 4250	98	K 3657	92	AUT PREP PHARMACEUTIQUES
55	PERFUME,CLEANING ETC PRD		5045		4756		5654		5845	PROD POUR PARFUM,TOILETTE
553	PERFUMERY,COSMETICS,ETC	W 340	2286	W 456	2231	W 346	2612	W 409	2747	PRODUITS DE PARFUMERIE
554	SOAP,CLEANSING ETC ; REPS	W 821	2054	W 845	2214	W 798	2404	W 1652	2619	SAVONS,PRODUITS DETERSIFS
5541	SOAPS	W 447	1078	W 345	900	W 354	931	W 453	994	SAVONS,PROD TENSIO–ACTIFS

4. General Imports C.I.F. by Commodities according to the S.I.T.C. (Rev. 2) in thousand U.S. Dollars
Importations Générales C.A.F. par Produits d'après la C.T.C.I. (Rév. 2) en milliers de Dollars E.U.

SITC CTCI	COMMODITY	1993 WEIGHT POIDS	1993 VALUE VALEUR	1994 WEIGHT POIDS	1994 VALUE VALEUR	1995 WEIGHT POIDS	1995 VALUE VALEUR	1996 WEIGHT POIDS	1996 VALUE VALEUR	PRODUIT
5542	WASHING PREPARATIONS ETC	W 299	699	W 381	899	W 372	1185	W 1096	1291	PROD ORG TENSIO–ACT NDA
58	PLASTIC MATERIALS ETC		1380		1272		1158		1497	MAT PLAST ARTIFICIELLES
583	POLYMERIZATION ETC PRODS	W 377	1167	W 309	1034	W 256	825	W 341	1231	PROD POLYMERISATION
59	CHEMICAL MATERIALS NES		2277		1942		1913		2321	MAT PROD CHIMIQUES NDA
591	PESTICIDES,DISINFECTANTS	W 163	711	W 262	652	W 126	625	W 509	868	DESINF,INSECT,FONG,HERB
598	MISCEL CHEM PRODUCTS NES	W 552	1178	W 538	993	W 213	917	W 357	1101	PROD DIV INDUST CHIM NDA
5989	CHEM PRODUCTS,PREPS NES	W 525	1117	W 505	928	W 163	732	W 191	700	PROD PREP CHIMIQUES NDA
59899	OTH CHEM PRODS,PREPS,NES	W 495	989	W 476	788	W 134	576	W 144	486	AUT PRODUITS CHIMIQUES NDA
6	BASIC MANUFACTURES		44770		41294		40444		50608	ART MANUFACTURES
62	RUBBER MANUFACTURES NES		2131		1658		2380		2637	CAOUTCHOUC MANUFACTURE
625	RUBBER TYRES, TUBES ETC		1171		1018	W 313	1609	W 408	1784	PNEUS CAOUTCHOUC VULCANISE
63	WOOD,CORK MANUFACTRS NES		3992		3934		3483		6116	OUVRAGES LIEGE ET BOIS
634	VENEERS,PLYWOOD,ETC	W 3817	2497	W 1563	1672	W 2178	1737	W 1521	2070	PLACAGES,CONTRE–PLAQUES
6342	PLYWOOD OF WOOD SHEETS	W 3228	1988	W 1014	1131	W 1831	1380	W 1014	1522	BOIS CONTRE–PLAQUES
635	WOOD MANUFACTURES NES		1486	W 274	2261	W 586	1595	W 1063	4011	ART MANUF EN BOIS NDA
6351	BOXES,CASES,CRATES,ETC	W 57	818	W 5	23	W 3	6	W 22	59	CAISSES EMBALLAGES BOIS
6353	BUILDERS WOODWRK,PREFABS		501	W 248	2124	W 555	1380	W 985	3723	OUVRAGES DE MENUISERIE
64	PAPER,PAPERBOARD AND MFR		5030		5734		6250		6118	PAPIERS,CARTONS & OUVRAGES
641	PAPER AND PAPERBOARD	W 691	1983	W 642	1589	W 968	2191	W 947	1735	PAPIERS ET CARTONS
6412	PRINTG,WRITING PAPER NES	W 221	870	W 271	576	W 51	126	W 20	99	PAPIERS POUR L'IMPRESSION
64122	— COATED,IMPREGNATD ETC	W 191	763	W 179	238	W 34	47	W 15	74	PAPIERS IMPRESSION COUCHES
6415	PAPER,PAPERBRD,BULK,NES	W 120	322	W 77	393	W 323	1167	W 331	980	PAPIERS,CARTONS ROULEAUX
64159	OTHER PAPER ETC,BULK,NES	W 115	302	W 73	372	W 321	1153	W 326	949	AUT PAPIER ROULEAUX FEUILLES
642	PAPER,ETC,PRECUT,ARTS OF	W 934	3047	W 1385	4145	W 890	4059	W 1332	4383	PAP,CARTONS DECOUPES
6421	PAPER ETC CONTAINERS	W 438	879	W 726	1553	W 432	1367	W 689	1669	BOITES,SACS EMBALLAGES
6428	PAPER ETC ARTICLES NES	W 199	1280	W 355	1477	W 232	1591	W 314	1567	OUVRAGES EN PATE A PAPIER
64285	PAPER ETC DIAPERS ETC	W 104	711	W 138	874	W 144	1106	W 216	1053	SERVIETTES HYGIENIQUES
65	TEXTILE YARN,FABRICS,ETC		4192		4047		5002		5158	FILS,TISSUS,ARTICLES TEXTILE
652	COTTON FABRICS,WOVEN		1549		907	W 130	1019	W 131	1206	TISSUS DE COTON
6522	WOVEN COTTON BLEACHD,ETC		874		613	W 97	762	W 103	917	TISSUS COTON BLANCHIS ETC
653	WOVN MAN–MADE FIB FABRIC		395		478	W 68	766	W 46	391	TISSUS FIBRES SYNTH,ARTIF
657	SPECIAL TXTL FABRC,PRODS		260		659	W 152	1119	W 187	1303	TISSUS SPECIAUX
658	TEXTILE ARTICLES NES		1377		1121	W 122	1140	W 162	1412	ART FACONNES MAT TEXTILES
6584	LINENS ETC		1004	N 93338	781	W 84	692	W 104	849	LINGE DE MAISON
66	NONMETAL MINERAL MFS NES		7575		7610		6412		8223	ART MIN NON METALLIQUES
661	LIME,CEMENT,BLDG PRODS	W 27300	2810	W 26780	2781	W 25989	2552	W 29110	3386	CHAUX,CIMENTS MAT CONSTR
6612	CEMENT	W 27188	2695	W 26741	2630	W 25915	2374	W 28859	2836	CIMENTS HYDRAULIQUES
662	CLAY,REFRACTORY BLDG PRD	W 1756	2146	W 2224	1866	W 1338	1317	W 1911	1648	MAT CONST REFRACTAIRES
6623	REFRACTORY BUILDING PROD	W 470	861	W 116	123	W 25	56	W 54	133	BRIQUES REFRACTAIRES
6624	BRICKS ETC NONREFRACTORY	W 1285	1284	W 2108	1743	W 1313	1261	W 1857	1515	BRIQUES ETC CERAM NON REFR
66245	GLAZED CERAMIC SETTS ETC	W 1175	1114	W 1910	1349	W 1034	878	W 1371	1102	AUT CARREAUX CERAMIQUE
664	GLASS		550		706	W 251	769	W 260	966	VERRE
665	GLASSWARE		1412		1533	W 477	1165	W 414	960	OUVRAGES EN VERRE
6651	BOTTLES ETC OF GLASS		897		1041	W 306	549	W 241	340	RECIPIENTS EN VERRE
66511	GLASS BOTTLES ETC NONVAC	W 1296	892	W 1358	1041	W 306	549	W 241	340	BONBONNES,BOUTEILLES,ETC
67	IRON AND STEEL		4339		5182		3824		4607	FER ET ACIER
673	IRON,STEEL SHAPES ETC	W 1321	1169	W 1805	1691	W 654	837	W 1519	1157	BARRES,PROFIL FER,ACIER
6733	IRON,STEEL PROFILES ETC	W 454	311	W 731	886	W 278	486	W 372	543	PROFILES,PALPLAN FER,ACIER
67336	IRN,SMPL STL SHEET PILNG	W 297	101	W 624	692	W 105	224	W 67	226	PALPLANCHES EN FER,ACIER
674	IRN,STL UNIV,PLATE,SHEET	W 1407	1647	W 1119	1505	W 1094	1587	W 1059	2115	LARGES PLATS,TOLES
6749	OTH IRN,STL PLATES,SHEET	W 1242	1451	W 942	1282	W 945	1375	W 850	1914	AUTRES TOLES FER,ACIER
67491	— OF IRON OR SIMPLE STL	W 1241	1443	W 915	1243	W 938	1358	W 719	1793	AUT TOLES AUTRES ACIER FIN
678	IRON,STL TUBES,PIPES,ETC	W 673	1182	W 1150	1713	W 270	1067	W 532	1110	TUBES,TUYAUX EN FONTE,FER
6783	IRON,STL TUBES,PIPES NES	W 289	415	W 991	1179	W 30	47	W 46	82	AUT TUBES,TUYAUX FER,ACIER
68	NON–FERROUS METALS		1356		1396		1480		1228	METAUX NON FERREUX
684	ALUMINIUM	W 200	1026	W 141	936	W 144	1004	W 143	880	ALUMINIUM
6842	ALUMINIUM,ALLOYS WORKED	W 199	1018	W 141	935	W 144	1004	W 117	780	ALUMINIUM,ALLIAGES OUVRE
69	METAL MANUFACTURES NES		16031		11674		11554		16503	ART MANUFACT EN METAL NDA
691	STRUCTURES AND PARTS NES	W 437	3645	W 732	2778	W 504	1692	W 1214	2204	CONSTRUCT FER,ACIER,ALU
6911	STRUCTURES,PARTS IRN,STL	W 235	869	W 696	2556	W 424	1159	W 1009	1435	CONSTRUCT FER,ACIER,FONTE
6912	STRUCTURES,PARTS ALUMNM	W 203	2776	W 36	222	W 80	533	W 205	769	CONSTRUCT ALUMINIUM
692	METAL TANKS,BOXES,ETC		6862		2886	W 2166	4168	W 3702	7367	RECIPIENTS METALLIQUES
6921	METAL STORAGE TANKS ETC	W 439	3206	W 8	58	W 12	169	W 21	99	CUVES EN FONTE,FER,ALU
69211	STEEL STORAGE TANKS ETC	W 381	2939	W 8	55	W 11	168	W 10	43	CUVES EN FONTE FER OU ACIER
6924	MTL TRANSPORT BOXES ETC		3657		2828	W 2153	3999	W 3681	7268	FUTS,TAMBOURS,BIDONS
69241	STL TRANSPORT BOXES ETC		3533		2687	W 2126	3871	W 3539	6958	FUTS,TAMBOURS,BIDONS FER
695	TOOLS	W 186	925	W 143	963	W 126	1095	W 99	894	OUTILS A MAIN
6953	OTHER HAND TOOLS	W 149	690	W 102	747	W 78	655	W 56	531	AUTRES OUTILS A MAIN
697	BASE MTL HOUSEHOLD EQUIP		1728		1599	W 247	1479	W 233	1482	ART MENAGE MET COMMUNS
6973	DMSTC HEATG,COOKG APPARA		637	N 2316	659	W 120	635	W 92	541	APPS CHAUF NON ELECTRIQ
699	BASE METAL MFRS NES		1723	W 415	2250	W 396	1983	W 472	2859	ART MANUFACTURES MET NDA
6991	LOCKSMITHS WARES,ETC	W 148	795	W 105	877	W 111	820	W 235	1349	ARTICLES DE SERRURERIE
6996	BASE MTL MISC ARTICLES	W 153	439	W 250	771	W 190	559	W 123	660	ART DIVERS METAUX COMMUNS
7	MACHINES,TRANSPORT EQUIP		60497		47817		68711		166141	MACHINES MATERIEL TRANSPORT
71	POWER GENERATING EQUIPMT		4706		2699		7672		10269	MACHINES GENERATRICES
713	INTRNL COMBUS PSTN ENGIN		1001		1233	W 121	3838	W 156	3899	MOTEURS EXPL COMB INT, PIECE
7131	AIRCRAFT PSTN ENGINS,PTS		10		85	W 8	1468	W 12	2137	MOTEURS EXPL P.AVIATION, PIE
71319	PTS NES OF ENGN OF 71311		10		85	W 7	1450	W 9	1686	PIECES POUR 713.11
7133	MARINE PISTON ENGINES	N 1083	646	N 78	431	W 70	1557	W 63	735	MOTEURS EXPL POUR BATEAUX
71331	—— OUTBOARD	N 1067	541	N 73	347	W 41	864	W 27	569	MOTEURS BATEAUX HORSBORD
716	ROTATING ELECTRIC PLANT		3173		1239	W 260	3487	W 610	6124	APP ELECTR ROTATIFS,PIECES
7161	DC MOTORS AND GENERATORS		1792	N 2	205	W 74	2187	W 554	5362	MOTEURS COURANT CONTINU
7162	AC MTRS,GENRTRS,GEN SETS		205		500	W 179	922	W 34	404	MOTEURS ELECTRIQUES
7169	PTS NES OF ROT ELEC PLNT		1177		490	W 7	379	W 22	357	PIECES MAC APP ROTATIFS
72	MACHS FOR SPCL INDUSTRYS		6079		5709		5286		4675	MAC SPECIALES POUR INDUST
721	AGRIC MACHY,EXC TRACTORS		489		1627	W 43	541	W 60	511	MACHINES AGRICOLES
7219	AGRICULTURE MACHINES NES		114		1337	W 20	172	W 12	102	ENGINS AGRICOLES NDA
72197	OTH AGRIC ETC MACHINERY		70		1287	W 18	151	W 7	66	AUT APP POUR AGRICULTURE
723	CIVIL ENGNEERG EQUIP ETC		731		1208	W 89	774	W 100	666	APPAREILS DE GENIE CIVIL
7234	CONST,MINING MACHNRY NES		655		1145	W 83	714	W 44	300	MACH POUR LA CONST, MINES
72342	SLFPRP SHOVELS,EXCAVATRS	N 14	397	N 1	1013	W 66	602	W 38	242	PELLES MECANIQUES
727	FOOD MACHRY NON–DOMESTIC		944		980	W 63	2584	W 108	2026	MACH INDUSTRIES ALIMENT
7272	OTH FOOD PROC MCHY,PARTS		941		976	W 63	2572	W 104	2016	AUT MACH IND ALIMENTAIRE
72722	INDUS FOOD PROC MACH NES		513	N 16430	344	W 54	2363	W 57	758	MACHINES BOULANGERIE
72729	PTS NES OF MCHY OF 72722		424		631	W 9	209	W 47	1259	PIECES MACH DU 727.22
728	OTH MACHY FOR SPCL INDUS		3394		944	W 165	1047	W 111	940	AUT MACH IND PARTICULIERES
7283	OTHR MINERAL WORKG MACHY		1976		226	W 134	672	W 46	377	MACH TRIER,CRIBLER,BROYER
72832	MINRL CRUSHING ETC MACHY		1111			W 109	427	W 1	3	MACH CONCASSER MAT MINER
7284	MACHY FOR SPCL INDUS NES		880		511	W 9	174	W 32	306	MACH SPEC IND PARTICUL.
73	METALWORKING MACHINERY		320		839		457		407	MACH TRAVAIL DES METAUX
736	METALWORKING MACH–TOOLS		237		661	W 52	329	W 22	254	MACH–OUTILS TRAVAIL METAUX

4. General Imports C.I.F. by Commodities according to the S.I.T.C. (Rev. 2) in thousand U.S. Dollars
Importations Générales C.A.F. par Produits d'après la C.T.C.I. (Rév. 2) en milliers de Dollars E.U.

SITC CTCI	COMMODITY	1993 WEIGHT POIDS	1993 VALUE VALEUR	1994 WEIGHT POIDS	1994 VALUE VALEUR	1995 WEIGHT POIDS	1995 VALUE VALEUR	1996 WEIGHT POIDS	1996 VALUE VALEUR	PRODUIT
74	GENRL INDUSTRL MACHY NES		6090		11549		10001		11385	MACH APP INDUSTRIE
741	HEATING,COOLING EQUIPMNT		2368		3214	W 290	2525	W 361	3353	MACH CHAUFFAGE,PIECES
7414	NONDOM REFRIG EQUIPT,PTS		453		1634	W 88	924	W 96	576	MAT PRODUCTION DU FROID
74141	REFRIG EQUIP NONDOMESTIC	N 210	388	N 115	1452	W 60	422	W 51	352	REFIG INDUSTRIELS
7415	AIR–CONDITIONING MACHNRY		1243	N 33	1110	W 141	1191	W 154	1244	GROUPES CONDITION AIR
7416	HEATING,COOLING EQU NES		389		323	W 43	235	W 97	1403	APP CHANGEMENT TEMP
742	PUMPS FOR LIQUIDS ETC		674		843	W 38	671	W 63	780	POMPES MOTO–POMPES
7428	OTHER PUMPS FOR LIQUIDS		146		701	W 30	500	W 39	515	AUTRES POMPES POUR LIQ
74288	PUMPS FR LIQUIDS NES ETC		130		692	W 30	498	W 39	510	POMPES POUR LIQUIDES NDA
743	PUMPS NES,CENTRFUGES ETC		572		883	W 61	909	W 101	1085	POMPES COMPRES,VENT ETC
744	MECHANICAL HANDLING EQU		1752		4334	W 147	1346	W 178	1705	EQUIP MANUTENTION PIECES
7441	FORK LIFT TRCKS,ETC,PTS		698		3616	W 69	406	W 35	309	CHARIOTS POUR USINES ETC
74419	PTS NES OF VEHC OF 74411		530		3306	W 8	137	W 7	118	PIECES POUR 744.11
7449	PTS NES OF MACHY OF 7442		635		632	W 33	565	W 49	612	PIECES DU 744.2
745	NONELEC MACHY,TOOLS NES		431		670	W 132	1694	W 292	3060	AUT MACH NON ELEC,PIECES
7452	OTH NONELEC MCHS,PTS NES		299		441	W 126	1572	W 273	2771	AUT MACH NON ELEC,PIECES
74522	PACKAGNG,BOTTLNG,ETC MCH		12		43	W 40	440	W 165	1370	MACH NETT BOUTEILLES,ETC
749	NONELEC MACH PTS,ACC NES		294		1605	W 204	2857	W 168	1402	PIECES MACH NON ELEC NDA
7492	COCKS,VALVES ETC NES		263		1262	W 64	599	W 53	569	ART ROB,SIM POUR TUYAUX
7499	OTH NONELEC MCHY PTS NES		19		93	W 112	1712	W 20	287	PIECES NON ELECT NDA
74992	METAL–PLASTIC GASKETS		6	N 3	56	W 99	1540	W 12	169	JOINTS METALLOPLASTIQUES
75	OFFICE MACHNES,ADP EQUIP		2944		3262		5393		4405	MACH BUREAU TRAIT AUTOM
751	OFFICE MACHINES		526		446	W 24	820	W 25	546	MACH,APPAREILS DE BUREAU
752	AUTOMTIC DATA PROC EQUIP		1861		2109	W 47	3135	W 45	1992	MACH TRAIT INFORMATION
7522	DIGITAL COMPUTERS	N 329	432	N 143	673	W 11	791	W 8	433	MACH DIGITALES COMPLETES
7525	ADP PERIPHERAL UNITS	N 361	387	N 139	426	W 17	1164	W 26	1108	UNITES PERIPHERIQUES
7528	OFF–LINE DATA PROC EQUIP		960	N 6635	587	W 12	550	W 7	256	M..CH AUXIL TRAIT INFORM
759	OFFICE,ADP MCH PTS,ACCES		557		706	W 33	1438	W 57	1868	PIECES DU 751 ET 752
7599	ACCTG,ETC,ADP MCH PTS,AC		342		408	W 20	982	W 44	1599	PIECES DU 751 ET 752
76	TELECOMM,SOUND EQUIPMENT		9954		5449		10825		14097	EQUIPMENT DE TELECOM
761	TELEVISION RECEIVERS	N 2917	1859	N 1224	604	W 94	1252	W 43	573	RECEPTEURS DE TELEVISION
7611	COLOUR TV RECEIVERS	N 2817	754	N 974	521	W 94	1246	W 41	550	RECEPTEURS COULEUR
7612	MONOCHROME TV RECEIVERS	N 100	1105	N 250	83		6	W 2	23	RECEPTEURS NOIR ET BLANC
763	SOUND RECORDRS,PHONOGRPH	N 4260	601	N 677	700	W 25	530	W 47	736	PHONO,APP ENREGISTREMENT
7638	OTHR SOUND APPARATUS ETC	N 4127	563	N 606	669	W 24	504	W 45	719	AUT APP D'ENREGIS,REPROD
764	TELECOM EQPT,PTS,ACC NES		7026		3716	W 161	8530	W 219	12352	EQUIP TELECOM,PIECES
7641	LINE TELEPHONE,ETC EQUIP	N 6236	4984	N 336	1762	W 70	4648	W 46	2259	APP TELEPHON PAR FIL
7648	TELECOMM EQUIPMENT NES		115	N 28	264	W 1	75	W 96	7248	APP TELECOM NDA
76483	RADAR APPARATUS ETC		46	N 2	79		2	W 94	7085	APP DE RADIOGUIDAGE ETC
7649	PTS NES OF EQUIPMT OF 76		1522		1170	W 77	3285	W 52	1751	PIECES DE LA DIV 76
76491	PTS NES OF APPAR OF 7641		838		616	W 67	2895	W 33	1440	PIECES POUR 764.1
77	ELECTRIC MACHNRY NES ETC		9139		8327		8912		10733	MACH APP ELECT NDA
771	ELECTRIC POWER MACHY NES		1496		397	W 30	314	W 38	237	MACH PROD,TRANS ELECTR
7712	OTH ELEC POWER MACHY NES		1276		193	W 3	50	W 5	65	AUT APP PROD TRANSF ELEC
77129	PTS NES OF MACHY OF 771		1254		167	W 1	5	W 1	13	PIECES MACH DU 771
772	SWITCHGEAR ETC,PARTS NES		1516		1452	W 87	1331	W 157	1710	APP COUPURE,SECT ETC
7721	SWITCHGEAR ETC		1177		1282	W 76	1008	W 151	1537	APP COUPURE,SECTIONMNT
773	ELECTR DISTRIBUTNG EQUIP		1273		953	W 251	1141	W 350	2196	EQUIPMT DISTRIBUTION ELECT
7731	INSULATED WIRE,CABLE ETC		1089		843	W 234	1040	W 334	2070	FILS,CABLES ISOLES ELECT
774	ELECTRO–MEDCL,XRAY EQUIP		916		11	W 1	21	W 4	62	APPAREILS MEDICAUX
7742	X–RAY APPARATUS ETC		915		6		1	W 1	13	APPAREILS A RAYONS X
775	HOUSEHOLD TYPE EQUIP NES		2389		2518	W 491	2991	W 1020	2694	MACH,APP USAGE DOMESTQUE
7752	DOM REFRIGERATRS,FREEZRS	N 3090	1024	N 3115	1066	W 273	1414	W 374	1107	REFRIG,CONGEL MENAGER
77521	DOMESTIC REFRIGERATORS	N 2012	657	N 2034	709	W 195	1009	W 324	760	REFRIGERATEURS
7758	ELECTRO–THERMIC APPL NES		717		642	W 95	767	W 89	781	APP ELECTROTHERMIQ NDA
776	TRANSISTORS,VALVES,ETC		35		980	W 16	989	W 24	1519	LAMPES,TUBES,VALVES
7764	ELECTRONIC MICROCIRCUITS		7		517	W 11	812	W 2	79	MICROSTRUCTURES ELECTRON
7768	ELCTRNC COMP PTS,CRYSTLS		1		10	W 1	68	W 18	1331	CRIST PIEZO–ELEC,PCS 776
77689	ELECTRNIC COMPON PTS NES		1		10	W 1	68	W 18	1331	PIECES DU GROUPE 776
778	ELECTRICAL MACHINERY NES		1514		2016	W 224	2126	W 252	2315	AUTRES MACH ELECT NDA
78	ROAD VEHICLES		16554		6161		12846		13482	VEHICULES ROUTIERS
781	PASS MOTOR VEH EXC BUSES	N 1210	5941	N 48	2022	W 492	4707	W 800	5660	AUTO TRANSPORT PERSONNES
782	LORRIES,SPCL MTR VEH NES	N 335	3670	N 56	2538	W 336	3238	W 209	2299	VEHICULES SPECIAUX,MARCH
7821	LORRIES,TRUCKS	N 306	2671	N 55	1318	W 193	1305	W 167	1635	VEHICULES TRANSP MARCHAND
7822	SPECIAL MOTOR VEHCLS NES	N 29	999	N 1	1220	W 144	1933	W 42	664	VEHICULES USAGES SPECIAUX
783	ROAD MOTOR VEHICLES NES	N 74	1832		102	W 271	663	W 171	1074	VEHICULES ROUTIERS NDA
7831	BUSES	N 71	1806	N 3	69	W 271	663	W 155	986	VOITURES TRANSPORT COMMUN
784	MOTOR VEH PRTS,ACCES NES		4681		964	W 295	3724	W 456	3956	PIECES 722,781,782,783
7849	OTHER MOTOR VEHCL PARTS		4583		905	W 272	3646	W 430	3853	PIECES 722,781,782,783
79	OTHR TRANSPORT EQUIPMENT		4710		3824		7319		96688	AUTRE MATERIEL TRANSPORT
792	AIRCRAFT ETC		3564		2951	W 10	1178	W 28	93330	APP NAVIGATION AERIENNE
7924	AIRCRFT NES OVER 15000KG							W 15	91049	AERODYNES PLUS 15000 KG
7929	AIRCRAFT PARTS NES		3528		2945	W 8	944	W 12	2280	PIECES DU 792
793	SHIPS AND BOATS ETC		1053		855	W 742	6095	W 620	3297	NAVIRES BATEAUX,ETC
7932	SHIPS AND BOATS NES	N 143	331		796	W 731	5931	W 607	3196	NAVIRES ET BATEAUX
79321	YACHTS,SPORTS VESSLS ETC	N 43	158	N 4	141	W 12	183	W 588	2793	BATEAUX DE PLAISANCE
79323	OTHER CARGO VESSELS	N 100	173		15	W 598	2304	W 3	76	AUT BATEAUX TRANS MARCH
79324	FISHING VESSELS ETC				641	W 122	3444	W 16	328	BATEAUX DE PECHE
8	MISC MANUFACTURED GOODS		35907		24806		27011		27418	ART MANUFACTURES DIVERS
812	*PLUMBG,HEATNG,LGHTNG EQ		1971		1277	W 204	1409	W 395	2617	APPAR SANITAIRES CHAUFFAGE
8122	CERAMIC PLUMBNG FIXTURES		736	W 112	585	W 126	665	W 250	1075	EVIERS,LAVABOS,CUVETTES
8124	LIGHTING EQUIPMENT NES		1223		632	W 74	705	W 117	1191	APPAREILS ECLAIRAGE ETC
81242	LAMPS,FITTINGS BASE METL		1156		515	W 54	472	W 99	1011	APPAREILS D'ECLAIRAGE
821	*FURNITURE,PARTS THEREOF		2513		2404	W 803	3035	W 1280	3961	MEUBLES ET PIECES
8212	MED FURN,STUFFD FURNSHGS		875		672	W 213	745	W 382	790	MOB MEDICO–CHIRUR,PIECES
82122	MATTRESSES ETC		733	N 2398	551	W 210	660	W 376	749	SOMMIERS,ARTICLES DE LITERIE
8219	FURNITURE AND PARTS NES		1517		1624	W 521	1993	W 829	2810	AUTRES MEUBLES ET PIECES
82192	WOOD FURNITURE NES		790		1001	W 351	1055	W 559	1572	MEUBLES NDA EN BOIS
84	CLOTHING AND ACCESSORIES		2824		2626		3595		3222	VETEMENTS
846	UNDER GARMENTS KNITTED	N 750855	1078	N 473470	816	W 158	1446	W 109	1159	SOUS VETS DE BONNETERIE
8462	— OF COTTON NON ELASTIC	N 674419	958	N 426195	673	W 138	1246	W 96	997	SOUS–VET BONNET COTON
84629	—— OTHER	N 672708	947	N 419895	645	W 135	1200	W 85	918	AUT SOUS–VET BONNET COTON
851	*FOOTWEAR	P 323729	1524	P 382658	2037	W 230	2270	W 181	2192	CHAUSSURES
85102	FOOTWEAR LEATHER	P 146300	756	P 199543	1285	W 159	1644	W 142	1766	CHAUS SEMELLES EN CUIR
87	PRECISION INSTRUMNTS NES		13634		3241		3210		2240	INSTRUM,APPAR SCIENT NDA
872	MEDICAL INSTRUMENTS NES		1024		1028	W 21	912	W 36	537	INSTR,APP MEDIC–CHIR NDA
87202	OTH MEDICAL INSTRUMENTS		964		1007	W 20	897	W 34	519	INSTRUM,APP MEDECINE
874	MEASURNG,CONTROLNG INSTR		12426		2025	W 74	2228		1511	INSTRUMENTS DE MESURE
8748	ELEC MEAS,CONTRL EQU NES		10697		1344	W 10	1067		421	APP ELEC ELECTRO MESURE
87483	OTH ELCTRNC MEAS ETC EQU		10300	N 70	1162	W 10	930	W 12	296	AUT APP ELECTRO DE MESURE
8749	INSTR PTS NES,ACCESSORYS		1104		87	W 8	386	W 4	66	PIECES 873,874.3,54,874.8

4. General Imports C.I.F. by Commodities according to the S.I.T.C. (Rev. 2) in thousand U.S. Dollars
Importations Générales C.A.F. par Produits d'après la C.T.C.I. (Rév. 2) en milliers de Dollars E.U.

SITC CTCI	COMMODITY	1993 WEIGHT POIDS	1993 VALUE VALEUR	1994 WEIGHT POIDS	1994 VALUE VALEUR	1995 WEIGHT POIDS	1995 VALUE VALEUR	1996 WEIGHT POIDS	1996 VALUE VALEUR	PRODUIT
88	PHOTO EQU,OPTICL GDS ETC		1399		1031		1192		1209	APP,FOURN PHOTO,OP,MONTR
89	MISC MANUFCTRD GOODS NES		11565		11772		11711		11537	ART MANUFACTURES DIVERS
892	PRINTED MATTER		2469		2818	W 302	2902	W 282	2312	IMPRIMES
8921	PRINTED BOOKS,GLOBES,ETC		1018		1184	W 105	976	W 99	785	LIVRES,BROCHURES,CARTES
89211	PRINTED BOOKS,PAMPHLETS		931		1135	W 100	927	W 90	725	LIVRES,BROCHURES
8928	PRINTED MATTER NES		1143		1220	W 132	1267	W 138	1100	IMPRIMES NDA
893	ARTICLES OF PLASTIC NES		4413		4009		4514		5139	OUVRAGES EN MAT DIVIS 58
8931	PLSTC PACKG CONTNRS,LIDS		1037		998	W 399	1729	W 460	2533	ART TRANSP EMBALLAGE ETC
8939	MISC PLASTIC ARTICLES		3286		2717	W 431	2614	W 586	2496	ART DIVERS EN MAT DIV 58
89399	OTHR PLASTC ARTICLES NES		3006		2483	W 399	2400	W 438	2167	AUT OUV MAT DIV 58
894	TOYS,SPORTING GOODS,ETC		2002		2167	W 837	1843	W 182	1712	VOITURES ENFANTS,JOUETS
8942	TOYS,INDOOR GAMES ETC		1621		1667	W 570	1090	W 136	1163	JOUETS,JEUX ETC
89423	TOYS NES		613		634	W 533	470	W 74	610	JOUETS,MODELES REDUITS
89424	INDOOR GAME EQUIPMENT		756		754	W 16	453	W 30	277	ART,JEUX DE SOCIETE
898	MUSICAL INSTRUMENTS,PTS		1068		643	W 45	845	W 43	663	INSTRUMENTS DE MUSIQUE
8983	SOUND RECRDNG TAPE,DISCS	N 300560	989	N 86576	584	W 42	767	W 40	602	SUPPORTS SON POUR 763
899	OTHER MANUFACTURED GOODS		731		1335		852		835	AUT ART MANUF DIVERS NDA
9	GOODS NOT CLASSD BY KIND		234		182		479		1745	ART TRANSACT NON CLASSES
931	*SPECIAL TRANSACTIONS	W 1	45		82		340		1598	TRANS.SPECIALES

5. General Exports F.O.B. by Commodities according to the S.I.T.C. (Rev. 2) in thousand U.S. Dollars
Exportations Générales F.O.B. par Produits d'après la C.T.C.I. (Rév. 2) en milliers de Dollars E.U.

SITC CTCI	COMMODITY	1993 WEIGHT POIDS	1993 VALUE VALEUR	1994 WEIGHT POIDS	1994 VALUE VALEUR	1995 WEIGHT POIDS	1995 VALUE VALEUR	1996 WEIGHT POIDS	1996 VALUE VALEUR	PRODUIT
	ALL COMMODITIES		51641		51772		53128		139354	TOUS PRODUITS
0	FOOD AND LIVE ANIMALS		15125		23585		23471		40783	ALIMENTS,ANIMAUX VIVANTS
02	DAIRY PRODCTS,BIRDS'EGGS		155		40		5		4	PRODUITS LAITIERS,OEUFS
022	MILK AND CREAM	W 51	155	W 5	8		1	W 1	4	LAIT ET CREME
0224	MILK,CREAM PRESERVED ETC	W 51	155	W 3	5					LAIT,CREME CONS,CONC
03	FISH AND PREPARATIONS		14397		22452		22667		39761	POISSONS ET PREPARATIONS
034	FISH,FRESH,CHILLED,FROZN	W 445	1798	W 438	1820	W 406	2125	W 496	2584	POISSON FRAIS, REFRIG,CONG
0341	FISH FRSH,CHLLD,EX FILLT	W 193	1146	W 246	1384	W 262	1744	W 297	2066	POISSON FRAIS,REFRIGERE
0342	FISH FROZEN,EXCL FILLETS	W 252	652	W 192	436	W 145	381	W 198	512	POISSONS CONGELES
035	FISH SALTED,DRIED,SMOKED	W 15	597	W 70	2584	W 17	655	W 131	808	POISSON SECHE,SALE,FUME
03503	FISH(EX COD)DRIED,SALTED	W 15	597	W 9	377	W 11	607	W 10	498	POISSONS SECHES,SALES
03504	FISH SMOKED			W 61	2206	W 6	48	W 16	121	POISSONS FUMES
036	SHELL FISH FRESH,FROZEN	W 68	644	W 39	371	W 131	1444	W 191	2195	CRUSTACES,MOLLUSQUES
037	FISH ETC PREPD,PRSVD NES	W 4466	11358	W 7362	17677	W 6291	18442	W 13019	34173	POIS,CRUST,MOL PREPARES
0371	FISH PREPARD,PRESRVD NES	W 4466	11358	W 7362	17677	W 6291	18442	W 13016	34150	CONSERVES DE POISSONS
07	COFFEE,TEA,COCOA,SPICES		462		516		752		962	CAFE,THE,CACAO,EPICES
075	SPICES	W 446	456	W 435	458	W 637	729	W 746	947	EPICES
0752	SPICES,EX PEPPER,PIMENTO	W 446	456	W 435	458	W 637	729	W 746	947	AUTRES EPICES
07522	CINNAMON,ETC	W 446	456	W 435	458	W 637	729	W 743	944	CANNELLE
081	*FEEDING STUFF FOR ANIML	W 196	65	W 1440	460					NOURRITURE POUR ANIMAUX
0814	MEAT OR FISH MEAL FODDER	W 196	65	W 1440	460					FARINES DE VIANDES,POISSONS
08142	FISH MEAL FODDER	W 196	65	W 1440	460					FARINES DE POISSONS
1	BEVERAGES AND TOBACCO		353		533		725		671	BOISSONS ET TABACS
11	BEVERAGES		277		393		481		503	BOISSONS
112	ALCOHOLIC BEVERAGES	W 93	258	W 107	353	W 102	465	W 92	399	BOISSONS ALCOOLIQUES
1124	DISTILLED ALCOHOLIC BEVS	W 30	192	W 73	271	W 42	355	W 43	297	ALCOOLS,EAUX–DE–VIE
11241	WHISKY	W 14	100	W 9	78	W 17	203	W 28	215	WHISKY
12	TOBACCO AND MANUFACTURES		75		141		244		168	TABACS BRUTS FABRIQUES
122	TOBACCO,MANUFACTURED	W 9	75	W 18	141	W 42	244	W 10	168	TABACS FABRIQUES
1222	CIGARETTES	W 8	74	W 17	124	W 42	193	W 9	147	CIGARETTES
2	CRUDE MATERLS,EXCL FUELS		240		117		225		146	MAT BRUTES NON COMESTIBLES
22	OIL SEEDS,OLEAGINOUS FRT		181		32		171		1	GRAINES,FRUITS OLEAGINEUX
223	SEEDS FOR OTH FIXED OILS	W 226	181	W 101	32	W 157	70		1	GRAINES AUTRES HUILES FIXES
2231	COPRA	W 226	181	W 101	32	W 157	70			COPRAH
3	MINERAL FUELS ETC		28466		23765		24824		30469	COMBUSTIBLES MINERAUX LUB
33	PETROLEUM AND PRODUCTS		28434		23765		24824		30469	PETROLE ET DERIVES
334	PETROLEUM PRODUCTS,REFIN	W 133816	28434	W 116151	23765	W 103916	24784	W 110050	30445	PRODUITS RAFFINES
3341	GASOLINE,OTH LIGHT OILS			W 116151	23765	W 103916	24784			ESSENCES POUR MOTEURS
3342	KEROSENE,OTH MEDIUM OILS	W 37923	8921					W 32580	10318	PETR LAMPANTS,AUT HUIL
33421	KEROSENE INCL JET FUEL	W 37923	8921					W 32580	10318	PETROLES LAMPANTS
3343	GAS OILS	W 92191	18645					W 72552	18478	GAS OILS
3344	FUEL OILS,NES	W 3062	414					W 3786	631	FUEL OILS
3345	LUBS,PETROLEUM OILS NES	W 640	454					W 1131	1019	HUILES LUBRIFIANTES
33451	LUBS(HIGH PETR CONT) ETC	W 640	454					W 1131	1019	HUILES LUBRIF,H LOURDES
5	CHEMCLS,RELATED PROD NES		139		60		253		255	PRODUITS CHIMIQUES
55	PERFUME,CLEANING ETC PRD		128		55		237		202	PROD POUR PARFUM,TOILETTE
553	PERFUMERY,COSMETICS,ETC	W 5	124	W 5	55	W 14	205	W 11	97	PRODUITS DE PARFUMERIE
6	BASIC MANUFACTURES		78		41		362		148	ART MANUFACTURES
66	NONMETAL MINERAL MFS NES		44		2		290		49	ART MIN NON METALLIQUES
661	LIME,CEMENT,BLDG PRODS	W 402	43	W 7	1	W 2023	289	W 29	14	CHAUX,CIMENTS MAT CONSTR
6612	CEMENT					W 2000	174			CIMENTS HYDRAULIQUES
7	MACHINES,TRANSPORT EQUIP		4012		1396		1576		64309	MACHINES MATERIEL TRANSPORT
71	POWER GENERATING EQUIPMT		19		215		89		282	MACHINES GENERATRICES
74	GENRL INDUSTRL MACHY NES		402		165		764		31	MACH APP INDUSTRIE
741	HEATING,COOLING EQUIPMNT					W 8	692		1	MACH CHAUFFAGE,PIECES
7413	INDUS FURNACES ETC,PARTS					W 7	661			FOURS IND,LABOR,PIECES
74132	INDUST FURNACES NONELECT					W 7	661			FOURS NON ELECTRIQUES
744	MECHANICAL HANDLING EQU		365		165				1	EQUIP MANUTENTION PIECES
7441	FORK LIFT TRCKS,ETC,PTS			W 5	164				1	CHARIOTS POUR USINES ETC
74419	PTS NES OF VEHC OF 74411			W 5	164				1	PIECES POUR 744.11
7449	PTS NES OF MACHY OF 7442		365		1					PIECES DU 744.2
76	TELECOMM,SOUND EQUIPMENT		2141		52		182		304	EQUIPMENT DE TELECOM
764	TELECOM EQPT,PTS,ACC NES		2136		46	W 1	166	W 3	150	EQUIP TELECOM,PIECES
7649	PTS NES OF EQUIPMT OF 76		2032		22	W 1	127	W 1	110	PIECES DE LA DIV 76
76499	PARTS ETC OF SOUND EQUIP		2002							PIECES NDA POUR 763
77	ELECTRIC MACHNRY NES ETC		32		77		94		10906	MACH APP ELECT NDA
778	ELECTRICAL MACHINERY NES		7		2		5	W 42	10867	AUTRES MACH ELECT NDA
7788	OTH ELEC MACHY,EQUIP NES		7				1	W 40	10864	AUT MACH APP ELEC NDA
77882	ELEC TRAFFIC CONTROL EQU							W 36	9508	APP ELECT SIGNAL,SECURITE ET
77886	OTH ELEC MACHINERY NES							W 4	1353	AUT MACH APP ELECTRIQUES
78	ROAD VEHICLES		20		13		16		1776	VEHICULES ROUTIERS
782	LORRIES,SPCL MTR VEH NES							W 34	1758	VEHICULES SPECIAUX,MARCH
7822	SPECIAL MOTOR VEHCLS NES							W 34	1758	VEHICULES USAGES SPECIAUX
79	OTHR TRANSPORT EQUIPMENT		1365		798		355		50993	AUTRE MATERIEL TRANSPORT
792	AIRCRAFT ETC		1365		797	W 16	336		50872	APP NAVIGATION AERIENNE
7924	AIRCRFT NES OVER 15000KG					W 15	6		49222	AERODYNES PLUS 15000 KG
7929	AIRCRAFT PARTS NES		1365		797	W 1	329	W 11	1650	PIECES DU 792
8	MISC MANUFACTURED GOODS		3219		2261		1686		2373	ART MANUFACTURES DIVERS
87	PRECISION INSTRUMNTS NES		2981		1799		1151		1760	INSTRUM,APPAR SCIENT NDA
874	MEASURNG,CONTROLNG INSTR		2975		1799	W 4	1147	W 8	1753	INSTRUMENTS DE MESURE
8741	SURVEYING INSTRUMENTS						76	W 4	666	INST GEODESIE,TOPO ETC
87412	SURVEY INSTR ETC NONELEC						74	W 4	666	INSTR GEODESIE,TOPO ETC
8748	ELEC MEAS,CONTRL EQU NES		397		1570	W 3	1069	W 4	1085	APP ELEC ELECTRO MESURE
87483	OTH ELCTRNC MEAS ETC EQU		397		1570	W 3	1021	W 3	1083	AUT APP ELECTRO DE MESURE
8749	INSTR PTS NES,ACCESSORYS		2578		130				1	PIECES 873,874.3,54,874.8
88	PHOTO EQU,OPTICL GDS ETC		71		119		173		162	APP,FOURN PHOTO,OP,MONTR
89	MISC MANUFCTRD GOODS NES		167		291		274		400	ART MANUFACTURES DIVERS
899	OTHER MANUFACTURED GOODS		77		214	W 4	116	W 3	61	AUT ART MANUF DIVERS NDA
8998	SMALLWARES,TOILETRYS ETC		75		213	W 3	100	W 3	58	ART MERCERIE,TOILETTE
89983	BUTTONS,STUDS,ETC		75		213	W 3	100	W 3	48	BOUTONS,BOUTONS–PRESSION

FOOT NOTES – NOTES

TABLE 1 –
1 In 1969, values for imports are estimated.
TABLEAU 1 –
1 En 1969 les valeurs des importations sont estimées.

1. HISTORICAL SERIES, 1961–1996 GENERAL TRADE, IMPORTS C.I.F., EXPORTS F.O.B. SERIES HISTORIQUES, 1961–1996 COMMERCE GENERAL, IMPORTATIONS C.A.F., EXPORTATIONS F.O.B

YEAR ANNEE	VALUE IN MILLION SINGAPOR.DOLLARS VALEUR EN MILLION SINGAPOR.DOLLARS MERCHANDISE–MARCHANDISE		GOLD–OR		CONVERSION FACTORS U.S. CENTS PER SINGAPORE DOLLAR FACTEURS DE CONVERSION CENTS E.U. PAR SINGAPORE DOLLAR		INDEX NUMBERS –INDICES QUANTUM		UNIT VALUE VALEUR UNITAIRE	
	IMPORTS	EXPORTS	IMPORTS	EXPORTS	IMPORTS	EXPORTS	IMPORTS	EXPORTS	IMPORTS	EXPORTS
1961	3963.00	3309.00			32.6667	32.6667				
1962	4036.00	3417.00	0.25	0.20	32.6667	32.6667				
1963	4279.00	3475.00	5.07		32.6667	32.6667				
1964	3479.00	2772.00	6.46		32.6667	32.6667				
1965	3807.00	3004.00	4.09		32.6667	32.6667				
1966	4066.00	3374.00	3.57	0.20	32.6667	32.6667				
1967	4407.00	3491.00	14.57		32.6667	32.6667				
1968	5084.00	3891.00	15.67		32.6667	32.6667				
1969	6244.00	4741.00	16.51		32.6667	32.6667				
1970	7534.00	4756.00	5.55		32.6667	32.6667				
1971	8664.00	5371.00			32.6667	32.6667				
1972	9538.00	6149.00			35.6248	35.6325	19	13	47	51
1973	12513.00	8907.00			41.1362	41.1643	22	16	54	62
1974	20405.00	14155.00			41.0666	41.0425	25	17	78	89
1975	19270.00	12758.00			42.2079	42.1395	23	16	78	87
1976	22404.00	16266.00			40.4830	40.4859	25	19	82	92
1977	25522.00	20090.00			41.0261	41.0185	27	22	88	100
1978	29601.00	22986.00			44.0811	44.0888	30	25	92	103
1979	38352.00	30940.00			46.0041	46.0026	35	29	99	110
1980	50481.00	41453.00			46.7290	46.7414	40	34	115	127
1981	58325.30	44290.80			47.3338	47.3398	45	35	128	146
1982	60244.50	44472.70			46.7552	46.7431	49	37	122	141
1983	59504.20	46154.90			47.3210	47.3027	49	40	119	134
1984	61133.60	51340.40			46.9654	46.9572	51	46	119	129
1985	57817.40	50178.70			45.4624	45.4633	50	46	105	114
1986	55543.01	48986.00			45.9306	45.9218	54	53	93	98
1987	68416.00	60266.00			47.5993	47.6089	62	62	101	101
1988	88228.00	79051.01			49.7149	49.7205	79	83	101	100
1989	96864.00	87117.01			51.2643	51.2659	87	92	101	100
1990	109806.00	95206.00			55.3467	55.3853	100	100	100	100
1991	114195.00	101880.00			57.8777	57.8760	107	113	97	95
1992	117530.00	103351.00			61.3735	61.3784	114	123	94	88
1993	137602.00	119475.00			61.9390	61.9441	137	145	92	86
1994	156397.00	147327.00			65.6471	65.7214				83
1995	176317.00	167515.00			70.6125	70.5984				81
1996	185183.00	176332.00			70.9244	70.9227				81

2. IMPORTS BY BROAD ECONOMIC CATEGORY AND EXPORTS BY INDUSTRIAL ORIGIN. (PERCENTAGE OF TOTAL VALUE) IMPORTATIONS PAR CATEGORIES ECONOMIQUES ET EXPORTATIONS PAR BRANCHE D'ACTIVITE.(EN POURCENTAGE DE LA VALEUR TOTALE)

IMPORTS – IMPORTATIONS

	1990	1991	1992	1993	1994	1995	1996
TOTAL IMPORTS–IMPORTATIONS TOTALES	100.	100.	100.	100.	100.	100.	100.
1 FOOD BEV–ALIMENTATION BOISSONS	4.8	5.1	4.9	4.4	4.1	3.6	3.6
11 PRIMARY–PRODUITS DE BASE	2.4	2.5	2.5	2.2	2.0	1.7	1.6
111 FOR INDUSTRY–POUR L'INDUSTRIE	0.7	0.7	0.7	0.6	0.6	0.5	0.4
112 FOR HOUSEHOLDS–POUR LES MENAGES	1.7	1.8	1.8	1.6	1.4	1.2	1.2
12 PROCESSED–PRODUITS ELABORES	2.4	2.6	2.5	2.1	2.0	1.9	2.0
121 FOR INDUSTRY–POUR L'INDUSTRIE	0.6	0.6	0.5	0.4	0.3	0.3	0.3
122 FOR HOUSEHOLDS–POUR LES MENAGES	1.8	2.0	2.0	1.8	1.7	1.6	1.7
2 IND SUPPLIES–APPROV INDUSTRIELS	23.4	23.2	22.9	21.2	19.6	19.9	17.5
21 PRIMARY–PRODUITS DE BASE	2.0	1.8	1.5	1.3	1.2	1.3	1.2
22 PROCESSED–PRODUITS ELABORES	21.5	21.5	21.4	19.9	18.5	18.6	16.3
3 FUELS–COMBUSTIBLES	15.8	14.1	12.7	10.9	8.8	8.1	9.4
31 PRIMARY–PRODUITS DE BASE	11.4	10.1	8.8	7.6	5.7	5.2	6.1
32 PROCESSED–PRODUITS ELABORES	4.4	4.0	3.9	3.3	3.1	2.9	3.3
321 MOTOR SPIRIT–ESSENCE	3.7	3.4	0.8	2.4	0.6		0.4
322 OTHER–AUTRES	0.7	0.6	3.1	1.0	2.5	2.9	2.9
4 MACHINERY–EQUIPEMENT	33.4	35.3	36.2	39.9	45.7	48.9	48.8
41 CAPITAL EQUIPMENT–MACHINES	19.6	21.1	21.0	22.7	24.9	23.6	24.5
42 PARTS–PIECES ACCESSOIRES	13.7	14.2	15.2	17.2	20.7	25.3	24.2
5 TRANSPORT–TRANSPORT	7.7	7.4	8.3	7.9	6.4	6.2	7.4
51 PASSENGER CARS–AUTOMOBILES			0.7		0.7	0.7	0.6
52 OTHER–AUTRES	3.7	4.0	3.8	4.5	2.8	2.7	3.8
521 INDUSTRIAL–INDUSTRIELS	3.5	3.8	3.6	4.3	2.7	2.7	3.7
522 NON INDUSTRIAL–NON INDUSTRIEL	0.2	0.2	0.2	0.2	0.1	0.1	0.1
53 PARTS–PIECES ACCESSOIRES	4.0	3.4	3.8	3.5	3.0	2.8	3.1
6 CONSUM GOODS–BIENS CONSOMMATION	13.7	13.8	13.8	14.6	13.9	12.3	12.4
61 DURABLE–DURABLES	6.1	6.1	5.6	6.5	6.4	5.2	5.0
62 SEMI DURABLE–SEMI DURABLES	5.3	5.4	5.7	5.4	5.1	4.9	5.3
63 NON DURABLE–NON DURABLES	2.3	2.3	2.5	2.7	2.4	2.1	2.1
7 GOODS NES–BIENS NDA	1.1	1.2	1.2	1.1	1.4	1.0	0.9

EXPORTS – EXPORTATIONS

	1990	1991	1992	1993	1994	1995	1996
TOTAL EXPORTS–EXPORTATIONS TOTALES	100.	100.	100.	100.	100.	100.	100.
1 AGRICULTURE	3.6	3.2	2.9	2.3	2.2	2.0	1.6
2 MINING QUARRY–INDUS EXTRACTIVES	0.4	0.5	0.4	0.4	0.3	0.3	0.4
3 MANUFACTURING–IND MANUFACTUR	96.0	96.3	96.7	97.3	97.4	97.6	98.0
31 FOOD BEV TOBACCO–ALIM BOISS TAB	3.6	3.9	4.0	3.6	3.1	2.7	2.7
32 TEXTILES–INDUSTRIES TEXTILES	4.9	5.0	4.8	4.0	3.2	2.7	2.4
33 WOOD & PRODUCTS–BOIS & PRODUITS	1.0	0.9	0.8	0.7	0.5	0.3	0.3
34 PAPER & PRODUCTS–PAPIER & PRODT	1.2	1.2	1.2	1.0	1.0	1.1	0.9
35 CHEMICALS–INDUSTRIES CHIMIQUES	25.7	24.9	20.9	19.9	16.4	14.0	14.6
36 NON METAL MIN–MIN NON METAL	0.4	0.5	0.5	0.5	0.5	0.5	0.4
37 BASIC METAL–IND METAL BASE	2.0	2.0	2.1	1.9	1.9	2.4	2.1
38 METAL MANUF–MANUF METAL	54.8	55.4	59.9	63.0	68.5	70.3	70.6
39 OTH MANUF IND–AUTRES MANUF	2.2	2.4	2.5	2.5	2.4	3.6	3.9

3. TRADE BY PRINCIPAL COUNTRIES OF PRODUCTION AND DESTINATION (VALUE IN THOUSAND U.S. DOLLARS)
ECHANGES SELON LES PRINCIPAUX PAYS DE PRODUCTION ET DE DESTINATION (VALEUR EN MILLIERS DE DOLLARS EU)

COUNTRIES–PAYS	GENERAL IMPORTS C.I.F. IMPORTATIONS GENERALES C.A.F				
	1992	1993	1994	1995	1996
World	72173675	85231076	102669327	124503489	131480211
Africa	550948	705680	637613	687145	707802
Americas	12993335	14969620	17017666	20375656	23578639
Northern America	12209427	14189920	16117595	19264395	22167674
LAIA	617240	497258	668028	877605	1095609
CACM	9530	13372	8484	13877	12586
Caribbean	82262	114289	49762	81941	98784
Rest of America	74876	154781	173798	137838	203987
As.ex F.USSR	46069196	55785018	67913778	82057029	83383410
Eur.x F.USSR	10949915	11910557	15110764	18946995	21338660
EU	9812243	10613470	13451396	16591057	19002471
EFTA	904489	1059957	1287908	1867839	1865482
East Europe	121619	163769	217984	313134	216303
Other Europe	70938	73361	153476	168227	249486
Former USSR	161521	162755	188338	382018	177863
Oceania	1448760	1697446	1801167	2054647	2293837
Japan/Japon	15200590	18650414	22597102	26330290	23867886
USA/Etats–Unis d'Amer	11879940	13852666	15701710	18740306	21574846
Malaysia/Malaisie	10615869	14041294	16805635	19267887	19743678
Thailand/Thaïlande	2680657	3515780	4904365	6423353	7183177
Saudi Arabia	3695766	3319404	3680851	3798805	4999573
Korea, Republic of	2375706	2742967	3929334	5405459	4517007
Germany/Allemagne	2357678	2603270	3459325	4326544	4799376
Hong Kong	2202760	2687439	3469732	4111065	4204272
China/Chine	2252223	2401459	2896345	4045769	4443732
United Kingdom	2014666	2225396	2839690	3309442	3597256
France,Monac	1797194	1939199	2178142	2798756	3727242
Australia/Australie	1226715	1476904	1570885	1804618	1986067
Italy/Italie	1282122	1135916	1450046	1772359	2263680
Switz.Liecht	738847	921423	1111771	1530740	1666391
United Arab Emirates	670810	900521	876572	1436803	2057426
Netherlands/Pays–Bas	663276	789783	1075516	1129836	1268943
Kuwait/Koweït	340408	684817	768616	1167805	1356997
Philippines	317438	503630	783160	1100439	1391279
India/Inde	532686	668721	792714	922170	1013056
Belgium–Luxembourg	446525	516431	612031	741662	711402
Sweden/Suède	386537	415052	513474	665881	773613
Iran (Islamic Rp. of)	507049	649631	591668	476488	362739
Canada	328885	337247	415883	524087	589533
Spain/Espagne	221471	259327	353264	554262	578759
Viet Nam	129309	352391	451448	449165	436573
Brazil/Brésil	255944	301468	353108	359971	338360
Finland/Finlande	134091	298862	351059	381442	419262
Qatar	227250	121133	112630	293250	604552
Brunei Darussalam	266126	216534	209147	223635	205950
Austria/Autriche	126397	121214	167971	356589	259796
Norway,SVD,JM	165642	138533	176137	337100	199091
Oman	228937	237510	98986	224174	225282
Denmark/Danemark	251791	132183	181805	218651	228939
New Zealand	185256	179702	191377	206879	236583
Ireland/Irlande	83840	132083	194626	262064	286512
Turkey/Turquie	121780	141106	208487	188550	247552
Israel/Israël	107758	126263	155853	232443	271719
Russian Federation	161521	129537	188338	311746	100881
Chile/Chili	133836	88360	136881	236061	292532
Myanmar	108048	111204	140841	211348	206229
Panama	68919	138925	134079	134171	202773
Malta/Malte	62506	65589	133617	158845	240836
Bahrain/Bahreïn	146776	127184	98130	108699	134883
Mexico/Mexique	46185	39475	61052	160201	305199
Yemen/Yémen	55812	15131	172744	234504	94138
Egypt/Egypte	70529	98788	122782	148447	110973
So. Africa Customs Un	5623	1058	38	248061	235674
Liberia/Libéria	48986	104730	68403	42150	149457
Cyprus/Chypre	10531	5438	9428	65223	315984
Romania/Roumanie	37909	45955	102212	127970	62036

COUNTRIES–PAYS	GENERAL EXPORTS F.O.B. EXPORTATIONS GENERALES F.O.B.				
	1992	1993	1994	1995	1996
Monde	63463155	74006830	96824598	118263152	125153077
Afrique	1337969	1317139	1420233	1548058	1517967
Amériques	14905643	16867194	20234805	23774038	25479333
Amérique du Nord	13863846	15548344	18783573	22168190	23496708
ALAI	528666	747363	828458	975223	1210651
MCAC	10168	51257	28746	33056	34265
Caraïbes	75040	101045	102512	116784	147342
Autre Amérique	427922	419184	491516	480785	590368
Asie l'URSS exclus	33777694	41106721	57182204	71564944	76087916
Europe l'URSS exclus	10771997	11767644	14045260	16829981	17323530
UE	9998224	10800813	13033958	15836178	16323297
AELE	506584	692610	650942	524433	523866
Europe de l'Est	162649	145348	176890	190932	205263
Autre de l'Europe	83792	128873	183470	256953	248311
Ancienne URSS	342152	552458	830624	977208	927213
Océanie	2327701	2395676	3111472	3568910	3817118
USA/Etats–Unis d'Amer	13392981	15062492	18177152	21589972	23088618
Malaysia/Malaisie	7938281	10494671	19118021	22679700	22537452
Hong Kong	4962910	6419816	8421698	10132454	11138053
Japan/Japon	4825263	5526244	6797276	9224553	10262841
Thailand/Thaïlande	3956299	4215256	5380144	6828219	7104375
Germany/Allemagne	2695296	2940322	3437122	4000311	3843224
United Kingdom	1844485	2214670	2619030	3072339	3538456
Korea, Republic of	1428130	2060122	2543983	3245093	3800540
Netherlands/Pays–Bas	1975791	1920318	2583430	3149529	2891948
China/Chine	1112345	1900141	2107493	2760863	3396603
Australia/Australie	1508893	1673680	2293874	2593802	2850004
Philippines	808968	1371611	1584833	1929222	2298628
France,Monac	972102	1089469	1313528	2013487	2486704
India/Inde	936195	949837	1267183	1878624	2078191
Viet Nam	385956	980234	1334344	1791178	1717999
Brunei Darussalam	663115	634651	819164	1466682	1712184
Ireland/Irlande	231174	500456	705418	1205265	1432444
United Arab Emirates	646641	681267	799616	849575	901956
Russian Federation	342152	489047	830624	911585	877232
Italy/Italie	654234	652547	690284	770398	508348
Canada	462435	480242	601078	571899	401409
Bangladesh	332095	347085	432573	589238	670573
Myanmar	262388	334972	392975	637898	722732
Panama	361440	385019	452966	465868	577705
Belgium–Luxembourg	412432	413208	477459	445449	414450
Switz.Liecht	406083	436561	516109	400521	400715
Democratic Kampuchea	249052	369115	384757	500540	517622
Saudi Arabia	412244	385992	330693	325776	380161
Sri Lanka	340207	311440	339071	376822	387735
Spain/Espagne	333408	297751	371871	339558	318204
New Zealand	293495	226790	316414	384392	384628
Brazil/Brésil	118868	293950	242173	436084	488206
Liberia/Libéria	223900	222658	411034	315469	315724
Pakistan	264115	261733	309398	308289	269837
Mexico/Mexique	108136	130718	204898	187290	388811
American Samoa	177398	157965	182347	209252	196696
Austria/Autriche	251305	181043	190249	154394	135109
So. Africa Customs Un	314	284	170	459405	437157
Israel/Israël	113472	113296	161492	234550	230100
Greece/Grèce	151656	175056	171349	169753	171093
Papua New Guinea	163734	154730	171135	172255	155430
Argentina/Argentine	145190	152184	186037	147776	154558
Sweden/Suède	163428	139057	157701	170949	136369
Malta/Malte	65368	98773	145396	233160	213717
Norway,SVD,JM	100501	256049	134833	123912	123152
Finland/Finlande	130635	96128	137158	168213	205832
Nigeria/Nigéria	220595	157942	73342	94546	102388
Denmark/Danemark	129683	122531	125112	116094	146678
Turkey/Turquie	130994	128377	68141	135744	170550
Iran (Islamic Rp. of)	186995	96921	64197	121977	117463

(VALUE AS PERCENTAGE OF WORLD TOTAL)(VALEURS EN POURCENTAGE DU TOTAL MONDIAL)

	1987	1988	1989	1990	1991	1992	1993	1994	1995	1996
Africa	1.1	0.7	0.9	0.7	0.6	0.8	0.8	0.6	0.6	0.5
Americas	15.9	17.2	18.9	17.8	17.6	18.0	17.6	16.6	16.4	17.9
Northern America	15.2	16.2	17.7	16.6	16.5	16.9	16.6	15.7	15.5	16.9
LAIA	0.6	1.0	1.0	1.0	1.0	0.9	0.6	0.7	0.7	0.8
CACM	0.0	0.0	0.0	0.0	0.0	0.0	0.0	0.0	0.0	0.0
Caribbean	0.0	0.0	0.1	0.0	0.1	0.1	0.1	0.0	0.1	0.1
Rest of America	0.0	0.1	0.1	0.2	0.1	0.1	0.2	0.2	0.1	0.2
As.ex F.USSR	66.0	64.9	62.9	63.4	64.7	63.8	65.5	66.1	65.9	63.4
Eur.x F.USSR	14.7	14.6	15.1	15.7	14.5	15.2	14.0	14.7	15.2	16.2
EU	13.1	12.9	13.5	13.8	13.1	13.6	12.5	13.1	13.3	14.5
EFTA	1.3	1.2	1.2	1.6	1.2	1.3	1.2	1.3	1.5	1.4
East Europe	0.2	0.3	0.3	0.3	0.2	0.2	0.2	0.2	0.3	0.2
Other Europe	0.1	0.1	0.1	0.1	0.1	0.1	0.1	0.1	0.1	0.2
Former USSR	0.1	0.2	0.3	0.2	0.3	0.2	0.2	0.2	0.3	0.1
Oceania	2.3	2.3	1.9	2.2	2.2	2.0	2.0	1.8	1.7	1.7
Japan/Japon	20.5	21.9	21.3	20.2	21.3	21.1	21.9	22.0	21.1	18.2
USA/Etats–Unis d'Amer	14.7	15.6	17.1	16.0	15.8	16.5	16.3	15.3	15.1	16.4
Malaysia/Malaisie	13.9	14.7	13.2	13.6	15.2	14.7	16.5	16.4	15.5	15.0
Thailand/Thaïlande	3.1	2.7	2.5	2.7	3.2	3.7	4.1	4.8	5.2	5.5
Saudi Arabia	4.1	4.4	4.8	5.3	5.1	5.1	3.9	3.6	3.1	3.8
Korea, Republic of	2.7	2.9	3.0	2.9	2.8	3.3	3.2	3.8	4.3	3.4
Germany/Allemagne	3.4	3.7	3.6	3.6	3.2	3.3	3.1	3.4	3.5	3.7
Hong Kong	2.6	2.8	2.8	3.1	3.0	3.1	3.2	3.4	3.3	3.2
China/Chine	4.3	3.8	3.4	3.4	3.4	3.1	2.8	2.8	3.2	3.4
United Kingdom	3.2	2.9	2.8	3.1	2.9	2.8	2.6	2.8	2.7	2.7

	1987	1988	1989	1990	1991	1992	1993	1994	1995	1996
Afrique	3.2	2.3	1.9	2.1	2.2	2.1	1.8	1.5	1.3	1.2
Amériques	26.9	26.3	25.5	23.5	22.2	23.5	22.8	20.9	20.1	20.4
Amérique du Nord	25.2	24.8	24.3	22.2	20.5	21.8	21.0	19.4	18.7	18.8
ALAI	0.7	0.7	0.6	0.5	0.7	0.8	1.0	0.9	0.8	1.0
MCAC	0.0	0.0	0.0	0.0	0.0	0.0	0.1	0.0	0.0	0.0
Caraïbes	0.2	0.1	0.1	0.1	0.2	0.1	0.1	0.1	0.1	0.1
Autre Amérique	0.8	0.7	0.6	0.7	0.7	0.7	0.6	0.5	0.4	0.5
Asie l'URSS exclus	51.3	52.3	52.5	53.3	55.2	53.2	55.5	59.1	60.5	60.8
Europe l'URSS exclus	13.7	15.0	15.3	16.5	16.2	17.0	15.9	14.5	14.2	13.8
UE	12.7	13.5	13.9	15.0	14.5	15.8	14.6	13.5	13.4	13.0
AELE	0.5	1.0	0.9	0.8	1.0	0.8	0.9	0.7	0.4	0.4
Europe de l'Est	0.2	0.3	0.3	0.4	0.4	0.3	0.2	0.2	0.2	0.2
Autre de l'Europe	0.3	0.2	0.3	0.3	0.2	0.1	0.2	0.2	0.2	0.2
Ancienne URSS	0.7	0.3	0.4	0.6	0.5	0.5	0.7	0.9	0.8	0.7
Océanie	4.2	3.8	4.2	3.9	3.7	3.7	3.2	3.2	3.0	3.0
USA/Etats–Unis d'Amer	24.4	23.8	23.3	21.3	19.8	21.1	20.4	18.8	18.3	18.4
Malaysia/Malaisie	14.2	13.6	13.7	13.1	15.0	12.5	14.2	19.7	19.2	18.0
Hong Kong	6.3	6.3	6.3	6.5	7.2	7.8	8.7	8.7	8.6	8.9
Japan/Japon	9.0	8.6	8.5	8.7	8.7	7.6	7.5	7.0	7.8	8.2
Thailand/Thaïlande	4.2	5.5	5.5	6.6	6.3	6.2	5.7	5.6	5.8	5.7
Germany/Allemagne	3.2	3.5	3.7	4.0	4.2	4.2	4.0	3.5	3.4	3.1
United Kingdom	2.8	2.9	3.4	3.2	3.0	2.9	3.0	2.7	2.6	2.8
Korea, Republic of	1.7	2.0	1.9	2.2	2.4	2.3	2.8	2.6	2.7	3.0
Netherlands/Pays–Bas	1.8	1.7	1.6	2.1	2.6	3.1	2.6	2.7	2.7	2.3
China/Chine	2.6	3.0	2.7	1.5	1.5	1.8	2.6	2.2	2.3	2.7

4. General Imports C.I.F. by Commodities according to the S.I.T.C. (Rev. 2) in thousand U.S. Dollars
Importations Générales C.A.F. par Produits d'après la C.T.C.I. (Rév. 2) en milliers de Dollars E.U.

SITC CTCI	COMMODITY	1993		1994		1995		1996		PRODUIT
		WEIGHT POIDS	VALUE VALEUR	WEIGHT POIDS	VALUE VALEUR	WEIGHT POIDS	VALUE VALEUR	WEIGHT POIDS	VALUE VALEUR	
	ALL COMMODITIES		85231076		102669327		124503489		131480211	TOUS PRODUITS
0	FOOD AND LIVE ANIMALS		3112276		3420883		3635719		3660886	ALIMENTS,ANIMAUX VIVANTS
02	DAIRY PRODCTS,BIRDS'EGGS		266333		262619		333909		328370	PRODUITS LAITIERS,OEUFS
03	FISH AND PREPARATIONS		558535		613032		656199		639584	POISSONS ET PREPARATIONS
04	CEREALS AND PREPARATIONS		342804		367236		398826		435599	CEREALES ET PRODUITS
05	VEGETABLES AND FRUIT		802452		813521		872238		873023	LEGUMES ET FRUITS
057	FRUIT,NUTS,FRESH,DRIED		358980		358726		374931		385421	FRUITS FRAIS OU SECS
07	COFFEE,TEA,COCOA,SPICES		328754		460429		423373		347638	CAFE,THE,CACAO,EPICES
1	BEVERAGES AND TOBACCO		1284626		1405708		1429254		1699268	BOISSONS ET TABACS
11	BEVERAGES		399845		508195		605410		738340	BOISSONS
112	ALCOHOLIC BEVERAGES	W 53228	356113	W 55006	458879	W 61540	534769	W 67193	665038	BOISSONS ALCOOLIQUES
1124	DISTILLED ALCOHOLIC BEVS	W 15367	288846	W 17550	372797	W 19475	426961	W 20480	381395	ALCOOLS,EAUX–DE–VIE
12	TOBACCO AND MANUFACTURES		884781		897513		823845		960928	TABACS BRUTS FABRIQUES
122	TOBACCO,MANUFACTURED	W 50260	842186	W 48869	833259	W 41925	755973	W 48547	884469	TABACS FABRIQUES
1222	CIGARETTES	W 47271	821913	W 44556	801883	W 38396	738650	W 46848	872026	CIGARETTES
2	CRUDE MATERLS,EXCL FUELS		1213556		1272405		1473211		1341085	MAT BRUTES NON COMESTIBLES
23	RUBBER, CRUDE		314434		349789		482815		392354	CAOUTCHOUC BRUT
232	NATURAL RUBBER,GUMS	W 351613	280750	W 308478	303815	W 298741	435893	W 260881	344875	LATEX CAOUTCHOUC NATUREL
3	MINERAL FUELS ETC		9259268		9081135		10063374		12327475	COMBUSTIBLES MINERAUX LUB
33	PETROLEUM AND PRODUCTS		9253521		9074970		10057762		12320871	PETROLE ET DERIVES
333	CRUDE PETROLEUM	MW 52627	6418672	MW 50947	5861668	MW 51159	6489189	MW 55192	7991607	HUILES BRUTES DE PETROLE
334	PETROLEUM PRODUCTS,REFIN		2808673	MW 25768	3186687	MW 26824	3536716	MW 30545	4303239	PRODUITS RAFFINES
3341	GASOLINE,OTH LIGHT OILS		2047529	W 4286954	720914			W 3524416	696306	ESSENCES POUR MOTEURS
33411	MOTOR,AVIATION SPIRIT		488057	W 2352562	407937			W 1583531	298689	ESSENCES MOTEURS D'AVIONS
3343	GAS OILS	W 3035389	550483	W 5164586	814338			W 4158661	813793	GAS OILS
3344	FUEL OILS,NES	W 64969	10445	MW 15574	1384392			MW 21583	2383920	FUEL OILS
4	ANIMAL,VEGETABLE OIL,FAT		516350		437984		549927		366976	HUILES,GRAISSES ANIM,VEG
431	*PROCESD ANML VEG OIL,ET	W 515718	309415	W 388063	223748		326258	W 114211	68411	HUILES,GRAISSES PREPAREES
4313	FATTY ACIDS ETC,RESIDUES	W 497093	287537	W 374425	208054		318189	W 106337	56301	ACIDES GRAS INDUST,RESIDUS
43131	FATTY ACIDS,ACID OILS	W 496836	287486	W 373913	207947	W 487806	318189	W 106332	56299	ACIDES GRAS INDUSTRIELS
5	CHEMCLS,RELATED PROD NES		5803415		6457884		7842411		7566608	PRODUITS CHIMIQUES
51	ORGANIC CHEMICALS		984299		1188693		1655534		1548744	PROD CHIMIQ ORGANIQUES
52	INORGANIC CHEMICALS		284070		305385		405027		403242	PROD CHIM INORGANIQUES
53	DYES,TANNING,COLOUR PROD		406538		464905		496367		494902	PROD TEINTURE,COLORANTS
541	*MEDICINAL,PHARM PRODUCT		434557		524400		661784		684474	PROD MEDICINAUX PHARMACEUT
55	PERFUME,CLEANING ETC PRD		549110		644365		780010		815879	PROD POUR PARFUM,TOILETTE
553	PERFUMERY,COSMETICS,ETC		388191		464604		560184		587050	PRODUITS DE PARFUMERIE
58	PLASTIC MATERIALS ETC		1194190		1480474		1759277		1602464	MAT PLAST ARTIFICIELLES
582	PROD OF CONDENSATION ETC	W 222589	442685	W 262137	541596	W 308842	727014	W 279883	685848	PROD CONDENS,POLYCOND
583	POLYMERIZATION ETC PRODS	W 576556	715014	W 617394	902454		990610	W 659425	878904	PROD POLYMERISATION
59	CHEMICAL MATERIALS NES		1908061		1811060		2045636		1964781	MAT PROD CHIMIQUES NDA
598	MISCEL CHEM PRODUCTS NES		1799783		1684402		1897569		1805832	PROD DIV INDUST CHIM NDA
5989	CHEM PRODUCTS,PREPS NES		1544488		1399448		1539484		1503853	PROD PREP CHIMIQUES NDA
59899	OTH CHEM PRODS,PREPS,NES	W 88672	1459817	W 68012	1307238	W 70008	1428786	W 75423	1389892	AUT PRODUITS CHIMIQUES NDA
6	BASIC MANUFACTURES		9947272		10899725		13599142		13030884	ART MANUFACTURES
62	RUBBER MANUFACTURES NES		430074		450552		572944		594571	CAOUTCHOUC MANUFACTURE
63	WOOD,CORK MANUFACTRS NES		308671		288260		255483		278728	OUVRAGES LIEGE ET BOIS
64	PAPER,PAPERBOARD AND MFR		818040		942087		1198401		1039152	PAPIERS,CARTONS & OUVRAGES
641	PAPER AND PAPERBOARD		521353		650378		873022		708811	PAPIERS ET CARTONS
642	PAPER,ETC,PRECUT,ARTS OF		296687		291709		325378		330341	PAP,CARTONS DECOUPES
65	TEXTILE YARN,FABRICS,ETC		1963833		2017347		2109102		1918250	FILS,TISSUS,ARTICLES TEXTILE
652	COTTON FABRICS,WOVEN		294215	A 273643	279708	A 229089	276581	A 183451	219303	TISSUS DE COTON
6522	WOVEN COTTON BLEACHD,ETC		281209	A 228474	258223	A 213412	261982	A 172955	207170	TISSUS COTON BLANCHIS ETC
65225	BLCHD COTN BLEND FAB NES	A 251198	271283	A 32834	39954	A 36616	48020	A 34601	53083	AUT TIS MOINS 85% COT BLANCH
653	WOVN MAN–MADE FIB FABRIC		647136	A 609075	661958	A 569588	643454	A 537720	569377	TISSUS FIBRES SYNTH,ARTIF
6532	DISC SYN TXTL FABRIC NES	A 287145	372595	A 287176	360877	A 252348	322704	A 252900	285454	TIS DISC MOINS 85% FIBR TEXT
655	KNITTED,ETC FABRICS	A 201179	324384	A 200211	283987	A 216467	305832	A 194442	264458	ETOF BONNETERIE PIECES ETC
6552	OTHER KNIT ETC FAB NONEL	A 201179	324384	A 200211	283987	A 216467	305832	A 194442	264458	ETOF BON NON ELAS NON SYNT
66	NONMETAL MINERAL MFS NES		1170933		1510222		1904323		2211883	ART MIN NON METALLIQUES
661	LIME,CEMENT,BLDG PRODS	W 3709092	242918	W 4332731	297120	W 4794007	367721	W 5689002	454471	CHAUX,CIMENTS MAT CONSTR
664	GLASS		184538		292927		337005		397481	VERRE
667	PEARL,PREC–,SEMI–P STONE		186740		261309		479772		607408	PERLES, PIERRES GEMMES
6672	DIAMONDS NONINDUST,UNSET		160282		240448		426375		533693	DIAMANTS BRUTS
66729	— CUT ETC NOT SET				239705		402943		523716	DIAMANTS TAILLES
67	IRON AND STEEL		2088430		2167596		2815282		2729507	FER ET ACIER
673	IRON,STEEL SHAPES ETC	W 1189406	491585	W 1426665	557552	W 1953427	822837	W 2068225	806398	BARRES,PROFIL FER,ACIER
6732	IRON,STEEL BARS ETC	W 85055	43996	W 740008	293788	W 882163	377848	W 1079628	417961	BARRES FER,ACIER
674	IRN,STL UNIV,PLATE,SHEET	W 1345797	731822	W 1298182	777037	W 1524442	1063035	W 1315275	892837	LARGES PLATS,TOLES
6744	IRN,STL HVY PLATE,ROLLED	W 667413	350118	W 492311	214789	W 581814	301360	W 507821	248457	TOLES LAMINEES PLUS 4.75 MM
67441	— OF IRON OR SIMPLE STL	W 633444	291651	W 468877	183680	W 566123	257668	W 491049	215783	TOLES NON ACIER FIN CARB
678	IRON,STL TUBES,PIPES,ETC	W 476324	496922	W 489236	525683	W 512713	590705	W 570464	707349	TUBES,TUYAUX EN FONTE,FER
68	NON–FERROUS METALS		1506972		1675166		2548830		1942757	METAUX NON FERREUX
681	SILVER,PLATINUM,ETC		280501		160033		154852		172664	ARGENT ET PLATINE
6811	SILVER UNWKD,PARTLY WRKD		263593		147202		141156		144049	ARGENT BRUT MI–OUVRE
682	COPPER EXC CEMENT COPPER	W 228626	643589	W 227089	794451	W 410809	1456578	W 335754	1066561	CUIVRE
6821	COPPER NES,ALLOYS,UNWRT	W 106643	212658	W 93805	293150	W 263138	778754	W 196245	483149	CUIVRE BRUT
68212	COPPER REFINED,UNWROUGHT	W 106430	211791	W 93497	291829	W 261523	773431	W 190834	468673	CUIVRE AFFINE BRUT
6822	COPPER,ALLOYS WORKED	W 121983	430931	W 133284	501302	W 147672	677824	W 139510	583412	CUIVRE,ALLIAGES OUVRES
684	ALUMINIUM	W 186268	362816	W 203804	457571	W 297596	742781	W 189927	496492	ALUMINIUM
6842	ALUMINIUM,ALLOYS WORKED	W 76263	225558	W 83351	282037	W 98904	379376	W 90593	335975	ALUMINIUM,ALLIAGES OUVRE
69	METAL MANUFACTURES NES		1560354		1719758		2069260		2190584	ART MANUFACT EN METAL NDA
695	TOOLS		295301		347345		420812		448682	OUTILS A MAIN
699	BASE METAL MFRS NES		559648		654512		761056		820196	ART MANUFACTURES MET NDA
7	MACHINES,TRANSPORT EQUIP		44545249		57890057		71991826		76023354	MACHINES MATERIEL TRANSPORT
71	POWER GENERATING EQUIPMT		2781325		2935499		2988235		2807958	MACHINES GENERATRICES
713	INTRNL COMBUS PSTN ENGIN		713157		821459		852419		776122	MOTEURS EXPL COMB INT, PIECE
7139	PISTON ENGINE PARTS NES		339530		377863		394601		386224	PIECES POUR 713.2,3,8
714	ENGINES AND MOTORS NES		792594		652403		306715		320954	MOTEURS NON ELECTRIQUES
7149	ENGINE & MOTOR PARTS NES		461623		445294		245523		224217	PIECES 714 ET 718.88
71491	PARTS NES OF 7144,71481				317920		148302		112977	PIECES DES PROPULSEURS
716	ROTATING ELECTRIC PLANT		1179368		1292694		1607827		1552357	APP ELECTR ROTATIFS,PIECES
7162	AC MTRS,GENRTRS,GEN SETS	MN 195896	1071129	MN 351906	988513	MN 485102	1229249	MN 442806	1261516	MOTEURS ELECTRIQUES
71621	AC MTRS,INC UNIVRSL MTRS	MN 195834	719906	MN 351852	754936	MN 485057	1008505	MN 442765	1049714	MOT ELEC NON COUR CONTINU
71623	GEN SETS WITH PISTN ENGN	N 30742	298717	N 20066	162310	N 12019	163151	N 11985	136159	GROUPES MOTEUR EXPLOSION
72	MACHS FOR SPCL INDUSTRYS		2632261		2997116		3801368		4645690	MAC SPECIALES POUR INDUST
723	CIVIL ENGNEERG EQUIP ETC		720025		700058		898593		1066948	APPAREILS DE GENIE CIVIL
7234	CONST,MINING MACHNRY NES	N 7880	251281	N 11888	301845	N 12474	438480	N 10377	490949	MACH POUR LA CONST, MINES
7239	CONSTR ETC MACHY PTS NES		459544		388188		445041		557108	PIECES 723.41–723.46
728	OTH MACHY FOR SPCL INDUS		1373904		1761142		2176794		2642515	AUT MACH IND PARTICULIERES
7284	MACHY FOR SPCL INDUS NES		1201345		1525620		1951284		2391937	MACH SPEC IND PARTICUL.
72848	OTH MCHY WITH INDIV FNCT	N 101661	741319	N 96410	869716	N 93985	1122778	N 358828	1506577	AUTRES MACHINES NDA

4. General Imports C.I.F. by Commodities according to the S.I.T.C. (Rev. 2) in thousand U.S. Dollars
Importations Générales C.A.F. par Produits d'après la C.T.C.I. (Rév. 2) en milliers de Dollars E.U.

SITC CTCI	COMMODITY	1993 WEIGHT POIDS	1993 VALUE VALEUR	1994 WEIGHT POIDS	1994 VALUE VALEUR	1995 WEIGHT POIDS	1995 VALUE VALEUR	1996 WEIGHT POIDS	1996 VALUE VALEUR	PRODUIT
72849	PTS OF MACHS OF 7284 ETC		6615		368648		535489		670234	PIECES DU 728.4 ETC
73	METALWORKING MACHINERY		493130		613749		759276		729243	MACH TRAVAIL DES METAUX
736	METALWORKING MACH–TOOLS		394268		481452		596120		591654	MACH–OUTILS TRAVAIL METAUX
74	GENRL INDUSTRL MACHY NES		3652444		4917602		5407420		6150167	MACH APP INDUSTRIE
741	HEATING,COOLING EQUIPMNT		809931		1068022		1134008		1234186	MACH CHAUFFAGE,PIECES
7415	AIR–CONDITIONING MACHNRY		426861	N 1607888	598659	N 1500397	598179	N 1563311	632341	GROUPES CONDITION AIR
742	PUMPS FOR LIQUIDS ETC		269759		364740		385842		425464	POMPES MOTO–POMPES
743	PUMPS NES,CENTRFUGES ETC		535187		672606		683201		773549	POMPES COMPRES,VENT ETC
744	MECHANICAL HANDLING EQU		567949		1039604		1195183		1498635	EQUIP MANUTENTION PIECES
7441	FORK LIFT TRCKS,ETC,PTS		257440		213901		263711		315399	CHARIOTS POUR USINES ETC
7442	LIFTING,LOADING MACH NES	N 222965	219525	N 337573	528243	N 423404	453074	N 205631	442351	APP LEVAGE,MANUTENTION
7449	PTS NES OF MACHY OF 7442		90984		297461		478397		740885	PIECES DU 744.2
749	NONELEC MACH PTS,ACC NES		1266891		1514476		1721609		1895029	PIECES MACH NON ELEC NDA
7491	BALL,ROLLER,ETC BEARINGS		447635		505094		683839		795960	ROULEMENTS BILLES ETC
7492	COCKS,VALVES ETC NES		345427	MN 53551	434393	MN 66035	412487	MN 43804	491447	ART ROB,SIM POUR TUYAUX
7499	OTH NONELEC MCHY PTS NES		249852		313010		370378		345500	PIECES NON ELECT NDA
75	OFFICE MACHNES,ADP EQUIP		7531636		9933484		13180517		15320093	MACH BUREAU TRAIT AUTOM
751	OFFICE MACHINES	MN 26500	398605	MN 32169	460011	MN 36689	488784	MN 44048	551394	MACH,APPAREILS DE BUREAU
752	AUTOMTIC DATA PROC EQUIP	MN 35191	3449338	MN 61971	5087308	MN 70709	5253050	MN 73838	6805570	MACH TRAIT INFORMATION
7522	DIGITAL COMPUTERS	N 1310909	389863	N 1317189	593516	N 1730910	617545	N 155580	234531	MACH DIGITALES COMPLETES
7523	DIGITL CENTRL PROCESSORS	N 87320	167384	N 186509	175370	N 251543	228174	N 417771	633167	UNITES CENTRALES
7524	DIGITL CENTRL STOR UNITS	N 811826	141699	MN 38509	3109701	MN 36125	2654688	MN 48554	4306666	UNITES MEMOIRE CENTRALES
7525	ADP PERIPHERAL UNITS	MN 32668	2641502	MN 16376	914880	MN 27411	1303491	MN 23623	1366583	UNITES PERIPHERIQUES
7528	OFF–LINE DATA PROC EQUIP	N 313282	107331	N 5581358	292732	N 5190660	448585	N 1087744	264622	MACH AUXIL TRAIT INFORM
759	OFFICE,ADP MCH PTS,ACCES		3683693		4386165		7438682		7963129	PIECES DU 751 ET 752
7599	ACCTG,ETC,ADP MCH PTS,AC		3547411		4239526		7238577		7778480	PIECES DU 751 ET 752
76	TELECOMM,SOUND EQUIPMENT		7618814		9115244		9203646		8128903	EQUIPMENT DE TELECOM
761	TELEVISION RECEIVERS	N 2985415	877056	N 4042706	1003309	N 3238531	854303	N 3547069	892975	RECEPTEURS DE TELEVISION
7611	COLOUR TV RECEIVERS	N 2875712	871091	N 3927143	996911	N 3160728	849773	N 3446735	883280	RECEPTEURS COULEUR
762	RADIO BROADCAST RECEIVRS	MN 24332	1112476	MN 32743	1447429	MN 22953	1229022	MN 15468	917742	RECEPTEURS RADIODIFFUSION
7622	PORTABLE RADIO RECEIVERS	MN 14886	486255	MN 21974	685061	MN 13867	520837	N 7647674	252091	RECEPT PORTATIFS RADIO
7628	OTHER RADIO RECEIVERS	N 5052658	422947	N 6327944	556731	N 4637768	447887	N 4598312	430899	AUTRES RECEPT RADIO
763	SOUND RECORDRS,PHONOGRPH	MN 26168	1665865	MN 24494	1687183	MN 12771	1135570	N 8698841	979396	PHONO,APP ENREGISTREMENT
7638	OTHR SOUND APPARATUS ETC	MN 25649	1642135	MN 24205	1678053	MN 12522	1125835	N 8687186	978423	AUT APP D'ENREGIS,REPROD
76381	TV IMAGE,SND RECRDRS ETC	N 3463274	711249	N 5883494	867734	N 4323352	731832	N 3840546	659370	APP ENREG,REPRO IMAG,SON
76388	DICTATING MACHINES ETC	MN 22186	930886	MN 18322	810319	N 8198607	394003	N 4846640	319053	MACHINES A DICTER
764	TELECOM EQPT,PTS,ACC NES		3963416		4977323		5984751		5338790	EQUIP TELECOM,PIECES
7641	LINE TELEPHONE,ETC EQUIP	MN 27435	597431	MN 32225	621860	MN 33237	662937	MN 24444	621832	APP TELEPHON PAR FIL
7642	MICROPH,LOUDSPKR,AMPLIFR	MN 107141	369259	MN 495588	441630	MN 121794	433970	MN 98030	398485	MICRO,HAUT–PARLEUR,AMPLI
7643	TV,RADIO TRANSMITTRS ETC	N 2524650	269396	N 1623481	250298	N 2317987	574204	N 5067079	654114	APP EMET TELE RADIO
7648	TELECOMM EQUIPMENT NES	MN 28468	358679	MN 15377	376931	MN 17120	573531	MN 15891	348991	APP TELECOM NDA
7649	PTS NES OF EQUIPMT OF 76		2368651		3286603		3740110		3315367	PIECES DE LA DIV 76
76491	PTS NES OF APPAR OF 7641		184605		252460		380318		396812	PIECES POUR 764.1
76493	TELECOMM EQUIPMT PTS NES		1012466		1318027		1229612		1282644	PIECES 761,762,764.3,8
76499	PARTS ETC OF SOUND EQUIP		1111729		1646810		2059741		1557087	PIECES NDA POUR 763
77	ELECTRIC MACHNRY NES ETC		14658387		22348483		30494657		30057377	MACH APP ELECT NDA
771	ELECTRIC POWER MACHY NES		775473		1135476		1418538		1402988	MACH PROD,TRANS ELECTR
7711	TRANSFORMERS,ELECTRICAL	MN 282398	308531	MN 544742	428787	MN 564752	428356	MN 430252	341449	TRANSFO ELECTRIQUES
77118	OTHER ELEC TRANSFORMERS	MN 277064	302113	MN 533999	401464	MN 559707	408449	MN 420730	329820	AUTRES TRANSFO ELECTRIQ
7712	OTH ELEC POWER MACHY NES		466942		706689		990181		1061539	AUT APP PROD TRANSF ELEC
77121	STATIC CONVERTERS ETC	MN 160198	122238	MN 311573	273399	MN 219925	413327	MN 161501	532912	CONVERTISSEURS STATIQUES
772	SWITCHGEAR ETC,PARTS NES		2144025		2914211		3470596		3468854	APP COUPURE,SECT ETC
7721	SWITCHGEAR ETC		1230149		1713252		2074193		2136245	APP COUPURE,SECTIONMNT
7722	PRINTED CIRCUITS,PTS NES		573969		736844		930807		943546	CIRCUITS ET PIECES
7723	FIXED,VARIABLE RESISTORS		339907		464114		465596		389063	POTENTIOMETRES PIECES
773	ELECTR DISTRIBUTNG EQUIP		639058		697621		743390		815159	EQUIPMT DISTRIBUTION ELECT
7731	INSULATED WIRE,CABLE ETC	W 106677	561586	W 127603	615145	W 119931	660048	W 109432	722836	FILS,CABLES ISOLES ELECT
775	HOUSEHOLD TYPE EQUIP NES		326960		375309		393557		422371	MACH,APP USAGE DOMESTQUE
776	TRANSISTORS,VALVES,ETC		9073772		14648957		21384510		21042443	LAMPES,TUBES,VALVES
7761	TV PICTURE TUBES	N 5347025	418904	N 5083337	376709	N 6124968	526981	N 5844515	567870	TUBES CATHODIQUES
7762	OTH ELECTRONIC TUBES ETC		224957		348914		412524		669984	AUT LAMPES ELECTRONIQUES
7763	DIODES,TRANSISTORS,ETC		861595		1570366		2170413		2286756	DIODES,TRANSISTORS
7764	ELECTRONIC MICROCIRCUITS		6431310		10716590		15573473		14754870	MICROSTRUCTURES ELECTRON
7768	ELCTRNC COMP PTS,CRYSTLS		1137006		1636377		2701119		2762964	CRIST PIEZO–ELEC,PCS 776
77681	PIEZO–ELEC CRYSTALS,MNTD		248949		341335		423698		362019	CRISTAUX PIEZO–ELECTRIQ
77689	ELECTRNIC COMPON PTS NES		888057		1295042		2277421		2400945	PIECES DU GROUPE 776
778	ELECTRICAL MACHINERY NES		1640181		2514338		3016370		2815283	AUTRES MACH ELECT NDA
7788	OTH ELEC MACHY,EQUIP NES		1149428		1865006		2296664		2083788	AUT MACH APP ELEC NDA
77884	ELECTRICAL CONDENSERS		761489		1154273		1381814		1235270	CONDENSATEURS ELECTRIQUES
77886	OTH ELEC MACHINERY NES		119718	MN 34181	252533		405944		455783	AUT MACH APP ELECTRIQUES
78	ROAD VEHICLES		2110352		2125566		2686562		2569086	VEHICULES ROUTIERS
781	PASS MOTOR VEH EXC BUSES			N 42588	695114	N 38229	853568	N 39323	768095	AUTO TRANSPORT PERSONNES
782	LORRIES,SPCL MTR VEH NES	N 72265	1005030	N 13422	284884	N 22056	451515	N 19008	454445	VEHICULES SPECIAUX,MARCH
7821	LORRIES,TRUCKS	N 71202	942339	N 12198	209112	N 20299	359956	N 16666	328959	VEHICULES TRANSP MARCHAND
784	MOTOR VEH PRTS,ACCES NES		637356		759876		972032		918331	PIECES 722,781,782,783
7849	OTHER MOTOR VEHCL PARTS		593772		703298		872875		860915	PIECES 722,781,782,783
785	CYCLES,ETC MOTRZD OR NOT		345698		274616		286992		316930	MOTOCYCLES SCOOTERS
79	OTHR TRANSPORT EQUIPMENT		3066900		2903315		3470145		5614837	AUTRE MATERIEL TRANSPORT
792	AIRCRAFT ETC		1755411		1627019		1677806		3014347	APP NAVIGATION AERIENNE
7924	AIRCRFT NES OVER 15000KG	N 11	1220062	N 9	1244288	N 8	922161	N 11	1592814	AERODYNES PLUS 15000 KG
7929	AIRCRAFT PARTS NES		496128		341169		673941		1344855	PIECES DU 792
793	SHIPS AND BOATS ETC	N 18719	1299427	N 14144	1228886	N 15277	1659272	N 21407	2571853	NAVIRES BATEAUX,ETC
7932	SHIPS AND BOATS NES	N 2690	1229430	N 3354	983591	N 1977	1554642	N 7663	2421077	NAVIRES ET BATEAUX
79322	TANKERS OF ALL KINDS	N 26	266897	N 21	211875	N 35	183952	N 56	1099258	BATEAUX–CITERNES
79323	OTHER CARGO VESSELS	N 207	936615	N 195	750279	N 229	1338318	N 229	1287364	AUT BATEAUX TRANS MARCH
8	MISC MANUFACTURED GOODS		8412984		10233959		12400396		13874547	ART MANUFACTURES DIVERS
821	*FURNITURE,PARTS THEREOF		287200		383461		446923		512024	MEUBLES ET PIECES
84	CLOTHING AND ACCESSORIES		1346495		1574521		1645168		1734068	VETEMENTS
843	WOMENS OUTERWEAR NONKNIT	MN 55187	286786	MN 51916	331536	MN 49277	336231	MN 48152	350923	VET DESSUS FEMMES MAT TEX
845	OUTERWEAR KNIT NONELASTC		404276	MN 118286	428007	MN 83192	422496	MN 81936	448580	VET DESSOUS,ACCES BONNET
8459	— OTHER,CLTHG ACCESRYS	MN 95314	264227	MN 86532	280297	MN 60966	286130	MN 56903	281215	AUT VET DESSUS DE BONNE
846	UNDER GARMENTS KNITTED	MN 128447	262989	MN 136773	314529	MN 126968	390677	MN 124674	410799	SOUS VETS DE BONNETERIE
87	PRECISION INSTRUMNTS NES		1561028		2068063		2508129		2628527	INSTRUM,APPAR SCIENT NDA
871	OPTICAL INSTRUMENTS		400700		649059		699892		539790	APPAR,INSTRUM D'OPTIQUE
87109	OPTICAL INSTRUMENTS NES		358520	MN 109797	611157	MN 137751	665777	MN 103414	493730	APP,INSTRUM OPTIQUE NDA
874	MEASURNG,CONTROLNG INSTR		948272		1164984		1550169		1814178	INSTRUMENTS DE MESURE
8742	MEASUR,DRAW ETC INST,PTS	MN 12786	168030		270721		385353		481701	INST DESSIN,TRACAGE,PCS
88	PHOTO EQU,OPTICL GDS ETC		1736146		2012148		2270701		2379202	APP,FOURN PHOTO,OP,MONTR
881	PHOTO APPARAT,EQUIPT NES		301456		324887		388639		451975	APP,EQUIP PHOTO NDA
882	PHOTO,CINEMA SUPPLIES		498597		604321		680657		637624	PRODUITS PHOTO,CINEMA
8822	PHOTO FILM EXC DEV CINMA		353579		402975		415373		360806	PLAQUES,PELLICULES,FILMS

4. General Imports C.I.F. by Commodities according to the S.I.T.C. (Rev. 2) in thousand U.S. Dollars
Importations Générales C.A.F. par Produits d'après la C.T.C.I. (Rév. 2) en milliers de Dollars E.U.

SITC CTCI	COMMODITY	1993 WEIGHT POIDS	1993 VALUE VALEUR	1994 WEIGHT POIDS	1994 VALUE VALEUR	1995 WEIGHT POIDS	1995 VALUE VALEUR	1996 WEIGHT POIDS	1996 VALUE VALEUR	PRODUIT
885	WATCHES AND CLOCKS		750892		921419		1019788		1094320	HORLOGERIE
8851	WATCHES,MOVEMENTS,CASES		578577		716017		845346		911740	MONTRES,MOUVEMENTS,BOITES
88511	WATCHES		530360		667636		806475		871100	MONTRES POCHE,BRACELET
89	MISC MANUFCTRD GOODS NES		2864158		3473243		4730120		5728015	ART MANUFACTURES DIVERS
892	PRINTED MATTER		269467		296318		345858		376557	IMPRIMES
893	ARTICLES OF PLASTIC NES		625512		722702		757004		774711	OUVRAGES EN MAT DIVIS 58
8939	MISC PLASTIC ARTICLES		421032		524738		549256		567178	ART DIVERS EN MAT DIV 58
89399	OTHR PLASTC ARTICLES NES		383776		493187		509900		527175	AUT OUV MAT DIV 58
894	TOYS,SPORTING GOODS,ETC		392271		419995		471457		494183	VOITURES ENFANTS,JOUETS
897	GOLD,SILVER WARE,JEWELRY		203631		419892		870965		1213950	BIJOUTERIE,ORFEVRERIE
8973	PREC JEWLRY,GLD–SILVWARE		177523		376480		836692		1181031	BIJOUX OR,ARGENT ORFEVRE
89731	PRECIOUS METAL JEWELLERY		146559		339369		789119		1119776	ART BIJOUTERIE,JOAILLER
898	MUSICAL INSTRUMENTS,PTS		1010704		1195032		1829551		2360327	INSTRUMENTS DE MUSIQUE
8983	SOUND RECRDNG TAPE,DISCS	MN 314519	958197	MN 393443	1133497	MN 532499	1758639	MN 936635	2281746	SUPPORTS SON POUR 763
89831	PREPD SND RECORDNG MEDIA	MN 281131	749840	MN 343211	863177	MN 490605	1347203	MN 802111	1986037	SUPPORTS PREPARES
89832	RECORDED DISCS,TAPES ETC	MN 33387	208357	MN 50232	270320	MN 41894	411436	MN 134524	295710	DISQUES,PHONO,BANDES
9	GOODS NOT CLASSD BY KIND		1136081		1569586		1518230		1589130	ART TRANSACT NON CLASSES
931	*SPECIAL TRANSACTIONS		885954		1282719		1193461		1185167	TRANS.SPECIALES
971	*GOLD,NON MONETARY NES	K 20304	219145	K 25714	276920	K 26813	318337	K 39766	397337	OR NON MONETAIRE

5. General Exports F.O.B. by Commodities according to the S.I.T.C. (Rev. 2) in thousand U.S. Dollars
Exportations Générales F.O.B. par Produits d'après la C.T.C.I. (Rév. 2) en milliers de Dollars E.U.

SITC CTCI	COMMODITY	1993 WEIGHT POIDS	1993 VALUE VALEUR	1994 WEIGHT POIDS	1994 VALUE VALEUR	1995 WEIGHT POIDS	1995 VALUE VALEUR	1996 WEIGHT POIDS	1996 VALUE VALEUR	PRODUIT
	ALL COMMODITIES		74006830		96824598		118263152		125153077	TOUS PRODUITS
0	FOOD AND LIVE ANIMALS		1799272		2324708		2506513		2264303	ALIMENTS,ANIMAUX VIVANTS
03	FISH AND PREPARATIONS		478664		562039		582000		540166	POISSONS ET PREPARATIONS
034	FISH,FRESH,CHILLED,FROZN		225261		253372		290833		280339	POISSON FRAIS, REFRIG,CONG
05	VEGETABLES AND FRUIT		290482		365965		399760		395661	LEGUMES ET FRUITS
07	COFFEE,TEA,COCOA,SPICES		449598		708188		753510		574623	CAFE,THE,CACAO,EPICES
071	COFFEE AND SUBSTITUTES	W 86025	82411	W 157922	317902	W 95997	282646	W 62663	137986	CAFE ET SUCCEDANES
0711	COFFEE GREEN,ROASTED,SUB	W 83876	77341	W 152160	302123	W 86133	247597	W 49703	94432	CAFE TORREFIE OU DECAFEINE
07111	COFFEE GREEN,HUSKS,SKINS	W 20	16	W 151773	299962	W 85511	244079	W 46798	84815	CAFE NON TORREFIE
1	BEVERAGES AND TOBACCO		1480086		1608508		1605597		1868244	BOISSONS ET TABACS
11	BEVERAGES		495097		566797		599592		585282	BOISSONS
112	ALCOHOLIC BEVERAGES	W 59034	390063	W 57025	465559		513345	W 69526	505745	BOISSONS ALCOOLIQUES
1124	DISTILLED ALCOHOLIC BEVS	W 10812	329227	W 13100	397348		421259	W 14733	406424	ALCOOLS,EAUX–DE–VIE
11242	DISTILLD WINE,GRAPE MARC	W 5443	298900	W 5702	354813	W 6574	366038	W 6639	346057	EAUX–DE–VIE NATURELLES
12	TOBACCO AND MANUFACTURES		984989		1041711		1006005		1282961	TABACS BRUTS FABRIQUES
122	TOBACCO,MANUFACTURED	W 51552	977989	W 55527	1034013	W 50715	998633	W 59333	1274245	TABACS FABRIQUES
1222	CIGARETTES	W 50596	971141	W 54425	1025784	W 49044	986548	W 56153	1252899	CIGARETTES
2	CRUDE MATERLS,EXCL FUELS		1315452		1440997		1697625		1410123	MAT BRUTES NON COMESTIBLES
23	RUBBER, CRUDE		500175		538312		692836		551897	CAOUTCHOUC BRUT
232	NATURAL RUBBER,GUMS	W 560970	482612	W 498389	515957	W 432330	669782	W 375798	528432	LATEX CAOUTCHOUC NATUREL
23202	OTHER NATURAL RUBBER	W 509349	435657	W 435778	453582	W 379904	590822	W 332913	470645	CAOUTCHOUC NATUREL
24	CORK AND WOOD		231810		209426		190727		156085	LIEGE ET BOIS
3	MINERAL FUELS ETC		9063443		9183066		8121050		9862211	COMBUSTIBLES MINERAUX LUB
33	PETROLEUM AND PRODUCTS		8947001		9040671		7968521		9666782	PETROLE ET DERIVES
334	PETROLEUM PRODUCTS,REFIN	MW 55855	8813624	MW 60543	8834833	MW 45074	7756843	MW 48530	9474638	PRODUITS RAFFINES
3341	GASOLINE,OTH LIGHT OILS	MW 39380	5535331	MW 16704	2975098			MW 17661	3773683	ESSENCES POUR MOTEURS
33411	MOTOR,AVIATION SPIRIT	W 5366952	1149694	W 5938455	1144824			W 6773522	1400701	ESSENCES MOTEURS D'AV'ONS
33412	SPIRIT TYPE JET FUEL	W 5704055	1142324	W 6265447	1123310			W 6685347	1566526	CARBUREACTEURS
33419	OTH LIGHT PETROLEUM OILS	W 4586722	778886	W 4500450	706965			W 4202568	806455	AUTRES HUILES LEGERES
3343	GAS OILS	MW 14620	2687899	MW 30706	4116862			MW 16318	3322495	GAS OILS
3344	FUEL OILS,NES	W 234220	36017	MW 11625	1190958			MW 12323	1550575	FUEL OILS
3345	LUBS,PETROLEUM OILS NES	W 861861	396666	W 978511	450849			W 1123074	566632	HUILES LUBRIFIANTES
33451	LUBS(HIGH PETR CONT) ETC	W 856485	384278	W 972430	433820			W 1111663	537994	HUILES LUBRIF,H LOURDES
4	ANIMAL,VEGETABLE OIL,FAT		377922		378027		511621		368872	HUILES,GRAISSES ANIM,VEG
431	*PROCESD ANML VEG OIL,ET	W 440879	236651	W 334757	214310	W 392168	311774	W 151970	114926	HUILES,GRAISSES PREPAREES
5	CHEMCLS,RELATED PROD NES		4667764		5412829		6902316		6869209	PRODUITS CHIMIQUES
51	ORGANIC CHEMICALS		1472488		1715076		2331322		2271613	PROD CHIMIQ ORGANIQUES
511	HYDROCARBONS NES,DERIVS		111386		300338		484487		361926	HYDROCARBURES NDA
5112	CYCLIC HYDROCARBONS	V 140118	43442	V 587643	223064	V 796809	406863	V 778842	285316	HYDROCARBURES CYCLIQUES
514	NITROGEN–FNCTN COMPOUNDS	W 69297	156210	W 85731	230793	W 125938	413465	W 136539	693393	COMPOSES FONCT AZOTEES
5148	OTH NITROGN–FNCTN CMPNDS	W 27708	61991	W 42439	107773	W 67527	258356	W 80153	501893	AUTRES COMPOSES AZOTES
515	ORG–INORG COMPOUNDS ETC	W 20799	867732	W 17946	715272	W 15651	766182	W 27328	628203	COMPOSES ORGANO–MINERAUX
5156	HETEROCYCLIC CMPDS ETC	W 8339	819737	W 6765	667420	W 4955	709505	W 6966	407827	COMPOSES HETEROCYCLIQUES
51569	OTH HETEROCYC CMPDS,ETC			W 5025	662202	W 3053	704154	W 5429	403775	AUT COMP HETEROCYCLIQUES
53	DYES,TANNING,COLOUR PROD		369595		466630		537505		495178	PROD TEINTURE,COLORANTS
533	PIGMENTS,PAINTS,ETC		246691		327824		387480		367443	PIGMENTS,PEINTURES,VERNIS
541	*MEDICINAL,PHARM PRODUCT		371137		494758		601196		616838	PROD MEDICINAUX PHARMACEUT
55	PERFUME,CLEANING ETC PRD		367982		485131		627127		715516	PROD POUR PARFUM,TOILETTE
553	PERFUMERY,COSMETICS,ETC		233009		302705		388008		433927	PRODUITS DE PARFUMERIE
58	PLASTIC MATERIALS ETC		1085980		1288281		1617886		1606175	MAT PLAST ARTIFICIELLES
582	PROD OF CONDENSATION ETC	W 211199	303703	W 250773	393633	W 268681	589802	W 291801	656500	PROD CONDENS,POLYCOND
583	POLYMERIZATION ETC PRODS	W 914492	764204	W 881126	873730	W 827729	1005553	W 815907	930116	PROD POLYMERISATION
5831	POLYETHYLENE	W 472308	318647	W 370199	286296	W 319871	326601	W 331583	296602	POLYETHYLENE
58311	— IN PRIMARY FORMS	W 417958	282149	W 358165	261217	W 311379	302952	W 326572	280217	POLYETHYLENE PRIMAIRES
59	CHEMICAL MATERIALS NES		819362		750329		968483		940195	MAT PROD CHIMIQUES NDA
598	MISCEL CHEM PRODUCTS NES		723920		640898		832710		793248	PROD DIV INDUST CHIM NDA
5982	ANTI–KNOCK PREPARTNS ETC	W 148302	261760	W 141462	251582	W 158284	293531	W 160830	290076	PREPARAT ANTIDETONANTES
5989	CHEM PRODUCTS,PREPS NES		442799		367866		515863		463859	PROD PREP CHIMIQUES NDA
59899	OTH CHEM PRODS,PREPS,NES	W 66679	375272	W 68712	291072	W 69953	400743	W 74037	357161	AUT PRODUITS CHIMIQUES NDA
6	BASIC MANUFACTURES		4817723		5846718		7525313		7192777	ART MANUFACTURES
62	RUBBER MANUFACTURES NES		222439		266236		344385		382679	CAOUTCHOUC MANUFACTURE
63	WOOD,CORK MANUFACTRS NES		310843		284955		222978		196265	OUVRAGES LIEGE ET BOIS
634	VENEERS,PLYWOOD,ETC		252642		210566		140704		107068	PLACAGES,CONTRE–PLAQUES
64	PAPER,PAPERBOARD AND MFR		380564		469010		581042		520580	PAPIERS,CARTONS & OUVRAGES
641	PAPER AND PAPERBOARD		240492		296457		366668		318002	PAPIERS ET CARTONS
65	TEXTILE YARN,FABRICS,ETC		1231731		1415844		1496054		1348339	FILS,TISSUS,ARTICLES TEXTILE
651	TEXTILE YARN	W 60216	228464	W 61752	274888	W 48573	267412	W 43861	248729	FILS TEXTILES
653	WOVN MAN–MADE FIB FABRIC		473954		540153		527389		470722	TISSUS FIBRES SYNTH,ARTIF
6532	DISC SYN TXTL FABRIC NES	A 228053	255907	A 251360	323703	A 236776	324318	A 231472	283684	TIS DISC MOINS 85% FIBR TEXT
66	NONMETAL MINERAL MFS NES		442117		518742		692465		806124	ART MIN NON METALLIQUES
67	IRON AND STEEL		619457		738061		894453		857306	FER ET ACIER
68	NON–FERROUS METALS		786119		1035746		1953383		1704423	METAUX NON FERREUX
682	COPPER EXC CEMENT COPPER	W 136131	336188	W 153203	436436	W 251272	828342	W 256108	702863	CUIVRE
6821	COPPER NES,ALLOYS,UNWRT	W 87734	177637	W 97835	216811	W 199118	586988	W 197161	496689	CUIVRE BRUT
68212	COPPER REFINED,UNWROUGHT	W 87642	177345	W 97733	216379	W 197122	581102	W 191887	481824	CUIVRE AFFINE BRUT
69	METAL MANUFACTURES NES		770112		1035835		1247799		1289229	ART MANUFACT EN METAL NDA
699	BASE METAL MFRS NES		319671		444124		520553		507221	ART MANUFACTURES MET NDA
7	MACHINES,TRANSPORT EQUIP		43138267		61828015		77567946		82455828	MACHINES MATERIEL TRANSPORT
71	POWER GENERATING EQUIPMT		1382527		1613795		1717009		1653773	MACHINES GENERATRICES
713	INTRNL COMBUS PSTN ENGIN		439564		436399		410021		398968	MOTEURS EXPL COMB INT, PIECE
714	ENGINES AND MOTORS NES		229581		218861		100452		73072	MOTEURS NON ELECTRIQUES
716	ROTATING ELECTRIC PLANT		679864		900720		1123505		1134268	APP ELECTR ROTATIFS,PIECES
7162	AC MTRS,GENRTRS,GEN SETS	MN 168434	573675	MN 392708	682873	MN 512563	855692	MN 424158	858168	MOTEURS ELECTRIQUES
71621	AC MTRS,INC UNIVRSL MTRS	MN 168398	339996	MN 392686	539426	MN 512539	730022	MN 424134	666263	MOT ELEC NON COUR CONTINU
72	MACHS FOR SPCL INDUSTRYS		1322496		1699567		2108604		2189910	MAC SPECIALES POUR INDUST
723	CIVIL ENGNEERG EQUIP ETC		511264		519154		718022		730422	APPAREILS DE GENIE CIVIL
7239	CONSTR ETC MACHY PTS NES		421187		396806		501140		487120	PIECES 723.41–723.46
728	OTH MACHY FOR SPCL INDUS		525012		851453		1015298		1000933	AUT MACH IND PARTICULIERES
7284	MACHY FOR SPCL INDUS NES		433927		696685		851200		860270	MACH SPEC IND PARTICUL.
72848	OTH MCHY WITH INDIV FNCT	N 61757	222917	N 42653	390410	N 44160	488021	N 42757	441332	AUTRES MACHINES NDA
73	METALWORKING MACHINERY		250745		374017		471279		440401	MACH TRAVAIL DES METAUX
736	METALWORKING MACH–TOOLS		208422		301472		370234		352137	MACH–OUTILS TRAVAIL METAUX
74	GENRL INDUSTRL MACHY NES		2337378		3267390		3602639		3845162	MACH APP INDUSTRIE
741	HEATING,COOLING EQUIPMNT		534577		666586		666072		690710	MACH CHAUFFAGE,PIECES
7415	AIR–CONDITIONING MACHNRY		387613	N 1018203	384137	N 1031921	416806	N 1061138	438318	GROUPES CONDITION AIR
743	PUMPS NES,CENTRFUGES ETC		513837		681252		677143		643918	POMPES COMPRES,VENT ETC
7431	PUMPS FOR GASES ETC	N 8977142	394114	MN 10513	485967	MN 9637	474629	MN 9045	440243	POMPES AIR A VIDE,COMPRES
744	MECHANICAL HANDLING EQU		234482		542590		622490		766802	EQUIP MANUTENTION PIECES
7449	PTS NES OF MACHY OF 7442		26576		244704		299561		388219	PIECES DU 744.2
749	NONELEC MACH PTS,ACC NES		840963		1062690		1279757		1344547	PIECES MACH NON ELEC NDA
7491	BALL,ROLLER,ETC BEARINGS		407933		473855		652509		708570	ROULEMENTS BILLES ETC

5. General Exports F.O.B. by Commodities according to the S.I.T.C. (Rev. 2) in thousand U.S. Dollars
Exportations Générales F.O.B. par Produits d'après la C.T.C.I. (Rév. 2) en milliers de Dollars E.U.

SITC CTCI	COMMODITY	1993		1994		1995		1996		PRODUIT
		WEIGHT POIDS	VALUE VALEUR	WEIGHT POIDS	VALUE VALEUR	WEIGHT POIDS	VALUE VALEUR	WEIGHT POIDS	VALUE VALEUR	
75	OFFICE MACHNES,ADP EQUIP		16511026		22567774		28962587		33107517	MACH BUREAU TRAIT AUTOM
751	OFFICE MACHINES	MN 17529	480689	MN 27471	522623	MN 30014	523283	MN 29633	535525	MACH,APPAREILS DE BUREAU
7512	CALCULATNG,ACCTG,ETC MCH	MN 15340	247284	MN 24802	302387	MN 27377	338303	MN 27507	406243	MACHINE A CALCULER ETC
75121	CALCULATING MACHINES	MN 15289	222365	MN 24698	261991	MN 27257	291348	MN 27288	342645	MACHINES A CALCULER
752	AUTOMTIC DATA PROC EQUIP	MN 68167	11951310	MN 104128	14668398	MN 107981	19538235	MN 118360	23104564	MACH TRAIT INFORMATION
7522	DIGITAL COMPUTFRS	N 3638877	2610104	N 3751669	2790348	N 3699420	3496367	N 1312255	1913416	MACH DIGITALES COMPLETES
7523	DIGITL CENTRL PROCESSORS	N 203277	148304	N 438570	461081	N 774173	691784	N 2336075	2202271	UNITES CENTRALES
7524	DIGITL CENTRL STOR UNITS	N 560284	140358	MN 59447	8924587	MN 68559	11460017	MN 79367	14252109	UNITES MEMOIRE CENTRALES
7525	ADP PERIPHERAL UNITS	MN 62203	8833747	MN 35887	1967628	MN 29726	2951130	MN 30343	3863712	UNITES PERIPHERIQUES
7528	OFF–LINE DATA PROC EQUIP	N 1561077	218769	N 4603959	524606	N 5222283	938915	N 5002273	873039	MACH AUXIL TRAIT INFORM
759	OFFICE,ADP MCH PTS,ACCES		4079027		7376753		8901068		9467428	PIECES DU 751 ET 752
7599	ACCTG,ETC,ADP MCH PTS,AC		3949210		7226769		8714285		9193462	PIECES DU 751 ET 752
76	TELECOMM,SOUND EQUIPMENT		8901993		12394274		12966582		11665299	EQUIPMENT DE TELECOM
761	TELEVISION RECEIVERS	N 6684799	1340385	N 7407270	1654788	N 7461391	1731298	N 7632702	1797089	RECEPTEURS DE TELEVISION
7611	COLOUR TV RECEIVERS	N 6614907	1335816	N 7318860	1649997	N 7415159	1728535	N 7586523	1793971	RECEPTEURS COULEUR
762	RADIO BROADCAST RECEIVRS	MN 27663	1879374	MN 29014	2303871	MN 23286	2098804	MN 20460	1912671	RECEPTEURS RADIODIFFUSION
7621	MTR VEHC RADIO RECEIVERS	N 3738233	265803	N 4646453	389504	N 4905489	426145	N 4908351	452883	RECEPTEURS RADIO AUTO
7622	PORTABLE RADIO RECEIVERS	MN 17040	740695	MN 16116	749063	MN 11818	601363	N 8821054	396631	RECEPT PORTATIFS RADIO
7628	OTHER RADIO RECEIVERS	N 6884616	872877	N 8251482	1165303	N 6562639	1071296	N 6730150	1063156	AUTRES RECEPT RADIO
763	SOUND RECORDRS,PHONOGRPH	MN 17401	1740997	MN 26632	2349129	MN 22143	2261977	MN 16227	1789432	PHONO,APP ENREGISTREMENT
7638	OTHR SOUND APPARATUS ETC	MN 17061	1726590	MN 26424	2341213	MN 21892	2254474	MN 16200	1787924	AUT APP D'ENREGIS,REPROD
76381	TV IMAGE,SND RECRDRS ETC	N 6166373	1136400	N 8953588	1480517	N 8986843	1515907	N 7763120	1307437	APP ENREG,REPRO IMAG,SON
76388	DICTATING MACHINES ETC	MN 10895	590190	MN 17471	860696	MN 12905	738567	N 8437166	480487	MACHINES A DICTER
764	TELECOM EQPT,PTS,ACC NES		3941237		6086487		6874503		6166107	EQUIP TELECOM,PIECES
7641	LINE TELEPHONE,ETC EQUIP	MN 11967	470096	MN 25890	695328	MN 29551	794318	MN 22986	611720	APP TELEPHON PAR FIL
7642	MICROPH,LOUDSPKR,AMPLIFR	MN 80606	275475	MN 156386	374933	MN 148269	406564	MN 138472	380736	MICRO,HAUT–PARLEUR,AMPLI
7643	TV,RADIO TRANSMITTRS ETC	N 2148957	158709		126990	N 5625410	287921	N 4730452	543358	APP EMET TELE RADIO
7648	TELECOMM EQUIPMENT NES	MN 21438	812052	MN 22744	848829	MN 28625	1253424	MN 24821	875129	APP TELECOM NDA
76481	RADIOTELEPHONE ETC RCVRS	N 5169895	646806	N 5737630	631932	N 8257415	921777	N 6436139	720727	RECEP RADIOTELEPHONIE
7649	PTS NES OF EQUIPMT OF 76		2224905		4040406		4132276		3755164	PIECES DE LA DIV 76
76493	TELECOMM EQUIPMT PTS NES		1239918		2001246		2079794		1831887	PIECES 761,762,764.3,8
76499	PARTS ETC OF SOUND EQUIP		860767		1688246		1722351		1546712	PIECES NDA POUR 763
77	ELECTRIC MACHNRY NES ETC		10485763		17838584		25511155		27049273	MACH APP ELECT NDA
771	ELECTRIC POWER MACHY NES		534098		819361		1046338		1073233	MACH PROD,TRANS ELECTR
7712	OTH ELEC POWER MACHY NES		381062		587451		787892		836511	AUT APP PROD TRANSF ELEC
772	SWITCHGEAR ETC,PARTS NES		1218149		2081200		2451411		2473271	APP COUPURE,SECT ETC
7721	SWITCHGEAR ETC		708730		1180758		1422311		1415313	APP COUPURE,SECTIONMNT
7722	PRINTED CIRCUITS,PTS NES		317456		492296		590738		618402	CIRCUITS ET PIECES
7723	FIXED,VARIABLE RESISTORS		191964		408146		438362		439556	POTENTIOMETRES PIECES
773	ELECTR DISTRIBUTNG EQUIP		286197		419182		504424		487019	EQUIPMT DISTRIBUTION ELECT
7731	INSULATED WIRE,CABLE ETC	W 45102	224954	W 61357	372837	W 54243	462482	W 47288	438552	FILS,CABLES ISOLES ELECT
775	HOUSEHOLD TYPE EQUIP NES		439150		492492		531696		558194	MACH,APP USAGE DOMESTQUE
7758	ELECTRO–THERMIC APPL NES		305226		312133		315358		321663	APP ELECTROTHERMIQ NDA
776	TRANSISTORS,VALVES,ETC		6852586		12053932		18392531		19772820	LAMPES,TUBES,VALVES
7761	TV PICTURE TUBES	N 8302302	609851	MN 9409	720691	MN 9351	775838	MN 9265	924881	TUBES CATHODIQUES
7762	OTH ELECTRONIC TUBES ETC		61350		218587		482877		594925	AUT LAMPES ELECTRONIQUES
7763	DIODES,TRANSISTORS,ETC		565092		1152454		2024787		2142691	DIODES,TRANSISTORS
7764	ELECTRONIC MICROCIRCUITS		5145504		9206183		14242129		14614095	MICROSTRUCTURES ELECTRON
7768	ELCTRNC COMP PTS,CRYSTLS		470788		756017		866900		1496228	CRIST PIEZO–ELEC,PCS 776
77689	ELECTRNIC COMPON PTS NES		422605		627672		673861		1308433	PIECES DU GROUPE 776
778	ELECTRICAL MACHINERY NES		1118481		1929452		2525216		2611136	AUTRES MACH ELECT NDA
7781	BATTERIES,ACCUMULATORS		207083		279663		372193		447597	PILES ET ACCUMULATEURS
7788	OTH ELEC MACHY,EQUIP NES		703100		1385042		1850230		1853937	AUT MACH APP ELEC NDA
77884	ELECTRICAL CONDENSERS		433791		933446		1310444		1319249	CONDENSATEURS ELECTRIQUES
78	ROAD VEHICLES		946573		967143		1193155		1290796	VEHICULES ROUTIERS
784	MOTOR VEH PRTS,ACCES NES		241933		287764		392514		488505	PIECES 722,781,782,783
7849	OTHER MOTOR VEHCL PARTS		237498		283504		387893		484294	PIECES 722,781,782,783
785	CYCLES,ETC MOTRZD OR NOT		426945		399537		393991		371053	MOTOCYCLES SCOOTERS
7853	INVAL CARR, PTS OF 785		317336		354825		348714		294942	FAUTEUILS INVALIDES,PIECES
78539	PARTS,ACCES NES OF 785		317086		354653		348447		294831	PIECES DU 785
79	OTHR TRANSPORT EQUIPMENT		999766		1105471		1034935		1213696	AUTRE MATERIEL TRANSPORT
792	AIRCRAFT ETC		251734		233282		380369		539680	APP NAVIGATION AERIENNE
7929	AIRCRAFT PARTS NES		238464		196581		268420		384330	PIECES DU 792
793	SHIPS AND BOATS ETC	N 2998	745468	N 5424	868568		650668	N 3992	671037	NAVIRES BATEAUX,ETC
7932	SHIPS AND BOATS NES	N 758	393599	N 1356	841507	N 1147	463684	N 1182	585614	NAVIRES ET BATEAUX
79323	OTHER CARGO VESSELS	N 120	356836	N 198	652720	N 156	318183	N 180	408342	AUT BATEAUX TRANS MARCH
7938	TUGS,SPECIAL VESSELS ETC	N 2058	348911	N 3911	23127	N 4346	184978	N 2673	82976	REMORQUEURS,BATEAUX SPEC
79382	SPECL PURPOSE VESSLS ETC	N 33	338246	N 20	1246	N 84	139832	N 21	43498	BAT–PHARES,–POMPES,DRAGUES
8	MISC MANUFACTURED GOODS		6109393		7438488		8971057		9400445	ART MANUFACTURES DIVERS
821	*FURNITURE,PARTS THEREOF		234255		250702		221567		206873	MEUBLES ET PIECES
84	CLOTHING AND ACCESSORIES		1548782		1526250		1464850		1400391	VETEMENTS
843	WOMENS OUTERWEAR NONKNIT	MN 40097	234448	MN 37234	212387	MN 33585	185459	MN 32001	164449	VET DESSUS FEMMES MAT TEX
845	OUTERWEAR KNIT NONELASTC	MN 141174	616644	MN 116007	553085	MN 105922	518903	MN 104391	541805	VET DESSOUS,ACCES BONNET
8459	— OTHER,CLTHG ACCESRYS	MN 95507	371357	MN 78664	343333	MN 73512	333230	MN 66909	317820	AUT VET DESSUS DE BONNE
846	UNDER GARMENTS KNITTED	MN 85386	304717	MN 85753	337952	MN 93063	372202	MN 87302	353458	SOUS VETS DE BONNETERIE
87	PRECISION INSTRUMNTS NES		1013290		1343807		1648064		1593011	INSTRUM,APPAR SCIENT NDA
872	MEDICAL INSTRUMENTS NES		381479		411976		506971		484853	INSTR,APP MEDIC–CHIR NDA
87202	OTH MEDICAL INSTRUMENTS		369439		403611		499901		475156	INSTRUM,APP MEDECINE
874	MEASURNG,CONTROLNG INSTR		521947		730030		866608		866798	INSTRUMENTS DE MESURE
88	PHOTO EQU,OPTICL GDS ETC		1098032		1368499		1768316		2040190	APP,FOURN PHOTO,OP,MONTR
882	PHOTO,CINEMA SUPPLIES		377219		493256		554002		572954	PRODUITS PHOTO,CINEMA
8822	PHOTO FILM EXC DEV CINMA		270944		315296		325679		277170	PLAQUES,PELLICULES,FILMS
885	WATCHES AND CLOCKS		438095		563801		815209		978358	HORLOGERIE
8851	WATCHES,MOVEMENTS,CASES		296281		400787		619144		752886	MONTRES,MOUVEMENTS,BOITES
88511	WATCHES		220412		329256		558655		729891	MONTRES POCHE,BRACELET
89	MISC MANUFCTRD GOODS NES		2035007		2731983		3574460		3810735	ART MANUFACTURES DIVERS
892	PRINTED MATTER		371777		483734		609057		595460	IMPRIMES
8921	PRINTED BOOKS,GLOBES,ETC		284019		355052		458792		438707	LIVRES,BROCHURES,CARTES
89211	PRINTED BOOKS,PAMPHLETS		249490		310501		419270		402564	LIVRES,BROCHURES
893	ARTICLES OF PLASTIC NES		410742		593148		665463		654164	OUVRAGES EN MAT DIVIS 58
8939	MISC PLASTIC ARTICLES		267959		415178		448262		467076	ART DIVERS EN MAT DIV 58
89399	OTHR PLASTC ARTICLES NES		238887		403627		432213		444191	AUT OUV MAT DIV 58
894	TOYS,SPORTING GOODS,ETC		298424		328199		463855		459391	VOITURES ENFANTS,JOUETS
897	GOLD,SILVER WARE,JEWELRY		135994		316716		658135		789097	BIJOUTERIE,ORFEVRERIE
8973	PREC JEWLRY,GLD–SILVWARE		127825		295881		646658		778505	BIJOUX OR,ARGENT ORFEVRE
89731	PRECIOUS METAL JEWELLERY		122056		280447		614792		746461	ART BIJOUTERIE,JOAILLER
898	MUSICAL INSTRUMENTS,PTS		575569		703840		841402		933250	INSTRUMENTS DE MUSIQUE
8983	SOUND RECRDNG TAPE,DISCS	MN 191446	550174	MN 282778	663360	MN 365446	800825	MN 406723	885882	SUPPORTS SON POUR 763
89831	PREPD SND RECORDNG MEDIA	MN 170385	202782	MN 251610	262845	MN 338259	347004	MN 384806	593242	SUPPORTS PREPARES
89832	RECORDED DISCS,TAPES ETC	MN 21061	347392	MN 31168	400516	MN 27187	453821	MN 21917	292640	DISQUES,PHONO,BANDES
9	GOODS NOT CLASSD BY KIND		1237508		1363241		2854116		3461065	ART TRANSACT NON CLASSES

5. General Exports F.O.B. by Commodities according to the S.I.T.C. (Rev. 2) in thousand U.S. Dollars
Exportations Générales F.O.B. par Produits d'après la C.T.C.I. (Rév. 2) en milliers de Dollars E.U.

SITC CTCI	COMMODITY	1993		1994		1995		1996		PRODUIT
		WEIGHT POIDS	VALUE VALEUR	WEIGHT POIDS	VALUE VALEUR	WEIGHT POIDS	VALUE VALEUR	WEIGHT POIDS	VALUE VALEUR	
931	*SPECIAL TRANSACTIONS		1079555		1189620		2639957		3099430	TRANS.SPECIALES

1. HISTORICAL SERIES, 1993–1996 GENERAL TRADE, IMPORTS F.O.B., EXPORTS F.O.B.
SERIES HISTORIQUES, 1993–1996 COMMERCE GENERAL, IMPORTATIONS F.O.B., EXPORTATIONS F.O.B

YEAR ANNEE	VALUE IN MILLION CZECH. KORUNY VALEUR EN MILLION CZECH. KORUNY MERCHANDISE –MARCHANDISE		GOLD –OR		CONVERSION FACTORS U.S. CENTS PER CZECH. KORUNA FACTEURS DE CONVERSION CENTS E.U. PAR CZECH. KORUNA		INDEX NUMBERS –INDICES QUANTUM		UNIT VALUE VALEUR UNITAIRE	
	IMPORTS	EXPORTS	IMPORTS	EXPORTS	IMPORTS	EXPORTS	IMPORTS	EXPORTS	IMPORTS	EXPORTS
1993	195034.00	167724.00			3.2610	3.2610				
1994	208227.00	211085.00			3.1230	3.1230				
1995	260791.00	255096.00			3.3693	3.3695				
1996	334139.90	270597.10			3.2583	3.2602				

2. IMPORTS BY BROAD ECONOMIC CATEGORY AND EXPORTS BY INDUSTRIAL ORIGIN. (PERCENTAGE OF TOTAL VALUE)
IMPORTATIONS PAR CATEGORIES ECONOMIQUES ET EXPORTATIONS PAR BRANCHE D'ACTIVITE.(EN POURCENTAGE DE LA VALEUR TOTALE)

IMPORTS – IMPORTATIONS

	1990	1991	1992	1993	1994	1995	1996
TOTAL IMPORTS–IMPORTATIONS TOTALES					100.		100.
1 FOOD BEV–ALIMENTATION BOISSONS					7.0		5.7
11 PRIMARY–PRODUITS DE BASE					3.3		2.4
111 FOR INDUSTRY–POUR L'INDUSTRIE					1.4		0.9
112 FOR HOUSEHOLDS–POUR LES MENAGES					1.9		1.5
12 PROCESSED–PRODUITS ELABORES					3.7		3.3
121 FOR INDUSTRY–POUR L'INDUSTRIE					0.3		0.2
122 FOR HOUSEHOLDS–POUR LES MENAGES					3.3		3.0
2 IND SUPPLIES–APPROV INDUSTRIELS					32.8		26.2
21 PRIMARY–PRODUITS DE BASE					4.3		3.3
22 PROCESSED–PRODUITS ELABORES					28.5		22.9
3 FUELS–COMBUSTIBLES					19.2		11.7
31 PRIMARY–PRODUITS DE BASE					18.0		9.8
32 PROCESSED–PRODUITS ELABORES					1.2		1.9
321 MOTOR SPIRIT–ESSENCE					0.6		
322 OTHER–AUTRES					0.6		1.9
4 MACHINERY–EQUIPEMENT					22.9		19.2
41 CAPITAL EQUIPMENT–MACHINES					19.9		16.4
42 PARTS–PIECES ACCESSOIRES					3.0		2.8
5 TRANSPORT–TRANSPORT					6.2		11.4
51 PASSENGER CARS–AUTOMOBILES					1.9		6.6
52 OTHER–AUTRES					1.7		2.0
521 INDUSTRIAL–INDUSTRIELS					1.6		2.0
522 NON INDUSTRIAL–NON INDUSTRIEL					0.1		0.1
53 PARTS–PIECES ACCESSOIRES					2.6		2.8
6 CONSUM GOODS–BIENS CONSOMMATION					11.3		10.8
61 DURABLE–DURABLES					2.2		2.3
62 SEMI DURABLE–SEMI DURABLES					4.6		4.0
63 NON DURABLE–NON DURABLES					4.5		4.5
7 GOODS NES–BIENS NDA					0.7		15.1

EXPORTS – EXPORTATIONS

	1990	1991	1992	1993	1994	1995	1996
TOTAL EXPORTS–EXPORTATIONS TOTALES					100.		100.
1 AGRICULTURE					2.9		1.7
2 MINING QUARRY–INDUS EXTRACTIVES					1.1		0.9
3 MANUFACTURING–IND MANUFACTUR					96.0		97.3
31 FOOD BEV TOBACCO–ALIM BOISS TAB					4.0		3.5
32 TEXTILES–INDUSTRIES TEXTILES					10.5		8.3
33 WOOD & PRODUCTS–BOIS & PRODUITS					3.1		2.6
34 PAPER & PRODUCTS–PAPIER & PRODT					5.1		5.8
35 CHEMICALS–INDUSTRIES CHIMIQUES					21.3		18.7
36 NON METAL MIN–MIN NON METAL					4.0		3.7
37 BASIC METAL–IND METAL BASE					19.5		8.6
38 METAL MANUF–MANUF METAL					28.1		30.7
39 OTH MANUF IND–AUTRES MANUF					0.5		15.5

3. TRADE BY PRINCIPAL COUNTRIES OF ORIGIN AND DESTINATION (VALUE IN THOUSAND U.S. DOLLARS)
ECHANGES SELON LES PRINCIPAUX PAYS D'ORIGINE ET DE DESTINATION (VALEUR EN MILLIERS DE DOLLARS EU)

COUNTRIES–PAYS	GENERAL IMPORTS F.O.B. IMPORTATIONS GENERALES F.O.B.				
	1992	1993	1994	1995	1996
World		6453672	6610959	8770403	10936305
Africa			34237	59600	57449
Americas		9000	271654	328136	415359
Northern America			201708	235550	322546
LAIA		9000	49035	61004	59918
CACM			16713	24968	23791
Caribbean			676	1477	2416
Rest of America			3522	5137	6687
As.ex F.USSR		41000	275866	466528	730389
Eur.x F.USSR		4115000	4610471	6180972	7489827
EU		1524000	2212664	3048664	4030489
EFTA			101905	166059	179133
East Europe		2546000	2244845	2892156	3193329
Other Europe			716	948	2141
Former USSR		1459000	1377956	1671835	2179959
Oceania			12045	17121	14657
Czech Republic		2321000	1957890	2433622	2681969
Russian Federation		1302000	1194664	1456009	1933069
Germany/Allemagne		746000	888082	1251502	1591169
Austria/Autriche		399000	381480	447650	509353
Italy/Italie		197000	289669	405782	650564
France,Monac		99000	147654	214778	348041
Poland/Pologne		127000	157523	243338	269511
USA/Etats–Unis d'Amer			187736	215295	293744
Hungary/Hongrie		86000	110753	193189	216971
Ukraine		157000	118596	122657	173272
United Kingdom		83000	105681	148240	203238
Netherlands/Pays–Bas			110088	150612	199221
Switz.Liecht			95058	148133	161325
Japan/Japon			81570	130665	189417
Belgium–Luxembourg			85067	109088	151735
Korea, Republic of			16761	37564	191354
Sweden/Suède			43266	101148	87624
Finland/Finlande			55158	73626	88544
China/Chine		31000	37631	57849	80975
Spain/Espagne			40038	61586	95598
Denmark/Danemark			40480	50877	62676
Slovenia/Slovénia			29576	48041	56368
Belarus/Bélarus			19024	39014	28024
India/Inde		10000	17844	31190	26207
Hong Kong			17301	32121	23162
Malaysia/Malaisie			8442	26626	36075
So. Africa Customs Un			16620	31217	22324
Turkey/Turquie			11764	26802	29275
Canada			11586	20235	28781
Ireland/Irlande			13928	18197	27513
Brazil/Brésil		9000	15641	15779	18526
Croatia/Croatie			17344	20256	21258
Yugoslavia/Yougoslavie		45000	408	224	5346
Kazakhstan			22490	14634	11509
Uzbekistan/Ouzbékistan			10831	21004	15662
Bulgaria/Bulgarie		12000	10325	11117	9653
Indonesia/Indonésie			8580	16350	17510
Norway,SVD,JM			6779	17649	17169
Australia/Australie			11015	15571	12057
Israel/Israël			7575	11279	18023
Cote d'Ivoire			10114	8949	17118
Thailand/Thaïlande			7762	12981	14034
Romania/Roumanie			7662	10635	15035
Costa Rica			7205	12697	12385
Greece/Grèce			9365	11696	10735
Colombia/Colombie			8418	9287	13376
Ecuador/Equateur			9441	8869	9049
Singapore/Singapour			7125	8170	11064
Honduras			7896	8349	6571
Peru/Pérou			4732	7606	8659

COUNTRIES–PAYS	GENERAL EXPORTS F.O.B. EXPORTATIONS GENERALES F.O.B.				
	1992	1993	1994	1995	1996
Monde		5392494	6690245	8577499	8824094
Afrique			54128	77665	49331
Amériques		2000	211188	189931	183102
Amérique du Nord			145711	127644	130160
ALAI		2000	56367	47940	38092
MCAC			5131	7426	5842
Caraïbes			3030	4664	7341
Autre Amérique			949	2257	1667
Asie l'URSS exclus		127000	331421	342181	312769
Europe l'URSS exclus		4212000	5619964	7343711	7629705
UE		1389000	2342995	3208250	3644876
AELE			53053	84932	106044
Europe de l'Est		2733000	3095580	3854574	3645807
Autre de l'Europe			664	746	2011
Ancienne URSS		396000	467088	612082	641097
Océanie			4017	4768	6574
Czech Republic		2310000	2501711	3024040	2737836
Germany/Allemagne		828000	1143911	1612496	1871065
Austria/Autriche		271000	351359	425880	533923
Hungary/Hongrie		247000	365742	390899	403341
Italy/Italie		148000	288329	413390	431432
Russian Federation		256000	277599	330783	307805
Poland/Pologne		159000	189296	378012	426877
Ukraine		140000	116707	190759	235893
France,Monac		87000	113341	171427	186820
Netherlands/Pays–Bas			118969	150793	166695
United Kingdom		55000	85613	112431	135346
USA/Etats–Unis d'Amer			108440	107581	118992
Belgium–Luxembourg			88372	93734	112171
Slovenia/Slovénia			45160	94803	87451
Switz.Liecht			46235	70375	95924
India/Inde		15000	61213	67064	64712
Croatia/Croatie			60645	72336	73351
Spain/Espagne			39770	61827	54347
Yugoslavia/Yougoslavie		90000	2614	3989	49119
China/Chine		65000	23078	16964	38622
Sweden/Suède			39726	58627	39800
Romania/Roumanie			26690	42619	57168
Syrian Arab Republic		47000	24551	17308	14815
Thailand/Thaïlande			52968	19024	21008
Finland/Finlande			21746	38163	32867
Turkey/Turquie			29287	40845	18958
Denmark/Danemark			19633	28496	31732
Greece/Grèce			20115	26230	32637
Belarus/Bélarus			18208	33569	24830
Canada			37271	20063	10935
Bulgaria/Bulgarie		17000	11647	18119	19666
Lithuania/Lituanie			18236	22621	25284
Egypt/Egypte			18838	21328	16785
Malaysia/Malaisie			20428	20024	13103
Indonesia/Indonésie			12394	10889	21993
Japan/Japon			6222	17671	19013
Saudi Arabia			5652	20321	16292
Tfyr Macedonia			16280	18449	6692
Israel/Israël			17835	14787	7856
Kazakhstan			16423	11200	10840
Lebanon/Liban			11529	14742	11928
Argentina/Argentine			10657	11631	13288
Mexico/Mexique			29061	2946	1199
Algeria/Algérie			6144	20180	6757
Korea, Republic of			17174	7017	7112
Iran (Islamic Rp. of)			6689	6891	15557
Norway,SVD,JM			5982	13644	9452
Singapore/Singapour			13836	10516	4182
United Arab Emirates			4630	11158	9155
Portugal			7046	9440	8452

(VALUE AS PERCENTAGE OF WORLD TOTAL)(VALEURS EN POURCENTAGE DU TOTAL MONDIAL)

	1987	1988	1989	1990	1991	1992	1993	1994	1995	1996
Africa								0.5	0.7	0.5
Americas							0.1	4.1	3.7	3.8
Northern America								3.1	2.7	2.9
LAIA							0.1	0.7	0.7	0.5
CACM								0.3	0.3	0.2
Caribbean								0.0	0.0	0.0
Rest of America								0.1	0.1	0.1
As.ex F.USSR							0.6	4.2	5.3	6.7
Eur.x F.USSR							63.8	69.7	70.5	68.5
EU							23.6	33.5	34.8	36.9
EFTA								1.5	1.9	1.6
East Europe							39.5	34.0	33.0	29.2
Other Europe								0.0	0.0	0.0
Former USSR							22.6	20.8	19.1	19.9
Oceania								0.2	0.2	0.1
Czech Republic							36.0	29.6	27.7	24.5
Russian Federation							20.2	18.1	16.6	17.7
Germany/Allemagne							11.6	13.4	14.3	14.5
Austria/Autriche							6.2	5.8	5.1	4.7
Italy/Italie							3.1	4.4	4.6	5.9
France,Monac							1.5	2.2	2.4	3.2
Poland/Pologne							2.0	2.4	2.8	2.5
USA/Etats–Unis d'Amer								2.8	2.5	2.7
Hungary/Hongrie							1.3	1.7	2.2	2.0
Ukraine							2.4	1.8	1.4	1.6

	1987	1988	1989	1990	1991	1992	1993	1994	1995	1996
Afrique								0.8	0.9	0.6
Amériques							0.0	3.2	2.2	2.1
Amérique du Nord								2.2	1.5	1.5
ALAI							0.0	0.8	0.6	0.4
MCAC								0.1	0.1	0.1
Caraïbes								0.0	0.1	0.1
Autre Amérique								0.0	0.0	0.0
Asie l'URSS exclus							2.4	5.0	4.0	3.5
Europe l'URSS exclus							78.1	84.0	85.6	86.5
UE							25.8	35.0	37.4	41.3
AELE								0.8	1.0	1.2
Europe de l'Est							50.7	46.3	44.9	41.3
Autre de l'Europe								0.0	0.0	0.0
Ancienne URSS							7.3	7.0	7.1	7.3
Océanie								0.1	0.1	0.1
Czech Republic							42.8	37.4	35.3	31.0
Germany/Allemagne							15.4	17.1	18.8	21.2
Austria/Autriche							5.0	5.3	5.0	6.1
Hungary/Hongrie							4.6	5.5	4.6	4.6
Italy/Italie							2.7	4.3	4.8	4.9
Russian Federation							4.7	4.1	3.9	3.5
Poland/Pologne							2.9	2.8	4.4	4.8
Ukraine							2.6	1.7	2.2	2.7
France,Monac							1.6	1.7	2.0	2.1
Netherlands/Pays–Bas								1.8	1.8	1.9

4. General Imports F.O.B. by Commodities according to the S.I.T.C. (Rev. 2) in thousand U.S. Dollars
Importations Générales F.O.B. par Produits d'après la C.T.C.I. (Rév. 2) en milliers de Dollars E.U.

SITC CTCI	COMMODITY	1993 WEIGHT POIDS	1993 VALUE VALEUR	1994 WEIGHT POIDS	1994 VALUE VALEUR	1995 WEIGHT POIDS	1995 VALUE VALEUR	1996 WEIGHT POIDS	1996 VALUE VALEUR	PRODUIT
	ALL COMMODITIES		6453672		6610959		8770403		10936305	TOUS PRODUITS
0	FOOD AND LIVE ANIMALS		472854		458015		594249		628899	ALIMENTS,ANIMAUX VIVANTS
02	DAIRY PRODCTS,BIRDS'EGGS				25292		25694		25309	PRODUITS LAITIERS,OEUFS
03	FISH AND PREPARATIONS				27789		30824		34236	POISSONS ET PREPARATIONS
04	CEREALS AND PREPARATIONS				54804		55887		87468	CEREA'ES ET PRODUITS
048	CEREAL ETC PREPARATIONS			W 20009	24723	W 26935	37738	W 45270	46168	PREPTNS A BASE CEREALES
05	VEGETABLES AND FRUIT				109035		158982		170652	LEGUMES ET FRUITS
054	VEG ETC FRSH,SMPLY PRSVD			W 140823	21519	W 122535	41242	W 89181	28406	LEGUMES FRAIS,CONG,SECS
057	FRUIT,NUTS,FRESH,DRIED			W 151723	63509	W 184994	81206	W 239124	93457	FRUITS FRAIS OU SECS
0573	BANANA,PLANTAIN,FRSH,DRY			W 56876	24012	W 74790	29935	W 78120	35999	BANANES FRAICHES,SECHEES
058	FRUIT PRESERVED,PREPARED			W 23458	19739	W 36128	30206	W 57938	40699	CONSERVES DE FRUITS
06	SUGAR AND PREPS,HONEY				25126		45099		25270	SUCRES ET PRODUITS
061	SUGAR AND HONEY			W 37973	14593	W 57334	29720	W 21021	10839	SUCRES ET MIEL
07	COFFEE,TEA,COCOA,SPICES				87411		114072		102332	CAFE,THE,CACAO,EPICES
071	COFFEE AND SUBSTITUTES				37118	W 13909	57000	W 13415	37611	CAFE ET SUCCEDANES
0711	COFFEE GREEN,ROASTED,SUB				33883	W 13324	50990	W 13297	37079	CAFE TORREFIE OU DECAFEINE
07111	COFFEE GREEN,HUSKS,SKINS			W 11823	26712	W 11523	42843	W 11356	29391	CAFE NON TORREFIE
073	CHOCOLATE AND PRODUCTS			W 10765	28366	W 10813	36224	W 12979	35141	CHOCOLAT
081	*FEEDING STUFF FOR ANIML			W 157124	55078	W 211626	73421	W 197458	84308	NOURRITURE POUR ANIMAUX
0813	OILCAKE AND OTH RESIDUES			W 110362	27336	W 134505	32573	W 134157	38054	TOURTEAUX
08131	— OF SOYA BEANS			W 105282	26161	W 134505	32573	W 134157	38054	TOURTEAUX DE SOJA
0819	FOOD WASTE AND FEED NES			W 29140	20501	W 61941	33407	W 47814	37489	DECHETS,ALIMENTS NDA
08199	FODDER NES,INCL SWEETNED			W 27824	20026	W 61599	33320	W 47451	37397	PREPARATIONS FOURRAGERES
09	MISC EDIBLE PRODUCTS				42241		52625		67862	PREP ALIMENTAIRES DIVERSES
098	EDIBLE PRODCTS,PREPS NES			W 19555	30944	W 21952	37111	W 30711	49790	PREP ALIMENTAIRES NDA
1	BEVERAGES AND TOBACCO		93757		85343		95602		111880	BOISSONS ET TABACS
11	BEVERAGES				37474		46699		55867	BOISSONS
112	ALCOHOLIC BEVERAGES				23863	W 79396	31428	W 94453	33666	BOISSONS ALCOOLIQUES
12	TOBACCO AND MANUFACTURES				47869		48903		56013	TABACS BRUTS FABRIQUES
122	TOBACCO,MANUFACTURED				36241	W 4688	38738	W 5495	45980	TABACS FABRIQUES
1222	CIGARETTES				34108	W 4607	38193	W 5455	45667	CIGARETTES
2	CRUDE MATERLS,EXCL FUELS		334363		348606		509590		517585	MAT BRUTES NON COMESTIBLES
23	RUBBER, CRUDE				44909		95715		84069	CAOUTCHOUC BRUT
232	NATURAL RUBBER,GUMS			W 13445	14360	W 19679	33365	W 20751	36541	LATEX CAOUTCHOUC NATUREL
23202	OTHER NATURAL RUBBER			W 12536	12978	W 19140	32256	W 19863	35104	CAOUTCHOUC NATUREL
233	RUBBER,SYNTHTIC,RECLAIMD			W 30837	30549	W 44793	62351	W 33666	47528	LATEX CAOUTCH SYNTH REGEN
2331	SYNTHETIC RUBBER ETC			W 29549	30017	W 43366	61611	W 32389	46840	LATEX CAOUTCH SYNTHETIQUE
251	*PULP AND WASTE PAPER			W 63259	19335	W 49088	31966	W 143421	49088	PATES A PAPIER,DECHETS
26	TEXTILE FIBRES AND WASTE				36475		39107		42917	FIBRES TEXTILES
27	CRUDE FERTLZR,MINRLS NES				37641		42591		45164	ENGRAIS MINERAUX BRUTS
278	OTHER CRUDE MINERALS			W 451262	23620	W 389967	25750	W 500723	30529	AUTRES MINERAUX BRUTS
28	METALLIFEROUS ORES,SCRAP				149259		220410		227118	MINERAIS METAL,DECHETS
281	IRON ORE,CONCENTRATES			W 4233539	90359	W 4888071	128772	W 4180036	113790	MINERAIS DE FER
2816	IRON ORE AGGLOMERATES			W 3408231	76522	W 4523565	111674	W 4129280	111443	MINERAIS AGGLOMERES
287	BASE METAL ORES,CONC NES			W 546745	44857	W 434239	63258	W 556615	93787	MINERAIS METAUX COMMUNS
2873	ALUMINIUM ORES,ALUMINA			W 198299	6557	W 242095	25403	W 354143	57499	MINERAIS D'ALUMINIUM
28732	ALUMINA(ALUMINIUM OXIDE)			W 7186	1526	W 103624	21466	W 222508	54036	ALUMINE (OXYDE ALUMINIUM)
2877	MANGANESE ORE,CONCENTRTE			W 195929	20298	W 80197	8118	W 120870	16084	MINERAIS DE MANGANESE
29	CRUDE ANIMAL,VEG MAT NES				22873		32143		33521	MATIERES BRUTES ANIM,VEGET
292	CRUDE VEG MATERIALS NES			W 13568	19730	W 8502	28087	W 7685	27259	MAT BRUTES VEGETALES NDA
3	MINERAL FUELS ETC		1364191		1280128		1045661		1277973	COMBUSTIBLES MINERAUX LUB
32	COAL,COKE AND BRIQUETTES				274113		310090		328143	HOUILLES,COKES,BRIQUETTES
322	COAL,LIGNITE AND PEAT			W 8604941	247300	W 8625242	289235	W 8524314	304081	HOUILLES,LIGNITES,TOURBE
3222	OTH COAL,NOT AGGLOMERATD			W 4956290	186758	W 4842520	221400	W 4994457	237749	AUTRES HOUILLES
3223	LIGNITE,NOT AGGLOMERATED			W 3460896	54013	W 3695506	64630	W 3355351	59256	LIGNITES
323	BRIQUETS,COKE,SEMI–COKE			W 519101	26813	W 256607	20855	W 274202	24062	BRIQUETTES
3232	COKE,SEMI–COKE,RTRT CRBN			W 265528	22253	W 200281	19380	W 237402	23065	COKES ET SEMI–COKES
33	PETROLEUM AND PRODUCTS				554577		703169		850051	PETROLE ET DERIVES
333	CRUDE PETROLEUM			W 4825407	498575	W 5301328	622603	W 5443068	762439	HUILES BRUTES DE PETROLE
334	PETROLEUM PRODUCTS,REFIN			W 262286	43907	W 368254	63525	W 354734	69159	PRODUITS RAFFINES
3341	GASOLINE,OTH LIGHT OILS			W 259937	37101					ESSENCES POUR MOTEURS
341	*GAS,NATURAL AND MANUFCT				441599	W 9013	2310	W 20318	3457	GAZ NATUREL,GAZ MANUFACT
3414	PETROLEUM GASES, GASEOUS			W 3688848	439699	W 1201	197		3	GAZ DE PETROLE GAZEUX
351	*ELECTRIC CURRENT				9839		30092		96321	ENERGIE ELECTRIQUE
5	CHEMCLS,RELATED PROD NES		730943		844268		1142235		1172280	PRODUITS CHIMIQUES
51	ORGANIC CHEMICALS				190702		261494		200372	PROD CHIMIQ ORGANIQUES
511	HYDROCARBONS NES,DERIVS			W 101473	32960	W 122198	54987	W 104133	40869	HYDROCARBURES NDA
5111	ACYCLIC HYDROCARBONS			W 42668	12669	W 55217	29559	W 53748	24554	HYDROCARBURES ACYCLIQUES
512	ALCOHOLS,PHENOLS ETC			W 147775	45944	W 57081	39342	W 35459	21204	PHENOLS,PHENOLS–ALCOOLS
5121	ACYCLIC ALCOHOLS,DERIVS			W 145158	41358	W 54027	33059	W 33328	17883	ALCOOLS ACYCLIQUES
513	CARBOXYLIC ACIDS ETC				38895	W 48016	61584	W 39571	39343	ACIDES CARBOXYLIQUES
5138	POLYACIDS AND DERIVATIVS				19068	W 26926	37105	W 21402	18695	ACIDES POLYCARBOXYLIQUES
514	NITROGEN–FNCTN COMPOUNDS				23595	W 26872	36724	W 37502	44177	COMPOSES FONCT AZOTEES
515	ORG–INORG COMPOUNDS ETC			W 29412	40697	W 29516	53936	W 18596	37543	COMPOSES ORGANO–MINERAUX
5156	HETEROCYCLIC CMPDS ETC			W 28853	37975	W 28484	49297	W 17211	31906	COMPOSES HETEROCYCLIQUES
51561	LACTAMS			W 27967	33594	W 27701	43051	W 16231	23670	LACTAMES .
52	INORGANIC CHEMICALS				76715		94992		98931	PROD CHIM INORGANIQUES
522	INORG ELEMNTS,OXIDES,ETC			W 214361	45312	W 235884	60747	W 239170	60035	ELEMENTS INORGANIQUES
523	OTHR INORG CHEMICALS ETC			W 111757	30656	W 105314	33039	W 126564	37548	AUT PRODUITS CHIMIQUES INORG
53	DYES,TANNING,COLOUR PROD				74405		89961		99207	PROD TEINTURE,COLORANTS
533	PIGMENTS,PAINTS,ETC			W 68336	60195	W 36105	75843	W 41217	82523	PIGMENTS,PEINTURES,VERNIS
5334	VARNISHES,DISTEMPERS ETC			W 48379	27370	W 15342	35016	W 15338	40846	PEINTURES A L'EAU
541	*MEDICINAL,PHARM PRODUCT			K 8284936	162028	MK 10396	266413	MK 10612	314325	PROD MEDICINAUX PHARMACEUT
5417	MEDICAMENTS			K 6050657	124807	K 7575683	209948	K 8318448	253478	MEDICAMENTS
54171	— CONTAINNG ANTIBIOTICS			K 385169	11881	K 576052	27539	K 609124	39254	MED CONTN ANTIBIOTIQUES
54172	— CONTAINING HORMONES			K 756212	17644	K 1245486	42206	K 1583689	58791	MED CONTENANT HORMONES
54179	— CONTNG OTH SUBSTANCES			K 4847488	94333	K 5702988	138787	K 6031773	150744	MED CONT AUT SUBSTANCES
55	PERFUME,CLEANING ETC PRD				84417		95639		104925	PROD POUR PARFUM,TOILETTE
553	PERFUMERY,COSMETICS,ETC			W 10955	39064	W 10759	44791	W 14459	55977	PRODUITS DE PARFUMERIE
554	SOAP,CLEANSING ETC PREPS				39476	W 46775	44223	W 45558	41341	SAVONS,PRODUITS DETERSIFS
5542	WASHING PREPARATIONS ETC			W 30104	31533	W 39341	34115	W 38096	31539	PROD ORG TENSIO–ACT NDA
562	*FERTILIZERS,MANUFACTURE			W 256445	24090	W 221849	24378	W 247791	35084	ENGRAIS MANUFACTURES
58	PLASTIC MATERIALS ETC				133425		193719		202304	MAT PLAST ARTIFICIELLES
582	PROD OF CONDENSATION ETC			W 21723	29382	W 19151	42086	W 20864	43540	PROD CONDENS,POLYCOND
583	POLYMERIZATION ETC PRODS			W 70210	99346	W 79089	146090	W 91204	153340	PROD POLYMERISATION
5834	POLYVINYL CHLORIDE			W 21969	25303	W 25759	40221	W 26672	37582	CHLORURE DE POLYVINYLE
5839	OTH POLYMRZTION ETC PROD			W 13147	32769	W 11984	41364	W 16785	48086	AUT PROD POLYMER COPOLYM
59	CHEMICAL MATERIALS NES				96691		112449		114006	MAT PROD CHIMIQUES NDA
591	PESTICIDES,DISINFECTANTS			W 6279	31083	W 7283	38964	W 8639	49573	DESINF,INSECT,FONG,HERB
598	MISCEL CHEM PRODUCTS NES				57862	W 51192	63664	W 34879	53145	PROD DIV INDUST CHIM NDA
5989	CHEM PRODUCTS,PREPS NES				46017	W 38456	51874	W 20339	38[illegible]11	PROD PREP CHIMIQUES NDA

4. General Imports F.O.B. by Commodities according to the S.I.T.C. (Rev. 2) in thousand U.S. Dollars
Importations Générales F.O.B. par Produits d'après la C.T.C.I. (Rév. 2) en milliers de Dollars E.U.

SITC CTCI	COMMODITY	1993		1994		1995		1996		PRODUIT
		WEIGHT POIDS	VALUE VALEUR	WEIGHT POIDS	VALUE VALEUR	WEIGHT POIDS	VALUE VALEUR	WEIGHT POIDS	VALUE VALEUR	
59899	OTH CHEM PRODS,PREPS,NES				26986	W 27170	33714	W 6668	15977	AUT PRODUITS CHIMIQUES NDA
6	BASIC MANUFACTURES		967226		1133441		1573526		1504671	ART MANUFACTURES
61	LEATHER,DRESSED FUR,ETC				25725		30780		48087	CUIRS,PELLETERIES
62	RUBBER MANUFACTURES NES				44576		59589		71807	CAOUTCHOUC MANUFACTURE
625	RUBBER TYRES, TUBES ETC			W 7929	18708	W 9121	27342	W 10794	33527	PNEUS CAOUTCHOUC VULCANISE
63	WOOD,CORK MANUFACTRS NES				31940		39819		35125	OUVRAGES LIEGE ET BOIS
64	PAPER,PAPERBOARD AND MFR				132937		196442		215077	PAPIERS,CARTONS & OUVRAGES
641	PAPER AND PAPERBOARD				88953	W 140199	134541	W 172497	148673	PAPIERS ET CARTONS
6412	PRINTG,WRITING PAPER NES			W 24147	22763	W 26503	33227	W 36147	37440	PAPIERS POUR L'IMPRESSION
64122	— COATED,IMPREGNATD ETC			W 23440	21676	W 24931	30143	W 34267	34593	PAPIERS IMPRESSION COUCHES
6415	PAPER,PAPERBRD,BULK,NES			W 36712	21255	W 42815	34878	W 61906	43979	PAPIERS,CARTONS ROULEAUX
64159	OTHER PAPER ETC,BULK,NES			W 32601	18965	W 40409	32238	W 51847	37959	AUT PAPIER ROULEAUX FEUILLES
6418	COATED ETC PAPER NES BLK			W 17053	19949	W 20254	31263	W 28035	36530	PAP,CARTONS COUCHES,ENDUITS
64189	COATED PAPER ETC NES			W 13394	14810	W 18875	27353	W 25564	31597	PAPIERS,CARTONS COUCHES
642	PAPER,ETC,PRECUT,ARTS OF			W 31596	43984	W 36060	61901	W 39348	66404	PAP,CARTONS DECOUPES
65	TEXTILE YARN,FABRICS,ETC				185523		215250		205397	FILS,TISSUS,ARTICLES TEXTILE
651	TEXTILE YARN			W 7861	30282	W 10997	39229	W 8635	32211	FILS TEXTILES
652	COTTON FABRICS,WOVEN				21299	W 3738	23672	W 3386	23059	TISSUS DE COTON
653	WOVN MAN–MADE FIB FABRIC				31626	W 3092	34397	W 3343	39287	TISSUS FIBRES SYNTH,ARTIF
657	SPECIAL TXTL FABRC,PRODS				54017	W 11334	67113	W 9044	55708	TISSUS SPECIAUX
6573	COATED ETC TEXTILES NES			W 7478	34929	W 7512	43640	W 6083	35386	TISSUS,ART MATIERE TEXT NDA
65733	RUBBERIZED TEXT NOT KNIT			W 5094	22050	W 4426	26242	W 2558	15899	TISSUS CAOUTCHOUTES
66	NONMETAL MINERAL MFS NES				105895		143437		169763	ART MIN NON METALLIQUES
662	CLAY,REFRACTORY BLDG PRD			W 78797	26045	W 67512	33157	W 98059	39630	MAT CONST REFRACTAIRES
663	MINERAL MANUFCTURES NES			W 87437	29592	W 106605	40967	W 134140	48974	ART MIN MANUF NDA
664	GLASS				22802	W 53997	33612	W 56558	39528	VERRE
67	IRON AND STEEL				300760		436276		308660	FER ET ACIER
671	PIG IRON ETC			W 59257	21702	W 43597	17181	W 41633	17833	FONTE,SPIEGEL,POUDRES
673	IRON,STEEL SHAPES ETC			W 247717	78424	W 371413	137774	W 196583	77944	BARRES,PROFIL FER,ACIER
6731	IRON,STEEL WIRE ROD			W 80150	23104	W 158599	51187	W 2309	880	FIL MACHINE FER,ACIER
67311	IRON,SIMPLE STL WIRE ROD			W 79729	22894	W 137981	41792	W 1850	565	FIL MACH AUT ACIER FIN
6732	IRON,STEEL BARS ETC			W 97833	33519	W 125732	55890	W 107358	46449	BARRES FER,ACIER
67326	IRN,OTH STL BARS HOTROLD			W 68781	18459	W 86015	28526	W 72617	20590	BARRES PLEINES FER,ACIER
6733	IRON,STEEL PROFILES ETC			W 69734	21801	W 87082	30698	W 86917	30614	PROFILES,PALPLAN FER,ACIER
674	IRN,STL UNIV,PLATE,SHEET			W 103907	51047	W 152971	85967	W 38371	35119	LARGES PLATS,TOLES
6744	IRN,STL HVY PLATE,ROLLED			W 59605	25899	W 99099	47965	W 12533	9923	TOLES LAMINEES PLUS 4.75 MM
67441	— OF IRON OR SIMPLE STL			W 58549	24182	W 97862	45305	W 10777	6053	TOLES NON ACIER FIN CARB
678	IRON,STL TUBES,PIPES,ETC				88806	W 146558	120955	W 144512	112402	TUBES,TUYAUX EN FONTE,FER
6782	IRON,STL SEAMLESS TUBES				23213	W 42282	31254	W 43722	33962	TUBES,TUYAUX SANS SOUDURE
6783	IRON,STL TUBES,PIPES NES			W 79408	53213	W 95443	73174	W 87998	55772	AUT TUBES,TUYAUX FER,ACIER
679	IRN,STL CASTINGS UNWORKD			W 18612	19963	W 23920	28347	W 29540	35977	OUVRAGES EN FONTE,FER,ACIER
68	NON–FERROUS METALS				127713		216066		168104	METAUX NON FERREUX
682	COPPER EXC CEMENT COPPER				35589	W 23647	74736	W 15922	45763	CUIVRE
6821	COPPER NES,ALLOYS,UNWRT			W 5351	10893	W 10523	28019	W 5820	13418	CUIVRE BRUT
68212	COPPER REFINED,UNWROUGHT			W 5330	10829	W 10059	27596	W 5784	13290	CUIVRE AFFINE BRUT
6822	COPPER,ALLOYS WORKED				24696	W 13124	46718	W 10102	32345	CUIVRE,ALLIAGES OUVRES
68221	COPPER BARS,WIRE,ETC			W 6939	17400	W 10842	34971	W 7639	20835	BARRES,PROFILES ET FILS
684	ALUMINIUM				58302	W 37138	92595	W 31642	82140	ALUMINIUM
6841	ALUMINIUM,ALLOYS,UNWRGHT			W 11983	16058	W 19658	32957	W 14876	22145	ALUMINIUM,ALLIAGES BRUTS
6842	ALUMINIUM,ALLOYS WORKED				42244	W 17480	59637	W 16766	59994	ALUMINIUM,ALLIAGES OUVRE
686	ZINC			W 24947	23056	W 26371	29401	W 25545	28204	ZINC
6861	ZINC,ALLOYS UNWROUGHT			W 24531	22474	W 26062	28935	W 25305	27731	ZINC ET ALLIAGES BRUTS
69	METAL MANUFACTURES NES				178371		235867		282651	ART MANUFACT EN METAL NDA
691	STRUCTURES AND PARTS NES			W 22422	23038	W 26433	27647	W 32693	39774	CONSTRUCT FER,ACIER,ALU
692	METAL TANKS,BOXES,ETC			W 14769	20574	W 13108	24445	W 14455	31516	RECIPIENTS METALLIQUES
695	TOOLS			W 2173	19113	W 2743	29915	W 3683	40310	OUTILS A MAIN
697	BASE MTL HOUSEHOLD EQUIP			W 5279	20207	W 5733	25866	W 7349	32878	ART MENAGE MET COMMUNS
699	BASE METAL MFRS NES			W 28964	72513	W 30956	90737	W 30990	91414	ART MANUFACTURES MET NDA
6991	LOCKSMITHS WARES,ETC			W 4189	24146	W 4503	29966	W 5082	35143	ARTICLES DE SERRURERIE
7	MACHINES,TRANSPORT EQUIP		1883731		1831818		2460343		3203313	MACHINES MATERIEL TRANSPORT
71	POWER GENERATING EQUIPMT				128334		100741		113038	MACHINES GENERATRICES
713	INTRNL COMBUS PSTN ENGIN			W 2859	20496	W 3401	28091	W 4043	35468	MOTEURS EXPL COMB INT, PIECE
716	ROTATING ELECTRIC PLANT			W 11624	37604	W 3076	19996	W 2870	25057	APP ELECTR ROTATIFS,PIECES
7169	PTS NES OF ROT ELEC PLNT			W 8434	22496	W 643	3839	W 319	4091	PIECES MAC APP ROTATIFS
718	OTH POWER GENERATG MACHY			W 2075	34124	W 1506	16495	W 1465	24589	AUTRES MOTEURS PARTIES
7187	NUCLEAR REACTORS,PTS NES			W 48	24526	W 157	7528	W 315	5851	REACTEURS NUCLEAIRES
72	MACHS FOR SPCL INDUSTRYS				274399		410044		509919	MAC SPECIALES POUR INDUST
721	AGRIC MACHY,EXC TRACTORS			W 9532	40974	W 13167	76154	W 12796	89643	MACHINES AGRICOLES
7212	HARVESTING ETC MACHINES			W 4723	17764	W 7381	43784	W 6829	47120	ENGINS POUR LA RECOLTE
723	CIVIL ENGNEERG EQUIP ETC				17693	W 5850	30394	W 7069	43059	APPAREILS DE GENIE CIVIL
7234	CONST,MINING MACHNRY NES				13210	W 5178	24858	W 5839	35271	MACH POUR LA CONST, MINES
724	TEXTILE,LEATHER MACHNRY				46082	W 3219	52568	W 3916	53516	MACH POUR INDUSTRIE TEXTILE
725	PAPER ETC MILL MACHINERY				16410	W 2762	29423	W 1987	38288	MACHINES FABR PATE PAPIER
726	PRINTG,BKBINDG MACHY,PTS			W 1286	24662	W 2382	53609	W 2208	46917	MACHINES POUR IMPRIMERIE
7264	PRINTING PRESSES			W 559	11157	W 1513	34846	W 1024	26187	MACHINES A IMPRIMER
72641	ROTARY PRINTING PRESSES			W 559	11157	W 1513	34846	W 1024	26187	MACH IMPRIMER ROTATIVES
727	FOOD MACHRY NON–DOMESTIC			W 2337	29182	W 2503	48103	W 3544	56353	MACH INDUSTRIES ALIMENT
7272	OTH FOOD PROC MCHY,PARTS			W 1738	26031	W 2296	46388	W 3322	54446	AUT MACH IND ALIMENTAIRE
72722	INDUS FOOD PROC MACH NES			W 1634	23220	W 2139	44975	W 3281	53808	MACHINES BOULANGERIE
728	OTH MACHY FOR SPCL INDUS			W 9495	93022	W 11561	109804	W 14322	162509	AUT MACH IND PARTICULIERES
7281	MACH–TOOLS FR SPCL INDUS			W 3560	24959	W 4316	35789	W 4345	39949	MACH–OUTILS SPEC IND PART
72812	MACH–TOOLS TO WORK WOOD			W 3070	20607	W 3853	31675	W 3319	30049	MACH–OUT POUR TRAVAIL BOIS
7284	MACHY FOR SPCL INDUS NES			W 3720	52818	W 3697	52730	W 6567	95632	MACH SPEC IND PARTICUL.
72842	RUBBER,PLASTICS WRKG MCH			W 1102	14859	W 1197	13617	W 2514	36971	MACH IND CAOUT MAT PLAST
73	METALWORKING MACHINERY				89326		113371		143180	MACH TRAVAIL DES METAUX
736	METALWORKING MACH–TOOLS			W 7771	67528	W 9713	68687	W 12309	92853	MACH–OUTILS TRAVAIL METAUX
7361	METAL CUTTING MACH–TOOLS			W 2681	41039	W 2229	22342	W 4750	36127	MACH–OUT ENLEVEMENT METAL
73619	OTH MTL CUTTNG MCH–TOOLS			W 815	22114	W 520	4922	W 1032	7226	MACH A AFFUTER ETC METAL
737	METALWORKING MACHNRY NES			W 5020	21798	W 9138	44684	W 7008	50326	MACH TRAV METAUX PIECES
74	GENRL INDUSTRL MACHY NES				332122		429958		547168	MACH APP INDUSTRIE
741	HEATING,COOLING EQUIPMNT				62303	W 8488	81587	W 11108	118494	MACH CHAUFFAGE,PIECES
742	PUMPS FOR LIQUIDS ETC			W 3197	30327	W 3034	39171	W 3779	47738	POMPES MOTO–POMPES
743	PUMPS NES,CENTRFUGES ETC			W 8108	70153	W 7457	78950	W 8917	87010	POMPES COMPRES,VENT ETC
7431	PUMPS FOR GASES ETC			W 3493	25370	W 2832	24277	W 2825	24186	POMPES AIR A VIDE,COMPRES
7436	GAS,LIQUID FILTERS ETC			W 2098	23970	W 2427	33388	W 3118	34589	APP POUR FILT DES LIQUIDES
744	MECHANICAL HANDLING EQU				50183	W 11148	58816	W 15649	68384	EQUIP MANUTENTION PIECES
7442	LIFTING,LOADING MACH NES			W 4559	23047	W 4048	21752	W 6144	28059	APP LEVAGE,MANUTENTION
745	NONELEC MACHY,TOOLS NES			W 2832	37671	W 3693	59588	W 5412	84024	AUT MACH NON ELEC,PIECES
7452	OTH NONELEC MCHS,PTS NES			W 2646	32705	W 3482	52070	W 5035	74962	AUT MACH NON ELEC,PIECES
74522	PACKAGNG,BOTTLNG,ETC MCH			W 675	14840	W 620	19637	W 1299	33295	MACH NETT BOUTEILLES,ETC
749	NONELEC MACH PTS,ACC NES			W 10510	81486	W 10959	111847	W 13971	141517	PIECES MACH NON ELEC NDA

4. General Imports F.O.B. by Commodities according to the S.I.T.C. (Rev. 2) in thousand U.S. Dollars
Importations Générales F.O.B. par Produits d'après la C.T.C.I. (Rév. 2) en milliers de Dollars E.U.

SITC CTCI	COMMODITY	1993 WEIGHT POIDS	1993 VALUE VALEUR	1994 WEIGHT POIDS	1994 VALUE VALEUR	1995 WEIGHT POIDS	1995 VALUE VALEUR	1996 WEIGHT POIDS	1996 VALUE VALEUR	PRODUIT
7492	COCKS,VALVES ETC NES			W 5443	42505	W 5360	62759	W 7252	84102	ART ROB,SIM POUR TUYAUX
75	OFFICE MACHNES,ADP EQUIP				203586		298221		106385	MACH BUREAU TRAIT AUTOM
751	OFFICE MACHINES			W 840	26659	W 1796	60943	W 1156	31910	MACH,APPAREILS DE BUREAU
7512	CALCULATNG,ACCTG,ETC MCH			W 197	7980	W 1149	42552	W 451	14800	MACHINE A CALCULER ETC
75123	CASH REGISTERS			W 121	4825	W 989	34839	W 154	5710	CAISSES ENREGISTREUSES
752	AUTOMTIC DATA PROC EQUIP			W 2250	146491	W 3206	198985	W 221	19512	MACH TRAIT INFORMATION
7522	DIGITAL COMPUTERS			W 490	48753	W 598	73382	W 19	1956	MACH DIGITALES COMPLETES
7525	ADP PERIPHERAL UNITS			W 1142	45117	W 1928	75043	W 46	2693	UNITES PERIPHERIQUES
759	OFFICE,ADP MCH PTS,ACCES			W 848	30436	W 1551	38293	W 1434	54962	PIECES DU 751 ET 752
7599	ACCTG,ETC,ADP MCH PTS,AC			W 644	23193	W 750	28870	W 1185	43709	PIECES DU 751 ET 752
76	TELECOMM,SOUND EQUIPMENT				135180		181844		208717	EQUIPMENT DE TELECOM
764	TELECOM EQPT,PTS,ACC NES				117703	W 2730	152065	W 2772	177481	EQUIP TELECOM,PIECES
7641	LINE TELEPHONE,ETC EQUIP			W 305	24766	W 427	30894	W 158	12460	APP TELEPHON PAR FIL
7643	TV,RADIO TRANSMITTRS ETC			W 158	22576	W 122	23485	W 175	31505	APP EMET TELE RADIO
7649	PTS NES OF EQUIPMT OF 76			W 1254	63773	W 1849	89029	W 1938	122834	PIECES DE LA DIV 76
76491	PTS NES OF APPAR OF 7641			W 781	52056	W 659	73629	W 841	99520	PIECES POUR 764.1
77	ELECTRIC MACHNRY NES ETC				324060		410049		431065	MACH APP ELECT NDA
771	ELECTRIC POWER MACHY NES				19828	W 3083	29599	W 4012	36145	MACH PROD,TRANS ELECTR
772	SWITCHGEAR ETC,PARTS NES				45502	W 3572	62568	W 4212	95759	APP COUPURE,SECT ETC
7721	SWITCHGEAR ETC				43052	W 3442	58559	W 4108	92157	APP COUPURE,SECTIONMNT
773	ELECTR DISTRIBUTNG EQUIP				42698	W 14545	52437	W 17838	62640	EQUIPMT DISTRIBUTION ELECT
7731	INSULATED WIRE,CABLE ETC			W 13705	38912	W 13321	47874	W 16370	57156	FILS,CABLES ISOLES ELECT
774	ELECTRO-MEDCL,XRAY EQUIP			W 381	63264	W 227	32368	W 242	32820	APPAREILS MEDICAUX
7742	X-RAY APPARATUS ETC			W 307	50055	W 128	17934	W 140	13902	APPAREILS A RAYONS X
775	HOUSEHOLD TYPE EQUIP NES			W 7220	38920	W 9234	55850	W 12465	75577	MACH,APP USAGE DOMESTQUE
776	TRANSISTORS,VALVES,ETC				44060	W 2861	79421	W 2260	31676	LAMPES,TUBES,VALVES
7764	ELECTRONIC MICROCIRCUITS				29124	W 279	55218	W 30	9708	MICROSTRUCTURES ELECTRON
778	ELECTRICAL MACHINERY NES				69788	W 17199	97806	W 12449	96448	AUTRES MACH ELECT NDA
7788	OTH ELEC MACHY,EQUIP NES				28349	W 6822	40854	W 3121	37882	AUT MACH APP ELEC NDA
78	ROAD VEHICLES				280822		459375		1077704	VEHICULES ROUTIERS
781	PASS MOTOR VEH EXC BUSES			W 21996	125720	W 28544	204233	W 94788	724184	AUTO TRANSPORT PERSONNES
782	LORRIES,SPCL MTR VEH NES			W 12481	41871	W 17084	68403	W 23299	108156	VEHICULES SPECIAUX,MARCH
7821	LORRIES,TRUCKS			W 8509	34108	W 12511	53809	W 18393	93786	VEHICULES TRANSP MARCHAND
783	ROAD MOTOR VEHICLES NES			W 4685	25141	W 7418	56155	W 8543	70082	VEHICULES ROUTIERS NDA
7832	TRACTORS FOR TR-TRAILERS			W 2202	12952	W 3050	30453	W 5686	53448	TRACTEURS ROUTIERS
784	MOTOR VEH PRTS,ACCES NES			W 13599	62787	W 17734	95765	W 22887	132381	PIECES 722,781,782,783
7849	OTHER MOTOR VEHCL PARTS			W 12300	58158	W 16500	89393	W 20874	119238	PIECES 722,781,782,783
79	OTHR TRANSPORT EQUIPMENT				63988		56739		66138	AUTRE MATERIEL TRANSPORT
791	RAILWAY VEHICLES			W 27351	34671	W 18213	33847	W 17008	44424	VEHIC MAT CHEMINS DE FER
7919	RY TRACK FIXT,ETC,PARTS			W 17631	30869	W 14274	26578	W 13486	32087	MATER FIXE VOIES FERREES
79199	PARTS NES OF 7911-7915			W 17027	30384	W 13645	25878	W 13062	31421	PIECES 791.1 ET 5
792	AIRCRAFT ETC			W 207	28615	W 158	22588	W 221	20685	APP NAVIGATION AERIENNE
7923	AIRCRFT NES2000-15000KG			W 33	23594	W 59	18208	W 33	493	AERODYNES 2000 A 15000 KG
8	MISC MANUFACTURED GOODS		579772		567080		708306		847337	ART MANUFACTURES DIVERS
812	*PLUMBG,HEATNG,LGHTNG EQ			W 15490	35099	W 15254	43003	W 17996	55441	APPAR SANITAIRES CHAUFFAGE
821	*FURNITURE,PARTS THEREOF			W 11890	36589	W 14952	45211	W 19870	68345	MEUBLES ET PIECES
8219	FURNITURE AND PARTS NES			W 8236	19819	W 10226	24916	W 14118	35592	AUTRES MEUBLES ET PIECES
84	CLOTHING AND ACCESSORIES				75998		86452		102347	VETEMENTS
851	*FOOTWEAR			W 4067	29832	W 5085	38635	W 6474	48896	CHAUSSURES
85102	FOOTWEAR LEATHER			W 2272	16685	W 3101	21755	W 4292	33300	CHAUS SEMELLES EN CUIR
87	PRECISION INSTRUMNTS NES				124278		157297		185512	INSTRUM,APPAR SCIENT NDA
872	MEDICAL INSTRUMENTS NES				26348	W 914	36896	W 1191	44020	INSTR,APP MEDIC-CHIR NDA
87202	OTH MEDICAL INSTRUMENTS				23424	W 689	29705	W 917	36806	INSTRUM,APP MEDECINE
874	MEASURNG,CONTROLNG INSTR				84982	W 3293	108202	W 3321	127497	INSTRUMENTS DE MESURE
8743	GAS,LIQUID CONTROL INSTR			W 2680	27546	W 909	32082	W 898	34759	APP,INSTR MESURE FLUIDES
8748	ELEC MEAS,CONTRL EQU NES				22584	W 290	27179	W 352	30562	APP ELEC ELECTRO MESURE
88	PHOTO EQU,OPTICL GDS ETC				34599		42676		47369	APP,FOURN PHOTO,OP,MONTR
89	MISC MANUFCTRD GOODS NES				224181		285647		327151	ART MANUFACTURES DIVERS
892	PRINTED MATTER				43081	W 8346	50827	W 9200	67818	IMPRIMES
893	ARTICLES OF PLASTIC NES				79592		104065		133257	OUVRAGES EN MAT DIVIS 58
8931	PLSTC PACKG CONTNRS,LIDS			W 9585	23099	W 11392	32632	W 16164	44617	ART TRANSP EMBALLAGE ETC
8939	MISC PLASTIC ARTICLES			W 17043	54490	W 15652	67648	W 19425	83669	ART DIVERS EN MAT DIV 58
89399	OTHR PLASTC ARTICLES NES			W 14229	49514	W 12776	61103	W 16070	75506	AUT OUV MAT DIV 58
894	TOYS,SPORTING GOODS,ETC				30669	W 4748	34011	W 6239	41478	VOITURES ENFANTS,JOUETS
8942	TOYS,INDOOR GAMES ETC			W 3363	21622	W 3231	22477	W 4030	25074	JOUETS,JEUX ETC
898	MUSICAL INSTRUMENTS,PTS				23623	W 1098	35472	W 923	12463	INSTRUMENTS DE MUSIQUE
8983	SOUND RECRDNG TAPE,DISCS				21843	W 1008	33519	W 808	9952	SUPPORTS SON POUR 763
899	OTHER MANUFACTURED GOODS				26407		35929		43472	AUT ART MANUF DIVERS NDA
9	GOODS NOT CLASSD BY KIND		11047		43779		624218		1656750	ART TRANSACT NON CLASSES
931	*SPECIAL TRANSACTIONS						608511		1526296	TRANS.SPECIALES
951	*WAR FIREARMS,AMMUNITION			W 765	40401	W 2198	7237	W 2382	118229	VEHIC BLINDES ARMES
95106	AMMUNITION NES			W 514	33700	W 124	779	W 1064	108876	PROJECTILES,MUNITIONS

5. General Exports F.O.B. by Commodities according to the S.I.T.C. (Rev. 2) in thousand U.S. Dollars
Exportations Générales F.O.B. par Produits d'après la C.T.C.I. (Rév. 2) en milliers de Dollars E.U.

SITC CTCI	COMMODITY	1993 WEIGHT POIDS	1993 VALUE VALEUR	1994 WEIGHT POIDS	1994 VALUE VALEUR	1995 WEIGHT POIDS	1995 VALUE VALEUR	1996 WEIGHT POIDS	1996 VALUE VALEUR	PRODUIT
	ALL COMMODITIES		5392494		6690245		8577499		8824094	TOUS PRODUITS
0	FOOD AND LIVE ANIMALS		296304		301317		421448		304534	ALIMENTS,ANIMAUX VIVANTS
001	*LIVE ANIMALS FOR FOOD			W 19812	27812	W 10404	19520	W 7689	13326	ANIMAUX VIVANTS
0011	BOVINE SPECIES,LIVE			W 17515	21742	W 8511	14456	W 6190	9228	ESPECE BOVINE
00119	— OTHR THAN FR BREEDING			W 16427	20297	W 6399	10738	W 5584	8253	BOVINS NON REPRODUCTEURS
02	DAIRY PRODCTS,BIRDS'EGGS				35807		45173		45974	PRODUITS LAITIERS,OEUFS
024	CHEESE AND CURD			W 9355	20592	W 9562	22570	W 10953	26223	FROMAGE ET CAILLEBOTTE
04	CEREALS AND PREPARATIONS				61963		177513		71895	CEREALES ET PRODUITS
041	WHEAT ETC UNMILLED			W 27792	3049	W 621868	77898	W 11205	1896	FROMENT,EPEAUTRE
0412	OTHER WHEAT ETC UNMILLED			W 19918	2073	W 539383	67805	W 10233	1758	AUTRE FROMENT NON MOULU
048	CEREAL ETC PREPARATIONS			W 76082	35472	W 171339	60673	W 113357	54712	PREPTNS A BASE CEREALES
0482	MALT INCLUDING FLOUR			W 55610	12049	W 149757	37478	W 80389	25424	MALT MEME TORREFIE
05	VEGETABLES AND FRUIT				76866		65065		59307	LEGUMES ET FRUITS
054	VEG ETC FRSH,SMPLY PRSVD			W 163056	50542	W 134714	43766	W 100512	37710	LEGUMES FRAIS,CONG,SECS
0545	OTHER FRESH VEGETABLES			W 63303	25253	W 53768	19169	W 40461	17372	AUTRES LEGUMES FRAIS,REF
05459	FRESH VEGETABLES NES			W 59757	23700	W 48204	17228	W 37734	16036	LEGUMES FRAIS,REFRI NDA
07	COFFEE,TEA,COCOA,SPICES				35062		43688		33838	CAFE,THE,CACAO,EPICES
073	CHOCOLATE AND PRODUCTS			W 10756	27735	W 10089	34931	W 11576	28635	CHOCOLAT
09	MISC EDIBLE PRODUCTS				12326		19219		32574	PREP ALIMENTAIRES DIVERSES
1	BEVERAGES AND TOBACCO		47583		62755		74034		58765	BOISSONS ET TABACS
11	BEVERAGES				35801		40226		35561	BOISSONS
112	ALCOHOLIC BEVERAGES			W 63031	32807	W 66888	36477	W 75745	31946	BOISSONS ALCOOLIQUES
12	TOBACCO AND MANUFACTURES				26954		33809		23203	TABACS BRUTS FABRIQUES
122	TOBACCO,MANUFACTURED				26700	W 4680	33809	W 3520	23203	TABACS FABRIQUES
1222	CIGARETTES				25154	W 4144	31262	W 2823	20896	CIGARETTES
2	CRUDE MATERLS,EXCL FUELS		265278		341551		409263		363358	MAT BRUTES NON COMESTIBLES
24	CORK AND WOOD				153442		190312		175104	LIEGE ET BOIS
247	OTH WOOD ROUGH,SQUARED			W 536833	35359	W 456669	32915	W 528887	34865	BOIS BRUTS EQUARRIS
2471	SAW–,VENEER–LOGS CONIFER			W 242489	20093	W 218894	18026	W 301244	22848	CONIFERES POUR SCIAGE,PLACAG
24711	— IN THE ROUGH			W 242489	20093	W 218894	18026	W 301244	22848	ECORCES OU DEGROSSIS
248	WOOD SHAPED,SLEEPERS			W 522622	115343	W 586095	153464	W 620247	135466	BOIS SIMPLEMENT TRAVAILLES
2482	LUMBER SHAPED CONIFER			W 364589	80702	W 382950	98150	W 445504	83922	CONIFERES SCIES,RABOTES
24821	LUMBER SAWN ETC CONIFER			W 361534	78741	W 380457	96020	W 441200	81179	CONIFERES SCIES LONGITUD
2483	LUMBER SHAPED NON–CONIFR			W 151132	33288	W 192805	52400	W 170650	50308	NON CONIFERES SCIES,RABOTES
24831	LUMBER SAWN ETC NON–CON			W 131827	26216	W 165083	40759	W 139421	36180	SCIES LONGITUDINALEMENT
251	*PULP AND WASTE PAPER			W 94181	40083	W 88322	65985	W 86821	37884	PATES A PAPIER,DECHETS
2517	SODA,SULPHATE WOOD PULP			W 74316	31218	W 68378	52343	W 66373	26866	PATES CHIMIQUES AU SULFATE
25172	— BLEACHED,NONDISSOLVNG			W 69915	30302	W 68016	52247	W 66075	26742	PATES BLANCHIES
27	CRUDE FERTLZR,MINRLS NES				47327		57644		60856	ENGRAIS MINERAUX BRUTS
278	OTHER CRUDE MINERALS			W 759352	39172	W 819037	49010	W 932393	52911	AUTRES MINERAUX BRUTS
2782	REFRACTORY MINERALS NES			W 588221	30624	W 682689	39917	W 797529	43029	ARGILE MINERAUX REFRACTAIRES
27824	MAGNESITE, ETC			W 162533	25106	W 259712	34926	W 249117	37226	CARBONATE DE MAGNESIUM
28	METALLIFEROUS ORES,SCRAP				44840		37874		28801	MINERAIS METAL,DECHETS
282	IRON AND STEEL SCRAP			W 2578321	22161	W 197836	20602	W 212688	18744	FERRAILLES
3	MINERAL FUELS ETC		265374		314312		358892		416752	COMBUSTIBLES MINERAUX LUB
33	PETROLEUM AND PRODUCTS				302835		345385		397857	PETROLE ET DERIVES
334	PETROLEUM PRODUCTS,REFIN			W 1845089	282947	W 1952382	329825	W 1983063	383258	PRODUITS RAFFINES
3341	GASOLINE,OTH LIGHT OILS			W 1841148	279015					ESSENCES POUR MOTEURS
5	CHEMCLS,RELATED PROD NES		648003		828006		1018603		935150	PRODUITS CHIMIQUES
51	ORGANIC CHEMICALS				168081		164272		142825	PROD CHIMIQ ORGANIQUES
511	HYDROCARBONS NES,DERIVS			W 247681	60286	W 134108	38743	W 98327	26643	HYDROCARBURES NDA
5112	CYCLIC HYDROCARBONS			W 156982	36921	W 57778	17086	W 54928	12918	HYDROCARBURES CYCLIQUES
512	ALCOHOLS,PHENOLS ETC			W 179055	40272	W 63010	42919	W 61488	33266	PHENOLS,PHENOLS–ALCOOLS
5121	ACYCLIC ALCOHOLS,DERIVS			W 121004	25106	W 31245	21704	W 26496	14208	ALCOOLS ACYCLIQUES
516	OTHER ORGANIC CHEMICALS			W 86233	44674	W 94110	70861	W 101054	60592	AUTRES PROD ORGANIQUES
5162	ALDEHYDE ETC FNCT CMPNDS			W 81766	41844	W 93953	69216	W 100872	58341	COMP FONCTION ALDEHYDE
51629	OTHER KETONES ETC,DERIVS			W 53809	33077	W 64982	54082	W 67664	48458	AUTRES CETONES
52	INORGANIC CHEMICALS				65131		55756		65022	PROD CHIM INORGANIQUES
522	INORG ELEMNTS,OXIDES,ETC			W 205950	45122	W 179532	37965	W 170206	39456	ELEMENTS INORGANIQUES
5221	CHEMICAL ELEMENTS			W 63725	21271	W 36615	7528	W 50034	12807	ELEMENTS CHIMIQUES
53	DYES,TANNING,COLOUR PROD				23957		29744		25667	PROD TEINTURE,COLORANTS
533	PIGMENTS,PAINTS,ETC			W 18521	22497	W 19612	28140	W 16097	23907	PIGMENTS,PEINTURES,VERNIS
5334	VARNISHES,DISTEMPERS ETC			W 16658	20830	W 17254	26012	W 14087	21874	PEINTURES A L'EAU
541	*MEDICINAL,PHARM PRODUCT				120242	K 6670109	138010	K 7280343	131487	PROD MEDICINAUX PHARMACEUT
5413	ANTIBIOTICS IN BULK			K 1971292	21216	K 604214	17804	K 541145	16117	ANTIBIOTIQUES NDA
5417	MEDICAMENTS				80736	K 5590985	107069	K 6287885	103940	MEDICAMENTS
54179	— CONTNG OTH SUBSTANCES			K 4228188	57249	K 4554133	72828	K 5174316	70316	MED CONT AUT SUBSTANCES
55	PERFUME,CLEANING ETC PRD				39197		44382		51047	PROD POUR PARFUM,TOILETTE
554	SOAP,CLEANSING ETC PREPS			W 28788	24906	W 32078	31980	W 78632	39898	SAVONS,PRODUITS DETERSIFS
5542	WASHING PREPARATIONS ETC			W 25794	21660	W 27264	27650	W 38327	34323	PROD ORG TENSIO–ACT NDA
562	*FERTILIZERS,MANUFACTURE			W 811189	77211	W 852177	103023	W 938783	112193	ENGRAIS MANUFACTURES
5621	CHEM NITROGENOUS FERTLZR			W 658956	54947	W 665364	72979	W 756543	83817	ENGRAIS AZOTES
56219	CHEM NITROG FERTILZR NES			W 495804	41776	W 511682	58757	W 573472	65609	ENGRAIS AZOTES NDA
5629	FERTILIZERS NES			W 146241	21601	W 186813	30043	W 182240	28376	ENGRAIS NDA
58	PLASTIC MATERIALS ETC				254908		363611		331426	MAT PLAST ARTIFICIELLES
582	PROD OF CONDENSATION ETC			W 44797	25922	W 63300	39808	W 99487	36969	PROD CONDENS,POLYCOND
583	POLYMERIZATION ETC PRODS				211514	W 314320	305026	W 277346	272689	PROD POLYMERISATION
5831	POLYETHYLENE			W 194514	103770	W 189058	142037	W 154430	131349	POLYETHYLENE
58311	— IN PRIMARY FORMS			W 179340	87493	W 172457	118583	W 134923	104563	POLYETHYLENE PRIMAIRES
5832	POLYPROPYLENE			W 44923	42886	W 50387	66342	W 54577	71663	POLYPROPYLENE
58321	— IN PRIMARY FORMS			W 37496	22819	W 42552	35193	W 45470	31176	POLYPROPYLENE PRIMAIRES
58322	— PLATES,FILM,STRIP,ETC			W 7427	20067	W 7835	31149	W 9108	40487	POLYPROPYLENE PLAQUES
5834	POLYVINYL CHLORIDE			W 45531	36161	W 54632	53840	W 55487	40955	CHLORURE DE POLYVINYLE
58341	— IN PRIMARY FORMS			W 42813	31517	W 51282	48005	W 53661	37071	SOUS FORMES PRIMAIRES
59	CHEMICAL MATERIALS NES				75284		114717		71390	MAT PROD CHIMIQUES NDA
598	MISCEL CHEM PRODUCTS NES			W 39155	53327	W 50962	89078	W 33075	51747	PROD DIV INDUST CHIM NDA
5989	CHEM PRODUCTS,PREPS NES			W 31782	41544	W 44556	70555	W 17842	31463	PROD PREP CHIMIQUES NDA
59899	OTH CHEM PRODS,PREPS,NES			W 26323	35426	W 38081	63282	W 12235	25040	AUT PRODUITS CHIMIQUES NDA
6	BASIC MANUFACTURES		2089783		2668503		3461864		2364846	ART MANUFACTURES
61	LEATHER,DRESSED FUR,ETC				37274		37899		38772	CUIRS,PELLETERIES
62	RUBBER MANUFACTURES NES				186467		264095		207417	CAOUTCHOUC MANUFACTURE
621	MATERIALS OF RUBBER			W 14012	22489	W 14080	30258	W 20855	31656	PRODUITS EN CAOUTCHOUC
62104	UNHARD VULC RUBBER,BASIC			W 11772	17818	W 11732	24414	W 19205	27044	PLAQUES,FEUILLES CAOUT
625	RUBBER TYRES, TUBES ETC			W 91656	119383	W 65189	170192	W 102310	165235	PNEUS CAOUTCHOUC VULCANISE
6251	TYRES NEW FOR MOTOR CARS			W 63005	56002	W 20591	56625	W 21873	62853	PNEUS POUR VOITURES
6252	TYRES,NEW,BUS OR LORRY			W 22572	54455	W 39554	102480	W 36063	92298	PNEUS POUR AUTOBUS,CAMIONS
628	RUBBER ARTICLES NES				44595	W 22389	63645	W 4792	10526	OUVRAGES CAOUTCHOUC NDA
6282	VULCANIZD RUBBER BELTING			W 13264	35647	W 16083	52808			COURROIES EN CAOUTCHOUC
63	WOOD,CORK MANUFACTRS NES				88668		109405		89326	OUVRAGES LIEGE ET BOIS
634	VENEERS,PLYWOOD,ETC				35685	W 64288	39672	W 17337	17848	PLACAGES,CONTRE–PLAQUES
6342	PLYWOOD OF WOOD SHEETS				22851	W 21855	25108	W 13549	15227	BOIS CONTRE–PLAQUES

5. General Exports F.O.B. by Commodities according to the S.I.T.C. (Rev. 2) in thousand U.S. Dollars
Exportations Générales F.O.B. par Produits d'après la C.T.C.I. (Rév. 2) en milliers de Dollars E.U.

SITC CTCI	COMMODITY	1993 WEIGHT POIDS	1993 VALUE VALEUR	1994 WEIGHT POIDS	1994 VALUE VALEUR	1995 WEIGHT POIDS	1995 VALUE VALEUR	1996 WEIGHT POIDS	1996 VALUE VALEUR	PRODUIT
635	WOOD MANUFACTURES NES			W 56461	52795	W 84957	69706	W 91278	71424	ART MANUF EN BOIS NDA
6353	BUILDERS WOODWRK,PREFABS			W 22305	37980	W 40642	52509	W 40674	53513	OUVRAGES DE MENUISERIE
64	PAPER,PAPERBOARD AND MFR				233044		339110		371169	PAPIERS,CARTONS & OUVRAGES
641	PAPER AND PAPERBOARD				170050	W 279357	244525	W 334598	247355	PAPIERS ET CARTONS
6412	PRINTG,WRITING PAPER NES			W 1574	1712	W 2475	3094	W 40887	31878	PAPIERS POUR L'IMPRESSION
64121	— UNCOATED			W 217	487	W 304	599	W 38691	29516	PAPIERS IMPRES NON COUCHES
6415	PAPER,PAPERBRD,BULK,NES			W 162455	90127	W 189051	153134	W 198435	112444	PAPIERS,CARTONS ROULEAUX
64151	SEMI-CHEM FLUTING PAPER			W 29362	9343	W 56148	27593	W 68334	29520	PAPIER FLUTING
64159	OTHER PAPER ETC,BULK,NES			W 131650	79454	W 131103	122935	W 128759	80697	AUT PAPIER ROULEAUX FEUILLES
6417	CORRUGATED PAPER ETC,BLK			W 23635	16909	W 27985	30460	W 41977	39636	PAPIERS,CARTONS ONDULES
64172	CREPED HSHOLD PAPER ETC			W 22892	16491	W 25659	28926	W 37561	36997	PAPIER NON KRAFT CREPE
6418	COATED ETC PAPER NES BLK			W 106075	46422	W 22139	35343	W 20859	42252	PAP,CARTONS COUCHES,ENDUITS
64181	PLASTIC COATED PAPER ETC			W 7003	19615	W 9223	29412	W 11867	38018	PAP,CARTONS ENDUITS,RESINES
64182	TARRED ETC PAPER,PAPERBD			W 97793	26034	W 11986	4167	W 7808	2797	PAPIERS,CARTONS GOUDRONNES
642	PAPER,ETC,PRECUT,ARTS OF				62994	W 70224	94585	W 86504	123815	PAP,CARTONS DECOUPES
6421	PAPER ETC CONTAINERS			W 24334	22098	W 30576	34303	W 29112	32359	BOITES,SACS EMBALLAGES
6424	PAPER ETC CT TO SIZE NES			W 28339	19862	W 25447	26061	W 36182	38382	PAP,CARTONS DECOUPES
64243	TOILET PAPER CUT TO SIZE			W 28081	19577	W 25181	25560	W 36030	37965	PAPIER HYGIENIQUE
6428	PAPER ETC ARTICLES NES			W 10516	16743	W 11212	27153	W 17835	46899	OUVRAGES EN PATE A PAPIER
64285	PAPER ETC DIAPERS ETC			W 3924	8165	W 3630	14768	W 7032	29308	SERVIETTES HYGIENIQUES
65	TEXTILE YARN,FABRICS,ETC				327645		370707		294832	FILS,TISSUS,ARTICLES TEXTILE
651	TEXTILE YARN				217133	W 86757	264663	W 62818	209126	FILS TEXTILES
6514	SYN FIB YRN,BULK,MONOFIL				161585	W 56824	186065	W 54879	174292	FILS CONT 85% FIB TEXT SYNTH
65141	— TEXTRD,CONT POLYAMIDE			W 8889	27716	W 4960	20513	W 5552	22457	FILS TEXT FIB CONT POLYAMID
65142	— NONTXT ETC CONT PAMID			W 31366	83571	W 33742	112703	W 33871	107171	FILS NON TEX FI CON POLYAMID
65144	— TEXTRD,CONT POLYESTER			W 14727	34368	W 11266	34190	W 9236	26324	FILS TEX FI CONT POLYESTERS
6517	REGEN FIBRE YARN,MONOFIL			W 6422	25556	W 7011	34396	W 5682	27368	FILS TEXT ART NON VENTE DT
65171	CONT VISCOSE RAYON YARN			W 5697	23864	W 6364	32887	W 5045	26422	FILS RAY,VIS NON VENTE DET
6519	TEXTILE FIBRE YARN NES			W 16053	21230	W 21307	36216	W 112	362	FILS TEXT NDA FILE FIB VER
65195	YARN ETC OF GLASS FIBRE			W 15575	19224	W 21120	35521			FILS DE FIBRES DE VERRE
652	COTTON FABRICS,WOVEN				21325	W 4519	18299	W 2976	17248	TISSUS DE COTON
653	WOVN MAN-MADE FIB FABRIC				18313	W 2552	25798	W 2588	29009	TISSUS FIBRES SYNTH,ARTIF
654	OTH WOVEN TEXTILE FABRIC			W 5538	26665	W 5291	25977	W 1394	8926	TISSUS AUT COTON SYNT,ARTIF
658	TEXTILE ARTICLES NES			W 4125	23262	W 3894	19526	W 3244	20667	ART FACONNES MAT TEXTILES
66	NONMETAL MINERAL MFS NES				272057		362482		314385	ART MIN NON METALLIQUES
661	LIME,CEMENT,BLDG PRODS			W 1722116	84442	W 1975128	131652	W 1784344	107407	CHAUX,CIMENTS MAT CONSTR
6612	CEMENT			W 1603145	76253	W 1760692	97400	W 1450918	76451	CIMENTS HYDRAULIQUES
6618	MNRL BLDG PRD UNFIRD NES			W 17722	3465	W 110942	29199	W 202257	25300	MAT CONST AMIANTE-CIMENT
662	CLAY,REFRACTORY BLDG PRD			W 215344	64088	W 249124	82835	W 288369	77523	MAT CONST REFRACTAIRES
6623	REFRACTORY BUILDING PROD			W 132065	43383	W 150519	58042	W 144059	54340	BRIQUES REFRACTAIRES
66232	REFRACTRY BRICKS ETC NES			W 126341	42097	W 141300	55686	W 130519	52021	BRIQUES ETC REFRACTAIRES
6624	BRICKS ETC NONREFRACTORY			W 83279	20705	W 98605	24793	W 144310	23183	BRIQUES ETC CERAM NON REFR
663	MINERAL MANUFCTURES NES				33556	W 368889	40123	W 296284	40480	ART MIN MANUF NDA
6633	MINRL MFS NES NONCERAMIC			W 315320	25371	W 341916	27251	W 268000	26916	OUVR MAT MINERALE NDA
66332	CEMENT,ARTFCL STONE PROD			W 314450	24003	W 337631	24329	W 263260	23316	OUVRAGES EN CIMENT
664	GLASS			W 18426	25311	W 20072	33715	W 19141	36134	VERRE
6649	GLASS NES			W 12536	19934	W 11969	22962	W 13151	26604	VERRE NDA
665	GLASSWARE			W 75543	56301	W 93199	72484	W 25186	50946	OUVRAGES EN VERRE
6651	BOTTLES ETC OF GLASS			W 64631	19355	W 82720	29649	W 13810	2873	RECIPIENTS EN VERRE
66511	GLASS BOTTLES ETC NONVAC			W 64110	17363	W 81805	25920	W 567	186	BONBONNES,BOUTEILLES,ETC
6652	HOUSEHLD,HOTEL ETC GLASS			W 10134	34953	W 9584	39216	W 10712	44370	OBJETS VERRE TABLE,CUISINE
67	IRON AND STEEL				1156438		1474320		454241	FER ET ACIER
671	PIG IRON ETC			W 175327	93446	W 139185	98916	W 113176	86102	FONTE,SPIEGEL,POUDRES
6716	FERRO-ALLOYS			W 168940	93050	W 139061	98859	W 113171	86098	FERRO-ALLIAGES
67162	FERRO-SILICON			W 48653	27045	W 35679	23657	W 66475	49778	FERRO-SILICIUM
67169	OTHER FERRO-ALLOYS			W 88144	50603	W 79570	61867	W 23164	23725	AUTRES FERRO-ALLIAGES
672	IRON,STEEL PRIMARY FORMS			W 1149600	291962	W 1079000	326784	W 130862	31116	LINGOTS FER,ACIER
6725	IRN,STL BLOOMS,SLABS,ETC			W 258161	54929	W 339666	86769	W 127427	30010	BLOOMS,BILLETTES FER ACIER
67251	IRN,SMPLE STL BLOOMS,ETC			W 258083	54815	W 339536	86667	W 127333	29953	BLOOMS ETC NON ACIER FIN
6727	IRN,STL COIL FR REROLLNG			W 886261	236511	W 739334	240014	W 3435	1106	EBAUCHES POUR TOLES FER
67271	IRON,SIMPLE STEEL COILS			W 881137	234933	W 736428	238968	W 3423	1096	EBAUCHES NON EN ACIER
674	IRN,STL UNIV,PLATE,SHEET			W 1840400	648083	W 2131471	875416	W 397537	212312	LARGES PLATS,TOLES
6744	IRN,STL HVY PLATE,ROLLED			W 404165	110957	W 332573	115145	W 17643	5621	TOLES LAMINEES PLUS 4.75 MM
67441	— OF IRON OR SIMPLE STL			W 402073	110319	W 332467	115038	W 17614	5580	TOLES NON ACIER FIN CARB
6745	IRN,STL MED PLATE,ROLLED			W 482433	147544	W 610302	209311	W 94651	30043	TOLES 3 A 4.75 MM
67451	— OF IRON OR SIMPLE STL			W 479226	146216	W 590313	198073	W 94647	30032	TOLES AUT NON ACIER FIN
6746	IRN,STL THIN PLATE,ROLLD			W 595269	225118	W 807445	337428	W 1890	839	TOLES LAM MOINS 3MM
67461	— OF IRON OR SIMPLE STL			W 592506	224012	W 806012	336653	W 1707	731	TOL NON AC FIN MOINS 3 MM
6747	TINNED PLATES,SHEETS			W 90509	55105	W 96530	71331	W 80000	60980	TOLES ETAMEES EN ACIER
6749	OTH IRN,STL PLATES,SHEET			W 268023	109360	W 284622	142200	W 203354	114829	AUTRES TOLES FER,ACIER
67491	— OF IRON OR SIMPLE STL			W 267875	109272	W 283964	141771	W 203353	114828	AUT TOLES AUTRES ACIER FIN
678	IRON,STL TUBES,PIPES,ETC			W 132208	70984	W 154165	100046	W 129174	89873	TUBES,TUYAUX EN FONTE,FER
6782	IRN,STL SEAMLESS TUBES			W 78682	40129	W 96552	61508	W 106438	67276	TUBES,TUYAUX SANS SOUDURE
679	IRN,STL CASTINGS UNWORKD			W 24873	17173	W 31946	27355	W 30297	29009	OUVRAGES EN FONTE,FER,ACIER
68	NON-FERROUS METALS				143268		207656		302756	METAUX NON FERREUX
682	COPPER EXC CEMENT COPPER				77172	W 104156	82709	W 29458	64790	CUIVRE
6821	COPPER NES,ALLOYS,UNWRT			W 9196	20935	W 6043	16857	W 2182	4748	CUIVRE BRUT
68212	COPPER REFINED,UNWROUGHT			W 9065	20771	W 5909	16446	W 2182	4747	CUIVRE AFFINE BRUT
6822	COPPER,ALLOYS WORKED				56238	W 98113	65852	W 27276	60042	CUIVRE,ALLIAGES OUVRES
68221	COPPER BARS,WIRE,ETC				48420	W 96266	57519	W 25598	53232	BARRES,PROFILES ET FILS
684	ALUMINIUM				61984	W 56645	114318	W 136443	233939	ALUMINIUM
6841	ALUMINIUM,ALLOYS,UNWRGHT			W 22853	32311	W 40613	76546	W 128598	214575	ALUMINIUM,ALLIAGES BRUTS
6842	ALUMINIUM,ALLOYS WORKED				29672	W 16032	37772	W 7845	19364	ALUMINIUM,ALLIAGES OUVRE
68421	ALUMINIUM BARS,WIRE,ETC			W 15169	26922	W 13941	34145	W 6394	15848	BARRES,PROFILES FILS ALU
69	METAL MANUFACTURES NES				223643		296190		291949	ART MANUFACT EN METAL NDA
691	STRUCTURES AND PARTS NES			W 50406	54856	W 60857	69888	W 58631	71086	CONSTRUCT FER,ACIER,ALU
6911	STRUCTURES,PARTS IRN,STL			W 48657	46994	W 59755	63799	W 57508	63829	CONSTRUCT FER,ACIER,FONTE
692	METAL TANKS,BOXES,ETC			W 30352	35026	W 34866	43798	W 30527	39557	RECIPIENTS METALLIQUES
6921	METAL STORAGE TANKS ETC			W 20962	21318	W 23191	25763	W 18481	20672	CUVES EN FONTE,FER,ALU
69211	STEEL STORAGE TANKS ETC			W 20936	21199	W 23182	25706	W 18474	20652	CUVES EN FONTE FER OU ACIER
693	WIRE PRODUCTS NON ELECTR			W 68326	34768	W 46855	44243	W 38686	39773	OUVRAGES FILS METALLIQUES
699	BASE METAL MFRS NES				60201	W 50724	89120	W 55422	85821	ART MANUFACTURES MET NDA
6997	IRON,STEEL ARTICLES NES				33513	W 40133	50305	W 45276	58103	OUV FONTE,FER,ACIER NDA
69979	IRN,STL MANUFACTURES NES				33381	W 39949	50056	W 45248	58045	AUT OUVRAGES EN FER NDA
7	MACHINES,TRANSPORT EQUIP		1046837		1274108		1587171		1992494	MACHINES MATERIEL TRANSPORT
71	POWER GENERATING EQUIPMT				121894		147478		168799	MACHINES GENERATRICES
713	INTRNL COMBUS PSTN ENGIN			W 3454	24181	W 3933	34461	W 4391	38355	MOTEURS EXPL COMB INT, PIECE
714	ENGINES AND MOTORS NES			W 807	24078	W 1038	7885	W 986	7389	MOTEURS NON ELECTRIQUES
716	ROTATING ELECTRIC PLANT			W 16597	52991	W 19412	81685	W 19584	85041	APP ELECTR ROTATIFS,PIECES
7162	AC MTRS,GENRTRS,GEN SETS			W 14746	45719	W 17080	73173	W 15907	75247	MOTEURS ELECTRIQUES
71621	AC MTRS,INC UNIVRSL MTRS			W 14620	45123	W 16997	72802	W 15800	74729	MOT ELEC NON CCUR CONTINU

5. General Exports F.O.B. by Commodities according to the S.I.T.C. (Rev. 2) in thousand U.S. Dollars
Exportations Générales F.O.B. par Produits d'après la C.T.C.I. (Rév. 2) en milliers de Dollars E.U.

SITC CTCI	COMMODITY	1993 WEIGHT POIDS	1993 VALUE VALEUR	1994 WEIGHT POIDS	1994 VALUE VALEUR	1995 WEIGHT POIDS	1995 VALUE VALEUR	1996 WEIGHT POIDS	1996 VALUE VALEUR	PRODUIT
72	MACHS FOR SPCL INDUSTRYS				111553		131280		148867	MAC SPECIALES POUR INDUST
722	TRACTORS NON–ROAD			W 5919	19889	W 5532	21730	W 6790	32110	TRACTEURS
7224	WHEELED TRACTORS NES			W 5907	19824	W 5457	21629	W 6757	32088	TRACTEURS A ROUES
723	CIVIL ENGNEERG EQUIP ETC			W 13387	39587	W 9995	35098	W 10289	37979	APPAREILS DE GENIE CIVIL
7234	CONST,MINING MACHNRY NES			W 11747	36348	W 8352	31835	W 7906	32468	MACH POUR LA CONST, MINES
72342	SLFPRP SHOVELS,EXCAVATRS			W 9210	27538	W 6785	25794	W 6209	26323	PELLES MECANIQUES
728	OTH MACHY FOR SPCL INDUS				18712	W 6307	32601	W 6589	29330	AUT MACH IND PARTICULIERES
73	METALWORKING MACHINERY				55277		92209		91183	MACH TRAVAIL DES METAUX
736	METALWORKING MACH–TOOLS			W 15885	46196	W 20223	73123	W 19275	74636	MACH–OUTILS TRAVAIL METAUX
7361	METAL CUTTING MACH–TOOLS			W 6007	20378	W 7026	27522	W 7482	30517	MACH–OUT ENLEVEMENT METAL
74	GENRL INDUSTRL MACHY NES				217278		283612		296002	MACH APP INDUSTRIE
744	MECHANICAL HANDLING EQU			W 21850	47308	W 29099	66967	W 30694	69423	EQUIP MANUTENTION PIECES
7449	PTS NES OF MACHY OF 7442			W 14315	28156	W 20225	43201	W 21098	45204	PIECES DU 744.2
749	NONELEC MACH PTS,ACC NES			W 105607	120215	W 24317	159588	W 22884	167545	PIECES MACH NON ELEC NDA
7491	BALL,ROLLER,ETC BEARINGS			W 11169	69151	W 13500	102463	W 13693	109000	ROULEMENTS BILLES ETC
7492	COCKS,VALVES ETC NES			W 4022	33020	W 2727	25789	W 2575	24202	ART ROB,SIM POUR TUYAUX
75	OFFICE MACHNES,ADP EQUIP				23954		17464		11401	MACH BUREAU TRAIT AUTOM
76	TELECOMM,SOUND EQUIPMENT				67864		83375		78106	EQUIPMENT DE TELECOM
761	TELEVISION RECEIVERS			W 1844	25695	W 1639	25503	W 1	5	RECEPTEURS DE TELEVISION
7611	COLOUR TV RECEIVERS			W 1826	25453	W 1638	25484	W 1	5	RECEPTEURS COULEUR
764	TELECOM EQPT,PTS,ACC NES			W 1906	39581	W 1910	56366	W 2131	76801	EQUIP TELECOM,PIECES
7641	LINE TELEPHONE,ETC EQUIP			W 416	18175	W 493	35547	W 486	42780	APP TELEPHON PAR FIL
7649	PTS NES OF EQUIPMT OF 76			W 1352	18793	W 1331	18205	W 1537	30426	PIECES DE LA DIV 76
77	ELECTRIC MACHNRY NES ETC				234944		307675		347903	MACH APP ELECT NDA
772	SWITCHGEAR ETC,PARTS NES			W 4212	30037	W 5139	35670	W 5201	37588	APP COUPURE,SECT ETC
7721	SWITCHGEAR ETC			W 4142	27750	W 4926	31220	W 4974	30344	APP COUPURE,SECTIONMNT
773	ELECTR DISTRIBUTNG EQUIP			W 21186	52731	W 31764	111578	W 40199	157895	EQUIPMT DISTRIBUTION ELECT
7731	INSULATED WIRE,CABLE ETC			W 17706	42768	W 28233	97684	W 36982	145808	FILS,CABLES ISOLES ELECT
775	HOUSEHOLD TYPE EQUIP NES			W 28998	89541	W 30015	105612	W 32150	111340	MACH,APP USAGE DOMESTQUE
7751	HOUSEHOLD LDRY EQUIP NES			W 5186	19395	W 11947	45067	W 13335	49413	MACH A LAVER ET SECHOIRS
77511	DOMESTIC WASHING MACHNES			W 5181	19358	W 11944	45044	W 13330	49387	MACH LAVER LINGE MOINS 6 KG
7752	DOM REFRIGERATRS,FREEZRS			W 15667	53083	W 11953	45613	W 13003	47169	REFRIG,CONGEL MENAGER
77521	DOMESTIC REFRIGERATORS			W 12356	40007	W 9815	35759	W 11223	39323	REFRIGERATEURS
778	ELECTRICAL MACHINERY NES				27467	W 9234	29120	W 4051	21497	AUTRES MACH ELECT NDA
78	ROAD VEHICLES				293640		369040		677385	VEHICULES ROUTIERS
781	PASS MOTOR VEH EXC BUSES			W 9945	69395	W 29394	66990	W 32115	274162	AUTO TRANSPORT PERSONNES
782	LORRIES,SPCL MTR VEH NES			W 27928	43524	W 14908	38298	W 10501	29322	VEHICULES SPECIAUX,MARCH
7821	LORRIES,TRUCKS			W 18278	26935	W 8288	23288	W 6115	18189	VEHICULES TRANSP MARCHAND
784	MOTOR VEH PRTS,ACCES NES			W 38340	134867	W 179221	194379	W 65666	300828	PIECES 722,781,782,783
7849	OTHER MOTOR VEHCL PARTS			W 34381	128187	W 174822	184535	W 59026	283043	PIECES 722,781,782,783
786	TRAILERS,NONMOTR VEH,NES			W 28627	31808	W 38038	53283	W 35349	54692	REMORQUES,CADRES,CONTAIN
7861	TRAILERS,TRANSP CONTAINR			W 22290	23351	W 26897	35214	W 25313	37446	REMORQUES TOUS VEHICULES
78613	CONTAINERS INC ROAD–RAIL			W 15357	15201	W 22927	28392	W 21971	30315	CADRES ET CONTAINERS
79	OTHR TRANSPORT EQUIPMENT				147705		155038		172847	AUTRE MATERIEL TRANSPORT
791	RAILWAY VEHICLES			W 51302	79325	W 62034	82430	W 52269	86268	VEHIC MAT CHEMINS DE FER
7915	FRT,MAINT CARS NOT POWRD			W 28627	38294	W 34997	32607	W 26591	34340	WAGONS DE SERVICE
79152	RAILWAY FREIGHT CARS NES			W 28078	36618	W 32769	28839	W 25705	25943	WAGONS MARCHANDISES
7919	RY TRACK FIXT,ETC,PARTS			W 19794	38622	W 16213	34433	W 13523	25040	MATER FIXE VOIES FERREES
79199	PARTS NES OF 7911–7915			W 19741	38537	W 16110	34291	W 13513	24991	PIECES 791.1 ET 5
793	SHIPS AND BOATS ETC			W 23920	60502	W 19038	68783	W 24511	83121	NAVIRES BATEAUX,ETC
7932	SHIPS AND BOATS NES			W 21991	60168	W 19038	68783	W 24511	83121	NAVIRES ET BATEAUX
79323	OTHER CARGO VESSELS			W 21546	59757	W 18993	68474	W 24454	82809	AUT BATEAUX TRANS MARCH
8	MISC MANUFACTURED GOODS		723172		832281		970664		982681	ART MANUFACTURES DIVERS
812	*PLUMBG,HEATNG,LGHTNG EQ				46339	W 19435	55635	W 22219	59494	APPAR SANITAIRES CHAUFFAGE
8121	CENTRAL HEATING EQUIPMNT			W 15662	21776	W 12992	25917	W 15794	30817	CHAUDIERES,RADIATEURS
8124	LIGHTING EQUIPMENT NES				23858	W 5894	28681	W 4427	26499	APPAREILS ECLAIRAGE ETC
821	*FURNITURE,PARTS THEREOF			W 178962	144123	W 97794	192431	W 189748	192643	MEUBLES ET PIECES
8211	CHAIRS,SEATS AND PARTS			W 16072	35825	W 21427	49703	W 21024	49321	SIEGES ET PIECES
82111	CHAIRS AND OTHER SEATS			W 13875	33444	W 16179	43231	W 15883	42084	SIEGES
8219	FURNITURE AND PARTS NES			W 161900	100078	W 74763	130496	W 73001	132384	AUTRES MEUBLES ET PIECES
82191	METAL FURNITURE NES			W 18658	25049	W 20226	31471	W 23409	30710	MEUBLES NDA EN METAL
82192	WOOD FURNITURE NES			W 38276	62503	W 42667	84654	W 38211	86340	MEUBLES NDA EN BOIS
84	CLOTHING AND ACCESSORIES				237497		256614		269394	VETEMENTS
842	MENS OUTERWEAR NOT KNIT			W 8603	105646	W 8700	113509	W 8525	114125	VET DESSUS POUR HOMMES
8422	— SUITS			W 931	21252	W 955	22993	W 1007	24613	COMPLETS HOMMES MAT TEXT
8423	— TROUSERS,BREECHES ETC			W 3250	32780	W 3509	33770	W 3720	34418	PANTALONS HOMMES MAT TEX
8424	— JACKETS,BLAZERS ETC			W 2233	31391	W 2192	36642	W 1965	36968	VESTES HOMMES MAT TEXTIL
843	WOMENS OUTERWEAR NONKNIT				53179	W 4630	62046	W 4609	63852	VET DESSUS FEMMES MAT TEX
8431	— COATS AND JACKETS			W 2526	27333	W 2042	28948	W 1975	28244	MANT,VEST FEM MAT TEXTIL
845	OUTERWEAR KNIT NONELASTC			W 3127	37181	W 3071	39202	W 3613	44454	VET DESSOUS,ACCES BONNET
8451	— JERSEYS,PULLOVERS ETC			W 1583	20065	W 1773	22641	W 2162	29031	CHANDAILS,PULL–OVERS ETC
846	UNDER GARMENTS KNITTED				21601	W 1944	20901	W 2537	23948	SOUS VETS DE BONNETERIE
8462	— OF COTTON NON ELASTIC			W 2015	20787	W 1879	19812	W 2423	22064	SOUS–VET BONNET COTON
84629	—— OTHER			W 2015	20787	W 1879	19812	W 2423	22064	AUT SOUS–VET BONNET COTON
851	*FOOTWEAR			W 11438	101907	W 10503	111018	W 10340	122998	CHAUSSURES
85102	FOOTWEAR LEATHER			W 7558	65640	W 8043	91838	W 8257	108340	CHAUS SEMELLES EN CUIR
85103	SHOES WOOD–,CORK–SOLED			W 1669	24284	W 385	6670	W 436	3788	CHAUS SEMELLES BOIS,LIEGE
87	PRECISION INSTRUMNTS NES				88498		101455		90417	INSTRUM,APPAR SCIENT NDA
872	MEDICAL INSTRUMENTS NES			W 3127	44621	W 3179	46229	W 2792	37406	INSTR,APP MEDIC–CHIR NDA
87201	DENTAL INSTRUMENTS			W 1006	26056	W 826	24421	W 526	17551	INSTRUM,APPAR DENTAIRE
873	METERS AND COUNTERS NES			W 2181	23292	W 2909	32329	W 2870	32589	COMPTEURS,INST DE MESURE
8731	GAS SUPPLY METERS ETC			W 2178	23215	W 2881	31914	W 2867	32051	COMPTEURS GAZ,LIQ ELECT
874	MEASURNG,CONTROLNG INSTR				20184	W 1276	22666	W 1206	20280	INSTRUMENTS DE MESURE
89	MISC MANUFCTRD GOODS NES				199328		238332		231128	ART MANUFACTURES DIVERS
892	PRINTED MATTER				70381	W 29518	86726	W 105974	101379	IMPRIMES
8921	PRINTED BOOKS,GLOBES,ETC				45132	W 18237	53945	W 18126	58802	LIVRES.BROCHURES,CARTES
89211	PRINTED BOOKS,PAMPHLETS				41844	W 17596	50355	W 17535	55205	LIVRES,BROCHURES
8922	NEWSPAPERS,PERIODICALS			W 9724	15348	W 9755	19759	W 85975	28513	JOURNAUX ET PERIODIQUES
893	ARTICLES OF PLASTIC NES				81670		96062		89455	OUVRAGES EN MAT DIVIS 58
8939	MISC PLASTIC ARTICLES				55812	W 91527	63572	W 25899	57720	ART DIVERS EN MAT DIV 58
89399	OTHR PLASTC ARTICLES NES				52713	W 86704	59381	W 23090	54829	AUT OUV MAT DIV 58
9	GOODS NOT CLASSD BY KIND		4630		61133		268000		1395559	ART TRANSACT NON CLASSES
931	*SPECIAL TRANSACTIONS						203210		1333197	TRANS.SPECIALES
951	*WAR FIREARMS,AMMUNITION			W 6005	58170	W 4859	61449	W 4839	58948	VEHIC BLINDES ARMES
95101	ARMORED FIGHTNG VEHICLES			W 5598	52365	W 3514	55025	W 3097	55106	CHARS DE COMBAT

1. HISTORICAL SERIES, 1992–1996 SPECIAL TRADE, IMPORTS C.I.F., EXPORTS F.O.B.
SERIES HISTORIQUES, 1992–1996 COMMERCE SPECIAL, IMPORTATIONS C.A.F., EXPORTATIONS F.O.B

YEAR ANNEE	VALUE IN MILLION U.S. DOLLARS VALEUR EN MILLION U.S. DOLLARS MERCHANDISE –MARCHANDISE		GOLD –OR		CONVERSION FACTORS FACTEURS DE CONVERSION CENTS E.U. PAR		INDEX NUMBERS –INDICES QUANTUM		UNIT VALUE VALEUR UNITAIRE	
	IMPORTS	EXPORTS	IMPORTS	EXPORTS	IMPORTS	EXPORTS	IMPORTS	EXPORTS	IMPORTS	EXPORTS
1992	6142.00	6681.00								
1993	6529.00	6083.00								
1994	7304.00	6828.00								
1995	9490.00	8315.00								
1996	9399.00	8123.00								

2. IMPORTS BY BROAD ECONOMIC CATEGORY AND EXPORTS BY INDUSTRIAL ORIGIN. (PERCENTAGE OF TOTAL VALUE)
IMPORTATIONS PAR CATEGORIES ECONOMIQUES ET EXPORTATIONS PAR BRANCHE D'ACTIVITE.(EN POURCENTAGE DE LA VALEUR TOTALE)

IMPORTS – IMPORTATIONS

	1990	1991	1992	1993	1994	1995	1996
TOTAL IMPORTS–IMPORTATIONS TOTALES			100.	100.	100.	100.	100.
1 FOOD BEV–ALIMENTATION BOISSONS			7.2	6.9	7.2	6.7	3.2
11 PRIMARY–PRODUITS DE BASE			3.2	3.3	3.5	2.9	1.4
111 FOR INDUSTRY–POUR L'INDUSTRIE			1.0	1.1	1.1	0.9	0.4
112 FOR HOUSEHOLDS–POUR LES MENAGES			2.2	2.2	2.4	2.0	1.0
12 PROCESSED–PRODUITS ELABORES			4.0	3.6	3.7	3.8	1.8
121 FOR INDUSTRY–POUR L'INDUSTRIE			0.5	0.6	0.5	0.6	0.3
122 FOR HOUSEHOLDS–POUR LES MENAGES			3.5	3.1	3.2	3.2	1.5
2 IND SUPPLIES–APPROV INDUSTRIELS			39.7	34.6	38.0	37.4	17.9
21 PRIMARY–PRODUITS DE BASE			4.4	3.3	4.0	3.9	1.7
22 PROCESSED–PRODUITS ELABORES			35.3	31.3	34.0	33.5	16.2
3 FUELS–COMBUSTIBLES			10.2	10.2	6.8	6.3	3.9
31 PRIMARY–PRODUITS DE BASE			5.8	5.8	2.1	2.3	1.1
32 PROCESSED–PRODUITS ELABORES			4.3	4.4	4.7	3.9	2.7
321 MOTOR SPIRIT–ESSENCE			1.7	1.6	2.1	1.6	1.1
322 OTHER–AUTRES			2.6	2.8	2.6	2.3	1.7
4 MACHINERY–EQUIPEMENT			16.2	16.8	18.5	18.6	9.2
41 CAPITAL EQUIPMENT–MACHINES			13.4	13.9	15.4	15.6	7.6
42 PARTS–PIECES ACCESSOIRES			2.8	2.9	3.1	3.0	1.6
5 TRANSPORT–TRANSPORT			10.2	13.7	13.5	15.6	8.0
51 PASSENGER CARS–AUTOMOBILES			3.1	7.1	5.9	6.4	3.3
52 OTHER–AUTRES			1.1	1.7	1.9	2.7	1.2
521 INDUSTRIAL–INDUSTRIELS			1.0	1.5	1.8	2.6	1.1
522 NON INDUSTRIAL–NON INDUSTRIEL			0.1	0.1	0.1	0.1	0.1
53 PARTS–PIECES ACCESSOIRES			6.0	4.9	5.7	6.5	3.5
6 CONSUM GOODS–BIENS CONSOMMATION			12.1	13.9	12.6	12.5	7.6
61 DURABLE–DURABLES			2.5	2.8	2.9	2.9	1.4
62 SEMI DURABLE–SEMI DURABLES			7.2	8.3	6.7	6.6	4.5
63 NON DURABLE–NON DURABLES			2.5	2.7	2.9	3.0	1.6
7 GOODS NES–BIENS NDA			4.5	4.0	3.3	2.9	0.2

EXPORTS – EXPORTATIONS

	1990	1991	1992	1993	1994	1995	1996
TOTAL EXPORTS–EXPORTATIONS TOTALES			100.	100.	100.	100.	100.
1 AGRICULTURE			1.5	1.0	1.0	0.7	0.4
2 MINING QUARRY–INDUS EXTRACTIVES			1.9	3.9	0.2	0.1	0.0
3 MANUFACTURING–IND MANUFACTUR			96.6	95.1	98.7	99.2	50.2
31 FOOD BEV TOBACCO–ALIM BOISS TAB			5.7	4.3	4.3	3.6	2.0
32 TEXTILES–INDUSTRIES TEXTILES			17.7	18.2	16.3	14.5	6.8
33 WOOD & PRODUCTS–BOIS & PRODUITS			4.4	4.5	4.8	4.7	2.3
34 PAPER & PRODUCTS–PAPIER & PRODT			5.4	5.0	5.4	6.0	2.6
35 CHEMICALS–INDUSTRIES CHIMIQUES			13.2	13.1	13.9	14.3	7.4
36 NON METAL MIN–MIN NON METAL			2.7	2.7	2.7	2.6	1.4
37 BASIC METAL–IND METAL BASE			5.7	5.3	6.0	6.9	3.2
38 METAL MANUF–MANUF METAL			40.8	40.0	43.2	44.4	23.6
39 OTH MANUF IND–AUTRES MANUF			1.1	2.0	2.0	2.2	0.8

3. TRADE BY PRINCIPAL COUNTRIES OF ORIGIN AND DESTINATION (VALUE IN THOUSAND U.S. DOLLARS)
ECHANGES SELON LES PRINCIPAUX PAYS D'ORIGINE ET DE DESTINATION (VALEUR EN MILLIERS DE DOLLARS EU)

COUNTRIES–PAYS	SPECIAL IMPORTS C.I.F. IMPORTATIONS SPECIALES C.A.F					COUNTRIES–PAYS	SPECIAL EXPORTS F.O.B. EXPORTATIONS SPECIALES F.O.B.				
	1992	1993	1994	1995	1996		1992	1993	1994	1995	1996
World	6140997	6500935	7303934	9491678	9420672	Monde	6681152	6082865	6827850	8315815	8309813
Africa	71450	86866	88863	113733	125651	Afrique	58126	39792	39330	58223	48548
Americas	235348	282004	321053	429100	478374	Amériques	245018	267940	325677	344038	316495
Northern America	186636	207253	232131	337896	365703	Amérique du Nord	224773	247316	292340	298733	278687
LAIA	43867	64771	80830	86422	107943	ALAI	16946	15821	22975	31136	35101
CACM	1060	964	817	1053	901	MCAC	62	582	1383	1342	1348
Caribbean	3335	7866	6354	1520	1773	Caraïbes	2118	2855	8064	10861	904
Rest of America	451	1151	920	2209	2055	Autre Amérique	1121	1366	915	1966	455
As.ex F.USSR	254614	437833	373222	505186	552597	Asie l'URSS exclus	236889	252374	189206	204225	202912
Eur.x F.USSR	5312591	5467719	6336625	8146532	7975376	Europe l'URSS exclus	5899376	5208035	5936959	7315555	7328700
EU	3659313	4265886	5052277	6531528	6358706	UE	4065667	3847098	4480231	5574540	5366750
EFTA	107118	135204	188191	237405	248500	AELE	64275	64997	74523	86720	82661
East Europe	327429	370474	501112	693914	647113	Europe de l'Est	259881	329236	339582	442657	489897
Other Europe	463	221	11073	12712	12553	Autre de l'Europe	1836	2241	2605	2845	4579
Former USSR	251399	216833	169451	274792	236364	Ancienne URSS	225648	297499	316293	374994	390184
Oceania	15544	9666	14692	22307	21682	Océanie	16035	17183	20345	18747	17013
Germany/Allemagne	1394321	1625974	1734248	2205965	2043931	Germany/Allemagne	1805438	1797619	2067742	2507772	2545381
Italy/Italie	838934	1051234	1258221	1611216	1591846	Italy/Italie	880114	755991	923625	1211838	1103291
Austria/Autriche	499685	553208	755520	918890	834729	Croatia/Croatie	951623	738515	737724	891077	855008
France,Monac	492588	521823	612678	798092	924539	France,Monac	616031	527754	586268	681503	598009
Croatia/Croatie	851605	595409	498217	575643	590438	Austria/Autriche	340689	303006	373328	534647	550562
USA/Etats–Unis d'Amer	167497	188146	197194	291429	325421	Russian Federation	200979	249121	264913	305235	298321
Russian Federation	245158	202480	147434	241418	208521	USA/Etats–Unis d'Amer	195300	216023	250318	261944	246215
Hungary/Hongrie	152186	164975	192604	266823	238590	United Kingdom	141129	148114	208240	229136	161527
Czech Republic		152171	177765	246859	236359	Tfyr Macedonia		198214	218041	189336	170528
Netherlands/Pays–Bas	104138	121957	167521	206640	194324	Yugoslavia/Yougoslavie	533272	7642	15678	9466	95722
Switz.Liecht	103202	129728	157151	202548	180105	Netherlands/Pays–Bas	92116	89835	99545	117191	124879
United Kingdom	73764	103015	129632	189921	208273	Poland/Pologne	69192	87405	96323	104850	141510
Japan/Japon	88123	125119	126199	156737	162545	Bosnia and Herzegovina	22823	20091	68574	118914	263554
Spain/Espagne	58777	70769	115398	224622	169983	Hungary/Hongrie	73026	87680	98678	114604	105417
Belgium–Luxembourg	60102	67199	88838	153766	153292	Czech Republic		86076	82512	132025	146559
Sweden/Suède	63549	65437	83541	100702	110515	Belgium–Luxembourg	48321	53824	60333	73737	78024
Yugoslavia/Yougoslavie	346318	266	184	1592	32003	Switz.Liecht	51840	53310	59942	74043	70418
Tfyr Macedonia		89324	80388	85677	70836	Sweden/Suède	45372	45411	50434	58482	54214
Korea, Republic of	27487	46993	47105	78363	91680	Spain/Espagne	28174	47957	36151	42393	43898
Algeria/Algérie	36859	42017	44013	62005	65229	Iran (Islamic Rp. of)	57694	59840	31660	20790	25414
Slovakia			58066	82340	91531	Canada	29455	31269	42022	36789	32471
Brazil/Brésil	21693	30084	43757	51208	54931	Denmark/Danemark	21528	23270	32267	42187	47225
China/Chine	20564	29406	37200	52936	49585	Slovakia			30330	51704	57213
Finland/Finlande	18316	24999	45486	39515	39086	Turkey/Turquie	31772	34130	7700	20545	24416
Denmark/Danemark	20521	24710	32439	46188	41782	Ukraine	8685	19045	24722	29245	33420
Canada	19125	19107	34815	46337	40146	Egypt/Egypte	24500	18434	20056	24521	25716
Norway,SVD,JM	3734	4688	30592	34364	67705	Greece/Grèce	19069	18207	16937	31866	22851
Poland/Pologne	17503	14034	22477	37678	48430	Japan/Japon	16404	25451	18159	20953	19075
Turkey/Turquie	13573	26863	21710	31769	32900	Bulgaria/Bulgarie	16526	45283	14301	12589	9307
Czechoslovakia	116528					Saudi Arabia	30752	17112	15297	15831	13588
Iran (Islamic Rp. of)	19663	87070	1083	1230	3967	Czechoslovakia	91933				
Bulgaria/Bulgarie	29920	22571	28642	23092	4149	Belarus/Bélarus	12386	15702	13264	16466	33063
Romania/Roumanie	8961	15705	20647	33370	24706	United Arab Emirates	22830	22060	16946	14419	14444
Ireland/Irlande	9728	20372	17998	19919	28630	Romania/Roumanie	7431	19006	12441	20973	22291
Indonesia/Indonésie	3350	13051	11960	21833	29805	Australia/Australie	14693	15917	17886	16850	15438
Australia/Australie	14792	8751	13635	21324	20527	Finland/Finlande	10721	9886	12562	17991	19603
Israel/Israël	3754	5684	20653	20772	25830	Norway,SVD,JM	12328	11480	14337	12377	11793
Thailand/Thaïlande	10756	11668	13303	17197	18055	Ireland/Irlande	11085	18313	6168	17002	4309
Hong Kong	8803	10729	13382	18512	18546	Korea, Republic of	7601	7571	11051	13125	9302
Argentina/Argentine	7673	16942	7409	9282	23684	Cyprus/Chypre	15349	17310	7095	3537	2434
Malaysia/Malaisie	6747	6229	8051	18421	25315	Portugal	5878	7912	6631	8797	12978
Libyan Arab Jamahiriya	13528	16967	802	4554	28399	India/Inde	3903	4585	7068	11511	11261
Bosnia and Herzegovina	20345	10935	5184	8062	15226	Hong Kong	3437	4676	5162	11204	12184
India/Inde	7680	9130	10824	16667	15448	Brazil/Brésil	611	1986	4281	10713	18027
Ecuador/Equateur	5713	9765	10093	13384	14264	Thailand/Thaïlande	6876	6520	5548	7807	7442
Egypt/Egypte	6814	7393	13471	14220	8046	Colombia/Colombie	6174	2764	5124	7657	7690
Portugal	22447	9888	4225	5396	5168	Israel/Israël	2186	4582	8007	7688	6655
Singapore/Singapour	7541	8098	6608	8849	9491	Syrian Arab Republic	3273	4108	4578	7354	9797
Greece/Grèce	2442	5301	6533	10698	12608	Singapore/Singapour	4669	6309	6243	6112	5729
Malta/Malte	452	188	10934	12589	12318	Lithuania/Lituanie	289	2259	5942	8826	11305

(VALUE AS PERCENTAGE OF WORLD TOTAL)(VALEURS EN POURCENTAGE DU TOTAL MONDIAL)

	1987	1988	1989	1990	1991	1992	1993	1994	1995	1996		1987	1988	1989	1990	1991	1992	1993	1994	1995	1996
Africa						1.2	1.3	1.2	1.2	1.3	Afrique						0.9	0.7	0.6	0.7	0.6
Americas						3.8	4.3	4.4	4.5	5.1	Amériques						3.7	4.4	4.8	4.1	3.8
Northern America						3.0	3.2	3.2	3.6	3.9	Amérique du Nord						3.4	4.1	4.3	3.6	3.4
LAIA						0.7	1.0	1.1	0.9	1.1	ALAI						0.3	0.3	0.3	0.4	0.4
CACM						0.0	0.0	0.0	0.0	0.0	MCAC						0.0	0.0	0.0	0.0	0.0
Caribbean						0.1	0.1	0.1	0.0	0.0	Caraïbes						0.0	0.0	0.1	0.1	0.0
Rest of America						0.0	0.0	0.0	0.0	0.0	Autre Amérique						0.0	0.0	0.0	0.0	0.0
As.ex F.USSR						4.1	6.7	5.1	5.3	5.9	Asie l'URSS exclus						3.5	4.1	2.8	2.5	2.4
Eur.x F.USSR						86.5	84.1	86.8	85.8	84.7	Europe l'URSS exclus						88.3	85.6	87.0	88.0	88.2
EU						59.6	65.6	69.2	68.8	67.5	UE						60.9	63.2	65.6	67.0	64.6
EFTA						1.7	2.1	2.6	2.5	2.6	AELE						1.0	1.1	1.1	1.0	1.0
East Europe						5.3	5.7	6.9	7.3	6.9	Europe de l'Est						3.9	5.4	5.0	5.3	5.9
Other Europe						0.0	0.0	0.2	0.1	0.1	Autre de l'Europe						0.0	0.0	0.0	0.0	0.1
Former USSR						4.1	3.3	2.3	2.9	2.5	Ancienne URSS						3.4	4.9	4.6	4.5	4.7
Oceania						0.3	0.1	0.2	0.2	0.2	Océanie						0.2	0.3	0.3	0.2	0.2
Germany/Allemagne						22.7	25.0	23.7	23.2	21.7	Germany/Allemagne						27.0	29.6	30.3	30.2	30.6
Italy/Italie						13.7	16.2	17.2	17.0	16.9	Italy/Italie						13.2	12.4	13.5	14.6	13.3
Austria/Autriche						8.1	8.5	10.3	9.7	8.9	Croatia/Croatie						14.2	12.1	10.8	10.7	10.3
France,Monac						8.0	8.0	8.4	8.4	9.8	France,Monac						9.2	8.7	8.6	8.2	7.2
Croatia/Croatie						13.9	9.2	6.8	6.1	6.3	Austria/Autriche						5.1	5.0	5.5	6.4	6.6
USA/Etats–Unis d'Amer						2.7	2.9	2.7	3.1	3.5	Russian Federation						3.0	4.1	3.9	3.7	3.6
Russian Federation						4.0	3.1	2.0	2.5	2.2	USA/Etats–Unis d'Amer						2.9	3.6	3.7	3.1	3.0
Hungary/Hongrie						2.5	2.5	2.6	2.8	2.5	United Kingdom						2.1	2.4	3.0	2.8	1.9
Czech Republic							2.3	2.4	2.6	2.5	Tfyr Macedonia							3.3	3.2	2.3	2.1
Netherlands/Pays–Bas						1.7	1.9	2.3	2.2	2.1	Yugoslavia/Yougoslavie						8.0	0.1	0.2	0.1	1.2

4. Special Imports C.I.F. by Commodities according to the S.I.T.C. (Rev. 2) in thousand U.S. Dollars
Importations Spéciales C.A.F. par Produits d'après la C.T.C.I. (Rév. 2) en milliers de Dollars E.U.

SITC CTCI	COMMODITY	1993 WEIGHT POIDS	1993 VALUE VALEUR	1994 WEIGHT POIDS	1994 VALUE VALEUR	1995 WEIGHT POIDS	1995 VALUE VALEUR	1996 WEIGHT POIDS	1996 VALUE VALEUR	PRODUIT
	ALL COMMODITIES		6500935		7303934		9491678		9420672	TOUS PRODUITS
0	FOOD AND LIVE ANIMALS		478560		555232		637447		637428	ALIMENTS,ANIMAUX VIVANTS
01	MEAT AND PREPARATIONS		64074		81161		75986		66451	VIANDES ET PREPARATIONS
011	MEAT FRESH,CHILLD,FROZEN	W 32944	56029	W 37438	73286	W 26933	64310	W 24403	57160	VIANDES FRAICHES,REF,CONGE
0113	PIG MEAT FRESH,CHLD,FRZN	W 23156	40107	W 24119	46534	W 19327	45003	W 18564	43717	VIANDE DE PORC
04	CEREALS AND PREPARATIONS		107353		105918		108456		140523	CEREALES ET PRODUITS
041	WHEAT ETC UNMILLED	W 162077	21287	W 125140	16591	W 82377	13672	W 64747	12823	FROMENT,EPEAUTRE
044	MAIZE UNMILLED	W 205471	28240	W 210344	28788	W 188841	24504	W 215317	43422	MAIS NON MOULU
048	CEREAL ETC PREPARATIONS	W 33619	32235	W 35119	37139	W 38826	47820	W 42763	49657	PREPTNS A BASE CEREALES
0484	BAKERY PRODUCTS	W 9990	21222	W 10849	23149	W 10791	28292	W 9391	26492	PRODUITS DE BOULANGERIE
05	VEGETABLES AND FRUIT		108196		122136		158845		157865	LEGUMES ET FRUITS
054	VEG ETC FRSH,SMPLY PRSVD	W 189529	44492	W 72795	45329	W 100961	61457	W 110803	61769	LEGUMES FRAIS,CONG,SECS
0545	OTHER FRESH VEGETABLES	W 42944	22140	W 40696	22319	W 43496	27425	W 41073	29737	AUTRES LEGUMES FRAIS,REF
057	FRUIT,NUTS,FRESH,DRIED	W 82624	38735	W 86681	46065	W 89580	57144	W 89729	61863	FRUITS FRAIS OU SECS
058	FRUIT PRESERVED,PREPARED	W 22146	16510	W 24991	22271	W 28201	29309	W 18632	23564	CONSERVES DE FRUITS
06	SUGAR AND PREPS,HONEY		26488		35800		42134		33220	SUCRES ET PRODUITS
061	SUGAR AND HONEY	W 52091	17348	W 59668	23140	W 70041	29929	W 55261	22490	SUCRES ET MIEL
07	COFFEE,TEA,COCOA,SPICES		49520		66087		76307		72317	CAFE,THE,CACAO,EPICES
071	COFFEE AND SUBSTITUTES	W 9368	16152	W 9714	29593	W 9030	33994	W 10265	32505	CAFE ET SUCCEDANES
0711	COFFEE GREEN,ROASTED,SUB	W 8895	15009	W 9244	27971	W 8542	31992	W 9659	29315	CAFE TORREFIE OU DECAFEINE
07111	COFFEE GREEN,HUSKS,SKINS	W 8116	12882	W 8597	24776	W 7852	27260	W 9154	26126	CAFE NON TORREFIE
073	CHOCOLATE AND PRODUCTS	W 6603	28868	W 7141	31291	W 7331	37153	W 7167	34363	CHOCOLAT
081	*FEEDING STUFF FOR ANIML	W 140650	43845	W 143078	46190	W 163149	52027	W 154912	56038	NOURRITURE POUR ANIMAUX
0813	OILCAKE AND OTH RESIDUES	W 99673	26418	W 104178	25297	W 116500	26496	W 110555	32105	TOURTEAUX
08131	— OF SOYA BEANS	W 92968	25354	W 96158	24085	W 103168	24554	W 93752	29302	TOURTEAUX DE SOJA
09	MISC EDIBLE PRODUCTS		38857		49510		64967		60932	PREP ALIMENTAIRES DIVERSES
098	EDIBLE PRODCTS,PREPS NES	W 9012	31586	W 11217	40988	W 13216	54717	W 13696	51154	PREP ALIMENTAIRES NDA
09809	MISC FOOD PREPRTIONS NES	W 5674	22899	W 7159	30034	W 8214	40653	W 8743	36125	PREP ALIMENTAIRES NDA
1	BEVERAGES AND TOBACCO		43789		46906		61027		60080	BOISSONS ET TABACS
11	BEVERAGES		22881		20842		36241		38096	BOISSONS
12	TOBACCO AND MANUFACTURES		20909		26063		24785		21984	TABACS BRUTS FABRIQUES
2	CRUDE MATERLS,EXCL FUELS		335957		462690		610266		471071	MAT BRUTES NON COMESTIBLES
21	HIDES,SKINS,FURS UNDRSSD		19310		23647		31545		27343	CUIRS,PEAUX BRUTS
211	HIDES,SKINS,EXC FURS,RAW	W 22995	18838	W 25436	23138	W 25699	30954	W 21654	27010	CUIRS ET PEAUX
23	RUBBER, CRUDE		34541		41155		63636		53713	CAOUTCHOUC BRUT
233	RUBBER,SYNTHTIC,RECLAIMD	W 22829	22757	W 24635	26613	W 27939	39948	W 25778	31259	LATEX CAOUTCH SYNTH REGEN
2331	SYNTHETIC RUBBER ETC	W 22389	22533	W 24367	26436	W 27624	39678	W 25254	30858	LATEX CAOUTCH SYNTHETIQUE
24	CORK AND WOOD		42016		61317		72075		58081	LIEGE ET BOIS
248	WOOD SHAPED,SLEEPERS	W 80239	34040	W 88943	42440	W 75171	47566	W 73955	47277	BOIS SIMPLEMENT TRAVAILLES
2483	LUMBER SHAPED NON–CONIFR	W 68479	27179	W 70162	31642	W 55949	33930	W 55712	34751	NON CONIFERES SCIES,RABOTES
24831	LUMBER SAWN ETC NON–CON	W 63945	21935	W 65311	25273	W 51992	27427	W 51636	27483	SCIES LONGITUDINALEMENT
251	*PULP AND WASTE PAPER	W 231606	61614	W 257436	95536	W 263979	158945	W 232721	84263	PATES A PAPIER,DECHETS
2511	WASTE PAPER,PPRBOARD ETC	W 108706	13295	W 115083	18544	W 125256	40988	W 103474	17654	DECHETS DE PAPIER
2517	SODA,SULPHATE WOOD PULP	W 71012	28458	W 83877	48345	W 90772	82755	W 88154	47704	PATES CHIMIQUES AU SULFATE
25172	— BLEACHED,NONDISSOLVNG	W 68177	27310	W 81726	47349	W 88919	81286	W 86444	46741	PATES BLANCHIES
2518	SULPHITE WOOD PULP	W 40661	16093	W 44494	23464	W 34156	27722	W 28233	13906	PATES AU BISULFITE
25182	— BLEACHED,NONDISSOLVNG	W 40545	16054	W 42761	22524	W 30994	25396	W 27878	13797	PATES BLANCHES
26	TEXTILE FIBRES AND WASTE		43481		54329		56560		45220	FIBRES TEXTILES
263	COTTON	W 12071	16950	W 13998	23382	W 11609	25849	W 10135	19765	COTON
27	CRUDE FERTLZR,MINRLS NES		41527		49960		65150		60202	ENGRAIS MINERAUX BRUTS
278	OTHER CRUDE MINERALS	W 241635	24808	W 315481	31850	W 387201	44449	W 344789	33226	AUTRES MINERAUX BRUTS
28	METALLIFEROUS ORES,SCRAP		63630		100985		116596		94621	MINERAIS METAL,DECHETS
282	IRON AND STEEL SCRAP	W 196268	22886	W 278290	46618	W 259960	63108	W 142581	34574	FERRAILLES
28209	— OF OTHR IRON OR STEEL	W 183535	18901	W 239773	32440	W 239103	38064	W 119951	16907	FERRAILLES DE FER
287	BASE METAL ORES,CONC NES	W 214740	34423	W 237759	39552	W 246356	43658	W 225541	42223	MINERAIS METAUX COMMUNS
2873	ALUMINIUM ORES,ALUMINA	W 169139	29921	W 169427	33336	W 160394	32510	W 155465	32438	MINERAIS D'ALUMINIUM
28732	ALUMINA(ALUMINIUM OXIDE)	W 160427	28802	W 140833	30120	W 145071	30934	W 140532	30721	ALUMINE (OXYDE ALUMINIUM)
29	CRUDE ANIMAL,VEG MAT NES		28445		34264		43500		44774	MATIERES BRUTES ANIM,VEGET
292	CRUDE VEG MATERIALS NES	W 11908	24628		29921	W 13070	38374	W 10595	39734	MAT BRUTES VEGETALES NDA
3	MINERAL FUELS ETC		706091		528197		632219		763923	COMBUSTIBLES MINERAUX LUB
32	COAL,COKE AND BRIQUETTES		21035		18140		27687		29042	HOUILLES,COKES,BRIQUETTES
33	PETROLEUM AND PRODUCTS		564261		410602		458895		595576	PETROLE ET DERIVES
333	CRUDE PETROLEUM	W 1997591	258084	W 410871	52927	W 515575	73239	W 460493	77748	HUILES BRUTES DE PETROLE
334	PETROLEUM PRODUCTS,REFIN	W 1419507	264422	W 1778199	325441	W 1800396	346995	W 2215621	482878	PRODUITS RAFFINES
3341	GASOLINE,OTH LIGHT OILS	W 568420	105908	W 754560	151913	W 770880	158081	W 917165	199135	ESSENCES POUR MOTEURS
33411	MOTOR,AVIATION SPIRIT	W 566176	103479	W 734530	147506	W 762598	153927	W 898434	194911	ESSENCES MOTEURS D'AVIONS
3343	GAS OILS	W 815021	128646	W 982104	142625	W 985632	154613	W 847067	165985	GAS OILS
3344	FUEL OILS,NES		34	W 2889	345	W 840	137	W 357374	69336	FUEL OILS
3345	LUBS,PETROLEUM OILS NES	W 14999	25058	W 15557	25733	W 16501	28265	W 27420	33176	HUILES LUBRIFIANTES
335	RESIDUAL PETRLM PROD NES	W 279645	41755	W 272395	32234	W 238375	38661	W 233804	34950	PRODUITS RESIDUELS NDA
3352	MINERAL TARS AND PRODCTS	W 90430	19781	W 44411	9170	W 50586	10231	W 11801	3089	GOUDRONS MINERAUX
341	*GAS,NATURAL AND MANUFCT	W 571368	105604	W 621910	92109	W 744701	126778	W 646267	117635	GAZ NATUREL,GAZ MANUFACT
3414	PETROLEUM GASES, GASEOUS	W 524778	98534	W 568344	85009	W 683447	115777	W 575675	101012	GAZ DE PETROLE GAZEUX
4	ANIMAL,VEGETABLE OIL,FAT		22467		29088		38001		38197	HUILES,GRAISSES ANIM,VEG
42	FIXED VEGETABLE OIL,FAT		16615		21072		29715		29009	HUILES VEGETALES FIXES
5	CHEMCLS,RELATED PROD NES		724382		862498		1109735		1083871	PRODUITS CHIMIQUES
51	ORGANIC CHEMICALS		126776		161787		213957		194078	PROD CHIMIQ ORGANIQUES
511	HYDROCARBONS NES,DERIVS		13401	W 34583	27245	W 33392	31060	W 34927	18850	HYDROCARBURES NDA
512	ALCOHOLS,PHENOLS ETC	W 36193	18755	W 25930	20780	W 25034	32582	W 27145	25887	PHENOLS,PHENOLS–ALCOOLS
513	CARBOXYLIC ACIDS ETC	W 20630	24013	W 25372	30202	W 22461	37992	W 24727	36348	ACIDES CARBOXYLIQUES
514	NITROGEN–FNCTN COMPOUNDS	W 8403	35976	W 9683	38800	W 11171	47538	W 12022	51557	COMPOSES FONCT AZOTEES
5148	OTH NITROGN–FNCTN CMPNDS	W 5965	25341	W 6581	26047	W 8460	35462	W 9018	36900	AUTRES COMPOSES AZOTES
515	ORG–INORG COMPOUNDS ETC	W 2626	24211	W 3688	34049	W 10160	51293	W 13021	48839	COMPOSES ORGANO–MINERAUX
5156	HETEROCYCLIC CMPDS ETC	W 1321	16127	W 2356	25939	W 8650	39261	W 11411	37420	COMPOSES HETEROCYCLIQUES
51569	OTH HETEROCYC CMPDS,ETC	W 642	14978	W 850	23630	W 909	26152	W 638	20845	AUT COMP HETEROCYCLIQUES
52	INORGANIC CHEMICALS		59345		64210		85232		88322	PROD CHIM INORGANIQUES
522	INORG ELEMNTS,OXIDES,ETC	W 96783	31601	W 94498	35438	W 129856	52529	W 134550	55306	ELEMENTS INORGANIQUES
523	OTHR INORG CHEMICALS ETC	W 82677	25403	W 78238	25922	W 73316	30438	W 71604	31375	AUT PRODUITS CHIMIQUES INORG
53	DYES,TANNING,COLOUR PROD		72646		80610		96251		92071	PROD TEINTURE,COLORANTS
531	SYNT DYE,NAT INDGO,LAKES	W 1467	20775	W 1754	23321	W 1960	23527	W 1827	21069	MAT COLOR ORGAN,LAQUES
533	PIGMENTS,PAINTS,ETC	W 16304	49750	W 19230	55050	W 32371	69832	W 38726	68106	PIGMENTS,PEINTURES,VERNIS
5334	VARNISHES,DISTEMPERS ETC	W 6528	26928	W 7547	31025	W 8152	37379	W 8043	36493	PEINTURES A L'EAU
53342	OTH PAINTS,VARNISHES ETC	W 4960	20577	W 5623	23141	W 5658	27040	W 4991	25169	AUTRES PEINTURES,VERNIS
541	*MEDICINAL,PHARM PRODUCT		114079		137136	K 4050886	165800		183658	PROD MEDICINAUX PHARMACEUT
5417	MEDICAMENTS	K 2293824	75676	K 3224312	90704	K 3255823	118227	K 2932892	131467	MEDICAMENTS
54179	— CONTNG OTH SUBSTANCES	K 1871009	51716	K 2495579	57449	K 2540351	75304	K 2446502	84712	MED CONT AUT SUBSTANCES
55	PERFUME,CLEANING ETC PRD		51912		63843		83366		87775	PROD POUR PARFUM,TOILETTE
553	PERFUMERY,COSMETICS,ETC	W 2645	17075	W 3366	22379	W 4399	32940	W 4344	32794	PRODUITS DE PARFUMERIE
554	SOAP,CLEANSING ETC PREPS	W 17098	28597	W 21346	33511	W 24302	42014	W 29189	46832	SAVONS,PRODUITS DETERSIFS
5542	WASHING PREPARATIONS ETC	W 15137	23627	W 19023	28093	W 21492	34855	W 26323	39019	PROD ORG TENSIO–ACT NDA
562	*FERTILIZERS,MANUFACTURE	W 180681	26413	W 196953	29656	W 219888	40280	W 222785	40575	ENGRAIS MANUFACTURES

4. Special Imports C.I.F. by Commodities according to the S.I.T.C. (Rev. 2) in thousand U.S. Dollars
Importations Spéciales C.A.F. par Produits d'après la C.T.C.I. (Rév. 2) en milliers de Dollars E.U.

SITC CTCI	COMMODITY	1993 WEIGHT POIDS	1993 VALUE VALEUR	1994 WEIGHT POIDS	1994 VALUE VALEUR	1995 WEIGHT POIDS	1995 VALUE VALEUR	1996 WEIGHT POIDS	1996 VALUE VALEUR	PRODUIT
58	PLASTIC MATERIALS ETC		182573		225636		301301		278994	MAT PLAST ARTIFICIELLES
582	PROD OF CONDENSATION ETC	W 42915	61337	W 56705	80021	W 55070	105133	W 44365	93501	PROD CONDENS,POLYCOND
583	POLYMERIZATION ETC PRODS	W 78552	114087	W 92979	137252	W 96521	186802	W 106144	176998	PROD POLYMERISATION
5831	POLYETHYLENE	W 26503	24943	W 31802	29745	W 33372	43528	W 37807	40185	POLYETHYLENE
58311	— IN PRIMARY FORMS	W 22685	16357	W 27360	20204	W 28320	30864	W 32561	29054	POLYETHYLENE PRIMAIRES
5833	POLYSTYRENE,ITS COPOLYMR	W 15048	18775	W 18211	23326	W 19339	32947	W 18741	26655	POLYPROPYLENE COPOLYMERES
58331	— IN PRIMARY FORMS	W 13362	16438	W 16179	20142	W 17884	29595	W 17694	24187	SOUS FORMES PRIMAIRES
5834	POLYVINYL CHLORIDE	W 15470	19011	W 17835	22777	W 18422	31862	W 20386	30707	CHLORURE DE POLYVINYLE
5839	OTH POLYMRZTION ETC PROD	W 7656	26537	W 8993	32774	W 9145	40277	W 10152	43237	AUT PROD POLYMER COPOLYM
59	CHEMICAL MATERIALS NES		88686		97661		121580		117084	MAT PROD CHIMIQUES NDA
598	MISCEL CHEM PRODUCTS NES	W 34480	61498	W 44633	70754	W 43946	84482	W 41350	81231	PROD DIV INDUST CHIM NDA
5989	CHEM PRODUCTS,PREPS NES	W 28428	53549	W 38390	61850	W 35871	73561	W 34470	71317	PROD PREP CHIMIQUES NDA
59899	OTH CHEM PRODS,PREPS,NES	W 19674	37760	W 24664	42078	W 23045	49275	W 18410	42777	AUT PRODUITS CHIMIQUES NDA
6	BASIC MANUFACTURES		1189957		1467830		1923846		1894708	ART MANUFACTURES
61	LEATHER,DRESSED FUR,ETC		66644		79723		73492		71317	CUIRS,PELLETERIES
611	LEATHER	W 4085	36910	W 3781	46009	W 2965	40349	W 2572	41323	CUIRS,PEAUX PREPARES
6114	LEATHR BOVINE NES,EQUINE	W 2285	26540	W 1788	30753	W 1442	29043	W 1603	32454	CUIRS DE BOVINS
612	LEATHER ETC MANUFACTURES	W 2258	28248	W 2207	31998	W 2188	32206	W 2191	28198	OUVRAGES EN CUIRS NDA
6123	PREPRD PARTS OF FOOTWEAR	W 2172	26689	W 2125	30890	W 2028	28720	W 1903	22915	PARTIES DE CHAUSSURES
62	RUBBER MANUFACTURES NES		41769		57039		85458		87005	CAOUTCHOUC MANUFACTURE
625	RUBBER TYRES, TUBES ETC	W 3728	12396	W 5289	19305	W 7131	34227	W 8578	33652	PNEUS CAOUTCHOUC VULCANISE
628	RUBBER ARTICLES NES	W 2053	18007	W 2447	21478	W 2980	28318	W 3547	29576	OUVRAGES CAOUTCHOUC NDA
63	WOOD,CORK MANUFACTRS NES		40702		51282		67982		68133	OUVRAGES LIEGE ET BOIS
634	VENEERS,PLYWOOD,ETC	W 28871	30986	W 43546	38784	W 42843	49278	W 41072	46665	PLACAGES,CONTRE–PLAQUES
64	PAPER,PAPERBOARD AND MFR		122546		147779		210837		203113	PAPIERS,CARTONS & OUVRAGES
641	PAPER AND PAPERBOARD	W 105672	77337	W 128486	98836	W 129199	143142	W 136384	133298	PAPIERS ET CARTONS
6415	PAPER,PAPERBRD,BULK,NES	W 48669	28188	W 58729	38056	W 54210	48250	W 60247	36692	PAPIERS,CARTONS ROULEAUX
64159	OTHER PAPER ETC,BULK,NES	W 32466	21722	W 41212	29438	W 37539	36527	W 52163	31570	AUT PAPIER ROULEAUX FEUILLES
6418	COATED ETC PAPER NES BLK	W 8351	15331	W 10295	18500	W 12536	35706	W 13331	39804	PAP,CARTONS COUCHES,ENDUITS
642	PAPER,ETC,PRECUT,ARTS OF	W 24083	45209	W 24779	48943	W 27011	67695	W 28390	69815	PAP,CARTONS DECOUPES
6421	PAPER ETC CONTAINERS	W 15821	25817	W 15041	24082	W 14154	29281	W 13516	27818	BOITES,SACS EMBALLAGES
65	TEXTILE YARN,FABRICS,ETC		223899		267792		345103		327309	FILS,TISSUS,ARTICLES TEXTILE
651	TEXTILE YARN	W 21591	76176	W 26933	92164	W 21991	103294	W 17162	84175	FILS TEXTILES
6514	SYN FIB YRN,BULK,MONOFIL	W 9689	27262	W 13745	37538	W 8647	37120	W 6214	32431	FILS CONT 85% FIB TEXT SYNTH
653	WOVN MAN–MADE FIB FABRIC	W 2069	28124	W 2566	32858	W 2268	38095	W 2017	34108	TISSUS FIBRES SYNTH,ARTIF
654	OTH WOVEN TEXTILE FABRIC	W 1747	19865	W 1491	20567	W 1696	28436	W 1408	23052	TISSUS AUT COTON SYNT,ARTIF
655	KNITTED,ETC FABRICS	W 789	10128	W 982	12408	W 1416	22733	W 2032	36194	ETOF BONNETERIE PIECES ETC
6552	OTHER KNIT ETC FAB NONEL	W 789	10128	W 982	12408	W 1416	22733	W 2032	36194	ETOF BON NON ELAS NON SYNT
657	SPECIAL TXTL FABRC,PRODS	W 5180	44656	W 5616	58979	W 8006	87183	W 8104	87640	TISSUS SPECIAUX
6573	COATED ETC TEXTILES NES	W 3285	30968	W 3878	43957	W 5685	67580	W 5688	66835	TISSUS,ART MATIERE TEXT NDA
65732	PLASTIC COATED TEXTILES	W 1588	18146	W 2285	32058	W 3544	50080	W 3748	51653	TISSUS IMPREGNES
66	NONMETAL MINERAL MFS NES		124500		142183		187720		187826	ART MIN NON METALLIQUES
662	CLAY,REFRACTORY BLDG PRD	W 80340	23642	W 79214	29263	W 108507	41108	W 90445	37068	MAT CONST REFRACTAIRES
663	MINERAL MANUFCTURES NES	W 48120	27389	W 43950	30798	W 51669	39773	W 59618	38341	ART MIN MANUF NDA
664	GLASS	W 28197	31243	W 32581	38140	W 34912	46896	W 37706	51891	VERRE
665	GLASSWARE	W 29713	22676	W 30105	22826	W 37675	31390	W 35518	30742	OUVRAGES EN VERRE
67	IRON AND STEEL		247618		311996		415490		394413	FER ET ACIER
672	IRON,STEEL PRIMARY FORMS	W 88123	25886	W 95092	30919	W 71774	30162	W 65918	25551	LINGOTS FER,ACIER
6727	IRN,STL COIL FR REROLLNG	W 67672	19315	W 85244	27589	W 68898	27963	W 63724	22308	EBAUCHES POUR TOLES FER
67271	IRON,SIMPLE STEEL COILS	W 65719	17937	W 83776	23396	W 67993	24829	W 62509	20480	EBAUCHES NON EN ACIER
673	IRON,STEEL SHAPES ETC	W 86673	37357	W 136809	56130	W 201058	85315	W 191886	82329	BARRES,PROFIL FER,ACIER
6731	IRON,STEEL WIRE ROD	W 45097	14886	W 69527	22879	W 90860	36507	W 85636	30831	FIL MACHINE FER,ACIER
6732	IRON,STEEL BARS ETC	W 21413	11379	W 42903	20255	W 84560	32902	W 80335	35985	BARRES FER,ACIER
674	IRN,STL UNIV,PLATE,SHEET	W 175891	118450		140223	W 214849	179888	W 232080	176145	LARGES PLATS,TOLES
6744	IRN,STL HVY PLATE,ROLLED	W 39218	21325	W 39541	24737	W 40245	32899	W 31345	20778	TOLES LAMINEES PLUS 4.75 MM
6746	IRN,STL THIN PLATE,ROLLD	W 70538	53026		65409	W 87143	81209	W 84141	75394	TOLES LAM MOINS 3MM
67461	— OF IRON OR SIMPLE STL	W 60635	32843		38237	W 68347	43704	W 61115	37068	TOL NON AC FIN MOINS 3 MM
6749	OTH IRN,STL PLATES,SHEET	W 39183	28420	W 44397	32033	W 44915	39000	W 54100	43398	AUTRES TOLES FER,ACIER
67491	— OF IRON OR SIMPLE STL	W 37335	26583	W 42996	30290	W 44581	38225	W 53098	41307	AUT TOLES AUTRES ACIER FIN
678	IRON,STL TUBES,PIPES,ETC	W 34773	34039	W 40744	39696	W 47642	58329	W 50252	59702	TUBES,TUYAUX EN FONTE,FER
68	NON–FERROUS METALS		139030		183908		227381		225864	METAUX NON FERREUX
682	COPPER EXC CEMENT COPPER	W 13112	36670	W 14063	43544	W 14568	59083	W 14003	50975	CUIVRE
6822	COPPER,ALLOYS WORKED	W 8180	28159	W 9074	34201	W 10984	49787	W 10303	42527	CUIVRE,ALLIAGES OUVRES
683	NICKEL	W 2797	15027	W 3503	20453	W 3327	26711	W 3515	30131	NICKEL
684	ALUMINIUM	W 32082	60933	W 39655	90605	W 36876	104985	W 44051	105168	ALUMINIUM
6841	ALUMINIUM,ALLOYS,UNWRGHT	W 21214	25646	W 27204	42802	W 25173	50846	W 29570	49040	ALUMINIUM,ALLIAGES BRUTS
6842	ALUMINIUM,ALLOYS WORKED	W 10868	35287	W 12451	47803	W 11703	54139	W 14481	56128	ALUMINIUM,ALLIAGES OUVRE
69	METAL MANUFACTURES NES		183250		226127		310383		329729	ART MANUFACT EN METAL NDA
691	STRUCTURES AND PARTS NES	W 5533	11272	W 8607	18424	W 12734	28379	W 15554	32630	CONSTRUCT FER,ACIER,ALU
692	METAL TANKS,BOXES,ETC	W 6802	18473	W 7702	24911	W 11072	39608	W 11550	40403	RECIPIENTS METALLIQUES
6924	MTL TRANSPORT BOXES ETC	W 6468	17339	W 7137	21253	W 10130	33916	W 11054	37158	FUTS,TAMBOURS,BIDONS
69241	STL TRANSPORT BOXES ETC	W 4152	11403	W 5743	16114	W 8644	27874	W 9898	31568	FUTS,TAMBOURS,BIDONS FER
693	WIRE PRODUCTS NON ELECTR	W 9957	18734	W 9290	19770	W 11283	27264	W 13067	28943	OUVRAGES FILS METALLIQUES
694	STL,COPPR NAILS,NUTS,ETC	W 3539	13893	W 4731	19251	W 6030	27442	W 7548	35518	CLOUS,VIS,ECROUS
69402	IRN,STL NUTS,BOLTS,ETC	W 2608	12875	W 3787	17796	W 4949	25861	W 5896	33617	BOULONS,VIS,ECROUS FER,AC
695	TOOLS	W 2163	30964	W 2120	31606	W 2134	41223	W 2606	46930	OUTILS A MAIN
6954	BLADES,TIPS,ETC FR TOOLS	W 1003	20625	W 660	20490	W 760	26462	W 1081	31546	OUTILS POUR MACHINE–OUTIL
699	BASE METAL MFRS NES	W 12817	67081		87423		117097	W 25419	114687	ART MANUFACTURES MET NDA
6991	LOCKSMITHS WARES,ETC	W 3917	25706	W 8630	34808	W 10272	45286	W 11310	48609	ARTICLES DE SERRURERIE
69913	BASE MTL DOOR,ETC FITTNG	W 3490	21028	W 8079	29113	W 9595	37863	W 10783	40582	GARNITURES POUR MEUBLES
6997	IRON,STEEL ARTICLES NES	W 4025	17348	W 5736	21980	W 7528	32580	W 6912	25817	OUV FONTE,FER,ACIER NDA
69979	IRN,STL MANUFACTURES NES	W 3994	17287	W 5707	21898	W 7449	32412	W 6686	25453	AUT OUVRAGES EN FER NDA
7	MACHINES,TRANSPORT EQUIP		1966350		2319844		3200764		3170398	MACHINES MATERIEL TRANSPORT
71	POWER GENERATING EQUIPMT		138376		150801		227153		254527	MACHINES GENERATRICES
713	INTRNL COMBUS PSTN ENGIN	W 7057	80411	W 13421	112630	W 15925	160739	W 11479	163537	MOTEURS EXPL COMB INT, PIECE
7132	MOTOR VEHCL PISTN ENGINS	W 6098	68819	W 12656	101265	W 14909	145452	W 10707	150949	MOTEURS EXPL POUR VEHICULES
716	ROTATING ELECTRIC PLANT	W 4113	25665	W 5712	30793	W 4419	35433	W 7004	56501	APP ELECTR ROTATIFS,PIECES
7162	AC MTRS,GENRTRS,GEN SETS	W 2089	15061	W 2820	18764	W 2640	21395	W 3938	31839	MOTEURS ELECTRIQUES
718	OTH POWER GENERATG MACHY	W 523	23616	W 424	4716	W 498	26855	W 480	27250	AUTRES MOTEURS PARTIES
72	MACHS FOR SPCL INDUSTRYS		197834		272644		376578		290668	MAC SPECIALES POUR INDUST
721	AGRIC MACHY,EXC TRACTORS	W 2304	9197	W 3353	17025	W 5327	28666	W 4540	25974	MACHINES AGRICOLES
722	TRACTORS NON–ROAD	W 7084	20368	W 5690	22425	W 6316	32882	W 5430	31088	TRACTEURS
7224	WHEELED TRACTORS NES	W 6998	19902	W 5653	21945	W 6261	32001	W 5349	30520	TRACTEURS A ROUES
723	CIVIL ENGNEERG EQUIP ETC	W 4441	15056	W 6557	27762	W 10211	49844	W 7672	37830	APPAREILS DE GENIE CIVIL
7234	CONST,MINING MACHNRY NES	W 3654	12544	W 5175	21879	W 8861	44057	W 6729	32320	MACH POUR LA CONST, MINES
72342	SLFPRP SHOVELS,EXCAVATRS	W 3167	9045	W 4469	15890	W 7470	32974	W 5311	21794	PELLES MECANIQUES
724	TEXTILE,LEATHER MACHNRY	W 4975	35974	W 6510	48340	W 6865	60475	W 3561	42092	MACH POUR INDUSTRIE TEXTILE
726	PRINTG,BKBINDG MACHY,PTS	W 1071	18357	W 1493	25274	W 1405	27796	W 1298	19903	MACHINES POUR IMPRIMERIE
728	OTH MACHY FOR SPCL INDUS	W 7022	81383	W 8104	98610	W 11717	137429	W 9456	106666	AUT MACH IND PARTICULIERES
7281	MACH–TOOLS FR SPCL INDUS	W 3080	18424	W 3127	23590	W 3568	34219	W 3236	29339	MACH–OUTILS SPEC IND PART
7284	MACHY FOR SPCL INDUS NES	W 3316	59456	W 4173	70448	W 5843	88615	W 4747	68350	MACH SPEC IND PARTICUL.

4. Special Imports C.I.F. by Commodities according to the S.I.T.C. (Rev. 2) in thousand U.S. Dollars
Importations Spéciales C.A.F. par Produits d'après la C.T.C.I. (Rév. 2) en milliers de Dollars E.U.

SITC CTCI	COMMODITY	1993 WEIGHT POIDS	1993 VALUE VALEUR	1994 WEIGHT POIDS	1994 VALUE VALEUR	1995 WEIGHT POIDS	1995 VALUE VALEUR	1996 WEIGHT POIDS	1996 VALUE VALEUR	PRODUIT
72848	OTH MCHY WITH INDIV FNCT	W 1415	25367	W 1838	39105	W 2440	46841	W 1855	32717	AUTRES MACHINES NDA
73	METALWORKING MACHINERY		45420		44481		66725		62290	MACH TRAVAIL DES METAUX
736	METALWORKING MACH–TOOLS	W 5049	35133	W 5076	36605	W 7754	52058	W 5117	42798	MACH–OUTILS TRAVAIL METAUX
74	GENRL INDUSTRL MACHY NES		267391		373600		422651		410307	MACH APP INDUSTRIE
741	HEATING,COOLING EQUIPMNT	W 5959	56994	W 5640	72425	W 6366	77566	W 6923	81660	MACH CHAUFFAGE,PIECES
7416	HEATING,COOLING EQU NES	W 1094	14020	W 1207	28454	W 1213	20007	W 1321	20035	APP CHANGEMENT TEMP
742	PUMPS FOR LIQUIDS ETC	W 1815	18829	W 1545	22097	W 1852	29775	W 1289	27516	POMPES MOTO–POMPES
743	PUMPS NES,CENTRFUGES ETC	W 9721	60241	W 18888	129671	W 16357	96478	W 15303	79655	POMPES COMPRES,VENT ETC
7431	PUMPS FOR GASES ETC	W 6479	33947	W 6933	33929	W 7379	43777	W 6412	37197	POMPES AIR A VIDE,COMPRES
7436	GAS,LIQUID FILTERS ETC	W 1181	15159	W 6355	79492	W 2169	30468	W 1311	19809	APP POUR FILT DES LIQUIDES
744	MECHANICAL HANDLING EQU	W 3667	20769	W 4922	25877	W 6433	41004	W 8142	52939	EQUIP MANUTENTION PIECES
7442	LIFTING,LOADING MACH NES	W 1522	11474	W 1947	12482	W 2839	20670	W 3789	29274	APP LEVAGE,MANUTENTION
745	NONELEC MACHY,TOOLS NES	W 1756	34059	W 1875	39904	W 2760	67339	W 2608	54396	AUT MACH NON ELEC,PIECES
7452	OTH NONELEC MCHS,PTS NES	W 1609	29624	W 1629	33651	W 2348	57367	W 2243	45002	AUT MACH NON ELEC,PIECES
74522	PACKAGNG,BOTTLNG,ETC MCH	W 424	12806	W 634	19213	W 1042	36155	W 724	22154	MACH NETT BOUTEILLES,ETC
749	NONELEC MACH PTS,ACC NES	W 5232	76498	W 6532	83625	W 8461	110489	W 8588	114141	PIECES MACH NON ELEC NDA
7492	COCKS,VALVES ETC NES	W 1940	31538	W 2194	32033	W 2374	43199	W 3259	49913	ART ROB,SIM POUR TUYAUX
75	OFFICE MACHNES,ADP EQUIP		151759		160406		223686		211621	MACH BUREAU TRAIT AUTOM
752	AUTOMTIC DATA PROC EQUIP	W 1537	100267	W 1525	101276	W 1948	143718	W 2321	150437	MACH TRAIT INFORMATION
7523	DIGITL CENTRL PROCESSORS	W 268	28808	W 182	27928	W 266	36395	W 391	36416	UNITES CENTRALES
7524	DIGITL CENTRL STOR UNITS	W 152	23850	W 159	22957	W 175	32090	W 205	29188	UNITES MEMOIRE CENTRALES
7525	ADP PERIPHERAL UNITS	W 967	35049	W 1073	36547	W 1408	53486	W 1454	49231	UNITES PERIPHERIQUES
759	OFFICE,ADP MCH PTS,ACCES	W 661	37226	W 778	44083	W 1013	58849	W 781	43942	PIECES DU 751 ET 752
7599	ACCTG,ETC,ADP MCH PTS,AC	W 604	34459	W 709	40959	W 915	54272	W 688	39776	PIECES DU 751 ET 752
76	TELECOMM,SOUND EQUIPMENT		98886		105143		173101		159209	EQUIPMENT DE TELECOM
764	TELECOM EQPT,PTS,ACC NES	W 1141	65549	W 1772	70327	W 1900	123697	W 2002	117900	EQUIP TELECOM,PIECES
7643	TV,RADIO TRANSMITTRS ETC	W 84	14537	W 69	21217	W 52	23066	W 77	28373	APP EMET TELE RADIO
7648	TELECOMM EQUIPMENT NES	W 100	18770	W 53	2951	W 153	34105	W 52	6923	APP TELECOM NDA
76483	RADAR APPARATUS ETC	W 87	17377	W 23	1333	W 77	28742	W 11	3995	APP DE RADIOGUIDAGE ETC
7649	PTS NES OF EQUIPMT OF 76	W 644	15786	W 1215	26144	W 1008	39328	W 1227	55263	PIECES DE LA DIV 76
77	ELECTRIC MACHNRY NES ETC		298426		390842		467244		516200	MACH APP ELECT NDA
771	ELECTRIC POWER MACHY NES	W 860	11393	W 992	15421	W 1466	24400	W 2082	29831	MACH PROD,TRANS ELECTR
772	SWITCHGEAR ETC,PARTS NES	W 2822	56027	W 3272	76166	W 3852	91454	W 3859	108224	APP COUPURE,SECT ETC
7721	SWITCHGEAR ETC	W 2682	51886	W 3185	71300	W 3703	82624	W 3633	98596	APP COUPURE,SECTIONMNT
773	ELECTR DISTRIBUTNG EQUIP	W 15416	71184	W 22215	94989	W 19431	106623	W 22039	112683	EQUIPMT DISTRIBUTION ELECT
7731	INSULATED WIRE,CABLE ETC	W 14860	67916	W 21584	90670	W 18835	101250	W 21213	105645	FILS,CABLES ISOLES ELECT
775	HOUSEHOLD TYPE EQUIP NES	W 5740	47377	W 6310	55376	W 7145	64705	W 6565	62207	MACH,APP USAGE DOMESTQUE
7758	ELECTRO–THERMIC APPL NES	W 2540	22133	W 2784	26591	W 2921	29942	W 2772	29266	APP ELECTROTHERMIQ NDA
776	TRANSISTORS,VALVES,ETC	W 1434	25020	W 2420	46293	W 1858	51978	W 3274	69788	LAMPES,TUBES,VALVES
7764	ELECTRONIC MICROCIRCUITS	W 45	12284	W 76	24111	W 66	29407	W 142	37813	MICROSTRUCTURES ELECTRON
778	ELECTRICAL MACHINERY NES	W 9069	71340	W 10124	82838	W 12125	112387	W 31112	113502	AUTRES MACH ELECT NDA
7783	AUTOMOTIVE ELECTR EQUIP	W 1658	17083	W 2234	23835	W 3051	33978	W 2956	33697	EQUIP ELECT MOTEURS EXPL
7788	OTH ELEC MACHY,EQUIP NES	W 3171	26287	W 4109	29445	W 3998	38856	W 3754	39756	AUT MACH APP ELEC NDA
78	ROAD VEHICLES		755024		799157		1194381		1197316	VEHICULES ROUTIERS
781	PASS MOTOR VEH EXC BUSES	W 54607	458545	W 53337	431697	W 64204	611131	W 64277	628444	AUTO TRANSPORT PERSONNES
782	LORRIES,SPCL MTR VEH NES	W 8387	51621	W 10273	66316	W 13902	110341	W 13074	108198	VEHICULES SPECIAUX,MARCH
7821	LORRIES,TRUCKS	W 7946	48866	W 9860	61232	W 13251	101603	W 12145	97555	VEHICULES TRANSP MARCHAND
783	ROAD MOTOR VEHICLES NES	W 5155	25987	W 4158	34116	W 5925	68797	W 2994	31567	VEHICULES ROUTIERS NDA
7832	TRACTORS FOR TR–TRAILERS	W 2538	17558	W 3436	26520	W 4345	43733	W 2148	19458	TRACTEURS ROUTIERS
784	MOTOR VEH PRTS,ACCES NES	W 29525	188807	W 31567	234997	W 40718	356172	W 58813	383483	PIECES 722,781,782,783
7849	OTHER MOTOR VEHCL PARTS	W 28495	185126	W 30809	233106	W 40213	354366	W 57934	377849	PIECES 722,781,782,783
786	TRAILERS,NONMOTR VEH,NES	W 6521	16878	W 6697	19398	W 7801	29299	W 6432	25251	REMORQUES,CADRES,CONTAIN
79	OTHR TRANSPORT EQUIPMENT		13233		22769		49246		68260	AUTRE MATERIEL TRANSPORT
792	AIRCRAFT ETC		5120	W 65	17007	W 286	33231	W 114	54029	APP NAVIGATION AERIENNE
7924	AIRCRFT NES OVER 15000KG							W 60	34952	AERODYNES PLUS 15000 KG
8	MISC MANUFACTURED GOODS		770910		785162		1000082		1261778	ART MANUFACTURES DIVERS
812	*PLUMBG,HEATNG,LGHTNG EQ	W 8405	28507	W 11206	37039	W 12965	49054	W 14186	57027	APPAR SANITAIRES CHAUFFAGE
821	*FURNITURE,PARTS THEREOF	W 16053	67531	W 16932	82703	W 22063	114108	W 23521	125062	MEUBLES ET PIECES
8211	CHAIRS,SEATS AND PARTS	W 7969	43504	W 8774	53444	W 9524	69179	W 11230	78356	SIEGES ET PIECES
82111	CHAIRS AND OTHER SEATS	W 2960	12473	W 4247	20219	W 6197	34398	W 6075	39509	SIEGES
82119	PTS NES OF CHAIRS ETC	W 5008	31030	W 4527	33226	W 3327	34781	W 5156	38847	PIECES DU 821.11
8219	FURNITURE AND PARTS NES	W 7293	18030	W 7175	22034	W 11034	34656	W 10674	36048	AUTRES MEUBLES ET PIECES
84	CLOTHING AND ACCESSORIES		231702		219589		261937		480982	VETEMENTS
842	MENS OUTERWEAR NOT KNIT	W 1625	38295	W 1652	39949	W 1594	42288	W 3714	104299	VET DESSUS POUR HOMMES
8423	— TROUSERS,BREECHES ETC	W 605	13135	W 667	14715	W 800	18972	W 1534	37504	PANTALONS HOMMES MAT TEX
843	WOMENS OUTERWEAR NONKNIT	W 2291	62987	W 2271	62682	W 2376	77007	W 4913	172891	VET DESSUS FEMMES MAT TEX
8431	— COATS AND JACKETS	W 518	15983	W 549	17880	W 520	19179	W 1368	55689	MANT,VEST FEM MAT TEXTIL
8439	— OTHER OUTER GARMENTS	W 1286	28541	W 1319	30030	W 1416	38631	W 2485	72950	AUT VET DES FEM MAT TEXT
845	OUTERWEAR KNIT NONELASTC	W 2537	42182	W 1845	39971	W 1940	53015	W 2706	73947	VET DESSOUS,ACCES BONNET
8451	— JERSEYS,PULLOVERS ETC	W 1268	16518	W 879	19623	W 926	25065	W 1436	35944	CHANDAILS,PULL–OVERS ETC
8459	— OTHER,CLTHG ACCESRYS	W 1214	23999	W 916	19019	W 967	26489	W 1158	33641	AUT VET DESSUS DE BONNE
846	UNDER GARMENTS KNITTED	W 3217	47532	W 2492	41414	W 2788	50336	W 4328	81281	SOUS VETS DE BONNETERIE
8462	— OF COTTON NON ELASTIC	W 1083	20343	W 1410	25386	W 1571	31858	W 1603	39998	SOUS–VET BONNET COTON
84629	—— OTHER	W 1083	20343	W 1410	25386	W 1571	31858	W 1603	39998	AUT SOUS–VET BONNET COTON
8463	— OF SYNTH FBR NONELAST	W 2060	23939	W 1003	12331	W 1131	14238	W 2472	27971	SOUS–VET BONNET FIB SYNT
84631	—— PANTY HOSE (TIGHTS)	W 1997	22408	W 956	11270	W 1076	12989	W 2393	26127	COLLANTS BON FIBR SYNT
851	*FOOTWEAR	W 3829	53691	W 3755	49031	W 4042	61528	W 3758	60233	CHAUSSURES
85102	FOOTWEAR LEATHER	W 2972	45806	W 2749	40454	W 2963	50273	W 2723	49173	CHAUS SEMELLES EN CUIR
87	PRECISION INSTRUMNTS NES		98971		117738		143246		145713	INSTRUM,APPAR SCIENT NDA
872	MEDICAL INSTRUMENTS NES	W 1170	33020	W 1358	39233	W 1562	42216	W 1692	40594	INSTR,APP MEDIC–CHIR NDA
87202	OTH MEDICAL INSTRUMENTS	W 1063	27198	W 1216	32050	W 1367	34434	W 1471	31836	INSTRUM,APP MEDECINE
874	MEASURNG,CONTROLNG INSTR	W 956	55481	W 1090	64744	W 1457	83770	W 1531	81777	INSTRUMENTS DE MESURE
88	PHOTO EQU,OPTICL GDS ETC		40859		47139		64974		64947	APP,FOURN PHOTO,OP,MONTR
89	MISC MANUFCTRD GOODS NES		240150		219710		289136		313640	ART MANUFACTURES DIVERS
892	PRINTED MATTER	W 4721	18977	W 6610	28658	W 7188	41365	W 8983	55539	IMPRIMES
893	ARTICLES OF PLASTIC NES		124619		87112		115785		123020	OUVRAGES EN MAT DIVIS 58
8931	PLSTC PACKG CONTNRS,LIDS	W 7680	21273	W 8352	22702	W 10039	33834	W 11489	30766	ART TRANSP EMBALLAGE ETC
8939	MISC PLASTIC ARTICLES	W 10194	99201	W 11577	59763	W 13457	76539	W 14167	85601	ART DIVERS EN MAT DIV 58
89399	OTHR PLASTC ARTICLES NES	W 8058	92793	W 8447	52673	W 10685	67452	W 11176	76326	AUT OUV MAT DIV 58
894	TOYS,SPORTING GOODS,ETC	W 3282	29455	W 2910	30959	W 3425	39551	W 3420	38881	VOITURES ENFANTS,JOUETS
8942	TOYS,INDOOR GAMES ETC	W 2581	21800	W 2028	21686	W 2194	24546	W 2181	24541	JOUETS,JEUX ETC
898	MUSICAL INSTRUMENTS,PTS	W 831	26016	W 822	25443	W 1036	37383	W 1096	40330	INSTRUMENTS DE MUSIQUE
8983	SOUND RECRDNG TAPE,DISCS	W 465	21834	W 527	20872	W 684	30360	W 790	34136	SUPPORTS SON POUR 763
89832	RECORDED DISCS,TAPES ETC	W 189	17327	W 235	16283	W 368	25104	W 424	28514	DISQUES,PHONO,BANDES
899	OTHER MANUFACTURED GOODS		23125		27981		32941		33390	AUT ART MANUF DIVERS NDA
9	GOODS NOT CLASSD BY KIND		262471		246488		278291		39219	ART TRANSACT NON CLASSES
931	*SPECIAL TRANSACTIONS	W 19659	256282	W 20531	239614	W 60012	272017	W 3908	29579	TRANS.SPECIALES

5. Special Exports F.O.B. by Commodities according to the S.I.T.C. (Rev. 2) in thousand U.S. Dollars
Exportations Spéciales F.O.B. par Produits d'après la C.T.C.I. (Rév. 2) en milliers de Dollars E.U.

SITC CTCI	COMMODITY	1993 WEIGHT POIDS	1993 VALUE VALEUR	1994 WEIGHT POIDS	1994 VALUE VALEUR	1995 WEIGHT POIDS	1995 VALUE VALEUR	1996 WEIGHT POIDS	1996 VALUE VALEUR	PRODUIT
	ALL COMMODITIES		6082865		6827850		8315815		8309813	TOUS PRODUITS
0	FOOD AND LIVE ANIMALS		239228		274515		263127		263862	ALIMENTS,ANIMAUX VIVANTS
01	MEAT AND PREPARATIONS		80828		87382		80455		83293	VIANDES ET PREPARATIONS
011	MEAT FRESH,CHILLD,FROZEN	W 26373	47463	W 17379	36724	W 14119	30919	W 13581	28580	VIANDES FRAICHES,REF,CONGE
0114	POULTRY FRESH CHLLD,FRZN	W 19746	26155	W 12251	18691	W 10462	16410	W 11377	19190	VOLAILLES MORTES
014	MEAT PREPD,PRSVD,NES ETC	W 11372	27863	W 16374	42657	W 14445	43468	W 15335	49181	CONSERVES DE VIANDES
0142	SAUSAGES INCLDING TINNED	W 5488	16563	W 7805	22724	W 6147	21360	W 10771	32759	SAUCISSES,SAUCISSONS
02	DAIRY PRODCTS,BIRDS'EGGS		25167		29157		36951		36424	PRODUITS LAITIERS,OEUFS
022	MILK AND CREAM	W 56056	18483	W 73566	22147	W 83979	29538	W 68538	28477	LAIT ET CREME
0223	MILK AND CREAM FRESH	W 46427	13432	W 62266	18590	W 77696	26257	W 65814	26536	LAIT,CREME FRAIS
04	CEREALS AND PREPARATIONS		15066		16828		14226		27861	CEREALES ET PRODUITS
05	VEGETABLES AND FRUIT		55661		64208		57463		44093	LEGUMES ET FRUITS
054	VEG ETC FRSH,SMPLY PRSVD	W 6862	24525	W 21564	32595	W 14237	23670	W 8057	16758	LEGUMES FRAIS,CONG,SECS
058	FRUIT PRESERVED,PREPARED	W 40818	20862	W 22220	19005	W 18604	19610	W 9134	12454	CONSERVES DE FRUITS
09	MISC EDIBLE PRODUCTS		18255		26701		28324		24091	PREP ALIMENTAIRES DIVERSES
098	EDIBLE PRODCTS,PREPS NES	W 7295	17886	W 9788	26371	W 10934	27994	W 12019	23680	PREP ALIMENTAIRES NDA
1	BEVERAGES AND TOBACCO		45149		49581		51085		72399	BOISSONS ET TABACS
11	BEVERAGES		36651		38076		41552		60683	BOISSONS
111	NON–ALCOHL BEVERAGES NES	W 1326769	12317	W 1964145	17042	W 1979467	18892	W 2111227	32956	BOISSONS NON ALCOOLIQUES
11102	FLAVORED WATERS NON–ALCO	W 20220	6825	W 33684	11401	W 26051	14035	W 36934	26900	LIMONADES,EAUX GAZEUSES
112	ALCOHOLIC BEVERAGES	W 128741	24334	W 45686	21035	W 43486	22660	W 47829	27726	BOISSONS ALCOOLIQUES
2	CRUDE MATERLS,EXCL FUELS		107415		130925		170511		138864	MAT BRUTES NON COMESTIBLES
24	CORK AND WOOD		67224		74941		84335		74143	LIEGE ET BOIS
248	WOOD SHAPED,SLEEPERS	W 212426	53938	W 232952	60673	W 221389	71579	W 199060	62319	BOIS SIMPLEMENT TRAVAILLES
2482	LUMBER SHAPED CONIFER	W 141424	34386	W 152081	37237	W 136406	42258	W 127593	36258	CONIFERES SCIES,RABOTES
24821	LUMBER SAWN ETC CONIFER	W 137404	31500	W 148161	34147	W 132764	39082	W 122927	33135	CONIFERES SCIES LONGITUD
2483	LUMBER SHAPED NON–CONIFR	W 71003	19550	W 80870	23436	W 84875	29314	W 71391	26020	NON CONIFERES SCIES,RABOTES
24831	LUMBER SAWN ETC NON–CON	W 69947	17953	W 79729	21997	W 84100	28065	W 70124	24370	SCIES LONGITUDINALEMENT
251	*PULP AND WASTE PAPER	W 30582	8646	W 46328	19519	W 57105	38165	W 39129	15574	PATES A PAPIER,DECHETS
2518	SULPHITE WOOD PULP	W 19481	7576	W 33139	18220	W 46505	36218	W 36209	15306	PATES AU BISULFITE
25182	— BLEACHED,NONDISSOLVNG	W 19111	7541	W 32952	18198	W 46505	36218	W 36197	15305	PATES BLANCHES
3	MINERAL FUELS ETC		314387		77378		99774		77913	COMBUSTIBLES MINERAUX LUB
33	PETROLEUM AND PRODUCTS		267487		22523		14292		26190	PETROLE ET DERIVES
333	CRUDE PETROLEUM	W 1818955	230174	W 94211	9116	W 179	26			HUILES BRUTES DE PETROLE
334	PETROLEUM PRODUCTS,REFIN	W 292738	35141	W 39855	11238	W 55973	13794	W 128051	25213	PRODUITS RAFFINES
3341	GASOLINE,OTH LIGHT OILS	W 121310	19036	W 27472	4532	W 43787	6873	W 111280	16517	ESSENCES POUR MOTEURS
351	*ELECTRIC CURRENT		42481		53081		84932		51199	ENERGIE ELECTRIQUE
5	CHEMCLS,RELATED PROD NES		541627		692892		852660		864720	PRODUITS CHIMIQUES
51	ORGANIC CHEMICALS		28527		84818		114685		77056	PROD CHIMIQ ORGANIQUES
513	CARBOXYLIC ACIDS ETC	W 12699	7452	W 27810	21420	W 27586	38383	W 34794	26490	ACIDES CARBOXYLIQUES
5138	POLYACIDS AND DERIVATIVS	W 11924	5861	W 27329	20510	W 27122	37456	W 34361	25683	ACIDES POLYCARBOXYLIQUES
515	ORG–INORG COMPOUNDS ETC	W 1211	17866	W 1428	49460	W 1466	56113	W 1261	39842	COMPOSES ORGANO–MINERAUX
5156	HETEROCYCLIC CMPDS ETC	W 1173	17713	W 1380	49191	W 1448	56014	W 1245	39774	COMPOSES HETEROCYCLIQUES
51569	OTH HETEROCYC CMPDS,ETC	W 1173	17713	W 1380	49191	W 1448	56014	W 1245	39773	AUT COMP HETEROCYCLIQUES
52	INORGANIC CHEMICALS		44213		52761		63995		76413	PROD CHIM INORGANIQUES
523	OTHR INORG CHEMICALS ETC	W 98932	35419	W 154482	37662	W 100517	43828	W 123533	57068	AUT PRODUITS CHIMIQUES INORG
5232	OTH MTL CMPD OF INRG ACD	W 36165	20029	W 63599	19627	W 45235	25204	W 72939	37710	SELS METALLIQUES
53	DYES,TANNING,COLOUR PROD		80903		83477		118485		124436	PROD TEINTURE,COLORANTS
533	PIGMENTS,PAINTS,ETC	W 44817	76739	W 52488	78986	W 63094	113328	W 72996	119117	PIGMENTS,PEINTURES,VERNIS
5331	COLOURING MATERIAL NES	W 21508	28874	W 25580	38329	W 25003	50200	W 21758	39557	AUT MATIERES COLORANTES
5334	VARNISHES,DISTEMPERS ETC	W 17145	39628	W 17960	31487	W 24699	48797	W 25937	53698	PEINTURES A L'EAU
53342	OTH PAINTS,VARNISHES ETC	W 11111	34417	W 7206	22397	W 10123	35330	W 11561	41876	AUTRES PEINTURES,VERNIS
541	*MEDICINAL,PHARM PRODUCT		234691		283071		318773		357708	PROD MEDICINAUX PHARMACEUT
5417	MEDICAMENTS	K 6713642	211543	K 6918050	253944	K 7870657	293833	K 8503636	338113	MEDICAMENTS
54171	— CONTAINNG ANTIBIOTICS	K 1944534	37244	K 1209309	39231	K 1487709	52397	K 1439649	68258	MED CONTN ANTIBIOTIQUES
54179	— CONTNG OTH SUBSTANCES	K 4559303	166317	K 5404577	204605	K 6148317	230951	K 6746341	251656	MED CONT AUT SUBSTANCES
55	PERFUME,CLEANING ETC PRD		60967		78598		85494		92700	PROD POUR PARFUM,TOILETTE
553	PERFUMERY,COSMETICS,ETC	W 5211	32376	W 14624	44585	W 8909	48757	W 11445	55205	PRODUITS DE PARFUMERIE
554	SOAP,CLEANSING ETC PREPS	W 22384	20488	W 26612	23652	W 26661	25000	W 27091	24830	SAVONS,PRODUITS DETERSIFS
58	PLASTIC MATERIALS ETC		51248		67874		110015		99330	MAT PLAST ARTIFICIELLES
582	PROD OF CONDENSATION ETC	W 47532	21708	W 40632	28129	W 121600	54184	W 93410	48285	PROD CONDENS,POLYCOND
583	POLYMERIZATION ETC PRODS	W 20337	29339	W 28507	39504	W 30590	55746	W 32084	50791	PROD POLYMERISATION
5839	OTH POLYMRZTION ETC PROD	W 9476	18369	W 10943	20608	W 11450	29257	W 12929	26806	AUT PROD POLYMER COPOLYM
59	CHEMICAL MATERIALS NES		35071		37564		37082		32646	MAT PROD CHIMIQUES NDA
598	MISCEL CHEM PRODUCTS NES	W 47450	20316	W 49427	19865	W 36682	17649	W 12695	10534	PROD DIV INDUST CHIM NDA
5989	CHEM PRODUCTS,PREPS NES	W 46109	19551	W 48744	19156	W 34925	16788	W 12206	9971	PROD PREP CHIMIQUES NDA
6	BASIC MANUFACTURES		1669425		1952511		2468511		2376681	ART MANUFACTURES
61	LEATHER,DRESSED FUR,ETC		89800		100292		99892		93961	CUIRS,PELLETERIES
611	LEATHER		60976	W 6311	68514	W 4952	61442	W 3048	55130	CUIRS,PEAUX PREPARES
6116	LEATHER OF OTH HIDE,SKIN		51278	W 2979	55814	W 2555	54247	W 2397	51375	PEAUX PREP D'AUTRES ANIMAUX
61169	LEATHER NES	W 3130	51278	W 2976	55804	W 2554	54223	W 2394	51323	PEAUX PREPAREES NDA
612	LEATHER ETC MANUFACTURES	W 2768	26951	W 3163	28347	W 3396	34424	W 2875	32448	OUVRAGES EN CUIRS NDA
6123	PREPRD PARTS OF FOOTWEAR	W 2636	23555	W 3009	25725	W 3134	29406	W 2531	26635	PARTIES DE CHAUSSURES
62	RUBBER MANUFACTURES NES		142893		155165		199740		199503	CAOUTCHOUC MANUFACTURE
625	RUBBER TYRES, TUBES ETC	W 39965	114813	W 58555	125257	W 46651	158047	W 42169	154344	PNEUS CAOUTCHOUC VULCANISE
6251	TYRES NEW FOR MOTOR CARS	W 18304	55326	W 16426	50715	W 18086	65223	W 16908	66059	PNEUS POUR VOITURES
6252	TYRES,NEW,BUS OR LORRY	W 13288	36829	W 21593	49643	W 20314	65746	W 18414	64178	PNEUS POUR AUTOBUS,CAMIONS
63	WOOD,CORK MANUFACTRS NES		220833		267407		315976		313279	OUVRAGES LIEGE ET BOIS
634	VENEERS,PLYWOOD,ETC	W 57592	29637	W 66568	36097	W 71218	48098	W 68758	43106	PLACAGES,CONTRE–PLAQUES
635	WOOD MANUFACTURES NES	W 115982	191125	W 121052	231260	W 113961	267846	W 117560	270146	ART MANUF EN BOIS NDA
6353	BUILDERS WOODWRK,PREFABS	W 100677	168695	W 105152	204178	W 97456	235500	W 99801	235380	OUVRAGES DE MENUISERIE
64	PAPER,PAPERBOARD AND MFR		246471		302465		408043		350383	PAPIERS,CARTONS & OUVRAGES
641	PAPER AND PAPERBOARD	W 235994	157671	W 289542	214316	W 302604	301737	W 298251	247349	PAPIERS ET CARTONS
6411	NEWSPRINT	W 17520	7585	W 18761	8758	W 32733	25744	W 29755	21890	PAPIER JOURNAL
6412	PRINTG,WRITING PAPER NES	W 63620	53764	W 66919	65367	W 59331	78817	W 63347	68088	PAPIERS POUR L'IMPRESSION
64122	— COATED,IMPREGNATD ETC	W 61671	52171	W 64961	63262	W 55955	74317	W 61083	65956	PAPIERS IMPRESSION COUCHES
6415	PAPER,PAPERBRD,BULK,NES	W 63660	41945	W 71239	55005	W 74129	81467	W 67145	57491	PAPIERS,CARTONS ROULEAUX
64159	OTHER PAPER ETC,BULK,NES	W 63341	41712	W 70272	54313	W 73393	80688	W 66609	56944	AUT PAPIER ROULEAUX FEUILLES
6418	COATED ETC PAPER NES BLK	W 57354	40200	W 90173	67458	W 97704	94673	W 101443	81992	PAP,CARTONS COUCHES,ENDUITS
64189	COATED PAPER ETC NES	W 57292	40125	W 90109	67389	W 97567	94460	W 101279	81491	PAPIERS,CARTONS COUCHES
642	PAPER,ETC,PRECUT,ARTS OF	W 76653	88801	W 74750	88149	W 70679	106306	W 67902	103034	PAP,CARTONS DECOUPES
6421	PAPER ETC CONTAINERS	W 14638	17187	W 18154	20089	W 17990	24953	W 15474	22535	BOITES,SACS EMBALLAGES
6424	PAPER ETC CT TO SIZE NES	W 27156	27045	W 26759	28995	W 26211	36829	W 23054	29831	PAP,CARTONS DECOUPES
64243	TOILET PAPER CUT TO SIZE	W 24723	22526	W 24917	24592	W 22011	26633	W 19681	21879	PAPIER HYGIENIQUE
6428	PAPER ETC ARTICLES NES	W 32763	40050	W 27013	34369	W 23604	37043	W 25875	42066	OUVRAGES EN PATE A PAPIER
64284	PAPER TISSUES,TOWELS ETC	W 27598	33304	W 21846	27239	W 19165	29504	W 20862	33181	MOUCHOIRS SERVIETTES EN PAP
65	TEXTILE YARN,FABRICS,ETC		246965		268806		321980		325131	FILS,TISSUS,ARTICLES TEXTILE
651	TEXTILE YARN	W 18354	61241		80005	W 21240	95288		99802	FILS TEXTILES
6514	SYN FIB YRN,BULK,MONOFIL	W 9715	32459	W 10948	39107	W 13363	56180	W 16555	67187	FILS CONT 85% FIB TEXT SYNTH
65141	— TEXTRD,CONT POLYAMIDE	W 6684	23874	W 6854	25919	W 6795	30145	W 11046	43887	FILS TEXT FIB CONT POLYAMID
652	COTTON FABRICS,WOVEN	W 3060	22795	W 4336	30181	W 5406	42541	W 5542	47347	TISSUS DE COTON

5. Special Exports F.O.B. by Commodities according to the S.I.T.C. (Rev. 2) in thousand U.S. Dollars
Exportations Spéciales F.O.B. par Produits d'après la C.T.C.I. (Rév. 2) en milliers de Dollars E.U.

SITC CTCI	COMMODITY	1993 WEIGHT POIDS	1993 VALUE VALEUR	1994 WEIGHT POIDS	1994 VALUE VALEUR	1995 WEIGHT POIDS	1995 VALUE VALEUR	1996 WEIGHT POIDS	1996 VALUE VALEUR	PRODUIT
6522	WOVEN COTTON BLEACHD,ETC	W 2658	21430	W 3004	23704	W 2868	29505	W 2814	32626	TISSUS COTON BLANCHIS ETC
65224	BLCHED COTTON FABRIC NES	W 2223	17344	W 2522	18951	W 2348	23380	W 2321	27225	AUT TIS PLUS 85% COT BLANCHI
653	WOVN MAN–MADE FIB FABRIC	W 5199	51885	W 5329	47713	W 6613	54469	W 4887	51972	TISSUS FIBRES SYNTH,ARTIF
657	SPECIAL TXTL FABRC,PRODS	W 9426	35124	W 11269	36589	W 11167	42540		44752	TISSUS SPECIAUX
658	TEXTILE ARTICLES NES	W 7023	48472	W 7215	49253	W 6242	57611	W 5342	52282	ART FACONNES MAT TEXTILES
6584	LINENS ETC	W 2710	25294	W 2599	26752	W 2535	30796	W 2085	26276	LINGE DE MAISON
66	NONMETAL MINERAL MFS NES		150490		165474		198430		213438	ART MIN NON METALLIQUES
663	MINERAL MANUFCTURES NES	W 160121	61402	W 139119	63175	W 266000	75596	W 155605	82621	ART MIN MANUF NDA
6631	GRINDING STONES ETC	W 6211	20006	W 6527	20183	W 7338	25554	W 8029	26918	PIERRES A AIGUISER,MEULES
6635	MINRL INSULATNG PROD NES	W 88661	25667	W 55322	26436	W 165963	29793	W 58080	32049	LAINES DE LAITIER
664	GLASS	W 17098	13587	W 22963	20022	W 22365	21353	W 22707	26770	VERRE
665	GLASSWARE	W 17160	46262	W 22142	48983	W 27084	64822	W 32235	68062	OUVRAGES EN VERRE
6652	HOUSEHLD,HOTEL ETC GLASS	W 9833	40066	W 12435	42299	W 17224	55443	W 16925	56090	OBJETS VERRE TABLE,CUISINE
67	IRON AND STEEL		155539		203563		311593		274494	FER ET ACIER
671	PIG IRON ETC	W 23673	16329	W 29195	19927	W 37387	31589	W 39213	32474	FONTE,SPIEGEL,POUDRES
6716	FERRO–ALLOYS	W 14159	12204	W 17210	14573	W 23683	24503	W 26011	25739	FERRO–ALLIAGES
672	IRON,STEEL PRIMARY FORMS	W 15607	9657	W 16403	9692	W 21262	26387	W 11302	9906	LINGOTS FER,ACIER
673	IRON,STEEL SHAPES ETC	W 97002	51874	W 100657	65537	W 97720	90032	W 82145	88506	BARRES,PROFIL FER,ACIER
6732	IRON,STEEL BARS ETC	W 83234	42567	W 77332	49406	W 80911	71185	W 72699	82901	BARRES FER,ACIER
67325	OTH ALLOY STEEL BARS ETC	W 39024	21645	W 50884	29917	W 54991	46016	W 50968	59304	BARRES NON ACIERS ALLIES
674	IRN,STL UNIV,PLATE,SHEET	W 64020	41444	W 89682	65266	W 87122	99971	W 69906	83829	LARGES PLATS,TOLES
6744	IRN,STL HVY PLATE,ROLLED	W 15929	6977	W 26922	13670	W 24890	27590	W 16661	28102	TOLES LAMINEES PLUS 4.75 MM
67443	— OF STAINLESS ETC STL	W 264	343	W 1193	1844	W 6589	15510	W 11127	24999	TOLES ACIER INOXYDABLE
6745	IRN,STL MED PLATE,ROLLED	W 34011	17776	W 40828	22634	W 42091	30491	W 25418	19583	TOLES 3 A 4.75 MM
67454	— OF OTHER ALLOY STEEL	W 31611	16372	W 34672	19698	W 35766	25341	W 23108	17301	TOLES NON ACIERS ALLIES
6746	IRN,STL THIN PLATE,ROLLD	W 12375	15131	W 18653	26039	W 18189	39039	W 22066	30804	TOLES LAM MOINS 3MM
67463	— OF STAINLESS ETC STL	W 8131	12556	W 13521	21908	W 13631	33494	W 11286	23794	TOL ACIER INOX MOINS 3 MM
678	IRON,STL TUBES,PIPES,ETC	W 34525	21176	W 87202	26301	W 52840	39836	W 51411	35823	TUBES,TUYAUX EN FONTE,FER
6783	IRON,STL TUBES,PIPES NES	W 30656	13363	W 82826	16977	W 47895	26237	W 45961	21405	AUT TUBES,TUYAUX FER,ACIER
68	NON–FERROUS METALS		165262		207865		263135		255663	METAUX NON FERREUX
684	ALUMINIUM	W 79535	122916	W 85199	157962	W 80088	208134	W 89609	199633	ALUMINIUM
6841	ALUMINIUM,ALLOYS,UNWRGHT	W 44599	53055	W 47317	71229	W 42101	86642	W 47750	83084	ALUMINIUM,ALLIAGES BRUTS
6842	ALUMINIUM,ALLOYS WORKED	W 34936	69861	W 37881	86733	W 37986	121491	W 41859	116549	ALUMINIUM,ALLIAGES OUVRE
68421	ALUMINIUM BARS,WIRE,ETC	W 12994	27700	W 16517	39450	W 15415	55997	W 15262	46554	BARRES,PROFILES FILS ALU
68422	ALUMNM PLATE,SHEET,STRIP	W 15709	28135	W 14272	30078	W 14955	40478	W 19692	47768	TOLES, PLANCHES EN ALU
69	METAL MANUFACTURES NES		251172		281474		349722		350829	ART MANUFACT EN METAL NDA
691	STRUCTURES AND PARTS NES	W 14668	29429	W 16251	40908	W 19075	56937	W 19291	56602	CONSTRUCT FER,ACIER,ALU
6911	STRUCTURES,PARTS IRN,STL	W 13663	22982	W 14783	29267	W 17046	40618	W 17713	41529	CONSTRUCT FER,ACIER,FONTE
695	TOOLS	W 6721	46064	W 7358	46073	W 7550	59404	W 6321	57315	OUTILS A MAIN
6953	OTHER HAND TOOLS	W 3605	21763	W 3842	26246	W 3690	32754	W 3191	30724	AUTRES OUTILS A MAIN
69539	HAND TOOLS ETC NES	W 3220	19080	W 3421	23709	W 3180	29039	W 2290	22296	OUTILLAGE A MAIN NDA
6954	BLADES,TIPS,ETC FR TOOLS	W 1276	18662	W 1426	13390	W 1934	19661	W 1625	20650	OUTILS POUR MACHINE–OUTIL
697	BASE MTL HOUSEHOLD EQUIP	W 13377	47409	W 8974	35064	W 7177	35702	W 7352	36656	ART MENAGE MET COMMUNS
6973	DMSTC HEATG,COOKG APPARA	W 6564	21609	W 3501	12472	W 2685	11536	W 2932	12094	APPS CHAUF NON ELECTRIQ
69731	IRN,STL DOM COOKG APPARA	W 5084	19696	W 2501	10763	W 1921	9575	W 1976	9176	APPS CUISSON FER,ACIER
699	BASE METAL MFRS NES	W 36883	100058	W 46229	122402	W 45394	149547	W 47152	151889	ART MANUFACTURES MET NDA
6991	LOCKSMITHS WARES,ETC	W 11184	44246	W 16721	60639	W 17178	69375	W 17781	69599	ARTICLES DE SERRURERIE
69913	BASE MTL DOOR,ETC FITTNG	W 9427	36194	W 14753	51640	W 15730	59404	W 16069	56966	GARNITURES POUR MEUBLES
7	MACHINES,TRANSPORT EQUIP		1662479		2065967		2612629		2771225	MACHINES MATERIEL TRANSPORT
71	POWER GENERATING EQUIPMT		154347		164605		213456		220447	MACHINES GENERATRICES
713	INTRNL COMBUS PSTN ENGIN	W 8927	39986	W 7609	28317	W 7474	41758	W 5638	28557	MOTEURS EXPL COMB INT, PIECE
7139	PISTON ENGINE PARTS NES	W 7260	22162	W 6557	16155	W 6056	22083	W 4937	18803	PIECES POUR 713.2,3,8
716	ROTATING ELECTRIC PLANT	W 21002	106491	W 21510	126458	W 21725	158811	W 23458	175785	APP ELECTR ROTATIFS,PIECES
7162	AC MTRS,GENRTRS,GEN SETS	W 6070	40951	W 6140	43766	W 5797	47915	W 6821	59511	MOTEURS ELECTRIQUES
71621	AC MTRS,INC UNIVRSL MTRS	W 6060	40863	W 6131	43682	W 5781	47842	W 6788	59299	MOT ELEC NON COUR CONTINU
7169	PTS NES OF ROT ELEC PLNT	W 13800	56469	W 13848	70968	W 13913	91610	W 14691	94107	PIECES MAC APP ROTATIFS
72	MACHS FOR SPCL INDUSTRYS		83150		89502		116399		127407	MAC SPECIALES POUR INDUST
728	OTH MACHY FOR SPCL INDUS	W 9493	42132	W 10002	44929	W 10086	56137	W 10643	56916	AUT MACH IND PARTICULIERES
7284	MACHY FOR SPCL INDUS NES	W 3684	21385	W 3248	21933	W 3971	25627	W 5219	29358	MACH SPEC IND PARTICUL.
73	METALWORKING MACHINERY		39437		42647		54126		64113	MACH TRAVAIL DES METAUX
736	METALWORKING MACH–TOOLS	W 4795	21331	W 4552	22091	W 6406	31237	W 5380	34749	MACH–OUTILS TRAVAIL METAUX
737	METALWORKING MACHNRY NES	W 4180	18106	W 5242	20556	W 5634	22889	W 6837	29364	MACH TRAV METAUX PIECES
74	GENRL INDUSTRL MACHY NES		185791		263079		348555		360710	MACH APP INDUSTRIE
741	HEATING,COOLING EQUIPMNT	W 4537	26261	W 5612	35398	W 6170	45845	W 7427	42008	MACH CHAUFFAGE,PIECES
743	PUMPS NES,CENTRFUGES ETC	W 7009	28150	W 15250	58119	W 14246	68504	W 16330	74101	POMPES COMPRES,VENT ETC
7431	PUMPS FOR GASES ETC	W 2285	9416	W 7725	29043	W 9349	42648	W 11141	47956	POMPES AIR A VIDE,COMPRES
7436	GAS,LIQUID FILTERS ETC	W 2939	12613	W 6039	23253	W 3395	18143	W 3746	18614	APP POUR FILT DES LIQUIDES
744	MECHANICAL HANDLING EQU	W 15288	47448	W 20600	58689	W 24666	88334	W 23925	94687	EQUIP MANUTENTION PIECES
7442	LIFTING,LOADING MACH NES	W 3981	16558	W 3813	15297	W 4740	23677	W 6380	31370	APP LEVAGE,MANUTENTION
7449	PTS NES OF MACHY OF 7442	W 9631	23489	W 15578	37753	W 17815	58189	W 15933	55992	PIECES DU 744.2
745	NONELEC MACHY,TOOLS NES	W 1802	14960	W 2139	20632	W 2110	24687	W 3145	31785	AUT MACH NON ELEC,PIECES
7452	OTH NONELEC MCHS,PTS NES	W 1715	12425	W 1998	16767	W 1878	19160	W 2972	26947	AUT MACH NON ELEC,PIECES
749	NONELEC MACH PTS,ACC NES	W 11954	59078	W 14870	74076	W 18249	97193	W 12451	94760	PIECES MACH NON ELEC NDA
7492	COCKS,VALVES ETC NES	W 3464	29741	W 4752	35838	W 4463	45200	W 5143	56595	ART ROB,SIM POUR TUYAUX
7493	SHAFT,CRANK,PULLEY ETC	W 7292	16412	W 8752	24454	W 12322	32082	W 4754	16415	ARBRES TRANS,VILEBREQUINS
76	TELECOMM,SOUND EQUIPMENT		56493		83983		116390		161824	EQUIPMENT DE TELECOM
761	TELEVISION RECEIVERS	W 1292	13198	W 2870	34174	W 2630	37024	W 4130	49111	RECEPTEURS DE TELEVISION
7611	COLOUR TV RECEIVERS	W 1290	13184	W 2870	34171	W 2629	36981	W 4128	49049	RECEPTEURS COULEUR
764	TELECOM EQPT,PTS,ACC NES	W 1241	42931	W 1461	49541	W 1376	79181	W 1648	112073	EQUIP TELECOM,PIECES
7641	LINE TELEPHONE,ETC EQUIP	W 155	9696	W 267	13119	W 212	12465	W 331	28464	APP TELEPHON PAR FIL
7649	PTS NES OF EQUIPMT OF 76	W 1055	30708	W 1167	34428	W 1132	63134	W 1280	78833	PIECES DE LA DIV 76
76491	PTS NES OF APPAR OF 7641	W 177	21585	W 280	22583	W 527	54426	W 788	73350	PIECES POUR 764.1
77	ELECTRIC MACHNRY NES ETC		547652		636876		759503		781192	MACH APP ELECT NDA
771	ELECTRIC POWER MACHY NES	W 3208	21561	W 3540	23545	W 2878	29440	W 3860	36611	MACH PROD,TRANS ELECTR
772	SWITCHGEAR ETC,PARTS NES	W 4242	64513	W 5241	76126	W 5440	89359	W 5187	95603	APP COUPURE,SECT ETC
7721	SWITCHGEAR ETC	W 3961	53822	W 4840	62876	W 4626	74743	W 4736	80730	APP COUPURE,SECTIONMNT
773	ELECTR DISTRIBUTNG EQUIP	W 1905	15392	W 3181	21680	W 3589	29457	W 3947	28378	EQUIPMT DISTRIBUTION ELECT
775	HOUSEHOLD TYPE EQUIP NES	W 77626	291146	W 84960	342328	W 87146	402120	W 91656	427559	MACH,APP USAGE DOMESTQUE
7751	HOUSEHOLD LDRY EQUIP NES	W 13288	36970	W 15362	41026	W 14904	46550	W 20666	67235	MACH A LAVER ET SECHOIRS
77511	DOMESTIC WASHING MACHNES	W 12948	35554	W 14869	39209	W 14320	43951	W 19976	64240	MACH LAVER LINGE MOINS 6 KG
7752	DOM REFRIGERATRS,FREEZRS	W 32618	111377	W 34829	123994	W 35568	146261	W 32106	135687	REFRIG,CONGEL MENAGER
77521	DOMESTIC REFRIGERATORS	W 21672	74294	W 24893	89506	W 26263	109172	W 24621	104501	REFRIGERATEURS
77522	DOMESTIC DEEP–FREEZERS	W 10946	37083	W 9936	34489	W 9305	37088	W 7484	31186	MEUBLES CONGELATEURS
7757	DOMESTIC ELECTRC EQU NES	W 4598	37794	W 6051	55744	W 6791	70409	W 7809	84228	APP ELECTR DOMEST NDA
77578	OTH DOMSTC ELEC APPL ETC	W 2022	17625	W 3030	31003	W 3201	37119	W 3321	42430	AUT APP ELECT USAGE DOM
7758	ELECTRO–THERMIC APPL NES	W 27049	104172	W 28653	120927	W 29853	138709	W 31063	140251	APP ELECTROTHERMIQ NDA
77586	ELECTROTHERM DOM APP NES	W 17258	64992	W 16325	67092	W 15427	74105	W 15460	79414	APP ELECTRO THERMIQUES
77589	ELECTRTHRMC APPL PTS NES	W 7788	27528	W 10089	39618	W 12092	47651	W 13203	42608	PIECES APP ELECTR THERM
778	ELECTRICAL MACHINERY NES	W 22690	147824	W 22597	161625		198756	W 26554	183853	AUTRES MACH ELECT NDA
7781	BATTERIES,ACCUMULATORS	W 13824	26680	W 13011	23030	W 16510	30136	W 16976	32583	PILES ET ACCUMULATEURS
77812	ELECTRIC ACCUMULATORS	W 11889	21922	W 10281	17283	W 12626	22329	W 14042	25064	ACCUMULATEURS ELECTRIQ

5. Special Exports F.O.B. by Commodities according to the S.I.T.C. (Rev. 2) in thousand U.S. Dollars
Exportations Spéciales F.O.B. par Produits d'après la C.T.C.I. (Rév. 2) en milliers de Dollars E.U.

SITC CTCI	COMMODITY	1993 WEIGHT POIDS	1993 VALUE VALEUR	1994 WEIGHT POIDS	1994 VALUE VALEUR	1995 WEIGHT POIDS	1995 VALUE VALEUR	1996 WEIGHT POIDS	1996 VALUE VALEUR	PRODUIT
7783	AUTOMOTIVE ELECTR EQUIP	W 5364	55008	W 5807	61904	W 6660	77129	W 6206	75042	EQUIP ELECT MOTEURS EXPL
77831	IGNITION,STARTING EQUIP	W 3634	35812	W 3950	40962	W 5077	56920	W 4547	53189	APP ELEC ALLUM,DEMARRAGE
77832	ELECT VEHICLE LGHTNG EQU	W 1730	19196	W 1857	20942	W 1583	20209	W 1659	21853	APP ELEC ECLAIR,SIGNAL AUTO
7784	ELECTRO–MECH HAND TOOLS	W 1740	18822	W 1968	27473	W 2076	32205	W 1484	23426	OUTILS ELECTROMEC,PIECES
7788	OTH ELEC MACHY,EQUIP NES	W 1535	42946	W 1569	44637		53281	W 1578	45964	AUT MACH APP ELEC NDA
77884	ELECTRICAL CONDENSERS	W 1081	26238	W 1055	31733	W 2143	36692	W 1124	31203	CONDENSATEURS ELECTRIQUES
78	ROAD VEHICLES		573664		729534		952273		1014429	VEHICULES ROUTIERS
781	PASS MOTOR VEH EXC BUSES	W 32700	315308	W 47351	513525	W 54260	698572	W 60391	782930	AUTO TRANSPORT PERSONNES
783	ROAD MOTOR VEHICLES NES	W 4173	38600	W 1823	14709	W 1963	21667	W 984	6067	VEHICULES ROUTIERS NDA
7831	BUSES	W 3819	36231	W 1648	13527	W 1901	21208	W 941	6016	VOITURES TRANSPORT COMMUN
784	MOTOR VEH PRTS,ACCES NES	W 24952	126456	W 24987	117622	W 27643	145115	W 27752	141650	PIECES 722,781,782,783
7849	OTHER MOTOR VEHCL PARTS	W 24484	123019	W 24726	115990	W 27407	144202	W 27495	139509	PIECES 722,781,782,783
785	CYCLES,ETC MOTRZD OR NOT	W 4523	22576	W 4530	24661	W 4047	26903	W 3131	24678	MOTOCYCLES SCOOTERS
786	TRAILERS,NONMOTR VEH,NES	W 17315	53288	W 14509	41552	W 54512	49536	W 11656	46812	REMORQUES,CADRES,CONTAIN
7861	TRAILERS,TRANSP CONTAINR	W 11991	42002	W 7545	28317	W 8664	34367	W 6502	33222	REMORQUES TOUS VEHICULES
78611	HOUSING,CAMPING TRAILERS	W 4719	28272	W 2989	18686	W 2920	20815	W 2919	23198	REMORQUES POUR CAMPING
79	OTHR TRANSPORT EQUIPMENT		12883		42050		39602		27026	AUTRE MATERIEL TRANSPORT
792	AIRCRAFT ETC	W 24	3438	W 138	32244	W 116	26030	W 78	12304	APP NAVIGATION AERIENNE
7924	AIRCRFT NES OVER 15000KG			W 105	29376	W 70	19746	W 50	5295	AERODYNES PLUS 15000 KG
8	MISC MANUFACTURED GOODS		1485351		1563158		1771268		1733424	ART MANUFACTURES DIVERS
812	*PLUMBG,HEATNG,LGHTNG EQ	W 11047	34274	W 12640	40635	W 17406	51346	W 11905	51285	APPAR SANITAIRES CHAUFFAGE
8124	LIGHTING EQUIPMENT NES	W 8684	27546	W 9773	32448	W 15269	44503	W 9820	45407	APPAREILS ECLAIRAGE ETC
81242	LAMPS,FITTINGS BASE METL	W 2852	12311	W 3413	15876	W 3823	25460	W 4061	26391	APPAREILS D'ECLAIRAGE
821	*FURNITURE,PARTS THEREOF	W 121527	321489	W 141740	374096	W 144579	454018	W 122336	473609	MEUBLES ET PIECES
8211	CHAIRS,SEATS AND PARTS	W 31005	149355	W 44706	178185	W 32806	226078	W 32189	252311	SIEGES ET PIECES
82111	CHAIRS AND OTHER SEATS	W 19380	81884	W 19960	84916	W 16219	81758	W 16164	83464	SIEGES
82119	PTS NES OF CHAIRS ETC	W 11626	67471	W 24746	93269	W 16586	144320	W 16024	168847	PIECES DU 821.11
8219	FURNITURE AND PARTS NES	W 88289	163887	W 95118	186684	W 109778	216240	W 87945	208293	AUTRES MEUBLES ET PIECES
82192	WOOD FURNITURE NES	W 57322	106885	W 61673	124017	W 61554	145271	W 56553	135372	MEUBLES NDA EN BOIS
82199	OTHR FURN,FURN PARTS NES	W 25632	44829	W 27080	48485	W 42420	55295	W 25705	56844	MEUBLES NDA AUTRES MATIERES
84	CLOTHING AND ACCESSORIES		642964		615744		659095		593563	VETEMENTS
842	MENS OUTERWEAR NOT KNIT	W 2613	129189	W 2524	127786	W 2110	131921	W 2241	122635	VET DESSUS POUR HOMMES
8422	— SUITS	W 555	30051	W 673	37440	W 497	38909	W 537	38411	COMPLETS HOMMES MAT TEXT
84221	—— OF WOOL,FINE HAIR	W 468	26833	W 558	33501	W 499	35689	W 507	37056	COMPLETS HOMMES LAINE
8423	— TROUSERS,BREECHES ETC	W 835	36423	W 786	34444	W 737	36382	W 834	33002	PANTALONS HOMMES MAT TEX
8424	— JACKETS,BLAZERS ETC	W 631	32955	W 614	32620	W 518	35189	W 500	30971	VESTES HOMMES MAT TEXTIL
843	WOMENS OUTERWEAR NONKNIT	W 8486	238389	W 6120	237604	W 6789	271701	W 4242	237384	VET DESSUS FEMMES MAT TEX
8431	— COATS AND JACKETS	W 3891	71456	W 3033	74903	W 3864	89121	W 1306	71436	MANT,VEST FEM MAT TEXTIL
8432	— SUITS AND COSTUMES	W 222	17617	W 283	22198	W 363	32830	W 374	32795	COSTUMES–TAIL MAT TEXIL
8435	— BLOUSES	W 350	27541	W 271	22660	W 232	21442	W 248	19611	BLOUSES FEM MAT TEXTILES
8439	— OTHER OUTER GARMENTS	W 3440	91765	W 2095	90206	W 1886	95995	W 1901	87204	AUT VET DES FEM MAT TEXT
844	UNDER GARMENTS NOT KNIT	W 804	32119	W 694	28379	W 500	24529	W 420	20959	VETEMENT DESSOUS MAT TEX
8441	— MENS SHIRTS	W 523	23559	W 369	18928	W 305	17700	W 305	16290	CHEMISES HOMMES MAT TEXT
84411	—— OF COTTON	W 355	18422	W 280	14919	W 247	14173	W 254	13893	CHEMISES HOMMES DE COTON
845	OUTERWEAR KNIT NONELASTC	W 2313	83628	W 2706	74002	W 1656	82984	W 1702	77823	VET DESSOUS,ACCES BONNET
8451	— JERSEYS,PULLOVERS ETC	W 1019	33345	W 1768	35408	W 835	35867	W 967	34206	CHANDAILS,PULL–OVERS ETC
8459	— OTHER,CLTHG ACCESRYS	W 1215	46328	W 865	35325	W 739	42598	W 670	40132	AUT VET DESSUS DE BONNE
846	UNDER GARMENTS KNITTED	W 4063	119894	W 3421	104335	W 3305	103186	W 2922	94755	SOUS VETS DE BONNETERIE
8462	— OF COTTON NON ELASTIC	W 733	27959	W 891	28644	W 838	32044	W 735	31939	SOUS–VET BONNET COTON
84629	—— OTHER	W 733	27959	W 891	28644	W 838	32044	W 735	31939	AUT SOUS–VET BONNET COTON
8463	— OF SYNTH FBR NONELAST	W 3055	64356	W 2243	46563	W 2164	39193	W 1908	34807	SOUS–VET BONNET FIB SYNT
84631	—— PANTY HOSE (TIGHTS)	W 2996	62535	W 2222	45475	W 2143	38016	W 1859	32468	COLLANTS BON FIBR SYNT
8465	CORSETS,GARTERS,ETC	W 275	27580	W 288	29128	W 303	31949	W 279	28009	CORSETS,GAINES ART SIM
84651	BRASSIERES	W 204	21680	W 198	21821	W 206	23099	W 191	20554	SOUTIENS–GORGE,BUSTIERS
848	HEADGEAR,NONTXTL CLOTHNG	W 415	24511		27148	W 464	26539	W 431	23454	VET ACCES MAT AUT QUE TEX
8481	LEATHER CLOTHES,ACCESSOR	W 225	18165	W 321	21769	W 286	20930	W 284	18296	VET ACCES MAT CUIR ARTIF
851	*FOOTWEAR	W 6167	133551	W 6344	137207	W 5459	129959	W 4552	104688	CHAUSSURES
85102	FOOTWEAR LEATHER	W 5076	118576	W 5128	119810	W 4397	113554	W 3934	93702	CHAUS SEMELLES EN CUIR
87	PRECISION INSTRUMNTS NES		115118		136516		158545		170355	INSTRUM,APPAR SCIENT NDA
871	OPTICAL INSTRUMENTS		18928		14820	W 4	751		6227	APPAR,INSTRUM D'OPTIQUE
87109	OPTICAL INSTRUMENTS NES	W 30	18902	W 23	14805	W 4	722	W 18	5967	APP,INSTRUM OPTIQUE NDA
873	METERS AND COUNTERS NES	W 2912	54066	W 3672	71109	W 4175	94273	W 4127	87843	COMPTEURS,INST DE MESURE
8731	GAS SUPPLY METERS ETC	W 2869	52450	W 3633	69552	W 4134	92016	W 4107	86564	COMPTEURS GAZ,LIQ ELECT
874	MEASURNG,CONTROLNG INSTR		37015	W 2446	42829	W 2145	52410	W 2345	61713	INSTRUMENTS DE MESURE
8743	GAS,LIQUID CONTROL INSTR	W 680	19108	W 769	21506	W 791	26781	W 874	31099	APP,INSTR MESURE FLUIDES
88	PHOTO EQU,OPTICL GDS ETC		40849		45428		57463		52629	APP,FOURN PHOTO,OP,MONTR
884	OPTICAL GOODS NES	W 196	18847	W 245	21147	W 205	23585	W 158	15926	ELEMENTS OPTIQ,ART LUNET
89	MISC MANUFCTRD GOODS NES		190144		204812		249563		276724	ART MANUFACTURES DIVERS
892	PRINTED MATTER	W 18604	54676	W 16194	51409	W 46270	57939	W 15252	67999	IMPRIMES
8921	PRINTED BOOKS,GLOBES,ETC	W 15626	40530	W 13390	38441	W 11549	43560	W 10727	39124	LIVRES,BROCHURES,CARTES
89211	PRINTED BOOKS,PAMPHLETS	W 14576	38413	W 13088	37705	W 11466	43203	W 10648	38703	LIVRES,BROCHURES
893	ARTICLES OF PLASTIC NES		57072	W 20698	67672	W 25270	93618		103033	OUVRAGES EN MAT DIVIS 58
8939	MISC PLASTIC ARTICLES	W 12215	35961	W 13712	43204	W 16395	60310	W 17861	65906	ART DIVERS EN MAT DIV 58
89399	OTHR PLASTC ARTICLES NES	W 9021	28896	W 10745	35447	W 12417	48517	W 12118	50354	AUT OUV MAT DIV 58
894	TOYS,SPORTING GOODS,ETC	W 4666	41839	W 4464	44425	W 4963	52042	W 4211	53459	VOITURES ENFANTS,JOUETS
8942	TOYS,INDOOR GAMES ETC	W 3545	16429	W 3588	21637	W 3834	27590	W 2651	21658	JOUETS,JEUX ETC
8947	OTH SPORT GDS,FAIR AMUSM	W 1097	25186	W 862	22691	W 1120	24359	W 1547	31698	AUT ART DE SPORT
89472	OTH OUTDOOR SPORT GOODS	W 1060	24917	W 860	22605	W 1087	24296	W 1508	31455	ART POUR JEUX PLEIN AIR
895	OFFICE SUPPLIES NES	W 4543	19009	W 5755	20840	W 8672	24214	W 5611	26759	ART PAPET NDA

1. HISTORICAL SERIES, 1960–1995 SPECIAL TRADE, IMPORTS C.I.F., EXPORTS F.O.B. # 1
SERIES HISTORIQUES, 1960–1995 COMMERCE SPECIAL, IMPORTATIONS C.A.F., EXPORTATIONS F.O.B

YEAR ANNEE	VALUE IN MILLION S.I. DOLLARS VALEUR EN MILLION S.I. DOLLARS MERCHANDISE –MARCHANDISE		GOLD –OR		CONVERSION FACTORS U.S. CENTS PER S.I. DOLLAR FACTEURS DE CONVERSION CENTS E.U. PAR S.I. DOLLAR		INDEX NUMBERS –INDICES QUANTUM		UNIT VALUE VALEUR UNITAIRE	
	IMPORTS	EXPORTS	IMPORTS	EXPORTS	IMPORTS	EXPORTS	IMPORTS	EXPORTS	IMPORTS	EXPORTS
1960	3.71	3.72			112.0000	112.0000				
1961	4.15	3.56			112.0000	112.0000				
1962	4.47	3.25			112.0000	112.0000				
1963	4.62	3.71			112.0000	112.0000				
1964	5.47	4.76			112.0000	112.0000				
1965	6.58	4.83		8.00	112.0000	112.0000				
1966	8.52	3.75		9.00	112.0000	112.0000				
1967	8.20	5.09		17.00	112.0000	112.0000				
1968	9.20	5.54		18.00	112.0000	112.0000				
1969	8.54	6.46		12.00	112.0000	112.0000				
1970	10.02	7.11		7.00	112.0000	112.0000				
1971	11.52	9.08		13.00	113.5720	112.8080				
1972	12.05	9.14		20.00	119.1000	119.1000		40		13
1973	11.26	9.55		61.00	142.6120	144.1660		47		11
1974	16.37	18.25		72.00	142.7390	144.8740		39		13
1975	21.77	11.82		45.00	130.9450	131.1830		43		25
1976	21.09	19.95		47.00	121.8460	121.3170		42		16
1977	25.75	29.61		56.00	110.9850	110.8880		47		25
1978	30.88	30.59		89.00	114.5150	114.5680		48		37
1979	50.57	59.26			111.6850	111.6030		57		35
1980	61.54	60.80			120.3530	120.4370		72		50
1981	65.78	57.55			114.9151	114.5287		74		49
1982	57.43	56.56			103.1025	102.5989		81		43
1983	70.63	71.22			86.7251	86.1231		77		44
1984	83.84	118.56			78.1544	78.4026		93		46
1985	102.67	103.86			67.1944	67.1541		103		69
1986	125.19	114.90			57.5333	56.9522		94		66
1987	162.08	128.30			50.2190	50.1490		116		59
1988	203.30	170.57			48.0443	47.7344		85		89
1989	262.50	171.45			43.5642	43.3447		94		107
1990	238.96	178.11			39.5887	39.5546		92		108
1991	299.60	228.71			36.7934	36.7658		100		100
1992	285.90	301.18			33.9819	34.0332		106		95
1993	321.10	411.44			31.4288	31.7276				
1994	468.11	467.87			30.3552	30.3772				
1995		573.15				29.3764				

2. IMPORTS BY BROAD ECONOMIC CATEGORY AND EXPORTS BY INDUSTRIAL ORIGIN. (PERCENTAGE OF TOTAL VALUE)
IMPORTATIONS PAR CATEGORIES ECONOMIQUES ET EXPORTATIONS PAR BRANCHE D'ACTIVITE.(EN POURCENTAGE DE LA VALEUR TOTALE)

IMPORTS – IMPORTATIONS

	1990	1991	1992	1993	1994	1995	1996
TOTAL IMPORTS–IMPORTATIONS TOTALES	100.						
1 FOOD BEV–ALIMENTATION BOISSONS	6.4						
11 PRIMARY–PRODUITS DE BASE							
111 FOR INDUSTRY–POUR L'INDUSTRIE							
112 FOR HOUSEHOLDS–POUR LES MENAGES							
12 PROCESSED–PRODUITS ELABORES	6.4						
121 FOR INDUSTRY–POUR L'INDUSTRIE	1.6						
122 FOR HOUSEHOLDS–POUR LES MENAGES	4.8						
2 IND SUPPLIES–APPROV INDUSTRIELS	0.3						
21 PRIMARY–PRODUITS DE BASE	0.3						
22 PROCESSED–PRODUITS ELABORES							
3 FUELS–COMBUSTIBLES							
31 PRIMARY–PRODUITS DE BASE							
32 PROCESSED–PRODUITS ELABORES							
321 MOTOR SPIRIT–ESSENCE							
322 OTHER–AUTRES							
4 MACHINERY–EQUIPEMENT	0.1						
41 CAPITAL EQUIPMENT–MACHINES	0.1						
42 PARTS–PIECES ACCESSOIRES							
5 TRANSPORT–TRANSPORT							
51 PASSENGER CARS–AUTOMOBILES							
52 OTHER–AUTRES							
521 INDUSTRIAL–INDUSTRIELS							
522 NON INDUSTRIAL–NON INDUSTRIEL							
53 PARTS–PIECES ACCESSOIRES							
6 CONSUM GOODS–BIENS CONSOMMATION	0.1						
61 DURABLE–DURABLES	0.1						
62 SEMI DURABLE–SEMI DURABLES							
63 NON DURABLE–NON DURABLES							
7 GOODS NES–BIENS NDA							

EXPORTS – EXPORTATIONS

	1990	1991	1992	1993	1994	1995	1996
TOTAL EXPORTS–EXPORTATIONS TOTALES	100.						
1 AGRICULTURE	6.2						
2 MINING QUARRY–INDUS EXTRACTIVES							
3 MANUFACTURING–IND MANUFACTUR	20.9						
31 FOOD BEV TOBACCO–ALIM BOISS TAB	15.5						
32 TEXTILES–INDUSTRIES TEXTILES							
33 WOOD & PRODUCTS–BOIS & PRODUITS							
34 PAPER & PRODUCTS–PAPIER & PRODT							
35 CHEMICALS–INDUSTRIES CHIMIQUES							
36 NON METAL MIN–MIN NON METAL							
37 BASIC METAL–IND METAL BASE							
38 METAL MANUF–MANUF METAL							
39 OTH MANUF IND–AUTRES MANUF	5.4						

3. TRADE BY PRINCIPAL COUNTRIES OF ORIGIN AND DESTINATION (VALUE IN THOUSAND U.S. DOLLARS)
ECHANGES SELON LES PRINCIPAUX PAYS D'ORIGINE ET DE DESTINATION (VALEUR EN MILLIERS DE DOLLARS EU)

COUNTRIES–PAYS	SPECIAL IMPORTS C.I.F. IMPORTATIONS SPECIALES C.A.F				
	1990	1991	1992	1993	1994
World	91420	112214	110988	137120	142099
Africa	249	297	529		
Americas	4754	6163	6927	7818	3998
Northern America	4754	6163	6927	7818	3998
LAIA					
CACM					
Caribbean					
Rest of America					
As.ex F.USSR	36251	41508	37408	49505	47892
Eur.x F.USSR	2399	5369	6285	3770	3602
EU	2396	5369	6186	3757	3591
EFTA	2		99	13	11
East Europe					
Other Europe					
Former USSR					
Oceania	44644	53587	54263	63968	69738
Australia/Australie	31744	40409	41684	48147	52929
Japan/Japon	14034	22199	16297	20081	24254
Singapore/Singapour	13899	12829	13163	16351	11968
New Zealand	8543	9149	9486	13218	13671
USA/Etats–Unis d'Amer	4754	6163	6927	7818	3998
China/Chine	3196	2597	3170	3778	3819
Hong Kong	2039	2539	2974	3416	2356
United Kingdom	1332	3154	1895	1982	1930
Papua New Guinea	2928	2657	1810	1358	1491
Thailand/Thaïlande	252	437	879	4252	3871
Germany/Allemagne	672	1711	3692	1477	1134
Korea, Republic of	2831	907	925	1627	1624
Fiji/Fidji	1429	1372	1283	1035	1076
Malawi	249	297	529		
Belgium–Luxembourg	68	200	373	152	210
Vanuatu				210	572
Sweden/Suède	222	115	75	93	77
Netherlands/Pays–Bas	54	127	134	38	228
Norway,SVD,JM	2		5	13	11

COUNTRIES–PAYS	SPECIAL EXPORTS F.O.B. EXPORTATIONS SPECIALES F.O.B.				
	1990	1991	1992	1993	1994
Monde	70354	83966	102322	130540	142127
Afrique					
Amériques	47	55	1506	908	688
Amérique du Nord	47	55	1506	908	688
ALAI					
MCAC					
Caraïbes					
Autre Amérique					
Asie l'URSS exclus	37355	45938	58657	84286	90900
Europe l'URSS exclus	22468	24597	29304	32477	34579
UE	22468	24361	29304	32477	34579
AELE		236			
Europe de l'Est					
Autre de l'Europe					
Ancienne URSS					
Océanie	9368	7921	5202	5480	3962
Japan/Japon	27579	23702	35579	54497	58406
United Kingdom	16474	12831	24141	18701	18568
Korea, Republic of	5576	5761	12491	21541	20018
Netherlands/Pays–Bas	959	6414		8495	12119
Thailand/Thaïlande	285	11566	2452	2033	6367
Singapore/Singapour	1443	1644	3868	4141	4852
Fiji/Fidji	5302	4280	1603	1540	857
Australia/Australie	3207	2344	2530	2776	2156
Germany/Allemagne	2846	2836	2833	2191	2084
Belgium–Luxembourg	2188	2279	2330	3089	1807
Hong Kong	916	2941	3810	2074	886
USA/Etats–Unis d'Amer	47	55	1506	908	688
India/Inde	1555	324	457		372
New Zealand	524	632	686	385	309
Papua New Guinea	290	519	169	677	436
Vanuatu	45	145	214	102	204
Norway,SVD,JM		236			

(VALUE AS PERCENTAGE OF WORLD TOTAL)(VALEURS EN POURCENTAGE DU TOTAL MONDIAL)

	1985	1986	1987	1988	1989	1990	1991	1992	1993	1994
Africa	0.7	0.6	0.5	0.2		0.3	0.3	0.5		
Americas	2.2	2.6	3.0	3.1		5.2	5.5	6.2	5.7	2.8
Northern America	2.1	2.3	3.0	3.0		5.2	5.5	6.2	5.7	2.8
LAIA	0.0	0.2	0.1	0.1						
CACM										
Caribbean		0.0	0.0	0.0						
Rest of America										
As.ex F.USSR	39.2	35.1	37.2	31.4		39.7	37.0	33.7	36.1	33.7
Eur.x F.USSR	6.3	10.5	6.8	8.0		2.6	4.8	5.7	2.7	2.5
EU	6.2	10.4	6.8	7.9		2.6	4.8	5.6	2.7	2.5
EFTA	0.0	0.0	0.0	0.1		0.0		0.1	0.0	0.0
East Europe	0.0	0.0	0.0	0.0						
Other Europe		0.0	0.0	0.0						
Former USSR	0.0	0.0	0.0	0.0						
Oceania	51.3	50.6	52.1	56.9		48.8	47.8	48.9	46.7	49.1
Australia/Australie	37.2	40.1	41.4	45.5		34.7	36.0	37.6	35.1	37.2
Japan/Japon	19.7	16.9	19.1	16.2		15.4	19.8	14.7	14.6	17.1
Singapore/Singapour	8.6	8.1	9.2	5.4		15.2	11.4	11.9	11.9	8.4
New Zealand	9.0	7.7	7.9	8.3		9.3	8.2	8.5	9.6	9.6
USA/Etats–Unis d'Amer	2.1	2.3	2.9	2.9		5.2	5.5	6.2	5.7	2.8
China/Chine	3.7	3.5	3.5	3.3		3.5	2.3	2.9	2.8	2.7
Hong Kong	3.0	3.0	2.5	2.7		2.2	2.3	2.7	2.5	1.7
United Kingdom	4.0	3.9	4.4	5.3		1.5	2.8	1.7	1.4	1.4
Papua New Guinea	3.4	1.5	1.9	1.4		3.2	2.4	1.6	1.0	1.0
Thailand/Thaïlande	1.7	0.8	0.1	0.1		0.3	0.4	0.8	3.1	2.7

	1985	1986	1987	1988	1989	1990	1991	1992	1993	1994
Afrique										
Amériques	2.5	0.1	7.2	4.2		0.1	0.1	1.5	0.7	0.5
Amérique du Nord	2.5	0.1	7.2	4.2		0.1	0.1	1.5	0.7	0.5
ALAI			0.0							
MCAC										
Caraïbes										
Autre Amérique										
Asie l'URSS exclus	63.0	70.0	57.2	56.6		53.1	54.7	57.3	64.6	64.0
Europe l'URSS exclus	29.6	17.6	23.2	22.3		31.9	29.3	28.6	24.9	24.3
UE	29.6	17.6	23.2	22.3		31.9	29.0	28.6	24.9	24.3
AELE				0.0			0.3			
Europe de l'Est										
Autre de l'Europe										
Ancienne URSS										
Océanie	4.9	12.3	12.3	16.9		13.3	9.4	5.1	4.2	2.8
Japan/Japon	51.9	37.0	35.6	34.5		39.2	28.2	34.8	41.7	41.1
United Kingdom	14.1	8.3	13.8	14.5		23.4	15.3	23.6	14.3	13.1
Korea, Republic of	2.4	4.3	6.0	3.2		7.9	6.9	12.2	16.5	14.1
Netherlands/Pays–Bas	10.4	2.5	2.0	1.7		1.4	7.6		6.5	8.5
Thailand/Thaïlande	8.4	23.1	12.2	14.6		0.4	13.8	2.4	1.6	4.5
Singapore/Singapour	0.1	0.6	0.9	1.1		2.1	2.0	3.8	3.2	3.4
Fiji/Fidji	0.2	5.4	2.7	4.2		7.5	5.1	1.6	1.2	0.6
Australia/Australie	2.3	4.0	3.7	4.7		4.6	2.8	2.5	2.1	1.5
Germany/Allemagne	1.5	3.4	4.2	2.9		4.0	3.4	2.8	1.7	1.5
Belgium–Luxembourg	1.3	2.1	2.2	1.2		3.1	2.7	2.3	2.4	1.3

4. Special Imports C.I.F. by Commodities according to the S.I.T.C. (Rev. 2) in thousand U.S. Dollars
Importations Spéciales C.A.F. par Produits d'après la C.T.C.I. (Rév. 2) en milliers de Dollars E.U.

SITC CTCI	COMMODITY	1991		1992		1993		1994		PRODUIT
		WEIGHT POIDS	VALUE VALEUR	WEIGHT POIDS	VALUE VALEUR	WEIGHT POIDS	VALUE VALEUR	WEIGHT POIDS	VALUE VALEUR	
	ALL COMMODITIES		112214		110988		137120		142099	TOUS PRODUITS
0	FOOD AND LIVE ANIMALS				15568		16654		18594	ALIMENTS,ANIMAUX VIVANTS
014	MEAT PREPD,PRSVD,NES ETC	W 204	585	W 228	559	W 393	861	W 435	1020	CONSERVES DE VIANDES
042	RICE	W 13943	5347	W 13084	6169	W 17749	6346	W 60543	7844	RIZ
0612	REFINED SUGAR ETC	W 1765	1093	W 2118	1020	W 2613	1000	W 2909	974	SUCRES RAFFINES
1	BEVERAGES AND TOBACCO				3220		1723		2080	BOISSONS ET TABACS
1123	BEER,ALE,STOUT,PORTER	W 2076	1670	W 2960	1876	W 917	705	W 919	726	BIERES
2	CRUDE MATERLS,EXCL FUELS				1342		846		1349	MAT BRUTES NON COMESTIBLES
3	MINERAL FUELS ETC				13396		12874		11611	COMBUSTIBLES MINERAUX LUB
3341	GASOLINE,OTH LIGHT OILS	W 9072	2340	W 8863000	1912	W 11974	1721	W 14814	2092	ESSENCES POUR MOTEURS
3343	GAS OILS	W 42094	9859			W 47647	8105	W 46612	6498	GAS OILS
3352	MINERAL TARS AND PRODCTS			MW 41030	8760					GOUDRONS MINERAUX
4	ANIMAL,VEGETABLE OIL,FAT				802		465		1047	HUILES,GRAISSES ANIM,VEG
5	CHEMCLS,RELATED PROD NES				5310		6514		7347	PRODUITS CHIMIQUES
562	*FERTILIZERS,MANUFACTURE	W 2522	606	W 990	187	W 1147	194	W 2288	512	ENGRAIS MANUFACTURES
6	BASIC MANUFACTURES				20241		28821		28317	ART MANUFACTURES
6612	CEMENT	W 23163	912	W 3459	622	W 7484	948	W 8207	1051	CIMENTS HYDRAULIQUES
7	MACHINES,TRANSPORT EQUIP				37972		54077		53956	MACHINES MATERIEL TRANSPORT
71331	—— OUTBOARD	N 1589	490	N 737	661	N 1501	929	N 998	1144	MOTEURS BATEAUX HORSBORD
72431	SEWING MACHINES	N 1925	104	N 1123	349	N 2626	215	N 2358	168	MACHINES A COUDRE
781	PASS MOTOR VEH EXC BUSES	N 81	681	N 120	1044	N 142	942	N 169	1116	AUTO TRANSPORT PERSONNES
8	MISC MANUFACTURED GOODS				11334		13378		13243	ART MANUFACTURES DIVERS
9	GOODS NOT CLASSD BY KIND				1802		1770			ART TRANSACT NON CLASSES

5. Special Exports F.O.B. by Commodities according to the S.I.T.C. (Rev. 2) in thousand U.S. Dollars
Exportations Spéciales F.O.B. par Produits d'après la C.T.C.I. (Rév. 2) en milliers de Dollars E.U.

SITC CTCI	COMMODITY	1991 WEIGHT POIDS	1991 VALUE VALEUR	1992 WEIGHT POIDS	1992 VALUE VALEUR	1993 WEIGHT POIDS	1993 VALUE VALEUR	1994 WEIGHT POIDS	1994 VALUE VALEUR	PRODUIT
	ALL COMMODITIES		83966		102322		130540		142127	TOUS PRODUITS
0	FOOD AND LIVE ANIMALS				38579		32998		34923	ALIMENTS,ANIMAUX VIVANTS
01	MEAT AND PREPARATIONS				3542		1003		783	VIANDES ET PREPARATIONS
011	MEAT FRESH,CHILLD,FROZEN				3542	W 316	1003	W 284	783	VIANDES FRAICHES,REF,CONGE
0118	MEAT NES FRESH,CHLD,FRZN				3542	W 316	1003	W 284	783	AUTRES VIANDES,ABATS
01189	OTHER MEAT NES FRESH,ETC			W 718	3542	W 316	1003	W 284	783	VIANDE,ABATS COMESTIBLES
03	FISH AND PREPARATIONS				30313		26499		30171	POISSONS ET PREPARATIONS
034	FISH,FRESH,CHILLED,FROZN	W 37624	24850	W 27845	16403	W 15507	9135	W 23173	10045	POISSON FRAIS, REFRIG,CONG
035	FISH SALTED,DRIED,SMOKED	W 409	1124		1422	W 699	2118	W 842	1782	POISSON SECHE,SALE,FUME
03503	FISH(EX COD)DRIED,SALTED	W 3	107	W 7	381	W 75	199	W 2	77	POISSONS SECHES,SALES
03504	FISH SMOKED			W 429	1041	W 624	1919	W 840	1705	POISSONS FUMES
036	SHELL FISH FRESH,FROZEN	W 622	2802							CRUSTACES,MOLLUSQUES
037	FISH ETC PREPD,PRSVD NES	W 5054	13201		12488	W 5661	15245	W 7712	18344	POIS,CRUST,MOL PREPARES
0371	FISH PREPARD,PRESRVD NES	W 5054	13201	W 5448	12488	W 5661	15245	W 7712	18344	CONSERVES DE POISSONS
07	COFFEE,TEA,COCOA,SPICES				4548		5332		3812	CAFE,THE,CACAO,EPICES
072	COCOA	W 4311	4946		4548	W 3936	5332	W 3683	3812	CACAO
0721	COCOA BEANS,RAW,ROASTED	W 4311	4946	W 4455	4548	W 3936	5332	W 3683	3812	CACAO EN FEVES
2	CRUDE MATERLS,EXCL FUELS				47694		81536		92984	MAT BRUTES NON COMESTIBLES
22	OIL SEEDS,OLEAGINOUS FRT				8379		6601		7313	GRAINES,FRUITS OLEAGINEUX
223	SEEDS FOR OTH FIXED OILS	W 31973	4316		8379	W 33406	6601	W 25093	7313	GRAINES AUTRES HUILES FIXES
2231	COPRA	W 27000	3807	W 25739	7744	W 26669	5880	W 19108	6006	COPRAH
2232	PALM NUTS AND KERNELS	W 4973	508	W 3742	634	W 6737	721	W 5985	1307	NOIX,AMANDES DE PALMISTE
24	CORK AND WOOD				37527		73518		84101	LIEGE ET BOIS
247	OTH WOOD ROUGH,SQUARED	W 242400	18757		37527	W 451	73518	W 502	84101	BOIS BRUTS EQUARRIS
2472	SAW–,VENEER–LOGS NON–CON				37527	W 451	73518	W 502	84101	NON CONIFERES SCIAGE,PLAC
248	WOOD SHAPED,SLEEPERS	W 3850	1506							BOIS SIMPLEMENT TRAVAILLES
2483	LUMBER SHAPED NON–CONIFR	W 3850	1506							NON CONIFERES SCIES,RABOTES
29	CRUDE ANIMAL,VEG MAT NES				1788		1418		1570	MATIERES BRUTES ANIM,VEGET
291	CRUDE ANIMAL MTRIALS NES	W 188	1238		1788	W 58	1418		1570	MATIERES BRUTES ANIMALES
2911	BONES,IVORY,HORNS,ETC	W 188	1238	W 139	1788	W 58	1418		1570	OS,CORNES,SABOTS
29115	CORAL, SHELLS, AND WASTE	W 186	1039	W 138	1621	W 58	1418		1570	CORAIL & SIMILAIRES
4	ANIMAL,VEGETABLE OIL,FAT				12246		12743		12735	HUILES,GRAISSES ANIM,VEG
42	FIXED VEGETABLE OIL,FAT				12246		12743		12735	HUILES VEGETALES FIXES
424	FIXED VEG OIL NONSOFT	W 23750	6691		12246	W 34432	12743	W 29217	12735	AUTRES HUILES VEG FIXES
4242	PALM OIL	W 21735	5999	W 30540	10870	W 30987	11361	W 28041	12124	HUILE DE PALME
4243	COCONUT (COPRA) OIL	W 2015	692	W 2499	1376	W 3445	1382	W 1176	611	HJUILE DE COPRAH
9	GOODS NOT CLASSD BY KIND				3721		3161		1387	ART TRANSACT NON CLASSES
931	*SPECIAL TRANSACTIONS		3985		3361		2018		953	TRANS.SPECIALES
971	*GOLD,NON MONETARY NES	K 50	460		360	K 28	301	K 8	94	OR NON MONETAIRE
97101	NONMON GLD UNWRT,SEMIMFD	K 50	460	K 37	360	K 28	301	K 8	94	OR,ALLIAGES D'OR BRUTS

FOOT NOTES – NOTES

TABLE 1 –

1 Prior to 1978, imports f.o.b.

TABLEAU 1 –

1 Avant 1978, les importations sont f.a.b.

1. HISTORICAL SERIES, 1961–1996 GENERAL TRADE, IMPORTS F.O.B., EXPORTS F.O.B.
SERIES HISTORIQUES, 1961–1996 COMMERCE GENERAL, IMPORTATIONS F.O.B., EXPORTATIONS F.O.B

YEAR ANNEE	VALUE IN MILLION RAND VALEUR EN MILLION RAND: MERCHANDISE –MARCHANDISE IMPORTS	MERCHANDISE –MARCHANDISE EXPORTS	GOLD –OR IMPORTS	GOLD –OR EXPORTS	CONVERSION FACTORS U.S. CENTS PER RAND FACTEURS DE CONVERSION CENTS E.U. PAR RAND: IMPORTS	EXPORTS	INDEX NUMBERS –INDICES: QUANTUM IMPORTS	QUANTUM EXPORTS	UNIT VALUE VALEUR UNITAIRE IMPORTS	UNIT VALUE VALEUR UNITAIRE EXPORTS
1961	1007.40	948.70	0.20	574.90	140.0000	140.0000	50	30	5	8
1962	1013.10	949.50	0.10	636.60	140.0000	140.0000	50	31	5	8
1963	1212.60	999.90	0.20	685.70	140.0000	140.0000	59	32	5	8
1964	1539.90	1041.50	0.10	730.50	140.0000	140.0000	74	32	5	8
1965	1756.40	1059.10	0.10	766.50	140.0000	140.0000	81	32	5	8
1966	1645.50	1206.30	0.10	776.20	140.0000	140.0000	72	36	5	8
1967	1919.30	1364.10	0.10	763.00	140.0000	140.0000	86	42	5	8
1968	1880.10	1506.30	0.20	771.20	140.0000	140.0000	88	47	5	8
1969	2134.60	1534.00	0.20	779.20	140.0000	140.0000	97	46	5	8
1970	2811.90	1536.50	0.20	837.00	140.0000	140.0000	114	45	5	8
1971	3184.40	1554.10	0.20	759.30	140.0000	140.0000	120	46	6	8
1972	2840.50	1955.30	0.20	1161.00	129.3730	129.2230	104	57	6	9
1973	3564.20	2375.80		1769.00	144.1460	144.0120	119	59	7	11
1974	5344.30	3016.90		2565.00	147.0020	146.9250	150	60	8	14
1975	5545.50	3408.10		2540.00	136.3360	136.0310	136	59	10	15
1976	5859.40	4331.90		2346.00	115.0000	115.0000	120	65	12	17
1977	5188.30	5863.20		2795.00	115.0000	115.0000	92	77	14	19
1978	6253.40	7333.30		3906.00	115.0000	115.0000	102	84	17	21
1979	9904.30	8808.70		6002.00	118.7930	118.9110	101	95	21	24
1980	14381.30	9774.80		10041.00	129.0110	128.3670	132	92	25	27
1981	18511.20	9675.50		8338.60	113.8625	114.4715	149	90	28	28
1982	18391.20	10440.90		8626.80	92.2800	92.2800	122	84	35	32
1983	16228.80	10779.00		9929.00	89.5183	89.7286	102	84	35	32
1984	21687.00	13671.00			68.9623	68.2741	124	85	42	40
1985	22707.70	20622.90			45.4447	45.2196	91	102	57	52
1986	29688.00	42011.30		16719.00	43.7375	43.7736	95	106	64	61
1987	31105.01	43202.00		17808.00	49.1760	49.1327	95	98	69	67
1988	42566.00	49723.90		19622.00	43.8696	43.8769	111	100	81	80
1989	48515.01	58198.80		19122.00	38.1184	38.0553	111	108	91	96
1990	47605.01	60928.50		18069.00	38.6506	38.6830	100	100	100	100
1991	52006.00	64354.90		19350.00	36.2071	36.1759	100	100	110	106
1992	56358.00	66773.90		18195.00	35.0245	35.1056	103	88	117	112
1993	65411.01	79279.01		22229.00	30.6410	30.6410	107	107	127	122
1994	83042.00	89907.01			28.1348	28.1502	123	116	141	131
1995	110826.00	101052.00			27.5624	27.5661	136	119	157	161
1996	129522.00	126102.00			23.3067	23.1775	155	169	166	177

2. IMPORTS BY BROAD ECONOMIC CATEGORY AND EXPORTS BY INDUSTRIAL ORIGIN. (PERCENTAGE OF TOTAL VALUE)
IMPORTATIONS PAR CATEGORIES ECONOMIQUES ET EXPORTATIONS PAR BRANCHE D'ACTIVITE.(EN POURCENTAGE DE LA VALEUR TOTALE)

IMPORTS – IMPORTATIONS

	1990	1991	1992	1993	1994	1995	1996
TOTAL IMPORTS–IMPORTATIONS TOTALES	100.	100.	100.	100.	100.	100.	
1 FOOD BEV–ALIMENTATION BOISSONS	2.8	2.9	4.8	4.8	5.2	5.1	
11 PRIMARY–PRODUITS DE BASE	1.4	1.5	2.3	2.3	2.0	2.1	
111 FOR INDUSTRY–POUR L'INDUSTRIE	1.1	1.1	1.2	1.5	1.0	1.1	
112 FOR HOUSEHOLDS–POUR LES MENAGES	0.3	0.4	1.1	0.8	1.1	1.0	
12 PROCESSED–PRODUITS ELABORES	1.4	1.4	2.5	2.5	3.1	3.0	
121 FOR INDUSTRY–POUR L'INDUSTRIE	0.3	0.5	0.8	0.8	0.8	0.8	
122 FOR HOUSEHOLDS–POUR LES MENAGES	1.0	0.9	1.7	1.7	2.3	2.2	
2 IND SUPPLIES–APPROV INDUSTRIELS	24.4	23.9	29.6	29.2	28.4	27.7	
21 PRIMARY–PRODUITS DE BASE	2.9	2.8	4.8	4.5	3.9	3.4	
22 PROCESSED–PRODUITS ELABORES	21.5	21.1	24.7	24.6	24.5	24.3	
3 FUELS–COMBUSTIBLES	0.0	0.0	0.3	0.5	0.4	10.0	
31 PRIMARY–PRODUITS DE BASE	0.0	0.0	0.2	0.1	0.1	9.7	
32 PROCESSED–PRODUITS ELABORES	0.0	0.0	0.1	0.3	0.2	0.3	
321 MOTOR SPIRIT–ESSENCE							
322 OTHER–AUTRES	0.0	0.0	0.1	0.3	0.2	0.3	
4 MACHINERY–EQUIPEMENT	3.8	3.6	27.9	28.9	32.5	30.8	
41 CAPITAL EQUIPMENT–MACHINES	1.3	0.9	22.5	23.0	26.5	24.9	
42 PARTS–PIECES ACCESSOIRES	2.5	2.7	5.4	5.9	6.0	5.9	
5 TRANSPORT–TRANSPORT	17.6	14.4	15.0	17.4	16.9	14.4	
51 PASSENGER CARS–AUTOMOBILES	5.0	4.2	3.4	5.1	4.4	3.9	
52 OTHER–AUTRES	3.5	2.7	4.8	5.2	4.8	4.3	
521 INDUSTRIAL–INDUSTRIELS	3.5	2.6	4.7	5.1	4.7	4.1	
522 NON INDUSTRIAL–NON INDUSTRIEL	0.0	0.0	0.1	0.1	0.1	0.1	
53 PARTS–PIECES ACCESSOIRES	9.0	7.5	6.8	7.0	7.8	6.3	
6 CONSUM GOODS–BIENS CONSOMMATION	6.7	7.5	10.0	10.3	9.8	9.3	
61 DURABLE–DURABLES	1.5	1.4	2.6	2.6	2.4	2.2	
62 SEMI DURABLE–SEMI DURABLES	3.1	3.8	4.2	4.5	4.2	4.3	
63 NON DURABLE–NON DURABLES	2.1	2.3	3.1	3.2	3.2	2.8	
7 GOODS NES–BIENS NDA	13.4	12.2	12.4	9.0	6.9	2.8	

EXPORTS – EXPORTATIONS

	1990	1991	1992	1993	1994	1995	1996
TOTAL EXPORTS–EXPORTATIONS TOTALES	100.	100.	100.	100.	100.	100.	
1 AGRICULTURE	1.0	0.0	4.4	4.1	7.9	4.7	
2 MINING QUARRY–INDUS EXTRACTIVES	19.4	20.8	18.7	22.1	39.5	18.8	
3 MANUFACTURING–IND MANUFACTUR	79.6	79.2	76.9	73.8	52.6	76.6	
31 FOOD BEV TOBACCO–ALIM BOISS TAB	3.5	3.7	3.9	3.4	4.9	4.1	
32 TEXTILES–INDUSTRIES TEXTILES	2.7	3.2	2.7	2.5	3.1	2.5	
33 WOOD & PRODUCTS–BOIS & PRODUITS	0.0	0.0	0.5	0.7	1.0	0.7	
34 PAPER & PRODUCTS–PAPIER & PRODT	3.0	2.9	2.9	2.5	4.0	4.6	
35 CHEMICALS–INDUSTRIES CHIMIQUES	3.4	4.1	5.9	5.4	9.4	10.6	
36 NON METAL MIN–MIN NON METAL	0.8	0.9	0.9	0.8	1.0	0.8	
37 BASIC METAL–IND METAL BASE	12.0	11.7	11.4	9.3	16.1	15.7	
38 METAL MANUF–MANUF METAL	6.3	7.3	8.4	8.8	12.3	12.4	
39 OTH MANUF IND–AUTRES MANUF	48.0	45.3	40.4	40.4	0.8	25.2	

3. TRADE BY PRINCIPAL COUNTRIES OF PRODUCTION AND LAST CONSIGNMENT (VALUE IN THOUSAND U.S. DOLLARS)
ECHANGES SELON LES PRINCIPAUX PAYS DE PRODUCTION ET DE DERNIERE CONSIGNATION (VALEUR EN MILLIERS DE DOLLARS EU)

COUNTRIES–PAYS	GENERAL IMPORTS F.O.B. IMPORTATIONS GENERALES F.O.B.					COUNTRIES–PAYS	GENERAL EXPORTS F.O.B. EXPORTATIONS GENERALES F.O.B.				
	1992	1993	1994	1995	1996		1992	1993	1994	1995	1996
World	18371648	18024554	21288033	27736968	26927967	Monde	23602294	23929709	25320871	27339868	29214006
Africa	420431	456756	585683	742406	773654	Afrique	2081962	2297985	2390871	3520096	4020089
Americas	3097257	2834431	3191742	4247404	4364207	Amériques	1967683	1909961	1963106	2576650	2441056
Northern America	2658588	2545111	2690612	3559299	3678898	Amérique du Nord	1649349	1565462	1374056	1982561	1762888
LAIA	422771	272508	475483	666121	626323	ALAI	284134	307610	494949	541197	600915
CACM	2351	3742	2961	7114	4581	MCAC	8327	8402	9811	12115	8442
Caribbean	11993	10559	20320	12394	19848	Caraïbes	19930	24793	77182	35349	32382
Rest of America	1554	2512	2366	2476	34558	Autre Amérique	5943	3693	7108	5429	36429
As.ex F.USSR	4148347	4777001	5188954	8380930	8042873	Asie l'URSS exclus	3780561	3989844	4282291	5423247	6021689
Eur.x F.USSR	8112945	8000547	10376325	13124460	12659311	Europe l'URSS exclus	5683283	4887796	7314944	9049651	8895251
EU	7606502	7511118	9766619	12335183	11863176	UE	5195647	4389952	5395897	7739817	7968446
EFTA	440695	426356	545314	694372	722766	AELE	384798	390383	1834904	1192592	850478
East Europe	60599	60336	61076	89577	68798	Europe de l'Est	80695	79360	66524	99078	68575
Other Europe	778	986	3226	2679	1913	Autre de l'Europe	14369	22991	17461	3491	1087
Former USSR	26250	34910	111275	50312	39199	Ancienne URSS	216779	162578	49589	91777	70888
Oceania	244765	235553	326986	489378	719669	Océanie	129937	159627	220253	427747	427767
Germany/Allemagne	3005903	2837959	3626850	4590842	4037349	United Kingdom	1553904	1143023	1654040	2381754	3036654
USA/Etats–Unis d'Amer	2512282	2392952	2390353	3276596	3452710	USA/Etats–Unis d'Amer	1572655	1509855	1238115	1812536	1579534
United Kingdom	1875251	1977483	2455315	2993363	3103205	Japan/Japon	1116103	1149867	1169516	1575371	1616475
Japan/Japon	1948278	2279104	2217753	2734857	2201735	Germany/Allemagne	1032700	922665	987735	1467051	1158596
Italy/Italie	645223	637057	837740	1115179	1182198	Zimbabwe	542362	752466	677997	1168799	1248869
France,Monac	717311	641344	778958	1049333	916251	Switz.Liecht	194830	215481	1703772	1051857	689196
China/Chine	228501	307043	360504	510546	1419000	Belgium–Luxembourg	454605	487869	727272	875401	839077
Netherlands/Pays–Bas	436791	424126	530408	638131	678636	Netherlands/Pays–Bas	609455	592218	591346	799455	784282
Switz.Liecht	428037	401363	520237	660783	685825	Italy/Italie	549800	421503	494403	874235	619246
Belgium–Luxembourg	413423	405986	508244	615076	541988	Hong Kong	448217	478632	418526	520110	601660
Iran (Islamic Rp. of)	5763	5160	13773	1206469	1229375	Korea, Republic of	294104	328173	489154	542365	667304
Hong Kong	309612	339857	410712	452655	424914	Spain/Espagne	314187	255302	339635	447841	634909
Australia/Australie	220679	210885	297331	452655	672545	Mozambique	238103	295541	388437	507094	550858
Korea, Republic of	247270	269649	303431	412644	542014	Zambia/Zambie	389776	399636	317809	358732	417401
Singapore/Singapour	225928	241569	275926	324568	327282	Israel/Israël	282220	452491	303390	349859	390494
Zimbabwe	267089	202855	281625	273568	274304	China/Chine	174014	183561	163006	246642	924387
Sweden/Suède	44578	72630	232227	400630	447827	France,Monac	322524	224668	281806	356223	415583
Canada	145262	150347	299798	282346	225790	Australia/Australie	115798	137696	186474	377359	381026
Brazil/Brésil	162514	169695	205773	249761	264472	Malawi	243673	181105	171294	182997	222962
Malaysia/Malaisie	125048	177969	210368	246085	251760	Singapore/Singapour	100872	129195	128928	251531	379568
Argentina/Argentine	182658	63134	160421	250826	232489	Brazil/Brésil	61339	101080	226369	262784	275723
Israel/Israël	105671	152768	171368	271548	171420	Thailand/Thaïlande	118387	120864	313924	165272	139531
Spain/Espagne	126221	115934	145348	215716	258454	Mauritius/Maurice	137258	144256	150249	184698	214121
Thailand/Thaïlande	135623	132812	156698	192318	167745	Angola	127573	80552	87111	112930	353277
Austria/Autriche	124032	112690	174715	175570	163547	Norway,SVD,JM	187100	174326	129796	113480	149363
India/Inde	38387	50441	114205	195860	257885	Kenya	52283	61984	185689	218808	220991
Ireland/Irlande	71568	96266	128645	168206	187627	Dem. Rep. of the Congo	101240	95834	104221	190510	222714
Finland/Finlande	55392	64104	175848	167356	156190	Canada	76611	55527	135356	169996	183354
Kuwait/ Koweït	270	417	219	172267	383294	India/Inde	6997	25532	136793	195366	244727
Denmark/Danemark	45972	67400	103275	129767	107754	Russian Federation	216779	162396	46664	86126	52190
Saudi Arabia	5893	11253	9966	208831	217421	Turkey/Turquie	118572	119347	65501	98224	135302
Dem. Rep. of the Congo	3979	80337	99486	100754	111815	Indonesia/Indonésie	44657	35759	79252	142876	175059
Indonesia/Indonésie	46495	57027	74303	100915	113408	Portugal	105801	85711	73588	106777	81557
Chile/Chili	61930	26522	84683	94446	54811	Malaysia/Malaisie	3086	8367	96160	177919	165615
Malawi	46907	48894	52031	56958	68818	Argentina/Argentine	75843	84480	77200	111223	92095
Portugal	38021	52233	56125	58798	67052	Ireland/Irlande	100165	98085	52171	115344	63348
Yemen/Yémen			10	220552	43434	Denmark/Danemark	14440	71469	74839	116557	151084
Turkey/Turquie	43518	47470	37056	52965	51137	Saudi Arabia	70064	97429	60594	88397	99210
United Arab Emirates	1653	8195	20967	61628	127789	United Arab Emirates	24015	64417	72027	102936	108305
Russian Federation	26250	34867	40345	40657	26509	Un. Rep. of Tanzania	9611	17942	50981	156177	127983
Egypt/Egypte	2085	1954	3507	101704	53074	Austria/Autriche	49220	37733	55822	106678	61768
New Zealand	23225	21960	26788	34954	45484	Chile/Chili	56148	51533	41141	56427	46421
Zambia/Zambie	15609	23314	29003	26302	40344	Philippines	45157	49624	46599	45337	57782
Cote d'Ivoire	16291	18048	24111	38291	30000	Sri Lanka	64045	43167	41578	41673	45584
Pakistan	12249	18656	26615	29581	33786	Greece/Grèce	62102	31712	28536	44150	54746
Mozambique	17855	18484	25815	33847	17454	Reunion/Réunion	63630	58418	41440	55605	
Philippines	18227	22825	23858	21525	25312	Pakistan	10811	9514	35913	74451	80846
Norway,SVD,JM	9479	20443	20868	27882	25577	Iran (Islamic Rp. of)	8430	1810	47968	39496	106588
Czech Republic		21624	21903	28361	20132	Mexico/Mexique	17712	19925	39314	33551	71898
Kenya	8311	9423	7865	31072	28656	Poland/Pologne	48871	29029	25333	42371	35027

(VALUE AS PERCENTAGE OF WORLD TOTAL)(VALEURS EN POURCENTAGE DU TOTAL MONDIAL)

	1987	1988	1989	1990	1991	1992	1993	1994	1995	1996
Africa						2.3	2.5	2.8	2.7	2.9
Americas						16.9	15.7	15.0	15.3	16.2
Northern America						14.5	14.1	12.6	12.8	13.7
LAIA						2.3	1.5	2.2	2.4	2.3
CACM						0.0	0.0	0.0	0.0	0.0
Caribbean						0.1	0.1	0.1	0.0	0.1
Rest of America						0.0	0.0	0.0	0.0	0.1
As.ex F.USSR						22.6	26.5	24.4	30.2	29.9
Eur.x F.USSR						44.2	44.4	48.7	47.3	47.0
EU						41.4	41.7	45.9	44.5	44.1
EFTA						2.4	2.4	2.6	2.5	2.7
East Europe						0.3	0.3	0.3	0.3	0.3
Other Europe						0.0	0.0	0.0	0.0	0.0
Former USSR						0.1	0.2	0.5	0.2	0.1
Oceania						1.3	1.3	1.5	1.8	2.7
Germany/Allemagne						16.4	15.7	17.0	16.6	15.0
USA/Etats–Unis d'Amer						13.7	13.3	11.2	11.8	12.8
United Kingdom						10.2	11.0	11.5	10.8	11.5
Japan/Japon						10.6	12.6	10.4	9.9	8.2
Italy/Italie						3.5	3.5	3.9	4.0	4.4
France,Monac						3.9	3.6	3.7	3.8	3.4
China/Chine						1.2	1.7	1.7	1.8	5.3
Netherlands/Pays–Bas						2.4	2.4	2.5	2.3	2.5
Switz.Liecht						2.3	2.2	2.4	2.4	2.5
Belgium–Luxembourg						2.3	2.3	2.4	2.2	2.0

	1987	1988	1989	1990	1991	1992	1993	1994	1995	1996
Afrique						8.8	9.6	9.4	12.9	13.8
Amériques						8.3	8.0	7.8	9.4	8.4
Amérique du Nord						7.0	6.5	5.4	7.3	6.0
ALAI						1.2	1.3	2.0	2.0	2.1
MCAC						0.0	0.0	0.0	0.0	0.0
Caraïbes						0.1	0.1	0.3	0.1	0.1
Autre Amérique						0.0	0.0	0.0	0.0	0.1
Asie l'URSS exclus						16.0	16.7	16.9	19.8	20.6
Europe l'URSS exclus						24.1	20.4	28.9	33.1	30.4
UE						22.0	18.3	21.3	28.3	27.3
AELE						1.6	1.6	7.2	4.4	2.9
Europe de l'Est						0.3	0.3	0.3	0.4	0.2
Autre de l'Europe						0.1	0.1	0.1	0.0	0.0
Ancienne URSS						0.9	0.7	0.2	0.3	0.2
Océanie						0.6	0.7	0.9	1.6	1.5
United Kingdom						6.6	4.8	6.5	8.7	10.4
USA/Etats–Unis d'Amer						6.7	6.3	4.9	6.6	5.4
Japan/Japon						4.7	4.8	4.6	5.8	5.5
Germany/Allemagne						4.4	3.9	3.9	5.4	4.0
Zimbabwe						2.3	3.1	2.7	4.3	4.3
Switz.Liecht						0.8	0.9	6.7	3.8	2.4
Belgium–Luxembourg						1.9	2.0	2.9	3.2	2.9
Netherlands/Pays–Bas						2.6	2.5	2.3	2.9	2.7
Italy/Italie						2.3	1.8	2.0	3.2	2.1
Hong Kong						1.9	2.0	1.7	1.9	2.1

4. General Imports F.O.B. by Commodities according to the S.I.T.C. (Rev. 2) in thousand U.S. Dollars
Importations Générales F.O.B. par Produits d'après la C.T.C.I. (Rév. 2) en milliers de Dollars E.U.

SITC CTCI	COMMODITY	1992 WEIGHT POIDS	1992 VALUE VALEUR	1993 WEIGHT POIDS	1993 VALUE VALEUR	1994 WEIGHT POIDS	1994 VALUE VALEUR	1995 WEIGHT POIDS	1995 VALUE VALEUR	PRODUIT
	ALL COMMODITIES		18371648		18024554		21288033		27736968	TOUS PRODUITS
0	FOOD AND LIVE ANIMALS		1156987		758351		868891		1247815	ALIMENTS,ANIMAUX VIVANTS
01	MEAT AND PREPARATIONS		77095		44697		171175		195844	VIANDES ET PREPARATIONS
011	MEAT FRESH,CHILLD,FROZEN		75968		43604	W 122491	121056		145092	VIANDES FRAICHES,REF,CONGE
03	FISH AND PREPARATIONS		51611		57002		56984		65756	POISSONS ET PREPARATIONS
04	CEREALS AND PREPARATIONS		675643		394717		258815		468307	CEREALES ET PRODUITS
041	WHEAT ETC UNMILLED	W 540017	69263		145396	W 728182	72782		155605	FROMENT,EPEAUTRE
0412	OTHER WHEAT ETC UNMILLED	W 517717	66430		141218	W 702697	67950		150007	AUTRE FROMENT NON MOULU
042	RICE	W 362083	105880		99444		126999		136823	RIZ
0422	RICE SEMI-MILLED,MILLED	W 245932	68820		70105	W 320349	87537		125144	RIZ POLI,GLACE INCL BRISURES
04221	RICE MILLED UNBROKEN	W 245439	68704		69765	W 317442	86855		117931	RIZ POLI,GLACE EXCL BRISURES
044	MAIZE UNMILLED	W 3594870	411943		103240	W 29760	11571		112692	MAIS NON MOULU
05	VEGETABLES AND FRUIT		89874		62035		68769		112564	LEGUMES ET FRUITS
054	VEG ETC FRSH,SMPLY PRSVD		57124		33346		35612		56005	LEGUMES FRAIS,CONG,SECS
07	COFFEE,TEA,COCOA,SPICES		67824		70137		103326		116939	CAFE,THE,CACAO,EPICES
081	*FEEDING STUFF FOR ANIML	W 401018	103682		58588	W 447854	116715		150501	NOURRITURE POUR ANIMAUX
0814	MEAT OR FISH MEAL FODDER	W 125658	60449	W 73196	27511	W 194785	70595		79798	FARINES DE VIANDES,POISSONS
08142	FISH MEAL FODDER	W 125164	60294	W 73195	27508	W 191867	69957		77403	FARINES DE POISSONS
1	BEVERAGES AND TOBACCO		184807		130912		156238		169937	BOISSONS ET TABACS
11	BEVERAGES		87158		78805		97760		106399	BOISSONS
112	ALCOHOLIC BEVERAGES		86405		78022		95709		104485	BOISSONS ALCOOLIQUES
1124	DISTILLED ALCOHOLIC BEVS		81579		73072		88845		95101	ALCOOLS,EAUX-DE-VIE
11241	WHISKY		70285		63656		75954		80557	WHISKY
12	TOBACCO AND MANUFACTURES		97649		52108		58478		63538	TABACS BRUTS FABRIQUES
121	TOBACCO UNMNFCTRD,REFUSE	W 25899	83155		40731	W 16232	45013		51423	TABACS BRUTS,DECHETS
2	CRUDE MATERLS,EXCL FUELS		621174		650846		695684		993680	MAT BRUTES NON COMESTIBLES
22	OIL SEEDS,OLEAGINOUS FRT		51081		62181		44358		69901	GRAINES,FRUITS OLEAGINEUX
222	SEEDS FOR'SOFT'FIXED OIL		48377		59778		41273		66623	GRAINES HUILES FIXES
23	RUBBER, CRUDE		73556		70626		85403		129421	CAOUTCHOUC BRUT
232	NATURAL RUBBER,GUMS		45988		45450		56351		87549	LATEX CAOUTCHOUC NATUREL
24	CORK AND WOOD		93713		115103		116165		130833	LIEGE ET BOIS
248	WOOD SHAPED,SLEEPERS		85578		109793		110916		120655	BOIS SIMPLEMENT TRAVAILLES
2483	LUMBER SHAPED NON-CONIFR	W 388569	76296		104428		101853		108472	NON CONIFERES SCIES,RABOTES
24831	LUMBER SAWN ETC NON-CON	W 386513	76081		104077		100613		105353	SCIES LONGITUDINALEMENT
26	TEXTILE FIBRES AND WASTE		149572		143277		153770		203521	FIBRES TEXTILES
263	COTTON	W 37822	50665	W 44581	52324	W 46750	65697		84588	COTON
27	CRUDE FERTLZR,MINRLS NES		89775		91582		97827		122254	ENGRAIS MINERAUX BRUTS
28	METALLIFEROUS ORES,SCRAP		84632		88830		92963		187212	MINERAIS METAL,DECHETS
287	BASE METAL ORES,CONC NES	W 333649	68203		71858		77693		165955	MINERAIS METAUX COMMUNS
2873	ALUMINIUM ORES,ALUMINA	W 310795	58972	W 339701	64677	W 329971	62684		129564	MINERAIS D'ALUMINIUM
28732	ALUMINA(ALUMINIUM OXIDE)	W 288737	57463	W 330890	63877	W 314278	61669		128408	ALUMINE (OXYDE ALUMINIUM)
29	CRUDE ANIMAL,VEG MAT NES		62459		57712		62007		81180	MATIERES BRUTES ANIM,VEGET
3	MINERAL FUELS ETC		102074		83270		78941		2833432	COMBUSTIBLES MINERAUX LUB
33	PETROLEUM AND PRODUCTS		59841		57806		48550		2788545	PETROLE ET DERIVES
333	CRUDE PETROLEUM								2635048	HUILES BRUTES DE PETROLE
334	PETROLEUM PRODUCTS,REFIN	W 2559	9237		9156		10877		90399	PRODUITS RAFFINES
4	ANIMAL,VEGETABLE OIL,FAT		144117		156473		267540		316482	HUILES,GRAISSES ANIM,VEG
42	FIXED VEGETABLE OIL,FAT		103393		111264		193130		226851	HUILES VEGETALES FIXES
423	FIXED VEG OILS,SOFT		45443		52187		127985		153136	HUILES VEGET DOUCES FIXES
4236	SUNFLOWER SEED OIL	W 114485	39492		29117	W 195834	116959		114931	HUILE DE TOURNESOL
424	FIXED VEG OIL NONSOFT		57950		59077		65145		73715	AUTRES HUILES VEG FIXES
5	CHEMCLS,RELATED PROD NES		2278354		2282369		2632617		3276589	PRODUITS CHIMIQUES
51	ORGANIC CHEMICALS		572969		563667		700126		904921	PROD CHIMIQ ORGANIQUES
511	HYDROCARBONS NES,DERIVS		57984		56581		68298		100191	HYDROCARBURES NDA
512	ALCOHOLS,PHENOLS ETC		67295		55606		84600		131498	PHENOLS,PHENOLS-ALCOOLS
5121	ACYCLIC ALCOHOLS,DERIVS		55595		42863		68654		111872	ALCOOLS ACYCLIQUES
513	CARBOXYLIC ACIDS ETC	W 125480	112948		117987		139530		214408	ACIDES CARBOXYLIQUES
5137	MONOACIDS AND DERIVATIVS	W 37210	45328		54587		59341		92285	ACIDES MONOCARBOXYLIQUES
5138	POLYACIDS AND DERIVATIVS	W 78861	43569		47404		61247		96680	ACIDES POLYCARBOXYLIQUES
51389	OTH POLYACIDS ETC,DERIVS	W 77192	42439		46735		60879		94681	ACIDES POLYCARBOXYLIQUES
514	NITROGEN-FNCTN COMPOUNDS		193295		191965		239187		256601	COMPOSES FONCT AZOTEES
5148	OTH NITROGN-FNCTN CMPNDS	W 78138	115404		113184		146996		168960	AUTRES COMPOSES AZOTES
51482	IMIDE-,IMIDE-FNCT CMPNDS	W 13209	72971		61874		81202		76452	COMPOSES A FONCTION IMIDE
515	ORG-INORG COMPOUNDS ETC	W 10686	92129		96457		112624		121827	COMPOSES ORGANO-MINERAUX
52	INORGANIC CHEMICALS		183798		181811		188950		231736	PROD CHIM INORGANIQUES
522	INORG ELEMNTS,OXIDES,ETC	W 119181	65023		67769		75556		85140	ELEMENTS INORGANIQUES
523	OTHR INORG CHEMICALS ETC		108655		105842		104331		136063	AUT PRODUITS CHIMIQUES INORG
5232	OTH MTL CMPD OF INRG ACD	W 215772	55294		58600		56368		73407	SELS METALLIQUES
53	DYES,TANNING,COLOUR PROD		147447		160697		183362		210278	PROD TEINTURE,COLORANTS
531	SYNT DYE,NAT INDGO,LAKES	W 5767	85786		93466	W 7989	100327		109365	MAT COLOR ORGAN,LAQUES
5311	SYNTHIC ORGNIC DYESTUFFS	W 4968	76498		81801	W 6482	88707		96196	MAT COLOR ORGAN SYNTHET
533	PIGMENTS,PAINTS,ETC		57289		63447		77805		95267	PIGMENTS,PEINTURES,VERNIS
541	*MEDICINAL,PHARM PRODUCT		384127		359007		441146		537001	PROD MEDICINAUX PHARMACEUT
5417	MEDICAMENTS		238905		230294		289330		352336	MEDICAMENTS
54179	— CONTNG OTH SUBSTANCES		154729		155338		187668		227299	MED CONT AUT SUBSTANCES
55	PERFUME,CLEANING ETC PRD		115723		110324		129515		148937	PROD POUR PARFUM,TOILETTE
551	ESSENTL OILS,PERFUME,ETC		57673		55008		65622		72636	HUILES ESSENTIELLES
58	PLASTIC MATERIALS ETC		420010		444523		488915		674126	MAT PLAST ARTIFICIELLES
582	PROD OF CONDENSATION ETC	W 58018	145981		166917		175100		230128	PROD CONDENS,POLYCOND
5824	POLYAMIDES	W 22217	51227	W 32137	67845	W 28134	58164		65394	POLYAMIDES
58241	— IN PRIMARY FORMS	W 22217	51227	W 32137	67845	W 28134	58164		65394	POLYAMIDES PRIMAIRES
583	POLYMERIZATION ETC PRODS		246898		250897		286959		412344	PROD POLYMERISATION
5831	POLYETHYLENE	W 36097	38394	W 43457	40387		46718		116724	POLYETHYLENE
58311	— IN PRIMARY FORMS	W 34150	33672	W 42464	36525	W 49314	41172		110452	POLYETHYLENE PRIMAIRES
5839	OTH POLYMRZTION ETC PROD	W 25958	85196		89322		95741		118569	AUT PROD POLYMER COPOLYM
59	CHEMICAL MATERIALS NES		397639		408814		446010		507704	MAT PROD CHIMIQUES NDA
591	PESTICIDES,DISINFECTANTS	W 9097	66298	W 12340	77522		84913		93785	DESINF,INSECT,FONG,HERB
598	MISCEL CHEM PRODUCTS NES		287004		286209		308303		358057	PROD DIV INDUST CHIM NDA
5982	ANTI-KNOCK PREPARTNS ETC	W 49378	122821		108004		119779		125491	PREPARAT ANTIDETONANTES
5989	CHEM PRODUCTS,PREPS NES		147499		158517		169723		211562	PROD PREP CHIMIQUES NDA
59899	OTH CHEM PRODS,PREPS,NES		93377		99023		105539		133925	AUT PRODUITS CHIMIQUES NDA
6	BASIC MANUFACTURES		2445150		2610836		3079643		3700302	ART MANUFACTURES
61	LEATHER,DRESSED FUR,ETC		72547		67303		107911		111402	CUIRS,PELLETERIES
611	LEATHER		55332		50861		91265		94608	CUIRS,PEAUX PREPARES
62	RUBBER MANUFACTURES NES		183003		172737		203877		261080	CAOUTCHOUC MANUFACTURE
625	RUBBER TYRES, TUBES ETC		88063		82680		97249		131319	PNEUS CAOUTCHOUC VULCANISE
628	RUBBER ARTICLES NES		67722		63307		75828		96500	OUVRAGES CAOUTCHOUC NDA
64	PAPER,PAPERBOARD AND MFR		350621		347053		412300		537354	PAPIERS,CARTONS & OUVRAGES
641	PAPER AND PAPERBOARD		307663		305331		364013		461827	PAPIERS ET CARTONS
6412	PRINTG,WRITING PAPER NES	W 90437	97077		91977		116721		153159	PAPIERS POUR L'IMPRESSION
64122	— COATED,IMPREGNATD ETC	W 87256	94122	W 93501	88486		114842		149664	PAPIERS IMPRESSION COUCHES

4. General Imports F.O.B. by Commodities according to the S.I.T.C. (Rev. 2) in thousand U.S. Dollars
Importations Générales F.O.B. par Produits d'après la C.T.C.I. (Rév. 2) en milliers de Dollars E.U.

SITC CTCI	COMMODITY	1992		1993		1994		1995		PRODUIT
		WEIGHT POIDS	VALUE VALEUR	WEIGHT POIDS	VALUE VALEUR	WEIGHT POIDS	VALUE VALEUR	WEIGHT POIDS	VALUE VALEUR	
6415	PAPER,PAPERBRD,BULK,NES		61552		68456		71271		92419	PAPIERS,CARTONS ROULEAUX
6418	COATED ETC PAPER NES BLK	W 58602	110295		101843		115571		150987	PAP,CARTONS COUCHES,ENDUITS
65	TEXTILE YARN,FABRICS,ETC		578386		550032		651856		744966	FILS,TISSUS,ARTICLES TEXTILE
651	TEXTILE YARN	W 19605	81447		87286		108649		114639	FILS TEXTILES
652	COTTON FABRICS,WOVEN		53299		47538		64014		87077	TISSUS DE COTON
653	WOVN MAN-MADE FIB FABRIC		230329		202526		204407		219104	TISSUS FIBRES SYNTH,ARTIF
6531	CONT SYNT WEAVES NONPILE		79598		98310		101169		92181	TISSUS FIBRES SYNTH CONTINUE
65315	CONT SYN TXTL FABRIC NES		71693		93972		94645		84996	TIS PLUS 85% TEXT SYNT CONT
6536	DISC REGN TXTL FABRC NES	A 54741	68723	A 45743	41276		30096		36432	TISSUS 85% TEXT ART DISC
654	OTH WOVEN TEXTILE FABRIC		23279		30255		68364		69210	TISSUS AUT COTON SYNT,ARTIF
657	SPECIAL TXTL FABRC,PRODS		88212		91134		93714		113790	TISSUS SPECIAUX
66	NONMETAL MINERAL MFS NES		345877		631849		707114		649471	ART MIN NON METALLIQUES
662	CLAY,REFRACTORY BLDG PRD		81177		77495		88007		125436	MAT CONST REFRACTAIRES
663	MINERAL MANUFCTURES NES		49381		54232		54938		73401	ART MIN MANUF NDA
667	PEARL,PREC-,SEMI-P STONE		81197		374677		422999		287682	PERLES, PIERRES GEMMES
6672	DIAMONDS NONINDUST,UNSET		77973		372595		421111		286237	DIAMANTS BRUTS
66721	— ROUGH,UNSORTED		55145				96456		40874	DIAMANTS BRUTS NON TRIES
66722	— SRTD,ROUGH,SIMPLY WKD		11549				308144		244660	DIAMANTS TRIES BRUTS
67	IRON AND STEEL		306740		259942		325961		421150	FER ET ACIER
674	IRN,STL UNIV,PLATE,SHEET		126269		105865		139660		163055	LARGES PLATS,TOLES
6749	OTH IRN,STL PLATES,SHEET	W 73235	59292		48034	W 65960	46506		53968	AUTRES TOLES FER,ACIER
678	IRON,STL TUBES,PIPES,ETC	W 65065	103383		77115		81395		118784	TUBES,TUYAUX EN FONTE,FER
6782	IRON,STL SEAMLESS TUBES	W 50309	60213		42193		40802		58068	TUBES,TUYAUX SANS SOUDURE
68	NON-FERROUS METALS		116790		122102		145812		324883	METAUX NON FERREUX
683	NICKEL	W 650	7539	W 428	5027		6141		107212	NICKEL
6831	NICKEL,ALLOYS UNWROUGHT	W 392	2446	W 155	902	W 201	1424		100533	NICKEL ET ALLIAGES BRUTS
684	ALUMINIUM	W 20044	56938		64750		69954		110990	ALUMINIUM
6842	ALUMINIUM,ALLOYS WORKED	W 19947	56746		64339		67574		108616	ALUMINIUM,ALLIAGES OUVRE
69	METAL MANUFACTURES NES		443403		416672		468012		579061	ART MANUFACT EN METAL NDA
695	TOOLS		119107		98330		119733		143736	OUTILS A MAIN
6954	BLADES,TIPS,ETC FR TOOLS		69853		50465		61521		71612	OUTILS POUR MACHINE-OUTIL
699	BASE METAL MFRS NES		144558		141253		161105		204971	ART MANUFACTURES MET NDA
7	MACHINES,TRANSPORT EQUIP		7582236		8010914		10172186		12142767	MACHINES MATERIEL TRANSPORT
71	POWER GENERATING EQUIPMT		561886		446610		485793		598705	MACHINES GENERATRICES
713	INTRNL COMBUS PSTN ENGIN		279817		231329		260849		311056	MOTEURS EXPL COMB INT, PIECE
7132	MOTOR VEHCL PISTN ENGINS	N 39211	79705	N 55801	45081	N 95074	52353		60158	MOTEURS EXPL POUR VEHICULES
7139	PISTON ENGINE PARTS NES		116619		116977		139829		160055	PIECES POUR 713.2,3,8
714	ENGINES AND MOTORS NES		82228		100864		94650		98418	MOTEURS NON ELECTRIQUES
7149	ENGINE & MOTOR PARTS NES		63013		75560		55751		70168	PIECES 714 ET 718.88
71491	PARTS NES OF 7144,71481		55370		68704		46876		58530	PIECES DES PROPULSEURS
716	ROTATING ELECTRIC PLANT		87731		79935		94770		115005	APP ELECTR ROTATIFS,PIECES
72	MACHS FOR SPCL INDUSTRYS		947806		973273		1401189		1864489	MAC SPECIALES POUR INDUST
721	AGRIC MACHY,EXC TRACTORS		37512		51077		73703		102163	MACHINES AGRICOLES
722	TRACTORS NON-ROAD	N 5521	33400	N 13728	70934	N 21628	130023		265122	TRACTEURS
7223	TRACK-LAYING TRACTORS	N 38	4598	N 30	5749	N 42	10267		131529	TRACTEURS A CHENILLES
7224	WHEELED TRACTORS NES	N 5483	28802	N 13698	65185	N 21586	119756		133593	TRACTEURS A ROUES
723	CIVIL ENGNEERG EQUIP ETC		160072		114822		163260		250182	APPAREILS DE GENIE CIVIL
7234	CONST,MINING MACHNRY NES	N 23090	150154		103406		145371		224830	MACH POUR LA CONST, MINES
72342	SLFPRP SHOVELS,EXCAVATRS	N 1511	69440	N 794	51094	N 1682	93100		165213	PELLES MECANIQUES
724	TEXTILE,LEATHER MACHNRY		212817		178832		228042		308343	MACH POUR INDUSTRIE TEXTILE
7244	SPINNING,EXTRDNG,ETC MCH		69299		42659		59148		78562	MACH POUR LE FILAGE
725	PAPER ETC MILL MACHINERY		40286		41893		117282		119014	MACHINES FABR PATE PAPIER
7251	PAPER,PULP MAKING MACHRY	N 114	7358	N 59	3034	N 4284	74838		29130	MACHINES FABR PATE CARTON
72511	CELLULOSE PULP MFG MACHY	N 31	1027	N 39	1203	N 4239	70404		13150	MACH FABR PATE CELLULOSE
726	PRINTG,BKBINDG MACHY,PTS		176408		211521		246081		311882	MACHINES POUR IMPRIMERIE
7267	OTH PRINTG & ANCILL MACH	N 219945	93681	N 230195	111532	N 273123	121598		165146	AUT MACH IMPRIMERIE,PIEC
72671	PRINTING MACHINERY NES	N 214109	86923	N 229547	96426	N 272727	118452		152290	AUT MACH IMPRIMERIE
727	FOOD MACHRY NON-DOMESTIC		45786		54148		53656		59274	MACH INDUSTRIES ALIMENT
728	OTH MACHY FOR SPCL INDUS		241524		250046		389142		448508	AUT MACH IND PARTICULIERES
7283	OTHR MINERAL WORKG MACHY		17931		17065		88909		55767	MACH TRIER,CRIBLER,BROYER
7284	MACHY FOR SPCL INDUS NES		190324		183218		245663		310697	MACH SPEC IND PARTICUL.
72842	RUBBER,PLASTICS WRKG MCH	N 10664	67954		57360	N 65293	94088		98646	MACH IND CAOUT MAT PLAST
72848	OTH MCHY WITH INDIV FNCT	N 948742	74131		81904	N 2168952	102144		121705	AUTRES MACHINES NDA
73	METALWORKING MACHINERY		196643		180342		402753		286966	MACH TRAVAIL DES METAUX
736	METALWORKING MACH-TOOLS		120053		102796		120004		170173	MACH-OUTILS TRAVAIL METAUX
737	METALWORKING MACHNRY NES		76590		77546		282749		116793	MACH TRAV METAUX PIECES
7372	ROLLING MILLS AND ROLLS		33602		30238		236527		64092	LAMINOIRS CYLINDRES PIEC
73721	ROLLING MILLS		17334		15721		226116		38551	LAMINOIRS ET TRAINS
74	GENRL INDUSTRL MACHY NES		1313336		1259908		1439009		1860229	MACH APP INDUSTRIE
741	HEATING,COOLING EQUIPMNT		245345		236794		236128		308148	MACH CHAUFFAGE,PIECES
7414	NONDOM REFRIG EQUIPT,PTS		42493		49711		62094		84924	MAT PRODUCTION DU FROID
7416	HEATING,COOLING EQU NES		141672		125527		94992		115472	APP CHANGEMENT TEMP
742	PUMPS FOR LIQUIDS ETC		111486		108378		123689		151366	POMPES MOTO-POMPES
743	PUMPS NES,CENTRFUGES ETC		193944		185257		216541		285608	POMPES COMPRES,VENT ETC
7431	PUMPS FOR GASES ETC	N 1413749	86051		85604		98885		128325	POMPES AIR A VIDE,COMPRES
744	MECHANICAL HANDLING EQU		153564		139344		165733		238415	EQUIP MANUTENTION PIECES
7449	PTS NES OF MACHY OF 7442		78160		65462		85729		114445	PIECES DU 744.2
745	NONELEC MACHY,TOOLS NES		144608		157489		187198		249090	AUT MACH NON ELEC,PIECES
7452	OTH NONELEC MCHS,PTS NES		125726		136929		162304		222330	AUT MACH NON ELEC,PIECES
74522	PACKAGNG,BOTTLNG,ETC MCH	N 32416	59197	N 85768	64512		81842		109043	MACH NETT BOUTEILLES,ETC
749	NONELEC MACH PTS,ACC NES		464389		432646		509720		627602	PIECES MACH NON ELEC NDA
7491	BALL,ROLLER,ETC BEARINGS		108109		94286		125435		147617	ROULEMENTS BILLES ETC
7492	COCKS,VALVES ETC NES		133536		126795		138424		181742	ART ROB,SIM POUR TUYAUX
7493	SHAFT,CRANK,PULLEY ETC		148502		136984		159262		206825	ARBRES TRANS,VILEBREQUINS
7499	OTH NONELEC MCHY PTS NES		74241		74581		86598		91418	PIECES NON ELECT NDA
75	OFFICE MACHNES,ADP EQUIP		808310		928175		1132091		1345714	MACH BUREAU TRAIT AUTOM
751	OFFICE MACHINES		83450		91672		117324		130589	MACH,APPAREILS DE BUREAU
7518	OFFICE MACHINES NES	N 1122081	55548	N 864613	62699	N 1016576	92508		101016	MACH,APP DE BUREAU NDA
75182	PHOTO,THERMOCOPY APPARAT	N 29191	44001	N 29240	51433	N 37494	76143		86047	APPAREILS DE PHOTOCOPIE
752	AUTOMTIC DATA PROC EQUIP	N 1462100	470177		521189		627494		710299	MACH TRAIT INFORMATION
7522	DIGITAL COMPUTERS	N 154870	135091		163934	N 313457	242571		238130	MACH DIGITALES COMPLETES
7523	DIGITL CENTRL PROCESSORS	N 83787	66469		79678	N 72216	83179		115661	UNITES CENTRALES
7524	DIGITL CENTRL STOR UNITS	N 442875	95353	N 385627	76816	N 279500	67676		59004	UNITES MEMOIRE CENTRALES
7525	ADP PERIPHERAL UNITS	N 750977	151473	N 960699	171943	N 1142563	202083		239798	UNITES PERIPHERIQUES
759	OFFICE,ADP MCH PTS,ACCES		254683		315313		387273		504826	PIECES DU 751 ET 752
7599	ACCTG,ETC,ADP MCH PTS,AC		227937		285357		344179		457664	PIECES DU 751 ET 752
76	TELECOMM,SOUND EQUIPMENT		454931		507322		863851		1038766	EQUIPMENT DE TELECOM
764	TELECOM EQPT,PTS,ACC NES		344001		390728		745579		895416	EQUIP TELECOM,PIECES
7641	LINE TELEPHONE,ETC EQUIP	N 1220901	125101	N 1076038	158786	N 1552984	231242		276288	APP TELEPHON PAR FIL
7643	TV,RADIO TRANSMITTRS ETC		58582	N 181710	54412	N 555885	267124		324279	APP EMET TELE RADIO
7649	PTS NES OF EQUIPMT OF 76		93227		104631		170989		177697	PIECES DE LA DIV 76

4. General Imports F.O.B. by Commodities according to the S.I.T.C. (Rev. 2) in thousand U.S. Dollars
Importations Générales F.O.B. par Produits d'après la C.T.C.I. (Rév. 2) en milliers de Dollars E.U.

SITC CTCI	COMMODITY	1992		1993		1994		1995		PRODUIT
		WEIGHT POIDS	VALUE VALEUR	WEIGHT POIDS	VALUE VALEUR	WEIGHT POIDS	VALUE VALEUR	WEIGHT POIDS	VALUE VALEUR	
76491	PTS NES OF APPAR OF 7641		34208		49145		94791		87771	PIECES POUR 764.1
76493	TELECOMM EQUIPMT PTS NES		51455		44364		64412		75865	PIECES 761,762,764.3,8
77	ELECTRIC MACHNRY NES ETC		1017802		1060551		1396615		1780063	MACH APP ELECT NDA
771	ELECTRIC POWER MACHY NES		64543		64322		89621		87579	MACH PROD,TRANS ELECTR
7712	OTH ELEC POWER MACHY NES		50362		48770		67325		68934	AUT APP PROD TRANSF ELEC
772	SWITCHGEAR ETC,PARTS NES		295511		294901		346498		395529	APP COUPURE,SECT ETC
7721	SWITCHGEAR ETC		263718		255845		307429		354428	APP COUPURE,SECTIONMNT
773	ELECTR DISTRIBUTNG EQUIP		54086		66713		78778		99070	EQUIPMT DISTRIBUTION ELECT
774	ELECTRO–MEDCL,XRAY EQUIP		62141		67900		68340		78891	APPAREILS MEDICAUX
775	HOUSEHOLD TYPE EQUIP NES		143404		139583		151778		174736	MACH,APP USAGE DOMESTQUE
7758	ELECTRO–THERMIC APPL NES		54170		57723		63826		76307	APP ELECTROTHERMIQ NDA
776	TRANSISTORS,VALVES,ETC		165576		183960		256294		324775	LAMPES,TUBES,VALVES
7764	ELECTRONIC MICROCIRCUITS	MN 69209	86642		112639		161633		218994	MICROSTRUCTURES ELECTRON
778	ELECTRICAL MACHINERY NES		232541		243172		405304		619483	AUTRES MACH ELECT NDA
7783	AUTOMOTIVE ELECTR EQUIP		63989		69214		80904		88541	EQUIP ELECT MOTEURS EXPL
7788	OTH ELEC MACHY,EQUIP NES		79773		77316		204304		395088	AUT MACH APP ELEC NDA
77886	OTH ELEC MACHINERY NES		34078		32578		153576		336361	AUT MACH APP ELECTRIQUES
78	ROAD VEHICLES		1796375		2180476		2658582		2876779	VEHICULES ROUTIERS
781	PASS MOTOR VEH EXC BUSES		617563		927260		926919		1073346	AUTO TRANSPORT PERSONNES
782	LORRIES,SPCL MTR VEH NES		368934		450570		563989		679302	VEHICULES SPECIAUX,MARCH
7821	LORRIES,TRUCKS		350054		435980		550576		659376	VEHICULES TRANSP MARCHAND
783	ROAD MOTOR VEHICLES NES		78796		74627	N 569580	105186		61199	VEHICULES ROUTIERS NDA
7832	TRACTORS FOR TR–TRAILERS	N 120026	44093		35873	N 525417	73303		16850	TRACTEURS ROUTIERS
784	MOTOR VEH PRTS,ACCES NES		683253		674491		1002609		985590	PIECES 722,781,782,783
7842	MOTOR VEHICLE BODIES	N 2666	14035	N 3972	16073	N 24264	51462		112209	CARROS 722,781,782,783
7849	OTHER MOTOR VEHCL PARTS		661092		644191		941639		856702	PIECES 722,781,782,783
79	OTHR TRANSPORT EQUIPMENT		485147		474257		392303		491056	AUTRE MATERIEL TRANSPORT
792	AIRCRAFT ETC		440640		437118		369551		458906	APP NAVIGATION AERIENNE
7923	AIRCRFT NES2000–15000KG	N 43	102465	N 52	142794	N 72	98613		243782	AERODYNES 2000 A 15000 KG
7924	AIRCRFT NES OVER 15000KG	N 7	246081	N 62	173117	N 54	156818		95206	AERODYNES PLUS 15000 KG
7929	AIRCRAFT PARTS NES		34467		80702		77136		75648	PIECES DU 792
8	MISC MANUFACTURED GOODS		1618238		1716779		1874256		2286592	ART MANUFACTURES DIVERS
84	CLOTHING AND ACCESSORIES		145710		143812		156679		140462	VETEMENTS
851	*FOOTWEAR		82152		111513		116564		166051	CHAUSSURES
85102	FOOTWEAR LEATHER		62548		89010		94811		135111	CHAUS SEMELLES EN CUIR
87	PRECISION INSTRUMNTS NES		499154		527134		557965		625159	INSTRUM,APPAR SCIENT NDA
872	MEDICAL INSTRUMENTS NES		123770		114851		132236		147078	INSTR,APP MEDIC–CHIR NDA
87202	OTH MEDICAL INSTRUMENTS		104603		101400		116269		124721	INSTRUM,APP MEDECINE
874	MEASURNG,CONTROLNG INSTR		337644		373721		384025		440827	INSTRUMENTS DE MESURE
8742	MEASUR,DRAW ETC INST,PTS		92413		78464		80637		94706	INST DESSIN,TRACAGE,PCS
87421	MEASURNG,DRAWNG ETC INST		81090		70215		71536		84451	INSTRUM DESSIN,TRACAGE
8743	GAS,LIQUID CONTROL INSTR		95409		92429		119858		140310	APP,INSTR MESURE FLUIDES
8745	MEAS,CONTRL,SCI INST NES		16897		54998		22126		17311	APP SCIENT MESURE NDA
8748	ELEC MEAS,CONTRL EQU NES		72240		76881		79174		100900	APP ELEC ELECTRO MESURE
87483	OTH ELCTRNC MEAS ETC EQU		63776		70552		71881		92943	AUT APP ELECTRO DE MESURE
88	PHOTO EQU,OPTICL GDS ETC		211426		209844		237705		255112	APP,FOURN PHOTO,OP,MONTR
882	PHOTO,CINEMA SUPPLIES		100206		100210		109003		122099	PRODUITS PHOTO,CINEMA
8822	PHOTO FILM EXC DEV CINMA		77561		76161		78861		85342	PLAQUES,PELLICULES,FILMS
89	MISC MANUFCTRD GOODS NES		576682		623510		681467		937854	ART MANUFACTURES DIVERS
892	PRINTED MATTER		147925		165583		164597		180453	IMPRIMES
8921	PRINTED BOOKS,GLOBES,ETC		114905		131646		124446		138902	LIVRES,BROCHURES,CARTES
89211	PRINTED BOOKS,PAMPHLETS		112706		128670		122352		135798	LIVRES,BROCHURES
893	ARTICLES OF PLASTIC NES		107442		115906		132348		165878	OUVRAGES EN MAT DIVIS 58
8939	MISC PLASTIC ARTICLES		88832		97349		108133		135215	ART DIVERS EN MAT DIV 58
89399	OTHR PLASTC ARTICLES NES		77491		85148		94788		120444	AUT OUV MAT DIV 58
894	TOYS,SPORTING GOODS,ETC		93486		91350		95196		116098	VOITURES ENFANTS,JOUETS
8942	TOYS,INDOOR GAMES ETC		62550		63601		58119		64811	JOUETS,JEUX ETC
898	MUSICAL INSTRUMENTS,PTS		98733		106517		137045		286965	INSTRUMENTS DE MUSIQUE
8983	SOUND RECRDNG TAPE,DISCS		87899		97315		125970		271526	SUPPORTS SON POUR 763
89832	RECORDED DISCS,TAPES ETC	N 6470674	56419		66570	N 6654338	94456		237447	DISQUES,PHONO,BANDES
899	OTHER MANUFACTURED GOODS		66207		73869		84512		94075	AUT ART MANUF DIVERS NDA
9	GOODS NOT CLASSD BY KIND		2238511		1623804		1462038		769370	ART TRANSACT NON CLASSES
931	*SPECIAL TRANSACTIONS		2236804		1619983		1457405		761847	TRANS.SPECIALES

5. General Exports F.O.B. by Commodities according to the S.I.T.C. (Rev. 2) in thousand U.S. Dollars
Exportations Générales F.O.B. par Produits d'après la C.T.C.I. (Rév. 2) en milliers de Dollars E.U.

SITC CTCI	COMMODITY	1992 WEIGHT POIDS	1992 VALUE VALEUR	1993 WEIGHT POIDS	1993 VALUE VALEUR	1994 WEIGHT POIDS	1994 VALUE VALEUR	1995 WEIGHT POIDS	1995 VALUE VALEUR	PRODUIT
	ALL COMMODITIES		23602294		23929709		25320871		27339868	TOUS PRODUITS
0	FOOD AND LIVE ANIMALS		1503839		1371355		1899659		1839547	ALIMENTS,ANIMAUX VIVANTS
01	MEAT AND PREPARATIONS		80472		74984		43588		70717	VIANDES ET PREPARATIONS
011	MEAT FRESH,CHILLD,FROZEN		76258		68831		38969		64852	VIANDES FRAICHES,REF,CONGE
03	FISH AND PREPARATIONS		178694		196383		250798		225683	POISSONS ET PREPARATIONS
034	FISH,FRESH,CHILLED,FROZN		95131		113972		159129		131308	POISSON FRAIS, REFRIG,CONG
0342	FISH FROZEN,EXCL FILLETS		70721		90660		117222		66879	POISSONS CONGELES
04	CEREALS AND PREPARATIONS		156114		103843		522352		254669	CEREALES ET PRODUITS
044	MAIZE UNMILLED		91779		41037	W 3760176	455297		154852	MAIS NON MOULU
05	VEGETABLES AND FRUIT		846116		808281		800212		926517	LEGUMES ET FRUITS
057	FRUIT,NUTS,FRESH,DRIED		562011		556057		545333		630041	FRUITS FRAIS OU SECS
0571	ORANGES, MANDARINS ETC		144437		125718	W 322314	120309		164046	ORANGES,MAND,CLEMENTINES
05711	ORANGES,FRESH OR DRIED		140506		120763	W 319933	118775		151245	ORANGES FRAICHES,SECHEES
0572	LEMONS,GRAPEFRUIT ETC		45259		39761		94692		34991	AUTRES AGRUMES FRAIS,SECS
05722	GRAPEFRUITS,FRESH,DRIED		27483		28754	W 189479	82175		19327	PAMPLEMOUSSES,POMELOS
0574	APPLES FRESH		155731		125200	W 245375	73991		109622	POMMES FRAICHES
0575	GRAPES FRESH OR DRIED		96079		125802	W 120380	144568		135192	RAISINS FRAIS OU SECS
05751	GRAPES FRESH		68136		93428	W 99899	122612		111446	RAISINS FRAIS
0579	FRUIT FRESH OR DRIED NES		117303		136100		106815		181108	FRUITS FRAIS,SECS NDA
05792	PEARS, QUINCES FRESH		53415		71653	W 98630	44375		108417	POIRES ET COINGS FRAIS
058	FRUIT PRESERVED,PREPARED		246281		217338		216071		252908	CONSERVES DE FRUITS
0585	FRUIT OR VEGETABLE JUICE		75277		62816	W 113411	65417		68150	JUS DE FRUITS
0589	FRUIT PREPRD,PRESRVD,NES		154513		145690		142139		168550	FRUITS PREPARES CONSERV
05899	FRUIT,NUTS NES,PRESERVED		154100		142871		137928		161498	FRUITS PREP CONSERV NDA
06	SUGAR AND PREPS,HONEY		127047		69699		151224		170947	SUCRES ET PRODUITS
061	SUGAR AND HONEY		109286		56602	W 922773	134246		155196	SUCRES ET MIEL
0611	RAW BEET AND CANE SUGAR		64763		33640	W 419766	91180		110242	SUCRES BRUTS
09	MISC EDIBLE PRODUCTS		27927		29641		28247		83320	PREP ALIMENTAIRES DIVERSES
1	BEVERAGES AND TOBACCO		159627		140921		194332		212917	BOISSONS ET TABACS
11	BEVERAGES		126606		112998		158035		174020	BOISSONS
112	ALCOHOLIC BEVERAGES		91833		83991	W 134163	125625		149713	BOISSONS ALCOOLIQUES
1121	WINE OF FRESH GRAPES ETC		42575		45554	W 52728	69385		91645	VINS DE RAISINS FRAIS
11212	WINE OF FRESH GRAPES		42526		45507	W 52714	69325		91496	VINS DE MOUTS DE RAISINS
2	CRUDE MATERLS,EXCL FUELS		2054361		1895493		4693419		2776446	MAT BRUTES NON COMESTIBLES
21	HIDES,SKINS,FURS UNDRSSD		73731		79706		76554		97064	CUIRS,PEAUX BRUTS
211	HIDES,SKINS,EXC FURS,RAW		73672		79606	W 30312	76546		97060	CUIRS ET PEAUX
24	CORK AND WOOD		29264		66015		116551		153255	LIEGE ET BOIS
246	PULPWOOD,CHIPS,WOODWASTE		69		19990	W 1180524	74652		109345	BOIS DE TRITURATION
24602	PULPWOOD CHIPS,PARTICLES				19989	W 1179619	74437		108963	EN FORME DE PLAQUETTES
251	*PULP AND WASTE PAPER		350884		294964	W 815820	370947		623375	PATES A PAPIER,DECHETS
2516	CHEM WOOD PULP DISSOLVNG		226855		191504	W 455545	220194		377555	PATES CHIMIQUES DE BOIS
2517	SODA,SULPHATE WOOD PULP		42147		38059	W 235927	116703		208632	PATES CHIMIQUES AU SULFATE
25172	— BLEACHED,NONDISSOLVNG		35161		20188	W 197041	103450		193792	PATES BLANCHIES
2518	SULPHITE WOOD PULP		78621		61458	W 104381	31535		34847	PATES AU BISULFITE
26	TEXTILE FIBRES AND WASTE		199998		135201		188657		212311	FIBRES TEXTILES
268	WOOL(EXC TOPS),ANML HAIR		187824		127024	W 46417	160449		177853	LAINES ET POILS
2681	WOOL GREASY,FLEECE–WSHED		73684		52408	W 26212	61448		60556	LAINE EN SUINT
27	CRUDE FERTLZR,MINRLS NES		336245		337215		2921608		251039	ENGRAIS MINERAUX BRUTS
277	NATURAL ABRASIVES NES		58366		46017		2741446		53108	ABRASIFS NATURELS NDA
2771	INDUSTRIAL DIAMONDS						2718414		15749	DIAMANTS INDUSTRIELS
278	OTHER CRUDE MINERALS		209283		234609		124027		138586	AUTRES MINERAUX BRUTS
2786	SLAG,SCALINGS,DROSS,ETC		74754		107786	W 56652	12605		14409	SCORIES,LAITIERS
27861	SLAG ETC FRM IRN,STL MFR		62693		107681	W 56110	12529		13099	SCORIES,LAITIER,BATTIT
28	METALLIFEROUS ORES,SCRAP		999902		915555		927394		1339669	MINERAIS METAL,DECHETS
281	IRON ORE,CONCENTRATES		273009		283751	MW 15998	257407		362473	MINERAIS DE FER
2816	IRON ORE AGGLOMERATES		272948		283741	MW 15998	257390		362377	MINERAIS AGGLOMERES
287	BASE METAL ORES,CONC NES		671585		526546	W 3694792	557018		777830	MINERAIS METAUX COMMUNS
2871	CPR ORE ETC,CEMENT COPPR		220068		123032	W 86646	119808		84119	MINERAIS DE CUIVRE,MATTES
28711	COPPER ORES,EXCL MATTE		91109		46411	W 31981	26306		20059	MINERAIS DE CUIVRE
28712	COPPER MATTE,CEMENT COPR		128959		76621	W 54665	93502		64060	MATTES DE CUIVRE
2872	NICKEL ORES,CONCENTRATES		134033		151697	W 54286	118708		150093	MINERAIS DE NICKEL
28722	NICKEL MATTE,SINTERS,ETC		134033		151697	W 54283	118671		150091	MATTES,SINTERS
2877	MANGANESE ORE,CONCENTRTE		175093		113695	W 1673004	108380		122074	MINERAIS DE MANGANESE
2879	OTH NONFER ORE,CONCNTRTE		109639		106948	W 1742897	161933		366921	MINERAIS D'AUTRES METAUX
28791	CHROMIUM ORE,CONCENTRATE		84320		69904	W 1061314	62295		119460	MINERAIS DE CHROME
28793	MOLYBD, NIOBIUM ETC ORES		24951		36712	W 658194	78753		143241	MINERAIS DE MOLYBDENE,TITANE
28799	OTH BASE MTL ORE,CON NES		316		256	W 23389	20884		104220	AUTRES MINERAIS
3	MINERAL FUELS ETC		1464379		1659884		1367915		2205406	COMBUSTIBLES MINERAUX LUB
32	COAL,COKE AND BRIQUETTES		1414068		1608897		1296062		1607050	HOUILLES,COKES,BRIQUETTES
322	COAL,LIGNITE AND PEAT		1408694		1601848	MW 52402	1289878		1603286	HOUILLES,LIGNITES,TOURBE
3221	ANTHRACITE,NOT AGGLOMRTD		72926		57922	W 937142	47151		42299	ANTHRACITE
3222	OTH COAL,NOT AGGLOMERATD		1335767		1543925	MW 51465	1242725		1560984	AUTRES HOUILLES
33	PETROLEUM AND PRODUCTS		47216		48608		64860		577608	PETROLE ET DERIVES
334	PETROLEUM PRODUCTS,REFIN		2145		6203	W 44090	3728		471499	PRODUITS RAFFINES
5	CHEMCLS,RELATED PROD NES		1241484		1114727		1562629		2097208	PRODUITS CHIMIQUES
51	ORGANIC CHEMICALS		135209		154224		264958		294438	PROD CHIMIQ ORGANIQUES
512	ALCOHOLS,PHENOLS ETC		41182		62041		153952		120258	PHENOLS,PHENOLS–ALCOOLS
5121	ACYCLIC ALCOHOLS,DERIVS		30071		44236		135528		94951	ALCOOLS ACYCLIQUES
51216	ETHYL ALC,DENATRD SPIRIT		10780		31046		114635		60609	ALCOOL ETHYLIQUE NON DENAT
52	INORGANIC CHEMICALS		575599		481281		705908		1012297	PROD CHIM INORGANIQUES
522	INORG ELEMNTS,OXIDES,ETC		235217		181664	W 1203656	379186		784227	ELEMENTS INORGANIQUES
5222	INORGANIC ACIDS ETC		6269		6707	W 449417	69200		102908	ACIDES INORGANIQUES
52224	PHOSPHORIC ACIDS ETC					W 417247	65391		99219	ACIDES PHOSPHORIQUES
5224	ZINC,IRON,LEAD ETC OXIDE		131839		79159	W 551215	206168		558034	OXYDES METALLIQUES
52245	COBALT OXIDES,HYDROXIDES		589		544	W 148	3016		215603	OXYDES,HYDROXYDES COBALT
52246	TITANIUM OXIDES		116530		64099	W 526276	182162		316822	OXYDES DE TITANE
523	OTHR INORG CHEMICALS ETC		242237		244441		284200		178050	AUT PRODUITS CHIMIQUES INORG
5231	METAL CMPD OF INORG ACID		132876		110759		144307		25895	SELS METALLIQUES
52312	CHLORIDES, BROMIDES ETC		97859		85290		118144		707	CHLORURES,OXYCHLORURES
5232	OTH MTL CMPD OF INRG ACD		85580		111378	W 1199815	120607		117768	SELS METALLIQUES
524	RADIOACTIVE ETC MATERIAL		98146		55176		42522		50020	MATIERES RADIOACTIVES
5241	RADIOACTIVE ELEMENTS ETC		98126		55154		42432		49626	RADIOELEMENTS,ISOTOPES
55	PERFUME,CLEANING ETC PRD		51179		44019		100511		83637	PROD POUR PARFUM,TOILETTE
562	*FERTILIZERS,MANUFACTURE		71651		79671	W 444937	84011		156963	ENGRAIS MANUFACTURES
5629	FERTILIZERS NES		34977		48479	W 217102	41329		82485	ENGRAIS NDA
58	PLASTIC MATERIALS ETC		166633		114124		127214		173478	MAT PLAST ARTIFICIELLES
583	POLYMERIZATION ETC PRODS		153282		100979		106970		132526	PROD POLYMERISATION
59	CHEMICAL MATERIALS NES		119027		127402		150580		226438	MAT PROD CHIMIQUES NDA
591	PESTICIDES,DISINFECTANTS		62711		74162	W 30783	82560		127069	DESINF,INSECT,FONG,HERB
598	MISCEL CHEM PRODUCTS NES		48746		46306		61442		93392	PROD DIV INDUST CHIM NDA
6	BASIC MANUFACTURES		5579706		5922889		6790895		8017158	ART MANUFACTURES

5. General Exports F.O.B. by Commodities according to the S.I.T.C. (Rev. 2) in thousand U.S. Dollars
Exportations Générales F.O.B. par Produits d'après la C.T.C.I. (Rév. 2) en milliers de Dollars E.U.

SITC CTCI	COMMODITY	1992 WEIGHT POIDS	1992 VALUE VALEUR	1993 WEIGHT POIDS	1993 VALUE VALEUR	1994 WEIGHT POIDS	1994 VALUE VALEUR	1995 WEIGHT POIDS	1995 VALUE VALEUR	PRODUIT
61	LEATHER,DRESSED FUR,ETC		67596		83275		126687		138790	CUIRS,PELLETERIES
611	LEATHER		64373		77441		120165		132940	CUIRS,PEAUX PREPARES
6116	LEATHER OF OTH HIDE,SKIN		38797		45875		70945		82078	PEAUX PREP D'AUTRES ANIMAUX
62	RUBBER MANUFACTURES NES		48139		57247		62749		98065	CAOUTCHOUC MANUFACTURE
63	WOOD,CORK MANUFACTRS NES		105161		127733		101368		76591	OUVRAGES LIEGE ET BOIS
634	VENEERS,PLYWOOD,ETC		66054		72975		19478		15802	PLACAGES,CONTRE-PLAQUES
635	WOOD MANUFACTURES NES		38780		54110		81534		60458	ART MANUF EN BOIS NDA
64	PAPER,PAPERBOARD AND MFR		309982		290477		343903		573832	PAPIERS,CARTONS & OUVRAGES
641	PAPER AND PAPERBOARD		267314		259288		253696		501765	PAPIERS ET CARTONS
6411	NEWSPRINT		73839		72410	W 228393	91023		134740	PAPIER JOURNAL
6413	KRAFT PAPER,PAPERBOARD		111692		110049	W 271297	94607		283185	PAPIER ET CARTON KRAFT
64131	KRAFT LINER IN BULK		109868		109379	W 268855	92948		280776	PAP KRAFT POUR COUVERTURES
642	PAPER,ETC,PRECUT,ARTS OF		42668		31189		90207		72067	PAP,CARTONS DECOUPES
6421	PAPER ETC CONTAINERS		25760		19540		76670		53592	BOITES,SACS EMBALLAGES
65	TEXTILE YARN,FABRICS,ETC		267174		220154		238306		250429	FILS,TISSUS,ARTICLES TEXTILE
651	TEXTILE YARN		169766		125589		123731		124835	FILS TEXTILES
6512	WOOL,HAIR YARN,INCL TOPS		90815		65560	W 14623	79805		63012	FILS DE LAINE,DE POILS
65121	WOOL TOPS		87877		62441	W 13831	76144		57698	RUBANS LAINE PEIGN,TOPS
66	NONMETAL MINERAL MFS NES		2222624		3057359		2837006		2495275	ART MIN NON METALLIQUES
661	LIME,CEMENT,BLDG PRODS		48478		53892		66579		91848	CHAUX,CIMENTS MAT CONSTR
667	PEARL,PREC-,SEMI-P STONE		2082489		2914002		2684943		2322284	PERLES, PIERRES GEMMES
6672	DIAMONDS NONINDUST,UNSET		2076726		2904948		2679509		2315852	DIAMANTS BRUTS
66721	— ROUGH,UNSORTED						145227		219462	DIAMANTS BRUTS NON TRIES
66722	— SRTD,ROUGH,SIMPLY WKD						2198288		1792758	DIAMANTS TRIES BRUTS
66729	— CUT ETC NOT SET						335994		301628	DIAMANTS TAILLES
67	IRON AND STEEL		1593931		1453279		2351276		2796129	FER ET ACIER
671	PIG IRON ETC		74036		64264	W 2115616	806490		1220650	FONTE,SPIEGEL,POUDRES
6712	PIG IRN,SPIEGELEISEN ETC		71969		61967	W 321592	53260		86405	FONTES BRUTES
6716	FERRO-ALLOYS					W 1786196	750112		1128945	FERRO-ALLIAGES
67161	FERRO-MANGANESE					W 419453	166497		208854	FERRO-MANGANESE
67169	OTHER FERRO-ALLOYS					W 1311183	555023		881311	AUTRES FERRO-ALLIAGES
672	IRON,STEEL PRIMARY FORMS		431967		388560	W 2568346	720420		519554	LINGOTS FER,ACIER
6725	IRN,STL BLOOMS,SLABS,ETC		139249		106079	W 481423	166975		234214	BLOOMS,BILLETTES FER ACIER
67251	IRN,SMPLE STL BLOOMS,ETC		99984		51797	W 339685	117778		105639	BLOOMS ETC NON ACIER FIN
67254	STNLS STL ETC BLOOMS ETC		1448		16346	W 21080	24121		86611	BLOOMS ETC ACIER INOXYD
6727	IRN,STL COIL FR REROLLNG		290094		280073	W 2086629	553192		282541	EBAUCHES POUR TOLES FER
67271	IRON,SIMPLE STEEL COILS		228245		227300	W 2008380	489045		229808	EBAUCHES NON EN ACIER
673	IRON,STEEL SHAPES ETC		436887		419043		228329		322424	BARRES,PROFIL FER,ACIER
6731	IRON,STEEL WIRE ROD		75441		76067	W 86671	26860		54351	FIL MACHINE FER,ACIER
67311	IRON,SIMPLE STL WIRE ROD		72968		71241	W 77654	23959		48437	FIL MACH AUT ACIER FIN
6732	IRON,STEEL BARS ETC		212300		144854		85623		70677	BARRES FER,ACIER
67326	IRN,OTH STL BARS HOTROLD		88588		65043	W 138398	36467		37260	BARRES PLEINES FER,ACIER
67327	IRN, OTH STL BARS FORGED		113021		67799	W 155185	41003		15594	BARRES FORGEES CREUSES
6733	IRON,STEEL PROFILES ETC		149146		198123		115846		197101	PROFILES,PALPLAN FER,ACIER
67333	OTH PRFILES HOTROLLD ETC		97105		120043	W 232579	64131		118572	AUT PROFILES LAMINES,FILES
674	IRN,STL UNIV,PLATE,SHEET		507155		447440		463729		580813	LARGES PLATS,TOLES
6744	IRN,STL HVY PLATE,ROLLED		144681		149664	W 318035	129296		86084	TOLES LAMINEES PLUS 4.75 MM
67441	— OF IRON OR SIMPLE STL		112160		107210	W 288811	87771		55349	TOLES NON ACIER FIN CARB
6746	IRN,STL THIN PLATE,ROLLD		133438		97551	W 307855	125448		103494	TOLES LAM MOINS 3MM
67461	— OF IRON OR SIMPLE STL		108627		85015	W 299155	114259		96562	TOL NON AC FIN MOINS 3 MM
6747	TINNED PLATES,SHEETS		29320		24600	W 71469	29703		180231	TOLES ETAMEES EN ACIER
6749	OTH IRN,STL PLATES,SHEET		138179		120717	W 300312	134610		168411	AUTRES TOLES FER,ACIER
67491	— OF IRON OR SIMPLE STL		137174		119628	W 299682	133848		166573	AUT TOLES AUTRES ACIER FIN
678	IRON,STL TUBES,PIPES,ETC		94079		91370		86792		100009	TUBES,TUYAUX EN FONTE,FER
6783	IRON,STL TUBES,PIPES NES		79767		80482		65885		67557	AUT TUBES,TUYAUX FER,ACIER
68	NON-FERROUS METALS		746791		419999		470301		1226618	METAUX NON FERREUX
681	SILVER,PLATINUM,ETC		230367		9165		9487		642770	ARGENT ET PLATINE
6812	METALS OF PLATINUM GROUP		222488		508		1393		634222	PLATINE
68122	ROLLED PLATINUM ETC		222488		508		1393		1685	PLAQUE PLATINE BRUT MI-OU
68123	PLATINUM,ALLOYS UNWRGHT								317547	PLATINE,ALLIAGES BRUTS
68125	PLAT GRP METALS SEMI-MFD								314990	METAUX MINE PLAT MI-OUVRES
682	COPPER EXC CEMENT COPPER		303236		250791		195764		235998	CUIVRE
6821	COPPER NES,ALLOYS,UNWRT		265726		215554	W 86511	151938		155541	CUIVRE BRUT
68211	COPPER UNREF,EXC CEMENT		105092		102601	W 37989	75340		30628	CUIVRE POUR AFFINAGE
68212	COPPER REFINED,UNWROUGHT		160610		112935	W 48514	76573		124749	CUIVRE AFFINE BRUT
683	NICKEL		90874		47371		46656		51177	NICKEL
6831	NICKEL,ALLOYS UNWROUGHT		90742		47265	W 7929	46486		50782	NICKEL ET ALLIAGES BRUTS
684	ALUMINIUM		41545		37361	W 95594	134121		191841	ALUMINIUM
6841	ALUMINIUM,ALLOYS,UNWRGHT					W 75870	95155		143851	ALUMINIUM,ALLIAGES BRUTS
69	METAL MANUFACTURES NES		218307		213366		259300		361429	ART MANUFACT EN METAL NDA
691	STRUCTURES AND PARTS NES		52375		46804	W 50346	48605		84343	CONSTRUCT FER,ACIER,ALU
7	MACHINES,TRANSPORT EQUIP		1571472		1680729		1710833		2392883	MACHINES MATERIEL TRANSPORT
71	POWER GENERATING EQUIPMT		73940		90076		90093		100918	MACHINES GENERATRICES
72	MACHS FOR SPCL INDUSTRYS		179632		171905		202671		337971	MAC SPECIALES POUR INDUST
728	OTH MACHY FOR SPCL INDUS		83824		91188		104098		219216	AUT MACH IND PARTICULIERES
7283	OTHR MINERAL WORKG MACHY		57823		58445		52244		89122	MACH TRIER,CRIBLER,BROYER
7284	MACHY FOR SPCL INDUS NES		22801		28877		46645		122610	MACH SPEC IND PARTICUL.
72848	OTH MCHY WITH INDIV FNCT		9519		15851		28439		102695	AUTRES MACHINES NDA
74	GENRL INDUSTRL MACHY NES		262742		300927		315572		555855	MACH APP INDUSTRIE
743	PUMPS NES,CENTRFUGES ETC		80361		102225		101828		146490	POMPES COMPRES,VENT ETC
7436	GAS,LIQUID FILTERS ETC		51606		72194		84532		126020	APP POUR FILT DES LIQUIDES
744	MECHANICAL HANDLING EQU		44579		62217		56611		193275	EQUIP MANUTENTION PIECES
7449	PTS NES OF MACHY OF 7442		22738		35058		30102		136588	PIECES DU 744.2
749	NONELEC MACH PTS,ACC NES		63626		57969		60636		84860	PIECES MACH NON ELEC NDA
76	TELECOMM,SOUND EQUIPMENT		54097		72225		60820		95884	EQUIPMENT DE TELECOM
77	ELECTRIC MACHNRY NES ETC		121529		153053		184243		288227	MACH APP ELECT NDA
772	SWITCHGEAR ETC,PARTS NES		34291		42457		45050		93147	APP COUPURE,SECT ETC
7721	SWITCHGEAR ETC		33032		41044		43096		91305	APP COUPURE,SECTIONMNT
78	ROAD VEHICLES		646398		671627		625725		748671	VEHICULES ROUTIERS
781	PASS MOTOR VEH EXC BUSES		158415		144097	N 27323	130153		147616	AUTO TRANSPORT PERSONNES
782	LORRIES,SPCL MTR VEH NES		66280		57777	N 112502	87342		114652	VEHICULES SPECIAUX,MARCH
7821	LORRIES,TRUCKS		63082		55899	N 101075	85020		108377	VEHICULES TRANSP MARCHAND
784	MOTOR VEH PRTS,ACCES NES		271324		288797		236422		270735	PIECES 722,781,782,783
7849	OTHER MOTOR VEHCL PARTS		265943		283156	W 39437	232502		267651	PIECES 722,781,782,783
786	TRAILERS,NONMOTR VEH,NES		136076		163685		154122		191927	REMORQUES,CADRES,CONTAIN
7861	TRAILERS,TRANSP CONTAINR		127800		151798	N 70445	145309		175624	REMORQUES TOUS VEHICULES
78613	CONTAINERS INC ROAD-RAIL		123910		146627	N 48377	142722		173333	CADRES ET CONTAINERS
79	OTHR TRANSPORT EQUIPMENT		164003		149582		155477		150780	AUTRE MATERIEL TRANSPORT
792	AIRCRAFT ETC		45082		45269		119991		110504	APP NAVIGATION AERIENNE
793	SHIPS AND BOATS ETC		92527		79271		15306		19950	NAVIRES BATEAUX,ETC
7932	SHIPS AND BOATS NES		92065		78374		13948		18704	NAVIRES ET BATEAUX

5. General Exports F.O.B. by Commodities according to the S.I.T.C. (Rev. 2) in thousand U.S. Dollars
Exportations Générales F.O.B. par Produits d'après la C.T.C.I. (Rév. 2) en milliers de Dollars E.U.

SITC CTCI	COMMODITY	1992 WEIGHT POIDS	1992 VALUE VALEUR	1993 WEIGHT POIDS	1993 VALUE VALEUR	1994 WEIGHT POIDS	1994 VALUE VALEUR	1995 WEIGHT POIDS	1995 VALUE VALEUR	PRODUIT
79323	OTHER CARGO VESSELS		77472		35185		334		2726	AUT BATEAUX TRANS MARCH
8	MISC MANUFACTURED GOODS		471209		553493		666881		904715	ART MANUFACTURES DIVERS
821	*FURNITURE,PARTS THEREOF		74658		82511		211531		383149	MEUBLES ET PIECES
8211	CHAIRS,SEATS AND PARTS		3077		6092		132608		280173	SIEGES ET PIECES
82119	PTS NES OF CHAIRS ETC		402		394	W 3341	126473		270974	PIECES DU 821.11
8219	FURNITURE AND PARTS NES		65589		67855		69661		95309	AUTRES MEUBLES ET PIECES
84	CLOTHING AND ACCESSORIES		172575		206644		124931		147942	VETEMENTS
842	MENS OUTERWEAR NOT KNIT		56917		73684		41367		51913	VET DESSUS POUR HOMMES
89	MISC MANUFCTRD GOODS NES		135329		167548		210957		225066	ART MANUFACTURES DIVERS
893	ARTICLES OF PLASTIC NES		40327		49226		53362		85124	OUVRAGES EN MAT DIVIS 58
9	GOODS NOT CLASSD BY KIND		9513518		9549639		6397171		6844984	ART TRANSACT NON CLASSES
931	*SPECIAL TRANSACTIONS		9421218		9523356				6704758	TRANS.SPECIALES
971	*GOLD,NON MONETARY NES		89790		23027		6393699		130700	OR NON MONETAIRE
97101	NONMON GLD UNWRT,SEMIMFD		84656		21183		6393494		69702	OR,ALLIAGES D'OR BRUTS

1. HISTORICAL SERIES, 1961–1996 SPECIAL TRADE, IMPORTS C.I.F., EXPORTS F.O.B.
SERIES HISTORIQUES, 1961–1996 COMMERCE SPECIAL, IMPORTATIONS C.A.F., EXPORTATIONS F.O.B

YEAR ANNEE	VALUE IN MILLION PESETAS # 1 VALEUR EN MILLION PESETAS # 1 MERCHANDISE –MARCHANDISE		GOLD –OR		CONVERSION FACTORS U.S. CENTS PER PESETA FACTEURS DE CONVERSION CENTS E.U. PAR PESETA		INDEX NUMBERS –INDICES QUANTUM		UNIT VALUE VALEUR UNITAIRE	
	IMPORTS	EXPORTS	IMPORTS	EXPORTS	IMPORTS	EXPORTS	IMPORTS	EXPORTS	IMPORTS	EXPORTS
1961	65.54	42.57	0.0		1.6670	1.6670	6	6	11	12
1962	94.17	44.16	0.0		1.6670	1.6670	9	6	11	13
1963	117.30	44.13	0.01		1.6670	1.6670	11	6	11	13
1964	134.64	57.27	0.89		1.6670	1.6670	12	8	12	13
1965	180.21	57.99	0.92		1.6670	1.6670	17	7	12	14
1966	214.34	75.21	1.10		1.6670	1.6670	19	9	12	15
1967	211.01	84.66	0.81		1.6360	1.6240	19	10	12	15
1968	245.15	111.24	1.40		1.4290	1.4290	21	13	13	15
1969	294.11	133.01	2.19	0.03	1.4290	1.4290	24	15	13	15
1970	330.04	167.09	2.25		1.4290	1.4290	25	18	14	16
1971	347.41	205.64	1.87		1.4290	1.4290	25	22	15	16
1972	437.57	245.21	2.04		1.5545	1.5534	31	25	15	17
1973	561.54	302.67	3.38		1.7218	1.7187	35	29	17	19
1974	883.66	407.89	5.03	0.08	1.7353	1.7355	36	31	26	23
1975	931.99	441.09			1.7419	1.7387	36	31	28	24
1976	1169.41	583.22			1.4933	1.4964	40	36	32	28
1977	1350.35	775.15			1.3215	1.3196	38	37	39	36
1978	1431.03	1001.38			1.3073	1.3097	36	46	43	37
1979	1704.01	1221.44			1.4925	1.4903	42	54	44	40
1980	2450.75	1493.19			1.3907	1.3877	43	53	63	51
1981	2975.97	1889.72			1.0826	1.0769	40	57	82	60
1982	3474.81	2233.93			0.9080	0.9080	42	59	92	67
1983	4177.03	2846.75			0.6991	0.6953	42	64	112	79
1984	4628.99	3778.07			0.6236	0.6243	41	73	125	91
1985	5073.24	4104.14			0.6109	0.6119	44	76	128	96
1986	4891.00	3802.00			0.7174	0.7162	52	72	105	95
1987	6030.00	4196.00			0.8146	0.8150	63	77	101	97
1988	7040.00	4686.00			0.8598	0.8609	78	85	101	99
1989	8396.00	5135.00			0.8451	0.8464	91	89	103	103
1990	8915.00	5643.00			0.9840	0.9861	100	100	100	100
1991	9637.00	6065.00			0.9650	0.9669	112	112	97	99
1992	10205.00	6658.00			0.9776	0.9740	122	117	96	100
1993	10131.00	7755.00			0.7872	0.7877	118	135	101	104
1994	12306.00	9747.00			0.7491	0.7482	131	160	107	109
1995	14107.00	11340.01			0.8033	0.8029			112	116
1996	15436.00	12930.99			0.7890	0.7888			114	119

2. IMPORTS BY BROAD ECONOMIC CATEGORY AND EXPORTS BY INDUSTRIAL ORIGIN. (PERCENTAGE OF TOTAL VALUE)
IMPORTATIONS PAR CATEGORIES ECONOMIQUES ET EXPORTATIONS PAR BRANCHE D'ACTIVITE.(EN POURCENTAGE DE LA VALEUR TOTALE)

IMPORTS – IMPORTATIONS

	1990	1991	1992	1993	1994	1995	1996
TOTAL IMPORTS–IMPORTATIONS TOTALES	100.	100.	100.	100.	100.	100.	100.
1 FOOD BEV–ALIMENTATION BOISSONS	9.1	10.1	10.4	11.4	11.5	11.6	10.7
11 PRIMARY–PRODUITS DE BASE	6.2	6.8	6.6	7.2	7.3	7.4	6.6
111 FOR INDUSTRY–POUR L'INDUSTRIE	2.1	2.2	2.1	2.4	2.5	2.9	2.4
112 FOR HOUSEHOLDS–POUR LES MENAGES	4.2	4.5	4.6	4.8	4.7	4.5	4.2
12 PROCESSED–PRODUITS ELABORES	2.9	3.3	3.8	4.2	4.2	4.2	4.1
121 FOR INDUSTRY–POUR L'INDUSTRIE	0.2	0.3	0.3	0.4	0.3	0.3	0.3
122 FOR HOUSEHOLDS–POUR LES MENAGES	2.7	3.1	3.5	3.8	3.8	3.9	3.8
2 IND SUPPLIES–APPROV INDUSTRIELS	29.3	28.3	27.3	27.2	29.5	31.5	29.5
21 PRIMARY–PRODUITS DE BASE	4.7	4.1	3.8	4.1	4.6	4.6	4.1
22 PROCESSED–PRODUITS ELABORES	24.6	24.2	23.5	23.1	24.9	26.9	25.3
3 FUELS–COMBUSTIBLES	11.6	10.7	10.0	10.8	9.3	8.2	9.0
31 PRIMARY–PRODUITS DE BASE	9.8	9.0	8.7	8.7	7.9	7.0	7.7
32 PROCESSED–PRODUITS ELABORES	1.8	1.7	1.3	2.0	1.4	1.2	1.3
321 MOTOR SPIRIT–ESSENCE	0.7	1.7	0.3	0.6	0.4	1.0	1.1
322 OTHER–AUTRES	1.1	0.0	1.0	1.4	0.9	0.2	0.2
4 MACHINERY–EQUIPEMENT	22.3	21.3	19.8	17.6	17.3	17.8	18.6
41 CAPITAL EQUIPMENT–MACHINES	18.6	17.7	16.2	14.0	13.7	14.4	15.1
42 PARTS–PIECES ACCESSOIRES	3.7	3.6	3.6	3.6	3.6	3.5	3.5
5 TRANSPORT–TRANSPORT	16.4	16.3	17.6	18.4	18.4	18.1	19.2
51 PASSENGER CARS–AUTOMOBILES	5.1	4.9	6.7	6.7	5.8	5.4	6.0
52 OTHER–AUTRES	4.4	4.5	3.4	2.4	2.5	2.4	2.8
521 INDUSTRIAL–INDUSTRIELS	4.0	4.1	2.9	2.0	2.2	2.2	2.6
522 NON INDUSTRIAL–NON INDUSTRIEL	0.4	0.4	0.5	0.4	0.2	0.2	0.2
53 PARTS–PIECES ACCESSOIRES	6.8	6.9	7.5	9.4	10.1	10.3	10.4
6 CONSUM GOODS–BIENS CONSOMMATION	11.2	13.1	14.9	14.5	14.0	12.7	13.0
61 DURABLE–DURABLES	4.2	4.5	4.5	4.5	4.1	3.5	3.4
62 SEMI DURABLE–SEMI DURABLES	5.1	6.5	7.7	6.9	6.5	5.9	6.4
63 NON DURABLE–NON DURABLES	1.8	2.2	2.6	3.1	3.3	3.4	3.2
7 GOODS NES–BIENS NDA	0.1	0.2	0.1	0.2	0.2	0.1	0.1

EXPORTS – EXPORTATIONS

	1990	1991	1992	1993	1994	1995	1996
TOTAL EXPORTS–EXPORTATIONS TOTALES	100.	100.	100.	100.	100.	100.	100.
1 AGRICULTURE	8.4	8.9	9.0	9.3	9.0	8.7	8.5
2 MINING QUARRY–INDUS EXTRACTIVES	0.7	0.6	0.6	0.6	0.5	0.5	0.5
3 MANUFACTURING–IND MANUFACTUR	90.8	90.5	90.4	90.1	90.5	90.8	90.9
31 FOOD BEV TOBACCO–ALIM BOISS TAB	7.1	7.3	6.9	7.2	7.5	7.5	7.8
32 TEXTILES–INDUSTRIES TEXTILES	7.6	6.7	6.5	6.7	7.1	7.1	7.1
33 WOOD & PRODUCTS–BOIS & PRODUITS	0.6	0.6	0.7	0.6	0.6	0.6	0.6
34 PAPER & PRODUCTS–PAPIER & PRODT	3.0	2.8	2.9	2.8	2.9	3.2	2.7
35 CHEMICALS–INDUSTRIES CHIMIQUES	16.6	14.6	13.2	13.3	13.2	13.1	13.5
36 NON METAL MIN–MIN NON METAL	3.3	3.2	3.5	3.6	3.7	3.7	3.6
37 BASIC METAL–IND METAL BASE	6.8	6.7	5.9	6.5	6.2	6.0	5.5
38 METAL MANUF–MANUF METAL	44.2	46.1	48.5	47.1	47.4	47.8	48.3
39 OTH MANUF IND–AUTRES MANUF	1.6	2.5	2.2	2.4	1.9	1.7	1.8

3. TRADE BY PRINCIPAL COUNTRIES OF PRODUCTION AND LAST CONSIGNMENT (VALUE IN THOUSAND U.S. DOLLARS)
ECHANGES SELON LES PRINCIPAUX PAYS DE PRODUCTION ET DE DERNIERE CONSIGNATION (VALEUR EN MILLIERS DE DOLLARS EU)

COUNTRIES–PAYS	SPECIAL IMPORTS C.I.F. IMPORTATIONS SPECIALES C.A.F				
	1992	1993	1994	1995	1996
World	99746780	79739372	92502444	113398635	121255430
Africa	6533490	4766761	5880705	6489222	7257034
Americas	12298089	9790917	11219589	13114215	13104218
Northern America	7955603	6217847	7183007	8195660	8178163
LAIA	4006462	3317775	3546337	4232812	4225271
CACM	83529	79363	175380	227094	203255
Caribbean	185448	132558	219143	327628	387764
Rest of America	67048	43375	95721	131021	109764
As.ex F.USSR	13155984	10755190	11540536	13973398	14771747
Eur.x F.USSR	66221271	52303899	62044826	77624909	84146967
EU	63395808	49649599	59293435	73895726	80379343
EFTA	2096768	2142776	1906490	2396272	2490431
East Europe	587179	412730	720491	1205658	1146822
Other Europe	46153	44821	55257	40233	51181
Former USSR	904242	1166986	1238756	1730567	1590053
Oceania	351175	309634	401379	429261	376276
France,Monac	15828104	13381308	16148239	19523929	21652333
Germany/Allemagne	16359669	11923404	13511519	17286234	17860905
Italy/Italie	9805427	6740582	8274220	10321442	11612671
United Kingdom	7281614	5930983	7259674	8812348	10038586
USA/Etats-Unis d'Amer	7380059	5818617	6750173	7526574	7524150
Netherlands/Pays-Bas	3460076	2738325	3606332	4889805	4753548
Japan/Japon	4649168	3419963	3295881	3793874	3441485
Belgium–Luxembourg	3175760	2766315	3090878	3866430	4303349
Portugal	2696104	2114719	2570879	3308973	3569524
China/Chine	1618540	1407653	1800490	2241068	2409879
Switz.Liecht	1538919	1687335	1363424	1686081	1553945
Sweden/Suède	1328928	980382	1213244	1413265	1823872
Nigeria/Nigéria	1303737	758551	1072730	1054845	1658579
Saudi Arabia	1081122	1050617	1115531	1210210	1288030
Russian Federation	826151	995430	1019954	1437873	1286832
Libyan Arab Jamahiriya	1242817	901726	1012805	1167965	1106624
Mexico/Mexique	1352989	1007328	960248	1018377	1004758
Brazil/Brésil	972243	862248	926768	1116966	1158627
Algeria/Algérie	1023266	791851	837069	987508	1169955
Austria/Autriche	747775	839363	975173	1012389	1226490
Ireland/Irlande	887589	692427	850258	1190000	1108436
Finland/Finlande	740606	710653	814693	992013	973424
Denmark/Danemark	836096	666817	744136	911877	1023783
Korea, Republic of	793274	632076	691585	968068	957217
Argentina/Argentine	632341	608102	688674	816134	854451
Iran (Islamic Rp. of)	357423	573017	643262	789235	962144
Indonesia/Indonésie	393019	395521	584936	695192	976360
So. Africa Customs Un	525274	468532	508679	730343	664954
Norway,SVD,JM	475474	386001	468045	642826	873161
Morocco/Maroc	472639	428265	511220	585419	626120
Canada	568954	394069	407611	637318	559575
Thailand/Thaïlande	490706	378215	442948	522657	631132
India/Inde	312973	299099	334381	470029	556132
Malaysia/Malaisie	294064	262508	321501	505383	482350
Chile/Chili	459697	307802	309784	417440	331761
Turkey/Turquie	416870	252452	272160	399251	447701
Cameroon/Cameroun	329698	318802	314400	316271	402776
Singapore/Singapour	322449	264543	320284	322783	315956
Greece/Grèce	248060	164321	234191	367022	432422
Israel/Israël	252723	210807	261221	318065	390344
Egypt/Egypte	396546	241565	297303	227574	208627
Australia/Australie	249907	228640	303349	288006	268464
Syrian Arab Republic	125014	290052	194235	274037	269995
Poland/Pologne	182899	141937	210680	322863	288018
Hungary/Hongrie	123218	81442	181394	380438	334034
Hong Kong	314144	213199	162596	197493	167542
Tunisia/Tunisie	141624	121723	258021	266658	231233
Colombia/Colombie	191078	154241	210084	236086	206153
Cote d'Ivoire	151287	136362	162856	223340	164139
Ecuador/Equateur	142559	125589	162679	208978	187200

COUNTRIES–PAYS	SPECIAL EXPORTS F.O.B. EXPORTATIONS SPECIALES F.O.B.				
	1992	1993	1994	1995	1996
Monde	64310953	60968531	73187932	89616115	100955530
Afrique	3141932	3126917	2986958	3445777	3453632
Amériques	6478396	7068531	8569499	9362685	10743289
Amérique du Nord	3421447	3293027	4053759	4257617	4765689
ALAI	2412251	3009787	3770730	4016060	4614761
MCAC	101095	122387	185798	194715	182769
Caraïbes	482318	577190	492294	796052	1094229
Autre Amérique	61284	66140	66917	98241	85842
Asie l'URSS exclus	4131832	5289765	6353570	7425080	8286777
Europe l'URSS exclus	49612342	44639335	54530532	68427515	76084630
UE	47185516	42076989	51717052	64773848	71966001
AELE	1339978	1264997	1150447	1586326	1564769
Europe de l'Est	402780	599229	872875	1028951	1473563
Autre de l'Europe	626705	630755	653910	784314	825035
Ancienne URSS	428089	342006	362650	482400	765066
Océanie	197222	200645	327341	414266	400661
France,Monac	13001993	11539710	14746520	18401499	20469396
Germany/Allemagne	10087503	8912043	10397360	13809793	14758780
Italy/Italie	7006336	5539987	6741399	8152604	8811128
United Kingdom	4925286	5021035	6016484	7160860	8584849
Portugal	4835535	4422658	5694397	7485732	8712213
USA/Etats-Unis d'Amer	3081720	2934377	3606618	3799655	4251343
Netherlands/Pays-Bas	2766438	2238680	3046281	3295966	3496658
Belgium–Luxembourg	2084869	1868487	2190625	2774727	2998133
Switz.Liecht	863249	790747	885293	998519	1152937
Japan/Japon	593035	562612	981916	1232867	1219575
Mexico/Mexique	879368	1180569	1372849	600177	534411
Argentina/Argentine	446669	617198	903989	956804	1300200
Algeria/Algérie	713561	786865	853190	1010514	689041
Morocco/Maroc	699850	759304	686337	742972	810410
Sweden/Suède	640091	691332	558746	797384	934297
Greece/Grèce	485610	498975	679472	895906	983298
Austria/Autriche	572054	548920	610473	719922	853000
China/Chine	269996	649885	800122	850513	532868
Turkey/Turquie	325308	468785	382418	616394	920245
Brazil/Brésil	164848	241195	359339	836876	953166
Denmark/Danemark	395756	373692	465735	616509	633106
Saudi Arabia	459598	462933	517933	480965	483389
Israel/Israël	248119	304416	459284	610085	712765
Hong Kong	276934	374589	497408	485458	572845
Korea, Republic of	205340	341190	555988	456733	629723
Andorra/Andorre	429760	381507	418592	494649	439807
Norway,SVD,JM	463765	448766	248326	558653	386461
Canada	338009	356826	420797	433933	439468
Russian Federation	413967	297170	292871	379275	589335
Chile/Chili	217540	262162	363561	465005	538041
Singapore/Singapour	214432	283907	342449	460779	530614
Poland/Pologne	158453	250488	344996	436886	621828
Cuba	200006	189751	289544	395947	465084
Ireland/Irlande	186352	252617	317861	327762	436545
Colombia/Colombie	231195	188728	237917	288362	312734
Australia/Australie	140193	146437	276007	355988	331687
Finland/Finlande	197694	168852	251699	335184	294598
Tunisia/Tunisie	184869	203735	216801	335319	287791
Iran (Islamic Rp. of)	269935	389475	133955	157294	256711
Egypt/Egypte	178769	205824	237636	287912	271949
Venezuela	284936	212071	163984	246984	241794
Indonesia/Indonésie	164760	153574	156085	180462	319454
So. Africa Customs Un	147044	139925	169571	229361	279714
Thailand/Thaïlande	103462	146035	170380	249616	282514
Gibraltar	154960	173469	184702	186266	226411
India/Inde	142927	154708	202613	215777	202343
Czech Republic		109532	172357	250232	355590
United Arab Emirates	129677	143074	166421	199808	236606
Hungary/Hongrie	93839	125076	239321	167538	244163
Liberia/Libéria	319244	294188	118635	3011	97719

(VALUE AS PERCENTAGE OF WORLD TOTAL)(VALEURS EN POURCENTAGE DU TOTAL MONDIAL)

	1987	1988	1989	1990	1991	1992	1993	1994	1995	1996
Africa	7.4	6.3	6.4	6.8	6.9	6.6	6.0	6.4	5.7	6.0
Americas	14.9	14.7	14.4	13.5	13.0	12.3	12.3	12.1	11.6	10.8
Northern America	8.7	9.3	9.5	8.8	8.4	8.0	7.8	7.8	7.2	6.7
LAIA	5.6	4.8	4.5	4.4	4.2	4.0	4.2	3.8	3.7	3.5
CACM	0.2	0.1	0.1	0.1	0.1	0.1	0.1	0.2	0.2	0.2
Caribbean	0.3	0.3	0.2	0.2	0.2	0.2	0.2	0.2	0.3	0.3
Rest of America	0.1	0.1	0.1	0.1	0.1	0.1	0.1	0.1	0.1	0.1
As.ex F.USSR	13.5	13.0	12.9	12.0	13.0	13.2	13.5	12.5	12.3	12.2
Eur.x F.USSR	60.8	63.2	63.6	65.6	65.7	66.4	65.6	67.1	68.5	69.4
EU	57.7	60.2	60.5	62.8	63.0	63.6	62.3	64.1	65.2	66.3
EFTA	2.1	2.0	2.2	2.0	2.0	2.1	2.7	2.1	2.1	2.1
East Europe	0.8	0.7	0.7	0.6	0.5	0.6	0.5	0.8	1.1	0.9
Other Europe	0.2	0.3	0.2	0.2	0.2	0.0	0.1	0.1	0.0	0.0
Former USSR	1.8	1.8	1.8	1.5	0.8	0.9	1.5	1.3	1.5	1.3
Oceania	0.8	0.7	0.6	0.3	0.3	0.4	0.4	0.4	0.4	0.3
France,Monac	12.8	13.5	13.7	14.7	15.2	15.9	16.8	17.5	17.2	17.9
Germany/Allemagne	16.1	16.2	16.1	16.4	16.2	16.4	15.0	14.6	15.2	14.7
Italy/Italie	8.8	9.6	10.4	10.1	10.0	9.8	8.5	8.9	9.1	9.6
United Kingdom	7.0	7.1	6.5	7.2	7.5	7.3	7.4	7.8	7.8	8.3
USA/Etats-Unis d'Amer	8.3	8.9	9.0	8.3	8.0	7.4	7.3	7.3	6.6	6.2
Netherlands/Pays-Bas	3.2	3.5	3.3	3.7	3.5	3.5	3.4	3.9	4.3	3.9
Japan/Japon	4.5	5.1	4.8	4.4	4.7	4.7	4.3	3.6	3.3	2.8
Belgium–Luxembourg	3.2	3.3	3.2	3.1	3.0	3.2	3.5	3.3	3.4	3.5
Portugal	1.7	2.1	2.3	2.5	2.7	2.7	2.7	2.8	2.9	2.9
China/Chine	0.5	0.6	0.7	0.8	1.2	1.6	1.8	1.9	2.0	2.0

	1987	1988	1989	1990	1991	1992	1993	1994	1995	1996
Afrique	5.9	5.4	4.6	4.7	4.5	4.9	5.1	4.1	3.8	3.4
Amériques	13.5	13.0	12.3	10.4	9.3	10.1	11.6	11.7	10.4	10.6
Amérique du Nord	9.2	9.1	8.2	6.5	5.5	5.3	5.4	5.5	4.8	4.7
ALAI	3.1	2.8	2.7	2.7	2.8	3.8	4.9	5.2	4.5	4.6
MCAC	0.2	0.2	0.2	0.2	0.1	0.2	0.2	0.3	0.2	0.2
Caraïbes	0.8	0.8	0.7	0.7	0.7	0.7	0.9	0.7	0.9	1.1
Autre Amérique	0.2	0.2	0.4	0.4	0.2	0.1	0.1	0.1	0.1	0.1
Asie l'URSS exclus	7.5	7.8	7.6	6.5	6.6	6.4	8.7	8.7	8.3	8.2
Europe l'URSS exclus	70.0	71.4	72.4	75.3	76.6	77.1	73.2	74.5	76.4	75.4
UE	66.0	67.7	68.7	71.4	73.1	73.4	69.0	70.7	72.3	71.3
AELE	2.3	2.1	2.0	2.2	1.9	2.1	2.1	1.6	1.8	1.5
Europe de l'Est	0.7	0.6	0.6	0.5	0.5	0.6	1.0	1.2	1.1	1.5
Autre de l'Europe	1.0	1.0	1.0	1.2	1.1	1.0	1.0	0.9	0.9	0.8
Ancienne URSS	0.9	0.7	0.9	0.7	0.9	0.7	0.6	0.5	0.5	0.8
Océanie	0.4	0.5	0.5	0.3	0.3	0.3	0.3	0.4	0.5	0.4
France,Monac	18.8	18.5	19.5	20.8	20.0	20.2	18.9	20.1	20.5	20.3
Germany/Allemagne	12.0	12.0	11.9	13.4	15.9	15.7	14.6	14.2	15.4	14.6
Italy/Italie	8.9	9.7	9.7	10.7	11.4	10.9	9.1	9.2	9.1	8.7
United Kingdom	9.5	9.8	10.0	9.0	7.7	7.7	8.2	8.2	8.0	8.5
Portugal	4.5	5.6	6.2	6.1	6.6	7.5	7.3	7.8	8.4	8.6
USA/Etats-Unis d'Amer	8.1	7.9	7.4	5.8	4.9	4.8	4.8	4.9	4.2	4.2
Netherlands/Pays-Bas	5.4	4.9	4.5	4.7	4.3	4.3	3.7	4.2	3.7	3.5
Belgium–Luxembourg	3.0	3.4	3.2	3.0	3.1	3.2	3.1	3.0	3.1	3.0
Switz.Liecht	1.8	1.7	1.5	1.6	1.6	1.3	1.3	1.2	1.1	1.1
Japan/Japon	1.1	1.2	1.4	1.1	1.0	0.9	0.9	1.3	1.4	1.2

4. Special Imports C.I.F. by Commodities according to the S.I.T.C. (Rev. 2) in thousand U.S. Dollars
Importations Spéciales C.A.F. par Produits d'après la C.T.C.I. (Rév. 2) en milliers de Dollars E.U.

SITC CTCI	COMMODITY	1993 WEIGHT POIDS	1993 VALUE VALEUR	1994 WEIGHT POIDS	1994 VALUE VALEUR	1995 WEIGHT POIDS	1995 VALUE VALEUR	1996 WEIGHT POIDS	1996 VALUE VALEUR	PRODUIT
	ALL COMMODITIES		79739372		92502444		113398635		121255430	TOUS PRODUITS
0	FOOD AND LIVE ANIMALS		8613681		9876783		11739245		11741789	ALIMENTS,ANIMAUX VIVANTS
001	*LIVE ANIMALS FOR FOOD	W 119073	335102	W 153922	450500		499117	W 165213	496271	ANIMAUX VIVANTS
0011	BOVINE SPECIES,LIVE	W 61098	209445	W 89596	306936	W 85983	328824	W 95614	301151	ESPECE BOVINE
01	MEAT AND PREPARATIONS		729028		802167		811284		811328	VIANDES ET PREPARATIONS
011	MEAT FRESH,CHILLD,FROZEN	W 232513	623296	W 258240	693943	W 224768	692833	W 243467	690443	VIANDES FRAICHES,REF,CONGE
0111	BOVINE MEAT FRESH,FROZEN	W 67859	299471	W 86864	348509	W 64231	341551	W 59723	305773	VIANDES BOVIN FRAI,REF
02	DAIRY PRODCTS,BIRDS'EGGS		696809		816706		874380		879547	PRODUITS LAITIERS,OEUFS
022	MILK AND CREAM	W 446672	374602	W 598243	461409	W 503780	462270	W 473590	442177	LAIT ET CREME
024	CHEESE AND CURD	W 57358	259029	W 103179	305226	W 80699	369827	W 81522	387042	FROMAGE ET CAILLEBOTTE
03	FISH AND PREPARATIONS		2368247		2601856		3065733		3082000	POISSONS ET PREPARATIONS
034	FISH,FRESH,CHILLED,FROZN	W 441370	1078471	W 497269	1175546	W 505752	1321341	W 542418	1383335	POISSON FRAIS, REFRIG,CONG
0341	FISH FRSH,CHLLD,EX FILLT	W 179864	598200	W 190369	609561	W 179183	663058	W 190743	684459	POISSON FRAIS,REFRIGERE
0342	FISH FROZEN,EXCL FILLETS	W 204087	343428	W 240274	407159	W 255999	461830	W 262713	448384	POISSONS CONGELES
036	SHELL FISH FRESH,FROZEN	W 267127	969490	W 316354	1089915	W 322418	1353796	W 322748	1286646	CRUSTACES,MOLLUSQUES
04	CEREALS AND PREPARATIONS		1198134		1321008		1851959		1689979	CEREALES ET PRODUITS
041	WHEAT ETC UNMILLED	W 1752923	382675	W 2049334	406240	W 2757498	581666	W 2103187	430218	FROMENT,EPEAUTRE
0412	OTHER WHEAT ETC UNMILLED	W 1624694	352546	W 1720619	341871	W 2358393	490286	W 1886113	385485	AUTRE FROMENT NON MOULU
044	MAIZE UNMILLED	W 2425172	397754	W 2339155	406853	W 2912371	461585	W 2031678	423113	MAIS NON MOULU
048	CEREAL ETC PREPARATIONS	W 123508	253067	W 137780	297176	W 154751	345743	W 271843	406917	PREPTNS A BASE CEREALES
05	VEGETABLES AND FRUIT		1146762		1464591		1786518		1802222	LEGUMES ET FRUITS
054	VEG ETC FRSH,SMPLY PRSVD	W 2595333	601617	W 2845326	715603	W 2195798	798990	W 2001726	679749	LEGUMES FRAIS,CONG,SECS
057	FRUIT,NUTS,FRESH,DRIED	W 406295	367604	W 557531	515537	W 670625	674097		757592	FRUITS FRAIS OU SECS
06	SUGAR AND PREPS,HONEY		347238		264912		386941		478477	SUCRES ET PRODUITS
061	SUGAR AND HONEY	W 588029	287655	W 488362	192400	W 620612	314772	W 804181	407208	SUCRES ET MIEL
07	COFFEE,TEA,COCOA,SPICES		516282		753980		1003673		866091	CAFE,THE,CACAO,EPICES
071	COFFEE AND SUBSTITUTES	W 188006	252107	W 183490	443951	W 185720	652718	W 207968	513077	CAFE ET SUCCEDANES
0711	COFFEE GREEN,ROASTED,SUB	W 183459	228821	W 180299	416053	W 181925	614754	W 203808	478492	CAFE TORREFIE OU DECAFEINE
07111	COFFEE GREEN,HUSKS,SKINS	W 180733	218751	W 176643	400662	W 176898	587780	W 197127	441025	CAFE NON TORREFIE
081	*FEEDING STUFF FOR ANIML	W 3837291	809793	W 3751752	840043	W 3893173	852763	W 3739146	971150	NOURRITURE POUR ANIMAUX
0813	OILCAKE AND OTH RESIDUES	W 2291932	443745	W 2364847	462592	W 2208230	399535	W 2076128	484544	TOURTEAUX
08131	— OF SOYA BEANS	W 1836906	386431	W 1978783	412168	W 1703720	333960	W 1709831	431293	TOURTEAUX DE SOJA
0819	FOOD WASTE AND FEED NES	W 1208904	298359	W 1041557	297275	W 1291536	363608	W 1169639	374984	DECHETS,ALIMENTS NDA
09	MISC EDIBLE PRODUCTS		466286		561020		606878		664724	PREP ALIMENTAIRES DIVERSES
098	EDIBLE PRODCTS,PREPS NES	W 105182	433157	W 128113	535567	W 126882	579215	W 148523	630423	PREP ALIMENTAIRES NDA
09809	MISC FOOD PREPRTIONS NES	W 58577	373545	W 77432	469710	W 75562	504435	W 91295	544245	PREP ALIMENTAIRES NDA
1	BEVERAGES AND TOBACCO		1233569		1494337		1870837		1584060	BOISSONS ET TABACS
11	BEVERAGES		860854		924247		1124485		1083821	BOISSONS
112	ALCOHOLIC BEVERAGES	W 312443	815031	W 371572	870396	W 593541	1068446	W 460259	1025230	BOISSONS ALCOOLIQUES
1124	DISTILLED ALCOHOLIC BEVS	W 121760	641158	W 109276	661340	W 137843	755519	W 148761	789447	ALCOOLS,EAUX–DE–VIE
11241	WHISKY	W 70948	446573	W 58281	448818	W 76626	486541	W 83523	506402	WHISKY
12	TOBACCO AND MANUFACTURES		372714		570090		746352		500240	TABACS BRUTS FABRIQUES
121	TOBACCO UNMNFCTRD,REFUSE	W 44767	224086	W 53510	282805	W 48413	262894	W 52782	296723	TABACS BRUTS,DECHETS
122	TOBACCO,MANUFACTURED	W 8605	148629	W 11143	287285	W 14198	483458	W 11403	203517	TABACS FABRIQUES
1222	CIGARETTES	W 2538	87194	W 5200	209392	W 7146	380605	W 7579	136538	CIGARETTES
2	CRUDE MATERLS,EXCL FUELS		4025705		5265888		6837211		6469479	MAT BRUTES NON COMESTIBLES
22	OIL SEEDS,OLEAGINOUS FRT		644682		687709		998769		972877	GRAINES,FRUITS OLEAGINEUX
222	SEEDS FOR'SOFT'FIXED OIL	W 2393443	635185	W 2430917	676789	W 3640399	986939	W 3028277	959803	GRAINES HUILES FIXES
2222	SOYA BEANS	W 2114528	517070	W 2019350	514408	W 2854706	714678	W 2322373	700869	FEVES DE SOJA
23	RUBBER, CRUDE		256582		326252		487840		479394	CAOUTCHOUC BRUT
24	CORK AND WOOD		544448		693291		912806		829986	LIEGE ET BOIS
248	WOOD SHAPED,SLEEPERS	W 891989	400589	W 998745	512911	W 1119726	642810	W 1175487	605609	BOIS SIMPLEMENT TRAVAILLES
2483	LUMBER SHAPED NON–CONIFR	W 387261	220175	W 423196	266618	W 508514	349677	W 535044	347952	NON CONIFERES SCIES,RABOTES
251	*PULP AND WASTE PAPER	W 1019719	269195	W 1211166	373450	W 1145541	560837	W 1204612	347061	PATES A PAPIER,DECHETS
2517	SODA,SULPHATE WOOD PULP	W 508382	203687	W 529964	265450	W 433557	356202	W 418082	218410	PATES CHIMIQUES AU SULFATE
25172	— BLEACHED,NONDISSOLVNG	W 498519	198991	W 519566	260218	W 425068	349763	W 410200	214513	PATES BLANCHIES
26	TEXTILE FIBRES AND WASTE		370938		537922		642338		616136	FIBRES TEXTILES
27	CRUDE FERTLZR,MINRLS NES		313009		377799		426357		454380	ENGRAIS MINERAUX BRUTS
28	METALLIFEROUS ORES,SCRAP		1213822		1718488		2066268		1996406	MINERAIS METAL,DECHETS
282	IRON AND STEEL SCRAP	W 4033327	537689	W 4622645	753745	W 4878557	963724	W 4433082	801184	FERRAILLES
28209	— OF OTHR IRON OR STEEL	W 3899020	473262	W 4329866	561556	W 4534198	675538	W 4003524	499015	FERRAILLES DE FER
287	BASE METAL ORES,CONC NES	W 2859833	418716	W 3272841	635622	W 3573624	714860	W 4377909	740500	MINERAIS METAUX COMMUNS
2871	CPR ORE ETC,CEMENT COPPR	W 476062	217638	W 518428	367670	W 465617	383231	W 736653	389697	MINERAIS DE CUIVRE,MATTES
28711	COPPER ORES,EXCL MATTE	W 476001	217533	W 518428	367670	W 465547	382928	W 736576	389403	MINERAIS DE CUIVRE
29	CRUDE ANIMAL,VEG MAT NES		290810		327853		508750		516298	MATIERES BRUTES ANIM,VEGET
292	CRUDE VEG MATERIALS NES	W 85019	228999	W 82909	256715	W 106282	425281		425159	MAT BRUTES VEGETALES NDA
3	MINERAL FUELS ETC		8719759		8733193		9480625		11136936	COMBUSTIBLES MINERAUX LUB
32	COAL,COKE AND BRIQUETTES		593108		565288		758165		650437	HOUILLES,COKES,BRIQUETTES
322	COAL,LIGNITE AND PEAT	MW 12731	582468	MW 11876	539957	MW 14062	676242	MW 12253	598701	HOUILLES,LIGNITES,TOURBE
3222	OTH COAL,NOT AGGLOMERATD	MW 12454	552969	MW 11482	502513	MW 13761	638104	MW 11846	555239	AUTRES HOUILLES
33	PETROLEUM AND PRODUCTS		7292666		7260815		7540150		9068627	PETROLE ET DERIVES
333	CRUDE PETROLEUM	MW 50565	5564187	MW 53567	5904275	MW 50032	6205422	MW 51955	7519638	HUILES BRUTES DE PETROLE
334	PETROLEUM PRODUCTS,REFIN	MW 11497	1576190	W 7525873	1184258	W 6647769	1113816	W 6759187	1304261	PRODUITS RAFFINES
3341	GASOLINE,OTH LIGHT OILS	W 3729303	479769	W 2285130	412878					ESSENCES POUR MOTEURS
33411	MOTOR,AVIATION SPIRIT	W 2738185	312728	W 750055	135811					ESSENCES MOTEURS D'AVIONS
3343	GAS OILS	W 4640934	714050	W 2966547	441978					GAS OILS
341	*GAS,NATURAL AND MANUFCT		799084		857990	W 7466047	1023857	W 8079814	1190886	GAZ NATUREL,GAZ MANUFACT
3413	PETROLM GASES,LIQUEFIED	W 5663707	783981	W 6163510	784483	W 6685493	918664	W 6999492	1042922	GAZ DE PETROLE LIQUEFIE
34139	OTH HYDROCARBON GAS LQFD	W 4447164	572115	W 5050021	600009	W 5644513	690055	W 5817952	777830	HYDROCARBURES GAZEUX NDA
4	ANIMAL,VEGETABLE OIL,FAT		287841		493765		807512		698452	HUILES,GRAISSES ANIM,VEG
42	FIXED VEGETABLE OIL,FAT		157429		338634		577782		522150	HUILES VEGETALES FIXES
423	FIXED VEG OILS,SOFT	W 89856	89366	W 213551	232635	W 225039	437956	W 184745	388301	HUILES VEGET DOUCES FIXES
4235	OLIVE OIL	W 40861	60189	W 125579	172543	W 137581	375196	W 101382	331139	HUILE D'OLIVE
5	CHEMCLS,RELATED PROD NES		8606158		10558181		13445847		13947552	PRODUITS CHIMIQUES
51	ORGANIC CHEMICALS		2314033		2850968		3626468		3515463	PROD CHIMIQ ORGANIQUES
511	HYDROCARBONS NES,DERIVS	W 530920	261890	W 592810	349436	W 693484	492826	W 635111	406444	HYDROCARBURES NDA
512	ALCOHOLS,PHENOLS ETC	W 603774	220791	W 682382	332617	W 749613	421285	W 742703	369560	PHENOLS,PHENOLS–ALCOOLS
5121	ACYCLIC ALCOHOLS,DERIVS	W 574282	177654	W 649693	285111	W 717599	360744	W 701125	306229	ALCOOLS ACYCLIQUES
513	CARBOXYLIC ACIDS ETC	W 304907	331898	W 381929	440813	W 387608	586146	W 347360	544905	ACIDES CARBOXYLIQUES
514	NITROGEN–FNCTN COMPOUNDS	W 210859	495110	W 278505	583954	W 338656	1015194	W 339523	1023983	COMPOSES FONCT AZOTEES
5148	OTH NITROGN–FNCTN CMPNDS	W 96285	131422	W 132060	170615	W 164486	540378	W 154333	497788	AUTRES COMPOSES AZOTES
515	ORG–INORG COMPOUNDS ETC	W 88475	762111	W 106265	871986	W 74522	757973	W 75519	805946	COMPOSES ORGANO–MINERAUX
5156	HETEROCYCLIC CMPDS ETC	W 47370	595304	W 58588	676000	W 24944	558649	W 23128	580018	COMPOSES HETEROCYCLIQUES
51569	OTH HETEROCYC CMPDS,ETC	W 40099	576544	W 46558	650236	W 18384	530996	W 18538	556365	AUT COMP HETEROCYCLIQUES
516	OTHER ORGANIC CHEMICALS	W 266577	242234	W 258207	272163	W 221057	353044	W 225446	364625	AUTRES PROD ORGANIQUES
52	INORGANIC CHEMICALS		698629		775785		946170		970900	PROD CHIM INORGANIQUES
522	INORG ELEMNTS,OXIDES,ETC	W 888298	251087	W 1226265	325287	W 1401751	452428	W 1310232	463532	ELEMENTS INORGANIQUES
53	DYES,TANNING,COLOUR PROD		533262		660322		791795		838615	PROD TEINTURE,COLORANTS
533	PIGMENTS,PAINTS,ETC	W 119787	334680	W 153319	420183	W 163931	527073	W 174390	556655	PIGMENTS,PEINTURES,VERNIS
541	*MEDICINAL,PHARM PRODUCT		1532783		1855244	MK 34234	2242289	MK 45734	2465603	PROD MEDICINAUX PHARMACEUT
5417	MEDICAMENTS	MK 11517	883355	MK 16301	1172203	MK 19465	1407256	MK 29319	1613743	MEDICAMENTS

4. Special Imports C.I.F. by Commodities according to the S.I.T.C. (Rev. 2) in thousand U.S. Dollars
Importations Spéciales C.A.F. par Produits d'après la C.T.C.I. (Rév. 2) en milliers de Dollars E.U.

SITC CTCI	COMMODITY	1993		1994		1995		1996		PRODUIT
		WEIGHT POIDS	VALUE VALEUR	WEIGHT POIDS	VALUE VALEUR	WEIGHT POIDS	VALUE VALEUR	WEIGHT POIDS	VALUE VALEUR	
54179	— CONTNG OTH SUBSTANCES	MK 9636	575949	MK 13993	809471	MK 16253	1026784	MK 25288	1142273	MED CONT AUT SUBSTANCES
55	PERFUME,CLEANING ETC PRD		686036		858276		999132		1047718	PROD POUR PARFUM,TOILETTE
553	PERFUMERY,COSMETICS,ETC	W 51974	373187	W 61663	476106	W 71827	568767	W 84133	617697	PRODUITS DE PARFUMERIE
562	*FERTILIZERS,MANUFACTURE	W 1676482	217058	W 2329528	324407	W 2347306	401818	W 2780992	487627	ENGRAIS MANUFACTURES
58	PLASTIC MATERIALS ETC		1547015		1973339		2866993		2927346	MAT PLAST ARTIFICIELLES
582	PROD OF CONDENSATION ETC	W 171478	405291	W 241295	539411	W 302017	806067	W 326791	829267	PROD CONDENS,POLYCOND
5823	ALKYDS,OTHER POLYESTERS	W 61308	158438	W 90811	210961	W 127092	349100	W 146241	349575	ALKYDES ET AUT POLYESTERS
583	POLYMERIZATION ETC PRODS	W 915687	1075317	W 1302334	1354913	W 1182832	1967343	W 1384542	1985267	PROD POLYMERISATION
5831	POLYETHYLENE	W 338442	255146	W 419978	321074	W 400262	469323	W 454896	475578	POLYETHYLENE
58311	— IN PRIMARY FORMS	W 295955	196191	W 367955	247309	W 343836	370089	W 392099	369672	POLYETHYLENE PRIMAIRES
5839	OTH POLYMRZTION ETC PROD	W 126858	295850	W 359444	359443	W 187984	496294	W 244509	561297	AUT PROD POLYMER COPOLYM
59	CHEMICAL MATERIALS NES		1069870		1251281		1552763		1678781	MAT PROD CHIMIQUES NDA
591	PESTICIDES,DISINFECTANTS	W 30953	180096	W 38021	221404	W 38563	295354	W 49361	364156	DESINF,INSECT,FONG,HERB
598	MISCEL CHEM PRODUCTS NES	W 344481	724931	W 355797	832581	W 418352	1009588	W 442770	1061235	PROD DIV INDUST CHIM NDA
5989	CHEM PRODUCTS,PREPS NES	W 213234	557798	W 216101	637964	W 243486	757777	W 252507	809127	PROD PREP CHIMIQUES NDA
59899	OTH CHEM PRODS,PREPS,NES	W 167779	443885	W 164620	509189	W 186982	604220	W 185535	638356	AUT PRODUITS CHIMIQUES NDA
6	BASIC MANUFACTURES		10191299		13042137		17648879		17712072	ART MANUFACTURES
61	LEATHER,DRESSED FUR,ETC		344689		541373		591434		593789	CUIRS,PELLETERIES
611	LEATHER	W 51684	300054	W 84827	489428	W 77027	538041	W 78877	534503	CUIRS,PEAUX PREPARES
62	RUBBER MANUFACTURES NES		848539		1068593		1432151		1500732	CAOUTCHOUC MANUFACTURE
625	RUBBER TYRES, TUBES ETC	W 119950	493891	W 154417	608078	W 194170	827999	W 226211	891760	PNEUS CAOUTCHOUC VULCANISE
6251	TYRES NEW FOR MOTOR CARS	W 59609	282887	W 71193	339114	W 91170	466724	W 118049	504094	PNEUS POUR VOITURES
63	WOOD,CORK MANUFACTRS NES		284660		337724		433040		432695	OUVRAGES LIEGE ET BOIS
64	PAPER,PAPERBOARD AND MFR		1744010		2146361		2969283		2801384	PAPIERS,CARTONS & OUVRAGES
641	PAPER AND PAPERBOARD	W 2146753	1428455	W 2521681	1818495	W 2574132	2549583	W 2871343	2359782	PAPIERS ET CARTONS
6412	PRINTG,WRITING PAPER NES	W 564747	440653	W 679558	562796	W 663248	782576	W 641449	642547	PAPIERS POUR L'IMPRESSION
64122	— COATED,IMPREGNATD ETC	W 498391	389392	W 598467	489880	W 582751	676270	W 561563	558626	PAPIERS IMPRESSION COUCHES
6413	KRAFT PAPER,PAPERBOARD	W 469578	242101	W 547539	317221	W 546655	439258	W 560634	378659	PAPIER ET CARTON KRAFT
6415	PAPER,PAPERBRD,BULK,NES	W 475258	282634	W 573064	377199	W 578520	532338	W 568624	474478	PAPIERS,CARTONS ROULEAUX
64159	OTHER PAPER ETC,BULK,NES	W 329333	218039	W 391579	290384	W 400799	411168	W 417159	387354	AUT PAPIER ROULEAUX FEUILLES
6418	COATED ETC PAPER NES BLK	W 138128	202483	W 196929	283586	W 212838	384518	W 217171	395625	PAP,CARTONS COUCHES,ENDUITS
642	PAPER,ETC,PRECUT,ARTS OF	W 145222	315554	W 170792	327865	W 186661	419700	W 184956	441602	PAP,CARTONS DECOUPES
65	TEXTILE YARN,FABRICS,ETC		1710276		2252166		2758329		2943800	FILS,TISSUS,ARTICLES TEXTILE
651	TEXTILE YARN	W 116875	453173	W 197521	674725		860534	W 205389	890211	FILS TEXTILES
6514	SYN FIB YRN,BULK,MONOFIL	W 54232	230349	W 86318	341326	W 97156	451324	W 110146	475428	FILS CONT 85% FIB TEXT SYNTH
653	WOVN MAN–MADE FIB FABRIC	W 38005	346033	W 52388	471084	W 60874	581588	W 59688	569911	TISSUS FIBRES SYNTH,ARTIF
657	SPECIAL TXTL FABRC,PRODS	W 43584	278814	W 65264	343460	W 65718	414994		470692	TISSUS SPECIAUX
66	NONMETAL MINERAL MFS NES		924827		1033518		1360008		1437482	ART MIN NON METALLIQUES
664	GLASS	W 191175	198916	W 197024	248674	W 298082	343246	W 287231	326710	VERRE
67	IRON AND STEEL		1776154		2386956		3766413		3713683	FER ET ACIER
671	PIG IRON ETC	W 516367	189546	W 774996	292168	W 829469	396986	W 880371	373001	FONTE,SPIEGEL,POUDRES
672	IRON,STEEL PRIMARY FORMS	W 1036643	303974	W 1131970	384098		766868	W 2170394	749756	LINGOTS FER,ACIER
6727	IRN,STL COIL FR REROLLNG	W 985176	284018	W 1066058	356430	W 1647043	664331	W 1710900	620383	EBAUCHES POUR TOLES FER
67271	IRON,SIMPLE STEEL COILS	W 976071	278355	W 1051095	348292	W 1628306	645914	W 1692299	599760	EBAUCHES NON EN ACIER
673	IRON,STEEL SHAPES ETC	W 489377	222955	W 652056	328702	W 970503	478055	W 817222	442509	BARRES,PROFIL FER,ACIER
674	IRN,STL UNIV,PLATE,SHEET	W 1257104	761394	W 1543607	945850	W 2032856	1482343	W 2122401	1447449	LARGES PLATS,TOLES
6746	IRN,STL THIN PLATE,ROLLD	W 385909	233776	W 423309	255530	W 584324	429538	W 518865	362018	TOLES LAM MOINS 3MM
6749	OTH IRN,STL PLATES,SHEET	W 471152	290409	W 583392	376652	W 709984	545592	W 868925	632917	AUTRES TOLES FER,ACIER
67491	— OF IRON OR SIMPLE STL	W 468747	284730	W 579389	368789	W 704276	530842	W 861154	618100	AUT TOLES AUTRES ACIER FIN
678	IRON,STL TUBES,PIPES,ETC	W 175850	222803	W 326976	335264	W 415999	506869	W 469907	559469	TUBES,TUYAUX EN FONTE,FER
68	NON–FERROUS METALS		970829		1308292		1947444		1713387	METAUX NON FERREUX
682	COPPER EXC CEMENT COPPER	W 167066	409247	W 178749	513183	W 233030	827219	W 200982	689697	CUIVRE
6822	COPPER,ALLOYS WORKED	W 97273	283933	W 130074	411361	W 170312	653812	W 159563	592260	CUIVRE,ALLIAGES OUVRES
684	ALUMINIUM	W 170741	372573	W 209427	465383	W 233332	685822	W 252740	683997	ALUMINIUM
6842	ALUMINIUM,ALLOYS WORKED	W 82371	265101	W 92885	294630	W 103518	422040	W 125146	475788	ALUMINIUM,ALLIAGES OUVRE
69	METAL MANUFACTURES NES		1587315		1967154		2390775		2575119	ART MANUFACT EN METAL NDA
695	TOOLS	W 32308	252453	W 37255	336718	W 125409	350250	W 38466	339378	OUTILS A MAIN
699	BASE METAL MFRS NES	W 118475	593306	W 155772	756387	W 180797	969187	W 239045	1075110	ART MANUFACTURES MET NDA
6991	LOCKSMITHS WARES,ETC	W 28461	228795	W 40268	316300	W 43995	402801	W 80573	425282	ARTICLES DE SERRURERIE
7	MACHINES,TRANSPORT EQUIP		28460847		32658683		40284063		45213354	MACHINES MATERIEL TRANSPORT
71	POWER GENERATING EQUIPMT		2868035		3443624		4145655		4616441	MACHINES GENERATRICES
713	INTRNL COMBUS PSTN ENGIN	W 216703	2161657	W 228395	2625054	W 255392	3174486	W 302607	3540058	MOTEURS EXPL COMB INT, PIECE
7132	MOTOR VEHCL PISTN ENGINS	W 155813	1659526	W 179940	2051171	W 192025	2456884	W 219078	2644979	MOTEURS EXPL POUR VEHICULES
7139	PISTON ENGINE PARTS NES	W 54361	422043	W 39637	430419	W 52832	509637	W 71172	692128	PIECES POUR 713.2,3,8
714	ENGINES AND MOTORS NES	W 4817	273042	W 3808	312630	W 3689	276448	W 3837	379720	MOTEURS NON ELECTRIQUES
716	ROTATING ELECTRIC PLANT	W 32935	278078	W 40956	339012	W 53111	484049	W 54590	490461	APP ELECTR ROTATIFS,PIECES
72	MACHS FOR SPCL INDUSTRYS		1692926		2032543		2673488		2991238	MAC SPECIALES POUR INDUST
722	TRACTORS NON–ROAD	W 24301	134622	W 45938	255740	W 51404	323009	W 72010	470945	TRACTEURS
7224	WHEELED TRACTORS NES	W 23558	131336	W 44368	248986	W 49671	314774	W 68952	456881	TRACTEURS A ROUES
723	CIVIL ENGNEERG EQUIP ETC	W 22347	155412	W 35920	230196	W 55399	377565	W 61784	386346	APPAREILS DE GENIE CIVIL
724	TEXTILE,LEATHER MACHNRY	W 13968	221057	W 19314	308847	W 20709	369531	W 18443	359625	MACH POUR INDUSTRIE TEXTILE
728	OTH MACHY FOR SPCL INDUS	W 41110	636972	W 46252	668229	W 59953	897717	W 59734	955071	AUT MACH IND PARTICULIERES
7284	MACHY FOR SPCL INDUS NES	W 24779	488443	W 25657	486000	W 33525	632296	W 33886	684020	MACH SPEC IND PARTICUL.
73	METALWORKING MACHINERY		430786		476653		623286		657264	MACH TRAVAIL DES METAUX
736	METALWORKING MACH–TOOLS	W 17057	251107	W 18243	297483	W 20049	346705	W 26847	475698	MACH–OUTILS TRAVAIL METAUX
74	GENRL INDUSTRL MACHY NES		3070143		3356727		4729792		5137281	MACH APP INDUSTRIE
741	HEATING,COOLING EQUIPMNT	W 61519	652019	W 74928	680372	W 95475	1022074	W 105012	1210836	MACH CHAUFFAGE,PIECES
7415	AIR–CONDITIONING MACHNRY	W 19937	252971	W 17624	240328	W 27183	428727	W 38266	543803	GROUPES CONDITION AIR
742	PUMPS FOR LIQUIDS ETC	W 22710	340518	W 21765	391257	W 27390	558171	W 34470	603301	POMPES MOTO–POMPES
743	PUMPS NES,CENTRFUGES ETC	W 50808	513640	W 60468	590922	W 73707	849270	W 76482	906776	POMPES COMPRES,VENT ETC
744	MECHANICAL HANDLING EQU	W 54765	398354	W 65809	421923	W 90048	678890	W 91333	665055	EQUIP MANUTENTION PIECES
745	NONELEC MACHY,TOOLS NES	W 22749	420085	W 25088	408653	W 29042	508246	W 34439	541046	AUT MACH NON ELEC,PIECES
7452	OTH NONELEC MCHS,PTS NES	W 21156	377898	W 22774	353445	W 26509	439220	W 31804	468041	AUT MACH NON ELEC,PIECES
749	NONELEC MACH PTS,ACC NES	W 73879	745527	W 83306	863600	W 96327	1113141	W 112868	1210267	PIECES MACH NON ELEC NDA
7492	COCKS,VALVES ETC NES	W 17850	262736	W 20582	300408	W 27228	407621	W 31592	448443	ART ROB,SIM POUR TUYAUX
75	OFFICE MACHNES,ADP EQUIP		2903111		3132820		3560979		3863138	MACH BUREAU TRAIT AUTOM
751	OFFICE MACHINES	W 10697	307361	W 10907	298622	W 11410	331404	W 11891	359877	MACH,APPAREILS DE BUREAU
752	AUTOMTIC DATA PROC EQUIP	W 47704	1434728	W 29625	1618890	W 33090	1938577	W 34440	2163750	MACH TRAIT INFORMATION
7523	DIGITL CENTRL PROCESSORS	W 4014	424590	W 4866	502365	W 4788	571464	W 4757	610879	UNITES CENTRALES
7524	DIGITL CENTRL STOR UNITS	W 3931	244384	W 3685	271983	W 5285	342049	W 2531	293611	UNITES MEMOIRE CENTRALES
7525	ADP PERIPHERAL UNITS	W 23847	373714	W 14658	479001	W 15480	571925	W 19035	642895	UNITES PERIPHERIQUES
7528	OFF–LINE DATA PROC EQUIP	W 14617	277780	W 5195	256514	W 5315	280504	W 7038	410932	MACH AUXIL TRAIT INFORM
759	OFFICE,ADP MCH PTS,ACCES	W 17464	1161022	W 21994	1215307	W 24230	1290998	W 26209	1339510	PIECES DU 751 ET 752
7599	ACCTG,ETC,ADP MCH PTS,AC	W 14124	1055796	W 18646	1106756	W 21093	1173985	W 21569	1198333	PIECES DU 751 ET 752
76	TELECOMM,SOUND EQUIPMENT		2199276		2575314		3233474		4155471	EQUIPMENT DE TELECOM
761	TELEVISION RECEIVERS	W 26557	372530	W 31470	436693	W 43743	506069	W 61399	473927	RECEPTEURS DE TELEVISION
7611	COLOUR TV RECEIVERS	W 25684	365205	W 30595	426226	W 43024	497075	W 60761	468068	RECEPTEURS COULEUR
762	RADIO BROADCAST RECEIVRS	W 17498	342841	W 20044	419750	W 23165	482385	W 21365	449881	RECEPTEURS RADIODIFFUSION
763	SOUND RECORDRS,PHONOGRPH	W 8128	283832	W 8335	302733	W 9485	330851	W 9660	381741	PHONO,APP ENREGISTREMENT
7638	OTHR SOUND APPARATUS ETC	W 7472	272061	W 7690	289639	W 8980	320155	W 9308	376402	AUT APP D'ENREGIS,REPROD
764	TELECOM EQPT,PTS,ACC NES	W 44024	1200074	W 41181	1416137	W 47593	1914169	W 42903	2849922	EQUIP TELECOM,PIECES

4. Special Imports C.I.F. by Commodities according to the S.I.T.C. (Rev. 2) in thousand U.S. Dollars
Importations Spéciales C.A.F. par Produits d'après la C.T.C.I. (Rév. 2) en milliers de Dollars E.U.

SITC CTCI	COMMODITY	1993			1994			1995			1996			PRODUIT
		WEIGHT POIDS		VALUE VALEUR	WEIGHT POIDS		VALUE VALEUR	WEIGHT POIDS		VALUE VALEUR	WEIGHT POIDS		VALUE VALEUR	
7641	LINE TELEPHONE,ETC EQUIP	W	8807	237352	W	5576	343415	W	5826	521728	W	5570	579193	APP TELEPHON PAR FIL
7643	TV,RADIO TRANSMITTRS ETC	W	2035	102673	W	784	107806	W	1272	209408	W	3047	679910	APP EMET TELE RADIO
7649	PTS NES OF EQUIPMT OF 76	W	22511	587363	W	23515	678642	W	23296	854144	W	21742	1381353	PIECES DE LA DIV 76
76491	PTS NES OF APPAR OF 7641	W	2539	189617	W	3154	226213	W	3963	392545	W	6297	892096	PIECES POUR 764.1
76493	TELECOMM EQUIPMT PTS NES	W	8856	285554	W	9666	305617	W	11897	313690	W	10010	349700	PIECES 761,762,764.3,8
77	ELECTRIC MACHNRY NES ETC			3909448			4653361			5834462			6019609	MACH APP ELECT NDA
772	SWITCHGEAR ETC,PARTS NES	W	35668	759231	W	44119	1006489	W	46946	1252525	W	67953	1288800	APP COUPURE,SECT ETC
7721	SWITCHGEAR ETC	W	28172	688772	W	38132	901929	W	42020	1149868	W	64507	1200290	APP COUPURE,SECTIONMNT
773	ELECTR DISTRIBUTNG EQUIP	W	38680	330200	W	44526	436035	W	76461	600466	W	63161	583425	EQUIPMT DISTRIBUTION ELECT
7731	INSULATED WIRE,CABLE ETC	W	32152	252592	W	34984	335370	W	60194	459548	W	50651	432039	FILS,CABLES ISOLES ELECT
775	HOUSEHOLD TYPE EQUIP NES	W	133239	784127	W	139330	830475	W	151807	954834	W	154627	987063	MACH,APP USAGE DOMESTQUE
7758	ELECTRO–THERMIC APPL NES	W	44872	318364	W	44057	334605	W	49271	369632	W	45321	363580	APP ELECTROTHERMIQ NDA
776	TRANSISTORS,VALVES,ETC	W	31839	563261	W	38146	666426	W	41118	854216	W	55848	970733	LAMPES,TUBES,VALVES
7764	ELECTRONIC MICROCIRCUITS	W	6212	303862	W	3381	353800	W	1783	421092	W	1521	516533	MICROSTRUCTURES ELECTRON
778	ELECTRICAL MACHINERY NES	W	128395	1125179	W	146359	1337958	W	216284	1747826	W	164388	1692336	AUTRES MACH ELECT NDA
7783	AUTOMOTIVE ELECTR EQUIP	W	33723	386197	W	40038	487563	W	89197	641076	W	40520	606850	EQUIP ELECT MOTEURS EXPL
77831	IGNITION,STARTING EQUIP	W	21793	238612	W	25774	300732	W	28271	392395	W	24578	362227	APP ELEC ALLUM,DEMARRAGE
7788	OTH ELEC MACHY,EQUIP NES	W	20516	340574	W	22065	387188	W	27864	508127	W	23306	493727	AUT MACH APP ELEC NDA
78	ROAD VEHICLES			10097942			11436172			13933901			15722094	VEHICULES ROUTIERS
781	PASS MOTOR VEH EXC BUSES	W	536145	5314808	W	584180	5378859	W	563617	6106114	W	657483	7208208	AUTO TRANSPORT PERSONNES
782	LORRIES,SPCL MTR VEH NES	W	57673	384985	W	74707	538552	W	108478	908546	W	130071	1086980	VEHICULES SPECIAUX,MARCH
7821	LORRIES,TRUCKS	W	46174	347787	W	68941	498058	W	102941	866144	W	121700	1024918	VEHICULES TRANSP MARCHAND
784	MOTOR VEH PRTS,ACCES NES	W	577092	3739087	W	801618	4860343	W	762594	6062972	W	923750	6504522	PIECES 722,781,782,783
7849	OTHER MOTOR VEHCL PARTS	W	571105	3677263	W	788384	4743848	W	742399	5860677	W	908234	6325534	PIECES 722,781,782,783
785	CYCLES,ETC MOTRZD OR NOT	W	48361	455231	W	31910	382577	W	29716	399965	W	28503	417400	MOTOCYCLES SCOOTERS
79	OTHR TRANSPORT EQUIPMENT			1289180			1551470			1549024			2050818	AUTRE MATERIEL TRANSPORT
792	AIRCRAFT ETC	W	3881	1042473	W	2166	1274861			1128420			1595916	APP NAVIGATION AERIENNE
7924	AIRCRFT NES OVER 15000KG	W	2854	761116	W	1285	954555	W	1156	736435	W	1851	1098276	AERODYNES PLUS 15000 KG
7929	AIRCRAFT PARTS NES	W	675	179725	W	582	185033	W	891	296080	W	924	365941	PIECES DU 792
793	SHIPS AND BOATS ETC	W	45742	173532	W	65042	193131	W	129181	334808			372914	NAVIRES BATEAUX,ETC
8	MISC MANUFACTURED GOODS			9381121			10059103			10803886			12280050	ART MANUFACTURES DIVERS
812	*PLUMBG,HEATNG,LGHTNG EQ	W	60155	311886	W	59284	323005	W	69938	384975	W	79231	406481	APPAR SANITAIRES CHAUFFAGE
821	*FURNITURE,PARTS THEREOF	W	94051	436087	W	103951	509254	W	105650	555110	W	133244	629829	MEUBLES ET PIECES
84	CLOTHING AND ACCESSORIES			2201262			2404660			2610163			2967548	VETEMENTS
842	MENS OUTERWEAR NOT KNIT	W	21692	427025	W	24732	488523	W	22998	504101	W	23637	564262	VET DESSUS POUR HOMMES
843	WOMENS OUTERWEAR NONKNIT	W	27268	490264	W	82320	520657	W	17896	561394	W	19126	623779	VET DESSUS FEMMES MAT TEX
845	OUTERWEAR KNIT NONELASTC	W	36819	406652	W	20433	453214	W	18827	502363	W	25435	616932	VET DESSOUS,ACCES BONNET
846	UNDER GARMENTS KNITTED	W	21545	350157	W	25004	395182	W	25269	472873	W	29200	542994	SOUS VETS DE BONNETERIE
8462	— OF COTTON NON ELASTIC	W	18274	250533	W	21107	278027	W	17306	278414	W	20881	313673	SOUS–VET BONNET COTON
851	*FOOTWEAR	W	22787	300753	W	24886	341827	W	30630	389384	W	32101	476214	CHAUSSURES
85102	FOOTWEAR LEATHER	W	16877	241487	W	17731	272828	W	22733	303454	W	21932	351097	CHAUS SEMELLES EN CUIR
87	PRECISION INSTRUMNTS NES			1520757			1696252			1944647			2027497	INSTRUM,APPAR SCIENT NDA
872	MEDICAL INSTRUMENTS NES	W	12414	430043	W	13763	450216	W	13874	516561	W	12015	579395	INSTR,APP MEDIC–CHIR NDA
87202	OTH MEDICAL INSTRUMENTS	W	10923	384252	W	12314	406781	W	12334	466634	W	10407	515762	INSTRUM,APP MEDECINE
874	MEASURNG,CONTROLNG INSTR	W	19069	972348	W	18692	1096311	W	19939	1248989	W	20055	1267927	INSTRUMENTS DE MESURE
8742	MEASUR,DRAW ETC INST,PTS	W	5282	250564	W	5490	300597	W	5762	320390	W	5740	325892	INST DESSIN,TRACAGE,PCS
8748	ELEC MEAS,CONTRL EQU NES	W	3088	293360	W	2724	301698	W	2153	309146	W	2268	313204	APP ELEC ELECTRO MESURE
87483	OTH ELCTRNC MEAS ETC EQU	W	2448	266250	W	2233	268232	W	1671	266572	W	1743	271711	AUT APP ELECTRO DE MESURE
88	PHOTO EQU,OPTICL GDS ETC			962758			1037566			1216793			1298161	APP,FOURN PHOTO,OP,MONTR
882	PHOTO,CINEMA SUPPLIES	W	29815	337836	W	34195	350620	W	37584	422477	W	36656	432104	PRODUITS PHOTO,CINEMA
8822	PHOTO FILM EXC DEV CINMA	W	19376	254394	W	22594	263323	W	24372	315689	W	22296	323364	PLAQUES,PELLICULES,FILMS
885	WATCHES AND CLOCKS			330123			374408			435300			441676	HORLOGERIE
8851	WATCHES,MOVEMENTS,CASES			272548			305774			354689			353995	MONTRES,MOUVEMENTS,BOITES
88511	WATCHES			260944			294949			341454			342388	MONTRES POCHE,BRACELET
89	MISC MANUFCTRD GOODS NES			3505025			3596586			3511128			4238522	ART MANUFACTURES DIVERS
892	PRINTED MATTER	W	51167	382055	W	68537	374628	W	53932	445578	W	53498	474532	IMPRIMES
893	ARTICLES OF PLASTIC NES			660279			801881			1064738			1179262	OUVRAGES EN MAT DIVIS 58
8939	MISC PLASTIC ARTICLES	W	131915	508542	W	153050	588110	W	175318	787283	W	184410	874687	ART DIVERS EN MAT DIV 58
89399	OTHR PLASTC ARTICLES NES	W	92950	477942	W	116383	550934	W	161930	738348	W	168692	816400	AUT OUV MAT DIV 58
894	TOYS,SPORTING GOODS,ETC	W	72499	691536	W	83731	701785	W	70666	558801	W	88048	830103	VOITURES ENFANTS,JOUETS
8942	TOYS,INDOOR GAMES ETC	W	55992	529945	W	62313	510708	W	48634	382417	W	64626	586832	JOUETS,JEUX ETC
896	WORKS OF ART ETC			568642			464110			100443			176540	OBJETS D'ART
89601	HAND PAINTINGS ETC NES			512710			405738			77467			122360	TABLEAUX,PEINTURES
898	MUSICAL INSTRUMENTS,PTS	W	27156	487020	W	24038	490188	W	23230	559777	W	23644	613958	INSTRUMENTS DE MUSIQUE
8983	SOUND RECRDNG TAPE,DISCS	W	23554	433086	W	20771	431452	W	19286	495087	W	20094	547882	SUPPORTS SON POUR 763
89832	RECORDED DISCS,TAPES ETC	W	8460	234934	W	8560	279642	W	6168	333703	W	7804	403967	DISQUES,PHONO,BANDES
899	OTHER MANUFACTURED GOODS			382879			416109			424798			523702	AUT ART MANUF DIVERS NDA
9	GOODS NOT CLASSD BY KIND			219393			320373			480530			471685	ART TRANSACT NON CLASSES

5. Special Exports F.O.B. by Commodities according to the S.I.T.C. (Rev. 2) in thousand U.S. Dollars
Exportations Spéciales F.O.B. par Produits d'après la C.T.C.I. (Rév. 2) en milliers de Dollars E.U.

SITC CTCI	COMMODITY	1993		1994		1995		1996		PRODUIT
		WEIGHT POIDS	VALUE VALEUR	WEIGHT POIDS	VALUE VALEUR	WEIGHT POIDS	VALUE VALEUR	WEIGHT POIDS	VALUE VALEUR	
	ALL COMMODITIES		60968531		73187932		89616115		100955530	TOUS PRODUITS
0	FOOD AND LIVE ANIMALS		7951734		9471846		11486256		12906698	ALIMENTS,ANIMAUX VIVANTS
01	MEAT AND PREPARATIONS		359439		500631		728734		1037927	VIANDES ET PREPARATIONS
011	MEAT FRESH,CHILLD,FROZEN		287193		390621	W 221550	576773	W 320966	830794	VIANDES FRAICHES,REF,CONGE
0113	PIG MEAT FRESH,CHLD,FRZN	W 45865	90119	W 83067	164450	W 101126	251871	W 161913	437641	VIANDE DE PORC
02	DAIRY PRODCTS,BIRDS'EGGS		159804		219008		316570		361808	PRODUITS LAITIERS,OEUFS
03	FISH AND PREPARATIONS		752033		1004055		1178414		1436383	POISSONS ET PREPARATIONS
034	FISH,FRESH,CHILLED,FROZN	W 179461	323180	W 251100	450645	W 271120	552087	W 304741	661670	POISSON FRAIS, REFRIG,CONG
0342	FISH FROZEN,EXCL FILLETS	W 131958	202954	W 193885	291908	W 203737	357646	W 217253	386507	POISSONS CONGELES
036	SHELL FISH FRESH,FROZEN	W 104649	238162	W 106195	324412	W 114045	317786	W 139811	431427	CRUSTACES,MOLLUSQUES
04	CEREALS AND PREPARATIONS		573634		682267		721635		844354	CEREALES ET PRODUITS
048	CEREAL ETC PREPARATIONS	W 107259	144262	W 172934	203577	W 213152	280009	W 255024	355070	PREPTNS A BASE CEREALES
05	VEGETABLES AND FRUIT		5335640		5922239		7044676		7489243	LEGUMES ET FRUITS
054	VEG ETC FRSH,SMPLY PRSVD	W 2137527	1737183	W 2576603	1951483		2475016		2595780	LEGUMES FRAIS,CONG,SECS
0544	TOMATOES FRESH	W 545496	420644	W 686249	535940	W 720753	636356	W 753599	662751	TOMATES FRAICHES
0545	OTHER FRESH VEGETABLES	W 1250356	1101552	W 1470674	1129989	W 1638248	1428535	W 1860615	1602403	AUTRES LEGUMES FRAIS,REF
05459	FRESH VEGETABLES NES	W 1034815	1004909	W 1208489	1017436	W 1352843	1299078	W 1572252	1480304	LEGUMES FRAIS,REFRI NDA
056	VEGTBLES ETC PRSVD,PREPD	W 225870	417474	W 265456	490312	W 241441	511564	W 263929	531766	CONSERVES DE LEGUMES
0565	VEGTBLES PRSVD,PREPD NES	W 214815	393996	W 250839	463603	W 226116	482517	W 254770	506999	LEGUMES PREPARES CONSERVE
05659	OTH VEG PRESVD,PREPD NES	W 210734	382685	W 243180	447493	W 218965	466671	W 244811	484390	LEGUM PREPAP,CONSERV NDA
057	FRUIT,NUTS,FRESH,DRIED	W 4096002	2754282	W 4205121	3033221	W 4193686	3518655	W 4318097	3797554	FRUITS FRAIS OU SECS
0571	ORANGES, MANDARINS ETC	W 2556906	1445226	W 2592324	1537526	W 2469240	1785998	W 2401980	1918020	ORANGES,MAND,CLEMENTINES
05711	ORANGES,FRESH OR DRIED	W 1415957	598829	W 1358746	621809	W 1361261	792248	W 1280818	815533	ORANGES FRAICHES,SECHEES
05712	MANDARINS ETC FRESH, DRY	W 1140950	846398	W 1233578	915717	W 1107979	993749	W 1121162	1102486	MANDARINES,CLEMENTINES
0572	LEMONS,GRAPEFRUIT ETC	W 472722	220204	W 374855	222596	W 347428	235337	W 373717	281291	AUTRES AGRUMES FRAIS,SECS
05721	LEMONS,LIMES,FRESH,DRIED	W 457253	213554	W 356087	213902	W 324253	223220	W 356181	272290	CITRONS ET LIMES
0577	NUTS EDIBLE,FRESH,DRIED	W 47941	207104	W 44510	195850	W 34593	174919	W 44495	243863	FRUITS A COQUES
0579	FRUIT FRESH OR DRIED NES	W 857319	755522	W 982809	898677	W 1066487	1063849	W 1182689	1101828	FRUITS FRAIS,SECS NDA
05793	STONE FRUIT FRESH NES	W 208147	223057	W 234393	260253	W 196237	280406	W 237028	308638	FRUITS A NOYAU NDA FRAIS
05794	BERRIES FRESH	W 123687	223611	W 159917	262023	W 173387	327050	W 160530	305943	BAIES FRAICHES
05798	OTHER FRESH FRUIT	W 447331	238873	W 479792	280165	W 590755	355972	W 665344	377797	AUTRES FRUITS FRAIS
058	FRUIT PRESERVED,PREPARED	W 487643	426701	W 540063	447223	W 525456	539440	W 545117	564143	CONSERVES DE FRUITS
0589	FRUIT PREPRD,PRESRVD,NES	W 225760	215850	W 256381	227075	W 253073	284760	W 261555	297555	FRUITS PREPARES CONSERV
05899	FRUIT,NUTS NES,PRESERVED	W 222483	204194	W 252836	214219	W 248133	265909	W 255021	275443	FRUITS PREP CONSERV NDA
06	SUGAR AND PREPS,HONEY		227867		367001		480092		475234	SUCRES ET PRODUITS
062	SUGAR CANDY NON–CHOCLATE	W 38794	139065	W 69099	219465	W 79467	292210	W 74154	294905	SUCRERIES
07	COFFEE,TEA,COCOA,SPICES		182584		280633		374271		414433	CAFE,THE,CACAO,EPICES
09	MISC EDIBLE PRODUCTS		177762		199795		271441		374996	PREP ALIMENTAIRES DIVERSES
098	EDIBLE PRODCTS,PREPS NES	W 83932	170342	W 97779	194735	W 117535	260481	W 165383	366025	PREP ALIMENTAIRES NDA
1	BEVERAGES AND TOBACCO		1006280		1162516		1353487		1570310	BOISSONS ET TABACS
11	BEVERAGES		964076		1101045		1250101		1453507	BOISSONS
112	ALCOHOLIC BEVERAGES	W 1073221	928149	W 926141	1026245	W 746804	1144206	W 814165	1362052	BOISSONS ALCOOLIQUES
1121	WINE OF FRESH GRAPES ETC	W 999306	796136	W 835716	849846	W 669296	992458	W 730113	1150630	VINS DE RAISINS FRAIS
11212	WINE OF FRESH GRAPES	W 952573	769344	W 775146	805717	W 626179	952020	W 672979	1092773	VINS DE MOUTS DE RAISINS
2	CRUDE MATERLS,EXCL FUELS		1190042		1522405		2078618		1968767	MAT BRUTES NON COMESTIBLES
251	*PULP AND WASTE PAPER	W 616421	206803	W 749961	319292	W 699525	539042	W 715780	325413	PATES A PAPIER,DECHETS
2517	SODA,SULPHATE WOOD PULP	W 563293	186549	W 688785	286242	W 617524	481520	W 624743	275960	PATES CHIMIQUES AU SULFATE
25172	— BLEACHED,NONDISSOLVNG	W 563269	186541	W 688693	286156	W 617344	481332	W 624743	275960	PATES BLANCHIES
27	CRUDE FERTLZR,MINRLS NES		246803		294432		353643		407701	ENGRAIS MINERAUX BRUTS
28	METALLIFEROUS ORES,SCRAP		194127		202426		259173		301230	MINERAIS METAL,DECHETS
29	CRUDE ANIMAL,VEG MAT NES		218333		274229		370058		346739	MATIERES BRUTES ANIM,VEGET
292	CRUDE VEG MATERIALS NES	W 51047	189538	W 71759	240912	W 80537	327114		293537	MAT BRUTES VEGETALES NDA
3	MINERAL FUELS ETC		1765388		1613813		1595913		2569869	COMBUSTIBLES MINERAUX LUB
33	PETROLEUM AND PRODUCTS		1703928		1566157		1488070		2468564	PETROLE ET DERIVES
334	PETROLEUM PRODUCTS,REFIN	MW 11502	1470306	MW 10036	1308820	W 8241197	1245504	MW 12281	2231606	PRODUITS RAFFINES
3341	GASOLINE,OTH LIGHT OILS	W 2824659	487488	W 2828129	459295					ESSENCES POUR MOTEURS
33411	MOTOR,AVIATION SPIRIT	W 1497115	269739	W 1777560	298479					ESSENCES MOTEURS D'AVIONS
33419	OTH LIGHT PETROLEUM OILS	W 1327544	217749	W 1050569	160816					AUTRES HUILES LEGERES
3343	GAS OILS	W 1541595	251207	W 1471657	209252					GAS OILS
3344	FUEL OILS,NES	W 6049537	482353	W 4816707	415844					FUEL OILS
335	RESIDUAL PETRLM PROD NES	W 1915764	233595	W 1756681	244286	W 1412358	240381	W 1330270	236946	PRODUITS RESIDUELS NDA
4	ANIMAL,VEGETABLE OIL,FAT		721491		932899		966863		1295839	HUILES,GRAISSES ANIM,VEG
42	FIXED VEGETABLE OIL,FAT		696343		899579		924248		1231818	HUILES VEGETALES FIXES
423	FIXED VEG OILS,SOFT		688739		865480	W 537669	887071	W 424501	1190888	HUILES VEGET DOUCES FIXES
4235	OLIVE OIL	W 219468	575595	W 266441	749826	W 175907	638801	W 211519	1059011	HUILE D'OLIVE
5	CHEMCLS,RELATED PROD NES		4619523		5894444		7424793		7841633	PRODUITS CHIMIQUES
51	ORGANIC CHEMICALS		943805		1186740		1374321		1419324	PROD CHIMIQ ORGANIQUES
514	NITROGEN–FNCTN COMPOUNDS	W 25016	149535	W 38575	236830	W 45499	299536	W 52095	352332	COMPOSES FONCT AZOTEES
515	ORG–INORG COMPOUNDS ETC	W 88174	318494	W 84661	337240	W 65610	285471	W 82077	358628	COMPOSES ORGANO–MINERAUX
5156	HETEROCYCLIC CMPDS ETC	W 67343	250176	W 61017	259180	W 40130	195019	W 54217	255623	COMPOSES HETEROCYCLIQUES
51569	OTH HETEROCYC CMPDS,ETC	W 15974	195182	W 19093	214525	W 9361	144322	W 7076	188696	AUT COMP HETEROCYCLIQUES
52	INORGANIC CHEMICALS		307952		350761		491898		477530	PROD CHIM INORGANIQUES
523	OTHR INORG CHEMICALS ETC	W 956538	200977	W 1046322	213453	W 1145349	263821	W 1226634	298033	AUT PRODUITS CHIMIQUES INORG
53	DYES,TANNING,COLOUR PROD		517995		607825		740869		847490	PROD TEINTURE,COLORANTS
533	PIGMENTS,PAINTS,ETC	W 292737	348157	W 419414	432087	W 506438	553282	W 500140	632040	PIGMENTS,PEINTURES,VERNIS
5335	GLAZES,DRIERS,PUTTY ETC	W 213387	197411	W 326712	251280	W 423436	340843	W 391816	376513	PREPTNS COLOR UTILISES CERAM
53351	PREPRD PIGMENT,GLAZE ETC	W 201521	165454	W 309741	211778	W 367916	282553	W 363743	314823	PIGMENTS OPACIFIANTS
541	*MEDICINAL,PHARM PRODUCT		837071	MK 36094	1061177	MK 42608	1164865	MK 53599	1365037	PROD MEDICINAUX PHARMACEUT
5413	ANTIBIOTICS IN BULK	K 3338040	332704	K 3645875	365273	K 4125162	407356	K 5253047	418835	ANTIBIOTIQUES NDA
54131	PENICILLINS AND DERIVTVS	K 2847230	193318	K 3086077	209969	K 3677091	262283	K 3806196	260529	PENICILLINES ET DERIVES
5417	MEDICAMENTS	MK 14856	378495	MK 26100	536237	MK 30963	567707	MK 39032	696027	MEDICAMENTS
54179	— CONTNG OTH SUBSTANCES	MK 12300	295374	MK 21956	423755	MK 25991	419697	MK 35014	526259	MED CONT AUT SUBSTANCES
55	PERFUME,CLEANING ETC PRD		467290		625695		825625		936128	PROD POUR PARFUM,TOILETTE
553	PERFUMERY,COSMETICS,ETC	W 35455	229598	W 50001	292271	W 58201	394767	W 61677	443837	PRODUITS DE PARFUMERIE
554	SOAP,CLEANSING ETC PREPS	W 161816	171953	W 259712	255085	W 300024	335593	W 361635	383663	SAVONS,PRODUITS DETERSIFS
58	PLASTIC MATERIALS ETC		1086816		1429588		2036887		1932820	MAT PLAST ARTIFICIELLES
582	PROD OF CONDENSATION ETC	W 218775	238585	W 299550	311863	W 330324	491562	W 384820	564179	PROD CONDENS,POLYCOND
583	POLYMERIZATION ETC PRODS	W 887228	805582	W 1103927	1068343		1488914	W 1064782	1311098	PROD POLYMERISATION
5831	POLYETHYLENE	W 352921	245387	W 364815	275398		387332	W 333053	318865	POLYETHYLENE
58311	— IN PRIMARY FORMS	W 337524	222863	W 335951	240960	W 334929	335900	W 305256	267820	POLYETHYLENE PRIMAIRES
5839	OTH POLYMRZTION ETC PROD	W 146167	224509	W 220966	303308	W 247744	419132	W 221991	381794	AUT PROD POLYMER COPOLYM
59	CHEMICAL MATERIALS NES		330873		480353		541621		632445	MAT PROD CHIMIQUES NDA
598	MISCEL CHEM PRODUCTS NES	W 219383	235034	W 409806	365257		372250	W 311644	424428	PROD DIV INDUST CHIM NDA
5989	CHEM PRODUCTS,PREPS NES	W 179495	197924	W 212277	227174	W 244959	313154	W 248643	350514	PROD PREP CHIMIQUES NDA
6	BASIC MANUFACTURES		12073375		14295577		17762433		19286646	ART MANUFACTURES
61	LEATHER,DRESSED FUR,ETC		510653		627225		686233		836762	CUIRS,PELLETERIES
611	LEATHER	W 16029	256009	W 16104	310049	W 16938	344205	W 19657	426082	CUIRS,PEAUX PREPARES
613	FUR SKINS TANNED,DRESSED	W 4534	191688	W 4278	234384	W 4117	242269	W 4946	315644	PELLETERIES
62	RUBBER MANUFACTURES NES		1134114		1366962		1676062		1896394	CAOUTCHOUC MANUFACTURE
625	RUBBER TYRES, TUBES ETC	W 276911	894183	W 320077	1060226	W 340439	1234234	W 351710	1387364	PNEUS CAOUTCHOUC VULCANISE
6251	TYRES NEW FOR MOTOR CARS	W 90487	393699	W 103156	443042	W 104847	497013	W 128669	591554	PNEUS POUR VOITURES

5. Special Exports F.O.B. by Commodities according to the S.I.T.C. (Rev. 2) in thousand U.S. Dollars
Exportations Spéciales F.O.B. par Produits d'après la C.T.C.I. (Rév. 2) en milliers de Dollars E.U.

SITC CTCI	COMMODITY	1993		1994		1995		1996		PRODUIT
		WEIGHT POIDS	VALUE VALEUR	WEIGHT POIDS	VALUE VALEUR	WEIGHT POIDS	VALUE VALEUR	WEIGHT POIDS	VALUE VALEUR	
6252	TYRES,NEW,BUS OR LORRY	W 74143	250567	W 89962	309233	W 99698	363456	W 104827	383938	PNEUS POUR AUTOBUS,CAMIONS
6259	OTH TYRES,TYRE CASES,ETC	W 107171	219957	W 122656	272807	W 131002	330921	W 112856	365256	AUTRES PNEUS RECHAPES FLAPS
62599	TYRES NES,TYRE CASES,ETC	W 106144	215796	W 121525	268953	W 130068	327106	W 112156	362321	PNEUS,FLAPS
63	WOOD,CORK MANUFACTRS NES		315064		373206		466092		548197	OUVRAGES LIEGE ET BOIS
64	PAPER,PAPERBOARD AND MFR		883177		1091100		1530808		1464795	PAPIERS,CARTONS & OUVRAGES
641	PAPER AND PAPERBOARD	W 942027	637199	W 1054458	776764	W 1095197	1120131		1012736	PAPIERS ET CARTONS
6418	COATED ETC PAPER NES BLK	W 186929	181861	W 234006	215160	W 226075	326202	W 150272	254150	PAP,CARTONS COUCHES,ENDUITS
642	PAPER,ETC,PRECUT,ARTS OF	W 144924	245979	W 182653	314336	W 198050	410678	W 231174	452059	PAP,CARTONS DECOUPES
65	TEXTILE YARN,FABRICS,ETC		1587259		1962251		2616668		2917982	FILS,TISSUS,ARTICLES TEXTILE
651	TEXTILE YARN	W 137204	482133	W 167013	623648		786768	W 167691	792929	FILS TEXTILES
652	COTTON FABRICS,WOVEN	W 34263	221826	W 37658	264389	W 42364	337582	W 46390	389657	TISSUS DE COTON
6522	WOVEN COTTON BLEACHD,ETC	W 29982	202659	W 31035	238208	W 36933	307416	W 43882	371661	TISSUS COTON BLANCHIS ETC
653	WOVN MAN–MADE FIB FABRIC	W 22641	266275	W 29239	340372	W 36683	501805	W 39070	579258	TISSUS FIBRES SYNTH,ARTIF
657	SPECIAL TXTL FABRC,PRODS	W 33780	182104		226048		325623		383821	TISSUS SPECIAUX
66	NONMETAL MINERAL MFS NES		2103330		2601687		3161239		3451320	ART MIN NON METALLIQUES
661	LIME,CEMENT,BLDG PRODS	W 4243576	462903	W 5719876	589158	W 5772719	735340	W 7134482	835752	CHAUX,CIMENTS MAT CONSTR
6613	BUILDING STONE ETC WORKD	W 628453	327894	W 746707	404318	W 811877	525124	W 834183	567762	PIERRES A BATIR
662	CLAY,REFRACTORY BLDG PRD	W 2146326	936000	W 2951531	1192841	W 3092252	1426488	W 3360694	1528420	MAT CONST REFRACTAIRES
6624	BRICKS ETC NONREFRACTORY	W 2056558	881172	W 2822366	1129025	W 2938827	1349134	W 3241056	1459589	BRIQUES ETC CERAM NON REFR
66245	GLAZED CERAMIC SETTS ETC	W 1905537	843427	W 2638670	1076477	W 2773399	1295883	W 3058601	1403259	AUT CARREAUX CERAMIQUE
663	MINERAL MANUFCTURES NES	W 241405	213611	W 343379	199959	W 410918	271103	W 409528	299669	ART MIN MANUF NDA
664	GLASS	W 145889	211328	W 248966	274706	W 244275	339016	W 299042	384478	VERRE
665	GLASSWARE	W 208856	169215	W 273931	222043	W 194981	254046	W 209286	265009	OUVRAGES EN VERRE
67	IRON AND STEEL		2836005		3258364		3853218		3784725	FER ET ACIER
672	IRON,STEEL PRIMARY FORMS	W 755361	275825	W 595774	321927	W 391326	413024	W 500953	407022	LINGOTS FER,ACIER
6727	IRN,STL COIL FR REROLLNG	W 528925	223058	W 486508	268782	W 294669	269624	W 255030	233892	EBAUCHES POUR TOLES FER
673	IRON,STEEL SHAPES ETC	W 2909543	983779	W 3006249	1077376	W 2652753	1266903	W 2750996	1152186	BARRES,PROFIL FER,ACIER
6731	IRON,STEEL WIRE ROD	W 594379	191123	W 535836	176676	W 464840	196281	W 537587	202162	FIL MACHINE FER,ACIER
6732	IRON,STEEL BARS ETC	W 1389697	493241	W 1587000	594773	W 1278500	699512	W 1290348	606162	BARRES FER,ACIER
67326	IRN,OTH STL BARS HOTROLD	W 1180577	325787	W 1321283	382763	W 946636	325145	W 993568	300693	BARRES PLEINES FER,ACIER
6733	IRON,STEEL PROFILES ETC	W 925466	299415	W 883413	305928	W 909413	371110	W 923062	343862	PROFILES,PALPLAN FER,ACIER
67332	LARGE U,I,H SECTIONS ETC	W 742691	226613	W 678457	226457	W 738727	285619	W 739864	258327	PROFILES PLUS 80MM
674	IRN,STL UNIV,PLATE,SHEET	W 1539335	994501	W 1713135	1164277	W 1427295	1328556	W 1623683	1328242	LARGES PLATS,TOLES
6746	IRN,STL THIN PLATE,ROLLD	W 535962	408878	W 647475	508760	W 483061	592396	W 488310	519491	TOLES LAM MOINS 3MM
67463	— OF STAINLESS ETC STL	W 171292	251534	W 200698	313585	W 175295	420930	W 200764	368500	TOL ACIER INOX MOINS 3 MM
6749	OTH IRN,STL PLATES,SHEET	W 354527	207122	W 490486	294763	W 396999	295180	W 459659	308879	AUTRES TOLES FER,ACIER
67491	— OF IRON OR SIMPLE STL	W 339914	183878	W 475458	271776	W 386640	271104	W 443930	280142	AUT TOLES AUTRES ACIER FIN
678	IRON,STL TUBES,PIPES,ETC	W 351884	409238	W 471091	433305	W 425908	543604	W 459966	596304	TUBES,TUYAUX EN FONTE,FER
6782	IRON,STL SEAMLESS TUBES	W 163659	202296	W 156481	165418	W 167264	255430	W 196665	316388	TUBES,TUYAUX SANS SOUDURE
68	NON–FERROUS METALS		1067014		1221119		1502625		1651497	METAUX NON FERREUX
682	COPPER EXC CEMENT COPPER	W 142118	328983	W 152307	380455	W 137250	452890	W 221203	587036	CUIVRE
6822	COPPER,ALLOYS WORKED	W 58428	184434	W 79599	234086	W 90230	344420	W 104366	336014	CUIVRE,ALLIAGES OUVRES
684	ALUMINIUM	W 333094	446817	W 472777	594159	W 283038	789568	W 317377	805387	ALUMINIUM
6841	ALUMINIUM,ALLOYS,UNWRGHT	W 167767	215357	W 146090	225476	W 119714	250444	W 137279	240266	ALUMINIUM,ALLIAGES BRUTS
6842	ALUMINIUM,ALLOYS WORKED	W 165327	231460	W 326687	368683	W 163323	539124	W 180098	565121	ALUMINIUM,ALLIAGES OUVRE
69	METAL MANUFACTURES NES		1636758		1793662		2269487		2734973	ART MANUFACT EN METAL NDA
691	STRUCTURES AND PARTS NES	W 84622	257175	W 101990	140995	W 105362	187969	W 141844	250129	CONSTRUCT FER,ACIER,ALU
6911	STRUCTURES,PARTS IRN,STL	W 82305	240041	W 98784	123590	W 100114	166080	W 137877	223972	CONSTRUCT FER,ACIER,FONTE
695	TOOLS	W 18538	234015	W 20557	302622	W 25372	328765	W 32218	413209	OUTILS A MAIN
697	BASE MTL HOUSEHOLD EQUIP	W 42127	199088	W 49798	216881	W 55738	274805	W 64795	321053	ART MENAGE MET COMMUNS
699	BASE METAL MFRS NES	W 123816	546020	W 170703	671247	W 185853	873760		1022418	ART MANUFACTURES MET NDA
6991	LOCKSMITHS WARES,ETC	W 23490	178996	W 29976	222560	W 35269	301554	W 48397	369080	ARTICLES DE SERRURERIE
7	MACHINES,TRANSPORT EQUIP		25356855		30806575		37969560		43035052	MACHINES MATERIEL TRANSPORT
71	POWER GENERATING EQUIPMT		1163939		1435356		1778792		2406418	MACHINES GENERATRICES
713	INTRNL COMBUS PSTN ENGIN	W 124862	749018	W 115422	931693	W 128877	1232194	W 188800	1806904	MOTEURS EXPL COMB INT, PIECE
7132	MOTOR VEHCL PISTN ENGINS	W 50742	445989	W 60981	630945	W 72371	881668	W 97033	1342511	MOTEURS EXPL POUR VEHICULES
7139	PISTON ENGINE PARTS NES	W 68479	228923	W 51598	269435	W 53542	308510	W 86491	410166	PIECES POUR 713.2,3,8
716	ROTATING ELECTRIC PLANT	W 21765	186095	W 35980	260585	W 30548	300163	W 27468	240412	APP ELECTR ROTATIFS,PIECES
72	MACHS FOR SPCL INDUSTRYS		975086		1085428		1334053		1536677	MAC SPECIALES POUR INDUST
724	TEXTILE,LEATHER MACHNRY	W 19750	207883	W 21618	224970	W 22945	275365		271571	MACH POUR INDUSTRIE TEXTILE
728	OTH MACHY FOR SPCL INDUS	W 37445	360584	W 42986	393290	W 58952	491798	W 56450	551059	AUT MACH IND PARTICULIERES
7284	MACHY FOR SPCL INDUS NES	W 15841	202019	W 16069	209498	W 20064	264713	W 21265	309127	MACH SPEC IND PARTICUL.
73	METALWORKING MACHINERY		418288		504227		655591		781926	MACH TRAVAIL DES METAUX
736	METALWORKING MACH–TOOLS	W 29039	286198	W 37226	313906	W 46590	455255	W 55436	606567	MACH–OUTILS TRAVAIL METAUX
74	GENRL INDUSTRL MACHY NES		2242216		2445526		3054496		3575693	MACH APP INDUSTRIE
741	HEATING,COOLING EQUIPMNT	W 47592	380337	W 51193	427987	W 60996	510279	W 77236	639816	MACH CHAUFFAGE,PIECES
742	PUMPS FOR LIQUIDS ETC	W 15524	168361	W 20258	223458	W 23910	272269	W 22059	359897	POMPES MOTO–POMPES
743	PUMPS NES,CENTRFUGES ETC	W 43195	305123	W 55704	389705	W 62371	479465	W 61554	492393	POMPES COMPRES,VENT ETC
744	MECHANICAL HANDLING EQU	W 63755	362593	W 77212	388465	W 92079	521976	W 100371	591609	EQUIP MANUTENTION PIECES
7442	LIFTING,LOADING MACH NES	W 30158	186984	W 40021	206197	W 45169	264135	W 49479	296887	APP LEVAGE,MANUTENTION
745	NONELEC MACHY,TOOLS NES	W 16539	232322	W 18303	265249	W 20044	342739	W 23465	406141	AUT MACH NON ELEC,PIECES
7452	OTH NONELEC MCHS,PTS NES	W 16286	227372	W 17879	260009	W 19687	336944	W 23103	399068	AUT MACH NON ELEC,PIECES
749	NONELEC MACH PTS,ACC NES	W 65605	793479	W 70408	750662	W 84812	927766	W 99949	1085837	PIECES MACH NON ELEC NDA
7492	COCKS,VALVES ETC NES	W 32262	477521	W 26857	324270	W 35676	427728	W 40715	491974	ART ROB,SIM POUR TUYAUX
75	OFFICE MACHNES,ADP EQUIP		1025986		1215124		1472249		1612033	MACH BUREAU TRAIT AUTOM
752	AUTOMTIC DATA PROC EQUIP	W 11508	661443	W 13719	838110	W 20072	1163146	W 22275	1247783	MACH TRAIT INFORMATION
7523	DIGITL CENTRL PROCESSORS	W 857	221958	W 478	88753	W 361	37436	W 750	77874	UNITES CENTRALES
7525	ADP PERIPHERAL UNITS	W 3861	217059	W 11045	539757	W 15574	775437	W 19080	901465	UNITES PERIPHERIQUES
759	OFFICE,ADP MCH PTS,ACCES	W 2752	323397	W 2503	299420	W 3111	226708	W 3945	288382	PIECES DU 751 ET 752
7599	ACCTG,ETC,ADP MCH PTS,AC	W 2206	308107	W 2153	285023	W 2588	208585	W 3072	268341	PIECES DU 751 ET 752
76	TELECOMM,SOUND EQUIPMENT		1260304		1518597		1996358		2029165	EQUIPMENT DE TELECOM
761	TELEVISION RECEIVERS	W 27961	414584	W 37008	473686	W 53501	708666	W 66179	830139	RECEPTEURS DE TELEVISION
7611	COLOUR TV RECEIVERS	W 27916	413650	W 36882	470934	W 53248	702833	W 65879	824170	RECEPTEURS COULEUR
764	TELECOM EQPT,PTS,ACC NES	W 19500	736096	W 24194	920854	W 29265	1133480	W 31099	1042014	EQUIP TELECOM,PIECES
7641	LINE TELEPHONE,ETC EQUIP	W 2822	276429	W 4627	363874	W 6943	568915	W 4703	308328	APP TELEPHON PAR FIL
7649	PTS NES OF EQUIPMT OF 76	W 8021	332757	W 8966	421392	W 9417	438202	W 11541	554878	PIECES DE LA DIV 76
76491	PTS NES OF APPAR OF 7641	W 3291	214316	W 4313	299893	W 3683	280291	W 5002	423458	PIECES POUR 764.1
77	ELECTRIC MACHNRY NES ETC		2651515		3342915		4097355		4639069	MACH APP ELECT NDA
772	SWITCHGEAR ETC,PARTS NES	W 19845	451429	W 29075	568902	W 36586	719781	W 41672	819157	APP COUPURE,SECT ETC
7721	SWITCHGEAR ETC	W 18308	373303	W 27386	478479	W 34849	602750	W 39659	666277	APP COUPURE,SECTIONMNT
773	ELECTR DISTRIBUTNG EQUIP	W 76883	482360	W 85608	616853	W 100374	766201	W 100562	753587	EQUIPMT DISTRIBUTION ELECT
7731	INSULATED WIRE,CABLE ETC	W 71868	434516	W 79186	560674	W 94062	694860	W 92762	681586	FILS,CABLES ISOLES ELECT
775	HOUSEHOLD TYPE EQUIP NES	W 112026	606859	W 132320	738456	W 145674	914954	W 192610	1093749	MACH,APP USAGE DOMESTQUE
7758	ELECTRO–THERMIC APPL NES	W 24702	168330	W 26860	206021	W 28437	249165	W 38976	313283	APP ELECTROTHERMIQ NDA
776	TRANSISTORS,VALVES,ETC	W 3073	180720	W 7595	263552	W 9712	297905	W 8935	298873	LAMPES,TUBES,VALVES
778	ELECTRICAL MACHINERY NES	W 121601	738587	W 151706	897694	W 186052	1138645	W 212295	1298477	AUTRES MACH ELECT NDA
7783	AUTOMOTIVE ELECTR EQUIP	W 26123	329584	W 37350	425804	W 42141	551521	W 44982	652672	EQUIP ELECT MOTEURS EXPL
77831	IGNITION,STARTING EQUIP	W 13249	179273	W 18341	211520	W 18330	277877	W 16436	319692	APP ELEC ALLUM,DEMARRAGE
77832	ELECT VEHICLE LGHTNG EQU	W 12874	150311	W 19008	214284	W 23811	273644	W 28546	332979	APP ELEC ECLAIR,SIGNAL AUTO
7788	OTH ELEC MACHY,EQUIP NES	W 32334	204142	W 31445	222007	W 49994	275418	W 53120	303580	AUT MACH APP ELEC NDA
78	ROAD VEHICLES		13330298		17075647		21534749		23722146	VEHICULES ROUTIERS

5. Special Exports F.O.B. by Commodities according to the S.I.T.C. (Rev. 2) in thousand U.S. Dollars
Exportations Spéciales F.O.B. par Produits d'après la C.T.C.I. (Rév. 2) en milliers de Dollars E.U.

SITC CTCI	COMMODITY	1993		1994		1995		1996		PRODUIT
		WEIGHT POIDS	VALUE VALEUR	WEIGHT POIDS	VALUE VALEUR	WEIGHT POIDS	VALUE VALEUR	WEIGHT POIDS	VALUE VALEUR	
781	PASS MOTOR VEH EXC BUSES	W 1153019	9883098	W 1394973	12296541	W 1551532	15097504	W 1683436	15937146	AUTO TRANSPORT PERSONNES
782	LORRIES,SPCL MTR VEH NES	W 112575	723351	W 165619	1149975	W 191907	1365130	W 266854	2132783	VEHICULES SPECIAUX,MARCH
7821	LORRIES,TRUCKS	W 108079	696762	W 160891	1114207	W 188990	1336931	W 263280	2080618	VEHICULES TRANSP MARCHAND
783	ROAD MOTOR VEHICLES NES	W 19528	199776	W 37886	345401	W 128937	533526	W 50097	447721	VEHICULES ROUTIERS NDA
7832	TRACTORS FOR TR–TRAILERS	W 13872	137216	W 30977	270566	W 120127	448284	W 40393	338887	TRACTEURS ROUTIERS
784	MOTOR VEH PRTS,ACCES NES	W 549598	2284558	W 720552	3011750	W 843210	4186055	W 911406	4796189	PIECES 722,781,782,783
7849	OTHER MOTOR VEHCL PARTS	W 522393	2254282	W 707717	2972915	W 836365	4131741	W 902372	4747049	PIECES 722,781,782,783
785	CYCLES,ETC MOTRZD OR NOT	W 13493	203267	W 14634	219743	W 17919	263970	W 19012	300848	MOTOCYCLES SCOOTERS
79	OTHR TRANSPORT EQUIPMENT		2289223		2183756		2045918		2731925	AUTRE MATERIEL TRANSPORT
791	RAILWAY VEHICLES	W 28440	63698	W 48571	246228	W 16021	143086	W 64397	225224	VEHIC MAT CHEMINS DE FER
792	AIRCRAFT ETC	W 2674	1104462	W 3169	1354823		1037785	W 2907	1235150	APP NAVIGATION AERIENNE
7923	AIRCRFT NES2000–15000KG	W 137	153297	W 397	349843	W 187	202425	W 259	181846	AERODYNES 2000 A 15000 KG
7924	AIRCRFT NES OVER 15000KG	W 995	442456	W 1291	507651	W 527	318840	W 1109	485749	AERODYNES PLUS 15000 KG
7929	AIRCRAFT PARTS NES	W 1484	506992	W 1447	490493	W 1448	507473	W 1490	555610	PIECES DU 792
793	SHIPS AND BOATS ETC	W 645309	1121062	W 381519	582705	W 375450	865046	W 335626	1271552	NAVIRES BATEAUX,ETC
7932	SHIPS AND BOATS NES	W 569292	822921	W 373060	556715	W 299535	802207	W 261441	689018	NAVIRES ET BATEAUX
79322	TANKERS OF ALL KINDS	W 284508	393460	W 24399	25517	W 102802	259621	W 138221	164015	BATEAUX–CITERNES
79323	OTHER CARGO VESSELS	W 223282	214906	W 305661	344818	W 166260	215954	W 96662	224354	AUT BATEAUX TRANS MARCH
79324	FISHING VESSELS ETC	W 44591	197277	W 28924	131654	W 22761	78251	W 19601	83297	BATEAUX DE PECHE
7938	TUGS,SPECIAL VESSELS ETC	W 75894	293193	W 6484	10481	W 26244	52900	W 71696	564177	REMORQUEURS,BATEAUX SPEC
79382	SPECL PURPOSE VESSLS ETC	W 75435	282466	W 6105	9201	W 24224	38158	W 69670	545834	BAT–PHARES,–POMPES,DRAGUES
8	MISC MANUFACTURED GOODS		5405767		6681069		8125889		9660897	ART MANUFACTURES DIVERS
812	*PLUMBG,HEATNG,LGHTNG EQ	W 53573	262465	W 73108	331729	W 81373	447255	W 88956	495471	APPAR SANITAIRES CHAUFFAGE
8124	LIGHTING EQUIPMENT NES	W 16425	188599	W 23946	235008	W 30432	327149	W 31989	354439	APPAREILS ECLAIRAGE ETC
821	*FURNITURE,PARTS THEREOF	W 127838	552528	W 184671	728586	W 200001	1037856	W 259736	1268543	MEUBLES ET PIECES
8211	CHAIRS,SEATS AND PARTS	W 39488	165529	W 45947	217459	W 42622	327442	W 52425	378189	SIEGES ET PIECES
8219	FURNITURE AND PARTS NES	W 84568	351753	W 132994	464406	W 152273	651965	W 200610	824369	AUTRES MEUBLES ET PIECES
82192	WOOD FURNITURE NES	W 43552	218080	W 78290	300380	W 89755	431878	W 121567	556995	MEUBLES NDA EN BOIS
84	CLOTHING AND ACCESSORIES		697387		835060		1115258		1369422	VETEMENTS
842	MENS OUTERWEAR NOT KNIT	W 3704	140734	W 3699	163491	W 5530	231151	W 7401	303198	VET DESSUS POUR HOMMES
845	OUTERWEAR KNIT NONELASTC	W 5893	160537	W 6242	188680	W 6583	239970	W 8656	304449	VET DESSOUS,ACCES BONNET
851	*FOOTWEAR	W 59417	1214630	W 87192	1649126	W 81539	1871003	W 90341	1999676	CHAUSSURES
85102	FOOTWEAR LEATHER	W 55242	1145910	W 80377	1548852	W 73619	1741462	W 80943	1857097	CHAUS SEMELLES EN CUIR
87	PRECISION INSTRUMNTS NES		539001		626062		670996		805693	INSTRUM,APPAR SCIENT NDA
874	MEASURNG,CONTROLNG INSTR		412148	W 10593	480889	W 7825	496058	W 8942	585349	INSTRUMENTS DE MESURE
8743	GAS,LIQUID CONTROL INSTR	W 3101	221837	W 3855	263167	W 3699	255891	W 3929	300169	APP,INSTR MESURE FLUIDES
88	PHOTO EQU,OPTICL GDS ETC		204907		237969		262853		299212	APP,FOURN PHOTO,OP,MONTR
89	MISC MANUFCTRD GOODS NES		1858912		2161801		2573913		3254299	ART MANUFACTURES DIVERS
892	PRINTED MATTER	W 126786	613375	W 165643	693524	W 181469	824960	W 215338	891119	IMPRIMES
8921	PRINTED BOOKS,GLOBES,ETC	W 71866	377031	W 100597	466800	W 102907	525512	W 125075	575872	LIVRES,BROCHURES,CARTES
89211	PRINTED BOOKS,PAMPHLETS	W 71384	374443	W 99397	461942	W 101839	513725	W 124053	568049	LIVRES,BROCHURES
893	ARTICLES OF PLASTIC NES		403692		506705		727284		949784	OUVRAGES EN MAT DIVIS 58
8939	MISC PLASTIC ARTICLES	W 56034	276327	W 71868	334245	W 98307	467119	W 110285	633466	ART DIVERS EN MAT DIV 58
89399	OTHR PLASTC ARTICLES NES	W 53805	268373	W 69253	325015	W 94995	452275	W 106927	616107	AUT OUV MAT DIV 58
894	TOYS,SPORTING GOODS,ETC	W 43851	405570	W 51063	411933	W 47186	416293	W 69075	610916	VOITURES ENFANTS,JOUETS
8942	TOYS,INDOOR GAMES ETC	W 32196	289307	W 37477	302070	W 31096	302965	W 48219	459726	JOUETS,JEUX ETC
9	GOODS NOT CLASSD BY KIND		878076		806788		852303		819818	ART TRANSACT NON CLASSES
931	*SPECIAL TRANSACTIONS	W 1122343	750756	W 1151863	588852	W 1071192	624518	W 2255278	609504	TRANS.SPECIALES

FOOT NOTES – NOTES

TABLE 1 –

1 Values are in thousand million pesetas.

TABLEAU 1 –

1 Les évaluations sont exprimées en milliards de pesetas.

1. HISTORICAL SERIES, 1961–1996 GENERAL TRADE, IMPORTS C.I.F., EXPORTS F.O.B.
SERIES HISTORIQUES, 1961–1996 COMMERCE GENERAL, IMPORTATIONS C.A.F., EXPORTATIONS F.O.B

YEAR ANNEE	VALUE IN MILLION SRI LANKA RUPEES VALEUR EN MILLION SRI LANKA RUPEES MERCHANDISE –MARCHANDISE		GOLD –OR		CONVERSION FACTORS U.S. CENTS PER SRI LANKA RUPEE FACTEURS DE CONVERSION CENTS E.U. PAR SRI LANKA RUPEE		INDEX NUMBERS –INDICES QUANTUM		UNIT VALUE VALEUR UNITAIRE	
	IMPORTS	EXPORTS	IMPORTS	EXPORTS	IMPORTS	EXPORTS	IMPORTS	EXPORTS	IMPORTS	EXPORTS
1961	1703.00	1733.00	1.90		21.0000	21.0000	71	61	12	28
1962	1660.00	1808.00	1.90		21.0000	21.0000	72	66	11	27
1963	1490.00	1731.00	1.90		21.0000	21.0000	62	63	12	27
1964	1975.00	1876.00	2.30		21.0000	21.0000	76	70	15	28
1965	1474.00	1949.00	1.90		21.0000	21.0000	57	72	14	28
1966	2028.00	1700.00	2.20		21.0000	21.0000	78	65	14	27
1967	1738.00	1690.00			20.7030	20.6040	15	72	2	4
1968	2173.00	2035.00			16.8010	16.8010	51	74	2	5
1969	2543.00	1916.00			16.8010	16.8010	54	70	2	5
1970	2313.00	2033.00			16.8010	16.8010	51	73	2	5
1971	1986.00	1947.00			16.8024	16.8024	45	71	2	5
1972	2064.00	2009.00			17.0176	16.8119	44	69	2	5
1973	2715.00	2617.00			15.5567	15.6169	40	70	3	6
1974	4554.00	3472.00			15.1098	15.0752	28	61	6	9
1975	5251.00	3933.00			14.3028	14.2154	35	73	7	9
1976	4689.00	4815.00			11.7836	11.7702	38	69	6	10
1977	6007.00	6638.00			11.7093	11.4932	49	64	7	16
1978	14663.00	13206.00			6.4034	6.4056	67	68	14	30
1979	22560.00	15273.00			6.4205	6.4202	48	64		
1980	33637.00	17273.00			6.0511	6.0311	56	68		
1981	35530.20	20199.10			5.2052	5.1702	97	69	39	38
1982	36875.40	21124.20			4.8040	4.8029	97	73	40	38
1983	42020.10	25182.70			4.2518	4.2330	106	68	42	48
1984	46913.30	37005.70			3.9335	3.9282	110	81	44	62
1985	49068.00	35035.00			3.6331	3.6398	105	83	48	55
1986	51281.50	34092.30			3.5666	3.5656	120	89	44	48
1987	59749.70	39860.59			3.3930	3.3826	106	87	53	60
1988	70320.40	47092.00			3.1436	3.1445	101	84	66	70
1989	75352.75	55511.17			2.7710	2.7545	95	86	79	83
1990	107729.00	76624.00			2.4961	2.4961	100	100	100	100
1991	126643.00	82225.01			2.4178	2.4178	114	104	104	102
1992	153555.00	107855.00			2.2826	2.2826	132	108	109	128
1993	193550.00	138175.00			2.0631	2.0631	154	124	115	140
1994	235576.00	158554.00			2.0237	2.0237	173	136	121	147
1995	272200.90	195117.00			1.9495	1.9464	178	145	140	169
1996	299424.00	226801.00			1.8074	1.8056	182	151	153	189

2. IMPORTS BY BROAD ECONOMIC CATEGORY AND EXPORTS BY INDUSTRIAL ORIGIN. (PERCENTAGE OF TOTAL VALUE)
IMPORTATIONS PAR CATEGORIES ECONOMIQUES ET EXPORTATIONS PAR BRANCHE D'ACTIVITE.(EN POURCENTAGE DE LA VALEUR TOTALE)

IMPORTS – IMPORTATIONS

	1990	1991	1992	1993	1994	1995	1996
TOTAL IMPORTS–IMPORTATIONS TOTALES	100.	100.	100.	100.	100.		
1 FOOD BEV–ALIMENTATION BOISSONS	18.0	16.0	14.7	12.2	14.1		
11 PRIMARY–PRODUITS DE BASE	6.3	6.6	5.4	3.1	5.9		
111 FOR INDUSTRY–POUR L'INDUSTRIE	3.4	2.7	2.0	0.2	2.9		
112 FOR HOUSEHOLDS–POUR LES MENAGES	2.9	3.8	3.4	2.8	2.9		
12 PROCESSED–PRODUITS ELABORES	11.7	9.4	9.3	9.2	8.2		
121 FOR INDUSTRY–POUR L'INDUSTRIE	6.2	4.7	4.1	4.8	4.8		
122 FOR HOUSEHOLDS–POUR LES MENAGES	5.5	4.7	5.2	4.3	3.4		
2 IND SUPPLIES–APPROV INDUSTRIELS	44.7	47.6	48.1	50.5	50.0		
21 PRIMARY–PRODUITS DE BASE	5.1	4.7	4.8	5.9	5.3		
22 PROCESSED–PRODUITS ELABORES	39.6	43.0	43.3	44.6	44.7		
3 FUELS–COMBUSTIBLES	12.6	10.9	8.8	7.7	6.2		
31 PRIMARY–PRODUITS DE BASE	10.9	8.6	4.9	5.8	5.0		
32 PROCESSED–PRODUITS ELABORES	1.7	2.3	3.9	1.9	1.2		
321 MOTOR SPIRIT–ESSENCE							
322 OTHER–AUTRES	1.7	2.3	3.9	1.9	1.2		
4 MACHINERY–EQUIPEMENT	10.7	10.0	12.6	12.4	12.6		
41 CAPITAL EQUIPMENT–MACHINES	9.2	8.5	10.9	10.9	10.9		
42 PARTS–PIECES ACCESSOIRES	1.5	1.5	1.7	1.6	1.6		
5 TRANSPORT–TRANSPORT	8.3	9.3	8.3	9.7	9.9		
51 PASSENGER CARS–AUTOMOBILES	1.3	0.7	1.0	1.0	1.9		
52 OTHER–AUTRES	4.4	5.6	4.7	4.6	4.1		
521 INDUSTRIAL–INDUSTRIELS	3.0	4.6	4.1	4.0	3.4		
522 NON INDUSTRIAL–NON INDUSTRIEL	1.4	1.0	0.6	0.6	0.6		
53 PARTS–PIECES ACCESSOIRES	2.7	3.0	2.6	4.0	3.9		
6 CONSUM GOODS–BIENS CONSOMMATION	5.5	6.0	7.3	7.2	7.0		
61 DURABLE–DURABLES	1.4	1.8	2.5	2.4	2.0		
62 SEMI DURABLE–SEMI DURABLES	1.7	2.2	2.3	2.6	2.6		
63 NON DURABLE–NON DURABLES	2.3	2.0	2.5	2.1	2.5		
7 GOODS NES–BIENS NDA	0.3	0.2	0.2	0.3	0.2		

EXPORTS – EXPORTATIONS

	1990	1991	1992	1993	1994	1995	1996
TOTAL EXPORTS–EXPORTATIONS TOTALES	100.	100.	100.	100.	100.		
1 AGRICULTURE	38.5	33.1	25.5	24.1	23.1		
2 MINING QUARRY–INDUS EXTRACTIVES	9.4	6.6	7.0	7.7	7.3		
3 MANUFACTURING–IND MANUFACTUR	52.1	60.3	67.5	68.2	69.6		
31 FOOD BEV TOBACCO–ALIM BOISS TAB	1.2	1.1	1.0	1.2	1.6		
32 TEXTILES–INDUSTRIES TEXTILES	35.5	43.7	52.6	52.6	52.6		
33 WOOD & PRODUCTS–BOIS & PRODUITS	0.6	1.0	0.6	0.6	0.7		
34 PAPER & PRODUCTS–PAPIER & PRODT	0.1	0.3	0.3	0.5	0.5		
35 CHEMICALS–INDUSTRIES CHIMIQUES	4.4	4.1	3.5	3.9	4.0		
36 NON METAL MIN–MIN NON METAL	0.8	1.2	1.2	1.2	1.3		
37 BASIC METAL–IND METAL BASE	0.1	0.1	0.1	0.1	0.1		
38 METAL MANUF–MANUF METAL	4.6	4.6	3.1	3.2	3.6		
39 OTH MANUF IND–AUTRES MANUF	4.9	4.3	5.0	4.9	5.2		

3. TRADE BY PRINCIPAL COUNTRIES OF PRODUCTION AND LAST CONSIGNMENT (VALUE IN THOUSAND U.S. DOLLARS)
ECHANGES SELON LES PRINCIPAUX PAYS DE PRODUCTION ET DE DERNIERE CONSIGNATION (VALEUR EN MILLIERS DE DOLLARS EU)

COUNTRIES–PAYS	GENERAL IMPORTS C.I.F. IMPORTATIONS GENERALES C.A.F					COUNTRIES–PAYS	GENERAL EXPORTS F.O.B. EXPORTATIONS GENERALES F.O.B.				
	1990	1991	1992	1993	1994		1990	1991	1992	1993	1994
World	2634129	3089699	3419249	3742919	4483360	Monde	1912604	1987230	2453990	2846947	3209669
Africa	116801	116672	78001	75105	84386	Afrique	104622	83775	68893	65370	88318
Americas	251435	215454	219653	168563	391107	Amériques	560359	629209	921047	1084778	1208024
Northern America	226683	190489	180671	145685	298470	Amérique du Nord	521584	590995	876796	1039961	1165729
LAIA	8398	24808	38084	17675	73913	ALAI	30587	35947	39631	38136	38061
CACM	11831	5	4	31	17078	MCAC	861	1031	1561	2075	1760
Caribbean	4523	61	871	661	1465	Caraïbes	6920	616	409	1153	482
Rest of America	1	91	23	4511	179	Autre Amérique	407	619	2650	3454	1993
As.ex F.USSR	1720541	2140912	2394688	2635170	2960471	Asie l'URSS exclus	549101	582911	508684	601517	711962
Eur.x F.USSR	467983	542902	618943	750838	898410	Europe l'URSS exclus	552388	594960	865518	951446	1069564
EU	410879	483086	537842	656057	804016	UE	505910	564197	825842	906783	1023175
EFTA	22575	28130	36098	40820	68149	AELE	17098	16714	18204	23428	24906
East Europe	24160	29407	43638	53700	24826	Europe de l'Est	22946	9554	18297	17458	19961
Other Europe	10370	2278	107	66	303	Autre de l'Europe	6433	4496	736	2112	184
Former USSR	3488	3668	19789	10371	7984	Ancienne URSS	40491	11547	8820	50376	37410
Oceania	73182	69151	87210	101953	140234	Océanie	30726	29062	30461	33760	34485
Japan/Japon	325367	357856	415764	451150	526517	USA/Etats–Unis d'Amer	492564	558972	837982	1003776	1114964
India/Inde	118082	220089	301993	341843	404375	Germany/Allemagne	126664	148850	211922	226862	222408
Hong Kong	120250	212711	241059	311479	316532	United Kingdom	115134	126208	170289	202920	285324
Korea, Republic of	127856	219088	209588	260806	326234	Belgium–Luxembourg	96897	78866	134964	176290	189063
USA/Etats–Unis d'Amer	207725	174539	159434	130871	284686	Japan/Japon	102396	101580	128076	147504	165209
United Kingdom	146027	167269	174236	186045	249575	Netherlands/Pays–Bas	48583	59042	97755	107288	112111
Singapore/Singapour	102498	134975	237743	207328	234000	France, Monac	43677	63517	90142	85862	85696
Malaysia/Malaisie	114356	139884	127763	171092	181172	Singapore/Singapour	49475	67493	33267	48543	76393
Iran (Islamic Rp. of)	222259	144775	117073	95770	90907	Iran (Islamic Rp. of)	64724	78034	48310	20209	16778
China/Chine	121229	101473	121030	149465	156442	United Arab Emirates	27845	36687	27629	66192	62375
Germany/Allemagne	83895	101948	127422	137934	169768	Italy/Italie	36589	37149	47350	42377	56132
Thailand/Thaïlande	85149	99082	96932	108853	122578	Egypt/Egypte	59098	36421	35046	25617	32145
Belgium–Luxembourg	56692	53957	77780	116456	127114	Canada	29017	32007	38803	36163	50749
So. Africa Customs Un	83430	87703	71376	48642	52094	Saudi Arabia	42255	38385	36586	29339	39610
Indonesia/Indonésie	39422	41110	65226	85820	84476	Jordan/Jordanie	16414	56263	31097	41403	39768
Pakistan	50817	73744	66005	55094	60693	Pakistan	32470	31987	28570	35348	43370
Australia/Australie	43422	36579	50920	59601	91755	Syrian Arab Republic	31219	16675	21965	31399	37068
Netherlands/Pays–Bas	19841	48071	42653	55077	70835	Australia/Australie	24237	24454	24080	27153	28062
France, Monac	42411	34842	43288	50379	55229	Hong Kong	17097	14868	24251	32039	35646
United Arab Emirates	14951	41367	25395	50456	72696	Korea, Republic of	5061	11253	27693	26697	38899
New Zealand	29488	32274	36035	42021	48163	Thailand/Thaïlande	21657	14011	17269	21472	31121
Switz.Liecht	18198	25901	32391	36493	60287	Russian Federation			8820	48227	35849
Italy/Italie	18932	19271	26076	43488	47833	Mexico/Mexique	18088	20274	19785	18254	14970
Romania/Roumanie	11546	18331	31596	43581	8012	Libyan Arab Jamahiriya	22809	28106	11194	15419	12791
Sweden/Suède	15852	19716	20651	24317	24338	India/Inde	20609	12627	11491	19701	23663
Turkey/Turquie	19038	23879	9230	18424	31113	Sweden/Suède	9962	13668	19424	16349	19179
Viet Nam	11878	28127	34979	16680	2558	Switz.Liecht	13936	12080	12715	17150	20226
Saudi Arabia	32750	9444	16052	11275	23369	Spain/Espagne	10012	12363	16441	15806	15832
Canada	18958	15951	21237	14800	13700	So. Africa Customs Un	12302	9811	12057	11057	13726
Brazil/Brésil	2601	7142	14434	7973	43635	Poland/Pologne	8190	5515	14843	13411	15786
Denmark/Danemark	7969	7713	8382	20638	19380	Former USSR/Anc. URSS	40491	11547			
Egypt/Egypte	1412	20215	1916	16680	16871	Maldives	7432	11249	8649	8836	10141
Maldives	6240	10066	9162	10875	14915	Denmark/Danemark	6608	10192	10616	8343	9689
Bahrain/Bahreïn	10916	4144	14664	5806	7404	Israel/Israël	6040	6705	7706	6273	16356
Bangladesh	8922	3875	14857	6907	8337	Malaysia/Malaisie	2727	26586	4524	3332	5807
Nepal/Népal	15	5298	23398	12175	920	Iraq	38830	1282	0	69	46
Chile/Chili	4065	7006	10553	5643	12490	Bangladesh	10301	4741	6787	7287	9484
Russian Federation			19789	9267	7465	Austria/Autriche	4016	5831	9533	8895	9762
Israel/Israël	5310	7159	5203	3326	14025	Chile/Chili	6955	6375	7509	7567	9392
Finland/Finlande	5229	4888	3347	4230	13433	Turkey/Turquie	4161	3790	8301	12269	8343
Jordan/Jordanie	6447	9008	9872	2915	1101	Lebanon/Liban	5819	10542	4290	5922	5651
Ireland/Irlande	6139	4082	5285	6198	7558	Yemen/Yémen		10363	8151	5812	6804
Guatemala	11831	5		18	16523	Greece/Grèce	1522	2165	7248	8534	10189
Oman	564	16855	2544	4901	2778	Kuwait/Koweït	5544	3476	3762	5192	5509
Spain/Espagne	2776	13724	2377	3233	4873	Norway, SVD, JM	3128	4411	5252	5802	4453
Ghana	23285	646	55	350	3	New Zealand	5089	3385	4725	4814	4354
Austria/Autriche	3594	4530	5320	4614	5043	Tunisia/Tunisie	3513	2762	3289	3517	6603
Philippines	3468	3147	2660	6533	6474	Philippines	1243	2639	1760	6619	7408
Norway, SVD, JM	4254	1974	3596	4152	7797	Ireland/Irlande	3183	2537	4439	3706	2944
Argentina/Argentine	791	6493	8484	2724	1692	Argentina/Argentine	1253	2818	4601	3433	3672

(VALUE AS PERCENTAGE OF WORLD TOTAL)(VALEURS EN POURCENTAGE DU TOTAL MONDIAL)

	1985	1986	1987	1988	1989	1990	1991	1992	1993	1994
Africa	2.0	5.5	5.4	5.8	6.0	4.4	3.8	2.3	2.0	1.9
Americas	10.6	10.2	7.8	10.1	8.3	9.5	7.0	6.4	4.5	8.7
Northern America	9.0	8.4	6.7	8.8	7.3	8.6	6.2	5.3	3.9	6.7
LAIA	1.0	1.0	0.7	1.0	1.0	0.3	0.8	1.1	0.5	1.6
CACM	0.4	0.6	0.2	0.2	0.0	0.4	0.0	0.0	0.0	0.4
Caribbean	0.1	0.0	0.1	0.2	0.0	0.2	0.0	0.0	0.0	0.0
Rest of America	0.0	0.1	0.1	0.0	0.0	0.0	0.0	0.0	0.1	0.0
As.ex F.USSR	64.1	61.7	63.4	61.2	62.1	65.3	69.3	70.0	70.4	66.0
Eur.x F.USSR	18.7	18.9	20.9	20.6	20.5	17.8	17.6	18.1	20.1	20.0
EU	17.2	16.9	19.4	19.0	17.8	15.6	15.6	15.7	17.5	17.9
EFTA	0.8	1.7	1.2	0.9	1.0	0.9	0.9	1.1	1.1	1.5
East Europe	0.5	0.3	0.3	0.6	1.6	0.9	1.0	1.3	1.4	0.6
Other Europe	0.3	0.1	0.1	0.1	0.2	0.4	0.1	0.0	0.0	0.0
Former USSR	0.4	1.1	0.6	0.1	0.1	0.1	0.1	0.6	0.3	0.2
Oceania	4.2	2.6	1.9	2.2	2.9	2.8	2.2	2.6	2.7	3.1
Japan/Japon	15.6	17.1	15.0	13.8	12.4	12.4	11.6	12.2	12.1	11.7
India/Inde	4.1	4.2	4.1	4.1	3.1	4.5	7.1	8.8	9.1	9.0
Hong Kong	3.2	4.6	6.4	5.3	5.3	4.6	6.9	7.1	8.3	7.1
Korea, Republic of	2.5	3.8	3.9	4.0	4.5	4.9	7.1	6.1	7.0	7.3
USA/Etats–Unis d'Amer	7.1	7.3	5.8	6.9	6.6	7.9	5.6	4.7	3.5	6.3
United Kingdom	5.5	5.5	6.9	5.7	6.0	5.5	5.4	5.1	5.0	5.6
Singapore/Singapour	4.1	3.8	4.9	4.2	4.5	3.9	4.4	7.0	5.5	5.2
Malaysia/Malaisie	1.6	2.2	2.9	2.8	2.9	4.3	4.5	3.7	4.6	4.0
Iran (Islamic Rp. of)	9.2	2.0	5.1	4.6	4.6	8.4	4.7	3.4	2.6	2.0
China/Chine	3.9	4.6	3.2	4.7	4.9	4.6	3.3	3.5	4.0	3.5

	1985	1986	1987	1988	1989	1990	1991	1992	1993	1994
Afrique	8.4	7.4	8.3	6.4	6.2	5.5	4.2	2.8	2.3	2.8
Amériques	25.5	29.2	29.5	28.0	29.9	29.3	31.7	37.5	38.1	37.6
Amérique du Nord	24.2	28.0	28.0	26.3	27.6	27.3	29.7	35.7	36.5	36.3
ALAI	1.2	1.1	1.1	1.5	1.8	1.6	1.8	1.6	1.3	1.2
MCAC	0.0	0.1	0.0	0.1	0.1	0.0	0.1	0.1	0.1	0.1
Caraïbes	0.1	0.0	0.0	0.0	0.4	0.4	0.0	0.0	0.0	0.0
Autre Amérique	0.0	0.0	0.3	0.1	0.1	0.0	0.0	0.1	0.1	0.1
Asie l'URSS exclus	32.4	28.2	29.0	33.0	28.7	28.7	29.3	20.7	21.1	22.2
Europe l'URSS exclus	22.6	27.0	25.8	26.4	28.8	28.9	29.9	35.3	33.4	33.3
UE	19.9	24.0	22.5	24.1	26.3	26.5	28.4	33.7	31.9	31.9
AELE	0.4	1.1	1.2	0.7	0.8	0.9	0.8	0.7	0.8	0.8
Europe de l'Est	1.9	1.6	1.9	1.3	1.4	1.2	0.5	0.7	0.6	0.6
Autre de l'Europe	0.4	0.3	0.2	0.2	0.3	0.3	0.2	0.0	0.1	0.0
Ancienne URSS	2.5	1.3	1.3	0.8	1.7	2.1	0.6	0.4	1.8	1.2
Océanie	1.8	1.8	1.6	1.7	1.5	1.6	1.5	1.2	1.2	1.1
USA/Etats–Unis d'Amer	22.3	26.1	26.2	24.8	26.0	25.8	28.1	34.1	35.3	34.7
Germany/Allemagne	5.5	6.8	7.5	7.0	6.2	6.6	7.5	8.6	8.0	6.9
United Kingdom	5.4	5.7	5.6	5.5	5.7	6.0	6.4	6.9	7.1	8.9
Belgium–Luxembourg	1.5	3.0	2.0	3.5	5.4	5.1	4.0	5.5	6.2	5.9
Japan/Japon	5.1	5.5	5.0	5.7	5.8	5.4	5.1	5.2	5.2	5.1
Netherlands/Pays–Bas	3.5	3.8	2.6	3.2	2.9	2.5	3.0	4.0	3.8	3.5
France, Monac	1.2	1.4	1.9	1.9	2.5	2.3	3.2	3.7	3.0	2.7
Singapore/Singapour	3.3	2.6	2.4	3.0	2.4	2.6	3.4	1.4	1.7	2.4
Iran (Islamic Rp. of)	1.3	1.3	2.1	2.1	2.2	3.4	3.9	2.0	0.7	0.5
United Arab Emirates	1.0	1.2	1.6	1.2	1.3	1.5	1.8	1.1	2.3	1.9

4. General Imports C.I.F. by Commodities according to the S.I.T.C. (Rev. 2) in thousand U.S. Dollars
Importations Générales C.A.F. par Produits d'après la C.T.C.I. (Rév. 2) en milliers de Dollars E.U.

SITC CTCI	COMMODITY	1991 WEIGHT POIDS	1991 VALUE VALEUR	1992 WEIGHT POIDS	1992 VALUE VALEUR	1993 WEIGHT POIDS	1993 VALUE VALEUR	1994 WEIGHT POIDS	1994 VALUE VALEUR	PRODUIT
	ALL COMMODITIES		3089699		3419249		3742919		4483360	TOUS PRODUITS
0	FOOD AND LIVE ANIMALS		497457		496836		434050		627544	ALIMENTS,ANIMAUX VIVANTS
02	DAIRY PRODCTS,BIRDS'EGGS		66333		65878		74286		85070	PRODUITS LAITIERS,OEUFS
022	MILK AND CREAM		63067	W 30474	62974	W 53417	71470	W 46002	81423	LAIT ET CREME
0224	MILK,CREAM PRESERVED ETC		62804	W 30400	62652	W 53364	71202	W 45812	80948	LAIT,CREME CONS,CONC
02242	MILK DRY,1.5% FAT OR LES		8061	W 3401	5812	W 3743	6259	W 8791	13748	LAIT POUDRE INF 1.5%
02243	MILK DRY,OVER 1.5% FAT		54595	W 25847	55757	W 32113	64340	W 36118	66521	LAIT POUDRE SUP 1.5%
03	FISH AND PREPARATIONS		50484		55849		50678		59794	POISSONS ET PREPARATIONS
035	FISH SALTED,DRIED,SMOKED		40720		41179		39872	W 47620	42341	POISSON SECHE,SALE,FUME
03503	FISH(EX COD)DRIED,SALTED		40650	W 44290	41010	W 64771	39649	W 47569	42126	POISSONS SECHES,SALES
037	FISH ETC PREPD,PRSVD NES		9410	W 11952	14090		10082	W 13168	16480	POIS,CRUST,MOL PREPARES
0371	FISH PREPARD,PRESRVD NES		9405	W 11949	14073	W 7458	10076	W 13145	16453	CONSERVES DE POISSONS
04	CEREALS AND PREPARATIONS		136625		145082		83670		154651	CEREALES ET PRODUITS
041	WHEAT ETC UNMILLED		81203	W 462307	65072	W 7322	1028	W 881814	120692	FROMENT,EPEAUTRE
0411	DURUM WHEAT UNMILLED		34334	W 14	9			W 681656	98870	FROMENT DUR NON MOULU
0412	OTHER WHEAT ETC UNMILLED		46869	W 462294	65064	W 7322	1028	W 200158	21822	AUTRE FROMENT NON MOULU
042	RICE		38416	W 237224	65094	W 208811	49222	W 58434	13261	RIZ
0422	RICE SEMI–MILLED,MILLED		38388	W 234119	63932	W 202707	47950	W 45675	10429	RIZ POLI,GLACE INCL BRISURES
04221	RICE MILLED UNBROKEN		11960	W 67662	19854	W 72582	18174	W 9877	2523	RIZ POLI,GLACE EXCL BRISURES
04222	RICE BROKEN		26428	W 166458	44078	W 130125	29775	W 35798	7906	BRISURES DE RIZ
044	MAIZE UNMILLED	W 53332	11725	W 34843	7687	W 80873	11040	W 84824	11894	MAIS NON MOULU
046	WHEAT ETC MEAL OR FLOUR		33		67	W 34420	11382	W 2545	349	SEMOULE FARINE,FROMENT
04601	FLOUR OF WHEAT OR MESLIN		33	W 93	67	W 34420	11382	W 2545	349	FARINE DE FROMENT
05	VEGETABLES AND FRUIT		62900		58999		55569		80153	LEGUMES ET FRUITS
054	VEG ETC FRSH,SMPLY PRSVD		53840		48556		43918		66571	LEGUMES FRAIS,CONG,SECS
0542	LEGUMINOUS VEGETBLES DRY		37065	W 76800	38612	W 78317	32140	W 106027	42909	LEGUMES A COSSE SECS
0545	OTHER FRESH VEGETABLES		15487	W 34093	8623	W 35327	8537		12451	AUTRES LEGUMES FRAIS,REF
05451	ALLIACEOUS VEGTBLS,FRESH		15413	W 33928	8430	W 35150	8363		11984	OIGNONS,ECHALOTES,AULX
06	SUGAR AND PREPS,HONEY		126923		116584		118896		183169	SUCRES ET PRODUITS
061	SUGAR AND HONEY		126678		115972		118416	W 498520	182555	SUCRES ET MIEL
0611	RAW BEET AND CANE SUGAR		121899	W 358597	109557	W 394753	116310	W 491546	179402	SUCRES BRUTS
07	COFFEE,TEA,COCOA,SPICES		20780		23366		17819		17968	CAFE,THE,CACAO,EPICES
075	SPICES		18560	W 38985	18819		10204	W 22990	13686	EPICES
0751	PEPPER AND PIMENTO		11714	W 6850	11027	W 944	1131	W 8314	6131	POIVRE,PIMENTS
081	*FEEDING STUFF FOR ANIML		14315		13281		17038	W 220291	25015	NOURRITURE POUR ANIMAUX
09	MISC EDIBLE PRODUCTS		16248		14874		13676		19390	PREP ALIMENTAIRES DIVERSES
098	EDIBLE PRODCTS,PREPS NES		15168		13413		12009		17251	PREP ALIMENTAIRES NDA
09809	MISC FOOD PREPRTIONS NES		9352		7481		5107	W 57263	8853	PREP ALIMENTAIRES NDA
1	BEVERAGES AND TOBACCO		22966		34638		36499		47168	BOISSONS ET TABACS
12	TOBACCO AND MANUFACTURES		16100		27795		28584		37174	TABACS BRUTS FABRIQUES
121	TOBACCO UNMNFCTRD,REFUSE		14149	W 2703	26763	W 1929	26700	W 2394	24900	TABACS BRUTS,DECHETS
1211	TOBACCO,NOT STRIPPED		14147	W 2687	26476	W 1929	26699	W 2389	24853	TABACS NON ECOTES
2	CRUDE MATERLS,EXCL FUELS		78830		84416		96070		111353	MAT BRUTES NON COMESTIBLES
26	TEXTILE FIBRES AND WASTE		41377		42381		47116		59186	FIBRES TEXTILES
263	COTTON		21800		22121		24664	W 18616	33715	COTON
2631	RAW COTTON,EXCL LINTERS		20272	W 13381	19546	W 15999	22435	W 17819	29921	COTON EN MASSE
266	SYNTHETIC FIBRES TO SPIN		7755		10741		13924	W 9571	15744	FIBRES SYNTHETIQUES
267	OTHER MAN–MADE FIBRES		11317		8311		7555	W 4282	8519	AUTR FIBR TEXT ARTIF SYNTH
2671	REGENERATD FIBRE TO SPIN		11317		8175	W 3245	7543	W 4278	8467	FIBRES TEXT ARTIFIC
26711	DISCN REGEN FIBRE UNCMBD		11317	W 4041	7955	W 2880	5906	W 3711	6233	FIBRES TEX ARTIF DISCONT
27	CRUDE FERTLZR,MINRLS NES		10200		14999		15230		14994	ENGRAIS MINERAUX BRUTS
29	CRUDE ANIMAL,VEG MAT NES		11595		12108		11320		12409	MATIERES BRUTES ANIM,VEGET
292	CRUDE VEG MATERIALS NES		10217		9896		9523	W 5002	10118	MAT BRUTES VEGETALES NDA
3	MINERAL FUELS ETC		339798		304581		289138		279484	COMBUSTIBLES MINERAUX LUB
33	PETROLEUM AND PRODUCTS		334504		294208		278753		266208	PETROLE ET DERIVES
333	CRUDE PETROLEUM		259983	W 1176367	158984	W 1614821	207062	W 1806309	211765	HUILES BRUTES DE PETROLE
334	PETROLEUM PRODUCTS,REFIN		71493	W 30484	132027		67966		50468	PRODUITS RAFFINES
4	ANIMAL,VEGETABLE OIL,FAT		17072		22961		46148		27807	HUILES,GRAISSES ANIM,VEG
42	FIXED VEGETABLE OIL,FAT		13116		18079		40520		22001	HUILES VEGETALES FIXES
424	FIXED VEG OIL NONSOFT		12888	W 42214	17672	W 83410	39480	W 44832	21157	AUTRES HUILES VEG FIXES
4242	PALM OIL		10791	W 38592	15376	W 44965	19340	W 41820	19231	HUILE DE PALME
4243	COCONUT (COPRA) OIL			W 300	185	W 29381	14812	W 1051	605	HJUILE DE COPRAH
5	CHEMCLS,RELATED PROD NES		282333		305063		328941		382141	PRODUITS CHIMIQUES
51	ORGANIC CHEMICALS		39717		34300		37747		37636	PROD CHIMIQ ORGANIQUES
515	ORG–INORG COMPOUNDS ETC		14993	W 3586	10349		9347		7900	COMPOSES ORGANO–MINERAUX
5154	ORGANO–SULPHUR CMPNDS		10243	W 1657	5119	W 1391	4068	W 580	3374	THIOCOMPOSES ORGANIQUES
52	INORGANIC CHEMICALS		24882		25832		25618		29304	PROD CHIM INORGANIQUES
522	INORG ELEMNTS,OXIDES,ETC		16600		16311		16332		17075	ELEMENTS INORGANIQUES
53	DYES,TANNING,COLOUR PROD		21951		35432		29459		32172	PROD TEINTURE,COLORANTS
531	SYNT DYE,NAT INDGO,LAKES		9720	W 11450	11680	W 11110	12731	W 2675	12713	MAT COLOR ORGAN,LAQUES
533	PIGMENTS,PAINTS,ETC		11599	W 5492	23177		16088	W 19372	18619	PIGMENTS,PEINTURES,VERNIS
5334	VARNISHES,DISTEMPERS ETC		3597	W 665	12474		4567	W 2240	5455	PEINTURES A L'EAU
541	*MEDICINAL,PHARM PRODUCT		38855		54821		49331		62567	PROD MEDICINAUX PHARMACEUT
5417	MEDICAMENTS		30730		46393		41609		53258	MEDICAMENTS
54179	— CONTNG OTH SUBSTANCES		24372	K 4857028	39091	K 4664337	34371		42911	MED CONT AUT SUBSTANCES
55	PERFUME,CLEANING ETC PRD		8971		12680		14453		18990	PROD POUR PARFUM,TOILETTE
562	*FERTILIZERS,MANUFACTURE		59432	W 293547	48474	W 440317	63766	W 413257	64805	ENGRAIS MANUFACTURES
5621	CHEM NITROGENOUS FERTLZR		39892	W 193358	29556	W 283090	38805	W 262371	39940	ENGRAIS AZOTES
56213	AMMONIUM SULPHATE		8577	W 69871	7302	W 102349	12326	W 76248	9450	SULFATE D'AMMONIUM
56216	UREA		30678	W 117945	20992	W 164366	24252	W 185370	30217	UREE
5623	CHEM POTASSIC FERTILIZER		6097	W 49405	9426	W 83127	12943	W 106419	16566	ENGRAIS POTASSIQUES
58	PLASTIC MATERIALS ETC		62217		62391		68770		89259	MAT PLAST ARTIFICIELLES
583	POLYMERIZATION ETC PRODS		53082		49684		56032		73683	PROD POLYMERISATION
5831	POLYETHYLENE		16722		14544		14223		18801	POLYETHYLENE
58311	— IN PRIMARY FORMS		16177	W 17494	13976	W 19165	13640	W 24915	17991	POLYETHYLENE PRIMAIRES
5834	POLYVINYL CHLORIDE		10579		8899		14650		17242	CHLORURE DE POLYVINYLE
58341	— IN PRIMARY FORMS		9113	W 30006	7571	W 14538	11288	W 18218	14889	SOUS FORMES PRIMAIRES
5839	OTH POLYMRZTION ETC PROD		13233		13831		15119		21118	AUT PROD POLYMER COPOLYM
59	CHEMICAL MATERIALS NES		24983		30209		39325		46550	MAT PROD CHIMIQUES NDA
591	PESTICIDES,DISINFECTANTS		11474	W 4672	14020	W 5757	18208	W 6671	20147	DESINF,INSECT,FONG,HERB
598	MISCEL CHEM PRODUCTS NES		10575		12608		16625	W 5885	20569	PROD DIV INDUST CHIM NDA
5989	CHEM PRODUCTS,PREPS NES		6244		8169		10565	W 1653	13725	PROD PREP CHIMIQUES NDA
6	BASIC MANUFACTURES		1049498		1228190		1415290		1672761	ART MANUFACTURES
61	LEATHER,DRESSED FUR,ETC		6842		7158		11579		18920	CUIRS,PELLETERIES
611	LEATHER		6059		5835		9623		15071	CUIRS,PEAUX PREPARES
62	RUBBER MANUFACTURES NES		19645		24626		32225		26221	CAOUTCHOUC MANUFACTURE
625	RUBBER TYRES, TUBES ETC		9992	N 1223402	11847	N 2004505	20444	N 1737007	13879	PNEUS CAOUTCHOUC VULCANISE
6252	TYRES,NEW,BUS OR LORRY		4556	N 151557	5866	N 269778	11293	N 128388	5745	PNEUS POUR AUTOBUS,CAMIONS
63	WOOD,CORK MANUFACTRS NES		12181		12958		16704		15475	OUVRAGES LIEGE ET BOIS
634	VENEERS,PLYWOOD,ETC		11441		11046		11453	W 19654	12518	PLACAGES,CONTRE–PLAQUES
6342	PLYWOOD OF WOOD SHEETS		10442	W 5351	10132		10364	W 17000	10956	BOIS CONTRE–PLAQUES

4. General Imports C.I.F. by Commodities according to the S.I.T.C. (Rev. 2) in thousand U.S. Dollars
Importations Générales C.A.F. par Produits d'après la C.T.C.I. (Rév. 2) en milliers de Dollars E.U.

SITC CTCI	COMMODITY	1991 WEIGHT POIDS	1991 VALUE VALEUR	1992 WEIGHT POIDS	1992 VALUE VALEUR	1993 WEIGHT POIDS	1993 VALUE VALEUR	1994 WEIGHT POIDS	1994 VALUE VALEUR	PRODUIT
64	PAPER,PAPERBOARD AND MFR		84163		85769		92204		107850	PAPIERS,CARTONS & OUVRAGES
641	PAPER AND PAPERBOARD		66818		67426		69055		82080	PAPIERS ET CARTONS
6411	NEWSPRINT		16075	W 19098	9844	W 25666	12744	W 25546	12189	PAPIER JOURNAL
6412	PRINTG,WRITING PAPER NES		13999	W 43560	17783	W 45562	18628	W 26620	20209	PAPIERS POUR L'IMPRESSION
64122	— COATED,IMPREGNATD ETC		13525	W 43023	16823	W 44381	17243	W 25953	18715	PAPIERS IMPRESSION COUCHES
6413	KRAFT PAPER,PAPERBOARD		12826	W 24620	14020	W 24558	12326	W 59435	18102	PAPIER ET CARTON KRAFT
6415	PAPER,PAPERBRD,BULK,NES		18667	W 93999	21364	W 75970	19817		22675	PAPIERS,CARTONS ROULEAUX
64159	OTHER PAPER ETC,BULK,NES		15380	W 84997	17535	W 66840	16179	W 12369	17711	AUT PAPIER ROULEAUX FEUILLES
642	PAPER,ETC,PRECUT,ARTS OF		17346		18343		23150		25770	PAP,CARTONS DECOUPES
6428	PAPER ETC ARTICLES NES		8263		8856		12421		14883	OUVRAGES EN PATE A PAPIER
65	TEXTILE YARN,FABRICS,ETC		610845		737574		851630		1024153	FILS,TISSUS,ARTICLES TEXTILE
651	TEXTILE YARN		73759		78901		84001		95074	FILS TEXTILES
6513	COTTON YARN		21974		23319		27397	W 704	35376	FILS DE COTON
6514	SYN FIB YRN,BULK,MONOFIL		32021	W 9685	29757	W 5790	22943		24342	FILS CONT 85% FIB TEXT SYNTH
65142	— NONTXT ETC CONT PAMID		16059	W 918	4177	W 749	3593	W 1386	4742	FILS NON TEX FI CON POLYAMID
6516	DISCON SYN FIB BLEND YRN		10880		16372		20056	W 4761	22464	FILS FIBR TEX SYNT DIS MOINS
65166	DISCON SYN FIB–COTTN YRN		2819	W 1416	6128		11559	W 2392	9383	FILS TEXT SYNT MELANGE COTON
652	COTTON FABRICS,WOVEN		141773		203900		240143	A 112492	256739	TISSUS DE COTON
6521	GREY WOVEN COTTON FABRIC		34224		42647		56204	A 12318	53186	TISSUS COT ECRUS NON MERCER
65214	GREY WOVEN COTTON NES		26700		32845		45690	A 94	41094	AUT TISSUS 85% COTON ECRUS
6522	WOVEN COTTON BLEACHD,ETC		107548		161253		183939	A 100174	203553	TISSUS COTON BLANCHIS ETC
65224	BLCHED COTTON FABRIC NES		92899		137068		163125	A 97867	182589	AUT TIS PLUS 85% COT BLANCHI
65225	BLCHD COTN BLEND FAB NES		10999	A 12521	18952		15617	A 410	15553	AUT TIS MOINS 85% COT BLANCH
653	WOVN MAN–MADE FIB FABRIC		205758		236886		255272		320519	TISSUS FIBRES SYNTH,ARTIF
6531	CONT SYNT WEAVES NONPILE		41480		42172		50543	A 659	60016	TISSUS FIBRES SYNTH CONTINUE
65315	CONT SYN TXTL FABRIC NES		40446		40607		48919	A 398	57786	TIS PLUS 85% TEXT SYNT CONT
6532	DISC SYN TXTL FABRIC NES		57200		52187		69135	A 208	81992	TIS DISC MOINS 85% FIBR TEXT
6534	DISC SYN BLEND FABRC NES		66154		85945		79127	A 9991	95647	TISSUS FIBRES SYNTH DISCONT
65341	DISC SYN FIB–COTTN FABRC		58238		71493		65462	A 147	78104	TISSUS FIB SYNT DIS MEL COTO
65349	OTH DISC SYN BLEND FABRC		6074		11132		9612	A 7755	12346	TISSUS FIB SYNT MEL MAT AUT
6536	DISC REGN TXTL FABRC NES		29522		41510	A 24119	44656		68575	TISSUS 85% TEXT ART DISC
654	OTH WOVEN TEXTILE FABRIC		7823		8599		14975		21391	TISSUS AUT COTON SYNT,ARTIF
655	KNITTED,ETC FABRICS		111513	A 68622	128497	A 142632	163542		195811	ETOF BONNETERIE PIECES ETC
6552	OTHER KNIT ETC FAB NONEL		111513	A 68622	128497	A 142632	163542		195811	ETOF BON NON ELAS NON SYNT
656	LACE,RIBBONS,TULLE,ETC		18606		26117		37029		51637	TULLES,BRODERIE
65601	NARROW FABRICS NES		7625		9990		12237		19817	RUBANS SANS TRAME EN FILS
657	SPECIAL TXTL FABRC,PRODS		41160		47669		52967		75068	TISSUS SPECIAUX
6573	COATED ETC TEXTILES NES		24433		25127	A 12171	27360		42583	TISSUS,ART MATIERE TEXT NDA
65732	PLASTIC COATED TEXTILES		14025	A 8885	16201	A 9110	19101		31461	TISSUS IMPREGNES
66	NONMETAL MINERAL MFS NES		136388		164347		215135		234467	ART MIN NON METALLIQUES
661	LIME,CEMENT,BLDG PRODS		41311		52351		58491		68954	CHAUX,CIMENTS MAT CONSTR
6612	CEMENT		41079	W 830362	50419	W 933196	56249	W 1091954	65577	CIMENTS HYDRAULIQUES
664	GLASS		10644		13552		10993		11819	VERRE
665	GLASSWARE		7386		10741		13160		9871	OUVRAGES EN VERRE
667	PEARL,PREC–,SEMI–P STONE		70617		77717		124807		133477	PERLES, PIERRES GEMMES
6672	DIAMONDS NONINDUST,UNSET		65397		75206		122370		127876	DIAMANTS BRUTS
66722	— SRTD,ROUGH,SIMPLY WKD		58619		60086		112355		121560	DIAMANTS TRIES BRUTS
66729	— CUT ETC NOT SET		6755		15076		9985		6266	DIAMANTS TAILLES
67	IRON AND STEEL		91173		101635		102508		127866	FER ET ACIER
672	IRON,STEEL PRIMARY FORMS		15280		13743		15302	W 91639	25639	LINGOTS FER,ACIER
6725	IRN,STL BLOOMS,SLABS,ETC		14120		12191		13961	W 87102	23123	BLOOMS,BILLETTES FER ACIER
67251	IRN,SMPLE STL BLOOMS,ETC		14114	W 48404	12169	W 48317	13938	W 87043	23073	BLOOMS ETC NON ACIER FIN
673	IRON,STEEL SHAPES ETC		22508		29428		31011	W 161100	34693	BARRES,PROFIL FER,ACIER
6732	IRON,STEEL BARS ETC		10473		11681	W 141121	14217	W 106757	12195	BARRES FER,ACIER
674	IRN,STL UNIV,PLATE,SHEET		28809		27709		26610	W 53678	34463	LARGES PLATS,TOLES
678	IRON,STL TUBES,PIPES,ETC		14361		20113		15666	W 17696	18700	TUBES,TUYAUX EN FONTE,FER
68	NON–FERROUS METALS		32815		25646		28868		29787	METAUX NON FERREUX
684	ALUMINIUM		21948		13134		14539	W 7326	16022	ALUMINIUM
6842	ALUMINIUM,ALLOYS WORKED		19819		11374		12097	W 5635	13315	ALUMINIUM,ALLIAGES OUVRE
69	METAL MANUFACTURES NES		55446		68477		64435		88023	ART MANUFACT EN METAL NDA
691	STRUCTURES AND PARTS NES		5757	W 2796	12226		8749		20174	CONSTRUCT FER,ACIER,ALU
6911	STRUCTURES,PARTS IRN,STL		5100	W 2367	10911	W 2603	6841		14340	CONSTRUCT FER,ACIER,FONTE
695	TOOLS		11909	MN 85125	13949	MN 15686	11967	MN 12024	11044	OUTILS A MAIN
699	BASE METAL MFRS NES		17889		20172		23803		29749	ART MANUFACTURES MET NDA
7	MACHINES,TRANSPORT EQUIP		607634		725804		859868		1046636	MACHINES MATERIEL TRANSPORT
71	POWER GENERATING EQUIPMT		46892		47832		63785		99855	MACHINES GENERATRICES
713	INTRNL COMBUS PSTN ENGIN		17077		16607	N 656350	13248	N 725503	12198	MOTEURS EXPL COMB INT, PIECE
714	ENGINES AND MOTORS NES		15894	N 5113	11746		30793	N 24485	62702	MOTEURS NON ELECTRIQUES
7149	ENGINE & MOTOR PARTS NES		13608	N 5106	11620		30664	N 24438	62477	PIECES 714 ET 718.88
71491	PARTS NES OF 7144,71481		13439	N 3605	11153	N 6116	29576	N 22580	61376	PIECES DES PROPULSEURS
716	ROTATING ELECTRIC PLANT		11160	N 468861	17710	N 557836	15772	N 537843	21437	APP ELECTR ROTATIFS,PIECES
72	MACHS FOR SPCL INDUSTRYS		102724		147214		178037		154813	MAC SPECIALES POUR INDUST
722	TRACTORS NON–ROAD		9640	N 5537	9753	N 5734	11388	N 6613	18469	TRACTEURS
7224	WHEELED TRACTORS NES		9523	N 5395	9264	N 5700	11208	N 6589	18386	TRACTEURS A ROUES
723	CIVIL ENGNEERG EQUIP ETC		2903	N 9461	4801	N 15096	24118	N 42677	11707	APPAREILS DE GENIE CIVIL
7234	CONST,MINING MACHNRY NES		2292	N 2070	4114	N 13369	23031	N 39614	10878	MACH POUR LA CONST, MINES
72341	SELF–PROPELLD DOZERS,ETC	N 10	392	N 38	704	N 169	11676	N 197	2352	BULLDOZERS
724	TEXTILE,LEATHER MACHNRY		46625	MN 37010	76126		75752	MN 104408	58784	MACH POUR INDUSTRIE TEXTILE
7243	SEWING MACHS,NEEDLES ETC		21479	MN 21043	36983		33090	MN 87585	23669	MACHINES A COUDRE,PIECES
72431	SEWING MACHINES		18900	N 6278562	32437		27593	N 2351597	17867	MACHINES A COUDRE
7244	SPINNING,EXTRDNG,ETC MCH		5447	N 717872	12081	N 2691004	7063	N 6451423	5747	MACH POUR LE FILAGE
7245	WEAVING,FELT MFG,ETC MCH		7369	N 116490	12326		17060	N 269703	8983	METIERS A TISSER,PIECES
7247	TEXTILE MACHINERY NES		9083	N 275257	7890		12067	N 218960	13862	MACH LAVAGE,TEINTURE TEX
726	PRINTG,BKBINDG MACHY,PTS		11185	N 78666	13884		12812	N 928386	10442	MACHINES POUR IMPRIMERIE
727	FOOD MACHRY NON–DOMESTIC		6154	N 282282	8224		13418	N 405484	10832	MACH INDUSTRIES ALIMENT
7272	OTH FOOD PROC MCHY,PARTS		4868	N 23236	7307		12213	N 41081	9330	AUT MACH IND ALIMENTAIRE
728	OTH MACHY FOR SPCL INDUS		22193	N 1764062	28292		33937	MN 45751	38240	AUT MACH IND PARTICULIERES
7283	OTHR MINERAL WORKG MACHY		2467	N 87672	5873		11449	N 6539690	9337	MACH TRIER,CRIBLER,BROYER
7284	MACHY FOR SPCL INDUS NES		15555	N 641076	17699		18565	N 5243499	24357	MACH SPEC IND PARTICUL.
73	METALWORKING MACHINERY		9649		7516		9877		11943	MACH TRAVAIL DES METAUX
74	GENRL INDUSTRL MACHY NES		71227		97747		95975		114026	MACH APP INDUSTRIE
741	HEATING,COOLING EQUIPMNT		10467		21127		24099		25827	MACH CHAUFFAGE,PIECES
743	PUMPS NES,CENTRFUGES ETC		11312		10656		14558	N 1188342	15365	POMPES COMPRES,VENT ETC
744	MECHANICAL HANDLING EQU		13137	N 132777	16429		12541	N 67211	21368	EQUIP MANUTENTION PIECES
7442	LIFTING,LOADING MACH NES		8943	N 26139	12271		8144	N 31768	14094	APP LEVAGE,MANUTENTION
745	NONELEC MACHY,TOOLS NES		7250		12371		10148	N 5465240	9982	AUT MACH NON ELEC,PIECES
7452	OTH NONELEC MCHS,PTS NES		6862		11888		9342	N 5461988	9301	AUT MACH NON ELEC,PIECES
749	NONELEC MACH PTS,ACC NES		22775	MN 40584	27382	MN 92065	27178	MN 143615	32360	PIECES MACH NON ELEC NDA
75	OFFICE MACHNES,ADP EQUIP		25120		36975		37578		47761	MACH BUREAU TRAIT AUTOM
752	AUTOMTIC DATA PROC EQUIP		10750	N 25698	13148	N 59589	14999	N 34121	19508	MACH TRAIT INFORMATION
759	OFFICE,ADP MCH PTS,ACCES		8131	MN 51906	15195	MN 47871	15609	MN 42894	20904	PIECES DU 751 ET 752

4. General Imports C.I.F. by Commodities according to the S.I.T.C. (Rev. 2) in thousand U.S. Dollars
Importations Générales C.A.F. par Produits d'après la C.T.C.I. (Rév. 2) en milliers de Dollars E.U.

SITC CTCI	COMMODITY	1991 WEIGHT POIDS	1991 VALUE VALEUR	1992 WEIGHT POIDS	1992 VALUE VALEUR	1993 WEIGHT POIDS	1993 VALUE VALEUR	1994 WEIGHT POIDS	1994 VALUE VALEUR	PRODUIT
7599	ACCTG,ETC,ADP MCH PTS,AC		7121	MN 50864	13967	MN 47788	14204	MN 42739	19777	PIECES DU 751 ET 752
76	TELECOMM,SOUND EQUIPMENT		32797		65039		73473		111349	EQUIPMENT DE TELECOM
761	TELEVISION RECEIVERS		10786	N 110531	12904	N 103689	13802	N 152570	17936	RECEPTEURS DE TELEVISION
7611	COLOUR TV RECEIVERS		5253	N 36234	7906	N 48304	10664	N 69593	13686	RECEPTEURS COULEUR
764	TELECOM EQPT,PTS,ACC NES		15824	MN 620011	44789	MN 667398	48624	MN 539329	83029	EQUIP TELECOM,PIECES
7641	LINE TELEPHONE,ETC EQUIP		3923	N 604052	22528	N 182131	22239	N 518135	23334	APP TELEPHON PAR FIL
7643	TV,RADIO TRANSMITTRS ETC		2484	N 4019	10553	N 24158	8497	N 27334	32458	APP EMET TELE RADIO
7649	PTS NES OF EQUIPMT OF 76		5603	MN 619194	9577	MN 666729	13206	MN 536928	20988	PIECES DE LA DIV 76
77	ELECTRIC MACHNRY NES ETC		76949		87805		109643		164436	MACH APP ELECT NDA
771	ELECTRIC POWER MACHY NES		6531	MN 15925	5401	MN 29316	14850	MN 39588	20292	MACH PROD,TRANS ELECTR
772	SWITCHGEAR ETC,PARTS NES		27359	MN 119246	26948	MN 131795	31810	MN 263936	44703	APP COUPURE,SECT ETC
7721	SWITCHGEAR ETC		21958	MN 48502	19796	MN 60181	24396	MN 97729	36719	APP COUPURE,SECTIONMNT
773	ELECTR DISTRIBUTNG EQUIP		7601		10814		13244		33133	EQUIPMT DISTRIBUTION ELECT
7731	INSULATED WIRE,CABLE ETC		6841	W 4047	6057	W 4627	10467		29097	FILS,CABLES ISOLES ELECT
775	HOUSEHOLD TYPE EQUIP NES		8270	N 696839	13311		16271	MN 85113	19005	MACH,APP USAGE DOMESTQUE
778	ELECTRICAL MACHINERY NES		19992	MN 277298	23642		26733	MN 947921	33813	AUTRES MACH ELECT NDA
78	ROAD VEHICLES		199407		205693		240532		338189	VEHICULES ROUTIERS
781	PASS MOTOR VEH EXC BUSES		21183	N 7815	35415	N 14352	39024	N 16261	85224	AUTO TRANSPORT PERSONNES
782	LORRIES,SPCL MTR VEH NES		60632	N 12909	76366	N 12706	89214	N 4413	113549	VEHICULES SPECIAUX,MARCH
7821	LORRIES,TRUCKS		59187	N 12596	74227	N 12185	84863	N 4314	109627	VEHICULES TRANSP MARCHAND
783	ROAD MOTOR VEHICLES NES		52639	N 3694	37319	N 2390	16044	N 10011	36404	VEHICULES ROUTIERS NDA
7831	BUSES		51128	N 2618	33040	N 1125	11207	N 9662	33292	VOITURES TRANSPORT COMMUN
784	MOTOR VEH PRTS,ACCES NES		21990	N 2491986	24357	N 1957409	60561	N 2677184	59994	PIECES 722,781,782,783
7841	MOTOR VEHICLE CHASSIS	N 419	4654	N 545	2881	N 2208	28814	N 981	12112	CHASSIS 722,781,782,783
7842	MOTOR VEHICLE BODIES		3376	N 1475	8009	N 1221	17001	N 7558	24832	CARROS 722,781,782,783
7849	OTHER MOTOR VEHCL PARTS		13960	N 2489966	13468	N 1953980	14745	N 2668645	23050	PIECES 722,781,782,783
785	CYCLES,ETC MOTRZD OR NOT		42061	MN 34779	30629	MN 42132	33705		40896	MOTOCYCLES SCOOTERS
7851	MOTORCYCLES ETC		31052	N 64655	21683	N 58504	22071		27394	MOTO VELO MOTEUR AUXIL
7853	INVAL CARR, PTS OF 785		10429	MN 34698	8580	MN 42030	10381	MN 59560	12927	FAUTEUILS INVALIDES,PIECES
78539	PARTS,ACCES NES OF 785		10389	MN 34638	8514	MN 42029	10325	MN 59559	12856	PIECES DU 785
79	OTHR TRANSPORT EQUIPMENT		42869		29983		50969		4264	AUTRE MATERIEL TRANSPORT
791	RAILWAY VEHICLES		28828		25316	N 610307	42318		1549	VEHIC MAT CHEMINS DE FER
7912	OTH RAIL LOCOMOTIVES ETC	N 20	14983	N 4	971					AUTRES LOCOMOTIVES
7913	MECHAN–PROPELLED RY CARS	N 12	2		14078	N 25	5474			AUTOMOTRICES,DRAISINES
7914	RY COACHES NES NOT POWRD	N 50	11289	N 42	9259	N 188	34854			VOITURES A VOYAGEURS
8	MISC MANUFACTURED GOODS		183741		210871		212742		257021	ART MANUFACTURES DIVERS
84	CLOTHING AND ACCESSORIES		21775		25417		33372		43278	VETEMENTS
847	TEXTILE CLTHNG ACCES NES		5201	MN 22787	9297	MN 42898	11744	MN 34404	12002	ACCES VET MAT TEXT NDA
848	HEADGEAR,NONTXTL CLOTHNG		9495		10279		13728		16108	VET ACCES MAT AUT QUE TEX
87	PRECISION INSTRUMNTS NES		30660		54763		31000		41532	INSTRUM,APPAR SCIENT NDA
872	MEDICAL INSTRUMENTS NES		7341		26992	MN 18672	4958	MN 16189	10800	INSTR,APP MEDIC–CHIR NDA
87202	OTH MEDICAL INSTRUMENTS		6788	MN 1008337	26543	MN 18580	4700	MN 16154	7989	INSTRUM,APP MEDECINE
874	MEASURNG,CONTROLNG INSTR		18922	N 2754367	20364		21265	N 2950998	25213	INSTRUMENTS DE MESURE
88	PHOTO EQU,OPTICL GDS ETC		15276		17609		18357		17486	APP,FOURN PHOTO,OP,MONTR
882	PHOTO,CINEMA SUPPLIES		10177		11023		10945		11639	PRODUITS PHOTO,CINEMA
89	MISC MANUFCTRD GOODS NES		105373		102209		115821		137879	ART MANUFACTURES DIVERS
892	PRINTED MATTER		13674	MN 746735	20937	MN 874510	22879	MN 1235183	27781	IMPRIMES
8928	PRINTED MATTER NES		7970	MN 729329	13273	MN 859950	15972	MN 1204842	17783	IMPRIMES NDA
893	ARTICLES OF PLASTIC NES		15570		21627		28563		34183	OUVRAGES EN MAT DIVIS 58
8939	MISC PLASTIC ARTICLES		10590		15380		17781		24077	ART DIVERS EN MAT DIV 58
89399	OTHR PLASTC ARTICLES NES		9832		14278		16855	N 65901	22560	AUT OUV MAT DIV 58
899	OTHER MANUFACTURED GOODS		63262		41744		43593		53979	AUT ART MANUF DIVERS NDA
8998	SMALLWARES,TOILETRYS ETC		58049	MN 1139340	36402	MN 3510801	39006	MN 1629029	47535	ART MERCERIE,TOILETTE
89983	BUTTONS,STUDS,ETC		34444	MN 1022534	22995	MN 1359276	20725	MN 1430854	24078	BOUTONS,BOUTONS–PRESSION
89984	SLIDE FASTENERS,PARTS		23359	MN 103663	13114	MN 2123780	18000	MN 159345	23021	FERMETURES A GLISSIERE
9	GOODS NOT CLASSD BY KIND		10368		5890		24173		31444	ART TRANSACT NON CLASSES
971	*GOLD,NON MONETARY NES		4620	MK 9711	2996		21260		28554	OR NON MONETAIRE
97101	NONMON GLD UNWRT,SEMIMFD		4620	MK 9491	2867		21260	K 9	27784	OR,ALLIAGES D'OR BRUTS

5. General Exports F.O.B. by Commodities according to the S.I.T.C. (Rev. 2) in thousand U.S. Dollars
Exportations Générales F.O.B. par Produits d'après la C.T.C.I. (Rév. 2) en milliers de Dollars E.U.

SITC CTCI	COMMODITY	1991		1992		1993		1994		PRODUIT
		WEIGHT POIDS	VALUE VALEUR	WEIGHT POIDS	VALUE VALEUR	WEIGHT POIDS	VALUE VALEUR	WEIGHT POIDS	VALUE VALEUR	
	ALL COMMODITIES		1987230		2453990		2846947		3209669	TOUS PRODUITS
0	FOOD AND LIVE ANIMALS		567942		500207		576250		635775	ALIMENTS,ANIMAUX VIVANTS
03	FISH AND PREPARATIONS		21337		30308		43871		63564	POISSONS ET PREPARATIONS
034	FISH,FRESH,CHILLED,FROZN		3354		6746		16517	W 2536	15638	POISSON FRAIS, REFRIG,CONG
0342	FISH FROZEN,EXCL FILLETS		1055		2809	W 2442	10695	W 2158	9147	POISSONS CONGELES
036	SHELL FISH FRESH,FROZEN		16275	W 2121	19709	W 2107	24003	W 1100	44832	CRUSTACES,MOLLUSQUES
04	CEREALS AND PREPARATIONS		1105		1359		2094		15242	CEREALES ET PRODUITS
042	RICE		386	W 474	367	W 756	609	W 60299	13648	RIZ
0422	RICE SEMI–MILLED,MILLED		289	W 318	245	W 531	434	W 60157	13537	RIZ POLI,GLACE INCL BRISURES
05	VEGETABLES AND FRUIT		66294		81615		66921		75543	LEGUMES ET FRUITS
054	VEG ETC FRSH,SMPLY PRSVD		9720	W 12491	7057		10118	W 13601	14700	LEGUMES FRAIS,CONG,SECS
0546	VEGETABLES SIMPLY PRESVD		4630	W 6294	3909	W 9949	6468	W 12140	10631	LEGUMES CONG,CONSER
05462	VEG PRSVD UNFRZN UNTINND		4582	W 6209	3831	W 9923	6427	W 12115	10563	LEGUMES CONSER PROVISOIR
057	FRUIT,NUTS,FRESH,DRIED		52059		67034		46626		51911	FRUITS FRAIS OU SECS
0577	NUTS EDIBLE,FRESH,DRIED		50378		65239		44442		49358	FRUITS A COQUES
05771	COCONUTS FRESH OR DRIED		41057		59069		37114		46717	NOIX DE COCO
05773	CASHEW NUTS,FRESH,DRIED		7005	W 1062	5399	W 1384	7053	W 390	2268	NOIX DE CAJOU
07	COFFEE,TEA,COCOA,SPICES		472288		379053		451087		467089	CAFE,THE,CACAO,EPICES
074	TEA AND MATE		429256	W 181263	336614	W 217700	404347	W 228986	416774	THE ET MATE
0741	TEA		429256	W 181263	336611	W 217700	404347	W 228986	416774	THE
075	SPICES		40966		40913		45605	W 14252	42432	EPICES
0752	SPICES,EX PEPPER,PIMENTO		37540		38069		37327	W 10780	36019	AUTRES EPICES
07522	CINNAMON,ETC		34724	W 8238	34785	W 8756	33941	W 9054	32957	CANNELLE
09	MISC EDIBLE PRODUCTS		4686		5489		9261		8800	PREP ALIMENTAIRES DIVERSES
098	EDIBLE PRODCTS,PREPS NES		4642		5458		9224		8774	PREP ALIMENTAIRES NDA
1	BEVERAGES AND TOBACCO		13471		42700		40652		39430	BOISSONS ET TABACS
12	TOBACCO AND MANUFACTURES		13033		42348		40186		38853	TABACS BRUTS FABRIQUES
121	TOBACCO UNMNFCTRD,REFUSE		5884	W 4279	39106	W 4353	36441		32629	TABACS BRUTS,DECHETS
1212	TOBACCO STRIPPED OR PART		3580	W 3536	32585	W 3465	29501		26563	TABACS PART ECOTES
122	TOBACCO,MANUFACTURED		7149	W 856	3243	W 828	3745	W 1057	6224	TABACS FABRIQUES
1222	CIGARETTES		7148	W 842	2845	W 826	3564	W 1016	4099	CIGARETTES
2	CRUDE MATERLS,EXCL FUELS		115279		126595		121706		135785	MAT BRUTES NON COMESTIBLES
23	RUBBER, CRUDE		64658		68761		63776		73062	CAOUTCHOUC BRUT
232	NATURAL RUBBER,GUMS		63845	W 78612	67550	W 69620	63674	W 69141	72468	LATEX CAOUTCHOUC NATUREL
23202	OTHER NATURAL RUBBER		31684	W 39594	31970	W 36485	31045	W 34540	34965	CAOUTCHOUC NATUREL
23203	BALATA,GUTTA–PERCHA, ETC		31902	W 35041	33102	W 31457	31293	W 31947	35270	BALATA,GUTTA–PERCHA
26	TEXTILE FIBRES AND WASTE		16357		17130		15989		21334	FIBRES TEXTILES
265	VEG FIBRE,EXCL COTN,JUTE		13902	W 74165	16069		14879	W 94286	19498	FIBRES VEGETALES
2659	VEG TEXT FIBRE,WASTE,NES		13897	W 74165	16069		14870	W 94247	19487	FIBRES TEXTILES VEGET NDA
26591	COIR FIBRE AND WASTE		13897	W 74161	16066	W 101109	14857	W 94160	19474	FIBRES DE COCO
27	CRUDE FERTLZR,MINRLS NES		8001		11191		9312		6102	ENGRAIS MINERAUX BRUTS
28	METALLIFEROUS ORES,SCRAP		5285		7055		11722		13092	MINERAIS METAL,DECHETS
29	CRUDE ANIMAL,VEG MAT NES		12048		13381		15475		15266	MATIERES BRUTES ANIM,VEGET
292	CRUDE VEG MATERIALS NES		10895	W 16537	12469	W 18008	14161	W 14251	13640	MAT BRUTES VEGETALES NDA
3	MINERAL FUELS ETC		27466		13104		17868		22393	COMBUSTIBLES MINERAUX LUB
33	PETROLEUM AND PRODUCTS		27464		13102		17867		22390	PETROLE ET DERIVES
334	PETROLEUM PRODUCTS,REFIN		8275	W 6	7		1177		7126	PRODUITS RAFFINES
335	RESIDUAL PETRLM PROD NES		19189		13094		16690		15264	PRODUITS RESIDUELS NDA
3352	MINERAL TARS AND PRODCTS	W 96417	19187	W 64154	13092	W 88219	16674		15264	GOUDRONS MINERAUX
33525	MINERAL TAR OILS ETC NES	W 96416	19187	W 64148	13090	W 88218	16674	W 117600	15264	AUTRES PRODUITS NDA
5	CHEMCLS,RELATED PROD NES		20172		24195		31640		27760	PRODUITS CHIMIQUES
59	CHEMICAL MATERIALS NES		13956		16444		16243		15379	MAT PROD CHIMIQUES NDA
598	MISCEL CHEM PRODUCTS NES		13336		15786		15692	W 13829	14582	PROD DIV INDUST CHIM NDA
5989	CHEM PRODUCTS,PREPS NES		13329		15760	W 13745	15649	W 13412	14378	PROD PREP CHIMIQUES NDA
59892	ACTIVTED NAT MINRL PROD		13297	W 14363	15645	W 13681	15561	W 13322	14249	CHARBONS ACTIVES
6	BASIC MANUFACTURES		273743		345932		424650		497036	ART MANUFACTURES
61	LEATHER,DRESSED FUR,ETC		23588		1046		1590		1898	CUIRS,PELLETERIES
611	LEATHER		23528		910		1010		970	CUIRS,PEAUX PREPARES
6114	LEATHR BOVINE NES,EQUINE	W 10807	23318	W 685	674		576	W 265	663	CUIRS DE BOVINS
62	RUBBER MANUFACTURES NES		19526		32014		40185		53939	CAOUTCHOUC MANUFACTURE
625	RUBBER TYRES, TUBES ETC		10867		20377	N 5768438	25207	N 7375624	37530	PNEUS CAOUTCHOUC VULCANISE
6259	OTH TYRES,TYRE CASES,ETC		10846		20226	N 5684265	24912	N 7251032	37222	AUTRES PNEUS RECHAPES FLAPS
62599	TYRES NES,TYRE CASES,ETC		10842	N 3044004	20179	N 5301860	24846	N 7000001	36921	PNEUS,FLAPS
628	RUBBER ARTICLES NES		7547		10903		14336		14740	OUVRAGES CAOUTCHOUC NDA
6289	OTH RUBBER ARTICLES NES		7463		10718	W 20506	13810		13968	AUT OUVR CAOUTCHOUC NDA
62898	UNHARD RUBBER PRODS NES		7463		10710	W 20496	13794		13959	OUV CAOUT VULC NON DURCI
63	WOOD,CORK MANUFACTRS NES		19329		13754		17662		21809	OUVRAGES LIEGE ET BOIS
635	WOOD MANUFACTURES NES		19245		13742		17422		21586	ART MANUF EN BOIS NDA
6354	WOOD MFRS DOMESTIC ETC		15331		10597		13880		17829	ART MANUF USAGE DOMESTIQUE
63549	WOOD MFRS,DOMESTIC NES		15314	MN 14517	10532	MN 22187	13844	MN 23257	17810	OUVRAGES DE TABLETTERIE
65	TEXTILE YARN,FABRICS,ETC		41382		81118		103231		132922	FILS,TISSUS,ARTICLES TEXTILE
651	TEXTILE YARN		8084		24127		31904		34905	FILS TEXTILES
6516	DISCON SYN FIB BLEND YRN		3858		19682		25145		26454	FILS FIBR TEX SYNT DIS MOINS
65166	DISCON SYN FIB–COTTN YRN		3568		19547		24900	W 183	25975	FILS TEXT SYNT MELANGE COTON
652	COTTON FABRICS,WOVEN		2205		6712		9428		18126	TISSUS DE COTON
6521	GREY WOVEN COTTON FABRIC		751		3643		6074		13529	TISSUS COT ECRUS NON MERCER
65214	GREY WOVEN COTTON NES		722		1259		3221		10566	AUT TISSUS 85% COTON ECRUS
653	WOVN MAN–MADE FIB FABRIC		4524		9223		18722		23348	TISSUS FIBRES SYNTH,ARTIF
6536	DISC REGN TXTL FABRC NES		1783	A 1882	5466	A 7729	9887		5825	TISSUS 85% TEXT ART DISC
658	TEXTILE ARTICLES NES		20701		33765		30827		44337	ART FACONNES MAT TEXTILES
6582	MADE–UP CANVAS GOODS		5212	N 187869	9770	N 730228	13853	N 661063	25385	BACHES,TENTES ETC
6584	LINENS ETC		12919		21432	MN 2293666	13157	MN 24780	12767	LINGE DE MAISON
65841	BED LINEN OF COTTON		2465	N 2360156	7498	N 1573620	3176	N 854598	1585	LINGE DE LIT DE COTON
65845	OTHER LINEN OF COTTON		8624	MN 36897	12981	MN 2291287	8380	MN 22845	7928	LINGE DE TOILETTE COTON
66	NONMETAL MINERAL MFS NES		144879		[illegible]9005		244714		265297	ART MIN NON METALLIQUES
666	POTTERY		17002	MN 26699	23712		27068	MN 30437	29609	POTERIE
6664	PORCELN,CHINA HOUSE WARE		7057	MN 10702	9478		11927	MN 14828	14215	VAISSELLE,ARTS MEN PORC
6666	CERAMIC ORNAMENTS ETC		9754	MN 15580	13604	MN 13243	14280	MN 15447	15020	OBJETS PORCELAINE,CERAM
667	PEARL,PREC–,SEMI–P STONE		121730		158803		209761		225996	PERLES, PIERRES GEMMES
6672	DIAMONDS NONINDUST,UNSET		65060		101779		137150		144996	DIAMANTS BRUTS
66722	— SRTD,ROUGH,SIMPLY WKD		20287		17656		23803		39889	DIAMANTS TRIES BRUTS
66729	— CUT ETC NOT SET		44726		84122		112592		105101	DIAMANTS TAILLES
6673	PREC–,SEMI–PR STONES NES		56664		56784		71276		79325	AUTRES PIERRES NON SERTIES
69	METAL MANUFACTURES NES		18750		21856		8191		9351	ART MANUFACT EN METAL NDA
694	STL,COPPR NAILS,NUTS,ETC		8093		10668		1981	W 301	256	CLOUS,VIS,ECROUS
69402	IRN,STL NUTS,BOLTS,ETC		8092		10658		1921	W 219	195	BOULONS,VIS,ECROUS FER,AC
695	TOOLS		6265		5704		447	N 20203	176	OUTILS A MAIN
6953	OTHER HAND TOOLS		6055		5600		412	N 19414	102	AUTRES OUTILS A MAIN
69532	WRENCHES AND SPANNERS		5990	N 2087529	5556		361	N 3908	20	CLES DE SERRAGE
7	MACHINES,TRANSPORT EQUIP		63916		44876		68860		82208	MACHINES MATERIEL TRANSPORT
72	MACHS FOR SPCL INDUSTRYS		2973		2082		15920		6047	MAC SPECIALES POUR INDUST

5. General Exports F.O.B. by Commodities according to the S.I.T.C. (Rev. 2) in thousand U.S. Dollars
Exportations Générales F.O.B. par Produits d'après la C.T.C.I. (Rév. 2) en milliers de Dollars E.U.

SITC CTCI	COMMODITY	1991		1992		1993		1994		PRODUIT
		WEIGHT POIDS	VALUE VALEUR	WEIGHT POIDS	VALUE VALEUR	WEIGHT POIDS	VALUE VALEUR	WEIGHT POIDS	VALUE VALEUR	
728	OTH MACHY FOR SPCL INDUS		1701		663		14553		2622	AUT MACH IND PARTICULIERES
7284	MACHY FOR SPCL INDUS NES		1437	N 495	528		14446		2463	MACH SPEC IND PARTICUL.
72848	OTH MCHY WITH INDIV FNCT		1367	N 1	220		13905		2034	AUTRES MACHINES NDA
74	GENRL INDUSTRL MACHY NES		12062		2345		2606		4487	MACH APP INDUSTRIE
744	MECHANICAL HANDLING EQU		10610		865		307		1558	EQUIP MANUTENTION PIECES
7442	LIFTING,LOADING MACH NES		10554		338		156		1411	APP LEVAGE,MANUTENTION
74428	OTH HANDLING ETC MCH NES		9514	N 1	133	N 2	7			AUT APP LEVAGE ETC
75	OFFICE MACHNES,ADP EQUIP		5338		15363		19086		18871	MACH BUREAU TRAIT AUTOM
759	OFFICE,ADP MCH PTS,ACCES		5218		15125		18722	MN 152731	18693	PIECES DU 751 ET 752
7599	ACCTG,ETC,ADP MCH PTS,AC		5114	MN 92837	15064	MN 2214164	18694	MN 152215	18650	PIECES DU 751 ET 752
77	ELECTRIC MACHNRY NES ETC		17222		20138		26430		40752	MACH APP ELECT NDA
772	SWITCHGEAR ETC,PARTS NES		8361	MN 39849	9365		7847	MN 26904	16590	APP COUPURE,SECT ETC
7721	SWITCHGEAR ETC		6579	MN 15553	6897	MN 16103	5049	MN 11337	11530	APP COUPURE,SECTIONMNT
778	ELECTRICAL MACHINERY NES		7465		8502		13513	MN 24351	11456	AUTRES MACH ELECT NDA
7782	ELECTRIC LAMPS,BULBS		4596	N 1451331	7849	N 2718204	12455	N 4030660	8926	LAMPES, TUBES ELECTRIQUES
77822	ELEC DISCHARGE LAMPS NES		4593	N 1444422	7830	N 2231034	12428	N 2101930	8651	LAMPES NON ULTRA–VIOLETS
79	OTHR TRANSPORT EQUIPMENT		21784		1674		1727		1424	AUTRE MATERIEL TRANSPORT
792	AIRCRAFT ETC		20885		707		957		431	APP NAVIGATION AERIENNE
7929	AIRCRAFT PARTS NES		20643		232		497		226	PIECES DU 792
8	MISC MANUFACTURED GOODS		848305		1302775		1502634		1704973	ART MANUFACTURES DIVERS
821	*FURNITURE,PARTS THEREOF		2061		2442		2409	N 681011	10789	MEUBLES ET PIECES
831	*TRAVEL GOODS,HANDBAGS		1753		9431	N 3831681	16166	N 7109747	34743	ARTICLES DE VOYAGE ETC
83102	TRAVEL GDS,TOILET–CASES	N 391641	1662	N 2963658	9166	N 3635655	14469	N 5396148	21021	ARTICLES DE VOYAGE
83109	OTHER TRAVEL BAGS,CASES		38		45	N 164233	1573	N 1438374	12617	AUT CONTENANTS SIMILAIRES
84	CLOTHING AND ACCESSORIES		790563		1183301		1355906		1484052	VETEMENTS
842	MENS OUTERWEAR NOT KNIT		141699		191463	MN 31546	216155	MN 36724	240932	VET DESSUS POUR HOMMES
8421	— OVERCOATS,OTHER COATS		10570		18911	N 1542278	25292	N 1759363	26134	MANTEAUX HOMMES MAT TEXT
84219	—— OF OTHER FIBRES		10489		18884	N 1485517	24510	N 1660859	24450	MANTEAUX HOMMES AUT FIBR
8423	— TROUSERS,BREECHES ETC		60179	MN 14641	75311	MN 15817	80653	MN 19589	86163	PANTALONS HOMMES MAT TEX
8424	— JACKETS,BLAZERS ETC		46959	N 7470912	72043	N 8166927	79240	N 8735613	93911	VESTES HOMMES MAT TEXTIL
8429	— OTHER OUTER GARMENTS		21900	N 5156825	21889	N 5204664	25664	N 5578749	28657	AUT VET DES HOM MAT TEX
843	WOMENS OUTERWEAR NONKNIT		291943	MN 3349806	462586		506253	MN 95632	557036	VET DESSUS FEMMES MAT TEX
8431	— COATS AND JACKETS		52021	N 8445410	82660	MN 9047	89425	MN 10098	90754	MANT,VEST FEM MAT TEXTIL
8432	— SUITS AND COSTUMES		7757	N 1244047	8611	N 1790189	11611	N 2436419	14232	COSTUMES–TAIL MAT TEXIL
8433	— DRESSES		24552	MN 3279591	48117	N 7171508	49663	MN 10742	70581	ROBES EN MAT–TEXTILES
8434	— SKIRTS		22607	N 6234444	43628	N 8134072	36747	N 7136978	34889	JUPES EN MAT TEXTILES
8435	— BLOUSES		102814	MN 31920	164856	MN 34334	181848	MN 34309	185514	BLOUSES FEM MAT TEXTILES
8439	— OTHER OUTER GARMENTS		82191	MN 22372	114713		136958	MN 30909	161066	AUT VET DES FEM MAT TEXT
844	UNDER GARMENTS NOT KNIT		84377		136694	MN 35042	166161	MN 33867	165311	VETEMENT DESSOUS MAT TEX
8441	— MENS SHIRTS		67219		110441	MN 27107	122975	MN 23848	109201	CHEMISES HOMMES MAT TEXT
84411	—— OF COTTON		47613	MN 15419	78472	MN 16307	82087	MN 12744	69005	CHEMISES HOMMES DE COTON
84412	—— OF SYNTHETIC FIBRES		19606		31969	MN 10801	40888	MN 11104	40196	CHEMISES HOMMES FIB SYNT
8442	— MENS,OTHR THAN SHIRTS		3232	N 898307	3946	N 2402681	10012	N 2386533	11850	SOUS–VET HOMMES MAT TEXT
8443	— WOMENS		13926	N 3395650	22307	N 5531934	33173	N 7632939	44260	VET DESSOUS FEM MAT TEXT
845	OUTERWEAR KNIT NONELASTC		115222	MN 28172	142511	MN 39968	179352	MN 42927	180462	VET DESSOUS,ACCES BONNET
8451	— JERSEYS,PULLOVERS ETC		26114	N 5783432	35238	N 6909613	39077	MN 10298	49726	CHANDAILS,PULL–OVERS ETC
8452	— WOMENS DRESSES ETC		17867	N 3522150	23895	N 4926950	25948	N 4822049	27384	ROBES,JUPES BONNETERIE
8459	— OTHER,CLTHG ACCESRYS		71241	MN 18867	83378	MN 28131	114327	MN 27807	103352	AUT VET DESSUS DE BONNE
846	UNDER GARMENTS KNITTED		103400	MN 79132	146503	MN 84574	171248	MN 90100	192319	SOUS VETS DE BONNETERIE
8462	— OF COTTON NON ELASTIC		38214	MN 22372	51691	MN 23729	60335	MN 29735	64989	SOUS–VET BONNET COTON
84629	—— OTHER		38214	MN 22372	51691	MN 23729	60335	MN 29735	64989	AUT SOUS–VET BONNET COTON
8463	— OF SYNTH FBR NONELAST		56970	MN 49267	82713	MN 52314	96707	MN 51137	108239	SOUS–VET BONNET FIB SYNT
84631	—— PANTY HOSE (TIGHTS)		18022	MN 37259	30314	MN 37075	29663	MN 32841	25708	COLLANTS BON FIBR SYNT
84632	—— MENS SHIRTS		38948	MN 12008	52400	MN 15239	67043	MN 18296	82531	CHEMISES DE BON FIB SYNMT
8465	CORSETS,GARTERS,ETC		8216	N 7492781	12098	N 8531645	14206	MN 9228	19090	CORSETS,GAINES ART SIM
84651	BRASSIERES		6639	N 5987301	9576	N 7240565	12261	N 8625983	17587	SOUTIENS–GORGE,BUSTIERS
847	TEXTILE CLTHNG ACCES NES		27955	MN 74018	42783	MN 82495	47228	MN 112675	58834	ACCES VET MAT TEXT NDA
8471	— NOT KNITTED		5828	N 2771943	9678	N 3786626	9350	MN 15788	13673	ACCES VET MAT TEX NON BON
8472	CLTHNG ACCESRYS ETC KNIT		22127	MN 71246	33105	MN 78708	37878	MN 96887	45161	ACCES VET BONNE NDA
84721	KNIT GLOVES,ETC NONELAST		17474	MN 65819	29564	MN 69401	33262	MN 86970	39071	GANTERIE BONNET NON ELAS
848	HEADGEAR,NONTXTL CLOTHNG		25968	MN 623665	60762		69510		89159	VET ACCES MAT AUT QUE TEX
8481	LEATHER CLOTHES,ACCESSOR		9065	N 2651900	12432	N 3128121	15783	N 3699411	15431	VET ACCES MAT CUIR ARTIF
8482	PLASTC,RUBBR CLTHG,ACCES		11135	MN 597947	28706	MN 546822	33620	MN 714099	49422	VET ACCES MAT PLAS ARTIF
84822	RUBBER CLOTHING,ACCESRYS		11096	MN 597350	28257	MN 545263	32027	MN 711842	47346	VET ACCES CAOUT VULCAN
8484	HEADGEAR		5767	MN 23067	19624		20103	MN 30404	24299	COIFFURES ET PARTIES NDA
84843	HEADGEAR TEXTILE NONFELT		5583	MN 16846	19301		19294	MN 24251	22815	CHAPEAUX EN BONNETERIE
851	*FOOTWEAR		10223	N 4470661	17168	N 5244029	25296	N 5216890	38164	CHAUSSURES
85102	FOOTWEAR LEATHER		8438	N 3179486	14236	N 3869432	21490	N 3851437	34455	CHAUS SEMELLES EN CUIR
89	MISC MANUFCTRD GOODS NES		41783		87861		99026		132799	ART MANUFACTURES DIVERS
893	ARTICLES OF PLASTIC NES		11088		11528		13911		15556	OUVRAGES EN MAT DIVIS 58
8931	PLSTC PACKG CONTNRS,LIDS		8269		7359		8398		9311	ART TRANSP EMBALLAGE ETC
894	TOYS,SPORTING GOODS,ETC		5389		32284	MN 60220	40852	MN 49217	47975	VOITURES ENFANTS,JOUETS
8942	TOYS,INDOOR GAMES ETC		4691	MN 32298	31137	MN 52443	38759	MN 37054	44768	JOUETS,JEUX ETC
89423	TOYS NES		3506	MN 25406	27943	MN 26339	34192	MN 26968	40068	JOUETS,MODELES REDUITS
897	GOLD,SILVER WARE,JEWELRY		7953		10640		12530		24731	BIJOUTERIE,ORFEVRERIE
8973	PREC JEWLRY,GLD–SILVWARE		7169		7175		7217		17855	BIJOUX OR,ARGENT ORFEVRE
89731	PRECIOUS METAL JEWELLERY		7168		6835		7161		16760	ART BIJOUTERIE,JOAILLER
899	OTHER MANUFACTURED GOODS		16271		29361		24559		33949	AUT ART MANUF DIVERS NDA
8997	BASKETWORK,BROOMS ETC		9961		21109		14670		17645	OUVRAGES VANNERIE NDA
89972	BRUSHES,BROOMS,MOPS ETC		9752	MN 72356	20975	MN 72654	14471	MN 76159	17539	BALAIS ET BALAYETTES
9	GOODS NOT CLASSD BY KIND		55767		50805		59702		60134	ART TRANSACT NON CLASSES
931	*SPECIAL TRANSACTIONS		55764	W 333960	50567	W 434259	59700	W 453119	59905	TRANS.SPECIALES

1. HISTORICAL SERIES, 1959–1994 GENERAL TRADE, IMPORTS C.I.F., EXPORTS F.O.B.
SERIES HISTORIQUES, 1959–1994 COMMERCE GENERAL, IMPORTATIONS C.A.F., EXPORTATIONS F.O.B

YEAR ANNEE	VALUE IN MILLION SURINAM.GUILDERS VALEUR EN MILLION SURINAM.GUILDERS MERCHANDISE –MARCHANDISE IMPORTS	EXPORTS	GOLD –OR IMPORTS	EXPORTS	CONVERSION FACTORS U.S. CENTS PER SURINAME GUILDER FACTEURS DE CONVERSION CENTS E.U. PAR SURINAME GUILDER IMPORTS	EXPORTS	INDEX NUMBERS –INDICES QUANTUM IMPORTS	EXPORTS	UNIT VALUE VALEUR UNITAIRE IMPORTS	EXPORTS
1959	84.86	77.01			53.0264	53.0264				
1960	101.80	82.48			53.0264	53.0264				
1961	101.09	77.99			53.0264	53.0264				
1962	102.87	79.98			53.0264	53.0264				
1963	110.14	87.48			53.0264	53.0264				
1964	152.00	90.13			53.0264	53.0264				
1965	179.10	110.45			53.0264	53.0264				
1966	168.71	171.24			53.0264	53.0264				
1967	193.42	198.16			53.0264	53.0264				
1968	188.50	216.53			53.0264	53.0264				
1969	207.56	249.26			53.0264	53.0264				
1970	217.70	257.70			53.0264	53.0264				
1971	237.80	296.74			53.0432	53.0426				
1972	258.20	308.20			55.9039	55.9039				
1973	281.00	322.20			56.0221	56.0221				
1974	410.50	467.90			55.9620	55.9633				
1975	454.10	468.50			56.0220	56.0220				
1976	525.50	508.30			56.0220	56.0220				
1977	709.90	589.30			56.0223	56.0223				
1978	724.50	702.40			56.0224	56.0223				
1979	738.80	792.70			56.0224	56.0224				
1980	925.30	894.50			56.0224	56.0224				
1981	1010.60	815.20			56.0224	56.0224				
1982	936.40	735.70			56.0224	56.0224				
1983	785.90	623.50			56.0224	56.0224				
1984	698.90	650.50			56.0224	56.0224				
1985	603.60	587.00			56.0224	56.0224				
1986	584.40	597.77			56.0224	56.0224				
1987	525.37	546.26			56.0224	56.0224				
1988	626.36	730.63			56.0224	56.0224				
1989	790.60	966.50			56.0224	56.0224				
1990	842.50	843.30			56.0224	56.0224				
1991	909.00	648.10			56.0220	56.0220				
1992	1142.08	644.82			56.0220	56.0220				
1993	1798.44	2318.84			56.0289	56.0289				
1994	59609.51	60225.58			0.9106	0.8651				

2. IMPORTS BY BROAD ECONOMIC CATEGORY AND EXPORTS BY INDUSTRIAL ORIGIN. (PERCENTAGE OF TOTAL VALUE)
IMPORTATIONS PAR CATEGORIES ECONOMIQUES ET EXPORTATIONS PAR BRANCHE D'ACTIVITE.(EN POURCENTAGE DE LA VALEUR TOTALE)

IMPORTS – IMPORTATIONS

	1990	1991	1992	1993	1994	1995	1996
TOTAL IMPORTS–IMPORTATIONS TOTALES	100.	100.	100.				
1 FOOD BEV–ALIMENTATION BOISSONS	10.5	11.3	7.3				
11 PRIMARY–PRODUITS DE BASE	4.0	3.5	1.9				
111 FOR INDUSTRY–POUR L'INDUSTRIE	1.9	1.3	0.9				
112 FOR HOUSEHOLDS–POUR LES MENAGES	2.1	2.2	1.0				
12 PROCESSED–PRODUITS ELABORES	6.6	7.7	5.4				
121 FOR INDUSTRY–POUR L'INDUSTRIE	1.8	2.4	1.4				
122 FOR HOUSEHOLDS–POUR LES MENAGES	4.8	5.4	4.1				
2 IND SUPPLIES–APPROV INDUSTRIELS	36.3	30.0	32.2				
21 PRIMARY–PRODUITS DE BASE	2.1	2.0	1.7				
22 PROCESSED–PRODUITS ELABORES	34.1	28.0	30.6				
3 FUELS–COMBUSTIBLES	17.9	17.0	13.3				
31 PRIMARY–PRODUITS DE BASE	3.4	2.9	2.4				
32 PROCESSED–PRODUITS ELABORES	14.4	14.2	10.9				
321 MOTOR SPIRIT–ESSENCE	3.4	3.1	2.5				
322 OTHER–AUTRES	11.0	11.1	8.4				
4 MACHINERY–EQUIPEMENT	15.0	17.5	14.0				
41 CAPITAL EQUIPMENT–MACHINES	12.4	15.0	12.1				
42 PARTS–PIECES ACCESSOIRES	2.6	2.5	1.9				
5 TRANSPORT–TRANSPORT	9.7	12.1	24.1				
51 PASSENGER CARS–AUTOMOBILES	2.9	4.9	18.5				
52 OTHER–AUTRES	3.1	3.6	2.8				
521 INDUSTRIAL–INDUSTRIELS	2.7	3.3	2.3				
522 NON INDUSTRIAL–NON INDUSTRIEL	0.5	0.3	0.5				
53 PARTS–PIECES ACCESSOIRES	3.6	3.6	2.8				
6 CONSUM GOODS–BIENS CONSOMMATION	10.2	11.3	8.9				
61 DURABLE–DURABLES	2.6	2.6	2.4				
62 SEMI DURABLE–SEMI DURABLES	5.1	5.2	3.9				
63 NON DURABLE–NON DURABLES	2.5	3.5	2.6				
7 GOODS NES–BIENS NDA	0.5	0.8	0.1				

EXPORTS – EXPORTATIONS

	1990	1991	1992	1993	1994	1995	1996
TOTAL EXPORTS–EXPORTATIONS TOTALES	100.	100.	100.				
1 AGRICULTURE	15.4	17.7	16.9				
2 MINING QUARRY–INDUS EXTRACTIVES	1.5	0.0	1.3				
3 MANUFACTURING–IND MANUFACTUR	83.1	82.3	81.8				
31 FOOD BEV TOBACCO–ALIM BOISS TAB	0.6	0.6	1.0				
32 TEXTILES–INDUSTRIES TEXTILES	0.0	0.0	0.0				
33 WOOD & PRODUCTS–BOIS & PRODUITS	0.0		0.3				
34 PAPER & PRODUCTS–PAPIER & PRODT	0.2	0.2	0.0				
35 CHEMICALS–INDUSTRIES CHIMIQUES	73.6	71.5	66.9				
36 NON METAL MIN–MIN NON METAL	0.0	0.0	0.0				
37 BASIC METAL–IND METAL BASE	0.0	0.0	12.2				
38 METAL MANUF–MANUF METAL	8.7	9.9	1.3				
39 OTH MANUF IND–AUTRES MANUF	0.0	0.0	0.0				

3. TRADE BY PRINCIPAL COUNTRIES OF FIRST AND LAST CONSIGNMENT (VALUE IN THOUSAND U.S. DOLLARS)
ECHANGES SELON LES PRINCIPAUX PAYS DE PREMIERE ET DE DERNIERE CONSIGNATION (VALEUR EN MILLIERS DE DOLLARS EU)

COUNTRIES–PAYS	GENERAL IMPORTS C.I.F. IMPORTATIONS GENERALES C.A.F				
	1990	1991	1992	1993	1994
World	469283	509239	639815	1007648	542804
Africa	42	3	5		
Americas	301664	313231	379319	791157	363931
Northern America	194372	198527	255395	447807	260828
LAIA	27806	22557	23469	126857	27659
CACM	454	5781	15523	982	
Caribbean	71195	82138	78349	206210	66674
Rest of America	7837	4228	6583	9302	8771
As.ex F.USSR	27983	38957	114638		
Eur.x F.USSR	139581	157032	145810	149832	144018
EU	137588	153827	143831	145710	139283
EFTA	1491	2515	1871	4122	4735
East Europe	147	69	107		
Other Europe	356	621	0		
Former USSR					
Oceania	13	16	2		
USA/Etats–Unis d'Amer	193975	195773	254254	441381	258031
Netherlands/Pays–Bas	110207	112812	124747	129209	96553
Trinidad and Tobago	42137	57063	62724	186971	56331
Venezuela	1984	3172	5858	115649	16380
Japan/Japon	13330	19008	99759		
Netherlands Antilles	24687	17770	8896	12938	7341
Brazil/Brésil	20207	15380	13324	7965	6589
United Kingdom	5613	8270	6588	5700	24635
Germany/Allemagne	9658	7604	5017	169	7168
Belgium–Luxembourg	8957	6752	3964	2376	2607
Italy/Italie	1039	12581	221	2025	6037
Guatemala	2	2450	14395	982	
Panama	2561	3061	2939	4150	4984
Guyana	4908	729	2969	4389	3216
Jamaica/Jamaïque	2573	3999	4429	2164	2871
Hong Kong	4998	5893	4040		
France,Monac	785	3997	1936	5397	1814
Canada	397	2751	1140	6426	2797
Colombia/Colombie	3769	2125	2373	1973	3222
Dominican Republic	1432	3212	1601	4049	118
Switz.Liecht	1169	1713	783	3242	1520
Korea, Republic of	1361	4334	1302		
Norway,SVD,JM	322	803	1088	880	3216
China/Chine	1566	1619	2958		
Mexico/Mexique	652	1187	1785	1224	971
Honduras	1	2948	1002		
Thailand/Thaïlande	208	1369	1260		
French Guiana	368	439	675	763	571
Argentina/Argentine	1144	329	53	46	496
Indonesia/Indonésie	238	546	1169		
India/Inde	916	483	379		
Denmark/Danemark	180	388	322	481	347
Singapore/Singapour	226	727	643		
Barbados/Barbade	281	91	659	89	13
Ireland/Irlande	66	952	1		
Fm Yugoslav	350	621			
Spain/Espagne	546	137	20	31	28
Costa Rica	421	232	104		
Finland/Finlande	23	124	601		
Malaysia/Malaisie	629	4	8		
Sweden/Suède	106	70	101	289	73
Austria/Autriche	165	125	312	33	0
Peru/Pérou		169	76		
Portugal	200	17			8
Turkey/Turquie	10	12	176		
Korea Dem People's Rp	51		138		
Ecuador/Equateur	51	133			
El Salvador	30	151			
Former GDR	128				
Greece/Grèce	42				12

COUNTRIES–PAYS	GENERAL EXPORTS F.O.B. EXPORTATIONS GENERALES F.O.B.				
	1990	1991	1992	1993	1994
Monde	475264	363079	361243	1299218	521012
Afrique	1			2	
Amériques	86459	87471	95198	587861	160951
Amérique du Nord	54065	46371	40912	343530	90106
ALAI	22658	29427	38135	205087	32262
MCAC				14	
Caraïbes	9372	11073	15821	36508	38067
Autre Amérique	365	600	330	2722	517
Asie l'URSS exclus	32020	27984	18889	30000	36324
Europe l'URSS exclus	356784	245587	247135	668594	320348
UE	175629	122829	170672	395694	168300
AELE	168012	122756	76463	272900	152048
Europe de l'Est		2	1		
Autre de l'Europe	13142				
Ancienne URSS		2038			3259
Océanie	1				
Netherlands/Pays–Bas	137134	94525	104159	349879	117679
Norway,SVD,JM	168010	122756	76463	272750	151697
USA/Etats–Unis d'Amer	54063	46324	40911	343451	90098
Brazil/Brésil	22657	29427	38058	205000	32255
Japan/Japon	31987	27967	18866	29983	36185
France,Monac	22336	8369	50050	14308	7426
Spain/Espagne	3483	6450	2971	22981	33755
Netherlands Antilles	373	559	9172	19468	26858
Trinidad and Tobago	7232	8664	4667	15092	9356
United Kingdom	10324	6395	9620	7708	7651
Fm Yugoslav	13142				
Martinique	1603	1721	1706	1403	1175
Portugal	1900	463	3592	13	
Former USSR/Anc. URSS		2038			3259
Germany/Allemagne	119	2841	189	217	332
Belgium–Luxembourg	26	1451	43	583	1409
French Guiana	258	338	124	1926	356
Sweden/Suède	278	2237			
Guyana	106	260	203	796	161
Guadeloupe	139	125	264	436	438
Switz.Liecht	2	0		150	352
Barbados/Barbade	0		3	67	220
Italy/Italie		88	48		48
Venezuela	0	1	67	82	6
Canada	1	47	1	79	8
Philippines					101
Hong Kong	29	12	6	6	
Jamaica/Jamaïque		0	1	42	0
Dominican Republic	19				19
Austria/Autriche	28	10		1	
Korea, Republic of		2	5	10	1
China/Chine	3	0	6		8
Singapore/Singapour		0			15
Colombia/Colombie	0		11	4	0
Guatemala				14	
Denmark/Danemark	3			4	
Panama		1	2		0
Poland/Pologne		2			
India/Inde		2			
Mexico/Mexique				1	0
Grenada/Grenade				1	
Ghana	1				
Iran (Islamic Rp. of)			1		

(VALUE AS PERCENTAGE OF WORLD TOTAL)(VALEURS EN POURCENTAGE DU TOTAL MONDIAL)

	1985	1986	1987	1988	1989	1990	1991	1992	1993	1994
Africa			0.0			0.0	0.0	0.0		
Americas		65.4	66.7	62.0	65.8	64.3	61.5	59.3	78.5	67.0
Northern America		32.1	33.2	37.7	44.0	41.4	39.0	39.9	44.4	48.1
LAIA		10.5	11.6	7.2	6.6	5.9	4.4	3.7	12.6	5.1
CACM		0.3	0.4	0.1	0.0	0.1	1.1	2.4	0.1	
Caribbean		22.0	20.9	15.9	14.2	15.2	16.1	12.2	20.5	12.3
Rest of America		0.5	0.7	1.1	1.0	1.7	0.8	1.0	0.9	1.6
As.ex F.USSR		4.4	4.2	5.4	7.7	6.0	7.7	17.9		
Eur.x F.USSR		27.7	28.4	32.5	26.5	29.7	30.8	22.8	14.9	26.5
EU		27.0	28.2	31.3	26.3	29.3	30.2	22.5	14.5	25.7
EFTA		0.7	0.2	1.2	0.2	0.3	0.5	0.3	0.4	0.9
East Europe				0.0	0.0	0.0	0.0	0.0		
Other Europe		0.0	0.0	0.0	0.0	0.1	0.1	0.0		
Former USSR				0.0						
Oceania		0.0		0.0		0.0	0.0	0.0		
USA/Etats–Unis d'Amer		31.7	32.8	37.3	43.9	41.3	38.4	39.7	43.8	47.5
Netherlands/Pays–Bas		16.2	17.5	23.6	20.1	23.5	22.2	19.5	12.8	17.8
Trinidad and Tobago		9.2	12.9	7.5	9.4	9.0	11.2	9.8	18.6	10.4
Venezuela		1.4	2.2	0.4	0.6	0.4	0.6	0.9	11.5	3.0
Japan/Japon		2.4	1.9	1.5	4.2	2.8	3.7	15.6		
Netherlands Antilles		11.8	5.5	6.4	3.6	5.3	3.5	1.4	1.3	1.4
Brazil/Brésil		7.4	8.6	5.9	5.1	4.3	3.0	2.1	0.8	1.2
United Kingdom		3.3	4.2	2.9	1.5	1.2	1.6	1.0	0.6	4.5
Germany/Allemagne		2.8	2.7	2.2	1.2	2.1	1.5	0.8	0.0	1.3
Belgium–Luxembourg		1.0	1.2	0.5	0.8	1.9	1.3	0.6	0.2	0.5

	1985	1986	1987	1988	1989	1990	1991	1992	1993	1994
Afrique		0.2	0.0	0.5	1.3	0.0			0.0	
Amériques		31.1	29.2	28.8	27.2	18.2	24.1	26.4	45.2	30.9
Amérique du Nord		15.7	18.6	19.5	13.3	11.4	12.8	11.3	26.4	17.3
ALAI		12.4	8.4	6.5	6.1	4.8	8.1	10.6	15.8	6.2
MCAC		0.0	0.0	0.0					0.0	
Caraïbes		2.4	1.7	2.5	7.7	2.0	3.0	4.4	2.8	7.3
Autre Amérique		0.6	0.6	0.2	0.1	0.1	0.2	0.1	0.2	0.1
Asie l'URSS exclus		11.0	10.2	6.2	5.6	6.7	7.7	5.2	2.3	7.0
Europe l'URSS exclus		57.7	60.5	64.5	65.9	75.1	67.6	68.4	51.5	61.5
UE		39.8	35.1	38.1	35.2	37.0	33.8	47.2	30.5	32.3
AELE		17.9	25.2	26.4	29.0	35.4	33.8	21.2	21.0	29.2
Europe de l'Est					1.4		0.0	0.0		
Autre de l'Europe			0.2		0.4	2.8				
Ancienne URSS							0.6			0.6
Océanie						0.0				
Netherlands/Pays–Bas		20.6	20.8	26.6	24.7	28.9	26.0	28.8	26.9	22.6
Norway,SVD,JM		17.3	24.8	26.4	29.0	35.4	33.8	21.2	21.0	29.1
USA/Etats–Unis d'Amer		15.4	17.6	19.5	13.3	11.4	12.8	11.3	26.4	17.3
Brazil/Brésil		8.8	7.7	6.5	6.1	4.8	8.1	10.5	15.8	6.2
Japan/Japon		10.9	10.2	6.2	5.2	6.7	7.7	5.2	2.3	6.9
France,Monac		4.0	2.4	1.7	1.5	4.7	2.3	13.9	1.1	1.4
Spain/Espagne		0.2	0.2		0.5	0.7	1.8	0.8	1.8	6.5
Netherlands Antilles		0.4	0.0	0.2	0.1	0.1	0.2	2.5	1.5	5.2
Trinidad and Tobago		0.0	0.2	0.9	7.0	1.5	2.4	1.3	1.2	1.8
United Kingdom		5.4	4.5	4.9	4.6	2.2	1.8	2.7	0.6	1.5

4. General imports C.I.F. by Commodities according to the S.I.T.C. (Rev. 2) in thousand U.S. Dollars
Importations Générales C.A.F. par Produits d'après la C.T.C.I. (Rév. 2) en milliers de Dollars E.U.

SITC CTCI	COMMODITY	1989		1990		1991		1992		PRODUIT
		WEIGHT POIDS	VALUE VALEUR	WEIGHT POIDS	VALUE VALEUR	WEIGHT POIDS	VALUE VALEUR	WEIGHT POIDS	VALUE VALEUR	
	ALL COMMODITIES		442953		469283		509239		639815	TOUS PRODUITS
0	FOOD AND LIVE ANIMALS		36684		41541		46375		36713	ALIMENTS,ANIMAUX VIVANTS
01	MEAT AND PREPARATIONS		675		1631		2353		992	VIANDES ET PREPARATIONS
02	DAIRY PRODCTS,BIRDS'EGGS		7962		5860		8947		5592	PRODUITS LAITIERS,OEUFS
022	MILK AND CREAM	W 2551	4120	W 1016	1804	W 3281	5771	W 934	2824	LAIT ET CREME
0223	MILK AND CREAM FRESH	W 7	4	W 5	5	W 966	1801	W 2	1	LAIT,CREME FRAIS
0224	MILK,CREAM PRESERVED ETC	W 2544	4116	W 1011	1799	W 2315	3970	W 932	2823	LAIT,CREME CONS,CONC
02242	MILK DRY,1.5% FAT OR LES	W 2353	3871	W 787	1546	W 1982	3616	W 814	2598	LAIT POUDRE INF 1.5%
025	EGGS,BIRDS,FRESH,PRSRVD	W 668	3130	W 706	3233	W 420	1954	W 112	980	OEUFS
0251	— IN SHELL	W 668	3129	W 701	3214	W 418	1950	W 112	979	OEUFS EN COQUILLE
03	FISH AND PREPARATIONS		1245		1527		4683		2270	POISSONS ET PREPARATIONS
035	FISH SALTED,DRIED,SMOKED	W 12	61	W 23	71	W 726	1967	W 60	495	POISSON SECHE,SALE,FUME
037	FISH ETC PREPD,PRSVD NES	W 580	1178	W 789	1438	W 1383	2712	W 447	1764	POIS,CRUST,MOL PREPARES
0371	FISH PREPARD,PRESRVD NES	W 580	1177	W 789	1437	W 1383	2710	W 447	1764	CONSERVES DE POISSONS
04	CEREALS AND PREPARATIONS		11288		10891		8726		7379	CEREALES ET PRODUITS
041	WHEAT ETC UNMILLED	W 51596	10039	W 138505	8468	W 38644	6248	W 11447	5512	FROMENT,EPEAUTRE
0412	OTHER WHEAT ETC UNMILLED	W 51596	10039	W 138505	8468	W 38644	6248	W 11447	5512	AUTRE FROMENT NON MOULU
048	CEREAL ETC PREPARATIONS	W 873	1120	W 1222	1716	W 1387	1647	W 403	1417	PREPTNS A BASE CEREALES
05	VEGETABLES AND FRUIT		4289		5980		5345		5229	LEGUMES ET FRUITS
054	VEG ETC FRSH,SMPLY PRSVD	W 6880	3285	W 8924	4475	W 7389	3970	W 3531	3661	LEGUMES FRAIS,CONG,SECS
0542	LEGUMINOUS VEGETBLES DRY	W 2168	1487	W 2586	2065	W 1761	1063	W 492	640	LEGUMES A COSSE SECS
06	SUGAR AND PREPS,HONEY		4715		6822		7280		6139	SUCRES ET PRODUITS
061	SUGAR AND HONEY	W 11707	4409	W 13121	6164	W 16138	6402	W 6707	5542	SUCRES ET MIEL
0611	RAW BEET AND CANE SUGAR	W 2330	459	W 3516	1282	W 8341	3197	W 4546	3524	SUCRES BRUTS
0612	REFINED SUGAR ETC	W 9301	3894	W 9506	4801	W 7725	3146	W 2046	1669	SUCRES RAFFINES
07	COFFEE,TEA,COCOA,SPICES		1225		1617		2115		1208	CAFE,THE,CACAO,EPICES
09	MISC EDIBLE PRODUCTS		4917		5983		5581		6719	PREP ALIMENTAIRES DIVERSES
098	EDIBLE PRODCTS,PREPS NES	W 1482	4682	W 1666	5706	W 1773	5215	W 893	6440	PREP ALIMENTAIRES NDA
09802	TEA,ETC EXTRACT,ESSENCE	W 105	1422	W 93	1139	W 102	1398	W 54	2481	EXTRAITS DE THE
09809	MISC FOOD PREPRTIONS NES	W 444	1246	W 846	2527	W 724	1988	W 414	2308	PREP ALIMENTAIRES NDA
1	BEVERAGES AND TOBACCO		4554		5906		6839		11823	BOISSONS ET TABACS
11	BEVERAGES		3164		3767		5054		7562	BOISSONS
112	ALCOHOLIC BEVERAGES	W 1456	3139	W 2131	3458	W 3210	4650	W 3038	6503	BOISSONS ALCOOLIQUES
1123	BEER,ALE,STOUT,PORTER	W 137	88	W 599	352	W 1623	1007	W 1533	2095	BIERES
1124	DISTILLED ALCOHOLIC BEVS	W 1174	2657	W 1344	2747	W 1267	3219	W 1384	4055	ALCOOLS,EAUX–DE–VIE
11241	WHISKY	W 1029	2151	W 1148	2142	W 1098	2631	W 602	3116	WHISKY
12	TOBACCO AND MANUFACTURES		1390		2139		1785		4261	TABACS BRUTS FABRIQUES
121	TOBACCO UNMNFCTRD,REFUSE	W 409	1228	W 475	1561	W 161	616	W 348	2746	TABACS BRUTS,DECHETS
1211	TOBACCO,NOT STRIPPED	W 409	1228	W 475	1561	W 161	616	W 348	2746	TABACS NON ECOTES
2	CRUDE MATERLS,EXCL FUELS		9256		7648		8811		7160	MAT BRUTES NON COMESTIBLES
27	CRUDE FERTLZR,MINRLS NES		4889		4836		6621		6659	ENGRAIS MINERAUX BRUTS
273	STONE,SAND AND GRAVEL	W 145370	2904	W 168251	3569	W 193779	4755	W 206440	5004	PIERRES,SABLES,GRAVIERS
2734	GRAVEL,CRUSHED STONE,ETC	W 144170	2862	W 168248	3566	W 189881	4575	W 206308	4916	PIERRES CONCASSEES
278	OTHER CRUDE MINERALS	W 10646	1960	W 4674	1230	W 6157	1528	W 6854	1587	AUTRES MINERAUX BRUTS
2789	MINERALS CRUDE NES	W 7925	1443	W 1069	498	W 3115	910	W 4965	1131	MINERAUX BRUTS NDA
28	METALLIFEROUS ORES,SCRAP		3706		1662		1452			MINERAIS METAL,DECHETS
287	BASE METAL ORES,CONC NES	W 152228	3706	W 59809	1662	W 35952	1452			MINERAIS METAUX COMMUNS
2873	ALUMINIUM ORES,ALUMINA	W 152228	3706	W 59809	1662	W 35952	1452			MINERAIS D'ALUMINIUM
28731	ALUMINIUM ORE,CONCNTRATE	W 152228	3706	W 59809	1662	W 35932	1449			MINERAIS D'ALUMINIUM
3	MINERAL FUELS ETC		72464		84117		87704		86598	COMBUSTIBLES MINERAUX LUB
32	COAL,COKE AND BRIQUETTES		6927		6285		6770		7355	HOUILLES,COKES,BRIQUETTES
323	BRIQUETS,COKE,SEMI–COKE	W 16969	6924	W 15921	6284	W 14831	6768	W 17843	7354	BRIQUETTES
33	PETROLEUM AND PRODUCTS		59627		67991		73141		71387	PETROLE ET DERIVES
334	PETROLEUM PRODUCTS,REFIN	W 366734	59227	W 387642	67661	W 432496	72135	W 344046	69652	PRODUITS RAFFINES
3341	GASOLINE,OTH LIGHT OILS	W 60561	14710	W 71704	16831	W 69810	16463	W 41243	16269	ESSENCES POUR MOTEURS
33411	MOTOR,AVIATION SPIRIT	W 50322	12070	W 48283	10780	W 64858	14820	W 37258	14546	ESSENCES MOTEURS D'AVIONS
33419	OTH LIGHT PETROLEUM OILS	W 9262	2167	W 21143	5251	W 3543	1032	W 3618	1373	AUTRES HUILES LEGERES
3344	FUEL OILS,NES	W 296783	38853	W 306253	43686	W 350526	45589	W 296961	44009	FUEL OILS
3345	LUBS,PETROLEUM OILS NES	W 6820	5165	W 7295	6451	W 9767	9496	W 4515	8850	HUILES LUBRIFIANTES
33451	LUBS(HIGH PETR CONT) ETC	W 682	615	W 862	1060	W 870	1570	W 226	670	HUILES LUBRIF,H LOURDES
33452	LUBS (LOW PETRLM CONTNT)	W 6138	4550	W 6433	5391	W 8897	7926	W 4289	8180	PREPARATIONS LUBRIFIANTES
341	*GAS,NATURAL AND MANUFCT	W 13803	5910	W 17439	9842	W 15864	7793	W 10054	7856	GAZ NATUREL,GAZ MANUFACT
3414	PETROLEUM GASES, GASEOUS	W 13796	5887	W 17433	9794	W 15537	7723	W 10052	7835	GAZ DE PETROLE GAZEUX
4	ANIMAL,VEGETABLE OIL,FAT		3573		5544		7733		5364	HUILES,GRAISSES ANIM,VEG
42	FIXED VEGETABLE OIL,FAT		2589		4822		7560		3495	HUILES VEGETALES FIXES
423	FIXED VEG OILS,SOFT	W 2845	2560	W 4550	3667	W 7224	6981	W 2020	3354	HUILES VEGET DOUCES FIXES
4232	SOYA BEAN OIL	W 2845	2558	W 4549	3666	W 7210	6975	W 2014	3345	HUILE DE SOJA
5	CHEMCLS,RELATED PROD NES		117259		101681		90249		81741	PRODUITS CHIMIQUES
51	ORGANIC CHEMICALS		2309		1189		1672		1439	PROD CHIMIQ ORGANIQUES
516	OTHER ORGANIC CHEMICALS	W 868	1869	W 244	1037	W 516	1608	W 330	1347	AUTRES PROD ORGANIQUES
5169	ORGANIC CHEMICALS,NES	W 868	1869	W 244	1037	W 516	1608	W 330	1347	PROD CHIM ORGANIQUES NDA
51699	OTHER ORGANIC COMPOUNDS	W 867	1845	W 226	914	W 497	1560	W 329	1329	AUTRES COMPOS ORGANIQUES
52	INORGANIC CHEMICALS		81919		63145		53152		39188	PROD CHIM INORGANIQUES
522	INORG ELEMNTS,OXIDES,ETC	W 479899	81919	W 337156	63134	W 270028	53150		39181	ELEMENTS INORGANIQUES
5225	INORGANIC BASES ETC NES	W 478963	81470	W 335971	62573	W 267668	52285	W 232020	38263	AUTRES BASES OXYDES METAL
52253	SODIUM HYDROXIDE, OTHER	W 478963	81470	W 335971	62573	W 267668	52285	W 232020	38263	HYDROXYDE SODIUM AQUEUX
53	DYES,TANNING,COLOUR PROD		2864		4234		5238		6548	PROD TEINTURE,COLORANTS
533	PIGMENTS,PAINTS,ETC	W 1124	2864	W 1783	4234	W 6294	5238	W 2211	6548	PIGMENTS,PEINTURES,VERNIS
5334	VARNISHES,DISTEMPERS ETC	W 811	1954	W 1318	3030	W 5212	4006	W 1515	4164	PEINTURES A L'EAU
541	*MEDICINAL,PHARM PRODUCT	K 467963	6856	K 366405	8161	K 224494	8489		10019	PROD MEDICINAUX PHARMACEUT
5411	PROVITAMINS AND VITAMINS	K 300897	2949	K 16058	4542	K 4962	1697	K 5226	3941	PROVITAMINES,VITAMINES
5417	MEDICAMENTS	K 137970	3438	K 120862	2272	K 202214	6197		5550	MEDICAMENTS
54179	— CONTNG OTH SUBSTANCES	K 130066	2915	K 119726	1926	K 199834	5386	K 84841	5415	MED CONT AUT SUBSTANCES
55	PERFUME,CLEANING ETC PRD		2775		3509		5327		4109	PROD POUR PARFUM,TOILETTE
553	PERFUMERY,COSMETICS,ETC	W 281	734	W 333	1438	W 489	1781	W 237	2104	PRODUITS DE PARFUMERIE
554	SOAP,CLEANSING ETC PREPS	W 1076	1537	W 1274	1924	W 2895	3366	W 668	1655	SAVONS,PRODUITS DETERSIFS
5541	SOAPS	W 225	368	W 1052	1264	W 2012	2327	W 515	1137	SAVONS,PROD TENSIO–ACTIFS
562	*FERTILIZERS,MANUFACTURE	W 14194	3829	W 19704	4617	W 7368	2410	W 7384	3667	ENGRAIS MANUFACTURES
5621	CHEM NITROGENOUS FERTLZR	W 12515	3356	W 17672	4169	W 6802	2077	W 7383	3665	ENGRAIS AZOTES
56216	UREA	W 11524	3017	W 15707	3551	W 3306	845	W 4536	2265	UREE
58	PLASTIC MATERIALS ETC		5638		4294		3728		5756	MAT PLAST ARTIFICIELLES
583	POLYMERIZATION ETC PRODS	W 3804	5408	W 3861	3454	W 1753	2949	W 1039	4138	PROD POLYMERISATION
5831	POLYETHYLENE	W 1746	2754	W 3064	2125	W 854	1662	W 540	1600	POLYETHYLENE
5839	OTH POLYMRZTION ETC PROD	W 1916	2408	W 231	720	W 834	1126	W 380	2189	AUT PROD POLYMER COPOLYM
59	CHEMICAL MATERIALS NES		10795		11684		9506		10430	MAT PROD CHIMIQUES NDA
591	PESTICIDES,DISINFECTANTS	W 1216	4144	W 1745	4224	W 1432	3152	W 753	4352	DESINF,INSECT,FONG,HERB
5911	INSECTICIDES,FOR RETAIL	W 849	3209	W 990	4110	W 955	2426	W 660	3554	INSECTICIDES VENTE DET
598	MISCEL CHEM PRODUCTS NES	W 3496	6233	W 3644	7047	W 3378	5948	W 2371	5775	PROD DIV INDUST CHIM NDA
5989	CHEM PRODUCTS,PREPS NES	W 3034	5568	W 2835	6112	W 3109	5523	W 2117	5064	PROD PREP CHIMIQUES NDA
59899	OTH CHEM PRODS,PREPS,NES	W 2827	5173	W 2691	5746	W 2954	5007	W 2009	4491	AUT PRODUITS CHIMIQUES NDA
6	BASIC MANUFACTURES		64147		69847		70588		100687	ART MANUFACTURES

4. General Imports C.I.F. by Commodities according to the S.I.T.C. (Rev. 2) in thousand U.S. Dollars
Importations Générales C.A.F. par Produits d'après la C.T.C.I. (Rév. 2) en milliers de Dollars E.U.

SITC CTCI	COMMODITY	1989 WEIGHT POIDS	1989 VALUE VALEUR	1990 WEIGHT POIDS	1990 VALUE VALEUR	1991 WEIGHT POIDS	1991 VALUE VALEUR	1992 WEIGHT POIDS	1992 VALUE VALEUR	PRODUIT
62	RUBBER MANUFACTURES NES		7043		6175		9160		6581	CAOUTCHOUC MANUFACTURE
625	RUBBER TYRES, TUBES ETC	W 1785	4199	W 2551	3462	W 1431	5353	W 569	3119	PNEUS CAOUTCHOUC VULCANISE
6251	TYRES NEW FOR MOTOR CARS	W 1191	1552	W 2259	2135	W 893	2811	W 311	1620	PNEUS POUR VOITURES
6259	OTH TYRES,TYRE CASES,ETC	W 462	1976	W 218	985	W 412	1970	W 175	1009	AUTRES PNEUS RECHAPES FLAPS
62599	TYRES NES,TYRE CASES,ETC	W 400	1760	W 195	890	W 334	1737	W 149	825	PNEUS,FLAPS
628	RUBBER ARTICLES NES	W 364	2034	W 292	1915	W 267	2649	W 200	2573	OUVRAGES CAOUTCHOUC NDA
6289	OTH RUBBER ARTICLES NES	W 125	834	W 165	1182	W 148	1751	W 85	1658	AUT OUVR CAOUTCHOUC NDA
62898	UNHARD RUBBER PRODS NES	W 124	825	W 164	1174	W 148	1749	W 76	1574	OUV CAOUT VULC NON DURCI
64	PAPER,PAPERBOARD AND MFR		9694		11488		9169		8511	PAPIERS,CARTONS & OUVRAGES
641	PAPER AND PAPERBOARD	W 4351	4381	W 5720	5828	W 3368	3580	W 1278	2469	PAPIERS ET CARTONS
6412	PRINTG,WRITING PAPER NES	W 1230	852	W 3638	3551	W 1032	1067	W 62	134	PAPIERS POUR L'IMPRESSION
64121	— UNCOATED	W 234	381	W 1748	2696	W 402	639	W 62	134	PAPIERS IMPRES NON COUCHES
6417	CORRUGATED PAPER ETC,BLK	W 1176	1734	W 856	1406	W 522	1208	W 474	1398	PAPIERS,CARTONS ONDULES
64173	OTHER CREPED ETC PAPER	W 1174	1718	W 843	1362	W 475	1138	W 453	1330	AUT PAPIER CREPE,PLISSE
642	PAPER,ETC,PRECUT,ARTS OF	W 5028	5312	W 2855	5660	W 4080	5589	W 2981	6042	PAP,CARTONS DECOUPES
6421	PAPER ETC CONTAINERS	W 3563	2387	W 1579	1783	W 3090	2472	W 1107	2406	BOITES,SACS EMBALLAGES
6423	EXERCISE BOOKS ETC	W 652	1130	W 762	2226	W 427	1444	W 311	1266	REGISTRES,CAHIERS,CARNETS
65	TEXTILE YARN,FABRICS,ETC		12250		11266		10293		10685	FILS,TISSUS,ARTICLES TEXTILE
651	TEXTILE YARN		1850	W 806	2707	W 357	1728	W 197	2855	FILS TEXTILES
6515	YARN OF 6514 FOR RETAIL	W 294	1766	W 709	2451	W 221	1506	W 192	2778	FILS CONT 85% FI SYNTHETIQ
652	COTTON FABRICS,WOVEN	W 876	4522	W 659	3732	W 647	3885	W 278	3110	TISSUS DE COTON
6521	GREY WOVEN COTTON FABRIC	W 876	4522	W 659	3732	W 647	3885	W 278	3110	TISSUS COT ECRUS NON MERCER
657	SPECIAL TXTL FABRC,PRODS	W 843	3406	W 375	1639	W 335	2517	W 201	1487	TISSUS SPECIAUX
6575	CORDAGE AND MANUFACTURES	W 664	2509	W 126	596	W 196	683	W 96	713	FICELLES,CORDES,CORDAGES
65752	NETTING OF ROPE,TWINE	W 359	1463	W 56	251	W 63	317	W 18	166	FILETS MAT DU 657.51
658	TEXTILE ARTICLES NES		1802	W 674	2270	W 267	1262	W 438	2361	ART FACONNES MAT TEXTILES
66	NONMETAL MINERAL MFS NES		8208		9648		10528		34415	ART MIN NON METALLIQUES
661	LIME,CEMENT,BLDG PRODS	W 47627	3681	W 61649	4664	W 55336	5870	W 32605	6298	CHAUX,CIMENTS MAT CONSTR
6612	CEMENT	W 47396	2953	W 61383	4199	W 54607	5098	W 32415	5408	CIMENTS HYDRAULIQUES
662	CLAY,REFRACTORY BLDG PRD	W 2922	1984	W 1481	1037	W 1806	1526	W 1850	2829	MAT CONST REFRACTAIRES
6624	BRICKS ETC NONREFRACTORY	W 1439	984	W 1418	963	W 1470	1198	W 1315	1929	BRIQUES ETC CERAM NON REFR
664	GLASS	W 726	1042	W 1148	1499	W 782	950	W 507	1095	VERRE
665	GLASSWARE		664	W 1480	1471	W 864	920	W 32289	23054	OUVRAGES EN VERRE
6651	BOTTLES ETC OF GLASS	W 604	596	W 1448	1223	W 850	771	W 32281	22879	RECIPIENTS EN VERRE
66511	GLASS BOTTLES ETC NONVAC	W 604	594	W 1444	1136	W 850	770	W 32281	22878	BONBONNES,BOUTEILLES,ETC
67	IRON AND STEEL		12154		12446		12665		18580	FER ET ACIER
672	IRON,STEEL PRIMARY FORMS	W 2344	1927	W 2200	1838	W 2681	1434	W 1649	2138	LINGOTS FER,ACIER
6725	IRN,STL BLOOMS,SLABS,ETC	W 2344	1927	W 2200	1838	W 2681	1434	W 1649	2138	BLOOMS,BILLETTES FER ACIER
673	IRON,STEEL SHAPES ETC	W 7283	4310	W 6680	4234	W 3446	3391	W 3160	2763	BARRES,PROFIL FER,ACIER
6732	IRON,STEEL BARS ETC	W 7283	4310	W 6680	4234	W 3446	3391	W 3160	2763	BARRES FER,ACIER
674	IRN,STL UNIV,PLATE,SHEET	W 2755	2683	W 5438	3058	W 4253	4702	W 2191	3783	LARGES PLATS,TOLES
6749	OTH IRN,STL PLATES,SHEET	W 2002	1959	W 5157	2791	W 4140	4536	W 2049	3636	AUTRES TOLES FER,ACIER
678	IRON,STL TUBES,PIPES,ETC	W 2168	3071	W 2849	3107	W 2378	2951	W 5954	9458	TUBES,TUYAUX EN FONTE,FER
6781	CAST IRON TUBES,PIPES	W 1376	1859	W 1896	1676	W 1654	1889	W 5439	8451	TUBES,TUYAUX EN FONTE
6783	IRON,STL TUBES,PIPES NES	W 792	1212	W 953	1431	W 724	1062	W 516	1007	AUT TUBES,TUYAUX FER,ACIER
68	NON–FERROUS METALS		1516		1717		1522		1445	METAUX NON FERREUX
69	METAL MANUFACTURES NES		12470		16253		15725		19285	ART MANUFACT EN METAL NDA
691	STRUCTURES AND PARTS NES	W 402	762	W 664	2062	W 517	1950	W 451	1964	CONSTRUCT FER,ACIER,ALU
693	WIRE PRODUCTS NON ELECTR		1797	W 918	1909	W 929	2144	W 625	5513	OUVRAGES FILS METALLIQUES
6931	WIRE CABLES, ROPES ETC	W 538	1434	W 521	1319	W 625	1523	W 463	5031	CORDAGES EN FILS DE FER
69311	IRN,STEEL CABLE,ROPE ETC	W 527	1357	W 504	1260	W 617	1502	W 370	4195	CORDAGES FILS FER,ACIER
694	STL,COPPR NAILS,NUTS,ETC	W 240	1308	W 518	1437	W 622	1744	W 361	1627	CLOUS,VIS,ECROUS
695	TOOLS	W 169	1557	W 278	1797	W 244	1602	W 153	1885	OUTILS A MAIN
6953	OTHER HAND TOOLS	W 147	1449	W 224	1631	W 176	1442	W 119	1679	AUTRES OUTILS A MAIN
697	BASE MTL HOUSEHOLD EQUIP	W 369	1573	W 607	2414	W 1072	1905	W 412	2304	ART MENAGE MET COMMUNS
6974	BASE MTL DMSTC ARTIC NES	W 163	957	W 194	1440	W 255	978	W 161	977	ARTICLES NDA FONTE,FER,ETC
699	BASE METAL MFRS NES	W 1240	3841	W 2422	5235	W 2327	5144	W 793	4833	ART MANUFACTURES MET NDA
6996	BASE MTL MISC ARTICLES	W 620	1048	W 1624	1713	W 517	1366	W 275	1232	ART DIVERS METAUX COMMUNS
6997	IRON,STEEL ARTICLES NES	W 410	1373	W 455	1651	W 1479	1826	W 367	2023	OUV FONTE,FER,ACIER NDA
69979	IRN,STL MANUFACTURES NES	W 410	1373	W 455	1651	W 1479	1826	W 367	2023	AUT OUVRAGES EN FER NDA
7	MACHINES,TRANSPORT EQUIP		109430		118860		150496		247789	MACHINES MATERIEL TRANSPORT
71	POWER GENERATING EQUIPMT		7107		9499		9792		10918	MACHINES GENERATRICES
713	INTRNL COMBUS PSTN ENGIN	W 437	4536	W 751	5908	W 556	5816	W 380	6147	MOTEURS EXPL COMB INT, PIECE
7132	MOTOR VEHCL PISTN ENGINS	W 272	928	W 477	1532	W 378	1066	W 250	1656	MOTEURS EXPL POUR VEHICULES
7133	MARINE PISTON ENGINES	W 81	1587	W 169	1927	W 89	2260	W 61	2260	MOTEURS EXPL POUR BATEAUX
7138	PISTON ENGINES NES	W 71	1339	W 99	1920	W 79	1743	W 65	1862	MOTEURS A PISTONS NDA
716	ROTATING ELECTRIC PLANT	W 179	1830	W 266	2520	W 376	3369	W 267	3165	APP ELECTR ROTATIFS,PIECES
72	MACHS FOR SPCL INDUSTRYS		15730		13846		30987		33628	MAC SPECIALES POUR INDUST
721	AGRIC MACHY,EXC TRACTORS	W 539	3878	W 164	602	W 212	1456	W 447	9842	MACHINES AGRICOLES
7211	CULTIVATING MACHINERY	W 500	3443	W 150	449	W 205	1391	W 426	9516	MACH PREPARATION DU SOL
72118	OTH AGRIC,HORTIC MACHNRY	W 500	3443	W 150	449	W 205	1391	W 426	9516	AUT MACHINES AGRICOLES
722	TRACTORS NON–ROAD	W 490	1749	W 75	279	W 1235	9937	W 368	5910	TRACTEURS
7224	WHEELED TRACTORS NES	W 289	790	W 73	260	W 1154	9181	W 351	5747	TRACTEURS A ROUES
723	CIVIL ENGNEERG EQUIP ETC	W 2886	8002	W 1599	8094	W 3412	17182	W 2012	16442	APPAREILS DE GENIE CIVIL
7234	CONST,MINING MACHNRY NES	W 2886	8001	W 1597	8088	W 3408	17139	W 2012	16441	MACH POUR LA CONST, MINES
72342	SLFPRP SHOVELS,EXCAVATRS	W 2026	5129	W 531	3159	W 1225	6760	W 546	6527	PELLES MECANIQUES
72343	SLFPRP CONST ETC MCH NES	W 860	2872	W 1066	4929	W 2183	10379	W 1466	9914	AUT MACH EXTR,TERRASSEM
728	OTH MACHY FOR SPCL INDUS	W 712	1804	W 797	3794	W 130	1215	W 44	976	AUT MACH IND PARTICULIERES
7283	OTHR MINERAL WORKG MACHY	W 712	1804	W 797	3794	W 130	1215	W 44	976	MACH TRIER,CRIBLER,BROYER
72831	MINRAL SORTING ETC MACHY	W 712	1804	W 797	3794	W 130	1215	W 44	976	MACH TRIER MAT MINERALES
74	GENRL INDUSTRL MACHY NES		19228		25590		24469		24049	MACH APP INDUSTRIE
741	HEATING,COOLING EQUIPMNT	W 240	1663	W 430	2937		2553	W 306	4292	MACH CHAUFFAGE,PIECES
7415	AIR–CONDITIONING MACHNRY	W 181	1087	W 233	1664	W 144	1232	W 179	2607	GROUPES CONDITION AIR
742	PUMPS FOR LIQUIDS ETC	W 318	5139	W 428	9591	W 483	6434	W 349	5886	POMPES MOTO–POMPES
7428	OTHER PUMPS FOR LIQUIDS	W 318	5139	W 428	9591	W 483	6434	W 349	5886	AUTRES POMPES POUR LIQ
74288	PUMPS FR LIQUIDS NES ETC	W 306	4998	W 404	9275	W 467	6242	W 342	5763	POMPES POUR LIQUIDES NDA
744	MECHANICAL HANDLING EQU	W 522	3767	W 854	3367	W 770	5667	W 1010	4942	EQUIP MANUTENTION PIECES
7441	FORK LIFT TRCKS,ETC,PTS	W 522	3767	W 854	3367	W 770	5667	W 1010	4942	CHARIOTS POUR USINES ETC
74411	FORK LIFT TRUCKS ETC	W 522	3767	W 854	3367	W 770	5667	W 1010	4942	CHARIOTS POUR LES GARES
745	NONELEC MACHY,TOOLS NES	W 354	3245	W 364	2771	W 336	3675	W 214	2392	AUT MACH NON ELEC,PIECES
7451	POWER TOOLS NONELEC, PTS	W 300	2398	W 321	2231	W 274	2718	W 180	1871	OUT MACH PNEUM A MOTEUR
74511	POWER HAND TOOLS NONELEC	W 300	2398	W 321	2231	W 274	2718	W 180	1871	OUT MACH PNEUM A MOTEUR
749	NONELEC MACH PTS,ACC NES	W 361	5415	W 557	6925	W 553	6141	W 340	6537	PIECES MACH NON ELEC NDA
7492	COCKS,VALVES ETC NES	W 112	1455	W 168	1991	W 148	1851	W 161	2518	ART ROB,SIM POUR TUYAUX
7493	SHAFT,CRANK,PULLEY ETC	W 182	2599	W 297	3397	W 299	2755	W 127	2387	ARBRES TRANS,VILEBREQUINS
75	OFFICE MACHNES,ADP EQUIP		2578		3711		4097		4221	MACH BUREAU TRAIT AUTOM
751	OFFICE MACHINES	W 117	2578	W 174	3711	W 186	4097	W 215	4221	MACH,APPAREILS DE BUREAU
7518	OFFICE MACHINES NES	W 111	2415	W 162	3469	W 176	3847	W 211	4067	MACH,APP DE BUREAU NDA
75188	OTHR OFFICE MACHINES NES	W 65	2027	W 87	2989	W 130	3334	W 189	3420	AUTRES MACH DE BUREAU
76	TELECOMM,SOUND EQUIPMENT		8065		8755		8981		7639	EQUIPMENT DE TELECOM
764	TELECOM EQPT,PTS,ACC NES	W 164	6417	W 175	6237	W 152	5972	W 88	3790	EQUIP TELECOM,PIECES

4. General Imports C.I.F. by Commodities according to the S.I.T.C. (Rev. 2) in thousand U.S. Dollars
Importations Générales C.A.F. par Produits d'après la C.T.C.I. (Rév. 2) en milliers de Dollars E.U.

SITC CTCI	COMMODITY	1989		1990		1991		1992		PRODUIT
		WEIGHT POIDS	VALUE VALEUR	WEIGHT POIDS	VALUE VALEUR	WEIGHT POIDS	VALUE VALEUR	WEIGHT POIDS	VALUE VALEUR	
7643	TV,RADIO TRANSMITTRS ETC	W 64	4658	W 90	4869	W 61	4767	W 59	2184	APP EMET TELE RADIO
77	ELECTRIC MACHNRY NES ETC		19800		23835		22105		25022	MACH APP ELECT NDA
772	SWITCHGEAR ETC,PARTS NES	W 76	1684	W 89	2165	W 164	2328	W 72	2817	APP COUPURE,SECT ETC
7721	SWITCHGEAR ETC	W 68	1479	W 82	2001	W 158	2179	W 65	2619	APP COUPURE,SECTIONMNT
773	ELECTR DISTRIBUTNG EQUIP	W 987	3138	W 1008	4977	W 949	4467	W 398	2656	EQUIPMT DISTRIBUTION ELECT
7731	INSULATED WIRE,CABLE ETC	W 975	3065	W 976	4889	W 867	4276	W 361	2405	FILS,CABLES ISOLES ELECT
775	HOUSEHOLD TYPE EQUIP NES	W 812	4083	W 1527	5903	W 1248	5923	W 830	6861	MACH,APP USAGE DOMESTQUE
7752	DOM REFRIGERATRS,FREEZRS	W 295	1070	W 479	1432	W 418	1643	W 326	2114	REFRIG,CONGEL MENAGER
77521	DOMESTIC REFRIGERATORS	W 295	1070	W 479	1432	W 418	1643	W 326	2114	REFRIGERATEURS
7757	DOMESTIC ELECTRC EQU NES	W 220	1001	W 481	1642	W 366	1691	W 202	1744	APP ELECTR DOMEST NDA
7758	ELECTRO–THERMIC APPL NES	W 148	1416	W 279	1756	W 250	1644	W 138	1750	APP ELECTROTHERMIQ NDA
77586	ELECTROTHERM DOM APP NES	W 138	1363	W 272	1704	W 222	1517	W 120	1630	APP ELECTRO THERMIQUES
778	ELECTRICAL MACHINERY NES	W 1335	10805	W 1377	10665	W 1212	9325	W 1842	12617	AUTRES MACH ELECT NDA
7781	BATTERIES,ACCUMULATORS	W 235	771	W 509	1490	W 416	1148	W 458	1955	PILES ET ACCUMULATEURS
7784	ELECTRO–MECH HAND TOOLS	W 103	980	W 87	1563	W 57	1070	W 30	937	OUTILS ELECTROMEC,PIECES
7788	OTH ELEC MACHY,EQUIP NES	W 827	7450	W 542	5625	W 571	5446	W 1215	7699	AUT MACH APP ELEC NDA
77886	OTH ELEC MACHINERY NES	W 826	7409	W 542	5614	W 571	5437	W 1211	7657	AUT MACH APP ELECTRIQUES
78	ROAD VEHICLES		33088		30595		46655		137261	VEHICULES ROUTIERS
781	PASS MOTOR VEH EXC BUSES	W 3179	12781	W 2005	13815	W 4971	24916	W 19754	118600	AUTO TRANSPORT PERSONNES
782	LORRIES,SPCL MTR VEH NES	W 2566	7354	W 2808	8461	W 2933	13116	W 1526	8540	VEHICULES SPECIAUX,MARCH
7821	LORRIES,TRUCKS	W 2455	7005	W 2740	8154	W 2875	11761	W 1427	7837	VEHICULES TRANSP MARCHAND
783	ROAD MOTOR VEHICLES NES	W 955	6701	W 321	896	W 147	1055	W 148	1003	VEHICULES ROUTIERS NDA
7831	BUSES	W 955	6701	W 321	896	W 147	1055	W 148	1003	VOITURES TRANSPORT COMMUN
784	MOTOR VEH PRTS,ACCES NES	W 492	4095	W 660	4663	W 689	4802	W 516	5053	PIECES 722,781,782,783
7849	OTHER MOTOR VEHCL PARTS	W 478	3970	W 658	4652	W 680	4789	W 492	4727	PIECES 722,781,782,783
785	CYCLES,ETC MOTRZD OR NOT	W 350	1763	W 410	2257	W 566	1875	W 550	3319	MOTOCYCLES SCOOTERS
7852	CYCLES, ETC NON–MOTOR	W 247	1324	W 205	1017	W 426	1122	W 435	2393	VELOCIPEDES SANS MOTEUR
79	OTHR TRANSPORT EQUIPMENT		3574		2717		3053		4570	AUTRE MATERIEL TRANSPORT
792	AIRCRAFT ETC	W 19	1376	W 23	1239	W 7	714	W 4	439	APP NAVIGATION AERIENNE
793	SHIPS AND BOATS ETC	W 359	2158		1296	W 679	2226		3433	NAVIRES BATEAUX,ETC
7932	SHIPS AND BOATS NES	W 247	1419	W 182	1182	W 110	798	W 450	709	NAVIRES ET BATEAUX
7938	TUGS,SPECIAL VESSELS ETC		12		63	W 550	1366		2615	REMORQUEURS,BATEAUX SPEC
79381	TUGS		12	W 25	63			W 315	2609	BATEAUX REMORQUEURS
8	MISC MANUFACTURED GOODS		24024		32856		36607		61695	ART MANUFACTURES DIVERS
821	*FURNITURE,PARTS THEREOF	W 133	611	W 246	1080	W 501	1851	W 258	2065	MEUBLES ET PIECES
84	CLOTHING AND ACCESSORIES		4141		5536		7763		8394	VETEMENTS
842	MENS OUTERWEAR NOT KNIT	W 106	661	W 132	1255	W 255	1807	W 257	1964	VET DESSUS POUR HOMMES
8429	— OTHER OUTER GARMENTS	W 106	661	W 132	1255	W 255	1807	W 257	1964	AUT VET DES HOM MAT TEX
843	WOMENS OUTERWEAR NONKNIT		616		1016	W 173	2073	W 71	2009	VET DESSUS FEMMES MAT TEX
8439	— OTHER OUTER GARMENTS		616		1016	W 173	2073	W 71	2009	AUT VET DES FEM MAT TEXT
845	OUTERWEAR KNIT NONELASTC	W 147	1344	W 300	1441	W 213	1843	W 98	2138	VET DESSOUS,ACCES BONNET
8459	— OTHER,CLTHG ACCESRYS	W 147	1344	W 300	1441	W 213	1843	W 98	2138	AUT VET DESSUS DE BONNE
851	*FOOTWEAR	W 577	2249	W 1614	4086	W 605	5592	W 251	3600	CHAUSSURES
85102	FOOTWEAR LEATHER	W 32	599	W 96	1329	W 81	1707	W 31	682	CHAUS SEMELLES EN CUIR
85104	FOOTWEAR NES	W 426	1049	W 201	1548	W 264	2214	W 108	1716	CHAUS SEMELLES AUT MAT
87	PRECISION INSTRUMNTS NES		4922		5409		5181		4579	INSTRUM,APPAR SCIENT NDA
872	MEDICAL INSTRUMENTS NES	W 43	1335	W 72	1718	W 45	887	W 29	1240	INSTR,APP MEDIC–CHIR NDA
874	MEASURNG,CONTROLNG INSTR	W 60	3191	W 91	3388	W 109	4204	W 46	3289	INSTRUMENTS DE MESURE
8748	ELEC MEAS,CONTRL EQU NES	W 27	1797	W 66	1983	W 80	2705	W 23	1707	APP ELEC ELECTRO MESURE
87489	ELEC MEASUR ETC INST NES	W 15	984	W 60	1504	W 72	1369	W 16	1199	AUT INSTRUM ELEC NDA
88	PHOTO EQU,OPTICL GDS ETC		1400		2179		2447		28770	APP,FOURN PHOTO,OP,MONTR
882	PHOTO,CINEMA SUPPLIES	W 60	536	W 162	1084	W 106	824		27613	PRODUITS PHOTO,CINEMA
8822	PHOTO FILM EXC DEV CINMA	W 34	387	W 127	897	W 58	629		27357	PLAQUES,PELLICULES,FILMS
88221	PHOTO FILM FLAT UNEXPOSD	W 15	243	W 26	419	W 21	352		27209	PLAQUES PHOTO,FILMS SENS
89	MISC MANUFCTRD GOODS NES		9551		13320		12903		13046	ART MANUFACTURES DIVERS
892	PRINTED MATTER	W 204	1477	W 281	3255	W 401	2578	W 249	3380	IMPRIMES
8921	PRINTED BOOKS,GLOBES,ETC	W 151	1267	W 227	2063	W 360	1854	W 169	1903	LIVRES,BROCHURES,CARTES
89211	PRINTED BOOKS,PAMPHLETS	W 150	1244	W 226	2030	W 360	1850	W 169	1898	LIVRES,BROCHURES
893	ARTICLES OF PLASTIC NES		5148		6696		6139		6333	OUVRAGES EN MAT DIVIS 58
8939	MISC PLASTIC ARTICLES		4573		6186		5457		5928	ART DIVERS EN MAT DIV 58
9	GOODS NOT CLASSD BY KIND		1564		1283		3838		245	ART TRANSACT NON CLASSES
961	*COIN NONGOLD,NONCURRENT	W 36	1420	W 3	344	W 29	3564		2	MONNAIES NON EMISES

5. General Exports F.O.B. by Commodities according to the S.I.T.C. (Rev. 2) in thousand U.S. Dollars
Exportations Générales F.O.B. par Produits d'après la C.T.C.I. (Rév. 2) en milliers de Dollars E.U.

SITC CTCI	COMMODITY	1989		1990		1991		1992		PRODUIT
		WEIGHT POIDS	VALUE VALEUR	WEIGHT POIDS	VALUE VALEUR	WEIGHT POIDS	VALUE VALEUR	WEIGHT POIDS	VALUE VALEUR	
	ALL COMMODITIES		546721		475264		363079		361243	TOUS PRODUITS
0	FOOD AND LIVE ANIMALS		81927		76124		66473		63983	ALIMENTS,ANIMAUX VIVANTS
03	FISH AND PREPARATIONS		32603		36757		32693		25580	POISSONS ET PREPARATIONS
034	FISH,FRESH,CHILLED,FROZN	N 3011240	32569	N 3931238	36712	N 3519481	32601	N 886638	2368	POISSON FRAIS, REFRIG,CONG
0341	FISH FRSH,CHLLD,EX FILLT	N 3011240	32569	N 3931238	36712	N 3519481	32601	N 785336	2194	POISSON FRAIS,REFRIGERE
036	SHELL FISH FRESH,FROZEN	N 90	1					N 1937523	23117	CRUSTACES,MOLLUSQUES
04	CEREALS AND PREPARATIONS		843		2013		1330		26500	CEREALES ET PRODUITS
042	RICE	N 1660566	685	N 5214891	1779	N 2812398	1041	MN 53409	26492	RIZ
0421	RICE IN HUSK OR HUSKED	N 361254	118	N 494216	104	N 434136	182	MN 46200	23075	RIZ SANS AUTRE PREPARATION
04212	RICE HUSKED	N 361254	118	N 494216	104	N 434136	182	MN 46200	23075	RIZ CARGO
0422	RICE SEMI–MILLED,MILLED	N 1299312	567	N 4720675	1675	N 2378262	859	N 7209214	3417	RIZ POLI,GLACE INCL BRISURES
04221	RICE MILLED UNBROKEN	N 512926	190	N 3947650	1355	N 1025243	316	N 5661714	3185	RIZ POLI,GLACE EXCL BRISURES
05	VEGETABLES AND FRUIT		47418		35592		31378		11700	LEGUMES ET FRUITS
054	VEG ETC FRSH,SMPLY PRSVD	MN 125276	47360		35380	MN 81506	31372	N 2133071	1529	LEGUMES FRAIS,CONG,SECS
0545	OTHER FRESH VEGETABLES	MN 44648	15628		10594	MN 28779	9364	N 1735408	1187	AUTRES LEGUMES FRAIS,REF
05451	ALLIACEOUS VEGTBLS,FRESH	MN 44213	15416	MN 28325	10331	MN 28196	9138			OIGNONS,ECHALOTES,AULX
05459	FRESH VEGETABLES NES	N 435373	212		263	N 583482	226	N 1735408	1187	LEGUMES FRAIS,REFRI NDA
0546	VEGETABLES SIMPLY PRESVD	MN 78637	31035	MN 60433	23548	MN 50066	20429			LEGUMES CONG,CONSER
05462	VEG PRSVD UNFRZN UNTINND	MN 78637	31035	MN 60433	23548	MN 50066	20429			LEGUMES CONSER PROVISOIR
0548	EDIBLE VEG NES FRESH,DRY	N 1971557	689	N 2365491	1229	N 2589541	1553	N 356139	310	RACINES,TUBERCULES
05488	VEG PRODTS NES FRESH,DRY	N 1691669	540	N 2117087	1101	N 2586636	1552	N 177558	228	PROD VEGET ALIM HUMAINE
057	FRUIT,NUTS,FRESH,DRIED	W 278	38		10	N 15848	6	MN 30803	10164	FRUITS FRAIS OU SECS
0579	FRUIT FRESH OR DRIED NES					N 250	1	MN 30357	9887	FRUITS FRAIS,SECS NDA
05793	STONE FRUIT FRESH NES							MN 30001	9657	FRUITS A NOYAU NDA FRAIS
2	CRUDE MATERLS,EXCL FUELS		30		20		120		242307	MAT BRUTES NON COMESTIBLES
28	METALLIFEROUS ORES,SCRAP								241484	MINERAIS METAL,DECHETS
287	BASE METAL ORES,CONC NES							N 1509624	241484	MINERAIS METAUX COMMUNS
2873	ALUMINIUM ORES,ALUMINA							N 1509624	241484	MINERAIS D'ALUMINIUM
28732	ALUMINA(ALUMINIUM OXIDE)							N 1509624	241484	ALUMINE (OXYDE ALUMINIUM)
3	MINERAL FUELS ETC		408556		356742		259623		4639	COMBUSTIBLES MINERAUX LUB
32	COAL,COKE AND BRIQUETTES				7091				4639	HOUILLES,COKES,BRIQUETTES
323	BRIQUETS,COKE,SEMI–COKE			W 9567	7091			MN 35256	4639	BRIQUETTES
33	PETROLEUM AND PRODUCTS		408556		349652		259619			PETROLE ET DERIVES
334	PETROLEUM PRODUCTS,REFIN		408556		349652		259619			PRODUITS RAFFINES
3342	KEROSENE,OTH MEDIUM OILS		402516		349652		253440			PETR LAMPANTS,AUT HUIL
33429	OTH MEDIUM PETROLEUM OIL		402516		349652		253440			AUTRES HUILES MOYENNES
3345	LUBS,PETROLEUM OILS NES		6038				6179			HUILES LUBRIFIANTES
33451	LUBS(HIGH PETR CONT) ETC		6038				6179			HUILES LUBRIF,H LOURDES
6	BASIC MANUFACTURES		2535		1097		1249		45483	ART MANUFACTURES
64	PAPER,PAPERBOARD AND MFR		2417		741		730		10	PAPIERS,CARTONS & OUVRAGES
68	NON–FERROUS METALS		1				11		43695	METAUX NON FERREUX
684	ALUMINIUM							MN 32210	43125	ALUMINIUM
6841	ALUMINIUM,ALLOYS,UNWRGHT							MN 32210	43125	ALUMINIUM,ALLIAGES BRUTS
7	MACHINES,TRANSPORT EQUIP		53359		40485		34127		3588	MACHINES MATERIEL TRANSPORT
75	OFFICE MACHNES,ADP EQUIP		52241		39079		32193		377	MACH BUREAU TRAIT AUTOM
751	OFFICE MACHINES		52241		39079		32193		377	MACH,APPAREILS DE BUREAU
7518	OFFICE MACHINES NES		52026		38865		32183		376	MACH,APP DE BUREAU NDA
75188	OTHR OFFICE MACHINES NES		52026		38858		32183		376	AUTRES MACH DE BUREAU
8	MISC MANUFACTURED GOODS		256		715		1452		912	ART MANUFACTURES DIVERS
87	PRECISION INSTRUMNTS NES		132		486		1170		244	INSTRUM,APPAR SCIENT NDA
874	MEASURNG,CONTROLNG INSTR	W 1	125	W 2	484	W 5	1170	W 1	244	INSTRUMENTS DE MESURE

1. HISTORICAL SERIES, 1961–1996 GENERAL TRADE, IMPORTS C.I.F., EXPORTS F.O.B.
SERIES HISTORIQUES, 1961–1996 COMMERCE GENERAL, IMPORTATIONS C.A.F., EXPORTATIONS F.O.B

YEAR ANNEE	VALUE IN MILLION SWEDISH KRONOR / VALEUR EN MILLION SWEDISH KRONOR — MERCHANDISE –MARCHANDISE IMPORTS	EXPORTS	GOLD –OR IMPORTS	EXPORTS	CONVERSION FACTORS U.S. CENTS PER SWEDISH KRONA / FACTEURS DE CONVERSION CENTS E.U. PAR SWEDISH KRONA — IMPORTS	EXPORTS	INDEX NUMBERS –INDICES — QUANTUM IMPORTS	EXPORTS	UNIT VALUE / VALEUR UNITAIRE IMPORTS	EXPORTS
1961	15151.00	14197.00	13.00	11.10	19.3300	19.3300	27	24	18	18
1962	16154.00	15129.00	71.50	12.00	19.3300	19.3300	28	26	18	17
1963	17552.00	16568.00	33.30	12.40	19.3300	19.3300	30	28	18	17
1964	19946.00	19014.00	36.70	14.10	19.3300	19.3300	33	31	19	18
1965	22644.00	20541.00	53.60	13.50	19.3300	19.3300	37	33	19	19
1966	23704.00	22071.00	42.20	12.90	19.3300	19.3300	38	35	20	19
1967	24319.00	23422.00	37.40	15.20	19.3300	19.3300	39	37	20	19
1968	26516.00	25553.00	24.00	11.90	19.3300	19.3300	43	40	20	19
1969	30546.00	29445.00	25.30	13.70	19.3300	19.3300	48	44	20	20
1970	36251.00	35150.00	15.80	12.80	19.3300	19.3300	53	49	22	21
1971	36192.00	38224.00	10.70	49.00	19.5700	19.5600	50	50	23	22
1972	38618.00	41749.00	13.50	9.00	21.0001	21.0045	52	53	23	23
1973	46336.00	53153.00	25.00	17.00	22.9481	22.9562	56	62	26	26
1974	72800.00	70514.00	42.00	29.00	22.6028	22.6017	64	64	36	33
1975	74000.00	72012.00			24.1370	24.1378	62	57	38	38
1976	84000.00	80195.00			23.0161	22.9878	65	60	40	40
1977	90220.00	85680.00			22.3444	22.2837	63	60	45	42
1978	92750.00	98210.00			22.2014	22.1916	59	65	49	45
1979	122960.00	118210.00			23.3698	23.3525	69	70	56	50
1980	141700.00	131010.00			23.6598	23.6390	70	69	64	57
1981	146040.00	144880.00			19.7517	19.7845	65	70	71	62
1982	173930.00	168130.00			15.8664	15.9504	68	72	80	70
1983	200368.00	210500.00			13.0361	13.0478	70	81	91	78
1984	218570.00	242810.50			12.0859	12.0993	73	87	94	83
1985	244654.20	260480.70			11.6830	11.7052	80	90	96	86
1986	232479.00	265104.00			14.0645	14.0577	83	93	88	86
1987	257386.00	281332.90			15.8164	15.8209	89	96	91	88
1988	280649.90	305040.10			16.3398	16.3552	94	99	94	92
1989	316590.00	332570.10			15.5189	15.5175	100	101	99	98
1990	320379.90	340039.90			16.9380	16.9221	100	100	100	100
1991	301260.00	332800.00			16.5973	16.5951	93	98	101	101
1992	290510.00	326040.00			17.2283	17.2230	95	99	99	98
1993	332489.90	388300.00			12.8385	12.8417	97	107	112	108
1994	397410.00	471600.10			13.0173	13.0093	108	114	117	113
1995	458299.90	568499.90			14.0622	14.0579	109	112	124	125
1996	446599.90	566599.90			14.9170	14.9165	102	105	120	120

2. IMPORTS BY BROAD ECONOMIC CATEGORY AND EXPORTS BY INDUSTRIAL ORIGIN. (PERCENTAGE OF TOTAL VALUE)
IMPORTATIONS PAR CATEGORIES ECONOMIQUES ET EXPORTATIONS PAR BRANCHE D'ACTIVITE.(EN POURCENTAGE DE LA VALEUR TOTALE)

IMPORTS – IMPORTATIONS

	1990	1991	1992	1993	1994	1995	1996
TOTAL IMPORTS–IMPORTATIONS TOTALES	100.	100.	100.	100.	100.	100.	100.
1 FOOD BEV–ALIMENTATION BOISSONS	5.4	6.2	6.6	6.8	7.0	6.0	6.5
11 PRIMARY–PRODUITS DE BASE	2.5	2.9	2.9	2.8	2.9	2.9	3.0
111 FOR INDUSTRY–POUR L'INDUSTRIE	0.5	0.5	0.4	0.5	0.7	0.7	0.6
112 FOR HOUSEHOLDS–POUR LES MENAGES	2.0	2.4	2.5	2.3	2.2	2.2	2.4
12 PROCESSED–PRODUITS ELABORES	3.0	3.3	3.7	4.0	4.0	3.1	3.5
121 FOR INDUSTRY–POUR L'INDUSTRIE	0.4	0.4	0.4	0.4	0.5	0.4	0.4
122 FOR HOUSEHOLDS–POUR LES MENAGES	2.6	2.9	3.3	3.5	3.5	2.7	3.1
2 IND SUPPLIES–APPROV INDUSTRIELS	26.8	26.5	26.5	26.9	27.8	28.1	25.2
21 PRIMARY–PRODUITS DE BASE	2.5	2.6	2.9	2.7	2.8	2.9	2.3
22 PROCESSED–PRODUITS ELABORES	24.2	23.9	23.6	24.3	25.0	25.2	22.9
3 FUELS–COMBUSTIBLES	8.9	8.6	8.5	8.9	7.3	5.7	7.4
31 PRIMARY–PRODUITS DE BASE	5.9	5.5	5.3	5.8	4.6	4.0	5.4
32 PROCESSED–PRODUITS ELABORES	3.0	3.1	3.2	3.1	2.7	1.7	2.0
321 MOTOR SPIRIT–ESSENCE	1.2	1.2	1.1	1.0	0.6	0.5	0.5
322 OTHER–AUTRES	1.9	1.8	2.0	2.1	2.1	1.1	1.5
4 MACHINERY–EQUIPEMENT	25.2	24.3	24.3	25.6	26.6	29.8	29.4
41 CAPITAL EQUIPMENT–MACHINES	19.7	18.9	18.8	19.6	20.4	22.7	22.5
42 PARTS–PIECES ACCESSOIRES	5.5	5.4	5.6	6.0	6.2	7.0	6.9
5 TRANSPORT–TRANSPORT	14.2	13.5	12.7	11.5	12.2	13.4	13.9
51 PASSENGER CARS–AUTOMOBILES	3.9	3.5	3.6	2.8	3.3	3.0	3.6
52 OTHER–AUTRES	4.3	3.7	2.7	2.1	2.1	2.0	2.2
521 INDUSTRIAL–INDUSTRIELS	4.1	3.5	2.5	1.9	1.9	1.8	2.0
522 NON INDUSTRIAL–NON INDUSTRIEL	0.2	0.2	0.2	0.2	0.2	0.1	0.2
53 PARTS–PIECES ACCESSOIRES	5.9	6.3	6.4	6.6	6.8	8.4	8.1
6 CONSUM GOODS–BIENS CONSOMMATION	18.4	19.8	20.3	19.3	18.1	15.5	15.6
61 DURABLE–DURABLES	4.9	5.2	4.7	4.5	4.4	3.7	3.7
62 SEMI DURABLE–SEMI DURABLES	9.9	10.5	11.1	10.2	9.5	8.0	8.0
63 NON DURABLE–NON DURABLES	3.6	4.1	4.5	4.6	4.2	3.8	4.0
7 GOODS NES–BIENS NDA	1.0	0.9	1.0	0.7	1.0	1.5	2.0

EXPORTS – EXPORTATIONS

	1990	1991	1992	1993	1994	1995	1996
TOTAL EXPORTS–EXPORTATIONS TOTALES	100.	100.	100.	100.	100.	100.	100.
1 AGRICULTURE	0.8	0.8	0.7	0.5	0.6	0.7	0.8
2 MINING QUARRY–INDUS EXTRACTIVES	1.5	1.3	1.4	1.4	1.1	1.1	1.0
3 MANUFACTURING–IND MANUFACTUR	97.7	97.8	97.9	98.2	98.3	98.2	98.2
31 FOOD BEV TOBACCO–ALIM BOISS TAB	1.8	1.7	1.6	1.8	2.0	1.8	2.0
32 TEXTILES–INDUSTRIES TEXTILES	2.0	2.0	2.0	1.8	1.7	1.6	1.7
33 WOOD & PRODUCTS–BOIS & PRODUITS	4.2	4.0	4.3	4.7	5.1	4.6	4.2
34 PAPER & PRODUCTS–PAPIER & PRODT	14.9	14.7	14.2	12.9	12.2	12.9	11.4
35 CHEMICALS–INDUSTRIES CHIMIQUES	12.0	13.5	14.0	15.3	13.8	10.8	11.1
36 NON METAL MIN–MIN NON METAL	0.9	1.0	1.0	1.0	1.0	0.9	0.9
37 BASIC METAL–IND METAL BASE	8.0	7.7	7.5	7.5	8.0	7.3	6.8
38 METAL MANUF–MANUF METAL	52.2	52.0	52.1	52.1	53.5	50.1	52.4
39 OTH MANUF IND–AUTRES MANUF	1.8	1.4	1.0	0.9	1.0	8.1	7.7

3. TRADE BY PRINCIPAL COUNTRIES OF ORIGIN AND LAST DESTINATION (VALUE IN THOUSAND U.S. DOLLARS)
ECHANGES SELON LES PRINCIPAUX PAYS D'ORIGINE ET DE DERNIERE DESTINATION (VALEUR EN MILLIERS DE DOLLARS EU)

COUNTRIES–PAYS	GENERAL IMPORTS C.I.F. IMPORTATIONS GENERALES C.A.F				
	1992	1993	1994	1995	1996
World	49870270	42652224	51773522	61646717	63986841
Africa	410276	203002	379210	324327	435790
Americas	5360500	4830834	5629682	4660934	4861227
Northern America	4643813	4129058	4744460	3854630	4100310
LAIA	587877	499311	720855	650416	575591
CACM	51428	43359	53219	59974	43784
Caribbean	22892	97652	56638	47046	44204
Rest of America	54490	61454	54509	48867	97339
As.ex F.USSR	6225399	5685049	6571001	5427444	5289131
Eur.x F.USSR	36796227	30961747	37432695	49778677	51824005
EU	31374943	26650894	32201993	42646391	44195914
EFTA	4396496	3633546	4130476	6011573	6480379
East Europe	768956	577877	829449	1025773	1059799
Other Europe	21590	8246	13891	7505	3832
Former USSR	796790	687906	1153683	1262446	1336159
Oceania	192791	176090	157805	192889	240529
Germany/Allemagne	9236951	7625996	9433909	12725538	12500846
United Kingdom	4298340	4015490	4954882	6087413	6654878
USA/Etats–Unis d'Amer	4365666	3885596	4413418	3520195	3859966
Denmark/Danemark	3796853	3037825	3413098	4597448	4984552
Norway,SVD,JM	3419634	2752619	3124268	4620633	5194281
Finland/Finlande	3087027	2646502	3249764	3821560	3755826
Netherlands/Pays–Bas	2139718	1981359	2089629	4671277	4993760
France, Monac	2555736	2280137	2883706	3414807	3730809
Japan/Japon	2521041	2132772	2448877	1872780	1573446
Belgium–Luxembourg	1763574	1476916	1789016	2409657	2426225
Italy/Italie	1914033	1523058	1988695	1992965	2135219
Switz.Liecht	950437	865175	985812	1364268	1255837
Spain/Espagne	699150	614518	715466	727500	862584
China/Chine	735871	827473	1090620	415558	446425
Austria/Autriche	673701	554801	637180	742522	742269
Hong Kong	409248	328740	341641	863364	914890
Ireland/Irlande	389022	346086	428152	858244	785221
Portugal	688396	458701	509747	494528	476709
Russian Federation	547478	431179	652334	479709	446426
Poland/Pologne	414614	319271	462848	591209	592411
Korea, Republic of	370032	301306	384735	273101	272920
Canada	266354	237034	321042	267867	239755
Saudi Arabia	280051	392968	296264	185024	125962
Latvia/Lettonie	90507	102719	228827	406133	386140
Iran (Islamic Rp. of)	229690	188487	192715	265604	242744
Brazil/Brésil	214641	179640	298008	210372	174038
Estonia/Estonie	97324	94395	166823	293775	396163
India/Inde	135498	132324	189276	195055	187836
Singapore/Singapour	170974	152490	185253	162654	152045
Thailand/Thaïlande	182892	153414	188570	136013	158305
Malaysia/Malaisie	140585	157292	223005	120091	105561
Australia/Australie	144682	127259	113357	139935	194643
Hungary/Hongrie	147171	102588	140794	148837	168230
Greece/Grèce	132444	89505	108749	102932	147017
Czech Republic		95723	129622	163269	185412
Venezuela	88664	101110	102169	138370	138084
Turkey/Turquie	109124	77630	95469	106964	130879
Chile/Chili	94286	80684	89315	115325	94430
Indonesia/Indonésie	70468	64677	85326	72352	162914
Israel/Israël	75750	61952	85978	93059	107796
Colombia/Colombie	75419	62844	118607	97433	66613
Egypt/Egypte	50180	36392	48980	109054	175954
Nigeria/Nigéria	98315	18421	128462	68993	71287
Croatia/Croatie	135457	24824	178563	15189	14352
Lithuania/Lituanie	53903	51850	81568	75217	93172
Pakistan	80046	64117	70294	70263	70075
Panama	52237	60696	53799	48277	96867
Slovenia/Slovénia	37846	61100	70814	67630	59935
Argentina/Argentine	47253	27476	40836	34034	52938
Philippines	46062	40022	42132	40939	28747

COUNTRIES–PAYS	GENERAL EXPORTS F.O.B. EXPORTATIONS GENERALES F.O.B.				
	1992	1993	1994	1995	1996
Monde	56018671	49858443	61299713	77436374	82880544
Afrique	740062	1013722	828789	1243134	1354696
Amériques	6389525	5790290	6354430	8752217	9629190
Amérique du Nord	5313263	4811342	5249842	7208890	7853438
ALAI	945986	858389	1039326	1431844	1669031
MCAC	29099	25780	23807	49371	32008
Caraïbes	84489	85853	33225	49130	53583
Autre Amérique	16688	8927	8229	12982	21129
Asie l'URSS exclus	5475468	6081841	6880174	9641469	11612437
Europe l'URSS exclus	41929579	35466014	41110925	55184001	57520702
UE	34895228	29393938	34018668	45399121	46492194
AELE	5965791	5072856	5802090	7816669	8791327
Europe de l'Est	898742	844264	1111245	1717111	1927126
Autre de l'Europe	23253	16769	14652	24790	19419
Ancienne URSS	520115	597249	825998	1291420	1473768
Océanie	797024	757280	849568	1323839	1289700
Germany/Allemagne	8351504	7140657	7648053	10249473	9886504
United Kingdom	5402274	5101369	5744890	7559074	8003649
USA/Etats–Unis d'Amer	4639095	4192882	4625639	6302479	7011397
Norway,SVD,JM	4709095	4050367	4672306	6102596	7146250
Denmark/Danemark	3989902	3296706	4016581	5077152	5188121
Netherlands/Pays–Bas	3125996	2523959	3037856	4365780	4673269
France, Monac	3232487	2671698	2918635	4118558	3933498
Finland/Finlande	2887074	2274436	2733449	3966924	4305498
Belgium–Luxembourg	2370130	2064429	2878084	3352061	3733897
Italy/Italie	2458207	1848039	2220596	2856973	2731599
Japan/Japon	1136496	1230441	1542895	2333667	2709691
Spain/Espagne	1248273	937749	1096613	1631869	1774137
Switz.Liecht	1145247	935703	1028587	1585966	1503978
China/Chine	429686	624710	971082	1158884	1391531
Australia/Australie	708745	650189	729242	1135312	1128565
Austria/Autriche	844302	674964	752514	966994	923263
Canada	629818	566622	621114	897655	840375
Poland/Pologne	373680	422294	562081	928145	1067793
Korea, Republic of	349641	372225	453034	640196	652383
Russian Federation	329241	332674	407127	667268	724126
Singapore/Singapour	331826	401778	523699	532112	629122
Hong Kong	263339	283640	357465	579551	802911
Thailand/Thaïlande	260660	328787	367571	557283	643418
Ireland/Irlande	343802	314444	392742	471979	543133
Saudi Arabia	440897	380761	351119	417660	376811
Malaysia/Malaisie	206300	253094	377850	527934	564054
Brazil/Brésil	200392	212332	311681	538313	641168
Turkey/Turquie	245340	347713	189153	435032	661558
Portugal	374653	269899	240555	409890	435496
Greece/Grèce	266625	275590	338100	372395	360130
Indonesia/Indonésie	178440	273529	159142	281930	524106
India/Inde	158687	145524	247505	288033	512241
Hungary/Hongrie	192995	179687	279254	319033	289096
Israel/Israël	164972	257238	170608	351884	307501
So. Africa Customs Un	33124	72727	198425	394256	467271
Mexico/Mexique	306197	211981	221484	155233	188476
Egypt/Egypte	186091	187261	174164	262434	272022
Czech Republic		142678	180604	295997	364847
Argentina/Argentine	121119	130189	190464	222475	283217
Estonia/Estonie	72757	104425	190830	237123	262909
Iran (Islamic Rp. of)	321626	163897	61063	79955	130899
United Arab Emirates	115735	110843	113006	154491	194655
Latvia/Lettonie	57007	72603	102462	183410	207496
New Zealand	81872	103568	115251	166101	153893
Chile/Chili	80029	84539	70592	176254	199333
Iceland/Islande	111450	86786	101198	128107	141100
Colombia/Colombie	64092	75040	110434	158516	142619
Morocco/Maroc	115730	101011	88834	138311	98052
Philippines	35128	51353	64282	97197	253832
Pakistan	107497	93762	71253	75082	127678

(VALUE AS PERCENTAGE OF WORLD TOTAL)(VALEURS EN POURCENTAGE DU TOTAL MONDIAL)

	1987	1988	1989	1990	1991	1992	1993	1994	1995	1996
Africa	0.7	0.4	0.4	0.5	0.7	0.8	0.5	0.7	0.5	0.7
Americas	9.6	10.4	11.2	11.2	10.8	10.7	11.3	10.9	7.6	7.6
Northern America	7.6	8.4	9.1	9.4	9.2	9.3	9.7	9.2	6.3	6.4
LAIA	1.6	1.7	1.6	1.3	1.3	1.2	1.2	1.4	1.1	0.9
CACM	0.2	0.2	0.2	0.1	0.1	0.1	0.1	0.1	0.1	0.1
Caribbean	0.1	0.1	0.1	0.2	0.1	0.0	0.2	0.1	0.1	0.1
Rest of America	0.1	0.1	0.3	0.1	0.1	0.1	0.1	0.1	0.1	0.2
As.ex F.USSR	11.3	12.2	12.0	11.4	12.4	12.5	13.3	12.7	8.8	8.3
Eur.x F.USSR	76.2	74.9	74.1	75.0	74.4	73.8	72.6	72.3	80.7	81.0
EU	65.6	64.3	63.0	63.1	63.1	62.9	62.5	62.2	69.2	69.1
EFTA	8.1	8.1	8.9	9.9	9.5	8.8	8.5	8.0	9.8	10.1
East Europe	2.2	2.1	1.9	1.7	1.4	1.5	1.4	1.6	1.7	1.7
Other Europe	0.4	0.4	0.3	0.3	0.3	0.0	0.0	0.0	0.0	0.0
Former USSR	1.9	1.6	1.6	1.4	1.1	1.6	1.6	2.2	2.0	2.1
Oceania	0.4	0.4	0.5	0.3	0.4	0.4	0.4	0.3	0.3	0.4
Germany/Allemagne	21.8	21.3	20.1	19.4	18.8	18.5	17.9	18.2	20.6	19.5
United Kingdom	9.1	8.6	8.1	8.1	8.3	8.6	9.4	9.6	9.9	10.4
USA/Etats–Unis d'Amer	6.9	7.5	8.2	8.7	8.5	8.8	9.1	8.5	5.7	6.0
Denmark/Danemark	6.7	6.6	6.8	7.5	7.6	7.6	7.1	6.6	7.5	7.8
Norway,SVD,JM	5.9	6.1	7.0	7.9	7.7	6.9	6.5	6.0	7.5	8.1
Finland/Finlande	6.9	7.0	6.7	6.8	7.0	6.2	6.2	6.3	6.2	5.9
Netherlands/Pays–Bas	4.1	4.1	4.2	4.1	4.3	4.3	4.6	4.0	7.6	7.8
France, Monac	5.1	5.0	5.3	5.0	4.9	5.1	5.3	5.6	5.5	5.8
Japan/Japon	6.0	6.4	6.1	5.1	5.1	5.1	5.0	4.7	3.0	2.5
Belgium–Luxembourg	3.0	3.2	3.1	3.0	3.2	3.5	3.5	3.5	3.9	3.8

	1987	1988	1989	1990	1991	1992	1993	1994	1995	1996
Afrique	2.3	1.9	1.8	1.6	1.5	1.3	2.0	1.4	1.6	1.6
Amériques	14.2	13.4	12.6	12.0	11.1	11.4	11.6	10.4	11.3	11.6
Amérique du Nord	12.4	11.6	11.0	10.2	9.4	9.5	9.7	8.6	9.3	9.5
ALAI	1.5	1.5	1.4	1.6	1.6	1.7	1.7	1.7	1.8	2.0
MCAC	0.0	0.1	0.1	0.1	0.0	0.1	0.1	0.0	0.1	0.0
Caraïbes	0.1	0.2	0.1	0.1	0.1	0.2	0.2	0.1	0.1	0.1
Autre Amérique	0.1	0.0	0.0	0.0	0.0	0.0	0.0	0.0	0.0	0.0
Asie l'URSS exclus	8.0	8.6	8.7	9.1	10.6	9.8	12.2	11.2	12.5	14.0
Europe l'URSS exclus	73.7	74.0	74.4	74.9	74.6	74.8	71.1	67.1	71.3	69.4
UE	58.4	60.0	61.6	62.1	62.0	62.3	59.0	55.5	58.6	56.1
AELE	13.3	12.0	10.7	10.9	10.9	10.6	10.2	9.5	10.1	10.6
Europe de l'Est	1.4	1.5	1.5	1.4	1.4	1.6	1.7	1.8	2.2	2.3
Autre de l'Europe	0.5	0.6	0.6	0.5	0.3	0.0	0.0	0.0	0.0	0.0
Ancienne URSS	0.6	0.6	0.7	0.7	0.7	0.9	1.2	1.3	1.7	1.8
Océanie	1.2	1.3	1.5	1.5	1.2	1.4	1.5	1.4	1.7	1.6
Germany/Allemagne	11.9	12.1	12.7	13.9	15.1	14.9	14.3	12.5	13.2	11.9
United Kingdom	10.2	11.2	11.2	10.1	9.3	9.6	10.2	9.4	9.8	9.7
USA/Etats–Unis d'Amer	10.8	9.9	9.3	8.6	8.1	8.3	8.4	7.5	8.1	8.5
Norway,SVD,JM	10.8	9.3	8.2	8.3	8.4	8.4	8.1	7.6	7.9	8.6
Denmark/Danemark	7.4	6.9	6.6	6.8	7.0	7.1	6.6	6.6	6.6	6.3
Netherlands/Pays–Bas	4.9	4.8	5.0	5.3	5.4	5.6	5.1	5.0	5.6	5.6
France, Monac	5.4	5.3	5.3	5.4	5.5	5.8	5.4	4.8	5.3	4.7
Finland/Finlande	6.2	6.5	7.0	6.8	5.7	5.2	4.6	4.5	5.1	5.2
Belgium–Luxembourg	4.1	4.1	3.8	3.8	3.8	4.2	4.1	4.7	4.3	4.5
Italy/Italie	3.8	4.0	4.4	4.7	4.5	4.4	3.7	3.6	3.7	3.3

4. General Imports C.I.F. by Commodities according to the S.I.T.C. (Rev. 2) in thousand U.S. Dollars
Importations Générales C.A.F. par Produits d'après la C.T.C.I. (Rév. 2) en milliers de Dollars E.U.

SITC CTCI	COMMODITY	1993		1994		1995		1996		PRODUIT
		WEIGHT POIDS	VALUE VALEUR	WEIGHT POIDS	VALUE VALEUR	WEIGHT POIDS	VALUE VALEUR	WEIGHT POIDS	VALUE VALEUR	
	ALL COMMODITIES		42652224		51773522		61646717		63986841	TOUS PRODUITS
0	FOOD AND LIVE ANIMALS		2676202		3247895		3496385		3836501	ALIMENTS,ANIMAUX VIVANTS
01	MEAT AND PREPARATIONS		151913		189679		293609		337805	VIANDES ET PREPARATIONS
011	MEAT FRESH,CHILLD,FROZEN	W 22432	93666		134377	W 40732	219683	W 52754	259688	VIANDES FRAICHES,REF,CONGE
03	FISH AND PREPARATIONS		359342		438627		537231		592930	POISSONS ET PREPARATIONS
034	FISH,FRESH,CHILLED,FROZN	W 41291	139991		171856	W 74398	272331	W 83355	271437	POISSON FRAIS, REFRIG,CONG
04	CEREALS AND PREPARATIONS		220942		256039		256801		304988	CEREALES ET PRODUITS
048	CEREAL ETC PREPARATIONS	W 99736	161218		181132	W 113940	208659	W 139363	232756	PREPTNS A BASE CEREALES
05	VEGETABLES AND FRUIT		920844		1054178		1062475		1192625	LEGUMES ET FRUITS
054	VEG ETC FRSH,SMPLY PRSVD	W 290229	276730		306657	W 392870	371176	W 398115	391905	LEGUMES FRAIS,CONG,SECS
0545	OTHER FRESH VEGETABLES	W 147308	151690		147714	W 159034	169875	W 164709	195971	AUTRES LEGUMES FRAIS,REF
05459	FRESH VEGETABLES NES	W 117298	131578		124704	W 122488	144219	W 128139	173009	LEGUMES FRAIS,REFRI NDA
057	FRUIT,NUTS,FRESH,DRIED	W 512037	394245	W 533203	452572	W 464176	434279	W 512223	528404	FRUITS FRAIS OU SECS
058	FRUIT PRESERVED,PREPARED	W 150735	177193	W 146153	213562	W 99615	179034	W 110314	188863	CONSERVES DE FRUITS
07	COFFEE,TEA,COCOA,SPICES		363205		546085		573570		528603	CAFE,THE,CACAO,EPICES
071	COFFEE AND SUBSTITUTES	W 99494	208328		357305	W 90781	371200	W 101560	327844	CAFE ET SUCCEDANES
0711	COFFEE GREEN,ROASTED,SUB	W 96797	179792		321831	W 88738	336379	W 98624	289753	CAFE TORREFIE OU DECAFEINE
07111	COFFEE GREEN,HUSKS,SKINS	W 88366	155305		281316	W 84265	307679	W 91467	259871	CAFE NON TORREFIE
081	*FEEDING STUFF FOR ANIML	W 730096	221295	W 846568	258156	W 830062	249857		283549	NOURRITURE POUR ANIMAUX
0819	FOOD WASTE AND FEED NES	W 334741	143865	W 284083	149451	W 340127	150145	W 286109	154877	DECHETS,ALIMENTS NDA
09	MISC EDIBLE PRODUCTS		220277		242487		255498		286320	PREP ALIMENTAIRES DIVERSES
098	EDIBLE PRODCTS,PREPS NES	W 75799	208828		231999		243377	W 72942	272968	PREP ALIMENTAIRES NDA
09809	MISC FOOD PREPRTIONS NES	W 36550	138011		156280	W 29266	162537	W 35198	186309	PREP ALIMENTAIRES NDA
1	BEVERAGES AND TOBACCO		460218		621989		388898		559396	BOISSONS ET TABACS
11	BEVERAGES		351525		491771		305022		460129	BOISSONS
112	ALCOHOLIC BEVERAGES	W 172985	336333	W 248022	473370		287894	W 219622	434643	BOISSONS ALCOOLIQUES
1121	WINE OF FRESH GRAPES ETC	W 105022	179872	W 160358	273763		178266	W 139212	283674	VINS DE RAISINS FRAIS
11212	WINE OF FRESH GRAPES	W 102695	174076	W 156001	263466	W 91472	174327	W 135126	273202	VINS DE MOUTS DE RAISINS
2	CRUDE MATERLS,EXCL FUELS		1387839		1857784		2333598		1960598	MAT BRUTES NON COMESTIBLES
24	CORK AND WOOD		264186		459940		624508		420254	LIEGE ET BOIS
247	OTH WOOD ROUGH,SQUARED	W 3622283	169503	W 5684540	318937	W 6864052	457474	W 4533287	269561	BOIS BRUTS EQUARRIS
2471	SAW–,VENEER–LOGS CONIFER	W 2038849	100567	W 3086191	176075	W 3279541	222889	W 2173298	134174	CONIFERES POUR SCIAGE,PLACAG
24711	— IN THE ROUGH	W 2038849	100567	W 3086191	176075	W 3279541	222889	W 2173298	134174	ECORCES OU DEGROSSIS
2472	SAW–,VENEER–LOGS NON–CON	W 1583434	68937	W 2598349	142863	W 3584511	234585	W 2359989	135386	NON CONIFERES SCIAGE,PLAC
24721	— IN THE ROUGH	W 1583434	68937	W 2598349	142863	W 3584511	234585	W 2359989	135386	BRUTS ECORCES DEGROSSIS
251	*PULP AND WASTE PAPER	W 744314	98317		157832		305490	W 772137	166731	PATES A PAPIER,DECHETS
27	CRUDE FERTLZR,MINRLS NES		205685		234488		275750		261942	ENGRAIS MINERAUX BRUTS
278	OTHER CRUDE MINERALS	W 2000400	158833	W 2166792	174071	W 2328971	200821		190525	AUTRES MINERAUX BRUTS
28	METALLIFEROUS ORES,SCRAP		369780		503096		624775		576241	MINERAIS METAL,DECHETS
282	IRON AND STEEL SCRAP	W 464645	132647	W 653370	186870	W 338419	209616	W 322760	170536	FERRAILLES
28202	— OF ALLOY STEEL	W 144086	96103	W 183693	128327	W 195516	189896	W 149224	147984	FERRAILLES D'ACIERS ALLIES
288	NONFERR METAL SCRAP NES	W 156631	116947	W 176403	143178	W 175296	188603	W 154110	192185	DECHETS NON FERREUX
29	CRUDE ANIMAL,VEG MAT NES		297478		299580		245147		283484	MATIERES BRUTES ANIM,VEGET
292	CRUDE VEG MATERIALS NES	W 170313	264871		265238		222037		260707	MAT BRUTES VEGETALES NDA
2926	LIVE PLANTS,BULBS,ETC	W 41737	137371	W 41478	138832	W 39017	114768	W 39831	130065	BULBES,TUBERCULES
3	MINERAL FUELS ETC		3950117		3850222		3620665		4776628	COMBUSTIBLES MINERAUX LUB
32	COAL,COKE AND BRIQUETTES		193350		217284		266477		244094	HOUILLES,COKES,BRIQUETTES
322	COAL,LIGNITE AND PEAT	W 3268001	165484	W 3116107	151913	W 3607210	204795	W 3391470	194373	HOUILLES,LIGNITES,TOURBE
3222	OTH COAL,NOT AGGLOMERATD	W 3180866	160302	W 3011646	145742	W 3447685	194121	W 3139894	179370	AUTRES HOUILLES
33	PETROLEUM AND PRODUCTS		3476164		3417152		3193660		4278595	PETROLE ET DERIVES
333	CRUDE PETROLEUM	MW 17803	2185981	MW 17954	2113250	MW 16411	2110652	MW 21342	3000646	HUILES BRUTES DE PETROLE
334	PETROLEUM PRODUCTS,REFIN	W 6567407	1234370	W 7036367	1246618	W 4987280	972238		1229981	PRODUITS RAFFINES
3341	GASOLINE,OTH LIGHT OILS	W 2135970	413435	W 1567825	297415	W 1665660	334676		347799	ESSENCES POUR MOTEURS
33411	MOTOR,AVIATION SPIRIT	W 1526205	305166	W 1464905	275159	W 1511931	305924	W 1461147	317560	ESSENCES MOTEURS D'AVIONS
3342	KEROSENE,OTH MEDIUM OILS	W 1876514	386730	W 2030719	390850	W 1028206	211971	W 965042	229468	PETR LAMPANTS,AUT HUIL
33421	KEROSENE INCL JET FUEL	W 1876178	386540	W 2030719	390850	W 1024005	210453	W 960948	227547	PETROLES LAMPANTS
3343	GAS OILS	W 1083835	207216	W 976383	164228					GAS OILS
3344	FUEL OILS,NES	W 1282065	126688	W 204603	19729	W 1110374	121385	W 1828664	250915	FUEL OILS
3345	LUBS,PETROLEUM OILS NES	W 189022	100302	W 2256837	374397	W 1183040	304205	W 1446536	401800	HUILES LUBRIFIANTES
33451	LUBS(HIGH PETR CONT) ETC	W 177460	80187	W 2242940	348568	W 1173229	272343	W 1436004	372574	HUILES LUBRIF,H LOURDES
341	*GAS,NATURAL AND MANUFCT		116622		125072	W 2841172	160528	W 1421668	253939	GAZ NATUREL,GAZ MANUFACT
3413	PETROLM GASES,LIQUEFIED		116420		124802	W 2828826	158163	W 1421641	253791	GAZ DE PETROLE LIQUEFIE
5	CHEMCLS,RELATED PROD NES		4742189		5570741		6405524		6405993	PRODUITS CHIMIQUES
51	ORGANIC CHEMICALS		830416		1057048		1097724		1110886	PROD CHIMIQ ORGANIQUES
511	HYDROCARBONS NES,DERIVS		165604		195480		143091		114627	HYDROCARBURES NDA
512	ALCOHOLS,PHENOLS ETC		117502		174102		57056	W 56930	63135	PHENOLS,PHENOLS–ALCOOLS
514	NITROGEN–FNCTN COMPOUNDS		76418		434051		601810	W 75149	654486	COMPOSES FONCT AZOTEES
5148	OTH NITROGN–FNCTN CMPNDS	W 11696	29702		378559		521092	W 24025	574047	AUTRES COMPOSES AZOTES
51482	IMIDE–,IMIDE–FNCT CMPNDS	W 105	1957		346752	W 10548	488225	W 11960	537988	COMPOSES A FONCTION IMIDE
515	ORG–INORG COMPOUNDS ETC	W 14814	295081		51897	W 14038	59328	W 14778	52553	COMPOSES ORGANO–MINERAUX
5156	HETEROCYCLIC CMPDS ETC	W 10647	272294		28672	W 3615	30652	W 3448	25763	COMPOSES HETEROCYCLIQUES
51569	OTH HETEROCYC CMPDS,ETC	W 10402	271676		27851	W 3205	29392	W 3193	24868	AUT COMP HETEROCYCLIQUES
52	INORGANIC CHEMICALS		435678		508888		655762		525332	PROD CHIM INORGANIQUES
522	INORG ELEMNTS,OXIDES,ETC		183800		234128		257170		228778	ELEMENTS INORGANIQUES
523	OTHR INORG CHEMICALS ETC		123975		159750		191900		158007	AUT PRODUITS CHIMIQUES INORG
524	RADIOACTIVE ETC MATERIAL		127902		115010		206692		138547	MATIERES RADIOACTIVES
5241	RADIOACTIVE ELEMENTS ETC		126484		112756		204372		136969	RADIOELEMENTS,ISOTOPES
53	DYES,TANNING,COLOUR PROD		327049		389419		471904		477555	PROD TEINTURE,COLORANTS
533	PIGMENTS,PAINTS,ETC	W 108622	256299	W 112233	294169	W 120220	352634	W 128063	360806	PIGMENTS,PEINTURES,VERNIS
541	*MEDICINAL,PHARM PRODUCT	MK 32106	879205		1004333		1167071		1350504	PROD MEDICINAUX PHARMACEUT
5417	MEDICAMENTS	MK 27086	648856		747009	MK 24884	911190	MK 35380	1038020	MEDICAMENTS
54179	— CONTNG OTH SUBSTANCES	MK 25190	482338	MK 23964	578193	MK 18603	715335	MK 30745	793106	MED CONT AUT SUBSTANCES
55	PERFUME,CLEANING ETC PRD		484765		509877		527427		540751	PROD POUR PARFUM,TOILETTE
553	PERFUMERY,COSMETICS,ETC	W 31534	240370	W 34355	258446	W 38840	248282	W 38331	250421	PRODUITS DE PARFUMERIE
554	SOAP,CLEANSING ETC PREPS	W 173717	220347	W 178441	220718	W 237129	245504	W 178922	256009	SAVONS,PRODUITS DETERSIFS
5542	WASHING PREPARATIONS ETC	W 157924	187133	W 163297	188664	W 223442	212005	W 158397	212775	PROD ORG TENSIO–ACT NDA
58	PLASTIC MATERIALS ETC		1058042		1333991		1649567		1530956	MAT PLAST ARTIFICIELLES
582	PROD OF CONDENSATION ETC	W 125919	264060	W 209845	339391	W 165376	437753	W 164709	408739	PROD CONDENS,POLYCOND
5823	ALKYDS,OTHER POLYESTERS	W 46514	120346	W 59413	152861	W 64946	206674	W 66528	194144	ALKYDES ET AUT POLYESTERS
583	POLYMERIZATION ETC PRODS		768855		963626	W 711017	1178113	W 743194	1091483	PROD POLYMERISATION
5831	POLYETHYLENE	W 271598	232515	W 303040	288343	W 262269	321758	W 273018	284341	POLYETHYLENE
58311	— IN PRIMARY FORMS	W 240079	170142	W 268796	216494	W 235463	261378	W 242720	221791	POLYETHYLENE PRIMAIRES
5839	OTH POLYMRZTION ETC PROD	W 86649	193724	W 104497	243688	W 136854	332764	W 144704	321057	AUT PROD POLYMER COPOLYM
59	CHEMICAL MATERIALS NES		586509		679562		755727		785620	MAT PROD CHIMIQUES NDA
598	MISCEL CHEM PRODUCTS NES	W 665223	414898		466541		519426	W 484398	528142	PROD DIV INDUST CHIM NDA
5989	CHEM PRODUCTS,PREPS NES	W 415855	304101	W 387403	335105	W 206921	384915	W 212758	384144	PROD PREP CHIMIQUES NDA
59899	OTH CHEM PRODS,PREPS,NES	W 175227	210238	W 178820	240354	W 126109	285922	W 148290	274026	AUT PRODUITS CHIMIQUES NDA
6	BASIC MANUFACTURES		6707338		8511811		10326100		9869513	ART MANUFACTURES
62	RUBBER MANUFACTURES NES		534738		665185		862357		880424	CAOUTCHOUC MANUFACTURE
625	RUBBER TYRES, TUBES ETC	W 79586	288625	W 94892	353286	W 110354	453144	W 110359	492668	PNEUS CAOUTCHOUC VULCANISE
6251	TYRES NEW FOR MOTOR CARS	W 36229	153920	W 42839	184273	W 43355	206266	W 44369	237303	PNEUS POUR VOITURES

4. General Imports C.I.F. by Commodities according to the S.I.T.C. (Rev. 2) in thousand U.S. Dollars
Importations Générales C.A.F. par Produits d'après la C.T.C.I. (Rév. 2) en milliers de Dollars E.U.

SITC CTCI	COMMODITY	1993		1994		1995		1996		PRODUIT
		WEIGHT POIDS	VALUE VALEUR	WEIGHT POIDS	VALUE VALEUR	WEIGHT POIDS	VALUE VALEUR	WEIGHT POIDS	VALUE VALEUR	
628	RUBBER ARTICLES NES	W 15097	150570	W 18482	189368	W 29361	267945	W 19508	251444	OUVRAGES CAOUTCHOUC NDA
6289	OTH RUBBER ARTICLES NES	W 11880	117132	W 14458	145551	W 25568	213631	W 15686	199213	AUT OUVR CAOUTCHOUC NDA
62898	UNHARD RUBBER PRODS NES	W 11838	116768	W 14344	144940	W 17334	212016	W 15389	198006	OUV CAOUT VULC NON DURCI
63	WOOD,CORK MANUFACTRS NES		225453		274935		344999		343623	OUVRAGES LIEGE ET BOIS
634	VENEERS,PLYWOOD,ETC	W 195003	115354	W 245791	162026	W 264929	199437	W 290209	207509	PLACAGES,CONTRE-PLAQUES
64	PAPER,PAPERBOARD AND MFR		697703		831415		1006239		995448	PAPIERS,CARTONS & OUVRAGES
641	PAPER AND PAPERBOARD	W 419844	364596	W 540582	474890	W 491440	576893	W 531251	595089	PAPIERS ET CARTONS
6418	COATED ETC PAPER NES BLK	W 79843	142846	W 96037	173012	W 85885	183743	W 89165	179659	PAP,CARTONS COUCHES,ENDUITS
642	PAPER,ETC,PRECUT,ARTS OF	W 161475	333107	W 163705	356525		429346	W 167236	400358	PAP,CARTONS DECOUPES
6428	PAPER ETC ARTICLES NES	W 93868	184893	W 89897	195473		249821	W 90441	210609	OUVRAGES EN PATE A PAPIER
65	TEXTILE YARN,FABRICS,ETC		940558		1087283		1157778		1155232	FILS,TISSUS,ARTICLES TEXTILE
651	TEXTILE YARN	W 24069	136599		175443		223985		205936	FILS TEXTILES
657	SPECIAL TXTL FABRC,PRODS	W 27203	186670		214628		229397		233242	TISSUS SPECIAUX
658	TEXTILE ARTICLES NES	W 21015	160147		182821		201740		219072	ART FACONNES MAT TEXTILES
659	FLOOR COVERINGS,ETC	W 33328	140125	W 34299	148623	W 30027	131925		142628	COUVRE-PARQUETS,TAPIS ETC
66	NONMETAL MINERAL MFS NES		679498		758374		809384		782889	ART MIN NON METALLIQUES
663	MINERAL MANUFCTURES NES	W 261309	160199		178993	W 250773	213210	W 202583	202801	ART MIN MANUF NDA
664	GLASS	W 112219	161608		190432		227921		217982	VERRE
67	IRON AND STEEL		1419757		2085417		2795951		2611817	FER ET ACIER
671	PIG IRON ETC	W 167736	132666		195817	W 239315	269811	W 217328	205929	FONTE,SPIEGEL,POUDRES
6716	FERRO-ALLOYS	W 135015	124126	W 178372	179827	W 186486	251444	W 167130	189800	FERRO-ALLIAGES
67169	OTHER FERRO-ALLOYS	W 91462	98645	W 120677	143890	W 134666	209930	W 111651	143183	AUTRES FERRO-ALLIAGES
672	IRON,STEEL PRIMARY FORMS	W 160209	130662	W 385312	340898	W 322122	313964	W 421071	463270	LINGOTS FER,ACIER
6725	IRN,STL BLOOMS,SLABS,ETC	W 96051	83230	W 329903	305840	W 245611	277336	W 334185	420533	BLOOMS,BILLETTES FER ACIER
67254	STNLS STL ETC BLOOMS ETC	W 64022	68401	W 246890	263671	W 122977	210955	W 300508	383186	BLOOMS ETC ACIER INOXYD
673	IRON,STEEL SHAPES ETC	W 495576	245310	W 590015	336738	W 703922	502141	W 590933	398079	BARRES,PROFIL FER,ACIER
6732	IRON,STEEL BARS ETC	W 159884	105903	W 199937	148935	W 268807	252530	W 222939	194563	BARRES FER,ACIER
674	IRN,STL UNIV,PLATE,SHEET	W 870318	516466	W 1042119	700376	W 1159278	1007444	W 1109497	925114	LARGES PLATS,TOLES
6746	IRN,STL THIN PLATE,ROLLD	W 217613	146661	W 255488	202438	W 249283	273979	W 230974	228025	TOLES LAM MOINS 3MM
6749	OTH IRN,STL PLATES,SHEET	W 365158	211185	W 450980	289661	W 555396	438987	W 532158	421817	AUTRES TOLES FER,ACIER
67491	— OF IRON OR SIMPLE STL	W 359924	199176	W 445338	276195	W 549535	425157	W 525403	409665	AUT TOLES AUTRES ACIER FIN
678	IRON,STL TUBES,PIPES,ETC	W 258803	261683	W 316395	348314	W 364807	511886	W 306532	445744	TUBES,TUYAUX EN FONTE,FER
6783	IRON,STL TUBES,PIPES NES	W 198178	138567	W 227528	181571	W 253837	265193	W 217569	229845	AUT TUBES,TUYAUX FER,ACIER
68	NON-FERROUS METALS		828572		1189469		1421630		1196341	METAUX NON FERREUX
682	COPPER EXC CEMENT COPPER	W 98897	258364		319284	W 120093	435346	W 97356	311566	CUIVRE
6821	COPPER NES,ALLOYS,UNWRT	W 57983	115724		130923	W 67773	205905	W 50214	117669	CUIVRE BRUT
68212	COPPER REFINED,UNWROUGHT	W 57744	115123		129965	W 67467	204782	W 48517	112950	CUIVRE AFFINE BRUT
6822	COPPER,ALLOYS WORKED	W 40914	142640	W 50550	188362	W 52320	229441	W 47142	193897	CUIVRE,ALLIAGES OUVRES
684	ALUMINIUM	W 152874	341588	W 263471	582756	W 206384	639451	W 221094	578603	ALUMINIUM
6841	ALUMINIUM,ALLOYS,UNWRGHT	W 64050	81531	W 157387	260805	W 89206	195959	W 105523	182099	ALUMINIUM,ALLIAGES BRUTS
6842	ALUMINIUM,ALLOYS WORKED	W 88823	260057	W 106084	321951	W 117178	443492	W 115571	396503	ALUMINIUM,ALLIAGES OUVRE
68422	ALUMNM PLATE,SHEET,STRIP	W 53530	126756	W 66137	167453	W 75811	244917	W 77297	221124	TOLES, PLANCHES EN ALU
69	METAL MANUFACTURES NES		1303484		1533714		1845075		1822356	ART MANUFACT EN METAL NDA
694	STL,COPPR NAILS,NUTS,ETC	W 44780	165760	W 56357	216611	W 70004	297667	W 63072	265747	CLOUS,VIS,ECROUS
69402	IRN,STL NUTS,BOLTS,ETC	W 37363	147178	W 47779	195044	W 59179	273597	W 53065	243572	BOULONS,VIS,ECROUS FER,AC
695	TOOLS	W 18899	301392	W 21099	345139	W 22624	428875	W 22653	463857	OUTILS A MAIN
6954	BLADES,TIPS,ETC FR TOOLS	W 8390	191701	W 8794	209410	W 8579	276922	W 10833	307593	OUTILS POUR MACHINE-OUTIL
69541	PARTS TO INSERT IN TOOLS	W 7731	156673	W 7862	160298	W 7210	191602	W 9878	233129	OUTILS DE FORAGE
699	BASE METAL MFRS NES	W 87298	508474		612133		723598		686242	ART MANUFACTURES MET NDA
6991	LOCKSMITHS WARES,ETC	W 24421	213175	W 28051	251747	W 37416	316082	W 30345	310255	ARTICLES DE SERRURERIE
69913	BASE MTL DOOR,ETC FITTNG	W 17855	145432	W 21480	174476	W 27079	222952	W 23640	212336	GARNITURES POUR MEUBLES
7	MACHINES,TRANSPORT EQUIP		15316163		19538292		25719303		26734114	MACHINES MATERIEL TRANSPORT
71	POWER GENERATING EQUIPMT		1146685		1303403		2035480		1986910	MACHINES GENERATRICES
713	INTRNL COMBUS PSTN ENGIN	W 39976	432386	W 56090	599440	W 81473	822942	W 72777	759800	MOTEURS EXPL COMB INT, PIECE
7139	PISTON ENGINE PARTS NES	W 31132	312306	W 44863	447471	W 69568	653975	W 62826	621887	PIECES POUR 713.2,3,8
714	ENGINES AND MOTORS NES	W 5731	289238	W 8121	235372	W 6917	627655	W 7869	707387	MOTEURS NON ELECTRIQUES
7149	ENGINE & MOTOR PARTS NES	W 5579	217857	W 8004	181176	W 6369	345295	W 7416	409777	PIECES 714 ET 718.88
71491	PARTS NES OF 7144,71481	W 572	177114	W 447	126309	W 668	262892	W 909	335969	PIECES DES PROPULSEURS
716	ROTATING ELECTRIC PLANT	W 21168	235895	W 26231	282788		344652		346745	APP ELECTR ROTATIFS,PIECES
7162	AC MTRS,GENRTRS,GEN SETS	W 13119	143796	W 15160	172757	W 18058	226288		219466	MOTEURS ELECTRIQUES
71621	AC MTRS,INC UNIVRSL MTRS	W 11758	124812	W 14086	156592	W 17012	207286	W 14631	199923	MOT ELEC NON COUR CONTINU
718	OTH POWER GENERATG MACHY	W 2757	159732		134922	W 3454	158948	W 3193	154085	AUTRES MOTEURS PARTIES
72	MACHS FOR SPCL INDUSTRYS		1054874		1300355		1776544		2021245	MAC SPECIALES POUR INDUST
721	AGRIC MACHY,EXC TRACTORS	W 17923	119705		161806		183861		199063	MACHINES AGRICOLES
725	PAPER ETC MILL MACHINERY	W 9882	142222	W 9026	148056	W 15943	243424	W 23374	348891	MACHINES FABR PATE PAPIER
7259	PTS NES OF MACHS OF 725	W 6604	90571	W 5944	81789	W 11844	164423	W 15604	218075	PIECES GROUPE 725
72591	PTS NES OF MACHS OF 7251	W 5916	75001	W 5283	64704	W 10981	143648	W 14588	193195	PIECES DU 725.1
726	PRINTG,BKBINDG MACHY,PTS	W 4986	137227	W 5497	164520	W 5548	182678	W 6714	210911	MACHINES POUR IMPRIMERIE
728	OTH MACHY FOR SPCL INDUS	W 28253	409986		496186	W 37455	746705		815311	AUT MACH IND PARTICULIERES
7284	MACHY FOR SPCL INDUS NES	W 14084	314646		370643	W 22433	606817		664513	MACH SPEC IND PARTICUL.
72848	OTH MCHY WITH INDIV FNCT	W 6958	160519	W 7548	171866	W 12072	345570	W 21070	384053	AUTRES MACHINES NDA
73	METALWORKING MACHINERY		258308		439697		527780		594353	MACH TRAVAIL DES METAUX
736	METALWORKING MACH-TOOLS	W 11955	201027		342173		419797	W 22395	475803	MACH-OUTILS TRAVAIL METAUX
74	GENRL INDUSTRL MACHY NES		2363844		3012789		3936287		3847709	MACH APP INDUSTRIE
741	HEATING,COOLING EQUIPMNT	W 20335	297915	W 27723	386151	W 32424	493523	W 30924	507808	MACH CHAUFFAGE,PIECES
742	PUMPS FOR LIQUIDS ETC	W 15775	262572	W 18880	331391	W 21930	455114	W 22458	459624	POMPES MOTO-POMPES
743	PUMPS NES,CENTRFUGES ETC	W 33346	386401	W 39537	487561	W 47816	637725	W 44365	582712	POMPES COMPRES,VENT ETC
7431	PUMPS FOR GASES ETC	W 13552	141913	W 16395	184008	W 19337	231961	W 18796	236715	POMPES AIR A VIDE,COMPRES
744	MECHANICAL HANDLING EQU	W 59948	337754	W 71004	411833	W 93256	522353	W 92911	536063	EQUIP MANUTENTION PIECES
7442	LIFTING,LOADING MACH NES	W 17016	157237	W 18250	170101	W 20047	187650	W 22297	187123	APP LEVAGE,MANUTENTION
7449	PTS NES OF MACHY OF 7442	W 39241	154878	W 47438	205628	W 66008	282407	W 62336	287567	PIECES DU 744.2
745	NONELEC MACHY,TOOLS NES		304492	W 14501	317574	W 16131	349716	W 17292	367169	AUT MACH NON ELEC,PIECES
7452	OTH NONELEC MCHS,PTS NES	W 10167	245312	W 11744	262825	W 13281	282668	W 14630	302823	AUT MACH NON ELEC,PIECES
749	NONELEC MACH PTS,ACC NES	W 66514	774709	W 92016	1078280	W 116545	1477856	W 111150	1394332	PIECES MACH NON ELEC NDA
7491	BALL,ROLLER,ETC BEARINGS	W 19134	193540	W 29068	326154	W 36265	502998	W 29840	422424	ROULEMENTS BILLES ETC
7492	COCKS,VALVES ETC NES	W 11346	241951	W 13749	306376	W 15008	383831	W 14619	395498	ART ROB,SIM POUR TUYAUX
7493	SHAFT,CRANK,PULLEY ETC	W 29562	221811	W 41758	307177	W 54583	407316	W 56378	390454	ARBRES TRANS,VILEBREQUINS
75	OFFICE MACHNES,ADP EQUIP		2220074		2647049		3549012		3478565	MACH BUREAU TRAIT AUTOM
751	OFFICE MACHINES	W 4310	134514		178107		165152		150775	MACH,APPAREILS DE BUREAU
752	AUTOMTIC DATA PROC EQUIP	W 17772	1396681	W 20327	1715220	W 29972	2370033	W 29220	2364344	MACH TRAIT INFORMATION
7522	DIGITAL COMPUTERS	W 1415	164935	W 1731	229512	W 1524	272187	W 1452	314174	MACH DIGITALES COMPLETES
7523	DIGITL CENTRL PROCESSORS	W 3892	421274	W 6278	656292	W 8363	1007157	W 7666	957355	UNITES CENTRALES
7524	DIGITL CENTRL STOR UNITS	W 892	171180	W 966	198640	W 1428	277209	W 2103	287545	UNITES MEMOIRE CENTRALES
7525	ADP PERIPHERAL UNITS	W 10752	533560	W 10551	523168	W 16772	625095	W 15996	580068	UNITES PERIPHERIQUES
7528	OFF-LINE DATA PROC EQUIP	W 785	102342	W 783	104677	W 1869	184563	W 1955	217721	MACH AUXIL TRAIT INFORM
759	OFFICE,ADP MCH PTS,ACCES	W 7525	688879	W 8200	753722	W 8805	1013827	W 9481	963446	PIECES DU 751 ET 752
7599	ACCTG,ETC,ADP MCH PTS,AC	W 5842	621679	W 6497	677022	W 6348	879497	W 7295	865802	PIECES DU 751 ET 752
76	TELECOMM,SOUND EQUIPMENT		1428238		2012956		2874450		2909971	EQUIPMENT DE TELECOM
761	TELEVISION RECEIVERS	W 15062	200224	W 19937	276968		284735	W 15695	255252	RECEPTEURS DE TELEVISION
7611	COLOUR TV RECEIVERS	W 15031	198266	W 19902	275165	W 17470	282780	W 15651	253346	RECEPTEURS COULEUR
762	RADIO BROADCAST RECEIVRS	W 4911	125908	W 7695	197092	W 6920	210820	W 5894	189865	RECEPTEURS RADIODIFFUSION

4. General Imports C.I.F. by Commodities according to the S.I.T.C. (Rev. 2) in thousand U.S. Dollars
Importations Générales C.A.F. par Produits d'après la C.T.C.I. (Rév. 2) en milliers de Dollars E.U.

SITC CTCI	COMMODITY	1993 WEIGHT POIDS	1993 VALUE VALEUR	1994 WEIGHT POIDS	1994 VALUE VALEUR	1995 WEIGHT POIDS	1995 VALUE VALEUR	1996 WEIGHT POIDS	1996 VALUE VALEUR	PRODUIT
763	SOUND RECORDRS,PHONOGRPH	W 4503	163505		176681	W 4448	194313	W 3883	211811	PHONO,APP ENREGISTREMENT
7638	OTHR SOUND APPARATUS ETC	W 4377	161522	W 4176	175782	W 4338	192217	W 3851	211182	AUT APP D'ENREGIS,REPROD
764	TELECOM EQPT,PTS,ACC NES	W 15213	938601	W 17810	1362214	W 22620	2184581	W 21139	2253042	EQUIP TELECOM,PIECES
7641	LINE TELEPHONE,ETC EQUIP	W 2670	202221	W 2958	250395	W 3687	308597	W 3547	313987	APP TELEPHON PAR FIL
7643	TV,RADIO TRANSMITTRS ETC	W 951	195026	W 1185	319933	W 1096	328422	W 1212	371823	APP EMET TELE RADIO
7649	PTS NES OF EQUIPMT OF 76	W 7046	418390	W 8849	652971	W 12653	1367554	W 11660	1436414	PIECES DE LA DIV 76
76491	PTS NES OF APPAR OF 7641	W 2246	181970	W 2210	243161	W 2475	405080	W 2212	359102	PIECES POUR 764.1
76493	TELECOMM EQUIPMT PTS NES	W 3459	220264	W 4738	388270	W 8221	940080	W 7993	1056873	PIECES 761,762,764.3,8
77	ELECTRIC MACHNRY NES ETC		3194558		4030653		5111287		5362182	MACH APP ELECT NDA
771	ELECTRIC POWER MACHY NES	W 20411	211508	W 22739	278540	W 24902	399710	W 21202	392885	MACH PROD,TRANS ELECTR
7712	OTH ELEC POWER MACHY NES	W 8420	138297	W 9938	192445	W 10154	286396	W 10707	294370	AUT APP PROD TRANSF ELEC
772	SWITCHGEAR ETC,PARTS NES	W 17877	684066	W 19566	864468	W 22390	1115015	W 22851	1137016	APP COUPURE,SECT ETC
7721	SWITCHGEAR ETC	W 16813	569014	W 18199	703171	W 20373	895800	W 20878	904699	APP COUPURE,SECTIONMNT
773	ELECTR DISTRIBUTNG EQUIP	W 31915	284121	W 38430	346352	W 45132	467827	W 40070	454698	EQUIPMT DISTRIBUTION ELECT
7731	INSULATED WIRE,CABLE ETC	W 26092	251476	W 32284	311843	W 39013	422949	W 31906	400330	FILS,CABLES ISOLES ELECT
775	HOUSEHOLD TYPE EQUIP NES	W 56896	402923	W 62144	448580		453389		531753	MACH,APP USAGE DOMESTQUE
7758	ELECTRO–THERMIC APPL NES	W 19634	154753	W 20394	173643		179975		201630	APP ELECTROTHERMIQ NDA
776	TRANSISTORS,VALVES,ETC	W 2664	689813		905565		1236477	W 3547	1323521	LAMPES,TUBES,VALVES
7764	ELECTRONIC MICROCIRCUITS	W 862	527603	W 1017	683102	W 1916	883446	W 1280	1041225	MICROSTRUCTURES ELECTRON
778	ELECTRICAL MACHINERY NES	W 77614	814797	W 91545	1070267	W 96695	1315251	W 122055	1392986	AUTRES MACH ELECT NDA
7781	BATTERIES,ACCUMULATORS	W 30014	158507	W 36799	218017	W 37701	277039	W 64584	286370	PILES ET ACCUMULATEURS
77812	ELECTRIC ACCUMULATORS	W 21537	97953	W 28341	154164	W 29075	210890	W 53789	201042	ACCUMULATEURS ELECTRIQ
7783	AUTOMOTIVE ELECTR EQUIP	W 12277	208237	W 15089	254569	W 18208	335582	W 16208	319630	EQUIP ELECT MOTEURS EXPL
7788	OTH ELEC MACHY,EQUIP NES	W 25099	274719	W 26128	381782	W 28141	461585	W 27158	528605	AUT MACH APP ELEC NDA
78	ROAD VEHICLES		2884740		4028595		5031547		5552196	VEHICULES ROUTIERS
781	PASS MOTOR VEH EXC BUSES	W 111208	1195949	W 158114	1724212	W 155139	1837616	W 194601	2319892	AUTO TRANSPORT PERSONNES
782	LORRIES,SPCL MTR VEH NES	W 16605	148860	W 26499	267224	W 37362	372482	W 39970	417581	VEHICULES SPECIAUX,MARCH
7821	LORRIES,TRUCKS	W 15140	131502	W 24800	247727	W 35505	353949	W 36649	386292	VEHICULES TRANSP MARCHAND
784	MOTOR VEH PRTS,ACCES NES	W 201263	1282089	W 275362	1716585	W 356338	2506631	W 320405	2442035	PIECES 722,781,782,783
7849	OTHER MOTOR VEHCL PARTS	W 200426	1275161	W 273911	1706419	W 354767	2491074	W 317782	2415635	PIECES 722,781,782,783
785	CYCLES,ETC MOTRZD OR NOT	W 9844	128793	W 13085	152597	W 7963	120599	W 11035	155857	MOTOCYCLES SCOOTERS
79	OTHR TRANSPORT EQUIPMENT		764841		762794		876916		980983	AUTRE MATERIEL TRANSPORT
792	AIRCRAFT ETC	W 1281	553403		340613		696119		724145	APP NAVIGATION AERIENNE
7923	AIRCRFT NES2000–15000KG	W 85	6969	W 25	3863	W 541	267464	W 507	302427	AERODYNES 2000 A 15000 KG
7924	AIRCRFT NES OVER 15000KG	W 347	316445	W 199	115897	W 619	157477	W 185	137494	AERODYNES PLUS 15000 KG
7929	AIRCRAFT PARTS NES	W 784	205926	W 763	180026	W 824	254008	W 721	242853	PIECES DU 792
793	SHIPS AND BOATS ETC		152889		341596		105101	W 7528	141992	NAVIRES BATEAUX,ETC
7932	SHIPS AND BOATS NES		140969		328675		94236	W 5009	130646	NAVIRES ET BATEAUX
79323	OTHER CARGO VESSELS		99847	V 354	271789	V 1920	71431	W 3072	107421	AUT BATEAUX TRANS MARCH
8	MISC MANUFACTURED GOODS		7007922		7946410		8249549		8458490	ART MANUFACTURES DIVERS
812	*PLUMBG,HEATNG,LGHTNG EQ	W 27690	195867	W 28427	217722	W 27833	253340	W 30873	258195	APPAR SANITAIRES CHAUFFAGE
8124	LIGHTING EQUIPMENT NES	W 17337	161252	W 19214	184468	W 20321	218344	W 22465	219960	APPAREILS ECLAIRAGE ETC
821	*FURNITURE,PARTS THEREOF	W 167111	616600	W 198089	763616	W 176832	760254	W 172580	750502	MEUBLES ET PIECES
8211	CHAIRS,SEATS AND PARTS	W 37790	222428	W 43711	263494	W 39511	260061	W 43679	283597	SIEGES ET PIECES
82111	CHAIRS AND OTHER SEATS	W 30500	159273	W 34768	186858	W 30580	189020	W 32456	192093	SIEGES
8219	FURNITURE AND PARTS NES	W 119370	295824	W 143134	379417	W 126581	383337	W 118461	353579	AUTRES MEUBLES ET PIECES
82192	WOOD FURNITURE NES	W 80769	192032	W 93710	245898	W 82253	237114	W 74285	218713	MEUBLES NDA EN BOIS
84	CLOTHING AND ACCESSORIES		1926819		2117418		2129454		2172076	VETEMENTS
842	MENS OUTERWEAR NOT KNIT	W 13117	325174		453367	W 19417	504854	W 16903	474744	VET DESSUS POUR HOMMES
8423	— TROUSERS,BREECHES ETC	W 5940	121375	W 9831	208987	W 10218	245983	W 9477	240502	PANTALONS HOMMES MAT TEX
843	WOMENS OUTERWEAR NONKNIT	W 17595	525547		530599	W 19913	514765	W 16979	518042	VET DESSUS FEMMES MAT TEX
8439	— OTHER OUTER GARMENTS	W 10461	255586		227616	W 10090	214224	W 9475	230695	AUT VET DES FEM MAT TEXT
845	OUTERWEAR KNIT NONELASTC	W 20906	485163		479656	W 18713	412293	W 18389	454236	VET DESSOUS,ACCES BONNET
8451	— JERSEYS,PULLOVERS ETC	W 12418	276080	W 13079	274981	W 10519	227329	W 10361	255019	CHANDAILS,PULL–OVERS ETC
8459	— OTHER,CLTHG ACCESRYS	W 7482	177056		165398	W 6671	143033	W 6861	163076	AUT VET DESSUS DE BONNE
846	UNDER GARMENTS KNITTED	W 14053	253860		270185	W 15820	300199	W 15643	337445	SOUS VETS DE BONNETERIE
8462	— OF COTTON NON ELASTIC	W 11616	183214		192977	W 13210	219939	W 12536	230147	SOUS–VET BONNET COTON
84629	—— OTHER	W 11616	183214		192977	W 13210	219939	W 12536	230147	AUT SOUS–VET BONNET COTON
848	HEADGEAR,NONTXTL CLOTHNG	W 9332	162716	W 14619	184641		180832	W 10438	175162	VET ACCES MAT AUT QUE TEX
851	*FOOTWEAR	W 20733	365232	W 25351	433834	W 21364	384945	W 21615	403371	CHAUSSURES
85102	FOOTWEAR LEATHER	W 15477	311693	W 19036	369011	W 15988	323997	W 15198	325835	CHAUS SEMELLES EN CUIR
87	PRECISION INSTRUMNTS NES		1093562		1306359		1539867		1547401	INSTRUM,APPAR SCIENT NDA
872	MEDICAL INSTRUMENTS NES	W 5203	198374	W 5044	227759	W 11881	303479	W 5372	308876	INSTR,APP MEDIC–CHIR NDA
87202	OTH MEDICAL INSTRUMENTS	W 4573	176176	W 4540	207147	W 11023	249256	W 4548	260441	INSTRUM,APP MEDECINE
874	MEASURNG,CONTROLNG INSTR	W 7129	743763		891660		1057503		1073350	INSTRUMENTS DE MESURE
8743	GAS,LIQUID CONTROL INSTR	W 2357	234279	W 2825	291348	W 4243	370047	W 3323	388937	APP,INSTR MESURE FLUIDES
8748	ELEC MEAS,CONTRL EQU NES	W 1207	159108	W 1326	187197	W 1391	242751	W 1227	233613	APP ELEC ELECTRO MESURE
87483	OTH ELCTRNC MEAS ETC EQU	W 996	142575	W 1159	169436	W 1247	225641	W 1083	212694	AUT APP ELECTRO DE MESURE
88	PHOTO EQU,OPTICL GDS ETC		507044		564749		611169		636973	APP,FOURN PHOTO,OP,MONTR
882	PHOTO,CINEMA SUPPLIES	W 23751	256439		281895		316765		328352	PRODUITS PHOTO,CINEMA
8822	PHOTO FILM EXC DEV CINMA	W 18073	210040		228063		245105		260303	PLAQUES,PELLICULES,FILMS
89	MISC MANUFCTRD GOODS NES		2216262		2443754		2467528		2579148	ART MANUFACTURES DIVERS
892	PRINTED MATTER	W 110611	452212	W 111256	462084		382281		400087	IMPRIMES
8921	PRINTED BOOKS,GLOBES,ETC	W 31903	166305	W 31719	170745	W 23760	151050	W 26667	162222	LIVRES,BROCHURES,CARTES
89211	PRINTED BOOKS,PAMPHLETS	W 30799	159786	W 30301	163407	W 22318	143889	W 25432	155504	LIVRES,BROCHURES
8928	PRINTED MATTER NES	W 55208	195648	W 53851	197484		155079		140741	IMPRIMES NDA
893	ARTICLES OF PLASTIC NES		630855		720563		803105		831799	OUVRAGES EN MAT DIVIS 58
8931	PLSTC PACKG CONTNRS,LIDS	W 49106	173187	W 53418	194249	W 51853	226677	W 56860	221200	ART TRANSP EMBALLAGE ETC
8939	MISC PLASTIC ARTICLES	W 132711	445449	W 100339	511336	W 90820	557266	W 95513	590596	ART DIVERS EN MAT DIV 58
89399	OTHR PLASTC ARTICLES NES	W 61098	389245	W 81937	452832	W 70711	485848	W 71612	508752	AUT OUV MAT DIV 58
894	TOYS,SPORTING GOODS,ETC	W 36621	333853		370141	W 38394	345270	W 39571	379143	VOITURES ENFANTS,JOUETS
8942	TOYS,INDOOR GAMES ETC	W 27797	230561	W 28112	232563	W 27186	209534	W 27498	220361	JOUETS,JEUX ETC
898	MUSICAL INSTRUMENTS,PTS	W 14325	357997		412825		452687		467399	INSTRUMENTS DE MUSIQUE
8983	SOUND RECRDNG TAPE,DISCS	W 13314	329686	W 13437	380876	W 12686	421803	W 12405	436106	SUPPORTS SON POUR 763
89832	RECORDED DISCS,TAPES ETC	W 6307	246569	W 6520	295159	W 6404	346196	W 6165	355709	DISQUES,PHONO,BANDES
899	OTHER MANUFACTURED GOODS		238306		278913		301683		316175	AUT ART MANUF DIVERS NDA
9	GOODS NOT CLASSD BY KIND		308026		494027		935095		1250777	ART TRANSACT NON CLASSES
931	*SPECIAL TRANSACTIONS	W 85337	153666		325878	W 2423335	883362	W 2119628	1209282	TRANS.SPECIALES

5. General Exports F.O.B. by Commodities according to the S.I.T.C. (Rev. 2) in thousand U.S. Dollars
Exportations Générales F.O.B. par Produits d'après la C.T.C.I. (Rév. 2) en milliers de Dollars E.U.

SITC CTCI	COMMODITY	1993		1994		1995		1996		PRODUIT
		WEIGHT POIDS	VALUE VALEUR	WEIGHT POIDS	VALUE VALEUR	WEIGHT POIDS	VALUE VALEUR	WEIGHT POIDS	VALUE VALEUR	
	ALL COMMODITIES		49858443		61299713		77436374		82880544	TOUS PRODUITS
0	FOOD AND LIVE ANIMALS		768176		991431		1416618		1710519	ALIMENTS,ANIMAUX VIVANTS
03	FISH AND PREPARATIONS		88145		120390		244787		286308	POISSONS ET PREPARATIONS
04	CEREALS AND PREPARATIONS		156678		227990		259202		400571	CEREALES ET PRODUITS
07	COFFEE,TEA,COCOA,SPICES		144865		192071		236205		241845	CAFE,THE,CACAO,EPICES
09	MISC EDIBLE PRODUCTS		110094		183036		245208		262655	PREP ALIMENTAIRES DIVERSES
1	BEVERAGES AND TOBACCO		124214		242179		216506		261623	BOISSONS ET TABACS
11	BEVERAGES		102213		217488		192951		233218	BOISSONS
112	ALCOHOLIC BEVERAGES	W 78743	92027		205445	W 72928	179789	W 53703	216337	BOISSONS ALCOOLIQUES
1124	DISTILLED ALCOHOLIC BEVS	W 67169	85293		195534	W 62319	173043	W 42918	207898	ALCOOLS,EAUX–DE–VIE
11249	OTH ALCOHOLC BEVS,CMPNDS	W 67165	85279		195330	W 62263	172720	W 42720	205822	BOISSONS ALCOOLIQUES NDA
2	CRUDE MATERLS,EXCL FUELS		3943611		4812188		6003391		5225815	MAT BRUTES NON COMESTIBLES
24	CORK AND WOOD		1904370		2509530		2807304		2668514	LIEGE ET BOIS
248	WOOD SHAPED,SLEEPERS	W 5318819	1843535	W 5557911	2431794	W 5385942	2640875	W 5794830	2512969	BOIS SIMPLEMENT TRAVAILLES
2482	LUMBER SHAPED CONIFER	W 5296215	1833160	W 5527397	2417459	W 5360885	2626721	W 5767431	2495200	CONIFERES SCIES,RABOTES
24821	LUMBER SAWN ETC CONIFER	W 5241535	1796871	W 5462403	2366985	W 5297569	2570281	W 5710344	2448774	CONIFERES SCIES LONGITUD
251	*PULP AND WASTE PAPER	W 3001137	1133467		1345034		2047984	W 2855918	1444160	PATES A PAPIER,DECHETS
2517	SODA,SULPHATE WOOD PULP	W 2363243	941766	W 2314120	1102190	W 2056454	1659037	W 2223711	1196515	PATES CHIMIQUES AU SULFATE
25172	— BLEACHED,NONDISSOLVNG	W 2265165	909251	W 2206653	1062039	W 1955922	1588419	W 2099056	1142659	PATES BLANCHIES
28	METALLIFEROUS ORES,SCRAP		683684		701481		870516		819808	MINERAIS METAL,DECHETS
281	IRON ORE,CONCENTRATES	MW 16442	421960	MW 15393	387133	MW 16918	497234	MW 15173	488551	MINERAIS DE FER
2815	IRON ORE,CONC,NOT AGGLOM	W 8945063	183417	W 8481106	166788	W 7661554	162608	W 6092751	145102	MINERAIS NON AGGLOMERES
2816	IRON ORE AGGLOMERATES	W 7473273	238533	W 6912076	220345	MW 9256	334615	MW 9080	343449	MINERAIS AGGLOMERES
3	MINERAL FUELS ETC		1695347		1557064		1470865		1735231	COMBUSTIBLES MINERAUX LUB
33	PETROLEUM AND PRODUCTS		1539422		1379883		1434149		1680400	PETROLE ET DERIVES
334	PETROLEUM PRODUCTS,REFIN	MW 9215	1468240		1292037	W 8394185	1316333	W 8440555	1541785	PRODUITS RAFFINES
3341	GASOLINE,OTH LIGHT OILS	W 1779792	346550		306230	W 2002566	366634	W 1877767	387293	ESSENCES POUR MOTEURS
33411	MOTOR,AVIATION SPIRIT	W 1529292	299924	W 1681911	280965	W 1796148	331568	W 1627964	337367	ESSENCES MOTEURS D'AVIONS
3343	GAS OILS	W 3902972	672284	W 3598344	543698					GAS OILS
3344	FUEL OILS,NES	W 3238774	325435	W 3190	356	W 2709643	307958	W 2794850	356503	FUEL OILS
3345	LUBS,PETROLEUM OILS NES	W 290000	123453	W 3395818	441329	W 3670809	639267	W 3670740	776355	HUILES LUBRIFIANTES
33451	LUBS(HIGH PETR CONT) ETC	W 288390	117485	W 3393392	432103	W 3665399	620435	W 3665178	755993	HUILES LUBRIF,H LOURDES
5	CHEMCLS,RELATED PROD NES		4859963		5565704		4940550		5470887	PRODUITS CHIMIQUES
51	ORGANIC CHEMICALS		494752		621824		369827		399670	PROD CHIMIQ ORGANIQUES
52	INORGANIC CHEMICALS		219733		279689		161319		181092	PROD CHIM INORGANIQUES
523	OTHR INORG CHEMICALS ETC		147872		195509		84944		96174	AUT PRODUITS CHIMIQUES INORG
53	DYES,TANNING,COLOUR PROD		214347		285035		369927		407315	PROD TEINTURE,COLORANTS
533	PIGMENTS,PAINTS,ETC	W 113979	204768		262901		332094	W 171850	374020	PIGMENTS,PEINTURES,VERNIS
541	*MEDICINAL,PHARM PRODUCT	MK 19730	2177766		2467487		2546158		2959131	PROD MEDICINAUX PHARMACEUT
5417	MEDICAMENTS	MK 16545	2050392		2323632	MK 16683	2358510	MK 26509	2777712	MEDICAMENTS
54172	— CONTAINING HORMONES	K 119663	298677		320491	K 103914	259441	K 146932	410630	MED CONTENANT HORMONES
54179	— CONTNG OTH SUBSTANCES	MK 15544	1715140	MK 16776	1946418	MK 14629	2057468	MK 22873	2271974	MED CONT AUT SUBSTANCES
55	PERFUME,CLEANING ETC PRD		197434		234319		287044		321770	PROD POUR PARFUM,TOILETTE
58	PLASTIC MATERIALS ETC		1036758		1096635		628496		616655	MAT PLAST ARTIFICIELLES
583	POLYMERIZATION ETC PRODS		813659		842191		451529		447268	PROD POLYMERISATION
5831	POLYETHYLENE		463240		524367	W 66497	157253	W 72983	154928	POLYETHYLENE
58311	— IN PRIMARY FORMS		352272		383365					POLYETHYLENE PRIMAIRES
59	CHEMICAL MATERIALS NES		428395		498650		500884		520622	MAT PROD CHIMIQUES NDA
598	MISCEL CHEM PRODUCTS NES		289986		341335	W 164609	400303	W 160453	404624	PROD DIV INDUST CHIM NDA
5989	CHEM PRODUCTS,PREPS NES	W 209752	228867		258090	W 106553	347403	W 89217	344660	PROD PREP CHIMIQUES NDA
59899	OTH CHEM PRODS,PREPS,NES	W 1185	98490		210020	W 77481	282831	W 59688	282577	AUT PRODUITS CHIMIQUES NDA
6	BASIC MANUFACTURES		12271591		15016982		18477668		18790406	ART MANUFACTURES
62	RUBBER MANUFACTURES NES		372498		456357		567881		611136	CAOUTCHOUC MANUFACTURE
628	RUBBER ARTICLES NES				194223	W 21248	252139	W 28891	244427	OUVRAGES CAOUTCHOUC NDA
63	WOOD,CORK MANUFACTRS NES		507653		695686		910712		952999	OUVRAGES LIEGE ET BOIS
635	WOOD MANUFACTURES NES	W 224353	450306	W 297909	621252	W 315105	814554	W 321461	847845	ART MANUF EN BOIS NDA
6353	BUILDERS WOODWRK,PREFABS	W 153291	363608	W 214112	507972	W 243104	691674	W 248769	712566	OUVRAGES DE MENUISERIE
64	PAPER,PAPERBOARD AND MFR		5112700		5864200		7674474		7762467	PAPIERS,CARTONS & OUVRAGES
641	PAPER AND PAPERBOARD	W 7344520	4634060		5334565	W 7771543	6964261	W 7734396	6995504	PAPIERS ET CARTONS
6411	NEWSPRINT	W 1884896	830170	W 2030184	931191	W 1983414	1202104	W 1958026	1364849	PAPIER JOURNAL
6412	PRINTG,WRITING PAPER NES	W 1044990	856151	W 1127783	987265	W 978745	1218930	W 1071346	1231046	PAPIERS POUR L'IMPRESSION
64121	— UNCOATED	W 278904	207304	W 231544	185548	W 174608	233223	W 178803	198516	PAPIERS IMPRES NON COUCHES
64122	— COATED,IMPREGNATD ETC	W 766086	648847	W 896239	801717	W 804137	985707	W 892543	1032530	PAPIERS IMPRESSION COUCHES
6413	KRAFT PAPER,PAPERBOARD	W 2205647	1151046	W 2380692	1270476	W 2292075	1797623	W 2191265	1626438	PAPIER ET CARTON KRAFT
64131	KRAFT LINER IN BULK	W 1215544	493598	W 1366136	589546	W 1343304	913930	W 1324543	776187	PAP KRAFT POUR COUVERTURES
64132	SACK KRAFT PAPER IN BULK	W 519408	316443	W 571864	351933	W 476418	398602	W 448821	406131	PAPIER KRAFT POUR SACS
64139	KRAFT PAPER PAPERBD,NES	W 470694	341005	W 442692	328997	W 472353	485091	W 417901	444121	PAPIER,CARTON KRAFT NDA
6415	PAPER,PAPERBRD,BULK,NES	W 1163753	712674		885514	W 1377627	1254518	W 1381605	1262225	PAPIERS,CARTONS ROULEAUX
64159	OTHER PAPER ETC,BULK,NES	W 894561	601481	W 1083524	767948	W 1104845	1073960	W 1121429	1120288	AUT PAPIER ROULEAUX FEUILLES
6418	COATED ETC PAPER NES BLK	W 867436	895002	W 986824	1032407	W 922835	1217751	W 920500	1240992	PAP,CARTONS COUCHES,ENDUITS
64181	PLASTIC COATED PAPER ETC	W 356157	462205	W 396048	524348	W 437908	721439	W 405129	709788	PAP,CARTONS ENDUITS,RESINES
64189	COATED PAPER ETC NES	W 478071	401441	W 554230	472609	W 440225	446848	W 454595	474838	PAPIERS,CARTONS COUCHES
642	PAPER,ETC,PRECUT,ARTS OF	W 244772	478640	W 250579	529635		710214		766963	PAP,CARTONS DECOUPES
6428	PAPER ETC ARTICLES NES	W 125410	267788	W 114476	274525	W 129486	360413	W 137810	387212	OUVRAGES EN PATE A PAPIER
65	TEXTILE YARN,FABRICS,ETC		530608		623545		766228		825237	FILS,TISSUS,ARTICLES TEXTILE
657	SPECIAL TXTL FABRC,PRODS	W 27100	198273		230848		288318		285185	TISSUS SPECIAUX
66	NONMETAL MINERAL MFS NES		483383		581810		672641		692411	ART MIN NON METALLIQUES
664	GLASS	W 204666	175204		195944		250348		261897	VERRE
67	IRON AND STEEL		2883743		3836842		4282629		4285303	FER ET ACIER
671	PIG IRON ETC	W 268392	172108		223080	W 39148	26902	W 86964	31218	FONTE,SPIEGEL,POUDRES
672	IRON,STEEL PRIMARY FORMS	W 719072	295453		591306	W 532188	458923		715572	LINGOTS FER,ACIER
6725	IRN,STL BLOOMS,SLABS,ETC	W 285884	166378	W 153748	184529	W 83587	163944	W 103317	150510	BLOOMS,BILLETTES FER ACIER
6727	IRN,STL COIL FR REROLLNG	W 416424	120103		393075	W 427382	273092	W 728154	548421	EBAUCHES POUR TOLES FER
67274	STNLESS STEEL ETC COILS			W 173862	209046	W 30548	82374	W 248428	365746	EBAUCHES ACIER INOXYDBLE
673	IRON,STEEL SHAPES ETC	W 639149	500921		682963	W 662391	869111		772759	BARRES,PROFIL FER,ACIER
6732	IRON,STEEL BARS ETC	W 515053	340464	W 601070	449242	W 470054	542673	W 465413	500148	BARRES FER,ACIER
67325	OTH ALLOY STEEL BARS ETC	W 162827	163692	W 235255	227096	W 196729	279836	W 196134	261706	BARRES NON ACIERS ALLIES
674	IRN,STL UNIV,PLATE,SHEET	W 1715154	1318757		1557460		1883244	W 1698240	1734999	LARGES PLATS,TOLES
6744	IRN,STL HVY PLATE,ROLLED	W 426145	166778		486576		457255	W 414623	390604	TOLES LAMINEES PLUS 4.75 MM
67441	— OF IRON OR SIMPLE STL	W 426145	166778		193446		228796	W 351178	171517	TOLES NON ACIER FIN CARB
67443	— OF STAINLESS ETC STL			W 91602	211891	W 46306	159876	W 54295	154100	TOLES ACIER INOXYDABLE
6746	IRN,STL THIN PLATE,ROLLD	W 310692	146614		603118		846670	W 715152	791474	TOLES LAM MOINS 3MM
67461	— OF IRON OR SIMPLE STL	W 310692	146614		185359		197849	W 354507	230396	TOL NON AC FIN MOINS 3 MM
67463	— OF STAINLESS ETC STL			W 79805	240381	W 98331	405994	W 94866	325440	TOL ACIER INOX MOINS 3 MM
67464	— OF OTHER ALLOY STEEL			W 239951	177379	W 267955	242828	W 265780	235637	TOL NON AC ALL MOINS 3 MM
6749	OTH IRN,STL PLATES,SHEET	W 403373	232047		317205		397183	W 429457	386228	AUTRES TOLES FER,ACIER
67491	— OF IRON OR SIMPLE STL	W 403373	232047		282488		349727	W 415545	342959	AUT TOLES AUTRES ACIER FIN
677	IRN,STL WIRE(EXCL W ROD)	W 64258	143310	W 81487	187466	W 90903	250201	W 83370	231772	FILS EN FER,ACIER
678	IRON,STL TUBES,PIPES,ETC		436134		570703		772548	W 243225	772745	TUBES,TUYAUX EN FONTE,FER
6782	IRON,STL SEAMLESS TUBES	W 99524	220985	W 134569	309228	W 138887	421586	W 126573	421528	TUBES,TUYAUX SANS SOUDURE
6783	IRON,STL TUBES,PIPES NES	W 81952	144192		177049		244532	W 103193	243197	AUT TUBES,TUYAUX FER,ACIER

5. General Exports F.O.B. by Commodities according to the S.I.T.C. (Rev. 2) in thousand U.S. Dollars
Exportations Générales F.O.B. par Produits d'après la C.T.C.I. (Rév. 2) en milliers de Dollars E.U.

SITC CTCI	COMMODITY	1993 WEIGHT POIDS	1993 VALUE VALEUR	1994 WEIGHT POIDS	1994 VALUE VALEUR	1995 WEIGHT POIDS	1995 VALUE VALEUR	1996 WEIGHT POIDS	1996 VALUE VALEUR	PRODUIT
68	NON-FERROUS METALS		804508		990433		1280496		1250629	METAUX NON FERREUX
682	COPPER EXC CEMENT COPPER		384688		450922	W 166389	607864		576361	CUIVRE
6822	COPPER,ALLOYS WORKED		338130		407708	W 145639	549633	W 141003	502867	CUIVRE,ALLIAGES OUVRES
68221	COPPER BARS,WIRE,ETC	W 61619	127449	W 70206	162534	W 83927	247376	W 78371	195493	BARRES,PROFILES ET FILS
684	ALUMINIUM	W 121345	311660	W 143614	398523	W 148400	524905	W 158710	503958	ALUMINIUM
6842	ALUMINIUM,ALLOYS WORKED	W 68357	241221	W 88366	315553	W 91497	398090	W 88045	376855	ALUMINIUM,ALLIAGES OUVRE
69	METAL MANUFACTURES NES		1518386		1901083		2253272		2339107	ART MANUFACT EN METAL NDA
691	STRUCTURES AND PARTS NES	W 63788	170705	W 73356	222317	W 75819	288666	W 81661	323917	CONSTRUCT FER,ACIER,ALU
695	TOOLS	W 24118	632811		755771		820214	W 20599	794936	OUTILS A MAIN
6953	OTHER HAND TOOLS	W 12505	171299		201274		211587	W 12289	197131	AUTRES OUTILS A MAIN
6954	BLADES,TIPS,ETC FR TOOLS	W 10804	451864		541575	W 7277	590530	W 7061	579715	OUTILS POUR MACHINE-OUTIL
69541	PARTS TO INSERT IN TOOLS			W 8456	241927	W 3339	175559	W 2818	182273	OUTILS DE FORAGE
69543	CARBIDE TOOL TIPS ETC			W 931	271917	W 1140	385210	W 1143	366047	PLAQUETTES,POINTES D'OUTILS
699	BASE METAL MFRS NES	W 96628	414384		534985		665519		697890	ART MANUFACTURES MET NDA
7	MACHINES,TRANSPORT EQUIP		21543596		27591580		32593586		36750133	MACHINES MATERIEL TRANSPORT
71	POWER GENERATING EQUIPMT		1539699		2036239		2810192		3013026	MACHINES GENERATRICES
713	INTRNL COMBUS PSTN ENGIN	W 69770	772008	W 102348	1226711		1434662		1623853	MOTEURS EXPL COMB INT, PIECE
7132	MOTOR VEHCL PSTN ENGINS	W 36685	362876	W 56849	692666	W 77802	847444	W 71316	1041146	MOTEURS EXPL POUR VEHICULES
7139	PISTON ENGINE PARTS NES	W 17772	218371	W 28314	299924	W 18883	335824	W 17379	316715	PIECES POUR 713.2,3,8
714	ENGINES AND MOTORS NES	W 2838	302237	W 1950	275004	W 3028	642156	W 2732	677987	MOTEURS NON ELECTRIQUES
7149	ENGINE & MOTOR PARTS NES	W 1838	237639	W 1702	235239	W 2613	439462	W 2264	497750	PIECES 714 ET 718.88
71491	PARTS NES OF 7144,71481	W 197	183223	W 170	160624	W 293	340215	W 461	397583	PIECES DES PROPULSEURS
716	ROTATING ELECTRIC PLANT	W 17132	220104	W 21716	301114		450836		394782	APP ELECTR ROTATIFS,PIECES
718	OTH POWER GENERATG MACHY	W 4080	187670		181204	W 7385	236846	W 7334	261102	AUTRES MOTEURS PARTIES
72	MACHS FOR SPCL INDUSTRYS		2417397		2660886		2667534		2759970	MAC SPECIALES POUR INDUST
721	AGRIC MACHY,EXC TRACTORS	W 20659	238447		337994		198577		160327	MACHINES AGRICOLES
723	CIVIL ENGNEERG EQUIP ETC		847095		755011	W 37104	329433	W 36047	367598	APPAREILS DE GENIE CIVIL
7234	CONST,MINING MACHNRY NES		455126	W 35486	543173	W 15610	207901	W 15162	232558	MACH POUR LA CONST, MINES
72342	SLFPRP SHOVELS,EXCAVATRS		342490	W 21702	413136	W 534	2083	W 557	2081	PELLES MECANIQUES
7239	CONSTR ETC MACHY PTS NES	W 33034	323075		114398	W 3532	2748	W 1993	2352	PIECES 723.41-723.46
724	TEXTILE,LEATHER MACHNRY	W 10680	168827		192199		228468		225738	MACH POUR INDUSTRIE TEXTILE
725	PAPER ETC MILL MACHINERY	W 24026	303589	W 26203	347398	W 48326	634615	W 39035	694086	MACHINES FABR PATE PAPIER
7251	PAPER,PULP MAKING MACHRY	W 10223	117111	W 13165	159854	W 22127	284026	W 15497	293635	MACHINES FABR PATE CARTON
7259	PTS NES OF MACHS OF 725	W 11300	156315	W 11093	153809	W 22761	289019	W 20149	316744	PIECES GROUPE 725
72591	PTS NES OF MACHS OF 7251	W 9892	145556	W 10266	140536	W 20493	273167	W 19101	299773	PIECES DU 725.1
728	OTH MACHY FOR SPCL INDUS	W 57922	679999	W 57659	818323		1059824		1083295	AUT MACH IND PARTICULIERES
7284	MACHY FOR SPCL INDUS NES	W 30779	498650	W 32520	622147		798130		810145	MACH SPEC IND PARTICUL.
72848	OTH MCHY WITH INDIV FNCT	W 16736	258749	W 17688	304441	W 18678	366775	W 13609	327454	AUTRES MACHINES NDA
72849	PTS OF MACHS OF 7284 ETC	W 5047	124461	W 7823	189485	W 7212	204908	W 8581	241716	PIECES DU 728.4 ETC
73	METALWORKING MACHINERY		512815		582321		743771		931560	MACH TRAVAIL DES METAUX
736	METALWORKING MACH-TOOLS	W 24195	288263		303172		339541		420536	MACH-OUTILS TRAVAIL METAUX
737	METALWORKING MACHNRY NES	W 30163	224551		279149		404230	W 36235	511024	MACH TRAV METAUX PIECES
7373	WELDING,BRAZING,ETC MCHS	W 6991	151560	W 9145	204328	W 13497	314736	W 16263	407036	MACH SOUDAGE ETC PIECES
73732	ELECTRIC WELDERS,ETC	W 6928	150288	W 9086	202915	W 13210	307931	W 16101	403474	MACH ELECT POUR SOUDER
74	GENRL INDUSTRL MACHY NES		3531679		4834268		4778739		5187105	MACH APP INDUSTRIE
741	HEATING,COOLING EQUIPMNT	W 53756	631615	W 54180	733633	W 52990	694770	W 62406	791460	MACH CHAUFFAGE,PIECES
7416	HEATING,COOLING EQU NES	W 22522	253835	W 28739	409798	W 25463	323534	W 33483	380768	APP CHANGEMENT TEMP
742	PUMPS FOR LIQUIDS ETC	W 21024	322614	W 23733	391813	W 26923	470222	W 30682	513391	POMPES MOTO-POMPES
743	PUMPS NES,CENTRFUGES ETC	W 24772	399124	W 24878	436419	W 27575	489724	W 27611	478817	POMPES COMPRES,VENT ETC
744	MECHANICAL HANDLING EQU	W 114593	828399		1408658		1221092	W 150340	1390877	EQUIP MANUTENTION PIECES
7441	FORK LIFT TRCKS,ETC,PTS	W 40365	214342	W 44693	278676	W 48833	341920	W 53669	416829	CHARIOTS POUR USINES ETC
74411	FORK LIFT TRUCKS ETC	W 40224	212939	W 44414	275344	W 48536	338931	W 53491	414074	CHARIOTS POUR LES GARES
7442	LIFTING,LOADING MACH NES	W 55411	435106		567814		583137	W 64121	629015	APP LEVAGE,MANUTENTION
74428	OTH HANDLING ETC MCH NES	W 39569	365119		500921	W 71113	515825	W 55501	546054	AUT APP LEVAGE ETC
7449	PTS NES OF MACHY OF 7442	W 18818	178951		562167	W 28118	296035	W 32550	345033	PIECES DU 744.2
745	NONELEC MACHY,TOOLS NES	W 23654	674309		912303	W 34143	702198	W 24375	753513	AUT MACH NON ELEC,PIECES
7451	POWER TOOLS NONELEC,PTS	W 8098	307951		416586	W 4309	148959	W 4703	192001	OUT MACH PNEUM A MOTEUR
74511	POWER HAND TOOLS NONELEC				334443	W 1543	56048	W 2505	99563	OUT MACH PNEUM A MOTEUR
7452	OTH NONELEC MCHS,PTS NES	W 15556	366358	W 19449	495717	W 29834	553239	W 19671	561512	AUT MACH NON ELEC,PIECES
74522	PACKAGNG,BOTTLNG,ETC MCH	W 4976	183382	W 7123	246949	W 17204	313239	W 6841	320319	MACH NETT BOUTEILLES,ETC
749	NONELEC MACH PTS,ACC NES	W 54531	675617	W 71782	951443	W 84652	1200733	W 85161	1259048	PIECES MACH NON ELEC NDA
7491	BALL,ROLLER,ETC BEARINGS	W 23480	275144	W 31807	424308	W 35787	541553	W 36525	550343	ROULEMENTS BILLES ETC
7492	COCKS,VALVES ETC NES	W 9440	219441	W 10994	276907	W 11090	316543	W 12548	353153	ART ROB,SIM POUR TUYAUX
7493	SHAFT,CRANK,PULLEY ETC	W 16171	92532	W 22674	141657	W 32873	235870	W 31211	231038	ARBRES TRANS,VILEBREQUINS
75	OFFICE MACHNES,ADP EQUIP		809309		832159		962187		1036497	MACH BUREAU TRAIT AUTOM
752	AUTOMTIC DATA PROC EQUIP	W 5266	402109	W 3601	344245	W 4001	395362	W 4397	425283	MACH TRAIT INFORMATION
7525	ADP PERIPHERAL UNITS	W 3071	212700	W 1424	99045	W 1825	116530	W 2134	110687	UNITES PERIPHERIQUES
759	OFFICE,ADP MCH PTS,ACCES	W 3245	308790	W 4113	362980	W 4837	429100	W 5250	456272	PIECES DU 751 ET 752
7599	ACCTG,ETC,ADP MCH PTS,AC	W 2403	264726	W 2839	302966	W 2872	327821	W 3190	355568	PIECES DU 751 ET 752
76	TELECOMM,SOUND EQUIPMENT		2881821		4344122		6727963		8578973	EQUIPMENT DE TELECOM
764	TELECOM EQPT,PTS,ACC NES	W 22897	2801265		4192645		6527833		8356232	EQUIP TELECOM,PIECES
7641	LINE TELEPHONE,ETC EQUIP	W 1311	187952	W 2529	329682	W 3178	435013	W 3849	718515	APP TELEPHON PAR FIL
7643	TV,RADIO TRANSMITTRS ETC	W 1832	738437	W 3162	1322945	W 5323	2488729	W 7828	3357472	APP EMET TELE RADIO
7649	PTS NES OF EQUIPMT OF 76	W 18490	1820739		2475896		3509795		4189784	PIECES DE LA DIV 76
76491	PTS NES OF APPAR OF 7641	W 10542	1080957	W 12242	1203611	W 13325	1412016	W 11157	1324841	PIECES POUR 764.1
76493	TELECOMM EQUIPMT PTS NES	W 7792	736917	W 15272	1267331	W 21711	2090994	W 23926	2853663	PIECES 761,762,764.3,8
77	ELECTRIC MACHNRY NES ETC		2275368		2976543		3597492		4700821	MACH APP ELECT NDA
771	ELECTRIC POWER MACHY NES	W 17141	259140	W 21791	329233	W 22475	426932	W 25072	810777	MACH PROD,TRANS ELECTR
7712	OTH ELEC POWER MACHY NES	W 5290	139710	W 5821	176199	W 7094	263961	W 9147	597161	AUT APP PROD TRANSF ELEC
77121	STATIC CONVERTERS ETC	W 2289	92367	W 2873	127187	W 3717	196196	W 5253	502931	CONVERTISSEURS STATIQUES
772	SWITCHGEAR ETC,PARTS NES	W 15570	497282	W 16655	650651		755899		1072138	APP COUPURE,SECT ETC
7721	SWITCHGEAR ETC	W 15211	449296	W 16222	547319	W 18400	631356	W 20996	785729	APP COUPURE,SECTIONMNT
7722	PRINTED CIRCUITS,PTS NES	W 163	41742	W 252	95813	W 270	111616	W 855	273182	CIRCUITS ET PIECES
773	ELECTR DISTRIBUTNG EQUIP	W 54349	244977	W 73665	355152		401278	W 76478	503195	EQUIPMT DISTRIBUTION ELECT
7731	INSULATED WIRE,CABLE ETC	W 52615	230517	W 71866	338028	W 69583	375287	W 74181	476186	FILS,CABLES ISOLES ELECT
774	ELECTRO-MEDCL,XRAY EQUIP	W 1529	185705	W 1841	204534	W 3726	289492	W 1845	255548	APPAREILS MEDICAUX
775	HOUSEHOLD TYPE EQUIP NES	W 69770	505835		610511	W 115869	721454		741804	MACH,APP USAGE DOMESTQUE
7758	ELECTRO-THERMIC APPL NES	W 23156	199003		248934	W 58642	289745		293845	APP ELECTROTHERMIQ NDA
77586	ELECTROTHERM DOM APP NES	W 19337	153100	W 22647	186234	W 53148	211835	W 34435	202770	APP ELECTRO THERMIQUES
776	TRANSISTORS,VALVES,ETC	W 374	175657		269585		309188		497519	LAMPES,TUBES,VALVES
7764	ELECTRONIC MICROCIRCUITS	W 199	142748	W 529	217535	W 559	234664	W 989	419740	MICROSTRUCTURES ELECTRON
778	ELECTRICAL MACHINERY NES		406772		556877		693249		819839	AUTRES MACH ELECT NDA
7788	OTH ELEC MACHY,EQUIP NES		141074		195420	W 7003	255585		318111	AUT MACH APP ELEC NDA
78	ROAD VEHICLES		6205378		8074348		8713652		9016378	VEHICULES ROUTIERS
781	PASS MOTOR VEH EXC BUSES	W 246172	2986522	W 252603	3403785	W 282329	4261321	W 266963	4162695	AUTO TRANSPORT PERSONNES
782	LORRIES,SPCL MTR VEH NES		1217181		1428518	W 40452	219604	W 33130	193853	VEHICULES SPECIAUX,MARCH
7821	LORRIES,TRUCKS		1178396		1389211	W 37256	198254	W 29166	159023	VEHICULES TRANSP MARCHAND
783	ROAD MOTOR VEHICLES NES	W 10846	42355	W 11693	66100	W 39127	400534	W 54541	569153	VEHICULES ROUTIERS NDA
7832	TRACTORS FOR TR-TRAILERS	W 4106	22636	W 5594	36944	W 32584	349985	W 49981	556636	TRACTEURS ROUTIERS
784	MOTOR VEH PRTS,ACCES NES	W 263276	1850709	W 392555	3050028	W 490334	3687916	W 437253	3928355	PIECES 722,781,782,783
7841	MOTOR VEHICLE CHASSIS	W 25561	268347	W 28197	322006	W 28488	349251	W 29539	375885	CHASSIS 722,781,782,783

5. General Exports F.O.B. by Commodities according to the S.I.T.C. (Rev. 2) in thousand U.S. Dollars
Exportations Générales F.O.B. par Produits d'après la C.T.C.I. (Rév. 2) en milliers de Dollars E.U.

SITC CTCI	COMMODITY	1993		1994		1995		1996		PRODUIT
		WEIGHT POIDS	VALUE VALEUR	WEIGHT POIDS	VALUE VALEUR	WEIGHT POIDS	VALUE VALEUR	WEIGHT POIDS	VALUE VALEUR	
7842	MOTOR VEHICLE BODIES	W 10419	96062	W 20015	227193	W 35413	390176	W 35287	447314	CARROS 722,781,782,783
7849	OTHER MOTOR VEHCL PARTS	W 227295	1486300	W 344343	2500829	W 426434	2948490	W 372428	3105157	PIECES 722,781,782,783
79	OTHR TRANSPORT EQUIPMENT		1370130		1250694		1592056		1525803	AUTRE MATERIEL TRANSPORT
792	AIRCRAFT ETC	W 808	365184		431540		1297030		1221163	APP NAVIGATION AERIENNE
7923	AIRCRFT NES2000–15000KG	W 261	201447	W 248	205545	W 811	632365	W 1038	841214	AERODYNES 2000 A 15000 KG
7924	AIRCRFT NES OVER 15000KG	W 198	35186	W 108	73630	W 389	368943	W 176	39460	AERODYNES PLUS 15000 KG
7929	AIRCRAFT PARTS NES	W 289	122372	W 261	141401	W 797	284443	W 470	331945	PIECES DU 792
793	SHIPS AND BOATS ETC		873966		720731		128979		107062	NAVIRES BATEAUX,ETC
7932	SHIPS AND BOATS NES		797960		535055		98181	W 5887	87256	NAVIRES ET BATEAUX
79322	TANKERS OF ALL KINDS		218190	V 25	1676	V 991	88			BATEAUX–CITERNES
79323	OTHER CARGO VESSELS		496198	V 843	442602	V 2171	1752	W 1417	4639	AUT BATEAUX TRANS MARCH
8	MISC MANUFACTURED GOODS		4271164		5044550		6151295		6663833	ART MANUFACTURES DIVERS
812	*PLUMBG,HEATNG,LGHTNG EQ	W 27077	189434		238969		286136	W 37320	317852	APPAR SANITAIRES CHAUFFAGE
821	*FURNITURE,PARTS THEREOF	W 266424	849575	W 306106	1012959	W 323939	1274016	W 434596	1440812	MEUBLES ET PIECES
8211	CHAIRS,SEATS AND PARTS	W 28315	171521	W 31664	207966	W 38614	295735	W 45971	316246	SIEGES ET PIECES
82111	CHAIRS AND OTHER SEATS	W 24085	147253	W 25645	172945	W 30375	236561	W 36671	252809	SIEGES
8219	FURNITURE AND PARTS NES	W 222581	568890	W 256394	671867	W 267562	814825	W 370751	950519	AUTRES MEUBLES ET PIECES
82192	WOOD FURNITURE NES	W 136393	334842	W 156143	420820	W 152879	491505	W 169255	585160	MEUBLES NDA EN BOIS
84	CLOTHING AND ACCESSORIES		290853		327855		375446		464726	VETEMENTS
87	PRECISION INSTRUMNTS NES		1162336		1294911		1596967		1696983	INSTRUM,APPAR SCIENT NDA
872	MEDICAL INSTRUMENTS NES	W 9511	378265	W 6661	396779	W 6673	492927	W 7633	565655	INSTR,APP MEDIC–CHIR NDA
87202	OTH MEDICAL INSTRUMENTS	W 8651	278258	W 5801	299585	W 5353	318215	W 6369	403659	INSTRUM,APP MEDECINE
874	MEASURNG,CONTROLNG INSTR	W 6737	748691		850999		1042992		1066003	INSTRUMENTS DE MESURE
8743	GAS,LIQUID CONTROL INSTR	W 1588	194202		168264	W 1175	194853	W 1225	204823	APP,INSTR MESURE FLUIDES
8748	ELEC MEAS,CONTRL EQU NES	W 1097	239300		295961		364398		343132	APP ELEC ELECTRO MESURE
87483	OTH ELCTRNC MEAS ETC EQU	W 1007	219094		277096	W 1013	314466	W 1133	283357	AUT APP ELECTRO DE MESURE
88	PHOTO EQU,OPTICL GDS ETC		170124		213035		275036		260383	APP,FOURN PHOTO,OP,MONTR
89	MISC MANUFCTRD GOODS NES		1552517		1891120		2266191		2406404	ART MANUFACTURES DIVERS
892	PRINTED MATTER	W 34584	198251	W 42828	236636		249795		259830	IMPRIMES
893	ARTICLES OF PLASTIC NES		670552		846456		1120516		1199301	OUVRAGES EN MAT DIVIS 58
8931	PLSTC PACKG CONTNRS,LIDS	W 47525	140803	W 49735	165553	W 64084	253270	W 65947	255369	ART TRANSP EMBALLAGE ETC
8939	MISC PLASTIC ARTICLES	W 123638	503818	W 153373	647091	W 200059	828847	W 223323	900696	ART DIVERS EN MAT DIV 58
89391	PVC FLOORING TILES ETC	W 65304	162635	W 88076	230738	W 128415	330042	W 144614	364941	CHLORURE POLYVINYL PLAQ
89399	OTHR PLASTC ARTICLES NES	W 56192	329719	W 62482	399955	W 68656	482682	W 75099	514085	AUT OUV MAT DIV 58
894	TOYS,SPORTING GOODS,ETC	W 15345	151673		173923		204397		215918	VOITURES ENFANTS,JOUETS
898	MUSICAL INSTRUMENTS,PTS	W 5610	160709		157694		182741		190134	INSTRUMENTS DE MUSIQUE
8983	SOUND RECRDNG TAPE,DISCS	W 5331	153574	W 5224	146354	W 5042	169739		175780	SUPPORTS SON POUR 763
899	OTHER MANUFACTURED GOODS		243875		282606		406247		450748	AUT ART MANUF DIVERS NDA
8996	HEARING,ORTHOPAEDIC AIDS		173457		197903		287885		325203	APPAREILS D'ORTHOPEDIE
89962	ORTHOPAEDIC ETC GOODS		171848		195469		284486		322632	APPAREILS D'ORTHOPEDIE
9	GOODS NOT CLASSD BY KIND		295226		363860		6093589		6204062	ART TRANSACT NON CLASSES
931	*SPECIAL TRANSACTIONS	W 488	6501		114539	W 2638994	5924864	W 2603475	6002564	TRANS.SPECIALES
951	*WAR FIREARMS,AMMUNITION	W 2562	183072		130780		21161		23717	VEHIC BLINDES ARMES

1. HISTORICAL SERIES, 1961–1996 SPECIAL TRADE, IMPORTS C.I.F., EXPORTS F.O.B.
SERIES HISTORIQUES, 1961–1996 COMMERCE SPECIAL, IMPORTATIONS C.A.F., EXPORTATIONS F.O.B

YEAR ANNEE	VALUE IN MILLION SWISS FRANCS / VALEUR EN MILLION SWISS FRANCS: MERCHANDISE – MARCHANDISE		GOLD – OR		CONVERSION FACTORS U.S. CENTS PER SWISS FRANC / FACTEURS DE CONVERSION CENTS E.U. PAR SWISS FRANC		INDEX NUMBERS – INDICES: QUANTUM		UNIT VALUE / VALEUR UNITAIRE	
	IMPORTS	EXPORTS	IMPORTS	EXPORTS	IMPORTS	EXPORTS	IMPORTS	EXPORTS	IMPORTS	EXPORTS
1961	11635.00	8773.00	10.00	49.00	23.2700	23.2700	20	20	56	43
1962	12977.00	9524.00	8.00	56.00	23.2700	23.2700	22	21	57	45
1963	13978.00	10378.00	11.00	64.00	23.2700	23.2700	23	22	58	46
1964	15512.00	11367.00	28.00	89.00	23.2700	23.2700	25	24	59	48
1965	15929.00	12861.00	42.00	143.00	23.2700	23.2700	26	27	60	49
1966	17004.00	14204.00	55.00	135.00	23.2700	23.2700	27	29	62	51
1967	17786.00	15165.00	43.00	139.00	23.2700	23.2700	14	14	52	41
1968	19425.00	17349.00	29.00	304.00	23.2700	23.2700	15	16	52	41
1969	22734.00	20009.00	19.00	131.00	23.2700	23.2700	17	19	53	42
1970	27873.00	22140.00	25.00	104.00	23.2700	23.2700	42	43	69	58
1971	29642.00	23617.00	20.00	103.00	24.1500	24.5200	44	45	70	60
1972	32372.00	26188.00	30.00	124.00	26.1934	26.2005	48	47	71	63
1973	36589.00	29948.00	29.00	170.00	31.7768	31.8118	50	52	76	65
1974	42929.00	35353.00	61.00	456.00	33.6461	33.7418	50	55	90	73
1975	34268.00	33430.00	104.00	180.00	38.8194	38.7588	41	50	87	76
1976	36871.00	37045.00			40.0689	40.0737	47	56	82	75
1977	43026.00	42159.00			41.7872	41.9408	51	63	87	76
1978	42300.00	41779.00			56.2753	56.3936	56	66	78	74
1979	48730.00	44024.00			60.2375	60.2100	62	67	83	76
1980	60859.00	49608.00			59.7383	59.7366	68	71	100	84
1981	60094.10	52821.90			51.0799	51.1953	65	72	97	86
1982	58059.70	52658.70			49.3802	49.4196	64	69	96	90
1983	61064.50	53723.50			47.6858	47.6425	67	69	96	91
1984	69024.40	60654.10			42.6942	42.6404	72	77	101	92
1985	74750.30	66623.70			41.1001	41.2028	75	82	105	95
1986	73513.01	67004.00			55.8451	55.9428	82	86	94	92
1987	75171.01	67477.01			67.3161	67.3916	88	86	90	92
1988	82399.01	74064.00			68.4131	68.4703	93	91	93	93
1989	95209.01	84268.00			61.1358	61.1571	98	96	101	99
1990	96611.01	88257.01			72.1357	72.2812	100	100	100	100
1991	95032.00	87947.01			69.9788	69.9652	99	99	100	103
1992	86739.01	86148.00			71.2051	71.2762	94	103	102	103
1993	83767.01	86659.01			67.7145	67.7300	93	104	100	103
1994	87279.01	90213.01			73.4250	73.4244	102	109	95	102
1995	90775.01	92012.00			84.8318	84.8394	109	114	93	100
1996	91967.01	94174.00			80.9740	80.9183	110	115	94	101

2. IMPORTS BY BROAD ECONOMIC CATEGORY AND EXPORTS BY INDUSTRIAL ORIGIN. (PERCENTAGE OF TOTAL VALUE)
IMPORTATIONS PAR CATEGORIES ECONOMIQUES ET EXPORTATIONS PAR BRANCHE D'ACTIVITE.(EN POURCENTAGE DE LA VALEUR TOTALE)

IMPORTS – IMPORTATIONS

	1990	1991	1992	1993	1994	1995	1996
TOTAL IMPORTS–IMPORTATIONS TOTALES	100.	100.	100.	100.	100.	100.	100.
1 FOOD BEV–ALIMENTATION BOISSONS	5.6	5.9	6.0	6.0	6.2	5.8	5.9
11 PRIMARY–PRODUITS DE BASE	2.7	2.8	2.8	2.8	2.9	2.6	2.6
111 FOR INDUSTRY–POUR L'INDUSTRIE	0.5	0.5	0.5	0.5	0.5	0.6	0.5
112 FOR HOUSEHOLDS–POUR LES MENAGES	2.1	2.3	2.3	2.3	2.4	2.1	2.1
12 PROCESSED–PRODUITS ELABORES	2.9	3.1	3.2	3.2	3.2	3.2	3.3
121 FOR INDUSTRY–POUR L'INDUSTRIE	0.3	0.3	0.3	0.3	0.3	0.3	0.3
122 FOR HOUSEHOLDS–POUR LES MENAGES	2.6	2.8	2.9	2.9	2.9	2.9	2.9
2 IND SUPPLIES–APPROV INDUSTRIELS	33.4	32.1	32.5	33.1	32.8	31.8	30.8
21 PRIMARY–PRODUITS DE BASE	6.1	5.8	5.9	6.3	5.4	3.8	4.6
22 PROCESSED–PRODUITS ELABORES	27.2	26.3	26.6	26.8	27.4	28.0	26.3
3 FUELS–COMBUSTIBLES	4.5	4.6	4.2	3.9	3.3	2.9	3.5
31 PRIMARY–PRODUITS DE BASE	1.3	1.7	1.5	1.6	1.4	1.3	1.7
32 PROCESSED–PRODUITS ELABORES	3.2	2.9	2.7	2.3	1.9	1.5	1.8
321 MOTOR SPIRIT–ESSENCE	1.3	1.2	1.1	0.9	0.7	0.6	0.7
322 OTHER–AUTRES	1.9	1.8	1.6	1.4	1.2	0.9	1.1
4 MACHINERY–EQUIPEMENT	21.1	20.3	20.5	20.5	21.0	22.6	22.2
41 CAPITAL EQUIPMENT–MACHINES	17.3	16.7	16.8	16.6	16.9	18.1	17.9
42 PARTS–PIECES ACCESSOIRES	3.8	3.6	3.6	3.8	4.2	4.5	4.3
5 TRANSPORT–TRANSPORT	11.4	12.4	11.6	10.2	10.8	12.0	12.5
51 PASSENGER CARS–AUTOMOBILES	6.5	6.4	6.5	5.7	6.3	6.2	6.2
52 OTHER–AUTRES	2.6	3.5	2.7	2.0	2.1	3.3	3.4
521 INDUSTRIAL–INDUSTRIELS	2.2	3.2	2.3	1.6	1.8	3.0	3.1
522 NON INDUSTRIAL–NON INDUSTRIEL	0.4	0.4	0.4	0.4	0.4	0.3	0.3
53 PARTS–PIECES ACCESSOIRES	2.3	2.4	2.5	2.5	2.4	2.5	2.9
6 CONSUM GOODS–BIENS CONSOMMATION	23.7	24.2	24.8	26.0	25.6	24.6	24.9
61 DURABLE–DURABLES	9.0	8.6	8.3	8.3	8.2	7.4	7.7
62 SEMI DURABLE–SEMI DURABLES	10.7	11.5	11.9	12.3	11.9	11.4	11.2
63 NON DURABLE–NON DURABLES	3.9	4.2	4.6	5.4	5.5	5.9	6.0
7 GOODS NES–BIENS NDA	0.4	0.4	0.4	0.4	0.3	0.3	0.2

EXPORTS – EXPORTATIONS

	1990	1991	1992	1993	1994	1995	1996
TOTAL EXPORTS–EXPORTATIONS TOTALES	100.	100.	100.	100.	100.	100.	100.
1 AGRICULTURE	0.5	0.5	0.5	0.4	0.4	0.4	0.4
2 MINING QUARRY–INDUS EXTRACTIVES	4.7	4.3	3.8	4.4	3.4	2.3	2.4
3 MANUFACTURING–IND MANUFACTUR	94.8	95.3	95.7	95.1	96.2	97.2	97.1
31 FOOD BEV TOBACCO–ALIM BOISS TAB	2.7	2.8	2.9	2.9	3.0	3.0	2.9
32 TEXTILES–INDUSTRIES TEXTILES	5.6	5.3	5.0	4.7	4.5	4.1	3.8
33 WOOD & PRODUCTS–BOIS & PRODUITS	0.4	0.4	0.4	0.4	0.4	0.4	0.4
34 PAPER & PRODUCTS–PAPIER & PRODT	2.5	2.5	2.5	2.3	2.5	2.7	2.5
35 CHEMICALS–INDUSTRIES CHIMIQUES	23.2	24.1	25.4	26.4	27.1	27.6	28.6
36 NON METAL MIN–MIN NON METAL	0.9	0.9	0.9	1.0	1.0	1.0	1.0
37 BASIC METAL–IND METAL BASE	3.6	3.7	3.6	3.2	3.5	3.4	3.2
38 METAL MANUF–MANUF METAL	49.8	50.2	49.5	48.1	48.7	50.4	50.5
39 OTH MANUF IND–AUTRES MANUF	6.2	5.2	5.4	6.1	5.5	4.6	4.3

Switzerland including Liechtenstein

Suisse y compris Liechtenstein

3. TRADE BY PRINCIPAL COUNTRIES OF PRODUCTION AND CONSUMPTION (VALUE IN THOUSAND U.S. DOLLARS)
ECHANGES SELON LES PRINCIPAUX PAYS DE PRODUCTION ET DE COMSOMMATION (VALEUR EN MILLIERS DE DOLLARS EU)

COUNTRIES–PAYS	SPECIAL IMPORTS C.I.F. IMPORTATIONS SPECIALES C.A.F				
	1992	1993	1994	1995	1996
World	65743872	60828174	67997375	80152044	79264462
Africa	721175	803330	831762	1035244	1331262
Americas	5642880	4918712	5458259	6340114	6881699
Northern America	4927979	4314043	4719300	5456197	6028086
LAIA	466607	386307	504191	674346	574309
CACM	66920	68649	61817	107722	81704
Caribbean	57588	33925	61374	53214	91374
Rest of America	123787	115787	111577	48636	106225
As.ex F.USSR	6445542	5990327	6342570	7043599	6758853
Eur.x F.USSR	52465755	48712757	54701727	65115589	63765896
EU	51575645	47950171	53876735	63963036	62640784
EFTA	371299	281599	226631	283961	247797
East Europe	383243	376385	466081	707036	718940
Other Europe	17224	16216	28881	43615	49391
Former USSR	268811	280924	407889	475078	358213
Oceania	158105	122121	137800	142376	168510
Germany/Allemagne	21977155	19805101	22273642	27023346	24886704
France,Monac	7111345	6645245	7466541	9129761	9155752
Italy/Italie	6576477	5948451	6706013	8121147	8507793
USA/Etats–Unis d'Amer	4195908	3923185	4498009	5130359	5686876
United Kingdom	3799192	4393134	4501256	4447644	5090644
Netherlands/Pays–Bas	2921072	2743559	3174024	3680251	3753127
Austria/Autriche	2569151	2473462	2786865	3388945	3145708
Belgium–Luxembourg	2526200	2178595	2564798	2842015	2797000
Japan/Japon	2835578	2349351	2298464	2532198	2138370
Sweden/Suède	1145838	952315	1155109	1447982	1279895
Spain/Espagne	900102	837616	963856	1157036	1306962
China/Chine	623150	733728	840269	912339	987428
Denmark/Danemark	723906	678183	756606	899981	833599
Ireland/Irlande	491453	527085	651385	725828	895115
Hong Kong	533148	542945	492881	545017	506019
Finland/Finlande	445707	370323	445634	550535	475641
Thailand/Thaïlande	352814	350740	377682	406727	452345
Portugal	292546	313132	342059	441802	420029
Russian Federation	239953	254635	365290	430684	305828
Korea, Republic of	266995	216998	247440	319451	311827
Canada	252149	198358	221256	325144	338691
Libyan Arab Jamahiriya	256963	200664	242952	297981	332355
India/Inde	218245	214461	243037	285890	300992
Israel/Israël	256927	201413	263777	290580	223536
Norway,SVD,JM	333115	233518	192770	234214	204476
Brazil/Brésil	218867	182626	232155	249789	232335
So. Africa Customs Un	193389	184149	159403	244856	296242
Saudi Arabia	169686	186316	185531	235471	217038
Turkey/Turquie	159793	145527	186630	214073	225212
Hungary/Hongrie	152420	139737	147273	188198	202265
Singapore/Singapour	137765	154320	183696	167883	182838
Nigeria/Nigéria	52660	76867	121975	181228	257565
Czech Republic		107409	143940	212037	219621
Bermuda/Bermudes	479758	192490	18	506	1373
Malaysia/Malaisie	75585	82990	101209	154442	116574
Poland/Pologne	70678	71998	90363	142465	128635
Panama	123394	114770	111009	48011	105928
Australia/Australie	115983	79653	90084	83488	99743
Greece/Grèce	95500	83965	88945	106763	92813
Argentina/Argentine	87379	64296	72830	179507	59939
Algeria/Algérie	36801	112161	80824	54902	165364
Lebanon/Liban	48475	58589	98878	79965	155835
Indonesia/Indonésie	63747	66640	83449	98704	106457
Slovenia/Slovénia	56312	50933	60552	73371	70818
Slovakia		27650	41247	116195	122296
Colombia/Colombie	54494	45610	57867	43187	94254
Iran (Islamic Rp. of)	46911	53336	66134	59110	54964
Mexico/Mexique	31427	36016	53811	79903	76623
New Zealand	41822	41738	46616	58003	67966
Iceland/Islande	38185	48081	33861	49747	43321

COUNTRIES–PAYS	SPECIAL EXPORTS F.O.B. EXPORTATIONS SPECIALES F.O.B.				
	1992	1993	1994	1995	1996
Monde	65675003	63184619	70360083	81641172	80842780
Afrique	1208609	1213437	1258872	1484457	1439012
Amériques	7795932	7892140	8693454	9777237	10446223
Amérique du Nord	5993327	6139102	6741429	7722702	8261424
ALAI	1481784	1427534	1637955	1773913	1899225
MCAC	79632	88875	80613	86249	79184
Caraïbes	103668	91377	99551	87158	91479
Autre Amérique	137522	145250	133906	107215	114911
Asie l'URSS exclus	11163682	12068631	13023418	15703126	15906503
Europe l'URSS exclus	43106928	41056953	44474690	53256869	51677549
UE	41507816	39457072	42662402	50896285	49145959
AELE	362669	366134	363229	434665	479515
Europe de l'Est	1002729	1011744	1152685	1576269	1620516
Autre de l'Europe	32631	32476	32146	51716	57924
Ancienne URSS	279078	352911	483565	516338	558509
Océanie	581445	600274	719228	903143	814848
Germany/Allemagne	15043101	14494692	16157734	19437555	18314586
France,Monac	6015651	5759406	6192733	7776176	7577566
USA/Etats–Unis d'Amer	5462530	5640377	6265263	7073593	7593166
Italy/Italie	5640258	4913976	5127228	6192591	6075256
United Kingdom	4229539	4341099	4566924	4972105	5090730
Japan/Japon	2394844	2181604	2657165	3262061	3369444
Austria/Autriche	2362928	2405236	2484407	2908868	2481642
Hong Kong	1802074	1980718	2251394	2411673	2211391
Netherlands/Pays–Bas	1767499	1732818	1837979	2196313	2113251
Belgium–Luxembourg	1765798	1589744	1715006	1828207	1911864
Spain/Espagne	1532802	1269173	1368191	1729193	1815927
Sweden/Suède	940573	867532	972066	1130582	1161372
Singapore/Singapour	598200	887974	890753	1077475	1185435
Saudi Arabia	775226	1010073	790989	1008342	738831
Israel/Israël	694049	797736	846292	822128	1012634
Denmark/Danemark	702732	665123	717341	963466	824483
Korea, Republic of	470846	417416	657607	826910	951859
Turkey/Turquie	462532	583942	405682	803362	938973
Thailand/Thaïlande	507106	536728	652057	743313	734133
China/Chine	439499	638401	627737	715408	727952
Australia/Australie	492260	503025	605530	762551	684431
Canada	488685	468962	468451	644384	664001
Brazil/Brésil	337511	369760	493531	682180	744851
Portugal	487235	454049	461028	575090	572578
So. Africa Customs Un	326428	424689	485092	600735	581706
Greece/Grèce	419705	396540	403646	474955	465633
Finland/Finlande	412575	363855	385252	492318	502925
India/Inde	249060	274171	388544	559547	546378
Norway,SVD,JM	344208	343692	349049	419821	456025
Poland/Pologne	290970	271744	320396	474340	540886
Mexico/Mexique	425323	365852	395552	328253	368127
United Arab Emirates	369844	311427	355805	368419	422331
Malaysia/Malaisie	199964	251806	359860	545571	443844
Indonesia/Indonésie	229645	253373	289647	386062	356538
Hungary/Hongrie	261772	278319	298520	319414	301110
Czech Republic		269587	298708	408374	447528
Russian Federation	186339	221593	307471	309577	351806
Iran (Islamic Rp. of)	338672	282221	165195	172948	196133
Ireland/Irlande	187419	203828	272867	218867	238146
Argentina/Argentine	186599	204879	225306	217403	278146
Egypt/Egypte	176388	155829	164383	214646	255687
Pakistan	209538	170463	144622	201722	181866
Philippines	108875	151849	148487	217789	202821
Colombia/Colombie	141083	135749	162100	153623	146268
Panama	135739	142342	130854	102060	112021
Lebanon/Liban	99671	101807	125210	143144	151855
Slovenia/Slovénia	74912	94258	128678	159180	152165
Chile/Chili	103964	105096	108671	111842	107133
Venezuela	133989	117345	90028	101553	92694
Bahrain/Bahreïn	172043	99103	102094	83763	74941

(VALUE AS PERCENTAGE OF WORLD TOTAL)(VALEURS EN POURCENTAGE DU TOTAL MONDIAL)

	1987	1988	1989	1990	1991	1992	1993	1994	1995	1996
Africa	1.9	1.9	1.8	1.7	1.6	1.1	1.3	1.2	1.3	1.7
Americas	8.0	8.2	9.0	8.5	9.7	8.6	8.1	8.0	7.9	8.7
Northern America	6.5	7.0	7.8	7.4	8.6	7.5	7.1	6.9	6.8	7.6
LAIA	0.8	0.9	0.8	0.8	0.8	0.7	0.6	0.7	0.8	0.7
CACM	0.2	0.1	0.1	0.1	0.1	0.1	0.1	0.1	0.1	0.1
Caribbean	0.1	0.0	0.1	0.0	0.1	0.1	0.1	0.1	0.1	0.1
Rest of America	0.3	0.2	0.2	0.2	0.1	0.2	0.2	0.2	0.1	0.1
As.ex F.USSR	9.1	9.9	9.5	9.5	9.8	9.8	9.8	9.3	8.8	8.5
Eur.x F.USSR	80.3	79.5	79.1	79.6	77.9	79.8	80.1	80.4	81.2	80.4
EU	78.6	77.8	77.3	78.1	76.6	78.4	78.8	79.2	79.8	79.0
EFTA	0.6	0.6	0.7	0.7	0.6	0.6	0.5	0.3	0.4	0.3
East Europe	0.9	0.8	0.8	0.7	0.6	0.6	0.6	0.7	0.9	0.9
Other Europe	0.2	0.2	0.2	0.2	0.2	0.0	0.0	0.0	0.1	0.1
Former USSR	0.5	0.4	0.4	0.4	0.8	0.4	0.5	0.6	0.6	0.5
Oceania	0.2	0.2	0.2	0.2	0.2	0.2	0.2	0.2	0.2	0.2
Germany/Allemagne	34.3	34.0	33.5	33.7	32.8	33.4	32.6	32.8	33.7	31.4
France,Monac	10.8	10.6	10.9	11.1	10.9	10.8	10.9	11.0	11.4	11.6
Italy/Italie	10.2	10.1	10.2	10.5	10.0	10.0	9.8	9.9	10.1	10.7
USA/Etats–Unis d'Amer	5.3	5.5	6.4	6.1	7.3	6.4	6.4	6.6	6.4	7.2
United Kingdom	6.1	5.7	5.6	5.3	5.5	5.8	7.2	6.6	5.5	6.4
Netherlands/Pays–Bas	4.0	4.2	4.1	4.1	4.1	4.4	4.5	4.7	4.6	4.7
Austria/Autriche	3.9	3.9	3.8	3.9	3.8	3.9	4.1	4.1	4.2	4.0
Belgium–Luxembourg	3.4	3.4	3.5	3.6	3.5	3.8	3.6	3.8	3.5	3.5
Japan/Japon	4.6	5.0	4.5	4.4	4.3	4.3	3.9	3.4	3.2	2.7
Sweden/Suède	2.0	2.1	2.0	1.9	1.8	1.7	1.6	1.7	1.8	1.6

	1987	1988	1989	1990	1991	1992	1993	1994	1995	1996
Afrique	2.5	2.4	2.1	2.1	2.1	1.8	1.9	1.8	1.8	1.8
Amériques	12.9	12.6	12.5	11.2	11.7	11.9	12.5	12.4	12.0	12.9
Amérique du Nord	9.9	9.7	9.8	8.8	9.1	9.1	9.7	9.6	9.5	10.2
ALAI	2.4	2.4	2.2	2.0	2.2	2.3	2.3	2.3	2.2	2.3
MCAC	0.1	0.1	0.1	0.1	0.1	0.1	0.1	0.1	0.1	0.1
Caraïbes	0.2	0.2	0.2	0.2	0.2	0.2	0.1	0.1	0.1	0.1
Autre Amérique	0.3	0.2	0.2	0.2	0.2	0.2	0.2	0.2	0.1	0.1
Asie l'URSS exclus	16.5	17.1	17.2	17.8	17.3	17.0	19.1	18.5	19.2	19.7
Europe l'URSS exclus	66.0	65.9	66.1	66.8	67.3	65.6	65.0	63.2	65.2	63.9
UE	62.4	62.3	62.7	63.9	64.7	63.2	62.4	60.6	62.3	60.8
AELE	0.8	0.7	0.6	0.6	0.6	0.6	0.6	0.5	0.5	0.6
Europe de l'Est	2.2	2.3	2.1	1.6	1.5	1.5	1.6	1.6	1.9	2.0
Autre de l'Europe	0.7	0.7	0.7	0.7	0.5	0.0	0.1	0.0	0.1	0.1
Ancienne URSS	1.1	1.1	1.1	1.2	0.7	0.4	0.6	0.7	0.6	0.7
Océanie	1.0	0.9	1.0	1.0	0.9	0.9	1.0	1.0	1.1	1.0
Germany/Allemagne	21.3	20.9	20.3	21.9	23.8	22.9	22.9	23.0	23.8	22.7
France,Monac	9.1	9.4	9.8	9.9	9.6	9.2	9.1	8.8	9.5	9.4
USA/Etats–Unis d'Amer	8.9	8.6	8.9	8.0	8.2	8.3	8.9	8.9	8.7	9.4
Italy/Italie	8.3	8.3	8.5	8.9	8.7	8.6	7.8	7.3	7.6	7.5
United Kingdom	7.5	7.9	8.2	7.4	6.6	6.4	6.9	6.5	6.1	6.3
Japan/Japon	3.8	4.3	4.2	4.8	4.3	3.6	3.5	3.8	4.0	4.2
Austria/Autriche	3.8	3.6	3.5	3.7	3.8	3.6	3.8	3.5	3.6	3.1
Hong Kong	2.1	2.3	2.6	2.6	2.6	2.7	3.1	3.2	3.0	2.7
Netherlands/Pays–Bas	2.8	2.8	2.7	2.7	2.7	2.7	2.7	2.6	2.7	2.6
Belgium–Luxembourg	2.4	2.2	2.3	2.3	2.4	2.7	2.5	2.4	2.2	2.4

4. Special Imports C.I.F. by Commodities according to the S.I.T.C. (Rev. 2) in thousand U.S. Dollars
Importations Spéciales C.A.F. par Produits d'après la C.T.C.I. (Rév. 2) en milliers de Dollars E.U.

SITC CTCI	COMMODITY	1993		1994		1995		1996		PRODUIT
		WEIGHT POIDS	VALUE VALEUR	WEIGHT POIDS	VALUE VALEUR	WEIGHT POIDS	VALUE VALEUR	WEIGHT POIDS	VALUE VALEUR	
	ALL COMMODITIES		60828174		67997375		80152044		79264462	TOUS PRODUITS
0	FOOD AND LIVE ANIMALS		3253217		3674645		3974842		3961328	ALIMENTS,ANIMAUX VIVANTS
01	MEAT AND PREPARATIONS		362821		408326		425527		478351	VIANDES ET PREPARATIONS
011	MEAT FRESH,CHILLD,FROZEN	W 67769	287958	W 71240	326447	W 67996	337096	W 81270	384108	VIANDES FRAICHES,REF,CONGE
02	DAIRY PRODCTS,BIRDS'EGGS		249526		269973		306899		320564	PRODUITS LAITIERS,OEUFS
03	FISH AND PREPARATIONS		336272		371722		405957		390798	POISSONS ET PREPARATIONS
04	CEREALS AND PREPARATIONS		313097		325688		372091		362753	CEREALES ET PRODUITS
048	CEREAL ETC PREPARATIONS	W 168790	204861	W 142829	217935	W 139648	229519	W 154970	237123	PREPTNS A BASE CEREALES
05	VEGETABLES AND FRUIT		1129024		1291375		1319975		1286470	LEGUMES ET FRUITS
054	VEG ETC FRSH,SMPLY PRSVD	W 251084	350053	W 310593	406542	W 338240	436523	W 286068	418460	LEGUMES FRAIS,CONG,SECS
0545	OTHER FRESH VEGETABLES	W 142524	229012	W 159488	249933	W 168145	269002	W 155357	273211	AUTRES LEGUMES FRAIS,REF
05459	FRESH VEGETABLES NES	W 133257	215031	W 148146	234687	W 152989	249490	W 144427	256399	LEGUMES FRAIS,REFRI NDA
057	FRUIT,NUTS,FRESH,DRIED	W 423946	555608	W 457543	639113	W 441354	617537	W 427841	609527	FRUITS FRAIS OU SECS
0579	FRUIT FRESH OR DRIED NES	W 132202	204806	W 146657	225335	W 142022	232701	W 138962	213753	FRUITS FRAIS,SECS NDA
07	COFFEE,TEA,COCOA,SPICES		294549		371663		456221		414529	CAFE,THE,CACAO,EPICES
081	*FEEDING STUFF FOR ANIML	W 436368	224940	W 439413	242355	W 415832	240952	W 476498	251644	NOURRITURE POUR ANIMAUX
09	MISC EDIBLE PRODUCTS		201507		233670		265543		280489	PREP ALIMENTAIRES DIVERSES
098	EDIBLE PRODCTS,PREPS NES	W 58005	196775	W 53920	229820	W 59195	260552	W 64794	275479	PREP ALIMENTAIRES NDA
1	BEVERAGES AND TOBACCO		769523		865159		1007302		1085716	BOISSONS ET TABACS
11	BEVERAGES		589889		662988		816983		854021	BOISSONS
112	ALCOHOLIC BEVERAGES	W 251213	525188	W 254337	581446	W 264844	712426	W 265211	738824	BOISSONS ALCOOLIQUES
1121	WINE OF FRESH GRAPES ETC	W 177200	410037	W 176295	458459	W 188695	573061	W 185890	611431	VINS DE RAISINS FRAIS
11212	WINE OF FRESH GRAPES	W 175664	408454	W 174634	456587	W 187372	570946	W 184773	609228	VINS DE MOUTS DE RAISINS
2	CRUDE MATERLS,EXCL FUELS		1482431		1717614		2016249		1767281	MAT BRUTES NON COMESTIBLES
24	CORK AND WOOD		242447		307233		357517		293457	LIEGE ET BOIS
248	WOOD SHAPED,SLEEPERS	W 276945	187290	W 335943	243569	W 346103	281255	W 303962	231257	BOIS SIMPLEMENT TRAVAILLES
251	*PULP AND WASTE PAPER	W 542875	187083	W 599017	247779	W 612448	393304	W 598539	255363	PATES A PAPIER,DECHETS
2517	SODA,SULPHATE WOOD PULP	W 327073	143434	W 350198	186692	W 348756	296666	W 357478	202148	PATES CHIMIQUES AU SULFATE
25172	— BLEACHED,NONDISSOLVNG	W 304135	133107	W 325527	174823	W 323288	277266	W 337961	191084	PATES BLANCHIES
27	CRUDE FERTLZR,MINRLS NES		255512		280429		304030		283009	ENGRAIS MINERAUX BRUTS
29	CRUDE ANIMAL,VEG MAT NES		439564		493682		565634		560143	MATIERES BRUTES ANIM,VEGET
292	CRUDE VEG MATERIALS NES	W 90210	388828	W 99126	434661	W 108024	501507	W 109382	499219	MAT BRUTES VEGETALES NDA
3	MINERAL FUELS ETC		2399424		2310884		2349103		2837525	COMBUSTIBLES MINERAUX LUB
33	PETROLEUM AND PRODUCTS		2036456		1938938		1909593		2390280	PETROLE ET DERIVES
333	CRUDE PETROLEUM	W 4499304	630085	W 4766577	607513	W 4544005	641184	W 5290311	886033	HUILES BRUTES DE PETROLE
334	PETROLEUM PRODUCTS,REFIN	W 6678149	1352605	W 6941008	1279253	W 6326300	1207021	W 6320385	1446237	PRODUITS RAFFINES
3341	GASOLINE,OTH LIGHT OILS	W 2651616	553159	W 2614010	494658	W 2586671	503117	W 2631092	586738	ESSENCES POUR MOTEURS
33411	MOTOR,AVIATION SPIRIT	W 2592119	538794	W 2571023	483829	W 2561187	495239	W 2609086	579296	ESSENCES MOTEURS D'AVIONS
3343	GAS OILS	W 3687582	678246	W 4125787	684235	W 3514166	591139	W 3564432	763487	GAS OILS
341	*GAS,NATURAL AND MANUFCT	W 1931747	332354	W 1853166	337020	W 1959193	397902	W 2176852	413935	GAZ NATUREL,GAZ MANUFACT
3414	PETROLEUM GASES, GASEOUS	W 1904710	324286	W 1821310	328250	W 1925201	387770	W 2146562	404164	GAZ DE PETROLE GAZEUX
5	CHEMCLS,RELATED PROD NES		8261562		9513103		11407067		11418807	PRODUITS CHIMIQUES
51	ORGANIC CHEMICALS		2190507		2483232		2938303		3267356	PROD CHIMIQ ORGANIQUES
512	ALCOHOLS,PHENOLS ETC	W 170109	177691	W 199178	234259	W 189445	278020	W 196514	256397	PHENOLS,PHENOLS–ALCOOLS
513	CARBOXYLIC ACIDS ETC	W 192099	287321	W 211977	338856	W 222696	473723	W 206394	502970	ACIDES CARBOXYLIQUES
514	NITROGEN–FNCTN COMPOUNDS	W 143940	759301	W 161571	841668	W 148162	928604	W 155176	1147168	COMPOSES FONCT AZOTEES
5145	AMINE–FUNCTION COMPOUNDS	W 82973	165817	W 96283	184751	W 83863	197418	W 85326	238109	COMPOSES FONCTION AMINE
5148	OTH NITROGN–FNCTN CMPNDS	W 31867	327845	W 34803	347349	W 34810	493617	W 36704	617764	AUTRES COMPOSES AZOTES
51482	IMIDE–,IMIDE–FNCT CMPNDS	W 16904	219629	W 18262	227162	W 18858	344947	W 19043	468515	COMPOSES A FONCTION IMIDE
515	ORG–INORG COMPOUNDS ETC	W 48634	484328	W 52185	548046	W 53645	620896	W 54634	734593	COMPOSES ORGANO–MINERAUX
5156	HETEROCYCLIC CMPDS ETC	W 41800	394178	W 43618	441946	W 44681	502486	W 44876	586299	COMPOSES HETEROCYCLIQUES
51569	OTH HETEROCYC CMPDS,ETC	W 11102	325052	W 10800	364915	W 10966	391916	W 12592	508905	AUT COMP HETEROCYCLIQUES
516	OTHER ORGANIC CHEMICALS	W 211472	388478	W 228736	424250	W 217840	519127	W 230766	529732	AUTRES PROD ORGANIQUES
5162	ALDEHYDE ETC FNCT CMPNDS	W 70526	170152	W 77666	194796	W 87733	253073	W 91027	244311	COMP FONCTION ALDEHYDE
52	INORGANIC CHEMICALS		259293		293365		346277		387616	PROD CHIM INORGANIQUES
53	DYES,TANNING,COLOUR PROD		852294		965212		1119028		1036797	PROD TEINTURE,COLORANTS
531	SYNT DYE,NAT INDGO,LAKES	W 29764	527453	W 32708	593398	W 30301	696915	W 31673	640926	MAT COLOR ORGAN,LAQUES
5311	SYNTHIC ORGNIC DYESTUFFS	W 26753	513200	W 28611	566949	W 27968	671770	W 29356	611208	MAT COLOR ORGAN SYNTHET
533	PIGMENTS,PAINTS,ETC	W 274463	321708	W 308523	367545	W 313116	418207	W 266201	390866	PIGMENTS,PEINTURES,VERNIS
541	*MEDICINAL,PHARM PRODUCT	MK 28534	2107535	MK 26738	2414973	MK 29077	2862357	MK 31634	2877153	PROD MEDICINAUX PHARMACEUT
5416	GLYCOSIDES,GLANDS,SERA	K 1094103	411738	K 1167308	606637	K 1600653	499322	K 1945872	374398	HETEROSIDES
54164	ANTISERA,MICROB VACCINES	K 594722	352318	K 804109	570500	K 1043656	455469	K 1490758	343475	SERUMS,VACCINS
5417	MEDICAMENTS	MK 15504	1180668	MK 18367	1386237	MK 20284	1929825	MK 22839	1996083	MEDICAMENTS
54171	— CONTAINNG ANTIBIOTICS	K 1560288	179782	K 1464729	204338	K 1470882	285746	K 1381982	259404	MED CONTN ANTIBIOTIQUES
54179	— CONTNG OTH SUBSTANCES	MK 13181	941544	MK 15875	1100225	MK 17863	1503137	MK 20487	1592322	MED CONT AUT SUBSTANCES
55	PERFUME,CLEANING ETC PRD		665050		814834		948620		905696	PROD POUR PARFUM,TOILETTE
553	PERFUMERY,COSMETICS,ETC	W 27542	388570	W 30987	509281	W 35456	593260	W 37917	571216	PRODUITS DE PARFUMERIE
58	PLASTIC MATERIALS ETC		1439013		1684176		2131325		1858766	MAT PLAST ARTIFICIELLES
582	PROD OF CONDENSATION ETC	W 204175	429386	W 222523	512900	W 237399	686066	W 233736	602306	PROD CONDENS,POLYCOND
5823	ALKYDS,OTHER POLYESTERS	W 82466	205281	W 93188	246580	W 101455	333961	W 99332	278917	ALKYDES ET AUT POLYESTERS
583	POLYMERIZATION ETC PRODS	W 619465	969665	W 683736	1122059	W 666914	1387697	W 650699	1201169	PROD POLYMERISATION
5831	POLYETHYLENE	W 225920	213476	W 247399	242419	W 232029	310683	W 212280	247794	POLYETHYLENE
5839	OTH POLYMRZTION ETC PROD	W 69868	257535	W 80595	309301	W 89249	379317	W 90769	350830	AUT PROD POLYMER COPOLYM
59	CHEMICAL MATERIALS NES		669009		779992		965298		998175	MAT PROD CHIMIQUES NDA
598	MISCEL CHEM PRODUCTS NES	W 571730	478993	W 703555	567818	W 764573	705434	W 725076	730148	PROD DIV INDUST CHIM NDA
5989	CHEM PRODUCTS,PREPS NES	W 540965	434523	W 669769	515979	W 731521	644312	W 692163	672805	PROD PREP CHIMIQUES NDA
59899	OTH CHEM PRODS,PREPS,NES	W 496218	343779	W 622375	404162	W 686567	526852	W 648638	561022	AUT PRODUITS CHIMIQUES NDA
6	BASIC MANUFACTURES		12549317		13658304		15487536		14710513	ART MANUFACTURES
62	RUBBER MANUFACTURES NES		492616		543289		641682		608058	CAOUTCHOUC MANUFACTURE
625	RUBBER TYRES, TUBES ETC	W 58738	307699	W 62638	331002	W 66611	385134	W 64793	374961	PNEUS CAOUTCHOUC VULCANISE
6251	TYRES NEW FOR MOTOR CARS	W 38437	220018	W 40634	235844	W 42393	271660	W 41731	264307	PNEUS POUR VOITURES
63	WOOD,CORK MANUFACTRS NES		486916		609091		750287		703496	OUVRAGES LIEGE ET BOIS
634	VENEERS,PLYWOOD,ETC	W 196728	181737	W 244232	228569	W 264432	277590	W 248237	238023	PLACAGES,CONTRE–PLAQUES
635	WOOD MANUFACTURES NES	W 126441	279927	W 156541	354380	W 170797	442054	W 166990	437880	ART MANUF EN BOIS NDA
6353	BUILDERS WOODWRK,PREFABS	W 71257	185438	W 90128	242031	W 98765	308233	W 95420	311038	OUVRAGES DE MENUISERIE
64	PAPER,PAPERBOARD AND MFR		1302686		1483367		1829129		1741561	PAPIERS,CARTONS & OUVRAGES
641	PAPER AND PAPERBOARD	W 791967	805360	W 916052	944623	W 915102	1178544	W 895364	1069298	PAPIERS ET CARTONS
6412	PRINTG,WRITING PAPER NES	W 259959	268854	W 306636	315541	W 289914	390880	W 296245	352401	PAPIERS POUR L'IMPRESSION
64122	— COATED,IMPREGNATD ETC	W 215763	215683	W 258430	257100	W 237757	307915	W 238009	271223	PAPIERS IMPRESSION COUCHES
6418	COATED ETC PAPER NES BLK	W 113663	203404	W 110132	213705	W 111355	248934	W 110712	235975	PAP,CARTONS COUCHES,ENDUITS
642	PAPER,ETC,PRECUT,ARTS OF	W 196098	497325	W 212307	538744	W 214347	650585	W 229709	672263	PAP,CARTONS DECOUPES
6428	PAPER ETC ARTICLES NES	W 78801	195541	W 85340	218535	W 85353	259286	W 88993	260775	OUVRAGES EN PATE A PAPIER
65	TEXTILE YARN,FABRICS,ETC		1589899		1760141		1937968		1756799	FILS,TISSUS,ARTICLES TEXTILE
651	TEXTILE YARN	W 49956	327946	W 55360	366745	W 56579	427218	W 47314	355540	FILS TEXTILES
653	WOVN MAN–MADE FIB FABRIC	W 10646	184379	W 11483	205478	W 10513	211312	W 9617	182201	TISSUS FIBRES SYNTH,ARTIF
658	TEXTILE ARTICLES NES	W 14806	223938	W 16108	251768	W 17280	296303	W 17433	290961	ART FACONNES MAT TEXTILES
659	FLOOR COVERINGS,ETC	W 37855	284008	W 39027	303267	W 37947	304648	W 35962	280062	COUVRE–PARQUETS,TAPIS ETC
66	NONMETAL MINERAL MFS NES		3878007		3766445		3294554		3827442	ART MIN NON METALLIQUES
663	MINERAL MANUFCTURES NES	W 424378	224212	W 513364	260860	W 583963	324239	W 626163	311970	ART MIN MANUF NDA
664	GLASS	W 145505	195297	W 156548	217735	W 158879	268241	W 163169	256046	VERRE
665	GLASSWARE	W 103057	239563	W 114682	279554	W 106189	317683	W 126623	318426	OUVRAGES EN VERRE

4. Special Imports C.I.F. by Commodities according to the S.I.T.C. (Rev. 2) in thousand U.S. Dollars
Importations Spéciales C.A.F. par Produits d'après la C.T.C.I. (Rév. 2) en milliers de Dollars E.U.

SITC CTCI	COMMODITY	1993		1994		1995		1996		PRODUIT
		WEIGHT POIDS	VALUE VALEUR	WEIGHT POIDS	VALUE VALEUR	WEIGHT POIDS	VALUE VALEUR	WEIGHT POIDS	VALUE VALEUR	
667	PEARL,PREC–,SEMI–P STONE		2809635		2538876		1853145		2436565	PERLES, PIERRES GEMMES
6672	DIAMONDS NONINDUST,UNSET		2314020		2070122		1520471		2051497	DIAMANTS BRUTS
66722	— SRTD,ROUGH,SIMPLY WKD		1582706		1362722		911942		1228958	DIAMANTS TRIES BRUTS
66729	— CUT ETC NOT SET		730686		706735		607462		822320	DIAMANTS TAILLES
6673	PREC–,SEMI–PR STONES NES		457677		441067		301943		326224	AUTRES PIERRES NON SERTIES
67	IRON AND STEEL		1466912		1755227		2369171		1790105	FER ET ACIER
673	IRON,STEEL SHAPES ETC	W 503689	323223	W 569721	378386	W 646067	542914	W 530046	414031	BARRES,PROFIL FER,ACIER
6732	IRON,STEEL BARS ETC	W 198363	141472	W 242340	178346	W 311958	278008	W 244515	214305	BARRES FER,ACIER
674	IRN,STL UNIV,PLATE,SHEET	W 837046	594061	W 936308	703565	W 984352	977871	W 765291	675627	LARGES PLATS,TOLES
6746	IRN,STL THIN PLATE,ROLLD	W 246476	203860	W 274178	243188	W 301567	385133	W 241553	257975	TOLES LAM MOINS 3MM
678	IRON,STL TUBES,PIPES,ETC	W 148856	281146	W 198662	359941	W 188590	423724	W 153854	350097	TUBES,TUYAUX EN FONTE,FER
68	NON–FERROUS METALS		1426744		1558831		2014114		1760814	METAUX NON FERREUX
681	SILVER,PLATINUM,ETC		562398		451530		548258		535947	ARGENT ET PLATINE
6812	METALS OF PLATINUM GROUP		550585		438117		534565		526217	PLATINE
68123	PLATINUM,ALLOYS UNWRGHT		329263		279139		382340		345668	PLATINE,ALLIAGES BRUTS
682	COPPER EXC CEMENT COPPER	W 97726	338887	W 109155	407889	W 117313	551374	W 107109	444594	CUIVRE
6822	COPPER,ALLOYS WORKED	W 90800	322875	W 101165	387048	W 108830	522735	W 99772	424181	CUIVRE,ALLIAGES OUVRES
68221	COPPER BARS,WIRE,ETC	W 55856	147042	W 61188	173621	W 65391	245141	W 61720	196681	BARRES,PROFILES ET FILS
684	ALUMINIUM	W 183831	425530	W 247713	579882	W 249486	762607	W 235111	650820	ALUMINIUM
6841	ALUMINIUM,ALLOYS,UNWRGHT	W 91034	124104	W 137164	211391	W 130833	264676	W 117406	203537	ALUMINIUM,ALLIAGES BRUTS
6842	ALUMINIUM,ALLOYS WORKED	W 92798	301426	W 110549	368491	W 118652	497931	W 117705	447282	ALUMINIUM,ALLIAGES OUVRE
69	METAL MANUFACTURES NES		1759508		2020755		2494541		2373193	ART MANUFACT EN METAL NDA
691	STRUCTURES AND PARTS NES	W 114096	336884	W 131303	388950	W 143483	462315	W 139921	447762	CONSTRUCT FER,ACIER,ALU
6911	STRUCTURES,PARTS IRN,STL	W 104537	245327	W 120568	284160	W 132417	338082	W 128146	327262	CONSTRUCT FER,ACIER,FONTE
694	STL,COPPR NAILS,NUTS,ETC	W 35867	173108	W 43451	202407	W 52144	268534	W 45653	235231	CLOUS,VIS,ECROUS
69402	IRN,STL NUTS,BOLTS,ETC	W 31354	154981	W 37954	180884	W 46687	242646	W 40692	211566	BOULONS,VIS,ECROUS FER,AC
695	TOOLS	W 12166	306433	W 14051	360531	W 16407	499175	W 16141	474541	OUTILS A MAIN
6954	BLADES,TIPS,ETC FR TOOLS	W 4824	196976	W 5659	222911	W 6424	309329	W 6603	294022	OUTILS POUR MACHINE–OUTIL
697	BASE MTL HOUSEHOLD EQUIP	W 28959	210917	W 32011	237655	W 31288	266784	W 31109	277614	ART MENAGE MET COMMUNS
699	BASE METAL MFRS NES	W 70668	541309	W 79094	611999	W 82720	734244	W 80039	693846	ART MANUFACTURES MET NDA
6991	LOCKSMITHS WARES,ETC	W 19691	186468	W 22775	215464	W 24095	249457	W 20802	214143	ARTICLES DE SERRURERIE
7	MACHINES,TRANSPORT EQUIP		17961594		20906344		26770118		26478816	MACHINES MATERIEL TRANSPORT
71	POWER GENERATING EQUIPMT		851061		955373		1098961		1191272	MACHINES GENERATRICES
714	ENGINES AND MOTORS NES	W 2520	182693	W 2881	208230	W 3379	233153	W 5468	399118	MOTEURS NON ELECTRIQUES
716	ROTATING ELECTRIC PLANT	W 19581	312816	W 22519	357822	W 24204	434387	W 22441	412163	APP ELECTR ROTATIFS,PIECES
7162	AC MTRS,GENRTRS,GEN SETS	W 12061	192258	W 14186	218897	W 15700	274662	W 14743	264160	MOTEURS ELECTRIQUES
71621	AC MTRS,INC UNIVRSL MTRS	W 10479	169478	W 12621	195165	W 13820	245042	W 12917	236464	MOT ELEC NON COUR CONTINU
72	MACHS FOR SPCL INDUSTRYS		1585152		1755801		2341994		2188576	MAC SPECIALES POUR INDUST
723	CIVIL ENGNEERG EQUIP ETC	W 15131	116632	W 21450	170392	W 28230	240919	W 23046	198590	APPAREILS DE GENIE CIVIL
724	TEXTILE,LEATHER MACHNRY	W 15096	253639	W 15866	243662	W 21884	333480	W 21219	307884	MACH POUR INDUSTRIE TEXTILE
726	PRINTG,BKBINDG MACHY,PTS	W 12619	202685	W 14063	229508	W 17000	286630	W 17479	319385	MACHINES POUR IMPRIMERIE
728	OTH MACHY FOR SPCL INDUS	W 44179	621198	W 39097	638003	W 49711	910691	W 44770	851307	AUT MACH IND PARTICULIERES
7284	MACHY FOR SPCL INDUS NES	W 20594	425537	W 21014	467175	W 27124	674420	W 25781	639276	MACH SPEC IND PARTICUL.
72848	OTH MCHY WITH INDIV FNCT	W 11096	236030	W 11477	262392	W 13462	375496	W 12399	339778	AUTRES MACHINES NDA
73	METALWORKING MACHINERY		436113		471392		777087		768197	MACH TRAVAIL DES METAUX
736	METALWORKING MACH–TOOLS	W 22288	363510	W 25363	395602	W 35853	671841	W 33728	650647	MACH–OUTILS TRAVAIL METAUX
74	GENRL INDUSTRL MACHY NES		2501727		2777152		3626705		3408043	MACH APP INDUSTRIE
741	HEATING,COOLING EQUIPMNT	W 28323	419079	W 33218	482077	W 38752	627395	W 37436	579734	MACH CHAUFFAGE,PIECES
7416	HEATING,COOLING EQU NES	W 12042	170639	W 15624	204391	W 16544	262140	W 15211	227652	APP CHANGEMENT TEMP
742	PUMPS FOR LIQUIDS ETC	W 9090	182643	W 9949	202144	W 12848	269807	W 10827	229521	POMPES MOTO–POMPES
743	PUMPS NES,CENTRFUGES ETC	W 22545	358015	W 23961	376109	W 30210	514491	W 28136	479657	POMPES COMPRES,VENT ETC
744	MECHANICAL HANDLING EQU	W 48318	429322	W 56420	474815	W 65969	640584	W 61470	581492	EQUIP MANUTENTION PIECES
7442	LIFTING,LOADING MACH NES	W 24447	220671	W 27045	235326	W 32809	329138	W 30119	296955	APP LEVAGE,MANUTENTION
745	NONELEC MACHY,TOOLS NES	W 15727	404797	W 17426	428801	W 18963	513185	W 18501	489193	AUT MACH NON ELEC,PIECES
7452	OTH NONELEC MCHS,PTS NES	W 14941	375815	W 16488	392851	W 17896	470064	W 17595	453564	AUT MACH NON ELEC,PIECES
749	NONELEC MACH PTS,ACC NES	W 38975	707870	W 46182	813205	W 48805	1061242	W 47450	1048447	PIECES MACH NON ELEC NDA
7492	COCKS,VALVES ETC NES	W 12966	302869	W 14999	345329	W 15871	422871	W 15294	402695	ART ROB,SIM POUR TUYAUX
7493	SHAFT,CRANK,PULLEY ETC	W 13514	165221	W 17016	194458	W 18556	262976	W 16910	251277	ARBRES TRANS,VILEBREQUINS
75	OFFICE MACHNES,ADP EQUIP		2758604		3309706		3924559		3885678	MACH BUREAU TRAIT AUTOM
751	OFFICE MACHINES	W 5088	184539	W 5118	212530	W 5338	242307	W 5441	226746	MACH,APPAREILS DE BUREAU
752	AUTOMTIC DATA PROC EQUIP	W 18862	1821817	W 23177	2160765	W 27404	2576976	W 28213	2627009	MACH TRAIT INFORMATION
7522	DIGITAL COMPUTERS	W 546	127808	W 618	166047	W 763	207581	W 1032	290992	MACH DIGITALES COMPLETES
7523	DIGITL CENTRL PROCESSORS	W 5456	818564	W 6562	975955	W 7754	1127653	W 7666	1094249	UNITES CENTRALES
7524	DIGITL CENTRL STOR UNITS	W 1349	276374	W 1487	304311	W 1573	385678	W 1753	406806	UNITES MEMOIRE CENTRALES
7525	ADP PERIPHERAL UNITS	W 11004	496749	W 13840	590586	W 16500	722946	W 17110	688096	UNITES PERIPHERIQUES
759	OFFICE,ADP MCH PTS,ACCES	W 6428	752249	W 7653	936411	W 8759	1105276	W 9770	1031923	PIECES DU 751 ET 752
7599	ACCTG,ETC,ADP MCH PTS,AC	W 4701	660940	W 5649	831900	W 6441	956383	W 7430	918968	PIECES DU 751 ET 752
76	TELECOMM,SOUND EQUIPMENT		1262716		1510727		1824639		1896058	EQUIPMENT DE TELECOM
761	TELEVISION RECEIVERS	W 11796	201000	W 13393	236987	W 13438	273279	W 13298	266769	RECEPTEURS DE TELEVISION
7611	COLOUR TV RECEIVERS	W 11726	198359	W 13327	233675	W 13380	270266	W 13222	263867	RECEPTEURS COULEUR
764	TELECOM EQPT,PTS,ACC NES	W 9865	747715	W 10917	917423	W 11740	1181434	W 12525	1260909	EQUIP TELECOM,PIECES
7641	LINE TELEPHONE,ETC EQUIP	W 1471	182467	W 1932	239051	W 2854	417554	W 3509	525108	APP TELEPHON PAR FIL
7649	PTS NES OF EQUIPMT OF 76	W 3533	251152	W 3550	316723	W 3478	331737	W 3556	340767	PIECES DE LA DIV 76
77	ELECTRIC MACHNRY NES ETC		2976663		3496672		4332247		4091150	MACH APP ELECT NDA
771	ELECTRIC POWER MACHY NES	W 11925	239728	W 12875	267920	W 15727	370047	W 16710	382618	MACH PROD,TRANS ELECTR
7712	OTH ELEC POWER MACHY NES	W 7366	176423	W 8577	206579	W 10254	277229	W 10878	286690	AUT APP PROD TRANSF ELEC
772	SWITCHGEAR ETC,PARTS NES	W 17450	790723	W 19784	908153	W 22364	1144837	W 22587	1102047	APP COUPURE,SECT ETC
7721	SWITCHGEAR ETC	W 16659	703610	W 18798	808866	W 21247	1020827	W 21492	985779	APP COUPURE,SECTIONMNT
773	ELECTR DISTRIBUTNG EQUIP	W 23537	173327	W 26955	198893	W 30862	261375	W 30882	255726	EQUIPMT DISTRIBUTION ELECT
775	HOUSEHOLD TYPE EQUIP NES	W 53040	516000	W 57415	582169	W 57658	656026	W 57952	625396	MACH,APP USAGE DOMESTQUE
7758	ELECTRO–THERMIC APPL NES	W 20778	240751	W 22001	263901	W 21718	294057	W 21518	277355	APP ELECTROTHERMIQ NDA
776	TRANSISTORS,VALVES,ETC	W 1095	425459	W 1260	592507	W 1504	771381	W 1449	708491	LAMPES,TUBES,VALVES
7764	ELECTRONIC MICROCIRCUITS	W 418	302173	W 488	429441	W 599	571810	W 615	533301	MICROSTRUCTURES ELECTRON
778	ELECTRICAL MACHINERY NES	W 34366	697669	W 37061	780541	W 38834	929862	W 38559	824452	AUTRES MACH ELECT NDA
7788	OTH ELEC MACHY,EQUIP NES	W 8665	308915	W 7983	336185	W 8500	422893	W 7646	360433	AUT MACH APP ELEC NDA
78	ROAD VEHICLES		4790965		5846759		6867442		6630597	VEHICULES ROUTIERS
781	PASS MOTOR VEH EXC BUSES	W 291238	3446814	W 332577	4276247	W 331511	4974681	W 345297	4923715	AUTO TRANSPORT PERSONNES
782	LORRIES,SPCL MTR VEH NES	W 30945	336112	W 42122	491934	W 50060	594771	W 45243	517932	VEHICULES SPECIAUX,MARCH
7821	LORRIES,TRUCKS	W 28923	312447	W 39721	458656	W 47314	557500	W 42686	477121	VEHICULES TRANSP MARCHAND
784	MOTOR VEH PRTS,ACCES NES	W 42410	455342	W 43268	461037	W 44785	547137	W 44966	515529	PIECES 722,781,782,783
7849	OTHER MOTOR VEHCL PARTS	W 36931	426654	W 37437	436617	W 38368	516534	W 37820	485233	PIECES 722,781,782,783
785	CYCLES,ETC MOTRZD OR NOT	W 16296	317074	W 15504	328479	W 15031	351640	W 14782	348135	MOTOCYCLES SCOOTERS
79	OTHR TRANSPORT EQUIPMENT		798594		782763		1976485		2419246	AUTRE MATERIEL TRANSPORT
791	RAILWAY VEHICLES	W 21720	142372	W 19841	101687	W 18410	215985	W 28276	335190	VEHIC MAT CHEMINS DE FER
792	AIRCRAFT ETC	W 1309	594996	W 1575	614286	W 2388	1694633	W 2728	2017992	APP NAVIGATION AERIENNE
7923	AIRCRFT NES2000–15000KG	W 111	90443	W 263	162198	W 322	234947	W 321	348944	AERODYNES 2000 A 15000 KG
7924	AIRCRFT NES OVER 15000KG	W 216	201768	W 167	134735	W 772	895680	W 828	891893	AERODYNES PLUS 15000 KG
7929	AIRCRAFT PARTS NES	W 795	251286	W 1027	275526	W 994	456712	W 1313	714663	PIECES DU 792
8	MISC MANUFACTURED GOODS		13726692		14873232		16688694		16733732	ART MANUFACTURES DIVERS
812	*PLUMBG,HEATNG,LGHTNG EQ	W 28472	290147	W 33855	339966	W 35920	410082	W 36294	408120	APPAR SANITAIRES CHAUFFAGE
8124	LIGHTING EQUIPMENT NES	W 12981	203328	W 14737	233671	W 16335	280670	W 16386	282874	APPAREILS ECLAIRAGE ETC

4. Special Imports C.I.F. by Commodities according to the S.I.T.C. (Rev. 2) in thousand U.S. Dollars
Importations Spéciales C.A.F. par Produits d'après la C.T.C.I. (Rév. 2) en milliers de Dollars E.U.

SITC CTCI	COMMODITY	1993			1994			1995			1996			PRODUIT
		WEIGHT POIDS		VALUE VALEUR	WEIGHT POIDS		VALUE VALEUR	WEIGHT POIDS		VALUE VALEUR	WEIGHT POIDS		VALUE VALEUR	
821	*FURNITURE,PARTS THEREOF	W	261355	1385529	W	289746	1575519	W	308006	1875665	W	305980	1825640	MEUBLES ET PIECES
8211	CHAIRS,SEATS AND PARTS	W	51668	416452	W	53565	451980	W	59268	537545	W	56722	520906	SIEGES ET PIECES
82111	CHAIRS AND OTHER SEATS	W	47033	387083	W	48845	422340	W	54470	501191	W	52103	486736	SIEGES
8219	FURNITURE AND PARTS NES	W	198717	814598	W	224376	950191	W	236592	1147219	W	236577	1111940	AUTRES MEUBLES ET PIECES
82192	WOOD FURNITURE NES	W	133059	556414	W	152881	655199	W	159852	781451	W	155003	747774	MEUBLES NDA EN BOIS
831	*TRAVEL GOODS,HANDBAGS	W	11748	255605	W	12899	294892	W	13696	332099	W	12963	300709	ARTICLES DE VOYAGE ETC
84	CLOTHING AND ACCESSORIES			3327419			3470547			3823221			3733179	VETEMENTS
842	MENS OUTERWEAR NOT KNIT	W	16342	585946	W	16533	637779	W	15524	668305	W	16249	693845	VET DESSUS POUR HOMMES
8423	— TROUSERS,BREECHES ETC	W	10083	265330	W	9699	268959	W	9111	286216	W	9632	308934	PANTALONS HOMMES MAT TEX
843	WOMENS OUTERWEAR NONKNIT	W	15253	1007082	W	15521	1060060	W	15892	1203739	W	16127	1117350	VET DESSUS FEMMES MAT TEX
8431	— COATS AND JACKETS	W	2562	220189	W	2473	229148	W	2581	263106	W	2484	241012	MANT,VEST FEM MAT TEXTIL
8435	— BLOUSES	W	2650	198051	W	2789	213549	W	2589	223209	W	2532	191618	BLOUSES FEM MAT TEXTILES
8439	— OTHER OUTER GARMENTS	W	7228	361337	W	7600	396591	W	7466	425438	W	8019	423409	AUT VET DES FEM MAT TEXT
845	OUTERWEAR KNIT NONELASTC	W	25431	957278	W	23938	940481	W	23158	1027983	W	24209	1021751	VET DESSOUS,ACCES BONNET
8451	— JERSEYS,PULLOVERS ETC	W	16642	583257	W	15928	586396	W	15026	622225	W	16110	638046	CHANDAILS,PULL–OVERS ETC
8459	— OTHER,CLTHG ACCESRYS	W	7539	306640	W	6881	287997	W	6842	320737	W	6990	308396	AUT VET DESSUS DE BONNE
846	UNDER GARMENTS KNITTED	W	7085	287924	W	7028	300188	W	7857	356332	W	8025	354819	SOUS VETS DE BONNETERIE
848	HEADGEAR,NONTXTL CLOTHNG	W	5975	204837	W	6732	222976	W	6617	224456	W	6630	218391	VET ACCES MAT AUT QUE TEX
851	*FOOTWEAR	W	25450	638042	W	26182	669107	W	26575	742320	W	26273	721721	CHAUSSURES
85102	FOOTWEAR LEATHER	W	20005	564460	W	20579	591064	W	20522	647885	W	20060	629970	CHAUS SEMELLES EN CUIR
87	PRECISION INSTRUMNTS NES			1148481			1211133			1451607			1514053	INSTRUM,APPAR SCIENT NDA
872	MEDICAL INSTRUMENTS NES	W	3553	216297	W	3948	249239	W	4086	293901	W	4303	314598	INSTR,APP MEDIC–CHIR NDA
87202	OTH MEDICAL INSTRUMENTS	W	2637	183426	W	2988	215409	W	3024	250133	W	3142	267228	INSTRUM,APP MEDECINE
874	MEASURNG,CONTROLNG INSTR	W	7322	763992	W	8076	810393	W	8895	983231	W	8638	983387	INSTRUMENTS DE MESURE
8748	ELEC MEAS,CONTRL EQU NES	W	885	186150	W	935	203527	W	1091	233263	W	1019	224222	APP ELEC ELECTRO MESURE
88	PHOTO EQU,OPTICL GDS ETC			1056600			1139179			1272123			1228400	APP,FOURN PHOTO,OP,MONTR
882	PHOTO,CINEMA SUPPLIES	W	16145	257576	W	15877	258906	W	15132	285627	W	14973	267105	PRODUITS PHOTO,CINEMA
8822	PHOTO FILM EXC DEV CINMA	W	8981	212944	W	9262	216326	W	8615	230771	W	8703	219715	PLAQUES,PELLICULES,FILMS
885	WATCHES AND CLOCKS			517550			577930			630891			607827	HORLOGERIE
8851	WATCHES,MOVEMENTS,CASES			301857			342024			360359			375895	MONTRES,MOUVEMENTS,BOITES
8852	CLOCKS,CLOCK,WATCH PARTS			215693			235906			270532			231931	HORLOGES,MOUV,PARTIES
89	MISC MANUFCTRD GOODS NES			5624870			6172889			6781577			7001909	ART MANUFACTURES DIVERS
892	PRINTED MATTER	W	133453	1013525	W	139980	1144346	W	151039	1361364	W	158103	1354265	IMPRIMES
8921	PRINTED BOOKS,GLOBES,ETC	W	37010	399687	W	35849	449718	W	34284	508566	W	34621	496814	LIVRES,BROCHURES,CARTES
89211	PRINTED BOOKS,PAMPHLETS	W	36039	391119	W	34948	441349	W	33386	498801	W	33654	487232	LIVRES,BROCHURES
8922	NEWSPAPERS,PERIODICALS	W	45640	264906	W	48979	303761	W	52982	377337	W	49763	349272	JOURNAUX ET PERIODIQUES
8928	PRINTED MATTER NES	W	49643	325555	W	54000	365551	W	62488	447375	W	72591	480684	IMPRIMES NDA
89286	TRADE ADV MATRL,CATALOGS	W	41642	216648	W	44641	240418	W	53285	311293	W	62990	331821	IMPRIMES PUBLICITAIRES
893	ARTICLES OF PLASTIC NES			919171			1078520			1260943			1175954	OUVRAGES EN MAT DIVIS 58
8931	PLSTC PACKG CONTNRS,LIDS	W	64322	262323	W	76953	313377	W	74509	351050	W	65607	297852	ART TRANSP EMBALLAGE ETC
8939	MISC PLASTIC ARTICLES	W	97220	627590	W	110040	731272	W	113115	863264	W	112952	831412	ART DIVERS EN MAT DIV 58
89399	OTHR PLASTC ARTICLES NES	W	86494	579226	W	99127	679143	W	101770	802367	W	101420	771000	AUT OUV MAT DIV 58
894	TOYS,SPORTING GOODS,ETC	W	36894	548582	W	38666	558818	W	41278	667818	W	41093	648266	VOITURES ENFANTS,JOUETS
8942	TOYS,INDOOR GAMES ETC	W	25169	346549	W	26218	356270	W	27123	418373	W	26294	379441	JOUETS,JEUX ETC
896	WORKS OF ART ETC			447892			589029			430398			695021	OBJETS D'ART
89601	HAND PAINTINGS ETC NES			222571			342652			270203			508600	TABLEAUX,PEINTURES
897	GOLD,SILVER WARE,JEWELRY			1570012			1598122			1680955			1694189	BIJOUTERIE,ORFEVRERIE
8973	PREC JEWLRY,GLD–SILVWARE			1504742			1522517			1588575			1616453	BIJOUX OR,ARGENT ORFEVRE
89731	PRECIOUS METAL JEWELLERY			1357607			1371096			1412638			1479885	ART BIJOUTERIE,JOAILLER
898	MUSICAL INSTRUMENTS,PTS	W	16436	658968	W	16224	721374	W	16022	825701	W	15708	873111	INSTRUMENTS DE MUSIQUE
8983	SOUND RECRDNG TAPE,DISCS	W	14048	575019	W	13742	633058	W	13684	731318	W	13535	786066	SUPPORTS SON POUR 763
89832	RECORDED DISCS,TAPES ETC	W	8516	480191	W	8577	543995	W	9710	653400	W	10039	708444	DISQUES,PHONO,BANDES
899	OTHER MANUFACTURED GOODS			352051			357329			406233			421689	AUT ART MANUF DIVERS NDA
9	GOODS NOT CLASSD BY KIND			342349			374303			334840			162198	ART TRANSACT NON CLASSES
971	*GOLD,NON MONETARY NES	K	55502	178072	K	60499	221435	K	69391	198678	K	113737	72520	OR NON MONETAIRE

5. Special Exports F.O.B. by Commodities according to the S.I.T.C. (Rev. 2) in thousand U.S. Dollars
Exportations Spéciales F.O.B. par Produits d'après la C.T.C.I. (Rév. 2) en milliers de Dollars E.U.

SITC CTCI	COMMODITY	1993		1994		1995		1996		PRODUIT
		WEIGHT POIDS	VALUE VALEUR	WEIGHT POIDS	VALUE VALEUR	WEIGHT POIDS	VALUE VALEUR	WEIGHT POIDS	VALUE VALEUR	
	ALL COMMODITIES		63184619		70360083		81641172		80842780	TOUS PRODUITS
0	FOOD AND LIVE ANIMALS		1465934		1618209		1864484		1799531	ALIMENTS,ANIMAUX VIVANTS
02	DAIRY PRODCTS,BIRDS'EGGS		408692		409869		487941		428044	PRODUITS LAITIERS,OEUFS
024	CHEESE AND CURD	W 60477	387845	W 59276	401617	W 63965	460567	W 57065	403791	FROMAGE ET CAILLEBOTTE
07	COFFEE,TEA,COCOA,SPICES		297144		363855		429854		425396	CAFE,THE,CACAO,EPICES
073	CHOCOLATE AND PRODUCTS	W 52053	231524	W 58576	273136	W 61399	322404	W 63197	322080	CHOCOLAT
09	MISC EDIBLE PRODUCTS		317950		363532		387419		400694	PREP ALIMENTAIRES DIVERSES
098	EDIBLE PRODCTS,PREPS NES	W 75570	316881	W 78532	362590	W 74403	386194	W 75669	399320	PREP ALIMENTAIRES NDA
09809	MISC FOOD PREPRTIONS NES	W 31125	195361	W 35339	239270	W 33113	253625	W 32744	272569	PREP ALIMENTAIRES NDA
1	BEVERAGES AND TOBACCO		388113		513890		545023		541453	BOISSONS ET TABACS
12	TOBACCO AND MANUFACTURES		299299		396860		431580		426175	TABACS BRUTS FABRIQUES
122	TOBACCO,MANUFACTURED	W 19054	257792	W 24730	353411	W 27359	377146	W 30200	379414	TABACS FABRIQUES
1222	CIGARETTES	W 17983	245939	W 23033	335145	W 24822	356706	W 26011	350383	CIGARETTES
2	CRUDE MATERLS,EXCL FUELS		654440		791448		983013		824105	MAT BRUTES NON COMESTIBLES
28	METALLIFEROUS ORES,SCRAP		147516		191842		278929		243511	MINERAIS METAL,DECHETS
5	CHEMCLS,RELATED PROD NES		15484608		17646655		20837160		21597957	PRODUITS CHIMIQUES
51	ORGANIC CHEMICALS		3995388		4648768		5587855		5844766	PROD CHIMIQ ORGANIQUES
513	CARBOXYLIC ACIDS ETC	W 35951	310684	W 43142	376755	W 44613	399695	W 49755	427149	ACIDES CARBOXYLIQUES
5139	OXY-FNCT ACIDS,DERIVATVS	W 21210	185614	W 29005	234911	W 30100	293713	W 32784	327112	ACIDES CARBOXYLIQUES
514	NITROGEN-FNCTN COMPOUNDS	W 84681	2055843	W 77078	2370842	W 81867	2925603	W 82712	3018187	COMPOSES FONCT AZOTEES
5145	AMINE-FUNCTION COMPOUNDS	W 7392	145317	W 7220	162636	W 8703	255459	W 6715	304862	COMPOSES FONCTION AMINE
5146	OXYGEN-FNCT AMINO-CMPNDS	W 6643	417682	W 7904	465021	W 7174	507043	W 8026	484936	COMP AMINES FONCT OXYGEN
5147	AMIDE-FNCT CMPD,EXC UREA	W 47227	383184	W 36922	472138	W 44643	516104	W 48695	521408	COMPOSES CARBOXYAMIDE
5148	OTH NITROGN-FNCTN CMPNDS	W 23418	1109661	W 25032	1271047	W 21347	1646997	W 19276	1706982	AUTRES COMPOSES AZOTES
51482	IMIDE-,IMIDE-FNCT CMPNDS	W 13795	962270	W 14657	1110634	W 14963	1484572	W 13183	1532336	COMPOSES A FONCTION IMIDE
515	ORG-INORG COMPOUNDS ETC	W 24055	1228105	W 26150	1424055	W 25724	1699779	W 27795	1840957	COMPOSES ORGANO-MINERAUX
5156	HETEROCYCLIC CMPDS ETC	W 14255	1023406	W 13999	1194229	W 13582	1452640	W 14929	1534356	COMPOSES HETEROCYCLIQUES
51569	OTH HETEROCYC CMPDS,ETC	W 14037	970402	W 13736	1131079	W 13242	1353318	W 14577	1413231	AUT COMP HETEROCYCLIQUES
516	OTHER ORGANIC CHEMICALS	W 26293	268578	W 28840	311333	W 29112	366942	W 30315	355285	AUTRES PROD ORGANIQUES
52	INORGANIC CHEMICALS		192567		223497		251670		246618	PROD CHIM INORGANIQUES
53	DYES,TANNING,COLOUR PROD		2007422		2191716		2415905		2234332	PROD TEINTURE,COLORANTS
531	SYNT DYE,NAT INDGO,LAKES	W 64746	1567764	W 63160	1670453	W 60743	1823272	W 68144	1650175	MAT COLOR ORGAN,LAQUES
5311	SYNTHIC ORGNIC DYESTUFFS	W 56319	1434968	W 54422	1528730	W 52463	1676078	W 58488	1518036	MAT COLOR ORGAN SYNTHET
533	PIGMENTS,PAINTS,ETC	W 65824	434792	W 72098	517393	W 78175	587356	W 87502	580215	PIGMENTS,PEINTURES,VERNIS
541	*MEDICINAL,PHARM PRODUCT	MK 71764	5661952		6324945	MK 79981	7589834	MK 79423	8411217	PROD MEDICINAUX PHARMACEUT
5411	PROVITAMINS AND VITAMINS	MK 31740	615534	MK 32510	688913	MK 31923	785964	MK 31293	711887	PROVITAMINES,VITAMINES
5413	ANTIBIOTICS IN BULK	K 444360	270225	K 433550	266986	K 323563	291386	K 300407	300499	ANTIBIOTIQUES NDA
54139	OTHER ANTIBIOTICS	K 354452	264476	K 368081	262050	K 278299	287140	K 243556	292684	AUTRES ANTIBIOTIQUES
5416	GLYCOSIDES,GLANDS,SERA	K 1647631	394032	K 1829399	535681	K 1818036	889859	K 1984818	920089	HETEROSIDES
54164	ANTISERA,MICROB VACCINES	K 827482	300131	K 932904	438733	K 1065306	794305	K 1199269	812811	SERUMS,VACCINS
5417	MEDICAMENTS	MK 34354	3607640	MK 37061	4067360	MK 42455	4713982	MK 42247	5483280	MEDICAMENTS
54171	— CONTAINING ANTIBIOTICS	K 3068018	421977	K 3390455	444625	K 3220461	525735	K 2549173	512422	MED CONTN ANTIBIOTIQUES
54172	— CONTAINING HORMONES	K 617677	345596	K 630176	347346	K 746606	506376	K 745773	664407	MED CONTENANT HORMONES
54179	— CONTNG OTH SUBSTANCES	MK 30210	2715379	MK 32381	3139264	MK 37830	3531575	MK 38335	4144794	MED CONT AUT SUBSTANCES
5419	PHARMACEUTICAL GOODS NES	K 3374595	467144	K 3013516	457429	K 3146978	570237	K 3267194	582637	PREP,ART PHARMACEUTIQUES
54191	BANDAGES PREPARED ETC	K 2936178	387393	K 2556768	359479	K 2689808	436898	K 2868817	461876	OUATES,GAZES,BANDES
55	PERFUME,CLEANING ETC PRD		1203510		1412542		1597608		1493630	PROD POUR PARFUM,TOILETTE
551	ESSENTL OILS,PERFUME,ETC	W 22312	512393	W 24559	623984	W 24224	707859	W 24305	674691	HUILES ESSENTIELLES
5514	MIXED PERFUME SUBSTANCES	W 21526	491026	W 23684	597558	W 23280	676768	W 23426	642830	MELANGES SUBSTAN ODORIFER
553	PERFUMERY,COSMETICS,ETC	W 38049	517732	W 43299	607615	W 28922	685761	W 26449	618615	PRODUITS DE PARFUMERIE
58	PLASTIC MATERIALS ETC		1253772		1450484		1736739		1605877	MAT PLAST ARTIFICIELLES
582	PROD OF CONDENSATION ETC	W 139928	571393	W 163085	677121	W 180177	828426	W 197710	875685	PROD CONDENS,POLYCOND
5826	EPOXIDE RESINS	W 44177	153423	W 55264	189810	W 59105	221839	W 70153	278564	RESINES EPOXYDES
58261	— IN PRIMARY FORMS	W 44177	153423	W 55264	189810	W 59105	221839	W 70153	278564	EPOXYDES PRIMAIRES
583	POLYMERIZATION ETC PRODS	W 250952	668071	W 282735	757068	W 278180	887081	W 223435	708221	PROD POLYMERISATION
5839	OTH POLYMRZTION ETC PROD	W 99918	375532	W 107269	409998	W 105114	465323	W 73931	345290	AUT PROD POLYMER COPOLYM
59	CHEMICAL MATERIALS NES		1154909		1375070		1626234		1729198	MAT PROD CHIMIQUES NDA
591	PESTICIDES,DISINFECTANTS	W 46242	496854	W 45737	555376	W 48080	723428	W 48222	764575	DESINF,INSECT,FONG,HERB
5912	FUNGICIDES,FOR RETAIL	W 10059	186672	W 11195	228767	W 10796	256335	W 13022	297882	FONGICIDES VENTE AU DET
5913	HERBICIDES,FOR RETAIL	W 20393	173838	W 19748	177065	W 19059	261358	W 18295	269479	HERBICIDES VENTE AU DET
598	MISCEL CHEM PRODUCTS NES	W 210832	576514	W 226297	710318	W 197865	768855	W 233215	804923	PROD DIV INDUST CHIM NDA
5989	CHEM PRODUCTS,PREPS NES	W 101531	525818	W 109321	651144	W 104387	698827	W 107085	737099	PROD PREP CHIMIQUES NDA
59899	OTH CHEM PRODS,PREPS,NES	W 67254	428388	W 73199	536133	W 66298	568272	W 61729	600817	AUT PRODUITS CHIMIQUES NDA
6	BASIC MANUFACTURES		10919594		11719422		12885405		12328278	ART MANUFACTURES
63	WOOD,CORK MANUFACTRS NES		240787		251271		302123		287772	OUVRAGES LIEGE ET BOIS
64	PAPER,PAPERBOARD AND MFR		912542		1099360		1465551		1433916	PAPIERS,CARTONS & OUVRAGES
641	PAPER AND PAPERBOARD	W 745063	682955	W 847857	828758	W 861390	1116372	W 948661	1091858	PAPIERS ET CARTONS
6412	PRINTG,WRITING PAPER NES	W 132390	123913	W 196115	210485	W 203483	311398	W 217148	245648	PAPIERS POUR L'IMPRESSION
64122	— COATED,IMPREGNATD ETC	W 119861	107906	W 180913	190800	W 187128	274875	W 200169	220284	PAPIERS IMPRESSION COUCHES
6415	PAPER,PAPERBRD,BULK,NES	W 283225	167047	W 313494	211238	W 329867	310387	W 361713	274244	PAPIERS,CARTONS ROULEAUX
64159	OTHER PAPER ETC,BULK,NES	W 274969	145430	W 304432	186159	W 321523	282648	W 354487	241042	AUT PAPIER ROULEAUX FEUILLES
6418	COATED ETC PAPER NES BLK	W 155265	226860	W 158108	233572	W 141172	268613	W 166870	338529	PAP,CARTONS COUCHES,ENDUITS
642	PAPER,ETC,PRECUT,ARTS OF	W 86688	229587	W 102783	270602	W 116946	349179	W 122359	342058	PAP,CARTONS DECOUPES
65	TEXTILE YARN,FABRICS,ETC		1966165		2116252		2266776		2010502	FILS,TISSUS,ARTICLES TEXTILE
651	TEXTILE YARN	W 119723	620630	W 122871	658892	W 117173	710435	W 110892	600324	FILS TEXTILES
6514	SYN FIB YRN,BULK,MONOFIL	W 72543	296916	W 81004	332770	W 82787	384240	W 77248	316647	FILS CONT 85% FIB TEXT SYNTH
65142	— NONTXT ETC CONT PAMID	W 60500	215804	W 69729	252483	W 73317	304197	W 69555	253651	FILS NON TEX FI CON POLYAMID
652	COTTON FABRICS,WOVEN	W 18682	295779	W 19967	317412	W 17417	325200	W 10982	262534	TISSUS DE COTON
6522	WOVEN COTTON BLEACHD,ETC	W 14851	248527	W 15770	264533	W 13448	271326	W 8342	224373	TISSUS COTON BLANCHIS ETC
65224	BLCHED COTTON FABRIC NES	W 13423	196620	W 14593	221632	W 12437	233828	W 7459	195223	AUT TIS PLUS 85% COT BLANCHI
653	WOVN MAN-MADE FIB FABRIC	W 7093	201807	W 7695	218236	W 6566	229443	W 6542	202134	TISSUS FIBRES SYNTH,ARTIF
657	SPECIAL TXTL FABRC,PRODS	W 13331	271074	W 14136	303463	W 12684	351832	W 13660	331075	TISSUS SPECIAUX
66	NONMETAL MINERAL MFS NES		3328319		3004896		2664402		2734973	ART MIN NON METALLIQUES
663	MINERAL MANUFCTURES NES	W 45325	180740	W 51622	210906	W 50553	257752	W 57544	260479	ART MIN MANUF NDA
665	GLASSWARE	W 33253	160639	W 25970	202143	W 30811	256042	W 42578	251814	OUVRAGES EN VERRE
667	PEARL,PREC-,SEMI-P STONE		2812634		2404839		1927077		2022230	PERLES, PIERRES GEMMES
6672	DIAMONDS NONINDUST,UNSET		2265667		1956034		1617271		1691692	DIAMANTS BRUTS
66722	— SRTD,ROUGH,SIMPLY WKD		1547129		1353364		1091446		1080578	DIAMANTS TRIES BRUTS
66729	— CUT ETC NOT SET		718405		601860		525715		610523	DIAMANTS TAILLES
6673	PREC-,SEMI-PR STONES NES		492575		393082		236585		225627	AUTRES PIERRES NON SERTIES
67	IRON AND STEEL		865971		926210		1095579		892792	FER ET ACIER
673	IRON,STEEL SHAPES ETC	W 683107	277211	W 549343	268387	W 386949	288909	W 332829	218763	BARRES,PROFIL FER,ACIER
678	IRON,STL TUBES,PIPES,ETC	W 218953	375753	W 253475	426016	W 256084	518231	W 232651	432827	TUBES,TUYAUX EN FONTE,FER
6783	IRON,STL TUBES,PIPES NES	W 195177	218103	W 226499	263586	W 235216	345006	W 216889	294321	AUT TUBES,TUYAUX FER,ACIER
68	NON-FERROUS METALS		1110283		1502706		1677193		1657972	METAUX NON FERREUX
681	SILVER,PLATINUM,ETC		430003		688752		639444		680752	ARGENT ET PLATINE
6812	METALS OF PLATINUM GROUP		403158		636553		599665		639071	PLATINE
68123	PLATINUM,ALLOYS UNWRGHT		163426		331738		351556		405536	PLATINE,ALLIAGES BRUTS
684	ALUMINIUM	W 120588	515169	W 143958	608537	W 145926	781709	W 147144	738845	ALUMINIUM
6842	ALUMINIUM,ALLOYS WORKED	W 114917	504583	W 136359	592981	W 138465	760830	W 138671	720352	ALUMINIUM,ALLIAGES OUVRE
68422	ALUMNM PLATE,SHEET,STRIP	W 44333	137502	W 57814	191226	W 61371	266400	W 61088	244199	TOLES, PLANCHES EN ALU

5. Special Exports F.O.B. by Commodities according to the S.I.T.C. (Rev. 2) in thousand U.S. Dollars
Exportations Spéciales F.O.B. par Produits d'après la C.T.C.I. (Rév. 2) en milliers de Dollars E.U.

SITC CTCI	COMMODITY	1993 WEIGHT POIDS	1993 VALUE VALEUR	1994 WEIGHT POIDS	1994 VALUE VALEUR	1995 WEIGHT POIDS	1995 VALUE VALEUR	1996 WEIGHT POIDS	1996 VALUE VALEUR	PRODUIT
68423	ALUMINIUM FOIL	W 42335	249127	W 43867	260176	W 45524	315897	W 44970	293895	FEUILLES,BANDES MINCES AL
69	METAL MANUFACTURES NES		2267078		2559280		3121176		3046074	ART MANUFACT EN METAL NDA
691	STRUCTURES AND PARTS NES	W 69899	225722	W 67683	213257	W 75462	255291	W 71016	246758	CONSTRUCT FER,ACIER,ALU
694	STL,COPPR NAILS,NUTS,ETC	W 33501	410637	W 38326	495410	W 40823	617972	W 40821	591201	CLOUS,VIS,ECROUS
69402	IRN,STL NUTS,BOLTS,ETC	W 28073	305577	W 32558	372789	W 35643	476850	W 35540	455229	BOULONS,VIS,ECROUS FER,AC
695	TOOLS	W 13493	595248	W 14590	696694	W 16533	891175	W 17129	889196	OUTILS A MAIN
6953	OTHER HAND TOOLS	W 8079	247268	W 8673	286769	W 9863	361325	W 9962	360710	AUTRES OUTILS A MAIN
6954	BLADES,TIPS,ETC FR TOOLS	W 5181	335585	W 5688	396535	W 6424	513698	W 6883	512256	OUTILS POUR MACHINE–OUTIL
69541	PARTS TO INSERT IN TOOLS	W 4609	275981	W 4999	323337	W 5642	418144	W 5981	415498	OUTILS DE FORAGE
697	BASE MTL HOUSEHOLD EQUIP	W 14580	225115	W 15199	229096	W 13490	236328	W 13540	233439	ART MENAGE MET COMMUNS
699	BASE METAL MFRS NES	W 58662	581324	W 65925	664692		809155		770946	ART MANUFACTURES MET NDA
7	MACHINES,TRANSPORT EQUIP		18334902		20801112		25624408		25636305	MACHINES MATERIEL TRANSPORT
71	POWER GENERATING EQUIPMT		1338928		1430434		1741209		1887569	MACHINES GENERATRICES
714	ENGINES AND MOTORS NES	W 6852	366073	W 7302	426497	W 4749	534584	W 7474	652036	MOTEURS NON ELECTRIQUES
7149	ENGINE & MOTOR PARTS NES	W 6804	351379	W 7261	410994	W 4724	523266	W 7438	634830	PIECES 714 ET 718.88
71499	PARTS NES,OF 71488,71888	W 6771	337310	W 7187	386866	W 4660	495348	W 7381	610281	PIECES 714.88 ET 718.88
716	ROTATING ELECTRIC PLANT	W 22596	524326	W 26139	598710	W 27774	768396	W 28629	778469	APP ELECTR ROTATIFS,PIECES
7162	AC MTRS,GENRTRS,GEN SETS	W 5558	221342	W 6454	271245	W 8002	354681	W 8178	348734	MOTEURS ELECTRIQUES
71621	AC MTRS,INC UNIVRSL MTRS	W 5101	202663	W 5824	251876	W 7198	326652	W 7516	340687	MOT ELEC NON COUR CONTINU
72	MACHS FOR SPCL INDUSTRYS		4929676		5601106		6924944		6510761	MAC SPECIALES POUR INDUST
724	TEXTILE,LEATHER MACHNRY	W 63816	1704349	W 63984	1809532	W 78638	2285555	W 70512	2008506	MACH POUR INDUSTRIE TEXTILE
7244	SPINNING,EXTRDNG,ETC MCH	W 24836	550477	W 20294	494482	W 30409	715087	W 28237	663827	MACH POUR LE FILAGE
72442	FIBRE PROCESSNG MACH NES	W 13168	205949	W 9463	147272	W 14001	250865	W 11676	200475	MACH PREP MAT TEXTILES
72449	PTS NES OF MACHS OF 7244	W 3748	179698	W 3794	197147	W 5422	238382	W 6232	245047	PIECES DES MACH DU 724.4
7245	WEAVING,FELT MFG,ETC MCH	W 21455	460829	W 25627	579595	W 29528	738671	W 24416	579141	METIERS A TISSER,PIECES
72451	WEAVING MACHINES (LOOMS)	W 16902	354157	W 20661	455719	W 22098	568447	W 16266	397044	METIERS A TISSER
7246	AUXIL TXTL MCH,PARTS NES	W 7296	396073	W 7788	420124	W 9095	499022	W 7546	447258	MACH PR 724.51,52,53,61
72469	LOOM,KNT MCH ETC PTS NES	W 5833	322055	W 6066	344976	W 6965	396481	W 5626	354556	PIECES 724.51,52,53,61
725	PAPER ETC MILL MACHINERY	W 14356	393727	W 16525	465901	W 18525	627806	W 16998	550490	MACHINES FABR PATE PAPIER
7252	PAPER ETC PRODCT MFG MCH	W 9449	271359	W 10446	308407	W 12254	415786	W 11651	365807	AUT MACH TRAVAIL PAP,CAR
726	PRINTG,BKBINDG MACHY,PTS	W 28882	874521	W 30797	1025710	W 33884	1177490	W 31437	1048210	MACHINES POUR IMPRIMERIE
7264	PRINTING PRESSES	W 7294	210881	W 9722	348570	W 8475	283397	W 8693	271648	MACHINES A IMPRIMER
72641	ROTARY PRINTING PRESSES	W 7294	210881	W 9722	348570	W 8475	283397	W 8693	271648	MACH IMPRIMER ROTATIVES
7267	OTH PRINTG & ANCILL MACH	W 8084	337586	W 6040	302311	W 7246	394530	W 5623	287282	AUT MACH IMPRIMERIE,PIEC
72672	MACH ANCILLARY TO PRINTG	W 5.'75	262105	W 4211	230062	W 4777	275857	W 4127	220951	APP AUXIL D'IMPRIMERIE
727	FOOD MACHRY NON–DOMESTIC	W 12581	331197	W 12286	354183	W 12116	416516	W 15205	440188	MACH INDUSTRIES ALIMENT
7272	OTH FOOD PROC MCHY,PARTS	W 6280	189256	W 6153	194572	W 6849	259987	W 8014	261497	AUT MACH IND ALIMENTAIRE
72722	INDUS FOOD PROC MACH NES	W 6239	188023	W 6150	194383	W 6825	259448	W 7982	260749	MACHINES BOULANGERIE
728	OTH MACHY FOR SPCL INDUS	W 52356	1494571	W 55197	1814805	W 61075	2258424	W 61145	2307290	AUT MACH IND PARTICULIERES
7281	MACH–TOOLS FR SPCL INDUS	W 8278	182769	W 9877	225310	W 12216	284533	W 11849	268323	MACH–OUTILS SPEC IND PART
7284	MACHY FOR SPCL INDUS NES	W 31712	1212025	W 34222	1497680	W 38794	1871295	W 40812	1945035	MACH SPEC IND PARTICUL.
72842	RUBBER,PLASTICS WRKG MCH	W 9606	287294	W 10267	365831	W 10106	379613	W 9828	368890	MACH IND CAOUT MAT PLAST
72848	OTH MCHY WITH INDIV FNCT	W 15002	601422	W 15735	754514	W 17414	997069	W 19733	1054467	AUTRES MACHINES NDA
72849	PTS OF MACHS OF 7284 ETC	W 5615	253425	W 6678	306615	W 7306	380842	W 9270	422992	PIECES DU 728.4 ETC
73	METALWORKING MACHINERY		1839374		2239868		2898410		2760145	MACH TRAVAIL DES METAUX
736	METALWORKING MACH–TOOLS	W 43730	1486753	W 51661	1860733	W 55383	2325192	W 52144	2230614	MACH–OUTILS TRAVAIL METAUX
7361	METAL CUTTING MACH–TOOLS	W 21806	714920	W 24788	925277	W 27901	1181710	W 25688	1129054	MACH–OUT ENLEVEMENT METAL
73611	ULTRASNC ETC MTLWKG MCHS	W 5080	198626	W 6982	310178	W 7420	364716	W 6773	319380	MACH–OUT ELECTRO–EROSION
73619	OTH MTL CUTTNG MCH–TOOLS	W 5340	213266	W 6505	254018	W 6720	333455	W 7426	376042	MACH A AFFUTER ETC METAL
7362	METAL FORMING MACH–TOOLS	W 10257	222900	W 13199	271229	W 11852	317050	W 10752	279501	MACH–OUTILS DEFORM METAL
7367	OTH METALWRKG MACH–TOOLS	W 4195	186967	W 5114	219608	W 4623	229484	W 4592	241391	AUT MACH–OUT POUR METAUX
7369	PTS NES OF TOOLS OF 736	W 6247	282328	W 7040	338281	W 9268	443462	W 9363	420733	PIECES GROUPE 736
737	METALWORKING MACHNRY NES	W 10049	352622	W 9396	379135	W 12136	573217	W 10763	529531	MACH TRAV METAUX PIECES
7373	WELDING,BRAZING,ETC MCHS	W 3749	265510	W 4019	285407	W 4532	415079	W 4408	413238	MACH SOUDAGE ETC PIECES
73732	ELECTRIC WELDERS,ETC	W 3577	262002	W 3878	281674	W 4457	411231	W 4338	409967	MACH ELECT POUR SOUDER
74	GENRL INDUSTRL MACHY NES		3757148		4285576		5124537		5141032	MACH APP INDUSTRIE
741	HEATING,COOLING EQUIPMNT	W 24882	644081	W 26216	706927	W 27733	848920	W 27613	816257	MACH CHAUFFAGE,PIECES
7416	HEATING,COOLING EQU NES	W 12649	414890	W 15442	478389	W 17017	566994	W 17454	554785	APP CHANGEMENT TEMP
742	PUMPS FOR LIQUIDS ETC	W 8669	222543	W 10206	257660	W 12605	343648	W 11647	335537	POMPES MOTO–POMPES
743	PUMPS NES,CENTRFUGES ETC	W 20964	657803	W 21918	723895	W 24185	884010	W 26493	969244	POMPES COMPRES,VENT ETC
7431	PUMPS FOR GASES ETC	W 8765	267250	W 9038	285445	W 11351	361240	W 12317	399850	POMPES AIR A VIDE,COMPRES
7439	PTS NES OF APP OF 7435,6	W 5191	223785	W 5389	248065	W 5255	292635	W 6260	322739	PIECES 743.5 ET 743.6
744	MECHANICAL HANDLING EQU	W 33085	512828	W 38670	583813	W 39563	654944	W 42955	660160	EQUIP MANUTENTION PIECES
7442	LIFTING,LOADING MACH NES	W 14796	255830	W 17259	278817	W 16857	311971	W 21326	370881	APP LEVAGE,MANUTENTION
74428	OTH HANDLING ETC MCH NES	W 9033	210313	W 10079	234979	W 9780	249922	W 8023	238245	AUT APP LEVAGE ETC
7449	PTS NES OF MACHY OF 7442	W 16493	243163	W 18914	286887	W 20874	327106	W 18867	268198	PIECES DU 744.2
745	NONELEC MACHY,TOOLS NES	W 18249	769446	W 19690	925175	W 19520	1002604	W 19517	968150	AUT MACH NON ELEC,PIECES
7452	OTH NONELEC MCHS,PTS NES	W 17926	746045	W 19381	900569	W 19152	971935	W 19123	939763	AUT MACH NON ELEC,PIECES
74522	PACKAGNG,BOTTLNG,ETC MCH	W 5079	300901	W 5210	365064	W 5284	380349	W 5586	378102	MACH NETT BOUTEILLES,ETC
74527	SPRAYING MACHINERY	W 6266	203708	W 7566	244529	W 7460	272781	W 6718	260245	APP PROJETER ETC LIQUID
749	NONELEC MACH PTS,ACC NES	W 49575	950446	W 54066	1088107	W 57556	1390412	W 55944	1391684	PIECES MACH NON ELEC NDA
7492	COCKS,VALVES ETC NES	W 10810	440119	W 11973	507650	W 13038	652653	W 12654	629487	ART ROB,SIM POUR TUYAUX
7493	SHAFT,CRANK,PULLEY ETC	W 17416	214513	W 19743	249408	W 22064	315344	W 23033	322855	ARBRES TRANS,VILEBREQUINS
7499	OTH NONELEC MCHY PTS NES	W 19899	228056	W 20452	253356	W 20109	315771	W 18157	316816	PIECES NON ELECT NDA
75	OFFICE MACHNES,ADP EQUIP		675296		714486		1014502		1087496	MACH BUREAU TRAIT AUTOM
752	AUTOMTIC DATA PROC EQUIP	W 2456	368001	W 2218	361014	W 2679	518912	W 2656	577146	MACH TRAIT INFORMATION
7523	DIGITL CENTRL PROCESSORS	W 890	197901	W 1000	232866	W 1300	363731	W 1266	408754	UNITES CENTRALES
759	OFFICE,ADP MCH PTS,ACCES	W 2098	213154	W 2040	251070	W 2005	324626	W 1974	313550	PIECES DU 751 ET 752
7599	ACCTG,ETC,ADP MCH PTS,AC	W 1703	194240	W 1755	232388	W 1718	299632	W 1684	286639	PIECES DU 751 ET 752
76	TELECOMM,SOUND EQUIPMENT		583527		698794		803358		816508	EQUIPMENT DE TELECOM
764	TELECOM EQPT,PTS,ACC NES	W 5066	512280	W 5129	622843	W 5125	718936	W 5717	729974	EQUIP TELECOM,PIECES
7641	LINE TELEPHONE,ETC EQUIP	W 1201	122509	W 951	116543	W 1464	247271	W 1999	247195	APP TELEPHON PAR FIL
7649	PTS NES OF EQUIPMT OF 76	W 2877	218548	W 2774	262377	W 2533	297250	W 2931	332181	PIECES DE LA DIV 76
77	ELECTRIC MACHNRY NES ETC		4006504		4583414		5500505		5443892	MACH APP ELECT NDA
771	ELECTRIC POWER MACHY NES	W 18214	330440	W 19760	351893	W 23644	440455	W 24343	441390	MACH PROD,TRANS ELECTR
7712	OTH ELEC POWER MACHY NES	W 12627	220787	W 13162	232686	W 16402	302937	W 17676	319134	AUT APP PROD TRANSF ELEC
772	SWITCHGEAR ETC,PARTS NES	W 20936	1501198	W 24042	1734760	W 26562	2153207	W 26763	2156928	APP COUPURE,SECT ETC
7721	SWITCHGEAR ETC	W 20435	1402008	W 23329	1615011	W 25679	1978972	W 25935	1991524	APP COUPURE,SECTIONMNT
773	ELECTR DISTRIBUTNG EQUIP	W 24303	257524	W 27894	296707	W 31867	383762	W 35128	416009	EQUIPMT DISTRIBUTION ELECT
7731	INSULATED WIRE,CABLE ETC	W 21707	207118	W 25141	235308	W 29167	312793	W 31776	329423	FILS,CABLES ISOLES ELECT
775	HOUSEHOLD TYPE EQUIP NES	W 15655	281101	W 16164	290756	W 15072	286121	W 13406	241541	MACH,APP USAGE DOMESTQUE
7758	ELECTRO–THERMIC APPL NES	W 12914	226312	W 11880	222323	W 9164	199331	W 7597	172059	APP ELECTROTHERMIQ NDA
776	TRANSISTORS,VALVES,ETC	W 631	285747	W 717	327498	W 904	439610	W 934	461026	LAMPES,TUBES,VALVES
7764	ELECTRONIC MICROCIRCUITS	W 282	186092	W 385	211199	W 410	286125	W 332	313030	MICROSTRUCTURES ELECTRON
778	ELECTRICAL MACHINERY NES		1219762		1444118	W 48609	1635830	W 53008	1576269	AUTRES MACH ELECT NDA
7784	ELECTRO–MECH HAND TOOLS	W 23123	634840	W 27187	773122	W 28352	856101	W 26689	791640	OUTILS ELECTROMEC,PIECES
7788	OTH ELEC MACHY,EQUIP NES		398938		462271	W 9445	558420	W 9373	568972	AUT MACH APP ELEC NDA
78	ROAD VEHICLES		688457		760635		777409		789482	VEHICULES ROUTIERS
782	LORRIES,SPCL MTR VEH NES	W 24765	174564	W 23374	218662	W 23654	195364	W 29227	183572	VEHICULES SPECIAUX,MARCH
784	MOTOR VEH PRTS,ACCES NES	W 27445	237586	W 36342	291223	W 37803	348262	W 40414	363397	PIECES 722,781,782,783
7849	OTHER MOTOR VEHCL PARTS	W 25107	209436	W 33557	256912	W 35381	315854	W 38030	338118	PIECES 722,781,782,783

5. Special Exports F.O.B. by Commodities according to the S.I.T.C. (Rev. 2) in thousand U.S. Dollars
Exportations Spéciales F.O.B. par Produits d'après la C.T.C.I. (Rév. 2) en milliers de Dollars E.U.

SITC CTCI	COMMODITY	1993		1994		1995		1996		PRODUIT
		WEIGHT POIDS	VALUE VALEUR	WEIGHT POIDS	VALUE VALEUR	WEIGHT POIDS	VALUE VALEUR	WEIGHT POIDS	VALUE VALEUR	
79	OTHR TRANSPORT EQUIPMENT		515993		486798		839533		1199419	AUTRE MATERIEL TRANSPORT
791	RAILWAY VEHICLES	W 11298	237587	W 13184	233789	W 11310	240204	W 14877	400585	VEHIC MAT CHEMINS DE FER
792	AIRCRAFT ETC	W 623	264958	W 739	239921	W 1776	587954	W 1419	790473	APP NAVIGATION AERIENNE
7924	AIRCRFT NES OVER 15000KG	W 201	83680	W 98	21936	W 720	163385	W 632	331821	AERODYNES PLUS 15000 KG
8	MISC MANUFACTURED GOODS		15523516		16933594		18402446		17789638	ART MANUFACTURES DIVERS
812	*PLUMBG,HEATNG,LGHTNG EQ	W 30263	204121	W 31852	244870	W 29314	261935	W 30401	252276	APPAR SANITAIRES CHAUFFAGE
821	*FURNITURE,PARTS THEREOF	W 80302	629334	W 83514	660166	W 88861	785529	W 98447	766247	MEUBLES ET PIECES
8212	MED FURN,STUFFD FURNSHGS	W 6221	217678	W 6665	232539	W 6892	267092	W 6840	254265	MOB MEDICO–CHIRUR,PIECES
8219	FURNITURE AND PARTS NES	W 65850	288850	W 69292	311359	W 73597	388253	W 82992	391959	AUTRES MEUBLES ET PIECES
84	CLOTHING AND ACCESSORIES		626609		668142		715010		698082	VETEMENTS
842	MENS OUTERWEAR NOT KNIT	W 2067	164731	W 2286	190708	W 2233	242528	W 2469	250078	VET DESSUS POUR HOMMES
851	*FOOTWEAR	W 5485	232688	W 4967	226187	W 4529	204331	W 3576	169419	CHAUSSURES
85102	FOOTWEAR LEATHER	W 3665	197332	W 3298	192290	W 3306	175752	W 2375	144743	CHAUS SEMELLES EN CUIR
87	PRECISION INSTRUMNTS NES		2403824		2686147		3111061		3071984	INSTRUM,APPAR SCIENT NDA
872	MEDICAL INSTRUMENTS NES	W 3679	371384	W 3835	452740	W 3933	556850	W 4277	594409	INSTR,APP MEDIC–CHIR NDA
87202	OTH MEDICAL INSTRUMENTS	W 3397	346309	W 3597	417626	W 3742	518551	W 4079	555570	INSTRUM,APP MEDECINE
874	MEASURNG,CONTROLNG INSTR	W 11746	1799394	W 12352	1969640	W 12205	2267770	W 12292	2181403	INSTRUMENTS DE MESURE
8742	MEASUR,DRAW ETC INST,PTS	W 2245	430190	W 2352	462400	W 2355	544383	W 2149	511755	INST DESSIN,TRACAGE,PCS
87421	MEASURNG,DRAWNG ETC INST	W 1869	336005	W 1984	353944	W 1908	401935	W 1764	374596	INSTRUM DESSIN,TRACAGE
8743	GAS,LIQUID CONTROL INSTR	W 3242	405399	W 3189	436759	W 2859	473550	W 2777	438772	APP,INSTR MESURE FLUIDES
8748	ELEC MEAS,CONTRL EQU NES	W 2063	393113	W 2201	438692	W 2025	513970	W 2147	526072	APP ELEC ELECTRO MESURE
87483	OTH ELCTRNC MEAS ETC EQU	W 1832	364448	W 2012	412389	W 1838	481871	W 1941	494590	AUT APP ELECTRO DE MESURE
8749	INSTR PTS NES,ACCESSORYS	W 2333	176096	W 2724	195223	W 3275	244365	W 3478	244601	PIECES 873,874.3,54,874.8
88	PHOTO EQU,OPTICL GDS ETC		5457140		6161958		6861514		6553925	APP,FOURN PHOTO,OP,MONTR
882	PHOTO,CINEMA SUPPLIES	W 8114	204384	W 7809	196709	W 9571	230933	W 8110	200667	PRODUITS PHOTO,CINEMA
885	WATCHES AND CLOCKS		5044740		5732864		6368841		6045830	HORLOGERIE
8851	WATCHES,MOVEMENTS,CASES		4653473		5288478		5878391		5646427	MONTRES,MOUVEMENTS,BOITES
88511	WATCHES		4472738		5098988		5662347		5464907	MONTRES POCHE,BRACELET
8852	CLOCKS,CLOCK,WATCH PARTS		391267		444385		490451		399403	HORLOGES,MOUV,PARTIES
88529	CLOCK,WATCH PARTS NES		320719		370305		396494		310126	FOURNIT D HORLOG NDA
89	MISC MANUFCTRD GOODS NES		5872835		6148871		6326789		6161923	ART MANUFACTURES DIVERS
892	PRINTED MATTER	W 91522	521575	W 96171	571937	W 87845	584359	W 81316	550570	IMPRIMES
8921	PRINTED BOOKS,GLOBES,ETC	W 16839	181958	W 16892	223240	W 13632	188370	W 12399	167210	LIVRES,BROCHURES,CARTES
89211	PRINTED BOOKS,PAMPHLETS	W 15746	170317	W 15936	211356	W 12727	176311	W 11715	154726	LIVRES,BROCHURES
8928	PRINTED MATTER NES	W 59885	247100	W 64417	250723	W 59480	279658	W 57176	275587	IMPRIMES NDA
893	ARTICLES OF PLASTIC NES		881397		1033635		1232016		1209908	OUVRAGES EN MAT DIVIS 58
8931	PLSTC PACKG CONTNRS,LIDS	W 43354	219142	W 48021	245409	W 51618	303639	W 57372	295924	ART TRANSP EMBALLAGE ETC
8939	MISC PLASTIC ARTICLES	W 70490	578136	W 74360	677239	W 76939	808423	W 83569	809013	ART DIVERS EN MAT DIV 58
89399	OTHR PLASTC ARTICLES NES	W 57822	528051	W 60382	617900	W 63198	739678	W 69379	738810	AUT OUV MAT DIV 58
894	TOYS,SPORTING GOODS,ETC	W 18921	337699	W 21410	369285	W 20433	374918	W 22954	417402	VOITURES ENFANTS,JOUETS
8942	TOYS,INDOOR GAMES ETC	W 15197	230905	W 17965	271330	W 16600	267032	W 19561	283629	JOUETS,JEUX ETC
89423	TOYS NES	W 13086	201830	W 15840	241355	W 14699	237356	W 18003	258775	JOUETS,MODELES REDUITS
896	WORKS OF ART ETC		942954		830463		604630		720002	OBJETS D'ART
89601	HAND PAINTINGS ETC NES		607759		505304		352733		452773	TABLEAUX,PEINTURES
897	GOLD,SILVER WARE,JEWELRY		1992404		1997390		2040756		1735650	BIJOUTERIE,ORFEVRERIE
8973	PREC JEWLRY,GLD–SILVWARE		1974798		1968149		2016752		1702833	BIJOUX OR,ARGENT ORFEVRE
89731	PRECIOUS METAL JEWELLERY		1800546		1798310		1829574		1551924	ART BIJOUTERIE,JOAILLER
898	MUSICAL INSTRUMENTS,PTS	W 7026	372243	W 5566	411288	W 5636	379951	W 5694	406115	INSTRUMENTS DE MUSIQUE
8983	SOUND RECRDNG TAPE,DISCS	W 6455	344038	W 4933	378945	W 4954	344618	W 5040	371833	SUPPORTS SON POUR 763
89832	RECORDED DISCS,TAPES ETC	W 5824	320423	W 4581	369034	W 4659	336111	W 4644	360454	DISQUES,PHONO,BANDES
899	OTHER MANUFACTURED GOODS		704234		794180		927332		939530	AUT ART MANUF DIVERS NDA
8996	HEARING,ORTHOPAEDIC AIDS		590803		674453		795125		812300	APPAREILS D'ORTHOPEDIE
89962	ORTHOPAEDIC ETC GOODS		528632		599823		706835		732357	APPAREILS D'ORTHOPEDIE
9	GOODS NOT CLASSD BY KIND		280165		192301		355796		171598	ART TRANSACT NON CLASSES
971	*GOLD,NON MONETARY NES	K 103420	200084	K 18464	89076	K 43001	301357	K 60844	86504	OR NON MONETAIRE
97101	NONMON GLD UNWRT,SEMIMFD	K 23890	190094	K 9206	79271	K 25479	287306	K 7644	68344	OR,ALLIAGES D'OR BRUTS

1. HISTORICAL SERIES, 1961–1996 SPECIAL TRADE, IMPORTS C.I.F., EXPORTS F.O.B.
SERIES HISTORIQUES, 1961–1996 COMMERCE SPECIAL, IMPORTATIONS C.A.F., EXPORTATIONS F.O.B

YEAR ANNEE	VALUE IN MILLION SYRIAN POUNDS / VALEUR EN MILLION SYRIAN POUNDS — MERCHANDISE –MARCHANDISE		GOLD –OR		CONVERSION FACTORS U.S. CENTS PER SYRIAN POUND FACTEURS DE CONVERSION CENTS E.U. PAR SYRIAN POUND		INDEX NUMBERS –INDICES — QUANTUM		UNIT VALUE VALEUR UNITAIRE	
	IMPORTS	EXPORTS	IMPORTS	EXPORTS	IMPORTS	EXPORTS	IMPORTS	EXPORTS	IMPORTS	EXPORTS
1961	711.30	392.80	0.02	1.90	27.9700	27.9700	92	31	69	68
1962	862.20	616.90	0.03	0.27	27.0300	26.9600	109	45	66	73
1963	896.20	720.60	0.01	0.35	26.1780	26.1780	90	54	77	63
1964	896.40	672.40	2.03	0.16	26.1780	26.1780	89	51	80	63
1965	810.10	640.80	2.09	2.92	26.1780	26.1780	80	47	78	64
1966	1101.50	661.30	1.99	0.11	26.1780	26.1780	106	48	77	64
1967	1008.60	581.40	0.49	0.04	26.1780	26.1780	84	37	78	64
1968	1156.90	658.40	30.24		26.1780	26.1780	94	37	83	67
1969	1405.40	789.90	5.92		26.1780	26.1780	128	47	81	67
1970	1365.60	775.30	9.03		26.1780	26.1780	114	46	83	65
1971	1677.30	743.50	2.67		26.1780	26.1780	38	39	18	11
1972	2060.60	1097.60			26.1780	26.1780	38	48	22	13
1973	2342.10	1341.30			26.1838	26.1732	45	45	27	16
1974	4570.90	2914.00			26.9009	26.8951	56	43	37	30
1975	6235.40	3440.90	62.79		27.0270	27.0270	88	53	42	26
1976	9203.30	4141.30	150.90		25.7169	25.7175	89	56	52	33
1977	10496.70	4199.00			25.3165	25.3165	111	54	48	36
1978	9658.70	4159.80			25.4770	25.4770	100	58	52	38
1979	13066.70	6453.30			25.4770	25.4770	112	53	64	50
1980	16188.10	8272.70			25.4777	25.4777				
1981	19781.00	8253.70			25.4777	25.4777	174	49	82	116
1982	15757.20	7953.60			25.4777	25.4777	150	53	77	101
1983	17829.00	7547.50			25.4777	25.4777	164	52	188	95
1984	16154.50	7274.80			25.4777	25.4777	153	48	82	97
1985	15570.50	6426.50			25.4777	25.4777	161	45	69	95
1986	10709.00	5198.90			25.4777	25.4777	152	43	82	70
1987	27915.01	15191.60			8.8889	8.8889				
1988	25040.00	15092.70			8.9087	8.9087				
1989	23543.81	33739.60			8.9087	8.9087	92	78	99	77
1990	26940.00	47280.00			8.9087	8.9087	100	100	100	100
1991	31070.00	38500.00			8.9087	8.9087	107	109	115	81
1992	39178.00	34720.00			8.9087	8.9087	143	105	98	68
1993	46467.70	35319.20			8.9087	8.9087	225	158	93	67
1994	61370.00	39820.00			8.9087	8.9087	276	171	105	72
1995	51820.00	44560.00			8.9087	8.9087	248	167	118	90
1996	58860.00	44890.00			8.9087	8.9087				89

2. IMPORTS BY BROAD ECONOMIC CATEGORY AND EXPORTS BY INDUSTRIAL ORIGIN. (PERCENTAGE OF TOTAL VALUE)
IMPORTATIONS PAR CATEGORIES ECONOMIQUES ET EXPORTATIONS PAR BRANCHE D'ACTIVITE.(EN POURCENTAGE DE LA VALEUR TOTALE)

IMPORTS – IMPORTATIONS

	1990	1991	1992	1993	1994	1995	1996
TOTAL IMPORTS–IMPORTATIONS TOTALES	100.		100.				
1 FOOD BEV–ALIMENTATION BOISSONS	26.3		16.7				
11 PRIMARY–PRODUITS DE BASE	12.5		7.9				
111 FOR INDUSTRY–POUR L'INDUSTRIE	10.6		6.0				
112 FOR HOUSEHOLDS–POUR LES MENAGES	1.9		1.9				
12 PROCESSED–PRODUITS ELABORES	13.9		8.8				
121 FOR INDUSTRY–POUR L'INDUSTRIE	7.6		4.8				
122 FOR HOUSEHOLDS–POUR LES MENAGES	6.3		4.0				
2 IND SUPPLIES–APPROV INDUSTRIELS	45.0		41.2				
21 PRIMARY–PRODUITS DE BASE	3.4		1.8				
22 PROCESSED–PRODUITS ELABORES	41.6		39.4				
3 FUELS–COMBUSTIBLES	3.0		3.8				
31 PRIMARY–PRODUITS DE BASE	2.3		1.0				
32 PROCESSED–PRODUITS ELABORES	0.7		2.9				
321 MOTOR SPIRIT–ESSENCE	0.0		0.0				
322 OTHER–AUTRES	0.7		2.9				
4 MACHINERY–EQUIPEMENT	15.5		17.9				
41 CAPITAL EQUIPMENT–MACHINES	13.0		15.0				
42 PARTS–PIECES ACCESSOIRES	2.5		2.9				
5 TRANSPORT–TRANSPORT	5.6		16.2				
51 PASSENGER CARS–AUTOMOBILES	0.3		2.0				
52 OTHER–AUTRES	1.3		8.7				
521 INDUSTRIAL–INDUSTRIELS	1.3		8.7				
522 NON INDUSTRIAL–NON INDUSTRIEL	0.0		0.0				
53 PARTS–PIECES ACCESSOIRES	3.9		5.5				
6 CONSUM GOODS–BIENS CONSOMMATION	3.5		3.4				
61 DURABLE–DURABLES	0.9		1.4				
62 SEMI DURABLE–SEMI DURABLES	1.0		0.9				
63 NON DURABLE–NON DURABLES	1.6		1.1				
7 GOODS NES–BIENS NDA	1.1		0.7				

EXPORTS – EXPORTATIONS

	1990	1991	1992	1993	1994	1995	1996
TOTAL EXPORTS–EXPORTATIONS TOTALES	100.		100.				
1 AGRICULTURE	14.7		18.1				
2 MINING QUARRY–INDUS EXTRACTIVES	35.8		61.3				
3 MANUFACTURING–IND MANUFACTUR	49.5		20.6				
31 FOOD BEV TOBACCO–ALIM BOISS TAB	3.2		1.4				
32 TEXTILES–INDUSTRIES TEXTILES	21.4		7.6				
33 WOOD & PRODUCTS–BOIS & PRODUITS	0.0		0.0				
34 PAPER & PRODUCTS–PAPIER & PRODT	0.2		0.1				
35 CHEMICALS–INDUSTRIES CHIMIQUES	23.6		10.1				
36 NON METAL MIN–MIN NON METAL	0.7		0.6				
37 BASIC METAL–IND METAL BASE	0.0		0.0				
38 METAL MANUF–MANUF METAL	0.3		0.7				
39 OTH MANUF IND–AUTRES MANUF	0.1		0.1				

3. TRADE BY PRINCIPAL COUNTRIES OF ORIGIN AND DESTINATION (VALUE IN THOUSAND U.S. DOLLARS)
ECHANGES SELON LES PRINCIPAUX PAYS D'ORIGINE ET DE DESTINATION (VALEUR EN MILLIERS DE DOLLARS EU)

COUNTRIES–PAYS	SPECIAL IMPORTS C.I.F. IMPORTATIONS SPECIALES C.A.F					COUNTRIES–PAYS	SPECIAL EXPORTS F.O.B. EXPORTATIONS SPECIALES F.O.B.				
	1990	1991	1992	1993	1994		1990	1991	1992	1993	1994
World	2399653	2767705	3490274	4139775	5467633	Monde	4213726	3430316	3093082	3279885	3547309
Africa	53950	52412	84402	109685	130045	Afrique	121971	121061	99884	85520	132528
Americas	343249	376095	348232	397986	480316	Amériques	37907	20674	53092	96265	50668
Northern America	265890	270580	230131	279939	332419	Amérique du Nord	36479	19015	24873	89347	46754
LAIA	52975	82961	94576	103192	135498	ALAI	1408	1658	7148	6918	3914
CACM	2463		1089			MCAC	14		12		
Caribbean	21921	22554	22378	14856	12399	Caraïbes	6		21059		1
Rest of America			58			Autre Amérique					
As.ex F.USSR	638098	580461	1114653	904405	1335715	Asie l'URSS exclus	821223	776951	788039	787385	960746
Eur.x F.USSR	1270695	1478209	1834776	2123391	2462541	Europe l'URSS exclus	1835580	1843974	2094084	2010076	2048137
EU	1063272	1145126	1365251	1629761	1931833	UE	1755964	1648426	1953747	1912393	1979142
EFTA	20700	20309	29856	28317	51128	AELE	16619	18781	16911	17267	936
East Europe	147278	252887	419058	450011	466538	Europe de l'Est	57008	169953	123252	70157	67625
Other Europe	39446		119			Autre de l'Europe	5990		8		
Former USSR	68263	37226	73988	145683	114214	Ancienne URSS	1376024	646760	55437	87662	245154
Oceania	1174		5067			Océanie	20342		48		
Germany/Allemagne	214907	278853	352054	421383	465781	Italy/Italie	877154	768187	1083631	967611	956062
Italy/Italie	152797	201081	285577	340148	474326	France,Monac	538022	606816	574279	481108	440401
Japan/Japon	79302	125068	346861	338386	552860	Former USSR/Anc. URSS	1376024	646760			
USA/Etats–Unis d'Amer	257708	259060	217131	266608	314838	Lebanon/Liban	266135	329205	401518	331207	389857
France,Monac	305015	186238	220625	293154	270664	Saudi Arabia	270463	199423	133459	154046	195854
Turkey/Turquie	184671	262964	216588	224446	259930	Spain/Espagne	28677	23537	109767	244134	240683
Romania/Roumanie	21764	74052	151331	185706	210417	United Kingdom	83375	64974	64672	101989	189143
Belgium–Luxembourg	79471	94732	108629	140123	153347	Turkey/Turquie	113588	92332	42937	67870	87486
United Kingdom	63457	72237	103751	111164	194953	Germany/Allemagne	91522	101125	76014	34800	88387
Bulgaria/Bulgarie	39027	77195	149043	118971	108229	Russian Federation			47582	87662	245154
China/Chine	41311	56332	88641	93953	200206	Jordan/Jordanie	24487	68460	44697	73105	96408
Netherlands/Pays–Bas	56865	70672	101062	110457	114577	Netherlands/Pays–Bas	89246	53796	21812	51613	26696
Russian Federation			73682	145683	114214	Bulgaria/Bulgarie	34878	79523	73684	30639	14098
Spain/Espagne	42957	49206	39978	54355	76365	Kuwait/ Koweït	12377	16777	61607	56034	51094
Sweden/Suède	46978	61798	45132	46393	59909	USA/Etats–Unis d'Amer	36103	18572	24282	60102	42626
Brazil/Brésil	12339	38496	53911	59677	71394	United Arab Emirates	58984	36790	14598	22353	35557
Saudi Arabia	32829	36672	43713	47264	74985	Romania/Roumanie	6889	60339	33608	22520	29258
Austria/Autriche	40528	44125	42837	43153	48725	Libyan Arab Jamahiriya	15998	34690	18233	25708	50451
Argentina/Argentine	34147	44465	31644	43515	64104	Tunisia/Tunisie	32084	22998	30014	25632	19784
Egypt/Egypte	20197	26293	42900	54434	69438	Cyprus/Chypre	6515	9128	47898	29638	36855
Lebanon/Liban	16802	29434	46616	65332	55077	Egypt/Egypte	47671	13589	16909	12859	22307
Czechoslovakia	19348	33599	54986	63475		Algeria/Algérie	15544	35129	16028	10611	24262
Greece/Grèce	28898	38104	27384	34916	33719	Greece/Grèce	36563	20778	12422	7620	21966
Poland/Pologne	28673	42523	27640	36132	23747	Switz.Liecht	16605	18778	16889	17258	914
Hungary/Hongrie	22557	25519	32435	45727	27417	Qatar	29706	8294	8628	8093	12373
Sri Lanka	27651	24641	21980	34303	35214	Poland/Pologne	3961	19696	12373	13759	16924
Switz.Liecht	18535	19223	28618	24989	46658	Morocco/Maroc	5856	13947	9619	7521	11744
Jordan/Jordanie	16215	15744	22505	20918	60286	Japan/Japon	2854	2537	9158	9479	11243
India/Inde	11511	18606	24142	37680	32011	Canada	376	444	591	29245	4127
Tunisia/Tunisie	28172	19126	20476	26730	25573	Portugal	820	932	478	20013	11398
Korea, Republic of	21928		85304			India/Inde	530	0	1	11338	16860
Former USSR/Anc. URSS	68263	37226				Bahrain/Bahreïn	6248	5610	1768	7403	4915
Fm Yugoslav	39302	59887				Cuba			21059		1
Iran (Islamic Rp. of)	32579	1504	12067	19225	31739	Australia/Australie	20342		41		
Czech Republic					96728	Hong Kong		0	762	9732	9792
Cuba	21919	22554	22246	14856	12399	Iran (Islamic Rp. of)	13582	2228	855	349	1849
Finland/Finlande	13887	20240	15523	16298	20843	Yemen/Yémen			2224	6376	9888
Malaysia/Malaisie	29455		45722			Czechoslovakia	2881	9545	2729	2166	
Denmark/Danemark	11321	23082	12331	11724	12746	Sudan/Soudan	305	702	8283	2960	3942
Thailand/Thaïlande	41625		27954			Brazil/Brésil	943	1362	1275	6333	3533
Canada	8183	11520	13000	13331	17581	Austria/Autriche	4493	4980	2487	687	578
Yugoslavia/Yougoslavie			20492	15301	13042	Fm Yugoslav	5990	6814			
Libyan Arab Jamahiriya	3913	5443	4929	11133	12231	Yugoslavia/Yougoslavie			165	10259	434
Bangladesh	11049		25937			Belgium–Luxembourg	935	1907	2696	1455	1408
Kuwait/ Koweït	24589	232	3381	2752	3751	Sri Lanka	3974	3622	6	171	627
United Arab Emirates	4261	4294	5365	6600	13397	Former GDR	8301				
Cyprus/Chypre	6885	1486	3890	5650	8094	Korea, Republic of	7148		756		
Morocco/Maroc	365	236	172	8645	14012	Hungary/Hongrie	98	850	720	1073	3798
Indonesia/Indonésie	4800		14555			Sweden/Suède	2510	1316	509	840	871
Ireland/Irlande	4337	2238	8067	4542		Ukraine			5858		

(VALUE AS PERCENTAGE OF WORLD TOTAL)(VALEURS EN POURCENTAGE DU TOTAL MONDIAL)

	1985	1986	1987	1988	1989	1990	1991	1992	1993	1994		1985	1986	1987	1988	1989	1990	1991	1992	1993	1994
Africa	7.6	6.2	6.7	1.0	1.1	2.2	1.9	2.4	2.6	2.4	Afrique	2.1	1.5	1.0	2.4	2.0	2.9	3.5	3.2	2.6	3.7
Americas	8.4	7.9	7.6	8.0	10.1	14.3	13.6	10.0	9.6	8.8	Amériques	0.0	0.3	1.3	1.7	2.8	0.9	0.6	1.7	2.9	1.4
Northern America	7.0	4.6	5.7	6.6	8.1	11.1	9.8	6.6	6.8	6.1	Amérique du Nord	0.0	0.0	1.3	1.7	2.4	0.9	0.6	0.8	2.7	1.3
LAIA	0.8	2.8	1.3	0.9	1.2	2.2	3.0	2.7	2.5	2.5	ALAI	0.0	0.3	0.0	0.0	0.4	0.0	0.0	0.2	0.2	0.1
CACM	0.1	0.0	0.0		0.0	0.1		0.0			MCAC	0.0					0.0		0.0		
Caribbean	0.5	0.4	0.6	0.5	0.7	0.9	0.8	0.6	0.4	0.2	Caraïbes		0.0	0.0	0.0	0.0	0.0		0.7		0.0
Rest of America								0.0			Autre Amérique										
As.ex F.USSR	31.6	25.1	24.7	28.9	29.2	26.6	21.0	31.9	21.8	24.4	Asie l'URSS exclus	6.9	13.2	12.8	19.8	20.8	19.5	22.6	25.5	24.0	27.1
Eur.x F.USSR	46.6	49.6	52.1	49.9	54.0	53.0	53.4	52.6	51.3	45.0	Europe l'URSS exclus	74.1	55.3	64.1	46.6	38.4	43.6	53.8	67.7	61.3	57.7
EU	36.9	39.9	39.2	39.4	45.2	44.3	41.4	39.1	39.4	35.3	UE	45.9	35.1	47.4	33.6	31.3	41.7	48.1	63.2	58.3	55.8
EFTA	1.2	1.3	3.5	1.6	1.2	0.9	0.7	0.9	0.7	0.9	AELE	0.1	4.4	1.0	0.9	0.7	0.4	0.5	0.5	0.5	0.0
East Europe	7.6	8.0	8.7	8.2	6.4	6.1	9.1	12.0	10.9	8.5	Europe de l'Est	28.1	15.6	15.4	11.8	6.2	1.4	5.0	4.0	2.1	1.9
Other Europe	0.8	0.4	0.7	0.3	1.2	1.6		0.0			Autre de l'Europe	0.1	0.2	0.2	0.1	0.2	0.1		0.0		
Former USSR	4.9	10.0	8.3	8.5	4.4	2.8	1.3	2.1	3.5	2.1	Ancienne URSS	16.8	29.7	20.8	28.9	35.7	32.7	18.9	1.8	2.7	6.9
Oceania	0.3	0.4	0.3	0.1	0.1	0.0		0.1			Océanie	0.0			0.0	0.3	0.5		0.0		
Germany/Allemagne	8.2	9.2	8.2	7.9	10.6	9.0	10.1	10.1	10.2	8.5	Italy/Italie	31.3	12.1	31.1	20.0	15.5	20.8	22.4	35.0	29.5	27.0
Italy/Italie	6.9	7.5	6.8	6.1	7.0	6.4	7.3	8.2	8.2	8.7	France,Monac	5.2	9.4	9.9	7.0	9.6	12.8	17.7	18.6	14.7	12.4
Japan/Japon	2.8	5.3	3.0	11.0	4.2	3.3	4.5	9.9	8.2	10.1	Former USSR/Anc. URSS	16.8	29.7	20.8	28.9	35.7	32.7	18.9			
USA/Etats–Unis d'Amer	6.2	4.4	5.3	6.3	7.9	10.7	9.4	6.2	6.4	5.8	Lebanon/Liban	0.2	1.1	0.8	3.8	4.5	6.3	9.6	13.0	10.1	11.0
France,Monac	4.5	8.7	9.8	10.4	11.4	12.7	6.7	6.3	7.1	5.0	Saudi Arabia	1.2	2.3	1.7	3.7	6.0	6.4	5.8	4.3	4.7	5.5
Turkey/Turquie	1.5	2.6	2.9	5.9	7.7	7.7	9.5	6.2	5.4	4.8	Spain/Espagne	2.8	3.5	0.5	0.2	0.8	0.7	0.7	3.5	7.4	6.8
Romania/Roumanie	1.6	2.9	2.4	2.5	1.9	0.9	2.7	4.3	4.5	3.8	United Kingdom	2.7	4.2	1.1	0.6	0.9	2.0	1.9	2.1	3.1	5.3
Belgium–Luxembourg	2.4	2.2	1.6	2.6	4.0	3.3	3.4	3.1	3.4	2.8	Turkey/Turquie	0.7	1.1	0.4	0.3	0.9	2.7	2.7	1.4	2.1	2.5
United Kingdom	2.8	3.2	2.6	2.3	2.9	2.6	2.6	3.0	2.7	3.6	Germany/Allemagne	1.1	4.1	0.9	1.1	2.0	2.2	2.9	2.5	1.1	2.5
Bulgaria/Bulgarie	1.1	0.6	0.6	1.5	1.1	1.6	2.8	4.3	2.9	2.0	Russian Federation								1.5	2.7	6.9

4. Special Imports C.I.F. by Commodities according to the S.I.T.C. (Rev. 2) in thousand U.S. Dollars
Importations Spéciales C.A.F. par Produits d'après la C.T.C.I. (Rév. 2) en milliers de Dollars E.U.

SITC CTCI	COMMODITY	1991 WEIGHT POIDS	1991 VALUE VALEUR	1992 WEIGHT POIDS	1992 VALUE VALEUR	1993 WEIGHT POIDS	1993 VALUE VALEUR	1994 WEIGHT POIDS	1994 VALUE VALEUR	PRODUIT
	ALL COMMODITIES		2767705		3490274		4139775		5467633	TOUS PRODUITS
0	FOOD AND LIVE ANIMALS		623201		588983		641040		804403	ALIMENTS,ANIMAUX VIVANTS
001	*LIVE ANIMALS FOR FOOD				121654		122654		95450	ANIMAUX VIVANTS
0012	SHEEP AND GOATS,LIVE			N 1801847	116406					ESPECES OVINE ET CAPRINE
00121	SHEEP,LIVE	N 1114000	70082	N 1801172	116404	W 2351	115595	N 1350000	87127	ESPECE OVINE
02	DAIRY PRODCTS,BIRDS'EGGS		14777		21138		33668		31589	PRODUITS LAITIERS,OEUFS
022	MILK AND CREAM			W 6368	10895					LAIT ET CREME
0224	MILK,CREAM PRESERVED ETC			W 6368	10895					LAIT,CREME CONS,CONC
02242	MILK DRY,1.5% FAT OR LES	W 5353	9102			W 7019	14785	W 10976	17374	LAIT POUDRE INF 1.5%
023	BUTTER			W 4735	9593	W 9930	17862	W 6746	12524	BEURRE
04	CEREALS AND PREPARATIONS		256745		170251		199328		145467	CEREALES ET PRODUITS
041	WHEAT ETC UNMILLED	W 751874	85117	W 88750	10555	W 79007	11390			FROMENT,EPEAUTRE
0411	DURUM WHEAT UNMILLED			W 88750	10555					FROMENT DUR NON MOULU
042	RICE			W 125051	43360					RIZ
0421	RICE IN HUSK OR HUSKED			W 125051	43360					RIZ SANS AUTRE PREPARATION
04212	RICE HUSKED	W 109201	42930			W 143826	45161	W 115861	42302	RIZ CARGO
043	BARLEY UNMILLED	W 198578	28296	W 82157	5791					ORGE NON MONDEE
044	MAIZE UNMILLED	W 262234	43636	W 104099	16747	W 347585	44978	W 399962	54301	MAIS NON MOULU
046	WHEAT ETC MEAL OR FLOUR			W 437659	92921					SEMOULE FARINE,FROMENT
04601	FLOUR OF WHEAT OR MESLIN	W 301535	56619	W 437659	92921	W 404154	88814	W 279487	48650	FARINE DE FROMENT
05	VEGETABLES AND FRUIT		21201		28178		31614		210437	LEGUMES ET FRUITS
057	FRUIT,NUTS,FRESH,DRIED			W 11222	18042					FRUITS FRAIS OU SECS
0577	NUTS EDIBLE,FRESH,DRIED			W 5911	17020					FRUITS A COQUES
05779	NUTS EDIBLE,FRSH,DRY,NES	W 1395	6957	W 2830	12925	W 3129	17609	W 4323	32062	FRUITS A COQUES NDA
06	SUGAR AND PREPS,HONEY		140152		105468		113397		142317	SUCRES ET PRODUITS
061	SUGAR AND HONEY			W 334817	105463					SUCRES ET MIEL
0611	RAW BEET AND CANE SUGAR	W 146687	38095	W 88250	24390	W 82559	23454	W 84100	21148	SUCRES BRUTS
0612	REFINED SUGAR ETC	W 275902	94004	W 228844	75129	W 270978	83661	W 345336	116435	SUCRES RAFFINES
07	COFFEE,TEA,COCOA,SPICES		64572		58725		71998		88992	CAFE,THE,CACAO,EPICES
071	COFFEE AND SUBSTITUTES			W 10449	14490					CAFE ET SUCCEDANES
0711	COFFEE GREEN,ROASTED,SUB			W 10202	11945			W 10837	26228	CAFE TORREFIE OU DECAFEINE
07111	COFFEE GREEN,HUSKS,SKINS	W 9807	13975	W 10166	11907	W 13220	17204			CAFE NON TORREFIE
074	TEA AND MATE			W 29335	38043					THE ET MATE
0741	TEA	W 21409	35486	W 22338	30298	W 20755	35325	W 23518	36283	THE
0742	MATE	W 7484	8792	W 6997	7745	W 6937	7669	W 8004	13178	MATE
081	*FEEDING STUFF FOR ANIML			W 162898	48886		54762		59577	NOURRITURE POUR ANIMAUX
0813	OILCAKE AND OTH RESIDUES	W 77692	25093	W 125339	33270	W 112610	26446	W 180065	42288	TOURTEAUX
08199	FODDER NES,INCL SWEETNED	W 27854	12777	W 19786	9114	W 35690	15878	W 21281	9379	PREPARATIONS FOURRAGERES
09	MISC EDIBLE PRODUCTS		5356		33017		10378		15841	PREP ALIMENTAIRES DIVERSES
091	MARGARINE AND SHORTENING			W 35526	27412					MARGARINE ET GRAISSES
0914	MARGARINE,EDIBLE FAT NES			W 35501	27346					MARGARINES,SIMILI SAINDOUX
1	BEVERAGES AND TOBACCO		1712		4663		20288		55387	BOISSONS ET TABACS
12	TOBACCO AND MANUFACTURES		374		38		16355		51834	TABACS BRUTS FABRIQUES
2	CRUDE MATERLS,EXCL FUELS		65621		111833		117778		155405	MAT BRUTES NON COMESTIBLES
22	OIL SEEDS,OLEAGINOUS FRT		5467		15564		10255		9289	GRAINES,FRUITS OLEAGINEUX
222	SEEDS FOR'SOFT'FIXED OIL			W 17730	14643					GRAINES HUILES FIXES
2225	SESAME SEEDS	W 7366	5220	W 17530	14488	W 15846	10040	W 10636	6639	GRAINES DE SESAME
24	CORK AND WOOD		21880		43995		57853		92097	LIEGE ET BOIS
248	WOOD SHAPED,SLEEPERS			W 106030	42523					BOIS SIMPLEMENT TRAVAILLES
2482	LUMBER SHAPED CONIFER	W 49609	20684			W 141137	55969			CONIFERES SCIES,RABOTES
24821	LUMBER SAWN ETC CONIFER							W 153640	89927	CONIFERES SCIES LONGITUD
2483	LUMBER SHAPED NON–CONIFR			W 106029	42523					NON CONIFERES SCIES,RABOTES
24831	LUMBER SAWN ETC NON–CON			W 106029	42523					SCIES LONGITUDINALEMENT
27	CRUDE FERTLZR,MINRLS NES		8547		8366		6857		7305	ENGRAIS MINERAUX BRUTS
28	METALLIFEROUS ORES,SCRAP		6975		12635		11606		13870	MINERAIS METAL,DECHETS
282	IRON AND STEEL SCRAP			W 79433	12295					FERRAILLES
29	CRUDE ANIMAL,VEG MAT NES		8302		12292		8391		10344	MATIERES BRUTES ANIM,VEGET
292	CRUDE VEG MATERIALS NES			W 2922	12215					MAT BRUTES VEGETALES NDA
2925	SEEDS,ETC FOR PLANTING	W 733	7249	W 832	10673	W 752	6541	W 682	7106	SEMENCES NDA
3	MINERAL FUELS ETC		65491		135879		179800		89239	COMBUSTIBLES MINERAUX LUB
33	PETROLEUM AND PRODUCTS		31745		101941		161759		64581	PETROLE ET DERIVES
334	PETROLEUM PRODUCTS,REFIN			W 447247	99875					PRODUITS RAFFINES
3343	GAS OILS			W 403661	80782					GAS OILS
3345	LUBS,PETROLEUM OILS NES			W 43323	18742					HUILES LUBRIFIANTES
33451	LUBS(HIGH PETR CONT) ETC			W 42521	17874					HUILES LUBRIF,H LOURDES
341	*GAS,NATURAL AND MANUFCT			W 120941	33514		17246	W 109306	23749	GAZ NATUREL,GAZ MANUFACT
3413	PETROLM GASES,LIQUEFIED			W 120941	33514					GAZ DE PETROLE LIQUEFIE
3414	PETROLEUM GASES, GASEOUS	W 96125	33061		1	W 74422	17228			GAZ DE PETROLE GAZEUX
4	ANIMAL,VEGETABLE OIL,FAT		68472		54647		95411		90085	HUILES,GRAISSES ANIM,VEG
411	*ANIMAL OILS AND FATS			W 1931	299		29223		37735	HUILES,GRAISSES ANIMALES
41139	ANIMAL OILS,FATS NES	W 38834	26759			W 38143	28862			GRAISSES,HUILES ANIM NDA
42	FIXED VEGETABLE OIL,FAT		31554		20985		53693		42376	HUILES VEGETALES FIXES
423	FIXED VEG OILS,SOFT			W 21540	17074					HUILES VEGET DOUCES FIXES
4232	SOYA BEAN OIL	W 11735	10375	W 21403	16783	W 31079	23628	W 35854	28113	HUILE DE SOJA
4233	COTTON SEED OIL	W 24857	16808	W 106	265	W 45104	28006	W 17238	10999	HUILE DE COTON
431	*PROCESD ANML VEG OIL,ET			W 55991	33363		12496		9973	HUILES,GRAISSES PREPAREES
4312	HYDROGENATED OIL,FAT			W 32791	21634					HUILES HYDROGENEES
4313	FATTY ACIDS ETC,RESIDUES			W 22634	11134					ACIDES GRAS INDUST,RESIDUS
43131	FATTY ACIDS,ACID OILS	W 14609	7511	W 22495	11043	W 25976	11918	W 20452	8678	ACIDES GRAS INDUSTRIELS
5	CHEMCLS,RELATED PROD NES		429612		446188		453133		462302	PRODUITS CHIMIQUES
51	ORGANIC CHEMICALS		56767		55461		74039		54354	PROD CHIMIQ ORGANIQUES
513	CARBOXYLIC ACIDS ETC			W 8672	10744					ACIDES CARBOXYLIQUES
514	NITROGEN–FNCTN COMPOUNDS			W 148216	31574					COMPOSES FONCT AZOTEES
5147	AMIDE–FNCT CMPD,EXC UREA	W 148235	29364	W 144619	25043	W 304300	40193	W 73759	13409	COMPOSES CARBOXYAMIDE
52	INORGANIC CHEMICALS		33677		40830		41233		40677	PROD CHIM INORGANIQUES
522	INORG ELEMNTS,OXIDES,ETC			W 28519	15004					ELEMENTS INORGANIQUES
523	OTHR INORG CHEMICALS ETC			W 68959	25444					AUT PRODUITS CHIMIQUES INORG
5232	OTH MTL CMPD OF INRG ACD			W 47205	17574					SELS METALLIQUES
53	DYES,TANNING,COLOUR PROD		26403		32119		34236		38992	PROD TEINTURE,COLORANTS
531	SYNT DYE,NAT INDGO,LAKES			W 1703	16157					MAT COLOR ORGAN,LAQUES
5312	SYNTH LUMIN,INDIGO,LAKES			W 1703	16157					LUMINOPHORES ORGAN SYNTH
53121	SYN ORG LUMIN ETC,INDIGO	W 1794	14118	W 1702	16155	W 2206	16669	W 2125	15386	PROD ORGANIQ SYNTH LUMIN
533	PIGMENTS,PAINTS,ETC			W 9844	14024					PIGMENTS,PEINTURES,VERNIS
541	*MEDICINAL,PHARM PRODUCT			K 3286909	39566		27964		34923	PROD MEDICINAUX PHARMACEUT
5413	ANTIBIOTICS IN BULK	K 70000	5781	K 136260	15610	K 113000	8680	K 138000	11933	ANTIBIOTIQUES NDA
5417	MEDICAMENTS			K 2736865	14000					MEDICAMENTS
54179	— CONTNG OTH SUBSTANCES	K 2398000	25073			K 2080000	6851	K 2907000	9534	MED CONT AUT SUBSTANCES
55	PERFUME,CLEANING ETC PRD		37239		15857		16336		18219	PROD POUR PARFUM,TOILETTE
5514	MIXED PERFUME SUBSTANCES	W 513	28372	W 610	5956	W 634	5460	W 918	6154	MELANGES SUBSTAN ODORIFER
562	*FERTILIZERS,MANUFACTURE			W 536048	78562		69155		65199	ENGRAIS MANUFACTURES
5621	CHEM NITROGENOUS FERTLZR	W 148537	20873	W 183702	22457	W 43207	5189	W 130205	18485	ENGRAIS AZOTES

4. Special Imports C.I.F. by Commodities according to the S.I.T.C. (Rev. 2) in thousand U.S. Dollars
Importations Spéciales C.A.F. par Produits d'après la C.T.C.I. (Rév. 2) en milliers de Dollars E.U.

SITC CTCI	COMMODITY	1991		1992		1993		1994		PRODUIT
		WEIGHT POIDS	VALUE VALEUR	WEIGHT POIDS	VALUE VALEUR	WEIGHT POIDS	VALUE VALEUR	WEIGHT POIDS	VALUE VALEUR	
5622	CHEM PHOSPHATIC FERTILZR	W 335842	52037	W 351514	54767	W 394741	57887	W 173964	43082	ENGRAIS PHOSPHATES
58	PLASTIC MATERIALS ETC		93772		111573		118735		136106	MAT PLAST ARTIFICIELLES
582	PROD OF CONDENSATION ETC			W 15253	16539			W 19291	20345	PROD CONDENS,POLYCOND
5829	OTH CONDNSATION,ETC PROD	W 13964	12379			W 19482	17590			AUT PROD CONDENSATION
583	POLYMERIZATION ETC PRODS			W 95528	83516					PROD POLYMERISATION
5831	POLYETHYLENE			W 40531	32504					POLYETHYLENE
58311	— IN PRIMARY FORMS	W 30879	26787			W 50376	35323	W 50625	33864	POLYETHYLENE PRIMAIRES
5832	POLYPROPYLENE			W 16592	14190					POLYPROPYLENE
58321	— IN PRIMARY FORMS	W 13509	14346			W 20490	15104	W 22911	18038	POLYPROPYLENE PRIMAIRES
58341	— IN PRIMARY FORMS	W 10394	8829			W 17570	13048	W 18543	14067	SOUS FORMES PRIMAIRES
58351	— IN PRIMARY FORMS	W 17642	20353			W 21738	25664			SOUS FORMES PRIMAIRES
5839	OTH POLYMRZTION ETC PROD			W 14483	9302			W 29348	32220	AUT PROD POLYMER COPOLYM
59	CHEMICAL MATERIALS NES		57899		66424		71435		73832	MAT PROD CHIMIQUES NDA
591	PESTICIDES,DISINFECTANTS			W 4398	20052					DESINF,INSECT,FONG,HERB
5913	HERBICIDES,FOR RETAIL	W 1568	10038			W 4582	18733	W 3394	27911	HERBICIDES VENTE AU DET
598	MISCEL CHEM PRODUCTS NES			W 20861	42479					PROD DIV INDUST CHIM NDA
5982	ANTI–KNOCK PREPARTNS ETC	W 1895	9060	W 1091	3921	W 2146	6872	W 1654	1983	PREPARAT ANTIDETONANTES
5989	CHEM PRODUCTS,PREPS NES			W 19262	37059					PROD PREP CHIMIQUES NDA
59899	OTH CHEM PRODS,PREPS,NES	W 17431	27364	W 18425	35320	W 21375	31373	W 19526	31454	AUT PRODUITS CHIMIQUES NDA
6	BASIC MANUFACTURES		838179		925183		1084275		1520027	ART MANUFACTURES
62	RUBBER MANUFACTURES NES		44832		61655		61544		68652	CAOUTCHOUC MANUFACTURE
625	RUBBER TYRES, TUBES ETC			W 15882	46348					PNEUS CAOUTCHOUC VULCANISE
6252	TYRES,NEW,BUS OR LORRY	W 5733	17393	W 6476	18901	W 9669	21808	W 9120	23127	PNEUS POUR AUTOBUS,CAMIONS
6253	TYRES NEW FOR AIRCRAFT			W 6722	19934					PNEUS POUR AVIONS
64	PAPER,PAPERBOARD AND MFR		78429		61382		69035		100702	PAPIERS,CARTONS & OUVRAGES
641	PAPER AND PAPERBOARD			W 99662	54481					PAPIERS ET CARTONS
6412	PRINTG,WRITING PAPER NES			W 15786	11363					PAPIERS POUR L'IMPRESSION
64121	— UNCOATED	W 27543	22188	W 15786	11358	W 17123	10873			PAPIERS IMPRES NON COUCHES
64122	— COATED,IMPREGNATD ETC	W 26808	15232		4	W 32330	18541	W 38299	21393	PAPIERS IMPRESSION COUCHES
6413	KRAFT PAPER,PAPERBOARD			W 21678	11996					PAPIER ET CARTON KRAFT
64159	OTHER PAPER ETC,BULK,NES			W 6995	6718			W 33353	24106	AUT PAPIER ROULEAUX FEUILLES
6418	COATED ETC PAPER NES BLK			W 32700	17709					PAP,CARTONS COUCHES,ENDUITS
64189	COATED PAPER ETC NES			W 32343	17473					PAPIERS,CARTONS COUCHES
65	TEXTILE YARN,FABRICS,ETC		212682		258024		343381		378518	FILS,TISSUS,ARTICLES TEXTILE
651	TEXTILE YARN			W 58402	157160					FILS TEXTILES
6514	SYN FIB YRN,BULK,MONOFIL			W 40382	107362			W 77645	162526	FILS CONT 85% FIB TEXT SYNTH
65147	— OF OTH CONT SYN FIBRE	W 14166	45887			W 25038	80734			FILS AUT FI TEXT SYNT CONT
65148	— OF DISCONT SYN FIBRES			W 9710	36520					FILS CONT 85% FI TEXT SYNTH
6516	DISCON SYN FIB BLEND YRN			W 12645	29154					FILS FIBR TEX SYNT DIS MOINS
65168	OTH DISC SYN BLEND YARN			W 11196	26219					FILS TEXT SYNT MELANGE AUT F
653	WOVN MAN–MADE FIB FABRIC			W 14118	43734					TISSUS FIBRES SYNTH,ARTIF
6531	CONT SYNT WEAVES NONPILE	W 698	5423	W 1876	13119	W 2352	19279	W 5093	57177	TISSUS FIBRES SYNTH CONTINUE
65315	CONT SYN TXTL FABRIC NES			W 1876	13119					TIS PLUS 85% TEXT SYNT CONT
6532	DISC SYN TXTL FABRIC NES			W 3466	18286					TIS DISC MOINS 85% FIBR TEXT
6534	DISC SYN BLEND FABRC NES	W 2288	14376			W 4154	42014	W 3168	24492	TISSUS FIBRES SYNTH DISCONT
6535	CONT REGN WEAVES NONPILE	W 873	6249	W 7462	2092	W 2120	14737	W 2537	36432	TISSUS FIB TEXT ART CONTINU
657	SPECIAL TXTL FABRC,PRODS			W 13963	20706					TISSUS SPECIAUX
6573	COATED ETC TEXTILES NES			W 11394	13807					TISSUS,ART MATIERE TEXT NDA
65732	PLASTIC COATED TEXTILES	W 8114	8843	W 10237	11826	W 12853	14554	W 11121	12645	TISSUS IMPREGNES
658	TEXTILE ARTICLES NES			W 55344	26723					ART FACONNES MAT TEXTILES
6581	BAGS,SACKS OF TEXTILES	W 23203	12467	W 55216	26583	W 42596	19613	W 25013	16578	SACS EMBALLAGE TEXTILES
66	NONMETAL MINERAL MFS NES		30150		39533		47496		96488	ART MIN NON METALLIQUES
662	CLAY,REFRACTORY BLDG PRD			W 17355	14251					MAT CONST REFRACTAIRES
6623	REFRACTORY BUILDING PROD			W 15583	13198					BRIQUES REFRACTAIRES
66232	REFRACTRY BRICKS ETC NES	W 9541	8245	W 13846	11895	W 15201	7816	W 14426	8596	BRIQUES ETC REFRACTAIRES
67	IRON AND STEEL		351710		314307		413918		589498	FER ET ACIER
672	IRON,STEEL PRIMARY FORMS	W 59244	14225	W 43829	20928	W 20317	5128	W 7033	1746	LINGOTS FER,ACIER
6724	IRN,STL INGOTS,LUMPS,ETC			W 13929	12560					FER,ACIER LINGOTS,MASSES
67242	HIGH CARBON STEEL INGOTS			W 13629	12515					LINGOTS EN ACIER FIN
673	IRON,STEEL SHAPES ETC	W 153054	55667	W 163895	55172	W 392738	129207			BARRES,PROFIL FER,ACIER
6732	IRON,STEEL BARS ETC			W 88395	29338			W 604404	286163	BARRES FER,ACIER
6733	IRON,STEEL PROFILES ETC			W 75148	25695					PROFILES,PALPLAN FER,ACIER
674	IRN,STL UNIV,PLATE,SHEET	W 210138	88403	W 167060	79127	W 281362	126005			LARGES PLATS,TOLES
6744	IRN,STL HVY PLATE,ROLLED							W 158777	68800	TOLES LAMINEES PLUS 4.75 MM
6746	IRN,STL THIN PLATE,ROLLD			W 117394	46679					TOLES LAM MOINS 3MM
6749	OTH IRN,STL PLATES,SHEET			W 40663	24182					AUTRES TOLES FER,ACIER
67491	— OF IRON OR SIMPLE STL							W 52474	30343	AUT TOLES AUTRES ACIER FIN
675	IRON,STEEL HOOP,STRIP			W 37342	15359					FEUILLARDS LAMINES
67501	IRN,SMPLE STL HOOP,STRIP			W 37342	15359					FEUILLARDS NON ACIER FIN
677	IRN,STL WIRE(EXCL W ROD)			W 41425	15700					FILS EN FER,ACIER
67701	IRON, SIMPLE STEEL WIRE	W 14034	13787	W 41425	15700	W 11709	11287	W 10225	10869	FILS NON ACIER FIN CARBONE
67705	OTHER ALLOY STEEL WIRE	W 42042	13898			W 41946	13715	W 35638	16618	FILS ACIER AUT ACIERS ALLIES
678	IRON,STL TUBES,PIPES,ETC			W 112953	115051					TUBES,TUYAUX EN FONTE,FER
6783	IRON,STL TUBES,PIPES NES	W 123714	122223	W 91843	87574	W 70958	63433	W 95297	86911	AUT TUBES,TUYAUX FER,ACIER
6785	IRON,STEEL TUBE FITTINGS	W 10075	17000	W 9452	15442	W 10574	24879	W 9548	20359	ACCESSOIRES DE TUYAUTERIE
68	NON–FERROUS METALS		24308		36462		36678		38249	METAUX NON FERREUX
682	COPPER EXC CEMENT COPPER			W 6017	17166					CUIVRE
6822	COPPER,ALLOYS WORKED			W 5963	17077					CUIVRE,ALLIAGES OUVRES
68221	COPPER BARS,WIRE,ETC	W 1921	4721	W 4174	11019	W 4386	9072	W 3264	7528	BARRES,PROFILES ET FILS
684	ALUMINIUM			W 8189	16406					ALUMINIUM
6842	ALUMINIUM,ALLOYS WORKED			W 5163	13884					ALUMINIUM,ALLIAGES OUVRE
69	METAL MANUFACTURES NES		90525		146388		102621		232906	ART MANUFACT EN METAL NDA
691	STRUCTURES AND PARTS NES			W 3998	15249					CONSTRUCT FER,ACIER,ALU
6911	STRUCTURES,PARTS IRN,STL	W 4094	17109	W 3985	15173	W 4879	8585	W 20904	103147	CONSTRUCT FER,ACIER,FONTE
692	METAL TANKS,BOXES,ETC			W 8263	52028					RECIPIENTS METALLIQUES
6921	METAL STORAGE TANKS ETC	W 6237	9227	W 1044	3341	W 4284	4056			CUVES EN FONTE,FER,ALU
69211	STEEL STORAGE TANKS ETC			W 1044	3341			W 7216	17888	CUVES EN FONTE FER OU ACIER
6924	MTL TRANSPORT BOXES ETC			W 7219	48687					FUTS,TAMBOURS,BIDONS
69242	ALUMNM TRNSPRT BOXES ETC	W 704	5049	W 5890	45820	W 4581	7023	W 1909	8318	FUTS,TAMBOURS,BIDONS ALU
694	STL,COPPR NAILS,NUTS,ETC			W 7923	11813					CLOUS,VIS,ECROUS
695	TOOLS			W 3762	16500					OUTILS A MAIN
699	BASE METAL MFRS NES			W 19500	34918					ART MANUFACTURES MET NDA
6991	LOCKSMITHS WARES,ETC			W 5126	14887					ARTICLES DE SERRURERIE
6996	BASE MTL MISC ARTICLES			W 10618	12214					ART DIVERS METAUX COMMUNS
7	MACHINES,TRANSPORT EQUIP		598893		1092273		1412177		2033991	MACHINES MATERIEL TRANSPORT
71	POWER GENERATING EQUIPMT		70056		90394		100886		264708	MACHINES GENERATRICES
713	INTRNL COMBUS PSTN ENGIN			W 22610	72031					MOTEURS EXPL COMB INT, PIECE
7131	AIRCRAFT PSTN ENGINS,PTS	W 21	7435	W 639	14082	W 7	77	W 17	5119	MOTEURS EXPL P.AVIATION, PIE
71319	PTS NES OF ENGN OF 71311			W 630	12509					PIECES POUR 713.11
7132	MOTOR VEHCL PISTN ENGINS	W 14960	24019	W 15689	26855	W 18734	25677	W 12451	32829	MOTEURS EXPL POUR VEHICULES
7139	PISTON ENGINE PARTS NES	W 3069	21964	W 3183	25630	W 3467	24940	W 3586	31835	PIECES POUR 713.2,3,8

4. Special Imports C.I.F. by Commodities according to the S.I.T.C. (Rev. 2) in thousand U.S. Dollars
Importations Spéciales C.A.F. par Produits d'après la C.T.C.I. (Rév. 2) en milliers de Dollars E.U.

SITC CTCI	COMMODITY	1991		1992		1993		1994		PRODUIT
		WEIGHT POIDS	VALUE VALEUR	WEIGHT POIDS	VALUE VALEUR	WEIGHT POIDS	VALUE VALEUR	WEIGHT POIDS	VALUE VALEUR	
716	ROTATING ELECTRIC PLANT			W 2999	16013					APP ELECTR ROTATIFS,PIECES
7161	DC MOTORS AND GENERATORS	W 2232	6936	W 1787	11162	W 2833	8674	W 2280	9607	MOTEURS COURANT CONTINU
7162	AC MTRS,GENRTRS,GEN SETS	W 553	2939	W 1212	4851	W 6204	33359			MOTEURS ELECTRIQUES
71622	AC GENERATORS							W 4937	61684	GENER COURANT ALTERNATIF
72	MACHS FOR SPCL INDUSTRYS		95123		195317		197578		260804	MAC SPECIALES POUR INDUST
722	TRACTORS NON–ROAD	W 19336	22494	W 19248	23416	W 20420	25153	W 20791	23066	TRACTEURS
723	CIVIL ENGNEERG EQUIP ETC			W 10927	51159					APPAREILS DE GENIE CIVIL
7234	CONST,MINING MACHNRY NES			W 10098	49627					MACH POUR LA CONST, MINES
724	TEXTILE,LEATHER MACHNRY			W 10087	64707					MACH POUR INDUSTRIE TEXTILE
7243	SEWING MACHS,NEEDLES ETC	W 2370	11301	W 2527	13012	W 2706	10527			MACHINES A COUDRE,PIECES
72431	SEWING MACHINES			W 2394	12517			W 2655	11072	MACHINES A COUDRE
7244	SPINNING,EXTRDNG,ETC MCH	W 121	775	W 989	8608	W 2614	5775	W 6616	58768	MACH POUR LE FILAGE
7245	WEAVING,FELT MFG,ETC MCH			W 3306	23889					METIERS A TISSER,PIECES
72452	KNITTING MACHINES	W 595	6554	W 1634	16251	W 1619	15006	W 1736	10360	METIERS A BONNETERIE
7246	AUXIL TXTL MCH,PARTS NES	W 271	6736	W 593	10686	W 533	7997	W 1012	16683	MACH PR 724.51,52,53,61
728	OTH MACHY FOR SPCL INDUS			W 4139	38076					AUT MACH IND PARTICULIERES
7284	MACHY FOR SPCL INDUS NES			W 3127	29282					MACH SPEC IND PARTICUL.
72848	OTH MCHY WITH INDIV FNCT	W 1430	13618	W 3127	29282	W 3297	30084	W 7171	54886	AUTRES MACHINES NDA
73	METALWORKING MACHINERY		8835		16013		15973		12424	MACH TRAVAIL DES METAUX
736	METALWORKING MACH–TOOLS			W 4888	14067					MACH–OUTILS TRAVAIL METAUX
7361	METAL CUTTING MACH–TOOLS			W 4561	12904					MACH–OUT ENLEVEMENT METAL
73732	ELECTRIC WELDERS,ETC	W 3516	7637			W 4185	14255	W 4072	11243	MACH ELECT POUR SOUDER
74	GENRL INDUSTRL MACHY NES		167371		180942		308571		458742	MACH APP INDUSTRIE
741	HEATING,COOLING EQUIPMNT			W 4252	23952					MACH CHAUFFAGE,PIECES
742	PUMPS FOR LIQUIDS ETC			W 5689	31663					POMPES MOTO–POMPES
7428	OTHER PUMPS FOR LIQUIDS			W 5165	28611					AUTRES POMPES POUR LIQ
74288	PUMPS FR LIQUIDS NES ETC	W 4107	15921	W 5150	28164	W 2623	15036	W 4007	16972	POMPES POUR LIQUIDES NDA
7429	PTS NES OF PUMPS OF 742	W 1104	8679			W 1349	12932	W 4015	56566	PIECES POUR GROUPE 742
743	PUMPS NES,CENTRFUGES ETC			W 5125	33456					POMPES COMPRES,VENT ETC
7431	PUMPS FOR GASES ETC	W 2864	14262	W 198	2907	W 4030	21000	W 7060	90462	POMPES AIR A VIDE,COMPRES
7434	FANS,BLOWERS,ETC,PARTS			W 3836	23063					VENTILATEURS,SIMIL,PIECES
74421	PULLEY TACKLE,WINCHS ETC	W 4189	22197			W 20746	79298	W 19215	45091	PALANS,TREUILS
74422	SHIP DERRICKS,CRANES ETC	W 1633	12247			W 4186	33438	W 48	1251	GRUES,PONTS ROULANTS
745	NONELEC MACHY,TOOLS NES			W 775	13174					AUT MACH NON ELEC,PIECES
7452	OTH NONELEC MCHS,PTS NES			W 741	12638					AUT MACH NON ELEC,PIECES
749	NONELEC MACH PTS,ACC NES			W 7953	70148					PIECES MACH NON ELEC NDA
7491	BALL,ROLLER,ETC BEARINGS			W 1694	11987					ROULEMENTS BILLES ETC
7492	COCKS,VALVES ETC NES	W 3121	26240	W 3778	34128	W 4479	31728	W 6243	66857	ART ROB,SIM POUR TUYAUX
7493	SHAFT,CRANK,PULLEY ETC	W 977	6710	W 1757	13529	W 1263	10484	W 983	9671	ARBRES TRANS,VILEBREQUINS
7499	OTH NONELEC MCHY PTS NES			W 723	10504					PIECES NON ELECT NDA
74999	MACH PARTS NONELEC NES	W 1329	8564			W 1934	11276	W 1830	11443	PIECES MACHINES NDA
75	OFFICE MACHNES,ADP EQUIP		10592		13382		19394		20049	MACH BUREAU TRAIT AUTOM
76	TELECOMM,SOUND EQUIPMENT		12903		52172		150447		89594	EQUIPMENT DE TELECOM
762	RADIO BROADCAST RECEIVRS			W 1551	12982					RECEPTEURS RADIODIFFUSION
7628	OTHER RADIO RECEIVERS			W 1376	10707					AUTRES RECEPT RADIO
764	TELECOM EQPT,PTS,ACC NES			W 854	32291					EQUIP TELECOM,PIECES
7641	LINE TELEPHONE,ETC EQUIP			W 524	25269					APP TELEPHON PAR FIL
76491	PTS NES OF APPAR OF 7641	W 54	1861			W 3724	126969	W 1515	45509	PIECES POUR 764.1
77	ELECTRIC MACHNRY NES ETC		79133		109404		130841		272023	MACH APP ELECT NDA
771	ELECTRIC POWER MACHY NES			W 3731	10827					MACH PROD,TRANS ELECTR
7711	TRANSFORMERS,ELECTRICAL	W 1085	2619	W 1506	3689	W 2271	3170	W 4964	42853	TRANSFO ELECTRIQUES
772	SWITCHGEAR ETC,PARTS NES			W 2331	24230					APP COUPURE,SECT ETC
7721	SWITCHGEAR ETC	W 1880	16827	W 2322	24095	W 3076	26216	W 6665	86612	APP COUPURE,SECTIONMNT
773	ELECTR DISTRIBUTNG EQUIP			W 5306	22021	W 13317	42031			EQUIPMT DISTRIBUTION ELECT
7731	INSULATED WIRE,CABLE ETC	W 3105	18231	W 5064	21011			W 8535	31039	FILS,CABLES ISOLES ELECT
778	ELECTRICAL MACHINERY NES			W 5218	36972					AUTRES MACH ELECT NDA
7788	OTH ELEC MACHY,EQUIP NES			W 1520	16353					AUT MACH APP ELEC NDA
77882	ELEC TRAFFIC CONTROL EQU	W 876	17016	W 22	475	W 949	14566			APP ELECT SIGNAL,SECURITE ET
77889	ELEC PARTS OF MACHY NES			W 288	10627			W 1681	21258	PIECES ELEC DE MACH NDA
78	ROAD VEHICLES		141418		418836		466887		634422	VEHICULES ROUTIERS
781	PASS MOTOR VEH EXC BUSES			W 5577	69903	W 12755	102088	W 9499	67460	AUTO TRANSPORT PERSONNES
782	LORRIES,SPCL MTR VEH NES			W 29281	190361					VEHICULES SPECIAUX,MARCH
7821	LORRIES,TRUCKS	W 7000	59715	W 27641	177762	W 40235	289621	W 44232	422227	VEHICULES TRANSP MARCHAND
7822	SPECIAL MOTOR VEHCLS NES	W 721	6986	W 1639	12599	W 1029	7754	W 1140	16423	VEHICULES USAGES SPECIAUX
783	ROAD MOTOR VEHICLES NES			W 13936	99447					VEHICULES ROUTIERS NDA
7831	BUSES	W 1756	6588	W 13556	97346	W 2463	2543	W 650	11838	VOITURES TRANSPORT COMMUN
784	MOTOR VEH PRTS,ACCES NES			W 17028	46850					PIECES 722,781,782,783
7849	OTHER MOTOR VEHCL PARTS	W 3924	23852	W 15674	38047	W 16457	42647	W 14883	78567	PIECES 722,781,782,783
79	OTHR TRANSPORT EQUIPMENT		13462		15814		21600		20691	AUTRE MATERIEL TRANSPORT
8	MISC MANUFACTURED GOODS		52197		104892		98664		159271	ART MANUFACTURES DIVERS
87	PRECISION INSTRUMNTS NES		23623		45004		42157		78313	INSTRUM,APPAR SCIENT NDA
872	MEDICAL INSTRUMENTS NES			W 453	11126					INSTR,APP MEDIC–CHIR NDA
87201	DENTAL INSTRUMENTS			W 429	10900					INSTRUM,APPAR DENTAIRE
874	MEASURNG,CONTROLNG INSTR			W 970	28447					INSTRUMENTS DE MESURE
8743	GAS,LIQUID CONTROL INSTR	W 420	6867	W 228	7508	W 473	11116	W 1802	34943	APP,INSTR MESURE FLUIDES
8748	ELEC MEAS,CONTRL EQU NES			W 282	12353					APP ELEC ELECTRO MESURE
87483	OTH ELCTRNC MEAS ETC EQU	W 94	5626			W 254	11825	W 815	31473	AUT APP ELECTRO DE MESURE
88	PHOTO EQU,OPTICL GDS ETC		6399		16619		19423		22122	APP,FOURN PHOTO,OP,MONTR
89	MISC MANUFCTRD GOODS NES		18781		32547		30273		46498	ART MANUFACTURES DIVERS
893	ARTICLES OF PLASTIC NES			W 2317	11152					OUVRAGES EN MAT DIVIS 58
8939	MISC PLASTIC ARTICLES			W 2175	10799					ART DIVERS EN MAT DIV 58
9	GOODS NOT CLASSD BY KIND				25733		37209		97524	ART TRANSACT NON CLASSES
931	*SPECIAL TRANSACTIONS				24295				97089	TRANS.SPECIALES

5. Special Exports F.O.B. by Commodities according to the S.I.T.C. (Rev. 2) in thousand U.S. Dollars
Exportations Spéciales F.O.B. par Produits d'après la C.T.C.I. (Rév. 2) en milliers de Dollars E.U.

SITC CTCI	COMMODITY	1991 WEIGHT POIDS	1991 VALUE VALEUR	1992 WEIGHT POIDS	1992 VALUE VALEUR	1993 WEIGHT POIDS	1993 VALUE VALEUR	1994 WEIGHT POIDS	1994 VALUE VALEUR	PRODUIT
	ALL COMMODITIES		3430316		3093082		3279885		3547309	TOUS PRODUITS
0	FOOD AND LIVE ANIMALS		391333		400711		455950		567749	ALIMENTS,ANIMAUX VIVANTS
001	*LIVE ANIMALS FOR FOOD				116092		93635		76434	ANIMAUX VIVANTS
0012	SHEEP AND GOATS,LIVE			N 1250186	112216					ESPECES OVINE ET CAPRINE
00121	SHEEP,LIVE	N 1190000	100829	N 1163825	107370	W 1045	82559	N 806000	62823	ESPECE OVINE
00122	GOATS,LIVE	N 1188000	17760	N 86361	4846	W 132	6895	N 164000	8432	ESPECE CAPRINE
02	DAIRY PRODCTS,BIRDS'EGGS		6243		5477		9704		11538	PRODUITS LAITIERS,OEUFS
04	CEREALS AND PREPARATIONS		7313		10487		22083		39940	CEREALES ET PRODUITS
05	VEGETABLES AND FRUIT		227883		245902		293578		381302	LEGUMES ET FRUITS
054	VEG ETC FRSH,SMPLY PRSVD			W 240042	133788					LEGUMES FRAIS,CONG,SECS
0541	POTATOES FRSH EXCL SWEET	W 267051	31263	W 135399	70369	W 67365	19524	W 49928	18731	POMMES DE TERRE
0542	LEGUMINOUS VEGETBLES DRY	W 45133	14733	W 21104	12141	W 67049	24050	W 126393	66400	LEGUMES A COSSE SECS
0544	TOMATOES FRESH	W 29622	14103	W 25470	9753	W 64255	24707	W 93176	51875	TOMATES FRAICHES
0545	OTHER FRESH VEGETABLES			W 58011	41488					AUTRES LEGUMES FRAIS,REF
05451	ALLIACEOUS VEGTBLS,FRESH	W 34917	12986	W 27511	23106	W 11982	6937	W 16985	11585	OIGNONS,ECHALOTES,AULX
05459	FRESH VEGETABLES NES	W 26851	15745	W 30501	18382	W 83762	70425	W 75587	61528	LEGUMES FRAIS,REFRI NDA
0548	EDIBLE VEG NES FRESH,DRY			W 48	26			W 6253	42291	RACINES,TUBERCULES
057	FRUIT,NUTS,FRESH,DRIED			W 115202	96773					FRUITS FRAIS OU SECS
05751	GRAPES FRESH	W 5940	2350	W 12601	7581	W 11716	7444	W 16928	14313	RAISINS FRAIS
0577	NUTS EDIBLE,FRESH,DRIED			W 10017	24662					FRUITS A COQUES
05774	ALMONDS,FRESH OR DRIED			W 7773	16111					AMANDES FRAICHES,SECHES
05779	NUTS EDIBLE,FRSH,DRY,NES	W 4211	17705	W 2149	8496	W 9828	34566	W 6669	24131	FRUITS A COQUES NDA
0579	FRUIT FRESH OR DRIED NES			W 83699	59777					FRUITS FRAIS,SECS NDA
05793	STONE FRUIT FRESH NES	W 3801	2488	W 14733	8066	W 24557	20338	W 22854	23874	FRUITS A NOYAU NDA FRAIS
05798	OTHER FRESH FRUIT	W 54016	30202	W 66130	50492	W 41813	17597	W 34828	14359	AUTRES FRUITS FRAIS
058	FRUIT PRESERVED,PREPARED			W 12025	12133					CONSERVES DE FRUITS
0583	FRUIT JAMS,JELLIES ETC			W 11798	11985	W 631	5677			PATES DE FRUITS CONFITURES
0586	FRUIT TEMPORARILY PRESVD	W 9773	48060	W 4	2					FRUITS CONSERV TEMPORAIRE
06	SUGAR AND PREPS,HONEY		6980		5796		10728		11237	SUCRES ET PRODUITS
07	COFFEE,TEA,COCOA,SPICES		17076		16433		24788		46274	CAFE,THE,CACAO,EPICES
075	SPICES			W 6950	12843					EPICES
0752	SPICES,EX PEPPER,PIMENTO			W 6933	12814					AUTRES EPICES
07525	SEEDS OF ANISE,CUMIN,ETC	W 5867	8836	W 6060	12135	W 15636	19594	W 22508	36532	GRAINES ANIS,FENOUIL
1	BEVERAGES AND TOBACCO		60095		5176		9099		7013	BOISSONS ET TABACS
11	BEVERAGES		19375		3216		4607		2788	BOISSONS
12	TOBACCO AND MANUFACTURES		40720		1960		4492		4225	TABACS BRUTS FABRIQUES
1211	TOBACCO,NOT STRIPPED	W 6397	16577			W 1990	4184	W 1602	4023	TABACS NON ECOTES
1222	CIGARETTES	W 796	24028	W 5	110					CIGARETTES
2	CRUDE MATERLS,EXCL FUELS		237157		249012		227848		270992	MAT BRUTES NON COMESTIBLES
21	HIDES,SKINS,FURS UNDRSSD		8433		17137		6236		7833	CUIRS,PEAUX BRUTS
211	HIDES,SKINS,EXC FURS,RAW	W 2725	4417	W 5295	17076	W 2985	5771			CUIRS ET PEAUX
2119	SKIN NES,WASTE,USED LTHR			W 4469	10743					CUIRS ET PEAUX NDA
21199	HIDES AND SKINS NES,RAW			W 3980	10739					CUIRS,PEAUX NDA
22	OIL SEEDS,OLEAGINOUS FRT		385		1215		16604		14189	GRAINES,FRUITS OLEAGINEUX
2223	COTTON SEEDS					W 127892	15409	W 107353	13244	GRAINES DE COTON
26	TEXTILE FIBRES AND WASTE		182477		179896		182749		206082	FIBRES TEXTILES
263	COTTON			W 155237	176970					COTON
2631	RAW COTTON,EXCL LINTERS	W 81202	171121	W 134924	170330	W 158923	174238	W 150595	194308	COTON EN MASSE
27	CRUDE FERTLZR,MINRLS NES		35009		44871		16539		19004	ENGRAIS MINERAUX BRUTS
271	FERTILIZERS,CRUDE			W 1239513	43472					ENGRAIS BRUTS
2713	NAT CALCM PHOSPHATES ETC	W 1140385	33231	W 1239512	43471	W 821423	15391	W 881756	16978	PHOSPHATES DE CALCIUM
29	CRUDE ANIMAL,VEG MAT NES		10823		5681		5012		17615	MATIERES BRUTES ANIM,VEGET
3	MINERAL FUELS ETC		1831887		2152353		2098965		1994753	COMBUSTIBLES MINERAUX LUB
33	PETROLEUM AND PRODUCTS		1830318		2152149		2098954		1994742	PETROLE ET DERIVES
333	CRUDE PETROLEUM			MW 14606	1850645					HUILES BRUTES DE PETROLE
334	PETROLEUM PRODUCTS,REFIN			W 2378700	294753					PRODUITS RAFFINES
3341	GASOLINE,OTH LIGHT OILS			W 573595	121976					ESSENCES POUR MOTEURS
33411	MOTOR,AVIATION SPIRIT			W 571376	121541					ESSENCES MOTEURS D'AVIONS
3344	FUEL OILS,NES			W 1763427	165400					FUEL OILS
5	CHEMCLS,RELATED PROD NES		101945		7204		13709		15412	PRODUITS CHIMIQUES
55	PERFUME,CLEANING ETC PRD		101109		5095		4609		8700	PROD POUR PARFUM,TOILETTE
553	PERFUMERY,COSMETICS,ETC	W 2628	97493	W 1215	2959	W 931	1667	W 799	3349	PRODUITS DE PARFUMERIE
6	BASIC MANUFACTURES		510514		131245		140386		203557	ART MANUFACTURES
61	LEATHER,DRESSED FUR,ETC		1339		357		15558		19865	CUIRS,PELLETERIES
61161	LEATHER FROM GOAT,KID				1	W 2056	15464	W 1756	19244	PEAUX DE CAPRINS PREPAREES
65	TEXTILE YARN,FABRICS,ETC		483727		102131		93934		148569	FILS,TISSUS,ARTICLES TEXTILE
651	TEXTILE YARN			W 2045	10093					FILS TEXTILES
6513	COTTON YARN	W 2748	12074	W 1872	9971	W 469	2079	W 15662	10093	FILS DE COTON
652	COTTON FABRICS,WOVEN			W 1821	10015					TISSUS DE COTON
65224	BLCHED COTTON FABRIC NES	W 4817	18248	W 980	6500	W 937	8079	W 347	4496	AUT TIS PLUS 85% COT BLANCHI
653	WOVN MAN–MADE FIB FABRIC			W 1919	36168					TISSUS FIBRES SYNTH,ARTIF
6531	CONT SYNT WEAVES NONPILE	W 3358	278077	W 1144	24012	W 952	7484	W 893	10954	TISSUS FIBRES SYNTH CONTINUE
65315	CONT SYN TXTL FABRIC NES			W 1144	24012					TIS PLUS 85% TEXT SYNT CONT
6532	DISC SYN TXTL FABRIC NES	W 87	1032	W 154	1186	W 503	3863	W 919	16857	TIS DISC MOINS 85% FIBR TEXT
655	KNITTED,ETC FABRICS	W 3234	141367	W 3989	31845	W 7293	43652			ETOF BONNETERIE PIECES ETC
6551	KNIT ETC SYNTH FAB NONEL			W 3700	30567					ETOFFES BON NON ELAS TEXT
6552	OTHER KNIT ETC FAB NONEL			W 278	1185			W 7781	56976	ETOF BON NON ELAS NON SYNT
65843	TABLE LINEN OF COTTON	W 543	4327			W 964	6615	W 811	12011	LINGE DE TABLE DE COTON
66	NONMETAL MINERAL MFS NES		15883		18745		7375		5496	ART MIN NON METALLIQUES
661	LIME,CEMENT,BLDG PRODS			W 572169	17301					CHAUX,CIMENTS MAT CONSTR
6612	CEMENT	W 437827	13522	W 561763	16291	W 152183	3848	W 1537	182	CIMENTS HYDRAULIQUES
69	METAL MANUFACTURES NES		6698		7576		12715		17076	ART MANUFACT EN METAL NDA
7	MACHINES,TRANSPORT EQUIP		7080		9035		86736		22405	MACHINES MATERIEL TRANSPORT
74	GENRL INDUSTRL MACHY NES		1973		1996		23852		7850	MACH APP INDUSTRIE
78	ROAD VEHICLES		181		705		44400		1598	VEHICULES ROUTIERS
8	MISC MANUFACTURED GOODS		289914		137540		246516		464171	ART MANUFACTURES DIVERS
84	CLOTHING AND ACCESSORIES		266516		109530		202993		402429	VETEMENTS
842	MENS OUTERWEAR NOT KNIT	W 2520	81217	W 1783	21778	W 2834	38719			VET DESSUS POUR HOMMES
843	WOMENS OUTERWEAR NONKNIT	W 1734	37199	W 1386	20586	W 2848	39674			VET DESSUS FEMMES MAT TEX
845	OUTERWEAR KNIT NONELASTC			W 2527	28220					VET DESSOUS,ACCES BONNET
8459	— OTHER,CLTHG ACCESRYS	W 3664	113897			W 6112	64671	W 1464	34688	AUT VET DESSUS DE BONNE
846	UNDER GARMENTS KNITTED			W 2484	28361					SOUS VETS DE BONNETERIE
8462	— OF COTTON NON ELASTIC			W 1757	17726					SOUS–VET BONNET COTON
84621	—— MENS SHIRTS	W 1427	19258			W 2514	26484			CHEMISES DE COTON
8463	— OF SYNTH FBR NONELAST			W 659	9466					SOUS–VET BONNET FIB SYNT
84632	—— MENS SHIRTS							W 2360	22553	CHEMISES DE BON FIB SYNMT
84721	KNIT GLOVES,ETC NONELAST	W 155	2328	W 53	659	W 389	4218	W 648	15230	GANTERIE BONNET NON ELAS
84723	KNIT ARTICLES NES ELASTC							W 6704	153763	ART NDA DE BONNET ELAST
851	*FOOTWEAR			W 2536	8097		12744		34462	CHAUSSURES
85102	FOOTWEAR LEATHER	W 867	3443	W 2048	6625	W 924	2536	W 831	12143	CHAUS SEMELLES EN CUIR
85104	FOOTWEAR NES			W 2	4			W 2125	10903	CHAUS SEMELLES AUT MAT

5. Special Exports F.O.B. by Commodities according to the S.I.T.C. (Rev. 2) in thousand U.S. Dollars
Exportations Spéciales F.O.B. par Produits d'après la C.T.C.I. (Rév. 2) en milliers de Dollars E.U.

SITC CTCI	COMMODITY	1991		1992		1993		1994		PRODUIT
		WEIGHT POIDS	VALUE VALEUR	WEIGHT POIDS	VALUE VALEUR	WEIGHT POIDS	VALUE VALEUR	WEIGHT POIDS	VALUE VALEUR	
89	MISC MANUFCTRD GOODS NES		7268		7557		16353		11461	ART MANUFACTURES DIVERS

1. HISTORICAL SERIES, 1992–1996 GENERAL TRADE, IMPORTS C.I.F., EXPORTS F.O.B.
SERIES HISTORIQUES, 1992–1996 COMMERCE GENERAL, IMPORTATIONS C.A.F., EXPORTATIONS F.O.B

YEAR ANNEE	VALUE IN MILLION U.S. DOLLARS VALEUR EN MILLION U.S. DOLLARS MERCHANDISE – MARCHANDISE IMPORTS	MERCHANDISE – MARCHANDISE EXPORTS	GOLD – OR IMPORTS	GOLD – OR EXPORTS	CONVERSION FACTORS FACTEURS DE CONVERSION CENTS E.U. PAR IMPORTS	CONVERSION FACTORS EXPORTS	INDEX NUMBERS – INDICES QUANTUM IMPORTS	QUANTUM EXPORTS	UNIT VALUE VALEUR UNITAIRE IMPORTS	UNIT VALUE VALEUR UNITAIRE EXPORTS
1992	132.00	111.00								
1993	532.11	349.77								
1994	546.99	491.90								
1995	809.92	748.59								
1996	668.10	770.09								

2. IMPORTS BY BROAD ECONOMIC CATEGORY AND EXPORTS BY INDUSTRIAL ORIGIN. (PERCENTAGE OF TOTAL VALUE)
IMPORTATIONS PAR CATEGORIES ECONOMIQUES ET EXPORTATIONS PAR BRANCHE D'ACTIVITE. (EN POURCENTAGE DE LA VALEUR TOTALE)

IMPORTS – IMPORTATIONS

	1990	1991	1992	1993	1994	1995	1996
TOTAL IMPORTS–IMPORTATIONS TOTALES							
1 FOOD BEV–ALIMENTATION BOISSONS							
11 PRIMARY–PRODUITS DE BASE							
111 FOR INDUSTRY–POUR L'INDUSTRIE							
112 FOR HOUSEHOLDS–POUR LES MENAGES							
12 PROCESSED–PRODUITS ELABORES							
121 FOR INDUSTRY–POUR L'INDUSTRIE							
122 FOR HOUSEHOLDS–POUR LES MENAGES							
2 IND SUPPLIES–APPROV INDUSTRIELS							
21 PRIMARY–PRODUITS DE BASE							
22 PROCESSED–PRODUITS ELABORES							
3 FUELS–COMBUSTIBLES							
31 PRIMARY–PRODUITS DE BASE							
32 PROCESSED–PRODUITS ELABORES							
321 MOTOR SPIRIT–ESSENCE							
322 OTHER–AUTRES							
4 MACHINERY–EQUIPEMENT							
41 CAPITAL EQUIPMENT–MACHINES							
42 PARTS–PIECES ACCESSOIRES							
5 TRANSPORT–TRANSPORT							
51 PASSENGER CARS–AUTOMOBILES							
52 OTHER–AUTRES							
521 INDUSTRIAL–INDUSTRIELS							
522 NON INDUSTRIAL–NON INDUSTRIEL							
53 PARTS–PIECES ACCESSOIRES							
6 CONSUM GOODS–BIENS CONSOMMATION							
61 DURABLE–DURABLES							
62 SEMI DURABLE–SEMI DURABLES							
63 NON DURABLE–NON DURABLES							
7 GOODS NES–BIENS NDA							

EXPORTS – EXPORTATIONS

	1990	1991	1992	1993	1994	1995	1996
TOTAL EXPORTS–EXPORTATIONS TOTALES							
1 AGRICULTURE							
2 MINING QUARRY–INDUS EXTRACTIVES							
3 MANUFACTURING–IND MANUFACTUR							
31 FOOD BEV TOBACCO–ALIM BOISS TAB							
32 TEXTILES–INDUSTRIES TEXTILES							
33 WOOD & PRODUCTS–BOIS & PRODUITS							
34 PAPER & PRODUCTS–PAPIER & PRODT							
35 CHEMICALS–INDUSTRIES CHIMIQUES							
36 NON METAL MIN–MIN NON METAL							
37 BASIC METAL–IND METAL BASE							
38 METAL MANUF–MANUF METAL							
39 OTH MANUF IND–AUTRES MANUF							

3. TRADE BY PRINCIPAL COUNTRIES OF ORIGIN AND DESTINATION (VALUE IN THOUSAND U.S. DOLLARS)
ECHANGES SELON LES PRINCIPAUX PAYS D'ORIGINE ET DE DESTINATION (VALEUR EN MILLIERS DE DOLLARS EU)

COUNTRIES–PAYS	GENERAL IMPORTS C.I.F. IMPORTATIONS GENERALES C.A.F				
	1992	1993	1994	1995	1996
World	160694	532108	546988	810000	668096
Africa		305	47		62
Americas		8780	33321	30900	18036
Northern America		8760	32993	30900	8861
LAIA		20			
CACM					
Caribbean					9175
Rest of America			328		
As.ex F.USSR		15684	25442	5000	45616
Eur.x F.USSR		245110	239531	257800	214644
EU		227012	129657	202800	107768
EFTA		9566	106909	53200	99792
East Europe		7622	2885	1800	7026
Other Europe		910	80		58
Former USSR	123838	261488	248557	487500	389733
Oceania		741	88		
Uzbekistan/Ouzbékistan	13660	65397	83216	251400	198858
Russian Federation	57867	83757	60689	136000	74410
United Kingdom		16380	67975	153900	78348
Switz.Liecht		4276	100347	45300	99792
Kazakhstan	15143	65470	32848	26600	52406
Turkmenistan/Turkménistn	18015	26037	39419	57400	26297
Netherlands/Pays–Bas		115582	16397	3800	5328
USA/Etats–Unis d'Amer		8733	31916	25300	7416
Belgium–Luxembourg		21003	22814	25100	282
Ukraine	8991	4352	13620	2200	19213
Germany/Allemagne		9350	5378	14200	9082
France,Monac		25371	1541	600	7422
Turkey/Turquie		4429	16688	3900	5312
Austria/Autriche		9916	9617	1400	558
Lithuania/Lituanie	826	4339	13636	700	1879
Sweden/Suède		18375	2480		16
Norway,SVD,JM		5290	6562	7900	
China/Chine		10522	4759	400	1318
Kyrgyzstan/Kirghizistan	2490	2088	1013	2700	7243
Belarus/Bélarus	3437	6756	1293	400	2972
Iran (Islamic Rp. of)			129		10462
Estonia/Estonie	425	263	810	4600	3892
Latvia/Lettonie	747	1073	1070	5100	1467
British Virgin Islds					8556
Canada		27	1077	5600	1445
Korea, Republic of		118	615	100	7103
Pakistan			1775		6021
Italy/Italie		5449	761		1436
Finland/Finlande		4224	4		3303
Ireland/Irlande			1904	3800	1512
United Arab Emirates					6638
Czech Republic		609	2409	1400	1371
Bulgaria/Bulgarie		13	329		4860
Poland/Pologne		3975	117		103
Afghanistan		217	1250		2308
Hungary/Hongrie		3025	30	300	102
Azerbaijan	1362	1078	203	200	44
Korea Dem People's Rp		26	209		2484
Denmark/Danemark		1299	758		15
Cyprus/Chypre		10			2016
Georgia/Géorgie	267	332	411		768
Japan/Japon		319			1120
Republic of Moldova	360	448	103		194
Malta/Malte		910	80		58
Armenia/Arménie	248	98	226	200	90
New Zealand		741	88		
Bahamas					619
Viet Nam				600	
Greece/Grèce		63	28		451
Slovakia					493

COUNTRIES–PAYS	GENERAL EXPORTS F.O.B. EXPORTATIONS GENERALES F.O.B.				
	1992	1993	1994	1995	1996
Monde	192487	349773	491904	748600	770087
Afrique		19	138		91
Amériques		15143	27114	14800	10779
Amérique du Nord		15143	27114	14800	10779
ALAI					
MCAC					
Caraïbes					
Autre Amérique					
Asie l'URSS exclus		26555	27541	35300	45365
Europe l'URSS exclus		173456	327036	412600	366943
UE		165694	259358	346600	265851
AELE		5822	57080	42600	84087
Europe de l'Est		1940	10598	19500	15662
Autre de l'Europe					
Ancienne URSS	85364	134588	110073	284300	346903
Océanie		10			
Netherlands/Pays–Bas		1064	147565	255100	218048
Uzbekistan/Ouzbékistan	7638	20262	22679	132000	190716
Russian Federation	40588	62525	46236	95300	78977
United Kingdom		119866	30274	20700	15212
Switz.Liecht		5822	44943	37200	83520
Belgium–Luxembourg		15235	30466	32700	5527
Kazakhstan	12524	16252	10099	7000	24290
USA/Etats–Unis d'Amer		15143	27114	14800	10779
Finland/Finlande		7798	18124	20100	8928
Latvia/Lettonie	720	7223	3387	21000	9503
Austria/Autriche		10797	16723	9700	3490
Ukraine	10011	4940	5090	9300	10747
Korea, Republic of		934	2855	9300	24919
Japan/Japon		17711	10977	8200	162
Lithuania/Lituanie	203	4476	13620	9000	5603
Hungary/Hongrie		5	3366	13500	10448
Turkey/Turquie		5156	7594	8100	1912
Kyrgyzstan/Kirghizistan	1981	4141	1934	2600	10496
Germany/Allemagne		719	12948	4700	2559
Belarus/Bélarus	3530	6685	3105	2300	4333
Turkmenistan/Turkménistn	3664	3457	1750	2200	8462
Norway,SVD,JM			12137	5400	567
China/Chine		147	1422	5600	6193
Italy/Italie		2535	428	2400	6648
Korea Dem People's Rp		542		3300	5138
Sweden/Suède		7600	774		
Azerbaijan	3294	1071	158	900	2582
Slovakia			3418	700	3795
Republic of Moldova	359	3364	1420		68
Romania/Roumanie			1542	2200	1215
France,Monac				200	4424
Estonia/Estonie	391	146	582	2700	796
Czech Republic		1465	780	2200	138
Yugoslavia/Yougoslavie				3900	
Afghanistan		775	780	300	1519
Iran (Islamic Rp. of)			1385		1714
Viet Nam			1217	300	729
Pakistan		775			1446
Greece/Grèce		80	1633		131
Bulgaria/Bulgarie		454	709	400	66
Spain/Espagne			423	700	296
Slovenia/Slovénia					1343
Poland/Pologne		16	783	500	
Ireland/Irlande				300	539
Iraq		50	734		
Mongolia/Mongolie		426	314		
Sri Lanka					534
Georgia/Géorgie	120	46			327
Cyprus/Chypre		10			405
Hong Kong					390

(VALUE AS PERCENTAGE OF WORLD TOTAL)(VALEURS EN POURCENTAGE DU TOTAL MONDIAL)

	1987	1988	1989	1990	1991	1992	1993	1994	1995	1996
Africa							0.1	0.0		0.0
Americas							1.7	6.1	3.8	2.7
Northern America							1.6	6.0	3.8	1.3
LAIA							0.0			
CACM										
Caribbean										1.4
Rest of America								0.1		
As.ex F.USSR							2.9	4.7	0.6	6.8
Eur.x F.USSR							46.1	43.8	31.8	32.1
EU							42.7	23.7	25.0	16.1
EFTA							1.8	19.5	6.6	14.9
East Europe							1.4	0.5	0.2	1.1
Other Europe							0.2	0.0		0.0
Former USSR						77.1	49.1	45.4	60.2	58.3
Oceania							0.1	0.0		
Uzbekistan/Ouzbékistan						8.5	12.3	15.2	31.0	29.8
Russian Federation						36.0	15.7	11.1	16.8	11.1
United Kingdom							3.1	12.4	19.0	11.7
Switz.Liecht							0.8	18.3	5.6	14.9
Kazakhstan						9.4	12.3	6.0	3.3	7.8
Turkmenistan/Turkménistn						11.2	4.9	7.2	7.1	3.9
Netherlands/Pays–Bas							21.7	3.0	0.5	0.8
USA/Etats–Unis d'Amer							1.6	5.8	3.1	1.1
Belgium–Luxembourg							3.9	4.2	3.1	0.0
Ukraine						5.6	0.8	2.5	0.3	2.9

	1987	1988	1989	1990	1991	1992	1993	1994	1995	1996
Afrique							0.0	0.0		0.0
Amériques							4.3	5.5	2.0	1.4
Amérique du Nord							4.3	5.5	2.0	1.4
ALAI										
MCAC										
Caraïbes										
Autre Amérique										
Asie l'URSS exclus							7.6	5.6	4.7	5.9
Europe l'URSS exclus							49.6	66.5	55.1	47.6
UE							47.4	52.7	46.3	34.5
AELE							1.7	11.6	5.7	10.9
Europe de l'Est							0.6	2.2	2.6	2.0
Autre de l'Europe										
Ancienne URSS						44.3	38.5	22.4	38.0	45.0
Océanie							0.0			
Netherlands/Pays–Bas							0.3	30.0	34.1	28.3
Uzbekistan/Ouzbékistan						4.0	5.8	4.6	17.6	24.8
Russian Federation						21.1	17.9	9.4	12.7	10.3
United Kingdom							34.3	6.2	2.8	2.0
Switz.Liecht							1.7	9.1	5.0	10.8
Belgium–Luxembourg							4.4	6.2	4.4	0.7
Kazakhstan						6.5	4.6	2.1	0.9	3.2
USA/Etats–Unis d'Amer							4.3	5.5	2.0	1.4
Finland/Finlande							2.2	3.7	2.7	1.2
Latvia/Lettonie						0.4	2.1	0.7	2.8	1.2

4. General Imports C.I.F. by Commodities according to the S.I.T.C. (Rev. 2) in thousand U.S. Dollars
Importations Générales C.A.F. par Produits d'après la C.T.C.I. (Rév. 2) en milliers de Dollars E.U.

SITC CTCI	COMMODITY	1992		1993		1994		1995		PRODUIT
		WEIGHT POIDS	VALUE VALEUR	WEIGHT POIDS	VALUE VALEUR	WEIGHT POIDS	VALUE VALEUR	WEIGHT POIDS	VALUE VALEUR	
	ALL COMMODITIES								810000	TOUS PRODUITS

5. General Exports F.O.B. by Commodities according to the S.I.T.C. (Rev. 2) in thousand U.S. Dollars
Exportations Générales F.O.B. par Produits d'après la C.T.C.I. (Rév. 2) en milliers de Dollars E.U.

SITC CTCI	COMMODITY	1992		1993		1994		1995		PRODUIT
		WEIGHT POIDS	VALUE VALEUR	WEIGHT POIDS	VALUE VALEUR	WEIGHT POIDS	VALUE VALEUR	WEIGHT POIDS	VALUE VALEUR	
	ALL COMMODITIES								748600	TOUS PRODUITS

The former Yugoslav Republic of Macedonia

L'ex–République Yugoslave de Macédoine

1. HISTORICAL SERIES, 1993–1995 GENERAL TRADE, IMPORTS F.O.B., EXPORTS F.O.B.
SERIES HISTORIQUES, 1993–1995 COMMERCE GENERAL, IMPORTATIONS F.O.B., EXPORTATIONS F.O.B

YEAR ANNEE	VALUE IN MILLION U.S. DOLLARS VALEUR EN MILLION U.S. DOLLARS MERCHANDISE –MARCHANDISE		GOLD –OR		CONVERSION FACTORS FACTEURS DE CONVERSION CENTS E.U. PAR		INDEX NUMBERS –INDICES QUANTUM		UNIT VALUE VALEUR UNITAIRE	
	IMPORTS	EXPORTS	IMPORTS	EXPORTS	IMPORTS	EXPORTS	IMPORTS	EXPORTS	IMPORTS	EXPORTS
1993	1199.35	1055.30								
1994	1484.09	1086.34								
1995	1718.90	1204.05								

2. IMPORTS BY BROAD ECONOMIC CATEGORY AND EXPORTS BY INDUSTRIAL ORIGIN. (PERCENTAGE OF TOTAL VALUE)
IMPORTATIONS PAR CATEGORIES ECONOMIQUES ET EXPORTATIONS PAR BRANCHE D'ACTIVITE.(EN POURCENTAGE DE LA VALEUR TOTALE)

IMPORTS – IMPORTATIONS

	1990	1991	1992	1993	1994	1995	1996
TOTAL IMPORTS–IMPORTATIONS TOTALES							
1 FOOD BEV–ALIMENTATION BOISSONS							
11 PRIMARY–PRODUITS DE BASE							
111 FOR INDUSTRY–POUR L'INDUSTRIE							
112 FOR HOUSEHOLDS–POUR LES MENAGES							
12 PROCESSED–PRODUITS ELABORES							
121 FOR INDUSTRY–POUR L'INDUSTRIE							
122 FOR HOUSEHOLDS–POUR LES MENAGES							
2 IND SUPPLIES–APPROV INDUSTRIELS							
21 PRIMARY–PRODUITS DE BASE							
22 PROCESSED–PRODUITS ELABORES							
3 FUELS–COMBUSTIBLES							
31 PRIMARY–PRODUITS DE BASE							
32 PROCESSED–PRODUITS ELABORES							
321 MOTOR SPIRIT–ESSENCE							
322 OTHER–AUTRES							
4 MACHINERY–EQUIPEMENT							
41 CAPITAL EQUIPMENT–MACHINES							
42 PARTS–PIECES ACCESSOIRES							
5 TRANSPORT–TRANSPORT							
51 PASSENGER CARS–AUTOMOBILES							
52 OTHER–AUTRES							
521 INDUSTRIAL–INDUSTRIELS							
522 NON INDUSTRIAL–NON INDUSTRIEL							
53 PARTS–PIECES ACCESSOIRES							
6 CONSUM GOODS–BIENS CONSOMMATION							
61 DURABLE–DURABLES							
62 SEMI DURABLE–SEMI DURABLES							
63 NON DURABLE–NON DURABLES							
7 GOODS NES–BIENS NDA							

EXPORTS – EXPORTATIONS

	1990	1991	1992	1993	1994	1995	1996
TOTAL EXPORTS–EXPORTATIONS TOTALES							
1 AGRICULTURE							
2 MINING QUARRY–INDUS EXTRACTIVES							
3 MANUFACTURING–IND MANUFACTUR							
31 FOOD BEV TOBACCO–ALIM BOISS TAB							
32 TEXTILES–INDUSTRIES TEXTILES							
33 WOOD & PRODUCTS–BOIS & PRODUITS							
34 PAPER & PRODUCTS–PAPIER & PRODT							
35 CHEMICALS–INDUSTRIES CHIMIQUES							
36 NON METAL MIN–MIN NON METAL							
37 BASIC METAL–IND METAL BASE							
38 METAL MANUF–MANUF METAL							
39 OTH MANUF IND–AUTRES MANUF							

3. TRADE BY PRINCIPAL COUNTRIES OF PRODUCTION AND CONSIGNMENT (VALUE IN THOUSAND U.S. DOLLARS)
ECHANGES SELON LES PRINCIPAUX PAYS DE PRODUCTION ET DE CONSIGNATION (VALEUR EN MILLIERS DE DOLLARS EU)

COUNTRIES–PAYS	GENERAL IMPORTS F.O.B. IMPORTATIONS GENERALES F.O.B.					COUNTRIES–PAYS	GENERAL EXPORTS F.O.B. EXPORTATIONS GENERALES F.O.B.				
	1991	1992	1993	1994	1995		1991	1992	1993	1994	1995
World			1199351	1484092	1718904	Monde			1055299	1086343	1204048
Africa			26438	5721	6716	Afrique			9155	8073	11775
Americas			35273	64049	83267	Amériques			63182	41103	36276
Northern America			28460	52346	63905	Amérique du Nord			62836	40998	36220
LAIA			6597	11676	19070	ALAI			184	105	56
CACM			210	27	284	MCAC			19		
Caribbean			6		8	Caraïbes			143		
Rest of America						Autre Amérique					
As.ex F.USSR			66294	109115	112419	Asie l'URSS exclus			84993	82432	67469
Eur.x F.USSR			838784	1114908	1372608	Europe l'URSS exclus			689918	800586	958575
EU			412537	550640	689542	UE			372543	361141	407768
EFTA			20646	24697	20043	AELE			29947	34103	37103
East Europe			186458	317921	329183	Europe de l'Est			159916	303975	324370
Other Europe						Autre de l'Europe					
Former USSR			138142	46424	62848	Ancienne URSS			114883	76404	87233
Oceania			8661	5136	12228	Océanie			1402	1050	757
Germany/Allemagne			160324	254376	282969	Bulgaria/Bulgarie			82751	239693	256034
Bulgaria/Bulgarie			130940	241651	255946	Germany/Allemagne			148289	145964	153075
Slovenia/Slovénia			173729	162188	116489	Italy/Italie			93753	125807	118405
Italy/Italie			77842	109939	179300	Russian Federation			114883	76404	87233
Russian Federation			138142	46424	62848	Slovenia/Slovénia			89258	71440	72424
Croatia/Croatie			45414	59462	56279	USA/Etats–Unis d'Amer			61732	39507	35560
Yugoslavia/Yougoslavie					161072	Turkey/Turquie			43789	35382	38274
Turkey/Turquie			34303	47678	55170	Croatia/Croatie			38254	29927	32125
USA/Etats–Unis d'Amer			26365	49528	57801	Switz.Liecht			28956	33978	36925
Austria/Autriche			23272	42546	44953	Albania/Albanie			35666	27976	24678
Greece/Grèce			52222	23504	28893	Yugoslavia/Yougoslavie					84785
Netherlands/Pays–Bas			15498	39956	43376	Greece/Grèce			49614	12724	14177
France,Monac			19022	35153	36102	Korea, Republic of			13667	31044	24998
Switz.Liecht			20258	24442	19663	France,Monac			21314	23649	23487
Belgium–Luxembourg			24567	16645	15387	Austria/Autriche			15821	19191	30342
Romania/Roumanie			12561	17356	16772	Netherlands/Pays–Bas			13850	14630	29741
Slovakia				24668	21300	United Kingdom			13038	5855	21086
Japan/Japon			9556	12724	14562	Romania/Roumanie			9554	11161	13401
Hungary/Hongrie			7984	12194	14949	Hungary/Hongrie			9115	11697	10765
United Kingdom			12436	2408	20208	Egypt/Egypte			8178	7213	8530
Korea, Republic of			1387	11499	20404	Belgium–Luxembourg			6890	5418	10045
Spain/Espagne			7695	7489	18001	Slovakia				6564	10764
Sweden/Suède			8311	12267	11259	Czechoslovakia			17204		
Poland/Pologne			12358	9378	9310	Poland/Pologne			5626	3442	4427
Australia/Australie			8168	4886	11679	Japan/Japon			10681	1201	1122
Albania/Albanie			7314	8172	8173	Spain/Espagne			4125	3420	2348
Libyan Arab Jamahiriya			20008	1256	1154	Cyprus/Chypre				9258	
Iran (Islamic Rp. of)			12603	2857	6388	Czech Republic				3442	4301
Denmark/Danemark			9699	4813	6561	Denmark/Danemark			2245	2243	2812
Brazil/Brésil			1871	7575	9401	Sweden/Suède			2151	2140	2184
Cyprus/Chypre				18546		China/Chine			5716	8	28
Jordan/Jordanie			3703	6105	7709	Jordan/Jordanie			3228	1071	809
Czechoslovakia			15301			Iran (Islamic Rp. of)			2693	954	1088
China/Chine			3168	5416	4711	Syrian Arab Republic			1425	1926	343
Egypt/Egypte			4860	3706	3272	Canada			1104	1491	660
Canada			2095	2818	6104	Australia/Australie			1402	1044	757
Ecuador/Equateur			1228	1915	4201	India/Inde			2719	466	1
Czech Republic				4502	2733	Morocco/Maroc					2569
Argentina/Argentine			326	1629	2653	Kuwait/ Koweït			594	671	711
India/Inde			214	1995	2107	Nigeria/Nigéria			853	229	588
Ireland/Irlande			1327	1083	1763	Finland/Finlande			1275	58	66
Malaysia/Malaisie			452	2032	307	Norway,SVD,JM			991	125	178
Mexico/Mexique			1137	136	1428	Saudi Arabia			205	376	16
Sudan/Soudan			619	516	1478	Libyan Arab Jamahiriya			124	335	6
Colombia/Colombie			462	421	1275	Algeria/Algérie				296	82
Chile/Chili			1573		112	Lebanon/Liban			228	75	5
Finland/Finlande			322	461	770	Ireland/Irlande			178	42	
Syrian Arab Republic			385	161	1002	Mexico/Mexique			25	71	56
New Zealand			493	250	549	Jamaica/Jamaïque			143		
Morocco/Maroc			951	167	108	Chile/Chili			123	10	

(VALUE AS PERCENTAGE OF WORLD TOTAL)(VALEURS EN POURCENTAGE DU TOTAL MONDIAL)

	1986	1987	1988	1989	1990	1991	1992	1993	1994	1995		1986	1987	1988	1989	1990	1991	1992	1993	1994	1995
Africa								2.2	0.4	0.4	Afrique								0.9	0.7	1.0
Americas								2.9	4.3	4.8	Amériques								6.0	3.8	3.0
Northern America								2.4	3.5	3.7	Amérique du Nord								6.0	3.8	3.0
LAIA								0.6	0.8	1.1	ALAI								0.0	0.0	0.0
CACM								0.0	0.0	0.0	MCAC								0.0		
Caribbean								0.0		0.0	Caraïbes								0.0		
Rest of America											Autre Amérique										
As.ex F.USSR								5.5	7.4	6.5	Asie l'URSS exclus								8.1	7.6	5.6
Eur.x F.USSR								69.9	75.1	79.9	Europe l'URSS exclus								65.4	73.7	79.6
EU								34.4	37.1	40.1	UE								35.3	33.2	33.9
EFTA								1.7	1.7	1.2	AELE								2.8	3.1	3.1
East Europe								15.5	21.4	19.2	Europe de l'Est								15.2	28.0	26.9
Other Europe											Autre de l'Europe										
Former USSR								11.5	3.1	3.7	Ancienne URSS								10.9	7.0	7.2
Oceania								0.7	0.3	0.7	Océanie								0.1	0.1	0.1
Germany/Allemagne								13.4	17.1	16.5	Bulgaria/Bulgarie								7.8	22.1	21.3
Bulgaria/Bulgarie								10.9	16.3	14.9	Germany/Allemagne								14.1	13.4	12.7
Slovenia/Slovénia								14.5	10.9	6.8	Italy/Italie								8.9	11.6	9.8
Italy/Italie								6.5	7.4	10.4	Russian Federation								10.9	7.0	7.2
Russian Federation								11.5	3.1	3.7	Slovenia/Slovénia								8.5	6.6	6.0
Croatia/Croatie								3.8	4.0	3.3	USA/Etats–Unis d'Amer								5.8	3.6	3.0
Yugoslavia/Yougoslavie										9.4	Turkey/Turquie								4.1	3.3	3.2
Turkey/Turquie								2.9	3.2	3.2	Croatia/Croatie								3.6	2.8	2.7
USA/Etats–Unis d'Amer								2.2	3.3	3.4	Switz.Liecht								2.7	3.1	3.1
Austria/Autriche								1.9	2.9	2.6	Albania/Albanie								3.4	2.6	2.0

4. General Imports F.O.B. by Commodities according to the S.I.T.C. (Rev. 2) in thousand U.S. Dollars
Importations Générales F.O.B. par Produits d'après la C.T.C.I. (Rév. 2) en milliers de Dollars E.U.

SITC CTCI	COMMODITY	1992 WEIGHT POIDS	1992 VALUE VALEUR	1993 WEIGHT POIDS	1993 VALUE VALEUR	1994 WEIGHT POIDS	1994 VALUE VALEUR	1995 WEIGHT POIDS	1995 VALUE VALEUR	PRODUIT
	ALL COMMODITIES				1199351		1484092		1718904	TOUS PRODUITS
0	FOOD AND LIVE ANIMALS				206297		282272		280729	ALIMENTS,ANIMAUX VIVANTS
001	*LIVE ANIMALS FOR FOOD				11975		3377		6057	ANIMAUX VIVANTS
00119	— OTHR THAN FR BREEDING			W 6973	4892					BOVINS NON REPRODUCTEURS
01	MEAT AND PREPARATIONS				48104		66218		64536	VIANDES ET PREPARATIONS
01112	BOVINE MEAT BONELESS			W 300	9091					VIANDES BOVIN DESOSSEES
0114	POULTRY FRESH CHLLD,FRZN			W 9588	11572			W 13500	11503	VOLAILLES MORTES
0142	SAUSAGES INCLDING TINNED			W 3482	8358			W 8938	21195	SAUCISSES,SAUCISSONS
02	DAIRY PRODCTS,BIRDS'EGGS				17430		23207		20849	PRODUITS LAITIERS,OEUFS
022	MILK AND CREAM							W 13447	7381	LAIT ET CREME
024	CHEESE AND CURD			W 6365	10030			W 1853	3764	FROMAGE ET CAILLEBOTTE
03	FISH AND PREPARATIONS				9177		5408		6814	POISSONS ET PREPARATIONS
04	CEREALS AND PREPARATIONS				27303		47827		30736	CEREALES ET PRODUITS
041	WHEAT ETC UNMILLED							W 45398	5393	FROMENT,EPEAUTRE
0411	DURUM WHEAT UNMILLED			W 27327	6795					FROMENT DUR NON MOULU
04601	FLOUR OF WHEAT OR MESLIN			W 31761	7484					FARINE DE FROMENT
05	VEGETABLES AND FRUIT				30882		61035		71610	LEGUMES ET FRUITS
0561	VEG DRIED EXC LEGUMINOUS							W 784	7148	LEGUM DESSECH,DESHYDRAT
05659	OTH VEG PRESVD,PREPD NES							W 5728	5385	LEGUM PREPAP,CONSERV NDA
0573	BANANA,PLANTAIN,FRSH,DRY							W 18493	5847	BANANES FRAICHES,SECHEES
0585	FRUIT OR VEGETABLE JUICE							W 6054	6174	JUS DE FRUITS
06	SUGAR AND PREPS,HONEY				15048		27281		28263	SUCRES ET PRODUITS
061	SUGAR AND HONEY			W 29737	10384					SUCRES ET MIEL
0612	REFINED SUGAR ETC							W 50853	21864	SUCRES RAFFINES
07	COFFEE,TEA,COCOA,SPICES				20610		20116		24155	CAFE,THE,CACAO,EPICES
07111	COFFEE GREEN,HUSKS,SKINS							W 3810	7121	CAFE NON TORREFIE
07112	COFFEE ROASTED			W 598	7915					CAFE TORREFIE
073	CHOCOLATE AND PRODUCTS			W 2025	5889			W 2238	6718	CHOCOLAT
081	*FEEDING STUFF FOR ANIML				9240		12025		11331	NOURRITURE POUR ANIMAUX
08131	— OF SOYA BEANS			W 13017	4725					TOURTEAUX DE SOJA
09	MISC EDIBLE PRODUCTS				16528		15778		16378	PREP ALIMENTAIRES DIVERSES
09806	YEASTS,BAKING POWDERS			W 148	5799					LEVURES
09809	MISC FOOD PREPRTIONS NES			W 1019	4579			W 1703	6837	PREP ALIMENTAIRES NDA
1	BEVERAGES AND TOBACCO				31504		24456		17370	BOISSONS ET TABACS
12	TOBACCO AND MANUFACTURES				28847		21560		14206	TABACS BRUTS FABRIQUES
1211	TOBACCO,NOT STRIPPED			W 7417	20334			W 5807	9908	TABACS NON ECOTES
2	CRUDE MATERLS,EXCL FUELS				66685		75217		78777	MAT BRUTES NON COMESTIBLES
21	HIDES,SKINS,FURS UNDRSSD				6025		7055		11550	CUIRS,PEAUX BRUTS
24	CORK AND WOOD				5920		7604		7108	LIEGE ET BOIS
26	TEXTILE FIBRES AND WASTE				25532		26111		25138	FIBRES TEXTILES
2631	RAW COTTON,EXCL LINTERS			W 4669	6052			W 3965	9726	COTON EN MASSE
26659	— OTHER							W 10157	10471	FIBRES AUTRES
27	CRUDE FERTLZR,MINRLS NES				13707		20971		16475	ENGRAIS MINERAUX BRUTS
27131	— UNGROUND			W 89182	7011			W 105002	8388	PHOSPHATES NON MOULUS
28	METALLIFEROUS ORES,SCRAP				7585		868		2797	MINERAIS METAL,DECHETS
2815	IRON ORE,CONC,NOT AGGLOM			W 43808	4882					MINERAIS NON AGGLOMERES
29	CRUDE ANIMAL,VEG MAT NES				1583		4300		7385	MATIERES BRUTES ANIM,VEGET
3	MINERAL FUELS ETC				191136		160952		198963	COMBUSTIBLES MINERAUX LUB
32	COAL,COKE AND BRIQUETTES				13748		13506		13337	HOUILLES,COKES,BRIQUETTES
3221	ANTHRACITE,NOT AGGLOMRTD			W 63086	6858					ANTHRACITE
3232	COKE,SEMI–COKE,RTRT CRBN			W 45485	5821			W 53902	8739	COKES ET SEMI–COKES
33	PETROLEUM AND PRODUCTS				176181		144861		181378	PETROLE ET DERIVES
333	CRUDE PETROLEUM			W 933301	123064			W 159190	22464	HUILES BRUTES DE PETROLE
3341	GASOLINE,OTH LIGHT OILS			W 74687	18506			W 192405	44534	ESSENCES POUR MOTEURS
3343	GAS OILS			W 94696	16514			W 574290	90123	GAS OILS
3345	LUBS,PETROLEUM OILS NES			W 8595	9054			W 9946	11506	HUILES LUBRIFIANTES
5	CHEMCLS,RELATED PROD NES				186198		196894		205015	PRODUITS CHIMIQUES
51	ORGANIC CHEMICALS				32718		42119		50892	PROD CHIMIQ ORGANIQUES
51215	ETHYLENE GLYCOL							W 5534	5347	ETHYLENE–GLYCOL
51384	TEREPHTHALIC ACID ESTERS							W 11724	13117	ESTERS DE L'ACIDE TEREPHTALI
51483	ACRYLONITRILE			W 12603	8133			W 9962	10603	ACRYLONITRILE
52	INORGANIC CHEMICALS				16925		15367		12649	PROD CHIM INORGANIQUES
53	DYES,TANNING,COLOUR PROD				22694		18409		14474	PROD TEINTURE,COLORANTS
541	*MEDICINAL,PHARM PRODUCT				27073		31370		34971	PROD MEDICINAUX PHARMACEUT
5417	MEDICAMENTS							K 1106000	14439	MEDICAMENTS
55	PERFUME,CLEANING ETC PRD				24847		20176		18230	PROD POUR PARFUM,TOILETTE
562	*FERTILIZERS,MANUFACTURE				9595		10706		7311	ENGRAIS MANUFACTURES
572	*EXPLOSIVES,PYROTECH PRO				22957		26189		34023	EXPLOSIFS
58	PLASTIC MATERIALS ETC				6754		7902		9193	MAT PLAST ARTIFICIELLES
59	CHEMICAL MATERIALS NES				22635		24656		23272	MAT PROD CHIMIQUES NDA
6	BASIC MANUFACTURES				203885		204059		269205	ART MANUFACTURES
61	LEATHER,DRESSED FUR,ETC				6551		3834		5436	CUIRS,PELLETERIES
62	RUBBER MANUFACTURES NES				15732		12414		15136	CAOUTCHOUC MANUFACTURE
6252	TYRES,NEW,BUS OR LORRY			W 3685	8306			W 1908	6294	PNEUS POUR AUTOBUS,CAMIONS
63	WOOD,CORK MANUFACTRS NES				10112		9742		8752	OUVRAGES LIEGE ET BOIS
64	PAPER,PAPERBOARD AND MFR				27033		36073		40900	PAPIERS,CARTONS & OUVRAGES
65	TEXTILE YARN,FABRICS,ETC				50318		37994		41448	FILS,TISSUS,ARTICLES TEXTILE
6513	COTTON YARN			W 3525	7747			W 1827	5646	FILS DE COTON
65316	CONT SYN BLEND FABRC NES			W 18	6209					TIS SYNTH MOINS 85% MAT TEX
65751	CORDAGE,CABLE,ROPE,TWINE			W 2118	7864					CORDAGES TRESSES OU NON
66	NONMETAL MINERAL MFS NES				13088		16982		23079	ART MIN NON METALLIQUES
67	IRON AND STEEL				45203		38111		75870	FER ET ACIER
67326	IRN,OTH STL BARS HOTROLD			W 28891	8105			W 22840	6165	BARRES PLEINES FER,ACIER
6745	IRN,STL MED PLATE,ROLLED							W 24554	6632	TOLES 3 A 4.75 MM
68	NON–FERROUS METALS				15648		22156		31957	METAUX NON FERREUX
686	ZINC							W 66458	15590	ZINC
69	METAL MANUFACTURES NES				20200		26753		26627	ART MANUFACT EN METAL NDA
691	STRUCTURES AND PARTS NES			W 2030	5629					CONSTRUCT FER,ACIER,ALU
6997	IRON,STEEL ARTICLES NES			W 282	5460					OUV FONTE,FER,ACIER NDA
7	MACHINES,TRANSPORT EQUIP				199589		292138		334637	MACHINES MATERIEL TRANSPORT
71	POWER GENERATING EQUIPMT				10733		18595		7192	MACHINES GENERATRICES
7132	MOTOR VEHCL PISTN ENGINS			W 339	6114					MOTEURS EXPL POUR VEHICULES
72	MACHS FOR SPCL INDUSTRYS				33346		34545		43782	MAC SPECIALES POUR INDUST
72842	RUBBER,PLASTICS WRKG MCH							W 387	5745	MACH IND CAOUT MAT PLAST
72843	TOBACCO WORKING MACH NES			W 81	7038					MACH POUR IND DU TABAC
74	GENRL INDUSTRL MACHY NES				51222		41361		51385	MACH APP INDUSTRIE
74132	INDUST FURNACES NONELECT			W 2	6133					FOURS NON ELECTRIQUES
74522	PACKAGNG,BOTTLNG,ETC MCH			W 81	9261			W 208	6044	MACH NETT BOUTEILLES,ETC
75	OFFICE MACHNES,ADP EQUIP				11178		16015		18621	MACH BUREAU TRAIT AUTOM
752	AUTOMTIC DATA PROC EQUIP							W 74	6841	MACH TRAIT INFORMATION
76	TELECOMM,SOUND EQUIPMENT				10764		20711		18253	EQUIPMENT DE TELECOM

4. General Imports F.O.B. by Commodities according to the S.I.T.C. (Rev. 2) in thousand U.S. Dollars
Importations Générales F.O.B. par Produits d'après la C.T.C.I. (Rév. 2) en milliers de Dollars E.U.

SITC CTCI	COMMODITY	1992		1993		1994		1995		PRODUIT
		WEIGHT POIDS	VALUE VALEUR	WEIGHT POIDS	VALUE VALEUR	WEIGHT POIDS	VALUE VALEUR	WEIGHT POIDS	VALUE VALEUR	
77	ELECTRIC MACHNRY NES ETC				27245		32074		34200	MACH APP ELECT NDA
78	ROAD VEHICLES				52138		125386		155964	VEHICULES ROUTIERS
781	PASS MOTOR VEH EXC BUSES			W 1583	13164			W 11453	96208	AUTO TRANSPORT PERSONNES
7821	LORRIES,TRUCKS			W 1766	4669			W 3617	18668	VEHICULES TRANSP MARCHAND
7822	SPECIAL MOTOR VEHCLS NES							W 715	5546	VEHICULES USAGES SPECIAUX
7832	TRACTORS FOR TR–TRAILERS			W 2058	10124			W 2293	11876	TRACTEURS ROUTIERS
8	MISC MANUFACTURED GOODS				79099		144196		154217	ART MANUFACTURES DIVERS
821	*FURNITURE,PARTS THEREOF				11201		9149		9320	MEUBLES ET PIECES
84	CLOTHING AND ACCESSORIES				30550		76174		74703	VETEMENTS
8424	— JACKETS,BLAZERS ETC							W 480	8217	VESTES HOMMES MAT TEXTIL
8439	— OTHER OUTER GARMENTS							W 1464	18605	AUT VET DES FEM MAT TEXT
84411	—— OF COTTON			W 1064	5303			W 907	11674	CHEMISES HOMMES DE COTON
851	*FOOTWEAR				8005		23099		24036	CHAUSSURES
85102	FOOTWEAR LEATHER							W 1265	13924	CHAUS SEMELLES EN CUIR
87	PRECISION INSTRUMNTS NES				8696		11169		14904	INSTRUM,APPAR SCIENT NDA
88	PHOTO EQU,OPTICL GDS ETC				2602		4554		4736	APP,FOURN PHOTO,OP,MONTR
89	MISC MANUFCTRD GOODS NES				15780		17235		23252	ART MANUFACTURES DIVERS
8931	PLSTC PACKG CONTNRS,LIDS							W 2207	5203	ART TRANSP EMBALLAGE ETC
9	GOODS NOT CLASSD BY KIND				33231		102352		175993	ART TRANSACT NON CLASSES

5. General Exports F.O.B. by Commodities according to the S.I.T.C. (Rev. 2) in thousand U.S. Dollars
Exportations Générales F.O.B. par Produits d'après la C.T.C.I. (Rév. 2) en milliers de Dollars E.U.

SITC CTCI	COMMODITY	1992 WEIGHT POIDS	1992 VALUE VALEUR	1993 WEIGHT POIDS	1993 VALUE VALEUR	1994 WEIGHT POIDS	1994 VALUE VALEUR	1995 WEIGHT POIDS	1995 VALUE VALEUR	PRODUIT
	ALL COMMODITIES				1055299		1086343		1204048	TOUS PRODUITS
0	FOOD AND LIVE ANIMALS				116300		110334		131828	ALIMENTS,ANIMAUX VIVANTS
001	*LIVE ANIMALS FOR FOOD				5337		847		380	ANIMAUX VIVANTS
01	MEAT AND PREPARATIONS				9644		7853		10246	VIANDES ET PREPARATIONS
0111	BOVINE MEAT FRESH,FROZEN			W 1582	5658					VIANDES BOVIN FRAI,REF
0112	MUTTON ETC FRSH,CHLD,FRN			W 1152	3384			W 1810	7811	VIANDE DE MOUTON
02	DAIRY PRODCTS,BIRDS'EGGS				4411		3906		3350	PRODUITS LAITIERS,OEUFS
04	CEREALS AND PREPARATIONS				12678		5163		11266	CEREALES ET PRODUITS
04221	RICE MILLED UNBROKEN			W 9001	6233					RIZ POLI,GLACE EXCL BRISURES
05	VEGETABLES AND FRUIT				54826		70721		88428	LEGUMES ET FRUITS
0544	TOMATOES FRESH							W 17902	7126	TOMATES FRAICHES
05459	FRESH VEGETABLES NES							W 1221	6066	LEGUMES FRAIS,REFRI NDA
0561	VEG DRIED EXC LEGUMINOUS							W 1023	10895	LEGUM DESSECH,DESHYDRAT
0574	APPLES FRESH							W 25736	9316	POMMES FRAICHES
0585	FRUIT OR VEGETABLE JUICE							W 4707	5190	JUS DE FRUITS
06	SUGAR AND PREPS,HONEY				4081		3563		3977	SUCRES ET PRODUITS
07	COFFEE,TEA,COCOA,SPICES				15410		11824		10295	CAFE,THE,CACAO,EPICES
073	CHOCOLATE AND PRODUCTS							W 2151	6876	CHOCOLAT
09	MISC EDIBLE PRODUCTS				6874		5898		3565	PREP ALIMENTAIRES DIVERSES
1	BEVERAGES AND TOBACCO				100415		62043		88023	BOISSONS ET TABACS
11	BEVERAGES				29622		18959		30929	BOISSONS
1121	WINE OF FRESH GRAPES ETC			W 45416	17580			W 69372	28088	VINS DE RAISINS FRAIS
12	TOBACCO AND MANUFACTURES				70793		43084		57094	TABACS BRUTS FABRIQUES
1211	TOBACCO,NOT STRIPPED			W 41219	43676			W 12065	41583	TABACS NON ECOTES
1222	CIGARETTES			W 4308	26807			W 1483	15212	CIGARETTES
2	CRUDE MATERLS,EXCL FUELS				64605		77146		92999	MAT BRUTES NON COMESTIBLES
21	HIDES,SKINS,FURS UNDRSSD				5493		6010		7663	CUIRS,PEAUX BRUTS
2116	SHEEP SKIN WITH WOOL							W 1363	5002	PEAUX LAINEES D'OVINS
24	CORK AND WOOD				16684		21363		20740	LIEGE ET BOIS
24831	LUMBER SAWN ETC NON–CON			W 49165	14559			W 55111	15620	SCIES LONGITUDINALEMENT
26	TEXTILE FIBRES AND WASTE				18387		23243		27989	FIBRES TEXTILES
26652	— POLYESTER							W 3737	6623	FIBRES EN POLYESTERS
27	CRUDE FERTLZR,MINRLS NES				6711		6451		9345	ENGRAIS MINERAUX BRUTS
27312	MARBLE,ETC BLDG STONE			W 13484	4293			W 13049	7484	MARBRES,TRAVERTINS
28	METALLIFEROUS ORES,SCRAP				12706		14456		20041	MINERAIS METAL,DECHETS
2871	CPR ORE ETC,CEMENT COPPR							W 16480	6549	MINERAIS DE CUIVRE,MATTES
2874	LEAD ORES,CONCENTRATES			W 24094	8038			W 26548	8000	MINERAIS DE PLOMB
29	CRUDE ANIMAL,VEG MAT NES				3227		4291		6429	MATIERES BRUTES ANIM,VEGET
3	MINERAL FUELS ETC				1855		1402		4840	COMBUSTIBLES MINERAUX LUB
33	PETROLEUM AND PRODUCTS				1674		1382		4727	PETROLE ET DERIVES
5	CHEMCLS,RELATED PROD NES				47457		47474		66702	PRODUITS CHIMIQUES
51	ORGANIC CHEMICALS				2114		3753		4870	PROD CHIMIQ ORGANIQUES
52	INORGANIC CHEMICALS				10401		9421		17175	PROD CHIM INORGANIQUES
52229	OTH INORGANIC ACIDS ETC			W 8286	8603					AUTRES ACIDES INORGANIQUES
541	*MEDICINAL,PHARM PRODUCT				21390		22884		25399	PROD MEDICINAUX PHARMACEUT
5417	MEDICAMENTS							K 751000	21064	MEDICAMENTS
55	PERFUME,CLEANING ETC PRD				1715		2269		4649	PROD POUR PARFUM,TOILETTE
572	*EXPLOSIVES,PYROTECH PRO				3221		3279		4204	EXPLOSIFS
58	PLASTIC MATERIALS ETC				2728		1617		4674	MAT PLAST ARTIFICIELLES
59	CHEMICAL MATERIALS NES				1670		2337		3916	MAT PROD CHIMIQUES NDA
6	BASIC MANUFACTURES				362528		409315		441181	ART MANUFACTURES
61	LEATHER,DRESSED FUR,ETC				5696		8197		7575	CUIRS,PELLETERIES
62	RUBBER MANUFACTURES NES				9023		12330		15310	CAOUTCHOUC MANUFACTURE
63	WOOD,CORK MANUFACTRS NES				3318		3382		5996	OUVRAGES LIEGE ET BOIS
65	TEXTILE YARN,FABRICS,ETC				76063		72649		71363	FILS,TISSUS,ARTICLES TEXTILE
6513	COTTON YARN			W 3026	7583			W 897	8403	FILS DE COTON
65152	— OF DISCONTIN FIBRES			W 1229	4032					FILS CONT 85% FI TEXT SYNT
65214	GREY WOVEN COTTON NES			W 2233	5782					AUT TISSUS 85% COTON ECRUS
65499	PILE,CHENILLE FABRIC NES			W 593	5524					VELOURS NDA
655	KNITTED,ETC FABRICS			W 1451	8308			W 1769	6121	ETOF BONNETERIE PIECES ETC
65751	CORDAGE,CABLE,ROPE,TWINE			W 5853	11230			W 5926	11880	CORDAGES TRESSES OU NON
65841	BED LINEN OF COTTON			W 2019	6594			W 1377	4344	LINGE DE LIT DE COTON
66	NONMETAL MINERAL MFS NES				21892		18079		20341	ART MIN NON METALLIQUES
67	IRON AND STEEL				114118		79106		104018	FER ET ACIER
67162	FERRO–SILICON			W 46941	22605			W 55181	30814	FERRO–SILICIUM
67169	OTHER FERRO–ALLOYS			W 18789	30686			W 17505	48070	AUTRES FERRO–ALLIAGES
6744	IRN,STL HVY PLATE,ROLLED			W 13520	24948					TOLES LAMINEES PLUS 4.75 MM
678	IRON,STL TUBES,PIPES,ETC			W 3340	3695			W 7324	5154	TUBES,TUYAUX EN FONTE,FER
68	NON–FERROUS METALS				105156		185916		183926	METAUX NON FERREUX
68212	COPPER REFINED,UNWROUGHT			W 21359	35623			W 39609	96736	CUIVRE AFFINE BRUT
6841	ALUMINIUM,ALLOYS,UNWRGHT							W 3620	5903	ALUMINIUM,ALLIAGES BRUTS
68512	REF LEAD(EXC ALLOY)UNWRT			W 25329	12978			W 20416	12305	PLOMB AFFINE BRUT
6863	ZINC,ALLOYS WKD,INC DUST			W 57509	32827			W 39639	21125	ZINC ET ALLIAGES OUVRES
68915	MAGNESIUM UNWROUGHT			W 12237	5256					MAGNESIUM BRUT
69	METAL MANUFACTURES NES				26231		28350		29543	ART MANUFACT EN METAL NDA
69741	— OF IRON OR STEEL			W 2820	7706					ART NDA EN FONTE,FER
7	MACHINES,TRANSPORT EQUIP				170945		133500		155719	MACHINES MATERIEL TRANSPORT
71	POWER GENERATING EQUIPMT				5010		5381		18353	MACHINES GENERATRICES
72	MACHS FOR SPCL INDUSTRYS				4957		4057		6263	MAC SPECIALES POUR INDUST
73	METALWORKING MACHINERY				6006		3573		7247	MACH TRAVAIL DES METAUX
74	GENRL INDUSTRL MACHY NES				9695		11309		19238	MACH APP INDUSTRIE
77	ELECTRIC MACHNRY NES ETC				95727		72751		77403	MACH APP ELECT NDA
7711	TRANSFORMERS,ELECTRICAL			W 21676	52854					TRANSFO ELECTRIQUES
7712	OTH ELEC POWER MACHY NES							W 16147	43454	AUT APP PROD TRANSF ELEC
77521	DOMESTIC REFRIGERATORS			W 4073	13315			W 1358	4218	REFRIGERATEURS
77812	ELECTRIC ACCUMULATORS			W 4714	8211					ACCUMULATEURS ELECTRIQ
78	ROAD VEHICLES				47962		34691		21576	VEHICULES ROUTIERS
7831	BUSES			W 3740	35656			W 369	3329	VOITURES TRANSPORT COMMUN
7849	OTHER MOTOR VEHCL PARTS			W 1751	9394			W 2145	9833	PIECES 722,781,782,783
79	OTHR TRANSPORT EQUIPMENT				1279		1256		4509	AUTRE MATERIEL TRANSPORT
8	MISC MANUFACTURED GOODS				190598		242312		220785	ART MANUFACTURES DIVERS
812	*PLUMBG,HEATNG,LGHTNG EQ				8080		4531		4811	APPAR SANITAIRES CHAUFFAGE
821	*FURNITURE,PARTS THEREOF				23729		50120		41402	MEUBLES ET PIECES
82192	WOOD FURNITURE NES			W 5128	13859			W 2831	7195	MEUBLES NDA EN BOIS
84	CLOTHING AND ACCESSORIES				129847		115357		112755	VETEMENTS
8423	— TROUSERS,BREECHES ETC			W 1231	9843			W 992	5799	PANTALONS HOMMES MAT TEX
8424	— JACKETS,BLAZERS ETC			W 867	8001			W 693	8532	VESTES HOMMES MAT TEXTIL
8431	— COATS AND JACKETS							W 737	8378	MANT,VEST FEM MAT TEXTIL
8439	— OTHER OUTER GARMENTS							W 1952	18344	AUT VET DES FEM MAT TEXT
84411	—— OF COTTON			W 1801	16013			W 2524	19458	CHEMISES HOMMES DE COTON
84419	—— OF OTHER FIBRES			W 855	10907			W 679	5329	CHEMISES HOMMES AUT FIBR

5. General Exports F.O.B. by Commodities according to the S.I.T.C. (Rev. 2) in thousand U.S. Dollars
Exportations Générales F.O.B. par Produits d'après la C.T.C.I. (Rév. 2) en milliers de Dollars E.U.

SITC CTCI	COMMODITY	1992		1993		1994		1995		PRODUIT
		WEIGHT POIDS	VALUE VALEUR	WEIGHT POIDS	VALUE VALEUR	WEIGHT POIDS	VALUE VALEUR	WEIGHT POIDS	VALUE VALEUR	
8451	— JERSEYS,PULLOVERS ETC			W 464	6076					CHANDAILS,PULL–OVERS ETC
8483	FUR ETC,CLOTHES,PRODUCTS			W 385	6212			W 247	4515	VETEMENTS DE FOURRURE
851	*FOOTWEAR				22014		66047		53843	CHAUSSURES
85102	FOOTWEAR LEATHER			W 1359	17145			W 3073	44837	CHAUS SEMELLES EN CUIR
89	MISC MANUFCTRD GOODS NES				4950		9086		6572	ART MANUFACTURES DIVERS

1. HISTORICAL SERIES, 1961–1996 GENERAL TRADE, IMPORTS C.I.F., EXPORTS F.O.B.
SERIES HISTORIQUES, 1961–1996 COMMERCE GENERAL, IMPORTATIONS C.A.F., EXPORTATIONS F.O.B

YEAR ANNEE	VALUE IN MILLION BAHT # 1 VALEUR EN MILLION BAHT # 1 MERCHANDISE – MARCHANDISE		GOLD – OR		CONVERSION FACTORS U.S. CENTS PER BAHT FACTEURS DE CONVERSION CENTS E.U. PAR BAHT		INDEX NUMBERS – INDICES QUANTUM		UNIT VALUE VALEUR UNITAIRE	
	IMPORTS	EXPORTS	IMPORTS	EXPORTS	IMPORTS	EXPORTS	IMPORTS	EXPORTS	IMPORTS	EXPORTS
1961	10.29	10.00	0.13		4.7710	4.7710	8	10	21	26
1962	11.50	9.53	0.16		4.7640	4.8460	9	9	20	25
1963	12.80	9.68	0.15		4.8200	4.8200	10	10	20	25
1964	14.25	12.34	0.10		4.8077	4.8077	12	12	20	25
1965	16.18	12.94	0.14		4.8077	4.8077	12	13	20	25
1966	25.35	14.31	0.12		4.8077	4.8077	15	13	20	26
1967	22.19	14.17	0.15		4.8077	4.8077	18	13	19	26
1968	24.10	13.68	0.18		4.8077	4.8077	21	13	19	26
1969	26.89	14.72	0.14		4.8077	4.8077	23	14	18	27
1970	27.01	14.77	0.11		4.8077	4.8077	22	14	20	25
1971	26.79	17.28	0.03		4.8077	4.8077	21	18	21	24
1972	30.88	22.49			4.8077	4.8077	23	22	22	25
1973	42.18	32.23			4.8571	4.8516	26	20	26	39
1974	64.04	50.25			4.9080	4.9080	25	21	41	59
1975	66.84	48.44			4.9071	4.9070	23	21	46	52
1976	72.88	60.80			4.9020	4.9020	24	30	48	51
1977	94.18	71.20			4.9261	4.8899	29	34	52	52
1978	108.90	83.07			4.9411	4.9056	19	19	32	37
1979	146.16	108.18			4.9190	4.8878	23	20	37	44
1980	188.69	133.20			4.8829	4.8839	38	41	81	79
1981	216.75	153.00			4.5911	4.5998	37	46	95	81
1982	196.62	159.73			4.3478	4.3478	32	52	98	76
1983	236.61	146.47			4.3478	4.3478	41	47	92	77
1984	245.15	175.24			4.2412	4.2302	43	57	93	77
1985	251.17	193.36			3.6803	3.6830	41	59	102	81
1986	241.36	233.38			3.8039	3.8044	40	48	76	82
1987	334.21	301.45			3.8880	3.8884	49	57	81	88
1988	513.11	403.57			3.9533	3.9529	26	30	72	75
1989	662.68	516.31			3.8888	3.8888	31	37	77	77
1990	844.45	589.81			3.9116	3.9116	100	100	100	100
1991	958.83	725.63			3.9192	3.9192	109	119	104	103
1992	1033.24	824.64			3.9371	3.9371	117	134	105	105
1993	1166.60	935.86			3.9496	3.9496	130	150	105	106
1994	1369.02	1137.60			3.9764	3.9764	151	177	107	109
1995	1829.40	1400.10			4.0137	4.0133	170	243	122	118
1996	1820.45	1407.20			3.9464	3.9459				120

2. IMPORTS BY BROAD ECONOMIC CATEGORY AND EXPORTS BY INDUSTRIAL ORIGIN. (PERCENTAGE OF TOTAL VALUE)
IMPORTATIONS PAR CATEGORIES ECONOMIQUES ET EXPORTATIONS PAR BRANCHE D'ACTIVITE.(EN POURCENTAGE DE LA VALEUR TOTALE)

IMPORTS – IMPORTATIONS

	1990	1991	1992	1993	1994	1995	1996
TOTAL IMPORTS–IMPORTATIONS TOTALES	100.	100.	100.	100.	100.	100.	
1 FOOD BEV–ALIMENTATION BOISSONS	4.2	4.6	4.3	3.6	3.3	2.8	
11 PRIMARY–PRODUITS DE BASE	2.8	3.2	2.9	2.2	2.0	1.6	
111 FOR INDUSTRY–POUR L'INDUSTRIE	0.3	0.4	0.5	0.4	0.4	0.4	
112 FOR HOUSEHOLDS–POUR LES MENAGES	2.4	2.8	2.4	1.8	1.5	1.2	
12 PROCESSED–PRODUITS ELABORES	1.4	1.3	1.4	1.3	1.3	1.2	
121 FOR INDUSTRY–POUR L'INDUSTRIE	0.2	0.2	0.2	0.2	0.2	0.2	
122 FOR HOUSEHOLDS–POUR LES MENAGES	1.2	1.1	1.2	1.1	1.1	1.0	
2 IND SUPPLIES–APPROV INDUSTRIELS	39.0	40.3	38.7	36.5	36.0	36.0	
21 PRIMARY–PRODUITS DE BASE	7.9	9.1	5.7	5.4	4.9	4.7	
22 PROCESSED–PRODUITS ELABORES	31.1	31.2	33.0	31.1	31.1	31.3	
3 FUELS–COMBUSTIBLES	9.3	9.2	8.2	7.5	6.8	6.7	
31 PRIMARY–PRODUITS DE BASE	4.8	4.1	4.4	4.0	4.1	4.2	
32 PROCESSED–PRODUITS ELABORES	4.5	5.2	3.8	3.4	2.7	2.5	
321 MOTOR SPIRIT–ESSENCE	0.3	0.4	0.5	0.4	0.2	0.1	
322 OTHER–AUTRES	4.2	4.8	3.4	3.1	2.4	2.4	
4 MACHINERY–EQUIPEMENT	29.4	31.9	31.1	33.5	36.0	36.6	
41 CAPITAL EQUIPMENT–MACHINES	20.7	22.9	21.3	23.1	23.8	23.8	
42 PARTS–PIECES ACCESSOIRES	8.7	8.9	9.9	10.4	12.2	12.8	
5 TRANSPORT–TRANSPORT	11.5	7.6	10.3	11.3	11.1	11.1	
51 PASSENGER CARS–AUTOMOBILES	1.2	1.3	2.3	3.3	2.8	2.2	
52 OTHER–AUTRES	2.8	1.2	3.4	2.1	1.1	2.2	
521 INDUSTRIAL–INDUSTRIELS	2.8	1.1	3.4	2.1	1.0	2.2	
522 NON INDUSTRIAL–NON INDUSTRIEL	0.0	0.0	0.0	0.0	0.0	0.0	
53 PARTS–PIECES ACCESSOIRES	7.4	5.2	4.5	6.0	7.1	6.7	
6 CONSUM GOODS–BIENS CONSOMMATION	4.2	4.2	4.9	5.1	5.5	5.5	
61 DURABLE–DURABLES	1.5	1.3	1.6	1.5	1.4	1.4	
62 SEMI DURABLE–SEMI DURABLES	1.7	1.8	2.2	2.3	2.9	2.9	
63 NON DURABLE–NON DURABLES	1.0	1.1	1.2	1.2	1.2	1.2	
7 GOODS NES–BIENS NDA	2.4	2.3	2.4	2.6	1.5	1.3	

EXPORTS – EXPORTATIONS

	1990	1991	1992	1993	1994	1995	1996
TOTAL EXPORTS–EXPORTATIONS TOTALES	100.	100.	100.	100.	100.	100.	
1 AGRICULTURE	15.6	14.4	14.1	12.2	12.0	11.4	
2 MINING QUARRY–INDUS EXTRACTIVES	4.6	4.2	3.2	3.1	2.9	2.6	
3 MANUFACTURING–IND MANUFACTUR	79.8	81.4	82.7	84.7	85.1	86.0	
31 FOOD BEV TOBACCO–ALIM BOISS TAB	17.8	16.7	16.2	13.2	13.2	12.8	
32 TEXTILES–INDUSTRIES TEXTILES	20.8	21.3	19.8	18.5	17.2	15.0	
33 WOOD & PRODUCTS–BOIS & PRODUITS	0.9	0.8	0.7	0.8	0.8	0.7	
34 PAPER & PRODUCTS–PAPIER & PRODT	0.3	0.3	0.3	0.4	0.6	1.1	
35 CHEMICALS–INDUSTRIES CHIMIQUES	5.0	5.5	5.7	8.3	7.3	10.1	
36 NON METAL MIN–MIN NON METAL	1.0	1.0	1.2	1.5	1.4	1.3	
37 BASIC METAL–IND METAL BASE	1.1	0.8	0.7	0.8	0.8	1.1	
38 METAL MANUF–MANUF METAL	26.0	28.5	31.1	34.6	38.2	38.3	
39 OTH MANUF IND–AUTRES MANUF	6.9	6.5	6.8	6.8	5.5	5.5	

3. TRADE BY PRINCIPAL COUNTRIES OF PRODUCTION AND CONSIGNMENT (VALUE IN THOUSAND U.S. DOLLARS)
ECHANGES SELON LES PRINCIPAUX PAYS DE PRODUCTION ET DE CONSIGNATION (VALEUR EN MILLIERS DE DOLLARS EU)

COUNTRIES–PAYS	GENERAL IMPORTS C.I.F. IMPORTATIONS GENERALES C.A.F				
	1991	1992	1993	1994	1995
World	37588335	40686804	46239317	54437152	70780784
Africa	520338	614962	678004	703640	831150
Americas	5010888	5869817	6443766	7654215	10126872
Northern America	4341529	5181997	5810835	6839321	8995628
LAIA	652231	623377	566590	766896	1079442
CACM	4774	2979	2260	6407	3243
Caribbean	2349	8053	13346	10248	16469
Rest of America	10005	53412	50736	31343	32091
As.ex F.USSR	23752335	25168873	28048837	33389909	43275494
Eur.x F.USSR	7050319	7413969	8787744	9490880	12841166
EU	5918819	6449917	7694209	8186684	11291429
EFTA	756266	639361	696095	907946	1224395
East Europe	341925	307218	381174	383897	308267
Other Europe	33310	377	5815	1673	2952
Former USSR	251754	328078	628318	946977	1308751
Oceania	780612	1085591	1137702	1306997	1597945
Japan/Japon	11036762	11906825	13962017	16435117	21622162
USA/Etats–Unis d'Amer	3990066	4775255	5381455	6448071	8509819
Singapore/Singapour	2990119	2970593	2969623	3437290	4161446
Germany/Allemagne	2095773	2164103	2482232	3182157	3749069
Malaysia/Malaisie	1190268	1595854	1674018	2647930	3234316
Korea, Republic of	1593808	1785904	1947780	1978047	2474141
China/Chine	1149166	1219894	1090477	1387658	2094647
United Kingdom	849199	944416	1055316	1150638	1455474
France,Monac	520268	943670	917300	751168	1946594
Australia/Australie	656871	912231	951081	1074507	1320951
Italy/Italie	544053	622812	906912	838739	1086776
Switz.Liecht	658243	549349	575268	754867	979193
Hong Kong	776048	492988	536244	689824	745793
Russian Federation		328078	620738	930335	1264588
India/Inde	937630	334923	522592	528146	629224
Belgium–Luxembourg	564989	384395	544041	478646	651972
Saudi Arabia	413344	518896	484355	527133	572198
Netherlands/Pays–Bas	326233	427782	403002	501331	698212
United Arab Emirates	296627	316004	447041	569829	678306
Indonesia/Indonésie	220493	291085	512200	451538	672731
Brazil/Brésil	374538	457815	341673	456559	501949
Sweden/Suède	317118	327251	416348	456587	585428
Canada	351450	405938	427621	389140	479273
Oman	160507	232717	300495	396015	682634
Philippines	97618	121183	180595	353273	579435
Finland/Finlande	111244	140806	309472	236752	375749
Brunei Darussalam	187471	218596	214117	182732	289376
Denmark/Danemark	154062	174353	231275	198556	256997
Spain/Espagne	146187	136656	174995	201407	255648
Myanmar	187494	140948	154998	157175	221191
Israel/Israël	119169	116487	124609	229373	219922
New Zealand	113776	136917	139166	155899	203842
Austria/Autriche	237988	113878	166453	105864	97992
Zambia/Zambie	109208	149598	143367	158740	159423
So. Africa Customs Un	46449	144154	150984	126912	219484
Norway,SVD,JM	95337	87338	113701	142262	228577
Poland/Pologne	126263	88437	114961	133495	138529
Iran (Islamic Rp. of)	149600	30151	67437	91075	223078
Chile/Chili	42920	43216	82114	148793	178950
Democratic Kampuchea	11567	93149	96370	126322	160008
Pakistan	112504	157513	83346	52095	64483
Mexico/Mexique	74814	53611	59591	75794	182904
Argentina/Argentine	129216	43313	56865	44673	172428
Czech Republic			162487	165342	81938
Viet Nam	116382	80252	84747	39178	43103
Turkey/Turquie	45988	95173	38806	81192	65921
Lao People's Dem. Rp.	47043	41120	63148	69112	69748
Ghana	15910	50076	58909	87290	64812
Cote d'Ivoire	52429	40680	62271	57214	47282
Former USSR/Anc. URSS	251754				

COUNTRIES–PAYS	GENERAL EXPORTS F.O.B. EXPORTATIONS GENERALES F.O.B.				
	1991	1992	1993	1994	1995
Monde	28420896	32474432	37166867	45235529	56439377
Afrique	801873	823723	969191	994947	1196834
Amériques	6852867	8161643	8928877	10620617	11273383
Amérique du Nord	6463808	7749182	8526097	10088501	10692045
ALAI	176948	220076	215955	330058	363719
MCAC	5059	7398	9070	8952	13779
Caraïbes	41484	25004	37805	43897	68876
Autre Amérique	165568	159983	139949	149209	134964
Asie l'URSS exclus	12983646	15055520	18619156	23890984	32070479
Europe l'URSS exclus	7026029	7469944	7415655	8012338	9832956
UE	6175815	6663015	6467871	7070101	8517171
AELE	355741	380119	405594	443391	552086
Europe de l'Est	470677	411086	530458	481949	743454
Autre de l'Europe	23796	8658	8790	9474	10885
Ancienne URSS	73215	192486	258180	337362	483908
Océanie	552508	638465	625554	766996	931202
USA/Etats–Unis d'Amer	6067462	7302024	8006474	9519618	10078335
Japan/Japon	5132837	5686126	6299927	7725177	9475371
Singapore/Singapour	2335427	2822944	4457711	6165411	7919084
Hong Kong	1347943	1507108	1958730	2385443	2920754
Germany/Allemagne	1468791	1427735	1479693	1591807	1638070
Netherlands/Pays–Bas	1246141	1404362	1156896	1257662	1801190
United Kingdom	1027705	1171854	1188386	1344748	1618870
Malaysia/Malaisie	683928	841757	1039851	1098713	1554117
France,Monac	699046	739751	773461	810332	977895
China/Chine	335153	385954	538675	927938	1640141
Australia/Australie	462868	525072	511889	642150	777587
Belgium–Luxembourg	391819	458201	582912	660966	744879
Korea, Republic of	459331	533314	461526	571502	800129
United Arab Emirates	383225	359416	476511	578425	1008593
Italy/Italie	525092	544001	463722	471292	572276
Canada	395868	446468	518178	568185	613020
Saudi Arabia	445262	384471	501891	434661	567534
Poland/Pologne	447366	364768	436818	389234	599071
Indonesia/Indonésie	213319	283171	202257	440156	811334
Switz.Liecht	311313	328370	355458	384638	491611
Spain/Espagne	281411	313827	271787	307890	450664
Russian Federation		192486	251555	303870	403322
Philippines	104998	154635	197817	223178	414549
Lao People's Dem. Rp.	76739	121056	175046	291322	354435
Viet Nam	22276	76693	115773	253701	467716
Myanmar	57920	80565	151575	238782	347525
Democratic Kampuchea	4630	65764	179322	260165	334063
Sweden/Suède	147186	154150	136745	153779	147247
Panama	163487	157320	136940	143361	126868
India/Inde	63336	65398	73885	192652	290236
Denmark/Danemark	123737	140099	112170	135525	170051
So. Africa Customs Un	46415	97886	133671	180252	217934
Iran (Islamic Rp. of)	76311	194054	134999	68720	190155
Israel/Israël	77532	93143	125107	136540	182166
Sri Lanka	83501	97686	88482	120269	216998
Pakistan	76022	70527	76416	142983	204928
Austria/Autriche	85791	90853	108674	105479	80981
Mexico/Mexique	94210	104252	88462	112062	52962
Bangladesh	38859	52416	72059	83480	192163
Portugal	59711	84659	72571	78534	77135
Yemen/Yémen	95003	105418	53425	64918	53543
Jordan/Jordanie	92976	98771	71700	46172	59351
Egypt/Egypte	51684	46966	73990	88111	99919
Finland/Finlande	61559	63256	59557	73949	88467
Kuwait/ Koweït	25612	52864	67939	89215	111060
New Zealand	46938	70950	62880	72090	92727
Brazil/Brésil	26256	19162	40825	98121	160699
Nigeria/Nigéria	96480	61610	73721	54075	57593
Nepal/Népal	15440	24046	63705	99696	129094
Benin/Bénin	52446	70122	89441	52006	64764

(VALUE AS PERCENTAGE OF WORLD TOTAL)(VALEURS EN POURCENTAGE DU TOTAL MONDIAL)

	1986	1987	1988	1989	1990	1991	1992	1993	1994	1995
Africa	1.6	1.7	1.5	1.2	1.0	1.4	1.5	1.5	1.3	1.2
Americas	17.3	15.4	16.8	14.9	13.9	13.3	14.4	13.9	14.1	14.3
Northern America	15.6	13.6	14.9	12.6	11.9	11.6	12.7	12.6	12.6	12.7
LAIA	1.6	1.7	1.9	2.2	2.0	1.7	1.5	1.2	1.4	1.5
CACM	0.0	0.0	0.0	0.0	0.0	0.0	0.0	0.0	0.0	0.0
Caribbean	0.0	0.0	0.0	0.0	0.0	0.0	0.0	0.0	0.0	0.0
Rest of America	0.1	0.0	0.0	0.0	0.0	0.0	0.1	0.1	0.1	0.0
As.ex F.USSR	58.0	59.8	58.7	62.2	62.7	63.2	61.9	60.7	61.3	61.1
Eur.x F.USSR	19.7	20.1	20.1	18.3	19.2	18.8	18.2	19.0	17.4	18.1
EU	16.5	16.8	16.6	15.1	15.9	15.7	15.9	16.6	15.0	16.0
EFTA	2.1	1.7	1.9	1.9	2.1	2.0	1.6	1.5	1.7	1.7
East Europe	1.1	1.5	1.4	1.2	1.1	0.9	0.8	0.8	0.7	0.4
Other Europe	0.1	0.1	0.2	0.1	0.1	0.1	0.0	0.0	0.0	0.0
Former USSR	0.2	0.3	0.3	0.3	0.5	0.7	0.8	1.4	1.7	1.8
Oceania	2.4	2.2	2.1	2.4	2.0	2.1	2.7	2.5	2.4	2.3
Japan/Japon	26.4	26.0	29.0	30.3	30.4	29.4	29.3	30.2	30.2	30.5
USA/Etats–Unis d'Amer	14.4	12.5	13.6	11.3	10.8	10.6	11.7	11.6	11.8	12.0
Singapore/Singapour	6.6	7.8	7.4	7.7	7.4	8.0	7.3	6.4	6.3	5.9
Germany/Allemagne	5.8	6.0	5.4	5.1	4.9	5.6	5.3	5.4	5.8	5.3
Malaysia/Malaisie	4.2	3.8	2.1	2.6	3.4	3.2	3.9	3.6	4.9	4.6
Korea, Republic of	2.4	2.4	2.8	2.9	3.1	4.2	4.4	4.2	3.6	3.5
China/Chine	2.9	3.9	3.4	2.9	3.3	3.1	3.0	2.4	2.5	3.0
United Kingdom	3.2	3.2	3.0	2.6	2.7	2.3	2.3	2.3	2.1	2.1
France,Monac	1.6	1.5	2.4	1.6	2.4	1.4	2.3	2.0	1.4	2.8
Australia/Australie	1.8	1.8	1.7	2.0	1.7	1.7	2.2	2.1	2.0	1.9

	1986	1987	1988	1989	1990	1991	1992	1993	1994	1995
Afrique	3.4	3.3	3.5	3.0	2.5	2.8	2.5	2.6	2.2	2.1
Amériques	20.6	20.9	22.7	24.4	25.5	24.1	25.1	24.0	23.5	20.0
Amérique du Nord	19.5	20.1	21.9	23.2	24.0	22.7	23.9	22.9	22.3	18.9
ALAI	0.8	0.1	0.1	0.3	0.5	0.6	0.7	0.6	0.7	0.6
MCAC	0.0	0.0	0.0	0.0	0.0	0.0	0.0	0.0	0.0	0.0
Caraïbes	0.1	0.2	0.3	0.3	0.2	0.1	0.1	0.1	0.1	0.1
Autre Amérique	0.2	0.5	0.4	0.6	0.7	0.6	0.5	0.4	0.3	0.2
Asie l'URSS exclus	49.1	48.5	47.6	46.8	44.5	45.7	46.4	50.1	52.8	56.8
Europe l'URSS exclus	23.9	24.7	23.4	21.9	24.9	24.7	23.0	20.0	17.7	17.4
UE	22.2	23.2	21.8	20.2	22.6	21.7	20.5	17.4	15.6	15.1
AELE	1.2	1.1	1.2	1.3	1.4	1.3	1.2	1.1	1.0	1.0
Europe de l'Est	0.3	0.2	0.2	0.3	0.7	1.7	1.3	1.4	1.1	1.3
Autre de l'Europe	0.1	0.1	0.2	0.2	0.1	0.1	0.0	0.0	0.0	0.0
Ancienne URSS	0.8	0.3	0.4	1.3	0.4	0.3	0.6	0.7	0.7	0.9
Océanie	2.1	2.1	2.1	2.2	1.9	1.9	2.0	1.7	1.7	1.6
USA/Etats–Unis d'Amer	18.1	18.6	20.1	21.7	22.7	21.3	22.5	21.5	21.0	17.9
Japan/Japon	14.2	14.9	16.0	17.0	17.2	18.1	17.5	17.0	17.1	16.8
Singapore/Singapour	8.9	9.0	7.7	7.1	7.3	8.2	8.7	12.0	13.6	14.0
Hong Kong	4.0	4.2	4.5	4.0	4.5	4.7	4.6	5.3	5.3	5.2
Germany/Allemagne	4.6	4.9	4.6	4.1	5.2	5.2	4.4	4.0	3.5	2.9
Netherlands/Pays–Bas	7.3	6.7	5.5	4.9	4.8	4.4	4.3	3.1	2.8	3.2
United Kingdom	3.2	3.6	3.7	3.7	4.1	3.6	3.6	3.2	3.0	2.9
Malaysia/Malaisie	4.3	3.3	3.0	2.9	2.5	2.4	2.6	2.8	2.4	2.8
France,Monac	2.3	2.4	2.4	2.2	2.4	2.5	2.3	2.1	1.8	1.7
China/Chine	3.1	3.3	3.0	2.7	1.2	1.2	1.2	1.4	2.1	2.9

4. General Imports C.I.F. by Commodities according to the S.I.T.C. (Rev. 2) in thousand U.S. Dollars
Importations Générales C.A.F. par Produits d'après la C.T.C.I. (Rév. 2) en milliers de Dollars E.U.

SITC CTCI	COMMODITY	1992 WEIGHT POIDS	1992 VALUE VALEUR	1993 WEIGHT POIDS	1993 VALUE VALEUR	1994 WEIGHT POIDS	1994 VALUE VALEUR	1995 WEIGHT POIDS	1995 VALUE VALEUR	PRODUIT
	ALL COMMODITIES		40686804		46239317		54437152		70780784	TOUS PRODUITS
0	FOOD AND LIVE ANIMALS		1935142		1847297		2016980		2243389	ALIMENTS,ANIMAUX VIVANTS
02	DAIRY PRODCTS,BIRDS'EGGS		219736		204375		247413		332654	PRODUITS LAITIERS,OEUFS
022	MILK AND CREAM	W 98375	188012	W 92157	177390	W 123095	209488	W 140676	285772	LAIT ET CREME
0224	MILK,CREAM PRESERVED ETC	W 95625	183621	W 89606	172612	W 117596	201686	W 134386	275074	LAIT,CREME CONS,CONC
03	FISH AND PREPARATIONS		890622		735046		689002		697145	POISSONS ET PREPARATIONS
034	FISH,FRESH,CHILLED,FROZN	W 558281	816503	W 539383	644045	W 566141	555957	W 611929	500388	POISSON FRAIS, REFRIG,CONG
0342	FISH FROZEN,EXCL FILLETS	W 516809	775179	W 510082	622934	W 516983	529165	W 547954	460707	POISSONS CONGELES
04	CEREALS AND PREPARATIONS		264394		235028		271422		348820	CEREALES ET PRODUITS
05	VEGETABLES AND FRUIT		106436		139101		178110		194056	LEGUMES ET FRUITS
081	*FEEDING STUFF FOR ANIML	W 1178273	335726	W 1274083	413221	W 1612181	483539	W 1487461	496070	NOURRITURE POUR ANIMAUX
0813	OILCAKE AND OTH RESIDUES	W 999830	210086	W 992601	223868	W 1230757	256811	W 1065875	231636	TOURTEAUX
08131	— OF SOYA BEANS	W 633868	160344	W 598844	160960	W 902708	201389	W 688516	165938	TOURTEAUX DE SOJA
1	BEVERAGES AND TOBACCO		211777		242474		240884		262254	BOISSONS ET TABACS
11	BEVERAGES		132020		153037		148979		161809	BOISSONS
112	ALCOHOLIC BEVERAGES	W 14848	131089	W 17104	150761	W 19388	147433	W 20498	159030	BOISSONS ALCOOLIQUES
1124	DISTILLED ALCOHOLIC BEVS	W 12345	123458	W 14111	142346	W 16212	137766	W 14916	139536	ALCOOLS,EAUX–DE–VIE
2	CRUDE MATERLS,EXCL FUELS		2423411		2517713		2790374		3475584	MAT BRUTES NON COMESTIBLES
21	HIDES,SKINS,FURS UNDRSSD		166918		183519		156455		174351	CUIRS,PEAUX BRUTS
211	HIDES,SKINS,EXC FURS,RAW	W 99254	166748	W 115743	183519	W 131184	156454	W 99423	174328	CUIRS ET PEAUX
2111	BOVINE,EQUINE HIDES,RAW	W 93705	160257	W 112585	179229	W 128462	152367	W 96462	169086	PEAUX DE BOVINS
24	CORK AND WOOD		722967		744895		945786		1086756	LIEGE ET BOIS
247	OTH WOOD ROUGH,SQUARED	W 1532884	285402		233369	W 1380602	294574	W 1075884	402439	BOIS BRUTS EQUARRIS
2472	SAW–,VENEER–LOGS NON–CON	W 1531131	285036	W 1025551	233342	W 1352967	287261	W 1045151	394701	NON CONIFERES SCIAGE,PLAC
24721	— IN THE ROUGH	W 1531131	285036	W 1025551	233342	W 1352967	287261	W 1045151	394701	BRUTS ECORCES DEGROSSIS
248	WOOD SHAPED,SLEEPERS	W 1351945	435832	W 2801029	509479	W 2185672	649023	W 1535141	681977	BOIS SIMPLEMENT TRAVAILLES
2483	LUMBER SHAPED NON–CONIFR	W 1328583	426451	W 2753567	499355	W 2111256	627844	W 1457187	647796	NON CONIFERES SCIES,RABOTES
24831	LUMBER SAWN ETC NON–CON	W 1323612	424787	W 2744290	496305	W 2103486	624835	W 1444654	642991	SCIES LONGITUDINALEMENT
251	*PULP AND WASTE PAPER	W 613522	208336	W 714914	225879	W 850048	290900	W 1025542	525281	PATES A PAPIER,DECHETS
2517	SODA,SULPHATE WOOD PULP	W 146421	75970	W 235640	106652	W 206915	106601	W 252520	216062	PATES CHIMIQUES AU SULFATE
26	TEXTILE FIBRES AND WASTE		742114		614033		714840		868200	FIBRES TEXTILES
263	COTTON	W 450251	567640	W 313064	462782	W 347561	568427	W 346831	679990	COTON
2631	RAW COTTON,EXCL LINTERS	W 414089	542833	W 275490	441339	W 321608	548734	W 326750	660973	COTON EN MASSE
27	CRUDE FERTLZR,MINRLS NES		160771		162280		164328		179479	ENGRAIS MINERAUX BRUTS
28	METALLIFEROUS ORES,SCRAP		242033		411826		309106		312132	MINERAIS METAL,DECHETS
282	IRON AND STEEL SCRAP	W 865435	200169	W 1458506	361464	W 1158764	257217	W 1035683	229063	FERRAILLES
28209	— OF OTHR IRON OR STEEL	W 826599	195189	W 1448217	359365	W 1155884	256803	W 1012022	224783	FERRAILLES DE FER
3	MINERAL FUELS ETC		3368077		3483200		3738117		4844548	COMBUSTIBLES MINERAUX LUB
33	PETROLEUM AND PRODUCTS		3337515		3426920		3656201		4744961	PETROLE ET DERIVES
333	CRUDE PETROLEUM	MW 12526	1744977	MW 14491	1804610	MW 14820	2145591	MW 21273	2851532	HUILES BRUTES DE PETROLE
334	PETROLEUM PRODUCTS,REFIN	MW 9215	1536492	MW 9193	1564415	MW 9539	1428073	MW 10458	1758587	PRODUITS RAFFINES
3341	GASOLINE,OTH LIGHT OILS	W 804481	188668	W 760463	166713	W 1147580	124960	W 690439	93959	ESSENCES POUR MOTEURS
33411	MOTOR,AVIATION SPIRIT	W 804481	188668	W 760463	166713	W 1147580	124960	W 690439	93959	ESSENCES MOTEURS D'AVIONS
3343	GAS OILS	W 3593645	695768	W 4366199	824562	W 4289028	648003	W 4935468	811067	GAS OILS
3344	FUEL OILS,NES	W 3878034	360763	W 3115378	260667	W 3176092	330265	W 3393567	404176	FUEL OILS
3345	LUBS,PETROLEUM OILS NES	W 415649	184218	W 431018	206152	W 627145	255686	W 1285451	420935	HUILES LUBRIFIANTES
33451	LUBS(HIGH PETR CONT) ETC	W 402680	146556	W 412149	157503	W 606878	197438	W 1262774	351444	HUILES LUBRIF,H LOURDES
5	CHEMCLS,RELATED PROD NES		4202866		4599568		5516468		7191780	PRODUITS CHIMIQUES
51	ORGANIC CHEMICALS		1119717		1277668		1657742		2512614	PROD CHIMIQ ORGANIQUES
511	HYDROCARBONS NES,DERIVS	W 646251	296921	W 783923	335735	W 922097	511759	W 1004125	754355	HYDROCARBURES NDA
5111	ACYCLIC HYDROCARBONS	W 266681	112756	W 285607	101415	W 379592	178639	W 366626	200147	HYDROCARBURES ACYCLIQUES
5112	CYCLIC HYDROCARBONS	W 202960	89347	W 219752	90700	W 256317	139134	W 328094	300239	HYDROCARBURES CYCLIQUES
5113	HALOG DERIV OF HYDROCARB	W 174231	92121	W 277588	141894	W 285111	192122	W 308480	251854	DERIVES HALOGENES HYDROCAR
512	ALCOHOLS,PHENOLS ETC		110966		130104		186268		291592	PHENOLS,PHENOLS–ALCOOLS
5121	ACYCLIC ALCOHOLS,DERIVS		91605		102924		153322		250343	ALCOOLS ACYCLIQUES
513	CARBOXYLIC ACIDS ETC	W 389935	289331	W 484273	346014	W 533344	435064	W 597520	725052	ACIDES CARBOXYLIQUES
5138	POLYACIDS AND DERIVATIVS	W 286544	182694	W 376715	241778	W 398955	306909	W 459015	528808	ACIDES POLYCARBOXYLIQUES
51389	OTH POLYACIDS ETC,DERIVS	W 220764	144408	W 298585	196955	W 317376	250021	W 364128	419813	ACIDES POLYCARBOXYLIQUES
514	NITROGEN–FNCTN COMPOUNDS	W 71207	171757	W 79040	184777	W 94202	201525	W 120448	305792	COMPOSES FONCT AZOTEES
515	ORG–INORG COMPOUNDS ETC	W 56752	174767	W 65107	181859	W 77526	189530	W 81975	268149	COMPOSES ORGANO–MINERAUX
5156	HETEROCYCLIC CMPDS ETC	W 46850	132018	W 53230	133995	W 66231	144001	W 66756	204796	COMPOSES HETEROCYCLIQUES
52	INORGANIC CHEMICALS		250635		270961		287597		358121	PROD CHIM INORGANIQUES
523	OTHR INORG CHEMICALS ETC	W 503959	142139	W 502669	148798		159351	W 623825	204946	AUT PRODUITS CHIMIQUES INORG
53	DYES,TANNING,COLOUR PROD		429924		452791		488850		585445	PROD TEINTURE,COLORANTS
531	SYNT DYE,NAT INDGO,LAKES	W 13819	161187	W 15758	170507	W 16119	165066	W 18625	200736	MAT COLOR ORGAN,LAQUES
5311	SYNTHIC ORGNIC DYESTUFFS	W 11977	142385	W 13969	151663	W 14141	147252	W 16054	178217	MAT COLOR ORGAN SYNTHET
533	PIGMENTS,PAINTS,ETC	W 103001	258622	W 102642	271307	W 116497	312642	W 123542	370396	PIGMENTS,PEINTURES,VERNIS
541	*MEDICINAL,PHARM PRODUCT		313814	MK 12673	326862	MK 14424	383879	MK 16814	469182	PROD MEDICINAUX PHARMACEUT
5417	MEDICAMENTS	K 8210497	130468	K 6108530	140270	K 7885584	173832	MK 9732	220851	MEDICAMENTS
55	PERFUME,CLEANING ETC PRD		184022		215455		253940		302533	PROD POUR PARFUM,TOILETTE
562	*FERTILIZERS,MANUFACTURE	W 2863418	494818	W 3262196	539764	W 3015364	537879	W 3152555	633394	ENGRAIS MANUFACTURES
5621	CHEM NITROGENOUS FERTLZR	W 1042675	140232	W 1150400	148694	W 945062	129899	W 1095875	183686	ENGRAIS AZOTES
5629	FERTILIZERS NES	W 1679922	333079	W 1970745	370404	W 1923398	385384	W 1851682	418655	ENGRAIS NDA
56291	NIT–PHOS–POT FERTLZR NES	W 842543	171969	W 1187840	228366	W 1062550	221334	W 1111800	247161	ENGRAIS CONT N P K
56292	NITROG–PHOS FERTILZR NES	W 820990	157332	W 776533	141072	W 849287	161403	W 731586	169286	ENGRAIS NDA CONT N P
58	PLASTIC MATERIALS ETC		915666		957698		1253396		1505669	MAT PLAST ARTIFICIELLES
582	PROD OF CONDENSATION ETC	W 97290	225664	W 110198	274942	W 124578	320222	W 169151	453693	PROD CONDENS,POLYCOND
583	POLYMERIZATION ETC PRODS	W 470548	657678	W 435572	646744	W 606407	893022		1004642	PROD POLYMERISATION
5833	POLYSTYRENE,ITS COPOLYMR	W 93045	120670	W 101177	124994	W 118876	155971	W 134064	240014	POLYPROPYLENE COPOLYMERES
58331	— IN PRIMARY FORMS	W 92300	118457	W 100108	122025	W 117761	152601	W 132271	234520	SOUS FORMES PRIMAIRES
5839	OTH POLYMRZTION ETC PROD	W 107533	277797	W 111847	289923	W 133076	362267	W 139861	408637	AUT PROD POLYMER COPOLYM
59	CHEMICAL MATERIALS NES		490173		551687		646510		801924	MAT PROD CHIMIQUES NDA
591	PESTICIDES,DISINFECTANTS	W 26189	129401	W 25165	120554	W 30048	127824	W 32344	145569	DESINF,INSECT,FONG,HERB
598	MISCEL CHEM PRODUCTS NES		310809		367435	W 286429	437668	W 330095	558408	PROD DIV INDUST CHIM NDA
5989	CHEM PRODUCTS,PREPS NES	W 165765	225748	W 191820	256300	W 214258	312366	W 247972	407275	PROD PREP CHIMIQUES NDA
59899	OTH CHEM PRODS,PREPS,NES	W 134496	171349	W 155861	204420	W 173580	248966	W 197112	328797	AUT PRODUITS CHIMIQUES NDA
6	BASIC MANUFACTURES		8269923		8944561		10331866		13811754	ART MANUFACTURES
61	LEATHER,DRESSED FUR,ETC		284568		290405		328303		319660	CUIRS,PELLETERIES
611	LEATHER	W 22383	239859	W 20769	243961	W 22481	273441	W 19632	260002	CUIRS,PEAUX PREPARES
6114	LEATHR BOVINE NES,EQUINE	W 18554	183646	W 17430	186328	W 19598	201399	W 16876	183173	CUIRS DE BOVINS
62	RUBBER MANUFACTURES NES		174662		214770		263627		331950	CAOUTCHOUC MANUFACTURE
628	RUBBER ARTICLES NES	W 11188	107728	W 13085	129726	W 13709	166768	W 19846	212768	OUVRAGES CAOUTCHOUC NDA
64	PAPER,PAPERBOARD AND MFR		444425		510792		566907		761016	PAPIERS,CARTONS & OUVRAGES
641	PAPER AND PAPERBOARD	W 446289	366909	W 530242	422646	W 534949	452832	W 483040	617109	PAPIERS ET CARTONS
6418	COATED ETC PAPER NES BLK	W 65270	116630	W 63055	130227	W 68827	159658	W 78677	221726	PAP,CARTONS COUCHES,ENDUITS
65	TEXTILE YARN,FABRICS,ETC		1209681		1306295		1359287		1533580	FILS,TISSUS,ARTICLES TEXTILE
651	TEXTILE YARN	W 42193	198779	W 42767	189734	W 48196	209330	W 74749	272231	FILS TEXTILES
652	COTTON FABRICS,WOVEN	A 131869	190116	A 133154	202279		210584	W 20268	197429	TISSUS DE COTON
6522	WOVEN COTTON BLEACHD,ETC	A 116491	180751	A 114130	189914		196512	W 17925	183996	TISSUS COTON BLANCHIS ETC
65224	BLCHED COTTON FABRIC NES	A 90848	129838	A 83557	136664		136288	W 14206	135337	AUT TIS PLUS 85% COT BLANCHI
653	WOVN MAN–MADE FIB FABRIC	A 355743	375610	A 496173	426563		419502	W 66830	465599	TISSUS FIBRES SYNTH,ARTIF

4. General Imports C.I.F. by Commodities according to the S.I.T.C. (Rev. 2) in thousand U.S. Dollars
Importations Générales C.A.F. par Produits d'après la C.T.C.I. (Rév. 2) en milliers de Dollars E.U.

SITC CTCI	COMMODITY	1992 WEIGHT POIDS	1992 VALUE VALEUR	1993 WEIGHT POIDS	1993 VALUE VALEUR	1994 WEIGHT POIDS	1994 VALUE VALEUR	1995 WEIGHT POIDS	1995 VALUE VALEUR	PRODUIT
6531	CONT SYNT WEAVES NONPILE	A 135417	182968	A 155608	188747		200466	W 26042	209854	TISSUS FIBRES SYNTH CONTINUE
65315	CONT SYN TXTL FABRIC NES	A 132638	177919	A 153522	184753		196235	W 25666	203720	TIS PLUS 85% TEXT SYNT CONT
655	KNITTED,ETC FABRICS	W 15748	158264	W 18527	174869	W 18325	186702	W 19226	215944	ETOF BONNETERIE PIECES ETC
6552	OTHER KNIT ETC FAB NONEL	W 15748	158264	W 18527	174869	W 18325	186702	W 19226	215944	ETOF BON NON ELAS NON SYNT
657	SPECIAL TXTL FABRC,PRODS	W 29169	193258	W 37235	204656	W 31986	199425	W 31723	219012	TISSUS SPECIAUX
6573	COATED ETC TEXTILES NES	W 21700	126374	W 28039	131636	W 19748	117255	W 19752	120550	TISSUS,ART MATIERE TEXT NDA
66	NONMETAL MINERAL MFS NES		1071243		1161973		1299352		1663665	ART MIN NON METALLIQUES
661	LIME,CEMENT,BLDG PRODS	W 3037496	175468	W 13205	11168	W 127396	16503	W 529270	43027	CHAUX,CIMENTS MAT CONSTR
6612	CEMENT	W 3029443	167334	W 2987	1252	W 116351	6089	W 516736	31292	CIMENTS HYDRAULIQUES
663	MINERAL MANUFCTURES NES	W 28080	114680	W 30391	158084	W 38142	160202	W 49246	186057	ART MIN MANUF NDA
664	GLASS	W 48178	99672	W 74126	132869		167137		243314	VERRE
667	PEARL,PREC--,SEMI--P STONE		622035		799324		884768		1074438	PERLES, PIERRES GEMMES
6672	DIAMONDS NONINDUST,UNSET		463806		630698		736365		894861	DIAMANTS BRUTS
66721	— ROUGH,UNSORTED		67486		144122		158774		197380	DIAMANTS BRUTS NON TRIES
66722	— SRTD,ROUGH,SIMPLY WKD		172191		182216		189320		178641	DIAMANTS TRIES BRUTS
66729	— CUT ETC NOT SET		224129		304360		388271		518840	DIAMANTS TAILLES
6673	PREC--,SEMI--PR STONES NES		136946		150880		126174		137725	AUTRES PIERRES NON SERTIES
67	IRON AND STEEL		3278251		3343383		3753106		5223335	FER ET ACIER
672	IRON,STEEL PRIMARY FORMS	W 3000712	949037	W 2912949	907485	W 4765723	1166473	W 5339195	1747949	LINGOTS FER,ACIER
6725	IRN,STL BLOOMS,SLABS,ETC	W 1224036	315503	W 1167072	296480	W 3209330	580063	W 3428055	908710	BLOOMS,BILLETTES FER ACIER
67251	IRN,SMPLE STL BLOOMS,ETC	W 1223846	314952	W 1166844	295927	W 3208612	578815	W 3427278	907275	BLOOMS ETC NON ACIER FIN
6727	IRN,STL COIL FR REROLLNG	W 1776646	633476	W 1745866	610993	W 1556371	586383	W 1911073	839085	EBAUCHES POUR TOLES FER
67271	IRON,SIMPLE STEEL COILS	W 1717496	594031	W 1677365	575433	W 1472962	508431	W 1811457	726632	EBAUCHES NON EN ACIER
673	IRON,STEEL SHAPES ETC	W 1933150	759173	W 1658783	697068	W 1929636	791703	W 1703677	831761	BARRES,PROFIL FER,ACIER
6731	IRON,STEEL WIRE ROD	W 663539	260631	W 581544	241800	W 693262	288621	W 774818	360075	FIL MACHINE FER,ACIER
67311	IRON,SIMPLE STL WIRE ROD	W 422205	138451	W 280938	100403	W 308675	108567	W 358095	133802	FIL MACH AUT ACIER FIN
6732	IRON,STEEL BARS ETC	W 863704	328745	W 664747	287292	W 645011	286386	W 322509	232393	BARRES FER,ACIER
67326	IRN,OTH STL BARS HOTROLD	W 794732	257126	W 579603	194393	W 548764	174897	W 189249	74552	BARRES PLEINES FER,ACIER
6733	IRON,STEEL PROFILES ETC	W 405907	169797	W 412492	167976	W 591364	216697	W 606349	239293	PROFILES,PALPLAN FER,ACIER
674	IRN,STL UNIV,PLATE,SHEET	W 2018787	1327496	W 2352156	1456200	W 2440486	1380116	W 3252352	2076892	LARGES PLATS,TOLES
6744	IRN,STL HVY PLATE,ROLLED	W 448265	205404	W 435053	179745	W 558955	205596	W 704328	311833	TOLES LAMINEES PLUS 4.75 MM
67441	— OF IRON OR SIMPLE STL	W 435367	186811	W 418688	152350	W 541108	182233	W 678615	266401	TOLES NON ACIER FIN CARB
6746	IRN,STL THIN PLATE,ROLLD	W 1071248	757645	W 1373033	902477	W 1322035	782936	W 1827452	1199599	TOLES LAM MOINS 3MM
67461	— OF IRON OR SIMPLE STL	W 1010122	610573	W 1281216	708022	W 1242646	639045	W 1737030	1002655	TOL NON AC FIN MOINS 3 MM
67463	— OF STAINLESS ETC STL	W 57986	143108	W 87140	189354	W 73297	138269	W 69571	180652	TOL ACIER INOX MOINS 3 MM
6749	OTH IRN,STL PLATES,SHEET	W 283448	218927	W 304725	226280	W 369399	265854	W 440883	374228	AUTRES TOLES FER,ACIER
67491	— OF IRON OR SIMPLE STL	W 282026	214686	W 303463	220817	W 367212	258463	W 430805	357143	AUT TOLES AUTRES ACIER FIN
678	IRON,STL TUBES,PIPES,ETC	W 110381	132525	W 145473	159919	W 180811	249849	W 276363	353367	TUBES,TUYAUX EN FONTE,FER
68	NON--FERROUS METALS		798836		911851		1183142		1801483	METAUX NON FERREUX
682	COPPER EXC CEMENT COPPER	W 125410	369027	W 159219	405656	W 233166	579724	W 221583	793118	CUIVRE
6821	COPPER NES,ALLOYS,UNWRT	W 91319	223867	W 122545	247113	W 177013	368281	W 154091	461617	CUIVRE BRUT
68212	COPPER REFINED,UNWROUGHT	W 91268	223665	W 122443	246755	W 176954	368055	W 153976	461016	CUIVRE AFFINE BRUT
6822	COPPER,ALLOYS WORKED	W 34092	145160	W 36674	158543	W 56153	211444	W 67492	331501	CUIVRE,ALLIAGES OUVRES
684	ALUMINIUM	W 179728	332235	W 220169	385070	W 234418	462582	W 316096	780634	ALUMINIUM
6841	ALUMINIUM,ALLOYS,UNWRGHT	W 148506	217027	W 181623	246864	W 184547	282960	W 254158	511327	ALUMINIUM,ALLIAGES BRUTS
6842	ALUMINIUM,ALLOYS WORKED	W 31222	115208	W 38545	138206	W 49871	179623	W 61938	269307	ALUMINIUM,ALLIAGES OUVRE
69	METAL MANUFACTURES NES		964326		1167075		1527840		2096959	ART MANUFACT EN METAL NDA
694	STL,COPPR NAILS,NUTS,ETC	W 24457	181250	W 37938	254341	W 38828	306188	W 40112	357881	CLOUS,VIS,ECROUS
69402	IRN,STL NUTS,BOLTS,ETC	W 22810	175678	W 36286	249126	W 36406	298195	W 37768	345497	BOULONS,VIS,ECROUS FER,AC
695	TOOLS		188128		214996	W 25440	272013	W 30369	409885	OUTILS A MAIN
6954	BLADES,TIPS,ETC FR TOOLS	W 3592	131261	W 4259	146034	W 5938	190968	W 7453	303706	OUTILS POUR MACHINE--OUTIL
69541	PARTS TO INSERT IN TOOLS	W 2763	102836	W 3315	109882	W 4778	151089	W 6037	251073	OUTILS DE FORAGE
699	BASE METAL MFRS NES		430910	W 102436	542036	W 123328	743199	W 124301	1022286	ART MANUFACTURES MET NDA
6997	IRON,STEEL ARTICLES NES	W 31721	195207	W 31908	244401	W 57842	383665	W 58535	608788	OUV FONTE,FER,ACIER NDA
69979	IRN,STL MANUFACTURES NES	W 31705	195127	W 31668	244002	W 57734	383264	W 58443	608604	AUT OUVRAGES EN FER NDA
7	MACHINES,TRANSPORT EQUIP		17020091		20773295		25495389		33551734	MACHINES MATERIEL TRANSPORT
71	POWER GENERATING EQUIPMT		1085266		1612288		1456684		1690462	MACHINES GENERATRICES
713	INTRNL COMBUS PSTN ENGIN		426182		506633		583165		619430	MOTEURS EXPL COMB INT, PIECE
7132	MOTOR VEHCL PISTN ENGINS	N 1752041	162622	N 2476338	115338	N 3165911	116153	N 964830	130639	MOTEURS EXPL POUR VEHICULES
7139	PISTON ENGINE PARTS NES	W 30610	230600	W 108657	347615	W 87146	410958	W 39768	431149	PIECES POUR 713.2,3,8
716	ROTATING ELECTRIC PLANT		528933		967306		751425		847211	APP ELECTR ROTATIFS,PIECES
7161	DC MOTORS AND GENERATORS		67529		357203	N 5227213	257706	N 1488868	198365	MOTEURS COURANT CONTINU
7162	AC MTRS,GENRTRS,GEN SETS	MN 49395	144558		190874		276623		363638	MOTEURS ELECTRIQUES
71621	AC MTRS,INC UNIVRSL MTRS	MN 49301	115777		154018	MN 84494	236531	MN 92643	315519	MOT ELEC NON COUR CONTINU
7169	PTS NES OF ROT ELEC PLNT	MN 370169	316434	MN 512087	418956	W 10023	216705	W 11560	284793	PIECES MAC APP ROTATIFS
72	MACHS FOR SPCL INDUSTRYS		2456018		2595172		3124050		4186252	MAC SPECIALES POUR INDUST
722	TRACTORS NON--ROAD	N 9543	140299	N 15495	164723	N 55519	212068	N 85455	244871	TRACTEURS
723	CIVIL ENGNEERG EQUIP ETC		332332		414608		602410		725377	APPAREILS DE GENIE CIVIL
7234	CONST,MINING MACHNRY NES	N 10904	261149	N 8016	306253		431491	N 14270	523191	MACH POUR LA CONST, MINES
72342	SLFPRP SHOVELS,EXCAVATRS	N 3627	186606	N 4326	247546	N 11411	301590	N 6507	395613	PELLES MECANIQUES
724	TEXTILE,LEATHER MACHNRY		637495		567192		545282		641900	MACH POUR INDUSTRIE TEXTILE
7244	SPINNING,EXTRDNG,ETC MCH		230476		155102		220603		258433	MACH POUR LE FILAGE
7245	WEAVING,FELT MFG,ETC MCH		153645		172548		125792		155123	METIERS A TISSER,PIECES
7247	TEXTILE MACHINERY NES		143187		107715		89184		98237	MACH LAVAGE,TEINTURE TEX
725	PAPER ETC MILL MACHINERY		122286		245173		75889		176923	MACHINES FABR PATE PAPIER
726	PRINTG,BKBINDG MACHY,PTS		129137		115364		168292		235747	MACHINES POUR IMPRIMERIE
727	FOOD MACHRY NON--DOMESTIC		110402		144110		95099		165721	MACH INDUSTRIES ALIMENT
728	OTH MACHY FOR SPCL INDUS		953870		915854		1394998		1930396	AUT MACH IND PARTICULIERES
7281	MACH--TOOLS FR SPCL INDUS		85387		79553		171614		230869	MACH--OUTILS SPEC IND PART
7283	OTHR MINERAL WORKG MACHY		188950		86136		185469		239310	MACH TRIER,CRIBLER,BROYER
7284	MACHY FOR SPCL INDUS NES		679533		750165		1037914		1460217	MACH SPEC IND PARTICUL.
72842	RUBBER,PLASTICS WRKG MCH	N 7034	206858	N 11830	275139		291823	N 27529	396162	MACH IND CAOUT MAT PLAST
72848	OTH MCHY WITH INDIV FNCT	N 171031	267187	N 252453	309990	N 946399	567761	N 1047118	848027	AUTRES MACHINES NDA
72849	PTS OF MACHS OF 7284 ETC	W 7127	145851	W 4142	91799	W 3648	82631	W 5183	88325	PIECES DU 728.4 ETC
73	METALWORKING MACHINERY		568557		890262		856111		1140950	MACH TRAVAIL DES METAUX
736	METALWORKING MACH--TOOLS		435623		477179		549423		829163	MACH--OUTILS TRAVAIL METAUX
7361	METAL CUTTING MACH--TOOLS	N 76350	214144		208067		281066	N 123188	397923	MACH--OUT ENLEVEMENT METAL
7362	METAL FORMING MACH--TOOLS	N 9955	136763	N 22493	137401	N 18969	147917	N 33646	245595	MACH--OUTILS DEFORM METAL
737	METALWORKING MACHNRY NES		132934		413083		306688		311786	MACH TRAV METAUX PIECES
7372	ROLLING MILLS AND ROLLS		50750		301248		169277		125185	LAMINOIRS CYLINDRES PIEC
73729	ROLL--MILL PTS NES, ROLLS	W 2864	27049	W 15152	170757		36184		50055	CYLINDRES DE LAMINOIRS
74	GENRL INDUSTRL MACHY NES		2385553		2855977		3463561		4753838	MACH APP INDUSTRIE
741	HEATING,COOLING EQUIPMNT		572357		774092		863998		1309342	MACH CHAUFFAGE,PIECES
7413	INDUS FURNACES ETC,PARTS		149626		113526		132354		208043	FOURS IND,LABOR,PIECES
7416	HEATING,COOLING EQU NES		263168		498179		485003		841659	APP CHANGEMENT TEMP
742	PUMPS FOR LIQUIDS ETC		217625		270100		339923		396596	POMPES MOTO--POMPES
7428	OTHER PUMPS FOR LIQUIDS	N 2863370	93045	N 1881043	135766	N 2252284	184375	N 2199063	241960	AUTRES POMPES POUR LIQ
74288	PUMPS FR LIQUIDS NES ETC	N 2852512	72959	N 1843730	108631	N 1953879	153185	N 2005134	214075	POMPES POUR LIQUIDES NDA
743	PUMPS NES,CENTRFUGES ETC		362926		460919		550403		766137	POMPES COMPRES,VENT ETC
7431	PUMPS FOR GASES ETC	N 3489172	212461	N 4891936	226455	N 8104986	311848	N 7064492	409922	POMPES AIR A VIDE,COMPRES
744	MECHANICAL HANDLING EQU		456004		428443		545127		684469	EQUIP MANUTENTION PIECES

4. General Imports C.I.F. by Commodities according to the S.I.T.C. (Rev. 2) in thousand U.S. Dollars
Importations Générales C.A.F. par Produits d'après la C.T.C.I. (Rév. 2) en milliers de Dollars E.U.

SITC CTCI	COMMODITY	1992		1993		1994		1995		PRODUIT
		WEIGHT POIDS	VALUE VALEUR	WEIGHT POIDS	VALUE VALEUR	WEIGHT POIDS	VALUE VALEUR	WEIGHT POIDS	VALUE VALEUR	
7442	LIFTING,LOADING MACH NES	N 365876	250802		279904		382729		416492	APP LEVAGE,MANUTENTION
74428	OTH HANDLING ETC MCH NES	N 287851	76451	N 392972	116119		169142		202388	AUT APP LEVAGE ETC
7449	PTS NES OF MACHY OF 7442	W 23504	132721	W 12849	81293	W 13846	63739	W 15484	82078	PIECES DU 744.2
745	NONELEC MACHY,TOOLS NES		164952		213202		269420		384469	AUT MACH NON ELEC,PIECES
7452	OTH NONELEC MCHS,PTS NES		152746		199168		248233		354955	AUT MACH NON ELEC,PIECES
749	NONELEC MACH PTS,ACC NES		611687		709221		894691		1212825	PIECES MACH NON ELEC NDA
7491	BALL,ROLLER,ETC BEARINGS	W 9826	164221	W 10955	176341	MN 273791	210106	MN 288197	276826	ROULEMENTS BILLES ETC
7492	COCKS,VALVES ETC NES	W 11020	141988	W 25022	185352	W 32152	228642	W 17767	290179	ART ROB,SIM POUR TUYAUX
7493	SHAFT,CRANK,PULLEY ETC	W 14195	145912	W 16946	174112	MN 227322	203556	MN 356106	270950	ARBRES TRANS,VILEBREQUINS
7499	OTH NONELEC MCHY PTS NES		159567		173416	W 17456	252388	W 11880	374869	PIECES NON ELECT NDA
74991	FOUNDRY MOULDS ETC NES	N 764918	120158	N 729964	131838	W 15129	199771	W 9345	288217	MOULES POUR METAUX
75	OFFICE MACHNES,ADP EQUIP		1619802		1750285		2389750		2978970	MACH BUREAU TRAIT AUTOM
752	AUTOMTIC DATA PROC EQUIP	N 1275106	337188	N 1803944	375740		509984		631042	MACH TRAIT INFORMATION
7525	ADP PERIPHERAL UNITS	N 465219	143647	N 896638	178659	N 1192196	207631	N 977038	251987	UNITES PERIPHERIQUES
759	OFFICE,ADP MCH PTS,ACCES	W 8647	1200459	W 15687	1269437	W 12742	1733994	W 17382	2170321	PIECES DU 751 ET 752
7599	ACCTG,ETC,ADP MCH PTS,AC	W 7131	1171150	W 13907	1228066	W 10397	1679954	W 11072	2090456	PIECES DU 751 ET 752
76	TELECOMM,SOUND EQUIPMENT		1303572		1507986		2118730		2395419	EQUIPMENT DE TELECOM
764	TELECOM EQPT,PTS,ACC NES		1058800		1271990		1799337		1978838	EQUIP TELECOM,PIECES
7641	LINE TELEPHONE,ETC EQUIP	N 5410146	103127	MN 10334	207803	MN 15434	372685	MN 13798	329882	APP TELEPHON PAR FIL
7643	TV,RADIO TRANSMITTRS ETC	N 328028	159974	N 439391	245433	N 1345162	474836	N 1901622	507604	APP EMET TELE RADIO
7649	PTS NES OF EQUIPMT OF 76	W 23578	704582	W 27352	691679	W 24851	809230	W 24766	949990	PIECES DE LA DIV 76
76491	PTS NES OF APPAR OF 7641	W 4770	148163	W 2709	185949	W 6097	153390	W 2063	150274	PIECES POUR 764.1
76493	TELECOMM EQUIPMT PTS NES	W 10187	266816	W 16362	284588	W 9527	349914	W 11713	475994	PIECES 761,762,764.3,8
76499	PARTS ETC OF SOUND EQUIP	W 4646	269213	W 3923	191863	W 3913	273719	W 6067	291364	PIECES NDA POUR 763
77	ELECTRIC MACHNRY NES ETC		3970681		5036985		6885488		9499762	MACH APP ELECT NDA
771	ELECTRIC POWER MACHY NES		217502		306262		373663		517764	MACH PROD,TRANS ELECTR
7711	TRANSFORMERS,ELECTRICAL		104087	MN 56017	156042	MN 68895	160611	MN 85796	179816	TRANSFO ELECTRIQUES
7712	OTH ELEC POWER MACHY NES		113415		150220		213052		337948	AUT APP PROD TRANSF ELEC
772	SWITCHGEAR ETC,PARTS NES	MN 17059850	749948	MN 18591506	907840	W 74153	1277237	W 52123	1755749	APP COUPURE,SECT ETC
7721	SWITCHGEAR ETC	MN 10607853	559565	MN 11310119	702279	W 54512	960072	W 40423	1191977	APP COUPURE,SECTIONMNT
7722	PRINTED CIRCUITS,PTS NES	MN 300644	129806	MN 373775	133727	W 6808	195604	W 6122	395468	CIRCUITS ET PIECES
773	ELECTR DISTRIBUTNG EQUIP	W 30336	256113	W 39176	313226	W 45972	372345	W 61407	481333	EQUIPMT DISTRIBUTION ELECT
7731	INSULATED WIRE,CABLE ETC	W 18169	196725	W 27242	240509	W 33330	290928	W 47506	383886	FILS,CABLES ISOLES ELECT
776	TRANSISTORS,VALVES,ETC		1899456		2460707		3493265		4993628	LAMPES,TUBES,VALVES
7761	TV PICTURE TUBES	N 3574330	184040	N 4139767	209555	MN 16878	336067	MN 19238	608476	TUBES CATHODIQUES
7763	DIODES,TRANSISTORS,ETC	MN 2031694	131303	MN 2180018	168738	MN 4447089	277129	MN 7373259	420683	DIODES,TRANSISTORS
7764	ELECTRONIC MICROCIRCUITS	MN 686589	602931	MN 1184621	929691	MN 1968549	1427544	MN 2315878	1870516	MICROSTRUCTURES ELECTRON
7768	ELCTRNC COMP PTS,CRYSTLS		917096		1071725		1377899		2045779	CRIST PIEZO–ELEC,PCS 776
77689	ELECTRNIC COMPON PTS NES	W 9033	897989	W 8892	1049053	W 5539	1345669	W 13509	2007141	PIECES DU GROUPE 776
778	ELECTRICAL MACHINERY NES		691543		860669		1141709		1454969	AUTRES MACH ELECT NDA
7783	AUTOMOTIVE ELECTR EQUIP		98348		142550		177239		229718	EQUIP ELECT MOTEURS EXPL
7788	OTH ELEC MACHY,EQUIP NES		470464		563027		778746		983129	AUT MACH APP ELEC NDA
77884	ELECTRICAL CONDENSERS	MN 3894108	172670	MN 4262837	188100	W 9235	290128	W 8946	426373	CONDENSATEURS ELECTRIQUES
77886	OTH ELEC MACHINERY NES		183550		200990		226811		316714	AUT MACH APP ELECTRIQUES
78	ROAD VEHICLES		2481064		3480906		4042162		5237210	VEHICULES ROUTIERS
781	PASS MOTOR VEH EXC BUSES	N 151538	935491	N 296296	1501809	N 394648	1537811	N 437203	1549558	AUTO TRANSPORT PERSONNES
782	LORRIES,SPCL MTR VEH NES		266573	N 12136	149862	N 17056	159249	N 13322	196832	VEHICULES SPECIAUX,MARCH
7821	LORRIES,TRUCKS		245773	N 10658	111901	N 16400	119056	N 13060	159619	VEHICULES TRANSP MARCHAND
784	MOTOR VEH PRTS,ACCES NES		1036454		1545208		1977042		3021561	PIECES 722,781,782,783
7841	MOTOR VEHICLE CHASSIS		511401	N 259358	605544	N 370180	867014		1318036	CHASSIS 722,781,782,783
7849	OTHER MOTOR VEHCL PARTS	W 85547	516191	W 130274	930623	W 228644	1103182	W 197155	1692669	PIECES 722,781,782,783
785	CYCLES,ETC MOTRZD OR NOT		192339		246205		289898		379650	MOTOCYCLES SCOOTERS
7853	INVAL CARR, PTS OF 785		189273		242978		286604		375541	FAUTEUILS INVALIDES,PIECES
78539	PARTS,ACCES NES OF 785	W 28345	189242	W 23859	242814	W 35578	286321	W 65382	375212	PIECES DU 785
79	OTHR TRANSPORT EQUIPMENT		1149578		1043434		1158851		1668870	AUTRE MATERIEL TRANSPORT
792	AIRCRAFT ETC		988135		827180		905720		1327025	APP NAVIGATION AERIENNE
7924	AIRCRFT NES OVER 15000KG	N 17	919370	N 10	518056	N 1	149792	N 8	941119	AERODYNES PLUS 15000 KG
7929	AIRCRAFT PARTS NES	W 109	15551	W 630	221440	W 973	746436	W 720	331559	PIECES DU 792
793	SHIPS AND BOATS ETC		137182		118799		243072		306781	NAVIRES BATEAUX,ETC
7932	SHIPS AND BOATS NES		79836		94925		158064		231267	NAVIRES ET BATEAUX
8	MISC MANUFACTURED GOODS		2007642		2352039		3078195		3938743	ART MANUFACTURES DIVERS
87	PRECISION INSTRUMNTS NES		424624		498085		696075		940165	INSTRUM,APPAR SCIENT NDA
874	MEASURNG,CONTROLNG INSTR		329490		358778		524079		703043	INSTRUMENTS DE MESURE
8742	MEASUR,DRAW ETC INST,PTS		149323		135889		202332		260292	INST DESSIN,TRACAGE,PCS
87421	MEASURNG,DRAWNG ETC INST	N 1151411	135632	N 1145085	128291	N 5680400	195284	N 6199589	248567	INSTRUM DESSIN,TRACAGE
88	PHOTO EQU,OPTICL GDS ETC		464082		492354		535609		612751	APP,FOURN PHOTO,OP,MONTR
885	WATCHES AND CLOCKS		260412		248943		256103		284567	HORLOGERIE
8852	CLOCKS,CLOCK,WATCH PARTS		176715		159426		158687		168078	HORLOGES,MOUV,PARTIES
88529	CLOCK,WATCH PARTS NES		153216		132467		127588		125193	FOURNIT D HORLOG NDA
89	MISC MANUFCTRD GOODS NES		1001719		1228650		1672660		2154491	ART MANUFACTURES DIVERS
893	ARTICLES OF PLASTIC NES		514071		555344		744631		904805	OUVRAGES EN MAT DIVIS 58
8939	MISC PLASTIC ARTICLES	W 36145	467770	W 42521	485692	W 56941	672002	W 69410	820129	ART DIVERS EN MAT DIV 58
89399	OTHR PLASTC ARTICLES NES	W 34924	464018	W 40610	480426	W 54431	665414	W 67411	814698	AUT OUV MAT DIV 58
898	MUSICAL INSTRUMENTS,PTS		150951		269304		503447		717482	INSTRUMENTS DE MUSIQUE
8983	SOUND RECRDNG TAPE,DISCS	MN 339868	130790	MN 115121	247666	MN 1747253	478798	MN 2493075	686846	SUPPORTS SON POUR 763
89831	PREPD SND RECORDNG MEDIA	MN 334364	105728	MN 96521	208945	MN 1682729	405075	MN 2449330	510815	SUPPORTS PREPARES
9	GOODS NOT CLASSD BY KIND		1195294		1426109		1173572		1380169	ART TRANSACT NON CLASSES
931	*SPECIAL TRANSACTIONS	W 355846	956963	W 348270	1120512	W 175686	751625		851834	TRANS.SPECIALES
971	*GOLD,NON MONETARY NES	K 45866	220326		285985	K 51462	391642	K 247984	472375	OR NON MONETAIRE
97101	NONMON GLD UNWRT,SEMIMFD	K 45127	220144	K 51068	285604	K 51445	391610	K 247848	472272	OR,ALLIAGES D'OR BRUTS

5. General Exports F.O.B. by Commodities according to the S.I.T.C. (Rev. 2) in thousand U.S. Dollars
Exportations Générales F.O.B. par Produits d'après la C.T.C.I. (Rév. 2) en milliers de Dollars E.U.

SITC CTCI	COMMODITY	1992 WEIGHT POIDS	1992 VALUE VALEUR	1993 WEIGHT POIDS	1993 VALUE VALEUR	1994 WEIGHT POIDS	1994 VALUE VALEUR	1995 WEIGHT POIDS	1995 VALUE VALEUR	PRODUIT
	ALL COMMODITIES		32474432		37166867		45235529		56439377	TOUS PRODUITS
0	FOOD AND LIVE ANIMALS		8279014		7939198		9305424		10689324	ALIMENTS,ANIMAUX VIVANTS
01	MEAT AND PREPARATIONS		466687		434231		499254		550430	VIANDES ET PREPARATIONS
011	MEAT FRESH,CHILLD,FROZEN	W 180589	427289	W 164265	370162	W 159393	409309	W 157644	411682	VIANDES FRAICHES,REF,CONGE
0114	POULTRY FRESH CHLLD,FRZN	W 180261	426509	W 163828	369127	W 158941	408219	W 156943	409470	VOLAILLES MORTES
03	FISH AND PREPARATIONS		3071809		3402331		4187969		4447132	POISSONS ET PREPARATIONS
034	FISH,FRESH,CHILLED,FROZN	W 294299	328829	W 285625	335509	W 300967	349132	W 314827	410041	POISSON FRAIS, REFRIG,CONG
0342	FISH FROZEN,EXCL FILLETS	W 131509	180334	W 130215	184161	W 144548	206833	W 169350	249880	POISSONS CONGELES
0344	FISH FILLETS,FROZEN	W 38395	108890	W 35505	111528	W 35187	100099	W 32832	110884	FILETS CONGELES
036	SHELL FISH FRESH,FROZEN	W 222468	1565949	W 222703	1825695	W 267616	2326004	W 246511	2411601	CRUSTACES,MOLLUSQUES
037	FISH ETC PREPD,PRSVD NES	W 412216	1150728	W 411883	1204729	W 474864	1489074	W 437239	1590667	POIS,CRUST,MOL PREPARES
0371	FISH PREPARD,PRESRVD NES	W 345597	724684	W 346881	732879	W 401282	853995	W 354126	820680	CONSERVES DE POISSONS
0372	SHELL FISH PREPRD,PRESVD	W 66619	426044	W 65001	471850	W 73582	635078	W 83113	769987	CRUSTACES,COQUIL PREPARES
04	CEREALS AND PREPARATIONS		1578145		1489650		1777730		2163498	CEREALES ET PRODUITS
042	RICE	W 5151477	1426098	W 4989225	1301963	W 4858638	1558244	W 6197991	1951537	RIZ
0422	RICE SEMI–MILLED,MILLED	W 5081088	1407051	W 4899817	1279509	W 4735397	1524026	W 6103303	1922628	RIZ POLI,GLACE INCL BRISURES
04221	RICE MILLED UNBROKEN	W 4681287	1326797	W 4338217	1179959	W 4266909	1428299	W 5533482	1783545	RIZ POLI,GLACE EXCL BRISURES
05	VEGETABLES AND FRUIT		1911079		1608940		1491559		1491525	LEGUMES ET FRUITS
054	VEG ETC FRSH,SMPLY PRSVD	W 8497685	1058289	W 6852190	799415	W 4905802	612541	W 3379050	545061	LEGUMES FRAIS,CONG,SECS
0548	EDIBLE VEG NES FRESH,DRY	W 8332853	951583	W 6675984	678564	W 4730773	485496	W 3226212	415769	RACINES,TUBERCULES
05481	ROOTS,TUBERS FRESH,DRY	W 8332296	950306	W 6674743	676995	W 4730184	484386	W 3225613	413137	RACINES DE MANIOC ETC
056	VEGTBLES ETC PRSVD,PREPD	W 435762	201054	W 413401	183545	W 493113	222167	W 383653	240244	CONSERVES DE LEGUMES
0565	VEGTBLES PRSVD,PREPD NES	W 155332	130226	W 151342	125650	W 191732	142641	W 184516	167797	LEGUMES PREPARES CONSERVE
05659	OTH VEG PRESVD,PREPD NES	W 113133	98067	W 128110	104569	W 148782	116085	W 151548	134887	LEGUM PREPAP,CONSERV NDA
058	FRUIT PRESERVED,PREPARED	W 735751	583969	W 792205	550293	W 1001004	546073	W 700915	566696	CONSERVES DE FRUITS
0585	FRUIT OR VEGETABLE JUICE	W 101495	100672	W 139101	105370	W 126115	105804	W 138512	128031	JUS DE FRUITS
0589	FRUIT PREPRD,PRESRVD,NES	W 601266	428430	W 618554	386094	W 837713	375981	W 524030	369811	FRUITS PREPARES CONSERV
05899	FRUIT,NUTS NES,PRESERVED	W 597527	424104	W 614222	381764	W 831517	369587	W 519713	365492	FRUITS PREP CONSERV NDA
06	SUGAR AND PREPS,HONEY		815596		530205		765548		1269288	SUCRES ET PRODUITS
061	SUGAR AND HONEY	W 4885757	795675	W 2798535	507747	W 3459455	732655	W 4962412	1229070	SUCRES ET MIEL
0611	RAW BEET AND CANE SUGAR	W 2476627	465769	W 1680800	356779	W 1902062	487697	W 2800616	832375	SUCRES BRUTS
0612	REFINED SUGAR ETC	W 1280720	279310	W 538186	124548	W 708762	196345	W 958614	322195	SUCRES RAFFINES
07	COFFEE,TEA,COCOA,SPICES		81360		72434		106805		215965	CAFE,THE,CACAO,EPICES
071	COFFEE AND SUBSTITUTES	W 70523	51652	W 58878	51789	W 68598	88661	W 76769	189909	CAFE ET SUCCEDANES
0711	COFFEE GREEN,ROASTED,SUB	W 69893	49088	W 58483	49360	W 68150	85597	W 76144	185206	CAFE TORREFIE OU DECAFEINE
07111	COFFEE GREEN,HUSKS,SKINS	W 69875	48989	W 58421	49020	W 68089	85377	W 76104	185014	CAFE NON TORREFIE
081	*FEEDING STUFF FOR ANIML	W 305383	189782	W 288954	202889	W 272329	204898	W 281383	235660	NOURRITURE POUR ANIMAUX
0819	FOOD WASTE AND FEED NES	W 156289	171690	W 166952	187084	W 177051	191268	W 167394	221049	DECHETS,ALIMENTS NDA
08199	FODDER NES,INCL SWEETNED	W 153544	171188	W 165156	186747	W 175454	190961	W 165014	220684	PREPARATIONS FOURRAGERES
09	MISC EDIBLE PRODUCTS		138272		167922		228212		269827	PREP ALIMENTAIRES DIVERSES
098	EDIBLE PRODCTS,PREPS NES		138229		167818		228032		269633	PREP ALIMENTAIRES NDA
09809	MISC FOOD PREPRTIONS NES	W 49592	78589	W 58726	99500	W 119396	143389	W 114964	171630	PREP ALIMENTAIRES NDA
1	BEVERAGES AND TOBACCO		169367		150424		164688		143724	BOISSONS ET TABACS
12	TOBACCO AND MANUFACTURES		144416		105896		91568		58135	TABACS BRUTS FABRIQUES
121	TOBACCO UNMNFCTRD,REFUSE	W 58344	141726	W 45907	104338	W 38645	87753	W 21985	56255	TABACS BRUTS,DECHETS
1212	TOBACCO STRIPPED OR PART	W 36136	117577	W 29293	80602	W 28025	68522	W 14763	41603	TABACS PART ECOTES
2	CRUDE MATERLS,EXCL FUELS		1567351		1597898		2207627		3232874	MAT BRUTES NON COMESTIBLES
23	RUBBER, CRUDE		1140268		1154532		1669052		2462039	CAOUTCHOUC BRUT
232	NATURAL RUBBER,GUMS	W 1463604	1139055	W 1492889	1152836	W 1735557	1663093	W 1747396	2458755	LATEX CAOUTCHOUC NATUREL
23201	NATURAL RUBBER LATEX	W 115170	71310	W 242557	156699	W 246359	168965	W 287128	288472	LATEX NATUREL
23202	OTHER NATURAL RUBBER	W 1078000	847923	W 983222	783311	W 1102983	1142662	W 1089677	1628632	CAOUTCHOUC NATUREL
23203	BALATA,GUTTA–PERCHA, ETC	W 270434	219821	W 267109	212826	W 386215	351465	W 370591	541651	BALATA,GUTTA–PERCHA
26	TEXTILE FIBRES AND WASTE		92689		95619		123069		213990	FIBRES TEXTILES
27	CRUDE FERTLZR,MINRLS NES		100048		117753		127975		141281	ENGRAIS MINERAUX BRUTS
29	CRUDE ANIMAL,VEG MAT NES		124001		118947		118656		122137	MATIERES BRUTES ANIM,VEGET
292	CRUDE VEG MATERIALS NES	W 52906	99665	W 50776	97054		96245		92790	MAT BRUTES VEGETALES NDA
3	MINERAL FUELS ETC		321102		397146		352269		409583	COMBUSTIBLES MINERAUX LUB
33	PETROLEUM AND PRODUCTS		181777		287685		223128		257207	PETROLE ET DERIVES
334	PETROLEUM PRODUCTS,REFIN	W 807556	180506	W 1307947	286666	W 829693	221834	W 1322195	252266	PRODUITS RAFFINES
3341	GASOLINE,OTH LIGHT OILS	W 544135	109999	W 692386	143137	W 440786	116062	W 497730	79917	ESSENCES POUR MOTEURS
33411	MOTOR,AVIATION SPIRIT	W 544018	109950	W 692362	143130	W 440693	116012	W 497493	79854	ESSENCES MOTEURS D'AVIONS
341	*GAS,NATURAL AND MANUFCT	W 829596	139312	W 653291	109424	W 830029	129092	W 924251	152363	GAZ NATUREL,GAZ MANUFACT
3413	PETROLM GASES,LIQUEFIED	W 826125	138802	W 635893	106993	W 801151	124296	W 924195	152318	GAZ DE PETROLE LIQUEFIE
34139	OTH HYDROCARBON GAS LQFD	W 826125	138802	W 635865	106969	W 801063	124221	W 923919	152100	HYDROCARBURES GAZEUX NDA
5	CHEMCLS,RELATED PROD NES		815606		1040202		1256130		2126656	PRODUITS CHIMIQUES
51	ORGANIC CHEMICALS		136690		134881		131051		238797	PROD CHIMIQ ORGANIQUES
53	DYES,TANNING,COLOUR PROD		82992		156239		189084		461951	PROD TEINTURE,COLORANTS
533	PIGMENTS,PAINTS,ETC	W 14189	38016	W 21869	105660	W 30152	147132	W 39105	414601	PIGMENTS,PEINTURES,VERNIS
5335	GLAZES,DRIERS,PUTTY ETC	W 1574	15279	W 2326	73910	W 4967	104023	W 8737	330769	PREPTNS COLOR UTILISES CERAM
53352	ARTISTS COLOURS	W 184	12906	W 476	70588	W 661	92389	W 2633	314549	COULEURS PEINT ARTISTIQUE
541	*MEDICINAL,PHARM PRODUCT	K 6031545	58011	MK 10596	126842	MK 9698	86999	MK 11121	126105	PROD MEDICINAUX PHARMACEUT
58	PLASTIC MATERIALS ETC		215382		297345		417480		713291	MAT PLAST ARTIFICIELLES
583	POLYMERIZATION ETC PRODS	W 180243	198055	W 233203	246697	W 277404	328645	W 484563	564272	PROD POLYMERISATION
5839	OTH POLYMRZTION ETC PROD	W 45557	88368	W 90668	133621	W 87849	144547	W 74507	153638	AUT PROD POLYMER COPOLYM
59	CHEMICAL MATERIALS NES		200129		186483		269215		370094	MAT PROD CHIMIQUES NDA
592	STARCH,INULIN,GLUTEN,ETC	W 505771	159526	W 416927	138995		204295	W 668749	271966	AMIDONS,INUL,GLUT FROM
6	BASIC MANUFACTURES		3926928		4563171		5514483		6741364	ART MANUFACTURES
61	LEATHER,DRESSED FUR,ETC		302386		341142		417213		472929	CUIRS,PELLETERIES
611	LEATHER	W 7133	137203	W 9960	169026	W 15462	227911	W 17564	269610	CUIRS,PEAUX PREPARES
6114	LEATHR BOVINE NES,EQUINE	W 3818	78810	W 5279	99970	W 8202	137961	W 9605	158852	CUIRS DE BOVINS
612	LEATHER ETC MANUFACTURES	W 38920	164891	W 37864	172020	W 41598	188965	W 43767	202712	OUVRAGES EN CUIRS NDA
6129	LEATHER MANUFACTURES NES	W 36301	108877	W 34896	101410	W 38380	111238	W 39968	131412	AUT OUV CUIR NAT,ARTIF
62	RUBBER MANUFACTURES NES		249956		301449		354041		436002	CAOUTCHOUC MANUFACTURE
625	RUBBER TYRES, TUBES ETC	MN 68277	140949	MN 87105	165593		192601	MN 102842	232336	PNEUS CAOUTCHOUC VULCANISE
63	WOOD,CORK MANUFACTRS NES		181130		222527		259952		296891	OUVRAGES LIEGE ET BOIS
635	WOOD MANUFACTURES NES	W 53753	164407	W 68991	190869	W 68755	225433	W 80668	262549	ART MANUF EN BOIS NDA
6354	WOOD MFRS DOMESTIC ETC	W 35320	117303	W 37667	130543	W 39486	152902	W 44443	177498	ART MANUF USAGE DOMESTIQUE
64	PAPER,PAPERBOARD AND MFR		72932		88845		167961		342325	PAPIERS,CARTONS & OUVRAGES
642	PAPER,ETC,PRECUT,ARTS OF	W 22865	46322	W 23277	52741	W 29452	92859	W 38637	196603	PAP,CARTONS DECOUPES
65	TEXTILE YARN,FABRICS,ETC		1290145		1397266		1690210		1987284	FILS,TISSUS,ARTICLES TEXTILE
651	TEXTILE YARN	W 111262	291334	W 137416	322775	W 201096	508629	W 171319	565671	FILS TEXTILES
6514	SYN FIB YRN,BULK,MONOFIL	W 17435	54365	W 33575	73689	W 62831	164452	W 53384	163913	FILS CONT 85% FIB TEXT SYNTH
6516	DISCON SYN FIB BLEND YRN	W 26981	94046	W 33470	106675	W 47550	145317	W 38283	125929	FILS FIBR TEX SYNT DIS MOINS
652	COTTON FABRICS,WOVEN	A 269462	190623	A 278576	201063		229560	W 36374	268994	TISSUS DE COTON
6521	GREY WOVEN COTTON FABRIC	A 196641	103685	A 198445	109356		122582	W 20650	108907	TISSUS COT ECRUS NON MERCER
653	WOVN MAN–MADE FIB FABRIC		462907		491648		502233		637685	TISSUS FIBRES SYNTH,ARTIF
6531	CONT SYNT WEAVES NONPILE	A 104381	79254	A 142678	100062		123679	W 25316	172684	TISSUS FIBRES SYNTH CONTINUE
6534	DISC SYN BLEND FABRC NES	A 421982	225904	A 237028	192923		192999	W 33708	232146	TISSUS FIBRES SYNTH DISCONT
65341	DISC SYN FIB–COTTN FABRC	A 208767	145693	A 180139	118375		133923	W 24672	172670	TISSUS FIB SYNT DIS MEL COTO
657	SPECIAL TXTL FABRC,PRODS		71869		93564		146895	W 38871	174628	TISSUS SPECIAUX
658	TEXTILE ARTICLES NES	W 48434	167915	W 49184	168466	W 46986	171122	W 44998	183618	ART FACONNES MAT TEXTILES

5. General Exports F.O.B. by Commodities according to the S.I.T.C. (Rev. 2) in thousand U.S. Dollars
Exportations Générales F.O.B. par Produits d'après la C.T.C.I. (Rév. 2) en milliers de Dollars E.U.

SITC CTCI	COMMODITY	1992 WEIGHT POIDS	1992 VALUE VALEUR	1993 WEIGHT POIDS	1993 VALUE VALEUR	1994 WEIGHT POIDS	1994 VALUE VALEUR	1995 WEIGHT POIDS	1995 VALUE VALEUR	PRODUIT
66	NONMETAL MINERAL MFS NES		1185598		1436054		1639718		1861012	ART MIN NON METALLIQUES
664	GLASS	W 129176	91352	W 210698	112655		131801		153884	VERRE
666	POTTERY	W 43303	111364	W 55642	146016	W 62258	172466	W 59225	173031	POTERIE
667	PEARL,PREC–,SEMI–P STONE		843715		949135		1061529		1201022	PERLES, PIERRES GEMMES
6672	DIAMONDS NONINDUST,UNSET		373161		473976		587434		754016	DIAMANTS BRUTS
66729	— CUT ETC NOT SET		359188		451332		558693		703632	DIAMANTS TAILLES
6673	PREC–,SEMI–PR STONES NES		436829		450278		450380		423360	AUTRES PIERRES NON SERTIES
67	IRON AND STEEL		163088		236794		278512		485008	FER ET ACIER
678	IRON,STL TUBES,PIPES,ETC	W 175822	132918	W 269518	185876	W 276140	207248	W 324729	251265	TUBES,TUYAUX EN FONTE,FER
6783	IRON,STL TUBES,PIPES NES	W 119428	65965	W 210364	112376	W 200793	113868	W 212763	121110	AUT TUBES,TUYAUX FER,ACIER
69	METAL MANUFACTURES NES		408950		482760		631387		747089	ART MANUFACT EN METAL NDA
699	BASE METAL MFRS NES		113588	W 48626	135545	W 69009	189239	W 79871	237518	ART MANUFACTURES MET NDA
7	MACHINES,TRANSPORT EQUIP		8587812		11027768		15062407		18989519	MACHINES MATERIEL TRANSPORT
71	POWER GENERATING EQUIPMT		196621		259385		384551		536709	MACHINES GENERATRICES
716	ROTATING ELECTRIC PLANT		143610		189527		306874		427411	APP ELECTR ROTATIFS,PIECES
7162	AC MTRS,GENRTRS,GEN SETS		128241		161092		266332		323940	MOTEURS ELECTRIQUES
71621	AC MTRS,INC UNIVRSL MTRS		127239	MN 50048	157266	MN 84923	264387	MN 110224	320859	MOT ELEC NON COUR CONTINU
72	MACHS FOR SPCL INDUSTRYS		104121		173758		159011		169891	MAC SPECIALES POUR INDUST
74	GENRL INDUSTRL MACHY NES		758097		1181023		1245438		1715388	MACH APP INDUSTRIE
741	HEATING,COOLING EQUIPMNT		326661		377837		596458		888330	MACH CHAUFFAGE,PIECES
7415	AIR–CONDITIONING MACHNRY	N 1339971	289155	N 1616330	328870	N 2442228	536470		809775	GROUPES CONDITION AIR
743	PUMPS NES,CENTRFUGES ETC		104611		125737		169460		236061	POMPES COMPRES,VENT ETC
749	NONELEC MACH PTS,ACC NES		280923		613977		370993		437212	PIECES MACH NON ELEC NDA
7491	BALL,ROLLER,ETC BEARINGS	W 2873	212084	W 3526	220855		215530	MN 769325	262072	ROULEMENTS BILLES ETC
7499	OTH NONELEC MCHY PTS NES		25387		339734	W 4592	101794	W 4926	104723	PIECES NON ELECT NDA
74992	METAL–PLASTIC GASKETS	W 235	5441	W 8332	309509	W 2419	74826	W 1536	65030	JOINTS METALLOPLASTIQUES
75	OFFICE MACHNES,ADP EQUIP		2409849		2822541		4129929		5692576	MACH BUREAU TRAIT AUTOM
751	OFFICE MACHINES		215884		321470		415719		479010	MACH,APPAREILS DE BUREAU
7512	CALCULATNG,ACCTG,ETC MCH		164819		208553	MN 47473	245792		313026	MACHINE A CALCULER ETC
75121	CALCULATING MACHINES	MN 35808	164783	MN 45724	208407	MN 47469	245573	MN 44402	312374	MACHINES A CALCULER
7518	OFFICE MACHINES NES		49646	N 707280	111760	N 1164366	169672	N 1395651	165629	MACH,APP DE BUREAU NDA
75182	PHOTO,THERMOCOPY APPARAT	N 92357	45735	N 237048	109448	N 412403	164123	N 411614	157868	APPAREILS DE PHOTOCOPIE
752	AUTOMTIC DATA PROC EQUIP		508943		948266		2117623		2869471	MACH TRAIT INFORMATION
7524	DIGITL CENTRL STOR UNITS	N 6975483	433955	MN 10744	756623	MN 23863	1683006		1966596	UNITES MEMOIRE CENTRALES
7525	ADP PERIPHERAL UNITS	N 419580	57496	N 1118686	173516	N 2153691	342969	N 3972132	628135	UNITES PERIPHERIQUES
7528	OFF–LINE DATA PROC EQUIP	N 558626	10469	N 555524	13997	N 2029493	83385	N 2873425	253759	MACH AUXIL TRAIT INFORM
759	OFFICE,ADP MCH PTS,ACCES	W 25527	1685023	W 31394	1552804	W 44444	1596587		2344095	PIECES DU 751 ET 752
7599	ACCTG,ETC,ADP MCH PTS,AC	W 24912	1675323	W 30257	1539107	W 41887	1562959		2294792	PIECES DU 751 ET 752
76	TELECOMM,SOUND EQUIPMENT		1928654		1987854		2717170		3032308	EQUIPMENT DE TELECOM
761	TELEVISION RECEIVERS	N 5668727	669986	N 4679274	720443	N 5653821	882825	N 6027983	955215	RECEPTEURS DE TELEVISION
7611	COLOUR TV RECEIVERS	N 5664159	669576	N 4648086	719673	N 5616027	880999	N 5669492	946099	RECEPTEURS COULEUR
763	SOUND RECORDRS,PHONOGRPH		420884		341130		594400		520808	PHONO,APP ENREGISTREMENT
7638	OTHR SOUND APPARATUS ETC	N 6303775	420759	N 5143708	322578		547782	N 5425120	446292	AUT APP D'ENREGIS,REPROD
76381	TV IMAGE,SND RECRDRS ETC	N 2513533	346478	N 2107257	264848	N 5545404	503760	N 3869803	416327	APP ENREG,REPRO IMAG,SON
764	TELECOM EQPT,PTS,ACC NES		821117		916257		1233687		1539802	EQUIP TELECOM,PIECES
7641	LINE TELEPHONE,ETC EQUIP		315562	MN 16886	329294	MN 19657	355869	MN 50758	438671	APP TELEPHON PAR FIL
7649	PTS NES OF EQUIPMT OF 76	W 19281	400718	W 25245	456503	W 39522	684068	W 43553	902661	PIECES DE LA DIV 76
76493	TELECOMM EQUIPMT PTS NES	W 6551	123229	W 9240	158017	W 12757	265064	W 16315	345488	PIECES 761,762,764.3,8
76499	PARTS ETC OF SOUND EQUIP	W 11112	241961	W 14559	263177	W 24185	368135	W 24828	495791	PIECES NDA POUR 763
77	ELECTRIC MACHNRY NES ETC		2702353		3673921		4921156		6370149	MACH APP ELECT NDA
771	ELECTRIC POWER MACHY NES		112784		221345		336898		564385	MACH PROD,TRANS ELECTR
7711	TRANSFORMERS,ELECTRICAL	MN 53494	52387		87770	MN 96405	142753		269754	TRANSFO ELECTRIQUES
77118	OTHER ELEC TRANSFORMERS	MN 52932	49834	MN 78439	84822	MN 72641	130299		216655	AUTRES TRANSFO ELECTRIQ
7712	OTH ELEC POWER MACHY NES		60397		133574		194145		294631	AUT APP PROD TRANSF ELEC
772	SWITCHGEAR ETC,PARTS NES	MN 1949469	309267	MN 2494746	385030	W 13038	631792	W 16973	972054	APP COUPURE,SECT ETC
7721	SWITCHGEAR ETC	MN 354360	78959	MN 487667	121967	W 6274	180867	W 8510	378727	APP COUPURE,SECTIONMNT
7722	PRINTED CIRCUITS,PTS NES	MN 104650	209348	MN 148184	233136	W 4489	401861	W 6672	557308	CIRCUITS ET PIECES
773	ELECTR DISTRIBUTNG EQUIP	W 26438	281659	W 38755	426464	W 43336	478502	W 40065	519216	EQUIPMT DISTRIBUTION ELECT
7731	INSULATED WIRE,CABLE ETC	W 25602	269474	W 37231	409143	W 40757	451374	W 36611	478716	FILS,CABLES ISOLES ELECT
775	HOUSEHOLD TYPE EQUIP NES		409505		451750		521611		628408	MACH,APP USAGE DOMESTQUE
7752	DOM REFRIGERATRS,FREEZRS	N 458728	109072	N 562456	136094	N 744959	161272	N 1251751	251365	REFRIG,CONGEL MENAGER
77521	DOMESTIC REFRIGERATORS	N 437403	105319	N 543669	131167	N 720797	155232	N 1232447	245770	REFRIGERATEURS
7758	ELECTRO–THERMIC APPL NES		216112		210255		231759		277497	APP ELECTROTHERMIQ NDA
77586	ELECTROTHERM DOM APP NES	N 3614467	176386	N 3602001	167320	N 3822980	190162	N 4201714	224711	APP ELECTRO THERMIQUES
776	TRANSISTORS,VALVES,ETC		1332565		1709216		2244036		2935022	LAMPES,TUBES,VALVES
7761	TV PICTURE TUBES	N 708986	37109	N 1429796	88795	N 2250767	135705	N 2815839	174223	TUBES CATHODIQUES
7763	DIODES,TRANSISTORS,ETC	MN 2410023	131261	MN 3678372	160419	MN 5387006	230323	MN 7689469	312400	DIODES,TRANSISTORS
7764	ELECTRONIC MICROCIRCUITS	MN 1605913	647743	MN 2090663	1049775	MN 3008615	1456307	MN 4000114	1939384	MICROSTRUCTURES ELECTRON
7768	ELCTRNC COMP PTS,CRYSTLS		514164		408124		418577		506662	CRIST PIEZO–ELEC,PCS 776
77689	ELECTRNIC COMPON PTS NES	W 3305	491223	W 3679	369668	W 2961	360537	W 3434	417883	PIECES DU GROUPE 776
778	ELECTRICAL MACHINERY NES		255216		477639		706807		748078	AUTRES MACH ELECT NDA
7783	AUTOMOTIVE ELECTR EQUIP		32838		211298		352963		208701	EQUIP ELECT MOTEURS EXPL
77831	IGNITION,STARTING EQUIP	N 4420031	25609		178552		229600	MN 9436	58898	APP ELEC ALLUM,DEMARRAGE
7788	OTH ELEC MACHY,EQUIP NES		146362		175882		254048		411713	AUT MACH APP ELEC NDA
78	ROAD VEHICLES		332215		632728		858514		724394	VEHICULES ROUTIERS
784	MOTOR VEH PRTS,ACCES NES		49978		183115		383473		140009	PIECES 722,781,782,783
7849	OTHER MOTOR VEHCL PARTS	W 9509	49834	W 23619	182834	W 46006	382964	W 17931	138921	PIECES 722,781,782,783
785	CYCLES,ETC MOTRZD OR NOT		110430		205604		290108		393433	MOTOCYCLES SCOOTERS
7853	INVAL CARR, PTS OF 785		27853		70755		127861		217577	FAUTEUILS INVALIDES,PIECES
78539	PARTS,ACCES NES OF 785	W 5633	27788	W 8636	70173	W 15614	127854	W 21560	217445	PIECES DU 785
786	TRAILERS,NONMOTR VEH,NES		137200		134235		89971		90961	REMORQUES,CADRES,CONTAIN
7861	TRAILERS,TRANSP CONTAINR	N 40719	134687	N 90881	130703	N 145655	86392		88929	REMORQUES TOUS VEHICULES
78613	CONTAINERS INC ROAD–RAIL	N 38700	134581	N 89367	130649	N 140272	86209	N 50456	88518	CADRES ET CONTAINERS
79	OTHR TRANSPORT EQUIPMENT		110188		242659		566938		632919	AUTRE MATERIEL TRANSPORT
792	AIRCRAFT ETC		77787		225444		489241		557461	APP NAVIGATION AERIENNE
7929	AIRCRAFT PARTS NES	W 125	76288	W 1834	221378	W 1184	470091	W 4235	557152	PIECES DU 792
8	MISC MANUFACTURED GOODS		8441507		9867444		10997304		13529600	ART MANUFACTURES DIVERS
821	*FURNITURE,PARTS THEREOF		485824		593966		707796		752779	MEUBLES ET PIECES
8211	CHAIRS,SEATS AND PARTS		194416		244693		296801		294363	SIEGES ET PIECES
82111	CHAIRS AND OTHER SEATS	MN 17959	174231	MN 25491	213838	MN 31736	266683	MN 25867	268342	SIEGES
8219	FURNITURE AND PARTS NES	W 117079	257397	W 142786	290563		349623		403308	AUTRES MEUBLES ET PIECES
82192	WOOD FURNITURE NES	W 73203	158261	W 100189	194863	MN 13220	231508	MN 16365	265974	MEUBLES NDA EN BOIS
831	*TRAVEL GOODS,HANDBAGS	W 31493	306511	W 37772	354663		419420		452587	ARTICLES DE VOYAGE ETC
83102	TRAVEL GDS,TOILET–CASES	W 20734	136595	W 25602	161328	MN 28014	216180	MN 27404	245192	ARTICLES DE VOYAGE
84	CLOTHING AND ACCESSORIES		3791917		4213396		4539958		5043143	VETEMENTS
842	MENS OUTERWEAR NOT KNIT	MN 187710	897001	MN 209033	975261	MN 227967	1055095		882636	VET DESSUS POUR HOMMES
8423	— TROUSERS,BREECHES ETC	MN 128154	512141	MN 145255	553413	MN 129267	539251	MN 96156	433229	PANTALONS HOMMES MAT TEX
8424	— JACKETS,BLAZERS ETC	N 8539887	124674	MN 9648	123972	MN 16371	137372	MN 9613	134911	VESTES HOMMES MAT TEXTIL
8429	— OTHER OUTER GARMENTS	MN 42527	210879	MN 48684	248206	MN 76212	331099		262956	AUT VET DES HOM MAT TEX
843	WOMENS OUTERWEAR NONKNIT	MN 179487	927066	MN 183937	922032		1149517	MN 167131	1132645	VET DESSUS FEMMES MAT TEX
8431	— COATS AND JACKETS	N 7505049	130217	N 7236530	124923	N 7035637	124985	N 6355691	131168	MANT,VEST FEM MAT TEXTIL

5. General Exports F.O.B. by Commodities according to the S.I.T.C. (Rev. 2) in thousand U.S. Dollars
Exportations Générales F.O.B. par Produits d'après la C.T.C.I. (Rév. 2) en milliers de Dollars E.U.

SITC CTCI	COMMODITY	1992		1993		1994		1995		PRODUIT
		WEIGHT POIDS	VALUE VALEUR	WEIGHT POIDS	VALUE VALEUR	WEIGHT POIDS	VALUE VALEUR	WEIGHT POIDS	VALUE VALEUR	
8433	— DRESSES	MN 34456	149938	MN 32619	163367	MN 49927	268697	MN 46917	264887	ROBES EN MAT–TEXTILES
8435	— BLOUSES	MN 32871	149026	MN 29918	151712	MN 35398	176692	MN 24789	141295	BLOUSES FEM MAT TEXTILES
8439	— OTHER OUTER GARMENTS	MN 87495	419884	MN 100098	408018		506730	MN 74330	503708	AUT VET DES FEM MAT TEXT
844	UNDER GARMENTS NOT KNIT	MN 80263	295196	MN 98608	358849	MN 142383	517121		418300	VETEMENT DESSOUS MAT TEX
8441	— MENS SHIRTS	MN 64919	259107	MN 73735	312688	MN 101091	446069	MN 69940	348547	CHEMISES HOMMES MAT TEXT
84411	—— OF COTTON	MN 29703	140747	MN 38862	187778	MN 68641	317346	MN 40811	221873	CHEMISES HOMMES DE COTON
84412	—— OF SYNTHETIC FIBRES	MN 35216	118359	MN 34873	124910	MN 32450	128723	MN 29129	126674	CHEMISES HOMMES FIB SYNT
845	OUTERWEAR KNIT NONELASTC	MN 190962	781574	MN 190607	749776		727402		963273	VET DESSOUS,ACCES BONNET
8451	— JERSEYS,PULLOVERS ETC	MN 38900	288529	MN 36404	256985	MN 34785	234365	MN 36307	247132	CHANDAILS,PULL–OVERS ETC
8459	— OTHER,CLTHG ACCESRYS	MN 141460	444202	MN 144507	448111		461114		660035	AUT VET DESSUS DE BONNE
846	UNDER GARMENTS KNITTED	MN 262953	573862	MN 266791	620988		683330		828596	SOUS VETS DE BONNETERIE
8462	— OF COTTON NON ELASTIC	MN 191820	353797	MN 180093	347380	MN 173665	332524	MN 188361	462396	SOUS–VET BONNET COTON
84629	—— OTHER	MN 191820	353797	MN 180093	347380	MN 173665	332524	MN 188361	462396	AUT SOUS–VET BONNET COTON
8463	— OF SYNTH FBR NONELAST	MN 39343	164967	MN 41307	187390		225526		243475	SOUS–VET BONNET FIB SYNT
84632	—— MENS SHIRTS	MN 32801	161256	MN 37345	185103	MN 43675	221326	MN 39758	234500	CHEMISES DE BON FIB SYNMT
848	HEADGEAR,NONTXTL CLOTHNG		229369		504375		306751		708228	VET ACCES MAT AUT QUE TEX
8482	PLASTC,RUBBR CLTHG,ACCES		144325		406498		201668		593450	VET ACCES MAT PLAS ARTIF
84821	PLASTIC CLTHG,INC GLOVES	W 3323	31368	W 8816	256320	W 3824	42916	W 7649	199694	VET ACCES MAT PLAS ARTIF
84822	RUBBER CLOTHING,ACCESRYS	MP 1650508	112957	MP 2653659	150177	MP 2717864	158752		393756	VET ACCES CAOUT VULCAN
851	*FOOTWEAR	MP 168187	955541	MP 167602	1035103	MP 267899	1485804	MP 287407	2088797	CHAUSSURES
85101	FOOTWEAR RUBBER,PLASTIC	MP 57767	202436	MP 66448	236922	MP 185586	703873	MP 218874	1342635	CHAUS SEMELLES CAOUTCH
85102	FOOTWEAR LEATHER	MP 108532	742133	MP 99430	785538	MP 79821	764080	MP 66738	731206	CHAUS SEMELLES EN CUIR
87	PRECISION INSTRUMNTS NES		157557		208899		258250		311339	INSTRUM,APPAR SCIENT NDA
88	PHOTO EQU,OPTICL GDS ETC		460444		413631		545790		685531	APP,FOURN PHOTO,OP,MONTR
885	WATCHES AND CLOCKS		325033		274397		376082		446201	HORLOGERIE
8851	WATCHES,MOVEMENTS,CASES		141222		89987		97947		125511	MONTRES,MOUVEMENTS,BOITES
8852	CLOCKS,CLOCK,WATCH PARTS		183811		184411		278135		320690	HORLOGES,MOUV,PARTIES
88529	CLOCK,WATCH PARTS NES		160542		154888		237102		260373	FOURNIT D HORLOG NDA
89	MISC MANUFCTRD GOODS NES		2207467		2949679		2916360		4064904	ART MANUFACTURES DIVERS
892	PRINTED MATTER		24354		42057	W 9489	89337		182032	IMPRIMES
893	ARTICLES OF PLASTIC NES		357154		1008814		749958		1588923	OUVRAGES EN MAT DIVIS 58
8931	PLSTC PACKG CONTNRS,LIDS	W 118259	182679	W 134962	273534	W 155440	246166	W 145642	322775	ART TRANSP EMBALLAGE ETC
8939	MISC PLASTIC ARTICLES	W 50416	172889	W 79377	715920	W 68360	497838	W 465422	1191111	ART DIVERS EN MAT DIV 58
89399	OTHR PLASTC ARTICLES NES	W 47528	168452	W 75355	699597	W 64024	481172	W 454088	1022448	AUT OUV MAT DIV 58
894	TOYS,SPORTING GOODS,ETC		713577		635400		680798		744100	VOITURES ENFANTS,JOUETS
8942	TOYS,INDOOR GAMES ETC		538891		435497		440315		482698	JOUETS,JEUX ETC
89423	TOYS NES	W 45446	298005	W 42478	262817	MN 611074	289994	MN 314565	321248	JOUETS,MODELES REDUITS
89425	XMAS DECORATIONS ETC	W 31168	138979	W 20588	81042	W 20770	77365	W 23205	90376	ART DIVERTIS,FETES
8947	OTH SPORT GDS,FAIR AMUSM		164432		177183		222325		247714	AUT ART DE SPORT
89472	OTH OUTDOOR SPORT GOODS	MN 47054	137516	MN 51471	150013		191152		217861	ART POUR JEUX PLEIN AIR
897	GOLD,SILVER WARE,JEWELRY		720088		790346		829925		928825	BIJOUTERIE,ORFEVRERIE
8973	PREC JEWLRY,GLD–SILVWARE		650438		722287		760126		853344	BIJOUX OR,ARGENT ORFEVRE
89731	PRECIOUS METAL JEWELLERY		637727		701510		738295		837180	ART BIJOUTERIE,JOAILLER
898	MUSICAL INSTRUMENTS,PTS		87919		121009		214994		222976	INSTRUMENTS DE MUSIQUE
8983	SOUND RECRDNG TAPE,DISCS	MN 80925	77885	MN 137858	107696	MN 242777	175506	MN 321456	180156	SUPPORTS SON POUR 763
89831	PREPD SND RECORDNG MEDIA	MN 69581	69892	MN 123250	102235	MN 223948	166569	MN 289670	170699	SUPPORTS PREPARES
899	OTHER MANUFACTURED GOODS		263975		310867		302862		308089	AUT ART MANUF DIVERS NDA
8999	OTHER MANUF GOODS NES		122857		133364	W 14541	135900	W 8498	134645	OUVRAGES DIVERS NDA
9	GOODS NOT CLASSD BY KIND		358164		574602		349876		552917	ART TRANSACT NON CLASSES
931	*SPECIAL TRANSACTIONS	W 91993	337921	W 189738	553240	W 23950	311028		480769	TRANS.SPECIALES

FOOT NOTES – NOTES

TABLE 1 –
1 Values are in thousand million baht.
TABLEAU 1 –
1 Les évaluations sont exprimées en milliards de baht.

1. HISTORICAL SERIES, 1961–1996 SPECIAL TRADE, IMPORTS C.I.F., EXPORTS F.O.B.
SERIES HISTORIQUES, 1961–1996 COMMERCE SPECIAL, IMPORTATIONS C.A.F., EXPORTATIONS F.O.B

YEAR ANNEE	VALUE IN MILLION C.F.A. FRANCS VALEUR EN MILLION C.F.A. FRANCS MERCHANDISE –MARCHANDISE		GOLD –OR		CONVERSION FACTORS U.S. CENTS PER C.F.A. FRANC FACTEURS DE CONVERSION CENTS E.U. PAR C.F.A. FRANC		INDEX NUMBERS –INDICES QUANTUM		UNIT VALUE VALEUR UNITAIRE	
	IMPORTS	EXPORTS	IMPORTS	EXPORTS	IMPORTS	EXPORTS	IMPORTS	EXPORTS	IMPORTS	EXPORTS
1961	6476.00	4615.00			0.4051	0.4051				
1962	6724.00	4239.00			0.4051	0.4051				
1963	7167.00	4509.00			0.4051	0.4051				
1964	10286.00	7448.00			0.4051	0.4051				
1965	11100.00	6679.00			0.4051	0.4051				
1966	11668.00	8872.00			0.4051	0.4051				
1967	11133.00	7894.00			0.4051	0.4051				
1968	11623.00	9549.00			0.4051	0.4051				
1969	14572.00	11477.00			0.3870	0.3895				
1970	17928.00	15176.00			0.3601	0.3601				
1971	19455.00	13626.00			0.3601	0.3601				
1972	21381.00	12659.00			0.3967	0.3960				
1973	22388.00	13755.00			0.4492	0.4465				
1974	28612.00	45174.00			0.4163	0.4183				
1975	37270.00	26922.00			0.4666	0.4698				
1976	44419.00	24914.00			0.4180	0.4222				
1977	69834.00	39115.00			0.4072	0.4075				
1978	100898.00	54238.00			0.4462	0.4434				
1979	110208.00	46432.00			0.4704	0.4704				
1980	116357.00	71285.00			0.4731	0.4698				
1981	117763.30	57438.40			0.3680	0.3680				
1982	128354.00	58173.00			0.3043	0.3043				
1983	108140.80	61921.10			0.2624	0.2624				
1984	118460.10	83588.00			0.2289	0.2289				
1985	129406.00	85380.00			0.2226	0.2226				
1986	107983.00	70551.01			0.2888	0.2888				
1987	127308.00	73212.00			0.3327	0.3327				
1988	145170.00	72209.01			0.3357	0.3357				
1989	150533.00	78188.00			0.3135	0.3135				
1990	158287.00	72942.00			0.3673	0.3673				
1991	125220.00	71433.01			0.3545	0.3545				
1992	104461.00	72779.01			0.3778	0.3778				
1993	50810.00	38512.00			0.3532	0.3532				
1994	123265.00	90053.01			0.1801	0.1801				
1995	191812.00	104218.00			0.2008	0.2009				
1996	206564.00	122090.00			0.1955	0.1955				

2. IMPORTS BY BROAD ECONOMIC CATEGORY AND EXPORTS BY INDUSTRIAL ORIGIN. (PERCENTAGE OF TOTAL VALUE)
IMPORTATIONS PAR CATEGORIES ECONOMIQUES ET EXPORTATIONS PAR BRANCHE D'ACTIVITE.(EN POURCENTAGE DE LA VALEUR TOTALE)

IMPORTS – IMPORTATIONS

	1990	1991	1992	1993	1994	1995	1996
TOTAL IMPORTS–IMPORTATIONS TOTALES	100.	100.					
1 FOOD BEV–ALIMENTATION BOISSONS	17.0	18.5					
11 PRIMARY–PRODUITS DE BASE	6.7	7.0					
111 FOR INDUSTRY–POUR L'INDUSTRIE	3.8	2.9					
112 FOR HOUSEHOLDS–POUR LES MENAGES	2.9	4.0					
12 PROCESSED–PRODUITS ELABORES	10.3	11.6					
121 FOR INDUSTRY–POUR L'INDUSTRIE	1.1	2.2					
122 FOR HOUSEHOLDS–POUR LES MENAGES	9.1	9.4					
2 IND SUPPLIES–APPROV INDUSTRIELS	33.8	26.3					
21 PRIMARY–PRODUITS DE BASE	1.6	1.8					
22 PROCESSED–PRODUITS ELABORES	32.3	24.5					
3 FUELS–COMBUSTIBLES	8.0	9.7					
31 PRIMARY–PRODUITS DE BASE	0.1	0.1					
32 PROCESSED–PRODUITS ELABORES	7.9	9.6					
321 MOTOR SPIRIT–ESSENCE	3.3	9.6					
322 OTHER–AUTRES	4.6	0.0					
4 MACHINERY–EQUIPEMENT	10.0	15.5					
41 CAPITAL EQUIPMENT–MACHINES	8.5	13.7					
42 PARTS–PIECES ACCESSOIRES	1.4	1.8					
5 TRANSPORT–TRANSPORT	11.2	11.6					
51 PASSENGER CARS–AUTOMOBILES	3.3	3.3					
52 OTHER–AUTRES	4.1	5.0					
521 INDUSTRIAL–INDUSTRIELS	3.6	4.4					
522 NON INDUSTRIAL–NON INDUSTRIEL	0.5	0.7					
53 PARTS–PIECES ACCESSOIRES	3.7	3.3					
6 CONSUM GOODS–BIENS CONSOMMATION	19.5	17.6					
61 DURABLE–DURABLES	2.7	1.8					
62 SEMI DURABLE–SEMI DURABLES	5.1	4.6					
63 NON DURABLE–NON DURABLES	11.7	11.2					
7 GOODS NES–BIENS NDA	0.6	0.9					

EXPORTS – EXPORTATIONS

	1990	1991	1992	1993	1994	1995	1996
TOTAL EXPORTS–EXPORTATIONS TOTALES	100.	100.	100.	100.			
1 AGRICULTURE	35.6	31.8	35.1	47.1			
2 MINING QUARRY–INDUS EXTRACTIVES	44.6	49.3	47.0	34.5			
3 MANUFACTURING–IND MANUFACTUR	19.8	18.9	17.9	18.4			
31 FOOD BEV TOBACCO–ALIM BOISS TAB	8.9	8.1	9.3	7.0			
32 TEXTILES–INDUSTRIES TEXTILES	2.8	0.7	0.3	0.9			
33 WOOD & PRODUCTS–BOIS & PRODUITS	0.1	0.0					
34 PAPER & PRODUCTS–PAPIER & PRODT	0.6	0.5	0.5	0.7			
35 CHEMICALS–INDUSTRIES CHIMIQUES	0.6	5.3	2.5	4.3			
36 NON METAL MIN–MIN NON METAL	2.6	1.2	1.5	0.3			
37 BASIC METAL–IND METAL BASE	1.3	0.3	0.1	0.1			
38 METAL MANUF–MANUF METAL	1.0	1.8	2.7	4.4			
39 OTH MANUF IND–AUTRES MANUF	1.9	0.9	0.7	0.7			

3. TRADE BY PRINCIPAL COUNTRIES OF PRODUCTION AND LAST CONSIGNMENT (VALUE IN THOUSAND U.S. DOLLARS)
ECHANGES SELON LES PRINCIPAUX PAYS DE PRODUCTION ET DE DERNIERE CONSIGNATION (VALEUR EN MILLIERS DE DOLLARS EU)

COUNTRIES–PAYS	SPECIAL IMPORTS C.I.F. IMPORTATIONS SPECIALES C.A.F				
	1990	1991	1992	1993	1994
World	581380	443908	394652	179460	222001
Africa	101329	68991	53008	38143	46500
Americas	44690	36837	9507	12502	16704
Northern America	37461	29102	3767	11188	12703
LAIA	6665	2795	5210	812	2950
CACM	24	18	40	2	77
Caribbean	509	4276	388	398	546
Rest of America	31	646	102	101	429
As.ex F.USSR	86025	78344	58662	32577	30077
Eur.x F.USSR	346091	258544	236446	93012	125448
EU	332673	248792	230223	87792	119876
EFTA	10818	8825	4310	2419	4144
East Europe	2540	687	1634	2801	1419
Other Europe	60	239	279	0	1
Former USSR	1210	115	263	5	51
Oceania	758	269	1290	865	1022
France,Monac	177230	146852	134907	50058	53301
Netherlands/Pays–Bas	52663	33488	23764	9422	11495
Germany/Allemagne	35039	18519	23082	10621	21937
Cote d'Ivoire	46901	16812	11900	7494	13883
Japan/Japon	25009	29701	20529	8033	7847
USA/Etats–Unis d'Amer	30819	28526	3476	11020	12182
United Kingdom	21836	16250	9071	3228	7484
Hong Kong	14918	10908	11000	7951	7381
Nigeria/Nigéria	13096	12774	9933	9891	5661
Italy/Italie	13256	13992	10727	5161	6635
Belgium–Luxembourg	10372	9122	9473	3212	6754
China/Chine	8896	6027	9481	6744	5858
Spain/Espagne	9561	4930	7874	2807	5948
Mauritania/Mauritanie	3049	3143	5184	4130	11428
Benin/Bénin	5694	4034	4670	5442	3276
Ghana	7699	5328	4320	1793	1997
Singapore/Singapour	7350	5601	3083	915	662
Norway,SVD,JM	7727	3560	1281	1346	3304
Thailand/Thaïlande	4416	4557	4384	1940	846
Korea, Republic of	5117	3612	3051	1592	2131
Cameroon/Cameroun	544	12482	2202	28	144
Gabon	5772	3431	1719	1465	1526
Denmark/Danemark	5679	1859	2079	1066	2818
Switz.Liecht	3091	5265	3029	1073	745
Pakistan	3171	2264	3213	2032	1952
So. Africa Customs Un	54	640	3556	4841	3540
Senegal/Sénégal	5451	1587	1323	1456	1572
Brazil/Brésil	1707	1885	3274	736	1561
Greece/Grèce	1503	637	4468	692	1086
Canada	6622	576	205	169	520
Burkina Faso	2115	1587	1348	537	626
Austria/Autriche	2166	1122	1591	817	496
Angola	3750	1165	413	27	800
Argentina/Argentine	3128	808	760	52	624
Mauritius/Maurice	18	2556	2615	6	
Finland/Finlande	1228	250	1885	447	1275
Turkey/Turquie	1343	624	565	319	2052
Tunisia/Tunisie	2520	666	810	12	890
Netherlands Antilles	287	4158			
Viet Nam	1519	1206	750	792	38
Venezuela	1726	2	1113	12	742
Morocco/Maroc	1318	1073	578	156	440
Bulgaria/Bulgarie	0	3	20	2305	1190
India/Inde	478	1492	318	526	606
Niger	835	398	957	282	78
Ireland/Irlande	698	949	400	140	318
Romania/Roumanie	817	167	929	459	93
Pacific Isld (Tr Terr.)	12		839	462	730
Portugal	747	421	659	55	159
Korea Dem People's Rp	406	334	380	501	160

COUNTRIES–PAYS	SPECIAL EXPORTS F.O.B. EXPORTATIONS SPECIALES F.O.B.				
	1990	1991	1992	1993	1994
Monde	267911	253228	274961	136024	162185
Afrique	46226	48210	68742	25699	26670
Amériques	42402	47665	58010	31464	44040
Amérique du Nord	36380	28867	57006	18097	27689
ALAI	5957	18747	952	13367	16333
MCAC		0			
Caraïbes	65	51		0	18
Autre Amérique			53		0
Asie l'URSS exclus	46999	58247	39988	27860	27711
Europe l'URSS exclus	118423	82306	80755	30332	37005
UE	109559	74576	63402	28172	32075
AELE	3391	3000	1820	321	886
Europe de l'Est	3120	3839	15534	1838	4036
Autre de l'Europe	2353	892			8
Ancienne URSS	12558	10383			48
Océanie	1167	25	3987	732	4988
Canada	33378	28700	56225	17881	27507
France,Monac	26278	17005	14050	6664	8081
Nigeria/Nigéria	8770	19418	25572	8672	6235
Spain/Espagne	17111	17156	11848	660	1577
Philippines	11482	12455	5408	9831	8779
India/Inde	14147	6513	15609	3679	2940
Netherlands/Pays–Bas	8778	2233	10133	8890	5830
Thailand/Thaïlande	1654	9329	12864	6583	5167
Italy/Italie	14180	10372	6389	2040	2508
Germany/Allemagne	9959	7101	6169	2619	2637
Poland/Pologne	3108	3625	15534	1810	4035
Benin/Bénin	5687	5105	6162	4364	4267
Mexico/Mexique	4279	17882		1217	1606
Br. Indian Ocean Terr	3207	4591	14335	2578	
Burkina Faso	8849	5703	4895	1428	3790
Portugal	14640	4015	1540	1473	2921
Former USSR/Anc. URSS	12558	10383			48
Indonesia/Indonésie	2198	4136	1394	4032	9180
Greece/Grèce	3839	7976	3486	1451	2129
Belgium–Luxembourg	5853	2128	4214	2684	3329
Ghana	4136	2869	4193	2337	3466
Bolivia/Bolivie				4155	12361
Morocco/Maroc	2517	1739	3158	2417	2795
Niger	3642	3314	3457	1145	644
United Kingdom	3891	3895	1469	853	1187
Denmark/Danemark	3817	2286	1699	382	1161
Switz.Liecht	3389	2979	1820	321	832
Brazil/Brésil		20	34	7042	1563
Singapore/Singapour	836	3618	2337	413	
Malaysia/Malaisie	1519	1760	1275	982	1448
Bangladesh	5656	486		383	
China/Chine	173	4607		1644	6
Australia/Australie	1167		1196		3309
Guinea/Guinée	3719	187	1180	118	63
Pacific Isld (Tr Terr.)			2791	732	1678
Uruguay	1678	845	898	953	802
USA/Etats–Unis d'Amer	3002	168	781	216	182
Mali	729	758	1236	774	415
So. Africa Customs Un	15	57	5		3550
Ireland/Irlande	35	239	2403	454	487
Congo	264	924	2014	124	98
Gabon	672	532	509	1050	505
Tunisia/Tunisie	1379	1730			33
Cote d'Ivoire	947	560	643	73	114
Fm Yugoslav	1165	869			
Sweden/Suède	1177	170	3		227
Senegal/Sénégal	237	258	459	203	82
Malta/Malte	1188	23			8
Cyprus/Chypre	1167	0			
Korea, Republic of	504		486	24	

(VALUE AS PERCENTAGE OF WORLD TOTAL)(VALEURS EN POURCENTAGE DU TOTAL MONDIAL)

	1985	1986	1987	1988	1989	1990	1991	1992	1993	1994
Africa	9.1	5.4	12.0	10.3	12.5	17.4	15.5	13.4	21.3	20.9
Americas	8.4	4.9	5.1	8.1	8.0	7.7	8.3	2.4	7.0	7.5
Northern America	5.3	4.2	4.8	7.2	7.0	6.4	6.6	1.0	6.2	5.7
LAIA	1.0	0.2	0.2	0.8	0.8	1.1	0.6	1.3	0.5	1.3
CACM		0.0	0.0	0.0	0.0	0.0	0.0	0.0	0.0	0.0
Caribbean	1.9	0.3	0.0	0.0	0.1	0.1	1.0	0.1	0.2	0.2
Rest of America	0.2	0.3	0.0	0.0	0.0	0.0	0.1	0.0	0.1	0.2
As.ex F.USSR	15.9	15.4	13.7	15.1	15.0	14.8	17.6	14.9	18.2	13.5
Eur.x F.USSR	65.7	73.5	68.6	66.0	64.3	59.5	58.2	59.9	51.8	56.5
EU	64.1	69.5	66.8	64.6	62.3	57.2	56.0	58.3	48.9	54.0
EFTA	0.9	2.4	0.9	0.8	0.7	1.9	2.0	1.1	1.3	1.9
East Europe	0.3	1.2	0.5	0.4	0.9	0.4	0.2	0.4	1.6	0.6
Other Europe	0.4	0.5	0.3	0.2	0.3	0.0	0.1	0.1	0.0	0.0
Former USSR	0.4	0.6	0.4	0.4	0.0	0.2	0.0	0.1	0.0	0.0
Oceania	0.0	0.1	0.0	0.0	0.0	0.1	0.1	0.3	0.5	0.5
France,Monac	30.8	32.0	32.7	31.0	29.6	30.5	33.1	34.2	27.9	24.0
Netherlands/Pays–Bas	10.2	11.2	9.3	10.6	11.8	9.1	7.5	6.0	5.3	5.2
Germany/Allemagne	9.1	11.3	8.8	6.5	7.6	6.0	4.2	5.8	5.9	9.9
Cote d'Ivoire	6.1	2.3	5.5	2.4	2.6	8.1	3.8	3.0	4.2	6.3
Japan/Japon	6.6	5.4	5.0	3.9	4.2	4.3	6.7	5.2	4.5	3.5
USA/Etats–Unis d'Amer	4.3	2.3	3.6	5.8	5.9	5.3	6.4	0.9	6.1	5.5
United Kingdom	6.3	6.7	7.1	6.3	4.2	3.8	3.7	2.3	1.8	3.4
Hong Kong	2.2	0.9	1.6	1.9	2.1	2.6	2.5	2.8	4.4	3.3
Nigeria/Nigéria	0.4	0.2	0.8	2.0	1.7	2.3	2.9	2.5	5.5	2.5
Italy/Italie	2.9	2.3	2.5	2.6	3.0	2.3	3.2	2.7	2.9	3.0

	1985	1986	1987	1988	1989	1990	1991	1992	1993	1994
Afrique	7.0	8.6	11.1	11.5	14.0	17.3	19.0	25.0	18.9	16.4
Amériques	5.1	13.8	13.5	13.6	14.5	15.8	18.8	21.1	23.1	27.2
Amérique du Nord	4.8	13.0	13.0	12.9	12.6	13.6	11.4	20.7	13.3	17.1
ALAI	0.2	0.8	0.4	0.7	1.9	2.2	7.4	0.3	9.8	10.1
MCAC							0.0			
Caraïbes		0.0	0.0			0.0	0.0		0.0	0.0
Autre Amérique	0.0			0.0				0.0		0.0
Asie l'URSS exclus	2.0	8.1	10.5	9.8	15.3	17.5	23.0	14.5	20.5	17.1
Europe l'URSS exclus	84.1	65.1	57.6	58.8	49.8	44.2	32.5	29.4	22.3	22.8
UE	65.6	56.1	52.0	51.8	43.8	40.9	29.5	23.1	20.7	19.8
AELE	5.7	1.6	0.8	1.0	0.6	1.3	1.2	0.7	0.2	0.5
Europe de l'Est	3.9	3.0	3.9	4.9	4.4	1.2	1.5	5.6	1.4	2.5
Autre de l'Europe	8.9	4.3	0.9	1.0	1.0	0.9	0.4			0.0
Ancienne URSS	1.5	3.9	6.6	4.0	2.0	4.7	4.1			0.0
Océanie	0.1		0.0	2.1	4.4	0.4	0.0	1.4	0.5	3.1
Canada	1.0	1.0	5.7	12.7	12.5	12.5	11.3	20.4	13.1	17.0
France,Monac	21.4	11.8	7.7	8.1	8.7	9.8	6.7	5.1	4.9	5.0
Nigeria/Nigéria	0.2	1.0	1.0	0.8	2.5	3.3	7.7	9.3	6.4	3.8
Spain/Espagne	2.6	2.4	7.4	7.3	7.7	6.4	6.8	4.3	0.5	1.0
Philippines	0.0		1.6	3.3	5.0	4.3	4.9	2.0	7.2	5.4
India/Inde	0.5	1.5	1.6	2.2	3.2	5.3	2.6	5.7	2.7	1.8
Netherlands/Pays–Bas	16.0	20.5	14.8	11.7	6.3	3.3	0.9	3.7	6.5	3.6
Thailand/Thaïlande	0.2	0.1	0.3	0.5	1.2	0.6	3.7	4.7	4.8	3.2
Italy/Italie	5.6	6.1	7.0	5.2	7.5	5.3	4.1	2.3	1.5	1.5
Germany/Allemagne	7.1	6.1	3.7	2.5	1.4	3.7	2.8	2.2	1.9	1.6

4. Special imports C.I.F. by Commodities according to the S.I.T.C. (Rev. 2) in thousand U.S. Dollars
Importations Spéciales C.A.F. par Produits d'après la C.T.C.I. (Rév. 2) en milliers de Dollars E.U.

SITC CTCI	COMMODITY	1990 WEIGHT POIDS	1990 VALUE VALEUR	1991 WEIGHT POIDS	1991 VALUE VALEUR	1992 WEIGHT POIDS	1992 VALUE VALEUR	1993 WEIGHT POIDS	1993 VALUE VALEUR	PRODUIT
	ALL COMMODITIES		581380		443908		394652		179460	TOUS PRODUITS
0	FOOD AND LIVE ANIMALS		86090		72368		83769		41806	ALIMENTS,ANIMAUX VIVANTS
001	*LIVE ANIMALS FOR FOOD	W 1536	2155	W 1919	1507		1042		455	ANIMAUX VIVANTS
01	MEAT AND PREPARATIONS		1897		732		3066		1544	VIANDES ET PREPARATIONS
011	MEAT FRESH,CHILLD,FROZEN	W 155	451	W 42	142		1670		1348	VIANDES FRAICHES,REF,CONGE
0114	POULTRY FRESH CHLLD,FRZN	W 113	143		7		1143	W 1608	1138	VOLAILLES MORTES
02	DAIRY PRODCTS,BIRDS'EGGS		6175		5599		5708		2524	PRODUITS LAITIERS,OEUFS
022	MILK AND CREAM	W 3712	5027	W 3654	4870	W 3968	5010	W 2124	2243	LAIT ET CREME
0223	MILK AND CREAM FRESH	W 761	593	W 1074	917	W 959	950	W 691	605	LAIT,CREME FRAIS
0224	MILK,CREAM PRESERVED ETC	W 2951	4434	W 2579	3952	W 3009	4060	W 1433	1638	LAIT,CREME CONS,CONC
02243	MILK DRY,OVER 1.5% FAT	W 320	720	W 339	616	W 1361	2057	W 461	718	LAIT POUDRE SUP 1.5%
02249	MILK(EX DRY) PRSVD,SWEET	W 2310	3252	W 1706	2299	W 1648	2003	W 936	884	LAIT CONS,CONC SUCRE
03	FISH AND PREPARATIONS		15252		16626		15782		9149	POISSONS ET PREPARATIONS
034	FISH,FRESH,CHILLED,FROZN	W 20802	11456	W 26495	14646		14585		8753	POISSON FRAIS, REFRIG,CONG
0341	FISH FRSH,CHLLD,EX FILLT	W 27	44	W 1282	595		165	W 2879	1182	POISSON FRAIS,REFRIGERE
0342	FISH FROZEN,EXCL FILLETS	W 20774	11408	W 25213	14050	W 26029	14418		7571	POISSONS CONGELES
037	FISH ETC PREPD,PRSVD NES	W 1337	1968	W 934	1372		670		251	POIS,CRUST,MOL PREPARES
0371	FISH PREPARD,PRESRVD NES	W 1335	1961	W 933	1369		660		249	CONSERVES DE POISSONS
04	CEREALS AND PREPARATIONS		33447		21502		35091		14791	CEREALES ET PRODUITS
041	WHEAT ETC UNMILLED	W 81388	19442	W 56693	11261	W 116926	25721	W 131247	6706	FROMENT,EPEAUTRE
0411	DURUM WHEAT UNMILLED	W 76601	17660	W 52793	10340	W 114247	24852	W 127498	5578	FROMENT DUR NON MOULU
0412	OTHER WHEAT ETC UNMILLED	W 4786	1783	W 3900	921	W 2679	870	W 3749	1128	AUTRE FROMENT NON MOULU
042	RICE	W 26816	7819	W 25811	6398	W 24017	6002	W 30219	6648	RIZ
0422	RICE SEMI–MILLED,MILLED	W 26552	7729	W 25736	6369	W 23201	5816	W 29836	6559	RIZ POLI,GLACE INCL BRISURES
04221	RICE MILLED UNBROKEN	W 9833	2976	W 14556	3429	W 13794	3758	W 16529	3841	RIZ POLI,GLACE EXCL BRISURES
04222	RICE BROKEN	W 16720	4753	W 11180	2940	W 9407	2058	W 13307	2718	BRISURES DE RIZ
046	WHEAT ETC MEAL OR FLOUR	W 5881	1648	W 1542	568	W 2566	1285	W 803	365	SEMOULE FARINE,FROMENT
048	CEREAL ETC PREPARATIONS	W 3813	3069	W 4205	2719		1296		764	PREPTNS A BASE CEREALES
0483	MACARONI,SPAGHETTI ETC	W 2076	1695	W 2484	1959	W 542	558	W 355	301	PATES ALMENTAIRES
05	VEGETABLES AND FRUIT		8178		6167		5159		3679	LEGUMES ET FRUITS
054	VEG ETC FRSH,SMPLY PRSVD	W 7094	1307	W 7593	5057		932		610	LEGUMES FRAIS,CONG,SECS
0546	VEGETABLES SIMPLY PRESVD	W 9	17	W 3900	4441	W 70	36		7	LEGUMES CONG,CONSER
05461	VEGETABLES FROZEN	W 8	15	W 3756	4417	W 38	31	W 1	1	LEGUMES CONGELES
056	VEGTBLES ETC PRSVD,PREPD	W 4482	5753	W 410	337		3717		2864	CONSERVES DE LEGUMES
0565	VEGTBLES PRSVD,PREPD NES	W 4465	5716	W 344	308		3533		2831	LEGUMES PREPARES CONSERVE
05659	OTH VEG PRESVD,PREPD NES	W 4456	5693	W 295	257		3521		2820	LEGUM PREPAP,CONSERV NDA
06	SUGAR AND PREPS,HONEY		9600		7724		7020		3484	SUCRES ET PRODUITS
061	SUGAR AND HONEY	W 14900	8744	W 15286	7128		6597		3262	SUCRES ET MIEL
0611	RAW BEET AND CANE SUGAR	W 60	48	W 8965	4670	W 4591	2505	W 2696	1279	SUCRES BRUTS
0612	REFINED SUGAR ETC	W 14738	8631	W 6124	2332	W 8877	4049	W 4838	1961	SUCRES RAFFINES
07	COFFEE,TEA,COCOA,SPICES		1314		977		686		717	CAFE,THE,CACAO,EPICES
09	MISC EDIBLE PRODUCTS		7563		11015		9428		5195	PREP ALIMENTAIRES DIVERSES
098	EDIBLE PRODCTS,PREPS NES	W 2977	6455	W 6592	10150		8422		4863	PREP ALIMENTAIRES NDA
09805	SOUPS AND BROTHS	W 1847	3782	W 6018	9143	W 3759	6575	W 2499	3197	SOUPES,POTAGES,BOUILLONS
09809	MISC FOOD PREPRTIONS NES	W 633	1691	W 133	370	W 1189	1325		1325	PREP ALIMENTAIRES NDA
1	BEVERAGES AND TOBACCO		35483		25195		19483		10214	BOISSONS ET TABACS
11	BEVERAGES		10340		7103		5684		3084	BOISSONS
112	ALCOHOLIC BEVERAGES	W 4089	9929	W 3777	6715	W 2497	5369	W 2201	2943	BOISSONS ALCOOLIQUES
1121	WINE OF FRESH GRAPES ETC	W 2159	3553	W 2491	2606	W 1399	1499	W 1527	1217	VINS DE RAISINS FRAIS
11212	WINE OF FRESH GRAPES	W 1977	3177	W 1411	1696	W 504	637	W 828	755	VINS DE MOUTS DE RAISINS
1124	DISTILLED ALCOHOLIC BEVS	W 1870	6311	W 1257	4069	W 1053	3822	W 673	1724	ALCOOLS,EAUX–DE–VIE
11241	WHISKY	W 380	1907	W 339	1640	W 191	1148	W 186	738	WHISKY
11249	OTH ALCOHOLC BEVS,CMPNDS	W 1415	4200	W 912	2381	W 859	2661	W 486	980	BOISSONS ALCOOLIQUES NDA
12	TOBACCO AND MANUFACTURES		25143		18092		13799		7130	TABACS BRUTS FABRIQUES
122	TOBACCO,MANUFACTURED	W 1341	24920	W 1130	17940		13795		7120	TABACS FABRIQUES
1222	CIGARETTES	W 1327	24713	W 1096	17719	W 800	13785	W 496	7103	CIGARETTES
2	CRUDE MATERLS,EXCL FUELS		10945		9007		7930		1325	MAT BRUTES NON COMESTIBLES
24	CORK AND WOOD		2066		2261		1423		486	LIEGE ET BOIS
248	WOOD SHAPED,SLEEPERS	W 16801	2013	W 10941	1204		805		483	BOIS SIMPLEMENT TRAVAILLES
2483	LUMBER SHAPED NON–CONIFR	W 16421	1937	W 10790	1167		579		456	NON CONIFERES SCIES,RABOTES
24831	LUMBER SAWN ETC NON–CON	W 16421	1937	W 10790	1167		578	W 2143	456	SCIES LONGITUDINALEMENT
26	TEXTILE FIBRES AND WASTE		5053		3511		4143		29	FIBRES TEXTILES
269	WASTE OF TEXTILE FABRICS	W 7154	4997	W 5413	3233	W 6519	4019	W 8	14	FRIPERIE DRILLES,CHIFFONS
26901	BULK TEXT WSTE,OLD CLTHG	W 7045	4936	W 5348	3213	W 6366	3962	W 2	10	ART ET ACCESS D'HABILLEMENT
27	CRUDE FERTLZR,MINRLS NES		3525		3146		1949		753	ENGRAIS MINERAUX BRUTS
278	OTHER CRUDE MINERALS	W 55402	2855	W 41710	2448		1161		571	AUTRES MINERAUX BRUTS
2783	COMMON SALT,ETC	W 14658	1456	W 17442	1597	W 8784	874	W 939	245	SEL
3	MINERAL FUELS ETC		48051		43560		25178		14274	COMBUSTIBLES MINERAUX LUB
33	PETROLEUM AND PRODUCTS		47713		43308		24715		14115	PETROLE ET DERIVES
334	PETROLEUM PRODUCTS,REFIN	W 177199	45922	W 173521	42654		24410		13974	PRODUITS RAFFINES
3341	GASOLINE,OTH LIGHT OILS	W 65227	19335	W 173518	42643					ESSENCES POUR MOTEURS
33411	MOTOR,AVIATION SPIRIT	W 65205	19321							ESSENCES MOTEURS D'AVIONS
33419	OTH LIGHT PETROLEUM OILS	W 22	14	W 173518	42643					AUTRES HUILES LEGERES
3342	KEROSENE,OTH MEDIUM OILS	W 15225	5264							PETR LAMPANTS,AUT HUIL
33421	KEROSENE INCL JET FUEL	W 14483	4217							PETROLES LAMPANTS
3343	GAS OILS	W 43463	10058							GAS OILS
3344	FUEL OILS,NES	W 50133	7502							FUEL OILS
3345	LUBS,PETROLEUM OILS NES	W 3151	3763	W 3	11		14		6	HUILES LUBRIFIANTES
33451	LUBS(HIGH PETR CONT) ETC	W 3141	3724							HUILES LUBRIF,H LOURDES
335	RESIDUAL PETRLM PROD NES	W 8815	1791	W 766	654	W 547	305	W 123	141	PRODUITS RESIDUELS NDA
4	ANIMAL,VEGETABLE OIL,FAT		8429		4773		4607		1417	HUILES,GRAISSES ANIM,VEG
42	FIXED VEGETABLE OIL,FAT		8295		4749		4596		1417	HUILES VEGETALES FIXES
423	FIXED VEG OILS,SOFT	W 2064	1928	W 3924	2904		2705		959	HUILES VEGET DOUCES FIXES
4232	SOYA BEAN OIL	W 1299	1262	W 1238	975	W 1235	1210	W 548	474	HUILE DE SOJA
4234	GROUNDNUT(PEANUT) OIL	W 704	552	W 2445	1790	W 633	591	W 319	241	HUILE D'ARACHIDE
424	FIXED VEG OIL NONSOFT	W 9928	6368	W 2657	1846		1891		458	AUTRES HUILES VEG FIXES
4249	FIXED VEGETABLE OILS NES	W 7570	5434	W 1726	1269	W 1263	1215	W 55	40	HUILES VEGET FIXES NDA
5	CHEMCLS,RELATED PROD NES		71862		52700		47648		29296	PRODUITS CHIMIQUES
52	INORGANIC CHEMICALS		2347		1468		1208		478	PROD CHIM INORGANIQUES
53	DYES,TANNING,COLOUR PROD		2695		1162		1279		544	PROD TEINTURE,COLORANTS
533	PIGMENTS,PAINTS,ETC	W 687	1887	W 549	1073		1159		472	PIGMENTS,PEINTURES,VERNIS
541	*MEDICINAL,PHARM PRODUCT	K 1754091	30026	K 1212167	21017		26017		10118	PROD MEDICINAUX PHARMACEUT
5416	GLYCOSIDES,GLANDS,SERA	K 20323	2611	K 22307	614		1289		828	HETEROSIDES
54164	ANTISERA,MICROB VACCINES	K 19196	2482	K 22012	606		1057		616	SERUMS,VACCINS
5417	MEDICAMENTS	K 1559282	25436	K 1145939	19702		24365		9039	MEDICAMENTS
54171	— CONTAINNG ANTIBIOTICS	K 1370672	23620	K 898826	16488		18746		420	MED CONTN ANTIBIOTIQUES
54172	— CONTAINING HORMONES	K 3253	38	K 86008	1496	K 36000	567		411	MED CONTENANT HORMONES
54179	— CONTNG OTH SUBSTANCES	K 184480	1762	K 158981	1682	K 335000	5019	K 541000	8195	MED CONT AUT SUBSTANCES
5419	PHARMACEUTICAL GOODS NES	K 124967	1932	K 41676	694		360		243	PREP,ART PHARMACEUTIQUES
55	PERFUME,CLEANING ETC PRD		6046		4575		3886		2606	PROD POUR PARFUM,TOILETTE
553	PERFUMERY,COSMETICS,ETC	W 2227	2312	W 2260	1623		1744		964	PRODUITS DE PARFUMERIE

4. Special Imports C.I.F. by Commodities according to the S.I.T.C. (Rev. 2) in thousand U.S. Dollars
Importations Spéciales C.A.F. par Produits d'après la C.T.C.I. (Rév. 2) en milliers de Dollars E.U.

SITC CTCI	COMMODITY	1990		1991		1992		1993		PRODUIT
		WEIGHT POIDS	VALUE VALEUR	WEIGHT POIDS	VALUE VALEUR	WEIGHT POIDS	VALUE VALEUR	WEIGHT POIDS	VALUE VALEUR	
554	SOAP,CLEANSING ETC PREPS	W 4043	3560	W 3540	2455		1793	W 1306	1524	SAVONS,PRODUITS DETERSIFS
5541	SOAPS	W 3029	2101	W 3061	1625	W 1699	1137	W 948	954	SAVONS,PROD TENSIO–ACTIFS
562	*FERTILIZERS,MANUFACTURE	W 16356	4667	W 17266	4851		4686		7843	ENGRAIS MANUFACTURES
5621	CHEM NITROGENOUS FERTLZR	W 3721	766	W 14008	3810	W 6831	1500		2367	ENGRAIS AZOTES
56216	UREA	W 3600	681	W 14008	3810	W 6810	1490	W 8169	2333	UREE
5629	FERTILIZERS NES	W 11368	3414	W 3256	1038		3181	W 23954	5454	ENGRAIS NDA
56291	NIT–PHOS–POT FERTLZR NES	W 11365	3401	W 3250	1036	W 23	3139	W 3232	702	ENGRAIS CONT N P K
56292	NITROG–PHOS FERTILZR NES					W 98	28	W 17722	4034	ENGRAIS NDA CONT N P
56299	OTHER FERTILIZERS NES	W 3	14	W 6	3		14	W 3000	718	AUTRES ENGRAIS NDA
58	PLASTIC MATERIALS ETC		3192		4203		3843		1687	MAT PLAST ARTIFICIELLES
582	PROD OF CONDENSATION ETC	W 1817	1823	W 2675	1937		1367		780	PROD CONDENS,POLYCOND
5826	EPOXIDE RESINS	W 1740	1663	W 2650	1901	W 1932	1334	W 963	767	RESINES EPOXYDES
58261	— IN PRIMARY FORMS	W 1739	1659	W 2650	1901	W 1932	1334	W 963	767	EPOXYDES PRIMAIRES
583	POLYMERIZATION ETC PRODS	W 709	1334	W 966	2266		2257		892	PROD POLYMERISATION
5839	OTH POLYMRZTION ETC PROD	W 147	366	W 885	1956	W 740	1896		829	AUT PROD POLYMER COPOLYM
59	CHEMICAL MATERIALS NES		21618		14514		6012		5700	MAT PROD CHIMIQUES NDA
591	PESTICIDES,DISINFECTANTS	W 3047	19776	W 2597	13112	W 1559	5054	W 1625	4931	DESINF,INSECT,FONG,HERB
5911	INSECTICIDES,FOR RETAIL	W 2475	18878	W 1728	9609	W 812	3117	W 1075	3910	INSECTICIDES VENTE DET
5914	DISINFECTANTS,ETC,FR RET	W 554	781	W 844	3201	W 709	1733	W 508	505	DESINFECTANTS VENTE DET
59149	RAT POISONS ETC FR RTAIL	W 155	373	W 835	3191	W 698	1707	W 484	439	ANTIPARASITES VENTE DET
6	BASIC MANUFACTURES		146207		78480		78949		23864	ART MANUFACTURES
62	RUBBER MANUFACTURES NES		7170		5434		7872		1292	CAOUTCHOUC MANUFACTURE
625	RUBBER TYRES, TUBES ETC	W 1202	4422	W 984	2946	W 836	2360		929	PNEUS CAOUTCHOUC VULCANISE
6252	TYRES,NEW,BUS OR LORRY	W 545	2612	W 466	1944	W 417	1630	W 21	556	PNEUS POUR AUTOBUS,CAMIONS
628	RUBBER ARTICLES NES	W 309	2056	W 383	2048		4847		257	OUVRAGES CAOUTCHOUC NDA
6282	VULCANIZD RUBBER BELTING	W 244	1325	W 318	1557	W 915	4301	W 505	107	COURROIES EN CAOUTCHOUC
63	WOOD,CORK MANUFACTRS NES		1826		867		502		88	OUVRAGES LIEGE ET BOIS
64	PAPER,PAPERBOARD AND MFR		11067		7964		8669		3250	PAPIERS,CARTONS & OUVRAGES
641	PAPER AND PAPERBOARD	W 1352	1481	W 1929	1969		2447		758	PAPIERS ET CARTONS
642	PAPER,ETC,PRECUT,ARTS OF	W 5269	9586	W 3464	5994		6221		2491	PAP,CARTONS DECOUPES
6421	PAPER ETC CONTAINERS	W 3089	5222	W 1909	2831	W 1927	4071		1547	BOITES,SACS EMBALLAGES
6424	PAPER ETC CT TO SIZE NES	W 1393	2232	W 896	1044		597		436	PAP,CARTONS DECOUPES
65	TEXTILE YARN,FABRICS,ETC		61219		29975		22329		8569	FILS,TISSUS,ARTICLES TEXTILE
652	COTTON FABRICS,WOVEN	W 5222	49307	W 2999	23135		14003		3606	TISSUS DE COTON
6522	WOVEN COTTON BLEACHD,ETC	W 4827	48000	W 2314	22525		13550		3074	TISSUS COTON BLANCHIS ETC
65224	BLCHED COTTON FABRIC NES	W 4499	47014	W 2247	22407		13305		2960	AUT TIS PLUS 85% COT BLANCHI
653	WOVN MAN–MADE FIB FABRIC	W 2834	4302	W 1523	2532		2478		2054	TISSUS FIBRES SYNTH,ARTIF
6534	DISC SYN BLEND FABRC NES	W 761	1131	W 1204	1918		1862	W 1232	1714	TISSUS FIBRES SYNTH DISCONT
65341	DISC SYN FIB–COTTN FABRC	W 332	443	W 752	1160		918	W 919	1292	TISSUS FIB SYNT DIS MEL COTO
6538	DISC REG BLEND FABRC NES	W 1331	2068	W 78	207		155	W 39	47	TIS MOINS 85% TEXT ART DISC
657	SPECIAL TXTL FABRC,PRODS	W 896	3150	W 562	2123		1976		1332	TISSUS SPECIAUX
6575	CORDAGE AND MANUFACTURES	W 468	2426	W 368	1703		1680		971	FICELLES,CORDES,CORDAGES
65752	NETTING OF ROPE,TWINE	W 251	2017	W 181	1308	W 191	1310		740	FILETS MAT DU 657.51
658	TEXTILE ARTICLES NES	W 1906	3414	W 597	1354		3182		1281	ART FACONNES MAT TEXTILES
6581	BAGS,SACKS OF TEXTILES	W 1413	1393	W 281	566		2193		515	SACS EMBALLAGE TEXTILES
6584	LINENS ETC	W 377	1184	W 252	594		849	W 395	630	LINGE DE MAISON
66	NONMETAL MINERAL MFS NES		30008		12847		18357		5344	ART MIN NON METALLIQUES
661	LIME,CEMENT,BLDG PRODS	W 474990	23854	W 168236	8688		15855	W 391255	4319	CHAUX,CIMENTS MAT CONSTR
6612	CEMENT	W 471085	22270	W 163607	7077		13952	W 389490	3783	CIMENTS HYDRAULIQUES
6618	MNRL BLDG PRD UNFIRD NES	W 2840	1215	W 4002	1389	W 4905	1577	W 1390	425	MAT CONST AMIANTE–CIMENT
66183	ASBESTOS–,FIBRE–CMNT PRD	W 2374	862	W 3590	1029	W 4687	1378	W 1340	384	OUVRAGES AMIANTE–CIMENT
662	CLAY,REFRACTORY BLDG PRD	W 4972	2800	W 2613	1444	W 2086	1121	W 898	329	MAT CONST REFRACTAIRES
6624	BRICKS ETC NONREFRACTORY	W 4856	2592	W 2580	1352	W 1990	979	W 816	307	BRIQUES ETC CERAM NON REFR
67	IRON AND STEEL		16413		8624		10610		2412	FER ET ACIER
672	IRON,STEEL PRIMARY FORMS	W 9747	5537	W 477	154		69		48	LINGOTS FER,ACIER
6725	IRN,STL BLOOMS,SLABS,ETC	W 4618	1767	W 81	43		2			BLOOMS,BILLETTES FER ACIER
67251	IRN,SMPLE STL BLOOMS,ETC	W 4618	1767	W 81	43					BLOOMS ETC NON ACIER FIN
6727	IRN,STL COIL FR REROLLNG	W 5128	3769	W 396	111		67	W 106	48	EBAUCHES POUR TOLES FER
67271	IRON,SIMPLE STEEL COILS	W 5128	3769	W 396	111		67	W 106	48	EBAUCHES NON EN ACIER
673	IRON,STEEL SHAPES ETC	W 7106	3302	W 6087	2183		2611		805	BARRES,PROFIL FER,ACIER
6732	IRON,STEEL BARS ETC	W 6291	2810	W 5212	1731		2120		729	BARRES FER,ACIER
67326	IRN,OTH STL BARS HOTROLD	W 5883	2604	W 103	71	W 3104	1232	W 2865	648	BARRES PLEINES FER,ACIER
67327	IRN, OTH STL BARS FORGED	W 407	197	W 4322	1359		865		81	BARRES FORGEES CREUSES
674	IRN,STL UNIV,PLATE,SHEET	W 2806	2694	W 4509	3391		5167		786	LARGES PLATS,TOLES
6747	TINNED PLATES,SHEETS			W 209	373	W 2825	2432	W 87	151	TOLES ETAMEES EN ACIER
6749	OTH IRN,STL PLATES,SHEET	W 718	1166	W 1882	1495		2151			AUTRES TOLES FER,ACIER
67491	— OF IRON OR SIMPLE STL	W 702	1105	W 1867	1479	W 3314	2121			AUT TOLES AUTRES ACIER FIN
678	IRON,STL TUBES,PIPES,ETC	W 1094	1582	W 1769	1973		996		334	TUBES,TUYAUX EN FONTE,FER
68	NON–FERROUS METALS		1605		2483		1092		161	METAUX NON FERREUX
69	METAL MANUFACTURES NES		16820		10176		9456		2685	ART MANUFACT EN METAL NDA
691	STRUCTURES AND PARTS NES	W 1803	4048	W 1218	1851	W 1443	1265	W 48	137	CONSTRUCT FER,ACIER,ALU
6911	STRUCTURES,PARTS IRN,STL	W 1659	3513	W 1083	1424	W 1389	1052	W 19	73	CONSTRUCT FER,ACIER,FONTE
692	METAL TANKS,BOXES,ETC	W 671	2144	W 1001	911		568		218	RECIPIENTS METALLIQUES
694	STL,COPPR NAILS,NUTS,ETC	W 570	1544	W 307	1247		1317		341	CLOUS,VIS,ECROUS
697	BASE MTL HOUSEHOLD EQUIP	W 3007	3650	W 4063	1663		1675		878	ART MENAGE MET COMMUNS
6974	BASE MTL DMSTC ARTIC NES	W 1280	2514	W 3929	1368		1424		811	ARTICLES NDA FONTE,FER,ETC
69741	— OF IRON OR STEEL	W 1208	2363	W 3873	1279	W 1356	1312		786	ART NDA EN FONTE,FER
699	BASE METAL MFRS NES	W 847	3063	W 631	2142		3118		555	ART MANUFACTURES MET NDA
7	MACHINES,TRANSPORT EQUIP		131164		125544		98597		39017	MACHINES MATERIEL TRANSPORT
71	POWER GENERATING EQUIPMT		4431		9267		3341		1114	MACHINES GENERATRICES
713	INTRNL COMBUS PSTN ENGIN	W 289	2369	W 231	1513		1516		270	MOTEURS EXPL COMB INT, PIECE
7139	PISTON ENGINE PARTS NES	W 62	1883	W 55	890		929	W 4	200	PIECES POUR 713.2,3,8
716	ROTATING ELECTRIC PLANT	W 144	1890	W 439	7595		1537		750	APP ELECTR ROTATIFS,PIECES
7162	AC MTRS,GENRTRS,GEN SETS	W 61	642	W 363	6534		465		467	MOTEURS ELECTRIQUES
71623	GEN SETS WITH PISTN ENGN	W 46	468	W 336	6151		126	W 82	243	GROUPES MOTEUR EXPLOSION
72	MACHS FOR SPCL INDUSTRYS		13049		14465		11345		2951	MAC SPECIALES POUR INDUST
722	TRACTORS NON–ROAD	W 187	992	W 660	3241		902	W 85	212	TRACTEURS
7223	TRACK–LAYING TRACTORS	W 83	513	W 546	2862	W 49	188	W 3	1	TRACTEURS A CHENILLES
723	CIVIL ENGNEERG EQUIP ETC	W 754	4500	W 389	2159		4159		118	APPAREILS DE GENIE CIVIL
7234	CONST,MINING MACHNRY NES	W 518	1797	W 352	1756		2778	W 3	7	MACH POUR LA CONST, MINES
7239	CONSTR ETC MACHY PTS NES	W 236	2683	W 37	403	W 120	1245		99	PIECES 723.41–723.46
724	TEXTILE,LEATHER MACHNRY	W 353	1270	W 392	2095		1967		848	MACH POUR INDUSTRIE TEXTILE
7244	SPINNING,EXTRDNG,ETC MCH	W 23	570	W 55	986		1209		663	MACH POUR LE FILAGE
72449	PTS NES OF MACHS OF 7244	W 23	569	W 52	969		1209		663	PIECES DES MACH DU 724.4
727	FOOD MACHRY NON–DOMESTIC	W 331	962	W 582	3756		770		408	MACH INDUSTRIES ALIMENT
7271	GRAIN WORKING MCHY,PARTS	W 290	509	W 386	3522	W 298	712	W 283	385	MACH POUR MINOTERIE,PIEC
72711	GRAIN MILLING ETC MACHRY	W 274	452	W 379	3478	W 268	620	W 260	295	MACHINES POUR MINOTERIE
728	OTH MACHY FOR SPCL INDUS	W 581	3633	W 185	2437		2671		702	AUT MACH IND PARTICULIERES
7283	OTHR MINERAL WORKG MACHY	W 450	2310	W 72	1559		1874	W 37	251	MACH TRIER,CRIBLER,BROYER
73	METALWORKING MACHINERY		1062		661		387		565	MACH TRAVAIL DES METAUX
74	GENRL INDUSTRL MACHY NES		20215		17628		13506		4322	MACH APP INDUSTRIE

4. Special Imports C.I.F. by Commodities according to the S.I.T.C. (Rev. 2) in thousand U.S. Dollars
Importations Spéciales C.A.F. par Produits d'après la C.T.C.I. (Rév. 2) en milliers de Dollars E.U.

SITC CTCI	COMMODITY	1990		1991		1992		1993		PRODUIT
		WEIGHT POIDS	VALUE VALEUR	WEIGHT POIDS	VALUE VALEUR	WEIGHT POIDS	VALUE VALEUR	WEIGHT POIDS	VALUE VALEUR	
741	HEATING,COOLING EQUIPMNT	W 254	2625	W 210	1905		1286		719	MACH CHAUFFAGE,PIECES
7415	AIR–CONDITIONING MACHNRY	W 197	1952	W 158	1288		986		529	GROUPES CONDITION AIR
742	PUMPS FOR LIQUIDS ETC	W 94	1795	W 130	1666		1395		1062	POMPES MOTO–POMPES
7428	OTHER PUMPS FOR LIQUIDS	W 43	960	W 71	1253		945	W 66	934	AUTRES POMPES POUR LIQ
74288	PUMPS FR LIQUIDS NES ETC	W 24	470	W 60	924		692	W 61	781	POMPES POUR LIQUIDES NDA
743	PUMPS NES,CENTRFUGES ETC	W 184	3676	W 133	2024		1960		681	POMPES COMPRES,VENT ETC
744	MECHANICAL HANDLING EQU	W 717	5708	W 843	4707		2515		302	EQUIP MANUTENTION PIECES
7441	FORK LIFT TRCKS,ETC,PTS	W 264	2041	W 163	916		113	W 6	11	CHARIOTS POUR USINES ETC
7442	LIFTING,LOADING MACH NES	W 323	1883	W 348	1847		796		231	APP LEVAGE,MANUTENTION
74428	OTH HANDLING ETC MCH NES	W 95	677	W 274	1453		629		177	AUT APP LEVAGE ETC
7449	PTS NES OF MACHY OF 7442	W 130	1785	W 331	1943	W 172	1606		61	PIECES DU 744.2
745	NONELEC MACHY,TOOLS NES	W 100	1159	W 108	2451		1312		1128	AUT MACH NON ELEC,PIECES
7452	OTH NONELEC MCHS,PTS NES	W 92	1037	W 106	2394		1283		1127	AUT MACH NON ELEC,PIECES
74522	PACKAGNG,BOTTLNG,ETC MCH	W 23	113	W 71	1373		798	W 5	443	MACH NETT BOUTEILLES,ETC
749	NONELEC MACH PTS,ACC NES	W 343	5252	W 285	4876		5036		429	PIECES MACH NON ELEC NDA
7491	BALL,ROLLER,ETC BEARINGS	W 60	1077	W 89	1293		1366		137	ROULEMENTS BILLES ETC
7493	SHAFT,CRANK,PULLEY ETC	W 116	2365	W 109	2369		2782		113	ARBRES TRANS,VILEBREQUINS
75	OFFICE MACHNES,ADP EQUIP		6245		4824		4438		1940	MACH BUREAU TRAIT AUTOM
752	AUTOMTIC DATA PROC EQUIP	W 38	3932	W 29	2438		2428		1275	MACH TRAIT INFORMATION
7528	OFF–LINE DATA PROC EQUIP	W 17	1686	W 12	1086	W 26	1193	W 13	863	MACH AUXIL TRAIT INFORM
76	TELECOMM,SOUND EQUIPMENT		11755		16662		5601		4332	EQUIPMENT DE TELECOM
761	TELEVISION RECEIVERS	W 368	3435	W 309	2121	W 288	1740	W 146	752	RECEPTEURS DE TELEVISION
7611	COLOUR TV RECEIVERS	W 368	3435	W 187	1683	W 176	1335	W 81	593	RECEPTEURS COULEUR
762	RADIO BROADCAST RECEIVRS	W 202	4392	W 190	596	W 72	354	W 44	107	RECEPTEURS RADIODIFFUSION
7622	PORTABLE RADIO RECEIVERS	W 183	3095	W 41	41	W 6	112	W 30	73	RECEPT PORTATIFS RADIO
763	SOUND RECORDRS,PHONOGRPH	W 38	758	W 52	584		360		1342	PHONO,APP ENREGISTREMENT
7638	OTHR SOUND APPARATUS ETC	W 34	722	W 51	575		346		1328	AUT APP D'ENREGIS,REPROD
76388	DICTATING MACHINES ETC	W 19	396	W 30	169		131		1236	MACHINES A DICTER
764	TELECOM EQPT,PTS,ACC NES	W 74	3170	W 265	13361		3147		2131	EQUIP TELECOM,PIECES
7641	LINE TELEPHONE,ETC EQUIP	W 15	1220	W 199	11829		1687		644	APP TELEPHON PAR FIL
7643	TV,RADIO TRANSMITTRS ETC	W 2	138	W 9	428		224		983	APP EMET TELE RADIO
77	ELECTRIC MACHNRY NES ETC		18038		16806		12439		5899	MACH APP ELECT NDA
772	SWITCHGEAR ETC,PARTS NES	W 122	2622	W 175	2618		2281		646	APP COUPURE,SECT ETC
7721	SWITCHGEAR ETC	W 117	2535	W 173	2562		2196		641	APP COUPURE,SECTIONMNT
773	ELECTR DISTRIBUTNG EQUIP	W 729	3170	W 867	4972		2699		954	EQUIPMT DISTRIBUTION ELECT
7731	INSULATED WIRE,CABLE ETC	W 690	2948	W 851	4918		2665		454	FILS,CABLES ISOLES ELECT
775	HOUSEHOLD TYPE EQUIP NES	W 521	2101	W 329	1434		1146		588	MACH,APP USAGE DOMESTQUE
778	ELECTRICAL MACHINERY NES	W 5230	8754	W 3816	5999		5473		3258	AUTRES MACH ELECT NDA
7781	BATTERIES,ACCUMULATORS	W 4984	6900	W 3675	4730		4481		2778	PILES ET ACCUMULATEURS
77811	PRIMARY BATTERIES,CELLS	W 4664	5789	W 3436	3716		3351		2338	PILES ELECTRIQUES,PIECES
78	ROAD VEHICLES		49637		41369		45048		16421	VEHICULES ROUTIERS
781	PASS MOTOR VEH EXC BUSES	W 4470	19454	W 3684	14476	W 4568	15504	W 2522	6156	AUTO TRANSPORT PERSONNES
782	LORRIES,SPCL MTR VEH NES	W 1468	6133	W 1226	4038	W 1530	4161		1506	VEHICULES SPECIAUX,MARCH
7821	LORRIES,TRUCKS	W 1333	5194	W 893	2276	W 1517	4091		404	VEHICULES TRANSP MARCHAND
7822	SPECIAL MOTOR VEHCLS NES	W 135	939	W 332	1762	W 13	70	W 89	1101	VEHICULES USAGES SPECIAUX
783	ROAD MOTOR VEHICLES NES	W 1361	5421	W 2071	6282	W 1720	5783	W 969	2683	VEHICULES ROUTIERS NDA
7831	BUSES	W 1009	4606	W 1648	4942	W 1197	4531	W 704	2352	VOITURES TRANSPORT COMMUN
7832	TRACTORS FOR TR–TRAILERS	W 352	815	W 423	1340	W 523	1252	W 265	331	TRACTEURS ROUTIERS
784	MOTOR VEH PRTS,ACCES NES	W 404	5700	W 343	4094	W 631	5094		814	PIECES 722,781,782,783
7849	OTHER MOTOR VEHCL PARTS	W 379	5399	W 322	3729	W 605	5031		803	PIECES 722,781,782,783
785	CYCLES,ETC MOTRZD OR NOT	W 927	3389	W 970	3660		3879		1230	MOTOCYCLES SCOOTERS
7851	MOTORCYCLES ETC	W 561	2168	W 747	2641	W 987	3311	W 242	950	MOTO VELO MOTEUR AUXIL
786	TRAILERS,NONMOTR VEH,NES	W 4847	9540	W 4517	8820	W 10226	10627	W 5836	4031	REMORQUES,CADRES,CONTAIN
7861	TRAILERS,TRANSP CONTAINR	W 4739	9155	W 3918	8348	W 9863	10264	W 5665	3902	REMORQUES TOUS VEHICULES
78613	CONTAINERS INC ROAD–RAIL	W 4469	8818	W 3821	8151	W 9645	9499	W 5577	3856	CADRES ET CONTAINERS
79	OTHR TRANSPORT EQUIPMENT		6732		3860		2492		1473	AUTRE MATERIEL TRANSPORT
792	AIRCRAFT ETC	W 27	6593	W 18	3254		1746		1439	APP NAVIGATION AERIENNE
7929	AIRCRAFT PARTS NES	W 27	6509	W 17	3242	W 6	1736		1438	PIECES DU 792
8	MISC MANUFACTURED GOODS		40416		28571		24501		17785	ART MANUFACTURES DIVERS
821	*FURNITURE,PARTS THEREOF	W 487	3200	W 404	1580		1268		411	MEUBLES ET PIECES
8219	FURNITURE AND PARTS NES	W 363	2378	W 299	1033	W 222	994	W 85	287	AUTRES MEUBLES ET PIECES
831	*TRAVEL GOODS,HANDBAGS	W 684	1690	W 557	906		915		543	ARTICLES DE VOYAGE ETC
84	CLOTHING AND ACCESSORIES		9663		7287		7111		6001	VETEMENTS
842	MENS OUTERWEAR NOT KNIT	W 550	2291	W 122	363		564		339	VET DESSUS POUR HOMMES
8429	— OTHER OUTER GARMENTS	W 474	2015	W 35	139		162		54	AUT VET DES HOM MAT TEX
845	OUTERWEAR KNIT NONELASTC	W 385	1437	W 265	962		1531		1588	VET DESSOUS,ACCES BONNET
8459	— OTHER,CLTHG ACCESRYS	W 378	1364	W 245	882		1009		1535	AUT VET DESSUS DE BONNE
84594	—— OF REGENERTD FIBRES	W 3	12				3	W 7	695	AUT VET DESSUS FIB ARTIF
846	UNDER GARMENTS KNITTED	W 1148	3100	W 1810	3978		2954		2810	SOUS VETS DE BONNETERIE
8462	— OF COTTON NON ELASTIC	W 222	793	W 1697	3655		1575	W 836	1759	SOUS–VET BONNET COTON
84629	—— OTHER	W 87	356	W 1642	3439		1236	W 763	1590	AUT SOUS–VET BONNET COTON
8463	— OF SYNTH FBR NONELAST	W 517	894	W 102	272		895	W 269	732	SOUS–VET BONNET FIB SYNT
84633	—— MENS NES	W 43	162			W 228	760	W 238	613	SOUS–VET BON FIB SYN
847	TEXTILE CLTHNG ACCES NES	W 204	1109	W 137	862		1197		333	ACCES VET MAT TEXT NDA
851	*FOOTWEAR	W 2881	6332	W 2065	3396		3417		5105	CHAUSSURES
85101	FOOTWEAR RUBBER,PLASTIC	W 1635	2291	W 1497	2312		2288		3440	CHAUS SEMELLES CAOUTCH
85102	FOOTWEAR LEATHER	W 1242	4007	W 518	1031		818		1508	CHAUS SEMELLES EN CUIR
87	PRECISION INSTRUMNTS NES		4246		3142		2806		1539	INSTRUM,APPAR SCIENT NDA
872	MEDICAL INSTRUMENTS NES	W 117	2036	W 254	1334		749		770	INSTR,APP MEDIC–CHIR NDA
87202	OTH MEDICAL INSTRUMENTS	W 115	2011	W 246	833	W 22	240		757	INSTRUM,APP MEDECINE
874	MEASURNG,CONTROLNG INSTR	W 60	1822	W 51	1308		1475		441	INSTRUMENTS DE MESURE
89	MISC MANUFCTRD GOODS NES		12967		10372		7481		3759	ART MANUFACTURES DIVERS
892	PRINTED MATTER	W 560	5642	W 247	3481		3073		1207	IMPRIMES
8921	PRINTED BOOKS,GLOBES,ETC	W 170	2315	W 90	1903		1915		508	LIVRES,BROCHURES,CARTES
89211	PRINTED BOOKS,PAMPHLETS	W 167	2298	W 87	1878	W 254	1911		502	LIVRES,BROCHURES
8928	PRINTED MATTER NES	W 283	2358	W 104	784	W 62	374		251	IMPRIMES NDA
893	ARTICLES OF PLASTIC NES	W 1134	3429		3048		2299		1018	OUVRAGES EN MAT DIVIS 58
8931	PLSTC PACKG CONTNRS,LIDS	W 101	342	W 448	1161	W 1768	1191		420	ART TRANSP EMBALLAGE ETC
8939	MISC PLASTIC ARTICLES	W 997	2910	W 493	1846		1057		580	ART DIVERS EN MAT DIV 58
89399	OTHR PLASTC ARTICLES NES	W 945	2711	W 420	1643		933		529	AUT OUV MAT DIV 58
894	TOYS,SPORTING GOODS,ETC	W 116	971	W 152	1402		227		705	VOITURES ENFANTS,JOUETS
8946	NON–MILITARY ARMS,AMMO			W 30	893		1		618	ARMES NON MILITAIRES
89463	HUNTNG,SPORTNG AMMUNTION			W 23	257			W 55	616	MUNITIONS
9	GOODS NOT CLASSD BY KIND		2733		3710		3990		462	ART TRANSACT NON CLASSES
951	*WAR FIREARMS,AMMUNITION	W 67	1273	W 115	3707		5		396	VEHIC BLINDES ARMES
95101	ARMORED FIGHTNG VEHICLES	W 3	211	W 82	1938	W 1	3	W 6	283	CHARS DE COMBAT
95104	SIDEARMS AND PARTS NES			W 32	1585					ARMES BLANCHES

5. Special Exports F.O.B. by Commodities according to the S.I.T.C. (Rev. 2) in thousand U.S. Dollars
Exportations Spéciales F.O.B. par Produits d'après la C.T.C.I. (Rév. 2) en milliers de Dollars E.U.

SITC CTCI	COMMODITY	1990 WEIGHT POIDS	1990 VALUE VALEUR	1991 WEIGHT POIDS	1991 VALUE VALEUR	1992 WEIGHT POIDS	1992 VALUE VALEUR	1993 WEIGHT POIDS	1993 VALUE VALEUR	PRODUIT
	ALL COMMODITIES		267911		253228		274961		136024	TOUS PRODUITS
0	FOOD AND LIVE ANIMALS		57285		43612		63592		26137	ALIMENTS,ANIMAUX VIVANTS
001	*LIVE ANIMALS FOR FOOD	W 3	7			W 5	16	W 3290	648	ANIMAUX VIVANTS
0011	BOVINE SPECIES,LIVE							W 3290	648	ESPECE BOVINE
03	FISH AND PREPARATIONS		813		557		499		614	POISSONS ET PREPARATIONS
036	SHELL FISH FRESH,FROZEN	W 163	773	W 94	525	W 113	447		414	CRUSTACES,MOLLUSQUES
04	CEREALS AND PREPARATIONS		17289		9233		19077		2429	CEREALES ET PRODUITS
041	WHEAT ETC UNMILLED	W 938	353	W 9693	2237	W 42505	11513			FROMENT,EPEAUTRE
0411	DURUM WHEAT UNMILLED	W 878	338	W 9693	2237	W 42505	11513			FROMENT DUR NON MOULU
042	RICE	W 12669	3639	W 399	145	W 252	58			RIZ
0422	RICE SEMI-MILLED,MILLED	W 12669	3639	W 399	145	W 251	58			RIZ POLI,GLACE INCL BRISURES
04221	RICE MILLED UNBROKEN	W 12634	3634	W 399	145	W 251	58			RIZ POLI,GLACE EXCL BRISURES
046	WHEAT ETC MEAL OR FLOUR	W 22173	12306	W 16094	6826	W 18018	7442	W 1677	2141	SEMOULE FARINE,FROMENT
04601	FLOUR OF WHEAT OR MESLIN	W 22173	12306	W 16094	6826	W 18018	7442	W 1677	2141	FARINE DE FROMENT
07	COFFEE,TEA,COCOA,SPICES		33541		20626		29033		16039	CAFE,THE,CACAO,EPICES
071	COFFEE AND SUBSTITUTES	W 14330	17809	W 9290	9050		17970		10595	CAFE ET SUCCEDANES
0711	COFFEE GREEN,ROASTED,SUB	W 14330	17809	W 9290	9050	W 19	17967	W 13100	10592	CAFE TORREFIE OU DECAFEINE
07111	COFFEE GREEN,HUSKS,SKINS	W 14330	17809	W 9290	9050	W 19	17967	W 13099	10587	CAFE NON TORREFIE
072	COCOA	W 7820	15185	W 6279	10966	W 6142	10181	W 5446	5140	CACAO
0721	COCOA BEANS,RAW,ROASTED	W 7820	15185	W 6279	10966	W 6142	10181	W 5446	5140	CACAO EN FEVES
075	SPICES	W 124	525	W 200	570	W 254	881		304	EPICES
0752	SPICES,EX PEPPER,PIMENTO	W 44	351	W 155	430	W 250	871	W 118	304	AUTRES EPICES
081	*FEEDING STUFF FOR ANIML	W 32958	3107	W 28119	2329		2887	W 16539	1713	NOURRITURE POUR ANIMAUX
0813	OILCAKE AND OTH RESIDUES	W 15720	2487	W 15116	1740		2517	W 13019	1564	TOURTEAUX
08133	— OF COTTON SEEDS	W 15720	2487	W 15116	1740	W 4516	2501	W 13019	1564	TOURTEAUX DE COTON
09	MISC EDIBLE PRODUCTS		1626		9981		10886		4169	PREP ALIMENTAIRES DIVERSES
091	MARGARINE AND SHORTENING	W 7	4	W 653	729	W 708	905	W 591	449	MARGARINE ET GRAISSES
0914	MARGARINE,EDIBLE FAT NES	W 7	4	W 653	729	W 708	905	W 591	449	MARGARINES,SIMILI SAINDOUX
09149	OTH PREPARED EDIBLE FATS			W 653	729	W 708	905	W 591	449	SIMILI-SAINDOUX
098	EDIBLE PRODCTS,PREPS NES	W 797	1622	W 5476	9253		9982		3720	PREP ALIMENTAIRES NDA
09805	SOUPS AND BROTHS	W 624	1261	W 5385	9090	W 4938	9670	W 2145	3560	SOUPES,POTAGES,BOUILLONS
1	BEVERAGES AND TOBACCO		424		177		887		279	BOISSONS ET TABACS
2	CRUDE MATERLS,EXCL FUELS		178942		186626		185279		96517	MAT BRUTES NON COMESTIBLES
22	OIL SEEDS,OLEAGINOUS FRT		1801		386		1028		137	GRAINES,FRUITS OLEAGINEUX
223	SEEDS FOR OTH FIXED OILS	W 5786	1801	W 1241	383	W 4441	1028	W 1112	137	GRAINES AUTRES HUILES FIXES
2232	PALM NUTS AND KERNELS	W 4759	1469			W 1850	105			NOIX,AMANDES DE PALMISTE
26	TEXTILE FIBRES AND WASTE		55652		60437		57577		50710	FIBRES TEXTILES
263	COTTON	W 33289	55586	W 35832	55447	W 38577	55790		47065	COTON
2631	RAW COTTON,EXCL LINTERS	W 33260	55582	W 35643	55216	W 38577	55790	W 42342	47065	COTON EN MASSE
266	SYNTHETIC FIBRES TO SPIN			W 1781	2963			W 2181	3169	FIBRES SYNTHETIQUES
2666	CONTIN FILAMNT TOW SYNTH			W 1781	2963			W 2181	3169	CABLES POUR DISCONTINUS
26662	— OF POLYESTER FIBRES			W 1781	2963			W 2181	3169	DE FIBRES EN POLYESTERS
269	WASTE OF TEXTILE FABRICS	W 60	66	W 228	1964	W 205	1787	W 53	475	FRIPERIE DRILLES,CHIFFONS
26901	BULK TEXT WSTE,OLD CLTHG	W 60	66	W 228	1964	W 205	1787	W 53	475	ART ET ACCESS D'HABILLEMENT
27	CRUDE FERTLZR,MINRLS NES		119551		124657		126345		44592	ENGRAIS MINERAUX BRUTS
271	FERTILIZERS,CRUDE	W 2560625	119145	W 3114911	122790	W 2835000	125614	W 1435000	44548	ENGRAIS BRUTS
2713	NAT CALCM PHOSPHATES ETC	W 2560625	119145	W 3114911	122790	W 2835000	125614	W 1435000	44548	PHOSPHATES DE CALCIUM
27131	— UNGROUND	W 2560625	119145	W 3114911	122790	W 2835000	125614	W 1435000	44548	PHOSPHATES NON MOULUS
278	OTHER CRUDE MINERALS	W 7442	231	W 58297	1798		569	W 732	23	AUTRES MINERAUX BRUTS
2785	QUARTZ,MICA,FELSPAR,ETC			W 52223	1597					QUARTZ,MICA,FELDSPATH
27852	MICA,MICA WASTE			W 52223	1597					MICA
29	CRUDE ANIMAL,VEG MAT NES		1814		1060		230		1073	MATIERES BRUTES ANIM,VEGET
291	CRUDE ANIMAL MTRIALS NES	W 3	1					W 566	1073	MATIERES BRUTES ANIMALES
2919	OTH ANIMAL MATERIALS NES							W 566	1073	MAT ORIGINE ANIMALE NDA
29192	BRUSH-MAKING HAIR,ETC							W 266	692	SOIES DE PORC
292	CRUDE VEG MATERIALS NES	W 611	1813	W 455	1060		229			MAT BRUTES VEGETALES NDA
2924	VEG USED IN PHARMACY ETC	W 492	1533							PLANTES MEDICINALES
2925	SEEDS,ETC FOR PLANTING			W 349	876					SEMENCES NDA
3	MINERAL FUELS ETC		70		5942		467		361	COMBUSTIBLES MINERAUX LUB
33	PETROLEUM AND PRODUCTS		10		5825		442		360	PETROLE ET DERIVES
334	PETROLEUM PRODUCTS,REFIN	W 28	10	W 21013	5817	W 2089	414	W 1950	360	PRODUITS RAFFINES
3341	GASOLINE,OTH LIGHT OILS			W 21013	5816					ESSENCES POUR MOTEURS
33419	OTH LIGHT PETROLEUM OILS			W 21013	5816					AUTRES HUILES LEGERES
4	ANIMAL,VEGETABLE OIL,FAT		1998		674		2847		212	HUILES,GRAISSES ANIM,VEG
42	FIXED VEGETABLE OIL,FAT		1996		674		2847		182	HUILES VEGETALES FIXES
424	FIXED VEG OIL NONSOFT	W 1079	1314	W 271	153		2845	W 190	126	AUTRES HUILES VEG FIXES
4249	FIXED VEGETABLE OILS NES	W 1077	1312	W 20	3	W 213	2239	W 1	1	HUILES VEGET FIXES NDA
5	CHEMCLS,RELATED PROD NES		1022		2740		5813		1687	PRODUITS CHIMIQUES
58	PLASTIC MATERIALS ETC		443		2138		4941		1500	MAT PLAST ARTIFICIELLES
582	PROD OF CONDENSATION ETC	W 197	230	W 1086	873	W 1300	887		194	PROD CONDENS,POLYCOND
5826	EPOXIDE RESINS	W 197	230	W 1076	838	W 1221	805	W 272	194	RESINES EPOXYDES
58261	— IN PRIMARY FORMS	W 197	230	W 1076	838	W 1221	805	W 272	194	EPOXYDES PRIMAIRES
583	POLYMERIZATION ETC PRODS	W 96	212	W 633	1243		1407	W 527	1298	PROD POLYMERISATION
5839	OTH POLYMRZTION ETC PROD	W 1	3	W 554	1151	W 276	927	W 369	1192	AUT PROD POLYMER COPOLYM
6	BASIC MANUFACTURES		19490		7744		6834		2593	ART MANUFACTURES
64	PAPER,PAPERBOARD AND MFR		1509		1299		1345		932	PAPIERS,CARTONS & OUVRAGES
642	PAPER,ETC,PRECUT,ARTS OF	W 863	1506	W 1291	1292		1312		913	PAP,CARTONS DECOUPES
6421	PAPER ETC CONTAINERS	W 847	1457	W 1186	1184	W 694	1080	W 504	754	BOITES,SACS EMBALLAGES
65	TEXTILE YARN,FABRICS,ETC		6480		1078		627		813	FILS,TISSUS,ARTICLES TEXTILE
658	TEXTILE ARTICLES NES	W 4419	5685	W 560	544		44		458	ART FACONNES MAT TEXTILES
6581	BAGS,SACKS OF TEXTILES	W 4416	5677	W 552	486			W 545	390	SACS EMBALLAGE TEXTILES
66	NONMETAL MINERAL MFS NES		6986		3032		4077		420	ART MIN NON METALLIQUES
661	LIME,CEMENT,BLDG PRODS	W 125484	6906	W 68949	3008	W 86129	4030	W 8372	362	CHAUX,CIMENTS MAT CONSTR
6612	CEMENT	W 125480	6901	W 68926	3003	W 86107	4015	W 8372	362	CIMENTS HYDRAULIQUES
67	IRON AND STEEL		3481		765		122		25	FER ET ACIER
673	IRON,STEEL SHAPES ETC	W 1987	1455	W 98	14	W 6	24			BARRES,PROFIL FER,ACIER
6732	IRON,STEEL BARS ETC	W 1933	1417	W 1	4	W 1	14			BARRES FER,ACIER
67326	IRN,OTH STL BARS HOTROLD	W 1933	1417							BARRES PLEINES FER,ACIER
674	IRN,STL UNIV,PLATE,SHEET	W 1548	1904	W 245	370	W 10	10	W 19	3	LARGES PLATS,TOLES
6746	IRN,STL THIN PLATE,ROLLD	W 1037	1167					W 19	3	TOLES LAM MOINS 3MM
67461	— OF IRON OR SIMPLE STL	W 1037	1167					W 19	3	TOL NON AC FIN MOINS 3 MM
69	METAL MANUFACTURES NES		607		1361		462		199	ART MANUFACT EN METAL NDA
693	WIRE PRODUCTS NON ELECTR			W 930	996	W 14	5	W 155	149	OUVRAGES FILS METALLIQUES
6935	METAL FENCING,GAUZE,ETC			W 926	990	W 14	5	W 155	149	TOILES EN FER,ACIER,CUIVRE
69351	IRN,STL FENCNG,GAUZE ETC			W 926	990	W 14	5	W 155	149	TOILES EN FER,ACIER
7	MACHINES,TRANSPORT EQUIP		1828		2582		5554		4558	MACHINES MATERIEL TRANSPORT
72	MACHS FOR SPCL INDUSTRYS		629		270		393		2491	MAC SPECIALES POUR INDUST
723	CIVIL ENGNEERG EQUIP ETC	W 162	416	W 18	183		311	W 154	791	APPAREILS DE GENIE CIVIL
7234	CONST,MINING MACHNRY NES	W 156	406	W 15	178		256	W 133	674	MACH POUR LA CONST, MINES
728	OTH MACHY FOR SPCL INDUS	W 44	59	W 5	14	W 2	45	W 251	1436	AUT MACH IND PARTICULIERES
7283	OTHR MINERAL WORKG MACHY	W 19	26	W 4	12			W 234	1307	MACH TRIER,CRIBLER,BROYER

5. Special Exports F.O.B. by Commodities according to the S.I.T.C. (Rev. 2) in thousand U.S. Dollars
Exportations Spéciales F.O.B. par Produits d'après la C.T.C.I. (Rév. 2) en milliers de Dollars E.U.

SITC CTCI	COMMODITY	1990		1991		1992		1993		PRODUIT
		WEIGHT POIDS	VALUE VALEUR	WEIGHT POIDS	VALUE VALEUR	WEIGHT POIDS	VALUE VALEUR	WEIGHT POIDS	VALUE VALEUR	
72834	MINRL MOULDING ETC MACHY	W 8	5					W 70	599	MACH AGGLO CIMENT ETC
72839	PTS NES OF MACHY OF 7283							W 163	697	PIECES MACH DU 728.3
76	TELECOMM,SOUND EQUIPMENT		159		330		2161		165	EQUIPMENT DE TELECOM
761	TELEVISION RECEIVERS	W 26	146	W 27	241	W 46	1066	W 15	125	RECEPTEURS DE TELEVISION
763	SOUND RECORDRS,PHONOGRPH		2	W 4	38		881			PHONO,APP ENREGISTREMENT
7638	OTHR SOUND APPARATUS ETC		2	W 4	38		881			AUT APP D'ENREGIS,REPROD
76388	DICTATING MACHINES ETC			W 4	34		881			MACHINES A DICTER
78	ROAD VEHICLES		450		1206		1358		1276	VEHICULES ROUTIERS
782	LORRIES,SPCL MTR VEH NES	W 1	1	W 60	139	W 54	452	W 98	440	VEHICULES SPECIAUX,MARCH
8	MISC MANUFACTURED GOODS		2014		3131		3643		3666	ART MANUFACTURES DIVERS
821	*FURNITURE,PARTS THEREOF	W 17	64	W 82	479		1181		1238	MEUBLES ET PIECES
8212	MED FURN,STUFFD FURNSHGS			W 6	7		35	W 75	862	MOB MEDICO–CHIRUR,PIECES
82121	MEDICAL FURNITURE,PARTS			W 6	7	W 3	35	W 68	855	MOBILIER MED,TABLE OPER ETC
8219	FURNITURE AND PARTS NES	W 11	38	W 70	409	W 147	1122		371	AUTRES MEUBLES ET PIECES
82192	WOOD FURNITURE NES	W 10	36	W 67	384	W 137	1093		266	MEUBLES NDA EN BOIS
84	CLOTHING AND ACCESSORIES		992		426		393		1242	VETEMENTS
842	MENS OUTERWEAR NOT KNIT	W 78	816	W 28	124		44			VET DESSUS POUR HOMMES
843	WOMENS OUTERWEAR NONKNIT	W 4	22	W 2	7		36	W 126	1107	VET DESSUS FEMMES MAT TEX
8439	— OTHER OUTER GARMENTS	W 1	5	W 2	7	W 5	21	W 126	1107	AUT VET DES FEM MAT TEXT
84399	—— OF OTHER FIBRES	W 1	5			W 3	13	W 120	1064	VET DES FEM NDA AUT FIBR
89	MISC MANUFCTRD GOODS NES		727		2102		1562		1128	ART MANUFACTURES DIVERS
893	ARTICLES OF PLASTIC NES	W 215	510	W 1145	1777		928		1014	OUVRAGES EN MAT DIVIS 58
8939	MISC PLASTIC ARTICLES	W 155	370	W 1142	1773	W 195	855		888	ART DIVERS EN MAT DIV 58
89399	OTHR PLASTC ARTICLES NES	W 155	370	W 1142	1773	W 195	855		888	AUT OUV MAT DIV 58
9	GOODS NOT CLASSD BY KIND		4839							ART TRANSACT NON CLASSES
931	*SPECIAL TRANSACTIONS		4825							TRANS.SPECIALES

1. HISTORICAL SERIES, 1960–1995 GENERAL TRADE, IMPORTS C.I.F., EXPORTS F.O.B.
SERIES HISTORIQUES, 1960–1995 COMMERCE GENERAL, IMPORTATIONS C.A.F., EXPORTATIONS F.O.B

YEAR ANNEE	VALUE IN MILLION PA'ANGA VALEUR EN MILLION PA'ANGA MERCHANDISE –MARCHANDISE IMPORTS	EXPORTS	GOLD –OR IMPORTS	EXPORTS	CONVERSION FACTORS U.S. CENTS PER PA'ANGA FACTEURS DE CONVERSION CENTS E.U. PAR PA'ANGA IMPORTS	EXPORTS	INDEX NUMBERS –INDICES QUANTUM IMPORTS	EXPORTS	UNIT VALUE VALEUR UNITAIRE IMPORTS	EXPORTS
1960	3.30	3.40			112.0000	112.0000				
1961	2.80	2.80			112.0000	112.0000				
1962	2.50	1.70			112.0000	112.0000				
1963	2.40	1.90			112.0000	112.0000				
1964	3.90	2.30			112.0000	112.0000				
1965	3.40	2.50			112.0000	112.0000				
1966	4.10	3.60			112.0000	112.0000				
1967	5.70	3.60			112.0000	112.0000				
1968	5.20	3.80			112.0000	112.0000				
1969	5.10	3.40			112.0000	112.0000				
1970	5.50	2.70			112.0000	112.0000				
1971	6.30	2.20			112.0000	112.0000				
1972	7.50	2.10			119.1000	119.1000				
1973	8.00	3.20			142.2690	142.2690				
1974	11.80	4.60			143.5400	144.4000				
1975	13.00	4.60			131.4840	131.4970				
1976	11.70	3.20			122.4950	122.2410				
1977	17.70	6.30			111.0240	110.8930				
1978	22.30	5.10			114.5410	114.7780				
1979	26.20	6.90			111.7600	111.4260				
1980	30.10	6.90			114.2140	114.0920				
1981	35.10	6.30			114.1400	114.1400				
1982	41.20	4.30			100.8997	101.1425				
1983	41.70	6.60			90.1371	89.8909				
1984	46.60	10.40			87.9600	87.9600				
1985	58.90	7.80			69.9997	70.1367				
1986	60.82	8.71			66.7995	66.6049				
1987	68.46	8.80			70.2228	69.7457				
1988	70.69	9.50			78.9162	79.5745				
1989	68.34	11.63			78.7337	78.7810				
1990	78.99	14.46			78.1020	77.7020				
1991	76.82	17.99			77.0898	76.7370				
1992	84.29	17.40			74.2620	73.4164				
1993	84.93	23.43			72.2432	71.9736				
1994	91.21	18.37			75.9378	76.9754				
1995	98.03	18.44			78.7142	78.8349				

2. IMPORTS BY BROAD ECONOMIC CATEGORY AND EXPORTS BY INDUSTRIAL ORIGIN. (PERCENTAGE OF TOTAL VALUE)
IMPORTATIONS PAR CATEGORIES ECONOMIQUES ET EXPORTATIONS PAR BRANCHE D'ACTIVITE.(EN POURCENTAGE DE LA VALEUR TOTALE)

IMPORTS – IMPORTATIONS

	1990	1991	1992	1993	1994	1995	1996
TOTAL IMPORTS–IMPORTATIONS TOTALES	100.	100.	100.	100.	100.		
1 FOOD BEV–ALIMENTATION BOISSONS	24.9	23.2	23.3	25.2	26.5		
11 PRIMARY–PRODUITS DE BASE	6.8	6.4	6.8	7.8	7.2		
111 FOR INDUSTRY–POUR L'INDUSTRIE	0.3	0.4	0.3	0.4	0.5		
112 FOR HOUSEHOLDS–POUR LES MENAGES	6.5	6.0	6.5	7.3	6.7		
12 PROCESSED–PRODUITS ELABORES	18.1	16.8	16.5	17.4	19.3		
121 FOR INDUSTRY–POUR L'INDUSTRIE	4.1	3.9	3.9	3.6	3.8		
122 FOR HOUSEHOLDS–POUR LES MENAGES	14.0	12.9	12.6	13.9	15.5		
2 IND SUPPLIES–APPROV INDUSTRIELS	26.3	25.6	31.5	30.4	33.4		
21 PRIMARY–PRODUITS DE BASE	3.1	2.8	3.0	3.5	3.9		
22 PROCESSED–PRODUITS ELABORES	23.1	22.8	28.5	26.9	29.4		
3 FUELS–COMBUSTIBLES	13.2	15.8	12.7	13.6	12.0		
31 PRIMARY–PRODUITS DE BASE	0.6	0.7	0.8	0.8	0.8		
32 PROCESSED–PRODUITS ELABORES	12.6	15.1	11.9	12.8	11.2		
321 MOTOR SPIRIT–ESSENCE	3.6	4.6	3.3	4.6	4.4		
322 OTHER–AUTRES	9.0	10.4	8.6	8.2	6.8		
4 MACHINERY–EQUIPEMENT	8.9	8.3	10.6	10.9	7.3		
41 CAPITAL EQUIPMENT–MACHINES	7.3	7.5	9.0	8.4	6.1		
42 PARTS–PIECES ACCESSOIRES	1.5	0.8	1.6	2.5	1.3		
5 TRANSPORT–TRANSPORT	7.7	9.4	7.4	6.9	6.9		
51 PASSENGER CARS–AUTOMOBILES	2.1	2.0	1.1	1.1	1.2		
52 OTHER–AUTRES	3.4	4.8	4.3	2.9	3.5		
521 INDUSTRIAL–INDUSTRIELS	3.3	4.8	4.1	2.8	3.4		
522 NON INDUSTRIAL–NON INDUSTRIEL	0.1	0.1	0.1	0.1	0.1		
53 PARTS–PIECES ACCESSOIRES	2.2	2.6	2.0	2.9	2.2		
6 CONSUM GOODS–BIENS CONSOMMATION	17.6	17.1	14.1	12.7	13.4		
61 DURABLE–DURABLES	3.4	2.5	2.7	2.4	3.1		
62 SEMI DURABLE–SEMI DURABLES	7.5	8.0	5.9	5.6	5.3		
63 NON DURABLE–NON DURABLES	6.7	6.5	5.5	4.7	5.0		
7 GOODS NES–BIENS NDA	1.4	0.6	0.4	0.3	0.4		

EXPORTS – EXPORTATIONS

	1990	1991	1992	1993	1994	1995	1996
TOTAL EXPORTS–EXPORTATIONS TOTALES	100.	100.	100.	100.	100.		
1 AGRICULTURE	70.9	81.9	76.9	82.5	83.6		
2 MINING QUARRY–INDUS EXTRACTIVES			0.0	0.1	0.4		
3 MANUFACTURING–IND MANUFACTUR	29.1	18.1	23.1	17.4	16.0		
31 FOOD BEV TOBACCO–ALIM BOISS TAB	3.2	2.6	6.1	4.7	9.4		
32 TEXTILES–INDUSTRIES TEXTILES	16.1	9.5	10.4	5.4	1.9		
33 WOOD & PRODUCTS–BOIS & PRODUITS			0.0		0.1		
34 PAPER & PRODUCTS–PAPIER & PRODT		0.0	0.0	0.0	0.0		
35 CHEMICALS–INDUSTRIES CHIMIQUES		0.6	0.2	0.2	0.4		
36 NON METAL MIN–MIN NON METAL	0.4	0.0					
37 BASIC METAL–IND METAL BASE							
38 METAL MANUF–MANUF METAL	3.5	1.9	4.1	5.1	2.2		
39 OTH MANUF IND–AUTRES MANUF	5.9	3.5	2.2	1.9	2.0		

3. TRADE BY PRINCIPAL COUNTRIES OF PRODUCTION AND LAST CONSIGNMENT (VALUE IN THOUSAND U.S. DOLLARS)
ECHANGES SELON LES PRINCIPAUX PAYS DE PRODUCTION ET DE DERNIERE CONSIGNATION (VALEUR EN MILLIERS DE DOLLARS EU)

COUNTRIES–PAYS	GENERAL IMPORTS C.I.F. IMPORTATIONS GENERALES C.A.F				
	1990	1991	1992	1993	1994
World	61782	59321	62581	61577	69075
Africa				2	1
Americas	6848	6269	5770	5888	6046
Northern America	6802	5916	5197	5529	5717
LAIA	45	310	565	354	320
CACM					
Caribbean	1	7	8	5	9
Rest of America		36			
As.ex F.USSR	12903	9735	13846	7616	8913
Eur.x F.USSR	1197	1307	1723	2181	765
EU	1005	1300	1701	2161	720
EFTA	23	3	19	14	40
East Europe	170	2	3	6	5
Other Europe		3			
Former USSR	27	23	0		
Oceania	40807	41987	41242	45891	53351
New Zealand	20067	17548	18713	24227	30917
Australia/Australie	13384	15143	14866	13917	16938
Fiji/Fidji	7070	9202	7451	7282	5332
USA/Etats–Unis d'Amer	6794	5887	5172	5498	5674
Japan/Japon	4032	5351	7835	4279	4611
Singapore/Singapour	5259	873	342	580	817
China/Chine	931	1085	3259	699	1142
Hong Kong	1027	907	892	535	589
United Kingdom	698	589	924	1143	291
Germany/Allemagne	160	287	315	667	190
Thailand/Thaïlande	481	207	201	200	376
Korea, Republic of	220	313	269	313	283
Chile/Chili	27	191	516	339	300
Indonesia/Indonésie	64	44	253	282	441
Samoa	220	79	158	450	132
Pakistan	264	123	118	47	15
Malaysia/Malaisie	9	91	133	152	172
France,Monac	19	283	205	23	10
Italy/Italie	13	56	39	201	82
Sweden/Suède	26	23	92	27	57
Former GDR	170				
Canada	9	29	25	31	43
Denmark/Danemark	21	1	43	33	7
Former USSR/Anc. URSS	27	23			
Bangladesh		11	11		
Kiribati	1				8
Spain/Espagne	0			2	6
American Samoa				3	
Norway,SVD,JM		1	1	0	

COUNTRIES–PAYS	GENERAL EXPORTS F.O.B. EXPORTATIONS GENERALES F.O.B.				
	1990	1991	1992	1993	1994
Monde	11967	16494	12781	16896	14045
Afrique					6
Amériques	2807	2638	2297	2851	3357
Amérique du Nord	2807	2638	2297	2851	3357
ALAI					
MCAC					
Caraïbes					
Autre Amérique					
Asie l'URSS exclus	3819	9645	6607	9824	8228
Europe l'URSS exclus	211	259	45	139	53
UE	211	259	45	139	53
AELE			0		
Europe de l'Est	0				
Autre de l'Europe					
Ancienne URSS					
Océanie	5130	3953	3831	4083	2400
Japan/Japon	3817	9572	6539	9449	7140
USA/Etats–Unis d'Amer	2807	2638	2297	2850	3330
New Zealand	2511	1414	1391	2030	848
Australia/Australie	1913	1475	1434	1194	622
Samoa	482	612	668	713	541
Fiji/Fidji	195	421	299	120	287
Hong Kong	2	1	67	362	565
France,Monac	201	236		89	
Singapore/Singapour				0	275
United Kingdom	9	10	30	48	38
Kiribati	3	2		0	32
Canada				1	27
Italy/Italie		9	15		
Korea, Republic of		1		3	19
Malaysia/Malaisie		15		0	
Spain/Espagne					14
Germany/Allemagne		3			1
Sweden/Suède		1	0		0
Former GDR	0				

(VALUE AS PERCENTAGE OF WORLD TOTAL)(VALEURS EN POURCENTAGE DU TOTAL MONDIAL)

	1985	1986	1987	1988	1989	1990	1991	1992	1993	1994
Africa	0.1			0.0					0.0	0.0
Americas	0.0	3.9	5.1	7.8	11.6	11.1	10.6	9.2	9.6	8.8
Northern America		3.9	4.8	7.6	11.5	11.0	10.0	8.3	9.0	8.3
LAIA		0.0	0.2	0.2	0.1	0.1	0.5	0.9	0.6	0.5
CACM										
Caribbean	0.0	0.0	0.0			0.0	0.0	0.0	0.0	0.0
Rest of America							0.1			
As.ex F.USSR	7.7	17.8	17.3	20.3	23.2	20.9	16.4	22.1	12.4	12.9
Eur.x F.USSR	11.9	4.1	6.5	2.2	2.7	1.9	2.2	2.8	3.5	1.1
EU	10.7	4.1	6.4	2.2	2.6	1.6	2.2	2.7	3.5	1.0
EFTA	1.2	0.0	0.1	0.0	0.0	0.0	0.0	0.0	0.0	0.1
East Europe		0.0	0.0	0.0	0.0	0.3	0.0	0.0	0.0	0.0
Other Europe	0.0						0.0			
Former USSR	13.9		0.0		0.1	0.0	0.0	0.0		
Oceania	66.2	74.1	71.1	69.7	62.4	66.0	70.8	65.9	74.5	77.2
New Zealand	42.2	38.6	35.9	30.2	30.5	32.5	29.6	29.9	39.3	44.8
Australia/Australie		28.5	25.7	28.6	22.3	21.7	25.5	23.8	22.6	24.5
Fiji/Fidji	23.5	6.6	8.7	10.2	9.2	11.4	15.5	11.9	11.8	7.7
USA/Etats–Unis d'Amer		3.8	4.8	7.6	11.5	11.0	9.9	8.3	8.9	8.2
Japan/Japon	5.2	11.4	8.8	7.6	7.2	6.5	9.0	12.5	6.9	6.7
Singapore/Singapour		2.0	4.0	4.9	8.7	8.5	1.5	0.5	0.9	1.2
China/Chine		1.4	1.6	2.9	1.3	1.5	1.8	5.2	1.1	1.7
Hong Kong	1.1	1.1	1.0	1.6	1.9	1.7	1.5	1.4	0.9	0.9
United Kingdom	2.6	2.8	4.3	1.1	1.4	1.1	1.0	1.5	1.9	0.4
Germany/Allemagne	1.6	0.9	0.9	0.6	0.8	0.3	0.5	0.5	1.1	0.3

	1985	1986	1987	1988	1989	1990	1991	1992	1993	1994
Afrique										0.0
Amériques	0.0	17.1	16.2	29.2	22.8	23.5	16.0	18.0	16.9	23.9
Amérique du Nord		17.1	16.2	29.2	22.8	23.5	16.0	18.0	16.9	23.9
ALAI										
MCAC										
Caraïbes	0.0									
Autre Amérique										
Asie l'URSS exclus	2.7	0.4	5.4	4.9	16.7	31.9	58.5	51.7	58.1	58.6
Europe l'URSS exclus	4.7	3.2	0.2	0.5	0.2	1.8	1.6	0.4	0.8	0.4
UE	3.7	2.1	0.2	0.5	0.2	1.8	1.6	0.4	0.8	0.4
AELE	1.0	1.2						0.0		
Europe de l'Est						0.0				
Autre de l'Europe										
Ancienne URSS	30.5									
Océanie	62.0	79.3	77.0	65.4	60.4	42.9	24.0	30.0	24.2	17.1
Japan/Japon	0.7	0.2	1.6	4.4	16.4	31.9	58.0	51.2	55.9	50.8
USA/Etats–Unis d'Amer		16.5	14.7	29.0	22.7	23.5	16.0	18.0	16.9	23.7
New Zealand	57.3	41.0	40.1	33.0	31.9	21.0	8.6	10.9	12.0	6.0
Australia/Australie		28.1	26.2	18.2	21.9	16.0	8.9	11.2	7.1	4.4
Samoa	0.1	8.9	0.3	0.8	0.4	4.0	3.7	5.2	4.2	3.9
Fiji/Fidji	4.5	1.0	0.5	5.2	1.5	1.6	2.6	2.3	0.7	2.0
Hong Kong	0.6	0.1	0.0	0.0	0.0	0.0	0.0	0.5	2.1	4.0
France,Monac	0.1	0.1		0.0		1.7	1.4		0.5	
Singapore/Singapour					0.0				0.0	2.0
United Kingdom	1.4	1.7	0.0	0.3	0.0	0.1	0.1	0.2	0.3	0.3

4. General Imports C.I.F. by Commodities according to the S.I.T.C. (Rev. 2) in thousand U.S. Dollars
Importations Générales C.A.F. par Produits d'après la C.T.C.I. (Rév. 2) en milliers de Dollars E.U.

SITC CTCI	COMMODITY	1991		1992		1993		1994		PRODUIT
		WEIGHT POIDS	VALUE VALEUR	WEIGHT POIDS	VALUE VALEUR	WEIGHT POIDS	VALUE VALEUR	WEIGHT POIDS	VALUE VALEUR	
	ALL COMMODITIES # 1		59321		62581		61577		69075	TOUS PRODUITS
0	FOOD AND LIVE ANIMALS		12757		13495		14189		17043	ALIMENTS,ANIMAUX VIVANTS
01	MEAT AND PREPARATIONS		4911		5166		5982		6694	VIANDES ET PREPARATIONS
011	MEAT FRESH,CHILLD,FROZEN	W 3901	3097	W 4462	3435	W 4742	4029	W 5181	4091	VIANDES FRAICHES,REF,CONGE
0111	BOVINE MEAT FRESH,FROZEN	W 132	198	W 74	136	W 192	249	W 138	248	VIANDES BOVIN FRAI,REF
0112	MUTTON ETC FRSH,CHLD,FRN	W 2638	2011	W 3119	2275	W 3376	2703	W 3950	2662	VIANDE DE MOUTON
0114	POULTRY FRESH CHLLD,FRZN	W 1115	864	W 1204	940	W 1131	1010	W 1039	1108	VOLAILLES MORTES
014	MEAT PREPD,PRSVD,NES ETC		1684	W 587	1655	W 648	1895	W 804	2508	CONSERVES DE VIANDES
0149	OTH PREPARD,PRESRVD MEAT	W 514	1605	W 533	1581	W 599	1813	W 697	2332	AUTRES PREP DE VIANDES
02	DAIRY PRODCTS,BIRDS'EGGS		1098		1229		1373		1753	PRODUITS LAITIERS,OEUFS
022	MILK AND CREAM	W 436	587	W 582	631	W 625	730	W 766	967	LAIT ET CREME
0224	MILK,CREAM PRESERVED ETC	W 399	557	W 456	502	W 536	631	W 696	892	LAIT,CREME CONS,CONC
02241	WHEY	W 159	168	W 301	247	W 344	289	W 546	479	LACTOSERUM (PETIT LAIT)
02242	MILK DRY,1.5% FAT OR LES	W 240	388	W 155	255	W 192	342	W 150	413	LAIT POUDRE INF 1.5%
023	BUTTER	W 244	427	W 263	500	W 247	488	W 310	634	BEURRE
03	FISH AND PREPARATIONS		365		334		479		543	POISSONS ET PREPARATIONS
037	FISH ETC PREPD,PRSVD NES	W 243	278	W 165	209	W 273	376	W 399	455	POIS,CRUST,MOL PREPARES
0371	FISH PREPARD,PRESRVD NES					W 273	375	W 397	452	CONSERVES DE POISSONS
04	CEREALS AND PREPARATIONS		2806		3056		2545		3316	CEREALES ET PRODUITS
046	WHEAT ETC MEAL OR FLOUR	W 4902	1680	W 5388	1860	W 4387	1555	W 5265	1941	SEMOULE FARINE,FROMENT
04601	FLOUR OF WHEAT OR MESLIN					W 4386	1555	W 5264	1940	FARINE DE FROMENT
048	CEREAL ETC PREPARATIONS		993		1055		913		1221	PREPTNS A BASE CEREALES
0481	PREPD BREAKFAST FOOD ETC	W 86	209	W 260	200	W 117	84	W 171	144	CEREALES TRAVAILLEES
0483	MACARONI,SPAGHETTI ETC	W 103	171	W 172	240	W 161	243	W 200	331	PATES ALMENTAIRES
0484	BAKERY PRODUCTS		236		245		232		361	PRODUITS DE BOULANGERIE
0488	OTH CEREAL PREPS,MALT EX	W 258	377	W 140	370	W 130	354	W 123	386	EXTRAITS DE MALT
05	VEGETABLES AND FRUIT		646		736		739		1046	LEGUMES ET FRUITS
057	FRUIT,NUTS,FRESH,DRIED	W 80	98	W 138	147	W 148	147	W 234	220	FRUITS FRAIS OU SECS
058	FRUIT PRESERVED,PREPARED	W 238	276	W 292	311	W 281	317	W 408	527	CONSERVES DE FRUITS
0585	FRUIT OR VEGETABLE JUICE	W 103	123	W 175	176	W 178	185	W 294	362	JUS DE FRUITS
06	SUGAR AND PREPS,HONEY		1115		1007		1037		1183	SUCRES ET PRODUITS
061	SUGAR AND HONEY	W 2246	738	W 2370	756		683	W 2415	828	SUCRES ET MIEL
0612	REFINED SUGAR ETC	W 2229	720	W 2361	748	W 2142	671	W 2396	809	SUCRES RAFFINES
062	SUGAR CANDY NON–CHOCLATE	W 165	377	W 122	251	W 200	354	W 183	355	SUCRERIES
07	COFFEE,TEA,COCOA,SPICES		479		238		330		529	CAFE,THE,CACAO,EPICES
081	*FEEDING STUFF FOR ANIML		254		285		289		497	NOURRITURE POUR ANIMAUX
0819	FOOD WASTE AND FEED NES	W 517	200	W 615	219	W 571	199	W 672	234	DECHETS,ALIMENTS NDA
08193	BEET–PULP,BAGASSE,ETC	W 516	196	W 614	213	W 570	195	W 672	234	PULPES,AUTRES DECHETS
09	MISC EDIBLE PRODUCTS		1078		1434		1411		1472	PREP ALIMENTAIRES DIVERSES
091	MARGARINE AND SHORTENING	W 194	191	W 247	201	W 240	221	W 144	166	MARGARINE ET GRAISSES
0914	MARGARINE,EDIBLE FAT NES	W 193	190	W 247	201	W 237	218	W 143	164	MARGARINES,SIMILI SAINDOUX
098	EDIBLE PRODCTS,PREPS NES		888		1233		1191		1306	PREP ALIMENTAIRES NDA
09806	YEASTS,BAKING POWDERS	W 103	168	W 90	211	W 94	193	W 103	216	LEVURES
09809	MISC FOOD PREPRTIONS NES		602		865		846		871	PREP ALIMENTAIRES NDA
1	BEVERAGES AND TOBACCO		2411		2412		2755		3068	BOISSONS ET TABACS
11	BEVERAGES		1140		1204		1442		1643	BOISSONS
111	NON–ALCOHL BEVERAGES NES	W 1002	559	W 1066	600	W 1156	740	W 1181	798	BOISSONS NON ALCOOLIQUES
11101	WATERS,ICE AND SNOW	W 992	553	W 1057	596	W 1098	714	W 1140	779	EAU,EAUX MINERALES
112	ALCOHOLIC BEVERAGES	W 509	580	W 574	603	W 656	702	W 776	845	BOISSONS ALCOOLIQUES
1123	BEER,ALE,STOUT,PORTER	W 468	465	W 522	520	W 607	608	W 739	760	BIERES
12	TOBACCO AND MANUFACTURES		1272		1208		1313		1424	TABACS BRUTS FABRIQUES
122	TOBACCO,MANUFACTURED	W 99	1271	W 91	1208	W 99	1313	W 97	1424	TABACS FABRIQUES
1222	CIGARETTES	W 77	973	W 61	795	W 68	884	W 64	901	CIGARETTES
1223	OTH MANUFACTURED TOBACCO	W 21	298	W 29	413	W 30	430	W 34	524	TABACS FUMER,CHIQUER,PRISER
2	CRUDE MATERLS,EXCL FUELS		2794		2995		2746		3778	MAT BRUTES NON COMESTIBLES
21	HIDES,SKINS,FURS UNDRSSD		124		252		20		6	CUIRS,PEAUX BRUTS
211	HIDES,SKINS,EXC FURS,RAW	W 16	124	W 51	220	W 1	20	W 1	6	CUIRS ET PEAUX
2119	SKIN NES,WASTE,USED LTHR	W 16	124	W 51	220	W 1	20	W 1	6	CUIRS ET PEAUX NDA
21199	HIDES AND SKINS NES,RAW	W 16	124	W 51	220	W 1	20	W 1	6	CUIRS,PEAUX NDA
24	CORK AND WOOD		1516		1403		1425		1999	LIEGE ET BOIS
248	WOOD SHAPED,SLEEPERS		1487	W 3858	1367	W 3222	1245	W 4401	1857	BOIS SIMPLEMENT TRAVAILLES
26	TEXTILE FIBRES AND WASTE		280		304		278		285	FIBRES TEXTILES
269	WASTE OF TEXTILE FABRICS	W 312	243	W 231	295	W 183	264	W 187	285	FRIPERIE DRILLES,CHIFFONS
26902	RAGS,WASTE CORDAGE ETC					W 183	264			DRILLES ET CHIFFONS
27	CRUDE FERTLZR,MINRLS NES		223		345		338		361	ENGRAIS MINERAUX BRUTS
273	STONE,SAND AND GRAVEL	W 66	9	W 4119	223					PIERRES,SABLES,GRAVIERS
278	OTHER CRUDE MINERALS		141		113	W 780	291		331	AUTRES MINERAUX BRUTS
2789	MINERALS CRUDE NES		84		46	W 525	219		236	MINERAUX BRUTS NDA
27896	NATURAL ASPHALT,BITUMEN	W 434	78	W 68	42	W 525	219	W 494	236	BITUMES,ASPHALTES NATURELS
29	CRUDE ANIMAL,VEG MAT NES		492		637		602		1084	MATIERES BRUTES ANIM,VEGET
292	CRUDE VEG MATERIALS NES		492		637		602		1084	MAT BRUTES VEGETALES NDA
2925	SEEDS,ETC FOR PLANTING	W 33	461	W 24	581			W 118	1079	SEMENCES NDA
2929	OTH CRUDE VEG MATERIALS						581			MATIERES VEGETALES NDA
29298	OTH CRD VEG MATERIAL NES						501			PRODUITS ORIGINE VEGET NDA
3	MINERAL FUELS ETC		9381		7988		8373		8339	COMBUSTIBLES MINERAUX LUB
33	PETROLEUM AND PRODUCTS		9015		7563		7909		7805	PETROLE ET DERIVES
334	PETROLEUM PRODUCTS,REFIN		8945		7432	W 1758776	7895	W 29818	7764	PRODUITS RAFFINES
3341	GASOLINE,OTH LIGHT OILS	W 12670	4444	W 10843	3335	W 13334	3822	W 14479	3892	ESSENCES POUR MOTEURS
33411	MOTOR,AVIATION SPIRIT	W 8128	2752	W 6402	2035	W 9710	2815	W 11367	3051	ESSENCES MOTEURS D'AVIONS
33412	SPIRIT TYPE JET FUEL	W 4542	1692	W 4441	1300	W 3624	1008	W 3112	842	CARBUREACTEURS
3343	GAS OILS	W 13073	4144	W 13889	3775	W 12338	3270	W 15012	3567	GAS OILS
3344	FUEL OILS,NES					W 1732682	436			FUEL OILS
3345	LUBS,PETROLEUM OILS NES		358		321	W 421	367	W 326	305	HUILES LUBRIFIANTES
33451	LUBS(HIGH PETR CONT) ETC	W 376	341	W 409	317	W 414	359	W 321	297	HUILES LUBRIF,H LOURDES
341	*GAS,NATURAL AND MANUFCT	W 557	366	W 755	424	W 742	463	W 861	534	GAZ NATUREL,GAZ MANUFACT
3413	PETROLM GASES,LIQUEFIED	W 557	366	W 755	424	W 742	463	W 861	534	GAZ DE PETROLE LIQUEFIE
4	ANIMAL,VEGETABLE OIL,FAT		144		145		190		272	HUILES,GRAISSES ANIM,VEG
5	CHEMCLS,RELATED PROD NES		4804		3842		4330		5726	PRODUITS CHIMIQUES
51	ORGANIC CHEMICALS		205		34		25		56	PROD CHIMIQ ORGANIQUES
516	OTHER ORGANIC CHEMICALS		182		15		19		21	AUTRES PROD ORGANIQUES
5169	ORGANIC CHEMICALS,NES		182		15		19		21	PROD CHIM ORGANIQUES NDA
53	DYES,TANNING,COLOUR PROD		362		444		303		418	PROD TEINTURE,COLORANTS
533	PIGMENTS,PAINTS,ETC		356		437		287		405	PIGMENTS,PEINTURES,VERNIS
5335	GLAZES,DRIERS,PUTTY ETC		241		289		287		295	PREPTNS COLOR UTILISES CERAM
53351	PREPRD PIGMENT,GLAZE ETC						287			PIGMENTS OPACIFIANTS
541	*MEDICINAL,PHARM PRODUCT		1056		710		1286		1522	PROD MEDICINAUX PHARMACEUT
5411	PROVITAMINS AND VITAMINS		170		195				11	PROVITAMINES,VITAMINES
5419	PHARMACEUTICAL GOODS NES		886		514		1286		1511	PREP,ART PHARMACEUTIQUES
54199	OTH PHARMACEUTICAL GOODS						1286			AUT PREP PHARMACEUTIQUES
55	PERFUME,CLEANING ETC PRD		1236		1337		1251		1448	PROD POUR PARFUM,TOILETTE
553	PERFUMERY,COSMETICS,ETC		396		440		448		465	PRODUITS DE PARFUMERIE

4. General Imports C.I.F. by Commodities according to the S.I.T.C. (Rev. 2) in thousand U.S. Dollars
Importations Générales C.A.F. par Produits d'après la C.T.C.I. (Rév. 2) en milliers de Dollars E.U.

SITC CTCI	COMMODITY	1991 WEIGHT POIDS	1991 VALUE VALEUR	1992 WEIGHT POIDS	1992 VALUE VALEUR	1993 WEIGHT POIDS	1993 VALUE VALEUR	1994 WEIGHT POIDS	1994 VALUE VALEUR	PRODUIT
554	SOAP,CLEANSING ETC PREPS		833		889		803		948	SAVONS,PRODUITS DETERSIFS
5542	WASHING PREPARATIONS ETC	W 386	643	W 429	700	W 325	574	W 408	720	PROD ORG TENSIO–ACT NDA
562	*FERTILIZERS,MANUFACTURE	W 2354	595	W 1519	478	W 2685	605	W 3905	1274	ENGRAIS MANUFACTURES
5629	FERTILIZERS NES	W 2354	595	W 1519	478	W 2685	605	W 3905	1274	ENGRAIS NDA
58	PLASTIC MATERIALS ETC		317		244		250		247	MAT PLAST ARTIFICIELLES
585	PLASTIC MATERIAL NES		203		161		186		244	RESINES ARTIFICIELLES
5852	OTH ART PLASTIC MTLS NES						186			AUT MAT PLAST ARTIFICIEL
58529	OTH HIGH POLYMRS ETC,NES						186			AUT HAUTS POLYMERES
59	CHEMICAL MATERIALS NES		869		509		524		671	MAT PROD CHIMIQUES NDA
591	PESTICIDES,DISINFECTANTS		624		341				463	DESINF,INSECT,FONG,HERB
598	MISCEL CHEM PRODUCTS NES		96		62		366		71	PROD DIV INDUST CHIM NDA
5989	CHEM PRODUCTS,PREPS NES		1				325			PROD PREP CHIMIQUES NDA
59899	OTH CHEM PRODS,PREPS,NES						319			AUT PRODUITS CHIMIQUES NDA
6	BASIC MANUFACTURES		9194		14235		12038		13698	ART MANUFACTURES
61	LEATHER,DRESSED FUR,ETC		427		432		284		144	CUIRS,PELLETERIES
611	LEATHER		238		243		250		122	CUIRS,PEAUX PREPARES
6112	COMPOSITION LEATHER		129		222				101	CUIRS ARTIF,RECONS PLAQUES
6118	LEATHER SPECIALLY FINSHD						197			CUIRS,PEAUX TANNES
61181	CHAMOIS–DRESSED LEATHER						197			CUIRS,PEAUX CHAMOISES
62	RUBBER MANUFACTURES NES		223		349		319		369	CAOUTCHOUC MANUFACTURE
625	RUBBER TYRES, TUBES ETC	N 7997	175	N 16203	292	N 22918	271	N 18356	289	PNEUS CAOUTCHOUC VULCANISE
63	WOOD,CORK MANUFACTRS NES		665		1332		1118		1529	OUVRAGES LIEGE ET BOIS
634	VENEERS,PLYWOOD,ETC		482	V 1831	999	V 1670	766	V 1600	820	PLACAGES,CONTRE–PLAQUES
6341	VENEER SHEETS ETC		482	V 1831	999			V 1600	820	BOIS SIMPLEMENT SCIES
6344	WOOD–BASED PANELS NES					V 1670	766			PANNEAUX SUPPORT BOIS NDA
63443	CELLULAR WOOD PANELS					V 1670	766			PANNEAUX CELLULAIRES
635	WOOD MANUFACTURES NES		183		332		352		707	ART MANUF EN BOIS NDA
6353	BUILDERS WOODWRK,PREFABS		3		71		146		461	OUVRAGES DE MENUISERIE
64	PAPER,PAPERBOARD AND MFR		1969		1739		2312		2859	PAPIERS,CARTONS & OUVRAGES
641	PAPER AND PAPERBOARD		409		393		336		349	PAPIERS ET CARTONS
6412	PRINTG,WRITING PAPER NES		308		313		248		143	PAPIERS POUR L'IMPRESSION
642	PAPER,ETC,PRECUT,ARTS OF		1559		1347		1976		2509	PAP,CARTONS DECOUPES
6421	PAPER ETC CONTAINERS		813		539		1219		1566	BOITES,SACS EMBALLAGES
6423	EXERCISE BOOKS ETC		259		107				178	REGISTRES,CAHIERS,CARNETS
6424	PAPER ETC CT TO SIZE NES		480		690				730	PAP,CARTONS DECOUPES
6428	PAPER ETC ARTICLES NES						757			OUVRAGES EN PATE A PAPIER
64282	PUNCHED CARD MACH CARDS						757			CARTES POUR MACHINES
65	TEXTILE YARN,FABRICS,ETC		1202		1260		996		970	FILS,TISSUS,ARTICLES TEXTILE
651	TEXTILE YARN		238		106		50		43	FILS TEXTILES
6519	TEXTILE FIBRE YARN NES		238		106		50		43	FILS TEXT NDA FILE FIB VER
65199	VEG FIBRE YARN NES ETC		238		106		46		43	FILS AUT FIB TEXT VEG
652	COTTON FABRICS,WOVEN		178	A 147	198	A 205	296	A 180	222	TISSUS DE COTON
6521	GREY WOVEN COTTON FABRIC		168	A 138	178			A 177	217	TISSUS COT ECRUS NON MERCER
6522	WOVEN COTTON BLEACHD,ETC	A 6	11	A 9	20	A 205	296	A 3	5	TISSUS COTON BLANCHIS ETC
65221	COTTON GAUZE BLEACHD,ETC					A 204	288			TISSUS COTON POINT DE GAZE
654	OTH WOVEN TEXTILE FABRIC		316		433		219		220	TISSUS AUT COTON SYNT,ARTIF
6549	WOVEN FABRICS NES	A 8	17	A 2	5		219	A 2	4	TISSUS NDA
65499	PILE,CHENILLE FABRIC NES						219			VELOURS NDA
659	FLOOR COVERINGS,ETC		190		163		180		178	COUVRE–PARQUETS,TAPIS ETC
6591	LINOLEUM ETC	A 41	182	A 43	161	A 37	176	A 40	172	LINO COUVRE–PARQUETS
66	NONMETAL MINERAL MFS NES		1250		1781		1299		2086	ART MIN NON METALLIQUES
661	LIME,CEMENT,BLDG PRODS		683		1239		721		1215	CHAUX,CIMENTS MAT CONSTR
6612	CEMENT	W 7056	673	W 12750	1227	W 8471	707	W 9699	1165	CIMENTS HYDRAULIQUES
663	MINERAL MANUFCTURES NES		109		210		103		195	ART MIN MANUF NDA
6631	GRINDING STONES ETC		87		204		100		180	PIERRES A AIGUISER,MEULES
664	GLASS		285		180		209		282	VERRE
6649	GLASS NES						186			VERRE NDA
66494	GLASS FIBRE AND PROD NES						186			LAINE DE VERRE,FIBRES
67	IRON AND STEEL		711		4512		978		1076	FER ET ACIER
672	IRON,STEEL PRIMARY FORMS		215	W 112	58	W 319	205	W 574	344	LINGOTS FER,ACIER
6724	IRN,STL INGOTS,LUMPS,ETC		215	W 112	58	W 319	205	W 574	344	FER,ACIER LINGOTS,MASSES
673	IRON,STEEL SHAPES ETC		75		1055		335		328	BARRES,PROFIL FER,ACIER
678	IRON,STL TUBES,PIPES,ETC		374	W 4395	3330	W 561	421	W 465	360	TUBES,TUYAUX EN FONTE,FER
6785	IRON,STEEL TUBE FITTINGS		374	W 4395	3330	W 561	421	W 465	360	ACCESSOIRES DE TUYAUTERIE
69	METAL MANUFACTURES NES		2729		2792		4619		4534	ART MANUFACT EN METAL NDA
691	STRUCTURES AND PARTS NES		740	W 800	762	W 1457	1816	W 1450	1702	CONSTRUCT FER,ACIER,ALU
6911	STRUCTURES,PARTS IRN,STL		221	W 170	207	W 539	850	W 794	1076	CONSTRUCT FER,ACIER,FONTE
6912	STRUCTURES,PARTS ALUMNM	W 564	519	W 630	555	W 918	966	W 656	626	CONSTRUCT ALUMINIUM
692	METAL TANKS,BOXES,ETC		134		203		429		151	RECIPIENTS METALLIQUES
6924	MTL TRANSPORT BOXES ETC		88		160		364		81	FUTS,TAMBOURS,BIDONS
69241	STL TRANSPORT BOXES ETC		22		113		322		18	FUTS,TAMBOURS,BIDONS FER
693	WIRE PRODUCTS NON ELECTR		337		378		374		472	OUVRAGES FILS METALLIQUES
6932	IRON,STEEL FENCING WIRE		216	W 292	219	W 425	255	W 528	324	RONCES DE FER OU ACIER
694	STL,COPPR NAILS,NUTS,ETC		422		389		750		365	CLOUS,VIS,ECROUS
69401	IRON,STEEL NAILS ETC		242		191		428		271	CLOUS,POINTES FER,ACIER
69402	IRN,STL NUTS,BOLTS,ETC		180		198		322		94	BOULONS,VIS,ECROUS FER,AC
695	TOOLS		321		329		486		551	OUTILS A MAIN
6951	HAND TOOLS,AGRIC,FOREST		144		102		297		202	BECHES,PELLES,PIOCHES
6953	OTHER HAND TOOLS		178		228		189		350	AUTRES OUTILS A MAIN
697	BASE MTL HOUSEHOLD EQUIP		340		283		199		301	ART MENAGE MET COMMUNS
6978	BASE MTL HOUSE EQUIP NES		340		283		199		301	ART MENAGE MET COMMUNS
69782	BASE MTL DECOR ARTICLES		339		278		189		294	AUT OBJETS ORNEM INTERIEUR
699	BASE METAL MFRS NES		284		349		468		885	ART MANUFACTURES MET NDA
6998	MFRS NES OF CPR,NIKL,ETC		143		118		236		586	OUVRAGES EN CU,NI,AL,PB,ZN
69985	ZINC MANUFACTURES NES		80		88		155		500	OUVRAGES EN ZINC
7	MACHINES,TRANSPORT EQUIP		11294		12056		11625		11645	MACHINES MATERIEL TRANSPORT
71	POWER GENERATING EQUIPMT		163		251		342		247	MACHINES GENERATRICES
713	INTRNL COMBUS PSTN ENGIN		98		194		230		207	MOTEURS EXPL COMB INT, PIECE
72	MACHS FOR SPCL INDUSTRYS		933		986		499		687	MAC SPECIALES POUR INDUST
721	AGRIC MACHY,EXC TRACTORS		277		280		218		213	MACHINES AGRICOLES
7219	AGRICULTURE MACHINES NES		189		243		138		107	ENGINS AGRICOLES NDA
722	TRACTORS NON–ROAD		622		631		224		391	TRACTEURS
74	GENRL INDUSTRL MACHY NES		774		1064		1846		1070	MACH APP INDUSTRIE
741	HEATING,COOLING EQUIPMNT		200		203		254		215	MACH CHAUFFAGE,PIECES
743	PUMPS NES,CENTRFUGES ETC		239		95		187		252	POMPES COMPRES,VENT ETC
749	NONELEC MACH PTS,ACC NES		335		767		1405		602	PIECES MACH NON ELEC NDA
7499	OTH NONELEC MCHY PTS NES		335		767		1405		602	PIECES NON ELECT NDA
74999	MACH PARTS NONELEC NES						1405			PIECES MACHINES NDA
75	OFFICE MACHNES,ADP EQUIP		440		675		514		714	MACH BUREAU TRAIT AUTOM
751	OFFICE MACHINES		440		675		508		714	MACH,APPAREILS DE BUREAU
7512	CALCULATNG,ACCTG,ETC MCH		357		618		453		645	MACHINE A CALCULER ETC

4. General Imports C.I.F. by Commodities according to the S.I.T.C. (Rev. 2) in thousand U.S. Dollars
Importations Générales C.A.F. par Produits d'après la C.T.C.I. (Rév. 2) en milliers de Dollars E.U.

SITC CTCI	COMMODITY	1991		1992		1993		1994		PRODUIT
		WEIGHT POIDS	VALUE VALEUR	WEIGHT POIDS	VALUE VALEUR	WEIGHT POIDS	VALUE VALEUR	WEIGHT POIDS	VALUE VALEUR	
76	TELECOMM,SOUND EQUIPMENT		836		1730		1690		787	EQUIPMENT DE TELECOM
762	RADIO BROADCAST RECEIVRS		227		245		303		212	RECEPTEURS RADIODIFFUSION
764	TELECOM EQPT,PTS,ACC NES		587		1405		1356		537	EQUIP TELECOM,PIECES
77	ELECTRIC MACHNRY NES ETC		2488		2710		2465		3107	MACH APP ELECT NDA
772	SWITCHGEAR ETC,PARTS NES		470		341		537		610	APP COUPURE,SECT ETC
773	ELECTR DISTRIBUTNG EQUIP		614		900		439		602	EQUIPMT DISTRIBUTION ELECT
7732	ELECTRC INSULATING EQUIP		614		900		439		602	EQUIP ISOL ELECTRIQUE
775	HOUSEHOLD TYPE EQUIP NES		422		611		437		696	MACH,APP USAGE DOMESTQUE
7752	DOM REFRIGERATRS,FREEZRS	N 915	252	N 1144	344	N 978	253	N 1437	414	REFRIG,CONGEL MENAGER
778	ELECTRICAL MACHINERY NES		973		854		1037		1164	AUTRES MACH ELECT NDA
7781	BATTERIES,ACCUMULATORS		318		360		337		466	PILES ET ACCUMULATEURS
77811	PRIMARY BATTERIES,CELLS		246		274		284		400	PILES ELECTRIQUES,PIECES
7782	ELECTRIC LAMPS,BULBS		127		228		191		440	LAMPES, TUBES ELECTRIQUES
7788	OTH ELEC MACHY,EQUIP NES		528		266		509		258	AUT MACH APP ELEC NDA
77886	OTH ELEC MACHINERY NES		488		241		482		216	AUT MACH APP ELECTRIQUES
78	ROAD VEHICLES		4515		3900		3159		3929	VEHICULES ROUTIERS
781	PASS MOTOR VEH EXC BUSES	N 475	1186	N 490	716	N 390	654	N 494	834	AUTO TRANSPORT PERSONNES
782	LORRIES,SPCL MTR VEH NES		2515	N 487	2344	N 367	1441	N 475	2124	VEHICULES SPECIAUX,MARCH
7821	LORRIES,TRUCKS	N 347	1928	N 286	1141	N 56	201	N 213	1019	VEHICULES TRANSP MARCHAND
7822	SPECIAL MOTOR VEHCLS NES		586	N 201	1203	N 311	1240	N 262	1105	VEHICULES USAGES SPECIAUX
783	ROAD MOTOR VEHICLES NES	N 31	181	N 28	127	N 24	220	N 11	133	VEHICULES ROUTIERS NDA
784	MOTOR VEH PRTS,ACCES NES		381		451		655		628	PIECES 722,781,782,783
7849	OTHER MOTOR VEHCL PARTS		377		422		571		625	PIECES 722,781,782,783
79	OTHR TRANSPORT EQUIPMENT		1058		594		1069		1011	AUTRE MATERIEL TRANSPORT
792	AIRCRAFT ETC		724		153		504		280	APP NAVIGATION AERIENNE
7928	AIRCRAFT NES,ASSOC EQUIP		724		153		504		280	APP NAVIG AERIENNE NDA
79282	BALLOONS AND AIRSHIPS		724		153		504		280	AEROSTATS
793	SHIPS AND BOATS ETC		329		440		561		708	NAVIRES BATEAUX,ETC
7933	VESSELS FOR BREAKING UP	N 29	184	N 34	67	N 53	434		493	BATEAUX A DEPECER
7938	TUGS,SPECIAL VESSELS ETC		146		374		127		215	REMORQUEURS,BATEAUX SPEC
8	MISC MANUFACTURED GOODS		6235		5178		5132		5229	ART MANUFACTURES DIVERS
812	*PLUMBG,HEATNG,LGHTNG EQ		213		303		302		324	APPAR SANITAIRES CHAUFFAGE
8122	CERAMIC PLUMBNG FIXTURES		70		139		195		194	EVIERS,LAVABOS,CUVETTES
821	*FURNITURE,PARTS THEREOF		469		443		567		785	MEUBLES ET PIECES
8219	FURNITURE AND PARTS NES						258			AUTRES MEUBLES ET PIECES
84	CLOTHING AND ACCESSORIES		942		696		747		700	VETEMENTS
842	MENS OUTERWEAR NOT KNIT		185		183		219		119	VET DESSUS POUR HOMMES
844	UNDER GARMENTS NOT KNIT		235		129		116		150	VETEMENT DESSOUS MAT TEX
848	HEADGEAR,NONTXTL CLOTHNG		496		348		365		380	VET ACCES MAT AUT QUE TEX
8482	PLASTC,RUBBR CLTHG,ACCES		466		306		347		363	VET ACCES MAT PLAS ARTIF
84822	RUBBER CLOTHING,ACCESRYS		466		306		347		363	VET ACCES CAOUT VULCAN
851	*FOOTWEAR	P 139385	407	P 171289	416	P 140755	370		369	CHAUSSURES
87	PRECISION INSTRUMNTS NES		407		868		641		363	INSTRUM,APPAR SCIENT NDA
874	MEASURNG,CONTROLNG INSTR		303		723		614		206	INSTRUMENTS DE MESURE
88	PHOTO EQU,OPTICL GDS ETC		220		254		201		400	APP,FOURN PHOTO,OP,MONTR
881	PHOTO APPARAT,EQUIPT NES		104		95		53		265	APP,EQUIP PHOTO NDA
89	MISC MANUFCTRD GOODS NES		3524		2150		2271		2240	ART MANUFACTURES DIVERS
892	PRINTED MATTER		581		326		370		323	IMPRIMES
8921	PRINTED BOOKS,GLOBES,ETC		506		263		305		266	LIVRES,BROCHURES,CARTES
893	ARTICLES OF PLASTIC NES		1265		592		699		753	OUVRAGES EN MAT DIVIS 58
894	TOYS,SPORTING GOODS,ETC		494		482		304		311	VOITURES ENFANTS,JOUETS
8947	OTH SPORT GDS,FAIR AMUSM		415		231		187		226	AUT ART DE SPORT
89473	AMUSEMENTS ETC FOR FAIRS		283		107		34		29	MANEGES,BALANCOIRES
895	OFFICE SUPPLIES NES		483		421		594		536	ART PAPET NDA
8951	BASE MTL OFFICE SUPPLIES		74		37		187		64	MAT BUREAU METAUX COMMUNS
8959	OTHER OFFICE SUPPLIES		325		270		298		396	AUT ART DE PAPETERIE
89592	SLATES FOR WRITING		325		270		296		392	ARDOISES
899	OTHER MANUFACTURED GOODS		547		264		234		259	AUT ART MANUF DIVERS NDA
8999	OTHER MANUF GOODS NES		250		49		31		10	OUVRAGES DIVERS NDA
9	GOODS NOT CLASSD BY KIND		306		237		200		277	ART TRANSACT NON CLASSES
931	*SPECIAL TRANSACTIONS		305		194		200		243	TRANS.SPECIALES

5. General Exports F.O.B. by Commodities according to the S.I.T.C. (Rev. 2) in thousand U.S. Dollars
Exportations Générales F.O.B. par Produits d'après la C.T.C.I. (Rév. 2) en milliers de Dollars E.U.

SITC CTCI	COMMODITY	1991		1992		1993		1994		PRODUIT
		WEIGHT POIDS	VALUE VALEUR	WEIGHT POIDS	VALUE VALEUR	WEIGHT POIDS	VALUE VALEUR	WEIGHT POIDS	VALUE VALEUR	
	ALL COMMODITIES # 1		16494		12781		16896		14045	TOUS PRODUITS
0	FOOD AND LIVE ANIMALS		13582		10202		14566		12536	ALIMENTS,ANIMAUX VIVANTS
03	FISH AND PREPARATIONS		1193		1542		2407		3031	POISSONS ET PREPARATIONS
034	FISH,FRESH,CHILLED,FROZN	W 344	1104	W 366	1081	W 391	1709	W 384	1646	POISSON FRAIS, REFRIG,CONG
036	SHELL FISH FRESH,FROZEN	W 1	10	W 1	10			W 17	76	CRUSTACES,MOLLUSQUES
037	FISH ETC PREPD,PRSVD NES	W 17	79	W 67	452	W 58	698	W 107	1309	POIS,CRUST,MOL PREPARES
0372	SHELL FISH PREPRD,PRESVD					W 57	696	W 106	1304	CRUSTACES,COQUIL PREPARES
05	VEGETABLES AND FRUIT		10166		7120		10172		7467	LEGUMES ET FRUITS
054	VEG ETC FRSH,SMPLY PRSVD		9968	W 10657	6863	W 19900	9989	W 18489	7384	LEGUMES FRAIS,CONG,SECS
0545	OTHER FRESH VEGETABLES	W 18502	9586	W 9962	6394			W 17266	6832	AUTRES LEGUMES FRAIS,REF
05451	ALLIACEOUS VEGTBLS,FRESH	W 18502	9586	W 9962	6394			W 17266	6832	OIGNONS,ECHALOTES,AULX
0548	EDIBLE VEG NES FRESH,DRY	W 815	365	W 693	467	W 19900	9988	W 1223	545	RACINES,TUBERCULES
05488	VEG PRODTS NES FRESH,DRY					W 19900	9988			PROD VEGET ALIM HUMAINE
057	FRUIT,NUTS,FRESH,DRIED	W 756	198		255		183	W 443	83	FRUITS FRAIS OU SECS
0577	NUTS EDIBLE,FRESH,DRIED	W 477	75	W 1421	232	W 856	151	W 401	63	FRUITS A COQUES
05771	COCONUTS FRESH OR DRIED	W 477	75	W 1421	232	W 856	151	W 401	63	NOIX DE COCO
0579	FRUIT FRESH OR DRIED NES	W 279	123	W 27	16	W 48	32	W 42	20	FRUITS FRAIS,SECS NDA
05794	BERRIES FRESH	W 277	121	W 25	15			W 20	11	BAIES FRAICHES
07	COFFEE,TEA,COCOA,SPICES		2195		1530		1986		2035	CAFE,THE,CACAO,EPICES
075	SPICES	W 37	2195	W 25	1530	W 36	1986	W 37	2035	EPICES
0752	SPICES,EX PEPPER,PIMENTO	W 37	2195	W 25	1530	W 36	1986	W 37	2035	AUTRES EPICES
07521	VANILLA					W 36	1986			VANILLE
2	CRUDE MATERLS,EXCL FUELS		30		83		88		578	MAT BRUTES NON COMESTIBLES
27	CRUDE FERTLZR,MINRLS NES				7		19		59	ENGRAIS MINERAUX BRUTS
277	NATURAL ABRASIVES NES				7		19		59	ABRASIFS NATURELS NDA
2772	OTHER NATURAL ABRASIVES				7		19		59	AUTR ABRASIFS NATURELS NDA
29	CRUDE ANIMAL,VEG MAT NES		11		47		69		520	MATIERES BRUTES ANIM,VEGET
292	CRUDE VEG MATERIALS NES	W 3	11		47	W 53	69		520	MAT BRUTES VEGETALES NDA
2924	VEG USED IN PHARMACY ETC	W 3	11	W 4	25			W 235	508	PLANTES MEDICINALES
2926	LIVE PLANTS,BULBS,ETC					W 53	69			BULBES,TUBERCULES
29269	LIVE PLANTS NES					W 53	69			AUTRES PLANTES VIVANTES
4	ANIMAL,VEGETABLE OIL,FAT		321		321		90			HUILES,GRAISSES ANIM,VEG
42	FIXED VEGETABLE OIL,FAT		321		321		90			HUILES VEGETALES FIXES
424	FIXED VEG OIL NONSOFT	V 1256	321	V 829	321	V 320	90			AUTRES HUILES VEG FIXES
4243	COCONUT (COPRA) OIL	V 1256	321	V 829	321	V 320	90			HJUILE DE COPRAH
5	CHEMCLS,RELATED PROD NES		99		30		36		57	PRODUITS CHIMIQUES
53	DYES,TANNING,COLOUR PROD		99		25		35		55	PROD TEINTURE,COLORANTS
533	PIGMENTS,PAINTS,ETC		99		25		35		55	PIGMENTS,PEINTURES,VERNIS
5335	GLAZES,DRIERS,PUTTY ETC		99		25		35		55	PREPTNS COLOR UTILISES CERAM
6	BASIC MANUFACTURES		1269		903		562		337	ART MANUFACTURES
61	LEATHER,DRESSED FUR,ETC		1081		815		468		264	CUIRS,PELLETERIES
612	LEATHER ETC MANUFACTURES		1081		815		468		264	OUVRAGES EN CUIRS NDA
6121	LEATHER BELTING ETC		673		522		309		204	ARTICLES EN CUIR ETC
6122	HARNESS–MAKERS GOODS	N 26349	308	N 19963	197	N 9906	83			ART SELLERIE,BOURRELLERIE
6129	LEATHER MANUFACTURES NES		99		96		76		60	AUT OUV CUIR NAT,ARTIF
69	METAL MANUFACTURES NES		152		75		91		56	ART MANUFACT EN METAL NDA
692	METAL TANKS,BOXES,ETC		135		42		43		28	RECIPIENTS METALLIQUES
6924	MTL TRANSPORT BOXES ETC	N 1113	128	N 514	25		32	N 682	18	FUTS,TAMBOURS,BIDONS
69244	ALUMNM COMP GAS CYLINDRS	N 1113	128	N 514	25	N 970	20	N 682	18	RECIP ALU GAZ COMPRIMES
7	MACHINES,TRANSPORT EQUIP		154		448		779		249	MACHINES MATERIEL TRANSPORT
71	POWER GENERATING EQUIPMT		92		251		497		92	MACHINES GENERATRICES
711	STEAM BOILERS & AUX PLNT		23		83		433		72	GENERATEURS VAPEUR EAU ETC
7111	STEAM BOILERS ETC		23		83		433		72	GENERATEURS VAPEUR EAU
716	ROTATING ELECTRIC PLANT		70		169		64		20	APP ELECTR ROTATIFS,PIECES
78	ROAD VEHICLES		37		42		30		52	VEHICULES ROUTIERS
781	PASS MOTOR VEH EXC BUSES	N 7	37	N 5	41	N 3	26	N 6	52	AUTO TRANSPORT PERSONNES
79	OTHR TRANSPORT EQUIPMENT		24		155		252		104	AUTRE MATERIEL TRANSPORT
791	RAILWAY VEHICLES		9		145				6	VEHIC MAT CHEMINS DE FER
7919	RY TRACK FIXT,ETC,PARTS		9		145				6	MATER FIXE VOIES FERREES
79199	PARTS NES OF 7911–7915		9		145				6	PIECES 791.1 ET 5
792	AIRCRAFT ETC				3		77		1	APP NAVIGATION AERIENNE
7928	AIRCRAFT NES,ASSOC EQUIP				3		77		1	APP NAVIG AERIENNE NDA
79282	BALLOONS AND AIRSHIPS				3		77		1	AEROSTATS
793	SHIPS AND BOATS ETC	N 1	15	N 3	6		175	N 8	97	NAVIRES BATEAUX,ETC
7932	SHIPS AND BOATS NES	N 1	15	N 3	6		175	N 8	97	NAVIRES ET BATEAUX
8	MISC MANUFACTURED GOODS		743		679		505		117	ART MANUFACTURES DIVERS
84	CLOTHING AND ACCESSORIES		369		503		442			VETEMENTS
842	MENS OUTERWEAR NOT KNIT				3		160			VET DESSUS POUR HOMMES
847	TEXTILE CLTHNG ACCES NES		369		499		282			ACCES VET MAT TEXT NDA
8471	— NOT KNITTED				227		208			ACCES VET MAT TEX NON BON
8472	CLTHNG ACCESRYS ETC KNIT		369		273		75			ACCES VET BONNE NDA
851	*FOOTWEAR	P 40450	80	P 453	1	P 812	6	P 1074	4	CHAUSSURES
89	MISC MANUFCTRD GOODS NES		293		175		56		113	ART MANUFACTURES DIVERS
899	OTHER MANUFACTURED GOODS		285		172		53		109	AUT ART MANUF DIVERS NDA
8991	CARVED,MOULDED GOODS		126		32		17		13	MAT A TAILLER,A MOULER
8997	BASKETWORK,BROOMS ETC		120		90		33		59	OUVRAGES VANNERIE NDA
8999	OTHER MANUF GOODS NES		39		50		3		36	OUVRAGES DIVERS NDA
9	GOODS NOT CLASSD BY KIND		296		115		272		170	ART TRANSACT NON CLASSES
931	*SPECIAL TRANSACTIONS		296		115		272		170	TRANS.SPECIALES

FOOT NOTES – NOTES

TABLE 4 –

1 The data presented according to SITC, Revision 2 have been estimated from data reported according to the national classification.

TABLE 5 –

1 The data presented according to SITC, Revision 2 have been estimated from data reported according to the national classification.

TABLEAU 4 –

1 Les données qui se présentent conformément à C TCI, Révision 2 sont les estimations des données rapportées d'après la classification nationale.

TABLEAU 5 –

1 Les données qui se présentent conformément à C TCI, Révision 2 sont les estimations des données rapportées d'après la classification nationale.

1. HISTORICAL SERIES, 1961–1996 SPECIAL TRADE, IMPORTS C.I.F., EXPORTS F.O.B.
SERIES HISTORIQUES, 1961–1996 COMMERCE SPECIAL, IMPORTATIONS C.A.F., EXPORTATIONS F.O.B

YEAR ANNEE	VALUE IN MILLION T.T. DOLLARS / VALEUR EN MILLION T.T. DOLLARS — MERCHANDISE – MARCHANDISE		GOLD – OR		CONVERSION FACTORS U.S. CENTS PER T.T. DOLLAR / FACTEURS DE CONVERSION CENTS E.U. PAR T.T. DOLLAR		INDEX NUMBERS # 1 – INDICES — QUANTUM		UNIT VALUE / VALEUR UNITAIRE	
	IMPORTS	EXPORTS	IMPORTS	EXPORTS	IMPORTS	EXPORTS	IMPORTS	EXPORTS	IMPORTS	EXPORTS
1961	584.00	593.50			58.3300	58.3300				
1962	605.60	592.00			58.3300	58.3300				
1963	646.40	640.70			58.3300	58.3300				
1964	730.60	699.00			58.3300	58.3300				
1965	817.00	690.50			58.3300	58.3300				
1966	777.70	735.10			58.3300	58.3300				
1967	723.90	763.40			57.5600	57.6200	57	90	4	5
1968	854.50	943.30			50.0000	50.0000	63	99	5	6
1969	966.40	947.70			50.0000	50.0000	67	101	5	6
1970	1084.90	960.60			50.0000	50.0000	73	101	5	6
1971	1326.70	1038.70			50.0000	50.0000	85	98	5	6
1972	1467.60	1068.40			52.2057	52.2335	82	100	6	6
1973	1536.30	1368.30			50.6524	50.6026	84	100	7	[illegible]
1974	3777.60	4165.90			48.9015	48.9279	112	107	16	22
1975	3243.90	3878.50			45.3567	45.2311	83	94	18	26
1976	4826.90	5393.50			40.9433	41.0367	114	110	21	30
1977	4340.40	5231.50			41.6670	41.6670	94	103	22	32
1978	4752.00	4902.00			41.6670	41.6670	97	93	23	33
1979	5067.00	6265.00			41.6670	41.6670	109	91	26	43
1980	7664.90	9804.10			41.6670	41.6670	124	88	39	69
1981	7462.00	9033.50			41.6670	41.6670	116	78	44	76
1982	8878.40	7372.40			41.6670	41.6670	114	80	50	72
1983	6190.90	5632.10			41.6668	41.6668	128	78	50	72
1984	4605.90	5216.20			41.6667	41.6667	145	90	50	71
1985	3731.00	5236.00			41.0083	40.7656	128	95	50	68
1986	4860.20	4988.60			27.7780	27.7780	131	94	68	66
1987	4387.50	5264.60			27.7780	27.7780	103	92	77	70
1988	4310.30	5424.20			26.1589	26.0473	87	95	86	66
1989	5190.40	6706.90			23.5290	23.5290	106	94	99	84
1990	4712.30	8330.70			23.5290	23.5290	100	100	100	100
1991	5993.90	7541.80			23.5290	23.5290				89
1992	4963.50	7188.30			23.5294	23.5294				84
1993	7495.30	8800.90			19.5173	18.8856				90
1994	6700.90	11055.20			16.8689	16.8830				95
1995	10191.10	14608.60			16.8153	16.8092				95
1996	12880.30	15014.70			16.6646	16.6503				96

2. IMPORTS BY BROAD ECONOMIC CATEGORY AND EXPORTS BY INDUSTRIAL ORIGIN. (PERCENTAGE OF TOTAL VALUE)
IMPORTATIONS PAR CATEGORIES ECONOMIQUES ET EXPORTATIONS PAR BRANCHE D'ACTIVITE.(EN POURCENTAGE DE LA VALEUR TOTALE)

IMPORTS – IMPORTATIONS

	1990	1991	1992	1993	1994	1995	1996
TOTAL IMPORTS–IMPORTATIONS TOTALES	100.	100.	100.	100.	100.	100.	
1 FOOD BEV–ALIMENTATION BOISSONS	16.3	13.3	15.1	13.4	13.9	11.3	
11 PRIMARY–PRODUITS DE BASE	8.5	6.4	7.2	6.4	7.3	5.3	
111 FOR INDUSTRY–POUR L'INDUSTRIE	4.6	3.2	3.7	3.6	4.5	3.4	
112 FOR HOUSEHOLDS–POUR LES MENAGES	3.9	3.2	3.5	2.9	2.8	1.9	
12 PROCESSED–PRODUITS ELABORES	7.9	6.9	7.9	7.0	6.6	6.0	
121 FOR INDUSTRY–POUR L'INDUSTRIE	1.3	1.4	1.3	1.0	1.1	1.1	
122 FOR HOUSEHOLDS–POUR LES MENAGES	6.6	5.6	6.6	6.0	5.5	4.9	
2 IND SUPPLIES–APPROV INDUSTRIELS	36.8	33.9	34.4	27.8	24.8	22.5	
21 PRIMARY–PRODUITS DE BASE	6.1	4.4	4.7	2.8	6.5	5.3	
22 PROCESSED–PRODUITS ELABORES	30.6	29.6	29.7	25.0	18.3	17.2	
3 FUELS–COMBUSTIBLES	11.3	14.6	9.0	15.9	0.6	0.5	
31 PRIMARY–PRODUITS DE BASE	9.5	13.1	8.2	15.5	0.0	0.0	
32 PROCESSED–PRODUITS ELABORES	1.8	1.5	0.8	0.4	0.5	0.4	
321 MOTOR SPIRIT–ESSENCE		0.0	0.0	0.0	0.0	0.0	
322 OTHER–AUTRES	1.8	1.5	0.8	0.4	0.5	0.4	
4 MACHINERY–EQUIPEMENT	20.6	19.4	22.2	27.3	20.1	27.1	
41 CAPITAL EQUIPMENT–MACHINES	16.6	15.6	18.6	24.2	18.4	25.6	
42 PARTS–PIECES ACCESSOIRES	4.0	3.7	3.7	3.1	1.6	1.5	
5 TRANSPORT–TRANSPORT	4.1	8.5	8.0	6.6	6.6	6.4	
51 PASSENGER CARS–AUTOMOBILES	0.7	2.5	3.2	2.0	2.3	2.5	
52 OTHER–AUTRES	0.8	2.3	1.8	2.1	1.6	1.7	
521 INDUSTRIAL–INDUSTRIELS	0.7	2.2	1.7	2.0	1.5	1.6	
522 NON INDUSTRIAL–NON INDUSTRIEL	0.0	0.1	0.0	0.1	0.0	0.1	
53 PARTS–PIECES ACCESSOIRES	2.6	3.7	3.1	2.6	2.8	2.2	
6 CONSUM GOODS–BIENS CONSOMMATION	10.4	9.5	10.4	8.6	10.1	9.8	
61 DURABLE–DURABLES	1.5	2.0	2.5	1.9	1.9	2.2	
62 SEMI DURABLE–SEMI DURABLES	3.7	3.4	3.1	2.9	3.6	3.4	
63 NON DURABLE–NON DURABLES	5.2	4.1	4.8	3.8	4.5	4.2	
7 GOODS NES–BIENS NDA	0.5	0.7	0.8	0.4	23.9	22.6	

EXPORTS – EXPORTATIONS

	1990	1991	1992	1993	1994	1995	1996
TOTAL EXPORTS–EXPORTATIONS TOTALES	100.	100.	100.	100.	100.	100.	
1 AGRICULTURE	0.6	0.5	0.6	1.0	0.8	0.7	
2 MINING QUARRY–INDUS EXTRACTIVES	37.0	31.7	25.9	24.0	19.8	18.4	
3 MANUFACTURING–IND MANUFACTUR	62.4	67.7	73.5	75.0	79.4	80.9	
31 FOOD BEV TOBACCO–ALIM BOISS TAB	5.0	5.4	5.7	6.9	6.1	6.5	
32 TEXTILES–INDUSTRIES TEXTILES	0.5	0.5	0.6	0.9	0.8	0.8	
33 WOOD & PRODUCTS–BOIS & PRODUITS	0.2	0.2	0.2	0.3	0.3	0.4	
34 PAPER & PRODUCTS–PAPIER & PRODT	0.7	0.9	1.2	1.7	1.4	1.4	
35 CHEMICALS–INDUSTRIES CHIMIQUES	45.1	50.8	54.0	51.0	46.1	45.7	
36 NON METAL MIN–MIN NON METAL	1.0	1.2	1.4	1.7	1.5	1.3	
37 BASIC METAL–IND METAL BASE	6.9	6.5	7.9	8.6	1.5	2.3	
38 METAL MANUF–MANUF METAL	2.8	2.0	2.3	3.8	2.4	3.4	
39 OTH MANUF IND–AUTRES MANUF	0.2	0.3	0.2	0.2	19.3	19.2	

3. TRADE BY PRINCIPAL COUNTRIES OF PRODUCTION AND LAST CONSIGNMENT (VALUE IN THOUSAND U.S. DOLLARS)
ECHANGES SELON LES PRINCIPAUX PAYS DE PRODUCTION ET DE DERNIERE CONSIGNATION (VALEUR EN MILLIERS DE DOLLARS EU)

COUNTRIES–PAYS	SPECIAL IMPORTS C.I.F. IMPORTATIONS SPECIALES C.A.F				
	1992	1993	1994	1995	1996
World	1435561	1462873	1133740	1723657	2204467
Africa	2168	745	2011	7202	17794
Americas	984792	1013252	787362	1178531	1555119
Northern America	678773	650889	612698	960284	919803
LAIA	211621	292842	113416	146640	534784
CACM	4847	5176	5889	8438	8149
Caribbean	72962	50121	45290	48740	50738
Rest of America	16588	14223	10069	14429	41645
As.ex F.USSR	167471	126504	127385	159144	206076
Eur.x F.USSR	260263	303542	199734	358265	406431
EU	238104	292520	183495	330043	378556
EFTA	17624	9662	12674	20475	16274
East Europe	4393	1336	3538	7550	11507
Other Europe	62	20	3	120	93
Former USSR	123	202	255	1480	781
Oceania	18554	15975	14155	13037	15609
USA/Etats–Unis d'Amer	605012	578574	547412	872086	840086
Venezuela	139130	246288	32850	49862	268264
United Kingdom	112199	118747	94200	124742	131823
Canada	73758	72303	65285	88192	79713
Germany/Allemagne	37128	96346	23459	101591	110445
Japan/Japon	96659	56056	52200	55690	89025
Brazil/Brésil	49472	32050	59711	69966	73309
Colombia/Colombie	4483	3934	3114	6730	153883
Netherlands/Pays–Bas	20571	16110	15451	24374	41433
Korea, Republic of	15390	15719	16944	33326	35323
Jamaica/Jamaïque	30984	20668	20805	20381	19328
China/Chine	14766	15817	17785	22418	31960
Barbados/Barbade	20523	19126	17795	15692	16797
France,Monac	17103	20253	10575	15822	20748
Ireland/Irlande	14315	13820	10209	11069	16216
Italy/Italie	11755	7728	8514	17090	18054
Switz.Liecht	15232	7015	11192	14129	11700
Mexico/Mexique	6675	5015	9313	14546	20043
New Zealand	11363	9983	9293	7666	11606
Guyana	7012	6696	7076	9966	12452
Belgium–Luxembourg	7536	6498	6003	8938	8701
Suriname/Suriname	3996	4264	214	140	25175
Spain/Espagne	3374	2775	3193	7374	11802
Argentina/Argentine	8587	3416	4339	3305	7336
Australia/Australie	6317	5992	4862	5288	4003
Hong Kong	5074	4662	4915	4998	5072
India/Inde	2967	3588	3886	6304	7177
Sweden/Suède	3692	2200	3052	7874	6410
Denmark/Danemark	4547	3424	2529	4155	4876
Austria/Autriche	4072	2512	3568	4049	4389
Norway,SVD,JM	2389	2600	1479	6335	4574
Netherlands Antilles	6264	1827	1058	3104	3875
Malaysia/Malaisie	2397	2975	2611	3889	3771
Singapore/Singapour	4901	3343	1861	2744	2732
Thailand/Thaïlande	1375	1288	4411	4011	4330
Belize/Bélize	5161	2145	1925	2069	2681
Indonesia/Indonésie	2535	2335	2497	2435	3225
Nigeria/Nigéria	271	11	35	30	12507
Poland/Pologne	1697	368	2129	3216	4737
Czech Republic		780	1232	3664	6085
Guatemala	2784	2242	1065	3596	1658
Dominica/Dominique	1923	1931	1923	2617	2387
Dominican Republic	1928	1594	1475	3128	2500
So. Africa Customs Un	40	106	358	6654	3462
Honduras	402	1544	3573	3652	1422
Saint Lucia/St. Lucie	1550	1834	1401	2609	2596
Costa Rica	1280	1356	1242	1181	4664
Ecuador/Equateur	104	315	12	222	8901
St Vincent & Grenadines	5359	1648			2359
Peru/Pérou	2615	1448	3486	553	667

COUNTRIES–PAYS	SPECIAL EXPORTS F.O.B. EXPORTATIONS SPECIALES F.O.B.				
	1992	1993	1994	1995	1996
Monde	1868943	1662107	1954282	2466984	2569251
Afrique	32971	28778	17204	15364	8647
Amériques	1646735	1471909	1709305	2122020	2277988
Amérique du Nord	942711	826089	983642	1110058	1311512
ALAI	127465	87076	167675	212457	190569
MCAC	18897	18281	18059	18401	20127
Caraïbes	408246	387795	381140	586799	585751
Autre Amérique	149416	152667	158789	194306	170030
Asie l'URSS exclus	42963	52012	52759	42583	10088
Europe l'URSS exclus	110323	84471	156007	261668	247617
UE	109283	80491	150373	249881	247086
AELE	991	3942	1331	3224	376
Europe de l'Est	26	9	4	305	150
Autre de l'Europe	23	29	26	4337	5
Ancienne URSS	121	326	7	4	64
Océanie	5317	2461	629	1706	1359
USA/Etats–Unis d'Amer	908221	792259	907114	1058550	1253968
Jamaica/Jamaïque	30897	71843	119302	207931	220742
Barbados/Barbade	64113	72814	70537	85422	89563
Guyana	42300	59726	59807	80649	90174
France,Monac	34764	25004	54306	70574	136234
Netherlands Antilles	120713	52978	29146	38213	33900
Canada	34469	33732	74410	46538	57524
Suriname/Suriname	41726	37047	37616	49574	68917
United Kingdom	31985	33643	36632	61572	48037
Colombia/Colombie	33730	31168	52718	58672	33841
Dominican Republic	33848	31134	23342	55026	45980
French Guiana	48198	38415	37949	46968	
Saint Lucia/St. Lucie	29558	30946	33038	35944	40757
Mexico/Mexique	26316	18959	29822	44744	39514
Venezuela	31471	14339	32184	29995	48559
Grenada/Grenade	21185	28901	25141	31657	36113
Brazil/Brésil	18953	2665	16149	38627	24806
Netherlands/Pays–Bas	9945	1548	28837	42231	18311
Antigua and Barbuda	15501	14705	21322	17386	16238
Cuba	11986	8902	6729	20382	26252
Saint–Kitts–Nevis	14315	15465	10714	14338	15349
Chile/Chili	6352	8644	17016	18188	17226
Panama	12852	13843	19425	12401	7224
St Vincent & Grenadines	18094	20999			26311
Dominica/Dominique	10501	10090	11083	13740	15971
Martinique	6127	8623	11937	28122	
Italy/Italie	2456	391	15719	26601	8131
Guadeloupe	9568	9451	10412	20532	
Japan/Japon	19274	18395	4552	651	6448
Germany/Allemagne	6479	9104	5386	18912	9364
Cote d'Ivoire	26562	11767	7569		
Korea, Republic of	5508	16229	17407	6532	29
Ecuador/Equateur	10019	7944	7150	8356	7540
Spain/Espagne	4100	2651	3382	12943	11381
Belgium–Luxembourg	13020	5228	177	7213	8503
Costa Rica	7380	5667	6759	4269	4018
Peru/Pérou	469	2559	7648	11025	3398
Aruba	11912	5686	1867	2881	2332
Guatemala	7253	6062	5409	3535	721
Argentina/Argentine	114	74	4961	2692	14307
Honduras	3919	3320	3252	2583	8308
Belize/Bélize	4340	3637	3991	4714	3715
Nigeria/Nigéria	1216	10137	1	19	4944
Haiti/Haïti	0	802	436	7892	6073
Indonesia/Indonésie	3210	7028	3386	0	
Senegal/Sénégal	2	2872		7093	3466
Nicaragua		387	872	5415	5692
Montserrat	2701	1888	2493	3054	2087
Bahamas	5292	1541			4443
Morocco/Maroc	1125	3820	5151		

(VALUE AS PERCENTAGE OF WORLD TOTAL)(VALEURS EN POURCENTAGE DU TOTAL MONDIAL)

	1987	1988	1989	1990	1991	1992	1993	1994	1995	1996
Africa	0.1	4.4	2.9	4.6	1.2	0.2	0.1	0.2	0.4	0.8
Americas	63.0	60.9	72.2	68.5	69.8	68.6	69.3	69.4	68.4	70.5
Northern America	48.7	43.3	55.1	46.4	44.5	47.3	44.5	54.0	55.7	41.7
LAIA	7.9	9.2	7.7	14.5	19.1	14.7	20.0	10.0	8.5	24.3
CACM	0.8	0.9	0.6	0.3	0.5	0.3	0.4	0.5	0.5	0.4
Caribbean	4.7	6.4	7.7	6.2	4.8	5.1	3.4	4.0	2.8	2.3
Rest of America	0.8	1.1	1.1	1.2	0.9	1.2	1.0	0.9	0.8	1.9
As.ex F.USSR	10.6	10.1	5.2	7.9	10.2	11.7	8.6	11.2	9.2	9.3
Eur.x F.USSR	23.9	21.9	18.0	17.2	16.7	18.1	20.7	17.6	20.8	18.4
EU	22.9	20.7	17.1	16.5	15.7	16.6	20.0	16.2	19.1	17.2
EFTA	1.0	1.1	0.7	0.6	0.8	1.2	0.7	1.1	1.2	0.7
East Europe	0.1	0.1	0.2	0.2	0.2	0.3	0.1	0.3	0.4	0.5
Other Europe	0.0	0.0	0.0	0.0	0.0	0.0	0.0	0.0	0.0	0.0
Former USSR	0.0	0.5	0.0	0.0	0.3	0.0	0.0	0.0	0.1	0.0
Oceania	2.1	1.6	1.5	1.6	1.3	1.3	1.1	1.2	0.8	0.7
USA/Etats–Unis d'Amer	42.1	38.0	50.1	40.5	39.6	42.1	39.6	48.3	50.6	38.1
Venezuela	1.4	2.6	3.0	7.5	13.9	9.7	16.8	2.9	2.9	12.2
United Kingdom	9.2	9.9	7.6	7.5	7.4	7.8	8.1	8.3	7.2	6.0
Canada	6.7	5.3	5.0	5.8	4.9	5.1	4.9	5.8	5.1	3.6
Germany/Allemagne	5.8	2.7	2.0	2.4	1.9	2.6	6.6	2.1	5.9	5.0
Japan/Japon	5.3	5.2	2.1	3.5	5.6	6.7	3.8	4.6	3.2	4.0
Brazil/Brésil	3.4	2.8	3.2	4.1	3.8	3.4	2.2	5.3	4.1	3.3
Colombia/Colombie	2.2	1.5	0.2	1.3	0.3	0.3	0.3	0.3	0.4	7.0
Netherlands/Pays–Bas	2.2	3.1	2.3	1.7	1.8	1.4	1.1	1.4	1.4	1.9
Korea, Republic of	1.0	0.7	0.6	0.6	0.7	1.1	1.1	1.5	1.9	1.6

	1987	1988	1989	1990	1991	1992	1993	1994	1995	1996
Afrique	0.2	0.7	0.7	0.6	1.0	1.8	1.7	0.9	0.6	0.3
Amériques	82.4	86.1	86.5	86.5	84.8	88.1	88.6	87.5	86.0	88.7
Amérique du Nord	60.3	60.1	57.1	58.3	51.7	50.4	49.7	50.3	45.0	51.0
ALAI	3.3	3.3	2.7	3.1	7.7	6.8	5.2	8.6	8.6	7.4
MCAC	0.6	0.6	0.4	0.2	0.3	1.0	1.1	0.9	0.7	0.8
Caraïbes	13.6	17.1	20.2	19.2	18.4	21.8	23.3	19.5	23.8	22.8
Autre Amérique	4.7	5.0	6.1	5.7	6.7	8.0	9.2	8.1	7.9	6.6
Asie l'URSS exclus	3.4	2.9	2.2	1.8	3.2	2.3	3.1	2.7	1.7	0.4
Europe l'URSS exclus	12.7	8.9	9.6	9.7	9.6	5.9	5.1	8.0	10.6	9.6
UE	12.6	8.8	9.1	8.5	9.5	5.8	4.8	7.7	10.1	9.6
AELE	0.0	0.0	0.1	0.6	0.0	0.1	0.2	0.1	0.1	0.0
Europe de l'Est	0.0	0.0	0.0	0.0	0.0	0.0	0.0	0.0	0.0	0.0
Autre de l'Europe	0.0	0.0	0.3	0.7	0.0	0.0	0.0	0.0	0.2	0.0
Ancienne URSS	0.0	0.1	0.0			0.0	0.0	0.0	0.0	0.0
Océanie	0.0	0.0	0.0	0.2	0.0	0.3	0.1	0.0	0.1	0.1
USA/Etats–Unis d'Amer	58.4	57.6	56.1	56.9	50.0	48.6	47.7	46.4	42.9	48.8
Jamaica/Jamaïque	2.5	2.5	3.7	2.7	2.1	1.7	4.3	6.1	8.4	8.6
Barbados/Barbade	3.1	3.4	3.9	3.5	3.3	3.4	4.4	3.6	3.5	3.5
Guyana	0.5	0.7	1.5	1.3	1.5	2.3	3.6	3.1	3.3	3.5
France,Monac	1.4	1.8	2.2	1.1	1.4	1.9	1.5	2.8	2.9	5.3
Netherlands Antilles	1.0	1.8	2.1	3.0	4.2	6.5	3.2	1.5	1.5	1.3
Canada	1.9	2.2	1.0	1.4	1.8	1.8	2.0	3.8	1.9	2.2
Suriname/Suriname	2.3	2.0	2.1	2.1	1.9	2.2	2.2	1.9	2.0	2.7
United Kingdom	3.1	2.7	2.5	2.8	2.2	1.7	2.0	1.9	2.5	1.9
Colombia/Colombie	0.2	0.7	0.2	0.2	1.6	1.8	1.9	2.7	2.4	1.3

4. Special Imports C.I.F. by Commodities according to the S.I.T.C. (Rev. 2) in thousand U.S. Dollars
Importations Spéciales C.A.F. par Produits d'après la C.T.C.I. (Rév. 2) en milliers de Dollars E.U.

SITC CTCI	COMMODITY	1993 WEIGHT POIDS	1993 VALUE VALEUR	1994 WEIGHT POIDS	1994 VALUE VALEUR	1995 WEIGHT POIDS	1995 VALUE VALEUR	1996 WEIGHT POIDS	1996 VALUE VALEUR	PRODUIT
	ALL COMMODITIES		1462873		1133740		1723657		2204467	TOUS PRODUITS
0	FOOD AND LIVE ANIMALS		183215		136852		184788		242059	ALIMENTS,ANIMAUX VIVANTS
01	MEAT AND PREPARATIONS		19907		15663		15800		18060	VIANDES ET PREPARATIONS
011	MEAT FRESH,CHILLD,FROZEN	W 9189	15147	W 6912	11827	W 10630	10281	W 7047	12068	VIANDES FRAICHES,REF,CONGE
0111	BOVINE MEAT FRESH,FROZEN	W 3998	7927	W 2896	6167	W 2097	4098	W 2124	4636	VIANDES BOVIN FRAI,REF
01112	BOVINE MEAT BONELESS	W 3485	7285	W 2684	5604	W 1910	3725	W 2042	4374	VIANDES BOVIN DESOSSEES
02	DAIRY PRODCTS,BIRDS'EGGS		39839		25676		35202		46240	PRODUITS LAITIERS,OEUFS
022	MILK AND CREAM	W 13183	28011	W 12657	21287	W 13203	29510	W 11127	27853	LAIT ET CREME
0224	MILK,CREAM PRESERVED ETC	W 12979	27609	W 12529	21093	W 13055	29235	W 11021	27593	LAIT,CREME CONS,CONC
02242	MILK DRY,1.5% FAT OR LES	W 2768	6190	W 3515	5994	W 4305	9611	W 3480	8110	LAIT POUDRE INF 1.5%
02243	MILK DRY,OVER 1.5% FAT	W 8986	20178	W 7133	13335	W 7101	17782	W 6146	17858	LAIT POUDRE SUP 1.5%
024	CHEESE AND CURD	W 3430	7024				344	W 4104	12005	FROMAGE ET CAILLEBOTTE
03	FISH AND PREPARATIONS		4323		4916		5152		5981	POISSONS ET PREPARATIONS
04	CEREALS AND PREPARATIONS		57641		45325		66551		78231	CEREALES ET PRODUITS
041	WHEAT ETC UNMILLED	W 120210	20267	W 85120	16037	W 130877	27323	W 105549	24873	FROMENT,EPEAUTRE
0412	OTHER WHEAT ETC UNMILLED	W 120210	20267	W 74413	14312	W 130877	27323	W 105549	24872	AUTRE FROMENT NON MOULU
042	RICE	W 59786	12692	W 16612	11287	W 41109	16088	W 59963	15537	RIZ
0422	RICE SEMI–MILLED,MILLED	W 58974	12433	W 11584	9608	W 37964	15159	W 55419	13537	RIZ POLI,GLACE INCL BRISURES
04221	RICE MILLED UNBROKEN	W 58674	12386	W 11027	9509	W 36890	14936	W 48876	12412	RIZ POLI,GLACE EXCL BRISURES
044	MAIZE UNMILLED	W 88597	13394	W 41875	9861	W 86008	13970	W 88903	18285	MAIS NON MOULU
048	CEREAL ETC PREPARATIONS	W 8348	7903	W 2628	5330	W 3268	6064	W 12360	15776	PREPTNS A BASE CEREALES
0488	OTH CEREAL PREPS,MALT EX	W 1116	3043	W 2030	4314	W 1869	4319	W 2419	5967	EXTRAITS DE MALT
05	VEGETABLES AND FRUIT		29418		21591		25158		36209	LEGUMES ET FRUITS
054	VEG ETC FRSH,SMPLY PRSVD	W 47753	22530	W 35490	15419	W 49505	16878	W 55441	25140	LEGUMES FRAIS,CONG,SECS
0541	POTATOES FRSH EXCL SWEET	W 19046	5662	W 23969	6764	W 31984	6254	W 24592	5797	POMMES DE TERRE
0542	LEGUMINOUS VEGETBLES DRY	W 10624	5476					W 14527	8098	LEGUMES A COSSE SECS
0545	OTHER FRESH VEGETABLES	W 13269	6989	W 7370	4543	W 8485	5532	W 10571	6166	AUTRES LEGUMES FRAIS,REF
05451	ALLIACEOUS VEGTBLS,FRESH	W 8185	4600	W 7325	4523	W 8482	5530	W 7607	4654	OIGNONS,ECHALOTES,AULX
0546	VEGETABLES SIMPLY PRESVD	W 3601	3816	W 4095	3993	W 8908	4932	W 5067	4603	LEGUMES CONG,CONSER
05461	VEGETABLES FROZEN	W 3554	3740	W 4087	3970	W 8894	4913	W 5063	4594	LEGUMES CONGELES
06	SUGAR AND PREPS,HONEY		3230		790		9030		17653	SUCRES ET PRODUITS
061	SUGAR AND HONEY	W 6574	2576	W 7	10	W 24641	8260	W 33429	16514	SUCRES ET MIEL
0611	RAW BEET AND CANE SUGAR	W 4983	1531	W 1	4	W 24609	8235	W 30958	13158	SUCRES BRUTS
07	COFFEE,TEA,COCOA,SPICES		5818		2881		3760		6744	CAFE,THE,CACAO,EPICES
081	*FEEDING STUFF FOR ANIML	W 41799	9894	W 51940	12928	W 41062	14153	W 39395	12085	NOURRITURE POUR ANIMAUX
0819	FOOD WASTE AND FEED NES	W 27829	9115	W 43624	12071	W 32716	12594	W 26863	9431	DECHETS,ALIMENTS NDA
08199	FODDER NES,INCL SWEETNED	W 27824	9112	W 43624	12071	W 32716	12594	W 26863	9431	PREPARATIONS FOURRAGERES
09	MISC EDIBLE PRODUCTS		12503		6583		9050		20292	PREP ALIMENTAIRES DIVERSES
098	EDIBLE PRODCTS,PREPS NES	W 3059	9667	W 1734	3479	W 3047	4808	W 4918	16604	PREP ALIMENTAIRES NDA
09809	MISC FOOD PREPRTIONS NES	W 1252	6556	W 233	365	W 559	721	W 3102	12303	PREP ALIMENTAIRES NDA
1	BEVERAGES AND TOBACCO		5933		6838		7427		11768	BOISSONS ET TABACS
11	BEVERAGES		3181		3896		4722		7510	BOISSONS
2	CRUDE MATERLS,EXCL FUELS		65813		96884		107184		124072	MAT BRUTES NON COMESTIBLES
22	OIL SEEDS,OLEAGINOUS FRT		30115		32887		28984		32857	GRAINES,FRUITS OLEAGINEUX
222	SEEDS FOR'SOFT'FIXED OIL	W 95555	29950	W 78525	32548	W 94737	28479	W 85434	32256	GRAINES HUILES FIXES
2222	SOYA BEANS	W 92781	27235	W 75531	29607	W 91527	25274	W 79889	28417	FEVES DE SOJA
24	CORK AND WOOD		8199		736		1030		14172	LIEGE ET BOIS
248	WOOD SHAPED,SLEEPERS	W 13089	6947	W 1277	717	W 1540	1005	W 19767	12717	BOIS SIMPLEMENT TRAVAILLES
2482	LUMBER SHAPED CONIFER	W 12780	6785	W 1205	672	W 1372	856	W 19020	12347	CONIFERES SCIES,RABOTES
24821	LUMBER SAWN ETC CONIFER	W 12650	6707					W 17870	11553	CONIFERES SCIES LONGITUD
27	CRUDE FERTLZR,MINRLS NES		5408		4449		7532		10130	ENGRAIS MINERAUX BRUTS
28	METALLIFEROUS ORES,SCRAP		16268		55709		65538		60624	MINERAIS METAL,DECHETS
281	IRON ORE,CONCENTRATES	W 199417	15280	W 1450539	54969	W 1531650	65020	W 1183178	59431	MINERAIS DE FER
2816	IRON ORE AGGLOMERATES	W 89719	12149	W 1450539	54969	W 1531650	65020	W 1183178	59431	MINERAIS AGGLOMERES
3	MINERAL FUELS ETC		233235		7652		9393		423445	COMBUSTIBLES MINERAUX LUB
33	PETROLEUM AND PRODUCTS		232459		6499		7778		421782	PETROLE ET DERIVES
333	CRUDE PETROLEUM	W 2345857	226015		8		19	W 2905392	405957	HUILES BRUTES DE PETROLE
334	PETROLEUM PRODUCTS,REFIN	W 6463	5537	W 11557	5491	W 16797	6771	W 48831	14603	PRODUITS RAFFINES
3345	LUBS,PETROLEUM OILS NES	W 6285	5366	W 6904	4306	W 9463	5215	W 12019	7273	HUILES LUBRIFIANTES
33451	LUBS(HIGH PETR CONT) ETC	W 5831	4198	W 6766	3767	W 9315	4464	W 11836	6556	HUILES LUBRIF,H LOURDES
4	ANIMAL,VEGETABLE OIL,FAT		5823		7877		5789		11633	HUILES,GRAISSES ANIM,VEG
42	FIXED VEGETABLE OIL,FAT		1601		5478		2474		6749	HUILES VEGETALES FIXES
423	FIXED VEG OILS,SOFT	W 506	877	W 3940	4893	W 733	1128	W 4258	5344	HUILES VEGET DOUCES FIXES
4232	SOYA BEAN OIL			W 3302	3963	W 46	48	W 3317	4066	HUILE DE SOJA
5	CHEMCLS,RELATED PROD NES		157894		75186		108022		216409	PRODUITS CHIMIQUES
51	ORGANIC CHEMICALS		10708		1759		2358		14737	PROD CHIMIQ ORGANIQUES
511	HYDROCARBONS NES,DERIVS	W 4153	4593	W 691	981	W 927	1420	W 4713	5450	HYDROCARBURES NDA
52	INORGANIC CHEMICALS		17060		7910		11357		21835	PROD CHIM INORGANIQUES
522	INORG ELEMNTS,OXIDES,ETC	W 9381	5167	W 7289	4134	W 10898	6476	W 9993	7407	ELEMENTS INORGANIQUES
523	OTHR INORG CHEMICALS ETC	W 22998	11768	W 12037	3775	W 14697	4881	W 47547	14296	AUT PRODUITS CHIMIQUES INORG
5232	OTH MTL CMPD OF INRG ACD	W 13903	5300	W 11441	2867	W 14174	4160	W 12715	6465	SELS METALLIQUES
53	DYES,TANNING,COLOUR PROD		7912		6221		7762		11451	PROD TEINTURE,COLORANTS
533	PIGMENTS,PAINTS,ETC	W 1790	6375	W 2201	4424	W 2631	6228	W 5490	10139	PIGMENTS,PEINTURES,VERNIS
541	*MEDICINAL,PHARM PRODUCT	K 2000398	31613		28962		29509	K 2439310	36059	PROD MEDICINAUX PHARMACEUT
5417	MEDICAMENTS	K 1605552	27412	K 1700377	26218	K 1309709	26293	K 2054126	30994	MEDICAMENTS
54179	— CONTNG OTH SUBSTANCES	K 1459977	21961	K 1526489	19921	K 1211005	20742	K 1925642	23905	MED CONT AUT SUBSTANCES
55	PERFUME,CLEANING ETC PRD		17221		14134		34547		21288	PROD POUR PARFUM,TOILETTE
553	PERFUMERY,COSMETICS,ETC	W 1899	6909	W 1959	6300	W 2362	25035	W 2497	9481	PRODUITS DE PARFUMERIE
554	SOAP,CLEANSING ETC PREPS	W 4330	7094	W 4539	7297	W 5197	8724	W 5626	8111	SAVONS,PRODUITS DETERSIFS
5542	WASHING PREPARATIONS ETC	W 3173	4990	W 2902	4590	W 3244	4958	W 3441	4259	PROD ORG TENSIO–ACT NDA
58	PLASTIC MATERIALS ETC		33844		654		3448		50234	MAT PLAST ARTIFICIELLES
582	PROD OF CONDENSATION ETC	W 10297	14030	W 185	400	W 1453	3104	W 11390	16136	PROD CONDENS,POLYCOND
5823	ALKYDS,OTHER POLYESTERS							W 7513	12032	ALKYDES ET AUT POLYESTERS
58231	— IN PRIMARY FORMS							W 7513	12032	SOUS FORMES PRIMAIRES
5829	OTH CONDNSATION,ETC PROD	W 7701	10277							AUT PROD CONDENSATION
583	POLYMERIZATION ETC PRODS	W 12379	19206	W 42	176	W 70	233	W 21778	33613	PROD POLYMERISATION
5831	POLYETHYLENE	W 3763	6348							POLYETHYLENE
5839	OTH POLYMRZTION ETC PROD	W 4159	8433					W 19217	31554	AUT PROD POLYMER COPOLYM
59	CHEMICAL MATERIALS NES		36565		13019		15741		56683	MAT PROD CHIMIQUES NDA
591	PESTICIDES,DISINFECTANTS	W 1822	7905	W 1892	7356	W 1768	8298	W 2009	9987	DESINF,INSECT,FONG,HERB
5911	INSECTICIDES,FOR RETAIL	W 945	4027	W 1011	3863	W 849	5059	W 1125	6478	INSECTICIDES VENTE DET
598	MISCEL CHEM PRODUCTS NES	W 8440	25525	W 1457	2437	W 1671	3643	W 13057	42983	PROD DIV INDUST CHIM NDA
5982	ANTI–KNOCK PREPARTNS ETC	W 2510	9188					W 2916	10639	PREPARAT ANTIDETONANTES
5989	CHEM PRODUCTS,PREPS NES	W 5683	15921	W 1212	2223	W 1332	3212	W 9747	31827	PROD PREP CHIMIQUES NDA
59898	COMPOUND CATALYSTS	W 644	2348					W 1377	7688	CATALYSEURS COMPOSITES
59899	OTH CHEM PRODS,PREPS,NES	W 4374	12397	W 156	1048	W 135	1257	W 7146	22138	AUT PRODUITS CHIMIQUES NDA
6	BASIC MANUFACTURES		243206		171620		246984		358734	ART MANUFACTURES
62	RUBBER MANUFACTURES NES		15571		13733		15465		20133	CAOUTCHOUC MANUFACTURE
625	RUBBER TYRES, TUBES ETC	W 5416	8178	W 4551	10357	W 7486	11787	W 6297	11069	PNEUS CAOUTCHOUC VULCANISE
6251	TYRES NEW FOR MOTOR CARS	W 1326	3065	W 1112	3993	W 2429	4491	W 1392	3855	PNEUS POUR VOITURES
6259	OTH TYRES,TYRE CASES,ETC	W 3582	3659	W 2983	4579	W 3686	4139	W 4114	4011	AUTRES PNEUS RECHAPES FLAPS

4. Special Imports C.I.F. by Commodities according to the S.I.T.C. (Rev. 2) in thousand U.S. Dollars
Importations Spéciales C.A.F. par Produits d'après la C.T.C.I. (Rév. 2) en milliers de Dollars E.U.

SITC CTCI	COMMODITY	1993 WEIGHT POIDS	1993 VALUE VALEUR	1994 WEIGHT POIDS	1994 VALUE VALEUR	1995 WEIGHT POIDS	1995 VALUE VALEUR	1996 WEIGHT POIDS	1996 VALUE VALEUR	PRODUIT
62599	TYRES NES,TYRE CASES,ETC	W 3468	3343	W 2868	4274	W 3534	3751	W 3239	3670	PNEUS,FLAPS
63	WOOD,CORK MANUFACTRS NES		9210		10200		3143		13702	OUVRAGES LIEGE ET BOIS
634	VENEERS,PLYWOOD,ETC	W 11331	8195	W 956	580	W 1488	1312	W 12939	10522	PLACAGES,CONTRE–PLAQUES
6342	PLYWOOD OF WOOD SHEETS	W 10957	7895					W 11890	9737	BOIS CONTRE–PLAQUES
635	WOOD MANUFACTURES NES	W 583	965	W 1101	9621	W 1198	1831	W 1084	3102	ART MANUF EN BOIS NDA
6353	BUILDERS WOODWRK,PREFABS	W 227	448	W 803	9130	W 73	936	W 219	2093	OUVRAGES DE MENUISERIE
64	PAPER,PAPERBOARD AND MFR		48402		28530		41466		68728	PAPIERS,CARTONS & OUVRAGES
641	PAPER AND PAPERBOARD	W 40203	36293	W 13839	14803	W 18291	23135	W 48269	52404	PAPIERS ET CARTONS
6411	NEWSPRINT	W 4451	4050	W 4384	3655	W 8993	7752	W 6289	6619	PAPIER JOURNAL
6413	KRAFT PAPER,PAPERBOARD	W 14815	9584					W 15789	12882	PAPIER ET CARTON KRAFT
64139	KRAFT PAPER PAPERBD,NES							W 15789	12882	PAPIER,CARTON KRAFT NDA
6415	PAPER,PAPERBRD,BULK,NES	W 7137	6836	W 33	123	W 26	164	W 12451	12340	PAPIERS,CARTONS ROULEAUX
64159	OTHER PAPER ETC,BULK,NES	W 6956	6489	W 33	123	W 26	164	W 10297	9689	AUT PAPIER ROULEAUX FEUILLES
6417	CORRUGATED PAPER ETC,BLK	W 6726	7997	W 8240	8589	W 7627	10639	W 6545	9489	PAPIERS,CARTONS ONDULES
64172	CREPED HSHOLD PAPER ETC	W 5694	7105	W 7920	8142	W 7358	10203	W 6139	9184	PAPIER NON KRAFT CREPE
6418	COATED ETC PAPER NES BLK	W 4838	5258	W 1076	2221	W 1244	3765	W 5574	9104	PAP,CARTONS COUCHES,ENDUITS
64189	COATED PAPER ETC NES	W 787	1759	W 984	2032	W 1141	3441	W 5477	8835	PAPIERS,CARTONS COUCHES
642	PAPER,ETC,PRECUT,ARTS OF	W 24221	12109	W 8801	13727	W 9696	18331	W 7575	16324	PAP,CARTONS DECOUPES
6421	PAPER ETC CONTAINERS	W 22754	8230	W 6614	8433	W 7816	12154	W 5785	10106	BOITES,SACS EMBALLAGES
65	TEXTILE YARN,FABRICS,ETC		45723		27987		31817		52842	FILS,TISSUS,ARTICLES TEXTILE
652	COTTON FABRICS,WOVEN	W 1184	5822	W 1330	6118	W 904	5065	W 1079	5944	TISSUS DE COTON
6522	WOVEN COTTON BLEACHD,ETC	W 1153	5657	W 1242	5730	W 878	4849	W 1060	5805	TISSUS COTON BLANCHIS ETC
65224	BLCHED COTTON FABRIC NES	W 1040	5013	W 1130	4977	W 761	4061	W 851	4470	AUT TIS PLUS 85% COT BLANCHI
653	WOVN MAN–MADE FIB FABRIC	W 2811	17382	W 1762	10957	W 2224	14330	W 3128	21530	TISSUS FIBRES SYNTH,ARTIF
6532	DISC SYN TXTL FABRIC NES	W 995	6604	W 905	5686	W 1082	7397	W 1427	10486	TIS DISC MOINS 85% FIBR TEXT
6534	DISC SYN BLEND FABRC NES	W 820	4702					W 1072	6595	TISSUS FIBRES SYNTH DISCONT
655	KNITTED,ETC FABRICS	W 808	5304					W 934	6204	ETOF BONNETERIE PIECES ETC
6552	OTHER KNIT ETC FAB NONEL	W 808	5304					W 934	6204	ETOF BON NON ELAS NON SYNT
657	SPECIAL TXTL FABRC,PRODS	W 1531	7657	W 768	4550	W 824	5012	W 1401	7400	TISSUS SPECIAUX
66	NONMETAL MINERAL MFS NES		17075		13933		18557		37053	ART MIN NON METALLIQUES
662	CLAY,REFRACTORY BLDG PRD	W 8621	5165	W 3672	2427	W 9847	5046	W 28296	18286	MAT CONST REFRACTAIRES
6623	REFRACTORY BUILDING PROD	W 5031	3219	W 3566	2313	W 9839	5026	W 18929	13203	BRIQUES REFRACTAIRES
66232	REFRACTRY BRICKS ETC NES	W 3498	2345					W 7899	7628	BRIQUES ETC REFRACTAIRES
664	GLASS	W 9531	4050	W 4861	5251	W 4137	5247	W 6812	5506	VERRE
67	IRON AND STEEL		49509		31893		80021		83138	FER ET ACIER
671	PIG IRON ETC	W 3964	1669	W 6062	3490	W 8355	4602	W 8072	7153	FONTE,SPIEGEL,POUDRES
6716	FERRO–ALLOYS	W 3931	1641	W 5963	3394	W 8348	4593	W 8031	7024	FERRO–ALLIAGES
672	IRON,STEEL PRIMARY FORMS		1022	W 1567	1195	W 5811	2629	W 21569	7913	LINGOTS FER,ACIER
673	IRON,STEEL SHAPES ETC	W 9499	4264	W 1040	895	W 6681	4074	W 16173	9777	BARRES,PROFIL FER,ACIER
6733	IRON,STEEL PROFILES ETC	W 9205	3898	W 643	578	W 5575	3298	W 14707	8694	PROFILES,PALPLAN FER,ACIER
674	IRN,STL UNIV,PLATE,SHEET	W 16944	12741	W 16155	12937	W 29252	26526	W 25832	21593	LARGES PLATS,TOLES
6744	IRN,STL HVY PLATE,ROLLED	W 4456	2753	W 4062	2710	W 9242	8148	W 5897	3489	TOLES LAMINEES PLUS 4.75 MM
67441	— OF IRON OR SIMPLE STL	W 4454	2740	W 4047	2684	W 8460	7623	W 5391	3072	TOLES NON ACIER FIN CARB
6749	OTH IRN,STL PLATES,SHEET	W 9411	7792	W 9857	8406	W 16921	15489	W 13701	12388	AUTRES TOLES FER,ACIER
67491	— OF IRON OR SIMPLE STL	W 7290	6164	W 8912	7656	W 15469	14084	W 12126	10909	AUT TOLES AUTRES ACIER FIN
678	IRON,STL TUBES,PIPES,ETC	W 22535	28346	W 4693	13046	W 16627	41575	W 21656	34842	TUBES,TUYAUX EN FONTE,FER
6782	IRON,STL SEAMLESS TUBES	W 13709	5717	W 9	46	W 10	48	W 5841	6966	TUBES,TUYAUX SANS SOUDURE
6783	IRON,STL TUBES,PIPES NES	W 7711	17220	W 4161	9971	W 15675	36492	W 14231	21123	AUT TUBES,TUYAUX FER,ACIER
6785	IRON,STEEL TUBE FITTINGS	W 1108	5369	W 523	3029	W 941	5035	W 1583	6753	ACCESSOIRES DE TUYAUTERIE
68	NON–FERROUS METALS		12646		2976		5831		20393	METAUX NON FERREUX
684	ALUMINIUM	W 1847	8021	W 6	94	W 9	129	W 2823	13381	ALUMINIUM
6842	ALUMINIUM,ALLOYS WORKED	W 1626	7563	W 6	94	W 9	129	W 2528	12694	ALUMINIUM,ALLIAGES OUVRE
68423	ALUMINIUM FOIL	W 1329	6490					W 1510	9166	FEUILLES,BANDES MINCES AL
69	METAL MANUFACTURES NES		44286		41708		50264		61806	ART MANUFACT EN METAL NDA
691	STRUCTURES AND PARTS NES	W 1683	5066	W 2350	5169	W 6988	4596	W 4880	6467	CONSTRUCT FER,ACIER,ALU
6911	STRUCTURES,PARTS IRN,STL	W 979	2201	W 1984	3489	W 6713	3570	W 4734	5954	CONSTRUCT FER,ACIER,FONTE
692	METAL TANKS,BOXES,ETC	W 4281	9384	W 5445	8714	W 4292	7740	W 4159	11425	RECIPIENTS METALLIQUES
6924	MTL TRANSPORT BOXES ETC	W 4071	9120	W 5405	8547	W 4080	7266	W 4109	11161	FUTS,TAMBOURS,BIDONS
69241	STL TRANSPORT BOXES ETC	W 2795	5087	W 4962	7475	W 3740	6334	W 2956	6235	FUTS,TAMBOURS,BIDONS FER
694	STL,COPPR NAILS,NUTS,ETC	W 830	3591	W 954	3617	W 1167	4557	W 1156	5313	CLOUS,VIS,ECROUS
695	TOOLS	W 560	5629	W 565	6485	W 620	10098	W 774	8576	OUTILS A MAIN
6954	BLADES,TIPS,ETC FR TOOLS	W 233	3050	W 134	3772	W 101	5208	W 101	4384	OUTILS POUR MACHINE–OUTIL
697	BASE MTL HOUSEHOLD EQUIP	W 1211	4902	W 1156	4083	W 1085	4792	W 2025	6242	ART MENAGE MET COMMUNS
699	BASE METAL MFRS NES	W 3143	12950	W 2568	10175	W 4923	12891	W 5286	18054	ART MANUFACTURES MET NDA
6991	LOCKSMITHS WARES,ETC	W 933	4462	W 280	1610	W 307	1927	W 953	5376	ARTICLES DE SERRURERIE
7	MACHINES,TRANSPORT EQUIP		480263		288629		561967		675009	MACHINES MATERIEL TRANSPORT
71	POWER GENERATING EQUIPMT		21226		34278		36973		46852	MACHINES GENERATRICES
712	STEAM ENGINES,TURBINES	W 11	1182	W 40	5682	W 25	1390	W 45	1646	MACHINES A VAPEUR D'EAU PIEC
7129	STM ENGINE ETC PARTS NES	W 9	1139	W 33	4933	W 24	1234	W 27	1083	PARTIES,PIECES DU 712.6
713	INTRNL COMBUS PSTN ENGIN	W 2201	7087	W 2182	9339	W 2826	9514	W 2850	13238	MOTEURS EXPL COMB INT, PIECE
714	ENGINES AND MOTORS NES	W 48	8803	W 58	14172	W 116	18502	W 180	21075	MOTEURS NON ELECTRIQUES
7149	ENGINE & MOTOR PARTS NES	W 41	7643	W 42	9911	W 77	13819	W 151	16011	PIECES 714 ET 718.88
71499	PARTS NES,OF 71488,71888	W 35	5614	W 33	7862	W 62	9545	W 138	14508	PIECES 714.88 ET 718.88
716	ROTATING ELECTRIC PLANT	W 276	3013	W 339	4326	W 543	7461	W 1465	8039	APP ELECTR ROTATIFS,PIECES
7162	AC MTRS,GENRTRS,GEN SETS	W 180	1923	W 250	2998	W 397	5331	W 550	5867	MOTEURS ELECTRIQUES
72	MACHS FOR SPCL INDUSTRYS		48592		21802		38643		49667	MAC SPECIALES POUR INDUST
723	CIVIL ENGNEERG EQUIP ETC	W 1168	13107	W 610	2389	W 633	4645	W 1601	7702	APPAREILS DE GENIE CIVIL
7234	CONST,MINING MACHNRY NES	W 1022	11033	W 524	1748	W 582	3787	W 1387	4712	MACH POUR LA CONST, MINES
72346	OTH CONST,MINING MCH NES	W 899	10427	W 14	46	W 35	130	W 4	37	AUT MACH EXTRACTION,EXCAV ET
728	OTH MACHY FOR SPCL INDUS	W 1181	26791	W 655	10801	W 1258	19908	W 1763	28195	AUT MACH IND PARTICULIERES
7283	OTHR MINERAL WORKG MACHY	W 178	2556	W 343	3546	W 395	4020	W 511	7138	MACH TRIER,CRIBLER,BROYER
7284	MACHY FOR SPCL INDUS NES	W 674	20510	W 313	7255	W 862	15889	W 1152	19758	MACH SPEC IND PARTICUL.
72848	OTH MCHY WITH INDIV FNCT	W 308	14461	W 187	3808	W 537	8587	W 654	8488	AUTRES MACHINES NDA
72849	PTS OF MACHS OF 7284 ETC	W 157	3414	W 119	3365	W 260	6822	W 283	7717	PIECES DU 728.4 ETC
73	METALWORKING MACHINERY		3000		3620		4908		11142	MACH TRAVAIL DES METAUX
737	METALWORKING MACHNRY NES	W 244	1474	W 392	3496	W 1458	4598	W 3126	9132	MACH TRAV METAUX PIECES
74	GENRL INDUSTRL MACHY NES		196141		85999		241240		198609	MACH APP INDUSTRIE
741	HEATING,COOLING EQUIPMNT	W 14013	105376	W 9725	42727	W 22781	179511	W 12330	92772	MACH CHAUFFAGE,PIECES
7413	INDUS FURNACES ETC,PARTS	W 4527	16478	W 5261	18682	W 3826	23872	W 730	10143	FOURS IND,LABOR,PIECES
74132	INDUST FURNACES NONELECT	W 4433	15945	W 5235	18402	W 3807	23678	W 700	9531	FOURS NON ELECTRIQUES
7416	HEATING,COOLING EQU NES	W 9055	86111	W 3087	19788	W 18120	150217	W 9975	74934	APP CHANGEMENT TEMP
742	PUMPS FOR LIQUIDS ETC	W 1510	27385	W 1066	9643	W 1686	11526	W 1375	12370	POMPES MOTO–POMPES
7428	OTHER PUMPS FOR LIQUIDS	W 831	21381	W 672	3447	W 906	5420	W 845	4836	AUTRES POMPES POUR LIQ
74288	PUMPS FR LIQUIDS NES ETC	W 811	20857	W 662	3198	W 896	5174	W 838	4691	POMPES POUR LIQUIDES NDA
7429	PTS NES OF PUMPS OF 742	W 315	4917	W 228	4895	W 496	4368	W 341	5744	PIECES POUR GROUPE 742
743	PUMPS NES,CENTRFUGES ETC	W 732	9247	W 1028	12151	W 1145	13079	W 2059	19362	POMPES COMPRES,VENT ETC
7431	PUMPS FOR GASES ETC	W 230	2583	W 425	3663	W 511	4696	W 858	6770	POMPES AIR A VIDE,COMPRES
7439	PTS NES OF APP OF 7435,6	W 98	3171	W 182	4759	W 137	3420	W 317	4754	PIECES 743.5 ET 743.6
744	MECHANICAL HANDLING EQU		12845	W 3082	14529	W 3001	22958	W 4219	26915	EQUIP MANUTENTION PIECES
7441	FORK LIFT TRCKS,ETC,PTS	W 213	625	W 268	1063	W 965	2363	W 1145	6970	CHARIOTS POUR USINES ETC
74411	FORK LIFT TRUCKS ETC	W 212	577	W 266	1027	W 964	2319	W 1143	6922	CHARIOTS POUR LES GARES

4. Special Imports C.I.F. by Commodities according to the S.I.T.C. (Rev. 2) in thousand U.S. Dollars
Importations Spéciales C.A.F. par Produits d'après la C.T.C.I. (Rév. 2) en milliers de Dollars E.U.

SITC CTCI	COMMODITY	1993		1994		1995		1996		PRODUIT
		WEIGHT POIDS	VALUE VALEUR	WEIGHT POIDS	VALUE VALEUR	WEIGHT POIDS	VALUE VALEUR	WEIGHT POIDS	VALUE VALEUR	
7442	LIFTING,LOADING MACH NES	W 705	3823	W 1060	3250	W 1121	5375	W 2158	6483	APP LEVAGE,MANUTENTION
7449	PTS NES OF MACHY OF 7442		8398	W 1754	10216	W 915	15220	W 916	13462	PIECES DU 744.2
745	NONELEC MACHY,TOOLS NES	W 1500	8821	W 462	5305	W 1114	12013	W 560	9386	AUT MACH NON ELEC,PIECES
7452	OTH NONELEC MCHS,PTS NES	W 1482	8317	W 413	4713	W 830	10635	W 464	7751	AUT MACH NON ELEC,PIECES
74522	PACKAGNG,BOTTLNG,ETC MCH	W 350	5304	W 78	2110	W 327	6486	W 156	3094	MACH NETT BOUTEILLES,ETC
749	NONELEC MACH PTS,ACC NES		32467	W 132	1645	W 76	2153	W 3255	37805	PIECES MACH NON ELEC NDA
7492	COCKS,VALVES ETC NES	W 4982	12486					W 1298	17705	ART ROB,SIM POUR TUYAUX
7493	SHAFT,CRANK,PULLEY ETC	W 273	7542					W 544	8889	ARBRES TRANS,VILEBREQUINS
7499	OTH NONELEC MCHY PTS NES		9359	W 132	1645	W 76	2153	W 736	5805	PIECES NON ELECT NDA
74992	METAL–PLASTIC GASKETS		6590					W 265	2111	JOINTS METALLOPLASTIQUES
75	OFFICE MACHNES,ADP EQUIP		19018		23372		35557		42154	MACH BUREAU TRAIT AUTOM
751	OFFICE MACHINES	W 101	2581	W 112	3502	W 168	4622	W 179	4444	MACH,APPAREILS DE BUREAU
752	AUTOMTIC DATA PROC EQUIP	W 190	11403	W 366	14231	W 388	21490	W 1127	26668	MACH TRAIT INFORMATION
7522	DIGITAL COMPUTERS	W 79	5737	W 87	8957	W 166	12055	W 240	13415	MACH DIGITALES COMPLETES
7525	ADP PERIPHERAL UNITS	W 73	3027	W 237	3072	W 136	4957	W 216	9381	UNITES PERIPHERIQUES
759	OFFICE,ADP MCH PTS,ACCES	W 122	5034	W 234	5640	W 147	9445	W 497	11042	PIECES DU 751 ET 752
7599	ACCTG,ETC,ADP MCH PTS,AC	W 61	4100	W 210	4716	W 113	7937	W 448	9300	PIECES DU 751 ET 752
76	TELECOMM,SOUND EQUIPMENT		27900		24158		41670		33787	EQUIPMENT DE TELECOM
761	TELEVISION RECEIVERS	W 412	3984	W 403	2319	W 669	6505	W 712	6777	RECEPTEURS DE TELEVISION
7611	COLOUR TV RECEIVERS	W 400	3898	W 397	2300	W 661	6438	W 701	6685	RECEPTEURS COULEUR
764	TELECOM EQPT,PTS,ACC NES	W 349	21525	W 490	20454	W 698	32023	W 550	22630	EQUIP TELECOM,PIECES
7641	LINE TELEPHONE,ETC EQUIP	W 186	15824	W 212	11449	W 424	22775	W 250	11953	APP TELEPHON PAR FIL
7643	TV,RADIO TRANSMITTRS ETC	W 41	1948	W 63	4200	W 76	3699	W 41	3152	APP EMET TELE RADIO
77	ELECTRIC MACHNRY NES ETC		39279		44375		53752		67585	MACH APP ELECT NDA
771	ELECTRIC POWER MACHY NES	W 389	2795	W 1117	6254	W 931	5859	W 946	6738	MACH PROD,TRANS ELECTR
7711	TRANSFORMERS,ELECTRICAL	W 173	1124	W 840	4186	W 626	3496	W 642	3404	TRANSFO ELECTRIQUES
77118	OTHER ELEC TRANSFORMERS	W 173	1117	W 833	4124	W 616	3478	W 638	3392	AUTRES TRANSFO ELECTRIQ
772	SWITCHGEAR ETC,PARTS NES	W 383	7993	W 374	8653	W 563	9442	W 1076	13392	APP COUPURE,SECT ETC
7721	SWITCHGEAR ETC	W 377	7540	W 366	8269	W 553	8692	W 1068	12584	APP COUPURE,SECTIONMNT
773	ELECTR DISTRIBUTNG EQUIP	W 1000	5100		8609	W 1661	9183	W 4675	10514	EQUIPMT DISTRIBUTION ELECT
7731	INSULATED WIRE,CABLE ETC	W 864	4289	W 2729	6948	W 1517	7382	W 1913	9369	FILS,CABLES ISOLES ELECT
775	HOUSEHOLD TYPE EQUIP NES	W 2080	10143	W 2895	9697		14911	W 4394	16905	MACH,APP USAGE DOMESTQUE
7752	DOM REFRIGERATRS,FREEZRS	W 936	4486	W 1078	3699	W 1547	6477	W 1586	7320	REFRIG,CONGEL MENAGER
778	ELECTRICAL MACHINERY NES	W 2532	11891	W 2390	11141	W 4118	14141	W 5369	18264	AUTRES MACH ELECT NDA
7788	OTH ELEC MACHY,EQUIP NES	W 1428	4449	W 1909	6459	W 2612	7786	W 3825	7737	AUT MACH APP ELEC NDA
77887	ELECTRICAL CARBONS	W 1378	3010	W 1882	5813	W 2498	6982	W 3667	4167	PIECES CHARBON,GRAPHITE
78	ROAD VEHICLES		48317		41775		64891		113268	VEHICULES ROUTIERS
781	PASS MOTOR VEH EXC BUSES	W 3673	28579	W 2432	26008	W 4736	43265	W 7239	70410	AUTO TRANSPORT PERSONNES
782	LORRIES,SPCL MTR VEH NES	W 984	7081	W 1878	11597	W 2498	17518	W 2741	18663	VEHICULES SPECIAUX,MARCH
7821	LORRIES,TRUCKS	W 728	4772	W 1761	11024	W 2148	15742	W 2498	16362	VEHICULES TRANSP MARCHAND
784	MOTOR VEH PRTS,ACCES NES	W 2304	8863	W 1	24	W 1	15	W 7957	18471	PIECES 722,781,782,783
7842	MOTOR VEHICLE BODIES	W 1	4					W 2742	7150	CARROS 722,781,782,783
7849	OTHER MOTOR VEHCL PARTS	W 2302	8858					W 5100	11162	PIECES 722,781,782,783
79	OTHR TRANSPORT EQUIPMENT		76790		9250		44333		111946	AUTRE MATERIEL TRANSPORT
792	AIRCRAFT ETC	W 108	24245	W 128	7538	W 138	7577	W 151	74453	APP NAVIGATION AERIENNE
7921	HELICOPTERS	W 10	5261	W 2	1037	W 2	987	W 4	517	HELICOPTERES
7924	AIRCRFT NES OVER 15000KG	W 69	13559	W 100	843	W 100	754	W 110	69591	AERODYNES PLUS 15000 KG
7929	AIRCRAFT PARTS NES	W 29	5417	W 26	5641	W 31	5788	W 37	4331	PIECES DU 792
793	SHIPS AND BOATS ETC	W 7464	52532	W 964	1712		36756	W 9050	37365	NAVIRES BATEAUX,ETC
7932	SHIPS AND BOATS NES	W 277	771	W 6	43		5944	W 280	2275	NAVIRES ET BATEAUX
79323	OTHER CARGO VESSELS	W 65	263			W 82	5660	W 139	1980	AUT BATEAUX TRANS MARCH
7938	TUGS,SPECIAL VESSELS ETC	W 7161	51582	W 958	1653	W 7117	30808	W 8770	35082	REMORQUEURS,BATEAUX SPEC
79382	SPECL PURPOSE VESSLS ETC	W 7111	50596	W 918	1323	W 6996	30096	W 8725	34566	BAT–PHARES,–POMPES,DRAGUES
8	MISC MANUFACTURED GOODS		83483		72789		105148		133146	ART MANUFACTURES DIVERS
821	*FURNITURE,PARTS THEREOF	W 1369	4301	W 944	3526	W 1615	6034	W 1882	6821	MEUBLES ET PIECES
84	CLOTHING AND ACCESSORIES		3120		2703		6266		8063	VETEMENTS
851	*FOOTWEAR	W 586	5287	W 795	6380	W 1238	8930	W 1202	11151	CHAUSSURES
85102	FOOTWEAR LEATHER	W 370	3856	W 447	4423	W 757	6201	W 803	8876	CHAUS SEMELLES EN CUIR
87	PRECISION INSTRUMNTS NES		16925		14545		25244		32281	INSTRUM,APPAR SCIENT NDA
874	MEASURNG,CONTROLNG INSTR		15035	W 546	12355	W 950	21867	W 636	28212	INSTRUMENTS DE MESURE
8741	SURVEYING INSTRUMENTS	W 26	2550	W 33	3271	W 51	5290	W 50	2798	INST GEODESIE,TOPO ETC
8743	GAS,LIQUID CONTROL INSTR		2664	W 31	1035	W 69	1378	W 279	7132	APP,INSTR MESURE FLUIDES
8748	ELEC MEAS,CONTRL EQU NES	W 164	5865	W 132	3355	W 126	9034	W 62	6723	APP ELEC ELECTRO MESURE
87483	OTH ELCTRNC MEAS ETC EQU	W 164	5847	W 130	3251	W 125	8964	W 61	6676	AUT APP ELECTRO DE MESURE
88	PHOTO EQU,OPTICL GDS ETC		4772		3391		4333		7881	APP,FOURN PHOTO,OP,MONTR
89	MISC MANUFCTRD GOODS NES		45534		39222		51380		62192	ART MANUFACTURES DIVERS
892	PRINTED MATTER	W 1808	14391	W 1173	11466	W 1186	12141	W 2149	16819	IMPRIMES
8921	PRINTED BOOKS,GLOBES,ETC	W 1140	9891	W 1112	8936	W 1082	8668	W 1377	9689	LIVRES,BROCHURES,CARTES
89211	PRINTED BOOKS,PAMPHLETS	W 1097	9580	W 1068	8701	W 1034	8377	W 1334	9346	LIVRES,BROCHURES
893	ARTICLES OF PLASTIC NES	W 5548	18542		18136		26098		27516	OUVRAGES EN MAT DIVIS 58
8931	PLSTC PACKG CONTNRS,LIDS	W 2618	9807	W 4910	9944	W 5445	13651	W 3650	13861	ART TRANSP EMBALLAGE ETC
8939	MISC PLASTIC ARTICLES	W 2753	8403	W 2991	7938	W 4496	11946	W 4309	13088	ART DIVERS EN MAT DIV 58
89399	OTHR PLASTC ARTICLES NES	W 1819	7244	W 1910	6696	W 2652	10005	W 2825	11244	AUT OUV MAT DIV 58
9	GOODS NOT CLASSD BY KIND		4009		269413		386954		8193	ART TRANSACT NON CLASSES
931	*SPECIAL TRANSACTIONS	W 2319	3761		268823		385959	W 3345	7828	TRANS.SPECIALES

5. Special Exports F.O.B. by Commodities according to the S.I.T.C. (Rev. 2) in thousand U.S. Dollars
Exportations Spéciales F.O.B. par Produits d'après la C.T.C.I. (Rév. 2) en milliers de Dollars E.U.

SITC CTCI	COMMODITY	1993		1994		1995		1996		PRODUIT
		WEIGHT POIDS	VALUE VALEUR	WEIGHT POIDS	VALUE VALEUR	WEIGHT POIDS	VALUE VALEUR	WEIGHT POIDS	VALUE VALEUR	
	ALL COMMODITIES		1662107		1954282		2466984		2569251	TOUS PRODUITS
0	FOOD AND LIVE ANIMALS		94711		87800		116147		140848	ALIMENTS,ANIMAUX VIVANTS
02	DAIRY PRODCTS,BIRDS'EGGS		4275		5693		9757		7878	PRODUITS LAITIERS,OEUFS
022	MILK AND CREAM	W 3125	4045	W 3352	5509	W 7554	9434	W 4663	7779	LAIT ET CREME
0224	MILK,CREAM PRESERVED ETC	W 1695	3026	W 3297	5442	W 7535	9381	W 2785	6145	LAIT,CREME CONS,CONC
03	FISH AND PREPARATIONS		6228		5909		6429		12366	POISSONS ET PREPARATIONS
034	FISH,FRESH,CHILLED,FROZN	W 2601	3900	W 3784	5595	W 4097	6168	W 5077	9541	POISSON FRAIS, REFRIG,CONG
04	CEREALS AND PREPARATIONS		14215		8680		11891		31937	CEREALES ET PRODUITS
048	CEREAL ETC PREPARATIONS	W 7762	13831	W 2976	8584	W 3271	10163	W 11975	29580	PREPTNS A BASE CEREALES
0481	PREPD BREAKFAST FOOD ETC	W 1831	4580	W 2173	5662	W 2564	7426	W 2964	9595	CEREALES TRAVAILLEES
0484	BAKERY PRODUCTS	W 4032	7064					W 6500	14073	PRODUITS DE BOULANGERIE
04841	BREAD,BISCUIT,COM WAFERS							W 3111	7755	PAINS,BISCUITS DE MER
05	VEGETABLES AND FRUIT		7853		7067		8333		13464	LEGUMES ET FRUITS
06	SUGAR AND PREPS,HONEY		30449		34223		51575		34021	SUCRES ET PRODUITS
061	SUGAR AND HONEY	W 51592	27540	W 57277	30602	W 86065	45461	W 49436	28138	SUCRES ET MIEL
0611	RAW BEET AND CANE SUGAR	W 51074	27223	W 52109	28014	W 67119	41783	W 44990	27519	SUCRES BRUTS
07	COFFEE,TEA,COCOA,SPICES		10230		6082		6475		10023	CAFE,THE,CACAO,EPICES
081	*FEEDING STUFF FOR ANIML	W 49363	11761	W 59313	12511	W 54430	12085	W 60272	16820	NOURRITURE POUR ANIMAUX
0813	OILCAKE AND OTH RESIDUES	W 42520	10743	W 49065	10650	W 37350	7928	W 45193	13005	TOURTEAUX
08131	— OF SOYA BEANS	W 42520	10743	W 49065	10650	W 37350	7928	W 45193	13005	TOURTEAUX DE SOJA
09	MISC EDIBLE PRODUCTS		8039		5981		7462		11074	PREP ALIMENTAIRES DIVERSES
098	EDIBLE PRODCTS,PREPS NES	W 4576	6386	W 3506	4170	W 4527	5386	W 6819	8328	PREP ALIMENTAIRES NDA
1	BEVERAGES AND TOBACCO		32141		39731		53032		61700	BOISSONS ET TABACS
11	BEVERAGES		31723		39429		51935		59819	BOISSONS
111	NON–ALCOHL BEVERAGES NES	W 17824	12240	W 25737	14773	W 68477	35466	W 67821	33889	BOISSONS NON ALCOOLIQUES
11102	FLAVORED WATERS NON–ALCO	W 17736	12191	W 25518	14657	W 68156	35322	W 65853	33644	LIMONADES,EAUX GAZEUSES
112	ALCOHOLIC BEVERAGES	W 21875	19484	W 31360	24655	W 21411	16469	W 30642	25931	BOISSONS ALCOOLIQUES
1123	BEER,ALE,STOUT,PORTER	W 10283	9333	W 21280	13450	W 15093	8706	W 13421	9261	BIERES
1124	DISTILLED ALCOHOLIC BEVS	W 11590	10142	W 10052	11177	W 6272	7708	W 17008	16562	ALCOOLS,EAUX–DE–VIE
11249	OTH ALCOHOLC BEVS,CMPNDS	W 11574	10122	W 10052	11176	W 6271	7705	W 17007	16560	BOISSONS ALCOOLIQUES NDA
2	CRUDE MATERLS,EXCL FUELS		4050		2682		4811		9450	MAT BRUTES NON COMESTIBLES
3	MINERAL FUELS ETC		957504		960731		1180832		1291494	COMBUSTIBLES MINERAUX LUB
33	PETROLEUM AND PRODUCTS		920827		926551		1118060		1238712	PETROLE ET DERIVES
333	CRUDE PETROLEUM	W 2760088	361868	W 2788688	352794	W 2986937	391348	W 2657375	439512	HUILES BRUTES DE PETROLE
334	PETROLEUM PRODUCTS,REFIN	W 4772378	553750	W 4811338	569788	W 5075580	722257	W 5091425	794720	PRODUITS RAFFINES
3341	GASOLINE,OTH LIGHT OILS	W 604323	112265	W 648379	109928	W 808367	134366	W 527430	117791	ESSENCES POUR MOTEURS
33411	MOTOR,AVIATION SPIRIT	W 604323	112265	W 648379	109928	W 808367	134366	W 525721	117399	ESSENCES MOTEURS D'AVIONS
3342	KEROSENE,OTH MEDIUM OILS	W 359593	66068	W 455312	78609	W 493795	84035	W 409288	86919	PETR LAMPANTS,AUT HUIL
33421	KEROSENE INCL JET FUEL	W 358917	65847	W 454640	78380	W 493790	84032	W 398089	84584	PETROLES LAMPANTS
3343	GAS OILS	W 775117	130524	W 23131	4320	W 26103	4732	W 1287527	236570	GAS OILS
3344	FUEL OILS,NES	W 2997493	230158	W 3602692	342591	W 3715033	478948	W 2781745	321904	FUEL OILS
3345	LUBS,PETROLEUM OILS NES	W 35852	14735	W 81824	34340	W 32283	20177	W 85433	31536	HUILES LUBRIFIANTES
33451	LUBS(HIGH PETR CONT) ETC	W 35843	14727	W 81824	34339	W 32268	20126	W 85426	31508	HUILES LUBRIF,H LOURDES
335	RESIDUAL PETRLM PROD NES	W 31856	5209	W 23329	3969	W 25832	4455	W 24989	4480	PRODUITS RESIDUELS NDA
341	*GAS,NATURAL AND MANUFCT	W 196086	36677	W 207833	34180	W 195364	62772	W 214361	52780	GAZ NATUREL,GAZ MANUFACT
3413	PETROLM GASES,LIQUEFIED	W 196085	36668	W 207833	34180	W 195364	62772	W 214361	52765	GAZ DE PETROLE LIQUEFIE
34131	LIQUEFIED PROPANE,BUTANE	W 179779	33123	W 160208	26953	W 95272	41598	W 97024	31190	PROPANE,BUTANE LIQUEFIES
34139	OTH HYDROCARBON GAS LQFD	W 16306	3544	W 47624	7227	W 100092	21174	W 117337	21575	HYDROCARBURES GAZEUX NDA
5	CHEMCLS,RELATED PROD NES		278591		315551		386003		583487	PRODUITS CHIMIQUES
51	ORGANIC CHEMICALS		40523		143		354		123769	PROD CHIMIQ ORGANIQUES
512	ALCOHOLS,PHENOLS ETC	W 391852	39663	W 98	119	W 277	296	W 697393	123116	PHENOLS,PHENOLS–ALCOOLS
5121	ACYCLIC ALCOHOLS,DERIVS	W 391852	39663	W 98	119	W 277	296	W 697390	123103	ALCOOLS ACYCLIQUES
51211	METHYL ALCOHOL(METHANOL)	W 391822	39622					W 697106	122671	ALCOOLS METHYLIQUES
52	INORGANIC CHEMICALS		149069		230999		261719		301751	PROD CHIM INORGANIQUES
522	INORG ELEMNTS,OXIDES,ETC	W 1399213	149006	W 1588193	230936	W 1465591	261633	W 1749252	301579	ELEMENTS INORGANIQUES
5225	INORGANIC BASES ETC NES	W 1397729	148425	W 1587467	230331	W 1443946	260936	W 1748138	300869	AUTRES BASES OXYDES METAL
52251	AMMONIA,ANHYDROUS ETC	W 1397724	148421	W 1587465	230330	W 1443942	260930	W 1748120	300852	AMMONIAC LIQUEFIE
55	PERFUME,CLEANING ETC PRD		18298		18178		18540		21859	PROD POUR PARFUM,TOILETTE
553	PERFUMERY,COSMETICS,ETC	W 1310	5516	W 1049	4256	W 706	5255	W 1220	5543	PRODUITS DE PARFUMERIE
554	SOAP,CLEANSING ETC PREPS	W 9661	12779	W 14061	13920	W 12570	13248	W 13678	16303	SAVONS,PRODUITS DETERSIFS
5542	WASHING PREPARATIONS ETC	W 7474	8695	W 11978	9912	W 11058	10587	W 11950	12648	PROD ORG TENSIO–ACT NDA
562	*FERTILIZERS,MANUFACTURE	W 513830	59225	W 341833	58777	W 512230	96293	W 606801	115665	ENGRAIS MANUFACTURES
5621	CHEM NITROGENOUS FERTLZR	W 511367	58961	W 340298	58383	W 502171	93928	W 603844	114816	ENGRAIS AZOTES
56216	UREA	W 511315	58952	W 340296	58382	W 502152	93926	W 603026	114201	UREE
6	BASIC MANUFACTURES		209536		105848		151370		324999	ART MANUFACTURES
63	WOOD,CORK MANUFACTRS NES		5023		5839		8984		9563	OUVRAGES LIEGE ET BOIS
635	WOOD MANUFACTURES NES	W 1308	4914	W 1613	5776	W 2647	8955	W 2619	8166	ART MANUF EN BOIS NDA
6353	BUILDERS WOODWRK,PREFABS	W 1164	4623	W 1317	5387	W 2529	8547	W 2431	7559	OUVRAGES DE MENUISERIE
64	PAPER,PAPERBOARD AND MFR		20098		26052		33213		35775	PAPIERS,CARTONS & OUVRAGES
642	PAPER,ETC,PRECUT,ARTS OF	W 9165	18779	W 14285	24846	W 13943	30946	W 14373	33603	PAP,CARTONS DECOUPES
6421	PAPER ETC CONTAINERS	W 4794	3587	W 5473	5293	W 7045	9690	W 7196	11144	BOITES,SACS EMBALLAGES
6428	PAPER ETC ARTICLES NES	W 2769	10802	W 5698	13149	W 3638	13880	W 3694	14734	OUVRAGES EN PATE A PAPIER
64285	PAPER ETC DIAPERS ETC	W 2526	10104	W 5235	11903	W 3165	12376	W 3133	13542	SERVIETTES HYGIENIQUES
65	TEXTILE YARN,FABRICS,ETC		5498		6026		6983		8915	FILS,TISSUS,ARTICLES TEXTILE
66	NONMETAL MINERAL MFS NES		26655		28795		32401		33568	ART MIN NON METALLIQUES
661	LIME,CEMENT,BLDG PRODS	W 329239	16518	W 461447	16050	W 305720	17310	W 358992	20428	CHAUX,CIMENTS MAT CONSTR
6612	CEMENT	W 329210	16432	W 461412	16027	W 305715	17305	W 358941	20297	CIMENTS HYDRAULIQUES
665	GLASSWARE	W 19281	8889	W 24877	11339	W 27318	12741	W 18658	9386	OUVRAGES EN VERRE
6651	BOTTLES ETC OF GLASS	W 19226	8863	W 24854	11322	W 27276	12714	W 18637	9342	RECIPIENTS EN VERRE
66511	GLASS BOTTLES ETC NONVAC	W 19226	8863	W 24854	11322	W 27276	12714	W 18637	9342	BONBONNES,BOUTEILLES,ETC
67	IRON AND STEEL		142198		28206		53445		212542	FER ET ACIER
671	PIG IRON ETC	W 155533	15097	W 232400	22644	W 325211	40514	W 163508	25827	FONTE,SPIEGEL,POUDRES
6713	IRON,STL POWDER,SHOT,ETC	W 155533	15097	W 232400	22644	W 325211	40514	W 163508	25827	POUDRES,GREN FER,ACIER
67133	SPONGE IRON OR STEEL	W 155533	15097	W 232395	22640	W 325163	40471	W 163508	25827	FER,ACIER SPONGIEUX AUT POUD
673	IRON,STEEL SHAPES ETC	W 401755	122345	W 10892	3973	W 18734	6072	W 620457	181037	BARRES,PROFIL FER,ACIER
6731	IRON,STEEL WIRE ROD	W 372852	111218	W 2	1	W 4	2	W 582742	166877	FIL MACHINE FER,ACIER
67311	IRON,SIMPLE STL WIRE ROD							W 582740	166874	FIL MACH AUT ACIER FIN
67314	STNLESS STL ETC WIRE ROD	W 372849	111215							FIL MACH ACIER INOXYDABLE
6732	IRON,STEEL BARS ETC	W 28530	10820	W 10793	3824	W 18545	5839	W 35708	13439	BARRES FER,ACIER
67322	HIGH CARBON STL BARS ETC	W 32	14					W 21824	8027	BARRES ACIER FIN CARBONE
67324	STNLESS STL ETC BARS ETC	W 21919	8148						1	BARRES ACIER INOXYDABLE
69	METAL MANUFACTURES NES		8434		9673		13789		18224	ART MANUFACT EN METAL NDA
7	MACHINES,TRANSPORT EQUIP		46017		28094		48712		96825	MACHINES MATERIEL TRANSPORT
74	GENRL INDUSTRL MACHY NES		4836		7543		13317		22986	MACH APP INDUSTRIE
741	HEATING,COOLING EQUIPMNT	W 478	3522	W 732	6475	W 3912	9285	W 1522	11916	MACH CHAUFFAGE,PIECES
76	TELECOMM,SOUND EQUIPMENT		7926		2796		2805		3140	EQUIPMENT DE TELECOM
764	TELECOM EQPT,PTS,ACC NES	W 77	6000		1420	W 109	1610	W 29	1488	EQUIP TELECOM,PIECES
77	ELECTRIC MACHNRY NES ETC		9551		3423		5446		10402	MACH APP ELECT NDA
79	OTHR TRANSPORT EQUIPMENT		17207		6373		19989		51722	AUTRE MATERIEL TRANSPORT
792	AIRCRAFT ETC	W 45	14241	W 100	4762	W 117	18678	W 82	11527	APP NAVIGATION AERIENNE
7921	HELICOPTERS			W 4	188	W 99	18336			HELICOPTERES

5. Special Exports F.O.B. by Commodities according to the S.I.T.C. (Rev. 2) in thousand U.S. Dollars
Exportations Spéciales F.O.B. par Produits d'après la C.T.C.I. (Rév. 2) en milliers de Dollars E.U.

SITC CTCI	COMMODITY	1993			1994			1995			1996			PRODUIT
		WEIGHT POIDS		VALUE VALEUR	WEIGHT POIDS		VALUE VALEUR	WEIGHT POIDS		VALUE VALEUR	WEIGHT POIDS		VALUE VALEUR	
7924	AIRCRFT NES OVER 15000KG	W	17	12866	W	74	4221				W	75	11399	AERODYNES PLUS 15000 KG
793	SHIPS AND BOATS ETC	W	2703	2965	W	230	1612	W	132	1311	W	7328	40194	NAVIRES BATEAUX,ETC
7938	TUGS,SPECIAL VESSELS ETC	W	2530	2229	W	100	823	W	22	16	W	6813	38497	REMORQUEURS,BATEAUX SPEC
79382	SPECL PURPOSE VESSLS ETC	W	2500	2185	W	97	796				W	6370	37323	BAT–PHARES,–POMPES,DRAGUES
8	MISC MANUFACTURED GOODS			35377			34599			48510			53422	ART MANUFACTURES DIVERS
84	CLOTHING AND ACCESSORIES			8599			9590			11483			11438	VETEMENTS
87	PRECISION INSTRUMNTS NES			1956			1833			10798			8534	INSTRUM,APPAR SCIENT NDA
874	MEASURNG,CONTROLNG INSTR	W	26	1875	W	37	1801	W	152	10751			8525	INSTRUMENTS DE MESURE
89	MISC MANUFCTRD GOODS NES			19508			17375			19614			25368	ART MANUFACTURES DIVERS
892	PRINTED MATTER			7637	W	216	2113	W	179	2412	W	883	6242	IMPRIMES
8928	PRINTED MATTER NES			5745	W	36	196	W	29	264	W	465	3408	IMPRIMES NDA
893	ARTICLES OF PLASTIC NES	W	3429	7536	W	5359	10774			12077			13027	OUVRAGES EN MAT DIVIS 58
8939	MISC PLASTIC ARTICLES	W	1667	3089	W	3191	6552	W	3705	6665	W	2958	6530	ART DIVERS EN MAT DIV 58
89399	OTHR PLASTC ARTICLES NES	W	1655	3066	W	3185	6542	W	3638	6514	W	2793	6208	AUT OUV MAT DIV 58
9	GOODS NOT CLASSD BY KIND			1526			375016			471729			538	ART TRANSACT NON CLASSES
931	*SPECIAL TRANSACTIONS	W	451	1515			375001			471719	W	113	531	TRANS.SPECIALES

FOOT NOTES – NOTES

TABLE 1 –

1 Export indices relate to national exports.

TABLEAU 1 –

1 Les indices des exportations se rapportent aux exportations nationales.

1. HISTORICAL SERIES, 1961–1996 GENERAL TRADE, IMPORTS C.I.F., EXPORTS F.O.B. # 1
SERIES HISTORIQUES, 1961–1996 COMMERCE GENERAL, IMPORTATIONS C.A.F., EXPORTATIONS F.O.B

YEAR ANNEE	VALUE IN MILLION TUNISIAN DINARS / VALEUR EN MILLION TUNISIAN DINARS — MERCHANDISE–MARCHANDISE IMPORTS	EXPORTS	GOLD–OR IMPORTS	EXPORTS	CONVERSION FACTORS U.S. CENTS PER TUNISIAN DINAR / FACTEURS DE CONVERSION CENTS E.U. PAR TUNISIAN DINAR IMPORTS	EXPORTS	INDEX NUMBERS–INDICES QUANTUM IMPORTS	EXPORTS	UNIT VALUE / VALEUR UNITAIRE IMPORTS	EXPORTS
1961	88.45	46.35			238.1000	238.1000	48	98	20	12
1962	90.89	48.69			238.1000	238.1000	48	100	20	12
1963	93.66	52.92			238.1000	238.1000	48	111	21	12
1964	110.85	57.30			219.9400	221.6100	52	129	23	11
1965	129.06	62.92			190.5000	190.5000	51	116	27	13
1966	131.22	76.39			190.5000	190.5000	53	134	27	14
1967	137.09	78.36			190.5000	190.5000	57	138	26	14
1968	114.50	82.83			190.5000	190.5000	48	146	26	14
1969	139.78	86.96			190.5000	190.5000	60	149	25	14
1970	160.40	95.80			190.4750	190.4750	28	75	17	9
1971	179.96	113.30			192.5840	193.1270	34	81	17	10
1972	222.22	150.33			209.5850	209.5090	39	105	18	10
1973	286.10	178.80			238.8350	235.5800	39	92	21	13
1974	488.66	397.70			230.8460	231.6810	50	95	29	27
1975	572.82	345.58			248.5570	247.5730	50	87	33	27
1976	656.72	338.26			232.8750	232.9480	57	92	31	24
1977	782.47	398.25			233.1700	233.0380	75	88	32	25
1978	899.73	468.42			240.2780	240.4260	79	102	33	27
1979	1156.70	726.70			246.2620	246.4110	97	108	37	37
1980	1428.40	904.80			246.9210	246.9610	92	102	48	53
1981	1866.00	1234.00			203.1444	202.8433	94	100	54	61
1982	2001.90	1169.40			169.9572	169.8244	98	100	59	67
1983	2106.40	1280.50			147.2836	146.1933	93	92	61	69
1984	2508.90	1399.10			128.2434	128.4135	100	91	66	76
1985	2287.00	1443.00			113.5613	112.7762	77	82	71	76
1986	2295.10	1403.70			125.9538	125.3746	93	92	70	68
1987	2509.10	1770.70			121.1012	120.7976	68	95	77	78
1988	3167.00	2055.40			116.4737	116.5065	85	96	81	83
1989	4163.60	2782.00			105.3758	105.3051	101	110	89	95
1990	4826.40	3087.40			114.2170	114.2412	100	100	100	100
1991	4789.00	3417.10			108.3609	108.2603	107	110	99	98
1992	5688.80	3549.70			113.0507	113.2195	104	111	94	95
1993	6237.20	3818.10			99.6265	99.5838	116	121	94	96
1994	6647.30	4696.60			98.9991	99.1623	120	137		101
1995	7464.10	5172.90			105.8798	105.8455				102
1996	7542.70	5372.00			102.7002	102.7102				103

2. IMPORTS BY BROAD ECONOMIC CATEGORY AND EXPORTS BY INDUSTRIAL ORIGIN. (PERCENTAGE OF TOTAL VALUE)
IMPORTATIONS PAR CATEGORIES ECONOMIQUES ET EXPORTATIONS PAR BRANCHE D'ACTIVITE.(EN POURCENTAGE DE LA VALEUR TOTALE)

IMPORTS – IMPORTATIONS

	1990	1991	1992	1993	1994	1995	1996
TOTAL IMPORTS–IMPORTATIONS TOTALES	100.	100.	100.	100.	100.	100.	100.
1 FOOD BEV–ALIMENTATION BOISSONS	8.6	6.0	6.2	6.3	7.8	10.5	7.4
11 PRIMARY–PRODUITS DE BASE	4.9	2.9	2.8	3.0	3.8	6.5	3.7
111 FOR INDUSTRY–POUR L'INDUSTRIE	3.7	1.7	1.8	1.8	2.6	5.4	2.9
112 FOR HOUSEHOLDS–POUR LES MENAGES	1.2	1.2	1.0	1.2	1.2	1.1	0.8
12 PROCESSED–PRODUITS ELABORES	3.7	3.1	3.4	3.3	4.0	4.0	3.7
121 FOR INDUSTRY–POUR L'INDUSTRIE	1.6	1.6	1.3	1.4	1.9	1.8	1.9
122 FOR HOUSEHOLDS–POUR LES MENAGES	2.2	1.5	2.0	1.9	2.0	2.1	1.8
2 IND SUPPLIES–APPROV INDUSTRIELS	43.8	44.6	45.4	42.8	43.4	44.4	44.2
21 PRIMARY–PRODUITS DE BASE	6.2	5.7	4.7	3.9	4.5	4.8	4.6
22 PROCESSED–PRODUITS ELABORES	37.6	39.0	40.6	38.9	38.9	39.6	39.6
3 FUELS–COMBUSTIBLES	9.0	8.1	7.4	7.7	7.5	7.2	8.3
31 PRIMARY–PRODUITS DE BASE	3.3	2.5	3.0	2.8	3.4	4.1	3.6
32 PROCESSED–PRODUITS ELABORES	5.6	5.6	4.4	5.0	4.2	3.1	4.6
321 MOTOR SPIRIT–ESSENCE	5.3	0.6	0.7	0.8	0.7	0.6	0.8
322 OTHER–AUTRES	0.4	5.0	3.7	4.2	3.5	2.5	3.8
4 MACHINERY–EQUIPEMENT	18.6	22.3	20.8	22.0	19.8	17.8	19.3
41 CAPITAL EQUIPMENT–MACHINES	15.6	19.2	17.7	18.8	16.9	15.2	16.6
42 PARTS–PIECES ACCESSOIRES	3.0	3.1	3.1	3.2	2.9	2.6	2.7
5 TRANSPORT–TRANSPORT	9.3	7.7	9.5	10.3	9.6	8.1	7.9
51 PASSENGER CARS–AUTOMOBILES	1.9	0.6	1.3	2.6	3.2	3.0	3.2
52 OTHER–AUTRES	3.3	3.2	4.3	3.2	3.2	2.3	1.6
521 INDUSTRIAL–INDUSTRIELS	3.1	3.1	4.3	3.2	3.1	2.2	1.6
522 NON INDUSTRIAL–NON INDUSTRIEL	0.2	0.1	0.0	0.0	0.0	0.0	0.0
53 PARTS–PIECES ACCESSOIRES	4.1	3.9	3.9	4.5	3.2	2.8	3.1
6 CONSUM GOODS–BIENS CONSOMMATION	10.6	11.2	10.7	10.6	11.8	12.0	12.8
61 DURABLE–DURABLES	2.2	1.9	1.5	1.4	1.4	1.4	1.4
62 SEMI DURABLE–SEMI DURABLES	5.1	5.6	5.7	6.1	7.0	7.4	8.2
63 NON DURABLE–NON DURABLES	3.3	3.7	3.5	3.1	3.4	3.1	3.2
7 GOODS NES–BIENS NDA	0.1	0.1	0.0	0.2	0.1	0.1	0.0

EXPORTS – EXPORTATIONS

	1990	1991	1992	1993	1994	1995	1996
TOTAL EXPORTS–EXPORTATIONS TOTALES	100.	100.	100.	100.	100.	100.	100.
1 AGRICULTURE	5.8	4.8	4.1	4.7	4.0	3.6	3.1
2 MINING QUARRY–INDUS EXTRACTIVES	16.8	13.1	14.0	10.9	8.8	8.3	9.8
3 MANUFACTURING–IND MANUFACTUR	77.4	82.1	81.9	84.4	87.2	88.2	87.1
31 FOOD BEV TOBACCO–ALIM BOISS TAB	5.5	10.5	6.2	6.8	9.0	6.4	4.4
32 TEXTILES–INDUSTRIES TEXTILES	38.2	38.8	43.4	46.4	47.5	49.8	50.9
33 WOOD & PRODUCTS–BOIS & PRODUITS	0.2	0.1	0.1	0.3	0.1	0.1	0.2
34 PAPER & PRODUCTS–PAPIER & PRODT	0.7	0.9	0.8	0.9	0.6	0.8	0.6
35 CHEMICALS–INDUSTRIES CHIMIQUES	17.4	16.8	15.9	13.6	14.2	14.4	16.0
36 NON METAL MIN–MIN NON METAL	2.9	2.1	2.5	2.0	1.6	2.1	1.5
37 BASIC METAL–IND METAL BASE	1.2	1.4	1.4	0.9	2.2	1.3	1.2
38 METAL MANUF–MANUF METAL	10.9	11.0	11.0	12.9	11.4	12.6	11.5
39 OTH MANUF IND–AUTRES MANUF	0.4	0.5	0.5	0.6	0.6	0.5	0.7

3. TRADE BY PRINCIPAL COUNTRIES OF PRODUCTION AND LAST DESTINATION (VALUE IN THOUSAND U.S. DOLLARS)
ECHANGES SELON LES PRINCIPAUX PAYS DE PRODUCTION ET DE DERNIERE DESTINATION (VALEUR EN MILLIERS DE DOLLARS EU)

COUNTRIES–PAYS	GENERAL IMPORTS C.I.F. IMPORTATIONS GENERALES C.A.F					COUNTRIES–PAYS	GENERAL EXPORTS F.O.B. EXPORTATIONS GENERALES F.O.B.				
	1992	1993	1994	1995	1996		1992	1993	1994	1995	1996
World	6431558	6213959	6483889	7903050	7698160	Monde	4039903	3804499	4584453	5474626	5517367
Africa	356644	273526	372588	540216	514971	Afrique	364545	322501	331886	462987	394936
Americas	508513	487771	597022	588397	541154	Amériques	67444	54830	83579	117429	121190
Northern America	382600	387326	462482	474835	357908	Amérique du Nord	35858	32534	50036	71207	76535
LAIA	109618	90371	125165	98964	168938	ALAI	24695	11552	24815	24241	27386
CACM	702	51	601	1963	332	MCAC	14	143	923	3	11
Caribbean	15579	9974	8492	12176	13826	Caraïbes	4027	10571	7566	21615	16336
Rest of America	14	49	283	460	149	Autre Amérique	2850	29	238	363	922
As.ex F.USSR	440188	444368	495102	573393	632334	Asie l'URSS exclus	290593	246132	266866	310141	343326
Eur.x F.USSR	4965053	4787480	4858522	5916148	5846323	Europe l'URSS exclus	3230774	3077282	3747557	4411765	4483310
EU	4711181	4602271	4665020	5642001	5569837	UE	3165067	3022076	3666438	4324121	4419202
EFTA	83073	84466	103722	123503	112056	AELE	15134	22724	53592	54115	31692
East Europe	139053	88550	76489	121881	153756	Europe de l'Est	41350	30539	20111	27984	24752
Other Europe	223	6903	9839	21794	6647	Autre de l'Europe	792	1363	5384	4537	4391
Former USSR	82849	98887	104138	230599	98538	Ancienne URSS	13966	8407	2792	1530	9648
Oceania	7949	4007	8932	11087	6906	Océanie	195	469	1362	2755	6653
France, Monac	1637840	1668226	1779589	2024585	1878489	France, Monac	1094025	1142804	1232176	1536353	1419768
Italy/Italie	1168236	1134365	999816	1208985	1451796	Italy/Italie	689606	620748	885921	1021370	1143395
Germany/Allemagne	901262	807662	791923	993687	976577	Germany/Allemagne	686000	660847	712824	860978	862337
USA/Etats–Unis d'Amer	320095	358394	426936	399994	320506	Belgium–Luxembourg	278917	276451	297729	357095	395451
Belgium–Luxembourg	302645	268504	283183	354322	348003	Libyan Arab Jamahiriya	176057	188520	156468	192377	195900
Spain/Espagne	213554	201432	233336	329432	303464	Spain/Espagne	110820	96030	216846	221489	199401
Netherlands/Pays–Bas	142320	136306	137471	206167	179698	Netherlands/Pays–Bas	103423	117293	141091	156071	171492
Japan/Japon	147317	143181	151804	140924	163635	Algeria/Algérie	97804	66622	106069	185464	96099
United Kingdom	113843	140506	144260	159182	144409	India/Inde	75511	49268	81204	98293	119327
Algeria/Algérie	151998	99032	124931	179838	127111	United Kingdom	72762	50375	68841	81569	106364
Libyan Arab Jamahiriya	51297	52139	120765	203876	234678	USA/Etats–Unis d'Amer	33771	31657	47979	69065	75403
Russian Federation	82849	98887	104138	228460	82893	Turkey/Turquie	37127	51182	42133	33658	49354
Switz.Liecht	75776	77769	96012	114376	103651	Greece/Grèce	84202	2761	54340	31441	37706
Turkey/Turquie	58067	57100	84595	105921	100430	Morocco/Maroc	46061	35065	27764	26798	37536
Sweden/Suède	70204	80615	69489	82678	84231	Switz.Liecht	12107	20385	49399	48187	27230
Morocco/Maroc	74372	48612	46737	59740	58641	China/Chine	28980	11287	24848	31133	18551
Greece/Grèce	39574	52200	45135	71964	66026	Indonesia/Indonésie	28515	27842	10535	18889	14877
China/Chine	48915	49126	49012	54659	61021	Saudi Arabia	16529	19979	16206	15616	23114
Brazil/Brésil	39962	43390	63801	43877	59092	Syrian Arab Republic	20814	24876	15925	25174	3085
Finland/Finlande	38624	48025	52529	64861	44561	Iran (Islamic Rp. of)	29638	7320	6571	15778	26264
Argentina/Argentine	50776	37136	44185	23611	84661	Poland/Pologne	13930	21696	14369	16953	15464
Canada	62505	28930	35475	74841	37392	Egypt/Egypte	7155	6648	16214	24536	26815
Poland/Pologne	67826	44267	39705	32349	38079	Denmark/Danemark	22049	15108	14174	14034	14032
Portugal	7603	7295	54904	60949	29260	Brazil/Brésil	12518	6994	16446	15749	18647
Syrian Arab Republic	27491	26207	24221	45629	32525	Japan/Japon	10313	6901	15558	16212	17306
Denmark/Danemark	34941	22399	27120	41611	25550	Ireland/Irlande	6065	22074	10765	10892	16053
Saudi Arabia	20909	19717	28332	44860	34648	Portugal	3567	4920	7231	11159	32273
Austria/Autriche	30483	22586	37836	29415	25929	Cuba	3850	8943	5841	19507	15925
Korea, Republic of	20784	26880	24686	34001	35703	Sweden/Suède	8745	7201	7874	10823	9532
Egypt/Egypte	23003	24050	25385	30188	30720	Pakistan	4557	17	0	20332	18086
Cote d'Ivoire	30654	26654	24593	26626	23296	Bahrain/Bahreïn	6173	10382	6883	5782	10393
Romania/Roumanie	3756	2352	4739	28408	68863	Bulgaria/Bulgarie	23747	4338	3396	5067	2720
Czech Republic		21539	15183	28857	19801	Lebanon/Liban	5257	4437	6430	12446	8543
Bulgaria/Bulgarie	17452	9038	11165	24295	18602	Cameroon/Cameroun	8512	7832	6994	7942	5299
India/Inde	15064	12234	11164	13100	23192	Jordan/Jordanie	8367	8241	14008	1644	1338
Malaysia/Malaisie	8327	9616	12702	18661	24143	Russian Federation	13966	8407	2792	1527	2377
Hong Kong	15073	12398	11097	13358	21090	Austria/Autriche	3188	3352	5403	6634	8780
Singapore/Singapour	11884	12132	13332	13637	7546	United Arab Emirates	3103	3594	4297	4515	8940
Ireland/Irlande	10052	12150	8428	14163	11844	Cote d'Ivoire	3744	4295	3208	5720	7097
Cuba	14335	9809	7597	10688	12690	Finland/Finlande	1696	2113	11224	4215	2621
Yugoslavia/Yougoslavie	31523	5289	3452	6969	3935	Venezuela	6465	4043	4647	5116	
Hungary/Hongrie	11854	11346	5697	7971	8411	Bangladesh	7160	6085	5706	0	
Malta/Malte	156	6837	9600	21262	6542	Ghana	7027	2698	2158	2130	2613
Thailand/Thaïlande	5306	6909	12422	5565	10960	Malta/Malte	783	1127	5339	4510	4391
Indonesia/Indonésie	5749	5536	7434	10347	11889	Romania/Roumanie	2401	3383	914	3425	5426
Norway, SVD, JM	7281	6677	7543	9048	8344	Yugoslavia/Yougoslavie	8431	580	2033	1008	3273
Czechoslovakia	38166					So. Africa Customs Un			651	4973	8915
Ecuador/Equateur	1872	3880	7909	13050	9343	Norway, SVD, JM	2123	1620	2737	3866	2439
Bahrain/Bahreïn	4222	6589	4097	7415	7652	Korea, Republic of	0	124	6462	2618	1654
Mexico/Mexique	1622	1272	513	11970	12248	Senegal/Sénégal	1095	2225	1907	2308	3182

(VALUE AS PERCENTAGE OF WORLD TOTAL)(VALEURS EN POURCENTAGE DU TOTAL MONDIAL)

	1987	1988	1989	1990	1991	1992	1993	1994	1995	1996		1987	1988	1989	1990	1991	1992	1993	1994	1995	1996
Africa	5.9	5.6	5.9	4.9	4.8	5.5	4.4	5.7	6.8	6.7	Afrique	5.3	5.7	8.2	8.8	9.4	9.0	8.5	7.2	8.5	7.2
Americas	9.7	12.2	9.5	8.1	8.0	7.9	7.8	9.2	7.4	7.0	Amériques	2.6	1.6	3.2	1.8	1.5	1.7	1.4	1.8	2.1	2.2
Northern America	8.0	9.4	6.3	6.1	6.4	5.9	6.2	7.1	6.0	4.6	Amérique du Nord	1.9	1.1	2.4	0.9	0.8	0.9	0.9	1.1	1.3	1.4
LAIA	1.3	2.6	2.7	1.5	1.4	1.7	1.5	1.9	1.3	2.2	ALAI	0.3	0.3	0.4	0.7	0.5	0.6	0.3	0.5	0.4	0.5
CACM	0.0	0.0	0.0	0.1	0.0	0.0	0.0	0.0	0.0	0.0	MCAC		0.0	0.1	0.0	0.1	0.0	0.0	0.0	0.0	0.0
Caribbean	0.3	0.2	0.5	0.3	0.2	0.2	0.2	0.1	0.2	0.2	Caraïbes	0.4	0.0	0.3	0.2	0.1	0.1	0.3	0.2	0.4	0.3
Rest of America	0.0	0.0	0.0	0.0	0.0	0.0	0.0	0.0	0.0	0.0	Autre Amérique	0.0	0.1	0.0	0.0	0.0	0.1	0.0	0.0	0.0	0.0
As.ex F.USSR	7.2	7.4	8.8	7.7	7.1	6.8	7.2	7.6	7.3	8.2	Asie l'URSS exclus	7.4	11.5	10.8	7.6	6.8	7.2	6.5	5.8	5.7	6.2
Eur.x F.USSR	75.9	73.1	73.6	77.0	78.1	77.2	77.0	74.9	74.9	75.9	Europe l'URSS exclus	81.7	77.7	75.7	79.1	78.9	80.0	80.9	81.7	80.6	81.3
EU	70.3	68.5	68.9	72.4	74.1	73.3	74.1	71.9	71.4	72.4	UE	78.4	75.0	74.0	78.1	76.9	78.3	79.4	80.0	79.0	80.1
EFTA	1.6	1.4	1.2	1.3	1.6	1.3	1.4	1.6	1.6	1.5	AELE	0.9	0.5	0.3	0.4	0.5	0.4	0.6	1.2	1.0	0.6
East Europe	3.4	2.8	3.2	2.5	2.0	2.2	1.4	1.2	1.5	2.0	Europe de l'Est	1.4	1.6	0.9	0.3	1.1	1.0	0.8	0.4	0.5	0.4
Other Europe	0.7	0.5	0.4	0.7	0.4	0.0	0.1	0.2	0.3	0.1	Autre de l'Europe	0.9	0.6	0.4	0.2	0.4	0.0	0.0	0.1	0.1	0.1
Former USSR	0.9	1.1	1.7	1.7	1.4	1.3	1.6	1.6	2.9	1.3	Ancienne URSS	1.7	1.1	0.7	1.2	1.1	0.3	0.2	0.1	0.0	0.2
Oceania	0.1	0.2	0.2	0.0	0.1	0.1	0.1	0.1	0.1	0.1	Océanie	0.0	0.0	0.0	0.0	0.0	0.0	0.0	0.0	0.1	0.1
France, Monac	27.5	24.8	26.3	27.9	26.1	25.5	26.8	27.4	25.6	24.4	France, Monac	21.6	25.8	24.6	26.6	25.3	27.1	30.0	26.9	28.1	25.7
Italy/Italie	11.4	13.3	13.7	15.9	17.5	18.2	18.3	15.4	15.3	18.9	Italy/Italie	16.5	18.9	18.7	21.2	19.7	17.1	16.3	19.3	18.7	20.7
Germany/Allemagne	12.7	12.6	11.7	12.5	14.3	14.0	13.0	12.2	12.6	12.7	Germany/Allemagne	19.6	14.1	12.9	15.1	16.4	17.0	17.4	15.5	15.7	15.6
USA/Etats–Unis d'Amer	6.0	7.1	5.1	5.2	4.8	5.0	5.8	6.6	5.1	4.2	Belgium–Luxembourg	6.5	5.9	6.1	7.0	6.2	6.9	7.3	6.5	6.5	7.2
Belgium–Luxembourg	4.6	4.8	4.7	4.8	5.4	4.7	4.3	4.4	4.5	4.5	Libyan Arab Jamahiriya	0.4	1.6	4.1	4.6	5.5	4.4	5.0	3.4	3.5	3.6
Spain/Espagne	4.6	4.6	3.8	3.1	3.1	3.3	3.2	3.6	4.2	3.9	Spain/Espagne	2.6	3.4	2.7	2.6	3.7	2.7	2.5	4.7	4.0	3.6
Netherlands/Pays–Bas	2.4	2.4	2.4	2.6	2.2	2.2	2.2	2.1	2.6	2.3	Netherlands/Pays–Bas	3.2	2.9	2.5	2.5	2.7	2.6	3.1	3.1	2.9	3.1
Japan/Japon	0.9	1.3	1.4	1.8	2.3	2.3	2.3	2.3	1.8	2.1	Algeria/Algérie	3.1	2.5	2.2	2.3	2.1	2.4	1.8	2.3	3.4	1.7
United Kingdom	1.7	1.7	1.5	1.7	1.8	1.8	2.3	2.2	2.0	1.9	India/Inde	1.0	3.4	2.8	1.2	1.8	1.9	1.3	1.8	1.8	2.2
Algeria/Algérie	3.4	2.4	2.3	2.0	1.9	2.4	1.6	1.9	2.3	1.7	United Kingdom	0.9	1.6	1.5	1.6	1.3	1.8	1.3	1.5	1.5	1.9

4. General Imports C.I.F. by Commodities according to the S.I.T.C. (Rev. 2) in thousand U.S. Dollars
Importations Générales C.A.F. par Produits d'après la C.T.C.I. (Rév. 2) en milliers de Dollars E.U.

SITC CTCI	COMMODITY	1993 WEIGHT POIDS	1993 VALUE VALEUR	1994 WEIGHT POIDS	1994 VALUE VALEUR	1995 WEIGHT POIDS	1995 VALUE VALEUR	1996 WEIGHT POIDS	1996 VALUE VALEUR	PRODUIT
	ALL COMMODITIES		6213959		6483889		7903050		7698160	TOUS PRODUITS
0	FOOD AND LIVE ANIMALS		385202		478292		787583		541774	ALIMENTS,ANIMAUX VIVANTS
01	MEAT AND PREPARATIONS		19590		13705		12472		8457	VIANDES ET PREPARATIONS
011	MEAT FRESH,CHILLD,FROZEN	W 11709	19533	W 8162	13569	W 6191	12355	W 2951	8437	VIANDES FRAICHES,REF,CONGE
02	DAIRY PRODCTS,BIRDS'EGGS		61316		45283		57605		30835	PRODUITS LAITIERS,OEUFS
022	MILK AND CREAM	W 38238	41878	W 28332	29743	W 19135	38075	W 12346	21063	LAIT ET CREME
0224	MILK,CREAM PRESERVED ETC	W 20686	34440	W 16516	24988	W 19113	38029	W 10197	19931	LAIT,CREME CONS,CONC
04	CEREALS AND PREPARATIONS		135794		183362		442480		265169	CEREALES ET PRODUITS
041	WHEAT ETC UNMILLED	W 714857	90020	W 851996	98693	W 1652381	301548	W 860299	184409	FROMENT,EPEAUTRE
0411	DURUM WHEAT UNMILLED	W 28714	4748	W 49492	11342	W 687345	145987	W 205003	54143	FROMENT DUR NON MOULU
0412	OTHER WHEAT ETC UNMILLED	W 686143	85272	W 802503	87351	W 965035	155561	W 655296	130265	AUTRE FROMENT NON MOULU
043	BARLEY UNMILLED	W 29803	2925	W 454239	36844	W 687203	79695	W 31757	4319	ORGE NON MONDEE
044	MAIZE UNMILLED	W 289959	36504	W 254076	32218	W 328896	45475	W 314762	59725	MAIS NON MOULU
05	VEGETABLES AND FRUIT		21006		34167		75669		35043	LEGUMES ET FRUITS
054	VEG ETC FRSH,SMPLY PRSVD	W 55591	12678	W 49654	17306	W 100872	49769	W 55645	19555	LEGUMES FRAIS,CONG,SECS
0541	POTATOES FRSH EXCL SWEET	W 52870	11602	W 37084	12380	W 64022	26348	W 31263	13061	POMMES DE TERRE
06	SUGAR AND PREPS,HONEY		61638		91486		72737		89883	SUCRES ET PRODUITS
061	SUGAR AND HONEY	W 212520	59958	W 283534	90266	W 186794	70324	W 241700	88343	SUCRES ET MIEL
0611	RAW BEET AND CANE SUGAR	W 55052	13031	W 85161	25003	W 55522	17167	W 69300	20640	SUCRES BRUTS
0612	REFINED SUGAR ETC	W 153996	45126	W 192803	62629	W 125900	50292	W 165213	63735	SUCRES RAFFINES
07	COFFEE,TEA,COCOA,SPICES		31105		44188		50359		45386	CAFE,THE,CACAO,EPICES
071	COFFEE AND SUBSTITUTES	W 5664	7169	W 9141	17296	W 8401	30024	W 7484	20779	CAFE ET SUCCEDANES
0711	COFFEE GREEN,ROASTED,SUB	W 5451	5684	W 8861	14819	W 8045	25804	W 7096	16517	CAFE TORREFIE OU DECAFEINE
07111	COFFEE GREEN,HUSKS,SKINS	W 5449	5664	W 8857	14788	W 8040	25738	W 6997	16340	CAFE NON TORREFIE
081	*FEEDING STUFF FOR ANIML	W 147410	34721	W 213470	44705	W 227008	45867	W 157821	43673	NOURRITURE POUR ANIMAUX
0813	OILCAKE AND OTH RESIDUES	W 143791	31124	W 148864	33377	W 139075	30479	W 153599	41325	TOURTEAUX
08131	— OF SOYA BEANS	W 143791	31124	W 148851	33372	W 139075	30479	W 153599	41325	TOURTEAUX DE SOJA
1	BEVERAGES AND TOBACCO		55980		54745		65365		64348	BOISSONS ET TABACS
12	TOBACCO AND MANUFACTURES		49574		46839		58478		58199	TABACS BRUTS FABRIQUES
121	TOBACCO UNMNFCTRD,REFUSE	W 7088	20116	W 5665	13634	W 6417	17016	W 6234	18456	TABACS BRUTS,DECHETS
122	TOBACCO,MANUFACTURED	W 3613	29458	W 3768	33205	W 4308	41462	W 4273	39743	TABACS FABRIQUES
1222	CIGARETTES	W 3552	29042	W 3482	31549	W 3988	39787	W 3662	36493	CIGARETTES
2	CRUDE MATERLS,EXCL FUELS		297167		372218		486096		402807	MAT BRUTES NON COMESTIBLES
24	CORK AND WOOD		74215		104359		111891		84510	LIEGE ET BOIS
248	WOOD SHAPED,SLEEPERS	W 182831	66456	W 215517	90609	W 191130	96293	W 169401	73663	BOIS SIMPLEMENT TRAVAILLES
2482	LUMBER SHAPED CONIFER	W 159198	54886	W 190343	76117	W 166303	81248	W 152595	64963	CONIFERES SCIES,RABOTES
24821	LUMBER SAWN ETC CONIFER	W 159196	54870	W 190341	76096	W 166300	81227	W 152591	64935	CONIFERES SCIES LONGITUD
251	*PULP AND WASTE PAPER	W 51758	17989	W 46013	19458	W 67715	48275	W 56492	24973	PATES A PAPIER,DECHETS
2517	SODA,SULPHATE WOOD PULP	W 32957	12922	W 28228	12706	W 46886	37523	W 38819	18805	PATES CHIMIQUES AU SULFATE
25172	— BLEACHED,NONDISSOLVNG	W 20911	9200	W 12077	5884	W 24291	24709	W 22869	13329	PATES BLANCHIES
26	TEXTILE FIBRES AND WASTE		83332		104430		140291		125042	FIBRES TEXTILES
263	COTTON	W 26349	32382	W 29431	44944	W 33230	68749	W 28262	53625	COTON
2631	RAW COTTON,EXCL LINTERS	W 26325	32265	W 29412	44899	W 33225	68721	W 28218	53589	COTON EN MASSE
269	WASTE OF TEXTILE FABRICS	W 38506	27273	W 44079	30171	W 43624	37939	W 50004	47171	FRIPERIE DRILLES,CHIFFONS
26901	BULK TEXT WSTE,OLD CLTHG	W 37970	27028	W 43920	29904	W 43497	37676	W 49763	46993	ART ET ACCESS D'HABILLEMENT
27	CRUDE FERTLZR,MINRLS NES		95754		112896		140166		120817	ENGRAIS MINERAUX BRUTS
274	SULPHUR,UNRSTD IRN PYRTE	W 1270178	63818	W 1454797	81370	W 1419179	100654	W 1443472	80594	SOUFRE ET PYRITES
2741	SULPHUR,EX SULP IN 52215	W 1270168	63811	W 1454787	81365	W 1419169	100646	W 1443453	80572	SOUFRE
278	OTHER CRUDE MINERALS	W 142459	23489	W 135966	20493	W 134027	23239	W 163800	26479	AUTRES MINERAUX BRUTS
3	MINERAL FUELS ETC		488034		496264		575193		647859	COMBUSTIBLES MINERAUX LUB
33	PETROLEUM AND PRODUCTS		352260		340785		358723		472943	PETROLE ET DERIVES
333	CRUDE PETROLEUM	W 371947	48756	W 608253	74380	W 917883	121233	W 757987	118870	HUILES BRUTES DE PETROLE
334	PETROLEUM PRODUCTS,REFIN	W 2362326	294892	W 2011645	257635	W 1512456	228236	W 1947358	341847	PRODUITS RAFFINES
3341	GASOLINE,OTH LIGHT OILS	W 292935	58329	W 346805	57178	W 310376	54868	W 336042	73744	ESSENCES POUR MOTEURS
33411	MOTOR,AVIATION SPIRIT	W 227843	45308	W 247963	40676	W 228667	39043	W 246161	52942	ESSENCES MOTEURS D'AVIONS
3344	FUEL OILS,NES	W 2003602	212701	W 1588083	173079	W 1142202	148938	W 1552325	239727	FUEL OILS
3345	LUBS,PETROLEUM OILS NES	W 65750	23780	W 76691	27290	W 59854	24393	W 58980	28343	HUILES LUBRIFIANTES
33451	LUBS(HIGH PETR CONT) ETC	W 64507	20856	W 75287	24340	W 58562	21052	W 57615	24426	HUILES LUBRIF,H LOURDES
341	*GAS,NATURAL AND MANUFCT	W 1284242	120808	W 2219295	142480	W 2950647	198467	W 2064548	159627	GAZ NATUREL,GAZ MANUFACT
3413	PETROLM GASES,LIQUEFIED	W 157735	30995	W 160214	27040	W 169649	39205	W 193241	50050	GAZ DE PETROLE LIQUEFIE
34139	OTH HYDROCARBON GAS LQFD	W 157735	30995	W 160214	27039	W 169638	39185	W 193241	50048	HYDROCARBURES GAZEUX NDA
3414	PETROLEUM GASES, GASEOUS	W 1126506	89812	W 2059080	115440	W 2780998	159261	W 1871307	109576	GAZ DE PETROLE GAZEUX
4	ANIMAL,VEGETABLE OIL,FAT		71694		98759		127879		128697	HUILES,GRAISSES ANIM,VEG
42	FIXED VEGETABLE OIL,FAT		65374		89363		117546		115614	HUILES VEGETALES FIXES
423	FIXED VEG OILS,SOFT	W 134045	61625	W 144571	83762	W 168322	111086	W 183682	106739	HUILES VEGET DOUCES FIXES
4232	SOYA BEAN OIL	W 116989	53305	W 141418	81889	W 134679	90095	W 116946	67694	HUILE DE SOJA
4239	OTH FIXED VEG OILS,SOFT	W 17051	8311	W 3150	1860	W 33641	20983	W 66736	39045	AUTRES HUILES FIXES
42391	RAPE,COLZA,MUSTARD OILS	W 17051	8311	W 3150	1860	W 33641	20982	W 66736	39045	H NAVETTE COLZA MOUTARDE
5	CHEMCLS,RELATED PROD NES		499168		549736		700259		686495	PRODUITS CHIMIQUES
51	ORGANIC CHEMICALS		41571		50736		73109		68664	PROD CHIMIQ ORGANIQUES
513	CARBOXYLIC ACIDS ETC	W 10427	11950	W 11884	14976	W 12517	24379	W 13338	19425	ACIDES CARBOXYLIQUES
52	INORGANIC CHEMICALS		78335		76329		102467		110344	PROD CHIM INORGANIQUES
522	INORG ELEMNTS,OXIDES,ETC	W 435155	57081	W 335963	57366	W 356346	80059	W 402966	87329	ELEMENTS INORGANIQUES
5225	INORGANIC BASES ETC NES	W 407320	48190	W 308738	46705	W 341253	67930	W 380833	74529	AUTRES BASES OXYDES METAL
52251	AMMONIA,ANHYDROUS ETC	W 316150	36876	W 228710	36803	W 266044	54541	W 298299	58576	AMMONIAC LIQUEFIE
523	OTHR INORG CHEMICALS ETC	W 56005	20863	W 59218	18481	W 80434	21861	W 79271	22505	AUT PRODUITS CHIMIQUES INORG
53	DYES,TANNING,COLOUR PROD		40490		41241		52185		48014	PROD TEINTURE,COLORANTS
533	PIGMENTS,PAINTS,ETC	W 15851	27163	W 16508	29337	W 16171	36873	W 14728	33212	PIGMENTS,PEINTURES,VERNIS
541	*MEDICINAL,PHARM PRODUCT	K 8696784	129516	K 6923140	144171	K 7541878	161442	K 5415518	160438	PROD MEDICINAUX PHARMACEUT
5417	MEDICAMENTS	K 7986622	109398	K 6197105	122231	K 6812524	131219	K 4604180	131240	MEDICAMENTS
54179	— CONTNG OTH SUBSTANCES	K 7650339	97292	K 5807243	105748	K 6318346	112020	K 4203942	111740	MED CONT AUT SUBSTANCES
55	PERFUME,CLEANING ETC PRD		21170		25317		33406		29468	PROD POUR PARFUM,TOILETTE
58	PLASTIC MATERIALS ETC		121174		137859		192978		175672	MAT PLAST ARTIFICIELLES
582	PROD OF CONDENSATION ETC	W 16130	24941	W 15293	25736	W 15987	32672	W 15018	29791	PROD CONDENS,POLYCOND
583	POLYMERIZATION ETC PRODS	W 95909	90564	W 107376	105725	W 108803	152484	W 126587	137473	PROD POLYMERISATION
5831	POLYETHYLENE	W 44489	35033	W 45371	36583	W 47658	57025	W 54428	51710	POLYETHYLENE
58311	— IN PRIMARY FORMS	W 43461	32730	W 43962	33822	W 45988	52685	W 53319	48907	POLYETHYLENE PRIMAIRES
5834	POLYVINYL CHLORIDE	W 23451	21865	W 28782	29785	W 27440	36301	W 32355	32488	CHLORURE DE POLYVINYLE
58341	— IN PRIMARY FORMS	W 21616	15720	W 26989	24002	W 25394	28898	W 30182	24480	SOUS FORMES PRIMAIRES
59	CHEMICAL MATERIALS NES		61125		65531		74945		86280	MAT PROD CHIMIQUES NDA
591	PESTICIDES,DISINFECTANTS	W 1894	13349	W 2086	14228	W 1812	11339	W 3127	23884	DESINF,INSECT,FONG,HERB
598	MISCEL CHEM PRODUCTS NES	W 21945	39623	W 21760	42177	W 24081	51261	W 26945	50475	PROD DIV INDUST CHIM NDA
5989	CHEM PRODUCTS,PREPS NES	W 15934	27431	W 16749	31222	W 17031	35300	W 20482	35943	PROD PREP CHIMIQUES NDA
59899	OTH CHEM PRODS,PREPS,NES	W 11186	18586	W 11686	18877	W 11072	22748	W 13580	23801	AUT PRODUITS CHIMIQUES NDA
6	BASIC MANUFACTURES		1805037		1845061		2268412		2236150	ART MANUFACTURES
61	LEATHER,DRESSED FUR,ETC		78962		98723		130947		151401	CUIRS,PELLETERIES
611	LEATHER	W 4742	56561	W 5461	73750	W 6674	99195	W 7089	110352	CUIRS,PEAUX PREPARES
6114	LEATHR BOVINE NES,EQUINE	W 2867	37865	W 3264	47966	W 3966	60964	W 4276	68877	CUIRS DE BOVINS
612	LEATHER ETC MANUFACTURES	W 1947	20201	W 2750	24504	W 3716	31605	W 4758	40514	OUVRAGES EN CUIRS NDA
6123	PREPRD PARTS OF FOOTWEAR	W 1893	17349	W 2702	21492	W 3670	30400	W 4703	38926	PARTIES DE CHAUSSURES
62	RUBBER MANUFACTURES NES		43738		40698		64977		71477	CAOUTCHOUC MANUFACTURE

4. General Imports C.I.F. by Commodities according to the S.I.T.C. (Rev. 2) in thousand U.S. Dollars
Importations Générales C.A.F. par Produits d'après la C.T.C.I. (Rév. 2) en milliers de Dollars E.U.

SITC CTCI	COMMODITY	1993			1994			1995			1996		PRODUIT
		WEIGHT POIDS		VALUE VALEUR	WEIGHT POIDS		VALUE VALEUR	WEIGHT POIDS		VALUE VALEUR	WEIGHT POIDS	VALUE VALEUR	
621	MATERIALS OF RUBBER	W	2392	10592	W	2222	9927	W 3671		24942	W 2901	12670	PRODUITS EN CAOUTCHOUC
625	RUBBER TYRES, TUBES ETC	W	3398	14430	W	2953	12009	W 4184		17783	W 9247	34095	PNEUS CAOUTCHOUC VULCANISE
628	RUBBER ARTICLES NES	W	2284	18717	W	2197	18763	W 2118		22252	W 2687	24712	OUVRAGES CAOUTCHOUC NDA
63	WOOD,CORK MANUFACTRS NES			18930			60433			22761		18513	OUVRAGES LIEGE ET BOIS
635	WOOD MANUFACTURES NES	W	2506	3692	W	9517	47667	W 3545		10764	W 3281	5443	ART MANUF EN BOIS NDA
6353	BUILDERS WOODWRK,PREFABS	W	387	1030	W	7650	43985	W 1126		7051	W 551	1741	OUVRAGES DE MENUISERIE
64	PAPER,PAPERBOARD AND MFR			81715			84301			126907		99292	PAPIERS,CARTONS & OUVRAGES
641	PAPER AND PAPERBOARD	W	82268	64741	W	80887	63197	W 91101		99680	W 178387	77351	PAPIERS ET CARTONS
6413	KRAFT PAPER,PAPERBOARD	W	28570	14473	W	24692	10902	W 31307		25087	W 21027	13018	PAPIER ET CARTON KRAFT
6418	COATED ETC PAPER NES BLK	W	16919	25518	W	15213	22148	W 14282		26454	W 28970	23890	PAP,CARTONS COUCHES,ENDUITS
64189	COATED PAPER ETC NES	W	15551	23298	W	14075	19906	W 12394		22997	W 27676	21508	PAPIERS,CARTONS COUCHES
642	PAPER,ETC,PRECUT,ARTS OF	W	7241	16975	W	8779	21103	W 9658		27227	W 8690	21941	PAP,CARTONS DECOUPES
65	TEXTILE YARN,FABRICS,ETC			979129			1063377			1288552		1295146	FILS,TISSUS,ARTICLES TEXTILE
651	TEXTILE YARN	W	18234	99339	W	19101	107746	W 19357		123880	W 18402	116922	FILS TEXTILES
6514	SYN FIB YRN,BULK,MONOFIL	W	9367	52932	W	9261	55067	W 9950		65096	W 9895	62648	FILS CONT 85% FIB TEXT SYNTH
65141	— TEXTRD,CONT POLYAMIDE	W	1451	19183	W	1400	19986	W 1452		23704	W 1746	23827	FILS TEXT FIB CONT POLYAMID
6516	DISCON SYN FIB BLEND YRN	W	4301	19164	W	4351	21080	W 4110		21781	W 2665	14864	FILS FIBR TEX SYNT DIS MOINS
652	COTTON FABRICS,WOVEN	W	46980	441837	W	52761	478024	W 54447		587157	W 56904	605188	TISSUS DE COTON
6521	GREY WOVEN COTTON FABRIC	W	2818	31098	W	3014	30123	W 2915		38635	W 4453	48190	TISSUS COT ECRUS NON MERCER
65214	GREY WOVEN COTTON NES	W	2370	25873	W	2640	26243	W 2489		32469	W 3291	38026	AUT TISSUS 85% COTON ECRUS
6522	WOVEN COTTON BLEACHD,ETC	W	44163	410739	W	49746	447901	W 51532		548522	W 52451	556998	TISSUS COTON BLANCHIS ETC
65224	BLCHED COTTON FABRIC NES	W	39513	360102	W	44589	390157	W 46651		485314	W 46943	494089	AUT TIS PLUS 85% COT BLANCHI
65225	BLCHD COTN BLEND FAB NES	W	3890	42268	W	4327	47438	W 4034		50756	W 4748	51716	AUT TIS MOINS 85% COT BLANCH
653	WOVN MAN–MADE FIB FABRIC	W	18637	252524	W	20823	284666	W 23218		363927	W 24061	349217	TISSUS FIBRES SYNTH,ARTIF
6531	CONT SYNT WEAVES NONPILE	W	4444	51572	W	3938	47785	W 4308		63887	W 4175	57460	TISSUS FIBRES SYNTH CONTINUE
65315	CONT SYN TXTL FABRIC NES	W	3541	36688	W	3367	41862	W 3934		55868	W 3799	49254	TIS PLUS 85% TEXT SYNT CONT
6532	DISC SYN TXTL FABRIC NES	W	2734	35765	W	4097	55853	W 4811		71751	W 5641	79645	TIS DISC MOINS 85% FIBR TEXT
6534	DISC SYN BLEND FABRC NES	W	7217	100277	W	8515	112812	W 9293		137440	W 9537	131611	TISSUS FIBRES SYNTH DISCONT
65341	DISC SYN FIB–COTTN FABRC	W	4311	45838	W	5356	61280	W 5739		71545	W 5602	64955	TISSUS FIB SYNT DIS MEL COTO
65349	OTH DISC SYN BLEND FABRC	W	1698	31223	W	2108	32661	W 2497		44951	W 2613	41765	TISSUS FIB SYNT MEL MAT AUT
6536	DISC REGN TXTL FABRC NES	W	837	18173	W	838	18713	W 1190		26962	W 1276	23909	TISSUS 85% TEXT ART DISC
6538	DISC REG BLEND FABRC NES	W	2108	29618	W	2058	30441	W 2275		41483	W 2419	42347	TIS MOINS 85% TEXT ART DISC
65383	DISC REG–CONT MAN–MD FAB	W	1310	20042	W	1586	23895	W 1824		33880	W 1359	22536	TISSUS TEX ART CONT MEL SYNT
654	OTH WOVEN TEXTILE FABRIC	W	3152	35439	W	2989	40347	W 1696		39466	W 2068	44477	TISSUS AUT COTON SYNT,ARTIF
6543	WOVEN WOOL ETC FABRC NES	W	934	16976	W	981	17479	W 981		21034	W 1264	28500	TISSUS LAINE,POILS FINS NDA
655	KNITTED,ETC FABRICS	W	2478	37598	W	2664	37826	W 2908		44049	W 3346	46670	ETOF BONNETERIE PIECES ETC
6552	OTHER KNIT ETC FAB NONEL	W	2478	37598	W	2664	37826	W 2908		44049	W 3346	46670	ETOF BON NON ELAS NON SYNT
656	LACE,RIBBONS,TULLE,ETC	W	1848	41961	W	2043	45400	W 2352		53964	W 2204	53472	TULLES,BRODERIE
65601	NARROW FABRICS NES	W	769	17439	W	893	18845	W 1148		24320	W 1122	22660	RUBANS SANS TRAME EN FILS
657	SPECIAL TXTL FABRC,PRODS	W	6758	62473	W	6947	61838	W 7116		68385	W 6765	64127	TISSUS SPECIAUX
6572	BONDED FIBRE TEXTLS NES	W	3142	30806	W	3440	30583	W 3312		31601	W 2991	26070	TISSUS NON TISSES
6573	COATED ETC TEXTILES NES	W	2370	19686	W	2217	19024	W 2427		23758	W 2398	25657	TISSUS,ART MATIERE TEXT NDA
66	NONMETAL MINERAL MFS NES			51856			59465			75182		68694	ART MIN NON METALLIQUES
67	IRON AND STEEL			347369			230193			294413		267102	FER ET ACIER
672	IRON,STEEL PRIMARY FORMS	W	85252	23667	W	101680	26080	W 72167		26960	W 101941	29149	LINGOTS FER,ACIER
673	IRON,STEEL SHAPES ETC	W	243308	76480	W	110834	37947	W 291749		94637	W 232084	78999	BARRES,PROFIL FER,ACIER
6732	IRON,STEEL BARS ETC	W	147939	45303	W	28952	11660	W 207873		62650	W 134753	43748	BARRES FER,ACIER
67326	IRN,OTH STL BARS HOTROLD	W	140717	40436	W	20343	5915	W 197644		54576	W 123812	35391	BARRES PLEINES FER,ACIER
674	IRN,STL UNIV,PLATE,SHEET	W	107338	59833	W	162468	78174	W 201142		113196	W 165861	93910	LARGES PLATS,TOLES
6746	IRN,STL THIN PLATE,ROLLD	W	38515	18357	W	97311	37443	W 130102		57221	W 97404	40136	TOLES LAM MOINS 3MM
67461	— OF IRON OR SIMPLE STL	W	37054	15204	W	95546	34185	W 128391		52440	W 95530	35176	TOL NON AC FIN MOINS 3 MM
678	IRON,STL TUBES,PIPES,ETC	W	156563	180472	W	58813	72782	W 24037		41269	W 28550	48835	TUBES,TUYAUX EN FONTE,FER
6782	IRON,STL SEAMLESS TUBES	W	16334	21588	W	39514	43324	W 17984		24186	W 18679	29174	TUBES,TUYAUX SANS SOUDURE
6783	IRON,STL TUBES,PIPES NES	W	136047	141640	W	16345	16524	W 3703		4842	W 4410	4925	AUT TUBES,TUYAUX FER,ACIER
68	NON–FERROUS METALS			64035			69806			91189		97012	METAUX NON FERREUX
682	COPPER EXC CEMENT COPPER	W	14193	34183	W	11640	31759	W 12752		45404	W 18086	55014	CUIVRE
6822	COPPER,ALLOYS WORKED	W	12722	31203	W	10095	27849	W 10697		38409	W 14991	46279	CUIVRE,ALLIAGES OUVRES
68221	COPPER BARS,WIRE,ETC	W	10401	24410	W	8661	21914	W 9444		31404	W 13325	37959	BARRES,PROFILES ET FILS
684	ALUMINIUM	W	8944	22347	W	6554	18926	W 10333		32697	W 8988	26014	ALUMINIUM
69	METAL MANUFACTURES NES			139303			138064			173483		167512	ART MANUFACT EN METAL NDA
695	TOOLS	W	1872	21436	W	1460	18958	W 1415		20621	W 1490	22815	OUTILS A MAIN
699	BASE METAL MFRS NES	W	9440	60203	W	9975	64784	W 10891		74473	W 11812	76608	ART MANUFACTURES MET NDA
7	MACHINES,TRANSPORT EQUIP			1987455			1893682			2043249		2095248	MACHINES MATERIEL TRANSPORT
71	POWER GENERATING EQUIPMT			237866			135379			106659		131729	MACHINES GENERATRICES
711	STEAM BOILERS & AUX PLNT	W	1772	16519	W	2185	19924	W 719		6332	W 1878	14850	GENERATEURS VAPEUR EAU ETC
713	INTRNL COMBUS PSTN ENGIN	W	5108	53555	W	5588	56245	W 13370		61156	W 4791	59430	MOTEURS EXPL COMB INT, PIECE
7132	MOTOR VEHCL PISTN ENGINS	W	2878	19287	W	3724	21332	W 2636		18492	W 2488	16672	MOTEURS EXPL POUR VEHICULES
7139	PISTON ENGINE PARTS NES	W	1952	30824	W	1616	30683	W 10271		36213	W 1955	37004	PIECES POUR 713.2,3,8
714	ENGINES AND MOTORS NES	W	3727	133114	W	238	16508	W 252		13394	W 1127	31628	MOTEURS NON ELECTRIQUES
7144	REACTION ENGINES	W	1137	64031			2	W 4		50	W 1	67	PROPULSEURS A REACTION
7148	GAS TURBINES NES	W	2274	57641	W	21	808	W 144		1975	W 173	8316	TURBINES A GAZ
71488	OTHER GAS TURBINES NES	W	2272	55743	W	21	808	W 144		1972	W 173	8316	AUTRES TURBINES A GAZ
7149	ENGINE & MOTOR PARTS NES	W	317	11442	W	217	15698	W 103		11370	W 953	23245	PIECES 714 ET 718.88
716	ROTATING ELECTRIC PLANT	W	2373	27132	W	1983	23368	W 1921		20211	W 1996	20254	APP ELECTR ROTATIFS,PIECES
7162	AC MTRS,GENRTRS,GEN SETS	W	1694	20990	W	1574	19996	W 1355		16333	W 1448	15136	MOTEURS ELECTRIQUES
72	MACHS FOR SPCL INDUSTRYS			371686			288892			351816		400034	MAC SPECIALES POUR INDUST
721	AGRIC MACHY,EXC TRACTORS	W	5735	30217	W	3084	18128	W 2131		13363	W 3552	19362	MACHINES AGRICOLES
7212	HARVESTING ETC MACHINES	W	3166	20943	W	1499	10049	W 474		4604	W 1517	10158	ENGINS POUR LA RECOLTE
722	TRACTORS NON–ROAD	W	11781	59236	W	4839	26999	W 5278		30020	W 6046	37544	TRACTEURS
7224	WHEELED TRACTORS NES	W	11709	58979	W	4818	26904	W 5261		29966	W 5934	37213	TRACTEURS A ROUES
723	CIVIL ENGNEERG EQUIP ETC	W	10315	63778	W	9053	48101	W 11559		67946	W 11625	72519	APPAREILS DE GENIE CIVIL
7234	CONST,MINING MACHNRY NES	W	8162	49270	W	7973	38246	W 10391		52751	W 10046	58039	MACH POUR LA CONST, MINES
72342	SLFPRP SHOVELS,EXCAVATRS	W	5804	30718	W	5169	24552	W 6053		29108	W 7829	43924	PELLES MECANIQUES
724	TEXTILE,LEATHER MACHNRY	W	6482	95209	W	5780	87889	W 6651		100629	W 7114	110406	MACH POUR INDUSTRIE TEXTILE
7243	SEWING MACHS,NEEDLES ETC	W	2258	43934	W	1975	45083	W 1845		48698	W 1953	50336	MACHINES A COUDRE,PIECES
72431	SEWING MACHINES	W	1990	36049	W	1717	36992	W 1576		38331	W 1573	38157	MACHINES A COUDRE
7247	TEXTILE MACHINERY NES	W	1435	14849	W	1535	15870	W 1902		21844	W 2564	25035	MACH LAVAGE,TEINTURE TEX
726	PRINTG,BKBINDG MACHY,PTS	W	1260	23231	W	1036	20362	W 711		14218	W 787	16398	MACHINES POUR IMPRIMERIE
727	FOOD MACHRY NON–DOMESTIC	W	1537	13956	W	1050	15015	W 1286		24229	W 2224	33056	MACH INDUSTRIES ALIMENT
7272	OTH FOOD PROC MCHY,PARTS	W	1409	11327	W	965	13537	W 998		22211	W 1925	30172	AUT MACH IND ALIMENTAIRE
728	OTH MACHY FOR SPCL INDUS	W	10576	75265	W	8476	66544	W 12509		93596	W 11562	102490	AUT MACH IND PARTICULIERES
7283	OTHR MINERAL WORKG MACHY	W	3388	19345	W	3064	20904	W 4911		22941	W 5746	32663	MACH TRIER,CRIBLER,BROYER
7284	MACHY FOR SPCL INDUS NES	W	5975	48623	W	4666	40968	W 5565		57377	W 4383	58134	MACH SPEC IND PARTICUL.
72848	OTH MCHY WITH INDIV FNCT	W	3898	22790	W	2957	22950	W 4126		32330	W 2317	23859	AUTRES MACHINES NDA
73	METALWORKING MACHINERY			27236			26445			28554		28294	MACH TRAVAIL DES METAUX
736	METALWORKING MACH–TOOLS	W	3377	20299	W	2708	18480	W 2876		22121	W 2138	21186	MACH–OUTILS TRAVAIL METAUX
74	GENRL INDUSTRL MACHY NES			367876			338264			393996		395665	MACH APP INDUSTRIE
741	HEATING,COOLING EQUIPMNT			88399	W	8976	77702	W 11849		108039	W 10720	96282	MACH CHAUFFAGE,PIECES
7414	NONDOM REFRIG EQUIPT,PTS	W	3626	22338	W	4587	29131	W 6139		40422	W 5470	37484	MAT PRODUCTION DU FROID
74141	REFRIG EQUIP NONDOMESTIC	W	1535	12040	W	1304	15177	W 1582		20387	W 1989	23142	REFIG INDUSTRIELS
7416	HEATING,COOLING EQU NES	W	2613	35549	W	1610	23635	W 2179		34425	W 2332	31525	APP CHANGEMENT TEMP

4. General Imports C.I.F. by Commodities according to the S.I.T.C. (Rev. 2) in thousand U.S. Dollars
Importations Générales C.A.F. par Produits d'après la C.T.C.I. (Rév. 2) en milliers de Dollars E.U.

SITC CTCI	COMMODITY	1993 WEIGHT POIDS	1993 VALUE VALEUR	1994 WEIGHT POIDS	1994 VALUE VALEUR	1995 WEIGHT POIDS	1995 VALUE VALEUR	1996 WEIGHT POIDS	1996 VALUE VALEUR	PRODUIT
742	PUMPS FOR LIQUIDS ETC	W 2127	32791	W 2187	45701	W 4642	38294	W 2325	40316	POMPES MOTO–POMPES
743	PUMPS NES,CENTRFUGES ETC	W 5600	62207	W 5606	60262	W 6287	71820	W 5270	67501	POMPES COMPRES,VENT ETC
7431	PUMPS FOR GASES ETC	W 3138	26200	W 3428	23886	W 3456	28118	W 2556	22060	POMPES AIR A VIDE,COMPRES
7436	GAS,LIQUID FILTERS ETC	W 1644	20413	W 1430	20227	W 2101	27715	W 1790	27819	APP POUR FILT DES LIQUIDES
744	MECHANICAL HANDLING EQU	W 6315	41060	W 4915	31588	W 6785	41715	W 6262	42093	EQUIP MANUTENTION PIECES
7442	LIFTING,LOADING MACH NES	W 3521	22611	W 2666	18580	W 3854	23559	W 3540	23877	APP LEVAGE,MANUTENTION
745	NONELEC MACHY,TOOLS NES	W 2324	31730	W 1662	30821	W 2007	34206	W 1790	38340	AUT MACH NON ELEC,PIECES
7452	OTH NONELEC MCHS,PTS NES	W 2179	30020	W 1587	29323	W 1938	32676	W 1678	36171	AUT MACH NON ELEC,PIECES
74522	PACKAGNG,BOTTLNG,ETC MCH	W 550	13474	W 648	17885	W 632	21470	W 711	25689	MACH NETT BOUTEILLES,ETC
749	NONELEC MACH PTS,ACC NES	W 8713	111690	W 7606	92191	W 13152	99922	W 11060	111133	PIECES MACH NON ELEC NDA
7492	COCKS,VALVES ETC NES	W 4433	55053	W 2290	36522	W 2319	37349	W 2717	38891	ART ROB,SIM POUR TUYAUX
7493	SHAFT,CRANK,PULLEY ETC	W 2846	29076	W 4018	29751	W 9376	33981	W 6681	38493	ARBRES TRANS,VILEBREQUINS
75	OFFICE MACHNES,ADP EQUIP		76929		76774		94311		93199	MACH BUREAU TRAIT AUTOM
752	AUTOMTIC DATA PROC EQUIP	W 724	54193	W 800	52533	W 888	61334	W 990	66285	MACH TRAIT INFORMATION
76	TELECOMM,SOUND EQUIPMENT		107548		98065		118293		127482	EQUIPMENT DE TELECOM
764	TELECOM EQPT,PTS,ACC NES	W 2363	99128	W 2705	86577	W 3634	102843	W 3754	114677	EQUIP TELECOM,PIECES
7641	LINE TELEPHONE,ETC EQUIP	W 372	31133	W 420	32392	W 839	44774	W 633	53906	APP TELEPHON PAR FIL
7643	TV,RADIO TRANSMITTRS ETC	W 257	29132	W 174	20087	W 153	12344	W 264	20123	APP EMET TELE RADIO
7649	PTS NES OF EQUIPMT OF 76	W 1534	33689	W 1914	26971	W 2319	32081	W 2611	34648	PIECES DE LA DIV 76
76493	TELECOMM EQUIPMT PTS NES	W 1021	22596	W 947	14068	W 1122	17598	W 1144	14633	PIECES 761,762,764.3,8
77	ELECTRIC MACHNRY NES ETC		324750		364903		415787		433821	MACH APP ELECT NDA
771	ELECTRIC POWER MACHY NES	W 2988	31956	W 2332	36947	W 3671	43218	W 3279	41363	MACH PROD,TRANS ELECTR
7712	OTH ELEC POWER MACHY NES	W 1591	20719	W 1645	26048	W 2518	34373	W 2396	31439	AUT APP PROD TRANSF ELEC
772	SWITCHGEAR ETC,PARTS NES	W 4121	98050	W 5642	115335	W 5034	120097	W 5263	128273	APP COUPURE,SECT ETC
7721	SWITCHGEAR ETC	W 3577	86298	W 4908	100394	W 4289	106398	W 4580	111232	APP COUPURE,SECTIONMNT
773	ELECTR DISTRIBUTNG EQUIP	W 8582	70703	W 8558	66283	W 9255	87094	W 11266	111648	EQUIPMT DISTRIBUTION ELECT
7731	INSULATED WIRE,CABLE ETC	W 7597	62695	W 7243	54882	W 8504	75984	W 10115	99283	FILS,CABLES ISOLES ELECT
776	TRANSISTORS,VALVES,ETC	W 2593	38169	W 2815	47368	W 2562	43881	W 2130	41996	LAMPES,TUBES,VALVES
7761	TV PICTURE TUBES	W 2169	22183	W 2221	21310	W 2050	23192	W 1705	19615	TUBES CATHODIQUES
778	ELECTRICAL MACHINERY NES	W 6002	63031	W 5700	76665	W 6014	83130	W 5661	82450	AUTRES MACH ELECT NDA
7783	AUTOMOTIVE ELECTR EQUIP	W 2486	22016	W 1891	21590	W 1827	22389	W 2049	22581	EQUIP ELECT MOTEURS EXPL
7788	OTH ELEC MACHY,EQUIP NES	W 1031	24500	W 988	35551	W 1441	39843	W 1066	38435	AUT MACH APP ELEC NDA
77886	OTH ELEC MACHINERY NES	W 129	12452	W 255	23094	W 290	23801	W 372	25938	AUT MACH APP ELECTRIQUES
78	ROAD VEHICLES		379835		395784		441657		469700	VEHICULES ROUTIERS
781	PASS MOTOR VEH EXC BUSES	W 19645	158468	W 28323	209507	W 24481	238883	W 20764	244215	AUTO TRANSPORT PERSONNES
782	LORRIES,SPCL MTR VEH NES	W 17266	95279	W 16701	67491	W 17461	80061	W 13487	97747	VEHICULES SPECIAUX,MARCH
7821	LORRIES,TRUCKS	W 14940	74378	W 15369	55503	W 15609	63871	W 11868	85080	VEHICULES TRANSP MARCHAND
7822	SPECIAL MOTOR VEHCLS NES	W 2326	20901	W 1332	11988	W 1852	16191	W 1619	12667	VEHICULES USAGES SPECIAUX
784	MOTOR VEH PRTS,ACCES NES	W 10449	100290	W 9270	94324	W 21190	96361	W 9272	100702	PIECES 722,781,782,783
7841	MOTOR VEHICLE CHASSIS	W 2674	21472	W 1658	15463	W 2159	18989	W 2108	21780	CHASSIS 722,781,782,783
7849	OTHER MOTOR VEHCL PARTS	W 7363	75708	W 7106	74702	W 18584	73995	W 7025	78045	PIECES 722,781,782,783
79	OTHR TRANSPORT EQUIPMENT		93728		169176		92175		15324	AUTRE MATERIEL TRANSPORT
792	AIRCRAFT ETC	W 95	78568	W 162	116534	W 115	78486	W 12	3137	APP NAVIGATION AERIENNE
7924	AIRCRFT NES OVER 15000KG	W 80	75593	W 153	114519	W 95	75630			AERODYNES PLUS 15000 KG
793	SHIPS AND BOATS ETC	W 1824	9163	W 17608	49645	W 2772	7281	W 5408	8485	NAVIRES BATEAUX,ETC
7938	TUGS,SPECIAL VESSELS ETC	W 509	5555	W 10461	43036	W 1124	3985	W 288	548	REMORQUEURS,BATEAUX SPEC
79382	SPECL PURPOSE VESSLS ETC	W 75	1013	W 10362	42627	W 1030	3412			BAT–PHARES,–POMPES,DRAGUES
8	MISC MANUFACTURED GOODS		614443		671388		828393		875632	ART MANUFACTURES DIVERS
812	*PLUMBG,HEATNG,LGHTNG EQ	W 6737	18387	W 6009	20110	W 6646	24478	W 6754	24408	APPAR SANITAIRES CHAUFFAGE
84	CLOTHING AND ACCESSORIES		268101		335635		434879		475483	VETEMENTS
842	MENS OUTERWEAR NOT KNIT	W 5355	75031	W 5544	75485	W 5954	91591	W 6720	107694	VET DESSUS POUR HOMMES
8423	— TROUSERS,BREECHES ETC	W 2202	33926	W 2204	32235	W 2278	36081	W 3384	54862	PANTALONS HOMMES MAT TEX
8429	— OTHER OUTER GARMENTS	W 2786	32589	W 2839	30896	W 2979	37089	W 2850	36076	AUT VET DES HOM MAT TEX
843	WOMENS OUTERWEAR NONKNIT	W 1969	31461	W 2684	38995	W 2792	47641	W 3421	61096	VET DESSUS FEMMES MAT TEX
8439	— OTHER OUTER GARMENTS	W 1113	19063	W 1424	25652	W 1323	30002	W 1960	41717	AUT VET DES FEM MAT TEXT
844	UNDER GARMENTS NOT KNIT	W 2749	48490	W 3771	70696	W 4713	98835	W 5202	110640	VETEMENT DESSOUS MAT TEX
8441	— MENS SHIRTS	W 2282	42962	W 3258	60887	W 4187	88525	W 4504	97879	CHEMISES HOMMES MAT TEXT
84412	—— OF SYNTHETIC FIBRES	W 2089	37508	W 3037	55307	W 3893	79842	W 4205	88254	CHEMISES HOMMES FIB SYNT
845	OUTERWEAR KNIT NONELASTC	W 1906	35358	W 3191	50559	W 4012	60454	W 3946	57699	VET DESSOUS,ACCES BONNET
8451	— JERSEYS,PULLOVERS ETC	W 1087	13802	W 2275	28652	W 3136	37519	W 3090	38216	CHANDAILS,PULL–OVERS ETC
846	UNDER GARMENTS KNITTED	W 2685	48187	W 3295	67672	W 4604	98371	W 5678	103577	SOUS VETS DE BONNETERIE
8462	— OF COTTON NON ELASTIC	W 2251	28008	W 2655	30069	W 3837	49947	W 4773	61005	SOUS–VET BONNET COTON
84629	—— OTHER	W 2251	28008	W 2655	30069	W 3837	49947	W 4773	61005	AUT SOUS–VET BONNET COTON
8465	CORSETS,GARTERS,ETC	W 349	17930	W 626	37299	W 751	48152	W 736	42067	CORSETS,GAINES ART SIM
84651	BRASSIERES	W 298	15701	W 547	34156	W 635	43429	W 645	38766	SOUTIENS–GORGE,BUSTIERS
847	TEXTILE CLTHNG ACCES NES	W 1021	17204	W 1223	20946	W 1261	23978	W 1358	24599	ACCES VET MAT TEXT NDA
87	PRECISION INSTRUMNTS NES		95535		86301		105321		108315	INSTRUM,APPAR SCIENT NDA
874	MEASURNG,CONTROLNG INSTR	W 1359	71626	W 1476	60509	W 1577	76993	W 1449	78734	INSTRUMENTS DE MESURE
88	PHOTO EQU,OPTICL GDS ETC		34204		35616		36439		39248	APP,FOURN PHOTO,OP,MONTR
89	MISC MANUFCTRD GOODS NES		187162		182176		212041		212529	ART MANUFACTURES DIVERS
892	PRINTED MATTER		44117	W 3593	31560	W 3818	34485	W 4102	35610	IMPRIMES
8928	PRINTED MATTER NES		23010	W 757	9627	W 869	11002	W 896	9506	IMPRIMES NDA
893	ARTICLES OF PLASTIC NES		57187		63636	W 12232	85890		84770	OUVRAGES EN MAT DIVIS 58
8939	MISC PLASTIC ARTICLES	W 6448	43874	W 6643	45931	W 8334	61004	W 9136	60984	ART DIVERS EN MAT DIV 58
89399	OTHR PLASTC ARTICLES NES	W 5901	42555	W 6191	44930	W 7800	59226	W 8582	59423	AUT OUV MAT DIV 58
899	OTHER MANUFACTURED GOODS		52889		51369		57861		58742	AUT ART MANUF DIVERS NDA
8998	SMALLWARES,TOILETRYS ETC	W 2114	43075	W 2369	43124	W 2400	47276	W 2238	47575	ART MERCERIE,TOILETTE
89983	BUTTONS,STUDS,ETC	W 1068	25867	W 1171	27514	W 1175	29203	W 1075	29007	BOUTONS,BOUTONS–PRESSION
9	GOODS NOT CLASSD BY KIND		9777		23744		20622		19150	ART TRANSACT NON CLASSES

5. General Exports F.O.B. by Commodities according to the S.I.T.C. (Rev. 2) in thousand U.S. Dollars
Exportations Générales F.O.B. par Produits d'après la C.T.C.I. (Rév. 2) en milliers de Dollars E.U.

SITC CTCI	COMMODITY	1993 WEIGHT POIDS	1993 VALUE VALEUR	1994 WEIGHT POIDS	1994 VALUE VALEUR	1995 WEIGHT POIDS	1995 VALUE VALEUR	1996 WEIGHT POIDS	1996 VALUE VALEUR	PRODUIT
	ALL COMMODITIES		3804499		4584453		5474626		5517367	TOUS PRODUITS
0	FOOD AND LIVE ANIMALS		213309		224541		247084		234903	ALIMENTS,ANIMAUX VIVANTS
03	FISH AND PREPARATIONS		85854		79001		76691		88946	POISSONS ET PREPARATIONS
034	FISH,FRESH,CHILLED,FROZN	W 2758	26487	W 2445	24255	W 1528	18736	W 2125	21468	POISSON FRAIS, REFRIG,CONG
0341	FISH FRSH,CHLLD,EX FILLT	W 2633	25403	W 2289	23098	W 1344	17943	W 1984	20759	POISSON FRAIS,REFRIGERE
036	SHELL FISH FRESH,FROZEN	W 12190	58220	W 10661	54033	W 8035	56973	W 10310	66151	CRUSTACES,MOLLUSQUES
04	CEREALS AND PREPARATIONS		20340		34115		42832		36285	CEREALES ET PRODUITS
048	CEREAL ETC PREPARATIONS	W 5455	12512	W 11603	15695	W 6240	14884	W 6441	17029	PREPTNS A BASE CEREALES
05	VEGETABLES AND FRUIT		70207		72654		85264		74663	LEGUMES ET FRUITS
057	FRUIT,NUTS,FRESH,DRIED	W 44509	62379	W 44263	66719	W 48196	76192	W 42220	60072	FRUITS FRAIS OU SECS
0579	FRUIT FRESH OR DRIED NES	W 19557	48860	W 22284	56876	W 22336	63135	W 19825	49033	FRUITS FRAIS,SECS NDA
05796	DATES,FRESH OR DRIED	W 18510	47496	W 20782	55486	W 20872	61689	W 18216	47919	DATTES FRAICHES OU SECHES
1	BEVERAGES AND TOBACCO		36107		58812		56986		46844	BOISSONS ET TABACS
11	BEVERAGES		14712		24105		19195		17360	BOISSONS
112	ALCOHOLIC BEVERAGES	W 8957	12813	W 15037	22174	W 11689	16731	W 9696	14412	BOISSONS ALCOOLIQUES
12	TOBACCO AND MANUFACTURES		21395		34707		37791		29483	TABACS BRUTS FABRIQUES
122	TOBACCO,MANUFACTURED	W 1951	20594	W 2776	31935	W 1857	31021	W 3063	28588	TABACS FABRIQUES
1222	CIGARETTES	W 1304	17137	W 1918	26759	W 1042	26663	W 2244	24647	CIGARETTES
2	CRUDE MATERLS,EXCL FUELS		71200		80519		115805		116253	MAT BRUTES NON COMESTIBLES
26	TEXTILE FIBRES AND WASTE		7007		9724		16215		18954	FIBRES TEXTILES
269	WASTE OF TEXTILE FABRICS	W 9113	4303	W 9875	5476	W 16532	11306	W 21580	16805	FRIPERIE DRILLES,CHIFFONS
27	CRUDE FERTLZR,MINRLS NES		40723		41242		44929		50106	ENGRAIS MINERAUX BRUTS
271	FERTILIZERS,CRUDE	W 1121792	32318	W 1296052	32113	W 1308203	33895	W 1205749	36681	ENGRAIS BRUTS
2713	NAT CALCM PHOSPHATES ETC	W 1121792	32318	W 1296052	32113	W 1308203	33895	W 1205749	36681	PHOSPHATES DE CALCIUM
27131	—UNGROUND	W 1121792	32318	W 1296052	32113	W 1308203	33895	W 1205749	36681	PHOSPHATES NON MOULUS
28	METALLIFEROUS ORES,SCRAP		7107		12142		35181		25437	MINERAIS METAL,DECHETS
287	BASE METAL ORES,CONC NES	W 4566	819	W 19926	3723	W 97609	22736	W 82613	18979	MINERAIS METAUX COMMUNS
2875	ZINC ORES,CONCENTRATES	W 4566	819	W 17856	3353	W 87636	20742	W 73938	16530	MINERAIS DE ZINC
3	MINERAL FUELS ETC		436182		434566		463669		579868	COMBUSTIBLES MINERAUX LUB
33	PETROLEUM AND PRODUCTS		434250		434112		462515		578889	PETROLE ET DERIVES
333	CRUDE PETROLEUM	W 3138211	368138	W 3233453	352195	W 3123982	377811	W 3147701	461957	HUILES BRUTES DE PETROLE
334	PETROLEUM PRODUCTS,REFIN	W 549150	66102	W 666168	81918	W 620148	84688	W 802287	116907	PRODUITS RAFFINES
3341	GASOLINE,OTH LIGHT OILS			W 101816	23464	W 101041	23385	W 116995	31545	ESSENCES POUR MOTEURS
33411	MOTOR,AVIATION SPIRIT			W 101816	23464	W 101041	23385	W 116995	31544	ESSENCES MOTEURS D'AVIONS
3344	FUEL OILS,NES	W 385062	37462	W 473681	43081	W 417425	44518	W 601536	68490	FUEL OILS
3345	LUBS,PETROLEUM OILS NES	W 163456	28481	W 90443	15292	W 73706	13325	W 83757	16873	HUILES LUBRIFIANTES
33451	LUBS(HIGH PETR CONT) ETC	W 163453	28472	W 90427	15230	W 73650	13224	W 83683	16702	HUILES LUBRIF,H LOURDES
4	ANIMAL,VEGETABLE OIL,FAT		179275		302179		230465		123560	HUILES,GRAISSES ANIM,VEG
42	FIXED VEGETABLE OIL,FAT		179140		301811		230147		123398	HUILES VEGETALES FIXES
423	FIXED VEG OILS,SOFT	W 126258	179140	W 197786	301766	W 90825	230147	W 30529	123368	HUILES VEGET DOUCES FIXES
4235	OLIVE OIL	W 126240	179134	W 197783	301756	W 90825	230144	W 30529	123368	HUILE D'OLIVE
5	CHEMCLS,RELATED PROD NES		421372		527582		651236		700817	PRODUITS CHIMIQUES
52	INORGANIC CHEMICALS		177567		223012		271527		306813	PROD CHIM INORGANIQUES
522	INORG ELEMNTS,OXIDES,ETC	W 897068	121450	W 1143453	167102	W 1166124	204567	W 1202359	224965	ELEMENTS INORGANIQUES
5222	INORGANIC ACIDS ETC	W 896462	120578	W 1143090	166644	W 1165790	204184	W 1202128	224357	ACIDES INORGANIQUES
52224	PHOSPHORIC ACIDS ETC	W 895368	120388	W 1141989	166150	W 1128388	201923	W 1198458	224144	ACIDES PHOSPHORIQUES
523	OTHR INORG CHEMICALS ETC	W 129449	56116	W 166843	55887	W 149761	66936	W 164872	81775	AUT PRODUITS CHIMIQUES INORG
5231	METAL CMPD OF INORG ACID	W 28305	20140	W 48341	16556	W 35962	21415	W 32176	25727	SELS METALLIQUES
52311	FLUORIDES ETC	W 26549	19629	W 26170	15340	W 32330	20448	W 29601	24850	FLUORURES
5232	OTH MTL CMPD OF INRG ACD	W 101145	35976	W 118500	39302	W 113743	45473	W 132659	56020	SELS METALLIQUES
52322	PHOSPHITES,PHOSPHATES	W 98752	35258	W 114364	38414	W 111762	44889	W 130906	55471	PHOSPHITES,PHOSPHATES
541	*MEDICINAL,PHARM PRODUCT	K 321659	12954	K 258229	23437	K 145453	12733	K 229713	6365	PROD MEDICINAUX PHARMACEUT
5417	MEDICAMENTS	K 292906	12586	K 203415	22699	K 75263	11819	K 180672	5307	MEDICAMENTS
54179	— CONTNG OTH SUBSTANCES	K 292126	12294	K 181764	19322	K 71756	11594	K 177045	5111	MED CONT AUT SUBSTANCES
55	PERFUME,CLEANING ETC PRD		25179		26015		26735		29017	PROD POUR PARFUM,TOILETTE
553	PERFUMERY,COSMETICS,ETC	W 2213	16131	W 2288	14733	W 1662	13395	W 1718	16633	PRODUITS DE PARFUMERIE
562	*FERTILIZERS,MANUFACTURE	W 1439008	183360	W 1534987	229783	W 1619119	298105	W 1628099	327370	ENGRAIS MANUFACTURES
5622	CHEM PHOSPHATIC FERTILZR	W 1393468	178713	W 869455	112088	W 801150	123727	W 751346	128001	ENGRAIS PHOSPHATES
56222	SUPERPHOSPHATES	W 635300	74738	W 776498	100506	W 743728	116958	W 704737	122896	SUPERPHOSPHATES
56229	CHEM PHOSPH FERTILZR NES	W 758168	103974	W 92957	11583	W 57422	6769	W 46609	5105	ENGRAIS PHOSPHATES NDA
5629	FERTILIZERS NES			W 646138	115365	W 748044	163810	W 844709	193650	ENGRAIS NDA
56292	NITROG–PHOS FERTILZR NES			W 646138	115365	W 748044	163810	W 844709	193650	ENGRAIS NDA CONT N P
6	BASIC MANUFACTURES		419752		557837		660541		549483	ART MANUFACTURES
61	LEATHER,DRESSED FUR,ETC		67709		94561		110808		126340	CUIRS,PELLETERIES
612	LEATHER ETC MANUFACTURES	W 2463	64534	W 3273	81961	W 3053	101732	W 3308	114484	OUVRAGES EN CUIRS NDA
6123	PREPRD PARTS OF FOOTWEAR	W 2423	62643	W 3215	79272	W 2999	98567	W 3212	109852	PARTIES DE CHAUSSURES
62	RUBBER MANUFACTURES NES		16202		27199		35161		42156	CAOUTCHOUC MANUFACTURE
625	RUBBER TYRES, TUBES ETC	W 3423	12628	W 7453	21864	W 8224	28542	W 10158	35625	PNEUS CAOUTCHOUC VULCANISE
6252	TYRES,NEW,BUS OR LORRY	W 1372	5881	W 2174	7899	W 2682	10517	W 6106	21165	PNEUS POUR AUTOBUS,CAMIONS
64	PAPER,PAPERBOARD AND MFR		24069		19518		28708		23536	PAPIERS,CARTONS & OUVRAGES
642	PAPER,ETC,PRECUT,ARTS OF	W 17960	21038	W 9707	13896	W 13518	21310	W 11620	18676	PAP,CARTONS DECOUPES
6421	PAPER ETC CONTAINERS	W 16373	15898	W 7980	7940	W 11894	14621	W 10168	12044	BOITES,SACS EMBALLAGES
65	TEXTILE YARN,FABRICS,ETC		125837		153689		165456		151042	FILS,TISSUS,ARTICLES TEXTILE
651	TEXTILE YARN	W 2767	10575	W 5787	29060	W 5054	28926	W 4146	22313	FILS TEXTILES
652	COTTON FABRICS,WOVEN	W 13937	57261	W 13094	52564	W 13922	62492	W 11955	58744	TISSUS DE COTON
6522	WOVEN COTTON BLEACHD,ETC	W 12245	49658	W 11632	46216	W 12742	55690	W 10406	49614	TISSUS COTON BLANCHIS ETC
65224	BLCHED COTTON FABRIC NES	W 12187	49113	W 11559	45433	W 12684	55058	W 10373	49274	AUT TIS PLUS 85% COT BLANCHI
653	WOVN MAN–MADE FIB FABRIC	W 3058	17671	W 4812	26386	W 5089	30011	W 4145	23920	TISSUS FIBRES SYNTH,ARTIF
6534	DISC SYN BLEND FABRC NES	W 2344	12741	W 3305	19987	W 3890	23404	W 2274	12073	TISSUS FIBRES SYNTH DISCONT
657	SPECIAL TXTL FABRC,PRODS	W 1899	12865	W 2020	11320	W 2119	8403	W 2265	7312	TISSUS SPECIAUX
658	TEXTILE ARTICLES NES	W 1786	12851	W 2893	21091	W 2433	23916	W 2356	29910	ART FACONNES MAT TEXTILES
6589	OTH TEXTILE ARTICLES NES	W 989	9329	W 1162	11655	W 1188	15803	W 1064	21670	AUT ART EN TEXTILES NDA
66	NONMETAL MINERAL MFS NES		75773		75726		118640		85115	ART MIN NON METALLIQUES
661	LIME,CEMENT,BLDG PRODS	W 754927	40806	W 988518	39501	W 1727857	75880	W 1053334	46404	CHAUX,CIMENTS MAT CONSTR
6612	CEMENT	W 750228	38932	W 986069	38642	W 1723426	74171	W 1047972	44147	CIMENTS HYDRAULIQUES
67	IRON AND STEEL		25135		91932		57445		54061	FER ET ACIER
674	IRN,STL UNIV,PLATE,SHEET	W 25235	10475	W 60675	22903	W 83542	36297	W 83100	36270	LARGES PLATS,TOLES
6749	OTH IRN,STL PLATES,SHEET	W 23584	9906	W 60479	22809	W 82864	35906	W 83065	36183	AUTRES TOLES FER,ACIER
67491	— OF IRON OR SIMPLE STL	W 23584	9905	W 60479	22809	W 82863	35899	W 83065	36183	AUT TOLES AUTRES ACIER FIN
678	IRON,STL TUBES,PIPES,ETC	W 6614	5555	W 102815	62274	W 18166	13983	W 14224	13999	TUBES,TUYAUX EN FONTE,FER
6783	IRON,STL TUBES,PIPES NES	W 5549	3805	W 99010	56519	W 11928	9627	W 12243	9077	AUT TUBES,TUYAUX FER,ACIER
69	METAL MANUFACTURES NES		67502		81750		122705		44533	ART MANUFACT EN METAL NDA
699	BASE METAL MFRS NES	W 9498	53259	W 12633	66951	W 13704	107351	W 9534	27522	ART MANUFACTURES MET NDA
6997	IRON,STEEL ARTICLES NES	W 1236	39517	W 1123	50953	W 1495	72792	W 1272	6206	OUV FONTE,FER,ACIER NDA
69979	IRN,STL MANUFACTURES NES	W 1223	39492	W 1121	50946	W 1495	72791	W 1272	6204	AUT OUVRAGES EN FER NDA
7	MACHINES,TRANSPORT EQUIP		366400		392478		515115		538721	MACHINES MATERIEL TRANSPORT
71	POWER GENERATING EQUIPMT		34016		12026		17315		15932	MACHINES GENERATRICES
714	ENGINES AND MOTORS NES		24596	W 20	1542		159	W 27	1085	MOTEURS NON ELECTRIQUES
7144	REACTION ENGINES	W 36	16458	W 4	966					PROPULSEURS A REACTION
72	MACHS FOR SPCL INDUSTRYS		11333		13237		18726		22330	MAC SPECIALES POUR INDUST
74	GENRL INDUSTRL MACHY NES		27352		27897		40949		44324	MACH APP INDUSTRIE

5. General Exports F.O.B. by Commodities according to the S.I.T.C. (Rev. 2) in thousand U.S. Dollars
Exportations Générales F.O.B. par Produits d'après la C.T.C.I. (Rév. 2) en milliers de Dollars E.U.

SITC CTCI	COMMODITY	1993		1994		1995		1996		PRODUIT
		WEIGHT POIDS	VALUE VALEUR	WEIGHT POIDS	VALUE VALEUR	WEIGHT POIDS	VALUE VALEUR	WEIGHT POIDS	VALUE VALEUR	
749	NONELEC MACH PTS,ACC NES	W 3498	16126	W 6620	18374	W 5666	22049	W 5508	21567	PIECES MACH NON ELEC NDA
7493	SHAFT,CRANK,PULLEY ETC	W 3091	10951	W 6129	14432	W 5063	15341	W 4885	15624	ARBRES TRANS,VILEBREQUINS
76	TELECOMM,SOUND EQUIPMENT		32397		38662		36666		37401	EQUIPMENT DE TELECOM
764	TELECOM EQPT,PTS,ACC NES	W 823	31234	W 1292	33213	W 1355	30339	W 1657	33054	EQUIP TELECOM,PIECES
7649	PTS NES OF EQUIPMT OF 76	W 487	22820	W 566	23925	W 421	18222	W 490	19960	PIECES DE LA DIV 76
76493	TELECOMM EQUIPMT PTS NES	W 476	20144	W 538	22297	W 404	16429	W 462	18848	PIECES 761,762,764.3,8
77	ELECTRIC MACHNRY NES ETC		222674		267902		355044		383697	MACH APP ELECT NDA
771	ELECTRIC POWER MACHY NES	W 2678	26517	W 3417	32670	W 4294	55604	W 3941	47484	MACH PROD,TRANS ELECTR
7712	OTH ELEC POWER MACHY NES	W 891	19120	W 1427	24503	W 2155	43739	W 2233	38522	AUT APP PROD TRANSF ELEC
77122	INDUCTORS	W 885	17326	W 1417	22455	W 2140	39435	W 2150	34802	BOBINES REACTANCE,SELFS
772	SWITCHGEAR ETC,PARTS NES	W 3250	55786	W 2864	70023	W 2633	90665	W 2875	99576	APP COUPURE,SECT ETC
7721	SWITCHGEAR ETC	W 3110	49267	W 2652	60242	W 2150	71467	W 2376	77931	APP COUPURE,SECTIONMNT
773	ELECTR DISTRIBUTNG EQUIP	W 6760	103702	W 8084	119936	W 9073	149809	W 13346	181580	EQUIPMT DISTRIBUTION ELECT
7731	INSULATED WIRE,CABLE ETC	W 6707	102786	W 7917	118148	W 9036	149213	W 13334	181505	FILS,CABLES ISOLES ELECT
775	HOUSEHOLD TYPE EQUIP NES	W 3183	12547	W 2924	10604	W 2747	11386	W 851	6144	MACH,APP USAGE DOMESTQUE
7752	DOM REFRIGERATRS,FREEZRS	W 3080	12147	W 2723	10072	W 2002	8543	W 273	1160	REFRIG,CONGEL MENAGER
778	ELECTRICAL MACHINERY NES	W 2215	22693	W 3793	32178	W 3883	45499	W 4247	47474	AUTRES MACH ELECT NDA
7788	OTH ELEC MACHY,EQUIP NES	W 192	14946	W 378	22969	W 510	36198	W 481	36256	AUT MACH APP ELEC NDA
77886	OTH ELEC MACHINERY NES	W 95	12016	W 162	19754	W 188	25961	W 195	26560	AUT MACH APP ELECTRIQUES
78	ROAD VEHICLES		27988		25148		37106		28505	VEHICULES ROUTIERS
784	MOTOR VEH PRTS,ACCES NES	W 3007	13705	W 2907	15276	W 2575	17389	W 2142	19628	PIECES 722,781,782,783
7849	OTHER MOTOR VEHCL PARTS	W 2964	13613	W 2896	15193	W 2567	17349	W 2084	19417	PIECES 722,781,782,783
8	MISC MANUFACTURED GOODS		1656857		2005919		2533722		2626918	ART MANUFACTURES DIVERS
831	*TRAVEL GOODS,HANDBAGS	W 806	12840	W 793	11708	W 829	24537	W 716	19139	ARTICLES DE VOYAGE ETC
84	CLOTHING AND ACCESSORIES		1503899		1839509		2322078		2396420	VETEMENTS
842	MENS OUTERWEAR NOT KNIT	W 47721	698722	W 52716	870233	W 54178	1068744	W 57690	1127152	VET DESSUS POUR HOMMES
8423	— TROUSERS,BREECHES ETC	W 34170	488016	W 36738	585034	W 37058	711219	W 40595	778425	PANTALONS HOMMES MAT TEX
8424	— JACKETS,BLAZERS ETC	W 643	21287	W 803	27243	W 969	39958	W 934	39284	VESTES HOMMES MAT TEXTIL
8429	— OTHER OUTER GARMENTS	W 12687	183914	W 14920	250352	W 15928	308283	W 15988	301790	AUT VET DES HOM MAT TEX
843	WOMENS OUTERWEAR NONKNIT	W 16059	353608	W 17892	441835	W 20828	580546	W 22300	609494	VET DESSUS FEMMES MAT TEX
8431	— COATS AND JACKETS	W 2886	66912	W 3415	84928	W 3257	93398	W 3129	92445	MANT,VEST FEM MAT TEXTIL
8433	— DRESSES	W 1046	27189	W 1139	29863	W 2199	61794	W 2141	59400	ROBES EN MAT–TEXTILES
8434	— SKIRTS	W 3117	62999	W 3050	74584	W 3392	91336	W 3082	76084	JUPES EN MAT TEXTILES
8435	— BLOUSES	W 1536	39953	W 2016	57055	W 2179	76172	W 2156	70821	BLOUSES FEM MAT TEXTILES
8439	— OTHER OUTER GARMENTS	W 7268	149247	W 8071	188050	W 9620	250674	W 11539	299980	AUT VET DES FEM MAT TEXT
844	UNDER GARMENTS NOT KNIT	W 4372	105525	W 5328	130902	W 5454	155253	W 5252	149043	VETEMENT DESSOUS MAT TEX
8441	— MENS SHIRTS	W 3321	85591	W 3897	101848	W 4081	119735	W 3953	114724	CHEMISES HOMMES MAT TEXT
84411	—— OF COTTON	W 2292	62753	W 2655	69773	W 3048	90254	W 3168	93432	CHEMISES HOMMES DE COTON
84412	—— OF SYNTHETIC FIBRES	W 1029	22838	W 1242	32075	W 1034	29481	W 785	21292	CHEMISES HOMMES FIB SYNT
8442	— MENS,OTHR THAN SHIRTS	W 617	12675	W 999	19049	W 935	22120	W 861	22404	SOUS–VET HOMMES MAT TEXT
845	OUTERWEAR KNIT NONELASTC	W 6191	158174	W 7216	165418	W 8811	209535	W 8520	212729	VET DESSOUS,ACCES BONNET
8451	— JERSEYS,PULLOVERS ETC	W 2001	33829	W 3510	60781	W 4596	83042	W 4891	102736	CHANDAILS,PULL–OVERS ETC
8452	— WOMENS DRESSES ETC	W 802	21289	W 733	17986	W 784	21614	W 623	17539	ROBES,JUPES BONNETERIE
8459	— OTHER,CLTHG ACCESRYS	W 3387	103057	W 2973	86651	W 3431	104878	W 3006	92454	AUT VET DESSUS DE BONNE
846	UNDER GARMENTS KNITTED	W 5226	149238	W 6023	190093	W 7391	262212	W 8327	255386	SOUS VETS DE BONNETERIE
8462	— OF COTTON NON ELASTIC	W 3884	76236	W 4455	79809	W 5420	111085	W 6498	124850	SOUS–VET BONNET COTON
84629	—— OTHER	W 3884	76236	W 4455	79809	W 5420	111085	W 6498	124850	AUT SOUS–VET BONNET COTON
8463	— OF SYNTH FBR NONELAST	W 633	17438	W 486	15635	W 583	21019	W 523	14727	SOUS–VET BONNET FIB SYNT
84632	—— MENS SHIRTS	W 590	16128	W 390	11611	W 479	15266	W 389	9236	CHEMISES DE BON FIB SYNMT
8465	CORSETS,GARTERS,ETC	W 709	55564	W 1083	94648	W 1389	130108	W 1306	115810	CORSETS,GAINES ART SIM
84651	BRASSIERES	W 550	47833	W 927	87627	W 1255	122916	W 1166	108752	SOUTIENS–GORGE,BUSTIERS
847	TEXTILE CLTHNG ACCES NES	W 1060	21445	W 1235	23654	W 1215	25098	W 1416	25027	ACCES VET MAT TEXT NDA
8472	CLTHNG ACCESRYS ETC KNIT	W 750	16536	W 874	18681	W 830	20053	W 934	18523	ACCES VET BONNE NDA
84722	KNIT SOCKS,ETC NONELASTC	W 650	15706	W 815	18350	W 754	19330	W 884	17956	CHAUSSETTES BON. NON ELAS
848	HEADGEAR,NONTXTL CLOTHNG	W 610	17186	W 446	17375	W 504	20689	W 446	17588	VET ACCES MAT AUT QUE TEX
851	*FOOTWEAR	W 4198	54802	W 6126	73898	W 6976	99124	W 7270	110408	CHAUSSURES
85102	FOOTWEAR LEATHER	W 3719	51275	W 5348	68811	W 6673	93735	W 6881	101646	CHAUS SEMELLES EN CUIR
87	PRECISION INSTRUMNTS NES		21263		12282		16406		13583	INSTRUM,APPAR SCIENT NDA
874	MEASURNG,CONTROLNG INSTR		21022	W 243	11550	W 232	14174	W 183	9974	INSTRUMENTS DE MESURE
8741	SURVEYING INSTRUMENTS		17331	W 9	1458	W 18	4070	W 22	1742	INST GEODESIE,TOPO ETC
87411	NAVIG INSTR NONELEC ETC		17306	W 1	379	W 1	192	W 1	131	INSTR NAVIGATION
88	PHOTO EQU,OPTICL GDS ETC		17313		22144		20768		23924	APP,FOURN PHOTO,OP,MONTR
89	MISC MANUFCTRD GOODS NES		34617		34847		37290		45257	ART MANUFACTURES DIVERS
893	ARTICLES OF PLASTIC NES	W 2533	11431	W 2039	9278	W 3677	11944	W 3249	17548	OUVRAGES EN MAT DIVIS 58

FOOT NOTES – NOTES

TABLE 1 –

1 Prior to 1974, special trade.

TABLEAU 1 –

1 Avant 1974, commerce spécial.

1. HISTORICAL SERIES, 1961–1996 SPECIAL TRADE, IMPORTS C.I.F., EXPORTS F.O.B.
SERIES HISTORIQUES, 1961–1996 COMMERCE SPECIAL, IMPORTATIONS C.A.F., EXPORTATIONS F.O.B

YEAR ANNEE	VALUE IN MILLION U.S. DOLLARS / VALEUR EN MILLION U.S. DOLLARS: MERCHANDISE – MARCHANDISE		GOLD – OR		CONVERSION FACTORS FACTEURS DE CONVERSION CENTS E.U. PAR		INDEX NUMBERS – INDICES: QUANTUM		UNIT VALUE VALEUR UNITAIRE	
	IMPORTS	EXPORTS	IMPORTS	EXPORTS	IMPORTS	EXPORTS	IMPORTS	EXPORTS	IMPORTS	EXPORTS
1961	509.50	346.70								
1962	622.20	381.20								
1963	690.70	368.10								
1964	542.00	410.80								
1965	577.00	458.92								
1966	724.60	490.50								
1967	690.70	522.30								
1968	770.40	496.40					34	20	118	119
1969	753.90	536.80					32	20	120	120
1970	893.94	588.47					20	18	23	38
1971	1087.40	676.59					24	18	25	41
1972	1507.87	884.97					31	20	26	44
1973	2036.66	1317.08					35	23	31	55
1974	3719.72	1532.18					43	19	46	75
1975	4738.58	1401.08					46	18	52	71
1976	5128.64	1960.21					50	24	52	74
1977	5796.28	1753.01					52	20	57	81
1978	4599.01	2288.16					34	25	65	86
1979	5069.37	2291.44					29	20	77	101
1980	7910.00	2910.00					34	20	118	119
1981	8933.00	4703.00					41	31	115	106
1982	8843.00	5746.00					42	38	90	75
1983	9235.00	5728.00					49	40	105	95
1984	10757.00	7134.00					60	50	101	88
1985	11343.00	7958.00					68	65	102	84
1986	11105.00	7457.00					76	71	86	82
1987	14158.00	10190.00					86	88	92	94
1988	14335.00	11662.00					87	101	92	90
1989	15792.00	11625.00					87	95	95	91
1990	22302.00	12959.00					100	100	100	100
1991	21047.01	13594.00					96	107	97	99
1992	22872.00	14716.00					98	110	95	100
1993	29174.00	15343.00					134	117	89	98
1994	23270.00	18106.00					105	134	90	94
1995	35710.00	21639.01					135	140	105	107
1996	42465.01	23083.01								106

2. IMPORTS BY BROAD ECONOMIC CATEGORY AND EXPORTS BY INDUSTRIAL ORIGIN. (PERCENTAGE OF TOTAL VALUE)
IMPORTATIONS PAR CATEGORIES ECONOMIQUES ET EXPORTATIONS PAR BRANCHE D'ACTIVITE.(EN POURCENTAGE DE LA VALEUR TOTALE)

IMPORTS – IMPORTATIONS

	1990	1991	1992	1993	1994	1995	1996
TOTAL IMPORTS–IMPORTATIONS TOTALES	100.	100.	100.	100.	100.	100.	100.
1 FOOD BEV–ALIMENTATION BOISSONS	6.0	3.6	3.7	3.7	3.6	5.6	4.8
11 PRIMARY–PRODUITS DE BASE	3.0	1.5	1.5	2.1	1.3	3.0	2.6
111 FOR INDUSTRY–POUR L'INDUSTRIE	2.7	1.1	1.1	1.6	1.0	2.4	2.3
112 FOR HOUSEHOLDS–POUR LES MENAGES	0.3	0.4	0.4	0.4	0.3	0.5	0.3
12 PROCESSED–PRODUITS ELABORES	3.0	2.1	2.2	1.6	2.3	2.6	2.1
121 FOR INDUSTRY–POUR L'INDUSTRIE	0.7	0.9	0.8	0.8	1.0	0.9	0.7
122 FOR HOUSEHOLDS–POUR LES MENAGES	2.3	1.2	1.4	0.8	1.3	1.7	1.4
2 IND SUPPLIES–APPROV INDUSTRIELS	35.7	37.3	38.3	37.9	41.2	43.4	38.2
21 PRIMARY–PRODUITS DE BASE	6.1	6.5	7.0	7.1	8.3	8.1	7.3
22 PROCESSED–PRODUITS ELABORES	29.6	30.8	31.3	30.8	32.8	35.3	30.8
3 FUELS–COMBUSTIBLES	20.6	17.7	16.2	13.3	16.2	12.8	13.7
31 PRIMARY–PRODUITS DE BASE	19.0	15.8	15.0	11.7	14.8	11.8	12.3
32 PROCESSED–PRODUITS ELABORES	1.5	1.9	1.2	1.5	1.4	1.0	1.4
321 MOTOR SPIRIT–ESSENCE	0.2	0.3	0.3	0.4	0.4	0.3	0.4
322 OTHER–AUTRES	1.4	1.6	0.9	1.2	1.0	0.7	1.0
4 MACHINERY–EQUIPEMENT	23.6	26.7	24.9	24.2	24.0	21.8	25.2
41 CAPITAL EQUIPMENT–MACHINES	19.6	21.8	20.2	20.1	19.9	18.6	21.8
42 PARTS–PIECES ACCESSOIRES	4.0	4.9	4.8	4.2	4.0	3.2	3.4
5 TRANSPORT–TRANSPORT	8.8	8.5	11.3	15.1	10.2	11.4	10.9
51 PASSENGER CARS–AUTOMOBILES	2.5	1.2	1.6	2.5	1.0	0.9	2.4
52 OTHER–AUTRES	2.5	3.3	4.7	7.9	5.6	6.3	4.6
521 INDUSTRIAL–INDUSTRIELS	2.4	3.1	4.6	7.8	5.5	6.3	4.5
522 NON INDUSTRIAL–NON INDUSTRIEL	0.1	0.2	0.1	0.2	0.1	0.0	0.1
53 PARTS–PIECES ACCESSOIRES	3.7	4.0	5.0	4.7	3.7	4.2	4.0
6 CONSUM GOODS–BIENS CONSOMMATION	5.1	5.7	5.2	5.3	4.4	4.8	6.4
61 DURABLE–DURABLES	1.4	1.4	1.5	1.5	1.2	1.4	2.2
62 SEMI DURABLE–SEMI DURABLES	1.3	1.6	1.7	1.6	1.5	1.8	2.5
63 NON DURABLE–NON DURABLES	2.4	2.6	2.0	2.2	1.7	1.5	1.7
7 GOODS NES–BIENS NDA	0.1	0.6	0.4	0.5	0.4	0.3	0.9

EXPORTS – EXPORTATIONS

	1990	1991	1992	1993	1994	1995	1996
TOTAL EXPORTS–EXPORTATIONS TOTALES	100.	100.	100.	100.	100.	100.	100.
1 AGRICULTURE	18.1	19.5	14.9	15.4	13.1	10.2	11.0
2 MINING QUARRY–INDUS EXTRACTIVES	2.7	2.2	1.9	1.6	1.5	1.9	1.0
3 MANUFACTURING–IND MANUFACTUR	79.2	78.4	83.2	83.1	85.4	88.0	88.0
31 FOOD BEV TOBACCO–ALIM BOISS TAB	6.3	8.4	8.7	8.6	9.5	9.9	9.7
32 TEXTILES–INDUSTRIES TEXTILES	37.1	36.6	39.8	39.2	38.4	40.6	38.9
33 WOOD & PRODUCTS–BOIS & PRODUITS	0.3	0.3	0.3	0.3	0.4	0.4	0.3
34 PAPER & PRODUCTS–PAPIER & PRODT	0.5	0.5	0.5	0.5	0.7	0.7	0.7
35 CHEMICALS–INDUSTRIES CHIMIQUES	9.9	8.7	8.3	7.4	7.9	8.3	7.6
36 NON METAL MIN–MIN NON METAL	3.0	3.4	3.5	3.0	3.2	3.2	3.4
37 BASIC METAL–IND METAL BASE	13.3	10.9	10.4	12.9	12.9	10.6	9.8
38 METAL MANUF–MANUF METAL	8.6	9.4	11.4	11.0	11.9	13.8	15.8
39 OTH MANUF IND–AUTRES MANUF	0.2	0.3	0.2	0.3	0.4	0.4	1.8

3. TRADE BY PRINCIPAL COUNTRIES OF PRODUCTION AND LAST CONSIGNMENT (VALUE IN THOUSAND U.S. DOLLARS)
ECHANGES SELON LES PRINCIPAUX PAYS DE PRODUCTION ET DE DERNIERE CONSIGNATION (VALEUR EN MILLIERS DE DOLLARS EU)

COUNTRIES–PAYS	SPECIAL IMPORTS C.I.F. IMPORTATIONS SPECIALES C.A.F				
	1992	1993	1994	1995	1996
World	22871045	29429324	23267998	35707461	42930306
Africa	807955	715857	860749	1384456	2028028
Americas	3119605	4036137	2922993	4723180	4395100
Northern America	2705836	3491495	2566403	4016730	3622451
LAIA	398357	523258	329222	658141	662356
CACM	5770	4301	2029	3068	13227
Caribbean	3516	5806	5755	2280	33759
Rest of America	6126	11278	19583	42962	63308
As.ex F.USSR	5089022	6390008	4798183	6647099	7593481
Eur.x F.USSR	12420861	15659679	12221480	18932544	25146881
EU	10656521	13874109	10914943	16862469	22704798
EFTA	791107	727144	561643	892037	1223386
East Europe	848982	968463	671538	1054167	1105460
Other Europe	5163	7615	11620	28545	6796
Former USSR	1244688	2284528	1834241	3361803	3074145
Oceania	158207	261253	301255	344795	410417
Germany/Allemagne	3754465	4533048	3645582	5547588	7583028
USA/Etats–Unis d'Amer	2600462	3350719	2429413	3723983	3287628
Italy/Italie	1918569	2558299	2008507	3193123	4245106
France,Monac	1350851	1952375	1458163	1995845	2739534
United Kingdom	1187332	1546017	1169690	1829761	2486301
Russian Federation	1040816	1542330	1044910	2082376	1900235
Saudi Arabia	1664991	1499746	1228812	1382990	1706342
Japan/Japon	1112677	1620788	967545	1399956	1414487
Netherlands/Pays–Bas	698094	869931	739982	1084328	1416741
Belgium–Luxembourg	551216	682976	531677	911895	1114858
Switz.Liecht	687947	650509	471692	816276	1126283
Iran (Islamic Rp. of)	364883	667027	692409	689476	805291
Spain/Espagne	320486	430735	380156	592606	989026
Ukraine	90003	472706	535071	856340	744531
Korea, Republic of	372767	621193	285259	566126	714636
Sweden/Suède	221942	427552	283198	517848	655433
China/Chine	172366	255226	257870	539019	551298
Libyan Arab Jamahiriya	445496	131021	319576	385220	476304
Austria/Autriche	282463	318836	210730	294016	540263
Romania/Roumanie	256112	300775	228911	367870	437401
Bulgaria/Bulgarie	224542	243244	195431	402014	358043
Algeria/Algérie	10162	23025	94677	447970	727938
Brazil/Brésil	199309	250832	206008	267874	290455
Australia/Australie	112839	206476	226337	235422	304112
United Arab Emirates	354188	314467	338755	41987	22979
Canada	105234	140774	136990	292681	334378
Malaysia/Malaisie	141147	159658	170478	272303	233610
So. Africa Customs Un	170363	208353	160609	132198	256070
Finland/Finlande	103165	178039	142488	240856	253139
India/Inde	100244	151853	110849	222872	254881
Greece/Grèce	88151	120461	105065	200673	283382
Egypt/Egypte	58844	105067	124210	210648	270771
Syrian Arab Republic	53718	68466	43867	258101	309880
Israel/Israël	97076	121793	125891	166635	192038
Denmark/Danemark	104607	135925	96280	188769	170046
Argentina/Argentine	116148	146165	49757	208617	152341
Hong Kong	78096	86367	73899	138574	199703
Ireland/Irlande	51014	71487	101082	192995	144334
Czech Republic		222986	94688	104531	107597
Indonesia/Indonésie	42101	78793	55225	132733	149408
Norway,SVD,JM	102577	76495	89560	74884	93254
Pakistan	43688	115628	36773	153625	82409
Kuwait/ Koweït	68265	84479	76900	97164	103449
Singapore/Singapour	88330	86098	41664	66249	130142
Hungary/Hongrie	97117	86684	55462	69904	94319
Poland/Pologne	86650	91096	69108	65264	78516
New Zealand	43024	54770	73879	106281	105658
Turkmenistan/Turkménistn	21181	76893	65560	111826	99890
Thailand/Thaïlande	35278	72264	31603	62973	87086
Mexico/Mexique	14669	25474	22020	84506	130664

COUNTRIES–PAYS	SPECIAL EXPORTS F.O.B. EXPORTATIONS SPECIALES F.O.B.				
	1992	1993	1994	1995	1996
Monde	14714629	15348934	18106058	21598657	23047758
Afrique	782034	706326	842668	1063869	1154655
Amériques	986770	1127600	1733821	1752062	1872802
Amérique du Nord	919304	1036210	1600077	1608283	1717101
ALAI	39435	83008	99330	92788	102814
MCAC	2654	773	3805	2964	4269
Caraïbes	9481	4194	19009	44396	30018
Autre Amérique	15896	3416	11601	3631	18600
Asie l'URSS exclus	3266939	3685905	3871571	3567444	3844351
Europe l'URSS exclus	8876575	8608059	9795677	12628715	12986056
UE	7934021	7602763	8637071	11076776	11467360
AELE	298429	247753	276894	293347	334962
Europe de l'Est	531548	622217	751063	1065592	987834
Autre de l'Europe	30884	53276	30702	51058	24932
Ancienne URSS	685743	1047946	1423422	2094453	2666575
Océanie	32251	27090	42275	53302	64440
Germany/Allemagne	3660428	3654327	3934285	5033584	5152197
USA/Etats–Unis d'Amer	865026	986466	1520678	1512552	1616833
Italy/Italie	942713	750326	1033619	1455799	1438411
United Kingdom	796311	835107	888890	1134456	1246701
France,Monac	808880	771289	851187	1032596	1041945
Russian Federation	441886	505332	820250	1232101	1494500
Netherlands/Pays–Bas	499785	517038	621037	736358	764419
Saudi Arabia	485942	652397	609395	467331	430111
Belgium–Luxembourg	289920	295375	371003	451397	487665
Iran (Islamic Rp. of)	455286	289691	249816	265574	296397
Spain/Espagne	298578	198853	233594	360307	366084
Syrian Arab Republic	216187	238884	253887	270666	308689
Austria/Autriche	229038	226624	248973	275109	287747
Poland/Pologne	186304	234810	249452	272387	252946
Switz.Liecht	222771	215919	238900	237839	274799
Libyan Arab Jamahiriya	246502	246267	179427	238245	243636
China/Chine	146717	511927	354841	66961	65083
Egypt/Egypte	173499	191421	194520	245205	314392
Romania/Roumanie	173073	151681	175342	301596	312723
Algeria/Algérie	107565	82190	237556	268958	277953
Greece/Grèce	145705	118151	168854	209736	235553
Japan/Japon	162408	158462	186501	179916	166628
Israel/Israël	89851	80236	178078	239553	253958
Hong Kong	47903	117652	236483	216563	219352
Cyprus/Chypre	148781	153727	130191	197118	200883
Iraq	212012	160118	140972	119215	187973
United Arab Emirates	96791	129463	184643	188577	210557
Singapore/Singapour	98417	121014	184575	142735	247949
Azerbaijan	102246	68214	132124	160695	239221
Lebanon/Liban	99202	99597	160612	159255	182943
Uzbekistan/Ouzbékistan	54492	213531	64531	138087	229859
Jordan/Jordanie	164150	105005	111737	169445	147757
Bulgaria/Bulgarie	72234	86235	133663	183035	152984
Ukraine	35848	39452	76285	198111	267043
Korea, Republic of	190854	91407	93692	99879	101738
Denmark/Danemark	92517	84360	91618	133296	147362
Kazakhstan	19379	67850	131803	149855	163323
Kuwait/ Koweït	65978	103671	128266	118706	106879
Sweden/Suède	83536	67091	86061	105512	120513
Malaysia/Malaisie	19004	62159	113683	99668	133642
Hungary/Hongrie	26964	37508	58280	159592	102632
Canada	54125	49732	79389	95703	100231
Yemen/Yémen	61949	100810	58140	81920	69486
Tunisia/Tunisie	47250	55553	74307	79281	94402
Pakistan	44034	43383	56527	89781	77735
Turkmenistan/Turkménistn	7495	83886	84153	56265	65284
Georgia/Géorgie	11617	34514	67071	67707	110198
Czech Republic		58453	62166	75724	92819
So. Africa Customs Un	51755	57456	45931	66887	65714
Thailand/Thaïlande	59155	25650	34212	86467	75718

(VALUE AS PERCENTAGE OF WORLD TOTAL)(VALEURS EN POURCENTAGE DU TOTAL MONDIAL)

	1987	1988	1989	1990	1991	1992	1993	1994	1995	1996
Africa	6.3	4.7	6.7	6.0	3.6	3.5	2.4	3.7	3.9	4.7
Americas	13.0	14.6	17.2	13.5	13.5	13.6	13.7	12.6	13.2	10.2
Northern America	10.9	12.3	14.4	11.1	11.5	11.8	11.9	11.0	11.2	8.4
LAIA	2.1	2.3	2.7	2.4	2.0	1.7	1.8	1.4	1.8	1.5
CACM	0.0	0.0	0.0	0.0	0.0	0.0	0.0	0.0	0.0	0.0
Caribbean	0.0	0.0	0.0	0.0	0.0	0.0	0.0	0.0	0.0	0.1
Rest of America	0.0	0.0	0.1	0.1	0.0	0.0	0.0	0.1	0.1	0.1
As.ex F.USSR	26.9	24.7	21.0	22.7	23.1	22.3	21.7	20.6	18.6	17.7
Eur.x F.USSR	50.4	51.4	49.8	51.5	54.0	54.3	53.2	52.5	53.0	58.6
EU	42.8	44.1	41.0	44.4	47.0	46.6	47.1	46.9	47.2	52.9
EFTA	2.9	2.7	3.1	2.7	2.6	3.5	2.5	2.4	2.5	2.8
East Europe	3.3	3.0	3.3	3.3	3.7	3.7	3.3	2.9	3.0	2.6
Other Europe	1.3	1.6	2.4	1.2	0.7	0.0	0.0	0.0	0.1	0.0
Former USSR	2.2	3.1	3.8	5.6	5.2	5.4	7.8	7.9	9.4	7.2
Oceania	1.2	1.6	1.0	0.7	0.6	0.7	0.9	1.3	1.0	1.0
Germany/Allemagne	14.9	14.3	14.0	15.7	15.4	16.4	15.4	15.7	15.5	17.7
USA/Etats–Unis d'Amer	9.7	10.6	13.3	10.2	10.7	11.4	11.4	10.4	10.4	7.7
Italy/Italie	7.6	7.0	6.8	7.7	8.8	8.4	8.7	8.6	8.9	9.9
France,Monac	4.3	5.8	4.7	6.0	5.8	5.9	6.6	6.3	5.6	6.4
United Kingdom	4.9	5.2	4.6	4.5	5.5	5.2	5.3	5.0	5.1	5.8
Russian Federation						4.6	5.2	4.5	5.8	4.4
Saudi Arabia	1.2	1.6	1.3	3.2	8.7	7.3	5.1	5.3	3.9	4.0
Japan/Japon	6.1	3.9	3.4	5.0	5.2	4.9	5.5	4.2	3.9	3.3
Netherlands/Pays–Bas	2.6	2.7	2.8	2.6	3.0	3.1	3.0	3.2	3.0	3.3
Belgium–Luxembourg	2.8	3.3	2.8	2.3	2.6	2.4	2.3	2.3	2.6	2.6

	1987	1988	1989	1990	1991	1992	1993	1994	1995	1996
Afrique	4.7	6.7	6.6	5.8	6.0	5.3	4.6	4.7	4.9	5.0
Amériques	7.9	7.4	9.3	8.3	7.6	6.7	7.3	9.6	8.1	8.1
Amérique du Nord	7.6	7.0	8.9	8.0	7.1	6.2	6.8	8.8	7.4	7.5
ALAI	0.3	0.3	0.2	0.2	0.4	0.3	0.5	0.5	0.4	0.4
MCAC	0.0	0.0	0.0	0.0	0.0	0.0	0.0	0.0	0.0	0.0
Caraïbes	0.0	0.0	0.1	0.0	0.1	0.1	0.0	0.1	0.2	0.1
Autre Amérique	0.0	0.0	0.0	0.1	0.1	0.1	0.0	0.1	0.0	0.1
Asie l'URSS exclus	29.9	31.9	22.7	19.8	21.4	22.2	24.0	21.4	16.5	16.7
Europe l'URSS exclus	55.6	51.4	53.3	61.6	60.1	60.3	56.1	54.1	58.5	56.3
UE	50.4	46.1	48.7	55.4	54.0	53.9	49.5	47.7	51.3	49.8
AELE	3.6	2.4	1.7	2.6	2.1	2.0	1.6	1.5	1.4	1.5
Europe de l'Est	1.4	2.4	2.1	2.4	3.3	3.6	4.1	4.1	4.9	4.3
Autre de l'Europe	0.2	0.6	0.9	1.2	0.7	0.2	0.3	0.2	0.2	0.1
Ancienne URSS	1.7	2.3	6.1	4.1	4.5	4.7	6.8	7.9	9.7	11.6
Océanie	0.2	0.2	0.4	0.2	0.2	0.2	0.2	0.2	0.2	0.3
Germany/Allemagne	21.4	18.4	18.7	23.6	25.1	24.9	23.8	21.7	23.3	22.4
USA/Etats–Unis d'Amer	7.0	6.5	8.4	7.5	6.7	5.9	6.4	8.4	7.0	7.0
Italy/Italie	8.3	8.2	8.4	8.5	7.1	6.4	4.9	5.7	6.7	6.2
United Kingdom	5.3	4.9	5.3	5.7	5.0	5.4	5.4	4.9	5.3	5.4
France,Monac	4.9	4.3	5.1	5.7	5.1	5.5	5.0	4.7	4.8	4.5
Russian Federation						3.0	3.3	4.5	5.7	6.5
Netherlands/Pays–Bas	2.7	3.0	3.5	3.4	3.5	3.4	3.4	3.4	3.4	3.3
Saudi Arabia	4.0	3.1	3.1	2.6	3.6	3.3	4.3	3.4	2.2	1.9
Belgium–Luxembourg	3.1	2.3	2.2	2.4	2.1	2.0	1.9	2.0	2.1	2.1
Iran (Islamic Rp. of)	4.3	4.7	4.8	3.8	3.6	3.1	1.9	1.4	1.2	1.3

4. Special Imports C.I.F. by Commodities according to the S.I.T.C. (Rev. 2) in thousand U.S. Dollars
Importations Spéciales C.A.F. par Produits d'après la C.T.C.I. (Rév. 2) en milliers de Dollars E.U.

SITC CTCI	COMMODITY	1993 WEIGHT POIDS	1993 VALUE VALEUR	1994 WEIGHT POIDS	1994 VALUE VALEUR	1995 WEIGHT POIDS	1995 VALUE VALEUR	1996 WEIGHT POIDS	1996 VALUE VALEUR	PRODUIT
	ALL COMMODITIES		29429324		23267998		35707461		42930306	TOUS PRODUITS
0	FOOD AND LIVE ANIMALS		838593		465146		1480181		1748885	ALIMENTS,ANIMAUX VIVANTS
001	*LIVE ANIMALS FOR FOOD	W 69593	102801	W 9483	22702	W 178306	341881	W 74547	165145	ANIMAUX VIVANTS
0011	BOVINE SPECIES,LIVE	W 69413	95176	W 9190	14434	W 176530	330257	W 73303	152241	ESPECE BOVINE
00111	— PURE BRED FR BREEDING	W 18703	36836	W 3528	7441	W 36304	107366	W 26374	77182	BOVINS REPRODUCTEURS
00119	— OTHR THAN FR BREEDING	W 50710	58340	W 5662	6993	W 140226	222891	W 46929	75059	BOVINS NON REPRODUCTEURS
04	CEREALS AND PREPARATIONS		354580		164943		470539		785485	CEREALES ET PRODUITS
041	WHEAT ETC UNMILLED	W 1220982	178894	W 495905	75945	W 1253331	243678	W 2146930	485099	FROMENT,EPEAUTRE
0412	OTHER WHEAT ETC UNMILLED	W 976011	140078	W 336288	40459	W 1128724	213045	W 1997962	444930	AUTRE FROMENT NON MOULU
042	RICE	W 298394	85799	W 197993	56256	W 307846	109431	W 211482	82083	RIZ
044	MAIZE UNMILLED	W 101881	16005	W 14878	3747	W 623975	92463	W 897440	175688	MAIS NON MOULU
05	VEGETABLES AND FRUIT		101093		47600		87509		93504	LEGUMES ET FRUITS
06	SUGAR AND PREPS,HONEY		10202		10372		202742		293097	SUCRES ET PRODUITS
061	SUGAR AND HONEY	W 23157	8700	W 14673	8706	W 432591	199644	W 772302	286760	SUCRES ET MIEL
0612	REFINED SUGAR ETC	W 17037	5629	W 569	279	W 402159	189089	W 581219	242429	SUCRES RAFFINES
081	*FEEDING STUFF FOR ANIML	W 459709	110766	W 314925	85052	W 436439	101073	W 428409	149727	NOURRITURE POUR ANIMAUX
1	BEVERAGES AND TOBACCO		336232		152519		173320		290551	BOISSONS ET TABACS
12	TOBACCO AND MANUFACTURES		327284		139819		159967		272009	TABACS BRUTS FABRIQUES
121	TOBACCO UNMNFCTRD,REFUSE	W 12497	93666	W 16693	86442	W 21639	134397	W 42962	240020	TABACS BRUTS,DECHETS
1212	TOBACCO STRIPPED OR PART	W 12449	93657	W 13676	85334	W 18602	131636	W 33953	223203	TABACS PART ECOTES
122	TOBACCO,MANUFACTURED	W 13927	233618	W 6623	53377		25570	W 6973	31990	TABACS FABRIQUES
1222	CIGARETTES	W 10414	214894	W 1710	32725	W 130	2415	W 37	547	CIGARETTES
2	CRUDE MATERLS,EXCL FUELS		2489960		2272462		3512184		3538103	MAT BRUTES NON COMESTIBLES
21	HIDES,SKINS,FURS UNDRSSD		214873		281517		464313		675537	CUIRS,PEAUX BRUTS
211	HIDES,SKINS,EXC FURS,RAW	W 129752	214426	W 122805	281237	W 171702	462749	W 253079	672174	CUIRS ET PEAUX
2116	SHEEP SKIN WITH WOOL	W 66462	86720	W 80593	130937	W 92647	213375	W 151689	387825	PEAUX LAINEES D'OVINS
2117	SHEEP SKIN WITHOUT WOOL	W 26282	93219	W 25372	127941	W 27703	164373	W 33053	181462	PEAUX EPILEES D'OVINS
22	OIL SEEDS,OLEAGINOUS FRT		72004		75466		204484		249821	GRAINES,FRUITS OLEAGINEUX
222	SEEDS FOR'SOFT'FIXED OIL	W 277650	71525	W 265343	75041	W 612309	203631	W 823917	249358	GRAINES HUILES FIXES
2224	SUNFLOWER SEEDS	W 66069	19149	W 94664	30140	W 357035	120406	W 640373	183012	GRAINES DE TOURNESOL
23	RUBBER, CRUDE		145481		130735		241415		239545	CAOUTCHOUC BRUT
232	NATURAL RUBBER,GUMS	W 81600	74046	W 64654	68907	W 83759	135538	W 86379	127216	LATEX CAOUTCHOUC NATUREL
23202	OTHER NATURAL RUBBER	W 70116	63984	W 52832	57986	W 71008	118141	W 72976	109132	CAOUTCHOUC NATUREL
24	CORK AND WOOD		344951		160721		145276		182575	LIEGE ET BOIS
247	OTH WOOD ROUGH,SQUARED	W 1911195	304864	W 933915	148095	W 622345	118198	W 788904	138065	BOIS BRUTS EQUARRIS
2471	SAW–,VENEER–LOGS CONIFER	W 1439614	205140	W 599554	88113	W 465038	70290	W 502755	68062	CONIFERES POUR SCIAGE,PLACAG
24711	— IN THE ROUGH	W 1439614	205140	W 599554	88113	W 465038	70290	W 502755	68062	ECORCES OU DEGROSSIS
2472	SAW–,VENEER–LOGS NON–CON	W 471581	99724	W 334361	59982	W 157307	47908	W 286149	70003	NON CONIFERES SCIAGE,PLAC
24721	— IN THE ROUGH	W 471581	99724	W 334361	59982	W 157307	47908	W 286149	70003	BRUTS ECORCES DEGROSSIS
251	*PULP AND WASTE PAPER	W 302892	103589	W 240226	102242	W 315838	246086	W 228908	126582	PATES A PAPIER,DECHETS
2517	SODA,SULPHATE WOOD PULP	W 203981	82615	W 185992	89267	W 235691	214430	W 189973	110558	PATES CHIMIQUES AU SULFATE
25172	— BLEACHED,NONDISSOLVNG	W 192485	78461	W 178493	86956	W 231771	211936	W 187945	109225	PATES BLANCHIES
26	TEXTILE FIBRES AND WASTE		578181		489703		808671		695313	FIBRES TEXTILES
263	COTTON	W 201666	247694	W 149063	240000	W 187303	383292	W 169168	302217	COTON
2631	RAW COTTON,EXCL LINTERS	W 200880	247256	W 147059	238970	W 182561	381045	W 166747	299718	COTON EN MASSE
266	SYNTHETIC FIBRES TO SPIN	W 96895	139181	W 60593	84677	W 62220	118750	W 72926	114079	FIBRES SYNTHETIQUES
267	OTHER MAN–MADE FIBRES	W 50516	87539	W 55087	85535	W 77671	159062	W 69571	168913	AUTR FIBR TEXT ARTIF SYNTH
2671	REGENERATD FIBRE TO SPIN	W 43078	83464	W 49786	82622	W 67275	151723	W 63226	164235	FIBRES TEXT ARTIFIC
268	WOOL(EXC TOPS),ANML HAIR	W 44875	93189	W 27376	65004	W 43315	133065	W 40238	99566	LAINES ET POILS
27	CRUDE FERTLZR,MINRLS NES		89167		81009		117958		125577	ENGRAIS MINERAUX BRUTS
28	METALLIFEROUS ORES,SCRAP		893326		908205		1218589		1171065	MINERAIS METAL,DECHETS
281	IRON ORE,CONCENTRATES	W 1710261	57002	W 1951330	46608	W 3221358	107442	W 2991253	115971	MINERAIS DE FER
282	IRON AND STEEL SCRAP	W 6372843	819657	W 5917325	848850	W 6851971	1081232	W 7042138	991315	FERRAILLES
28209	— OF OTHR IRON OR STEEL	W 6358358	817882	W 5916852	848794	W 6848247	1079174	W 7027321	987768	FERRAILLES DE FER
3	MINERAL FUELS ETC		3989557		3837938		4657702		5940981	COMBUSTIBLES MINERAUX LUB
32	COAL,COKE AND BRIQUETTES		336518		401888		321266		623499	HOUILLES,COKES,BRIQUETTES
322	COAL,LIGNITE AND PEAT	W 6112400	306510	W 7339517	377819	W 5159675	287749	W 8821653	580697	HOUILLES,LIGNITES,TOURBE
3222	OTH COAL,NOT AGGLOMERATD	W 5377818	274198	W 6582088	344676	W 4330834	238026	W 7842637	519571	AUTRES HOUILLES
33	PETROLEUM AND PRODUCTS		3065831		2807482		3329431		4042875	PETROLE ET DERIVES
333	CRUDE PETROLEUM	MW 21740	2550340	MW 21181	2432133	MW 23605	2917173	MW 22767	3415917	HUILES BRUTES DE PETROLE
334	PETROLEUM PRODUCTS,REFIN	W 2429204	421150	W 1884316	302105	W 1756626	330235	W 2426066	534565	PRODUITS RAFFINES
3341	GASOLINE,OTH LIGHT OILS	W 618777	111524	W 545853	88209	W 627746	111450	W 803315	169936	ESSENCES POUR MOTEURS
33411	MOTOR,AVIATION SPIRIT	W 430939	81039	W 301706	51192	W 349967	62166	W 767892	162549	ESSENCES MOTEURS D'AVIONS
3343	GAS OILS	W 1285400	211579	W 665190	97826	W 560199	86645			GAS OILS
3344	FUEL OILS,NES	W 417546	39535	W 571078	55870	W 457656	53033	W 1533653	280519	FUEL OILS
335	RESIDUAL PETRLM PROD NES	W 2234711	94341	W 1544099	73245	W 1504274	82023	W 1710893	92392	PRODUITS RESIDUELS NDA
341	*GAS,NATURAL AND MANUFCT		587208		628568		1007005	MW 11995	1262788	GAZ NATUREL,GAZ MANUFACT
3413	PETROLM GASES,LIQUEFIED	W 1424035	237468	W 1842077	256883	W 3139134	484710	W 6369723	741686	GAZ DE PETROLE LIQUEFIE
34139	OTH HYDROCARBON GAS LQFD	W 1424034	237466	W 1842077	256883	W 3138231	484582	W 6367693	740983	HYDROCARBURES GAZEUX NDA
3414	PETROLEUM GASES, GASEOUS	MV 5040428	349740	MV 5048399	371684	MV 5660032	522293	W 5625323	521103	GAZ DE PETROLE GAZEUX
4	ANIMAL,VEGETABLE OIL,FAT		407951		458964		638006		490349	HUILES,GRAISSES ANIM,VEG
42	FIXED VEGETABLE OIL,FAT		354885		404040		537117		383090	HUILES VEGETALES FIXES
423	FIXED VEG OILS,SOFT	W 390494	181493	W 426714	253908	W 462889	311132	W 309251	181626	HUILES VEGET DOUCES FIXES
4232	SOYA BEAN OIL	W 232124	104756	W 137756	80885	W 141153	93328	W 105766	61362	HUILE DE SOJA
4236	SUNFLOWER SEED OIL	W 153999	74690	W 287624	171299	W 305594	206452	W 191724	112531	HUILE DE TOURNESOL
424	FIXED VEG OIL NONSOFT	W 374333	173392	W 281660	150131	W 321295	225985	W 310373	201464	AUTRES HUILES VEG FIXES
4242	PALM OIL	W 215671	88771	W 201239	96824	W 200473	135276	W 174776	101831	HUILE DE PALME
5	CHEMCLS,RELATED PROD NES		3481103		3145166		5236269		5599862	PRODUITS CHIMIQUES
51	ORGANIC CHEMICALS		864962		890141		1521044		1386319	PROD CHIMIQ ORGANIQUES
511	HYDROCARBONS NES,DERIVS	W 325278	132662	W 321756	155766	W 379141	244796	W 386356	182646	HYDROCARBURES NDA
5112	CYCLIC HYDROCARBONS	W 166425	60261	W 161752	85348	W 176833	128615	W 165903	74367	HYDROCARBURES CYCLIQUES
512	ALCOHOLS,PHENOLS ETC		76819		99012		166407	W 303859	166783	PHENOLS,PHENOLS–ALCOOLS
5121	ACYCLIC ALCOHOLS,DERIVS		67638		91182		154177	W 295711	154996	ALCOOLS ACYCLIQUES
513	CARBOXYLIC ACIDS ETC	W 179517	161894	W 180399	178168	W 234607	344441	W 274923	320204	ACIDES CARBOXYLIQUES
5137	MONOACIDS AND DERIVATIVS	W 114184	90800	W 116072	101823	W 127544	176719	W 141697	151560	ACIDES MONOCARBOXYLIQUES
5138	POLYACIDS AND DERIVATIVS	W 58064	41457	W 56257	49529	W 94528	116286	W 120399	117946	ACIDES POLYCARBOXYLIQUES
514	NITROGEN–FNCTN COMPOUNDS	W 128101	251736	W 144770	242047	W 183760	424281	W 167037	384449	COMPOSES FONCT AZOTEES
5148	OTH NITROGN–FNCTN CMPNDS	W 102571	161366	W 117238	156258	W 155021	311557	W 137381	268577	AUTRES COMPOSES AZOTES
51483	ACRYLONITRILE	W 64087	41963	W 82137	54712	W 111339	146510	W 89633	74313	ACRYLONITRILE
515	ORG–INORG COMPOUNDS ETC	W 26739	182886	W 26280	163159	W 33583	253795	W 28663	248654	COMPOSES ORGANO–MINERAUX
5156	HETEROCYCLIC CMPDS ETC	W 17290	122363	W 18376	113722	W 22796	178275	W 17526	168813	COMPOSES HETEROCYCLIQUES
51569	OTH HETEROCYC CMPDS,ETC	W 3944	103950	W 2794	92940	W 4338	136812	W 4652	142119	AUT COMP HETEROCYCLIQUES
52	INORGANIC CHEMICALS		356211		282812		441542		476952	PROD CHIM INORGANIQUES
522	INORG ELEMNTS,OXIDES,ETC		235589		173860		287881	W 1038159	290086	ELEMENTS INORGANIQUES
5225	INORGANIC BASES ETC NES	W 826805	109682	W 484971	82899	W 616534	150753	W 557022	128648	AUTRES BASES OXYDES METAL
52251	AMMONIA,ANHYDROUS ETC	W 708674	86485	W 378634	60104	W 504819	113360	W 414180	85937	AMMONIAC LIQUEFIE
523	OTHR INORG CHEMICALS ETC	W 162725	114869	W 152369	102630	W 196269	146584	W 262478	178777	AUT PRODUITS CHIMIQUES INORG
53	DYES,TANNING,COLOUR PROD		436177		392850		560966		640029	PROD TEINTURE,COLORANTS
531	SYNT DYE,NAT INDGO,LAKES	W 21110	247733	W 20613	228084	W 25064	299577	W 33494	344842	MAT COLOR ORGAN,LAQUES
5311	SYNTHIC ORGNIC DYESTUFFS	W 19962	236872	W 19481	217289	W 23557	284840	W 31507	327340	MAT COLOR ORGAN SYNTHET
533	PIGMENTS,PAINTS,ETC	W 68148	178830	W 57697	157556	W 77557	249032	W 90713	274572	PIGMENTS,PEINTURES,VERNIS

4. Special Imports C.I.F. by Commodities according to the S.I.T.C. (Rev. 2) in thousand U.S. Dollars
Importations Spéciales C.A.F. par Produits d'après la C.T.C.I. (Rév. 2) en milliers de Dollars E.U.

SITC CTCI	COMMODITY	1993		1994		1995		1996		PRODUIT
		WEIGHT POIDS	VALUE VALEUR	WEIGHT POIDS	VALUE VALEUR	WEIGHT POIDS	VALUE VALEUR	WEIGHT POIDS	VALUE VALEUR	
541	*MEDICINAL,PHARM PRODUCT	K 4949918	394893	K 4917751	357074	K 5769920	550816	K 5026284	634945	PROD MEDICINAUX PHARMACEUT
5413	ANTIBIOTICS IN BULK	K 752289	123292	K 545938	100539	K 731139	138413	K 685414	147920	ANTIBIOTIQUES NDA
5417	MEDICAMENTS	K 1930970	132367	K 2143112	133954	K 2419026	227629	K 1760347	282146	MEDICAMENTS
54179	— CONTNG OTH SUBSTANCES	K 1452291	86165	K 1562147	88093	K 1960728	146728	K 1358266	186441	MED CONT AUT SUBSTANCES
55	PERFUME,CLEANING ETC PRD		140943		134353		219826		306293	PROD POUR PARFUM,TOILETTE
551	ESSENTL OILS,PERFUME,ETC	W 3132	49478	W 3715	58528	W 4990	89517	W 6887	136244	HUILES ESSENTIELLES
5514	MIXED PERFUME SUBSTANCES	W 2909	47474	W 3497	56531	W 4711	85598	W 6508	132034	MELANGES SUBSTAN ODORIFER
562	*FERTILIZERS,MANUFACTURE	W 3015006	309487	W 1402353	168611	W 2489070	362223	W 2003364	330735	ENGRAIS MANUFACTURES
5621	CHEM NITROGENOUS FERTLZR	W 1819726	148419	W 793128	67549	W 1700703	198959	W 1431325	200912	ENGRAIS AZOTES
5629	FERTILIZERS NES	W 1019511	140849	W 451772	82927	W 636342	143164	W 430451	109939	ENGRAIS NDA
56292	NITROG–PHOS FERTILZR NES	W 988680	132141	W 435337	77795	W 624931	136314	W 416898	101084	ENGRAIS NDA CONT N P
58	PLASTIC MATERIALS ETC		655083		626028		1129923		1276901	MAT PLAST ARTIFICIELLES
582	PROD OF CONDENSATION ETC	W 92059	189119	W 79011	162238	W 112147	290072	W 123875	326568	PROD CONDENS,POLYCOND
583	POLYMERIZATION ETC PRODS	W 522005	434000	W 404445	435874	W 539447	796203	W 735010	901544	PROD POLYMERISATION
5831	POLYETHYLENE	W 137192	80470	W 92881	77580	W 103617	131193	W 169939	175967	POLYETHYLENE
58311	— IN PRIMARY FORMS	W 133192	71917	W 88242	66639	W 97284	112742	W 162471	155596	POLYETHYLENE PRIMAIRES
5832	POLYPROPYLENE	W 133567	78986	W 118118	100658	W 184642	220350	W 247670	238303	POLYPROPYLENE
58321	— IN PRIMARY FORMS	W 126457	63514	W 110864	83788	W 175491	190305	W 238822	209777	POLYPROPYLENE PRIMAIRES
5833	POLYSTYRENE,ITS COPOLYMR	W 77201	75516	W 66785	71397	W 86609	139027	W 110005	132694	POLYPROPYLENE COPOLYMERES
58331	— IN PRIMARY FORMS	W 76549	73657	W 66308	70240	W 85948	137130	W 109402	130777	SOUS FORMES PRIMAIRES
5839	OTH POLYMRZTION ETC PROD	W 46326	96537	W 43205	85751	W 63611	152570	W 72831	174263	AUT PROD POLYMER COPOLYM
59	CHEMICAL MATERIALS NES		318454		286973		441750		537715	MAT PROD CHIMIQUES NDA
598	MISCEL CHEM PRODUCTS NES	W 127903	212343	W 204804	202891	W 192819	301123	W 188978	368153	PROD DIV INDUST CHIM NDA
5989	CHEM PRODUCTS,PREPS NES	W 94303	154570	W 82117	129586	W 123777	218338	W 138679	277621	PROD PREP CHIMIQUES NDA
59899	OTH CHEM PRODS,PREPS,NES	W 72034	105557	W 62469	91155	W 100677	147705	W 110815	196004	AUT PRODUITS CHIMIQUES NDA
6	BASIC MANUFACTURES		5053977		4063188		6732221		7186658	ART MANUFACTURES
61	LEATHER,DRESSED FUR,ETC		183489		182664		235865		290283	CUIRS,PELLETERIES
611	LEATHER	W 10897	152213	W 11493	157119	W 12892	195666	W 14882	222055	CUIRS,PEAUX PREPARES
6115	LEATHER FROM SHEEP,LAMBS	W 5674	85273	W 6500	94389	W 5619	95104	W 6955	127832	PEAUX D'OVINS PREPAREES
62	RUBBER MANUFACTURES NES		184244		115199		170504		255699	CAOUTCHOUC MANUFACTURE
64	PAPER,PAPERBOARD AND MFR		466647		309363		706858		726199	PAPIERS,CARTONS & OUVRAGES
641	PAPER AND PAPERBOARD		413943		246823		604877	W 741087	610953	PAPIERS ET CARTONS
6411	NEWSPRINT	W 256287	121496	W 124703	54868	W 218286	173630	W 254980	169693	PAPIER JOURNAL
6413	KRAFT PAPER,PAPERBOARD	W 112344	53653	W 54418	29550	W 134195	110916	W 129423	86091	PAPIER ET CARTON KRAFT
6415	PAPER,PAPERBRD,BULK,NES	W 171730	111245	W 83642	66149	W 89194	110603	W 117969	111647	PAPIERS,CARTONS ROULEAUX
64159	OTHER PAPER ETC,BULK,NES	W 149059	95535	W 70082	55278	W 64153	86921	W 91426	88016	AUT PAPIER ROULEAUX FEUILLES
65	TEXTILE YARN,FABRICS,ETC		1026868		1121664		1834345		1966336	FILS,TISSUS,ARTICLES TEXTILE
651	TEXTILE YARN	W 189286	515706	W 153521	464460	W 216382	771638	W 214051	737404	FILS TEXTILES
6513	COTTON YARN	W 62133	167796	W 53289	167247	W 58795	221608	W 41058	142645	FILS DE COTON
6514	SYN FIB YRN,BULK,MONOFIL	W 59583	180011	W 44326	137268	W 67244	250738	W 70478	258188	FILS CONT 85% FIB TEXT SYNTH
65142	— NONTXT ETC CONT PAMID	W 36198	115585	W 28954	97993	W 42679	173587	W 45041	179536	FILS NON TEX FI CON POLYAMID
6517	REGEN FIBRE YARN,MONOFIL	W 22459	57987	W 22053	68145	W 32470	118500	W 30690	112576	FILS TEXT ART NON VENTE DT
652	COTTON FABRICS,WOVEN	W 29183	127590	W 35586	185844	W 55511	346890	W 41590	303100	TISSUS DE COTON
6521	GREY WOVEN COTTON FABRIC	W 17270	56560	W 21458	81086	W 28616	134366	W 17487	86332	TISSUS COT ECRUS NON MERCER
65214	GREY WOVEN COTTON NES	W 17183	55713	W 17915	59563	W 26104	117718	W 15671	73705	AUT TISSUS 85% COTON ECRUS
6522	WOVEN COTTON BLEACHD,ETC	W 11912	71030	W 14128	104758	W 26895	212523	W 24102	216768	TISSUS COTON BLANCHIS ETC
65224	BLCHED COTTON FABRIC NES	W 9940	61641	W 12543	92581	W 23781	185946	W 21305	189183	AUT TIS PLUS 85% COT BLANCHI
653	WOVN MAN–MADE FIB FABRIC	W 34789	189355	W 42989	223396	W 74776	421070	W 70564	462535	TISSUS FIBRES SYNTH,ARTIF
6531	CONT SYNT WEAVES NONPILE	W 12876	76946	W 13500	66033	W 23602	108851	W 22475	139152	TISSUS FIBRES SYNTH CONTINUE
65315	CONT SYN TXTL FABRIC NES	W 12384	73400	W 13134	64069	W 22767	103051	W 21682	132308	TIS PLUS 85% TEXT SYNT CONT
6536	DISC REGN TXTL FABRC NES	W 8948	33263	W 17779	72440	W 27685	128600	W 23575	104261	TISSUS 85% TEXT ART DISC
655	KNITTED,ETC FABRICS	W 5580	33796	W 15435	90588	W 8334	64204	W 10555	90281	ETOF BONNETERIE PIECES ETC
6552	OTHER KNIT ETC FAB NONEL	W 5580	33796	W 15435	90588	W 8334	64204	W 10555	90281	ETOF BON NON ELAS NON SYNT
657	SPECIAL TXTL FABRC,PRODS		87953		87101		125076	W 25339	163256	TISSUS SPECIAUX
66	NONMETAL MINERAL MFS NES		276881		199330		343007		431838	ART MIN NON METALLIQUES
67	IRON AND STEEL		2003072		1315849		2115336		1940663	FER ET ACIER
671	PIG IRON ETC	W 845846	156704	W 729103	154797	W 758425	196346	W 576953	182915	FONTE,SPIEGEL,POUDRES
6712	PIG IRN,SPIEGELEISEN ETC	W 698494	85218	W 563513	76873	W 585407	99995	W 395423	67989	FONTES BRUTES
6716	FERRO–ALLOYS	W 141355	68683	W 163537	76088	W 169226	92927	W 177360	110898	FERRO–ALLIAGES
672	IRON,STEEL PRIMARY FORMS	W 3277412	730701	W 2007134	424612	W 2103465	612924	W 1858132	488776	LINGOTS FER,ACIER
6725	IRN,STL BLOOMS,SLABS,ETC	W 2517986	515339	W 1620415	313468	W 1009621	240027	W 838039	197613	BLOOMS,BILLETTES FER ACIER
67251	IRN,SMPLE STL BLOOMS,ETC	W 2511410	509992	W 1615472	308504	W 880100	206091	W 819497	185737	BLOOMS ETC NON ACIER FIN
6727	IRN,STL COIL FR REROLLNG	W 759385	215287	W 386700	111110	W 1093278	372460	W 1020061	291045	EBAUCHES POUR TOLES FER
67271	IRON,SIMPLE STEEL COILS	W 721801	200697	W 353183	96927	W 1040631	345996	W 984986	274502	EBAUCHES NON EN ACIER
673	IRON,STEEL SHAPES ETC	W 464419	166220	W 262806	104094	W 277786	154982	W 277202	159466	BARRES,PROFIL FER,ACIER
674	IRN,STL UNIV,PLATE,SHEET	W 1640681	775548	W 808367	434796	W 1543394	959688	W 1293450	836518	LARGES PLATS,TOLES
6744	IRN,STL HVY PLATE,ROLLED	W 320053	95287	W 137927	48865	W 358362	140651	W 213984	98642	TOLES LAMINEES PLUS 4.75 MM
67441	— OF IRON OR SIMPLE STL	W 311994	81751	W 131761	38395	W 352572	124434	W 203885	74993	TOLES NON ACIER FIN CARB
6745	IRN,STL MED PLATE,ROLLED	W 229076	92791	W 148451	68201	W 202661	117163	W 212222	113577	TOLES 3 A 4.75 MM
6746	IRN,STL THIN PLATE,ROLLD	W 917140	468261	W 415253	240033	W 771742	523790	W 559817	385910	TOLES LAM MOINS 3MM
67461	— OF IRON OR SIMPLE STL	W 839341	316956	W 361669	139919	W 708593	344358	W 480354	211194	TOL NON AC FIN MOINS 3 MM
67463	— OF STAINLESS ETC STL	W 74506	143445	W 51052	96067	W 60507	173102	W 74537	167926	TOL ACIER INOX MOINS 3 MM
6749	OTH IRN,STL PLATES,SHEET	W 87266	64198	W 54497	43809	W 73447	72786	W 190696	146050	AUTRES TOLES FER,ACIER
67491	— OF IRON OR SIMPLE STL	W 83073	52992	W 51817	36865	W 71668	66857	W 188912	141347	AUT TOLES AUTRES ACIER FIN
678	IRON,STL TUBES,PIPES,ETC	W 103675	118968	W 114573	132895	W 90000	141895	W 161602	230130	TUBES,TUYAUX EN FONTE,FER
68	NON–FERROUS METALS		408393		399115		752260		768719	METAUX NON FERREUX
682	COPPER EXC CEMENT COPPER	W 92206	132380	W 83087	166458	W 94330	295593	W 121355	306512	CUIVRE
6821	COPPER NES,ALLOYS,UNWRT	W 70803	75173	W 58899	104145	W 63690	179665	W 84072	185533	CUIVRE BRUT
68212	COPPER REFINED,UNWROUGHT	W 18335	31529	W 26248	55952	W 42054	114549	W 51956	113593	CUIVRE AFFINE BRUT
6822	COPPER,ALLOYS WORKED	W 21403	57207	W 24188	62313	W 30640	115928	W 37283	120979	CUIVRE,ALLIAGES OUVRES
684	ALUMINIUM	W 136109	209571	W 93875	169276	W 142913	343538	W 151509	328164	ALUMINIUM
6841	ALUMINIUM,ALLOYS,UNWRGHT	W 120923	161349	W 67462	102465	W 101577	219431	W 99312	173429	ALUMINIUM,ALLIAGES BRUTS
6842	ALUMINIUM,ALLOYS WORKED	W 15187	48222	W 26413	66811	W 41336	124107	W 52197	154735	ALUMINIUM,ALLIAGES OUVRE
69	METAL MANUFACTURES NES		474235		391692		531039		749054	ART MANUFACT EN METAL NDA
695	TOOLS	W 5327	89057	W 4450	58238	W 5712	71017	W 7675	102457	OUTILS A MAIN
699	BASE METAL MFRS NES	W 29504	168126	W 35636	174024	W 36845	225820	W 44109	302621	ART MANUFACTURES MET NDA
7	MACHINES,TRANSPORT EQUIP		11196247		7657021		11470312		15169561	MACHINES MATERIEL TRANSPORT
71	POWER GENERATING EQUIPMT		705128		444620		594470		890718	MACHINES GENERATRICES
713	INTRNL COMBUS PSTN ENGIN	W 31907	358596	W 16939	207265	W 27448	368178	W 34248	479405	MOTEURS EXPL COMB INT, PIECE
7132	MOTOR VEHCL PISTN ENGINS	W 14485	154892	W 7495	82301	W 15981	190109	W 19389	239903	MOTEURS EXPL POUR VEHICULES
7139	PISTON ENGINE PARTS NES	W 12326	149879	W 6649	87796	W 6855	110661	W 6891	127840	PIECES POUR 713.2,3,8
714	ENGINES AND MOTORS NES	W 2095	93677	W 582	76107	W 1674	60492	W 1276	87198	MOTEURS NON ELECTRIQUES
716	ROTATING ELECTRIC PLANT	W 10094	132741	W 8475	124223	W 8366	114251	W 16794	183561	APP ELECTR ROTATIFS,PIECES
7162	AC MTRS,GENRTRS,GEN SETS	W 6946	69688	W 6183	59315	W 6501	71652	W 13714	133328	MOTEURS ELECTRIQUES
72	MACHS FOR SPCL INDUSTRYS		2245224		1456944		2583052		4195369	MAC SPECIALES POUR INDUST
723	CIVIL ENGNEERG EQUIP ETC	W 30272	182620	W 12915	81859	W 23302	155921	W 49608	313870	APPAREILS DE GENIE CIVIL
7234	CONST,MINING MACHNRY NES	W 27753	161763	W 11639	69668	W 21635	142482	W 46342	289801	MACH POUR LA CONST, MINES
72342	SLFPRP SHOVELS,EXCAVATRS	W 20794	99363	W 8181	45650	W 17225	98044	W 37867	216129	PELLES MECANIQUES
724	TEXTILE,LEATHER MACHNRY	W 75730	1111228	W 50144	685160	W 91040	1541171	W 148793	2410774	MACH POUR INDUSTRIE TEXTILE
7243	SEWING MACHS,NEEDLES ETC	W 5011	97821	W 3105	57514	W 6912	148690	W 7119	170462	MACHINES A COUDRE,PIECES
72431	SEWING MACHINES	W 4588	85705	W 2925	48622	W 6674	133702	W 6734	153657	MACHINES A COUDRE

4. Special Imports C.I.F. by Commodities according to the S.I.T.C. (Rev. 2) in thousand U.S. Dollars
Importations Spéciales C.A.F. par Produits d'après la C.T.C.I. (Rév. 2) en milliers de Dollars E.U.

SITC CTCI	COMMODITY	1993 WEIGHT POIDS		1993 VALUE VALEUR	1994 WEIGHT POIDS		1994 VALUE VALEUR	1995 WEIGHT POIDS		1995 VALUE VALEUR	1996 WEIGHT POIDS		1996 VALUE VALEUR	PRODUIT
7244	SPINNING,EXTRDNG,ETC MCH	W	27392	429080	W	21970	274891	W	33849	593206	W	52045	842418	MACH POUR LE FILAGE
72442	FIBRE PROCESSNG MACH NES	W	10053	134561	W	4599	56827	W	10754	165994	W	17665	227799	MACH PREP MAT TEXTILES
72443	SPINNING,REELING,ETC MCH	W	14678	231942	W	12195	133342	W	20594	345445	W	30102	494855	MACH POUR LA FILATURE
7245	WEAVING,FELT MFG,ETC MCH	W	26334	340881	W	14032	183306	W	36833	515496	W	61365	845752	METIERS A TISSER,PIECES
72451	WEAVING MACHINES (LOOMS)	W	14043	120211	W	6773	58756	W	23977	256943	W	37541	363683	METIERS A TISSER
72452	KNITTING MACHINES	W	6811	126204	W	4633	85335	W	7263	168964	W	10883	280976	METIERS A BONNETERIE
72453	GIMPING,WARPING ETC MCHS	W	4865	89193	W	2551	37789	W	5369	87558	W	12620	198005	METIERS A TULLE ETC
7247	TEXTILE MACHINERY NES	W	12962	177928	W	8516	118573	W	9683	189511	W	21660	398386	MACH LAVAGE,TEINTURE TEX
72474	OTH TEXTILE MACHNERY NES	W	10053	156022	W	6286	99013	W	7988	165894	W	18064	344965	MACH LAVAGE ETC MAT TEXT
726	PRINTG,BKBINDG MACHY,PTS	W	8605	183551	W	4906	80485	W	6446	133993	W	12067	266704	MACHINES POUR IMPRIMERIE
7264	PRINTING PRESSES	W	5474	98176	W	2994	29761	W	3735	57156	W	6332	111355	MACHINES A IMPRIMER
72641	ROTARY PRINTING PRESSES	W	5474	98176	W	2994	29761	W	3735	57156	W	6332	111355	MACH IMPRIMER ROTATIVES
727	FOOD MACHRY NON-DOMESTIC	W	2795	54981	W	3033	53297	W	2758	57604	W	5630	154836	MACH INDUSTRIES ALIMENT
7272	OTH FOOD PROC MCHY,PARTS	W	2198	50388	W	2530	50478	W	2719	57215	W	5440	151235	AUT MACH IND ALIMENTAIRE
728	OTH MACHY FOR SPCL INDUS	W	38432	624178	W	32479	507508	W	30292	563987	W	52315	847220	AUT MACH IND PARTICULIERES
7283	OTHR MINERAL WORKG MACHY	W	10480	95409	W	8606	82957	W	6531	60823	W	13899	137056	MACH TRIER,CRIBLER,BROYER
7284	MACHY FOR SPCL INDUS NES	W	24260	475959	W	20876	380130	W	20528	453749	W	33430	635524	MACH SPEC IND PARTICUL.
72842	RUBBER,PLASTICS WRKG MCH	W	10383	123010	W	7606	113535	W	7841	122459	W	12359	207718	MACH IND CAOUT MAT PLAST
72848	OTH MCHY WITH INDIV FNCT	W	9886	234269	W	8873	166410	W	8445	206415	W	11079	224744	AUTRES MACHINES NDA
73	METALWORKING MACHINERY			348802			317307			373670			378508	MACH TRAVAIL DES METAUX
736	METALWORKING MACH-TOOLS	W	26676	264703	W	13247	160280	W	17954	223478	W	28605	306224	MACH-OUTILS TRAVAIL METAUX
7361	METAL CUTTING MACH-TOOLS	W	11584	95472	W	5543	71040	W	7865	87589	W	15480	127590	MACH-OUT ENLEVEMENT METAL
7362	METAL FORMING MACH-TOOLS	W	10393	105024	W	4736	39447	W	5240	67847	W	5622	57688	MACH-OUTILS DEFORM METAL
737	METALWORKING MACHNRY NES	W	12893	84099	W	8384	157027	W	5952	150192	W	6063	72283	MACH TRAV METAUX PIECES
7372	ROLLING MILLS AND ROLLS	W	10054	27682	W	5969	104381	W	4191	110143	W	3574	20648	LAMINOIRS CYLINDRES PIEC
73721	ROLLING MILLS	W	7873	19518	W	4080	80130	W	2437	84373	W	488	7750	LAMINOIRS ET TRAINS
74	GENRL INDUSTRL MACHY NES			1489963			1271610			1584566			2137152	MACH APP INDUSTRIE
741	HEATING,COOLING EQUIPMNT	W	27263	315197	W	20707	265633	W	31256	354095	W	37882	515700	MACH CHAUFFAGE,PIECES
7413	INDUS FURNACES ETC,PARTS	W	5649	75743	W	5666	88187	W	6761	70985	W	8637	139362	FOURS IND,LABOR,PIECES
74132	INDUST FURNACES NONELECT	W	4076	46423	W	4832	74711	W	5075	48831	W	6830	111648	FOURS NON ELECTRIQUES
7415	AIR-CONDITIONING MACHNRY	W	6293	74560	W	3025	42322	W	6150	84814	W	10379	131461	GROUPES CONDITION AIR
7416	HEATING,COOLING EQU NES	W	6119	81941	W	5632	76026	W	6782	95145	W	7909	108774	APP CHANGEMENT TEMP
742	PUMPS FOR LIQUIDS ETC	W	7174	129633	W	5595	102000	W	6989	143443	W	8856	189240	POMPES MOTO-POMPES
743	PUMPS NES,CENTRFUGES ETC	W	17755	209154	W	14456	188085	W	19780	309206	W	25507	371198	POMPES COMPRES,VENT ETC
7436	GAS,LIQUID FILTERS ETC	W	4889	86660	W	4345	83010	W	4074	74987	W	8453	167538	APP POUR FILT DES LIQUIDES
7439	PTS NES OF APP OF 7435,6	W	1410	26826	W	1099	25061	W	3740	113682	W	2243	54942	PIECES 743.5 ET 743.6
744	MECHANICAL HANDLING EQU	W	25608	206351	W	17980	164677	W	16965	166008	W	33006	258267	EQUIP MANUTENTION PIECES
7442	LIFTING,LOADING MACH NES	W	15461	134923	W	11707	119822	W	8692	107783	W	15677	136919	APP LEVAGE,MANUTENTION
74428	OTH HANDLING ETC MCH NES	W	8936	89595	W	7599	83502	W	4941	62125	W	7216	85894	AUT APP LEVAGE ETC
745	NONELEC MACHY,TOOLS NES	W	9758	190641	W	6602	180339	W	5864	165806	W	8043	262222	AUT MACH NON ELEC,PIECES
7452	OTH NONELEC MCHS,PTS NES	W	8984	178286	W	6204	172676	W	5207	149288	W	7089	233492	AUT MACH NON ELEC,PIECES
74522	PACKAGNG,BOTTLNG,ETC MCH	W	3245	108176	W	2961	103462	W	2627	100649	W	3930	152734	MACH NETT BOUTEILLES,ETC
749	NONELEC MACH PTS,ACC NES	W	26067	438986	W	21494	370876	W	22226	446008	W	30058	540526	PIECES MACH NON ELEC NDA
7491	BALL,ROLLER,ETC BEARINGS	W	7062	105271	W	4898	72550	W	6254	108922	W	8246	130442	ROULEMENTS BILLES ETC
7492	COCKS,VALVES ETC NES	W	5700	113699	W	4630	86385	W	5530	119557	W	7335	151474	ART ROB,SIM POUR TUYAUX
7493	SHAFT,CRANK,PULLEY ETC	W	9987	136942	W	7564	108234	W	7583	124548	W	8043	130640	ARBRES TRANS,VILEBREQUINS
7499	OTH NONELEC MCHY PTS NES	W	3317	83074	W	4402	103707	W	2858	92981	W	6433	127970	PIECES NON ELECT NDA
74991	FOUNDRY MOULDS ETC NES	W	2213	56074	W	2638	74927	W	1471	58185	W	4917	88162	MOULES POUR METAUX
75	OFFICE MACHNES,ADP EQUIP			587762			398366			686925			770414	MACH BUREAU TRAIT AUTOM
752	AUTOMTIC DATA PROC EQUIP	W	6159	392350	W	4319	276233	W	9263	481566	W	9694	530942	MACH TRAIT INFORMATION
7523	DIGITL CENTRL PROCESSORS	W	949	111719	W	641	74991	W	1891	128431	W	963	120529	UNITES CENTRALES
7525	ADP PERIPHERAL UNITS	W	3279	140269	W	2279	95722	W	5254	189559	W	6471	217422	UNITES PERIPHERIQUES
759	OFFICE,ADP MCH PTS,ACCES	W	1708	129160	W	1024	79157	W	1441	130352	W	2589	140574	PIECES DU 751 ET 752
7599	ACCTG,ETC,ADP MCH PTS,AC	W	1528	120737	W	828	71743	W	1217	119482	W	2317	127004	PIECES DU 751 ET 752
76	TELECOMM,SOUND EQUIPMENT			440740			537302			633780			834390	EQUIPMENT DE TELECOM
764	TELECOM EQPT,PTS,ACC NES	W	13908	407374	W	9851	513525	W	12003	590783	W	15059	673020	EQUIP TELECOM,PIECES
7643	TV,RADIO TRANSMITTRS ETC	W	553	74734	W	1026	134927	W	849	256433	W	905	267742	APP EMET TELE RADIO
7648	TELECOMM EQUIPMENT NES	W	478	73039	W	1009	183587	W	1025	61539	W	1492	60233	APP TELECOM NDA
76483	RADAR APPARATUS ETC	W	283	49168	W	647	136628	W	267	23007	W	608	27363	APP DE RADIOGUIDAGE ETC
7649	PTS NES OF EQUIPMT OF 76	W	9672	164046	W	5546	125659	W	6591	159584	W	7494	215105	PIECES DE LA DIV 76
76493	TELECOMM EQUIPMT PTS NES	W	7439	102946	W	4361	97198	W	5553	117850	W	6670	131956	PIECES 761,762,764.3,8
77	ELECTRIC MACHNRY NES ETC			1505477			1173100			1469364			2030305	MACH APP ELECT NDA
771	ELECTRIC POWER MACHY NES	W	4858	74516	W	3044	69869	W	4153	69041	W	7302	100440	MACH PROD,TRANS ELECTR
772	SWITCHGEAR ETC,PARTS NES	W	9535	295472	W	8515	267127	W	7672	311377	W	9513	394806	APP COUPURE,SECT ETC
7721	SWITCHGEAR ETC	W	8545	259578	W	7820	242564	W	7133	284532	W	8786	360426	APP COUPURE,SECTIONMNT
773	ELECTR DISTRIBUTNG EQUIP	W	16095	127960	W	9236	98929	W	10095	118105	W	11528	127076	EQUIPMT DISTRIBUTION ELECT
7731	INSULATED WIRE,CABLE ETC	W	13125	103064	W	7129	66817	W	8461	89886	W	8200	85101	FILS,CABLES ISOLES ELECT
774	ELECTRO-MEDCL,XRAY EQUIP	W	740	55831	W	954	55073	W	816	68336	W	1427	137512	APPAREILS MEDICAUX
775	HOUSEHOLD TYPE EQUIP NES	W	23464	147954	W	14911	87949	W	20807	135588	W	45329	287847	MACH,APP USAGE DOMESTQUE
776	TRANSISTORS,VALVES,ETC	W	32584	398414	W	22445	258252	W	31732	356086	W	42676	483306	LAMPES,TUBES,VALVES
7761	TV PICTURE TUBES	W	30402	166215	W	21172	114353	W	30526	181066	W	41376	254062	TUBES CATHODIQUES
7764	ELECTRONIC MICROCIRCUITS	W	1406	164996	W	796	93441	W	567	117475	W	550	160442	MICROSTRUCTURES ELECTRON
778	ELECTRICAL MACHINERY NES	W	48216	405329	W	39654	335901	W	46997	410831	W	54665	499317	AUTRES MACH ELECT NDA
7788	OTH ELEC MACHY,EQUIP NES	W	34509	242800	W	28634	215477	W	29696	222585	W	26761	254524	AUT MACH APP ELEC NDA
77887	ELECTRICAL CARBONS	W	29730	76279	W	24898	71371	W	25904	85873	W	23117	81591	PIECES CHARBON,GRAPHITE
78	ROAD VEHICLES			2008650			871097			1521723			2623588	VEHICULES ROUTIERS
781	PASS MOTOR VEH EXC BUSES	W	102787	734229	W	24781	222011	W	43026	327141	W	77390	1017933	AUTO TRANSPORT PERSONNES
782	LORRIES,SPCL MTR VEH NES	W	63620	398422	W	20007	140972	W	26380	178054	W	59499	397705	VEHICULES SPECIAUX,MARCH
7821	LORRIES,TRUCKS	W	50966	288569	W	14227	84611	W	21464	127566	W	53331	325841	VEHICULES TRANSP MARCHAND
7822	SPECIAL MOTOR VEHCLS NES	W	12655	109853	W	5779	56362	W	4917	50488	W	6168	71864	VEHICULES USAGES SPECIAUX
783	ROAD MOTOR VEHICLES NES	W	8540	88534	W	3349	39043	W	15924	191768	W	27901	302462	VEHICULES ROUTIERS NDA
7832	TRACTORS FOR TR-TRAILERS	W	3451	32072	W	2146	26662	W	11865	159964	W	18820	233456	TRACTEURS ROUTIERS
784	MOTOR VEH PRTS,ACCES NES	W	75656	694251	W	46098	425644	W	84531	767751	W	87949	798431	PIECES 722,781,782,783
7849	OTHER MOTOR VEHCL PARTS	W	74163	678347	W	45137	413639	W	77482	742455	W	82617	771990	PIECES 722,781,782,783
79	OTHR TRANSPORT EQUIPMENT			1864500			1186675			2022762			1309117	AUTRE MATERIEL TRANSPORT
791	RAILWAY VEHICLES	W	7311	122105	W	3665	104885	W	4482	109743	W	7148	189023	VEHIC MAT CHEMINS DE FER
7913	MECHAN-PROPELLED RY CARS	W	2402	80186	W	2255	93285	W	1426	95538	W	2577	163538	AUTOMOTRICES,DRAISINES
792	AIRCRAFT ETC			1404863			802382			1377558	W	1834	763169	APP NAVIGATION AERIENNE
7923	AIRCRFT NES2000-15000KG	N	37	174346	N	18	25809	N	65	450426	W	124	155794	AERODYNES 2000 A 15000 KG
7924	AIRCRFT NES OVER 15000KG	N	34	1158762	N	21	691437	N	26	706407	W	1347	502336	AERODYNES PLUS 15000 KG
7929	AIRCRAFT PARTS NES	W	97	44538	W	197	59842	W	162	121715	W	303	90850	PIECES DU 792
793	SHIPS AND BOATS ETC			337533			279408			535461			356925	NAVIRES BATEAUX,ETC
7932	SHIPS AND BOATS NES			314918			255723			483392			329434	NAVIRES ET BATEAUX
79323	OTHER CARGO VESSELS			271676			237170			451489			241369	AUT BATEAUX TRANS MARCH
8	MISC MANUFACTURED GOODS			1506473			1130745			1727132			2376158	ART MANUFACTURES DIVERS
812	*PLUMBG,HEATNG,LGHTNG EQ	W	16657	68184	W	10805	43374	W	21520	104499	W	19591	138694	APPAR SANITAIRES CHAUFFAGE
821	*FURNITURE,PARTS THEREOF	W	10747	61263	W	8698	42956	W	12552	77957	W	19293	139516	MEUBLES ET PIECES
84	CLOTHING AND ACCESSORIES			45690			35272			49013			152459	VETEMENTS
87	PRECISION INSTRUMNTS NES			527767			417196			566113			647668	INSTRUM,APPAR SCIENT NDA
872	MEDICAL INSTRUMENTS NES	W	3252	172678	W	2526	127080	W	3639	176696	W	3460	182322	INSTR,APP MEDIC-CHIR NDA
87202	OTH MEDICAL INSTRUMENTS	W	2832	160564	W	2256	119081	W	3225	163854	W	2982	166961	INSTRUM,APP MEDECINE

4. Special Imports C.I.F. by Commodities according to the S.I.T.C. (Rev. 2) in thousand U.S. Dollars
Importations Spéciales C.A.F. par Produits d'après la C.T.C.I. (Rév. 2) en milliers de Dollars E.U.

SITC CTCI	COMMODITY	1993 WEIGHT POIDS	1993 VALUE VALEUR	1994 WEIGHT POIDS	1994 VALUE VALEUR	1995 WEIGHT POIDS	1995 VALUE VALEUR	1996 WEIGHT POIDS	1996 VALUE VALEUR	PRODUIT
874	MEASURNG,CONTROLNG INSTR	W 5170	318634	W 4156	243222	W 6369	341280	W 6518	396507	INSTRUMENTS DE MESURE
88	PHOTO EQU,OPTICL GDS ETC		224533		159769		246638		322076	APP,FOURN PHOTO,OP,MONTR
882	PHOTO,CINEMA SUPPLIES	W 10647	105655	W 8431	79740	W 11594	113737	W 12869	130992	PRODUITS PHOTO,CINEMA
8822	PHOTO FILM EXC DEV CINMA	W 8043	89682	W 6253	66997	W 8711	96342	W 9594	107035	PLAQUES,PELLICULES,FILMS
89	MISC MANUFCTRD GOODS NES		547155		409566		642550		878820	ART MANUFACTURES DIVERS
892	PRINTED MATTER	W 39081	123012	W 24787	81783	W 11779	76289	W 9008	86312	IMPRIMES
8921	PRINTED BOOKS,GLOBES,ETC	W 34425	91909	W 19686	50828	W 6976	33704	W 4233	36123	LIVRES,BROCHURES,CARTES
893	ARTICLES OF PLASTIC NES		174248		134124		243534		345474	OUVRAGES EN MAT DIVIS 58
8939	MISC PLASTIC ARTICLES	W 22985	145823	W 17850	110457	W 28648	194699	W 38440	286860	ART DIVERS EN MAT DIV 58
89399	OTHR PLASTC ARTICLES NES	W 20119	139320	W 15527	104745	W 24612	184989	W 31727	268873	AUT OUV MAT DIV 58
899	OTHER MANUFACTURED GOODS		90318		80498		103536		142413	AUT ART MANUF DIVERS NDA
9	GOODS NOT CLASSD BY KIND		129231		84850		80134		589198	ART TRANSACT NON CLASSES
931	*SPECIAL TRANSACTIONS						2		354126	TRANS.SPECIALES
951	*WAR FIREARMS,AMMUNITION		128660		84027		78945	W 2205	36714	VEHIC BLINDES ARMES
95101	ARMORED FIGHTNG VEHICLES	W 6451	118914	W 4413	70190	W 2031	42979			CHARS DE COMBAT
971	*GOLD,NON MONETARY NES	K 1701	167	K 900	173	K 109	116	K 16097	197670	OR NON MONETAIRE
97101	NONMON GLD UNWRT,SEMIMFD	K 466	128	K 171	149	K 60	104	K 16097	197670	OR,ALLIAGES D'OR BRUTS

5. Special Exports F.O.B. by Commodities according to the S.I.T.C. (Rev. 2) in thousand U.S. Dollars
Exportations Spéciales F.O.B. par Produits d'après la C.T.C.I. (Rév. 2) en milliers de Dollars E.U.

SITC CTCI	COMMODITY	1993		1994		1995		1996		PRODUIT
		WEIGHT POIDS	VALUE VALEUR	WEIGHT POIDS	VALUE VALEUR	WEIGHT POIDS	VALUE VALEUR	WEIGHT POIDS	VALUE VALEUR	
	ALL COMMODITIES		15348934		18106058		21598657		23047758	TOUS PRODUITS
0	FOOD AND LIVE ANIMALS		2793676		3298233		3414854		3552333	ALIMENTS,ANIMAUX VIVANTS
001	*LIVE ANIMALS FOR FOOD	W 71972	281701	W 85554	221722	W 40612	130276	W 24107	83260	ANIMAUX VIVANTS
0012	SHEEP AND GOATS,LIVE	W 71952	281533	W 85526	221360	W 40602	130061	W 24093	83091	ESPECES OVINE ET CAPRINE
00121	SHEEP,LIVE	W 71837	281132	W 83239	216593	W 40246	129004	W 24058	82992	ESPECE OVINE
03	FISH AND PREPARATIONS		53944		70133		84742		101445	POISSONS ET PREPARATIONS
04	CEREALS AND PREPARATIONS		284640		383056		450247		515366	CEREALES ET PRODUITS
041	WHEAT ETC UNMILLED	W 648653	75494	W 980029	88470	W 232587	22630	W 7494	1905	FROMENT,EPEAUTRE
0412	OTHER WHEAT ETC UNMILLED	W 585157	68602	W 892181	79671	W 232165	22424	W 7140	1765	AUTRE FROMENT NON MOULU
046	WHEAT ETC MEAL OR FLOUR	W 379299	82040	W 564750	107629	W 629146	143731	W 570576	175366	SEMOULE FARINE,FROMENT
04601	FLOUR OF WHEAT OR MESLIN	W 359479	74827	W 538712	99077	W 610268	135861	W 551355	166808	FARINE DE FROMENT
048	CEREAL ETC PREPARATIONS	W 114872	91650	W 163544	123886	W 241524	232732	W 306386	309208	PREPTNS A BASE CEREALES
0484	BAKERY PRODUCTS	W 42421	60497	W 65795	81435	W 122341	171813	W 172289	237721	PRODUITS DE BOULANGERIE
04842	PASTRY, CAKES ETC	W 36258	52234	W 53167	67066	W 108080	152226	W 139516	192741	PATISSERIE ETC.
05	VEGETABLES AND FRUIT		1671008		2003341		2176776		2215945	LEGUMES ET FRUITS
054	VEG ETC FRSH,SMPLY PRSVD	W 1098888	444748	W 1096199	452688	W 833241	470409	W 1379638	608329	LEGUMES FRAIS,CONG,SECS
0541	POTATOES FRSH EXCL SWEET	W 244102	48042	W 229095	36865	W 103515	23866	W 240701	29857	POMMES DE TERRE
0542	LEGUMINOUS VEGETBLES DRY	W 440602	184561	W 411667	166610	W 282624	198342	W 502249	269002	LEGUMES A COSSE SECS
0545	OTHER FRESH VEGETABLES	W 166863	56347	W 131125	50778	W 178464	65197	W 281241	77606	AUTRES LEGUMES FRAIS,REF
0546	VEGETABLES SIMPLY PRESVD	W 152222	109119	W 194180	145791	W 158748	134982	W 225622	176772	LEGUMES CONG,CONSER
05461	VEGETABLES FROZEN	W 148817	104335	W 189670	140339	W 153576	126684	W 218462	164246	LEGUMES CONGELES
056	VEGTBLES ETC PRSVD,PREPD	W 123844	134369	W 173896	187011	W 159860	194101	W 162120	183967	CONSERVES DE LEGUMES
0565	VEGTBLES PRSVD,PREPD NES	W 106708	95979	W 149638	128360	W 140572	142436	W 140211	131221	LEGUMES PREPARES CONSERVE
05651	VEGTBLS,FRUIT IN VINEGAR	W 83675	63960	W 121435	94724	W 107323	93356	W 112099	90675	LEGUM CONSERV AU VINAIGRE
057	FRUIT,NUTS,FRESH,DRIED	W 747562	897590	W 941518	1079878	W 986293	1211198	W 944058	1103492	FRUITS FRAIS OU SECS
0571	ORANGES, MANDARINS ETC	W 140323	55580	W 196444	76596	W 206074	73499	W 210033	82137	ORANGES,MAND,CLEMENTINES
0572	LEMONS,GRAPEFRUIT ETC	W 135995	56471	W 192963	79972	W 186712	79729	W 158990	76903	AUTRES AGRUMES FRAIS,SECS
05721	LEMONS,LIMES,FRESH,DRIED	W 102667	42976	W 153462	64615	W 140663	63819	W 110440	59659	CITRONS ET LIMES
0575	GRAPES FRESH OR DRIED	W 146316	145403	W 199504	188887	W 194930	204576	W 200278	205925	RAISINS FRAIS OU SECS
05752	GRAPES DRIED(RAISINS)	W 123767	134078	W 173246	176189	W 169701	189933	W 171868	188322	RAISINS SECS
0576	FIGS,FRESH OR DRIED	W 34605	64133	W 40218	66564	W 40703	77865	W 40704	75021	FIGUES FRAICHES,SECHES
0577	NUTS EDIBLE,FRESH,DRIED	W 151796	440458	W 141138	523834	W 196380	610349	W 154228	469678	FRUITS A COQUES
05775	HAZELNUTS,FRESH OR DRIED	W 144862	426261	W 134251	509910	W 185712	590792	W 144018	444375	NOISETTES FRAICHES,SECHES
0579	FRUIT FRESH OR DRIED NES	W 95707	118020	W 138673	130261	W 133668	153094	W 123350	159598	FRUITS FRAIS,SECS NDA
05799	OTHER DRIED FRUIT	W 35446	85912	W 47671	91767	W 53395	102705	W 47371	111349	AUTRES FRUITS SECHES
058	FRUIT PRESERVED,PREPARED	W 115262	194301	W 150324	283764	W 151474	301068	W 188440	320157	CONSERVES DE FRUITS
0585	FRUIT OR VEGETABLE JUICE	W 29738	25252	W 45135	36538	W 52535	66709	W 75730	84406	JUS DE FRUITS
05857	JUICE OF OTHER FRUIT,VEG	W 29199	24686	W 42929	35028	W 48795	64424	W 70323	80413	JUS AUTRES FRUITS,LEGUMES
0589	FRUIT PREPRD,PRESRVD,NES	W 56442	125501	W 65229	178657	W 70249	181957	W 77100	178308	FRUITS PREPARES CONSERV
05891	NUTS ROASTD(INCL PEANUT)	W 40581	101478	W 47384	154773	W 50627	154687	W 49142	141117	FRUITS A COQUE GRILLES
06	SUGAR AND PREPS,HONEY		214232		314891		195936		210161	SUCRES ET PRODUITS
061	SUGAR AND HONEY		153734	W 486084	171483	W 20827	10208	W 11069	15348	SUCRES ET MIEL
0612	REFINED SUGAR ETC		145097	W 456971	162437	W 4090	1718	W 3955	2718	SUCRES RAFFINES
062	SUGAR CANDY NON–CHOCLATE	W 23614	60498	W 60143	143408	W 74132	185728	W 74074	194813	SUCRERIES
07	COFFEE,TEA,COCOA,SPICES		128149		96087		125351		144310	CAFE,THE,CACAO,EPICES
073	CHOCOLATE AND PRODUCTS	W 17521	37915	W 23133	48501	W 37684	80046	W 39860	87550	CHOCOLAT
09	MISC EDIBLE PRODUCTS		119489		140641		197532		206477	PREP ALIMENTAIRES DIVERSES
091	MARGARINE AND SHORTENING	W 105402	80939	W 110112	89638	W 140921	140394	W 131824	124472	MARGARINE ET GRAISSES
0914	MARGARINE,EDIBLE FAT NES	W 105402	80939	W 110112	89638	W 140921	140394	W 131803	124448	MARGARINES,SIMILI SAINDOUX
09141	MARGARINE	W 102789	79100	W 106874	86992	W 140765	140243	W 130598	122993	MARGARINE
098	EDIBLE PRODCTS,PREPS NES		38550		51003		57138	W 56824	82005	PREP ALIMENTAIRES NDA
09806	YEASTS,BAKING POWDERS		30496	W 39596	42249	W 45367	44030	W 49255	69626	LEVURES
1	BEVERAGES AND TOBACCO		465586		471136		467341		738165	BOISSONS ET TABACS
11	BEVERAGES		24561		47501		85930		104663	BOISSONS
12	TOBACCO AND MANUFACTURES		441025		423635		381411		633502	TABACS BRUTS FABRIQUES
121	TOBACCO UNMNFCTRD,REFUSE	W 91352	395561	W 103712	395166	W 82590	244544	W 162027	538549	TABACS BRUTS,DECHETS
1211	TOBACCO,NOT STRIPPED	W 78518	387030	W 86471	384755	W 72967	240031	W 151449	529214	TABACS NON ECOTES
122	TOBACCO,MANUFACTURED	W 5779	45465		28470	W 61008	136867	W 12746	94954	TABACS FABRIQUES
1222	CIGARETTES	W 3503	42944	W 2510	12593	W 8525	37474	W 10529	88932	CIGARETTES
1223	OTH MANUFACTURED TOBACCO	W 2276	2520	W 9294	15876	W 52483	99393	W 2121	4750	TABACS FUMER,CHIQUER,PRISER
2	CRUDE MATERLS,EXCL FUELS		554535		604863		774166		680754	MAT BRUTES NON COMESTIBLES
26	TEXTILE FIBRES AND WASTE		198363		152908		167313		277925	FIBRES TEXTILES
263	COTTON	W 180991	159993	W 79147	56552	W 59861	47881	W 146850	171357	COTON
2631	RAW COTTON,EXCL LINTERS	W 132355	144472	W 27149	31364	W 2911	6080	W 76035	124059	COTON EN MASSE
266	SYNTHETIC FIBRES TO SPIN	W 21087	30697	W 54336	78404	W 52003	99855	W 53047	82954	FIBRES SYNTHETIQUES
27	CRUDE FERTLZR,MINRLS NES		201268		215002		248866		112226	ENGRAIS MINERAUX BRUTS
278	OTHER CRUDE MINERALS		178111	W 1846801	189811	W 2442963	220057	W 1694440	80650	AUTRES MINERAUX BRUTS
2789	MINERALS CRUDE NES		131021	W 850717	131225	W 1020239	147538	W 350517	17910	MINERAUX BRUTS NDA
27894	CRUDE NATURAL BORATES		120520	W 622346	120881	W 683584	133751	W 1	1	BORATES NATURELS BRUTS
28	METALLIFEROUS ORES,SCRAP		51619		92602		193606		154271	MINERAIS METAL,DECHETS
287	BASE METAL ORES,CONC NES	W 517110	40880	W 740026	54142	W 1261794	161238	W 836434	119683	MINERAIS METAUX COMMUNS
2879	OTH NONFER ORE,CONCNTRTE	W 321818	19471	W 604541	34273	W 1022291	94639	W 541195	63085	MINERAIS D'AUTRES METAUX
28791	CHROMIUM ORE,CONCENTRATE	W 321818	19471	W 602100	33548	W 1013303	93214	W 527697	60084	MINERAIS DE CHROME
29	CRUDE ANIMAL,VEG MAT NES		68056		73884		99428		77394	MATIERES BRUTES ANIM,VEGET
3	MINERAL FUELS ETC		177600		245680		290638		269468	COMBUSTIBLES MINERAUX LUB
33	PETROLEUM AND PRODUCTS		168120		233886		279792		243738	PETROLE ET DERIVES
334	PETROLEUM PRODUCTS,REFIN	W 1832158	160951	W 2310558	226222	W 2537823	264527	W 2121273	237287	PRODUITS RAFFINES
3344	FUEL OILS,NES	W 1666096	125435	W 2060290	176933	W 2096508	187186	W 1646920	156008	FUEL OILS
4	ANIMAL,VEGETABLE OIL,FAT		186846		182063		324540		231048	HUILES,GRAISSES ANIM,VEG
42	FIXED VEGETABLE OIL,FAT		97890		97447		204325		126933	HUILES VEGETALES FIXES
423	FIXED VEG OILS,SOFT	W 41687	40880	W 60236	63247	W 107024	170587	W 44767	93427	HUILES VEGET DOUCES FIXES
4235	OLIVE OIL	W 7071	12023	W 14472	20975	W 58203	120606	W 23277	74358	HUILE D'OLIVE
424	FIXED VEG OIL NONSOFT	W 58590	57010	W 34700	34200	W 27665	33738	W 29455	33507	AUTRES HUILES VEG FIXES
4249	FIXED VEGETABLE OILS NES	W 58479	56959	W 34599	34105	W 27550	33600	W 29229	33320	HUILES VEGET FIXES NDA
431	*PROCESD ANML VEG OIL,ET	W 97051	87284	W 82987	82432	W 102738	113311	W 103438	95900	HUILES,GRAISSES PREPAREES
4312	HYDROGENATED OIL,FAT	W 92593	84497	W 78481	79731	W 98120	109610	W 91836	90287	HUILES HYDROGENEES
5	CHEMCLS,RELATED PROD NES		605640		724513		874406		868299	PRODUITS CHIMIQUES
51	ORGANIC CHEMICALS		73993		113310		121359		102644	PROD CHIMIQ ORGANIQUES
52	INORGANIC CHEMICALS		115307		145789		150847		25049	PROD CHIM INORGANIQUES
523	OTHR INORG CHEMICALS ETC		93304	W 442252	106489	W 468838	115223	W 70464	15926	AUT PRODUITS CHIMIQUES INORG
5232	OTH MTL CMPD OF INRG ACD	W 302820	72889	W 358147	85274	W 367525	89054	W 6113	2196	SELS METALLIQUES
52328	BORATES AND PERBORATES	W 167655	52583	W 202535	63009	W 204934	64763	W 3443	1229	BORATES ET PERBORATES
53	DYES,TANNING,COLOUR PROD		29236		34391		52085		74736	PROD TEINTURE,COLORANTS
541	*MEDICINAL,PHARM PRODUCT	K 4894488	76369	K 6951046	78090	K 5577256	63211	K 4751668	96938	PROD MEDICINAUX PHARMACEUT
5417	MEDICAMENTS	K 1627400	70191	K 3431469	66548	K 1935473	45483	K 1489270	60130	MEDICAMENTS
55	PERFUME,CLEANING ETC PRD		90384		118280		223192		315849	PROD POUR PARFUM,TOILETTE
554	SOAP,CLEANSING ETC PREPS	W 96045	78554	W 119833	101634	W 212129	195320	W 296736	270927	SAVONS,PRODUITS DETERSIFS
5541	SOAPS	W 63732	51621	W 78269	69813	W 104934	109441	W 140383	148247	SAVONS,PROD TENSIO–ACTIFS
5542	WASHING PREPARATIONS ETC	W 32122	26569	W 41073	30714	W 105934	83399	W 153722	116935	PROD ORG TENSIO–ACT NDA
58	PLASTIC MATERIALS ETC		158972		163735		194867		182868	MAT PLAST ARTIFICIELLES
583	POLYMERIZATION ETC PRODS	W 155807	111695	W 141334	118895	W 75792	128798	W 73591	118808	PROD POLYMERISATION

5. Special Exports F.O.B. by Commodities according to the S.I.T.C. (Rev. 2) in thousand U.S. Dollars
Exportations Spéciales F.O.B. par Produits d'après la C.T.C.I. (Rév. 2) en milliers de Dollars E.U.

SITC CTCI	COMMODITY	1993 WEIGHT POIDS	1993 VALUE VALEUR	1994 WEIGHT POIDS	1994 VALUE VALEUR	1995 WEIGHT POIDS	1995 VALUE VALEUR	1996 WEIGHT POIDS	1996 VALUE VALEUR	PRODUIT
5831	POLYETHYLENE	W 85750	53497	W 70479	38907	W 17210	17111	W 11854	11424	POLYETHYLENE
58311	— IN PRIMARY FORMS	W 84528	51937	W 69912	37750	W 16284	15474	W 10740	9026	POLYETHYLENE PRIMAIRES
6	BASIC MANUFACTURES		4486404		5707397		6262862		6573839	ART MANUFACTURES
62	RUBBER MANUFACTURES NES		193481		231027		276843		251924	CAOUTCHOUC MANUFACTURE
625	RUBBER TYRES, TUBES ETC	W 60420	169222	W 73506	200840	W 82041	227461	W 71135	203786	PNEUS CAOUTCHOUC VULCANISE
6251	TYRES NEW FOR MOTOR CARS	W 21863	61090	W 30367	83597	W 38147	109118	W 34705	102217	PNEUS POUR VOITURES
6252	TYRES,NEW,BUS OR LORRY	W 23037	66752	W 25538	71701	W 24554	68596	W 19335	55515	PNEUS POUR AUTOBUS,CAMIONS
64	PAPER,PAPERBOARD AND MFR		50696		109035		128223		129406	PAPIERS,CARTONS & OUVRAGES
641	PAPER AND PAPERBOARD		29662		81813		81357	W 55525	65144	PAPIERS ET CARTONS
65	TEXTILE YARN,FABRICS,ETC		1592181		2194699		2526640		2722679	FILS,TISSUS,ARTICLES TEXTILE
651	TEXTILE YARN	W 122297	347151	W 218751	597698	W 154317	505759	W 169380	512420	FILS TEXTILES
6513	COTTON YARN	W 31620	75242	W 86807	250488	W 39733	137879	W 44534	139213	FILS DE COTON
6514	SYN FIB YRN,BULK,MONOFIL	W 48517	113667	W 75763	155692	W 65611	174002	W 74894	174796	FILS CONT 85% FIB TEXT SYNTH
65142	— NONTXT ETC CONT PAMID	W 32139	70072	W 52985	100035	W 53432	128085	W 57008	118247	FILS NON TEX FI CON POLYAMID
6516	DISCON SYN FIB BLEND YRN	W 26615	113061	W 35547	133993	W 32309	140054	W 34743	148963	FILS FIBR TEX SYNT DIS MOINS
65168	OTH DISC SYN BLEND YARN	W 19209	78808	W 26904	97078	W 24192	97364	W 28207	112175	FILS TEXT SYNT MELANGE AUT F
652	COTTON FABRICS,WOVEN	W 38937	184442	W 68599	341022	W 56328	372805	W 59693	392417	TISSUS DE COTON
6521	GREY WOVEN COTTON FABRIC	W 17566	61735	W 35243	137326	W 20211	105079	W 17270	84667	TISSUS COT ECRUS NON MERCER
65214	GREY WOVEN COTTON NES	W 17520	61417	W 31372	116528	W 17581	88993	W 15281	71268	AUT TISSUS 85% COTON ECRUS
6522	WOVEN COTTON BLEACHD,ETC	W 21371	122706	W 33356	203696	W 36117	267726	W 42423	307750	TISSUS COTON BLANCHIS ETC
65224	BLCHED COTTON FABRIC NES	W 20104	109154	W 30434	172997	W 32385	234344	W 38579	270618	AUT TIS PLUS 85% COT BLANCHI
653	WOVN MAN-MADE FIB FABRIC	W 23957	246285	W 34810	326586	W 40877	547498	W 41533	478312	TISSUS FIBRES SYNTH,ARTIF
6531	CONT SYNT WEAVES NONPILE	W 3913	44750	W 7464	64015	W 7549	150434	W 6267	71535	TISSUS FIBRES SYNTH CONTINUE
65315	CONT SYN TXTL FABRIC NES	W 3850	44016	W 7205	61905	W 6896	144529	W 5897	68404	TIS PLUS 85% TEXT SYNT CONT
6534	DISC SYN BLEND FABRC NES	W 7117	89033	W 7635	75485	W 8290	101434	W 9563	130585	TISSUS FIBRES SYNTH DISCONT
65349	OTH DISC SYN BLEND FABRC	W 4957	59201	W 5299	55986	W 6369	77023	W 5519	71470	TISSUS FIB SYNT MEL MAT AUT
6536	DISC REGN TXTL FABRC NES	W 4371	35812	W 8983	85838	W 9214	107099	W 10533	116959	TISSUS 85% TEXT ART DISC
6538	DISC REG BLEND FABRC NES	W 1400	15159	W 3489	37024	W 7940	99318	W 7536	85902	TIS MOINS 85% TEXT ART DISC
65383	DISC REG-CONT MAN-MD FAB	W 1053	11445	W 2859	30703	W 6975	90429	W 5983	75442	TISSUS TEX ART CONT MEL SYNT
654	OTH WOVEN TEXTILE FABRIC	W 1317	32498	W 2156	42577	W 3019	67903	W 8215	82376	TISSUS AUT COTON SYNT,ARTIF
655	KNITTED,ETC FABRICS	W 9958	63098	W 25839	140588	W 13127	84387	W 19399	123437	ETOF BONNETERIE PIECES ETC
6552	OTHER KNIT ETC FAB NONEL	W 9958	63098	W 25839	140588	W 13127	84387	W 19399	123437	ETOF BON NON ELAS NON SYNT
656	LACE,RIBBONS,TULLE,ETC	W 2364	31420	W 3349	43333	W 4146	58089	W 5864	73184	TULLES,BRODERIE
657	SPECIAL TXTL FABRC,PRODS		82937		77029		115578	W 23625	150139	TISSUS SPECIAUX
6573	COATED ETC TEXTILES NES	W 13774	71503	W 13801	68174	W 18896	103120	W 18510	97853	TISSUS,ART MATIERE TEXT NDA
65733	RUBBERIZED TEXT NOT KNIT	W 12635	67614	W 12889	65151	W 17450	96755	W 15282	84398	TISSUS CAOUTCHOUTES
658	TEXTILE ARTICLES NES	W 54783	312329	W 65834	372467	W 78681	523263	W 98186	603071	ART FACONNES MAT TEXTILES
6581	BAGS,SACKS OF TEXTILES	W 20589	50662	W 27037	67559	W 33960	105932	W 41843	124751	SACS EMBALLAGE TEXTILES
6584	LINENS ETC	W 23154	180858	W 24862	204925	W 28478	275405	W 34100	310832	LINGE DE MAISON
65841	BED LINEN OF COTTON	W 7503	59417	W 7938	64172	W 8023	80312	W 10138	92185	LINGE DE LIT DE COTON
65845	OTHER LINEN OF COTTON	W 7811	60511	W 8323	67437	W 10913	103312	W 13734	120531	LINGE DE TOILETTE COTON
65849	OTH FURN ART OF OTH FIBR	W 6190	45669	W 6870	54718	W 7290	62278	W 6897	62998	AUT ART AMEUBLEMENT AUT FIBR
6589	OTH TEXTILE ARTICLES NES	W 6364	63704	W 8488	81749	W 10488	122254	W 14133	138069	AUT ART EN TEXTILES NDA
65898	KNITTED ETC ARTICLES NES	W 6263	62292	W 8302	80915	W 10330	120185	W 13957	136690	ART BONNET NON ELASTIQUE
659	FLOOR COVERINGS,ETC	W 23823	292021	W 27819	253398	W 30169	251357	W 41524	307322	COUVRE-PARQUETS,TAPIS ETC
6592	CARPETS ETC KNOTTED	W 2769	185815	W 3391	126704	W 2769	108659	W 3255	138969	TAPIS POINTS NOUES,ENROULES
65921	— OF WOOL OR FINE HAIR	W 2477	106238	W 3235	93885	W 2654	89606	W 2819	104612	TAP NOUES,ENROULES LAINE
65929	— OF OTHER TEXTILE MTLS	W 292	79578	W 156	32819	W 115	19053	W 436	34357	TAP NOUES AUT MAT TEXT
6595	MAN-MADE TXTL CARPTS NES	W 15985	66168	W 18754	85892	W 23373	110986	W 33892	135031	TAPIS MAT TEXT SYNT ARTIF
65952	— WOVEN	W 13215	59546	W 16017	77202	W 21845	106037	W 27080	118860	TAPIS MAT TEXT SYNT TISSES
66	NONMETAL MINERAL MFS NES		421972		529688		632460		712903	ART MIN NON METALLIQUES
661	LIME,CEMENT,BLDG PRODS	W 2855175	137588	W 4711980	202535	W 4339744	211523	W 3414517	220548	CHAUX,CIMENTS MAT CONSTR
6612	CEMENT	W 2741761	90150	W 4569740	145158	W 4173593	141198	W 3216286	135122	CIMENTS HYDRAULIQUES
6613	BUILDING STONE ETC WORKD	W 77727	39966	W 105330	50767	W 130546	63603	W 170322	79195	PIERRES A BATIR
66132	BUILDING STONE WORKED	W 76514	39915	W 105190	50755	W 129585	63514	W 169927	79142	OUVR EN PIERRES DE TAILLE
662	CLAY,REFRACTORY BLDG PRD	W 247745	90487	W 267989	99967	W 409974	142489	W 525501	175513	MAT CONST REFRACTAIRES
6624	BRICKS ETC NONREFRACTORY	W 217791	77365	W 248360	90672	W 350167	129566	W 473820	160756	BRIQUES ETC CERAM NON REFR
66245	GLAZED CERAMIC SETTS ETC	W 210851	76555	W 238656	88316	W 335055	126528	W 437797	153108	AUT CARREAUX CERAMIQUE
664	GLASS	W 168555	64280	W 178342	88753	W 168385	100743	W 178940	103593	VERRE
665	GLASSWARE	W 100545	114612	W 108671	117901	W 103524	143467	W 121405	170522	OUVRAGES EN VERRE
6652	HOUSEHLD,HOTEL ETC GLASS	W 55528	94472	W 62278	99283	W 76190	129123	W 94698	153820	OBJETS VERRE TABLE,CUISINE
67	IRON AND STEEL		1828795		2160104		1997593		1954182	FER ET ACIER
671	PIG IRON ETC	W 176586	50081	W 195519	60666	W 70750	73531	W 184941	77412	FONTE,SPIEGEL,POUDRES
6716	FERRO-ALLOYS	W 92355	41409	W 102729	48692	W 69924	73149	W 93427	61782	FERRO-ALLIAGES
67169	OTHER FERRO-ALLOYS	W 92301	41342	W 102692	48654	W 68507	72184	W 92953	61274	AUTRES FERRO-ALLIAGES
672	IRON,STEEL PRIMARY FORMS	W 2025243	491594	W 2659809	599750	W 1887884	483416	W 1362837	344327	LINGOTS FER,ACIER
6725	IRN,STL BLOOMS,SLABS,ETC	W 1765281	416831	W 2128551	452179	W 1747468	430754	W 1045218	254465	BLOOMS,BILLETTES FER ACIER
67251	IRN,SMPLE STL BLOOMS,ETC	W 1758448	412045	W 2100357	437575	W 1725406	416994	W 1023483	241010	BLOOMS ETC NON ACIER FIN
6727	IRN,STL COIL FR REROLLNG	W 259913	74743	W 515218	145884	W 140291	52587	W 317617	89860	EBAUCHES POUR TOLES FER
67271	IRON,SIMPLE STEEL COILS	W 259868	74725	W 515159	145782	W 140149	52274	W 317592	89839	EBAUCHES NON EN ACIER
673	IRON,STEEL SHAPES ETC	W 4004154	1135334	W 4961988	1284574	W 3848104	1094607	W 4320701	1198300	BARRES,PROFIL FER,ACIER
6731	IRON,STEEL WIRE ROD	W 642746	177853	W 788545	201771	W 637613	182087	W 822883	230315	FIL MACHINE FER,ACIER
67311	IRON,SIMPLE STL WIRE ROD	W 642742	177850	W 788528	201742	W 636701	181764	W 819643	229203	FIL MACH AUT ACIER FIN
6732	IRON,STEEL BARS ETC	W 3017467	852281	W 4009081	1036144	W 2909950	811354	W 3332539	913515	BARRES FER,ACIER
67326	IRN,OTH STL BARS HOTROLD	W 2989449	842819	W 3959657	1015773	W 2820918	770794	W 3255837	882085	BARRES PLEINES FER,ACIER
6733	IRON,STEEL PROFILES ETC	W 343941	105200	W 164361	46659	W 300541	101167	W 165279	54470	PROFILES,PALPLAN FER,ACIER
67331	SMALL U,I,H SECTIONS ETC	W 296230	89524	W 154441	42942	W 253674	84672	W 150428	47736	PROFILES MOINS 80MM
674	IRN,STL UNIV,PLATE,SHEET	W 50276	19479	W 105840	42099	W 127554	57891	W 221446	95241	LARGES PLATS,TOLES
678	IRON,STL TUBES,PIPES,ETC	W 213707	116480	W 315153	153693	W 448009	245796	W 351262	190205	TUBES,TUYAUX EN FONTE,FER
6783	IRON,STL TUBES,PIPES NES	W 210732	109714	W 310239	139825	W 439371	230916	W 341324	171432	AUT TUBES,TUYAUX FER,ACIER
68	NON-FERROUS METALS		145371		167401		271351		297813	METAUX NON FERREUX
682	COPPER EXC CEMENT COPPER	W 44183	91351	W 35971	88009	W 48118	148961	W 62836	165725	CUIVRE
6822	COPPER,ALLOYS WORKED	W 27926	61188	W 30865	77419	W 44301	139822	W 52716	142788	CUIVRE,ALLIAGES OUVRES
68221	COPPER BARS,WIRE,ETC	W 27694	60477	W 30325	75986	W 44149	139011	W 51960	140075	BARRES,PROFILES ET FILS
684	ALUMINIUM	W 23718	53262	W 34640	77390	W 41003	118475	W 50753	126817	ALUMINIUM
6842	ALUMINIUM,ALLOYS WORKED	W 19046	48540	W 27453	67306	W 29541	97314	W 35338	103244	ALUMINIUM,ALLIAGES OUVRE
69	METAL MANUFACTURES NES		205346		237230		333644		402271	ART MANUFACT EN METAL NDA
691	STRUCTURES AND PARTS NES	W 18874	33026	W 25973	43134	W 46836	69415	W 67345	100937	CONSTRUCT FER,ACIER,ALU
6911	STRUCTURES,PARTS IRN,STL	W 17693	24898	W 22612	29330	W 43598	48313	W 61949	70970	CONSTRUCT FER,ACIER,FONTE
697	BASE MTL HOUSEHOLD EQUIP	W 17024	62807	W 24721	73643	W 25857	86343	W 32252	95196	ART MENAGE MET COMMUNS
699	BASE METAL MFRS NES	W 14377	30340	W 18008	41991	W 29509	68903	W 34126	81991	ART MANUFACTURES MET NDA
7	MACHINES,TRANSPORT EQUIP		1290662		1696362		2373949		2890154	MACHINES MATERIEL TRANSPORT
71	POWER GENERATING EQUIPMT		69161		131252		171154		198052	MACHINES GENERATRICES
713	INTRNL COMBUS PSTN ENGIN	W 3606	47844	W 5243	83991	W 7111	113053	W 11686	117005	MOTEURS EXPL COMB INT, PIECE
7139	PISTON ENGINE PARTS NES	W 3211	44823	W 4898	81853	W 6690	110080	W 10673	108767	PIECES POUR 713.2,3,8
72	MACHS FOR SPCL INDUSTRYS		92390		117417		122383		157746	MAC SPECIALES POUR INDUST
74	GENRL INDUSTRL MACHY NES		114615		195871		246694		299049	MACH APP INDUSTRIE
741	HEATING,COOLING EQUIPMNT	W 3608	23252	W 7999	57532	W 11952	77907	W 10915	73641	MACH CHAUFFAGE,PIECES
744	MECHANICAL HANDLING EQU	W 10363	20104	W 15055	29382	W 24797	46150	W 32702	70296	EQUIP MANUTENTION PIECES
749	NONELEC MACH PTS,ACC NES	W 4537	27312	W 5195	45950	W 6884	55069	W 11086	74118	PIECES MACH NON ELEC NDA
76	TELECOMM,SOUND EQUIPMENT		184851		199343		243032		300658	EQUIPMENT DE TELECOM

5. Special Exports F.O.B. by Commodities according to the S.I.T.C. (Rev. 2) in thousand U.S. Dollars
Exportations Spéciales F.O.B. par Produits d'après la C.T.C.I. (Rév. 2) en milliers de Dollars E.U.

SITC CTCI	COMMODITY	1993		1994		1995		1996		PRODUIT
		WEIGHT POIDS	VALUE VALEUR	WEIGHT POIDS	VALUE VALEUR	WEIGHT POIDS	VALUE VALEUR	WEIGHT POIDS	VALUE VALEUR	
761	TELEVISION RECEIVERS	W 12777	135919	W 16761	152952	W 19850	201554	W 21018	216559	RECEPTEURS DE TELEVISION
7611	COLOUR TV RECEIVERS	W 12777	135919	W 16761	152949	W 19844	201521	W 21018	216557	RECEPTEURS COULEUR
764	TELECOM EQPT,PTS,ACC NES	W 1196	44299	W 1700	42981	W 1498	40523	W 2618	83217	EQUIP TELECOM,PIECES
77	ELECTRIC MACHNRY NES ETC		432181		526916		748031		965652	MACH APP ELECT NDA
771	ELECTRIC POWER MACHY NES	W 8497	52275	W 12545	70744	W 15649	81962	W 24814	127717	MACH PROD,TRANS ELECTR
7711	TRANSFORMERS,ELECTRICAL	W 7683	46952	W 11969	65063	W 14939	73471	W 23785	117174	TRANSFO ELECTRIQUES
77111	LIQUID DIELEC TRANSFRMRS	W 5820	28000	W 9993	48398	W 12252	48958	W 18696	78649	TRANSFO DIELEC LIQUIDE
772	SWITCHGEAR ETC,PARTS NES	W 2106	28237	W 3421	44154	W 4241	57670	W 5622	86607	APP COUPURE,SECT ETC
7721	SWITCHGEAR ETC	W 2066	19549	W 3356	32582	W 4176	49841	W 5532	76502	APP COUPURE,SECTIONMNT
773	ELECTR DISTRIBUTNG EQUIP	W 31193	201810	W 39070	218434	W 51269	308276	W 65182	402464	EQUIPMT DISTRIBUTION ELECT
7731	INSULATED WIRE,CABLE ETC	W 31035	200411	W 38784	216370	W 50352	305226	W 64723	399539	FILS,CABLES ISOLES ELECT
775	HOUSEHOLD TYPE EQUIP NES	W 38460	117513	W 49482	152580	W 74670	237392	W 80778	259818	MACH,APP USAGE DOMESTQUE
7752	DOM REFRIGERATRS,FREEZRS	W 24221	66612	W 29975	87226	W 46001	132056	W 37984	115438	REFRIG,CONGEL MENAGER
77521	DOMESTIC REFRIGERATORS	W 24016	65898	W 29416	85333	W 43897	125305	W 34295	103327	REFRIGERATEURS
7758	ELECTRO–THERMIC APPL NES	W 12681	42011	W 17091	55202	W 23546	84890	W 36943	118655	APP ELECTROTHERMIQ NDA
77586	ELECTROTHERM DOM APP NES	W 10316	34104	W 13263	41175	W 17288	63218	W 22935	82274	APP ELECTRO THERMIQUES
778	ELECTRICAL MACHINERY NES	W 10232	30461	W 12376	37047	W 19110	59774	W 24591	81148	AUTRES MACH ELECT NDA
78	ROAD VEHICLES		295333		413751		725889		843729	VEHICULES ROUTIERS
781	PASS MOTOR VEH EXC BUSES	W 6559	48918	W 10923	70801	W 30990	251170	W 32123	269578	AUTO TRANSPORT PERSONNES
783	ROAD MOTOR VEHICLES NES	W 9323	89317	W 20100	119006	W 11203	142680	W 24828	244228	VEHICULES ROUTIERS NDA
7831	BUSES	W 9323	89317	W 20082	118917	W 11162	142395	W 24782	244104	VOITURES TRANSPORT COMMUN
784	MOTOR VEH PRTS,ACCES NES	W 26981	90779	W 41097	117014	W 60774	181803	W 61104	193695	PIECES 722,781,782,783
7849	OTHER MOTOR VEHCL PARTS	W 25934	87399	W 40025	114358	W 59728	177394	W 59150	186169	PIECES 722,781,782,783
786	TRAILERS,NONMOTR VEH,NES	W 42207	48523	W 83072	84310	W 82796	91010	W 72358	85807	REMORQUES,CADRES,CONTAIN
7861	TRAILERS,TRANSP CONTAINR	W 41799	47785	W 82335	82389	W 82284	89026	W 71395	83152	REMORQUES TOUS VEHICULES
78613	CONTAINERS INC ROAD–RAIL	W 40109	41126	W 81787	81417	W 81562	87502	W 70444	80422	CADRES ET CONTAINERS
79	OTHR TRANSPORT EQUIPMENT		75862		78932		74648		68289	AUTRE MATERIEL TRANSPORT
793	SHIPS AND BOATS ETC		74780		53779		67362		57247	NAVIRES BATEAUX,ETC
7932	SHIPS AND BOATS NES		74769		53655		58235		48779	NAVIRES ET BATEAUX
79323	OTHER CARGO VESSELS		49867		50945		47161		39062	AUT BATEAUX TRANS MARCH
8	MISC MANUFACTURED GOODS		4779159		5165525		6801137		6962952	ART MANUFACTURES DIVERS
812	*PLUMBG,HEATNG,LGHTNG EQ	W 39041	71048	W 46457	84691	W 59241	105525	W 73238	122137	APPAR SANITAIRES CHAUFFAGE
821	*FURNITURE,PARTS THEREOF	W 14309	47440	W 20360	55608	W 25127	75539	W 26146	80139	MEUBLES ET PIECES
84	CLOTHING AND ACCESSORIES		4339695		4581782		6118763		6070806	VETEMENTS
842	MENS OUTERWEAR NOT KNIT	W 17574	333852	W 21902	366779	W 25527	525464	W 24879	500095	VET DESSUS POUR HOMMES
8423	— TROUSERS,BREECHES ETC	W 10617	153723	W 12383	162672	W 16301	261330	W 16823	281569	PANTALONS HOMMES MAT TEX
8429	— OTHER OUTER GARMENTS	W 4999	115755	W 5274	103721	W 5362	142585	W 3595	85721	AUT VET DES HOM MAT TEX
843	WOMENS OUTERWEAR NONKNIT	W 36759	779201	W 42891	846576	W 52073	1220722	W 60169	1255342	VET DESSUS FEMMES MAT TEX
8431	— COATS AND JACKETS	W 2325	76272	W 3947	103170	W 5243	154947	W 6236	169932	MANT,VEST FEM MAT TEXTIL
8433	— DRESSES	W 1562	40740	W 1626	39074	W 3894	122762	W 3778	113713	ROBES EN MAT–TEXTILES
8434	— SKIRTS	W 1879	43018	W 2271	51830	W 3468	96616	W 3475	82513	JUPES EN MAT TEXTILES
8435	— BLOUSES	W 5344	147595	W 6267	172176	W 6978	229579	W 7433	217330	BLOUSES FEM MAT TEXTILES
8439	— OTHER OUTER GARMENTS	W 25216	461090	W 28115	467518	W 31696	591150	W 38526	654640	AUT VET DES FEM MAT TEXT
844	UNDER GARMENTS NOT KNIT	W 11373	225158	W 13947	260060	W 16974	382768	W 14747	323470	VETEMENT DESSOUS MAT TEX
8441	— MENS SHIRTS	W 8291	183684	W 9869	207489	W 12311	315293	W 10216	262936	CHEMISES HOMMES MAT TEXT
84411	—— OF COTTON	W 6427	141801	W 8125	172350	W 10563	273764	W 8691	232509	CHEMISES HOMMES DE COTON
845	OUTERWEAR KNIT NONELASTC	W 73742	1492417	W 82240	1520446	W 84185	1990949	W 98472	2014230	VET DESSOUS,ACCES BONNET
8451	— JERSEYS,PULLOVERS ETC	W 26792	553989	W 36957	705339	W 35476	860241	W 50467	1036686	CHANDAILS,PULL–OVERS ETC
8452	— WOMENS DRESSES ETC	W 8121	185919	W 6258	125573	W 8001	216732	W 5585	136592	ROBES,JUPES BONNETERIE
8459	— OTHER,CLTHG ACCESRYS	W 38828	752509	W 39026	689533	W 40708	913976	W 42420	840952	AUT VET DESSUS DE BONNE
846	UNDER GARMENTS KNITTED	W 45257	879449	W 53488	946602	W 61965	1308835	W 70231	1384477	SOUS VETS DE BONNETERIE
8462	— OF COTTON NON ELASTIC	W 39929	790701	W 45424	805063	W 51042	1086182	W 59044	1169930	SOUS–VET BONNET COTON
84629	—— OTHER	W 39929	790701	W 45424	805063	W 51042	1086182	W 59044	1169930	AUT SOUS–VET BONNET COTON
8463	— OF SYNTH FBR NONELAST	W 5123	83119	W 7722	131408	W 10281	199599	W 10554	195025	SOUS–VET BONNET FIB SYNT
84632	—— MENS SHIRTS	W 3291	63873	W 5444	104437	W 7833	164768	W 7436	150760	CHEMISES DE BON FIB SYNMT
847	TEXTILE CLTHNG ACCES NES	W 11821	131284	W 14201	167403	W 15794	218331	W 17283	237121	ACCES VET MAT TEXT NDA
8472	CLTHNG ACCESRYS ETC KNIT	W 9083	98209	W 10439	119729	W 12286	163504	W 13681	182022	ACCES VET BONNE NDA
84722	KNIT SOCKS,ETC NONELASTC	W 9064	97996	W 10405	119433	W 12227	162168	W 13632	180757	CHAUSSETTES BON. NON ELAS
848	HEADGEAR,NONTXTL CLOTHNG		498333		473916		471693	W 5478	356072	VET ACCES MAT AUT QUE TEX
8481	LEATHER CLOTHES,ACCESSOR	W 7599	440692	W 6758	410386	W 5862	406516	W 4477	308620	VET ACCES MAT CUIR ARTIF
8483	FUR ETC,CLOTHES,PRODUCTS	W 742	55794	W 794	61186	W 630	60226	W 361	41379	VETEMENTS DE FOURRURE
84831	ARTICLES OF FURSKIN,NES	W 738	55697	W 793	61152	W 625	59931	W 360	41359	PELLETERIES OUVREES NDA
851	*FOOTWEAR	W 9005	93377	W 13283	158751	W 12331	112589	W 16197	148746	CHAUSSURES
85102	FOOTWEAR LEATHER	W 4926	63355	W 6780	121381	W 5311	70520	W 7147	91097	CHAUS SEMELLES EN CUIR
89	MISC MANUFCTRD GOODS NES		177509		233178		328449		463224	ART MANUFACTURES DIVERS
893	ARTICLES OF PLASTIC NES		39640		73351		123548		159617	OUVRAGES EN MAT DIVIS 58
8931	PLSTC PACKG CONTNRS,LIDS	W 5695	12542	W 16704	35052	W 31184	68268	W 44066	90885	ART TRANSP EMBALLAGE ETC
897	GOLD,SILVER WARE,JEWELRY		26917		49292		65728		116127	BIJOUTERIE,ORFEVRERIE
8973	PREC JEWLRY,GLD–SILVWARE		25990		47981		64468		114760	BIJOUX OR,ARGENT ORFEVRE
89731	PRECIOUS METAL JEWELLERY		24516		45999		62065		111523	ART BIJOUTERIE,JOAILLER
898	MUSICAL INSTRUMENTS,PTS		67727		67300		83872	W 19633	114995	INSTRUMENTS DE MUSIQUE
8983	SOUND RECRDNG TAPE,DISCS	W 8010	66995	W 9767	66671	W 17067	83079	W 19532	114062	SUPPORTS SON POUR 763
89831	PREPD SND RECORDNG MEDIA	W 7524	36082	W 8919	41110	W 16241	73415	W 18199	91218	SUPPORTS PREPARES
9	GOODS NOT CLASSD BY KIND		8824		10287		14764		280745	ART TRANSACT NON CLASSES
931	*SPECIAL TRANSACTIONS			W 5	39		2		258900	TRANS.SPECIALES

1. HISTORICAL SERIES, 1986–1996 GENERAL TRADE, IMPORTS C.I.F., EXPORTS F.O.B.
SERIES HISTORIQUES, 1986–1996 COMMERCE GENERAL, IMPORTATIONS C.A.F., EXPORTATIONS F.O.B

YEAR ANNEE	VALUE IN MILLION UGANDA SHILLINGS VALEUR EN MILLION UGANDA SHILLINGS MERCHANDISE –MARCHANDISE IMPORTS	EXPORTS	GOLD –OR IMPORTS	EXPORTS	CONVERSION FACTORS U.S. CENTS PER UGANDA SHILLING FACTEURS DE CONVERSION CENTS E.U. PAR UGANDA SHILLING IMPORTS	EXPORTS	INDEX NUMBERS –INDICES QUANTUM IMPORTS	EXPORTS	UNIT VALUE VALEUR UNITAIRE IMPORTS	EXPORTS
1986	4298.00	6104.00			7.1429	7.1429				
1987	23775.86	13684.00			2.3343	2.3343				
1988	94112.00	29074.00			0.9422	0.9422				
1989	87851.98	55674.00			0.4438	0.4482				
1990	125060.00	64652.00			0.2342	0.2352				100
1991	137000.00	147000.00			0.1428	0.1360				99
1992	580999.90	159000.00			0.0886	0.0897				85
1993		214000.00				0.0836				96
1994	850000.10	394000.10			0.1034	0.1040				185
1995	1024000.00	446000.10			0.1031	0.1033				244
1996	1247000.00	614000.10			0.0953	0.0957				180

2. IMPORTS BY BROAD ECONOMIC CATEGORY AND EXPORTS BY INDUSTRIAL ORIGIN. (PERCENTAGE OF TOTAL VALUE)
IMPORTATIONS PAR CATEGORIES ECONOMIQUES ET EXPORTATIONS PAR BRANCHE D'ACTIVITE.(EN POURCENTAGE DE LA VALEUR TOTALE)

IMPORTS – IMPORTATIONS

	1990	1991	1992	1993	1994	1995	1996
TOTAL IMPORTS–IMPORTATIONS TOTALES							
1 FOOD BEV–ALIMENTATION BOISSONS							
11 PRIMARY–PRODUITS DE BASE							
111 FOR INDUSTRY–POUR L'INDUSTRIE							
112 FOR HOUSEHOLDS–POUR LES MENAGES							
12 PROCESSED–PRODUITS ELABORES							
121 FOR INDUSTRY–POUR L'INDUSTRIE							
122 FOR HOUSEHOLDS–POUR LES MENAGES							
2 IND SUPPLIES–APPROV INDUSTRIELS							
21 PRIMARY–PRODUITS DE BASE							
22 PROCESSED–PRODUITS ELABORES							
3 FUELS–COMBUSTIBLES							
31 PRIMARY–PRODUITS DE BASE							
32 PROCESSED–PRODUITS ELABORES							
321 MOTOR SPIRIT–ESSENCE							
322 OTHER–AUTRES							
4 MACHINERY–EQUIPEMENT							
41 CAPITAL EQUIPMENT–MACHINES							
42 PARTS–PIECES ACCESSOIRES							
5 TRANSPORT–TRANSPORT							
51 PASSENGER CARS–AUTOMOBILES							
52 OTHER–AUTRES							
521 INDUSTRIAL–INDUSTRIELS							
522 NON INDUSTRIAL–NON INDUSTRIEL							
53 PARTS–PIECES ACCESSOIRES							
6 CONSUM GOODS–BIENS CONSOMMATION							
61 DURABLE–DURABLES							
62 SEMI DURABLE–SEMI DURABLES							
63 NON DURABLE–NON DURABLES							
7 GOODS NES–BIENS NDA							

EXPORTS – EXPORTATIONS

	1990	1991	1992	1993	1994	1995	1996
TOTAL EXPORTS–EXPORTATIONS TOTALES							
1 AGRICULTURE							
2 MINING QUARRY–INDUS EXTRACTIVES							
3 MANUFACTURING–IND MANUFACTUR							
31 FOOD BEV TOBACCO–ALIM BOISS TAB							
32 TEXTILES–INDUSTRIES TEXTILES							
33 WOOD & PRODUCTS–BOIS & PRODUITS							
34 PAPER & PRODUCTS–PAPIER & PRODT							
35 CHEMICALS–INDUSTRIES CHIMIQUES							
36 NON METAL MIN–MIN NON METAL							
37 BASIC METAL–IND METAL BASE							
38 METAL MANUF–MANUF METAL							
39 OTH MANUF IND–AUTRES MANUF							

3. TRADE BY PRINCIPAL COUNTRIES OF PRODUCTION AND LAST CONSIGNMENT (VALUE IN THOUSAND U.S. DOLLARS)
ECHANGES SELON LES PRINCIPAUX PAYS DE PRODUCTION ET DE DERNIERE CONSIGNATION (VALEUR EN MILLIERS DE DOLLARS EU)

COUNTRIES–PAYS	GENERAL IMPORTS C.I.F. IMPORTATIONS GENERALES C.A.F				
	1988	1989	1990	1991	1992
World	531801	578287	551095	522689	524433
Africa	108165	101708	86902	97381	136667
Americas	40139	52196	39849	19322	36969
Northern America	21139	33296	34219	17891	36579
LAIA					
CACM					
Caribbean	19000	18900	5630	1431	390
Rest of America					
As.ex F.USSR	130759	109858	86011	126184	156758
Eur.x F.USSR	201722	225706	242815	208942	161926
EU	184476	219140	235760	200985	153333
EFTA	5192	4980	4640	6409	8410
East Europe					
Other Europe					
Former USSR					
Oceania					
Kenya	102807	92987	71133	82751	118357
United Kingdom	68701	73731	81312	72572	52186
Germany/Allemagne	37398	61790	54105	33325	26794
Japan/Japon	30568	33632	29449	46940	51674
Italy/Italie	36593	23892	50713	28235	14985
USA/Etats–Unis d'Amer	19073	27620	31034	15300	25314
India/Inde	12032	18755	13686	14543	23854
China/Chine	21240	11411	5256	19683	20521
France,Monac	5801	11141	13679	16811	13663
Pakistan	13427	16268	5972	19234	2175
Belgium–Luxembourg	9167	10596	10000	13562	11214
Spain/Espagne	5992	15600	1393	17472	12980
Un. Rep. of Tanzania	4583	6927	9541	13162	16959
Cuba	19000	18900	5630	1431	390
Netherlands/Pays–Bas	11900	8442	8819	4927	8798
Hong Kong	5335	8596	8539	9408	7671
Malaysia/Malaisie	33866	584	78	838	2525
United Arab Emirates	4120	4739	5920	5330	14767
Singapore/Singapour	6022	5369	2713	3837	15982
Denmark/Danemark	4066	9788	4833	3897	5332
Korea, Republic of	2437	4926	12338	4397	3326
Switz.Liecht	4623	3388	4341	5489	7890
Canada	2066	5676	3185	2591	11265
Fm Yugoslav	12054	1586	2415	1548	183
Austria/Autriche	1130	853	7753	4955	2612
Bahrain/Bahreïn	462	534	606	668	12790
Sweden/Suède	2443	2604	2197	4018	3311
Zimbabwe	775	1794	6228	1468	1351
Saudi Arabia	1250	5044	1454	1306	1473
Finland/Finlande	1285	703	956	1211	1458
Norway,SVD,JM	569	1592	299	920	520

COUNTRIES–PAYS	GENERAL EXPORTS F.O.B. EXPORTATIONS GENERALES F.O.B.				
	1988	1989	1990	1991	1992
Monde	300091	298133	190102	196009	171353
Afrique	1833	3961	8187	15193	19036
Amériques	37889	36293	20375	21355	15669
Amérique du Nord	37889	36265	20375	21355	15669
ALAI		28			
MCAC					
Caraïbes					
Autre Amérique					
Asie l'URSS exclus	8843	11216	6617	9399	4685
Europe l'URSS exclus	225044	197219	135186	129263	108943
UE	225044	197219	135186	129263	108943
AELE					
Europe de l'Est					
Autre de l'Europe					
Ancienne URSS					
Océanie					
United Kingdom	44145	22335	14545	30767	35557
Spain/Espagne	38192	40551	27183	17436	15859
USA/Etats–Unis d'Amer	37238	36264	19348	19708	13961
France,Monac	26803	23638	23229	24643	10912
Belgium–Luxembourg	25349	23636	16906	11392	21139
Italy/Italie	21595	22328	25207	21586	7290
Netherlands/Pays–Bas	37009	26539	14943	9122	8914
Germany/Allemagne	27809	28875	8030	8813	7408
Kenya	1833	3961	8187	15193	19036
Japan/Japon	7753	9037	4395	4043	984
Portugal	3425	8927	3933	1739	862
Greece/Grèce	717	390	1210	3765	1002
Canada	651	1	1027	1647	1708
Korea, Republic of	130	1897	189	329	2225
Hong Kong	146	183	196	2668	739
Singapore/Singapour	814	19	231	1127	141
Saudi Arabia		58	964	574	427
United Arab Emirates		22	642	658	169

(VALUE AS PERCENTAGE OF WORLD TOTAL)(VALEURS EN POURCENTAGE DU TOTAL MONDIAL)

	1983	1984	1985	1986	1987	1988	1989	1990	1991	1992
Africa	39.8	39.4				20.3	17.6	15.8	18.6	26.1
Americas	2.6	2.0				7.5	9.0	7.2	3.7	7.0
Northern America	2.3	1.6				4.0	5.8	6.2	3.4	7.0
LAIA	0.3	0.4								
CACM										
Caribbean	0.0	0.0				3.6	3.3	1.0	0.3	0.1
Rest of America										
As.ex F.USSR	17.7	15.5				24.6	19.0	15.6	24.1	29.9
Eur.x F.USSR	39.7	40.7				37.9	39.0	44.1	40.0	30.9
EU	38.0	39.0				34.7	37.9	42.8	38.5	29.2
EFTA	1.6	1.6				1.0	0.9	0.8	1.2	1.6
East Europe	0.0	0.0								
Other Europe	0.1	0.0								
Former USSR	0.1	2.3								
Oceania	0.0									
Kenya	36.2	39.4				19.3	16.1	12.9	15.8	22.6
United Kingdom	10.9	14.7				12.9	12.7	14.8	13.9	10.0
Germany/Allemagne	11.7	7.1				7.0	10.7	9.8	6.4	5.1
Japan/Japon	5.2	6.6				5.7	5.8	5.3	9.0	9.9
Italy/Italie	4.0	4.2				6.9	4.1	9.2	5.4	2.9
USA/Etats–Unis d'Amer	1.4	1.2				3.6	4.8	5.6	2.9	4.8
India/Inde	6.8					2.3	3.2	2.5	2.8	4.5
China/Chine						4.0	2.0	1.0	3.8	3.9
France,Monac	3.2	4.8				1.1	1.9	2.5	3.2	2.6
Pakistan	0.7	0.3				2.5	2.8	1.1	3.7	0.4

	1983	1984	1985	1986	1987	1988	1989	1990	1991	1992
Afrique	0.4	0.5				0.6	1.3	4.3	7.8	11.1
Amériques	31.8	24.4				12.6	12.2	10.7	10.9	9.1
Amérique du Nord	31.8	24.3				12.6	12.2	10.7	10.9	9.1
ALAI							0.0			
MCAC										
Caraïbes	0.1	0.0								
Autre Amérique										
Asie l'URSS exclus	8.8	9.7				2.9	3.8	3.5	4.8	2.7
Europe l'URSS exclus	56.4	61.9				75.0	66.2	71.1	65.9	63.6
UE	55.6	61.4				75.0	66.2	71.1	65.9	63.6
AELE	0.5	0.5								
Europe de l'Est										
Autre de l'Europe	0.3	0.0								
Ancienne URSS	2.3	3.4								
Océanie	0.2	0.2								
United Kingdom	12.8	15.5				14.7	7.5	7.7	15.7	20.8
Spain/Espagne	10.5	10.9				12.7	13.6	14.3	8.9	9.3
USA/Etats–Unis d'Amer	31.7	24.1				12.4	12.2	10.2	10.1	8.1
France,Monac	11.2	10.1				8.9	7.9	12.2	12.6	6.4
Belgium–Luxembourg						8.4	7.9	8.9	5.8	12.3
Italy/Italie	6.3	7.4				7.2	7.5	13.3	11.0	4.3
Netherlands/Pays–Bas	3.4	4.4				12.3	8.9	7.9	4.7	5.2
Germany/Allemagne	9.3	9.7				9.3	9.7	4.2	4.5	4.3
Kenya	0.3	0.3				0.6	1.3	4.3	7.8	11.1
Japan/Japon	5.1	7.3				2.6	3.0	2.3	2.1	0.6

4. General Imports C.I.F. by Commodities according to the S.I.T.C. (Rev. 2) in thousand U.S. Dollars
Importations Générales C.A.F. par Produits d'après la C.T.C.I. (Rév. 2) en milliers de Dollars E.U.

SITC CTCI	COMMODITY	1989		1990		1991		1992		PRODUIT
		WEIGHT POIDS	VALUE VALEUR	WEIGHT POIDS	VALUE VALEUR	WEIGHT POIDS	VALUE VALEUR	WEIGHT POIDS	VALUE VALEUR	
	ALL COMMODITIES		578287		551095		522689		524433	TOUS PRODUITS
0	FOOD AND LIVE ANIMALS		33262		19812		18667		21195	ALIMENTS,ANIMAUX VIVANTS
001	*LIVE ANIMALS FOR FOOD		2016		829		646		571	ANIMAUX VIVANTS
01	MEAT AND PREPARATIONS		4814		3392		2311		3373	VIANDES ET PREPARATIONS
03	FISH AND PREPARATIONS		1576		39		1754		119	POISSONS ET PREPARATIONS
04	CEREALS AND PREPARATIONS		6705		4394		6134		8182	CEREALES ET PRODUITS
06	SUGAR AND PREPS,HONEY		15154		8380		5203		6343	SUCRES ET PRODUITS
09	MISC EDIBLE PRODUCTS		2997		2778		978		1671	PREP ALIMENTAIRES DIVERSES
1	BEVERAGES AND TOBACCO		3031		3710		1801		2777	BOISSONS ET TABACS
11	BEVERAGES		3031		3709		1801		2483	BOISSONS
2	CRUDE MATERLS,EXCL FUELS		12869		10911		12925		21868	MAT BRUTES NON COMESTIBLES
26	TEXTILE FIBRES AND WASTE		6386		5954		8965		12689	FIBRES TEXTILES
27	CRUDE FERTLZR,MINRLS NES		5296		4196		3456		8017	ENGRAIS MINERAUX BRUTS
3	MINERAL FUELS ETC		96350		99367		81499		70409	COMBUSTIBLES MINERAUX LUB
33	PETROLEUM AND PRODUCTS		95719		98745		81223		69965	PETROLE ET DERIVES
4	ANIMAL,VEGETABLE OIL,FAT		9471		15241		10145		30362	HUILES,GRAISSES ANIM,VEG
411	*ANIMAL OILS AND FATS		6510		6937		6005		10215	HUILES,GRAISSES ANIMALES
42	FIXED VEGETABLE OIL,FAT								16185	HUILES VEGETALES FIXES
5	CHEMCLS,RELATED PROD NES		38425		38806		37655		43770	PRODUITS CHIMIQUES
53	DYES,TANNING,COLOUR PROD		2812		2789		1565		2277	PROD TEINTURE,COLORANTS
541	*MEDICINAL,PHARM PRODUCT		13732		15062		8845		18269	PROD MEDICINAUX PHARMACEUT
55	PERFUME,CLEANING ETC PRD		4138		4691		6463		3092	PROD POUR PARFUM,TOILETTE
562	*FERTILIZERS,MANUFACTURE		1784		239		945		889	ENGRAIS MANUFACTURES
58	PLASTIC MATERIALS ETC		5194		4801		6403		7833	MAT PLAST ARTIFICIELLES
59	CHEMICAL MATERIALS NES		7352		7261		10550		6633	MAT PROD CHIMIQUES NDA
6	BASIC MANUFACTURES		111075		86552		110631		114680	ART MANUFACTURES
61	LEATHER,DRESSED FUR,ETC		8899		9456		9927		13278	CUIRS,PELLETERIES
64	PAPER,PAPERBOARD AND MFR		7737		7065		8225		11437	PAPIERS,CARTONS & OUVRAGES
65	TEXTILE YARN,FABRICS,ETC		29472		19101		30499		12344	FILS,TISSUS,ARTICLES TEXTILE
66	NONMETAL MINERAL MFS NES		15639		14181		15984		19595	ART MIN NON METALLIQUES
67	IRON AND STEEL		22150		18445		27286		34315	FER ET ACIER
69	METAL MANUFACTURES NES		27178		18304		18710		20737	ART MANUFACT EN METAL NDA
7	MACHINES,TRANSPORT EQUIP		211310		217913		198898		168994	MACHINES MATERIEL TRANSPORT
8	MISC MANUFACTURED GOODS		47291		51970		46396		49109	ART MANUFACTURES DIVERS
84	CLOTHING AND ACCESSORIES		6484		10268		7033		3231	VETEMENTS
851	*FOOTWEAR		4397		7362		8096		4522	CHAUSSURES
89	MISC MANUFCTRD GOODS NES		29613		25054		21377		26572	ART MANUFACTURES DIVERS
9	GOODS NOT CLASSD BY KIND		15203		6813		4072		1268	ART TRANSACT NON CLASSES
931	*SPECIAL TRANSACTIONS		15203		6813		4072		1268	TRANS.SPECIALES

5. General Exports F.O.B. by Commodities according to the S.I.T.C. (Rev. 2) in thousand U.S. Dollars
Exportations Générales F.O.B. par Produits d'après la C.T.C.I. (Rév. 2) en milliers de Dollars E.U.

SITC CTCI	COMMODITY	1992		1993		1994		1995		PRODUIT
		WEIGHT POIDS	VALUE VALEUR	WEIGHT POIDS	VALUE VALEUR	WEIGHT POIDS	VALUE VALEUR	WEIGHT POIDS	VALUE VALEUR	
	ALL COMMODITIES		171353		201192		463959		560505	TOUS PRODUITS
0	FOOD AND LIVE ANIMALS		117205							ALIMENTS,ANIMAUX VIVANTS
03	FISH AND PREPARATIONS		5487		8943		12263		17541	POISSONS ET PREPARATIONS
04	CEREALS AND PREPARATIONS		4690							CEREALES ET PRODUITS
044	MAIZE UNMILLED	W 29623	3894	W 160438	23319	W 95453	30169	W 98283	19302	MAIS NON MOULU
05	VEGETABLES AND FRUIT		3187							LEGUMES ET FRUITS
0542	LEGUMINOUS VEGETBLES DRY	W 9327	2782	W 47532	12580	W 35329	11913	W 25936	10847	LEGUMES A COSSE SECS
071	COFFEE AND SUBSTITUTES	W 119006	95372	W 114169	106775	W 194360	342763	W 168858	384122	CAFE ET SUCCEDANES
0711	COFFEE GREEN,ROASTED,SUB	W 119006	95372	W 114169	106775	W 194360	342763	W 168858	384122	CAFE TORREFIE OU DECAFEINE
072	COCOA		225	W 1313	714	W 680	639	W 509	442	CACAO
0721	COCOA BEANS,RAW,ROASTED			W 1313	714	W 680	639	W 509	442	CACAO EN FEVES
074	TEA AND MATE	W 7816	7721			W 10972	11802	W 10681	8698	THE ET MATE
0741	TEA	W 7816	7721	W 10175	11141	W 10972	11802	W 10681	8698	THE
1	BEVERAGES AND TOBACCO		4730							BOISSONS ET TABACS
12	TOBACCO AND MANUFACTURES		4372		6943					TABACS BRUTS FABRIQUES
121	TOBACCO UNMNFCTRD,REFUSE			W 3854	6943	W 4082	8043	W 3525	7397	TABACS BRUTS,DECHETS
2	CRUDE MATERLS,EXCL FUELS		40953							MAT BRUTES NON COMESTIBLES
21	HIDES,SKINS,FURS UNDRSSD		7655							CUIRS,PEAUX BRUTS
2111	BOVINE,EQUINE HIDES,RAW	W 3561	3375	W 5259	5228	W 7697	12852	W 4359	8924	PEAUX DE BOVINS
2114	GOAT AND KID SKINS,RAW		664	W 486	619					PEAUX DE CAPRINS
22	OIL SEEDS,OLEAGINOUS FRT		22305							GRAINES,FRUITS OLEAGINEUX
2222	SOYA BEANS			W 7076	2056	W 1802	773	W 2211	880	FEVES DE SOJA
2225	SESAME SEEDS	W 12863	6478	W 8372	2776	W 4245	1565	W 8235	5282	GRAINES DE SESAME
26	TEXTILE FIBRES AND WASTE		8941							FIBRES TEXTILES
263	COTTON	W 7536	8218	W 7961	5534	W 3841	3590	W 5580	9696	COTON
2631	RAW COTTON,EXCL LINTERS	W 7536	8218	W 7961	5534	W 3841	3590	W 5580	9696	COTON EN MASSE
29	CRUDE ANIMAL,VEG MAT NES		1929							MATIERES BRUTES ANIM,VEGET
3	MINERAL FUELS ETC		5149							COMBUSTIBLES MINERAUX LUB
33	PETROLEUM AND PRODUCTS		3612							PETROLE ET DERIVES
351	*ELECTRIC CURRENT	H 281827	1537	W 256182	728	H 245651	2237	H 195500	2414	ENERGIE ELECTRIQUE
5541	SOAPS			W 2597	1302	W 2452	1774	W 3907	2630	SAVONS,PROD TENSIO–ACTIFS
6	BASIC MANUFACTURES		689							ART MANUFACTURES
69	METAL MANUFACTURES NES		534							ART MANUFACT EN METAL NDA
6951	HAND TOOLS,AGRIC,FOREST		462		381		1015		2160	BECHES,PELLES,PIOCHES
7	MACHINES,TRANSPORT EQUIP		1512							MACHINES MATERIEL TRANSPORT
8	MISC MANUFACTURED GOODS		757							ART MANUFACTURES DIVERS
89	MISC MANUFCTRD GOODS NES		665							ART MANUFACTURES DIVERS
931	*SPECIAL TRANSACTIONS								56124	TRANS.SPECIALES
971	*GOLD,NON MONETARY NES	K 8	48	K 11	89	K 1	224	K 20	23197	OR NON MONETAIRE

1. HISTORICAL SERIES, 1992–1996 GENERAL TRADE, IMPORTS C.I.F., EXPORTS F.O.B. #1
SERIES HISTORIQUES, 1992–1996 COMMERCE GENERAL, IMPORTATIONS C.A.F., EXPORTATIONS F.O.B

YEAR ANNEE	VALUE IN MILLION U.S. DOLLARS / VALEUR EN MILLION U.S. DOLLARS — MERCHANDISE – MARCHANDISE: IMPORTS	MERCHANDISE – MARCHANDISE: EXPORTS	GOLD – OR: IMPORTS	GOLD – OR: EXPORTS	CONVERSION FACTORS FACTEURS DE CONVERSION CENTS E.U. PAR: IMPORTS	CONVERSION FACTORS: EXPORTS	INDEX NUMBERS – INDICES — QUANTUM: IMPORTS	QUANTUM: EXPORTS	UNIT VALUE / VALEUR UNITAIRE: IMPORTS	UNIT VALUE / VALEUR UNITAIRE: EXPORTS
1992	2219.00	3774.00								
1993	2651.00	3222.00								
1994	10748.00	10305.00								
1995	16052.30	13166.80								
1996	18639.10	14441.20								

2. IMPORTS BY BROAD ECONOMIC CATEGORY AND EXPORTS BY INDUSTRIAL ORIGIN. (PERCENTAGE OF TOTAL VALUE)
IMPORTATIONS PAR CATEGORIES ECONOMIQUES ET EXPORTATIONS PAR BRANCHE D'ACTIVITE.(EN POURCENTAGE DE LA VALEUR TOTALE)

IMPORTS – IMPORTATIONS

	1990	1991	1992	1993	1994	1995	1996
TOTAL IMPORTS–IMPORTATIONS TOTALES							
1 FOOD BEV–ALIMENTATION BOISSONS							
11 PRIMARY–PRODUITS DE BASE							
111 FOR INDUSTRY–POUR L'INDUSTRIE							
112 FOR HOUSEHOLDS–POUR LES MENAGES							
12 PROCESSED–PRODUITS ELABORES							
121 FOR INDUSTRY–POUR L'INDUSTRIE							
122 FOR HOUSEHOLDS–POUR LES MENAGES							
2 IND SUPPLIES–APPROV INDUSTRIELS							
21 PRIMARY–PRODUITS DE BASE							
22 PROCESSED–PRODUITS ELABORES							
3 FUELS–COMBUSTIBLES							
31 PRIMARY–PRODUITS DE BASE							
32 PROCESSED–PRODUITS ELABORES							
321 MOTOR SPIRIT–ESSENCE							
322 OTHER–AUTRES							
4 MACHINERY–EQUIPEMENT							
41 CAPITAL EQUIPMENT–MACHINES							
42 PARTS–PIECES ACCESSOIRES							
5 TRANSPORT–TRANSPORT							
51 PASSENGER CARS–AUTOMOBILES							
52 OTHER–AUTRES							
521 INDUSTRIAL–INDUSTRIELS							
522 NON INDUSTRIAL–NON INDUSTRIEL							
53 PARTS–PIECES ACCESSOIRES							
6 CONSUM GOODS–BIENS CONSOMMATION							
61 DURABLE–DURABLES							
62 SEMI DURABLE–SEMI DURABLES							
63 NON DURABLE–NON DURABLES							
7 GOODS NES–BIENS NDA							

EXPORTS – EXPORTATIONS

	1990	1991	1992	1993	1994	1995	1996
TOTAL EXPORTS–EXPORTATIONS TOTALES							
1 AGRICULTURE							
2 MINING QUARRY–INDUS EXTRACTIVES							
3 MANUFACTURING–IND MANUFACTUR							
31 FOOD BEV TOBACCO–ALIM BOISS TAB							
32 TEXTILES–INDUSTRIES TEXTILES							
33 WOOD & PRODUCTS–BOIS & PRODUITS							
34 PAPER & PRODUCTS–PAPIER & PRODT							
35 CHEMICALS–INDUSTRIES CHIMIQUES							
36 NON METAL MIN–MIN NON METAL							
37 BASIC METAL–IND METAL BASE							
38 METAL MANUF–MANUF METAL							
39 OTH MANUF IND–AUTRES MANUF							

3. TRADE BY PRINCIPAL COUNTRIES OF ORIGIN AND DESTINATION (VALUE IN THOUSAND U.S. DOLLARS)
ECHANGES SELON LES PRINCIPAUX PAYS D'ORIGINE ET DE DESTINATION (VALEUR EN MILLIERS DE DOLLARS EU)

COUNTRIES–PAYS	GENERAL IMPORTS C.I.F. # 1 IMPORTATIONS GENERALES C.A.F				
	1992	1993	1994	1995	1996
World	1953458	9533000	10748000	16052300	18639100
Africa	25509	78000	10000	99100	140800
Americas	120457	343700	243000	745600	916700
Northern America	105713	231000	243000	448500	608200
LAIA	8333	76700		159300	159600
CACM	91			16800	25100
Caribbean	3949	36000		117100	121200
Rest of America	2371			3900	2600
As.ex F.USSR	407824	210300	120000	539700	653300
Eur.x F.USSR	1398168	1786300	1775700	3795000	4358800
EU	716179	1099000	1160300	2314100	2814600
EFTA	22491	234000	78400	171900	144100
East Europe	588463	436000	521000	1236300	1333800
Other Europe	103			1000	6900
Former USSR		7099700	8002000	10233800	11391000
Oceania	1472	2000	13000	20000	24200
Russian Federation		4999000	6349000	8249100	8686100
Turkmenistan/Turkménistn		1339000	688000	680500	1604900
Germany/Allemagne	291501	462000	655000	958300	1155200
Belarus/Bélarus		288000	340000	526400	382400
USA/Etats–Unis d'Amer	100109	224000	220000	419300	562100
Poland/Pologne	101744	77000	123000	476700	505900
Italy/Italie	233864	96000	127000	271800	341600
Kazakhstan		82000	165000	323300	242700
Hungary/Hongrie	117091	115000	100000	169600	233900
France,Monac	44526	157000	65000	195900	244300
Austria/Autriche	53256	121000	99000	132600	169000
Bulgaria/Bulgarie	156380	93000	69000	128400	124800
Czech Republic		46000	128000	157100	206600
Lithuania/Lituanie		167000	68000	129500	155400
Switz.Liecht	13759	225000	33400	139200	94000
Netherlands/Pays–Bas	19629	88000	63000	149200	179300
Slovakia		68000	75000	152800	182100
United Kingdom	14941	53000	59000	142800	189100
China/Chine	92146	53000	33000	83700	89700
Republic of Moldova		33000	172000	61100	71700
Japan/Japon	41562	44000	30000	106900	114900
Brazil/Brésil	7145	74000		137500	111700
Romania/Roumanie	23243	37000	26000	151500	80400
Belgium–Luxembourg	12627	15000	21000	112700	135500
Korea, Republic of	194830	4000	5000	27500	47900
Latvia/Lettonie		31000	70000	81800	91600
Finland/Finlande	21554	22000	25000	88400	95700
Uzbekistan/Ouzbékistan		53000	55000	73400	61100
Turkey/Turquie	26322	12000	9000	67600	109500
India/Inde	13447	15000	24000	74300	93200
Guinea/Guinée	10806	69000		51900	71600
Cuba	1442	35000		44200	117100
Czechoslovakia	190005				
Azerbaijan		55700	41000	53200	30700
Greece/Grèce	6715	24000		84500	59900
Denmark/Danemark	8098	8000	17000	49000	67400
Sweden/Suède	1766	10000	1300	46900	66700
Spain/Espagne	7307	4000	6000	46500	58700
Ireland/Irlande	343	13000	22000	33900	49400
Norway,SVD,JM	8732	9000	17000	32600	49400
Estonia/Estonie		22000	27000	26600	38400
Canada	5604	7000	23000	29000	46100
Yugoslavia/Yougoslavie	70864		16000	1700	13300
Israel/Israël	1463	5000		39900	49600
Slovenia/Slovénia		6000		31300	34700
Anguilla		1000		63200	2500
Australia/Australie	1189	2000	13000	19300	23000
Singapore/Singapour	8314	14000		16200	19600
Cyprus/Chypre	273	28000		10400	8800
Indonesia/Indonésie	11			17600	27500

COUNTRIES–PAYS	GENERAL EXPORTS F.O.B. # 1 EXPORTATIONS GENERALES F.O.B.				
	1992	1993	1994	1995	1996
Monde	3173388	7817000	10305000	13166800	14441200
Afrique	63638	131500	58000	251600	211700
Amériques	58967	231000	395000	407000	594900
Amérique du Nord	31174	178000	393000	283100	381600
ALAI	17676	30000		55400	101100
MCAC	745	3000		100	800
Caraïbes	9004	3000	2000	61500	107400
Autre Amérique	368	17000		6900	4000
Asie l'URSS exclus	1273851	875900	870000	2363200	2573900
Europe l'URSS exclus	1771404	1805900	2075000	2777500	3191000
UE	649365	840000	948000	1408200	1593800
AELE	23750	297000	338000	76000	137500
Europe de l'Est	1016324	647000	773000	1254000	1405300
Autre de l'Europe	92	1000		6800	4400
Ancienne URSS		4701000	5924000	7187000	7623200
Océanie	3274	10000	10000	31800	18500
Russian Federation		3544800	4065000	5697900	5527700
China/Chine	723509	271000	506000	755400	769200
Belarus/Bélarus		350000	542000	545900	732700
Turkey/Turquie	295921	142000	116000	453000	410800
Germany/Allemagne	140639	172000	283000	338700	418700
Italy/Italie	133892	141000	200000	425700	345900
USA/Etats–Unis d'Amer	27843	164000	359000	273100	367400
Hungary/Hongrie	142765	181000	170000	298100	373800
Poland/Pologne	87875	123000	150000	274500	362500
Turkmenistan/Turkménistn		195000	222000	270200	271600
Republic of Moldova		76000	489000	151900	236400
Bulgaria/Bulgarie	340733	144000	130000	179200	138600
Switz.Liecht	19468	225000	326000	66700	126500
Slovakia		45000	125000	216400	231500
Austria/Autriche	41867	201000	171000	77300	101800
Romania/Roumanie	43347	74000	72000	167300	156700
Lithuania/Lituanie		62000	193000	127300	130400
Thailand/Thaïlande	7015	52000		124800	325200
Czech Republic		80000	126000	118100	142100
India/Inde	29681	65000	54000	231400	82000
Uzbekistan/Ouzbékistan		93000	73000	114100	176700
United Kingdom	24180	36000	77000	176000	134600
Netherlands/Pays–Bas	57033	121000	36000	113300	100000
Kazakhstan		114000	119000	94400	89700
Czechoslovakia	401477				
Azerbaijan		185200	79000	41500	88600
Egypt/Egypte	19087	69000	58000	106300	96900
Lebanon/Liban	16272	6000		141600	154400
Syrian Arab Republic	990	4000	17000	83800	196000
Japan/Japon	93596	19000	26000	65600	81300
France,Monac	50174	30000	37000	45200	112800
Belgium–Luxembourg	52244	21000	46000	72900	79500
Latvia/Lettonie		33000	94000	63900	78400
Greece/Grèce	69506	41000		39700	96900
Korea, Republic of	6536	28000	67000	79300	59500
Georgia/Géorgie		14000	9000	18000	185000
Cyprus/Chypre	5745	118000		35000	39500
Ireland/Irlande	478	51000	64000	9300	64400
Spain/Espagne	6978	12000	18000	64100	84000
Philippines	5821	12900		86000	55100
Iran (Islamic Rp. of)	1240	7000		34900	116200
Israel/Israël	3313	8000		59900	65400
British Virgin Islds				36800	92300
Yugoslavia/Yougoslavie	81873		16000	800	25500
Estonia/Estonie		11000	19000	36000	53500
Norway,SVD,JM	4282	72000	12000	4200	10700
Indonesia/Indonésie	3108	3000		40600	49200
Finland/Finlande	36436	10000	3000	22900	22000
Hong Kong	6276	54000		22500	7700
Viet Nam	9928	5000	17000	27800	28800

(VALUE AS PERCENTAGE OF WORLD TOTAL)(VALEURS EN POURCENTAGE DU TOTAL MONDIAL)

	1987	1988	1989	1990	1991	1992	1993	1994	1995	1996
Africa						1.3	0.8	0.1	0.6	0.8
Americas						6.2	3.6	2.3	4.6	4.9
Northern America						5.4	2.4	2.3	2.8	3.3
LAIA						0.4	0.8		1.0	0.9
CACM						0.0			0.1	0.1
Caribbean						0.2	0.4		0.7	0.7
Rest of America						0.1			0.0	0.0
As.ex F.USSR						20.9	2.2	1.1	3.4	3.5
Eur.x F.USSR						71.6	18.7	16.5	23.6	23.4
EU						36.7	11.5	10.8	14.4	15.1
EFTA						1.2	2.5	0.7	1.1	0.8
East Europe						30.1	4.6	4.8	7.7	7.2
Other Europe						0.0			0.0	0.0
Former USSR							74.5	74.5	63.8	61.1
Oceania						0.1	0.0	0.1	0.1	0.1
Russian Federation							52.4	59.1	51.4	46.6
Turkmenistan/Turkménistn							14.0	6.4	4.2	8.6
Germany/Allemagne						14.9	4.8	6.1	6.0	6.2
Belarus/Bélarus							3.0	3.2	3.3	2.1
USA/Etats–Unis d'Amer						5.1	2.3	2.0	2.6	3.0
Poland/Pologne						5.2	0.8	1.1	3.0	2.7
Italy/Italie						12.0	1.0	1.2	1.7	1.8
Kazakhstan							0.9	1.5	2.0	1.3
Hungary/Hongrie						6.0	1.2	0.9	1.1	1.3
France,Monac						2.3	1.6	0.6	1.2	1.3

	1987	1988	1989	1990	1991	1992	1993	1994	1995	1996
Afrique						2.0	1.7	0.6	1.9	1.5
Amériques						1.9	3.0	3.8	3.1	4.1
Amérique du Nord						1.0	2.3	3.8	2.2	2.6
ALAI						0.6	0.4		0.4	0.7
MCAC						0.0	0.0		0.0	0.0
Caraïbes						0.3	0.0	0.0	0.5	0.7
Autre Amérique						0.0	0.2		0.1	0.0
Asie l'URSS exclus						40.1	11.2	8.4	17.9	17.8
Europe l'URSS exclus						55.8	23.1	20.1	21.1	22.1
UE						20.5	10.7	9.2	10.7	11.0
AELE						0.7	3.8	3.3	0.6	1.0
Europe de l'Est						32.0	8.3	7.5	9.5	9.7
Autre de l'Europe						0.0	0.0		0.1	0.0
Ancienne URSS							60.1	57.5	54.6	52.8
Océanie						0.1	0.1	0.1	0.2	0.1
Russian Federation							45.3	39.4	43.3	38.3
China/Chine						22.8	3.5	4.9	5.7	5.3
Belarus/Bélarus							4.5	5.3	4.1	5.1
Turkey/Turquie						9.3	1.8	1.1	3.4	2.8
Germany/Allemagne						4.4	2.2	2.7	2.6	2.9
Italy/Italie						4.2	1.8	1.9	3.2	2.4
USA/Etats–Unis d'Amer						0.9	2.1	3.5	2.1	2.5
Hungary/Hongrie						4.5	2.3	1.6	2.3	2.6
Poland/Pologne						2.8	1.6	1.5	2.1	2.5
Turkmenistan/Turkménistn							2.5	2.2	2.1	1.9

4. General Imports C.I.F. by Commodities according to the S.I.T.C. (Rev. 2) in thousand U.S. Dollars
Importations Générales C.A.F. par Produits d'après la C.T.C.I. (Rév. 2) en milliers de Dollars E.U.

SITC CTCI	COMMODITY	1992		1993		1994		1995		PRODUIT
		WEIGHT POIDS	VALUE VALEUR	WEIGHT POIDS	VALUE VALEUR	WEIGHT POIDS	VALUE VALEUR	WEIGHT POIDS	VALUE VALEUR	
	ALL COMMODITIES						10748000		16052300	TOUS PRODUITS

5. General Exports F.O.B. by Commodities according to the S.I.T.C. (Rev. 2) in thousand U.S. Dollars
Exportations Générales F.O.B. par Produits d'après la C.T.C.I. (Rév. 2) en milliers de Dollars E.U.

SITC CTCI	COMMODITY	1992		1993		1994		1995		PRODUIT
		WEIGHT POIDS	VALUE VALEUR	WEIGHT POIDS	VALUE VALEUR	WEIGHT POIDS	VALUE VALEUR	WEIGHT POIDS	VALUE VALEUR	
	ALL COMMODITIES						10305000		13166800	TOUS PRODUITS

FOOT NOTES – NOTES

TABLE 1 –
1 Excludes trade with the Commonwealth of Independent States in 1992.
TABLE 3 –
1 Excludes trade with the Commonwealth of Independent States in 1992.
TABLEAU 1 –
1 En 1992 le commerce avec la confédération des états indépendants est exclu.
TABLEAU 3 –
1 En 1992 le commerce avec la confédération des états indépendants est exclu.

1. HISTORICAL SERIES, 1969–1993 GENERAL TRADE, IMPORTS C.I.F., EXPORTS F.O.B.
SERIES HISTORIQUES, 1969–1993 COMMERCE GENERAL, IMPORTATIONS C.A.F., EXPORTATIONS F.O.B

YEAR ANNEE	VALUE IN MILLION U.A.E. DIRHAMS / VALEUR EN MILLION U.A.E. DIRHAMS — MERCHANDISE # 1 –MARCHANDISE		GOLD –OR		CONVERSION FACTORS U.S. CENTS PER U.A.E. DIRHAM FACTEURS DE CONVERSION CENTS E.U. PAR U.A.E. DIRHAM		INDEX NUMBERS –INDICES — QUANTUM		UNIT VALUE VALEUR UNITAIRE	
	IMPORTS	EXPORTS	IMPORTS	EXPORTS	IMPORTS	EXPORTS	IMPORTS	EXPORTS	IMPORTS	EXPORTS
1969	1461.90	2038.10			21.0000	21.0000				
1970	1272.40	2619.10			21.0000	21.0000				
1971	1469.30	4623.80			21.0000	21.0000				
1972	2113.10	4745.60			22.8000	22.8000				
1973	3278.90	7175.00			25.1105	25.1011				
1974	6750.00	25305.00			25.2580	25.2580				
1975	10571.00	27609.00			25.2440	25.2440				
1976	13150.00	34328.00			25.2970	25.2970				
1977	19703.00	37890.00			25.6193	25.6193				
1978	20765.00	35433.00			25.8530	25.8360				
1979	26527.00	51807.00			26.2392	26.2424				
1980	32425.00	76627.00			26.9920	26.9854				
1981	35410.00	74302.00			27.2400	27.2400				
1982	34577.00	63350.00			27.2400	27.2400				
1983	30676.00	53582.00			27.2400	27.2400				
1984	25856.00	50743.00			27.2400	27.2400				
1985	24931.00	48180.00			27.2400	27.2400				
1986	23575.01	58138.99			27.2401	27.2405				
1987	26526.00	37962.00			27.2400	27.2405				
1988	31282.00	10219.74			27.2400	27.2405				
1989	36746.00	57703.00			27.2400	27.2405				
1990	41111.01	14482.39			27.2400	27.2405				
1991	50462.00				27.2400					
1992	63912.00				27.2400					
1993	71659.01	13818.65			27.2403	27.2404				

2. IMPORTS BY BROAD ECONOMIC CATEGORY AND EXPORTS BY INDUSTRIAL ORIGIN. (PERCENTAGE OF TOTAL VALUE)
IMPORTATIONS PAR CATEGORIES ECONOMIQUES ET EXPORTATIONS PAR BRANCHE D'ACTIVITE.(EN POURCENTAGE DE LA VALEUR TOTALE)

IMPORTS – IMPORTATIONS

	1990	1991	1992	1993	1994	1995	1996
TOTAL IMPORTS–IMPORTATIONS TOTALES	100.	100.	100.	100.			
1 FOOD BEV–ALIMENTATION BOISSONS	13.5	10.2	9.8	9.3			
11 PRIMARY–PRODUITS DE BASE	7.2	5.6	6.0	5.8			
111 FOR INDUSTRY–POUR L'INDUSTRIE	0.9	1.4	2.4	1.9			
112 FOR HOUSEHOLDS–POUR LES MENAGES	6.3	4.2	3.6	3.9			
12 PROCESSED–PRODUITS ELABORES	6.2	4.5	3.8	3.5			
121 FOR INDUSTRY–POUR L'INDUSTRIE	1.5	0.3	0.2	0.4			
122 FOR HOUSEHOLDS–POUR LES MENAGES	4.7	4.2	3.6	3.1			
2 IND SUPPLIES–APPROV INDUSTRIELS	29.7	29.3	28.1	30.8			
21 PRIMARY–PRODUITS DE BASE	1.9	0.9	0.9	1.3			
22 PROCESSED–PRODUITS ELABORES	27.8	28.5	27.2	29.5			
3 FUELS–COMBUSTIBLES	3.2	1.8	1.2	1.5			
31 PRIMARY–PRODUITS DE BASE	0.0	0.0	0.0	0.0			
32 PROCESSED–PRODUITS ELABORES	3.2	1.8	1.2	1.4			
321 MOTOR SPIRIT–ESSENCE		0.0	0.1	0.1			
322 OTHER–AUTRES	3.2	1.8	1.2	1.3			
4 MACHINERY–EQUIPEMENT	16.8	14.8	16.1	15.1			
41 CAPITAL EQUIPMENT–MACHINES	16.8	13.1	14.2	12.9			
42 PARTS–PIECES ACCESSOIRES		1.6	1.9	2.2			
5 TRANSPORT–TRANSPORT	14.1	12.6	15.3	13.3			
51 PASSENGER CARS–AUTOMOBILES		4.6	5.4	4.7			
52 OTHER–AUTRES	2.4	2.6	4.7	3.8			
521 INDUSTRIAL–INDUSTRIELS	2.4	2.5	4.5	3.6			
522 NON INDUSTRIAL–NON INDUSTRIEL		0.2	0.2	0.2			
53 PARTS–PIECES ACCESSOIRES	11.7	5.3	5.1	4.8			
6 CONSUM GOODS–BIENS CONSOMMATION	22.1	31.3	29.3	30.0			
61 DURABLE–DURABLES	8.5	13.8	12.4	12.7			
62 SEMI DURABLE–SEMI DURABLES	10.7	13.7	13.4	13.8			
63 NON DURABLE–NON DURABLES	2.9	3.7	3.6	3.5			
7 GOODS NES–BIENS NDA	0.6	0.1	0.1	0.0			

EXPORTS – EXPORTATIONS

	1990	1991	1992	1993	1994	1995	1996
TOTAL EXPORTS–EXPORTATIONS TOTALES	100.	100.	100.	100.			
1 AGRICULTURE	9.7	1.3	2.4	0.4			
2 MINING QUARRY–INDUS EXTRACTIVES	0.9	0.3	0.4	0.1			
3 MANUFACTURING–IND MANUFACTUR	89.4	98.4	97.2	25.1			
31 FOOD BEV TOBACCO–ALIM BOISS TAB	8.6	5.5	5.8	1.7			
32 TEXTILES–INDUSTRIES TEXTILES	19.4	16.9	22.4	6.3			
33 WOOD & PRODUCTS–BOIS & PRODUITS	1.0	0.7	0.4	0.0			
34 PAPER & PRODUCTS–PAPIER & PRODT	1.2	1.7	1.6	0.4			
35 CHEMICALS–INDUSTRIES CHIMIQUES	9.4	8.6	11.8	3.0			
36 NON METAL MIN–MIN NON METAL	2.0	1.5	1.5	0.4			
37 BASIC METAL–IND METAL BASE	12.0	50.0	38.3	8.3			
38 METAL MANUF–MANUF METAL	27.7	12.2	14.3	4.7			
39 OTH MANUF IND–AUTRES MANUF	8.1	1.3	1.2	0.3			

3. TRADE BY PRINCIPAL COUNTRIES OF ORIGIN AND DESTINATION (VALUE IN THOUSAND U.S. DOLLARS)
ECHANGES SELON LES PRINCIPAUX PAYS D'ORIGINE ET DE DESTINATION (VALEUR EN MILLIERS DE DOLLARS EU)

COUNTRIES–PAYS	GENERAL IMPORTS C.I.F. IMPORTATIONS GENERALES C.A.F				
	1989	1990	1991	1992	1993
World	9390477	11580189	10381330	12951896	13764825
Africa	44347	82532	59045	58804	109777
Americas	1014142	1215005	1059274	1181248	1234262
Northern America	913995	1083851	964467	1072444	1114179
LAIA	91803	122192	85872	99658	111301
CACM	7613	7798	7980	8120	7818
Caribbean	511	1134	908	994	919
Rest of America	221	30	47	31	45
As.ex F.USSR	4874903	5871230	5978845	7092659	7988658
Eur.x F.USSR	3179790	4101229	2974382	4233271	4071382
EU	2921280	3744998	2680252	3905673	3749441
EFTA	133781	218374	215524	226879	215294
East Europe	83281	88435	50937	72201	90124
Other Europe	41448	49421	27668	3995	3310
Former USSR	3228	16991	6046	5813	21910
Oceania	260035	259841	267176	322308	253962
Japan/Japon	1369315	1639872	1724128	1976968	1922364
USA/Etats–Unis d'Amer	883353	1050330	928830	1027875	1073367
United Kingdom	858006	1146297	724860	926671	980728
China/Chine	385073	571831	818242	1042571	1187073
Germany/Allemagne	674786	869247	588383	962817	861214
Korea, Republic of	486971	504776	618136	769027	899140
India/Inde	356897	489603	573667	745631	958283
Italy/Italie	431408	521176	370737	535466	605188
France, Monac	318927	410781	369170	684790	506999
Thailand/Thaïlande	301121	314079	331038	369982	389987
Australia/Australie	237197	237384	242007	291626	230060
Malaysia/Malaisie	131560	184707	237528	288638	372549
Singapore/Singapour	211491	215050	209501	220022	275637
Indonesia/Indonésie	121278	143324	240697	282182	343183
Netherlands/Pays–Bas	211702	256932	189876	240175	215387
Saudi Arabia	288175	415107	101629	141250	162720
Iran (Islamic Rp. of)	139961	169073	196007	201949	213906
Switz.Liecht	111005	183374	193781	204797	193863
Pakistan	125634	139684	131960	193563	208496
Hong Kong	156852	119543	121438	146208	170697
Belgium–Luxembourg	101320	149459	119006	154577	164210
Bahrain/Bahreïn	95284	132723	103051	65971	98705
Spain/Espagne	84504	95334	85815	99033	104340
Turkey/Turquie	102827	90654	48049	69513	88508
Sweden/Suède	66019	83797	73684	80417	92502
Denmark/Danemark	65293	75565	63449	64023	70957
Brazil/Brésil	57434	75090	49313	60999	71937
Austria/Autriche	42133	55445	23661	78230	58215
Qatar	96080	129351	7873	4020	8097
Canada	30635	33513	35637	44570	40709
Lebanon/Liban	51413	53605	13528	21304	29170
Ireland/Irlande	20553	29622	30849	37113	39067
Jordan/Jordanie	54142	69254	11753	11599	10330
Sri Lanka	3887	30113	38111	28842	54953
Poland/Pologne	17589	20223	17075	28489	42355
New Zealand	22531	22430	25114	30572	23856
Norway,SVD,JM	22775	34995	21653	22013	21416
Kuwait/ Koweït	41606	38796	3655	10097	28140
Fm Yugoslav	39224	45752	25356		
Chile/Chili	20184	33832	18582	14639	20178
Greece/Grèce	23620	23627	21682	19984	18186
Finland/Finlande	18945	20098	11424	12805	24204
Egypt/Egypte	14230	21217	11780	16198	19212
Philippines	7445	27569	11002	14758	20988
Hungary/Hongrie	14876	21274	12303	16764	16027
Somalia/Somalie	13608	24535	19671	12371	7695
So. Africa Customs Un	1201	12226	2015	11347	49018
Romania/Roumanie	26457	11844	7695	11673	16606
Syrian Arab Republic	19370	25541	2301	4513	7946
Czechoslovakia	16323	14055	12442	11836	

COUNTRIES–PAYS	GENERAL EXPORTS F.O.B. # 1 EXPORTATIONS GENERALES F.O.B.				
	1989	1990	1991	1992	1993
Monde	753981	3945076	758656	899341	3764200
Afrique	11862		21272	9084	243062
Amériques	60150		27986	48548	108619
Amérique du Nord	60084		27985	48483	104496
ALAI	66		1	1	3575
MCAC					56
Caraïbes				61	349
Autre Amérique				2	142
Asie l'URSS exclus	609128		575614	610118	2873754
Europe l'URSS exclus	71855		133422	229639	492920
UE	70696		123567	226754	423971
AELE	788		9162	2145	20169
Europe de l'Est	15		603	664	44079
Autre de l'Europe	356		89	24	2913
Ancienne URSS				63	20838
Océanie	442		362	1888	3214
Iran (Islamic Rp. of)	3267		9192	9893	918337
Japan/Japon	211300		244253	148704	140969
Saudi Arabia	114152		19112	35048	215007
Kuwait/ Koweït	31777		19952	36459	266929
Oman	52072		70466	72927	73507
Bahrain/Bahreïn	24308		34735	43262	147363
USA/Etats–Unis d'Amer	55028		26075	45699	101139
Germany/Allemagne	6478		45688	54262	112582
Qatar	58232		10499	8323	137403
United Kingdom	8617		27975	89924	87646
Hong Kong	3350		6108	13245	176562
India/Inde	20614		12378	22099	143830
Yemen/Yémen			20191	35510	129660
Pakistan	11348		15178	14881	140169
Netherlands/Pays–Bas	21916		9232	35496	108605
Korea, Republic of	8388		35255	42411	56681
Singapore/Singapour	1564		5226	12172	99772
Thailand/Thaïlande	7657		21964	19215	38864
France, Monac	8187		22926	20276	26197
Belgium–Luxembourg	2542		4243	10966	38803
Nigeria/Nigéria			15	7	50862
Italy/Italie	6277		9464	9617	16814
Somalia/Somalie	1072		330	1244	38505
Poland/Pologne			330	102	33250
Switz.Liecht	257		8459	1759	18509
Un. Rep. of Tanzania	638		884	1486	24812
Indonesia/Indonésie	2326		3635	5916	12384
Afghanistan	29		5	52	23953
Kenya	2026		646	1219	19773
Mozambique				25	23157
Sri Lanka	405		913	5532	14543
China/Chine	931		2451	7102	10446
Congo			17655	38	707
Egypt/Egypte	349		582	1023	15783
Lebanon/Liban	1798		203	383	14604
Russian Federation				63	15996
Jordan/Jordanie	2848		2372	283	8617
Libyan Arab Jamahiriya	1572		79	593	11397
Turkey/Turquie	3623		851	223	8690
Canada	5056		1911	2784	3357
Austria/Autriche	94		449	905	11521
Spain/Espagne	1635		951	1650	7543
Syrian Arab Republic	6871		510	509	3157
Cyprus/Chypre	184		561	886	9188
Bangladesh	129		231	2063	7534
Djibouti	139		84	300	8732
Sweden/Suède	4341		753	239	3922
Portugal	7596		319	427	707
Philippines	886		1010	1934	4174
So. Africa Customs Un				66	7886

(VALUE AS PERCENTAGE OF WORLD TOTAL) (VALEURS EN POURCENTAGE DU TOTAL MONDIAL)

	1984	1985	1986	1987	1988	1989	1990	1991	1992	1993
Africa	0.7	0.7	0.5	0.4	0.8	0.5	0.7	0.6	0.5	0.8
Americas	10.9	11.6	7.1	9.4	11.1	10.8	10.5	10.2	9.1	9.0
Northern America	9.7	10.5	6.3	8.5	9.7	9.7	9.4	9.3	8.3	8.1
LAIA	1.1	1.1	0.8	0.9	1.2	1.0	1.1	0.8	0.8	0.8
CACM	0.0	0.1	0.1	0.1	0.1	0.1	0.1	0.1	0.1	0.1
Caribbean	0.0	0.0	0.0	0.0	0.0	0.0	0.0	0.0	0.0	0.0
Rest of America	0.0	0.0	0.0	0.0	0.0	0.0	0.0	0.0	0.0	0.0
As.ex F.USSR	41.7	45.5	40.0	44.4	50.9	51.9	50.7	57.6	54.8	58.0
Eur.x F.USSR	35.2	35.5	29.6	41.8	34.7	33.9	35.4	28.7	32.7	29.6
EU	33.0	33.5	27.7	38.9	32.2	31.1	32.3	25.8	30.2	27.2
EFTA	1.2	1.4	1.4	2.1	1.4	1.4	1.9	2.1	1.8	1.6
East Europe	0.7	0.4	0.3	0.5	0.8	0.9	0.8	0.5	0.6	0.7
Other Europe	0.3	0.2	0.1	0.2	0.4	0.4	0.4	0.3	0.0	0.0
Former USSR	0.0	0.0	0.0	0.0	0.1	0.0	0.1	0.1	0.0	0.2
Oceania	2.5	2.8	3.3	2.3	2.5	2.8	2.2	2.6	2.5	1.8
Japan/Japon	17.4	19.1	15.6	17.1	16.4	14.6	14.2	16.6	15.3	14.0
USA/Etats–Unis d'Amer	9.5	10.2	6.2	8.2	9.4	9.4	9.1	8.9	7.9	7.8
United Kingdom	8.7	10.1	8.5	11.0	9.6	9.1	9.9	7.0	7.2	7.1
China/Chine	1.4	1.7	1.6	1.3	3.2	4.1	4.9	7.9	8.0	8.6
Germany/Allemagne	6.1	6.8	6.5	9.5	7.1	7.2	7.5	5.7	7.4	6.3
Korea, Republic of	1.8	2.1	2.7	4.4	5.0	5.2	4.4	6.0	5.9	6.5
India/Inde	2.7	3.4	2.8	3.3	3.7	3.8	4.2	5.5	5.8	7.0
Italy/Italie	6.5	4.7	2.5	5.0	4.5	4.6	4.5	3.6	4.1	4.4
France, Monac	4.3	3.9	4.2	5.3	3.4	3.4	3.5	3.6	5.3	3.7
Thailand/Thaïlande	0.9	1.3	1.4	2.9	2.3	3.2	2.7	3.2	2.9	2.8

	1984	1985	1986	1987	1988	1989	1990	1991	1992	1993
Afrique						1.6		2.8	1.0	6.5
Amériques						8.0		3.7	5.4	2.9
Amérique du Nord						8.0		3.7	5.4	2.8
ALAI						0.0		0.0	0.0	0.1
MCAC										0.0
Caraïbes									0.0	0.0
Autre Amérique									0.0	0.0
Asie l'URSS exclus						80.8		75.9	67.8	76.3
Europe l'URSS exclus						9.5		17.6	25.5	13.1
UE						9.4		16.3	25.2	11.3
AELE						0.1		1.2	0.2	0.5
Europe de l'Est						0.0		0.1	0.1	1.2
Autre de l'Europe						0.0		0.0	0.0	0.1
Ancienne URSS									0.0	0.6
Océanie						0.1		0.0	0.2	0.1
Iran (Islamic Rp. of)						0.4		1.2	1.1	24.4
Japan/Japon						28.0		32.2	16.5	3.7
Saudi Arabia						15.1		2.5	3.9	5.7
Kuwait/ Koweït						4.2		2.6	4.1	7.1
Oman						6.9		9.3	8.1	2.0
Bahrain/Bahreïn						3.2		4.6	4.8	3.9
USA/Etats–Unis d'Amer						7.3		3.4	5.1	2.7
Germany/Allemagne						0.9		6.0	6.0	3.0
Qatar						7.7		1.4	0.9	3.7
United Kingdom						1.1		3.7	10.0	2.3

4. General Imports C.I.F. by Commodities according to the S.I.T.C. (Rev. 2) in thousand U.S. Dollars
Importations Générales C.A.F. par Produits d'après la C.T.C.I. (Rév. 2) en milliers de Dollars E.U.

SITC CTCI	COMMODITY	1990 WEIGHT POIDS	1990 VALUE VALEUR	1991 WEIGHT POIDS	1991 VALUE VALEUR	1992 WEIGHT POIDS	1992 VALUE VALEUR	1993 WEIGHT POIDS	1993 VALUE VALEUR	PRODUIT
	ALL COMMODITIES # 1		11580189		10381330		12951896		13764825	TOUS PRODUITS
0	FOOD AND LIVE ANIMALS		1506354		996419		1213873		1204798	ALIMENTS,ANIMAUX VIVANTS
001	*LIVE ANIMALS FOR FOOD	W 51145	62963	W 32709	44082	W 26294	38416	W 26835	35234	ANIMAUX VIVANTS
0012	SHEEP AND GOATS,LIVE			W 31451	38064	W 24397	28364	W 25037	29527	ESPECES OVINE ET CAPRINE
01	MEAT AND PREPARATIONS		196463		118433		127572		138304	VIANDES ET PREPARATIONS
011	MEAT FRESH,CHILLD,FROZEN	W 113587	185403	W 57877	105723	W 63895	117087	W 72834	125422	VIANDES FRAICHES,REF,CONGE
0112	MUTTON ETC FRSH,CHLD,FRN			W 16554	38108	W 19958	49123	W 20981	50648	VIANDE DE MOUTON
0114	POULTRY FRESH CHLLD,FRZN			W 29947	42470	W 34643	45401	W 38671	47145	VOLAILLES MORTES
02	DAIRY PRODCTS,BIRDS'EGGS		160857		115845		113582		121405	PRODUITS LAITIERS,OEUFS
022	MILK AND CREAM	W 58839	102673	W 33889	60190	W 32134	59444	W 35877	65026	LAIT ET CREME
0224	MILK,CREAM PRESERVED ETC			W 30891	54409	W 29330	53820	W 31794	55638	LAIT,CREME CONS,CONC
04	CEREALS AND PREPARATIONS		212872		133852		316289		251915	CEREALES ET PRODUITS
041	WHEAT ETC UNMILLED	W 106892	20686	W 45	17	W 648987	95641	W 183270	27085	FROMENT,EPEAUTRE
0411	DURUM WHEAT UNMILLED			W 45	17	W 648987	95641	W 183270	27085	FROMENT DUR NON MOULU
042	RICE	W 309182	132420	W 214203	88857	W 328041	135113	W 471964	169009	RIZ
0421	RICE IN HUSK OR HUSKED							W 471964	169009	RIZ SANS AUTRE PREPARATION
048	CEREAL ETC PREPARATIONS	W 23028	41385	W 22305	38510	W 18661	36792	W 18729	35032	PREPTNS A BASE CEREALES
05	VEGETABLES AND FRUIT		466140		264664		285623		313914	LEGUMES ET FRUITS
054	VEG ETC FRSH,SMPLY PRSVD	W 374419	151815	W 216036	77555	W 263470	86797	W 287773	93921	LEGUMES FRAIS,CONG,SECS
0545	OTHER FRESH VEGETABLES			W 158691	47203	W 187036	48785	W 191297	48252	AUTRES LEGUMES FRAIS,REF
057	FRUIT,NUTS,FRESH,DRIED	W 549659	267219	W 341340	141126	W 346780	146387	W 405251	188283	FRUITS FRAIS OU SECS
0577	NUTS EDIBLE,FRESH,DRIED			W 28713	61854	W 31014	63043	W 33594	80952	FRUITS A COQUES
05779	NUTS EDIBLE,FRSH,DRY,NES			W 13788	37825	W 12516	36997	W 17479	55886	FRUITS A COQUES NDA
0579	FRUIT FRESH OR DRIED NES			W 212586	52312	W 211835	54857	W 243141	69413	FRUITS FRAIS,SECS NDA
06	SUGAR AND PREPS,HONEY		161033		114310		127876		82552	SUCRES ET PRODUITS
061	SUGAR AND HONEY	W 314013	139639	W 224389	86476	W 274757	93996	W 171557	57493	SUCRES ET MIEL
0612	REFINED SUGAR ETC			W 216544	80989	W 268954	89782	W 164206	52760	SUCRES RAFFINES
07	COFFEE,TEA,COCOA,SPICES		129237		133633		130322		161667	CAFE,THE,CACAO,EPICES
074	TEA AND MATE	W 17831	49544	W 19980	52441	W 12903	33038	W 33096	73405	THE ET MATE
0741	TEA			W 19975	52432	W 12784	32814	W 33053	73344	THE
075	SPICES	W 54513	47724	W 50233	46473	W 59789	60796	W 55058	55341	EPICES
0752	SPICES,EX PEPPER,PIMENTO			W 45790	42341	W 56799	57578	W 51208	51467	AUTRES EPICES
081	*FEEDING STUFF FOR ANIML	W 178004	41757	W 49999	10316	W 55471	11256	W 43322	10848	NOURRITURE POUR ANIMAUX
09	MISC EDIBLE PRODUCTS		60515		43171		46866		68841	PREP ALIMENTAIRES DIVERSES
098	EDIBLE PRODCTS,PREPS NES	W 26605	56394	W 18357	37822	W 20959	43526	W 45212	62547	PREP ALIMENTAIRES NDA
1	BEVERAGES AND TOBACCO		121894		94443		114220		113935	BOISSONS ET TABACS
11	BEVERAGES		59306		50883		66958		68568	BOISSONS
112	ALCOHOLIC BEVERAGES	W 36118	51413	W 34925	48990	W 41626	63112	W 44960	64489	BOISSONS ALCOOLIQUES
12	TOBACCO AND MANUFACTURES		62588		43560		47262		45367	TABACS BRUTS FABRIQUES
122	TOBACCO,MANUFACTURED	W 7379	62272	W 5173	43508	W 5862	47072	W 6217	45025	TABACS FABRIQUES
1222	CIGARETTES			W 4002	40073	W 4344	42421	W 3968	37189	CIGARETTES
2	CRUDE MATERLS,EXCL FUELS		261614		258991		227795		315530	MAT BRUTES NON COMESTIBLES
24	CORK AND WOOD		63164		57071		72332		86365	LIEGE ET BOIS
248	WOOD SHAPED,SLEEPERS	W 172283	61471	W 143972	54724	W 163972	66328	W 189243	81800	BOIS SIMPLEMENT TRAVAILLES
2482	LUMBER SHAPED CONIFER			W 121	175	W 381	359	W 189243	81800	CONIFERES SCIES,RABOTES
24821	LUMBER SAWN ETC CONIFER							W 188916	81364	CONIFERES SCIES LONGITUD
2483	LUMBER SHAPED NON–CONIFR			W 143851	54548	W 163590	65969			NON CONIFERES SCIES,RABOTES
24831	LUMBER SAWN ETC NON–CON			W 143851	54548	W 163590	65969			SCIES LONGITUDINALEMENT
28	METALLIFEROUS ORES,SCRAP		124002		141036		88585		158648	MINERAIS METAL,DECHETS
287	BASE METAL ORES,CONC NES	W 367452	104447	W 560998	135011	W 458669	78851	W 511070	92620	MINERAIS METAUX COMMUNS
2873	ALUMINIUM ORES,ALUMINA			W 560382	132962	W 458132	77342	W 510787	92070	MINERAIS D'ALUMINIUM
28732	ALUMINA(ALUMINIUM OXIDE)			W 512774	132039	W 419032	76490	W 484801	91739	ALUMINE (OXYDE ALUMINIUM)
289	PREC MTAL ORES,WASTE NES							K 5	54849	MINERAIS,DECHETS MET PREC
28902	PREC METAL SCRAP, WASTE							K 5	54849	CENDRES D'ORFEVRERIE
3	MINERAL FUELS ETC		366927		249043		216862		225890	COMBUSTIBLES MINERAUX LUB
33	PETROLEUM AND PRODUCTS		365625		248485		216346		224998	PETROLE ET DERIVES
334	PETROLEUM PRODUCTS,REFIN	W 1633213	332907	W 1282952	187377	W 888052	158627	W 927280	198419	PRODUITS RAFFINES
3342	KEROSENE,OTH MEDIUM OILS			W 196104	52816	W 384754	86286	W 404360	88242	PETR LAMPANTS,AUT HUIL
33421	KEROSENE INCL JET FUEL			W 196104	52816	W 384754	86286	W 404360	88242	PETROLES LAMPANTS
3343	GAS OILS			W 194029	42627	W 117439	21813	W 183769	34054	GAS OILS
3344	FUEL OILS,NES			W 876355	79417	W 331122	27780	W 157649	12731	FUEL OILS
3345	LUBS,PETROLEUM OILS NES			W 15600	12116	W 13849	11431	W 108516	46117	HUILES LUBRIFIANTES
33451	LUBS(HIGH PETR CONT) ETC			W 15345	11252	W 13244	10266	W 108051	44886	HUILES LUBRIF,H LOURDES
335	RESIDUAL PETRLM PROD NES	W 172964	32718	W 231950	61108	W 220479	57719	W 176330	26579	PRODUITS RESIDUELS NDA
4	ANIMAL,VEGETABLE OIL,FAT		35878		38695		32785		38424	HUILES,GRAISSES ANIM,VEG
42	FIXED VEGETABLE OIL,FAT		35065		36513		31221		35541	HUILES VEGETALES FIXES
5	CHEMCLS,RELATED PROD NES		832295		602095		712927		726616	PRODUITS CHIMIQUES
51	ORGANIC CHEMICALS		26940		27074		38420		42372	PROD CHIMIQ ORGANIQUES
52	INORGANIC CHEMICALS		45388		37981		42059		43083	PROD CHIM INORGANIQUES
53	DYES,TANNING,COLOUR PROD		48057		40861		45432		42357	PROD TEINTURE,COLORANTS
533	PIGMENTS,PAINTS,ETC	W 19383	44824	W 14988	36587	W 15574	39646	W 15487	36198	PIGMENTS,PEINTURES,VERNIS
541	*MEDICINAL,PHARM PRODUCT	K 6897910	97646	K 5067644	99349	K 4963288	120879	K 5074757	105213	PROD MEDICINAUX PHARMACEUT
5417	MEDICAMENTS			K 4376965	92763	K 4129020	109968	K 4423448	94013	MEDICAMENTS
54171	— CONTAINNG ANTIBIOTICS							K 4423448	94013	MED CONTN ANTIBIOTIQUES
55	PERFUME,CLEANING ETC PRD		196960		160437		207071		232255	PROD POUR PARFUM,TOILETTE
553	PERFUMERY,COSMETICS,ETC	W 20091	144053	W 16692	121532	W 21528	165071	W 24407	178143	PRODUITS DE PARFUMERIE
554	SOAP,CLEANSING ETC PREPS	W 29651	44984	W 18427	27590	W 19622	29223	W 30020	38364	SAVONS,PRODUITS DETERSIFS
58	PLASTIC MATERIALS ETC		250560		141989		147399		145972	MAT PLAST ARTIFICIELLES
582	PROD OF CONDENSATION ETC	W 141674	175863	W 30983	41517	W 32330	43171	W 33514	44968	PROD CONDENS,POLYCOND
583	POLYMERIZATION ETC PRODS	W 78857	73680	W 87690	94285	W 97909	97164	W 95917	96067	PROD POLYMERISATION
59	CHEMICAL MATERIALS NES		157916		85816		99965		100032	MAT PROD CHIMIQUES NDA
598	MISCEL CHEM PRODUCTS NES	W 391366	129596	W 34163	59244	W 34729	67022	W 35874	69391	PROD DIV INDUST CHIM NDA
5989	CHEM PRODUCTS,PREPS NES			W 19035	36232	W 20513	39799	W 18996	44536	PROD PREP CHIMIQUES NDA
6	BASIC MANUFACTURES		2829798		2706948		3374576		3836990	ART MANUFACTURES
62	RUBBER MANUFACTURES NES		140171		171754		196274		193724	CAOUTCHOUC MANUFACTURE
625	RUBBER TYRES, TUBES ETC	W 41288	116533	W 53029	152410	W 66351	171246	W 70960	164158	PNEUS CAOUTCHOUC VULCANISE
6251	TYRES NEW FOR MOTOR CARS			W 35262	106635	W 46135	122770	W 49853	116088	PNEUS POUR VOITURES
63	WOOD,CORK MANUFACTRS NES		86684		86297		108740		127394	OUVRAGES LIEGE ET BOIS
634	VENEERS,PLYWOOD,ETC	W 132464	76389	W 120509	77533	W 159354	100141	W 164534	118803	PLACAGES,CONTRE–PLAQUES
6342	PLYWOOD OF WOOD SHEETS			W 118141	75604	W 156194	97731	W 160600	115482	BOIS CONTRE–PLAQUES
64	PAPER,PAPERBOARD AND MFR		178639		143833		146214		134381	PAPIERS,CARTONS & OUVRAGES
641	PAPER AND PAPERBOARD	W 122021	99185	W 95135	71430	W 97085	71382	W 123889	80802	PAPIERS ET CARTONS
642	PAPER,ETC,PRECUT,ARTS OF	W 37974	79455	W 30517	72402	W 31949	74832	W 24333	53579	PAP,CARTONS DECOUPES
6428	PAPER ETC ARTICLES NES			W 12831	35369	W 10845	29677	W 7916	20313	OUVRAGES EN PATE A PAPIER
65	TEXTILE YARN,FABRICS,ETC		1009369		1242554		1549696		1764119	FILS,TISSUS,ARTICLES TEXTILE
652	COTTON FABRICS,WOVEN	W 9733	63816	W 17046	107158	W 21083	133011	W 27173	144477	TISSUS DE COTON
6521	GREY WOVEN COTTON FABRIC			W 11431	75959	W 15637	103824			TISSUS COT ECRUS NON MERCER
6522	WOVEN COTTON BLEACHD,ETC			W 5615	31199	W 5446	29187	W 27169	144393	TISSUS COTON BLANCHIS ETC
65224	BLCHED COTTON FABRIC NES							W 22627	124751	AUT TIS PLUS 85% COT BLANCHI
653	WOVN MAN–MADE FIB FABRIC	W 66136	648213	W 82257	818552	W 103568	1024580	W 142412	1205761	TISSUS FIBRES SYNTH,ARTIF
6531	CONT SYNT WEAVES NONPILE			W 69859	712937	W 85232	889514	W 121007	1070061	TISSUS FIBRES SYNTH CONTINUE

4. General Imports C.I.F. by Commodities according to the S.I.T.C. (Rev. 2) in thousand U.S. Dollars
Importations Générales C.A.F. par Produits d'après la C.T.C.I. (Rév. 2) en milliers de Dollars E.U.

SITC CTCI	COMMODITY	1990 WEIGHT POIDS	1990 VALUE VALEUR	1991 WEIGHT POIDS	1991 VALUE VALEUR	1992 WEIGHT POIDS	1992 VALUE VALEUR	1993 WEIGHT POIDS	1993 VALUE VALEUR	PRODUIT
6534	DISC SYN BLEND FABRC NES			W 6547	42328	W 11198	64552	W 12723	60635	TISSUS FIBRES SYNTH DISCONT
6536	DISC REGN TXTL FABRC NES			W 3840	35914	W 4638	33881			TISSUS 85% TEXT ART DISC
654	OTH WOVEN TEXTILE FABRIC	W 4743	27720	W 8319	32343	W 5405	36936	W 7488	42513	TISSUS AUT COTON SYNT,ARTIF
655	KNITTED,ETC FABRICS	W 4669	25607	W 5115	28691	W 7248	39019	W 7954	41545	ETOF BONNETERIE PIECES ETC
6552	OTHER KNIT ETC FAB NONEL			W 5115	28691	W 7248	39019	W 7954	41545	ETOF BON NON ELAS NON SYNT
656	LACE,RIBBONS,TULLE,ETC	W 1231	20940	W 2296	34395	W 3003	49891	W 3870	55111	TULLES,BRODERIE
658	TEXTILE ARTICLES NES	W 21195	91307	W 25317	97991	W 27037	119663	W 32797	129196	ART FACONNES MAT TEXTILES
6584	LINENS ETC			W 1047	6909	W 1113	8370	W 18023	74231	LINGE DE MAISON
6589	OTH TEXTILE ARTICLES NES			W 11704	50983	W 14136	65428	W 773	3483	AUT ART EN TEXTILES NDA
659	FLOOR COVERINGS,ETC	W 21270	85913	W 18215	75209	W 17456	76927	W 17661	68727	COUVRE–PARQUETS,TAPIS ETC
6594	WOOL CARPETS ETC NES			W 10239	44582	W 8472	41796			TAPIS DE LAINE
66	NONMETAL MINERAL MFS NES		228794		196577		272464		319763	ART MIN NON METALLIQUES
661	LIME,CEMENT,BLDG PRODS	W 96035	34927	W 43475	27845	W 64389	41904	W 414449	64193	CHAUX,CIMENTS MAT CONSTR
662	CLAY,REFRACTORY BLDG PRD	W 107336	56541	W 50952	25327	W 63503	28825	W 69933	30401	MAT CONST REFRACTAIRES
664	GLASS	W 30359	36623	W 25741	27849	W 29940	31251	W 33227	33018	VERRE
665	GLASSWARE	W 40314	44068	W 24426	46063	W 38526	69540	W 49641	87593	OUVRAGES EN VERRE
6652	HOUSEHLD,HOTEL ETC GLASS			W 15165	28630	W 22021	45632	W 30325	58008	OBJETS VERRE TABLE,CUISINE
666	POTTERY	W 14054	21381	W 22249	32571	W 28034	44829	W 24190	34522	POTERIE
6664	PORCELN,CHINA HOUSE WARE			W 21833	30042	W 26745	40485	W 20582	27139	VAISSELLE,ARTS MEN PORC
667	PEARL,PREC–,SEMI–P STONE		20081		23682		38076		50008	PERLES, PIERRES GEMMES
6672	DIAMONDS NONINDUST,UNSET				21581		30834		42994	DIAMANTS BRUTS
67	IRON AND STEEL		477911		276945		300371		395671	FER ET ACIER
672	IRON,STEEL PRIMARY FORMS	W 1725	1096	W 72715	34827	W 78777	33957	W 537	348	LINGOTS FER,ACIER
6727	IRN,STL COIL FR REROLLNG			W 70754	33388	W 76535	32109			EBAUCHES POUR TOLES FER
673	IRON,STEEL SHAPES ETC	W 500288	185788	W 157697	67556	W 207366	73679	W 410812	149687	BARRES,PROFIL FER,ACIER
6732	IRON,STEEL BARS ETC			W 51829	19617	W 121630	38650	W 272181	95656	BARRES FER,ACIER
6733	IRON,STEEL PROFILES ETC			W 94936	43009	W 72718	30288	W 106813	43058	PROFILES,PALPLAN FER,ACIER
674	IRN,STL UNIV,PLATE,SHEET	W 132645	84918	W 66610	49938	W 73045	48289	W 233168	112066	LARGES PLATS,TOLES
6749	OTH IRN,STL PLATES,SHEET							W 75955	47897	AUTRES TOLES FER,ACIER
67491	— OF IRON OR SIMPLE STL							W 75955	47897	AUT TOLES AUTRES ACIER FIN
678	IRON,STL TUBES,PIPES,ETC	W 174206	186797	W 111649	109800	W 118432	125402	W 118518	108210	TUBES,TUYAUX EN FONTE,FER
6782	IRON,STL SEAMLESS TUBES			W 47782	41763	W 42831	36729	W 52791	35944	TUBES,TUYAUX SANS SOUDURE
6783	IRON,STL TUBES,PIPES NES			W 49406	35828	W 59086	52917	W 49649	39777	AUT TUBES,TUYAUX FER,ACIER
6785	IRON,STEEL TUBE FITTINGS			W 14421	32152	W 16462	35685	W 15613	32140	ACCESSOIRES DE TUYAUTERIE
68	NON–FERROUS METALS		342187		243945		321811		416964	METAUX NON FERREUX
681	SILVER,PLATINUM,ETC		235257		165746		216287		315181	ARGENT ET PLATINE
6811	SILVER UNWKD,PARTLY WRKD				165603		216223		315139	ARGENT BRUT MI–OUVRE
68113	SILVER UNWROUGHT								313156	ARGENT ET ALLIAGES BRUTS
682	COPPER EXC CEMENT COPPER	W 11493	37947	W 8493	27651	W 15814	51659	W 14793	40467	CUIVRE
6822	COPPER,ALLOYS WORKED			W 8481	27612	W 15423	50786	W 14498	40012	CUIVRE,ALLIAGES OUVRES
684	ALUMINIUM	W 19410	51106	W 12881	33756	W 19299	42335	W 25352	49348	ALUMINIUM
69	METAL MANUFACTURES NES		364092		342476		474337		476106	ART MANUFACT EN METAL NDA
691	STRUCTURES AND PARTS NES	W 35971	55826	W 15877	29319	W 38447	81163	W 36485	73942	CONSTRUCT FER,ACIER,ALU
6911	STRUCTURES,PARTS IRN,STL			W 14663	23492	W 37623	76667	W 35761	69938	CONSTRUCT FER,ACIER,FONTE
695	TOOLS	W 6396	46953	W 6789	57237	W 10796	95075	W 10515	76168	OUTILS A MAIN
6954	BLADES,TIPS,ETC FR TOOLS			W 1518	34025	W 2629	64492	W 1575	44718	OUTILS POUR MACHINE–OUTIL
696	CUTLERY	W 5211	36517	W 5219	37507	W 5984	44540	W 7512	47605	COUTELLERIE
697	BASE MTL HOUSEHOLD EQUIP	W 11082	52014	W 11763	48404	W 13502	56307	W 17647	61998	ART MENAGE MET COMMUNS
699	BASE METAL MFRS NES	W 56004	110306	W 51704	112746	W 57963	138209	W 69262	151355	ART MANUFACTURES MET NDA
6991	LOCKSMITHS WARES,ETC			W 10924	42721	W 14296	55623	W 16598	58669	ARTICLES DE SERRURERIE
6997	IRON,STEEL ARTICLES NES			W 22146	29532	W 21132	33439	W 31750	43786	OUV FONTE,FER,ACIER NDA
7	MACHINES,TRANSPORT EQUIP		3694776		3345117		4552448		4439182	MACHINES MATERIEL TRANSPORT
71	POWER GENERATING EQUIPMT		231277		204070		356302		248180	MACHINES GENERATRICES
713	INTRNL COMBUS PSTN ENGIN	W 5680	115804	W 6138	79353	W 7446	86395	W 7497	89543	MOTEURS EXPL COMB INT, PIECE
7139	PISTON ENGINE PARTS NES			W 2425	44293	W 2502	48282	W 2775	52022	PIECES POUR 713.2,3,8
714	ENGINES AND MOTORS NES	W 1062	46365	W 2184	64533	W 7883	182046	W 2989	89044	MOTEURS NON ELECTRIQUES
7148	GAS TURBINES NES			W 739	26548	W 4621	97095	W 2970	88307	TURBINES A GAZ
71488	OTHER GAS TURBINES NES			W 738	26491	W 4621	97095			AUTRES TURBINES A GAZ
7149	ENGINE & MOTOR PARTS NES			W 1445	37978	W 3257	79047	W 20	737	PIECES 714 ET 718.88
716	ROTATING ELECTRIC PLANT	W 5229	54685	W 6187	57278	W 7477	55126	W 6137	49937	APP ELECTR ROTATIFS,PIECES
7162	AC MTRS,GENRTRS,GEN SETS			W 2176	23928	W 1508	14904	W 5631	42033	MOTEURS ELECTRIQUES
72	MACHS FOR SPCL INDUSTRYS		357998		310814		399110		274079	MAC SPECIALES POUR INDUST
723	CIVIL ENGNEERG EQUIP ETC	W 26726	197533	W 20775	182516	W 19430	222765	W 17665	80705	APPAREILS DE GENIE CIVIL
7234	CONST,MINING MACHNRY NES			W 13132	75772	W 11349	69529	W 16445	75490	MACH POUR LA CONST, MINES
7239	CONSTR ETC MACHY PTS NES			W 7643	106745	W 8081	153237			PIECES 723.41–723.46
728	OTH MACHY FOR SPCL INDUS	W 8127	60426	W 5630	66095	W 8039	79633	W 9411	99220	AUT MACH IND PARTICULIERES
7284	MACHY FOR SPCL INDUS NES			W 3876	54125	W 4477	52933	W 5579	71126	MACH SPEC IND PARTICUL.
72848	OTH MCHY WITH INDIV FNCT			W 1924	30082	W 2482	28657	W 3490	43374	AUTRES MACHINES NDA
74	GENRL INDUSTRL MACHY NES		557545		526108		652531		827824	MACH APP INDUSTRIE
741	HEATING,COOLING EQUIPMNT	W 27278	165113	W 20106	147720	W 24538	175324	W 24775	166483	MACH CHAUFFAGE,PIECES
7415	AIR–CONDITIONING MACHNRY			W 16782	108780	W 20258	130964	W 19429	122244	GROUPES CONDITION AIR
742	PUMPS FOR LIQUIDS ETC	W 9828	75463	W 6509	55640	W 7720	74810	W 8229	74483	POMPES MOTO–POMPES
7428	OTHER PUMPS FOR LIQUIDS			W 5396	41023	W 5879	46134	W 5924	51943	AUTRES POMPES POUR LIQ
74288	PUMPS FR LIQUIDS NES ETC							W 5924	51943	POMPES POUR LIQUIDES NDA
743	PUMPS NES,CENTRFUGES ETC	W 6951	58678	W 6716	68808	W 8272	74781	W 11256	85227	POMPES COMPRES,VENT ETC
7431	PUMPS FOR GASES ETC			W 3252	33924	W 3938	34389	W 4251	28560	POMPES AIR A VIDE,COMPRES
744	MECHANICAL HANDLING EQU	W 22910	98354	W 18130	114029	W 23790	143373	W 41478	292915	EQUIP MANUTENTION PIECES
7442	LIFTING,LOADING MACH NES			W 13771	87636	W 19694	115448	W 29467	135496	APP LEVAGE,MANUTENTION
7449	PTS NES OF MACHY OF 7442			W 1232	13462	W 709	14059	W 7714	140598	PIECES DU 744.2
745	NONELEC MACHY,TOOLS NES	W 2541	31146	W 2315	28441	W 3001	35407	W 3645	43592	AUT MACH NON ELEC,PIECES
749	NONELEC MACH PTS,ACC NES	W 11067	128790	W 11272	111469	W 15408	148835	W 20890	165123	PIECES MACH NON ELEC NDA
7491	BALL,ROLLER,ETC BEARINGS			W 3208	26951	W 4574	36640	W 8521	46657	ROULEMENTS BILLES ETC
7492	COCKS,VALVES ETC NES			W 5483	54676	W 7567	76300	W 8639	74119	ART ROB,SIM POUR TUYAUX
75	OFFICE MACHNES,ADP EQUIP		149835		141834		189646		209710	MACH BUREAU TRAIT AUTOM
751	OFFICE MACHINES	W 1778	41998	W 2407	57152	W 2672	61425	W 1820	34853	MACH,APPAREILS DE BUREAU
7518	OFFICE MACHINES NES			W 1656	35506	W 1902	38956	W 477	7768	MACH,APP DE BUREAU NDA
752	AUTOMTIC DATA PROC EQUIP	W 613	46698	W 627	39203	W 944	52214	W 944	61919	MACH TRAIT INFORMATION
7521	ANALOG,HYBRID COMPUTERS							W 944	61919	MACH POUR TRAIT INFORMAT
759	OFFICE,ADP MCH PTS,ACCES	W 963	61139	W 940	45479	W 1305	76006	W 2893	112938	PIECES DU 751 ET 752
7599	ACCTG,ETC,ADP MCH PTS,AC			W 940	45479	W 1305	76006	W 1735	84599	PIECES DU 751 ET 752
76	TELECOMM,SOUND EQUIPMENT		565458		716045		710461		846334	EQUIPMENT DE TELECOM
761	TELEVISION RECEIVERS	W 12585	138445	W 15262	177918	W 18748	197528	W 20471	208678	RECEPTEURS DE TELEVISION
7611	COLOUR TV RECEIVERS			W 12017	163204	W 13275	174797	W 15311	190411	RECEPTEURS COULEUR
762	RADIO BROADCAST RECEIVRS	W 9032	103982	W 13530	150222	W 16358	172383	W 17335	169067	RECEPTEURS RADIODIFFUSION
7621	MTR VEHC RADIO RECEIVERS			W 13530	150222	W 16358	172383			RECEPTEURS RADIO AUTO
7628	OTHER RADIO RECEIVERS							W 17335	169067	AUTRES RECEPT RADIO
763	SOUND RECORDRS,PHONOGRPH	W 6211	159909	W 7363	192243	W 5254	127099	W 6194	149693	PHONO,APP ENREGISTREMENT
7638	OTHR SOUND APPARATUS ETC			W 7242	188950	W 5226	125923	W 6166	148468	AUT APP D'ENREGIS,REPROD
76381	TV IMAGE,SND RECRDRS ETC			W 5731	164768	W 3401	100438	W 3648	114349	APP ENREG,REPRO IMAG,SON
764	TELECOM EQPT,PTS,ACC NES	W 4904	163121	W 5888	195662	W 7235	213451	W 11664	318896	EQUIP TELECOM,PIECES
7641	LINE TELEPHONE,ETC EQUIP			W 2707	95680	W 2933	114748	W 4073	152977	APP TELEPHON PAR FIL

4. General Imports C.I.F. by Commodities according to the S.I.T.C. (Rev. 2) in thousand U.S. Dollars
Importations Générales C.A.F. par Produits d'après la C.T.C.I. (Rév. 2) en milliers de Dollars E.U.

SITC CTCI	COMMODITY	1990 WEIGHT POIDS	1990 VALUE VALEUR	1991 WEIGHT POIDS	1991 VALUE VALEUR	1992 WEIGHT POIDS	1992 VALUE VALEUR	1993 WEIGHT POIDS	1993 VALUE VALEUR	PRODUIT
7648	TELECOMM EQUIPMENT NES			W 462	39514	W 362	37025	W 518	58009	APP TELECOM NDA
76482	TELEVISION CAMERAS			W 383	34671	W 310	32632	W 479	53980	APP PRISE DE VUES TELE
7649	PTS NES OF EQUIPMT OF 76			W 1499	22273	W 2567	36890	W 5608	73693	PIECES DE LA DIV 76
76493	TELECOMM EQUIPMT PTS NES			W 1051	16262	W 2093	31323	W 5039	67394	PIECES 761,762,764.3,8
77	ELECTRIC MACHNRY NES ETC		533407		470914		662550		579821	MACH APP ELECT NDA
771	ELECTRIC POWER MACHY NES	W 7495	38733	W 5758	20964	W 10874	57899	W 9099	39121	MACH PROD,TRANS ELECTR
7711	TRANSFORMERS,ELECTRICAL			W 3224	13046	W 9092	49268	W 6331	28519	TRANSFO ELECTRIQUES
772	SWITCHGEAR ETC,PARTS NES	W 8143	95838	W 7776	83223	W 10686	179264	W 9036	115774	APP COUPURE,SECT ETC
7721	SWITCHGEAR ETC			W 7749	82627	W 10602	177291	W 8982	114679	APP COUPURE,SECTIONMNT
773	ELECTR DISTRIBUTNG EQUIP	W 31663	94036	W 21368	67758	W 20959	77171	W 18478	54658	EQUIPMT DISTRIBUTION ELECT
7731	INSULATED WIRE,CABLE ETC			W 20362	62850	W 20116	70847	W 17660	49120	FILS,CABLES ISOLES ELECT
775	HOUSEHOLD TYPE EQUIP NES	W 34023	168305	W 35269	177949	W 38480	207235	W 44619	221534	MACH,APP USAGE DOMESTQUE
7752	DOM REFRIGERATRS,FREEZRS			W 9961	46636	W 9345	42306	W 9053	41738	REFRIG,CONGEL MENAGER
77521	DOMESTIC REFRIGERATORS			W 9401	43592	W 8743	39614	W 8008	36868	REFRIGERATEURS
7757	DOMESTIC ELECTRC EQU NES			W 13061	59818	W 15163	78994	W 20906	95017	APP ELECTR DOMEST NDA
7758	ELECTRO–THERMIC APPL NES			W 6592	39578	W 8065	52428	W 9144	52907	APP ELECTROTHERMIQ NDA
778	ELECTRICAL MACHINERY NES	W 26287	120550	W 25486	110112	W 26831	131191	W 34670	135570	AUTRES MACH ELECT NDA
7781	BATTERIES,ACCUMULATORS			W 16665	37097	W 15847	37529	W 20634	43317	PILES ET ACCUMULATEURS
78	ROAD VEHICLES		1018649		829396		1174920		1187326	VEHICULES ROUTIERS
781	PASS MOTOR VEH EXC BUSES	W 66447	585638	W 52245	478733	W 73019	705049	W 71166	644469	AUTO TRANSPORT PERSONNES
782	LORRIES,SPCL MTR VEH NES	W 35386	172736	W 28952	137676	W 40883	215240	W 50241	244800	VEHICULES SPECIAUX,MARCH
7821	LORRIES,TRUCKS			W 26244	121278	W 37087	189889	W 44955	216836	VEHICULES TRANSP MARCHAND
783	ROAD MOTOR VEHICLES NES	W 4376	22335	W 4809	25507	W 6193	34994	W 9553	52185	VEHICULES ROUTIERS NDA
784	MOTOR VEH PRTS,ACCES NES	W 22478	209982	W 17328	154156	W 19252	177869	W 22859	197718	PIECES 722,781,782,783
7849	OTHER MOTOR VEHCL PARTS			W 15300	142237	W 18384	172590	W 22237	193857	PIECES 722,781,782,783
79	OTHR TRANSPORT EQUIPMENT		253951		116562		372689		228480	AUTRE MATERIEL TRANSPORT
792	AIRCRAFT ETC	W 711	205640	W 297	102714	W 586	357237	W 342	212915	APP NAVIGATION AERIENNE
7924	AIRCRFT NES OVER 15000KG			W 172	71425	W 426	311857	W 177	162465	AERODYNES PLUS 15000 KG
7929	AIRCRAFT PARTS NES			W 120	31145	W 149	43736	W 161	48827	PIECES DU 792
793	SHIPS AND BOATS ETC	W 8885	47362	W 2617	13840	W 7329	15429	W 4292	15526	NAVIRES BATEAUX,ETC
8	MISC MANUFACTURED GOODS		1853190		2070472		2491750		2858301	ART MANUFACTURES DIVERS
812	*PLUMBG,HEATNG,LGHTNG EQ	W 20580	90586	W 16331	72872	W 19923	96683	W 24958	102609	APPAR SANITAIRES CHAUFFAGE
8124	LIGHTING EQUIPMENT NES			W 10423	60418	W 12939	81117	W 14751	80048	APPAREILS ECLAIRAGE ETC
81241	LIGHTING ETC GLASSWARE							W 10659	57484	VERRERIE D'ECLAIRAGE
821	*FURNITURE,PARTS THEREOF	W 36605	126278	W 34564	107847	W 41035	141495	W 37844	121903	MEUBLES ET PIECES
8219	FURNITURE AND PARTS NES			W 29737	84108	W 35523	111708	W 31652	92029	AUTRES MEUBLES ET PIECES
82191	METAL FURNITURE NES			W 29737	84108	W 35523	111708			MEUBLES NDA EN METAL
82199	OTHR FURN,FURN PARTS NES							W 31652	92029	MEUBLES NDA AUTRES MATIERES
831	*TRAVEL GOODS,HANDBAGS	W 10513	53037	W 13272	66468	W 13457	71660	W 17112	85021	ARTICLES DE VOYAGE ETC
83102	TRAVEL GDS,TOILET–CASES							W 17112	85021	ARTICLES DE VOYAGE
84	CLOTHING AND ACCESSORIES		528198		634909		734157		783051	VETEMENTS
842	MENS OUTERWEAR NOT KNIT	W 24134	205788	W 19833	183688	W 20858	195101	W 24755	188028	VET DESSUS POUR HOMMES
8422	— SUITS			W 18560	172959	W 19406	182518			COMPLETS HOMMES MAT TEXT
8423	— TROUSERS,BREECHES ETC							W 24473	185451	PANTALONS HOMMES MAT TEX
843	WOMENS OUTERWEAR NONKNIT	W 13526	133905	W 12581	127935	W 16170	148951	W 20133	165416	VET DESSUS FEMMES MAT TEX
8431	— COATS AND JACKETS			W 117	1801	W 39	412	W 14865	120304	MANT,VEST FEM MAT TEXTIL
8432	— SUITS AND COSTUMES			W 9485	97324	W 12866	117878			COSTUMES–TAIL MAT TEXIL
844	UNDER GARMENTS NOT KNIT	W 6554	54854	W 18032	132443	W 19851	145168	W 22306	144200	VETEMENT DESSOUS MAT TEX
8441	— MENS SHIRTS			W 6883	70565	W 8333	82360	W 10424	82684	CHEMISES HOMMES MAT TEXT
8443	— WOMENS			W 7202	39840	W 7611	38441	W 8051	39413	VET DESSOUS FEM MAT TEXT
845	OUTERWEAR KNIT NONELASTC	W 5956	46814	W 3014	25935	W 4052	37802	W 5642	43537	VET DESSOUS,ACCES BONNET
846	UNDER GARMENTS KNITTED	W 1854	14743	W 13723	94570	W 20244	115844	W 26519	136561	SOUS VETS DE BONNETERIE
8462	— OF COTTON NON ELASTIC			W 12729	84502	W 18403	100516	W 24767	120768	SOUS–VET BONNET COTON
84629	—— OTHER			W 12729	84502	W 18403	100516	W 24767	120768	AUT SOUS–VET BONNET COTON
847	TEXTILE CLTHNG ACCES NES	W 4300	48945	W 5193	52040	W 7048	68908	W 9613	78452	ACCES VET MAT TEXT NDA
8471	— NOT KNITTED			W 3391	32100	W 4049	38942	W 6019	48851	ACCES VET MAT TEX NON BON
851	*FOOTWEAR	W 22698	125347	W 27161	146903	W 36732	194969	W 41634	201879	CHAUSSURES
85101	FOOTWEAR RUBBER,PLASTIC							W 20601	89027	CHAUS SEMELLES CAOUTCH
85102	FOOTWEAR LEATHER							W 7571	77296	CHAUS SEMELLES EN CUIR
87	PRECISION INSTRUMNTS NES		96803		71095		91688		104376	INSTRUM,APPAR SCIENT NDA
874	MEASURNG,CONTROLNG INSTR	W 2214	71680	W 1635	51339	W 2449	64673	W 2480	72353	INSTRUMENTS DE MESURE
88	PHOTO EQU,OPTICL GDS ETC		257272		260360		284529		329436	APP,FOURN PHOTO,OP,MONTR
881	PHOTO APPARAT,EQUIPT NES	W 902	37442	W 680	28953	W 700	32639	W 965	41795	APP,EQUIP PHOTO NDA
882	PHOTO,CINEMA SUPPLIES	W 4963	60595	W 4501	52172	W 3024	37338	W 3603	47935	PRODUITS PHOTO,CINEMA
8822	PHOTO FILM EXC DEV CINMA			W 2583	42851	W 1796	28545	W 2444	40195	PLAQUES,PELLICULES,FILMS
885	WATCHES AND CLOCKS		143010		162122		192340		215059	HORLOGERIE
8851	WATCHES,MOVEMENTS,CASES				145481		170101		188789	MONTRES,MOUVEMENTS,BOITES
88511	WATCHES				144130		168467		186856	MONTRES POCHE,BRACELET
89	MISC MANUFCTRD GOODS NES		575668		710017		876570		1130025	ART MANUFACTURES DIVERS
893	ARTICLES OF PLASTIC NES	W 23122	72442	W 31747	99559	W 39480	121811	W 44030	127584	OUVRAGES EN MAT DIVIS 58
8939	MISC PLASTIC ARTICLES			W 24741	77877	W 30782	94233	W 34143	99421	ART DIVERS EN MAT DIV 58
89399	OTHR PLASTC ARTICLES NES			W 19043	68481	W 23143	81082	W 20501	67340	AUT OUV MAT DIV 58
894	TOYS,SPORTING GOODS,ETC	W 13980	70199	W 21411	110491	W 23216	131530	W 31734	157176	VOITURES ENFANTS,JOUETS
8942	TOYS,INDOOR GAMES ETC			W 18290	92196	W 19874	110142	W 26949	132226	JOUETS,JEUX ETC
89423	TOYS NES							W 18489	80201	JOUETS,MODELES REDUITS
895	OFFICE SUPPLIES NES	W 3602	30673	W 4485	33820	W 6468	44817	W 7407	52716	ART PAPET NDA
8952	PENS,PENCILS,FOUNTN PENS			W 3035	27073	W 4844	37110	W 5704	43932	PLUMES,CRAYONS,STYLOS
897	GOLD,SILVER WARE,JEWELRY		245217		309101		385536		562580	BIJOUTERIE,ORFEVRERIE
8973	PREC JEWLRY,GLD–SILVWARE				295691		369236		548813	BIJOUX OR,ARGENT ORFEVRE
89731	PRECIOUS METAL JEWELLERY				293133		366050		545442	ART BIJOUTERIE,JOAILLER
898	MUSICAL INSTRUMENTS,PTS	W 7263	57196	W 7973	63286	W 8635	71216	W 10259	84252	INSTRUMENTS DE MUSIQUE
8983	SOUND RECRDNG TAPE,DISCS			W 7412	53148	W 7995	59013	W 9747	76104	SUPPORTS SON POUR 763
89831	PREPD SND RECORDNG MEDIA			W 7186	45702	W 7575	44513	W 9148	56528	SUPPORTS PREPARES
899	OTHER MANUFACTURED GOODS	W 15042	71829		71829		95136		115032	AUT ART MANUF DIVERS NDA
9	GOODS NOT CLASSD BY KIND		77462		19109		14660		5159	ART TRANSACT NON CLASSES
951	*WAR FIREARMS,AMMUNITION	W 724	59419	W 98	759	W 100	668	W 7	198	VEHIC BLINDES ARMES

5. General Exports F.O.B. by Commodities according to the S.I.T.C. (Rev. 2) in thousand U.S. Dollars
Exportations Générales F.O.B. par Produits d'après la C.T.C.I. (Rév. 2) en milliers de Dollars E.U.

SITC CTCI	COMMODITY	1990 WEIGHT POIDS	1990 VALUE VALEUR	1991 WEIGHT POIDS	1991 VALUE VALEUR	1992 WEIGHT POIDS	1992 VALUE VALEUR	1993 WEIGHT POIDS	1993 VALUE VALEUR	PRODUIT
	ALL COMMODITIES # 1		3945076		758656		899341		3764200	TOUS PRODUITS
0	FOOD AND LIVE ANIMALS		535646		29824		50353		56629	ALIMENTS,ANIMAUX VIVANTS
01	MEAT AND PREPARATIONS		25231		5086		11262		15518	VIANDES ET PREPARATIONS
011	MEAT FRESH,CHILLD,FROZEN	W 19053	23832	W 348	566	W 592	1297	W 978	1822	VIANDES FRAICHES,REF,CONGE
014	MEAT PREPD,PRSVD,NES ETC	W 520	1259	W 1496	4518	W 3548	9957	W 4746	13639	CONSERVES DE VIANDES
0149	OTH PREPARD,PRESRVD MEAT			W 1430	4233	W 3500	9822	W 4716	13529	AUTRES PREP DE VIANDES
02	DAIRY PRODCTS,BIRDS'EGGS		8823		6556		7775		11203	PRODUITS LAITIERS,OEUFS
022	MILK AND CREAM	W 2733	5444	W 3162	6552	W 3752	7775	W 5833	10825	LAIT ET CREME
0223	MILK AND CREAM FRESH			W 3124	6500	W 3739	7759	W 5832	10825	LAIT,CREME FRAIS
03	FISH AND PREPARATIONS		22843		7864		13251		7644	POISSONS ET PREPARATIONS
034	FISH,FRESH,CHILLED,FROZN	W 8625	9380	W 504	1281	W 1148	3126	W 903	2575	POISSON FRAIS, REFRIG,CONG
035	FISH SALTED,DRIED,SMOKED	W 230	3799	W 533	5051	W 557	8471	W 347	5037	POISSON SECHE,SALE,FUME
04	CEREALS AND PREPARATIONS		92665		3945		3539		4405	CEREALES ET PRODUITS
042	RICE	W 173613	67287							RIZ
046	WHEAT ETC MEAL OR FLOUR	W 44354	12410	W 1547	540	W 3842	1288	W 5104	1661	SEMOULE FARINE,FROMENT
048	CEREAL ETC PREPARATIONS	W 8663	8974	W 2095	3301	W 1412	2173	W 2061	2619	PREPTNS A BASE CEREALES
05	VEGETABLES AND FRUIT		198884		3787		10230		9097	LEGUMES ET FRUITS
054	VEG ETC FRSH,SMPLY PRSVD	W 122918	36777	W 1099	1074	W 15937	5730	W 15227	5295	LEGUMES FRAIS,CONG,SECS
0544	TOMATOES FRESH			W 229	159	W 11492	4002	W 13268	4070	TOMATES FRAICHES
057	FRUIT,NUTS,FRESH,DRIED	W 217377	144963	W 2293	1529	W 2737	1797	W 3711	1780	FRUITS FRAIS OU SECS
058	FRUIT PRESERVED,PREPARED	W 13846	12937	W 961	830	W 2375	1791	W 1384	1235	CONSERVES DE FRUITS
06	SUGAR AND PREPS,HONEY		69985		1046		609		482	SUCRES ET PRODUITS
061	SUGAR AND HONEY	W 135202	64860	W 26	15	W 21	59	W 2	2	SUCRES ET MIEL
07	COFFEE,TEA,COCOA,SPICES		75394		156		74		93	CAFE,THE,CACAO,EPICES
073	CHOCOLATE AND PRODUCTS	W 3900	14268	W 10	16	W 27	73	W 31	93	CHOCOLAT
074	TEA AND MATE	W 6510	21220							THE ET MATE
075	SPICES	W 40477	37759	W 147	140	W 2	1			EPICES
09	MISC EDIBLE PRODUCTS		30279		1286		3563		8068	PREP ALIMENTAIRES DIVERSES
091	MARGARINE AND SHORTENING	W 5429	4704	W 759	932	W 3699	3344	W 7490	7409	MARGARINE ET GRAISSES
0914	MARGARINE,EDIBLE FAT NES			W 759	932	W 3699	3344	W 7490	7409	MARGARINES,SIMILI SAINDOUX
09149	OTH PREPARED EDIBLE FATS			W 495	574	W 3680	3317	W 7484	7400	SIMILI–SAINDOUX
098	EDIBLE PRODCTS,PREPS NES	W 21176	25575	W 233	355	W 162	219	W 454	658	PREP ALIMENTAIRES NDA
1	BEVERAGES AND TOBACCO		108771		17256		17114		15951	BOISSONS ET TABACS
11	BEVERAGES		25315		17222		17073		15935	BOISSONS
111	NON–ALCOHL BEVERAGES NES	W 66892	22289	W 51692	17222	W 61222	17073	W 61160	15935	BOISSONS NON ALCOOLIQUES
11101	WATERS,ICE AND SNOW			W 33044	5707	W 38472	6314			EAU,EAUX MINERALES
11102	FLAVORED WATERS NON–ALCO			W 18648	11515	W 22751	10759			LIMONADES,EAUX GAZEUSES
12	TOBACCO AND MANUFACTURES		83456		34		41		16	TABACS BRUTS FABRIQUES
122	TOBACCO,MANUFACTURED	W 20389	83329			W 4	3	W 11	6	TABACS FABRIQUES
2	CRUDE MATERLS,EXCL FUELS		158267		36320		40070		33456	MAT BRUTES NON COMESTIBLES
21	HIDES,SKINS,FURS UNDRSSD		13211		2517		2321		892	CUIRS,PEAUX BRUTS
211	HIDES,SKINS,EXC FURS,RAW	W 5702	13208	W 1560	2517	W 1500	2321	W 569	892	CUIRS ET PEAUX
26	TEXTILE FIBRES AND WASTE		53255							FIBRES TEXTILES
269	WASTE OF TEXTILE FABRICS	W 36778	41730							FRIPERIE DRILLES,CHIFFONS
28	METALLIFEROUS ORES,SCRAP		56053		30501		33731		29483	MINERAIS METAL,DECHETS
282	IRON AND STEEL SCRAP	W 94888	16752	W 61968	16096	W 97038	16421	W 96092	14484	FERRAILLES
28201	— OF PIG OR CAST IRON			W 61968	16096	W 97038	16421	W 96092	14484	FERRAILLES DE FONTE
288	NONFERR METAL SCRAP NES	W 55195	36951	W 25185	13959	W 32645	17134	W 28315	13799	DECHETS NON FERREUX
2881	METALIFEROUS NONFER WSTE			W 1298	460	W 4242	2758	W 2355	1232	CENDRES ET RESIDUS
2882	OTHER BASE MTL SCRAP NES			W 23887	13500	W 28403	14376	W 25961	12567	AUTRES DECHETS
28821	COPPER WASTE AND SCRAP			W 10462	8944	W 10014	7619	W 7141	5718	DECHETS DE CUIVRE
28823	ALUMINIUM WSTE AND SCRAP			W 7689	2974	W 11655	5035	W 12478	5156	DECHETS D'ALUMINIUM
3	MINERAL FUELS ETC		60824		35442		51997		52859	COMBUSTIBLES MINERAUX LUB
33	PETROLEUM AND PRODUCTS		59593		34652		49494		49026	PETROLE ET DERIVES
334	PETROLEUM PRODUCTS,REFIN	W 76697	56641	W 40174	33737	W 60197	48567	W 61666	48868	PRODUITS RAFFINES
3345	LUBS,PETROLEUM OILS NES			W 39897	33684	W 58364	47713	W 60352	48596	HUILES LUBRIFIANTES
33451	LUBS(HIGH PETR CONT) ETC			W 39894	33679	W 58346	47698	W 60352	48596	HUILES LUBRIF,H LOURDES
5	CHEMCLS,RELATED PROD NES		184660		23152		45186		54280	PRODUITS CHIMIQUES
53	DYES,TANNING,COLOUR PROD		16159		7457		10394		11836	PROD TEINTURE,COLORANTS
533	PIGMENTS,PAINTS,ETC	W 13688	16012	W 5042	7457	W 7909	10381	W 8018	11826	PIGMENTS,PEINTURES,VERNIS
5334	VARNISHES,DISTEMPERS ETC			W 5035	7447	W 7433	10278	W 7996	11797	PEINTURES A L'EAU
53341	WATER–THINNED PAINTS			W 1762	2201	W 6791	8740			PEINTURES DILUEES
53342	OTH PAINTS,VARNISHES ETC			W 3171	5010	W 640	1531			AUTRES PEINTURES,VERNIS
541	*MEDICINAL,PHARM PRODUCT	K 4930835	17238	K 106676	421	K 473352	1951	K 237965	2410	PROD MEDICINAUX PHARMACEUT
55	PERFUME,CLEANING ETC PRD		53939		4657		13912		17644	PROD POUR PARFUM,TOILETTE
553	PERFUMERY,COSMETICS,ETC	W 3800	37127	W 211	1569	W 1345	8571	W 1208	9885	PRODUITS DE PARFUMERIE
554	SOAP,CLEANSING ETC PREPS	W 11982	10704	W 2660	3088	W 5170	5300	W 7902	7750	SAVONS,PRODUITS DETERSIFS
5542	WASHING PREPARATIONS ETC			W 2562	2813	W 5045	5095	W 7188	7080	PROD ORG TENSIO–ACT NDA
58	PLASTIC MATERIALS ETC		53042		5551		11722		10965	MAT PLAST ARTIFICIELLES
582	PROD OF CONDENSATION ETC	W 28401	43694	W 542	2074	W 1682	6941	W 1680	6235	PROD CONDENS,POLYCOND
5823	ALKYDS,OTHER POLYESTERS			W 539	2055	W 1598	6783	W 1680	6229	ALKYDES ET AUT POLYESTERS
58231	— IN PRIMARY FORMS			W 539	2055	W 1598	6783	W 1680	6229	SOUS FORMES PRIMAIRES
583	POLYMERIZATION ETC PRODS	W 6869	9247	W 2828	3128	W 4622	4621	W 6384	4693	PROD POLYMERISATION
59	CHEMICAL MATERIALS NES		32858		4488		6222		9957	MAT PROD CHIMIQUES NDA
598	MISCEL CHEM PRODUCTS NES	W 45951	29956	W 3708	4432	W 6504	6003	W 9308	9712	PROD DIV INDUST CHIM NDA
5989	CHEM PRODUCTS,PREPS NES			W 3507	4271	W 6184	5715	W 9269	9698	PROD PREP CHIMIQUES NDA
6	BASIC MANUFACTURES		1170542		428615		403897		391279	ART MANUFACTURES
62	RUBBER MANUFACTURES NES		54726		65		10		216	CAOUTCHOUC MANUFACTURE
625	RUBBER TYRES, TUBES ETC	W 17933	53618					W 48	37	PNEUS CAOUTCHOUC VULCANISE
63	WOOD,CORK MANUFACTRS NES		25936		5048		3558		1357	OUVRAGES LIEGE ET BOIS
634	VENEERS,PLYWOOD,ETC	W 37343	21068							PLACAGES,CONTRE–PLAQUES
635	WOOD MANUFACTURES NES	W 2793	4854	W 732	5048	W 1530	3558	W 586	1357	ART MANUF EN BOIS NDA
6353	BUILDERS WOODWRK,PREFABS			W 732	5048	W 1529	3556	W 580	1264	OUVRAGES DE MENUISERIE
64	PAPER,PAPERBOARD AND MFR		39676		11398		12681		14363	PAPIERS,CARTONS & OUVRAGES
642	PAPER,ETC,PRECUT,ARTS OF	W 27146	33115	W 5886	11023	W 9058	12198	W 12102	13226	PAP,CARTONS DECOUPES
6421	PAPER ETC CONTAINERS			W 4562	7843	W 7923	9846	W 11075	11524	BOITES,SACS EMBALLAGES
6428	PAPER ETC ARTICLES NES			W 1121	2590	W 909	1620	W 792	1258	OUVRAGES EN PATE A PAPIER
65	TEXTILE YARN,FABRICS,ETC		402668		5727		7314		8977	FILS,TISSUS,ARTICLES TEXTILE
653	WOVN MAN–MADE FIB FABRIC	W 22625	197695			W 16	192	W 31	95	TISSUS FIBRES SYNTH,ARTIF
658	TEXTILE ARTICLES NES	W 5507	18663	W 848	4657	W 1689	7059	W 2147	8533	ART FACONNES MAT TEXTILES
6589	OTH TEXTILE ARTICLES NES			W 838	4529	W 1670	6986	W 419	1767	AUT ART EN TEXTILES NDA
659	FLOOR COVERINGS,ETC	W 2829	176933					W 2	4	COUVRE–PARQUETS,TAPIS ETC
66	NONMETAL MINERAL MFS NES		100246		11057		12911		12602	ART MIN NON METALLIQUES
661	LIME,CEMENT,BLDG PRODS	W 1094569	45349	W 97005	6637	W 81330	6881	W 63273	4821	CHAUX,CIMENTS MAT CONSTR
6612	CEMENT			W 96208	6147	W 80116	6251	W 62034	4496	CIMENTS HYDRAULIQUES
667	PEARL,PREC–,SEMI–P STONE		25728				32			PERLES, PIERRES GEMMES
67	IRON AND STEEL		53892		10006		13039		3757	FER ET ACIER
673	IRON,STEEL SHAPES ETC	W 52355	21485	W 21246	9996	W 25022	12090	W 5823	2559	BARRES,PROFIL FER,ACIER
6731	IRON,STEEL WIRE ROD			W 6603	2774					FIL MACHINE FER,ACIER
6732	IRON,STEEL BARS ETC			W 14549	7111	W 24548	11721	W 5646	2328	BARRES FER,ACIER
678	IRON,STL TUBES,PIPES,ETC	W 28682	23892		3	W 274	354	W 696	959	TUBES,TUYAUX EN FONTE,FER

5. General Exports F.O.B. by Commodities according to the S.I.T.C. (Rev. 2) in thousand U.S. Dollars
Exportations Générales F.O.B. par Produits d'après la C.T.C.I. (Rév. 2) en milliers de Dollars E.U.

SITC CTCI	COMMODITY	1990		1991		1992		1993		PRODUIT
		WEIGHT POIDS	VALUE VALEUR	WEIGHT POIDS	VALUE VALEUR	WEIGHT POIDS	VALUE VALEUR	WEIGHT POIDS	VALUE VALEUR	
68	NON–FERROUS METALS		403770		366973		328551		307099	METAUX NON FERREUX
681	SILVER,PLATINUM,ETC		98694		17					ARGENT ET PLATINE
684	ALUMINIUM	W 178341	301947	W 236597	365603	W 249039	327869	W 243037	305130	ALUMINIUM
6841	ALUMINIUM,ALLOYS,UNWRGHT			W 236155	364677	W 248454	326483	W 242554	304420	ALUMINIUM,ALLIAGES BRUTS
69	METAL MANUFACTURES NES		86397		18220		25753		42881	ART MANUFACT EN METAL NDA
691	STRUCTURES AND PARTS NES	W 22277	29025	W 4306	8533	W 4563	9681	W 15165	31911	CONSTRUCT FER,ACIER,ALU
6911	STRUCTURES,PARTS IRN,STL			W 3716	6636	W 3965	7243	W 13868	26685	CONSTRUCT FER,ACIER,FONTE
692	METAL TANKS,BOXES,ETC	W 4885	8260	W 1733	6073	W 6510	11043	W 4577	6618	RECIPIENTS METALLIQUES
6924	MTL TRANSPORT BOXES ETC			W 1486	5130	W 6162	10502	W 4496	6409	FUTS,TAMBOURS,BIDONS
69241	STL TRANSPORT BOXES ETC			W 426	640	W 2369	4453			FUTS,TAMBOURS,BIDONS FER
69242	ALUMNM TRNSPRT BOXES ETC			W 604	3407	W 199	1260			FUTS,TAMBOURS,BIDONS ALU
69244	ALUMNM COMP GAS CYLINDRS			W 199	755	W 2919	4060			RECIP ALU GAZ COMPRIMES
693	WIRE PRODUCTS NON ELECTR	W 36331	6189	W 1881	2528	W 3378	3039	W 2732	1958	OUVRAGES FILS METALLIQUES
699	BASE METAL MFRS NES	W 12067	16554	W 250	782	W 266	1457	W 401	1994	ART MANUFACTURES MET NDA
7	MACHINES,TRANSPORT EQUIP		793968		35848		60758		97964	MACHINES MATERIEL TRANSPORT
71	POWER GENERATING EQUIPMT		16767				9			MACHINES GENERATRICES
72	MACHS FOR SPCL INDUSTRYS		99988				3		2	MAC SPECIALES POUR INDUST
723	CIVIL ENGNEERG EQUIP ETC	W 19382	80552				3			APPAREILS DE GENIE CIVIL
74	GENRL INDUSTRL MACHY NES		74746		2743		1911		2050	MACH APP INDUSTRIE
741	HEATING,COOLING EQUIPMNT	W 4711	26708	W 366	2701	W 634	1741	W 269	1737	MACH CHAUFFAGE,PIECES
744	MECHANICAL HANDLING EQU	W 7479	16210						2	EQUIP MANUTENTION PIECES
749	NONELEC MACH PTS,ACC NES	W 2054	17434	W 1	10	W 3	67	W 4	257	PIECES MACH NON ELEC NDA
75	OFFICE MACHNES,ADP EQUIP		21001				13		126	MACH BUREAU TRAIT AUTOM
76	TELECOMM,SOUND EQUIPMENT		161623		8		4			EQUIPMENT DE TELECOM
761	TELEVISION RECEIVERS	W 4750	53566							RECEPTEURS DE TELEVISION
762	RADIO BROADCAST RECEIVRS	W 1575	18533							RECEPTEURS RADIODIFFUSION
763	SOUND RECORDRS,PHONOGRPH	W 12791	83159							PHONO,APP ENREGISTREMENT
77	ELECTRIC MACHNRY NES ETC		129501		13247		19697		15617	MACH APP ELECT NDA
773	ELECTR DISTRIBUTNG EQUIP	W 5565	14973	W 3931	12394	W 6764	17746	W 6363	14237	EQUIPMT DISTRIBUTION ELECT
7731	INSULATED WIRE,CABLE ETC			W 3916	12348	W 6764	17746	W 6363	14237	FILS,CABLES ISOLES ELECT
775	HOUSEHOLD TYPE EQUIP NES	W 10530	53917	W 76	379	W 178	774	W 259	755	MACH,APP USAGE DOMESTQUE
778	ELECTRICAL MACHINERY NES	W 18236	51667							AUTRES MACH ELECT NDA
78	ROAD VEHICLES		270297		534		353		167	VEHICULES ROUTIERS
781	PASS MOTOR VEH EXC BUSES	W 17231	148296							AUTO TRANSPORT PERSONNES
782	LORRIES,SPCL MTR VEH NES	W 9397	30796							VEHICULES SPECIAUX,MARCH
784	MOTOR VEH PRTS,ACCES NES	W 9700	82309	W 42	437	W 26	192	W 28	147	PIECES 722,781,782,783
79	OTHR TRANSPORT EQUIPMENT		14939		19312		38767		79999	AUTRE MATERIEL TRANSPORT
793	SHIPS AND BOATS ETC	W 3767	10617	W 5362	19312	W 3457	38767	W 13053	79999	NAVIRES BATEAUX,ETC
7938	TUGS,SPECIAL VESSELS ETC			W 5300	17655	W 3250	38041	W 12971	79702	REMORQUEURS,BATEAUX SPEC
79382	SPECL PURPOSE VESSLS ETC			W 5300	17655	W 3250	38041	W 12971	79702	BAT–PHARES,–POMPES,DRAGUES
8	MISC MANUFACTURED GOODS		653178		147213		228379		257323	ART MANUFACTURES DIVERS
821	*FURNITURE,PARTS THEREOF	W 12328	24883	W 2660	7698	W 3612	8912	W 3350	7963	MEUBLES ET PIECES
8211	CHAIRS,SEATS AND PARTS			W 966	3137	W 939	2562	W 666	1357	SIEGES ET PIECES
8219	FURNITURE AND PARTS NES			W 1386	3892	W 2332	5378	W 2331	5447	AUTRES MEUBLES ET PIECES
82191	METAL FURNITURE NES			W 1386	3892	W 2332	5378			MEUBLES NDA EN METAL
84	CLOTHING AND ACCESSORIES		269059		121508		193937		227093	VETEMENTS
842	MENS OUTERWEAR NOT KNIT	W 24298	171800	W 1823	20408	W 2349	24743	W 3467	26811	VET DESSUS POUR HOMMES
8422	— SUITS			W 1421	14543	W 2147	21497			COMPLETS HOMMES MAT TEXT
8423	— TROUSERS,BREECHES ETC							W 3432	26517	PANTALONS HOMMES MAT TEX
8429	— OTHER OUTER GARMENTS			W 389	5659	W 193	3198			AUT VET DES HOM MAT TEX
843	WOMENS OUTERWEAR NONKNIT	W 5325	45733	W 1722	20325	W 2646	27197	W 3456	33677	VET DESSUS FEMMES MAT TEX
8431	— COATS AND JACKETS			W 18	232		7	W 2278	20568	MANT,VEST FEM MAT TEXTIL
8432	— SUITS AND COSTUMES			W 933	10422	W 1980	18852			COSTUMES–TAIL MAT TEXIL
8435	— BLOUSES			W 654	8011	W 588	7436	W 1004	11446	BLOUSES FEM MAT TEXTILES
844	UNDER GARMENTS NOT KNIT	W 1762	15836	W 3955	39418	W 3720	36995	W 6499	52236	VETEMENT DESSOUS MAT TEX
8441	— MENS SHIRTS			W 3746	38218	W 3608	35965	W 6321	50666	CHEMISES HOMMES MAT TEXT
845	OUTERWEAR KNIT NONELASTC	W 1657	12816	W 581	6479	W 1381	12077	W 1500	11486	VET DESSOUS,ACCES BONNET
8451	— JERSEYS,PULLOVERS ETC			W 196	2174	W 1019	8287	W 1074	7449	CHANDAILS,PULL–OVERS ETC
8459	— OTHER,CLTHG ACCESRYS			W 310	3485	W 202	1698	W 305	2660	AUT VET DESSUS DE BONNE
846	UNDER GARMENTS KNITTED	W 182	711	W 4117	34571	W 11968	92573	W 14004	102184	SOUS VETS DE BONNETERIE
8462	— OF COTTON NON ELASTIC			W 3577	29321	W 11716	90086	W 13774	100123	SOUS–VET BONNET COTON
84629	—— OTHER			W 3577	29321	W 11716	90086	W 13774	100123	AUT SOUS–VET BONNET COTON
8463	— OF SYNTH FBR NONELAST			W 538	5245	W 251	2485	W 229	2027	SOUS–VET BONNET FIB SYNT
84632	—— MENS SHIRTS			W 538	5245	W 251	2485	W 229	2027	CHEMISES DE BON FIB SYNMT
848	HEADGEAR,NONTXTL CLOTHNG	W 2956	13661	W 2	3	W 4	29	W 5	119	VET ACCES MAT AUT QUE TEX
851	*FOOTWEAR	W 3158	16399		3	W 38	277	W 26	91	CHAUSSURES
88	PHOTO EQU,OPTICL GDS ETC		79279		332		266		154	APP,FOURN PHOTO,OP,MONTR
881	PHOTO APPARAT,EQUIPT NES	W 671	14482							APP,EQUIP PHOTO NDA
882	PHOTO,CINEMA SUPPLIES	W 2458	35597	W 29	332	W 18	266	W 17	130	PRODUITS PHOTO,CINEMA
885	WATCHES AND CLOCKS		28158							HORLOGERIE
89	MISC MANUFCTRD GOODS NES		240232		17240		24677		20918	ART MANUFACTURES DIVERS
893	ARTICLES OF PLASTIC NES	W 11655	24560	W 2930	6431	W 5943	10703	W 4886	8364	OUVRAGES EN MAT DIVIS 58
8939	MISC PLASTIC ARTICLES			W 2306	5171	W 4245	8063	W 3583	6083	ART DIVERS EN MAT DIV 58
89399	OTHR PLASTC ARTICLES NES			W 2306	5171	W 4244	8062	W 3352	5602	AUT OUV MAT DIV 58
894	TOYS,SPORTING GOODS,ETC	W 3627	13597	W 4	4	W 1	1	W 8	31	VOITURES ENFANTS,JOUETS
897	GOLD,SILVER WARE,JEWELRY		34461		9846		10984		9732	BIJOUTERIE,ORFEVRERIE
8973	PREC JEWLRY,GLD–SILVWARE				9846		10984		9731	BIJOUX OR,ARGENT ORFEVRE
89731	PRECIOUS METAL JEWELLERY				9843		10971		9731	ART BIJOUTERIE,JOAILLER
898	MUSICAL INSTRUMENTS,PTS	W 1900	16572	W 46	352	W 161	1927	W 104	1116	INSTRUMENTS DE MUSIQUE
899	OTHER MANUFACTURED GOODS	W 45835	137197	W 13	46	W 26	125	W 53	210	AUT ART MANUF DIVERS NDA
9	GOODS NOT CLASSD BY KIND		271109		4219		44			ART TRANSACT NON CLASSES
931	*SPECIAL TRANSACTIONS	W 19998	126201							TRANS.SPECIALES
971	*GOLD,NON MONETARY NES		141710	K 921	4219	K 145	23			OR NON MONETAIRE
97103	GOLD SWEEPINGS,WASTE ETC			K 921	4219	K 145	23			CENDRES ORFEVR,DECHET OR

FOOT NOTES – NOTES

TABLE 1 –

1 Excludes exports of most crude petroleum in 1990, 1991, 1992 and 1993.

TABLE 3 –

1 Excludes exports of most crude petroleum in 1990, 1991, 1992 and 1993. Excludes re–exports in 1989, 1991 and 1992.

TABLE 4 –

1 Because of the conversion from SITC Rev.3 to SITC Rev.2, not all data for 1991, 1992 and 1993 are comparable with those for previous years. For further details see the Introduction.

Foot Notes (Continued) – Notes (Suite)

TABLE 5 –
1 Excludes exports of most crude petroleum; excludes re–exports in 1991 and 1992. Because of the conversion from SITC Rev.3 to SITC Rev.2, not all data for 1991, 1992 and 1993 are comparable with those for previous years. For further details see the introduction.
TABLEAU 1 –
1 La plupart des exportations du pétrole brut est exclue en 1990, 1991, 1992 et 1993.
TABLEAU 3 –
1 La plupart des exportations du pétrole brut est exclue en 1990, 1991, 1992 et 1993.
TABLEAU 4 –
1 A cause de la conversion de la CTCI Rev.3 à la CTCI Rev.2, toutes les données pour 1991, 1992 et 1993 ne sont pas comparables à celles des années précédentes. Se référer aux explications supplémentaires dans l'introduction.
TABLEAU 5 –
1 La plupart des exportations du pétrole brut est exclue. A cause de la conversion de la CTCI Rev.3 à la CTCI Rev. 2, toutes les données pour 1991, 1992 et 1993 ne sont pas comparables à celles des années précédentes. S e référer aux explications supplémentaires dans l'introduction.

1. HISTORICAL SERIES, 1961–1996 GENERAL TRADE, IMPORTS C.I.F., EXPORTS F.O.B.
SERIES HISTORIQUES, 1961–1996 COMMERCE GENERAL, IMPORTATIONS C.A.F., EXPORTATIONS F.O.B

YEAR ANNEE	VALUE IN MILLION POUNDS STERLING VALEUR EN MILLION POUNDS STERLING MERCHANDISE –MARCHANDISE IMPORTS	EXPORTS	GOLD –OR IMPORTS	EXPORTS	CONVERSION FACTORS U.S. CENTS PER POUND STERLING FACTEURS DE CONVERSION CENTS E.U. PAR POUND STERLING IMPORTS	EXPORTS	INDEX NUMBERS –INDICES QUANTUM IMPORTS	EXPORTS	UNIT VALUE VALEUR UNITAIRE IMPORTS	EXPORTS
1961	4546.00	3955.00	637.90	321.80	280.0000	280.0000	23	26	11	13
1962	4628.00	4062.00	434.60	372.50	280.0000	280.0000	24	27	11	13
1963	4983.00	4365.00	436.30	251.20	280.0000	280.0000	25	28	12	13
1964	5659.00	4565.00	520.30	256.90	280.0000	280.0000	28	29	12	13
1965	5751.00	4901.00	504.90	993.50	280.0000	280.0000	29	31	12	14
1966	5947.00	5241.00	337.50	485.40	280.0000	280.0000	29	32	12	14
1967	6434.00	5214.00	444.50	821.80	275.0000	275.8000	31	32	12	14
1968	7890.00	6402.00	672.20	836.90	240.0000	240.0000	35	36	14	15
1969	8315.00	7298.00	222.00	196.00	240.0000	240.0000	35	40	14	16
1970	9040.00	8076.00	448.30	288.20	240.0000	240.0000	37	41	15	17
1971	9821.00	9187.00	485.70	341.00	243.4790	243.6190	39	44	16	18
1972	11143.00	9759.00	317.50	321.00	249.7390	249.7950	43	45	16	19
1973	15852.00	12505.00	482.40	673.00	245.0120	245.1590	50	52	21	21
1974	23234.00	16600.00	645.40	1558.00	234.2090	234.2540	49	54	31	27
1975	24046.00	19607.00			221.6850	221.4390	46	53	35	34
1976	31084.00	25277.00			179.3690	179.5010	49	58	43	40
1977	36219.00	31990.00			174.4810	174.6370	50	62	50	48
1978	39533.00	35380.00			191.8700	191.9490	53	64	51	52
1979	46925.00	40637.00			212.4490	212.6690	58	66	56	58
1980	49773.00	47357.00			232.1860	232.5720	55	67	64	65
1981	51168.60	50998.10			200.7584	201.6149	53	66	69	71
1982	56978.20	55557.80			174.9931	174.7287	56	68	75	76
1983	66101.10	60684.30			151.6394	151.5036	61	70	82	82
1984	78967.40	70488.30			134.1827	134.0828	68	75	89	88
1985	84789.60	85027.00			128.8708	129.3632	70	80	93	93
1986	86176.00	72988.00			146.6377	146.5649	75	83	89	86
1987	94026.00	79849.01			164.2177	164.3225	80	87	91	89
1988	106571.00	81655.01			178.0212	178.1671	65	70	87	86
1989	121699.00	93771.01			163.6989	163.4824	70	75	91	90
1990	126086.00	103692.00			178.0931	178.7275	100	100	100	100
1991	118786.00	104877.00			176.6736	176.6890	95	101	101	101
1992	125867.00	108508.00			176.0892	175.6021	101	103	102	103
1993	137404.00	120936.00			150.1562	150.1285	101	103	112	116
1994	147564.00	133030.00			153.2705	153.3559	108	116	115	118
1995	168055.00	153353.00			157.8776	157.8292	112	125	127	126
1996	184113.00	167764.00			156.1557	156.2306	122	135	127	128

2. IMPORTS BY BROAD ECONOMIC CATEGORY AND EXPORTS BY INDUSTRIAL ORIGIN. (PERCENTAGE OF TOTAL VALUE)
IMPORTATIONS PAR CATEGORIES ECONOMIQUES ET EXPORTATIONS PAR BRANCHE D'ACTIVITE.(EN POURCENTAGE DE LA VALEUR TOTALE)

IMPORTS – IMPORTATIONS

	1990	1991	1992	1993	1994	1995	1996
TOTAL IMPORTS–IMPORTATIONS TOTALES	100.	100.	100.	100.	100.	100.	100.
1 FOOD BEV–ALIMENTATION BOISSONS	9.1	9.6	9.9	9.5	9.2	9.0	8.9
11 PRIMARY–PRODUITS DE BASE	3.6	3.7	3.8	3.7	3.6	3.5	3.4
111 FOR INDUSTRY–POUR L'INDUSTRIE	0.7	0.6	0.7	0.7	0.7	0.6	0.6
112 FOR HOUSEHOLDS–POUR LES MENAGES	3.0	3.1	3.1	2.9	2.8	2.8	2.8
12 PROCESSED–PRODUITS ELABORES	5.5	5.9	6.1	5.9	5.6	5.5	5.5
121 FOR INDUSTRY–POUR L'INDUSTRIE	0.8	0.9	0.9	0.9	0.9	0.9	0.9
122 FOR HOUSEHOLDS–POUR LES MENAGES	4.7	5.0	5.2	4.9	4.7	4.6	4.6
2 IND SUPPLIES–APPROV INDUSTRIELS	29.3	28.9	27.8	26.5	27.8	29.0	27.3
21 PRIMARY–PRODUITS DE BASE	4.3	4.2	3.8	4.3	4.0	4.0	4.0
22 PROCESSED–PRODUITS ELABORES	24.9	24.7	23.9	22.2	23.8	25.0	23.3
3 FUELS–COMBUSTIBLES	6.2	6.3	5.5	5.3	4.0	3.5	3.8
31 PRIMARY–PRODUITS DE BASE	4.2	4.4	4.0	3.9	2.7	2.4	2.7
32 PROCESSED–PRODUITS ELABORES	1.9	1.9	1.5	1.4	1.3	1.1	1.1
321 MOTOR SPIRIT–ESSENCE	0.6	0.5	0.3	0.3	0.3	0.2	0.2
322 OTHER–AUTRES	1.3	1.4	1.2	1.1	1.1	0.9	0.9
4 MACHINERY–EQUIPEMENT	21.9	22.6	23.2	24.5	24.7	26.1	26.6
41 CAPITAL EQUIPMENT–MACHINES	16.0	16.4	16.8	18.0	17.9	18.8	18.6
42 PARTS–PIECES ACCESSOIRES	5.8	6.2	6.4	6.5	6.8	7.3	8.0
5 TRANSPORT–TRANSPORT	14.9	13.8	15.0	16.0	16.6	15.6	16.3
51 PASSENGER CARS–AUTOMOBILES	5.8	4.6	5.3	6.2	6.2	5.9	6.2
52 OTHER–AUTRES	3.1	2.1	1.9	2.3	2.9	2.0	2.1
521 INDUSTRIAL–INDUSTRIELS	2.9	1.9	1.8	2.1	2.8	1.8	1.9
522 NON INDUSTRIAL–NON INDUSTRIEL	0.2	0.2	0.2	0.2	0.2	0.2	0.2
53 PARTS–PIECES ACCESSOIRES	5.9	7.1	7.8	7.6	7.5	7.6	8.0
6 CONSUM GOODS–BIENS CONSOMMATION	16.1	16.6	17.2	17.1	16.9	15.9	15.9
61 DURABLE–DURABLES	5.8	5.2	5.2	5.0	5.2	4.5	4.5
62 SEMI DURABLE–SEMI DURABLES	7.7	8.4	8.9	8.9	8.4	8.0	8.2
63 NON DURABLE–NON DURABLES	2.6	3.0	3.1	3.2	3.3	3.4	3.2
7 GOODS NES–BIENS NDA	2.6	1.6	1.5	1.0	0.8	1.0	1.1

EXPORTS – EXPORTATIONS

	1990	1991	1992	1993	1994	1995	1996
TOTAL EXPORTS–EXPORTATIONS TOTALES	100.	100.	100.	100.	100.	100.	100.
1 AGRICULTURE	1.8	1.9	2.1	1.6	1.5	1.5	1.4
2 MINING QUARRY–INDUS EXTRACTIVES	7.6	6.7	6.3	6.1	7.3	6.8	7.2
3 MANUFACTURING–IND MANUFACTUR	90.5	91.2	91.6	92.4	91.3	91.7	91.4
31 FOOD BEV TOBACCO–ALIM BOISS TAB	5.5	5.9	6.5	6.4	6.4	6.3	5.8
32 TEXTILES–INDUSTRIES TEXTILES	5.0	4.8	4.9	4.9	4.9	4.7	4.8
33 WOOD & PRODUCTS–BOIS & PRODUITS	0.2	0.2	0.2	0.1	0.2	0.2	0.2
34 PAPER & PRODUCTS–PAPIER & PRODT	2.7	2.8	2.9	3.0	2.9	2.9	2.7
35 CHEMICALS–INDUSTRIES CHIMIQUES	17.5	18.1	18.6	19.7	18.7	18.0	17.7
36 NON METAL MIN–MIN NON METAL	1.3	1.3	1.3	1.3	1.2	1.3	1.2
37 BASIC METAL–IND METAL BASE	5.3	5.0	4.6	4.5	4.6	4.9	4.3
38 METAL MANUF–MANUF METAL	48.0	49.1	48.4	49.0	48.9	50.3	51.8
39 OTH MANUF IND–AUTRES MANUF	5.1	4.1	4.3	3.4	3.5	3.1	2.9

3. TRADE BY PRINCIPAL COUNTRIES OF FIRST AND LAST CONSIGNMENT (VALUE IN THOUSAND U.S. DOLLARS)
ECHANGES SELON LES PRINCIPAUX PAYS DE PREMIERE ET DE DERNIERE CONSIGNATION (VALEUR EN MILLIERS DE DOLLARS EU)

COUNTRIES–PAYS	GENERAL IMPORTS C.I.F. IMPORTATIONS GENERALES C.A.F					COUNTRIES–PAYS	GENERAL EXPORTS F.O.B. EXPORTATIONS GENERALES F.O.B.				
	1992	1993	1994	1995	1996		1992	1993	1994	1995	1996
World	221658146	211726218	224551907	262572088	283851257	Monde	190480813	171699761	202857933	239948047	259277030
Africa	4736521	4692116	4733439	5516471	6084550	Afrique	6327995	5909698	6213990	7478100	7841697
Americas	31881017	33841818	34349450	40832275	45447855	Amériques	27643919	29454397	33432413	36360016	39237294
Northern America	27692099	29651165	30200151	35906239	39993038	Amérique du Nord	24588726	26150092	29464001	31962866	34593974
LAIA	3174309	3185265	3153905	3850232	4175053	ALAI	2142214	2363177	2976714	3046983	3525377
CACM	92927	131142	188554	194546	211718	MCAC	136844	117238	123703	157802	157691
Caribbean	682163	641456	585747	643359	801180	Caraïbes	597820	635175	694228	966484	736505
Rest of America	239520	232790	221093	237899	266865	Autre Amérique	178315	188715	173768	225882	223747
As.ex F.USSR	37544140	41978757	40822437	47533399	53259093	Asie l'URSS exclus	28270622	29926990	32535672	38796286	43579684
Eur.x F.USSR	141989626	126037472	139233065	162673842	171935768	Europe l'URSS exclus	122714041	101605726	124729657	150423605	160663997
EU	126096322	109202935	123305774	144117746	151892947	UE	114198938	92845683	114388948	138047466	146654835
EFTA	14166157	14790293	13435836	15369035	16687999	AELE	5892449	5914740	7033543	7727866	8499148
East Europe	1333534	1648854	2048429	2671381	2747354	Europe de l'Est	1936995	2109557	2453422	3430860	4418855
Other Europe	175599	193081	227069	268124	342145	Autre de l'Europe	469580	504375	464892	608123	569102
Former USSR	1344212	1830636	2071676	2408007	3127063	Ancienne URSS	835865	1137738	1482440	1890035	2379334
Oceania	2780924	2655464	2695993	2979513	3348897	Océanie	2965601	2982334	3635114	4123182	4675340
Germany/Allemagne	33520433	28972869	32773364	40247264	40827555	Germany/Allemagne	26705227	21944700	25810704	31141074	31573918
USA/Etats–Unis d'Amer	24333304	26638873	27290243	32129380	36088766	USA/Etats–Unis d'Amer	21756391	23342026	26486310	29071848	31472744
France,Monac	21526151	19626928	22612077	25038900	26533182	France,Monac	20160918	16540873	20139674	23390210	25904451
Netherlands/Pays–Bas	17448085	12712427	14981431	17628919	18744668	Netherlands/Pays–Bas	14927051	11377241	14296865	18867533	20308576
Japan/Japon	13106046	13810264	13551529	15177976	14041648	Ireland/Irlande	10074357	8692029	10660834	12564003	13974932
Italy/Italie	11914798	9798651	11012169	12982675	14606469	Belgium–Luxembourg	10032617	7139723	10909050	12744837	12916480
Belgium–Luxembourg	10110339	9508080	10592163	12338159	12906151	Italy/Italie	10792312	8306297	10160409	12009882	12240481
Ireland/Irlande	8928617	7955762	8677073	10800793	10962112	Spain/Espagne	7942720	6164548	7708786	9636317	10470330
Switz.Liecht	6901474	7639397	7383275	8142507	8488286	Sweden/Suède	4281499	4341899	5134399	6148201	6738037
Norway,SVD,JM	6842884	6746909	5685823	6828857	7781513	Japan/Japon	3917251	3983771	4587119	5970649	6661036
Sweden/Suède	5781008	5860883	6375874	6780492	7151466	Switz.Liecht	3238134	3413054	3766187	4355050	5029696
Spain/Espagne	5325804	4758911	5581958	6858276	7771336	Hong Kong	2831477	3257960	3523446	4192893	4567152
Hong Kong	4221869	4849970	4720136	5586978	6358552	Saudi Arabia	3454328	2741527	2323728	2595291	3879109
Denmark/Danemark	4200059	3083491	3230654	3398873	3620120	Australia/Australie	2416729	2399592	2935910	3348136	3852011
Finland/Finlande	2952608	3081523	3453568	3717678	3890363	Canada	2780527	2768089	2939317	2859828	3084757
Canada	3340683	3000011	2882927	3756874	3878020	Denmark/Danemark	2739602	2196702	2716501	3324201	3437675
Singapore/Singapour	2100687	2613179	2907375	3482444	4016271	Norway,SVD,JM	2492589	2281161	3099136	3154848	3228900
China/Chine	1679252	2147102	2516392	3059446	3437827	Singapore/Singapour	2010548	2146326	2712161	3264848	3350589
Malaysia/Malaisie	1943820	2259197	1845417	2349023	3715768	So. Africa Customs Un	1951749	1733965	2211117	2946019	2991927
Korea, Republic of	1644670	1743622	1680164	2465649	3182256	Finland/Finlande	1750111	1696034	1989432	2574072	2761559
Portugal	2061921	1792357	1921532	2269179	2531580	India/Inde	1659850	1696448	2011255	2655824	2666195
India/Inde	1518209	1761582	1975564	2266292	2515041	Portugal	2043531	1831537	1881431	2294821	2576395
So. Africa Customs Un	1679657	1767766	1625736	1899981	2083599	United Arab Emirates	1626484	1973556	1707736	1868925	2177982
Australia/Australie	1784903	1611632	1629653	1753140	2023312	Turkey/Turquie	1214739	1571101	1247584	1827323	2446432
Austria/Autriche	1671050	1571140	1560108	1397137	1749640	Malaysia/Malaisie	1116240	1448718	2001603	1877521	1812283
Brazil/Brésil	1559647	1461783	1409107	1557486	1534696	Austria/Autriche	1395781	1368663	1587079	1686100	1937464
Thailand/Thaïlande	1130458	1246845	1399567	1641681	1854472	Korea, Republic of	1158597	1195593	1489052	1819966	2036525
Russian Federation	1183700	1330081	1233547	1524884	1990158	Israel/Israël	1029124	1315621	1582088	1749478	1977491
Saudi Arabia	1697010	2061927	1133590	1137949	1174946	Greece/Grèce	1353211	1245436	1393784	1666216	1814537
Indonesia/Indonésie	944004	1133365	1199412	1426997	1531010	Poland/Pologne	1063237	1077624	1077649	1490978	2110616
Turkey/Turquie	804740	860711	962705	1254947	1456380	Thailand/Thaïlande	836229	989911	1143402	1320443	1521760
Israel/Israël	854249	890145	877282	1092754	1298652	Russian Federation	801703	828518	1085145	1373735	1576731
New Zealand	755259	803034	826759	910210	986618	China/Chine	754613	1110176	1295650	1301158	1153765
Poland/Pologne	627535	726935	835214	1007376	936488	Brazil/Brésil	479428	623137	805487	1064568	1322477
Philippines	423844	447855	374510	556398	1398008	Nigeria/Nigéria	1093004	952847	702242	681052	676423
Greece/Grèce	655448	479913	533804	659400	598306	Indonesia/Indonésie	549076	497067	561337	829396	1293986
Pakistan	481342	524727	550056	573201	610299	Iran (Islamic Rp. of)	1022629	745470	443293	524966	619539
Mauritius/Maurice	480081	455203	448323	544911	537295	Kuwait/ Koweït	460370	467904	478527	869439	904711
United Arab Emirates	584542	406815	353550	443699	594655	New Zealand	464846	499773	630641	687949	737114
Chile/Chili	362314	399330	298195	473565	589419	Czech Republic		431721	574245	896355	1116425
Hungary/Hongrie	207163	246253	367964	586624	660835	Oman	422531	458781	555346	706956	649517
Iceland/Islande	421799	403987	366738	397672	418200	Egypt/Egypte	442853	506090	564349	605345	674005
Czech Republic		396804	426553	507570	581999	Brunei Darussalam	371234	487064	640323	401334	878619
Mexico/Mexique	268040	268148	367450	470668	522626	Pakistan	547302	508306	544502	537227	538216
Brunei Darussalam	222535	497576	450900	198795	455411	Philippines	359803	459613	544614	682454	617586
Egypt/Egypte	241279	304731	386553	389353	439473	Mexico/Mexique	511426	504239	597013	436800	495911
Morocco/Maroc	217019	295062	307435	400615	474593	Cyprus/Chypre	389485	354197	376017	485230	454209
Algeria/Algérie	286277	302670	280259	385660	316026	Hungary/Hongrie	283525	308802	397482	466955	542285
Argentina/Argentine	219433	228350	262046	398268	445695	Libyan Arab Jamahiriya	400726	411429	298898	358857	388723
Kuwait/ Koweït	224051	382590	366866	238989	280801	Ghana	305623	321397	292334	378920	468357

(VALUE AS PERCENTAGE OF WORLD TOTAL)(VALEURS EN POURCENTAGE DU TOTAL MONDIAL)

	1987	1988	1989	1990	1991	1992	1993	1994	1995	1996
Africa	2.4	2.2	2.1	2.4	2.3	2.1	2.2	2.1	2.1	2.1
Americas	13.4	13.9	14.9	15.0	15.1	14.4	16.0	15.3	15.6	16.0
Northern America	11.5	12.1	13.1	13.3	13.3	12.5	14.0	13.4	13.7	14.1
LAIA	1.5	1.3	1.4	1.3	1.3	1.4	1.5	1.4	1.5	1.5
CACM	0.0	0.0	0.0	0.1	0.0	0.0	0.1	0.1	0.1	0.1
Caribbean	0.3	0.3	0.3	0.4	0.3	0.3	0.3	0.3	0.2	0.3
Rest of America	0.1	0.1	0.1	0.1	0.1	0.1	0.1	0.1	0.1	0.1
As.ex F.USSR	14.7	15.4	15.2	14.8	16.1	16.9	19.8	18.2	18.1	18.8
Eur.x F.USSR	66.7	65.9	65.3	65.1	64.0	64.1	59.5	62.0	62.0	60.6
EU	58.4	58.1	57.8	57.4	56.4	56.9	51.6	54.9	54.9	53.5
EFTA	7.2	6.8	6.5	6.9	6.9	6.4	7.0	6.0	5.9	5.9
East Europe	0.9	0.8	0.8	0.6	0.5	0.6	0.8	0.9	1.0	1.0
Other Europe	0.3	0.2	0.2	0.2	0.2	0.1	0.1	0.1	0.1	0.1
Former USSR	0.9	0.7	0.7	0.7	0.8	0.6	0.9	0.9	0.9	1.1
Oceania	1.3	1.2	1.2	1.3	1.2	1.3	1.3	1.2	1.1	1.2
Germany/Allemagne	16.8	16.6	16.5	15.8	14.9	15.1	13.7	14.6	15.3	14.4
USA/Etats–Unis d'Amer	9.8	10.2	11.2	11.5	11.6	11.0	12.6	12.2	12.2	12.7
France,Monac	8.9	8.8	8.9	9.4	9.3	9.7	9.3	10.1	9.5	9.3
Netherlands/Pays–Bas	7.6	7.8	7.9	8.3	8.4	7.9	6.0	6.7	6.7	6.6
Japan/Japon	5.8	6.1	5.8	5.4	5.7	5.9	6.5	6.0	5.8	4.9
Italy/Italie	5.5	5.5	5.5	5.3	5.4	5.4	4.6	4.9	4.9	5.1
Belgium–Luxembourg	4.6	4.7	4.7	4.5	4.6	4.6	4.5	4.7	4.7	4.5
Ireland/Irlande	3.7	3.6	3.5	3.6	3.7	4.0	3.8	3.9	4.1	3.9
Switz.Liecht	3.5	3.7	3.4	3.4	3.2	3.1	3.6	3.3	3.1	3.0
Norway,SVD,JM	3.5	2.9	3.0	3.3	3.6	3.1	3.2	2.5	2.6	2.7

	1987	1988	1989	1990	1991	1992	1993	1994	1995	1996
Afrique	4.2	4.1	3.6	3.6	3.5	3.3	3.4	3.1	3.1	3.0
Amériques	18.2	17.4	17.1	16.1	14.2	14.5	17.2	16.5	15.2	15.1
Amérique du Nord	16.3	15.7	15.5	14.5	12.5	12.9	15.2	14.5	13.3	13.3
ALAI	1.3	1.2	1.0	1.1	1.1	1.1	1.4	1.5	1.3	1.4
MCAC	0.1	0.1	0.1	0.1	0.1	0.1	0.1	0.1	0.1	0.1
Caraïbes	0.5	0.4	0.4	0.4	0.4	0.3	0.4	0.3	0.4	0.3
Autre Amérique	0.1	0.1	0.1	0.1	0.1	0.1	0.1	0.1	0.1	0.1
Asie l'URSS exclus	15.1	15.2	15.6	14.8	14.6	14.8	17.4	16.0	16.2	16.8
Europe l'URSS exclus	59.2	59.6	59.7	62.1	65.1	64.4	59.2	61.5	62.7	62.0
UE	54.0	54.6	54.9	57.3	60.6	60.0	54.1	56.4	57.5	56.6
AELE	3.9	3.7	3.6	3.6	3.4	3.1	3.4	3.5	3.2	3.3
Europe de l'Est	0.8	0.8	0.7	0.6	0.7	1.0	1.2	1.2	1.4	1.7
Autre de l'Europe	0.5	0.5	0.5	0.5	0.4	0.2	0.3	0.2	0.3	0.2
Ancienne URSS	0.6	0.6	0.7	0.6	0.3	0.4	0.7	0.7	0.8	0.9
Océanie	2.1	2.1	2.3	2.0	1.6	1.6	1.7	1.8	1.7	1.8
Germany/Allemagne	11.8	11.7	11.9	12.7	14.0	14.0	12.8	12.7	13.0	12.2
USA/Etats–Unis d'Amer	13.8	13.2	13.1	12.6	10.9	11.4	13.6	13.1	12.1	12.1
France,Monac	9.8	10.1	10.2	10.5	11.1	10.6	9.6	9.9	9.7	10.0
Netherlands/Pays–Bas	7.3	6.8	7.1	7.3	7.9	7.8	6.6	7.0	7.9	7.8
Ireland/Irlande	4.8	5.0	5.0	5.1	5.1	5.3	5.1	5.3	5.2	5.4
Belgium–Luxembourg	4.8	5.2	5.2	5.5	5.6	5.3	4.2	5.4	5.3	5.0
Italy/Italie	5.2	5.0	4.9	5.4	5.9	5.7	4.8	5.0	5.0	4.7
Spain/Espagne	2.8	3.4	3.4	3.6	4.2	4.2	3.6	3.8	4.0	4.0
Sweden/Suède	2.9	2.7	2.6	2.6	2.4	2.2	2.5	2.5	2.6	2.6
Japan/Japon	1.9	2.1	2.5	2.5	2.2	2.1	2.3	2.3	2.5	2.6

4. General Imports C.I.F. by Commodities according to the S.I.T.C. (Rev. 2) in thousand U.S. Dollars
Importations Générales C.A.F. par Produits d'après la C.T.C.I. (Rév. 2) en milliers de Dollars E.U.

SITC CTCI	COMMODITY	1993 WEIGHT POIDS	1993 VALUE VALEUR	1994 WEIGHT POIDS	1994 VALUE VALEUR	1995 WEIGHT POIDS	1995 VALUE VALEUR	1996 WEIGHT POIDS	1996 VALUE VALEUR	PRODUIT
	ALL COMMODITIES		211726218		224551907		262572088		283851257	TOUS PRODUITS
0	FOOD AND LIVE ANIMALS		18295719		18380948		20975647		22321153	ALIMENTS,ANIMAUX VIVANTS
01	MEAT AND PREPARATIONS		3075991		2889229		3618801		3939042	VIANDES ET PREPARATIONS
011	MEAT FRESH,CHILLD,FROZEN	W 565226	1676561	W 571132	1551897	W 665635	1889561	W 691035	2110780	VIANDES FRAICHES,REF,CONGE
012	MEAT DRIED,SALTED,SMOKED	W 205527	696247		630933	W 229378	851457	W 262780	1062176	VIANDE,ABATS SALES,SECHES
0121	PIG MEAT DRIED,SLTD,SMKD	W 205162	693710		625825	W 228694	847895	W 262417	1060178	LARD,JAMBONS
014	MEAT PREPD,PRSVD,NES ETC	W 231742	703183	W 224409	706399	W 258610	877783	W 229868	766086	CONSERVES DE VIANDES
02	DAIRY PRODCTS,BIRDS'EGGS		1513231		1514693		1588651		1710330	PRODUITS LAITIERS,OEUFS
024	CHEESE AND CURD	W 189045	795972	W 210361	812131	W 209655	841712	W 310656	983353	FROMAGE ET CAILLEBOTTE
03	FISH AND PREPARATIONS		1580370		1550647		1775151		1901001	POISSONS ET PREPARATIONS
034	FISH,FRESH,CHILLED,FROZN	W 243079	690063	W 266841	667474	W 266283	715705	W 301843	808150	POISSON FRAIS, REFRIG,CONG
037	FISH ETC PREPD,PRSVD NES	W 171684	715342	W 151833	629768	W 178488	793571	W 193871	851242	POIS,CRUST,MOL PREPARES
04	CEREALS AND PREPARATIONS		1838447		1751842		1849670		2025064	CEREALES ET PRODUITS
048	CEREAL ETC PREPARATIONS	W 570609	821739	W 460610	865306	W 508465	977918	W 531962	1125413	PREPTNS A BASE CEREALES
05	VEGETABLES AND FRUIT		4809100		5085949		6082935		6489458	LEGUMES ET FRUITS
054	VEG ETC FRSH,SMPLY PRSVD	W 1870833	1545832	W 2371968	1771592	W 2973950	2214464	W 2511957	2218793	LEGUMES FRAIS,CONG,SECS
0545	OTHER FRESH VEGETABLES	W 586064	690249	W 746942	760602	W 840778	927740	W 871629	986343	AUTRES LEGUMES FRAIS,REF
05459	FRESH VEGETABLES NES	W 408598	612304	W 514297	659108	W 577267	800005	W 653648	894735	LEGUMES FRAIS,REFRI NDA
057	FRUIT,NUTS,FRESH,DRIED	W 2475411	2160112	W 2556733	2259988	W 2641393	2515006	W 2773690	2812590	FRUITS FRAIS OU SECS
058	FRUIT PRESERVED,PREPARED	W 650223	804846	W 651892	772309	W 707696	933715	W 750074	1017623	CONSERVES DE FRUITS
06	SUGAR AND PREPS,HONEY		1232507		1214192		1309042		1355017	SUCRES ET PRODUITS
061	SUGAR AND HONEY	W 2191938	1078609		1060666		1158516	W 2340911	1202696	SUCRES ET MIEL
0611	RAW BEET AND CANE SUGAR	W 1198052	804154	W 1232162	777014	W 1203783	840612	W 1232829	856196	SUCRES BRUTS
07	COFFEE,TEA,COCOA,SPICES		1574311		1858755		1986350		1976760	CAFE,THE,CACAO,EPICES
081	*FEEDING STUFF FOR ANIML	W 4712775	1307229		1180151	W 5293894	1255179	W 4956126	1335142	NOURRITURE POUR ANIMAUX
09	MISC EDIBLE PRODUCTS		1151416		1141188		1268875		1280202	PREP ALIMENTAIRES DIVERSES
098	EDIBLE PRODCTS,PREPS NES	W 316032	1078302	W 345808	1052472	W 412157	1173645	W 337559	1179136	PREP ALIMENTAIRES NDA
09809	MISC FOOD PREPRTIONS NES	W 201048	853334	W 217394	777067	W 294960	899832	W 218492	927212	PREP ALIMENTAIRES NDA
1	BEVERAGES AND TOBACCO		3343679		3356982		3854150		4455158	BOISSONS ET TABACS
11	BEVERAGES		2661429		2775938		3096976		3482441	BOISSONS
112	ALCOHOLIC BEVERAGES	W 1525364	2487228	W 1598057	2598264	W 1545404	2860624	W 1683598	3264179	BOISSONS ALCOOLIQUES
1121	WINE OF FRESH GRAPES ETC	W 837788	1653895	W 905530	1773390	W 873062	1969965	W 950170	2296128	VINS DE RAISINS FRAIS
11212	WINE OF FRESH GRAPES	W 782087	1581354	W 849998	1718582	W 798757	1887845	W 879619	2201260	VINS DE MOUTS DE RAISINS
12	TOBACCO AND MANUFACTURES		682250		581044		757175		972717	TABACS BRUTS FABRIQUES
2	CRUDE MATERLS,EXCL FUELS		7625537		8398746		9799070		9611654	MAT BRUTES NON COMESTIBLES
24	CORK AND WOOD		1782616		2135928		1864513		1897675	LIEGE ET BOIS
248	WOOD SHAPED,SLEEPERS	W 3778761	1671750	W 4415847	2011752	W 3116420	1691201	W 3358647	1707515	BOIS SIMPLEMENT TRAVAILLES
2482	LUMBER SHAPED CONIFER	W 3362899	1306565	W 3992707	1617046	W 2752534	1307328	W 2935929	1324944	CONIFERES SCIES,RABOTES
24821	LUMBER SAWN ETC CONIFER	W 3313686	1267922	W 3942351	1575958	W 2726268	1275294	W 2907986	1284050	CONIFERES SCIES LONGITUD
251	*PULP AND WASTE PAPER	W 1878061	859887		978386		1655148		1091851	PATES A PAPIER,DECHETS
2517	SODA,SULPHATE WOOD PULP	W 1396442	623202	W 1503144	727978	W 1536836	1243662	W 1460455	817146	PATES CHIMIQUES AU SULFATE
25172	— BLEACHED,NONDISSOLVNG	W 1367786	611121	W 1442695	696788	W 1453236	1175362	W 1363098	765930	PATES BLANCHIES
26	TEXTILE FIBRES AND WASTE		624154		916920		1015938		1012896	FIBRES TEXTILES
27	CRUDE FERTLZR,MINRLS NES		799166		550747		578707		574873	ENGRAIS MINERAUX BRUTS
2771	INDUSTRIAL DIAMONDS		814500		86521		18001		21465	DIAMANTS INDUSTRIELS
28	METALLIFEROUS ORES,SCRAP		1858895		1779409		2351961		2517387	MINERAIS METAL,DECHETS
29	CRUDE ANIMAL,VEG MAT NES		866788		967407		1085821		1137322	MATIERES BRUTES ANIM,VEGET
292	CRUDE VEG MATERIALS NES	W 217501	716549	W 251595	804106	W 242477	930320	W 267309	977164	MAT BRUTES VEGETALES NDA
3	MINERAL FUELS ETC		11439710		9144969		9323317		11011684	COMBUSTIBLES MINERAUX LUB
32	COAL,COKE AND BRIQUETTES		1099169		938169		984386		1112310	HOUILLES,COKES,BRIQUETTES
322	COAL,LIGNITE AND PEAT	MW 16140	1014003		879940		916207		1016359	HOUILLES,LIGNITES,TOURBE
3222	OTH COAL,NOT AGGLOMERATD	MW 14452	850188	MW 13379	708522	MW 13955	724364	MW 16472	880448	AUTRES HOUILLES
33	PETROLEUM AND PRODUCTS		8974702		7146873		7431190		8981029	PETROLE ET DERIVES
333	CRUDE PETROLEUM	MW 48993	6598443	MW 39838	4637700	MW 40349	5109659	MW 40996	6296519	HUILES BRUTES DE PETROLE
334	PETROLEUM PRODUCTS,REFIN	MW 14634	2180333	MW 17495	2347539	MW 14507	2170491	MW 14461	2518768	PRODUITS RAFFINES
3341	GASOLINE,OTH LIGHT OILS	W 3738476	737671	W 3778700	651547	W 2273542	429504	W 2750549	580214	ESSENCES POUR MOTEURS
3344	FUEL OILS,NES	W 8409821	868349	MW 9697	929697	W 8657147	960972	W 8119906	1029881	FUEL OILS
341	*GAS,NATURAL AND MANUFCT	W 4011227	676239	W 3007072	464547	W 1573999	262935	W 1670694	307845	GAZ NATUREL,GAZ MANUFACT
351	*ELECTRIC CURRENT		689600		595379		644806		610500	ENERGIE ELECTRIQUE
4	ANIMAL,VEGETABLE OIL,FAT		697311		807177		959599		1072099	HUILES,GRAISSES ANIM,VEG
5	CHEMCLS,RELATED PROD NES		17535429		21318401		27161225		27847749	PRODUITS CHIMIQUES
51	ORGANIC CHEMICALS		4546221		5300596		7492852		7542344	PROD CHIMIQ ORGANIQUES
511	HYDROCARBONS NES,DERIVS	W 756362	394926		645451		1041155		792966	HYDROCARBURES NDA
512	ALCOHOLS,PHENOLS ETC	W 724803	505157		679468		941574		888521	PHENOLS,PHENOLS–ALCOOLS
513	CARBOXYLIC ACIDS ETC	W 445951	701661		879672		1176640		1116828	ACIDES CARBOXYLIQUES
514	NITROGEN–FNCTN COMPOUNDS	W 330111	1472234		1703579		2046449		2304505	COMPOSES FONCT AZOTEES
5148	OTH NITROGN–FNCTN CMPNDS	W 45178	572676	W 80591	609773	W 114993	829299	W 401639	1000506	AUTRES COMPOSES AZOTES
515	ORG–INORG COMPOUNDS ETC		1033755		829367		1611729		1758160	COMPOSES ORGANO–MINERAUX
5156	HETEROCYCLIC CMPDS ETC		796361	W 29507	352486	W 43606	1214001	W 41396	1140102	COMPOSES HETEROCYCLIQUES
51569	OTH HETEROCYC CMPDS,ETC		656021	W 25331	325636	W 37685	775231	W 35287	977014	AUT COMP HETEROCYCLIQUES
52	INORGANIC CHEMICALS		1170658		1659977		1773220		1995242	PROD CHIM INORGANIQUES
522	INORG ELEMNTS,OXIDES,ETC	W 1432647	553953		676489		852747		904996	ELEMENTS INORGANIQUES
53	DYES,TANNING,COLOUR PROD		1043480		1206872		1461108		1550612	PROD TEINTURE,COLORANTS
533	PIGMENTS,PAINTS,ETC	W 224791	696540		715238		895850	W 387669	965321	PIGMENTS,PEINTURES,VERNIS
541	*MEDICINAL,PHARM PRODUCT	MK 81174	3200098		3467450		4325691		4719376	PROD MEDICINAUX PHARMACEUT
5417	MEDICAMENTS	MK 64165	2114131	MK 40219	2367887	MK 47994	2990228	MK 62078	3217023	MEDICAMENTS
54179	— CONTNG OTH SUBSTANCES	MK 54301	1574663	MK 32244	1864866	MK 35251	2249321	MK 39743	2284196	MED CONT AUT SUBSTANCES
55	PERFUME,CLEANING ETC PRD		1600342		1795734		2142071		2265332	PROD POUR PARFUM,TOILETTE
553	PERFUMERY,COSMETICS,ETC	W 94696	836269	W 130167	935840	W 135208	1141125	W 195418	1208202	PRODUITS DE PARFUMERIE
58	PLASTIC MATERIALS ETC		3501775		5172564		6746587		6214336	MAT PLAST ARTIFICIELLES
582	PROD OF CONDENSATION ETC	W 386902	1005934	W 500266	1320147	W 603195	1745208	W 573644	1630501	PROD CONDENS,POLYCOND
5823	ALKYDS,OTHER POLYESTERS	W 169660	432249	W 198133	522033	W 269860	789583	W 240146	669641	ALKYDES ET AUT POLYESTERS
583	POLYMERIZATION ETC PRODS	W 1738884	2398699		3709548		4837382	W 3225230	4405764	PROD POLYMERISATION
5831	POLYETHYLENE	W 301453	324858	W 1036339	874106	W 953672	1201184	W 982045	1037082	POLYETHYLENE
58311	— IN PRIMARY FORMS	W 249202	195906	W 952150	726451	W 885367	1017655	W 911875	855671	POLYETHYLENE PRIMAIRES
5834	POLYVINYL CHLORIDE	W 470509	624836	W 698596	730103	W 550060	877946	W 530214	726020	CHLORURE DE POLYVINYLE
5839	OTH POLYMRZTION ETC PROD	W 398552	759179	W 719363	938123	W 577441	1249562	W 597350	1222533	AUT PROD POLYMER COPOLYM
59	CHEMICAL MATERIALS NES		2085237		2182501		2554782		2777077	MAT PROD CHIMIQUES NDA
598	MISCEL CHEM PRODUCTS NES	W 865619	1287057		1361172		1575409	W 830125	1725849	PROD DIV INDUST CHIM NDA
5989	CHEM PRODUCTS,PREPS NES	W 580480	971431		1017563	W 554003	1207553	W 532442	1353530	PROD PREP CHIMIQUES NDA
59899	OTH CHEM PRODS,PREPS,NES	W 453090	685633	W 396440	737562	W 427747	886550	W 399048	1031304	AUT PRODUITS CHIMIQUES NDA
6	BASIC MANUFACTURES		34210993		36808389		44106640		45107387	ART MANUFACTURES
62	RUBBER MANUFACTURES NES		1687076		1879336		2237268		2361731	CAOUTCHOUC MANUFACTURE
625	RUBBER TYRES, TUBES ETC	W 279833	1077547	W 311112	1166337	W 367765	1394175	W 408790	1501399	PNEUS CAOUTCHOUC VULCANISE
6251	TYRES NEW FOR MOTOR CARS	W 133011	588338	W 150447	654840	W 180491	799298	W 194076	879831	PNEUS POUR VOITURES
63	WOOD,CORK MANUFACTRS NES		1298363		1431626		1503983		1628298	OUVRAGES LIEGE ET BOIS
634	VENEERS,PLYWOOD,ETC	W 1362330	798041		842706		857772		839110	PLACAGES,CONTRE–PLAQUES
64	PAPER,PAPERBOARD AND MFR		6003947		6544022		8246054		7903197	PAPIERS,CARTONS & OUVRAGES
641	PAPER AND PAPERBOARD	W 6440495	4994312	W 7335217	5491307	W 6913201	6958008	W 7181277	6643659	PAPIERS ET CARTONS
6411	NEWSPRINT	W 1353395	666955	W 1696477	804972	W 1553070	1022132	W 1525272	1134809	PAPIER JOURNAL
6412	PRINTG,WRITING PAPER NES	W 1498997	1340347	W 1736343	1499512	W 1586319	1952003	W 1582113	1663830	PAPIERS POUR L'IMPRESSION

4. General Imports C.I.F. by Commodities according to the S.I.T.C. (Rev. 2) in thousand U.S. Dollars
Importations Générales C.A.F. par Produits d'après la C.T.C.I. (Rév. 2) en milliers de Dollars E.U.

SITC CTCI	COMMODITY	1993 WEIGHT POIDS	1993 VALUE VALEUR	1994 WEIGHT POIDS	1994 VALUE VALEUR	1995 WEIGHT POIDS	1995 VALUE VALEUR	1996 WEIGHT POIDS	1996 VALUE VALEUR	PRODUIT
64122	— COATED,IMPREGNATD ETC	W 1262612	1152630	W 1496848	1283918	W 1396493	1706642	W 1420032	1485725	PAPIERS IMPRESSION COUCHES
6415	PAPER,PAPERBRD,BULK,NES	W 1352725	1034766	W 1610816	1211405	W 1622654	1616100	W 1819274	1567795	PAPIERS,CARTONS ROULEAUX
64159	OTHER PAPER ETC,BULK,NES	W 1231733	933539	W 1470860	1086962	W 1521479	1488807	W 1712193	1454592	AUT PAPIER ROULEAUX FEUILLES
6418	COATED ETC PAPER NES BLK	W 813804	972013	W 866524	1021570	W 758909	1134314	W 799433	1115199	PAP,CARTONS COUCHES,ENDUITS
64189	COATED PAPER ETC NES	W 586633	695669	W 650614	736992	W 529421	746034	W 593762	765391	PAPIERS,CARTONS COUCHES
642	PAPER,ETC,PRECUT,ARTS OF	W 354246	1009635	W 357494	1052716	W 380828	1288046	W 419207	1259538	PAP,CARTONS DECOUPES
65	TEXTILE YARN,FABRICS,ETC		6130063		6783839		7581471		7946809	FILS,TISSUS,ARTICLES TEXTILE
651	TEXTILE YARN	W 320121	1396439		1653162	W 385045	1819783	W 396564	1848642	FILS TEXTILES
6514	SYN FIB YRN,BULK,MONOFIL	W 130896	590878	W 173604	724576	W 190930	840758	W 202813	858213	FILS CONT 85% FIB TEXT SYNTH
652	COTTON FABRICS,WOVEN	W 134034	855037	W 142288	896978	W 140677	989374	W 145395	1043392	TISSUS DE COTON
653	WOVN MAN–MADE FIB FABRIC	W 158044	1436535	W 172058	1521722	W 180153	1738161	W 186441	1706282	TISSUS FIBRES SYNTH,ARTIF
657	SPECIAL TXTL FABRC,PRODS	W 109192	645512	W 130272	687433	W 128088	799130	W 139865	869044	TISSUS SPECIAUX
659	FLOOR COVERINGS,ETC	W 186596	643994	W 215377	712836	W 217375	747500	W 267710	837969	COUVRE–PARQUETS,TAPIS ETC
66	NONMETAL MINERAL MFS NES		6075821		6317478		7055206		7740114	ART MIN NON METALLIQUES
664	GLASS	W 489796	638350		654863		788852	W 545803	748754	VERRE
667	PEARL,PREC–,SEMI–P STONE		4079005		4038049		4517820		5170033	PERLES, PIERRES GEMMES
6672	DIAMONDS NONINDUST,UNSET		3976401		3961566		4434895		5074205	DIAMANTS BRUTS
66721	— ROUGH,UNSORTED		1117543		821783		764476		778898	DIAMANTS BRUTS NON TRIES
66722	— SRTD,ROUGH,SIMPLY WKD		2527644		2726734		3223626		3686481	DIAMANTS TRIES BRUTS
67	IRON AND STEEL		4037683		4513174		5829548		5663852	FER ET ACIER
672	IRON,STEEL PRIMARY FORMS	W 1130612	676560	W 1223016	576017	W 1807826	1050591	W 1301312	909279	LINGOTS FER,ACIER
673	IRON,STEEL SHAPES ETC	W 1038047	622411	W 1347028	743804	W 1459955	983335	W 1241558	823679	BARRES,PROFIL FER,ACIER
674	IRN,STL UNIV,PLATE,SHEET	W 2349359	1609457	W 2717364	1838965	W 2621157	2097896	W 2752633	2056155	LARGES PLATS,TOLES
678	IRON,STL TUBES,PIPES,ETC	W 446554	601524	W 616781	746716	W 667263	905100		1079057	TUBES,TUYAUX EN FONTE,FER
68	NON–FERROUS METALS		4599758		4552750		6021476		5924034	METAUX NON FERREUX
681	SILVER,PLATINUM,ETC		648020		706627		1208427		822761	ARGENT ET PLATINE
6811	SILVER UNWKD,PARTLY WRKD		210933		309514		804587		523991	ARGENT BRUT MI–OUVRE
682	COPPER EXC CEMENT COPPER	W 536313	1359048	W 448084	1206380	W 459492	1598055	W 515754	1555958	CUIVRE
6821	COPPER NES,ALLOYS,UNWRT	W 393296	837958	W 270685	614968	W 280187	814825	W 338052	816661	CUIVRE BRUT
68212	COPPER REFINED,UNWROUGHT	W 382661	814516	W 260808	589023	W 277507	802251	W 330629	795539	CUIVRE AFFINE BRUT
684	ALUMINIUM	W 918557	1788569		1744309		2133545	W 1062963	2453705	ALUMINIUM
6841	ALUMINIUM,ALLOYS,UNWRGHT	W 589100	808561	W 477326	662407	W 388089	751812	W 653109	1108508	ALUMINIUM,ALLIAGES BRUTS
6842	ALUMINIUM,ALLOYS WORKED	W 329457	980008	W 385040	1081903	W 388062	1381733	W 409854	1345197	ALUMINIUM,ALLIAGES OUVRE
68422	ALUMNM PLATE,SHEET,STRIP	W 220910	591511	W 275374	685441	W 270339	855355	W 273667	813661	TOLES, PLANCHES EN ALU
69	METAL MANUFACTURES NES		3913125		4254850		5068727		5320907	ART MANUFACT EN METAL NDA
695	TOOLS	W 52948	665364	W 58061	758577	W 65939	953694	W 61948	896701	OUTILS A MAIN
699	BASE METAL MFRS NES	W 341206	1506467	W 342974	1583813	W 340642	1859958	W 337991	2047789	ART MANUFACTURES MET NDA
7	MACHINES,TRANSPORT EQUIP		84524739		91512749		107873869		120046323	MACHINES MATERIEL TRANSPORT
71	POWER GENERATING EQUIPMT		6308056		5975499		7097403		8146517	MACHINES GENERATRICES
713	INTRNL COMBUS PSTN ENGIN	W 297524	2035690	W 275204	2101444	W 336370	2664481	W 325378	2692420	MOTEURS EXPL COMB INT, PIECE
7132	MOTOR VEHCL PISTN ENGINS	W 58775	646347	W 65460	712904	W 69233	870886	W 83076	958690	MOTEURS EXPL POUR VEHICULES
7139	PISTON ENGINE PARTS NES	W 161330	960573	W 177354	1016910	W 236682	1363007	W 208956	1295285	PIECES POUR 713.2,3,8
714	ENGINES AND MOTORS NES	W 15648	3364627	W 12549	2949161	W 10355	3211510	W 16333	4187996	MOTEURS NON ELECTRIQUES
7144	REACTION ENGINES	W 1465	939487	W 1370	803601	W 1433	804160	W 2315	1152039	PROPULSEURS A REACTION
7148	GAS TURBINES NES	W 4189	665446	W 2901	531580	W 1939	508765	W 2140	593760	TURBINES A GAZ
7149	ENGINE & MOTOR PARTS NES	W 9994	1759693	W 8278	1613981	W 6983	1898585	W 11878	2442197	PIECES 714 ET 718.88
71491	PARTS NES OF 7144,71481	W 1717	1039117	W 1555	1028489	W 1822	1223885	W 2662	1579405	PIECES DES PROPULSEURS
71499	PARTS NES,OF 71488,71888	W 8277	720576	W 6723	585493	W 5161	674700	W 9216	862792	PIECES 714.88 ET 718.88
716	ROTATING ELECTRIC PLANT	W 54920	685463	W 57244	675678	W 61118	846345	W 62616	894296	APP ELECTR ROTATIFS,PIECES
72	MACHS FOR SPCL INDUSTRYS		4760965		5104170		6260883		6198528	MAC SPECIALES POUR INDUST
723	CIVIL ENGNEERG EQUIP ETC	W 83162	573645	W 117476	741092	W 124552	899990	W 113962	789393	APPAREILS DE GENIE CIVIL
726	PRINTG,BKBINDG MACHY,PTS	W 24981	730697	W 27573	813156	W 35861	1069081	W 35401	1059640	MACHINES POUR IMPRIMERIE
728	OTH MACHY FOR SPCL INDUS	W 85516	1432095	W 93404	1535346	W 97086	1876819	W 100889	2045849	AUT MACH IND PARTICULIERES
7284	MACHY FOR SPCL INDUS NES	W 55866	1182986	W 60309	1235736	W 58824	1521934	W 65412	1678271	MACH SPEC IND PARTICUL.
73	METALWORKING MACHINERY		900551		1086530		1523752		1619170	MACH TRAVAIL DES METAUX
736	METALWORKING MACH–TOOLS	W 37286	703859		812847	W 70425	1204330	W 72764	1327207	MACH–OUTILS TRAVAIL METAUX
74	GENRL INDUSTRL MACHY NES		7317041		8226690		9735407		10430814	MACH APP INDUSTRIE
741	HEATING,COOLING EQUIPMNT	W 73986	1034232	W 96032	1152086	W 99607	1406136	W 108664	1556021	MACH CHAUFFAGE,PIECES
742	PUMPS FOR LIQUIDS ETC	W 40414	875467	W 46508	983929	W 50051	1164504	W 50724	1176581	POMPES MOTO–POMPES
743	PUMPS NES,CENTRFUGES ETC	W 78221	1094784	W 99906	1255302	W 129510	1501483	W 143523	1743510	POMPES COMPRES,VENT ETC
744	MECHANICAL HANDLING EQU	W 161894	1200793	W 206556	1404883	W 296812	1829780	W 326509	1899805	EQUIP MANUTENTION PIECES
7449	PTS NES OF MACHY OF 7442	W 83654	620074	W 110439	690322	W 173516	913451	W 145275	925072	PIECES DU 744.2
745	NONELEC MACHY,TOOLS NES	W 43965	947163	W 48548	1036920	W 53121	1089139	W 55791	1208042	AUT MACH NON ELEC,PIECES
7452	OTH NONELEC MCHS,PTS NES	W 39343	810036	W 42835	877036	W 46902	933745	W 50962	1052642	AUT MACH NON ELEC,PIECES
749	NONELEC MACH PTS,ACC NES	W 160695	2164601	W 203933	2393570	W 226755	2744367	W 344854	2846856	PIECES MACH NON ELEC NDA
7492	COCKS,VALVES ETC NES	W 58249	886463	W 63628	974051	W 62359	1044387	W 96123	1153159	ART ROB,SIM POUR TUYAUX
75	OFFICE MACHNES,ADP EQUIP		16153696		16235451		19334385		19924189	MACH BUREAU TRAIT AUTOM
751	OFFICE MACHINES	W 28225	758839	W 31502	780820	W 31629	911263	W 33669	822751	MACH,APPAREILS DE BUREAU
752	AUTOMTIC DATA PROC EQUIP	W 128046	10461205	W 146063	9919331	W 158339	11945445	W 163849	11988543	MACH TRAIT INFORMATION
7522	DIGITAL COMPUTERS	W 6322	961543	W 8805	929984	W 9365	1421250	W 15330	1903449	MACH DIGITALES COMPLETES
7523	DIGITL CENTRL PROCESSORS	W 16672	2498300	W 18591	2581893	W 23119	3042096	W 25272	2682004	UNITES CENTRALES
7524	DIGITL CENTRL STOR UNITS	W 11655	2327436	W 14935	2336609	W 17773	3397477	W 17826	3429298	UNITES MEMOIRE CENTRALES
7525	ADP PERIPHERAL UNITS	W 77251	2792449	W 81059	2449525	W 77062	2477853	W 86427	2584530	UNITES PERIPHERIQUES
7528	OFF–LINE DATA PROC EQUIP	W 15942	1774598	W 22375	1546328	W 30727	1508928	W 17974	1232259	MACH AUXIL TRAIT INFORM
759	OFFICE,ADP MCH PTS,ACCES	W 83768	4933652	W 102474	5535299	W 83544	6477676	W 92494	7112895	PIECES DU 751 ET 752
7599	ACCTG,ETC,ADP MCH PTS,AC	W 41452	4328677	W 62911	4953703	W 46380	5815130	W 60469	6407427	PIECES DU 751 ET 752
76	TELECOMM,SOUND EQUIPMENT		6560583		7663722		9887334		11745591	EQUIPMENT DE TELECOM
761	TELEVISION RECEIVERS	W 40156	642047	W 34253	527773	W 41032	650223	W 46972	758987	RECEPTEURS DE TELEVISION
762	RADIO BROADCAST RECEIVRS	W 37509	828952	W 52863	890437	W 43870	965411	W 43393	860070	RECEPTEURS RADIODIFFUSION
763	SOUND RECORDRS,PHONOGRPH	W 22853	981851	W 22781	1011018	W 22810	1095424	W 29774	1454572	PHONO,APP ENREGISTREMENT
7638	OTHR SOUND APPARATUS ETC	W 21274	956144	W 20560	988655	W 21046	1067621	W 28152	1425539	AUT APP D'ENREGIS,REPROD
76381	TV IMAGE,SND RECRDRS ETC	W 11669	618211	W 12054	666034	W 11205	668377	W 15346	1076999	APP ENREG,REPRO IMAG,SON
764	TELECOM EQPT,PTS,ACC NES	W 78911	4107733		5234493		7176277		8671961	EQUIP TELECOM,PIECES
7641	LINE TELEPHONE,ETC EQUIP	W 13569	876698	W 19315	1214157	W 23080	2135986	W 28137	3197736	APP TELEPHON PAR FIL
7643	TV,RADIO TRANSMITTRS ETC	W 601	721257		1019391		1520922		2003701	APP EMET TELE RADIO
7648	TELECOMM EQUIPMENT NES	W 2652	662295		663608		709382		571805	APP TELECOM NDA
7649	PTS NES OF EQUIPMT OF 76	W 37239	1605009	W 68207	2051640	W 83046	2456761	W 59538	2539207	PIECES DE LA DIV 76
76491	PTS NES OF APPAR OF 7641	W 4704	460995	W 9870	661686	W 7037	786760	W 9641	917282	PIECES POUR 764.1
76493	TELECOMM EQUIPMT PTS NES	W 16082	756660	W 19499	911438	W 26741	1147252	W 25969	1063079	PIECES 761,762,764.3,8
77	ELECTRIC MACHNRY NES ETC		14603391		16065123		20577806		24046510	MACH APP ELECT NDA
771	ELECTRIC POWER MACHY NES	W 38511	663469	W 45258	803286	W 48727	1025229	W 75074	1344137	MACH PROD,TRANS ELECTR
7712	OTH ELEC POWER MACHY NES	W 29040	507928	W 34077	620899	W 35600	821253	W 55283	1104157	AUT APP PROD TRANSF ELEC
772	SWITCHGEAR ETC,PARTS NES	W 69229	2431528	W 79610	2587040	W 87977	3124349	W 92992	3286395	APP COUPURE,SECT ETC
7721	SWITCHGEAR ETC	W 60685	1863829	W 68939	1961301	W 73800	2368127	W 76934	2491399	APP COUPURE,SECTIONMNT
773	ELECTR DISTRIBUTNG EQUIP	W 144130	875502		1054104	W 540133	1352289	W 244630	1524180	EQUIPMT DISTRIBUTION ELECT
7731	INSULATED WIRE,CABLE ETC	W 139252	806727	W 168289	965210	W 533644	1252382	W 235732	1422991	FILS,CABLES ISOLES ELECT
775	HOUSEHOLD TYPE EQUIP NES	W 242714	1547102		1593759	W 305587	1818875	W 279006	1764205	MACH,APP USAGE DOMESTQUE
7758	ELECTRO–THERMIC APPL NES	W 81111	662739		638549	W 89074	709868	W 90017	709258	APP ELECTROTHERMIQ NDA
776	TRANSISTORS,VALVES,ETC	W 120861	5356792	W 139373	5626029	W 113579	7918774	W 124762	10888319	LAMPES,TUBES,VALVES
7763	DIODES,TRANSISTORS,ETC	W 4616	522941	W 3876	621626	W 6044	811706	W 5440	770783	DIODES,TRANSISTORS
7764	ELECTRONIC MICROCIRCUITS	W 7770	3990472	W 8406	4035596	W 11569	5894177	W 20196	8722669	MICROSTRUCTURES ELECTRON

4. General Imports C.I.F. by Commodities according to the S.I.T.C. (Rev. 2) in thousand U.S. Dollars
Importations Générales C.A.F. par Produits d'après la C.T.C.I. (Rév. 2) en milliers de Dollars E.U.

SITC CTCI	COMMODITY	1993		1994		1995		1996		PRODUIT
		WEIGHT POIDS	VALUE VALEUR	WEIGHT POIDS	VALUE VALEUR	WEIGHT POIDS	VALUE VALEUR	WEIGHT POIDS	VALUE VALEUR	
778	ELECTRICAL MACHINERY NES	W 210140	3394041		4076267		4951534	W 312870	4789090	AUTRES MACH ELECT NDA
7788	OTH ELEC MACHY,EQUIP NES	W 39230	1721434	W 46643	2304471	W 95715	2720175	W 71535	2632451	AUT MACH APP ELEC NDA
77886	OTH ELEC MACHINERY NES	W 1175	554792	W 1287	662819	W 12810	862441	W 13386	907910	AUT MACH APP ELECTRIQUES
78	ROAD VEHICLES		22612573		24665945		28489343		32177635	VEHICULES ROUTIERS
781	PASS MOTOR VEH EXC BUSES	W 1215084	13043211	W 1311667	13957376	W 1361527	15580713	W 1544335	17727601	AUTO TRANSPORT PERSONNES
782	LORRIES,SPCL MTR VEH NES	W 147802	1242792		1793426		2247326	W 224875	2091721	VEHICULES SPECIAUX,MARCH
7821	LORRIES,TRUCKS	W 114672	990082	W 171974	1489593	W 233542	2151269	W 215000	2001950	VEHICULES TRANSP MARCHAND
784	MOTOR VEH PRTS,ACCES NES	W 1087740	7283119	W 1201019	7655102	W 1456205	9272215	W 1457193	10861817	PIECES 722,781,782,783
7849	OTHER MOTOR VEHCL PARTS	W 1067342	7094872	W 1177444	7446179	W 1438442	9116458	W 1439889	10730996	PIECES 722,781,782,783
79	OTHR TRANSPORT EQUIPMENT		5307884		6489619		4967556		5757369	AUTRE MATERIEL TRANSPORT
791	RAILWAY VEHICLES	W 28819	384970	W 47041	1117058	W 22667	346833	W 12284	133519	VEHIC MAT CHEMINS DE FER
792	AIRCRAFT ETC		4821059		5280068		4128063		5398036	APP NAVIGATION AERIENNE
7924	AIRCRFT NES OVER 15000KG		2452602	W 2	2695801		1047503		1919061	AERODYNES PLUS 15000 KG
7929	AIRCRAFT PARTS NES		2162034		2356812		2756364		3124786	PIECES DU 792
8	MISC MANUFACTURED GOODS		32000822		33022619		36093717		39734212	ART MANUFACTURES DIVERS
821	*FURNITURE,PARTS THEREOF	W 800368	1614420	W 440269	1745587	W 427511	1915108	W 476445	2209419	MEUBLES ET PIECES
8219	FURNITURE AND PARTS NES	W 330142	1021111	W 317342	1115669	W 314347	1209258	W 350039	1370577	AUTRES MEUBLES ET PIECES
84	CLOTHING AND ACCESSORIES		7455316		7359565		8273546		9616918	VETEMENTS
842	MENS OUTERWEAR NOT KNIT	W 63720	1229791	W 64607	1203818	W 61791	1307978	W 66401	1500808	VET DESSUS POUR HOMMES
843	WOMENS OUTERWEAR NONKNIT	W 69393	1708550	W 87746	1763699	W 77572	2041916	W 87701	2370361	VET DESSUS FEMMES MAT TEX
8439	— OTHER OUTER GARMENTS	W 33931	692069	W 34484	637529	W 32928	713850	W 39341	876646	AUT VET DES FEM MAT TEXT
844	UNDER GARMENTS NOT KNIT	W 37222	658275	W 39572	658900	W 48800	827418	W 48712	846889	VETEMENT DESSOUS MAT TEX
845	OUTERWEAR KNIT NONELASTC	W 106625	1915360	W 107051	1791815	W 94029	1834611	W 108534	2222795	VET DESSOUS,ACCES BONNET
8451	— JERSEYS,PULLOVERS ETC	W 56903	1049938	W 59008	996482	W 52113	1065798	W 59305	1236429	CHANDAILS,PULL–OVERS ETC
8459	— OTHER,CLTHG ACCESRYS	W 41828	733928	W 41624	674696	W 37302	656572	W 44631	861792	AUT VET DESSUS DE BONNE
846	UNDER GARMENTS KNITTED	W 72180	1183643	W 70650	1112885	W 80386	1336369	W 91002	1636584	SOUS VETS DE BONNETERIE
8462	— OF COTTON NON ELASTIC	W 52120	750519	W 50846	705059	W 55949	852513	W 63983	1044711	SOUS–VET BONNET COTON
84629	—— OTHER	W 52120	750519	W 50846	705059	W 55949	852513	W 63983	1044711	AUT SOUS–VET BONNET COTON
851	*FOOTWEAR	W 117745	1763075	W 142804	2002749	W 140994	2188549	W 155223	2522212	CHAUSSURES
85102	FOOTWEAR LEATHER	W 46576	633489	W 81881	1320636	W 109382	1876717	W 115554	2105774	CHAUS SEMELLES EN CUIR
85103	SHOES WOOD–,CORK–SOLED	W 47801	923737	W 30910	429694	W 1723	28415	W 1791	34416	CHAUS SEMELLES BOIS,LIEGE
87	PRECISION INSTRUMNTS NES		4608729		4550322		5358482		5955920	INSTRUM,APPAR SCIENT NDA
872	MEDICAL INSTRUMENTS NES	W 31564	741213	W 25346	772395	W 24716	900392	W 27409	990275	INSTR,APP MEDIC–CHIR NDA
87202	OTH MEDICAL INSTRUMENTS	W 29521	673333	W 19192	691928	W 21006	799473	W 23370	871248	INSTRUM,APP MEDECINE
874	MEASURNG,CONTROLNG INSTR	W 36045	3402948	W 38183	3301265	W 53082	3847975	W 47940	4319359	INSTRUMENTS DE MESURE
8741	SURVEYING INSTRUMENTS	W 2587	715548	W 3778	663911	W 3844	783701	W 3987	958527	INST GEODESIE,TOPO ETC
8748	ELEC MEAS,CONTRL EQU NES	W 4402	558939	W 3813	620655	W 5753	749866	W 5083	852582	APP ELEC ELECTRO MESURE
8749	INSTR PTS NES,ACCESSORYS	W 10408	733879	W 9989	675632	W 10577	721814	W 12418	778047	PIECES 873,874.3,54,874.8
88	PHOTO EQU,OPTICL GDS ETC		2821239		2908248		3253380		3480341	APP,FOURN PHOTO,OP,MONTR
882	PHOTO,CINEMA SUPPLIES	W 87903	1226331	W 91267	1273420	W 95081	1442349	W 100989	1460966	PRODUITS PHOTO,CINEMA
8822	PHOTO FILM EXC DEV CINMA	W 55876	958471	W 57692	990965	W 60389	1092966	W 63524	1130523	PLAQUES,PELLICULES,FILMS
885	WATCHES AND CLOCKS		712161		709182		782556		849769	HORLOGERIE
89	MISC MANUFCTRD GOODS NES		12600984		13204975		13699799		14293646	ART MANUFACTURES DIVERS
892	PRINTED MATTER	W 352033	1498562		1578153		1774835	W 318696	2094162	IMPRIMES
8921	PRINTED BOOKS,GLOBES,ETC	W 173147	839506	W 168218	870415	W 175005	1043765	W 152664	1004667	LIVRES,BROCHURES,CARTES
89211	PRINTED BOOKS,PAMPHLETS	W 159658	792162	W 155305	826013	W 163108	995485	W 140626	954851	LIVRES,BROCHURES
893	ARTICLES OF PLASTIC NES	W 604934	2220354		2489998		2834353		2881229	OUVRAGES EN MAT DIVIS 58
8931	PLSTC PACKG CONTNRS,LIDS	W 239312	747315	W 284346	826317	W 351964	981161	W 466520	983627	ART TRANSP EMBALLAGE ETC
8939	MISC PLASTIC ARTICLES	W 362319	1428373	W 356282	1614209	W 353751	1795565	W 381081	1839354	ART DIVERS EN MAT DIV 58
89399	OTHR PLASTC ARTICLES NES	W 318600	1284658	W 302411	1452328	W 298750	1621982	W 319736	1665414	AUT OUV MAT DIV 58
894	TOYS,SPORTING GOODS,ETC	W 253927	2539180		2045933	W 279995	2303514	W 301666	2490981	VOITURES ENFANTS,JOUETS
8942	TOYS,INDOOR GAMES ETC	W 217817	2132713	W 209982	1641152	W 223330	1792446	W 239903	1911660	JOUETS,JEUX ETC
89423	TOYS NES	W 116670	851034	W 111127	799824	W 113285	851367	W 118566	902642	JOUETS,MODELES REDUITS
89424	INDOOR GAME EQUIPMENT	W 62151	1015188	W 54277	543715	W 53149	559143	W 67691	658176	ART,JEUX DE SOCIETE
896	WORKS OF ART ETC		1718037		1966823		1619830		1235345	OBJETS D'ART
89601	HAND PAINTINGS ETC NES		1049958		1165522		1016412		673468	TABLEAUX,PEINTURES
897	GOLD,SILVER WARE,JEWELRY		1384307		1858446		1624300		1887706	BIJOUTERIE,ORFEVRERIE
8973	PREC JEWLRY,GLD–SILVWARE		1264504		1728764		1476820		1738581	BIJOUX OR,ARGENT ORFEVRE
89731	PRECIOUS METAL JEWELLERY		1191590		1653242		1416512		1663476	ART BIJOUTERIE,JOAILLER
898	MUSICAL INSTRUMENTS,PTS	W 110708	2183891	W 109980	2085544	W 103700	2141777	W 127099	2204996	INSTRUMENTS DE MUSIQUE
8983	SOUND RECRDNG TAPE,DISCS	W 96026	2011459	W 92370	1897431	W 92267	1951500	W 116867	1997247	SUPPORTS SON POUR 763
89831	PREPD SND RECORDNG MEDIA	W 64017	809528	W 62264	687930	W 67528	699568	W 88671	659265	SUPPORTS PREPARES
89832	RECORDED DISCS,TAPES ETC	W 32009	1201931	W 30106	1209501	W 24740	1251931	W 28196	1337982	DISQUES,PHONO,BANDES
899	OTHER MANUFACTURED GOODS		680525		763209		885105		972731	AUT ART MANUF DIVERS NDA
9	GOODS NOT CLASSD BY KIND		2052280		1800927		2424853		2643838	ART TRANSACT NON CLASSES
931	*SPECIAL TRANSACTIONS		1359591		1037357	W 132860	1593293		1834973	TRANS.SPECIALES

5. General Exports F.O.B. by Commodities according to the S.I.T.C. (Rev. 2) in thousand U.S. Dollars
Exportations Générales F.O.B. par Produits d'après la C.T.C.I. (Rév. 2) en milliers de Dollars E.U.

SITC CTCI	COMMODITY	1993 WEIGHT POIDS	1993 VALUE VALEUR	1994 WEIGHT POIDS	1994 VALUE VALEUR	1995 WEIGHT POIDS	1995 VALUE VALEUR	1996 WEIGHT POIDS	1996 VALUE VALEUR	PRODUIT
	ALL COMMODITIES		171699761		202857933		239948047		259277030	TOUS PRODUITS
0	FOOD AND LIVE ANIMALS		8185446		9329620		10939481		10652272	ALIMENTS,ANIMAUX VIVANTS
01	MEAT AND PREPARATIONS		1343202		1744896		2259580		1620208	VIANDES ET PREPARATIONS
011	MEAT FRESH,CHILLD,FROZEN	W 483351	1214936	W 605905	1579975	W 767218	2108681	W 545445	1444584	VIANDES FRAICHES,REF,CONGE
0111	BOVINE MEAT FRESH,FROZEN	W 182656	534794	W 231141	736933	W 271824	937636	W 63061	219239	VIANDES BOVIN FRAI,REF
02	DAIRY PRODCTS,BIRDS'EGGS		905220		994365		1192832		1055357	PRODUITS LAITIERS,OEUFS
03	FISH AND PREPARATIONS		845922		992702		1091058		1110764	POISSONS ET PREPARATIONS
04	CEREALS AND PREPARATIONS		1955611		1882566		2232526		2638002	CEREALES ET PRODUITS
041	WHEAT ETC UNMILLED	W 3897589	654597	W 3410671	522560	W 3038440	556601	W 3865808	707837	FROMENT,EPEAUTRE
0412	OTHER WHEAT ETC UNMILLED	W 3895190	654053	W 3410671	522560	W 3038440	556590	W 3865708	707611	AUTRE FROMENT NON MOULU
048	CEREAL ETC PREPARATIONS	W 789297	1044164	W 859058	1085508	W 886499	1230639	W 1028865	1515484	PREPTNS A BASE CEREALES
0484	BAKERY PRODUCTS	W 205320	546078	W 233309	529477	W 251160	591729	W 281741	705308	PRODUITS DE BOULANGERIE
07	COFFEE,TEA,COCOA,SPICES		852509		989175		1061596		1052638	CAFE,THE,CACAO,EPICES
1	BEVERAGES AND TOBACCO		4880408		5697158		6524352		6810583	BOISSONS ET TABACS
11	BEVERAGES		3914152		4340635		4728801		4913493	BOISSONS
112	ALCOHOLIC BEVERAGES	W 889479	3783040	W 1012986	4153661	W 1089406	4492636	W 1200874	4652050	BOISSONS ALCOOLIQUES
1124	DISTILLED ALCOHOLIC BEVS	W 636002	3519973	W 655318	3803246	W 723842	4096229	W 731398	4083927	ALCOOLS,EAUX–DE–VIE
11241	WHISKY	W 558105	3188497	W 550769	3388808	W 601509	3647362	W 604066	3609077	WHISKY
12	TOBACCO AND MANUFACTURES		966256		1356523		1795550		1897090	TABACS BRUTS FABRIQUES
122	TOBACCO,MANUFACTURED	W 56682	951109	W 77892	1336293	W 99626	1775646	W 105629	1870783	TABACS FABRIQUES
1222	CIGARETTES	W 44566	854734	W 63209	1209641	W 83215	1620478	W 87566	1685117	CIGARETTES
2	CRUDE MATERLS,EXCL FUELS		2957976		3528779		4211620		3929966	MAT BRUTES NON COMESTIBLES
26	TEXTILE FIBRES AND WASTE		620573		777392		886280		862425	FIBRES TEXTILES
27	CRUDE FERTLZR,MINRLS NES		629030		657291		765515		776426	ENGRAIS MINERAUX BRUTS
278	OTHER CRUDE MINERALS	W 3967288	521081		505879		605022		602569	AUTRES MINERAUX BRUTS
28	METALLIFEROUS ORES,SCRAP		899102		1008413		1192450		1029112	MINERAIS METAL,DECHETS
3	MINERAL FUELS ETC		12222745		13628919		14621553		17170252	COMBUSTIBLES MINERAUX LUB
33	PETROLEUM AND PRODUCTS		11588138		13029570		13780641		16161466	PETROLE ET DERIVES
333	CRUDE PETROLEUM	MW 59642	7509689	MW 77612	9193106	MW 79065	10144444	MW 76484	11683473	HUILES BRUTES DE PETROLE
334	PETROLEUM PRODUCTS,REFIN	MW 23317	3857777		3611572		3348761		4139039	PRODUITS RAFFINES
3341	GASOLINE,OTH LIGHT OILS	MW 17446	2724137	W 8059224	1379198	W 7879863	1426843	W 8867788	1805534	ESSENCES POUR MOTEURS
33411	MOTOR,AVIATION SPIRIT	W 5606284	1045528	W 6341127	1081085	W 5864814	1049801	W 7319638	1478418	ESSENCES MOTEURS D'AVIONS
33412	SPIRIT TYPE JET FUEL	MW 10085	1357640	W 8	13	W 103	140	W 210	168	CARBUREACTEURS
3343	GAS OILS	W 6695527	1103559	W 6233450	919493	W 5553256	858602	W 5016593	943433	GAS OILS
3344	FUEL OILS,NES	W 6134056	592923	W 6126074	533525	W 4000810	437459	W 4858222	594845	FUEL OILS
341	*GAS,NATURAL AND MANUFCT	W 3237426	526637	W 3329823	484620	W 4068154	719732	W 4492706	866115	GAZ NATUREL,GAZ MANUFACT
5	CHEMCLS,RELATED PROD NES		24561347		27912281		32281914		33905441	PRODUITS CHIMIQUES
51	ORGANIC CHEMICALS		6134239		7140179		7751265		8094282	PROD CHIMIQ ORGANIQUES
511	HYDROCARBONS NES,DERIVS	W 2634543	1119068		1148777		1408366		1176390	HYDROCARBURES NDA
5111	ACYCLIC HYDROCARBONS	W 1470838	523811	W 1547724	554432	W 1646631	791099	W 1544506	642044	HYDROCARBURES ACYCLIQUES
513	CARBOXYLIC ACIDS ETC	W 1010821	947536		1159740		1617661		1308333	ACIDES CARBOXYLIQUES
514	NITROGEN–FNCTN COMPOUNDS	W 423159	2092450		2167811		2108753		2622882	COMPOSES FONCT AZOTEES
5148	OTH NITROGN–FNCTN CMPNDS	W 32219	726907	W 147192	869337	W 128779	818762	W 148587	1066209	AUTRES COMPOSES AZOTES
51482	IMIDE–,IMIDE–FNCT CMPNDS	W 10367	648841	W 10117	695869	W 11351	582240	W 10500	776761	COMPOSES A FONCTION IMIDE
515	ORG–INORG COMPOUNDS ETC	W 80090	1023665		1671004		1509158	W 107874	1804765	COMPOSES ORGANO–MINERAUX
5156	HETEROCYCLIC CMPDS ETC	W 39939	825661	W 61521	1413373	W 72879	1190640	W 56481	1403380	COMPOSES HETEROCYCLIQUES
51569	OTH HETEROCYC CMPDS,ETC	W 39666	818101	W 61300	1405692	W 72563	1180175	W 56135	1381757	AUT COMP HETEROCYCLIQUES
516	OTHER ORGANIC CHEMICALS	W 188673	577070		567203		649217		647763	AUTRES PROD ORGANIQUES
52	INORGANIC CHEMICALS		1786954		1716834		1939968		1870294	PROD CHIM INORGANIQUES
523	OTHR INORG CHEMICALS ETC	W 504182	702366		664133		789565		761811	AUT PRODUITS CHIMIQUES INORG
524	RADIOACTIVE ETC MATERIAL		628995		562783		537495		543341	MATIERES RADIOACTIVES
5241	RADIOACTIVE ELEMENTS ETC		620369		536235		508755		508754	RADIOELEMENTS,ISOTOPES
53	DYES,TANNING,COLOUR PROD		2079052		2247198		2548693		2557370	PROD TEINTURE,COLORANTS
531	SYNT DYE,NAT INDGO,LAKES	W 78545	779944		785282		881078	W 98182	889802	MAT COLOR ORGAN,LAQUES
5311	SYNTHIC ORGNIC DYESTUFFS	W 67806	703756	W 41485	371416	W 8438	79265	W 85679	826992	MAT COLOR ORGAN SYNTHET
533	PIGMENTS,PAINTS,ETC	W 507019	1259369		1418823		1620264		1615736	PIGMENTS,PEINTURES,VERNIS
541	*MEDICINAL,PHARM PRODUCT	MK 116274	5476915		6079974		7720013		8320133	PROD MEDICINAUX PHARMACEUT
5417	MEDICAMENTS	MK 85534	4169591	MK 101954	4732076	MK 96231	6135241	MK 111653	6752716	MEDICAMENTS
54171	— CONTAINNG ANTIBIOTICS	MK 11228	742876	MK 11735	854146	MK 12344	1008913	MK 15760	1071865	MED CONTN ANTIBIOTIQUES
54179	— CONTNG OTH SUBSTANCES	MK 71737	3048204	MK 87364	3436939	MK 80348	4599515	MK 91354	4924100	MED CONT AUT SUBSTANCES
55	PERFUME,CLEANING ETC PRD		2481421		3015170		3325291		3766377	PROD POUR PARFUM,TOILETTE
553	PERFUMERY,COSMETICS,ETC	W 227267	1372801	W 295908	1787276	W 339041	1873432	W 427461	2269833	PRODUITS DE PARFUMERIE
554	SOAP,CLEANSING ETC PREPS	W 495576	741614	W 542531	781655	W 636594	927842	W 609085	896602	SAVONS,PRODUITS DETERSIFS
5542	WASHING PREPARATIONS ETC	W 387861	527754	W 435368	576217	W 519507	693137	W 497160	665848	PROD ORG TENSIO–ACT NDA
58	PLASTIC MATERIALS ETC		3198158		3774091		4546853		4492469	MAT PLAST ARTIFICIELLES
582	PROD OF CONDENSATION ETC	W 385593	812211	W 471315	979078	W 503862	1214781	W 508269	1185247	PROD CONDENS,POLYCOND
5823	ALKYDS,OTHER POLYESTERS	W 212247	443275	W 266457	555247	W 291863	729604	W 293759	679838	ALKYDES ET AUT POLYESTERS
583	POLYMERIZATION ETC PRODS	W 1303727	2327720		2746629		3278015		3253864	PROD POLYMERISATION
59	CHEMICAL MATERIALS NES		3209976		3742676		4233038		4528645	MAT PROD CHIMIQUES NDA
591	PESTICIDES,DISINFECTANTS	W 133823	953385	W 145976	981694	W 152415	1130584	W 159150	1259628	DESINF,INSECT,FONG,HERB
598	MISCEL CHEM PRODUCTS NES	W 879325	2102555		2543103		2860912		3007956	PROD DIV INDUST CHIM NDA
5982	ANTI–KNOCK PREPARTNS ETC	W 218092	627019	W 339755	875640	W 333111	919797	W 337437	989414	PREPARAT ANTIDETONANTES
5989	CHEM PRODUCTS,PREPS NES	W 611340	1393285	W 681049	1567642	W 792929	1941217	W 785092	1908244	PROD PREP CHIMIQUES NDA
59899	OTH CHEM PRODS,PREPS,NES	W 496946	1043324	W 554544	1147729	W 559362	1388849	W 647076	1467958	AUT PRODUITS CHIMIQUES NDA
6	BASIC MANUFACTURES		23352859		29852250		35676356		36423398	ART MANUFACTURES
62	RUBBER MANUFACTURES NES		1582784		1794476		2079537		2235335	CAOUTCHOUC MANUFACTURE
625	RUBBER TYRES, TUBES ETC	W 252578	969577	W 292241	1125719	W 308066	1273224	W 325505	1326030	PNEUS CAOUTCHOUC VULCANISE
64	PAPER,PAPERBOARD AND MFR		2738372		3042851		3656896		3652693	PAPIERS,CARTONS & OUVRAGES
641	PAPER AND PAPERBOARD	W 1605229	2041494	W 1742670	2242011	W 1664343	2635575	W 1708399	2548009	PAPIERS ET CARTONS
6415	PAPER,PAPERBRD,BULK,NES	W 548068	590145	W 556747	654114	W 544461	766344	W 567783	725070	PAPIERS,CARTONS ROULEAUX
64159	OTHER PAPER ETC,BULK,NES	W 516506	553113	W 516756	605742	W 507790	710934	W 525275	674838	AUT PAPIER ROULEAUX FEUILLES
6418	COATED ETC PAPER NES BLK	W 285255	589894	W 332360	598916	W 346290	740933	W 340189	711584	PAP,CARTONS COUCHES,ENDUITS
642	PAPER,ETC,PRECUT,ARTS OF	W 280714	696878	W 1333561	800840	W 421216	1021321	W 363267	1104685	PAP,CARTONS DECOUPES
65	TEXTILE YARN,FABRICS,ETC		3876897		4498728		5173511		5403765	FILS,TISSUS,ARTICLES TEXTILE
651	TEXTILE YARN	W 211175	1069183		1262866		1480714		1497273	FILS TEXTILES
6514	SYN FIB YRN,BULK,MONOFIL	W 92395	529458	W 96224	600863	W 85369	472893	W 43717	268718	FILS CONT 85% FIB TEXT SYNTH
657	SPECIAL TXTL FABRC,PRODS	W 83031	615318	W 89934	699522	W 89343	836339	W 94716	881781	TISSUS SPECIAUX
66	NONMETAL MINERAL MFS NES		3664994		6746850		7510177		8087302	ART MIN NON METALLIQUES
663	MINERAL MANUFCTURES NES	W 413475	575983	W 512427	692283	W 739745	882154	W 877803	860927	ART MIN MANUF NDA
667	PEARL,PREC–,SEMI–P STONE		1603068		4322158		4585168		5141130	PERLES, PIERRES GEMMES
6672	DIAMONDS NONINDUST,UNSET		1562910		4273442		4526954		5088539	DIAMANTS BRUTS
66721	— ROUGH,UNSORTED		201		463860		380497		858637	DIAMANTS BRUTS NON TRIES
66722	— SRTD,ROUGH,SIMPLY WKD		1490286		3569602		3804063		3879991	DIAMANTS TRIES BRUTS
67	IRON AND STEEL		4829625		5670738		7107475		6628211	FER ET ACIER
672	IRON,STEEL PRIMARY FORMS	W 1974258	832794	W 2013208	914151	W 1789482	1186961	W 2041681	1125596	LINGOTS FER,ACIER
6725	IRN,STL BLOOMS,SLABS,ETC	W 1220222	603741	W 1164983	616024	W 1103884	862163	W 1150227	807494	BLOOMS,BILLETTES FER ACIER
673	IRON,STEEL SHAPES ETC	W 3218254	1313809	W 3554070	1599806	W 3663998	1921421	W 3565632	1577681	BARRES,PROFIL FER,ACIER
6733	IRON,STEEL PROFILES ETC	W 1687648	646079	W 1710687	739051	W 1688781	818875	W 1684485	760276	PROFILES,PALPLAN FER,ACIER
674	IRN,STL UNIV,PLATE,SHEET	W 2296446	1451102	W 2457798	1764276	W 2468447	2244744	W 2589362	2045969	LARGES PLATS,TOLES
6749	OTH IRN,STL PLATES,SHEET	W 717183	447849	W 858372	573503	W 870605	720636	W 891434	712151	AUTRES TOLES FER,ACIER
678	IRON,STL TUBES,PIPES,ETC	W 564785	697524		817436		1025860		1148174	TUBES,TUYAUX EN FONTE,FER

5. General Exports F.O.B. by Commodities according to the S.I.T.C. (Rev. 2) in thousand U.S. Dollars
Exportations Générales F.O.B. par Produits d'après la C.T.C.I. (Rév. 2) en milliers de Dollars E.U.

SITC CTCI	COMMODITY	1993 WEIGHT POIDS	1993 VALUE VALEUR	1994 WEIGHT POIDS	1994 VALUE VALEUR	1995 WEIGHT POIDS	1995 VALUE VALEUR	1996 WEIGHT POIDS	1996 VALUE VALEUR	PRODUIT
68	NON–FERROUS METALS		2808093		3402577		4491799		4189240	METAUX NON FERREUX
681	SILVER,PLATINUM,ETC		827218		849211		875190		1042275	ARGENT ET PLATINE
6812	METALS OF PLATINUM GROUP		516423		483911		537754		518737	PLATINE
682	COPPER EXC CEMENT COPPER	W 172938	545145		771350		1009700	W 252580	889293	CUIVRE
6822	COPPER,ALLOYS WORKED	W 147631	490028	W 201326	665777	W 227349	917878	W 220537	808489	CUIVRE,ALLIAGES OUVRES
684	ALUMINIUM	W 376593	907742		1164862		1773570	W 507566	1399482	ALUMINIUM
6842	ALUMINIUM,ALLOYS WORKED	W 247651	724333	W 281643	798307	W 312204	1086836	W 302286	1033397	ALUMINIUM,ALLIAGES OUVRE
69	METAL MANUFACTURES NES		3159554		3841616		4638804		4965495	ART MANUFACT EN METAL NDA
695	TOOLS	W 57783	554961	W 48259	670600	W 53753	800546	W 54323	907493	OUTILS A MAIN
699	BASE METAL MFRS NES	W 211630	1060505	W 259907	1354894	W 284630	1658722	W 298004	1830699	ART MANUFACTURES MET NDA
7	MACHINES,TRANSPORT EQUIP		70968379		83824412		102470290		114371131	MACHINES MATERIEL TRANSPORT
71	POWER GENERATING EQUIPMT		8974417		9359593		10195458		11225621	MACHINES GENERATRICES
713	INTRNL COMBUS PSTN ENGIN	W 242364	2635204	W 284841	3068815	W 331162	3611823	W 323878	3728213	MOTEURS EXPL COMB INT, PIECE
7132	MOTOR VEHCL PISTN ENGINS	W 120674	1299147	W 141834	1526893	W 159628	1730884	W 151825	1701272	MOTEURS EXPL POUR VEHICULES
7139	PISTON ENGINE PARTS NES	W 64541	756011	W 79777	909391	W 95586	1046129	W 97132	1173361	PIECES POUR 713.2,3,8
714	ENGINES AND MOTORS NES	W 29979	4914831	W 23465	4634747	W 23692	4861251	W 26454	5604114	MOTEURS NON ELECTRIQUES
7144	REACTION ENGINES	W 2898	2200970	W 2517	2228873	W 4086	2194871	W 5551	2316584	PROPULSEURS A REACTION
7148	GAS TURBINES NES	W 12412	707378	W 6760	557152	W 4200	522682	W 2585	535972	TURBINES A GAZ
71488	OTHER GAS TURBINES NES	W 12183	634242	W 6482	471570	W 4058	420286	W 2206	407271	AUTRES TURBINES A GAZ
7149	ENGINE & MOTOR PARTS NES	W 14669	2006483	W 14188	1848723	W 15406	2143697	W 18318	2751558	PIECES 714 ET 718.88
71491	PARTS NES OF 7144,71481	W 2727	1189291	W 2136	1094135	W 1986	1196332	W 2740	1756579	PIECES DES PROPULSEURS
71499	PARTS NES,OF 71488,71888	W 11942	817192	W 12052	754587	W 13419	947366	W 15578	994979	PIECES 714.88 ET 718.88
716	ROTATING ELECTRIC PLANT	W 114196	1019114	W 117174	1115626	W 125631	1217091	W 128096	1311644	APP ELECTR ROTATIFS,PIECES
7162	AC MTRS,GENRTRS,GEN SETS	W 86226	739650	W 84185	768452	W 88579	838189	W 95120	952359	MOTEURS ELECTRIQUES
72	MACHS FOR SPCL INDUSTRYS		5894689		6770991		8083329		8591552	MAC SPECIALES POUR INDUST
722	TRACTORS NON–ROAD	W 194300	943140	W 225192	1178785	W 244665	1438839	W 269059	1728710	TRACTEURS
7224	WHEELED TRACTORS NES	W 194130	942536	W 225019	1178588	W 244434	1438179	W 268914	1727679	TRACTEURS A ROUES
723	CIVIL ENGNEERG EQUIP ETC	W 230513	1287731		1548108		1928087		1870439	APPAREILS DE GENIE CIVIL
7234	CONST,MINING MACHNRY NES	W 182300	896842	W 216212	1157416		1493172	W 236783	1372193	MACH POUR LA CONST, MINES
72342	SLFPRP SHOVELS,EXCAVATRS	W 152646	676170	W 190393	960026	W 233476	1249611	W 202014	1108008	PELLES MECANIQUES
724	TEXTILE,LEATHER MACHNRY	W 43623	637956	W 45512	664846	W 40820	713689	W 35867	624334	MACH POUR INDUSTRIE TEXTILE
726	PRINTG,BKBINDG MACHY,PTS	W 247730	781798	W 52078	873728	W 54498	915871	W 33293	889634	MACHINES POUR IMPRIMERIE
728	OTH MACHY FOR SPCL INDUS	W 129600	1480322	W 141429	1653544	W 152780	2053592	W 165345	2303378	AUT MACH IND PARTICULIERES
7284	MACHY FOR SPCL INDUS NES	W 61761	1050952	W 69888	1189204	W 74728	1487225	W 83638	1682977	MACH SPEC IND PARTICUL.
73	METALWORKING MACHINERY		969752		1181187		1435622		1649926	MACH TRAVAIL DES METAUX
736	METALWORKING MACH–TOOLS	W 64615	716165	W 71486	833929	W 77359	1067612	W 74511	1230762	MACH–OUTILS TRAVAIL METAUX
74	GENRL INDUSTRL MACHY NES		7334846		8575970		10524569		11682236	MACH APP INDUSTRIE
741	HEATING,COOLING EQUIPMNT	W 78979	1079157	W 83938	1168089	W 101910	1503485	W 126525	1705839	MACH CHAUFFAGE,PIECES
742	PUMPS FOR LIQUIDS ETC	W 32744	715674	W 41429	855277	W 49850	976851	W 58386	1103262	POMPES MOTO–POMPES
743	PUMPS NES,CENTRFUGES ETC	W 90439	1380649	W 111828	1651514	W 129679	2094853	W 139865	2275677	POMPES COMPRES,VENT ETC
7436	GAS,LIQUID FILTERS ETC	W 39400	419735	W 49495	576114	W 52568	799613	W 59345	855915	APP POUR FILT DES LIQUIDES
744	MECHANICAL HANDLING EQU	W 198478	1269931	W 251701	1573309	W 300466	2010213	W 317090	2307690	EQUIP MANUTENTION PIECES
7441	FORK LIFT TRCKS,ETC,PTS	W 98875	450763	W 126472	583325	W 156758	825078	W 162478	961358	CHARIOTS POUR USINES ETC
74411	FORK LIFT TRUCKS ETC	W 97134	441107	W 124281	571274	W 154812	809646	W 160359	944567	CHARIOTS POUR LES GARES
745	NONELEC MACHY,TOOLS NES	W 34411	749239	W 38558	895251	W 40065	1003793	W 44028	1127534	AUT MACH NON ELEC,PIECES
7452	OTH NONELEC MCHS,PTS NES	W 30298	649815	W 34817	775165	W 36664	890059	W 40950	1014277	AUT MACH NON ELEC,PIECES
749	NONELEC MACH PTS,ACC NES	W 151346	2140194	W 168143	2432531	W 271667	2935373	W 190158	3162235	PIECES MACH NON ELEC NDA
7492	COCKS,VALVES ETC NES	W 49611	907746	W 50343	985926	W 55812	1159517	W 59822	1263088	ART ROB,SIM POUR TUYAUX
75	OFFICE MACHNES,ADP EQUIP		11910809		14419956		18317568		18951198	MACH BUREAU TRAIT AUTOM
751	OFFICE MACHINES	W 38731	947974	W 43531	1067168	W 39144	1060884	W 47004	1100118	MACH,APPAREILS DE BUREAU
7518	OFFICE MACHINES NES	W 32060	756226	W 37998	892794	W 33942	866913	W 40195	903559	MACH,APP DE BUREAU NDA
75188	OTHR OFFICE MACHINES NES	W 19049	520892	W 20890	600741	W 19271	585366	W 24283	601683	AUTRES MACH DE BUREAU
752	AUTOMTIC DATA PROC EQUIP	W 89861	7267973	W 107990	8663048	W 116497	11531201	W 139246	11931944	MACH TRAIT INFORMATION
7522	DIGITAL COMPUTERS	W 3958	761551	W 3108	588772	W 3993	1012371	W 8923	1979628	MACH DIGITALES COMPLETES
7523	DIGITL CENTRL PROCESSORS	W 24597	3271285	W 33801	4075791	W 38953	5402456	W 44976	4895164	UNITES CENTRALES
7524	DIGITL CENTRL STOR UNITS	W 5464	1045286	W 8794	1520412	W 11185	2418460	W 8771	1853232	UNITES MEMOIRE CENTRALES
7525	ADP PERIPHERAL UNITS	W 50449	1510188	W 55767	1813152	W 56700	1958132	W 66160	2054342	UNITES PERIPHERIQUES
7528	OFF–LINE DATA PROC EQUIP	W 4478	552342	W 5420	584631	W 5044	651960	W 9257	921702	MACH AUXIL TRAIT INFORM
759	OFFICE,ADP MCH PTS,ACCES	W 34953	3694862	W 40204	4689740	W 61719	5725483	W 45467	5919136	PIECES DU 751 ET 752
7599	ACCTG,ETC,ADP MCH PTS,AC	W 26519	3360942	W 28926	4223213	W 36479	5271034	W 32056	5401933	PIECES DU 751 ET 752
76	TELECOMM,SOUND EQUIPMENT		5327671		7284173		9978361		11826351	EQUIPMENT DE TELECOM
761	TELEVISION RECEIVERS	W 66877	968339	W 88613	1231374	W 88416	1342886	W 119706	1864290	RECEPTEURS DE TELEVISION
7611	COLOUR TV RECEIVERS	W 66645	958531	W 88339	1219527	W 88093	1329926	W 118697	1854363	RECEPTEURS COULEUR
763	SOUND RECORDRS,PHONOGRPH	W 13487	565404	W 13702	712619	W 14733	787931	W 17555	1005258	PHONO,APP ENREGISTREMENT
7638	OTHR SOUND APPARATUS ETC	W 13191	557752	W 13443	705203	W 14333	776034	W 17072	989887	AUT APP D'ENREGIS,REPROD
76381	TV IMAGE,SND RECRDRS ETC	W 10439	399286	W 10590	526635	W 11383	581645	W 14417	811650	APP ENREG,REPRO IMAG,SON
764	TELECOM EQPT,PTS,ACC NES	W 58585	3527997		5020485		7432057		8552028	EQUIP TELECOM,PIECES
7641	LINE TELEPHONE,ETC EQUIP	W 7787	595937	W 9837	1010583	W 13705	2040227	W 22214	2834389	APP TELEPHON PAR FIL
7643	TV,RADIO TRANSMITTRS ETC	W 2072	918317		1711600		2488349		2649807	APP EMET TELE RADIO
7649	PTS NES OF EQUIPMT OF 76	W 27887	1271425	W 112847	1489249	W 42319	1925108	W 37981	2167759	PIECES DE LA DIV 76
76491	PTS NES OF APPAR OF 7641	W 2918	262331	W 5239	441919	W 4407	463241	W 5934	797289	PIECES POUR 764.1
76493	TELECOMM EQUIPMT PTS NES	W 16260	883068	W 15425	917118	W 17040	1276597	W 25026	1211816	PIECES 761,762,764.3,8
77	ELECTRIC MACHNRY NES ETC		11822766		14808284		18381689		19466231	MACH APP ELECT NDA
771	ELECTRIC POWER MACHY NES	W 29216	434638	W 31438	522833	W 37589	787341	W 65684	955618	MACH PROD,TRANS ELECTR
772	SWITCHGEAR ETC,PARTS NES	W 47819	1783324	W 62188	2117825	W 74486	2600680	W 81745	2941622	APP COUPURE,SECT ETC
7721	SWITCHGEAR ETC	W 44130	1436759	W 56932	1694825	W 68186	1993430	W 61972	2258433	APP COUPURE,SECTIONMNT
773	ELECTR DISTRIBUTNG EQUIP	W 116203	638726	W 127445	764144	W 153368	952458	W 158903	1023061	EQUIPMT DISTRIBUTION ELECT
7731	INSULATED WIRE,CABLE ETC	W 107539	534515	W 118115	641656	W 138766	789757	W 143090	871591	FILS,CABLES ISOLES ELECT
775	HOUSEHOLD TYPE EQUIP NES	W 98596	780411	W 114967	963087	W 146308	1188599	W 152311	1278503	MACH,APP USAGE DOMESTQUE
7758	ELECTRO–THERMIC APPL NES	W 44865	432833	W 49526	509140	W 70927	668018	W 83029	800081	APP ELECTROTHERMIQ NDA
776	TRANSISTORS,VALVES,ETC	W 54237	4952228		6345567		8054951		7828488	LAMPES,TUBES,VALVES
7763	DIODES,TRANSISTORS,ETC	W 1700	525638	W 2053	628014	W 2882	795171	W 4765	774001	DIODES,TRANSISTORS
7764	ELECTRONIC MICROCIRCUITS	W 3895	3895589	W 4734	5139763	W 8334	6535491	W 9495	6321420	MICROSTRUCTURES ELECTRON
778	ELECTRICAL MACHINERY NES	W 161169	2813046		3739129		4362071	W 236051	5003809	AUTRES MACH ELECT NDA
7788	OTH ELEC MACHY,EQUIP NES	W 22870	1646814		2243948	W 46828	2758079	W 48702	3027824	AUT MACH APP ELEC NDA
77886	OTH ELEC MACHINERY NES	W 1452	668462		862603	W 14529	1094415	W 12509	1300393	AUT MACH APP ELECTRIQUES
78	ROAD VEHICLES		12254402		14293210		18486992		22524632	VEHICULES ROUTIERS
781	PASS MOTOR VEH EXC BUSES	W 620045	6530277	W 711467	7765020	W 953226	11008466	W 1137975	13428327	AUTO TRANSPORT PERSONNES
782	LORRIES,SPCL MTR VEH NES	W 206091	1510580		1167488		1290151	W 237049	1703921	VEHICULES SPECIAUX,MARCH
7821	LORRIES,TRUCKS	W 141262	1140504	W 107005	754877	W 161149	1076096	W 213839	1494513	VEHICULES TRANSP MARCHAND
784	MOTOR VEH PRTS,ACCES NES	W 505267	3636566	W 675628	4600261	W 782618	5240417	W 917300	6280623	PIECES 722,781,782,783
7849	OTHER MOTOR VEHCL PARTS	W 480056	3446210	W 644844	4392509	W 747790	4967777	W 867211	5901924	PIECES 722,781,782,783
79	OTHR TRANSPORT EQUIPMENT		6479028		7131049		7066702		8453385	AUTRE MATERIEL TRANSPORT
791	RAILWAY VEHICLES	W 16232	193444	W 31960	650690	W 15114	163101	W 18342	197125	VEHIC MAT CHEMINS DE FER
792	AIRCRAFT ETC		5917773		5712978		6209586		7359595	APP NAVIGATION AERIENNE
7923	AIRCRFT NES2000–15000KG		693254		865506		799435		1099490	AERODYNES 2000 A 15000 KG
7924	AIRCRFT NES OVER 15000KG		680699		738515		998765		819280	AERODYNES PLUS 15000 KG
7929	AIRCRAFT PARTS NES		4234185		3866481		4210852		5083657	PIECES DU 792
793	SHIPS AND BOATS ETC		367811		767380		694015	W 32261	896665	NAVIRES BATEAUX,ETC
8	MISC MANUFACTURED GOODS		21903017		26403497		29743166		32465581	ART MANUFACTURES DIVERS
821	*FURNITURE,PARTS THEREOF	W 193519	916165	W 416107	1108520	W 318758	1337411	W 822267	1552183	MEUBLES ET PIECES

5. General Exports F.O.B. by Commodities according to the S.I.T.C. (Rev. 2) in thousand U.S. Dollars
Exportations Générales F.O.B. par Produits d'après la C.T.C.I. (Rév. 2) en milliers de Dollars E.U.

SITC CTCI	COMMODITY	1993			1994			1995			1996			PRODUIT
		WEIGHT POIDS		VALUE VALEUR	WEIGHT POIDS		VALUE VALEUR	WEIGHT POIDS		VALUE VALEUR	WEIGHT POIDS		VALUE VALEUR	
8219	FURNITURE AND PARTS NES	W	159778	563383	W	265473	713211	W	265872	852567	W	732436	993351	AUTRES MEUBLES ET PIECES
84	CLOTHING AND ACCESSORIES			3208781			3966676			4454601			4940630	VETEMENTS
842	MENS OUTERWEAR NOT KNIT	W	19097	518484	W	40510	642514	W	23859	666285	W	22667	684235	VET DESSUS POUR HOMMES
843	WOMENS OUTERWEAR NONKNIT	W	21800	806933	W	24607	969927	W	28572	1081829	W	31786	1229126	VET DESSUS FEMMES MAT TEX
845	OUTERWEAR KNIT NONELASTC	W	24448	808525	W	30760	1057930	W	32918	1107351	W	34940	1254932	VET DESSOUS,ACCES BONNET
8451	— JERSEYS,PULLOVERS ETC	W	13144	456993	W	17043	625919	W	18114	640357	W	19291	718677	CHANDAILS,PULL–OVERS ETC
851	*FOOTWEAR	W	24140	551157	W	28922	671946	W	28862	748751	W	33050	886646	CHAUSSURES
85102	FOOTWEAR LEATHER	W	9908	217063	W	16897	424433	W	23963	673381	W	27940	806917	CHAUS SEMELLES EN CUIR
87	PRECISION INSTRUMNTS NES			4883476			5587006			6485358			7179153	INSTRUM,APPAR SCIENT NDA
872	MEDICAL INSTRUMENTS NES	W	21923	729615	W	23550	875517	W	26739	1021598	W	32496	1187983	INSTR,APP MEDIC–CHIR NDA
87202	OTH MEDICAL INSTRUMENTS	W	19306	601247	W	20349	714982	W	22747	820646	W	27186	942035	INSTRUM,APP MEDECINE
874	MEASURNG,CONTROLNG INSTR	W	38576	3631476	W	56527	4083292	W	54021	4792518	W	65489	5273508	INSTRUMENTS DE MESURE
8741	SURVEYING INSTRUMENTS	W	3420	677215	W	2787	694906	W	2970	783431	W	3365	946858	INST GEODESIE,TOPO ETC
87411	NAVIG INSTR NONELEC ETC	W	1001	527909	W	846	556512	W	1036	625859	W	920	750307	INSTR NAVIGATION
8743	GAS,LIQUID CONTROL INSTR	W	7439	501886	W	20158	569220	W	15495	671625	W	25811	783958	APP,INSTR MESURE FLUIDES
8748	ELEC MEAS,CONTRL EQU NES	W	5977	874223	W	6946	981500	W	6550	1179523	W	6640	1328725	APP ELEC ELECTRO MESURE
87483	OTH ELCTRNC MEAS ETC EQU	W	5111	758825	W	6193	866089	W	5562	1029083	W	5133	1031785	AUT APP ELECTRO DE MESURE
8749	INSTR PTS NES,ACCESSORYS	W	9455	696090	W	11637	788160	W	13345	977706	W	13301	987722	PIECES 873,874.3,54,874.8
88	PHOTO EQU,OPTICL GDS ETC			2089560			2537439			2795278			2995715	APP,FOURN PHOTO,OP,MONTR
882	PHOTO,CINEMA SUPPLIES	W	136517	1389680	W	164619	1610184	W	165651	1822246	W	162717	1888975	PRODUITS PHOTO,CINEMA
8822	PHOTO FILM EXC DEV CINMA	W	104580	1272158	W	125519	1457765	W	122395	1601462	W	117728	1651700	PLAQUES,PELLICULES,FILMS
88222	PHOTO FILM ROLL UNEXPOSD	W	15140	543361	W	18619	591254	W	20166	652064	W	21634	716458	PEL SENSIB PERF OU NON
89	MISC MANUFCTRD GOODS NES			9785795			11999345			13311863			14155784	ART MANUFACTURES DIVERS
892	PRINTED MATTER	W	405295	2395893			2795718			3149325	W	332870	3439177	IMPRIMES
8921	PRINTED BOOKS,GLOBES,ETC	W	200461	1348756	W	160508	1508096	W	152145	1710252	W	161973	1837425	LIVRES,BROCHURES,CARTES
89211	PRINTED BOOKS,PAMPHLETS	W	196886	1308988	W	156605	1465940	W	148638	1665680	W	157411	1786236	LIVRES,BROCHURES
8928	PRINTED MATTER NES	W	131087	532982	W	62408	609345	W	68263	700921	W	78450	839972	IMPRIMES NDA
893	ARTICLES OF PLASTIC NES	W	364788	1617426			2008608			2450971			2650690	OUVRAGES EN MAT DIVIS 58
8939	MISC PLASTIC ARTICLES	W	227752	1033789	W	262396	1317897	W	325149	1632620	W	318092	1765998	ART DIVERS EN MAT DIV 58
89399	OTHR PLASTC ARTICLES NES	W	164629	864246	W	188185	1116724	W	242784	1397206	W	238973	1515221	AUT OUV MAT DIV 58
894	TOYS,SPORTING GOODS,ETC	W	74294	832129			1109371	W	118438	1344608	W	113695	1423836	VOITURES ENFANTS,JOUETS
8942	TOYS,INDOOR GAMES ETC	W	59767	603492	W	93252	842155	W	92720	1036202	W	79100	1064095	JOUETS,JEUX ETC
896	WORKS OF ART ETC			1817252			1964307			2038980			1834203	OBJETS D'ART
89601	HAND PAINTINGS ETC NES			1030368			1015612			1067812			868173	TABLEAUX,PEINTURES
89606	ANTIQUES NES			527056			618893			695401			654544	OBJETS D'ANTIQUITE
897	GOLD,SILVER WARE,JEWELRY			1078533			1545479			1449184			1623573	BIJOUTERIE,ORFEVRERIE
8973	PREC JEWLRY,GLD–SILVWARE			929457			1355083			1269582			1453937	BIJOUX OR,ARGENT ORFEVRE
89731	PRECIOUS METAL JEWELLERY			868427			1257287			1104865			1304948	ART BIJOUTERIE,JOAILLER
898	MUSICAL INSTRUMENTS,PTS	W	57007	1247962	W	63799	1594218	W	118561	1751633	W	76622	1928505	INSTRUMENTS DE MUSIQUE
8983	SOUND RECRDNG TAPE,DISCS	W	51664	1170017	W	59347	1507333	W	114805	1648656	W	73030	1839731	SUPPORTS SON POUR 763
89832	RECORDED DISCS,TAPES ETC	W	23610	833821	W	31027	1148617	W	81981	1240284	W	42132	1433929	DISQUES,PHONO,BANDES
899	OTHER MANUFACTURED GOODS			523085			653107			743878			847004	AUT ART MANUF DIVERS NDA
9	GOODS NOT CLASSD BY KIND			2500416			2400190			3090831			3231812	ART TRANSACT NON CLASSES
931	*SPECIAL TRANSACTIONS			1105276			1268601	W	92426	1319707			1443262	TRANS.SPECIALES
951	*WAR FIREARMS,AMMUNITION			863925			667921			1156155			1230852	VEHIC BLINDES ARMES
95101	ARMORED FIGHTNG VEHICLES			220945			154493	W	7812	723165	W	6962	624745	CHARS DE COMBAT

1. HISTORICAL SERIES, 1961–1996 GENERAL TRADE, IMPORTS C.I.F., EXPORTS F.O.B.
SERIES HISTORIQUES, 1961–1996 COMMERCE GENERAL, IMPORTATIONS C.A.F., EXPORTATIONS F.O.B

YEAR ANNEE	VALUE IN MILLION TANZ.SHILLINGS VALEUR EN MILLION TANZ.SHILLINGS MERCHANDISE –MARCHANDISE IMPORTS	EXPORTS	GOLD # 1 –OR IMPORTS	EXPORTS	CONVERSION FACTORS U.S. CENTS PER TANZ.SHILLING FACTEURS DE CONVERSION CENTS E.U. PAR TANZ.SHILLING IMPORTS	EXPORTS	INDEX NUMBERS –INDICES QUANTUM IMPORTS	EXPORTS	UNIT VALUE VALEUR UNITAIRE IMPORTS	EXPORTS
1961	1005.80	1057.00		25.00	14.0000	14.0000				
1962	1030.00	1116.20		25.40	14.0000	14.0000				
1963	1055.20	1371.20	0.40	25.60	14.0000	14.0000				
1964	1193.20	1530.70	0.40	23.40	14.0000	14.0000				
1965	1333.80	1399.80	0.80	22.80	14.0000	14.0000				
1966	1612.10	1785.20	1.00	14.20	14.0000	14.0000				
1967	1576.70	1667.60	0.20	4.60	14.0000	14.0000				
1968	1833.80	1717.80		4.80	14.0000	14.0000				
1969	1710.00	1792.40		4.80	14.0000	14.0000				
1970	2274.20	1851.90		2.00	14.0000	14.0000				
1971	2725.60	1988.80	0.20		14.0000	14.0000				
1972	2956.10	2276.60			14.0000	14.0000				
1973	3478.90	2586.80			14.2860	14.2160				
1974	5257.90	2860.60			14.0000	14.0000				
1975	5694.20	2763.80			13.5806	13.4653				
1976	4752.00	3846.00			11.9235	11.9387				
1977	6161.00	4198.00			12.1397	12.1391				
1978	8798.00	3669.00			12.9859	13.0059				
1979	8885.00	4216.00			12.1221	12.1239				
1980	10046.40	4160.50			12.2029	12.2028				
1981	10047.00	5087.00			12.0673	12.0572				
1982	10519.00	4230.00			10.7530	10.7520				
1983	9207.00	4130.00			8.9309	8.8700				
1984	13373.00	6135.00			6.8618	6.5676				
1985	16966.00	6173.00			5.7418	5.7274				
1986	30576.99	11285.00			2.9180	2.9190				
1987	59340.00	18512.00			1.5240	1.5230				
1988	80828.00	27040.99			0.9960	0.9960				
1989	146705.20	52777.01			0.6800	0.7075				
1990	265984.00	64571.01			0.5129	0.5128				
1991	338990.00	74708.00			0.4561	0.4573				
1992	449479.90	123966.00			0.3232	0.3324				
1993	615990.00	181147.00			0.2431	0.2485				
1994	765756.90	265177.00			0.1965	0.1958				
1995	968910.00	390377.90			0.1733	0.1754				
1996	804948.90	441344.00			0.1721	0.1718				

2. IMPORTS BY BROAD ECONOMIC CATEGORY AND EXPORTS BY INDUSTRIAL ORIGIN. (PERCENTAGE OF TOTAL VALUE)
IMPORTATIONS PAR CATEGORIES ECONOMIQUES ET EXPORTATIONS PAR BRANCHE D'ACTIVITE.(EN POURCENTAGE DE LA VALEUR TOTALE)

IMPORTS – IMPORTATIONS

	1990	1991	1992	1993	1994	1995	1996
TOTAL IMPORTS–IMPORTATIONS TOTALES							
1 FOOD BEV–ALIMENTATION BOISSONS							
11 PRIMARY–PRODUITS DE BASE							
111 FOR INDUSTRY–POUR L'INDUSTRIE							
112 FOR HOUSEHOLDS–POUR LES MENAGES							
12 PROCESSED–PRODUITS ELABORES							
121 FOR INDUSTRY–POUR L'INDUSTRIE							
122 FOR HOUSEHOLDS–POUR LES MENAGES							
2 IND SUPPLIES–APPROV INDUSTRIELS							
21 PRIMARY–PRODUITS DE BASE							
22 PROCESSED–PRODUITS ELABORES							
3 FUELS–COMBUSTIBLES							
31 PRIMARY–PRODUITS DE BASE							
32 PROCESSED–PRODUITS ELABORES							
321 MOTOR SPIRIT–ESSENCE							
322 OTHER–AUTRES							
4 MACHINERY–EQUIPEMENT							
41 CAPITAL EQUIPMENT–MACHINES							
42 PARTS–PIECES ACCESSOIRES							
5 TRANSPORT–TRANSPORT							
51 PASSENGER CARS–AUTOMOBILES							
52 OTHER–AUTRES							
521 INDUSTRIAL–INDUSTRIELS							
522 NON INDUSTRIAL–NON INDUSTRIEL							
53 PARTS–PIECES ACCESSOIRES							
6 CONSUM GOODS–BIENS CONSOMMATION							
61 DURABLE–DURABLES							
62 SEMI DURABLE–SEMI DURABLES							
63 NON DURABLE–NON DURABLES							
7 GOODS NES–BIENS NDA							

EXPORTS – EXPORTATIONS

	1990	1991	1992	1993	1994	1995	1996
TOTAL EXPORTS–EXPORTATIONS TOTALES							
1 AGRICULTURE							
2 MINING QUARRY–INDUS EXTRACTIVES							
3 MANUFACTURING–IND MANUFACTUR							
31 FOOD BEV TOBACCO–ALIM BOISS TAB							
32 TEXTILES–INDUSTRIES TEXTILES							
33 WOOD & PRODUCTS–BOIS & PRODUITS							
34 PAPER & PRODUCTS–PAPIER & PRODT							
35 CHEMICALS–INDUSTRIES CHIMIQUES							
36 NON METAL MIN–MIN NON METAL							
37 BASIC METAL–IND METAL BASE							
38 METAL MANUF–MANUF METAL							
39 OTH MANUF IND–AUTRES MANUF							

3. TRADE BY PRINCIPAL COUNTRIES OF CONSIGNMENT (VALUE IN THOUSAND U.S. DOLLARS)
ECHANGES SELON LES PRINCIPAUX PAYS DE CONSIGNATION (VALEUR EN MILLIERS DE DOLLARS EU)

COUNTRIES–PAYS	GENERAL IMPORTS C.I.F. IMPORTATIONS GENERALES C.A.F				
	1986	1987	1988	1989	1990
World	838493	943386	1495215	997614	1021407
Africa	51634	50475	62280	44214	37163
Americas	47397	46192	60158	39889	45657
Northern America	36424	45430	57609	36536	36082
LAIA	2385	716	2440	952	8263
CACM					
Caribbean	8587	46	110	2400	1312
Rest of America					
As.ex F.USSR	288281	287167	465132	330065	265194
Eur.x F.USSR	438637	541691	878611	544415	629565
EU	396488	507568	815196	507511	576306
EFTA	21299	26533	42250	25561	24266
East Europe	1936	1661	8506	7460	23667
Other Europe		5928			
Former USSR	6567	1615	3337	4910	2097
Oceania	3255	4846	4631	1666	7792
United Kingdom	101388	136962	258631	162602	174817
Germany/Allemagne	89883	117180	176491	96771	102822
Japan/Japon	97403	105994	187517	96859	79074
Italy/Italie	56433	87615	116363	90726	68642
Netherlands/Pays–Bas	33282	47793	75905	40154	44694
United Arab Emirates	46386	42702	51971	52034	45421
Denmark/Danemark	29156	43952	70875	32307	28813
Kenya	35246	30800	38376	28152	18110
Sweden/Suède	26771	27798	46443	14287	31310
Belgium–Luxembourg	27417	16170	27808	30831	32847
Iran (Islamic Rp. of)	20962	30	37499	30022	44125
USA/Etats–Unis d'Amer	26687	33757	30448	14559	15952
France,Monac	13217	10577	19741	21236	43858
India/Inde	12628	14874	28496	18748	17613
Canada	9738	11674	27161	21978	20130
Bahrain/Bahreïn	2133	19507	36782	22732	2045
China/Chine	13161	11628	25976	12607	18761
Switz.Liecht	12909	15530	25836	14593	11528
Qatar	28	11247	5289	37094	25041
Kuwait/ Koweït	31514	32004	2699	4046	846
Singapore/Singapour	8643	7940	22798	15293	9042
Saudi Arabia	13217	5166	23187	16980	5095
Norway,SVD,JM	8391	11003	16414	10968	12738
Finland/Finlande	11842	11887	13307	5698	11026
Fm Yugoslav	18914	5928	12659	3883	5326
Hong Kong	6903	6797	15020	6249	5280
Thailand/Thaïlande	19980	5334	10219	1258	1517
Zambia/Zambie	8250	6477	9591	8140	5177
Ireland/Irlande	561	1173	1793	768	27168
Bangladesh	9485	6568	3914	4862	3040
Former GDR	702	686	1813	2856	17680
Australia/Australie	3199	4846	4442	1618	7592
Zimbabwe	2638	3277	4452	3924	4665
Former USSR/Anc. URSS	6567	1615	3337	4910	2097
Spain/Espagne	4967	2896	1922	884	5772
Austria/Autriche	1291	3307	3914	3325	3019
Korea Dem People's Rp	281	4831	3366	3924	1297
Czechoslovakia	281	168	4870	2230	4988
Pakistan	1796	1829	1504	1394	2891
So. Africa Customs Un	393	1387	2102	1856	3035
Brazil/Brésil	2357	655	1912	911	2748
Portugal	140	122	797	4148	1240
Turkey/Turquie	1291	396	2052	2380	267
Korea, Republic of	28	3597	1534	530	236
Israel/Israël	505	3810	1444	34	21
Argentina/Argentine	28		169	27	5516
Indonesia/Indonésie	1347	792	847	1754	923
Malaysia/Malaisie	253	564	2370	360	2081
Greece/Grèce	140	137	1205	3774	277
Burundi	337	3962	219	286	41

COUNTRIES–PAYS	GENERAL EXPORTS F.O.B. EXPORTATIONS GENERALES F.O.B.				
	1986	1987	1988	1989	1990
Monde	344826	290939	337106	371387	415955
Afrique	21219	33491	32151	50155	34794
Amériques	8350	7204	10040	13405	29161
Amérique du Nord	7945	7173	10030	13348	29146
ALAI	249			49	10
MCAC					
Caraïbes	156	30	10	7	5
Autre Amérique					
Asie l'URSS exclus	61568	76165	79053	89372	140814
Europe l'URSS exclus	233623	164484	173951	176799	179677
UE	229323	155453	169748	172190	167511
AELE	3116	3610	1803	1421	7611
Europe de l'Est	561	3655	1116	1287	2716
Autre de l'Europe		1767			
Ancienne URSS	717	1995	657	686	1015
Océanie	1184	1401	1504	1280	1076
Germany/Allemagne	83441	37984	47788	52474	51475
United Kingdom	42593	30262	34183	44308	43962
India/Inde	15672	21870	21573	9184	69326
Netherlands/Pays–Bas	24116	23850	19661	21161	22309
Finland/Finlande	29102	29546	13884	4249	4592
Japan/Japon	15143	11148	15498	17251	16092
Italy/Italie	16825	10493	16305	17449	11972
Singapore/Singapour	13678	10082	9263	19117	13146
USA/Etats–Unis d'Amer	6886	6275	8655	11581	28162
Portugal	8631	8468	13605	11927	15713
Hong Kong	5484	7219	12968	15554	11162
Kenya	3240	8163	10976	14762	12136
Pakistan	5608	5970	10647	11093	12777
Belgium–Luxembourg	7758	5909	11783	10471	7011
France,Monac	10376	1462	3267	4044	3142
Spain/Espagne	1246	4173	6454	3804	4961
Uganda/Ouganda	5920	2772	3396	3959	3997
Switz.Liecht	2150	3427	1793	1046	7421
Malaysia/Malaisie	1277	1919	936	5599	2732
Dem. Rep. of the Congo	935	1097	2709	5670	1635
Nigeria/Nigéria		30	896	9219	625
Indonesia/Indonésie	935	1523	2341	1534	4085
Zambia/Zambie	966	1691	3914	1725	1988
Turkey/Turquie	249	1965	976	2326	3869
Algeria/Algérie		9108	169		
Burundi	1745	883	1753	2885	1220
Sudan/Soudan	1309	731	1345	1796	2286
Fm Yugoslav	623	1767	1285	1902	1840
Zimbabwe	436	503	1504	1485	3434
Egypt/Egypte	1807	2178	608	1018	1655
Malawi	280	350	1932	3422	866
United Arab Emirates	561	716	1554	1831	1999
Mozambique	312	3823	90	1478	871
Denmark/Danemark	2898	1020	727	905	856
Canada	1059	899	1374	1767	984
Thailand/Thaïlande	93	487	209	2793	2357
China/Chine	1963	1873	1056	205	15
Former USSR/Anc. URSS	717	1995	657	686	1015
Australia/Australie	623	1234	1116	749	717
Saudi Arabia	405	1249	1036	559	1010
Sweden/Suède	841	990	687	665	810
Hungary/Hongrie	31	868	717	686	907
Somalia/Somalie	1028	228	239	445	1086
Angola	2056	61	717		
Czechoslovakia		2711			
Ireland/Irlande	841	548	468	325	507
Greece/Grèce	623	396	647	396	164
Sri Lanka	93	1691	110	297	5
Mauritius/Maurice	312	91	508	686	451
New Zealand	561	168	388	530	359

(VALUE AS PERCENTAGE OF WORLD TOTAL)(VALEURS EN POURCENTAGE DU TOTAL MONDIAL)

	1981	1982	1983	1984	1985	1986	1987	1988	1989	1990
Africa	2.5	1.6	1.9	3.9	4.3	6.2	5.4	4.2	4.4	3.6
Americas	9.3	8.5	8.9	7.1	6.9	5.7	4.9	4.0	4.0	4.5
Northern America	8.0	7.6	7.5	6.3	6.3	4.3	4.8	3.9	3.7	3.5
LAIA	1.3	0.9	1.4	0.8	0.6	0.3	0.1	0.2	0.1	0.8
CACM										
Caribbean				0.0	0.0	1.0	0.0	0.0	0.2	0.1
Rest of America	0.0									
As.ex F.USSR	24.6	27.3	29.7	31.6	38.2	34.4	30.4	31.1	33.1	26.0
Eur.x F.USSR	62.3	61.4	58.8	53.6	48.1	52.3	57.4	58.8	54.6	61.6
EU	56.3	55.8	52.8	49.7	44.0	47.3	53.8	54.5	50.9	56.4
EFTA	3.6	4.8	5.1	2.6	2.2	2.5	2.8	2.8	2.6	2.4
East Europe	0.6	0.1	0.2	0.5	0.6	0.2	0.2	0.6	0.7	2.3
Other Europe	1.7	0.7	0.7	0.4			0.6			
Former USSR	1.0	1.0	0.4	1.5	0.8	0.8	0.2	0.2	0.5	0.2
Oceania	0.3	0.1	0.2	0.3	0.4	0.4	0.5	0.3	0.2	0.8
United Kingdom	20.9	14.9	15.4	11.5	11.1	12.1	14.5	17.3	16.3	17.1
Germany/Allemagne	9.5	9.3	10.8	9.8	8.9	10.7	12.4	11.8	9.7	10.1
Japan/Japon	12.0	11.6	12.9	10.6	8.9	11.6	11.2	12.5	9.7	7.7
Italy/Italie	4.1	5.2	6.8	8.7	8.4	6.7	9.3	7.8	9.1	6.7
Netherlands/Pays–Bas	4.3	4.9	3.9	4.7	3.9	4.0	5.1	5.1	4.0	4.4
United Arab Emirates	0.4	0.1	0.1	0.8	2.2	5.5	4.5	3.5	5.2	4.4
Denmark/Danemark	2.0	2.0	2.5	2.3	2.2	3.5	4.7	4.7	3.2	2.8
Kenya	1.8	1.5	1.6	1.2	2.3	4.2	3.3	2.6	2.8	1.8
Sweden/Suède	4.9	5.1	3.7	4.0	3.0	3.2	2.9	3.1	1.4	3.1
Belgium–Luxembourg				2.1	2.9	3.3	1.7	1.9	3.1	3.2

	1981	1982	1983	1984	1985	1986	1987	1988	1989	1990
Afrique	2.3	3.0	2.8	6.4	5.5	6.2	11.5	9.5	13.5	8.4
Amériques	4.6	7.5	4.2	3.8	2.1	2.4	2.5	3.0	3.6	7.0
Amérique du Nord	4.5	7.4	4.2	3.8	2.1	2.3	2.5	3.0	3.6	7.0
ALAI	0.0	0.0	0.0	0.0		0.1			0.0	0.0
MCAC										
Caraïbes	0.0	0.0	0.0	0.0		0.0	0.0	0.0	0.0	0.0
Autre Amérique	0.0	0.0	0.0	0.0						
Asie l'URSS exclus	37.0	31.6	31.0	18.2	24.9	17.9	26.2	23.5	24.1	33.9
Europe l'URSS exclus	47.1	54.2	54.8	65.5	57.8	67.8	56.5	51.6	47.6	43.2
UE	43.9	51.2	53.1	62.2	55.4	66.5	53.4	50.4	46.4	40.3
AELE	0.8	0.9	0.8	2.3	0.8	0.9	1.2	0.5	0.4	1.8
Europe de l'Est	0.0	0.5	0.0	0.2	1.2	0.2	1.3	0.3	0.3	0.7
Autre de l'Europe	2.3	1.6	0.8	0.4			0.6			
Ancienne URSS	8.4	3.4	6.7	1.7	0.4	0.2	0.7	0.2	0.2	0.2
Océanie	0.5	0.3	0.5	0.8	0.4	0.3	0.5	0.4	0.3	0.3
Germany/Allemagne	15.3	17.0	16.8	22.7	19.4	24.2	13.1	14.2	14.1	12.4
United Kingdom	9.2	7.4	9.5	13.9	15.4	12.4	10.4	10.1	11.9	10.6
India/Inde	10.4	12.4	13.3	2.8	3.3	4.5	7.5	6.4	2.5	16.7
Netherlands/Pays–Bas	4.2	5.8	5.3	5.5	5.7	7.0	8.2	5.8	5.7	5.4
Finland/Finlande	0.9	2.2	2.9	3.3	4.2	8.4	10.2	4.1	1.1	1.1
Japan/Japon	3.4	3.9	4.3	4.3	3.1	4.4	3.8	4.6	4.6	3.9
Italy/Italie	5.4	6.1	6.7	7.1	4.3	4.9	3.6	4.8	4.7	2.9
Singapore/Singapour	3.0	4.2	5.5	2.8	7.5	4.0	3.5	2.7	5.1	3.2
USA/Etats–Unis d'Amer	3.7	6.9	3.8	3.0	1.7	2.0	2.2	2.6	3.1	6.8
Portugal	1.2	1.8	1.8	2.6	1.8	2.5	2.9	4.0	3.2	3.8

4. General Imports C.I.F. by Commodities according to the S.I.T.C. (Rev. 2) in thousand U.S. Dollars
Importations Générales C.A.F. par Produits d'après la C.T.C.I. (Rév. 2) en milliers de Dollars E.U.

SITC CTCI	COMMODITY	1991		1992		1993		1994		PRODUIT
		WEIGHT POIDS	VALUE VALEUR	WEIGHT POIDS	VALUE VALEUR	WEIGHT POIDS	VALUE VALEUR	WEIGHT POIDS	VALUE VALEUR	
	ALL COMMODITIES		1546810		1452719		1497471		1504713	TOUS PRODUITS
0	FOOD AND LIVE ANIMALS		55160		47957		93754		127240	ALIMENTS,ANIMAUX VIVANTS
3	MINERAL FUELS ETC		164031		146142		169214		148891	COMBUSTIBLES MINERAUX LUB
65	TEXTILE YARN,FABRICS,ETC		304977		330066		216276		231983	FILS,TISSUS,ARTICLES TEXTILE
69	METAL MANUFACTURES NES		125761		112100		110190		107327	ART MANUFACT EN METAL NDA
7	MACHINES,TRANSPORT EQUIP		712401		524986		529943		546246	MACHINES MATERIEL TRANSPORT
781	PASS MOTOR VEH EXC BUSES		280677		223021		170971		163803	AUTO TRANSPORT PERSONNES
9	GOODS NOT CLASSD BY KIND		170820		291468		378092			ART TRANSACT NON CLASSES

5. General Exports F.O.B. by Commodities according to the S.I.T.C. (Rev. 2) in thousand U.S. Dollars
Exportations Générales F.O.B. par Produits d'après la C.T.C.I. (Rév. 2) en milliers de Dollars E.U.

SITC CTCI	COMMODITY	1991		1992		1993		1994		PRODUIT
		WEIGHT POIDS	VALUE VALEUR	WEIGHT POIDS	VALUE VALEUR	WEIGHT POIDS	VALUE VALEUR	WEIGHT POIDS	VALUE VALEUR	
	ALL COMMODITIES		340893		412063		450151		519216	TOUS PRODUITS
05773	CASHEW NUTS,FRESH,DRIED		16071		21561		22695		51901	NOIX DE CAJOU
071	COFFEE AND SUBSTITUTES		75536		57507		97978		115061	CAFE ET SUCCEDANES
0711	COFFEE GREEN,ROASTED,SUB		75536		57507		97978		115061	CAFE TORREFIE OU DECAFEINE
07523	CLOVES		3276		5216		4636			GIROFLES
263	COTTON		62198		94291		78768		104607	COTON
2631	RAW COTTON,EXCL LINTERS		62198		94291		78768		104607	COTON EN MASSE
265	VEG FIBRE,EXCL COTN,JUTE				1300		3580		5175	FIBRES VEGETALES
2654	SISAL,AGAVE FIBRES,WASTE		2186		1300		3580		5175	SISAL,AUTRES AGAVES
27	CRUDE FERTLZR,MINRLS NES		38690							ENGRAIS MINERAUX BRUTS
33	PETROLEUM AND PRODUCTS				8267		13995		5465	PETROLE ET DERIVES
334	PETROLEUM PRODUCTS,REFIN		6251		8267		13995		5465	PRODUITS RAFFINES
6	BASIC MANUFACTURES		56672							ART MANUFACTURES
8	MISC MANUFACTURED GOODS		80012							ART MANUFACTURES DIVERS

FOOT NOTES – NOTES

TABLE 1 –
1 The gold trade includes refined and unrefined or partly–worked gold and excludes gold specie. The gold exports are national exports only.
TABLEAU 1 –
1 Le commerce de l'or comprend l'or raffiné ou non et l'or partiellement travaillé mais exclut les pièces de monnaie. Les exportations d'or ne concernent que les exportations nationales.

1. HISTORICAL SERIES, 1961–1996 GENERAL TRADE, IMPORTS C.I.F., EXPORTS F.O.B. #1
SERIES HISTORIQUES, 1961–1996 COMMERCE GENERAL, IMPORTATIONS C.A.F., EXPORTATIONS F.O.B

YEAR ANNEE	VALUE IN MILLION U.S. DOLLARS VALEUR EN MILLION U.S. DOLLARS MERCHANDISE –MARCHANDISE		GOLD –OR		CONVERSION FACTORS U.S. CENTS PER U.S. DOLLAR FACTEURS DE CONVERSION CENTS E.U. PAR U.S. DOLLAR		INDEX NUMBERS –INDICES QUANTUM		UNIT VALUE VALEUR UNITAIRE	
	IMPORTS	EXPORTS	IMPORTS	EXPORTS	IMPORTS	EXPORTS	IMPORTS	EXPORTS	IMPORTS	EXPORTS
1961	14761.00	21036.00	56.00	775.00			15	22	19	25
1962	16457.00	21715.00	151.00	381.00			17	23	19	25
1963	17211.00	23389.00	44.00	204.00			18	24	19	25
1964	18750.00	26652.00	41.00	423.00			19	28	19	25
1965	21431.00	27532.00	102.00	1285.00			22	28	19	26
1966	25620.00	30434.00	42.00	457.00			25	30	20	26
1967	26892.00	31627.00	33.00	1005.00			26	31	20	27
1968	33226.00	34636.00	226.00	839.00			32	33	20	27
1969	36043.00	38006.00	237.00	12.00			34	35	21	28
1970	39756.00	42590.00	237.00	38.00			35	38	22	30
1971	45516.00	43498.00	284.00	51.00			38	37	24	31
1972	55282.00	48959.00	358.00	63.00			43	41	25	32
1973	68656.00	70246.00	356.00	146.00			46	51	30	37
1974	107112.00	97144.00	397.00	228.00			44	55	45	47
1975	105880.00	108113.00	434.00	569.00			39	54	48	53
1976	132498.00	115413.00	331.00	342.00			48	56	50	54
1977	160411.00	121293.00	532.00	1043.00			53	56	54	57
1978	186044.00	143766.00	862.00	1123.00			59	63	59	61
1979	222228.00	182025.00	1468.00	4929.00			59	70	70	69
1980	256984.00	220786.00	2717.00	3705.00			54	74	88	78
1981	273352.20	233666.10	2126.00	3111.00			56	72	92	85
1982	254884.50	212277.20	1830.00	1115.60			53	64	91	86
1983	269878.30	200537.60	1897.10	1349.00			58	60	87	87
1984	341176.80	223999.00					72	64	89	89
1985	361626.40	218828.00					79	63	87	88
1986	382295.00	227158.00					87	63	84	88
1987	424442.10	254122.00					90	71	89	90
1988	459542.00	322426.80					93	84	94	97
1989	492922.10	363812.10					98	93	97	99
1990	516986.80	393592.00					100	100	100	100
1991	508363.00	421730.00					98	106	100	101
1992	553923.00	448163.00					106	113	101	101
1993	603438.00	464773.10					117	116	100	101
1994	689214.90	512626.90					131	126	102	104
1995	770852.10	584742.90					140	137	106	109
1996	822024.90	625072.90					148	145	107	109

2. IMPORTS BY BROAD ECONOMIC CATEGORY AND EXPORTS BY INDUSTRIAL ORIGIN. (PERCENTAGE OF TOTAL VALUE)
IMPORTATIONS PAR CATEGORIES ECONOMIQUES ET EXPORTATIONS PAR BRANCHE D'ACTIVITE.(EN POURCENTAGE DE LA VALEUR TOTALE)

IMPORTS – IMPORTATIONS

	1990	1991	1992	1993	1994	1995	1996
TOTAL IMPORTS–IMPORTATIONS TOTALES	100.	100.	100.	100.	100.	100.	100.
1 FOOD BEV–ALIMENTATION BOISSONS	5.5	5.5	5.3	4.9	4.8	4.5	4.6
11 PRIMARY–PRODUITS DE BASE	3.0	3.1	2.9	2.7	2.6	2.5	2.4
111 FOR INDUSTRY–POUR L'INDUSTRIE	0.7	0.8	0.7	0.7	0.7	0.8	0.7
112 FOR HOUSEHOLDS–POUR LES MENAGES	2.2	2.3	2.1	2.0	1.9	1.7	1.7
12 PROCESSED–PRODUITS ELABORES	2.6	2.5	2.5	2.2	2.1	2.0	2.2
121 FOR INDUSTRY–POUR L'INDUSTRIE	0.5	0.4	0.4	0.4	0.3	0.3	0.4
122 FOR HOUSEHOLDS–POUR LES MENAGES	2.1	2.1	2.1	1.8	1.8	1.7	1.8
2 IND SUPPLIES–APPROV INDUSTRIELS	18.9	18.6	18.3	18.3	18.9	19.4	19.2
21 PRIMARY–PRODUITS DE BASE	2.4	2.4	2.3	2.2	2.2	2.2	2.2
22 PROCESSED–PRODUITS ELABORES	16.5	16.2	16.1	16.0	16.8	17.2	16.9
3 FUELS–COMBUSTIBLES	13.2	11.4	10.6	9.8	8.7	8.1	9.4
31 PRIMARY–PRODUITS DE BASE	9.7	8.6	8.2	7.7	6.8	6.6	7.4
32 PROCESSED–PRODUITS ELABORES	3.5	2.8	2.4	2.1	1.8	1.5	2.0
321 MOTOR SPIRIT–ESSENCE	1.3	0.9	1.0	0.8	0.6	0.5	0.8
322 OTHER–AUTRES	2.2	1.9	1.4	1.3	1.2	1.0	1.2
4 MACHINERY–EQUIPEMENT	20.8	21.9	22.5	24.0	25.6	27.8	26.9
41 CAPITAL EQUIPMENT–MACHINES	15.3	15.9	16.2	17.0	17.4	17.8	17.8
42 PARTS–PIECES ACCESSOIRES	5.5	6.0	6.3	7.0	8.2	10.0	9.0
5 TRANSPORT–TRANSPORT	19.2	19.2	18.7	18.6	18.6	17.4	17.1
51 PASSENGER CARS–AUTOMOBILES	9.2	9.3	8.7	8.9	9.1	8.6	8.4
52 OTHER–AUTRES	2.7	2.8	3.0	2.9	2.7	2.6	2.6
521 INDUSTRIAL–INDUSTRIELS	2.6	2.6	2.8	2.6	2.5	2.4	2.4
522 NON INDUSTRIAL–NON INDUSTRIEL	0.2	0.2	0.2	0.2	0.2	0.2	0.2
53 PARTS–PIECES ACCESSOIRES	7.2	7.0	7.0	6.8	6.7	6.2	6.2
6 CONSUM GOODS–BIENS CONSOMMATION	19.3	20.2	21.3	21.2	20.3	19.6	19.5
61 DURABLE–DURABLES	5.7	6.0	6.2	6.1	6.0	5.7	5.6
62 SEMI DURABLE–SEMI DURABLES	12.1	12.5	13.3	13.3	12.5	12.1	12.0
63 NON DURABLE–NON DURABLES	1.5	1.7	1.9	1.9	1.7	1.8	1.9
7 GOODS NES–BIENS NDA	3.2	3.2	3.3	3.1	3.2	3.2	3.3

EXPORTS – EXPORTATIONS

	1990	1991	1992	1993	1994	1995	1996
TOTAL EXPORTS–EXPORTATIONS TOTALES	100.	100.	100.	100.	100.	100.	100.
1 AGRICULTURE	7.8	7.0	7.0	6.6	6.1	6.6	6.7
2 MINING QUARRY–INDUS EXTRACTIVES	2.5	3.0	2.1	1.7	1.6	1.7	1.7
3 MANUFACTURING–IND MANUFACTUR	89.7	90.0	90.9	91.7	92.3	91.6	91.6
31 FOOD BEV TOBACCO–ALIM BOISS TAB	5.2	5.0	5.2	5.2	5.4	5.1	5.0
32 TEXTILES–INDUSTRIES TEXTILES	2.4	2.5	2.7	2.8	2.8	2.8	2.9
33 WOOD & PRODUCTS–BOIS & PRODUITS	1.0	1.0	1.0	1.1	1.0	0.9	0.9
34 PAPER & PRODUCTS–PAPIER & PRODT	3.2	3.2	3.2	3.0	3.1	3.5	3.0
35 CHEMICALS–INDUSTRIES CHIMIQUES	14.0	13.5	13.7	13.6	13.7	14.0	13.7
36 NON METAL MIN–MIN NON METAL	0.8	0.8	0.8	0.9	0.9	0.8	0.9
37 BASIC METAL–IND METAL BASE	2.5	2.6	2.2	2.0	2.0	2.5	2.2
38 METAL MANUF–MANUF METAL	55.1	56.3	57.1	58.2	58.7	57.4	58.6
39 OTH MANUF IND–AUTRES MANUF	5.6	5.0	5.0	5.0	4.9	4.6	4.6

3. TRADE BY PRINCIPAL COUNTRIES OF PRODUCTION AND LAST CONSIGNMENT (VALUE IN THOUSAND U.S. DOLLARS)
ECHANGES SELON LES PRINCIPAUX PAYS DE PRODUCTION ET DE DERNIERE CONSIGNATION (VALEUR EN MILLIERS DE DOLLARS EU)

COUNTRIES–PAYS	GENERAL IMPORTS C.I.F. IMPORTATIONS GENERALES C.A.F				
	1992	1993	1994	1995	1996
World	553496521	603153642	689029975	770821511	817627201
Africa	15085851	15729884	15099282	16241734	19457032
Americas	173091994	191362168	223549848	256319206	285821400
Northern America	101279925	113608970	131935889	148299770	159709576
LAIA	61465773	66586232	79291286	94430923	110692313
CACM	4059340	4607418	5150221	6266535	7285605
Caribbean	5776248	6022625	6595713	6690148	7441887
Rest of America	510708	536923	576739	631829	692018
As.ex F.USSR	244498853	268858641	304987103	336422844	338417366
Eur.x F.USSR	114401500	119849352	135995657	151101761	162942317
EU	104565276	109253516	123883255	136815074	147426671
EFTA	8006900	8463978	9368252	11377529	12334160
East Europe	1212018	1532536	2138970	2263140	2424352
Other Europe	123066	118318	108762	146159	225764
Former USSR	917236	2246092	4122603	5245670	4957020
Oceania	5501079	5107488	5275483	5490243	6031745
Canada	101241410	113580396	131916214	148277904	159691182
Japan/Japon	100217447	110417685	122468049	127195339	117962870
Mexico/Mexique	35865045	40720678	50333546	62745632	74108156
China/Chine	27450243	33673216	41345785	48505594	54396461
Germany/Allemagne	29594947	29461110	32688442	38041614	39989239
United Kingdom	20666304	22361803	25817696	27663761	29669200
Korea, Republic of	17362353	17778975	20374349	24890539	23297384
France,Monac	15260822	15689819	17315972	17768152	19202776
Singapore/Singapour	11560071	13049157	15656272	18897166	20648255
Italy/Italie	12843214	13829278	15442024	17304719	19000971
Malaysia/Malaisie	8594720	10922502	14418623	17980832	18330710
Hong Kong	10265146	10000129	10141439	10744722	10261980
Thailand/Thaïlande	7926801	8982305	10799183	11854385	11798399
Venezuela	8636476	8707318	8989442	10427906	13718876
Saudi Arabia	11285706	8431510	8306799	8897841	9442679
Brazil/Brésil	8144452	8021271	9307312	9428294	9296201
Indonesia/Indonésie	4914130	5886851	7020217	7954815	8742580
Switz.Liecht	5769564	6184051	6604447	7878334	8023424
Philippines	4623000	5175524	6025150	7364299	8496428
Netherlands/Pays–Bas	5531939	5722785	6358440	6768952	7011824
Belgium–Luxembourg	4847253	5598076	6861727	6478680	7185336
Sweden/Suède	4876899	4689988	5243119	6467306	7375398
India/Inde	4065573	4882977	5663210	6090549	6528524
Nigeria/Nigéria	5299500	5609208	4705888	5055022	6171331
Israel/Israël	3902532	4526870	5336565	5840414	6545809
Spain/Espagne	3185832	3204289	3809617	4160243	4563117
Australia/Australie	3949975	3513847	3423536	3560509	4117730
Colombia/Colombie	3063989	3270287	3406603	3992018	4525007
Ireland/Irlande	2314978	2574382	2952694	4149457	4870396
Dominican Republic	2452307	2757531	3187783	3511103	3676944
Russian Federation	709322	1844569	3432696	4269197	3744556
Norway,SVD,JM	2062898	2035875	2499259	3251098	4057958
Angola	2435715	2237487	2209202	2390159	2855055
So. Africa Customs Un	1881631	1994680	2279322	2443620	2588202
Chile/Chili	1625934	1692618	2072392	2196961	2580453
Denmark/Danemark	1736438	1740754	2211483	2032760	2222863
Finland/Finlande	1265867	1720476	1928025	2391230	2464212
Ecuador/Equateur	1494566	1562862	1937016	2157910	2121348
Alger'a/Algérie	1693780	1710782	1664330	1807210	2270363
Costc Rica	1541566	1672515	1775545	1997828	2121131
Austria/Autriche	1346634	1456691	1810979	2034121	2268953
Argentina/Argentine	1369506	1297647	1819577	1881138	2450569
Turkey/Turquie	1183423	1279992	1692910	1925591	1883045
New Zealand	1334855	1325571	1544894	1595966	1608293
Guatemala	1182117	1301094	1386145	1632331	1785542
Kuwait/ Koweït	309894	2003396	1597607	1468838	1782120
Gabon	983524	1008652	1237784	1557557	2067015
Honduras	850932	984940	1174940	1541724	1899840
Sri Lanka	857553	1076697	1172791	1343019	1476842
Bangladesh	899602	952964	1160602	1345305	1422828

COUNTRIES–PAYS	GENERAL EXPORTS F.O.B. # 1 EXPORTATIONS GENERALES F.O.B.				
	1992	1993	1994	1995	1996
Monde	447330200	464757280	512336974	582964826	622784272
Afrique	9882479	9285919	9204010	9908124	10595706
Amériques	165808518	178630884	206843804	222341728	241457616
Amérique du Nord	90401649	100456929	114556540	126323223	132867286
ALAI	63514605	65007898	78198980	79739829	92229022
MCAC	4291894	4773971	5350561	6026901	6353369
Caraïbes	6044440	6502203	6918988	7987802	8164179
Autre Amérique	1555929	1889883	1818735	2263973	1843762
Asie l'URSS exclus	141065589	150416094	163906647	199888979	210153646
Europe l'URSS exclus	115770292	112165866	116877875	133655776	140813367
UE	107725735	101472233	107745094	123604668	127915259
AELE	5930140	8152076	6983005	7710624	10193099
Europe de l'Est	1714385	2123518	1737117	1896889	2186367
Autre de l'Europe	87759	195325	115877	142042	162766
Ancienne URSS	3782807	3980215	3564087	3809719	5068354
Océanie	10719043	9934764	11686553	12795296	14066356
Canada	90155345	100188899	114253038	126021757	132579563
Japan/Japon	47748665	47932754	53453451	64259700	67514646
Mexico/Mexique	40508996	41602726	50834162	46309290	56758566
United Kingdom	22805689	26369767	26831618	28826387	30914905
Germany/Allemagne	21229891	18946105	19226245	22370011	23468779
Korea, Republic of	14629697	14775545	18028330	25413125	26582877
Netherlands/Pays–Bas	13739608	12839177	13590423	16557327	16614041
France,Monac	14580974	13272548	13627679	14249971	14836401
Singapore/Singapour	9622403	11675142	13021557	15318106	16685334
Hong Kong	9068011	9870757	11444732	14218934	13954961
Belgium–Luxembourg	10048674	9436880	11172480	12832442	12760404
Australia/Australie	8912376	8271588	9779898	10788365	11991575
China/Chine	7469573	8767097	9286688	11748112	11977748
Brazil/Brésil	5740148	6045448	8118394	11443587	12699214
Italy/Italie	8697858	6460301	7195598	8867741	8791160
Malaysia/Malaisie	4395829	6064453	6964614	8818398	8521250
Saudi Arabia	7163291	6665609	6010501	6084971	7295231
Switz.Liecht	4530367	6793527	5601487	6245775	8377076
Thailand/Thaïlande	3982311	3768475	4861003	6401911	7211287
Spain/Espagne	5486771	4180908	4624758	5529309	5485841
Israel/Israël	4074156	4420242	5006021	5593227	6009016
Venezuela	5438166	4597945	4041700	4641209	4740822
Philippines	2753097	3529093	3888329	5294147	6124680
Argentina/Argentine	3221618	3770008	4466339	4189343	4515614
Colombia/Colombie	3282033	3229143	4070251	4628235	4708712
Ireland/Irlande	2852585	2730609	3415484	4094805	3659501
Indonesia/Indonésie	2777844	2770002	2811002	3356044	3964958
Chile/Chili	2454956	2605347	2775905	3613109	4131529
Russian Federation	3133586	2966990	2578751	2826172	3340130
Egypt/Egypte	3087348	2762594	2843824	2985292	3146113
Turkey/Turquie	2729728	3433612	2753535	2727201	2886099
Sweden/Suède	2843966	2353480	2519832	3076594	3428598
India/Inde	1914403	2761095	2296323	3295744	3318093
Dominican Republic	2098160	2349537	2799459	3016614	3183175
So. Africa Customs Un	2512469	2247625	2220478	2818220	3161953
United Arab Emirates	1552378	1811282	1593026	1993694	2526892
Costa Rica	1350946	1547291	1866626	1739056	1813564
Austria/Autriche	1256136	1324721	1372145	2016736	2008248
New Zealand	1307251	1247273	1508323	1692820	1726880
Guatemala	1203784	1310272	1354603	1646429	1564322
Denmark/Danemark	1476518	1091939	1215278	1517499	1729690
Peru/Pérou	1002031	1069154	1405949	1775060	1766606
Kuwait/ Koweït	1326910	1008953	1175081	1416231	1979067
Norway,SVD,JM	1280699	1211725	1269593	1294282	1559043
Finland/Finlande	786643	847091	1069163	1248424	2437383
Panama	1100281	1190682	1276338	1391032	1377793
Ecuador/Equateur	998978	1098182	1196058	1538370	1257355
Jamaica/Jamaïque	938464	1112802	1066408	1420887	1490726
Honduras	808255	897665	1011794	1280724	1641015
Greece/Grèce	896467	883917	829841	1518910	819900

(VALUE AS PERCENTAGE OF WORLD TOTAL)(VALEURS EN POURCENTAGE DU TOTAL MONDIAL)

	1987	1988	1989	1990	1991	1992	1993	1994	1995	1996
Africa	3.0	2.5	3.0	3.3	2.9	2.7	2.6	2.2	2.1	2.4
Americas	28.4	29.4	30.3	31.1	31.3	31.3	31.7	32.4	33.3	35.0
Northern America	16.9	17.7	18.1	18.1	18.4	18.3	18.8	19.1	19.2	19.5
LAIA	10.0	10.2	10.6	11.4	11.1	11.1	11.0	11.5	12.3	13.5
CACM	0.5	0.5	0.5	0.5	0.6	0.7	0.8	0.7	0.8	0.9
Caribbean	1.0	0.9	0.9	1.0	1.1	1.0	1.0	1.0	0.9	0.9
Rest of America	0.1	0.1	0.1	0.1	0.1	0.1	0.1	0.1	0.1	0.1
As.ex F.USSR	43.7	43.8	43.8	42.4	43.7	44.2	44.6	44.3	43.6	41.4
Eur.x F.USSR	23.7	23.0	21.5	21.9	20.8	20.7	19.9	19.7	19.6	19.9
EU	21.7	21.0	19.6	20.0	18.9	18.9	18.1	18.0	17.7	18.0
EFTA	1.5	1.4	1.4	1.5	1.5	1.4	1.4	1.4	1.5	1.5
East Europe	0.4	0.4	0.3	0.3	0.2	0.2	0.3	0.3	0.3	0.3
Other Europe	0.2	0.2	0.2	0.2	0.2	0.0	0.0	0.0	0.0	0.0
Former USSR	0.1	0.1	0.2	0.2	0.2	0.2	0.4	0.6	0.7	0.6
Oceania	1.1	1.2	1.2	1.2	1.1	1.0	0.8	0.8	0.7	0.7
Canada	16.9	17.7	18.1	18.1	18.4	18.3	18.8	19.1	19.2	19.5
Japan/Japon	20.8	20.2	19.7	18.1	18.8	18.1	18.3	17.8	16.5	14.4
Mexico/Mexique	4.8	5.1	5.6	5.9	6.2	6.5	6.8	7.3	8.1	9.1
China/Chine	1.6	2.0	2.6	3.1	4.0	5.0	5.6	6.0	6.3	6.7
Germany/Allemagne	6.6	6.0	5.2	5.6	5.3	5.3	4.9	4.7	4.9	4.9
United Kingdom	4.2	4.1	3.8	4.0	3.7	3.7	3.7	3.7	3.6	3.6
Korea, Republic of	4.2	4.6	4.2	3.7	3.5	3.1	2.9	3.0	3.2	2.8
France,Monac	2.6	2.8	2.7	2.6	2.7	2.8	2.6	2.5	2.3	2.3
Singapore/Singapour	1.5	1.8	1.9	2.0	2.0	2.1	2.2	2.3	2.5	2.5
Italy/Italie	2.7	2.7	2.6	2.6	2.4	2.3	2.3	2.2	2.2	2.3

	1987	1988	1989	1990	1991	1992	1993	1994	1995	1996
Afrique	2.2	2.2	2.1	2.0	2.1	2.2	2.0	1.8	1.7	1.7
Amériques	37.2	35.4	35.0	34.9	35.2	37.1	38.4	40.4	38.1	38.8
Amérique du Nord	23.6	21.9	21.6	21.2	20.2	20.2	21.6	22.4	21.7	21.3
ALAI	10.7	10.9	10.7	11.1	12.4	14.2	14.0	15.3	13.7	14.8
MCAC	0.7	0.7	0.7	0.7	0.8	1.0	1.0	1.0	1.0	1.0
Caraïbes	1.7	1.5	1.6	1.5	1.4	1.4	1.4	1.4	1.4	1.3
Autre Amérique	0.4	0.4	0.4	0.4	0.3	0.3	0.4	0.4	0.4	0.3
Asie l'URSS exclus	28.2	30.7	31.6	31.2	31.6	31.5	32.4	32.0	34.3	33.7
Europe l'URSS exclus	26.7	26.6	27.3	28.4	27.8	25.9	24.1	22.8	22.9	22.6
UE	24.6	24.5	25.2	26.3	25.7	24.1	21.8	21.0	21.2	20.5
AELE	1.6	1.6	1.7	1.6	1.7	1.3	1.8	1.4	1.3	1.6
Europe de l'Est	0.3	0.3	0.3	0.3	0.3	0.4	0.5	0.3	0.3	0.4
Autre de l'Europe	0.2	0.2	0.2	0.2	0.1	0.0	0.0	0.0	0.0	0.0
Ancienne URSS	0.6	0.9	1.2	0.8	0.8	0.8	0.9	0.7	0.7	0.8
Océanie	2.6	2.5	2.7	2.5	2.3	2.4	2.1	2.3	2.2	2.3
Canada	23.5	21.8	21.5	21.1	20.2	20.2	21.6	22.3	21.6	21.3
Japan/Japon	10.9	11.6	12.3	12.4	11.4	10.7	10.3	10.4	11.0	10.8
Mexico/Mexique	5.7	6.4	6.9	7.2	7.9	9.1	9.0	9.9	7.9	9.1
United Kingdom	5.5	5.7	5.7	6.0	5.2	5.1	5.7	5.2	4.9	5.0
Germany/Allemagne	4.5	4.4	4.6	4.8	5.0	4.7	4.1	3.8	3.8	3.8
Korea, Republic of	3.0	3.3	3.7	3.7	3.7	3.3	3.2	3.5	4.4	4.3
Netherlands/Pays–Bas	3.2	3.1	3.1	3.3	3.2	3.1	2.8	2.7	2.8	2.7
France,Monac	3.1	3.1	3.2	3.5	3.6	3.3	2.9	2.7	2.4	2.4
Singapore/Singapour	1.6	1.8	2.0	2.0	2.1	2.2	2.5	2.5	2.6	2.7
Hong Kong	1.6	1.8	1.7	1.7	1.9	2.0	2.1	2.2	2.4	2.2

4. General Imports C.I.F. by Commodities according to the S.I.T.C. (Rev. 2) in thousand U.S. Dollars
Importations Générales C.A.F. par Produits d'après la C.T.C.I. (Rév. 2) en milliers de Dollars E.U.

SITC CTCI	COMMODITY	1993 WEIGHT POIDS	1993 VALUE VALEUR	1994 WEIGHT POIDS	1994 VALUE VALEUR	1995 WEIGHT POIDS	1995 VALUE VALEUR	1996 WEIGHT POIDS	1996 VALUE VALEUR	PRODUIT
	ALL COMMODITIES		603153642		689029975		770821511		817627201	TOUS PRODUITS
0	FOOD AND LIVE ANIMALS		24955042		27500103		29317866		31114016	ALIMENTS,ANIMAUX VIVANTS
01	MEAT AND PREPARATIONS		2984351		2812677		2486959		2469019	VIANDES ET PREPARATIONS
011	MEAT FRESH,CHILLD,FROZEN	W 977112	2406854	W 961089	2240344	W 898160	1936728	W 897442	1940402	VIANDES FRAICHES,REF,CONGE
0111	BOVINE MEAT FRESH,FROZEN	W 714840	1828431	W 696695	1650925	W 640581	1327288	W 640890	1230270	VIANDES BOVIN FRAI,REF
03	FISH AND PREPARATIONS		6156038		6939258		7100775		7026875	POISSONS ET PREPARATIONS
034	FISH,FRESH,CHILLED,FROZN	W 650249	2175584	W 659413	2250674	W 716359	2457786	W 743169	2510644	POISSON FRAIS, REFRIG,CONG
036	SHELL FISH FRESH,FROZEN	W 373793	3005727	W 395027	3613010	W 378944	3535397	W 382459	3309393	CRUSTACES,MOLLUSQUES
05	VEGETABLES AND FRUIT		6570827		7020058		7576169		8599998	LEGUMES ET FRUITS
054	VEG ETC FRSH,SMPLY PRSVD	W 2480020	1692309	W 2561506	1861513	W 3094520	2159211	W 3554145	2487994	LEGUMES FRAIS,CONG,SECS
057	FRUIT,NUTS,FRESH,DRIED	W 5367738	2887575	W 5721292	3043961	W 5881258	3263497	W 6248328	3570110	FRUITS FRAIS OU SECS
07	COFFEE,TEA,COCOA,SPICES		3192056		4145057		5012971		4899379	CAFE,THE,CACAO,EPICES
071	COFFEE AND SUBSTITUTES	W 1120450	1634691	W 934100	2571866	W 991945	3356841	W 1125113	2884042	CAFE ET SUCCEDANES
0711	COFFEE GREEN,ROASTED,SUB	W 1095094	1538397	W 910097	2432903	W 968163	3169156	W 1097855	2692448	CAFE TORREFIE OU DECAFEINE
07111	COFFEE GREEN,HUSKS,SKINS	W 1081441	1482464	W 892346	2347372	W 953158	3067124	W 1076140	2573549	CAFE NON TORREFIE
1	BEVERAGES AND TOBACCO		5854600		5518033		5673719		7031386	BOISSONS ET TABACS
11	BEVERAGES		4234295		4610942		4902597		5647126	BOISSONS
112	ALCOHOLIC BEVERAGES	W 1682622	3914488	W 1859097	4210960	W 1947724	4498130	W 2175470	5164695	BOISSONS ALCOOLIQUES
2	CRUDE MATERLS,EXCL FUELS		16692327		19140605		22311338		22871335	MAT BRUTES NON COMESTIBLES
23	RUBBER, CRUDE		1483384		1664252		2399037		2198642	CAOUTCHOUC BRUT
24	CORK AND WOOD		5998808		7070012		6552086		7927346	LIEGE ET BOIS
248	WOOD SHAPED,SLEEPERS		5824373		6878594		6302334		7689366	BOIS SIMPLEMENT TRAVAILLES
2482	LUMBER SHAPED CONIFER		5453375		6433399		5855924		7246068	CONIFERES SCIES,RABOTES
24821	LUMBER SAWN ETC CONIFER	MW 22251	5126670	MW 22972	6106714	MW 24357	5543168	MW 25518	6862432	CONIFERES SCIES LONGITUD
251	*PULP AND WASTE PAPER	W 5042886	2018895	W 5370499	2453177	W 5886600	3983803	W 5618410	2791517	PATES A PAPIER,DECHETS
2517	SODA,SULPHATE WOOD PULP	W 4167270	1672027	W 4389972	2079340	W 4716589	3479632	W 4478109	2382784	PATES CHIMIQUES AU SULFATE
25172	— BLEACHED,NONDISSOLVNG	W 4064275	1636611	W 4232617	2000758	W 4589770	3397933	W 4342095	2315257	PATES BLANCHIES
28	METALLIFEROUS ORES,SCRAP		3276479		3514771		4314692		4377191	MINERAIS METAL,DECHETS
3	MINERAL FUELS ETC		59272317		60150800		63051731		77126286	COMBUSTIBLES MINERAUX LUB
33	PETROLEUM AND PRODUCTS		53143842		52765331		56113413		69065816	PETROLE ET DERIVES
333	CRUDE PETROLEUM	MW 347433	41001607	MW 369773	40930163	MW 369781	45481859	MW 364442	53331068	HUILES BRUTES DE PETROLE
334	PETROLEUM PRODUCTS,REFIN	MW 86583	11889631	MW 86842	11408750	MW 69606	10191038	MW 86603	15152461	PRODUITS RAFFINES
3341	GASOLINE,OTH LIGHT OILS	MW 25368	4699847	MW 26473	4448704	MW 22396	4036786	MW 31737	6841109	ESSENCES POUR MOTEURS
33411	MOTOR,AVIATION SPIRIT	MW 10624	2181949	MW 13847	2479877	MW 9420	1882023	MW 17188	3854980	ESSENCES MOTEURS D'AVIONS
33419	OTH LIGHT PETROLEUM OILS	MW 14590	2483741	MW 12577	1958779	MW 12698	2102865	MW 14514	2977764	AUTRES HUILES LEGERES
3344	FUEL OILS,NES	MW 44644	4522778	MW 41559	4168690	MW 29736	3370734	MW 35798	4761483	FUEL OILS
341	*GAS,NATURAL AND MANUFCT		4874858		5677878		5266788		6455064	GAZ NATUREL,GAZ MANUFACT
3413	PETROLM GASES,LIQUEFIED		1613547		1734283		2000549		2507500	GAZ DE PETROLE LIQUEFIE
3414	PETROLEUM GASES, GASEOUS	MV 63602807	3261304	MV 72561264	3943595	MV 81301227	3266239	MV 82812782	3947564	GAZ DE PETROLE GAZEUX
5	CHEMCLS,RELATED PROD NES		29945960		34812017		41345628		45799477	PRODUITS CHIMIQUES
51	ORGANIC CHEMICALS		9674781		11236875		13866741		15383104	PROD CHIMIQ ORGANIQUES
514	NITROGEN–FNCTN COMPOUNDS	W 353434	2941102	W 376847	3234406	W 370172	3715336	W 410263	4377105	COMPOSES FONCT AZOTEES
515	ORG–INORG COMPOUNDS ETC	W 177249	2286799	W 210797	2555126	W 203065	3408399	W 223039	4231525	COMPOSES ORGANO–MINERAUX
5156	HETEROCYCLIC CMPDS ETC	W 71453	1600578	W 94092	1862253	W 88948	2367202	W 106323	2916203	COMPOSES HETEROCYCLIQUES
51569	OTH HETEROCYC CMPDS,ETC	W 57595	1548238	W 67550	1793844	W 67304	2292414	W 76174	2831012	AUT COMP HETEROCYCLIQUES
52	INORGANIC CHEMICALS		3536226		4400028		4995102		5272740	PROD CHIM INORGANIQUES
522	INORG ELEMNTS,OXIDES,ETC		1581549		2118973		2574209		2548231	ELEMENTS INORGANIQUES
541	*MEDICINAL,PHARM PRODUCT		4198335		4755058		5605343	MK 92203	7150378	PROD MEDICINAUX PHARMACEUT
5417	MEDICAMENTS	K 5153121	1951510	K 4667786	2224547		2830787	MK 32882	3686651	MEDICAMENTS
55	PERFUME,CLEANING ETC PRD		1871269		2063411		2391271		2511335	PROD POUR PARFUM,TOILETTE
58	PLASTIC MATERIALS ETC		4559955		5608689		6730071		6989745	MAT PLAST ARTIFICIELLES
583	POLYMERIZATION ETC PRODS	W 2079442	3251665	W 2663691	3977105	W 2849803	4785675	W 3106082	4858386	PROD POLYMERISATION
59	CHEMICAL MATERIALS NES		2834118		3149741		3876415		4492358	MAT PROD CHIMIQUES NDA
598	MISCEL CHEM PRODUCTS NES		1776481		2009304		2563343		2980113	PROD DIV INDUST CHIM NDA
5989	CHEM PRODUCTS,PREPS NES	W 373745	1441335	W 432252	1688317	W 493331	2190551	W 620703	2593253	PROD PREP CHIMIQUES NDA
6	BASIC MANUFACTURES		70383101		83921956		94766902		96861256	ART MANUFACTURES
62	RUBBER MANUFACTURES NES		4368471		5036661		5418498		5423542	CAOUTCHOUC MANUFACTURE
625	RUBBER TYRES, TUBES ETC	MN 134404	2902985	MN 157236	3218015	MN 164460	3328453	MN 156539	3242882	PNEUS CAOUTCHOUC VULCANISE
63	WOOD,CORK MANUFACTRS NES		3162913		3638356		4004509		4352333	OUVRAGES LIEGE ET BOIS
64	PAPER,PAPERBOARD AND MFR		9203654		9727690		13174020		12353628	PAPIERS,CARTONS & OUVRAGES
641	PAPER AND PAPERBOARD		8174821		8466329		11512435		10454216	PAPIERS ET CARTONS
6411	NEWSPRINT	W 7061513	3774146	W 7149976	3517531	W 7082891	4597693	W 6305744	4221181	PAPIER JOURNAL
6415	PAPER,PAPERBRD,BULK,NES		1905447		2065435	W 3592713	3042260	W 3308408	2629087	PAPIERS,CARTONS ROULEAUX
64159	OTHER PAPER ETC,BULK,NES		1795569		1924290	W 3291886	2855751	W 3033121	2491134	AUT PAPIER ROULEAUX FEUILLES
65	TEXTILE YARN,FABRICS,ETC		8885435		9688392		10474949		10731475	FILS,TISSUS,ARTICLES TEXTILE
658	TEXTILE ARTICLES NES	W 269423	1810554	W 296628	2126954	W 342917	2534433	W 347398	2497486	ART FACONNES MAT TEXTILES
66	NONMETAL MINERAL MFS NES		12073018		13975833		15128783		16394049	ART MIN NON METALLIQUES
667	PEARL,PREC–,SEMI–P STONE		5762359		6448865		6686949		7430986	PERLES, PIERRES GEMMES
6672	DIAMONDS NONINDUST,UNSET		5116461		5754818		5984324		6600659	DIAMANTS BRUTS
66729	— CUT ETC NOT SET		4503074		4957636		5334940		5840042	DIAMANTS TAILLES
67	IRON AND STEEL		11105562		15664308		15634403		16693291	FER ET ACIER
672	IRON,STEEL PRIMARY FORMS	W 7173826	2205993	MW 12072	3962810	W 8358858	3361266	MW 11709	3994379	LINGOTS FER,ACIER
673	IRON,STEEL SHAPES ETC	W 3206291	1783194	W 4097774	2168694	W 4535061	2509631	W 4915140	2666818	BARRES,PROFIL FER,ACIER
674	IRN,STL UNIV,PLATE,SHEET	W 5165582	3447438	W 8398575	5061246	W 6748360	4528281	W 7238574	4575382	LARGES PLATS,TOLES
68	NON–FERROUS METALS		9022530		11818787		14822902		13881251	METAUX NON FERREUX
682	COPPER EXC CEMENT COPPER	W 709217	1785844	W 877127	2360877	W 904608	3057100	W 1052085	3021561	CUIVRE
684	ALUMINIUM	W 2342955	3358720	W 3132715	5067479		5947763		4945961	ALUMINIUM
6841	ALUMINIUM,ALLOYS,UNWRGHT	W 1860740	2222071	W 2495871	3571379	W 1979827	3838057	W 1950993	3150291	ALUMINIUM,ALLIAGES BRUTS
69	METAL MANUFACTURES NES		11044089		12637892		14326962		15245566	ART MANUFACT EN METAL NDA
694	STL,COPPR NAILS,NUTS,ETC	W 1063082	1760507	W 1154978	2080437	W 1230124	2336159	W 1219709	2302331	CLOUS,VIS,ECROUS
695	TOOLS		1976332		2150776		2463865		2513235	OUTILS A MAIN
699	BASE METAL MFRS NES		4008007		4705060		5206643		5860467	ART MANUFACTURES MET NDA
7	MACHINES,TRANSPORT EQUIP		265419019		314381283		357625478		368994301	MACHINES MATERIEL TRANSPORT
71	POWER GENERATING EQUIPMT		17489170		19945685		20922921		22870520	MACHINES GENERATRICES
713	INTRNL COMBUS PSTN ENGIN		8567626		10392347		11436870		12280595	MOTEURS EXPL COMB INT, PIECE
7132	MOTOR VEHCL PISTN ENGINS	N 3501699	4897037	N 4584948	5991627	N 4299247	6334608	N 4370053	7093037	MOTEURS EXPL POUR VEHICULES
7139	PISTON ENGINE PARTS NES	W 503933	2479233	W 565141	2952677	W 660039	3337524	W 513514	3479214	PIECES POUR 713.2,3,8
714	ENGINES AND MOTORS NES		5765333		5809182		5353966		6274595	MOTEURS NON ELECTRIQUES
7144	REACTION ENGINES	N 1457	2276342	N 967	2411611	N 1225	1477732	N 2499	1584004	PROPULSEURS A REACTION
7149	ENGINE & MOTOR PARTS NES		3127746		3078051		3519952		4231853	PIECES 714 ET 718.88
71491	PARTS NES OF 7144,71481		2508014		2381773		2653698		3334954	PIECES DES PROPULSEURS
716	ROTATING ELECTRIC PLANT		2620106		3103325		3401794		3431214	APP ELECTR ROTATIFS,PIECES
72	MACHS FOR SPCL INDUSTRYS		13370312		16384871		18616299		18095783	MAC SPECIALES POUR INDUST
723	CIVIL ENGNEERG EQUIP ETC	N 477910	1705115	N 668074	2649655		2740895		2667174	APPAREILS DE GENIE CIVIL
7234	CONST,MINING MACHNRY NES	N 79889	1472063	N 153063	2356884	N 139894	2389074	N 126700	2242681	MACH POUR LA CONST, MINES
724	TEXTILE,LEATHER MACHNRY		2715062		2763606		2715435		2329484	MACH POUR INDUSTRIE TEXTILE
728	OTH MACHY FOR SPCL INDUS		4368017		5418431		6703998		6938034	AUT MACH IND PARTICULIERES
7284	MACHY FOR SPCL INDUS NES		3440898		4329754		5346695		5344307	MACH SPEC IND PARTICUL.
73	METALWORKING MACHINERY		3717784		4653835		5985895		6843941	MACH TRAVAIL DES METAUX
736	METALWORKING MACH–TOOLS		2908923		3744597		4801089		5285801	MACH–OUTILS TRAVAIL METAUX
74	GENRL INDUSTRL MACHY NES		17435072		21983892		24951199		26096075	MACH APP INDUSTRIE

4. General Imports C.I.F. by Commodities according to the S.I.T.C. (Rev. 2) in thousand U.S. Dollars
Importations Générales C.A.F. par Produits d'après la C.T.C.I. (Rév. 2) en milliers de Dollars E.U.

SITC CTCI	COMMODITY	1993 WEIGHT POIDS	1993 VALUE VALEUR	1994 WEIGHT POIDS	1994 VALUE VALEUR	1995 WEIGHT POIDS	1995 VALUE VALEUR	1996 WEIGHT POIDS	1996 VALUE VALEUR	PRODUIT
741	HEATING,COOLING EQUIPMNT		2013059		2485462		2754518		3298798	MACH CHAUFFAGE,PIECES
743	PUMPS NES,CENTRFUGES ETC		2941932		3704613		4202383		4436376	POMPES COMPRES,VENT ETC
744	MECHANICAL HANDLING EQU		2800310		3607295		4242684		4358064	EQUIP MANUTENTION PIECES
745	NONELEC MACHY,TOOLS NES		1974941		2257179		2478606		2736193	AUT MACH NON ELEC,PIECES
749	NONELEC MACH PTS,ACC NES		6119310		8071462		9224732		9129717	PIECES MACH NON ELEC NDA
7492	COCKS,VALVES ETC NES	W 77432	2277336	W 95118	2737827		3108073		3291365	ART ROB,SIM POUR TUYAUX
7493	SHAFT,CRANK,PULLEY ETC		1803119		2289139		2699850		2718002	ARBRES TRANS,VILEBREQUINS
75	OFFICE MACHNES,ADP EQUIP		43958290		53004752		63962696		67549609	MACH BUREAU TRAIT AUTOM
751	OFFICE MACHINES	MN 105997	3374394	MN 124081	3939315	MN 144411	4585948	MN 130670	4500501	MACH,APPAREILS DE BUREAU
7518	OFFICE MACHINES NES	MN 24969	2267610	MN 30016	2766129	MN 35201	3492832	MN 39111	3419425	MACH,APP DE BUREAU NDA
75182	PHOTO,THERMOCOPY APPARAT	N 1031846	1724994	N 1279580	2078057	N 1576128	2492634	N 1530372	2358013	APPAREILS DE PHOTOCOPIE
752	AUTOMTIC DATA PROC EQUIP	MN 172008	26929341	MN 209594	30614507	MN 259645	35422920	MN 270210	39934622	MACH TRAIT INFORMATION
7522	DIGITAL COMPUTERS	N 1911084	2485358	N 1947987	2355146	N 1446058	2244432	N 2340974	3451686	MACH DIGITALES COMPLETES
7523	DIGITL CENTRL PROCESSORS	N 3845589	3141099	N 2903653	2984842	N 2501373	2759889	MN 15356	4125330	UNITES CENTRALES
7524	DIGITL CENTRL STOR UNITS	MN 59011	9436252	MN 77397	11116763	MN 97602	14451002	MN 112633	16621451	UNITES MEMOIRE CENTRALES
7525	ADP PERIPHERAL UNITS	MN 73412	9767005	MN 88191	11727887	MN 107017	12936205	MN 113519	13071373	UNITES PERIPHERIQUES
7528	OFF–LINE DATA PROC EQUIP	MN 33819	2089774	MN 39144	2418693	MN 51065	3020873	MN 26328	2638412	MACH AUXIL TRAIT INFORM
759	OFFICE,ADP MCH PTS,ACCES		13654555		18450929		23953829		23114487	PIECES DU 751 ET 752
7599	ACCTG,ETC,ADP MCH PTS,AC		11947743		16584905		22156955		21324437	PIECES DU 751 ET 752
76	TELECOMM,SOUND EQUIPMENT		27797179		33068537		35007739		34700827	EQUIPMENT DE TELECOM
761	TELEVISION RECEIVERS	MN 16732	2799725	MN 20248	3632449	MN 20277	3820491	MN 20831	4025512	RECEPTEURS DE TELEVISION
7611	COLOUR TV RECEIVERS	MN 14443	2670919	MN 18146	3503740	MN 18681	3710974	MN 19395	3917157	RECEPTEURS COULEUR
762	RADIO BROADCAST RECEIVRS	MN 105647	4897681	MN 125716	6053281	MN 119991	6142471	MN 126081	5457642	RECEPTEURS RADIODIFFUSION
7621	MTR VEHC RADIO RECEIVERS	MN 19675	1837245	MN 23395	2284891	MN 21879	2366361	MN 23127	2339863	RECEPTEURS RADIO AUTO
763	SOUND RECORDRS,PHONOGRPH	MN 64090	5775638	MN 77637	6352338	MN 77672	6397405	MN 74601	7404680	PHONO,APP ENREGISTREMENT
7638	OTHR SOUND APPARATUS ETC	MN 63017	5702067	MN 76380	6270918	MN 77109	6351082	MN 74240	7358730	AUT APP D'ENREGIS,REPROD
76381	TV IMAGE,SND RECRDRS ETC	MN 16593	3279369	MN 19342	3575438	MN 20209	3530938	MN 22009	4814505	APP ENREG,REPRO IMAG,SON
76388	DICTATING MACHINES ETC	MN 46424	2422697	MN 57038	2695480	MN 56901	2820144	MN 52231	2544225	MACHINES A DICTER
764	TELECOM EQPT,PTS,ACC NES		14324135		17030469		18647372		17812993	EQUIP TELECOM,PIECES
7641	LINE TELEPHONE,ETC EQUIP	MN 106027	3143924	MN 116309	3618337	MN 147884	3695090		5197214	APP TELEPHON PAR FIL
7643	TV,RADIO TRANSMITTRS ETC		3236574		4543847		5023873		4019163	APP EMET TELE RADIO
7648	TELECOMM EQUIPMENT NES		2511535		2511290		2844057		1150367	APP TELECOM NDA
76482	TELEVISION CAMERAS	N 4124701	2027792	N 4422923	2004951	N 5129342	2246920	N 1546489	484822	APP PRISE DE VUES TELE
7649	PTS NES OF EQUIPMT OF 76		4238259		4812367		5424998		5701559	PIECES DE LA DIV 76
76493	TELECOMM EQUIPMT PTS NES		2276216		2544556		2747145		2663189	PIECES 761,762,764.3,8
77	ELECTRIC MACHNRY NES ETC		48317438		59444625		77109059		77394378	MACH APP ELECT NDA
771	ELECTRIC POWER MACHY NES		2555237		2814847		3653624		5037357	MACH PROD,TRANS ELECTR
7712	OTH ELEC POWER MACHY NES		1974714		2218327		2942620		4287039	AUT APP PROD TRANSF ELEC
77121	STATIC CONVERTERS ETC		1140054		1340441		1727104	MN 179521	2996983	CONVERTISSEURS STATIQUES
772	SWITCHGEAR ETC,PARTS NES	MN 38082639	7163592	MN 47422621	8474942		9698619		9860382	APP COUPURE,SECT ETC
7721	SWITCHGEAR ETC	MN 2646561	5312711	MN 2953185	6328964		7073827		7308944	APP COUPURE,SECTIONMNT
773	ELECTR DISTRIBUTNG EQUIP		3969394		4970411		5567940		6109109	EQUIPMT DISTRIBUTION ELECT
7731	INSULATED WIRE,CABLE ETC	W 78497	3864021	W 99738	4848525		5430550		5967880	FILS,CABLES ISOLES ELECT
774	ELECTRO–MEDCL,XRAY EQUIP		2062427		1917033		2071919		2157841	APPAREILS MEDICAUX
775	HOUSEHOLD TYPE EQUIP NES		4007863		4380610		4618256		4916963	MACH,APP USAGE DOMESTQUE
7758	ELECTRO–THERMIC APPL NES		2113312		2244374		2349793		2411437	APP ELECTROTHERMIQ NDA
776	TRANSISTORS,VALVES,ETC		20813672		27631714		40956517		38410546	LAMPES,TUBES,VALVES
7763	DIODES,TRANSISTORS,ETC	MN 14852479	1653725	MN 17114917	1987660	MN 21779001	2553505	MN 20945979	2657025	DIODES,TRANSISTORS
7764	ELECTRONIC MICROCIRCUITS	MN 9598197	17336952	MN 10684578	23382923	MN 12970935	35487039	MN 13420557	33010495	MICROSTRUCTURES ELECTRON
778	ELECTRICAL MACHINERY NES		7745252		9255070		10542184		10902181	AUTRES MACH ELECT NDA
7788	OTH ELEC MACHY,EQUIP NES		3771010		4530129		5417556		5364795	AUT MACH APP ELEC NDA
78	ROAD VEHICLES		85323935		97209730		102639870		105477516	VEHICULES ROUTIERS
781	PASS MOTOR VEH EXC BUSES	N 3811513	53454937	N 4103564	62648606	N 4121023	66126954	N 4070205	68087912	AUTO TRANSPORT PERSONNES
782	LORRIES,SPCL MTR VEH NES	N 748454	10020362	N 733937	9673192	N 675477	10192838	N 706649	10964638	VEHICULES SPECIAUX,MARCH
7821	LORRIES,TRUCKS	N 747929	9959899	N 732940	9592916	N 674533	10075965	N 705708	10807694	VEHICULES TRANSP MARCHAND
784	MOTOR VEH PRTS,ACCES NES		18650207		20707598		21155994		21382074	PIECES 722,781,782,783
7849	OTHER MOTOR VEHCL PARTS		18235045		20271533		20713386	W 3948065	20874172	PIECES 722,781,782,783
785	CYCLES,ETC MOTRZD OR NOT	MN 14278	1882820	MN 13338	1937777		2340808		2213581	MOTOCYCLES SCOOTERS
79	OTHR TRANSPORT EQUIPMENT		8009840		8685356		8429799		9965652	AUTRE MATERIEL TRANSPORT
792	AIRCRAFT ETC		6383505		6818233		6387220		7709466	APP NAVIGATION AERIENNE
7924	AIRCRFT NES OVER 15000KG	N 64	2062480	N 49	1722570	N 54	1623036	N 57	1398251	AERODYNES PLUS 15000 KG
7929	AIRCRAFT PARTS NES		2559281		2626081		2592279	W 27612	3441561	PIECES DU 792
8	MISC MANUFACTURED GOODS		108781458		118656780		129077334		136597885	ART MANUFACTURES DIVERS
812	*PLUMBG,HEATNG,LGHTNG EQ	MN 326224	1798271	MN 400528	2103201		2359114		2625844	APPAR SANITAIRES CHAUFFAGE
821	*FURNITURE,PARTS THEREOF		6905130		8290294		9128199		10200143	MEUBLES ET PIECES
8211	CHAIRS,SEATS AND PARTS		3053417		3726631		4042164		4579127	SIEGES ET PIECES
82111	CHAIRS AND OTHER SEATS	MN 70183	1682856	MN 84376	2241694	MN 79066	2286025	MN 82677	2530738	SIEGES
8219	FURNITURE AND PARTS NES		3392944		4023660		4558917		5080713	AUTRES MEUBLES ET PIECES
82192	WOOD FURNITURE NES		1967421		2429180		2702811		3042100	MEUBLES NDA EN BOIS
831	*TRAVEL GOODS,HANDBAGS		2836282		3290758		3629623		3790867	ARTICLES DE VOYAGE ETC
84	CLOTHING AND ACCESSORIES		35833018		38859968		41582222		43506221	VETEMENTS
842	MENS OUTERWEAR NOT KNIT	W 291913	5333533	W 331496	6049116	W 354384	6577775	W 362582	6966784	VET DESSUS POUR HOMMES
8423	— TROUSERS,BREECHES ETC	W 180269	2653674	W 203775	3025719	W 236627	3589834	W 246805	3840528	PANTALONS HOMMES MAT TEX
8429	— OTHER OUTER GARMENTS	W 91149	1838024	W 104996	2083511	W 95784	1964725	W 94219	2045106	AUT VET DES HOM MAT TEX
843	WOMENS OUTERWEAR NONKNIT	W 462234	10955369	W 493822	11210125	W 490288	11345764	W 508275	11913276	VET DESSUS FEMMES MAT TEX
8435	— BLOUSES	W 89465	2749480	W 89060	2480421	W 76421	2078620	W 73338	2008311	BLOUSES FEM MAT TEXTILES
8439	— OTHER OUTER GARMENTS	W 284175	5055845	W 309310	5451097	W 308969	5630218	W 319514	5939563	AUT VET DES FEM MAT TEXT
844	UNDER GARMENTS NOT KNIT	W 161244	3536354	W 178379	3622963	W 189810	3863670	W 175812	3559397	VETEMENT DESSOUS MAT TEX
8441	— MENS SHIRTS	W 131514	2905855	W 144776	2958401	W 154038	3168339	W 137912	2829199	CHEMISES HOMMES MAT TEXT
84411	—— OF COTTON	W 98061	2050028	W 112073	2231448	W 121444	2479956	W 107388	2241639	CHEMISES HOMMES DE COTON
845	OUTERWEAR KNIT NONELASTC	W 437879	8263645	W 482142	9128550	W 485808	9619235	W 489583	9996568	VET DESSOUS,ACCES BONNET
8451	— JERSEYS,PULLOVERS ETC	W 273145	5030145	W 301309	5612013	W 294738	5750796	W 291526	5982088	CHANDAILS,PULL–OVERS ETC
8459	— OTHER,CLTHG ACCESRYS	W 149982	2862063	W 165927	3144434	W 174661	3439954	W 179903	3552579	AUT VET DESSUS DE BONNE
846	UNDER GARMENTS KNITTED	W 182614	3255573	W 230152	4049770	W 309814	5384334	W 369249	6049708	SOUS VETS DE BONNETERIE
8462	— OF COTTON NON ELASTIC	W 119974	1612246	W 149224	1982303	W 197232	2632720	W 247297	3153251	SOUS–VET BONNET COTON
84629	—— OTHER	W 119974	1612246	W 149224	1982303	W 197232	2632720	W 247297	3153251	AUT SOUS–VET BONNET COTON
848	HEADGEAR,NONTXTL CLOTHNG		3679820		3876637		3792450		3968977	VET ACCES MAT AUT QUE TEX
8481	LEATHER CLOTHES,ACCESSOR		1940099		2010692		1769427		1692505	VET ACCES MAT CUIR ARTIF
851	*FOOTWEAR		11182766		11697379	MP 1416870	12176970	MP 1385068	12760965	CHAUSSURES
85101	FOOTWEAR RUBBER,PLASTIC	MP 482337	2690276	MP 469447	2604264	MP 474513	2749238	MP 489280	2850793	CHAUS SEMELLES CAOUTCH
85102	FOOTWEAR LEATHER	MP 834994	8391520	MP 920628	8993229	MP 907684	9341645	MP 862635	9822635	CHAUS SEMELLES EN CUIR
87	PRECISION INSTRUMNTS NES		8703255		10265079		11948265		12814022	INSTRUM,APPAR SCIENT NDA
872	MEDICAL INSTRUMENTS NES		2072150		2199945		2496787		2735568	INSTR,APP MEDIC–CHIR NDA
874	MEASURNG,CONTROLNG INSTR		5322370		6237375		7345269		7896012	INSTRUMENTS DE MESURE
88	PHOTO EQU,OPTICL GDS ETC		8494171		9062277		9926744		10230898	APP,FOURN PHOTO,OP,MONTR
881	PHOTO APPARAT,EQUIPT NES		2044610		2389399		2690542		2911703	APP,EQUIP PHOTO NDA
882	PHOTO,CINEMA SUPPLIES		2313468		2400688		2578649		2485827	PRODUITS PHOTO,CINEMA
885	WATCHES AND CLOCKS		2557706		2645647		2749174		2798759	HORLOGERIE
8851	WATCHES,MOVEMENTS,CASES		2134171		2202025		2299710		2345209	MONTRES,MOUVEMENTS,BOITES
88511	WATCHES		2066528		2134716		2221670		2262843	MONTRES POCHE,BRACELET
89	MISC MANUFCTRD GOODS NES		33028566		35087824		38326196		40668926	ART MANUFACTURES DIVERS

4. General Imports C.I.F. by Commodities according to the S.I.T.C. (Rev. 2) in thousand U.S. Dollars
Importations Générales C.A.F. par Produits d'après la C.T.C.I. (Rév. 2) en milliers de Dollars E.U.

SITC CTCI	COMMODITY	1993		1994		1995		1996		PRODUIT
		WEIGHT POIDS	VALUE VALEUR	WEIGHT POIDS	VALUE VALEUR	WEIGHT POIDS	VALUE VALEUR	WEIGHT POIDS	VALUE VALEUR	
892	PRINTED MATTER		2116613		2329043		2701967		2811672	IMPRIMES
893	ARTICLES OF PLASTIC NES		4763201		5453283		6195669		6435977	OUVRAGES EN MAT DIVIS 58
8939	MISC PLASTIC ARTICLES		3780057		4350763		4834507		4991614	ART DIVERS EN MAT DIV 58
89399	OTHR PLASTC ARTICLES NES	W 72471	3597928	W 123172	4118548		4559756		4687212	AUT OUV MAT DIV 58
894	TOYS,SPORTING GOODS,ETC		12307770		12631886		13900482		15531614	VOITURES ENFANTS,JOUETS
8942	TOYS,INDOOR GAMES ETC		9984341		9805874		10880424		12606534	JOUETS,JEUX ETC
89423	TOYS NES		3801995		4173151		4681371		5580410	JOUETS,MODELES REDUITS
89424	INDOOR GAME EQUIPMENT		3922390		3159183		3066643		3668147	ART,JEUX DE SOCIETE
8947	OTH SPORT GDS,FAIR AMUSM		1900784		2343627		2607388		2514076	AUT ART DE SPORT
896	WORKS OF ART ETC		2662536		2437433		2684152		2793138	OBJETS D'ART
897	GOLD,SILVER WARE,JEWELRY		4044859		4595902		4470298		4501982	BIJOUTERIE,ORFEVRERIE
8973	PREC JEWLRY,GLD–SILVWARE		3389183		3693805		3846665		3951901	BIJOUX OR,ARGENT ORFEVRE
89731	PRECIOUS METAL JEWELLERY		3116094		3426111		3552248		3742416	ART BIJOUTERIE,JOAILLER
898	MUSICAL INSTRUMENTS,PTS	MN 1749461	3527529	MN 1884935	3696359		3989169		4170826	INSTRUMENTS DE MUSIQUE
8983	SOUND RECRDNG TAPE,DISCS	MN 1691420	2634070	MN 1810243	2768414		2922338		3128207	SUPPORTS SON POUR 763
89831	PREPD SND RECORDNG MEDIA	MN 1689453	1998702	MN 1807392	1990234		1975648		2105932	SUPPORTS PREPARES
899	OTHER MANUFACTURED GOODS		2562547		2780952		3150898		3195020	AUT ART MANUF DIVERS NDA
9	GOODS NOT CLASSD BY KIND		20778943		23663694		26203547		29580237	ART TRANSACT NON CLASSES
931	*SPECIAL TRANSACTIONS		18184857		21115300		23492123		26293732	TRANS.SPECIALES
971	*GOLD,NON MONETARY NES # 1	K 175996	2016154	K 174199	1933878	K 185364	2154212	K 245935	2738991	OR NON MONETAIRE
97101	NONMON GLD UNWRT,SEMIMFD	K 148076	1941332	K 151306	1818946	K 170260	2030087	K 232591	2635221	OR,ALLIAGES D'OR BRUTS

5. General Exports F.O.B. by Commodities according to the S.I.T.C. (Rev. 2) in thousand U.S. Dollars
Exportations Générales F.O.B. par Produits d'après la C.T.C.I. (Rév. 2) en milliers de Dollars E.U.

SITC CTCI	COMMODITY	1993		1994		1995		1996		PRODUIT
		WEIGHT POIDS	VALUE VALEUR	WEIGHT POIDS	VALUE VALEUR	WEIGHT POIDS	VALUE VALEUR	WEIGHT POIDS	VALUE VALEUR	
	ALL COMMODITIES		464757280		512336974		582964826		622784272	TOUS PRODUITS
0	FOOD AND LIVE ANIMALS		33816480		35453986		42223185		45773661	ALIMENTS,ANIMAUX VIVANTS
01	MEAT AND PREPARATIONS		4377042*		5211887		6481892		7007293	VIANDES ET PREPARATIONS
011	MEAT FRESH,CHILLD,FROZEN	W 1946500	4001352	W 2543236	4795079	W 3241497	5995222	W 3685414	6426623	VIANDES FRAICHES,REF,CONGE
0111	BOVINE MEAT FRESH,FROZEN	W 412305	1944991	W 518943	2255129	W 583442	2596576	W 598430	2381711	VIANDES BOVIN FRAI,REF
01112	BOVINE MEAT BONELESS	W 358737	1739543	W 456579	2034005	W 515822	2316499	W 520785	2099577	VIANDES BOVIN DESOSSEES
0114	POULTRY FRESH CHLLD,FRZN	W 1018520	952893	W 1463908	1425093	W 1940278	1843365	W 2306203	2311172	VOLAILLES MORTES
03	FISH AND PREPARATIONS		3098625		3153115		3298059		3058564	POISSONS ET PREPARATIONS
034	FISH,FRESH,CHILLED,FROZN	W 658983	1782285	W 653821	1842558	W 692340	2078142	W 717911	1902442	POISSON FRAIS, REFRIG,CONG
04	CEREALS AND PREPARATIONS		12102962		11570032		16285862		18437311	CEREALES ET PRODUITS
041	WHEAT ETC UNMILLED	MW 35666	4667808	MW 30572	4061192	MW 32417	5457780	MW 31154	6306954	FROMENT,EPEAUTRE
0412	OTHER WHEAT ETC UNMILLED	MW 34432	4478836	MW 29360	3825348	MW 31289	5226376	MW 30144	6092373	AUTRE FROMENT NON MOULU
044	MAIZE UNMILLED	MW 40365	4473932	MW 35877	4187101	MW 60238	7534947	MW 52407	8626039	MAIS NON MOULU
05	VEGETABLES AND FRUIT		6400815		7138756		7537870		7781656	LEGUMES ET FRUITS
054	VEG ETC FRSH,SMPLY PRSVD	W 2676121	1660139	W 3056975	1872280	W 3087824	1996884	W 3102536	1941563	LEGUMES FRAIS,CONG,SECS
057	FRUIT,NUTS,FRESH,DRIED	W 3430552	3181081	W 3855408	3549810	W 3842471	3871086	W 3829554	4047757	FRUITS FRAIS OU SECS
081	*FEEDING STUFF FOR ANIML	MW 18758	3583441	MW 17710	3458686	MW 20200	3798680	MW 18437	4387099	NOURRITURE POUR ANIMAUX
0819	FOOD WASTE AND FEED NES	W 8976710	1842914	MW 9052	1929248	MW 10349	2123172	W 8714425	2235421	DECHETS,ALIMENTS NDA
09	MISC EDIBLE PRODUCTS		1873790		2283270		2167616		2512302	PREP ALIMENTAIRES DIVERSES
098	EDIBLE PRODCTS,PREPS NES		1758262		2135969		1989712		2361909	PREP ALIMENTAIRES NDA
09809	MISC FOOD PREPRTIONS NES	W 560625	1374918	W 288851	1649292	W 593089	1507104	W 664687	1830584	PREP ALIMENTAIRES NDA
1	BEVERAGES AND TOBACCO		6596767		8015417		8086068		8024804	BOISSONS ET TABACS
12	TOBACCO AND MANUFACTURES		5583652		6740696		6668137		6663686	TABACS BRUTS FABRIQUES
122	TOBACCO,MANUFACTURED		4262026		5423635		5263840		5267814	TABACS FABRIQUES
1222	CIGARETTES		3933935		5011349	W 235289	4812078	W 246172	4764702	CIGARETTES
2	CRUDE MATERLS,EXCL FUELS		24613539		27256857		34758560		32252876	MAT BRUTES NON COMESTIBLES
21	HIDES,SKINS,FURS UNDRSSD		1309857		1551149		1776639		1711135	CUIRS,PEAUX BRUTS
22	OIL SEEDS,OLEAGINOUS FRT		4979519		4724769		5920963		7855075	GRAINES,FRUITS OLEAGINEUX
222	SEEDS FOR'SOFT'FIXED OIL	MW 20020	4916699	MW 18777	4669078	MW 23692	5869305	MW 26467	7796918	GRAINES HUILES FIXES
2222	SOYA BEANS	MW 19512	4631380	MW 18126	4354778	MW 22842	5427678	MW 25961	7457720	FEVES DE SOJA
24	CORK AND WOOD		5798805		5580782		5666198		5542647	LIEGE ET BOIS
247	OTH WOOD ROUGH,SQUARED		2670617		2445916	MW 11141	2450674	MW 10508	2286560	BOIS BRUTS EQUARRIS
2471	SAW–,VENEER–LOGS CONIFER		2395652		2138240	MW 9926	2150611	MW 9484	2026627	CONIFERES POUR SCIAGE,PLACAG
24711	— IN THE ROUGH		2395652		2138240	MW 9926	2150611	MW 9484	2026627	ECORCES OU DEGROSSIS
248	WOOD SHAPED,SLEEPERS		2684084		2655939		2638255		2671915	BOIS SIMPLEMENT TRAVAILLES
2482	LUMBER SHAPED CONIFER		1512850		1452725		1341865		1324480	CONIFERES SCIES,RABOTES
24821	LUMBER SAWN ETC CONIFER	W 3491961	1401041	W 3093384	1351066	W 2853403	1266236	W 2717725	1227599	CONIFERES SCIES LONGITUD
251	*PULP AND WASTE PAPER	MW 11396	3006155	MW 13302	3838819	MW 17189	6279499	MW 13246	4079035	PATES A PAPIER,DECHETS
2517	SODA,SULPHATE WOOD PULP	W 4811117	1771464	W 4971183	2175334	W 6004967	3641927	W 5201087	2391176	PATES CHIMIQUES AU SULFATE
25172	— BLEACHED,NONDISSOLVNG	W 4689578	1737185	W 4819432	2122349	W 5679394	3529942	W 5010693	2331517	PATES BLANCHIES
26	TEXTILE FIBRES AND WASTE		2662110		3953389		5359231		4372733	FIBRES TEXTILES
263	COTTON	W 1240556	1581354	W 1885712	2723954	W 2173018	3765358	W 1612194	2801319	COTON
2631	RAW COTTON,EXCL LINTERS	W 1140766	1528871	W 1747443	2655543	W 2043758	3686704	W 1498497	2717662	COTON EN MASSE
27	CRUDE FERTLZR,MINRLS NES		1408676		1553305		1577020		1581066	ENGRAIS MINERAUX BRUTS
28	METALLIFEROUS ORES,SCRAP		3342051		3771659		5592318		4381259	MINERAIS METAL,DECHETS
3	MINERAL FUELS ETC		10007758		9210623		10720528		12512415	COMBUSTIBLES MINERAUX LUB
32	COAL,COKE AND BRIQUETTES		3200697		2963752		3714215		3852645	HOUILLES,COKES,BRIQUETTES
322	COAL,LIGNITE AND PEAT	MW 67702	3092612	MW 64972	2861602		3575362		3698712	HOUILLES,LIGNITES,TOURBE
3222	OTH COAL,NOT AGGLOMERATD	MW 67239	3060003	MW 64480	2825229		3518538		3634837	AUTRES HOUILLES
33	PETROLEUM AND PRODUCTS		6149096		5669391		6212634		7833676	PETROLE ET DERIVES
334	PETROLEUM PRODUCTS,REFIN	MW 28270	4957760	MW 24512	4265437		4528097		5450610	PRODUITS RAFFINES
3341	GASOLINE,OTH LIGHT OILS	MW 12172	2277254	MW 10250	1715355	MW 9218	1667918	MW 9997	2126838	ESSENCES POUR MOTEURS
335	RESIDUAL PETRLM PROD NES	MW 19805	1171115	MW 20124	1350628	MW 21406	1679497	MW 22183	1914015	PRODUITS RESIDUELS NDA
4	ANIMAL,VEGETABLE OIL,FAT		1400593		1780297		2428393		1743099	HUILES,GRAISSES ANIM,VEG
5	CHEMCLS,RELATED PROD NES		44741188		51138110		60220040		61202044	PRODUITS CHIMIQUES
51	ORGANIC CHEMICALS		11256278		13078656		16411063		15067446	PROD CHIMIQ ORGANIQUES
511	HYDROCARBONS NES,DERIVS		2396312	W 5757015	2887646	W 6132476	3726632		3024075	HYDROCARBURES NDA
5112	CYCLIC HYDROCARBONS		961028	W 2648130	1215270	W 3026972	1773827		1269576	HYDROCARBURES CYCLIQUES
512	ALCOHOLS,PHENOLS ETC		1097551	W 2189761	1461527		2096736		1846578	PHENOLS,PHENOLS–ALCOOLS
513	CARBOXYLIC ACIDS ETC	W 1974996	1795487	W 2055878	2042031	W 2094054	2721293	W 1877659	2097127	ACIDES CARBOXYLIQUES
514	NITROGEN–FNCTN COMPOUNDS	W 1421792	2996362	W 1734181	3400919	W 1754582	3819685	W 1815746	3585100	COMPOSES FONCT AZOTEES
5148	OTH NITROGN–FNCTN CMPNDS	W 879647	1622007	W 1126532	1933674	W 1114678	2338567	W 1105536	1985881	AUTRES COMPOSES AZOTES
515	ORG–INORG COMPOUNDS ETC	W 331480	1714711	W 410450	1911352	W 467150	2301643	W 505905	2623639	COMPOSES ORGANO–MINERAUX
516	OTHER ORGANIC CHEMICALS	W 1261331	1255855	W 1393387	1375181	W 1294581	1745074		1890927	AUTRES PROD ORGANIQUES
52	INORGANIC CHEMICALS		3884799		4147734		4573663		4728612	PROD CHIM INORGANIQUES
523	OTHR INORG CHEMICALS ETC		1443094		1535043		1817490		1878464	AUT PRODUITS CHIMIQUES INORG
53	DYES,TANNING,COLOUR PROD		1989197		2305089		2568682		2720271	PROD TEINTURE,COLORANTS
533	PIGMENTS,PAINTS,ETC		1516328		1759993		1999741		2086523	PIGMENTS,PEINTURES,VERNIS
541	*MEDICINAL,PHARM PRODUCT		5841792		6184490		6553981	MK 207384	7330070	PROD MEDICINAUX PHARMACEUT
5416	GLYCOSIDES,GLANDS,SERA	MK 10205	1471904	MK 9547	1600009		1762696	MK 26624	2077414	HETEROSIDES
5417	MEDICAMENTS		2058707		2333616		2295175	MK 99026	2802575	MEDICAMENTS
55	PERFUME,CLEANING ETC PRD		3142182		3644218		3943008		4436610	PROD POUR PARFUM,TOILETTE
553	PERFUMERY,COSMETICS,ETC	W 75194	1503669	W 116370	1808330		1970176		2275063	PRODUITS DE PARFUMERIE
562	*FERTILIZERS,MANUFACTURE		1823271		2706303		3226334		3076447	ENGRAIS MANUFACTURES
5629	FERTILIZERS NES		1823271		2706303		3226334		3076447	ENGRAIS NDA
56299	OTHER FERTILIZERS NES		1823271		2706303		3226334		3076447	AUTRES ENGRAIS NDA
58	PLASTIC MATERIALS ETC		9865264		11486329		13854287		14185495	MAT PLAST ARTIFICIELLES
582	PROD OF CONDENSATION ETC	W 1269565	3032173	W 1536676	3560941	W 1721958	4206213	W 1760961	4386380	PROD CONDENS,POLYCOND
583	POLYMERIZATION ETC PRODS		6119507		7118288		8765977		8947529	PROD POLYMERISATION
5831	POLYETHYLENE	W 1517853	1345684	W 1592690	1542256	W 1699576	2041229	W 2056586	2112943	POLYETHYLENE
5839	OTH POLYMRZTION ETC PROD		2257975		2601404		3078886		3167084	AUT PROD POLYMER COPOLYM
59	CHEMICAL MATERIALS NES		6699552		7344881		8853633		9344324	MAT PROD CHIMIQUES NDA
598	MISCEL CHEM PRODUCTS NES		5054368	W 2091887	5506401	W 2366314	6717052		7023648	PROD DIV INDUST CHIM NDA
5989	CHEM PRODUCTS,PREPS NES	W 849279	3495829	W 1022343	4009274	W 1223924	4990906	W 1331570	5351135	PROD PREP CHIMIQUES NDA
59899	OTH CHEM PRODS,PREPS,NES	W 530447	2377814	W 703440	2740330	W 832673	3438267	W 884644	3735454	AUT PRODUITS CHIMIQUES NDA
6	BASIC MANUFACTURES		39935525		44913107		54444180		57025158	ART MANUFACTURES
62	RUBBER MANUFACTURES NES		2739620		3111497		3570436		3875334	CAOUTCHOUC MANUFACTURE
625	RUBBER TYRES, TUBES ETC	MN 37439	1486271	MN 41972	1646299	MN 43877	1901039	MN 45404	2009043	PNEUS CAOUTCHOUC VULCANISE
63	WOOD,CORK MANUFACTRS NES		1701373		1826871		1916873		2055942	OUVRAGES LIEGE ET BOIS
64	PAPER,PAPERBOARD AND MFR		6684288		7721358		9888103		10191284	PAPIERS,CARTONS & OUVRAGES
641	PAPER AND PAPERBOARD		4702237		5443967		7221453		7206323	PAPIERS ET CARTONS
6413	KRAFT PAPER,PAPERBOARD	W 3309506	1307512	W 3584804	1469532	W 3931265	2185918	W 4407608	2032597	PAPIER ET CARTON KRAFT
6418	COATED ETC PAPER NES BLK	W 1348457	1318728	W 1547238	1495942	W 1909036	1959357	W 1994045	2007334	PAP,CARTONS COUCHES,ENDUITS
642	PAPER,ETC,PRECUT,ARTS OF		1982051		2277392		2666650		2984961	PAP,CARTONS DECOUPES
65	TEXTILE YARN,FABRICS,ETC		6038135		6617475		7404737		8022992	FILS,TISSUS,ARTICLES TEXTILE
657	SPECIAL TXTL FABRC,PRODS		1403164	W 244388	1563488	W 242734	1722054		1788234	TISSUS SPECIAUX
66	NONMETAL MINERAL MFS NES		5429204		6159540		6928255		7555942	ART MIN NON METALLIQUES
664	GLASS		1541880		1717384		1934016		2233094	VERRE
667	PEARL,PREC–,SEMI–P STONE		1850762		2189286		2471006		2659759	PERLES, PIERRES GEMMES
6672	DIAMONDS NONINDUST,UNSET		1635138		1939551		2181606		2398521	DIAMANTS BRUTS
66729	— CUT ETC NOT SET		1440909		1738312		2010001		2179075	DIAMANTS TAILLES

5. General Exports F.O.B. by Commodities according to the S.I.T.C. (Rev. 2) in thousand U.S. Dollars
Exportations Générales F.O.B. par Produits d'après la C.T.C.I. (Rév. 2) en milliers de Dollars E.U.

SITC CTCI	COMMODITY	1993 WEIGHT POIDS	1993 VALUE VALEUR	1994 WEIGHT POIDS	1994 VALUE VALEUR	1995 WEIGHT POIDS	1995 VALUE VALEUR	1996 WEIGHT POIDS	1996 VALUE VALEUR	PRODUIT
67	IRON AND STEEL		3908282		4233907		6151428		5716235	FER ET ACIER
678	IRON,STL TUBES,PIPES,ETC	W 672570	1181781	W 926193	1419577	W 1076608	1765865	W 1077863	1872309	TUBES,TUYAUX EN FONTE,FER
68	NON–FERROUS METALS		4706063		5387657		7521762		7194776	METAUX NON FERREUX
684	ALUMINIUM	W 1138069	2328177	W 1257869	2797139	W 1407199	3814135	W 1360463	3534633	ALUMINIUM
6842	ALUMINIUM,ALLOYS WORKED	W 700259	1742208	W 870577	2193072	W 958982	3000196	W 913873	2810255	ALUMINIUM,ALLIAGES OUVRE
68422	ALUMNM PLATE,SHEET,STRIP	W 522512	1196203	W 638613	1527171	W 709080	2174628	W 646831	1911380	TOLES, PLANCHES EN ALU
69	METAL MANUFACTURES NES		7653070		8831881		10019153		11251907	ART MANUFACT EN METAL NDA
695	TOOLS		1431090		1601816		1806605		1904855	OUTILS A MAIN
699	BASE METAL MFRS NES		3301529		3939490		4520746		5136464	ART MANUFACTURES MET NDA
7	MACHINES,TRANSPORT EQUIP		224630500		252062735		281184372		305748604	MACHINES MATERIEL TRANSPORT
71	POWER GENERATING EQUIPMT		19675588		20870112		22429871		23169023	MACHINES GENERATRICES
713	INTRNL COMBUS PSTN ENGIN		7401543		8263842		8833323		9028772	MOTEURS EXPL COMB INT, PIECE
7132	MOTOR VEHCL PISTN ENGINS	N 1645945	3248329	N 1511953	3326027	N 1733053	3734708	N 1637695	3629747	MOTEURS EXPL POUR VEHICULES
7139	PISTON ENGINE PARTS NES	W 272625	2850416	W 337690	3318768	W 262520	3436439	W 304754	3742508	PIECES POUR 713.2,3,8
714	ENGINES AND MOTORS NES		8387262		8517434		8756911		9277727	MOTEURS NON ELECTRIQUES
7144	REACTION ENGINES	N 17937	2248171	N 5955	2379857	N 13460	1658905	N 9004	2068567	PROPULSEURS A REACTION
7149	ENGINE & MOTOR PARTS NES		4908719		5095749		5594511		6118521	PIECES 714 ET 718.88
71491	PARTS NES OF 7144,71481		3414447		3495124		3839562		4204340	PIECES DES PROPULSEURS
71499	PARTS NES,OF 71488,71888		1494272		1600624		1754949		1914181	PIECES 714.88 ET 718.88
716	ROTATING ELECTRIC PLANT		2612613		2677779		3077045		3052699	APP ELECTR ROTATIFS,PIECES
72	MACHS FOR SPCL INDUSTRYS		17638555		19712992		23339400		25605591	MAC SPECIALES POUR INDUST
721	AGRIC MACHY,EXC TRACTORS		1917081		2048824		2125233		2453058	MACHINES AGRICOLES
723	CIVIL ENGNEERG EQUIP ETC	N 417751	5407903	N 827751	5953843		6274718		7060290	APPAREILS DE GENIE CIVIL
7234	CONST,MINING MACHNRY NES	N 96186	2020663	N 117607	2533701		2388013		2436574	MACH POUR LA CONST, MINES
7239	CONSTR ETC MACHY PTS NES	N 318454	3296629	N 706345	3311611		3765967		4511209	PIECES 723.41–723.46
728	OTH MACHY FOR SPCL INDUS		5698831		6882980		9392102		10297970	AUT MACH IND PARTICULIERES
7284	MACHY FOR SPCL INDUS NES		4759706		5847715		8194678		9098437	MACH SPEC IND PARTICUL.
72848	OTH MCHY WITH INDIV FNCT	N 43935	2398456	N 54116	2947987	N 938433	4788756	N 1004705	5297439	AUTRES MACHINES NDA
72849	PTS OF MACHS OF 7284 ETC		1588693		2002872		2375944		2715546	PIECES DU 728.4 ETC
73	METALWORKING MACHINERY		3202167		3922034		4601510		5216747	MACH TRAVAIL DES METAUX
736	METALWORKING MACH–TOOLS		2383032		2987049		3682108		4261715	MACH–OUTILS TRAVAIL METAUX
74	GENRL INDUSTRL MACHY NES		20912622		23579674		26141228		28549391	MACH APP INDUSTRIE
741	HEATING,COOLING EQUIPMNT		4486562		4970435		5656059		6033314	MACH CHAUFFAGE,PIECES
7415	AIR–CONDITIONING MACHNRY	N 2361386	1690889	N 3162572	1792062		1945682		2101798	GROUPES CONDITION AIR
742	PUMPS FOR LIQUIDS ETC		2085551		2267276		2418776		2563057	POMPES MOTO–POMPES
743	PUMPS NES,CENTRFUGES ETC		4151755		4655303		5205141		5826903	POMPES COMPRES,VENT ETC
7431	PUMPS FOR GASES ETC	N 4154000	1367318	N 5247501	1628503	N 5870285	1747834	N 8618395	1958228	POMPES AIR A VIDE,COMPRES
7436	GAS,LIQUID FILTERS ETC	N 230712	1465409	N 245093	1648766		1767729		2031223	APP POUR FILT DES LIQUIDES
744	MECHANICAL HANDLING EQU		3516485		4048977		4667268		5213150	EQUIP MANUTENTION PIECES
7449	PTS NES OF MACHY OF 7442		2252376		2527366		2758750		3054899	PIECES DU 744.2
745	NONELEC MACHY,TOOLS NES		2350151		2671636		2790717		3052164	AUT MACH NON ELEC,PIECES
7452	OTH NONELEC MCHS,PTS NES		1985982		2210151		2307814		2553728	AUT MACH NON ELEC,PIECES
749	NONELEC MACH PTS,ACC NES		4322117		4966047		5403267		5860802	PIECES MACH NON ELEC NDA
7492	COCKS,VALVES ETC NES		1712713		1964777		2238455		2500287	ART ROB,SIM POUR TUYAUX
75	OFFICE MACHNES,ADP EQUIP		31347941		35396164		41947095		45751285	MACH BUREAU TRAIT AUTOM
752	AUTOMTIC DATA PROC EQUIP	MN 23654	18027349	MN 31145	20427266	MN 33660	23077534	MN 36792	25220065	MACH TRAIT INFORMATION
7522	DIGITAL COMPUTERS	N 588455	1826689	N 1016623	1893387	N 1085680	2022392	N 1459484	2551591	MACH DIGITALES COMPLETES
7523	DIGITL CENTRL PROCESSORS	N 2338865	6018779	N 3000386	6821389	N 3114544	7273961	MN 9853	10346662	UNITES CENTRALES
7524	DIGITL CENTRL STOR UNITS	N 7235625	4164639	MN 9131	4537404	MN 10383	5150348	MN 9255	3559255	UNITES MEMOIRE CENTRALES
7525	ADP PERIPHERAL UNITS	MN 10357	4034470	MN 12856	4314795	MN 13144	4747528	N 8428398	2613588	UNITES PERIPHERIQUES
7528	OFF–LINE DATA PROC EQUIP	N 3048109	1620083	N 5027040	2358433	N 5821162	3401205	N 7564980	5362999	MACH AUXIL TRAIT INFORM
759	OFFICE,ADP MCH PTS,ACCES		12362910		14017934		17767915		19350620	PIECES DU 751 ET 752
7599	ACCTG,ETC,ADP MCH PTS,AC		11514698		13120672		16811500		18238838	PIECES DU 751 ET 752
76	TELECOMM,SOUND EQUIPMENT		14236843		17128578		20331591		21414382	EQUIPMENT DE TELECOM
764	TELECOM EQPT,PTS,ACC NES		12262435		14810293		17842320		18734996	EQUIP TELECOM,PIECES
7641	LINE TELEPHONE,ETC EQUIP	N 3778798	2079976	N 3724156	2548708		3247828		3887656	APP TELEPHON PAR FIL
7643	TV,RADIO TRANSMITTRS ETC		3046207		4153130		5275388		5215323	APP EMET TELE RADIO
7649	PTS NES OF EQUIPMT OF 76		5371255		5947173		7072587		7186613	PIECES DE LA DIV 76
76491	PTS NES OF APPAR OF 7641		1864701		2189664		2494415		2710836	PIECES POUR 764.1
76493	TELECOMM EQUIPMT PTS NES		3185530		3448403		4188613		3954888	PIECES 761,762,764.3,8
77	ELECTRIC MACHNRY NES ETC		43045189		52771219		65452241		69983697	MACH APP ELECT NDA
771	ELECTRIC POWER MACHY NES		1538382		1873897		2153193		2510287	MACH PROD,TRANS ELECTR
7712	OTH ELEC POWER MACHY NES		1266396		1589611		1816323		2078840	AUT APP PROD TRANSF ELEC
772	SWITCHGEAR ETC,PARTS NES	MN 3946654	5882377	MN 8650843	7235841		8319059		9168689	APP COUPURE,SECT ETC
7721	SWITCHGEAR ETC	MN 900280	4465917	MN 4370226	5365607		6175007		6893123	APP COUPURE,SECTIONMNT
773	ELECTR DISTRIBUTNG EQUIP		3263408		3643022		4102422		4545884	EQUIPMT DISTRIBUTION ELECT
7731	INSULATED WIRE,CABLE ETC	W 194896	2911185	W 234664	3263818		3679439		4121002	FILS,CABLES ISOLES ELECT
774	ELECTRO–MEDCL,XRAY EQUIP		2660026		2958179		3349185		3803063	APPAREILS MEDICAUX
7741	ELECTRO–MEDICAL EQUIPMNT		1683556		1808752		2012581		2437210	APP ELECTRICITE MEDICALE
775	HOUSEHOLD TYPE EQUIP NES		2290695		2384774		2464999		2633860	MACH,APP USAGE DOMESTQUE
776	TRANSISTORS,VALVES,ETC		20077905		26452135		35711214		37451160	LAMPES,TUBES,VALVES
7763	DIODES,TRANSISTORS,ETC	MN 2081224	1442857	MN 3896721	1685357	MN 5346029	2332023	MN 5576293	2505554	DIODES,TRANSISTORS
7764	ELECTRONIC MICROCIRCUITS	MN 11712777	16990570	MN 12625404	22589384	MN 14553772	30588949	MN 14051114	31889025	MICROSTRUCTURES ELECTRON
778	ELECTRICAL MACHINERY NES		7332395		8223372		9352168		9870754	AUTRES MACH ELECT NDA
7783	AUTOMOTIVE ELECTR EQUIP	MN 1012365	1703619	MN 54884	1697418		1528976		1640187	EQUIP ELECT MOTEURS EXPL
7788	OTH ELEC MACHY,EQUIP NES		3845948		4456118		5586749		5878628	AUT MACH APP ELEC NDA
78	ROAD VEHICLES		41177870		46304809		49221785		51702767	VEHICULES ROUTIERS
781	PASS MOTOR VEH EXC BUSES	N 1107497	14824306	N 1224954	16661996	N 1232604	16799209	N 1239379	17175950	AUTO TRANSPORT PERSONNES
782	LORRIES,SPCL MTR VEH NES	N 239614	3991094	N 353207	4598984	N 327799	5318340	N 396251	6762934	VEHICULES SPECIAUX,MARCH
7821	LORRIES,TRUCKS	N 232707	3457073	N 347721	4176449	N 319633	4839844	N 388582	6274168	VEHICULES TRANSP MARCHAND
784	MOTOR VEH PRTS,ACCES NES		19710968		22106129		23816631		24628129	PIECES 722,781,782,783
7849	OTHER MOTOR VEHCL PARTS		19318589		21674879	W 3293723	23373033	W 3260132	24110676	PIECES 722,781,782,783
79	OTHR TRANSPORT EQUIPMENT		33393726		32377153		27719652		34355721	AUTRE MATERIEL TRANSPORT
792	AIRCRAFT ETC		31856291		30431247		25612616		32456698	APP NAVIGATION AERIENNE
7923	AIRCRFT NES2000–15000KG	N 422	1639456	N 438	1382615		1147688	N 558	3510808	AERODYNES 2000 A 15000 KG
7924	AIRCRFT NES OVER 15000KG	N 328	19327181	N 314	18068235	N 192	12656663	N 285	15842940	AERODYNES PLUS 15000 KG
7929	AIRCRAFT PARTS NES		9575108		9872404		10567930	W 53372	11953055	PIECES DU 792
8	MISC MANUFACTURED GOODS		51836549		56496642		62106121		67819587	ART MANUFACTURES DIVERS
821	*FURNITURE,PARTS THEREOF		3308637		3728791		3806367		4085829	MEUBLES ET PIECES
8211	CHAIRS,SEATS AND PARTS		1398941		1644234		1793663		1867493	SIEGES ET PIECES
84	CLOTHING AND ACCESSORIES		4957477		5620652		6657274		7520075	VETEMENTS
846	UNDER GARMENTS KNITTED	W 80558	1243058	W 94929	1355430	W 133385	1707544	W 157957	1946805	SOUS VETS DE BONNETERIE
87	PRECISION INSTRUMNTS NES		15724513		17177437		19358806		21463077	INSTRUM,APPAR SCIENT NDA
872	MEDICAL INSTRUMENTS NES		3559998		3860578		4294542		4914505	INSTR,APP MEDIC–CHIR NDA
87202	OTH MEDICAL INSTRUMENTS		3134181		3405188		3791125		4397879	INSTRUM,APP MEDECINE
874	MEASURNG,CONTROLNG INSTR		11045252		11848421		13484843		14673609	INSTRUMENTS DE MESURE
8742	MEASUR,DRAW ETC INST,PTS		1167168		1379691		1699843		2284856	INST DESSIN,TRACAGE,PCS
87421	MEASURNG,DRAWNG ETC INST		964376		1128097		1370404		1918732	INSTRUM DESSIN,TRACAGE
8743	GAS,LIQUID CONTROL INSTR	MN 27976	2193999	MN 35113	2450478		2623471		2554653	APP,INSTR MESURE FLUIDES
8748	ELEC MEAS,CONTRL EQU NES	MN 13857	4017514	MN 12278	4276026		4887700		5388463	APP ELEC ELECTRO MESURE
87483	OTH ELCTRNC MEAS ETC EQU	MN 11907	3709410	MN 9779	3944097		4560636		5008447	AUT APP ELECTRO DE MESURE

5. General Exports F.O.B. by Commodities according to the S.I.T.C. (Rev. 2) in thousand U.S. Dollars
Exportations Générales F.O.B. par Produits d'après la C.T.C.I. (Rév. 2) en milliers de Dollars E.U.

SITC CTCI	COMMODITY	1993		1994		1995		1996		PRODUIT
		WEIGHT POIDS	VALUE VALEUR	WEIGHT POIDS	VALUE VALEUR	WEIGHT POIDS	VALUE VALEUR	WEIGHT POIDS	VALUE VALEUR	
8749	INSTR PTS NES,ACCESSORYS		1701470		1758966		2196274		2266683	PIECES 873,874.3,54,874.8
88	PHOTO EQU,OPTICL GDS ETC		4042610		4229134		4690858		5315315	APP,FOURN PHOTO,OP,MONTR
882	PHOTO,CINEMA SUPPLIES		2063036		2115815		2420464		2789733	PRODUITS PHOTO,CINEMA
8822	PHOTO FILM EXC DEV CINMA		1695389		1689045		1833076		2240346	PLAQUES,PELLICULES,FILMS
89	MISC MANUFCTRD GOODS NES		22267949		24043874		25828879		27608045	ART MANUFACTURES DIVERS
892	PRINTED MATTER		4110941		4089269		4406556		4428163	IMPRIMES
8921	PRINTED BOOKS,GLOBES,ETC	MN 938018	1839471	MN 951721	1894741		2017343		2051321	LIVRES,BROCHURES,CARTES
89211	PRINTED BOOKS,PAMPHLETS	MN 902092	1805431	MN 919493	1861525	MN 1035132	1988107	MN 1001831	2022381	LIVRES,BROCHURES
8928	PRINTED MATTER NES		1400456		1234905		1331655		1317817	IMPRIMES NDA
893	ARTICLES OF PLASTIC NES		4190993		4963385		5393895		6221174	OUVRAGES EN MAT DIVIS 58
8939	MISC PLASTIC ARTICLES		3032736		3636449		3851195		4535624	ART DIVERS EN MAT DIV 58
89399	OTHR PLASTC ARTICLES NES	W 108983	2794498	W 149232	3381310		3599359		4251928	AUT OUV MAT DIV 58
894	TOYS,SPORTING GOODS,ETC		3291727		3689598		4230536		4287598	VOITURES ENFANTS,JOUETS
8942	TOYS,INDOOR GAMES ETC		1887654		2176283		2269748		2313082	JOUETS,JEUX ETC
896	WORKS OF ART ETC		1912143		1693425		1487120		1508054	OBJETS D'ART
898	MUSICAL INSTRUMENTS,PTS		5664769		6266319		6584540		6874328	INSTRUMENTS DE MUSIQUE
8983	SOUND RECRDNG TAPE,DISCS		5280167		5846657		6139128		6408640	SUPPORTS SON POUR 763
89831	PREPD SND RECORDNG MEDIA		1953906		2045906		2250161		2861372	SUPPORTS PREPARES
89832	RECORDED DISCS,TAPES ETC	MN 15898	3326262	MN 15278	3800751		3888967	MN 254178	3547268	DISQUES,PHONO,BANDES
899	OTHER MANUFACTURED GOODS		1673062		1853098		2034051		2287421	AUT ART MANUF DIVERS NDA
9	GOODS NOT CLASSD BY KIND		27178381		26009200		26793381		30682024	ART TRANSACT NON CLASSES
931	*SPECIAL TRANSACTIONS		15084508		16675386		17699968		19342450	TRANS.SPECIALES
951	*WAR FIREARMS,AMMUNITION		2998014		3625877		3953443		4612504	VEHIC BLINDES ARMES
95101	ARMORED FIGHTNG VEHICLES		923016		1677318		1619060		2221933	CHARS DE COMBAT
95106	AMMUNITION NES		1691886	MN 14568995	1295264		1848654		1509885	PROJECTILES,MUNITIONS
971	*GOLD,NON MONETARY NES	K 1715092	9063300	K 501752	5676508	K 461805	5098440	K 585745	6671293	OR NON MONETAIRE
97101	NONMON GLD UNWRT,SEMIMFD	K 734502	8428273	K 404682	4898543	K 358861	4307303	K 483771	5795330	OR,ALLIAGES D'OR BRUTS

FOOT NOTES – NOTES

TABLE 1 –
1 Prior to 1974, imports f.o.b.
TABLE 3 –
1 Export data for certain countries exclude some special category shipments consisting mostly of military supplies which, for security reasons, are not reported by country of destination.
TABLE 4 –
1 Imports individually valued at $250 or less are recorded on a sample basis are included in SITC 931.
TABLE 5 –
1 All shipments valued under $100 are included in SITC 931.
TABLEAU 1 –
1 Avant 1974, les importations sont f.a.b.
TABLEAU 3 –
1 Les données pour certains pays excluent certaines fournitures spéciales consistant surtout en matériel militaire qui pour des raisons de sécurité nationale ne sont pas ventilées par pays de destination.
TABLEAU 4 –
1 Les importations estimeées invividuellement à moins de 250 dollars et qui sont reprises sur la base d'un sondage statistique sont comprises dans le groupe 931 de la CTCI.
TABLEAU 5 –
1 Toutes les livraisons évaluées à moins de 100 dollars sont comprises dans le groupe 931 de la CTCI.

1. H # 1TORICAL SERIES, 1961–1996 SPECIAL TRADE, IMPORTS C.I.F., EXPORTS F.O.B.
SERIES HISTORIQUES, 1961–1996 COMMERCE SPECIAL, IMPORTATIONS C.A.F., EXPORTATIONS F.O.B

YEAR ANNEE	VALUE IN MILLION U.S. DOLLARS / VALEUR EN MILLION U.S. DOLLARS — MERCHANDISE – MARCHANDISE		GOLD – OR		CONVERSION FACTORS FACTEURS DE CONVERSION CENTS E.U. PAR		INDEX NUMBERS – INDICES — QUANTUM		UNIT VALUE / VALEUR UNITAIRE	
	IMPORTS	EXPORTS	IMPORTS	EXPORTS	IMPORTS	EXPORTS	IMPORTS	EXPORTS	IMPORTS	EXPORTS
1961	210.90	174.70								38
1962	230.50	153.40								33
1963	176.90	165.20								35
1964	198.40	178.90								33
1965	150.40	191.20								37
1966	164.00	185.80								36
1967	171.40	158.70								33
1968	157.40	179.20								41
1969	197.30	200.30								43
1970	230.90	232.70								47
1971	228.90	205.70								43
1972	211.60	214.10								35
1973	284.80	321.50								
1974	486.70	382.10								
1975	556.40	383.80								
1976	587.20	546.50								
1977	729.90	607.50								
1978	774.30	686.10								70
1979	1206.30	788.10								88
1980	1680.30	1058.50								99
1981	1641.10	1215.40								101
1982	1110.00	1022.90								89
1983	787.50	1045.10								
1984	775.70	924.60								
1985	707.80	853.60								
1986	870.00	1087.80								
1987	1141.90	1189.20								
1988	1157.20	1404.50								
1989	1202.80	1598.80								
1990	1342.90	1692.90								100
1991	1636.50	1604.70								102
1992	2045.10	1702.50								97
1993	2325.70	1645.30								93
1994	2786.10	1913.40								87
1995	2866.90	2106.00								89
1996	3322.80	2397.20								86

2. IMPORTS BY BROAD ECONOMIC CATEGORY AND EXPORTS BY INDUSTRIAL ORIGIN. (PERCENTAGE OF TOTAL VALUE)
IMPORTATIONS PAR CATEGORIES ECONOMIQUES ET EXPORTATIONS PAR BRANCHE D'ACTIVITE.(EN POURCENTAGE DE LA VALEUR TOTALE)

IMPORTS – IMPORTATIONS

	1990	1991	1992	1993	1994	1995	1996
TOTAL IMPORTS–IMPORTATIONS TOTALES	100.	100.	100.	100.	100.	100.	100.
1 FOOD BEV–ALIMENTATION BOISSONS	5.8	6.5	8.1	7.1	9.4	9.4	9.5
11 PRIMARY–PRODUITS DE BASE	3.5	3.5	4.5	3.2	3.7	3.1	3.3
111 FOR INDUSTRY–POUR L'INDUSTRIE	0.5	0.8	2.1	0.7	1.1	0.5	0.8
112 FOR HOUSEHOLDS–POUR LES MENAGES	3.0	2.7	2.4	2.5	2.5	2.6	2.4
12 PROCESSED–PRODUITS ELABORES	2.3	3.0	3.6	3.9	5.7	6.3	6.2
121 FOR INDUSTRY–POUR L'INDUSTRIE	0.6	1.1	1.1	1.0	1.4	1.4	1.4
122 FOR HOUSEHOLDS–POUR LES MENAGES	1.7	1.9	2.5	2.9	4.3	4.9	4.8
2 IND SUPPLIES–APPROV INDUSTRIELS	37.9	36.9	30.9	29.6	31.9	31.9	33.3
21 PRIMARY–PRODUITS DE BASE	4.0	3.7	2.7	2.2	3.1	3.4	3.1
22 PROCESSED–PRODUITS ELABORES	33.9	33.2	28.2	27.4	28.8	28.5	30.2
3 FUELS–COMBUSTIBLES	18.0	15.6	10.4	8.5	8.1	10.1	10.8
31 PRIMARY–PRODUITS DE BASE	14.3	13.5	7.5	1.7	0.6	6.6	7.2
32 PROCESSED–PRODUITS ELABORES	3.7	2.1	2.8	6.7	7.6	3.5	3.6
321 MOTOR SPIRIT–ESSENCE	3.5	1.9	0.2	1.5	1.9		1.7
322 OTHER–AUTRES	0.2	0.2	2.6	5.2	5.6	3.5	1.8
4 MACHINERY–EQUIPEMENT	19.1	17.3	16.1	17.9	16.8	18.0	19.4
41 CAPITAL EQUIPMENT–MACHINES	17.4	15.7	14.6	16.2	15.3	16.5	17.9
42 PARTS–PIECES ACCESSOIRES	1.6	1.7	1.6	1.7	1.5	1.5	1.6
5 TRANSPORT–TRANSPORT	10.0	12.2	15.8	17.9	16.4	14.2	11.6
51 PASSENGER CARS–AUTOMOBILES	5.8	7.2	7.9	10.6	10.1	7.1	4.6
52 OTHER–AUTRES	1.7	2.1	4.6	4.0	3.2	4.3	4.3
521 INDUSTRIAL–INDUSTRIELS	1.3	1.6	3.9	3.1	2.2	3.5	3.6
522 NON INDUSTRIAL–NON INDUSTRIEL	0.4	0.4	0.7	0.9	1.0	0.8	0.7
53 PARTS–PIECES ACCESSOIRES	2.5	2.9	3.2	3.2	3.2	2.7	2.6
6 CONSUM GOODS–BIENS CONSOMMATION	9.2	11.5	18.7	19.1	17.4	16.4	15.4
61 DURABLE–DURABLES	3.6	3.9	10.3	8.8	6.5	5.3	4.6
62 SEMI DURABLE–SEMI DURABLES	3.1	4.5	5.4	7.1	7.3	7.1	6.8
63 NON DURABLE–NON DURABLES	2.6	3.0	3.0	3.2	3.5	4.0	4.1
7 GOODS NES–BIENS NDA	0.0	0.0	0.0	0.1	0.0	0.0	0.0

EXPORTS – EXPORTATIONS

	1990	1991	1992	1993	1994	1995	1996
TOTAL EXPORTS–EXPORTATIONS TOTALES	100.	100.	100.	100.	100.	100.	100.
1 AGRICULTURE	16.5	16.4	14.5	14.9	13.8	17.2	14.7
2 MINING QUARRY–INDUS EXTRACTIVES	0.2	0.2	0.3	0.2	0.2	0.2	0.2
3 MANUFACTURING–IND MANUFACTUR	83.3	83.4	85.2	84.9	85.9	82.6	85.1
31 FOOD BEV TOBACCO–ALIM BOISS TAB	31.8	30.1	28.3	29.6	31.2	30.9	35.4
32 TEXTILES–INDUSTRIES TEXTILES	35.9	37.7	40.0	33.9	30.3	30.9	30.4
33 WOOD & PRODUCTS–BOIS & PRODUITS	0.0	0.0	0.1	0.1	0.2	0.3	0.3
34 PAPER & PRODUCTS–PAPIER & PRODT	0.8	1.7	1.5	1.6	1.4	1.5	1.9
35 CHEMICALS–INDUSTRIES CHIMIQUES	9.8	8.2	8.1	7.9	7.5	8.9	8.6
36 NON METAL MIN–MIN NON METAL	1.4	1.4	1.7	2.0	1.6	1.3	1.4
37 BASIC METAL–IND METAL BASE	0.5	0.8	0.6	0.6	0.6	0.9	1.1
38 METAL MANUF–MANUF METAL	2.5	2.8	4.2	8.7	12.6	7.3	5.6
39 OTH MANUF IND–AUTRES MANUF	0.6	0.7	0.6	0.6	0.5	0.5	0.3

3. TRADE BY PRINCIPAL COUNTRIES OF FIRST AND LAST CONSIGNMENT (VALUE IN THOUSAND U.S. DOLLARS)
ECHANGES SELON LES PRINCIPAUX PAYS DE PREMIERE ET DE DERNIERE CONSIGNATION (VALEUR EN MILLIERS DE DOLLARS EU)

COUNTRIES–PAYS	SPECIAL IMPORTS C.I.F. IMPORTATIONS SPECIALES C.A.F				
	1992	1993	1994	1995	1996
World	2009862	2332868	2707189	2865745	3322393
Africa	40375	22261	17028	41567	86032
Americas	1150447	1416909	1789234	1799852	2096171
Northern America	199267	249250	285390	303309	431062
LAIA	933123	1142763	1468044	1469171	1641818
CACM	272	306	1033	751	1449
Caribbean	2389	6271	6127	6016	6669
Rest of America	15395	18319	28640	20605	15173
As.ex F.USSR	407321	305087	296652	343098	381846
Eur.x F.USSR	366605	561998	563998	640821	691365
EU	329944	522695	514458	597536	644913
EFTA	28540	26236	29090	28973	33461
East Europe	7667	12623	19952	13894	12708
Other Europe	56	90	226	249	21
Former USSR	901	14103	23606	1008	19669
Oceania	32523	3350	11117	3482	7933
Brazil/Brésil	474866	608058	745728	698458	745452
Argentina/Argentine	345809	432116	608855	608587	690701
USA/Etats–Unis d'Amer	187064	210612	262510	283948	405706
Italy/Italie	68605	234884	137753	147804	171426
Germany/Allemagne	90575	79474	93732	104126	100437
Japan/Japon	100218	124954	78565	73263	72079
France,Monac	60967	71295	78960	100256	117860
Spain/Espagne	32148	51851	83094	106294	103337
Korea, Republic of	122269	43687	50517	49887	61745
Chile/Chili	33809	36465	45491	49291	55401
Mexico/Mexique	37851	46410	39172	41533	48918
United Kingdom	38673	37281	41733	41103	52403
Iran (Islamic Rp. of)	82297	18532	25	33392	62657
Hong Kong	27070	38972	45788	37735	38478
China/Chine	9781	15637	28127	34557	49463
Switz.Liecht	27807	25335	28210	28140	27903
Nigeria/Nigéria	35988		7	30388	61720
Venezuela	23935	3795	11335	25194	63683
Canada	12203	38568	22717	18296	25286
Panama	15395	18319	28637	20605	15173
Netherlands/Pays–Bas	14178	16211	20837	24485	22304
Sweden/Suède	6067	3535	18586	24063	28837
Paraguay	10860	6466	8599	13553	25259
India/Inde	2877	6657	16044	16426	18553
Belgium–Luxembourg	6134	9032	13580	16535	14832
Russian Federation	901	13722	22391		17739
Singapore/Singapour	9978	11129	12591	11757	7311
Australia/Australie	31273	1784	6889	3482	4099
Israel/Israël	6880	5392	8982	10687	12504
Denmark/Danemark	3342	6752	6130	12183	13937
So. Africa Customs Un	4289	5906	11988	7701	8793
Saudi Arabia		8	3476	23599	92
Austria/Autriche	3948	4589	4810	5469	3286
Malaysia/Malaisie	2516	2531	6221	6107	4662
Ecuador/Equateur	307	697	2390	18415	
Finland/Finlande	2808	2580	6130	3711	6192
Colombia/Colombie	1276	1748	3009	8993	5359
Poland/Pologne	2076	2958	5825	3839	3980
Romania/Roumanie	2393	2115	6170	5212	1311
Peru/Pérou	3662	2537	2970	3227	4665
Greece/Grèce	918	2337	4329	4664	4045
Turkey/Turquie	1791	2562	2859	2801	4357
Cuba	2078	353	5498	5184	1106
Indonesia/Indonésie	1484	1711	2572	2903	5158
Morocco/Maroc		5200	2436	691	5351
Hungary/Hongrie	1380	4590	3751	1425	2438
Thailand/Thaïlande	732	1974	3554	2571	3463
Ireland/Irlande	768	1922	2379	3072	3963
Egypt/Egypte		10569	350	225	144
United Arab Emirates	11091	1	15		30

COUNTRIES–PAYS	SPECIAL EXPORTS F.O.B. EXPORTATIONS SPECIALES F.O.B.				
	1992	1993	1994	1995	1996
Monde	1620189	1606533	1918178	2106098	2397448
Afrique	6970	4602	4708	15213	19996
Amériques	865516	981171	1183783	1201148	1604098
Amérique du Nord	186572	157668	146255	139524	159838
ALAI	671999	813344	1025443	1053406	1435254
MCAC	1434	2284	1128	5473	3233
Caraïbes	4926	7542	10544	2186	3178
Autre Amérique	585	333	413	559	2595
Asie l'URSS exclus	254703	237373	284693	538063	313381
Europe l'URSS exclus	462845	360574	414790	324513	426520
UE	433337	344749	400456	307615	407038
AELE	7207	6573	10854	10234	11546
Europe de l'Est	22109	8760	3199	6029	6678
Autre de l'Europe	97	315	66	182	364
Ancienne URSS	2884	3599	11717	7434	14949
Océanie	3194	1693	972	3661	4083
Brazil/Brésil	284317	366159	494111	660090	908354
Argentina/Argentine	249705	279075	377449	257665	267937
USA/Etats–Unis d'Amer	172942	146926	131341	123296	144147
Germany/Allemagne	131814	104360	121716	85262	93805
China/Chine	91008	88049	115907	123391	116175
Italy/Italie	74697	49109	60638	54769	73664
United Kingdom	65627	64590	71987	56399	53944
Chile/Chili	49755	52269	41914	29347	115669
Singapore/Singapour	6798	3896	3599	260484	2588
Hong Kong	46458	41086	33940	44700	86198
Netherlands/Pays–Bas	53290	47230	48571	33723	39638
Mexico/Mexique	42108	40303	46775	14910	26918
Spain/Espagne	32718	18961	33339	32166	37834
Israel/Israël	38178	45615	57083	4480	5746
Peru/Pérou	17614	37128	22561	35982	36532
France,Monac	37968	28914	25195	18869	18850
Paraguay	10285	16114	24124	24684	49513
Sweden/Suède	11090	6606	12869	10060	62112
Japan/Japon	20151	13668	20907	18414	24786
Canada	13630	10741	14914	16228	13971
Colombia/Colombie	8364	14863	12563	18296	15148
Saudi Arabia	13858	11788	18959	9769	9320
Iran (Islamic Rp. of)	14900	10488	2523	15148	19497
Belgium–Luxembourg	12934	12019	14244	1613	15435
Korea, Republic of	6436	4473	7788	9668	11150
Russian Federation	2884	3478	10218	7043	14084
Venezuela	5274	3725	2464	10340	12905
Poland/Pologne	19424	4969	1284	2091	3610
Malaysia/Malaisie	636	434	172	17243	12552
Switz.Liecht	5702	4153	7645	4158	3112
Turkey/Turquie	724	2826	4282	9910	6630
Norway,SVD,JM	1505	2419	3209	6076	8424
Portugal	3714	6076	3154	2227	5494
Senegal/Sénégal			2053	8541	7920
India/Inde	2955	1107	2254	5752	2228
Denmark/Danemark	2762	2669	3665	3427	1761
Finland/Finlande	1915	1179	1616	6033	2408
Australia/Australie	3109	1666	915	3564	3743
Dominican Republic	3014	2938	3786	1094	1120
Bolivia/Bolivie	3074	1991	1939	2092	2278
So. Africa Customs Un	1197	892	1112	3754	4005
Austria/Autriche	2205	1243	1387	2543	700
Thailand/Thaïlande	592	1238	2183	2049	1081
Greece/Grèce	2360	1712	1886	343	798
Haiti/Haïti		2167	4489	41	111
Guatemala	121	347	221	4101	1472
Czech Republic		1258	857	2548	1244
Morocco/Maroc	2551	15	70	2034	483
United Arab Emirates	147	878	1303	1234	1201
Ecuador/Equateur	1502	1717	1543		

(VALUE AS PERCENTAGE OF WORLD TOTAL)(VALEURS EN POURCENTAGE DU TOTAL MONDIAL)

	1987	1988	1989	1990	1991	1992	1993	1994	1995	1996
Africa	5.4	2.1	3.3	1.0	5.7	2.0	1.0	0.6	1.5	2.6
Americas	58.4	59.7	63.5	60.1	59.7	57.2	60.7	66.1	62.8	63.1
Northern America	9.4	8.4	13.0	10.8	10.5	9.9	10.7	10.5	10.6	13.0
LAIA	48.6	50.4	49.6	48.7	48.4	46.4	49.0	54.2	51.3	49.4
CACM	0.0	0.0		0.0	0.0	0.0	0.0	0.0	0.0	0.0
Caribbean	0.0	0.6	0.5	0.1	0.0	0.1	0.3	0.2	0.2	0.2
Rest of America	0.3	0.3	0.5	0.5	0.7	0.8	0.8	1.1	0.7	0.5
As.ex F.USSR	10.3	9.7	9.1	12.3	13.7	20.3	13.1	11.0	12.0	11.5
Eur.x F.USSR	25.2	26.6	23.5	23.4	20.5	18.2	24.1	20.8	22.4	20.8
EU	22.5	23.3	20.5	20.2	18.3	16.4	22.4	19.0	20.9	19.4
EFTA	1.9	2.0	1.8	2.4	1.7	1.4	1.1	1.1	1.0	1.0
East Europe	0.7	1.3	1.2	0.8	0.5	0.4	0.5	0.7	0.5	0.4
Other Europe	0.0	0.0	0.0	0.0	0.0	0.0	0.0	0.0	0.0	0.0
Former USSR	0.3	1.7	0.3	3.0	0.2	0.0	0.6	0.9	0.0	0.6
Oceania	0.5	0.1	0.3	0.1	0.1	1.6	0.1	0.4	0.1	0.2
Brazil/Brésil	24.4	26.1	26.5	23.3	24.0	23.6	26.1	27.5	24.4	22.4
Argentina/Argentine	13.7	15.2	15.4	15.5	17.5	17.2	18.5	22.5	21.2	20.8
USA/Etats–Unis d'Amer	8.0	7.9	12.1	9.9	9.9	9.3	9.0	9.7	9.9	12.2
Italy/Italie	2.2	2.5	2.8	3.5	2.9	3.4	10.1	5.1	5.2	5.2
Germany/Allemagne	8.1	6.4	6.2	6.5	4.9	4.5	3.4	3.5	3.6	3.0
Japan/Japon	3.2	3.0	2.9	3.2	3.8	5.0	5.4	2.9	2.6	2.2
France,Monac	3.4	4.4	3.1	2.9	3.3	3.0	3.1	2.9	3.5	3.5
Spain/Espagne	2.0	2.1	1.7	1.7	1.9	1.6	2.2	3.1	3.7	3.1
Korea, Republic of	0.5	0.7	0.8	0.9	1.2	6.1	1.9	1.9	1.7	1.9
Chile/Chili	1.5	1.9	1.7	1.4	1.7	1.7	1.6	1.7	1.7	1.7

	1987	1988	1989	1990	1991	1992	1993	1994	1995	1996
Afrique	1.7	2.2	1.2	1.6	0.6	0.4	0.3	0.2	0.7	0.8
Amériques	46.4	40.1	50.1	51.2	52.5	53.4	61.1	61.7	57.0	66.9
Amérique du Nord	15.7	12.0	12.0	10.9	11.1	11.5	9.8	7.6	6.6	6.7
ALAI	30.3	27.1	36.9	39.2	40.3	41.5	50.6	53.5	50.0	59.9
MCAC	0.0	0.0	0.1	0.1	0.1	0.1	0.1	0.1	0.3	0.1
Caraïbes	0.4	0.9	1.1	1.0	1.0	0.3	0.5	0.5	0.1	0.1
Autre Amérique	0.1	0.0	0.0	0.0	0.0	0.0	0.0	0.0	0.0	0.1
Asie l'URSS exclus	13.8	21.0	16.1	13.2	15.6	15.7	14.8	14.8	25.5	13.1
Europe l'URSS exclus	33.4	30.5	27.4	27.3	26.9	28.6	22.4	21.6	15.4	17.8
UE	29.5	26.9	24.2	25.1	25.4	26.7	21.5	20.9	14.6	17.0
AELE	1.4	0.8	0.5	0.4	0.5	0.4	0.4	0.6	0.5	0.5
Europe de l'Est	2.4	2.7	2.5	1.6	0.9	1.4	0.5	0.2	0.3	0.3
Autre de l'Europe	0.1	0.1	0.2	0.2	0.1	0.0	0.0	0.0	0.0	0.0
Ancienne URSS	3.4	5.7	4.1	5.2	3.2	0.2	0.2	0.6	0.4	0.6
Océanie	0.8	0.3	0.1	0.1	0.3	0.2	0.1	0.1	0.2	0.2
Brazil/Brésil	17.3	16.4	27.6	29.6	24.4	17.5	22.8	25.8	31.3	37.9
Argentina/Argentine	9.5	7.3	4.9	4.8	10.4	15.4	17.4	19.7	12.2	11.2
USA/Etats–Unis d'Amer	14.9	11.2	11.1	9.4	10.1	10.7	9.1	6.8	5.9	6.0
Germany/Allemagne	10.2	8.3	7.7	7.7	8.7	8.1	6.5	6.3	4.0	3.9
China/Chine	3.8	9.8	4.7	3.9	6.4	5.6	5.5	6.0	5.9	4.8
Italy/Italie	5.0	3.8	3.5	4.4	3.9	4.6	3.1	3.2	2.6	3.1
United Kingdom	4.6	4.0	4.0	4.1	3.8	4.1	4.0	3.8	2.7	2.3
Chile/Chili	0.7	0.8	1.0	1.0	1.4	3.1	3.3	2.2	1.4	4.8
Singapore/Singapour	0.2	0.2	0.4	0.3	0.3	0.4	0.2	0.2	12.4	0.1
Hong Kong	1.4	1.5	1.5	1.0	1.9	2.9	2.6	1.8	2.1	3.6

4. Special Imports C.I.F. by Commodities according to the S.I.T.C. (Rev. 2) in thousand U.S. Dollars
Importations Spéciales C.A.F. par Produits d'après la C.T.C.I. (Rév. 2) en milliers de Dollars E.U.

SITC CTCI	COMMODITY	1993		1994		1995		1996		PRODUIT
		WEIGHT POIDS	VALUE VALEUR	WEIGHT POIDS	VALUE VALEUR	WEIGHT POIDS	VALUE VALEUR	WEIGHT POIDS	VALUE VALEUR	
	ALL COMMODITIES		2332868		2707189		2865745		3322393	TOUS PRODUITS
0	FOOD AND LIVE ANIMALS		147253		238951		246906		292991	ALIMENTS,ANIMAUX VIVANTS
01	MEAT AND PREPARATIONS		5257		8736		8195		10662	VIANDES ET PREPARATIONS
04	CEREALS AND PREPARATIONS		26514		53754		32716		49425	CEREALES ET PRODUITS
041	WHEAT ETC UNMILLED	W 55749	9623	W 66819	9991	W 477	145	W 37714	8369	FROMENT,EPEAUTRE
0411	DURUM WHEAT UNMILLED	W 46777	6878	W 62292	9265	W 340	97	W 494	287	FROMENT DUR NON MOULU
044	MAIZE UNMILLED	W 46618	7657	W 139446	18726	W 66441	11848	W 54097	12225	MAIS NON MOULU
048	CEREAL ETC PREPARATIONS	W 4499	6997	W 6853	11106	W 15913	14435	W 14412	18773	PREPTNS A BASE CEREALES
0484	BAKERY PRODUCTS	W 2313	3868	W 3318	5699	W 8642	8754	W 8297	11480	PRODUITS DE BOULANGERIE
05	VEGETABLES AND FRUIT		36541		51256		51750		54450	LEGUMES ET FRUITS
054	VEG ETC FRSH,SMPLY PRSVD	W 66745	16270	W 61710	16834	W 28098	14754	W 46514	16178	LEGUMES FRAIS,CONG,SECS
0541	POTATOES FRSH EXCL SWEET	W 43569	8239	W 33094	5388	W 8027	3406	W 16946	4303	POMMES DE TERRE
057	FRUIT,NUTS,FRESH,DRIED	W 55442	12067	W 60284	19519		20268	W 56033	23295	FRUITS FRAIS OU SECS
0573	BANANA,PLANTAIN,FRSH,DRY	W 48701	7123	W 47760	11552	W 35470	13989	W 47285	16054	BANANES FRAICHES,SECHEES
058	FRUIT PRESERVED,PREPARED	W 4380	4384	W 9959	8411	W 11075	10242	W 8835	7971	CONSERVES DE FRUITS
06	SUGAR AND PREPS,HONEY		20925		34520		35658		40910	SUCRES ET PRODUITS
061	SUGAR AND HONEY	W 67749	17528	W 88712	28306	W 88456	29041	W 107816	33397	SUCRES ET MIEL
0611	RAW BEET AND CANE SUGAR	W 54689	14282	W 75222	26261	W 81845	27743	W 93724	29697	SUCRES BRUTS
07	COFFEE,TEA,COCOA,SPICES		34168		46259		55448		56769	CAFE,THE,CACAO,EPICES
073	CHOCOLATE AND PRODUCTS	W 1178	3516	W 2276	7710	W 3672	9022	W 3687	11053	CHOCOLAT
074	TEA AND MATE		26180	W 23657	29956	W 24515	35468	W 25986	35892	THE ET MATE
0742	MATE	W 19542	24957	W 22995	28416	W 23747	33836	W 25304	34286	MATE
081	*FEEDING STUFF FOR ANIML		5494	W 39180	9058	W 24397	7544	W 55125	15013	NOURRITURE POUR ANIMAUX
09	MISC EDIBLE PRODUCTS		11023		26831		45759		53891	PREP ALIMENTAIRES DIVERSES
098	EDIBLE PRODCTS,PREPS NES	W 4433	10201	W 6960	25289		43269	W 14293	50923	PREP ALIMENTAIRES NDA
09809	MISC FOOD PREPRTIONS NES	W 2608	7376	W 4097	21242	W 33944	38327	W 9148	44138	PREP ALIMENTAIRES NDA
1	BEVERAGES AND TOBACCO		27537		33848		28926		42561	BOISSONS ET TABACS
11	BEVERAGES		18042		24574		23600		26024	BOISSONS
112	ALCOHOLIC BEVERAGES	W 8279	16040	W 10933	17949		18213	W 17360	21673	BOISSONS ALCOOLIQUES
1124	DISTILLED ALCOHOLIC BEVS	W 2142	10363	W 2320	10655	W 1850	9708	W 4290	12675	ALCOOLS,EAUX–DE–VIE
11241	WHISKY	W 1911	9886	W 2042	10017	W 1678	8047	W 3931	12033	WHISKY
12	TOBACCO AND MANUFACTURES		9494		9274		5326		16537	TABACS BRUTS FABRIQUES
121	TOBACCO UNMNFCTRD,REFUSE	W 4348	9236	W 4233	9035	W 1855	4778	W 5836	15783	TABACS BRUTS,DECHETS
1211	TOBACCO,NOT STRIPPED	W 3481	6907	W 3714	7555	W 1684	4256	W 5157	14055	TABACS NON ECOTES
2	CRUDE MATERLS,EXCL FUELS		65877		94364		126496		125019	MAT BRUTES NON COMESTIBLES
23	RUBBER, CRUDE		12666		17511		24530		23089	CAOUTCHOUC BRUT
233	RUBBER,SYNTHTIC,RECLAIMD		9574	W 10554	13894		19811	W 13043	19096	LATEX CAOUTCH SYNTH REGEN
2331	SYNTHETIC RUBBER ETC	W 8187	9562	W 10519	13882		19807	W 13023	19081	LATEX CAOUTCH SYNTHETIQUE
23312	OTH SYNTHTC RUBBER LATEX	W 1131	1277	W 1941	2226		8973	W 6817	9708	AUTRES LATEX CAOUT SYNTH
24	CORK AND WOOD		11445		9716		9870		11709	LIEGE ET BOIS
248	WOOD SHAPED,SLEEPERS	W 26568	11075	W 28661	9445		9559	W 25761	11258	BOIS SIMPLEMENT TRAVAILLES
26	TEXTILE FIBRES AND WASTE		18008		37198		57744		47218	FIBRES TEXTILES
263	COTTON	W 5394	6559	W 7876	11264	W 4906	8906	W 4928	8145	COTON
2631	RAW COTTON,EXCL LINTERS	W 4733	6148	W 6746	10549	W 4508	8432	W 4323	7670	COTON EN MASSE
268	WOOL(EXC TOPS),ANML HAIR	W 3221	4596	W 9957	18911	W 16731	42803	W 14841	30866	LAINES ET POILS
2681	WOOL GREASY,FLEECE–WSHED	W 3195	4355	W 9895	18660	W 16457	41989	W 14813	30590	LAINE EN SUINT
27	CRUDE FERTLZR,MINRLS NES		8738		10731		8013		12070	ENGRAIS MINERAUX BRUTS
29	CRUDE ANIMAL,VEG MAT NES		6245		7063		8409		10658	MATIERES BRUTES ANIM,VEGET
3	MINERAL FUELS ETC		202476		226088		291228		362351	COMBUSTIBLES MINERAUX LUB
33	PETROLEUM AND PRODUCTS		190929		210788		280548		346792	PETROLE ET DERIVES
333	CRUDE PETROLEUM	W 253325	28892				177269	W 1505118	225214	HUILES BRUTES DE PETROLE
334	PETROLEUM PRODUCTS,REFIN	W 612896	157324	W 747314	204486	W 539687	101342	W 541457	118195	PRODUITS RAFFINES
3341	GASOLINE,OTH LIGHT OILS	W 206949	35766	W 300143	52105			W 389020	81966	ESSENCES POUR MOTEURS
33411	MOTOR,AVIATION SPIRIT	W 201179	34817	W 280038	49217			W 3326	1439	ESSENCES MOTEURS D'AVIONS
33412	SPIRIT TYPE JET FUEL							W 103822	24416	CARBUREACTEURS
33419	OTH LIGHT PETROLEUM OILS	W 5770	950	W 20105	2888			W 281872	56111	AUTRES HUILES LEGERES
3342	KEROSENE,OTH MEDIUM OILS	W 50601	9714	W 75643	13127					PETR LAMPANTS,AUT HUIL
33421	KEROSENE INCL JET FUEL	W 50542	9656	W 75638	13119					PETROLES LAMPANTS
3343	GAS OILS	W 273305	83297	W 281714	104391					GAS OILS
3344	FUEL OILS,NES	W 63582	13393	W 73913	18316			W 143663	28562	FUEL OILS
3345	LUBS,PETROLEUM OILS NES	W 18458	15154	W 15901	16547	W 1313	3027	W 8774	7667	HUILES LUBRIFIANTES
33451	LUBS(HIGH PETR CONT) ETC	W 17301	12511	W 14326	12840			W 7039	4119	HUILES LUBRIF,H LOURDES
341	*GAS,NATURAL AND MANUFCT	W 55759	11493		15230		10435	W 55595	15322	GAZ NATUREL,GAZ MANUFACT
3413	PETROLM GASES,LIQUEFIED	W 55759	11489	W 78909	15230	W 44020	10432	W 55513	15271	GAZ DE PETROLE LIQUEFIE
34139	OTH HYDROCARBON GAS LQFD	W 55547	11400	W 53278	9646	W 44020	10432	W 55513	15271	HYDROCARBURES GAZEUX NDA
4	ANIMAL,VEGETABLE OIL,FAT		13350		19144		17992		19353	HUILES,GRAISSES ANIM,VEG
42	FIXED VEGETABLE OIL,FAT		10422		15971		13755		13530	HUILES VEGETALES FIXES
423	FIXED VEG OILS,SOFT	W 13966	7927	W 16094	12761		10307	W 11186	10040	HUILES VEGET DOUCES FIXES
4236	SUNFLOWER SEED OIL	W 10933	6186	W 15011	11489	W 9648	9121	W 10739	8758	HUILE DE TOURNESOL
5	CHEMCLS,RELATED PROD NES		317952		395227		425926		543828	PRODUITS CHIMIQUES
51	ORGANIC CHEMICALS		55318		61477		72982		67991	PROD CHIMIQ ORGANIQUES
512	ALCOHOLS,PHENOLS ETC	W 15453	7869	W 11775	7630		7594	W 10820	8489	PHENOLS,PHENOLS–ALCOOLS
513	CARBOXYLIC ACIDS ETC	W 12117	10550	W 12983	12116	W 11442	17775	W 12712	14448	ACIDES CARBOXYLIQUES
5137	MONOACIDS AND DERIVATIVS	W 7418	6152	W 8405	7367	W 6669	9913	W 8309	9470	ACIDES MONOCARBOXYLIQUES
514	NITROGEN–FNCTN COMPOUNDS	W 1607	15827	W 2667	17855		19637	W 1864	17672	COMPOSES FONCT AZOTEES
5148	OTH NITROGN–FNCTN CMPNDS	W 1023	11724	W 1275	13249	W 1179	14907	W 1121	12373	AUTRES COMPOSES AZOTES
51482	IMIDE–,IMIDE–FNCT CMPNDS	W 118	7021	W 108	8027	W 103	9996	W 131	7687	COMPOSES A FONCTION IMIDE
515	ORG–INORG COMPOUNDS ETC	W 832	12212		12680	W 826	13478	W 886	15137	COMPOSES ORGANO–MINERAUX
5156	HETEROCYCLIC CMPDS ETC	W 420	8100		8937	W 335	9470	W 299	10681	COMPOSES HETEROCYCLIQUES
51569	OTH HETEROCYC CMPDS,ETC	W 415	7908		8500	W 332	9317	W 295	10444	AUT COMP HETEROCYCLIQUES
52	INORGANIC CHEMICALS		17581		19714		20187		21101	PROD CHIM INORGANIQUES
523	OTHR INORG CHEMICALS ETC	W 34258	12795	W 42008	15076		14914	W 29893	15137	AUT PRODUITS CHIMIQUES INORG
53	DYES,TANNING,COLOUR PROD		27802		33507		30637		32525	PROD TEINTURE,COLORANTS
531	SYNT DYE,NAT INDGO,LAKES	W 914	12595	W 1139	14367	W 933	11922	W 1343	12817	MAT COLOR ORGAN,LAQUES
5311	SYNTHIC ORGNIC DYESTUFFS	W 786	11187	W 1030	13553	W 798	11163	W 1053	11905	MAT COLOR ORGAN SYNTHET
533	PIGMENTS,PAINTS,ETC	W 4408	11608	W 6105	15366		16407	W 6331	16505	PIGMENTS,PEINTURES,VERNIS
541	*MEDICINAL,PHARM PRODUCT		53053		64525		81096		97414	PROD MEDICINAUX PHARMACEUT
5413	ANTIBIOTICS IN BULK	K 56522	6914	K 40048	6072	K 86957	10952	K 112743	13912	ANTIBIOTIQUES NDA
5417	MEDICAMENTS	K 1369139	36283	K 1912181	45391		55109	K 2721582	63855	MEDICAMENTS
54171	— CONTAINNG ANTIBIOTICS	K 98538	6426	K 105021	6703		8913	K 222536	9818	MED CONTN ANTIBIOTIQUES
54179	— CONTNG OTH SUBSTANCES	K 1175823	23309	K 1593970	30720	K 4699858	35945	K 2326128	43328	MED CONT AUT SUBSTANCES
55	PERFUME,CLEANING ETC PRD		26260		36544		44801		58698	PROD POUR PARFUM,TOILETTE
551	ESSENTL OILS,PERFUME,ETC	W 300	5685	W 332	7011	W 333	8673	W 401	9000	HUILES ESSENTIELLES
553	PERFUMERY,COSMETICS,ETC	W 2936	11987	W 3844	17146		21741	W 7613	27710	PRODUITS DE PARFUMERIE
554	SOAP,CLEANSING ETC PREPS	W 5273	8588	W 7770	12387	W 9588	14387	W 19241	21989	SAVONS,PRODUITS DETERSIFS
5542	WASHING PREPARATIONS ETC	W 3853	6254	W 5613	8891	W 5442	9698	W 14154	15341	PROD ORG TENSIO–ACT NDA
562	*FERTILIZERS,MANUFACTURE	W 176292	24877	W 195351	38012		19906	W 362889	80739	ENGRAIS MANUFACTURES
5621	CHEM NITROGENOUS FERTLZR	W 44275	6116	W 68508	10861		8822	W 85117	17914	ENGRAIS AZOTES
56216	UREA	W 42444	5878	W 66655	10517	W 37896	8332	W 82581	17243	UREE
5629	FERTILIZERS NES	W 102583	15024	W 100234	23123	W 32389	7737	W 214661	51469	ENGRAIS NDA
56292	NITROG–PHOS FERTILZR NES	W 62919	8966	W 60785	15249	W 20929	4841	W 204210	48764	ENGRAIS NDA CONT N P

4. Special Imports C.I.F. by Commodities according to the S.I.T.C. (Rev. 2) in thousand U.S. Dollars
Importations Spéciales C.A.F. par Produits d'après la C.T.C.I. (Rév. 2) en milliers de Dollars E.U.

SITC CTCI	COMMODITY	1993 WEIGHT POIDS	1993 VALUE VALEUR	1994 WEIGHT POIDS	1994 VALUE VALEUR	1995 WEIGHT POIDS	1995 VALUE VALEUR	1996 WEIGHT POIDS	1996 VALUE VALEUR	PRODUIT
58	PLASTIC MATERIALS ETC		70212		82300		98579		105605	MAT PLAST ARTIFICIELLES
582	PROD OF CONDENSATION ETC	W 8500	13484	W 8562	14067		20117	W 9900	17454	PROD CONDENS,POLYCOND
5823	ALKYDS,OTHER POLYESTERS	W 5479	6643	W 5105	6742		13445	W 7084	10156	ALKYDES ET AUT POLYESTERS
58231	— IN PRIMARY FORMS	W 5403	5940	W 4997	5919	W 5590	12059	W 6899	8850	SOUS FORMES PRIMAIRES
583	POLYMERIZATION ETC PRODS	W 51388	50863	W 67238	62819		72397	W 72292	80520	PROD POLYMERISATION
5831	POLYETHYLENE	W 26144	20555	W 33297	24928	W 26574	28255	W 30404	31638	POLYETHYLENE
58311	— IN PRIMARY FORMS	W 25646	19257	W 32446	22764	W 24196	25904	W 29431	29186	POLYETHYLENE PRIMAIRES
5832	POLYPROPYLENE	W 5163	6510	W 7012	8275	W 7104	11167	W 9863	13084	POLYPROPYLENE
5834	POLYVINYL CHLORIDE	W 9716	8705	W 14256	12192		14727	W 18525	14956	CHLORURE DE POLYVINYLE
58341	— IN PRIMARY FORMS	W 9387	5937	W 13823	10909	W 13386	12840	W 17802	12797	SOUS FORMES PRIMAIRES
5839	OTH POLYMRZTION ETC PROD	W 4111	7650	W 5910	8558	W 5393	8308	W 5756	9656	AUT PROD POLYMER COPOLYM
59	CHEMICAL MATERIALS NES		42423		58810		57473		79342	MAT PROD CHIMIQUES NDA
591	PESTICIDES,DISINFECTANTS	W 4031	16542	W 5439	23282	W 4052	24553	W 8735	36239	DESINF,INSECT,FONG,HERB
5913	HERBICIDES,FOR RETAIL	W 1477	6870	W 1756	9096	W 623	11882	W 3811	18289	HERBICIDES VENTE AU DET
598	MISCEL CHEM PRODUCTS NES		20381	W 17887	29867		26717	W 16365	34404	PROD DIV INDUST CHIM NDA
5989	CHEM PRODUCTS,PREPS NES		15862	W 14671	22213		20132	W 12366	24503	PROD PREP CHIMIQUES NDA
59899	OTH CHEM PRODS,PREPS,NES	W 8146	12547	W 12107	16822	W 9950	14834	W 8813	18198	AUT PRODUITS CHIMIQUES NDA
6	BASIC MANUFACTURES		374836		428272		468402		551893	ART MANUFACTURES
61	LEATHER,DRESSED FUR,ETC		36311		30980		32555		49959	CUIRS,PELLETERIES
611	LEATHER	W 1814	25315	W 2417	28250		29706	W 5010	45291	CUIRS,PEAUX PREPARES
6114	LEATHR BOVINE NES,EQUINE	W 1471	21881	W 2046	24471		27398	W 4814	42751	CUIRS DE BOVINS
612	LEATHER ETC MANUFACTURES	W 3141	10755	W 400	2357		2478	W 597	4439	OUVRAGES EN CUIRS NDA
6123	PREPRD PARTS OF FOOTWEAR	W 3137	10679	W 395	2235		2362	W 589	4316	PARTIES DE CHAUSSURES
62	RUBBER MANUFACTURES NES		22912		26896		28904		32025	CAOUTCHOUC MANUFACTURE
625	RUBBER TYRES, TUBES ETC	W 3690	14342	W 4748	17045		18795	W 6080	20889	PNEUS CAOUTCHOUC VULCANISE
63	WOOD,CORK MANUFACTRS NES		8165		15816		14211		12921	OUVRAGES LIEGE ET BOIS
635	WOOD MANUFACTURES NES	W 6574	4633	W 14487	11438		9298	W 10532	7752	ART MANUF EN BOIS NDA
6353	BUILDERS WOODWRK,PREFABS	W 5687	3639	W 13357	10063		7793	W 8740	6045	OUVRAGES DE MENUISERIE
64	PAPER,PAPERBOARD AND MFR		48806		67579		86229		101844	PAPIERS,CARTONS & OUVRAGES
641	PAPER AND PAPERBOARD	W 44678	31916	W 56319	39541		50622	W 69520	59908	PAPIERS ET CARTONS
6411	NEWSPRINT	W 13973	8312	W 15093	8413	W 10026	6994	W 13063	10584	PAPIER JOURNAL
6415	PAPER,PAPERBRD,BULK,NES	W 8625	6478	W 11975	8077		13380	W 19762	14671	PAPIERS,CARTONS ROULEAUX
64159	OTHER PAPER ETC,BULK,NES	W 7756	5843	W 8402	6789	W 8635	9902	W 11088	10864	AUT PAPIER ROULEAUX FEUILLES
6418	COATED ETC PAPER NES BLK	W 6412	7986	W 7369	9966		14099	W 10773	17508	PAP,CARTONS COUCHES,ENDUITS
64189	COATED PAPER ETC NES	W 6134	7399	W 6305	6985		8420	W 8273	9624	PAPIERS,CARTONS COUCHES
642	PAPER,ETC,PRECUT,ARTS OF	W 8968	16890	W 17761	28038		35607	W 22395	41936	PAP,CARTONS DECOUPES
6421	PAPER ETC CONTAINERS	W 3681	4214	W 10184	9869		12314	W 10699	13745	BOITES,SACS EMBALLAGES
6428	PAPER ETC ARTICLES NES	W 2980	7962	W 4457	11985		16459	W 7947	19270	OUVRAGES EN PATE A PAPIER
64285	PAPER ETC DIAPERS ETC	W 2044	5768	W 3118	8825	W 3904	12030	W 5626	14613	SERVIETTES HYGIENIQUES
65	TEXTILE YARN,FABRICS,ETC		76260		83008		94720		102936	FILS,TISSUS,ARTICLES TEXTILE
651	TEXTILE YARN	W 6253	10941	W 2742	14269		17365	W 3505	18976	FILS TEXTILES
652	COTTON FABRICS,WOVEN	W 1667	10547	W 2074	13734		14503	W 2389	16059	TISSUS DE COTON
6522	WOVEN COTTON BLEACHD,ETC	W 1598	10218	W 1929	13106		13607	W 2259	15230	TISSUS COTON BLANCHIS ETC
65224	BLCHED COTTON FABRIC NES	W 1227	7115	W 1493	9742		9524	W 1869	11879	AUT TIS PLUS 85% COT BLANCHI
653	WOVN MAN–MADE FIB FABRIC	W 1515	13468	W 1460	14843		17927	W 1906	18478	TISSUS FIBRES SYNTH,ARTIF
654	OTH WOVEN TEXTILE FABRIC	W 1576	15247	W 2284	8200		6866	W 1545	5997	TISSUS AUT COTON SYNT,ARTIF
6543	WOVEN WOOL ETC FABRC NES	W 113	7975	W 252	3437		1837	W 197	2559	TISSUS LAINE,POILS FINS NDA
657	SPECIAL TXTL FABRC,PRODS	W 1892	10228	W 2562	10090		10893	W 2448	12237	TISSUS SPECIAUX
658	TEXTILE ARTICLES NES	W 1678	6699		11531		16052	W 4273	19176	ART FACONNES MAT TEXTILES
6584	LINENS ETC	W 484	3286	W 867	6614		8840	W 1118	9245	LINGE DE MAISON
66	NONMETAL MINERAL MFS NES		38329		55482		59077		60698	ART MIN NON METALLIQUES
661	LIME,CEMENT,BLDG PRODS	W 83350	7843	W 82988	15982		16234	W 243433	17294	CHAUX,CIMENTS MAT CONSTR
6612	CEMENT	W 75205	4433	W 68540	10272	W 137072	9837	W 226831	10563	CIMENTS HYDRAULIQUES
662	CLAY,REFRACTORY BLDG PRD	W 33337	7866	W 51738	10407		11143	W 55748	11831	MAT CONST REFRACTAIRES
6624	BRICKS ETC NONREFRACTORY	W 31031	6230	W 50274	9450		10262	W 54204	10774	BRIQUES ETC CERAM NON REFR
664	GLASS	W 8651	8321	W 12521	12021		11951	W 14241	12032	VERRE
665	GLASSWARE	W 6051	7196	W 12530	9806		12029	W 18322	11178	OUVRAGES EN VERRE
67	IRON AND STEEL		58162		63613		68682		89862	FER ET ACIER
673	IRON,STEEL SHAPES ETC	W 36354	12345	W 48418	17973		15143	W 31111	12772	BARRES,PROFIL FER,ACIER
674	IRN,STL UNIV,PLATE,SHEET	W 59785	31461	W 63182	34479		38997	W 62621	39728	LARGES PLATS,TOLES
6746	IRN,STL THIN PLATE,ROLLD	W 31024	15802	W 32341	16505	W 28618	20309	W 32512	20860	TOLES LAM MOINS 3MM
67461	— OF IRON OR SIMPLE STL	W 29357	12406	W 30975	13689	W 25761	13459	W 27540	13269	TOL NON AC FIN MOINS 3 MM
678	IRON,STL TUBES,PIPES,ETC	W 4086	6878	W 3807	5210		6798	W 22127	29202	TUBES,TUYAUX EN FONTE,FER
6781	CAST IRON TUBES,PIPES	W 302	993	W 446	310		2514	W 16323	20545	TUBES,TUYAUX EN FONTE
68	NON–FERROUS METALS		18011		20927		25040		25559	METAUX NON FERREUX
682	COPPER EXC CEMENT COPPER	W 2808	7594	W 3225	9368		10525	W 3227	10660	CUIVRE
6822	COPPER,ALLOYS WORKED	W 2798	7553	W 3219	9338		10404	W 3205	10617	CUIVRE,ALLIAGES OUVRES
684	ALUMINIUM	W 3882	7913	W 4252	9018		11970	W 5229	12110	ALUMINIUM
69	METAL MANUFACTURES NES		67880		63971		58984		76088	ART MANUFACT EN METAL NDA
695	TOOLS	W 1085	8638	W 1609	9796		9188	W 1766	8884	OUTILS A MAIN
697	BASE MTL HOUSEHOLD EQUIP	W 2530	27846	W 3401	13254		11653	W 3594	14153	ART MENAGE MET COMMUNS
6973	DMSTC HEATG,COOKG APPARA	W 1397	21183	W 2094	7556		7008	W 2272	8261	APPS CHAUF NON ELECTRIQ
69731	IRN,STL DOM COOKG APPARA	W 1084	9942	W 1540	4640		4071	W 1717	5711	APPS CUISSON FER,ACIER
69732	IRN,STL DOM HEATG APPARA	W 305	11137	W 520	2604		2802	W 534	2385	POELES,RECHAUDS NON ELECTRS
699	BASE METAL MFRS NES	W 2392	12128	W 2969	15451		14596	W 4208	19523	ART MANUFACTURES MET NDA
7	MACHINES,TRANSPORT EQUIP		956099		1002500		987976		1075344	MACHINES MATERIEL TRANSPORT
71	POWER GENERATING EQUIPMT		22431		17785		23211		23763	MACHINES GENERATRICES
713	INTRNL COMBUS PSTN ENGIN	W 1125	9072	W 1389	7882		8616	W 2026	9619	MOTEURS EXPL COMB INT, PIECE
72	MACHS FOR SPCL INDUSTRYS		126377		102767		131115		172262	MAC SPECIALES POUR INDUST
721	AGRIC MACHY,EXC TRACTORS	W 4505	16117	W 5175	19340		26050	W 10086	41704	MACHINES AGRICOLES
7211	CULTIVATING MACHINERY	W 2601	4511	W 2941	6354		9468	W 5972	15653	MACH PREPARATION DU SOL
7212	HARVESTING ETC MACHINES	W 1420	8325	W 1996	10972		12787	W 3763	21249	ENGINS POUR LA RECOLTE
722	TRACTORS NON–ROAD	W 2900	13019	W 3863	16236		20797	W 6903	33887	TRACTEURS
7224	WHEELED TRACTORS NES	W 2849	12887	W 3847	16173		20765	W 6848	33672	TRACTEURS A ROUES
723	CIVIL ENGNEERG EQUIP ETC	W 4496	17685	W 3181	8914		8155	W 3186	12728	APPAREILS DE GENIE CIVIL
7234	CONST,MINING MACHNRY NES	W 3417	14766	W 3008	7985		7063	W 2850	11258	MACH POUR LA CONST, MINES
72342	SLFPRP SHOVELS,EXCAVATRS	W 2017	7743	W 2241	5282		3832	W 1773	6038	PELLES MECANIQUES
724	TEXTILE,LEATHER MACHNRY	W 2042	40308		15415		18763	W 1134	18145	MACH POUR INDUSTRIE TEXTILE
7244	SPINNING,EXTRDNG,ETC MCH	W 557	19294		3491		6442	W 260	6111	MACH POUR LE FILAGE
72442	FIBRE PROCESSNG MACH NES	W 342	13975		487		1868	W 87	2388	MACH PREP MAT TEXTILES
7245	WEAVING,FELT MFG,ETC MCH	W 390	11277	W 162	3244		3394	W 138	1918	METIERS A TISSER,PIECES
725	PAPER ETC MILL MACHINERY	W 179	1682	W 300	4810		12250	W 846	10351	MACHINES FABR PATE PAPIER
726	PRINTG,BKBINDG MACHY,PTS	W 264	4697	W 336	6901		8909	W 473	7451	MACHINES POUR IMPRIMERIE
727	FOOD MACHRY NON–DOMESTIC	W 1718	14475	W 517	7811		8291	W 1009	12694	MACH INDUSTRIES ALIMENT
7272	OTH FOOD PROC MCHY,PARTS	W 1669	13965	W 495	7339		6299	W 750	11171	AUT MACH IND ALIMENTAIRE
72722	INDUS FOOD PROC MACH NES	W 1601	12819	W 480	6915		5729	W 714	10702	MACHINES BOULANGERIE
728	OTH MACHY FOR SPCL INDUS	W 2151	18395	W 3060	23340		27900	W 5980	35303	AUT MACH IND PARTICULIERES
7284	MACHY FOR SPCL INDUS NES	W 1340	13508	W 2214	19017		19313	W 4381	26786	MACH SPEC IND PARTICUL.
72848	OTH MCHY WITH INDIV FNCT	W 927	9084	W 1408	8984		12240	W 3441	17221	AUTRES MACHINES NDA
73	METALWORKING MACHINERY		8238		6033		5322		7741	MACH TRAVAIL DES METAUX
74	GENRL INDUSTRL MACHY NES		118324		110735		129741		152375	MACH APP INDUSTRIE

4. Special Imports C.I.F. by Commodities according to the S.I.T.C. (Rev. 2) in thousand U.S. Dollars
Importations Spéciales C.A.F. par Produits d'après la C.T.C.I. (Rév. 2) en milliers de Dollars E.U.

SITC CTCI	COMMODITY	1993		1994		1995		1996		PRODUIT
		WEIGHT POIDS	VALUE VALEUR	WEIGHT POIDS	VALUE VALEUR	WEIGHT POIDS	VALUE VALEUR	WEIGHT POIDS	VALUE VALEUR	
741	HEATING,COOLING EQUIPMNT		28469	W 3957	29874		43386	W 7674	51888	MACH CHAUFFAGE,PIECES
7413	INDUS FURNACES ETC,PARTS	W 536	4652	W 430	3133		9642	W 1732	7134	FOURS IND,LABOR,PIECES
74132	INDUST FURNACES NONELECT	W 456	3868	W 216	1508		8884	W 1669	6479	FOURS NON ELECTRIQUES
7414	NONDOM REFRIG EQUIPT,PTS	W 1248	9016	W 2045	13204		16738	W 3168	19411	MAT PRODUCTION DU FROID
74141	REFRIG EQUIP NONDOMESTIC	W 1127	8099	W 1728	11682		15594	W 2705	17364	REFIG INDUSTRIELS
7416	HEATING,COOLING EQU NES	W 775	8447	W 765	5801		8312	W 1748	14842	APP CHANGEMENT TEMP
742	PUMPS FOR LIQUIDS ETC	W 682	9610	W 558	7492		9902	W 909	10561	POMPES MOTO-POMPES
743	PUMPS NES,CENTRFUGES ETC	W 1743	20289	W 1816	14153		13457	W 2155	16235	POMPES COMPRES,VENT ETC
7431	PUMPS FOR GASES ETC	W 856	10369	W 725	4806		4545	W 792	5077	POMPES AIR A VIDE,COMPRES
744	MECHANICAL HANDLING EQU	W 3187	13799	W 4715	12026		12028	W 4356	19403	EQUIP MANUTENTION PIECES
745	NONELEC MACHY,TOOLS NES	W 1104	23454	W 2273	22176		27936	W 2068	27537	AUT MACH NON ELEC,PIECES
7452	OTH NONELEC MCHS,PTS NES	W 1023	21576	W 1384	19949		24421	W 1863	23682	AUT MACH NON ELEC,PIECES
74522	PACKAGNG,BOTTLNG,ETC MCH	W 369	10322	W 313	10051		14763	W 365	12274	MACH NETT BOUTEILLES,ETC
74527	SPRAYING MACHINERY	W 452	7902	W 681	4912		4573	W 1221	7353	APP PROJETER ETC LIQUID
749	NONELEC MACH PTS,ACC NES	W 2737	22703	W 1806	25014		23032	W 2895	26750	PIECES MACH NON ELEC NDA
7492	COCKS,VALVES ETC NES	W 826	10412	W 637	9398	W 4307	9555	W 1249	12433	ART ROB,SIM POUR TUYAUX
75	OFFICE MACHNES,ADP EQUIP		42119		43804		59723		75203	MACH BUREAU TRAIT AUTOM
751	OFFICE MACHINES	W 337	8215	W 346	7929		7171	W 412	9797	MACH,APPAREILS DE BUREAU
752	AUTOMTIC DATA PROC EQUIP	W 511	26712	W 558	29271		43031	W 1420	52515	MACH TRAIT INFORMATION
7523	DIGITL CENTRL PROCESSORS	W 240	12075	W 255	12950		16133	W 353	16757	UNITES CENTRALES
7525	ADP PERIPHERAL UNITS	W 168	6571	W 216	8747	W 166	12879	W 731	19179	UNITES PERIPHERIQUES
759	OFFICE,ADP MCH PTS,ACCES	W 107	7192	W 129	6604		9521	W 400	12891	PIECES DU 751 ET 752
7599	ACCTG,ETC,ADP MCH PTS,AC	W 87	6023	W 103	5474		7702	W 340	10852	PIECES DU 751 ET 752
76	TELECOMM,SOUND EQUIPMENT		83328		136013		114267		150847	EQUIPMENT DE TELECOM
761	TELEVISION RECEIVERS	W 2553	34349	W 2791	35157		27476	W 2339	25280	RECEPTEURS DE TELEVISION
7611	COLOUR TV RECEIVERS	W 2371	29015	W 2617	32767		26636	W 2256	24526	RECEPTEURS COULEUR
762	RADIO BROADCAST RECEIVRS	W 895	13691	W 1375	19444		16415	W 1040	13320	RECEPTEURS RADIODIFFUSION
7628	OTHER RADIO RECEIVERS	W 560	8737	W 899	12723		9540	W 519	6986	AUTRES RECEPT RADIO
763	SOUND RECORDRS,PHONOGRPH	W 365	12593		10883		7623	W 173	5186	PHONO,APP ENREGISTREMENT
7638	OTHR SOUND APPARATUS ETC	W 340	12370		10694		7580	W 168	5158	AUT APP D'ENREGIS,REPROD
76381	TV IMAGE,SND RECRDRS ETC	W 281	10905	W 237	9039		6015	W 115	3659	APP ENREG,REPRO IMAG,SON
764	TELECOM EQPT,PTS,ACC NES	W 654	22695	W 1294	70528		62753	W 1914	107062	EQUIP TELECOM,PIECES
7641	LINE TELEPHONE,ETC EQUIP	W 187	10049	W 280	11056		10170	W 607	31030	APP TELEPHON PAR FIL
7643	TV,RADIO TRANSMITTRS ETC	W 46	3643	W 64	9276	W 186	22512	W 379	39857	APP EMET TELE RADIO
7649	PTS NES OF EQUIPMT OF 76	W 230	5312	W 643	44627		25088	W 580	31320	PIECES DE LA DIV 76
76491	PTS NES OF APPAR OF 7641	W 164	3621	W 501	41453	W 1346	21992	W 294	22617	PIECES POUR 764.1
77	ELECTRIC MACHNRY NES ETC		173721		184065		158767		154880	MACH APP ELECT NDA
771	ELECTRIC POWER MACHY NES	W 406	5282	W 1168	9012		15430	W 1612	10428	MACH PROD,TRANS ELECTR
7711	TRANSFORMERS,ELECTRICAL	W 237	3700	W 691	4395		10766	W 824	4672	TRANSFO ELECTRIQUES
77111	LIQUID DIELEC TRANSFRMRS	W 162	2555	W 434	1737	W 700	9505	W 668	3082	TRANSFO DIELEC LIQUIDE
772	SWITCHGEAR ETC,PARTS NES	W 1140	21968	W 1771	33792		25222	W 1941	27935	APP COUPURE,SECT ETC
7721	SWITCHGEAR ETC	W 1128	21423	W 1760	33041		23968	W 1843	26428	APP COUPURE,SECTIONMNT
773	ELECTR DISTRIBUTNG EQUIP	W 2462	16923	W 6942	26611		12812	W 3647	12668	EQUIPMT DISTRIBUTION ELECT
7731	INSULATED WIRE,CABLE ETC	W 1927	15666	W 6504	25345	W 4250	12359	W 3259	11895	FILS,CABLES ISOLES ELECT
775	HOUSEHOLD TYPE EQUIP NES	W 12259	87435	W 13554	60647		55114	W 13131	57070	MACH,APP USAGE DOMESTQUE
7751	HOUSEHOLD LDRY EQUIP NES	W 3616	17769	W 4933	14277		12177	W 4085	12091	MACH A LAVER ET SECHOIRS
77511	DOMESTIC WASHING MACHNES	W 3535	17356	W 4831	13722		11691	W 4012	11740	MACH LAVER LINGE MOINS 6 KG
7752	DOM REFRIGERATRS,FREEZRS	W 3557	17132	W 4444	21069		17692	W 4531	19580	REFRIG,CONGEL MENAGER
77521	DOMESTIC REFRIGERATORS	W 2554	13062	W 3338	16075		13404	W 3452	15207	REFRIGERATEURS
7757	DOMESTIC ELECTRC EQU NES	W 2191	11287	W 2247	11317		10882	W 2239	10065	APP ELECTR DOMEST NDA
7758	ELECTRO-THERMIC APPL NES	W 2747	39922	W 1822	12758		12829	W 2137	13927	APP ELECTROTHERMIQ NDA
77586	ELECTROTHERM DOM APP NES	W 2340	35131	W 1042	8254		8242	W 1496	10098	APP ELECTRO THERMIQUES
778	ELECTRICAL MACHINERY NES		33945	W 6822	46048		40342	W 6975	41682	AUTRES MACH ELECT NDA
7781	BATTERIES,ACCUMULATORS	W 2311	7639	W 3203	9067		10715	W 3965	11428	PILES ET ACCUMULATEURS
7783	AUTOMOTIVE ELECTR EQUIP	W 771	8329	W 1403	14041		7958	W 1016	9399	EQUIP ELECT MOTEURS EXPL
77831	IGNITION,STARTING EQUIP	W 522	5158	W 1035	10299		4781	W 562	5614	APP ELEC ALLUM,DEMARRAGE
7788	OTH ELEC MACHY,EQUIP NES		10505	W 417	10863		10841	W 493	8699	AUT MACH APP ELEC NDA
77886	OTH ELEC MACHINERY NES	W 56	7294	W 164	6236		5051	W 142	4708	AUT MACH APP ELECTRIQUES
78	ROAD VEHICLES		362900		398645		361165		333455	VEHICULES ROUTIERS
781	PASS MOTOR VEH EXC BUSES	W 32496	248078	W 35561	272562		203712	W 22546	153917	AUTO TRANSPORT PERSONNES
782	LORRIES,SPCL MTR VEH NES	W 6773	40106	W 8773	47420		76898	W 14914	95589	VEHICULES SPECIAUX,MARCH
7821	LORRIES,TRUCKS	W 6209	37233	W 8006	45215		72716	W 14311	92266	VEHICULES TRANSP MARCHAND
783	ROAD MOTOR VEHICLES NES	W 1077	9576	W 832	6310		15206	W 1703	13839	VEHICULES ROUTIERS NDA
7831	BUSES	W 805	7535	W 425	3235		5887	W 746	5617	VOITURES TRANSPORT COMMUN
7832	TRACTORS FOR TR-TRAILERS	W 272	2040	W 408	3075		9319	W 956	8222	TRACTEURS ROUTIERS
784	MOTOR VEH PRTS,ACCES NES	W 4286	31183	W 5583	37753		33225	W 5805	36925	PIECES 722,781,782,783
7849	OTHER MOTOR VEHCL PARTS	W 4268	31039	W 5532	37395		32674	W 5661	36121	PIECES 722,781,782,783
785	CYCLES,ETC MOTRZD OR NOT	W 3413	25791	W 4886	31051		27046	W 4878	26052	MOTOCYCLES SCOOTERS
7851	MOTORCYCLES ETC	W 1902	20495	W 2665	23926		20750	W 2774	20718	MOTO VELO MOTEUR AUXIL
786	TRAILERS,NONMOTR VEH,NES	W 2402	8166	W 1790	3548		5078	W 3640	7133	REMORQUES,CADRES,CONTAIN
79	OTHR TRANSPORT EQUIPMENT		18659		2654		4665		4818	AUTRE MATERIEL TRANSPORT
791	RAILWAY VEHICLES	W 1127	16377	W 31	706		128	W 15	60	VEHIC MAT CHEMINS DE FER
7912	OTH RAIL LOCOMOTIVES ETC	W 674	11960							AUTRES LOCOMOTIVES
8	MISC MANUFACTURED GOODS		226311		268048		271088		308159	ART MANUFACTURES DIVERS
821	*FURNITURE,PARTS THEREOF	W 8425	20580	W 13774	26145		24148	W 11678	25428	MEUBLES ET PIECES
8211	CHAIRS,SEATS AND PARTS	W 2042	10291	W 3136	7908		6223	W 2223	6652	SIEGES ET PIECES
82111	CHAIRS AND OTHER SEATS	W 1949	9505	W 3046	7577		5839	W 2113	6212	SIEGES
8219	FURNITURE AND PARTS NES	W 6235	8794	W 10314	15221		14197	W 8793	14871	AUTRES MEUBLES ET PIECES
82192	WOOD FURNITURE NES	W 5394	6213	W 8533	10076		9995	W 6955	9631	MEUBLES NDA EN BOIS
84	CLOTHING AND ACCESSORIES		48504		51951		45703		47473	VETEMENTS
842	MENS OUTERWEAR NOT KNIT	W 541	7121	W 929	11791		7471	W 331	5878	VET DESSUS POUR HOMMES
843	WOMENS OUTERWEAR NONKNIT	W 685	11746	W 425	8492		9018	W 377	7474	VET DESSUS FEMMES MAT TEX
8439	— OTHER OUTER GARMENTS	W 566	8865	W 225	3626		3149	W 228	3662	AUT VET DES FEM MAT TEXT
845	OUTERWEAR KNIT NONELASTC	W 327	14621	W 531	11452		11465	W 571	12573	VET DESSOUS,ACCES BONNET
8451	— JERSEYS,PULLOVERS ETC	W 127	11063	W 232	5966		6521	W 278	6977	CHANDAILS,PULL-OVERS ETC
846	UNDER GARMENTS KNITTED	W 325	6214	W 417	7883		7441	W 562	10470	SOUS VETS DE BONNETERIE
851	*FOOTWEAR		21148	W 2883	23750		24858	W 4360	32048	CHAUSSURES
85102	FOOTWEAR LEATHER	W 2320	13606	W 1740	16357		17229	W 2607	20872	CHAUS SEMELLES EN CUIR
87	PRECISION INSTRUMNTS NES		25271		31193		34684		44239	INSTRUM,APPAR SCIENT NDA
872	MEDICAL INSTRUMENTS NES	W 344	9067	W 344	10865		14587	W 472	12910	INSTR,APP MEDIC-CHIR NDA
87202	OTH MEDICAL INSTRUMENTS	W 287	7847	W 293	9629	W 1382	12994	W 396	11702	INSTRUM,APP MEDECINE
874	MEASURNG,CONTROLNG INSTR	W 446	14191	W 472	16185		16524	W 673	26163	INSTRUMENTS DE MESURE
88	PHOTO EQU,OPTICL GDS ETC		19993		22592		21684		24333	APP,FOURN PHOTO,OP,MONTR
882	PHOTO,CINEMA SUPPLIES	W 762	9538	W 834	10064		10788	W 1137	12316	PRODUITS PHOTO,CINEMA
8822	PHOTO FILM EXC DEV CINMA	W 488	7412	W 530	7799		8207	W 788	9448	PLAQUES,PELLICULES,FILMS
89	MISC MANUFCTRD GOODS NES		83775		100812		107661		120415	ART MANUFACTURES DIVERS
893	ARTICLES OF PLASTIC NES		32175		39747		47557	W 15832	54236	OUVRAGES EN MAT DIVIS 58
8931	PLSTC PACKG CONTNRS,LIDS	W 3190	12157	W 5535	17215		21543	W 8542	25373	ART TRANSP EMBALLAGE ETC
8939	MISC PLASTIC ARTICLES	W 3844	19768	W 6203	21951		25193	W 7145	28156	ART DIVERS EN MAT DIV 58
89399	OTHR PLASTC ARTICLES NES	W 3258	18173	W 5565	20218		23454	W 6126	26110	AUT OUV MAT DIV 58
894	TOYS,SPORTING GOODS,ETC	W 2490	19448	W 4161	24410		23543	W 5510	24051	VOITURES ENFANTS,JOUETS

4. Special Imports C.I.F. by Commodities according to the S.I.T.C. (Rev. 2) in thousand U.S. Dollars
Importations Spéciales C.A.F. par Produits d'après la C.T.C.I. (Rév. 2) en milliers de Dollars E.U.

SITC CTCI	COMMODITY	1993 WEIGHT POIDS	1993 VALUE VALEUR	1994 WEIGHT POIDS	1994 VALUE VALEUR	1995 WEIGHT POIDS	1995 VALUE VALEUR	1996 WEIGHT POIDS	1996 VALUE VALEUR	PRODUIT
8942	TOYS,INDOOR GAMES ETC	W 1901	12506	W 3249	18563		16166	W 4078	17362	JOUETS,JEUX ETC
89423	TOYS NES	W 993	5738	W 1959	10347		9182	W 2297	9724	JOUETS,MODELES REDUITS
898	MUSICAL INSTRUMENTS,PTS	W 504	7728	W 675	10131		10224	W 712	11164	INSTRUMENTS DE MUSIQUE
8983	SOUND RECRDNG TAPE,DISCS	W 436	6459	W 583	8855		8726	W 618	9780	SUPPORTS SON POUR 763
899	OTHER MANUFACTURED GOODS		12034		15032		13528		16223	AUT ART MANUF DIVERS NDA

5. Special Exports F.O.B. by Commodities according to the S.I.T.C. (Rev. 2) in thousand U.S. Dollars
Exportations Spéciales F.O.B. par Produits d'après la C.T.C.I. (Rév. 2) en milliers de Dollars E.U.

SITC CTCI	COMMODITY	1993 WEIGHT POIDS	1993 VALUE VALEUR	1994 WEIGHT POIDS	1994 VALUE VALEUR	1995 WEIGHT POIDS	1995 VALUE VALEUR	1996 WEIGHT POIDS	1996 VALUE VALEUR	PRODUIT
	ALL COMMODITIES		1606533		1918178		2106098		2397448	TOUS PRODUITS
0	FOOD AND LIVE ANIMALS		640439		770526		905976		1070269	ALIMENTS,ANIMAUX VIVANTS
001	*LIVE ANIMALS FOR FOOD	W 15581	13436	W 59593	46393	W 103866	95281	W 31832	33032	ANIMAUX VIVANTS
0011	BOVINE SPECIES,LIVE	W 7598	8533	W 40535	34923	W 97284	90634	W 20369	25413	ESPECE BOVINE
00119	— OTHR THAN FR BREEDING	W 7531	8385	W 40403	34651	W 96549	88613	W 20335	25331	BOVINS NON REPRODUCTEURS
0012	SHEEP AND GOATS,LIVE	W 6383	4049	W 17183	10401	W 5357	3979	W 10381	6945	ESPECES OVINE ET CAPRINE
00121	SHEEP,LIVE	W 6383	4049	W 17183	10401	W 5357	3979	W 10381	6945	ESPECE OVINE
01	MEAT AND PREPARATIONS		199541		265628		279450		356818	VIANDES ET PREPARATIONS
011	MEAT FRESH,CHILLD,FROZEN	W 76128	174565	W 111440	243273	W 102200	255657	W 157868	334054	VIANDES FRAICHES,REF,CONGE
0111	BOVINE MEAT FRESH,FROZEN	W 55359	134714	W 89414	204563	W 102200	255657	W 131769	280174	VIANDES BOVIN FRAI,REF
01111	BOVINE MEAT WITH BONE IN	W 3521	3272	W 17990	20242			W 40965	48511	VIANDES BOVIN NON DESOSS
01112	BOVINE MEAT BONELESS	W 51838	131441	W 71424	184320	W 102200	255657	W 90804	231663	VIANDES BOVIN DESOSSEES
0112	MUTTON ETC FRSH,CHLD,FRN	W 11301	19350	W 10927	18726			W 13532	30110	VIANDE DE MOUTON
0115	HORSE MEAT FRSH,CHLD,FRN	W 5224	11386	W 4560	9625			W 4568	10353	VIANDES DE CHEVAL
0116	EDIBLE OFFAL FRESH,CH,FR	W 3099	6557	W 4952	8270			W 4789	10105	ABATS COMESTIBLES
014	MEAT PREPD,PRSVD,NES ETC	W 7610	23825	W 7168	20822	W 7700	23793	W 9589	21331	CONSERVES DE VIANDES
0149	OTH PREPARD,PRESRVD MEAT	W 7487	22476	W 7027	19928	W 7439	22239	W 9392	20513	AUTRES PREP DE VIANDES
02	DAIRY PRODCTS,BIRDS'EGGS		76404		102511		103963		143696	PRODUITS LAITIERS,OEUFS
022	MILK AND CREAM	W 83000	43743	W 80412	51726	W 62721	54498	W 95307	72221	LAIT ET CREME
0223	MILK AND CREAM FRESH	W 70213	19939	W 62373	17062	W 47129	18163	W 76587	28080	LAIT,CREME FRAIS
0224	MILK,CREAM PRESERVED ETC	W 12787	23804	W 18039	34663	W 15593	36335	W 18721	44141	LAIT,CREME CONS,CONC
02242	MILK DRY,1.5% FAT OR LES	W 3576	7568	W 10643	20123	W 10888	25574	W 9539	21633	LAIT POUDRE INF 1.5%
02243	MILK DRY,OVER 1.5% FAT	W 5136	10171	W 7397	14540	W 4348	10448	W 8534	21006	LAIT POUDRE SUP 1.5%
02249	MILK(EX DRY) PRSVD,SWEET	W 4075	6064			W 104	96	W 625	1483	LAIT CONS,CONC SUCRE
023	BUTTER	W 2856	5136	W 9614	16863	W 5944	12901	W 9583	20186	BEURRE
024	CHEESE AND CURD	W 8878	27394	W 11285	33337	W 11041	35925	W 16289	50670	FROMAGE ET CAILLEBOTTE
03	FISH AND PREPARATIONS		73662		81977		94292		95616	POISSONS ET PREPARATIONS
034	FISH,FRESH,CHILLED,FROZN	W 62215	66879	W 70745	73403	W 77723	81400	W 86027	80211	POISSON FRAIS, REFRIG,CONG
0341	FISH FRSH,CHLLD,EX FILLT	W 13886	5769	W 10327	4886	W 21717	10225	W 30576	14796	POISSON FRAIS,REFRIGERE
0342	FISH FROZEN,EXCL FILLETS	W 29621	23888	W 46933	41712	W 39378	36130	W 36282	29689	POISSONS CONGELES
0344	FISH FILLETS,FROZEN	W 18705	37211	W 13484	26802	W 16625	35039	W 19170	35726	FILETS CONGELES
036	SHELL FISH FRESH,FROZEN	W 2461	2403	W 1458	2960	W 2890	5484	W 5480	8839	CRUSTACES,MOLLUSQUES
037	FISH ETC PREPD,PRSVD NES	W 1996	4063	W 2150	5498	W 2343	7262	W 2074	5973	POIS,CRUST,MOL PREPARES
04	CEREALS AND PREPARATIONS		212704		197755		252233		351413	CEREALES ET PRODUITS
041	WHEAT ETC UNMILLED					W 58820	13126	W 69883	9938	FROMENT,EPEAUTRE
0412	OTHER WHEAT ETC UNMILLED					W 58817	13122	W 69883	9938	AUTRE FROMENT NON MOULU
042	RICE	W 501983	150057	W 419729	152135	W 482919	162976	W 642521	228537	RIZ
0421	RICE IN HUSK OR HUSKED	W 171899	43350	W 99483	29320	W 133144	35357	W 223276	62757	RIZ SANS AUTRE PREPARATION
04211	RICE IN THE HUSK	W 43778	7719	W 34589	7624	W 67068	13956	W 112181	24851	RIZ PADDY
04212	RICE HUSKED	W 128120	35630	W 64893	21696	W 66076	21402	W 111095	37905	RIZ CARGO
0422	RICE SEMI–MILLED,MILLED	W 330085	106707	W 320246	122814	W 349776	127619	W 419245	165780	RIZ POLI,GLACE INCL BRISURES
04221	RICE MILLED UNBROKEN	W 307432	102863	W 285621	116619	W 298606	117242	W 363999	153365	RIZ POLI,GLACE EXCL BRISURES
04222	RICE BROKEN	W 22652	3844	W 34625	6195	W 51170	10376	W 55246	12415	BRISURES DE RIZ
043	BARLEY UNMILLED	W 89043	19763	W 3026	524	W 375	61	W 78043	18946	ORGE NON MONDEE
046	WHEAT ETC MEAL OR FLOUR	W 2258	510	W 108	25	W 7017	2229	W 19346	7270	SEMOULE FARINE,FROMENT
04601	FLOUR OF WHEAT OR MESLIN	W 2258	510	W 108	25	W 7016	2229	W 19346	7270	FARINE DE FROMENT
048	CEREAL ETC PREPARATIONS	W 104848	42229	W 125486	45025	W 158320	72736	W 165293	85871	PREPTNS A BASE CEREALES
0482	MALT INCLUDING FLOUR	W 99545	29425	W 120419	33255	W 150073	54402	W 154534	65086	MALT MEME TORREFIE
0484	BAKERY PRODUCTS	W 1718	3664	W 2000	4372	W 5421	11501	W 6275	11313	PRODUITS DE BOULANGERIE
04841	BREAD,BISCUIT,COM WAFERS	W 1630	3500	W 1754	3864	W 3891	7933	W 4838	8270	PAINS,BISCUITS DE MER
0488	OTH CEREAL PREPS,MALT EX	W 3202	8797	W 2411	6793	W 1654	5438	W 2688	7781	EXTRAITS DE MALT
05	VEGETABLES AND FRUIT		47029		60604		61884		65370	LEGUMES ET FRUITS
057	FRUIT,NUTS,FRESH,DRIED	W 121348	42705	W 146979	56227	W 128200	55447	W 137383	58481	FRUITS FRAIS OU SECS
0571	ORANGES, MANDARINS ETC	W 95428	33100	W 116211	44047	W 94507	40486	W 108406	45425	ORANGES,MAND,CLEMENTINES
05711	ORANGES,FRESH OR DRIED	W 77230	23229	W 93465	31230	W 76521	29088	W 77030	27746	ORANGES FRAICHES,SECHEES
05712	MANDARINS ETC FRESH, DRY	W 18198	9870	W 22746	12818	W 17986	11398	W 31376	17679	MANDARINES,CLEMENTINES
0572	LEMONS,GRAPEFRUIT ETC	W 21180	7604	W 28787	11362	W 30023	13089	W 21502	9086	AUTRES AGRUMES FRAIS,SECS
05721	LEMONS,LIMES,FRESH,DRIED	W 15961	5498	W 22058	8801	W 25050	10906	W 16627	7121	CITRONS ET LIMES
06	SUGAR AND PREPS,HONEY		9024		8193		10925		13899	SUCRES ET PRODUITS
061	SUGAR AND HONEY	W 12516	8261	W 13346	7547	W 14536	10604	W 13505	13078	SUCRES ET MIEL
0616	NATURAL HONEY	W 6169	5703	W 4833	3932	W 7147	7419	W 6466	10152	MIEL NATUREL
081	*FEEDING STUFF FOR ANIML	W 40432	5521	W 41972	5840	W 23145	5099	W 26362	7148	NOURRITURE POUR ANIMAUX
1	BEVERAGES AND TOBACCO		2711		6431		9655		25516	BOISSONS ET TABACS
11	BEVERAGES		2255		5555		7999		6600	BOISSONS
112	ALCOHOLIC BEVERAGES	W 6326	2215	W 10840	5536	W 16835	7578	W 26863	6574	BOISSONS ALCOOLIQUES
1123	BEER,ALE,STOUT,PORTER	W 6190	1964	W 10684	5201	W 16502	7035	W 25893	5339	BIERES
12	TOBACCO AND MANUFACTURES		457		876		1656		18916	TABACS BRUTS FABRIQUES
122	TOBACCO,MANUFACTURED	W 66	457	W 107	876	W 185	1656	W 3688	18910	TABACS FABRIQUES
1222	CIGARETTES	W 66	455	W 107	876	W 185	1656	W 3688	18910	CIGARETTES
2	CRUDE MATERLS,EXCL FUELS		103933		122187		129127		140143	MAT BRUTES NON COMESTIBLES
21	HIDES,SKINS,FURS UNDRSSD		8451		11520		6471		9993	CUIRS,PEAUX BRUTS
211	HIDES,SKINS,EXC FURS,RAW	W 5868	8160	W 6044	11226	W 2870	6287	W 4615	9378	CUIRS ET PEAUX
22	OIL SEEDS,OLEAGINOUS FRT		3589		4740		9815		11831	GRAINES,FRUITS OLEAGINEUX
222	SEEDS FOR'SOFT'FIXED OIL	W 13933	3286	W 6048	4619	W 12005	9597	W 47810	11428	GRAINES HUILES FIXES
2224	SUNFLOWER SEEDS	W 13933	3286	W 2136	3734	W 12005	9597	W 47810	11428	GRAINES DE TOURNESOL
24	CORK AND WOOD		5529		11740		30442		35358	LIEGE ET BOIS
247	OTH WOOD ROUGH,SQUARED	W 34101	3396	W 89189	7923	W 245218	24932	W 389480	27557	BOIS BRUTS EQUARRIS
2472	SAW–,VENEER–LOGS NON–CON	W 32686	3222	W 82269	6688	W 237401	23909	W 384911	26854	NON CONIFERES SCIAGE,PLAC
24721	— IN THE ROUGH	W 32686	3222	W 82269	6688	W 237401	23909	W 384911	26854	BRUTS ECORCES DEGROSSIS
248	WOOD SHAPED,SLEEPERS	W 14797	2133	W 22216	3804	W 29519	5510	W 36412	7801	BOIS SIMPLEMENT TRAVAILLES
26	TEXTILE FIBRES AND WASTE		65556		68585		55808		55571	FIBRES TEXTILES
268	WOOL(EXC TOPS),ANML HAIR	W 32502	60833	W 32550	63930	W 18028	48815	W 20919	49284	LAINES ET POILS
2681	WOOL GREASY,FLEECE–WSHED	W 17025	33447	W 16311	34275	W 7759	25779	W 8003	21046	LAINE EN SUINT
2682	WOOL DEGREASED,UNCOMBED	W 9193	19280	W 8786	20235	W 4642	14487	W 6617	18384	LAINE DEGRAISSEE
2686	WASTE OF WOOL,HAIR NES	W 5914	7806	W 7112	9080	W 5382	8198	W 6019	9566	DECHETS LAINE ET POILS
26861	— NOT PULLD OR GARNETTD	W 5761	7632	W 6993	8886	W 5311	8094	W 5930	9420	DECHETS LAINE ET POILS
29	CRUDE ANIMAL,VEG MAT NES		15203		18616		17547		20628	MATIERES BRUTES ANIM,VEGET
291	CRUDE ANIMAL MTRIALS NES	W 13225	13455	W 16496	15861	W 18050	15668	W 20808	18184	MATIERES BRUTES ANIMALES
2919	OTH ANIMAL MATERIALS NES	W 12746	13301	W 15846	15612	W 17771	15557	W 20554	18104	MAT ORIGINE ANIMALE NDA
29193	GUT,BLADDERS,ETC NONFISH	W 6600	10448	W 6632	12103	W 6291	12886	W 7961	15107	BOYAUX,VESSIES
3	MINERAL FUELS ETC		751		693		18806		27392	COMBUSTIBLES MINERAUX LUB
33	PETROLEUM AND PRODUCTS		751		693		18806		24305	PETROLE ET DERIVES
334	PETROLEUM PRODUCTS,REFIN	W 499	613	W 550	688	W 109681	18780	W 155028	24295	PRODUITS RAFFINES
3341	GASOLINE,OTH LIGHT OILS							W 45365	8007	ESSENCES POUR MOTEURS
3344	FUEL OILS,NES							W 102139	13112	FUEL OILS
4	ANIMAL,VEGETABLE OIL,FAT		5162		8447		9170		12049	HUILES,GRAISSES ANIM,VEG
411	*ANIMAL OILS AND FATS	W 12723	4289	W 19361	6967	W 19247	7624	W 24084	8995	HUILES,GRAISSES ANIMALES
4113	ANIML OIL,FAT,GREASE NES	W 12611	4238	W 19323	6957	W 19178	7598	W 24030	8971	HUILES,GRAISSES ANIMALES NDA
41132	FATS OF BOVINE,SHEEP,ETC	W 12373	3944	W 19044	6717	W 18659	7207	W 23254	8418	SUIFS BRUTS FONDUS
5	CHEMCLS,RELATED PROD NES		86365		101544		116686		129340	PRODUITS CHIMIQUES
51	ORGANIC CHEMICALS		4931		5631		5373		6256	PROD CHIMIQ ORGANIQUES

5. Special Exports F.O.B. by Commodities according to the S.I.T.C. (Rev. 2) in thousand U.S. Dollars
Exportations Spéciales F.O.B. par Produits d'après la C.T.C.I. (Rév. 2) en milliers de Dollars E.U.

SITC CTCI	COMMODITY	1993 WEIGHT POIDS	1993 VALUE VALEUR	1994 WEIGHT POIDS	1994 VALUE VALEUR	1995 WEIGHT POIDS	1995 VALUE VALEUR	1996 WEIGHT POIDS	1996 VALUE VALEUR	PRODUIT
52	INORGANIC CHEMICALS		7355		9044		7839		8105	PROD CHIM INORGANIQUES
523	OTHR INORG CHEMICALS ETC	W 8792	5843	W 10080	6615	W 7708	5106	W 8310	5889	AUT PRODUITS CHIMIQUES INORG
5231	METAL CMPD OF INORG ACID	W 8644	5783	W 9343	6357	W 7190	5009	W 8286	5869	SELS METALLIQUES
52319	OTH SULPHATES,PERSLPHTES	W 8252	5650	W 9227	6309	W 6881	4922	W 7512	5703	AUTRE SULFATES,ALUNS
53	DYES,TANNING,COLOUR PROD		11312		14444		16116		15386	PROD TEINTURE,COLORANTS
533	PIGMENTS,PAINTS,ETC	W 2668	5922	W 5513	9625	W 4386	10487	W 5209	11032	PIGMENTS,PEINTURES,VERNIS
5334	VARNISHES,DISTEMPERS ETC	W 2525	5523	W 5214	9258	W 4066	9380	W 5052	10557	PEINTURES A L'EAU
541	*MEDICINAL,PHARM PRODUCT		12788		13970		23993	K 1213282	22333	PROD MEDICINAUX PHARMACEUT
5417	MEDICAMENTS	K 292577	8612	K 298837	9538	K 547770	18744	K 1008981	16293	MEDICAMENTS
54171	— CONTAINNG ANTIBIOTICS	K 45387	4176	K 38183	3288	K 73006	7761	K 128920	8323	MED CONTN ANTIBIOTIQUES
54179	— CONTNG OTH SUBSTANCES	K 246910	4411	K 260266	6192	K 467974	10835	K 872852	7666	MED CONT AUT SUBSTANCES
55	PERFUME,CLEANING ETC PRD		6623		11963		9581		6573	PROD POUR PARFUM,TOILETTE
554	SOAP,CLEANSING ETC PREPS	W 4535	5154	W 10569	9480	W 7874	7299	W 5661	4424	SAVONS,PRODUITS DETERSIFS
5542	WASHING PREPARATIONS ETC	W 2807	2862	W 7337	5994	W 6681	5857	W 4881	3436	PROD ORG TENSIO–ACT NDA
562	*FERTILIZERS,MANUFACTURE	W 17623	2408	W 34902	5495	W 32970	6436	W 64283	14256	ENGRAIS MANUFACTURES
5629	FERTILIZERS NES	W 9303	1612	W 19904	4026	W 16985	4251	W 48034	11950	ENGRAIS NDA
56291	NIT–PHOS–POT FERTLZR NES	W 6032	993	W 8899	1726	W 10287	2460	W 38235	9198	ENGRAIS CONT N P K
58	PLASTIC MATERIALS ETC		24611		26183		31136		39338	MAT PLAST ARTIFICIELLES
582	PROD OF CONDENSATION ETC	W 5465	8462	W 6011	9097	W 5453	11499	W 7845	11610	PROD CONDENS,POLYCOND
5823	ALKYDS,OTHER POLYESTERS	W 4551	6334	W 5048	7060	W 4980	10246	W 7447	10249	ALKYDES ET AUT POLYESTERS
58231	— IN PRIMARY FORMS	W 4549	6317	W 5048	7060	W 4980	10243	W 7447	10249	SOUS FORMES PRIMAIRES
583	POLYMERIZATION ETC PRODS	W 12111	16106	W 12771	17036	W 12259	19571	W 20569	27670	PROD POLYMERISATION
5834	POLYVINYL CHLORIDE	W 3905	5418	W 4953	7099	W 2928	5495	W 9273	11218	CHLORURE DE POLYVINYLE
58341	— IN PRIMARY FORMS	W 3532	4504	W 4426	5622	W 2286	3589	W 8551	9488	SOUS FORMES PRIMAIRES
59	CHEMICAL MATERIALS NES		16338		14813		16214		17093	MAT PROD CHIMIQUES NDA
591	PESTICIDES,DISINFECTANTS	W 960	6748	W 720	4223	W 703	3916	W 1103	5148	DESINF,INSECT,FONG,HERB
592	STARCH,INULIN,GLUTEN,ETC	W 1473	6183	W 1354	5788	W 1336	6709	W 1332	6633	AMIDONS,INUL,GLUT FROM
5922	ALBUMINOID SUBSTAN,GLUES	W 1466	6180	W 1354	5788	W 1331	6705	W 1332	6633	MAT ALBUMIN,COLLES
59221	CASEIN AND DERIVATVS,ETC	W 858	4928	W 966	4884	W 1022	5605	W 897	5343	CASEINES,CASEINATES
6	BASIC MANUFACTURES		441088		490496		589212		669655	ART MANUFACTURES
61	LEATHER,DRESSED FUR,ETC		107598		139210		187121		210773	CUIRS,PELLETERIES
611	LEATHER	W 12303	100441	W 16726	122732	W 19266	159447	W 24541	177016	CUIRS,PEAUX PREPARES
6114	LEATHR BOVINE NES,EQUINE	W 11809	97689	W 15852	119280	W 18635	156125	W 24425	176133	CUIRS DE BOVINS
612	LEATHER ETC MANUFACTURES	W 120	3900	W 420	3237	W 823	4118	W 1448	8399	OUVRAGES EN CUIRS NDA
613	FUR SKINS TANNED,DRESSED	W 204	3258	W 738	13241	W 1016	23556	W 959	25358	PELLETERIES
62	RUBBER MANUFACTURES NES		26532		31834		35092		37378	CAOUTCHOUC MANUFACTURE
621	MATERIALS OF RUBBER	W 7660	14556	W 11216	20199	W 9494	21963	W 11476	23910	PRODUITS EN CAOUTCHOUC
62104	UNHARD VULC RUBBER,BASIC	W 7652	14532	W 11200	20173	W 9483	21935	W 11406	23786	PLAQUES,FEUILLES CAOUT
625	RUBBER TYRES, TUBES ETC	W 3864	11906	W 3763	11602	W 4220	13105	W 3868	13401	PNEUS CAOUTCHOUC VULCANISE
6252	TYRES,NEW,BUS OR LORRY	W 2490	7692	W 2912	9053	W 2824	9607	W 2647	9148	PNEUS POUR AUTOBUS,CAMIONS
64	PAPER,PAPERBOARD AND MFR		20579		21488		26610		34186	PAPIERS,CARTONS & OUVRAGES
641	PAPER AND PAPERBOARD	W 20555	14586	W 19791	14842	W 14939	15684	W 21626	21932	PAPIERS ET CARTONS
6412	PRINTG,WRITING PAPER NES	W 328	362	W 808	1010	W 1013	1432	W 6452	7534	PAPIERS POUR L'IMPRESSION
6415	PAPER,PAPERBRD,BULK,NES	W 12130	9468	W 10427	8601	W 7862	9782	W 12178	12424	PAPIERS,CARTONS ROULEAUX
64159	OTHER PAPER ETC,BULK,NES	W 11970	9305	W 10202	8392	W 7786	9679	W 11803	11945	AUT PAPIER ROULEAUX FEUILLES
642	PAPER,ETC,PRECUT,ARTS OF	W 6104	5992	W 7280	6646	W 9985	10927	W 11673	12254	PAP,CARTONS DECOUPES
6421	PAPER ETC CONTAINERS	W 5226	4193	W 6102	4957	W 9011	9343	W 8101	8865	BOITES,SACS EMBALLAGES
65	TEXTILE YARN,FABRICS,ETC		244062		252500		290517		327146	FILS,TISSUS,ARTICLES TEXTILE
651	TEXTILE YARN		173006	W 44401	183305	W 37896	210547	W 51486	253410	FILS TEXTILES
6512	WOOL,HAIR YARN,INCL TOPS	W 43903	165687	W 43235	177507	W 36143	201361	W 49228	242409	FILS DE LAINE,DE POILS
65121	WOOL TOPS	W 43838	165031	W 43167	176790	W 36107	200760	W 49191	241943	RUBANS LAINE PEIGN,TOPS
6517	REGEN FIBRE YARN,MONOFIL		5065	W 863	4410	W 1305	6626	W 1876	8696	FILS TEXT ART NON VENTE DT
65171	CONT VISCOSE RAYON YARN		4519	W 666	3464	W 1180	6067	W 1768	8280	FILS RAY,VIS NON VENTE DET
653	WOVN MAN–MADE FIB FABRIC	W 752	7316	W 648	7095	W 709	8695	W 914	10355	TISSUS FIBRES SYNTH,ARTIF
654	OTH WOVEN TEXTILE FABRIC	W 2390	53805	W 2423	51939	W 2453	57110	W 2151	48671	TISSUS AUT COTON SYNT,ARTIF
6542	WOVEN WOOL,HAIR NONPILE	W 2301	52605	W 2095	47605	W 2199	52409	W 1899	42703	TIS PLUS 85% LAINE,POILS
65422	WOVN COMB WOOL,FINE HAIR	W 2077	49350	W 1942	45466	W 2069	50611	W 1682	39896	TISSUS 85% LAINE,PLS PEIG
66	NONMETAL MINERAL MFS NES		29375		28323		24588		28312	ART MIN NON METALLIQUES
662	CLAY,REFRACTORY BLDG PRD	W 32003	13128	W 23757	10426	W 18507	8683	W 25582	9859	MAT CONST REFRACTAIRES
6624	BRICKS ETC NONREFRACTORY	W 31931	13112	W 23612	10377	W 18348	8614	W 25355	9737	BRIQUES ETC CERAM NON REFR
66245	GLAZED CERAMIC SETTS ETC	W 30514	12741	W 22179	9941	W 17942	8482	W 24619	9558	AUT CARREAUX CERAMIQUE
665	GLASSWARE	W 10358	6451	W 13375	7542	W 11651	7070	W 13939	8090	OUVRAGES EN VERRE
6651	BOTTLES ETC OF GLASS	W 10316	5792	W 13332	6714	W 11603	6593	W 13876	7655	RECIPIENTS EN VERRE
66511	GLASS BOTTLES ETC NONVAC	W 10316	5792	W 13329	6701	W 11603	6593	W 13876	7655	BONBONNES,BOUTEILLES,ETC
67	IRON AND STEEL		7662		8336		10789		17063	FER ET ACIER
678	IRON,STL TUBES,PIPES,ETC	W 5492	5913	W 6070	5762	W 4859	7813	W 7964	12957	TUBES,TUYAUX EN FONTE,FER
6783	IRON,STL TUBES,PIPES NES	W 5380	5730	W 6062	5750	W 4835	7768	W 7909	12850	AUT TUBES,TUYAUX FER,ACIER
68	NON–FERROUS METALS		2031		4016		7076		9159	METAUX NON FERREUX
684	ALUMINIUM	W 371	1994	W 928	3907	W 1860	6737	W 1777	6797	ALUMINIUM
6842	ALUMINIUM,ALLOYS WORKED	W 371	1994	W 928	3907	W 1860	6737	W 1776	6795	ALUMINIUM,ALLIAGES OUVRE
69	METAL MANUFACTURES NES		3195		4720		7390		5430	ART MANUFACT EN METAL NDA
7	MACHINES,TRANSPORT EQUIP		129959		223900		125772		106837	MACHINES MATERIEL TRANSPORT
72	MACHS FOR SPCL INDUSTRYS		3782		4276		8168		7325	MAC SPECIALES POUR INDUST
77	ELECTRIC MACHNRY NES ETC		10618		16114		15875		13578	MACH APP ELECT NDA
775	HOUSEHOLD TYPE EQUIP NES	W 627	4734	W 610	4380	W 931	6919	W 1315	9010	MACH,APP USAGE DOMESTQUE
778	ELECTRICAL MACHINERY NES	W 447	3984	W 867	9694	W 381	4296	W 245	696	AUTRES MACH ELECT NDA
7783	AUTOMOTIVE ELECTR EQUIP	W 221	3428	W 660	9303	W 267	3815	W 2	30	EQUIP ELECT MOTEURS EXPL
77831	IGNITION,STARTING EQUIP	W 221	3428	W 659	9301	W 266	3810	W 2	30	APP ELEC ALLUM,DEMARRAGE
78	ROAD VEHICLES		110587		198050		92117		71049	VEHICULES ROUTIERS
781	PASS MOTOR VEH EXC BUSES	W 8497	84658	W 13818	166803	W 5388	66798	W 3767	42480	AUTO TRANSPORT PERSONNES
784	MOTOR VEH PRTS,ACCES NES	W 1849	22261	W 2395	27549	W 2089	21750	W 2837	25025	PIECES 722,781,782,783
7849	OTHER MOTOR VEHCL PARTS	W 1849	22260	W 2394	27548	W 2055	21482	W 2835	24993	PIECES 722,781,782,783
8	MISC MANUFACTURED GOODS		187414		188176		191047		209674	ART MANUFACTURES DIVERS
821	*FURNITURE,PARTS THEREOF	W 185	876		5799	W 6419	13067	W 7131	12724	MEUBLES ET PIECES
8211	CHAIRS,SEATS AND PARTS	W 138	478	W 2264	3770	W 4797	8409	W 4874	7800	SIEGES ET PIECES
82111	CHAIRS AND OTHER SEATS	W 137	388	W 2264	3770	W 4797	8409	W 4874	7800	SIEGES
84	CLOTHING AND ACCESSORIES		138387		136922		131371		141351	VETEMENTS
842	MENS OUTERWEAR NOT KNIT	W 918	29740	W 794	28551	W 670	24536	W 780	27244	VET DESSUS POUR HOMMES
8421	— OVERCOATS,OTHER COATS	W 151	5037	W 190	6765	W 190	6239	W 160	4924	MANTEAUX HOMMES MAT TEXT
84211	—— OF WOOL,FINE HAIR	W 139	4432	W 171	5883	W 174	5457	W 150	4447	MANTEAUX HOMMES DE LAINE
8422	— SUITS	W 97	5126	W 30	1892	W 33	2088	W 66	3716	COMPLETS HOMMES MAT TEXT
8423	— TROUSERS,BREECHES ETC	W 277	5869	W 294	6645	W 228	5914	W 301	6803	PANTALONS HOMMES MAT TEX
8424	— JACKETS,BLAZERS ETC	W 164	8705	W 175	9237	W 155	7890	W 205	10079	VESTES HOMMES MAT TEXTIL
8429	— OTHER OUTER GARMENTS	W 229	5003	W 104	4012	W 64	2405	W 48	1723	AUT VET DES HOM MAT TEX
843	WOMENS OUTERWEAR NONKNIT	W 754	23635	W 544	20857	W 526	25650	W 646	31104	VET DESSUS FEMMES MAT TEX
8431	— COATS AND JACKETS	W 437	14008	W 379	14119	W 332	14987	W 407	18262	MANT,VEST FEM MAT TEXTIL
8439	— OTHER OUTER GARMENTS	W 254	6586	W 112	3912	W 119	6049	W 140	6745	AUT VET DES FEM MAT TEXT
845	OUTERWEAR KNIT NONELASTC	W 519	18678	W 351	17475	W 1111	17201	W 469	17545	VET DESSOUS,ACCES BONNET
8451	— JERSEYS,PULLOVERS ETC	W 472	15697	W 318	15063	W 1090	15373	W 435	15710	CHANDAILS,PULL–OVERS ETC
848	HEADGEAR,NONTXTL CLOTHNG	W 1261	59239	W 1237	61823	W 1243	56008	W 939	57211	VET ACCES MAT AUT QUE TEX
8481	LEATHER CLOTHES,ACCESSOR	W 541	25523	W 420	21607	W 618	18846	W 321	16208	VET ACCES MAT CUIR ARTIF

5. Special Exports F.O.B. by Commodities according to the S.I.T.C. (Rev. 2) in thousand U.S. Dollars
Exportations Spéciales F.O.B. par Produits d'après la C.T.C.I. (Rév. 2) en milliers de Dollars E.U.

SITC CTCI	COMMODITY	1993		1994		1995		1996		PRODUIT
		WEIGHT POIDS	VALUE VALEUR	WEIGHT POIDS	VALUE VALEUR	WEIGHT POIDS	VALUE VALEUR	WEIGHT POIDS	VALUE VALEUR	
8483	FUR ETC,CLOTHES,PRODUCTS	W 693	33454	W 787	39847	W 597	36675	W 583	40185	VETEMENTS DE FOURRURE
84831	ARTICLES OF FURSKIN,NES	W 693	33454	W 787	39846	W 597	36675	W 583	40185	PELLETERIES OUVREES NDA
851	*FOOTWEAR	W 1834	24516	W 1810	20735	W 1406	17083	W 1593	19949	CHAUSSURES
85102	FOOTWEAR LEATHER	W 893	20273	W 725	16222	W 524	11825	W 834	15023	CHAUS SEMELLES EN CUIR
89	MISC MANUFCTRD GOODS NES		15559		15240		19461		22433	ART MANUFACTURES DIVERS
892	PRINTED MATTER	W 2465	4339	W 2170	4008	W 1925	4111	W 4371	9812	IMPRIMES
8928	PRINTED MATTER NES	W 1966	2899	W 1798	2917	W 1909	4016	W 4360	9746	IMPRIMES NDA
89286	TRADE ADV MATRL,CATALOGS	W 1963	2852	W 1795	2837	W 1856	3526	W 4293	9295	IMPRIMES PUBLICITAIRES
893	ARTICLES OF PLASTIC NES	W 2368	7240		5039	W 1796	8551	W 1886	7591	OUVRAGES EN MAT DIVIS 58
8939	MISC PLASTIC ARTICLES	W 982	3012	W 857	3082	W 1389	6927	W 997	4636	ART DIVERS EN MAT DIV 58
9	GOODS NOT CLASSD BY KIND		8710		5777		10646		6573	ART TRANSACT NON CLASSES

1. HISTORICAL SERIES, 1992–1996 GENERAL TRADE, IMPORTS C.I.F., EXPORTS F.O.B.
SERIES HISTORIQUES, 1992–1996 COMMERCE GENERAL, IMPORTATIONS C.A.F., EXPORTATIONS F.O.B

YEAR ANNEE	VALUE IN MILLION U.S. DOLLARS VALEUR EN MILLION U.S. DOLLARS MERCHANDISE –MARCHANDISE		GOLD –OR		CONVERSION FACTORS FACTEURS DE CONVERSION CENTS E.U. PAR		INDEX NUMBERS –INDICES QUANTUM		UNIT VALUE VALEUR UNITAIRE	
	IMPORTS	EXPORTS	IMPORTS	EXPORTS	IMPORTS	EXPORTS	IMPORTS	EXPORTS	IMPORTS	EXPORTS
1992	929.30	869.30								
1993	958.00	721.00								
1994	2479.00	3044.00								
1995	2900.00	3100.00								
1996	4721.10	4590.20								

2. IMPORTS BY BROAD ECONOMIC CATEGORY AND EXPORTS BY INDUSTRIAL ORIGIN. (PERCENTAGE OF TOTAL VALUE)
IMPORTATIONS PAR CATEGORIES ECONOMIQUES ET EXPORTATIONS PAR BRANCHE D'ACTIVITE.(EN POURCENTAGE DE LA VALEUR TOTALE)

IMPORTS – IMPORTATIONS

	1990	1991	1992	1993	1994	1995	1996
TOTAL IMPORTS–IMPORTATIONS TOTALES							
1 FOOD BEV–ALIMENTATION BOISSONS							
11 PRIMARY–PRODUITS DE BASE							
111 FOR INDUSTRY–POUR L'INDUSTRIE							
112 FOR HOUSEHOLDS–POUR LES MENAGES							
12 PROCESSED–PRODUITS ELABORES							
121 FOR INDUSTRY–POUR L'INDUSTRIE							
122 FOR HOUSEHOLDS–POUR LES MENAGES							
2 IND SUPPLIES–APPROV INDUSTRIELS							
21 PRIMARY–PRODUITS DE BASE							
22 PROCESSED–PRODUITS ELABORES							
3 FUELS–COMBUSTIBLES							
31 PRIMARY–PRODUITS DE BASE							
32 PROCESSED–PRODUITS ELABORES							
321 MOTOR SPIRIT–ESSENCE							
322 OTHER–AUTRES							
4 MACHINERY–EQUIPEMENT							
41 CAPITAL EQUIPMENT–MACHINES							
42 PARTS–PIECES ACCESSOIRES							
5 TRANSPORT–TRANSPORT							
51 PASSENGER CARS–AUTOMOBILES							
52 OTHER–AUTRES							
521 INDUSTRIAL–INDUSTRIELS							
522 NON INDUSTRIAL–NON INDUSTRIEL							
53 PARTS–PIECES ACCESSOIRES							
6 CONSUM GOODS–BIENS CONSOMMATION							
61 DURABLE–DURABLES							
62 SEMI DURABLE–SEMI DURABLES							
63 NON DURABLE–NON DURABLES							
7 GOODS NES–BIENS NDA							

EXPORTS – EXPORTATIONS

	1990	1991	1992	1993	1994	1995	1996
TOTAL EXPORTS–EXPORTATIONS TOTALES							
1 AGRICULTURE							
2 MINING QUARRY–INDUS EXTRACTIVES							
3 MANUFACTURING–IND MANUFACTUR							
31 FOOD BEV TOBACCO–ALIM BOISS TAB							
32 TEXTILES–INDUSTRIES TEXTILES							
33 WOOD & PRODUCTS–BOIS & PRODUITS							
34 PAPER & PRODUCTS–PAPIER & PRODT							
35 CHEMICALS–INDUSTRIES CHIMIQUES							
36 NON METAL MIN–MIN NON METAL							
37 BASIC METAL–IND METAL BASE							
38 METAL MANUF–MANUF METAL							
39 OTH MANUF IND–AUTRES MANUF							

3. TRADE BY PRINCIPAL COUNTRIES OF PURCHASE AND DESTINATION (VALUE IN THOUSAND U.S. DOLLARS)
ECHANGES SELON LES PRINCIPAUX PAYS D'ACHAT ET DE DESTINATION (VALEUR EN MILLIERS DE DOLLARS EU)

COUNTRIES–PAYS	GENERAL IMPORTS C.I.F. IMPORTATIONS GENERALES C.A.F				
	1991	1992	1993	1994	1995
World		929338		2479000	2892700
Africa				300	100
Americas		58974		101400	33100
Northern America		37640		101400	33100
LAIA		21333			
CACM					
Caribbean					
Rest of America					
As.ex F.USSR		168278		212200	624400
Eur.x F.USSR		146217		471000	932700
EU		73346		340500	705000
EFTA		19817		6300	26000
East Europe		45805		124200	201600
Other Europe					
Former USSR				1415600	1291800
Oceania		5012		24400	3100
Russian Federation				764000	720000
Germany/Allemagne		21631		176800	374700
Korea, Republic of		1357		26400	429600
Tajikistan/Tadjikistan				307200	73000
Kazakhstan				148500	217800
Italy/Italie		8059		23700	221000
Hungary/Hongrie		12366		87500	145600
Turkmenistan/Turkménistn				95700	98700
Turkey/Turquie		35060		67500	85600
China/Chine		67626		88100	23400
USA/Etats–Unis d'Amer		37601		94600	30400
Ukraine				46600	61400
Netherlands/Pays–Bas		2401		51900	35500
Japan/Japon		5691		23700	44800
Belarus/Bélarus				11600	50000
Kyrgyzstan/Kirghizistan				25900	34100
United Kingdom		13958		18100	27900
Switz.Liecht		19817		6300	26000
Austria/Autriche		14598		27000	10100
Czech Republic				16200	33400
Poland/Pologne		15157		17300	4500
Lithuania/Lituanie				7700	28400
Afghanistan		32342		400	1400
Australia/Australie		5012		24400	3100
France,Monac		5064		11200	15500
Syrian Arab Republic		778			25200
Sweden/Suède		7119		12300	2800
Argentina/Argentine		21333			
Belgium–Luxembourg				15200	4300
India/Inde		1008		4100	13900
Czechoslovakia		16885			
Indonesia/Indonésie		16675			
Denmark/Danemark		20		1700	9900
Bulgaria/Bulgarie		1239		2900	6300
Latvia/Lettonie				6500	3700
Romania/Roumanie		158			10000
Canada		40		6800	2700
Fm Yugoslav		7249			
Korea Dem People's Rp		2406		2000	500
Finland/Finlande		160		1500	1100
Republic of Moldova				700	1900
Ireland/Irlande				1100	1500
Slovakia				300	1800
Azerbaijan				600	1200
Cyprus/Chypre		1417			
Estonia/Estonie				200	1000
Hong Kong		1020			
Singapore/Singapour		982			
Spain/Espagne		212			700
Georgia/Géorgie				300	500

COUNTRIES–PAYS	GENERAL EXPORTS F.O.B. EXPORTATIONS GENERALES F.O.B.				
	1991	1992	1993	1994	1995
Monde		869309		3044000	3109000
Afrique		29		300	
Amériques		62443		20800	12800
Amérique du Nord		37818		20700	12700
ALAI		24518			
MCAC					
Caraïbes		108		100	100
Autre Amérique					
Asie l'URSS exclus		223919		177000	317100
Europe l'URSS exclus		466966		579300	685600
UE		321414		441300	556500
AELE		15933		102300	74000
Europe de l'Est		122520		35700	55100
Autre de l'Europe					
Ancienne URSS				1683500	1318100
Océanie		3470			
Russian Federation				476500	584800
Kazakhstan				370000	238100
Tajikistan/Tadjikistan				410700	156100
United Kingdom		117317		175000	236600
Netherlands/Pays–Bas		20199		153000	156800
Turkmenistan/Turkménistn				99300	150400
Ukraine				186100	45000
Turkey/Turquie		77321		42400	109700
Switz.Liecht		15933		102300	74000
Korea, Republic of		3246		40100	146800
Germany/Allemagne		94023		32400	35800
China/Chine		39529		77000	35500
Kyrgyzstan/Kirghizistan				77500	68300
Italy/Italie		11403		26400	80900
Austria/Autriche		29290		41600	41100
Poland/Pologne		47796		21500	27100
USA/Etats–Unis d'Amer		37641		20700	12700
Belarus/Bélarus				37200	31700
Afghanistan		40256		4200	17200
Hungary/Hongrie		51814		1500	1900
France,Monac		39330		1200	600
Bulgaria/Bulgarie		12672		8000	13000
Lithuania/Lituanie				16100	10400
Argentina/Argentine		24500			
Latvia/Lettonie				6600	15900
Indonesia/Indonésie		22387			
Israel/Israël		13808			
Japan/Japon		4570		5200	1600
India/Inde		1092		4200	5100
Estonia/Estonie				500	9300
Slovakia				1400	6700
Czechoslovakia		8062			
Belgium–Luxembourg				7500	300
Fm Yugoslav		7099			
Romania/Roumanie		2175		300	4600
Ireland/Irlande		5725			800
Denmark/Danemark		1250		2900	2300
Korea Dem People's Rp		2133		2700	700
Syrian Arab Republic		4322		900	100
Azerbaijan				1200	4000
Czech Republic				3000	1800
Spain/Espagne		2394		1000	1300
Republic of Moldova				1400	3100
Cyprus/Chypre		3910			
Australia/Australie		3470			
Pakistan		3453			
Hong Kong		3206			
Mongolia/Mongolie		1824		300	100
Georgia/Géorgie				400	900
Viet Nam		942			300

(VALUE AS PERCENTAGE OF WORLD TOTAL)(VALEURS EN POURCENTAGE DU TOTAL MONDIAL)

	1986	1987	1988	1989	1990	1991	1992	1993	1994	1995
Africa									0.0	0.0
Americas							6.3		4.1	1.1
Northern America							4.1		4.1	1.1
LAIA							2.3			
CACM										
Caribbean										
Rest of America										
As.ex F.USSR							18.1		8.6	21.6
Eur.x F.USSR							15.7		19.0	32.2
EU							7.9		13.7	24.4
EFTA							2.1		0.3	0.9
East Europe							4.9		5.0	7.0
Other Europe										
Former USSR									57.1	44.7
Oceania							0.5		1.0	0.1
Russian Federation									30.8	24.9
Germany/Allemagne							2.3		7.1	13.0
Korea, Republic of							0.1		1.1	14.9
Tajikistan/Tadjikistan									12.4	2.5
Kazakhstan									6.0	7.5
Italy/Italie							0.9		1.0	7.6
Hungary/Hongrie							1.3		3.5	5.0
Turkmenistan/Turkménistn									3.9	3.4
Turkey/Turquie							3.8		2.7	3.0
China/Chine							7.3		3.6	0.8

	1986	1987	1988	1989	1990	1991	1992	1993	1994	1995
Afrique							0.0		0.0	
Amériques							7.2		0.7	0.4
Amérique du Nord							4.4		0.7	0.4
ALAI							2.8			
MCAC										
Caraïbes							0.0		0.0	0.0
Autre Amérique										
Asie l'URSS exclus							25.8		5.8	10.2
Europe l'URSS exclus							53.7		19.0	22.1
UE							37.0		14.5	17.9
AELE							1.8		3.4	2.4
Europe de l'Est							14.1		1.2	1.8
Autre de l'Europe										
Ancienne URSS									55.3	42.4
Océanie							0.4			
Russian Federation									15.7	18.8
Kazakhstan									12.2	7.7
Tajikistan/Tadjikistan									13.5	5.0
United Kingdom							13.5		5.7	7.6
Netherlands/Pays–Bas							2.3		5.0	5.0
Turkmenistan/Turkménistn									3.3	4.8
Ukraine									6.1	1.4
Turkey/Turquie							8.9		1.4	3.5
Switz.Liecht							1.8		3.4	2.4
Korea, Republic of							0.4		1.3	4.7

4. General Imports C.I.F. by Commodities according to the S.I.T.C. (Rev. 2) in thousand U.S. Dollars
Importations Générales C.A.F. par Produits d'après la C.T.C.I. (Rév. 2) en milliers de Dollars E.U.

SITC CTCI	COMMODITY	1992		1993		1994		1995		PRODUIT
		WEIGHT POIDS	VALUE VALEUR	WEIGHT POIDS	VALUE VALEUR	WEIGHT POIDS	VALUE VALEUR	WEIGHT POIDS	VALUE VALEUR	
	ALL COMMODITIES						2479000		2892700	TOUS PRODUITS

5. General Exports F.O.B. by Commodities according to the S.I.T.C. (Rev. 2) in thousand U.S. Dollars
Exportations Générales F.O.B. par Produits d'après la C.T.C.I. (Rév. 2) en milliers de Dollars E.U.

SITC CTCI	COMMODITY	1992		1993		1994		1995		PRODUIT
		WEIGHT POIDS	VALUE VALEUR	WEIGHT POIDS	VALUE VALEUR	WEIGHT POIDS	VALUE VALEUR	WEIGHT POIDS	VALUE VALEUR	
	ALL COMMODITIES						3044000		3109000	TOUS PRODUITS

1. HISTORICAL SERIES, 1961–1996 SPECIAL TRADE, IMPORTS C.I.F., EXPORTS F.O.B. # 1
SERIES HISTORIQUES, 1961–1996 COMMERCE SPECIAL, IMPORTATIONS C.A.F., EXPORTATIONS F.O.B

YEAR ANNEE	VALUE IN MILLION VATU VALEUR EN MILLION VATU MERCHANDISE –MARCHANDISE		GOLD –OR		CONVERSION FACTORS U.S. CENTS PER VATU FACTEURS DE CONVERSION CENTS E.U. PAR VATU		INDEX NUMBERS –INDICES QUANTUM		UNIT VALUE VALEUR UNITAIRE	
	IMPORTS	EXPORTS	IMPORTS	EXPORTS	IMPORTS	EXPORTS	IMPORTS	EXPORTS	IMPORTS	EXPORTS
1961	650.50	424.40			1.1140	1.1140				
1962	559.80	495.60			1.1140	1.1140				
1963	543.60	579.40			1.1140	1.1140				
1964	605.50	810.80			1.1140	1.1140				
1965	647.20	819.50			1.1140	1.1140				
1966	735.20	931.80			1.1140	1.1140				
1967	864.60	1063.00			1.1140	1.1140				
1968	908.10	1043.20			1.1140	1.1140				
1969	1057.20	1002.20			1.0730	1.0730				
1970	1310.70	1161.50			0.9902	0.9902				
1971	1814.20	1284.90			0.9902	0.9902				
1972	2372.50	1206.20			1.0905	1.0905				
1973	2489.80	1498.10			1.2391	1.2391				
1974	3857.40	2370.50			1.1462	1.1473				
1975	2622.10	789.70			1.2837	1.2828				
1976	2628.10	1291.80			1.1465	1.1305				
1977	4155.00	2914.00			1.2505	1.2505				
1978	4614.00	3082.00			1.3538	1.3538				
1979	5020.00	3240.00			1.4463	1.4463				
1980	4922.00	2449.00			1.4426	1.4445				
1981	5116.00	2832.00			1.1407	1.1450				
1982	5663.00	2201.00			1.0479	1.0464				
1983	6292.00	2940.00			1.0049	1.0027				
1984	6811.00	4395.00			1.0083	1.0117				
1985	7378.00	3263.00			0.9459	0.9430				
1986	6105.00	1841.00			0.9327	0.9337				
1987	7638.00	1943.00			0.9121	0.9141				
1988	7361.00	2066.00			0.9579	0.9582				
1989	8250.00	2560.00			0.8575	0.8469				
1990	11211.00	2202.00			0.8549	0.8538				
1991	9216.00	2035.00			0.8968	0.8954				
1992	9276.00	2677.00			0.8819	0.8835				
1993	9581.00	2758.00			0.8226	0.8224				
1994	10404.00	2911.00			0.8402	0.8632				
1995	10659.00	3173.00			0.8917	0.8908				
1996	10888.00	3368.00			0.8954	0.8964				

2. IMPORTS BY BROAD ECONOMIC CATEGORY AND EXPORTS BY INDUSTRIAL ORIGIN. (PERCENTAGE OF TOTAL VALUE)
IMPORTATIONS PAR CATEGORIES ECONOMIQUES ET EXPORTATIONS PAR BRANCHE D'ACTIVITE.(EN POURCENTAGE DE LA VALEUR TOTALE)

IMPORTS – IMPORTATIONS

	1990	1991	1992	1993	1994	1995	1996
TOTAL IMPORTS–IMPORTATIONS TOTALES				100.			
1 FOOD BEV–ALIMENTATION BOISSONS				19.4			
11 PRIMARY–PRODUITS DE BASE				7.3			
111 FOR INDUSTRY–POUR L'INDUSTRIE				4.7			
112 FOR HOUSEHOLDS–POUR LES MENAGES				2.6			
12 PROCESSED–PRODUITS ELABORES				12.2			
121 FOR INDUSTRY–POUR L'INDUSTRIE				3.0			
122 FOR HOUSEHOLDS–POUR LES MENAGES				9.2			
2 IND SUPPLIES–APPROV INDUSTRIELS				20.5			
21 PRIMARY–PRODUITS DE BASE				0.7			
22 PROCESSED–PRODUITS ELABORES				19.9			
3 FUELS–COMBUSTIBLES				9.1			
31 PRIMARY–PRODUITS DE BASE				0.8			
32 PROCESSED–PRODUITS ELABORES				8.4			
321 MOTOR SPIRIT–ESSENCE				8.4			
322 OTHER–AUTRES				0.0			
4 MACHINERY–EQUIPEMENT				15.0			
41 CAPITAL EQUIPMENT–MACHINES				14.0			
42 PARTS–PIECES ACCESSOIRES				1.0			
5 TRANSPORT–TRANSPORT				13.0			
51 PASSENGER CARS–AUTOMOBILES							
52 OTHER–AUTRES				7.7			
521 INDUSTRIAL–INDUSTRIELS				7.6			
522 NON INDUSTRIAL–NON INDUSTRIEL				0.1			
53 PARTS–PIECES ACCESSOIRES				5.4			
6 CONSUM GOODS–BIENS CONSOMMATION				20.2			
61 DURABLE–DURABLES				4.6			
62 SEMI DURABLE–SEMI DURABLES				9.3			
63 NON DURABLE–NON DURABLES				6.3			
7 GOODS NES–BIENS NDA				2.6			

EXPORTS – EXPORTATIONS

	1990	1991	1992	1993	1994	1995	1996
TOTAL EXPORTS–EXPORTATIONS TOTALES	100.	100.		100.			
1 AGRICULTURE	54.7	51.7		53.1			
2 MINING QUARRY–INDUS EXTRACTIVES							
3 MANUFACTURING–IND MANUFACTUR	45.3	48.3		46.9			
31 FOOD BEV TOBACCO–ALIM BOISS TAB	27.4	24.7		24.9			
32 TEXTILES–INDUSTRIES TEXTILES	1.8	8.5		0.1			
33 WOOD & PRODUCTS–BOIS & PRODUITS	5.7	5.6		8.0			
34 PAPER & PRODUCTS–PAPIER & PRODT	0.0			0.0			
35 CHEMICALS–INDUSTRIES CHIMIQUES	1.8	0.1		0.0			
36 NON METAL MIN–MIN NON METAL		0.0					
37 BASIC METAL–IND METAL BASE				0.7			
38 METAL MANUF–MANUF METAL	2.7	1.8		2.1			
39 OTH MANUF IND–AUTRES MANUF	5.9	7.7		11.1			

3. TRADE BY PRINCIPAL COUNTRIES OF FIRST AND LAST CONSIGNMENT (VALUE IN THOUSAND U.S. DOLLARS)
ECHANGES SELON LES PRINCIPAUX PAYS DE PREMIERE ET DE DERNIERE CONSIGNATION (VALEUR EN MILLIERS DE DOLLARS EU)

COUNTRIES–PAYS	SPECIAL IMPORTS C.I.F. IMPORTATIONS SPECIALES C.A.F					COUNTRIES–PAYS	SPECIAL EXPORTS F.O.B. EXPORTATIONS SPECIALES F.O.B.				
	1992	1993	1994	1995	1996		1992	1993	1994	1995	1996
World	81133	73521	85423	92560	94107	Monde	22424	17602	20198	28627	30191
Africa		8				Afrique		61	17		
Americas		901	1596			Amériques		61	320		
Northern America		802	1386			Amérique du Nord		49			
LAIA		99	210			ALAI					
CACM						MCAC					
Caribbean		0				Caraïbes			320		
Rest of America						Autre Amérique		12			
As.ex F.USSR	12449	14652	20484	14596	10530	Asie l'URSS exclus	4248	8220	9014	8589	12881
Eur.x F.USSR	6427	6302	7982	5046	5856	Europe l'URSS exclus		5567	6567		
EU	6427	6248	7906	5046	5856	UE		5564	6542		
EFTA		54	76			AELE			25		
East Europe						Europe de l'Est		3			
Other Europe						Autre de l'Europe					
Former USSR						Ancienne URSS					
Oceania	47187	51642	55075	61601	66385	Océanie	2888	3693	3675	3916	1291
Australia/Australie	29673	31137	32440	37094	40723	Japan/Japon	3321	5129	4810	5540	3935
New Zealand	8150	10066	10738	11217	10861	Bangladesh		1694	3153	2346	7494
Japan/Japon	7376	5966	7940	7109	5095	Australia/Australie	1819	1862	1539	2391	861
New Caledonia	5126	4790	6125	7523	7853	Netherlands/Pays–Bas		3214	4036		
France,Monac	6427	4583	5898	5046	5856	New Caledonia	980	1175	1127	1380	430
Fiji/Fidji	4238	4218	3705	5766	6948	Korea, Republic of	927	740	673	704	1452
Hong Kong	2805	2554	5033	2757	2874	United Kingdom		1928	1480		
Singapore/Singapour	2268	1982	2672	4730	2561	Germany/Allemagne		51	883		
Papua New Guinea		1085	1781			Solomon Isls		287	505		
China/Chine		1092	1017			New Zealand	88	179	135	144	
USA/Etats–Unis d'Amer		785	1243			France,Monac		357	126		
Malaysia/Malaisie		101	1580			Wallis and Futuna Is		124	202		
Korea, Republic of		771	790			Hong Kong		135	185		
Thailand/Thaïlande		734	697			Netherlands Antilles			320		
United Kingdom		563	773			Fiji/Fidji		22	101		
Italy/Italie		358	655			Singapore/Singapour			84		
India/Inde		389	370			China/Chine			50		
Indonesia/Indonésie		350	294			Papua New Guinea		11	34		
Germany/Allemagne		319	168			USA/Etats–Unis d'Amer		37			
Solomon Isls		205	269			Switz.Liecht			25		
Chile/Chili		83	168			Canada		12			
Netherlands/Pays–Bas		135	101			Philippines		9			
Sweden/Suède		86	143			Belgium–Luxembourg			8		
Philippines		149	34			Malaysia/Malaisie		8			
Denmark/Danemark		127	42			Spain/Espagne		4			
Canada		17	143			Thailand/Thaïlande		3			
Switz.Liecht		49	42			Italy/Italie		3			
Belgium–Luxembourg		55	8			India/Inde		0			
Spain/Espagne		11	34								
Norway,SVD,JM		4	34								
Wallis and Futuna Is		13	8								
Portugal		4									

(VALUE AS PERCENTAGE OF WORLD TOTAL)(VALEURS EN POURCENTAGE DU TOTAL MONDIAL)

	1987	1988	1989	1990	1991	1992	1993	1994	1995	1996
Africa		0.0					0.0			
Americas	0.2	1.5					1.2	1.9		
Northern America		1.2					1.1	1.6		
LAIA	0.2	0.3					0.1	0.2		
CACM										
Caribbean							0.0			
Rest of America										
As.ex F.USSR	15.9	18.9	11.6	12.2	15.6	15.3	19.9	24.0	15.8	11.2
Eur.x F.USSR	17.5	26.6	5.4	7.6	7.5	7.9	8.6	9.3	5.5	6.2
EU	14.5	19.9	5.4	7.6	7.5	7.9	8.5	9.3	5.5	6.2
EFTA	3.0	6.6					0.1	0.1		
East Europe										
Other Europe										
Former USSR										
Oceania	54.8	46.6	64.4	59.3	60.1	58.2	70.2	64.5	66.6	70.5
Australia/Australie	32.4	31.7	39.1	37.1	35.9	36.6	42.4	38.0	40.1	43.3
New Zealand	11.1	9.5	13.0	10.3	11.1	10.0	13.7	12.6	12.1	11.5
Japan/Japon	9.3	12.0	11.6	12.2	8.1	9.1	8.1	9.3	7.7	5.4
New Caledonia	4.4	2.0	3.0	2.7	5.0	6.3	6.5	7.2	8.1	8.3
France,Monac	5.9	4.0	5.4	7.6	7.5	7.9	6.2	6.9	5.5	6.2
Fiji/Fidji	6.8	3.4	9.3	9.2	8.1	5.2	5.7	4.3	6.2	7.4
Hong Kong	3.3	3.2			3.9	3.5	3.5	5.9	3.0	3.1
Singapore/Singapour	3.2	3.5			3.6	2.8	2.7	3.1	5.1	2.7
Papua New Guinea							1.5	2.1		
China/Chine							1.5	1.2		

	1987	1988	1989	1990	1991	1992	1993	1994	1995	1996
Afrique	0.0	0.0					0.3	0.1		
Amériques	0.3	19.4		0.0	0.0		0.3	1.6		
Amérique du Nord		19.1		0.0	0.0		0.3			
ALAI	0.2	0.2								
MCAC	0.1									
Caraïbes								1.6		
Autre Amérique							0.1			
Asie l'URSS exclus	23.5	17.9	18.7	23.3	29.8	18.9	46.7	44.6	30.0	42.7
Europe l'URSS exclus	27.5	52.3	55.0	52.5	48.9		31.6	32.5		
UE	26.9	51.6	55.0	52.5	48.9		31.6	32.4		
AELE	0.6	0.7						0.1		
Europe de l'Est							0.0			
Autre de l'Europe										
Ancienne URSS										
Océanie	12.0	4.6	17.8	24.1	21.2	12.9	21.0	18.2	13.7	4.3
Japan/Japon	18.9	15.3	18.5	18.2	22.0	14.8	29.1	23.8	19.4	13.0
Bangladesh	0.3	0.4					9.6	15.6	8.2	24.8
Australia/Australie	7.4	3.0	10.1	12.3	13.3	8.1	10.6	7.6	8.4	2.9
Netherlands/Pays–Bas	4.8	22.6	28.6	25.7	38.5		18.3	20.0		
New Caledonia	3.3	1.5	7.7	7.7	5.2	4.4	6.7	5.6	4.8	1.4
Korea, Republic of	3.8	0.6		3.7	7.5	4.1	4.2	3.3	2.5	4.8
United Kingdom	0.1	0.1		0.9	1.0		11.0	7.3		
Germany/Allemagne	16.6	19.0		16.6	2.1		0.3	4.4		
Solomon Isls				0.8	0.5		1.6	2.5		
New Zealand	0.2	0.1		0.3	0.2	0.4	1.0	0.7	0.5	

4. Special Imports C.I.F. by Commodities according to the S.I.T.C. (Rev. 2) in thousand U.S. Dollars
Importations Spéciales C.A.F. par Produits d'après la C.T.C.I. (Rév. 2) en milliers de Dollars E.U.

SITC CTCI	COMMODITY	1993 WEIGHT POIDS	1993 VALUE VALEUR	1994 WEIGHT POIDS	1994 VALUE VALEUR	1995 WEIGHT POIDS	1995 VALUE VALEUR	1996 WEIGHT POIDS	1996 VALUE VALEUR	PRODUIT
	ALL COMMODITIES		73521		85423		92560		94107	TOUS PRODUITS
0	FOOD AND LIVE ANIMALS		12444		13107		14542		19108	ALIMENTS,ANIMAUX VIVANTS
01	MEAT AND PREPARATIONS		1153							VIANDES ET PREPARATIONS
011	MEAT FRESH,CHILLD,FROZEN	W 333	638							VIANDES FRAICHES,REF,CONGE
0114	POULTRY FRESH CHLLD,FRZN	W 316	588							VOLAILLES MORTES
012	MEAT DRIED,SALTED,SMOKED	W 56	251							VIANDE,ABATS SALES,SECHES
0121	PIG MEAT DRIED,SLTD,SMKD	W 56	251							LARD,JAMBONS
014	MEAT PREPD,PRSVD,NES ETC	W 141	264							CONSERVES DE VIANDES
0149	OTH PREPARD,PRESRVD MEAT	W 127	224							AUTRES PREP DE VIANDES
02	DAIRY PRODCTS,BIRDS'EGGS		860							PRODUITS LAITIERS,OEUFS
022	MILK AND CREAM	W 398	505							LAIT ET CREME
0223	MILK AND CREAM FRESH	W 283	245							LAIT,CREME FRAIS
0224	MILK,CREAM PRESERVED ETC	W 116	261							LAIT,CREME CONS,CONC
02242	MILK DRY,1.5% FAT OR LES	W 113	253							LAIT POUDRE INF 1.5%
03	FISH AND PREPARATIONS		733							POISSONS ET PREPARATIONS
037	FISH ETC PREPD,PRSVD NES	W 626	631							POIS,CRUST,MOL PREPARES
0371	FISH PREPARD,PRESRVD NES	W 624	609							CONSERVES DE POISSONS
04	CEREALS AND PREPARATIONS		5234							CEREALES ET PRODUITS
042	RICE	W 7713	3310							RIZ
0421	RICE IN HUSK OR HUSKED	W 7713	3310							RIZ SANS AUTRE PREPARATION
04211	RICE IN THE HUSK	W 7713	3310							RIZ PADDY
046	WHEAT ETC MEAL OR FLOUR	W 2398	874							SEMOULE FARINE,FROMENT
04601	FLOUR OF WHEAT OR MESLIN	W 2398	874							FARINE DE FROMENT
048	CEREAL ETC PREPARATIONS	W 1367	1009							PREPTNS A BASE CEREALES
0481	PREPD BREAKFAST FOOD ETC	W 215	267							CEREALES TRAVAILLEES
04812	CEREAL ROASTED, PUFFED	W 212	262							PRODTS BASE CEREALES
0484	BAKERY PRODUCTS	W 207	416							PRODUITS DE BOULANGERIE
04841	BREAD,BISCUIT,COM WAFERS	W 207	416							PAINS,BISCUITS DE MER
05	VEGETABLES AND FRUIT		1459							LEGUMES ET FRUITS
054	VEG ETC FRSH,SMPLY PRSVD	W 850	511							LEGUMES FRAIS,CONG,SECS
0545	OTHER FRESH VEGETABLES	W 555	290							AUTRES LEGUMES FRAIS,REF
056	VEGTBLES ETC PRSVD,PREPD	W 816	322							CONSERVES DE LEGUMES
0564	FLOUR ETC OF FRUIT,VEGET	W 771	256							FARINES,SEMOULES,FLOCONS
05643	POTATO FLOUR,MEAL,FLAKES	W 770	255							FLOCONS DE POMMES DE TERRE
057	FRUIT,NUTS,FRESH,DRIED	W 231	298							FRUITS FRAIS OU SECS
058	FRUIT PRESERVED,PREPARED	W 1107	328							CONSERVES DE FRUITS
06	SUGAR AND PREPS,HONEY		891							SUCRES ET PRODUITS
061	SUGAR AND HONEY	W 1375	648							SUCRES ET MIEL
0611	RAW BEET AND CANE SUGAR	W 1371	640							SUCRES BRUTS
062	SUGAR CANDY NON–CHOCLATE	W 80	242							SUCRERIES
07	COFFEE,TEA,COCOA,SPICES		555							CAFE,THE,CACAO,EPICES
073	CHOCOLATE AND PRODUCTS	W 83	323							CHOCOLAT
081	*FEEDING STUFF FOR ANIML	W 1347	533							NOURRITURE POUR ANIMAUX
0819	FOOD WASTE AND FEED NES	W 1347	533							DECHETS,ALIMENTS NDA
08199	FODDER NES,INCL SWEETNED	W 1347	533							PREPARATIONS FOURRAGERES
09	MISC EDIBLE PRODUCTS		957							PREP ALIMENTAIRES DIVERSES
091	MARGARINE AND SHORTENING	W 160	265							MARGARINE ET GRAISSES
0914	MARGARINE,EDIBLE FAT NES	W 159	264							MARGARINES,SIMILI SAINDOUX
09141	MARGARINE	W 159	264							MARGARINE
098	EDIBLE PRODCTS,PREPS NES	W 492	692							PREP ALIMENTAIRES NDA
09809	MISC FOOD PREPRTIONS NES	W 224	319							PREP ALIMENTAIRES NDA
1	BEVERAGES AND TOBACCO		2981		3554		3370		3573	BOISSONS ET TABACS
11	BEVERAGES		2161							BOISSONS
111	NON–ALCOHL BEVERAGES NES	W 633	470							BOISSONS NON ALCOOLIQUES
11102	FLAVORED WATERS NON–ALCO	W 540	400							LIMONADES,EAUX GAZEUSES
112	ALCOHOLIC BEVERAGES	W 1200	1691							BOISSONS ALCOOLIQUES
1121	WINE OF FRESH GRAPES ETC	W 317	731							VINS DE RAISINS FRAIS
11212	WINE OF FRESH GRAPES	W 315	718							VINS DE MOUTS DE RAISINS
1123	BEER,ALE,STOUT,PORTER	W 757	588							BIERES
1124	DISTILLED ALCOHOLIC BEVS	W 125	369							ALCOOLS,EAUX–DE–VIE
11249	OTH ALCOHOLC BEVS,CMPNDS	W 125	369							BOISSONS ALCOOLIQUES NDA
12	TOBACCO AND MANUFACTURES		820							TABACS BRUTS FABRIQUES
122	TOBACCO,MANUFACTURED		820							TABACS FABRIQUES
1221	CIGARS,CHEROOTS,ETC	W 19	609							CIGARES
2	CRUDE MATERLS,EXCL FUELS		718		529		982		1263	MAT BRUTES NON COMESTIBLES
3	MINERAL FUELS ETC		6831		5646		7785		8712	COMBUSTIBLES MINERAUX LUB
33	PETROLEUM AND PRODUCTS		6266							PETROLE ET DERIVES
334	PETROLEUM PRODUCTS,REFIN		6159							PRODUITS RAFFINES
341	*GAS,NATURAL AND MANUFCT	W 938	558							GAZ NATUREL,GAZ MANUFACT
3413	PETROLM GASES,LIQUEFIED	W 938	558							GAZ DE PETROLE LIQUEFIE
34139	OTH HYDROCARBON GAS LQFD	W 938	558							HYDROCARBURES GAZEUX NDA
4	ANIMAL,VEGETABLE OIL,FAT		309		302		351		537	HUILES,GRAISSES ANIM,VEG
42	FIXED VEGETABLE OIL,FAT		270							HUILES VEGETALES FIXES
5	CHEMCLS,RELATED PROD NES		4407		5663		6343		6402	PRODUITS CHIMIQUES
53	DYES,TANNING,COLOUR PROD		731							PROD TEINTURE,COLORANTS
533	PIGMENTS,PAINTS,ETC	W 418	712							PIGMENTS,PEINTURES,VERNIS
5334	VARNISHES,DISTEMPERS ETC	W 350	612							PEINTURES A L'EAU
53341	WATER–THINNED PAINTS	W 144	393							PEINTURES DILUEES
541	*MEDICINAL,PHARM PRODUCT		1298							PROD MEDICINAUX PHARMACEUT
5417	MEDICAMENTS		1158							MEDICAMENTS
54171	— CONTAINNG ANTIBIOTICS		1158							MED CONTN ANTIBIOTIQUES
55	PERFUME,CLEANING ETC PRD		1236							PROD POUR PARFUM,TOILETTE
553	PERFUMERY,COSMETICS,ETC	W 82	660							PRODUITS DE PARFUMERIE
554	SOAP,CLEANSING ETC PREPS	W 623	568							SAVONS,PRODUITS DETERSIFS
5541	SOAPS	W 349	238							SAVONS,PROD TENSIO–ACTIFS
5542	WASHING PREPARATIONS ETC	W 268	311							PROD ORG TENSIO–ACT NDA
59	CHEMICAL MATERIALS NES		698							MAT PROD CHIMIQUES NDA
591	PESTICIDES,DISINFECTANTS	W 169	394							DESINF,INSECT,FONG,HERB
5911	INSECTICIDES,FOR RETAIL	W 169	394							INSECTICIDES VENTE DET
6	BASIC MANUFACTURES		13195		16602		18840		15992	ART MANUFACTURES
62	RUBBER MANUFACTURES NES		1143							CAOUTCHOUC MANUFACTURE
621	MATERIALS OF RUBBER	W 42	333							PRODUITS EN CAOUTCHOUC
62104	UNHARD VULC RUBBER,BASIC	W 37	261							PLAQUES,FEUILLES CAOUT
625	RUBBER TYRES, TUBES ETC	W 177	706							PNEUS CAOUTCHOUC VULCANISE
6251	TYRES NEW FOR MOTOR CARS	W 158	650							PNEUS POUR VOITURES
63	WOOD,CORK MANUFACTRS NES		890							OUVRAGES LIEGE ET BOIS
634	VENEERS,PLYWOOD,ETC		250							PLACAGES,CONTRE–PLAQUES
635	WOOD MANUFACTURES NES	W 214	638							ART MANUF EN BOIS NDA
6353	BUILDERS WOODWRK,PREFABS	W 34	463							OUVRAGES DE MENUISERIE
64	PAPER,PAPERBOARD AND MFR		1581							PAPIERS,CARTONS & OUVRAGES
641	PAPER AND PAPERBOARD	W 432	711							PAPIERS ET CARTONS

4. Special Imports C.I.F. by Commodities according to the S.I.T.C. (Rev. 2) in thousand U.S. Dollars
Importations Spéciales C.A.F. par Produits d'après la C.T.C.I. (Rév. 2) en milliers de Dollars E.U.

SITC CTCI	COMMODITY	1993		1994		1995		1996		PRODUIT
		WEIGHT POIDS	VALUE VALEUR	WEIGHT POIDS	VALUE VALEUR	WEIGHT POIDS	VALUE VALEUR	WEIGHT POIDS	VALUE VALEUR	
6412	PRINTG,WRITING PAPER NES	W 210	397							PAPIERS POUR L'IMPRESSION
64121	— UNCOATED	W 208	387							PAPIERS IMPRES NON COUCHES
642	PAPER,ETC,PRECUT,ARTS OF	W 353	870							PAP,CARTONS DECOUPES
6423	EXERCISE BOOKS ETC	W 93	366							REGISTRES,CAHIERS,CARNETS
6424	PAPER ETC CT TO SIZE NES	W 174	269							PAP,CARTONS DECOUPES
65	TEXTILE YARN,FABRICS,ETC		1727							FILS,TISSUS,ARTICLES TEXTILE
652	COTTON FABRICS,WOVEN	W 79	507							TISSUS DE COTON
6521	GREY WOVEN COTTON FABRIC	W 68	440							TISSUS COT ECRUS NON MERCER
65215	GREY WOVN COTN BLEND NES	W 51	320							AUT TIS MOINS 85% COT ECRUS
653	WOVN MAN–MADE FIB FABRIC	W 70	261							TISSUS FIBRES SYNTH,ARTIF
658	TEXTILE ARTICLES NES	W 90	571							ART FACONNES MAT TEXTILES
6589	OTH TEXTILE ARTICLES NES	W 79	475							AUT ART EN TEXTILES NDA
65898	KNITTED ETC ARTICLES NES	W 78	473							ART BONNET NON ELASTIQUE
66	NONMETAL MINERAL MFS NES		2202							ART MIN NON METALLIQUES
661	LIME,CEMENT,BLDG PRODS	W 11055	1331							CHAUX,CIMENTS MAT CONSTR
6612	CEMENT	W 10918	1179							CIMENTS HYDRAULIQUES
662	CLAY,REFRACTORY BLDG PRD	W 450	355							MAT CONST REFRACTAIRES
6624	BRICKS ETC NONREFRACTORY	W 418	328							BRIQUES ETC CERAM NON REFR
66245	GLAZED CERAMIC SETTS ETC	W 341	260							AUT CARREAUX CERAMIQUE
67	IRON AND STEEL		1850							FER ET ACIER
673	IRON,STEEL SHAPES ETC	W 999	622							BARRES,PROFIL FER,ACIER
6732	IRON,STEEL BARS ETC	W 665	400							BARRES FER,ACIER
674	IRN,STL UNIV,PLATE,SHEET	W 744	589							LARGES PLATS,TOLES
6745	IRN,STL MED PLATE,ROLLED	W 534	443							TOLES 3 A 4.75 MM
67454	— OF OTHER ALLOY STEEL	W 532	440							TOLES NON ACIERS ALLIES
68	NON–FERROUS METALS		316							METAUX NON FERREUX
69	METAL MANUFACTURES NES		3444							ART MANUFACT EN METAL NDA
691	STRUCTURES AND PARTS NES	W 800	964							CONSTRUCT FER,ACIER,ALU
6911	STRUCTURES,PARTS IRN,STL	W 764	770							CONSTRUCT FER,ACIER,FONTE
692	METAL TANKS,BOXES,ETC	W 242	366							RECIPIENTS METALLIQUES
6924	MTL TRANSPORT BOXES ETC	W 227	343							FUTS,TAMBOURS,BIDONS
693	WIRE PRODUCTS NON ELECTR	W 308	349							OUVRAGES FILS METALLIQUES
6935	METAL FENCING,GAUZE,ETC	W 237	237							TOILES EN FER,ACIER,CUIVRE
69351	IRN,STL FENCNG,GAUZE ETC	W 234	233							TOILES EN FER,ACIER
694	STL,COPPR NAILS,NUTS,ETC	W 162	341							CLOUS,VIS,ECROUS
695	TOOLS	W 60	454							OUTILS A MAIN
6953	OTHER HAND TOOLS	W 33	235							AUTRES OUTILS A MAIN
697	BASE MTL HOUSEHOLD EQUIP	W 90	394							ART MENAGE MET COMMUNS
699	BASE METAL MFRS NES		457							ART MANUFACTURES MET NDA
7	MACHINES,TRANSPORT EQUIP		21924		25719		27282		22045	MACHINES MATERIEL TRANSPORT
71	POWER GENERATING EQUIPMT		1083							MACHINES GENERATRICES
713	INTRNL COMBUS PSTN ENGIN		408							MOTEURS EXPL COMB INT, PIECE
7131	AIRCRAFT PSTN ENGINS,PTS		309							MOTEURS EXPL P.AVIATION, PIE
716	ROTATING ELECTRIC PLANT		498							APP ELECTR ROTATIFS,PIECES
7162	AC MTRS,GENRTRS,GEN SETS		274							MOTEURS ELECTRIQUES
7169	PTS NES OF ROT ELEC PLNT		225							PIECES MAC APP ROTATIFS
72	MACHS FOR SPCL INDUSTRYS		2295							MAC SPECIALES POUR INDUST
721	AGRIC MACHY,EXC TRACTORS		349							MACHINES AGRICOLES
723	CIVIL ENGNEERG EQUIP ETC		1334							APPAREILS DE GENIE CIVIL
7234	CONST,MINING MACHNRY NES		1334							MACH POUR LA CONST, MINES
72341	SELF–PROPELLD DOZERS,ETC		1021							BULLDOZERS
74	GENRL INDUSTRL MACHY NES		2136							MACH APP INDUSTRIE
741	HEATING,COOLING EQUIPMNT		421							MACH CHAUFFAGE,PIECES
7415	AIR–CONDITIONING MACHNRY		300							GROUPES CONDITION AIR
742	PUMPS FOR LIQUIDS ETC		385							POMPES MOTO–POMPES
7428	OTHER PUMPS FOR LIQUIDS		385							AUTRES POMPES POUR LIQ
74281	GARAGE–TYPE FUEL PUMPS		385							POMPES DISTRIB CARBURNTS
743	PUMPS NES,CENTRFUGES ETC		230							POMPES COMPRES,VENT ETC
744	MECHANICAL HANDLING EQU		588							EQUIP MANUTENTION PIECES
7449	PTS NES OF MACHY OF 7442		372							PIECES DU 744.2
745	NONELEC MACHY,TOOLS NES		223							AUT MACH NON ELEC,PIECES
749	NONELEC MACH PTS,ACC NES		289							PIECES MACH NON ELEC NDA
75	OFFICE MACHNES,ADP EQUIP		1451							MACH BUREAU TRAIT AUTOM
751	OFFICE MACHINES		383							MACH,APPAREILS DE BUREAU
7518	OFFICE MACHINES NES		272							MACH,APP DE BUREAU NDA
75182	PHOTO,THERMOCOPY APPARAT		241							APPAREILS DE PHOTOCOPIE
752	AUTOMTIC DATA PROC EQUIP		934							MACH TRAIT INFORMATION
7521	ANALOG,HYBRID COMPUTERS		934							MACH POUR TRAIT INFORMAT
76	TELECOMM,SOUND EQUIPMENT		2814							EQUIPMENT DE TELECOM
762	RADIO BROADCAST RECEIVRS		818							RECEPTEURS RADIODIFFUSION
7622	PORTABLE RADIO RECEIVERS		818							RECEPT PORTATIFS RADIO
764	TELECOM EQPT,PTS,ACC NES		1607							EQUIP TELECOM,PIECES
7641	LINE TELEPHONE,ETC EQUIP		437							APP TELEPHON PAR FIL
7643	TV,RADIO TRANSMITTRS ETC		605							APP EMET TELE RADIO
7649	PTS NES OF EQUIPMT OF 76		476							PIECES DE LA DIV 76
76493	TELECOMM EQUIPMT PTS NES		440							PIECES 761,762,764.3,8
77	ELECTRIC MACHNRY NES ETC		3858							MACH APP ELECT NDA
772	SWITCHGEAR ETC,PARTS NES		741							APP COUPURE,SECT ETC
7721	SWITCHGEAR ETC		730							APP COUPURE,SECTIONMNT
773	ELECTR DISTRIBUTNG EQUIP		544							EQUIPMT DISTRIBUTION ELECT
7731	INSULATED WIRE,CABLE ETC		514							FILS,CABLES ISOLES ELECT
774	ELECTRO–MEDCL,XRAY EQUIP		504							APPAREILS MEDICAUX
7741	ELECTRO–MEDICAL EQUIPMNT		453							APP ELECTRICITE MEDICALE
775	HOUSEHOLD TYPE EQUIP NES		975							MACH,APP USAGE DOMESTQUE
7752	DOM REFRIGERATRS,FREEZRS		678							REFRIG,CONGEL MENAGER
77521	DOMESTIC REFRIGERATORS		678							REFRIGERATEURS
778	ELECTRICAL MACHINERY NES		919							AUTRES MACH ELECT NDA
7781	BATTERIES,ACCUMULATORS		549							PILES ET ACCUMULATEURS
77811	PRIMARY BATTERIES,CELLS		390							PILES ELECTRIQUES,PIECES
78	ROAD VEHICLES		5692							VEHICULES ROUTIERS
782	LORRIES,SPCL MTR VEH NES		4390							VEHICULES SPECIAUX,MARCH
7821	LORRIES,TRUCKS		4265							VEHICULES TRANSP MARCHAND
783	ROAD MOTOR VEHICLES NES		400							VEHICULES ROUTIERS NDA
7831	BUSES		400							VOITURES TRANSPORT COMMUN
784	MOTOR VEH PRTS,ACCES NES		772							PIECES 722,781,782,783
7849	OTHER MOTOR VEHCL PARTS		757							PIECES 722,781,782,783
79	OTHR TRANSPORT EQUIPMENT		2380							AUTRE MATERIEL TRANSPORT
792	AIRCRAFT ETC		1694							APP NAVIGATION AERIENNE
7929	AIRCRAFT PARTS NES		1598							PIECES DU 792
793	SHIPS AND BOATS ETC		685							NAVIRES BATEAUX,ETC
7932	SHIPS AND BOATS NES		605							NAVIRES ET BATEAUX

4. Special Imports C.I.F. by Commodities according to the S.I.T.C. (Rev. 2) in thousand U.S. Dollars
Importations Spéciales C.A.F. par Produits d'après la C.T.C.I. (Rév. 2) en milliers de Dollars E.U.

SITC CTCI	COMMODITY	1993		1994		1995		1996		PRODUIT
		WEIGHT POIDS	VALUE VALEUR	WEIGHT POIDS	VALUE VALEUR	WEIGHT POIDS	VALUE VALEUR	WEIGHT POIDS	VALUE VALEUR	
79321	YACHTS,SPORTS VESSLS ETC		278							BATEAUX DE PLAISANCE
79323	OTHER CARGO VESSELS		327							AUT BATEAUX TRANS MARCH
8	MISC MANUFACTURED GOODS		8836		9965		11109		14210	ART MANUFACTURES DIVERS
812	*PLUMBG,HEATNG,LGHTNG EQ		357							APPAR SANITAIRES CHAUFFAGE
8124	LIGHTING EQUIPMENT NES		256							APPAREILS ECLAIRAGE ETC
821	*FURNITURE,PARTS THEREOF		679							MEUBLES ET PIECES
8219	FURNITURE AND PARTS NES		434							AUTRES MEUBLES ET PIECES
82191	METAL FURNITURE NES		434							MEUBLES NDA EN METAL
831	*TRAVEL GOODS,HANDBAGS	W 36	246							ARTICLES DE VOYAGE ETC
83102	TRAVEL GDS,TOILET–CASES	W 36	246							ARTICLES DE VOYAGE
84	CLOTHING AND ACCESSORIES		1683							VETEMENTS
842	MENS OUTERWEAR NOT KNIT	W 41	323							VET DESSUS POUR HOMMES
8422	— SUITS	W 37	305							COMPLETS HOMMES MAT TEXT
84221	—— OF WOOL,FINE HAIR	W 37	305							COMPLETS HOMMES LAINE
845	OUTERWEAR KNIT NONELASTC	W 35	330							VET DESSOUS,ACCES BONNET
846	UNDER GARMENTS KNITTED	W 68	560							SOUS VETS DE BONNETERIE
8462	— OF COTTON NON ELASTIC	W 55	430							SOUS–VET BONNET COTON
84629	—— OTHER	W 55	430							AUT SOUS–VET BONNET COTON
851	*FOOTWEAR	W 78	394							CHAUSSURES
87	PRECISION INSTRUMNTS NES		550							INSTRUM,APPAR SCIENT NDA
874	MEASURNG,CONTROLNG INSTR		450							INSTRUMENTS DE MESURE
88	PHOTO EQU,OPTICL GDS ETC		519							APP,FOURN PHOTO,OP,MONTR
882	PHOTO,CINEMA SUPPLIES	W 20	232							PRODUITS PHOTO,CINEMA
89	MISC MANUFCTRD GOODS NES		4408							ART MANUFACTURES DIVERS
892	PRINTED MATTER		911							IMPRIMES
8921	PRINTED BOOKS,GLOBES,ETC	W 72	546							LIVRES,BROCHURES,CARTES
89211	PRINTED BOOKS,PAMPHLETS	W 64	483							LIVRES,BROCHURES
893	ARTICLES OF PLASTIC NES	W 509	1235							OUVRAGES EN MAT DIVIS 58
8931	PLSTC PACKG CONTNRS,LIDS	W 170	363							ART TRANSP EMBALLAGE ETC
8939	MISC PLASTIC ARTICLES	W 324	828							ART DIVERS EN MAT DIV 58
89399	OTHR PLASTC ARTICLES NES	W 226	578							AUT OUV MAT DIV 58
894	TOYS,SPORTING GOODS,ETC		924							VOITURES ENFANTS,JOUETS
8942	TOYS,INDOOR GAMES ETC		558							JOUETS,JEUX ETC
89423	TOYS NES		322							JOUETS,MODELES REDUITS
8947	OTH SPORT GDS,FAIR AMUSM		354							AUT ART DE SPORT
89472	OTH OUTDOOR SPORT GOODS		279							ART POUR JEUX PLEIN AIR
895	OFFICE SUPPLIES NES		344							ART PAPET NDA
898	MUSICAL INSTRUMENTS,PTS		515							INSTRUMENTS DE MUSIQUE
8983	SOUND RECRDNG TAPE,DISCS		396							SUPPORTS SON POUR 763
89832	RECORDED DISCS,TAPES ETC		283							DISQUES,PHONO,BANDES
899	OTHER MANUFACTURED GOODS		266							AUT ART MANUF DIVERS NDA
9	GOODS NOT CLASSD BY KIND		1878				1955		2265	ART TRANSACT NON CLASSES
931	*SPECIAL TRANSACTIONS		1817							TRANS.SPECIALES

5. Special Exports F.O.B. by Commodities according to the S.I.T.C. (Rev. 2) in thousand U.S. Dollars
Exportations Spéciales F.O.B. par Produits d'après la C.T.C.I. (Rév. 2) en milliers de Dollars E.U.

SITC CTCI	COMMODITY	1993		1994		1995		1996		PRODUIT
		WEIGHT POIDS	VALUE VALEUR	WEIGHT POIDS	VALUE VALEUR	WEIGHT POIDS	VALUE VALEUR	WEIGHT POIDS	VALUE VALEUR	
	ALL COMMODITIES		17602		20198		28627		30191	TOUS PRODUITS
0	FOOD AND LIVE ANIMALS		6638							ALIMENTS,ANIMAUX VIVANTS
01	MEAT AND PREPARATIONS		3894							VIANDES ET PREPARATIONS
011	MEAT FRESH,CHILLD,FROZEN	W 1634	3894					W 1247	3855	VIANDES FRAICHES,REF,CONGE
0111	BOVINE MEAT FRESH,FROZEN	W 1620	3874		3902		3852	W 1247	3855	VIANDES BOVIN FRAI,REF
01111	BOVINE MEAT WITH BONE IN	W 209	537							VIANDES BOVIN NON DESOSS
01112	BOVINE MEAT BONELESS	W 1411	3337							VIANDES BOVIN DESOSSEES
03	FISH AND PREPARATIONS		125							POISSONS ET PREPARATIONS
036	SHELL FISH FRESH,FROZEN	W 25	117							CRUSTACES,MOLLUSQUES
05	VEGETABLES AND FRUIT		1244							LEGUMES ET FRUITS
054	VEG ETC FRSH,SMPLY PRSVD	W 1503	1243							LEGUMES FRAIS,CONG,SECS
0545	OTHER FRESH VEGETABLES	W 1456	1060							AUTRES LEGUMES FRAIS,REF
05459	FRESH VEGETABLES NES	W 1456	1060							LEGUMES FRAIS,REFRI NDA
0548	EDIBLE VEG NES FRESH,DRY	W 47	184							RACINES,TUBERCULES
05482	SUGAR BEET FRSH DRY,CANE	W 44	178							BETTERAVES,CANNES A SUCRE
07	COFFEE,TEA,COCOA,SPICES		1290							CAFE,THE,CACAO,EPICES
072	COCOA	W 1401	1243		1951		1137	W 1584	1479	CACAO
0721	COCOA BEANS,RAW,ROASTED	W 1401	1243					W 1584	1479	CACAO EN FEVES
09	MISC EDIBLE PRODUCTS		78							PREP ALIMENTAIRES DIVERSES
098	EDIBLE PRODCTS,PREPS NES	W 27	78							PREP ALIMENTAIRES NDA
09809	MISC FOOD PREPRTIONS NES	W 27	78							PREP ALIMENTAIRES NDA
2	CRUDE MATERLS,EXCL FUELS		8019							MAT BRUTES NON COMESTIBLES
21	HIDES,SKINS,FURS UNDRSSD		205							CUIRS,PEAUX BRUTS
211	HIDES,SKINS,EXC FURS,RAW	W 356	205							CUIRS ET PEAUX
2111	BOVINE,EQUINE HIDES,RAW				371		505	W 73	421	PEAUX DE BOVINS
2112	CALF AND KIP SKINS,RAW	W 356	205							PEAUX DE VEAUX
22	OIL SEEDS,OLEAGINOUS FRT		5817							GRAINES,FRUITS OLEAGINEUX
223	SEEDS FOR OTH FIXED OILS	W 28140	5817					W 30026	11115	GRAINES AUTRES HUILES FIXES
2231	COPRA	W 28140	5817		7717		9924	W 30026	11115	COPRAH
24	CORK AND WOOD		1785							LIEGE ET BOIS
245	FUEL WOOD NES, CHARCOAL	W 543	246							BOIS DE CHAUFFAGE
24502	WOOD CHARCOAL	W 543	246							CHARBON DE BOIS
247	OTH WOOD ROUGH,SQUARED	W 4126	616					W 337	3191	BOIS BRUTS EQUARRIS
2471	SAW–,VENEER–LOGS CONIFER	W 4126	616					W 337	3191	CONIFERES POUR SCIAGE,PLACAG
24711	— IN THE ROUGH	W 4126	616					W 337	3191	ECORCES OU DEGROSSIS
248	WOOD SHAPED,SLEEPERS	W 1205	923		2659		2274			BOIS SIMPLEMENT TRAVAILLES
2482	LUMBER SHAPED CONIFER	W 356	194							CONIFERES SCIES,RABOTES
24821	LUMBER SAWN ETC CONIFER	W 356	194							CONIFERES SCIES LONGITUD
2483	LUMBER SHAPED NON–CONIFR	W 849	729							NON CONIFERES SCIES,RABOTES
24831	LUMBER SAWN ETC NON–CON	W 738	524							SCIES LONGITUDINALEMENT
24832	LUMBER PLANED ETC NONCON	W 111	204							RABOTES,RAINES,LANGUETES
29	CRUDE ANIMAL,VEG MAT NES		198							MATIERES BRUTES ANIM,VEGET
291	CRUDE ANIMAL MTRIALS NES	W 200	192					W 7259	807	MATIERES BRUTES ANIMALES
2911	BONES,IVORY,HORNS,ETC	W 19	150					W 7259	807	OS,CORNES,SABOTS
29115	CORAL, SHELLS, AND WASTE	W 19	150		777		911	W 7259	807	CORAIL & SIMILAIRES
2924	VEG USED IN PHARMACY ETC				492		433	W 64	654	PLANTES MEDICINALES
6	BASIC MANUFACTURES		611							ART MANUFACTURES
63	WOOD,CORK MANUFACTRS NES		488							OUVRAGES LIEGE ET BOIS
634	VENEERS,PLYWOOD,ETC	W 937	448							PLACAGES,CONTRE–PLAQUES
6341	VENEER SHEETS ETC	W 354	119							BOIS SIMPLEMENT SCIES
6342	PLYWOOD OF WOOD SHEETS	W 221	129							BOIS CONTRE–PLAQUES
6349	WOOD SIMPLY SHAPED NES	W 293	178							BOIS SIMPL TRAVAILLES NDA
63491	HOOPWOOD,SPLIT POLES ETC	W 293	178							BOIS ETC
68	NON–FERROUS METALS		123							METAUX NON FERREUX
682	COPPER EXC CEMENT COPPER	W 218	123							CUIVRE
6822	COPPER,ALLOYS WORKED	W 218	123							CUIVRE,ALLIAGES OUVRES
68221	COPPER BARS,WIRE,ETC	W 218	123							BARRES,PROFILES ET FILS
7	MACHINES,TRANSPORT EQUIP		350							MACHINES MATERIEL TRANSPORT
77	ELECTRIC MACHNRY NES ETC		349							MACH APP ELECT NDA
776	TRANSISTORS,VALVES,ETC	W 6	349							LAMPES,TUBES,VALVES
7764	ELECTRONIC MICROCIRCUITS	W 6	349							MICROSTRUCTURES ELECTRON
8	MISC MANUFACTURED GOODS		609							ART MANUFACTURES DIVERS
89	MISC MANUFCTRD GOODS NES		595							ART MANUFACTURES DIVERS
899	OTHER MANUFACTURED GOODS	W 55	589							AUT ART MANUF DIVERS NDA
8991	CARVED,MOULDED GOODS	W 22	192							MAT A TAILLER,A MOULER
89911	GOODS OF ANML CARVNG MTL	W 22	192							ECAILLE,NACRE,IVOIRE ETC
8998	SMALLWARES,TOILETRYS ETC	W 34	397							ART MERCERIE,TOILETTE
89983	BUTTONS,STUDS,ETC	W 34	397							BOUTONS,BOUTONS–PRESSION
9	GOODS NOT CLASSD BY KIND		1364							ART TRANSACT NON CLASSES
931	*SPECIAL TRANSACTIONS	W 182	1364				3916			TRANS.SPECIALES

FOOT NOTES – NOTES

TABLE 1 –
1 Prior to 1980, general trade.
TABLEAU 1 –
1 Avant 1980, commerce général.

1. HISTORICAL SERIES, 1961–1996 GENERAL TRADE, IMPORTS F.O.B., EXPORTS F.O.B.
SERIES HISTORIQUES, 1961–1996 COMMERCE GENERAL, IMPORTATIONS F.O.B., EXPORTATIONS F.O.B

YEAR ANNEE	VALUE IN MILLION BOLIVARES VALEUR EN MILLION BOLIVARES MERCHANDISE –MARCHANDISE		GOLD –OR		CONVERSION FACTORS U.S. CENTS PER BOLIVAR FACTEURS DE CONVERSION CENTS E.U. PAR BOLIVAR		INDEX NUMBERS –INDICES QUANTUM		UNIT VALUE VALEUR UNITAIRE	
	IMPORTS	EXPORTS	IMPORTS	EXPORTS	IMPORTS	EXPORTS	IMPORTS	EXPORTS	IMPORTS	EXPORTS
1961	3522.00	8092.00	28.86		27.6800	29.8500				
1962	3871.00	8689.00	21.16	0.07	25.2900	29.8500				
1963	3703.00	8807.00	19.24	0.03	29.8500	29.8500				
1964	4886.00	9241.00	30.17		23.1900	29.2500				
1965	5590.00	12076.00	36.93	0.10	23.2100	22.7300				
1966	5120.00	11941.00	34.03		23.2100	22.7300				
1967	5632.00	11238.00	39.78		22.2207	22.7300				
1968	6532.00	11175.00	33.26		22.2242	22.2192				
1969	6748.00	11104.00	23.29		22.2247	22.2262				
1970	7382.00	14379.00	27.68	7.30	22.2247	22.2307			5	1
1971	8252.00	13996.00	28.92	0.30	22.2187	22,2198			5	1
1972	9471.00	12993.00	30.41	0.20	22.7272	22.7279			5	1
1973	10856.00	20431.00			23.2331	23.2731			5	2
1974	16249.00	47435.00			23.3383	23.3370			6	4
1975	22834.00	39876.00			23.3383	23.3370			7	5
1976	25841.00	41057.00			23.3083	23.3094			8	5
1977	41971.00	43506.00			23.2962	23.2962			8	6
1978	45599.00	41957.00			23.2964	23.2964			9	5
1979	41323.00	64024.00			23.2964	23.2964			10	8
1980	45804.00	85501.00			23.2964	23.2964			11	12
1981	50706.00	86388.00			23.2964	23.2964			12	13
1982	50093.00	70583.00			23.2964	23.2964			13	12
1983	33739.00	64470.00			23.2704	23.2694			14	11
1984	47566.00	99934.00			14.4527	14.3466			17	16
1985	55637.00	94034.00			13.3333	13.3333			19	16
1986	67427.10	77842.99			12.7547	11.1250			23	10
1987	115135.50	123353.00			7.5658	8.5746			38	19
1988	213008.00	154703.00			5.3877	6.5370			44	20
1989	239964.90	448466.90			2.9295	2.8691			83	60
1990	347899.90	831200.00			2.1394	2.1394			100	100
1991	637700.10	863000.00			1.7651	1.7651			119	94
1992	961900.00	975399.90			1.4705	1.4705			140	109
1993	1107200.00	1311800.00			1.1081	1.1081			189	127
1994	1324000.00	2409799.00			0.7018	0.7018			341	209
1995	2087200.00	3288100.00			0.5731	0.5623			514	278
1996	4179899.00	8810598.00			0.2342	0.2352			1098	331

2. IMPORTS BY BROAD ECONOMIC CATEGORY AND EXPORTS BY INDUSTRIAL ORIGIN. (PERCENTAGE OF TOTAL VALUE)
IMPORTATIONS PAR CATEGORIES ECONOMIQUES ET EXPORTATIONS PAR BRANCHE D'ACTIVITE.(EN POURCENTAGE DE LA VALEUR TOTALE)

IMPORTS – IMPORTATIONS

	1990	1991	1992	1993	1994	1995	1996
TOTAL IMPORTS–IMPORTATIONS TOTALES	100.	100.	100.	100.	100.	100.	
1 FOOD BEV–ALIMENTATION BOISSONS	8.3	8.5	7.8	8.4	10.5	11.2	
11 PRIMARY–PRODUITS DE BASE	3.8	3.2	2.9	3.2	4.1	4.4	
111 FOR INDUSTRY–POUR L'INDUSTRIE	2.9	2.1	1.9	2.0	2.8	2.8	
112 FOR HOUSEHOLDS–POUR LES MENAGES	0.9	1.0	1.0	1.2	1.4	1.7	
12 PROCESSED–PRODUITS ELABORES	4.5	5.3	4.8	5.2	6.4	6.8	
121 FOR INDUSTRY–POUR L'INDUSTRIE	2.0	1.6	1.5	1.5	2.5	2.8	
122 FOR HOUSEHOLDS–POUR LES MENAGES	2.5	3.7	3.4	3.7	3.9	4.0	
2 IND SUPPLIES–APPROV INDUSTRIELS	38.9	37.9	30.6	30.6	33.7	39.6	
21 PRIMARY–PRODUITS DE BASE	4.7	3.5	3.0	3.6	3.9	4.7	
22 PROCESSED–PRODUITS ELABORES	34.2	34.3	27.6	27.0	29.8	34.9	
3 FUELS–COMBUSTIBLES	2.4	1.7	0.8	0.6	1.1	0.5	
31 PRIMARY–PRODUITS DE BASE	0.1	0.2	0.3	0.1	0.0	0.0	
32 PROCESSED–PRODUITS ELABORES	2.3	1.4	0.5	0.5	1.1	0.5	
321 MOTOR SPIRIT–ESSENCE	2.1	0.5	0.0	0.0	0.2	0.0	
322 OTHER–AUTRES	0.2	0.9	0.4	0.5	0.9	0.5	
4 MACHINERY–EQUIPEMENT	33.8	32.3	33.2	32.8	31.8	24.7	
41 CAPITAL EQUIPMENT–MACHINES	27.4	26.4	28.9	28.5	27.0	19.9	
42 PARTS–PIECES ACCESSOIRES	6.4	5.9	4.3	4.3	4.7	4.8	
5 TRANSPORT–TRANSPORT	9.3	12.4	19.0	17.9	13.2	12.4	
51 PASSENGER CARS–AUTOMOBILES	2.7	4.5	8.8	8.6	6.4	5.9	
52 OTHER–AUTRES	2.6	3.1	4.8	4.7	3.6	2.9	
521 INDUSTRIAL–INDUSTRIELS	2.5	3.0	4.7	4.5	3.6	2.8	
522 NON INDUSTRIAL–NON INDUSTRIEL	0.1	0.1	0.1	0.2	0.1	0.1	
53 PARTS–PIECES ACCESSOIRES	4.0	4.8	5.4	4.5	3.2	3.6	
6 CONSUM GOODS–BIENS CONSOMMATION	6.5	7.0	8.4	9.6	9.6	11.6	
61 DURABLE–DURABLES	1.4	1.8	2.2	2.5	2.1	2.7	
62 SEMI DURABLE–SEMI DURABLES	3.5	3.4	4.4	4.8	4.5	5.9	
63 NON DURABLE–NON DURABLES	1.6	1.7	1.8	2.3	2.9	3.0	
7 GOODS NES–BIENS NDA	0.9	0.3	0.2	0.1	0.1	0.1	

EXPORTS – EXPORTATIONS

	1990	1991	1992	1993	1994	1995	1996
TOTAL EXPORTS–EXPORTATIONS TOTALES	100.	100.	100.	100.	100.	100.	
1 AGRICULTURE	1.1	1.1	1.2	1.4	1.3	1.0	
2 MINING QUARRY–INDUS EXTRACTIVES	82.0	53.4	52.9	49.8	50.6	46.3	
3 MANUFACTURING–IND MANUFACTUR	16.9	45.6	45.9	48.8	48.1	52.7	
31 FOOD BEV TOBACCO–ALIM BOISS TAB	1.1	1.2	1.5	1.5	1.7	1.9	
32 TEXTILES–INDUSTRIES TEXTILES	0.9	0.4	0.5	0.6	0.6	0.6	
33 WOOD & PRODUCTS–BOIS & PRODUITS	0.0	0.0	0.0	0.0	0.0	0.0	
34 PAPER & PRODUCTS–PAPIER & PRODT	0.5	0.4	0.4	0.4	0.5	0.7	
35 CHEMICALS–INDUSTRIES CHIMIQUES	2.4	32.7	32.1	33.4	31.5	36.2	
36 NON METAL MIN–MIN NON METAL	0.6	0.8	0.8	0.9	1.1	1.1	
37 BASIC METAL–IND METAL BASE	8.5	8.0	8.0	7.7	8.5	8.2	
38 METAL MANUF–MANUF METAL	2.7	2.0	2.6	4.0	4.2	3.9	
39 OTH MANUF IND–AUTRES MANUF	0.1	0.0	0.1	0.2	0.1	0.1	

3. TRADE BY PRINCIPAL COUNTRIES OF FIRST AND LAST CONSIGNMENT (VALUE IN THOUSAND U.S. DOLLARS)
ECHANGES SELON LES PRINCIPAUX PAYS DE PREMIERE ET DE DERNIERE CONSIGNATION (VALEUR EN MILLIERS DE DOLLARS EU)

COUNTRIES–PAYS	GENERAL IMPORTS F.O.B. IMPORTATIONS GENERALES F.O.B.				
	1991	1992	1993	1994	1995
World	10037555	12668057	11266624	8036709	10791286
Africa	45454	46074	26734	60521	29775
Americas	6617354	8226120	7275854	5394753	7706721
Northern America	5072253	6184097	5567657	3998426	5052036
LAIA	1272927	1665791	1474881	1208534	2291011
CACM	6511	24889	20751	33571	77124
Caribbean	123970	143852	87811	60369	83438
Rest of America	141693	207490	124753	93853	203112
As.ex F.USSR	755900	1343248	1304979	738152	912435
Eur.x F.USSR	2525451	2958795	2599264	1794193	2067042
EU	2371370	2830569	2475450	1694880	1935817
EFTA	108549	113941	111224	90338	110768
East Europe	43432	13081	10554	8379	19618
Other Europe	2099	4	15	21	32
Former USSR	17167	48993	18442	2629	13631
Oceania	76103	44612	41320	46405	61660
USA/Etats–Unis d'Amer	4793301	5901270	5201374	3704478	4594523
Japan/Japon	499190	944075	860822	450024	473707
Germany/Allemagne	698883	819422	625775	445049	521295
Colombia/Colombie	289533	487123	469580	401199	818801
Italy/Italie	474613	605917	533457	299118	323758
Brazil/Brésil	452491	496247	398180	254013	415521
Canada	278416	282397	366112	293632	457317
United Kingdom	268434	294126	286863	207617	217075
France,Monac	225852	241180	328392	217778	249720
Mexico/Mexique	149614	250560	219257	181601	351636
Spain/Espagne	236930	285625	235009	138270	250041
Argentina/Argentine	215892	226343	213125	190780	292905
Netherlands/Pays–Bas	150761	168462	167234	154265	135332
Panama	129575	201821	116813	93132	200975
Belgium–Luxembourg	158555	227597	137305	105345	111773
Peru/Pérou	89491	103779	82953	77072	154946
Switz.Liecht	93780	97000	97351	82235	93826
Korea, Republic of	53515	89406	99506	63064	102490
Chile/Chili	48410	68417	74577	64706	119691
Hong Kong	43652	93996	114271	40649	62029
Sweden/Suède	39214	90540	66502	38733	30479
New Zealand	64233	33093	30771	42191	53654
Netherlands Antilles	26171	39918	37080	24238	45545
Denmark/Danemark	41611	36434	30088	32146	29520
Trinidad and Tobago	57709	30540	15969	20959	22342
Finland/Finlande	25981	27901	28379	23269	29291
So. Africa Customs Un	26811	32234	19872	26716	27038
Paraguay	10009	8973	2899	21993	82941
Singapore/Singapour	9296	22196	26881	24321	26024
Austria/Autriche	27327	15820	17328	18220	17181
Israel/Israël	15191	18842	15918	19589	19636
Russian Federation		48993	18442	373	12824
Guatemala	2812	844	2563	19677	53626
Norway,SVD,JM	14759	16940	13871	8067	16935
Poland/Pologne	34168	8650	5572	6013	12444
Ecuador/Equateur	6647	13785	7880	7940	29561
Malaysia/Malaisie	7547	7683	18556	9018	18627
Jamaica/Jamaïque	9367	26522	17010	3839	1761
Indonesia/Indonésie	10403	5407	11331	11673	16438
Ireland/Irlande	12305	10629	7454	7709	11490
Cuba	17901	19887	3343	5081	2344
India/Inde	3583	5601	13147	10832	14977
Turkey/Turquie	5388	7203	4695	10079	18491
Australia/Australie	11705	11371	10195	4066	5402
Uruguay	7283	9382	5295	5588	12327
El Salvador	212	8344	7747	10434	10387
Portugal	6498	5657	9632	6848	8182
Costa Rica	3149	5570	9214	3204	10524
Guyana	11008	5075	6873	489	1859
Anguilla	7698	8940	2462	1421	3448

COUNTRIES–PAYS	GENERAL EXPORTS F.O.B. EXPORTATIONS GENERALES F.O.B.				
	1991	1992	1993	1994	1995
Monde	15129868	14235322	15208136	16649658	18914219
Afrique	26785	37480	51143	15414	35682
Amériques	11451539	11855820	13236641	14488419	16493805
Amérique du Nord	8461381	7871923	8596376	8863071	9892312
ALAI	1153589	1284228	1823039	2390319	3940953
MCAC	238775	344771	376011	406637	377420
Caraïbes	1562375	2089791	2130003	1868290	1802065
Autre Amérique	35419	265107	311212	960102	481054
Asie l'URSS exclus	538583	541519	391375	366592	374959
Europe l'URSS exclus	1954601	1555086	1326463	1519575	1742327
UE	1898375	1521698	1281209	1490710	1722290
AELE	38208	28548	44932	21372	19266
Europe de l'Est	16731	3904	300	7438	765
Autre de l'Europe	1288	31	21	29	
Ancienne URSS	15069	1592	3790	10483	43882
Océanie	4514	4688	8514	1358	441
USA/Etats–Unis d'Amer	7872766	7709923	8472113	8648713	9645719
Netherlands Antilles	923828	1343675	1358582	1051159	927279
Colombia/Colombie	307785	497599	910079	1174901	1423247
Brazil/Brésil	340119	261233	376987	568150	1683907
Germany/Allemagne	648426	345053	342522	342239	345141
Netherlands/Pays–Bas	395793	562705	335499	244242	317505
Suriname/Suriname	2763	206027	249428	888389	388973
Japan/Japon	415535	361114	223680	283075	292775
United Kingdom	181967	103627	262531	437155	531776
Canada	588615	149839	123464	211082	215753
Dominican Republic	124215	134870	195412	315344	242598
Mexico/Mexique	132215	193325	224351	251906	177604
Trinidad and Tobago	261723	256754	183773	154829	75887
Anguilla	97207	106718	102750	125544	305351
Chile/Chili	146591	116228	128388	106104	138723
Peru/Pérou	89949	119098	89402	97171	239419
Italy/Italie	131504	88131	64600	128750	158053
Belgium–Luxembourg	165028	124486	84911	100944	61386
Guatemala	75557	88858	110366	108582	143011
Ecuador/Equateur	45530	47693	44463	146110	215206
El Salvador	66781	92461	108828	118317	63826
Cuba	48503	79380	120313	89622	111749
Spain/Espagne	134109	84186	47608	103572	78238
France,Monac	125488	102815	59234	41700	81662
Costa Rica	69245	50827	60178	87299	129453
Sweden/Suède	93064	48357	54610	75474	104233
Jamaica/Jamaïque	62028	62764	70446	67731	49027
Nicaragua	2829	97897	86527	81247	18660
Panama	26860	40525	48607	61838	61809
Bahamas	944	59200	57815	30312	46403
Argentina/Argentine	60357	22330	31210	34986	35973
Korea, Republic of	17576	17370	21898	22279	36082
Portugal	1911	52150	11973	13287	33862
Norway,SVD,JM	20688	21509	31265	8690	10535
Uruguay	28655	21775	9527	7857	16907
Honduras	24363	14728	10111	11191	22471
Singapore/Singapour	178	59974	12076	8982	1399
Barbados/Barbade	5090	17617	18148	18988	6574
Switz.Liecht	17520	7039	13632	12682	8731
India/Inde	185	9161	34431	9091	5836
Russian Federation		1592	3790	10483	41941
Egypt/Egypte	16661	7726	19265	0	8391
Bermuda/Bermudes		12161	800	3275	30841
Guyana	5495	13560	8807	9611	7728
Guadeloupe	11240	12663	6132	4982	9344
Haiti/Haïti	13757	4055	1227	2838	18415
Hong Kong	17749	9984	2406	1180	6465
Thailand/Thaïlande	14932	5851	10381	4744	1678
Yemen/Yémen		15921	11764	6828	
Finland/Finlande	14949	7537	7963	201	3547

(VALUE AS PERCENTAGE OF WORLD TOTAL)(VALEURS EN POURCENTAGE DU TOTAL MONDIAL)

	1986	1987	1988	1989	1990	1991	1992	1993	1994	1995
Africa	0.4	0.5	0.6	0.5	0.4	0.5	0.4	0.2	0.8	0.3
Americas	58.5	59.0	58.5	59.1	63.4	65.9	64.9	64.6	67.1	71.4
Northern America	48.5	47.3	45.8	46.5	49.6	50.5	48.8	49.4	49.8	46.8
LAIA	8.1	9.2	10.0	9.3	11.1	12.7	13.1	13.1	15.0	21.2
CACM	0.1	0.1	0.1	0.1	0.0	0.1	0.2	0.2	0.4	0.7
Caribbean	0.3	1.1	1.2	1.7	1.4	1.2	1.1	0.8	0.8	0.8
Rest of America	1.5	1.3	1.4	1.4	1.3	1.4	1.6	1.1	1.2	1.9
As.ex F.USSR	9.3	8.4	7.9	6.5	6.5	7.5	10.6	11.6	9.2	8.5
Eur.x F.USSR	30.3	31.4	32.1	32.9	28.8	25.2	23.4	23.1	22.3	19.2
EU	28.3	28.8	29.5	30.5	27.0	23.6	22.3	22.0	21.1	17.9
EFTA	1.5	2.0	2.1	1.8	1.6	1.1	0.9	1.0	1.1	1.0
East Europe	0.5	0.6	0.5	0.5	0.2	0.4	0.1	0.1	0.1	0.2
Other Europe	0.0	0.0	0.1	0.2	0.0	0.0	0.0	0.0	0.0	0.0
Former USSR	0.0	0.0	0.0	0.4	0.1	0.2	0.4	0.2	0.0	0.1
Oceania	0.3	0.6	0.8	0.6	0.9	0.8	0.4	0.4	0.6	0.6
USA/Etats–Unis d'Amer	45.9	44.6	42.6	44.3	46.7	47.8	46.6	46.2	46.1	42.6
Japan/Japon	6.8	6.1	5.4	4.1	3.9	5.0	7.5	7.6	5.6	4.4
Germany/Allemagne	7.3	8.6	9.1	7.9	9.9	7.0	6.5	5.6	5.5	4.8
Colombia/Colombie	1.1	1.2	1.4	1.4	2.2	2.9	3.8	4.2	5.0	7.6
Italy/Italie	4.7	5.0	6.1	7.3	4.8	4.7	4.8	4.7	3.7	3.0
Brazil/Brésil	4.3	4.3	4.8	4.0	4.0	4.5	3.9	3.5	3.2	3.9
Canada	2.6	2.7	3.2	2.2	2.9	2.8	2.2	3.2	3.7	4.2
United Kingdom	4.1	3.4	2.8	3.0	3.0	2.7	2.3	2.5	2.6	2.0
France,Monac	4.4	3.5	3.3	3.0	3.5	2.3	1.9	2.9	2.7	2.3
Mexico/Mexique	0.8	1.1	1.2	0.9	1.5	1.5	2.0	1.9	2.3	3.3

	1986	1987	1988	1989	1990	1991	1992	1993	1994	1995
Afrique	0.2	0.1	0.2	0.3	0.1	0.2	0.3	0.3	0.1	0.2
Amériques	65.8	21.4	60.4	75.3	69.5	75.7	83.3	87.0	87.0	87.2
Amérique du Nord	56.7	6.5	50.3	59.2	54.2	55.9	55.3	56.5	53.2	52.3
ALAI	4.4	5.8	5.7	5.5	6.7	7.6	9.0	12.0	14.4	20.8
MCAC	2.0	2.5	2.0	1.9	2.0	1.6	2.4	2.5	2.4	2.0
Caraïbes	2.0	5.9	2.2	8.4	6.3	10.3	14.7	14.0	11.2	9.5
Autre Amérique	0.7	0.6	0.3	0.3	0.3	0.2	1.9	2.0	5.8	2.5
Asie l'URSS exclus	4.3	3.3	5.1	4.6	4.4	3.6	3.8	2.6	2.2	2.0
Europe l'URSS exclus	15.1	2.2	16.5	16.8	14.2	12.9	10.9	8.7	9.1	9.2
UE	14.9	1.6	13.9	15.0	14.0	12.5	10.7	8.4	9.0	9.1
AELE	0.1	0.7	2.5	1.6	0.2	0.3	0.2	0.3	0.1	0.1
Europe de l'Est	0.0	0.0	0.2	0.2	0.1	0.1	0.0	0.0	0.0	0.0
Autre de l'Europe	0.0		0.0		0.0	0.0	0.0	0.0	0.0	
Ancienne URSS			0.1	0.0	0.0	0.1	0.0	0.0	0.1	0.2
Océanie	0.0	0.0	0.0	0.1	0.1	0.0	0.0	0.1	0.0	0.0
USA/Etats–Unis d'Amer	53.0	6.5	47.0	55.3	51.6	52.0	54.2	55.7	51.9	51.0
Netherlands Antilles		0.3	0.4	6.3	0.3	6.1	9.4	8.9	6.3	4.9
Colombia/Colombie	1.3	1.3	1.6	1.9	2.1	2.0	3.5	6.0	7.1	7.5
Brazil/Brésil	1.1	1.3	1.8	1.6	1.9	2.2	1.8	2.5	3.4	8.9
Germany/Allemagne	4.9	0.0	4.4	4.7	3.7	4.3	2.4	2.3	2.1	1.8
Netherlands/Pays–Bas	2.6	0.8	3.6	3.8	3.9	2.6	4.0	2.2	1.5	1.7
Suriname/Suriname	0.0	0.1	0.0	0.0	0.1	0.0	1.4	1.6	5.3	2.1
Japan/Japon	3.3	2.5	4.5	4.0	2.8	2.7	2.5	1.5	1.7	1.5
United Kingdom	1.8	0.1	1.2	1.4	0.9	1.2	0.7	1.7	2.6	2.8
Canada	3.7	0.1	3.3	3.9	2.6	3.9	1.1	0.8	1.3	1.1

4. General Imports F.O.B. by Commodities according to the S.I.T.C. (Rev. 2) in thousand U.S. Dollars
Importations Générales F.O.B. par Produits d'après la C.T.C.I. (Rév. 2) en milliers de Dollars E.U.

SITC CTCI	COMMODITY	1992		1993		1994		1995		PRODUIT
		WEIGHT POIDS	VALUE VALEUR	WEIGHT POIDS	VALUE VALEUR	WEIGHT POIDS	VALUE VALEUR	WEIGHT POIDS	VALUE VALEUR	
	ALL COMMODITIES		12668057		11266624		8036709		10791286	TOUS PRODUITS
0	FOOD AND LIVE ANIMALS		912641		930906		800618		1164985	ALIMENTS,ANIMAUX VIVANTS
02	DAIRY PRODCTS,BIRDS'EGGS		134051		102987		124998		177659	PRODUITS LAITIERS,OEUFS
022	MILK AND CREAM	W 57029	105147	W 43746	79334	W 60128	114716	W 71130	152562	LAIT ET CREME
0224	MILK,CREAM PRESERVED ETC	W 55996	103257	W 41883	77209	W 58055	111085	W 68684	148894	LAIT,CREME CONS,CONC
02243	MILK DRY,OVER 1.5% FAT	W 51959	97278	W 36482	67537	W 40926	78623	W 64934	142707	LAIT POUDRE SUP 1.5%
04	CEREALS AND PREPARATIONS		352629		409026		350059		428168	CEREALES ET PRODUITS
041	WHEAT ETC UNMILLED	W 1176324	179773	W 1110375	186969	W 1063447	183067	W 1036179	193776	FROMENT,EPEAUTRE
0411	DURUM WHEAT UNMILLED	W 416665	64486	W 333957	56421	W 437731	80573	W 305432	64451	FROMENT DUR NON MOULU
0412	OTHER WHEAT ETC UNMILLED	W 759660	115287	W 776418	130548	W 625715	102495	W 730748	129326	AUTRE FROMENT NON MOULU
044	MAIZE UNMILLED	W 821907	100066	W 1180445	155446	W 791594	106896	W 1055210	144550	MAIS NON MOULU
048	CEREAL ETC PREPARATIONS	W 230095	69077	W 229867	61385	W 191735	47088	W 166563	63818	PREPTNS A BASE CEREALES
0482	MALT INCLUDING FLOUR	W 210726	53528	W 211224	47080	W 174501	33967	W 146098	43319	MALT MEME TORREFIE
05	VEGETABLES AND FRUIT		133029		142934		122990		179213	LEGUMES ET FRUITS
054	VEG ETC FRSH,SMPLY PRSVD	W 231236	81270	W 251350	91820	W 188035	80795	W 245234	125778	LEGUMES FRAIS,CONG,SECS
0542	LEGUMINOUS VEGETBLES DRY	W 84601	42164	W 87724	46846	W 66869	38714	W 111111	73865	LEGUMES A COSSE SECS
057	FRUIT,NUTS,FRESH,DRIED	W 54118	32658	W 52526	33865	W 34796	31589	W 38787	36954	FRUITS FRAIS OU SECS
06	SUGAR AND PREPS,HONEY		94057		78545		88428		171232	SUCRES ET PRODUITS
061	SUGAR AND HONEY	W 333768	88146	W 231585	66621	W 251633	81046	W 440350	156292	SUCRES ET MIEL
0611	RAW BEET AND CANE SUGAR	W 190458	49561	W 184351	50936	W 203358	62912	W 346581	123861	SUCRES BRUTS
081	*FEEDING STUFF FOR ANIML	W 564636	134918	W 575642	148394	W 319521	82239	W 501939	126058	NOURRITURE POUR ANIMAUX
0813	OILCAKE AND OTH RESIDUES	W 543034	125764	W 549250	133198	W 291006	68592	W 480388	111082	TOURTEAUX
08131	— OF SOYA BEANS	W 523613	123010	W 549213	133178	W 291004	68581	W 480381	111037	TOURTEAUX DE SOJA
1	BEVERAGES AND TOBACCO		141050		173879		98918		105117	BOISSONS ET TABACS
11	BEVERAGES		134337		164974		90117		88569	BOISSONS
112	ALCOHOLIC BEVERAGES	W 37885	131029	W 46846	164090	W 21699	89869	W 20646	88271	BOISSONS ALCOOLIQUES
1124	DISTILLED ALCOHOLIC BEVS	W 20549	105593	W 29924	137480	W 16269	80558	W 14945	78473	ALCOOLS,EAUX–DE–VIE
11241	WHISKY	W 14072	81025	W 23464	116639	W 13539	71321	W 11368	66936	WHISKY
2	CRUDE MATERLS,EXCL FUELS		487810		431730		374232		671025	MAT BRUTES NON COMESTIBLES
22	OIL SEEDS,OLEAGINOUS FRT		38551		30046		32009		66687	GRAINES,FRUITS OLEAGINEUX
222	SEEDS FOR'SOFT'FIXED OIL	W 152582	37653	W 114870	28439	W 123572	31202	W 234035	65979	GRAINES HUILES FIXES
2222	SOYA BEANS	W 148771	34381	W 112624	26158	W 122101	29494	W 230827	62780	FEVES DE SOJA
23	RUBBER, CRUDE		69601		66165		54566		100455	CAOUTCHOUC BRUT
232	NATURAL RUBBER,GUMS	W 23519	22322	W 23908	24774	W 19204	22440	W 24242	40283	LATEX CAOUTCHOUC NATUREL
233	RUBBER,SYNTHTIC,RECLAIMD	W 41688	47279	W 39979	41392	W 31979	32126	W 43560	60172	LATEX CAOUTCH SYNTH REGEN
2331	SYNTHETIC RUBBER ETC	W 41307	46983	W 39562	41153	W 31436	31856	W 42449	59550	LATEX CAOUTCH SYNTHETIQUE
23315	POLYBUTADIENE–STYRN(SBR)	W 23001	21094	W 23855	20711	W 19322	15988	W 26198	33081	POLYBUTADIENE–STYRENE
251	*PULP AND WASTE PAPER	W 395051	141199	W 400733	123126	W 362136	129483	W 440830	254724	PATES A PAPIER,DECHETS
2511	WASTE PAPER,PPRBOARD ETC	W 205652	40186	W 188458	28892	W 184417	34156	W 238540	79307	DECHETS DE PAPIER
2517	SODA,SULPHATE WOOD PULP	W 184457	97749	W 198406	86417	W 168015	90757	W 198091	171711	PATES CHIMIQUES AU SULFATE
25172	— BLEACHED,NONDISSOLVNG	W 149326	81010	W 160327	69126	W 138484	76932	W 166796	147247	PATES BLANCHIES
26	TEXTILE FIBRES AND WASTE		59965		44606		41401		93368	FIBRES TEXTILES
263	COTTON	W 26837	42129	W 19926	26400	W 20835	28595	W 34316	74404	COTON
2631	RAW COTTON,EXCL LINTERS	W 26592	39378	W 19767	26077	W 20755	28542	W 34008	73813	COTON EN MASSE
27	CRUDE FERTLZR,MINRLS NES		66626		64188		55831		74521	ENGRAIS MINERAUX BRUTS
278	OTHER CRUDE MINERALS	W 378674	51194	W 546464	50052	W 372878	42823	W 492280	58063	AUTRES MINERAUX BRUTS
2782	REFRACTORY MINERALS NES	W 107079	26659	W 116976	27336	W 134611	22883	W 236284	34322	ARGILE MINERAUX REFRACTAIRES
28	METALLIFEROUS ORES,SCRAP		67534		73976		37974		49131	MINERAIS METAL,DECHETS
287	BASE METAL ORES,CONC NES	W 1524709	60476		62525	W 127136	16608	W 366602	22039	MINERAIS METAUX COMMUNS
2873	ALUMINIUM ORES,ALUMINA	W 1465031	50649	W 1662644	56365	W 35094	8435	W 241729	11917	MINERAIS D'ALUMINIUM
28731	ALUMINIUM ORE,CONCNTRATE	W 1460717	45721	W 1657500	51598	W 26792	2674	W 232889	5899	MINERAIS D'ALUMINIUM
3	MINERAL FUELS ETC		167235		138201		123609		125003	COMBUSTIBLES MINERAUX LUB
33	PETROLEUM AND PRODUCTS		118778		114941		113562		105662	PETROLE ET DERIVES
334	PETROLEUM PRODUCTS,REFIN	W 123731	49185	W 97861	43062	W 381963	79208	W 46298	35952	PRODUITS RAFFINES
3345	LUBS,PETROLEUM OILS NES	W 122750	48381	W 59737	38475	W 88127	36322	W 45434	35109	HUILES LUBRIFIANTES
33451	LUBS(HIGH PETR CONT) ETC	W 120785	43429	W 58708	35839	W 86687	32630	W 43532	30063	HUILES LUBRIF,H LOURDES
335	RESIDUAL PETRLM PROD NES	W 353563	69570	W 374853	71780	W 213920	34291	W 379799	69657	PRODUITS RESIDUELS NDA
3354	PETROLM BITUMEN,COKE ETC	W 258614	36491	W 283262	42276	W 178635	22125	W 283448	37356	BITUME,COKE DE PETROLE
33542	PETROLEUM COKE	W 237751	32120	W 282049	40441	W 151823	17989	W 282570	36396	COKE DE PETROLE
4	ANIMAL,VEGETABLE OIL,FAT		167443		154746		139102		205282	HUILES,GRAISSES ANIM,VEG
411	*ANIMAL OILS AND FATS	W 81492	25566	W 84333	26209	W 53428	21374	W 79678	35972	HUILES,GRAISSES ANIMALES
4113	ANIML OIL,FAT,GREASE NES	W 81408	25416	W 84247	25887	W 53359	21089	W 79514	35525	HUILES,GRAISSES ANIMALES NDA
41132	FATS OF BOVINE,SHEEP,ETC	W 81180	24777	W 84030	25384	W 53299	20832	W 79400	35082	SUIFS BRUTS FONDUS
42	FIXED VEGETABLE OIL,FAT		137499		126171		114044		161401	HUILES VEGETALES FIXES
423	FIXED VEG OILS,SOFT	W 287177	125848	W 236694	118401	W 180438	108127	W 214813	149107	HUILES VEGET DOUCES FIXES
4232	SOYA BEAN OIL	W 132232	55551	W 115206	51996	W 137941	81113	W 155042	104282	HUILE DE SOJA
4236	SUNFLOWER SEED OIL	W 151878	66826	W 118967	62818	W 38762	23503	W 54296	37655	HUILE DE TOURNESOL
5	CHEMCLS,RELATED PROD NES		1507784		1356576		1085218		1735020	PRODUITS CHIMIQUES
51	ORGANIC CHEMICALS		414303		372937		311353		507023	PROD CHIMIQ ORGANIQUES
511	HYDROCARBONS NES,DERIVS	W 136023	56399	W 117340	47542	W 105199	43766	W 88201	64025	HYDROCARBURES NDA
5112	CYCLIC HYDROCARBONS	W 32577	15595	W 43439	17978	W 71518	28017	W 55222	43751	HYDROCARBURES CYCLIQUES
512	ALCOHOLS,PHENOLS ETC	W 210589	60239	W 228281	51698	W 83021	35975	W 40423	50218	PHENOLS,PHENOLS–ALCOOLS
5121	ACYCLIC ALCOHOLS,DERIVS	W 200712	49635	W 220717	42733	W 77716	28192	W 30759	36157	ALCOOLS ACYCLIQUES
513	CARBOXYLIC ACIDS ETC	W 74707	73068	W 59446	68558	W 56012	63513	W 84821	122009	ACIDES CARBOXYLIQUES
5137	MONOACIDS AND DERIVATIVS	W 34738	36595	W 28601	33812	W 21349	27453	W 30234	50323	ACIDES MONOCARBOXYLIQUES
5138	POLYACIDS AND DERIVATIVS	W 35518	24057	W 25555	17915	W 29903	24202	W 48273	54973	ACIDES POLYCARBOXYLIQUES
51389	OTH POLYACIDS ETC,DERIVS	W 26653	18470	W 21402	15272	W 27233	21435	W 40269	44968	ACIDES POLYCARBOXYLIQUES
514	NITROGEN–FNCTN COMPOUNDS	W 25109	89979	W 24062	83054	W 19334	65065	W 24819	97762	COMPOSES FONCT AZOTEES
5148	OTH NITROGN–FNCTN CMPNDS	W 15279	51201	W 13195	45082	W 9968	34170	W 12287	52043	AUTRES COMPOSES AZOTES
515	ORG–INORG COMPOUNDS ETC	W 12632	87774	W 12552	88263	W 10593	70747	W 13713	89007	COMPOSES ORGANO–MINERAUX
5156	HETEROCYCLIC CMPDS ETC	W 5926	54172	W 3854	45575	W 3438	36382	W 5650	51067	COMPOSES HETEROCYCLIQUES
51569	OTH HETEROCYC CMPDS,ETC	W 2496	48379	W 2330	43217	W 1662	34012	W 2656	46188	AUT COMP HETEROCYCLIQUES
516	OTHER ORGANIC CHEMICALS	W 45949	46844	W 28591	33821	W 26817	32288	W 121781	84003	AUTRES PROD ORGANIQUES
5161	ETHERS,EPOXIDES,ACETALS	W 21468	19266	W 15753	14146	W 16178	15064	W 108242	56478	ETHERS–OXYDES,ALCOOLS
51611	ETHERS,ETHER–ALCOHOL,ETC	W 10407	8796	W 7573	7384	W 7366	7395	W 97432	44867	ETHERS–OXYDES
52	INORGANIC CHEMICALS		216504		197495		103651		204580	PROD CHIM INORGANIQUES
522	INORG ELEMNTS,OXIDES,ETC	W 343099	97217	W 385831	59330	W 151699	39018	W 416557	97981	ELEMENTS INORGANIQUES
5225	INORGANIC BASES ETC NES	W 219005	51285	W 281090	25038	W 26687	6687	W 306850	54960	AUTRES BASES OXYDES METAL
52252	SODIUM HYDROXIDE, SOLID	W 127579	31651	W 111371	8985	W 2409	828	W 286942	44824	HYDROXYDE DE SODIUM
523	OTHR INORG CHEMICALS ETC	W 340509	118295		137329	W 171207	63851	W 336454	105877	AUT PRODUITS CHIMIQUES INORG
5231	METAL CMPD OF INORG ACID	W 120638	56549	W 119658	59763	W 44710	24728	W 92461	46164	SELS METALLIQUES
5232	OTH MTL CMPD OF INRG ACD	W 214267	55388		71919	W 123409	35371	W 237851	52953	SELS METALLIQUES
52323	NEUTRAL SODIUM CARBONATE	W 179990	31817	W 207219	34023	W 87011	14498	W 208996	33868	CARBONATE NEUTRE SODIUM
53	DYES,TANNING,COLOUR PROD		95773		82207		59610		99097	PROD TEINTURE,COLORANTS
531	SYNT DYE,NAT INDGO,LAKES	W 2621	39322	W 3019	30259	W 2621	24008	W 2998	31232	MAT COLOR ORGAN,LAQUES
533	PIGMENTS,PAINTS,ETC	W 19125	49292	W 18805	48138	W 12375	31027	W 22378	61454	PIGMENTS,PEINTURES,VERNIS
541	*MEDICINAL,PHARM PRODUCT	K 6018465	142832	K 8175265	152411	K 8511513	144053	MK 11155	206132	PROD MEDICINAUX PHARMACEUT
5413	ANTIBIOTICS IN BULK	K 487850	41002	K 429869	33765	K 282425	26528	K 539764	45696	ANTIBIOTIQUES NDA
54139	OTHER ANTIBIOTICS	K 293975	27495	K 277130	23548	K 187957	19212	K 354410	36453	AUTRES ANTIBIOTIQUES
5417	MEDICAMENTS	K 3384507	47208	K 4707712	60511	K 6204359	68351	K 7874380	94520	MEDICAMENTS
54179	— CONTNG OTH SUBSTANCES	K 3044563	26357	K 3984959	33938	K 5933876	42915	K 7327202	56010	MED CONT AUT SUBSTANCES

4. General Imports F.O.B. by Commodities according to the S.I.T.C. (Rev. 2) in thousand U.S. Dollars
Importations Générales F.O.B. par Produits d'après la C.T.C.I. (Rév. 2) en milliers de Dollars E.U.

SITC CTCI	COMMODITY	1992 WEIGHT POIDS	1992 VALUE VALEUR	1993 WEIGHT POIDS	1993 VALUE VALEUR	1994 WEIGHT POIDS	1994 VALUE VALEUR	1995 WEIGHT POIDS	1995 VALUE VALEUR	PRODUIT
55	PERFUME,CLEANING ETC PRD		82552		80430		72076		120709	PROD POUR PARFUM,TOILETTE
551	ESSENTL OILS,PERFUME,ETC	W 2373	43735	W 2663	39903	W 1891	31428	W 2256	38598	HUILES ESSENTIELLES
5514	MIXED PERFUME SUBSTANCES	W 2098	39312	W 2175	36206	W 1630	28252	W 1970	33083	MELANGES SUBSTAN ODORIFER
553	PERFUMERY,COSMETICS,ETC	W 2212	23516	W 3056	23830	W 4651	23005	W 10105	40784	PRODUITS DE PARFUMERIE
554	SOAP,CLEANSING ETC PREPS	W 11088	15300	W 10025	16697	W 11573	17643	W 28272	41327	SAVONS,PRODUITS DETERSIFS
562	*FERTILIZERS,MANUFACTURE	W 414160	66176	W 193967	26128	W 97015	11692	W 152586	25344	ENGRAIS MANUFACTURES
58	PLASTIC MATERIALS ETC		232463		214078		162712		276895	MAT PLAST ARTIFICIELLES
582	PROD OF CONDENSATION ETC	W 23796	56640	W 19489	48306	W 14985	37027	W 21113	58781	PROD CONDENS,POLYCOND
583	POLYMERIZATION ETC PRODS	W 148207	150925	W 132660	140515	W 76836	97484	W 121162	181414	PROD POLYMERISATION
5834	POLYVINYL CHLORIDE	W 48467	32970	W 32258	23009	W 23396	20952	W 43120	48267	CHLORURE DE POLYVINYLE
58341	— IN PRIMARY FORMS	W 47704	30876	W 31545	20958	W 22734	18815	W 41563	42666	SOUS FORMES PRIMAIRES
5839	OTH POLYMRZTION ETC PROD	W 26800	41543	W 25696	43491	W 12736	27931	W 16715	44333	AUT PROD POLYMER COPOLYM
584	CELLULOSE DERIVATIVS ETC	W 6868	22256	W 8179	23260	W 10105	26556	W 10990	32726	CEL REGEN NIT ACETATE
59	CHEMICAL MATERIALS NES		252267		224915		213858		285017	MAT PROD CHIMIQUES NDA
591	PESTICIDES,DISINFECTANTS	W 3797	19140	W 3740	19626	W 3613	17667	W 6937	37845	DESINF,INSECT,FONG,HERB
598	MISCEL CHEM PRODUCTS NES	W 82041	210524	W 76524	186700	W 91801	178603	W 73411	225565	PROD DIV INDUST CHIM NDA
5982	ANTI–KNOCK PREPARTNS ETC	W 21918	77199	W 22525	71712	W 51410	68871	W 21987	89601	PREPARAT ANTIDETONANTES
5989	CHEM PRODUCTS,PREPS NES	W 50827	119014	W 45674	103891	W 32919	99980	W 41324	121083	PROD PREP CHIMIQUES NDA
59898	COMPOUND CATALYSTS	W 8431	28171	W 9777	32812	W 8943	43379	W 8119	42978	CATALYSEURS COMPOSITES
59899	OTH CHEM PRODS,PREPS,NES	W 31757	76341	W 26166	57798	W 16095	45210	W 24368	64242	AUT PRODUITS CHIMIQUES NDA
6	BASIC MANUFACTURES		1784756		1466417		1174891		1808737	ART MANUFACTURES
61	LEATHER,DRESSED FUR,ETC		30009		26953		16794		35111	CUIRS,PELLETERIES
62	RUBBER MANUFACTURES NES		96914		91160		65030		105078	CAOUTCHOUC MANUFACTURE
625	RUBBER TYRES, TUBES ETC	W 21541	46831	W 17232	45259	W 10334	30477	W 16384	55263	PNEUS CAOUTCHOUC VULCANISE
628	RUBBER ARTICLES NES	W 4013	37213	W 4417	35376	W 2593	25617	W 3387	36719	OUVRAGES CAOUTCHOUC NDA
64	PAPER,PAPERBOARD AND MFR		202850		206420		159106		245584	PAPIERS,CARTONS & OUVRAGES
641	PAPER AND PAPERBOARD	W 214007	166901	W 197093	158285	W 163233	123750	W 169632	168611	PAPIERS ET CARTONS
6411	NEWSPRINT	W 135162	75479	W 126496	75880	W 107219	59108	W 106298	76837	PAPIER JOURNAL
6418	COATED ETC PAPER NES BLK	W 25114	36875	W 23899	35291	W 20569	29377	W 23814	36527	PAP,CARTONS COUCHES,ENDUITS
642	PAPER,ETC,PRECUT,ARTS OF	W 16208	35949	W 21705	48135	W 19809	35355	W 28847	76973	PAP,CARTONS DECOUPES
6421	PAPER ETC CONTAINERS	W 3031	3170	W 5460	7135	W 6558	8087	W 10443	34104	BOITES,SACS EMBALLAGES
65	TEXTILE YARN,FABRICS,ETC		264681		231015		173772		276150	FILS,TISSUS,ARTICLES TEXTILE
651	TEXTILE YARN	W 8034	37944		21220	W 5258	22086	W 8534	40572	FILS TEXTILES
652	COTTON FABRICS,WOVEN	W 7468	35579	W 8932	39176	W 5866	27356	W 10016	60411	TISSUS DE COTON
6522	WOVEN COTTON BLEACHD,ETC	W 6914	32686	W 8364	36718	W 5316	24821	W 9513	58060	TISSUS COTON BLANCHIS ETC
65224	BLCHED COTTON FABRIC NES	W 4519	22439	W 5681	27695	W 3712	19212	W 7104	45872	AUT TIS PLUS 85% COT BLANCHI
653	WOVN MAN–MADE FIB FABRIC	W 9972	70239	W 10356	63095	W 7188	44931	W 9224	66577	TISSUS FIBRES SYNTH,ARTIF
6531	CONT SYNT WEAVES NONPILE	W 6526	43764	W 5977	37061	W 3609	22733	W 4858	34006	TISSUS FIBRES SYNTH CONTINUE
65315	CONT SYN TXTL FABRIC NES	W 6014	41337	W 5381	34720	W 3346	21590	W 4425	31165	TIS PLUS 85% TEXT SYNT CONT
657	SPECIAL TXTL FABRC,PRODS	W 6799	39314	W 7638	41906	W 7159	46458	W 9485	57890	TISSUS SPECIAUX
6573	COATED ETC TEXTILES NES	W 3601	16019	W 4395	20275	W 3713	25957	W 5770	32408	TISSUS,ART MATIERE TEXT NDA
65733	RUBBERIZED TEXT NOT KNIT	W 2944	13270	W 3888	18587	W 3337	24180	W 5394	30117	TISSUS CAOUTCHOUTES
66	NONMETAL MINERAL MFS NES		136170		135203		108029		120704	ART MIN NON METALLIQUES
662	CLAY,REFRACTORY BLDG PRD	W 52630	29747	W 59369	35318	W 58753	37962		40174	MAT CONST REFRACTAIRES
6623	REFRACTORY BUILDING PROD	W 16454	15683	W 18443	19554	W 21912	24754	W 20290	29561	BRIQUES REFRACTAIRES
663	MINERAL MANUFCTURES NES	W 19450	38668	W 10125	27985	W 9390	22343	W 11799	29562	ART MIN MANUF NDA
67	IRON AND STEEL		520637		307476		304941		463348	FER ET ACIER
672	IRON,STEEL PRIMARY FORMS	W 68317	27751	W 26127	10716	W 22623	8064	W 128596	43081	LINGOTS FER,ACIER
673	IRON,STEEL SHAPES ETC	W 121247	63266	W 64182	40512	W 65151	33178	W 101009	56627	BARRES,PROFIL FER,ACIER
674	IRN,STL UNIV,PLATE,SHEET	W 237207	164738	W 131673	91955	W 122598	68389	W 172866	119089	LARGES PLATS,TOLES
6744	IRN,STL HVY PLATE,ROLLED	W 85461	46107	W 40924	22884	W 25191	12337	W 111224	59126	TOLES LAMINEES PLUS 4.75 MM
67441	— OF IRON OR SIMPLE STL	W 84522	44103	W 39372	20020	W 24382	10562	W 110520	56991	TOLES NON ACIER FIN CARB
6746	IRN,STL THIN PLATE,ROLLD	W 64416	41575	W 49066	34754	W 81647	41414	W 31815	30575	TOLES LAM MOINS 3MM
67461	— OF IRON OR SIMPLE STL	W 52666	24686	W 42778	21851	W 76484	31504	W 26426	15510	TOL NON AC FIN MOINS 3 MM
678	IRON,STL TUBES,PIPES,ETC	W 187037	213405	W 92229	124764	W 171347	165433	W 189473	206165	TUBES,TUYAUX EN FONTE,FER
6782	IRON,STL SEAMLESS TUBES	W 133314	140562	W 61864	73038	W 153560	131054	W 164784	157391	TUBES,TUYAUX SANS SOUDURE
6783	IRON,STL TUBES,PIPES NES	W 44942	41499	W 23250	28459	W 11564	13080	W 15895	18533	AUT TUBES,TUYAUX FER,ACIER
68	NON–FERROUS METALS		227158		178193		144759		270460	METAUX NON FERREUX
682	COPPER EXC CEMENT COPPER	W 33154	86876	W 25198	62189	W 21757	54030	W 33480	110958	CUIVRE
6821	COPPER NES,ALLOYS,UNWRT	W 19956	46041	W 13240	28359	W 14275	30606	W 22968	71033	CUIVRE BRUT
68212	COPPER REFINED,UNWROUGHT	W 18790	44528	W 13144	28061	W 14203	30380	W 22883	70693	CUIVRE AFFINE BRUT
6822	COPPER,ALLOYS WORKED	W 13198	40836	W 11959	33830	W 7481	23424	W 10513	39926	CUIVRE,ALLIAGES OUVRES
684	ALUMINIUM	W 34847	94915	W 31054	77484	W 25378	60655	W 31025	102845	ALUMINIUM
6842	ALUMINIUM,ALLOYS WORKED	W 32118	90663	W 27831	73576	W 24921	59297	W 30470	100750	ALUMINIUM,ALLIAGES OUVRE
68422	ALUMNM PLATE,SHEET,STRIP	W 28008	74236	W 23969	57478	W 21899	48215	W 25974	77032	TOLES, PLANCHES EN ALU
686	ZINC	W 20353	27740	W 20575	22738	W 16077	17839	W 32646	35187	ZINC
6861	ZINC,ALLOYS UNWROUGHT	W 18665	24559	W 19069	20264	W 15034	16079	W 32092	33897	ZINC ET ALLIAGES BRUTS
69	METAL MANUFACTURES NES		268706		261476		183517		263269	ART MANUFACT EN METAL NDA
695	TOOLS	W 8719	67197	W 7312	60072	W 4117	47138	W 5762	72477	OUTILS A MAIN
6954	BLADES,TIPS,ETC FR TOOLS	W 1941	32282	W 1609	30023	W 1305	28922	W 1494	40332	OUTILS POUR MACHINE–OUTIL
69541	PARTS TO INSERT IN TOOLS	W 1314	23436	W 925	22885	W 763	22919	W 919	32479	OUTILS DE FORAGE
699	BASE METAL MFRS NES	W 18963	91255	W 17850	91622	W 12105	69173	W 21624	96495	ART MANUFACTURES MET NDA
7	MACHINES,TRANSPORT EQUIP		6525858		5684473		3583456		3983219	MACHINES MATERIEL TRANSPORT
71	POWER GENERATING EQUIPMT		584416		479676		345296		297686	MACHINES GENERATRICES
713	INTRNL COMBUS PSTN ENGIN	W 44935	149385	W 37821	109848	W 24962	80045	W 27677	117190	MOTEURS EXPL COMB INT, PIECE
7139	PISTON ENGINE PARTS NES	W 7436	83567	W 6024	65496	W 4232	51788	W 5640	75246	PIECES POUR 713.2,3,8
714	ENGINES AND MOTORS NES	W 5517	196322	W 3179	143354	W 457	44124	W 558	55595	MOTEURS NON ELECTRIQUES
7148	GAS TURBINES NES	W 4866	127158	W 2415	99291	W 96	10497	W 149	14866	TURBINES A GAZ
71488	OTHER GAS TURBINES NES	W 4826	126515	W 2409	99136	W 90	10272	W 136	14211	AUTRES TURBINES A GAZ
7149	ENGINE & MOTOR PARTS NES	W 646	69040	W 568	36745	W 318	28028	W 366	33203	PIECES 714 ET 718.88
71499	PARTS NES,OF 71488,71888	W 608	68484	W 523	36081	W 311	27688	W 362	32148	PIECES 714.88 ET 718.88
716	ROTATING ELECTRIC PLANT	W 17861	166067	W 15830	158694	W 15236	160182	W 9966	84200	APP ELECTR ROTATIFS,PIECES
7161	DC MOTORS AND GENERATORS	W 5261	82008	W 3358	61411	W 4675	75737	W 697	7883	MOTEURS COURANT CONTINU
7162	AC MTRS,GENRTRS,GEN SETS	W 10889	71201	W 10741	84109	W 8969	73193	W 8173	63219	MOTEURS ELECTRIQUES
71621	AC MTRS,INC UNIVRSL MTRS	W 5611	38986	W 5850	43224	W 3776	32551	W 4687	34352	MOT ELEC NON COUR CONTINU
71622	AC GENERATORS	W 4634	26239	W 4064	32307	W 4525	33376	W 2852	21763	GENER COURANT ALTERNATIF
718	OTH POWER GENERATG MACHY	W 2949	29665	W 2860	36681	W 2442	38216	W 1337	24934	AUTRES MOTEURS PARTIES
7188	WIND,WATER,ETC ENGINES	W 2922	29588	W 2822	36370	W 2336	36436	W 1316	24854	MOT MACHINES MOTRICES NDA
71882	OTH HYDRAULIC ENGNS,MTRS	W 2668	26642	W 2646	32428	W 2185	32957	W 1137	19442	MACH MOTRICES HYDRAULQUES
72	MACHS FOR SPCL INDUSTRYS		1048767		777090		278916		356700	MAC SPECIALES POUR INDUST
722	TRACTORS NON–ROAD	W 16668	53208	W 7121	15431	W 1589	3531	W 2007	9740	TRACTEURS
7224	WHEELED TRACTORS NES	W 13728	47488	W 5376	11524	W 1268	2048	W 1528	6983	TRACTEURS A ROUES
723	CIVIL ENGNEERG EQUIP ETC	W 43963	158908	W 14828	71216	W 10079	53919	W 14103	88091	APPAREILS DE GENIE CIVIL
7234	CONST,MINING MACHNRY NES	W 39207	120346	W 12726	47986	W 7474	26050	W 11357	45330	MACH POUR LA CONST, MINES
72342	SLFPRP SHOVELS,EXCAVATRS	W 23315	65466	W 7748	33446	W 3063	16185	W 3356	17105	PELLES MECANIQUES
7239	CONSTR ETC MACHY PTS NES	W 3123	33184	W 1690	22357	W 2525	27699	W 2616	42006	PIECES 723.41–723.46
724	TEXTILE,LEATHER MACHNRY	W 9437	86645	W 6349	56751	W 3600	28553	W 3837	39702	MACH POUR INDUSTRIE TEXTILE
725	PAPER ETC MILL MACHINERY	W 2099	30211	W 2921	39933	W 2172	24565	W 663	11838	MACHINES FABR PATE PAPIER
726	PRINTG,BKBINDG MACHY,PTS	W 4199	62330	W 2680	49854	W 1069	17897	W 906	18408	MACHINES POUR IMPRIMERIE
727	FOOD MACHRY NON–DOMESTIC	W 2731	41452	W 3016	40965	W 3147	36941	W 2222	39284	MACH INDUSTRIES ALIMENT
7272	OTH FOOD PROC MCHY,PARTS	W 2130	33225	W 2497	31154	W 2738	32571	W 1884	33570	AUT MACH IND ALIMENTAIRE

4. General Imports F.O.B. by Commodities according to the S.I.T.C. (Rev. 2) in thousand U.S. Dollars
Importations Générales F.O.B. par Produits d'après la C.T.C.I. (Rév. 2) en milliers de Dollars E.U.

SITC CTCI	COMMODITY	1992			1993			1994			1995			PRODUIT
			WEIGHT POIDS	VALUE VALEUR		WEIGHT POIDS	VALUE VALEUR		WEIGHT POIDS	VALUE VALEUR		WEIGHT POIDS	VALUE VALEUR	
72722	INDUS FOOD PROC MACH NES	W	1860	32462	W	2222	30313	W	1844	29896	W	1492	30035	MACHINES BOULANGERIE
728	OTH MACHY FOR SPCL INDUS	W	66201	594009	W	44129	489435	W	9073	103465	W	17565	138026	AUT MACH IND PARTICULIERES
7283	OTHR MINERAL WORKG MACHY	W	14061	160663	W	6001	62659	W	2060	16687	W	2503	25088	MACH TRIER,CRIBLER,BROYER
72834	MINRL MOULDING ETC MACHY	W	7704	119858	W	1769	42166	W	145	605	W	209	4043	MACH AGGLO CIMENT ETC
7284	MACHY FOR SPCL INDUS NES	W	50517	422575	W	34110	409589	W	6094	82888	W	14186	107247	MACH SPEC IND PARTICUL.
72842	RUBBER,PLASTICS WRKG MCH	W	3701	44294	W	2316	25149	W	1703	11675	W	1759	16978	MACH IND CAOUT MAT PLAST
72848	OTH MCHY WITH INDIV FNCT	W	32458	199336	W	20954	249276	W	2806	39179	W	10639	52969	AUTRES MACHINES NDA
72849	PTS OF MACHS OF 7284 ETC	W	13235	158664	W	9739	120140	W	1123	16585	W	1242	22464	PIECES DU 728.4 ETC
73	METALWORKING MACHINERY			133539			91139			48747			79691	MACH TRAVAIL DES METAUX
736	METALWORKING MACH–TOOLS	W	14104	84441	W	8121	57849	W	4896	28112	W	4224	32587	MACH–OUTILS TRAVAIL METAUX
737	METALWORKING MACHNRY NES	W	11448	49098	W	7786	33291	W	4791	20634	W	6827	47105	MACH TRAV METAUX PIECES
74	GENRL INDUSTRL MACHY NES			1127722			1080004			897058			914195	MACH APP INDUSTRIE
741	HEATING,COOLING EQUIPMNT	W	26679	239848	W	42464	315248	W	56272	398133	W	23654	184353	MACH CHAUFFAGE,PIECES
7413	INDUS FURNACES ETC,PARTS	W	3414	36911	W	1955	19590	W	2698	28720	W	1865	11582	FOURS IND,LABOR,PIECES
7415	AIR–CONDITIONING MACHNRY	W	5632	29835	W	6148	34830	W	3991	18643	W	6391	34581	GROUPES CONDITION AIR
7416	HEATING,COOLING EQU NES	W	15686	149544	W	32310	243858	W	48440	341074	W	13167	117211	APP CHANGEMENT TEMP
742	PUMPS FOR LIQUIDS ETC	W	7967	117944	W	7515	106270	W	7430	83521	W	9684	119240	POMPES MOTO–POMPES
7428	OTHER PUMPS FOR LIQUIDS	W	3381	34145	W	2598	26831	W	2220	23503	W	3053	34292	AUTRES POMPES POUR LIQ
74288	PUMPS FR LIQUIDS NES ETC	W	3300	31909	W	2593	26726	W	2187	23330	W	2944	32510	POMPES POUR LIQUIDES NDA
7429	PTS NES OF PUMPS OF 742	W	1781	46174	W	1833	27703	W	3083	31993	W	3505	42311	PIECES POUR GROUPE 742
743	PUMPS NES,CENTRFUGES ETC	W	25093	219905	W	19292	209501	W	9689	93966	W	15744	160690	POMPES COMPRES,VENT ETC
7431	PUMPS FOR GASES ETC	W	17135	115783	W	13467	130408	W	4766	28361	W	10042	85014	POMPES AIR A VIDE,COMPRES
7439	PTS NES OF APP OF 7435,6	W	3880	59002	W	2778	43812	W	1850	33688	W	2095	37769	PIECES 743.5 ET 743.6
744	MECHANICAL HANDLING EQU	W	24963	124803	W	18561	102460	W	10082	60044	W	16692	115959	EQUIP MANUTENTION PIECES
7442	LIFTING,LOADING MACH NES	W	10518	54427	W	8862	47406	W	4473	25012	W	9881	69921	APP LEVAGE,MANUTENTION
74428	OTH HANDLING ETC MCH NES	W	3977	28086	W	2338	18301	W	1387	9951	W	6633	57385	AUT APP LEVAGE ETC
745	NONELEC MACHY,TOOLS NES	W	4289	87504	W	4086	70193	W	2571	45501	W	3325	65686	AUT MACH NON ELEC,PIECES
7452	OTH NONELEC MCHS,PTS NES	W	3893	78934	W	3511	60495	W	2306	40583	W	2999	57930	AUT MACH NON ELEC,PIECES
74522	PACKAGNG,BOTTLNG,ETC MCH	W	1417	45030	W	1231	28881	W	766	22631	W	1055	29986	MACH NETT BOUTEILLES,ETC
749	NONELEC MACH PTS,ACC NES	W	24442	337717	W	21199	276331	W	13100	215894	W	15607	268267	PIECES MACH NON ELEC NDA
7491	BALL,ROLLER,ETC BEARINGS	W	3690	50550	W	3125	42101	W	2454	33837	W	3004	48223	ROULEMENTS BILLES ETC
7492	COCKS,VALVES ETC NES	W	10006	123487	W	8870	102216	W	4421	76139	W	5311	93818	ART ROB,SIM POUR TUYAUX
7493	SHAFT,CRANK,PULLEY ETC	W	7408	101061	W	6825	86431	W	4390	62561	W	5071	75518	ARBRES TRANS,VILEBREQUINS
7499	OTH NONELEC MCHY PTS NES	W	3338	62620	W	2379	45583	W	1835	43357	W	2221	50708	PIECES NON ELECT NDA
75	OFFICE MACHNES,ADP EQUIP			313628			345231			195114			341253	MACH BUREAU TRAIT AUTOM
751	OFFICE MACHINES	W	4324	61781	W	3919	65139	W	2181	36890	W	2238	46916	MACH,APPAREILS DE BUREAU
7518	OFFICE MACHINES NES	W	1622	36993	W	1534	37735	W	969	24520	W	1221	31563	MACH,APP DE BUREAU NDA
752	AUTOMTIC DATA PROC EQUIP	W	3982	193388	W	4331	219584	W	2900	123256	W	4299	218801	MACH TRAIT INFORMATION
7522	DIGITAL COMPUTERS	W	947	71055	W	1185	85122	W	871	52772	W	1361	86598	MACH DIGITALES COMPLETES
7525	ADP PERIPHERAL UNITS	W	1330	46700	W	1514	47234	W	1313	38946	W	1737	62856	UNITES PERIPHERIQUES
759	OFFICE,ADP MCH PTS,ACCES	W	2313	58459	W	2177	60509	W	1467	34968	W	1793	75537	PIECES DU 751 ET 752
7599	ACCTG,ETC,ADP MCH PTS,AC	W	1851	43355	W	1786	46459	W	1165	26654	W	1559	64708	PIECES DU 751 ET 752
76	TELECOMM,SOUND EQUIPMENT			492271			433766			283980			305426	EQUIPMENT DE TELECOM
761	TELEVISION RECEIVERS	W	8663	41687	W	7073	40074	W	4424	24888	W	5900	49161	RECEPTEURS DE TELEVISION
7611	COLOUR TV RECEIVERS	W	6868	37039	W	5641	36059	W	3726	22838	W	5413	46905	RECEPTEURS COULEUR
764	TELECOM EQPT,PTS,ACC NES	W	10238	398324	W	8649	332400	W	4463	226717	W	4304	195957	EQUIP TELECOM,PIECES
7641	LINE TELEPHONE,ETC EQUIP	W	3025	180428	W	2368	108011	W	1105	48625	W	981	46963	APP TELEPHON PAR FIL
7643	TV,RADIO TRANSMITTRS ETC	W	2022	111648	W	1602	106454	W	1054	93662	W	1140	97722	APP EMET TELE RADIO
7649	PTS NES OF EQUIPMT OF 76	W	2792	82639	W	2875	98388	W	1362	64971	W	1182	36374	PIECES DE LA DIV 76
76491	PTS NES OF APPAR OF 7641	W	753	49549	W	858	53862	W	242	22545	W	76	8057	PIECES POUR 764.1
76493	TELECOMM EQUIPMT PTS NES	W	1308	23386	W	1340	35583	W	734	37004	W	643	21653	PIECES 761,762,764.3,8
77	ELECTRIC MACHNRY NES ETC			542942			555483			426089			514032	MACH APP ELECT NDA
771	ELECTRIC POWER MACHY NES	W	8476	63489	W	5543	46244	W	4991	47787	W	5598	50495	MACH PROD,TRANS ELECTR
7711	TRANSFORMERS,ELECTRICAL	W	5431	43694	W	3162	25722	W	3132	33343	W	3731	32592	TRANSFO ELECTRIQUES
772	SWITCHGEAR ETC,PARTS NES	W	8137	154228	W	6872	143712	W	5134	110421	W	4711	98801	APP COUPURE,SECT ETC
7721	SWITCHGEAR ETC	W	7615	146255	W	6336	132334	W	4985	102375	W	4580	92219	APP COUPURE,SECTIONMNT
773	ELECTR DISTRIBUTNG EQUIP	W	6421	39825	W	13268	71900	W	9968	58508	W	6610	47674	EQUIPMT DISTRIBUTION ELECT
7731	INSULATED WIRE,CABLE ETC	W	3660	27879	W	10166	59697	W	8168	50324	W	5105	41578	FILS,CABLES ISOLES ELECT
775	HOUSEHOLD TYPE EQUIP NES	W	20440	73564	W	22106	74624	W	13231	46086	W	23099	95651	MACH,APP USAGE DOMESTQUE
7752	DOM REFRIGERATRS,FREEZRS	W	7376	24237	W	6552	22207	W	5488	15255	W	11731	41938	REFRIG,CONGEL MENAGER
77521	DOMESTIC REFRIGERATORS	W	6966	22476	W	6069	19923	W	5192	13424	W	10968	37369	REFRIGERATEURS
776	TRANSISTORS,VALVES,ETC	W	1701	33482	W	1161	39930	W	616	28486	W	609	35138	LAMPES,TUBES,VALVES
778	ELECTRICAL MACHINERY NES	W	40401	159954	W	34510	157772	W	29049	127017	W	36094	170968	AUTRES MACH ELECT NDA
7788	OTH ELEC MACHY,EQUIP NES	W	23860	72587	W	17213	68443	W	15433	59224	W	18605	73107	AUT MACH APP ELEC NDA
77887	ELECTRICAL CARBONS	W	20376	37831	W	14969	37740	W	14016	36067	W	17326	45998	PIECES CHARBON,GRAPHITE
78	ROAD VEHICLES			2055918			1667097			807881			1061723	VEHICULES ROUTIERS
781	PASS MOTOR VEH EXC BUSES	W	140977	1112887	W	119504	972528	W	70695	512293	W	92027	637348	AUTO TRANSPORT PERSONNES
782	LORRIES,SPCL MTR VEH NES	W	97391	392996	W	70878	298150	W	31768	168021	W	48190	249702	VEHICULES SPECIAUX,MARCH
7821	LORRIES,TRUCKS	W	83831	346003	W	62846	263000	W	30290	158023	W	45561	231400	VEHICULES TRANSP MARCHAND
7822	SPECIAL MOTOR VEHCLS NES	W	13559	46992	W	8032	35150	W	1478	9998	W	2629	18302	VEHICULES USAGES SPECIAUX
783	ROAD MOTOR VEHICLES NES	W	34322	92227	W	21586	62753	W	3332	17911	W	1653	14355	VEHICULES ROUTIERS NDA
7831	BUSES	W	16508	57527	W	12135	46782	W	2571	15936	W	1163	9488	VOITURES TRANSPORT COMMUN
784	MOTOR VEH PRTS,ACCES NES	W	59079	406983	W	48773	283203	W	24207	90652	W	31469	136817	PIECES 722,781,782,783
7841	MOTOR VEHICLE CHASSIS	W	8090	44546	W	3864	24992	W	1836	11679	W	1456	11202	CHASSIS 722,781,782,783
7849	OTHER MOTOR VEHCL PARTS	W	50435	360429	W	43862	257534	W	21747	76790	W	28790	120733	PIECES 722,781,782,783
785	CYCLES,ETC MOTRZD OR NOT	W	11890	36654	W	10921	37787	W	4365	14207	W	4054	16951	MOTOCYCLES SCOOTERS
79	OTHR TRANSPORT EQUIPMENT			226654			254985			300376			112512	AUTRE MATERIEL TRANSPORT
791	RAILWAY VEHICLES			23148	W	3038	50734	W	4933	68421	W	4210	10109	VEHIC MAT CHEMINS DE FER
7914	RY COACHES NES NOT POWRD	W	1	11	W	894	43362	W	1002	49773			1	VOITURES A VOYAGEURS
792	AIRCRAFT ETC	W	947	48261	W	461	23533	W	560	19451	W	178	21971	APP NAVIGATION AERIENNE
793	SHIPS AND BOATS ETC	W	27029	155246	W	62907	180718	W	58598	212504	W	22019	80432	NAVIRES BATEAUX,ETC
7932	SHIPS AND BOATS NES	W	11020	36235	W	32891	63087	W	14801	17485	W	6261	14963	NAVIRES ET BATEAUX
79323	OTHER CARGO VESSELS	W	7130	8762	W	30245	37629	W	13241	9575	W	4668	3216	AUT BATEAUX TRANS MARCH
7938	TUGS,SPECIAL VESSELS ETC	W	15498	116318	W	29988	117412	W	42925	190367	W	15745	65389	REMORQUEURS,BATEAUX SPEC
79382	SPECL PURPOSE VESSLS ETC	W	11783	109830	W	25722	109756	W	37889	181403	W	13845	62177	BAT–PHARES,–POMPES,DRAGUES
8	MISC MANUFACTURED GOODS			958937			924024			653412			988704	ART MANUFACTURES DIVERS
821	*FURNITURE,PARTS THEREOF	W	7885	29281	W	10861	40862	W	8092	31329	W	8278	31686	MEUBLES ET PIECES
84	CLOTHING AND ACCESSORIES			237212			196590			135147			275323	VETEMENTS
842	MENS OUTERWEAR NOT KNIT	W	6583	49217	W	4866	33054	W	3241	22707	W	5244	51275	VET DESSUS POUR HOMMES
8423	— TROUSERS,BREECHES ETC	W	5693	40925	W	3963	25760	W	2629	17916	W	4661	43305	PANTALONS HOMMES MAT TEX
843	WOMENS OUTERWEAR NONKNIT	W	6289	52166	W	4980	45109	W	2896	29495	W	3938	50256	VET DESSUS FEMMES MAT TEX
844	UNDER GARMENTS NOT KNIT	W	3893	25994	W	3907	20906	W	2127	18106	W	3198	35753	VETEMENT DESSOUS MAT TEX
846	UNDER GARMENTS KNITTED	W	5553	58254	W	4286	51642	W	3188	35011	W	4842	85343	SOUS VETS DE BONNETERIE
8462	— OF COTTON NON ELASTIC	W	4512	43498	W	3141	36464	W	2358	25590	W	3763	60149	SOUS–VET BONNET COTON
84629	—— OTHER	W	4512	43498	W	3141	36464	W	2260	24636	W	3615	58464	AUT SOUS–VET BONNET COTON
851	*FOOTWEAR	W	7060	43342	W	7401	47238	W	3251	19862	W	5145	39314	CHAUSSURES
87	PRECISION INSTRUMNTS NES			220185			192664			152637			189052	INSTRUM,APPAR SCIENT NDA
872	MEDICAL INSTRUMENTS NES	W	1990	46573	W	1648	38179	W	1576	26081	W	2333	35385	INSTR,APP MEDIC–CHIR NDA
87202	OTH MEDICAL INSTRUMENTS	W	1487	41737	W	1348	33560	W	1405	23688	W	2077	31555	INSTRUM,APP MEDECINE
874	MEASURNG,CONTROLNG INSTR	W	5100	161890	W	4266	142509	W	3336	118875	W	3931	142006	INSTRUMENTS DE MESURE
8743	GAS,LIQUID CONTROL INSTR	W	1161	32094	W	1302	31122	W	1000	28872	W	1052	34366	APP,INSTR MESURE FLUIDES

 Venezuela

4. General Imports F.O.B. by Commodities according to the S.I.T.C. (Rev. 2) in thousand U.S. Dollars
Importations Générales F.O.B. par Produits d'après la C.T.C.I. (Rév. 2) en milliers de Dollars E.U.

SITC CTCI	COMMODITY	1992		1993		1994		1995		PRODUIT
		WEIGHT POIDS	VALUE VALEUR	WEIGHT POIDS	VALUE VALEUR	WEIGHT POIDS	VALUE VALEUR	WEIGHT POIDS	VALUE VALEUR	
8748	ELEC MEAS,CONTRL EQU NES	W 1398	59414	W 685	50112	W 513	32971	W 555	40526	APP ELEC ELECTRO MESURE
87483	OTH ELCTRNC MEAS ETC EQU	W 1132	49237	W 507	42286	W 355	25289	W 327	31695	AUT APP ELECTRO DE MESURE
88	PHOTO EQU,OPTICL GDS ETC		117905		107513		67236		93501	APP,FOURN PHOTO,OP,MONTR
882	PHOTO,CINEMA SUPPLIES	W 4770	54910	W 6497	52261	W 3547	36605	W 4191	49287	PRODUITS PHOTO,CINEMA
8822	PHOTO FILM EXC DEV CINMA	W 2569	41005	W 4584	38749	W 1946	26485	W 2576	33761	PLAQUES,PELLICULES,FILMS
89	MISC MANUFCTRD GOODS NES		284696		312614		225292		326244	ART MANUFACTURES DIVERS
892	PRINTED MATTER	W 11081	66744	W 12120	75228	W 9529	56750	W 9348	67054	IMPRIMES
8921	PRINTED BOOKS,GLOBES,ETC	W 5188	40771	W 5508	41527	W 4548	32601	W 4714	39637	LIVRES,BROCHURES,CARTES
89211	PRINTED BOOKS,PAMPHLETS	W 5020	39963	W 5360	41074	W 4396	32179	W 4552	38626	LIVRES,BROCHURES
893	ARTICLES OF PLASTIC NES		65607		80911		62128		90345	OUVRAGES EN MAT DIVIS 58
8939	MISC PLASTIC ARTICLES	W 10909	52360	W 12513	62678	W 8365	45807	W 11975	68200	ART DIVERS EN MAT DIV 58
89399	OTHR PLASTC ARTICLES NES	W 10049	50318	W 11657	60401	W 7884	44451	W 11143	64790	AUT OUV MAT DIV 58
894	TOYS,SPORTING GOODS,ETC	W 15821	59820	W 15238	61773	W 9294	40205	W 12384	67684	VOITURES ENFANTS,JOUETS
8942	TOYS,INDOOR GAMES ETC	W 12603	45587	W 11955	48061	W 7512	32246	W 8625	48650	JOUETS,JEUX ETC
898	MUSICAL INSTRUMENTS,PTS	W 4268	41981	W 4511	41337	W 3082	28861	W 2470	44734	INSTRUMENTS DE MUSIQUE
8983	SOUND RECRDNG TAPE,DISCS	W 2701	32194	W 3220	34897	W 2410	25284	W 2129	41646	SUPPORTS SON POUR 763

5. General Exports F.O.B. by Commodities according to the S.I.T.C. (Rev. 2) in thousand U.S. Dollars
Exportations Générales F.O.B. par Produits d'après la C.T.C.I. (Rév. 2) en milliers de Dollars E.U.

SITC CTCI	COMMODITY	1992 WEIGHT POIDS	1992 VALUE VALEUR	1993 WEIGHT POIDS	1993 VALUE VALEUR	1994 WEIGHT POIDS	1994 VALUE VALEUR	1995 WEIGHT POIDS	1995 VALUE VALEUR	PRODUIT
	ALL COMMODITIES		14235322		15208136		16649658		18914219	TOUS PRODUITS
0	FOOD AND LIVE ANIMALS		233656		307325		334426		347730	ALIMENTS,ANIMAUX VIVANTS
03	FISH AND PREPARATIONS		74654		88196		88537		75676	POISSONS ET PREPARATIONS
04	CEREALS AND PREPARATIONS		29013		54548		64409		95187	CEREALES ET PRODUITS
05	VEGETABLES AND FRUIT		60506		64506		46993		50037	LEGUMES ET FRUITS
057	FRUIT,NUTS,FRESH,DRIED	W 112290	44968	W 108262	50205	W 81693	32512	W 121386	31897	FRUITS FRAIS OU SECS
07	COFFEE,TEA,COCOA,SPICES		23817		46444		42386		20944	CAFE,THE,CACAO,EPICES
1	BEVERAGES AND TOBACCO		110201		80300		104685		162319	BOISSONS ET TABACS
11	BEVERAGES		16726		24135		48312		86191	BOISSONS
112	ALCOHOLIC BEVERAGES	W 15804	12487	W 20007	17630	W 46621	37738	W 102261	66118	BOISSONS ALCOOLIQUES
12	TOBACCO AND MANUFACTURES		93475		56165		56373		76129	TABACS BRUTS FABRIQUES
122	TOBACCO,MANUFACTURED	W 10476	91497	W 8190	56114	W 9135	56216	W 12888	75549	TABACS FABRIQUES
1222	CIGARETTES	W 10041	90332	W 7605	54943	W 8287	54682	W 11897	70881	CIGARETTES
2	CRUDE MATERLS,EXCL FUELS		331100		149665		286840		189187	MAT BRUTES NON COMESTIBLES
28	METALLIFEROUS ORES,SCRAP		293652		80573		227824		134563	MINERAIS METAL,DECHETS
281	IRON ORE,CONCENTRATES		227956				139072	W 984	20	MINERAIS DE FER
2815	IRON ORE,CONC,NOT AGGLOM		227956				139072	W 984	20	MINERAIS NON AGGLOMERES
287	BASE METAL ORES,CONC NES	W 202466	33810	W 304013	49448	W 260731	43326	W 391064	70084	MINERAIS METAUX COMMUNS
2873	ALUMINIUM ORES,ALUMINA	W 202219	33730	W 302836	49041	W 260243	43117	W 389620	68972	MINERAIS D'ALUMINIUM
28732	ALUMINA(ALUMINIUM OXIDE)	W 202219	33730	W 302836	49041	W 260243	43117	W 351140	68010	ALUMINE (OXYDE ALUMINIUM)
3	MINERAL FUELS ETC		11376956		11928733		12644441		14559283	COMBUSTIBLES MINERAUX LUB
32	COAL,COKE AND BRIQUETTES		88168		130220		116305		117466	HOUILLES,COKES,BRIQUETTES
322	COAL,LIGNITE AND PEAT	W 2395483	85308	W 4361311	129478	W 3591169	116301	W 3648845	117466	HOUILLES,LIGNITES,TOURBE
3222	OTH COAL,NOT AGGLOMERATD	W 2395383	85290	W 4361311	129478	W 3591169	116301	W 3648845	117466	AUTRES HOUILLES
33	PETROLEUM AND PRODUCTS		11288788		11785866		12528110		14441814	PETROLE ET DERIVES
333	CRUDE PETROLEUM		7189504		7318833		8004330		8576341	HUILES BRUTES DE PETROLE
334	PETROLEUM PRODUCTS,REFIN		4099284		4467017		4523685		5862997	PRODUITS RAFFINES
3345	LUBS,PETROLEUM OILS NES	W 39	120		4467017					HUILES LUBRIFIANTES
33451	LUBS(HIGH PETR CONT) ETC				4466871					HUILES LUBRIF,H LOURDES
5	CHEMCLS,RELATED PROD NES		383938		431068		504114		788861	PRODUITS CHIMIQUES
51	ORGANIC CHEMICALS		150446		158341		222153		336845	PROD CHIMIQ ORGANIQUES
512	ALCOHOLS,PHENOLS ETC	W 1116	649	W 33183	10807	W 348493	95177	W 604589	156840	PHENOLS,PHENOLS–ALCOOLS
5121	ACYCLIC ALCOHOLS,DERIVS	W 943	434	W 32579	9969	W 339955	92766	W 604339	156411	ALCOOLS ACYCLIQUES
51211	METHYL ALCOHOL(METHANOL)	W 486	67	W 8	3	W 301567	76063	W 574989	137926	ALCOOLS METHYLIQUES
516	OTHER ORGANIC CHEMICALS	W 372006	126400	W 412035	120811	W 449608	104774	W 332209	99061	AUTRES PROD ORGANIQUES
5161	ETHERS,EPOXIDES,ACETALS	W 371091	125961	W 411215	120498	W 449100	104252	W 332033	98842	ETHERS–OXYDES,ALCOOLS
51611	ETHERS,ETHER–ALCOHOL,ETC	W 371077	125937	W 411190	120436	W 449062	104196	W 332033	98841	ETHERS–OXYDES
52	INORGANIC CHEMICALS		42657		54562		53279		83752	PROD CHIM INORGANIQUES
522	INORG ELEMNTS,OXIDES,ETC	W 75132	19095	W 140390	28791	W 80931	27344	W 220316	56919	ELEMENTS INORGANIQUES
562	*FERTILIZERS,MANUFACTURE	W 352713	43946	W 358295	38614	W 17810	2998	W 400753	75722	ENGRAIS MANUFACTURES
5621	CHEM NITROGENOUS FERTLZR	W 352688	43923	W 357301	38355	W 715	161	W 390502	74402	ENGRAIS AZOTES
56216	UREA	W 352688	43923	W 357247	38305	W 713	155	W 390336	74365	UREE
58	PLASTIC MATERIALS ETC		49833		67990		102844		154421	MAT PLAST ARTIFICIELLES
583	POLYMERIZATION ETC PRODS	W 44719	37809	W 68508	48944	W 98641	83048	W 127862	114430	PROD POLYMERISATION
59	CHEMICAL MATERIALS NES		55489		55340		61645		58495	MAT PROD CHIMIQUES NDA
598	MISCEL CHEM PRODUCTS NES	W 67106	45441	W 52339	39675	W 58474	41468	W 43136	36055	PROD DIV INDUST CHIM NDA
6	BASIC MANUFACTURES		1490743		1597829		1893232		2135292	ART MANUFACTURES
64	PAPER,PAPERBOARD AND MFR		52313		57310		75321		119139	PAPIERS,CARTONS & OUVRAGES
641	PAPER AND PAPERBOARD	W 58482	42056	W 59781	39531	W 93078	53296	W 101458	80122	PAPIERS ET CARTONS
65	TEXTILE YARN,FABRICS,ETC		35586		54920		59193		61985	FILS,TISSUS,ARTICLES TEXTILE
66	NONMETAL MINERAL MFS NES		121982		146405		187156		203969	ART MIN NON METALLIQUES
661	LIME,CEMENT,BLDG PRODS	W 1268891	40731	W 1567829	51696	W 1893584	69328	W 3139651	96301	CHAUX,CIMENTS MAT CONSTR
6612	CEMENT	W 1260880	37309	W 1549995	46561	W 1885563	66087	W 3130970	92545	CIMENTS HYDRAULIQUES
67	IRON AND STEEL		472067		585036		639090		621762	FER ET ACIER
671	PIG IRON ETC	W 760627	75335	W 1085322	104819	W 1074697	114614	W 1180099	143754	FONTE,SPIEGEL,POUDRES
6713	IRON,STL POWDER,SHOT,ETC	W 712097	51162	W 1023695	77676	W 1016868	91079	W 1105516	104169	POUDRES,GREN FER,ACIER
67133	SPONGE IRON OR STEEL	W 712082	51147	W 1023694	77675	W 1016832	91063	W 1105458	104143	FER,ACIER SPONGIEUX AUT POUD
672	IRON,STEEL PRIMARY FORMS	W 892998	143343	W 1182284	175108	W 1260367	252812	W 803679	167880	LINGOTS FER,ACIER
6724	IRN,STL INGOTS,LUMPS,ETC	W 466276	40713	W 656450	51569	W 506089	59447	W 342033	44168	FER,ACIER LINGOTS,MASSES
67245	IRN,STL BLOCKS,LUMPS,ETC	W 466105	40587	W 620816	51114	W 505991	59409	W 341864	44135	FER,ACIER EN MASSES
6725	IRN,STL BLOOMS,SLABS,ETC	W 284758	63601	W 357776	79375	W 449354	101798	W 356638	87286	BLOOMS,BILLETTES FER ACIER
67251	IRN,SMPLE STL BLOOMS,ETC	W 284746	63592	W 357719	79319	W 449353	101795	W 356573	87240	BLOOMS ETC NON ACIER FIN
6727	IRN,STL COIL FR REROLLNG	W 141964	39029	W 168058	44164	W 304924	91567	W 105009	36426	EBAUCHES POUR TOLES FER
67271	IRON,SIMPLE STEEL COILS	W 141520	38917	W 165767	43267	W 302680	90459	W 104468	36197	EBAUCHES NON EN ACIER
673	IRON,STEEL SHAPES ETC	W 233116	67327	W 313284	93925	W 311522	97076	W 284082	89379	BARRES,PROFIL FER,ACIER
6731	IRON,STEEL WIRE ROD	W 110280	31714	W 183771	55287	W 173111	52128	W 148435	45789	FIL MACHINE FER,ACIER
67311	IRON,SIMPLE STL WIRE ROD	W 109879	31598	W 183007	54988	W 172143	51840	W 147804	45554	FIL MACH AUT ACIER FIN
674	IRN,STL UNIV,PLATE,SHEET	W 357403	146129	W 429381	173510	W 344038	142686	W 368469	183116	LARGES PLATS,TOLES
6746	IRN,STL THIN PLATE,ROLLD	W 297228	119839	W 307133	120246	W 225738	87515	W 256479	121668	TOLES LAM MOINS 3MM
67461	— OF IRON OR SIMPLE STL	W 297214	119827	W 307067	120162	W 225710	87497	W 256262	121542	TOL NON AC FIN MOINS 3 MM
68	NON–FERROUS METALS		663455		566931		748948		929328	METAUX NON FERREUX
684	ALUMINIUM	W 562240	655095	W 478909	555058	W 556872	734374	W 500282	913672	ALUMINIUM
6841	ALUMINIUM,ALLOYS,UNWRGHT	W 484733	541414	W 408058	459905	W 459870	581912	W 407724	728370	ALUMINIUM,ALLIAGES BRUTS
6842	ALUMINIUM,ALLOYS WORKED	W 77507	113682	W 70851	95153	W 97003	152461	W 92558	185302	ALUMINIUM,ALLIAGES OUVRE
68421	ALUMINIUM BARS,WIRE,ETC	W 54605	74751	W 51353	62703	W 57186	85332	W 52669	91576	BARRES,PROFILES FILS ALU
68422	ALUMNM PLATE,SHEET,STRIP	W 20569	33166	W 18015	29022	W 35700	58635	W 33945	78269	TOLES, PLANCHES EN ALU
69	METAL MANUFACTURES NES		113249		127522		112884		114321	ART MANUFACT EN METAL NDA
7	MACHINES,TRANSPORT EQUIP		209749		428091		516503		536972	MACHINES MATERIEL TRANSPORT
78	ROAD VEHICLES		123298		321950		416416		440264	VEHICULES ROUTIERS
781	PASS MOTOR VEH EXC BUSES	W 4836	38039	W 14524	151017	W 20884	205027	W 19288	228845	AUTO TRANSPORT PERSONNES
782	LORRIES,SPCL MTR VEH NES	W 1063	6022	W 8328	57797	W 15426	96210	W 14848	105173	VEHICULES SPECIAUX,MARCH
7821	LORRIES,TRUCKS	W 436	2313	W 7885	56364	W 15153	95319	W 14513	104150	VEHICULES TRANSP MARCHAND
784	MOTOR VEH PRTS,ACCES NES	W 46061	71968	W 54963	92245	W 50335	85485	W 53605	96595	PIECES 722,781,782,783
7849	OTHER MOTOR VEHCL PARTS	W 46029	71692	W 54909	92060	W 49991	83610	W 53420	95346	PIECES 722,781,782,783
8	MISC MANUFACTURED GOODS		83635		90719		89756		89207	ART MANUFACTURES DIVERS
89	MISC MANUFCTRD GOODS NES		40187		47054		52675		54327	ART MANUFACTURES DIVERS
9	GOODS NOT CLASSD BY KIND		10480		185664		272706		100040	ART TRANSACT NON CLASSES
971	*GOLD,NON MONETARY NES	K 933	10380	K 16485	185274	K 37233	272411	K 8013	100000	OR NON MONETAIRE
97101	NONMON GLD UNWRT,SEMIMFD	K 933	10380	K 16485	185274	K 22233	272407	K 8013	100000	OR,ALLIAGES D'OR BRUTS

1. HISTORICAL SERIES, 1975–1995 GENERAL TRADE, IMPORTS C.I.F., EXPORTS F.O.B.
SERIES HISTORIQUES, 1975–1995 COMMERCE GENERAL, IMPORTATIONS C.A.F., EXPORTATIONS F.O.B

YEAR ANNEE	VALUE IN MILLION U.S. DOLLARS VALEUR EN MILLION U.S. DOLLARS MERCHANDISE – MARCHANDISE		GOLD – OR		CONVERSION FACTORS FACTEURS DE CONVERSION CENTS E.U. PAR		INDEX NUMBERS – INDICES QUANTUM		UNIT VALUE VALEUR UNITAIRE	
	IMPORTS	EXPORTS	IMPORTS	EXPORTS	IMPORTS	EXPORTS	IMPORTS	EXPORTS	IMPORTS	EXPORTS
1975	1040.06	202.85								
1976	799.90	230.11								
1977	1141.84	456.08								
1978	1160.00	482.00								
1979	1225.00	535.00								
1986	2155.00	823.00								
1987	2455.00	854.00								
1988	2757.00	1038.00								
1989	2566.00	1946.00								
1990	2752.00	2404.00								
1991	2338.00	2087.00								
1992	2540.00	2580.00								
1993	3924.00	2985.00								
1994	5825.00	4054.00								
1995	7500.00	5200.00								

2. IMPORTS BY BROAD ECONOMIC CATEGORY AND EXPORTS BY INDUSTRIAL ORIGIN. (PERCENTAGE OF TOTAL VALUE)
IMPORTATIONS PAR CATEGORIES ECONOMIQUES ET EXPORTATIONS PAR BRANCHE D'ACTIVITE. (EN POURCENTAGE DE LA VALEUR TOTALE)

IMPORTS – IMPORTATIONS

	1990	1991	1992	1993	1994	1995	1996
TOTAL IMPORTS–IMPORTATIONS TOTALES							
1 FOOD BEV–ALIMENTATION BOISSONS							
11 PRIMARY–PRODUITS DE BASE							
111 FOR INDUSTRY–POUR L'INDUSTRIE							
112 FOR HOUSEHOLDS–POUR LES MENAGES							
12 PROCESSED–PRODUITS ELABORES							
121 FOR INDUSTRY–POUR L'INDUSTRIE							
122 FOR HOUSEHOLDS–POUR LES MENAGES							
2 IND SUPPLIES–APPROV INDUSTRIELS							
21 PRIMARY–PRODUITS DE BASE							
22 PROCESSED–PRODUITS ELABORES							
3 FUELS–COMBUSTIBLES							
31 PRIMARY–PRODUITS DE BASE							
32 PROCESSED–PRODUITS ELABORES							
321 MOTOR SPIRIT–ESSENCE							
322 OTHER–AUTRES							
4 MACHINERY–EQUIPEMENT							
41 CAPITAL EQUIPMENT–MACHINES							
42 PARTS–PIECES ACCESSOIRES							
5 TRANSPORT–TRANSPORT							
51 PASSENGER CARS–AUTOMOBILES							
52 OTHER–AUTRES							
521 INDUSTRIAL–INDUSTRIELS							
522 NON INDUSTRIAL–NON INDUSTRIEL							
53 PARTS–PIECES ACCESSOIRES							
6 CONSUM GOODS–BIENS CONSOMMATION							
61 DURABLE–DURABLES							
62 SEMI DURABLE–SEMI DURABLES							
63 NON DURABLE–NON DURABLES							
7 GOODS NES–BIENS NDA							

EXPORTS – EXPORTATIONS

	1990	1991	1992	1993	1994	1995	1996
TOTAL EXPORTS–EXPORTATIONS TOTALES							
1 AGRICULTURE							
2 MINING QUARRY–INDUS EXTRACTIVES							
3 MANUFACTURING–IND MANUFACTUR							
31 FOOD BEV TOBACCO–ALIM BOISS TAB							
32 TEXTILES–INDUSTRIES TEXTILES							
33 WOOD & PRODUCTS–BOIS & PRODUITS							
34 PAPER & PRODUCTS–PAPIER & PRODT							
35 CHEMICALS–INDUSTRIES CHIMIQUES							
36 NON METAL MIN–MIN NON METAL							
37 BASIC METAL–IND METAL BASE							
38 METAL MANUF–MANUF METAL							
39 OTH MANUF IND–AUTRES MANUF							

3. TRADE BY PRINCIPAL COUNTRIES OF PURCHASE AND SALE (VALUE IN THOUSAND U.S. DOLLARS)
ECHANGES SELON LES PRINCIPAUX PAYS D'ACHAT ET DE VENTE (VALEUR EN MILLIERS DE DOLLARS EU)

COUNTRIES–PAYS	GENERAL IMPORTS C.I.F. IMPORTATIONS GENERALES C.A.F				
	1989	1990	1991	1992	1993
World	2565800	2752400	2338100	2540800	3924000
Africa			13300		
Americas	10100	7900	10400	24800	27000
Northern America	2400	1000	6900	16000	22500
LAIA					
CACM					
Caribbean	7700	6900	3500	8800	4500
Rest of America					
As.ex F.USSR	285400	625400	1337600	1589800	2295840
Eur.x F.USSR	239500	256100	346603	310500	488806
EU	62600	53900	301200	255400	445500
EFTA			503	39500	23400
East Europe	176900	202200	44500	14900	19906
Other Europe					
Former USSR	1532900	1194100	100100	100280	167600
Oceania	11000	3600	11000	19800	33000
Singapore/Singapour	41300	428200	722200	821600	1058300
Russian Federation	1532900	1194100		100100	144300
Japan/Japon	105600	98300	157700	239400	452300
Korea, Republic of	15600	27500	152100	211200	281500
France,Monac	52500	40000	147900	161700	267400
Hong Kong	102600	48900	194800	142900	145400
Germany/Allemagne	5200	8700	101200	40600	72000
Indonesia/Indonésie	500	2600	49400	39800	84500
Former GDR	68200	96800			
Thailand/Thaïlande	2300	6800	14200	41200	99500
China/Chine		1100	18400	31800	85500
Hungary/Hongrie	32800	51400	13600	3200	4700
Former USSR/Anc. URSS			100100		
Czechoslovakia	43900	26600	18900	4300	
Poland/Pologne	20800	20300	8400	6700	15200
Australia/Australie	11000	3600	9600	15800	30300
Malaysia/Malaisie			6200	35900	24800
Lao People's Dem. Rp.	2800	2100	3300	7700	41900
Switz.Liecht			500	39500	13400
Netherlands/Pays–Bas			8400	16200	25800
Italy/Italie	3000	2800	1200	6000	34800
Sweden/Suède			14200	12800	18500
Canada	2400	1000	5800	14000	18700
India/Inde	10000	4100	2400	9000	8100
Cuba	7700	6900	3500	8800	4500
Democratic Kampuchea	4600	5700	5200	6700	7600
Belgium–Luxembourg	1200	2100	6800	5000	8100
Ukraine				180	22200
Finland/Finlande			10000	5500	5300
Austria/Autriche			2500	3900	13600
United Kingdom	700	300	9000	3700	
Egypt/Egypte			13300		
Philippines			10600	500	1900
Bulgaria/Bulgarie	6600	3800	1000		6
Norway,SVD,JM			3		10000
New Zealand			1400	4000	2700
Korea Dem People's Rp	100	100	1100	2100	4500
Albania/Albanie	1300	2700	2600	700	
USA/Etats–Unis d'Amer			1100	2000	3800
Romania/Roumanie	3300	600			
Republic of Moldova					1100
Yugoslavia/Yougoslavie				700	
Fm Yugoslav			400		

COUNTRIES–PAYS	GENERAL EXPORTS F.O.B. EXPORTATIONS GENERALES F.O.B.				
	1989	1990	1991	1992	1993
Monde	1946000	2404000	2087100	2580700	2985200
Afrique			13300	23000	6300
Amériques	16600	12600	6000	21400	37600
Amérique du Nord	3900	1100	1300	2700	6000
ALAI					
MCAC					
Caraïbes	12700	11500	4700	18700	31600
Autre Amérique					
Asie l'URSS exclus	518600	503900	1544100	1834300	2015530
Europe l'URSS exclus	324000	180000	139800	262400	265100
UE	93100	49800	119400	239800	229800
AELE			1600	6400	10700
Europe de l'Est	230900	130200	16500	15800	24600
Autre de l'Europe					
Ancienne URSS	548600	856700	214500	105700	136700
Océanie	800	2300	5200	21400	54700
Japan/Japon	261000	287600	719300	833900	936900
Russian Federation	548600	856700		104800	135400
Singapore/Singapour	70700	111100	425000	401700	380300
Hong Kong	78900	47600	223300	201700	169000
France,Monac	79700	42500	83100	132300	95000
Korea, Republic of	25000	13200	51300	93500	99400
China/Chine	300	100	19300	95600	135800
Thailand/Thaïlande	15200	19600	57700	71500	71800
Former USSR/Anc. URSS			214500		
Malaysia/Malaisie			14500	68400	55800
Democratic Kampuchea	10900	5900	6300	6400	96200
Poland/Pologne	89200	8400	4200	6100	9700
Germany/Allemagne	8700	3400	6700	34400	50100
Czechoslovakia	43800	48300	4200	2100	2900
Former GDR	57600	27300			
Australia/Australie	800	2300	5200	21400	54700
Indonesia/Indonésie	31000	1500	16500	10900	22900
Cuba	12700	11500	4700	18700	31600
India/Inde	16100	9500	5500	19400	18900
Netherlands/Pays–Bas			16200	20100	28100
United Kingdom	1500	1900	2400	27500	23000
Hungary/Hongrie	20100	15800	5000	6200	8700
Lao People's Dem. Rp.	2700	3200	3600	16000	14400
Iraq	6300	4000	700	14200	12500
Algeria/Algérie			13300	10000	6100
Bulgaria/Bulgarie	9000	11500	3100	1200	3300
Austria/Autriche			5900	10700	10000
Italy/Italie	2800	1800	3800	7200	8100
Romania/Roumanie	7500	14900			
Belgium–Luxembourg	400	200	100	6400	11800
Switz.Liecht			800	5700	10600
Canada	3900	1100	400	2600	5900
Libyan Arab Jamahiriya				13000	200
Albania/Albanie	3700	4000		200	
Sweden/Suède			1200	1200	3700
Philippines			700	1000	1600
Fm Yugoslav			2300		
Ukraine				800	900
Norway,SVD,JM			800	700	100
Korea Dem People's Rp	500	600	300	100	30
USA/Etats–Unis d'Amer			900	100	100
Belarus/Bélarus				100	400
Yugoslavia/Yougoslavie				400	

(VALUE AS PERCENTAGE OF WORLD TOTAL)(VALEURS EN POURCENTAGE DU TOTAL MONDIAL)

	1984	1985	1986	1987	1988	1989	1990	1991	1992	1993
Africa								0.6		
Americas	6.1		0.3	0.4	0.3	0.4	0.3	0.4	1.0	0.7
Northern America	5.3			0.0		0.1	0.0	0.3	0.6	0.6
LAIA	0.8									
CACM										
Caribbean			0.3	0.4	0.3	0.3	0.3	0.1	0.3	0.1
Rest of America										
As.ex F.USSR	61.6		10.5	8.4	8.8	11.1	22.7	57.2	62.6	58.5
Eur.x F.USSR	31.5		11.1	10.3	11.2	9.3	9.3	14.8	12.2	12.5
EU	17.9		1.6	1.9	3.6	2.4	2.0	12.9	10.1	11.4
EFTA	0.3							0.0	1.6	0.6
East Europe	13.3		9.5	8.3	7.6	6.9	7.3	1.9	0.6	0.5
Other Europe	0.0									
Former USSR	0.4		66.6	70.4	65.3	59.7	43.4	4.3	3.9	4.3
Oceania	0.4		0.5	0.4	0.1	0.4	0.1	0.5	0.8	0.8
Singapore/Singapour	15.9		1.4	1.0	1.3	1.6	15.6	30.9	32.3	27.0
Russian Federation			66.6	70.4	65.3	59.7	43.4		3.9	3.7
Japan/Japon	26.4		5.6	4.2	5.0	4.1	3.6	6.7	9.4	11.5
Korea, Republic of			0.3	0.3	0.2	0.6	1.0	6.5	8.3	7.2
France,Monac	6.2		1.3	1.5	3.3	2.0	1.5	6.3	6.4	6.8
Hong Kong	16.3		1.8	1.4	1.1	4.0	1.8	8.3	5.6	3.7
Germany/Allemagne	1.8		0.2	0.2	0.3	0.2	0.3	4.3	1.6	1.8
Indonesia/Indonésie	0.4		0.8	0.9	0.4	0.0	0.1	2.1	1.6	2.2
Former GDR			2.6	2.3	2.2	2.7	3.5			
Thailand/Thaïlande	1.9			0.0	0.1	0.1	0.2	0.6	1.6	2.5

	1984	1985	1986	1987	1988	1989	1990	1991	1992	1993
Afrique	4.3							0.6	0.9	0.2
Amériques	0.7		1.8	1.4	1.5	0.9	0.5	0.3	0.8	1.3
Amérique du Nord	0.7		0.0	0.1	0.0	0.2	0.0	0.1	0.1	0.2
ALAI	0.0									
MCAC										
Caraïbes			1.7	1.3	1.4	0.7	0.5	0.2	0.7	1.1
Autre Amérique										
Asie l'URSS exclus	73.5		21.3	20.5	20.3	26.6	21.0	74.0	71.1	67.5
Europe l'URSS exclus	20.1		19.2	22.6	19.4	16.6	7.5	6.7	10.2	8.9
UE	7.8		3.0	3.6	3.3	4.8	2.1	5.7	9.3	7.7
AELE	0.4							0.1	0.2	0.4
Europe de l'Est	11.9		16.2	18.9	16.1	11.9	5.4	0.8	0.6	0.8
Autre de l'Europe										
Ancienne URSS	1.3		34.3	39.2	38.3	28.2	35.6	10.3	4.1	4.6
Océanie	0.1		0.4	0.6	0.4	0.0	0.1	0.2	0.8	1.8
Japan/Japon	18.8		4.1	6.0	5.8	13.4	12.0	34.5	32.3	31.4
Russian Federation			34.3	39.2	38.3	28.2	35.6		4.1	4.5
Singapore/Singapour	18.0		7.7	6.7	5.9	3.6	4.6	20.4	15.6	12.7
Hong Kong	32.4		5.5	5.8	6.3	4.1	2.0	10.7	7.8	5.7
France,Monac	3.0		2.3	3.3	2.9	4.1	1.8	4.0	5.1	3.2
Korea, Republic of			2.5	0.5	0.7	1.3	0.5	2.5	3.6	3.3
China/Chine						0.0	0.0	0.9	3.7	4.5
Thailand/Thaïlande	0.2		0.0	0.0	0.1	0.8	0.8	2.8	2.8	2.4
Former USSR/Anc. URSS	1.3							10.3		
Malaysia/Malaisie	3.1							0.7	2.7	1.9

4. General Imports C.I.F. by Commodities according to the S.I.T.C. (Rev. 2) in thousand U.S. Dollars
Importations Générales C.A.F. par Produits d'après la C.T.C.I. (Rév. 2) en milliers de Dollars E.U.

SITC CTCI	COMMODITY	1990		1991		1992		1993		PRODUIT
		WEIGHT POIDS	VALUE VALEUR	WEIGHT POIDS	VALUE VALEUR	WEIGHT POIDS	VALUE VALEUR	WEIGHT POIDS	VALUE VALEUR	
	ALL COMMODITIES		2752400		2338100		2540800		3924000	TOUS PRODUITS
0	FOOD AND LIVE ANIMALS		114300		138000		140100		205800	ALIMENTS,ANIMAUX VIVANTS
541	*MEDICINAL,PHARM PRODUCT		41000		42100		61400		86000	PROD MEDICINAUX PHARMACEUT
5417	MEDICAMENTS		35700							MEDICAMENTS
5911	INSECTICIDES,FOR RETAIL		9000							INSECTICIDES VENTE DET
7	MACHINES,TRANSPORT EQUIP		179400		119600		216200		634600	MACHINES MATERIEL TRANSPORT
87	PRECISION INSTRUMNTS NES		134500		71000		155900			INSTRUM,APPAR SCIENT NDA

5. General Exports F.O.B. by Commodities according to the S.I.T.C. (Rev. 2) in thousand U.S. Dollars
Exportations Générales F.O.B. par Produits d'après la C.T.C.I. (Rév. 2) en milliers de Dollars E.U.

SITC CTCI	COMMODITY	1990		1991		1992		1993		PRODUIT
		WEIGHT POIDS	VALUE VALEUR	WEIGHT POIDS	VALUE VALEUR	WEIGHT POIDS	VALUE VALEUR	WEIGHT POIDS	VALUE VALEUR	
	ALL COMMODITIES		2404000		2087100		2580700		2985200	TOUS PRODUITS
03	FISH AND PREPARATIONS		239100		285400		307700		427200	POISSONS ET PREPARATIONS
24	CORK AND WOOD		126500		175500		140800		97500	LIEGE ET BOIS
656	LACE,RIBBONS,TULLE,ETC		50900							TULLES,BRODERIE
8	MISC MANUFACTURED GOODS		635800		300100		349500		526500	ART MANUFACTURES DIVERS
84	CLOTHING AND ACCESSORIES		178100							VETEMENTS
8997	BASKETWORK,BROOMS ETC		44000							OUVRAGES VANNERIE NDA

1. HISTORICAL SERIES, 1986–1995 GENERAL TRADE, IMPORTS C.I.F., EXPORTS F.O.B.
SERIES HISTORIQUES, 1986–1995 COMMERCE GENERAL, IMPORTATIONS C.A.F., EXPORTATIONS F.O.B

YEAR ANNEE	VALUE IN MILLION YEMENI RIALS / VALEUR EN MILLION YEMENI RIALS: MERCHANDISE # 1 – MARCHANDISE		GOLD – OR		CONVERSION FACTORS U.S. CENTS PER YEMENI RIAL / FACTEURS DE CONVERSION CENTS E.U. PAR YEMENI RIAL		INDEX NUMBERS – INDICES: QUANTUM		UNIT VALUE / VALEUR UNITAIRE	
	IMPORTS	EXPORTS	IMPORTS	EXPORTS	IMPORTS	EXPORTS	IMPORTS	EXPORTS	IMPORTS	EXPORTS
1986	166.81	10.02			289.5200	289.5200				
1987	169.70	24.28			289.5200	289.5200				
1988	225.62	28.11			289.5200	289.5200				
1989	202.49	27.20			289.5199	289.5197				
1990	18867.09	8315.50			8.4160	8.4216				
1991	23509.52	7684.78			8.3263	8.3263				
1992	31075.62	5693.35			8.3263	8.3263				
1993	33883.23	4494.60			8.3263	8.3263				
1994	25070.22	11215.60			8.3263	8.3263				
1995	64590.68	74785.12			1.9984	1.9984				

2. IMPORTS BY BROAD ECONOMIC CATEGORY AND EXPORTS BY INDUSTRIAL ORIGIN. (PERCENTAGE OF TOTAL VALUE)
IMPORTATIONS PAR CATEGORIES ECONOMIQUES ET EXPORTATIONS PAR BRANCHE D'ACTIVITE. (EN POURCENTAGE DE LA VALEUR TOTALE)

IMPORTS – IMPORTATIONS

	1990	1991	1992	1993	1994	1995	1996
TOTAL IMPORTS–IMPORTATIONS TOTALES		100.					
1 FOOD BEV–ALIMENTATION BOISSONS		25.8					
11 PRIMARY–PRODUITS DE BASE		11.1					
111 FOR INDUSTRY–POUR L'INDUSTRIE		6.7					
112 FOR HOUSEHOLDS–POUR LES MENAGES		4.4					
12 PROCESSED–PRODUITS ELABORES		14.7					
121 FOR INDUSTRY–POUR L'INDUSTRIE		3.7					
122 FOR HOUSEHOLDS–POUR LES MENAGES		10.9					
2 IND SUPPLIES–APPROV INDUSTRIELS		16.8					
21 PRIMARY–PRODUITS DE BASE		1.2					
22 PROCESSED–PRODUITS ELABORES		15.6					
3 FUELS–COMBUSTIBLES		40.5					
31 PRIMARY–PRODUITS DE BASE							
32 PROCESSED–PRODUITS ELABORES		40.5					
321 MOTOR SPIRIT–ESSENCE		12.5					
322 OTHER–AUTRES		28.0					
4 MACHINERY–EQUIPEMENT		5.0					
41 CAPITAL EQUIPMENT–MACHINES		4.7					
42 PARTS–PIECES ACCESSOIRES		0.3					
5 TRANSPORT–TRANSPORT		6.4					
51 PASSENGER CARS–AUTOMOBILES		1.8					
52 OTHER–AUTRES		0.7					
521 INDUSTRIAL–INDUSTRIELS		0.7					
522 NON INDUSTRIAL–NON INDUSTRIEL		0.0					
53 PARTS–PIECES ACCESSOIRES		3.9					
6 CONSUM GOODS–BIENS CONSOMMATION		5.5					
61 DURABLE–DURABLES		1.4					
62 SEMI DURABLE–SEMI DURABLES		1.2					
63 NON DURABLE–NON DURABLES		2.9					
7 GOODS NES–BIENS NDA		0.0					

EXPORTS – EXPORTATIONS

	1990	1991	1992	1993	1994	1995	1996
TOTAL EXPORTS–EXPORTATIONS TOTALES		100.					
1 AGRICULTURE		8.0					
2 MINING QUARRY–INDUS EXTRACTIVES		0.4					
3 MANUFACTURING–IND MANUFACTUR		91.6					
31 FOOD BEV TOBACCO–ALIM BOISS TAB		1.0					
32 TEXTILES–INDUSTRIES TEXTILES		0.4					
33 WOOD & PRODUCTS–BOIS & PRODUITS							
34 PAPER & PRODUCTS–PAPIER & PRODT		0.0					
35 CHEM'CALS–INDUSTRIES CHIMIQUES		89.4					
36 NON METAL MIN–MIN NON METAL							
37 BASIC METAL–IND METAL BASE		0.1					
38 METAL MANUF–MANUF METAL		0.6					
39 OTH MANUF IND–AUTRES MANUF							

3. TRADE BY PRINCIPAL COUNTRIES OF FIRST AND LAST CONSIGNMENT (VALUE IN THOUSAND U.S. DOLLARS)
ECHANGES SELON LES PRINCIPAUX PAYS DE PREMIERE ET DE DERNIERE CONSIGNATION (VALEUR EN MILLIERS DE DOLLARS EU)

COUNTRIES–PAYS	GENERAL IMPORTS C.I.F. # 1 IMPORTATIONS GENERALES C.A.F				
	1991	1992	1993	1994	1995
World	770333	2587884	2821253	2087448	1290780
Africa	28232	117091	143007	127657	59341
Americas	23522	309583	343908	217570	150100
Northern America	7643	250659	274978	197772	102877
LAIA	15879	58924	68803	19798	45297
CACM			45		40
Caribbean			82		1
Rest of America					1884
As.ex F.USSR	477085	1283320	1300266	996700	742137
Eur.x F.USSR	166139	757485	921846	655612	327533
EU	143963	722154	869579	626578	308496
EFTA	528	7096	7047	5190	3318
East Europe	21299	25924	43892	23095	12496
Other Europe	349	209	147	332	1290
Former USSR	47221	20991	8130	6185	5566
Oceania	25872	51248	49974	51512	5432
United Arab Emirates	84176	213154	272002	218973	183178
USA/Etats–Unis d'Amer	6722	238024	270775	188563	98858
Saudi Arabia	23885	192534	196376	215633	124911
United Ki..gdom	37142	142705	147350	116351	61967
France, Monac	21870	91569	199885	123111	54461
Japan/Japon	21766	180881	131516	93196	51234
Malaysia/Malaisie	39776	109435	141673	99115	83038
Singapore/Singapour	31164	127741	111256	74629	44893
Turkey/Turquie	4704	100436	141974	95316	46162
Italy/Italie	7215	132869	95116	85697	43750
Netherlands/Pays–Bas	12200	111648	125186	85502	25875
Belgium–Luxembourg	19098	97530	103054	92542	27874
Germany/Allemagne	20811	88185	108863	62029	42303
China/Chine	34522	76000	92436	44235	45586
Brazil/Brésil	15879	54351	63613	17389	43984
Australia/Australie	24610	51205	43123	51511	5014
Thailand/Thaïlande	23478	92648	30266	17647	8631
Kuwait/ Koweït	106403	1462	10250	5809	47864
India/Inde	17820	46331	47755	29873	20624
Somalia/Somalie	9952	49207	43767	28767	18879
Korea, Republic of	7268	44172	42969	29621	19037
Djibouti	6120	21072	49045	48401	7351
Egypt/Egypte	3352	25037	34400	27038	17060
Jordan/Jordanie	2859	22104	25174	13452	16907
Denmark/Danemark	20369	17696	18099	11681	9246
Greece/Grèce	332	14602	23008	25482	12666
Romania/Roumanie	10600	13802	28040	17517	4654
Former USSR/Anc. URSS	47221	20991			
Iraq	57489	1			
Bahrain/Bahreïn	9085	20458	11408	15807	454
Indonesia/Indonésie	503	11544	12877	9019	16943
Hong Kong	2347	16862	7348	11002	10592
Sweden/Suède	2447	5253	16496	8632	9425
Austria/Autriche	1086	10549	14059	7686	3589
Sri Lanka	5879	13361	6281	6684	4208
Sudan/Soudan	6354	2779	7051	16615	1961
Canada	921	12500	4203	9209	4019
Hungary/Hongrie	1041	6221	8258	3932	3936
Switz.Liecht	387	7002	6962	4763	3295
Pakistan	635	3779	5607	3227	8027
Kenya	1812	4998	4276	3826	4908
Russian Federation			8130	6185	4811
Bulgaria/Bulgarie	8199	254	6332	705	2667
Spain/Espagne	628	3451	8033	1654	4375
Ireland/Irlande	578	3894	5740	733	3586
Finland/Finlande	168	2202	4688	5460	1233
Syrian Arab Republic	56	2226	5723	3617	1561
Ethiopia/Ethiopie	620	10108	957	1062	342
Oman	481	291	1936	4810	2135
Cyprus/Chypre	590	3481	3100	884	986

COUNTRIES–PAYS	GENERAL EXPORTS F.O.B. # 1 EXPORTATIONS GENERALES F.O.B.				
	1991	1992	1993	1994	1995
Monde	202300	328983	374239	933856	1587407
Afrique	19200	27345	23662	96674	165359
Amériques	18234	116636	3827	130044	142076
Amérique du Nord	18234	116230	3710	113384	4977
ALAI		406	116	16476	137035
MCAC					
Caraïbes					7
Autre Amérique				184	57
Asie l'URSS exclus	82541	104049	297151	616508	1250667
Europe l'URSS exclus	79333	58111	45750	83639	17435
UE	78540	57642	45702	63391	17251
AELE	794			8622	7
Europe de l'Est			48	11626	177
Autre de l'Europe		225			
Ancienne URSS					47
Océanie				14	76
Korea, Republic of	72	485	21459	195049	303736
Japan/Japon	17779	55506	98031	123973	194491
China/Chine			52948	22908	370453
Singapore/Singapour	9095	7162	53611	133594	160665
USA/Etats–Unis d'Amer	9994	116230	3415	113384	3926
Egypt/Egypte	6243	222	55	64047	103298
Brazil/Brésil		406	116	16476	137035
Saudi Arabia	33	22377	28681	37702	27320
Thailand/Thaïlande				101	108208
India/Inde	28739	505	22523	19135	2113
Malaysia/Malaisie		4304	1127	25935	33963
France, Monac	6137	4920	17028	29048	7997
Netherlands/Pays–Bas	46829	3286	2	10453	2463
Bahrain/Bahreïn		5894	3945	29926	22444
Somalia/Somalie	1204	11702	14034	21694	8604
Italy/Italie	11962	8312	5861	22298	4367
So. Africa Customs Un					46894
United Arab Emirates	4038	4133	7114	13980	15599
Germany/Allemagne	88	39191	972	12	318
Austria/Autriche			19857		
Djibouti	4863	4650	6269	511	852
Sudan/Soudan	4066	8578	387	1006	764
Ethiopia/Ethiopie	2452	1756	2371	6272	1191
Greece/Grèce	13428				
Kuwait/ Koweït	151	1		8306	4524
Pakistan	8856	745	795	904	424
Bulgaria/Bulgarie				11561	
Iraq	9822				
Switz.Liecht	794			8622	0
Jordan/Jordanie		1653	2737	2817	1197
Bermuda/Bermudes	8240				
Turkey/Turquie	277		1399	314	3016
Eritrea/Erythrée				2321	2127
United Kingdom	95	1276	895	717	1113
Sri Lanka	3586				1
Hong Kong		663	1460	799	254
Syrian Arab Republic		581	782	812	850
Spain/Espagne		416	859	592	620
Morocco/Maroc		437	239	505	577
Canada			296		1052
Oman		20	7		1171
Belgium–Luxembourg		241	229	259	344
Nigeria/Nigéria			232	297	253
Lebanon/Liban			528	204	15
Un. Rep. of Tanzania	308		29		287
Poland/Pologne			48	65	159
Yugoslavia/Yougoslavie		245			
Panama				184	57
Malta/Malte		225			
Seychelles	64				153

(VALUE AS PERCENTAGE OF WORLD TOTAL)(VALEURS EN POURCENTAGE DU TOTAL MONDIAL)

	1986	1987	1988	1989	1990	1991	1992	1993	1994	1995
Africa					5.6	3.7	4.5	5.1	6.1	4.6
Americas					6.9	3.1	12.0	12.2	10.4	11.6
Northern America					6.0	1.0	9.7	9.7	9.5	8.0
LAIA					0.8	2.1	2.3	2.4	0.9	3.5
CACM								0.0		0.0
Caribbean								0.0		0.0
Rest of America										0.1
As.ex F.USSR					41.4	61.9	49.6	46.1	47.7	57.5
Eur.x F.USSR					34.6	21.6	29.3	32.7	31.4	25.4
EU					32.7	18.7	27.9	30.8	30.0	23.9
EFTA					0.4	0.1	0.3	0.2	0.2	0.3
East Europe					1.3	2.8	1.0	1.6	1.1	1.0
Other Europe						0.0	0.0	0.0	0.0	0.1
Former USSR					3.8	6.1	0.8	0.3	0.3	0.4
Oceania					5.6	3.4	2.0	1.8	2.5	0.4
United Arab Emirates					3.7	10.9	8.2	9.6	10.5	14.2
USA/Etats–Unis d'Amer					5.5	0.9	9.2	9.6	9.0	7.7
Saudi Arabia					8.0	3.1	7.4	7.0	10.3	9.7
United Kingdom					5.8	4.8	5.5	5.2	5.6	4.8
France, Monac					6.9	2.8	3.5	7.1	5.9	4.2
Japan/Japon					4.1	2.8	7.0	4.7	4.5	4.0
Malaysia/Malaisie					3.0	5.2	4.2	5.0	4.7	6.4
Singapore/Singapour					3.2	4.0	4.9	3.9	3.6	3.5
Turkey/Turquie					0.8	0.6	3.9	5.0	4.6	3.6
Italy/Italie					2.3	0.9	5.1	3.4	4.1	3.4

	1986	1987	1988	1989	1990	1991	1992	1993	1994	1995
Afrique					4.5	9.5	8.3	6.3	10.4	10.4
Amériques					41.2	9.0	35.5	1.0	13.9	9.0
Amérique du Nord					41.2	9.0	35.3	1.0	12.1	0.3
ALAI							0.1	0.0	1.8	8.6
MCAC										
Caraïbes					0.0					0.0
Autre Amérique									0.0	0.0
Asie l'URSS exclus					14.2	40.8	31.6	79.4	66.0	78.8
Europe l'URSS exclus					37.3	39.2	17.7	12.2	9.0	1.1
UE					36.6	38.8	17.5	12.2	6.8	1.1
AELE					0.1	0.4			0.9	0.0
Europe de l'Est					0.6			0.0	1.2	0.0
Autre de l'Europe					0.0		0.1			
Ancienne URSS					0.4					0.0
Océanie									0.0	0.0
Korea, Republic of					0.0	0.0	0.1	5.7	20.9	19.1
Japan/Japon					1.7	8.8	16.9	26.2	13.3	12.3
China/Chine								14.1	2.5	23.3
Singapore/Singapour					2.0	4.5	2.2	14.3	14.3	10.1
USA/Etats–Unis d'Amer					37.2	4.9	35.3	0.9	12.1	0.2
Egypt/Egypte					0.0	3.1	0.1	0.0	6.9	6.5
Brazil/Brésil							0.1	0.0	1.8	8.6
Saudi Arabia					2.9	0.0	6.8	7.7	4.0	1.7
Thailand/Thaïlande									0.0	6.8
India/Inde					2.4	14.2	0.2	6.0	2.0	0.1

4. General Imports C.I.F. by Commodities according to the S.I.T.C. (Rev. 2) in thousand U.S. Dollars
Importations Générales C.A.F. par Produits d'après la C.T.C.I. (Rév. 2) en milliers de Dollars E.U.

SITC CTCI	COMMODITY	1992		1993		1994		1995		PRODUIT
		WEIGHT POIDS	VALUE VALEUR	WEIGHT POIDS	VALUE VALEUR	WEIGHT POIDS	VALUE VALEUR	WEIGHT POIDS	VALUE VALEUR	
	ALL COMMODITIES		2587884		2821253		2087448		1290780	TOUS PRODUITS
0	FOOD AND LIVE ANIMALS		727977		737473		674930		285187	ALIMENTS,ANIMAUX VIVANTS
001	*LIVE ANIMALS FOR FOOD		56441		49876		47118	W 13956	20287	ANIMAUX VIVANTS
0011	BOVINE SPECIES,LIVE							W 8675	11947	ESPECE BOVINE
0012	SHEEP AND GOATS,LIVE							W 5224	7418	ESPECES OVINE ET CAPRINE
01	MEAT AND PREPARATIONS		30652		55613		59153		20669	VIANDES ET PREPARATIONS
011	MEAT FRESH,CHILLD,FROZEN							W 22343	20563	VIANDES FRAICHES,REF,CONGE
0114	POULTRY FRESH CHLLD,FRZN							W 17787	16979	VOLAILLES MORTES
02	DAIRY PRODCTS,BIRDS'EGGS		85509		134402		75387		30418	PRODUITS LAITIERS,OEUFS
022	MILK AND CREAM							W 16347	20234	LAIT ET CREME
0224	MILK,CREAM PRESERVED ETC							W 16332	20220	LAIT,CREME CONS,CONC
02242	MILK DRY,1.5% FAT OR LES							W 14670	18822	LAIT POUDRE INF 1.5%
024	CHEESE AND CURD							W 2682	3962	FROMAGE ET CAILLEBOTTE
025	EGGS,BIRDS,FRESH,PRSRVD							W 2692	5545	OEUFS
0251	— IN SHELL							W 2681	5511	OEUFS EN COQUILLE
04	CEREALS AND PREPARATIONS		310897		257014		297575		94116	CEREALES ET PRODUITS
041	WHEAT ETC UNMILLED							W 754461	36426	FROMENT,EPEAUTRE
042	RICE							W 124937	15420	RIZ
0422	RICE SEMI–MILLED,MILLED							W 124937	15420	RIZ POLI,GLACE INCL BRISURES
044	MAIZE UNMILLED							W 58893	5786	MAIS NON MOULU
046	WHEAT ETC MEAL OR FLOUR							W 523257	31918	SEMOULE FARINE,FROMENT
04601	FLOUR OF WHEAT OR MESLIN							W 523237	31909	FARINE DE FROMENT
05	VEGETABLES AND FRUIT		42680		43754		44068		22518	LEGUMES ET FRUITS
054	VEG ETC FRSH,SMPLY PRSVD							W 20287	6371	LEGUMES FRAIS,CONG,SECS
0542	LEGUMINOUS VEGETBLES DRY							W 19052	5960	LEGUMES A COSSE SECS
056	VEGTBLES ETC PRSVD,PREPD							W 13397	8564	CONSERVES DE LEGUMES
0565	VEGTBLES PRSVD,PREPD NES							W 11799	8172	LEGUMES PREPARES CONSERVE
05659	OTH VEG PRESVD,PREPD NES							W 11473	7876	LEGUM PREPAP,CONSERV NDA
058	FRUIT PRESERVED,PREPARED							W 8053	4314	CONSERVES DE FRUITS
06	SUGAR AND PREPS,HONEY		138424		134499		88584		67194	SUCRES ET PRODUITS
061	SUGAR AND HONEY							W 187205	64861	SUCRES ET MIEL
0611	RAW BEET AND CANE SUGAR							W 11025	4414	SUCRES BRUTS
0612	REFINED SUGAR ETC							W 163621	56986	SUCRES RAFFINES
07	COFFEE,TEA,COCOA,SPICES		33957		21721		31092		17192	CAFE,THE,CACAO,EPICES
074	TEA AND MATE							W 8265	10382	THE ET MATE
0741	TEA							W 8265	10382	THE
075	SPICES							W 5607	6028	EPICES
0752	SPICES,EX PEPPER,PIMENTO							W 4477	4768	AUTRES EPICES
081	*FEEDING STUFF FOR ANIML		10448		18054		9057	W 12751	4237	NOURRITURE POUR ANIMAUX
09	MISC EDIBLE PRODUCTS		15310		18493		16939		6559	PREP ALIMENTAIRES DIVERSES
098	EDIBLE PRODCTS,PREPS NES							W 4212	6559	PREP ALIMENTAIRES NDA
1	BEVERAGES AND TOBACCO		49286		50120		49000		27173	BOISSONS ET TABACS
12	TOBACCO AND MANUFACTURES		47418		43682		47988		26428	TABACS BRUTS FABRIQUES
121	TOBACCO UNMNFCTRD,REFUSE							W 9232	25639	TABACS BRUTS,DECHETS
1213	TOBACCO REFUSE							W 9232	25639	DECHETS DE TABACS
2	CRUDE MATERLS,EXCL FUELS		93316		90507		62073		36769	MAT BRUTES NON COMESTIBLES
22	OIL SEEDS,OLEAGINOUS FRT		7963		14712		10619		3593	GRAINES,FRUITS OLEAGINEUX
24	CORK AND WOOD		64173		63461		40042		25476	LIEGE ET BOIS
248	WOOD SHAPED,SLEEPERS							W 102956	23864	BOIS SIMPLEMENT TRAVAILLES
2482	LUMBER SHAPED CONIFER							W 73375	19273	CONIFERES SCIES,RABOTES
2483	LUMBER SHAPED NON–CONIFR							W 29581	4591	NON CONIFERES SCIES,RABOTES
27	CRUDE FERTLZR,MINRLS NES		14740		5764		5498		2254	ENGRAIS MINERAUX BRUTS
3	MINERAL FUELS ETC		156914		188009		108324		101832	COMBUSTIBLES MINERAUX LUB
33	PETROLEUM AND PRODUCTS		156582		187649		108235		101319	PETROLE ET DERIVES
334	PETROLEUM PRODUCTS,REFIN							W 835643	100743	PRODUITS RAFFINES
3341	GASOLINE,OTH LIGHT OILS							W 174735	20625	ESSENCES POUR MOTEURS
33411	MOTOR,AVIATION SPIRIT							W 174536	20562	ESSENCES MOTEURS D'AVIONS
3343	GAS OILS							W 262751	22503	GAS OILS
3344	FUEL OILS,NES							W 359486	35120	FUEL OILS
3345	LUBS,PETROLEUM OILS NES							W 38191	22282	HUILES LUBRIFIANTES
33451	LUBS(HIGH PETR CONT) ETC							W 37385	21986	HUILES LUBRIF,H LOURDES
4	ANIMAL,VEGETABLE OIL,FAT		55501		62479		39505		57653	HUILES,GRAISSES ANIM,VEG
42	FIXED VEGETABLE OIL,FAT		51726		55103		39340		57391	HUILES VEGETALES FIXES
423	FIXED VEG OILS,SOFT							W 40117	20732	HUILES VEGET DOUCES FIXES
4232	SOYA BEAN OIL							W 29968	14933	HUILE DE SOJA
4234	GROUNDNUT(PEANUT) OIL							W 8006	5148	HUILE D'ARACHIDE
424	FIXED VEG OIL NONSOFT							W 70501	36660	AUTRES HUILES VEG FIXES
4242	PALM OIL							W 23667	10142	HUILE DE PALME
4249	FIXED VEGETABLE OILS NES							W 46291	26188	HUILES VEGET FIXES NDA
5	CHEMCLS,RELATED PROD NES		171908		211700		161543		105966	PRODUITS CHIMIQUES
51	ORGANIC CHEMICALS		6070		9278		2744		3633	PROD CHIMIQ ORGANIQUES
52	INORGANIC CHEMICALS		11172		16777		7895		9641	PROD CHIM INORGANIQUES
522	INORG ELEMNTS,OXIDES,ETC							W 10794	3884	ELEMENTS INORGANIQUES
523	OTHR INORG CHEMICALS ETC							W 29725	5748	AUT PRODUITS CHIMIQUES INORG
53	DYES,TANNING,COLOUR PROD		7790		11386		8574		6320	PROD TEINTURE,COLORANTS
533	PIGMENTS,PAINTS,ETC							W 3789	6081	PIGMENTS,PEINTURES,VERNIS
541	*MEDICINAL,PHARM PRODUCT		53321		69464		62913	K 3367773	29231	PROD MEDICINAUX PHARMACEUT
5417	MEDICAMENTS							K 3202602	27945	MEDICAMENTS
55	PERFUME,CLEANING ETC PRD		11190		12866		13882		12008	PROD POUR PARFUM,TOILETTE
554	SOAP,CLEANSING ETC PREPS							W 9790	6429	SAVONS,PRODUITS DETERSIFS
5542	WASHING PREPARATIONS ETC							W 9384	5848	PROD ORG TENSIO–ACT NDA
562	*FERTILIZERS,MANUFACTURE		6264		4160		1173	W 25487	6363	ENGRAIS MANUFACTURES
58	PLASTIC MATERIALS ETC		45415		44479		43307		22243	MAT PLAST ARTIFICIELLES
583	POLYMERIZATION ETC PRODS							W 24985	19677	PROD POLYMERISATION
59	CHEMICAL MATERIALS NES		27445		36845		19049		15895	MAT PROD CHIMIQUES NDA
591	PESTICIDES,DISINFECTANTS							W 2121	5531	DESINF,INSECT,FONG,HERB
598	MISCEL CHEM PRODUCTS NES							W 9068	8057	PROD DIV INDUST CHIM NDA
5989	CHEM PRODUCTS,PREPS NES							W 7889	7336	PROD PREP CHIMIQUES NDA
59899	OTH CHEM PRODS,PREPS,NES							W 6813	6206	AUT PRODUITS CHIMIQUES NDA
6	BASIC MANUFACTURES		626491		671804		444144		296568	ART MANUFACTURES
62	RUBBER MANUFACTURES NES		49588		61629		43386		27620	CAOUTCHOUC MANUFACTURE
625	RUBBER TYRES, TUBES ETC							W 13320	23381	PNEUS CAOUTCHOUC VULCANISE
6251	TYRES NEW FOR MOTOR CARS							W 11898	20403	PNEUS POUR VOITURES
63	WOOD,CORK MANUFACTRS NES		37330		36555		20989		9608	OUVRAGES LIEGE ET BOIS
634	VENEERS,PLYWOOD,ETC							W 84172	8925	PLACAGES,CONTRE–PLAQUES
6342	PLYWOOD OF WOOD SHEETS							W 84090	8894	BOIS CONTRE–PLAQUES
64	PAPER,PAPERBOARD AND MFR		57367		57112		41379		35515	PAPIERS,CARTONS & OUVRAGES
641	PAPER AND PAPERBOARD							W 38176	26050	PAPIERS ET CARTONS
6411	NEWSPRINT							W 15782	12019	PAPIER JOURNAL
6412	PRINTG,WRITING PAPER NES							W 9334	5119	PAPIERS POUR L'IMPRESSION
6415	PAPER,PAPERBRD,BULK,NES							W 9692	5194	PAPIERS,CARTONS ROULEAUX

4. General Imports C.I.F. by Commodities according to the S.I.T.C. (Rev. 2) in thousand U.S. Dollars
Importations Générales C.A.F. par Produits d'après la C.T.C.I. (Rév. 2) en milliers de Dollars E.U.

SITC CTCI	COMMODITY	1992 WEIGHT POIDS	1992 VALUE VALEUR	1993 WEIGHT POIDS	1993 VALUE VALEUR	1994 WEIGHT POIDS	1994 VALUE VALEUR	1995 WEIGHT POIDS	1995 VALUE VALEUR	PRODUIT
642	PAPER,ETC,PRECUT,ARTS OF							W 7386	9466	PAP,CARTONS DECOUPES
6421	PAPER ETC CONTAINERS							W 5359	4470	BOITES,SACS EMBALLAGES
65	TEXTILE YARN,FABRICS,ETC		53076		66522		50405		31234	FILS,TISSUS,ARTICLES TEXTILE
653	WOVN MAN-MADE FIB FABRIC							W 3244	10269	TISSUS FIBRES SYNTH,ARTIF
657	SPECIAL TXTL FABRC,PRODS							W 4021	4590	TISSUS SPECIAUX
658	TEXTILE ARTICLES NES							W 6185	6821	ART FACONNES MAT TEXTILES
659	FLOOR COVERINGS,ETC							W 7108	5708	COUVRE-PARQUETS,TAPIS ETC
66	NONMETAL MINERAL MFS NES		99435		82304		58460		33320	ART MIN NON METALLIQUES
661	LIME,CEMENT,BLDG PRODS							W 345123	18610	CHAUX,CIMENTS MAT CONSTR
6612	CEMENT							W 343125	17766	CIMENTS HYDRAULIQUES
662	CLAY,REFRACTORY BLDG PRD							W 22243	6555	MAT CONST REFRACTAIRES
6624	BRICKS ETC NONREFRACTORY							W 22144	6458	BRIQUES ETC CERAM NON REFR
665	GLASSWARE							W 7106	4385	OUVRAGES EN VERRE
67	IRON AND STEEL		225406		256801		144977		98261	FER ET ACIER
673	IRON,STEEL SHAPES ETC							W 206278	39177	BARRES,PROFIL FER,ACIER
6731	IRON,STEEL WIRE ROD							W 151403	28921	FIL MACHINE FER,ACIER
6732	IRON,STEEL BARS ETC							W 32235	6074	BARRES FER,ACIER
6733	IRON,STEEL PROFILES ETC							W 22641	4182	PROFILES,PALPLAN FER,ACIER
674	IRN,STL UNIV,PLATE,SHEET							W 42342	20889	LARGES PLATS,TOLES
678	IRON,STL TUBES,PIPES,ETC							W 40667	34872	TUBES,TUYAUX EN FONTE,FER
6781	CAST IRON TUBES,PIPES							W 20195	21117	TUBES,TUYAUX EN FONTE
6782	IRON,STL SEAMLESS TUBES							W 12562	7086	TUBES,TUYAUX SANS SOUDURE
68	NON-FERROUS METALS		37709		34179		32101		15446	METAUX NON FERREUX
684	ALUMINIUM							W 7583	14834	ALUMINIUM
6842	ALUMINIUM,ALLOYS WORKED							W 6483	14824	ALUMINIUM,ALLIAGES OUVRE
68421	ALUMINIUM BARS,WIRE,ETC							W 2303	5869	BARRES,PROFILES FILS ALU
68423	ALUMINIUM FOIL							W 2703	7397	FEUILLES,BANDES MINCES AL
69	METAL MANUFACTURES NES		64586		74558		50888		43962	ART MANUFACT EN METAL NDA
691	STRUCTURES AND PARTS NES							W 9815	14083	CONSTRUCT FER,ACIER,ALU
6911	STRUCTURES,PARTS IRN,STL							W 9762	13970	CONSTRUCT FER,ACIER,FONTE
692	METAL TANKS,BOXES,ETC							W 5516	6830	RECIPIENTS METALLIQUES
6924	MTL TRANSPORT BOXES ETC							W 5056	5585	FUTS,TAMBOURS,BIDONS
69243	IRN,STL COMP GAS CYLINDR							W 4265	4366	RECIP FER,ACIER GAZ COMP
695	TOOLS							W 1278	4899	OUTILS A MAIN
697	BASE MTL HOUSEHOLD EQUIP							W 2579	4349	ART MENAGE MET COMMUNS
699	BASE METAL MFRS NES							W 8785	8647	ART MANUFACTURES MET NDA
7	MACHINES,TRANSPORT EQUIP		564544		638028		427893		298102	MACHINES MATERIEL TRANSPORT
71	POWER GENERATING EQUIPMT		28447		39312		32834		16813	MACHINES GENERATRICES
713	INTRNL COMBUS PSTN ENGIN							W 1743	7347	MOTEURS EXPL COMB INT, PIECE
7139	PISTON ENGINE PARTS NES							W 460	4267	PIECES POUR 713.2,3,8
716	ROTATING ELECTRIC PLANT							W 1213	9110	APP ELECTR ROTATIFS,PIECES
7162	AC MTRS,GENRTRS,GEN SETS							W 1163	7141	MOTEURS ELECTRIQUES
72	MACHS FOR SPCL INDUSTRYS		81783		140468		74822		32187	MAC SPECIALES POUR INDUST
723	CIVIL ENGNEERG EQUIP ETC							W 4282	21640	APPAREILS DE GENIE CIVIL
7234	CONST,MINING MACHNRY NES							W 2449	7525	MACH POUR LA CONST, MINES
7239	CONSTR ETC MACHY PTS NES							W 1789	13993	PIECES 723.41-723.46
728	OTH MACHY FOR SPCL INDUS							W 1198	6163	AUT MACH IND PARTICULIERES
7284	MACHY FOR SPCL INDUS NES							W 608	4089	MACH SPEC IND PARTICUL.
74	GENRL INDUSTRL MACHY NES		113309		128780		58470		57046	MACH APP INDUSTRIE
741	HEATING,COOLING EQUIPMNT							W 1319	6363	MACH CHAUFFAGE,PIECES
742	PUMPS FOR LIQUIDS ETC							W 2705	9766	POMPES MOTO-POMPES
7428	OTHER PUMPS FOR LIQUIDS							W 1674	6469	AUTRES POMPES POUR LIQ
743	PUMPS NES,CENTRFUGES ETC							W 981	4486	POMPES COMPRES,VENT ETC
744	MECHANICAL HANDLING EQU							W 1221	7270	EQUIP MANUTENTION PIECES
7442	LIFTING,LOADING MACH NES							W 781	6178	APP LEVAGE,MANUTENTION
74422	SHIP DERRICKS,CRANES ETC							W 163	4532	GRUES,PONTS ROULANTS
745	NONELEC MACHY,TOOLS NES							W 940	6616	AUT MACH NON ELEC,PIECES
7452	OTH NONELEC MCHS,PTS NES							W 848	5897	AUT MACH NON ELEC,PIECES
74522	PACKAGNG,BOTTLNG,ETC MCH							W 284	3889	MACH NETT BOUTEILLES,ETC
749	NONELEC MACH PTS,ACC NES							W 2969	22545	PIECES MACH NON ELEC NDA
7492	COCKS,VALVES ETC NES							W 2333	14089	ART ROB,SIM POUR TUYAUX
7499	OTH NONELEC MCHY PTS NES							W 481	6772	PIECES NON ELECT NDA
74992	METAL-PLASTIC GASKETS							W 69	4273	JOINTS METALLOPLASTIQUES
75	OFFICE MACHNES,ADP EQUIP		14729		16019		10958		13425	MACH BUREAU TRAIT AUTOM
751	OFFICE MACHINES							W 249	8319	MACH,APPAREILS DE BUREAU
7518	OFFICE MACHINES NES							W 170	7514	MACH,APP DE BUREAU NDA
75182	PHOTO,THERMOCOPY APPARAT							W 82	7200	APPAREILS DE PHOTOCOPIE
76	TELECOMM,SOUND EQUIPMENT		31009		50675		23501		16144	EQUIPMENT DE TELECOM
761	TELEVISION RECEIVERS							W 472	3988	RECEPTEURS DE TELEVISION
764	TELECOM EQPT,PTS,ACC NES							W 830	10301	EQUIP TELECOM,PIECES
7641	LINE TELEPHONE,ETC EQUIP							W 172	3988	APP TELEPHON PAR FIL
7649	PTS NES OF EQUIPMT OF 76							W 146	4228	PIECES DE LA DIV 76
77	ELECTRIC MACHNRY NES ETC		76605		88121		85857		67399	MACH APP ELECT NDA
772	SWITCHGEAR ETC,PARTS NES							W 1940	15048	APP COUPURE,SECT ETC
773	ELECTR DISTRIBUTNG EQUIP							W 6358	15910	EQUIPMT DISTRIBUTION ELECT
7731	INSULATED WIRE,CABLE ETC							W 6106	15157	FILS,CABLES ISOLES ELECT
774	ELECTRO-MEDCL,XRAY EQUIP							W 244	6139	APPAREILS MEDICAUX
7741	ELECTRO-MEDICAL EQUIPMNT							W 198	4959	APP ELECTRICITE MEDICALE
775	HOUSEHOLD TYPE EQUIP NES							W 3779	9308	MACH,APP USAGE DOMESTQUE
778	ELECTRICAL MACHINERY NES							W 11219	18006	AUTRES MACH ELECT NDA
7781	BATTERIES,ACCUMULATORS							W 9179	10726	PILES ET ACCUMULATEURS
77811	PRIMARY BATTERIES,CELLS							W 6931	4798	PILES ELECTRIQUES,PIECES
77812	ELECTRIC ACCUMULATORS							W 2202	5788	ACCUMULATEURS ELECTRIQ
78	ROAD VEHICLES		182833		157204		130605		85464	VEHICULES ROUTIERS
781	PASS MOTOR VEH EXC BUSES							W 12418	31184	AUTO TRANSPORT PERSONNES
782	LORRIES,SPCL MTR VEH NES							W 9668	26331	VEHICULES SPECIAUX,MARCH
7821	LORRIES,TRUCKS							W 9162	22055	VEHICULES TRANSP MARCHAND
7822	SPECIAL MOTOR VEHCLS NES							W 506	4276	VEHICULES USAGES SPECIAUX
783	ROAD MOTOR VEHICLES NES							W 2319	5399	VEHICULES ROUTIERS NDA
7831	BUSES							W 2256	4839	VOITURES TRANSPORT COMMUN
784	MOTOR VEH PRTS,ACCES NES							W 4373	18879	PIECES 722,781,782,783
7849	OTHER MOTOR VEHCL PARTS							W 4311	18724	PIECES 722,781,782,783
79	OTHR TRANSPORT EQUIPMENT		32713		13003		8169		6807	AUTRE MATERIEL TRANSPORT
792	AIRCRAFT ETC							W 36	6683	APP NAVIGATION AERIENNE
7929	AIRCRAFT PARTS NES							W 35	6682	PIECES DU 792
8	MISC MANUFACTURED GOODS		140553		170353		119906		81173	ART MANUFACTURES DIVERS
812	*PLUMBG,HEATNG,LGHTNG EQ		9440		8517		8280	W 5780	6994	APPAR SANITAIRES CHAUFFAGE
8124	LIGHTING EQUIPMENT NES							W 2371	3990	APPAREILS ECLAIRAGE ETC
821	*FURNITURE,PARTS THEREOF		12475		20824		5550	W 3238	6199	MEUBLES ET PIECES
8219	FURNITURE AND PARTS NES							W 2783	5458	AUTRES MEUBLES ET PIECES
82192	WOOD FURNITURE NES							W 2356	4259	MEUBLES NDA EN BOIS

4. General Imports C.I.F. by Commodities according to the S.I.T.C. (Rev. 2) in thousand U.S. Dollars
Importations Générales C.A.F. par Produits d'après la C.T.C.I. (Rév. 2) en milliers de Dollars E.U.

SITC CTCI	COMMODITY	1992		1993		1994		1995		PRODUIT
		WEIGHT POIDS	VALUE VALEUR	WEIGHT POIDS	VALUE VALEUR	WEIGHT POIDS	VALUE VALEUR	WEIGHT POIDS	VALUE VALEUR	
84	CLOTHING AND ACCESSORIES		30907		37012		40652		18819	VETEMENTS
842	MENS OUTERWEAR NOT KNIT							W 3721	10054	VET DESSUS POUR HOMMES
8429	— OTHER OUTER GARMENTS							W 3721	10054	AUT VET DES HOM MAT TEX
843	WOMENS OUTERWEAR NONKNIT							W 191	5739	VET DESSUS FEMMES MAT TEX
8439	— OTHER OUTER GARMENTS							W 191	5739	AUT VET DES FEM MAT TEXT
851	*FOOTWEAR		12998		12858		13653	W 4206	8238	CHAUSSURES
85102	FOOTWEAR LEATHER							W 1622	4155	CHAUS SEMELLES EN CUIR
87	PRECISION INSTRUMNTS NES		33566		29343		14045		6867	INSTRUM,APPAR SCIENT NDA
874	MEASURNG,CONTROLNG INSTR							W 170	4035	INSTRUMENTS DE MESURE
88	PHOTO EQU,OPTICL GDS ETC		4318		10743		2809		2852	APP,FOURN PHOTO,OP,MONTR
89	MISC MANUFCTRD GOODS NES		35503		48852		33436		30278	ART MANUFACTURES DIVERS
893	ARTICLES OF PLASTIC NES							W 7814	15970	OUVRAGES EN MAT DIVIS 58
8939	MISC PLASTIC ARTICLES							W 5063	11464	ART DIVERS EN MAT DIV 58
89391	PVC FLOORING TILES ETC							W 3719	9207	CHLORURE POLYVINYL PLAQ
899	OTHER MANUFACTURED GOODS								6254	AUT ART MANUF DIVERS NDA

5. General Exports F.O.B. by Commodities according to the S.I.T.C. (Rev. 2) in thousand U.S. Dollars
Exportations Générales F.O.B. par Produits d'après la C.T.C.I. (Rév. 2) en milliers de Dollars E.U.

SITC CTCI	COMMODITY	1992 WEIGHT POIDS	1992 VALUE VALEUR	1993 WEIGHT POIDS	1993 VALUE VALEUR	1994 WEIGHT POIDS	1994 VALUE VALEUR	1995 WEIGHT POIDS	1995 VALUE VALEUR	PRODUIT
	ALL COMMODITIES		328983		374239		933856		1587407	TOUS PRODUITS
0	FOOD AND LIVE ANIMALS		36303		47236		61544		37834	ALIMENTS,ANIMAUX VIVANTS
02	DAIRY PRODCTS,BIRDS'EGGS		793		2847		3287		699	PRODUITS LAITIERS,OEUFS
03	FISH AND PREPARATIONS		6129		8503		8548		9413	POISSONS ET PREPARATIONS
04	CEREALS AND PREPARATIONS		5261		5513		6811		1843	CEREALES ET PRODUITS
05	VEGETABLES AND FRUIT		1658		2834		1865		2551	LEGUMES ET FRUITS
07	COFFEE,TEA,COCOA,SPICES		21464		26180		37695		21900	CAFE,THE,CACAO,EPICES
071	COFFEE AND SUBSTITUTES							W 3876	21794	CAFE ET SUCCEDANES
0711	COFFEE GREEN,ROASTED,SUB							W 3876	21794	CAFE TORREFIE OU DECAFEINE
07111	COFFEE GREEN,HUSKS,SKINS							W 3548	20580	CAFE NON TORREFIE
1	BEVERAGES AND TOBACCO		3580		3354		3220		3077	BOISSONS ET TABACS
11	BEVERAGES		1285		1869		1274		707	BOISSONS
12	TOBACCO AND MANUFACTURES		2295		1485		1946		2370	TABACS BRUTS FABRIQUES
2	CRUDE MATERLS,EXCL FUELS		33290		24989		24178		17637	MAT BRUTES NON COMESTIBLES
21	HIDES,SKINS,FURS UNDRSSD		16078		8085		9374		3262	CUIRS,PEAUX BRUTS
27	CRUDE FERTLZR,MINRLS NES		1382		2720				1702	ENGRAIS MINERAUX BRUTS
28	METALLIFEROUS ORES,SCRAP		7442		5361		2254		6106	MINERAIS METAL,DECHETS
29	CRUDE ANIMAL,VEG MAT NES		7866		8269		12164		6163	MATIERES BRUTES ANIM,VEGET
291	CRUDE ANIMAL MTRIALS NES							W 346	5728	MATIERES BRUTES ANIMALES
3	MINERAL FUELS ETC		244739		285035		830839		1497055	COMBUSTIBLES MINERAUX LUB
33	PETROLEUM AND PRODUCTS		241679		285033		830383		1496945	PETROLE ET DERIVES
333	CRUDE PETROLEUM							MW 13724	1423818	HUILES BRUTES DE PETROLE
334	PETROLEUM PRODUCTS,REFIN							W 452995	34168	PRODUITS RAFFINES
3342	KEROSENE,OTH MEDIUM OILS							W 50084	5675	PETR LAMPANTS,AUT HUIL
33421	KEROSENE INCL JET FUEL							W 50084	5675	PETROLES LAMPANTS
3344	FUEL OILS,NES							W 377234	25317	FUEL OILS
335	RESIDUAL PETRLM PROD NES							W 422536	38960	PRODUITS RESIDUELS NDA
3352	MINERAL TARS AND PRODCTS							W 422536	38960	GOUDRONS MINERAUX
341	*GAS,NATURAL AND MANUFCT		3045		1		457	W 1281	93	GAZ NATUREL,GAZ MANUFACT
4	ANIMAL,VEGETABLE OIL,FAT		3082		1979		2569		1625	HUILES,GRAISSES ANIM,VEG
42	FIXED VEGETABLE OIL,FAT		2971		1974		2568		1056	HUILES VEGETALES FIXES
5	CHEMCLS,RELATED PROD NES		5089		4620		4974		1929	PRODUITS CHIMIQUES
55	PERFUME,CLEANING ETC PRD		4995		4328		4963		1660	PROD POUR PARFUM,TOILETTE
6	BASIC MANUFACTURES		1057		3243		2178		7508	ART MANUFACTURES
7	MACHINES,TRANSPORT EQUIP		346		170		461		14313	MACHINES MATERIEL TRANSPORT
8	MISC MANUFACTURED GOODS		1246		3611		3869		6418	ART MANUFACTURES DIVERS
851	*FOOTWEAR		491		1650		1474	W 373	602	CHAUSSURES
89	MISC MANUFCTRD GOODS NES		365		1621		1766		1098	ART MANUFACTURES DIVERS

FOOT NOTES – NOTES

TABLE 1 –

1 In 1986, 1987, 1988 and 1989 data comprise trade of the former Democratic Yemen only.

TABLE 3 –

1 In 1991 data comprise trade of the former Democratic Yemen only.

TABLEAU 1 –

1 Les données se rapportent seulement au commerce de l'ancien Yémen démocratique en 1986, 1987, 1988 et 1989.

TABLEAU 3 –

1 Les données se rapportent seulement au commerce de l'ancien Yémen démocratique en 1991.

1. HISTORICAL SERIES, 1992–1996 SPECIAL TRADE, IMPORTS C.I.F., EXPORTS F.O.B.
SERIES HISTORIQUES, 1992–1996 COMMERCE SPECIAL, IMPORTATIONS C.A.F., EXPORTATIONS F.O.B

YEAR ANNEE	VALUE IN MILLION U.S. DOLLARS VALEUR EN MILLION U.S. DOLLARS MERCHANDISE –MARCHANDISE		GOLD –OR		CONVERSION FACTORS FACTEURS DE CONVERSION CENTS E.U. PAR		INDEX NUMBERS –INDICES QUANTUM		UNIT VALUE VALEUR UNITAIRE	
	IMPORTS	EXPORTS	IMPORTS	EXPORTS	IMPORTS	EXPORTS	IMPORTS	EXPORTS	IMPORTS	EXPORTS
1992	3630.00	2480.00							116	90
1995	3984.00	2539.00							126	93
1996	4102.00	1842.00							126	91

2. IMPORTS BY BROAD ECONOMIC CATEGORY AND EXPORTS BY INDUSTRIAL ORIGIN. (PERCENTAGE OF TOTAL VALUE)
IMPORTATIONS PAR CATEGORIES ECONOMIQUES ET EXPORTATIONS PAR BRANCHE D'ACTIVITE.(EN POURCENTAGE DE LA VALEUR TOTALE)

IMPORTS – IMPORTATIONS

	1990	1991	1992	1993	1994	1995	1996
TOTAL IMPORTS–IMPORTATIONS TOTALES							100.
1 FOOD BEV–ALIMENTATION BOISSONS							12.2
11 PRIMARY–PRODUITS DE BASE							6.2
111 FOR INDUSTRY–POUR L'INDUSTRIE							2.1
112 FOR HOUSEHOLDS–POUR LES MENAGES							4.1
12 PROCESSED–PRODUITS ELABORES							6.0
121 FOR INDUSTRY–POUR L'INDUSTRIE							1.7
122 FOR HOUSEHOLDS–POUR LES MENAGES							4.4
2 IND SUPPLIES–APPROV INDUSTRIELS							43.0
21 PRIMARY–PRODUITS DE BASE							7.3
22 PROCESSED–PRODUITS ELABORES							35.8
3 FUELS–COMBUSTIBLES							14.0
31 PRIMARY–PRODUITS DE BASE							6.0
32 PROCESSED–PRODUITS ELABORES							8.0
321 MOTOR SPIRIT–ESSENCE							
322 OTHER–AUTRES							8.0
4 MACHINERY–EQUIPEMENT							14.3
41 CAPITAL EQUIPMENT–MACHINES							12.3
42 PARTS–PIECES ACCESSOIRES							2.1
5 TRANSPORT–TRANSPORT							6.2
51 PASSENGER CARS–AUTOMOBILES							2.3
52 OTHER–AUTRES							1.7
521 INDUSTRIAL–INDUSTRIELS							1.6
522 NON INDUSTRIAL–NON INDUSTRIEL							0.0
53 PARTS–PIECES ACCESSOIRES							2.2
6 CONSUM GOODS–BIENS CONSOMMATION							9.3
61 DURABLE–DURABLES							2.6
62 SEMI DURABLE–SEMI DURABLES							5.0
63 NON DURABLE–NON DURABLES							1.8
7 GOODS NES–BIENS NDA							0.9

EXPORTS – EXPORTATIONS

	1990	1991	1992	1993	1994	1995	1996
TOTAL EXPORTS–EXPORTATIONS TOTALES							100.
1 AGRICULTURE							9.7
2 MINING QUARRY–INDUS EXTRACTIVES							1.0
3 MANUFACTURING–IND MANUFACTUR							89.3
31 FOOD BEV TOBACCO–ALIM BOISS TAB							19.7
32 TEXTILES–INDUSTRIES TEXTILES							7.6
33 WOOD & PRODUCTS–BOIS & PRODUITS							3.0
34 PAPER & PRODUCTS–PAPIER & PRODT							0.9
35 CHEMICALS–INDUSTRIES CHIMIQUES							14.2
36 NON METAL MIN–MIN NON METAL							3.0
37 BASIC METAL–IND METAL BASE							19.5
38 METAL MANUF–MANUF METAL							18.7
39 OTH MANUF IND–AUTRES MANUF							2.5

3. TRADE BY PRINCIPAL COUNTRIES OF ORIGIN AND LAST DESTINATION (VALUE IN THOUSAND U.S. DOLLARS)
ECHANGES SELON LES PRINCIPAUX PAYS D'ORIGINE ET DE DERNIERE DESTINATION (VALEUR EN MILLIERS DE DOLLARS EU)

COUNTRIES–PAYS	SPECIAL IMPORTS C.I.F. IMPORTATIONS SPECIALES C.A.F				
	1992	1993	1994	1995	1996
World				3859229	4101851
Africa				55904	106036
Americas				343448	348296
Northern America				200150	125953
LAIA				119416	181244
CACM				6257	5431
Caribbean				10893	34854
Rest of America				6732	814
As.ex F.USSR				346517	327772
Eur.x F.USSR				2491135	3011875
EU				1689494	1724860
EFTA				91326	118391
East Europe				710315	657570
Other Europe					1579
Former USSR				600955	296171
Oceania				11863	11597
Germany/Allemagne				578790	523831
Russian Federation				580834	224551
Italy/Italie				370303	434586
Bulgaria/Bulgarie				187358	219040
Romania/Roumanie				197050	123020
Austria/Autriche				164524	123520
Greece/Grèce				140041	147747
USA/Etats–Unis d'Amer				145507	119363
France,Monac				125797	134431
Hungary/Hongrie				114606	128474
Bosnia and Herzegovina					230021
Tfyr Macedonia					212683
United Kingdom				106540	97979
Switz.Liecht				88816	112279
Slovakia				122832	46426
Poland/Pologne				86661	58074
Netherlands/Pays–Bas				58173	76003
China/Chine				81813	48035
Sweden/Suède				32820	85988
Japan/Japon				58310	57640
Brazil/Brésil				56396	57743
Belgium–Luxembourg				58437	51280
Libyan Arab Jamahiriya				40285	68251
Czech Republic					79653
Iran (Islamic Rp. of)				42357	35658
Turkey/Turquie				36980	40247
Ukraine				17629	55036
Cyprus/Chypre				21557	42314
Canada				54596	6582
Peru/Pérou				23816	35814
Slovenia/Slovénia					55730
Ecuador/Equateur				7090	41997
Cuba				10721	33666
Korea, Republic of				16024	17521
Denmark/Danemark				16823	13912
Spain/Espagne				12556	17703
Argentina/Argentine				11007	18122
Israel/Israël				13630	13207
Australia/Australie				10314	10874
India/Inde				9681	10475
Colombia/Colombie				8298	10268
Finland/Finlande				6364	11918
Hong Kong				10893	7243
Malaysia/Malaisie				8295	8821
Ireland/Irlande				11498	5449
Indonesia/Indonésie				3307	12147
Egypt/Egypte				5299	9582
Singapore/Singapour				4929	8265
So. Africa Customs Un				1909	10439
Belarus/Bélarus				2492	8652

COUNTRIES–PAYS	SPECIAL EXPORTS F.O.B. EXPORTATIONS SPECIALES F.O.B.				
	1992	1993	1994	1995	1996
Monde				2538506	1841746
Afrique				100216	38564
Amériques				108972	43553
Amérique du Nord				104997	36924
ALAI				2265	2354
MCAC				2	263
Caraïbes				782	2239
Autre Amérique				926	1773
Asie l'URSS exclus				245882	90986
Europe l'URSS exclus				1531374	1489945
UE				1113516	586404
AELE				50461	92594
Europe de l'Est				363052	188822
Autre de l'Europe				4345	97
Ancienne URSS				547166	177448
Océanie				4865	1250
Russian Federation				538193	156445
Germany/Allemagne				417022	146424
Italy/Italie				301971	180613
Bosnia and Herzegovina					380469
Romania/Roumanie				193952	62464
Tfyr Macedonia					211750
Greece/Grèce				103765	94876
USA/Etats–Unis d'Amer				100216	33141
Bulgaria/Bulgarie				64966	62898
Switz.Liecht				38924	83834
France,Monac				60373	55343
Austria/Autriche				68924	26669
Cyprus/Chypre				46831	36777
United Kingdom				49679	27468
Hungary/Hongrie				45103	29666
Netherlands/Pays–Bas				53276	21400
Turkey/Turquie				45227	12039
Egypt/Egypte				36514	20565
Belgium–Luxembourg				16913	20222
Kuwait/ Koweït				35289	165
Iran (Islamic Rp. of)				30986	1354
Slovakia				24665	6517
Poland/Pologne				23512	6158
Slovenia/Slovénia					28749
Libyan Arab Jamahiriya				22159	1208
Ukraine				5950	14892
China/Chine				9477	10785
Norway,SVD,JM				11453	8712
Sweden/Suède				15018	3563
Syrian Arab Republic				16188	2360
Albania/Albanie				10854	6720
India/Inde				9594	7332
Czech Republic					14399
Nigeria/Nigéria				13226	734
Israel/Israël				6288	7565
Saudi Arabia				12598	302
Denmark/Danemark				10130	2643
Lebanon/Liban				9585	2305
Algeria/Algérie				9042	1352
Spain/Espagne				8239	1116
Liberia/Libéria				797	8386
Tunisia/Tunisie				8392	279
Canada				4781	3733
Belarus/Bélarus				3023	3482
Ireland/Irlande				2259	4034
Finland/Finlande				4063	2032
Morocco/Maroc				5412	122
So. Africa Customs Un				1123	3924
Hong Kong				1120	3385
Australia/Australie				3514	986

(VALUE AS PERCENTAGE OF WORLD TOTAL)(VALEURS EN POURCENTAGE DU TOTAL MONDIAL)

	1987	1988	1989	1990	1991	1992	1993	1994	1995	1996
Africa									1.4	2.6
Americas									8.9	8.5
Northern America									5.2	3.1
LAIA									3.1	4.4
CACM									0.2	0.1
Caribbean									0.3	0.8
Rest of America									0.2	0.0
As.ex F.USSR									9.0	8.0
Eur.x F.USSR									64.6	73.4
EU									43.8	42.1
EFTA									2.4	2.9
East Europe									18.4	16.0
Other Europe										0.0
Former USSR									15.6	7.2
Oceania									0.3	0.3
Germany/Allemagne									15.0	12.8
Russian Federation									15.1	5.5
Italy/Italie									9.6	10.6
Bulgaria/Bulgarie									4.9	5.3
Romania/Roumanie									5.1	3.0
Austria/Autriche									4.3	3.0
Greece/Grèce									3.6	3.6
USA/Etats–Unis d'Amer									3.8	2.9
France,Monac									3.3	3.3
Hungary/Hongrie									3.0	3.1

	1987	1988	1989	1990	1991	1992	1993	1994	1995	1996
Afrique									3.9	2.1
Amériques									4.3	2.4
Amérique du Nord									4.1	2.0
ALAI									0.1	0.1
MCAC									0.0	0.0
Caraïbes									0.0	0.1
Autre Amérique									0.0	0.1
Asie l'URSS exclus									9.7	4.9
Europe l'URSS exclus									60.3	80.9
UE									43.9	31.8
AELE									2.0	5.0
Europe de l'Est									14.3	10.3
Autre de l'Europe									0.2	0.0
Ancienne URSS									21.6	9.6
Océanie									0.2	0.1
Russian Federation									21.2	8.5
Germany/Allemagne									16.4	8.0
Italy/Italie									11.9	9.8
Bosnia and Herzegovina										20.7
Romania/Roumanie									7.6	3.4
Tfyr Macedonia										11.5
Greece/Grèce									4.1	5.2
USA/Etats–Unis d'Amer									3.9	1.8
Bulgaria/Bulgarie									2.6	3.4
Switz.Liecht									1.5	4.6

4. Special Imports C.I.F. by Commodities according to the S.I.T.C. (Rev. 2) in thousand U.S. Dollars
Importations Spéciales C.A.F. par Produits d'après la C.T.C.I. (Rév. 2) en milliers de Dollars E.U.

SITC CTCI	COMMODITY	1993		1994		1995		1996		PRODUIT
		WEIGHT POIDS	VALUE VALEUR	WEIGHT POIDS	VALUE VALEUR	WEIGHT POIDS	VALUE VALEUR	WEIGHT POIDS	VALUE VALEUR	
	ALL COMMODITIES								4101851	TOUS PRODUITS
0	FOOD AND LIVE ANIMALS								501343	ALIMENTS,ANIMAUX VIVANTS
01	MEAT AND PREPARATIONS								34192	VIANDES ET PREPARATIONS
011	MEAT FRESH,CHILLD,FROZEN							W 19715	29120	VIANDES FRAICHES,REF,CONGE
0111	BOVINE MEAT FRESH,FROZEN							W 7013	12846	VIANDES BOVIN FRAI,REF
02	DAIRY PRODCTS,BIRDS'EGGS								21149	PRODUITS LAITIERS,OEUFS
03	FISH AND PREPARATIONS								18916	POISSONS ET PREPARATIONS
034	FISH,FRESH,CHILLED,FROZN								13185	POISSON FRAIS, REFRIG,CONG
04	CEREALS AND PREPARATIONS								33943	CEREALES ET PRODUITS
048	CEREAL ETC PREPARATIONS							W 11166	12451	PREPTNS A BASE CEREALES
05	VEGETABLES AND FRUIT								134201	LEGUMES ET FRUITS
054	VEG ETC FRSH,SMPLY PRSVD							W 104908	26373	LEGUMES FRAIS,CONG,SECS
057	FRUIT,NUTS,FRESH,DRIED								93952	FRUITS FRAIS OU SECS
0571	ORANGES, MANDARINS ETC							W 33355	13785	ORANGES,MAND,CLEMENTINES
0573	BANANA,PLANTAIN,FRSH,DRY							W 66244	59234	BANANES FRAICHES,SECHEES
06	SUGAR AND PREPS,HONEY								81792	SUCRES ET PRODUITS
061	SUGAR AND HONEY							W 166997	72633	SUCRES ET MIEL
0611	RAW BEET AND CANE SUGAR							W 120484	47184	SUCRES BRUTS
0612	REFINED SUGAR ETC							W 45931	24776	SUCRES RAFFINES
07	COFFEE,TEA,COCOA,SPICES								79912	CAFE,THE,CACAO,EPICES
071	COFFEE AND SUBSTITUTES							W 10666	33869	CAFE ET SUCCEDANES
0711	COFFEE GREEN,ROASTED,SUB							W 10589	33133	CAFE TORREFIE OU DECAFEINE
07111	COFFEE GREEN,HUSKS,SKINS							W 10550	32891	CAFE NON TORREFIE
073	CHOCOLATE AND PRODUCTS							W 8758	29927	CHOCOLAT
081	*FEEDING STUFF FOR ANIML							W 119969	65494	NOURRITURE POUR ANIMAUX
0813	OILCAKE AND OTH RESIDUES							W 62791	20563	TOURTEAUX
08131	— OF SOYA BEANS							W 60358	20234	TOURTEAUX DE SOJA
0814	MEAT OR FISH MEAL FODDER							W 47499	38439	FARINES DE VIANDES,POISSONS
08142	FISH MEAL FODDER							W 47475	38429	FARINES DE POISSONS
09	MISC EDIBLE PRODUCTS								26913	PREP ALIMENTAIRES DIVERSES
098	EDIBLE PRODCTS,PREPS NES								25164	PREP ALIMENTAIRES NDA
09809	MISC FOOD PREPRTIONS NES							W 2967	21365	PREP ALIMENTAIRES NDA
1	BEVERAGES AND TOBACCO								36489	BOISSONS ET TABACS
11	BEVERAGES								25808	BOISSONS
112	ALCOHOLIC BEVERAGES								15105	BOISSONS ALCOOLIQUES
2	CRUDE MATERLS,EXCL FUELS								425606	MAT BRUTES NON COMESTIBLES
22	OIL SEEDS,OLEAGINOUS FRT								34454	GRAINES,FRUITS OLEAGINEUX
222	SEEDS FOR'SOFT'FIXED OIL							W 101357	34027	GRAINES HUILES FIXES
2222	SOYA BEANS							W 67654	22635	FEVES DE SOJA
23	RUBBER, CRUDE								26731	CAOUTCHOUC BRUT
233	RUBBER,SYNTHTIC,RECLAIMD							W 11745	18044	LATEX CAOUTCH SYNTH REGEN
2331	SYNTHETIC RUBBER ETC							W 11423	17800	LATEX CAOUTCH SYNTHETIQUE
24	CORK AND WOOD								66110	LIEGE ET BOIS
248	WOOD SHAPED,SLEEPERS							W 191540	53619	BOIS SIMPLEMENT TRAVAILLES
2482	LUMBER SHAPED CONIFER							W 150258	39211	CONIFERES SCIES,RABOTES
24821	LUMBER SAWN ETC CONIFER							W 149346	38860	CONIFERES SCIES LONGITUD
2483	LUMBER SHAPED NON–CONIFR							W 40579	14175	NON CONIFERES SCIES,RABOTES
251	*PULP AND WASTE PAPER								15325	PATES A PAPIER,DECHETS
26	TEXTILE FIBRES AND WASTE								46963	FIBRES TEXTILES
263	COTTON							W 8807	16417	COTON
2631	RAW COTTON,EXCL LINTERS							W 8075	15554	COTON EN MASSE
266	SYNTHETIC FIBRES TO SPIN								13863	FIBRES SYNTHETIQUES
27	CRUDE FERTLZR,MINRLS NES								41556	ENGRAIS MINERAUX BRUTS
278	OTHER CRUDE MINERALS							W 310133	23529	AUTRES MINERAUX BRUTS
2783	COMMON SALT,ETC							W 200191	12674	SEL
28	METALLIFEROUS ORES,SCRAP								182377	MINERAIS METAL,DECHETS
281	IRON ORE,CONCENTRATES							W 987662	33043	MINERAIS DE FER
2815	IRON ORE,CONC,NOT AGGLOM							W 798294	25105	MINERAIS NON AGGLOMERES
287	BASE METAL ORES,CONC NES								136009	MINERAIS METAUX COMMUNS
2871	CPR ORE ETC,CEMENT COPPR							W 189580	115301	MINERAIS DE CUIVRE,MATTES
28711	COPPER ORES,EXCL MATTE							W 189580	115301	MINERAIS DE CUIVRE
3	MINERAL FUELS ETC								575003	COMBUSTIBLES MINERAUX LUB
32	COAL,COKE AND BRIQUETTES								56676	HOUILLES,COKES,BRIQUETTES
323	BRIQUETS,COKE,SEMI–COKE							W 431958	51145	BRIQUETTES
3232	COKE,SEMI–COKE,RTRT CRBN							W 409154	50374	COKES ET SEMI–COKES
33	PETROLEUM AND PRODUCTS								478144	PETROLE ET DERIVES
333	CRUDE PETROLEUM							W 1321098	228819	HUILES BRUTES DE PETROLE
334	PETROLEUM PRODUCTS,REFIN							W 1045557	236363	PRODUITS RAFFINES
335	RESIDUAL PETRLM PROD NES								12962	PRODUITS RESIDUELS NDA
351	*ELECTRIC CURRENT								30971	ENERGIE ELECTRIQUE
5	CHEMCLS,RELATED PROD NES								563927	PRODUITS CHIMIQUES
51	ORGANIC CHEMICALS								84598	PROD CHIMIQ ORGANIQUES
513	CARBOXYLIC ACIDS ETC							W 10602	17179	ACIDES CARBOXYLIQUES
514	NITROGEN–FNCTN COMPOUNDS							W 5954	23950	COMPOSES FONCT AZOTEES
5148	OTH NITROGN–FNCTN CMPNDS							W 2724	13474	AUTRES COMPOSES AZOTES
515	ORG–INORG COMPOUNDS ETC								13427	COMPOSES ORGANO–MINERAUX
52	INORGANIC CHEMICALS								63849	PROD CHIM INORGANIQUES
522	INORG ELEMNTS,OXIDES,ETC								25187	ELEMENTS INORGANIQUES
523	OTHR INORG CHEMICALS ETC								38168	AUT PRODUITS CHIMIQUES INORG
5231	METAL CMPD OF INORG ACID							W 22875	14565	SELS METALLIQUES
5232	OTH MTL CMPD OF INRG ACD								20295	SELS METALLIQUES
53	DYES,TANNING,COLOUR PROD								50778	PROD TEINTURE,COLORANTS
531	SYNT DYE,NAT INDGO,LAKES							W 1194	13150	MAT COLOR ORGAN,LAQUES
533	PIGMENTS,PAINTS,ETC							W 13242	35522	PIGMENTS,PEINTURES,VERNIS
5334	VARNISHES,DISTEMPERS ETC							W 6107	18635	PEINTURES A L'EAU
53342	OTH PAINTS,VARNISHES ETC							W 4717	14623	AUTRES PEINTURES,VERNIS
541	*MEDICINAL,PHARM PRODUCT								61004	PROD MEDICINAUX PHARMACEUT
5417	MEDICAMENTS								32797	MEDICAMENTS
54179	— CONTNG OTH SUBSTANCES							K 362	16725	MED CONT AUT SUBSTANCES
55	PERFUME,CLEANING ETC PRD								50325	PROD POUR PARFUM,TOILETTE
554	SOAP,CLEANSING ETC PREPS							W 30470	31566	SAVONS,PRODUITS DETERSIFS
5542	WASHING PREPARATIONS ETC							W 27316	26403	PROD ORG TENSIO–ACT NDA
562	*FERTILIZERS,MANUFACTURE								31515	ENGRAIS MANUFACTURES
5623	CHEM POTASSIC FERTILIZER								12902	ENGRAIS POTASSIQUES
56231	POTASSIUM CHLORIDE							W 101419	12900	CHLORURE DE POTASSIUM
58	PLASTIC MATERIALS ETC								127312	MAT PLAST ARTIFICIELLES
582	PROD OF CONDENSATION ETC							W 9307	22994	PROD CONDENS,POLYCOND
583	POLYMERIZATION ETC PRODS								99249	PROD POLYMERISATION
5831	POLYETHYLENE								29079	POLYETHYLENE
58311	— IN PRIMARY FORMS							W 30781	27883	POLYETHYLENE PRIMAIRES
5832	POLYPROPYLENE							W 15424	17004	POLYPROPYLENE

4. Special Imports C.I.F. by Commodities according to the S.I.T.C. (Rev. 2) in thousand U.S. Dollars
Importations Spéciales C.A.F. par Produits d'après la C.T.C.I. (Rév. 2) en milliers de Dollars E.U.

SITC CTCI	COMMODITY	1993		1994		1995		1996		PRODUIT
		WEIGHT POIDS	VALUE VALEUR	WEIGHT POIDS	VALUE VALEUR	WEIGHT POIDS	VALUE VALEUR	WEIGHT POIDS	VALUE VALEUR	
58321	— IN PRIMARY FORMS							W 14314	12834	POLYPROPYLENE PRIMAIRES
5834	POLYVINYL CHLORIDE							W 19232	20234	CHLORURE DE POLYVINYLE
58341	— IN PRIMARY FORMS							W 16879	15225	SOUS FORMES PRIMAIRES
5839	OTH POLYMRZTION ETC PROD							W 5758	14286	AUT PROD POLYMER COPOLYM
59	CHEMICAL MATERIALS NES								94540	MAT PROD CHIMIQUES NDA
591	PESTICIDES,DISINFECTANTS							W 1743	23390	DESINF,INSECT,FONG,HERB
598	MISCEL CHEM PRODUCTS NES							W 27147	63708	PROD DIV INDUST CHIM NDA
5982	ANTI-KNOCK PREPARTNS ETC							W 3336	13911	PREPARAT ANTIDETONANTES
5989	CHEM PRODUCTS,PREPS NES							W 20120	44946	PROD PREP CHIMIQUES NDA
59899	OTH CHEM PRODS,PREPS,NES							W 15038	32623	AUT PRODUITS CHIMIQUES NDA
6	BASIC MANUFACTURES								829084	ART MANUFACTURES
61	LEATHER,DRESSED FUR,ETC								19149	CUIRS,PELLETERIES
612	LEATHER ETC MANUFACTURES								14546	OUVRAGES EN CUIRS NDA
6123	PREPRD PARTS OF FOOTWEAR							W 1337	14488	PARTIES DE CHAUSSURES
62	RUBBER MANUFACTURES NES								36390	CAOUTCHOUC MANUFACTURE
625	RUBBER TYRES, TUBES ETC							W 14940	24579	PNEUS CAOUTCHOUC VULCANISE
6252	TYRES,NEW,BUS OR LORRY							W 4242	15485	PNEUS POUR AUTOBUS,CAMIONS
63	WOOD,CORK MANUFACTRS NES								20014	OUVRAGES LIEGE ET BOIS
64	PAPER,PAPERBOARD AND MFR								157417	PAPIERS,CARTONS & OUVRAGES
641	PAPER AND PAPERBOARD							W 128236	117178	PAPIERS ET CARTONS
6411	NEWSPRINT							W 18070	13019	PAPIER JOURNAL
6412	PRINTG,WRITING PAPER NES							W 17592	20525	PAPIERS POUR L'IMPRESSION
64122	— COATED,IMPREGNATD ETC							W 14604	16861	PAPIERS IMPRESSION COUCHES
6413	KRAFT PAPER,PAPERBOARD							W 36275	25340	PAPIER ET CARTON KRAFT
64132	SACK KRAFT PAPER IN BULK							W 23757	17250	PAPIER KRAFT POUR SACS
6415	PAPER,PAPERBRD,BULK,NES							W 29992	30312	PAPIERS,CARTONS ROULEAUX
64159	OTHER PAPER ETC,BULK,NES							W 25299	26547	AUT PAPIER ROULEAUX FEUILLES
6418	COATED ETC PAPER NES BLK							W 8136	15010	PAP,CARTONS COUCHES,ENDUITS
642	PAPER,ETC,PRECUT,ARTS OF							W 23445	40239	PAP,CARTONS DECOUPES
6421	PAPER ETC CONTAINERS							W 12884	15749	BOITES,SACS EMBALLAGES
65	TEXTILE YARN,FABRICS,ETC								234412	FILS,TISSUS,ARTICLES TEXTILE
651	TEXTILE YARN								23580	FILS TEXTILES
652	COTTON FABRICS,WOVEN							W 102992	151614	TISSUS DE COTON
6521	GREY WOVEN COTTON FABRIC							W 95953	127012	TISSUS COT ECRUS NON MERCER
65215	GREY WOVN COTN BLEND NES							W 95456	125623	AUT TIS MOINS 85% COT ECRUS
6522	WOVEN COTTON BLEACHD,ETC							W 7038	24602	TISSUS COTON BLANCHIS ETC
65224	BLCHED COTTON FABRIC NES							W 6398	20020	AUT TIS PLUS 85% COT BLANCHI
653	WOVN MAN-MADE FIB FABRIC							W 1959	13263	TISSUS FIBRES SYNTH,ARTIF
657	SPECIAL TXTL FABRC,PRODS								23557	TISSUS SPECIAUX
66	NONMETAL MINERAL MFS NES								64425	ART MIN NON METALLIQUES
662	CLAY,REFRACTORY BLDG PRD							W 73926	14223	MAT CONST REFRACTAIRES
663	MINERAL MANUFCTURES NES								12590	ART MIN MANUF NDA
664	GLASS							W 20496	17914	VERRE
67	IRON AND STEEL								171306	FER ET ACIER
671	PIG IRON ETC							W 15468	12944	FONTE,SPIEGEL,POUDRES
672	IRON,STEEL PRIMARY FORMS							W 99577	23569	LINGOTS FER,ACIER
6725	IRN,STL BLOOMS,SLABS,ETC							W 91410	21004	BLOOMS,BILLETTES FER ACIER
67251	IRN,SMPLE STL BLOOMS,ETC							W 90546	19872	BLOOMS ETC NON ACIER FIN
673	IRON,STEEL SHAPES ETC								43421	BARRES,PROFIL FER,ACIER
6731	IRON,STEEL WIRE ROD								22347	FIL MACHINE FER,ACIER
67311	IRON,SIMPLE STL WIRE ROD							W 76097	22038	FIL MACH AUT ACIER FIN
6732	IRON,STEEL BARS ETC							W 31917	15701	BARRES FER,ACIER
674	IRN,STL UNIV,PLATE,SHEET							W 56657	43444	LARGES PLATS,TOLES
678	IRON,STL TUBES,PIPES,ETC							W 30349	32035	TUBES,TUYAUX EN FONTE,FER
6782	IRON,STL SEAMLESS TUBES							W 16629	19606	TUBES,TUYAUX SANS SOUDURE
68	NON-FERROUS METALS								64670	METAUX NON FERREUX
682	COPPER EXC CEMENT COPPER							W 11349	28841	CUIVRE
6821	COPPER NES,ALLOYS,UNWRT							W 10248	25690	CUIVRE BRUT
68211	COPPER UNREF,EXC CEMENT							W 8035	20659	CUIVRE POUR AFFINAGE
684	ALUMINIUM							W 6811	23051	ALUMINIUM
6842	ALUMINIUM,ALLOYS WORKED							W 5467	20908	ALUMINIUM,ALLIAGES OUVRE
69	METAL MANUFACTURES NES								61301	ART MANUFACT EN METAL NDA
699	BASE METAL MFRS NES								18923	ART MANUFACTURES MET NDA
7	MACHINES,TRANSPORT EQUIP								795672	MACHINES MATERIEL TRANSPORT
71	POWER GENERATING EQUIPMT								25743	MACHINES GENERATRICES
713	INTRNL COMBUS PSTN ENGIN								17096	MOTEURS EXPL COMB INT, PIECE
72	MACHS FOR SPCL INDUSTRYS								102092	MAC SPECIALES POUR INDUST
727	FOOD MACHRY NON-DOMESTIC								15551	MACH INDUSTRIES ALIMENT
7272	OTH FOOD PROC MCHY,PARTS							W 936	14007	AUT MACH IND ALIMENTAIRE
72722	INDUS FOOD PROC MACH NES							W 925	13575	MACHINES BOULANGERIE
728	OTH MACHY FOR SPCL INDUS								39195	AUT MACH IND PARTICULIERES
7284	MACHY FOR SPCL INDUS NES								25575	MACH SPEC IND PARTICUL.
72842	RUBBER,PLASTICS WRKG MCH							W 2326	13341	MACH IND CAOUT MAT PLAST
73	METALWORKING MACHINERY								14354	MACH TRAVAIL DES METAUX
74	GENRL INDUSTRL MACHY NES								115345	MACH APP INDUSTRIE
741	HEATING,COOLING EQUIPMNT							W 2970	24748	MACH CHAUFFAGE,PIECES
743	PUMPS NES,CENTRFUGES ETC							W 2168	18435	POMPES COMPRES,VENT ETC
744	MECHANICAL HANDLING EQU								13524	EQUIP MANUTENTION PIECES
745	NONELEC MACHY,TOOLS NES								27035	AUT MACH NON ELEC,PIECES
7452	OTH NONELEC MCHS,PTS NES								24318	AUT MACH NON ELEC,PIECES
74522	PACKAGNG,BOTTLNG,ETC MCH							W 768	19515	MACH NETT BOUTEILLES,ETC
749	NONELEC MACH PTS,ACC NES								23066	PIECES MACH NON ELEC NDA
75	OFFICE MACHNES,ADP EQUIP								73852	MACH BUREAU TRAIT AUTOM
752	AUTOMTIC DATA PROC EQUIP								46639	MACH TRAIT INFORMATION
7525	ADP PERIPHERAL UNITS							W 1061	21401	UNITES PERIPHERIQUES
759	OFFICE,ADP MCH PTS,ACCES								20069	PIECES DU 751 ET 752
7599	ACCTG,ETC,ADP MCH PTS,AC							W 635	18828	PIECES DU 751 ET 752
76	TELECOMM,SOUND EQUIPMENT								160500	EQUIPMENT DE TELECOM
762	RADIO BROADCAST RECEIVRS								36153	RECEPTEURS RADIODIFFUSION
7622	PORTABLE RADIO RECEIVERS							W 251	34045	RECEPT PORTATIFS RADIO
764	TELECOM EQPT,PTS,ACC NES								115516	EQUIP TELECOM,PIECES
7641	LINE TELEPHONE,ETC EQUIP							W 587	82650	APP TELEPHON PAR FIL
7649	PTS NES OF EQUIPMT OF 76								18277	PIECES DE LA DIV 76
76491	PTS NES OF APPAR OF 7641							W 144	13330	PIECES POUR 764.1
77	ELECTRIC MACHNRY NES ETC								101961	MACH APP ELECT NDA
772	SWITCHGEAR ETC,PARTS NES								21964	APP COUPURE,SECT ETC
7721	SWITCHGEAR ETC							W 748	19879	APP COUPURE,SECTIONMNT
776	TRANSISTORS,VALVES,ETC								16205	LAMPES,TUBES,VALVES
778	ELECTRICAL MACHINERY NES								33387	AUTRES MACH ELECT NDA
7788	OTH ELEC MACHY,EQUIP NES								15120	AUT MACH APP ELEC NDA
78	ROAD VEHICLES								184274	VEHICULES ROUTIERS

4. Special Imports C.I.F. by Commodities according to the S.I.T.C. (Rev. 2) in thousand U.S. Dollars
Importations Spéciales C.A.F. par Produits d'après la C.T.C.I. (Rév. 2) en milliers de Dollars E.U.

SITC CTCI	COMMODITY	1993 WEIGHT POIDS	1993 VALUE VALEUR	1994 WEIGHT POIDS	1994 VALUE VALEUR	1995 WEIGHT POIDS	1995 VALUE VALEUR	1996 WEIGHT POIDS	1996 VALUE VALEUR	PRODUIT
781	PASS MOTOR VEH EXC BUSES							W 21689	95564	AUTO TRANSPORT PERSONNES
782	LORRIES,SPCL MTR VEH NES							W 10044	25311	VEHICULES SPECIAUX,MARCH
7821	LORRIES,TRUCKS							W 9661	22980	VEHICULES TRANSP MARCHAND
783	ROAD MOTOR VEHICLES NES							W 4758	24821	VEHICULES ROUTIERS NDA
7832	TRACTORS FOR TR–TRAILERS							W 3071	19392	TRACTEURS ROUTIERS
784	MOTOR VEH PRTS,ACCES NES							W 3254	23817	PIECES 722,781,782,783
7849	OTHER MOTOR VEHCL PARTS							W 2862	20455	PIECES 722,781,782,783
79	OTHR TRANSPORT EQUIPMENT								17551	AUTRE MATERIEL TRANSPORT
8	MISC MANUFACTURED GOODS								327227	ART MANUFACTURES DIVERS
821	*FURNITURE,PARTS THEREOF							W 12498	33530	MEUBLES ET PIECES
8219	FURNITURE AND PARTS NES							W 9808	23688	AUTRES MEUBLES ET PIECES
82192	WOOD FURNITURE NES							W 6900	14959	MEUBLES NDA EN BOIS
84	CLOTHING AND ACCESSORIES								75020	VETEMENTS
843	WOMENS OUTERWEAR NONKNIT							W 1843	40799	VET DESSUS FEMMES MAT TEX
8431	— COATS AND JACKETS							W 937	27170	MANT,VEST FEM MAT TEXTIL
851	*FOOTWEAR							W 4792	48355	CHAUSSURES
85102	FOOTWEAR LEATHER							W 4223	43573	CHAUS SEMELLES EN CUIR
87	PRECISION INSTRUMNTS NES								64220	INSTRUM,APPAR SCIENT NDA
872	MEDICAL INSTRUMENTS NES								37465	INSTR,APP MEDIC–CHIR NDA
87202	OTH MEDICAL INSTRUMENTS							W 776	33625	INSTRUM,AP° MEDECINE
874	MEASURNG,CONTROLNG INSTR								22213	INSTRUMENTS DE MESURE
88	PHOTO EQU,OPTICL GDS ETC								17106	APP,FOURN PHOTO,OP,MONTR
89	MISC MANUFCTRD GOODS NES								81121	ART MANUFACTURES DIVERS
893	ARTICLES OF PLASTIC NES								37326	OUVRAGES EN MAT DIVIS 58
8939	MISC PLASTIC ARTICLES							W 4525	26045	ART DIVERS EN MAT DIV 58
89399	OTHR PLASTC ARTICLES NES							W 3749	24039	AUT OUV MAT DIV 58
899	OTHER MANUFACTURED GOODS								15855	AUT ART MANUF DIVERS NDA
9	GOODS NOT CLASSD BY KIND								36603	ART TRANSACT NON CLASSES
931	*SPECIAL TRANSACTIONS							W 5870	34966	TRANS.SPECIALES

5. Special Exports F.O.B. by Commodities according to the S.I.T.C. (Rev. 2) in thousand U.S. Dollars
Exportations Spéciales F.O.B. par Produits d'après la C.T.C.I. (Rév. 2) en milliers de Dollars E.U.

SITC CTCI	COMMODITY	1993 WEIGHT POIDS	1993 VALUE VALEUR	1994 WEIGHT POIDS	1994 VALUE VALEUR	1995 WEIGHT POIDS	1995 VALUE VALEUR	1996 WEIGHT POIDS	1996 VALUE VALEUR	PRODUIT
	ALL COMMODITIES								1841746	TOUS PRODUITS
0	FOOD AND LIVE ANIMALS								406322	ALIMENTS,ANIMAUX VIVANTS
01	MEAT AND PREPARATIONS								30787	VIANDES ET PREPARATIONS
011	MEAT FRESH,CHILLD,FROZEN							W 2353	5760	VIANDES FRAICHES,REF,CONGE
014	MEAT PREPD,PRSVD,NES ETC							W 8324	23951	CONSERVES DE VIANDES
0142	SAUSAGES INCLDING TINNED							W 6439	14922	SAUCISSES,SAUCISSONS
0149	OTH PREPARD,PRESRVD MEAT							W 1885	9029	AUTRES PREP DE VIANDES
04	CEREALS AND PREPARATIONS								146900	CEREALES ET PRODUITS
041	WHEAT ETC UNMILLED							W 446008	70724	FROMENT,EPEAUTRE
0411	DURUM WHEAT UNMILLED							W 335126	55135	FROMENT DUR NON MOULU
0412	OTHER WHEAT ETC UNMILLED							W 110882	15589	AUTRE FROMENT NON MOULU
044	MAIZE UNMILLED							W 255155	44318	MAIS NON MOULU
046	WHEAT ETC MEAL OR FLOUR							W 55408	13774	SEMOULE FARINE,FROMENT
04601	FLOUR OF WHEAT OR MESLIN							W 55099	13687	FARINE DE FROMENT
048	CEREAL ETC PREPARATIONS							W 12722	16093	PREPTNS A BASE CEREALES
0484	BAKERY PRODUCTS							W 4150	11061	PRODUITS DE BOULANGERIE
04842	PASTRY, CAKES ETC							W 2808	7908	PATISSERIE ETC.
05	VEGETABLES AND FRUIT								157918	LEGUMES ET FRUITS
054	VEG ETC FRSH,SMPLY PRSVD							W 31813	28451	LEGUMES FRAIS,CONG,SECS
0545	OTHER FRESH VEGETABLES							W 8109	12644	AUTRES LEGUMES FRAIS,REF
05459	FRESH VEGETABLES NES							W 6045	12235	LEGUMES FRAIS,REFRI NDA
0546	VEGETABLES SIMPLY PRESVD							W 9725	11948	LEGUMES CONG,CONSER
05461	VEGETABLES FROZEN							W 8456	6467	LEGUMES CONGELES
056	VEGTBLES ETC PRSVD,PREPD							W 4513	16446	CONSERVES DE LEGUMES
0561	VEG DRIED EXC LEGUMINOUS							W 1164	11997	LEGUM DESSECH,DESHYDRAT
058	FRUIT PRESERVED,PREPARED							W 96346	107770	CONSERVES DE FRUITS
0585	FRUIT OR VEGETABLE JUICE							W 9127	18200	JUS DE FRUITS
05857	JUICE OF OTHER FRUIT,VEG							W 7515	16763	JUS AUTRES FRUITS,LEGUMES
0586	FRUIT TEMPORARILY PRESVD							W 83165	85187	FRUITS CONSERV TEMPORAIRE
05861	FRUIT,FRZN WITHOUT SUGAR							W 80262	83210	FRUITS CONG SANS SUCRE
06	SUGAR AND PREPS,HONEY								6357	SUCRES ET PRODUITS
07	COFFEE,TEA,COCOA,SPICES								15998	CAFE,THE,CACAO,EPICES
073	CHOCOLATE AND PRODUCTS							W 2997	11148	CHOCOLAT
081	*FEEDING STUFF FOR ANIML							W 145815	22804	NOURRITURE POUR ANIMAUX
0819	FOOD WASTE AND FEED NES							W 105568	15553	DECHETS,ALIMENTS NDA
08193	BEET–PULP,BAGASSE,ETC							W 79972	7325	PULPES,AUTRES DECHETS
08199	FODDER NES,INCL SWEETNED							W 25549	8197	PREPARATIONS FOURRAGERES
09	MISC EDIBLE PRODUCTS								15617	PREP ALIMENTAIRES DIVERSES
098	EDIBLE PRODCTS,PREPS NES							W 8844	13267	PREP ALIMENTAIRES NDA
09809	MISC FOOD PREPRTIONS NES							W 6086	7886	PREP ALIMENTAIRES NDA
1	BEVERAGES AND TOBACCO								100984	BOISSONS ET TABACS
11	BEVERAGES								30051	BOISSONS
112	ALCOHOLIC BEVERAGES								25406	BOISSONS ALCOOLIQUES
1123	BEER,ALE,STOUT,PORTER							W 39636	14713	BIERES
1124	DISTILLED ALCOHOLIC BEVS								6029	ALCOOLS,EAUX–DE–VIE
12	TOBACCO AND MANUFACTURES								70933	TABACS BRUTS FABRIQUES
121	TOBACCO UNMNFCTRD,REFUSE							W 3283	7797	TABACS BRUTS,DECHETS
122	TOBACCO,MANUFACTURED							W 5594	63136	TABACS FABRIQUES
1222	CIGARETTES							W 5545	63074	CIGARETTES
2	CRUDE MATERLS,EXCL FUELS								86620	MAT BRUTES NON COMESTIBLES
21	HIDES,SKINS,FURS UNDRSSD								7622	CUIRS,PEAUX BRUTS
211	HIDES,SKINS,EXC FURS,RAW							W 6010	7622	CUIRS ET PEAUX
2111	BOVINE,EQUINE HIDES,RAW							W 4159	5592	PEAUX DE BOVINS
24	CORK AND WOOD								45956	LIEGE ET BOIS
248	WOOD SHAPED,SLEEPERS							W 105022	41802	BOIS SIMPLEMENT TRAVAILLES
2483	LUMBER SHAPED NON–CONIFR							W 96139	39084	NON CONIFERES SCIES,RABOTES
24831	LUMBER SAWN ETC NON–CON							W 91674	36147	SCIES LONGITUDINALEMENT
26	TEXTILE FIBRES AND WASTE								6132	FIBRES TEXTILES
28	METALLIFEROUS ORES,SCRAP								5908	MINERAIS METAL,DECHETS
29	CRUDE ANIMAL,VEG MAT NES								8474	MATIERES BRUTES ANIM,VEGET
292	CRUDE VEG MATERIALS NES								7299	MAT BRUTES VEGETALES NDA
3	MINERAL FUELS ETC								39853	COMBUSTIBLES MINERAUX LUB
33	PETROLEUM AND PRODUCTS								28920	PETROLE ET DERIVES
334	PETROLEUM PRODUCTS,REFIN							W 134954	23721	PRODUITS RAFFINES
4	ANIMAL,VEGETABLE OIL,FAT								7917	HUILES,GRAISSES ANIM,VEG
5	CHEMCLS,RELATED PROD NES								162328	PRODUITS CHIMIQUES
51	ORGANIC CHEMICALS								19969	PROD CHIMIQ ORGANIQUES
511	HYDROCARBONS NES,DERIVS								7216	HYDROCARBURES NDA
513	CARBOXYLIC ACIDS ETC								7636	ACIDES CARBOXYLIQUES
5137	MONOACIDS AND DERIVATIVS							W 6216	7563	ACIDES MONOCARBOXYLIQUES
51371	ACETIC ACID,ITS SALTS							W 6095	7348	ACIDE ACETIQUE,SELS
52	INORGANIC CHEMICALS								13049	PROD CHIM INORGANIQUES
522	INORG ELEMNTS,OXIDES,ETC								6220	ELEMENTS INORGANIQUES
523	OTHR INORG CHEMICALS ETC								6827	AUT PRODUITS CHIMIQUES INORG
53	DYES,TANNING,COLOUR PROD								10299	PROD TEINTURE,COLORANTS
533	PIGMENTS,PAINTS,ETC								8763	PIGMENTS,PEINTURES,VERNIS
5334	VARNISHES,DISTEMPERS ETC							W 2606	6818	PEINTURES A L'EAU
53342	OTH PAINTS,VARNISHES ETC							W 1693	5604	AUTRES PEINTURES,VERNIS
541	*MEDICINAL,PHARM PRODUCT								46268	PROD MEDICINAUX PHARMACEUT
5416	GLYCOSIDES,GLANDS,SERA							K 54	6052	HETEROSIDES
5417	MEDICAMENTS							K 1764	38347	MEDICAMENTS
54171	— CONTAINNG ANTIBIOTICS							K 263	6788	MED CONTN ANTIBIOTIQUES
54172	— CONTAINING HORMONES							K 138	6015	MED CONTENANT HORMONES
54179	— CONTNG OTH SUBSTANCES							K 1348	25124	MED CONT AUT SUBSTANCES
55	PERFUME,CLEANING ETC PRD								9038	PROD POUR PARFUM,TOILETTE
562	*FERTILIZERS,MANUFACTURE								13602	ENGRAIS MANUFACTURES
5621	CHEM NITROGENOUS FERTLZR							W 45029	6372	ENGRAIS AZOTES
5629	FERTILIZERS NES							W 27651	5774	ENGRAIS NDA
56291	NIT–PHOS–POT FERTLZR NES							W 25167	5592	ENGRAIS CONT N P K
58	PLASTIC MATERIALS ETC								40048	MAT PLAST ARTIFICIELLES
583	POLYMERIZATION ETC PRODS								35953	PROD POLYMERISATION
5831	POLYETHYLENE								26377	POLYETHYLENE
58311	— IN PRIMARY FORMS							W 37067	25971	POLYETHYLENE PRIMAIRES
5832	POLYPROPYLENE							W 9308	6329	POLYPROPYLENE
58321	— IN PRIMARY FORMS							W 9271	6182	POLYPROPYLENE PRIMAIRES
59	CHEMICAL MATERIALS NES								9898	MAT PROD CHIMIQUES NDA
6	BASIC MANUFACTURES								618121	ART MANUFACTURES
61	LEATHER,DRESSED FUR,ETC								17826	CUIRS,PELLETERIES
611	LEATHER								11082	CUIRS,PEAUX PREPARES
6114	LEATHR BOVINE NES,EQUINE							W 2275	8508	CUIRS DE BOVINS
62	RUBBER MANUFACTURES NES								52333	CAOUTCHOUC MANUFACTURE

5. Special Exports F.O.B. by Commodities according to the S.I.T.C. (Rev. 2) in thousand U.S. Dollars
Exportations Spéciales F.O.B. par Produits d'après la C.T.C.I. (Rév. 2) en milliers de Dollars E.U.

SITC CTCI	COMMODITY	1993 WEIGHT POIDS	1993 VALUE VALEUR	1994 WEIGHT POIDS	1994 VALUE VALEUR	1995 WEIGHT POIDS	1995 VALUE VALEUR	1996 WEIGHT POIDS	1996 VALUE VALEUR	PRODUIT
621	MATERIALS OF RUBBER								8097	PRODUITS EN CAOUTCHOUC
625	RUBBER TYRES, TUBES ETC								37928	PNEUS CAOUTCHOUC VULCANISE
6251	TYRES NEW FOR MOTOR CARS							W 8065	23327	PNEUS POUR VOITURES
6259	OTH TYRES,TYRE CASES,ETC							W 4502	10855	AUTRES PNEUS RECHAPES FLAPS
62599	TYRES NES,TYRE CASES,ETC							W 3678	8620	PNEUS,FLAPS
628	RUBBER ARTICLES NES							W 1692	6308	OUVRAGES CAOUTCHOUC NDA
63	WOOD,CORK MANUFACTRS NES								13741	OUVRAGES LIEGE ET BOIS
634	VENEERS,PLYWOOD,ETC							W 11832	7587	PLACAGES,CONTRE-PLAQUES
635	WOOD MANUFACTURES NES							W 5242	6137	ART MANUF EN BOIS NDA
64	PAPER,PAPERBOARD AND MFR								12100	PAPIERS,CARTONS & OUVRAGES
641	PAPER AND PAPERBOARD							W 5859	6072	PAPIERS ET CARTONS
642	PAPER,ETC,PRECUT,ARTS OF								6028	PAP,CARTONS DECOUPES
65	TEXTILE YARN,FABRICS,ETC								46080	FILS,TISSUS,ARTICLES TEXTILE
651	TEXTILE YARN								11440	FILS TEXTILES
653	WOVN MAN-MADE FIB FABRIC								6379	TISSUS FIBRES SYNTH,ARTIF
658	TEXTILE ARTICLES NES								7907	ART FACONNES MAT TEXTILES
659	FLOOR COVERINGS,ETC								9500	COUVRE-PARQUETS,TAPIS ETC
66	NONMETAL MINERAL MFS NES								53731	ART MIN NON METALLIQUES
661	LIME,CEMENT,BLDG PRODS							W 117918	10258	CHAUX,CIMENTS MAT CONSTR
6612	CEMENT							W 102162	7345	CIMENTS HYDRAULIQUES
662	CLAY,REFRACTORY BLDG PRD							W 128884	25572	MAT CONST REFRACTAIRES
6623	REFRACTORY BUILDING PROD							W 27756	15445	BRIQUES REFRACTAIRES
66232	REFRACTRY BRICKS ETC NES							W 23176	13425	BRIQUES ETC REFRACTAIRES
6624	BRICKS ETC NONREFRACTORY							W 101128	10127	BRIQUES ETC CERAM NON REFR
66242	ROOFNG TILES ETC,CERAMIC							W 67177	6521	TUILES,ORNEMENTS ARCH
665	GLASSWARE								6497	OUVRAGES EN VERRE
67	IRON AND STEEL								95814	FER ET ACIER
671	PIG IRON ETC							W 7662	17470	FONTE,SPIEGEL,POUDRES
6716	FERRO-ALLOYS							W 6499	17328	FERRO-ALLIAGES
67169	OTHER FERRO-ALLOYS							W 6487	17311	AUTRES FERRO-ALLIAGES
672	IRON,STEEL PRIMARY FORMS								37885	LINGOTS FER,ACIER
6727	IRN,STL COIL FR REROLLNG							W 145268	37773	EBAUCHES POUR TOLES FER
67271	IRON,SIMPLE STEEL COILS							W 145019	37664	EBAUCHES NON EN ACIER
674	IRN,STL UNIV,PLATE,SHEET								24426	LARGES PLATS,TOLES
6746	IRN,STL THIN PLATE,ROLLD							W 40506	14144	TOLES LAM MOINS 3MM
67461	— OF IRON OR SIMPLE STL							W 40124	13874	TOL NON AC FIN MOINS 3 MM
6749	OTH IRN,STL PLATES,SHEET							W 11249	5640	AUTRES TOLES FER,ACIER
678	IRON,STL TUBES,PIPES,ETC							W 8802	9662	TUBES,TUYAUX EN FONTE,FER
6785	IRON,STEEL TUBE FITTINGS							W 2785	6454	ACCESSOIRES DE TUYAUTERIE
68	NON-FERROUS METALS								263367	METAUX NON FERREUX
681	SILVER,PLATINUM,ETC								7079	ARGENT ET PLATINE
6811	SILVER UNWKD,PARTLY WRKD								7020	ARGENT BRUT MI-OUVRE
68113	SILVER UNWROUGHT								7015	ARGENT ET ALLIAGES BRUTS
682	COPPER EXC CEMENT COPPER								151686	CUIVRE
6821	COPPER NES,ALLOYS,UNWRT								103812	CUIVRE BRUT
68212	COPPER REFINED,UNWROUGHT							W 74352	103795	CUIVRE AFFINE BRUT
6822	COPPER,ALLOYS WORKED							W 21229	47874	CUIVRE,ALLIAGES OUVRES
68221	COPPER BARS,WIRE,ETC							W 12176	23490	BARRES,PROFILES ET FILS
68222	COPPER PLATE,SHEET,STRIP							W 4725	11056	TOLES DE PLUS 0.15 MM
68225	COPPER TUBES,PIPES,ETC							W 3928	12008	TUBES,TUYAUX EN CUIVRE
684	ALUMINIUM								62794	ALUMINIUM
6841	ALUMINIUM,ALLOYS,UNWRGHT							W 39140	54192	ALUMINIUM,ALLIAGES BRUTS
6842	ALUMINIUM,ALLOYS WORKED								8602	ALUMINIUM,ALLIAGES OUVRE
685	LEAD							W 25794	14966	PLOMB
6851	LEAD,ALLOYS UNWROUGHT							W 25612	14837	PLOMB,ALLIAGES BRUTS
68512	REF LEAD(EXC ALLOY)UNWRT							W 25140	14485	PLOMB AFFINE BRUT
686	ZINC							W 23967	19487	ZINC
6861	ZINC,ALLOYS UNWROUGHT							W 22308	18829	ZINC ET ALLIAGES BRUTS
689	NON-FER BASE METALS NES								7278	AUT METAUX NON FERREUX
6891	TUNGST,MOLYB,TANTAL,MAGN								7128	TUNG,MOLYB,TANT,MAG BRUTS
68915	MAGNESIUM UNWROUGHT							W 2926	7113	MAGNESIUM BRUT
69	METAL MANUFACTURES NES								63129	ART MANUFACT EN METAL NDA
691	STRUCTURES AND PARTS NES							W 5794	9350	CONSTRUCT FER,ACIER,ALU
6911	STRUCTURES,PARTS IRN,STL							W 5476	7358	CONSTRUCT FER,ACIER,FONTE
695	TOOLS								14068	OUTILS A MAIN
6954	BLADES,TIPS,ETC FR TOOLS								12662	OUTILS POUR MACHINE-OUTIL
69541	PARTS TO INSERT IN TOOLS							W 443	11561	OUTILS DE FORAGE
697	BASE MTL HOUSEHOLD EQUIP								8420	ART MENAGE MET COMMUNS
6973	DMSTC HEATG,COOKG APPARA							W 4352	6302	APPS CHAUF NON ELECTRIQ
699	BASE METAL MFRS NES								20795	ART MANUFACTURES MET NDA
6991	LOCKSMITHS WARES,ETC							W 913	13905	ARTICLES DE SERRURERIE
69913	BASE MTL DOOR,ETC FITTNG							W 743	12580	GARNITURES POUR MEUBLES
7	MACHINES,TRANSPORT EQUIP								220465	MACHINES MATERIEL TRANSPORT
71	POWER GENERATING EQUIPMT								15411	MACHINES GENERATRICES
713	INTRNL COMBUS PSTN ENGIN								6369	MOTEURS EXPL COMB INT, PIECE
716	ROTATING ELECTRIC PLANT								7665	APP ELECTR ROTATIFS,PIECES
7162	AC MTRS,GENRTRS,GEN SETS							W 1938	6691	MOTEURS ELECTRIQUES
71621	AC MTRS,INC UNIVRSL MTRS							W 1917	6530	MOT ELEC NON COUR CONTINU
72	MACHS FOR SPCL INDUSTRYS								18256	MAC SPECIALES POUR INDUST
73	METALWORKING MACHINERY								10426	MACH TRAVAIL DES METAUX
736	METALWORKING MACH-TOOLS								8840	MACH-OUTILS TRAVAIL METAUX
7361	METAL CUTTING MACH-TOOLS								5588	MACH-OUT ENLEVEMENT METAL
74	GENRL INDUSTRL MACHY NES								41036	MACH APP INDUSTRIE
744	MECHANICAL HANDLING EQU								5529	EQUIP MANUTENTION PIECES
749	NONELEC MACH PTS,ACC NES								24217	PIECES MACH NON ELEC NDA
7491	BALL,ROLLER,ETC BEARINGS							W 1034	9128	ROULEMENTS BILLES ETC
7492	COCKS,VALVES ETC NES							W 2042	12072	ART ROB,SIM POUR TUYAUX
77	ELECTRIC MACHNRY NES ETC								73701	MACH APP ELECT NDA
772	SWITCHGEAR ETC,PARTS NES								6256	APP COUPURE,SECT ETC
7721	SWITCHGEAR ETC							W 355	6240	APP COUPURE,SECTIONMNT
773	ELECTR DISTRIBUTNG EQUIP							W 14844	43839	EQUIPMT DISTRIBUTION ELECT
7731	INSULATED WIRE,CABLE ETC							W 14271	41815	FILS,CABLES ISOLES ELECT
775	HOUSEHOLD TYPE EQUIP NES								9223	MACH,APP USAGE DOMESTQUE
7758	ELECTRO-THERMIC APPL NES								7593	APP ELECTROTHERMIQ NDA
778	ELECTRICAL MACHINERY NES								9989	AUTRES MACH ELECT NDA
7781	BATTERIES,ACCUMULATORS							W 2945	7217	PILES ET ACCUMULATEURS
77812	ELECTRIC ACCUMULATORS							W 2901	7035	ACCUMULATEURS ELECTRIQ
78	ROAD VEHICLES								31679	VEHICULES ROUTIERS
781	PASS MOTOR VEH EXC BUSES							W 1630	8444	AUTO TRANSPORT PERSONNES
784	MOTOR VEH PRTS,ACCES NES							W 3528	18168	PIECES 722,781,782,783
7849	OTHER MOTOR VEHCL PARTS							W 3503	18079	PIECES 722,781,782,783

5. Special Exports F.O.B. by Commodities according to the S.I.T.C. (Rev. 2) in thousand U.S. Dollars
Exportations Spéciales F.O.B. par Produits d'après la C.T.C.I. (Rév. 2) en milliers de Dollars E.U.

SITC CTCI	COMMODITY	1993		1994		1995		1996		PRODUIT
		WEIGHT POIDS	VALUE VALEUR	WEIGHT POIDS	VALUE VALEUR	WEIGHT POIDS	VALUE VALEUR	WEIGHT POIDS	VALUE VALEUR	
79	OTHR TRANSPORT EQUIPMENT								25857	AUTRE MATERIEL TRANSPORT
792	AIRCRAFT ETC								12492	APP NAVIGATION AERIENNE
7924	AIRCRFT NES OVER 15000KG							W 84	12000	AERODYNES PLUS 15000 KG
793	SHIPS AND BOATS ETC							W 6375	11143	NAVIRES BATEAUX,ETC
7932	SHIPS AND BOATS NES							W 6173	10848	NAVIRES ET BATEAUX
79323	OTHER CARGO VESSELS							W 6097	10709	AUT BATEAUX TRANS MARCH
8	MISC MANUFACTURED GOODS								163829	ART MANUFACTURES DIVERS
812	*PLUMBG,HEATNG,LGHTNG EQ							W 3581	6853	APPAR SANITAIRES CHAUFFAGE
821	*FURNITURE,PARTS THEREOF							W 18580	45901	MEUBLES ET PIECES
8211	CHAIRS,SEATS AND PARTS							W 10024	21713	SIEGES ET PIECES
82111	CHAIRS AND OTHER SEATS							W 9945	21635	SIEGES
8219	FURNITURE AND PARTS NES							W 6892	20489	AUTRES MEUBLES ET PIECES
82192	WOOD FURNITURE NES							W 5303	16742	MEUBLES NDA EN BOIS
84	CLOTHING AND ACCESSORIES								57349	VETEMENTS
842	MENS OUTERWEAR NOT KNIT							W 1335	12986	VET DESSUS POUR HOMMES
843	WOMENS OUTERWEAR NONKNIT							W 3579	25324	VET DESSUS FEMMES MAT TEX
8431	— COATS AND JACKETS							W 1670	10271	MANT,VEST FEM MAT TEXTIL
8439	— OTHER OUTER GARMENTS							W 983	8072	AUT VET DES FEM MAT TEXT
845	OUTERWEAR KNIT NONELASTC								5585	VET DESSOUS,ACCES BONNET
851	*FOOTWEAR							W 3550	21946	CHAUSSURES
85102	FOOTWEAR LEATHER							W 2318	16018	CHAUS SEMELLES EN CUIR
89	MISC MANUFCTRD GOODS NES								26550	ART MANUFACTURES DIVERS
893	ARTICLES OF PLASTIC NES								9541	OUVRAGES EN MAT DIVIS 58
8939	MISC PLASTIC ARTICLES							W 2334	6386	ART DIVERS EN MAT DIV 58
899	OTHER MANUFACTURED GOODS								5910	AUT ART MANUF DIVERS NDA
9	GOODS NOT CLASSD BY KIND								35307	ART TRANSACT NON CLASSES
931	*SPECIAL TRANSACTIONS							W 12805	33772	TRANS.SPECIALES

1. HISTORICAL SERIES, 1960–1995 GENERAL TRADE, IMPORTS F.O.B., EXPORTS F.O.B.
SERIES HISTORIQUES, 1960–1995 COMMERCE GENERAL, IMPORTATIONS F.O.B., EXPORTATIONS F.O.B

YEAR ANNEE	VALUE IN MILLION ZAMBIAN KWACHA / VALEUR EN MILLION ZAMBIAN KWACHA — MERCHANDISE #2 – MARCHANDISE: IMPORTS	MERCHANDISE #2 – MARCHANDISE: EXPORTS	GOLD – OR: IMPORTS	GOLD – OR: EXPORTS	CONVERSION FACTORS U.S. CENTS PER ZAMBIAN KWACHA / FACTEURS DE CONVERSION CENTS E.U. PAR ZAMBIAN KWACHA: IMPORTS	CONVERSION FACTORS: EXPORTS	INDEX NUMBERS #1 – INDICES — QUANTUM: IMPORTS	QUANTUM: EXPORTS	UNIT VALUE / VALEUR UNITAIRE: IMPORTS	UNIT VALUE / VALEUR UNITAIRE: EXPORTS
1960	176.70	206.00			140.0000	140.0000				
1961		239.38			140.0000	140.0000				
1962		239.21			140.0000	140.0000				
1963		257.97			140.0000	140.0000				
1964	156.44	335.52			140.0000	140.0000				
1965	210.74	380.29			140.0000	140.0000				
1966	246.11	493.46			140.0000	140.0000				
1967	306.26	470.01			140.0000	140.0000				
1968	325.17	544.42			140.0000	140.0000				
1969	311.77	766.49			140.0000	140.0000				
1970	340.71	714.96			140.0000	140.0000				
1971	399.28	485.18			140.0000	140.0000				
1972	402.47	541.56			140.0000	140.0000				
1973	346.87	741.96			154.2040	154.6520				
1974	506.64	905.09			155.4090	155.4090				
1975	597.60	521.05			155.4090	155.4090				
1976	468.70	751.90			139.7610	138.3850				
1977	529.30	708.00			126.6550	126.7530				
1978	492.60	686.80			127.5140	126.5610				
1979	593.70	593.60			126.3180	126.2210				
1980	876.70	1023.30			126.7030	126.9670				
1981	924.40	936.50			114.8568	114.6455				
1982	930.00	950.50			107.5856	107.5536				
1983	893.20	1047.50			78.7534	78.7268				
1984	1107.90	1188.10			54.8574	55.1157				
1985	2133.00	1508.00			33.4604	36.2879				
1986	4447.69	5366.58			13.5540	13.1141				
1987	6627.47	8058.70			11.1551	10.8293				
1988	6898.13	9786.20			12.1651	12.0411				
1989	10901.80	18434.00			7.1433	7.2921				
1990	37627.60	39143.30			3.3475	3.3505				100
1991	60000.00	69600.00			1.6018	1.5468				198
1992	172900.00	193600.00			0.5620	0.6083				456
1993	553400.00	448199.90			0.2276	0.2232				878
1994	805299.90	713799.90			0.1343	0.1343				1131
1995	1284600.00	1024900.00			0.1185	0.1187				1290

2. IMPORTS BY BROAD ECONOMIC CATEGORY AND EXPORTS BY INDUSTRIAL ORIGIN. (PERCENTAGE OF TOTAL VALUE)
IMPORTATIONS PAR CATEGORIES ECONOMIQUES ET EXPORTATIONS PAR BRANCHE D'ACTIVITE. (EN POURCENTAGE DE LA VALEUR TOTALE)

IMPORTS – IMPORTATIONS

	1990	1991	1992	1993	1994	1995	1996
TOTAL IMPORTS–IMPORTATIONS TOTALES							
1 FOOD BEV–ALIMENTATION BOISSONS							
11 PRIMARY–PRODUITS DE BASE							
111 FOR INDUSTRY–POUR L'INDUSTRIE							
112 FOR HOUSEHOLDS–POUR LES MENAGES							
12 PROCESSED–PRODUITS ELABORES							
121 FOR INDUSTRY–POUR L'INDUSTRIE							
122 FOR HOUSEHOLDS–POUR LES MENAGES							
2 IND SUPPLIES–APPROV INDUSTRIELS							
21 PRIMARY–PRODUITS DE BASE							
22 PROCESSED–PRODUITS ELABORES							
3 FUELS–COMBUSTIBLES							
31 PRIMARY–PRODUITS DE BASE							
32 PROCESSED–PRODUITS ELABORES							
321 MOTOR SPIRIT–ESSENCE							
322 OTHER–AUTRES							
4 MACHINERY–EQUIPEMENT							
41 CAPITAL EQUIPMENT–MACHINES							
42 PARTS–PIECES ACCESSOIRES							
5 TRANSPORT–TRANSPORT							
51 PASSENGER CARS–AUTOMOBILES							
52 OTHER–AUTRES							
521 INDUSTRIAL–INDUSTRIELS							
522 NON INDUSTRIAL–NON INDUSTRIEL							
53 PARTS–PIECES ACCESSOIRES							
6 CONSUM GOODS–BIENS CONSOMMATION							
61 DURABLE–DURABLES							
62 SEMI DURABLE–SEMI DURABLES							
63 NON DURABLE–NON DURABLES							
7 GOODS NES–BIENS NDA							

EXPORTS – EXPORTATIONS

	1990	1991	1992	1993	1994	1995	1996
TOTAL EXPORTS–EXPORTATIONS TOTALES				100.			
1 AGRICULTURE				2.1			
2 MINING QUARRY–INDUS EXTRACTIVES				0.8			
3 MANUFACTURING–IND MANUFACTUR				97.1			
31 FOOD BEV TOBACCO–ALIM BOISS TAB				2.2			
32 TEXTILES–INDUSTRIES TEXTILES				1.3			
33 WOOD & PRODUCTS–BOIS & PRODUITS				0.1			
34 PAPER & PRODUCTS–PAPIER & PRODT				0.1			
35 CHEMICALS–INDUSTRIES CHIMIQUES				0.9			
36 NON METAL MIN–MIN NON METAL				1.4			
37 BASIC METAL–IND METAL BASE				88.8			
38 METAL MANUF–MANUF METAL				1.0			
39 OTH MANUF IND–AUTRES MANUF				1.5			

3. TRADE BY PRINCIPAL COUNTRIES OF PRODUCTION AND LAST CONSIGNMENT (VALUE IN THOUSAND U.S. DOLLARS)
ECHANGES SELON LES PRINCIPAUX PAYS DE PRODUCTION ET DE DERNIERE CONSIGNATION (VALEUR EN MILLIERS DE DOLLARS EU)

COUNTRIES–PAYS	GENERAL IMPORTS F.O.B. IMPORTATIONS GENERALES F.O.B.				
	1989	1990	1991	1992	1993
World	1258321	1237717			
Africa	386461	390213			
Americas	78344	136925			
Northern America	77460	134212			
LAIA	885	2554			
CACM		63			
Caribbean		18			
Rest of America		77			
As.ex F.USSR	153647	208752			
Eur.x F.USSR	636414	497459			
EU	612776	479517			
EFTA	18429	14449			
East Europe	1093	2654			
Other Europe	858	672			
Former USSR	215	168			
Oceania	305	254			
So. Africa Customs Un	286500	224177			
United Kingdom	256049	200365			
Germany/Allemagne	184038	144015			
USA/Etats–Unis d'Amer	67071	125522			
Japan/Japon	105590	82627			
Zimbabwe	73948	57866			
Italy/Italie	38706	30289			
Madagascar	82	66700			
Finland/Finlande	29627	23184			
India/Inde	29302	22930			
Sweden/Suède	24553	19213			
Netherlands/Pays–Bas	19771	15472			
Iran (Islamic Rp. of)		35134			
Kuwait/ Koweït		33697			
Belgium–Luxembourg	17496	13694			
France,Monac	15937	12471			
Switz.Liecht	14433	11294			
Denmark/Danemark	14338	11220			
Algeria/Algérie		20451			
Dem. Rep. of the Congo	11455	8964			
Canada	10270	8611			
Bangladesh	15	11073			
Kenya	5783	4526			
Malawi	5489	4295			
Saudi Arabia	5036	3941			
China/Chine	4407	3449			
Ireland/Irlande	4228	3309			
Norway,SVD,JM	3996	3127			
Israel/Israël	3805	2977			
Greece/Grèce	3502	2741			
Un. Rep. of Tanzania	2872	2247			
Austria/Autriche	2464	1928			
Thailand/Thaïlande		4258			
Spain/Espagne	1929	1509			
Fm Yugoslav	3257	167			
Brazil/Brésil	872	2436			
Hong Kong	1834	1435			
Singapore/Singapour	473	2068			
Korea, Republic of	893	1559			
Malaysia/Malaisie	1045	818			
Bulgaria/Bulgarie		1693			
Czechoslovakia	946	740			
United Arab Emirates	870	680			
Pakistan	233	1305			
Malta/Malte	858	672			
Libyan Arab Jamahiriya		623			
Australia/Australie	303	235			
Former USSR/Anc. URSS	215	168			
Korea Dem People's Rp	70	292			
Uganda/Ouganda	174	136			

COUNTRIES–PAYS	GENERAL EXPORTS F.O.B. EXPORTATIONS GENERALES F.O.B.				
	1989	1990	1991	1992	1993
Monde	667811	594765			920536
Afrique	55975	46215			73545
Amériques	13902	9844			3325
Amérique du Nord	13786	9755			3325
ALAI	116	83			
MCAC		6			
Caraïbes					
Autre Amérique					
Asie l'URSS exclus	363052	351273			566353
Europe l'URSS exclus	231873	187339			276775
UE	227240	181874			273954
AELE	3702	5465			2408
Europe de l'Est	238				413
Autre de l'Europe					
Ancienne URSS					
Océanie	93	87			538
Japan/Japon	223194	184268			122023
France,Monac	98121	81008			94938
Belgium–Luxembourg	48619	34405			99429
Saudi Arabia	38732	31977			64017
India/Inde	44141	36443			52383
Malaysia/Malaisie	27689	22860			74058
Thailand/Thaïlande		40673			61538
Pakistan	433	516			83319
Indonesia/Indonésie	24070	19872			28593
Zimbabwe	21833	18025			27359
Italy/Italie	32243	26620			7638
Greece/Grèce	19648	16221			29367
Singapore/Singapour	161	11004			51504
United Kingdom	14712	12147			14072
Netherlands/Pays–Bas	7893	6517			24359
Dem. Rep. of the Congo	10105	8342			11677
USA/Etats–Unis d'Amer	13781	9752			3317
So. Africa Customs Un	2972	2454			17795
Kenya	9360	7728			5281
Malawi	5215	4306			5559
Switz.Liecht	3512	5308			2407
Hong Kong	1386	1144			8624
Germany/Allemagne	4705	3884			1953
Un. Rep. of Tanzania	3779	3120			1147
Korea, Republic of	3223	2504			
Burundi	1478	1218			2175
Spain/Espagne	428	353			1991
United Arab Emirates		1			2142
Angola	1108	914			62
Mozambique	100	82			1901
Israel/Israël	13	11			1956
Australia/Australie	87	86			538
Ireland/Irlande	321	265			117
Fm Yugoslav	693				
Portugal	225	186			5
Norway,SVD,JM	190	157			1
Finland/Finlande	164	136			2
Albania/Albanie					294
Sweden/Suède	139	115			38
Mali					246
Czechoslovakia	238				
Rwanda	4				197
Brazil/Brésil	116	82			
Nigeria/Nigéria	0	0			89
Austria/Autriche	14	12			46
Uganda/Ouganda	14	11			29
Canada	5	3			9
Denmark/Danemark	7	6			
Cyprus/Chypre	9				
Ethiopia/Ethiopie	1	7			

(VALUE AS PERCENTAGE OF WORLD TOTAL)(VALEURS EN POURCENTAGE DU TOTAL MONDIAL)

	1984	1985	1986	1987	1988	1989	1990	1991	1992	1993
Africa	14.6	16.7	16.3	19.2	16.8	30.7	31.5			
Americas	14.0	14.7	11.5	12.6	17.9	6.2	11.1			
Northern America	12.4	13.2	11.1	12.3	17.6	6.2	10.8			
LAIA	1.7	1.5	0.4	0.4	0.3	0.1	0.2			
CACM	0.0	0.0		0.0	0.0		0.0			
Caribbean	0.0	0.0	0.0	0.0	0.0		0.0			
Rest of America	0.0	0.0					0.0			
As.ex F.USSR	36.8	25.1	21.6	16.0	18.3	12.2	16.9			
Eur.x F.USSR	33.7	42.9	50.4	51.8	46.5	50.6	40.2			
EU	30.0	38.9	47.7	49.4	43.9	48.7	38.7			
EFTA	3.1	2.9	1.9	2.0	1.8	1.5	1.2			
East Europe	0.2	0.2	0.2	0.1	0.5	0.1	0.2			
Other Europe	0.3	0.3	0.1	0.2	0.2	0.1	0.1			
Former USSR	0.3	0.3	0.0	0.0	0.1	0.0	0.0			
Oceania	0.3	0.2	0.1	0.2	0.2	0.0	0.0			
So. Africa Customs Un	10.9	13.2	9.3	9.4	9.8	22.8	18.1			
United Kingdom	14.2	20.2	21.7	18.8	15.5	20.3	16.2			
Germany/Allemagne	5.7	6.3	7.4	10.4	8.3	14.6	11.6			
USA/Etats–Unis d'Amer	11.3	12.3	9.4	10.0	15.4	5.3	10.1			
Japan/Japon	5.0	9.3	9.1	7.6	9.6	8.4	6.7			
Zimbabwe	2.6	2.3	5.1	7.7	5.6	5.9	4.7			
Italy/Italie	1.6	1.6	3.2	2.6	4.3	3.1	2.4			
Madagascar			0.0	0.0	0.0	0.0	5.4			
Finland/Finlande	0.6	0.6	1.9	2.2	2.1	2.4	1.9			
India/Inde	0.7	0.5	1.1	1.0	2.0	2.3	1.9			

	1984	1985	1986	1987	1988	1989	1990	1991	1992	1993
Afrique	3.3	4.1	6.8	4.8	4.4	8.4	7.8			8.0
Amériques	13.5	6.6	7.2	5.3	11.6	2.1	1.7			0.4
Amérique du Nord	13.2	6.3	6.9	5.2	11.5	2.1	1.6			0.4
ALAI	0.3	0.3	0.3	0.1	0.1	0.0	0.0			
MCAC	0.0		0.0	0.0			0.0			
Caraïbes		0.0	0.0		0.0					
Autre Amérique	0.0		0.0	0.0						
Asie l'URSS exclus	41.4	45.4	45.9	51.7	48.6	54.4	59.1			61.5
Europe l'URSS exclus	41.6	43.5	40.0	38.0	35.2	34.7	31.5			30.1
UE	37.9	41.8	38.2	34.8	32.0	34.0	30.6			29.8
AELE	0.4	0.3	0.5	1.7	1.3	0.6	0.9			0.3
Europe de l'Est	0.3	0.3	0.2	0.1		0.0				0.0
Autre de l'Europe	1.6	0.8	0.6	1.2	1.5					
Ancienne URSS	0.1	0.3	0.0							
Océanie	0.1	0.1	0.2	0.2	0.2	0.0	0.0			0.1
Japan/Japon	24.8	29.4	17.5	23.2	28.8	33.4	31.0			13.3
France,Monac	7.3	8.9	10.1	8.2	6.6	14.7	13.6			10.3
Belgium–Luxembourg	2.7	1.5	7.0	7.1	5.5	7.3	5.8			10.8
Saudi Arabia	0.0	0.5	5.5	4.9	3.9	5.8	5.4			7.0
India/Inde	3.0	3.9	11.8	10.8	2.7	6.6	6.1			5.7
Malaysia/Malaisie	3.1	2.2	0.8	2.0	2.4	4.1	3.8			8.0
Thailand/Thaïlande	1.6	2.1	4.7	6.3	3.1		6.8			6.7
Pakistan	0.0	0.0	0.1	0.1	0.0	0.1	0.1			9.1
Indonesia/Indonésie	1.4	1.7	1.3	2.0	2.7	3.6	3.3			3.1
Zimbabwe	1.1	1.2	1.6	1.9	2.7	3.3	3.0			3.0

4. General Imports F.O.B. by Commodities according to the S.I.T.C. (Rev. 2) in thousand U.S. Dollars
Importations Générales F.O.B. par Produits d'après la C.T.C.I. (Rév. 2) en milliers de Dollars E.U.

SITC CTCI	COMMODITY	1983		1984		1985		1986		PRODUIT
		WEIGHT POIDS	VALUE VALEUR	WEIGHT POIDS	VALUE VALEUR	WEIGHT POIDS	VALUE VALEUR	WEIGHT POIDS	VALUE VALEUR	
	ALL COMMODITIES				595610		713768		602839	TOUS PRODUITS
0	FOOD AND LIVE ANIMALS				27727		25279			ALIMENTS,ANIMAUX VIVANTS
02	DAIRY PRODCTS,BIRDS'EGGS				1372		3928		1181	PRODUITS LAITIERS,OEUFS
04	CEREALS AND PREPARATIONS				20996		14342		10141	CEREALES ET PRODUITS
081	*FEEDING STUFF FOR ANIML				1736		2930		1713	NOURRITURE POUR ANIMAUX
09	MISC EDIBLE PRODUCTS				1997		3275		2398	PREP ALIMENTAIRES DIVERSES
2	CRUDE MATERLS,EXCL FUELS				13110		10868			MAT BRUTES NON COMESTIBLES
23	RUBBER, CRUDE				3576		2814		2343	CAOUTCHOUC BRUT
26	TEXTILE FIBRES AND WASTE				1400		1426		1837	FIBRES TEXTILES
27	CRUDE FERTLZR,MINRLS NES				3820		4208		2772	ENGRAIS MINERAUX BRUTS
3	MINERAL FUELS ETC				180588		156062			COMBUSTIBLES MINERAUX LUB
32	COAL,COKE AND BRIQUETTES				4782		2359		1551	HOUILLES,COKES,BRIQUETTES
33	PETROLEUM AND PRODUCTS				174976		153698		80068	PETROLE ET DERIVES
333	CRUDE PETROLEUM							W 570000	71657	HUILES BRUTES DE PETROLE
4	ANIMAL,VEGETABLE OIL,FAT				4092		1403			HUILES,GRAISSES ANIM,VEG
5	CHEMCLS,RELATED PROD NES				82794		106003			PRODUITS CHIMIQUES
51	ORGANIC CHEMICALS				8596		4654		3671	PROD CHIMIQ ORGANIQUES
52	INORGANIC CHEMICALS				10950		12129		6168	PROD CHIM INORGANIQUES
53	DYES,TANNING,COLOUR PROD				3561		3551		3295	PROD TEINTURE,COLORANTS
541	*MEDICINAL,PHARM PRODUCT				6950		10780		8432	PROD MEDICINAUX PHARMACEUT
55	PERFUME,CLEANING ETC PRD				4688		6190		2402	PROD POUR PARFUM,TOILETTE
562	*FERTILIZERS,MANUFACTURE				24157		29234		3010	ENGRAIS MANUFACTURES
572	*EXPLOSIVES,PYROTECH PRO				2136		1191		571	EXPLOSIFS
58	PLASTIC MATERIALS ETC				9457		15623		9848	MAT PLAST ARTIFICIELLES
59	CHEMICAL MATERIALS NES				12300		22650		18569	MAT PROD CHIMIQUES NDA
6	BASIC MANUFACTURES				99033		115964			ART MANUFACTURES
62	RUBBER MANUFACTURES NES				9556		17569		15982	CAOUTCHOUC MANUFACTURE
64	PAPER,PAPERBOARD AND MFR				8720		11088		7369	PAPIERS,CARTONS & OUVRAGES
65	TEXTILE YARN,FABRICS,ETC				25480		19643		14491	FILS,TISSUS,ARTICLES TEXTILE
66	NONMETAL MINERAL MFS NES				7825		10160		8303	ART MIN NON METALLIQUES
67	IRON AND STEEL				27353		25373		20552	FER ET ACIER
68	NON–FERROUS METALS				3488		6019		7695	METAUX NON FERREUX
69	METAL MANUFACTURES NES				15486		24950		25472	ART MANUFACT EN METAL NDA
7	MACHINES,TRANSPORT EQUIP				174140		232067			MACHINES MATERIEL TRANSPORT
71	POWER GENERATING EQUIPMT				11945		17588		18196	MACHINES GENERATRICES
72	MACHS FOR SPCL INDUSTRYS				35820		59966		46784	MAC SPECIALES POUR INDUST
73	METALWORKING MACHINERY				2274		2353		1463	MACH TRAVAIL DES METAUX
74	GENRL INDUSTRL MACHY NES				46641		57768		56539	MACH APP INDUSTRIE
75	OFFICE MACHNES,ADP EQUIP				2934		6864		5123	MACH BUREAU TRAIT AUTOM
76	TELECOMM,SOUND EQUIPMENT				9891		6536		20759	EQUIPMENT DE TELECOM
77	ELECTRIC MACHNRY NES ETC				16429		21529		24066	MACH APP ELECT NDA
78	ROAD VEHICLES				42305		52292		74212	VEHICULES ROUTIERS
79	OTHR TRANSPORT EQUIPMENT				5900		7171		7692	AUTRE MATERIEL TRANSPORT
8	MISC MANUFACTURED GOODS				13040		23791			ART MANUFACTURES DIVERS
84	CLOTHING AND ACCESSORIES				1491		967		2165	VETEMENTS
851	*FOOTWEAR				1452		1027		2229	CHAUSSURES
87	PRECISION INSTRUMNTS NES				5205		6655		8536	INSTRUM,APPAR SCIENT NDA
89	MISC MANUFCTRD GOODS NES				2302		11228		6738	ART MANUFACTURES DIVERS

5. General Exports F.O.B. by Commodities according to the S.I.T.C. (Rev. 2) in thousand U.S. Dollars
Exportations Générales F.O.B. par Produits d'après la C.T.C.I. (Rév. 2) en milliers de Dollars E.U.

SITC CTCI	COMMODITY	1990 WEIGHT POIDS	1990 VALUE VALEUR	1991 WEIGHT POIDS	1991 VALUE VALEUR	1992 WEIGHT POIDS	1992 VALUE VALEUR	1993 WEIGHT POIDS	1993 VALUE VALEUR	PRODUIT
	ALL COMMODITIES								920536	TOUS PRODUITS
0	FOOD AND LIVE ANIMALS								24345	ALIMENTS,ANIMAUX VIVANTS
04	CEREALS AND PREPARATIONS								4369	CEREALES ET PRODUITS
044	MAIZE UNMILLED							W 7031	3997	MAIS NON MOULU
05	VEGETABLES AND FRUIT								3280	LEGUMES ET FRUITS
054	VEG ETC FRSH,SMPLY PRSVD							W 3201	2941	LEGUMES FRAIS,CONG,SECS
06	SUGAR AND PREPS,HONEY								13530	SUCRES ET PRODUITS
061	SUGAR AND HONEY							W 8983	13527	SUCRES ET MIEL
0611	RAW BEET AND CANE SUGAR							W 8235	13260	SUCRES BRUTS
1	BEVERAGES AND TOBACCO								7766	BOISSONS ET TABACS
12	TOBACCO AND MANUFACTURES								7173	TABACS BRUTS FABRIQUES
121	TOBACCO UNMNFCTRD,REFUSE							W 5831	7080	TABACS BRUTS,DECHETS
1211	TOBACCO,NOT STRIPPED							W 1378	2785	TABACS NON ECOTES
1212	TOBACCO STRIPPED OR PART							W 3707	3654	TABACS PART ECOTES
2	CRUDE MATERLS,EXCL FUELS								11992	MAT BRUTES NON COMESTIBLES
26	TEXTILE FIBRES AND WASTE								6231	FIBRES TEXTILES
266	SYNTHETIC FIBRES TO SPIN							W 1051	4676	FIBRES SYNTHETIQUES
2666	CONTIN FILAMNT TOW SYNTH							W 998	4558	CABLES POUR DISCONTINUS
26661	— OF POLYAMIDE FIBRES							W 721	3503	DE FIBRES EN POLYAMIDES
3	MINERAL FUELS ETC								15769	COMBUSTIBLES MINERAUX LUB
351	*ELECTRIC CURRENT							H 17927	13482	ENERGIE ELECTRIQUE
5	CHEMCLS,RELATED PROD NES								3618	PRODUITS CHIMIQUES
6	BASIC MANUFACTURES								845851	ART MANUFACTURES
65	TEXTILE YARN,FABRICS,ETC								10608	FILS,TISSUS,ARTICLES TEXTILE
651	TEXTILE YARN							W 5735	9896	FILS TEXTILES
6513	COTTON YARN							W 4498	8548	FILS DE COTON
66	NONMETAL MINERAL MFS NES								17459	ART MIN NON METALLIQUES
661	LIME,CEMENT,BLDG PRODS							W 167848	6650	CHAUX,CIMENTS MAT CONSTR
6611	LIME,QUICK,SLKD,HYDRAULC							W 121459	3612	CHAUX ORDINAIRE,HYDRAUL
6612	CEMENT							W 46386	3029	CIMENTS HYDRAULIQUES
664	GLASS								5777	VERRE
6645	CAST,ROLLED GLASS UNWRKD							A 3	5762	VERRE COULE NON TRAVAILLE
667	PEARL,PREC-,SEMI-P STONE								4855	PERLES, PIERRES GEMMES
6673	PREC-,SEMI-PR STONES NES								3081	AUTRES PIERRES NON SERTIES
68	NON-FERROUS METALS								810306	METAUX NON FERREUX
682	COPPER EXC CEMENT COPPER							W 411173	787876	CUIVRE
6821	COPPER NES,ALLOYS,UNWRT							W 407578	766012	CUIVRE BRUT
68212	COPPER REFINED,UNWROUGHT							W 407578	766012	CUIVRE AFFINE BRUT
6822	COPPER,ALLOYS WORKED							W 3595	21865	CUIVRE,ALLIAGES OUVRES
68221	COPPER BARS,WIRE,ETC							W 2199	20418	BARRES,PROFILES ET FILS
686	ZINC							W 4156	5393	ZINC
6861	ZINC,ALLOYS UNWROUGHT							W 4156	5393	ZINC ET ALLIAGES BRUTS
689	NON-FER BASE METALS NES							W 876	14692	AUT METAUX NON FERREUX
6899	BASE METALS NES,CERMETS							W 876	14692	METAUX COMMUNS NDA
68999	BASE MTL NES UNWRT,WASTE							W 876	14692	AUT METAUX COM BRUTS NDA
69	METAL MANUFACTURES NES								6096	ART MANUFACT EN METAL NDA
699	BASE METAL MFRS NES								5943	ART MANUFACTURES MET NDA
6999	OTHR BASE METAL MFRS ETC							W 1	5791	OUVRAGES EN TUNGST,MOLYB
69999	BASE MTLS NES WRGHT,MFRS							W 1	5791	MET COMMUNS OUVRES NDA
7	MACHINES,TRANSPORT EQUIP								7094	MACHINES MATERIEL TRANSPORT
77	ELECTRIC MACHNRY NES ETC								3911	MACH APP ELECT NDA
773	ELECTR DISTRIBUTNG EQUIP							W 601	3672	EQUIPMT DISTRIBUTION ELECT
7731	INSULATED WIRE,CABLE ETC							W 601	3672	FILS,CABLES ISOLES ELECT

FOOT NOTES – NOTES

TABLE 1 –

1 The export indices relate to national exports only.

2 Prior to 1964, the merchandise exports are national exports only.

TABLEAU 1 –

1 Les indices des exportations se rapportent aux exportations nationales seulement.

2 Avant 1964, les exportations de marchandises ne concernent que les exportations nationales.

Zimbabwe

1. HISTORICAL SERIES, 1960–1995 GENERAL TRADE, IMPORTS F.O.B., EXPORTS F.O.B.
SERIES HISTORIQUES, 1960–1995 COMMERCE GENERAL, IMPORTATIONS F.O.B., EXPORTATIONS F.O.B

YEAR ANNEE	VALUE IN MILLION ZIMB. DOLLARS / VALEUR EN MILLION ZIMB. DOLLARS — MERCHANDISE –MARCHANDISE: IMPORTS	EXPORTS	GOLD –OR: IMPORTS	EXPORTS	CONVERSION FACTORS U.S. CENTS PER ZIMB. DOLLAR / FACTEURS DE CONVERSION CENTS E.U. PAR ZIMB. DOLLAR: IMPORTS	EXPORTS	INDEX NUMBERS –INDICES — QUANTUM: IMPORTS	EXPORTS	UNIT VALUE / VALEUR UNITAIRE: IMPORTS	EXPORTS
1960	313.60	123.86			140.0000	140.0000				
1961	310.00	142.50			140.0000	140.0000				
1962	286.00	145.64			140.0000	140.0000				
1963	269.60	150.18			140.0000	140.0000				
1964	216.47	274.85			140.0000	140.0000				34
1965	239.58	322.82			140.0000	140.0000				36
1966	169.41	200.80			140.0000	140.0000				32
1967	187.05	194.37			140.0000	140.0000				31
1968	207.05	187.77			140.0000	140.0000				32
1969	199.43	231.86			140.0000	140.0000				34
1970	234.88	262.23			140.0000	140.0000				12
1971	282.38	284.02			140.0000	140.0000				13
1972	274.59	341.33			151.9950	151.9950				13
1973	308.60	389.10			178.0000	178.0000				14
1974	438.30	531.20			177.5990	177.5990				18
1975	461.90	531.30			173.7000	173.7000				19
1976	382.70	557.40			162.0000	162.0000				20
1977	388.10	550.80			160.2500	160.2500				21
1978	403.70	609.30			146.6430	146.2120				22
1979	549.30	715.70			170.5940	170.0230				26
1980	809.40	909.20			159.4310	156.5030				34
1981	1017.70	971.70			144.6500	144.6500				38
1982	1081.80	968.40			132.1764	131.4394				37
1983	1061.60	1150.20			99.0609	98.0913				41
1984	1200.70	1453.00			79.9061	79.0148				54
1985	1446.50	1795.50			62.0425	61.7810				64
1986	1886.50	2170.30			60.0580	59.9465				66
1987	2003.00	2371.40			60.1372	60.0821				
1988	2349.70	2966.40			55.5000	55.5000				
1989	3438.10	3267.30			47.3200	47.3200				
1990	4528.20	4231.40			40.8500	40.8500				100
1991	7443.10	5546.50			27.3624	27.5909				106
1992	11232.30	7365.70			19.6003	19.5754				136
1993	11798.40	10164.20			15.4029	15.3949				151
1994	18270.61	15364.70			12.2667	12.2414				188
1995	23049.38	18359.10			11.5465	11.5183				188

2. IMPORTS BY BROAD ECONOMIC CATEGORY AND EXPORTS BY INDUSTRIAL ORIGIN. (PERCENTAGE OF TOTAL VALUE)
IMPORTATIONS PAR CATEGORIES ECONOMIQUES ET EXPORTATIONS PAR BRANCHE D'ACTIVITE. (EN POURCENTAGE DE LA VALEUR TOTALE)

IMPORTS – IMPORTATIONS

	1990	1991	1992	1993	1994	1995	1996
TOTAL IMPORTS–IMPORTATIONS TOTALES	100.	100.	100.	100.	100.	100.	
1 FOOD BEV–ALIMENTATION BOISSONS	2.4	1.1	6.2	6.0	3.8	4.8	
11 PRIMARY–PRODUITS DE BASE	1.7	0.5	2.2	2.7	1.6	2.3	
111 FOR INDUSTRY–POUR L'INDUSTRIE	1.6	0.4	2.0	1.9	0.9	1.5	
112 FOR HOUSEHOLDS–POUR LES MENAGES	0.1	0.1	0.3	0.7	0.7	0.8	
12 PROCESSED–PRODUITS ELABORES	0.7	0.6	4.0	3.3	2.2	2.4	
121 FOR INDUSTRY–POUR L'INDUSTRIE	0.2	0.3	2.3	2.0	1.1	1.0	
122 FOR HOUSEHOLDS–POUR LES MENAGES	0.5	0.3	1.7	1.3	1.1	1.4	
2 IND SUPPLIES–APPROV INDUSTRIELS	35.9	37.2	38.7	36.9	35.3	33.4	
21 PRIMARY–PRODUITS DE BASE	2.3	2.9	12.7	7.6	1.9	2.4	
22 PROCESSED–PRODUITS ELABORES	33.6	34.2	26.0	29.4	33.4	31.0	
3 FUELS–COMBUSTIBLES	15.1	12.2	11.7	14.3	9.7	8.9	
31 PRIMARY–PRODUITS DE BASE	0.4	0.3	0.3	0.1	0.2	0.1	
32 PROCESSED–PRODUITS ELABORES	14.7	11.9	11.4	14.2	9.5	8.7	
321 MOTOR SPIRIT–ESSENCE	3.6	3.1	2.6	4.3	2.2	2.6	
322 OTHER–AUTRES	11.1	8.8	8.8	9.9	7.3	6.1	
4 MACHINERY–EQUIPEMENT	22.7	24.9	24.3	22.5	27.7	27.9	
41 CAPITAL EQUIPMENT–MACHINES	19.1	21.7	21.6	19.5	24.1	25.0	
42 PARTS–PIECES ACCESSOIRES	3.6	3.2	2.7	3.0	3.6	2.9	
5 TRANSPORT–TRANSPORT	15.4	17.4	12.5	14.2	14.6	15.0	
51 PASSENGER CARS–AUTOMOBILES	1.2	2.4	1.7	2.7	3.4	2.9	
52 OTHER–AUTRES	8.8	9.8	6.6	6.8	7.5	8.6	
521 INDUSTRIAL–INDUSTRIELS	8.7	9.7	6.5	6.6	7.4	8.5	
522 NON INDUSTRIAL–NON INDUSTRIEL	0.1	0.1	0.1	0.2	0.2	0.1	
53 PARTS–PIECES ACCESSOIRES	5.5	5.1	4.2	4.7	3.7	3.6	
6 CONSUM GOODS–BIENS CONSOMMATION	5.6	4.2	4.0	4.3	6.6	6.5	
61 DURABLE–DURABLES	1.4	1.2	1.7	1.2	2.2	1.9	
62 SEMI DURABLE–SEMI DURABLES	2.0	1.0	0.8	1.3	1.9	2.4	
63 NON DURABLE–NON DURABLES	2.1	1.9	1.5	1.7	2.5	2.2	
7 GOODS NES–BIENS NDA	3.0	3.1	2.5	1.7	2.3	3.5	

EXPORTS – EXPORTATIONS

	1990	1991	1992	1993	1994	1995	1996
TOTAL EXPORTS–EXPORTATIONS TOTALES	100.	100.	100.	100.	100.	100.	
1 AGRICULTURE	43.4	47.5	42.0	39.4	49.6	38.0	
2 MINING QUARRY–INDUS EXTRACTIVES	6.7	5.6	7.7	6.3	4.6	6.3	
3 MANUFACTURING–IND MANUFACTUR	49.8	46.9	50.3	54.4	45.8	55.7	
31 FOOD BEV TOBACCO–ALIM BOISS TAB	7.6	6.8	5.1	8.4	10.3	10.4	
32 TEXTILES–INDUSTRIES TEXTILES	6.6	7.9	10.6	10.3	8.6	9.2	
33 WOOD & PRODUCTS–BOIS & PRODUITS	0.6	0.6	1.0	1.3	1.6	2.0	
34 PAPER & PRODUCTS–PAPIER & PRODT	0.5	0.5	0.6	1.9	1.3	1.0	
35 CHEMICALS–INDUSTRIES CHIMIQUES	2.1	2.3	3.5	4.0	2.4	3.8	
36 NON METAL MIN–MIN NON METAL	1.0	0.9	0.9	1.0	0.8	0.9	
37 BASIC METAL–IND METAL BASE	24.2	22.2	21.4	17.6	12.6	18.7	
38 METAL MANUF–MANUF METAL	5.7	4.3	5.4	8.0	6.5	7.1	
39 OTH MANUF IND–AUTRES MANUF	1.6	1.4	1.6	2.0	1.7	2.6	

3. TRADE BY PRINCIPAL COUNTRIES OF PRODUCTION AND LAST CONSIGNMENT (VALUE IN THOUSAND U.S. DOLLARS)
ECHANGES SELON LES PRINCIPAUX PAYS DE PRODUCTION ET DE DERNIERE CONSIGNATION (VALEUR EN MILLIERS DE DOLLARS EU)

COUNTRIES–PAYS	GENERAL IMPORTS F.O.B. IMPORTATIONS GENERALES F.O.B.				
	1991	1992	1993	1994	1995
World	2030095	2213301	1817329	2241267	2661253
Africa	623440	627549	582838	814114	1139846
Americas	147901	441467	213054	165272	208978
Northern America	129103	212760	174638	129578	145827
LAIA	18397	227868	37544	33452	61582
CACM	3	409	7	16	1
Caribbean	361	366	863	2225	1329
Rest of America	38	64	2	1	239
As.ex F.USSR	222973	213385	222694	312784	391575
Eur.x F.USSR	804793	697774	570731	693364	724766
EU	749874	642301	518852	609047	668475
EFTA	48202	50775	39971	74997	48113
East Europe	5313	4225	11853	8504	7531
Other Europe	1404	3	2	322	23
Former USSR	744	1129	453	70598	2726
Oceania	23957	20326	19480	20396	23091
So. Africa Customs Un	585243	583807	553126	782417	1092243
United Kingdom	309949	265554	183690	230409	214421
Japan/Japon	122059	130755	124959	144101	195472
USA/Etats–Unis d'Amer	110994	198204	161957	118929	119854
Germany/Allemagne	191637	141581	88629	131643	135140
France, Monac	61441	37455	44756	45875	99937
Argentina/Argentine	2331	195152	22509	10688	39804
Switz.Liecht	43828	38826	34970	67087	39268
Italy/Italie	48154	46240	27497	43483	49234
Netherlands/Pays–Bas	34503	33540	46827	43461	46034
Sweden/Suède	25079	22799	37597	31208	33019
Belgium–Luxembourg	23566	27290	24593	27080	33199
China/Chine	15784	21951	32147	20597	27829
Hong Kong	11060	9508	12354	24319	32755
Brazil/Brésil	12137	24055	13501	19696	19791
Australia/Australie	21075	18629	15576	15513	16018
Canada	18107	14550	12681	10649	25684
Finland/Finlande	10630	25227	17073	12031	9143
Austria/Autriche	18400	16527	13252	11443	12260
Russian Federation		828	374	70298	128
Denmark/Danemark	8474	14135	12627	15831	16310
Korea, Republic of	4245	4052	6612	24304	27192
Zambia/Zambie	11353	14100	14053	6557	15400
India/Inde	9727	7128	6986	13370	16995
Spain/Espagne	9572	5316	17101	9220	9237
Malaysia/Malaisie	6838	8154	7895	15555	10120
Mauritius/Maurice	7052	5600	5033	6730	12894
Norway,SVD,JM	4169	11763	4883	6955	8766
Singapore/Singapour	9988	6168	1993	6206	9367
Saudi Arabia	3084	152	2173	10719	11764
Kenya	6025	4170	3971	4076	3581
Mozambique	5094	5042	728	5323	4615
Portugal	3806	1906	3010	3411	6590
New Zealand	2773	1089	3682	4869	6186
Malawi	2889	2678	2142	3957	5473
Pakistan	608	161	837	7452	7663
Ireland/Irlande	4117	4316	1869	2816	3265
Czech Republic			7790	4585	697
Un. Rep. of Tanzania	2795	6055	1393	702	1773
Thailand/Thaïlande	946	835	948	2176	4428
Korea Dem People's Rp	1565	224	431	3169	3544
Mexico/Mexique	610	6122	509	248	319
Viet Nam		0	7530	17	103
Indonesia/Indonésie	471	241	555	2821	3174
Kuwait/ Koweït	0	2	6	3430	3463
Poland/Pologne	1875	842	354	1602	1919
Romania/Roumanie	302	540	2912	1443	1359
Cyprus/Chypre	42	35	48	1683	4494
Bangladesh	1278	1365	710	369	2317
Chile/Chili	1724	1694	633	965	581

COUNTRIES–PAYS	GENERAL EXPORTS F.O.B. EXPORTATIONS GENERALES F.O.B.				
	1991	1992	1993	1994	1995
Monde	1289186	1251549	1318922	1967464	1845627
Afrique	397820	418125	498486	653121	601139
Amériques	84695	95659	113685	150425	109723
Amérique du Nord	78873	83813	97516	144180	91394
ALAI	5511	8441	15843	5895	17188
MCAC	48	0	63	35	43
Caraïbes	263	3383	263	201	1000
Autre Amérique	0	21	0	113	97
Asie l'URSS exclus	188655	199516	193853	304554	303261
Europe l'URSS exclus	604370	524278	501950	833895	807241
UE	548801	433775	439818	724499	743436
AELE	36500	70856	51494	56693	27403
Europe de l'Est	8065	15225	8458	49942	29471
Autre de l'Europe	11003	1102	0	35	40
Ancienne URSS	144	1312	1819	1906	1115
Océanie	13131	11610	8845	22988	15531
So. Africa Customs Un	219718	239230	268130	356956	340763
United Kingdom	177803	142202	145679	254359	237189
Germany/Allemagne	136246	86278	78941	140258	151859
Japan/Japon	93102	82366	95506	124975	145532
USA/Etats–Unis d'Amer	75237	80244	94210	124438	87622
Zambia/Zambie	45917	48045	66855	65667	92905
Italy/Italie	46114	46671	48790	58432	87629
Netherlands/Pays–Bas	38594	40433	46281	88900	65189
Malawi	42668	40348	42709	78275	49864
Mozambique	35364	42295	54018	60830	51590
Belgium–Luxembourg	54168	31177	32736	48054	54097
China/Chine	38314	43398	22832	47106	56385
Switz.Liecht	27704	62623	44382	43472	20772
France, Monac	19337	17824	19815	31978	31641
Spain/Espagne	22760	22134	17227	26277	31030
Portugal	14000	8366	10890	28619	36396
Indonesia/Indonésie	7352	11966	12509	26601	22635
Philippines	3999	15428	10904	30390	10743
Poland/Pologne	4152	9564	7489	25479	18234
Kenya	13316	17288	12180	14419	3382
Hong Kong	14595	15248	9875	5794	13353
Australia/Australie	10350	8508	7690	18922	11954
Denmark/Danemark	9277	12729	2850	13046	10985
Un. Rep. of Tanzania	3715	3022	4950	25217	9705
Sweden/Suède	8287	4039	9971	10180	11790
Greece/Grèce	10282	8388	10553	8320	6431
Norway,SVD,JM	8743	8211	7112	13220	6631
Dem. Rep. of the Congo	8070	3381	3916	18311	8463
India/Inde	3548	6028	9036	8390	13185
Angola	7301	4459	3224	10660	11660
Austria/Autriche	5862	5426	11906	6270	7748
Egypt/Egypte	5947	31	20832	334	9126
Canada	3633	3540	3306	19738	3761
Ireland/Irlande	3883	7045	3781	7455	9570
Singapore/Singapour	5237	4214	5367	6561	7578
Thailand/Thaïlande	1405	1755	1939	9782	7595
Iran (Islamic Rp. of)	2108	1046	5306	13385	42
Mauritius/Maurice	695	3020	4696	5766	5974
Brazil/Brésil	1062	1329	3503	2731	10004
Mexico/Mexique	2376	5421	7747	956	1500
Uganda/Ouganda	1879	4113	2756	5188	3790
Hungary/Hongrie	18	721	408	9154	4764
Bulgaria/Bulgarie	44	1519	83	7863	4798
Korea, Republic of	2874	2761	1693	2315	3429
Malaysia/Malaisie	873	1183	1973	4707	3278
Ghana	1883	2592	2014	2402	2733
New Zealand	1467	2455	890	3703	2768
Libyan Arab Jamahiriya	2272	3799	460	1444	2804
Saudi Arabia	706	1801	1143	6278	779
Fm Yugoslav	10655				

(VALUE AS PERCENTAGE OF WORLD TOTAL)(VALEURS EN POURCENTAGE DU TOTAL MONDIAL)

	1986	1987	1988	1989	1990	1991	1992	1993	1994	1995
Africa	29.7	30.0	21.9	18.2	26.3	30.7	28.4	32.1	36.3	42.8
Americas	9.7	11.0	8.9	13.9	13.8	7.3	19.9	11.7	7.4	7.9
Northern America	9.3	10.8	8.2	10.5	12.5	6.4	9.6	9.6	5.8	5.5
LAIA	0.3	0.2	0.8	3.4	1.2	0.9	10.3	2.1	1.5	2.3
CACM	0.0				0.0	0.0	0.0	0.0	0.0	0.0
Caribbean	0.0			0.0	0.0	0.0	0.0	0.0	0.1	0.0
Rest of America	0.0				0.0	0.0	0.0	0.0	0.0	0.0
As.ex F.USSR	8.6	6.6	6.8	7.9	10.5	11.0	9.6	12.3	14.0	14.7
Eur.x F.USSR	40.8	39.2	47.2	43.2	33.3	39.6	31.5	31.4	30.9	27.2
EU	35.4	35.2	43.4	39.2	30.0	36.9	29.0	28.6	27.2	25.1
EFTA	3.4	3.1	3.5	3.5	2.3	2.4	2.3	2.2	3.3	1.8
East Europe	1.8	0.9	0.3	0.5	0.9	0.3	0.2	0.7	0.4	0.3
Other Europe	0.1	0.0		0.0	0.1	0.1	0.0	0.0	0.0	0.0
Former USSR	0.1				0.1	0.0	0.1	0.0	3.1	0.1
Oceania	1.1	0.5	0.7	1.3	2.8	1.2	0.9	1.1	0.9	0.9
So. Africa Customs Un	26.3	28.0	20.2	16.0	24.1	28.8	26.4	30.4	34.9	41.0
United Kingdom	10.9	11.6	13.3	8.2	11.5	15.3	12.0	10.1	10.3	8.1
Japan/Japon	4.3	4.1	4.5	4.0	4.6	6.0	5.9	6.9	6.4	7.3
USA/Etats–Unis d'Amer	8.3	9.6	6.4	9.4	11.4	5.5	9.0	8.9	5.3	4.5
Germany/Allemagne	9.9	9.1	11.7	11.3	7.3	9.4	6.4	4.9	5.9	5.1
France, Monac	3.3	3.7	4.7	4.8	2.1	3.0	1.7	2.5	2.0	3.8
Argentina/Argentine	0.0	0.0	0.0	0.0	0.2	0.1	8.8	1.2	0.5	1.5
Switz.Liecht	2.9	2.2	2.0	2.5	2.0	2.2	1.8	1.9	3.0	1.5
Italy/Italie	4.3	3.1	2.4	2.8	2.2	2.4	2.1	1.5	1.9	1.9
Netherlands/Pays–Bas	1.6	2.8	3.6	3.6	2.0	1.7	1.5	2.6	1.9	1.7

	1986	1987	1988	1989	1990	1991	1992	1993	1994	1995
Afrique	31.7	22.3	14.8	14.5	32.3	30.9	33.4	37.8	33.2	32.6
Amériques	6.5	6.1	8.8	9.3	8.0	6.6	7.6	8.6	7.6	5.9
Amérique du Nord	6.1	5.9	8.6	8.9	7.3	6.1	6.7	7.4	7.3	5.0
ALAI	0.3	0.1	0.2	0.4	0.7	0.4	0.7	1.2	0.3	0.9
MCAC	0.0				0.0	0.0	0.0	0.0	0.0	0.0
Caraïbes	0.1	0.0	0.0	0.0	0.0	0.0	0.3	0.0	0.0	0.1
Autre Amérique	0.0	0.0	0.0	0.0	0.0	0.0	0.0	0.0	0.0	0.0
Asie l'URSS exclus	12.3	8.3	9.7	12.7	12.5	14.6	15.9	14.7	15.5	16.4
Europe l'URSS exclus	48.1	34.8	43.3	42.6	45.8	46.9	41.9	38.1	42.4	43.7
UE	42.6	32.4	41.5	40.9	42.2	42.6	34.7	33.3	36.8	40.3
AELE	1.7	1.0	0.9	1.0	2.0	2.8	5.7	3.9	2.9	1.5
Europe de l'Est	3.3	1.4	0.9	0.3	0.6	0.6	1.2	0.6	2.5	1.6
Autre de l'Europe	0.5	0.0		0.0	1.0	0.9	0.1	0.0	0.0	0.0
Ancienne URSS	0.2				0.0	0.0	0.1	0.1	0.1	0.1
Océanie	1.2	0.7	9.1	9.8	1.2	1.0	0.9	0.7	1.2	0.8
So. Africa Customs Un	17.1	12.2	7.5	7.4	15.1	17.0	19.1	20.3	18.1	18.5
United Kingdom	12.0	10.1	10.4	11.6	10.9	13.8	11.4	11.0	12.9	12.9
Germany/Allemagne	8.4	8.0	10.3	10.4	11.8	10.6	6.9	6.0	7.1	8.2
Japan/Japon	4.4	4.0	6.5	6.5	5.5	7.2	6.6	7.2	6.4	7.9
USA/Etats–Unis d'Amer	5.6	5.6	8.2	8.4	6.5	5.8	6.4	7.1	6.3	4.7
Zambia/Zambie	2.8	2.3	2.2	2.0	3.5	3.6	3.8	5.1	3.3	5.0
Italy/Italie	5.8	3.5	6.6	5.5	4.6	3.6	3.7	3.7	3.0	4.7
Netherlands/Pays–Bas	5.9	2.9	4.7	3.2	4.3	3.0	3.2	3.5	4.5	3.5
Malawi	2.9	1.5	1.5	1.2	4.8	3.3	3.2	3.2	4.0	2.7
Mozambique	3.2	3.0	1.5	1.4	3.7	2.7	3.4	4.1	3.1	2.8

4. General Imports F.O.B. by Commodities according to the S.I.T.C. (Rev. 2) in thousand U.S. Dollars
Importations Générales F.O.B. par Produits d'après la C.T.C.I. (Rév. 2) en milliers de Dollars E.U.

SITC CTCI	COMMODITY	1992 WEIGHT POIDS	1992 VALUE VALEUR	1993 WEIGHT POIDS	1993 VALUE VALEUR	1994 WEIGHT POIDS	1994 VALUE VALEUR	1995 WEIGHT POIDS	1995 VALUE VALEUR	PRODUIT
	ALL COMMODITIES		2213301		1817329		2241267		2661253	TOUS PRODUITS
0	FOOD AND LIVE ANIMALS		317117		152140		53915		97872	ALIMENTS,ANIMAUX VIVANTS
03	FISH AND PREPARATIONS		2781		7603		10023		13319	POISSONS ET PREPARATIONS
034	FISH,FRESH,CHILLED,FROZN	W 178	518	W 8248	4879	W 13363	7562	W 14421	8561	POISSON FRAIS, REFRIG,CONG
0342	FISH FROZEN,EXCL FILLETS	W 140	289	W 7883	4355	W 13117	7083	W 14168	7748	POISSONS CONGELES
04	CEREALS AND PREPARATIONS		257477		113204		23036		45102	CEREALES ET PRODUITS
041	WHEAT ETC UNMILLED	W 67	16	W 85689	23894		13053	W 80890	29429	FROMENT,EPEAUTRE
0412	OTHER WHEAT ETC UNMILLED	W 67	16	W 85618	23708	W 16665	13053	W 80890	29429	AUTRE FROMENT NON MOULU
042	RICE	W 13392	4316	W 10846	7847	W 25721	7053	W 29080	9879	RIZ
0422	RICE SEMI–MILLED,MILLED	W 13390	4310	W 10843	7844	W 25525	6991	W 28950	9817	RIZ POLI,GLACE INCL BRISURES
04221	RICE MILLED UNBROKEN	W 13341	4283	W 10782	7816	W 23584	6432	W 27293	9297	RIZ POLI,GLACE EXCL BRISURES
044	MAIZE UNMILLED	W 1208060	237438		69981	W 1289	884	W 2266	700	MAIS NON MOULU
047	OTHER CEREAL MEALS,FLOUR	W 37374	9522	W 3536	1395	W 22	23	W 5	8	AUTRES SEMOULES,FARINES
04702	MEAL OR GROATS NON–WHEAT	W 37369	9520	W 3517	1375	W 16	14	W 1	2	GRUAUX,SEMOULES DE CEREALES
048	CEREAL ETC PREPARATIONS	W 562	530	W 2924	7500	W 971	1350	W 1439	2323	PREPTNS A BASE CEREALES
0481	PREPD BREAKFAST FOOD ETC	W 182	156	W 2588	7059	W 215	377	W 181	559	CEREALES TRAVAILLEES
04811	CEREAL FLAKED,ROLLED,ETC	W 79	92	W 2538	6908	W 110	117	W 12	30	GRAINS GERMES DE CEREALES
05	VEGETABLES AND FRUIT		5502		9053		10478		14985	LEGUMES ET FRUITS
054	VEG ETC FRSH,SMPLY PRSVD	W 7479	4793	W 13564	7836	W 8452	7041		9780	LEGUMES FRAIS,CONG,SECS
0542	LEGUMINOUS VEGETBLES DRY	W 6260	3853	W 11004	6495	W 6694	3477	W 7016	4842	LEGUMES A COSSE SECS
06	SUGAR AND PREPS,HONEY		25864		19230		806		1849	SUCRES ET PRODUITS
061	SUGAR AND HONEY	W 97771	25822	W 60506	19075		308	W 12533	1073	SUCRES ET MIEL
0611	RAW BEET AND CANE SUGAR	W 69056	22211	W 40981	16583			W 785	261	SUCRES BRUTS
081	*FEEDING STUFF FOR ANIML	W 28073	4234	W 3407	675	W 6723	2429	W 54650	12922	NOURRITURE POUR ANIMAUX
0813	OILCAKE AND OTH RESIDUES	W 17352	2618	W 50	23	W 636	173	W 46591	9260	TOURTEAUX
09	MISC EDIBLE PRODUCTS		19759		638		2250		3110	PREP ALIMENTAIRES DIVERSES
098	EDIBLE PRODCTS,PREPS NES	W 11493	19695	W 199	637	W 948	2154	W 1026	2957	PREP ALIMENTAIRES NDA
09809	MISC FOOD PREPRTIONS NES	W 11457	19612	W 67	308	W 494	989	W 326	1197	PREP ALIMENTAIRES NDA
1	BEVERAGES AND TOBACCO		6818		5490		8349		10736	BOISSONS ET TABACS
11	BEVERAGES		6635		3705		7438		9127	BOISSONS
2	CRUDE MATERLS,EXCL FUELS		106741		91674		73127		92400	MAT BRUTES NON COMESTIBLES
22	OIL SEEDS,OLEAGINOUS FRT		43485		8332		3667		5827	GRAINES,FRUITS OLEAGINEUX
222	SEEDS FOR'SOFT'FIXED OIL	W 39844	37377	W 4130	8323	W 5520	3622	W 12916	5710	GRAINES HUILES FIXES
2221	GROUNDNUTS,GREEN	W 2077	3846	W 3996	8157	W 4212	3162	W 424	163	ARACHIDES NON GRILLEES
2222	SOYA BEANS	W 37209	32135	W 41	4			W 5775	4066	FEVES DE SOJA
23	RUBBER, CRUDE		13162		9565		13529		16778	CAOUTCHOUC BRUT
232	NATURAL RUBBER,GUMS	W 7846	8199	W 4959	5327	W 6221	7865	W 5319	9984	LATEX CAOUTCHOUC NATUREL
23201	NATURAL RUBBER LATEX	W 6193	6900	W 1320	1367	W 1056	1169	W 777	1244	LATEX NATUREL
251	*PULP AND WASTE PAPER	W 8924	4049		7038	W 30165	10353	W 20991	9848	PATES A PAPIER,DECHETS
26	TEXTILE FIBRES AND WASTE		18657		14783		13892		15899	FIBRES TEXTILES
263	COTTON	W 6089	8511	W 4752	6917	W 451	34	W 3047	6360	COTON
2631	RAW COTTON,EXCL LINTERS	W 5570	8431	W 4438	6900	W 3	6	W 3015	6226	COTON EN MASSE
27	CRUDE FERTLZR,MINRLS NES		12974		12280		13822		13432	ENGRAIS MINERAUX BRUTS
278	OTHER CRUDE MINERALS	W 52313	6214		9269		8492		8122	AUTRES MINERAUX BRUTS
2783	COMMON SALT,ETC	W 46477	3962	W 61043	5487	W 59893	4899	W 67181	5038	SEL
28	METALLIFEROUS ORES,SCRAP		4303		32788		10250		22900	MINERAIS METAL,DECHETS
287	BASE METAL ORES,CONC NES		4152		32614		10123		22802	MINERAIS METAUX COMMUNS
2871	CPR ORE ETC,CEMENT COPPR	W 9178	3296	W 18839	31441	W 4388	7549		21653	MINERAIS DE CUIVRE,MATTES
28712	COPPER MATTE,CEMENT COPR	W 956	2854	W 14202	31069	W 3988	7528	W 3530	21653	MATTES DE CUIVRE
3	MINERAL FUELS ETC		262305		267398		222369		240080	COMBUSTIBLES MINERAUX LUB
33	PETROLEUM AND PRODUCTS		251901		265190		215659		234012	PETROLE ET DERIVES
334	PETROLEUM PRODUCTS,REFIN	W 1017946	247790	W 1554000	256771		210164		228840	PRODUITS RAFFINES
3341	GASOLINE,OTH LIGHT OILS	W 233695	57440	W 777065	77138	W 173955	50103	W 358642	68425	ESSENCES POUR MOTEURS
33411	MOTOR,AVIATION SPIRIT	W 231526	56247	W 775451	76271	W 170522	48739	W 356921	67483	ESSENCES MOTEURS D'AVIONS
3342	KEROSENE,OTH MEDIUM OILS	W 122787	39984	W 191347	41807	W 335168	32577	W 155085	28577	PETR LAMPANTS,AUT HUIL
33421	KEROSENE INCL JET FUEL	W 120341	39414	W 191346	41807	W 335070	32565	W 155078	28575	PETROLES LAMPANTS
3343	GAS OILS	W 621160	129156	W 549766	110133		109069		114554	GAS OILS
3345	LUBS,PETROLEUM OILS NES	W 25580	19178	W 36207	27504		18168		17260	HUILES LUBRIFIANTES
33451	LUBS(HIGH PETR CONT) ETC	W 24709	17189	W 35422	26158		16657		16489	HUILES LUBRIF,H LOURDES
335	RESIDUAL PETRLM PROD NES	W 7825	4086	W 20547	8415		5491		5145	PRODUITS RESIDUELS NDA
4	ANIMAL,VEGETABLE OIL,FAT		25866		36607		42161		44340	HUILES,GRAISSES ANIM,VEG
411	*ANIMAL OILS AND FATS	W 27039	12833	W 31165	15356	W 40946	18660	W 24353	15986	HUILES,GRAISSES ANIMALES
4113	ANIML OIL,FAT,GREASE NES	W 27012	12804	W 31161	15342	W 40919	18632	W 24311	15944	HUILES,GRAISSES ANIMALES NDA
41132	FATS OF BOVINE,SHEEP,ETC	W 26969	12672	W 31147	15275	W 40868	18508	W 24274	15845	SUIFS BRUTS FONDUS
42	FIXED VEGETABLE OIL,FAT		11045		19616		22520		26173	HUILES VEGETALES FIXES
423	FIXED VEG OILS,SOFT	W 8006	6612	W 16059	12201	W 18856	12850	W 26512	21308	HUILES VEGET DOUCES FIXES
4232	SOYA BEAN OIL	W 5158	4952	W 14852	10965	W 18821	12795	W 21005	16611	HUILE DE SOJA
424	FIXED VEG OIL NONSOFT	W 7005	4433	W 12297	7416	W 16792	9671	W 7143	4865	AUTRES HUILES VEG FIXES
4242	PALM OIL	W 4225	1979	W 9386	2549	W 14541	7968	W 6355	4089	HUILE DE PALME
5	CHEMCLS,RELATED PROD NES		254222		248919		360505		358488	PRODUITS CHIMIQUES
51	ORGANIC CHEMICALS		25845		24956		40349		32241	PROD CHIMIQ ORGANIQUES
511	HYDROCARBONS NES,DERIVS		8175		4901		6441		6920	HYDROCARBURES NDA
513	CARBOXYLIC ACIDS ETC	W 4529	5823	W 3951	5233	W 5760	7040	W 3657	6668	ACIDES CARBOXYLIQUES
514	NITROGEN–FNCTN COMPOUNDS	W 826	4144	W 1487	5594	W 1540	7641	W 1782	7916	COMPOSES FONCT AZOTEES
515	ORG–INORG COMPOUNDS ETC	W 824	2550	W 1062	3903	W 4017	12397	W 1691	4669	COMPOSES ORGANO–MINERAUX
5154	ORGANO–SULPHUR CMPNDS	W 634	1149	W 805	1840	W 3606	10106	W 1397	2896	THIOCOMPOSES ORGANIQUES
52	INORGANIC CHEMICALS		43691		44413		54126		56418	PROD CHIM INORGANIQUES
522	INORG ELEMNTS,OXIDES,ETC		18441		21013		26369		30413	ELEMENTS INORGANIQUES
5225	INORGANIC BASES ETC NES		11161		12991		15037		20878	AUTRES BASES OXYDES METAL
52251	AMMONIA,ANHYDROUS ETC	W 19736	3192	W 41270	6708		9838		13132	AMMONIAC LIQUEFIE
523	OTHR INORG CHEMICALS ETC		25048		23305		27621		25868	AUT PRODUITS CHIMIQUES INORG
5231	METAL CMPD OF INORG ACID	W 9719	7053	W 15840	8049	W 15324	8208	W 14577	7816	SELS METALLIQUES
5232	OTH MTL CMPD OF INRG ACD	W 32372	15499	W 26694	11508	W 36272	16522	W 31279	15219	SELS METALLIQUES
52325	CYANIDES,COMPLEX CYANIDE	W 11436	7419	W 6426	5300	W 6913	6976	W 5151	6660	CYANURES SIMPLES,COMPLEXES
53	DYES,TANNING,COLOUR PROD		18666		19020		45957		21217	PROD TEINTURE,COLORANTS
531	SYNT DYE,NAT INDGO,LAKES	W 1173	10138	W 1104	11292	W 2283	35868	W 916	9233	MAT COLOR ORGAN,LAQUES
5311	SYNTHIC ORGNIC DYESTUFFS	W 1028	8888	W 991	10241	W 2165	34667	W 857	8446	MAT COLOR ORGAN SYNTHET
533	PIGMENTS,PAINTS,ETC		6631		6702		9337		11019	PIGMENTS,PEINTURES,VERNIS
541	*MEDICINAL,PHARM PRODUCT		22929		27430		33952		34861	PROD MEDICINAUX PHARMACEUT
5417	MEDICAMENTS		10518		11212		13266		17025	MEDICAMENTS
54173	— CONTAINING ALKALOIDS		1101		3176		5469		8400	MED CONTEN ALCALOIDES
54179	— CONTNG OTH SUBSTANCES		6489		6457		5741		5182	MED CONT AUT SUBSTANCES
55	PERFUME,CLEANING ETC PRD		9580		7074		14092		20132	PROD POUR PARFUM,TOILETTE
551	ESSENTL OILS,PERFUME,ETC	W 403	4975	W 427	3980	W 753	6776	W 1481	11777	HUILES ESSENTIELLES
5514	MIXED PERFUME SUBSTANCES	W 374	4414	W 385	3398	W 686	5917	W 1416	10907	MELANGES SUBSTAN ODORIFER
562	*FERTILIZERS,MANUFACTURE		11751	W 129647	19179	W 142778	27383	W 99859	22947	ENGRAIS MANUFACTURES
5621	CHEM NITROGENOUS FERTLZR		1649	W 26757	4866	W 74467	10641	W 50703	11897	ENGRAIS AZOTES
5623	CHEM POTASSIC FERTILIZER	W 38653	9690	W 102330	14142	W 55142	13914	W 34820	7701	ENGRAIS POTASSIQUES
56231	POTASSIUM CHLORIDE	W 22187	4616	W 37162	3161	W 41541	7924	W 12281	2565	CHLORURE DE POTASSIUM
56232	POTASSIUM SULPHATE NES	W 16444	5049	W 65163	10981	W 13601	5990	W 22539	5135	SULFATE DE POTASSIUM
572	*EXPLOSIVES,PYROTECH PRO		8474		13851		13094		14804	EXPLOSIFS

4. General Imports F.O.B. by Commodities according to the S.I.T.C. (Rev. 2) in thousand U.S. Dollars
Importations Générales F.O.B. par Produits d'après la C.T.C.I. (Rév. 2) en milliers de Dollars E.U.

SITC CTCI	COMMODITY	1992		1993		1994		1995		PRODUIT
		WEIGHT POIDS	VALUE VALEUR	WEIGHT POIDS	VALUE VALEUR	WEIGHT POIDS	VALUE VALEUR	WEIGHT POIDS	VALUE VALEUR	
5721	PREPARED EXPLOSIVES		6	W 6974	7184	W 7205	6703	W 6647	6682	POUDRES,EXPLOSIFS
57212	PREPARED EXPLOSIVES NES			W 6945	6935	W 7181	6630	W 6557	6339	EXPLOSIFS PREPARES
5722	FUSES,PRIMERS,DETONATORS	W 741	8454	W 685	6649	W 558	6314	W 655	7977	MECHES,CORDEAUX,AMORCES
58	PLASTIC MATERIALS ETC		55889		49740		72299		89508	MAT PLAST ARTIFICIELLES
582	PROD OF CONDENSATION ETC	W 6502	10956	W 6264	8789	W 8815	12217	W 9248	13897	PROD CONDENS,POLYCOND
583	POLYMERIZATION ETC PRODS	W 38894	42740	W 41021	39422	W 62027	57935	W 57867	73548	PROD POLYMERISATION
5831	POLYETHYLENE	W 14437	12860	W 16492	14160	W 22390	18113	W 24565	27296	POLYETHYLENE
58311	— IN PRIMARY FORMS	W 14427	12757	W 16446	13921	W 22277	17706	W 24190	26716	POLYETHYLENE PRIMAIRES
5832	POLYPROPYLENE	W 8281	8365	W 9203	7632	W 14570	12744	W 14496	17428	POLYPROPYLENE
58321	— IN PRIMARY FORMS	W 7819	7322	W 8866	6611	W 13882	11209	W 13690	15350	POLYPROPYLENE PRIMAIRES
5834	POLYVINYL CHLORIDE	W 9331	7649	W 8386	6745	W 15890	12600	W 9768	11389	CHLORURE DE POLYVINYLE
58341	— IN PRIMARY FORMS	W 9142	7017	W 8296	6476	W 15756	12280	W 9581	10767	SOUS FORMES PRIMAIRES
5839	OTH POLYMRZTION ETC PROD	W 4114	8643	W 2731	5505	W 4573	8213	W 3718	9296	AUT PROD POLYMER COPOLYM
59	CHEMICAL MATERIALS NES		57396		43256		59252		66361	MAT PROD CHIMIQUES NDA
591	PESTICIDES,DISINFECTANTS	W 12126	29377	W 4813	21242	W 5358	27690	W 11953	29308	DESINF,INSECT,FONG,HERB
5911	INSECTICIDES,FOR RETAIL	W 1737	12612	W 2038	10136	W 1943	11981	W 2331	15837	INSECTICIDES VENTE DET
5913	HERBICIDES,FOR RETAIL	W 10052	14076	W 2188	6784	W 2086	10296	W 1834	9162	HERBICIDES VENTE AU DET
598	MISCEL CHEM PRODUCTS NES		26594		20626		28041		33865	PROD DIV INDUST CHIM NDA
5982	ANTI–KNOCK PREPARTNS ETC	W 3936	9282	W 2859	6509	W 4281	7722	W 2784	6564	PREPARAT ANTIDETONANTES
5989	CHEM PRODUCTS,PREPS NES		12130		11193		17594		19932	PROD PREP CHIMIQUES NDA
59899	OTH CHEM PRODS,PREPS,NES		6993	W 2	6660		10544		11714	AUT PRODUITS CHIMIQUES NDA
6	BASIC MANUFACTURES		316868		268567		369411		458270	ART MANUFACTURES
62	RUBBER MANUFACTURES NES		25642		23003		29570		34539	CAOUTCHOUC MANUFACTURE
625	RUBBER TYRES, TUBES ETC	W 4178	14453	W 2333	14034	W 3685	14588	W 5181	18720	PNEUS CAOUTCHOUC VULCANISE
6252	TYRES,NEW,BUS OR LORRY	W 1207	3920	W 613	7654	W 1152	4801	W 2331	7867	PNEUS POUR AUTOBUS,CAMIONS
6259	OTH TYRES,TYRE CASES,ETC	W 2235	7091	W 1150	3601	W 1846	6369	W 2021	7022	AUTRES PNEUS RECHAPES FLAPS
628	RUBBER ARTICLES NES		8490		6898		11146		11704	OUVRAGES CAOUTCHOUC NDA
6289	OTH RUBBER ARTICLES NES	W 231	5421	W 232	4530	W 460	7176	W 326	6746	AUT OUVR CAOUTCHOUC NDA
62898	UNHARD RUBBER PRODS NES	W 229	5399	W 230	4506	W 446	7112	W 322	6679	OUV CAOUT VULC NON DURCI
64	PAPER,PAPERBOARD AND MFR		36429		27833		48115		52225	PAPIERS,CARTONS & OUVRAGES
641	PAPER AND PAPERBOARD	W 34726	32718	W 32454	24549	W 42604	38538	W 36629	41816	PAPIERS ET CARTONS
6413	KRAFT PAPER,PAPERBOARD	W 19566	12492	W 14453	7755	W 16241	10234	W 16226	14282	PAPIER ET CARTON KRAFT
64139	KRAFT PAPER PAPERBD,NES	W 8533	5339	W 5469	3098	W 5311	3546	W 12289	11173	PAPIER,CARTON KRAFT NDA
6415	PAPER,PAPERBRD,BULK,NES	W 5520	9422	W 6938	5770	W 7095	10414	W 5889	10426	PAPIERS,CARTONS ROULEAUX
64159	OTHER PAPER ETC,BULK,NES	W 5128	8642	W 6758	5342	W 6835	9913	W 5494	9662	AUT PAPIER ROULEAUX FEUILLES
6418	COATED ETC PAPER NES BLK	W 2802	4074	W 6275	6566	W 7773	8739	W 5183	7526	PAP,CARTONS COUCHES,ENDUITS
64189	COATED PAPER ETC NES	W 2459	3348	W 5835	5786	W 7241	7362	W 4361	5564	PAPIERS,CARTONS COUCHES
642	PAPER,ETC,PRECUT,ARTS OF		3710	W 1533	3285		9577		10409	PAP,CARTONS DECOUPES
65	TEXTILE YARN,FABRICS,ETC		64184		73360		96361		115638	FILS,TISSUS,ARTICLES TEXTILE
651	TEXTILE YARN	W 2671	12617	W 1633	7213	W 3672	13364	W 3494	13628	FILS TEXTILES
6514	SYN FIB YRN,BULK,MONOFIL	W 1607	6056	W 1104	4560	W 2509	7681	W 1755	6416	FILS CONT 85% FIB TEXT SYNTH
652	COTTON FABRICS,WOVEN	A 6405	9422	A 3673	10674	A 9745	18191	A 12185	27101	TISSUS DE COTON
6522	WOVEN COTTON BLEACHD,ETC	A 4758	7229	A 2747	9198	A 8725	16450	A 11424	25844	TISSUS COTON BLANCHIS ETC
65224	BLCHED COTTON FABRIC NES	A 4342	6600	A 2334	7599	A 6842	12411	A 9367	22039	AUT TIS PLUS 85% COT BLANCHI
653	WOVN MAN–MADE FIB FABRIC	A 9102	18225	A 6172	18671	A 13899	30778	A 14293	30561	TISSUS FIBRES SYNTH,ARTIF
6531	CONT SYNT WEAVES NONPILE	A 4174	7360	A 2780	7706	A 4403	8338	A 4800	10650	TISSUS FIBRES SYNTH CONTINUE
65315	CONT SYN TXTL FABRIC NES	A 3487	6140	A 2612	7082	A 3773	7409	A 4055	9360	TIS PLUS 85% TEXT SYNT CONT
6534	DISC SYN BLEND FABRC NES	A 2584	6753	A 1583	6213	A 5648	13090	A 4519	9525	TISSUS FIBRES SYNTH DISCONT
65349	OTH DISC SYN BLEND FABRC	A 635	1203	A 578	2188	A 3263	8792	A 2390	6056	TISSUS FIB SYNT MEL MAT AUT
655	KNITTED,ETC FABRICS	A 3359	6859	A 1353	5842	A 2025	5498	A 1606	5772	ETOF BONNETERIE PIECES ETC
6552	OTHER KNIT ETC FAB NONEL	A 3359	6859	A 1353	5842	A 2025	5498	A 1606	5772	ETOF BON NON ELAS NON SYNT
657	SPECIAL TXTL FABRC,PRODS		10646		14076		17929		20392	TISSUS SPECIAUX
6573	COATED ETC TEXTILES NES		7559		10154		12420		10306	TISSUS,ART MATIERE TEXT NDA
65733	RUBBERIZED TEXT NOT KNIT		5286	A 560	5800		6289	A 962	5615	TISSUS CAOUTCHOUTES
658	TEXTILE ARTICLES NES		918		12838		3054		6366	ART FACONNES MAT TEXTILES
6581	BAGS,SACKS OF TEXTILES	N 508041	619	N 3421052	12477	N 3051028	1597	N 7292904	5493	SACS EMBALLAGE TEXTILES
66	NONMETAL MINERAL MFS NES		36268		29129		32893		35413	ART MIN NON METALLIQUES
661	LIME,CEMENT,BLDG PRODS		14173	W 70454	6226		6637	W 45539	7288	CHAUX,CIMENTS MAT CONSTR
6612	CEMENT	W 177287	9181	W 39194	3449		2301	W 3299	558	CIMENTS HYDRAULIQUES
662	CLAY,REFRACTORY BLDG PRD		10076		8084		9587		9977	MAT CONST REFRACTAIRES
6623	REFRACTORY BUILDING PROD	W 7694	9144	W 6643	7487	W 7668	6840	W 8115	7058	BRIQUES REFRACTAIRES
66232	REFRACTRY BRICKS ETC NES	W 5106	6699	W 4434	5737	W 4623	4306	W 4724	4518	BRIQUES ETC REFRACTAIRES
664	GLASS		4014		7132		6943		6726	VERRE
67	IRON AND STEEL		94089		54900		84033		102436	FER ET ACIER
672	IRON,STEEL PRIMARY FORMS	W 9646	4979	W 13026	6256		8996		12220	LINGOTS FER,ACIER
6727	IRN,STL COIL FR REROLLNG	W 9604	4862	W 12979	6202	W 20167	8593	W 23142	11601	EBAUCHES POUR TOLES FER
67271	IRON,SIMPLE STEEL COILS	W 8997	3885	W 12656	5700	W 19821	8029	W 22511	10587	EBAUCHES NON EN ACIER
673	IRON,STEEL SHAPES ETC	W 17015	12197	W 9237	6186	W 43639	16695	W 49148	23668	BARRES,PROFIL FER.ACIER
6732	IRON,STEEL BARS ETC	W 2867	4995	W 3927	3328	W 7019	6734	W 15536	7763	BARRES FER,ACIER
6733	IRON,STEEL PROFILES ETC	W 14072	7159	W 4665	2431	W 23041	6428	W 14253	8057	PROFILES,PALPLAN FER,ACIER
674	IRN,STL UNIV,PLATE,SHEET	W 83620	52459		30385		40121	W 78424	48181	LARGES PLATS,TOLES
6744	IRN,STL HVY PLATE,ROLLED	W 23667	14438	W 12648	6309		8195	W 22520	12087	TOLES LAMINEES PLUS 4.75 MM
67441	— OF IRON OR SIMPLE STL	W 23513	14172	W 12589	6179		7557	W 22092	11598	TOLES NON ACIER FIN CARB
6745	IRN,STL MED PLATE,ROLLED	W 12933	7584	W 1266	2601	W 3894	5464	W 9405	4994	TOLES 3 A 4.75 MM
6746	IRN,STL THIN PLATE,ROLLD	W 28007	15249	W 20833	11775	W 22953	13088	W 27715	16858	TOLES LAM MOINS 3MM
67461	— OF IRON OR SIMPLE STL	W 27455	14548	W 20505	11345	W 22183	12323	W 27516	16533	TOL NON AC FIN MOINS 3 MM
6747	TINNED PLATES,SHEETS	W 10194	8812	W 3753	3108	W 6833	5830	W 6679	5723	TOLES ETAMEES EN ACIER
6749	OTH IRN,STL PLATES,SHEET	W 8819	6376		6592		7543	W 12105	8519	AUTRES TOLES FER,ACIER
67491	— OF IRON OR SIMPLE STL	W 8722	6187		6428		7291	W 11619	8031	AUT TOLES AUTRES ACIER FIN
678	IRON,STL TUBES,PIPES,ETC	W 13130	17516	W 5665	7844	W 7151	12251	W 7637	11787	TUBES,TUYAUX EN FONTE,FER
6782	IRON,STL SEAMLESS TUBES	W 6767	8110	W 1710	2419	W 3391	4465	W 2050	2859	TUBES,TUYAUX SANS SOUDURE
6783	IRON,STL TUBES,PIPES NES	W 5927	6748	W 3222	2830	W 3001	3478	W 4062	4098	AUT TUBES,TUYAUX FER,ACIER
68	NON–FERROUS METALS		15851		13290		17652		20215	METAUX NON FERREUX
684	ALUMINIUM	W 3211	10414	W 2564	5543	W 10811	9254	W 2944	7866	ALUMINIUM
6842	ALUMINIUM,ALLOYS WORKED	W 2196	7250	W 1688	4043	W 9291	6956	W 2319	6609	ALUMINIUM,ALLIAGES OUVRE
69	METAL MANUFACTURES NES		39778		41447		52176		86172	ART MANUFACT EN METAL NDA
691	STRUCTURES AND PARTS NES	W 800	1016	W 921	1215	W 1187	1742	W 6644	12320	CONSTRUCT FER,ACIER,ALU
6911	STRUCTURES,PARTS IRN,STL	W 797	1003	W 891	1006	W 1111	1375	W 6488	11750	CONSTRUCT FER,ACIER,FONTE
693	WIRE PRODUCTS NON ELECTR	W 2465	6584	W 3131	8018	W 2433	5083	W 4196	10352	OUVRAGES FILS METALLIQUES
6931	WIRE CABLES, ROPES ETC	W 2377	6013	W 3038	7336	W 1967	4171	W 3313	7786	CORDAGES EN FILS DE FER
695	TOOLS		10633		10093		20013		22452	OUTILS A MAIN
6953	OTHER HAND TOOLS	W 342	3536	W 556	4629	W 827	9500	W 2108	13121	AUTRES OUTILS A MAIN
6954	BLADES,TIPS,ETC FR TOOLS	W 274	7061	W 212	5309	W 692	10359	W 524	9159	OUTILS POUR MACHINE–OUTIL
69541	PARTS TO INSERT IN TOOLS	W 182	3529	W 162	3525	W 602	7830	W 427	6858	OUTILS DE FORAGE
699	BASE METAL MFRS NES		13134		13193		14233		19861	ART MANUFACTURES MET NDA
7	MACHINES,TRANSPORT EQUIP		805341		636781		934633		1107722	MACHINES MATERIEL TRANSPORT
71	POWER GENERATING EQUIPMT		41551		32525		60414		63917	MACHINES GENERATRICES
713	INTRNL COMBUS PSTN ENGIN		25794		17353		27380		26972	MOTEURS EXPL COMB INT, PIECE
7132	MOTOR VEHCL PISTN ENGINS	N 7261	6682	N 15350	3426	N 6941	6640	N 12714	7691	MOTEURS EXPL POUR VEHICULES
7139	PISTON ENGINE PARTS NES	W 510	11321	W 473	9782	W 579	11818	W 498	12905	PIECES POUR 713.2,3,8
716	ROTATING ELECTRIC PLANT		13051		9038		22534		23828	APP ELECTR ROTATIFS,PIECES

4. General Imports F.O.B. by Commodities according to the S.I.T.C. (Rev. 2) in thousand U.S. Dollars
Importations Générales F.O.B. par Produits d'après la C.T.C.I. (Rév. 2) en milliers de Dollars E.U.

SITC CTCI	COMMODITY	1992 WEIGHT POIDS	1992 VALUE VALEUR	1993 WEIGHT POIDS	1993 VALUE VALEUR	1994 WEIGHT POIDS	1994 VALUE VALEUR	1995 WEIGHT POIDS	1995 VALUE VALEUR	PRODUIT
7162	AC MTRS,GENRTRS,GEN SETS		9735		6417		19434		16397	MOTEURS ELECTRIQUES
71621	AC MTRS,INC UNIVRSL MTRS	N 13263	1985	N 39053	1636	N 75536	2413	N 71791	14489	MOT ELEC NON COUR CONTINU
71623	GEN SETS WITH PISTN ENGN	W 750	5940	W 601	4608	W 448	16694	W 141	1695	GROUPES MOTEUR EXPLOSION
72	MACHS FOR SPCL INDUSTRYS		190355		103418		183478		247202	MAC SPECIALES POUR INDUST
721	AGRIC MACHY,EXC TRACTORS		16419		4355		13798		13797	MACHINES AGRICOLES
7212	HARVESTING ETC MACHINES		11801		1451		8378		7332	ENGINS POUR LA RECOLTE
72124	AGRIC CLEAN,GRADING MACH		8607	W 1	173		4119		1896	MACH NETTOYAGE DES GRAINS
722	TRACTORS NON-ROAD	N 28144	30220	N 3079	16814	N 12467	38547	N 1475	25389	TRACTEURS
7224	WHEELED TRACTORS NES	N 28141	30132	N 3078	16804	N 12464	38470	N 1474	25386	TRACTEURS A ROUES
723	CIVIL ENGNEERG EQUIP ETC		28013		17130		40987		64896	APPAREILS DE GENIE CIVIL
7234	CONST,MINING MACHNRY NES		23835		14676		37105		60223	MACH POUR LA CONST, MINES
72341	SELF-PROPELLD DOZERS,ETC	N 76	6390	N 59	5730		12069		14378	BULLDOZERS
72342	SLFPRP SHOVELS,EXCAVATRS		11117	N 19	5030	N 151	20151		30746	PELLES MECANIQUES
72343	SLFPRP CONST ETC MCH NES		2666	W 38	1763	W 198	2213	W 690	12231	AUT MACH EXTR,TERRASSEM
724	TEXTILE,LEATHER MACHNRY		43645		20159		26206		21823	MACH POUR INDUSTRIE TEXTILE
7244	SPINNING,EXTRDNG,ETC MCH	W 505	11061	W 332	6950	W 143	4086	W 405	7014	MACH POUR LE FILAGE
7245	WEAVING,FELT MFG,ETC MCH		16338		4231		8654		2766	METIERS A TISSER,PIECES
72453	GIMPING,WARPING ETC MCHS	W 574	10447	W 68	817	W 64	761	W 19	218	METIERS A TULLE ETC
725	PAPER ETC MILL MACHINERY	W 235	2245	W 473	7106	W 433	2706	W 422	6241	MACHINES FABR PATE PAPIER
726	PRINTG,BKBINDG MACHY,PTS	W 410	11916	W 658	5080	W 349	6256	W 423	8607	MACHINES POUR IMPRIMERIE
727	FOOD MACHRY NON-DOMESTIC	W 947	14766	W 737	6180	W 716	8556	W 1369	19370	MACH INDUSTRIES ALIMENT
7272	OTH FOOD PROC MCHY,PARTS	W 900	13667	W 684	4647	W 526	5268	W 1073	14146	AUT MACH IND ALIMENTAIRE
72722	INDUS FOOD PROC MACH NES	W 840	12826	W 502	2910	W 513	5160	W 1073	14125	MACHINES BOULANGERIE
728	OTH MACHY FOR SPCL INDUS	W 3293	43131	W 2474	26592	W 6087	46422	W 11549	87079	AUT MACH IND PARTICULIERES
7281	MACH-TOOLS FR SPCL INDUS	W 560	8689	W 382	4041	W 611	4450	W 1658	14699	MACH-OUTILS SPEC IND PART
72812	MACH-TOOLS TO WORK WOOD	W 421	7386	W 335	2871	W 406	3458	W 1553	13471	MACH-OUT POUR TRAVAIL BOIS
7283	OTHR MINERAL WORKG MACHY	W 1186	12348	W 624	4355	W 1729	22907	W 7634	43467	MACH TRIER,CRIBLER,BROYER
72831	MINRAL SORTING ETC MACHY	W 72	1538	W 49	426	W 509	11545	W 820	6696	MACH TRIER MAT MINERALES
72832	MINRL CRUSHING ETC MACHY	W 225	1325	W 116	703	W 668	6182	W 4122	21358	MACH CONCASSER MAT MINER
72839	PTS NES OF MACHY OF 7283	W 451	2868	W 184	1321	W 230	2635	W 1873	10584	PIECES MACH DU 728.3
7284	MACHY FOR SPCL INDUS NES	W 1548	22094	W 1468	18195	W 3746	19065	W 2257	28913	MACH SPEC IND PARTICUL.
72842	RUBBER,PLASTICS WRKG MCH	W 582	11446	W 759	8480	W 2666	9541	W 820	9249	MACH IND CAOUT MAT PLAST
72848	OTH MCHY WITH INDIV FNCT	W 655	4764	W 217	2563	W 834	5192	W 1036	13926	AUTRES MACHINES NDA
73	METALWORKING MACHINERY		25430		14064		15473		11395	MACH TRAVAIL DES METAUX
736	METALWORKING MACH-TOOLS	W 2973	21940	W 1555	10001	W 1091	8383	W 1355	8893	MACH-OUTILS TRAVAIL METAUX
7361	METAL CUTTING MACH-TOOLS	W 1117	11174	W 645	4992	W 610	4050	W 517	3392	MACH-OUT ENLEVEMENT METAL
737	METALWORKING MACHNRY NES	W 503	3490	W 694	4063	W 699	7091	W 341	2503	MACH TRAV METAUX PIECES
74	GENRL INDUSTRL MACHY NES		163306		107876		162999		171012	MACH APP INDUSTRIE
741	HEATING,COOLING EQUIPMNT		53389		14556		18978		25626	MACH CHAUFFAGE,PIECES
7413	INDUS FURNACES ETC,PARTS	W 2160	44377	W 408	2205	W 524	3075	W 1161	6591	FOURS IND,LABOR,PIECES
74132	INDUST FURNACES NONELECT	W 2053	43070	W 224	1008	W 336	1809	W 276	3696	FOURS NON ELECTRIQUES
7415	AIR-CONDITIONING MACHNRY	W 272	4231	W 487	5496	W 590	4967	W 823	5412	GROUPES CONDITION AIR
7416	HEATING,COOLING EQU NES	W 255	3644	W 317	4765	W 503	6293	W 2010	8559	APP CHANGEMENT TEMP
742	PUMPS FOR LIQUIDS ETC	W 691	12330	W 1209	10605	W 1031	18149	W 1568	20463	POMPES MOTO-POMPES
7428	OTHER PUMPS FOR LIQUIDS	W 317	6120	W 896	5458	W 633	10126	W 1097	13208	AUTRES POMPES POUR LIQ
74288	PUMPS FR LIQUIDS NES ETC	W 307	5933	W 865	4918	W 535	8473	W 927	10221	POMPES POUR LIQUIDES NDA
743	PUMPS NES,CENTRFUGES ETC		22441		15549		25321		30860	POMPES COMPRES,VENT ETC
7431	PUMPS FOR GASES ETC	W 820	8125	W 627	7204	W 1210	10429	W 1363	11573	POMPES AIR A VIDE,COMPRES
7436	GAS,LIQUID FILTERS ETC	W 802	8056		4440		7565	W 1436	9002	APP POUR FILT DES LIQUIDES
744	MECHANICAL HANDLING EQU	W 3033	23399	W 2989	22551	W 3384	28009	W 4993	31049	EQUIP MANUTENTION PIECES
7442	LIFTING,LOADING MACH NES	W 1827	13285	W 1946	14741	W 1705	15775	W 2590	14129	APP LEVAGE,MANUTENTION
74424	LIFTS AND SKIP HOISTS	W 272	1766	W 721	5953	W 565	5528	W 149	1373	ASCENSEURS,MONTE-CHARGE
74428	OTH HANDLING ETC MCH NES	W 887	7248	W 563	5604	W 605	6921	W 1625	7796	AUT APP LEVAGE ETC
7449	PTS NES OF MACHY OF 7442	W 447	4766	W 654	5703	W 665	6357	W 1431	11327	PIECES DU 744.2
745	NONELEC MACHY,TOOLS NES		12644		9179		20582		17737	AUT MACH NON ELEC,PIECES
7452	OTH NONELEC MCHS,PTS NES		11894		8424		19532		16393	AUT MACH NON ELEC,PIECES
74522	PACKAGNG,BOTTLNG,ETC MCH	W 208	8933	W 180	3920	W 527	11720	W 214	5618	MACH NETT BOUTEILLES,ETC
749	NONELEC MACH PTS,ACC NES	W 2084	39104	W 2357	35435		51960	W 2815	45277	PIECES MACH NON ELEC NDA
7491	BALL,ROLLER,ETC BEARINGS	W 560	10762	W 565	8968	W 737	13148	W 583	11096	ROULEMENTS BILLES ETC
7492	COCKS,VALVES ETC NES	W 435	8419	W 433	9452	W 702	14771	W 737	10541	ART ROB,SIM POUR TUYAUX
7493	SHAFT,CRANK,PULLEY ETC	W 772	15540	W 1022	12686		16179	W 1144	18509	ARBRES TRANS,VILEBREQUINS
7499	OTH NONELEC MCHY PTS NES	W 316	4383	W 337	4329	W 606	7862	W 351	5131	PIECES NON ELECT NDA
75	OFFICE MACHNES,ADP EQUIP		29632		27566		38398		48896	MACH BUREAU TRAIT AUTOM
751	OFFICE MACHINES	N 27761	4196	N 74072	4951	N 27154	8107	N 83467	8699	MACH,APPAREILS DE BUREAU
752	AUTOMTIC DATA PROC EQUIP	N 15715	20777	N 16971	17341	N 21740	22813	N 46131	30318	MACH TRAIT INFORMATION
7522	DIGITAL COMPUTERS	N 8384	12297	N 4639	7569	N 4497	8595	N 10830	11757	MACH DIGITALES COMPLETES
7525	ADP PERIPHERAL UNITS	N 4116	4040	N 6088	4055	N 6074	6517	N 21937	8393	UNITES PERIPHERIQUES
759	OFFICE,ADP MCH PTS,ACCES	W 72	4659	W 90	5274		7478		9880	PIECES DU 751 ET 752
7599	ACCTG,ETC,ADP MCH PTS,AC	W 43	3719	W 72	4478		5526		8296	PIECES DU 751 ET 752
76	TELECOMM,SOUND EQUIPMENT		56052		61703		66472		79374	EQUIPMENT DE TELECOM
763	SOUND RECORDRS,PHONOGRPH	N 49301	18574	N 5022	4006	N 31550	3118	N 45816	3646	PHONO,APP ENREGISTREMENT
7638	OTHR SOUND APPARATUS ETC	N 48566	18484	N 4547	3861	N 28064	2947	N 31108	3406	AUT APP D'ENREGIS,REPROD
76381	TV IMAGE,SND RECRDRS ETC	N 46080	18026	N 4258	2132	N 12307	2277	N 17348	2349	APP ENREG,REPRO IMAG,SON
764	TELECOM EQPT,PTS,ACC NES		31915		50345		51975		64741	EQUIP TELECOM,PIECES
7641	LINE TELEPHONE,ETC EQUIP		20570	N 4	34760		15579		24900	APP TELEPHON PAR FIL
7643	TV,RADIO TRANSMITTRS ETC	N 5805	4488	N 19186	4438	N 9342	9091	N 32095	18549	APP EMET TELE RADIO
7648	TELECOMM EQUIPMENT NES		800		942		17448		12178	APP TELECOM NDA
76483	RADAR APPARATUS ETC		233	W 5	714		15713		10586	APP DE RADIOGUIDAGE ETC
7649	PTS NES OF EQUIPMT OF 76		5600		9383		9228		7937	PIECES DE LA DIV 76
76491	PTS NES OF APPAR OF 7641	W 113	3411	W 110	7945	W 16	1485	W 38	2813	PIECES POUR 764.1
76493	TELECOMM EQUIPMT PTS NES		1358		1274		7306		4843	PIECES 761,762,764.3,8
77	ELECTRIC MACHNRY NES ETC		68368		70212		131660		144769	MACH APP ELECT NDA
771	ELECTRIC POWER MACHY NES		16885		19813		10730		34925	MACH PROD,TRANS ELECTR
7711	TRANSFORMERS,ELECTRICAL		14756	N 84820	13102		4312	N 490892	28572	TRANSFO ELECTRIQUES
77111	LIQUID DIELEC TRANSFRMRS		6632	N 29271	5177		2089	N 42596	11184	TRANSFO DIELEC LIQUIDE
77118	OTHER ELEC TRANSFORMERS		8124	N 55549	7926	N 33547	2223	N 448296	17388	AUTRES TRANSFO ELECTRIQ
7712	OTH ELEC POWER MACHY NES		2129		6711		6418		6354	AUT APP PROD TRANSF ELEC
772	SWITCHGEAR ETC,PARTS NES		23060		22521		44915		37327	APP COUPURE,SECT ETC
7721	SWITCHGEAR ETC	W 964	22022	W 886	21077	W 1301	42075	W 1763	35458	APP COUPURE,SECTIONMNT
773	ELECTR DISTRIBUTNG EQUIP	W 1470	9073		8540		19350		23628	EQUIPMT DISTRIBUTION ELECT
7731	INSULATED WIRE,CABLE ETC	W 1261	6333	W 1585	6081	W 8372	17449	W 6478	19509	FILS,CABLES ISOLES ELECT
774	ELECTRO-MEDCL,XRAY EQUIP		1535		1180		13626		8012	APPAREILS MEDICAUX
7742	X-RAY APPARATUS ETC		869		780		12879		6993	APPAREILS A RAYONS X
775	HOUSEHOLD TYPE EQUIP NES		3181		4043		18355		13082	MACH,APP USAGE DOMESTQUE
7752	DOM REFRIGERATRS,FREEZRS	N 2223	503	N 2418	1004	N 46646	12296	N 16895	4251	REFRIG,CONGEL MENAGER
77521	DOMESTIC REFRIGERATORS	N 1337	335	N 2111	892	N 45689	11701	N 13465	3131	REFRIGERATEURS
778	ELECTRICAL MACHINERY NES		13560		12662		22160		24719	AUTRES MACH ELECT NDA
78	ROAD VEHICLES		160953		163481		256971		316896	VEHICULES ROUTIERS
781	PASS MOTOR VEH EXC BUSES	N 5763	36688	N 8696	48127		76664		75509	AUTO TRANSPORT PERSONNES
782	LORRIES,SPCL MTR VEH NES	N 15313	74554	N 5539	55993	N 48743	108248	N 64087	153700	VEHICULES SPECIAUX,MARCH
7821	LORRIES,TRUCKS	N 15268	72994	N 5472	48301	N 48645	101366	N 63987	140571	VEHICULES TRANSP MARCHAND

4. General Imports F.O.B. by Commodities according to the S.I.T.C. (Rev. 2) in thousand U.S. Dollars
Importations Générales F.O.B. par Produits d'après la C.T.C.I. (Rév. 2) en milliers de Dollars E.U.

SITC CTCI	COMMODITY	1992		1993		1994		1995		PRODUIT
		WEIGHT POIDS	VALUE VALEUR	WEIGHT POIDS	VALUE VALEUR	WEIGHT POIDS	VALUE VALEUR	WEIGHT POIDS	VALUE VALEUR	
7822	SPECIAL MOTOR VEHCLS NES	N 45	1560	N 67	7692	N 98	6882	N 100	13130	VEHICULES USAGES SPECIAUX
783	ROAD MOTOR VEHICLES NES	N 620	15910	N 758	17842	N 3504	46474		49589	VEHICULES ROUTIERS NDA
7831	BUSES	N 457	6913	N 557	8051	N 2724	24393		31009	VOITURES TRANSPORT COMMUN
7832	TRACTORS FOR TR–TRAILERS	N 163	8997	N 201	9791	N 780	22081		18580	TRACTEURS ROUTIERS
784	MOTOR VEH PRTS,ACCES NES		28274		34743		19099		27705	PIECES 722,781,782,783
7841	MOTOR VEHICLE CHASSIS	N 35	1285	N 231	8294	N 38	378	N 44	2301	CHASSIS 722,781,782,783
7849	OTHER MOTOR VEHCL PARTS	W 473	26913	W 235	26234		18720		25404	PIECES 722,781,782,783
785	CYCLES,ETC MOTRZD OR NOT		3577		5697		4345		4161	MOTOCYCLES SCOOTERS
79	OTHR TRANSPORT EQUIPMENT		69695		55937		18767		24261	AUTRE MATERIEL TRANSPORT
791	RAILWAY VEHICLES		22861		3415		2659		1850	VEHIC MAT CHEMINS DE FER
7912	OTH RAIL LOCOMOTIVES ETC	N 13	18738	N 23837	93		161		83	AUTRES LOCOMOTIVES
792	AIRCRAFT ETC		46702		52289		15980		22155	APP NAVIGATION AERIENNE
7921	HELICOPTERS	N 2	27800		75	N 9	4849	N 6	3918	HELICOPTERES
7923	AIRCRFT NES2000–15000KG	N 7	3381	N 167	38524	N 5	2562		8747	AERODYNES 2000 A 15000 KG
7929	AIRCRAFT PARTS NES	W 48	14798	W 19	8834	W 26	7803	W 40	8032	PIECES DU 792
8	MISC MANUFACTURED GOODS		55274		75265		120895		146133	ART MANUFACTURES DIVERS
87	PRECISION INSTRUMNTS NES		23303		30350		41640		46927	INSTRUM,APPAR SCIENT NDA
872	MEDICAL INSTRUMENTS NES		5587		7574		14126		15021	INSTR,APP MEDIC–CHIR NDA
87202	OTH MEDICAL INSTRUMENTS		5037		7116		13753		14155	INSTRUM,APP MEDECINE
874	MEASURNG,CONTROLNG INSTR		16397		17915		24664		28211	INSTRUMENTS DE MESURE
8743	GAS,LIQUID CONTROL INSTR		6087		6001		6245		5165	APP,INSTR MESURE FLUIDES
8748	ELEC MEAS,CONTRL EQU NES		4497		4835		5454		12479	APP ELEC ELECTRO MESURE
87483	OTH ELCTRNC MEAS ETC EQU		4061		4246		4322		11696	AUT APP ELECTRO DE MESURE
88	PHOTO EQU,OPTICL GDS ETC		5407		6326		9701		12163	APP,FOURN PHOTO,OP,MONTR
89	MISC MANUFCTRD GOODS NES		20972		28586		48463		60326	ART MANUFACTURES DIVERS
892	PRINTED MATTER		6079		8410		19443		17168	IMPRIMES
8921	PRINTED BOOKS,GLOBES,ETC		4610		6041		15105		11818	LIVRES,BROCHURES,CARTES
89211	PRINTED BOOKS,PAMPHLETS		4436		5916		15013		11273	LIVRES,BROCHURES
893	ARTICLES OF PLASTIC NES		5291		6460		9780		17891	OUVRAGES EN MAT DIVIS 58
8939	MISC PLASTIC ARTICLES		3751		4345		6304		12650	ART DIVERS EN MAT DIV 58
89399	OTHR PLASTC ARTICLES NES	W 499	3614		3715		5697		11947	AUT OUV MAT DIV 58
9	GOODS NOT CLASSD BY KIND		62748		34487		55901		105213	ART TRANSACT NON CLASSES
931	*SPECIAL TRANSACTIONS		46983		23920		39698		76165	TRANS.SPECIALES
971	*GOLD,NON MONETARY NES	K 1852	6839	K 1129	4585	K 4638	5237	K 19647	13156	OR NON MONETAIRE
97101	NONMON GLD UNWRT,SEMIMFD	K 1652	6839	K 1129	4585	K 4638	5237	K 19647	13156	OR,ALLIAGES D'OR BRUTS

5. General Exports F.O.B. by Commodities according to the S.I.T.C. (Rev. 2) in thousand U.S. Dollars
Exportations Générales F.O.B. par Produits d'après la C.T.C.I. (Rév. 2) en milliers de Dollars E.U.

SITC CTCI	COMMODITY	1992 WEIGHT POIDS	1992 VALUE VALEUR	1993 WEIGHT POIDS	1993 VALUE VALEUR	1994 WEIGHT POIDS	1994 VALUE VALEUR	1995 WEIGHT POIDS	1995 VALUE VALEUR	PRODUIT
	ALL COMMODITIES		1251549		1318922		1967464		1845627	TOUS PRODUITS
0	FOOD AND LIVE ANIMALS		86337		148836		389159		306107	ALIMENTS,ANIMAUX VIVANTS
001	*LIVE ANIMALS FOR FOOD	N 4013993	4068	N 4021729	6514	N 7517960	11083	N 8216425	10988	ANIMAUX VIVANTS
0014	LIVE POULTRY	N 4002311	1329	N 3962521	3097	N 7492638	6294	N 8194631	5693	VOLAILLES VIVANTES
01	MEAT AND PREPARATIONS		15047		24475		20183		24538	VIANDES ET PREPARATIONS
011	MEAT FRESH,CHILLD,FROZEN	W 10540	7077	W 16405	10845	W 11207	7922	W 15016	12430	VIANDES FRAICHES,REF,CONGE
0111	BOVINE MEAT FRESH,FROZEN	W 9342	4970	W 15654	9724	W 9002	5092	W 12247	6989	VIANDES BOVIN FRAI,REF
01112	BOVINE MEAT BONELESS	W 9342	4970	W 15644	9714	W 8950	5001	W 12224	6935	VIANDES BOVIN DESOSSEES
014	MEAT PREPD,PRSVD,NES ETC	W 3787	7945	W 4826	13486	W 4245	12213	W 3929	11985	CONSERVES DE VIANDES
0149	OTH PREPARD,PRESRVD MEAT	W 3732	7812	W 4819	13430	W 4232	12193	W 3915	11917	AUTRES PREP DE VIANDES
02	DAIRY PRODCTS,BIRDS'EGGS		4991		10100		13951		14147	PRODUITS LAITIERS,OEUFS
022	MILK AND CREAM	W 3144	3950	W 6581	7403	W 13351	9548	W 13501	11234	LAIT ET CREME
0224	MILK,CREAM PRESERVED ETC	W 3031	3885	W 5936	7049	W 9203	7553	W 13243	11079	LAIT,CREME CONS,CONC
02243	MILK DRY,OVER 1.5% FAT	W 2373	2642	W 4667	4960	W 8327	5679	W 11362	7634	LAIT POUDRE SUP 1.5%
04	CEREALS AND PREPARATIONS		13564		43263		171742		65469	CEREALES ET PRODUITS
041	WHEAT ETC UNMILLED					W 1577	506	W 86379	8355	FROMENT,EPEAUTRE
0412	OTHER WHEAT ETC UNMILLED					W 1500	472	W 70614	6904	AUTRE FROMENT NON MOULU
044	MAIZE UNMILLED	W 25345	9089	W 215827	31190	W 1279928	146222	W 287818	33468	MAIS NON MOULU
045	CEREALS NES UNMILLED	W 532	304	W 5192	1746	W 19916	8192	W 1954	552	AUTRES CEREALES NON MOULUES
0459	OTHER CEREALS UNMILLED	W 532	304	W 5192	1746	W 19916	8192	W 1954	552	SARRASIN,MILLET,SORGHO
04599	OTH CEREALS UNMILLED NES	W 29	22	W 59	17	W 13695	6675	W 255	18	AUTRES CEREALES NDA
046	WHEAT ETC MEAL OR FLOUR	W 66	32	W 5675	5340	W 16331	2812	W 31753	9569	SEMOULE FARINE,FROMENT
04601	FLOUR OF WHEAT OR MESLIN	W 60	28	W 5614	5317	W 16331	2812	W 31751	9569	FARINE DE FROMENT
047	OTHER CEREAL MEALS,FLOUR	W 240	70	W 643	142	W 40977	7389	W 19848	4038	AUTRES SEMOULES,FARINES
04702	MEAL OR GROATS NON-WHEAT	W 236	68	W 50	19	W 37572	6804	W 18774	3853	GRUAUX,SEMOULES DE CEREALES
048	CEREAL ETC PREPARATIONS	W 10077	4070	W 10476	4753	W 13223	6608	W 22946	9486	PREPTNS A BASE CEREALES
0482	MALT INCLUDING FLOUR	W 9404	3439	W 9287	3744	W 10710	4642	W 21265	7443	MALT MEME TORREFIE
05	VEGETABLES AND FRUIT		10757		15146		24673		40950	LEGUMES ET FRUITS
054	VEG ETC FRSH,SMPLY PRSVD	W 7232	4794	W 12431	9722	W 17483	14841	W 9996	24595	LEGUMES FRAIS,CONG,SECS
0545	OTHER FRESH VEGETABLES	W 3289	3098	W 4827	5262	W 6097	8505	W 4699	19424	AUTRES LEGUMES FRAIS,REF
05459	FRESH VEGETABLES NES	W 3152	3062	W 4619	5182	W 5297	8237	W 4552	19310	LEGUMES FRAIS,REFRI NDA
057	FRUIT,NUTS,FRESH,DRIED	W 9879	3648	W 8958	3185	W 16851	5042	W 28096	12260	FRUITS FRAIS OU SECS
0571	ORANGES, MANDARINS ETC	W 7063	1894	W 6318	1545	W 12535	2518	W 19263	5964	ORANGES,MAND,CLEMENTINES
05711	ORANGES,FRESH OR DRIED	W 7061	1893	W 6311	1542	W 12496	2507	W 19228	5945	ORANGES FRAICHES,SECHEES
06	SUGAR AND PREPS,HONEY		8078		4564		101832		83326	SUCRES ET PRODUITS
061	SUGAR AND HONEY	W 11181	4480	W 1880	327	W 243548	96704	W 151464	76217	SUCRES ET MIEL
0611	RAW BEET AND CANE SUGAR	W 1	2	W 352	230	W 182059	88540	W 129407	62063	SUCRES BRUTS
0612	REFINED SUGAR ETC	W 11134	4463	W 2	3	W 16475	4913	W 16737	13870	SUCRES RAFFINES
062	SUGAR CANDY NON-CHOCLATE	W 2965	3598	W 3058	4237	W 3827	5128	W 4126	7109	SUCRERIES
07	COFFEE,TEA,COCOA,SPICES		19865		18277		28922		41700	CAFE,THE,CACAO,EPICES
071	COFFEE AND SUBSTITUTES	W 10324	11713	W 4029	4893	W 4321	12453	W 10209	26453	CAFE ET SUCCEDANES
0711	COFFEE GREEN,ROASTED,SUB	W 10253	11628	W 4027	4891	W 4313	12412	W 10202	26423	CAFE TORREFIE OU DECAFEINE
07111	COFFEE GREEN,HUSKS,SKINS	W 10246	11612	W 4014	4843	W 4303	12347	W 10062	26061	CAFE NON TORREFIE
074	TEA AND MATE	W 6089	7332	W 8065	9961	W 9688	11302	W 9156	10962	THE ET MATE
0741	TEA	W 6089	7332	W 8065	9961	W 9688	11302	W 9156	10962	THE
081	*FEEDING STUFF FOR ANIML	W 15040	3761		19611	W 57905	9975	W 77757	16927	NOURRITURE POUR ANIMAUX
0812	BRAN,POLLARD,SHARPS,ETC	W 1	1		3364	W 8016	1946	W 27739	6724	SONS
08122	BRAN,ETC OF OTHR CEREALS			W 5729	3034	W 7931	1915	W 22855	5854	SONS D'AUTRES CEREALES
0813	OILCAKE AND OTH RESIDUES	W 13364	2782	W 62031	11500	W 22187	3656	W 5933	1434	TOURTEAUX
08131	— OF SOYA BEANS	W 13176	2742	W 54374	10142	W 10222	2085	W 5065	1314	TOURTEAUX DE SOJA
0819	FOOD WASTE AND FEED NES	W 1536	962	W 23762	3802	W 26223	4061	W 43711	8643	DECHETS,ALIMENTS NDA
08199	FODDER NES,INCL SWEETNED	W 1535	961	W 23762	3802	W 26195	4058	W 43171	8602	PREPARATIONS FOURRAGERES
09	MISC EDIBLE PRODUCTS		6024		6744		6705		7413	PREP ALIMENTAIRES DIVERSES
091	MARGARINE AND SHORTENING	W 4888	4333	W 6278	5066	W 5729	5044	W 3844	4953	MARGARINE ET GRAISSES
0914	MARGARINE,EDIBLE FAT NES	W 4888	4333	W 6278	5066	W 5729	5044	W 3844	4953	MARGARINES,SIMILI SAINDOUX
1	BEVERAGES AND TOBACCO		441753		393075		668957		485000	BOISSONS ET TABACS
11	BEVERAGES		1474		13623		3373		3360	BOISSONS
111	NON-ALCOHL BEVERAGES NES	W 430298	145	W 631798	10340	W 2624852	967	W 49169	1040	BOISSONS NON ALCOOLIQUES
11102	FLAVORED WATERS NON-ALCO	W 132	45	W 32957	10165	W 2360	672	W 8098	1008	LIMONADES,EAUX GAZEUSES
12	TOBACCO AND MANUFACTURES		440280		379452		665584		481640	TABACS BRUTS FABRIQUES
121	TOBACCO UNMNFCTRD,REFUSE	W 150488	434381	W 184290	370237	W 298896	649005	W 175966	470818	TABACS BRUTS,DECHETS
1211	TOBACCO,NOT STRIPPED	W 51326	165650	W 55143	102021	W 54187	133596	W 14258	47609	TABACS NON ECOTES
1212	TOBACCO STRIPPED OR PART	W 72836	260567	W 109684	261518	W 227087	509173	W 155063	420591	TABACS PART ECOTES
1213	TOBACCO REFUSE	W 26326	8163	W 19463	6698	W 17622	6236	W 6646	2618	DECHETS DE TABACS
122	TOBACCO,MANUFACTURED		5899	W 2556	9215	W 7880	16579	W 2085	10823	TABACS FABRIQUES
1222	CIGARETTES	W 1383	3228	W 622	4953	W 6458	13274	W 818	8418	CIGARETTES
1223	OTH MANUFACTURED TOBACCO	W 1297	1700	W 1934	4262	W 1422	3305	W 1267	2405	TABACS FUMER,CHIQUER,PRISER
2	CRUDE MATERLS,EXCL FUELS		153404		185049		217933		232829	MAT BRUTES NON COMESTIBLES
21	HIDES,SKINS,FURS UNDRSSD		8990		8193		8207		5351	CUIRS,PEAUX BRUTS
211	HIDES,SKINS,EXC FURS,RAW	W 5296	8990	W 6675	8159	W 3458	8200	W 1499	5350	CUIRS ET PEAUX
2111	BOVINE,EQUINE HIDES,RAW	W 3101	6464	W 4927	5495	W 3004	4747	W 1447	1781	PEAUX DE BOVINS
22	OIL SEEDS,OLEAGINOUS FRT		333		13090		12988		4403	GRAINES,FRUITS OLEAGINEUX
222	SEEDS FOR'SOFT'FIXED OIL	W 835	263	W 53215	13089	W 34653	12951	W 8045	3708	GRAINES HUILES FIXES
2222	SOYA BEANS	W 38	20	W 35919	8039	W 23377	6984	W 1404	620	FEVES DE SOJA
24	CORK AND WOOD		9929		15836		22006		27494	LIEGE ET BOIS
247	OTH WOOD ROUGH,SQUARED	W 38866	712	W 375322	4640	W 22244	1094	W 23889	1996	BOIS BRUTS EQUARRIS
2471	SAW-,VENEER-LOGS CONIFER	W 11395	151	W 369693	4271	W 19338	917	W 10342	1127	CONIFERES POUR SCIAGE,PLACAG
24711	— IN THE ROUGH	W 11395	151	W 369693	4271	W 19338	917	W 10342	1127	ECORCES OU DEGROSSIS
248	WOOD SHAPED,SLEEPERS	W 596702	7967	W 718646	10689	W 811998	20373	W 186038	24347	BOIS SIMPLEMENT TRAVAILLES
2482	LUMBER SHAPED CONIFER	W 595672	7671	W 716082	9958	W 785749	19117	W 129785	22014	CONIFERES SCIES,RABOTES
24821	LUMBER SAWN ETC CONIFER	W 539190	6701	W 446671	9040	W 636625	18048	W 120479	21417	CONIFERES SCIES LONGITUD
26	TEXTILE FIBRES AND WASTE		28038		25522		64265		53978	FIBRES TEXTILES
263	COTTON	W 15667	27305	W 18745	24162	W 48118	60445	W 28259	50447	COTON
2631	RAW COTTON,EXCL LINTERS	W 15516	27077	W 18361	23440	W 47102	58983	W 26755	45262	COTON EN MASSE
27	CRUDE FERTLZR,MINRLS NES		82574		73583		72904		96279	ENGRAIS MINERAUX BRUTS
273	STONE,SAND AND GRAVEL	W 107413	9458	W 172681	11380	W 147187	10569	W 242720	11596	PIERRES,SABLES,GRAVIERS
2731	BLDG,DIMENSION STONE	W 84700	9292	W 122000	11050	W 108154	10415	W 104581	11360	PIERRES DE TAILLE
27313	GRANITE,SANDSTONE,ETC	W 80619	8860	W 121450	10924	W 107458	10200	W 103660	11039	GYPSE,BASALTE,GRES
277	NATURAL ABRASIVES NES		9195	W 8040	376		285	W 504	34	ABRASIFS NATURELS NDA
2771	INDUSTRIAL DIAMONDS		9055							DIAMANTS INDUSTRIELS
278	OTHER CRUDE MINERALS	W 169009	63856	W 141584	61797	W 160288	61959		84636	AUTRES MINERAUX BRUTS
2782	REFRACTORY MINERALS NES	W 19316	5017	W 13120	3388	W 12518	3540	W 22789	3728	ARGILE MINERAUX REFRACTAIRES
27822	NATURAL GRAPHITE	W 11849	4690	W 8078	2985	W 9077	3009	W 12854	3112	GRAPHITE NATUREL
2784	ASBESTOS CRDE,SMPLY WRKD	W 128811	55789	W 105407	55300	W 129289	56418	W 174558	69958	AMIANTE (ASBESTE)
2789	MINERALS CRUDE NES	W 20024	2908	W 20289	2670	W 17578	1839	W 99208	9573	MINERAUX BRUTS NDA
27893	TALC,NATURAL STEATITE	W 95	11	W 430	44	W 82	9	W 67400	6069	STEATITE NATURELLE
28	METALLIFEROUS ORES,SCRAP		9568		16324		12045		7409	MINERAIS METAL,DECHETS
282	IRON AND STEEL SCRAP	W 22215	1290	W 81550	13232	W 77912	10245	W 61716	4389	FERRAILLES
28202	— OF ALLOY STEEL	W 5324	222	W 56377	11690	W 7556	582	W 14005	1091	FERRAILLES D'ACIERS ALLIES
28209	— OF OTHR IRON OR STEEL	W 12801	650	W 18842	1038	W 66219	9077	W 38250	2814	FERRAILLES DE FER
289	PREC MTAL ORES,WASTE NES	K 953	5877					K 4001	3	MINERAIS,DECHETS MET PREC

5. General Exports F.O.B. by Commodities according to the S.I.T.C. (Rev. 2) in thousand U.S. Dollars
Exportations Générales F.O.B. par Produits d'après la C.T.C.I. (Rév. 2) en milliers de Dollars E.U.

SITC CTCI	COMMODITY	1992		1993		1994		1995		PRODUIT
		WEIGHT POIDS	VALUE VALEUR	WEIGHT POIDS	VALUE VALEUR	WEIGHT POIDS	VALUE VALEUR	WEIGHT POIDS	VALUE VALEUR	
28901	PRECIOUS METAL ORES,CONC	K 917	5461							MINERAIS METAUX PRECIEUX
29	CRUDE ANIMAL,VEG MAT NES		13723		32394		25480		37874	MATIERES BRUTES ANIM,VEGET
292	CRUDE VEG MATERIALS NES		13545		31785		24944		37178	MAT BRUTES VEGETALES NDA
2927	CUT FLOWERS AND FOLIAGE		10827		26782		19310		32538	FLEURS,FEUILLAGES COUPES
29271	CUT FLOWERS		10779		26740		19298		32532	FLEURS ET BOUTONS
3	MINERAL FUELS ETC		4779		7626		14033		23622	COMBUSTIBLES MINERAUX LUB
32	COAL,COKE AND BRIQUETTES		3366		2360		10216		11179	HOUILLES,COKES,BRIQUETTES
323	BRIQUETS,COKE,SEMI-COKE	W 49281	2753	W 25642	1716	W 280061	8428	W 406928	9521	BRIQUETTES
3232	COKE,SEMI-COKE,RTRT CRBN	W 49281	2753	W 25642	1716	W 280061	8428	W 406928	9521	COKES ET SEMI-COKES
33	PETROLEUM AND PRODUCTS		1412		5264		3798		12381	PETROLE ET DERIVES
334	PETROLEUM PRODUCTS,REFIN		390	W 1296	1928	W 3505	2731	W 16267	6839	PRODUITS RAFFINES
3345	LUBS,PETROLEUM OILS NES	W 89	73	W 1266	1913	W 2496	2436	W 11472	6678	HUILES LUBRIFIANTES
33451	LUBS(HIGH PETR CONT) ETC	W 88	72	W 1259	1890	W 2258	2040	W 11298	6520	HUILES LUBRIF,H LOURDES
335	RESIDUAL PETRLM PROD NES	W 2100	1022	W 277456	3336		1065		5540	PRODUITS RESIDUELS NDA
5	CHEMCLS,RELATED PROD NES		36592		37643		36120		46605	PRODUITS CHIMIQUES
51	ORGANIC CHEMICALS		1553		1860		2109		6564	PROD CHIMIQ ORGANIQUES
512	ALCOHOLS,PHENOLS ETC		1257		1450		1243		5958	PHENOLS,PHENOLS-ALCOOLS
53	DYES,TANNING,COLOUR PROD		5109		4856		9042		8565	PROD TEINTURE,COLORANTS
532	DYES NES,TANNING PROD	W 5929	3752	W 5419	3847	W 8934	7585	W 8743	7108	EXTRAITS TEINTURE,TANNAGE
5322	DYE,TANN EXTRCTS,TANNINS	W 5857	3698	W 5419	3790	W 8933	7581	W 8742	7105	EXT TAN ORIG VEG,TANNINS
541	*MEDICINAL,PHARM PRODUCT		5411		5808		4961		5858	PROD MEDICINAUX PHARMACEUT
5417	MEDICAMENTS		4420		5035		4226		4125	MEDICAMENTS
54173	— CONTAINING ALKALOIDS		3990		4187		2363		1966	MED CONTEN ALCALOIDES
55	PERFUME,CLEANING ETC PRD		5913		6764		8159		9334	PROD POUR PARFUM,TOILETTE
554	SOAP,CLEANSING ETC PREPS	W 6230	5072	W 6962	5722	W 6791	6840	W 6283	7771	SAVONS,PRODUITS DETERSIFS
5541	SOAPS	W 5876	4697	W 6297	5188	W 6121	5986	W 5648	6745	SAVONS,PROD TENSIO-ACTIFS
562	*FERTILIZERS,MANUFACTURE	W 49563	10153	W 76010	10565		4026	W 27811	7090	ENGRAIS MANUFACTURES
5623	CHEM POTASSIC FERTILIZER	W 17580	3581	W 20118	4039	W 4765	1906	W 1987	487	ENGRAIS POTASSIQUES
58	PLASTIC MATERIALS ETC		4866		3544		2370		2431	MAT PLAST ARTIFICIELLES
6	BASIC MANUFACTURES		380527		370934		411994		531420	ART MANUFACTURES
61	LEATHER,DRESSED FUR,ETC		9719		7828		12402		21882	CUIRS,PELLETERIES
611	LEATHER	W 5705	8535	W 3399	5847	W 3014	10991	W 8466	20550	CUIRS,PEAUX PREPARES
6114	LEATHR BOVINE NES,EQUINE	W 5675	8113	W 3137	5201	W 2984	10938	W 8463	19818	CUIRS DE BOVINS
62	RUBBER MANUFACTURES NES		3846		5503		3300		5033	CAOUTCHOUC MANUFACTURE
63	WOOD,CORK MANUFACTRS NES		4250		6364		10629		12110	OUVRAGES LIEGE ET BOIS
634	VENEERS,PLYWOOD,ETC		2293		3514		4856		6554	PLACAGES,CONTRE-PLAQUES
64	PAPER,PAPERBOARD AND MFR		5956		6129		9522		15126	PAPIERS,CARTONS & OUVRAGES
641	PAPER AND PAPERBOARD	W 8536	4390	W 7368	4154	W 9221	5016	W 18746	10100	PAPIERS ET CARTONS
6415	PAPER,PAPERBRD,BULK,NES	W 6084	2310	W 4398	1684	W 5691	2761	W 8821	5614	PAPIERS,CARTONS ROULEAUX
65	TEXTILE YARN,FABRICS,ETC		60013		61678		76149		62722	FILS,TISSUS,ARTICLES TEXTILE
651	TEXTILE YARN	W 9832	19677	W 10605	19890	W 10052	24595	W 4135	26638	FILS TEXTILES
6513	COTTON YARN	W 9110	17955	W 10047	18083	W 9740	23454	W 3879	25459	FILS DE COTON
652	COTTON FABRICS,WOVEN	A 20643	15977	A 19613	23781	A 32804	33506	A 21615	20581	TISSUS DE COTON
6521	GREY WOVEN COTTON FABRIC	A 14908	9677	A 14273	17393	A 27963	26716	A 18348	13511	TISSUS COT ECRUS NON MERCER
65214	GREY WOVEN COTTON NES	A 13772	8495	A 8740	10135	A 14623	13503	A 17673	12928	AUT TISSUS 85% COTON ECRUS
65215	GREY WOVN COTN BLEND NES	A 1136	1182	A 5531	7088	A 13339	13213	A 674	583	AUT TIS MOINS 85% COT ECRUS
6522	WOVEN COTTON BLEACHD,ETC	A 5735	6300	A 5340	6387	A 4841	6791	A 3267	7070	TISSUS COTON BLANCHIS ETC
65224	BLCHED COTTON FABRIC NES	A 4186	5174	A 4367	5327	A 4477	6312	A 3078	6753	AUT TIS PLUS 85% COT BLANCHI
653	WOVN MAN-MADE FIB FABRIC		7121		3139		2311	A 1967	2426	TISSUS FIBRES SYNTH,ARTIF
658	TEXTILE ARTICLES NES		14622		11274		11134		6487	ART FACONNES MAT TEXTILES
6583	BLANKETS ETC NON ELECTRC	W 2030	3597	W 2166	4870	W 1887	4183	W 621	1478	COUVERTURES
65833	SYN FIB BLANKETS ETC NES	W 1055	1818	W 1713	4091	W 524	1427	W 537	1347	COUVERTURES FIBRES SYNTHET
6584	LINENS ETC	W 1444	7093	W 793	4288	W 796	5133	W 288	2398	LINGE DE MAISON
65845	OTHER LINEN OF COTTON	W 647	4557	W 338	2359	W 354	2914	W 148	1409	LINGE DE TOILETTE COTON
66	NONMETAL MINERAL MFS NES		14827		19589		21607		25985	ART MIN NON METALLIQUES
661	LIME,CEMENT,BLDG PRODS	W 96908	7544	W 114556	9002	W 156937	10744	W 177424	12416	CHAUX,CIMENTS MAT CONSTR
6612	CEMENT	W 93259	6165	W 109302	6967	W 149530	8078	W 167180	9227	CIMENTS HYDRAULIQUES
667	PEARL,PREC-,SEMI-P STONE		3949		6589		6270		9071	PERLES, PIERRES GEMMES
6672	DIAMONDS NONINDUST,UNSET		936		1574		3871		6868	DIAMANTS BRUTS
66721	— ROUGH,UNSORTED		936		1567		3854		6868	DIAMANTS BRUTS NON TRIES
6673	PREC-,SEMI-PR STONES NES		3011		5015		2398		2203	AUTRES PIERRES NON SERTIES
67	IRON AND STEEL		166593		155503		137437		234104	FER ET ACIER
671	PIG IRON ETC	W 187381	116634	W 174430	101802		115164		214055	FONTE,SPIEGEL,POUDRES
6713	IRON,STL POWDER,SHOT,ETC	W 649	3706	W 935	4565				2	POUDRES,GREN FER,ACIER
67131	IRON,STEEL SHOT,GRIT,ETC	W 645	3698	W 895	4565				1	GRENAILLE FER,ACIER
6716	FERRO-ALLOYS	W 186188	112792	W 172495	97122	W 209904	115164		214010	FERRO-ALLIAGES
67169	OTHER FERRO-ALLOYS	W 177137	111159	W 172495	97122	W 209901	115160	W 279343	214009	AUTRES FERRO-ALLIAGES
672	IRON,STEEL PRIMARY FORMS		38408	W 111109	24396		4996	W 43298	6079	LINGOTS FER,ACIER
6725	IRN,STL BLOOMS,SLABS,ETC		35055	W 89621	19368		3560	W 22726	3039	BLOOMS,BILLETTES FER ACIER
67251	IRN,SMPLE STL BLOOMS,ETC	W 215608	35054	W 89617	19360	W 26703	3557	W 22726	3039	BLOOMS ETC NON ACIER FIN
6727	IRN,STL COIL FR REROLLNG	W 15509	3331	W 21488	5028	W 8462	1358	W 20499	2950	EBAUCHES POUR TOLES FER
67271	IRON,SIMPLE STEEL COILS	W 15503	3325	W 21485	5019	W 8431	1345	W 20401	2907	EBAUCHES NON EN ACIER
673	IRON,STEEL SHAPES ETC	W 23627	7099		21197		7061	W 11079	5126	BARRES,PROFIL FER,ACIER
6731	IRON,STEEL WIRE ROD	W 9943	2759		15017	W 8432	3384	W 4477	2347	FIL MACHINE FER,ACIER
67312	HIGH CARBON STL WIRE ROD	W 3362	1059	W 38340	12241	W 1426	471	W 1139	456	FIL MACH ACIER FIN CARBONE
6732	IRON,STEEL BARS ETC	W 11559	3553	W 5368	4094		1893	W 2813	1200	BARRES FER,ACIER
68	NON-FERROUS METALS		96896		73929		109313		110219	METAUX NON FERREUX
682	COPPER EXC CEMENT COPPER	W 8992	16612		16030		19511	W 8447	16864	CUIVRE
6821	COPPER NES,ALLOYS,UNWRT	W 8555	16142	W 13758	15425	W 7896	14207	W 7499	14618	CUIVRE BRUT
68212	COPPER REFINED,UNWROUGHT	W 8387	15319	W 13638	15274	W 7867	14176	W 7474	14549	CUIVRE AFFINE BRUT
683	NICKEL		71172	W 10910	49615	W 17100	80533		87730	NICKEL
6831	NICKEL,ALLOYS UNWROUGHT	W 10810	71170	W 10909	49615	W 17100	80533	W 12859	87727	NICKEL ET ALLIAGES BRUTS
687	TIN	W 681	3802		2796		624			ETAIN
689	NON-FER BASE METALS NES	W 400	4566	W 529	4777	W 1093	7073	W 361	4385	AUT METAUX NON FERREUX
6899	BASE METALS NES,CERMETS	W 349	4250	W 353	3717	W 978	6293	W 361	4385	METAUX COMMUNS NDA
68999	BASE MTL NES UNWRT,WASTE	W 349	4250	W 353	3717	W 978	6293	W 361	4385	AUT METAUX COM BRUTS NDA
69	METAL MANUFACTURES NES		18427		34413		31636		44241	ART MANUFACT EN METAL NDA
691	STRUCTURES AND PARTS NES	W 4562	3427	W 4610	3811	W 4852	3472	W 4142	5882	CONSTRUCT FER,ACIER,ALU
6911	STRUCTURES,PARTS IRN,STL	W 4542	3371	W 4599	3779	W 4837	3420	W 4119	5816	CONSTRUCT FER,ACIER,FONTE
693	WIRE PRODUCTS NON ELECTR	W 6554	3902	W 8453	4170	W 7384	4439	W 8434	5851	OUVRAGES FILS METALLIQUES
694	STL,COPPR NAILS,NUTS,ETC	W 509	558	W 1102	872	W 1430	1108	W 2705	8523	CLOUS,VIS,ECROUS
69401	IRON,STEEL NAILS ETC	W 127	97	W 647	333	W 742	399	W 2218	7773	CLOUS,POINTES FER,ACIER
697	BASE MTL HOUSEHOLD EQUIP		6027		19564		16447		14896	ART MENAGE MET COMMUNS
6974	BASE MTL DMSTC ARTIC NES	W 2267	5434	W 2707	18549	W 2320	15709	W 1784	14060	ARTICLES NDA FONTE,FER,ETC
69741	— OF IRON OR STEEL	W 1648	2946	W 1943	15039	W 1794	3891	W 1177	2279	ART NDA EN FONTE,FER
69743	— OF ALUMINIUM	W 611	2383	W 752	3395	W 518	11751	W 602	11719	ARTICLES NDA EN ALUMINIUM
699	BASE METAL MFRS NES		2843		3495		3612		6770	ART MANUFACTURES MET NDA
7	MACHINES,TRANSPORT EQUIP		37801		39830		49278		49198	MACHINES MATERIEL TRANSPORT
71	POWER GENERATING EQUIPMT		2486		1643		5088		8001	MACHINES GENERATRICES
713	INTRNL COMBUS PSTN ENGIN		372		896		4649		6187	MOTEURS EXPL COMB INT, PIECE
7131	AIRCRAFT PSTN ENGINS,PTS		245		801		4573		5931	MOTEURS EXPL P.AVIATION, PIE

5. General Exports F.O.B. by Commodities according to the S.I.T.C. (Rev. 2) in thousand U.S. Dollars
Exportations Générales F.O.B. par Produits d'après la C.T.C.I. (Rév. 2) en milliers de Dollars E.U.

SITC CTCI	COMMODITY	1992 WEIGHT POIDS	1992 VALUE VALEUR	1993 WEIGHT POIDS	1993 VALUE VALEUR	1994 WEIGHT POIDS	1994 VALUE VALEUR	1995 WEIGHT POIDS	1995 VALUE VALEUR	PRODUIT
72	MACHS FOR SPCL INDUSTRYS		3996		4729		8579		9591	MAC SPECIALES POUR INDUST
74	GENRL INDUSTRL MACHY NES		3397		3322		2830		6811	MACH APP INDUSTRIE
76	TELECOMM,SOUND EQUIPMENT		1259		9091		1568		543	EQUIPMENT DE TELECOM
764	TELECOM EQPT,PTS,ACC NES		513		8557		835		140	EQUIP TELECOM,PIECES
7649	PTS NES OF EQUIPMT OF 76		307		8502		643		57	PIECES DE LA DIV 76
76493	TELECOMM EQUIPMT PTS NES		132		8439		216		37	PIECES 761,762,764.3,8
77	ELECTRIC MACHNRY NES ETC		9556		6695		9515		7304	MACH APP ELECT NDA
773	ELECTR DISTRIBUTNG EQUIP		6052	W 2092	3670		3430		3622	EQUIPMT DISTRIBUTION ELECT
7731	INSULATED WIRE,CABLE ETC	W 2642	5973	W 2076	3616	W 1710	3367	W 1480	3564	FILS,CABLES ISOLES ELECT
78	ROAD VEHICLES		10212		8314		12808		9995	VEHICULES ROUTIERS
782	LORRIES,SPCL MTR VEH NES	N 523	4620	N 44	377	N 319	5423	N 66	967	VEHICULES SPECIAUX,MARCH
7821	LORRIES,TRUCKS	N 521	4616	N 44	377	N 317	5376	N 65	893	VEHICULES TRANSP MARCHAND
786	TRAILERS,NONMOTR VEH,NES		3160		4303		2764		2205	REMORQUES,CADRES,CONTAIN
79	OTHR TRANSPORT EQUIPMENT		6066		5116		8241		4968	AUTRE MATERIEL TRANSPORT
791	RAILWAY VEHICLES		5749		4676		6428		2589	VEHIC MAT CHEMINS DE FER
7915	FRT,MAINT CARS NOT POWRD		4419		3618	N 927717	5869	N 39	1342	WAGONS DE SERVICE
79152	RAILWAY FREIGHT CARS NES		4419		3618	N 927717	5869	N 39	1342	WAGONS MARCHANDISES
8	MISC MANUFACTURED GOODS		84410		124811		159786		161881	ART MANUFACTURES DIVERS
812	*PLUMBG,HEATNG,LGHTNG EQ	W 25	262	W 95	300		441		7662	APPAR SANITAIRES CHAUFFAGE
8124	LIGHTING EQUIPMENT NES	W 9	223	W 26	191		334		7536	APPAREILS ECLAIRAGE ETC
81242	LAMPS,FITTINGS BASE METL	W 2	83	W 13	100		185		7300	APPAREILS D'ECLAIRAGE
821	*FURNITURE,PARTS THEREOF		7864		14317		31125		21286	MEUBLES ET PIECES
8219	FURNITURE AND PARTS NES	W 4332	7470	W 7127	12561	W 10529	29131	W 8700	19612	AUTRES MEUBLES ET PIECES
82191	METAL FURNITURE NES	W 1076	1430	W 1029	1352	W 2128	12309	W 1449	2157	MEUBLES NDA EN METAL
82192	WOOD FURNITURE NES	W 3063	5884	W 5413	9605	W 7850	14912	W 6729	15649	MEUBLES NDA EN BOIS
84	CLOTHING AND ACCESSORIES		50664		49681		63864		61162	VETEMENTS
842	MENS OUTERWEAR NOT KNIT	N 3282897	18404	N 4650154	21232	N 4637553	27185	N 3307289	23724	VET DESSUS POUR HOMMES
8423	— TROUSERS,BREECHES ETC	N 3104395	17295	N 4305876	19190	N 4325098	25354	N 3053702	21374	PANTALONS HOMMES MAT TEX
843	WOMENS OUTERWEAR NONKNIT	N 1277294	8579	N 649539	8448		14450	N 1469590	8584	VET DESSUS FEMMES MAT TEX
8433	— DRESSES	N 218673	1397	N 275487	2145	N 751360	7577	N 211479	1546	ROBES EN MAT–TEXTILES
8439	— OTHER OUTER GARMENTS	N 537211	3944	N 63927	4622		4778	N 536341	3906	AUT VET DES FEM MAT TEXT
844	UNDER GARMENTS NOT KNIT	N 643148	2611		2775	N 750266	3428	N 1125445	6396	VETEMENT DESSOUS MAT TEX
8441	— MENS SHIRTS	N 593646	2514		2236	N 703656	3322	N 1111429	6357	CHEMISES HOMMES MAT TEXT
845	OUTERWEAR KNIT NONELASTC	N 2281951	11129	N 584744	8438	N 524452	8413	N 1225198	8267	VET DESSOUS,ACCES BONNET
8459	— OTHER,CLTHG ACCESRYS	N 1916887	8538	N 156447	6317	N 97734	5811	N 662287	4777	AUT VET DESSUS DE BONNE
846	UNDER GARMENTS KNITTED		9507		8584		9924		13740	SOUS VETS DE BONNETERIE
8462	— OF COTTON NON ELASTIC	N 3810137	6633	N 3559487	5668	N 3554687	6720	N 3746020	8412	SOUS–VET BONNET COTON
84629	—— OTHER	N 3810137	6633	N 3559487	5668	N 3554687	6720	N 3746020	8412	AUT SOUS–VET BONNET COTON
851	*FOOTWEAR	P 2016621	8826	P 1201528	11220		10443	P 1675782	13672	CHAUSSURES
85102	FOOTWEAR LEATHER	P 1408067	5436	P 291710	5130		5481	P 938069	5260	CHAUS SEMELLES EN CUIR
85103	SHOES WOOD–,CORK–SOLED	P 370348	2646	P 855032	5915	P 1003644	4773	P 700528	8216	CHAUS SEMELLES BOIS,LIEGE
89	MISC MANUFCTRD GOODS NES		13508		46278		49846		52964	ART MANUFACTURES DIVERS
892	PRINTED MATTER		1740		18940		15673		2977	IMPRIMES
8928	PRINTED MATTER NES		199		17244		14418		1471	IMPRIMES NDA
89283	UNISSUED BANKNOTES ETC		75		17134		14213		1311	TIMBRES–POSTE FISCAUX
896	WORKS OF ART ETC		7324		8856		11811		14563	OBJETS D'ART
89603	ORIGINAL SCULPTURE ETC		1932		3025		4395		7140	PROD ORIG STATUAIRE
89605	COINS,NATURE COLLECTIONS		5375		5730		6916		7341	COLLECTIONS ZOOLOG,BOTAN
897	GOLD,SILVER WARE,JEWELRY		1701		13338		16289		27729	BIJOUTERIE,ORFEVRERIE
8973	PREC JEWLRY,GLD–SILVWARE		1635		13269		16271		27695	BIJOUX OR,ARGENT ORFEVRE
89731	PRECIOUS METAL JEWELLERY		1624		13264		16248		27687	ART BIJOUTERIE,JOAILLER
9	GOODS NOT CLASSD BY KIND		22751		7859		15355		6460	ART TRANSACT NON CLASSES
931	*SPECIAL TRANSACTIONS		8596		2042		347		1177	TRANS.SPECIALES
971	*GOLD,NON MONETARY NES	K 25227	12738	K 5622	2040	K 44986	8562	K 2648	433	OR NON MONETAIRE
97102	ROLLED GLD UNWKD,SEMIMFD	K 25197	12575	K 5622	2040	K 44532	3211	K 2648	433	MET COMMUNS PLAQUES OR

135,80 pet

كيفية الحصول على منشورات الأمم المتحدة

يمكن الحصول على منشورات الأمم المتحدة من المكتبات ودور التوزيع في جميع أنحاء العالم . استعلم عنها من المكتبة التي تتعامل معها أو اكتب إلى : الأمم المتحدة ، قسم البيع في نيويورك أو في جنيف .

如何购取联合国出版物

联合国出版物在全世界各地的书店和经售处均有发售。请向书店询问或写信到纽约或日内瓦的联合国销售组。

HOW TO OBTAIN UNITED NATIONS PUBLICATIONS

United Nations publications may be obtained from bookstores and distributors throughout the world. Consult your bookstore or write to: United Nations, Sales Section, New York or Geneva.

COMMENT SE PROCURER LES PUBLICATIONS DES NATIONS UNIES

Les publications des Nations Unies sont en vente dans les librairies et les agences dépositaires du monde entier. Informez-vous auprès de votre libraire ou adressez-vous à : Nations Unies, Section des ventes, New York ou Genève.

КАК ПОЛУЧИТЬ ИЗДАНИЯ ОРГАНИЗАЦИИ ОБЪЕДИНЕННЫХ НАЦИЙ

Издания Организации Объединенных Наций можно купить в книжных магазинах и агентствах во всех районах мира. Наводите справки об изданиях в вашем книжном магазине или пишите по адресу: Организация Объединенных Наций, Секция по продаже изданий, Нью-Йорк или Женева.

COMO CONSEGUIR PUBLICACIONES DE LAS NACIONES UNIDAS

Las publicaciones de las Naciones Unidas están en venta en librerías y casas distribuidoras en todas partes del mundo. Consulte a su librero o diríjase a: Naciones Unidas, Sección de Ventas, Nueva York o Ginebra.

Litho in United Nations, New York
93363—October 1997—3,780
ISBN 92-1-061172-1

United Nations publication
Sales No. E/F.98.XVII.2, vol. I
ST/ESA/STAT/SER.G/45